Cambridge-Eichborn German Dictionary

Economics
Law
Administration
Business
General

Volume 1

English-German

Cambridge University Press

Cambridge

London   New York   New Rochelle
Melbourne   Sydney

Published by the Press Syndicate of the University of Cambridge
The Pitt Building, Trumpington Street, Cambridge CB2 1RP
32 East 57th Street, New York, NY 10022, USA
296 Beaconsfield Parade, Middle Park, Melbourne 3206, Australia

© von Eichborn Siebenpunkt Verlag KG

First published in the Federal Republic of Germany 1981
First published by Cambridge University Press 1983

Printed in Great Britain at the University Press, Cambridge
and in the Federal Republic of Germany at Mohndruck Gütersloh

Library of Congress catalogue card number: 83–10144

British Library cataloguing in publication data

Cambridge-Eichborn German dictionary.
Vol. 1: English-German
1. German language–Dictionaries–English
2. English language–Dictionaries–German
433′.21   PF3640
ISBN 0 521 25845 6

45337

Cambridge-Eichborn German Dictionary

Meiner Frau
für 35 Jahre
gemeinsamen Lebens
mit dem Wörterbuch

Dictionaries are like watches;
the worst
is better than none,
and the best
cannot be expected to go quite true.
Samuel Johnson 1709-1784

Foreword

Thirty-five years ago in Stuttgart the Military Government of that time granted permission to the Deutsche Verlagsanstalt for the initial edition of 30,000 copies of the *Spezialwörterbuch für Handel und Wirtschaft* (Specialized Dictionary for Commerce and Industrial Economy). The author had to resist the temptation of this tenfold print run as compared to that of the average book of those days - even if he had been in a position to procure the requisite quantities of paper for his publisher. At that time the idea of elaborating a really reliable dictionary from existing English-language commercial and other specialized literature was an almost impossible task. Later on there was then a donation on the part of the American government of more than a hundred books intended for the advanced training by competent college and university teachers of those of their occupation forces who wished to become lawyers, judges, political scientists, business administrators, tax experts, transport economists, bankers, insurance agents or politicians. Exploitation and analysis of these and of several hundred more books gave birth to the vocabulary which forms the foundation of the present-day dictionary.

Sterling conveniently provided by an English cousin rendered possible the procurement of Webster's New International Dictionary of the English Language. Then came Funk & Wagnall's New Standard Dictionary of the English Language, the large Oxford Dictionary and the twenty-four volume Encyclopaedia Britannica. Following upon the change-over of the Deutsche Verlagsanstalt, where the Specialized Dictionary for Commerce and Industrial Economy had appeared in three editions and its vocabulary had already trebled, to *ECON*, where four editions of the *Wirtschaftswörterbuch* (Business Dictionary) have so far appeared, the *BUSINESS DICTIONARY*, published as a parallel edition by Prentice Hall of New York, led to the continuous obtainment of English-language trade and professional journals. Many years spent in exploiting the modern terminology of BUSINESS WEEK, FORTUNE, The FINANCIAL TIMES and the ECONOMIST, together with careful analysis of bank and insurance forms and blanks, income-tax returns and international balance-sheets as well as of numerous other technical English, Canadian and American documents, have enabled the vocabulary of the present-day *GROSSER EICHBORN* to expand to a good quarter-million entries. The provinces and subjects dealt with contain what a businessman or economist having connections with the English-speaking world will occasionally require to look up. Particular attention has been paid to enlarging the phraseological content of the work so as to cover a broad spectrum of the most modern aspect of colloquial language, a large number of slang expressions having likewise been incorporated. It is the author's fond hope that, in the course of the few decades involved, he will have succeeded in making some small contribution to a still closer mutual understanding between the German and the English-speaking world.

Burscheid, August 1981   Reinhart von Eichborn

Vorwort

Vor fünfunddreißig Jahren genehmigte die damalige Militärregierung in Stuttgart der Deutschen Verlagsanstalt eine Erstauflage von 30 000 Stück für das *Spezialwörterbuch für Handel und Wirtschaft*. Der Verfasser widerstand der Verlockung dieser zehnfachen Auflagenhöhe eines damaligen Durchschnittbuches, wenngleich er seinem Verleger auch diese Papiermenge hätte beschaffen können. Zu diesem Zeitpunkt waren die Möglichkeiten, ein zuverlässiges Wörterbuch aus der angelsächsischen Fachliteratur zu erarbeiten, einfach noch nicht gegeben.

Später gab es dann eine Spende von mehr als hundert Büchern, die Amerika's Regierung zur Fortbildung derjenigen ihrer Besatzungssoldaten von kompetenten Hochschullehrern veranstaltet hatte, die Anwälte, Richter, Volks- oder Betriebswirte, Steuerfachleute, Verkehrswirtschaftler, Banker, Versicherungsagenten oder Politiker werden wollten.

Die Auswertung dieser Bücher und vieler hundert anderer, ließen den Wortschatz entstehen, der die Grundlage des jetzt vorliegenden Wörterbuches bildet.

Von einem englischen Vetter gespendete Pfunde ermöglichten die Anschaffung von Webster's New International Dictionary of the English Language. Es folgten Funk & Wagnall's New Standard Dictionary of the English Language, das große Oxford Dictionary und die vierundzwanzigbändige Encyclopaedia Britannica.

Nach dem Wechsel von der Deutschen Verlagsanstalt, bei der das *Spezialwörterbuch für Handel und Wirtschaft* drei Auflagen erlebte und sein Wortschatz sich verdreifachte zu ECON, bei dem vier Auflagen des *Wirtschaftwörterbuches* erschienen, ermöglichte das als Parallelausgabe bei Prentice Hall, New York verlegte *BUSINESS DICTIONARY* den laufenden Bezug angelsächsischer Wirtschaftsfachzeitschriften. Die über viele Jahre vorgenommene Auswertung der modernen Terminologie von BUSINESS WEEK, FORTUNE, der FINANCIAL TIMES und des ECONOMIST sowie die Durchsicht von Bank- und Versicherungsformularen, Einkommensteuererklärungen und internationalen Bilanzen sowie zahlreicher anderer fachbezogener englischer, kanadischer und amerikanischer Unterlagen ließ den Wortschatz des jetzt vorliegenden GROSSER EICHBORN auf eine gute Viertelmillion Eintragungen anschwellen. Die behandelten Sachgebiete beinhalten das, was der in der Wirtschaft Tätige, sofern er mit der angelsächsischen Welt zu tun hat, gelegentlich nachschlagen will.

Besonderer Wert wurde darauf gelegt, die Phraselogie anzureichern, um das gesamte Spektrum der Umgangssprache des modernen Menschen zu erfassen. Zahlreiche Slangausdrücke wurden aufgenommen.

Der Verfasser hofft, daß es ihm im Lauf der Jahrzehnte gelungen ist, zum gegenseitigen Verständnis zwischen deutscher und angelsächsischer Welt ein wenig beizutragen.

Burscheid, August 1981   Reinhart von Eichborn

Danksagung

Ich danke allen denen, die mir bei der technischen Fertigstellung dieses Buches geholfen haben:

den Mitarbeitern unseres Satzstudios für ihre sorgfältige Arbeit

Mr. Percival Edgar Wrigley für seine unermüdliche Korrekturentätigkeit

Herrn Dr. Alfred Hopf für seine so geduldig gewährte juristische Beratung

meinen Töchtern Clarissa, Isabelle, Jacqueline und Evelyn für ihre zuverlässige und zeitsparende Tätigkeit beim selbständigen Einalphabetisieren

meiner Tochter Clarissa für ihre Satzarbeiten

meinem Sohn Wolfram für Satzarbeiten und seine Kurierfahrten mit Zetteln und Fahnen

meiner Tochter Isabelle für das Umzetteln und Abschreiben von Zetteln

meiner Tochter Evelyn für die grafische Gestaltung des Buches

meinem Sohn Holger für seine Mitarbeit in technischen Fragen des Satzstudios, für den Transport von Maschinen und Terminals und für seine Stärkung meines Durchhaltewillens

VORBEMERKUNG

I. Alphabetische Anordnung

1. Stichwörter sind grundsätzlich alphabetisch geordnet.

2. Pluralformen sind, soweit sie angeführt werden müssen, hinsichtlich ihrer alphabetischen Anordnung wie Singularformen behandelt.
   Selbständig behandelt sind lediglich die Pluralformen der Wörter auf -y.

3. Verben, bei denen auf die Partikel »to« verzichtet wird, sind durch (v.), Adjektive durch (a.) kenntlich gemacht.

4. Über die Einordnung eines Wortes als Stichwort oder seine Unterordnung unter ein Stichwort entschied der Grad seiner Selbständigkeit.

5. Die Untergruppen sind in nachstehender Reihenfolge angeordnet:

   a) reines Substantiv, ohne Beifügung;

   b) Substantiv, erweitert durch Synonyme und Hinweise auf seinen besonderen Anwendungsbereich (eingeklammerter Kursivtext, in alphabetischer Reihenfolge), z. B.
   abatement *(decrease)* [Ver]minderung, Abnahme, *(deduction)* Abzug, *(discount)* Abschlag, [Preis]nachlaß, Rabatt, *(law of real property)* widerrechtliche Besitzergreifung;

   c) Substantiv, erweitert durch Präposition, z. B. **for account and risk** auf Rechnung und Gefahr; **for third ~** für fremde Rechnung; **not taken into ~** unberücksichtigt;

   d) Substantiv, erweitert durch unverbundene adjektivische oder substantivische Appositionen, durch welche die Bedeutung des Substantivs modifiziert wird, z. B.
   account Konto; **advance ~** Vorschußkonto; **appropriation ~** Bereitstellungskonto; »**~ attached**« »Konto beschlagnahmt«; **bank ~** Bankkonto;

   e) Substantiv, erweitert durch verbundene, nachgestellte Appositionen (alphabetisch, ohne Berücksichtigung der Bindewörter, nach den Anfangsbuchstaben der Appositionen geordnet), z. B. **account | in arrears** Rechnungsrückstand; **~ in bank** Bankkonto; **~ of charges** Unkostenkonto; **~ with customers** Kundenkonto;

   f) Adjektiv (a.), das mit dem Stichwort-Substantiv gleichlautend ist;

   g) einfaches Verb (v.), das mit dem Stichwort-Substantiv gleichlautend ist;

   h) Verb, erweitert durch Synonyme und Hinweise auf seinen besonderen Anwendungsbereich (eingeklammerter Kursivtext, in alphabetischer Reihenfolge), z. B.
   abate *(v.)* *(decrease)* abnehmen, geringer werden, *(deduct)* herabsetzen, abziehen, nach-, ablassen, *(reduce legacies)* (Legate) verkürzen;

   i) Verb, erweitert zur Phrase durch beliebige grammatische Konstruktionen, alphabetisch geordnet nach dem Anfangsbuchstaben des jeweils wichtigsten Wortes dieser Konstruktion, z. B. **accept | (v.) a bill** Wechsel akzeptieren, mit Akzept versehen; **~ bills for collection (discount)** Wechsel zum Einzug (Diskont) hereinnehmen; **~ in blank** blanko akzeptieren;

   k) Substantiv, erweitert zur Phrase durch verbale Konstruktionen, in alphabetischer Reihenfolge dieser Verben, z. B. **to add to an account** einem Konto zuschlagen; **to age ~s** Konten nach ihrer Fälligkeit aufgliedern; **to appear in an ~** auf einer Rechnung stehen; **to audit ~s** Rechnungen überprüfen;

   l) Einfaches Kompositum des Stichworts, alphabetisch geordnet nach den Anfangsbuchstaben des jeweils nachgestellten (unbetonten) Kompositumgliedes, z. B.
   account | analysis Kontenanalyse; **~ book** Kontobuch; **~ day** *(stock exchange)* Abrechnungstag.

6. Die Untergruppen eines Stichworts sind im Text jeweils durch einen Absatz hervorgehoben.

II. Erläuterungen der angewandten Abkürzungen und Zeichen

1. Abkürzungen

a.	= Adjektiv	o.s.	= oneself
abbr.	= (abbreviation) = Abkürzung	pl.	= plural
Br.	= hauptsächlich in Großbritannien	pol.	= politisch
	= gebräuchlich	print.	= Buchdruck
coll.	= umgangssprachlich	sociol.	= Soziologie
dial.	= dialektisch	s. o.	= someone
el.	= elektrisch	s. th.	= something
[etwa]	= annähernd entsprechender	Scot.	= schottisch
	= Begriff	sl.	= Slang
fam.	= familiär	techn.	= Technik
fig.	= bildlich	tel.	= Telefon
j., jds.,		th.	= thing
jem.	= jemand, jemandes,	US	= hauptsächlich in den USA
	= jemandem		= gebräuchlich
lat.	= aus dem Lateinischen	v.	= Verb
mar.	= Schiffahrt	v. i.	= verbum intransitivum
math.	= Mathematik	v. t.	= verbum transitivum
med.	= Medizin	→	= siehe
mil.	= Militär		

2. Tildenzeichen

Fettgedruckte Stichwörter werden bei Wiederholungen innerhalb ihres Abschnittes durch eine Tilde (~) ersetzt, wobei sich die Tilde auf die Gesamtheit eines mehrteiligen Stichwortes bezieht. Beginnt das durch die Tilde ersetzte Wort im Gegensatz zum Stichwort mit einem großen Buchstaben oder umgekehrt, so wird dies durch einen Kreis über der Tilde (⌀) angedeutet.

3. Senkrechter Strich

Wird vom Ordnungswort eines mehrteiligen Stichwortes (z. B. **extension agreement**) eine Untergruppe abgeleitet (~ **course** = Fortbildungskursus), so wird das Ordnungswort dieses Stichwortes von seinem restlichen Teil durch einen dünnen senkrechten Strich (**extension | agreement**) abgetrennt.

4. Runde Klammern

a) Steht ein Buchstabe innerhalb eines Wortes in runden Klammern, z. B. bei **hono(u)r,** so deutet die Klammer eine zweite Schreibmöglichkeit an;

b) steht ein Wort innerhalb eines Ausdrucks in runden Klammern, so verweist die Klammer auf ein Synonym, z. B. **current account** laufendes (tägliches) Konto, **to audit (balance) accounts** Konten saldieren (ausgleichen).

5. Eckige Klammern

Sie bedeuten, daß die eingeklammerten Stellen (Buchstaben oder Wörter) mitgelesen oder ausgelassen werden können, z. B. **abandonment** [Verzicht]leistung; **abatement** *(remittance of tax)* [Steuer]erlaß, Nachlaß.

6. Während im Englischen die Wiederholung eines Wortes durch eine Tilde (~) bezeichnet wird, sind kurz nacheinander wiederholt auftretende deutsche Wörter oder Wortteile durch einen kurzen Strich (-) markiert, z. B. **able to earn** dienst-, unterhaltsfähig; **ability to pay** Zahlungs-, Leistungsfähigkeit; **bear account** Baissekonto, -position.

III. Rechtschreibung

Die amerikanische Rechtschreibung weicht häufig von der englischen ab. Den wesentlichen Abweichungen wurde durch nachfolgende Regelung Rechnung getragen;

1. Wörter, die im Amerikanischen verkürzt wiedergegeben werden, bekamen folgendes Druckbild; **hono(u)r, program(me).**
2. Die Wortendung **ise** oder **ize** wurde in Anlehnung an die vom Oxford Dictionary Dictionary durchgeführte Schreibweise meist mit **ise** wiedergegeben.
3. Die amtlichen Regeln für die englische Silbentrennung wurden strengstens beachtet und an Hand von Webster's New International Dictionary kontrolliert.
4. Die Verwendung der Bindestriche zwischen einzelnen selbständigen Substantiven ist heute zwiespaltiger denn je. In der englischen und amerikanischen Literatur finden sich alle Varianten (Bindestrich, kein Bindestrich, Zusammenschreibung).
   Da die Entwicklung mehr in die Richtung geht, den Bindestrich wegzulassen oder Wörter zusammenzuschreiben, wurde dieser Tendenz im allgemeinen entsprochen.

NOTES

I. Alphabetical Order

1. Catchwords are placed in alphabetical order.

2. The plural form has been treated, as far as it has to be mentioned, in the same alphabetical order as the singular. The plural form of words ending with a »y« has been treated separately.

3. Verbs have been marked with a (v.) where the participle »to« has been omitted.
Adjectives with an (a.).

4. The classification of a word as catchword has been decided according to the grade of its independency, or its sub-division under a catchword.

5. The sub-grouping is arranged in the following manner:

   a) pure substantives without attributes;

   b) nouns extended by synonyms and indication of their special use (in brackets, text in italics) are in alphabetical order, i.e. **abatement** *(decrease)* [Ver]minderung, Abnahme, *(deduction)* Abzug, *(discount)* Abschlag [Preis]nachlaß, Rabatt, *(law of real property)* widerrechtliche Besitzergreifung;

   c) nouns extended by prepositions, i. e. **for account and risk** auf Rechnung und Gefahr; **for third** ~ für fremde Rechnung; **not taken into** ~ unberücksichtigt;

   d) nouns extended by detached adjectival or substantival appositions in which the meaning of the nouns is modified, i.e.
   account Konto; **advance** ~ Vorschußkonto; **appropriation** ~ Bereitstellungskonto; **»~ attached«** »Konto beschlagnahmt«; **bank** ~ Bankkonto;

   e) nouns extended by joined following appositions (alphabetical order without any regard to the conjunction) are arranged according to the first letter of the apposition, i.e. **account|in arrears** Rechnungsrückstand; ~ **of charges** Unkostenkonto; ~ **with customers** Kundenkonto;

   f) adjectives (a.) which are of homonymous value with the catchword noun;

   g) simple verb (v.) which is of homonymous value with the catchword noun;

   h) verbs extended by synonyms and with explanations as to their special use (in brackets, text in italics) are in alphabetical order, i.e.
   abate *(v.) (decrease)* abnehmen, geringer werden, *(deduct)* herabsetzen, abziehen, nach-, ablassen, *(reduce legacies)* (Legate) verkürzen;

   i) verbs extended into phrases through any grammatical construction have been placed alphabetically according to the first letter of the most important word in this construction, i.e. **accept|** *(v.)* **a bill** Wechsel akzeptieren, mit Akzept versehen; ~ **bills for collection (discount)** Wechsel zum Einzug (Diskont) hereinnehmen; ~ **in blank** blanko akzeptieren;

   k) nouns extended into phrases by means of verbal construction have been placed in alphabetical order of the verbs, i. e. **to add|to an account** einem Konto zuschlagen; **to age** ~**s** Konten nach ihrer Fälligkeit aufgliedern; **to appear in an** ~ auf einer Rechnung stehen; **to audit** ~**s** Rechnungen überprüfen;

   l) simple compounds of the catchwords have been placed in alphabetical order according to the first letter of the following unaccentuated part of the compositum, i.e. **account|analysis** Kostenanalyse; ~ **book** Kontobuch; ~ **day** *(stock exchange)* Abrechnungstag.

6. The sub-grouping of a catchword is always shown in the text by a paragraph.

II. Explanation of the use of abbreviations and signs

I. Abbreviations

a.	=	adjective	o.s.	=	oneself
abbr.	=	abbreviation	pl.	=	plural
Br.	=	chiefly used in Great Britain	pol.	=	political
coll.	=	colloquial	print.	=	printing term
dial.	=	dialect	sociol.	=	sociological
el.	=	electrical	s. o.	=	someone
[etwa]	=	approximate translation	s. th.	=	something
fam.	=	familiar	Scot.	=	Scotch
fig.	=	figurative	sl.	=	slang
j., jds.,	=		techn.	=	technical
jem.	=	jemand, jemandes	tel.	=	telephone
	=	jemandem (someone,	th.	=	thing
	=	someone's, to someone)	US	=	chiefly used in the USA
lat	=	Latin	v.	=	verb
mar.	=	marine	v. i.	=	verbum intransitivum
math.	=	mathematical	v. t.	=	verbum transitivum
med.	=	medical	→	=	see

2. Repetition sign

Heavy typed catchwords when repeated in the paragraph are substituted by a repetition mark (~). When the catchword consists of one or more sections, this sign replaces the whole.

When in contrast with the catchword the repeated word begins with a capital letter or vice versa, this is indicated by a circle put over the repetition mark (⌒).

3. Perpendicular stroke

If however a subdivision is formed of a catchword consisting of one or more words (i. e. **extension agreement**) whose first part determines the alphabetically placed word of the whole the catchword is separated from the remaining part by a thin perpendicular stroke (**extension | agreement**).

4. Round brackets

a) If a letter is placed in round brackets, i. e. **hono(u)r,** then the bracket shows a second form of spelling;

b) if a word is placed in round brackets, then the bracket refers to the synonym, i. e. **current account** laufendes (tägliches) Konto, **to audit (balance) accounts** Konten saldieren (ausgleichen).

5. Square brackets

These mean that the bracketed letters (or words) can be read or omitted, i.e. **abandonment** Verzicht[leistung]; **abatement** *(remittance of tax)* [Steuer]erlaß, Nachlaß.

6. In order to save space the separation sign (-) is used frequently in the German text and it indicates that the same word is used before and after, i.e. **able to earn** dienst-, unterhaltsfähig; **ability to pay** Zahlungs-, Leistungsfähigkeit; **bear account** Baissekonto, -position.

III. Correct Spelling

The American spelling often differs from the English. The most important differances have been accounted for by the following scheme:

1. Words which are used by Americans in an abbreviated manner have been printed as follows: **hono(u)r, program(me).**

2. The Oxford Dictionary way of spelling has been adopted for words ending in **ise** and **ize.**

3. The recognized rules for dividing syllables in English have been most carefully followed and checked with the Webstar's New International Dictionary.

4. The use of the hyphen between single simple nouns is nowadays even more disputable than ever. One finds all sorts of variations in both English and American literature (hyphen, no hyphen, written together). Since the development tends more to leave the hyphen out or to write words together this tendency has generally been followed.

A

A 1 *(US)* erstklassig, ausgezeichnet, prima;
~ **at Lloyd's** erstklassige Schiffsbeschaffenheit.
ABC Anfangsgründe, *(Br.)* alphabetisches Kursbuch;
not to know the ~ **of finance** nicht einmal die Grundbegriffe des Finanzwesens begreifen;
~ **powers** ABC-Staaten; ~ **warfare** ABC-Kriegsführung; ~ **weapons** Atom-, biologische und chemische Waffen.
abandon Ungezwungenheit, *(underwriting)* Aufgabe (Verlassen) eines Schiffes;
~ *(v.)* *(balance sheet)* ausbuchen, *(customs)* abandonnieren, *(give up to)* überlassen, übergeben, *(possession, right)* aufgeben, *(wife)* verlassen;
~ **an action** Klage zurücknehmen; ~ **an appeal** Berufung zurücknehmen; ~ **an attempt** vom Versuch zurücktreten; ~ **a child** Kind aussetzen; ~ **a claim** auf einen Anspruch verzichten, Anspruch fallenlassen, von einer Forderung Abstand nehmen; ~ **the country-side** vom Lande wegziehen; ~ **the defence** Verteidigung niederlegen; ~ **a domicile** Wohnsitz aufgeben; ~ **an enterprise** Unternehmen aufgeben; ~ **foreign exchange controls** Devisenbewirtschaftung aufheben; ~ **the gold standard** Goldstandard aufgeben; ~ **the goods as a constructive total loss** Waren als Totalverlust reklamieren; ~ **an invention** Erfindung fallenlassen; ~ **a mine** Grube auflassen; ~ **a mortgaged estate** belastetes Grundstück aufgeben; ~ **an option** Optionsrecht aufgeben (nicht ausüben); ~ **a patent** Patent fallenlassen; ~ **a position to the enemy** Stellung dem Feind überlassen; ~ **a property to the insurer** Schiff dem Versicherer überlassen; ~ **a railway** Eisenbahnlinie stillegen; ~ **a right** Recht aufgeben, sich eines Rechtes begeben; ~ **a road** Straße einziehen; ~ **a scheme** Plan fallenlassen; ~ **a security** auf eine Sicherheit verzichten; ~ **a ship** Schiff aufgeben (verlassen); ~ **a ship covered by a policy** Schiff den Versicherern überlassen; ~ **a territory** Gebiet räumen; ~ **a legal title** auf einen Rechtsanspruch verzichten.
abandoned aufgegeben, verlassen, herrenlos;
~ **car** herrenloses (stehengelassenes) Auto; ~ **land** aufgegebenes Land; ~ **mine** stillgelegte (aufgelassene) Grube; ~ **property** herrenloses Gut; ~ **ship** Wrack, aufgegebenes Schiff.
abandonee Wracks auswertende Versicherungsgesellschaft, Schiffsabwracker.
abandonment *(accounting)* Ausbuchung, *(customs)* Zollabandonnierung, *(mil.)* befehlswidriges Verlassen, *(railway)* Stillegung, *(relinquishment of a claim)* Aufgabe, Verzicht[leistung], *(ship)* Preisgabe, Verlassen, *(surrender)* Überlassung, *(wife)* Verlassen;
~ **of action** Klagerücknahme; ~ **of appeal** Rücknahme der Berufung, Berufungsverzicht; ~ **of attempt** Rücktritt vom Versuch; ~ **of building restrictions** Aufhebung von Bebauungsvorschriften; ~ **of business** Geschäftsaufgabe; ~ **of cargo** *(marine insurance)* Abandon; ~ **of a child** Kindesaussetzung; ~ **of a claim** Anspruchsverzicht, Aufgabe eines Anspruchs; ~ **of domicile** Wohnsitzaufgabe; ~ **of an easement** Verzicht auf eine Grunddienstbarkeit; ~ **of an enterprise** Aufgabe eines Unternehmens; ~ **of a mortgaged estate** Aufgabe eines belasteten Grundstücks; ~ **of the gold standard** Abgang vom Goldstandard; ~ **of an invention** Fallenlassen einer Erfindung; ~ **of lines** Einstellung des Verkehrs; ~ **of a mine** Auflassung einer Grube; ~ **of an option** Nichtausübung einer Option; ~ **of the option money** Prämienaufgabe; ~ **of a patent** Fallenlassen eines Patents, Patentverzicht; ~ **of a public office** Verzicht auf ein Staatsamt; ~ **of a railway (railroad,** *US***)** Stillegung einer Eisenbahnlinie; ~ **of a road** Einziehung einer Straße; ~ **of security** Verzichtleistung auf (Preisgabe einer) Sicherheit; ~ **of a ship to the underwriters** Überlassung eines Schiffes an die Versicherungsgesellschaft; ~ **of taxing power** Verzicht auf ein Besteuerungsrecht; ~ **of a territory** Räumung eines Gebiets; ~ **of a legal title** Verzicht auf einen Rechtsanspruch; ~ **of trademarks** Nichtbenutzung von Warenzeichen; ~ **clause** Abandonklausel.
abase *(v.)* demütigen, entwürdigen, *(mil.)* degradieren.
abasement Demütigung.
abatable aufhebbar, abschaffbar;
~ **nuisance** zu beseitigender Mißstand.
abate *(v.)* *(decrease)* abnehmen, geringer werden, *(deduct)* herabsetzen, nachlassen, ablassen, *(intrude unlawfully)* sich widerrechtlich niederlassen, *(price)* herabsetzen, ermäßigen, mindern, reduzieren, *(reduce legacies)* verkürzen, *(remit*

taxes) [Steuern] erlassen, *(stay)* [Verfahren] einstellen, *(become void)* erlöschen, ungültig werden, *(make void)* umstoßen, aufheben, *(wind)* abnehmen, *(yield)* mit sich handeln lassen, nachgeben;
~ **an action** Prozeß einstellen; ~ **debts** Schulden [teilweise] erlassen; ~ **a fee** Gebühr niederschlagen (ermäßigen); ~ **income tax** Steuernachlaß gewähren; ~ **a legacy** Vermächtnis kürzen; ~ **legacies pro rata to pay debts** Legate anteilsmäßig zwecks Schuldentilgung kürzen; ~ **a nuisance** Mißstand beseitigen; ~ **proceedings** Verfahren einstellen; ~ **the purchase price** Kaufpreis herabsetzen (ermäßigen); ~ **a rent** Miete herabsetzen; ~ **a tax** Steuer erlassen; ~ **travel(l)ing expenses** Reisekosten abziehen.
abatement *(accounting)* [Bilanz]berichtigung, *(decrease)* [Ver]-minderung, Abnahme, *(deduction)* Abzug, Herabsetzung, Abstrich, *(discount)* Abschlag, [Preis]nachlaß, Preisermäßigung, -herabsetzung, -abschlag, *(duty)* Zollerlaß, *(nuisance)* Abstellung, Abschaffung, *(proceedings)* Aussetzung des Verfahrens, *(remittance of tax)* [Steuer]erlaß, -nachlaß;
no ~ feste Preise; **without** ~ ohne Preisnachlaß;
~ **of action** Einstellung des Verfahrens; ~ **of debts** teilweiser Schuldenerlaß; ~ **of fees** Gebührenermäßigung; ~ **of income tax** Einkommensteuernachlaß, -ermäßigung; ~ **of legacies** Vermächtniskürzung; ~ **of a nuisance** Beseitigung eines Mißstandes; ~ **of civil proceedings** Klageänderung; ~ **in proportion** proportionale Herabsetzung; ~ **of purchase money (price)** Kaufpreisminderung, Herabsetzung des Kaufpreises; ~ **of rent** Mietherabsetzung; ~ **and revival** Aussetzung des Verfahrens; ~ **of tax** Steuernachlaß;
to allow an ~ Nachlaß bewilligen, Rabatt gewähren;
~ **clause** Herabsetzungsklausel; ~ **limit** *(taxation)* Ermäßigungsgrenze.
abater Antrag auf Einstellung des Verfahrens.
abating│a nuisance Beseitigung eines Mißstandes; ~ **of the wind** Windabnahme.
abbreviate *(v.)* abkürzen.
abbreviation Abkürzung, Kurzbezeichnung, Kürzel.
abdicate *(v.)* abdanken, *(resign)* seinen Abschied nehmen;
~ **a child** Kind enterben; ~ **a throne** der Krone entsagen.
abdication Abdankung, *(disinheritance)* Enterbung, *(magistrate)* Amtsniederlegung, *(resignation)* Rücktritt;
~ **of the throne** Thronniederlegung, -entsagung.
abduct *(v.)* entführen, verschleppen.
abduction Entführung, Verschleppung, Menschenraub.
abductor Verschlepper.
aberration Abweichung, Abirrung, *(disorder of the mind)* geistige Verwirrung, Geistesstörung, -zerrüttung.
abet *(v.)* anstiften, begünstigen;
to aid and ~ Vorschub (Beihilfe) leisten.
abetment Aufhetzung, Anstiftung, Beihilfe, Vorschub;
~ **of crime** Verbrechensbegünstigung.
abettor Begünstiger.
abey *(v.)* unentschieden lassen.
abeyance *(state of suspension)* Schwebe[zustand], Unentschiedenheit;
in ~ in der Schwebe, *(goods)* herrenlos;
to be left in ~ in der Schwebe bleiben, unentschieden sein; **to fall into** ~ ruhen, zeitweilig außer Kraft treten.
abeyant unentschieden, in der Schwebe.
abidal Aufenthaltsort, Wohnstätte.
abidance by rules Befolgung von Regeln.
abide *(v.)* leben, wohnen, *(remain stable)* festhalten an;
~ **abroad** sich ständig im Ausland aufhalten; ~ **by an agreement** sich an eine Absprache halten; ~ **by an award** Schiedsspruch annehmen; ~ **by the consequences** Folgen auf sich nehmen; ~ **by a contract** Vertrag einhalten; ~ **by the law** dem Gesetz Folge leisten; ~ **by what I have said** bei meiner Aussage bleiben; ~ **and satisfy** vollstrecken.
abiding bleibend, dauernd;
law-~ gesetzestreu;
~ **conviction** unumstößliche Überzeugung von einer Schuld; ~ **place** Wohn-, Aufenthaltsort.
abilities geistige Anlagen, Fähigkeiten.
ability [Leistungs]fähigkeit, Befähigung, Vermögen, Können, Geschick, Talent, *(technics)* Leistungsfähigkeit;
to the best of one's ~ nach besten Kräften;

administrative ~ Organisationsfähigkeit; **coordinating (organizing)** ~ Organisationsfähigkeit, -talent; **executive** ~ Führereigenschaft; **specialized** ~ besondere Fachkenntnisse; **supervisory** ~ Überwachungsfähigkeit;

~ **to contract** Vertragsfähigkeit; ~ **to earn one's livelihood** Erwerbsfähigkeit; ~ **to express ideas in writing** Fähigkeit, seine Gedanken schriftlich zu formulieren; ~ **to inherit** Erbfähigkeit; ~ **to invest** Investitionsmöglichkeit; ~ **to make a will** Testierfähigkeit; ~ **to meet competition** Konkurrenzfähigkeit; ~ **to negotiate** Verhandlungsgeschick; ~ **to pay** Zahlungs-, Leistungsfähigkeit, Solvenz; ~ **to perform labo(u)r** Arbeitsfähigkeit; ~ **to shift focus** Wandlungsfähigkeit; ~ **to sue** Prozeßfähigkeit, Aktivlegitimation; ~ **to supply** Lieferfähigkeit; ~ **to survive** Überlebensfähigkeit; ~ **to type** Schreibmaschinenkenntnisse; ~ **to work** Arbeitsfähigkeit; ~ **to work independently** Fähigkeit, selbständig zu arbeiten;

~**-to-pay principle** *(taxation)* Steuerleistungsprinzip; ~ **requirements** Befähigungsnachweis.

abjuration [feierliche] Entsagung, Abschwörung;
~ **of allegiance** *(naturalized citizen, US)* Absage an frühere Treueverpflichtungen.

abjure *(v.)* entsagen, abschwören;
~ **the state** für immer außer Landes gehen.

able [leistungs]fähig, tauglich, begabt, *(law)* berechtigt, fähig;
~ **to contract** vertragsfähig; ~ **to dispose of property** verfügungsberechtigt, testierfähig; ~ **to deposit security** kautionsfähig; ~ **to earn one's livelihood** arbeits-, erwerbsfähig; ~ **to enter into contract** vertragsfähig; ~ **to inherit** erbfähig; ~ **to make a will** testierfähig; ~ **to meet competition** konkurrenzfähig; ~ **to pay** leistungs-, zahlungsfähig, solvent; ~ **to perform labo(u)r** arbeitsfähig; ~ **to purchase** zahlungskräftig; ~ **to shift focus** wandlungsfähig; ~ **to sue** aktiv legitimiert; ~ **to supply** lieferfähig; ~ **to work** arbeitsfähig;
to be ~ imstande (in der Lage) sein.

able-bodied körperlich leistungsfähig, kerngesund, *(mil.)* [dienst]tauglich, wehrfähig;
~ **seaman** *(Br.)* Vollmatrose.

able-bodiedness Tauglichkeit.

able-minded geistig beweglich.

abnegate *(v.)* *(right)* aufgeben, verzichten, entsagen.

abnegation Verzicht, Entsagung.

abnormal außergewöhnlich, regelwidrig, abnorm, anormal.

abnormality Regelwidrigkeit, Ungewöhnlichkeit, *(statistics)* Abnormalität, Anomalie.

aboard an Bord;
to go (get, US) ~ an Bord gehen, in ein Schiff einsteigen, sich einschiffen; **to go** ~ **a train** in einen Zug einsteigen;
all ~! alle Mann an Bord, *(US)* alles einsteigen.

abode Wohnort, Aufenthaltsort, Wohnung;
of (without) fixed ~ mit festem (ohne festen) Wohnsitz; **of unknown** ~ unbekannten Aufenthalts;
to make (set up, take up) one's ~ sich niederlassen, seinen Wohnsitz begründen; **to make one's** ~ **in the country** sich auf dem Lande niederlassen.

abolish *(v.)* aufheben, beseitigen, abstellen, abschaffen, widerrufen;
~ **an abuse** mit einem Mißbrauch aufräumen; ~ **customs** Zölle abschaffen; ~ **a government** Regierung stürzen; ~ **a law** Gesetz aufheben; ~ **an office (post)** Stelle einsparen (streichen); ~ **resale price maintenance** Preisbindung der zweiten Hand aufheben; ~ **a reserve** Vorbehalt aufheben; ~ **restrictions** Beschränkungen aufheben; ~ **a tax** Steuer abschaffen (beseitigen); ~ **visas** Visumzwang (Sichtvermerkzwang) aufheben.

abolishable abschaffbar, aufhebbar.

abolished *(post)* eingespart;
to be ~ wegfallen, fortfallen.

abolishment Abschaffung, Aufhebung, Beseitigung.

abolition Aufhebung, Abschaffung, Aufgabe, *(post)* Streichung, *(remission of punishment)* Niederschlagung eines schwebenden Verfahrens;
~ **of an abuse** Abstellung eines Mißbrauchs; ~ **of customs** Abschaffung von Zöllen; ~ **of debts** Schuldenannullierung; ~ **of a government** Regierungssturz; ~ **of a law** Aufhebung eines Gesetzes; ~ **of an office** Stelleneinsparung; ~ **of resale price maintenance** Aufhebung der Preisbindung der zweiten Hand; ~ **of restrictions** Aufhebung von Beschränkungen; ~ **of a tariff** Zollaufhebung; ~ **of a tax** Steueraufhebung, -beseitigung, Aufhebung einer Steuer; ~ **of visas** Aufhebung des Sichtvermerkzwanges.

aboriginal Ureinwohner, Eingeborener;
~ *(a.)* ureingesessen, eingeboren.

aborigenes Urbevölkerung.

abort Fehlgeburt;
~ *(v.)* Fehlgeburt haben, *(airforce, sl.)* herunterfallen, *(mil., sl.)* vermasseln.

abortion Abtreibung, Fehlgeburt, Frühgeburt, *(fig.)* Mißlingen;
elective ~ in besonderen Fällen erlaubte Abtreibung; **illegal** ~ unerlaubte Schwangerschaftsunterbrechung;
~ **in cases of rape** Abtreibung in Notzuchtsfällen;
to perform an ~ Schwangerschaft unterbrechen; **to prove an** ~ sich als Fehlschlag erweisen;
~ **clinic** Abtreibungsklinik; ~ **law** Abtreibungsgesetz; ~ **stipulations** Abtreibungsbestimmungen.

abortive gegenstandslos;
~ **coup** mißlungener Staatsstreich;
to prove ~ mißlingen.

abound *(v.)* Überfluß haben an, im Überfluß vorhanden sein;
~ **in one's own sense** nach seinem eigenen Kopf handeln.

abounding reichlich vorhanden.

about zirka, etwa, ungefähr;
to be ~ **s. th.** sich mit etw. befassen; **to be** ~ **early in the morning** früh auf sein; **to be** ~ **to take one's examination** dicht vor dem Examen stehen;
~**-face** Meinungswechsel; **to make an** ~**-face** seinen Standpunkt vollkommen ändern.

above, over and extra;
~ **average** überdurchschnittlich; ~**-mentioned** vor-, obenerwähnt; ~ **par** über pari; ~ **provisions** vorstehende Bestimmungen.

aboveboard ehrlich, redlich.

abovedeck auf Deck.

aboveground *(mining)* über Tage.

abovestairs in einem höheren Stockwerk, *(fig.)* bei der Herrschaft.

abrade *(v.)* abnutzen, verschleißen, *(fig.)* untergraben, zerstören.

abrasion *(of coin)* Abnutzung;
limit of ~ *(coins)* Abnutzungsgrenze.

abreast nebeneinander, *(fig.)* auf der Höhe;
to keep ~ **of one's field** sich auf seinem Gebiet auf dem laufenden halten.

abridge *(v.)* *(condense)* Auszug machen, *(shorten)* [ab]kürzen, zusammenfassen;
~ **damages** Schadensersatzansprüche beschränken; ~ **a party of its rights** Rechte einer Partei beeinträchtigen; ~ **a privilege** Sonderrecht einschränken.

abridged version gekürzte Ausgabe.

abridgement Beeinträchtigung, *(book)* Auszug, Abriß, Zusammenfassung, Leitfaden, *(shortening)* [Ab]kürzung;
~ **of damages** Beschränkung des Schadenersatzanspruchs; ~ **of patent** Patentschriftauszug; ~ **of time** Fristverkürzung.

abroad im Ausland, *(before the public)* öffentlich bekannt;
to be ~ außer Landes sein, *(rumo(u)r)* umgehen; **to go** ~ ins Ausland gehen; **to have got** ~ ruchbar geworden sein; **to live** ~ im Ausland leben; **to send** ~ ins Ausland schicken.

abrogate *(v.)* außer Kraft setzen, widerrufen, für ungültig erklären, abschaffen, *(immunology)* als Gegenmittel wirken;
~ **restrictions** Beschränkungen aufheben.

abrogation Abschaffung, *(of a law)* Widerruf, Außerkraftsetzung, Aufhebung.

abscond *(v.)* sich der Festnahme durch die Flucht entziehen, sich heimlich davonmachen, flüchtig werden.

absconder Flüchtling.

absconding flüchtig;
~ **in bail cases** Flucht nach Kautionsgestellung;
~ **debtor** unbekannt verzogener Schuldner.

absence Abwesenheit, Aus-, Fernbleiben, Nichterscheinen;
in the ~ **of** mangels, in Ermangelung; **in the** ~ **of evidence** in Ermangelung von Beweisen; **in the** ~ **of further information** aus Mangel an weiterer Information;
chronic ~ dauernde Abwesenheit; **occasional** ~ gelegentliche Abwesenheit;
~ **of authority** fehlende Vollmacht; ~ **of consideration** fehlende Gegenleistung; ~ **from duty** Dienstabwesenheit; ~ **with[out] leave** [un]entschuldigtes Fehlen, [un]genehmigter Urlaub; ~ **of leave** *(mil.)* Urlaubsüberschreitung; ~ **of mind** Geistesabwesenheit, Zerstreutheit; ~ **of quorum** nicht vorhandene Beschlußfähigkeit, Beschlußunfähigkeit; ~ **from work** Nichterscheinen am Arbeitsplatz.

absent *(v.)* o. s. fernbleiben;
~ **o. s. from a meeting** sich von einer Versammlung fernhalten;
~ *(a.)* abwesend, nicht erschienen;

~ on medical certificate ärztlich entschuldigt;
to be ~ fernbleiben, nicht erscheinen, abwesend sein; **to be ~ without good excuse** unentschuldigt fehlen; **to be ~ with[out] leave** [un]entschuldigt fehlen (fernbleiben), *(mil.)* sich [un]erlaubt entfernen; **to be ~ from school** in der Schule fehlen; **to be ~-minded** nicht bei der Sache sein; **~-mindedness** Geistesabwesenheit; ~ **voter** *(US)* Briefwähler; ~ **voting** *(US)* Briefwahl.

absentee Abwesender, Nichterschienener, *(landlord)* nicht ortsansässiger Grundeigentümer;
~ *(a.)* im Ausland lebend;
~s' list Abwesenheitsliste; ~ **ownership** Managerfunktion ohne Eigentümerrisiko; ~ **rate** *(workers)* Abwesenheitssatz; ~ **taxpayer** im Ausland wohnhafter Steuerflüchtiger.

absenteeism Wohnen im Ausland, *(labo(u)r)* Abwesenheit [vom Arbeitsplatz], fortgesetzte Nichtanwesenheit, Arbeitsversäumnis, unentschuldigtes Fernbleiben, Feier-, Fehlschichten;
~ **rate** Abwesenheitssatz.

absentia, in in Abwesenheit.

absolute unbeschränkt, absolut, unbedingt, endgültig, bedingungslos, *(unmixed)* unvermischt, unverdünnt;
to become ~ rechtskräftig werden;
~ **advantage** absoluter Kostenvorteil; ~ **altitude** absolute Höhe, Flughöhe über Grund; ~ **assignment** offene Forderungsabtretung; ~ **bar** prozeßhindernde Einrede; ~ **bill of sale** uneingeschränkte Übertragungsurkunde beweglicher Sachen; **decree ~** Endurteil [im Scheidungsverfahren]; ~ **delivery** *(instrument)* bedingungslose Aushändigung; ~ **deviation** *(statistics)* Absolutwert einer Abweichung; ~ **estate** unumschränktes Eigentum; ~ **frequency** *(statistics)* Anzahl, Häufigkeit; ~ **gift** Schenkung unter Lebenden; ~ **guarantee** selbstschuldnerische Bürgschaft; ~ **guarantor** selbstschuldnerischer Bürge; ~ **indorsement** unbeschränktes Giro; ~ **interest** unbeschränktes Eigentum; ~ **liability** unbeschränkte Haftpflicht; ~ **majority** absolute Majorität; ~ **monarchy** absolute Monarchie; ~ **numbers** absolute Zahlen; ~ **obligation** unabdingbare Verpflichtung; ~ **owner** unumschränkter Eigentümer; ~ **ownership** unumschränktes Eigentumsrecht; ~ **power** unumschränkte Gewalt; ~ **privilege** unabdingbares Vorrecht; ~ **proof** einwandfreier Beweis; ~ **right** unbeschränkt wirksames (uneingeschränktes) Recht; ~ **rule** strenge Vorschrift; ~ **ruler** Alleinherrscher; ~ **sale** bedingungsloser Verkauf; ~ **title** unumschränktes Eigentum; ~ **veto** unüberwindbares (absolutes) Vetorecht.

absolutely void null und nichtig.

absolution Freisprechung.

absolutism Absolutismus.

absolve *(v.)* befreien, entbinden, *(acquit)* freisprechen;
~ s. o. from an examination jem. eine Prüfung erlassen.

absorb *(v.)* aufsaugen, [in sich] aufnehmen, absorbieren, *(carrier)* Frachtnachlaß gewähren, *(prices)* auffangen, *(stocks)* aufnehmen;
~ s. o. j. völlig absorbieren; **~ a bank** Bank fusionieren; **~ border areas** Randgebiete eingemeinden; **~ buying power** Kaufkraft abschöpfen; **~ expenses** Unkosten übernehmen; **~ the extras** Sonderausgaben anderweitig ausgleichen; **~ part of the cost increase** Kostenerhöhungen teilweise selbst tragen; **~ freight charges** Frachtkosten übernehmen; **~ increase in costs (rising costs)** Kostenerhöhungen auffangen; **~ liquidity** Liquidität abschöpfen; **~ losses** Verluste auffangen; **~ its full share of overhead(s)** voll zur Deckung des Gemeinkostenanteils beitragen; **~ the whole of the available income** gesamte Einkünfte aufzehren; **~ new workers in the labo(u)r force** neue Kräfte in den Arbeitsprozeß eingliedern.

absorbed|in a book völlig in ein Buch vertieft sein; **~ by the public** *(stocks)* sofort abgesetzt werden;
~ expenses verrechnete Gemeinkosten.

absorbent paper saugfähiges Papier, Saugpost.

absorbing|capacity (power) Aufnahmefähigkeit, Absorptionsvermögen [des Marktes]; ~ **company** *(merger)* aufnehmende Gesellschaft; ~ **freight** sich nicht tragende Transportkosten.

absorption Abschöpfung, Absorption, *(amalgamation)* Fusion [durch Aufnahme], *(carrier)* Frachtnachlaß, *(point of saturation)* Sättigungspunkt, *(prices)* Auffangen;
cost ~ Kostenübernahme; **freight ~** Frachtkostennachlaß; ~ **of buying power** Abschöpfung der Kaufkraft; ~ **of charges** Gebührenübernahme; ~ **of extras** anderweitiger Ausgleich von Sonderausgaben; ~ **of liquidity** Liquiditätsabschöpfung, -entzug; ~ **of part of the cost increase** teilweise Selbsttragung von Kostenerhöhungen; ~ **of new workers in the labo(u)r force** Eingliederung neuer Kräfte in den Arbeitsprozeß;

~ **account** Wertberichtigungskonto; ~ **approach** *(balance of payment)* Absorptionstheorie; **to match output to the ~ capacities** Förderung den Absatzmöglichkeiten anpassen; ~ **capacity** *(market)* Aufnahmefähigkeit; ~ **costing** Kostenaufteilungsverfahren; ~ **power** Aufnahmefähigkeit, *(market)* Sättigungspunkt; ~ **value** berichtigter Wert.

abstain *(v.)* Abstand nehmen, entsagen, unterlassen;
~ in a vote (from voting) sich des Stimmrechts (der Stimme) enthalten.

abstainer Temperenzler;
total ~ Antialkoholiker.

abstemious enthaltsam, mäßig.

abstention Unterlassung, Verzicht, *(consumption)* Konsumverzicht;
~ **[from voting]** Stimmenthaltung.

abstinence theory of interest Wartetheorie des Zinses.

abstinent enthaltsam, mäßig.

abstract kurze Übersicht, *(art)* abstraktes Kunstwerk, *(books)* Auszug, Abriß, Kompendium;
in ~s auszugsweise; **in the ~** an und für sich, rein theoretisch betrachtet;
~ **of account** Konto-, Rechnungsauszug; **equated ~ of account** Staffelauszug; ~ **of balance sheet** Bilanzauszug; ~ **of records** kurzgefaßter Akteninhalt, Aktenauszug; ~ **of title** Eigentumsnachweis, Grundbuchauszug;
~ *(v.)* entziehen, absondern, abstrahieren, *(insurance contract)* zusammenfassen;
~ from Auszüge machen aus, ausziehen;
~ money from a till Geld aus der Ladenkasse stehlen; **~ a watch from s. o.** *(coll.)* jem. die Uhr klauen;
to make an ~ from an account Kontoauszug anfertigen; **to make ~s from the documents of title** [etwa] Grundbuchauszug anfertigen; **to verify an ~** *(Br.)* Kontoauszug prüfen;
~ **art** abstrakte Kunst; ~ **service** *(US)* Ausschnittsdienst.

abstracting Zusammenstellen von Tatsachen.

abstraction Absonderung, Entwendung;
~ **of bank funds** Unterschlagung von Bankgeldern; ~ **of documents** Urkundenunterschlagung.

abstruse schwer verständlich, unklar.

abundance Ergiebigkeit, Überfluß, Fülle, Menge;
in ~ in Hülle und Fülle;
~ **of labo(u)r supply** Überangebot an Arbeitskräften; ~ **of money** Geldschwemme, -überfluß, -überhang, -fülle; ~ **of seams** Flözreichtum;
~ **economy** Überflußgesellschaft.

abuse *(abusive language)* Kränkung, Beschimpfung, Schmähung, *(ill treatment)* Mißhandlung, Mißbrauch, mißbräuchliche Anwendung (Benutzung), *(civil law)* Substanzzerstörung, *(criminal law)* Notzucht, Schändung, Entehrung;
crying ~ grober Mißbrauch;
~ **of authority** Amtsmißbrauch, Mißbrauch der Ermessensfreiheit; ~ **of bail** Kautionsmißbrauch; ~ **of civil rights** Mißbrauch von Bürgerrechten; **~s in the civil service** Durchstechereien in der Beamtenschaft; ~ **of confidence** Vertrauensbruch; ~ **of discretion** Ermessensmißbrauch; ~ **of distress** Pfand-, Vollstreckungsmißbrauch; ~ **of language** Schimpfworte, Beschimpfung, Beleidigung; ~ **of monopoly** Mißbrauch einer Monopolstellung; ~ **of name** Namensmißbrauch, mißbräuchliche Verwendung eines Namens; ~ **of patent [privilege]** mißbräuchliche Patentbenutzung, Patentmißbrauch; ~ **of powers** Ermessensüberschreitung, -mißbrauch; ~ **of prisoners** Mißhandlung von Gefangenen; ~ **of process in court** Verfahrens-, Prozeßmißbrauch; ~ **of a fiduciary relationship** Mißbrauch eines Vertrauensverhältnisses; ~ **of rights** *(international law)* Rechtsmißbrauch; ~ **of trust** Vertrauensmißbrauch;
~ *(v.)* mißbrauchen, schlechten Gebrauch von etw. machen; **~ one's authority** seine Vollmacht mißbrauchen; **~ one's health** Raubbau mit seiner Gesundheit betreiben; **~ s. one's patience** jds. Geduld überstrapazieren; **~ prisoners** Gefangene mißhandeln;
to remedy crying ~s schreiende Mißstände abschaffen (abstellen).

abusive beleidigend.

abut *(v.)* anliegen, -grenzen.

abutment Angrenzen.

abutter Anlieger, Anrainer.

abutting anstoßend, anliegend, angrenzend;
~ **fields** anliegende Felder; ~ **letters** Anschlußbuchstaben; ~ **owner** Anlieger, Anrainer; ~ **piece of land** *(property)* Nachbargrundstück.

academic akademisch, *(classical)* allgemeinbildend, geisteswissenschaftlich;
~ **achievement** Leistung in den wissenschaftlichen Fächern; ~ **background** akademischer Werdegang; ~ **career** akademische-, Universitätslaufbahn; ~ **circles** Universitätskreise; ~ **credentials** akademische Würden; ~ **discussion** nutzlose (überflüssige) Diskussion; ~ **dress** akademische Tracht; ~ **field** akademischer Bereich; ~ **freedom** akademische Freiheit; ~ **position** Universitätsstellung, akademisches Amt; ~ **qualification** akademischer Grad; ~ **question** rein akademische Frage; ~ **rank** akademische Würde, Universitätsgrad; ~ **rating** Bildungsniveau; ~ **standards** akademisches Niveau; ~ **training** akademische Ausbildung, Universitätsstudium; ~ **year** Universitätsjahr.

academical akademisch;
to have strong ~ **credentials** hervorragende wissenschaftliche Laufbahn aufzuweisen haben; ~ **qualification** akademische Vorbildung; ~ **training** akademische Ausbildung (Vorbildung), Universitätsstudium.

academy Lehranstalt, Akademie, *(US, secondary school)* höhere Bildungsanstalt;
military ~ Militärakademie;
~ **of arts** Kunstakademie;
~ **award** Akademiepreis, *(film)* Oskar.

accede *(v.)* einwilligen, zustimmen, willfahren;
~ **to an international agreement** einem internationalen Abkommen beitreten; ~ **to an estate** Erbschaft antreten; ~ **to an office** Amt antreten; ~ **to an opinion** einer Meinung beipflichten; ~ **to a political party** einer politischen Partei beitreten; ~ **to a request** einem Gesuch stattgeben; ~ **to the throne** Thron besteigen.

accelerate *(v.)* *(traffic)* beschleunigen, Geschwindigkeit erhöhen;
~ **one's departure** seine Abfahrt vorverlegen; ~ **inflation** Inflationszunahme beschleunigen; ~ **proceedings** Verfahren beschleunigen; ~ **a pupil** *(US)* Schüler Klassen überspringen lassen.

accelerated beschleunigt, *(pupil)* überdurchschnittlich begabt;
~ **allowance** erhöhte Abschreibung; ~ **course** Schnellkurs; ~ **depreciation** [steuerbegünstigte] vorzeitige Abschreibung; ~ **express goods** beschleunigtes Eilgut.

accelerating premium produktionsgebundene Tantieme, progressive Leistungsprämie.

acceleration Beschleunigung, *(date)* Vorverlegung, *(school)* beschleunigter Fortschritt;
~ **of an increase in money supply** Beschleunigung der Geldvermehrung; ~ **of inflation** Inflationsbeschleunigung, Inflationszunahme; ~ **of maturity** frühzeitige Fälligstellung; ~ **of spending** Ausgabenbeschleunigung, gesteigertes Ausgabentempo;
~ **clause** *(instal(l)ment contract)* Fälligkeitsklausel; ~ **factor** *(Keynes)* Beschleunigungsfaktor; ~ **lane** Überholungsbahn; ~ **note** Schuldscheinverpflichtung mit dem Recht der vorzeitigen Rückzahlung; ~ **principle** *(investment)* Akzelerationsprinzip, Beschleunigungsprinzip.

accelerator Gaspedal, *(advertising agency)* Terminbearbeiter, Terminüberwacher, *(railway)* Postwagen;
to step on the ~ Gas geben, beschleunigen;
~ **pedal** Gaspedal; **to press down the** ~ **pedal** Gaspedal durchtreten.

accentuate *(v.)* hervorheben, betonen.

accept *(v.)* an-, entgegennehmen, akzeptieren, einverstanden sein, *(assume discharge of duty)* übernehmen;
~ **an agreement** seinen Vertragsbeitritt erklären; ~ **a bill** Wechsel akzeptieren (mit Akzept versehen); ~ **bills for collection (discount)** Wechsel zum Einzug (Diskont) hereinnehmen; ~ **in blank** blanko akzeptieren; ~ **a bribe** sich bestechen lassen; ~ **a check** *(US)* **(cheque,** *Br.)* Scheck entgegennehmen; ~ **combat** *(mil.)* sich zum Kampf stellen; ~ **s. one's conditions** in jds. Bedingungen einwilligen; ~ **[delivery of] goods** Waren[lieferung] abnehmen; ~ **a risk** Risiko übernehmen; ~ **the tender** Zuschlag erhalten; ~ **without dissent** ohne Beanstandung annehmen; ~ **an order** Auftrag annehmen; ~ **the terms** Bedingungen annehmen; ~ **the treasurer's account** Schatzmeister entlasten, dem Schatzmeister Entlastung erteilen; ~ **uncovered** ungedeckt akzeptieren.

acceptability Annehmbarkeit.

acceptable annehmbar, akzeptabel, *(as colleteral)* beleihbar, lombardfähig;
to be ~ **to s. o.** bei jem. ankommen;
~ **quality level** ausreichende (annehmbare) Qualität.

acceptance Annahme, Aufnahme, Empfang, *(approval)* Billigung, Genehmigung, *(bill of exchange)* Akzept, Akzeptierung, *(law)* Zustimmung, *(marine insurance)* Entgegennahme der Abandonerklärung, *(market)* Aufnahmefähigkeit;
against ~ gegen Annahme; **for** ~ **within seven days** dieses Angebot gilt sieben Tage; **returned for want of** ~ mangels Annahme zurück;
absolute ~ unbedingte Annahme; **accommodation** ~ Gefälligkeitsakzept; **anticipated** ~ vor Fälligkeit bezahltes Akzept; **approved** ~ formell gültiges Akzept; **banker's** ~ Bankakzept; **blank** ~ Blankoakzept; **clean** ~ reines Akzept, unbedingte Annahme; **collateral** ~ Wechselbürgschaft, *(in case of need)* Interventions-, Notakzept; **conditional** ~ bedingte Annahme; **consumer** ~ Aufnahmefreudigkeit [des Marktes]; ~ **declined** Annahme verweigert; **defensive** ~ ungern erteilte Zustimmung; **delayed** ~ Annahmeverzug; ~ **due** verfallenes Akzept; **express** ~ ausdrückliche Annahmeerklärung; **first-class** ~ erstklassiges Akzept; **foreign** ~ Außengeltung eines Akzeptes; **general** ~ unbedingtes (uneingeschränktes) Akzept; **implied** ~ Annahmevermutung; **local** ~ Platzakzept; **outstanding** ~ laufendes Akzept; **partial** ~ Teilannahme, *(bill)* Teilakzept; **physical** ~ tatsächliche Annahme, Abnahme; **qualified** ~ bedingte Annahme [eines Wechsels], Annahme unter Vorbehalt, bedingtes Akzept; **rebated** ~ vor Fälligkeit bezahltes Akzept; **refused** ~ Annahmeverweigerung [eines Wechsels]; **three-months'** ~ Dreimonatsakzept; **trade** ~ Waren-, Kundenakzept; **unconditional** ~ unbedingtes Akzept; **uncovered** ~ Blankoakzept; **unqualified (unreserved)** ~ unbedingte Annahme [eines Wechsels];
~ **of abandonment** Abandonakzept; ~ **by act** Vertragsannahme durch Vornahme einer Handlung; ~ **of an agreement** Beitrittserklärung zu einem Vertrag; ~ **of a bid** *(auction sale)* Zuschlag; ~ **of a bill** Wechselannahme, -akzept; ~ **in blank** Blankoakzept; ~ **of a bribe** Annahme einer Bestechung; ~ **in case of need** Notakzept; ~ **s on behalf of customers** Kundenakzepte; ~ **of deposits** Depositengeschäft, Depotentgegennahme; ~ **against documents** Akzept gegen Papiere; ~ **of freight** Frachtannahme; ~ **of a gift** Schenkungsannahme; ~ **of goods** Warenabnahme; ~ **for (upon) hono(u)r** Ehrenakzept, Akzept ehrenhalber, Interventionsakzept, Ehrenannahme, Interventionsannahme; ~ **of a judgment** Annahme eines Urteils; ~ **of money on current account** Entgegennahme von Kontokorrenteinlagen; ~ **of a motion** Antragsannahme; ~ **of an order** Auftragsannahme; ~ **of persons** Günstlingswirtschaft; ~ **by post** Annahme auf dem Postwege, Annahme durch die Post; ~ **of product** Produktaufnahme [im Markt]; ~ **of a proposal** Annahme eines Vorschlags; ~ **supra protest** Interventionsakzept; ~ **of rent** Mieteinnahme, Entgegennahme der Mietzahlung; ~ **of report** Entlastungserteilung; ~ **under reserve** Annahme unter Vorbehalt; ~ **of a risk** Risikoübernahme; ~ **of service** Empfangsbescheinigung einer Zustellungsurkunde; ~ **of shipment** Frachtabnahme; ~ **of tender** Zuschlag, Auftragserteilung; ~ **on trail** *(ship)* Abnahmefahrt; ~ **of the treasurer's account** Entlastung des Schatzmeisters; ~ **by wire** Drahtannahme;
to discharge ~**s** Akzepte einlösen; **to find** ~ **for one's proposal** mit seinem Vorschlag durchdringen; **to gain** ~ Anerkennung finden; **to meet with general** ~ allgemeine Zustimmung finden; **to hono(u)r (meet) an** ~ Akzept einlösen; **to obtain** ~ Akzept einholen; **to present for** ~ zur Annahme vorlegen; **to provide for** ~ Akzept decken; **to provide with** ~ mit Akzept versehen, akzeptieren; **to refuse** ~ **of a bill** Annahme eines Wechsels verweigern; **to secure** ~ Akzept einholen; **to telephone one's** ~ Angebot telefonisch annehmen;
~ **account** Akzeptkonto; ~ **bank** Akzeptbank; ~ **bill** Dokumentenwechsel; ~ **boundary** *(statistics)* Annahmegrenze; ~ **charge** *(banking)* Akzeptgebühr; ~ **commitments** Akzeptumlauf, Akzeptverbindlichkeiten, Akzeptschulden; ~ **committee** Abnahmekommission; ~ **corporation** Akzeptbank; ~ **credit** Akzept-, Trassierungs-, Rembourskredit; ~ **creditor** Akzeptgläubiger; ~ **criteria** Abnahmebewertungsmaßstäbe; ~ **debtor** Akzeptschuldner; ~ **flight** Abnahmeflug; ~ **house** Akzeptbank, -haus, Wechsel-, Diskontbank; ~ **ledger** Akzeptbuch, Obligobuch; ~ **liability** Akzeptverbindlichkeit; ~ **line** Höchstbetrag eines eingeräumten Akzeptkredits, Akzepthöchstkredit; ~ **maturity tickler** Wechselverfallbuch; ~ **note** Annahmebestätigung; ~ **number** *(statistics)* Annahmezahl; ~ **region** *(statistics)* Annahme-, Gutbereich; ~ **register** Akzept-, Obligobuch; ~ **rules** Aufnahmerichtlinien; ~ **sampling** Abnahme nach Stichproben, statistische Qualitätskontrolle; ~ **test** Abnahmeprüfung; ~ **tolerance** Abnahmetoleranz.

acceptancy Aufnahmefähigkeit.

acceptation *(ling.)* gebräuchlicher Sinn [eines Wortes], anerkannte Bedeutung;
literal ~ **of the law** Buchstabe des Gesetzes.

accepted angenommen, akzeptiert, *(bill)* mit Akzept versehen;
bills ~ Wechselschulden; **generally** ~ allgemeingültig, landläufig.

acceptilation freiwilliger formeller Erlaß einer geringfügigen Schuld.

accepting Annahme;
~ **banker** Akzeptbank; ~ **commission** Akzeptprovision; ~ **house** Akzeptbank; ~ **official** Abnahmebeamter.

acception, to find favo(u)rable Eingang (Abnahme) finden.

acceptor Akzeptant, Wechselverbundener, *(drawee)* Bezogener;
~ **dead** Akzeptant verstorben;
~ **of a bill** Wechselakzeptant; ~ **for hono(u)r** *(supra protest)* Ehrenakzeptant;
~**s' ledger** Akzeptanten-Kontokorrent.

access Zugang, Zugangsweg, Zutritt, Zufahrt,*(data processing)* Zugriff, *(divorced couple)* Verkehr mit den Kindern, *(illness)* Beginn, Anfang, *(politics)* freier Zugang;
difficult of ~ schwer zugänglich; **easy of** ~ leicht zugänglich; **safe** ~ sicherer Zugang; **tariff-free** ~ zollfreier Zugang;
~ **to airport** Flugplatznähe; ~ **to books and accounts** Einsichtnahme in Rechnungsbücher und Konten; ~ **to the children** *(divorce law)* Verkehr mit den Kindern; ~ **to information** Zugang zu Informationen; ~ **to the market** Marktzugang; ~ **to public records** Beiziehung (Benutzung) öffentlicher Unterlagen; ~ **to the sea** Zugang zum Meer; ~ **to studies** Zulassung zum Studium;
~ *(v.) (terminal)* Speicherzugriff veranlassen, ansteuern;
to deny ~ nicht zulassen, Zugang verweigern; **to gain** ~ Zutritt erhalten; **to gain** ~ **to capital** Zugang zum Kapitalmarkt haben; **to get free** ~ **to sterling credits** jederzeit Pfundkredite bewilligt bekommen; **to have** ~ **to the books of a company** Einsicht in die Bücher einer Firma haben; **to have** ~ **to the files** Akteneinsicht haben; **to lose** ~ **to the discount windows** *(US)* seine Refinanzierungsmöglichkeiten bei der Landeszentralbank verlieren;
~ **card** Einlaßkarte; ~ **control light** Zufahrt regelnde Verkehrsampel; ~ **point** *(freeway)* Autobahnauffahrt; ~ **road** Zufahrtsweg, [Fabrik]zufahrt, Zubringer, Zugangs-, Anliegerstraße; ~ **route** Anfahrts-, Zugangsweg; ~ **settlement** *(divorced couple)* Zugangsregelung; ~ **time** *(data processing)* Zugriffszeit.

accessibility Zugänglichkeit, Verkehrsgunst.

accessible zugänglich, verkehrsgünstig;
~ **to bribery** bestechlich; **to make the interior of a continent** ~ Inneres eines Kontinents erschließen;
~ **person** zugänglicher (ansprechbarer) Mensch; ~ **town** verkehrsgünstig gelegene Stadt.

accession *(addition)* Zuwachs, Zunahme, Vergrößerung, *(to agreement)* Beitritt, *(state)* Anwachsen, Anwachsung;
~**s** *(books)* Neuerwerbungen, -anschaffungen, *(labo(u)r force)* Zugänge [in der Belegschaft], Belegschaftszuwachs;
~ **to a confederacy** Eintritt in einen Bundesstaat; ~ **to an estate** Nachlaßübernahme, Erbschaftsantritt; ~ **of funds from abroad** ausländische Mittelzuflüsse; ~ **to knowledge** Erweiterung des Wissens; ~ **to office** Amtsantritt; ~ **to power** Machtübernahme; ~ **of property** Vermögenszuwachs, -anfall; ~ **of a state** Anschluß eines Staates; ~ **to the throne** Thronbesteigung, Besteigung des Thrones, Regierungsantritt; ~ **to a treaty** *(international law)* Vertragsbeitritt;
~ *(v.) (US, books in library)* eintragen, inventarisieren;
~ **book** *(library)* Zugangsliste; **to enter in the** ~ **book** Bücher inventarisieren; ~ **number** Zugangsnummer; ~ **rate** Zugangsrate, Einstellungsquote; ~ **record** Zugangsverzeichnis.

accessorial | agency nachgeordnete Behörde; ~ **services** *(carrier)* zusätzliche Dienstleistungen, Nebenleistungen.

accessories Zubehör, Beistellteile.

accessory Mitschuldiger, Teilnehmer, Mittäter, Komplize, *(adjunct)* Zubehör, Beiwerk;
~ **after the fact** Begünstigter, Hehler; ~ **before the fact** Anstifter; ~ **during the fact** Mittäter, Helfershelfer;
~ *(a.)* hinzukommend, untergeordnet, nebensächlich, akzessorisch, zusätzlich, *(criminal)* mitschuldig;
~ **advertising** zusätzliche Werbung, begleitende Werbeaktion, Ergänzungswerbung; ~ **charges** *(expenses)* Nebenausgaben; ~ **claim** Nebenforderung, -anspruch; ~ **contract** Zusatz-, Nebenvertrag; ~ **desk** Zusatzgerät; ~ **equipment** Beistellteile; ~ **obligation** Nebenverpflichtung, zusätzliche Verpflichtung.

accidency Glücksfall.

accident *(casualty)* Unglück, Unfall, *(event)* Zufall, Zufallserscheinung, Unvorhergesehenes, *(nonessential property)* Nebensache;
barring ~ Unfall ausgenommen; **by** ~ zufällig; **by** ~ **on purpose** *(sl.)* scheinbar beabsichtigt; **in case of an** ~ im Fall eines Unfalls;
automobile ~ Kraftfahrzeug-, Autounfall; **bad** ~ schwerer Unfall; **fatal** ~ tödlicher Unfall, Unfall mit tödlichem Ausgang; **fatigue** ~ auf Ermüdung zurückzuführender Unfall; **flying** ~ Flugzeugunglück; **hit-and-run** ~ Unfallfluchtsache; **industrial** ~ Betriebsunfall; **inevitable** ~ unvermeidlicher Unfall; **lost-time** ~ Unfall mit Arbeitsausfall (in der Arbeitszeit); **motor-vehicle** ~ Kraftfahrzeugunfall; **motorcar** ~ *(Br.)* Auto-, Kraftfahrzeugunfall; **noncompensable** ~ nicht zum Schadenersatz verpflichtender Unfall; **nonoccupational (off-the-job)** ~ Unfall außerhalb der Arbeitszeit; **on-the-job** ~ Betriebsunfall; **railway** ~ **(railroad,** *US)* Eisenbahnunglück; **road (street, traffic)** ~ Verkehrsunfall; **serious** ~ schwerer Unfall; **unavoidable** ~ unvermeidbarer Unfall; **working** ~ Betriebsunfall;
~ **at sea** Seeunfall, Schiffsunglück; ~ **to third parties** mittelbarer Unfall; ~ **at work** Arbeitsunfall;
to ascribe to an ~ einem Unfall zuschreiben; **to be at fault in an** ~ Unfall verschuldet haben, Unfallschuldiger sein; **to be killed in an** ~ bei einem Unfall den Tod finden; **to cause an** ~ Unfall herbeiführen (verursachen); **to draw up a report on an** ~ Unfallschaden melden; **to have a fatal** ~ tödlich verunglücken; **to meet with an** ~ Unfall haben (erleiden), verunglücken; **to prevent an** ~ Unfall verhüten; **to provide against** ~**s** Unfallverhütungsmaßnahmen ergreifen; **to report an** ~ **to the police** Unfall der Polizei melden; **to result from an** ~ aus einem Unfall herrühren, unfallbedingt sein; **to witness an** ~ bei einem Unfall zugegen sein;
~ **analysis** Unfallanalyse; ~ **annuity** Unfallrente; ~ **avoidance** Unfallvermeidung, -hütung; ~ **benefit** freiwillige Unfallzulage, Unfallentschädigung, -rente; ~ **black spot** typische Unfallstelle, Gefahrenstelle; ~ **book** *(Br.)* Unfallbuch [für Betriebsunfälle]; ~ **branch** *(insurance)* Gefahrenklasse; ~ **causes** Unfallgründe; ~ **claim** aus einem Unfall herrührende Schadenersatzforderung; ~ **costs** Unfallkosten; ~ **death** Unfalltod; ~**-free** unfallfrei; ~ **frequency** Unfallhäufigkeit; ~ **frequency rates** Unfall[häufigkeits]ziffern; ~ **hazard** Unfallsrisiko; ~ **indemnity** Unfallentschädigung; **[compulsory]** ~ **insurance** Unfall[zwangs]versicherung; **industrial** ~ **insurance** gewerbliche Unfallversicherung, Betriebsunfallversicherung; **personal** ~ **insurance** private Unfallversicherung; ~ **insurance contract** Unfallversicherungsvertrag; ~ **manager** Leiter einer Unfallversicherungsabteilung; ~ **payments** Unfallbeihilfe; ~ **policy** Unfallversicherungspolice; **general** ~ **portfolio** gesamtes Haftpflichtrisiko; ~ **prevention** Unfallverhütung; ~ **process** Unfallwahrscheinlichkeit; ~**-prone** unfallgefährdet, unfallanfällig; ~ **proneness** Unfallneigung, Unfallanfälligkeit; ~**-proof** unfallsicher; ~ **rates** Unfallziffern; ~ **recidivism** Unfallgefährdung; ~ **record (report)** Unfallbericht; ~ **record** unfallfreier Fahrrekord; ~ **reduction** Unfallbegrenzung; ~ **relief** Unfallunterstützung; ~ **report form** Unfallberichtsformular; ~ **risk** Unfallrisiko; ~ **severity** Unfallzeitverlust; ~ **source** Unfallquelle; ~ **statistics** Unfallstatistik; ~ **victim** Unfallopfer; **to reduce** ~ **waste** Unfallverluste begrenzen; ~ **welfare work** Unfallfürsorge.

accidental zufällig;
~ **collision damage** durch Autounfall entstandener Schaden; ~ **cover** *(mil.)* natürliche Deckung; ~ **damage** Unfallschaden; ~ **death** tödlicher Unfall, Unfalltod; ~ **injury** auf Unfall beruhender Schaden; ~ **killing** Unfalltod; ~ **loss** Unfallverlust; ~ **result** Zufallsergebnis; ~ **sampling** stichprobenartige Marktuntersuchung; ~ **visit** Gelegenheitsbesuch.

acclamation Zuruf, Akklamation.
to vote by ~ durch Zuruf abstimmen.

acclimatization Akklimatisierung.

acclimatize *(v.)* o. s. sich einleben (akklimatisieren).

accommodate *(v.) (adapt)* anpassen, *(conciliate)* [Streit] schlichten, *(fit out)* ausstatten, -rüsten, versorgen, *(furnish accommodation)* Raum bieten, unterbringen, bewirten, *(oblige)* Gefälligkeit erweisen;
~ o. s. sich fügen, schicken; ~ **s. o. with small change** jem. mit Kleingeld aushelfen; ~ **o. s. to circumstances** sich den Verhältnissen anpassen, sich auf die Umstände einstellen; ~ **a client** einem Kunden einen Dienst erweisen; ~ **conflicting interests** widerstreitende Interessen ausgleichen; ~ **differences** Mei-

nungsverschiedenheiten ausgleichen; ~ **with money** Geld leihen; ~ **one's statement to the fact** seine Darstellung mit den Tatsachen in Übereinstimmung bringen; ~ **local traffic** dem Ortsverkehr dienen; ~ **vessels of any draught** *(harbo(u)r)* Schiffe ohne Rücksicht auf den Tiefgang aufnehmen.

accommodated party Begünstigter.

accommodating gefällig, entgegen-, zuvorkommend, kulant, *(hospitable)* gastlich;
to be ~ Entgegenkommen zeigen, gefällig sein;
on ~ terms zu annehmbaren Bedingungen.

accommodation *(adaption)* Anpassung, *(convenience)* Bequemlichkeit, Komfort, *(favo(u)r)* Gefallen, Gefälligkeit, Hilfsbereitschaft, Kulanz, *(fitting out)* Ausrüstung, Ausstattung, Versorgung, *(loan)* finanzielle Unterstützung, *(lodgement, US)* Behausung, Unterbringung, Unterbringungsmöglichkeit, Unterkommen, -kunft, *(mil.)* Einquartierung, *(settlement)* Verständigung, Beilegung, Schlichtung, Ausgleich, Vergleich;
merely for ~ aus reiner Gefälligkeit;
average ~ Wohnraumunterbringung; **collective ~** Massenunterbringung; **group ~** Gruppenanpassung; **hotel ~** Hotelmöglichkeiten; **low-cost ~** billige Unterkunft; **married ~** Unterbringung für Verheiratete (ein Ehepaar); **rent-controlled ~** dem Mieterschutz unterliegende Wohnung; **rent-free ~** kostenlos zur Verfügung gestellte Unterkunft; **serviced ~** Unterbringung mit Bedienung; **single-room ~** Einzelzimmerreservierung; **sleeping ~** Schlafgelegenheit; **suitable alternative ~** zumutbare anderweitige Unterbringung;
~ to circumstances Anpassung an die Verhältnisse; **~ for clothing** Ankleidemöglichkeit; **~ arranged all on one floor** ebenerdig gelegener Wohn- und Versorgungsbereich; **~ of conflicting interests** Ausgleichung widerstreitender Interessen; **~ for the night** Nachtquartier; **~ in public housing** Unterbringung in Sozialwohnungen; **~ of a railway carriage** Laderaum eines Waggons; **~ provided of nominal rent** preiswerte Unterbringung;
to arrange for ~s für Unterkunft sorgen, Quartier beschaffen (besorgen); **to assist in finding ~s** bei der Wohnungssuche behilflich sein; **to come to an ~** Vergleich abschließen, zu einer gütlichen Verständigung kommen, sich verständigen; **to offer alternative ~** *(landlord)* für anderweitige Unterbringung sorgen; **to offer suitable alternative ~** ausreichenden und geeigneten anderen Wohnraum nachweisen; **to reserve ~** Hotelquartier besorgen; **to supply bank ~** bankmäßige Geschäfte besorgen;
~ acceptance Gefälligkeitsakzept, Gefälligkeitsannahme; **~ address** Hilfs-, Deck-, Gefälligkeitsadresse; **~ allowance** Wohnungsgeldzuschuß; **~ bill (draft)** Keller-, Gefälligkeitswechsel; **~ endorsement** Gefälligkeitsgiro; **~ endorsement loan** Kredit gegen Wechselbürgschaft; **~ endorser** Gefälligkeitsgirant; **~ ladder** Fallreep; **~ land** Spekulationsbauplatz; **~ loan** Überbrückungskredit; **~ maker** Aussteller eines Gefälligkeitswechsels, Gefälligkeitsaussteller; **~ note** *(Br.)* Gefälligkeitswechsel; **~ paper** Gefälligkeitspapier; **~ party** Gefälligkeitspartei; **~ quarters** Aufenthaltsraum; **~ registry** *(Br.)* Wohnungsnachweis; **~ road** private Zufahrtsstraße; **~ subsidies** Unterbringungszuschüsse; **~ train** *(US dial.)* Bummel-, Vorortzug; **~ unit** Wohnungseinheit; **~ works** Bahnanlagen für Gleisanlieger.

accompany *(v.)* begleiten, geleiten;
~ an account with receipts Abrechnung mit Quittungen belegen.

accompanying | address Begleitadresse; **~ colo(u)r** Schmuckfarbe; **~ documents** Begleitpapiere; **~ fire** *(mil.)* Sperrfeuer; **~ letter** Begleitbrief.

accomplice Mittäter, -schuldiger, Komplize, Helfershelfer, Gehilfe, Mitbeteiligter, Teilnehmer an einem Verbrechen.

accomplish *(v.)* *(finish)* vollenden, fertigstellen, beenden, bewältigen, *(make complete)* vervollständigen, *(perform)* ausführen, durchführen, bewerkstelligen, ausrichten, bewirken, effektuieren, zustande (zuwege) bringen, vollbringen;
~ just about nothing so gut wie nichts zustande bringen.

accomplished vollkommen, vollständig, fertig, *(trained)* perfekt ausgebildet;
~ fact vollendete Tatsache; **~ scholar** gebildeter Gelehrter; **~ villain** ausgemachter Schurke.

accomplishment Vollendung, *(achievement)* Leistung, *(performance)* Ausführung, Durchführung, Durchsetzung, Fertigstellung, Erfüllung, Bewältigung, Vollbringung;
~s Fertigkeiten, Leistungen, Kenntnisse;
industrial ~ wirtschaftlicher Erfolg.

accord *(v.)* Übereinstimmung, *(arrangement)* Abkommen, Abmachung, *(international law)* formloses Abkommen, Vereinbarung, *(settlement)* Vergleich;
of one's own ~ freiwillig, aus freiem Willen; **in ~ with** im Einklang mit; **with one ~** einstimmig;
~ and satisfaction Hingabe erfüllungshalber, vergleichsweise Erfüllung, außergerichtlicher Vergleich;
~ (v.) sich verständigen, *(concede)* zugestehen, einräumen, gewähren, bewilligen;
~ a commission Provision gewähren (einräumen); **~ a petition** einem Gesuch stattgeben; **~ a respite** Frist einräumen (gewähren, zugestehen), Stundung gewähren, stunden;
to be of ~ *(accounts)* übereinstimmen.

accordable vereinbar.

accordance Übereinstimmung, Einklang;
in ~ with laut, in Übereinstimmung (im Einvernehmen) mit; **in ~ with the accounts (books)** rechnungsmäßig; **in ~ with your instructions** weisungsgemäß; **in ~ with regulations** laut Vorschrift;
to be in ~ übereinstimmen, konform gehen.

accordant with, according to gemäß, übereinstimmend mit, nach Maßgabe.

according | to age nach dem Alter; **~ to the best authorities** in Übereinstimmung mit den Experten; **~ to circumstances** nach Lage der Dinge; **~ to contract** vertragsmäßig; **~ to directions** vorschriftsmäßig; **~ to law** von Rechtswegen, gesetzesmäßig; **~ to the orders** laut Verfügung; **~ to plan** planmäßig; **~ to their rank** ihrem Rang entsprechend.

accordion folding Leporellofalzung.

accost *(v.)* s. o. an j. herantreten.

account Soll und Haben, Konto, *(~ stated)* Kontobestätigung, *(advantage)* Vorteil, Gewinn, *(advertising agency)* Kunden-, Werbeetat, *(bill)* Rechnung, *(calculation)* Berechnung, *(client)* Kunde einer Werbeagentur, *(financial statement)* Jahresabschluß, *(against guardian)* Rechtsverfahren zwecks Rechnungslegung, *(invoice)* Faktura, *(importance)* Wichtigkeit, Ansehen, *(list)* Liste, Verzeichnis, Aufstellung, Übersicht, *(reason)* Grund, *(report)* Bericht, Erzählung, Darstellung, Beschreibung, *(statement of administration)* Rechnungslage, Rechenschaftsbericht, *(stock exchange)* Liquidationstermin, Abrechnungszeitraum, *(valuation)* Wertschätzung, Ansehen, Geltung;
as per ~ laut Rechnung (Aufstellung); **by all ~s** wie verlautet; **by his own ~** nach seiner eigenen Darstellung (Beschreibung); **for the ~ of** à conto; **for ~ only** *(check)* nur zur Verrechnung; **for one's own ~** auf Eigenrechnung; **for my sole ~** auf meine alleinige Rechnung; **for third ~** für fremde Rechnung; **for ~ and risk** auf Rechnung und Gefahr; **in full discharge of our ~** zum Ausgleich unserer Rechnung; **of no ~** ohne Belang (Bedeutung); **in settlement of an ~** zum Ausgleich eines Kontos; **not on any ~** unter keiner Bedingung; **not taken into ~** unberücksichtigt; **on ~** auf Rechnung (Abschlag), à conto; **on former ~** auf alte Rechnung; **on (for) joint ~** auf gemeinschaftliche (gemeinsame) Rechnung; **on no ~** um keinen Preis, auf keinen Fall; **on new ~** auf neue Rechnung; **~ payee only** *(check)* nur zur Verrechnung; **[as] per ~ rendered** laut eingeschickter Rechnung (Aufstellung); **received on ~** in Gegenrechnung empfangen, à conto; **taking all things into ~** bei Berücksichtigung des ganzen Sachverhalts; **to s. one's ~** auf jds. Rechnung; **to balance our ~s** zur Berichtigung unserer Rechnung (Bücher); **when opening an ~** bei der Eröffnung eines Kontos, bei Kontoeröffnung;
~s *(business records)* Bücher, Buchhaltungsunterlagen, Rechnungswerk, *(value)* Wert;
active ~ Konto mit hohen Umsätzen, umsatzträchtiges Konto; **adjunct ~** Hilfskonto; **adjustment of property ~** Wertberichtigungskonto; **advance ~** Vorschußkonto; **aging ~s** Einteilung der Außenstände nach Fälligkeit; **annual ~** Jahresabschluß; **appropriation ~** Bereitstellungskonto; **asset ~** Bestandskonto; **assigned ~** abgetretenes (zediertes) Konto; **~ attached** Konto beschlagnahmt; **auxiliary ~** Hilfskonto; **bad-debts collected ~** Konto für nachträglich eingegangene Dubiosen; **balanced ~** ausgeglichenes Konto; **bank[ing] ~** Bankkonto; **bear ~** Baissekonto, -position; **~ bearing [no] interest** [un]verzinsliches Konto; **benevolent ~** Unterstützungskonto; **bills overdue ~** Konto überfälliger Wechsel; **bills payable ~** Akzeptkonto; **bills receivable ~** Rimessenkonto; **blocked ~** Sperrguthaben, -konto, gesperrtes Konto; **broken ~** umsatzloses (unbewegtes) Konto; **bull ~** Hausseposition; **buying ~** Einkaufskonto; **capital ~** Kapitalkonto; **carriage ~** Frachtkonto; **cash ~** Kassenkonto; **checking ~** *(US)* Giro-

konto, laufendes (tägliches, offenes) Konto; **circumstantial ~** ausführlicher Bericht; **clear ~s** bezahlte Rechnungen; **clearing ~** Verrechnungskonto, Girokonto; **closed ~** [ab]geschlossenes Konto; **closed-end ~** *(depreciation method)* geschlossener Bestand; **commission ~** Provisionskonto, -rechnung; **companion ~** Nebenkonto; **consignment ~** Konsignationskonto; **consolidated ~** Konzernkonto; **consolidated ~s** konsolidierter Konzernabschluß; **contingency ~** Delkrederekonto; **continued ~** Übertrag [in Büchern]; **continuing ~** laufendes Konto, Kontokorrentkonto; **contra ~** Gegenkonto; **control ~** Gegenkonto; **controlling ~** Gegen-, Kontrollkonto; **corporate ~** Gesellschafts-, Firmenkonto; **cost ~** Unkostenkonto; **credit ~** laufendes Konto mit ständigem Kreditsaldo, Kreditkonto; **currency ~** Valuta-, Devisen-, Währungskonto; **current ~** laufende Rechnung, laufendes (tägliches, offenes) Konto, *(US)* Kontokorrent-, Girokonto, Sichteinlage, *(balance of payment)* Leistungsbilanz; **customer's ~** lebendes Konto, Kundenkonto; **dead ~** umsatzloses (unbewegliches) Konto; **debit ~** Debitoren-, Debetkonto, Schuldkonto, Soll; **deficiency ~** Verlustkonto; **delinquent ~** rückständiges Konto; **deposit ~** Depositen-, Guthaben-, Hinterlegungskonto, *(Br.)* Sparkonto, *(US)* festangelegtes Geld, Festgeld, Konto Termineinlagen; **depositor's ~** Kundenkonto; **depreciation ~** Konto Abschreibungen, Abschreibungskonto; **detailed ~** eingehender Bericht, *(itemized account)* spezifizierte Rechnung; **discount ~** Disagiokonto; **~ dormant ~** umsatzloses (unbewegtes) Konto; **doubtful ~s** dubiose Guthaben; **drawing ~** *(US)* Konto für Privatentnahmen, Scheckkonto, Verrechnungskonto, Girokonto; **duplicate ~** doppeltes Konto, Gegenkonto; **earmarked ~** zweckgebundenes Konto; **established ~** fester Kunde; **exact ~** genauer Bericht; **executorship ~** Testamentsvollstreckerkonto; **expense ~** Spesen-, [Un]kosten-, Ausgabenkonto; **eye-witness ~** Augenzeugenbericht; **fabricated ~** gefälschte Rechnung; **fictitious ~** fingiertes Konto, Deckkonto; **filled ~s** *(Scot.)* unwidersprochene Kontokorrentrechnung; **final ~** [Ab]schlußrechnung; **financial ~** Geschäftsbuchführung; **fixed-assets ~** Konto der Anlagewerte; **freight ~** Frachtrechnung, -nota; **frozen ~** eingefrorenes Konto; **furniture and fixtures ~** Inventar-, Sachkonto; **garnished ~** beim Drittschuldner gepfändetes Konto; **general ~** allgemeines Konto, Hauptkonto; **giro ~** *(Br.)* Postscheckkonto; **goods ~** Warenkonto; **group ~s** Konzernabschluß; **guaranty ~** Sicherstellungskonto; **half-yearly ~** Halbjahresrechnung; **head-office ~** Konto der Hauptniederlassung; **husband-and-wife joint ~** eheliches Gemeinschaftskonto; **impersonal ~** *(Br.)* unpersönliches Konto, Sachkonto; **inaccurate ~** unrichtige Rechnung; **inactive ~** umsatzloses (unbewegtes) Konto; **income ~** Ertragsrechnung; **income and expenditure ~s** Einnahme-Ausgabenkonto; **income statement ~** Erfolgskonto; **individual ~** Einzelkonto; **industrial ~s** Industriekundschaft; **inland ~** im Inland geführtes Konto; **inoperative ~** *(Br.)* umsatzloses (unbewegtes) Konto; **instalment ~** Abzahlungskonto; **prepaid insurance ~** Versicherungsvorauszahlungskonto; **intercompany ~s** interne Konten, Konten von Organgesellschaften; **interest ~** Zinsenkonto; **interest-bearing ~** zinstragendes Konto; **interim ~s** Zwischenabschluß; **intermediate ~** Zwischenbericht; **inventory ~** Sach-, Inventarkonto; **investment ~** Beteiligungskonto, *(National Savings Bank, Br.)* Postsparkonto; **itemized ~** spezifizierte (detaillierte) Rechnung; **joint ~** Gemeinschafts-, Konsortial-, Metakonto; **ledger ~** Hauptbuchkonto; **liability ~** Konto für kurzfristige Verbindlichkeiten; **loan ~** Kreditkonto, Darlehnskonto; **special loan ~** Kreditsonderkonto; **long ~** *(US)* Engagements der Hausseepartei; **loose-leaf ~s** Loseblattbuchhaltung; **manufacturing ~** Fabrikationskonto; **margin ~** *(US)* Einschußkonto; **mixed ~** gemischtes Konto; **mutual current ~** laufende gegenseitige Rechnung; **monthly ~** monatliche Rechnung, *(Br.)* Kunden-, Anschreibungskonto; **national ~s** volkswirtschaftliche Gesamtrechnung; **national giro ~** *(Br.)* Postscheckkonto; **negotiated order of withdrawal ~s** *(US)* verzinsliche Sichteinlagen; **next ~** nächste [Ab]rechnung, kommende Monatsabrechnung; **no ~** kein Konto; **nominal ~** totes Konto, Sachkonto; **non-interest-bearing ~** unverzinsliches Konto; **non-resident ~** Devisenausländerkonto; **numbered ~** Nummernkonto; **omnibus ~** Sammelkonto; **open ~** *(US)* laufende Rechnung, Kontokorrent, *(not closed)* offenstehendes (laufendes) Konto; **open-end ~** *(depreciation method)* offener Bestand; **operating ~** Gewinn- und Verlustrechnung; **operating ~s** Betriebsbuchführung; **negotiated order of withdrawal ~s** *(US)* [etwa] verzinsliche Sichteinlagen; **ordinary ~** *(National Savings Bank, Br.)* Postscheckkonto; **other ~s** *(balance sheet)* sonstige Forderungen; **our ~** *(US, balance sheet)* Nostroguthaben; **outstanding ~** offene Rechnung; **long outstanding ~** lange ausstehende Rechnung; **overdrawn ~** überzogenes Konto; **overextended ~** *(US)* ungenügend gedecktes Konto; **overhead charges ~** Gemeinkostenkonto, Handlungsunkostenkonto; **~s paid up** *(balance sheet)* geleistete Anzahlungen; **participating ~** Konsortial-, Beteiligungskonto; **participation ~** gemeinsames Konto; **partnership ~** Teilhaber-, Gesellschafterkonto; **past-due ~** überfällige (längst fällige) Rechnung; **~s payable** ausstehende Rechnungen, *(US, balance sheet)* Kreditoren, [Kreditoren aus] Buchforderungen; **other ~s payable** *(balance sheet)* sonstige Verbindlichkeiten; **~s payable for goods received and services accepted** *(balance sheet, US)* mittel- und kurzfristige Verbindlichkeiten; **~s payable for purchases and deliveries** *(balance sheet, US)* Verbindlichkeiten aus Lieferungen und Leistungen; **personal ~** Kunden-, Kreditkonto, *(private account)* Privatkonto; **post-office transfer ~** Postscheckkonto; **postal checking ~** *(US)* Postscheckkonto; **premises ~** Liegenschafts-, Immobilienkonto; **private ~** privates (persönliches) Konto, Geheim-, Privatkonto; **produce loan ~** Warenkreditkonto; **pro-forma ~** Proformarechnung, fingierte Rechnung; **profit and loss ~** Gewinn- und Verlustrechnung, Erfolgsrechnung; **profit and loss appropriation ~** Gewinn- und Verlustverteilungskonto; **property ~** Liegenschafts-, Immobilien-, Vermögens-, Anlagekonto; **proprietorship ~** Kapitalkonto; **provisional ~** vorläufiges Konto; **public ~** Konto für Gelder der öffentlichen Hand; **public ~s** öffentliches Rechnungswesen; **purchase ~** Wareneingangskonto, -rechnung; **real ~** Liegenschafts-, Grundstückskonto, Bestandskonto; **real ~s** Sachkonten; **realization ~** Liquidationskonto; **~s receivable** *(US, balance sheet)* ausstehende Gelder, Forderungsbestand, [Debitoren aus] Buchforderungen, ausstehende Forderungen; **aging ~s receivable** *(US)* Debitorenaufstellung nach Fälligkeit; **~s receivable discounted** *(US)* zedierter Debitorenstand, Verpflichtungen aus abgetretenen Debitoren; **pledged ~s receivable** *(US)* abgetretene Kundenforderungen; **~ receivable from affiliates** *(US)* Forderungen an verbundene Unternehmen; **~ receivable resulting from loans** *(US)* Forderungen aus gewährten Krediten; **~s receivable for sales and services** *(US)* Forderungen aus Lieferungen und Leistungen; **~ rendered** vorgelegte (ausstehende) Rechnung, *(statement)* Rechenschaftsbericht; **reserve ~** Rücklagenkonto; **reserve interest ~** Konto zweifelhafter Zinseingänge; **residuary ~s** Rechnungslegung über den Nachlaß; **revenue ~** Ertrags-, Gewinn- und Verlustkonto; **revolving ~** revolvierendes Konto; **~ ruled off** abgeschlossenes Konto; **running ~** laufende (offene) Rechnung, Kontokorrent, Girokonto; **salary ~** Gehaltskonto; **sales ~** Verkaufskonto, Warenausgangskonto; **returned sales and allowances ~** Retouren und Nachlaßkonto; **salt ~** gepfefferte Rechnung; **savings ~** Sparkonto, Sparguthaben; **savings-bank ~** Sparkassenkonto; **national savings ~** *(Br.)* Postsparkonto; **secured ~** abgesichertes (gedecktes) Konto; **securities ~** Stücke-, Depotkonto; **security ~** Wertpapier-, Depotkonto; **semiannual ~** Halbjahresrechnung; **separate ~s** *(pension scheme)* getrennte Anlagen; **settled ~** anerkannte Rechnungslegung, anerkannter Rechnungsabschluß, beglichene Rechnung, abgerechnetes Konto, regulierte Rechnung, schriftlich anerkanntes Kontokorrent; **settlement ~** Liquidationskonto; **share ~** Aktien-, Kapitalkonto; **short ~** *(Br.)* Baisseposition, Übersicht; **~ showing a credit balance** Guthabenkonto; **~ showing a debit balance** Verlustkonto; **simulated ~** fingierte Rechnung, Proformarechnung; **six-month ~** Halbjahresrechnung; **sole ~** alleinige Rechnung; **solicitor's client's ~** [Rechtsanwalts]anderkonto; **special ~** Sonderkonto; **special checking ~** *(US)* Scheckkonto mit Buchungsbelastung; **special drawing ~** *(International Monetary Fund)* Fonds im Rahmen der Sonderziehungsrechte; **specified ~** detaillierte Rechnung; **stated ~** bestätigter Kontoauszug, Kontoauszugsbestätigung, Schuldanerkenntnis; **sterling ~** Pfundkonto, Pfundguthaben; **stock ~** *(capital)* Kapitalkonto, *(inventory)* Lagerkonto, *(securities)* Effektenrechnung; **store ~** Lagerrechnung; **subsidiary ~** Unterkonto; **sundries (sundry persons') ~** *(Br.)* Konto für (pro) Diverse; **suspense ~** vorläufiges (transitorisches) Konto, Interims-, Berichtigungs-, Zwischenkonto; **suspense interest ~** *(Br.)* Konto zweifelhafter Zinseingänge; **syndicate ~** Beteiligungskonto; **their ~** *(US)* Vostroguthaben; **third-party ~** fremde Rechnung; **thrift ~** Sparkonto; **time ~** *(stock exchange)* Terminkonto; **trading ~** Firmenverkaufs-, Lieferkonto, Warenverkaufskonto, Betriebskonto; **trading ~s** Geschäftsbücher;

transferred ~ Übertrag; **transit** ~ Übergangskonto; **travelling** ~ Abrechnungskonto für Geschäftsreisende; **uncollectable** ~ nicht beitreibbare Rechnung; **undeclared foreign bank** ~ nicht angegebenes Auslandskonto; **unsecured** ~ ungedecktes Konto; **unsettled** ~ offenstehende Rechnung; **valuation** ~ Wertberichtigungskonto; **wage** ~ Lohnkonto; **warehouse** ~ Lagerrechnung, -konto; **well regarded** ~ als sicher angesehenes Konto; **working** ~ Betriebskonto; **worksheet** ~s (US) Loseblattbuchhaltung; **last year's** ~ vorjähriges Konto; **yearly** ~ Jahresrechnung;

~s **agreed upon** festgestellter Rechnungsabschluß; ~ **in arrears** Rechnungsrückstand; ~ **of assets and liabilities** Gewinn- und Verlustrechnung; ~ **in bank** Bankkonto; ~ **of a bankrupt** Bankkonto eines Gemeinschuldners; ~ **with an undischarged bankrupt** Konto eines nicht entlasteten Gemeinschuldners; ~ **of charges (costs)** Gebührenaufstellung, [Un]kostenkonto, Spesenrechnung, Kostenrechnung, [Kosten]liquidation; ~ **of conveyance** Speditionskonto; ~s **with creditors** Gläubigerkonten; ~s **of customers** Kundenkonten; ~ **of customs** Zollrechnung; ~s **having a debit balance** debitorische Konten; ~ **of disbursements** Auslagennota; ~ **of exchange** Wechselkonto; ~ **of expenses** Unkostenkonto; ~ **of goods purchased** Einkaufsrechnung; ~ **of interrogation** Vernehmungsprotokoll; ~ **of a journey** Reisebericht; **the** ~ **of Her Majesty's Exchequer** (Br.) Staatskonto bei der englischen Nationalbank; ~s **of the National Giro** (Br.) Postscheckkonten; ~ **opened without security** Blankokredit; ~ **in participation** gemeinsames Konto; ~ **[of] payee** (check) nur zur Gutschrift auf Konto des genannten Zahlungsempfängers; ~ **of proceedings** Verhandlungsbericht; ~ **of redraft** Rückrechnung eines Wechsels; ~ **of re-exchange** Rikambionota; ~ **of return** Rückrechnung; ~s **to be settled every six months** halbjährlicher Kontoabschluß; ~ **of settlement** Abschlußrechnung; ~ **for settlement with travel(l)ers** Abrechnungskonto für Geschäftsreisende; ~ **for tools and implements** Gerätekonto; ~ **of travelling expenses** (Br.) Reisekosten-, Spesenabrechnung; ~ **of a voyage** Reisebericht, Bericht über eine Seereise; ~ **of the winding up** Liquidationsabrechnung;

~ (v.) (give an account) Rechnung ablegen, abrechnen (place to account) buchen, (return unsold tickets) bei der Abrechnung zurückgeben;

~ **for** Rechenschaft ablegen; ~ **to** (auditing) Buchführung ermöglichen; ~ **for the bulk of goods** Massenabsatz von Erzeugnissen beeinflussen; ~ **for 30% of consumption** 30% des Verbrauchs betragen; ~ **for one's expenses** seine Spesen abrechnen;

to act on one's own ~ auf eigene Faust handeln; **to add to an** ~ einem Konto zuschlagen; **to adjust an** ~ Konto ausgleichen; **to age** ~s Konten nach ihrer Fälligkeit aufgliedern; **to agree** ~s Rechnungen in Übereinstimmung bringen; **to allow a rebate on an** ~ Rechnungsnachlaß gewähren; **to appear in an** ~ auf einer Rechnung stehen; **to approve an** ~ Konto entlasten; **to attach an** ~ Kontoguthaben pfänden; **to audit** ~s Rechnungen (Konten) überprüfen; **to balance an** ~ Konto saldieren (ausgleichen, abrechnen), Saldo eines Kontos ziehen; **to be assigned an** ~ Konto zugeteilt bekommen; **to be a no-**~ eine Null sein; **to be quick at** ~s gut kalkulieren können; **to block an** ~ Guthaben (Konto) sperren; **to bring** ~s **up to date** Konten auf den neuesten Stand bringen; **to buy for the** ~ auf Termin kaufen; **to buy s. th. on one's own** ~ etw. auf eigene Rechnung kaufen; **to call s. o. to** ~ von jem. Rechenschaft fordern; **to call over** ~s Konten ablesen; **to call up an** ~ Konto kündigen; **to carry to** ~ in Rechnung stellen (bringen); **to carry to new** ~ auf neue Rechnung vortragen; **to charge against an** ~ Konto belasten; **to charge [forward] to new** ~ auf neue Rechnung setzen; **to churn captive** ~s nicht für den Markt bestimmte Anlagekonten melden; **to clean up** ~s Konten bereinigen; **to clear** ~s abrechnen; **to close an** ~ Konto abschließen (aufheben, löschen); **to close and rule an** ~ Konto abschließen; **to comprise in an** ~ einrechnen; **to control special** ~s **on an imprest fund basis** Sonderkonten nach Portokassenrichtlinien überwachen; **to cook the** ~s bei der Kontoführung Unregelmäßigkeiten begehen; **to correct an** ~ Rechnung durch Nachrechnen berichtigen; **to credit an** ~ einem Konto gutschreiben, Konto erkennen; **to conduct a current** ~ Kontokorrentkonto führen; **to debate an** ~Rechnung anfechten; **to debit an** ~ Konto belasten; **to disallow an** ~ Rechnung zurückweisen; **to discharge an** ~ Konto ausgleichen (glattstellen), Rechnung begleichen; **to dot** ~s Rechnungsposten nachprüfen; **to draw on an** ~ von einem Konto abheben, Kontoabhebung vornehmen; **to draw up an** ~ Rechnung aufstellen; **to eliminate an** ~ (US) Konto

auflösen; **to enter in** ~ in Rechnung stellen; **to equalize** ~s Konten ausgleichen; **to even up an** ~ **in funds** Konto regulieren; **to examine an** ~ Rechnung (Konto) prüfen; **to find one's** ~ **in s. th.** bei etw. profitieren; **to foot up an** ~ Rechnungsbeträge addieren; **to freeze an** ~ Guthaben sperren; **to garnish an** ~ Kontoguthaben pfänden; **to get one's** ~s **square** seine Konten in Ordnung bringen; **to give** ~ Bericht erstatten, Rechenschaft (Rechnung) ablegen, abrechnen, ausweisen; **to give an** ~ **of one's journey** Reisebericht erstatten; **to give a circumstantial** ~ in allen Einzelheiten erzählen; **to give a good** ~ **of o. s.** sich bewähren; **to give an** ~ **to an attorney for collection** ausstehende Rechnung einem Anwalt zum Inkasso übertragen; **to go over an** ~ Konto durchsehen (überprüfen); **to handle an** ~ Werbeetat verantwortlich bearbeiten; **to have an** ~ **with a bank** Bankkonto haben, Konto bei einer Bank haben (führen); **to have an amount credited to s. one's** ~ Betrag auf jds. Konto anweisen (überweisen); **to have a current** ~ in laufender Rechnung (im Kontokorrentverkehr) stehen; **to have a current** ~ **opened** laufende Rechnung eröffnen; **to hold an** ~ **with a bank** Konto bei einer Bank unterhalten; **to hold an** ~ **under current check card arrangements** über sein Konto mittels Scheckkarte verfügen können; **to include in the** ~ mit einrechnen; **to initial** ~s Rechnungen abzeichnen; **to itemize an** ~ einzelne Rechnungsposten angeben; **to invest one's money to good** ~ sein Geld gut anlegen; **to keep for one's own** ~ für eigene Rechnung bezahlen; **to keep the** ~s ordentliche Buchführung unterhalten, Bücher führen, buchführen; **to keep an** ~ **with** Konto haben bei; **to keep an** ~ **of expenses** über Ausgaben Buch führen; **to keep a current** ~ **with s. o.** im Kontokorrentverkehr stehen; **to keep one's** ~ **within reasonable limits** sein Konto nur begrenzt überziehen; **to keep separate** ~s getrennte Rechnung haben; **to keep an** ~ **under constant observation** Kontostand laufend überwachen; **to keep a strict** ~ **of the expenses** Spesen genauestens überwachen; **to leave out of** ~ außer Betracht lassen; **to look over an** ~ Rechnung durchsehen; **to maintain an** ~ Konto unterhalten; **to make** ~s **agree** Konten abstimmen (in Übereinstimmung bringen); **to make out (up) an** ~ Rechnung ausstellen (aufstellen); **to make up one's** ~s Bilanz aufstellen, Jahresabschluß machen; **to make an extract of an** ~ Kontoauszug anfertigen; **to make up an** ~ **of the winding up** Liquidationsbericht vorlegen; **to merge** ~s Konten zusammenwerfen; **to nurse an** ~ (Br.) Konto sanieren; **to open an** ~ **[with]** Konto anlegen, Konto (Rechnung) eröffnen [bei]; **to open up one's own** ~ auf eigene Rechnung arbeiten; **to open an** ~ **with a bank** sich ein Bankkonto einrichten, Konto bei einer Bank eröffnen; **to operate on own** ~ auf eigene Rechnung betreiben; **to operate upon another person's** ~ über ein fremdes Konto verfügen; **to overdraw an** ~ Konto überziehen; **to pass an** ~ Rechnung in Ordnung befinden; **to pass to** ~ in Rechnung stellen; **to pass (place) to the credit of an** ~ einem Konto kreditieren (gutschreiben); **to pass (place) to the debit of an** ~ Konto debitieren (belasten); **to pay an** ~ Rechnung bezahlen; **to pay on** ~ anzahlen, Anzahlung leisten; **to pay into an** ~ auf ein Konto einzahlen; **to peruse an** ~ Rechnung durchgehen; **to place to** ~ in Rechnung stellen; **to place an** ~ **in funds** Konto dotieren (alimentieren); **to place an** ~ **with an attorney** ausstehende Rechnung einem Anwalt übergeben; **to place to new** ~ auf neue Rechnung vortragen; **to pool** ~s Konten zusammenlegen; **to prepare** ~s bilanzieren; **to present an** ~ Rechnung vorlegen; **to purchase on** ~ auf Rechnung (Kredit) kaufen; **to put to an** ~ einem Konto zurechnen (zuschreiben); **to put an** ~ **right** Rechnung in Ordnung bringen; **to put down to s. one's** ~ jem. in Anrechnung bringen; **to put paid to s. one's** ~ (fam.) jds. Rechnung begleichen; **to put to** ~ **every single item** jeden Posten verrechnen; **to readjust** ~s Konten in Übereinstimmung bringen; **to release blocked** ~s gesperrte Konten freigeben, Kontensperre aufheben; **to render an** ~ Bericht erstatten; **to render an** ~ **[of]** Rechnung legen [über], Abrechnung erteilen; **to run up an** ~ [Schuld]konto anwachsen (anschreiben) lassen; **to run up an** ~ **with a shop** auf Rechnung in einem Geschäft einkaufen, anschreiben lassen; **to salt an** ~ gepfefferte Rechnung aufmachen; **to send one's** ~s **for audit** seine Abrechnung zur Revision vorlegen; **to send out** ~s Rechnungen verschicken; **to set down to s. one's** ~ auf jem. Rechnung setzen; **to settle an** ~ Rechnung (Konto) begleichen (ausgleichen, glattstellen), abrechnen; **to solicit for an** ~ um Einrichtung eines Kontos nachsuchen; **to sign on s. one's** ~ über jem. Konto verfügen; **to square** ~s Konten ausgleichen; **to state an** ~ Rechnung spezifizieren; **to stop an** ~ Konto sperren, Kontensperrung vornehmen; **to straighten an** ~ Rechnung in Ordnung bringen; **to subjoin a statement of** ~ **for**

audit Kontoauszug zur Prüfung beifügen; **to take ~ of** in Rechnung stellen; **to take due ~** gebührend berücksichtigen; **to take into ~** berücksichtigen, einrechnen, in Betracht ziehen; **to take no ~ of** nicht beachten; **to take on future ~s** auf zukünftige Rechnung kaufen; **to take s. o. sufficiently into ~** j. in seine Kalkulationen entsprechend einbeziehen; **to tamper with the ~s** bei der Kontenführung Unregelmäßigkeiten begehen; **to trade for own ~** auf eigene Rechnung abschließen; **to turn to ~** gut ausnutzen; **to turn everything to ~** aus allem Vorteil ziehen; **to use an ~ for trade (business) purposes** Geschäftsverkehr über ein Konto abwickeln; **to verify an ~** Rechnung prüfen, Richtigkeit eines Kontos bestätigen; **to wipe off old ~s** alte Rechnungen erledigen; **to withdraw one's ~** sein Konto auflösen; **to withdraw from an ~** Kontoabhebung vornehmen; **to write out an ~** Rechnung ausschreiben; **special ~ agreement** besondere Kontoführungsvereinbarung; **~ analysis** Kostenanalyse; **~ balance** Kontoausgleich, Kontosaldo; **~ book** Kontobuch, Geschäfts-, Handelsbücher; **~s opened and closed book** (Br.) Kontenverzeichnis; **outstanding ~ book** Schuldbuch; **to muddle ~ books** Buchführung durcheinanderbringen; **current ~ business** Kontokorrentgeschäft; **~ card** Kontokarte; **~ [-carrying] charges** Kontospesen, Kontoführungsgebühr; **~ classification** Kontenaufgliederung; **~ clerk** Fakturist; **~s control** Rechnungskontrolle; **current ~ creditors** Kreditoren in laufender Rechnung; **current ~ customer** Kontokorrentkunde; **~ day** (stock exchange) Zahl-, Liquidations-, Abrechnungstag; **~s department** Buchhaltung; **~ deposits** Kontoguthaben, -einlagen; **~ duty** (Br.) Vermächtnissteuer, Nachlaßsteuer [für Gegenstände über 100 £]; **~ executive** (advertising agency) Bearbeiter von Kundenwerbungen, Sachbearbeiter eines Werbeetats, Kundenbearbeiter, -sachbearbeiter, -berater, -betreuer, Verbindungs-, Kontaktmann, Kontakter, (brokerage) Vertreter eines Maklerhauses; **~ files** Kontounterlagen; **~ folder** Kundenakte; **~ form** Kontoblatt; **~ heading** Kontobezeichnung; **~ holder** Kontoinhaber, Kontobesitzer, (National Giro, Br.) Inhaber eines Postscheckkontos; **~ manager** Kontoführer, Kundenbetreuer; **~ mandate** Kontoauftrag; **~ name** Kontoname; **~ number** Kontonummer; **~ operations** Kontoverwendung; **~ passbook** Kontobuch; **~s payable** (US) Kreditoren [aus Buch-, Lieferantenschulden]; **~s payable clerk** (US) Kreditorenbuchhalter; **~s payable department** (US) Kreditorenbuchhaltung; **~s payable ledger** (US) Kontokorrentbuch; **~ payee only** (Br.) nur zur Gutschrift des Zahlungsempfängers; **~ period** Rechnungszeit; **~ price** Ultimopreis; **~purchases** (A/P) Einkaufsabrechnung [des Einkaufskommissionärs]; **~s receivable clerk** (US) Debitorenbuchhalter; **~s receivable department** (US) Debitorenbuchhaltung; **~s receivable financing** (US) Finanzierung durch Abtretung der Debitoren; **~s receivable ledger** (US) Kontokorrentbuch, -konto; **~s receivable loan** (US) Kontokorrentkredit; **~s receivable statement** (US) Kontoauszug; **~ records** Kundenunterlagen; **~ sales** (US) Verkaufsabrechnung [eines Kommissionärs]; **~ render** Klage auf Rechnungslegung; **proforma ~ sales** fingierte Verkaufsrechnung; **~ saving** Kontensparen; **~ solicitation service** Bonitätsauskunft; **~ statement** Kontoauszug; **~ statement** (Br.) Rechnungsaufstellung; **~ supervisor** Kontenbearbeiter, Kontoführer, (advertising agency) leitender Kontakter; **to arrange ~ terms** Kundenkreditkonto eröffnen; **to grant open ~ terms** Kundenkreditkonto zugestehen; **~ title** Kontobezeichnung, -kopf, -überschrift; **~ transactions** Kontobewegungen; **~ turnover** Kontoumsatz; **~ year** Rechnungs-, Wirtschaftsjahr.

accountable haftbar, verantwortlich, nachweis-, rechenschaftspflichtig, (law) zurechnungsfähig;
~ to parliament dem Parlament verantwortlich;
to be ~ Rechenschaft schuldig sein, (bookkeeping) zur vollständigen Buchführung verpflichtet sein; **to be ~ to s. o.** jem. Rechenschaft ablegen müssen; **to be ~ for duty on a gift** schenkungssteuerpflichtig sein; **to be ~ for a sum of money** über einen Geldbetrag Rechnung abzulegen haben; **to hold ~** verantwortlich machen;
~ condition (event) Geschäftsvorfall, Buchungsvorgang; **~ person** Rechnungsleger; **~ receipt** Empfangs-, Belegquittung, Buchungsbeleg; **~ warrant** Auszahlungsanweisung.

accountability (employee) Haftung des Erfüllungsgehilfen, (liability) Haftpflicht, Verantwortlichkeit, (liability to give account) Rechenschafts-, Rechnungslegungspflicht, (measure of liability) Haftungsumfang;
management ~ Verantwortlichkeit der Betriebsführung; **property ~** Rechnungslegungspflicht über ein Vermögen; **~ unit** Umfang der Haftpflicht, Haftungsumfang.

accountancy Buchführungs-, Rechnungswesen, Buchführung, -haltung;
~ adjustment Buchkorrektur; **~ body** Gremium von Wirtschaftsprüfern; **~ field** Buchführungsgebiet; **~ firm** Wirtschaftsprüfungsgesellschaft; **~ practice** Wirtschaftsprüferpraxis; **~ profession** Wirtschaftsprüferberuf; **~ qualification** Wirtschaftsprüferausbildung; **~ service** Buchprüfungsdienst, Hilfe bei der Erstellung der Buchungsunterlagen; **~ student** Buchhaltungslehrling; **~ trainees** Buchhalternachwuchs.

accountant Rechnungsführer, -beamter, Bilanzbuchhalter, -prüfer, bilanzsicherer Buchhalter, (accounting expert) Buchsachverständiger, -haltungsfachmann, Bücherrevisor, (defendant) Beklagter im Prozeß auf Rechnungslegung, (officer in charge of public accounts) Rendant;
~ accounts payable (US) Lieferantenbuchhalter; **~ accounts receivable** (US) Kundenbuchhalter; **cash ~** Kassenbuchhalter; **certified ~** (Br.) Wirtschaftsprüfer; **certified public ~** (US) beeidigter (öffentlich zugelassener) Buch-, Wirtschafts-, Rechnungsprüfer; **chartered ~** (Br.) konzessionierter Buchprüfer, geprüfter (beeidigter) Bücherrevisor, vereidigter Rechnungsprüfer, Wirtschaftsprüfer; **chief ~** Buchhaltungsleiter, Chefbuchhalter, Hauptbuchhalter; **cost ~** [Betriebs]kalkulator, -buchhalter; **financial ~** Finanzbuchhalter; **~ general** Hauptbuchhalter, -rechnungsführer, Prokurist; **imprest ~** (Br.) Zuschußempfänger; **incorporated ~** (US) geprüfter Bücherrevisor, Wirtschaftsprüfer; **junior ~** Hilfsprüfer; **private ~** betriebseigener Prüfer; **public ~** Bücherrevisor, Wirtschaftsprüfer; **senior ~** Hauptprüfer, -revisor, leitender Buchhalter, Buchhaltungschef;
~ in charge aufsichtsführender Prüfer, leitender Außenrevisor (Prüfungsbeamter), Revisionsleiter; **~ of court** Gerichtsbuchhalter;
to call in a certified ~ (Br.) Bücherrevisor (Wirtschaftsprüfer) zuziehen; **to employ an expert ~** Buchsachverständigen zuziehen; **to employ a private ~ on a full-time basis** Wirtschaftsprüfer ganztags beschäftigen;
~'s certificate Prüfungsbescheinigung; **~'s Department** (Br.) Staatsschuldenregister; **~'s fee** Wirtschaftsprüfergebühren; **~'s report** Prüfungs-, Revisionsbericht; **~'s responsibility** Standespflichten eines Prüfers.

accountantship Amt (Stelle) eines Rechnungsführers.

accounting (bookkeeping) Führung der Bücher, Buchführung, -haltung, Rechnungswesen, Rechnungsführung, (internal auditing) Überwachung des Rechnungswesens, Revisionswesen, (rendition of account) Rechenschaftslegung, Rechnungslegung;
accrual ~ periodenechte Aufwands- und Ertragsrechnung; **activity ~** Sachkalkulation; **budgetary ~** Haushaltsrechnungsführung, Finanzplanung; **cash ~** Kassenbuchführung; **contribution margin ~** Deckungsbeitragsrechnung; **corporation ~** Rechnungswesen einer AG; **cost ~** betriebliches Rechnungswesen, [Selbst]kostenrechnung, Rentabilitätsberechnung; **cost centre ~** (Br.) Kostenstellenrechnung; **cost location ~** (US) Kostenstellenrechnung; **deliveries ~** wertmäßige Abrechnung; **department[al] ~** dezentralisiertes Rechnungswesen; **electronic ~** Elektronenbuchführung; **entity ~** Buchführung einer Konzerngesellschaft; **factory ~** Betriebsbuchhaltung; **family ~** Familienhaushaltsrechnung; **final ~** Schlußabrechnung; **financial ~** Finanzbuchhaltung; **general ~** allgemeine Buchführung; **good ~** ordnungsgemäße Buchführung; **government ~** kameralistische Buchführung, Staatsrechnungswesen; **head-office ~** Buchhaltungsprüfung der Hauptgeschäftsstelle; **historical ~** Buchführung nach angefallenen Istkosten; **industrial ~** betriebliche Buchführung, Betriebsbuchhaltung; **job order cost ~** Arbeitsauftragskostenrechnung, Stückerfolgsrechnung; **management ~** Rechnungswesen für besondere Betriebsprüfungsbedürfnisse; **manufacturing ~** Betriebsbuchhaltung, -führung; **municipal ~** kommunales Rechnungswesen; **national income ~** volkswirtschaftliche Gesamtrechnung; **online revenue ~** Buchführung über die Einnahmen aus dem Linienverkehr; **operational ~** Betriebsabrechnung; **personal ~** Privatbuchhaltung; **personnel ~** Lohn- und Gehaltsbuchhaltung, Personalbuchhaltung, Personalbuchführung; **plant ~** Anlagenbuchführung; **product cost ~** Erzeugniskostenrechnung; **property ~** Anlagenbuchhaltung; **public ~** öffentlicher Rechenschaftsbericht; **punched-card ~** Buchführung mittels Lochkarten; **shop ~** Betriebsabrechnung; **stock brokerage ~** Maklerbuchführung; **store ~** Lagerbuchführung; **subsidiary company ~** Buchführung einer Tochtergesellschaft; **tax ~** Steuerbuchhaltung; **uniform ~** standardisierte Buchführung;

~ for changing price levels inflationsbezogenes Rechnungswesen; **~ for income tax** Einkommensteuerbuchhaltung; **~ for units** Stück-, Einheitsrechnung;

~ abuses Buchführungsmißbräuche; **~ adviser** Betriebsberater; **~ agency** *(payments agreement, US)* Rechnungsführer; **~ axioms** Bilanzierungsgrundsätze; **~ changes** vorgenommene Änderungen in der Buchführung; **~ charge** buchhalterische Belastung; **~ classification** Rechnungssystem; **~ control** betriebsinterne Kontrolle der Buchführung, Überwachung der Buchhaltung; **~ costs** Kosten der Buchhaltung; **for conveniences** zur Erleichterung der Buchhaltung; **~ cycle** Buchungskreislauf; **~ date** [Bilanz]stichtag; **~ deficit** Rechnungsdefizit; **~ department (division)** Buchhaltungsabteilung, Rechnungsabteilung, Buchhalterei; **~ dollar** Verrechnungsdollar; **~ entity** selbständig bilanzierendes Unternehmen; **~ equation** Kontenabstimmung; **~ evidence** Buchhaltungs-, Rechnungsnachweis; **~ experience** Erfahrungen im Buchhaltungswesen; **~ expert** Rechnungs-, Buchsachverständiger; **principal ~ financial authority** Chef der Finanzbuchhaltung; **~ firm** Revisionsfirma; **~ form** Kontenblatt; **~ identity** Ausgleichung der Buchhaltung; **~ machine** Buchungsmaschine; **~ manoeuvre** angreifbares Buchungsverfahren; **~ manual** Handbuch für Betriebsprüfer; **~ method** Buchführungs-, Buchungsmethode; **~ office** Rechnungsstelle; **General Office** *(US)* Bundesrechnungshof; **~ operation** Rechnungsvorgang; **well-arranged ~ organization** gut organisierter Buchhaltungsapparat; **~ period** Rechnungsabschnitt, Rechnungsperiode, Veranlagungszeitraum, Buchungszeitraum, Abrechnungs-, Bilanzierungsperiode; **~ policy** Bilanzpolitik; **~ position** Rechnungsposition; **~ practice** Buchprüfertätigkeit; **consistently maintained sound ~ practices** ständig fehlerfreie Buchprüfung; **~ practitioner** Bilanzierungsfachmann, Bilanzexperte; **~ principles** Buchführungsgrundsätze, Bilanzierungsrichtlinien; **good ~ principles** Grundsätze ordnungsgemäßer Buchführung und Bilanzierung; **~ procedure** Buchungs-, Buchprüfungsverfahren; **~ process** Buchhaltungsvorgang; **~ profit** im Rechnungsabschnitt angefallener Gewinn; **for ~ purposes** zu Buchführungszwecken; **~ records** Buchführungsunterlagen, Buchungsunterlagen, Buchführungs-, Rechnungsbelege; **self-balancing ~ records** Buchhaltungsunterlagen für selbständige Bilanzierung; **to keep ~ records sufficient to show and explain its transactions** die zur Erläuterung von Geschäftstransaktionen erforderlichen Buchungsunterlagen aufheben; **~ reference date** Bilanzabschlußtermin; **~ service** Buchprüfungsdienst; **~ setup** Buchhaltung; **~ specialist** Buchprüfungsspezialist; **International Standards Committee** internationaler Ausschuß für Wirtschaftsprüferrichtlinien; **~ supervisor** Leiter des Rechnungswesens, Buchhaltungschef; **~ system** Kontenrahmen, Buchungsverfahren, Buchführungssystem; **uniform ~ system** einheitliches Buchführungssystem; **~ technique** Bilanzierungstechnik; **~ terms** Buchführungsbegriffe; **~ terminology** Buchführungsterminologie; **~ transaction** Buchhaltungsvorgang; **~ unit** Rechnungsposten, Verrechnungseinheit; **~ value** Buchwert; **~ work** Bilanzierungsarbeiten; **~ year** Rechnungsjahr.

accredit *(v.)* bevollmächtigen, akkreditieren, *(letter of credit)* Akkreditiv einräumen.

accredited beglaubigt, autorisiert, bevollmächtigt, akkreditiert; **~ advertising agency** anerkannte Werbeagentur; **~ broker** amtlich zugelassener Makler; **~ representative** bevollmächtigter Vertreter, Bevollmächtigter.

accreditee Akkreditivinhaber.

accreditif, dos-a-dos *(US)* Gegenakkreditiv.

accretion | to fixed assets Anlagenzugang; **~ of business** Geschäftszunahme, -ausweitung.

accrual Anfall, Zuwachs, Zugang, Anwachsung, *(funds)* Eingang, *(interests)* Auflaufen, *(balance sheet)* Zugänge; **depreciation ~s** entstandene Abschreibungen; **~s payable** entstandene (noch nicht fällige) Verbindlichkeiten; **~s receivable** entstandene (noch nicht fällige) Forderungen; **~ of a cause of action** Entstehung eines Klageanspruchs; **~ of a dividend** Stichtag für den Dividendenanspruch, Dividendenanfall; **~ of exchange** Devisenzugang; **~s to a fund** Fondszugänge; **~ of an inheritance** Anfall einer Erbschaft, Erbschaftsanfall; **~ of interest** fällig werdende Zinsen, *(accumulation)* Auflaufen (Anwachsen) von Zinsen, **~ of a right** Entstehung eines Rechts; **~ accounting** periodengetreue Aufwandsrechnung; **~ basis** Fälligkeitsbasis; **~ date** Fälligkeitstag; **~ method** Gewinnermittlung durch Betriebsvermögensvergleich.

accrue *(v.)* anwachsen, zuwachsen, *(interest)* auflaufen, fällig werden, *(liability)* eintreten, *(proceeds)* anfallen, *(taxation)* zufließen, *(become vested)* entstehen, erwachsen, zur Entstehung gelangen; **~ to employer** dem Arbeitgeber zufallen; **~ to an enterprise** einem Unternehmen zufließen; **~ by way of succession** im Erbgang anfallen.

accrued aufgelaufen, angewachsen, entstanden; **~ payable accounts** *(balance sheet, US)* entstandene [aber noch nicht fällige] Aufwendungen; **~ receivable accounts** *(balance sheet, US)* entstandene [aber noch nicht fällige] Forderungen; **~ amount** entstandener [noch nicht fälliger] Betrag; **~ assets** *(balance sheet)* antizipative Aktiva; **~ benefits** erworbene Leistungsberechtigung; **~ charges (costs)** aufgelaufene Kosten; **~ compensation** zuerkannte und fällige Entschädigung; **~ depreciation** *(US)* Wertberichtigung für Abnutzung; **~ dividend** noch nicht bezahlte Dividende; **~ expenses** *(balance sheet)* antizipatorische Passiva; **~ holiday remuneration** einklagbare Ferienvergütung, Urlaubsgeldrückstände; **~ income** *(balance sheet)* antizipative Erträge, entstandene [aber noch nicht ausgezahlte] Einkünfte; **~ interest** Stückzinsen, aufgelaufene (noch nicht ausgezahlte) Zinsen; **~ interest payable** *(balance sheet)* entstandene (noch nicht zur Auszahlung gelangende] Zinsverbindlichkeiten; **~ interest receivable** *(balance sheet)* entstandene [noch nicht ausgezahlte] Zinsforderungen; **~ liabilities** *(US)* entstandene Verpflichtungen (Verbindlichkeiten), antizipative Schulden; **~ payables** *(US)* antizipative Passiva; **~ payrolls** *(accounting)* fällige Löhne und Gehälter; **~ receivables** *(US)* antizipative Aktiva; **~ rent** aufgelaufener Mietzins, Mietrückstände; **~ revenue** antizipative Erträge; **~ royalty** entstandene Tantiemenforderung; **~ salaries** Gehaltsrückstände; **~ sales** getätigte Verkäufe; **~ taxes** *(balance sheet)* Steuerschulden; **~ wages** fällige Lohnforderungen, Lohnrückstände.

accruement Anwachs[ung], Zuwachs.

accruer Landzuwachs, *(inheritance)* Erbanfall.

accruing fällig werdend, entstehend; **~ amounts** anfallende Beträge; **~ costs** entstehende Kosten, Auflaufen von Kosten; **~ interest** fällig werdende (anfallende, entstehende) Zinsen; **~ items** entstandene, noch nicht fällige Posten; **~ right** Anwachsungsrecht.

accumulate *(v.)* anhäufen, aufhäufen, kumulieren, horten, *(electric power)* aufspeichern, *(funds)* ansammeln, *(interest)* auflaufen, ansammeln; **~ income** Einkünfte thesaurieren; **~ mountainous deferred tax provisions in the balance sheet** gewaltige Rückstellungen für Steuervorauszahlungen ansammeln; **~ reserves in foreign currencies** Devisenvorräte anhäufen.

accumulated | advertising effectiveness kumulierte Werbewirkung; **~ audience** kumulierte Leserschaft (Hörerschaft); **~ charges** aufgelaufene Kosten; **~ coverage** kumulierte Reichweite; **~ debt** aufgelaufene Schuld; **~ demand** Nachfrageballung, Nachholbedarf; **~ depreciation on fixed assets** *(balance sheet)* Wertberichtigung auf Posten des Anlagevermögens; **~ dividend** aufgelaufene (rückständige) Dividende; **~ earnings** *(US)* thesaurierter Gewinn, [etwa] gesetzliche Rücklagen; **~ income** Unternehmensertrag, nicht verteilter Gewinn, Gewinnvortrag; **~ interest** aufgelaufene Zinsen, Verzugszinsen; **~ profits** noch nicht ausgeschüttete Gewinne, thesaurierter Gewinn; **~ surplus** Gewinnvortrag; **~ value** Endwert.

accumulation *(amassing)* Ansammlung, Anhäufung, Haufen, Hortung, Thesaurierung, *(of capital)* Akkumulation, Akkumulierung, Kapitalansammlung, Festlegung von Kapitalbeträgen, *(electricity)* Aufspeicherung, *(of interest)* Auflaufen, *(life insurance)* Gewinnansammlung, *(stock exchange)* spekulativer Effektenaufkauf während einer Baisse; **excessive ~** *(trustee)* unzulässige Thesaurierung; **~ of an annuity** Endwert einer Annuität; **~ of arrears** Anhäufung von Rückständen; **~ of assets** Vermögensbildung; **~ of capital** Kapital-, Vermögensbildung, Kapitalansammlung; **~ of charges** Auflaufen von Kosten; **~ of currency reserves** Devisenanhäufung; **~ of debts** Anwachsen von Schulden; **~ of dividends** Dividendenansammlung; **~ of interest** Auflaufen von Zinsen; **~ for payment of debts** Akkumulierung zur Schuldentilgung; **~ of profits** Gewinnansammlung, -thesaurierung; **~ of property** Vermögensanhäufung; **~ of reserves** Rücklagen-, Reservenbildung; **~ of risks** Risiken-, Gefahrenhäufung; **~ of savings** Spareinlagenzunahme; **~ agreement** Kapitalansammlungsvertrag; **~ factor** Akkumulationsfaktor; **~ period** Thesaurierungszeitraum; **~ plan (schedule)** Kapitalansammlungsplan; **~ unit trust** Wachstumsfond.

accumulative *(v.)* *(sinking fund)* akkumulierend, *(stock)* kumulativ, sich anhäufend, wachsend;
~ **dividend** Dividende auf kumulative Vorzugsaktien; ~ **judgment** zunächst ausgesetztes Strafurteil; ~ **sentence** *(US)* zusätzliche Strafzumessung.

accumulator Akkumulator, Akku;
~ **battery** Sammlerbatterie.

accuracy Sorgfalt, [Grad an] Genauigkeit, Korrektheit, Exaktheit, *(data processing)* Ergebnisgenauigkeit;
~ **rate** Genauigkeitsquote; ~ **table** Fehlertabelle.

accurate genau, pünktlich, sorgfältig, einwandfrei, fehlerfrei, exakt;
~ **interest** genaue Zinsberechnung; ~ **translation** wortgetreue Übersetzung.

accusation Beschuldigung, Anklage, Strafanzeige;
false ~ falsche Anschuldigung; **self-**~ Selbstbeschuldigung; **to be under an** ~ **of theft** unter der Anklage des Diebstahls stehen; **to bring false** ~ **against s. o.** falsche Beschuldigungen gegen j. erheben; **to prefer an** ~ **against s. o.** j. anklagen, Anklage gegen j. erheben; **to rebut an** ~ Anklage widerlegen.

accusatory anklagend;
~ **part** Straftenor.

accuse *(v.)* beschuldigen, anklagen, Anklage erheben;
~ **s. o. of having committed a crime** j. eines Verbrechens beschuldigen.

accused Angeklagter, Beschuldigter;
~ *(a.)* angeklagt;
to be ~ **of theft** unter Anklage des Diebstahls stehen; **to bring the** ~ **face to face with a witness** Angeklagten mit einem Zeugen konfrontieren;
~ **person** Be-, Angeschuldigter, Angeklagter.

accuser Ankläger, Privatkläger.

accustom *(v.)* o. s. sich gewöhnen an, sich einleben.

accustomed gewohnt;
to be ~ **to do s. th.** etw. zu tun pflegen; **to get** ~ **to the climate** sich an das Klima gewöhnen.

achievable erreichbar.

achieve *(v.)* *(accomplish)* ausführen, vollenden, -bringen, leisten, *(acquire)* erlangen, *(reach end)* erreichen, erzielen;
~ **distinction in public life** öffentliche Anerkennung finden; ~ **the facile** leichte Lösungen erreichen; ~ **a purpose** Zweck erreichen; ~ **subject matter** patentfähig sein.

achievement *(accomplishment)* Arbeit, [bedeutende] Leistung, *(completion)* Vollbringung, Erziehung, Ausführung, *(great deed)* Errungenschaft, Großtat;
academic ~s Leistungen in den wissenschaftlichen Fächern; **exceptional** ~ außerordentliche Leistung; **industrial** ~s wirtschaftliche Leistungen; **no mean** ~ bedeutende Leistung; **outstanding** ~ überragende Leistung; **scientific** ~s Errungenschaften der Forschung; **socialist** ~s sozialistische Errungenschaften;
~ **age** Leistungsalter; ~ **quotient** Leistungsquotient; ~ **test** Leistungstest.

acetate nicht brennbarer Film, *(broadcasting)* Mutterplatte.

acid test Feuerprobe, Prüfstein, *(balance sheet)* Liquiditätsprüfung;
~ **ratio** *(US)* Flüssigkeitsverhältnis, Liquiditätsgrad, -kennziffer.

acknowledge *(v.)* *(certify)* notariell bescheinigen (beglaubigen), beurkunden, *(confess)* zugeben, eingestehen, einräumen, *(own with gratitude)* sich erkenntlich zeigen, *(receipt)* [Empfang] bestätigen, quittieren, *(recognize)* anerkennen;
~ **the corn** *(coll.)* seinen Fehler zugeben; ~ **a deed** Urkunde als echt anerkennen; ~ **a favo(u)r** Gunstbezeichnung dankbar annehmen; ~ **a secret marriage** Eheschließung legitimieren; ~ **receipt of letter** Brief bestätigen; ~ **service of a writ** [gerichtliche] Zustellung nachweisen; ~ **one's signature** seine Unterschrift anerkennen; ~ **a treaty** Völkerrechtsvertrag ratifizieren.

acknowledged anerkannt, geltend.

acknowledgement Anerkennung, Anerkenntnis, Zuerkennung, *(of account)* Richtigbefund, *(attestation)* Bestätigung, *(author)* Danksagung, *(formal certificate)* Beglaubigungsklausel, *(confessment)* Eingeständnis, *(receipt)* Empfangsbestätigung, Quittung, *(recognition in legal form)* [urkundliche, notarielle] Anerkennung (Bestätigung), Beglaubigung, offizielle Bescheinigung;
in ~ **of his service** in Anerkennung seiner Verdienste;
~s Danksagung;
ritual ~ feierliche Bestätigung; **written** ~ schriftliche Bestätigung;

author's ~ **of assistance** Danksagung des Verfassers für Mitarbeit; ~ **of a complaint** Entgegennahme einer Beschwerde; ~ **of a debt (indebtedness) in writing** schriftliches Schuldanerkenntnis; ~ **of liability** Haftpflichtanerkenntnis; ~ **of order** Auftragsbestätigung; ~ **of paternity** Vaterschaftsanerkennung; ~ **of receipt** Eingangsbestätigung, Empfangs-, Abnahmebescheinigung, Quittung; ~ **of receipt of a letter** Bestätigung eines Briefeingangs; ~ **of receipt of payment** Zahlungsbestätigung; ~ **by record** schriftliches Anerkenntnis; ~ **of satisfaction** Schuldbegleichungsurkunde; ~ **of service** Zustellungsnachweis;
to take ~ **of deeds** notariell bestätigen.

acme Gipfel, höchste Vollkommenheit.

acoustic advertising akustische Webung.

acquaint *(v.)* bekanntmachen mit, benachrichtigen, in Kenntnis setzen, *(advertising)* informieren;
~ **o. s. with a. th.** sich einarbeiten in (vertraut machen mit, unterrichten über) etw.; ~ **s. o. with his duties** j. in seinen Aufgabenkreis einführen.

acquaintance Bekanntschaft, Kenntnis, Vertrautsein, *(persons)* Bekanntenkreis;
casual ~ flüchtige Bekanntschaft; **personal** ~ persönliche Bekanntschaft; **speaking** ~ flüchtige Bekanntschaft;
to cultivate s. one's ~ jds. Bekanntschaft pflegen; **to drop s. one's** ~ Verkehr mit jem. abbrechen; **to form (make) an** ~ Bekanntschaft machen; **to have a nodding (bowing)** ~ **with s. o.** j. oberflächlich kennen; **to improve on** ~ bei näherer Bekanntschaft gewinnen; **to keep up** ~ **with s. o.** Umgang mit jem. haben; **to make** ~ **of s. o.** Bekanntschaft von jem. machen; **to pluck up** ~ **with s. o.** mit jem. Bekanntschaft schließen; **to renew an** ~ Bekanntschaft erneuern;
~ **factor** Bekanntschaftsmoment.

acquaintanceship Bekanntenkreis.

acquainted, intimately näher bekannt, vertraut;
~ **with a matter** sachkundig;
to be ~ kennen; **to be fully** ~ **with the facts of the case** alle Einzelheiten eines Falles kennen; **to be thoroughly** ~ genau wissen; **to become** ~ **with** kennenlernen.

acquest *(law)* Erwerb, Errungenschaft.

acquiesce *(v.)* dulden, stillschweigend genehmigen, ruhig hinnehmen, einwilligen;
~ **in an agreement** einer Vereinbarung zustimmen; ~ **in an arrangement** Anordnung billigen.

acquiescence Duldung, Einverständnis, Einwilligung, *(tacit agreement)* stillschweigende Genehmigung (Hinnahme).

acquirable erwerbbar.

acquire *(v.)* an-, beschaffen, erwerben, erlangen, sich zulegen (aneignen);
~ **only the assets of another business** lediglich die Anlagen eines anderen Betriebs kaufen; ~ **bona fide** gutgläubig erwerben; ~ **a controlling interest in a concern** Kapitalmehrheit eines Unternehmens erwerben; ~ **a customer** Kunden werben (gewinnen); ~ **a language** Sprache erlernen; ~ **a nationality** Staatsangehörigkeit erwerben; ~ **by purchase** käuflich erwerben; ~ **the title** Eigentumsrecht erwerben; ~ **for value without notice** gutgläubig erwerben.

acquired, duly wohlerworben;
~ **characters** erworbene Eigenschaften; ~ **nationality** erworbene Staatsangehörigkeit; ~ **rights** wohlerworbene Rechte.

acquirement Erwerbung, Erlangung, *(faculty)* erworbene Fertigkeit;
~s Kenntnisse, Bildung.

acquirer Erwerber, Ankäufer.

acquisition Erwerbung, Errungenschaft, *(purchase)* Erwerb, Beschaffung, Anschaffung, Ankauf, Abnahme, *(terminal)* Datenerfassung;
bona fide ~ gutgläubiger Erwerb; **derivative** ~ abgeleiteter Eigentumserwerb; **new** ~s Neuerwerbungen; **original** ~ originärer Eigentumserwerb, Ersterwerb; **recent** ~ Neuerwerbungen; **unprofitable individual** ~s *(bookseller)* unrentable Einzelbesorgungen;
~ **at birth** *(citizenship)* Erwerb durch Geburt; ~ **of capital assets** Anlagenerwerb, -kauf; **great** ~ **to a club** bedeutsame Bereicherung eines Vereins; ~ **of a 50-per-cent interest** fünfzigprozentiger Beteiligungserwerb; ~ **of land** Grunderwerb; ~ **of nationality** Erwerb der Staatsangehörigkeit; ~ **of property** Eigentumserwerb; ~ **with reservation of title** Erwerb unter Eigentumsvorbehalt; ~ **of securities** Beschaffung von Wertpapieren; ~ **of signal** *(aerospace)* Erfassen des Signals; ~ **of stock** Aktienerwerb; ~ **of territory** Gebietserwerb; ~ **of title** Eigentumserwerb;

~ **agreement** Übernahmevertrag; ~ **binge** Aufkauftour; ~ **commission** Abschlußprovision; ~ **cost (expense)** Anschaffungskosten, *(insurance)* Akquisitionskosten; ~ **fee** *(bookseller)* Besorgungsgebühr; **to play the ~ game** sich in immer größerem Ausmaß Beteiligungen zulegen; ~ **possibilities** Ankaufsmöglichkeiten; ~ **program(me)** Zukaufsplan, Zukunfts-, Akquisitionsprogramm; ~ **project** Ankaufsprojekt; ~ **prospects** Akquisitionschancen; ~ **radar** *(mil.)* Erfassungsradar; ~ **value** Erwerbswert, Anschaffungswert.

acquisitive auf Erwerb gerichtet, gewinn-, erwerbssüchtig; ~ **capital** Erwerbskapital; ~ **prescription** *(US)* Ersitzung; ~ **price** Anschaffungspreis.

acquisitiveness Erwerbstrieb, Gewinnsucht.

acquisitor Erwerber.

acquit *(v.)* *(discharge debt)* abtragen, abzahlen, erfüllen, begleichen, tilgen, *(release from debt)* von Verbindlichkeiten befreien, *(law)* freisprechen, auf Freispruch erkennen; ~ **o. s.** seine Sache gut machen; ~ **a debt** Schuld abtragen; ~ **o. s. of a duty** sich einer Verpflichtung entledigen; ~ **s. o. of manslaughter** j. von der Anklage des Totschlags freisprechen; ~ **o. s. successfully** sich einer Sache erfolgreich entledigen.

acquittal Freispruch, Freisprechung, *(debt)* Erlaß; **hono(u)rable ~** Freispruch wegen erwiesener Unschuld; ~ **in fact** Freispruch aus tatsächlichen Gründen; ~ **in law** Freispruch aus Rechtsgründen; **to appeal against an ~** gegen einen Freispruch Berufung einlegen; **to give s. o. a bare ~** j. mangels Beweisen freisprechen; **to pronounce an ~** freisprechen, Freispruch verkünden.

acquittance *(discharge of debts)* Entlastung, Schuldbefreiung, Tilgung, Abtragung, *(receipt)* [Ausgleich]quittung, *(release)* Erlaß von Schulden, Schuldenerlaß.

acre *(measure)* Flächenmaß von 40,4673 Ar, Morgen; **to own ~s of land** erheblichen Grundbesitz haben; ~ **produce** Ertrag pro Morgen.

acreage Anbaufläche, *(measure)* Flächeninhalt; **to reduce ~** Anbaufläche verringern; ~ **allotment** zugewiesene Anbaufläche; ~ **restriction** Anbaubeschränkung.

acred begütert.

across, all the way ganz weit verbreitet worden; **to put s. th. ~ to s. o.** jem. etw. klar machen; ~ **country** querfeldein.

across-the-board global; ~ **boost** Globalanstieg; ~ **broadcasting (commercial)** *(US)* Werbesendung jeweils zur gleichen Tageszeit jeden Wochentag; ~ **increase** genereller Lohnanstieg (Preisanstieg).

act Handlung[sweise], Werk, Tat, Leistung, *(broadcasting)* festes Rahmenprogramm, *(decision)* Beschluß, Resolution, *(deed)* Urkunde, Schriftstück, Instrument, Dokument, *(law)* Gesetz, Akt, Verfügung, Erlaß, *(legal transaction)* Rechtsgeschäft, *(theater)* Aufzug, Akt; **by ~ of law** kraft Gesetzes; **during the ~** auf offener Szene; **in the ~ of going** im Begriff, zu gehen; **in the very ~** auf frischer Tat; **within the meaning of the ~** im Sinne des Gesetzes; **Air Force ~** *(Br.)* Luftwaffengesetz; **Antitrust ~** *(US)* Kartellgesetz; **authorized ~** genehmigtes Rechtsgeschäft; **Bank ~** *(Br.)* Bankgesetz; **Bankruptcy ~** *(Br.)* Konkursordnung; **blanket ~** Blankettgesetz; **Bill of Exchange ~** *(Br.)* Wechselordnung; **Chandler ~** *(US)* Konkursordnung; **Companies ~** Aktiengesetz; **Copyright ~** Urhebergesetz; **criminal ~** strafbare Handlung, Straftat, Verbrechen; **Design ~** *(Br.)* Geschmacksmustergesetz; **elective ~** Wahlakt, -handlung; **Emergency Powers ~** *(Br.)* Notstandsgesetz; **Factor's ~** *(Br.)* Kommissionärsgesetz; **Factory ~** *(Br.)* Arbeitsschutzgesetz, Gewerbeordnung; **Fair Trade ~** *(US)* Gesetz über die Preisbindung von Markenartikeln; **Federal Credit Union ~** *(US)* Gesetz über das Bundesaufsichtsamt für Versicherungswesen; **Federal Reserve ~** *(US)* Landeszentralbankgesetz; **final ~** *(dipl.)* Schlußakte; **Finance ~** *(Br.)* Steuergesetz; **governmental ~** Staatsakt; **illegal ~** gesetzwidrige Handlung; **Income Tax ~** *(Br.)* Einkommensteuergesetz; **Judiciary ~** *(US)* Gerichtsverfassungsgesetz; **legal ~** Willenserklärung, Rechtshandlung; **legislative ~** Gesetzgebungsakt; **malicious ~** vorsätzliche, rechtswidrige Handlung; **Marriage ~** Ehegesetz; **ministerial ~** Ministerialverfügung, Verwaltungsmaßnahme; **National Insurance ~** Sozialversicherungsgesetz; **National Service ~** *(Br.)* Wehrpflichtgesetz; **Navigation ~** *(Br.)* Schiffahrtsakte, -gesetz; **negligent ~** fahrlässige Handlung; **Uniform Negotiable Instruments ~** *(US)* Wechselordnung, Wertpapiergesetz; **official ~** Amtshandlung; **overt ~** offenkundiger Tatbestand; **Patent ~** *(Br.)* Patentgesetz; **penal ~** strafbare Handlung;

preliminary ~ *(Br, collision of ships)* Tatbestandsurkunde; **Prevention of Crimes ~** Gewohnheitsverbrecher-, Kriminalverfügungsgesetz; **Prevention of Fraud ~** *(Br.)* Gesetz zur Verhütung von Kapitalanlagenbetrug; **private ~** Spezialgesetz [für eine Körperschaft]; **Probation of Offenders ~** *(Br.)* Bewährungsgesetz; **public ~** gesetzliche Vorschrift; **public ~s** *(Br.)* Gesetze allgemeinen Inhalts; **punishable ~** strafbare Handlung; **Rent Restriction ~** *(Br.)* Mieterschutzgesetz; **Revenue ~s** Steuergesetze; **Riot ~** *(Br.)* Aufruhrakt, Tumultgesetz; **Stamp ~** *(Br.)* Stempelsteuergesetz; **Social Security ~** *(US)* Sozialversicherungsgesetz; **supplemental ~** Ergänzungsgesetz; **tortious ~** unerlaubte Handlung; **Trademark Registration ~** Warenzeichenschutzgesetz; **unauthorized ~** unbefugte Tätigkeit, eigenmächtiges Handeln; **unfriendly ~** *(pol.)* unfreundliche Handlung; **unlawful ~** gesetzwidrige Handlung, verbotene Eigenmacht; **Vagrancy ~** *(Br.)* Gesetz gegen Landstreicherei; **wilful ~** vorsätzliche Handlung; **Workmen's Compensation ~** *(Br.)* [Arbeiter]unfallversicherungsgesetz; **wrongful ~** unerlaubte Handlung;

~ **of Adjournal** *(Scot.)* Verfahrensordnung; ~ **of aggression** Angriffshandlung, Aggressionsakt; ~ **of attainder** Achtung; ~ **of bankruptcy** Konkursvoraussetzung; ~ **of bonds** *(bill of exchange)* Intervention; ~ **of coercion** Zwangsanwendung; ~ **of Congress** *(US)* Bundesgesetz; ~ **of court** Maßnahme des Gerichts; ~ **of curatory** *(Scot.)* Vormundsbestellung; ~ **of disclaimer** Verzichtshandlung; ~ **of disobedience** Gehorsamsverweigerung; ~ **of the King's (Queen's) enemy** *(Br.)* Feindesgewalt; ~ **of faith** Autodafé, Ketzerverbrennung; ~ **of God** höhere Gewalt, Natur-, Elementarereignis; ~ **of grace** Gnadenakt, Gnadenerlaß, Amnestie; ~ **of hono(u)r** Ehreneintritt, Ehrenannahme, Notadresse; ~ **of hostility** *(international law)* feindseliger Akt; ~ **of illegality** rechtswidrige Handlung; ~ **of the imagination** Phantasiegebilde; ~ **of indemnity** Indemnitätsbeschluß, Amnestiegesetz; ~ **of insolvency** Konkurshandlung; ~ **of law** rechtsgestaltender Gesetzesakt; ~ **of negligence** fahrlässige Handlung, Fahrlässigkeit; ~**s and omissions** Handlungen und Unterlassungen; ~ **of oppression** Nötigungshandlung; ~ **of Parliament** *(Br.)* [Parlaments]gesetz, Parlamentsakte, -beschluß; ~ **of party** Willenserklärung einer Partei, Parteihandlung; ~ **of protest** Protest[aufnahme], -urkunde; ~ **of providence** unabwendbarer Zufall; ~ **capable of ratification** genehmigungsfähige Handlung; ~ **of sabotage** Sabotageakt, -handlung; ~ **of sale** Kaufvertrag, *(Louisiana)* notariell beurkundete Auflassung; ~ **of Settlement** *(Br.)* Thronfolgegesetz; ~ **of State** staatlicher Hoheitsakt, *(Br.)* Maßnahmen der Krone; ~ **of transfer** Abtretungserklärung; ~ **of violence** Gewaltverbrechen, -akt, -tat; ~ **of war** kriegerische Handlung, Kriegshandlung;

~ *(v.)* agieren, handeln, sich verhalten, *(as deputy)* stellvertretend amtieren, *(play a rôle)* spielen, darstellen, *(be apt for theatrical performance)* bühnenfähig sein, sich aufführen lassen;

~ **as** tätig sein, amtieren, fungieren; ~ **upon** ausführen; ~ **for s. o.** j. vertreten; ~ **in accordance with the rules** gemäß den Bestimmungen handeln; ~ **adversely to s. one's interests** gegen jds. Interessen handeln; ~ **on s. one's advice** jds. Ratschlag folgen; ~ **with assurance** sicher auftreten; ~ **aboveboard** ganz offen handeln; ~ **on one's own behalf** im eigenen Namen handeln; ~ **bona fide** gutgläubig handeln; ~ **in an advisory capacity** konsultative Funktionen ausüben, beratend tätig sein; ~ **in one's individual capacity** auf eigene Initiative handeln; ~ **in one's official capacity** offiziell tätig sein (werden), kraft seines Amtes handeln; ~ **carelessly** fahrlässig handeln; ~ **in a case** in einer Sache vorgehen; ~ **with caution** umsichtig handeln; ~ **conjointly** gemeinsam handeln; ~ **from conviction** aus innerster Überzeugung handeln; ~ **as correspondent** Korrespondenz führen, *(news agency)* als Berichterstatter tätig sein; ~ **as curtain** abschirmen; ~ **deliberately** vorsätzlich handeln; ~ **as deputy** als Stellvertreter fungieren; ~ **with diplomacy** diplomatisch vorgehen; ~ **under duress** unter Zwang handeln; ~ **in excess of one's powers** seine Vollmachten überschreiten; ~ **in good faith** gutgläubig handeln; ~ **as a father to s. o.** Vaterstelle an jem. vertreten; ~ **mala fide** bösgläubig handeln; ~ **independently** aus eigener Machtvollkommenheit handeln; ~ **contrary to law** sich einer Gesetzesübertretung schuldig machen; ~ **in lie** durch Handlungen bewußt irreführen; ~ **in a calculating manner** mit kühler Berechnung vorgehen; ~ **from interested motives** aus eigennützigen Motiven tätig werden; ~ **ex officio** von Amts wegen tätig werden; ~ **contrary to an order** Anordnung übertreten; ~ **upon an order** Auftrag ausführen; ~ **a part** Rolle spielen; **~ the part of a judge** richterliche Funktionen ausüben; **~ as principal and agent** mit sich selbst kontrahieren; **~ beyond the scope of one's authority** außerhalb seiner Vertretungsbefugnisse handeln, seine Vollmacht überschreiten; **~ within the scope of one's authority** innerhalb seiner Vertretungsmacht handeln; **~ as secretary** als Sekretär fungieren; **~ on the stage** auf der Bühne auftreten; **~ as one thinks fit** nach Gutdünken handeln; **~ in violation of a treaty** gegen einen Vertrag verstoßen; **~ ultra vires** in Überschreitung seiner Befugnisse handeln; **~ up** *(US)* angeben, sich aufspielen;

to be caught in the **~** auf frischer Tat betroffen werden; **to commit a fraudulent ~** sich eines Betruges schuldig machen; **to commit an available ~ of bankruptcy** Konkursvergehen begehen; **to do the hospitality ~** sich als Gastgeber aufspielen; **to get in on the ~** bei einer Sache einsteigen, sich in das Spiel einschalten, aktiv mitmachen;

~ book *(law court, Scot.)* Protokollbuch.

actable bühnengerecht, aufführbar.

acting tätig, handelnd, wirkend, amtierend, diensttuend, *(as deputy)* stellvertretend, *(managing)* geschäftsführend, verantwortlich;

~ for in Vertretung für;

~ career Schauspielerkarriere; **~ manager** stellvertretender Leiter, *(Br.)* geschäftsführendes Vorstandsmitglied; **~ officer** amtierender Beamter; **~ order** Handlungsvollmacht; **~ partner** tätiger (geschäftsführender) Teilhaber (Partner); **~ president** amtierender Präsident; **~ version** Bühnenausgabe.

action *(activity)* Tätigkeit, Aktion, Handlung, Vorgehen, *(US, Congress)* gesetzgebende Tätigkeit, *(deed)* Handlungs[weise], Handeln, Tat, *(dipl.)* Aktion, *(lawsuit)* Klage, Prozeß, Rechtsstreit, -sache, Rechtsverfahren, Rechtshandel, Sache, *(machine)* Gang, Funktionieren, *(mil.)* Gefecht, Kriegseinsatz, Kampfhandlung, Treffen, Kampf, *(rhetorics)* Vortragsweise, *(right to bring suit)* Klagegrund, *(share of stocks)* Aktie; „~" „zur Erledigung", *(film)* Achtung Aufnahme;

at the time the ~ was filed zum Zeitpunkt der Klageerhebung; **by bringing an ~** im Wege der Klage; **by way of ~** im Klagewege; **died in ~** gefallen; **for appropriate (further) ~** zur weiteren Veranlassung; **in ~** im Streit befangen, *(troops)* im Einsatz; **in full ~** in vollem Betrieb; **out of ~** *(machine)* außer Betrieb; **ready for ~** gerüstet, bereit;

take no ~! nichts unternehmen!;

abortive ~ gegenstandslos gewordene Klage; **accessory ~** Nebenverfahren; **administration ~** Klage auf Anordnung der Nachlaßverwaltung; **administrative ~** Verwaltungshandlung, -maßnahmen; **admiralty ~s** seerechtliche Streitigkeiten; **antitrust ~** *(US)* Kartellklage; **arbitrary ~** Willkürakt, Eigenmächtigkeit; **breach-of-contract ~** Klage wegen Vertragsverletzung, Schadensersatzklage, *(shareholder)* Aktionärsklage; **civil ~** Zivilprozeß, bürgerlicher Rechtsstreit, Klage in bürgerlichen Rechtsstreitigkeiten; **common ~** gemeinsames Vorgehen; **common law ~** bürgerlicher Rechtsstreit; **concerted ~** gemeinschaftliches (vereinbartes) Vorgehen, konzertierte Aktion; **corporate ~** Klage einer AG; **court ~** gerichtliches Vorgehen, gerichtliche Maßnahmen; **criminal ~** Strafverfahren, -prozeß; **cross ~** Gegen-, Widerklage; **declaratory ~** Feststellungsklage; **defamatory ~** Verleumdungs-, Beleidigungsklage; **derivative ~** *(shareholder)* Aktionärsklage; **diplomatic ~** diplomatischer Schritt, diplomatische Tätigkeit; **disciplinary ~** Disziplinarmaßnahmen; **discretionary ~** Ermessenshandlung; **equitable ~** auf Billigkeitsrecht gegründete Klage; **feigned ~** Scheinverfahren, -prozeß; **feint ~** Scheinverfahren; **fictitious ~** Prozeß zur Klärung einer Rechtslage; **first-of-a-kind ~** erstmalige Aktion; **foreclosure ~** *(US)* Zwangsvollstreckungsklage; **governmental ~** Verwaltungsmaßnahme, staatliche Maßnahmen, Regierungstätigkeit; **hypothecary ~** Klage auf Einleitung des Zwangsversteigerungsverfahrens; **industrial ~** Arbeitskampf; **joint ~** gemeinsames Vorgehen; **judicial ~** richterliche Tätigkeit; **legal ~** Rechtshandlung; **libel ~** Beleidigungs-, Verleumdungsklage; **local ~** Klage am Gerichtsstand der belegenen Sache; **mixed ~** schuldrechtliche und dingliche Klage; **mopping-up ~** *(mil.)* Säuberungsaktion; **nonviolent ~** gewaltloses Handeln; **passing-off ~** Klage wegen unlauteren Wettbewerbs; **penal ~** Strafverfahren; **pending ~** anhängiger Rechtsstreit, schwebendes Verfahren; **personal ~** obligatorische (schuldrechtliche) Klage, Leistungsklage; **petitory ~** *(Scot.)* Klage auf Herausgabe des Eigentums, Eigentums-, Herausgabeklage; **plenary ~** *(US)* Klage im ordentlichen Verfahren; **political ~** politische Maßnahmen; **popular ~** öffentliche Klage; **possessory ~** *(US)* Besitzstörungsklage; **private ~** privatrechtliche Klage; **real ~** dingliche

Klage; **redhibitory ~** Gewährleistungs-, Wandlungsklage; **replevin ~** Klage auf Freigabe gegen Sicherheitsleistung; **representative ~** *(shareholder)* Musterprozeß; **rescissory ~** *(Scot.)* Feststellungsklage; **revendication ~** Herausgabeklage, Klage auf Herausgabe des Eigentums; **revocatory ~** Vertragsaufhebungsklage; **secondary ~** Nebenwirkung; **separate ~** selbständige Klage; **slander ~** Beleidigungsklage; **speedy ~** Sofortmaßnahmen; **stockholder's representative ~** Klage auf Anfechtung von Hauptversammlungsbeschlüssen; **transitory ~** an keinen besonderen Gerichtsstand gebundene Klage; **vexatious ~** schikanöse Klage;

~ in abatement Klage wegen Kürzung des Pflichtteils; **~ for an account [for accounting]** Klage auf Rechnungslegung; **~ for affiliation** Vaterschaftsklage; **~ for annulment** Eheanfechtungsklage; **~ for assumpsit** Schadensersatzklage wegen Nichterfüllung, Erfüllungsklage; **~ for avoidance of contract** Anfechtungsklage; **~ on a bill of exchange** Wechselklage; **~ for breach of contract** Klage wegen Vertragsbruchs; **~ on a dishono(u)red bill** Wechselklage; **~ of book debt** Einklagung von Außenständen; **~ on the case** Besitzstörungsklage; **~ of character** Verleumdungsklage; **~ for conspiracy** Klage aus unerlaubter Handlung; **~ on contract** [auf Grund eines Vertrages angestrengte] Leistungsklage, Klage aus Vertrag; **~ for conversion** Schadensersatzklage wegen widerrechtlicher Aneignung, Klage auf Herausgabe; **~ for damages** Schadenersatzklage; **~ for damages to credit** Schadensersatzklage wegen Kreditschädigung; **~ for damages for deceit** Schadensersatzklage wegen arglistiger Täuschung; **~ for damages for breach of warranty** Schadensersatzklage wegen Verletzung der Gewährleistungspflicht; **~ for damages for nonacceptance** Schadensersatzklage bei Nichtannahme; **~ for damages for nondelivery** Schadensersatzklage wegen Nichterfüllung; **~ of debt** Klage auf Rückzahlung eines Darlehns; **~ in deceit** Betrugsverfahren; **~ for declarator** *(Scot.)* Feststellungsklage; **~ of detinue** Klage auf Herausgabe von Eigentum, Herausgabeklage; **~ for unfair dismissal** *(Br.)* Klage wegen Entlassung aus unsozialen Gründen; **~ for wrongful dismissal** Feststellungsklage auf Unwirksamkeit der Kündigung; **~s of the East-Indian Company** Aktien der Ostindischen Gesellschaft; **~ for ejectment** Räumungsklage; **~ in expropriation of real properties** Klage auf Herausgabe eines Grundstücks; **~ for failing to deliver goods** Klage wegen nicht erfolgter Übergabe von Sachen; **~ for foreclosure** *(US)* Zwangsvollstreckungsklage; **~ for forfeiture of a patent** Patentlöschungsklage; **~ for an illegitimate child to claim his status** Vaterschaftsklage; **~ for infringement of copyright** Klage wegen Urheberrechtsverletzung, Patentverletzungsklage; **~ of jactitation** negative Feststellungsklage; **~ on a foreign judgment** Verfahren zur Anerkennung und Vollstreckung ausländischer Urteile; **~ at law** gerichtliche Klage, Rechtsstreit, Prozeß[sache]; **~ at law for damages caused by nondelivery** Klage auf Schadenersatz wegen Nichterfüllung; **~ at law for damages for nonacceptance** Klage auf Schadenersatz wegen Nichtabnahme; **~ at law for the purchase price** Klage auf Zahlung des Kaufpreises; **~ for money had and received** *(Br.)* Klage auf Herausgabe der ungerechtfertigten Bereicherung, Bereicherungsklage; **~ for libel** Verleumdungsklage, Beleidigungsklage; **~ of negligence** fahrlässige Handlung, Schadensersatzklage wegen fahrlässigen Verhaltens; **~ of nullity** Nichtigkeitsklage; **~ of partition** Teilungsklage, -verfahren; **~ for payment** Klage auf Zahlung des Kaufpreises; **~ to claim specific performance of contract** Leistungs-, Erfüllungsklage; **~ in personam** obligatorische Klage; **~ for poinding** Zwangsvollstreckungsantrag; **~ for possession** *(Br.)* Räumungsklage; **~ for the price of goods** Klageanspruch auf Kaufpreisbezahlung; **~ for recovery of property** Herausgabeklage; **~ on a quantum meruit** Klage auf angemessene Vergütung; **~ to recover land** Räumungsklage; **~ for recovery of arrears** Klage wegen Mietrückständen; **~ for redemption** Klage auf Rückgabe der Pfandsache; **~ for relief** Sachantrag; **~ in rem** dingliche Klage; **~ for removing** *(Scot.)* Räumungsklage; **~ in replevin** Klage auf Rückgabe verpfändeter Gegenstände; **~ for rescission** Anfechtungsklage; **~ on the security** Klage aufgrund gewährter Sicherheiten; **~ for slander** Verleumdungsklage; **~ for support** *(US)* Unterhaltsklage; **~ to quiet title** Eigentumsfeststellungsklage; **~ in tort** Klage aus unerlaubter Handlung, **~ for the tort of defamation** Verleumdungsklage; **~ for tort of libel** Schadensersatzklage wegen Rufschädigung; **~ of trespass** Eigentums-, Besitzstörungsklage; **~ of trover [and conversion]** Bereicherungsklage; **~ for words** *(Br.)* Beleidigungsklage.

to allow an ~ einer Klage stattgeben; **to appear in an** ~ sich auf eine Klage einlassen; **to be brought into** ~ zum Einsatz kommen; **to be out of** ~ *(machine)* ausfallen; **to bring an** ~ **against s. o. j.** [bei Gericht] verklagen, Klage gegen j. anstrengen (erheben), gegen j. gerichtliche Schritte unternehmen, j. gerichtlich in Anspruch nehmen; **to bring s. o. into an** ~ j. in einen Prozeß hineinziehen; **to bring an** ~ **for infringement of a patent against s. o. j.** wegen Patentverletzung verklagen; **to bring an** ~ **for an injunction** auf Erlaß einer einstweiligen Verfügung klagen; **to bring an** ~ **for damages** auf Schadenersatz klagen; **to bring an** ~ **on a quantum meruit** Teilbetrag einklagen; **to bring an** ~ **for rescission of a contract** Wandlungs-, Anfechtungsklage erheben, auf Vertragsaufhebung klagen; **to bring an** ~ **for tort** aus unerlaubter Handlung klagen; **to close an** ~ Klage abweisen; **to come into** ~ in Gang kommen; **to declare an** ~ **admissible** Zulässigkeit einer Klage feststellen; **to defend an** ~ Klagebehauptung bestreiten; **to dismiss an** ~ Klage abweisen; **to drop an** ~ Klage fallen lassen; **to enter an** ~ **against s. o.** Klage gegen j. anstrengen; **to fight in an** ~ **at law** sich in einem Prozeß verteidigen; **to file an** ~ **against s. o. jem.** gerichtlich belangen; **to give rise to an** ~ Grund für eine Klage geben; **to go into** ~ zum Fronteinsatz kommen; **to have been killed in** ~ im Felde geblieben sein; **to institute an** ~ **against s. o. j.** verklagen, gerichtliche Schritte gegen j. einleiten; **to lie in** ~ zulässig sein; **to lose an** ~ Prozeß verlieren; **to maintain an** ~ Klage erheben, Prozeß führen, prozessieren; **to maintain an** ~ **in one's own name** im eigenen Namen klagen; **to prosecute an** ~ Prozeß betreiben; **to put into** ~ in die Tat umsetzen; **to put out of** ~ außer Gefecht setzen, kampfunfähig machen, *(mechanism)* abschalten, außer Betrieb setzen; **to raise an** ~ Prozeß anhängig machen; **to relinquish an** ~ Klage zurücknehmen; **to set in** ~ in Betrieb (Gang) setzen; **to sustain an** ~ Prozeß durchführen; **to swing into** ~ in Gang kommen; **to take** ~ Maßnahmen ergreifen, Schritte tun, einschreiten; **to take** ~ **at law** gerichtlich vorgehen, klagen; **to take** ~ **against s. o.** Klage gegen j. erheben, j. verklagen, Gerichtsverfahren gegen j. einleiten; **to take** ~ **against the demonstrators** gegen Demonstranten vorgehen (einschreiten); **to withdraw an** ~ Klage zurückziehen, -nehmen;

~ **area plan** *(Br.)* vordringliches Erschließungsprogramm; ~ **cycle** *(technics)* Arbeitsperiode; ~ **group** Aktionsgruppe; ~ **report** Tätigkeitsbericht; ~ **research** Aktionsforschung; ~ **space** Handlungsraum.

actionable [ein]klagbar, verklagbar, belangbar, prozeßfähig; ~ **fraud** arglistige Täuschung; ~ **loss** einklagbarer Schaden; ~ **misrepresentation** *(law of contract)* erhebliche falsche Angaben, gravierende Falschangaben; ~ **negligence** zum Schadenersatz verpflichtende (strafbare) Nachlässigkeit; ~ **nuisance** rechtserhebliche Belästigung; ~ **tort** zum Schadenersatz verpflichtende unerlaubte Handlung; ~ **words** *(law of libel)* beleidigende Äußerungen; ~ **wrong** schadensersatzpflichtige, unerlaubte Handlung.

actionary Aktionär.

activate *(v.)* aktivieren, *(chem.)* radioaktiv machen, *(mil.)* Einheit ausstatten.

activation | of trade Aktivierung des Handels; ~ **research** *(advertising)* Kaufentschlußanalyse, Erfolgsmessung.

active tätig, betriebsam, *(law)* gültig, *(lively)* aktiv, rührig, *(market)* lebhaft, *(share)* gängig; **to be** ~ Tätigkeit entfalten, tätig sein; ~ **account** Konto mit häufigen Umsätzen, Umsatzkonto; ~ **army** stehendes Heer; ~ **balance** Aktivsaldo; ~ **balance of trade** aktive Handelsbilanz; ~ **bonds** *(Br.)* festverzinsliche Obligationen, Prioritätsobligationen, *(US)* überdurchschnittlich gehandelte Obligationen; ~ **buyers** lebhafte Käufe; ~ **capital** flüssiges (schnell realisierbares) Kapital, Aktiva; ~ **circulation** Banknotenumlauf; ~ **commerce** lebhafter Handelsverkehr, *(export)* Aktivhandel, *(mercantile shipping on own ships)* Außenhandel mit eigenen Schiffen; ~ **competition** starke Konkurrenz; ~ **concealment** absichtliches Verschweigen; ~ **considerations** *(officialese)* ernsthafte Überlegungen; ~ **debts** Außenstände; ~ **demand** lebhafte Nachfrage; **on** ~ **duty** im aktiven Dienst; ~ **duty for training** *(US)* Wehrdienstübung; ~ **event** Veranstaltung, Feierlichkeit; ~ **line** *(television)* Abtastlinie; **on** ~ **list** im aktiven Dienst; ~ **market** lebhafte Börse; **to be an** ~ **member** aktiv sein; ~ **mind** geistige Beweglichkeit; ~ **owner (partner, Br.)** tätiger Teilhaber; ~ **part** aktive Teilnahme; **to take an** ~ **part in the research program(me)** sich an den Forschungsaufgaben aktiv beteiligen; ~ **securities** Effekten mit täglichen Börsenumsätzen; ~ **service** Front-

dienst; **to be on** ~ **service** aktiv dienen; ~ **service allowance** Frontzulage; ~ **service pay** Wehrsold; ~ **shares** gängige Aktien; ~ **side** *(balance sheet)* Aktivseite; ~ **stock** rege gehandelte Aktien; ~ **trade balance** aktive Handelsbilanz, Aktivbilanz.

activist *(pol.)* Aktivist.

activities Umtriebe, Tätigkeiten, Geschäfte, *(sphere of activity)* Bereich, Tätigkeitsbereich; **outside** ~ außerberufliche Tätigkeit; **principal** ~ **of a company** Haupttätigkeit einer Gesellschaft; **to come into s. one's** ~ zu jds. Aufgabenbereich gehören; **to sell off its peripheral** ~ seine Randgeschäfte aufgeben.

activity Tätigkeit, *(diligence)* Betriebsamkeit, Rührigkeit, Aktivität, *(active event)* Veranstaltung, *(functions)* Aufgabengebiet; **in full** ~ in vollem Gange, in Betrieb; **building** ~ Bautätigkeit; **business** ~ Geschäftstätigkeit; **economic** ~ geschäftliche Betätigung, konjunkturelle Belebung; **fiduciary** ~ treuhänderische Tätigkeit; **fifth-column** ~ Untergrundtätigkeit; **imaginative** ~ Wunschhandlung; **increased** ~ erhöhte Tätigkeit; **industrial** ~ gewerbliche (industrielle) Tätigkeit; **nonbanking** ~ bankfremde Geschäfte; **normal** ~ normaler Aufgabenkreis; **political** ~ politische Betätigung; **productive** ~ gewinnbringende Tätigkeit; **professional** ~ freiberufliche Tätigkeit; **subsidiary** ~ Nebentätigkeit; **subversive** ~ subversive Tätigkeit, Untergrundtätigkeit; **trade-union** ~ Gewerkschaftstätigkeit; ~ **of accounts** Kontenbewegung; ~ **in trade** geschäftliche Tätigkeit; **to be engaged in an** ~ Tätigkeit ausüben; **to be positively jumping with** ~ von hektischer Geschäftigkeit sein; **to buzz with** ~ voller Tatendrang stecken; **to resume** ~ Betrieb wieder aufnehmen; **to show renewed** ~ neuen Aufschwung nehmen; ~ **accounting** funktionale Kontenrechnung; ~ **rate** Erwerbsquote; ~ **report** Tätigkeitsbericht.

actor Handelnder, *(advocate in civil causes)* Anwalt, *(pleader)* Kläger, *(sociology)* Akteur, *(theater)* Schauspieler; **second-rate** ~ zweitklassiger Schauspieler; ~ **of character** zentrale Figur; **to become an** ~ zur Bühne gehen.

actual wirklich, effektiv, vorhanden, tatsächlich, eigentlich, *(present)* gegenwärtig, augenblicklich; ~ **amount** Effektiv-, Istbestand; ~ **assets** Reinvermögen; ~ **authority** Vertretungsmacht im Einzelfall; ~ **balance** Effektivbestand; ~ **bias** *(juror)* offensichtliches Vorurteil; ~ **business** effektives Geschäft, Effektivgeschäft; ~ **cash value** *(insurance)* Effektiv-, Versicherungswert; ~ **change of possession** unmittelbarer Besitzübergang; ~ **costs** Gestehungs-, Effektivkosten, Selbst-, Ist-, Herstellungskosten, Erwerbspreis; **to be caught in the** ~ **crime** auf frischer Tat ergriffen werden; ~ **damage** tatsächlich entstandener Schaden; ~ **deaths** *(insurance)* eingetretene Todesfälle; ~ **delivery** tatsächliche Übergabe, unmittelbare Besitzverschaffung; ~ **depreciation** wirkliche Wertminderung; ~ **displacement** *(vessel)* Wasserverdrängung; ~ **earnings** tatsächlicher Verdienst; ~ **eviction** Zwangsräumung; ~ **expenditure** Barauslagen; ~ **fact** Gegebenheit; ~ **fraud** vollendeter Betrug; ~ **goods** effektive Waren; ~ **hours** tatsächliche Arbeitsstunden, Istzeit; ~ **hourly earnings** Iststundenverdienst; ~ **loss** tatsächlicher Verlust; ~ **manhours** Iststunden; ~ **market** tatsächlicher Markt; ~ **market value** Markt-, Verkehrswert; ~ **notice** tatsächliche Kenntnis; ~ **number** Effektivzahl, *(mil.)* Iststärke; ~ **pay** reales Einkommen; ~ **practice** regelmäßige Berufsausübung; ~ **price** Markt-, Tagespreis, effektiver Preis; ~ **profit** echter Gewinn; ~ **rate of output** Istausstoß; ~ **receipts (takings)** Effektiveinnahmen; ~ **reserve** Istreserve; ~ **residence** gegenwärtiger Wohnort, ständiger Wohnsitz; ~ **sale** Verkaufsabschluß; ~ **situation** Sachverhalt; ~ **size** natürliche Größe; ~ **strength** *(mil.)* Iststärke; ~ **takings** Effektiveinnahmen; ~ **time** Istzeit; ~ **total loss** tatsächlicher Gesamtverlust, *(ship)* Totalverlust; ~ **value** Gegenwarts-, Real-, Effektivwert, effektiver Wert, Marktwert; ~ **violence** Gewaltanwendung.

actually outstanding *(securities)* tatsächlich begeben.

actuality Aktualität, Tatsächlichkeit, Wirklichkeit.

actualize *(v.)* verwirklichen.

actuals wirkliche-, Effektiveinnahmen.

actuarial versicherungstechnisch, -statistisch, -mathematisch; ~ **calculation** Versicherungskalkulation; ~ **consultant** versicherungstechnischer Berater; ~ **deficit** versicherungsmathematisches Defizit; ~ **department** Abteilung für Versicherungsstatistik; ~ **method** Tafelmethode; ~ **practice** Versi-

cherungstechnik; ~ **rate** Tafelziffer; ~ **reserve** Deckungskapital, Prämienreserve; ~ **science** Versicherungsmathematik; ~ **statistics** Versicherungsstatistik; ~ **tables** versiche-
rungsmathematische Tabellen; ~ **terms** Fachausdrücke der
Versicherungssprache; ~ **theory** Versicherungsmathematik;
~ **value** versicherungsmathematischer (rechnungsmäßiger)
Wert, Versicherungswert; ~ **valuation** Aufstellung einer
versicherungstechnischen Bilanz.
actuarially sound versicherungsmathematisch durchaus einwandfrei.
actuary *(filing clerk)* Registrator, *(insurance business)* Versi-
cherungsstatistiker, -fachmann, -mathematiker, -kalkulator,
(Br.) Urkundsbeamter, *(public clerk)* Gerichtsschreiber.
acute shortage kritischer Mangel.
ad *(abbr. for advertisement, US)* Anzeige, Inserat, Annonce;
four-colo(u)r-~ Vierfarbanzeige; **full-page** ~ ganzseitige
Anzeige; **small ~s** kleine Anzeigen, Anzeigenteil einer Zeitung; **two page** ~ zweiseitige Anzeige;
to run free ~s for jobseekers Stellengesuche kostenlos veröffentlichen; **to run ~s at lower local rates** billigere Anzeigen-
preise für Regionalausgaben berechnen;
~ **agency** Werbeagentur; ~ **budget** Werbeetat; **to allocate 80%
of its** ~ **budget to television** 80% seines Werbeaufwandes im
Fernsehsektor einsetzen; **~-checking bureau** Erfolgskontroll-
stelle; ~ **columns** Anzeigenteil; ~ **effectiveness** Werbewirksamkeit; ~ **man** Anzeigenfachmann; ~ **material** Werbematerial; **~-page audience** Beachtung pro Anzeigenseite;
~-page exposure Leserkontaktmöglichkeit je Anzeigenseite;
~-page traffic Blickverlauf auf einer Anzeigenseite; ~ **place-
ments** Stellenanzeigen; ~ **position** Anzeigenplazierung; ~ **rate**
Anzeigenpreis, -gebühr; ~ **representative** Anzeigenvertreter;
~ **revenues** Anzeigeneinnahmen; ~ **sales promotion manager**
Anzeigenwerbeleiter; ~ **salesman** Anzeigenvertreter; ~ **spender** Werbeaufwandträger; ~ **writer** Werbe-, Anzeigentexter.
ad interim | copyright vorläufiger Urheberschutz; ~ **duties**
einstweilige Aufgaben; ~ **referendum** *(law)* zur späteren
Ergänzung; ~ **report** Zwischenbericht; ~ **valorem** dem Wert
entsprechend.
Adam, not to know s. o. from keine Ahnung haben, wer jemand
ist.
adapt *(v.)* *(adjust)* anpassen, angleichen, adaptieren, *(change)*
umstellen, ändern, *(theater)* bearbeiten;
~ **o. s. to circumstances** sich den Verhältnissen anpassen; ~ **a
factory to the lines of other products** Fabrikationsbetrieb
umstellen; ~ **a play for broadcasting** Stück für den Rundfunk
umarbeiten; ~ **a room to office use** Zimmer als Büro einrichten
(herrichten); ~ **for sale** für den Verkauf herrichten.
adaptability Anpassungsfähigkeit, -vermögen, Verwendungsfähigkeit, *(range of application)* Verwendungsbereich.
adaptable anpassungs-, abänderungs-, verwendungsfähig;
~ **demand** anpassungsfähige Nachfrage.
adaptation Anpassung, Angleichung, Adaption, *(film, theater)*
Bearbeitung;
~ **to** *(building)* Umbau in;
social ~ soziale Anpassung;
~ **of a factory to the production of other lines** Umstellung des
Fabrikationsbetriebes; ~ **of a play for broadcasting** Umarbeitung eines Stücks für den Rundfunk; ~ **of prices** Anpassung
der Preise; ~ **of a room to office use** Herrichtung eines Zimmers als Büro;
~ **allowance** Anpassungsbeihilfe; ~ **level** Adaptionsniveau.
adapted bearbeitet, leicht verändert, angepaßt, *(statistics)*
bereinigt;
to be ~ to s. th. auf etw. zugeschnitten sein;
~ **figures** bereinigte Werte.
adapter Zusatzgerät, *(film, theater)* Bearbeiter.
adaptive anpassungsfähig;
~ **control** *(production method)* Optimierungsrechnung.
add *(v.)* addieren, zusammenzählen, hinzurechnen, -fügen,
beistellen, *(enclose)* beifügen, *(make a supplementary payment)* zuzahlen, nachschießen;
~ **to** zuzählen, nachfüllen; ~ **to a building** an ein Gebäude
anbauen; ~ **a column of figures** Zahlenkolonne zusammenrechnen; ~ **correctly** richtig addieren; ~ **the interest to the
capital** Zinsen zum Kapital schlagen; ~ **to a language** Sprache
bereichern; ~ **8% to the price** 8% auf den Preis aufschlagen; ~
a piece to one's collection Stück seiner Sammlung einverle-
ben; ~ **up** addieren, zusammenzählen, -rechnen, aufrechnen,
(assets) sich belaufen auf; ~ **a zero** Null anhängen;
~-ons miteinander verbundene Abzahlungsverträge; **~-on
unit** Vorsatzgerät.

added erhöht, verstärkt, zusätzlich;
~ **damages** über den verursachten Schaden hinausgehende
Entschädigung, Buße, Bußgeld; ~ **money** Zusatzwette,
zusätzlicher Wetterlös; ~ **performance** Zugabe; ~ **risk** Risikoerhöhung; ~ **value** Mehrwert.
addendum Nachtrag, Zusatz.
adder Addiermaschine.
addict Süchtiger;
drug ~ Rauschgiftsüchtiger; **film** ~ Filmnarr.
addicted to the bottle dem Trunk ergeben.
adding unter Hinzufügung von;
~ **[-listing] machine** Additionsmaschine, Addiermaschine mit
Schreibwerk.
addition *(adding up)* Zusammenrechnung, Hinzufügung, Zurechnung, *(balance sheet)* Zugang [beim Sachanlagever-
mögen], *(building, US)* Anbau, *(employees)* Zugänge, *(enlargement)* Vergrößerung *(land, US)* Landzukauf, *(mark of
designation to name)* Zusatz[name], berufliche Zusatzbe-
zeichnung, *(suburban area)* neu erschlossenes Wohngebiet,
(thing added) Zugabe, Beifügung;
in ~ zusätzlich, dazu, extra;
subsequent ~s *(balance sheet)* [Anlagen]zugänge;
~ **to one's collection** Einverleibung in seine Sammlung; ~ **at
cost** zusätzliche Leistungen zum Selbstkostenpreis; **~s and
improvements** Wertveränderungen; ~ **to a language** Sprachbe-
reicherung; **~s to management** Vorstandserweiterung; ~ **to
price** Zuschlag zum Verkaufspreis; ~ **to reserve** Zuführung
zum Reservefonds; ~ **to retained earnings** *(US)* Zuführung zur
Gewinnrücklage; ~ **to s. one's salary** Gehaltserhöhung, -zu-
lage, -aufbesserung; **~s to the staff** Vergrößerung der Belegschaft, Personalerweiterung; ~ **to [our] stocks** Lageranreicherung, -zugänge; ~ **to working capital** Betriebskapital-
erhöhung;
to make an ~ nachtragen; **to pay in** ~ zuzahlen; **to perform an** ~
Addition vornehmen;
~ **sign** Pluszeichen.
additional hinzugefügt, -kommend, zuzüglich, weiter, zusätzlich, nachträglich;
~ **agreement** Nebenabrede, Zusatzabkommen; ~ **allowance**
Zuschuß, Zulage; ~ **amount** Zuschußbetrag; ~ **annuity**
Zusatzrente; ~ **application** (Patent) Zusatzanmeldung; ~
article Zusatzartikel; ~ **assessment** Nachveranlagung; ~ **benefit** Zusatzunterstützung, -versorgung; ~ **burden** zusätzliche
Lasten; ~ **care** besondere Vorsicht; ~ **charges** Aufschlag,
Aufrechnung, Zuschlag, zusätzliche Kosten, Neben-, Mehrkosten, [Preis]zuschlag; ~ **claim** Nachforderung; ~ **clause**
Zusatzklausel, -bestimmung, Nachtrag; ~ **commission** Zusatzprovision; ~ **conditions** Neben-, Zusatzbedingungen; ~
consumption Mehrverbrauch; ~ **contribution** Zusatzbeitrag; ~
costs Mehrkosten; **to involve** ~ **costs** mit zusätzlichen Kosten
verbunden sein; ~ **cover** zusätzliche Deckung, Nachschußzahlung; **to furnish (put up)** ~ **cover** Nachschußzahlung leisten; ~ **credit** zusätzlicher Kredit; ~ **delivery** Zusatz-,
Nachlieferung; ~ **demand** Mehrbedarf, Nachforderung; ~
depreciation Sonderabschreibung; ~ **discount** Sonderrabatt; ~
dividend Zusatzdividende, Bonus; ~ **duty** Steuerzuschlag,
(customs) Nachzoll, Zollaufschlag; ~ **entry** Nachbuchung; ~
expenditure Mehrausgabe; ~ **expenses** zusätzliche Kosten,
Mehrkosten; ~ **fee** Zuschlagsgebühr, Gebührenzuschlag; ~
freight Frachtzuschlag, -aufschlag, Mehrfracht; ~ **income**
Nebeneinkommen, Nebenverdienst, -einkünfte; ~ **insertion**
zusätzliche Anzeige; ~ **insurance** Nachversicherung, Zusatzversicherung; ~ **insured** *(automobile insurance)* nachversicher-
ter Nichteigentümer; ~ **interest** Stückzinsen; ~ **invention**
Zusatzerfindung; ~ **leave** Nachurlaub; ~ **legacy** Zusatzvermächtnis; ~ **margin** *(US)* weitere Deckung, Nachschußzahlung; ~ **order** zusätzlicher Auftrag, Zusatzauftrag,
Nachbestellung; ~ **pay** Gehaltszulage; ~ **payment** Nachzahlung, Nachschuß; **to make an** ~ **payment** nachzahlen, zuzahlen, nachschießen; **to call for an** ~ **payment** Nachschuß
einfordern; ~ **plant** Nebenanlage; ~ **policy** Zusatz, Nachtragspolice; ~ **postage** Nach-, Mehrporto, Portozuschlag, Nachgebühr; ~ **premium** Prämienzuschlag; ~ **price** Aufpreis,
Preisaufschlag, Mehrpreis; ~ **profit** Mehrgewinn; ~ **proof**
Nebenbeweis; ~ **protocol** Zusatzprotokoll; ~ **provisions**
Zusatzbestimmungen; ~ **receipts** Mehreinnahmen; ~ **report**
Zusatzbericht; ~ **requirements** nachträglicher Bedarf, Mehrbedarf; ~ **respite** Nachfrist; ~ **security** zusätzliche Sicherheit;
~ **set** *(el.)* Zusatzaggregat; ~ **sum** Zusatzbetrag; ~ **tax** Steuerzuschlag; ~ **test** Nach-, Zusatztest; ~ **training** Zusatzausbil-
dung; ~ **work** zusätzliche Arbeitsleistungen.

additionally als Zusatz (Zugabe).

additive Zusatz.

address Adresse, *(law court, US)* Anrede des Gerichts, *(letter)* Anschrift, Aufschrift, *(petition)* Eingabe, Denk-, Bittschrift, *(speech)* Ansprache, Festrede, Vortrag, *(superscription of letter)* Anrede;
in case of change of ~ falls verzogen; of no fixed ~ ohne festen Wohnsitz;
abbreviated ~ Telegrammadresse; **accommodation** ~ Deckadresse; **brief** ~ kurze Adresse; **business** ~ Geschäftsanschrift, -adresse; **cable** ~ Drahtanschrift, Telegrammadresse; **ceremonial** ~ Festansprache; **code** ~ Deckadresse; **cover** ~ Deckanschrift, -adresse; **final** ~ Schlußansprache; **home** ~ Privatanschrift; **inaugural (inauguration)** ~ Antritts-, Einweihungsrede; **mailing** ~ Zustellanschrift, Postanschrift; **memorial** ~ Gedenk-, Gedächtnisrede; **official** ~ Büroanschrift; **opening** ~ Eröffnungsansprache, -rede; **permanent** ~ ständige Adresse; **post-office** ~ Postanschrift; **postal** ~ Postanschrift; **private** ~ Privatanschrift; **radio** ~ Rundfunkansprache; **registered** ~ Geschäftssitz; **return** ~ Absender; **telegram (telegraphic)** ~ Telegrammanschrift, -adresse; **television** ~ Fernsehansprache; **wrong** ~ falsche Adresse (Anschrift);
~ **in case of need** *(bill of exchange)* Notadresse; ~ **of convenience** Deckadresse; ~ **to the crown** *(parliament, Br.)* Dankesadresse; ~ **and rejoinder** Rede und Gegenrede; ~ **for service** *(Br.)* Zustellungswohnort, -adresse, Zustellanschrift; ~ **of thanks** Dankadresse; ~ **to the voters** Wahlrede; ~ **of welcome** Begrüßungsansprache;
~ *(v.)* Briefe senden, adressieren, *(direct)* richten an;
~ **an appeal** Aufruf richten an; ~ **envelopes** Briefumschläge beschriften; ~ **a gathering** Ansprache halten; ~ **the House** *(Br.)* das Wort ergreifen; ~ **a meeting** Wort in einer Versammlung ergreifen; ~ **notification** Mitteilung machen an;
to change the ~ umadressieren; **to deliver a short** ~ kurze Ansprache halten; **to depart without leaving one's** ~ ohne Adressenangabe abreisen; **to find out s. one's** ~ jds. Adresse ermitteln; **to give an** ~ Vortrag halten; **to leave one's** ~ seine Adresse hinterlassen; **to live at a good** ~ in einer guten Gegend wohnen; **to take down s. one's name on** ~ sich jds. Namen und Anschrift notieren; **to write an** ~ **down** sich eine Adresse notieren;
~ **book** Adressen-, Notizbuch; ~ **card** Geschäftskarte; ~ **changes** Adressenänderung; ~ **commission** Provision des Verladers, *(ship)* Schiffsüberführungsgebühr; ~ **control** Adressenkontrolle; ~ **label** Adressenzettel; ~ **office** Adressenbüro; ~ **point** Anschriftensammelpunkt; ~ **revision** Überprüfung des Adressenmaterials; ~ **source** Adressenquelle; **public** ~ **system** Rundsprech-, Lautsprecheranlage.

addressed bill Domizilwechsel.

addressee Empfänger, Adressat;
~ **firm** angeschriebene Firma.

addresser Adressant, Aussteller.

addressing machine Adressiermaschine.

addressograph Adressiermaschine, Adrema;
~ **plate** Adremaplatte.

adduce *(v.)* **evidence (proof)** Beweis erbringen.

adduction of evidence Beweiserbringung.

adeem *(v.)* **a legacy** Vermächtnis widerrufen.

ademption of a legacy Legatsentziehung, Vermächtniswiderruf.

adept Kenner, Kunstsachverständiger.

adequacy Angemessenheit;
~ **of service** zufriedenstellende Dienstleistung.

adequate hinlänglich, angemessen, zufriedenstellend;
~ **care** hinreichende (genügende) Sorgfalt; ~ **cause** adäquate Ursache; ~ **compensation** angemessene Abstandsumme; ~ **consideration** angemessene (gleichwertige) Gegenleistung; ~ **judge** zuständiger Richter; ~ **preparation** *(trial)* ausreichende Prozeßvorbereitung; ~ **price** angemessener Preis; ~ **provocation** schuldmindernde Provokationen der Gegenseite; ~ **remedy** ausreichender (genügender) Rechtsbehelf; ~ **remuneration** angemessene Belohnung; ~ **sample** repräsentative Marktuntersuchung, ausreichende Stichprobe; ~ **supply of provisions** ausreichende Vorräte.

adhere *(v.)* festhalten an, befolgen, einhalten, *(law, Scot.)* bestätigen;
~ **strictly to a clause** sich unnachgiebig an eine Vertragsbestimmung halten; ~ **to instructions** Vorschriften einhalten; ~ **to a party** sich einer Partei anschließen; ~ **to a plan** einem Plan treu bleiben; ~ **to rules** Regeln befolgen; ~ **to one's statement** seine Behauptung aufrechterhalten, bei seiner Aussage bleiben; ~ **to terms** Bedingungen einhalten.

adherence Festhalten, Beharren, *(adhesion)* Beitritt, *(Scot.)* Klage auf Wiederherstellung der ehelichen Lebensgemeinschaft;
~ **to a party** Parteizugehörigkeit.

adherent Anhänger;
~s [politischer] Anhang, Anhängerschaft, Gefolgschaft;
~ *(a.)* fest verbunden, anhänglich.

adhesion Beitritt, Anschluß, Assoziierung;
~ **to a policy** Festhalten an einer Politik;
to give in one's ~ seinen Beitritt erklären.

adhesive gummierte Briefmarke, *(US)* Klebestoff, Kleber;
~ *(a.)* anhaftend, *(US)* anhänglich, bleibend;
~ **binding** Klebebindung, Lumbecken; ~ **envelope** gummierter Briefumschlag; ~ **label** Klebevignette; ~ **postage stamp** gummiertes Postwertzeichen; ~ **stamp** Stempelmarke; ~ **stick** Klebestift.

adjacency Umgebung, *(broadcasting)* Beiprogramm.

adjacent anliegend, anstoßend, aneinandergrenzend, benachbart;
~ **land** Anlieger-, Nachbargrundstück, benachbartes Gebiet; ~ **owner** Anwohner, Anlieger, Grenznachbar; ~ **parts of land** angrenzende Grundstücke; ~ **rooms** angrenzende Zimmer; ~ **site** Nachbargrundstück; ~ **village** Nachbardorf; ~ **waters** Küstengewässer.

adjective Eigenschaftswort;
~ **law** Prozeß-, Verfahrensrecht, formelles Recht.

adjoin *(v.)* aneinandergrenzen.

adjoining angrenzend, anliegend, aneinandergrenzend, anstoßend, benachbart;
~ **estate** Nachbargrundstück; ~ **field** angrenzendes Feldstück; ~ **highway** vorbeiführende Landstraße; ~ **house** Nachbarhaus; ~ **land** Nachbargrundstück; ~ **owner** Anlieger, Grenznachbar; ~ **room** Nebenzimmer; ~ **table** nebenstehende Tabelle.

adjourn *(v.)* *(break off)* vertagen, [Sitzungsort] verlegen, *(postpone)* verschieben, aufschieben;
~ **a case** *(law court)* Sitzung unterbrechen; ~ **sine die** sich auf unbestimmt Zeit vertagen; ~ **a decision** Entscheidung aussetzen; ~ **a hearing** Verhandlung vertagen; ~ **over the holidays** sich bis nach den Ferien vertagen; ~ **for an hour** für eine Stunde unterbrechen; ~ **a general meeting** Hauptversammlung vertagen; ~ **a petition in bankruptcy** über einen Konkursantrag noch nicht entscheiden.

adjournable aufschiebbar.

adjournal *(Scot.)* Strafakten.

adjourned vertagt;
to move that a case may be ~ um Vertagung bitten, Vertagung beantragen; **to stand** ~ sich vertagen.

adjournment *(postponement)* Verschiebung, Aufschub, *(propagation)* Unterbrechung, Vertagung, Verlegung;
~ **sine die** Vertagung auf unbestimmte Zeit; ~ **of three days** dreitägige Vertagung; ~ **of a hearing** Aussetzen eines Termins; ~ **of a meeting** Sitzungsunterbrechung; ~ **of a petition in bankruptcy** Aufschub eines Konkursantrages;
to petition for ~ um Terminverlegung bitten; **to vote the** ~ **of a meeting** Vertagung (Verlegung) einer Versammlung beschließen;
~ **day** neuer Verhandlungstermin; ~ **day in error** *(Br.)* neuer Berufungstermin; ~ **deadline** äußerster Vertagungstermin; ~ **motion** Vertagungsantrag; ~ **term** verlängerte Sitzungsperiode.

adjudge *(v.)* gerichtlich (richterlich) entscheiden, *(award)* durch gerichtliche Entscheidung zusprechen (zuerkennen, -teilen);
~ **s. o. a bankrupt** Konkursverfahren über jds. Vermögen eröffnen; ~ **a complaint** einer Beschwerde abhelfen; ~ **damages** Schadenersatz zusprechen (zuerkennen); ~ **a prize to s. o.** jem. eine Belohnung (einen Preis) zuerkennen; ~ **a question of law** Rechtsfrage entscheiden.

adjudicate *(v.)* zuteilen, zuschlagen, *(decide upon)* [gerichtlich] entscheiden, Urteil fällen, Recht sprechen;
~ **s. o. judicially to be a bankrupt** über j. den Konkurs verhängen; ~ **a claim** Forderung anerkennen.

adjudicated | bankrupt Konkurs-, Gemeinschuldner; ~ **liquidation** Zwangsliquidation.

adjudication *(at auction)* Zuschlag[serteilung], *(award)* Zuerkennung, Zusprechung, *(of bankruptcy)* Konkurseröffnung, -verhängung, *(legal decision)* Rechtsspruch, richterliche Entscheidung, Gerichtsentscheidung, *(law, Scot.)* Nachlaßpfändung, *(of stamps)* Wertbemessung [für Stempelsteuer];
free ~ freihändige Auftragsvergabe;

~ in bankruptcy (of a bankrupt) Konkursverhängung, -eröffnung, -erklärung, Eröffnung des Konkursverfahrens; **~ of national claims commissions** Zuerkennung von Schadensersatzansprüchen durch staatliche Schadensregulierungsausschüsse; **~ in s. one's favo(u)r** Entscheidung für j.; **~ in implement** Klage auf Eigentumsverschaffung;
to annul an ~ Konkurseröffnung aufheben; **~ order** Konkurseröffnungsbeschluß; **~ process** Zuerkennungsverfahren.

adjudicative *(law)* deklaratorisch.
adjudicator Preis-, Schiedsrichter.
adjunct *(s. th. added)* Zusatz, Beigabe, Anfang, *(colleague)* Amtsgenosse, -gehilfe, Kollege, *(court)* Beigeordneter;
~ account Hilfskonto; **~ professor** *(US)* außerordentlicher Professor.
adjunction Beiordnung, *(accession)* Eigentumserwerb durch Vermischung, *(confusion)* Vermischung.
adjuration Beschwörung, dringende Bitte, *(solemn oath)* Vereidiung.
adjure *(v.)* beschwören, inständig bitten, *(bind by oath)* vereidigen.
adjust *(v.) (adapt)* anpassen, angleichen, abstimmen, *(balance)* ausgleichen, abwickeln, *(coin)* einer Münze das richtige Gewicht geben, *(determine amount of loss)* [Versicherungs-]ansprüche regulieren, *(gauge)* [Gewicht] eichen, *(income tax)* fortschreiben, *(settle)* [gütlich] beilegen, schlichten, Streitigkeit beilegen;
~ accounts Konten in Ordnung bringen (berichtigen, glattstellen, bereinigen); **~ advertising rates** Anzeigensätze anpassen; **~ the average** Versicherungsschaden durch Besichtigung feststellen, Dispache aufmachen; **~ the calender** Kalender angleichen; **~ the capital** Kapital berichtigen; **~ o. s. readily to circumstances** sich schnell auf veränderte Verhältnisse einstellen; **~ complaints** Beschwerden abhelfen; **~ currencies** Währungen angleichen; **~ damages** Schadenersatzansprüche regeln; **~ differences** Streitigkeiten schlichten; **~ an entry** Buchung berichtigen; **~ o. s. to one's environment** sich seiner Umgebung anpassen; **~ freight rates** Frachtsätze angleichen; **~ the interest** Zinsen anpassen; **~ a matter** Angelegenheit richtigstellen; **~ production** Produktionsangleichung vornehmen; **~ quotas** Quoten bereinigen (berichtigen); **~ the real-estate value** Grundstückswert fortschreiben; **~ existing wage rates** bestehende Lohnsätze ausgleichen; **~ a weight** Gewicht eichen; **~ prior year's profit** Vorjahresgewinn berichtigen.
adjustable ein-, verstellbar, *(insurance)* regulierbar;
~ peg *(exchange)* zugelassene Bandbreite.
adjusted berichtigt, bereinigt;
seasonally ~ saisonbereinigt;
~ to inflation inflationsbereinigt; **~ for price** preisbereinigt; **~ for seasonal variations** saisonbereinigt;
~ basis *(federal income tax)* bereinigte Besteuerungsgrundlage; **~ costs** auf den Tageswert umgerechnete Kosten; **~ cost basis** *(income tax)* bereinigter Selbstkostenpreis; **~ gross income** *(US)* berichtigtes Roheinkommen; **~ production index** bereinigter Produktionsindex.
adjuster, adjustor Regulierungs-, Feststellungsbeamter, Schadenssachverständiger, *(marine insurance)* Schadensregulierer, Regulierungsbeauftragter;
average ~ Dispacheur; **claim ~** *(insurance)* Schadenssachverständiger, Regulierungsbeauftragter.
adjusting|journal entry Berichtigungsbuchung; **~ shop** Zurichterei.
adjustment *(adaption)* Anpassung, Angleichung, *(balancing)* Ab-, Ausgleichung, Beilegung, Regulierung, *(balance sheet)* Wertberichtigung, *(bookkeeping)* Berichtigungsbuchung, *(correction)* Richtigstellung, Berichtigung, *(insurance)* Schadensfestsetzung, Regulierung, *(reorganization)* Sanierung, *(settlement)* gütlicher Vergleich, Schlichtung, gütliche Beilegung;
after ~ of inflation inflationsbereinigt;
amicable ~ gütlicher Vergleich; **average ~** Havarie-, Seeschadensberechnung, Dispache[aufmachung]; **capital ~** Kapitalberichtigung; **cash ~** Barausgleich, -regulierung; **currency ~** Währungsangleichung; **end-of-year ~** Rechnungsabgrenzung; **financial ~** Finanzausgleich, finanzieller Ausgleich; **foreign exchange ~** Devisenwertberichtigungen; **overall ~** Sammelwertberichtigung; **price ~** Preisregulierung, -angleichung, -anpassung; **prior period ~** Berichtigungsfortschreibung; **prior year ~s** Berichtigungen der Vorjahresbilanz; **~ released** aufgelöste Wertberichtigung; **salary ~** Gehaltsangleichung; **short-rate ~** Anpassung an den ermä-

ßigten Tarif, Preiskorrektur; **social ~** soziale Anpassung, sozialer Ausgleich; **social security ~** Anpassung der Sozialversicherungsleistungen; **supply-demand ~** Regulierung von Angebot und Nachfrage; **vocational ~** Einarbeitung; **wage ~** Lohnangleichung, -ausgleich;
~ of accounts Kontenabstimmung, -bereinigung, -glattstellung, -regulierung; **~ in advertising rates** Anpassung der Anzeigensätze; **~ of average** Havarie-, Seeschadensberechnung, Dispache; **~ of the calender** Kalenderangleichung; **~ of a complaint** Erledigung einer Beschwerde; **~ of currencies** Währungsangleichung; **~ of capital** Kapitalberichtigung; **~ of damages** Schadensregulierung, -feststellung; **~ of depreciations** Abschreibungskorrekturen; **~ of differences** Beilegung (Schlichtung) von Streitigkeiten; **~ with retroactive effect** rückwirkende Berichtigung; **~ of an entry** Abänderung einer Buchung; **~ of freight rates** Angleichung der Frachtsätze; **~ of frontier** Grenzberichtigung; **~ of incomes** Einkommensangleichung; **~ of an insurance claim** Regulierung eines Versicherungsfalles; **~ of interest** Zinsanpassung; **~ of a loss** Schadensregulierung; **~ of premium** Prämienangleichung; **~ of prices** Preisanpassung; **~ in production** Produktionsangleichung; **~ of prior year's profits** Berichtigung des vorjährigen Gewinns, Berichtigungen der Vorjahresbilanz; **~ of quotas** Quotenberichtigung; **~ [and relationship] of rates** *(customs)* Tarifanpassung, *(railway)* Angleichung der Frachtsätze; **~ for tax purposes** steuerlich notwendige Berichtigung; **automatic ~ of tax schedules to the rate of inflation** automatische Anpassung der Steuertabelle an die Inflationsrate; **~ of value** Einzelwertberichtigung; **~ of real-estate value** Fortschreibung des Grundstückswertes; **global ~ of value** Sammelwertberichtigung; **~ of existing wage rates** Angleichung der bestehenden Lohnsätze; **~ for wear and tear** Wertberichtigung für Abnutzung; **~ of weight** Gewichtseichung; **~ of a will** Testamentsabänderung;
to allow for ~ für Berichtigungen Vorsorge treffen; **to make ~s** Anpassungen durchführen;
~ account Berichtigungskonto; **~ action** Ausgleichsmaßnahmen; **~ board** Schlichtungskommission; **~ [income] bond** *(US)* Besserungsschein; **~ bureau** *(department store)* Abteilung zur Regulierung unbezahlter Rechnungen, Schadensbüro; **~ charges** Dispachekosten; **~ column** Berichtigungsspalte; **~ entry** berichtigende Buchung, Berichtigungseintrag, -buchung; **~ item** Ausgleichsposten, [Wert]berichtigungsposten; **~ letter** Beschwichtigungsbrief; **price ~ levy** *(European Community)* Abschöpfungsbetrag; **~ measures** *(European Community)* Ausgleichsmaßnahmen; **~ mechanism** Anpassungsmechanismus; **~ mortgage** Hypothek zur Sicherung von Inhaberschuldverschreibungen; **~ policy** Beschwichtigungspolitik; **~ procedure** außergerichtliches Vergleichsverfahren; **~ process** Regulierungsprozeß.
adjutancy Adjutantur.
adjutant Adjutant.
admag *(coll.)* Anzeigenblatt, -zeitschrift.
adman *(US)* Werbe-, Reklamefachmann, Anzeigenakquisiteur, -fachmann.
admarginate *(v.)* mit Randbemerkungen versehen.
admass Massenpublikum [bei Werbesendungen].
admeasure *(v.) (gauge)* ab-, ausmessen, eichen, *(law)* zuerkennen, zumessen;
~ a dower gesetzliches Erbrecht der Witwe festsetzen; **~ a legacy** Legat aussetzen.
admeasurement Ab-, Aus-, Vermessung, Eichung, *(punishment)* Zumessung;
~ of dowry Festsetzung des Witwenerbrechtes; **~ of legacy** Legataussetzung; **~ of pasture** Ausgleichsverfahren für Weidenutzungen.
adminicle *(law)* Nebenbeweis.
administer *(v.)* verwalten, handhaben, *(act as administrator)* als Nachlaßverwalter tätig sein, als Testamentsvollstrecker verwalten, *(manage)* verwalten, handhaben, *(price)* regulieren, kontrollieren, *(real estate)* bewirtschaften;
~ an affirmation eidesstattliche Erklärung abnehmen; **~ a bankrupt's estate** Konkurs verwalten (abwickeln); **~ custodianship accounts** Depots verwalten; **~ a debtor's estate summarily** Schuldnervermögen zwangsverwalten; **~ upon a decedent's estate** Nachlaß von jem. abwickeln; **~ the government** Regierungsgeschäfte wahrnehmen; **~ justice** Gesetze anwenden, Recht sprechen; **~ the law** Recht sprechen; **~ a medicine** Arznei (Medizin) eingeben; **~ an oath to s. o.** jem. einen Eid abnehmen, jem. vereidigen; **~ to the needs of the poor** der Not der Armen steuern; **~ poison** Gift beibringen;

property Vermögen verwalten; ~ **relief** Fürsorge angedeihen lassen; ~ **restrictions** Beschränkungen handhaben; ~ **a will** Testamentsbestimmungen durchführen.

administered│competition regulierter Wettbewerb; ~ **price** künstlich festgesetzter Preis, Richtpreis, regulierter Preis; ~ **rate of interest** von der Zentralbank regulierter Zinssatz.

administering│poison Giftbeibringung;
~ **authority** *(international law)* Verwaltungsmacht.

administrable verwaltbar.

administrant Verwaltungsbeamter, Verwalter.

administrate *(v.)* als Verwalter tätig sein.

administration Administration, Handhabung, Verwaltung, *(apparatus)* Verwaltungsapparat, -behörde, *(estate)* Nachlaßverwaltung, *(hospital)* Direktion, *(politics, US)* Ministerium, Regierung, Kabinett, *(term of office, US)* Amtsdauer eines Präsidenten, *(trustee)* treuhänderische Verwaltung, Vermögensverwaltung;

after the ~ of the oath nach der Eidesleistung;

ancillary ~ Nebennachlaßverwaltung; **bribable ~** korrupte Verwaltung; **business ~** *(US)* Betriebswirtschaftslehre; **central ~** Zentral-, Hauptverwaltung; **civil ~** Zivil-, Staatsverwaltung; **customs ~** Zollverwaltung; **Economic Cooperation ~** **(ECA)** Verwaltung für europäische wirtschaftliche Zusammenarbeit; **fiscal ~** Finanzverwaltung; **forest ~** Forstverwaltung; **general ~** Verwaltung des gesamten Nachlasses; **industrial ~** Betriebswirtschaft; **lame-duck ~** auslaufende Regierung; **local ~** Gemeindeverwaltung; **main ~** Hauptverwaltung; **municipal ~** Gemeindeverwaltung; **personnel ~** Personalverwaltung; **public ~** Regie, *(deceased's estate)* Abwesenheitspflegschaft; **public-business ~** Verwaltung öffentlich-rechtlicher Betriebe; **self-~** Selbstverwaltung; **special ~** auf einzelne Nachlaßgegenstände beschränkte Nachlaßverwaltung; **summary ~** Nachlaßverwaltung von Bagatellsachen; **tax ~** Steuerverwaltung; **trust ~** Treuhandverwaltung; **wage and salary ~** Lohn- und Gehaltswesen; **wasteful ~** aufwendige Verwaltung;

~ **of an affirmation** Abnahme einer eidesstaatlichen Erklärung; ~ **of assets** Nachlaßverwaltung; ~ **of a bankrupt's estate** Konkursverwaltung; ~ **of business** Geschäftsführung; ~ **by the Crown** *(Br.)* fiskalische Verwaltung; ~ **of custodianship accounts** Depotverwaltung; ~ **of [the] customs** Zollverwaltung; ~ **of an estate** Nachlaß-, Erbschaftsverwaltung; ~ **upon a decedent's estate** *(US)* Nachlaßverwaltung, Nachlaßabwicklung; ~ **of the government** Wahrnehmung der Regierungsgeschäfte; ~ **of income tax** Einkommensteuerbehörde; ~ **of justice** Rechtsprechung, Rechtspflege, Justizverwaltung; ~ **of the National Debt** Staatsschuldenverwaltung; ~ **of an oath** Eidesabnahme, Vereidigung; ~ **of office** Amtsführung; ~ **of property** Vermögensverwaltung; ~ **of restrictions** Handhabung von Beschränkungen; ~ **of the public revenue** Verwaltung der Staatsfinanzen; ~ **of stores** Magazinverwaltung; ~ **with the will annexed** gerichtlich angeordnete Nachlaßverwaltung, Testamentsvollstreckerbestellung;

to form an ~ *(US)* Regierung bilden;

~⁹ **of Estates Act** *(Br.)* Gesetz zur Regelung der gesetzlichen Erbfolge; ~⁹ **of Justice Act** *(Br.)* Justizverwaltungsgesetz; ~ **action** Klage auf ordnungsgemäße Nachlaßverwaltung; ~ **bill** von der Regierung eingebrachtes Gesetz; ~ **bond** Sicherheitsleistung des Nachlaßverwalters; ~ **building** Verwaltungsgebäude; ~ **burden** Verwaltungskostenlast; ~ **centre** *(Br.)* **(center,** *US*) Verwaltungszentrum; ~**'s commitments** *(US)* Regierungszusagen; ~ **economists** Wirtschaftsfachkräfte der Regierung; ~ **expenses** Nachlaßkosten, *(bankruptcy proceedings)* Konkursverwaltungskosten; ~ **machinery** Verwaltungsapparat; ~ **measure** Verwaltungsmaßnahme; ~ **office** Verwaltungsamt; ~ **opposition** Widerstand der Regierung; ~ **order** *(Br.)* Anordnung der Vermögensverwaltung; ~ **proposal** Regierungsvorschlag; ~ **regulations** Verwaltungsvorschriften; ~ **suit** Klage auf Anordnung der Nachlaßverwaltung, Nachlaßverfahren.

administration trainee *(civil service, Br.)* in Ausbildung befindlicher Beamter.

administrationist *(US)* Regierungsanhänger.

administrative verwaltend, verwaltungstechnisch, -mäßig;

good ~ ability Begabung für Verwaltungsaufgaben; ~ **act** Verwaltungshandlung, -akt, -maßnahme; **to put into effect by ~ action** im Verwaltungswege zur Durchführung bringen; ~ **activity** Verwaltungstätigkeit; ~ **agency** *(US)* Verwaltungsbehörde; ~ **agreement** Verwaltungsabkommen; ~ **aid** Amtshilfe; ~ **apparatus** Verwaltungsapparat; ~ **area** Verwaltungsbezirk, -gebiet; ~ **arrangement** Verwaltungsvereinbarung; ~ **author-**

ity Verwaltungsbehörde; ~ **autonomy** Selbstverwaltung; ~ **board** Verwaltungsstelle, Verwaltungsgremium, -körper, *(European Investment Bank)* Verwaltungsrat; **to appoint an ~ board** Verwaltungsausschuß einsetzen; ~ **body** Verwaltungsorgan, -gremium, *(government)* Regierungsbehörde; ~ **bond** Sicherheitsleistung des Nachlaßverwalters; ~ **business** Nachlaßangelegenheit; ~ **center** *(US)* **(centre,** *Br.*) Verwaltungszentrum; **through ~ channels** auf dem Verwaltungswege; ~ **charges** Verwaltungskosten, -gebühr; ~ **charges expended on the work to date** aufgeschlüsselte Verwaltungsunkosten; ~ **chief** Aufsichtsinstanz; ~ **company** Verwaltungsgesellschaft; ~ **costs** Verwaltungs-, Bewirtschaftungskosten, Verwaltungsaufwand; ~ **county** *(Br.)* Geschäfts-, Verwaltungsbezirk, [etwa] Landkreis; ~ **court** Verwaltungsgericht; ~ **decision** Verwaltungsentscheidung; ~ **department** Verwaltungsabteilung, -fach, -zweig, Dezernat; ~ **determination** Verwaltungsentscheidung; ~ **difficulties** Verwaltungsschwierigkeiten; ~ **directive** Verwaltungsanordnung; ~ **discretion** Ermessen der Verwaltungsbehörde; ~ **district** Regierungs-, Verwaltungsbezirk; ~ **division** Verwaltungsabteilung; ~ **duties** Verwaltungsaufgaben; ~ **establishment** Verwaltungsapparat; ~ **expenditure (expense)** Verwaltungskosten, Verwaltungsaufwand; ~ **experience** Verwaltungserfahrung; ~ **fee** Verwaltungsgebühr; ~ **fine** Ordnungsstrafe, Zwangsgeld; ~ **function** Verwaltungsfunktion, *(law court)* Gerichtstätigkeit; ~ **genius** Verwaltungsgenie; ~ **headquarters** Verwaltungssitz; ~ **jurisdiction** Verwaltungsgerichtbarkeit; ~ **law** Verwaltungsrecht; ~ **law judge** Verwaltungsrichter; **to pass on the ~ leadership** Leitung der Verwaltung abgeben; ~ **machinery** Verwaltungsapparat; ~ **manpower** Verwaltungskräfte; ~ **matter** Verwaltungsangelegenheit; ~ **measures** verwaltungstechnische Maßnahmen, Verwaltungsmaßnahmen; ~ **network** Versorgungsnetz; ~ **office** *(US)* Verwaltungsbüro; ~ **officer** Verwaltungsbeamter; ~ **order** *(Br.)* behördliche Anordnung, Verwaltungsanordnung, -verfügung, Anordnung der Vermögensverwaltung, *(probate court)* Verteilungsanordnung, *County Court Act, Br.)* Zwangsverwaltungsbeschluß; ~ **organ** Verwaltungsorgan; ~ **organization** Verwaltungsapparat; ~ **overheads** Verwaltungsgemeinkosten; ~ **personnel** Verwaltungspersonal; ~ **post** leitende Stellung; **to lodge ~ powers** Verwaltungsbefugnisse übertragen; ~ **practice** Verwaltungspraxis; ~ **procedure** Verwaltungsverfahren; ~ **process** Verwaltungsvorgang; ~ **regulation** Verwaltungsvorschrift; ~ **remedy** Abhilfe (Rechtsbehelf) im Verwaltungswege; ~ **report** Verwaltungsbericht; ~ **ruling** Verwaltungsverfügung, -entscheidung; ~ **science** Verwaltungswissenschaft; ~ **service** Verwaltungsdienst; **to provide ~ services** Verwaltungsdienstleistungen erstellen; ~ **setup** Verwaltungsapparat; ~ **staff** Verwaltungspersonal; ~ **supervision** Verwaltungsaufsicht; ~ **terminology** Verwaltungssprache; ~ **tribunal** *(US)* Verwaltungsgericht; ~ **unit** Verwaltungsbezirk, Gebietskörperschaft; ~ **work** Verwaltungsarbeit, -tätigkeit.

administratively, to review im Verwaltungswege überprüfen.

administrator Verwalter, Geschäftsführer, Verweser, Sequester, Kurator, *(of an estate)* Nachlaßverwalter, -pfleger, Testamentsvollstrecker;

ancillary ~ *(US)* Hilfsverwalter; **domestic ~** Nachlaßverwalter am letzten Wohnsitz des Erblassers; **foreign ~** ausländischer Nachlaßverwalter; **public ~** Abwesenheitspfleger;

~ **in bankruptcy** *(of a bankrupt's estate)* *(Br.)* Konkursverwalter; ~ **de bonis non** Ersatztestamentsvollstrecker, Teilnachlaßpfleger; ~ **of an estate** gesetzlich bestellter Nachlaßverwalter; ~ **in law** *(Scot.)* gesetzlicher Vertreter [seiner Kinder]; ~ **ad litem** Prozeßpfleger; ~ **with the will annexed** behördlich bestellter Nachlaßverwalter [bei Nichtantritt von testamentarisch vorgesehenen Parteien];

~**'s account** Nachlaßverwalterkonto; ~**'s bond** Kaution des Nachlaßverwalters.

administratorship Verwalteramt.

Admiralty *(Br.)* Admiralität, Marineamt, *(court of the admiral, Br.)* Seegericht, *(tribunal, US)* Schiffahrtsrecht;

~ **actions** seerechtliche Streitigkeiten; ~⁹ **bond** Garantieschein für Seetransport; ~⁹ **chart** Navigationskarte; ~ **court** Seegericht; ~⁹ **law** Seerecht.

admissibility Zulässigkeit, Statthaftigkeit;
~ **of evidence** Beweiszulässigkeit.

admissible *(allowable)* statthaft, zulässig, *(as evidence)* als Beweismittel zugelassen, *(to position)* zulassungsberechtigt;
~ **evidence** zulässiger Beweis, zulässiges Beweismittel.

admission *(acknowledgement)* Zugeständnis, Einräumung, Zulassung, *(action at law)* Nichtbestreiten, *(criminal)* Ge-

ständnis, *(entrance)* Eintritt, Zutritt, *(price of entrance)* Eintrittspreis, *(to society)* Aufnahme, Zulassung;
direct ~ *(culprit)* ausdrückliches Geständnis; **duty-free ~** Zulassung zur zollfreien Einfuhr; **~ free** Berechtigung zum freien Eintritt, Eintritt frei; **implied ~** Eingeständnis; **incidental ~** ungewolltes Eingeständnis; **judicial ~** Geständnis vor Gericht; **partial ~** Teilgeständnis; **plenary ~** umfassendes Geständnis;
~ of aliens into a country Aufnahme von Ausländern; **~ as attorney (to the bar)** *(US)* Zulassung zur Anwaltschaft, Anwaltszulassung; **~ to bail** Kautionsgewährung; **~ of a fact** Nichtbestreiten einer Tatsache; **~ of guilt** Schuldeingeständnis; **~ to a hospital** Krankenhausaufnahme; **~ to a mental hospital** Einweisung in eine Heil- und Pflegeanstalt; **~ by invitation only** Eintritt nur auf Grund besonderer Einladung; **~ to membership** Mitgliedsaufnahme; **~ into a partnership** Aufnahme eines Teilhabers, Gesellschafteraufnahme; **~ of the press** Zulassung der Presse; **~ of securities to the stock exchange** Zulassung von Effekten zum Börsenhandel, Börsenzulassung von Wertpapieren; **~ as solicitor** *(Br.)* Anwaltszulassung; **~ to the theatre** Einlaß ins Theater; **~ of a theft** Eingeständnis eines Diebstahls;
to be eligible for ~ Aufnahmebedingungen erfüllen; **to be qualified for ~ to a university** Berechtigung zum Universitätsbesuch haben; **to gain ~** sich Einlaß verschaffen; **to grant s. o. ~** jem. Eintritt gewähren; **to refuse s. o. ~** jem. die Einreise verweigern; **to seek ~** Zulassung beantragen;
~ charge Eintrittsgeld; **~ committee** Zulassungsausschuß; **~ fee** Zulassungsgebühr, Eintrittspreis; **~ officer** Einlassungsbeamter; **~ quota** Zulassungsquote; **~ tax** *(US)* Lustbarkeits-, Vergnügungssteuer; **~ test** Zulassungsprüfung; **~ ticket** Einlaß-, Eintrittskarte.

admit *(v.)* ein-, zulassen, *(acknowledge)* anerkennen, ein-, zugestehen, zugeben, Zutritt gewähren;
~ s. o. *(ticket)* zum Eintritt berechtigen; **~ an attorney to practise law (to the bar)** *(US)* Anwalt zulassen (in den Anwaltsstand aufnehmen); **~ a claim** Forderung anerkennen; **~ s. o. to a club** j. in einen Verein aufnehmen; **~ s. o. into one's confidence** j. ins Vertrauen ziehen; **~ of no doubt** keinem Zweifel unterliegen; **~ evidence** Beweismittel zulassen; **~ to an examination** zu einem Examen zulassen; **~ no exception** keine Ausnahme zulassen; **~ a fact** Tatsache nicht bestreiten; **~ one's guilt** seine Schuld zugeben; **into hospital** ins Krankenhaus einweisen; **~ to a mental hospital under compulsory powers** in eine Nervenheilanstalt zwangsweise einweisen; **~ into a house** in ein Haus einlassen; **~ of two interpretations** zwei Auslegungen zulassen; **~ the justification of a criticism** Berechtigung einer Kritik anerkennen; **~ new members** neue Mitglieder aufnehmen; **~ a statement to be true** Parteibehauptung anerkennen; **~ as partner** als Teilhaber aufnehmen; **~ for quotation on the stock exchange** zum Börsenhandel zulassen; **~ a solicitor** *(Br.)* als Anwalt zulassen; **~ visitors one at a time** Besucher einzeln einlassen; **~ in writing** schriftlich bestätigen.

admittance Zugang, Zu-, Eintritt, Einlaß, Eingang;
no ~ Zugang verboten; **no ~ except on business** Unbefugten ist der Eintritt verboten.
~ to a mental hospital under compulsory powers Zwangseinweisung in eine Nervenheilanstalt;
~ process Zulassungsverfahren.

admitted zulässig, *(acknowledged)* anerkannt, *(as member)* zugelassen;
generally ~ allgemeingültig;
~ by competitive examination zur Prüfung zugelassen; **~ to probate** *(will)* gerichtlich bestätigt; **~ to the stock exchange** börsenfähig;
to be ~ as attorney *(US)* **(solicitor,** *Br.)* als Anwalt zugelassen sein; **to be ~ to bail** als Bürge zugelassen werden; **to be ~ to the bar** als Anwalt zugelassen sein; **to be ~ to citizenship** naturalisiert werden; **to be ~ as partner** als Teilhaber eintreten;
~ [net] assets von der Versicherungsgesellschaft anerkanntes Vermögen; **~ claim** *(insurance)* anerkannter Versicherungsanspruch, Schadenersatzanspruch; **~ company** zugelassene Versicherungsgesellschaft; **~ fact** anerkannte Tatsache; **~ setoff** nicht bestrittener Aufrechnungsanspruch.

admittee *(US)* Zugelassener.
admitting of no legal appeal unter Ausschluß des Rechtsweges.
admix *(v.)* beimischen, beimengen.
admixture Beimischung, Beimengung, Zusatz.
admonish *(v.)* ermahnen, warnen, Verweis erteilen.
admonition Verweis, Rüge, Verwarnung.
admonitory letter Mahnbrief.

adolescence jugendliches Alter, Reifezeit.
adolescent Jugendlicher, Heranwachsender;
~ *(a.)* jugendlich, heranwachsend.
adopt *(v.)* annehmen, sich aneignen, *(improvements)* übernehmen [von], einführen;
~ a candidate *(Br.)* der Aufstellung eines Kandidaten zustimmen; **~ a child** Kind adoptieren, an Kindes Statt annehmen; **o. s. to circumstances** sich auf die Umstände einstellen; **~ a contract** Vertrag annehmen; **~ a new line** *(policy)* neuen Kurs einschlagen; **~ measures** Maßnahmen ergreifen; **~ a method** Methode anwenden; **~ a motion** Antrag annehmen; **~ a name** sich einen Namen zulegen (aneignen); **~ a proposal** Vorschlag annehmen; **~ a report** Bericht annehmen; **~ a resolution** Resolution annehmen, Vorschlag zum Beschluß erheben; **~ a route of transportation of mail** Postroute festlegen; **~ rules** Richtlinien aufstellen; **~ as it stands** unverändert annehmen; **~ a system** System einführen; **~ a transaction** einem Geschäftsabschluß zustimmen; **~ unanimously** einstimmig annehmen; **~ a view** sich einer Meinung anschließen.
adoptable annehmbar;
not to be ~ without considerable outlay for other trade sich nur nach bedeutendem Kostenaufwand anderweitig gewerblich nützen lassen.
adopted an Kindes Statt angenommen, adoptiert;
to be ~ *(proposal)* durchgehen; **to be ~ by unanimous vote** einstimmige Annahme erfahren;
~ child angenommenes Kind, Adoptivkind; **~ country** Wahlheimat; **~ son** Adoptivsohn; **~ street** vom Staat übernommene Straße.
adoptee *(US)* Adoptierte(r), Adoptivkind.
adopter Adoptierender.
adoption Annahme an Kindes Statt, Adoption, *(into society)* Aufnahme;
legal ~ Adoptionsvertrag; **unanimous ~** einstimmige Annahme;
~ of a candidate Kandidatenaufstellung; **~ of children** Kindesannahme; **~ of contract** Vertragsannahme; **~ of a foreign corporation** Aufnahme einer ausländischen Gesellschaft; **~ into hospital** Krankenhausaufnahme; **~ of measures** Ergreifung von Maßnahmen; **~ of a method** Anwendung einer Methode; **~ of a name** Zulegung eines Namens; **~ of opinion** Zustimmung zu einer Ansicht; **~ of a new policy** Beginn einer neuen Politik; **~ of a proposal** Vorschlagsannahme; **~ of a report** Annahme eines Berichts; **~ of a resolution** Beschluß-, Resolutionsannahme; **~ of a transaction** Zustimmung zu einem Geschäftsabschluß, Billigung eines Rechtsgeschäfts; **~ Act** *(Br.)* Adoptionsgesetz; **~ decree** Adoptionsbeschluß; **~ law** Adoptionsrecht; **~ notice** *(carrier)* Nachfolgeverpflichtungserklärung; **~ order** Adoptionsgenehmigungsbeschluß; **~ supplements** *(carrier)* Frachtzusätze.
adoptive | act *(Br.)* ermessungsmäßig im kommunalen Bereich angewendetes Gesetz, Übernahmegesetz; **~ brother** Adoptivbruder; **~ father** Adoptivvater; **~ parents** Adoptiveltern.
adrate *(US)* Anzeigengebühr.
adscript hinzugefügt, danebengeschrieben.
adstipulate *(v.)* zu einer geschäftlichen Abmachung hinzugezogen werden.
adult Erwachsener, Volljähriger;
~ age Erwachsenenalter; **~ education** berufliche Fortbildung, Erwachsenenfortbildung; **~ education courses** Volkshochschule; **~ fare** voller Fahrpreis; **~ person** Erwachsener; **~ school** Erwachsenen-, Abendschule, Volksbildungsstätte; **~ unemployment** Arbeitslosigkeit unter den Erwachsenen; **~ version** Fassung für Erwachsene.
adulterant Verfälschungsmittel.
adulterate *(v.)* [Nahrungsmittel] verfälschen;
~ *(a.)* ehebrecherisch.
adulterated verfälscht;
~ money falsches Geld, Falschgeld.
adulteration Verfälschung, *(product)* Fälschung, verfälschtes Produkt;
warranted free from ~ Reinheit garantiert;
~ of food Nahrungsmittelfälschung.
adulterator Fälscher, Ehebrecher, *(coins)* Falschmünzer;
to become an ~ ehebrüchig werden.
adulterous ehebrecherisch.
adultery, to commit ehebrechen, Ehebruch begehen.
advance Erhöhung, Steigen, *(auction sale)* höheres Gebot, Mehrgebot, *(budget)* Vorgriff, *(earnest money)* Handgeld, *(law of inheritance)* [Erb]voraus, *(loan)* Kredit, [offenes] Darlehn, *(mil.)* Vorrücken, Vormarsch, *(offer)* Anerbieten, *(pay-*

ment beforehand) Vorschuß[zahlung], Anzahlung, *(perfection)* Verbesserung, Vervollkommnung, Fortschritt, *(of prices)* Preissteigerung, -erhöhung, *(promotions)* Aufrücken, Beförderung, *(push)* Vorstoß, *(to consignee of a shipment of goods)* Warenbevorschussung, *(stock exchange)* Aufwärtsbewegung, Kursbesserung;

by way of ~ vorschußweise, als Vorschuß; **in** ~ pränumerando, vorab, im voraus, vorab; ~**s** Annäherungsversuche;

building ~ Baugeld-, Bauzwischenkredit; **cash** ~ Kassenvorschuß, Geldvorschuß; **collateral** ~ Lombardkredit, Effektenlombard; **covered** ~ besichertes Darlehn; **day-to-day** ~**s** kurzfristige Vorschüsse der Banken; **economic** ~ wirtschaftlicher Fortschritt; **fluctuating** ~ schwankender Debetsaldo; **freight** ~ Frachtvorschuß; **interest** ~ Zinsvorauszahlung; ~**s made** geleistete Vorschüsse; **obligatory** ~ Pflichteinlage; **overbid** ~ Übergebot; ~**s paid** geleistete Anzahlungen; **price** ~ Steigen der Preise, Preis-, Kurssteigerung; ~**s received** erhaltene Anzahlungen; **maximum** ~ **required** erforderliches Höchstdarlehen; **salary** ~ Gehaltsvorschuß; **scattered** ~**s** *(stock exchange)* vereinzelte Kurserhöhungen; **secured** ~ Lombardkredit; **self-liquidating** ~ kurzfristiger Warenkredit; **sharp** ~ *(stock exchange)* scharfer Kursanstieg; **short-term** ~ kurzfristiger Kredit; **technical** ~**s** technische Errungenschaften; **uncovered** ~ ungedeckter Kontokorrentvorschuß; **unsecured** ~ Blankovorlage;

~ **in the art** *(patent law)* gewerblicher (technischer) Fortschritt; **day-to-day** ~**s from banks** kurzfristige Bankvorschüsse; ~ **on the succeeding budget** Haushaltsvorgriff; **modest** ~ **in business** maßvoller Konjunkturanstieg; ~ **on costs (expenses)** Kostenvorschuß; ~ **on current account** Kontokorrentkredit; ~**s to customers and other accounts** *(balance sheet)* Schuldner in laufender Rechnung, an Kunden ausgeliehene Gelder, Lieferantenkredite; ~**s to employees** an Betriebsangehörige geleistete Vorschüsse; ~ **of fees** Gebührenvorschuß; ~ **to finance** Vorwegfinanzierung; ~ **to finance exports** Exportfinanzierungskredit; ~ **to finance imports** Einfuhrfinanzierungskredit; ~ **to a new high** Steigerung auf einen neuen Höchstkurs; ~ **brought into hotchpot** Anrechnung des Vorausempfangs; ~**s against [hypothecation of] merchandize** *(US)* Warenlombard, -vorschüsse; ~ **for imports** Einfuhrkredit; ~ **free of interest** zinsloses Darlehen; ~ **of knowledge** Fortschritt der Wissenschaften; ~ **of money** [Geld]vorschuß; ~ **upon mortgage** Hypothekardarlehen; ~ **of an offer** Mehrgebot; ~**s for plant** Anzahlungen auf Anlagen; ~ **in prices** Preissteigerung, -erhöhung, -aufschlag, *(stock exchange)* Kurssteigerung; **sudden** ~ **in prices** plötzlicher Preisaufschwung, plötzliche Kurssteigerung; ~ **against products** Warenbevorschussung; ~ **in profits** Gewinnzunahme, -steigerung; ~ **on the rent** Mietvorauszahlung; ~ **of the season** fortgeschrittene Saison; ~ **of (on) salary** Gehaltsvorschuß; ~**s on (against) securities** Effektenbeleihung, Lombardvorschüsse, -kredite; ~ **against marketable securities** *(Br.)* Darlehn aufgrund börsengängiger Wertpapiere; ~**s and loans on security of negotiable stock** Report- und Lombardvorschüsse; ~ **by seniority** Beförderung nach dem Dienstalter; ~ **against shipping documents** Bevorschussung von Verladepapieren; ~**s on the stock market** Aufwärtsbewegung am Aktienmarkt; ~ **toward** Tendenz hinzu; ~ **for travel(l)ing** Reisekostenvorschuß; ~ **for wages** zur Lohnauszahlung gewährte Darlehnsmittel; ~**s on warrants** Lagerscheinvorschüsse;

~ *(v.)* steigen, anziehen, gewinnen, *(building society)* zuteilen, *(get on)* voran-, vorwärtskommen, Fortschritte machen, *(lend)* [aus]leihen, [ver]borgen, *(mil.)* vorgehen, -dringen, vorrücken, *(pay money before due)* bevorschussen, Vorschuß leisten, vorauszahlen, vorstrecken, *(promote)* [be]fördern, *(be promoted)* befördert werden, aufrücken, avancieren, *(raise)* erhöhen, heben;

~ **s. o. j.** befördern; ~ **an amount** Betrag vorschießen (vorlegen); ~ **an argument** Argumente vorbringen; ~ **a child** einem Kind einen Erbvoraus gewähren; ~ **a claim** Anspruch erheben (vorbringen, geltend machen); ~ **a fraction** ein wenig anziehen; ~ **funds** Vorschüsse zahlen; ~ **one's interests** seine Eigeninteressen fördern; ~ **money** Geld vorstrecken (vorschießen), bevorschussen, Vorschuß leisten; ~ **money against s. one's life policy** jds. Lebensversicherungspolice beleihen; ~ **money on securities** Effekten beleihen (lombardieren); ~ **an opinion** Meinung äußern; ~ **the price (rate)** *(stock exchange)* Kurs hinaufsetzen; ~ **in price** im Kurs (Preis) steigen; ~ **against products** Waren bevorschussen; ~ **reasons** Gründe vorbringen; ~ **sale excessively** Vorverkauf übermäßig anheizen; ~ **sharply**

(prices) scharf anziehen; ~ **in the social scale** sozial aufsteigen; ~ **from the start in brisk dealings** bei Börseneröffnung mit lebhaften Umsätzen beginnen;

to allow a customer an ~ einem Kunden einen Kredit einräumen; **to ask for an** ~ um einen Vorschuß bitten, Vorschuß verlangen; **to be on the** ~ *(stock exchange)* anziehen, im Steigen begriffen sein; **to be covered by** ~**s** durch Vorschüsse gedeckt sein; **to be in the van of** ~ Aufwärtsbewegung anführen; **to close with small** ~**s** *(stock exchange)* mit kleinen Kursaufbesserungen schließen; **to continue its upward** ~ Aufwärtsbewegung fortsetzen; **to grant an** ~ Vorschuß bewilligen, bevorschussen; **to go in** ~ auf Vorschuß arbeiten; **to grant an** ~ bevorschussen; **to lag behind the** ~ der Aufwärtsbewegung nur langsam folgen; **to make** ~**s** Annäherungsversuche machen, *(US)* Vorschüsse gewähren; **to make** ~**s to s. o.** jem. gegenüber den ersten Schritt tun; **to make** ~**s to customers** *(US)* Kunden bevorschussen; **to make only a limited** ~ **on its share of the vote** seinen Stimmenanteil nur geringfügig vergrößern; **to make an** ~ **in stages against production of architect's certificate** Kredit etappenweise entsprechend den nachgewiesenen Bauleistungen auszahlen; **to obtain an** ~ **of money** Vorschuß erhalten; **to order in** ~ vorausbestellen; **to pay (make payments) in** ~ vor Verfall (pränumerando) zahlen, vorauszahlen; **to receive an** ~ *(law of inheritance)* [Erb]voraus erhalten; **to score an** ~ **of 5 points** Kursgewinn von 5 Punkten verzeichnen; **to stipulate s. th. in** ~ etw. im voraus ausbedingen;

~ **account** Vorschußkonto; ~ **agent** auf Vorschußbasis arbeitender Vertreter; ~ **authority** im voraus erteilte Vollmacht; ~ **bill** Vorschußwechsel; ~ **billing** *(carrier)* Rückvergütung; ~ **booking** [Karten]vorverkauf, Vorausbestellung; ~ **charge** *(carrier)* vorausbezahlte Frachtgebühr; ~ **command post** vorgeschobener Befehlsstand; ~ **commitment** Darlehns-, Kreditzusage; ~ **compensation** Schadensbevorschussung; ~ **copy** Vorabdruck, Vorausexemplar; ~ **corporation tax** *(Br.)* Körperschaftssteuervorauszahlung, vorausgezahlte Körperschaftssteuer; ~ **dating** Vorausdatierung; ~ **factory** *(Br.)* standardisiertes gewerbliches Gebäude; ~ **financing** Vorfinanzierung; ~ **freight** vorausbezahlte Fracht; ~ **guarantee** Anzahlungsgarantie; ~ **guard** *(mil.)* Vorhut; ~ **information** Vorausbenachrichtigung; ~ **money** *(US)* Vorschuß; ~ **note** *(Br.)* Vorschußanweisung; ~ **notice** Vorankündigung, -anzeige, Vorabinformation; ~ **order** Vor[aus]bestellung; ~ **party** Vorkommando; ~ **pay** Gehaltsvorschuß; ~ **payment** Vorkasse, Voraus[be]zahlung, *(downpayment)* Auszahlung; ~ **payment of corporation tax** Körperschaftssteuervorauszahlungen; **to receive** ~ **payments on salary** Gehaltsvorschuß erhalten; ~ **placement course** Fortbildungskursus; ~ **planning** Vorausplanung; ~ **position** *(mil.)* vorgeschobene Stellung; ~ **premium** Vorausprämie; ~ **publication** Vorabdruck, ~ **publicity** Vorschußlorbeeren; ~ **quota** Vorgriffskontingent; ~ **rental** Mietvorauszahlung; ~ **salary** Gehaltsvorschuß; ~ **sale** Vorverkauf; ~ **sheet** Aushängebogen, Druckfahne; ~ **sign** Abfahrtshinweis; ~ **ticket** Vorverkaufskarte; ~ **wages** Lohnvorschuß; ~ **warning** Vorwarnung; ~ **word** Vorausunterrichtung.

advanced fortgeschritten, fortschrittlich, modern, *(mil.)* vorgeschoben, *(beyond the elementary)* fortgeschritten;

~ **in years** in vorgerücktem Alter, bejahrt;

to be ~ befördert werden; **to recover money** ~ Vorschußleistungen zurückbekommen;

~ **age** vorgerücktes Alter; ~ **base** vorgeschobene Versorgungsbasis; ~ **capital** Einlage; ~ **charges** *(carrier)* verauslagte Kosten; ~ **cost of living** gestiegener Lebenshaltungsindex; ~ **countries** Industrieländer; ~ **course** Fortgeschrittenenkurs; ~ **freight** vorausbezahlte Fracht; ~ **ignition** Frühzündung; ~ **landing ground** Absprungplatz, -hafen; ~ **member** *(building society, Br.)* zugeteilter Bausparer; ~ **payment** Vorauszahlung; ~ **price** erhöhter (angehobener) Preis; ~ **student** Fortgeschrittener; ~ **studies** fortgeschrittenes Studium; **sums** ~ *(balance sheet)* Vorschüsse; ~ **tax payment** Steuervorauszahlung; ~ **thinking** Vorausdenken; ~ **units** *(mil.)* Voraustruppen; ~ **views** moderne Ansichten.

advancement *(gift of intestate during life)* Vor[aus]empfang eines Erben, [Erb]voraus, Vorversorgung, Zuwendung, *(money advanced)* Vorschuß, *(payment on advance, US)* An-, Vorschußzahlung, *(person)* Beförderung [in einer Stellung], Vorrücken im Amt, Erhöhung im Rang, *(plan)* Förderung, *(in social scale)* Emporkommen;

career ~ berufliche Förderung; **economic** ~ wirtschaftlicher Fortschritt; **future** ~ spätere Beförderung;

~ **of education** Förderung des Bildungswesens; **social ~ of labo(u)r** sozialer Aufstieg der Arbeiterklasse; ~ **by portion** Aussteuer, Pflichtteilsausstattung;
to groom s. o. for ~ jds. Aufstieg mit allen Mitteln fördern; ~ **costs** Fortbildungskosten; ~ **roster** Beförderungsplan, -liste.

advancer Förderer, Geld-, Darlehensgeber.

advancing | market Markt mit steigendem Preisniveau; ~ **prices** steigende Preise (Kurse); ~ **stocks** steigende Aktien.

advantage *(chance)* günstige Gelegenheit, *(precedence)* Vorteil, Überlegensein, *(preference)* Vorzug, *(profit)* Nutzen, Gewinn, Profit;
with the intent to gain ~ in gewinnsüchtiger Absicht; **commercial ~** Handelsvorteil; **cost ~** Kostenvorteil; **dearly bought ~** teuer erkaufter Vorteil; **improper ~** mißbräuchliche Ausnutzung; **incidental ~** Nebenvorteil; **nonmonetary ~** nicht geldwerte Vorteile; **special ~** Sondervorteil;
~**s accruing from the freedom of the press** aus der Pressefreiheit erwachsende Vorteile; ~ **of location** *(advertising)* Plazierungsvorteil; ~ **of saving** Sparvorteil;
to derive ~ from Nutzen ziehen aus; **to execute an order to the best ~** Auftrag bestens ausführen; **to follow up an ~** Vorteil ausnutzen (wahrnehmen); **to have the ~ of (in) numbers** zahlenmäßig überlegen sein; **to lay out one's money to ~** sein Geld vorteilhaft anlegen; **to offer an ~** Vorteil gewähren; **to press one's ~** seinen Vorteil rücksichtslos wahrnehmen; **to redound to s. one's ~** sich zu jds. Vorteil auswirken; **to sell to ~** etw. glänzend verkaufen; **to sell s. th. to good ~** etw. vorteilhaft verkaufen, mit Gewinn verkaufen; **to suck ~ of** Vorteil ziehen aus; **to take ~ of** Vorteil (Gewinn) ziehen [aus], günstige Gelegenheit benützen; **to take ~ of s. o.** jds. Gutgläubigkeit ausnützen; **to take full ~ of s. th.** etw. gründlich ausnützen; **to take undue ~** in sittenwidriger Weise ausnutzen; **to turn s. th. to ~** Profit von etw. erzielen, Nutzen aus etw. ziehen; **to use to good ~** nützlich verwenden.

advantageous *(profitable)* vorteilhaft, günstig, gewinnbringend, *(useful)* nützlich;
to be ~ Vorteile erbringen; ~ **position** günstige Stellung; **on ~ terms** zu vorteilhaften (günstigen) Bedingungen.

advent to power Machtübernahme.

adventitious | property Erbschaftsvermögen; ~ **value of land** zufälliger Grundstückswert.

adventure *(carrier)* Versand auf eigene Rechnung, *(hazardous enterprise)* gewagtes Unternehmen, *(risk)* Risiko, Wagnis, *(speculation)* Spekulation[s]geschäft, Risikogeschäft, *(travel)* Reiseabenteuer;
gross ~ Bodmereidarlehn; **joint ~** Gelegenheitsgesellschaft, Arbeitsgemeinschaft; **marine ~** Seerisiko, -gefahr;
~ **story** Abenteuergeschichte; **touch** Hauch von Abenteuer.

adventurer Abenteurer, Glücksritter, *(speculator)* Spekulant;
~ **in Co** Versand auf gemeinsame Rechnung.

adventurous gewagt, riskant.

adversary Gegner, Opponent, Widersacher, Feind, *(lawsuit)* Prozeßgegner;
~ **proceedings** kontradiktorisches Verfahren; ~**'s speech** gegnerisches Plädoyer.

adverse feindlich, gegnerisch, *(disadvantageous)* abträglich, nachteilig, ungünstig, defizitär, *(having opposite interests)* mit den eigenen Ansprüchen unvereinbar, entgegengesetzt;
~ **to health** gesundheitsschädlich;
~ **balance** Unterbilanz, Verlustsaldo, Defizit; ~ **balance of payments** passive Zahlungsbilanz; ~ **budget** unausgeglichener (defizitärer) Haushalt (Etat), Haushaltsdefizit, Defizithaushalt; ~ **circumstances** widrige Umstände; ~ **claim** entgegenstehender Anspruch; ~ **decision** abschlägiger Bescheid; ~ **fortune** unglückliches Schicksal; ~ **majority** Mehrheit gegen den Antrag; ~ **party** Gegenpartei, gegnerische Partei, Prozeßgegner; ~ **possession** Ersitzung; **to acquire by ~ possession** ersitzen; ~ **selection** *(insurance)* Antiselektion, Ausscheiden der besseren Risiken; ~ **solicitor** *(Br.)* gegnerischer Anwalt; ~ **trade balance** passive Handelsbilanz; ~ **witness** Zeuge der Gegenseite.

advertise, advertize *(US)* *(v.)* *(canvass)* werben, Werbung betreiben, Reklame machen, *(in newspaper)* [in der Zeitung] ankündigen, annoncieren, Anzeige (Annonce) aufgeben, durch Inserat suchen, inserieren, (einrücken [lassen], *(notify)* benachrichtigen, in Kenntnis setzen, *(publish)* [öffentlich, durch Anschlag] bekanntgeben, bekanntmachen, öffentlich ausschreiben, *(situation)* Stelle ausschreiben;

~ **o. s. (one's work)** für sich selbst Reklame machen; ~ **for bids** *(US)* ausschreiben; ~ **in a paper** in einer Zeitung inserieren (ein Inserat aufgeben); ~ **a reward** Belohnung aussetzen; ~ **a sale** Verkauf anzeigen; ~ **a vacancy** freie (offene) Stelle (Wohnung) ausschreiben, annoncieren; ~ **widely** großzügige Werbung veranstalten.

advertised | article Reklame-, Werbeartikel; ~ **price** Bezugspreis; ~ **route** angegebene Strecke.

advertisement Reklame, Werbung, *(announcement)* Ankündigung, Bekanntmachung, Bekanntgabe, Benachrichtigung, *(newspaper)* [Zeitungs]anzeige, Annonce, Inserat, *(poster)* Anschlag, *(situation)* Ausschreibung;
accessory (auxiliary) ~ begleitende Werbeaktion; **air ~** Werbung in der Luft, Himmelsschrift; **big-splurge ~** großformatige Anzeige; **boxed ~** umrandete Anzeige; **center** *(US)* **(centre,** *Br.***) -spread position ~** doppelseitige Anzeige in Heftmitte; **classified ~** kleine Anzeigen, nach Branchen geordnete Inserate; **consumer ~** Verbraucherreklame, -werbung; **direct ~** direkt gestreute Werbung; **display ~** Schlagzeilenwerbung, Repräsentationsinserat; **display-type ~** besonders gestaltete Anzeige, Schlagzeilenwerbung; **editorialized ~** redaktionell gestaltete Anzeige; **fixed-date ~** Terminanzeige; **flaring ~** marktschreierische Reklame; **following-on ~** Anzeige im Rahmen einer Serie; **foreign-language ~** fremdsprachliche Werbung; **full-page ~** ganzseitige Zeitungsreklame; **full-run edition ~s** Anzeigen in der Gesamtausgabe; **half-page ~** halbseitige Anzeige; **illustrated ~** mit Bildmotiven illustrierte Anzeige, Bildwerbung; **magazine ~** Zeitschriftenreklame, -werbung; **misleading ~** irreführende Reklame; **movie ~** *(US)* Lichtspielhauswerbung; **nation-wide ~** überregionale Werbung; **newspaper ~** Zeitungsinserat, Annonce; **official ~** amtliche Anzeige; **original ~** Einführungsreklame; **press ~** Zeitungsanzeige; **printed ~** gedruckte Anzeige; **puffing ~** marktschreierische Reklame; **reader ~** Textanzeige; **sample ~s** Musterwerbeanzeigen; **self-~** Eigenwerbung; **single ~** Einzelwerbung; **small ~s** kleine Anzeigen; **sole ~** einzeln stehende Anzeige; **space ~** seitenteilige Anzeige; **teaser ~** *(US)* Rätselreklame; **television ~** Werbefernsehanzeige; **two-page ~** zweiseitige Anzeige; **wall ~** Maueranschlag; **want ~** Suchanzeige; ~**s of appointments (for positions)** Stellenanzeigen; ~ **in black and white** Schwarz-Weißanzeige; ~ **for deposits** *(Br.)* Einlagenwerbung; ~ **in the Gazette** *(Br.)* [etwa] Veröffentlichung im Bundesanzeiger; ~ **in circulating magazines** Lesezirkelwerbung; ~ **to the reader** Textwerbung; ~ **of a sale** Verkaufsanzeige; ~ **in short story** feuilletonistische Anzeige; ~ **in feuilleton style** feuilletonistische Anzeige;
to issue an ~ in compliance with the requirements of the Council of Stock Exchange in London Inserat aufgrund der Bestimmungen der Londoner Börse bei der Aktieneinführung aufgeben; **to key an ~** Anzeige kennzeichnen; **to place ~s in various media** Anzeigen bei verschiedenen Werbeträgern unterbringen; **to put an ~ into the paper** Anzeige in die Zeitung einrücken lassen, Inserat aufgeben, inserieren; **to run ~s** Anzeigen laufen haben; **to run an ~ only once** Einzelinserat aufgeben;
~ **canvasser** Anzeigenakquisiteur; ~ **charges** Insertionsgebühren; ~ **column** Anzeigenspalte; ~ **columns** Anzeigen-, Inseratenteil; ~ **compositor** Anzeigensetzer; ~ **contractor** Akquisiteur, Werbebüro, -unternehmen; ~ **cost per line** Zeilenpreis für Inserate; ~ **department** Anzeigenabteilung, Inseratenannahme; ~ **director** Anzeigenleiter, -direktor; ~ **display** Großanzeige; ~ **height** Abdruckhöhe; ~ **lineage** Anzeigengröße; ~ **magazine** Anzeigenblatt; ~ **manager** Anzeigenleiter; ~ **material** Werbematerial; ~ **money** Beträge aus der Werbewirtschaft; ~ **office** Inseratenannahme, Anzeigenbüro; ~ **order** Werbe-, Anzeigenauftrag; ~ **page** Anzeigenseite; ~ **panel** Streifenanzeige; ~ **puff** überzogene Werbung; ~ **rate** *(Br.)* Anzeigentarif; ~ **rate card (schedule)** Anzeigentarif; ~ **representative** Anzeigenvertreter; ~ **sales promotion manager** Anzeigenwerbeleiter; ~ **size** Anzeigenformat; ~ **space salesman** Anzeigenakquisiteur; ~ **support** Unterstützung durch die Werbewirtschaft; ~ **type area** Anzeigenspiegel.

advertiser, advertizer *(US)* Inserent, Aufgeber einer Anzeige, Werbungstreibender, *(newspaper)* Anzeigenblatt;
business ~ Werbung treibende Firma; **consumer ~** Verbrauchwerber; **industrial ~** Wirtschaftsanzeigenblatt, Anzeigenblatt der Wirtschaft; **local ~** Lokalblatt; **national ~** Anzeigenkunde der Hauptausgabe; **regular ~** Dauerkunde für die Werbung;
~ **money** Beträge aus der Werbewirtschaft; ~ **support** Unterstützung durch die Werbewirtschaft.

advertising Reklame, Werbung, Inserieren, Anzeigenwesen; **above-the-line** ~ klassische Anzeigenwerbung; **accessory (auxiliary)** ~ Werbungszusatz, zusätzliche Werbung; **aerial** ~ Werbung in der Luft, Luftwerbung, Himmelschrift; **appealing** ~ ansprechende Werbung; **artistic** ~ künstlerische Werbung; **association** ~ Gemeinschaftswerbung; **audio-visual** ~ audio-visuelle Werbung; **bargain-sales** ~ Werbung für Gelegenheitskäufe; **billboard** ~ *(Br.)* Plakatwerbung; **black-and-white** ~ Schwarzweißanzeige; **brand** ~ Markenwerbung; **broadcast** ~ Rundfunkwerbung; **business** ~ Wirtschaftswerbung; **camouflaged** ~ Schleichwerbung; **cinema** ~ Filmwerbung, Kinoreklame; **classified** ~ nach Branchen gegliederte Inserate; **colo(u)r** ~ Farbanzeige; **commercial** ~ Wirtschaftswerbung; **comparative** ~ vergleichende Werbung; **competitive** ~ aggressive Werbung; **[large-scale] consumer** ~ [breit gestreute] Verkaufswerbung; **cooperative** ~ Gemeinschaftswerbung; **coordinated** ~ gleich gerichtete Werbung; **corporate [image]** ~ Firmen-, Prestigewerbung; **current** ~ gegenwärtig laufende Werbekampagne; **direct** ~ Einzel-, Direktwerbung; **direct mail** ~ direkte Werbung durch Drucksachenversand, Postwurfsendung, -streuung; **display** ~ Schlagzeilenwerbung; **dynamic** ~ schwungvolle Werbung; **editoralized** ~ redaktionell gestaltete Anzeige; **educational** ~ belehrende Werbung; **electric sign** ~ Leucht-, Lichtreklame; **ethical** ~ an ethischen Gesichtspunkten ausgerichtete Werbung; **false** ~ unwahre Werbung; **flaring** ~ marktschreierische (sensationell aufgemachte) Werbung; **follow-up** ~ Erinnerungswerbung; **foreign** ~ Auslandswerbung; **foreign-language** ~ fremdsprachige Werbung; **free-gift** ~ Werbung durch Musterverteilung; **guaranteed** ~ *(US)* von einer anderen Stelle überprüfte Reklameankündigungen; **high-pressure** ~ hochtönende Reklame; **house-to-house** ~ an den Haustüren verteilte Werbematerial; **in-house** ~ im eigenen Betrieb hergestellte Werbung; **illuminated** ~ Lichtreklame; **indirect-action** ~ Prestigewerbung; **individual** ~ Einzelwerbung; **industrial** ~ Wirtschaftswerbung, Werbung für Industrieerzeugnisse; **inside-the-store** ~ Werbung im Ladeninneren; **institutional** ~ firmenbetonte Werbung, Prestigewerbung; **keyed** ~ Werbung mit Kennziffern; **launch** ~ *(US)* Einführungswerbung; **local** ~ Anzeigenwerbung ortsansässiger Geschäfte; **low** ~ geringes Anzeigenaufkommen; **magazine** ~ Zeitschriftenwerbung; **mail-order** ~ Versandhausreklame; **masked** ~ Schleichwerbung; **mass** ~ Massenreklame, -werbung; **misleading** ~ irreführende Reklame (Werbung); **national** ~ Werbung auf Bundesebene; **nation-wide** ~ überregionale Werbung; **newspaper** ~ Zeitungsreklame, Werbung in den Tageszeitungen; **nonselective** ~ ungezielte Werbung; **novelty** ~ Werbung durch Musterverteilung; **offbeat** ~ ungewöhnliche Werbung; **opportunity** ~ gelegentliche Werbung; **original** ~ Einführungswerbung; **outdoor** ~ Außen-, Plakatwerbung, Werbung am Verkehrsstrom; **paid** ~ bezahlte Werbung; **patent** ~ Patentberühmung; **periodical** ~ Zeitschriftenwerbung; **persuasive** ~ überzogene Werbung; **pictorial** ~ Bildwerbung; **point-of-purchase** ~ Werbung innerhalb eines Einzelhandelsgeschäfts, Werbung am Kaufort, Werbung innerhalb des Ladens; **point-of-sale** ~ Werbung im Einzelhandelsgeschäft; **poster** ~ Plakatwerbung; **preplanned** ~ langfristig geplante Werbekampagne; **prestige** ~ Repräsentationswerbung; **print[ed]** ~ Drucksachenwerbung; **professional** ~ Werbung in Berufskreisen; **program(m)e** ~ Werbung in Verbindung mit einem Fernsehprogramm; **puffing** ~ marktschreierische Reklame (Werbung); ~ **pulling the best results** Werbung mit größter Durchschlagskraft; **radio** ~ Rundfunkwerbung; **railroad** *(US)* **(railway,** *Br.)* Eisenbahnreklame; **real-estate** ~ Grundstücksreklame; **reason-why** ~ *(US)* Aufklärungswerbung; **retail** ~ Einzelhandelswerbung; **roof** ~ Dachwerbung; **sample** ~ Werbung durch Ausgabe von Warensendungen; **seasonal** ~ Saisonwerbung; **selective** ~ gezielte Werbung; **sky-line** ~ Luftreklame; **small-size** ~ Kleinanzeige; **stop-gap** ~ Füllanzeige; **street-car** ~ Straßenbahnreklame; **subliminal** ~ unterschwellige Werbung; **television** ~ Fernsehwerbung; **tie-in** ~ eingeblendete Reklame; **tie-up** ~ kombinierte Werbeaktion; **tourist** ~ Fremdenverkehrswerbung; **trade** ~ Branchenwerbung; **tradepaper** ~ Fachzeitschriftenwerbung; **transportation** ~ Verkehrsmittelwerbung; **vertical cooperative** ~ Gemeinschaftswerbung von Hersteller und Händler; **window** ~ Schaufensterreklame, -werbung; ~ **getting (billing) the best results** wirksamste Werbung; **to be down in** ~ Werbeetat gekürzt haben; **to buy** ~ **at a discount** bei einer Werbekampagne Rabattsätze ausnutzen; **to place** ~ Werbung unterbringen; **to place** ~ **direct** unter Umgehung einer Agentur inserieren;

~ **accountability** Angemessenheit des Werbeaufwands; ~ **activity** Werbe-, Reklametätigkeit; **expert** ~ **advice** fachmännische Werbeberatung; ~ **adviser** Werbeberater; ~ **aeroplane** Reklame-, Werbeflugzeug; ~ **agency** Reklame-, Werbebüro, Anzeigen-, Werbeagentur, Anzeigenannahme, -vermittlung, Annoncenexpedition, Annoncenvertreter, -akquisiteur, Inseratenbüro; **accredited** ~ **agency** anerkannte Werbeagentur; ~ **agent** Werbungs-, Anzeigenvermittler, -vertreter, Annoncenvertreter, -akquisiteur; ~ **aids** Werbematerial; ~ **allowance** *(retailer)* Werberabatt, Reklamenachlaß, Werbezuschuß des Herstellers; ~ **alternative** Alternativen im Werbeplan; ~ **angle** werblicher Gesichtspunkt, Werbeargument, Werbe-, Reklamestandpunkt, Verkaufsstandpunkt, Aufhänger; ~ **announcement** Werbedurchsage; ~ **appeal** Anklang, Zug-, Werbekraft, Werbeappell; ~ **approach** Aufmerksamkeitserreger, Werbeansprache, Aufhänger; ~ **appropriation** *(US)* bewilligter Werbeetat, Reklamegelder, -fonds, Werbefonds, -mittel; ~ **area** Werbebereich; ~ **argot** Werbejargon; ~ **art** Werbe-, Gebrauchsgraphik; ~ **article** Werbematerial, Reklame-, Werbeartikel, Werbe-, Reklamegeschenk; ~ **artist** Reklame-, Werbezeichner, Werbegraphiker; ~ **association** Werbeverband; ~ **battle** Werbeschlacht; ~ **block** Anzeigenklischee; ~ **brochure** Werbebroschüre; ~ **budget** Werbeetat, Reklameetat; ~ **business** Werbewesen; ~ **budget procedure** Verfahren bei der Aufstellung des Werbeetats; ~ **campaign** Reklame-, Werbefeldzug, -aktion, -kampagne; **to run an** ~ **campaign** Werbefeldzug durchführen; ~ **canvasser** Anzeigenakquisiteur; ~ **card** Anzeigen-, Annoncentarif; ~ **cartoonist** Werbezeichner; ~ **censorship** Werbezensur; ~ **character** Reklamefigur; ~ **charges** Werbekosten, Anzeigengebühren, -preise, Anzeigen-, Annoncentarif; ~ **circular** Reklameschrift, -rundschreiben, Werberundschreiben; ~ **columns** Reklameteil [einer Zeitung], Anzeigenteil, -spalten; ~ **company** Werbegesellschaft; ~ **competition** Werbewettbewerb; ~ **composition** Anzeigensatz; ~ **concept** Werbekonzeption; ~ **consultant (counsel,** *US)* frei[beruflich]er Werbeberater; ~ **contest** Werbewettbewerb, -preisausschreiben; ~ **contract** Anzeigenabschluß, Insertionsvertrag; ~ **contractor** Werbefirma, Anzeigenvermittler; ~ **contribution** Werbe-, Reklamebeitrag; ~ **control** Werbeerfolgskontrolle; ~ **copy** Reklame-, Werbetext, Anzeigensatz; ~ **costs** Reklame-, Werbe[un]kosten; ~ **counsel(l)or** Werbeberater; **to rise and fall with the** ~ **cycle** mit seinen Einkünften vom Anzeigenvolumen abhängen; ~ **department** Anzeigen-, Werbeabteilung; ~ **design** Werbezeichnung; ~ **designer** Werbegraphiker; ~ **device** Werbemotto; ~ **devices** Werbemittel; ~ **director** Werbedirektor, Leiter der Werbeabteilung; ~ **directory** Adreßbuch der Werbewirtschaft, Werbeadressbuch; ~ **discount** Rückvergütung an die Agentur; ~ **display** Werbe-, Reklameauslage; ~ **division** Werbeabteilung; ~ **drawing** Werbeentwurf, -zeichnung; ~ **edition** Werbeausgabe; ~ **editorial** redaktionell gestaltete Anzeige; ~ **effect** Werbewirkung, -effekt; ~ **effectiveness** Werbewirksamkeit; ~ **effectiveness survey** Werbewirksamkeitsanalyse, -erfolgskontrolle; ~ **effort** Werbeanstrengung, -maßnahmen, -bemühungen; ~ **engineer** *(US)* Werbefachmann; ~ **enterprise** Werbeunternehmen; ~ **executive** Werbefachmann; ~ **executives** führende Werbefachleute; ~ **expenditure** Reklame-, Werbeausgaben, Werbeaufwand, -aufwendungen; ~ **expert** Werbefachmann; ~ **extravagance** Werbeauswüchse; ~ **fee** Anzeigen-, Insertionsgebühr; ~ **field** Werbegebiet; ~ **figure** Werbefigur; ~ **film** Werbefilm; ~ **filmlet** Werbekurzfilm; ~ **form** Anzeigenvordruck; ~ **function** Werbefunktion; ~ **gift** Werbegeschenk; ~ **growth** Anzeigenzunahme; ~ **headline** Reklameüberschrift, Schlagzeile einer Werbung; ~ **horizons** Werbemöglichkeiten; ~ **idea** Werbeidee; ~ **impact** Durchschlagskraft (Wirksamkeit) einer Werbung; **to test the** ~ **impact** Werbeerfolgskontrolle durchführen; ~ **industry** Werbeindustrie, -wirtschaft; ~ **inscription** Reklameaufschrift; ~ **investment** Werbeinvestitionen, -aufwand; ~ **kite** Reklamedrachen; ~ **label** Reklame-, Werbeaufschrift; ~ **law** Werbevorschriften; ~ **layout** Werbe-, Reklamegestaltung; ~ **letter** Werbebrief; ~ **lights** Reklamebeleuchtung; **to be in the** ~ **line** im Werbefach tätig sein; ~ **literature** Reklame-, Werbeliteratur; ~ **magazine** Werbefachzeitschrift; ~ **man** Werbefachmann; ~ **manager** Anzeigen-, Werbeleiter; ~ **material** Reklame-, Werbemittel; ~ **matter** Werbematerial, -drucksache, -manuskript; ~ **media selection** Medienauswahl; ~ **medium** Reklame-, Werbemittel, Werbeträger, -instrument; ~ **message** Werbeaussage; ~ **messages** Werbenachrichten; ~ **motive** Werbemotiv; ~ **motto** Werbemotto, Slogan; ~ **news** Werbenachricht; ~ **novelty** Werbeneuheit; **to detail one's ~ object** seinen Anzeigen-, Werbezweck konkret ansprechen; ~ **objective** Werbeziel; ~ **office** Anzeigen-, Werbe-, Annoncenbüro, -expedition; ~ **operator** Anzeigenvermittler, Werbeflächenpächter in öffentlichen Verkehrsmitteln; ~ **order** Anzeigen-, Werbeauftrag; ~ **page** Reklame-, Anzeigenseite; ~ **page plan** Anzeigenspiegel; ~ **pamphlet** Werbeschrift; ~ **part** Reklameteil; ~ **pavilion** Werbepavillon; ~ **performance** Werbefunktion; ~ **pillar** Anschlag-, Litfaß-, Plakatsäule, Anzeigenständer; ~ **plan** Werbeplan; ~ **point** Werbeargument, -gesichtspunkt; ~ **policy** Reklame-, Werbepolitik; ~ **practices** Werbebrauch, -usancen; ~ **practitioner** (Br.) freiberuflicher Werbeberater; ~ **premium** Zugabeartikel; ~ **printed matter** Reklamedrucksache, Werbeschrift; ~ **profession** Werbeberuf; ~ **program(me)** Werbeprogramm, -plan; ~ **promotion** Werbeförderung; ~ **proposal** Werbevorschlag; ~ **prospectus** Werbeschrift; ~ **provisions** Werbebestimmungen; ~ **psychology** Werbepsychologie; ~ **publication** Werbezeitschrift; ~ **purpose** Werbezweck, -ziel; ~ **rates** Anzeigentarif; **graded ~ rates** degressive Werbesätze; ~ **rate base** Anzeigenrichtsatz, -tarif; ~ **rate card** (book) Anzeigenpreisliste; ~ **rate schedule** Anzeigentarif; ~ **record** Werbenachweis; ~ **regulations** Werbebestimmungen; ~ **representative** Anzeigenvertreter; ~ **research** Werbevorbereitung; ~ **reservation** Anzeigenreservierung; ~ **result** Werbeerfolg; ~ **revenue** Einkünfte aus Publikationen, Werbe-, Anzeigeneinnahmen; ~ **sales executive (salesman,** US**)** Anzeigenvertreter; ~ **sales promoter** Anzeigenwerbeleiter; ~ **sample** Werbemuster; ~ **schedule** Terminkalender einer Werbeaktion, Einschalt-, Streu-, Werbe-, Erscheinungsplan, Datenschema; ~ **screen** Werbefilm, -streifen; ~ **section** Anzeigenteil; ~ **sector** Werbe-, Anzeigensektor; ~ **service** Werbe-, Anzeigendienst; ~ **sheet** Anzeigen-, Annoncenseite, Beiblatt mit Anzeigen; ~ **showcase** Werbevitrine; ~ **sketch** Werbekurzspiel, Werbesketch; ~ **slogan** Werbemotto, -slogan; ~ **solicitor** (US) Anzeigenakquisiteur; ~ **space** Anzeigenraum, -teil, Reklame-, Werbefläche, Inseratenteil; ~ **space buyer** Anzeigenexpedition; ~ **space salesman** Anzeigenraumvermittler; ~ **specialist** Werbefachmann, -spezialist; ~ **spot** (television) Werbespot; ~ **staff** Werbeabteilung; **outdoor ~ stand** Plakatanschlagfläche; ~ **standards** Lauterkeit der Werbung, Werbeethik; ~ **story** Werbegeschichte; ~ **studio** Werbestudio; ~ **supplement** Werbebeilage; ~ **support** werbliche Unterstützung, Werbeunterstützung; ~ **tactics** Werbestrategie; ~ **tape** Werbestreifband; ~ **tax** Reklamesteuer; ~ **technique** Werbe-, Reklametechnik; ~ **test** Versuchswerbung; ~ **text** Werbe-, Reklametext; ~ **theme** Werbethema; ~ **time** (broadcast, television) Werbezeit; ~ **trade** Werbegeschäft; ~ **type** Reklameschrift; ~ **type area** Anzeigenspiegel; ~ **value** Reklame-, Werbewert; ~ **van** Werbe-, Reklamewagen; ~ **vehicle** Werbeträger; ~ **volume** Anzeigenvolumen; ~ **writer** Werbetexter.

advertographer Akzidenzsetzer.

advertorial (US sl.) redaktionell aufgemachte Anzeige, Textanzeige.

advice (council) Empfehlung, Rat, Beratung, Ratserteilung, (information) Meldung, Nachricht, (notice) Bericht, Anzeige, Benachrichtigung, Mitteilung, Bescheid, Avis;
as per ~ aufgabegemäß, laut Aufgabe (Anweisung, Bericht); **for want of ~** mangels Bericht; **on the ~ of** auf Vorschlag (Anraten) von; **with the ~ and consent of** mit Zustimmung von; **without ~** ohne Bericht;
credit ~ Gutschrift[saufgabe], -anzeige; **debit ~** Belastungsanzeige, -aufgabe, Lastschrift; **expert ~** fachkundige Beratung; **financial ~** finanzielle Beratung; **independent ~** unparteiische Beratung; **invalid ~** Benachrichtigung über ungültige Geldanweisung; **legal ~** juristische Beratung, Rechtsberatung, -beistand; **medical ~** ärztlicher Rat, ärztlicher Beratung; **no ~** mangels Bericht; **preliminary ~** Voravis; **shipping ~** Versandanzeige; **special ~** Separatanzeige;
~s from abroad auswärtige Informationen; **immediate ~ of new publications** Neuerscheinungs-, Sofortdienst; ~ **of arrival** Eingangsanzeige; ~ **of collection** Einziehungsanzeige, -benachrichtigung, Inkassoanzeige; ~ **and consent** (US) Zustimmung; ~ **in due course** Aufgabe folgt; ~ **of credit** Gutschriftanzeige; ~ **of deal** (stock exchange, Br.) Ausführungsanzeige; ~ **of debit** Belastungsanzeige, Lastschrift; ~ **of delivery** (post) Zustellungsbenachrichtigung, Aufgaben-, Rückschein; **[provisional] ~ of despatch (dispatch)** [vorläufige] Versandanzeige; ~ **of draft** Trattenavis; ~ **without engagement** unverbindliche Benachrichtigung; ~ **of fate** Bezahltmeldung, Scheckbestätigung; ~ **on gifts** Testamentsberatung; ~ **of negotiation** Begebungsaviso; ~ **of goods** Warenavis; ~ **on invest-**

ment Effektenberatung; ~ **of nondelivery** Unbestellbarkeitsmeldung; ~ **of payment** Zahlungsanzeige; ~ **of receipt** Empfangsbestätigung; ~ **in return** Rückanzeige; ~ **of shipment** Verschiffungsanzeige, Versandnote, -anzeige;
to ask for ~ Rat einholen; **to give ~** beraten; **to give s. o. an ~** jem. einen Rat erteilen; **to seek s. one's ~** j. konsultieren; **to take s. one's ~** jds. Rat einholen; **to take a lawyer's ~** sich anwaltlich beraten lassen; **to take legal ~** sich juristisch beraten lassen; **to take medical ~** Arzt konsultieren;
~ **book** Kopierbuch für eingehende [und ausgehende] Avise; **covering ~ memorandum** beigefügte Kommissionsanzeige; ~ **note** Versandanzeige, Benachrichtigungsschreiben, (banking) Buchungsanzeige; ~ **slip** Aviszettel.

advisable angebracht, zweckmäßig.

advise (v.) (come forward) sich [als Gläubiger] melden, (counsel) [an]raten, beraten, empfehlen, (inform) unterrichten, benachrichtigen, informieren, verständigen, in Kenntnis setzen, (notify) anzeigen, avisieren;
~ **s. o. against s. th.** jem. von etw. abraten; ~ **and assist** mit Rat und Tat unterstützen; ~ **a client** Mandant beraten; ~ **in due course** rechtzeitig avisieren; ~ **a draft** Tratte anmelden; ~ **fate** (banking term) sofortige Auskunft über Deckung [für einen Scheck] erbeten; ~ **s. o. on legal points during a hearing** j. während einer Verhandlung in Rechtsfragen beraten;
~ **duration and charge call** Gespräch mit Gebührenansage.

advised benachrichtigt, informiert;
as ~ by laut Bericht (Aufgabe);
to be ~ by the court vom Gericht belehrt werden; **to be soundly ~** gut beraten sein; **to keep ~** auf dem laufenden halten.

advisedly überlegt, absichtlich.

adviser, advisor Berater, Ratgeber, (university, US) Studienberater;
domestic policy ~ innenpolitischer Berater; **economic ~** Wirtschaftsberater, wirtschaftlicher Berater; **foreign policy ~** außenpolitischer Berater; **legal ~** juristischer Berater, Rechtsberater; **scientific ~** wissenschaftlicher Berater; **tax ~** Steuerberater; **technical ~** technischer Berater; **vocational ~** Berufsberater;
~ **on foreign policy** außenpolitischer Berater; ~ **on national security** Sicherheitsbeauftragter, -berater; ~ **on security questions** Sicherheitsbeauftragter; ~ **on tax avoidance** Berater auf dem Gebiet der Steuerverminderung;
to override one's ~s sich über die Meinung seiner Berater hinwegsetzen.

advising bank Korrespondenzbank.

advisory beratend;
~ **board** Beratungsgremium, Beirat, -organ, -stelle; ~ **body** Beratungsgremium; ~ **capacity** beratende Funktion; **in an ~ capacity** in beratender Eigenschaft; ~ **committee** Gutachterkommission, Beratungsausschuß, Beirat; ~ **council** beratender Ausschuß; ~ **function** beratende Funktion; ~ **group** Beratergruppe; ~ **office** Beratungsstelle; ~ **opinion** Stellungnahme, [Rechts]gutachten; ~ **panel** beratender Ausschuß; ~ **post** Beraterposition, -vertrag; ~ **procedure** (international law) Gutachter-, Konsultationsverfahren; ~ **service** Beratungsdienst, Gutachtertätigkeit; **~ Conciliation and Arbitration Service** (Br.) Beratungs-, Schlichtungs- und Schiedsgerichtsstelle in arbeitsrechtlichen Streitigkeiten; ~ **service for customers** Kundenberatungsdienst.

advocacy Anwaltschaft, Anwaltstätigkeit, (act of advocating) Befürwortung, (act of pleading) Plädoyer.

advocate (pleader) Befürworter, Fürsprecher, Verfechter, (Scot.) [Rechts]anwalt, Rechtsbeistand, Advokat;
as an ~ in seiner Eigenschaft als Anwalt;
~-general (Br.) Rechtsberater der Krone, (EG) Generalanwalt; **Lord ~** (Br.) Generalstaatsanwalt, (Scot.) Kronanwalt; ~ **of devaluation** Abwertungsbefürworter; ~ **of peace** Friedensadvokat; ~ **of free trade** Freihandelsanhänger;
~ (v.) befürworten, vertreten, eintreten, verfechten;
~ **a referendum** Volksbefragung befürworten;
to become the ~ of a cause Sache vertreten, zum Anwalt einer Sache werden; **to enter the lists as an ~** zum Befürworter werden.

advocator Befürworter, Fürsprecher.

advowson Pfründenbesetzungsrecht.

aerial Antenne;
built-in ~ Einbauantenne; **electrically operated ~** (car) automatisch ausfahrbare Antenne; **synopsis ~** Gemeinschaftsantenne;
~ (a.) (airplane) fliegerisch, (fig.) schemenhaft, nur in der Vorstellung bestehend;

~ **advertising** Luftwerbung, Himmelsschrift; ~ **attack** Luftangriff; ~ **barrage** Flakfeuer, *(balloon)* Ballonsperre; ~ **bombardment** Luftbombardement; ~ **cable** Luftkabel; ~ **cableway** Drahtseilbahn; ~ **camera** Luftbildgerät, -kamera; ~ **combat** Luftkampf; ~ **defense** (defence, *Br.*) Luftabwehr; ~ **dominance** Luftherrschaft; ~ **incident** Luftzwischenfall; ~ **inspection** Luftüberwachung; ~ **ladder** Feuerwehrleiter; ~ **map** Luftbildkarte; ~ **mine** Luftmine; ~ **navigation** Luftfahrt; ~ **photo** Luftaufnahme, -bild; ~ **photography** Luftbildwesen; ~ **photomap** Luftbildkarte; ~ **piracy** Luftpiraterie, Flugzeugentführung; ~ **railway** Schwebebahn; **prohibited** ~ **space** Luftsperrgebiet; ~ **stunts** Luftakrobatik; ~ **survey** Luftansicht, -bildaufnahme; ~ **torpedo** Lufttorpedo; ~ **tramway** Schwebebahn; ~ **view** Luftbild, Flugzeugaufnahme; ~ **warfare** Luftkrieg; ~ **wire** Antennendraht.

aerobatics Kunstfliegen.
aeroboat Wasserflugzeug.
aerobus Großflugzeug.
aerocab Lufttaxi, Hubschrauber als Zubringerflugzeug.
aerodrome *(Br.)* Flugplatz, -hafen, -feld;
~ *(v.)* auf einem Flughafen unterbringen;
~ **beacon** Landelicht; ~ **forecast** Flugplatzwettervorhersage; ~ **meteorological minima** Flugplatzwettermindestbedingungen.
aeroengine production Flugmotorenherstellung.
aerogram Funkspruch;
~ **airmail** Luftpostleichtbrief.
aerograph Spritzpistole.
aeromancy Wettervorhersage.
aeromechanic Flugzeugmechaniker.
aeronaut Luftschiffer.
Aeronautic Board *(US)* Verkehrsluftfahrtbehörde.
aeronautical flugtechnisch;
~ **engineer** Flugzeugingenieur, Flugtechniker; ~ **research** [etwa] Luftfahrtforschung; ~ **station** Bodenfunkstelle; ~ **weather station** Flugwetterdienst, -warte.
aeronautics Wissenschaft vom Flugwesen, Flugtechnik, Luftschiffahrt, Aeronautik;
National ⁓ and Space Administration (NASA) *(US)* Bundesbehörde für Luft- und Raumfahrt; **Civil ⁓ Board** *(US)* Luftsicherheitsbehörde.
aeroplane Flugzeug;
commercial ~ Verkehrsflugzeug; **heavy transport cargo** ~ Frachtflugzeug; **short-take-off vertical-landing** ~ Kurzstreckensenkrechtstarter;
~ *(v.)* im Flugzeug reisen;
~ **hangar** Flugzeugschuppen; ~ **highjack** Flugzeugentführung; ~ **ticket** Flugschein, -karte.
aerosol can Sprühdose.
aerospace Raumfahrt;
~ **activity** Raumfahrtgebiet; ~ **company** Raumfahrtunternehmen; ~ **components** Raumfahrtzubehör; ~ **conglomerate** Raumfahrtkonzern; ~ **contract** Raumfahrtauftrag; ~ **contractor** Lieferant von Raumfahrterzeugnissen; ~ **cutback** Kürzung des Raumfahrtprogramms; ~ **employee** Angestellter in der Raumfahrtsindustrie; ~ **engineer** Raumfahrtingenieur; ~ **industry** Luft- und Raumfahrtindustrie; ~ **interests** Raumfahrtbeteiligungen; ~ **job** Stellung in der Raumfahrtsindustrie; ~ **job market** Stellenmarkt für Raumfahrtspezialisten; ~ **manufacturer** Raumfahrtunternehmen; ~ **outlook** Zukunftschancen der Raumfahrtindustrie; ~ **part** Raumfahrtanteil; ~ **project** Raumfahrtprojekt; ~ **side** Raumfahrtgebiet; ~ **subcontractors** Zulieferanten der Raumfahrtindustrie; ~ **subsidiary** im Raumfahrtgeschäft tätige Tochtergesellschaft; ~ **work** Raumfahrtaufträge.
aerotow flight Schleppflug.
aerotel *(US)* Flugplatzhotel.
affair *(business)* Geschäft, Handel, *(matter)* Sache, Angelegenheit, Affäre, *(mil.)* Treffen, kurzes Gefecht;
business (commercial, mercantile) ~s Handelssachen; **costly** ~ kostspielige Angelegenheit; **external (foreign)** ~s auswärtige Angelegenheiten; **family** ~s Familienangelegenheiten; **financial** ~ finanzielle Angelegenheit; **home** ~ innere Angelegenheiten; **internal** ~s interne Angelegenheiten; **legal** ~s Rechtsangelegenheiten; **love** ~ Liebesaffäre, -verhältnis; **maritime** ~s Schiffahrtsangelegenheiten; **mundane** ~s weltliche Angelegenheiten; **pecuniary** ~s Geldangelegenheiten; **private** ~s persönliche Angelegenheiten, Privatverhältnisse; **public** ~s öffentliche Angelegenheiten, öffentliches Leben, Staatsangelegenheiten; **stage** ~s hochoffizielle Angelegenheiten; **urban** ~s städtische Angelegenheiten;

~ **of hono(u)r** Ehrenangelegenheit; ~s **of state** Staatsangelegenheiten; **cultural** ~s **of a town** kulturelle Belange einer Stadt; **to attend to one's** ~s seinen eigenen Angelegenheiten nachgehen; **to be incapable of managing one's own** ~s seine eigenen Angelegenheiten nicht mehr besorgen können; **to have no hand in an** ~ mit einer Sache nichts zu tun haben; **to leave one's** ~s **in perfect order** alles in bester Ordnung hinterlassen; **to link s. o. with an** ~ j. mit einer Sache in Verbindung bringen; **to look after s. one's** ~s jds. Geschäfte besorgen; **to look closely into an** ~ Angelegenheit genauestens untersuchen; **to make an** ~ **of s. th.** wichtige Angelegenheit aus etw. machen; **to manage one's own** ~s seine eigenen Sachen selbst erledigen; **to put one's** ~s **in order** seine Angelegenheiten regeln; **to set one's** ~s **in order** seine Angelegenheiten in Ordnung bringen; **to settle an** ~ **among one's selves** Sache intern regeln; **to settle a pending** ~ laufende Geschäfte besorgen.
affect Affekt, Erregung;
~ *(v.)* beeinflussen, angehen, betreffen, berühren, in Mitleidenschaft ziehen, *(hypothecate)* belasten, *(Scot. law)* [Schuldnervermögen] beschlagnahmen, *(v/i)* sich affektiert benehmen;
~ **all classes** *(price rise)* alle Klassen der Bevölkerung treffen; ~ **the findings** maßgeblich auf die gerichtliche Entscheidung einwirken; ~ **the health** Gesundheit beeinträchtigen; ~ **the market** Markt beeinflussen; ~ **prejudicially** nachteilig beeinflussen, Nachteile zur Folge haben, in Mitleidenschaft ziehen; ~ **in considerable measure the rights of landlords** freie Kündigungsrechte des Vermieters weitgehend einschränken; ~ **the trade** Gewerbebetrieb beeinträchtigen; ~ **unfavo(u)rably** ungünstig beeinflussen.
affected beeindruckt, betroffen, *(pretending)* affektiert;
~ **adversely** ~ benachteiligt, in Mitleidenschaft gezogen; ~ **personally** persönlich betroffen;
~ **with a public interest** das öffentliche Interesse berührend; **to be** ~ **by a fall in prices** von einem Preisrückgang betroffen werden;
~ **estate** belastetes Grundstück; ~ **property** *(restitution)* entzogene Vermögensgegenstände.
affection Gemütsbewegung, Affekt, Erregungszustand, *(influence)* Beeinträchtigung, *(med.)* Erkrankung, Leiden, *(pawning)* Verpfändung;
natural ~ natürliche Zuneigung.
affiance Verlobung.
affiant Eidesleister, Abgeber einer eidesstaatlichen Erklärung.
affiche Plakat, Anschlag.
affidavit [etwa] eidesstattliche Versicherung;
~ **of increase** *(US)* Erklärung über erhöhte Geschäftsunkosten; ~ **of means** Offenbarungseid; ~ **of merits** beeidigtes Klagevorbringen; ~ **of service** beeidigte Zustellungserklärung; ~ **of support** *(US)* Bürgschaftserklärung für Einwanderer; ~ **of verification** eidesstattliche Erklärung über Urkundenechtheit;
to file an ~ an Eides Statt versichern; **to swear an** ~ eidliche Versicherung abgeben; **to verify by** ~ durch eidesstattliche Erklärung bestätigen.
affiliate Zweig-, Konzern-, Beteiligungs-, Tochtergesellschaft, Filiale, Zweigorganisation, angeschlossener Verband, *(confederate)* Verbündeter, Genosse, *(US, radio)* Nebensender;
nonconsolidated ~s nicht in den Konzernabschluß einbezogene Unternehmen;
~ *(v.)* angliedern, *(member)* aufnehmen, zulassen;
~ **with an association** sich einem Verband anschließen; ~ **a child [up] on [to] a putative father** jem. die Vaterschaft eines unehelichen Kindes zuschieben; ~ **a member to a society** als Mitglied in eine Gesellschaft aufnehmen; ~ **o. s. to (with) a society** einer Gesellschaft als Mitglied beitreten.
affiliated angeschlossen;
~ **company (corporation,** *US)* Konzern-, Tochtergesellschaft; ~ **firm** Zweigfirma, -niederlassung; ~ **group of corporations** *(US)* Konzern; ~ **institution** Zweiganstalt; ~ **office** Filialbüro; ~ **organization** Konzern-, Zweigbetrieb; ~ **society** Zweig-, Tochtergesellschaft, angeschlossener Verband.
affiliation Angliederung, angeschlossener Verband, *(of member)* Mitgliedsaufnahme, Zulassung, Anschluß, *(putative father)* Vaterschaftsermittlung, Zuschreibung der Vaterschaft;
labo(u)r union ~ Gewerkschaftszugehörigkeit; **political** ~s *(US)* politische Beziehungen;
~ **case** Vaterschaftsprozeß, Unterhaltssache; ~ **fee** Mitgliedsbeitrag; ~ **order** Unterhaltsverfügung; ~ **responsibilities** Unterhaltsverpflichtungen; ~ **want** Gesellschaftsbedürfnis.

affinity Verschwägerung, Schwägerschaft, Verwandtschaft, *(conformity)* Wahlverwandtschaft.

affirm *(v.)* zustimmen, bestätigen, genehmigen, bekräftigen, *(depose on oath, US)* eidesstattliche Erklärung abgeben, an Eides Statt versichern;
~ **a judgment** Urteil bestätigen; ~ **upon oath** eidlich bekräftigen.

affirmable bestätigungsfähig.

affirmance Bestätigung, Bekräftigung.

affirmant Erklärender.

affirmation Zustimmung, Bestätigung, Bekräftigung, Genehmigung, *(law)* feierliche Versicherung, eidesstattliche Erklärung, *(politics)* Amtseid;
~ **of a contract** Vertragsbestätigung; ~ **of fact** Zusicherung in tatsächlicher Hinsicht;
to administer an ~ Versicherung an Eides Statt abnehmen.

affirmative Bejahung, Zustimmung;
~ *(a.)* bestätigend, zustimmend, bejahend, *(radiotelephony)* genehmigt, ja;
~ **answer** zustimmende Antwort; ~ **authorization** ausdrückliche Ermächtigung; **to hold the** ~ **burden of proof** *(US)* beweispflichtig sein; ~ **defence** neues Gegenvorbringen; ~ **easement** positive Grunddienstbarkeit; ~ **relief** zuerkannte Unterstützung; ~ **vote** Jastimme; ~ **warranty** *(insurance)* positive Zusicherung.

affix *(v.)* befestigen, ankleben, *(subjoin)* beifügen;
~ **a seal to a document** Urkunde siegeln; ~ **one's signature to a document** Urkunde unterschreiben; ~ **a stamp** Brief-, Stempelmarke aufkleben.

affixed to land mit dem Grundstück fest verbunden.

affluence Reichtum, Fülle, Überfluß;
to rise to ~ zu Vermögen gelangen, wohlhabend werden.

afflicted person betroffene Person, Betroffener.

affluent reichlich, *(wealthy)* wohlhabend, reich;
to live in ~ **circumstances** im Wohlstand leben; ~ **society** Wohlstands-, Überflußgesellschaft; ~ **years** Überfluß-, Wohlstandsperiode.

afflux Zufluß.

afford *(v.)* gewähren, bewilligen, ermöglichen, *(have the means)* [Kosten] aufbringen, sich leisten (erschwingen) [können];
~ **an expense** sich eine Ausgabe leisten können; ~ **great pleasure** großes Vergnügen bereiten; ~ **a holiday** sich einen Urlaub leisten; ~ **protection** *(patent)* Schutz gewähren; ~ **time for a cinema** Zeit zum Besuch einer Filmvorführung aufbringen; ~ **o. s. a trip abroad** sich eine Auslandsreise leisten.

afforest *(v.)* aufforsten.

afforestation Aufforstung.

affranchise *(v.)* Wahlrecht gewähren.

affray Schlägerei, Handgemenge, Landfriedensbruch.

affreight *(v.)* Frachtschiff heuern (chartern).

affreightment Voll-, Raumcharter, Schiffsfrachtvertrag, Seefrachtgeschäft.

affront Beschimpfung, Beleidigung, Affront;
~ *(v.)* s. o. jem. die Stirn bieten;
to offer an ~ öffentlich beleidigen; **to swallow an** ~ Beleidigung einstecken.

afloat im Umlauf, zirkulierend, *(debts)* ohne Schulden, schuldenfrei, *(goods)* verschifft;
goods ~ unterwegs befindliche Ware; **life** ~ Seemannsleben; **to get a newspaper** ~ Zeitung gründen; **to get a ship** ~ **again** Schiff wieder flottmachen; **to keep** ~ *(fig.)* sich über Wasser halten; **to keep bills** ~ Wechsel im Umlauf haben; **to set** ~ in Umlauf bringen, in Gang setzen; **to stay** ~ sich über Wasser halten.

afoot, to set in die Wege leiten.

afoul im Zusammenstoß;
to run ~ zusammenstoßen; **to run** ~ **of the law** mit dem Gesetz in Konflikt kommen.

aforementioned, aforesaid vorerwähnt, vorgenannt.

aforethought vorbedacht, vorsätzlich;
malice ~ vorbedachte böse Absicht.

afraid of hard work faul, arbeitsscheu.

after|-acceptance spätere Annahme; **~-acquired clause** *(mortgage)* Nachverpfändungsklausel; **~-acquired property** *(wife)* nach der Heirat erworbenes Eigentum; **~-dinner speech** Tischrede; **~-tax profit** Gewinn nach Steuern.

afterborn nachgeboren.

aftercare Jugendfürsorge der Nachschulzeit, *(patients)* Nachbehandlung;
~ **for discharged prisoners** Entlassenenfürsorge;
~ **arrangement** Anordnung der Entlassenenbetreuung.

aftercareer spätere Karriere.

afterclaim Nachforderung.

aftercosts nachträglich berechnete Kosten.

afterdate *(v.)* nachdatieren, mit einem späteren Datum versehen.

afterdeck Achterdeck.

aftereffect Nachwirkung;
~s of a disease Folgewirkungen einer Krankheit.

afterhours Zeit nach den Bürostunden, nach Ladenschluß, *(stock exchange)* Nachbörse.

afterimage *(psychol.)* Nachbild.

aftermath Nachwirkungen, Nachspiel;
~ **of war** Kriegsnachwirkungen.

afternoon paper Nachmittagszeitung;
~ **session** Nachmittagssitzung.

afterreckoning Nachberechnung.

aftersales service Kundenbetreuung, Kundendienst.

afterseason Nachsaison.

afterservice for customers Werkstätten- und Pflegedienst.

afterthought spätere Überlegung, Nachüberlegung.

aftertime Folgezeit.

aftertreatment Nachbehandlung, Weiterverarbeitung.

agate *(US, printing)* Pariser Schrift;
~ **line** *(US, advertising)* Anzeigenmaß; ~ **rate** *(advertising, US)* Zeilenpreis.

age Lebensdauer, -zeit, Lebensalter, *(full age)* Mündigkeit, Volljährigkeit, *(generation)* Zeit-, Menschenalter, Epoche, Generation;
at the awkward ~ in einem schwierigen Alter; **at the** ~ **of discretion** in unterscheidungsfähigem Alter; **at an early** ~ frühzeitig; **for** ~**s** seit langer Zeit; **of** ~ mündig, volljährig; **of competent** ~ strafmündig; **of the same** ~ gleichaltrig; **not being of** ~ minderjährig; **of tender** ~ im Kindesalter; **on (at) his coming of** ~ bei Volljährigkeit; **over** ~ über der Altersgrenze; **under** ~ minderjährig, unmündig; **at the** ~ **of** im Alter von;
~ **admitted** *(insurance)* anerkannter Altersnachweis; **advanced** ~ vorgerücktes Alter; ~ **attained** erreichtes Alter; **average** ~ Durchschnittsalter; **insured** ~ Versicherungsalter; **lawful** ~ Volljährigkeit, Mündigkeit; **legal** ~ Wahlalter; **legal school** ~ schulpflichtiges Alter, Schulalter; **marriageable** ~ Ehemündigkeit, heiratsfähiges Alter; **minimum** ~ Mindestalter; **decrepit old** ~ Altersschwäche; **green old** ~ rüstiges Alter; **pensionable** ~ pensionsfähiges Alter, Pensionierungsgrenze; **preschool** ~ vorschulpflichtiges Alter; **the present** ~ das gegenwärtige Zeitalter; **probable** ~ *(ad, US)* erwünschtes Alter; **reproductive** ~ gebärfähiges Alter; **required** ~ erforderliches Alter; **retirement** ~ Pensionierungsalter; **school-leaving** ~ Schulentlassungsalter; **statutory** ~ vorgeschriebenes Alter; **voting** ~ Wahlalter; **workable** ~ erwerbsfähiges Alter;
~ **of capacity** Geschäftsfähigkeitsalter; ~ **of consent** Mündigkeitsalter; ~ **of consumerism** Konsumentenzeitalter; ~ **of discretion** Strafmündigkeit, unterscheidungsfähiges (verständiges) Alter; ~ **of enlightement** Aufklärungsalter; ~ **at entry** *(insurance)* Eintrittsalter; ~ **at exit** *(insurance)* Austrittsalter; ~ **at expiry** *(insurance)* Endalter; **~-in-grade** Rangdienstalter; ~ **of insured** Versicherungsalter; ~ **of retirement** Pensionierungsalter; **the** ~ **we live in** unser Zeitalter; ~ **of machines** Maschinenzeitalter; ~ **of marriage** Heiratsalter; **legal** ~ **to consent marriage** Ehemündigkeit; ~ **of criminal responsibilities** Strafmündigkeitsalter; **qualifying** ~ **of riders** Führerscheinalter; ~ **of withdrawal** *(insurance)* Austrittsalter;
~ *(v.)* altern, alt werden;
~ **accounts** Konten nach ihrer Fälligkeit aufgliedern;
to be of ~ volljährig sein; **to be of** ~ **to marry** heiratsfähig sein; **to be under** ~ minderjährig sein; **to be eligible of** ~ **to retire** im pensionsfähigen Alter sein; **to come of** ~ volljährig (mündig) werden; **to declare [to be] of** ~ für mündig erklären; **to have reached the** ~ **of understanding** unterscheidungsfähiges Alter erreicht haben; **to lay aside money for one's old** ~ für sein Alter sparen (zurücklegen); **to live to a grey** ~ hohes Alter erreichen; **to take** ~**s** Ewigkeit dauern;
~ **addition** *(Br.)* Alterszulage; ~ **allowance** *(taxation, Br.)* Altersfreibetrag; ~ **analysis** Fälligkeitsanalyse; **old-**~ **assistance** Altershilfe; ~ **barrier** Altersgrenze; **old-**~ **benefit** *(US)* Altersversorgung, Altersrente; ~ **bracket** Altersgruppe, -stufe, -klasse; ~ **bulge** geburtenstarker Jahrgang; ~ **class** Altersklasse, *(mil.)* Jahrgang; ~ **classification** Alterszusammensetzung; ~ **constitution** *(population)* Altersaufbau; ~ **contingencies** Altersbedingungen; ~ **data** Altersangaben; ~ **distribution** Altersaufbau, -zusammensetzung, -gliederung; **old-**~ **exemption** *(US)* Altersfreibetrag; **old-**~ **exemption limit**

(US) Altersfreibetragsgrenze; ~ **grade (group)** Altersklasse, -gruppe, Jahrgang; **to call an ~ group** Jahrgang aufrufen; ~ **grouping** Altersaufbau; **old-~ insurance** Altersversicherung; ~ **limit** Altersgrenze; ~ **mortality** Alterssterblichkeit; **~-specific mortality rate** nach Altersgruppen aufgegliederte Sterblichkeitsrate; **to work beyond the age limit** über die Altersgrenze hinaus tätig bleiben; ~ **norm** Altersnorm; **Old-~ Pension Act** (Br.) Altersversorgungs-gesetz; **old-~ pension fund** betriebliche Altersversicherung; **old-~ pensioner** Rentner; ~ **pyramid** Bevölkerungspyramide; ~ **relief** (taxation, Br.) altersbedingte Einkommensteuervergünstigung, Freibetrag für über 65jährige, Altersfreibetrag; ~ **requirement** Alterserfordernis; ~ **restrictions** Altersbeschränkungen; ~ **scale** Altersstaffelung; ~ **schedule** Alterstabelle; ~ **structure** Altersaufbau; **Old-~ Superannuation Act** (US) Altersversorgungsgesetz.

agencies | of socialization Sozialisierungsinstanzen; **to axe ~** Dienststellen abbauen.

agency (activity) Tätigkeit, Wirksamkeit, (US, authority) [Verwaltungs]behörde, Dienststelle, (branch) Außen-, Nebenstelle, Filiale, (branch of bank) Filiale, Depositenkasse, (broadcasting) Programmagentur, (business of agent) Handeln für andere, Agentur, Vertretung, (distribution centre) Verkaufsbüro, Lieferstelle, (district of agent) Vertreterbezirk, (place of business) Geschäftsstelle, Büro, (relationship between principal and agent) Vertrags-, Vertretungsverhältnis, Geschäftsführung fremder Geschäfte, (trading station) Faktorei, ausländische Niederlassung;

by the ~ of vermittels; **through the ~ of** durch Vermittlung von; **actual ~** wirkliche Stellvertretung; **advertising ~** Werbe-, Inseratenbüro; **central ~** Zentralstelle; **chief ~** Generalvertretung; **collection ~** Inkassobüro, -stelle; **commercial ~** Handelsvertretung; **commission ~** Kommissionsgeschäft; **communicating ~** (law of contract) Erfüllungsgehilfe; **consular ~** konsularische Vertretung; **domestic ~** Hausangestelltenvermittlung; **emigration ~** Auswanderungsbüro; **employment ~** Stellenvermittlung, Arbeitsnachweis; **enforcement ~** Ausführungsbehörde; **exclusive ~** Alleinvertretung, -vertrieb, Vertretungsmonopol; **extra-legal ~** mit besonderen Vollmachten ausgestattete Dienststelle; **forwarding ~** Speditionsgeschäft; **general (head) ~** Generalvertretung, Hauptagentur; **govern-ment[al] ~** (US) Regierungsstelle; **house ~** (advertising) vorgeschobene Agentur; **implementing ~** ausführende Dienststelle; **implied ~** stillschweigend erteilte Vollmacht; **industrial ~** Agentur für Industriewerbung; **insurance ~** Versicherungsagentur; **job-creating ~** Arbeitsbeschaffungsstelle; **joint ~** Gesamtvertretung; **lending ~** Geldverleiher; **literary ~** Verlagsmittler; **matrimonial ~** Heiratsvermittlung; **mercantile ~** Handelsvertretung, Handelsagentur, Auskunftei; **national ~** staatliche Agentur; **news (press) ~** Nachrichtenagentur; **ostensible ~** Vertretung ohne Vertretungsmacht; **own case ~** (insurance business) Hausagentur; **procurement ~** Bedarfsträger; **real-estate ~** Immobilienbüro; **recognized ~** anerkannte Werbeagentur; **regional ~** Bezirksagentur; **sales ~** Verkaufsorganisation, Absatzvertretung; **servants' ~** Dienstbotenvermittlung; **sole ~** Alleinvertretung, -vertrieb; **special ~** Sonderorganisation, -vertretung, Einzelvertretung; **specialized ~** (UNO) Sonderorganisation; **state buying ~** staatliche Einkaufsstelle; **supervisory ~** Überwachungsstelle; **transportation ~** Speditionsgesellschaft, -firma; **travel ~** Reisebüro, -agentur; **unauthorized ~** Vertretung ohne Vertretungsmacht; **undisclosed ~** verdeckte Stellvertretung; **withholding ~** Lohnsteuer einbehaltende Stelle;

~ of control Aufsichtsbehörde; **~ for International Development** (US) Behörde für Internationale Entwicklung; **~ by estoppel** durch schlüssiges Verhalten erteilte Vollmacht, Scheinvollmacht, Vertretung kraft Rechtsscheins; **~ coupled with an interest** gewinnbeteiligte Vertretung, Provisionsvertretung; **~ of necessity** Geschäftsführung ohne Auftrag, (wife) Schlüsselgewalt; **~ with full service** Agentur mit Beratung auf allen Gebieten; **~ of the United Nations** Hilfsorganisation der Vereinten Nationen;

to accept the ~ of a firm Vertretung einer Firma übernehmen; **to establish an ~** Vertretung einrichten; **to have free ~** nach freier Willensbestimmung handeln; **to resign an ~** Vertretung niederlegen; **to retain an ~** Werbeagentur beschäftigen; **to service an ~** sich eine Vertretung sichern; **to take up an ~** Vertretung übernehmen;

~ account Filialkonto; **special ~ account** Treuhandsonderkonto; **~ agreement** Geschäftsbesorgungs-, Agenturvertrag, Handelsvertretervereinbarung; **exclusive ~ agreement** Ausschließlichkeitsvertrag; **~ application** Agenturbewerbung,

Bewerbung um eine Vertretung; **~ appointment** Bestallung eines Vertreters; **~ background** Agenturerfahrungen; **on an ~ basis** kommissionsweise; **~ budget** Agenturetat, (government) Behördenetat; **~ business** (commission) Kommissionsgeschäft, (representative) Agenturgeschäft, Vertretung, Vertretertätigkeit, Kommissionsgeschäft; **general ~ business** Generalagentur, unabhängige Handelsvertretung; **~ car** Vertreterwagen; **~ commission** Vertreterprovision, (advertising) Agenturprovision, Mittlervergütung; **~ company** Verkaufs-, Vertriebsgesellschaft; **~ contract** Auftragsverhältnis, Agentur-, Vertretervertrag; **exclusive ~ contract** Alleinvertretungsvertrag; **~ cost** Kosten der Geschäftsstelle; **~ discount** Agenturskonto; **~ draft** Inkassotratte; **to carry out ~ duties** bestimmte Aufgaben wahrnehmen; **~ executives** führende Agenturleute; **~ expenses** Agenturunkosten; **~ experience** Agenturerfahrung; **~ fees** Vertretergebühr, Agenturkosten; **~ field** Agenturwesen; **~ head** (government) Stellen-, Behördenleiter; **~ law** Recht des Handelsvertreter; **~ manager** Agenturleiter; **~ office** Agentur, Vertretung, Zweigstelle; **~ relationship** Vertretungs-, Vollmachtsverhältnis; **to create an ~ relationship** Vollmachtsverhältnis begründen; **~ report** (US) Bericht einer [Kredit]auskunftei; **~ representative** Agenturvertreter; **~ service** Agenturtätigkeit, Dienstleistungsgeschäft; **~ service fee** Agenturvergütung; **~ shop** (Br.) gewerkschaftspflichtiger Betrieb, Fabrikbetrieb mit gewerkschaftlichem Beitrittszwang; **~ shop agreement** (Br.) Vereinbarung der Tarifpartner über gewerkschaftliche Zwangsbeiträge, Einzeltarifvertrag; **~ staff** Außenorganisation, (diplomacy) Personal einer diplomatischen Vertretung; **~ station** Speditionsniederlassung; **~ tariff** vom bevollmächtigten Vertreter vereinbarter Speditionstarif; **~ team** Agenturmannschaft; **~ work** Vertretertätigkeit; **~ world** Agenturwesen.

agenda Tagesordnung, Traktandenliste, Verhandlungsgegenstände, zu erledigende Punkte;

approved ~ endgültige Tagesordnung; **draft ~** Tagesordnungsentwurf; **economic-policy ~** konjunkturpolitische Verhandlungspunkte; **provisional ~** vorläufige Tagesordnung; **~ for discussion** Diskussionsgrundlage;

to adopt the ~ Tagesordnung annehmen; **to be on the ~** auf der Tagesordnung stehen; **to cut out an item from the ~** Punkt von der Tagesordnung absetzen; **to draw up (fix) the ~** Verhandlungspunkte (Tagesordnung) aufstellen, Tagesordnung festlegen; **to include in the ~** in die Tagesordnung aufnehmen, auf die Tagesordnung setzen; **to overload the ~** Tagesordnung überladen; **to place a question on the ~** Frage auf die Tagesordnung setzen; **to proceed to the ~** zur Tagesordnung übergehen; **to remove from the ~** von der Tagesordnung absetzen; **to send the ~ in advance** Tagesordnung vorher verteilen (verschicken); **to withdraw an item from the ~** Frage von der Tagesordnung absetzen;

~ committee Tagesordnungsausschuß; **~ paper** schriftliche Tagesordnung, Traktandenliste.

agent Agent, (go-between) Zwischenhändler, Vermittler, Makler, (mil.) Kampfstoff, (representative) Agent, Vertreter, Bevollmächtigter, Handlungsbeauftragter, Geschäftsführer [im Sinne des BGB], Kommissionär, (travel(l)er) Handelsreisender;

during the course of one's duties as ~ in seiner Vertreterzeit; **advance ~** auf Vorschußbasis arbeitender Vertreter; **advertising ~** Werbeagent; **apparent ~** Vertreter ohne Vertretungsmacht; **appointed ~** ständiger Vertreter; **duly (lawfully) appointed (authorized) ~** ordnungsgemäß bestellter Vertreter; **bank ~** Filialdirektor, -leiter; **bargaining ~** Tarifvertragsbevollmächtigter; **business ~** (US) Gewerkschaftsvertreter; **buying ~** Einkaufsvertreter; **cash ~** (insurance business) Vermittlungsagent; **casual ~** Gelegenheitsagent; **chartered patent ~** (Br.) eingetragener Patentanwalt; **chief ~** General-, Hauptvertreter; **claim ~** Inkassobüro, Vertreter; **closing ~** Abschlußagent; **collection ~** Inkassovertreter, -bevollmächtigter, -büro, -stelle; **commercial ~** Provisions-, Handelsvertreter; **commission ~** Kommissionär; **confidential ~** Vertrauensmann; **consular ~** Konsularvertreter; **credit ~** (insurance business) Abschlußagent; **diplomatic ~** diplomatischer Vertreter; **employment ~** Stellenvermittler; **estate ~** (Br.) Grundstücks-, Immobilienmakler; **exclusive ~** Alleinvertreter; **export ~** Exportagent, -vertreter; **fiscal ~** Vertreter des Fiskus; **forwarding (freight) ~** Spediteur; **free-lance ~** selbständiger Vertreter; **full-time ~** hauptberuflicher Vertreter; **general ~** Generalvertreter, -bevollmächtigter, Handlungsbevollmächtigter; **gratuitous ~** unentgeltlicher Vertreter; **head ~** Haupt-, Generalvertreter; **house ~** Immo-

bilienmakler; **import** ~ Einfuhragent, Importvertreter; **insurance** ~ Versicherungsvertreter; **joint** ~ gemeinsamer Vertreter; **land** ~ *(Br.)* Gutsinspektor, Domänenverwalter, *(broker)* Immobilienmakler; **law** ~ *(Scot.)* Anwalt; **legal** ~ Rechtsvertreter, gesetzlicher Vertreter; **loan** ~ Darlehensvermittler, Finanzmakler; **local** ~ Bezirks-, Platzvertreter; **managing** ~ Generalbevollmächtigter, Handlungsbevollmächtigter; ~ **manufacturer's** ~ Werks-, Firmenvertreter ~ *(Br.)* Handelsvertreter, Kommissionär; **no** ~**s** Vertreterbesuche verboten; **ostensible** ~ Vertreter ohne Vertretungsmacht; **own case** ~ *(insurance business)* Hausagentur; **parliamentary** ~ parlamentarischer Vertreter; **part-time** ~ nebenberuflich tätiger Vertreter; **patent** ~ *(Br.)* Patentanwalt; **paying** ~ Zahlstelle; **placement** ~ *(US)* Stellenvermittler; **police** ~ Polizeispitzel; **political** ~ politischer Agent; **press** ~ Nachrichtenvermittler; **principal** ~ Hauptvertreter; **private** ~ Bevollmächtigter, Vertrauensmann; ~ **provocateur** Lockspitzel; **public** ~ Staatsbeauftragter; **publicity** ~ Anzeigenexpedition, Annoncenbüro; **purchasing** ~ Einkäufer; **real-estate** ~ *(US)* Immobilien-, Grundstücksmakler; **recognized** ~ anerkannter Vertreter; **regular** ~ ständiger Vertreter; **revenue** ~ Steuerbeamter; **sales** ~ Handels-, Verkaufsvertreter; **secret** ~ Geheimagent; **selling** ~ Verkaufsvertreter; **shipping** ~ Schiffsmakler, *(US)* Verlader, Spediteur; **sole** ~ Alleinvertreter; **soliciting** ~ Vermittlungsagent; **special** ~ Sonderbevollmächtigter; **station** ~ *(US)* Stationsvorsteher; **statutory** ~ gesetzlicher Vertreter; **ticket** ~ Fahrkartenbüro; **transfer** ~ Bevollmächtigter für den Verkauf von Aktien; **transport** ~ Spediteur; **travel(l)ing** ~ Reisevertreter; **unauthorized** ~ Vertreter ohne Vertretungsmacht; **universal** ~ Generalbevollmächtigter; **withholding** ~ lohnsteuerabzugspflichtige Stelle;
~ **and patient** *(law)* Insichgeschäft; **principal and** ~ Auftraggeber und Auftragnehmer, Stellvertretung;
~ **of collection** Inkassoagent, -vertreter; ~**s of the crown** *(Br.)* Vertreter des Staates; ~ **for a particular duty** Vertreter mit begrenztem Aufgabenbereich; ~ **by estoppel** Scheinvertreter, Vertreter kraft Rechtsscheins; ~**s in the field** auswärtige Vertretungen; ~ **of necessity** Geschäftsführer ohne Auftrag; ~ **with limited power** Vertreter mit beschränkten Vollmachten; ~**s of production** Produktionsfaktoren; ~**s and servants** Versicherungsgehilfen; ~ **on the spot** Platzvertreter;
~ *(v.)* Firma vertreten, als Agent auftreten;
to act as (in the quality of) ~ in fremdem Namen handeln; **to act as principal and** ~ mit sich selbst kontrahieren; **to appoint an** ~ Vertreter bestellen (ernennen); **to be** ~ **for s. o.** j. vertreten; **to be a free** ~ freier Vertreter sein; **to be sole** ~ alleiniges Vertriebsrecht (Alleinvertretung) haben; **to employ an** ~ Vertreter einsetzen (beschäftigen); **to hold an** ~ sich an einen Vertreter halten; **to proclaim o. s.** ~ **for s. o.** sich als jds. Bevollmächtigten ausgeben; **to recall an** ~ Vertreter abberufen; **to retain an** ~ Vertreter beschäftigen; **to run an** ~ *(intelligence officer)* Agenten führen; **to send one's** ~ seinen Vertreter schicken;
~**'s authority** Vertretungsvollmacht, Vertretungsbefugnis; ~**'s business** Kommissionshandel; ~**'s commission** Vertreterprovision; ~ **middleman** unselbständiger Kommissionär; ~**'s report** Vertreterbericht; ~**'s territory** Vertreterbezirk.
agglomeration Anhäufung, Sammlung, Verdichtung, Zusammenballung;
~ **area** Ballungsraum, -gebiet, Verdichtungsraum; ~ **cost** Agglommerationskosten.
aggrandize *(v.)* vergrößern erweitern;
~ **a state** Machtbereich eines Staates erweitern.
aggrandizement Vergrößerung, Erweiterung, Zunahme;
territorial ~ territoriale Vergrößerung.
aggravate *(v.)* verschlimmern, erweitern;
~ **an offence** Straftat verschärfen; ~ **the situation** Lage verschärfen.
aggravated|assault schwere Körperverletzung; ~ **larceny** schwerer Diebstahl; ~ **risk** erhöhtes Risiko.
aggravating erschwerend, [straf]verschärfend;
~ **circumstances** gravierende (erschwerende) Umstände.
aggravation Erschwerung, Verschärfung, *(law)* erschwerender Umstand;
~ **of the disability** schadenersatzerhöhende Verletzungen; ~ **of risk** Risikoerhöhung; ~ **of the situation** Verschärfung der Lage.
aggregate Anhäufung, -sammlung, Gesamtsumme;
in the ~ alles zusammengerechnet, insgesamt;
~**s of capital** Kapitalzusammenballung;
~ *(v.)* sich belaufen auf, im ganzen betragen;
~ **s. o. to a society** j. in eine Körperschaft aufnehmen;
~ *(a.)* angesammelt, gesamt;

~ **amount** Gesamtbetrag; ~ **amount of purchase** Gesamtauftrag; ~ **corporation** aus mehreren Personen bestehende juristische Person; ~ **demand** Gesamtnachfrage; ~ **estate** Gesamtvermögen, -nachlaß; ~ **foreign trade** Gesamtaußenhandel; ~ **funding** *(pension plan)* Fundierung der Altersversorgungskosten; ~ **income** Gesamteinkommen; ~ **mortality table** *(insurance)* Aggregattafel; ~ **output** Gesamtausstoß; ~ **period of five years** Gesamtzeit von fünf Jahren; ~ **profit** Gesamtertrag; ~ **supply** gesamtwirtschaftliches Angebot; ~ **supply curve** Gesamtangebotskurve; ~ **value** Gesamtwert; ~ **wage tax** Lohnsummensteuer.
aggregated shipment Sammelladung.
aggregation Anhäufung, Ansammlung, *(patentable combination)* Zusammenfassung von Erfindungselementen, patentfähige Zusammensetzung;
~ **of assets** *(estate tax)* Zusammenveranlagung von Nachlaßgegenständen; ~ **for estate duty** einheitliche Behandlung für Erbschaftssteuerzwecke; ~ **of light** Lichtbündel; ~ **of people** Menschenansammlung;
to be exempt from ~ *(estate)* gesonderter Erbschaftssteuer unterliegen;
~ **exemption** bei der allgemeinen Erbschaftssteuerberechnung ausgenommene Nachlaßgegenstände.
aggression Aggression, Angriff[shandlung], Überfall;
unprovoked ~ nicht provozierter Angriff;
to vent ~ Agression abreagieren.
aggressive initiativ, aktiv, unternehmungslustig;
~ **action** Angriffs-, Aggressionshandlung; **to invite** ~ **action** zu Aggressionen herausfordern; ~ **management** unternehmerischer Vorstand; ~ **portion** *(investment trust, US)* risikoreicherer Teil, risikoreiche Effektenanlage; ~ **sales manager** draufgängerischer Verkaufsleiter; ~ **war** Angriffskrieg; ~ **weapons** Angriffswaffen.
aggressiveness Angriffslust, Aktivität.
aggressor Angreifer;
~ **nation** angreifender Staat.
aggrieve *(v.)* benachteiligen, kränken.
aggrieved *(law)* eines Rechtes beraubt, beschwert;
to feel ~ sich benachteiligt fühlen;
~ **party** beschwerte Partei; ~ **person** Geschädigter, Beschwerter.
aging Altern, *(technics)* Veredelung;
extreme ~ Überalterung;
~ **of the population** Überalterung der Bevölkerung;
~ **accounts receivable** *(US)* überfällige Außenstände; ~ **schedule** Debitoren-, Fälligkeitstabelle, Terminliste, -plan; ~ **statement** Fälligkeitsaufstellung, -tabelle.
agio Agio, Aufgeld, *(brokerage)* Maklergeschäft, *(of a coin)* Wertverlust durch Abnutzung;
~ **account** Aufgeldkonto.
agiotage Börsenspiel, Wechselgeschäft, *(speculation in stocks)* Aktienspekulation.
agitate *(v.)* aufwiegeln, -hetzen, erregen, beunruhigen;
~ **a question** Frage aufwerfen; ~ **for electoral reform** Wahlreform erwägen; ~ **for the repeal of a law** sich öffentlich für die Abschaffung eines Gesetzes einsetzen; ~ **for higher wages** höhere Löhne verlangen.
agitated *(market)* bewegt;
to be ~ **about s. one's health** sich über jds. Gesundheitszustand Sorgen machen.
agitating aufwieglerisch.
agitation Hetze, [Volks]aufwiegelung, Aufruhr, *(discussion)* Beratung;
war ~ Kriegshetze;
to be in ~ zur Beratung anstehen; **to carry on a long** ~ **against the big department stores** die Übermacht der Warenhäuser sorgenvoll diskutieren.
agitator Agitator, Rädelsführer, Volksaufwiegler, Hetzer;
war ~ Kriegshetzer.
agnate Blutsverwandter, Seitenverwandter im Mannesstamm;
~ *(a.)* väterlicherseits verwandt.
agnation Blutsverwandtschaft.
agog|with curiosity vor Neugierde platzend; ~ **for news** sensationssüchtig;
to be all ~ in großer Spannung sein; **to set a town** ~ Gerüchte in Umlauf setzen.
agony Todeskampf;
~ **of remorse** Gewissensqual;
to pile on the ~ aus Sensationslust übertreiben;
~ **column** *(Br.)* Seufzerspalte.
agora Versammlungsplatz.

agrarian *(US)* Befürworter landwirtschaftlicher Interessen;
~ *(a.)* landwirtschaftlich, agrarisch;
~ **city** Agrarstadt; ~ **country** Ackerbau treibendes Land; ~ **party** Landwirtschaftspartei; ~ **policy** Agrarpolitik; ~ **reform** Agrar-, Bodenreform; ~ **state** Agrarstaat.

agrarianism Bewegung zur Förderung landwirtschaftlicher Interessen.

agree *(v.)* beipflichten *(come to understanding)* abmachen, absprechen, Absprache treffen, vertraglich vereinbaren, übereinkommen, genehmigen, *(consent)* einwilligen, zustimmen, sich einigen, sich einverstanden erklären, einverstanden sein, genehmigen, *(make a contract)* [Vertrag] abschließen, *(think alike)* übereinstimmen;
~ **accounts** Konten abstimmen, Rechnungen in Übereinstimmung bringen; ~ **the books** Bücher abstimmen; ~ **upon (as to) certain conditions** bestimmte Bedingungen annehmen; ~ **formally** einer Sache formell zustimmen; ~ **upon a period of one month's notice** monatliche Kündigung vereinbaren; ~ **about (upon) a price** sich auf einen Preis einigen, Preisvereinbarung treffen; ~ **to a proposal** einem Vorschlag zustimmen; ~ **subject to one qualification** seine Zustimmung von einer Bedingung abhängig machen; ~ **subsequently** sich nachträglich einigen; ~ **in writing upon s. th.** etw. schriftlich vereinbaren;
to make ~ [Bücher] abstimmen.

agreeable angenehm, gefällig, übereinstimmend;
~ **to the order of the day** in Übereinstimmung mit der Tagesordnung;
to be ~ **with** einverstanden sein.

agreed abgemacht, vereinbart, einverstanden;
as ~ **upon** wie verabredet, verabredetermaßen, vertragsgemäß;
except as may be otherwise ~ **upon** mangels besonderer Abmachung;
to be ~ **with s. o.** mit jem. konform gehen; **to be** ~ **on the conditions** sich über die Bedingungen einig sein;
~ **case** Scheinprozeß; ~ **charges** *(railway rate, Br., Canada)* vereinbarter Sondertarif, ausgehandelte Frachtgebühren; ~ **damages** pauschalierter Schadenersatz; ~ **minutes** vereinbarte Niederschrift; ~ **price** abgemachter (vereinbarter) Preis; ~ **statement of facts** vereinbarter Sachverhalt; ~ **unanimously** einstimmig angenommen; ~ **value** (vereinbarter) Wert; ~**-value clause** Abschätzungsklausel; ~ **weight** *(carrier)* einverständlich festgelegtes Gewicht.

agreement *(arrangement)* Übereinkommen, -einkunft, Vereinbarung, Abkommen, Abmachung, Absprache, *(basis of contract)* Vertragsgrundlage, *(consent)* Einverständnis, -willigung, -vernehmen, Zustimmung, *(contract)* Vertrag, *(convention)* Konvention, *(diplomacy)* Agrement, *(harmony)* Einklang, Übereinstimmung, *(international law)* Vereinbarung, *(understanding)* Verständigung;
according to ~ laut Absprache; **against previous** ~**s** entgegen früheren Vereinbarungen; **as per** ~ vertragsvereinbarungsgemäß; **by** ~ laut Übereinkunft (Vertrag); **by mutual** ~ durch beiderseitiges Abkommen; **by way of** ~ vergleichsweise; **by between themselves** in gegenseitigem Einvernehmen; **contrary to** ~ vertragswidrig; **failing** ~ mangels Vereinbarung, mangels einer Einigung; **for the purpose of this** ~ im Sinne dieses Abkommens; **in** ~ **with** in Übereinstimmung, (in freiem Vernehmen) mit; **in wholehearted** ~ in vollständiger Übereinstimmung;
additional ~ Zusatzvertrag; **agency** ~ Agentur-, Geschäftsbesorgungsvertrag; **amicable** ~ gütliche Einigung (Abmachung); **arbitration** ~ Schiedsvereinbarung, Vertragsabkommen; **bare** ~ einfacher Vertrag; **armistice** ~ Waffenstillstandsabkommen; **bargaining** ~ Tarifabkommen, -vereinbarung; **barter** ~ Tauschhandelsabkommen; **basic** ~ Mantel-, Rahmenvertrag; **bilateral clearing** ~ zweiseitiges Verrechnungsabkommen; **bilateral transfer** ~ zweiseitiges Zahlungsabkommen; **binding** ~ unwiderrufliches Abkommen; **blocking** ~ Stillhalteabkommen, -vereinbarung; **business** ~ Wirtschaftsabkommen; **cartel** ~ Kartellvereinbarung; **ceasefire** ~ Waffenstillstandsabkommen; **civil aviation** ~ Luftfahrt-, -verkehrsabkommen; **clearing** ~ Verrechnungsabkommen; **collateral** ~ Nebenabrede; **collective** ~ Kollektiv-, Tarifvertrag; **commodity** ~ Warenabkommen; **conditional** ~ bedingter Vertrag; **continuing** ~ laufendes Abkommen; **contractual** ~ vertragliche Vereinbarung; **covering** ~ Mantelvertrag; **credit** ~ Kreditabkommen; **cultural** ~ Kulturabkommen; **currency** ~ Währungsabkommen; **current** ~ laufendes Abkommen; **mutual defence** ~ Verteidigungsabkommen; **draft** ~ Vertragsentwurf; **economic** ~ Wirtschafts-, Handelsabkommen; **exchange** ~ Abkommen über den Zahlungsverkehr; **executed** ~ beiderseits erfüllter Vertrag; **execu-**

tory ~ bedingter Vertrag; **express** ~ ausdrückliche Abmachung; **financial** ~ Vereinbarung über die Zahlungsmodalitäten, Finanzabkommen, finanzielles Abkommen; **financing** ~ Finanzierungsvereinbarung; **foreign exchange** ~ Devisenabkommen; **Four Power** ~ Viermächteabkommen; **gentleman's** ~ Gentlemanvereinbarung, Vereinbarung auf Treu und Glauben; **goods** ~ Warenabkommen; **hire-purchase** ~ *(Br.)* Ratenzahlungs-, Abzahlungsvertrag; **hold-harmless** ~ Vereinbarung über die Freistellung von Schadensersatzverpflichtungen; **implicit** ~ stillschweigende Vereinbarung; **industrial** ~ Lohntarif, Tarifabkommen; **industry-wide** ~ Manteltarifvertrag; **information-sharing** ~ Abkommen zur gegenseitigen Unterrichtung; **inter-insurer** ~ versicherungsinterne Vereinbarung; **interdepartmental** ~ Ressortabkommen; **international** ~ internationale Vereinbarung, zwischenstaatliche Abmachung; **invalid** ~ ungültige Vereinbarung; **joint** ~ *(trade union)* Manteltarifvertrag; **licensing** ~ Lizenzabkommen; **loan** ~ Darlehnsvertrag; **London** ~ Abkommen über deutsche Auslandsschulden; **marketing** ~ Marktabsprache; **master** ~ Mustertarifvertrag; **monetary** ~ Zahlungs-, Währungsabkommen; **multilateral** ~ mehrseitiges (multilaterales) Abkommen; **mutual** ~ zweiseitiger Vertrag, gegenseitige Vereinbarung; **naked** ~ einseitig verpflichtender Vertrag; **naval** ~ Flottenabkommen; **nonwaiver** ~ Vereinbarung über den Vorbehalt aller Rechte; **notional** ~ gedankliche Übereinstimmung; **no-strings** ~ nicht verklausuliertes Abkommen; **obligatory** ~ bindende Abmachung; **oral** ~ mündliche Vereinbarung; **original** ~ ursprüngliche Vereinbarung; **offset** ~ Devisenausgleichs-, Verrechnungsabkommen; **parol** ~ mündliche Vereinbarung, formloser Vertrag; **partial** ~ Zeitabkommen; **partnership** ~ Gesellschafter-, Teilhabervertrag; **pattern-setting** ~ beispielhafte Vereinbarung; **payments** ~ Zahlungsabkommen; **pocket** ~ Nebenabrede, Revers; **pooling** ~ Kartellabkommen, Poolvertrag, Interessengemeinschaft; **preliminary** ~ vorläufiger Vertrag, Vorvertrag, *(real estate)* Grundstücksvorvertrag; **present** ~ dieses Abkommen; **previous** ~ frühere Abrede; **price** ~ Preiskonvention, -vereinbarung, -absprache, -abkommen; **price-fixing** ~ Preiskartell, -konvention; **private** ~ gütlicher Vergleich, Privatabmachung; **prolongation** ~ Verlängerungsabkommen; **proposed** ~ Vergleichsvorschlag; **provisional** ~ vorläufiges Abkommen; **purchase and sales** ~ *(US)* Grundstückskaufvertrag; **real** ~ dinglicher Vertrag; **redemption** ~ Tilgungsvereinbarung; **registrable** ~ *(Restrictive Trade Practices, Br.)* eintragungspflichtige Vereinbarung; **registered** ~ *(Br.)* registrierte Kartellvereinbarung (Absprache); **repatriation** ~ Repatriierungsabkommen; **restrictive trading** ~ *(Br.)* wettbewerbsbeschränkende Vereinbarung; **sales** ~ Kaufvereinbarung, -vertrag; **mutually satisfactory** ~ alle Teile befriedigende Abmachung; **sealed** ~ förmlicher Vertrag; **secret** ~ Geheimvertrag, -abkommen; **security** ~ *(pol.)* Sicherheitsabkommen; **separate** ~ Sonderabkommen; **separation** ~ *(married couple)* Trennungsvereinbarung, Vereinbarung über das Getrenntleben; **settlement** ~ Auseinandersetzungsvertrag; **shop** ~ Betriebsvereinbarung; **silent (tacit)** ~ stillschweigendes Übereinkommen; **single-plant bargaining** ~ Betriebsvereinbarung, betrieblich ausgehandelter Tarifvertrag, Einzeltarifvertrag; **skeleton** ~ *(bargaining)* Rahmenvertrag, Manteltarif; **Smithonian** ~ *(Br.)* Washingtoner Währungsabkommen; **social** ~ gesellschaftliche Vereinbarung; **solemn** ~ förmlicher Vertrag; **special** ~ Separatvertrag, Sonderabkommen, Sondervereinbarung; **standard** ~ Einheitstarifvertrag; **standing** ~ laufendes Abkommen; **standstill** ~ Stillhalteabkommen, -vereinbarung; **subsidiary** ~ Nebenvereinbarung; **summit** ~ Gipfelabkommen; **supplementary** ~ Ergänzugsabkommen, Zusatzabkommen; **sweetheart** ~ *(US)* auf enge Zusammenarbeit abgestellter Tarifvertrag; **tacit** ~ stillschweigende Vereinbarung; **temporary** ~ vorübergehendes Abkommen; **trade** ~ Tarif, Handelsabkommen, Wirtschaftsvertrag; **collective trade** ~ Tarifkollektivvertrag; **reciprocal trade** ~ Gegenseitigkeitsabkommen; **transfer** ~ Verrechnungsabkommen; **transient** ~ befristetes Abkommen; **trust** ~ *(trustee)* Sicherungsübereignungsvertrag, Treuhandvertrag; **tying** ~ Ausschließlichkeitsvertrag, -abkommen; **underlying** ~ *(banking)* Rahmenkreditvertrag; **underwriting** ~ Emissions-, Konsortialvertrag; **union** ~ Abkommen mit den Gewerkschaften; **verbal** ~ mündliche Abmachung (Vereinbarung); **wage** ~ Tarifvertrag, Lohnabkommen; **working** ~ Interessengemeinschaft; **written** ~ schriftliche Vereinbarung, schriftliches Abkommen;
~ **of accounts** Kontenabstimmung; ~ **in arms control** Rüstungsbegrenzungsabkommen; ~ **of association** Gründungsvertrag; ~ **to build** Bauauftrag; ~ **of consolidation** Fusionsvertrag; ~

with one's creditors Akkord, [Gläubiger]vergleich; ~ **on Economic Cooperation** *(AEC)* Abkommen über wirtschaftliche Zusammenarbeit; ~ **of deposit** Hinterlegungsvertrag, -urkunde; ~ **for collective enforcement of conditions as to resale prices** Kartellvereinbarung zur Durchsetzung von gebundenen Wiederverkaufspreisen; ~ **under hand** formfreier (formloser) Vertrag, privatrechtliche Vereinbarung; ~ **by inference from the conduct of the parties** Vereinbarung auf Grund schlüssigen Parteiverhaltens; ~ **to insure (for insurance)** Versicherungsvorvertrag; ~ **of interests** Interessenabstimmung; ~ **on interest rates** Zinsabkommen; ~ **for a lease** Pachtvereinbarung, -vertrag; **legally binding** ~ **for the maintenance of children** rechtsverbindliche Unterhaltsvereinbarung; ~ **between the parties** Parteivereinbarung; ~ **by the piece** Stückakkord; ~ **on all points** Einstimmigkeit in allen Punkten; ~ **in principle** grundsätzliche Übereinkunft; ~ **between producers** Produktionsabkommen; ~ **subject to numerous qualifications** sehr bedingtes Übereinkommen; ~ **subject to registration** *(cartel law, Br.)* anmeldepflichtige Absprache; ~ **of renewal** Erneuerungsvertrag; ~ **in restraint of trade** *(US)* Kartell[vereinbarung], Wettbewerbsverbotsvertrag; ~ **for sale** Verkaufsvertrag, -vereinbarung; ~ **of sale and purchase** *(Br.)* Grundstückskaufvertrag; ~ **to sell** obligatorischer Kaufvertrag; ~ **to sell land** Vorvertrag für ein Grundstück; ~ **of service** Dienstvertrag; ~ **of submission** Schiedsgerichtsvereinbarung; ~ **of views** Meinungsübereinstimmung; ~ **by word of mouth** mündliche Vereinbarung; ~ **in writing** schriftliche Vereinbarung;
to abide by an ~ sich an eine Abmachung (einen Vertrag) halten, vertragstreu sein; **to accede to an international** ~ einem internationalen Abkommen beitreten; **to acquiesce in an** ~ einer Vereinbarung zustimmen; **to act in** ~ **with s. o.** im Einverständnis mit jem. handeln; **to arrive at an** ~ sich mit jem. verständigen, zu einer Verständigung gelangen; **to be in** ~ **with s. o.** sich mit jem. in Übereinstimmung befinden, mit jem. konform gehen; **to be in substantial** ~ sich im wesentlichen einig sein; **to be in** ~ **with a proposal** mit einem Vorschlag einverstanden sein; **to become party to an** ~ einem Vertrag beitreten; **to break an** ~ Abmachung brechen; **to bring about an** ~ Vereinbarung zustande bringen; **to cancel an** ~ Vertrag aufheben; **to carry out an** ~ Vereinbarung durchführen; **to come to (conclude, consummate) an** ~ Verständigung erzielen, sich verständigen, übereinkommen, zu einer Übereinkunft (zu einem Vertrag, zum Abschluß) gelangen, Abrede treffen; **to confirm an** ~ Übereinkommen bestätigen; **to constitute an indenture a valid, binding and legal** ~ Urkunde zu einem rechtsgültigen, bindenden und gesetzmächtigen Vertrag machen; **to denounce an** ~ **with tree months' notice** Vertrag mit vierteljährlicher Frist kündigen; **to dissent from an** ~ einem Abkommen nicht zustimmen; **to dissolve an** ~ Vertrag lösen; **to effect an** ~ Vertrag abschließen; **to enter into an** ~ Vertrag (Vereinbarung) abschließen (eingehen), übereinkommen; **to fall within the ambit of an** ~ in den Bereich eines Abkommens fallen; **to grant the** ~ Agreement erteilen; **to keep to the terms of an** ~ der Abrede gemäß handeln; **to make an** ~ Übereinkommen, Abkommen (Absprache) treffen; **to make an** ~ **as to one's remuneration** Honorarvereinbarung treffen; **to reach an** ~ Übereinstimmung (Abkommen) erzielen; **to rescind an** ~ Vertrag aufheben; **to rush into a quick** ~ zu einer sofortigen Vereinbarung gelangen; **to satisfy an** ~ Vertrag erfüllen; **to secure** ~ Zustimmung einholen; **to sign an (a legal)** ~ [Notariats]vertrag unterzeichnen; **to sign an** ~ **provisionally** Abkommen mit Vorbehalt unterzeichnen; **to sign an** ~ **under duress** Vereinbarung unter Druck unterzeichnen; **to stand by an** ~ sich an eine Vereinbarung halten; **to work by** ~ im Akkord arbeiten;
~ **country** Verrechnungsland; ~ **currency** Verrechnungswährung; ~ **restraining trade** *(US)* Wettbewerbsbeschränkungsvereinbarung.
agribusiness sector Agrarmarktbereich.
agricultural agrar-, landwirtschaftlich;
~ **advisory service** *(Br.)* landwirtschaftlicher Beratungsdienst; ~ **area** landwirtschaftliches Gebiet, Agrargebiet, landwirtschaftliche Betriebsfläche; ~ **assets** landwirtschaftliche Anlagen (Vermögenswerte); ~ **association** Landwirtschaftsverband; ~ **avalanche** Lawine landwirtschaftlicher Erzeugnisse; ~ **bank** Landwirtschaftsbank; ~ **bloc** *(parl.)* grüne Front; ~ **building** landwirtschaftliches Gebäude, Gutsgebäude, Wirtschaftsgebäude; ~ **buildings allowance** Abschreibung auf Wirtschaftsgebäude; ~ **charge** *(banking, Br.)* Verpfändung landwirtschaftlichen Betriebsvermögens, Belastung eines landwirtschaftlichen Besitzes; ~ **college** Landwirtschaftsschule; ~ **commerce** Handel mit landwirtschaftlichen Erzeug-

nissen; ~ **commodity** landwirtschaftliches Erzeugnis, Agrarerzeugnis; ~ **cooperative society (cooperation)** Agrargenossenschaft, landwirtschaftliche Betriebsgenossenschaft; ~ **country** Agrarland, -staat; ~ **credit** Agrarkredit, Landwirtschaftskredit; ~ **Credits Act** *(Br.)* Agrargenossenschaftsgesetz; ~ **credit society** landwirtschaftliche Genossenschaftsbank; ~ **crisis** Agrarkrise; ~ **department** *(US)* Landwirtschaftsministerium; ~ **depression** Darniederliegen der Landwirtschaft, landwirtschaftliche Notlage; ~ **duty** Agrarzoll; ~ **economics** Agrarwirtschaftslehre; ~ **economist** Agrarwirtschaftler, -wissenschaftler, Agronom; ~ **employment** landwirtschaftliche Beschäftigung; ~ **engineering** Agrartechnik; ~ **enterprise (estate)** landwirtschaftlicher Betrieb; ~ **exports** Agrarexporte; ~ **fair** Landwirtschaftsmesse; ~ **fixtures** Einbauten des Pächters; ~ **fluctuations** Agrarkonjunkturen; ~ **fund** Agrarfonds; ~ **holding** landwirtschaftlich genutzter Besitz, Bauernhof, *(Br.)* Pachtland, -gut; ~ **holdings Act** *(Br.)* Pachtgesetz; ~ **imports** Agrareinfuhren; ~ **income** Agrareinkommen; ~ **industry** Agrarwirtschaft; ~ **insurance** landwirtschaftliche Versicherung; ~ **labo(u)r** Landarbeit; ~ **labo(u)rer** Landarbeiter; ~ **land** *(Br.)* landwirtschaftlich genutztes Grundstück; ~ **Land Board** *(Br.)* Ackerbaubehörde; ~ **Land Tribunal** *(Br.)* Schiedsstelle für Enteignungsentschädigungen; ~ **levy** Agrarabschöpfung; ~ **lien** Erntepfandrecht; ~ **loan** landwirtschaftliche Anleihe; ~ **loan bank** Landwirtschaftsbank; ~ **machinery** landwirtschaftliche Maschinen; ~ **market** Markt für landwirtschaftliche Erzeugnisse, Agrarmarkt; ~ **marketing** Agrarmarktpolitik; ~ **marketing association** *(US)* landwirtschaftliche Absatzorganisation; ~ **Mortgage Corporation Limited** *(Br.)* Landwirtschaftsbank, [etwa] Bodenkreditanstalt; ~ **output** Gesamtproduktion der Landwirtschaft; ~ **paper** landwirtschaftliches Akzept; ~ **plant** landwirtschaftliche Betriebseinrichtung; ~ **common policy** gemeinsame Agrarpolitik; ~ **price** Agrarpreis; ~ **producer** Produzent landwirtschaftlicher Erzeugnisse; ~ **product** Agrarprodukt; ~ **production** Erzeugung landwirtschaftlicher Produkte; ~ **property** landwirtschaftliches Vermögen; ~ **publications** landwirtschaftliche Blätter; ~ **relief** *(US)* Agrarhilfe; ~ **show** Landwirtschaftsausstellung, -messe; ~ **sphere** Agrarsektor; ~ **statistics** Agrarstatistik; ~ **structure** Agrarstruktur; ~ **subsidies (support)** *(Br.)* Agrarhilfe, -zuschüsse, -subventionen; ~ **surplus** Agrarüberschuß; ~ **system** Agrarsystem; ~ **tenant** Pächter; ~ **trade** Handel mit Erzeugnissen der Landwirtschaft; ~ **unit** landwirtschaftliche Betriebseinheit; ~ **value** Wert des landwirtschaftlichen Vermögens; ~ **value relief** Erbschaftssteuernachlaß auf landwirtschaftliche Betriebsflächen; ~ **vehicle** Ackerschlepper; ~ **wage** Landarbeiterlohn; ~ **Wages Board** *(Br.)* Behörde zur Festsetzung von Landarbeiterlöhnen; ~ **worker** Landarbeiter; ~ **workforce** landwirtschaftliche Arbeitskräfte.
agriculture Landwirtschaft, Ackerwirtschaft, -bau, Ökonomie;
in the field of ~ auf landwirtschaftlichem Gebiet;
Board *(Br.)* **(Department, US) of** ~ Landwirtschaftsministerium.
agrimotor Schlepper, Traktor.
agrotat *(Br.)* Krankheitsattest.
aground gestrandet, *(fig.)* in Verlegenheit;
to be ~ festliegen, festgefahren sein; **to run** ~ auf Grund laufen.
ahead vorwärts, an der Spitze;
to buy ~ auf spätere Lieferung kaufen; **to date a check** *(US)* **(cheque, Br.)** ~ Scheck nachdatieren; **to get** ~ *(US coll.)* Karriere machen; **to get** ~ **of s. o.** j. überholen; **to sell** ~ blanko (für zukünftige Lieferung) verkaufen.
aid Hilfe, Hilfsdienst, Beistand, Unterstützung, *(law)* Rechtshilfe, *(person)* Gehilfe, Hilfsperson, Helfer, Assistent, Entwicklungshilfe;
in ~ **of** zugunsten von;
economic ~ Wirtschaftshilfe; **emergency** ~ Soforthilfe; **US-financed foreign** ~ amerikanische Auslandshilfe; **financial** ~ finanzielle Hilfe; **first** ~ erste Hilfe; **grant-in-**~ *(US)* *(municipal corporation)* öffentlicher Zuschuß, innerstaatliche Finanzzuweisung; **interim** ~ Übergangs-, Überbrückungshilfe; **legal** ~ *(Br.)* Armenrecht, *(US)* Rechtshilfe, unentgeltliche Rechtsberatung; **mechanical** ~s technische Hilfsmittel; **memory** ~ Gedächtnisstütze; **mutual** ~ gegenseitige Hilfeleistung, Unterstützung; **public** ~ öffentliche Unterstützung; **self** ~ Selbsthilfe; **short-term interim** ~ kurzfristige Zwischenfinanzierung; **spot** ~ Soforthilfe; **state** ~ staatliche Unterstützung; **stopgap** ~ Übergangs-, Überbrückungshilfe; **technical** ~ fachliche Unterstützung; **tied** ~ projektgebundene wirtschaftliche Unterstützung; **untied** ~ projektfreie Wirtschaftshilfe; **visual** ~ bildliche Verkaufsunterstützung;

~ **for abortions** Abtreibungsbeihilfe; ~ **to the blind** Blindenhilfe; ~ **for building** Bauzuschuß; ~ **to families with dependent children** Unterstützung für Familien mit abhängigen Familienangehörigen; ~ **to memory** Gedächtnisstütze; ~ **for modernization** Modernisierungsbeihilfe; ~ **for research** Forschungszuschuß;

~ *(v.)* helfen, unterstützen, Beihilfe leisten, beistehen, behilflich sein;

~ **and abet** Beihilfe (Vorschub) leisten, begünstigen; ~ **and comfort** [dem Feinde] Vorschub leisten; ~ **management** der Geschäftsleitung eine große Hilfe sein; ~ **s. o. with money** j. unterstützen, jem. mit Geld aushelfen; ~ **s. one's recovery** jem. beim Wiederaufbau helfen;

to act in ~ for the enemy Feindbegünstigung treiben; to call in the ~ of an attorney Anwalt zu Rate ziehen; to enlist the ~ of the court Hilfe des Gerichts in Anspruch nehmen; to extend financial ~ finanzielle Unterstützung gewähren, subventionieren; to lend one's ~ to s. th. einer Sache Unterstützung gewähren; to make ~ available for developing countries Hilfsmittel für Entwicklungsländer bereitstellen; to seek s. one's ~ j. um Hilfe bitten;

~ **appeal** Hilfsappell, -aufruf; ~ **appropriation** Mittelzuweisung für das Hilfsprogramm; ~ **bill** *(US)* Auslandshilfegesetz; ~ **budget** Auslandshilfeetat; ~ **center** *(US)* Hilfsstelle; ~ **cut** Kürzung des Hilfsprogramms; ~ **donor** *(development policy)* Wirtschaftshilfe gewährender Staat; ~ **expenditure** Hilfsaufwand; ~ **fund** Hilfs-, Unterstützungsfonds; ~ **grant** Hilfszusage; ~ **man** *(mil.)* Sanitäter; ~ **moneys** Hilfsgelder; ~ **official** Entwicklungshelfer; **mutual** ~ **plan** Hilfsabkommen auf Gegenseitigkeit; ~ **planner** Entwicklungsplaner; ~ **progam(me)** Hilfs-, Unterstützungsprogramm; ~-**to-education program(me)** Ausbildungsbeihilfeplan; **no-strings** ~ **program(me)** nicht verklausuliertes Hilfsprogramm; ~ **project** Hilfsprojekt; ~ **quantum** Hilfsvolumen; ~ **scheme** Hilfs-, Notdienst; **mutual** ~ **society** Hilfsverein auf Gegenseitigkeit; ~ **station** *(mil.)* Truppenverbandsplatz; **legal** ~ **system** *(Br.)* Armenrechtswesen, *(US)* unentgeltliche Rechtsberatung; ~ **tying** Bindung der Entwicklungshilfe.

aide *(mil.)* Hilfskraft, *(politics)* Berater;
personal ~ persönlicher Referent;
~-**memoire** Gedächtnisstütze, *(pol.)* Denkschrift.

aided recall Gedächtnisstütze, Erinnerungshilfe;
~ **survey** *(insurance)* Fragebogen mit vorgedruckten Antworten; ~ **technique** Methode zur Überprüfung des Erinnerungswertes einer Werbung; ~ **test** Erinnerungstest mit abgestuften Hilfen.

aider Helfer, Gehilfe, Beistand;
~ **and abettor** Gehilfe und Anstifter, Tatgehilfe; ~ **by verdict** durch Urteil geheilter Verfahrensmangel.

aiding *(criminal)* Begünstigung;
~ **and abetting** Beihilfe, Mittäterschaft; ~ **and comforting the enemy** Feindbegünstigung; ~ **an escape** Beihilfe zur Gefangenenbefreiung.

aileron *(airplane)* Querruder.

ailment Unpäßlichkeit.

aim Ziel, Zweck, Vorhaben, Bestreben, Bestrebung;
final ~ Endzweck; **long-term** ~ Ziel auf lange Sicht; ~ **of a letter** Briefzweck; ~**s of taxation** Besteuerungszweck; **to miss one's** ~ seinen Zweck verfehlen.

air Luft, Atmosphäre, *(appearance)* Auftreten, Allüren, *(melody)* Lied, Melodie, Weise, *(mining)* Wetter, *(outward appearance)* Augenschein, Schein;
by ~ auf dem Luftwege, per Flugzeug; **in the** ~ *(fig.)* in der Schwebe; **on the** ~ durch Rundfunk;
clean ~ saubere Luft; **foul** ~ schlechte Luft, *(mining)* schlagende Wetter; **impure** ~ unsaubere (schlechte) Luft; **tainted** ~ verpestete Luft; **upper** ~ obere Luftschichten; **vitiated** ~ verpestete Luft;
~ **of authority** autoritäres Auftreten; ~ **of impending doom** Weltuntergangsstimmung;
~ *(v.) (fig.)* der Diskussion zugänglich machen, an die Öffentlichkeit bringen, *(to go on the ~)* Rundfunkwerbung betreiben; ~ **a problem** Problem diskutieren; ~ **one's views** seine Ansicht bekanntgeben;
to be in the ~ *(rumo(u)r)* in der Luft liegen; **to be in the** ~ **for two hours** zwei Stunden fliegen; **to be on the** ~ *(broadcasting)* senden, über den Rundfunk sprechen, *(program(me))* gesendet werden; **to be given the** ~ *(sl.)* gefeuert werden; **to be put on the** ~ durch Rundfunk übertragen werden; **to be still up in the** ~ noch völlig in der Luft hängen; **to beat the** ~ sich erfolglos bemühen; **to be off the** ~ außer Betrieb sein; **to carry goods by** ~

Lufttransporte durchführen; **to charge the** ~ **with tension** Spannungsfeld erzeugen; **to give o. s.** ~**s** sich zieren; **to give s. o.the** ~ *(US sl.)* jem. den Laufpaß geben, j. an die frische Luft befördern; **to go by** ~ per Flugzeug reisen, fliegen; **to go off the** ~ Sendung beenden (einstellen); **to go on the** ~ Sendung beginnen, *(advertising)* Rundfunkkampagne starten; **to go on the** ~ **nationally** über alle Sender sprechen; **to have an** ~ **of comfort** *(house)* sehr komfortabel wirken; **to have an** ~ **of importance** bedeutend aussehen; **to infect (pollute) the** ~ Luft verpesten; **to put on the** ~ durch Rundfunk übertragen; **to ship by** ~ per Luftfracht versenden; **to stay on the** ~ weiterhin senden; **to take the** ~ frische Luft schöpfen, *(aircraft)* aufsteigen, starten; **to travel by** ~ fliegen, per Flugzeug reisen; **to tread (walk) on** ~ sich wie im siebenten Himmel fühlen;

~ **accident** Flugzeugunglück; ~ **advertisement** Luftwerbung; ~ **age** Flugzeugalter; ~ **alert** Fliegeralarm, *(troops)* Alarmbereitschaft; ~ **alert mission** Bereitschaftsauftrag; ~ **ambulance** Sanitätsflugzeug; ~ **arm** *(Br.)* Luftstreitkräfte; ~ **attaché** Luftattaché; ~ **attack** Fliegerangriff; ~ **barrage** Luftsperre; ~ **base** *(US)* Luftstützpunkt, Fliegerhorst; ~ **beacon** Leuchtfeuer; ~ **bed** *(Br.)* Luftmatratze; ~ **brake** Luftdruckbremse; ~ **brake parachute** Landefallschirm; ~ **bridge** Luftbrücke; ~ **brick** Luftziegel; ~ **broker** Luftfrachtmakler; ~ **bubble** Luftblase; ~ **bump** Bö; ~ **bumper** Luftpolster.

air cargo Luftfracht;
~ **business** Luftfrachtgewerbe, -geschäft; ~ **carrier** Lufttransportgesellschaft; ~ **equipment** Luftfrachtanlagen; ~ **market** Luftfrachtmarkt; ~ **rate** Luftfrachttarif; ~ **terminus** Luftfrachtbahnhof; ~ **terminus facilities** Einrichtungen eines Luftfrachthafens.

air|carriage Luftbeförderung; ~ **carrier** Lufttransportgesellschaft, Luftfrachtführer; ~ **carrier permit** Fluglizenz; ~ **castle** Luftschloß; ~ **cell** *(balloon)* Luftsack; ~ **charter** Charterfluggesellschaft; ~ **chartering** Luftchartergeschäft; ~ **chamber** Luftkammer; ~ **chief marshal** *(Br.)* Luftwaffengeneral; ~ **circulation** Luftzirkulation; ~ **circus** Flugschau; ~ **cleaner** Luftfilter; ~ **coach** *(US)* Airbus, Passagierflugzeug der Touristenklasse; ~ **commerce** Lufttransport; ~-**condition** *(v.)* klimatisieren; ~ **conditioner** Klimaanlage; ~ **conditioning** Klimatisierung, Klimaanlage; ~ **congestion** Verstopfung der Luftfahrtwege; ~ **automatically controlled high-pressure** ~ **conditioning sytem** automatisch gesteuerte Hochdruckklimaanlage; ~ **connection** Luftverbindung; ~ **consignment note** *(Br.)* Luftfrachtbegleitschein; ~ **conveyance** Lufttransport; ~-**cooled** luftgekühlt; ~ **cooling** Luftkühlung; ~ **corps** *(US)* Luftwaffe; ~ **corridor** Einflugschneise, Luftkorridor; ~ **council** *(Br.)* Luftwaffenamt; ~ **cover** *(mining)* Wetterweg; ~ **crash** Flugzeugunglück; ~ **crew** Flugzeugbesatzung; ~ **crew training** Ausbildung der Besatzungsmitglieder; ~ **current** Luftströmung; ~ **cushion** Luftkissen; ~-**cushion vehicle** Luftkissenfahrzeug; ~ **defence** Flugabwehr, Luftraumverteidigung; **passive** ~ **defence** Luftschutz; ~ **defence alert system** Luftwarnsystem; ~ **defence identification zone** Luftverteidigungs-, Luftüberwachungszone; **semi-automatic** ~ **defence network** halbautomatisches Flugabwehrnetz; ~ **display** Flugschau, -vorführung; ~-**dried** luftgetrocknet; ~-**dropped mine** Luftmine; ~ **edition** *(newspaper)* Luftpostausgabe; ~ **express** *(US)* Lufteilgut, -expreßfracht; ~ **express rates** *(US)* Luftexpreßtarif; ~ **fares** Flugtarif, Luftverkehrstarif, Flugpreise; ~ **fare savings** Ersparnisse beim Erwerb einer Flugkarte; ~ **fee** Luftpostgebühr, -zuschlag; ~ **feed** Luftversorgung, -verpflegung; ~ **fleet** Luftflotte; ~ **filter** Luftfilter; ~ **flap** Luftklappe; ~ **Force** Luftwaffe, Luftstreitkräfte; **Royal** ~ **Force** *(Br.)* Luftwaffe, -flotte, -streitkräfte; ~ **force base** Luftwaffenstützpunkt; ~ **force manoeuvre** Luftflottenmanöver; ~ **forwarder** Luftfrachtspediteur; ~-**ground** Bord-Boden; **Civil** ~ **Guard** *(Br.)* Luftschutzbund; ~ **hazard** Flugrisiko; ~ **hole** Luftloch, Fallbö; ~ **hostess** Stewardeß; ~ **incident** Luftzwischenfall; ~ **industry** Flugzeugindustrie; ~ **injection** Drucklufteinspritzung; ~ **jacket** Schwimmweste; ~-**landed operation** *(US)* Luftlandeunternehmen; ~ **lane** Luftkorridor; ~ **law** internationales Luftrecht; ~ **letter** *(US)* Luftpostleichtbrief; ~ **letter form** Luftpostformat; ~ **liaison officer** Luftverbindungsoffizier; ~ **links** Luftverbindung; ~ **lock** Luft-, Druckschleuse; ~ **mail** *(Br.)* Luftpost; **by** ~ **mail** *(Br.)* mit Luftpost; ~-**mail company** *(Br.)* Luftpostgesellschaft; ~-**mail envelope** *(Br.)* Luftpostkuvert, -umschlag; ~-**mail fee** *(Br.)* Luftpostporto, -gebühr; ~-**mail label** *(Br.)* Luftpostaufkleber; ~-**mail letter** *(Br.)* Luftpostbrief; ~-**mail newspaper** *(Br.)* Luftpostzeitungsgut; ~-**mail parcel post** *(Br.)* Luftpaketpost; ~-**mail printed paper** *(Br.)* Luftpostdrucksachen; ~-**mail printed paper rate** *(Br.)* Drucksachengebühr mit Luftpostzuschlag, Luftposttarif für Drucksachen; ~-**mail rate** *(Br.)* Luftposttarif, -bezugspreis; ~-**mail receipt** *(Br.)* Luftposteinlieferungsschein; ~-**mail service** *(Br.)* Luftpostverkehr, -dienst; ~-**mail stamp** *(Br.)* Luftpostmarke; ~-**mail zone** *(Br.)* Luftposttarifzone; ~ **mechanic** Bordmonteur; ~-**minded** flugbegeistert; ~ **mindedness** Flugbegeisterung; ~ **Ministry** *(Br.)* Luftfahrtministerium; ~-**to-~ missile** Luftkampfflugkörper; ~ **navigation** Flugnavigation, Luftfahrt; ~ **nozzle** Luftdüse; ~ **pact** Luftfahrtabkommen; ~ **parcel** *(Br.)* mit Luftpost versandtes Paket, Luftpostpaket; ~ **passage** Flug; ~ **passenger** Flugpassagier, Fluggast; ~ **passenger insurance** Fluggastversicherung; **to fly** ~ **patrols** Kontrollflüge durchführen; ~ **photo** Luftbild; ~ **pillow** Luftkissen; ~ **piracy** Luftpiraterie; ~ **plot** Kursaufzeichnung; ~ **pocket** Luftloch, Fallbö; ~ **policy** Luftfahrtpolitik; ~ **pollution** Luftverschmutzung; ~ **pollution control area** Emmissionsschutzgebiet; ~ **pollution plant** Luftverschmutzer; ~ **post** Luftpost; ~ **poster towing** Reklameschlepp; ~ **pressure** Luftdruck; ~-**to-ground radio** Bord-Boden-Funkverkehr; ~ **raft** Schlauchboot; ~ **reconnaissance** Flugaufklärung; ~ **regulations** Luftverkehrsvorschriften; ~ **resistance** Luftwiderstand; ~ **route** Luftweg, Luftverkehrslinie, Fluglinie, -route, -strecke; **internal** ~ **route** Inlandfluglinie; ~ **sabotage** Flugzeugsabotage; ~ **safety** Flugsicherheit; ~ **safety expert** Luftsicherheitsexperte; ~ **scape** Luft-, Flugaufnahme; ~ **scout** Beobachter, Luftspäher; ~ **service** Fluglinien-, Luftverkehr; **no-frills cheap** ~ **service** verbilligter Flugverkehr ohne Extraleistungen; **nonscheduled** ~ **service** *(US)* nichtplanmäßiger Luftverkehr; **scheduled** ~ **service** *(US)* fahrplanmäßiger Luftverkehr, Linienverkehr; **to inaugurate** ~ **service** Fluglinienverkehr aufnehmen; ~ **shipment** Luftfrachtsendung, -transport; ~ **show** Flugschau, -veranstaltung; ~ **shuttle** Luftpendelbus; ~ **sickness** Flugkrankheit; ~ **sortie** Feindflug; ~ **sovereignty** Lufthoheit; ~ **space** Luftraum; ~ **speed** Fluggeschwindigkeit; ~-**speed head** Fahrtgeber, -messer; ~-**speed indicator** Fahrtmesser; ~-**speeded** per Luftpost; ~ **staff** Flugpersonal; ~ **steward** Flugbegleiter, Steward; ~ **subsidies** *(US)* Beihilfen für Luftpostbeförderung; ~ **supply** Luftzufuhr; ~ **superiority (supremacy)** Luftherrschaft, -überlegenheit; ~ **support** Unterstützung durch die Luftwaffe; ~ **support for ground troops** Luftunterstützung für Erdkampftruppen; ~ **talks** Luftverkehrsverhandlungen; ~ **taxi** Lufttaxi; ~ **tee** Landekreuz; ~ **terminal** Großflughafen, *(building)* Flughafenabfertigungsgebäude; ~ **ticket** Flugkarte, -schein; ~ **time** *(broadcasting)* Sendezeit; ~ **tour** Flugreise; ~ **tourism** Flugtourismus; ~ **tourist** Flugreisender; ~ **traffic** Flug-, Luftverkehr, -betrieb; ~-**traffic control** Flugüberwachung, -sicherung; ~-**traffic control center** *(US)* Flugsicherungszentrale; ~-**traffic control purposes** Flugsicherungszwecke; ~-**traffic control service** Flugsicherungsdienst; ~-**traffic control staff** Flugsicherungspersonal; ~-**traffic controller** Flugsicherungsbeamter; ~-**traffic controller assistant** Gehilfe eines Flugsicherungsbeamten; ~-**traffic job** Luftverkehrsaufgabe; ~-**traffic regulations** Luftverkehrsbestimmungen; ~-**traffic rules** Luftverkehrsvorschriften; ~-**traffic safety** Flugverkehrssicherheit; ~ **train** Luftschleppzug, -beförderung; ~ **transport** Beförderung auf dem Luftwege, Lufttransport; **commercially scheduled** ~ **transport** *(US)* planmäßig gewerblicher Luftverkehr; ~-**transport company** Luftverkehrsgesellschaft; ~-**transport convention** Luftverkehrsabkommen; ~ **transport undertaking** Lufttransportunternehmen; ~ **transportation** Beförderung auf dem Luftwege, Lufttransport, -beförderung; ~ **travel** Flug; **corporate** ~ **travel** Flugverkehr mit Betriebsflugzeugen; **to diversify into** ~ **travel** sich dem Lufttransportgeschäft zuwenden; ~ **travel agreement** Luftverkehrsabkommen; ~-**travel bureau** Flugreisebüro; ~ **traveller** Flug[zeug]passagier, Flugreisender, -gast; ~ **trip** [Rund]flug, Flugreise; ~ **troops** Luftlandetruppen; ~ **tube** Luftschlauch; ~ **tunnel** festgelegte Fluglinie; ~ **umbrella** Luftschirm; ~ **vent** Entlüftungsrohr; ~ **vessel** Luftfahrzeug; ~ **war** Lufkrieg; ~ **wave** Funkwelle; ~ **well** Luftschacht.

airbill *(US)* Luftfrachtbrief;
   ~ **number** *(US)* Luftfrachtbriefnummer.
airborne durch die Luft, im Flugzeug befördert;
   to be ~ *(plane)* sich in der Luft befinden;
   ~ **division** Luftlandedivision; ~ **early warning** *(mil.)* fliegendes Frühwarngerät; ~ **firefighter** Löschflugzeug; ~ **office** fliegendes Büro; ~ **operation** Luftlandeunternehmen; ~ **transmitter** Bordsender; ~ **troops** Luftlandetruppen; ~ **warning and control system (Awacs)** fliegendes Frühwarn- und Kontrollsystem.
airbrush Spritzpistole;
   ~ **technique** Spritztechnik.

airbus Airbus, Luft[omni]bus, Kurzstreckenflugzeug.
aircast Rundfunksendung.
aircraft Flugzeug, Luftfahrzeug;
   free on ~ frei Flugzeug;
   ~**s** *(stock exchange)* Flugzeugwerte;
   carrier-borne ~ Bordflugzeug; **chartered** ~ Charterflugzeug; **civil** ~ Verkehrsflugzeug; **commuter** ~ im Pendelverkehr eingesetztes Flugzeug; **electronics-loaded** ~ mit elektronischen Einrichtungen voll ausgestattetes Flugzeug; **hostile** ~ Feindflugzeug; **jet** ~ Düsenflugzeug; **light** ~ Sportflugzeug; **nuclear** ~ atomangetriebenes Flugzeug; **pilotless** ~ unbemanntes Flugzeug; **projected** ~ in der Planung befindliches Flugzeug; **prototype** ~ Flugzeugmodell; **sea and land** ~ Landwasserflugzeug; **seaborne** ~ Marineflugzeug; **single-purpose** ~ Einzweckflugzeug; **turbine-powered** ~ Flugzeug mit Turbinenantrieb; **vertical take-off and landing** ~ senkrecht startendes und landendes Flugzeug;
   to bring (put) ~ **into action** Flugzeuge einsetzen (zum Einsatz bringen); **to follow the flight of an** ~ **by radar** Flugzeug auf dem Radarschirm verfolgen; **to pilot an** ~ Flugzeug steuern; **to write off an** ~ **as lost** Flugzeug als verunglückt abschreiben;
   ~ **business** Flugzeugindustrie; ~ **carrier** Flugzeugträger; ~ **communications** Flugnachrichtenverkehr; ~ **company** Flugzeugfirma; ~ **contract** Flugzeugauftrag; ~ **crash** Flugzeugunglück, -absturz; ~ **defect** Fabrikationsfehler bei der Flugzeugherstellung; ~ **departure time** Abflugzeit; ~ **designer** Flugzeugkonstrukteur; ~ **development** Flugzeugentwicklung; ~ **direction finding** Flugzeugortung; ~ **disaster** Flugzeugkatastrophe; ~ **display** Flug-, Luftfahrtschau; ~ **engine** Flugzeugmotor; ~ **engineer** Flugzeugingenieur; ~ **engineering** Flugzeugbau; ~ **export** Flugzeugexport; ~ **factory** Flugzeugfabrik; ~ **fleet** Flugzeugpark; ~ **hangar** Flugzeugschuppen; ~ **hijacker** Luftpirat; ~ **hull insurance** Luftkaskoversicherung; ~ **industry** Flugzeugindustrie; ~ **industry jobs** Arbeitsplätze in der Flugzeugindustrie; ~ **insurance** Flugzeug-, Luftfahrtversicherung; ~ **kilometer** Flugkilometer; ~ **maintenance** Flugzeugwartung; ~ **maker** Flugzeugfabrikant; ~ **manufacture** Flugzeugproduktion; ~ **manufacturer** Flugzeughersteller; ~ **market** Flugzeugmarkt; ~ **mechanic** Flugzeugmechaniker; ~ **nationalization** Verstaatlichung der Flugzeugindustrie; ~ **noise** Flugzeuggeräusch; ~ **operation** Flug[zeug]betrieb; ~ **parking** Abstellplatz für Flugzeuge; ~ **passenger** Fluggast; ~ **performance** fliegerische Leistung; ~ **production** Flugzeugproduktion; ~ **program(me)** Flugzeugprogramm; ~ **radio** Flugfunk, Bordfunkgerät; ~ **radio room** Bordstation; **to be within the** ~'**s range** im Aktionsbereich eines Flugzeuges liegen; ~ **recognition service** Flugzeugerkennungsdienst; ~ **register** Luftfahrzeugrolle; ~ **repair** Flugzeugreparatur; ~ **route** Flugstrecke, -route; ~ **shed** Flugzeugschuppen; ~ **transport** Luftfrachtverkehr; ~ **type** Flugzeugtyp; ~ **works** Flugzeugfabrik.
aircraftman *(Br.)* Flieger.
aircrew Flugzeugbesatzung, fliegendes Personal.
aircrewman Besatzungsmitglied.
airdrome *(US)* Flughafen, -platz.
airdrop Fallschirm-, Flugzeugabwurf;
   ~ *(v.)* mit Fallschirm abwerfen.
airfield Flugplatz, -hafen;
   auxiliary ~ Hilfsflugplatz; **civil** ~ Verkehrsflughafen; **military** ~ Militärflugplatz.
airflow Luftstrom.
airfoil Tragfläche.
airfreight Luftfracht;
   ~ **bill** Luftfrachtbrief; ~ **business** Luftfrachtgeschäft, -spedition; ~ **cargo equipment** Luftfrachtanlagen; ~ **facility** Luftfrachteinrichtungen; ~ **forwarder** Luftfrachtspediteur; ~ **forwarding** Luftfrachtgeschäft, -spedition; ~ **outfit** Luftfrachtunternehmer; ~ **rates** Luftfrachttarif; ~ **service** Luftfrachtdienst, Frachtflugverkehr, Frachtluftverkehr; ~ **terminus** Luftfrachtbahnhof; ~ **user** Luftfrachtbenutzer.
airfreighter Frachtflugzeug;
   ~ **corporation** Luftfrachtunternehmen, Luftfrachter.
airfrost Eisniederschlag.
airgraph Luftpostbeförderung von Mikrofilmbriefen.
airhead Luftlandekopf.
airing Spaziergang, -fahrt;
   to take an ~ frische Luft schöpfen;
   ~ **plant** Belüftungsanlage.
airlift Luftbrücke;
   ~ *(v.)* auf dem Luftwege (über eine Luftbrücke) befördern (transportieren).

airline Flug[verkehrs]linie, Flugstrecke, *(company)* Flug-, Luftverkehrsgesellschaft, -linie, *(network)* Luftverkehrsnetz; **bargain** ~ Billigfluggesellschaft; **commercial** ~ Linienfluggesellschaft; **commuter** ~ Flugzeugnahverkehrlinie; **national flag** ~ Linienfluggesellschaft; **nonscheduled** ~ *(US)* Chartergesellschaft; **regional** ~ Nahverkehrsgesellschaft; **scheduled** ~ *(US)* fahrplanmäßige Flugverkehrslinie; **state-owned** ~ staatliche Flugzeuggesellschaft; **supplemental** ~ auf Nebenstrecken (im Charterverkehr) zugelassene Fluggesellschaft; **US flag** ~ Luftverkehrsgesellschaft der USA;
to license an ~ Fluggesellschaft zum Luftverkehr zulassen; **to operate an** ~ Luftverkehrsunternehmen betreiben;
~ **accident** Flugzeugunfall; ~ **bag** Luftgepäck; ~ **bargaining** Aushandlung von Tarifen für Flugangestellte; ~ **carrier** Lufttransportgesellschaft; ~ **cartel** Absprachen der Fluggesellschaften; ~ **catering** Verproviantierung von Fluggesellschaften; ~ **company (corporation,** *US)* Luftverkehrsgesellschaft, -unternehmen; ~ **customer** Fluggast; ~ **earnings** Erträgnisse einer Fluggesellschaft; ~ **executive** leitender Angestellter einer Luftverkehrsgesellschaft; ~ **fare** Flugkarte, -preis; ~ **hostess** Stewardeß; ~ **industry** Flugverkehrsindustrie; **tightly regulated** ~ **industry** festes Preisgefüge der IATA angeschlossener Linienfluggesellschaften; ~ **network** Flug-, Luftverkehrsnetz; ~ **office** Flugbüro; ~ **official** Angestellter einer Luftfahrtgesellschaft; **long-distance** ~ **operation** Langstreckenflugbetrieb; ~ **passenger** Fluggast; ~ **pilot** Flug[zeug]kapitän, Flugzeugkommandant; ~ **rates** Luftverkehrstarif; ~ **reservation** Flugreservierung; ~ **seat** Flugzeugsitz, -platz; ~ **security** Sicherheit des Flugverkehrs; **[scheduled]** ~ **service** [fahrplanmäßiger] Luftverkehrsdienst; ~ **table** Flugplan; ~ **ticket** Flugkarte; ~ **ticket tax** *(US)* Flugscheingebühr; ~ **timetable** Flug-, Luftverkehrsplan; ~ **traffic** Fluglinienverkehr; ~ **travel** Flugreise; ~ **traveller** Fluggast.
airliner Passagier-, Linien-, Verkehrsflugzeug;
commercial ~ Linienflugzeug; **120 - 160 seat civil jet** ~ Düsenflugzeug des Linienflugdienstes mit 120 - 160 Sitzplätzen; **subsonic** ~ mit Unterschallgeschwindigkeit fliegendes Flugzeug; **to land an** ~ **safely** sichere Flugzeuglandung durchführen; ~'s **arrival** Flugzeugankunft.
airmail *(US)* Luft-, Flugpost;
by (per) ~ mit Luftpost;
~ *(v.)* **a letter** Luftpostbrief schicken, aufgeben;
~ **company** Luftpostgesellschaft; ~ **edition** Luftpostausgabe; ~ **envelope** Luftpostkuvert; ~ **fee** Luftpostgebühr; ~ **label** Luftpostaufkleber; ~ **letter** Luftpostbrief; ~ **printed paper** Luftpostdrucksachen; ~ **printed paper rate** Drucksachengebühr mit Luftpostzuschlag; ~ **parcel** Luftpostpaket; ~ **parcel post** Luftpaketpost; ~ **rate** Luftposttarif-, bezugspreis; ~ **receipt** Luftposteinlieferungsschein; ~ **service** Luftpostverkehr; ~ **stamps** Luftpostmarken; ~ **transfer** Luftpostüberweisung.
airmailing order *(US)* Luftpostauftrag.
airman Flieger;
basic ~ *(US mil.)* Flieger.
airmark *(v.)* mit Bodenmarkierungen versehen.
airmen Flugpersonal.
airpark Kleinflughafen.
airplane *(US)* Flugzeug;
company ~ Betriebsflugzeug; **private** ~ Privatflugzeug; **sophisticated** ~ technisch hochgezüchtetes Flugzeug;
to pilot an ~ Flugzeug fliegen; **to power-brake an** ~ Flugzeug durch Heckfallschirm abbremsen; **to redress an** ~ Flugzeug in die normale Lage zurückbringen; **to ride an** ~ Flugzeug benutzen; **to stabilize an** ~ Flugzeug stabilisieren; **to stunt an** ~ Flugkunststücke vorführen;
~ **accident** Flugzeugunglück; ~ **baggage** *(US)* Fluggepäck; ~ **banner** vom Flugzeug gezogene Werbefahne; ~ **carrier** Flugzeugträger; ~ **crash** Flugzeugunglück; ~ **engine** Flugzeugmotor; ~-**engine plant** Flugzeugmotorenfabrik; ~ **luggage** *(Br.)* Fluggepäck; **regulation** ~ **seat** verstellbarer Flugsitzplatz; ~ **undercarriage** Flugzeugfahrgestell.
airport [Verkehrs]flughafen, Flugplatz;
commercial ~ Verkehrsflughafen; **customs-free** ~ Freiflughafen; **domestic** ~ Binnenflughafen; **heavy-traffic** ~ häufig angeflogener Flugplatz; **phased-out** ~ aufgelassener Flugplatz; **secondary** ~ zweitrangiger Flugplatz;
~ **of arrival** Landeflughafen; ~ **of departure** Abflughafen; ~ **of entry** Zoll-, [Einreise]flughafen;
to maintain an ~ für die Instandhaltung eines Flugplatzes Sorge tragen; **to see s. o. off at the** ~ j. am Flugplatz verabschieden; **to serve an** ~ Flugplatz anfliegen; **to serve an** ~ **commercially** Flugplatz mit Linienflugzeugen anfliegen;

~ **banner** Schleppfahne; ~ **catering** Versorgung von Flugplatzgaststätten; ~ **commission** Flugplatzkommission; ~ **development** Flugplatzausbau; ~ **feeder** Flughafenzubringer; ~ **feeder service** Flughafenzubringerdienst; **special** ~ **feeder service rates** Spezialtarif im Rahmen des Flughafenzubringerdienstes; ~ **inn** Flughafenhotel; ~ **liability insurance** Flugplatzversicherung; ~ **lighting (lights)** Flugplatzbefeuerung; **door-to-door** ~ **limousine service** Flugplatzabholdienst; ~ **location** Flugplatzgelände; **to meet** ~ **noise rules** den Lärmvorschriften bei Benutzung von Flugplätzen gerecht werden; ~ **operator** Flugplatzverwaltung; ~ **page** Ausrufanlage auf einem Flugplatz; ~ **planning** Flugplatzplanung; ~ **property** Flughafengelände; ~ **reception** Flugabfertigung; ~ **restaurant** Flughafenrestaurant; ~ **runway** [Flughafen]rollbahn; ~ **security precautions** Sicherungsmaßnahmen auf einem Flugplatz; ~ **service charge** Fluggastgebühr; ~ **shutdown** Flugplatzschließung; ~ **tax** Flugzeug-, Flughafengebühr; ~ **terminal** Flughafenabfertigungsgebäude.
airproof luftdicht.
airraid Luftangriff;
~ **alarm** Flugalarm; ~ **precautions** Luftschutz; ~ **precaution measures** Luftschutzmaßnahmen; ~ **protection** Luftschutz; ~ **shelter** Luftschutzbunker, -raum; ~ **siren** Luftschutzsirene; ~ **warden** Luftschutzwart, -helfer; ~ **warning** Vorwarnung, Fliegeralarm; ~ **warning service** Flugwarndienst.
airraider angreifendes Flugzeug.
airscrew *(Br.)* Propeller, Luftschraube.
airship Luftschiff;
general purpose cargo ~ Mehrzweckflugzeug;
to walk an ~ **into the shed** Luftschiff in die Halle befördern; **to do** ~ **designs** sich mit Luftschiffbau beschäftigen.
airshipped auf dem Luftwege befördert.
airsick luftkrank.
airsickness Luftkrankheit.
airspace Luftgebiet, -raum;
territorial ~ Lufthoheitsgebiet.
airstop Hubschrauberlandeplatz.
airstrip Behelfsflugplatz, *(runway)* Start- und Landestreifen, Lande-, Rollbahn.
airtight luftdicht, hermetisch abgeschlossen;
~ **case** todsicherer Fall; ~ **door** luftdicht abgeschlossene Tür.
airtime Fernsehwerbezeiten.
airtrap Windfang.
airway Fluglinie, -strecke, -route, -straße, Luftverkehrslinie, -straße, *(mining)* Wetterstraße;
civil ~ Luftverkehrslinie; **purple** ~ *(Br.)* Flugroute einer königlichen Maschine;
~ **beacon** Flugstreckenfeuer; ~ **bill** Frachtbrief; ~ **bill fee** Luftfracht[brief]gebühr; ~**s corporation** Luftverkehrsgesellschaft; ~ **line** Luftverkehrslinie; ~**s station** Flugnachrichtenstelle; ~ **weather report** Streckenmeldung.
airworthiness Flugtüchtigkeit.
airworthy flugtüchtig, -tauglich, *(airplane)* zugelassen.
aisle *(shop)* Gang zwischen den Ladentischen;
~ **sitter** *(US)* Theaterkritiker.
akin [bluts]verwandt.
alarm Alarm, Alarmruf, *(attack)* Überfall, Angriff, *(clock)* Wecker, *(warning)* Warnvorrichtung, Alarmsignal, *(burglar)* Alarmanlagen, *(fear)* Furcht, Bestürzung, Angst;
airraid ~ Flieger-, Luftschutzalarm; **blue** ~ Voralarm; **false** ~ blinder Alarm; **fire** ~ Feueralarm; **police** ~ Alarmanlage;
~ *(v.)* alarmieren, Alarm schlagen, *(disturb)* beunruhigen, erschrecken;
to feel ~ **at the news** von Nachrichten beunruhigt werden; **to have s. th. wired to** ~ Alarmanlagen eingeschaltet haben; **to put the** ~ **on** Wecker stellen; **to raise the** ~ Alarmzeichen geben, alarmieren; **to ring an** ~ blinden Alarm schlagen; **to set off an** ~ Alarmanlage auslösen; **to set the mental** ~ **off** Verdacht auslösen; **to sound an** ~ Alarm schlagen;
~ **bell** Alarmglocke; ~ **clock** Wecker; **to set the** ~ **clock for six o'clock** Wecker auf 6 Uhr stellen; ~ **lamp** Warnlampe; ~ **post** *(mil.)* Alarm-, Sammelposten; ~ **signal** Warnzeichen; ~ **system** Gefahrenmeldeanlage; **automatic** ~ **system** automatische Alarmanlage; **visual** ~ **system** optische Alarmanlage; ~ **valve** Sicherheitsventil.
alarming beunruhigend.
alarmist Schwarzseher.
alcohol Alkohol;
~ **monopoly** Branntweinmonopol; ~ **test** Alkoholtest.
alcoholic Trinker, Alkoholsüchtiger;
~ **beverages** alkoholische Getränke; ~ **beverage tax** *(US)* Steuer auf alkoholische Getränke; ~ **strength** Alkoholgehalt.

alcoholism Alkoholismus, Alkoholvergiftung.
alcove Balkon;
   ~ **room** Balkonzimmer.
alderman *(Br.)* Ratsherr, Stadtrat.
aleatory mit Gefahr verbunden, riskant.
alehouse [Gast]wirtschaft.
alert [Alarm]bereitschaft, *(air force)* Einsatzbereitschaft,
   erhöhte Gefechtsbereitschaft, *(mil.)* Alarm, *(signal)* Alarmsignal;
   on the ~ in Alarmbereitschaft;
   air ~ Fliegeralarm;
   ~ *(v.)* Alarm schlagen, *(troops)* in Alarmzustand versetzen;
   ~ **the police of a break-in** Polizei auf einen Einbruch aufmerksam machen; ~ **to a situation** bei einer bestimmten Situation
   Alarm geben, *(mil.)* im bestimmten Fall alarmieren;
   to be on the ~ auf dem Posten sein; **to give the** ~ Alarm geben; **to
   place on full** ~ höchste Mobilmachungsstufe anordnen; **to
   sound the** ~ Alarm geben;
   ~ **phase** Bereitschaftsstufe.
alfresco lunch Mittagessen im Freien.
alias angenommener Name, Pseudonym;
   to travel under an ~ unter einem Pseudonym (anonym) reisen.
alibi Alibi, Aufenthaltsnachweis, *(coll.)* Ausrede;
   perfect ~ einwandfreies Alibi;
   to establish (produce) one's ~ sein Alibi beibringen.
alien Ausländer, Fremder;
   enemy ~ feindlicher Ausländer; **friendly** ~ befreundeter Ausländer; **undesirable** ~ unerwünschter (lästiger) Ausländer;
   ~ *(v.)* veräußern;
   to deport an undesirable ~ unerwünschten Ausländer abschieben; **to turn back an** ~ Ausländer abweisen;
   ~ *(a.)* ausländisch, fremd, *(fig.)* unsympatisch, zuwider;
   ⌐ **Agency Act** Gesetz zur Registrierung ausländischer Agenten; ~ **corporation** *(US)* ausländische Handelsgesellschaft; ~
   culture wesensfremde Kultur; ~**s' department** Fremdenpolizei;
   ~ **duty** Fremdensteuer; ~ **element** Fremdkörper; ~ **employee**
   Gast-, Fremdarbeiter; ⌐ **Immigration Act** Einwanderungsgesetz; ~**'s labo(u)r permit** Arbeitserlaubnis für Ausländer; ~**s
   laws** Ausländergesetzgebung; ~ **née** Ausländer von Geburt; ~**s
   order** *(Br.)* Ausländergesetz; ~ **property** Feind-, Ausländervermögen; ~ **property custodian** *(US)* ausländische Vermögensverwaltung; ~**s' registration** Ausländerkontrolle, -registrie-
   rung; ~**s' registration office** Ausländerpolizei; ~**'s residence
   permit** Aufenthaltsgenehmigung für Ausländer; ~ **resident**
   (US) ansässiger Ausländer.
alienability Veräußerlichkeit, *(transferability)* Übertragbarkeit,
   Abtretbarkeit.
alienable veräußerlich, *(transferable)* übertragbar, abtretbar.
alienage Ausländereigenschaft, -status.
alienate *(v.)* veräußern, *(estrange)* entfremden, *(property)*
   umschreiben, *(transfer)* übertragen, abtreten;
   ~ **affections** der ehelichen Zuneigung entfremden; ~ **capital**
   Kapital abziehen; ~ **customers** Kunden ausspannen (abwerben); ~ **an estate** Grundstücksumschreibung vornehmen; ~
   funds from their natural channels Gelder anderen als den vorgesehenen Zwecken zuführen; ~ **in mortmain** Grundstücke an die
   tote Hand veräußern; ~ **property** Vermögen übertragen; ~
   enemy property Feindvermögen beschlagnahmen.
alienation Ent-, Veräußerung, *(estrangement)* Entfremdung,
   Abneigung, Abgeneigtheit, *(transfer)* [Besitz]übertragung,
   Umschreibung;
   fraudulent ~ Vollstreckungsvereitelung; **mental** ~ Geistesgestörtheit, -krankheit;
   ~ **of affection** *(US)* Entfremdung ehelicher Zuneigung; ~ **from
   authority** Autoritätsentfremdung; ~ **of capital** Kapitalabzug;
   ~ **of customers** Kundenabwerbung; ~ **of an estate** Umschreibung eines Grundstücks, Grundstücksübertragung; ~ **of funds
   from their natural channels** zweckentfremdete Mittelzufüh-
   rung; ~ **of labo(u)r** entfremdete Arbeit; ~ **of land** Grundstücksveräußerung; **of mind** Geistesgestörtheit; ~ **in mortmain**
   Veräußerung an die tote Hand; ~ **of property** Vermögensübertragung.
alienator Veräußerer, *(transferer)* Zedent.
alienee Erwerber, neuer Eigentümer.
alienist Psychiater, Nervenarzt.
alienor Veräußerer, Übertragender.
alight *(v.)* aussteigen, *(plane)* landen;
   ~ **on the water** auf dem Wasser landen.
alighting Landung, Landen;
   ~ **on earth** Bodenlandung;
   ~ **run** Landestrecke.

align *(v.)* ausrichten, *(adjust lines)* Linie (Zeile) halten,
   ausschließen;
   ~ **o. s. with s. o.** sich an j. anschließen; ~ **nations against war**
   Verteidigungsblock zusammenbringen.
alignment *(adjusting a line)* Ausfluchtung, *(pol.)* Blockbildung,
   Gruppierung, *(railway)* Trasse;
   ~ **chart** Fluchtlinientafel.
aliment *(Scot.)* Unterhalt;
   ~ *(v.)* Unterhalt gewähren.
alimentary zum Unterhalt dienend;
   ~ **endorsement** Unterhaltspension; ~ **process** Unterhaltsprozeß.
alimentation Beköstigung, Ernährung, Verpflegung;
   ~ **of an account** Dotierung eines Kontos.
alimonied unterhalten, versorgt.
alimony *(US)* Unterhaltsbeitrag [an getrennt lebende (geschiedene) Ehefrau], Alimente, lebenslängliche Unterhaltsrente;
   entitled to ~ alimentations-, unterhaltsberechtigt; **liable to pay**
   ~ unterhaltsverpflichtet;
   permanent ~ laufender Unterhaltsbetrag, lebenslängliche
   Unterhaltsrente; **temporary** ~ *(US)* provisorischer Unterhalt;
   ~ **in gross** Alimenten-, Pauschalabfindung; ~ **pendente lite**
   vorläufiges Unterhaltsgeld; ~ **awarded to a wife** *(Br.)* für die
   Ehefrau festgesetzter Unterhaltsanspruch; ~ **granted to a wife**
   Unterhaltszahlung an die Ehefrau;
   to award ~ *(Br.)* Unterhalt zuerkennen; **to be entitled to** ~
   unterhaltsberechtigt sein; **to be under an obligation of** ~ unterhaltspflichtig sein; **to claim** ~ Unterhaltsansprüche geltend
   machen; **to pay** ~ Unterhalt gewähren; **to provide one's wife
   with** ~ Unterhalt für seine Ehefrau sicherstellen;
   to contest the ~ **claim** Unterhaltsanspruch bestreiten; ~ **payment** Unterhaltszahlung; ~ **suit** Unterhaltsprozeß.
aliquot ohne Rest aufgehend;
   ~ **part** gleicher Anteil, Bruchteil.
alive lebend, am Leben;
   ~ **and kicking** frisch und munter;
   to be ~ **and well** sich bester Gesundheit erfreuen.
all Alles, Hab und Gut;
   ~ *(a.)* gesamt, vollständig, ganz, alles;
   ~ **and singular** ausnahmslos, sämtlich;
   to be ~ **for it** ganz und gar dafür sein; **to be** ~ **in** völlig fertig
   sein; **to be** ~ **for making money** nur auf Geldverdienen aus sein;
   ~ **aboard!** einsteigen!; ~ **abroad** fehlerhaft; ~**-American** *(US)*
   repräsentativ für die USA; ~**-at-one price** Einheitspreis; ~**-
   cargo service** durchgehende Gepäckabfertigung; ~ **cases at law**
   sämtliche anhängige Verfahren; ~ **clear** Entwarnungssignal;
   ~**-commodity rate** Stückguttarif; ~**-day meeting** ganztägige Sitzung; ~**-duty tractor** Allzwecktraktor; ~ **ears** ganz Ohr
   sein; ~ **the estate** *(conveyancing)* Globalklausel; ~**-European
   course** gesamteuropäischer Kurs; ~**-European solution** gesamteuropäische Lösung; ~**-expense tour (trip,** *US)* kostenlose
   (vollbezahlte) Besichtigungsreise; **with** ~ **faults** Sachmänge-
   lausschluß, wie besehen; **to be on** ~ **fours** *(law suit)* identisch
   (gleichgelagert) mit einem früheren Rechtsstreit sein; ~**-freight
   cargo plane** Universalfrachtflugzeug; ~ **hands** gesamte Schiffsmannschaft; ~**-in** gesamt, global, *(Br.)* alles inbegriffen, *(sl.)*
   total erledigt; ~**-in insurance** Einheits-, Gesamt-, Globalversi-
   cherung; ~**-inclusive cover** Pauschalabdeckung; ~**-industry
   average** gesamter Industriequerschnitt; ~**-loss insurance** *(US)*
   Global-, Gesamtversicherung; ~**-metal** Ganzmetall; ~**-metal
   airplane** Ganzmetallflugzeug; ~**-metal construction** Ganzme-
   tallbauweise; ~**-night service** durchgehender Betrieb; ~**-night
   sitting** lange Nachtsitzung; ~**-out** gesamt, total, vollkommen,
   unbedingt, *(sl.)* völlig erledigt, *(greatly mistaken)* auf dem
   Holzweg; ~**-out demand** Gesamtnachfrage; ~**-out strike** Glo-
   balstreik; **to be an** ~**-outer** über Leichen gehen; ~**-party committee** Allparteienausschuß; ~**-party talks** Allparteienge-
   spräch; ~**-price** Pauschal-, Gesamtpreis; ~**-purpose authority**
   Allzweckbehörde; ~**-purpose corporation** Gemischtunterneh-
   men; ~**-purpose unit** Allzweckverwaltungseinheit; ~**-purpose
   vehicle** Mehrzweckfahrzeug; ~**-rail** lediglich im Bahntransport; ~**-red route** *(Br.)* Verkehrsverbindungen innerhalb des
   Commonwealth; ~ **risks whatever of the passage** sämtliche
   Gefahren der Schiffsreise; ~**-risk insurance** Globalversiche-
   rung; ~**-risk insurance policy** global Risikoversicherungspolice; ~ **round** durch die Bank; ~ **sales final** kein Umtausch; ~
   set in der richtigen Geistesverfassung; ~**-stage turnover tax** Pha-
   senumsatzsteuer; ~**-star band** mit Spitzenmusikern besetzte
   Kapelle; ~**-star cast** Starbesetzung; ~**-steel body** Ganzstahlka-
   rosserie; ~**-steel construction** Ganzstahlbauweise; ~**-terrain
   vehicle** geländegängiges Fahrzeug; ~**-time** ganztägig beschäf-

tigt; ~-**time high** *(US)* absoluter Höchststand; ~-**time low** *(US)* absoluter Tiefstand; ~-**time record** unerreichte Rekordleistung; ~-**up** *(postal service)* alles per Luftpost; ~-**up newspapers** Streifbandzeitungen, Luftpostzeitungsgut; ~-**up newspaper rates** Gebühren für Luftpostdrucksachen; ~-**up service** *(Br.)* generelle Luftpostbeförderung nach Europa; ~-**up weight** *(airplane)* Gesamtgewicht; ~-**volunteer armed force** nur aus Freiwilligen bestehendes Heer; ~-**water** Transport nur auf dem Wasserweg; ~-**wave receiving set** Allwellenempfänger; ~-**weather body** Allwetterkarosserie; ~-**weather capability** Allwettereigenschaft; ~-**wheel brake** Allradbremse; ~-**wheel drive** Allradantrieb; ~-**wing type** *(aircraft)* Nurflügelflugzeug; ~-**wood construction** Ganzholzbauweise; ~-**wool** *(US)* reine Wolle.

allegation Aufführung, -gabe, *(lawsuit)* [Partei]behauptung, -vorbringen, Aufzählung der Klagepunkte;
false ~ fälschliche Beschuldigung, Falschanschuldigung; **material** ~s tatsächliche Behauptungen, vorgebrachte Tatsachen;
~ **of faculties** *(alimony)* behauptete Leisungsfähigkeit; ~ **of fact** Sachvortrag.

allege *(v.)* angeben, aufführen, behaupten, *(plead)* bei Gericht vorbringen, einwenden;
~ **s. o. to be dead** j. für tot erklären lassen; ~ **one's good faith** sich auf seinen guten Glauben berufen; ~ **ill health as a reason** Krankheit als Grund angeben; ~ **an injury** Verletzung vorschützen.

alleged angeblich, vorgeblich, behauptet, *(presumed)* vermutlich;
~ **piece of information** angebliche Information; ~ **offence** zur Last gelegte Tat; ~ **thief** angeblicher Dieb.

allegiance Treuepflicht.

allegiant loyal.

allergy Allergie, *(sl.)* Abneigung.

alleviate *(v.)* erleichtern, mildern, lindern;
~ **unemployment** Arbeitslosigkeit beheben (beseitigen).

alleviation Erleichterung, Milderung, Linderung;
~ **of tension** Entspannung; ~ **of unemployment** Behebung (Beseitigung) der Arbeitslosigkeit.

alley Gasse, Weg.

alliance Bündnis, Allianz, Bund, *(relationship)* Verschwägerung, *(Br., trade union)* Gewerkschaftsverband;
defensive ~ Verteidigungspack; **military** ~ Militärbündnis; **offensive and defensive** ~ Schutz- und Trutzbündnis; **to enter into an** ~ sich liieren, Bündnis schließen.

allied verbündet;
~ **company** Tochter-, Konzerngesellschaft; ~ **Forces** alliierte Streitkräfte; ~ **industries** verwandte Industrien; ~ **services** verwandte Dienstleistungen.

alligation *(mint.)* Legierung;
~ **medial** Durchschnittsrechnung.

allision seitliche Schiffskollision.

allocable *(deferred charges)* zu-, aufteilbar.

allocate *(v.)* zuwenden, zuweisen, zuteilen, umlegen, bestimmen, *(adjudicate)* zuschlagen, vergeben, *(intergovernmental control)* zuteilen, rationieren, *(zoning ordinance)* ausweisen;
~ **an account** Konto dotieren; ~ **an amount to the reserve fund** Betrag dem Reservefonds zuführen (überweisen); ~ **to the highest bidder** dem Meistbietenden zuschlagen; ~ **duties** Pflichtenkreis zuweisen; ~ **expenses** Gemeinkosten umlegen; ~ **corporate overhead expenses to overseas subsidiaries in proportion to their share of sales** Gemeinkosten der Muttergesellschaft auf ihre Auslandstöchter entsprechend ihrem Umsatzanteil aufschlüsseln; ~ **export quotas** Export kontingentieren; ~ **foreign exchange** Devisen zuteilen; ~ **frequencies** Frequenzen zuteilen; ~ **a poor fund** Unterstützungsfonds ausstatten; ~ **labo(u)r (manpower)** Arbeitskräfte zuweisen; ~ **the market** Marktaufteilung vornehmen; ~ **to profits** *(corporation tax)* den Gewinnen zurechnen; ~ **to the published reserves** in die offenen Rücklagen einstellen; ~ **the reserve fund** Reservefonds dotieren; ~ **sales** Absatz kontingentieren; ~ **shares** Aktien zuteilen; ~ **the shares in a quota** Kontingent aufteilen; ~ **special drawing rights** *(International Monetary Fund)* Sonderziehungsrechte zuteilen; ~ **a sum to s. th.** Betrag für etw. bestimmen; ~ **a sum of money amongst several people** Betrag unter verschiedenen Leuten aufteilen; ~ **by tenders** im Submissionswege vergeben; ~ **to the lowest tenderer** billigstes Angebot berücksichtigen.

allocated dotiert;
~ **goods** rationierte Waren.

allocatee Bezugsberechtigter, Zuteilungsempfänger.

allocation Zuwendung, -weisung, -teilung, Verteilung, Bestimmung, *(of an account)* Dotierung, Zurechnung, *(adjudication)* Zuschlag[serteilung], *(allowance of balance item)* Anerkenntnis [eines Bilanzpostens], *(assignment of advertising expenditure)* Kostenverteilung, *(quota)* Kontingent, Quote;
foreign-exchange ~ Devisenzuteilung; **overhead** ~ Geschäftsunkostenverteilung; **reserve** ~ Rückstellungszuweisung; **special** ~ Sonderzuweisung;
~ **of an account** Dotierung eines Kontos, Kontendotierung; ~ **of advertising expenditure** Aufteilung des Werbeetats; ~ **of channels** Fernsehkanalzuweisung; ~ **of contract** Auftragsvergabe, -lenkung; ~ **to the highest bidder** Zuschlag an den Meistbietenden; ~ **of cost** Kostenverrechnung; ~ **of indirect costs** Umlage von Gemeinkosten; ~ **of currency** Devisenzuteilung; ~ **of duties** Pflichtenzuweisung; ~ **from the net earnings** Einstellung aus dem Jahresüberschuß; ~ **of expense** Umlegung von Gemeinkosten, Unkostenverteilung; ~ **of frequencies** Frequenzzuteilung; ~ **of export quotas** Exportkontingentierung; ~ **of funds** Kapital-, Mittel-, Geldbewilligung, Fondsausstattung; ~ **of labo(u)r (manpower)** Zuweisung von Arbeitskräften, Arbeitskräfteverteilung; ~ **of markets** Marktaufteilung; ~ **to the pension reserve** Sonderzuführung zur Pensionsrückstellung; ~ **of profits** *(taxation)* Gewinnzurechnung; ~ **to provisions for possible loan losses** *(bank balance)* Zuführung zu den Rückstellungen für das Kreditgeschäft; ~ **of quotas** Kontingentierung[szuweisung]; ~ **of relief** Steuernachlaßverteilung; ~ **to reserve fund** Zuweisung an den Rücklagenfonds, Zuführung zu den Rücklagen; ~ **to declared (published) reserves** Einstellung in die offenen Rücklagen; ~ **of resources** Mittelverwendung; ~ **of revenue** Abgabenverteilung; ~ **of sales** Absatzkontingentierung; ~ **of seats** Sitzverteilung; ~ **of shares** Aktienzuteilung; ~ **of shares in a quota** Kontingentsaufteilung; ~ **to staff pension and provident fund** Zuweisung an die Pensions- und Unterstützungskasse; ~ **to staff profit-sharing fund** Zuweisung an den Gewinnbeteilungsfonds; ~ **of a sum among several people** Aufteilung eines Betrags unter verschiedene Leute; ~ **to the lowest tenderer** Berücksichtigung des billigsten Angebots; ~ **by tenders** Vergabe im Submissionswege; ~ **of time** Zeiteinteilung;
to be under ~ bewirtschaftet sein, zugeteilt werden; **to cut an** ~ **as fine as possible** Zuteilung knappstens bemessen; **to change the** ~ **of profits** Gewinnverteilungsschlüssel ändern;
~ **committee** Zuteilungsausschuß; ~ **control** Bewilligungskontrollorgan; ~ **decision** Entscheidungsbefugnis; ~ **draft** Werbeetatsplan; ~ **scheme** Zuteilungsplan; ~ **system** Schrebergartensystem.

allocative function Verteilungsfunktion.

allocator Zuteilungsstelle.

allocatur *(lat.)* Kostenverteilung [bei Gericht], *(taxing master)* Kostenfestsetzungsbeschluß, Kostenbescheinigung.

allocute *(v.)* feierliche Ansprache halten.

allocution feierliche Ansprache.

allodial zinsfrei, erbeigen;
~ **lands** Allodialgüter.

allodium Erbgut.

allonge Verlängerungs-, Ansatzstück, Allonge.

allonym Deckname.

allot *(v.)* *(assign)* zuweisen, aus-, ver-, zuteilen, *(lottery)* durch Los zuteilen, verlosen, *(shares)* Aktion nach erfolgter Zeichnung zuteilen, repartieren, quotieren;
~ **to the highest bidder** dem Meistbietenden zuschlagen; ~ **duties to s. o.** jem. Aufgaben zuweisen; ~ **a house to live in** Haus zur Verfügung stellen; ~ **a portion of pay to a relative** auf ein Gehaltsteil zugunsten eines Verwandten verzichten; ~ **shares to all applicants** Aktien voll zuteilen.

allotment *(adjudication)* Zuerkennung, Zuschlag, *(auction)* Zuschlag, *(allocation)* Zuweisung, -teilung, *(lot)* [Grundstücks]parzelle, Kleingarten, Schrebergarten[land], *(lottery)* Verlosung, *(portion)* Anteil, *(repartition)* Verteilung, *(of shares)* Aktienzuteilung, -repartierung;
on ~ bei Zuteilung;
foreign-exchange ~ *(Br.)* Devisenzuteilung;
~ **of appropriation** Budgetaufschlüsselung; ~ **to the highest bidder** Zuschlag an den Meistbietenden; ~ **of estovers** Brennholzzuteilung; ~ **of loan** Anleihezuteilung; ~ **of pay** teilweiser Gehaltsverzicht; ~ **of seats (mandates)** Sitzverteilung; ~ **of shares** Aktienzuteilung; ~ **of shares to all applicants** volle Aktienzuteilung; ~ **of wages** Lohnanteilszuweisung;
to be subject to ~ der Zuteilung unterliegen; **to pay so much on** ~ seine Zuteilung in solcher Höhe in Anspruch nehmen; **to preclude from all** ~s von der Zuteilung ausschließen;

~ **certificate** Zuteilungsanzeige, -benachrichtigung, -schein [bei Effektenemission]; ~ **committee** Zuteilungsausschuß; **small** ~ **holder** *(Br.)* Besitzer von Kleingartenland, Schrebergärtner; ~ **letter** Zuteilungsanzeige; ~ **money** Zuteilungsbetrag; ~ **note** *(Br.)* Lohnanteilszuweisung, *(seaman)* Heuerabtretungsschein; ~ **notice** *(US)* Zuteilungsanzeige, -schein; **tender** ~ **price** Zuteilungskurs; ~ **rate** Zuteilungskurs; ~ **right** *(for new shares)* Zuteilungsanspruch; ~ **sheet** Aktienzeichnungsliste; ~ **system** *(Br.)* Schrebergartensystem; ~ **ticket** Lohnauszahlungsanweisung.

allotted zugeteilt;
~ **days** *(Br.)* für Haushaltssitzungen reservierte Tage.

allottee Empfänger einer Effektenzuteilung, Zuteilungsempfänger, Bezugsberechtigter, Zeichner.

allotter Zuteiler, Ausloser, *(tel.)* Wählersucher.

allotted, fully (partly) ganz (teilweise) zugeteilt.

allow *(v.)* *(admit)* zulassen, *(deduct)* in Abzug (Anrechnung) bringen, anrechnen, vergüten, *(grant)* Summe auswerfen, *(periodical)* Zuschuß gewähren, *(permit)* bewilligen, erlauben, gestatten, einräumen, *(take into consideration)* berücksichtigen, in Betracht ziehen;
~ **3%** 3% abziehen; ~ **for** vergüten für, anrechnen, in Abzug (Abschlag) bringen;
~ **an abatement** Rabatt gewähren; ~ **an advance to be taken as the various stages are completed** Darlehn ratenweise entsprechend den fertiggestellten Bauabschnitten auszahlen; ~ **an appeal** einer Berufung stattgeben; ~ **a bill to be protested** Wechsel zu Protest gehen lassen; ~ **extenuating circumstances** mildernde Umstände gewähren; ~ **a claim** Forderung (Anspruch) anerkennen, einem Anspruch stattgeben, *(bankruptcy proceedings)* Konkursforderung anerkennen; ~ **a complaint** Beschwerde zulassen; ~ **costs** für Unkosten in Abzug bringen; ~ **a credit** Kredit einräumen; ~ **for bad** *(US)* **(doubtful) debts** Rückstellung für Dubiose vornehmen; ~ **a debtor time to pay** einem Schuldner Zahlungsfrist gewähren; ~ **of no delay** keine Zeitverzögerung zulassen; ~ **4% on deposits** Einlagen mit 4% verzinsen; ~ **for depreciation** für Abschreibungen zurückstellen, abschreiben; ~ **a discount** Nachlaß gewähren, Diskont vergüten (einräumen); ~ **a discount for cash** Skonto gewähren; ~ **no discussion on s. th.** keine Diskussion über etw. zulassen; ~ **one's dividend to accumulate** seine Dividende sich ansammeln lassen; ~ **an item of expenditure** Sonderausgabe bewilligen, Unkostenposten anerkennen; ~ **3%** 3% abziehen (abrechnen, einräumen); ~ **in full** voll vergüten; ~ **for professional expenditure** für Werbungskosten abziehen; ~ **for special expenditure** Aufwandsentschädigung gewähren; ~ **for exchange fluctuations** Rückstellungen für Devisenschwankungen vornehmen; ~ **the garrison to leave free** einer Besatzung freien Abzug gewähren; ~ **grace** Frist gewähren; ~ **a week's holiday** Woche Urlaub genehmigen; ~ **for possible illness** Krankheitsrücklage bilden; ~ **for losses** *(income tax)* Steuerermäßigung für Verluste gewähren; ~ **a margin for errors** Fehlerquelle mit einkalkulieren; ~ **a reduced price to s. o.** jem. einen Preisabzug einräumen; ~ **for quarters** Wohnungsgeldzuschuß gewähren; ~ **for readjustments** für Berichtigungen Vorsorge treffen; ~ **respite** Aufschub gewähren; ~ **a reduction** Ermäßigung gewähren; ~ **for representation** Repräsentationszulage gewähren; ~ **one's daughter a stipend** seiner Tochter ein Nadelgeld zukommen lassen; ~ **for sums paid in advance** im voraus bezahlte Beträge in Anrechnung bringen; ~ **a sum for leakage** für Leckage in Abzug bringen; ~ **for [the] tare** Tara vergüten, Verpackungskosten abziehen; ~ **time** stunden, Aufschub (Frist) gewähren; ~ **s. o. £ 4000 a year** jem. eine Jahresrente von 4000 Pfund aussetzen; ~ **s. o. ten years seniority** jem. zehn Jahre Dienstzeit anrechnen.

allowable *(admissible)* zulässig, statthaft, erlaubt, *(deductible)* abziehbar, abzugsfähig;
~ **for tax purposes** steuerlich absetzbar;
~ **claim** zulässige Forderung; ~ **defects** zugelassene Fehlstücke; ~ **expense** abzugsfähige Ausgabe; ~ **tolerance** zulässige Abweichung.

allowance *(allotment)* Zuteilung, Zuwendung, *(balance sheet, Br.)* Abschreibung, *(board expenses)* Kostgeld, Deputat, *(of a claim)* Anerkennung, Billigung, Genehmigung, Erlaubnis, Einwilligung, Einräumung, Zulassung, *(compensation)* Vergütung, Entschädigung, *(consideration)* Berücksichtigung, *(dipl.)* Auslandszulage, *(discount)* Abzug, Abstrich, Rabatt, [Preis]ermäßigung, Nachlaß, Vergünstigung, *(for entertainment)* Aufwandsentschädigung, *(pocket money)* Taschengeld, *(ration)* Unterhaltszuschuß, *(taxation, Br.)* Steuerfreibetrag, -ermäßigung, *(tolerance)* Toleranz, *(weight)* Gutgewicht;

additional ~ Zusatzkontingent, *(allowance)* Nachbewilligung, *(taxation, Br.)* zusätzlicher Freibetrag für das Arbeitseinkommen der Ehefrau; **advertising** ~ Reklamenachlaß; **age** ~ *(Br.)* Altersfreibetrag; **higher age** ~ *(Br.)* [etwa] Altersentlastungsbetrag; **annual** ~ *(Br.)* jährliche Absetzung für Abnutzung, jährliche Abschreibung für Anlagegüter (AFA); **constant attendance** ~ *(taxation)* Sozialvergütung im Fall der Notwendigkeit einer Dauerpflegschaft; **balancing** ~ *(taxation)* Steuerabzug für unter Abschreibungswert veräußerte Anlagen, zusätzlich gewährter Abschreibungsbetrag; **blind-person's** ~ *(Br.)* Blindenfreibetrag; **capital** ~ *(Br.)* steuerlich zulässige Abschreibungen auf das Anlagevermögen; **child** ~ *(US)* Kindergeld; **child dependency** ~ *(Br.)* Freibetrag für ein in der Ausbildung befindliches Kind; **child's special** ~ *(national insurance, Br.)* Kinderzulage; **children's** ~ Kinderermäßigung, *(US)* Steuerfreibetrag für Kinder; **clothing** ~ Ausstattungszuschuß, Kleiderzulage; **coding** ~ *(Br.)* gesetzlich zugestandene Freibeträge; **combat** ~ *(mil.)* Front-, Kriegszulage; **constructive** ~ Vergütung für Leergut; **cost-of-living** ~ Lebenshaltungszuschuß; **daily** ~ Tagegeld; **daily** ~ *(parl.)* Diäten; **[daily] meal** ~ *(parl.)* [tägliches] Verpflegungsgeld, Tagessatz, -gelder, Diäten; **daily subsistence** ~ tägliches Verpflegungsgeld; **daughter's services** ~ *(Br.)* Freibetrag für im Haushalt mitarbeitende Tochter; **dependant's** ~ *(unemployment insurance)* Zuschußbetrag für Familiengehörige; **dependency** ~ Beihilfe für ein [unterstütztes] Familienmitglied; **depletion** ~ *(Br.)* Abschreibung für Substanzverzehr; **depreciation** ~ *(Br.)* Abschreibungsbetrag, -freiheit; **dress** ~ Kleidergeld, -zulage; **duty-free** ~ Zollfreibetrag; **duty-tour** ~ Dienstreisenvergütung; **earned-income** ~ *(Br.)* Freibetrag für Einkünfte aus freiberuflicher Tätigkeit; **education** ~ Ausbildungs-, Erziehungsbeihilfe; **entertainment** ~ Aufwandsentschädigung; **excess** ~ *(Br.)* steuerlich noch nicht ausgenutzte Abschreibungsbeträge; **expatriate inducement** ~ Gehaltszuschlag für Auslandtätigkeit; **expense** ~ Aufwandsentschädigung, Spesenzuschuß; **extra** ~ Sonderzuteilung, -vergütung; **family** ~ *(Br.)* Familienzulage, -beihilfe, Kindergeld, Sozialzulage; **family** ~s *(US)* Unterhalt [aus dem Nachlaß]; **field** ~ *(mil.)* Front-, Mobilmachungszulage; **first year** ~ *(FYA, Br.)* Abschreibung im Anschaffungsjahr; **fixed** ~ Fixum; **food** ~ Verpflegungszulage; **foreign service** ~ *(dipl.)* Auslandszulage; **free baggage** ~ *(US)* Freigepäcksgrenze; **full** ~ volle Ration, *(depreciation)* voller Abschreibungsbetrag; **gasoline** ~ *(US)* Kraftstoff-, Treibstoffzuteilung; **guardian's** ~ Freibetrag für die Tätigkeit als Vormund, Vormundsvergütung; **housekeeper** ~ *(Br.)* Freibetrag für eine Haushaltshilfe; **industrial building** ~ *(Br.)* Abschreibung auf gewerblich genutzte Gebäude (Industriebauten); **initial** ~ *(taxation, Br.)* Steuerabzug für Anschaffungskosten, Sonderabschreibung für Neuanschaffungen, erhöhte Sonderabschreibung; **Inner London** ~ Ortszuschlag für das Zentrum von London; **invalid-care** ~ Freibetrag für die Pflege eines Schwerbeschädigten; **investment** ~ Steuervergünstigung für Kapitalanlagen; **language** ~ Sprachenzulage; **life insurance** ~ *(income tax, Br.)* Freibetrag für Lebensversicherungsprämienzahlungen; **living** ~ Unterhaltszuschuß; **lodging** ~ Wohnungsgeldzuschuß; **maintenance** ~ Unterhaltsbeitrag; **marriage** ~ Ehegattenfreibetrag; **married** ~ *(Br.)* Steuerfreibetrag für Verheiratete; **married man's** ~ *(Br.)* Steuerfreibetrag des Ehemanns; **maximum** ~ *(Br.)* höchster Steuerfreibetrag; **meal** ~ Verpflegungsgeld; **mil(e)age** ~ Kilometergeld; **mills and factories** ~ *(Br.)* Abschreibung auf Fabrikgebäude; **mineral depletion** ~ Steuerfreibetrag für den Erwerb eines Bergwerks; **mining works** ~ Freibetrag für Grubenuntersuchungen; **mobility** ~ *(Br.)* Freibetrag für weitab wohnende Arbeitnehmer; **monthly** ~ monatlicher Unterhaltsbetrag, Monatszuschuß, Monatswechsel; **motor-vehicle advance and basic** ~ Anschaffungs und Unterhaltungszuschuß für ein Kraftfahrzeug; **moving** ~ *(US)* Umzugsbeihilfe, -kostenersatz, -erstattung; **national assistance** ~ *(Br.)* Sozialrente; **nil** ~s *(income tax, Br.)* kein Freibetrag; **notional** ~ rechnerisch angenommener Freibetrag; **obsolescence** ~ *(Br.)* Bewertungsfreibetrag bei Ersatzbeschaffung für veraltete Wirtschaftsgüter; **office** ~ Repräsentationsfonds, Aufwandsentschädigung; **orphans'** ~s Waisengeldzahlungen; **overnight** ~ Übernachtungskostenzuschuß; **overtime** ~ Überstundenvergütung; **per diem** ~ tägliche Vergütung, Tagegeld, Reisespesentagessatz; **personal** ~ *(Br.)* persönlicher Zuschuß, *(taxation, Br.)* Steuerfreibetrag, Freibetrag für Ehegatten und Kinder; **additional personal** ~ *(Br.)* zusätzlicher persönlicher Freibetrag; **ordinary personal** ~ *(Br.)* üblicher persönlicher Steuerfreibetrag; **promotion** ~ Werbe-, Vorzugsrabatt; **purchase** ~ Kaufpreisminderung, -nachlaß; **~s related back** in das vorangegangene Veranlagungsjahr zurückgebuchter Steuerfreibetrag; **dependent relatives ~** *(Br.)* Unterhaltsfreibetrag, Steuerfreibetrag für unterstützungsbedürftige Familienangehörige; **removal ~** *(Br.)* Umzugsbeihilfe, -kostenersatz, -kostenerstattung; **rental ~** Wohnungsgeld, -zuschuß; **repairs ~** 7b-Abschreibung; **representation ~** Aufwandsentschädigung; **residential ~** Ortszulage; **retiring ~** Pensionszuschuß; **secretarial ~** *(MP)* Sekretariatszuschuß; **seniority ~** Dienstalterszulage; **separation ~** Trennungszulage, -entschädigung; **service ~** Dienstleistungsrabatt; **short ~** knappe Ration; **sickness ~** Krankenbeihilfe, -geld; **single ~** *(income tax, Br.)* persönlicher Freibetrag, Steuerfreibetrag für Ledige; **single age ~** *(Br.)* Altersfreibetrag für Ledige; **small-income ~** *(Br.)* Freibetrag für niedrige Einkommen; **special ~** Sonderrabatt, *(Br., law court)* gerichtlich anerkannte erhöhte Kostenrechnung; **superannuation ~** Alterszulage; **supplementary ~** Nachbewilligung, zusätzliche Zuteilung, Zusatzkontingent, *(Br.)* Zusatzkontingent, Sozialrente; **tax ~** *(Br.)* Steuerfreibetrag; **tax-free ~** *(Br.)* Steuerfreibetrag; **temporary living-quarter ~** Freibetrag für eine vorübergehende Zweitwohnung; **total ~** Gesamtabschreibung; **total ~s due** *(income tax, Br.)* Gesamtheit der Steuerfreibeträge; **trade ~** Rabatt für Wiederverkäufer; **trade-in ~** Rabattgewährung bei Inzahlungnahme; **transfer ~** *(US)* Umzugskostenersatz, -erstattung, Umzugsbeihilfe; **transport ~** Fahrgeldzuschuß; **travel ~** *(Br.)* Tagessatz, Devisenfreibetrag für Ferienreisende; **travel(l)ing ~** Reisekostenentschädigung, Spesensatz; **unconsolidated ~** vorübergehend gewährter Ortszuschlag; **voluntary ~** unentgeltliche Zuwendung; **waiting ~** Karenzentschädigung; **wear-and-tear ~** Abschreibung für Abnutzung; **weekly ~** Wochengeld, wöchentliche Zuwendung; **widow's ~** Witwengeld; **widowed mother's ~** Zuschlag für Witwe mit Kindern; **wife's earned income (earnings) ~** *(Br.)* zusätzlicher Steuerfreibetrag für das Erwerbseinkommen der Ehefrau, Steuerfreibetrag der erwerbstätigen Ehefrau; **writing-down ~** Vollabschreibung, *(WDA, Br.)* laufender Abschreibungsbetrag [vom 2. Jahr an]; **future writing-down ~** zukünftige Abschreibungsbeträge;

~ of an appeal Stattgabe einer Berufung; **tax-free daily ~ for attendance** steuerfreies Anwesenheitsgeld; **~ for board** Verpflegungs-, Beköstigungsgeld; **statutory ~ to the board of directors** satzungsgemäße Vergütung an den Aufsichtsrat; **~ of a bonus** Prämiengewährung; **~ to cashier for errors** Nachlaß für Rechenfehler des Kassierers, Fehlgeld; **additional ~ for children** *(Br.)* zusätzlicher Kinderfreibetrag; **~ of extenuating circumstances** Gewährung mildernder Umstände; **~ of a claim** Anerkennung einer Forderung, Forderungsanerkennung; **~ of free coal** Kohlendeputat; **~ of costs** Kostenanerkenntnis; **~ for costs** Berücksichtigung von Kosten; **~ for cost of living** Teuerungszulage; **~ of credit** Krediteinräumung; **~ as a credit of a tax** Anerkennung einer auswärts gezahlten Steuer; **~ to debtor** an den Gemeinschuldner gezahlte Vergütung; **~ for dependants** *(Br.)* Steuerfreibetrag für Familienangehörige, Kinderfreibetrag; **~ for depreciation** Abschreibung für Abnutzung, Abschreibungs-, Entwertungsrücklage, Rückstellung für Abschreibungen; **systematic ~ for depreciation** laufender Abschreibungsbetrag; **~ of a discount** Diskonteinräumung, Nachlaßgewährung; **~ for doubtful** *(Br.)* **(bad, US) debts** Rückstellung für Dubiose; **~ for errors** Fehlgelder; **~ for exchange fluctuations** Rückstellung für Devisenschwankungen; **~ for professional expenditure** Abzüge für Werbungskosten; **~ for special expenditure** Aufwandsentschädigung; **~ for expenses** Abzug für Kosten; **civilian ~ for foreign travel** *(Br.)* Devisenzuteilung für private Auslandsreisen; **~ for hardship conditions** Härtezulage; **special ~ for irregular hours** Überstundenvergütung; **~ for possible illness** Krankheitsrücklage; **~s given against other income** sonst gewährte Steuerfreibeträge; **~ of income tax** Einkommensteuerermäßigung; **~ of interest** Vergütung von Zinsen, Zinsvergütung; **~ of 4% interest on deposits** Einlagenverzinsung mit 4%; **~ of items in an account** Rückstellung für einzelne Rechnungsposten; **~ of an item of expenditure** Unkostenpostenanerkennung; **~ in kind** Naturallohn, -leistung, Deputat, Sachbezüge, -leistungen; **~ for leakage** Leckageabzug; **~ for loss** Refaktie; **~ for losses** *(taxation)* Steuerermäßigungen für Verluste; **~ of a margin for errors** Einkalkulierung von Fehlerquellen; **~ in money** Barvergütung; **~ for moving** *(US)* Umzugsgeld; **~ for night duty** Nachtdienstentschädigung; **~ given against a pension** pensionsbezogener Freibetrag; **~ on plant** Abschreibungen auf Betriebsanlagen; **~ on premises** Grundstücks-, 7b-Abschreibung; **~ for quarters** Wohnungsgeldzuschuß; **~ of rations** Bewilligung von Rationen; **~ for readjustment** Vorsorge für Berichtigungen; **~ for**

removal *(Br.)* Umzugsgeld, -kostenbeihilfe; **~ for rent** Wohnungsgeldzuschuß; **~ for representation** Repräsentationszulage; **~ of respite** Aufschubgewährung; **~ of a stipend to one's daughter** Aussetzung eines Nadelgelds für seine Tochter; **~ for tare** Taravergütung; **~ for tax** Steuerrückstellungen; **~ as a tax credit** Steueranrechnung; **~ of time** Fristgewährung, Stundung; **~ for vacancies** Rückstellung für unvermietete Räume; **~ for wages** Absetzung für gezahlte Löhne; **~ for wear and tear** Absetzung für Abnutzung; **income-tax ~ for wife and child** Steuerfreibetrag für Familienangehörige; **~ for good will** Vergütung für den Firmenwert;

~ *(v.)* Rationen bewilligen, auf Rationen setzen, rationieren; **to be entitled to an ~** Anspruch auf Unterhalt haben; **to claim capital ~s** *(Br.)* steuerlich zulässige Abschreibungen in Anspruch nehmen; **to claim the ~ available in respect of a student on a full-time course** Freibetrag für ein auswärts studierendes Kind beantragen; **to claim ~ for wear and tear of a car** Abschreibungsbeträge für ein Kraftfahrzeug in Anspruch nehmen; **to compute ~** *(Br.)* zulässige Abschreibung berechnen; **to compute the writing-down ~ on the basis of 2% per year of the cost of the building** *(Br.)* 2% des Hauswertes pro Jahr für Abschreibungen zulassen; **to cut down s. one's monthly ~** jds. Monatswechsel beschneiden (verkürzen); **to grant an ~** Zuschuß gewähren; **to make ~** *(accounting)* Rücklage bilden, *(grant reduction)* [vom Preis] nachlassen (abziehen), Abschlag auf den Preis (Preisnachlaß) gewähren, Rabatt geben, erlassen, *(take into consideration)* in Anschlag bringen, in Betracht ziehen, etw. berücksichtigen; **to make ~ for age** Altersvergünstigungen gewähren; **to make ~ for losses** Verluste berücksichtigen; **to make full ~ for large orders** erhebliche Preisnachlässe bei Großaufträgen vorsehen; **to make one's sister an ~ of $1000 a year** seiner Schwester eine jährliche Rente von 1000 Dollar aussetzen; **to make one's son an ~ of 1,000,- DM a year** seinem Sohn 1000,- DM im Jahr zukommen lassen; **to make an ~ for the tare** Tara vergüten; **to make ~s for s. one's youth** jem. seine Jugend zugute halten; **to offer ~s on a sliding scale [basis]** gestaffelten Sonderrabatt (gestaffelte Rabattsätze) anbieten; **to put s. o. on short ~** jem. den Brotkorb höher hängen; **to qualify for an ~** *(Br.)* den Abschreibungsbestimmungen entsprechen, abschreibungsberechtigt sein; **to qualify for an ~ of 100%** voll abschreibungsfähig sein, zu 100% abgeschrieben werden können; **to split an ~** *(Br.)* Steuerfreibetrag aufteilen; **to spread an ~ over 17 years** *(Br.)* Abschreibungsbeträge auf siebzehn Jahre verteilen; **to stop s. one's ~** jem. den Unterhaltszuschuß sperren;

for ~ purposes *(US)* für Abschreibungszwecke; **children's ~ regulations** Kindergeldbestimmungen; **~ system** *(Br.)* Ortszuschlagswesen.

allowed zulässig, statthaft, erlaubt;
~ reductions gewährte Rabattsätze; **~ time** Erholungspause.
allowing for unter Berücksichtigung von.
alloy *(inferior metal)* Beisatz, Münzzusatz, *(mixture of metals)* Legierung, *(quality of gold)* Feingehalt;
of base ~ geringhaltig;
~ of gold Goldlegierung;
~ *(v.)* legieren, Metalle versetzen;
~ s. one's happiness jds. Zufriedenheit beeinträchtigen.
allround durch die Bank, *(tool)* generell verwendbar;
~ banking service umfassende bankgeschäftliche Betreuung; **~ defence** *(mil.)* Rundumverteidigung; **~ education** umfassende Bildung; **~ improvement** Verbesserung auf der ganzen Linie; **~ inquiry** Rundfrage; **~ knowledge** umfassende Kenntnisse; **~ man** vielseitiger Mann, Alleskönner, Tausendsassa; **~ price** Pauschal-, Gesamtpreis.
allroundedness Beschlagenheit auf jedem Gebiet.
allude *(v.)* **to s. th.** auf etw. anspielen.
alluded person Betroffener.
alluvion Anschwemmung.
ally Verbündeter, Bundesgenosse, Alliierter;
~ *(v.)* **o. s.** sich verbünden.
allure *(v.)* anziehen, anlocken, ködern;
~ customers to buy goods Kunden zum Kauf verleiten.
allurement Anziehungskraft, Köder;
~s of a big city Großstadtverlockungen.
allusion Anspielung, Andeutung.
almanac Almanach, Jahrbuch, Kalender.
almoner *(Br.)* Sozialpfleger, Betreuer, Fürsorgebeamter;
lady ~ Sozialpflegerin.
almonry *(Br.)* soziale Fürsorge.
alms Armenunterstützung, -hilfe, wohltätige Spende, Almosen;
to beg for ~ um Almosen betteln; **to bestow ~** Almosen geben,

spenden; **to dispense** ~ Almosen austeilen; **to live on** ~ von Almosen leben; **to spend money on** ~ Geld zur Unterstützung der Armen geben;

~ **bag** Klingelbeutel; ~ **basin** Opferteller; ~ **box** *(Br.)* **(chest)** Opferkasten; ~ **dish** Opferteller; ~**-fed** von Almosen lebend; ~ **fee** Peterspfennig; ~ **land** *(Br.)* Kirchengut; ~ **penny** Scherflein; ~ **priest** Armenpriester; ~ **purse** Armenkasse.

almsfolk Almosenempfänger.

almsgiver Almosengeber, Spender.

almsgiving Almosen, Spende.

almshouse *(Br.)* Armenhaus, Spital.

almsman Almosenempfänger.

alod Erb-, Freigut.

alodial erbeigen, zinsfrei.

alone, to go it auf eigene Faust handeln.

alongshore längs der Küste.

alongshoreman Werftarbeiter.

alongside längsseits;
~ **to the quay** längsseits Kai; ~ **the vessel** längsseits Schiff.

alpha error *(Hofstetter-Wendt)* Alpha-Fehler.

alphabetarian Abc-Schütze, Anfänger.

alphabetic⎮arrangement of customers alphabetisch angeordnete Kundenkartei; ~ **files** alphabetisch geführte Akten; ~ **filing** alphabetische Ablage.

alphabetical⎮index alphabetisches Verzeichnis; ~ **order** alphabetische Reihenfolge.

alphabetize *(v.)* alphabetisch ordnen, alphabetisieren.

alphaplus allerbestens, einzigartig.

also-ran *(sl.)* unbedeutende Person.

alter *(v.)* ab-, um-, verändern, *(document)* abändern;
~ **the conditions contained in the memorandum** Satzung ändern; ~ **the course** *(ship)* Kurs ändern; ~ **an entry** Buchung abändern; ~ **materially** *(bill of exchange)* nachträglich ändern; ~ **the time to summer time** Sommerzeit einführen;
~ **ego** zweites Selbst, *(crony)* Busenfreund.

alterable veränderlich, änderungsfähig.

alteration [Ver]änderung, *(company)* Satzungsänderung, *(written instrument)* Abänderung;
subject to ~**s** Änderungen vorbehalten;
author's ~**s** Textkorrektur; **material** ~ rechtserhebliche Änderung, *(bill of exchange)* nachträgliche Wechseländerung; **serious** ~**s** bedeutende Veränderungen;
~ **of amount** *(bill of exchange)* Änderung eines Wechselbetrages; ~ **of articles of an association** Satzungsänderung einer Gesellschaft; ~ **of borders** Grenzveränderung; ~ **of capital** Änderung des Grundkapitals, Kapitaländerung; ~ **of a check (cheque,** *Br.)* Scheckfälschung; ~ **in the constitution** Satzungsänderung; ~ **of contract** Vertragsänderung; ~ **of course** *(ship)* Kurswechsel, -änderung; ~ **of a date** Datumsänderung; ~ **of an instrument** unbefugte Urkundenänderung; ~ **of memorandum** Satzungsänderung; ~ **of the minutes** Protokolländerung; ~ **of name** Namensänderung; ~ **of objects clause** Änderung des Gesellschaftszwecks; ~ **of passport** unberechtigte Paßänderung; ~ **of priority** Rangänderung; ~ **of terms of supply** Änderung der Bezugsbedingungen; ~ **of title** Titeländerung; ~ **to a will** Testamentsänderung;
to initial an ~ Zusatz abzeichnen; **to make** ~**s to a suit of clothes** Kleid ändern.

alterative verändernd.

alternate *(law of nations)* Unterschriftsfolge, *(US pol.)* Stellvertreter;
~ *(a.)* abwechselnd, wechselseitig;
~ *(v.)* [sich] abwechseln, alternieren;
~ **aerodrome** Ausweichflughafen; ~ **currency** *(US)* Alternativwährung; ~ **deposit** gemeinschaftliches Depot; ~ **director** turnusmäßig zuständiger Direktor; ~ **heir** *(US)* Ersatzerbe; ~ **husbandry** Wechselwirtschaft; ~ **legacy** Wahlvermächtnis, Alternativvermächtnis; ~ **material** *(US)* Austauschwerkstoff; ~ **member** Ersatzmitglied; **on** ~ **Mondays** jeden zweiten Montag.

alternating abwechselnd;
~ **current** Wechselstrom.

alternation Abwechslung, Wechsel;
~ **of generations** Generationswechsel.

alternative Alternative, Wahl, Möglichkeit, Entweder-Oder;
to come up with an ~ mit einer Alternative herausrücken; **to have no** ~ keine Wahl haben;
~ *(a.)* einander ausschließend, alternativ, wechselweise;
~ **accommodation** Ersatzunterbringung; ~ **airfield** Ausweichflugplatz; ~ **application** Verwendung von Ausweichfrachtsätzen; ~ **costs** Alternativkosten, Wartekosten; ~ **currency** *(Br.)*

Alternativwährung; ~ **decision** Alternativentscheidung; ~ **draft** Gesamtentwurf; ~ **forecast** Alternativprognose; ~ **frequency** Ausweichfrequenz; ~ **hypothesis** *(statistics)* Alternativhypothese; ~ **material** Austauschwerkstoff; ~ **obligation** Alternativverpflichtung; ~ **plan** Ausweichplan; ~ **pleading** Hilfsantrag; ~ **proposal** Alternativ-, Gegenvorschlag; ~ **question** Alternativfrage; ~ **rate** Ausweichfrachtsatz; ~ **relief** Hilfsantrag; ~ **reply** Alternativantwort; ~ **route** Ausweichfrachtroute; ~ **solution** Alternativlösung; ~ **standard** Alternativwährung; ~ **tariff** Ausweichfrachtsatz; ~ **tender** Alternativangebot.

alternatively wechselweise, abwechselnd, ersatzweise.

altimeter Höhenbarometer.

altitude Höhe, Gipfel, *(aircraft)* Flughöhe, *(satellite)* Höhenumlaufbahn;
cruising ~ Reiseflughöhe;
~ **of barometer** Barometerhöhe;
~ **cabin** Überdruckkammer; ~ **range** *(satellite)* Höhenumlaufbahn.

alu *(arithmetic and logical unit)* Rechenwerk.

aluminium *(Br.)* **(aluminum,** *US)* **airframe** Außenhaut aus Aluminium.

alumnus *(US)* ehemaliger Student.

amalgamate *(v.)* zusammenlegen, -fassen, verschmelzen, fusionieren, amalgamieren, *(v. i.)* sich zusammenschließen;
~ **industries** Gewerbezweige wirtschaftlich zusammenfassen; ~ **shares** Aktien zusammenlegen.

amalgamated craft union Fachgewerkschaft, -verband.

amalgamation Vereinigung, Verschmelzung, Zusammenlegung, -schluß, Fusion[ierung], *(US)* Rassenmischung;
~ **of banks** Bankenfusion; ~ **of industries** wirtschaftliche Zusammenfassung von Gewerbezweigen; ~ **by share purchase** Fusion durch Aktienübernahme.

amass *(v.)* anhäufen, ansammeln;
~ **a fortune** Vermögen ansammeln; ~ **riches** Reichtum anhäufen.

amassing of capital Kapitalansammlung.

amateur Dilettant, Stümper, Nichtfachmann, *(sport)* Amateur;
~ **binding** Liebhabereinband; ~ **dramatics** Laienspielgruppe; ~ **edition** Liebhaberausgabe; ~ **flying** Sportfliegerei; ~ **gardener** Freizeitgärtner; ~ **photographer** Hobbyphotograph; ~ **status** Amateureigenschaft; ~ **theatrical** Amateuraufführung; ~ **transmitting licence** Amateurfunklizenz.

amateurish dilettantisch.

amateurism Dilettantismus.

ambassador Botschafter;
~ **extraordinary** außerordentlicher Botschafter, Sonderbotschafter; **goodwill** ~ Botschafter auf einer Goodwill Tour; **joint** ~ gemeinsamer Botschafter; ~ **plenipotentiary** außerordentlicher und bevollmächtigter Botschafter; **roving** ~ fliegender Botschafter;
~**-at-large** Sonderbotschafter;
the ~ **will be present** in Gegenwart des Botschafters;
to delegate s. o. as ~ j. als Botschafter entsenden; **to recall an** ~ **to report** Botschafter zur Berichterstattung zurückbeordern; ~**'s deputy** Botschaftstellvertreter; **on** ~ **level** auf Botschaftsebene, im Botschafterrang.

ambassadorial⎮appointment Bestellung zum Botschafter; ~ **conference** Botschafterkonferenz; ~ **group** Botschafterlenkungsausschuß; **on** ~ **level** auf Botschafterebene; ~ **post** Botschafterposten.

amber light signal (traffic lights) gelbes Licht, Wartesignal.

ambidexter *(law)* von beiden Seiten Bestochener.

ambiguity *(law)* Zweideutigkeit, Dissens;
latent ~ versteckter Dissens; **patent** ~ offener Dissens.

ambiguous zweideutig, mehrdeutig, doppelsinnig;
~ **question** mehrdeutige Frage.

ambit Anwendungsbereich, Gebiet, Zuständigkeitsgrenze, *(range of power)* Vollmachtsumfang;
~ **of a tax** Steueranwendungsgebiet;
to fall within the ~ **of an agreement** in den Bereich eines Abkommens fallen.

ambulance Unfall-, Rettungs-, Sanitäts-, Krankenwagen, Ambulanz, *(~ station)* Sanitätswache, Ambulanz;
motor ~ Krankenauto;
~ *(v.)* im Krankenwagen befördern;
~ **box** Verbandskasten; ~ **chaser** *(US)* auf Schadenersatzklagen ausgehender Anwalt; ~ **dog** Sanitätshund; ~ **plane** Sanitäts-, Rettungsflugzeug; ~ **room** Krankenbehandlungsraum; ~ **service** Unfallrettungsdienst; ~ **station** Unfallstation; ~ **train** Lazarettzug.

ambulant ambulant;
~ **boundaries** nicht festliegende Grenzen.
ambulatory *(US)* Wandelgang;
~ *(a.)* beweglich, *(out of bed)* nicht mehr bettlägerig, *(law)* jederzeit widerruflich;
~ **court** nicht ortsgebundenes Gericht; ~ **school** Wanderschule;
~ **will** widerrufliches Testament.
ambush Hinterhalt;
to fall into an ~ in einen Hinterhalt geraten; **to lie in** ~ im Hinterhalt liegen; **to prepare an** ~ Hinterhalt legen.
ameliorate *(v.)* verbessern.
ameliorating waste werterhöhende Veränderungen an der Grundstückssubstanz.
amelioration Bodenverbesserung, *(prices)* Preissteigerung;
~ **of the trade balance** Verbesserung der Handelsbilanz;
~ **works** Meliorationen.
amenability Zugänglichkeit.
amenable zugänglich;
~ **to advice** einem Rat zugänglich; ~ **to law** vor dem Gesetz (rechtlich) verantwortlich;
to be ~ **to jurisdiction** der Gerichtbarkeit unterworfen sein; **to find s. o.** ~ **to s. th.** j. einer Sache gegenüber sehr aufgeschlossen finden.
amend *(v.)* | **an appropriation bill** Haushaltungsvoranschlag abändern; ~ **a charter** Konzession ändern; ~ **a complaint** einer Beschwerde abhelfen; ~ **a judgment** Urteil ergänzen; ~ **a patent** Patent berichtigen; ~ **a statement of claim** Klage abändern; ~ **one's ways** seine Lebensweise zum Besseren ändern.
amendable abänderungsfähig.
amendatory legislation ergänzende Gesetzgebung.
amende Geldstrafe;
hono(u)rable ~ Ehrenerklärung.
amended version ergänzte Fassung.
amendment Änderungsvorschlag, Zusatz, Ergänzungsvorschlag, Novelle, *(law)* Abänderung, *(parl.)* Abänderungsvorschlag, Zusatzantrag, *(process)* Urteilsergänzung, *(rectification)* Verbesserung, Berichtigung;
~s *(US)* Zusatzartikel zur Verfassung;
constitutional ~ Verfassungsänderung, -zusatz; **first** ~ *(constitution)* Zusatzartikel; **hono(u)rable** ~ Ehrenerklärung; **opposed** ~ Abänderungsvorschlag;
~ **to an act** Gesetzesänderung; ~ **of an action** Klageänderung; ~ **to an** ~ Zusatzantrag; ~ **of a bill** Abänderung einer Gesetzesvorlage; ~ **of an appropriation bill** Abänderung eines Haushaltsvoranschlags; ~ **of a cause of action** Berichtigung eines Klagevorbringens; ~ **of a charter** Konzessionsänderung; ~ **of a complaint** Beschwerdeabhilfe; ~ **of a judgment** Urteilsergänzung; ~s **to a pleading** Klageänderung; ~ **of the constitution** Verfassungsänderung, -zusatz; ~ **of a passport** Paßänderung; ~ **of a patent** Patentberichtigung, -änderung; ~ **of a statement of claim** Klageabänderung; ~ **of a text** Berichtigung eines Textes, Textänderung;
to move an ~ **[to a bill]** Abänderungsgesetz (Zusatzantrag) einbringen; **to pass an** ~ Abänderungsantrag annehmen; **to table an** ~ Zusatzantrag (Gegenantrag) einbringen; **to vote on an** ~ über einen Änderungsantrag abstimmen;
~ **law** Anpassungsgesetz.
amends [Schaden]ersatz, Schadloshaltung, Entschädigung, Wiedergutmachung;
to make ~ Schadenersatz leisten, entschädigen, ersetzen, wiedergutmachen; **to make** ~ **for an injury** Schadenersatz wegen Körperverletzung leisten.
amenities persönliche Vorzüge;
~ **of life** Annehmlichkeiten des Lebens;
to provide the usual ~ üblichen Service bieten;
~ **center** *(US)* Freizeitzentrum.
amenity *(real estate)* besondere Vorzüge;
~ **of an area** Anziehungskraft (Attraktivität) eines Gebietes;
~ **value** Gebrauchswert, *(real estate)* Annehmlichkeitswert.
amerce | **s. o.** jem. eine Geldbuße auferlegen; ~ **an estate to the Crown** *(Br.)* Grundstück enteignen.
amerceable straffällig.
amercement *(US)* Geldstrafe, -buße;
~ **royal** *(Br.)* Disziplinarstrafe.
American | **Association of State Highway Officials** Vereinigung der staatlichen amerikanischen Straßenverwaltungen; ~ **Bankers Association** *(US)* Banken- und Bankiervereinigung; ~ **Bar Association** *(US)* Bundesanwaltskammer; ~ **clause** *(marine insurance)* Ausgleichsausschlußklausel; ~ **envelope** Versandtasche; ~ **Federation of Labor** Dachverband der amerikanischen Gewerkschaften; ~ **market** *(Br.)* Markt für amerikanische

Werte; ~ **plan** *(US)* Vollpensionssystem; ~ **rails** *(Br.)* amerikanische Eisenbahnwerte; ~ **Standard Association** Amerikanisches Normenbüro; ~ **way of life** amerikanische Lebensweise; ~ **term** *(grain exchange)* amerikanische Bedingungen.
Americanism Amerikanismus.
Americanization Amerikanisierung.
americanize *(v.)* amerikanisieren.
amiable composition *(international law)* Beilegungsverfahren.
amicable gütlich, freundschaftlich;
~ **action** Antrag auf Vorlage eines Vergleichs durch das Gericht; ~ **arrangement** gütliche Einigung, Vergleich; ~ **compounder** Schlichter; ~ **settlement** gütliche Beilegung.
amicably auf gütlichem Wege, außergerichtlich;
to settle a matter ~ sich gütlich einigen.
amidship mittschiffs.
amiss verfehlt, nicht in Ordnung.
ammunition Munition, *(depot)* Munitionslager;
~ **carrier** Munitionswagen.
ammunity depot Munitionsdepot.
amnesia Bewußtseinslücke, Gedächtnisverlust.
amnesty *(general)* Amnestie, allgemeiner Straferlaß;
tax ~ Steueramnestie;
~ *(v.)* amnestieren, begnadigen;
to be covered by an ~ unter eine Amnestie fallen; **to grant** ~ amnestieren; **to issue an** ~ Amnestie erlassen; **to vote an** ~ Amnestie beschließen.
amortizable amortisierbar.
amortization [Schulden]tilgung, Amortisation, Amortisierung, *(alienation in mortmain)* Veräußerung von Grundstücken an die tote Hand, *(depreciation)* Abschreibung;
~ **of a loan** Anleihetilgung;
to pay ~ Tilgungsraten leisten, amortisieren;
~ **charges** Abschreibungslasten; ~ **fund** Tilgungsstock, Amortisationsfonds; ~ **instal(l)ment** Amortisationsrate; ~ **loan** Amortisationsanleihe; ~ **method** Amortisationsmethode; ~ **mortgage** Amortisationshypothek; ~ **payment** Amortisationszahlung; ~ **plan** Tilgungsplan; ~ **quota** Amortisationsquote, Tilgungsrate; ~ **reserve** Rückstellung für Amortisationen; ~ **schedule** Amortisationstabelle, Amortisations-, Tilgungsplan.
amortize *(v.)* tilgen, amortisieren, *(depreciate)* abschreiben, *(mortmain)* Grundstücke an die tote Hand veräußern;
~ **costs over a period of 3 years** Unkosten über 3 Jahre verteilen.
amortized cost Kosten nach Abschreibungen.
amortizement Amortisierung.
amotion Besitzentziehung, *(corporation law, US)* Vorstandsentlastung.
amount Betrag, Summe, Menge, Höhe, *(accounting)* Kapital und Zinsen, *(fig.)* Inhalt, Kern, *(quantity)* Menge, *(significance)* Bedeutung, Wert, Umfang, *(total)* Gesamtsumme, -ergebnis;
for small ~s *(law court)* mit geringem Streitwert; **good for any** ~ gut für jeden Betrag; **in one** ~ auf einmal, in einer Summe; **in small** ~s in kleinen Mengen; **of little** ~ ziemlich wertlos; **[up] to the** ~ of bis zum Betrage (Höchstsatz) von; **with due** ~ **of care** mit der nötigen Sorgfalt;
~ **accrued** entstandener, noch nicht fälliger Betrag; **actual** ~ Ist-, Effektivbestand; ~ **advanced** Vorauszahlung, kreditierter Betrag; ~s **advised** avisierte Zahlungen; ~ **agreed upon** vereinbarter Betrag; **aggregate** ~ Gesamtsumme, -betrag; ~ **allowed** ausgesetzte Summe; **annual** ~ Jahresbetrag; **any** ~ beliebiger Betrag; **available** ~ verfügbarer Betrag; **average** ~ Durchschnittbetrag; **blocked** ~ gesperrter Betrag; ~ **booked** Buchungsbetrag; ~ **brought forward** vorgetragener Betrag; ~ **brought in** *(bookkeeping)* Vortrag aus vorjährigem Rechnungsjahr; ~ **carried (brought) forward** Vortrag auf neue Rechnung, Saldoübertrag; **considerable** ~ erhebliche Menge; **chief** ~ Hauptbetrag; ~ **clear** Reinertrag; ~ **covered** *(insurance)* von der Versicherung gedeckter Betrag, Deckungssumme; ~ **credited** ~ verfügbares Guthaben; ~ **debited** abgebuchter Betrag; **deposited** ~ hinterlegter Nominalbetrag; **depreciation** ~ Abnutzungsbetrag; **double the** ~ doppelter Betrag; ~ **due** geschuldeter fälliger Betrag, Schuldbetrag; ~ **entered twice** doppelt gebuchter Betrag; **entire** ~ Gesamtbetrag; **estimated** ~ veranschlagte Summe, Schätzwert; **exempted** ~ *(income tax)* Freibetrag; **exceeding** ~ überschießender Betrag, Mehrbetrag; **face** ~ Nominal-, Nennbetrag; **final** ~ ausmachender Betrag; **fractional** ~ *(stock exchange)* Spitzenbetrag; **full** ~ voller (ganzer) Betrag; **global** ~ Pauschalbetrag; **granted** ~ ausgesetzte Summe; **gross** ~ Bruttobetrag; ~ **guaranteed** *(caution money)* Garantiehöhe, Haftsumme; **indicated** ~ angegebener Betrag; **individual** ~s einzelne Beträge, Einzelbeträge; ~ **insured** Versi-

cherungsbetrag, -summe, -höhe; ~ **invested** [**in a company**] Anlagebetrag, Beteiligung; **invoiced** ~ Rechnungsbetrag; ~ **involved** Streitwert; **large** ~ große Summe; **maximum** ~ Höchstbetrag; **minimum** ~ Mindest-, Minimalbetrag; **missing** ~ fehlender Betrag, Fehlbetrag; **net** ~ Nettobetrag; **nominal** ~ proforma angesetzter Betrag; **original** ~ Grundbetrag; ~ **overdue** überfälliger Betrag; ~ **owing** geschuldete Summe, Schuldbetrag; **partial** ~ Teilbetrag; **principal** ~ Kapitalbetrag; **pro-rata** ~ anteiliger Betrag; ~ **realized** realisierter Betrag; ~ **received** Betrag erhalten; **remitted** ~ überwiesene Summe, überwiesener Betrag; ~ **set up** Ansatz; **smallest** ~**s** kleinste Beträge; **specific** ~ bestimmter Betrag; **subscribed** ~ gezeichneter Betrag, Zeichnungsbetrag; ~ **surrendered** abgeführter Gewinn; **tax** ~ Steuerbetrag; **tax-exempt** ~ Steuerfreibetrag; **total** ~ gesamter Betrag, Gesamtsumme, -betrag, ganze Summe; **uncovered** ~ offenstehender Betrag, offener Posten; **uneven** ~ *(stock exchange)* Spitzenbetrag; ~ **written off** abgeschriebener Betrag; Abschreibungsbetrag;
~ **paid on account** angezahlter Betrag; ~ **paid in advance** vorausgezahlter Betrag, Vorauszahlung; ~ **of an allowance** *(income tax, Br.)* Freibetragshöhe; ~ **of** [**ordinary**] **annuity due** Endwert einer vor[nach]schüssigen Rente; ~ **of appreciation** Wertzuwachsbetrag; ~ **of assets** Vermögensbetrag, -höhe; ~ **of balance** Saldo; ~ **due to banks** *(balance sheet)* Verbindlichkeiten gegenüber Banken; ~ **brought to debit of revenue account** auf Ertragskonto gutgeschriebener Betrag; ~ **of capital** Kapitalbetrag, -höhe; ~ **carried over** Übertrag; ~ **in cash** Barvorrat, -betrag, Kassenbestand; ~ **of cash held** unterhaltene Bargeldreserven; ~ **of claim** Forderungsbetrag, -bestand, *(insurance)* Höhe des Versicherungsanspruchs; ~ **of compensation** Abfindungssumme, -betrag, Entschädigungsbetrag; ~ **of compensation demanded** geforderter Entschädigungsbetrag; ~ **in controversy** Streitwert; ~ **of foreign currency** Devisenbetrag; ~ **of damage** Entschädigungs-, Ersatzbetrag, Schadenshöhe; ~ **of a debt** Schuldsumme, -betrag; ~ **of depreciation** Abschreibungsbetrag, -bedarf; ~ **of depreciation earned** verdiente Abschreibung; ~ **at disposal** verfügbare Summe; ~ **in dispute** streitiger Betrag; ~ **regarded as free for distribution** für die Ausschüttung frei verfügbarer Betrag; ~ **of expenses** Unkostenbetrag; ~ **in figures** Betrag in Zahlen; ~ **of freight** Frachtanteil; ~ **of guarantee** Kautions-, Bürgschaftssumme; ~ **of income** Einkommenshöhe, -betrag; ~ **of indebtedness** Höhe der Verschuldung; ~ **of inspection** Prüfungsumfang; ~ **of insurance** Versicherungsbetrag; ~ **of insurance carried** von der Versicherung gedeckter Betrag; ~ **of interest** Zinshöhe, -betrag; ~ **of invention** *(patent law)* Erfindungshöhe; ~ **of invoice** Rechnungsbetrag; ~ **at issue** strittiger Betrag; ~ **withdrawn from a letter of credit** einem Kreditbrief entnommener Betrag; ~ **of levy** *(EC)* Abschöpfungsbetrag; ~ **of** [**the**] **a loan** Anleihe-, Darlehnsbetrag; ~ **of loss** Schadensbetrag, -höhe; ~ **of maintenance** Unterhaltsbetrag; ~ **due at maturity** Fälligkeitsbetrag; ~ **of money** Geldbetrag, -summe; ~ **of notice** Kündigungszeitraum; ~ **of output** Produktionsmenge; ~ **of premium** Prämienhöhe; ~ **of production** Produktionsmenge; ~ **of redemption** Ablösungssumme; ~ **of rainfall** Niederschlagsmenge; ~ **of reduction** Kürzungsbetrag; ~ **qualifying for relief** *(Br.)* Steuerermäßigungs-, -abzugsbetrag; ~ **of rent** Miethöhe, -betrag; ~ **of reserves** Reservenhöhe; ~ **of revenue** Nutzungswert; **net** ~ **at risk** *(life insurance)* Risikobetrag, -summe; ~ **of security** Kautionsbetrag; ~ **of space** Anzeigenraum, *(retail shop)* Regalfläche; ~ **of stock** Kapitalanteil; ~**s of stock negotiable** durch Indossament übertragbare Aktienpakete; ~ **of tax deducted** abgezogener Steuerbetrag; ~ **of time required** erforderlicher Zeitaufwand; ~ **of traffic** Verkehrsumfang; ~**s due to vendors and employees** Vertretern und Angestellten geschuldete Beträge; ~ **to be withheld** einzuzahlender Betrag; ~ **in words** Betrag in Worten; ~ **written off** Abschreibungsbetrag;
~ *(v.)* **to** betragen, ausmachen, sich beziffern auf;
~ **to a confession of guilt** praktisch ein Schuldgeständnis darstellen; ~ **to invention** *(patent law)* Erfindungshöhe erreichen; ~ **to very little** nicht gerade bedeutend sein; ~ **to quite a lot of money** beträchtliche Summe ausmachen (darstellen); ~ **to the same** auf das Gleiche herauskommen;
to advance an ~ Betrag vorschießen; **to be of little** ~ praktisch wertlos sein; **to bring an** ~ **up to round figures** Betrag nach oben abrunden; **to charge an** ~ **to s. one's account** jds. Konto mit einem Betrag belasten; **to collect outstanding** ~**s** Außenstände einziehen; **to credit an** ~ Summe gutschreiben; **to deduct an** ~ Betrag abziehen; **to give a fair** ~ **of support to ...** *(stock exchange)* beträchtliches Interesse für ... zeigen; **to make up an**

~ Betrag abrunden; **to make any** ~ **of money** jede Menge Geld verdienen; **to pass an** ~ **to the credit of s. o.** jem. einen Betrag gutschreiben; **to pay an** ~ **to s. o.** Betrag an j. abführen; **to prorate an** ~ Betrag aufteilen; **to refer the** ~ **of rent to arbitration** Miethöhe schiedsgerichtlich festlegen (überprüfen) lassen.

amphibian *(airplane)* Amphibienflugzeug;
~ **landing** amphibische Operation; ~ **truck** Schwimmlastkraftwagen.

amphibious | **base** Land- u. Seestützpunkt; ~ **vehicle** Amphibienfahrzeug.

ample reichhaltig, *(sufficient)* ausreichend, genügend, hinreichend, *(vast)* reichlich;
~ **fortune** großes Vermögen; ~ **house** geräumiges Haus; ~ **means** reichliche Mittel; **to have** ~ **means at one's disposal** über beträchtliches Kapital verfügen, reichlich mit Mitteln versehen (kapitalkräftig) sein; **to have** ~ **money for building** ausreichendes Baukapital haben; **to have** ~ **resources** über umfangreiche Mittel verfügen; ~ **security** ausreichende Sicherheit.

ampliation Urteilsaussetzung.
amplification Vergrößerung, Erweiterung.
amplifier equipment Verstärkeranlage.
amplify *(v.) (radio)* verstärken;
~ **an account** Bericht vervollständigen.
amplitude Umfang, Fülle, Reichtum.
amply | **rewarded** reich belohnt; ~ **supplied with money** reichlich mit Geld versehen.
amputee *(US)* Amputierter.
amuck, to run Amok laufen.
amuse *(v.)* **o. s.** sich amüsieren (gut unterhalten).
amused, to keep s. o. j. angenehm unterhalten.
amusement Unterhaltung, Kurzweil, Zeitvertreib;
~ **caterer** Vergnügungsbetrieb; ~ **park** Vergnügungsgelände; ~ **place** Stimmungslokal; ~ **tax** Vergnügungs-, Lustbarkeitssteuer;
to drop the ~ **tax** Lustbarkeitssteuer niederschlagen.
anabetic wind Aufwind.
anachronism Anachronismus.
anafront Aufgleitfläche.
analogous analog, ähnlich, entsprechend, sinngemäß;
to treat s. th. ~**ly** in Analogie zu etw. anderem behandeln;
~ **articles** *(transport)* analog einzustufende Güter.
analogue computer Rechenmaschine, Analogrechner.
analogy, on the ~ **of** im Wege der Analogie;
to argue from ~ aus der Analogie schließen.
analyse *(v.)* analysieren, auswerten, *(picture)* abtasten;
~ **an account** Konto aufgliedern, ~ **a balance sheet** Bilanz zergliedern; ~ **an economic theory** volkswirtschaftliche Theorie analysieren; ~ **a graph** Diagramm auswerten; ~ **the market** Marktanalyse vornehmen.
analysis Analyse, Zer-, Aufgliederung, Auswertung;
market ~ Marktanalyse; **qualitative** ~ qualitative Analyse; ~ **of an account** Kontenaufgliederung; ~ **of the cost price** Selbstkostenberechnung; ~ **of data** Auswertung von Daten; ~ **of expenses** Kostenanalyse; ~ **of a graph** Diagrammauswertung; ~ **of the market** Marktanalyse; ~ **of subscribers** Abonnenten-, Bezieheranalyse; ~ **of surplus** Gewinnanalyse; ~ **of variance** Varianzanalyse;
~ **department** statische Abteilung einer Bank; ~ **sheet** Bilanzanalyse, -zergliederung.
analyst Analytiker;
food ~ Nahrungsmittelchemiker; **public** ~ Gerichtschemiker; **security** ~ Effektenberater.
anarchism Gesetzlosigkeit, Anarchismus.
anarchist Anarchist, Staatsfeind.
anarchistic anarchistisch, gesetzlos.
anarchy Regierungs-, Gesetzlosigkeit, Anarchie, Umsturz.
anastatic printing anastatischer Druck.
ancestor Vorfahre, Ahne, Erblasser;
~ **worship** Ahnenverehrung.
ancestral angestammt, ererbt;
~ **debt** Erbschaftsschulden; ~ **estate** ererbter Grundbesitz; ~ **home** geerbtes Haus; ~ **memory** überkommene Erinnerungen.
ancestry Abstammung, Vorfahren, Ahnen;
~ **research** Ahnenforschung.
anchor Anker, *(fig.)* Rettungsanker, Zuflucht;
~ *(v.)* verankern;
to cast ~ ankern, vor Anker gehen; **to take the** ~ **aboard** Anker einziehen;
~ **buoy** Ankerboje.

anchorage Anlegestelle, Ankerplatz, -grund, *(fee charged for ~)* Anker-, Hafengebühren, *(fig.)* sicherer Hafen, *(mooring)* Verankerung, *(Br.)* Ankergebühr.

anchorite Einsiedler.

ancient altertümlich, altmodisch, *(law)* durch Verjährung zu Recht bestehend;
  ~ **demesne** freies Kronland; ~ **house** historisches (unter Denkmalschutz stehendes) Bauwerk; ~ **lights** Recht auf Licht; ~ **Monuments Directorate** *(Br.)* Amt für Denkmalsschutz; ~ **water course** alter Wasserlauf; ~ **writings** über 30 Jahre alte Grundstücke.

ancillary untergeordnet, ergänzend, abhängig, *(subservient)* dienend;
  ~ **administration** Nebenerbschaftsverwaltung; ~ **administrator** Nachlaßverwalter für einen Auslandsverstorbenen; ~ **attachment** Ersatzpfändung; **substantial** ~ **benefits** erhebliche Nebenvergünstigungen; ~ **bill** Nebenverfahren; ~ **document** zusätzliche Urkunde; ~ **duties** untergeordnete Aufgaben; ~ **function** Hilfsfunktion; ~ **industries** Hilfsindustriezweige, Zulieferindustrie; ~ **information** *(statistics)* Nebeninformation; ~ **letter of credit** Hilfsakkreditiv; ~ **letters testamentary** *(US)* Hilfstestamentsvollstreckerzeugnis; ~ **object** Nebenzweck; ~ **papers** Beiakten; ~ **proceedings** Nebenverfahren; ~ **receiver** behördlich bestellter Verwalter in fremdem Gerichtsbezirk; ~ **relief** ersatzweises Klagevorbringen; ~ **restraint** wettbewerbsbeschränkende Nebenabrede; ~ **road** Entlastungs-, Nebenstraße; ~ **services** zusätzliche Dienstleistungen, Nebenleistungen; ~ **suit** Nebenprozeß; ~ **undertaking** Neben-, Hilfsbetrieb, Filiale; ~ **unit** Versorgungseinheit; ~ **workers** Hilfspersonal.

angel *(sl.)* geldgebender Außenseiter, finanzierender Hintermann.

angle *(fig.)* Gesichtspunkt, *(math.)* Winkel, *(method, US)* Methode;
  ~ *(v.)* **for an invitation to a party** sich um eine Einladung bemühen; ~ **news** Nachrichten tendenziös aufmachen;
  to consider all ~s of a question alle Seiten einer Frage erörtern; **equal-~ map** winkelgetreue Karte; ~-**parked** schräg geparkt.

angledozer Planierraupe.

anglophile englandfreundlich.

anglophobe englandfeindlich.

animadversion Rüge, Verweis.

animadvert *(v.)* Verweis erteilen, Rüge aussprechen.

animal, domesticated Haustier;
  to keep an ~ Tier halten;
  ~ **husbandry** Tierzucht; ~ **kingdom** Tierreich; ~ **shelter** Tierasyl.

animate *(v.)* beleben, anregen, aufmuntern;
  ~ **a cartoon** Trickfilm zeichnen (herstellen).

animated lebhaft, angeregt;
  ~ **cartoon** Zeichentrickfilm; ~ **electric sign advertising** bewegliche Lichtreklame; ~ **film** Trickfilm.

animation Lebhaftigkeit, Belebung;
  ~ **of buyers** Kaufbereitschaft, -lust; **little** ~ **among buyers** wenig Kauflust; ~ **of cartoons** Herstellung von Zeichentrickfilmen; ~ **studio** Trickfilmstudio.

animator Trickfilmzeichner.

animosity Feindseligkeit.

annalist Chronist, Jahrbuchverfasser.

annals Annalen, Jahrbücher.

annex Anhang, Zusatz, Nachtrag, *(building)* Nebengebäude, Anbau, Anbauten, *(document)* Anlage;
  ~ **to a hotel** Hotelanbau;
  ~ *(v.)* an-, hinzufügen, anhängen, *(sl.)* organisieren, *(unite)* annektieren, einverleiben;
  ~ **ten acres to one's farm** sein Gut um zehn Morgen vergrößern; ~ **a codicil** Testamentszusatz anfertigen; ~ **another company** sich eine weitere Gesellschaft einverleiben; ~ **a penalty to a prohibition** Verbot mit Strafe belegen; ~ **one's signature** seine Unterschrift darunter setzen; ~ **another territory** sich ein weiteres Gebiet einverleiben.

annexation Annexion, Aneignung, Einverleibung, Angliederung, *(fixtures)* Immobilisierung.

annexationist Annexionsanhänger;
  ~ **tendency** Annexionsgelüste.

annexed bei-, anliegend, anhängend, in der Anlage;
  the ~ **memorandum** das beigefügte Exposé.

annihilation Vernichtung, Zerstörung.

anniversary Jahrestag, Gedenkfeier, -tag, Stiftungsfest;
  ~ **publication** Jubiläumsausgabe, -zeitschrift; ~ **stamp** Jubiläumsbriefmarke; ~ **volume** Festschrift.

annotate *(v.)* kommentieren, mit einem Kommentar versehen, mit Anmerkungen (Erläuterungen) versehen.

annotated text kommentierter Text.

annotation Erläuterung, Kommentierung, Kommentar, Glosse.

annotator Kommentator.

announce *(v.)* ankündigen, bekanntmachen, -geben, *(broadcasting)* durchgeben, -sagen;
  ~ **s. th. to s. o.** jem. eine Eröffnung machen; ~ **a birth** Geburtsanzeige veröffentlichen; ~ **a marriage** Eheschließung anzeigen; ~ **publicly** öffentlich bekanntgeben, ankündigen; ~ **the result of the poll** Abstimmungsergebnis bekanntgeben;
  ~ **shares** Aktien auflegen;
  to be ~d *(advertising)* kann erscheinen.

announcement Ankündigung, [An]meldung, Bekanntmachung, -gabe, Veröffentlichung, *(broadcasting)* kurze Werbeeinblendung, -durchsage, *(newspaper)* Hinweis, Notiz;
  by public ~ im Wege öffentlicher Bekanntgabe;
  broadcast ~ Rundfunkdurchsage; **newspaper** ~ Zeitungsmeldung, -nachricht; **personal** ~ Familienanzeige; **preliminary (previous)** ~ Voranmeldung, -anzeige; **prestige** ~ Repräsentationsanzeige; **public** ~ öffentliche Bekanntmachung (Verlautbarung), Kundgabe; **spot** ~ kurze Werbeeinblendung; **surprise** ~ überraschende Bekanntmachung;
  ~ **of birth** Geburtsanzeige; ~ **of death** Todesanzeige; ~ **of the government** Erklärung der Regierung, Regierungserklärung; ~ **of marriage** Heiratsanzeige; ~ **of sale** Verkaufsangebot;
  to read out an official ~ amtliche Bekanntmachung verlesen;
  ~ **campaign** Einführungskampagne; ~ **effect** Ankündigungseffekt, Signalwirkung; ~ **procedure** Aufgebotsverfahren.

announcer Rundfunkansager, -sprecher.

annoyance and inconvenience Schikanen und Belästigungen.

annual *(book)* Taschen-, Jahrbuch, *(ground, Scot.)* Grund-, Erbpachtzins;
  ~ *(a.)* jährlich [wiederkehrend];
  ~ **Abstract of Statistics** *(Br.)* statistisches Jahrbuch; ~ **accounts** Jahresrechnung, Jahresauszug; ~ **allowance** jährlicher Abschreibungsbetrag, jährliche Absetzung für Abschreibung; ~ **amount** Jahresbetrag; ~ **audit** Jahresabschlußprüfung; ~ **average** Jahresdurchschnitt; ~ **average earnings** Jahresdurchschnittsverdienst; ~ **balance [sheet]** Jahresbilanz; ~ **budget** Jahreshaushalt[splan]; ~ **capacity** Jahreskapazität; ~ **charges** jährliche Belastung; ~ **conference** Jahrestagung; ~ **consumption** Jahresverbrauch; ~ **convention** Jahrestagung; ~ **deficit** Jahresdefizit; ~ **depreciation** jährliche Abschreibung auf das Anlagevermögen; ~ **dividend** Jahresdividende; ~ **earnings** Jahresverdienst; ~ **Estimates** *(Br.)* Haushaltsvoranschlag; ~ **expenses** Jahresausgaben; ~ **fee** Jahreshonorar; ~ **financial statement** Jahresabschluß; ~ **general meeting** *(company law, Br.)* Jahreshauptversammlung; ~ **grant** Jahreszuschuß; **[guaranteed]** ~ **income** [garantiertes] Jahreseinkommen; ~ **increment** *(salary)* jährliche Gehaltssteigerung; ~ **interest** Jahreszinsen; ~ **instal(l)ment** Jahresrate; ~ **leave** Jahresurlaub; ~ **list** Jahresverzeichnis; ~ **loss** Jahresverlust; ~ **meeting** *(Br.)* Hauptversammlung; ~ **meeting day** *(Br.)* Hauptversammlungstag; ~ **output** Jahresproduktion; ~ **pay** Jahresgehalt; ~ **payment** Jahreszahlung; ~ **peak** Jahreshöchststand; ~ **pension** Jahreseinnahme, -miete; ~ **policy** Jahresversicherung; ~ **premium** Jahresprämie; ~ **proceeds** Jahresertrag; ~ **production** Jahresproduktion; ~ **profit** Jahresgewinn, -ertrag; ~ **provision** jährliche Bereitstellung; ~ **rate of depreciation** jährlicher Abschreibungsbetrag; ~ **rate of increase** Jahressteigerungsrate; ~ **rate of interest** Jahreszinssatz; ~ **receipts** Jahreseinnahme; ~ **register** *(Br.)* Jahrbuch; ~ **rent** jährlich abgerechnete Darlehenszinsen; ~ **rental** Jahresmiete; ~ **report** *(Br.)* Tätigkeits-, Jahresbericht, -abschluß, jährlicher [Rechenschafts]bericht, Jahresausweis, -übersicht; **employees'** ~ **report** für die Angestellten zusammengestellter Jahresbericht; ~ **requirements** Jahresbedarf; ~ **return** Jahresrendite, *(company law, Br.)* Jahresbericht; ~ **revenue** jährliche Einkünfte; ~ **review** *(UNO)* Jahreserhebung; ~ **salary** Jahresgehalt; ~ **set (volume)** Jahrgang; ~ **settlement** Jahresabrechnung; ~ **statement** *(US)* Jahresausweis, -abschluß; ~ **subscription** Jahresbeitrag, -abonnement; ~ **ticket** Jahreskarte, -abonnement; ~ **turnover** Jahresumsatz; ~ **value** *(Br.)* jährlicher Ertragswert, Jahresertrag; **gross** ~ **value** *(Br.)* Bruttojahresertrag, jährlicher Ertragswert; ~ **wage** Jahreslohn; ~ **wage guarantee** garantierter Jahreslohn; ~ **yield** Jahresrendite.

annualist Jahrbuchherausgeber.

annualize *(v.)* Beitrag für ein Jahrbuch schreiben.

annuitant Rentenempfänger, Rentner;
  life ~ Leibrentner.

annuities Jahreszinsen, Renten[papiere];
   amortizable ~ Tilgungsrenten; **consolidated** ~ konsolidierte Staatsanleihe; **government** ~ Staatsanleihe; ~ **payable out of the public revenue** *(Br.)* Renten aus Staatstiteln;
   ~ **sales** Rentenabsatz.
annuity [Jahres]rente, Jahreseinkommen, *(annual payment)* Jahreszahlung, -zinsen, *(Br.)* Staatspapier, Annuität, *(legacy)* in Teilbeträgen auszugebendes Vermächtnis, *(patent office)* Jahresgebühr;
   cash-refund ~ Rente mit Barausschüttung nicht erschöpfter Prämienzahlungen; ~ **certain** Rente mit bestimmter Laufzeit, Zeitrente; **clear** ~ steuerfreie Rente; **complete** ~ Rente mit vollem Betrag im Todesjahr; **contingent** ~ Rente mit unbestimmter Laufzeit; **continuous** ~ stetige Rente; **convertible** ~ umwandlungsfähige Rente; **curtate** ~ Rente mit nicht vollem Betrag im Todesjahr; **deferred** [life] ~ aufgeschobene [Leib]rente, Anwartschaftsrente, in der Zukunft fällige Rente; **disablement** ~ Invalidenrente; ~ **due** vorschüssige Rente; **government** ~ Staatsrente; **group** ~ Gemeinschaftsrente; **guaranteed** ~ Leibrente für eine festgelegte Zeit; **immediate** ~ sofort fällige lebenslängliche Rente; **irredeemable** ~ unablösbare Rente; **joint** ~ Gemeinschaftsrente; **joint and** [last] **survivor** ~ gemeinsame Überlebensrente; **level** ~ gleichbleibende Rente; **life** ~ Lebens-, Leibrente, lebenslängliche Rente; **noncontributory** ~ beitragsfreie Rente; **old-age** ~ Altersrente; **ordinary** ~ nachschüssige Rente; **perpetual** ~ lebenslängliche (unablösbare, ewige) Rente; **redeemable** ~ ablösbare Rente; **reduced** ~ gekürzte Rente; **cash refund** [life] ~ Rente mit Barausschüttung nicht erschöpfter Prämienzahlungen; **modified refund** ~ Restbetragsrente; **reversionary** ~ in Zukunft fällige Rente, einseitige Überlebensrente, Anwartschaftsrente; **survivorship** ~ Überlebensrente; **temporary** [terminable] ~ abgekürzte Rente, Zeitrente, fundierte Annuitätenschuld; **temporary life** ~ abgekürzte Leibrente; **termed** ~ zeitlich befristete Rente; **two-life** ~ Rente einer Versicherung über verbundene Leben, Überlebensrente; **unearned** ~ Kapitalrente; **variable** ~ von Kursschwankungen abhängige Rentenzahlung; **widow's** ~ Witwenrente;
   ~ **in redemption of a debt** Tilgungsrente; ~ **in perpetuity** lebenslängliche Rente; ~ **on the last survivor** Überlebensrente;
   to buy an ~ sich in eine Rentenversicherung einkaufen; **to commute an** ~ Rente durch Pauschalzahlung ablösen; **to hold an** ~ Rente beziehen; **to invest money in an** ~ sich in eine Rentenversicherung einkaufen; **to pay s. o. an** ~ jem. eine Rente gewähren; **to redeem an** ~ Rente ablösen; **to remit an** ~ *(patent office)* Jahresgebühr erlassen; **to service an** ~ Rentenauszahlung sicherstellen; **to settle an** ~ **on s. o.** jem. eine Jahresrente aussetzen; **to sink money in an** ~ sich in eine Rentenversicherung einkaufen; **to transfer the cash value into an** ~ Kapitalwert in eine Rente umwandeln;
   ~ **agreement** Leibrentenvertrag; ~ **bank** Rentenbank; ~ **basis** Rentenbasis; ~ **bond** Rentenanleihe, -titel; ~ **certificate (coupon)** Rentenschein; ~ **charge** Rentenschuld; ~ **computation** Rentenberechnung; **life** ~ **company** Rentenanstalt; ~ **contract** [Leib]rentenvertrag; ~ **department** Rentenabteilung; ~ **gift** Rentenstiftung; ~ **holder** Rentenempfänger, -berechtigter, *(disability)* Sozial-, Invalidenrentner; ~ **insurance** Leibrentenversicherung; **group rent** ~ **insurance** kollektive Rentenversicherung; ~ **insurance contract** Leibrentenvertrag; ~ **option** Rentenwahlrecht; ~ [benefit] **payment** Rentenzahlung; ~ **policy** Leibrentenversicherungspolice; **survivorship** ~ **policy** Rentenversicherungspolice zugunsten eines überlebenden Dritten; ~ **sales** Rentenabsatz; ~ **trust** Rentenfonds; ~ **value** Rentenbarwert.
annul *(v.)* *(annihilate)* vernichten, *(cancel)* annullieren, wiederrufen, rückgängig machen, anfechten, umstoßen, *(declare null and void)* [für] nichtig (ungültig) erklären;
   ~ **a contract** Vertrag kündigen (aufheben); ~ **a judgment** Urteil aufheben; ~ **a law** Gesetz abschaffen; ~ **a marriage** Ehe aufheben, für ungültig erklären; ~ **judicial proceedings** Gerichtsverfahren für ungültig erklären; ~ **a sale by paying a fine** Kaufvertrag gegen Bezahlung einer Geldbuße annullieren; ~ **a scheme of arrangement** vergleichsweise Schuldenregelung aufheben; ~ **a train** Zug ausfallen lassen.
annullability Tilgbarkeit.
annullable aufhebbar, annullierbar.
annulment *(annihilation)* Vernichtung *(invalidation)* Abschaffung, Kraftlos-, Nichtigkeits-, Ungültigkeitserklärung, Aufhebung, Kassation, Annullierung;
   ~ **of an award** Aufhebung eines Schuldspruchs; ~ **of a contract** Vertragsaufhebung, Kündigung eines Vertrages; ~ **of a judg-**

ment Aufhebung eines Urteils; ~ **of a law** Abschaltung eines Gesetzes; ~ **of marriage** Ungültigkeitserklärung (Aufhebung) einer Ehe, Eheaufhebung, Ehenichtigkeitsurteil; ~ **of a scheme of arrangement** *(Br.)* Aufhebung einer vergleichsweisen Schuldenregelung; ~ **of a train** Zugausfall.
anonymous ohne Namensnennung, anonym, inkognito;
   to write ~**ly** unter einem Pseudonym schreiben;
   ~ **letter** anonymer Brief.
anonymity Anonymität.
anonymuncule unbedeutender Schriftsteller.
annunciator Nummeranzeiger.
anomaly Abweichung, Unregelmäßigkeit, *(stock exchange)* Kursanomalie.
another action pending Einrede der Rechtsfähigkeit.
answer Antwort, Beantwortung, Bescheid, Entgegnung, Erwiderung, *(to a charge)* Klagebeantwortung, -erwiderung, Gegenerklärung, Gegenschrift, Replik, *(fig.)* Reaktion;
   in ~ **to your letter** in Beantwortung Ihres geehrten Schreibens; **in** ~ **to a request** in Erledigung eines Gesuchs;
   affirmative ~ Bejahung; **direct** ~ klare Antwort; **favo(u)rable** ~ positive Antwort; **final** ~ entscheidende Antwort; **frivolous** ~ ungenügende Antwort, *(pleading)* offentsichtlich unschlüssiges Gegenvorbringen; **irrelevant** ~ irrelevantes Vorbringen; **negative** ~ abschlägige Antwort; **noncommittal (evasive)** ausweichende Antwort; **positive** ~ zustimmende Antwort; **preliminary** ~ Vorbescheid; ~ **prepaid (A. P.)** Antwort bezahlt; **prompt** ~ umgehende Antwort; **sham** ~ *(pleading)* Scheinvorbringen; **short** ~ barsche Antwort; **smart** ~ falsche Antwort; **stock** ~ stereotype Antwort; **the whole** ~ der Weisheit letzter Schluß;
   ~ **in the affirmative** bejahende Antwort, Zusage; ~ **to a charge** Klagebeantwortung; ~ **to a letter** Briefbeantwortung; ~ **in the negative** verneinende Antwort; ~ **by return of post** umgehende Antwort; ~ **by telephone** fernmündliche Antwort;
   ~ *(v.)* *(charge)* Klage beantworten, sich verteidigen, Einspruch erheben, *(correspond to)* entsprechen, *(reply)* beantworten, entgegnen, *(be responsible)* verantwortlich sein, Rede stehen für, Rechenschaft abgeben über;
   ~ **for** haften für; ~ **for s. o.** für j. bürgen;
   ~ **in the affirmative** mit einem Ja antworten; ~ **a bill of exchange** Wechsel einlösen (decken, honorieren); ~ **a charge** sich vor Gericht verantworten; ~ **a claim** Anspruch befriedigen, Forderung erfüllen; ~ **for the consequences** für die Folgen einstehen; ~ **for a debt** sich für eine Schuld verbürgen, für eine Schuld einstehen; ~ **the door** Tür öffnen; ~ **expectations** den Erwartungen entsprechen, nach Wunsch ausfallen; ~ **a purpose** einem Zweck entsprechen; ~ **the requirements** den Anforderungen entsprechen; ~ **by return of post** umgehend [be]antworten; ~ **a summons** einer Vorladung Folge leisten; ~ **the telephone** Telefonapparat abnehmen, Telefon[zentrale] bedienen; ~ **well** gut anschlagen; ~ **in writing** schriftlich beantworten;
   to announce in a Parliamentary ~ im Parlament bekanntgeben; **to come up with an** ~ Erklärung finden; **to have a complete** ~ **to an accusation** Anschuldigung hundertprozentig zurückweisen können; **to precede an** ~ **with** Antwort einleiten; **to press for an** ~ auf eine Antwort drängen; **to prompt s. o. with an** ~ jem. eine Antwort suggerieren;
   ~ **print** Originalfilm.
answerable beantwortbar, *(liable)* haftbar, -pflichtig, *(responsible)* verantwortlich;
   to be ~ **for** haften für, bürgen (einstehen) für; **to be** ~ **for damages** schadenersatzpflichtig sein; **to be** ~ **for a debt** haftpflichtig sein; **to be personally** ~ persönlich haftbar sein;
   ~ **argument** brauchbares Argument.
answering|service *(tel.)* telefonischer Auftragsdienst; ~ **station** Gegenfunkstelle; ~ **the telephone** Telefonbedienung.
antagonism Gegensätzlichkeit, Widerstreit, Antagonismus.
antagonist Gegenspieler, Widersacher, Feind.
antagonize *(v.)* bekämpfen, entgegenwirken.
ante *(v.)* *(sl.)* Unterstützung gewähren;
   ~ **up** *(US sl.)* seine Schulden bezahlen;
   to raise the ~ **on one's annual contract** Grundvergütung eines Jahresvertrages erhöhen.
antecede *(v.)* Vorrang haben.
antecedence Vorrang, Vortritt.
antecedent vorangehend, vorrängig;
   ~ **creditor** Gläubiger einer vor Vermögensübertragung entstandenen Forderung; ~ **debt** frühere Schuld.
antecedents Vergangenheit, Vorgeschichte, Vorleben [einer Person].

antecessor Vorgänger.
antedate Vor-, Zurückdatierung;
~ *(v.)* vorverlegen, vor-, zurückdatieren;
~ **a check (cheque,** *Br.)* Scheck zurück-, vordatieren.
antedated paper vordatierte Zeitung.
antedating Zurückdatieren, Einsetzen eines früheren Datums.
antenna Antenne;
dish ~ Parabolantenne; **fading-reducing** ~ schwundmindernde Antenne; **whiplash** ~ Peitschenantenne;
to be an ~ **for possible sales** für Verkaufsmöglichkeiten auf Empfang stehen.
antenuptial|debts voreheliche Schulden; ~ **settlement** Ehevorvertrag.
anteroom Vorraum, -zimmer, Vestibül, *(waiting room)* Wartezimmer.
antetype Prototyp.
anthem, national Nationalhymne.
antiaircraft|defence Flug-, Luftabwehr; ~ **equipment** Flugabwehranlagen; ~ **gun** Flak.
antiavoidance provisions gegen Steuerumgehungen gerichtete Vorschriften.
antiballistic missile Abwehrrakete.
antibiotic Antibiotikum.
antiboycott legislation Boykottverbotsgesetzgebung.
antibritish englandfeindlich.
antiburglar device Einbruchssicherung.
anticapitalism Antikapitalismus.
anticapitalistic antikapitalistisch.
anticartel kartellfeindlich;
~ **law** Kartellgesetz; ~ **people** Kartellgegner.
antichresis *(law)* Nutzungspfand.
anticipate *(v.)* vorwegnehmen, im Voraus tun, erwarten, *(pay in advance)* im voraus bezahlen, *(use in advance)* vorgreifen auf;
~ **one's arrival** seine Ankunft beschleunigen; ~ **a bill** Wechsel vor Verfall einlösen; ~ **one's income** sein Einkommen im voraus verbrauchen; ~ **payment** vor Verfallzeit Zahlung leisten; ~ **one's salary** Vorschuß nehmen.
anticipated im voraus, vorzeitig, vor Fälligkeit;
~ **acceptance** vor Fälligkeit bezahltes Akzept; ~ **bill of exchange** vor Verfall eingelöster Wechsel; ~ **bonus** *(insurance)* vorweggenommener Gewinnanteil; ~ **freight** zu erwartende Frachteinnahmen; ~ **interest** Antizipandozinsen; ~ **payment** Vorauszahlung, Zahlung im voraus; ~ **profit** erhoffter Gewinn; ~ **redemption** vorzeitiger Rückkauf; ~ **requirements** voraussichtlicher Bedarf.
anticipation Erwartung, *(using beforehand)* Vorwegnahme, Vorausnahme, Vorgriff, *(date)* Vorausdatierung, *(extra cash discount)* [Bar]rabatt, *(marketing)* Erwartungsstruktur, *(objection to patent)* Patenteinwand, *(prepayment)* Vorauszahlung, Abschlagszahlung, *(rebatement)* Kleinhandelsrabatt bei frühzeitiger Warenlieferung;
by ~ auf Abschlag; **contrary to** ~ wider Erwarten; **in** ~ **of** im Vorgriff auf; **thanking you in** ~ in dem ich Ihnen im voraus danke; **with pleasant** ~ in angenehmer Erwartung;
~ **of a bill** Wechseleinlösung vor Verfall; ~ **of demand** Bedarfsvorwegnahme; ~ **of an invention** neuheitsschädliche Vorwegnahme einer Erfindung; ~ **of life** mutmaßliche Lebensdauer; ~ **of payment** Zahlung vor Fälligkeit; ~ **of property** Vorausverfügung über Vermögenserträge; ~ **of salary** Gehaltsvorgriff; ~ **of tax payments** Steuervorgriff;
to save in ~ **of the future** für die Zukunft vorsorgen;
~ **rate** Rabattsatz; ~ **survey** Konjunkturbefragung; ~ **term** Erwartungsgröße, -wert.
anticipative vorgreifend, vorwegnehmend.
anticipatory vorweggenommen, *(patent)* neuheitsschädlich;
~ **breach of contract** Erfüllungsverweigerung, angekündigte Vertragsverletzung; ~ **credit** *(Br.)* Versandbereitstellungskredit; ~ **drawing of a draft** Vorausziehung einer Tratte; ~ **expenditure** [Ausgaben im] Vorgriff; ~ **interest** Antizipandozinsen.
anticlockwise entgegen dem Uhrzeigersinn.
anticolonialism Antikolonialismus.
anticommercial wirtschaftsfeindlich.
anticommunism Antikommunismus.
anticompetitive wettbewerbsbeschränkend.
anticonstitutional verfassungswidrig.
anticyclical|approach antizyklische Methode; ~ **measures** marktkonforme Mittel; ~ **policy resolutions** konjunkturpolitische Entschlüsse; ~ **program(me)** Konjunkturprogramm; **for** ~ **reasons** aus konjunkturpolitischen Gründen; ~ **policy resolutions** konjunkturpolitische Entschlüsse.
anticyclone Hochdruckgebiet, -zone.

antidazzle|lamp Blendschutzlampe; ~ **requirements** Abblendvorschriften; ~ **screen** Blendschutzscheibe.
antidistortion device Entzerrer.
antidote Gegengift, -mittel.
antidumping duty Antidumpingzoll.
antifading Schwundausgleich.
antifreeze Frostschutz;
~ **agent (fluid, solution)** Frostschutzmittel.
antigovernmental regierungsfeindlich.
antihalo *(film)* lichthoffrei;
~ **base** Lichthofschutz.
antiindustry stances industriefeindliche Einstellung.
antiinflation|plan Antiinflationsprogramm; ~ **powers** antiinflationistische Vollmachten; ~ **program(me)** Inflationsprogramm.
antiinflationary inflationsfeindlich;
~ **force** antiinflationistische Kräfte; **to build** ~ **forces into the economy** antiinflationistische Maßnahmen in der Konjunkturpolitik ergreifen; ~ **strategy** Inflationsbekämpfung.
antiknock *(motor)* klopffest;
~ **quality** Klopffestigkeit.
antilabo(u)r legislation gewerkschaftsfeindliche Gesetzgebung.
antileft forces rechtsoppositionelle Kräfte.
antimarketeer *(Br.)* Gegner der britischen Zugehörigkeit zur Europäischen Gemeinschaft.
antimissile missile *(mil.)* Antiraketenrakete.
antimode seltenster Wert.
antimonopoly legislation Kartellgesetzgebung.
antinomy Widerspruch zweier Gesetze.
antipathy to advertising Werbefeindlichkeit.
antipersonnel bomb Splitterbombe.
antiprogressive fortschrittsfeindlich.
antiquarian Zeichenpapier;
~ *(a.)* antiquarisch;
~ **bookseller** Antiquar; **bibliophile** ~ **bookselling** bibliophiles Antiquariat; ~ **bookshop** Antiquariat; ~ **collection** Antiquitätensammlung; ~**'s shop** Antiquitätenladen.
antiquated veraltet, altmodisch, überlebt;
to become *(law)* überholt sein.
antique alter Kunstgegenstand;
~**s** Antiquitäten;
to browse for ~**s** Antiquitätenläden abgrasen;
~ *(a.)* antik, *(bookbinding)* blindgeprägt;
~ **collector** Antiquitätensammler; ~ **dealer** Antiquitätenhändler; ~ **finish paper** Werkdruckpapier; ~ **market** Antiquitätenmarkt; ~ **shop** Antiquitätengeschäft.
antirecession package Maßnahmen zur Rezessionsbekämpfung.
antiroll device Schlingertank.
antisaloon league Blaukreuzlerverein.
antiskid rutschfest, schleudersicher.
antisocial gemeinschaftsfeindlich, asozial.
antistrike legislation Antistreikgesetzgebung.
antitank weapons Tankabwehrwaffen.
antiterrorist|force [etwa] Sonderbatallion des Grenzschutzes; ~ **squad** Terroristenbekämpfungseinheit.
antithesis Antithese, Gegensatz.
antitrust gesellschafts-, kartellfeindlich;
~ **Act** *(US)* Kartellgesetz; ~ **action** *(US)* Kartellklage; ~ **charge** *(US)* Kartellklage; ~ **Committee** *(US)* Kartellausschuß; ~ **division** *(US)* Kartellbehörde; ~ **expert** *(US)* Kartellfachmann; ~ **field** *(US)* Kartellgebiet, -wesen; ~ **fine** *(US)* vom Kartellamt verhängte Geldstrafe; **to chase up** ~ **injuries** *(US)* Verstöße gegen die Kartellgesetze vor Gericht bringen; ~ **law** *(US)* Kartellgesetz; ~ **lawyer** *(US)* Kartellanwalt; ~ **legislation** *(US)* Kartellgesetzgebung; ~ **official** *(US)* Beamter des Kartellamtes; ~ **policy** *(US)* Kartellpolitik; ~ **provisions** *(US)* Kartellvorschriften; ~ **specialist** *(US)* Kartellexperte, -fachmann, -spezialist; **to violate the** ~ **statutes** *(US)* Kartellamtsbestimmungen verletzen; ~ **suit** *(US)* Kartellklage, -verfahren; **to get through** ~ **suspicion** *(US)* Mißtrauen der Kartellbehörden zerstreuen; ~ **violation** *(US)* Verletzung der Bestimmungen des Kartellgesetzes.
antiunemployment measures Maßnahmen zur Bekämpfung der Arbeitslosigkeit.
antiunion attitude gewerkschaftsfeindliche Einstellung.
antiunionist Gewerkschaftsgegner;
~ *(a.)* gewerkschaftsfeindlich.
antiwar protestor Kriegsgegner.
anxious begierig, gespannt, *(agreement)* in dem Bestreben;
~ **to please** dienstbeflissen;
to be ~ **to succeed** unbedingt Erfolg haben wollen.

apart einzeln, getrennt, abgesondert;
~ **from** abgerechnet (abgesehen) von;
to live ~ getrennt leben; **to set** ~ *(bankruptcy proceedings)* absondern.

apartment *(US)* [Miet]wohnung, Etagenwohnung, Etage, Appartment, Zimmerflucht, *(room, Br.)* Zimmer;
~**s** *(Br.)* Zimmerflucht, Wohnung;
condominium ~ *(US)* Eigentumswohnung; **furnished** ~ möblierte Wohnung; **higher-bracket** ~ Wohnung für gehobenere Ansprüche; **individual** ~ eigene Wohnung; **state** ~ herrschaftliche Wohnung; **three-room** ~ Dreizimmerwohnung;
~ **on the ground floor** Parterrewohnung; ~**s to let** Zimmer zu vermieten;
to let furnished ~**s** möbliert vermieten; **to let off a house into** ~**s** Wohnungen in einem Haus einzeln vermieten; **to live in furnished** ~**s** möbliert wohnen; **to make a house over into several** ~**s** Einfamilienhaus etagenweise vermieten; **to move out of an** ~ aus einer Wohnung ausziehen; **to rent [a furnished]** ~ [möblierte] Wohnung mieten; **to rent an** ~ **and take over the furniture** Wohnung mieten und die Möbel mit übernehmen; **to unfurnish an** ~ Möbel aus einer Wohnung entfernen;
~ **block** *(US)* Wohnblock; ~ **building** *(US)* Mietshaus, Wohngebäude, Appartment-, Mehrfamilienhaus, Etagenwohnhaus; ~ **construction** Wohnungsbau; ~ **dweller** Appartmentbewohner; ~ **hotel** *(US)* Apartment-, Wohnhotel; ~ **house** *(US)* Wohn-, Rentenhaus, Mehrfamilienhaus mit Komfort; ~ **house site** *(US)* Miethausbaustelle; **four-story** ~ **house** *(US)* vierstöckiges Mietshaus; ~ **house construction** *(US)* Mietshausbau; ~ **house owner** *(US)* Mietshausbesitzer; ~ **project** Wohnhausprojekt; ~ **rent** *(US)* [Wohnungs]miete.

apathy, to reflect ~ **among the voters** Wahlmüdigkeit wiedergeben.

apex *(fig.)* Kulminationspunkt, Gipfel.

apolitical unpolitisch.

apologizer *(fig.)* Ehrenretter.

apology Entschuldigung, Ehrenerklärung, Rechtfertigung, *(coll.)* Notbehelf, Ersatz, Surrogat;
written ~ Entschuldigungsbrief;
to offer an ~ um Entschuldigung bitten.

apothecaries' weight Apothekergewicht.

apothecary Drogist.

appanage Apanage, Leibgedinge, Jahresrente, *(natural adjunct)* Merkmal, Eigenschaft, *(inheritance)* Erb-, Pflichtteil, *(territory)* abhängiges Gebiet.

apparatus Vorrichtung, Gerät, Apparat, Maschine;
copying ~ Lichtpausapparat.

apparel Kleidung;
necessary wearing ~ **and bedding** *(bankrupt)* notwendige Kleidungsstücke und Bettstücke;
~ *(v.)* *(US)* bekleiden;
~ **industry** *(US)* Konfektionsindustrie, Herstellung von Konfektionsware.

apparent offensichtlich, offenbar, sichtbar, augenscheinlich, wahrnehmbar, *(law)* rechtmäßig, *(seeming)* scheinbar, anscheinend;
~ **authority** Scheinvollmacht; ~ **danger** *(self-defence)* augenscheinliche (gegenwärtige) Gefahr; ~ **death** Scheintod; ~ **defect** offensichtlicher Fehler (Mangel); ~ **easement (servitude)** sichtbare Dienstbarkeit; ~ **good order** ordnungsgemäßer Zustand; ~ **heir** *(Br.)* rechtmäßiger (gesetzlicher) Erbe; ~ **necessity** offensichtliche Notwehrlage.

appeal *(customers)* Anklang, -reiz, Anziehungskraft, -moment, Aufforderung, Appell, Signalreiz, *(law)* Einspruch, Berufung[santrag], Berufungsklage, Rechtsmittel, Rechtsbehelf, Revision, *(entreaty)* Appell, Aufruf, *(criminal law)* Be-, Anschuldigung;
acquitted on ~ im Berufungsverfahren freigesprochen; **admitting of no** ~ unter Ausschluß des Rechtsweges;
on ~ in der Berufungsinstanz; **with possible** ~ rechtsmittelfähig, Berufung zulässig; **without** ~ Rechtsmittel ausgeschlossen, Berufung unzulässig;
appetizing ~ appetitanregende Aufmachung; **cross-**~ Anschlußberufung; **general** ~ allgemeiner Anklang; **Hitchcock** ~ kriminalistischer Stimmungseffekt; **last-minute** ~ Appell in letzter Minute; **mass-emotional** ~ auf Massenwirkung gerichtete Werbung; **price** ~ preislicher Anreiz; **rating** ~ *(goodwill)* Einspruch gegen zu hohe Einschätzung; **snob** ~ Ansprechen snobistischer Gefühle; **tax** ~ Steuereinspruch; **highly technical** ~ *(taxation)* komplizierter Steuereinspruch; **twin** ~ doppelte Anziehungskraft; **general voter** ~ allgemeiner Anklang bei den Wählern;

~ **to arbitration** Schiedsgerichtsantrag; ~ **to the arms** Zuflucht zu den Waffen; ~ **on behalf of charity** Spendenaufruf; ~ **against costs** Kostenanfechtung; ~ **to a higher court** Anrufung einer höheren Instanz; ~ **with (to) the Supreme Court** Revisionseinlegung; ~ **to the country** *(Br.)* Ausschreibung von Neuwahlen; ~ **against costs** Anfechtung einer Kostenentscheidung; ~ **to customers** Anziehungskraft auf den Kunden; ~ **by the Red Cross** Hilferuf des Roten Kreuzes; ~ **and error** Berufung und Revision; ~ **to force** Aufforderung zur Gewalt; ~ **for help** Hilfeersuchen; ~ **from a judgment** Berufung (Einspruch) einlegen, Urteil anfechten; ~ **for peace** Friedensappell; ~ **to the public** öffentlicher Aufruf;
~ *(v.)* Beschwerde führen, sich beschweren, *(law)* Berufung (Revision, Rechtsmittel) einlegen, *(v. t., US)* vor einen höheren Gerichtshof bringen;
~ **to arbitration** Schiedsgericht in Anspruch nehmen; ~ **to the arms** seine Zuflucht zu den Waffen nehmen; ~ **against an award** gegen einen Schiedsspruch Beschwerde einlegen; ~ **a case** *(US)* Berufung (Rechtsmittel) einlegen; ~ **to the country** *(Br.)* Neuwahlen ausschreiben; ~ **to another court** weitere (erneute) Berufung einlegen; ~ **to the court above** sich beschwerdeführend an das größere Gericht wenden; ~ **to a higher court** höhere Instanz anrufen; ~ **from a lower court** gegen das Urteil eines niedrigen Gerichtes bei einem höheren Berufung einlegen; ~ **to the Supreme Court** Revision einlegen; ~ **to customers** Kunden anziehen; ~ **against a decision** Beschwerde gegen eine Entscheidung einlegen; ~ **against a decision of the Inland Revenue** gegen eine Entscheidung des Finanzamtes Einspruch einlegen; ~ **for funds** Mittel erbitten, um Mittel werben; ~ **to s. o. for help** j. um Hilfe ansprechen; ~ **against an injunction** Berufung gegen den Erlaß einer einstweiligen Verfügung einlegen; ~ **to the law** Hilfe des Gerichtes anrufen; ~ **for mercy** um Gnade bitten; ~ **against a sentence** Berufung einlegen; ~ **a suit** *(US)* Rechtsmittel einlegen; ~ **to the sword** Kriegsglück entscheiden lassen; ~ **in writing** schriftliche Beschwerde einlegen;
to allow an ~ Berufung zulassen, einer Berufung stattgeben; **to be acquitted on** ~ in der Berufungsinstanz freigesprochen werden; **to dismiss s. one's** ~ jds. Beschwerde zurückweisen; **to file an** ~ Berufung einlegen; **to give notice of** ~ **to s. o.** bei jem. Beschwerde einlegen; **to grant leave to** ~ Berufung zulassen; **to have long-term** ~ *(securities)* für eine langfristige Anlage attraktiv sein; **to have no broad** ~ nicht überall Anklang finden; **to have universal** ~ generell ansprechen; **to hear an** ~ **against income-tax assessment** über einen Einspruch gegen eine Einkommenssteuererklärung verhandeln; **to judge without** ~ letztinstanzlich entscheiden; **to launch an** ~ Sammelaktion starten; **to lodge an** ~ **against** Berufung (Beschwerde) einlegen gegen; **to lodge an** ~ **with the Supreme Court** Revision einlegen; **to lose one's popular** ~ an Volkstümlichkeit verlieren; **to make an** ~ **to s. o.** bei jem. Anklang finden; **to make an** ~ **to charity** an die Nächstenliebe appellieren; **to make a public** ~ **for funds** Spendenappell an die Öffentlichkeit richten; **to quash a sentence on** ~ Beschluß (Urteil) in der Berufungsinstanz aufheben; **to take an** ~ *(US)* Rechtsmittel einlegen; **to refuse to take an** ~ Berufung nicht zulassen; **to treat an** ~ **as abandoned** Berufung als zurückgezogen behandeln; **to uphold a decision on** ~ einer Berufung stattgeben; **to withdraw an** ~ Berufung zurücknehmen;
~**s board** Beschwerdestelle; ~ **bond** Sicherheitsleistung; ~ **committee** Berufungsausschuß; ~**s court** Berufungsgericht; ~**s' court decision** Entscheidung des Berufungsgerichtes; ~ **fee** Rechtsmittelgebühr; ~ **hearing** *(inspector of taxes)* Steuereinspruchverfahren; ~ **letter** Beschwerdebrief; ~ **matter** Berufungssache; ~**s procedures** Rechtsmittelverfahren, *(personnel management)* Anrufungsverfahren, *(taxation)* Einspruchsverfahren; **to meet an** ~ **target** anvisierten Spendenbetrag hereinbekommen.

appealable beschwerde-, berufungs-, revisionsfähig, durch Rechtsmittel anfechtbar.

appealed | **case** *(US)* Beschwerde-, Berufungssache; ~ **decision** angefochtene Entscheidung.

appealer Berufungskläger.

appealing | **advertising** ansprechende Werbung; ~ **party** Berufungskläger, Beschwerdeführer.

appear *(v.)* sich einfinden (zeigen, einstellen), *(on account)* [auf einem Konto] erscheinen (figurieren), *(actor)* auftreten, *(answer a charge)* sich auf eine Klage einlassen, *(books)* erscheinen, herauskommen, *(law court)* vor Gericht erscheinen (auftreten), *(plead a cause)* flüssig vortragen;
~ **for s. o.** für j. vor Gericht auftreten;

~ **in an action** sich auf eine Klage einlassen; ~ **against s. o.** gegen j. vor Gericht auftreten; ~ **by counsel** *(Br.)* sich anwaltlich vertreten lassen; ~ **before court** vor Gericht erscheinen; ~ **on the debit side of the balance sheet** auf der Passivseite der Bilanz erscheinen; ~ **for the defense (defence,** *Br.,* **defendant)** als Prozeßbevollmächtigter für den Beklagten auftreten (erscheinen); ~ **in the gazette** *(Br.)* als Konkursfall veröffentlicht werden, in der Konkursliste erscheinen; ~ **in a list** in einer Liste stehen; ~ **in person** persönlich erscheinen; ~ **as plaintiff** als Kläger auftreten; ~ **for the plaintiff** als Prozeßbevollmächtigter für den Kläger auftreten (erscheinen); ~ **in print** gedruckt werden, im Druck erscheinen; ~ **in public** in der Öffentlichkeit erscheinen (auftreten); ~ **quarterly** vierteljährlich erscheinen; ~ **on record** aus den Akten hervorgehen, aktenkundig werden; ~ **on the scene** auf der Bildfläche erscheinen;
as it ~s from the judgment wie aus dem Urteil hervorgeht;
to fail to ~ *(law court)* ausbleiben, nicht erscheinen, Termin versäumen.

appearance Erscheinen, Vorkommen, *(actor)* Auftritt, Auftreten, *(coming into court)* Erscheinen (Auftreten) vor Gericht, *(joining issue)* [Klage]einlassung, Einlassungserklärung, *(outward state)* äußeres Erscheinungsbild, Äußeres, Aussehen, *(publication)* Veröffentlichung, Erscheinen, *(thing seen)* Phänomen, Erscheinung;
at first ~ beim ersten Anblick, Aussehen; **for ~'s sake** um den Schein zu wahren; **to all ~s** allem Anschein nach;
compulsory ~ gerichtlich angeordnetes persönliches Erscheinen; **corporal ~** persönliches Erscheinen unter Vorbehalt; **general ~** vorbehaltloses Klageerscheinen; **public ~** Auftreten in der Öffentlichkeit; **outward ~** äußeres Erscheinungsbild; **personal ~** persönliches Erscheinen; **special ~** beschränkte Klageeinlassung; **voluntary ~** persönlich freigestelltes Erscheinen;
~ **by attorney** Vertretung durch einen Anwalt; ~ **of consent** Zustimmungserklärung; ~ **on television** Fernsehauftritt;
to assume an ~ sich den Augenschein geben; **to attend for the sake of ~s** nur um sich zu zeigen erscheinen; **to default an ~** Termin versäumen; **to enter an ~** sich auf eine Klage einlassen; **to keep up ~s** den Schein wahren; **to make ~** *(bill of exchange)* vorgelegt werden; **to make a poor ~** armselig aussehen; **to make one's ~** sich zeigen, auf den Plan treten, *(law court)* vor Gericht erscheinen; **to make one's first ~** zum ersten Mal öffentlich auftreten; **to make default of ~** Termin versäumen; **to put in an ~** persönlich erscheinen, *(law court)* einer gerichtlichen Ladung Folge leisten;
~ **day** Gerichts-, Verhandlungstermin; ~ **design** *(product)* Formgebung; ~ **docket** Termin-, Verhandlungsliste; ~ **money** Tagegeld.

appease *(v.)* beschwichtigen, besänftigen, *(pacify)* befrieden;
~ **a mutiny** Meuterei unterdrücken.

appeasement Beschwichtigung, Befriedung, Beruhigung;
~ **group** Anhänger einer Beschwichtigungspolitik; ~ **policy** Befriedungs-, Beschwichtigungspolitik.

appeaser *(pol.)* Beschwichtigungspolitiker.

appellant Beschwerdeführer, Rechtsmittel-, Revisions-, Berufungskläger.

appellate rechtsmittel-, berufungsfähig;
~ **court** Rechtsmittelgericht, Berufungsgericht, Gericht zweiter Instanz, [etwa] Oberlandesgericht; ~ **division** Berufungsabteilung; ~ **jurisdiction** Berufungsgerichtsbarkeit, Zuständigkeit in Berufungssachen; **to have ~ jurisdiction** Rechtsmittelinstanz sein; ~ **procedure** Rechtsmittelverfahren.

appellation Benennung, Bezeichnung.

appellative name Gattungsname.

appellee *(US)* Beschwerdegegner, Revisions-, Berufungsbeklagter.

append *(v.)* anhängen, beifügen, hinzufügen;
~ **a document to a dossier** Urkunde einem Exposé beifügen; ~ **marginal notes** Randbemerkungen machen; ~ **a seal to an act** Siegel auf einem Gesetz anbringen; ~ **one's signature to a document** seine Unterschrift unter eine Urkunde setzen.

appendage *(building)* Nebengebäude, *(person)* ständiger Begleiter.

appendant Anhang, Anhängsel, Zusatz, Anhang, Zubehör, *(law)* zustehendes Recht, *(territory)* zugehöriges Gebiet;
~ *(a.)* zugehörig, verbunden, *(subjoined)* bei-, hinzugefügt.

appended document beiliegende Urkunde.

appendix Zubehör, *(supplement)* Anhang, Anlage.

appertain *(v.) (belong)* zustehen, betreffen, *(relate to)* zugehören, gehören zu;
~ **to an office** zu einem Amt gehören.

appertaining zugehörig.

appetite Verlangen, Begierde, Neigung, *(desire for food)* Appetit;
to have little ~ for advances wenig Darlehnswünsche äußern.

applaud *(v.)* applaudieren, Beifall spenden.

applause Beifall, Applaus, *(fig.)* Billigung, Zustimmung;
slight ~ schwacher Beifall;
to break into ~ in Beifall ausbrechen; **to meet with ~** Beifall finden; **to win the ~ of the audience** beim Publikum gut ankommen;
~ **mail** *(US)* Anerkennungsschreiben.

apple, long-keeping haltbarer Apfel;
the ~ of s. one's eye jds. ein und alles;
in ~-pie order alles in Butter.

applecart, to upset s. one's jds. Pläne zum Scheitern bringen (über den Haufen werfen).

appliance Anwendung, *(apparatus)* Vorrichtung, Einrichtung, Mittel, Apparat, Gerät;
~**s** Zubehör;
labo(u)r-saving ~ Hilfsgerät; **office ~s** Büroausrüstung, Büroeinrichtung;
~ **for rescuing sailors from a wrecked ship** Rettungseinrichtung für gestrandete Seeleute;
~ **producer** Gerätehersteller.

applicability Eignung, Anwendbarkeit.

applicable anwendbar, geeignet;
to be ~ to a case auf einen Fall zutreffen.

applicant Bewerber, Bitt-, Antragsteller, *(job)* Stellungsuchender, Stellenbewerber, *(patent law)* Anmelder, *(petition)* Bittsteller, *(subscriber)* Anteilszeichner;
ideal ~ Idealbewerber; **joint ~s** *(patent law)* gemeinsame Anmelder; **prior ~** *(patent law)* Voranmelder;
~**s for civil service jobs** Beamtenanwärter; ~ **for credit** Kreditsuchender; ~ **for an employment** Stellenbewerber, Stellungsuchender; ~ **for insurance** Versicherungsnehmer; ~ **of interpleader** Streitverkünder; ~ **for a patent** Patentbewerber, -anmelder; ~ **for a position** Stellenbewerber; ~ **for relief** Unterstützungssuchender; ~ **for shares** *(Br.)* Aktienzeichner;
~ **state** antragstellender Staat.

application *(appropriation)* Konkretisierung, *(customs)* Erhebung, Anwendungsgebiet, *(employment)* [Nutz]anwendung, Verwendung, Gebrauch, *(insurance)* Versicherungsaufnahmeantrag, *(patent law)* Patentanmeldung, *(for a position)* Bewerbung, Stellengesuch, Bewerbungsschreiben, *(request)* Ersuchen, Gesuch, Beantragung, Eingabe, Antrag, *(shares, Br.)* Zeichnung;
by ~ to the court durch Antrag beim Gericht; **on ~** auf Verlangen (Antrag, Ersuchen, Wunsch); **on ~ of three members** auf Ansuchen von drei Mitgliedern; **payable on ~** zahlbar bei Bestellung (Antragstellung); **upon the ~ of the debtor** auf Antrag des Schuldners;
analogical ~ sinngemäße Anwendung; ~ **blank** Bewerbungs-, Anmeldeformular, Anmeldeschein, -vordruck; **business ~** Antrag auf Erteilung einer Gewerbelizenz; **divisional ~s** *(patent law)* ausgeschiedene Anmeldungen; **due ~** rechtzeitige Anmeldung; **economic ~** wirtschaftliche Verwendung; **employment ~** Stellengesuch, Bewerbungsantrag, -schreiben; **only a few ~s** nur einzelne Bewerbungen; **formal ~** formelles Aufnahmegesuch; **handwritten ~** handschriftliche Bewerbung; **intent ~** ernsthafte Bewerbung; **interfering ~** *(patent law)* kollidierende Anmeldung; **loan ~** Kreditantrag; **mailed ~** schriftliche Bewerbung, schriftlicher Antrag; **membership ~** Mitglieds-, Aufnahme-, Zulassungsantrag; **mortgage-loan ~** Hypothekengesuch; **new ~s** Neuanmeldungen; **original ~** *(patent law)* Erstanmeldung; **ex-parte ~** Parteiantrag; **passport ~** Paßantrag; **peace-time ~** Friedensverwendung; **practical ~** praktische Anwendung, Nutzanwendung; **previous (prior) ~** *(patent law)* Voranmeldung, frühere Anmeldung; ~**s received so far** bisher vorliegende Anmeldungen; **restricted ~** begrenzte Anwendung; **territorial ~** räumlicher Geltungsbereich; **written ~** schriftliche Antrag, Bewerbungsschreiben;
~ **for an account** Kontoeröffnungsantrag; ~ **for adjournment** Vertagungsantrag; ~ **for admission** Aufnahmeantrag, -gesuch, Zulassungsgesuch, -antrag; ~ **to amend** Ergänzungsantrag; ~ **for an advance** Kreditantrag; ~ **for allotment** *(issue of shares)* Antrag auf Zuteilung, Zuteilungsantrag; ~ **for asylum** Asylgesuch; ~ **with full career details** Bewerbung mit vollständigem Lebenslauf; ~ **for change in classification** Einstufungs-, Abänderungsantrag; ~ **for copyright** Urheberschutzantrag; ~ **to the court** Antrag bei Gericht, Klageerhebung; ~ **for credit** Kreditantrag; ~ **of creditors** Gläubigerantrag; ~ **for discharge** Rehabilitierungsantrag [des Konkursschuldners]; ~ **for employ-**

ment Bewerbungsantrag; ~ **of funds** Kapital-, Mittelverwendung; ~ **for a grant** Zuschußantrag; ~ **for increase** Tariferhöhungsantrag; **industrial ~ of an invention** Nutzbarmachung einer Erfindung; ~ **for a job** Stellenbewerbung; ~ **to join** Beitrittsantrag; ~ **of a law** Rechts-, Gesetzesanwendung; ~ **for leave of absence** Urlaubsgesuch; ~ **for listing on the stock exchange** *(US)* Antrag auf offizielle Einführung [von Effekten] an der Börse; ~ **for a loan** Kredit-, Darlehnsantrag; ~ **for membership** Mitgliedschaftsantrag, Beitritts-, Aufnahmegesuch, -antrag; ~ **for a mortgage** Hypothekengesuch; ~ **for passport** Paßantrag; ~ **for a patent** Anmeldung eines Patents; ~ **for payment** Zahlungsersuchen, Mahnung; ~ **of payments** Zweckbestimmung von Zahlungen; ~ **of poison gas** Giftgasverwendung; ~ **for a position** *(post)* Stellenbewerbung, Stellungsgesuch; ~ **to postpone payment of tax** Steueraussetzungsantrag; ~ **for pority** Dringlichkeitsantrag; ~ **of proceeds** Verwendung des Gegenwertes, Mittelverwendung; **practical ~ of a process** Verfahrensanwendung; **continued ~ of provisions** Weitergeltung von Bestimmungen; ~ **for official quotation on the stock exchange** *(Br.)* Antrag auf offizielle Einführung von Aktien an der Börse, Börsenanmeldung; ~ **for receiver** Antrag auf Bestellung eines Konkursverwalters; ~ **for rediscount** Rediskontantrag; ~ **for registration** Eintragungsantrag; ~ **for registration of trademarks** Warenzeichenanmeldung; ~ **for release** Freigabeantrag; ~ **for relief** Unterstützungsgesuch; ~ **for renewal** Verlängerungsantrag; ~ **for respite** Stundungsgesuch; ~ **for revocation** *(patent, Br.)* Nichtigkeits-, Löschungsantrag; ~ **of a rule** Regelanwendung; ~ **for shares** *(Br.)* Aktienzeichnung; ~ **to the stock exchange for permission to deal** Börsenzulassungsantrag; ~ **of a system** Anwendung eines Systems; ~ **to stay proceedings** Antrag auf Verfahrenseinstellung; ~ **for a tariff** Zollanwendungsgebiet; ~ **for visa** Visumantrag; ~ **for winding up** Liquidationsantrag; ~ **in writing** schriftlicher Antrag;

to act on an ~ über einen Antrag entscheiden; **to approve an ~** einem Aufnahmeantrag stattgeben; **to back s. one's ~** jds. Bewerbung befürworten; **to consider an ~** Antrag berücksichtigen; **to draft an ~** Antrag aufsetzen; **to file an ~** Gesuch (Antrag, Anmeldung) einreichen; **to grant an ~ without objection** Gesuch anstandslos bewilligen; **to invite ~ for shares** *(Br.)* Öffentlichkeit zur Zeichnung von Aktien auffordern; **to make an ~ to the council of the stock exchange to be admitted to the official list** bei der Börsenzulassungsstelle offizielle Börseneinführung beantragen; **to make ~ to the court for directions** *(receiver)* Gericht um Weisungen bitten; **to make an ~ for membership** Aufnahmeantrag stellen, um seine Aufnahme einkommen; **to make ~ for receivership** Antrag auf Geschäftsaufsicht stellen; **to make ~ for the registration of a charge** Antrag auf Eintragung eines Grundpfandrechtes stellen; **to make ~ for shares** *(Br.)* Aktien zeichnen; **to reject an ~** Bewerbung (Bewerber) ablehnen, *(patent law)* Anmeldung zurückweisen; **to resubmit an ~** Antrag erneut vorlegen; **to secure an ~** [Versicherungs]antrag entgegenehmen; **to send in an ~** Gesuch einreichen; **to specify ~ of one's payments** Zahlungsaufforderung belegen; **to take charge of an ~** Antrag bearbeiten; **to withdraw an ~** *(patent law)* Anmeldung zurückziehen;

~ **backlogs** nicht bearbeitete Anträge, Antragsrückstände; ~ **call** erste Einzahlung [auf Aktien]; ~ **card** Anmeldekarte; ~ **close** Anmeldeschluß, letzter Bewerbungstag, -termin; ~ **date** *(patent)* Anmeldetag; ~ **documents** *(patent)* Anmeldeunterlagen; ~ **fee** Anmelde-, Antragsgebühr, *(subscription, Br.)* Zeichnungsgebühr; ~ **files** Bewerbungsakten, -unterlagen; ~ **form** Antrags-, Bewerbungsformular, -bogen, -vordruck, *(Br., deposit receipt)* Zeichnungs-, Einzahlungsformular, *(shares, Br.)* Zeichnungs-, Bezugsrechtsformular; ~ **formalities** Zuteilungsformalitäten; ~ **material** Bewerbungsunterlagen; ~ **money** *(Br.)* Hinterlegungs-, Zeichnungsbetrag [bei Aktienzeichnung]; ~ **papers** Bewerbungsunterlagen; ~ **procedure** Bewerbungsverfahren; ~ **receipt** *(Br.)* Zeichnungsbescheinigung; ~ **request** Verwendungsantrag, *(budget)* Etatsvorlage; ~ **right** *(Br.)* Zeichnungsberechtigung; ~ **slip** Antragszettel; ~ **stage** Antragsstadium; ~ **of funds statement** Ausweis über die Verwendung des Grundkapitals; ~ **techniques** Anwendungstechnik.

applied angewandt, praktisch;
~ **art** Gebrauchsgraphik; ~ **cost** verrechnete Gemeinkosten; ~ **mathematics** angewandte Mathematik; ~ **political economy** angewandte Volkswirtschaft.

apply *(v.)* **for** *(position)* sich bewerben um, nachsuchen, *(make request)* beantragen, ansuchen (einkommen), *(make use of)* verwenden, gebrauchen, anwenden, Anwendung finden;

~ **to s. o. for s. th.** j. um etw. angehen; **not to ~** *(law)* entfallen, nicht anwendbar sein;
~ **to an authority** bei einer Behörde vorstellig werden; ~ **the brake** Bremse betätigen, bremsen; ~ **to all cases** auf alle Fälle zutreffen; ~ **for consent** Genehmigung einholen; ~ **correctly** zweckentsprechend verwenden; ~ **to the consul for a visa** beim Konsulat ein Visum beantragen; ~ **to the court for directions** Gericht um Richtlinien ersuchen; ~ **for a credit line** Kreditantrag stellen; ~ **for an increase in salary** um eine Gehaltserhöhung einkommen, Gehaltszulage beantragen; ~ **for information** um Auskunft einkommen; ~ **for instructions** Informationen einholen; ~ **for a job** sich um eine Stelle bewerben; ~ **one's knowledge** seine Kenntnisse verwerten; ~ **the law** Gesetz (Recht) anwenden; ~ **by letter** schriftlich beantragen, schriftliches Gesuch einreichen; ~ **for a loan** Darlehen beantragen; ~ **to Mr. N.** bei Herrn N. zu erfragen; ~ **money for the benefit of poor people** Geld zur Steuerung der Armut zur Verfügung stellen; ~ **money to payment of debts** Geld für die Bezahlung von Schulden verwenden; ~ **at the office** sich im Büro melden; ~ **for a patent** Patent anmelden; ~ **a payment to a particular debt** Zahlung zur Begleichung einer bestimmten Schuld bestimmen; ~ **payments to the reduction of interest** Zahlungen zur Verkürzung der Zinsrückstände verwenden; ~ **for permission under the Bankruptcy Act** Antrag auf Eröffnung des Vergleichsverfahrens stellen; ~ **in person** sich persönlich bemühen; ~ **poison gas** Giftgas verwenden; ~ **for a position** sich um eine Stelle bewerben; ~ **for a purchasing permit** Bezugsschein beantragen; ~ **a rate of ...** in Anwendung bringen; ~ **a rule** Regel anwenden; ~ **for shares** *(Br.)* Aktien zeichnen; ~ **shares as collateral security** *(US)* Aktien als Kreditdeckung verwenden; ~ **to the stock exchange for permission to deal** Börsenzulassung beantragen; ~ **o. s. to one's studies** sich seinen Studien widmen; ~ **o. s. to a task** sich einer Sache verschreiben; ~ **the testimony to the case** Zeugenaussagen für ein Verfahren auswerten; ~ **without any time limit** zeitlich unbegrenzt Anwendung finden; ~ **o. s. to one's work** sich seiner Arbeit widmen; ~ **in writing** schriftliches Gesuch einreichen.

appoint *(v.)* *(date)* ansetzen, anberaumen, *(determine)* bestimmen, festsetzen, anordnen, vorschreiben, *(engage)* anstellen, *(fit out)* einrichten, ausrüsten, *(install)* bestellen, einsetzen, bestallen, *(nominate)* ernennen, berufen;
~ **an agent** Vertreter bestellen; ~ **s. o. during good behavio(u)r** j. nach einer Probezeit fest anstellen; ~ **as chairman** zum Vorsitzenden berufen; ~ **a committee** Ausschuß einsetzen, in einen Ausschuß berufen; ~ **correctly** zweckentsprechend verwenden; ~ **an executor** Testamentsvollstrecker einsetzen (vorsehen); ~ **an expert** Sachverständigen bestimmen; ~ **s. o. as governor** j. als Gouverneur einsetzen; ~ **as a guardian** zum Vormund bestellen; ~ **s. o. one's heir** *(US)* j. zu seinem Erben einsetzen; ~ **for life** auf Lebenszeit anstellen; ~ **a liquidator** Liquidator (Abwickler) einsetzen; ~ **s. o. [to be] manager** j. zum Vorstandsmitglied bestellen; ~ **s. o. as mayor** j. als Bürgermeister einsetzen; ~ **a meeting** Versammlungstermin festlegen; ~ **s. o. to a post** j. für einen Posten bestimmen; ~ **s. o. to a professorship** j. zum Professor ernennen, jem. eine Professur übertragen; ~ **a proxy** Bevollmächtigten ernennen; ~ **a receiver** Konkursverwalter bestellen; ~ **a time** Termin festsetzen; ~ **a trustee** Treuhänder einsetzen;
to draw per ~ per Saldo trassieren.

appointed ernannt, beauftragt, beamtet;
badly ~ schlecht ausgestattet; **permanently ~** fest angestellt; **time ~** festgesetzter Termin;
~ **by the articles** satzungsgemäß, bestallt; ~ **for life** auf Lebenszeit angestellt;
to be ~ judge zum Richter ernannt werden;
~ **agent** ständiger Vertreter; ~ **day** festgesetzter Tag, Termin, Stichtag; **on the ~ day** fristgerecht; ~ **dealer** Vertragshändler; ~ **space** *(advertising)* Platzvorschrift.

appointee *(US)* Kandidat, Ernannter, Beauftragter, *(beneficiary)* Nutznießer;
Cabinet-level ~ Beauftragter auf Kabinettsebene.

appointive term Beschäftigungszeit.

appointment *(appropriation of money)* Zweckbestimmung für einen Geldbetrag, *(commission)* Auftrag, *(date)* Anberaumung, *(decree)* Vorschrift, Verordnung, Beschluß, *(dentist)* Sitzung, *(designation of an heir)* Bestimmung des Erbberechtigten, *(determination)* Bestimmung, Festsetzung, *(employment)* Beschäftigung, *(engagement)* Verabredung, *(nomination)* Ernennung, Einsetzung, Bestallung, *(office)* Stelle, Anstellung, Amt, *(outfit)* Einrichtung, Mobiliar, *(power of ~)* Ausübung des Bestallungsrechtes;

after his ~ as professor nach seiner Berufung auf einen Lehrstuhl; by ~ nach Vereinbarung; by special ~ to His Majesty (Br.) königlicher Hoflieferant;

agency ~ Bestellung eines Vertreters; controversial ~ umstrittene Ernennung; definite ~ feste Anstellung; exclusive ~ ausschließliches Berufungsrecht; excessive ~ Vollmachtsüberschreitung; fraudulent ~ betrügerisch ausgeübte Vollmacht; honorary ~ Ehrenamt; mistaken ~ Fehlbesetzung; new ~ Neubesetzung; permanent ~ feste Anstellung, Dauerstellung; probationary ~ Einstellung auf Probe, Probeanstellung; public ~ staatliche Anstellung; senior ~ Einstellung eines leitenden Angestellten; temporary ~ Ernennung auf Widerruf;

~ of an administrator Testamentvollstreckereinsetzung; ~ of an agent Vertreterbestellung; ~ of auditors Bestellung der Revisoren; ~ of a committee Ausschußeinsetzung; ~ by the court gerichtliche Bestellung, Bestellung durch das Gericht; ~ of a director Vorstandsbestallung; ~ of a governor Einsetzung eines Gouverneurs; ~ of a guardian Bestellung eines Vormundes, Vormundsbestellung; ~ of an heir (US) Erbeinsetzung; ~s for a hotel Ausstattung eines Hotels; ~ for life Anstellung auf Lebenszeit, Lebensstellung; ~ of a liquidator Einsetzung eines Liquidators (Abwicklers); ~ as manager Bestellung zum Vorstandsmitglied; ~s of an office Amtseinkünfte, Dienstbezüge, Sporteln; ~ of a proxy Bestellung eines Bevollmächtigten; ~ of a receiver Bestellung eines Konkursverwalters; ~ of a trustee Treuhändereinsetzung, -bestellung, Einsetzung, Berufung eines Treuhänders, (in bankruptcy) Konkursverwalterbestellung; ~ by will testamentarische Einsetzung (Bestellung);

to ask for an ~ um eine Unterredung ersuchen; to be here on ~ bestellt sein; to break an ~ Verabredung nicht einhalten können (absagen); to confirm an ~ Ernennung bestätigen; to decline an ~ Übernahme eines Amtes ablehnen; to fix an ~ Verabredung treffen; to get an ~ Stelle bekommen; to have an ~ bestellt sein, Verabredung haben; to have an ~ for the evening abends verabredet sein; to hold an ~ Stelle innehaben; to keep an ~ Verabredung einhalten, Termin wahrnehmen; to make an ~ Verabredung treffen, Zusammenkunft festsetzen; to make the ~ in writing Anstellungsvertrag abschließen; to meet s. o. by ~ j. auf Verabredung treffen, sich mit jem. verabredet haben; to miss an ~ Verabredung verpassen; to obtain s. one's ~ for a post jds. Ernennung für eine Stelle durchsetzen; to receive one's ~ as minister seine Ernennungsurkunde als Minister erhalten; to take up an ~ in industry in der Industrie Verwendung finden; ~s board (Br.) amtliche Stellenvermittlung für leitende Angestellte, Büro für die Vermittlung von Führungskräften; ~s book Terminkalender; ~s card Terminplan, -zettel; ~ grant Anstellungszuschuß; ~s officer Personalsachbearbeiter; ~s schedule Terminkalender.

appointor Bestallender, Bestallungsbehörde, (law of inheritance) Erbe mit dem Recht der Nacherbenbestimmung.

apportion (v.) auf-, ver-, zuteilen, zumessen, zuweisen, (shares) repartieren, gleichmäßig verteilen;
~ the costs Kosten umlegen (aufteilen); ~ the costs to the sides Gerichtskosten anteilmäßig auf die Parteien verteilen; ~ losses evenly over the year Verluste gleichmäßig über das ganze Jahr verteilen; ~ part of profits to a particular tax year Gewinnteile steuerlich aufteilen; ~ a sum among several people Betrag unter verschiedene Leute [gleichmäßig] verteilen; ~ on a time basis zeitlich umlegen.

apportionable aufteilbar;
~ costs Gemein-, Schlüsselkosten.

apportioned, to be entfallen [auf];
~ tax (US) aufgeteilte Steuer.

apportionment Verteilung, Aufteilung, gleichmäßige Zuteilung, (shares) Repartierung;
prorata ~ anteilsmäßige Aufteilung;
~ of contract Sukzessivlieferungsvertrag; ~ of cost Kostenumlegung, -verteilung; ~ of income Einkommensverteilung; ~ of indirect cost Gemeinkostenumlage; ~ of the net profit Ausschüttung des Nettogewinns; ~ of directors' remuneration anteilsmäßige Verwaltungsrats-, Vorstandsvergütung; ~ of rent Aufteilung der Grundstückspacht; ~ of representatives (US) Festlegung der Abgeordnetenzahl für die Einzelstaaten; ~ of a tax Steueraufteilung;
~ clearance (inspector of taxes, Br.) Gewinnaufteilungsgenehmigung; ~ distribution (passenger traffic) Teilstreckenaufteilung; ~ sheet Aufteilungsbogen.

appose (v.) one's signature to a document seine Unterschrift unter eine Urkunde setzen.

apposition Beifügung, Zusatz.

appraisable abschätzbar, bewertbar.

appraisal [Ab]schätzung, (balance sheet) Bewertung, Wertbestimmung, -ansatz, -ermittlung, (appraised value) Taxwert, (performance) [Leistungs]beurteilung, (tariff) Zollbewertung;
business property ~ Bewertung eines Geschäftsgrundstücks; condemnation ~ Enteignungstaxe; critical ~ kritische Würdigung; dwelling ~ Wohngrundstücksschätzung; expert ~ Abschätzung (Bewertung) durch Sachverständige; income property ~ Vermögensschätzung; land ~ Grundstücksschätzung; leasehold ~ Pacht-, Miettaxe; property ~ Vermögensschätzung; real-estate ~ Grundstücksschätzung, -bewertung; research ~ Bewertung der Forschungstätigkeit; retrospective ~ Bewertung zu einem früheren Zeitpunkt;
~ of damage Schadensabschätzung; ~ for fixing of utility rates Abschätzung zur Festlegung öffentlicher Gebührnisse; ~ for inheritance taxation purposes Abschätzung zur Festsetzung der Erbschaftssteuer (zu Erbschaftssteuerzwecken); ~ for insurance Abschätzung (Bewertung) zu Versicherungszwecken; ~ of investment Anlagenbewertung; ~ of agricultural land Bewertung landwirtschaftlich genutzten Geländes; ~ for taxation purpose Abschätzung zu Steuerzwecken;
to make an ~ schätzen, Bewertung vornehmen;
~ clause (insurance) Abschätzungsklausel; ~ committee Schätzungskommission, Bewertungsausschuß; ~ company Bewertungs-, Schätzerfirma; ~ fees Schätzgebühren; ~ interview Bewertungsgespräch; ~ profile Bewertungsskala; ~ program(me) Programm zur Leistungsbeurteilung, Bewertungsprogramm; ~ questionnaire Bewertungsfragebogen; ~ report Schätzungsbericht; ~ surplus (US) aus Höherbewertung von Anlagegütern gebildete Rücklagen; ~ technique Bewertungsverfahren.

appraise (v.) abschätzen, bewerten, Wert bestimmen, berechnen, begutachten, taxieren;
~ a credit risk Kreditrisiko berechnen; ~ a loss by fire Feuerschaden abschätzen; ~ a patent Patent bewerten; ~ property for taxation Grundstück steuerlich veranlagen; ~ a stock of goods Warenlager bewerten (abschätzen).

appraised value Taxwert, Schätz[ungs]wert.

appraisement (valuation) [Ab]schätzung, Taxierung, Wertbestimmung, -ermittlung, -feststellung, Bewertung, (value) geschätzter Wert, Taxwert;
official ~ amtliche Schätzung, Bewertung durch Sachverständige;
~ of the productive capacity Bonitierung der Produktionskapazität;
~ committee Schätzungsausschuß, Bewertungskommission.

appraiser Schätzer, Taxator, (insurance) Schadensabschätzer, -bearbeiter, (US) beeidigter Schätzer, gerichtlich bestellter Sachverständiger;
general ~ (US) Zollsachverständiger; merchant ~ (US) sachverständiger Schätzer bei Zollwertfestsetzungen; official ~ amtlicher Schätzer, Abschätzungsbeamter; sworn ~ beeidigter Schätzer, vereidigter Gutachter;
~'s fees Taxgebühren, Schätzungskosten; ~'s store Zollager.

appreciable [ab]schätz-, taxier-, bewertbar;
not in any ~ degree kaum nennenswert.

appreciate (v.) (improve) sich im Wert verbessern, (raise in value) Wert erhöhen, im Wert steigen, Wertsteigerung erfahren, an Wert zunehmen, (valuate) bewerten, taxieren, [ab]schätzen;
~ fixed assets Anlagegüter höher bewerten; ~ the coinage Münzwert erhöhen; ~ a gift Geschenk zu schätzen wissen; ~ greatly (land) im Wert erheblich steigen; ~ a holiday Ferientag genießen.

appreciated surplus auf Neubewertung beruhender Gewinn.

appreciation (balance sheet) Aufwertung von Anlagen, (book) Würdigung, (investment fund) Wertzuwachs, (revaluation) Aufwertung, (rise in value) Wertzuwachs, -erhöhung, -steigerung, -zunahme, Preiserhöhung, (valuation) [Ab]schätzung, (just valuation) Wertschätzung, Würdigung;
musical ~ Musikverständnis; recorded ~ nachgewiesener Wertzuwachs; sincere ~ dankbare Würdigung; value ~ Wertabschätzung;
~ of fixed assets (US) Höherbewertung von Anlagegütern; ~ of a currency Währungsaufwertung; ~ in prices Steigen der Preise, Kurs-, Preissteigerung; ~ of real estate Wertzuwachs eines Grundstücks; ~ of stocks Höherbewertung der Lagervorräte; ~ in value Wertsteigerung;
to show an ~ im Wert gestiegen sein; to write an ~ of a new symphony neue Symphonie würdigen;
~ audience verständnisvolles Publikum; ~ people Kunstliebhaber; ~ possibilities (potentialities) Wertsteigerungsmöglichkeiten; ~ surplus Kapitalzuwachs aus Werterhöhungen.

appreciator Taxator.

apprehend *(v.)* *(criminal)* fassen, ergreifen, festnehmen, gefangennehmen, -setzen, verhaften, *(understand)* verstehen, begreifen, erfassen.

apprehensible verständlich, begreiflich, wahrnehmbar.

apprehension Ergreifung, Festnahme, Gefangennahme, Verhaftung, *(understanding)* Wahrnehmung, Auffassungsvermögen, Verständnis;
  according to popular ~ nach landläufigen Vorstellungen; **quick of ~** schnell auffassend;
  to be under some ~s about a matter Angelegenheit mit Beunruhigung betrachten; **to feel ~ for s. one's safety** Befürchtungen um jds. Sicherheit hegen.

apprehensive leicht auffassend, *(anxious)* ängstlich;
  to be ~ for one's life um sein Leben besorgt sein;
  ~ period *(insurance)* Zeitspanne erhöhter Gefahr.

apprentice Volontär, Eleve, Lehrling, Lehrjunge, -bursche, Auszubildender;
  commercial ~ Handelslehrling; **fresh ~** unerfahrener Lehrling; **girl ~** Lehrmädchen; **idle ~** fauler Lehrling; **infant ~** minderjähriger Lehrling; **outdoor ~** außerhalb wohnender Lehrling;
  ~ *(v.)* **s. o.** j. in die Lehre geben;
  to bind s. o. ~ j. in die Lehre geben; **to fasten an ~** Lehrlingsvertrag (Ausbildungsvertrag) abschließen; **to put out as ~** in die Lehre geben; **to recruit ~s** Lehrlinge einstellen; **to take an ~** Lehrling annehmen; **to turn over one's ~ to another master** seinen Lehrling an einen anderen Lehrherrn abtreten;
  ~ age Lehrlingsjahre, Ausbildungszeit; **~ compositor** Setzerlehrling; **~ fee** Lehrgeld; **~ machine fitter** Maschinenschlosserlehrling; **~ program(me)** [Lehrlings]ausbildungsprogramm; **~ rate (wages)** Lehrlingsgeld, -lohn, Ausbildungszuschuß; **~ teacher** [Lehrlings]ausbilder; **~ training** Lehrlingsausbildung.

apprenticeable | occupation Lehrberuf; **~ trade** erlernbares Handwerk, Beruf mit anerkannter Lehrlingsausbildung.

apprenticed, to be in der Lehre sein; **to become ~** als Lehrling eingestellt werden.

apprenticeship [kaufmännische] Lehre, Lehrzeit, -jahre, Lehrlingsstand;
  to be through one's ~ seine Lehre (Ausbildung) beendet haben; **to conclude one's ~** auslernen; **to enter into ~** mit der Lehrlingszeit beginnen; **to finish one's ~** seine Lehrzeit (Ausbildung) beenden; **to go through one's ~** seine Lehrzeit durchmachen; **to serve (be serving) one's ~ with** in der Lehre sein;
  ~ agreement Ausbildungs-, Lehrlingsvertrag; **~ committee** Lehrlingsausschuß; **~ contract** Ausbildungs-, Lehrlingsvertrag; **~ deed** Ausbildungs-, Lehrlingsvertrag; **~ executive** Lehrlingsausbilder; **~ period** Ausbildungszeit; **~ program(me)** Lehrlings-, Ausbildungsprogramm; **~ ratio** Lehrlingsquote; **~ regulations** Ausbildungsbestimmungen für Lehrlinge; **~ requirements** Vorbedingungen für die Annahme als Lehrling; **~ scheme** [Lehrlings]ausbildungsplan; **~ system** Lehrlingswesen; **~ training** Lehrlingsausbildung; **~ training agreement** Ausbildungs-, Lehrvertrag.

apprise *(v.)* in Kenntnis setzen, benachrichtigen.

approach Herangehen, Annäherung, *(access)* Auffahrt, Zufahrt, Zugang, Zutritt, *(advertising)* Aufmerksamkeitserreger, Aufhänger, Blickfänger im Anzeigentextanfang, *(airplane)* Anflug, *(manner of taking)* Verhalten, Herangehen, Stellungnahme, *(mil.)* Anmarschweg, Vormarschstraße, *(tentative steps)* Annäherungsversuch;
  easy of ~ leicht zugänglich;
  ~es Annäherungsversuche;
  advertising ~ Aufmerksamkeitserreger; **analytical ~** analytische Methode; **buy-and-hold ~** *(securities)* Durchhaltepolitik; **damn-the-torpedo ~** von möglichen Repressalien unbeeinflußte Einstellung; **elevated ~** Rampe; **fresh ~** unkonventionelle Einstellung; **go-slow ~** vorsichtiges Vorgehen; **literalist ~** buchstabengetreue Auslegung; **meat-axe ~** Fleischhackermethode; **missed ~** *(airplane)* Fehlanflug; **personal ~** persönliche Ansprache; **show-business ~** Annäherungsmethode; **velvet-glove ~** Samthandschuhmethode;
  ~ to the tax revenue Einschätzung des Steueraufkommens; **~ to a subject** Stellungnahme zu einem Thema; **planned ~ to training** planmäßige Anlernmethode;
  ~ *(v.)* herangehen, sich nähern, *(airplane)* anfliegen, *(make offer)* [mit einem Angebot] herantreten, sich wenden;
  ~ s. o. an j. herantreten; **~ s. o. with a bribe** sich j. mit Bestechungen zugänglich machen; **the city** sich der Stadt nähern; **~ one's employer about an increase in salary** seinem Arbeitgeber um Gehaltserhöhung ansprechen; **~ a purchaser** an einen Kunden herantreten; **~ a certain standard** bestimmte Norm

erreichen; **~ a subject** sich mit einem Thema befassen; **~ a task** an eine Aufgabe herangehen;
  to find a common ~ gemeinsame Basis finden; **to make ~es to s. o.** Annäherungsversuche bei jem. unternehmen; **to reflect the ~ of the Administration** Regierungsansicht widerspiegeln; **to restructure its whole ~ to the customer** Kundenwerbung auf eine völlig neue Basis stellen;
  ~ flight Zielanflug; **~ path** Anflugweg; **~ ramp** Zufahrtsrampe; **~ section** Annäherungsabschnitt; **~ surveyance radar** Anflugüberwachungsradar.

approachability Zugänglichkeit.

approachable zugänglich, erreichbar.

approbate *(v.)* Erlaubnis (Genehmigung) erteilen, anerkennen, genehmigen, *(doctor)* lizensieren, approbieren, *(gift)* annehmen.

approbation Zustimmung, Genehmigung, Billigung, *(doctor)* Approbation;
  on ~ zur Ansicht, auf Probe;
  to buy on ~ auf Probe kaufen.

appropriate *(v.)* *(allocate)* bewilligen, [Geld] zuweisen, [zweck-] bestimmen, einer Zweckbestimmung zuführen, *(bankruptcy proceedings)* aussondern, *(executor)* Nachlaß verteilen, *(take possession)* sich aneignen, Besitz ergreifen, beschlagnahmen, *(use)* verwenden;
  ~ to a debt auf eine Schuld anrechnen; **~ funds** Geldmittel bereitstellen; **~ goods to the contract** Eigentum konkretisieren; **~ s. one's ideas** sich jds. Ideen aneignen; **~ a piece of land** Stück Land in Besitz nehmen; **~ a payment** Zweckbestimmung einer Zahlung festlegen; **~ profits** Gewinne verwenden; **~ to free reserve** in die freie Rücklage einstellen; **~ £ 50.000 for the new school building** 50.000 £ für die Errichtung der Schulneubauten ansetzen; **~ unlawfully** sich rechtswidrig aneignen;
  ~ *(a.)* *(appurtenant)* eigen, *(suitable)* angemessen, passend, geeignet, gebührend, zugehörig, sachdienlich;
  for ~ action zur weiteren Veranlassung; **~ earnings** *(US)* den Rücklagen zugewiesene Gewinn; **~ funds** zweckgebundene Mittel; **to refer to the ~ quarter** an die zuständige Stelle weiterleiten; **to write a letter in ~ style** passenden Ton in einem Brief anschlagen; **at the ~ time** zur gegebenen Zeit.

appropriated | earnings *(US)* den Rücklagen zugewiesene Gewinne; **~ funds** *(US)* zweckgebundene (bereitgestellte) Mittel; **~ surplus** *(US)* zweckgebundene Rücklagen.

appropriateness Verwendbarkeit.

appropriation *(application)* Anwendung, *(bankruptcy proceedings)* Aussonderung, *(dedication)* Zueignung, *(funds set apart, US)* Bereitstellungsfonds, *(law of contract)* [Eigentums]konkretisierung, *(parl.)* Haushaltsmittelbereitstellung, *(seizure)* Aneignung, Inbesitznahme, *(setting apart of funds)* Bereitstellung, Zuweisung [von Mitteln], Geldbewilligung, -zuwendung, [Zweck]bestimmung, *(use)* Verwendung, Benutzung;
  ~s bereitgestellte Haushaltsmittel, *(US)* Rücklagen;
  advertising ~s genehmigte Werbefonds, genehmigte Werbemittel; **budgetary ~s** bewilligte Haushaltsmittel, Ansätze des Haushaltsplans; **contractual ~s** *(US)* satzungsmäßige Rücklagen; **discretionary ~s** *(US)* freie Rücklagen; **express ~** ausdrückliche Zweckbestimmung; **itemized (segregated) ~** *(US)* detaillierte Mittelzuweisung; **legal ~s** *(US)* gesetzliche Rücklagen; **new ~s** neu bereitgestellte Mittel; **specific ~** ausdrückliche Zweckbestimmung; **statutory ~s** *(US)* satzungsgemäße Rücklagen; **unbudgeted ~s** im Haushaltsplan nicht vorgesehene Posten; **unspent ~s** nicht ausgegebene Kapitalmittel, *(budgeting)* Haushaltsüberschüsse;
  ~ for advertising genehmigter Werbeetat, genehmigte Werbemittel; **~-in-aid** *(budgeting)* Eigenverwaltung haushaltsfreier Mittel; **~ to the contract** Konkretisierung des Eigentums; **~ by debtor** Zweckbestimmung durch den Schuldner; **~ of an estate** Nachlaßverteilung [durch den Testamentsvollstrecker]; **~ of funds** Zahlungsanweisung, Mittel-, Geldzuweisung, -bereitstellung, Zuweisung von Mitteln; **~ of unascertained goods** Konkretisierung einer Gattungsschuld; **~ of land** Bereitstellung von Grundstücken zum Gemeingebrauch; **~s for losses** Bereitstellungen für Verluste, Verlustrückstellungen; **~ of money to a debt** Verrechnung (Anrechnung) auf die Schuldsumme; **~ of payments** Zweckbestimmung von Zahlungen; **~ of a piece of land** Inbesitznahme eines Grundstückes; **~ of profit** Verwendung des Gewinns, Gewinnverwendung; **proposed ~ of profits** Gewinnverteilungsvorschlag; **~ of net profit** Verwendung des Reingewinns; **~ to free reserve** Rücklageneinstellung; **~s of surplus** Bildung von Rücklagen, *(US)* Rücklagen-, Reservenbildung; **~ of water** Wasserableitung aus öffentlichen Gewässern;

to make ~ for the payment of debts Vorkehrungen zur Schuldentilgung treffen; to trim one's ~ by 4 per cent bereitgestellte
Mittel um 4% kürzen; to vote the ~ Etat genehmigen;
~ account (US) Bereitstellungs-, Rückstellungskonto; ~ Act
(Br.) Haushaltsgesetz; ~ bill Kreditbewilligungsvorlage,
(parl.) Haushaltsvorlage, Ausgabebudget; ~ committee (US)
Haushaltsausschuß; ~ mark Verwendungsgrenze; ~ ordinance
Haushaltsverordnung; ~ request Vorlage des Haushaltsvoran-
schlages; ~ trust Investmentgesellschaft mit sofortiger Anlage
der zufließenden Mittel.

approval Zustimmung, Genehmigung, Gutbefund, Annahme,
Billigung, Entlastungserteilung, (of account) Richtigbefund,
in need of (subject to) ~ genehmigungsbedürftig, -pflichtig; on
~ versuchsweise, zur Ansicht (Probe); with the ~ of the authorities mit behördlicher Genehmigung;
court ~ Genehmigung durch das Gericht; House ~ (Br.)
Zustimmung des Plenums; lightning-like ~ sofortige Zustimmung; majority ~ Zustimmung der Mehrheit; official ~ amtliche Genehmigung; previous (prior) ~ [vorherige] Genehmigung; obligatory ~ Genehmigungsvorbehalt; qualified ~
bedingte Zustimmung; shareholders' (stockholders', US) ~
Genehmigung durch die Anteilseigner; written ~ schriftliche
Genehmigung;
~ of an account Kontoanerkennung; ~ of the acts of directors
Entlastung des Vorstands; ~ of the balance sheet Genehmigung der Bilanz, Bilanzverabschiedung; ~ by the court gerichtliche Genehmigung; ~ of minutes Genehmigung des
Protokolls; ~ of a nomination Bestätigung einer Ernennung; ~
of profit and loss account Genehmigung der Gewinn- und
Verlustrechnung;
to be subject to s. one's ~ von jds. Genehmigung abhängen; to
express one's ~ sich mit etw. einverstanden erklären; to give ~
Genehmigung erteilen, genehmigen, billigen; to meet with s.
one's ~ jds. Zustimmung finden; to meet with a lively ~ lebhaftes Echo finden; to receive s. one's ~ jds. Genehmigung erhalten; to seek s. one's ~ jds. Genehmigung einholen; to stamp ~
on a document einer Urkunde durch Siegelung Rechtskraft
verleihen; to submit for ~ zur Genehmigung vorlegen;
~ acquisition (bookseller) Ansichtsbesorgung; ~ book (philately) Ansichtsalbum; on-~ fee (bookseller) Ansichtsgebühr; ~
sale Kauf auf Probe; ~ sheet (philately) Ansichtssendung.

approve (v.) genehmigen, billigen, zustimmen, bestätigen, ratifizieren, gutheißen, entlasten;
~ of s. o. gute Meinung von jem. haben; ~ an account Richtigkeit einer Rechnung anerkennen; ~ of an appointment Ernennung bestätigen; ~ [of] the acts of directors dem Vorstand
Entlastung erteilen; ~ the amounts set aside to reserve Rücklagenzuführung bewilligen; ~ a balance sheet Bilanz[abschluß]
genehmigen; ~ a decision Urteil bestätigen; ~ the directors'
report dem Vorstand Entlastung erteilen; ~ a dissertation Dissertation annehmen; ~ into law Gesetzeskraft verleihen; ~ o. s.
as good lawyer sich als guter Jurist erweisen; ~ of a marriage
einer Heirat zustimmen; ~ the minutes Protokoll genehmigen;
~ a nomination Ernennung bestätigen; ~ profit and loss account
Gewinn- und Verlustrechnung genehmigen; ~ waste land
Brachland kultivieren.

approved anerkannt, erprobt, bewährt;
read and ~ gelesen und genehmigt; ~ by genehmigt durch;
federally ~ von der Regierung gebilligt;
to be ~ of Anklang finden, (proposal) angenommen sein; to
stand ~ ratifiziert sein;
~ acceptance einwandfreies Akzept; ~ bill einwandfreier
Wechsel; ~ friend bewährter Freund; ~ indorsed notes zusätzlich girierte Solawechsel; ~ price genehmigter Preis; ~ school
(Br.) Fürsorgeinternat, -anstalt, Hilfsschule, Besserungsanstalt; ~ stamp Genehmigungsstempel, -vermerk.

approver (Br., law) Kronzeuge.

approving the minutes Protokollgenehmigung.

approximate (v.) annähern, nahe kommen, fast erreichen,
angleichen;
~ progressively (EC) schrittweise angleichen;
~ (a.) annähernd, ungefähr, beiläufig;
~ amount ungefährer Wert (Betrag); ~ calculation annähernde
Schätzung, ungefähre Berechnung, Kostenüberschlag, Näherungsrechnung; ~ formula Faustformel; ~ result annähernd
richtiges Ergebnis; ~ value Annäherungswert.

approximation annähernde Berechnung, [An]näherungswert;
close ~ genaue Näherung;
~ of municipal laws (EC) Angleichung der innerstaatlichen
Rechtsvorschriften;
~ error Näherungsfehler; ~ method Näherungsverfahren.

appurtenance Anhängsel, Zusatz, Zubehör;
~s Gerätschaften, Ausrüstung, -stattung, (law) Realrechte.

appurtenant [da]zugehörig.

apron Talon, (airdrome) Hallenvorplatz, -feld, (car) Schutzblech, (footpath) Fußsteig, (runway) Landebahn;
to be tied to one's mother's ~ strings an Mutters Schürzenzipfel
hängen; to be tied to a woman's ~ strings unter dem Pantoffel
einer Frau stehen; ~-string tenure Nutznießungsrecht des Ehemannes am eingebrachten Gut.

apt geeignet, tauglich, fähig;
~ time geeigneter Zeitpunkt; ~ words zutreffende Formulierung.

aptitude Eignung, Befähigung, Begabung, Fähigkeit, Talent,
(intelligence) Auffassungsgabe, Intelligenz;
~ for work Arbeitseignung;
~ test Eignungsprüfung.

arable anbau-, kulturfähig, bestellbar;
~ land Ackerland, Anbaufläche.

arbiter Schlichter, Schiedsrichter, -mann;
industry-unions ~ Wirtschaftsschiedsrichter.

arbitrable schiedsgerichtsfähig, schiedsgerichtlich beilegbar.

arbitrage Arbitrage, (arbitration) Schiedsspruch, schiedsgerichtliche Entscheidung, Schiedsgerichtsverfahren;
compound ~ Mehrfacharbitrage, Arbitrage über mehrere Zwischenplätze; currency ~ Devisenarbitrage; direct (simple) ~
(Br.) Einfach-, direkte Arbitrage; indirect (triangular) ~ (US)
Arbitrage in drei verschiedenen Währungen, indirekte Arbitrage; interest ~ Zinsarbitrage; stock ~ Effektenarbitrage;
~ in bills [of exchange] Wechsel-, Devisenarbitrage; ~ in bullion
Goldarbitrage; ~ in securities Effektenarbitrage;
~ dealer Arbitragehändler; ~ dealings Arbitragegeschäft; ~
house Bankhaus, das besondere Arbitragegeschäfte betreibt; ~
stocks Arbitragewerte; ~ syndicate Arbitragesyndikat; ~
transaction Arbitragegeschäft.

arbitrager, arbitragist Arbitragehändler.

arbitral schiedsrichterlich;
~ award Schiedsspruch; to abide by an ~ award Schiedsspruch
anerkennen; ~ body Schiedsstelle, -instanz, Schiedsorgan; ~
case Schiedssache, -angelegenheit; ~ clause Schiedsklausel;
decree ~ Schiedsspruch; ~ facilities Schiedseinrichtungen; ~
jurisdiction Schiedsgerichtsbarkeit; ~ legislation schiedsgerichtliche Gesetzgebung; ~ settlement schiedsgerichtliche Beilegung; ~ tribunal Schiedsgerichtshof.

arbitrament schiedsgerichtliche Entscheidung.

arbitrariness Willkür[lichkeit].

arbitrary (transportation) festvereinbarter Tarif;
~ (a.) willkürlich, eigenmächtig, (discretionary) in das Ermessen gestellt;
~ action Willkürakt; ~ assessment auf Schätzungen beruhende
Veranlagung; ~ decision Ermessensentscheidung; ~ government Willkürherrschaft; ~ method of profit distribution (insurance) mechanisches Dividendensystem; ~ notice einseitige
(willkürliche) Kündigung; ~ number beliebige Zahl; ~ origin
(statistics) willkürlicher Nullpunkt; ~ power unbeschränkte
Ermessensbefugnis; ~ price willkürlicher Preis; ~ punishment
Strafe nach freiem Ermessen; ~ use willkürliche Anwendung.

arbitrate (v.) [durch Schiedsspruch] schlichten, Schiedsspruch
fällen, schiedsrichterlich entscheiden, (act as arbitrator) als
Schiedsrichter fungieren (amtieren), (stock exchange) durch
Kursvergleich feststellen;
~ a case über eine Sache schiedsrichterlich verhandeln; ~
between parties to a suit in einem schiedsgerichtlichen Verfahren tätig werden.

arbitration Schlichtungs-, Schiedsverfahren, schiedsrichterli-
ches Verfahren, (award) Schiedsspruch, schiedsrichterliche
Entscheidung;
by ~ schiedsrichterlich, schiedlich;
commercial ~ wirtschaftliches Schiedsgerichtswesen, Schiedsgerichtswesen der Wirtschaft, Handels[schieds]gerichtsbar-
keit; compound ~ Mehrfacharbitrage, Arbitrage über mehrere
Zwischenplätze; compulsory ~ Zwangsschlichtung, obligatorisches Schiedsverfahren; direct (simple) ~ (Br.) Einfach-,
direkte Arbitrage; indirect (triangular) ~ (US) Arbitrage in
drei verschiedenen Währungen; industrial ~ gewerbliche
Schiedsgerichtsbarkeit, Gewerbegerichtsbarkeit, Schlichtungsverfahren; international ~ internationales Schiedsgericht; labo(u)r ~ betriebliche Schiedsgerichtsbarkeit; stock ~
Effektenarbitrage; terminal ~ abschließendes Schiedsgerichtsverfahren; voluntary ~ vereinbarte (freiwillige) Schiedsgerichtsbarkeit, frei vereinbarte schiedsgerichtliche Regelung;
wage ~ Schiedsgericht in Lohnstreitigkeiten;

~ **of exchange** Arbitragerechnung, Wechselarbitrage, -kursvergleich, Devisenarbitrage;

to compromise to an ~ Schiedsvertrag eingehen; **to go to** ~ sich einem Schiedsgericht unterwerfen, schiedsgerichtliche Entscheidung einholen; **to have recourse to** ~ Schiedsgericht anrufen; **to leave a matter to** ~ Sache schiedsrichterlicher Erledigung überlassen; **to refer a dispute to** ~ an ein Schiedsgericht verweisen, Streitigkeit schiedsgerichtlich beilegen lassen; **to refer future disputes exclusively to English** ~ zukünftige Auseinandersetzungen ausschließlich englischer Schiedsgerichtstätigkeit unterstellen; **to settle by** ~ schiedsgerichtlich beilegen, schlichten; **to submit to** ~ sich einem schiedsrichterlichen Verfahren unterwerfen;

~ **Act** *(Br.)* Schiedsordnung; ~ **agency** Schlichtungsstelle; ~ **agreement** Schiedsvertrag, -vereinbarung, -abkommen; ~ **award** Schiedsspruch; ~ **board** *(US)* Schlichtungsausschuß, -amt, -stelle, Einigungsamt; ~ **board decision** Schiedsspruch; ~ **bond** schriftlich anerkannte Schiedsgerichtsvereinbarung; ~ **charges** Schiedsgerichtsgebühren; ~ **clause** Schieds[gericht s]klausel; **contractual** ~ **clause** vertraglich vereinbarte Schiedsgerichtsklausel; ~ **committee (commission)** Schlichtungs-, Vermittlungs-, Schiedsausschuß; ~ **condition** Schiedsbestimmung; ~ **court** Schiedsgericht[shof]; ~ **court for trade disputes** Gewerbegericht; **to belong before an** ~ **court** vor ein Schiedsgericht gehören; ~ **procedure governing disputed firings** Schiedsverfahren wegen strittiger Arbeiterentlassungen; ~ **hearing** Anhörung im Schiedsgerichtsverfahren; ~ **institutions** schiedsgerichtliche Einrichtungen; ~ **law** Schiedsrecht; ~ **medium** Schiedsorgan; ~ **panel** Schiedsgremium; ~ **proceedings** Schlichtungs-, Schiedsgerichtsverfahren; ~ **process** Schiedsgerichtsverfahren; ~ **rules** Richtlinien für die Abwicklung von Schiedssachen; ~ **service** Schiedstätigkeit; ~ **statute** Schiedsordnung; ~ **treaty** Schieds[gerichts]vertrag; ~ **tribunal** Schiedsgericht.

arbitrational schiedsgerichtlich, -richterlich.

arbitrative mit schiedsrichterlichen Funktionen ausgestattet, schiedsrichterlich.

arbitrator Schiedsrichter, -mann, Schlichter;

alternate ~ Schiedsmann-Stellvertreter; **party-appointed** ~ von einer Schiedspartei benannter Schiedsrichter; **third** ~ Schiedsobmann;

~ **of average** Dispacheur;

to act as ~ Schiedsrichter (schiedsrichterlich tätig) sein; **to appoint as** ~ als Schiedsrichter einsetzen; **to constitute s. o. as** j. als Schiedsrichter benennen; **to refer to an** ~ an einen Schiedsrichter verweisen;

~'**s award (finding)** Schiedsspruch, -urteil, schiedsgerichtliche Entscheidung.

arbitratorship Schiedsrichteramt.

arcade Arkadengang;

amusement ~ Arkadenviertel.

arcana of political intrigue Hintergründiges der politischen Intrige.

arch, triumphal Triumphbogen.

archetype Vorbild, Modell, Original, *(coins)* Justiergewicht.

archie *(Br., sl.)* Flak.

architect Architekt, Baumeister;

~'**s certificate** Baufortgangsbescheinigung; ~ **of one's own fortune** des eigenen Glückes Schmied.

architectural baulich, architektonisch;

~ **conservation** Denkmalschutz; ~ **design** Raumgestaltung; ~ **engineer** Bauingenieur; ~ **engineering** Hochbau; ~ **establishment** tonangebende Architektengruppe; ~ **planning** Gebäudeplanung; ~ **practice** Architekturbüro.

architecture bauliche Anordnung, Architektur, *(edifice)* Bauwerk, Baulichkeit, Gebäude.

archival *(a.)* urkundlich.

archives Archiv, Urkundensammelstelle, Dokumentensammlung;

family ~ Familienarchiv; **national** ~ Staatsarchiv.

archivist Archivleiter.

Arctic | Circle Polarkreis; ~ **smoke** Eisnebel.

arduous | efforts große Anstrengungen; ~ **enterprise** anstrengendes Unternehmen; ~ **worker** zäher Arbeiter.

area Fläche, Raum, *(region)* Region, Bezirk, [Geltungs]gebiet, Zone, Bereich, *(mil.)* Abschnitt, *(open space)* freier Platz, *(range)* Spielraum, *(tel.)* Gebührenzone;

in the ~ **of N** im Großraum von N; **in the railway station** ~ in der Gegend des Bahnhofs;

administrative ~ Verwaltungsgebiet, -bezirk; **agricultural** ~ landwirtschaftlich genutztes Gebiet; **all-white** ~ nur der wei-

ßen Bevölkerung vorbehaltenes Gebiet; **assembly** ~ *(mil.)* Aufmarschgebiet, Bereitstellungsraum; **backward** ~s in der Entwicklung zurückgebliebene Gebiete; **big-city** ~ Großstadtgebiet; **blighted** ~ heruntergekommenes Wohnviertel; **built-up** ~ bebautes Gelände, geschlossene Ortschaft, dichtbesiedeltes Gebiet, neuentstandenes Siedlungsgebiet; **closed** ~ *(mil.)* Sperrgebiet, -zone; **coastal** ~ Küstengebiet; **compulsory** ~ *(Br.)* grundbuchpflichtiger Bezirk; **congested** ~ dichtbesiedeltes Gebiet; **controlled** ~ Kontrollgebiet; **cultivated** ~ Anbaufläche, -gebiet; **currency** ~ Währungsgebiet, -bereich; **danger** ~ Gefahrenbereich; **depressed** ~ *(Br.)* Notstandsgebiet; **semi-permanently depressed** ~ nahezu ständiges Notstandsgebiet; **desert** ~s Wüstengebiete; **devastated** ~ verwüstetes Gebiet; **less developed** ~ Entwicklungsgebiet; **development** ~ *(Br.)* Fördergebiet; **disaster-prone** ~ katastrophengefährdetes Gebiet; **distressed** ~ *(Br.)* Notstandsgebiet, Gebiet mit großer Arbeitslosigkeit; **economic** ~ Wirtschaftsgebiet; **electoral** ~ Wahlbezirk; **evacuated** ~ geräumtes Gebiet; **free-trade** ~ Freihandelszone; **frontier** ~ Grenzgebiet; **high-cost** ~ hohe Akquisitionskosten forderndes Marktgebiet; **industrial** ~ Industriegegend; **intermediate** ~ *(Br.)* Förderungsgebiet; **judicial** ~ Gerichtsbezirk; **labo(u)r-short** ~ ungenügend mit Arbeitskräften versorgtes Gebiet; **larger** ~ Großraum; **linguistic** ~ Sprachgebiet; **low-mortality** ~ Gebiet mit niedriger Sterblichkeit; **midtown** ~ im Stadtzentrum gelegenes Gebiet; **monetary** ~ Währungsgebiet; **marketing** ~ Absatzgebiet; **natural** ~s gewachsene Gebiete; **no-grow** ~ Gebiet mit Anbauverbot; **no-parking** ~ Parkverbotszone; **nonbuilt-up** ~ nicht geschlossene Ortschaft; **occupied** ~ besetztes Gebiet; **sparsely populated** ~ dünnbesiedeltes Gebiet; **postal** ~ Postzustellungsbezirk; **problem** ~ Problemgebiet; **prohibited** ~ *(mil.)* Sperrgebiet, -zone; **restricted** ~ Stadtteil mit Geschwindigkeitsbeschränkung, *(building law)* Bebauungsbeschränkungen unterworfenes Gebiet, *(mil.)* militärischer Schutzbereich, Sperrgebiet; **rural** ~ ländliches Gebiet; **narrow sales** ~ beschränktes Absatzgebiet; **self-enclosed** ~ Enklave; **selling** ~ Absatz, Verkaufsgebiet; **sparsely settled** ~ dünnbesiedeltes Gebiet; **special (stricken)** ~ *(Br.)* Förder-, Notstandsgebiet; **speech** ~ Sprachgebiet; **suburban** ~ Vorstadtbezirk; **target** ~ luftgefährdetes Gebiet, Flächenziel; **tourist** ~ Fremdenverkehrsgebiet; **trading** ~ Wirtschaftsraum; **trouble** ~ *(car)* störanfälliger Bereich; **undeveloped** ~ unbebautes (noch nicht erschlossenes) Gelände; **underdeveloped** ~ *(regional planning)* zurückgebliebenes Gebiet; **uninhabited** ~s unbewohnte Gebiete; **heavily-unionized** ~ von den Gewerkschaften beherrschtes Gebiet; **urban** ~ Stadtgebiet; **urbanized** ~ verstädtertes Gebiet; **war-stricken** ~ vom Kriege betroffenes Gebiet; **large** ~ **of agreement** breite Verständigungsgrundlage; ~ **of applicability** räumlicher Geltungsbereich, Anwendungsbereich; ~ **of assessment** Veranlagungsbereich, Steuerbezirk; ~ **of Outstanding Natural Beauty** *(Br.)* Landschaftsschutzgebiet; ~ **rich in coal** kohlenreiches Gebiet; **line of communication** ~ *(mil.)* Etappengebiet; ~ **of multiple deprivation** unterversorgtes Gebiet; **principal** ~ **of consumption** Hauptverbrauchsgebiet; ~ **under cultivation** Anbaufläche; ~ **of destination** Verkaufs-, Absatzgebiet; ~ **of employment** Beschäftigungsbereich; ~s **for expansion** Expansionsgebiete; ~ **of friction** Spannungsgebiet; ~ **of information** Informationsbereich; ~ **of inquiry** Befragungsgebiet; **total** ~ **of land farmed** gesamtes Anbaugebiet; **white (unexplored)** ~ **on the map** weißer Fleck auf der Landkarte; ~ **of operations** Geschäftsbereich, Tätigkeitsgebiet, Tätigkeitsbereich, *(airplane)* Flugbereich; ~ **of operations of blockading naval force** Aktionsbereich von Blockadestreitkräften; ~ **of patents** Patentbereich; ~ **of low pressure** Tiefdruckgebiet; ~ **of production** *(US)* Produktionsgebiet; ~ **of responsibility** Verantwortungsbereich; ~ **of primary responsibility** *(antitrust law, US)* Verkaufsgebiet mit primärer Verantwortlichkeit; ~ **of a scheme of development** Siedlungsfläche; ~ **of search** Suchgebiet; ~ **of specialization** spezielles Sachgebiet; ~ **of supply** Auslieferungs-, Verbrauchsgebiet; ~ **of taxation** steuerliches Anwendungsgebiet, Besteuerungsgebiet; ~ **of tension** Spannungsgebiet;

to be located in the ~ **in which a law is valid** in den Geltungsbereich eines Gesetzes fallen; **to forbid an** ~ Gebiet sperren; **to patrol an** ~ Gebiet abfliegen; **to upgrade an** ~ Gebiet höher einstufen;

~ **agreement** *(bargaining)* Regional-, Bereichsabkommen; ~ **authority** Bezirksbehörde; ~ **board** *(banking)* Vorstand einer Kopffiliale, *(Health Service, Br.)* Bezirksstelle; ~ **bombing** *(mil.)* Flächenbombardierung; **equal** ~ **chart** flächengetreue Karte; ~ **command** *(US)* Militärbereich; ~ **composition** Fließ-, Mengensatz; ~**-development program(me)** Notstandsgebietsplan; ~ **director** Bereichsleiter; ~ **forecast** Gebietswettervorhersage; ~ **government** Bezirksregierung; ~ **headquarters** Bezirksgeschäftsstelle, -leitung, -zentrale; ~ **manager** Bezirksdirektor; ~ **office** Bezirksbüro; ~ **organizer** *(trade union)* Gebietsleiter; ~ **planning** Raumplanung; ~-**preserving** flächengetreu; ~ **pricing** Preisfestsetzung nach Zonengebieten, Zonentarif; ~ **sample** *(statistics)* Flächenstichprobe, regionale Marktuntersuchung; ~ **sampling** *(statistics)* regionale Marktuntersuchung, Flächenstichprobenverfahren; ~ **stripping** *(mining, US)* Abbau größerer Gebiete im Tagebau; ~ **superintendent** *(bank)* [etwa] Kopffilialleiter; ~ **target** *(mil.)* Flächenziel; ~ **thinking** Flächendenken; ~-**wide bargaining** Gesamttarifvertrag.

arena Arena *(sport)* Kampfbahn, -platz;
  ~ **of politics** politische Bühne;
  to climb down into the ~ zum Kampf antreten; **to enter the** ~ auf den Platz treten, in den Ring steigen.

argot Gaunersprache.

argue *(v.)* diskutieren, argumentieren, Gründe anführen, verhandeln, erörtern, beweisen, *(counsel)* vortragen, plädieren;
  ~ **s. o. out of s. th.** j. von etw. abbringen; ~ **a case** mündlich verhandeln; ~ **a case for the plaintiff** Auffassung des Klägers vortragen; ~ **a point of law** Rechtsfrage erörtern.

argument *(debate)* Erörterung, Argument, Streitfrage, Debatte, Verhandlung, Auseinandersetzung, *(pleading)* Parteivorbringen, Sachvortrag, *(reason advanced)* Beweis[grund], Beweisführung, *(summary)* Inhaltsangabe;
  answerable ~ brauchbares Argument; **clinching** ~ entscheidender Beweis; **emotional** ~ rein gefühlsbetontes Argument; **factual** ~**s** Sachausführungen; **feeble** ~ schwaches Argument; **legal** ~**s** Rechtsausführungen; **seeming (spurious)** ~ Scheinbeweis, -argument; **solid** ~**s** handfeste Argumente; **stock** ~ übliches Argument; **threadbare** ~**s** dürftige Argumentation; **tight** ~ hieb- und stichfestes Argument; **valid** ~ stichhaltiges Argument;
  ~ **by (from) analogy (from example)** Analogieschluß; ~ **of counsel** Plädoyer; ~ **for dismissing s. o.** Kündigungsgrund; ~**s of the parties** Parteivorbringen; ~**s of little substance** wenig stichhaltige Argumente;
  to clinch an ~ zwingende Beweisgründe anführen; **to conclude one's** ~ *(party)* Schlußanträge stellen; **to get the better of s. o. in an** ~ sich in einer Diskussion gegen j. durchsetzen; **to hold an** ~ Beweis aufrecht erhalten, *(law)* streitig verhandeln; **to invalidate an** ~ Argument entkräften; **to look the winning** ~ überzeugend klingen; **to produce several** ~**s** verschiedene Beweisgründe anführen; **to put out an** ~ Argument vorbringen; **to tear an** ~ **to shreds** Argument zerpflücken.

argumentation Beweisführung, Begründung, Schlußfolgerung.

argumentative streitsüchtig, polemisch.

arid regenarm.

arisal of a claim Entstehung eines Anspruchs, Anspruchsentstehung.

arise *(v.) (claim)* erwachsen, entstehen aus, *(demand)* sich einstellen;
  ~ **out of the employment** aus dem Arbeitsverhältnis erwachsen.

arising basis *(income tax, Br.)* Entstehungsgrundlage.

aristocracy Aristokratie, Adel;
  landed ~ Großgrundbesitzer.

arithmetic Rechnen, Arithmetik;
  business (commercial) ~ kaufmännisches Rechnen;
  ~ **of inventory** Lagermathematik;
  ~ **book** Rechenbuch; ~ **mean** *(statistics)* arithmetischer Mittelwert; ~ **progression** arithmetische Reihe; ~ **unit** Rechenwerk.

arithmetical system Zahlensystem.

arm *(fig.)* Macht, Gewalt, *(support)* Unterstützung;
  air ~ Luftwaffe;
  ~ **of the law** Arm des Gesetzes;
  ~ *(v.)* sich bewaffnen, [auf]rüsten;
  to have a long ~ weitreichende Beziehungen haben.

armament Bewaffnung, Rüstung, *(strength)* Kriegsstärke, Militärmacht, Kriegspotential;
  conventional ~ konventionelle Bewaffnung; **nuclear strategic** ~ strategische Nuklearbewaffnung;
  ~ **bill** *(Br.)* Finanzierungswechsel für Rüstungsaufträge; ~ **boom** Rüstungshochkonjunktur; ~ **company** *(Br.)* Rüstungsbetrieb; ~ **credit** *(Br.)* Rüstungsanleihe; ~ **industry** Rüstungsindustrie; ~ **issues** Rüstungswerte; ~ **magnate** Rüstungsindustrieller; ~ **maker** Waffenfabrikant; ~ **makers** Rüstungsbetrieb; ~ **order** Rüstungsauftrag; ~ **plant** Rüstungsbetrieb; ~ **production** Kriegsproduktion; ~-**program(me)** Aufrüstungsprogramm; ~ **race** Wettrüsten; ~ **supplies** Rüstungsgüter.

armchair am grünen Tisch, theoretisch;
  ~ **decision** Entscheidung am grünen Tisch; ~ **politician** Stammtisch-, Bierbankpolitiker; ~ **shopper** Schreibtischeinkäufer; ~ **strategist** Stammtischstratege.

armed|attack bewaffneter Angriff; ~ **car body** gepanzerte Karosserie; ~ **combat car** Panzerkampfwagen; ~ **conflict** bewaffneter Konflikt; ~ **demonstration** bewaffnete Demonstration; ~ **forces** bewaffnete Macht, Streitkräfte; **all volunteer** ~ **force** nur aus Freiwilligen bestehendes Heer; ~ **force sources** Armeekreise; ~ **intervention** bewaffnetes Eingreifen; ~ **merchant cruiser** Handelskreuzer; ~ **neutrality** bewaffnete Neutralität; ~ **resistance** bewaffneter Widerstand; ~ **services** Streitkräfte.

armful of parcels Arm voller Pakete.

arming Bewaffnung, Ausrüstung.

armistice Waffenstillstand;
  ~ **agreement** Waffenstillstandsabkommen; ~ **commission** Waffenstillstandskommission; ~ **delegation** Waffenstillstandsdelegation; ~ **negotiations** Waffenstillstandsverhandlungen; ~ **terms** Waffenstillstandsbedingungen.

armo(u)r|for self-preservation Selbsterhaltungstrieb;
  ~-**proof glass** kugelsicheres (bewehrtes) Glas, Panzerglas; ~ **ship** Panzerschiff.

armo(u)red|cable armiertes Kabel; ~ **car** gepanzertes Fahrzeug, gepanzertes Auto, Panzerwagen; ~ **concrete** Stahlbeton; ~ **cruiser** Panzerkreuzer; ~ **division** Panzergrenadierdivision.

arms Waffen;
  by force of ~ mit Waffengewalt; **in** ~ bewaffnet; **under** ~ *(mil.)* einsatzfähig; **up in** ~ in offenem Aufruf; **with** ~ mit Waffengewalt;
  small ~ Handfeuerwaffen;
  ~ **of courtesy** stumpfe Waffen;
  to be up in ~ zu den Waffen greifen, im Aufruhr sein; **to lay down** ~ Waffen niederlegen;
  ~ **agreement** Waffenabkommen; ~ **boom** Hochkonjunktur des Waffengeschäfts; ~ **build-up** Waffenansammlung; ~ **business** Waffengeschäft, -industrie; ~ **control** Rüstungsbeschränkung, -lenkung; ~ **control agreement** Rüstungsbeschränkungsabkommen; ~ **delivery** Waffenlieferung; ~ **embargo** Waffenembargo; ~ **export** Waffenexport, -ausfuhr; ~ **import** Waffeneinfuhr; ~ **limitation** Rüstungsbegrenzung, -beschränkung; ~ **limitation agreement** Waffenbegrenzungsabkommen; ~ **manufacturer** Waffenhersteller; **to move on the international** ~ **market** ins internationale Waffengeschäft einsteigen; ~ **moratorium** Waffenmoratorium; ~ **negotiations** Abrüstungsgespräche; ~ **procurement** Waffenbeschaffung; ~ **race** Rüstungswettlauf, Wettrüsten; ~ **reduction** Rüstungsverminderung; ~ **sales** Waffenverkäufe; ~ **selling process** Waffengeschäft; ~ **shipment** Waffenlieferung, -transporte; ~ **smuggler** Waffenschmuggler; ~ **welfare center** Heeresbetreuung; ~ **zone** Armeegebiet.

army Armee, Heer, Militär, Landstreitkräfte;
  regular (standing) ~ stehendes Heer, Berufsheer; **relieving** ~ Ersatzheer; **route** ~ marschbereite Armee; **Salvation** ~⁹ Heilsarmee; **Territorial** ~⁹ *(Br.)* Landwehr;
  ~ **of the jobless** Heer der Arbeitslosen; ~ **of liberation** Befreiungsarmee; ~ **of occupation** Besatzungsarmee; ~ **of workmen** Heer von Arbeitern;
  to be in the ~ Soldat sein; **to furnish an** ~ **with supplies** Armee verproviantieren; **to join the** ~ unter die Soldaten gehen, Soldat werden;
  ~ **agent** Heereslieferant; ~ **board** *(Br.)* Militärverwaltung; ~ **broker** Heereslieferant; ~ **commissary** Heeresverpflegungsamt; ~ **contract** Heeresauftrag; ~ **contractor** Heereslieferant; ~⁹ **Council** *(Br.)* Militärverwaltung; ~ **coup** Staatsstreich durch das Heer; ~ **group** Heeresgruppe; ~ **manual** Heeresdienstvorschrift; ~ **minister** Kriegsminister; ~ **patrol** Militär-, Heeresstreife; ~ **pay** Wehrsold; ~ **post office** Feldpostamt; ~ **procurement** Heeresbeschaffung; ~ **raid** militärischer Überfall; ~⁹ **Register** *(US)* Rangordnung; ~ **roadblock** militärische Straßensperre; ~ **service area** rückwärtiges Armeegebiet; ~ **supplies** Heereslieferant; ~ **takeover** Machtübernahme durch das Militär; ~ **training ground** Truppenübungsplatz; ~ **vote** Wahlstimmen der Armee; ~ **war college** *(US)* Kriegsakademie.

aromarama *(Br.)* Geruchsfilm.

around|-the-clock durchgehend, den ganzen Tag über;
  to travel ~ **from town to town** von Ort zu Ort reisen.

arouse *(v.)* auslösen.

arraign *(v.)* vor Gericht stellen, zur Anklage vernehmen, Hauptverfahren eröffnen.

arraigned on a charge of theft des Diebstahls angeklagt.

arraigner Ankläger.

arraignment Eröffnung des Hauptverfahrens.

arrange *(v.) (agree upon)* vereinbaren, verabreden, abmachen, *(decree)* festsetzen, anordnen, *(put into order)* einrichten, ordnen, gruppieren, arrangieren, aufbauen, *(plan)* Vorkehrungen treffen, veranstalten, *(settle dispute)* schlichten, beilegen;
~ **in alphabetical order** alphabetisch anordnen; ~ **amicably** gütlich beilegen; ~ **one's business affairs** sein Haus bestellen, seine Angelegenheiten ordnen; ~ **a case out of court** Sache außergerichtlich vergleichen; ~ **in classes** klassifizieren; ~ **with creditors** Gläubigervergleich schließen; ~ **the evidence against s. o.** Beweisergebnis zu jds. Ungunsten verfälschen; ~ **an exhibition** Ausstellung gestalten; ~ **for an extension of time** Zahlungsabkommen treffen; ~ **in groups** gruppieren; ~ **an insurance** Versicherung[svertrag] abschließen; ~ **a journey** Reise vorbereiten; ~ **for the manufacture** Vorkehrungen für die Herstellung treffen; ~ **to meet s. o.** sich mit jem. verabreden; ~ **a meeting** Tagung veranstalten; ~ **in order of values** wertmäßig anordnen; ~ **privately** sich außergerichtlich vergleichen; ~ **a settlement** Vergleich herbeiführen; ~ **on shelves** aufschichten, stapeln; ~ **according to size** der Größe nach ordnen; ~ **time and place for the next meeting** Zeit und Ort für die nächste Sitzung festsetzen; ~ **troops** Truppen aufstellen.

arranged, as laut Vereinbarung, wie vereinbart, programm-, abredegemäß.

arrangement *(agreement)* Ab-, Übereinkommen, Vereinbarung, Abmachung, Verabredung, Regelung, Verständigung, [gegenseitige] Übereinkunft, *(cartels, Br.)* abgestimmte Verhaltensweise, Abrede, *(compromise)* [Gläubiger]vergleich, *(of dispute)* Schlichtung, Beilegung, *(proceedings)* Vergleichsverfahren, *(instruction)* Anordnung, *(mil.)* Aufstellung, *(plan)* Plan, *(putting in proper order)* Anordnung, Aufbauen, Aufstellung, Einrichtung, Gestaltung, Gruppierung, Arrangement;
according to previous ~s verabredetermaßen; **against previous** ~s entgegen früheren Abmachungen; **as per** ~ vereinbarungs-, absprachegemäß; **pending** ~ bis zur Austragung der Sache;
~s *(measures taken in advance)* Vorkehrungen, Vorbereitungen, Maßnahmen;
amicable ~ gütliche Erledigung, außergerichtlicher Vergleich; **binding** ~ bindende Abmachung; **blocking** ~ Stillhalteabkommen; **contractual** ~ vertragliche Vereinbarung; **financial** ~s Vereinbarung über die Zahlungsmodalitäten, Zahlungsvereinbarungen; **follow-up** ~s anschließende Vorkehrungen; **general** ~ Generalplan; **internal** ~s interne Abmachungen; **joint purse** ~ Poolvereinbarung; **post-shutdown** ~ der Betriebsschließung folgende Vereinbarung; **previous** ~s frühere Abmachungen; **private** ~ Privatabmachung, außergerichtlicher Vergleich; **provisional** ~ vorläufige Anordnung, Zwischenregelung, Provisorium; **revised** ~ Neuregelung; **sanitary** ~s sanitäre Einrichtungen; **mutually satisfactory** ~ alle Teile befriedigende Abmachung; **special** ~ Sondervereinbarung; **temporary** ~ Provisorium, Übergangsregelung; **testamentary** ~ testamentarische Verfügung, Verfügung von Todes wegen; **transitional** ~ Übergangsregelung, -abkommen; **voluntary** ~ Vergleichsverfahren; **well ordered** ~ übersichtliche Anordnung;
~ **in alphabetical order** alphabetische Anordnung; ~ **outside bankruptcy** außerkonkursrechtlicher Vergleich; ~ **with the board of inland revenue** Vereinbarung mit der Finanzverwaltung; ~ **of claims** Rangfolge von Konkursforderungen; ~ **in classes** Klassifizierung; ~ **out of court** außergerichtliche Regelung; ~ **with one's creditors** Gläubigervergleich; ~ **with creditors in a voluntary liquidation** Liquidationsvergleich; ~ **of an exhibition** Gestaltung einer Ausstellung; ~ **for an extension of time** Zahlungsabkommen; ~ **of furniture in a new house** Möbelaufstellung in einem neuen Haus; ~ **in groups** Gruppierung; **generous** ~s **for home leave** großzügige Regelung des Heimaturlaubs; ~s **for a journey** Reisevorbereitungen; ~ **of a library** Anordnung einer Bibliothek; **equitable** ~ **between parties** Parteivergleich; **planned** ~ **of stock orders** Abwicklung von Lagerbestellungen; ~ **for subscription** Abonnementsvereinbarung;
to assent to an ~ einem Vergleich zustimmen; **to come to an** ~ zu einem Vergleich (einer Abmachung) gelangen, sich vergleichen; **to come to an** ~ **with one's creditors** sich mit seinen Gläubigern arrangieren; **to confirm an** ~ *(bankrupty)* Vergleich bestätigen; **to enter into an** ~ Übereinkommen treffen; **to file a petition for an** ~ Vergleichsverfahren beantragen; **to make an** ~ Vergleich schließen; **to make** ~s Vorkehrungen (Vorbereitungen) treffen, sich auf etw. einrichten, arrangieren; **to make an amicable** ~ sich gütlich einigen (vergleichen); **to make provisional** ~s vorläufige Vereinbarung treffen; **to make all necessary** ~s notwendige Anordnungen treffen; **to make** ~s **for cover** Vorkehrungen für die Deckung treffen; **to make an** ~ **with one's creditors** seine Gläubiger abfinden, mit seinen Gläubigern ein Abkommen schließen.

array *(jurors, US)* Einsetzung eines Geschworenengerichts, Geschworenenliste, *(mil.)* Gefechtsaufstellung, *(statistics)* Schema, Verteilung, Anordnung;
in holiday ~ in Ferienkluft;
~ **of shops** Einkaufszentrum; **imposing** ~ **of statistics** beeindruckende Präsentierung statistischen Materials; ~ **of switches** Schaltersystem;
~ *(v.)* **to a panel** Geschworene ernennen;
to challenge the ~ Geschworene ablehnen.

arrearage Restsumme, Rückstand, unbezahlter Restbetrag.

arrears Rückstand, rückständiger Betrag, [Zahlungs]rückstände, Restanten, Verzugszinsen, *(club)* rückständige Beiträge;
in ~ im Rückstand, rückständig;
rent ~ rückständige Miete, Pacht-, Mietrückstand; **salary** ~ Gehaltsrückstände; **tax** ~ Steuerrückstände;
~ **of annuity** Rentenrückstand; ~ **of correspondence** Briefschulden; ~ **of instalments** Ratenrückstände; ~ **of interest** Zinsrückstand, rückständige Zinsen; ~ **on interest** Verzugszinsen; ~ **of maintenance** rückständige Unterhaltszahlungen; ~ **of payment** Zahlungsrückstand; ~ **of premium** Prämienrückstand; ~ **of rent** Mietrückstand; ~ **of repairs** zurückgestellte Reparaturen; ~ **of taxes** Steuerrückstände, rückständige Steuern; ~ **of wages** rückständige Löhne, Lohnrückstand; ~ **of work** unerledigte Arbeit, Arbeitsrückstand;
to be in ~ [mit der Zahlung] im Rückstand sein; **to be in** ~ **with one's correspondence** Briefschulden haben; **to clear off** ~ **of work** liegengebliebene Arbeit erledigen; **to fall (get) into** ~ in Rückstand geraten; **to let the** ~ **run on** Rückstände entstehen lassen; **to make up** ~ [**of work**] Rückstände aufarbeiten; **to pay up** ~ Rückstände begleichen; **to remain in** ~ in Rückstand bleiben; **to work off** ~ Rückstände aufarbeiten;
~ **certificate** *(Br.)* Verpflichtungsschein über rückständige Obligationszinsen.

arrest *(attachment)* Beschlagnahme, Pfändung, *(detention)* Arrest, Festnahme, Ergreifung, Verhaftung, Inhaftierung, Gefangennahme, *(stoppage)* Hemmung, Stockung, Stillstand;
under ~ verhaftet, in Haft;
investigative ~ vorläufige Festnahme; **malicious** ~ Freiheitsberaubung; **mass** ~s Massenverhaftungen; **personal** ~ *(mil.)* Strafarrest;
~ **in civil practice** Arrest zur Vollziehung einer Beugestrafe; ~ **in criminal cases** Verhaftung im Strafverfahren; ~ **of debt** Pfändung einer Forderung; ~ **of development** *(child)* Entwicklungsstörung; ~ **of goods** Warenbeschlagnahme; ~ **of inquest** Antrag auf Einstellung des Untersuchungsverfahrens; ~ **of judgment** Aussetzung des Verfahrens, Urteilsaussetzung, -sistierung; ~ **of a vessel** Beschlagnahme (Arrest, Pfändung) eines Schiffs, Schiffsbeschlagnahme;
~ *(v.)* ergreifen, gefangennehmen, festnehmen, verhaften, in Haft nehmen, inhaftieren, *(attach)* beschlagnahmen, mit Beschlag belegen, pfänden, *(stop)* hemmen, anfallen;
~ **on charges** aufgrund von Beschuldigungen verhaften; ~ **a debt** Forderung pfänden; ~ **development** Entwicklung stören; ~ **a judgment** Urteilsfällung (gerichtliches Verfahren) aussetzen; ~ **a ship** Schiff mit Beschlag belegen; ~ **on the spot** vom Fleck weg verhaften; ~ **a thief** Dieb verhaften; ~ **immediately without warrant** vorläufig festnehmen;
to be put (placed, held) under ~ verhaftet werden; **to have had a previous** ~ schon einmal verhaftet gewesen sein; **to issue a warrant of** ~ Haftbefehl erlassen; **to make several** ~s mehrere Verhaftungen vornehmen; **to resist** ~ sich der Festnahme widersetzen, Widerstand gegen die Staatsgewalt leisten; **to warrant the** ~ **of a suspected criminal** Haftbefehl gegen einen Verdächtigen erlassen;
~ **squad** Festnahmegruppe; ~ **warrant** Haftbefehl.

arrestation Verhaftung.

arrested person Festgenommener, Verhafteter.

arrestee Pfandschuldner.

arresting officer festnehmender Beamter.

arrestment Beschlagnahme, Pfändung, *(attachment, Scot.)* Verhaftung, Festnahme.

arrester Pfandgläubiger.

arriage and carriage Hand- und Spanndienste.

arrival Ankunft, Ankommen, Eintreffen, *(airplane)* Landung, *(newcomer)* neuer Gast;
on ~ bei Ankunft;

~s *(goods)* Eingänge, Zufuhr, *(ships, trains)* eingelaufene Schiffe (Züge);

~s and departures Ankunfts- und Abfahrtszeiten, Ankunft und Abfahrt der Züge; ~ of goods Wareneingang, -zufuhr; ~ in power Machtantritt; ~ of a report Eingang eines Berichts; to notify the police of one's ~ sich polizeilich melden;

await ~ *(post)* nicht nachsenden!;

~ board Ankunftstafel; ~ book Fremdenbuch; ~ draft *(US)* Tratte mit beigefügten Verschiffungsdokumenten; ~ notice Eingangs-, Frachtbenachrichtigung; ~ platform Ankunftsbahnsteig; ~ side Ankunftshalle; ~ time Ankunftszeit; ~ track Einfahrgleis.

arrive *(v.)* *(letter, goods)* eingehen, *(order, ship)* einlaufen, *(person)* ankommen, eintreffen, *(be successful)* es in der Welt zu etw. bringen;

~ at an agreement zu einer Einigung gelangen; ~ in batches stoßweise eintreffen; ~ at a conclusion zu einem Schluß kommen; ~ at a decision zu einer Entscheidung gelangen; ~ in harbo(u)r im Hafen einlaufen; ~ linguistically in die Sprache aufgenommen werden; ~ on the minute auf die Minute (pünktlich) ankommen (eintreffen); ~ at a price Preis festsetzen.

arrived, to have arriviert sein.

arrivé Emporkömmling.

arrogate *(v.)* fordern, beanspruchen, verlangen;

~ property to o. s. sich etw. unrechtmäßig aneignen; ~ a right to o. s. sich ein Recht anmaßen.

arrogation *(adoption)* Adoption [eines Mündigen].

arrow filter signal Pfeil für Linksabbieger.

arsenal Waffenlager, -depot, Waffen-, Munitionsfabrik.

arson Brandlegung, -stiftung;

to commit ~ Brandstiftung begehen.

arsonist Brandstifter.

art künstlerisches Schaffen, Kunst, Künstlerarbeit, *(patent law)* Fachgebiet, -kenntnisse, *(science)* Wissenszweig;

applied ~ Kunstgewerbe; black ~ schwarze Kunst; colossal ~ Monumentalkunst; the fine ~s die schönen Künste; finished ~ Reinzeichnung, reproduktionsreife Vorlage; industrial ~ Gewerbegraphik; performing ~s darstellende Künste; prior ~ *(patent law)* Stand der Technik;

~s and crafts Kunstgewerbe; ~ and part Entwurf und Ausführung, *(Scot.)* Tatgehilfe; ~ of persuasion Überredungskunst; ~s and wiles of politics politische Tricks und Kniffe; ~ of surveying mines Markscheidekunst;

to be ~ and part in s. th. planend und ausführend an etw. beteiligt sein; to be skilled in ~ *(patent law)* auf einem Fachgebiet erfahren sein;

~ bug Kunstnarr; ~ buyer *(advertising)* Referent für freie Mitarbeiter; ~ calendar Kunstkalender; ~ cardboard Kunstdruckkarton; ~s center *(US)* Kulturzentrum; ~ collector Kunstsammler; ~ connoisseur Kunstkenner; ~s-and-crafts items kunsthandwerkliche Gegenstände; ~s-and-crafts shop Kunstgewerbeladen; ~ critic Kunstkritiker; ~ criticism Kunstkritik; ~ dealer Kunsthändler; ~ department graphisches Atelier; ~ design künstlerischer Entwurf; ~ designer Werbegestalter, -graphiker, Gebrauchsgraphiker; ~ director Gestalter, Leiter der Gestaltung, künstlerischer Leiter, Atelierleiter [einer Werbeagentur]; ~ exhibition Kunstausstellung; ~ expert Kunstsachverständiger; ~ expression Kunstausdruck; ~ gallery Gemäldegalerie; ~ journal Kunstzeitschrift; ~ league Kunstverein; ~ lessons Kunstunterricht; ~ literature Kunstliteratur; ~ market Kunstmarkt; ~ matt paper *(Br.)* mattes Kunstdruckpapier; ~s ministry Ministerium der schönen Künste; ~ museum Museum der schönen Künste; ~ paper Kunstdruckpapier; ~ period Kunstepoche; ~ possessions Kunstbesitz; ~ print Kunstblatt; ~ printing Kunstdruck; ~ pull *(Br.)* Abzug auf Kunstdruckpapier; ~ representative Künstleragentur; ~ representation Künstleragentur; ~ sale Kunstauktion; ~ school Handwerksschule; ~ shop Kunsthandlung; ~ show Kunstausstellung; ~ smuggling Schmuggel von Kunstgegenständen; ~ student Kunststudent; ~ studio Werbestudio, -atelier; ~ supplement Kunstbeilage; ~ teacher Kunstlehrer; ~ theft Kunstdiebstahl; ~ value künstlerischer Wert; ~ work Künstlerarbeit, Kunstgegenstand, *(advertising)* Druck-, Reprovorlage, Druckunterlagen, Gestaltung[sarbeit], gebrauchsgraphische Kompositionselemente; to order ~ work from freelancers Anzeigengestaltung an freiberuflich tätige Graphiker vergeben.

artefact Gebrauchsgegenstand.

arterial | highway *(US, local)* Durchgangs-, Fernverkehrsstraße; ~ railway Hauptstrecke; ~ road Ausfallstraße, Hauptverkehrsweg; ~ traffic Hauptverkehr.

arteries | of commerce Haupthandelsströme; ~ of traffic Hauptverkehrsstraßen;.

artery *(traffic)* Hauptverkehrsader, Hauptstrecke, -straße, *(waterway)* Hauptwasserstraße;

~ of commerce Handelsweg.

article *(agreement)* Vertrag, Kontrakt, *(clause)* Klausel, Bestimmung, Paragraph, Abschnitt, Absatz, *(commodity)* Artikel, Erzeugnis, Ware, *(brief composition)* Artikel, Aufsatz, *(item)* Posten, *(object)* Gegenstand, Sache, Ding, Stück, Artikel;

additional ~ Zusatzartikel; advertising (advertised) ~ Werbe-, Reklameartikel; amending ~ Ergänzungs-, Zusatzartikel; branded ~s Markenartikel; called ~ begehrter Artikel; ~ certain to sell sicher abzusetzende Ware; exceptionally cheap ~ spottbilliger Gegenstand; crowded-out ~ wegen Platzmangels zurückgestellter Zeitungsartikel; ~ demanded bestellter Artikel; domestic ~ Inlandserzeugnis; export ~ Ausfuhrartikel; feature ~ groß aufgemachter Zeitungsartikel; genuine ~ Markenartikel; high-class ~ Qualitätsware; imported ~ Importartikel; leading ~ Leitartikel; necessary ~ Bedarfsartikel; newspaper ~ Zeitungsartikel; patent[ed] ~ Markenartikel, *(patent law)* Patentgegenstand; personal ~ persönlicher Gebrauchsgegenstand; popular ~ Zugartikel, zugkräftiger Artikel; proprietary ~ patentiertes Monopolerzeugnis; reliable ~ zuverlässiger Artikel; seasonal ~ Saisonartikel; semifinished ~ Halbfabrikat; signed ~ signierter Zeitungsartikel; superior ~ Qualitätsware; syndicated ~ in mehreren Zeitungen zugleich erscheinender Artikel; tearsheet ~ Belegartikel; three-column ~ dreispaltiger Artikel; twenty-line ~ zwanzigzeiliger Artikel; wholly manufactured ~ Ganzfabrikat;

~ of an agreement Vertragsartikel; ~ of consumption Verbrauchsartikel, -gegenstand, Konsumgut; ~ of dress Bekleidungsstück; ~ of exportation Ausfuhrartikel; ~ of importation Einfuhrartikel; ~ of merchandise Handelsware; ~ of average quality Durchschnittsware; ~ of first quality Primaware; ~ of high quality hochwertiger Artikel; ~ of superior quality vorzügliche Ware; ~ hard to get rid of schwer verkäuflicher Artikel; ~ of sale Verkaufsgegenstand; ~ of quick sale Zugartikel, Verkaufsschlager; ~ to be supplied Liefergegenstand; ~ of everyday use täglicher Gebrauchsgegenstand;

~ *(v.)* *(bind as apprentice)* in die Lehre (Ausbildung) geben, *(charge specially)* schriftlich anklagen, Anklagepunkte vorbringen, *(formulate)* artikelweise abfassen, Punkt für Punkt darlegen;

~ a seaman for a voyage Seemann für eine Reise anheuern; to be out of an ~ Ware nicht mehr führen (auf Lager haben); to deal in an ~ Artikel führen; to fall within ~ 5 in Paragraph 5 geregelt sein; to get up an ~ for sale Artikel zum Verkauf aufmachen; to have (keep) an ~ in stock Artikel (Ware) führen; not to keep an ~ Artikel nicht führen; to place an ~ to s. one's credit j. für einen Posten erkennen; to place an order for an ~ with a firm Artikel bei einer Firma bestellen; to put an ~ on the market Artikel einführen; to rewrite an ~ Artikel umschreiben; to shorten an ~ Zeitungsartikel zusammenstreichen; to skim an ~ Zeitungsartikel überfliegen; to stock an ~ Artikel führen; to sub-edit an ~ Zeitungsartikel vor Veröffentlichung durchsehen.

articles Satzung, *(goods)* Güter, Waren, *(navy)* Heuervertrag; according to the ~ satzungsgemäß; against the ~ satzungswidrig; contrary to the ~ satzungswidrig;

appointed (provided) by the ~ vertraglich vorgesehen; under (in accordance with) the ~ nach den Vertragsbestimmungen;

~s approbatory *(Scot., law)* Klageerwiderung; choice ~ ausgesuchte Waren; corporate ~ *(US)* Gründungsurkunde; dangerous ~ gefährliche Waren; factory-produced ~ Fabrikware; good-class ~ erstklassige Ware; knock-down ~ Massenware; low-rate ~ niedrig verzollte Waren; mass-produced ~ seriengefertigter Artikel, Massenartikel, -ware; memorandum ~ vom Versicherungsschutz ausgeschlossene Gegenstände; price-controlled ~ der Preisüberwachung unterliegende Waren; price-maintained ~ Waren mit gleichbleibenden Preisen; proprietary ~ Markenerzeugnisse, -artikel; scarce ~ Mangelware; second-hand ~ gebrauchte Artikel; semifinished ~ Halbfertigfabrikate; ship's ~ Heuervertrag; stock ~ stets vorrätige Artikel; superior ~ erstklassige Ware; toilet ~ Toilettengegenstände; ~ wanted *(newspaper)* Kaufgesuche; well-introduced ~ gut eingeführte Waren;

~ of agreement [schriftliche] Vertragsabmachung, -bestimmungen, -punkte, *(company)* Gesellschaftsvertrag, Gründungsurkunde; ~ of apprenticeship Lehrvertrag; ~ of association *(Br.)* Gründungs-, Gesellschaftsvertrag, Statuten, Satzung; ~ made in bulk Massenartikel, -ware; ~ of clothing

Bekleidungsstücke; **~ of commission** Kommissionsgut; **~ of consumption** Bedarfsartikel, Verbrauchsgegenstände; **~ of contract** Vertragsbestimmungen; **~ of [co]partnership** Gesellschaftsstatuten, -vertrag, Kommanditvertrag; **~ of corporation** *(US)* Gesellschaftsstatut, Satzung; **~ in demand** gesuchte Waren; **~ of employment** Anstellungsvertrag; **~ of impeachment** *(parliament)* Parlamentsanklage, Anklageschrift; **~ of import** Importware; **~ of incorporation** *(US)* Gründungsurkunde, -vertrag (Satzung) einer AG; **~ of foreign manufacture** ausländische Erzeugnisse; **~ of marriage** Heiratsvertrag; **~ of merchandise** Handelsware; **~ of first necessity** lebenswichtige Artikel; **~ of organization** *(US)* Gründungsurkunde; **~ of partnership** Gesellschaftsvertrag, -statuten; **~ of average quality** Durchschnittsware; **~ of high quality** vollwertige Artikel, Qualitätsware; **~ of superior quality** vorzügliche Waren, hochwertige Qualitätserzeugnisse; **~ left for safe custody** Depotgegenstände; **~ of quick sale** Zugartikel, zugkräftige Waren, Verkaufsschlager, Waren mit hoher Umschlagsgeschwindigkeit; **~ of set** *(Scot. law)* Pachtvertrag; **~ of virtue** Kunstgegenstände; **~ of war** Militärstrafgesetzbuch; **~s shown in the window** Auslege-, Schaufensterware;
to arrange ~ in groups Paragraphen zusammenstellen; **to box ~ for sale** Ware für den Verkauf verpacken; **to get up ~ for sale** Waren für den Verkauf herausstellen; **to serve one's ~** als Lehrling dienen, seine Lehrjahre durchmachen (Ausbildungszeit absolvieren); **to sign the ship's ~** anheuern; **to write ~ for a newspaper** Beiträge für eine Zeitung liefern.
articled vertraglich gebunden, *(apprentice)* in der Lehre (Ausbildung);
~ clerk *(Br.)* Praktikant [in einer Anwaltskanzlei], Anwaltsgehilfe, *(chartered accountant)* Volontär, Praktikant.
articulate *(v.) (phonetics)* deutlich aussprechen, artikulieren;
~ *(a.)* deutlich, klar, artikuliert;
to be fully ~ sehr sicher und routiniert sein;
~ unrest *(workers)* spürbare Unruhe.
articulation Artikulierung, deutliche Aussprache, *(tel.)* Verständlichkeit.
artifact Gebrauchsgegenstand.
artifice Kniff, Kunstgriff, Trick, Täuschungsmanöver.
artificer *(artistic worker)* Kunstgewerbler, *(skilled worker)* Handwerker, *(master)* Handwerksmeister.
artificial synthetisch, nachgemacht, unecht, falsch, künstlich, *(feigned)* unwirklich, vorgetäuscht;
~ antenna Ersatzantenne; **~ capital** anderes Kapital als Grund und Boden; **~ daylight** künstliches Tageslicht, Kunstlicht; **~ fertilizer** Kunstdünger; **~ fibre** Kunstfaser; **~ language** Kunstsprache; **~ manure** Kunstdünger; **~ material** Werkstoff; **~ person** juristische Person; **~ presumption** gesetzliche Vermutung; **~ respiration** künstliche Beatmung; **~ silk** Kunstseide.
artificially, to be fed künstlich ernährt werden.
artisan Handwerker, Mechaniker.
artist *(advertising)* Mitarbeiter für graphische Werbegestaltung, Gebrauchsgraphiker, Layouter, *(artisan)* geschickter Handwerker, *(schemer)* Könner;
industrial ~ Kunstgewerbler; **free-lance ~** freier Graphiker; **no mean ~** bedeutender Künstler;
an ~ in his every fibre jeder Zoll ein Künstler;
~'s impression Modellskizze.
artistic|advertising künstlerische Werbung; **~ director** künstlerischer Leiter; **~ getup** künstlerische Ausstattung; **~ merit** künstlerischer Wert; **~ slang** Künstlersprache; **~ work** Kunstwerk.
artotype *(printing)* Lichtdruck.
as|-is merchandise Ausschußware; **~ of** *(US)* (at, *Br.*) Jan. 1, 1978 Stand am 1. 1. 1978.
ascend *(v.) (in rank)* aufsteigen;
~ to the throne Thron besteigen.
ascendancy Überlegenheit, Vorherrschaft;
in one's ~ auf dem Höhepunkt der Macht;
to gain ~ over a country bestimmenden Einfluß auf ein Land gewinnen; **to rise to ~** zur Macht gelangen, ans Ruder kommen.
ascendant Verwandter in aufsteigender Linie, Vorfahr, *(astrology)* Horoskop;
~ *(a.)* überlegen.
ascendency, ascendancy Machtstellung;
to be in the ~ im Aufsteigen begriffen sein; **to gain ~ over s. o.** über j. Übergewicht gewinnen.
ascender *(printing)* Oberlänge.
ascending|letter Großbuchstabe mit Oberlänge; **~ line** *(law of inheritance)* aufsteigende Linie.

ascent Rampe, Auffahrt, *(road)* Gefälle;
~ in a balloon Ballonfahrt; **~ of a mountain** Bergbesteigung.
ascertain *(v.)* feststellen, festsetzen, erfahren, ermitteln;
~ a balance Saldo vergleichen; **~ the costs** Kosten ermitteln; **~ the facts** Tatsachen feststellen, Tatbestand feststellen (ermitteln); **~ interest** Zinsen errechnen; **~ a price** Preis festsetzen; **~ the value** Wert ermitteln; **~ the rental value** Mietwert feststellen.
ascertainable nachweis-, feststellbar, zu ermitteln.
ascertained|damage festgestellter Schaden; **~ fact** festgestellte Tatsache; **~ goods** Speziessachen.
ascertainment Feststellung, Ermittlung;
~ of costs Kostenerfassung; **~ of damage** Schadensfeststellung; **~ of loss** Schadensfeststellung; **~ of price** Preisfestsetzung; **~ of profits** Gewinnfeststellung; **~ of returns** Erfolgsermittlung; **~ error** *(statistics)* Erhebungsfehler.
ascribable zuschreibbar;
to be ~ zurückzuführen sein.
ascribe *(v.)* beimessen, zuschreiben;
~ to an accident einem Unfall zuschreiben.
ash|barrel *(US)* Mülltonne; **~ bin** *(Br.)*; **~ can** *(US)* Mülltonne, -eimer, -kasten, Abfallkübel; **~ cart** *(US)* Müllwagen; **~ tray** Aschenbecher.
ashore auf See;
to be driven ~ stranden; **to go ~** an Land gehen.
aside *(Br.)* Nebeneffekt, -bemerkung;
to put ~ auf die Seite bringen; **to set ~ a verdict** Urteil aufheben.
ask *(v.)* ersuchen, bitten, [er]fragen, sich erkundigen;
~ for advice um Rat fragen; **~ the banns** Aufgebot bestellen; **~ s. o. to come** j. bestellen; **~ for larger credits** um größere Kredite nachsuchen; **~ for damages** Schadenersatz verlangen; **~ a dollar a dozen** pro Dutzend einen Dollar verlangen (berechnen); **~ a favo(u)r** um einen Gefallen bitten; **~ for a guaranty** Kaution verlangen; **~ a guest** Gast einladen; **~ about s. one's health** sich nach jds. Befinden erkundigen; **~ for help** um Hilfe ersuchen; **~ s. o. in** j. hereinbitten; **~ for it** etw. herausfordern; **~ for the manager** Geschäftsführer verlangen; **~ s. one's name** j. nach seinem Namen fragen; **~ out to dinner** zum Essen ausführen; **~ payment in advance** Vorauszahlung verlangen; **~ the price** sich nach dem Preis erkundigen; **~ moderate prices** niedrige Preise berechnen; **~ a question** Frage stellen; **~ £ 100 a month as rent** Monatsmiete von 100 Pfund verlangen; **~ to speak** sich zum Wort melden; **~ for trouble** etw. herausfordern, etw. heraufbeschwören; **~ the way** sich nach dem Weg erkundigen.
asked gefragt, gesucht, *(stock exchange)* Brief;
at the best possible ~ bestens; **[not] ~ for** [un]gefragt; **~ and bid** *(stock exchange)* Brief und Geld; **~ out for dinner** zum Essen eingeladen;
to be ~ out eingeladen sein;
~ price Preisforderung, *(stock exchange)* Briefkurs; **~ quotation** Briefkurs.
asker Frager, Bittsteller.
asking Fragen, Bitten, *(marriage)* Aufgebot;
to be had for the ~ mühelos (umsonst) zu haben sein.
asocial ungesellig, egoistisch.
aspect *(appearance)* Aussehen, Erscheinung, *(fig.)* Seite, Gesichtspunkt, Aspekt, *(piece of land)* Aussicht, Lage;
in all its ~s in jeder Hinsicht; **under its social ~** vom sozialen Gesichtspunkt aus; **with southern ~** mit Südlage; **~s of financial activities** gesamter Bereich des Finanzgeschäfts; **technical ~s of a job** fachliche Aspekte eines Berufs;
to have a southern ~ *(house)* nach Süden liegen;
~ ratio *(television)* Bildschirmformat, -kantenverhältnis.
asperse *(v.)* s. one's good name j. verleumden.
aspersion Verleumdung, Anschwärzung.
asphyxia Scheintod.
aspirant Bewerber, Anwärter, Kandidat, Aspirant;
~ for s. one's hand Heiratskandidat.
aspiration Bestreben.
asport *(v.)* widerrechtlich fortschaffen.
asportation widerrechtliche Wegnahme, widerrechtliches Fortschaffen.
assail *(v.)* angreifen, überfallen.
assailant Angreifer.
assart Rodung, Urbarmachung.
assassin Attentäter, Meuchelmörder;
hired ~ gedungener Mörder.
assassinate *(v.)* ermorden, meuchlerisch umbringen.
assassination Ermordung, Mord;
attempted ~ Mordanschlag, -versuch; **~ attempt** Mordversuch, -anschlag; **~ clause** Attentatsklausel.

assault Angriff, *(law, US)* Körperverletzung, Tätlichkeit, Gewaltanwendung, gewalttätiger (tätlicher) Angriff, *(mil.)* Sturm, Angriff;

aggravated ~ schwere Körperverletzung; **simple** ~ versuchte Körperverletzung;

~ **and battery** gewalttätiger Angriff, tätliche Beleidigung, Realinjurie; ~ **with intent to commit manslaughter** versuchter Totschlag; ~ **with intent to commit murder** Mordversuch; ~ **with intent to commit rape** versuchtes Notzuchtverbrechen; ~ **with intent to commit robbery** versuchter Raub; ~ **with intent to do grievous bodily injury** vorsätzliche schwere Körperverletzung;

~ **(v.)** *(law)* tätlich beleidigen, *(mil.)* angreifen;

~ **a fortress** Festung im Sturm nehmen; ~ **s. one's reputation** jds. guten Ruf attackieren;

to carry by ~ *(mil.)* erstürmen, im Sturm nehmen; **to commit an** ~ tätlich angreifen;

~ **boat** kleines Landungsboot; ~ **cable** Feldkabel; ~ **case** Beleidigungssache; ~ **ship** Landungsfahrzeug; ~ **wire** Feldkabel.

assay Metallprobe, -analyse, Probe auf Feinheit, Feingehaltsbestimmung;

~ **(v.)** prüfen, eichen, Feingehalt feststellen;

~ **balance** Goldwaage; ~ **cost** Münzgebühr; ~ **office** Laboratorium zur Bestimmung des Feingehalts von Metallen; ~ **office bar** amtlich auf Feingehalt geprüfter Goldbarren; ~ **office value** Feingehaltswert; ~ **sample** Probestück; ~ **ton** Probiergewicht; ~ **value** Feingehalts-, Münzwert.

assayer Münz-, Edelmetall prüfen.

assemblage Versammlung, Vereinigung, Menge, Haufen, Schar, *(fitting together)* Montage, Zusammenbau, Verbindung, Anschluß, *(real estate law)* Zusammenschreibungskosten;

political ~ politische Vereinigung;

~ **of building material** Bereitstellung von Baumaterialien; ~ **value** Sammelwert.

assemble *(v.)* *(convene)* zusammenrufen, einberufen, versammeln, *(fit together)* zusammensetzen, -bauen, aufstellen, montieren, *(machine)* zusammenbauen, *(parl.)* zusammentreten, *(stocks)* [Vorräte] ansammeln, bevorraten, *(train)* zusammenstellen;

~ **a motor-car** Wagen montieren; ~ **delegates** Delegierte einberufen; ~ **two parcels of land** zwei Grundstücksparzellen zusammenschreiben; ~ **railway cars** Zug zusammenstellen; ~ **troops** Truppen bereitstellen (zusammenziehen).

assembled examination gemeinsames Prüfungsverfahren.

assembler *(conference member)* Versammlungsteilnehmer, -mitglied, *(convoker)* Einberufer, *(data processing)* Programmumsetzer, *(fitter)* Monteur.

assembling Bevorratung, *(plots)* Baulandbeschaffung;

~ **parcels of land** Grundstückszusammenschreibung, Parzellenvereinigung; ~ **of plots** Baulandbeschaffung; ~ **of railway cars** Zugzusammenstellung;

~ **shop** Montagebetrieb.

assembly Versammlung, Zusammenkunft, *(fitting together)* Zusammenbau, Montierung, Montage, *(mil.)* Sammelruf, Bereitstellung, Zusammenziehung, *(politics)* beratende (gesetzgebende) Körperschaft, *(production unit)* Fertigungseinheit, *(training)* gemeinsame Unterrichtung, *(US, states)* Unterhaus;

annual ~ Jahresversammlung; **constituent** ~ konstituierende Versammlung; **conveyor-line** ~ Fließbandmontage; **directly elected** ~ direkt gewähltes Parlament; **eagerly listening** ~ aufmerksame Zuhörerschaft; **General** ⁓ Generalsynode, Generalversammlung, *(some US states)* Parlament, *(United Nation)* Vollversammlung; **legislative** ~ gesetzgebende Versammlung; **National** ⁓ Nationalversammlung; **permanent** ~ ständige Versammlung; **plenary** ~ Vollversammlung; **political** ~ politische Zuhörerschaft; **popular** ~ Volksversammlung; **progressive** ~ *(US)* Fließbandmontage; **regional legislative** ~ Regionalversammlung mit Gesetzgebungsbefugnissen; **secret** ~ geheime Zusammenkunft; **seditious** ~ *(Br.)* Parlamentsnötigung; **unlawful** ~ Zusammenrottung, Auflauf, Landfriedensbruch;

~ **of troops** Bereitstellung von Truppen, Truppenzusammenziehung;

to convene an ~ Versammlung abhalten;

~ **agreement** Montagevereinbarung; ~ **area** *(mil.)* Aufmarschgebiet, Bereitstellungsraum; ~ **capacity** Montagemöglichkeit; ~ **committee** Gesetzgebungsausschuß; ~ **costs** Montagekosten; ~ **cost system** Kostenrechnung für Montagebetrieb; ~ **department** Montageabteilung; **automated** ~ **facilities** automatische Montageeinrichtungen; ~ **fault** Montagefehler; ~ **hall** Werkstatt, Stadt-, Montagehalle; ~ **hangar** Helling.

assembly line laufendes Band, Montageband, Fließband, Fertigungsstraße;

to rumble off the ~ Fließband verlassen; **to stay away from the** ~ **in droves** scharenweise der Arbeit fernbleiben.

assembly-line | foreman Fließbandvorarbeiter; ~ **operator** Fließbandarbeiter; ~ **production** Fließbandfertigung, -produktion; ~ **technique** Produktion am laufenden Band, Fließbandproduktion; ~ **town** Fließbandstadt; ~ **work** Fließbandarbeit; ~ **worker** Fließbandarbeiter.

assembly | operation Montagetätigkeit, -betrieb; ~ **plant** Montagewerk; ~ **room** Versammlungsraum, Ball-, Festsaal, Aula, *(US)* Montagehalle; ~ **schedule** Montageplan; ~ **shop** Montagehalle, -werkstatt, -betrieb; ~ **trainee** Fließbandanlernling; ~ **work** Montagearbeit.

assemblyman *(US)* Mitglied einer gesetzgebenden Körperschaft, Abgeordneter.

assent Bejahung, Billigung, Einwilligung, Zustimmung[serklärung], Einverständnis, Genehmigung;

by common ~ mit allgemeiner Zustimmung; **with one** ~ einstimmig, einmütig; **express** ~ ausdrückliche Zustimmung; **implied** ~ gesetzlich vermutete Zustimmung; **mutual** ~ Willensübereinstimmung; **parental** ~ elterliche Zustimmung; **Royal** ~ königliche Genehmigung; **tacit** ~ stillschweigende Zustimmung; **unreserved** ~ uneingeschränkte Zustimmung; **vesting** ~ *(Br.)* Übertragungsurkunde; **written** ~ schriftliche Zustimmungserklärung;

~ **in writing** schriftliche Genehmigung;

~ **(v.)** **to** bei-, zustimmen, beipflichten, genehmigen, einwilligen in, einverstanden sein;

~ **to s. one's conditions** mit jds. Bedingungen einverstanden sein;

to secure the ~ Zustimmung herbeiführen; **to secure the** ~ **of two thirds of the senate** Zweidrittelmehrheit im Senat sicherstellen.

assented genehmigt;

~ **bonds (stocks, securities)** im Sammeldepot hinterlegte und im Sanierungsverfahren abgestempelte Wertpapiere; **to be** ~ **by a majority in number and value** von einer zahlen- und wertmäßigen Mehrheit gebilligt sein.

assentient Zustimmender.

assentor Beipflichtender, *(Br., politics)* Unterstützer eines Wahlvorschlags.

assert *(v.)* behaupten, erklären, versichern, vorbringen, geltend machen;

~ **o. s.** energisch auftreten, sich durchsetzen (zur Geltung bringen);

~ **a claim** Anspruch geltend machen; ~ **a patent claim** Patent verteidigen; ~ **one's good faith** seinen guten Glauben geltend machen; ~ **one's innocence** seine Unschuld beteuern; ~ **one's rights** seine Rechte durchsetzen.

assertible verfechtbar.

assertion Vorbringen, Feststellung, Behauptung;

positive ~ positive Behauptung;

~ **of a claim** Geltendmachung eines Anspruchs; ~ **of a right** Geltendmachung eines Rechtes;

to bear out an ~ jds. Behauptung bestätigen; **to make an** ~ Behauptung aufstellen.

assertory oath *(US)* Beteuerung unter Eid, Bekräftigungseid.

assess *(v.)* *(charge with a tax)* besteuern, [steuerlich] veranlagen (einschätzen), *(fix)* festsetzen, feststellen, *(members, US)* Vereinsbeitrag fordern (festsetzen), *(value)* [steuerlich] bewerten, einschätzen, abschätzen, taxieren, berechnen, bemessen;

~ **a building** Gebäude abschätzen (steuerlich veranschlagen), Einheitswert feststellen; ~ **the amount of damages** Entschädigungssumme bestimmen, Schadenshöhe (Entschädigungssumme) festsetzen; ~ **a business profit at a higher rate** Geschäftsgewinn mit einem höheren Steuersatz veranlagen; ~ **a claim** Anspruch bewerten; ~ **to corporation tax** körperschaftssteuerlich veranlagen; ~ **the damage** Schadensbetrag [der Höhe nach] feststellen, *(insurance)* Versicherungsschaden aufnehmen, *(ship)* Havarie aufmachen; ~ **death duties** zur Erbschaftssteuer veranlagen; ~ **duty** Zoll festsetzen; ~ **[the extent of] a loss** Verlust berechnen; ~ **a fine** Bußgeld festsetzen; ~ **income tax** einkommensteuerlich veranlagen; ~ **incorrectly** falsche Steuerveranlagung vornehmen; ~ **members of a society for expenses** Unkosten auf die Vereinsmitglieder umlegen; ~ **s. o. in (at) so much** j. steuerlich so hoch veranlagen; ~ **for additional payment** zu zusätzlichen Zahlungen heranziehen; ~ **a property** Vermögen bewerten; ~ **property for improvements** Einheitswert eines Grundstücks neu feststellen; ~ **property for taxation** zur Vermögenssteuer veranlagen; ~ **separately** *(income-tax return)* getrennt veranlagen; ~ **the starting salary** Anfangsgehalt festsetzen; ~ **s. o. a tax** *(US)* jem. eine Steuer auferlegen; ~ **for taxable value** nach dem Steuerwert abschätzen; ~ **a value** Wert festsetzen.

assessable taxierbar, [ab]schätzbar, bewertbar, *(liable to duty)* abgabesteuerpflichtig, steuerbar, veranlagungspflichtig; ~ **for tax** steuerpflichtig;
~ **income** steuerpflichtiges Einkommen; ~ **share of profit** steuerpflichtiger Gewinnanteil; ~ **stock** *(US)* nachschußpflichtige Aktien.

assessed Besteuerter;
~ *(a.)* veranlagt, bewertet;
illegally ~ unberechtigt veranlagt;
~ **income tax** veranlagte Einkommensteuer; ~ **price** Schätz-, Taxpreis; ~ **rental** steuerlicher Mietwert; ~ **taxes** direkte (im Veranlagungswege erhobene) Steuern; ~ **valuation** steuerliche Veranlagung, Abschätzung zu Steuerzwecken; ~ **value** Schätzwert, Veranlagungswert, veranlagter Wert, *(real estate)* Einheits-, Steuerwert.

assessee *(US)* Zahlungspflichtiger.
assessing death duties Erbschaftssteuerveranlagung.
assessment *(allocation)* anteilsmäßige Festsetzung, *(amount fixed)* veranlagter Steuerbetrag, *(apportionment of taxes)* Besteuerung, Steueranschlag, [Steuer]veranlagung, *(appraisal)* Einschätzung, [steuerliche] Bewertung, Wertfeststellung, Berechnung, *(campaign expenses, US)* Wahlbeitrag, *(capital stock, US)* Nachzahlungsveranlagung, *(contribution, US)* Umlage, Beitrag, *(of damages)* Festsetzung von Schadenersatz, *(duty)* Steuer, Abgabe, *(levying of a tax)* Steuererhebung, *(mutual life insurance)* Versicherungsnachzahlung, *(pol.)* Beurteilung, *(reorganization of stock corporation)* Zuzahlung [von Effekteninhabern], *(ship)* Havarieaufmachung, *(tax amount to a deficiency)* Steuernachzahlungsbetrag, *(tax system)* Steuersystem, -tarif, *(valuation of property)* Grundstücksbewertung;
additional ~ Nachveranlagung; **arbitrary** ~ aufgrund von Schätzungen vorgenommene Veranlagung; **capital-gains** ~ Besteuerung von Veräußerungsgewinnen; **fair and proper legal** ~ ordnungsgemäße Steuerveranlagung; **income-tax** ~ Einkommensteuerveranlagung; **jeopardy** ~ sofortige Einkommensteuerveranlagung; **net** ~ Nettoveranlagung; ~ **paid** Zuzahlung geleistet; **proportional** ~ anteilsmäßige Veranlagung; **rating** ~ Einschätzung der Kreditfähigkeit; **gross rating** ~ Veranlagung der Bruttoeinnahmen; **reduced** ~ niedrigere Bewertung, *(tax)* herabgesetzte Veranlagung; **self** ~ Selbstveranlagung, -einschätzung; **separate** ~ getrennte Veranlagung; **special** ~ Sonderumlage, *(real estate)* Anliegerbeiträge; **stock** ~ *(US)* Nachschußaufforderung; **subsequent** ~ Nachveranlagung; **tax** ~ Steuerveranlagung, -festsetzung, -bescheid; **union** ~ Gewerkschaftssonderbeitrag;
~ **of a balance sheet** Bilanzbewertung; ~ **on bank stocks** Nachschußzahlung auf Bankaktien im Sanierungsfall; ~ **of a building** Gebäudeabschätzung; ~ **of a claim** Anspruchsbewertung; ~ **of costs** Kostenfestsetzung; ~ **of damage** Schadensfeststellung, -bemessung; ~ **of damages** Festsetzung einer Entschädigung; ~ **of duty** Zollfestsetzung; ~ **of a fee** Gebührenansatz, -festsetzung; ~ **of income tax** Veranlagung zur Einkommensteuer, Einkommensteuerveranlagung; ~ **of personnel** *(US)* Personalbeurteilung; ~ **of profitability** Rentabilitätsschätzung; ~ **of (on) property** *(Br.)* Bewertung von Grundvermögen, *(US)* Veranlagung zur Vermögenssteuer, Vermögensteuerveranlagung; ~ **of landed property** *(Br.)* Grundsteuerveranlagung; ~ **of a remuneration** Festsetzung einer Vergütung; ~ **of risk** Risikoeinschätzung, -beurteilung; ~ **to tax** Steuerveranlagung; **equalizing** ~ Steuerausgleich; ~ **of value** Wertberechnung, Wertermittlung;
to appeal against a tax ~ Einspruch gegen einen Steuerbescheid einlegen; **to apply for a separate** ~ um getrennte Steuerveranlagung einkommen; **to be aggrieved by an** ~ durch eine Veranlagung benachteiligt werden; **to calculate an** ~ Veranlagung durchführen; **to claim separate** ~ *(spouses)* getrennte Steuerveranlagung beantragen; **to increase the** ~ Veranlagungsbetrag erhöhen; **to levy** ~ *(corporation, US)* zur Zahlung auf das Grundkapital auffordern; **to make a self-**~ sich selbst einschätzen (veranlagen); **to prepare an** ~ Steuerveranlagung durchführen; **to raise an estimated** ~ Steuerbescheid in Abweichung von der Steuererklärung festsetzen; **to reduce the** ~ **of a building** Einheitswert eines Hauses herabsetzen; **to reopen an** ~ neue Steuerveranlagung beantragen; **to revise an** ~ Neuveranlagung vornehmen, Veranlagung berichtigen;

~ **area** Veranlagungs-, Steuerbezirk; **pure** ~ **mutual association** Versicherungsverein auf Gegenseitigkeit, Gegenseitigkeitsverein; ~ **basis** Bemessungsgrundlage; **special** ~ **bonds** *(US)* kommunale Meliorations-Schuldverschreibungen; ~ **committee** Abschätzungskommission; ~ **committee act** Bewertungs-, Veranlagungsgesetz; ~ **company** *(insurance)* Sterbegeldverein mit Umlageverfahren; ~ **contract** Umlagevereinbarung; ~ **costs** Veranlagungskosten; ~ **directives** Veranlagungsrichtlinien; ~ **district** Steuer[veranlagungs]bezirk; ~ **fund** *(insurance)* Guthaben eines Versicherungsvereins auf Gegenseitigkeit, Umlagevermögen; **special** ~ **fund** kommunaler Meliorationsfonds; ~ **instal(l)ment** Steuerrate; ~ **insurance** Versicherung auf Gegenseitigkeit; ~ **list** Steuer-, Veranlagungsliste; ~ **machinery** Steuerveranlagungseinrichtungen; ~ **notice** Steuerbescheid; ~ **office** [Steuer]veranlagungsstelle; ~ **period** Veranlagungsperiode, -zeitraum, Bemessungszeitraum, Steuerperiode; ~ **principles** Bewertungsrichtlinien; ~ **procedure** *(staff)* Beurteilungsverfahren; ~ **roll** Steuerliste, -rolle, Veranlagungsliste; ~ **system** Umlageverfahren; ~ **work** *(mining, US)* jährliche Arbeit.

assessor *(adviser)* Berater, Assistent, *(assistant to judge, Br.)* [rechtskundiger] Beisitzer, *(colleague)* Kollege, Amtsbruder, *(insurance)* Taxator, Berechner, Schadensabschätzer, Regulierungsbeamter, *(taxation, Scot.)* Feststellungs-, Finanzbeamter, Veranlagungsstelle;
legal ~ *(Br.)* Sachverständiger, Beisitzer; **loss** ~ *(Br.)* Schadensabschätzer; **nautical** ~ *(Br.)* amtlich bestellter Schiffssachverständiger;
~ **of taxes** Steuer-, Finanzbeamter.

asset *(balance sheet)* Aktivposten, Posten auf der Aktivseite, Haben, Aktivum, *(estate)* Nachlaßgegenstand, *(merit)* wertvolle (nutzbringende) Eigenschaft, Vorzug, wichtiger Faktor, Stütze, *(possession)* Vermögensgegenstand, -wert;
to be an ~ zu den Pluspunkten zählen; **to discard an** ~ [Betriebs]-anlage außer Betrieb setzen; **to dispose of an** ~ Vermögensgegenstand veräußern; **to make an** ~ **viable on acquisition** Anlagegut beim Ankauf wirtschaftlich nutzbar machen; **to write up the value of an** ~ Wert einer Anlage heraufsetzen.

assets *(balance sheet)* Guthaben, Aktivvermögen, Aktiva, Deckungsforderungen, Werksanlagen, *(deceased estate)* Hinterlassenschaft, Erbschaftsmasse, zur Schuldendeckung ausreichender Nachlaß, *(insolvency)* [Konkurs]masse, Aktivmasse, -vermögen, *(of merchant)* Betriebsvermögen, *(property)* Vermögen[swerte], Vermögenskomplex, -bestand, Güter und Rechte;
active ~ produktives Betriebsvermögen, Aktivkapital; **actual** ~ effektiver Vermögenswert, Rein-, Nettovermögen; **admitted** ~ *(insurance law)* anerkannte Versicherungsansprüche; **after-acquired** ~ *(mortgage bonds)* später erworbene Anlagen; **attachable** ~ beschlagnahmefähige Werte; **available** ~ [frei] verfügbare (freie) Aktiva, unbelastete Anlagen, Aktivbestand; **bank** ~ Vermögenswerte einer Bank, Bankvermögen; **bankruptcy (bankrupt's)** ~ Vermögensmasse des Konkursschuldners, Konkursmasse; ~ **brought in** Einlage; **business** ~ Betriebsvermögen; **capital** ~ Anlagevermögen, -kapital, -güter, festliegende Aktiva, unbewegliches Vermögen; **cash** ~ *(balance sheet)* Barvermögen, Kassenbestand und Bankguthaben im Liquidationsfall; **chargeable** ~ steuerpflichtige Vermögenswerte; **chargeable** ~ **disposed of** veräußerte steuerpflichtige Vermögensgegenstände; **circulating** ~ flüssige Aktiva, Umlaufvermögen; **concealed** ~ stille Reserven, verschleierte Vermögenswerte; **contingent** ~ potentielle Aktivposten; **convertible** ~ konvertierbare Vermögenswerte; **corporate** ~ Vermögenswerte einer Aktiengesellschaft; **current** ~ kurzfristiges Umlaufvermögen; **dead** ~ totes Kapital, nicht realisierbare Wirtschaftsgüter, unproduktive Anlagen; **debtor's** ~ Konkursmasse; **deferred** ~ transitorische Aktiva; **disposable** ~ verfügbare Vermögenswerte (Guthaben); **distributed** ~ verteilte Konkursmasse; **doubtful** ~ ihrem Wert nach ungewisse Vermögenswerte; **dwindling** ~ Kapitalschwund, Vermögensverfall; **earning** ~ gewinnbringende [Kapital]anlagen; **economic** ~ Wirtschaftsgüter; **employed** ~ eingesetztes Aktivvermögen; **equitable** ~ aus dem Nachlaß aussonderungsfähige Vermögenswerte; **estimated** ~ veranschlagte Aktiva; **exempt** ~ pfändungsfreies Vermögen; **external** ~ Auslandsvermögen, Auslandswerte, Vermögenswerte im Ausland; **fictitious** ~ fingierte (fiktive) Vermögenswerte; **fixed** ~ *(accounting)* Anlagevermögen, -kapital, festliegende Aktiva, Sachanlagen; **floating** *(fluid, US)* ~ Betriebsmittel, Umlaufvermögen, -kapital; **foreign** ~ Auslandsanlagen, -guthaben, -vermögen; **frozen** ~ nicht flüssige (eingefrorene) Guthaben, blockierte Vermögens-

werte; **fund** ~ Fondsvermögen; **hidden** ~ stille Reserven; **his** ~ seine Vorteile; **household** ~ Haushaltsgegenstände, *(estate)* Dreißigster; **hypothecated** ~ sicherungsübereignete Vermögensgegenstände; **inadmitted** ~ *(income-tax return)* im Liquidationsfall geringwertige Anlagegüter; **income-earning** ~ gewinnbringende Kapitalanlagen; **individual** ~ *(partner)* Privatvermögen; **instalment option** ~ Nachlaßwerte, die in Raten erbschaftsversteuert werden können; **insufficient** ~ unzureichende Aktiva; **intangible** ~ immaterielle Anlagewerte; **intercompany** ~ Konzernguthaben; **investment-type** ~ kapitalähnliche Anlagewerte; **legal** ~ frei verwertbare Nachlaßaktiva; **limited-life** ~ Anlagewerte mit begrenzter Lebensdauer, kurzfristige Anlagegüter; **liquid** ~ *(accounting)* flüssige (liquide) Mittel, frei verfügbare Vermögenswerte, *(US, balance sheet)* Umlaufvermögen; **live** ~ ertragreiche (wohlfundierte) Anlagewerte; **long-lived** ~ langlebige Anlagegüter; **medium-term** ~ mittelfristige Anlagegüter; **medium-term and short-term** ~ mittel- und kurzfristiges Umlaufvermögen; **miscellaneous** ~ *(balance sheet)* verschiedene Anlagegüter; **net** ~ *(deceased)* reiner Nachlaß, Reinvermögen, *(insurance)* von der Versicherungsgesellschaft anerkanntes Vermögen; **no** ~ *(on bill of exchange)* kein Guthaben; **nominal** ~ Buchwerte; **nonledger** ~ in der Bilanz nicht aufgeführte Anlagegüter; **nonoperating** ~ außerbetriebliche Anlagen; **nonredeemable** ~ nicht voll einbringlich erscheinende Guthaben; **nonreplaceable** ~ in der Substanz abnehmende Anlagen; **operating** ~ Betriebsvermögen; **ordinary** ~ Geschäftsvermögen; **original** ~ Anfangsvermögen, -kapital; **other** ~ *(balance sheet)* sonstige Aktiva (Vermögenswerte); **jointly owned** ~ Gesamthandsvermögen; **partnership** ~ Gesellschaftsvermögen; **permanent** ~ *(accounting)* festliegende Ativa, Anlagevermögen, -kapital, *(property)* unbewegliches Vermögen; **personal** ~ Privatvermögen, *(bankrupt)* persönliches Vermögen des Gemeinschuldners, *(deceased person)* beweglicher Nachlaß; **physical** ~ Sachanlagevermögen; **fully pledged** ~ nur zur Deckung der Sicherungsübereignungsansprüche ausreichende Aktiva; **party pledged** ~ teilweise zur Masseverteilung verfügbare Aktiva; **private** ~ Privatvermögen; **quick** ~ sofort einlösbare Guthaben, leicht realisierbare Aktiva, flüssige (kurzfristige) Mittel, *(US, balance sheet)* Umlaufvermögen, -kapital; **ready** ~ verfügbare Vermögenswerte; **real** ~ Grundstückswerte, unbewegliches Vermögen, Immobiliarvermögen; **realizable** ~ Effektivbestand, effektiver Bestand; **easily realizable** ~ leicht greifbare Aktiva; **receivable** ~ ausstehende Guthaben; **remaining** ~ Restmasse; **service-yielding** ~ Dienstleistungsanlagen; **short-life (-lived)** ~ kurzlebige Anlage-, Wirtschaftsgüter; **slow** ~ schwer realisierbare Wirtschaftsgüter; **special** ~ Ausgleichsposten; **sticky** ~ nicht realisierbare Aktiva; **sundry** ~ *(balance sheet)* sonstige Aktivposten; **suspense** ~ transitorische Aktiva; **tangible** ~ greifbare (reale) Sachwerte, Vermögenswerte, Barsachvermögen; **tangible fixed** ~ Sachanlagen, -vermögen, Anlagevermögen; **total** ~ Gesamtvermögen; **trust** ~ Treuhandvermögen; **unattachable** ~ pfändungsfreies Vermögen; **unencumbered** ~ freies Vermögen; **unpledged** ~ zur Verteilung für die Masse verfügbare Aktiva; **unrealizable** ~ nicht realisierbare Vermögenswerte; **wasting** ~ in der Substanz abnehmende Anlagen, kurzlebige Wirtschaftsgüter; **watered** ~ Wirtschaftsgüter mit überhöhtem Buchwert; **working** ~ Aktiv-, Betriebskapital, Betriebsvermögen;
~ **held abroad** Auslandsbesitz, -guthaben, -vermögen; ~ **of a bank** Bankvermögen; ~ **of the banking department** *(Br.)* Guthaben der Bank von England; ~ **of a bankrupt's estate** Konkurs-, Aktivmasse, Konkursgegenstände, Vermögensmasse des Konkursschuldners; ~ **of a business** Firmenvermögen; ~ **for use in the business** dem Geschäftsbetrieb dienende Anlagen; ~ **exempt from capital gains tax** nicht der Kapitalgewinnsteuer unterliegende Vermögenswerte; ~ **pledged as collateral** verpfändete Aktiva; ~ **of a company** Gesellschaftsvermögen; ~ **per descent** vererbliches Vermögen; ~ **at disposal** freie Aktiva; ~ **relieved of estate duty** erbschaftssteuerfreie Vermögenswerte; ~ **of a fund** Fondsvermögen; ~ **acquired on hire purchase** *(Br.)* im Abzahlungswege erworbene Wirtschaftsgüter; ~ **in kind brought in** Sacheinlage; ~ **and liabilities** *(balance sheet)* Aktiva und Passiva, Vermögensbilanz; ~ **entre mains (in hand)** frei verfügbare Nachlaßmasse; ~ **of a partnership** Gesellschaftsvermögen; ~ **with rapid rates of cash return** Anlagegüter mit schnell erzielbarem Barerlöswert; ~ **under will** Nachlaßvermögen;
to arrange ~ **in the order of liquidity** Aktiva nach Liquiditätsgesichtspunkten aufführen; **to be long-term business** ~ zu den laufenden Aktivposten eines Unternehmens zählen; **to carry as**

~ auf der Aktivseite einer Bilanz aufführen, [in der Bilanz] aktivieren; **to conceal** ~ Vermögenswerte verschleiern; **to destroy the** ~ **of the debtor** Vermögensmasse des Gemeinschuldners aufbrauchen; **to discard** ~ Anlagen außer Betrieb nehmen; **to liquidate the** ~ **of a bankrupt** Konkursmasse liquidieren; **to marshal the** ~ Aktiva feststellen; **to pay out of the** ~ aus der [Konkurs]masse zahlen; **to realize** ~ Vermögenswerte flüssigmachen; **to redeploy** ~ **of a company** Vermögenswerte eines Unternehmens anderweitig einsetzen; **to replace fixed** ~ Anlagen erneuern; **to retire** ~ Anlagen außer Betrieb nehmen; **to write down** ~ Anlagen abschreiben.

asset | account Aktiv-, Bestandskonto; **fixed** ~ **account** Anlagenkonto, Konto der Anlagenwerte, Sachanlagenkonto; ~ **backing** Aufkauf von Industrieunternehmungen; **to build up the** ~ **base** Grundlagen für den Anlagenpark schaffen; ~ **costs** Kosten des Anlagevermögens; ~ **coverage** Deckung durch Aktiva; ~ **creating** vermögenswirksam; **fixed-**~ **financing** Anlagenfinanzierung; ~ **items** Aktiv-, Anlageposten; **useful** ~ **life** Nutzungsdauer einer Anlage; ~ **management** Anlagenverwaltung; ~ **management department** Anlagenverwaltungsabteilung; ~ **mortgage** Aktivhypothek; ~ **potential** Aktivpotential; ~ **purchases** Anlagenkäufe; ~ **replacement** Anlagenerneuerung; ~ **side** *(balance sheet)* Aktivseite; ~ **and liability statement** Gewinn- und Verlustrechnung; ~ **status** Anlagenstatus; ~ **strategy** Vermögensstrategie; ~ **stripping** Anlagenausschlachtung; ~ **transfer** Anlagenüberschreibung; **fixed-**~ **unit** Anlageneinheit; ~ **valuation** Anlagenbewertung; ~ **valuation reserve** Wertberichtigung für Wertänderungen; ~ **value** Substanzwert, *(investment fund)* Fondsvermögen; **net** ~ **value** Liquidations-, Inventarwert [eines Investmentfonds].

asseverate *(v.)* beteuern, feierlich versichern.
asseveration feierliche Versicherung, Beteuerung.
assiduate begeisterter Anhänger.
assiduity in one's duties Pflichteifer.
assiduous fleißig, emsig, eifrig.
assign Rechtsnachfolger, Zessionar, Forderungsübernehmer;
~ *(v.) (allot)* anweisen, zuweisen, zuteilen, *(fix)* bestimmen, angeben, festlegen, *(mil.)* abstellen, abkommandieren, *(place to)* [Stellung] übertragen, versetzen, *(transfer)* übertragen, -eignen, Eigentumsübertragung vornehmen, abtreten, zedieren;
~ **an account** Kontensaldo abtreten; ~ **advertising expenditure** Werbeetat aufteilen; ~ **in blank** blanko übertragen; ~ **business** *(law court)* Geschäftsverteilung vornehmen; ~ **a case** Fall zuweisen; ~ **choses in action** immaterielle Güter abtreten; ~ **claims** Ansprüche (Forderungen) abtreten (zedieren); ~ **costs** Kosten aufteilen; ~ **a counsel** Offizialverteidiger bestellen; ~ **a day for a hearing in court** Verhandlungstermin festsetzen, Verhandlung anberaumen; ~ **a debt** Forderung abtreten; ~ **a dower** Witwengeld festsetzen; ~ **a duty to s. o.** jem. einen Aufgabenbereich zuweisen; ~ **a flat to s. o.** j. in eine Wohnung einweisen; ~ **land** Land zuweisen; ~ **a life assurance policy** *(Br.)* Lebensversicherungspolice abtreten; ~ **a mortgage** Hypothekenforderung abtreten; ~ **a patent** Patentanspruch abtreten; **to a post** für einen Posten bestimmen; ~ **property** Vermögen übertragen; ~ **a reason** Grund angeben; ~ **a right** Recht abtreten (übertragen); ~ **a salary to an office** Gehalt für eine Stellung festsetzen; ~ **shares** *(stocks, US)* Aktien übertragen; ~ **a task** Aufgabe stellen (zuweisen).
assignability Abtretbarkeit, Übertragbarkeit, Zedierbarkeit.
assignable zuweisbar, *(alienable)* übertragbar, abtretbar, zedierbar, zessions-, abtretungsfähig, *(determinable)* bestimmbar; ~ **instrument** begebbares Papier.
assignation *(allotment)* Zuweisung, Zuteilung, Bestimmung, *(deed of assignment)* Übertretungs-, Abtretungsurkunde, *(transfer)* Übertragung, Zession;
~ **of choses in action** Abtretung immaterieller Güter; ~ **of a claim** Forderungsabtretung, Zession; ~ **of a patent** Patentabtretung; ~ **of shares** Aktienübertragung;
~ **house** *(US)* elegantes Bordell.
assigned *(allotted)* zugewiesen, -geteilt, *(transferred)* abgetreten, übertragen;
~ **account** abgetretenes Konto; ~ **book accounts** abgetretene Buchforderungen; ~ **counsel** Pflicht-, Offizialverteidiger; ~ **forces** *(mil.)* operativ unterstellte Kräfte; ~ **frequency** zugewiesene (zugeteilte) Frequenz, Sollfrequenz; ~ **siding** Verladegleis.
assignee Abtretungs-, Anweisungsempfänger, Zessionar, *(agent)* Beauftragter, Vertreter, *(legal successor)* Besitz-, Rechtsnachfolger, *(representative)* Bevollmächtigter, *(transferee)* Zessionar, Forderungsübernehmer;

~ **in bankruptcy (of a bankrupt)** vom Gemeinschuldner vorgeschlagener Konkursverwalter; ~ **for the benefit of creditors** *(in insolvency)* zugunsten der Gläubiger besteller Pfleger (Treuhänder); ~ **of a debt** Zessionar; ~ **in fact** Zessionar; ~ **in law** Forderungsübernehmer.

assigneeship Pflegschaft, Treuhandverwaltung.

assignment *(allotment)* Zu-, Anweisung, Zuteilung, *(bill)* Anweisung, trassierter Wechsel, *(deed)* Zessions-, Abtretungs-, Übertaragungsurkunde, *(journalism)* Bestimmung eines Vorfalls für einen Sonderbericht, *(patent law)* Patentübertragung, *(school)* Hausaufgabe, *(specifying)* Festlegung, -setzung, Bestimmung, *(task)* Aufgabe, Aufgabengebiet, -stellung, Auftrag, Verwendung, *(transfer)* Abtretung, Zession, Übertragung, -eignung, *(US)* Stellung, Posten;
absolute ~ offene Forderungsabtretung; **automatic** ~ automatischer Forderungsübergang; **binding** ~ gültige Abtretung; **conditional** ~ vom Eintritt eines Ereignisses abhängige Abtretung; **diplomatic** ~ diplomatischer Posten; **equitable** ~ formlose Forderungsabtretung, [etwa] stille [Forderungs]abtretung, *(policy)* zu Besicherungszwecken vorgenommene Abtretung; **foreign** ~ im Ausland vorgenommene Abtretung; **general** ~ *(banking)* vollständige Vermögensübertragung zugunsten der Gläubiger, Mantelzession; **invalid** ~ ungültige Abtretung; **involuntary** ~ *(bankrupt)* zwangsweise Vermögensübertragung; **irrevocable** ~ unwiderrufliche Übertragung; **legal** ~ rechtswirksame Abtretung, gesetzlicher Forderungsübergang; **overseas** ~ Überseeverwendung; **partial** ~ Teilabtretung; **pending** ~ bevorstehende Versetzung; **permanent** ~ *(US)* Dauerstellung; **re-**~ Rückabtretung; **statutory** ~ gesetzlicher Forderungsübergang; **subrogation** ~ Abtretung des Ersatzanspruches; **successive** ~ mehrfache Abtretung; **voluntary** ~ freiwillige Vermögensübertragung [im Konkurs];
~ **of account** Kontoabtretung; ~ **of accounts receivable** *(US)* Diskontierung von Buchforderungen, Debitoren-, Forderungsabtretung; ~ **of the balance of account** Saldenabtretung; ~ **of action** *(court)* Zuweisung einer Sache aufgrund der Geschäftsordnung; ~ **of activities** Arbeitszuordnung, -verteilung; ~ **of advertising expenditure** Aufteilung des Werbeetats; ~ **in bankruptcy** Abtretung im Konkursverfahren, Forderungsübergang auf den Konkursverwalter; ~ **for the benefit of creditors** außerkonkursliche Abwicklung zugunsten der Gläubiger, Liquidationsvergleich; ~ **in blank** Blankogiro, -indossament; ~ **of book debts** Abtretung von Buchforderungen; **unregistered general** ~ **of book debts** stille Zession aller Buchforderungen; ~ **of business** *(law court)* Geschäfteilung; ~ **of choses in action** Forderungsabtretung; ~ **of a claim** Forderungsabtretung, -übergang, Zession; ~ **of contract** Übertragung des gesamten Vertrages; ~ **of costs** Kostenaufteilung; ~ **for coverage** Betreuungsauftrag; ~ **of a customer's credit balance** Saldenabtretung eines Kundenkontos; ~ **on death** Forderungsübergang im Todesfall; ~ **of debt** Forderungsabtretung; **specific** ~ **of an existing debt** Abtretung einer bestimmten Forderung; ~ **of a future debt** Abtretung einer zukünftigen Forderung; ~ **of debts accruing due** Abtretung zukünftiger Forderungen; ~ **of dower** Festsetzung des Pflichtteilanspruchs der Witwe; ~ **of duties** Aufgabenzuweisung; ~ **of error** Berufungs-, Revisionsbegründung, Begründung einer Nichtigkeitsbeschwerde; ~ **of advertising expenditure** Aufteilung des Werbeetats; ~ **of funds** Mittelzuweisung, Guthabenübertragung; ~ **of interest** Anteilsübertragung; ~ **of land** Landzuweisung, -zuteilung; ~ **of lease** Abtretung der Mieteinkünfte, Miet-, Pachtabtretung; ~ **of mortgage** Hypothekenabtretung; ~ **of contractual obligation** Übertragung von Vertragsverpflichtungen; ~ **by operation of law** Forderungsübergang kraft Gesetzes; ~ **of a patent** Patentübertragung; ~ **of pension** Abtretung der Pensionsbezüge; ~ **of policy** Abtretung der Rechte aus einer Versicherung (der Versicherungsforderung), Policenabtretung; ~ **with preference** Vermögensübertragung auf den Konkursverwalter zwecks bevorzugter Befriedigung bevorrechtigter Gläubiger; ~ **of the proceeds of a policy** Abtretung des Versicherungsanspruches; ~ **of property** Grundstücks-, Vermögensübertragung; ~ **of retired pay** Abtretung des Ruhegehalts; ~ **of reasons** Aufführung (Angabe) von Gründen; ~ **of responsibility** Zuweisung des Verantwortungsbereichs; ~ **of revenue** Einnahmenübertragung; ~ **of a right** Rechtsübertragung; ~ **of a salary** Gehaltsfestsetzung; ~ **of a share in partnership** Abtretung eines Gesellschafteranteils; ~ **of stock** Aktienübertragung; ~ **of a task** Aufgabenzuweisung; ~ **of wages** Lohnabtretung; ~ **by way of security** zu Besicherungszwecken vorgenommene Zession; ~ **by way of charge** Abtretung von Forderungen gegen einen Sonderfonds;

to conduct an ~ Aufgabe durchführen; **to go on** ~ Auftrag durchführen; **to make an** ~ abtreten, übertragen, zedieren; **to take over an** ~ Aufgabe übernehmen; **to work on** ~ **abroad** seiner Arbeit im Ausland nachgehen, Stellung im Ausland haben;
~ **agreement** Zessionsvertrag; ~ **officer** *(Foreign Office)* Beamter der Personalabteilung; ~ **panel** Versetzungsgremium; ~ **problem** Zuordnungsproblem; ~ **sheet** Leitfaden für Interviews, Interviewanweisung.

assignor Zedent, Abtretender, Rechtsvorgänger.

assimilate *(v.)* anpassen, angleichen, assimilieren, *(stock exchange)* [Wertpapiere] aufnehmen;
~ **people from European countries** europäische Einwanderer assimilieren; ~ **properly** genau erfassen.

assimilation Anpassung, Angleichung, Assimilierung, *(stock exchange)* Aufnahme [von Wertpapieren].

assist *(v.)* Hilfe leisten, helfen, unterstützen, mitarbeiten, aushelfen;
to advise and ~ mit Rat und Tat unterstützen; ~ **in doing a job** bei einer Arbeit mithelfen; ~ **at a meeting** an einer Versammlung teilnehmen; ~ **s. o. with money** j. finanziell unterstützen; ~ **s. o. in advancing his position** jem. zu einer besseren Stellung verhelfen; ~ **a ship in distress** einem in Seenot geratenem Schiff Hilfe leisten; ~ **the voltage** Spannung erhöhen.

assistance Unterstützung, Hilfe, Hilfsdienst, Beistand;
in need of ~ hilfs-, fürsorgebedürftig; **with the** ~ **of** unter Hinzuziehung von;
cash ~ bar ausgezahlte Unterstützung; **financial** ~ Geldhilfe, finanzielle Unterstützung; **government** ~ staatliche Unterstützung; **hostile** ~ *(law of nations)* Beistandsleistung; **judicial** ~ Rechtshilfeverkehr; **medical** ~ Krankenfürsorge, ärztliche Hilfe; **military** ~ militärische Hilfeleistung; **mutual** ~ gegenseitige Hilfe, gegenseitige Unterstützung; **national** ~ *(Br.)* Fürsorge[unterstützung], Sozialhilfe; **pecuniary** ~ finanzielle Unterstützung; **public (social)** ~ *(US)* Sozialhilfe, Fürsorge[unterstützung]; **relocation** ~ Repatriierungsbeihilfe;
~ **of counsel** Bestellung eines Pflichtverteidigers; ~ **with removal expenses** Umzugsbeihilfe; ~ **to ships in distress** Hilfeleistung für in Seenot geratene Schiffe;
to afford ~ Hilfe gewähren; **to be in receipt of national** *(Br.)* **(public, US)** ~ Fürsorgeunterstützung (Sozialhilfe) beziehen; **to extend pecuniary** ~ finanzielle Unterstützung gewähren; **to get** ~ Hilfe finden; **to give (render)** ~ Hilfe angedeihen lassen, Hilfsdienst (Hilfe) leisten; **to live on national** ~ *(Br.)* Sozialhilfeempfänger sein; **to spring to s. one's** ~ jem. zu Hilfe eilen; **Public** ~ **Authority** *(US)* Sozial-, Fürsorgeamt; **public** ~ **benefits** *(US)* Fürsorgeleistungen; **national** ~ **committee** *(Br.)* Sozial-, Fürsorgeausschuß; ~ **effort** Hilfsbemühungen, -leistungen; **public** ~ **roll** *(US)* Fürsorgeempfängerliste; **to be put on public** ~ **rolls** *(US)* der Fürsorge (Sozialhilfe) anheimfallen; **mutual** ~ **treaty** Beistandspakt.

assistanceship Assistentenstelle.

assistant Mitarbeiter, Gehilfe, Hilfskraft, -person, Assistent, *(administration)* Substitut, *(deputy)* Stellvertreter, *(law court)* Beisitzer, Hilfsrichter, *(US, school)* Hilfslehrkraft;
legal ~ juristischer Mitarbeiter; **shop** ~ Verkäufer, Ladenangestellter; **unestablished** ~ wissenschaftlicher Hilfsarbeiter;
aids and ~s enge Mitarbeiter;
~ **to a manager** Vorstandssekretär; ~ **to memory** Gedächtnishilfe, -stütze; ~ **in the taxation department** Mitarbeiter in der Steuerabteilung;
~ *(a.)* behilflich, hilfreich, beistehend, *(deputizing)* stellvertretend, assistierend;
~ **accountant** Hilfsprüfer; ~ **agent** Vertretergehilfe; ~ **architect** Bauführer; ~ **auditor** Hilfsrevisor; ~ **bookkeeper** Hilfsbuchhalter, zweiter Buchhalter; ~ **cashier** zweiter Kassierer; ~ **chemist** Laborant; ~ **clerk** Buchhalterstellvertreter; ~ **controller** Hilfsrevisor; ~ **department head** stellvertretender Abteilungsleiter; ~ **deputy minister** [etwa] Staatssekretär; ~ **director** stellvertretender Direktor; ~ **driver** Hilfsfahrer; ~ **editor** Neben-, Hilfsredakteur; ~ **engineer** Hilfsingenieur; ~ **examiner** *(patent law)* Hilfsprüfer; ~ **judge** Hilfsrichter, Beisitzer, [Gerichts]assessor; ~ **librarian** Bibliothekskraft; ~ **manager** stellvertretender Direktor; ~ **master** Oberlehrer; ~ **member of a committee** Ersatzmitglied eines Ausschusses; ~ **overseer** Armenaufseher; ~ **paying teller** stellvertretender Kassierer; ~ **professor** *(Br.)* mit Teilaufgaben betrauter Professor; ~ **secretary** *(US)* Ministerialdirektor; ~ **Secretary of Defense** *(US mil.)* Abteilungsleiter im Verteidigungsministerium; ~ **teacher** Aushilfslehrer; ~ **treasurer** Schatzmeisterstellvertreter.

assistantship Assistentenstelle.

assisted | person *(Br.)* Fürsorge-, Sozialhilfeempfänger, *(law court)* Armenrechtspartei; ~ **take-off** *(plane)* Abflug mit Starthilfe.

assisting numbers Hilfsnummern.

assistor Beisitzer.

assize *(judicial decree)* gerichtliche Verfügung, *(ordinance)* Spruch, richterlicher Beschluß, Verdikt, *(sitting in court)* Gerichtssitzung, -tagung, Prozeß, Verhandlung, richterliche Untersuchung;
~s *(trial before jurymen)* Schwurgericht.

associate Gesellschafter, Teilhaber, Teilnehmer, Geschäftspartner, *(ally)* Bundesgenosse, Verbündeter, *(EC)* assoziiertes Mitglied, *(fellow)* Genosse, Kollege, *(membership)* Mitarbeiter, außerordentliches Mitglied, Beigeordneter, *(US, university)* Lehrbeauftragter;
business ~ Teilhaber, Geschäftspartner;
~ **of an academy** korrespondierendes Mitglied einer Akademie; ~s **to memory** Aide-Memoire; ~ **in office** Teilhaber, Partner;
~ *(v.)* sich verbinden, assoziieren, zusammentun;
~ **with others in business** sich geschäftlich zusammentun; ~ **with intelligent people** mit intelligenten Leuten verkehren; ~ **o. s. with a party** sich einer Partei anschließen; ~ **trademarks** Warenzeichen miteinander verbinden; ~ **o. s. with s. o. in an undertaking** jds. Teilhaber in einem Unternehmen werden;
~ *(a.)* eng verbunden, vereinigt, assoziiert, *(admitted)* beigeordnet, zugesellt;
~ **companies** *(Br.)* Konzernunternehmen; ~ **counsel** Sozius; ~ **director** stellvertretender Direktor; ~ **editor** Mitherausgeber; ~ **judge** Beisitzer; ~ **justice** beigeordneter Richter, *(US)* Richter am Obersten Gerichtshof; ~ **member** außerordentliches (korrespondierendes) Mitglied; ~ **professor** *(US)* außerordentlicher Professor; ~ **status** Assoziiertenstatus.

associated | advertising Gemeinschaftswerbung; ~ **agency** Vertragsagentur; ~ **banks** *(US)* Clearingbanken; ~ **buying office** gemeinsames Einkaufsbüro; ~ **company** *(Br.)* nahestehende (angegliederte) Gesellschaft, Schwester-, Konzern-, Beteiligungsgesellschaft; ~ **country** *(EC)* assoziiertes Land; ~ **house** wirtschaftlich verbundenes Unternehmen; ~ **operations** zusammenhängende Transaktionen; ~ **overseas territories** *(EC)* assoziierte überseeische Gebiete; ~ **state** assoziierter Staat; ~ **Television Company** *(Br.)* kommerzielles Fernsehen; ~ **trademarks** Sortiments-, Serienmarken.

associateship Teilhaberschaft, *(academy)* Akademiezugehörigkeit, *(membership)* auswärtige Mitgliedschaft.

association Assoziation, *(EC)* Assoziierung, *(corporation)* Gesellschaft, *(society)* Genossenschaft, [Handels]gesellschaft, Verband, Verein, *(with other people)* Umgang, Verkehr, Beisammensein, *(union)* Bund, Vereinigung, Verbindung, Assoziierung, Syndikat;
Automobile ~ Automobilverband; **national banking** ~ *(US)* im Gebiet der USA zugelassenes Bankinstitut; **building and loan** ~ *(US)* Bausparkasse; **collective bargaining** ~ Tarifverband, -vereinigung; **cooperative** ~ *(US)* Genossenschaft; **employee** ~ Arbeitnehmerverband; **employers'** ~ Arbeitgeberverband; **fraternity** ~ *(US)* Verein zur Förderung gemeinsamer Interessen; **homestead aid benefit** ~ *(US)* Bausparkasse; **incorporated** ~ eingetragener Verein; **industrial** ~ *(US)* Fach-, Industrie-, Wirtschaftsverband; **local** ~ Ortsverband; **membership** ~ nicht eingetragener Verein; **mining** ~ Bergwerksverein; **mutual-aid** ~ Gegenseitigkeitsverein; **nonprofit** ~ Idealverein; **parents'** ~ Elternvereinigung; **producers'** ~ Produktionskartell; **professional** ~ berufliche Vereinigung, Berufsgenossenschaft; **regional** ~ Gebietsverband; **registered** ~ eingetragener Verein; **trade** ~ Berufsgenossenschaft, -vereinigung, Fachschaft, *(employers, US)* Unternehmerverband; **trading** ~ Handelsgesellschaft; **unincorporated** ~ nicht eingetragener (nicht rechtsfähiger) Verein; **vocational** ~ Berufs-, Fachverband; **International Working Men's** ~ Internationale Arbeitervereinigung;
~ **for the Advancement of Science** Vereinigung zur Förderung der Wissenschaft, Stifterverband; ~ **of banks** Bankenvereinigung; ~ **of better business bureau** *(US)* Vereinigung zur Erzielung besserer Geschäftsmethoden; ~ **of chambers of commerce** Handelskammerverband; ~ **for consumer research** Verbraucherverband; ~ **of County Councils** *(Scotland)* kommunaler Spitzenverband; ~ **of creditors** Gläubigervereinigung, -konsortium; ~ **of a second doctor in a case** Hinzuziehung eines zweiten Arztes im Krankheitsfall; ~ **of employers** Vereinigung der Arbeitgeberverbände; ~ **of enterprises** Unternehmensverband; ~ **of Executive Recruiting Consultants** Unternehmensbe-

raterverband; ~ **of ideas** Ideenassoziation, Gedankenverbindung; ~ **of pension funds** Pensionskassenvereinigung; ~ **of real-estate boards** vereinigte Immobilienmaklerkammer; ~ **of Professional Executive, Clerical and Computer Staff** *(Br.)* Gewerkschaft für Fach- u. Führungskräfte, Büro- u. Computerangestellte; ~ **of stock and share dealers** Börsenmaklerverband; ~ **of trademarks** Verbindung von Warenzeichen;
to become member of (join) an ~ einem Verein beitreten; **to form an** ~ Verband gründen; **to withdraw from an** ~ aus einem Verein austreten;
~ **advertising** Verbund-, Gemeinschaftswerbung; ~ **agreement** Verbandsabkommen, *(bargaining)* Tarifvereinbarung, *(EC)* Assoziationsabkommen; ~ **attorney** Verbandssyndikus; ~ **clause** Beitrittsklausel; ~ **Committee** *(EC)* Assoziationsausschuß; ~**'s funds** Vereinsgelder; ~ **interference** assoziative Hemmung; ~ **negotiations** Assoziierungsverhandlungen; ~ **president** Verbandspräsident, -vorsitzender, -leiter; ~ **property** Vereinsvermögen; ~ **shop** Gemeinschaftsladen einer Händlervereinigung; ~ **test** *(advertising)* Werbewirksamkeitstest, *(statistics)* Assoziationstest.

associative marketing genossenschaftlicher Absatz, Genossenschaftsvertrieb.

assort *(v.)* gruppieren, passend zusammenstellen, sortieren, ordnen, *(furnish with assortment)* mit einem Sortiment beliefern, assortieren, *(replenish)* auffüllen, ergänzen;
~ **a cargo** Ladung zusammenstellen; ~ **samples** Muster zusammenstellen; ~ **a stock of goods** mit einem Warensortiment ausstatten.

assorted geordnet, zusammengestellt, sortiert;
well ~ **stock** reich sortiertes Lager.

assortment *(classification)* Zusammenstellung, Sortieren, *(set of goods)* Sortiment, Auswahl, Kollektion, [Waren]lager;
broken ~ unvollständiges Warensortiment; **cash-down** ~ Barsortiment; **fair** ~ mittelmäßige Auswahl; **large (rich)** ~ reiche Auswahl; **sample** ~ Musterkollektion;
~ **of goods (merchandise)** Warensortiment; ~ **of patterns** Musterkollektion; ~ **of tools** Werkzeugausstattung;
~ **composition** Zusammensetzung eines Sortiments.

assuage *(v.)* lindern, mildern.

assuetude Verkehrssitte.

assume *(v.)* annehmen, mutmaßen, voraussetzen, *(office)* übernehmen;
~ **a specified amount of each loss** Selbstbehalt in festgesetzter Höhe übernehmen; ~ **a threatening attitude** drohende Haltung annehmen; ~ **the chair** Verhandlungsleitung (Vorsitz) übernehmen; ~ **a contract** Vertrag annehmen; ~ **control** Leitung übernehmen; ~ **a debt** Schuld übernehmen; ~ **the defence** Verteidigung übernehmen; ~ **direction of a business** Geschäftsleitung übernehmen; ~ **a different look** anderes Aussehen bekommen; ~ **a mortgage** Hypothek übernehmen; ~ **a name** Namen annehmen; ~ **obligations** Verbindlichkeiten eingehen; ~ **an office** Amt übernehmen; ~ **ownership** Eigentum übernehmen, in Eigentumsrechte eintreten; ~ **power** Macht ergreifen; ~ **the reins of government** zu regieren beginnen; ~ **the responsibility** Verantwortung übernehmen; ~ **a right** sich ein Recht anmaßen; ~ **all risks** volles Risiko übernehmen; ~ **a succession** Erbschaft antreten; ~ **new trustees** weitere Treuhänder bestimmen.

assumed angenommen, mutmaßlich, *(fictitious)* fingiert;
~ **bond** mit zusätzlicher Dividendengarantie ausgestattetes Wertpapier; ~ **executor** Hilfstestamentsvollstrecker; ~ **liability** Schuldübernahme; ~ **name** angenommener Name, Deckname, Pseudonym; ~ **risk** Risikoübernahme; ~ **value** angenommener (fiktiver) Wert.

assumedly angenommenermaßen.

assuming anmaßend;
~ **of a mortgage** Hypothekenübernahme.

assumpsit *(US)* Verbindlichkeit, formloses Versprechen, *(action)* Erfüllungsklage;
common (general) ~ Schadenersatzklage aus vertragsähnlichem Verhältnis; **express** ~ Schuldenanerkenntnis; **special** ~ Schuldanerkennungsklage.

assumption *(supposition)* Annahme, Voraussetzung, Vermutung, *(taking upon o. s.)* Übernahme;
on the ~ unter der Annahme (Voraussetzung);
precarious ~ fragwürdige Annahme; **unauthorized** ~ Rechtsmißbrauch;
~ **of a specified amount of each loss** Selbstbehaltübernahme in festgesetzter Höhe; ~ **of authority** Amtsanmaßung; ~ **of costs** Kostenübernahme; ~ **of indebtedness** Schuldübernahme; ~ **of liability** Anerkennung der Haftung, Haftungsübernahme; ~ **of**

losses Verlustübernahme; ~ **of mortgage** Hypothekenübernahme; ~ **of a name** Annahme eines Namens; ~ **of office**
Amtsübernahme, -antritt, Dienstantritt; ~ **of power** Machtübernahme; **unauthorized** ~ **of a right** Rechtsmißbrauch; ~ **of**
risk Risikoübernahme; **voluntary** ~ **of risk** Handeln auf eigene
Gefahr; ~ **of skill** *(master)* Vermutung besseren Fachwissens;
~ **of succession** Nachlaßübernahme, Erbantritt; ~ **of new trus-**
tees Bestellung weiterer Treuhänder.
assumptive anmaßend, kritiklos.
assurable versicherungsfähig.
assurance Selbstsicherheit, sicheres Auftreten, *(conveyancing)*
Eigentumsübertragung[surkunde], *(formal guaranty)* Zusicherung, Zusage, Bürgschaft, Sicherstellung, *(life insurance,*
Br.) [Lebens]versicherung, Assekuranz;
child's deferred ~ *(Br.)* Kurzlebensversicherung mit möglicher
Prämienfortzahlung durch das Kind; **common** ~ *(Br.)* Übertragung von Grundstücksrechten, Auflassung; **convertible term** ~
(Br.) Risikoumtauschversicherung; **decreasing term** ~ *(Br.)*
Kurzlebensversicherung mit abnehmendem Auszahlungsbe-
trag; **deferred** ~ *(Br.)* aufgeschobene Lebensversicherung;
endowment ~ *(Br.)* [abgekürzte] Todesfallversicherung, Versicherung auf den Erlebensfall; **educational endowment** ~ *(Br.)*
Ausbildungsversicherung; **industrial** ~ *(Br.)* Kleinlebensversicherung; **limited payment** ~ *(Br.)* Lebensversicherung mit
begrenzter Prämienzahlung; **ordinary life** ~ *(Br.)* große
Lebensversicherung; **partnership** ~ *(Br.)* Teilhaberversicherung; **term (temporary)** ~ *(Br.)* abgekürzte Lebensversicherung, Kurzversicherung;
~ **payable at death** *(Br.)* Todesfallversicherung; ~ **of property**
Übertragung von Grundstücksrechten, Auflassung;
to have plenty of ~ selbstsicher auftreten; **to take out an endow-**
ment ~ **maturing at the age of 60** *(Br.)* sich mit Abkürzung auf
das 60. Jahr versichern; **to vest an** ~ **on one's own name** *(Br.)*
Lebensversicherung auf seinen eigenen Namen umschreiben;
-ℐ **Companies Winding-Up Act** *(Br.)* Gesetz über die Liquidation von Lebensversicherungsanstalten; ~ **company** *(Br.)*
Lebensversicherungsgesellschaft.
assure *(v.)* jem. etw. zusichern, beteuern, versichern, *(life in-*
surance, Br.) versichern, assekurieren, *(property)* auflassen,
[Vermögen] übertragen;
~ **delivery** Lieferung sicherstellen; ~ **one's life with a company**
(Br.) sein Leben bei einer Gesellschaft versichern, sich in eine
Lebensversicherung einkaufen; ~ **s. one's position** jds. Stellung
festigen; ~ **s. o. a definite salary** jem. ein bestimmtes Gehalt
zusichern; ~ **the success of one's work** Erfolg seiner Arbeit
garantieren.
assured [person] *(Br.)* Versicherungsnehmer, Versicherter;
~ *(a.)* versichert;
to have one's life ~ sich versichern lassen;
~ **market** zugesicherter Absatzmarkt.
assurer *(Br.)* Assekurant, Versicherer, Versicherungsträger.
asterisk *(print.)* Stern[chen].
astern achtern.
astray vom rechten Weg ab, irre;
to go ~ verloren gehen;
~ **freight** Stückgutfracht; ~ **waybill** Stückgutbegleitschein.
astrodome Vollsichtkuppel.
astrogation Raumfahrtwissenschaft.
astronaut Raumfahrer, Astronaut.
astronautics Astronautik, Raumfahrt, -schiffahrt.
asylum Asyl, Zufluchtsland, Freistätte, Pflegeanstalt, [Versor-
gungs]anstalt;
diplomatic ~ diplomatisches Asyl; **insane** ~ *(US)* Heil- und
Pflegeanstalt; **lunatic** ~ Irrenanstalt; **neutral** ~ Asylgewährung
durch ein neutrales Land; **orphan** ~ Waisenhaus; **pauper** ~
Asyl für Obdachlose; **political** ~ politisches Asyl;
~ **for the aged** Altersheim; ~ **for the blind** Blindenanstalt; ~ **for**
inebriates *(US)* Trinkerheilanstalt;
to ask for political ~ um politisches Asyl bitten; **to confine to an**
~ in eine Anstalt verbringen; **to grant** ~ Asyl gewähren;
~-**seeker** Asylsucher.
at-home bestimmter Empfangstag.
Atlantic | Charter Atlantikcharta; ~ **Community** Atlantische
Gemeinschaft; **to cut** ~ **fares** Atlantikflugpreise senken; ~ **Pact**
Atlantikpakt; ~ **port** Atlantikhafen.
atlas Atlas;
~ **folio** *(printing)* Atlasformat.
atmosphere Klima, *(fig.)* Einfluß, Stimmung, Atmosphäre.
atmospheric | conditions Wetterverhältnisse, -lage; ~ **distur-**
bances atmosphärische Störungen; ~**humidity** Luftfeuchtigkeit; ~
layer Luftschicht; ~ **pressure** Luftdruck.

atmospherics *(radio, Br.)* atmosphärische Störungen, Empfangs-
störungen.
atom | bomb *(v.)* Atombomben einsetzen; ~-**free zone** atom-
waffenfreie Zone.
atomic | age Atomzeitalter; ~ **base** Abschußbasis für Atomrake-
ten; ~ **bomb** Atombombe; -ℐ **Club** Atomklub; ~ **decay (disinte-**
griation) Atomzerfall; ~ **energy** Atomenergie; -ℐ **Energy**
Authority *(Br.)* Atomenergiebehörde; -ℐ **Energy Commission**
Atomenergiekommission; ~ **fallout** radioaktiver Niederschlag; ~-**fission trigger** Kernspaltungsauslöser; ~ **nucleus**
Atomkern; ~ **pile** Atommeiler; ~ **pool** Atomgemeinschaft; ~
power Atomkraft; ~ **power plant (station)** Atomkraftwerk; ~
power plant sides Atomkraftwerksgelände; ~-**powered** mit
Atomkraft angetrieben; ~-**powered submarine** Atom-U-Boot;
~ **reactor** Atomreaktor; ~ **rocket** Atomrakete; ~ **shares**
(stocks, *US)* Atomaktien; ~ **warfare** Atomkrieg; ~ **warhead**
Atomgefechtskopf; ~ **weapons** Atomwaffen; ~ **weight**
Atomgewicht.
atone *(v.)* Buße zahlen, Ersatz leisten.
atonement Buße, Wiedergutmachung;
to make ~ **for a fault** Fehler wiedergutmachen;
~ **money** Buße, Bußgeld, Reuegeld, *(restoration)* Wiedergutmachung.
atrocious entsetzlich, grausam;
~ **act** Greueltat; ~ **assault and battery** gefährliche Körperverletzung; ~ **crime** scheußliches Verbrechen, Greueltat.
atrocity Greueltat, *(coll.)* Geschmacklosigkeit;
~ **propaganda** Greuelpropaganda; ~ **stories** Schauerge-
schichten.
attach *(v.)* *(legal consequences)* eintreten, *(fasten)* bei-, anheften,
befestigen, beistellen, -fügen, *(fig.)* für sich einnehmen, *(risk)*
eintreten, entstehen, *(seize)* beschlagnahmen, pfänden, *(wag-*
(g)on) anhängen;
~ **o. s.** sich anschließen; ~ **to s. o.** *(suspicion)* jem. anhängen; ~
the balance of an account Konto pfänden; ~ **authentication** mit
einer Beglaubigungsklausel versehen; ~ **conditions to s. th.**
Bedingungen an etw. knüpfen; ~ **a debt** Forderung pfänden; ~
a document to a letter Urkunde einem Brief beifügen; ~ **impor-**
tance to an event einem Ereignis Bedeutung beimessen; ~ **a**
label to the luggage Gepäckanhänger festmachen; ~ **an officer**
Offizier abordnen; ~ **part of salary** Gehalt teilweise pfänden; ~
o. s. to a political party sich einer politischen Partei anschließen; ~ **to a regiment** zu einem Regiment abkommandieren,
einem Regiment zuteilen.
attachability Pfändbarkeit.
attachable beschlagnahmefähig, pfändbar;
not ~ nicht pfändbar, unpfändbar;
~ **yellow glass** *(photo)* aufsteckbarer Gelbfilter.
attaché Attaché;
air ~ Luftattaché; **commercial** ~ Handelsattaché; **military** ~
Militärattaché; **naval** ~ Marineattaché; **press** ~ Presseattaché;
~ **case** Aktentasche, -koffer, Stadtkoffer.
attached unbeweglich, fest, *(annexed)* angeheftet, beigeschlossen;
with a garage ~ mit angebauter Garage;
to be ~ **to old customs** alten Bräuchen anhängen;
~ **business value** Verkehrswert; ~ **debtor** festgenommener
Schuldner; ~ **person** Festgenommener; ~ **sample** beigefügtes
Muster.
attaching creditor Pfändungsgläubiger.
attachment Verbindung, Befestigung, *(argument attached)* An-,
Beifügung, *(affection)* Zuneigung, Sympathie, *(arrest)* Verhaftung, Festnahme, persönlicher Arrest, *(execution sales)* Arrest
[im Zwangsvollstreckungsverfahren], *(seizure)* Beschlagnahme, Pfändung, *(technical appliance)* Zusatzgerät, *(writ of ~)*
Haftbefehl;
economic ~ wirtschaftliche Angliederung; **uncompleted** ~ nicht
beendete Pfändung; **undue** ~ unberechtigt vorgenommene
Pfändung;
~ **of a bank account** Pfändung eines Bankkontos; ~ **of a debt**
Forderungspfändung; ~ **of earnings** Lohnpfändung aus
Unterhaltsklage, Gehaltspfändung; ~ **of funds** Geld-, Vermö-
genspfändung; ~ **to one's profession** Liebe zum Beruf; ~ **of**
property Vermögensbeschlagnahme; ~ **of real property** dinglicher Arrest; ~ **of risk** *(insurance)* Risikobeginn; ~ **against**
security Pfändung gegen Sicherheitsleistung;
to be subject to ~ der Beschlagnahme (Pfändung) unterliegen;
to discharge (release, vacate) an ~ Freigabe anordnen, Beschlagnahme aufheben; **to have an** ~ **for s. o.** Zuneigung für j. gefaßt
haben; **to issue an** ~ **against s. one's person and goods** Pfändung
gegen j. herausbringen;

~ bond (US) gerichtliche Sicherheitsleistung [für eine einstweilige Verfügung]; **~ cord** Steckerkabel; **~ execution** Vollstreckungsverfahren, Arrestvollziehung; **~ order** (US) Beschlagnahmeverfügung, Pfändungs- und Überweisungsbeschluß, Arrest; **~ of earnings order** Lohnpfändungsbeschluß; **to levy an ~ order** (US) Beschlagnahme anordnen, Pfändungsbeschluß erlassen; **~ proceedings** (US) Pfändungsverfahren.

attack Angriff, Attacke, Überfall, (work) Inangriffnahme;
accidental ~ Angriff aus Zufall; **aerial ~** Luftangriff; **collateral ~** im Nebenverfahren betriebene Urteilsanfechtung; **false ~** Scheinangriff; **heart ~** Herzanfall; **holding ~** (mil.) Scheinangriff; **large-scale ~** groß angelegter Angriff; **mock ~** (mil.) Scheinangriff; **nervous ~** Nervenkrise; **relay ~** (mil.) rollender Angriff; **surprise ~** (mil.) Überraschungsangriff, Überfall;
strong ~ against the government's policy scharfe Attacke gegen die Regierungspolitik; **~ of fever** Fieberanfall;
~ is the best form of defence Angriff ist die beste Verteidigung;
~ (v.) überfallen, angreifen, attackieren, (set to work) sich an die Arbeit machen;
~ the Prime Minister's proposals Vorschläge des Premierministers hart angreifen;
to be under ~ unter Beschuß stehen; **to lay o. s. open to ~** Angriffsfläche bieten;
~ dog abgerichteter Wachhund; **~ helicopter** Angriffshubschrauber; **~ plane** Schlachtflugzeug; **~ rate** Neuzugangs-, Neuerkrankungsziffer; **~ transport** Landungsschiff.

attain (v.) erlangen, erreichen;
~ the age limit Altersgrenze erreichen; **~ one's end** sein Ziel erreichen; **~ to man's estate** volljährig werden; **~ one's object** seinen Zweck erreichen; **~ to power** zur Macht gelangen.

attainder (law) Verlust der bürgerlichen Ehrenrechte.

attainment Erreichung, Erlangung;
difficult of ~ schwer erreichbar; **for the ~ of one's purpose** um zum Ziel zu gelangen.

attainments Kenntnisse, Fertigkeiten, Errungenschaften;
legal ~ Rechtskenntnisse; **linguistic ~** Sprachkenntnisse; **~ in Latin** gute Leistungen in Latein.

attaint zum Verlust der bürgerlichen Ehrenrechte verurteilen.

attempt Versuch, (attack) Angriff, Anschlag, Attentat, (effort) Bemühung, Bestreben, Unternehmen;
assassination ~ Mordversuch, -anschlag; **conjunct ~** gemeinsam unternommener Versuch; **criminal ~** Versuch einer strafbaren Handlung; **rescue ~** Rettungsunternehmen; **serious ~** ernsthafter Versuch; **vain ~** nutzloser Versuch;
~ to bribe Bestechungsversuch; **~ to commit a crime** Versuch der Begehung eines Verbrechens (einer strafbaren Handlung); **~ at escaping** (to escape) Fluchtversuch; **~ at explanation** Erklärungs-, Deutungsversuch; **~ to intimidate** (pol.) Einschüchterungsversuch; **~ against the liberty of the people** Anschlag auf die Freiheit des Volkes; **~ on s. one's life** Mordversuch, -anschlag; **~ to monopolize** Monopolversuch; **~ to obstruct the proceedings** Verschleppungsversuch; **~ to quit** Rücktrittsversuch; **~ to sabotage** Sabotageversuch; **~ to speak** Ansatz zum Reden, Redeversuch;
~ (v.) versuchen, unternehmen, wagen, probieren;
~ an enemy's camp feindliches Lager angreifen; **~ a bold flight** kühnen Fluchtversuch unternehmen, sein Heil in einer kühnen Flucht suchen; **~ s. one's life** Mordanschlag auf j. begehen; **~ to solve a problem** Versuch zur Lösung eines Problems unternehmen;
to abandon an ~ vom Versuch zurücktreten; **to constitute an act of ~** Tatbestand des Versuchs erfüllen; **to flout s. one's ~** sich über jds. Bemühungen hinwegsetzen; **to make an ~** Versuch unternehmen (machen); **to make an ~ on s. one's life** Attentat auf j. begehen.

attempted | blackmail Erpressungsversuch; **~ deceit** Täuschungsversuch; **~ murder** Mordanschlag; **~ suicide** Selbstmordversuch.

attend (v.) (be present) beiwohnen, anwesend sein, besuchen, (care for) erledigen, besorgen, (listen) achtgeben, hören, merken, (machinery) bedienen, warten, pflegen, (nurse) pflegen, warten, behandeln;
~ s. o. jem. seine Aufwartung machen, j. bedienen, (doctor) j. ärztlich behandeln; **~ to s. one's affairs** jds. Angelegenheiten besorgen; **~ strictly to business** sich nur ums Geschäft kümmern; **~ to the collection of a bill** Inkasso eines Wechsels besorgen; **~ upon a committee** einem Ausschuß zur Verfügung stehen; **~ to the correspondence** eingegangene Post erledigen; **~ personally in court** persönlich vor Gericht erscheinen; **~ a course of lectures** Vorlesung besuchen (hören); **~ to customers** Kunden bedienen; **~ to directions** auf Anweisungen achten; **~ a**

doctor Arzt aufsuchen; **~ to a hearing** mündliche Verhandlung wahrnehmen; **~ the House** einer Parlamentssitzung beiwohnen; **~ to one's interests** seine Interessen wahrnehmen; **~ machinery** überwachen; **~ to a matter of business** geschäftliche Besorgung erledigen; **~ a meeting** Versammlung besuchen, an einer Versammlung teilnehmen; **~ to an order** Auftrag ausführen; **~ a patient** Patienten besuchen; **~ promptly** schnell erledigen; **~ regularly** regelmäßig besuchen; **~ to a request** Gesuch in Betracht ziehen; **~ school** Schule besuchen, zur Schule gehen; **~ to one's track** sich seiner Arbeit widmen **~ to the unloading** Abladen übernehmen; **~ to the wants of customers** Kundenwünsche erfüllen;
to be unfit to ~ am Erscheinen verhindert sein.

attendance Gegenwart, Anwesenheit, (machinery) Bedienung, Wartung, (at meetings) Teilnahmefrequenz, Besucherzahl, Zuhörerschaft, (nursing) Pflege, Wartung, (retinue) Begleitung, Gefolge, (servants) Dienerschaft, (service) Bedienung, Aufwartung, Dienst, Bereitschaft;
in ~ (physician) in Bereitschaft, diensttuend; **~ included** einschließlich Bedienung;
all-over ~ Gesamtzuschauerzahl; **compulsory ~** zwangsweise Vorführung; **constant ~** dauernde Betreuung; **doctor's ~** ärztliche Behandlung; **low ~** niedrige Besucherzahl; **poor ~** schwacher Besuch; **record ~** Rekordbesuch; **regular ~** regelmäßige Teilnahme;
~ of a doctor Arztbesuch; **~ at a lecture** Besuch einer Vorlesung; **good ~ at a meeting** gut besuchte Versammlung; **good ~ at a performance** starker Besuch einer Vorstellung; **~ at school** Schulbesuch; **full-time ~ at school** Ganztagsunterricht; **~ on the stock exchange** Börsenbesuch; **~ of a witness** Zeugenanwesenheit, Erscheinen eines Zeugen;
to be in ~ anwesend sein; **to dance ~** antichambrieren;
constant ~ allowance (Br.) Sozialvergütung im Fall der Notwendigkeit von Dauerpflegschaft; **~ bonus** Anwesenheitsprämie; **~ book** Anwesenheitsbuch; **~ centre** (Br.) Freizeitarrest; **~ fee** Tage-, Präsenzgeld; **~ figure** Teilnehmerzahl; **~ money** Anwesenheitsvergütung; **~ record** Anwesenheitsnachweis, Besucherrekord; **~ register** Teilnehmerverzeichnis, Präsenzliste; **~ sheet** Anwesenheitsliste, -verzeichnis; **~ time** Wartezeit.

attendant (care) Wärter, (companion) Begleiter, Gesellschafter, Gefährte, Gefolgsmann, (fig.) Begleiterscheinung, (servant) Diener, Bediensteter, Wärter, (visitor) Besucher, Anwesender; **~s** Gefolge, Begleitung, Dienerschaft;
court ~ Gerichtsdiener; **medical ~** Arzt;
to be a constant ~ at a course of lectures Vorlesungen regelmäßig besuchen;
~ (a.) (law) abhängig, verpflichtet, (present) anwesend, begleitend, gegenwärtig, (purtenant) dazugehörig; **~ circumstances** Begleitumstände.

attended, well gut besucht;
~ with great difficulties mit großen Schwierigkeiten verbunden; **~ by some risk** nicht ganz risikolos.

attendee Teilnehmer.

attentate Attentat.

attention Aufmerksamkeit, Beachtung, (care) Wartung, Pflege, (mil.) Haltung, Grundstellung;
~ of zu Händen von; **for immediate ~** zur sofortigen Veranlassung; **for your ~** zur Einsichtnahme; **for your kind ~** zur gefälligen Kenntnisnahme;
~s Aufmerksamkeiten, Höflichkeitsbezeugungen;
medical ~ ärztliche Behandlung; **prompt ~** sofortige Erledigung;
~ of a conscientious businessman Sorgfalt eines gewissenhaften Kaufmanns; **~s paid to a stranger** einem Fremden erwiesene Aufmerksamkeiten;
to attract ~ Aufmerksamkeit erregen; **to be all ~** ganz Ohr sein; **to bestow one's ~ upon s. th.** seine Aufmerksamkeit zuwenden; **to come to the ~** zur Kenntnis gelangen; **to come to the ~ of a broader section of the investing public** in den Blickpunkt eines breiteren Anlagepublikums rücken; **to give one's best ~ to orders** Aufträge bestens (prompt) ausführen; **to give a matter prompt ~** Angelegenheit schnell erledigen; **to give a matter greater ~** sich näher mit etw. beschäftigen; **to give urgent ~** vordringlich behandeln; **to hold the ~ of an audience** seine Zuhörer in Bann halten; **to pay ~** beachten; **to receive ~** Berücksichtigung finden; **to receive perfunctory ~** oberflächliche Beachtung finden; **to stand to ~** (mil.) Haltung annehmen;
~ factor Aufmerksamkeitsfaktor; **~ getter** (advertising) Blickfang, Aufmerksamkeitserreger; **~ signal** Achtungssignal; **~ time** (time study) Beobachtungszeit; **~ value** (advertisement) Werbe-, Zugkraft, Reklamewirkung, Aufmerksamkeitswert.

attentive, to be ~ to [the need of] one's guests sich um seine Gäste kümmern.

attenuate *(fig.)* abschwächen, verringern, verkleinern.

attenuation *(fig.)* Abschwächung.

attest *(v.) (bear witness)* bezeugen, *(certify)* [amtlich] bestätigen, bescheinigen, beglaubigen, attestieren;
~ **a copy of record** Abschrift beglaubigen; ~ **the signature of a document** Unterschrift beglaubigen; ~ **the truth of a statement** Wahrheitsgehalt einer Aussage bestätigen.

attestant Zeuge.

attestation [Unterschrifts]beglaubigung, Bestätigung [einer Urkunde], Beurkundung, amtliche Bestätigung, Attest, *(evidence)* Zeugnis, Bescheinigung, *(Br., mil.)* Eidesleistung [der Rekruten], Vereidigung;
~ **of a deed** Urkundenbeglaubigung; ~ **of signature** Unterschriftsbeglaubigung; ~ **of a will** Zeugenschaft bei der Testamentserrichtung;
~ **clause** *(insurance)* Beglaubigungsformel, -vermerk, Zusicherungsklausel.

attested beglaubigt;
legally ~ amtlich beglaubigt;
~ **by a notary** notariell beglaubigt;
~ **copy** beglaubigte Abschrift; **duly ~ declaration** ordnungsgemäß beglaubigte Erklärung; ~ **signature** beglaubigte Unterschrift; ~ **will** von Zeugen unterschriebenes Testament.

attesting|notary beurkundender Notar; ~ **witness** Unterschriftszeuge.

attestor Beglaubigender, *(witness)* Zeuge;
~ **of a cautioner** Rückbürge.

attic Dachkammer, -geschoß, Mansarde, Mansardenzimmer;
~ **full of junk** mit Gerümpel angefüllte Dachkammer;
~ **flat** ausgebaute Mansardenwohnung; ~ **storey** Dachgeschoß.

attire Kleidung;
in holiday ~ in Ferienkluft;
casual ~ saloppe Kleidung; **official ~** Amtstracht.

attitude Einstellung, Haltung, Verhalten, Stellungnahme;
antiunion ~ gewerkschaftsfeindliche Einstellung; **critical ~** kritische Einstellung; **employee ~** Arbeitnehmerverhalten; **firm ~** *(pol.)* feste Haltung; **fundamental ~** Grundhaltung; **hands-off ~** distanzierte Haltung; **intransigent ~** unnachgiebige Haltung; **large ~** vorurteilslose Stellungnahme; **outworn ~** überwundene Einstellung; **political ~** politische Einstellung; **threatening ~** drohende Haltung; **unbending ~** unnachgiebige Haltung;
~ **of expectancy** abwartende Haltung; ~ **of flight** Fluglage; ~ **of mind** Geisteshaltung; **provincial ~ of mind** provinzielle Einstellung; ~ **toward work** Einstellung zur Arbeit;
to adopt a firm ~ feste Haltung einnehmen, fest bleiben; **to change one's ~** sich umstellen; **to declare one's ~** seine Stellungnahme bekanntgeben; **to depend on the ~ of s. o.** von jds. Gepflogenheiten abhängen; **to hold the affirmative ~** positive Lebenseinstellung haben; **to maintain (preserve) a firm ~** feste Haltung einnehmen, *(stock exchange)* fest bleiben; **to maintain a neutral ~** neutrale Haltung einnehmen; **to maintain a passive ~** sich passiv (abwartend) verhalten; **to strike an ~** theatralische Haltung einnehmen; **to take a negative ~** sich ablehnend verhalten;
~ **change** Einstellungs-, Verhaltensänderung; ~ **rating** Klassifizierung des Verhaltens; ~ **scale** Verhaltensskala; ~ **study (survey)** Verhaltensstudie, -prüfung.

attorn *(v.)* [neuen] Gutsherrn anerkennen;
~ **to the new owner** Mietverhältnis mit dem neuen Eigentümer fortsetzen.

attorney *(US, in court of law)* [Rechts]anwalt, Rechtsvertreter, *(representative)* Bevollmächtigter, Geschäftsführer, gesetzlicher Vertreter, Sachwalter, Berechtigter;
by ~ in Vertretung (Vollmacht), im Auftrag;
circuit (district) ~ *(US)* Staatsanwalt; **federal ~** *(US)* Bundesanwalt; ~ **General** *(Br.)* Kron-, Generalstaatsanwalt, *(US)* Justizminister; **patent ~** *(US)* Patentanwalt; **private ~** Sachverwalter, Beauftragter, Bevollmächtigter, Anwalt; **prosecuting ~** Staatsanwalt; **public ~** Prozeßanwalt, -bevollmächtigter;
~ **for the defendant** *(defense, US)* Verteidiger, Anwalt des Beklagten; ~ **ad hoc** Sonderbevollmächtigter; ~ **in fact** gesetzlicher Vertreter, Stellvertreter, Sonderbevollmächtigter; ~ **at large** *(US)* an allen Gerichten zugelassener Anwalt; ~ **at law** *(US)* [Rechts]anwalt; ~ **of record** *(US)* prozeßbevollmächtigter Anwalt, Prozeßbevollmächtigter;
to constitute s. o. one's ~ *(US)* j. zu seinem Anwalt bestellen; **to consult an ~** *(US)* Anwalt zuziehen; **to provide s. o. with an ~** *(US)* jem. einen Anwalt stellen;

~**'s certificate** *(US)* Zulassungsnachweis eines Anwalts; ~**client privilege** Anwaltsprivileg; ~**'s fee** *(US)* Anwaltsgebühr, -kosten, -honorar; ~**'s lien** *(US)* Zurückbehaltungsrecht des Anwalts.

attorneyship *(US)* Anwaltschaft, anwaltschaftliche Tätigkeit.

attornment to the new owner Fortsetzung des Mietverhältnisses mit dem neuen Eigentümer.

attract *(v.) (capital)* anziehen, *(customers)* anlocken, gewinnen;
~ **away** wegengagieren; ~ **s. o. strongly** starke Anziehungskraft auf j. ausüben.

attraction Anziehungskraft, *(advertising)* Zugkraft;
~ **of a country** Reiz eines Landes; ~ **of customers** Kundengewinnung;
to have little ~ geringen Reiz ausüben.

attractive anziehend, zugkräftig;
~ **advertising** zugkräftige Werbung; ~ **offer** reizvolles (vorteilhaftes) Angebot; ~ **power** Anziehungskraft; ~ **price** günstiger Preis.

attributable anrechenbar, zuschreibbar, *(income)* anfallend;
~ **to capital** steuerlich als Kapital zu behandeln.

attribute [charakteristische] Eigenschaft, [wesentliches] Merkmal, *(marketing)* qualitatives Merkmal;
statistical ~ festes Merkmal;
~ *(v.)* beimessen, beilegen;
~ **a disease to filth** Krankheit auf Verschmutzung zurückführen; ~ **a meaning to a passage** einer Textstelle eine Bedeutung beimessen; ~ **false motives to s. o.** jem. falsche Beweggründe unterschieben; ~ **profits** Gewinne [steuerlich] zurechnen; ~ **one's success to hard work** seinen Erfolg harter Arbeit zuschreiben;
to share an ~ über die gleiche Eigenschaft verfügen.

attributed to infection auf eine Infektion zurückzuführen.

attribution Zuerkennung, Zuweisung, Zuschreibung, *(ascribed quality)* zuerkannte Eigenschaft.

attrition Zermürbung, *(wear and tear)* Abnutzung, Verschleiß.

auction [öffentliche] Versteigerung, Auktion, Verkauf im Wege der Versteigerung;
Dutch ~ Versteigerung mit laufend erniedrigtem Anbietungspreis (bei Zuschlag unter Taxpreis); **mock ~** Scheinauktion; **public ~** öffentliche Versteigerung;
~ **of an estate** Nachlaßversteigerung;
~ *(v.)* **[off]** in die Auktion geben, verauktionieren, versteigern;
to be sold at *(US)* **(by, Br.)** ~ zur Auktion (Versteigerung) kommen; **to purchase at ~** ersteigern; **to put up at** *(US)* **(to, Br.)** ~ öffentlich versteigern, meistbietend verkaufen; **to sell at** *(US)* **(by, Br.)** ~ [öffentlich] versteigern, verauktionieren, in die Auktion geben;
~**'s Act** *(Br.)* Auktionsgesetz; **to spur ~ activity** Auktionsgeschäft beleben; ~ **bill** Auktionsliste, Versteigerungsliste; **to be on the ~ block** zum Verkauf anstehen; **to put on the ~ block** zur Versteigerung gebracht werden; ~ **buyer** Ersteigerer, Ersteher; ~ **charges** Versteigerungsgebühren; ~ **company** Versteigerungsfirma; ~ **day** Auktions-, Versteigerungstermin; ~ **fees** Auktionsgebühren, Versteigerungskosten, -gebühren; ~ **house** Auktionsfirma; ~ **lot** Auktionsposten; ~ **market** Auktionsmarkt; ~ **mart** Auktionslokal; ~ **notice** Auktionsankündigung; **to increase one's share of the bigger ~ pie** seinen Anteil am ausgeweiteten Auktionsumsätzen steigern; ~ **price** Auktions-, Versteigerungspreis; ~ **room** Auktionssaal, -lokal; ~ **sale** Auktion, Versteigerung; ~ **sign** Auktionsankündigung; ~ **terms** Auktions-, Versteigerungsbedingungen.

auctioneer Auktionator, öffentlicher Versteigerer;
~**'s fee** Auktionskosten, -gebühren.

auctioneering Versteigern.

audience Audienz, Empfang, *(attendance)* Zuhörer[schaft], Versammlung, Auditorium, Zuschauer[schaft], Publikum, *(formal hearing)* rechtliches Gehör, Anhörung, *(readers)* Hörer-, Leserkreis, Leserschaft;
accumulated ~ kumulierte Leserschaft (Hörerschaft); **average-issue ~** Leser einer Durchschnittsauflage; **critical ~** kritische Zuhörerschaft; **daytime ~** Fernsehpublikum während des Tages; **first ~** Antrittsaudienz; **high-income ~** wohlsituiertes Publikum; **inherited ~** *(television)* Zuschauer einer vorausgegangenen Fernsehsendung; **leave-taking ~** Abschiedsaudienz; **magazine ~** Zeitschriftenleserkreis; **private ~** Privataudienz; **public ~** öffentliche Audienz; **slim ~** dürftige Zuhörerschaft; **stand-in ~** vorgesehenes Publikum; **sympathetic ~** sympathisches Publikum; **undergraduate ~** aus Studenten bestehendes Publikum; **viewing ~** Fernsehpublikum;
~ **of s. o.** Audienz mit jem.; ~ **of students** Studentenzuhörerschaft, -publikum;

to find an attentive ~ aufmerksame Zuhörer finden; **to get across with the** ~ beim Publikum ankommen; **to grant an** ~ Audienz gewähren (erteilen); **to grip one's** ~ seine Zuhörer packen; **to have** ~ **with the king** Audienz beim König haben, vom König in Audienz empfangen werden; **to hold one's** ~ sein Publikum in Spannung halten (fesseln); **to please an** ~ Publikum zufriedenstellen; **to pull an** ~ Publikum anlocken; **to request an** ~ um eine Audienz nachsuchen (einkommen); **to sweep one's** ~ **along with one** Zuhörerschaft zu stürmischem Beifall hinreißen;

~ **analysis** Hörer-, Zuschauer-, Publikums-, Leseranalyse; ~ **attention** Leserschaftsinteresse; ~ **box** Zuhörerraum; ~ **builder** zugkräftige Sendung (Werbung), zugkräftiges Medium; ~ **chamber** Zuhörerraum, Verhandlungssaal; ~ **composition** Zusammenstellung (Zusammensetzung) des Leserkreises, demographische Struktur; ~ **data** Angaben über die Leserschaft; ~ **flow** Hörergesamtheit bei Programmende; ~ **interest** Publikumsinteresse; ~ **measurement** Feststellung der Hörerschaft (des Leserkreises) [zur Werbeerfolgskontrolle], Werbewirksamkeitsanalyse, Leserkreismaßstäbe; ~ **participation** Zuhörer, Publikumsbeteiligung; ~ **profile** Zusammensetzung des Publikums; ~ **rating** Messung des Leser-, Hörerverhaltens; ~ **research** Leser- und Höreranalyse, Leser-, Hörerforschung; ~ **taste** Publikumsgeschmack; ~ **turnover** Publikums-, Zuhörerbeteiligung, Teilnehmerzahl im Rundfunk (Fernsehen).

audio | control engineer Toningenieur, -meister; ~ **frequency** Tonfrequenz; ß **goods** audio-visuelle Güter, ~ **reception** Hörerempfang; ~ **surveillance war** Abhörerkrieg; ~ **typist** Phonotypist[in]; ~**-visual instruction** Unterricht mit Lehrfilmen.

audiovisual audio-visuell;
~ **advertising** audio-visuelle Werbung; ~ **age** Zeitalter der audio-visuellen Unterrichtsmethode; ~ **aids** audio-visuelle Verkaufshilfen; ~ **equipment** audio-visuelle Geräte.

audit [amtliche] Rechnungsprüfung, Buch-, Wirtschafts-, Bilanzprüfung, [Bücher]revision, Abschluß-, Bestandsprüfung, *(fig.)* Rechenschaftslegung, *(marketing)* Durchleuchtung, *(newspaper)* Auflagenprüfung, *(rent)* Mietabrechnung, Pachtzahlung, *(statement of accounts)* Bilanz, *(final statement)* Hauptrechenschaftsbericht;
before the close of the ~ vor Beendigung der Prüfung;
annual ~ [Jahres]abschlußprüfung; **balance-sheet** ~ Bilanzprüfung, -revision; **cash** ~ Kassenrevision, -prüfung, -aufnahme; **completed** ~ zum Jahresabschluß durchgeführte Revision; **continuous** ~ laufend durchgeführte Prüfung (Revision), laufende Revisionsarbeiten; **desk** ~ Buchprüfung auf Grund mitgenommener Belege; **detailed** ~ eingehende Revision; **external** ~ Buchprüfung durch [betriebsfremde] Berufsprüfer, außerbetriebliche (betriebsfremde) Revision; **general** ~ [Jahres]abschlußprüfung; **interim** ~ in der Berichtszeit vorgenommene Revision; **internal** ~ [betriebs]eigene Buchprüfung (Revision) Hausrevision, Betriebsrevision; **inventory** ~ Inventarprüfung; **limited** ~ abgekürzte Prüfung; **partial** ~ Teilrevision; **periodic** ~ laufend durchgeführte Revision; **post** ~ Rechnungsprüfung; **special** ~ außerplanmäßige Revision, Sonderprüfung; **surprise** ~ überraschende Revision; **tax** ~ *(US)* Steuerprüfung; **voucher** ~ Belegprüfung, Prüfung der Auszahlungsbelege (Buchungsunterlagen);
~ **of circulation** Auflagenüberwachung; ~ **for credit purposes** Kreditprüfung; ~**s of one's estate** Vermögenseinnahmen; ~ **of personnel** *(US)* Personalbeurteilung;
~ *(v.)* Rechnungen prüfen, [amtlich] revidieren, Revision durchführen, *(marketing)* durchleuchten, *(US, university)* an einem Lehrgang als Gasthörer teilnehmen;
~ **an abstract of account** Kontoauszug vergleichen; ~ **the accounts** Bücher (Rechnungsführung) prüfen (revidieren); ~ **a balance sheet** Bilanz prüfen; ~ **for credit purposes** zu Kreditzwecken überprüfen;
to conclude an ~ Buchführung (Revision) abschließen; **to make an** ~ Prüfung (Revision) durchführen; **to prosecute an** ~ Bilanzprüfung durchführen; **to stand an** ~ einer amtlichen Überprüfung standhalten;
~ **adjustment** durch die Revision veranlaßte Berichtigungsbuchung; ~ **book** Bilanz-, Revisionsbuch; ~ **Bureau of Circulations** *(US)* Auflagenüberwachungsstelle, freiwillige Auflagenselbstkontrolle; ~ **certificate** Bestätigungsvermerk, Revisionsbericht, Prüfungsbescheinigung, -bericht, -vermerk; ~ **commission** Buchprüfungskommission; ~ **date** Revisions-, Prüfungstermin; ~ **day** Abrechnungstag; **internal** ~ **department** betriebseigene Revisionsabteilung, Innenrevision; ~ **engagement** Prüfungs-, Revisionsauftrag; ~ **fees** Revisions-, Prüfungsgebühren; **internal** ~ **group** betriebseigene Revisions-

abteilung; ~ **instructions** Prüfungs-, Revisionsanweisungen; ~ **notebook** Revisionsunterlagen; ~ **office** Büro einer Revisionsgesellschaft, *(Commissioner of Audits)* Rechnungshof, -kammer, Oberrechnungskammer; ~ **period** Prüfungszeitraum, Berichtsperiode; **to land o. s. on the** ~ **pile** zur Steuerprüfung dran sein; ~ **privilege** Prüfungs-, Revisionsrecht; ~ **procedure** Prüfungsablauf, Revisionsverfahren; ~ **program(me)** Revisionsplan; ~ **qualification** einschränkender Bestätigungsvermerk, einschränkendes Testat eines Wirtschaftsprüfers; ~ **report** Prüfungs-, Wirtschaftsprüfer-, Revisionsbericht; **statutory** ~ **requirements** gesetzlich vorgeschriebene Revisionsvorschriften; ~ **routine** Prüfungsgang; ~ **services** Revisionstätigkeit; ~ **situation** Revisionslage; ~ **standards** Prüfungs-, Revisionsrichtlinien, -vorschriften; ~ **store** *(advertising)* Testladen; ~ **system** [Rechnungs]prüfungs-, Revisionswesen; **single** ~ **system of circulation** *(US)* Institut zur Auflagen- und Hörerschaftskontrolle; ~ **test** stichprobenartige Prüfung; ~ **work** Revisionsarbeiten; ~ **year** Prüfungs-, Revisionsjahr.

audited | accounts Revisionsbericht; ~ **balance sheet** geprüfte Bilanz; ~ **voucher** geprüfter Beleg.

auditing Wirtschafts-, Rechnungprüfung, Revision[swesen], Prüfungswesen;
when ~ **the books** bei der Rechnungsprüfung (Revision);
external ~ außerbetriebliche Revision; **internal** ~ betriebsinterne Revision, Innenrevision; **operational** ~ betriebsinterne Überprüfung der Arbeitsabläufe; **pre-**~ Vorprüfung;
~ **of accounts** Rechnungsprüfung; ~ **above local level** überörtliche Revision (Prüfung);
~ **commission** Prüfungs-, Revisionsausschuß; ~ **company** Prüfungs-, Revisionsgesellschaft, Treuhandbüro; ~ **department (division)** Revisionsabteilung; ~ **error** Revisionsfehler; ~ **expert** Buchsachverständiger, Prüfer, Revisor; ~ **fee** Prüfungs-, Revisionsgebühr, Buchprüfungskosten; ~ **order** Revisions-, Prüfungsauftrag; ~ **procedure** Prüfungsverfahren; ~ **profession** Revisoren-, Buchprüferberuf; **business** ~ **service** Buch- und Betriebsprüfung; ~ **staff** Prüferstab; ~ **technique** Revisionstechnik.

audition Sprechprobe;
~ *(v.) (theatre)* vorsprechen.

auditor Buch-, Kassen-, Rechnungsprüfer, Buchsachverständiger, Wirtschaftsprüfer, Bücherrevisor, *(court)* Beisitzer, *(firm)* Prüfungs-, Revisions-, Treuhandgesellschaft, *(investment fund)* Kontrollstelle, *(listener)* Zuhörer, Gesprächspartner, *(US, university)* Gasthörer;
field ~ Außenrevisor; ~ **general** [etwa] Präsident des Bundesrechnungshofes; ~ **government** ~ Beamter des Rechnungshofes; **internal** ~ innerbetrieblicher Revisionsbeamter, betriebseigener Revisor, Betriebsrevisor; **official** ~ Revisionsbeamter; **operational** ~ Betriebsrevisor; **professional (public)** ~ öffentlicher Bücherrevisor, Wirtschaftsprüfer; **state** ~ staatlicher Rechnungsprüfer; **travel(l)ing** ~ Reiserevisor;
~⁹**s of the Exchequer** *(Br.)* Kollegium der Rechnungskammer; **to have the** ~**s** in Betriebsprüfung haben;
~'s **certificate** Prüfungs-, Revisionsbericht, Prüfungs-, Bestätigungsvermerk; ~'s **office** Revisionsbüro; ~'s **report** Revisions-, Rechnungs-, Buchprüfungsbericht, Bericht des Wirtschaftsführers, Revisionsprotokoll; **to take exception to the** ~'s **report** Revisionsbericht beanstanden; ~'s **statement** Revisionsbericht.

auditorium Zuhörerraum, Auditorium, *(lecture room)* Vortrags-, Vorführungsraum.

auditorship Rechnungsprüferamt, Amt eines Revisors.

auditory Zuhörerschaft, *(lecture room)* Auditorium, Hörsaal;
~ **memory span** Erinnerungsvermögen.

augment *(v.) (grow)* zunehmen, anwachsen, sich vermehren, *(make greater)* vermehren, vergrößern;
~ **one's income by writing short stories** seine Einkünfte durch das Verfassen von Kurzgeschichten aufbessern.

augmentation Vermehrung, Vergrößerung, Zunahme, -wachs, Wachstum, *(addition)* Zusatz;
~ **of salary** Gehaltserhöhung.

aula Aula, Halle.

auricular witness Ohrenzeuge.

auspices, Vorzeichen, Auspizien;
under the ~ unter der Schirmherrschaft;
favo(u)rable ~ günstige Anzeichen.

austerity eingeschränkte Lebensweise, *(public financing)* Sparprogramm der öffentlichen Hand;
to lift the ~ **lid a bit** erste Maßnahmen zur Erleichterung in der Konsumbeschränkung treffen; ~ **measures** Einschränkungs-, Sanierungsmaßnahmen, Sparmaßnahmen; ~ **package for the**

economy Bündel von Sparmaßnahmen der öffentlichen Hand, für die Gesundung der Wirtschaft verordnetes Bündel von Sanierungsvorschlägen; ~ **policy** währungssichernde Politik der Ausgabenbeschränkung; ~ **program(me)** auf Konsumbeschränkung abgestelltes Wirtschaftssystem, Not-, Sanierungsprogramm.

autarchic, autarcic selbstregierend, selbstgenügsam, wirtschaftlich, unabhängig, autark.

autarchy Autarkie, wirtschaftliche Unabhängigkeit, (self-government) Selbstverwaltung;
economic ~ Wirtschaftsautarkie.

autarkical selbstgenügsam, wirtschaftlich, unabhängig, autark.

autarkist Befürworter der Autarkie, Autarkieanhänger.

autarky autarkes Wirtschaftssystem, Autarkie, wirtschaftliche Unabhängigkeit.

authentic maßgeblich, authentisch, (genuine) echt, (reliable) glaubwürdig, glaubhaft, verbürgt, zuverlässig, authentisch, (vested with legal formalities and duly attested) rechtsgültig ausgestellt und bestätigt;
~ **act** notarielle Beglaubigung; ~ **copy** ordnungsgemäß beglaubigte Abschrift; ~ **information** zuverlässige Information; ~ **interpretation** gültige Auslegung; ~ **record** verbürgte Überlieferung; ~ **text** authentischer (maßgebender) Text; ~ **translation** maßgebliche Übersetzung.

authenticate (v.) Echtheit feststellen, beglaubigen, beurkunden, amtlich bestätigen, (make valid) Gültigkeit verleihen;
~ **a claim** Anspruch glaubhaft machen; ~ **a signature** Unterschrift beglaubigen; ~ **by key word** mittels Schlüsselwort bestätigen.

authenticated (v.) **by seal** notariell beglaubigt;
~ **document** beglaubigte Urkunde; ~ **power of attorney** beglaubigte Vollmacht.

authentication Echtheitsbescheinigung, (attestation) Beurkundung, Beglaubigung, (genuineness) Rechtsgültigkeit, (legalization) Legalisierung;
~ **of claims** Glaubhaftmachung von Ansprüchen;
to attach ~ mit der Beglaubigungsklausel versehen.

authenticity Echtheit, Verbürgtheit, (truth) Glaubwürdigkeit, Glaubhaftmachung;
~ **of a signature** Rechtsgültigkeit einer Unterschrift.

author Verfasser, Autor, Schriftsteller, (originator) Urheber, Schöpfer;
with the compliments of the ~ mit den besten Empfehlungen des Verfassers; **with the sanctions of the** ~ mit Genehmigung des Autors;
anonymous ~ ungenannter Verfasser; **joint** ~**s** Mitverfasser; **sole** ~ alleiniger Verfasser; **standard** ~ anerkannt guter Schriftsteller;
to avow o. s. as the ~ sich als Verfasser bekennen; **to pull an** ~ **to pieces** Verfasser (Autor) in Grund und Boden verurteilen;
~**'s alterations** Text-, Autorenkorrekturen; ~ **catalog(ue)** Autorenkatalog; ~**'s copy** Autoren-, Handexemplar; ~**'s corrections** Autorenkorrektur; ~ **entry** Autoreneintrag, -aufführung; ~**'s fee** Autorenanteil, -honorar; ~**'s notes** Anmerkung des Verfassers; ~**'s proof** Autorenkorrekturen; ~**'s publication** Selbstverlag; ~**-publisher** Selbstverleger.

authoritarian autoritär;
~ **state** Obrigkeitsstaat.

authoritarianism autoritäres Regierungssystem.

authoritative (entitled) bevollmächtigt, (proceeding from competent authority) maßgebend, kompetent, gutachtlich, (possessing authority) autoritativ;
~ **document** öffentlichen Glauben genießende Urkunde; ~ **solution** autoritäre Lösung; ~ **statement** maßgebende Feststellung; ~ **system** autoritäres System.

authoritative|construction maßgebliche Auslegung; ~ **tone** diktatorischer Ton.

authoritativeness Bevollmächtigtsein, Kompetenz.

authorities Behörden, Dienststelle, Obrigkeit, Regierung;
city ~ Stadtbehörde; **customs** ~ Zollbehörde; **district** ~ Kreisbehörde; **fiscal** ~ Finanzbehörden; **health** ~ Gesundheitsamt; **leading** ~ Spitzen der Behörden; **local** ~ örtliche Behörden; **military** ~ Militärbehörden; **municipal** ~ Kommunalbehörden; **postal** ~ Postbehörden; **revenue** ~ Finanzbehörden; **responsible** ~ **for roads** Straßenbaubehörden;
to quote one's ~ seine Quellen ausführen.

authority (decision of court) gerichtliche Entscheidung, (decree) amtlicher Erlaß, (expert) Sachverständiger, Fachmann, Autorität, Kapazität, (government agency) [Verwaltungs]behörde, Regierung, (mil.) Befehlsgewalt, (power) Gewalt, Machtbefugnis, Autorität, Amtsgewalt, (delegated power) Befugnis,

Ermächtigung, Vertretungsmacht, Bevollmächtigung, Vollmacht, Mandat, (precedent) Vorgang, maßgebliche Gerichtsentscheidung, Präzedenzfall, (prestige) Ansehen, Autorität, Einfluß, Gewicht, (source) Quelle, Beleg, Gewährsmann;
beyond the scope of one's ~ außerhalb des Rahmens seiner Vertretungsmacht; **by** ~ mit obrigkeitlicher Erlaubnis, auf grund von; **by higher** ~ höheren Ortes; **from a competent** ~ aus berufenem Munde; **in virtue of my** ~ Kraft der mir erteilten Vollmacht; **of suspected** ~ unglaubwürdig; **of great** ~ von großem Ansehen; **of one's own** ~ aus eigener Machtbefugnis; **of unrequested** ~ unbedingt glaubwürdig; **on the** ~ **of** im Auftrag von; **on good** ~ von berufener (zuständiger) Stelle, aus sicherer Quelle, glaubwürdig; **printed by under** ~ **of** mit amtlicher Erlaubnis gedruckt; **signed on** ~ amtlich bescheinigt; **under the** ~ **of** im Auftrage von; **within the scope of one's** ~ innerhalb des Rahmens seiner Vertretungsmacht; **without** ~ unbefugt, unberechtigt, ohne Vollmacht;
actual ~ tatsächliche Vertretungsmacht, Vertretungsmacht im Einzelfall; **administrative** ~ vollziehende Gewalt, Verwaltungsbehörde; **advance** ~ von vornherein erteilte Vollmacht; **apparent** ~ scheinbare (Vertretung ohne) Vertretungsmacht; **appropriate** ~ zuständige Behörde; **approving** ~ Genehmigungsbehörde; **broad** ~ umfassende Vollmacht; **central** ~ Zentralbehörde; **civilian** ~ Zivilbehörde; **competent** ~ zuständige Behörde; **corporate** ~ handelsrechtliche Befugnis; **delegated** ~ übertragene Ermächtigung; **disciplinary** ~ Disziplinarbehörde; **executive** ~ vollziehende Gewalt; **express** ~ ausdrücklich erteilte Vollmacht; **general** ~ Generalvollmacht; **good** ~ zuverlässige Quelle; **governmental** ~ Regierungsbehörde; **High** ~ Hohe Behörde; **implied** ~ stillschweigend erteilte Vollmacht; **joint** ~ Gesamtvollmacht, (local government, Br.) Zweckverband; **judicial** ~ richterliche Gewalt; **legal** ~ Justiz-, Gerichtsbehörde; **limited** ~ beschränkte (begrenzte) Vollmachten; **local** ~ (Br.) örtliche Stelle, Kommunalkreis, Ortsbehörde; **mere** ~ jederzeit widerrufliche Vollmacht; **naked** ~ schlichte widerrufliche Vollmacht; **occupation** ~ Besatzungsbehörde; **operating** ~ Betriebsvollmacht; **ostensible** ~ Anscheinsvollmacht, scheinbare Vertretungsmacht; **parental (paternal)** ~ elterliche Gewalt; **port** ~ Hafenbehörde; **public** ~ öffentliche Gewalt, Staatsgewalt; **relevant** ~ betreffende Behörde; **reliable** ~ sicherer Gewährsmann; **reviewing** ~ Rechtsmittel-, Berufungsinstanz; **rightful** ~ ordnungsgemäße Vollmacht; **self-** ~ angemaßte Vollmacht; **special** ~ Einzel-, Sondervollmacht; **subordinate** ~ unterstellte Behörde; **superior (supervising)** ~ vorgesetzte Behörde, höhere Instanz, Aufsichtsbehörde; **taxation (taxing)** ~ Steuerbehörde; **terminated** ~ erloschene Vollmacht; **unlimited** ~ unbeschränkte Vertretungsmacht, Blankovollmacht; **vicarious** ~ stellvertretend ausgeübte Vollmacht; **written** ~ schriftliche Vollmacht;
~ **to act** Vertretungsbefugnis, Handlungsvollmacht; ~ **of an agent** Vertretungsmacht; ~ **to barter** Tauschbefugnis; ~ **to collect debts** Inkassovollmacht; ~ **to contract** Abschlußvollmacht; ~ **to convene** Einberufungsvollmacht; ~ **of the court** richterliche Gewalt; ~ **of directors** Vorstandsbefugnisse; ~ **to dispose** Verfügungsmacht; ~ **by estoppel** durch schlüssiges Verhalten erteilte Vollmacht, Vertretungsmacht kraft Rechtsscheins; ~ **beyond exception** unanfechtbare Vollmacht; ~ **to execute a deed** vollstreckbare Ausfertigung; ~ **of a father** väterliche Gewalt; **recognized** ~ **in his field** anerkannter Fachmann auf seinem Gebiet; ~ **to instruct** Weisungsrecht; ~ **coupled with an interest** Vollmacht mit Ausschluß der Selbstkontraktion; ~ **to negotiate** Verhandlungs-, Abschlußvollmacht, (banking) Ankaufsermächtigung; ~ **of partners** Gesellschaftervollmacht; ~ **to pay** Zahlungsvollmacht, (banking) Einlösungsermächtigung; ~ **to purchase** (export trade, US) Ankaufsvollmacht; ~ **to represent** Vertretungsbefugnis; ~ **to sell** Verkaufsvollmacht; ~ **to sign** Zeichnungsberechtigung, Unterschriftsvollmacht; ~ **to sign an account** Kontovollmacht; ~ **from the state** (US) staatliche Ermächtigung; ~ **to tax** Besteuerungsrecht; ~ **for a thesis** Beleg für eine These; ~ **for withdrawal** Abhebungsbefugnis; ~ **in writing** schriftliche Vollmacht;
to act on s. one's ~ auf Grund einer Vollmacht handeln; **to be in** ~ Gewalt in Händen haben; **to act within the actual limits of one's** ~ sich im Rahmen seiner Vollmacht halten; **to act beyond the scope of one's** ~ seine Befugnisse (Vollmacht) überschreiten; **to be an** ~ **on a subject** kompetent (Autorität auf einem Gebiet) sein; **to be of binding** ~ bindende Kraft haben; **to be given express** ~ ausdrückliche Vollmacht haben; **to be in** ~ Autoritätsperson sein, Gewalt in Händen haben; **to be invested with full** ~ mit Vollmacht versehen sein; **to be under paternal** ~ der väterlichen Gewalt unterliegen; **to be under the** ~ **of the**

Home Office *(Br.)* dem Innenministerium unterstehen; **to buck s. one's ~** jds. Autorität in Frage stellen; **to carry ~** Autorität genießen; **to conduct affairs without ~** ohne Vertretungsmacht handeln; **to confer ~ upon** Befugnisse auf j. übertragen; **to delegate ~** Vollmachten delegieren; **to divest o. s. of one's ~** seine Vollmacht zurückgeben; **to establish ~** Vollmacht erteilen; **to exceed one's ~** seine Vollmacht (Befugnisse, Kompetenz) überschreiten; **to exercise ~** Regierungsgewalt ausüben; **to exert one's ~** seine Autorität geltend machen; **to gird s. o. with ~** j. mit Autorität ausstatten; **to give s. o. ~ to do s. th.** jem. für etw. Vollmacht erteilen; **to have ~** befugt (ermächtigt, bevollmächtigt, berechtigt) sein, Vollmacht haben; **to have ~ to give cover for a class of business concerned** Vollmachten zur Erteilung von Deckungszusagen für bestimmte Versicherungssparten haben; **to have ~ over s. o.** jem. übergeordnet sein; **to have the ~ of the governor** im Auftrag des Gouverneurs handeln; **to have the ~ to make payments** auszahlungsberechtigt sein; **to have it on ~** aus sicherer Quelle wissen; **to have full ~ to act** volle Handlungsfreiheit haben; **to make one's ~ felt** seine Machtbefugnisse deutlich machen; **to misuse one's ~** Mißbrauch mit seiner Vollmacht treiben; **to project ~** Autorität ausstrahlen; **to quote s. o. as one's ~** j. als Gewährsmann angeben; **to recover one's ~** seine Autorität zurückgewinnen; **to refer to an ~** sich auf seine Quelle berufen; **to seek ~** Vollmacht erbitten (nachsuchen).

authorizable autorisierbar.

authorization Ermächtigung, *(approval)* Genehmigung, Erlaubnis, *(commission)* Bevollmächtigung, Vollmachtserteilung; **subject to ~** genehmigungspflichtig; **borrowing ~** Kreditaufnahmebefugnis; **contract ~** Vollmacht zur Auftragsvergabe auch außerhalb des Etatsjahres; **drawing ~** Abhebungsbefugnis, *(International Monetary Fund)* Ziehungsermächtigung; **government ~** amtliche Bescheinigung; **husband's ~** ehemännliche Genehmigung; **official ~** amtliche Genehmigung; **special ~** ausdrückliche Ermächtigung; **withholding ~** Vollmacht für die Einbehaltung von Lohnsteuerbeträgen; **written ~** schriftliche Vollmacht, Berechtigungsschein; **~ to fill in a blank** Blankettausfüllungsbefugnis; **~ to pay** Auszahlungsermächtigung; **~ to sign** Zeichnungsbefugnis, Unterschriftsvollmacht; **~ to transact insurance** Genehmigung zum Abschluß von Versicherungsverträgen; **~ in writing** schriftliche Vollmacht; **to give s. o. ~** j. ermächtigen; **~ bill** Ermächtigungsgesetz; **~ budget** genehmigungspflichtiger Etat; **~ card** Tarifvertragsvollmacht; **~ form** Vollmachtsformular; **~ request** Behördenanforderung.

authorize *(v.) (empower)* bevollmächtigen, Vollmacht erteilen, ermächtigen, autorisieren, *(sanction)* genehmigen, berechtigen, legitimieren, gutheißen, billigen; **~ s. o.** j. zum Bevollmächtigten einsetzen; **~ to fill in a blank** Blankettausfüllungsbefugnis zuerkennen; **~ s. o. to sign a contract** j. zur Vertragsunterschrift bevollmächtigen; **~ the issue of money** Banknotendruck authorisieren; **~ the levy of a tax** Steuererhebung zulassen; **~ the payment of a sum** Betrag zur Zahlung anweisen; **~ legal proceedings** gerichtliches Verfahren ermöglichen; **~ the sale of effects** Effektenverkaufsauftrag erteilen; **~ in writing** schriftlich bevollmächtigen.

authorized befugt, verfügungsberechtigt, ermächtigt, bevollmächtigt, beauftragt, autorisiert, berechtigt, legitimiert, *(sanctioned)* rechtsverbindlich, *(story)* verbürgt; **not ~** nicht bevollmächtigt; **~ to dispose** verfügungsberechtigt; **~ by usage** durch langen Gebrauch sanktioniert, durch Gewohnheitsrecht begründet; **to be ~** Befugnis besitzen; **to be ~ to act** bevollmächtigt sein; **to be duly ~** ordnungsgemäße Vollmacht haben; **to be ~ to negotiate** Verhandlungsvollmacht haben; **to be ~ to sign** unterschriftsberechtigt sein; **~ agent** Bevollmächtigter, bevollmächtigter Vertreter; **duly ~ agent** ordnungsgemäß bestellter Vertreter; **~ bank** *(Br.)* Devisenbank; **~ capital** *(Br.)* [**stock**, *US*] genehmigtes (bewilligtes) [Aktien]kapital, Stamm-, Grundkapital; **through ~ channels** auf dem Dienstwege; **~ clerk** *(stockbroker)* zugelassener Börsenmakler; **~ dealer** Vertragshändler; **~ dealer in gold** *(Br.)* konzessionierter Goldhändler; **~ depository** *(Br.)* Hinterlegungsstelle für Devisenwerte; **~ person** bevollmächtigte Person, Bevollmächtigter; **~ recipient** Zustellungsbevollmächtigter; **~ representation** bevollmächtigter Vertreter; **~ signer** Unterschriftsberechtigter; **~ strength** *(mil.)* Etats-, Sollstärke; **~ version** maßgebende Fassung.

authorizing body maßgebende Genehmigungsbehörde.

authorship Autorschaft, Verfasser-, Urheberschaft.

auto, junk ausrangiertes Auto, Schrottwagen; **pollution-free ~** abgasfreies Auto; **~ accident** Autounfall; **~ age** Autozeitalter; **~ assembler** Automontagewerk; **~ assembly** Automontage; **~ assembly plant** Automontagewerk, -fabrik; **~ bargaining contract** Autotarifvertragsverhandlungen; **~ bumper** Stoßdämpfer; **~ company** Autofirma; **~ bodily injury insurance** Autohaftpflichtversicherung gegen Personenschaden; **~ carrier** *(Br.)* Autoanhänger; **~ carrier service** Autofährdienst; **~ changer** Plattenwechsler; **~ components** Autozubehör; **~ components industry** Autozubehörindustrie, Autozulieferungsindustrie; **~ concern** Autokonzern; **~ court** Motel; **~ coverage** Autoversicherungsschutz; **~ dealer** Autohändler, -vertreter; **~ dealership** Autovertretung; **~ establishment** Auto[mobil]firma; **~ executives** Führungskräfte der Autoindustrie; **~ exhaust** Autoauspuff; **~ experts** Autofachleute; **~ factory** Autofabrik; **~ industry** Autoindustrie; **~ industry supplier** Autozulieferungsbetrieb; **~ insurance** Autoversicherung, Kraftfahrzeugversicherung; **commercial ~ insurance** Haftpflichtversicherung für Geschäftsfahrzeuge; **personal ~ insurance** Haftpflichtversicherung für Privatfahrzeuge; **~ insurance claim** Kraftfahrzeugversicherungsschadensersatzanspruch; **~ insurance customer** Kraftfahrzeugversicherungsnehmer; **voluntary ~ insurance market** Versicherungsmarkt für nicht haftpflichtbedingte Risiken; **~ insurance rates** Kraftfahrzeug-, Autoversicherungstarif; **~ insurance underwriter** Kraftfahrzeugversicherungsgesellschaft; **~ insurer** Kraftfahrzeug-, Kfz-Versicherungsgesellschaft; **~ liability costs** Kfz-Haftpflichtunkosten; **~ liability rates** Kfz-Haftpflichtversicherungstarif; **~ livery service** Autovermietung mit gestelltem Chauffeur; **~ loan** Autokredit; **~ maintenance** Kraftfahrzeugunterhaltung; **~ maker** Autohersteller; **~ manufacturer** Automobilproduzent, -hersteller; **~ manufacturing** Autoproduktion, -herstellung; **~ market** Automarkt; **~ mechanic** Kraftfahrzeug-, Automechaniker, Autoschlosser; **~ muffler** Schalldämpfer; **~ output** Autoausstoß, -produktion; **~ parts suppliers** Autozulieferungsindustrie; **~ pilot** *(plane)* automatische Kurssteuerung; **~ plant** Autofabrik; **~ premium** Kfz-Versicherungsprämie; **~ production** Autoproduktion; **~ property damage insurance** Autosachschadensversicherung; **~ repairs** Autoreparatur; **~ repair costs** Autoreparaturkosten; **~ sales** Umsätze der Autoindustrie; **~ schedule** Kraftfahrzeugproduktionsprogramm; **~ scrap** Auto-, Schrottauto, Schrottwagen; **~ servicing** Kundendienst; **~ show** Autoausstellung; **~ stage** im Linienverkehr eingesetztes Kraftfahrzeug; **~ stocks** *(US)* Autoaktien; **~ strike** Autoarbeiterstreik; **~ supplier** Autozulieferungsbetrieb; **~ supplier industries** Autozulieferungsindustrie; **~ supply** Autoangebot; **~ trial** Kraftfahrzeug-, Kfz-Abnahme; **~ underwriting** Kfz-Versicherungsgeschäft; **personal ~ underwriting** Versicherungsabschlüsse für Privatfahrzeuge; **~ wage settlement** Autotarifabkommen; **~ worker** Autoarbeiter; **~ workers union** *(US)* Gewerkschaft des Autoarbeiters.

autobiographer Autobiograph.

autobiography Selbst-, Autobiographie.

autobus Autobus, Omnibus.

autocade Autokolonne.

autocamp Campingplatz für Autos.

autocracy Selbstherrschaft, Autokratie.

autocrat Selbstherrscher, Autokrat.

autocycle Fahrrad mit Hilfsmotor, Moped.

autogiro Tragschrauber.

autograph eigenhändiges Manuskript, *(printing)* autographischer Abdruck, *(reproduction)* Vervielfältigung, *(signature)* Autogramm; **~ *(a.)*** selbstgeschrieben, eigenhändig unterschrieben, mit einem Autogramm versehen; **~ *(v.)*** eigenhändig unterschreiben, mit einem Autogramm versehen, *(printing)* autographieren; **~ a book** Buch mit einer Widmung versehen; **~ album** Unterschriftenverzeichnis; **~ book** Unterschriftenverzeichnis; **~ collector** Autogrammsammler; **~ hunter** Autogrammjäger; **~ market** Autogrammmarkt; **~ price** Autogrammpreis; **~ letter** eigenhändiger Brief.

autographic eigenhändig, *(self-recording)* hektographisch.

automat Automatenrestaurant.

automate *(v.)* automatisieren.

automated vollautomatisiert, automatisch.

automatic Automat, *(mil.)* Selbstladepistole; **~ *(a.)*** [voll]automatisiert, automatisch, selbsttätig; **~ aerial camera** Reihenbildgerät; **~ area** *(tel.)* Netz mit Wählbetrieb; **~ block signal** *(railway)* automatisches Haltesignal ~

checkoff *(US)* tarifvertraglich durchgeführter Gehaltsabzug von Gewerkschaftsbeiträgen; ~ **circuit breaker** *(el.)* Sicherungsautomat; ~ **coverage** *(insurance)* automatische Deckung; ~ **currency** elastische Währung; ~ **exchange** *(tel.)* Selbstwählamt; ~ **machine** Automat; ~ **pencil** *(US)* Druck-, Drehbleistift; ~ **pilot** *(airplane)* automatische Kurssteuerung; ~ **pistol** Selbstladepistole; ~ **salary increase** automatischer Gehaltsanstieg; ~ **selling** automatischer Verkauf, Automatenverkauf; ~ **selling machine** Automat; ~ **starter** *(car)* Selbstanlasser; ~ **teaching device** Lehrautomat, -roboter; ~ **telephone** Selbst[wähl]anschluß; ~ **telephone answering machine** automatischer Anrufbeantworter; ~ **telephone answering service** Fernsprechauftragsdienst; ~ **termination of cover** *(outbreak of war)* automatische Beendigung des Deckungsschutzes; ~ **transmission** *(car)* automatische Schaltung, automatisches Getriebe; ~ **typewriter** Schreibmaschine mit Lochstreifensteuerung; ~ **vending machine** Verkaufsautomat; ~ **volume control** *(wireless)* selbsttätiger Schwundausgleich, Fadingausgleich; ~ **wage adjustment** automatische Lohnregulierung; ~ **[wage] progression** automatische Lohnprogression; ~ **working** Automatik.

automation Automatisierung, Automation;
  process ~ automatische Weiterverarbeitung;
  ~ **sales** Umsatzgeschäft in der Automatenindustrie; ~ **spending** Automatisierungsaufwand.

automatize *(v.)* automatisieren.

automobile *(especially, US)* Kraftfahrzeug, -wagen, Auto[mobil;
  legally operating ~ zugelassenes Kraftfahrzeug; **pollution-free** ~ abgasfreies Auto;
  to operate s. one's ~ jds. Auto (Kfz) benutzen;
  ~ **accessories** Autozubehör; ~ **accident** Auto-, Kraftfahrzeugunfall; ~ **Association** *(Br.)* Kraftfahrerverband; ~ **battery** Autobatterie; ~ **bill** Autorechnung; ~ **body** Autokarosserie; ~ **business** Kraftfahrzeugbranche; ~ **collision insurance** Kraftfahrzeug-, Autohaftpflichtversicherung; ~ **dealer** Autohändler; ~ **deck** Autoverdeck; ~ **expense** Autounkosten; ~ **expressway** *(US)* Autobahn; ~ **ferry** Autofähre; ~ **garage** Autogarage; ~ **guest** Mitfahrer; ~ **industry** Kraftfahrzeugautoindustrie; ~**injury** Autounfall; ~ **insurance** *(US)* Kraftfahrzeugversicherung; ~ **insurance contract** Kraftfahrzeugversicherungsvertrag; ~ **manufacturing** Autoproduktion, Automobilbau; ~ **mechanic** Autoschlosser; ~ **operating costs** Kraftfahrzeug-, Autounterhaltungskosten; ~ **operation** Kraftfahrzeugbetrieb; ~ **owner** Kraftfahrzeugbesitzer, -halter; ~ **ownership documents** Kraftfahrzeugpapiere; ~ **public liability** Kraftfahrzeughaftung; **short-term** ~ **and hospitalization policy** kurzfristige Auto- und Krankenhausversicherung; **standard** ~ **public liability policy** allgemeine Kfz-Haftpflichtversicherungspolice; ~ **pool** Wagenpark; ~ **production** Autoproduktion; ~ **repair shop** Autoreparaturwerkstatt; ~ **service station** Autotankstelle; ~ **shares** *(US)* Autoaktien; ~ **show** Autoausstellung; ~ **tax** *(US)* Kraftfahrzeugsteuer; ~ **transportation** Kraftfahrzeugbeförderung; ~ **truck** Autoanhänger; ~ **underwriting** Kraftfahrzeugversicherungsgeschäft.

automobilist Kraftfahrer.

automotive|**austerity** Konsumbeschränkung auf dem Kfz-Sektor; ~ **components** Autozubehör; ~ **industry** *(US)* Autoindustrie; ~ **plant** Autofabrik; ~ **replacement parts** Autoersatzteile; ~ **supplier** Autozulieferungsbetrieb.

autonomic[al] sich selbst regierend, autonom.

autonomist demonstration Demonstrationszug der Autonomistenbewegung.

autonomous selbständig, autonom;
  ~ **investmnent** von wirtschaftlichen Überlegungen unabhängige Investition; ~ **tariff system** autonomer Zolltarif.

autonomy Selbstregierung, -verwaltung, Autonomie;
  to achieve ~ autonom werden; **to suspend** ~ Selbstverwaltung beseitigen.

autopsy Obduktion, Autopsie, Leichenöffnung, -schau, *(fig.)* kritische Zergliederung.

autoradiogram(me) Radioapparat mit Plattenwechsler.

autorist *(US)* Automobilist, Autofahrer.

autosilo Hochhausgarage, Autosilo.

autosled Motorschlitten.

autotruck *(US)* Lastkraftwagen.

autotype *(print.)* Rasterätzung, Autotypie, *(television)* Rasterbild.

autotypography autographischer Buchdruck.

autumn holidays Herbstferien.

auxiliaries *(mil.)* Hilfstruppen.

auxiliary Hilfskraft, *(navy)* Hilfskreuzer;
  ~ *(a.)* zusätzlich, helfend, mitwirkend;

~ **account** Hilfskonto; ~ **advertising** zusätzliche (unterstützende) Werbung, Zusatzwerbung; ~ **body** Hilfsorgan; ~ **book** Kladde, Hilfsbuch; ~ **capital** Produktivkapital; ~ **column** *(bookkeeping)* Hilfsspalte; ~ **committee** Hilfsausschuß; ~ **cruiser** Hilfskreuzer; ~ **department** Hilfsabteilung; ~ **engine** Hilfsmotor; ~ **function** Hilfsfunktion; ~ **goods** Produktionsgüter; ~ **personnel** Hilfspersonal; ~ **service** zusätzliche Dienstleistungen; ~ **troops** Hilfstruppen; ~ **worker** Hilfsarbeiter.

avail Nutzen, Vorteil, Gewinn;
  of no ~ nutzlos;
  ~ *(v.)* **o. s.** Gebrauch machen von, ausüben, sich zu Nutze machen (bedienen);
  to be of no ~ nutzlos (zwecklos) sein.

availability Nützlichkeit, Verfügbarkeit, Disponibilität, *(broadcasting)* noch verfügbare Werbezeit, *(politics, US)* Erfolgschance [eines Kandidaten], *(scope of validity)* Gültigkeitsbereich, *(ticket)* Gültigkeit;
  ~ **of access** Zugangsmöglichkeit; ~ **of flight** Flugmöglichkeit; ~ **of a loan for home purchase** Darlehensgewährung zum Zweck eines Eigenheimerwerbs; **reduced** ~ **of mortgage funds** verknappte Hypothekengelder; ~ **to travel** Reisebereitschaft; ~ **for work** *(unemployment compensation)* Bereitschaft, eine angemessene Arbeitsstelle anzutreten; ~ **date** *(US, banking)* Wert[stellung], Valuta.

available verfügbar, disponibel, erhältlich, vorhanden, *(law)* zulässig, statthaft, *(ticket)* gültig;
  not ~ *(ticket)* ungültig; **publicly** ~ allgemein zugänglich; **unconditionally** ~ uneingeschränkt verfügbar;
  ~ **for letting** in verpachtungsfähigem Zustand; ~ **for outright purchase only** lieferbar nur fest; ~ **in all sizes** in allen Größen lieferbar;
  to be ~ bereitstehen; **[not] to be** ~ **on appeal** [kein] Berufungsgrund sein; **to be** ~ **on call** für besondere Gelegenheiten zur Verfügung stehen; **to be** ~ **for one month** einen Monat gültig sein (Gültigkeit haben); **not to be** ~ **to talk to the press** sich der Presse nicht stellen; **to make** ~ bereitstellen, zur Verfügung stellen;
  ~ **assets** jederzeit greifbare Aktiva; ~ **audience** Gesamtzahl der eingeschalteten Rundfunk- und Fernsehgeräte; ~ **candidate** *(US, politics)* Kandidat mit Erfolgsaussichten; ~ **capital** flüssige Gelder, verfügbares Kapital; ~ **funds** verfügbare Guthaben, liquide Mittel; ~ **information** zur Verfügung stehende Nachrichten; ~ **means** verfügbare Mittel; ~ **plea** schlüssiger Einwand; **all** ~ **resources** alle verfügbaren Hilfsmittel; ~ **sites** verfügbarer Anschlagraum; ~ **surplus** *(balance sheet)* verfügbarer Reingewinn.

avails *(US)* Ertrag, Erlös, *(note)* Gegenwert;
  net ~ Nettoerlös;
  ~ **of a sale by auction** *(US)* Versteigerungserlös.

aval Wechselbürgschaft, Aval;
  ~ **account** Avalrechnung.

avalanche Lawine;
  ~ **of letters** Flut von Briefen; ~ **of selling** Verkaufslawine.

avenge *(v.)* [Verbrechen] ahnden, strafen;
  ~ **an insult** Beleidigung rächen.

avenue Zugang, Weg, Allee, *(US)* [Pracht]straße, Promenade;
  ~ **to fame** Weg zum Ruhm; ~**s to success** Erfolgsleiter;
  not to be the only ~ nicht die einzige Möglichkeit darstellen; **to provide new** ~**s for industry** der Wirtschaft neue Aufgaben stellen.

aver *(v.)* behaupten, versichern, als Tatsache hinstellen, *(law)* beweisen, Beweis erbringen, versichern.

average Durchschnitt, Mittelwert, *(charge in addition)* kleiner Frachtaufschlag, *(ship)* Havarie, Seeschaden, *(statistics)* arithmetisches Mittel;
  above ~ überdurchschnittlich; **all** ~ **recoverable** alle Schäden zu ersetzen; **below** ~ nicht ganz auf der Höhe, unterdurchschnittlich; **free of** ~ nicht gegen Havarie versichert, havariefrei; **free of all** ~ nicht gegen große und besondere Havarie versichert; **on an** ~ im Durchschnitt; **with** ~ *(marine insurance)* ohne Beschränkung;
  ~**s** *(stock exchange, US)* Aktienindex;
  ~ **accustomed** Havarie nach Seebrauch; **annual** ~ Jahresdurchschnitt; **fair** ~ guter Durchschnitt; **general (gross)** ~ große (gemeinschaftliche) Havarie; **foreign general** ~ große ausländische Havarie; **high-grade** ~ hohe Durchschnittnote; **monthly** ~ Monatsdurchschnitt; **market** ~ durchschnittliche Kursversicherung; **particular (simple)** ~ besondere (einfache) Havarie, Teilschaden, -Havarie; **petty** ~ Vergütung für kleinere Reisenkosten eines Schiffes; **rough** ~ annähernder Durchschnitt; **weighted** ~ gewogenes arithmetisches Mittel;

~ **of the class** Klassendurchschnitt; ~ **in fire insurance** verhältnismäßige Kürzung der Entschädigung im Fall einer Unterversicherung;

~ *(v. intr.)* durchschnittlich betragen (ergeben), *(v. tr.)* Mittelwert errechnen, *(divide proportionally)* anteilmäßig aufgliedern, *(income statement)* steuerlich verteilen;

~ **the amounts** Durchschnittszahl der Beträge ermitteln; ~ **down (up)** *(stock exchange)* seine Verluste durch An- und Verkauf reduzieren, Durchschnittskosten vermindern; ~ **as expected** erwarteten Durchschnitt erzielen; ~ **80 miles an hour** Durchschnittsgeschwindigkeit von 120 km erzielen; ~ **a loss** Schadensbetrag anteilmäßig aufgliedern; ~ **out** *(stock exchange)* Kursgeschäft ohne Verlust abschließen;

to adjust the ~ Havarie aufmachen, dispachieren; **to be up to the** ~ Durchschnitt erreichen; **to bear** ~ Havarie tragen; **to find the** ~ Durchschnitt berechnen; **to make** ~ Havarie machen; **to recover** ~ Ersatz für Havarie erhalten; **to rough in the** ~ durchschnittlich ergeben; **to settle the** ~ Havarie aufmachen; **to strike an** ~ Durchschnitt nehmen; **to suffer** ~ Havarie erleiden; **to take an** ~ **of results** durchschnittliches Ergebnis nehmen;

~ *(a.)* durchschnittlich, mittelmäßig;

~ **account** Havarierechnung; ~ **adjuster** Dispacheur, Havarievertreter; ~ **adjustment** Havarieberechnung, Dispache; ~ **age** Durchschnittsalter; ~ **agent** Havarieagent, Havarievertreter, -kommissar; ~ **agreement** Havarievertrag; ~ **amount** Durchschnittsbetrag; ~ **audience rating** durchschnittliche Leser-, Hörerbeteiligung; ~ **balance** Durchschnittsguthaben; ~ **bill** Havarierechnung; ~ **bond** Havarieschein, -revers; ~ **book** Durchschnittssaldenliste; ~ **burden rate** Durchschnittsgemeinkostensatz; ~ **capacity** Durchschnittskapazität, Durchschnittskapital; **general** ~ **cash deposit** Havarieeinschuß zur großen Havarie; ~ **charges** Havariegelder, *(transportation)* durchschnittliche Zoll- und Transportkosten; ~ **circulation** Durchschnittsauflage; ~ **citizen** Durchschnittsbürger; ~ **clause** Verhältnisklausel, *(sea damage)* Havarie-, Freizeichnungsklausel; **general** ~ **clause** große Havarieklausel; ~ **collection period** durchschnittliche Zahlungsfrist; ~ **consumer** Durchschnittsverbraucher, -kunde; ~ **consumption** Durchschnittsverbrauch; ~ **contribution** Havariebeitrag; ~ **cost** Durchschnittskosten, -aufwand; ~ **cost price** durchschnittlicher Gestehungspreis; ~ **cost pricing** Preisbildung auf Durchschnittskostenbasis; ~ **customer** Durchschnittskunde; ~ **date of posting** mittlere Anlaufzeit; ~ **days in receivables** Debitorenlaufzeit; ~ **deviation** mittlere Abweichung; ~ **due date** mittlerer Zahlungstermin, *(bill of exchange)* durchschnittlicher Verfalltag, Fälligkeitstermin; ~ **driver** Durchschnittsfahrer; ~ **duration of life** *(insurance)* durchschnittliche Lebensdauer; ~ **earnings** Durchschnittseinkommen, -verdienst; ~ **expenses** Havariegelder; ~ **figure** Durchschnittszahl; ~ **figure for world trade** Welthandelsdurchschnitt; ~ **goods** Havariewaren; ~ **haul** Durchschnittstransportkosten; ~ **hourly earnings** Durchschnittsstundenverdienst; ~ **human being** Durchschnittsmensch; ~ **income** Durchschnittseinkommen; ~ **interest** Durchschnittszinsen; ~ **issue** Durchschnittsauflage; ~ **kind and quality** mittlere Art und Güte; ~ **life** durchschnittliche Nutzungsdauer; ~ **loss** Havarieschaden; ~ **marrying age** durchschnittliches Heiratsalter; ~ **mechanic skilled in the art** *(patent law)* Durchschnittsfachmann; ~ **money** Havariegelder; ~ **net assets** Nettovermögen; ~ **net paid** Durchschnittsverkaufsauflage; ~ **number** Durchschnittszahl; ~ **number of impressions per reader** durchschnittliche Kontaktzahl der Leser; ~ **output** Durchschnittsproduktion; ~ **percentage** Durchschnittsprozentsatz; ~ **performance** Durchschnittsleistung; ~ **person** Durchschnittsmensch; ~ **pocket-book** Durchschnittsgeldbeutel; ~ **premium** Durchschnittsprämie; ~ **price** Durchschnittspreis, *(stock exchange)* Durchschnittskurs; ~ **price level** *(national product)* Gesamtpreisindex; ~ **production** Durchschnittserzeugung; ~ **productivity** Durchschnittsproduktivität; ~ **profit** Durchschnittsgewinn; ~ **proportion** Durchschnittsanteil; ~ **fair quality** Durchschnittsqualität; ~ **quantity** Durchschnittsmenge; ~ **quotation** Durchschnittsnotierung; ~ **rate** Durchschnittssatz, *(stock exchange)* Mittel-, Durchschnittskurs, *(taxation)* Durchschnittssteuersatz; ~ **earned rate** Durchschnittsverdienst; ~ **rate of wages** mittlerer Lohnsatz; ~ **ratio** Durchschnittsverhältnis; ~ **return** Durchschnittsertrag; ~ **revenue** Durchschnittseinnahmen; ~ **revenue per passenger mile** Durchschnittseinkünfte pro Beförderungsziffer; ~ **sacrifice** Havarieaufopferungen; ~ **sales** Durchschnittsumsatz; ~ **annual net sales** jährlicher Durchschnittsbruttoumsatz; ~ **shipping weight** Durchschnittsverladegewicht; ~ **sort** Mittelsorte; ~ **span of life** durchschnittliche Lebenszeit; ~ **speed** Durch-

schnittsgeschwindigkeit; ~ **statement** Dispache, Havarie-, Seeschadensberechnung; ~ **stater** Havarievertreter, Dispacheur; ~ **stock** durchschnittlicher Lagerbestand; ~ **sum** Durchschnittssumme, Pauschalbetrag; ~ **tare** Durchschnittstara; ~ **turnover** Durchschnittsumsatz; ~ **unit cost** Durchschnittskosten pro Einheit; ~ **value** Mittel-, Durchschnittswert; ~ **volume of transactions** durchschnittliches Kursniveau; ~ **voter** Durchschnittswähler; ~ **wage** Durchschnittslohn; ~ **working force** Durchschnittsbelegschaft; ~ **workman** Durchschnittsarbeiter; ~ **yield** Durchschnittsrendite, -ertrag.

averaging, cost Durchschnittskostenmethode; ~ **down** *(stock exchange)* Durchschnittskostenverminderung.

averment Sachvortrag, Beweisanerbieten, -antrag;
immaterial ~ unerhebliches Vorbringen; **particular** ~ substantiiertes Vorbringen;
~ **of notice** Zustellungsnachweis.

averse to labo(u)r arbeitsscheu, -unlustig.

aversion Abneigung, Abscheu, Widerwillen;
pet ~ besondere Abneigung;
~ **to labo(u)r** *(work)* Arbeitsscheu, -unlust;
to have a strong ~ **to getting up early** sehr gegen frühes Aufstehen eingestellt sein; **to take an** ~ **to s. o.** Abneigung gegen j. haben.

avert *(v.)* ablenken, abwenden;
~ **an accident** Unfall vermeiden; ~ **a catastrophe** Unglück verhüten; ~ **failure by hard work** Versagen durch harte Arbeit vermeiden.

aviation Luftfahrt, Flugwesen, -verkehr, Fliegerei, *(organization)* Luftfahrtorganisation;
civil ~ Passagierflugverkehr; **commercial** ~ Verkehrsluftfahrt; ~ **administration** Luftfahrtbehörde; [**civil**] ~ **agreement** Abkommen der Luftfahrtgesellschaften, Luftfahrtabkommen; ~ **badge** *(US)* Fliegerabzeichen; ~ **bailiewick** spezielles Flugverkehrsgebiet; ~ **beacon** Flugzeugbake; ~ **company** Luftverkehrsgesellschaft; ~ **experience** Flugerfahrung; ~ **facility** Luftverkehrsanlagen; ~ **fuel** Flugzeugbenzin; ~ **ground** Flugplatz; ~ **industry** Flugzeugindustrie; ~ **insurance** Flugzeug-, Luftfahrtversicherung; ~ **insurer** Flugzeugversicherungsgesellschaft; ~ **magazine** Luftfahrtmagazin, -zeitschrift; ~ **market** Markt für Flugzeugwerte; ~ **office** Luftamt; ~ **organization** Luftfahrtverband, -organisation; **civil** ~ **permit** Luftverkehrsgenehmigung; ~ **pioneer** Flugpionier; ~ **rally** Flugzeugralley; ~ **risk** Flugverkehrsrisiko; ~ **school** Fliegerschule; ~ **shares** Flugzeugaktien; ~ **spirit** Flugzeugbenzin, Sprit; ~ **state rules** Flugsicherungsbestimmungen; ~ **supply** Luftfahrtausrüstung; ~ **underwriter** Luftfahrtversicherungsgesellschaft; ~ **weather service** Flugwetterdienst.

aviator Flieger, Flugzeugführer, Pilot.

avigator Flugzeugführer, Pilot.

aviso Benachrichtigung, *(mar.)* Meldeboot.

avocation Nebenbeschäftigung, -beruf, Steckenpferd.

avocatory letter Rückberufungsschreiben.

avoid *(v.)* umwälzen, -stoßen, vermeiden, umgehen, *(escape)* entgehen, *(invalidate)* ungültig machen, anfechten, aufheben, annullieren;
~ **anomalies** Härten vermeiden; ~ **colliding** Zusammenstoß vermeiden; ~ **a contract** Vertrag anfechten; ~ **a punitive combination of high inflation and progressive taxation** einer Bestrafung gleichkommende Kombination hoher Inflationsraten mit progressiven Steuersätzen ausweichen; ~ **double taxation** Doppelbesteuerung vermeiden; ~ **liability** sich der Haftung entziehen; ~ **one's obligations** seinen Verpflichtungen nicht nachkommen; ~ **a patent** Patent anfechten; ~ **paying taxes** Steuerzahlungen vermeiden.

avoidable vermeidbar, zu umgehen, *(contract)* annullierbar, anfechtbar.

avoidance *(annulment)* Anfechtungserklärung, Annullierung, Widerruf, Aufhebung, *(benefice)* Freiwerden, Vakanz, *(evasion)* Vermeidung, Umgehung, *(invalidation)* Nichtigkeitserklärung;
subject to ~ anfechtbar;
confession and ~ Einrede ohne Leugnen des Klagegrundes;
~ **of an agreement** Annullierung einer Vereinbarung; ~ **of bankruptcy proceedings** Konkursabwendung; ~ **of a contract** Vertragsanfechtung, -annullierung; ~ **of contract owing to mistake** Vertragsanfechtung wegen Irrtums; ~ **of duty** Abgabenumgehung; ~ **of estate duty** Erbschaftssteuerumgehung; ~ **of liability** Umgehung von Haftungsbestimmungen; ~ **of taxes** Steuerumgehung;
to be conditioned for ~ Anfechtungsgrund abgeben;
~ **provisions** Umgehungsbestimmungen.

avoiding | a risk Risikovermeidung;
~ **provisions** Umgehungsbestimmungen.
avoirdupois [weight] Handelsgewicht.
avouch *(v.)* einstehen, garantieren, verbürgen, versichern.
avouchment Bescheinigung.
avow Geständnis;
~ *(v.)* offen bekennen, anerkennen, zugestehen;
~ **o. s. the author** sich als Autor bekennen; ~ **a fault** Fehler zugeben.
avowal Eingeständnis, Bekenntnis;
~ **of guaranty** Bürgschaftserklärung.
avulsion *(law)* Abschwemmen [von Land].
await | *(v.)* arrival *(letters)* nicht nachsenden; ~ **instructions** Anweisungen abwarten; ~ **orders** Aufträgen entgegensehen.
awaken *(v.)* **s. o. to his responsibilities** jem. seine Verantwortung klar machen.
award *(acceptance of bid for purchases of securities)* Akzeptierung eines Angebots auf Kauf eines Effektenpaketes, *(adjudgment)* Zuerkennung, Zubilligung, *(arbitration)* Schiedsspruch, -urteil, schiedsrichterliche Entscheidung, *(opinion)* Gutachten, *(insurance business)* zuerkannter Schadensersatz, *(prize show)* Preis, Prämie, Auszeichnung;
arbitration (arbitrator's) ~ Schiedsspruch, schiedsrichterliche Entscheidung; **commonly binding** ~ allgemein verbindlicher Schiedsspruch; **foreign** ~ ausländischer Schiedsspruch; **highest possible** ~ höchstmögliche Auszeichnung; **industrial** ~ Schiedsspruch in gewerblichem Schiedsverfahren; **legal** ~ *(insurance business)* rechtlich zuerkannter Schadensersatz; **partial** ~ parteiischer Schiedsspruch; **state** ~ staatlicher Schiedsspruch;
~ **of alimony (maintenance)** Zuerkennung von Unterhalt; ~ **of compensation** im Schiedswege zuerkannte Abfindung; ~ **of a contract** Auftragsvergabe; ~ **of damages** Zubilligung von Schadensersatz; ~ **to inventor** Erfinderprämie; ~ **of a loan** Anleihe-, Kreditgewährung; ~ **of maintenance** Zuerkennung von Unterhalt; ~ **of a prize** Zuerkennung eines Preises; ~ **of reference** Schiedsgutachten;
~ *(v.)* durch Schiedsspruch zuerkennen;
~ **alimony** *(US)* Unterhalt zuerkennen; ~ **a contract** [Fabrikations-, Lieferungs]auftrag (Zuschlag) erteilen; ~ **damages against** j. zur Leistung von Schadensersatz verurteilen, auf Schadensersatz gegen j. erkennen; ~ **heavy damages** zur Zahlung eines hohen Schadensersatzes verurteilen; ~ **s. o. a sum of damages** jem. Schadensersatz zuerkennen; ~ **s. o. £ 100 as damages** jem. 100 Pfund Schadenersatz zubilligen; ~ **an injunction** einstweilige Verfügung erlassen; ~ **a loan** Anleihe gewähren; ~ **maintenance** Unterhalt zuerkennen; ~ **a prize** prämieren; ~ **s. o. the first prize** jem. den ersten Preis zuerkennen; ~ **a prize of honour** Ehrenpreis gewähren;
to abide by an ~ Schiedsspruch anerkennen; **to enforce an** ~ Schiedsspruch durchsetzen (vollstrecken); **to enter for an** ~ sich um eine Auszeichnung bewerben; **to make an** ~ Schiedsspruch fällen, *(prize show)* Preis zuerkennen; **to offer an** ~ Belohnung aussetzen; **to receive an individual** ~ persönliche Auszeichnung erhalten; **to set aside an** ~ Schiedsspruch aufheben.
awarded damages zuerkannter Schadenersatz.
awarding | of contracts Auftragszuteilung; ~ **of travel grants** Reisezuschußgewährung.
aware *(agreement)* in Anbetracht, gewahr, in der Erkenntnis, in dem Bewußtsein;
to be dimly ~ nur ahnen; **to be well** ~ sich voll bewußt sein.
awareness Bewußtsein, Kenntnis.
away entfernt, weg;
to be ~ sich auf Reisen befinden; **to be** ~ **on leave** im Urlaub sein; **to work** ~ drauflosarbeiten;
~ **going crop** Ernte auf dem Halm.
awkward | age *(adolescents)* schwieriges Alter; ~ **customer** unangenehmer Kunde; **to be an** ~ **customer** mit jem. nicht gut Kirschen essen sein; ~ **street corner** gefährliche Straßenecke.
awning Plane, Zeltbahn, *(rooflike cover)* Markise.
axe, ax *(US) (cut in expenditure)* Etatkürzung, Sparkommission;
~ **of expenditure** Ausgabenbeschneidung;
~ *(v.)* Dienststellen abbauen, Ausgaben radikal herabsetzen;
~ **s. o. j.** absägen; ~ **expenditure** Ausgaben beschneiden; ~ **a number of officials** radikalen Beamtenabbau durchführen;
to apply the ~ **to public expenditure** Etatstreichungen durchführen; **to get the** ~ *(US coll.)* entlassen werden; **to have an** ~ **to grind** Privatinteressen verfolgen; **to set an** ~ **to s. th.** Axt an etw. legen.
axiom allgemein anerkannter Grundsatz;
~ **of law** Rechtsgrundsatz.
axis *(pol.)* Achse;
~ **of supply** *(mil.)* Nachschubachse.
axle load zugelassenes Achsengewicht.
aye *(politics)* Jastimme;
~**s and noes** *(parl.)* Stimmen für und wider, Ja- und Neinstimmen;
the ~**s have it** der Antrag ist angenommen.

B

b *(trade)* Güteklasse B, zweite Qualität;
  ~ girl Animierdame.
Babbit *(US)* Spießbürger.
babble *(v.)* **out secrets** Geheimnisse ausquatschen.
babe in the woods vertrauensselige Person.
babel babylonisches Sprachengewirr.
babloid *(US)* Boulevardzeitung, -blatt.
baby Kleinstkind, *(good performance, sl.)* tolle Sache;
  to be landed with (hold, carry) the ~ etw. ausbaden müssen; **to be left holding the ~** *(fam.)* im Stich gelassen sein; **to empty the ~ out with the bathwater** Kind mit dem Bad ausschütten; **to hold the ~** *(Br., sl.)* Kopf hinhalten;
  to plead the ~ act *(US)* Einwand der Minderjährigkeit erheben; ~ **bonds** *(US)* kleingestückelte Schuldverschreibungen, Wertpapiere mit geringem Nominalwert, Kleinobligationen; **postwar ~ boom** nachkriegsbedingter Kindersegen; ~ **car** Kleinwagen; ~ **carriage** *(US)* Kinderwagen; ~ **farm** Säuglingsheim; ~ **minder** Kindermädchen; ~ **nursery** Säuglingsheim; ~ **share** Kleinaktie; ~ **stock** *(US)* neu ausgegebene Aktie.
babysit *(v.)* Babysitter abgeben.
babysitter Kinderhüter, -wärter, Babysitter.
babysitting Kinderhüten.
bachelor Lediger;
  ♌ **of Commerce** *(Br.)* [etwa] Diplomkaufmann; ♌ **of Science** *(Br.)* Diplomphysiker;
  to remain a ~ ledig bleiben;
  ~ **apartment (flat)** Junggesellenwohnung; ~ **quarters** Junggesellenwohnung; ~**'s tax** Junggesellensteuer.
bachelordom Junggesellenstand.
bachelorhood Junggesellenstand.
back *(bill of exchange)* Rückseite, *(book, house)* Hinter-, Rückseite, Rücken, *(car)* Rücksitz, *(Br., stock exchange)* Prolongationsgebühr;
  at s. one's ~ zu jds Rückenstützung; **at the ~ of one's mind** in seinen verborgensten Gedanken; **behind s. one's ~** in jds. Abwesenheit, hinterrücks; **on giving ~** bei Rückgabe; **with one's ~ to the wall** mit dem Rücken zur Wand;
  ~ **of a book** Buchrücken;
  ~ *(v.)* unterstützen, befürworten, *(bill of exchange)* [fremde Wechsel] indossieren, girieren;
  ~ **s. o.** die Stange halten;
  ~ **s. o. in an argument** j. bei einer Debatte unterstützen; ~ **a car out of the garage** Auto rückwärts aus der Garage fahren; ~ **every £ 100 of extra cash which they hold with an extra £ 12.50 of reserve assets** Landeszentralbankguthaben in Höhe von 1/8 für besondere Barguthaben unterhalten; ~ **the currency** Währung stützen; ~ **down** Ansprüche aufgeben, klein beigeben; ~ **down from the position one took last week** andere Auffassung als in der vergangenen Woche vertreten; ~ **down from a statement** Aussage widerrufen; ~ **and fill** *(US)* unschlüssig sein, schwanken; ~ **s. o. financially** j. finanziell unterstützen; ~ **a horse** auf ein Pferd setzen (wetten); ~ **the wrong horse** auf die falsche Karte (aufs falsche Pferd) setzen; ~ **a motion** Antrag unterstützen; ~ **notes** Noten decken; ~ **out of s. th.** sich vor etw. drücken, sich einer Sache entziehen, kneifen; ~ **out of a bargain** sich aus einem Geschäft zurückziehen; ~ **out of a contract** sich vertraglich übernommenen Verbindlichkeiten entziehen; ~ **out of an obligation** Verpflichtung nicht mehr gelten lassen; ~ **up** unterstützen, befürworten; ~ **up a candidate** Kandidaten unterstützen; ~ **s. o. up throughout a discussion** jem. in einer Diskussion Hilfestellung geben; ~**-water** *(v.) (fig., US)* klein beigeben;
  to be at the ~ of s. th. hinter einer Sache stehen (stecken); **to be with one's ~ to the wall** mit dem Rücken zur Wand stehen, in einer schwierigen Lage sein; **to be ~ in one's rent** mit seiner Miete im Rückstand sein, Mietrückstände haben; **to be a little high ~** *(stocks)* stark zurückgefallen sein; **to be flat on one's ~** nicht aktionsfähig sein; **to be glad to see the ~ of s. o.** j. am liebsten von hinten sehen; **to be right ~ in s. th.** mit etw. wieder ganz vertraut sein; **to break her ~** *(ship)* auseinanderbrechen; **to get one's own ~ on s. o.** jem. etw. heimzahlen; **to give ~** zurückgeben; **to go behind s. one's ~** hinter jds. Rücken agieren; **to go ~ from one's engagement** seine Verbindlichkeiten nicht erfüllen; **to go ~ from one's word** sein Versprechen nicht halten; **to have s. o. on one's ~** j. auf dem Halse haben; **to have a strong ~** *(fig.)* breiten Rücken haben; **to have one's ~ up** *(sl.)* sehr wütend sein; **to have one's ~ to the wall** in Schwierigkeiten (bedrängter Lage) sein; **to have broken the ~ of s. th.** das

Schlimmste hinter sich haben; **to have broken the ~ of the work** über den Berg sein; **to hold the crowd ~** die Menschenmenge zurückhalten; **to pay ~** zurück[be]zahlen; **to put one's ~ into s. th.** mit ganzer Kraft und Energie arbeiten; **to say s. th. behind s. one's ~** hinter jds. Rücken über ihn reden; **to turn one's ~ on s. o.** j. im Stich lassen; **to turn one's ~ on s. th.** sich von einer Sache abwenden; **to take ~** zurücknehmen;
  ~ *(a.) (overdue)* rückständig, im Rückstand;
  ~ **alley** *(US)* Seitengäßchen; ~ **apartment** *(Br.)* nach hinten gelegenes Zimmer; ~ **bench** hintere Sitzreihe; ~ **bencher** gewöhnlicher Abgeordneter; ~ **bond** *(Scot.)* Urkunde über die Offenlegung bloßer Treuhänderschaft; ~**-of-envelope calculations** überschlägliche Kalkulationen; ~ **charges** Rückspesen; ~ **country** *(US)* Hinterland; ~ **cover** vierte Umschlagseite; ~**-to-~ credit** *(US)* Zweit-, Gegenakkreditiv; ~ **door** *(fig.)* Hintertür; ~**-door intrigues** heimliche Machenschaften; ~**-door operation** *(Bank of England, Br.)* verbilligter Schatzwechselankauf, Stützungskauf, Liquiditätsbeschaffung durch Schatzwechselverkauf; ~**-door pay supplements** Gehaltszuschüsse durchs Hintertürchen; ~**-door route into the market** Hintertürchen zur Inanspruchnahme der Börse im Notfall; ~ **entry** Hintereingang; ~ **freight** Rückfracht; ~**-handed compliment** zweischneidiges Kompliment; ~ **interest** Zinsrückstände; ~ **issue** alte Nummer (Ausgabe); ~ **land** billigeres Bauland; ~ **margin** Bundsteg; ~ **number** *(person)* rückständiger Mensch; ~ **numbers** *(of a journal)* alte Zeitungsnummern; ~**-off** Kurssturz; ~**-office personnel** Bürohilfspersonal; ~**-office system** interne Betriebsabwicklung; ~ **order** noch nicht erledigter Auftrag; ~ **page** Rückseite; ~ **pay** Lohn-, Gehaltsrückstand; ~ **payment** Nachzahlung; ~ **rent** rückständige Miete; ~ **road** Nebenweg; ~ **room** Hinterzimmer; **in a ~ room** hinter den Kulissen; ~**-room boy** *(US coll.)* wissenschaftlicher Experte; ~**-room work** *(US)* wissenschaftliche Tätigkeit, Expertenarbeit; ~ **seat** Rücksitz; **to take a ~ seat** *(fig.)* in den Hintergrund treten; **the ~ side of the coin** die andere Seite der Medaille; ~ **spread** Arbitragegeschäft; ~ **street** abgelegene Straße; ~**-street conspirator** Hinterhausverschwörer; ~ **taxes** Steuerrückstände; ~ **train** Rückzug; ~ **wheel** Hinterrad; ~**-to-work movement** Antistreikbewegung.
backbencher *(Br. politics)* Hinterbänkler, nicht zum Kabinett gehörender Abgeordneter.
backbite *(v.)* hinter dem Rücken reden, verleumden.
backbiter Verleumder.
backbiting Verleumdung.
backbone *(fig.)* Willenskraft, Rückgrat, *(book)* Buchrücken, *(business undertaking)* Stammpersonal;
  to the ~ ganz und gar, durch und durch;
  ~ **of the country** Rückgrat eines Staates.
backbreaker große Anstrengung.
backcap *(v.) (US)* verächtlich machen.
backchat *(sl.)* freche Antwort.
backdate *(v.)* rückdatieren.
backdated element Rückdatierungsbestandteil.
backdown Aufgabe von Ansprüchen.
backed | bill avalierter Wechsel; ~ **frame** gerasterter Rahmen; ~ **note** abgestempelter Ladeschein.
backer Hintermann, Helfer, Unterstützer, *(bill of exchange)* Wechselbürge, *(sheet)* Deckblatt;
  financial ~ Geldgeber.
backfire *(car)* Fehlzündung, *(mil.)* Gegenfeuer;
  ~ *(v.)* Fehlzündung haben, früh-, fehlzünden, *(plot)* fehlschlagen, mißlingen, ins Auge gehen, *(US)* Gegenfeuer legen.
backformation *(ling.)* Rückbildung.
background *(art)* Hinter-und Untergrund, *(film)* vergrößerter Bildhintergrund, *(music)* Geräuschkulisse, Tonuntermalung, *(of a person)* Vorgeschichte, Vergangenheit, Werdegang, Hintergrund material, *(radio)* Hintergrundgeräusch, *(window dressing)* Schaufensterhintergrund;
  academic ~ akademischer Werdegang; **business administration ~** betriebswirtschaftliche Ausbildung; **educational ~** Bildungsgang, Ausbildungsweg; **family ~** [Familien]herkunft; **financial ~** finanzieller Rückhalt; **political ~** politischer Werdegang; **social ~** gesellschaftliche Herkunft;
  sound ~ as a general economist solide Kenntnisse auf dem volkswirtschaftlichen Gebiet;
  to fill in the ~ Hintergrund erläutern; **to have a ~** Vorkenntnisse haben; **to have the same regional ~** aus der gleichen Gegend stammen; **to have a ~ in law enforcement** rudimentäre

Kenntnisse des Polizeiapparates haben; **to have a ~ in various parts of the world** auf verschiedenen Plätzen im Außendienst gewesen sein; **to keep in the ~** nicht hervortreten; **to keep s. th. in the ~** etw. wissentlich zurückhalten; **to push into the ~** in den Hintergrund abdrängen;
~ **briefings (material)** Hintergrundmaterial, -informationen; ~ **music** Geräuschkulisse, Tonuntermalung; ~ **noises** Geräuschkulisse; ~ **plate** Tonplatte; ~ **preparation** *(law suit)* Prozeßvorbereitung; ~ **sound** Tonuntermalung, musikalische Untermalung; ~ **story** Stimmungsbericht; ~ **study** Untersuchung der persönlichen Vergangenheit; ~ **stuff** Hintergrundmaterial.
backing Hilfe, Stütze, Unterstützung, *(bank notes)* Deckung, *(bill of exchange)* Giro, Indossament, *(stock exchange)* Stützungskäufe;
financial ~ finanzielle Unterstützung; **political ~** politische Unterstützung;
~ **a bill** Wechselindossierung; ~ **of currency** Stützung der Währung; ~ **of notes** Notendeckung; ~ **up** Hilfestellung, *(printing)* Bedrucken der Rückseite, Rückseitendruck; ~ **up of a candidate** Unterstützung eines Bewerbers;
to find a ~ for unter Dach und Fach bringen.
backlash toter Gang.
backletter *(US)* Ungültigkeitsvereinbarung.
backlog *(of orders, coll.)* unerledigter Auftragsbestand, unerledigte Aufträge, Angebotsüberhang;
~ **of money** Geldüberhang; ~ **of purchasing power** Kaufkraftüberhang;
to work ~s down Rückstände aufarbeiten;
~ **demand** Nachholbedarf, Bedarfsreserven; ~ **number** alte Zeitungsnummer.
backpedal *(v.)* Rückzieher machen.
backpedal(l)ing brake *(Br.)* Rücktrittsbremse.
backset Rückschlag.
backsight *(architecture)* Rückansicht.
backslap *(v.)* vertraulich auf die Schulter klopfen, sich anbiedern.
backslapper *(US sl.)* plump vertrauliche Person, Anbiederer.
backslide Rückfall;
~ *(v.)* auf die schiefe Bahn geraten.
backslider Rückfälliger.
backsliding into inflation Rückkehr zur Inflation.
backspacer *(typewriter)* Rücktaste.
backstage *(theater)* Hinterbühne;
~ *(adv.)* hinter den Kulissen;
~ **negotiations** hinter den Kulissen geführte Verhandlungen; ~ **plan** hinter den Kulissen ausgeführter Plan; ~ **pressure** hinter den Kulissen ausgeübter Druck.
backstairs Hintertreppe;
~ **influence** geheimer Einfluß; ~ **politics** Hintertreppenpolitik.
backstop *(fig.)* Sicherheitsfaktor.
backtrack *(v.)* Rückzieher machen, sich distanzieren, sich von einem Unternehmen zurückziehen.
backtracking Distanzierung, *(US)* Beibehaltung langjähriger Angestellter bei Entlassungen.
backup Zusatz, *(aerospace)* Ersatzmannschaft, -gerät, *(book)* Rückseitendruck, *(delivery)* Wartezeit, *(vehicle)* Rückwärtsbewegung;
~ **of goods** Warenanhäufung; ~ **with reserve capacity** Bereitstellung von Kapazitätsreserven;
~ **falicities** Rückgriffsmöglichkeit; ~ **missile** nachfolgender Flugkörper; ~ **pilot** *(US)* Reservepilot; ~ **system** Zusatzsystem.
backward zurückgeblieben, rückständig, hinterwäldlerisch;
to be ~ in one's duty seine Pflicht vernachlässigen; **not to be ~ in coming forward** um keine Antwort verlegen sein; **to be ~ in learning** schwer lernen;
~ **areas** in der Entwicklung zurückgebliebene Gebiete, Rückstandsgebiete; ~ **-bending supply curve** regressive Angebotskurve; ~ **country** rückständiges Land; ~ **integration** Geschäftsausweitung durch monopolartige Rohstofflieferungen, vertikales Betriebswachstum, vertikale Konzentration in vorgelagerte Produktionsstufen; ~ **s motion** Rückentwicklung; ~ **movement** Rückwärtsbewegung.
backwardation *(Br.)* Deport, Kursabschlag, *(Br., stock exchange)* Prolongationsgebühr;
~ **business** *(Br.)* Deport-, Kostgeschäft; ~ **rate** *(Br.)* Prolongationsgebühr, Deportsatz.
backwardness Rückständigkeit.
backwash *(fig.)* Nachwirkung.
backwater Stauwasser, *(fig.)* stagnierendes Nebengebiet;
 to live in an intellectual ~ völlig rückständige Ansichten haben.
backwoods settlement abgelegene Siedlung.

backyard *(US)* nach hinten heraus gelegener Garten.
bacon, to bring home the *(sl.)* Erfolg haben; **to save one's ~** sich aus der Patsche ziehen, mit heiler Haut davonkommen.
bacteriological warfare bakteriologische Kriegsführung.
bad Unglück, *(business)* Defizit;
in ~ *(US)* in Ungnade gefallen; **to the ~** ins Minus (Defizit); ~ *(a.)* schlecht, böse, übel, *(debt)* faul, dubios, minderwertig, *(fruit)* verdorben, schädlich, *(health)* angegriffen, *(soil)* unfruchtbar, *(unfavo(u)rable)* ungünstig;
to be in ~ with the boss *(US)* beim Chef schlecht angeschrieben sein; **to go ~** Havarie machen; **to go to the ~** auf die schiefe Bahn geraten; **to go from ~ to worse** immer schlimmer werden; ~ **accident** schwerer Unfall; ~ **bargain** schlechtes Geschäft; ~ **behavio(u)r** schlechte Führung; **in s. one's ~ books** schlecht angeschrieben bei jem.; ~ **business** unangenehme Sache; ~ **check** ungedeckter Scheck; ~ **claim** unbegründeter Anspruch; ~ **coin** falsche (schlechte) Münze, Falschgeld; ~ **cold** starke Erkältung; ~ **debts** *(US)* uneinbringliche Forderungen; ~ **debts account** *(US)* Dubiosenkonto; ~ **debts collected** *(US)* eingegangene, schon abgeschriebene Forderungen; ~ **-debts deductions** *(income tax, US)* Freibeträge für ungewisse Forderungen; ~ **debt losses** *(US)* aus zweifelhaften Forderungen herrührende Verluste; ~ **debts reserve** *(US)* Rückstellung für zweifelhafte Schulden; ~ **debtor** zahlungsunfähiger Schuldner; ~ **delivery** mangelhafte Lieferung; ~ **egg** *(sl.)* übler Kunde; ~ **faith** *(law)* schlechter (böser) Glaube; **in ~ faith** bösgläubig; ~ **faith taker** bösgläubiger Erwerber; ~ **form** schlechte Manieren; ~ **hat** *(Br., sl.)* übler Kunde; **a ~ job** unangenehme Sache; ~ **lands** *(US)* wüstes Land; **to make a ~ landing** schlecht landen; ~ **language** Schimpfworte, Zoten; ~ **lot** *(sl.)* übler Kunde; ~ **man** *(US sl.)* Schurke, Revolverheld, Bandit; **to come to a ~ market** sich schlecht verkaufen lassen; ~ **money** abgewertete Währung; **to call s. o. ~ names** j. beleidigen; ~ **news** schlechte Nachrichten; ~ **reputation** schlechter Ruf; ~ **risk** zweifelhaftes Risiko; **to be a ~ sailor** leicht seekrank werden; ~ **shot** *(fig.)* falsche Vermutung; ~ **taste** Geschmacklosigkeit; ~ **title** mangelhafter Rechtstitel; ~ **voting paper** ungültiger Stimmzettel; **to be in a ~ way** schlimm dran sein, Schwierigkeiten haben, *(goods)* schlecht gehen; ~ **will** schlechter Ruf.
badge [Rang]abzeichen, Dienst-, Amtszeichen;
party ~ Parteiabzeichen;
to flash a ~ Dienstmarke zücken; ~ **number** *(labo(u)rer)* Werknummer.
badgeman Abzeichenträger.
badly off (situated) in schlechten Verhältnissen, schlecht situiert.
baffle Verwirrung;
~ *(v.)* verwirren, vereiteln, durchkreuzen.
baffling wind umspringender Wind.
bag Sack, Beutel, *(Br.)* Geldbeutel, Börse, *(post)* Postsack, -beutel;
hand-~ Handkoffer; **sealed ~** versiegelter Behälter; **tool ~** Werkzeugtasche; **travelling ~** Reisesack;
~ **and baggage** mit Sack und Pack; ~ **of bones** *(lean person)* Bohnenstange; **the whole ~ of tricks** das ganze Repertoire;
~ *(v.)* einsacken, *(sl.)* klauen, organisieren;
to be in the ~ *(sl.)* in der Tasche haben; **to be a mixed ~** *(fam.)* reichlich verworrene Angelegenheit sein; **to give s. o. the ~** jem. den Laufpaß geben; **to have it in the ~** *(sl.)* etw. im Sack haben; **to hold the ~** *(US)* auf seiner Ware sitzenbleiben, *(fig.)* Kopf hinhalten, Sache ausbaden; **to let the cat out of the ~** Katze aus dem Sack lassen; **to park one's ~ at the station** sein Gepäck am Bahnhof lassen;
~ **cargo** Sackgut; ~ **list** *(postal service)* Abgangszettel.
bagatelle Bagatelle, Lappalie, Geringfügigkeit, Kleinigkeit.
baggage *(US)* [Reise]gepäck;
carry-on ~ Handgepäck; **checked** ~ aufgegebenes Gepäck; ~ **en route** unterwegs befindliches Gepäck; **excess** ~ Mehrgepäck, Gepäckzuschlag, *(US)* gebührenpflichtiges Gepäck; **heavy** ~ schweres Gepäck, Großgepäck; **overweight** ~ Gepäck mit Übergewicht; **registered** ~ aufgegebenes Gepäck;
to carry ~ **with one** Gepäck mit sich führen; **to check one's** ~ sein Gepäck aufbewahren lassen (aufgeben); **to check out the** ~ Gepäck abholen; **to collect one's** ~ sein Gepäck einlösen; **to deliver** ~ Gepäck ausfolgen; **to examine the** ~ Gepäck durchsuchen; **to run the** ~ **to the station** Gepäck zum Bahnhof fahren; **to see to the** ~ Gepäck besorgen; **to take charge of the** ~ sich um das Gepäck kümmern; **to transmit** ~ Gepäck befördern;
free ~ **allowance** Freigepäcksgrenze; ~ **car** Gepäckwagen; ~ **carrier** *(car)* Gepäckhalter; ~ **cart** Gepäckkarren; ~ **check** Gepäckschein, *(aerodrome)* Fluggepäckabschnitt; ~ **checkroom** Gepäckaufbewahrung; ~ **claim** Gepäckschein; ~ **clerk**

Gepäckausgeber; ~ **counter** Gepäckaufgabe, -schalter; ~ **delivery** Gepäckzustellung; ~ **dispatch** *(US)* Gepäckabfertigung; ~ **examination** [zollamtliche] Gepäckrevision; ~ **hall** Gepäckhalle; ~ **handler** Gepäckabfertiger; ~ **insurance** Gepäckversicherung; ~ **label** Gepäckanhänger; ~ **label holder** Gepäckanhänger; ~ **hall** Gepäckhalle; ~ **loss** Gepäckverlust; ~ **office** Gepäckannahme, -abfertigungsstelle, -schalter; ~ **office clerk** Abfertigungsbeamter; ~ **pickup** *(US)* Gepäckausgabe; ~ **platform** Gepäckbahnsteig; ~ **porter** Gepäckträger; ~ **rack** *(railway)* Gepäcknetz; ~ **room** Handgepäckaufbewahrung; **walk-in** ~ **room** betretbarer Gepäckraum; **to check one's** ~ **in the** ~ **room** sein Gepäck abgeben; ~ **service** *(airport)* Gepäckauslieferung; **self-claim** ~ **system** Gepäckselbstbedienung; ~ **tag** Gepäckstücknummer; ~**ticket** Gepäckschein; ~ **tracing** Gepäckermittlung; ~ **train** *(mil., Br.)* Troß; ~ **truck** Handgepäckwagen; ~ **van (waggon)** Gepäckwagen.

baggageman *(US)* Gepäckträger.

bagged in Säcken.

bagman *(Br.)* Handlungsreisender.

bail Bürge, *(marine insurance)* Sicherheitsleistung, *(prisoner)* Freilassung (Haftentlassung) gegen Sicherheitsleistung, *(security)* Bürgschaft, Kaution, Sicherheitsleistung;
free on ~ gegen Bürgschaft (Kaution) freigelassen; **released on** ~ gegen Kaution freigelassen;
~ **above** Prozeßbürge; ~ **absolute** Ausfallbürge; **additional** ~ Nebenbürge; **ample** ~ hohe Kaution; **common** ~ Bürgschaft für Erscheinen vor Gericht; **counter** ~ Rückbürgschaft; **good** ~ sichere Bürgschaft; **second** ~ Rück-, Nachbürgschaft; **special** ~ zugelassene Kaution, Prozeßbürge; **straw** ~ wertlose Kaution; **substantial** ~ sichere Bürgschaft;
~ **in error** Sicherheitsleistung des Revisionsklägers;
~ *(v.)* Bürgschaft leisten, sich verbürgen, bürgen, *(criminal law)* Kaution stellen, *(deposit)* [Waren] hinterlegen;
~ **goods to s. o.** jem. Waren vertragsgemäß übergeben; ~ **out** aus dem Flugzeug springen, *(criminal law)* durch Kautionsgestellung auf freien Fuß bringen, *(stock market)* aussteigen, seine Bestände verkaufen; ~ **out dud companies** erfolglose Unternehmen fallen lassen; ~ **out a prisoner** Freilassung (Haftentlassung) eines Gefangenen bewirken; ~ **out of public business** sich aus dem Geschäftsleben zurückziehen;
to admit s. o. to ~ j. gegen Kaution freilassen; **to be let out on** ~ gegen Kaution freigelassen werden; **to be out on** ~ sich gegen Kaution auf freiem Fuß befinden; **to be released on** ~ gegen Hinterlegung einer Kaution freigelassen werden; **to become** ~ **for s. o.** Bürgschaft (Kaution) für j. stellen; **to enlarge** ~ Kaution erhöhen; **to find** ~ Bürgen stellen, sich Bürgschaft verschaffen, Sicherheit leisten; **to forfeit one's** ~ Kaution verfallen lassen; **to furnish** ~ bürgen; **to give** ~ Bürgschaft leisten, Kaution stellen; **to go** ~ **for s. o.** für j. bürgen (Bürgschaft leisten); **to grant** ~ Kaution zulassen; **to hold to** ~ Stellung einer Kaution auferlegen; **to hold for** ~ bis zur Kautionsgestellung in Haft behalten; **to jump** ~ Kaution schießen lassen; **to let s. o. out on** ~ j. gegen Hinterlegung einer Kaution freilassen; **to put in** ~ **for s. o.** für j. bürgen (Bürgschaft leisten); **to raise** ~ Bürgschaft aufbringen; **to refuse [to grant]** ~ Sicherheitsleistung ablehnen; **to release (remand,** *Br.)* **s. o. out on** ~ j. gegen Kautionsgestellung freilassen; **to save one's** ~ vor Gericht erscheinen; **to ship** ~ Kaution verfallen lassen; **to stand** ~ sich verbürgen für, Bürgschaft leisten, als Bürge haften, Kaution leisten; **to surrender to one's** ~ rechtzeitig zum Termin erscheinen; **to take** ~ gegen Bürgschaft freilassen;
♀ **Act** *(Br.)* Kautionsgesetz; ~ **bond** anstelle einer Kaution abgegebene schriftliche Erklärung; ~ **conditions** Bürgschaftsbedingungen; ~ **jumping** *(US)* Verfall der Sicherheitsleistung, Kautionsverfall.

bailable bürgschafts-, kautionsfähig;
~ **offence** Straftat mit Haftverschonung gegen Kaution.

bailee Verwahrer, Gewahrsamsinhaber, Depositar, Pfandgläubiger, *(trustee)* Treuhänder, -nehmer;
gratuitous ~ unentgeltlicher Verwahrer;
~ **at law** Hinterlegungsstelle; ~ **for reward** entgeltlicher Verwahrer;
~ **clause** *(insurance)* Gewahrsamsklausel.

bailie *(Scot.)* Stadtverordneter, Magistratsmitglied, Ratsherr.

bailiewick *(US)* Amtsbezirk, *(fig.)* Spezialfach, -gebiet.

bailiff *(landholder's steward, Br.)* Gutsverwalter, Justizinspektor, Vogt, *(law, Br.)* Zustellungsbeamter, Gerichtsvollzieher, Büttel, *(US)* Justizwachtmeister;
farm ~ Domänen-, Gutsverwalter; **high** ~ *(Br.)* Obergerichtsvollzieher; **special** ~ *(Br.)* von der Prozeßpartei beauftragter Zustellungsbeamter.

bailment Bürgschafts-, Kautionsleistung, Kaution[sgestellung], *(delivery in trust)* Hinterlegung, Hinterlegungs-, Verwahrungs-, Treuhandvertrag, *(freight)* Frachtgut, *(pledging)* Verpfändung, *(release from prison)* Freilassung gegen Bürgschaft;
actual ~ tatsächliche Besitzverschaffung; **constructive** ~ mittelbare Besitzverschaffung; **gratuitous** ~ unentgeltliche Verwahrung, unentgeltlicher Hinterlegungsvertrag; **involuntary** ~ zufällig erlangter Fremdbesitz; **lucrative** ~ entgeltliche Verwahrung; **mutual-benefit** ~ zweiseitiger Hinterlegungsvertrag;
~ **for hire** entgeltlicher Verwahrungs-, Hinterlegungsvertrag; ~ **for repair** Werkvertrag; ~ **for the sole benefit of one party** einseitiges Verwahrungs-, Hinterlegungsgeschäft;
~ **agreement (contract)** Verwahrungs-, Hinterlegungsvertrag; ~ **lease** Verkauf unter Eigentumsvorbehalt; ~ **sale** Kommissionsverkauf mit Selbsteintritt.

bailor Hinterleger, Verpfänder.

bailsman Bürge;
to act (go) as ~ als Bürge auftreten; **to put in a** ~ Bürgschaft stellen.

bait *(advertising)* Lockartikel, Köder, *(goods)* billiges Warenangebot, *(on journey)* Imbiß, Erfrischungspause;
~ *(v.)* ködern, anlocken, *(Br.)* Rast machen, einkehren, Imbiß einnehmen;
~ **advertising** Werbung mit Lockartikeln.

baiting Einkehren.

baksheesh Bestechungsgeld.

balance Bilanz, *(counterpoise)* Gegengewicht, *(difference between Cr. and De.)* Rechnungs-, Abschluß-, [Konten]saldo, Saldoauszug, Rechnungsabschluß, Kontostand, Bestand, Überschuß, Rest-, Ausgleichsbetrag, *(equilibrium)* Gleichgewicht, Ausgewogenheit, *(remainder)* Differenz, Unterschied;
on ~ nach reiflicher Überlegung, wenn man alles berücksichtigt, per Saldo;
account ~ Kontoausgleich; **active** ~ Aktivsaldo; **actual** ~ effektiver Saldo, Effektivbestand; **adjusted** ~ berichtigter Saldo; **adjusted trial** ~ berichtigte Rohbilanz; **adverse** ~ passive Bilanz, Unterbilanz; **annual** ~ *(Br.)* jährliche Abrechnung, Jahresabschluß, -bilanz; **available** ~ verfügbares Guthaben; **bank** ~ Kontostand, Bankguthaben; **banker's** ~ Bankeinlagen, -depositen; **blocked** ~ Sperrguthaben; ~ **carried down** Saldovortrag; ~ **brought (carried) forward** vorgetragener Saldo, Saldovortrag, -übertrag, Vortrag auf neue Rechnung; **cash** ~ Kassenbestand; **credit** ~ Haben-, Kreditsaldo, Guthaben; **daily** ~ täglicher Saldo, Tagessaldo; **debit** ~ Soll-, Debetsaldo, Verlustabschluß; **disposable** ~ verfügbarer Saldo; **dormant** ~ ungenutzter Saldo; ~ **due** geschuldeter (noch ausstehender) Restbetrag, Debetsaldo; ~ **due to us** Guthabensaldo; **favo(u)rable** ~ aktive Bilanz, Aktivbilanz; **final** ~ Schlußbilanz; **foreign-exchange** ~ Devisenbilanz; **foreign-held** ~s Zahlungsmittel in fremder Hand; ~ **forward** Saldovortrag; **free** ~s frei verfügbare Guthaben; **general** ~ von der Haftung nicht erfaßte Restvermögen; **gross** ~ Bruttoüberschuß; **insufficient** ~ unzureichendes Guthaben; **interbank** ~s gegenseitige Bankforderungen; **invisible** ~ Leistungsbilanz; **letter** ~ *(Br.)* Briefwaage; **loss** ~ Verlustsaldo; **minimum** ~ Mindestguthaben; **monthly** ~ *(Br.)* Monatsbilanz; **net** ~ Saldobilanz, Nettosaldo; **nominal** ~ Sollbestand; ~ **owing** Restbetrag; ~ **payable** Debetsaldo; **profit** ~ Gewinnsaldo; ~ **receivable** Guthabensaldo; **remaining** ~ Restsaldo; **rough** ~ Rohbilanz, Bruttobilanz; ~ **struck** aufgestellter Saldo; **sufficient** ~ ausreichendes Guthaben; **total** ~ Gesamtmenge; **trade** ~ Handelsbilanz; **trial** ~ Salden-, Vor-, Probebilanz; **post-closing trial** ~ Rohbilanz ohne Aufwand und Ertrag; **unappropriated** ~ Gewinnvortrag; **unclaimed** ~ nicht abgehobenes Kontoguthaben; **uncovered** ~ ungedeckter Saldo; **unearned** ~ Debetsaldo; **unexpended** ~ noch zur Verfügung stehender Betrag; **unfavo(u)rable** ~ Passivbilanz; **unpaid** ~ überschießender Betrag; **visible** ~ außenwirtschaftliche Bilanz; **your credit** ~ Saldo zu Ihren Gunsten; **your debit** ~ Saldo zu Ihren Lasten;
~ **of an account** Restbetrag einer Rechnung; ~ **of accounts agreed upon** festgestellter Rechnungssaldo; ~ **of former accounts** Saldoübertrag; ~ **to net accounts** Saldoübertrag; ~ **passed to new account** Saldoübertrag; ~ **at bank on current account** Kontokorrentguthaben; ~ **at bank on deposit account** Festgeldguthaben; ~ **of the bank** Bankabschluß, -ausweis; ~ **with banks** *(bank balance)* Bankguthaben; ~ **with the bank of England** [etwa] Landeszentralbankguthaben; ~s **with banks for agreed periods** terminlich abgesprochene Bankguthaben; ~s **with home and foreign bankers** Nostroguthaben bei in- und ausländischen Bankfirmen; ~ **of the budget** ausgeglichener Haushalt; ~ **from previous business year** Vortrag aus dem

vorhergehenden Geschäftsjahr; ~ **on capital account** Kapital-
bilanz; ~ **in cash** Kassensaldo, -bestand, Barbestand; ~ **of
commitments** Lieferpflichtsaldo; ~ **of convenience** Verhältnis-
mäßigkeit einer Gerichtsentscheidung; ~ **standing to (in) your
credit** Ihr gegenwärtiges Guthaben; ~ **on current account**
[Dienst]leistungsbilanz; ~ **standing to your debit** Ihr gegenwärtiger Debetsaldo; ~ **in favo(u)r** Saldoguthaben; ~ **with financial
institutions** Guthaben bei Finanzinstituten; ~ **of foreign
exchange payments** Devisenbilanz; ~ **on giro account** *(Br.)*
Postscheckguthaben; ~ **on hand** Kassensaldo, -bestand; ~
actually in hand Istbestand; ~ **of indebtedness** Verschuldungs-
bilanz; ~ **of interest** Zinssaldo; ~ **of invoice** Rechnungssaldo; ~
at liquidation Liquidationssaldo, -bilanz; ~ **of merchandise
imports** Wareneinfuhrbilanz; ~ **outstanding on a mortgage** restliche Hypothekenvaluta; ~ **to be paid within one week** innerhalb einer Woche zu zahlender Restbetrag; ~ **of payments**
Zahlungs-, Außenhandelsbilanz; **favo(u)rable ~ of payments in
tourism** positive Tourismusbilanz; ~ **of power** Gleichgewicht
der Kräfte, politisches Gleichgewicht; ~ **of probabilities** Abwägen der Wahrscheinlichkeiten; ~ **on postal cheque accounts**
(Br.) Postscheckguthaben; ~ **of purchase price** Restkaufgeld; ~
of revenue Überschuß der Einnahmen über die Betriebsausgaben, Rohgewinn; ~ **of risk** *(insurance)* noch nicht plaziertes
Risiko; **adverse ~ of trade** defizitäre Handelsbilanz; **favo(u)ra-
ble ~ of trade** aktive Handelsbilanz; **unfavo(u)rable ~ of trade**
passive Handelsbilanz; ~ **of trade in goods and services** Waren-
und Dienstleistungsbilanz, Leistungsbilanz;
~ *(v.) (be in equipoise)* ausgeglichen sein, *(set off)* aufrechnen,
ausgleichen, *(settle and adjust)* bilanzieren, Bilanz machen,
ausgleichen, saldieren, abschließen;
~ **an account** *(by paying deficit)* Rechnung berichtigen (begleichen), *(by equalizing De. and Cr.)* Saldo ausgleichen, Konto
ausgleichen (saldieren, abschließen); ~ **our accounts** zur
Berichtigung unserer Rechnung; ~ **against** in die Waagschale
werfen; ~ **the books** Bücher abschließen, Bilanz ziehen; ~ **the
budget** Etat ausgleichen; ~ **in favo(u)r of s. o.** jem. einen Saldo
gutschreiben; ~ **one item against the other** einen Posten gegen
einen anderen aufrechnen; ~ **the ledger** Hauptbuch abschließen; ~ **one thing against the other** eine Sache gegen die andere
abwägen;
to be out of ~ nicht übereinstimmen; **to bring down a ~** Bilanz
abschließen; **to carry a ~ forward [to new account]** Saldo eines
Kontos auf ein anderes Konto übertragen; **to close the ~ of an
account into another account** Saldo eines Kontos auf ein anderes Konto übertragen; **to extend a ~** Saldo übertragen; **to hang
in the ~** ungewiß (in der Schwebe) sein; **to have a ~ in one's
favo(u)r** Summe (Betrag) guthaben; **to hold the ~** Züngeln an
der Waage bilden; **to keep one's ~** seine Fassung bewahren; **to
leave a ~ to one's debit** Debetsaldo stehenlassen; **to leave a ~ of
£ 100 to your debit** Saldo von 100 Pfund zu Ihren Lasten
ausweisen; **to lose one's ~** *(fig.)* Fassung verlieren; **to maintain
~s interest-free with the central bank** bei der Notenbank zinslose Guthaben unterhalten; **to make up a ~** Bilanz aufstellen,
bilanzieren; **to pay over the ~** Saldo auszahlen; **to pay the ~ in
instal(l)ments** Restschuld in Raten abzahlen; **to present a ~ of £
100 to your credit** Saldo von 100 Pfund zu Ihren Gunsten
ausweisen; **to remit the ~** Saldo überweisen; **to settle a ~**
Rechnungssaldo begleichen (bezahlen); **to show a ~** Guthaben
(Saldo) aufweisen; **to show in the ~** in der Bilanz aufführen; **to
strike a ~** Saldo ziehen (feststellen), Bilanz aufstellen (ziehen),
(fig.) Ausgleich finden; **to turn out a ~** Saldo ausweisen;
~ **account** Restbetrag, Bilanz-, Ausgleichskonto; ~ **bill** Saldo-
wechsel; ~ **book** Saldier-, Bilanzbuch; **daily ~ book** Tagesabschlußbuch; ~ **clerk** Bilanzbuchhalter; ~ **deficit** Verlustabschluß; ~ **figure** Ausgleichsziffer; ~ **ledger** Saldenliste; ~ **maker**
Bilanzaufsteller; ~ **order** *(winding up)* vollstreckbarer Nach-
zahlungsbeschluß; ~ **remittance** Ausgleichszahlung.
balance of payments Zahlungsbilanz;
~ **on current account** Waren- und Dienstleistungsbilanz; ~ **in
[dis]equilibrium** [un]ausgeglichene Zahlungsbilanz; **favo(u)ra-
ble ~ intourism** positive Fremdenverkehrsbilanz;
~ **adjustment** Zahlungsbilanzausgleich; ~ **aid** Zahlungsbilanz-
hilfe; ~ **benefits** Zahlungsbilanzvorteile; ~ **burden** Zahlungs-
bilanzverpflichtung; ~ **crisis** Zahlungsbilanzkrise; ~ **current
account** Zahlungsbilanzsaldo; ~ **deficit** Zahlungsbilanzdefizit,
Passivsaldo der Handelsbilanz; ~ **disequilibrium** Zahlungsbilanzungleichgewicht; ~ **financing** Zahlungsbilanzfinanzierung;
~ **gap** Zahlungsbilanzlücke; ~ **loan** Zahlungsbilanzdarlehen; ~
picture Zahlungsbilanzbild; **relaxed ~ situation** entspannte
Zahlungsbilanzsituation; ~ **surplus** Zahlungsbilanzüberschuß; ~ **theory** Zahlungsbilanztheorie.

balance sheet Bilanz[bogen], Rechnungsabschluß, Kassenbericht, aufgestellte Bilanz, Bilanzaufstellung;
shown by the ~ bilanzmäßig;
actual ~ Istbilanz; **annual ~** Jahresbilanz; **audited ~** geprüfte
Bilanz; **bank ~** Bankbilanz; **bankrupt's ~** Status eines Konkursschuldners; **company ~** Firmenbilanz; **comparative ~** Vergleichsbilanz; **condensed ~** abgekürzte Bilanz; **consolidated ~**
konsolidierter Jahresabschluß, zusammengezogene Bilanz,
Gesamtbilanz, Konzernbilanz; **corporate ~** Bilanz einer AG,
Gesellschaftsbilanz; **departmental ~** Warenhausbilanz; **false
(faked, fraudulent) ~** gefälschte (frisierte) Bilanz; **fund ~** Bilanz
einer Vermögensverwaltung; **initial (opening) ~** Eröffnungsbilanz; **monthly ~** monatlicher Bilanzbogen; **partnership ~** Firmenbilanz, Bilanz einer OHG; **postclosing ~** Jahresschluß-
bilanz; **pro-forma ~** fiktive Bilanz; **sample ~** Bilanzmuster,
-schema; **sole trader's ~** Bilanz eines Einzelkaufmanns; **tentative ~** Bilanzentwurf; **up-to-date ~** neueste Bilanz; **veiled
~** verschleierte Bilanz; **vertical-form ~** vertikal gegliederte
Bilanz; **window-dressed ~** frisierte Bilanz;
~ **that shows a deficit** Verlustbilanz;
to analyse a ~ Bilanz analysieren (zergliedern); **to approve a ~**
Bilanz genehmigen; **to assess a ~** Bilanzbewertung vornehmen;
to audit a ~ Bilanz überprüfen; **to break down a ~** Bilanz
analysieren (zergliedern); **to construct the ~on a current market
liquidation basis** Bilanzpositionen zu jederzeit realisierbaren
Verkaufswerten ansetzen; **to cook (doctor) a ~** Bilanz frisieren,
verschleiern; **to draw up a ~** Bilanz aufstellen; **to fake a ~** Bilanz
frisieren (verschleiern); **to include in the ~** in die Bilanz aufnehmen; **to interpret a ~** Bilanz analysieren; **to make out the ~**
Rechnungsabschluß machen, Bilanz aufstellen; **to make the ~s
public** Bilanzergebnis veröffentlichen; **to make up the ~** Bilanz
aufstellen; **to place on the ~ among the long-term liabilities** in
der Bilanz unter langfristigen Schulden aufführen; **to present
the ~** Jahresabschluß vorlegen; **to read the ~** Bilanz lesen; **to
show in the ~** bilanzieren, bilanzmäßig ausweisen; **to strike a
~** bilanzieren, Bilanz aufstellen; **to submit a ~** Bilanz vorlegen;
~ **account** Bestandskonto; ~ **assets** aus der Bilanz ersichtliche
Anlagen; ~ **audit** Bilanzprüfung; ~ **changes** Bilanzveränderun-
gen; ~ **contra item** bilanzmäßiger Gegenposten; ~ **data** Bilanzangaben; ~ **date** Bilanz[ierungsstich]tag; ~ **equation** Bilanz-
gleichung; ~ **figures** Bilanzziffern; ~ **growth** Bilanzwachstum;
~ **highlights** wesentliche Bilanzaussagen; **[consolidated] ~ item**
[konsoldierter] Bilanzposten, -position; ~ **layout** Bilanzgestal-
tung; ~ **projection** Bilanzprojektion; **for ~ purposes** für Bilan-
zierungszwecke; ~ **record** Bilanzbericht; **comparative ~ record
form** Vergleichsbilanzberichtsformular; ~ **reserves** bilanzmäßig ausgewiesene Rücklagen; ~ **section** Bilanzabschnitt; ~
structure Bilanzstruktur, Gliederung der Bilanz; ~ **term** Bi-
lanzausdruck; ~ **terminology** Bilanzfachsprache; ~ **ticket**
Skontozettel; ~ **total** Bilanzsumme, -volumen; ~ **value** Bilanzwert, -volumen.
balanced ausgewogen, ausgeglichen;
~ **in account** Gegenrechnung saldiert;
~ **budget** ausgeglichener (durch regelmäßige Einnahmen
gedeckter) Etat; ~ **fund** *(US)* aus Aktien und Obligationen
bestehender Investmentfonds; ~ **growth** gleichgewichtiges
Wachstum; ~ **sample** *(statistics)* gewichtete Stichprobe; ~
trade ausgeglichener Handelsverkehr.
balancing Saldieren, Saldierung, Bilanzziehung, Bilanzziehen,
Ausgleichen, Abstimmung;
~ **of accounts** Bücher-, Rechnungsabschluß; ~ **of the books**
Bücherabschluß, Jahresabschlußarbeiten; ~ **of the budget**
Budget-, Etatausgleich;
to be ~ the books for the year mit Jahresabschlußarbeiten
beschäftigt sein;
~ **adjustment** Bilanzausgleich; ~ **allowance** Ausgleichsbetrag
für Abschreibungsverluste; ~ **amount** Ausgleichsbetrag; ~
charge *(liquidation of assets)* aktivierte Abschreibungsbeträge,
Bilanzierungskosten; **built-in ~ effort** automatischer Ausgleich; ~ **entry** Ausgleichs-, Gegenbuchung; ~ **item** Ausgleichsposten.
balcony Balkon, *(mar.)* Hintergalerie, *(US, theater)* Balkon,
erster Rang.
baldheaded row *(US sl.)* vorderste Sperrsitzreihe.
bale Ballen[ware];
in ~s ballenweise;
running ~s nach dem tatsächlichen Gewicht verkaufte Ballen;
~ *(v.)* in Ballen verpacken, emballieren;
to make up in ~s in Ballen verpacken; **to sell in ~** Waren in
Ballen verkaufen;
~ **goods** Ballengut, -ware; ~ **mark** Ballenzeichen.

balecloth Verpackungsleinwand.
baled papers gebündelte Zeitungen.
baler Verpacker, *(machine)* Ballen-, Packpresse.
balk *(Br.)* Fehler, Schnitzer, *(obstacle)* Hindernis;
~ *(v.)* aufhalten, verhindern;
~ **at an expense** *(fam.)* Kosten scheuen; ~ **government demands** staatliche Forderungen ablehnen; ~ **s. one's plans** jds. Pläne durchkreuzen (vereiteln).
balked landing Fehllandung.
ball *(dance)* Tanzvergnügen, Ball;
on the ~ *(fig.)* auf dem laufenden;
fancy-dress ~ Kostümball; **late-night** ~ Mitternachtsball; **masked** ~ Maskenball;
~ **of soil** Erdballen;
to have a ~ Riesenspaß haben; **to have s. th. on the** ~ *(US sl.)* etw. auf dem Kasten haben; **to have the** ~ **on one's feet** *(Br.)* Herr der Lage sein, Spiel in der Hand haben; **to keep one's eye on the** ~ *(US sl.)* lausig aufpassen; **to keep the** ~ **rolling** Gespräch im Gang halten; **to open the** ~ *(fig.)* Diskussion eröffnen; **to play** ~ *(US coll.)* sich kooperativ verhalten, kooperieren; **to start the** ~ **rolling** Gespräch in Gang setzen; **to take the** ~ Initiative ergreifen;
~ **bearings** Kugellager; ~ **dress** Ballkleid; **a whole new** ~ **game** *(US)* eine ganz neue Szene; **to be a whole new** ~ **game** etw. völlig Neues sein; ~**-point pen** Kugelschreiber; ~ **room** Tanzsaal.
ballast Ballast[ladung], *(fig.)* sittlicher Halt;
in ~ ohne Ladung; **going in** ~ ballastgeladen;
shifting ~ fliegender Ballast;
~ *(v.)* mit Ballast beladen;
to discharge ~ Ballast abwerfen; **to take in** ~ Ballast einnehmen;
~ **engine** Baggermaschine; ~**-laden** ballastgeladen; ~ **lighter** Ballastschiff; ~ **passage** Ballastreise; ~ **tank** Ballasttank.
ballastage Ballastgebühren.
ballasting Ballasteinnahme.
balloon [Fessel]ballon, *(advertising film)* Test-, Sprechblase;
captive ~ Fesselballon; **observation** ~ Beobachtungsballon; **sounding** ~ Sondierungs-, Registrierballon;
~ *(v.)* im Ballon aufsteigen, *(airplane)* [bei der Landung] springen, *(stock exchange, US)* Börsenpapiere künstlich in die Höhe treiben;
~ **advertising** Fesselballonwerbung; ~ **apron** Fesselballonschutz; ~ **ascent** Ballonaufstieg; ~ **barrage** Ballonsperre; ~ **tyre** Ballonreifen.
ballooning Ballonluftfahrt, *(stock exchange, US)* Hervorrufung einer künstlichen Hausse.
balloonist Ballonflieger, -fahrer.
ballot geheime Abstimmung, [Zettel]wahl, *(little ball)* Wahlkugel, *(ticket)* Wahlzettel, Stimmzettel, *(votes)* abgegebene Wahlstimmen;
by ~ durch Abstimmung; **in (on) the first** ~ im ersten Wahlgang;
additional ~ engere Wahl, Stichwahl; **blanket** ~ Allparteienliste; **final** ~ engere Wahl; **invalid** ~ ungültige Stimme; **joint** ~ gemeinsame Abstimmung; **mail** ~ Briefwahl; **mutilated** ~ ungültiger Stimmzettel; **official** ~ amtlicher Wahlschein; **postal** ~ Briefwahl; **printed** ~ Wahlvordruck; **proportional** ~ Verhältniswahl; **second** ~ Stichwahl, engere Wahl, zweiter Wahlgang; **secret** ~ geheime Abstimmung; **split** ~ *(opinion research)* gegabelte Befragung; **test** ~ Probeabstimmung;
~ **on the recommendations** *(trade union)* Abstimmung über die Tarifempfehlungen;
~ *(v.)* geheim abstimmen;
~ **against s. o.** gegen j. stimmen; ~ **for a candidate** *(US)* für einen Kandidaten stimmen; ~ **the workforce on a productivity deal** an die Belegschaft ein an die Produktivität gekoppeltes Tarifangebot zur Abstimmung vorlegen;
to cast the ~ Stimmzettel abgeben; **to halt the** ~ Abstimmung verhindern; **to hold a second** ~ zum zweiten Wahlgang schreiten; **to mail** ~**s** *(US)* Wahlvorschläge versenden; **to open the** ~ Abstimmung eröffnen; **to put the company's plan to a** ~ **of the workforce** Vorschlag der Betriebsführung der Belegschaft zur Abstimmung vorlegen; **to remain on the** ~ Wahlkandidat bleiben; **to request a** ~ Abstimmung beantragen; **to take a** ~ geheim abstimmen; **to vote by** ~ in geheimer Wahl (durch Stimmzettel) abstimmen;
~ **box** [Wahl]urne; ~**-box stuffing** *(US)* Wahlschwindel; ~ **manipulations** Wahlmanipulierungen; ~ **order** Abstimmungsanweisung; ~ **paper** Wahlschein, -zettel, Stimmzettel; **to spoil one's** ~ **paper** seinen Wahlschein ungültig machen; ~ **vote** *(bargaining)* Urabstimmung.

balloting geheime Abstimmung, Wahlvorgang, Abstimmung durch Abgabe von Stimmzetteln;
~ **rewards** Wahlgewinne.
ballroom [Ball]saal.
ballyhoo laute Reklame, Mordspropaganda, marktschreierische (anreißerische) Werbung, Marktschreierei, Sensations-, Werberummel;
~ *(v.)* aufdringliche Reklame betreiben, Tamtam machen.
balneary Badeort.
Baltic and International Maritime Conference Schiffahrtskonferenz der Trampschiffahrt.
ban Verbot, *(banishment)* Ächtung, Acht, Landesverweisung, Verbannung, *(notice)* Bekanntmachung, öffentliche Aufforderung;
under a ~ verboten, geächtet;
driving ~ *(Br.)* Fahrverbot; **export** ~ Ausfuhrverbot; **hot-cargo** ~ Liefersperre für bestreikten Betrieb; **import** ~ Einfuhrverbot; **travel** ~ Reisesperre;
~ **of gathering** Versammlungsverbot; ~ **of imigration** Einwanderungssperre; ~ **on political meetings** Verbot politischer Versammlungen; ~ **of strikes** Streikverbot;
~ *(v.)* **a play** Theaterstück verbieten;
to impose a ~ Verbot erlassen; **to lift a** ~ Beschränkung (Verbot) aufheben; **to overturn a** ~ Verbot aufheben.
banc Richterbank, *(sitting)* Gerichtssitzung.
bancogiro bankinterne Kontoumbuchung.
band Band, Schnur, *(advertising)* Streifenanzeige, *(bookbinding)* Heftschnur, Bund, *(exchange system)* Bandbreite, *(group of persons)* bewaffnete Gruppe, Schar, Bande, *(medical)* Verband, Binde, Bandage, *(misic)* Kapelle, Unterhaltungsorchester, Band, *(radio)* Frequenzband;
endless ~ Endlosband, Band ohne Ende; **error** ~ *(statistics)* Fehlerbereich; **predatory** ~ Räuberbande; **rubber** ~ Gummiband;
~ **of fugitives** Flüchtlingsgruppe; ~ **of pickets** Streikgruppe; ~ **of robbers** Räuberbande; ~ **of youths** Bande Jugendlicher;
~ *(v.)* **together** sich zu einer Bande vereinigen, sich zusammenrotten;
to introduce a reduced ~ **of income tax at 20% for the first £ 225 of taxable income** verkürzten Anfangssteuersatz von 20% für Einkünfte bis zu 225 Pfund einführen;
~ **advertising** Werbung mittels Streifenanzeigen; ~ **conveyor** Transport-, Fließband; **wave** ~ **filter** *(radio)* Bandfilter; ~**[pass] width** *(radio)* Bandbreite; ~ **spread** *(radio)* Bandspreizung; ~ **switch** *(radio)* Wellenschalter.
bandage Bandage;
~ **case** Verbandskasten.
bandbox Hutschachtel.
bandit Räuber, Bandit;
one-armed ~ *(US)* Spiel-, Glücksautomat.
banditry Räuber-, Banditenwesen.
bandstand Orchesterpavillon.
bandstring Heftschnur.
bandwaggon Paradewagen, *(politics)* erfolgreiche politische Bewegung;
to climb (jump) onto the ~ *(US)* sich für j. (etw.) einsetzen (einer Sache anschließen), zur erfolgreichen Partei umschwenken, augenblicklichen Trend mitmachen, Mitläufer sein; **to get on the** ~ ins Geschäft einsteigen;
~ **effect** Mehrheitseinfluß, *(demand)* steigende Nachfragewirkung, externer Konsumeffekt, Mitläufereffekt, nachhaltige Wirkungen zeigen; ~ **personalities** Mitläufertypen.
bandwaggoner Mitläufer.
bandwork Gruppen-, Gemeinschaftsarbeit.
bandy *(v.)* kursieren lassen, herumposaunen;
~ **a story about** Geschichte verbreiten.
bang Krach, Bums, *(car)* lärmendes Auffahren;
sonic ~ Überschallknall;
~ *(v.)* **s. o. about** j. unsanft behandeln; ~ **the market** offene Baisseverkäufe durchführen; ~ **the prices** Preise drücken; ~ **one's fist on the table** mit der Faust auf den Tisch schlagen; **to go over with a** ~ *(US coll.)* Mordserfolg sein;
~**-free** überschallknallfrei; ~**-on** *(sl.)* tipp-topp, prima.
banging the market Durchführung offener Baisseverkäufe.
banian hospital Tierpflegeanstalt.
banish *(v.)* des Landes verweisen, ausweisen, verbannen, vertreiben.
banished person Ausgewiesener.
banishment Landesverweisung, Verbannung, *(criminal)* Aufenthaltsverbot;
to go into ~ in Exil gehen.

bank Bank[haus], Bankgeschäft, *(bench)* Bank, Sitz, *(full court)* Kammersitzung, *(dam)* Erdwall, Damm, *(mining)* Tagesfläche, *(reserve)* Reserve, Vorrat, *(on street)* Böschung, *(typewriter)* Tastatur;
at the ~ auf der Bank; **in** ~ *(law court)* in voller Besetzung; **payable at a** ~ bei einer Bank zahlbar; **the** ~ *(Br.)* Bank von England;
acceptance ~ Akzeptbank; **associated** ~ *(US)* dem Verrechnungsverkehr angeschlossene Bank; **authorized** ~ *(Br.)* Devisenbank; **big** ~ Großbank; **blood** ~ Blutbank; **branch** ~ Filialbank, Filiale; **businessmen's** ~ Geschäftsbank; **cashpaying** ~ barauszahlende Bank; **central** ~ Zentralbank; **Central Reserve** ~s *(US)* Nationalbanken in New York und Chicago; **chartered** ~ konzessionierte Bank; **check (cheque,** *Br.***)** Girobank; **clearing** ~ dem Abrechnungsverkehr angeschlossene Bank, Giro-, Verrechnungsbank; **closed** ~ geschlossene Bank; **collecting** ~ Inkassobank; **commercial** ~ Geschäftsbank; **cooperative** ~ Genossenschaftsbank; **country** ~ Regionalbank; **credit** ~ Darlehenskasse; **deposit** ~ Depositenbank; **depositary** ~ *(US)* als Hinterlegungsstelle fungierende Bank; **drawee** ~ bezogene Bank; **Export-Import** ~ **of Washington** Export-Import-Bank; **farmer's** ~ Landwirtschaftsbank; **Federal Land** ~ *(US)* staatliche Landwirtschaftsbank; **Federal Reserve** ~ *(US)* [etwa] Landeszentralbank; **foreign** ~ Auslandsbank; **full-service** ~ Bank mit Beratungsdienst auf allen Gebieten; **head** ~ Hauptbank; **housing** ~ Bank für Wohnungsbaufinanzierungen; **incorporated** ~ *(US)* Aktienbank; **industrial** ~ Industriekreditbank; **insolvent** ~ zahlungsunfähige Bank; **intermediary** ~ eingeschaltete (durchleitende) Bank; **investment** ~Effekten-, Emissionsbank; **issuing** ~ Emissionsbank; **joint-stock** ~ *(Br.)* Aktienbank; **joint-stock land** ~ *(US)* landwirtschaftliche Aktienbank; **labor** ~ *(US)* Gemeinwirtschaftsbank; **land** ~ landwirtschaftliche Bodenkreditbank; **lead[ing]** ~ führende Bank; **loan** ~ Darlehenskasse; **local** ~ örtliches Bankinstitut; **member** ~ *(US)* amLandeszentralbanksystem beteiligte Bank; **merged** ~ fusionierte Bank; **mortgage** ~ Hypothekenbank; **mutual savings** ~ *(US)* genossenschaftsähnliche Sparkasse, Genossenschaftsbank; **National** ~ *(US)* Nationalbank; **nonmember (outside,** *US***)** ~ Nichtmitgliedsbank des Federal Reserve Systems; **notifying** ~ avisierende Bank; **out-of-town** ~ auswärtige Bank; **overseas** ~ Bank für Überseehandel; **paying** ~ beauftragte Bank; **payor** ~ *(US)* beauftragte Bank; **penny** ~ Kleinsparkasse; **post-office savings** ~ *(Br.)* Postsparkasse; **private** ~ Privatbankhaus, -geschäft; **provincial** ~ Regionalbank; **public loan** ~ Anleihebank; **regional** ~ Regionalbank; **reporting** ~ korrespondierende Bank; **rival** ~ Konkurrenzbank; **rural** ~ Landwirtschaftsbank; **savings** ~ Sparkasse; **semi-private** ~ halbstaatliche Bank; **State** ~ *(US)* Landesbank; **state-chartered** ~ staatlich konzessionierte Bank; **top-drawer exclusive** ~ Bank der oberen Zehntausend; **works savings** ~ Betriebssparkasse; **wrecked** ~ ruinierte Bank;
~ **of circulation** Noten-, Emissionsbank; ~ **in failing condition** zahlungsunfähige Bank; ~ **for cooperatives** *(US)* Genossenschaftsbank; ~ **of deposit** Depositenbank; ~ **of discount** Diskontbank; ~ **of England** *(Br.)* Bank von England; ~ **of ideas** Ideenvorrat; ~ **of issue** Notenbank, -institut, Emissionsbank; **International** ~ **for Reconstruction and Development** Weltbank; ~ **for International Settlements** Bank für Internationalen Zahlungsausgleich; ~ **incorporated under public law** öffentlich-rechtliche Bank; ~ **of issue** Notenbank;
~ *(v.)* Banktätigkeit ausüben, Bankgeschäfte machen, Bank unterhalten, Bankier sein, Bankgeschäft betreiben, *(~ with s. o.)* mit einer Bank arbeiten, Bankkonto haben, *(deposit in a bank)* in eine Bank einzahlen, bei einer Bank hinterlegen, *(realize)* flüssigmachen, realisieren;
~ **on s. o.** seine Hoffnungen auf j. setzen; ~ **an amount** Geldbetrag bei einer Bank einzahlen; ~ **an estate** Grundstück realisieren; ~ **upon s. one's help** mit jds. Hilfe rechnen; ~ **a plane** Flugzeug in Schräglage bringen; ~ **half one's salary** Gehaltshälfte zur Bank tragen; ~ **outside the state** Bankverbindungen außerhalb des Landes unterhalten; ~ **the takings** Einnahmen zur Bank bringen;
to appoint a ~ **as bankers to the company** Bank zur Hausbank einer Firma bestimmen; **to approach a** ~ **for an overdraft** Bank auf Überziehungsmöglichkeiten ansprechen; **to ask a** ~ **for a line of credit** bei seiner Bank eine Kreditlinie beantragen; **to be deeply in hock to the** ~**s** stark bei den Banken verschuldet; **to be employed in a** ~ Bankangestellter sein; **to be overdrawn at the** ~ bei der Bank im Debet sein; **to break the** ~ [Spiel]bank sprengen; **to break one's piggy** ~ sein Sparschwein schlachten; **to**

charter a ~ Bankkonzession gewähren; **to commission one's** ~ **to pay one's taxes** seine Bank mit der Bezahlung anfallender Steuern beauftragen; **to deposit at a** ~ bei einer Bank hinterlegen; **to have (keep) an account with a** ~ Konto bei einer Bank (Bankkonto) unterhalten; **to have credit with a** ~ über einen Bankkredit verfügen; **to hold the** ~ [Spiel]bank halten; **to increase the borrowings at a** ~ Bank in erhöhtem Maße in Anspruch nehmen; **to instruct one's** ~ seine Bank anweisen; **to interpolate a** ~ Bank einschalten; **to keep the** ~ Bank halten; **keep money at a** ~ Geld bei einer Bank stehen haben; **to lie at the** ~ auf der Bank liegen; **to pay money into a** ~ Geldbetrag bei einer Bank einzahlen; **to remitthrough a** ~ vom Bankkonto überweisen; **to run on a** ~ Ansturm auf die Bankschalter machen; **to withdraw from a** ~ von der Bank (seinem Bankkonto) abheben;
~ **acceptance** Bankakzept, -wechsel; **fine** ~ **acceptance** *(Br.)* erstklassiges Bankakzept;~ **accommodation** Kundendarlehen einer Bank gegen Hingabe von Wechseln.
bank account Bankkonto, -guthaben;
special ~ Sonderkonto;
~ **fed by the husband** vom Ehemann alimentiertes Bankkonto; **to garnish (attach) a** ~ Bank-, Kontoguthaben pfänden; **to have a** ~ Bankkonto besitzen; **to open a** ~ Bankkonto eröffnen (errichten); **to overdraw one's** ~ sein [Bank]konto überziehen; **to touch s. one's** ~ sich an jds. Bankkonto vergreifen.
bank|accountant Bankbuchhalter; ~ **accounting** Bankbuchhaltung; ~ **Act** *(Br.)* Bankgesetz; ~ **advance** Bankdarlehen, -kredit, *(bank balance sheet)* Kundenkredite; **day-to-day-**~**advances**kurzfristige Bankvorschüsse;~ **agent** Bankvertreter, -vertretung, *(branch manager)* Filialleiter; ~ **agio** Bankprovision; ~ **annuities** *(Br.)* Staatspapiere, Konsols, ~ **assets** Bankvermögen, Vermögenswerte einer Bank; ~ **assistant** Bankangestellter; ~ **audit** Bankrevision; ~ **auditor** Bankrevisor; ~ **bag** Geldsack; **[dormant]** ~ **balance** [unbeanspruchtes] Bankguthaben; ~**-balance charges** Abschlußspesen; ~**'s balance sheet** Bankbilanz; ~ **bill** *(bank-note, US)* Banknote, *(bill of exchange)* Bankwechsel, -akzept, *(US)*Kassenanweisung; ~ **bonds** Bankschuldverschreibungen, -obligationen; **to be creditor on the** ~**'s books** Bankkonto besitzen; ~ **borrower** Bankkunde, -schuldner; ~ **borrowing** Bankdarlehn, Schuldenaufnahme bei Banken, Bankverschuldung; ~ **branch** Bankfiliale; ~ **broker** Bankagentur; ~ **building** Bankgebäude; ~ **burglary insurance** Bankeinbruchsversicherung; ~ **call** *(US)* Aufforderung zur Vorlage des Bankausweises; ~**'s capital** Kapital einer Bank; **outstanding** ~ **capital** ausgegebenes Aktienkapital einer Bank; ~ **cashier** Kassierer; ~ **charges** Bankspesen, Konto-, Bankunkosten, Bankprovision; ~ **charter** Bankprivileg, -konzession; ~ **Charter Act** *(Br.)* [etwa] Bankgesetz; ~ **cheque** *(Br.)* **(check,** *US***)** Bankscheck, -anweisung; ~**'s claim** Bankforderung; ~ **clearing** Bankenabrechnung; ~ **clearings** *(US)* der Verrechnungsstelle eingereichte Schecks und Wechsel; ~ **clearing system** bankinterner Abrechnungsverkehr; ~ **clerk** *(Br.)* Bankangestellter, -beamter; ~**'s client** Bankkunde; ~ **closure** Bankenschließung; ~**'s commission** Bankprovision, -spesen; ~ **Commissioner** *(US)* Bankenkommissar, Bankaufsichtsbehörde; ~**'s commitment** Bankengagement; ~ **communication** Bankverkehr; ~ **confirmation** Bestätigung des Kontoauszuges; ~ **consortium** Bankenkonsortium, Konsortium von Banken; ~ **court** *(Br.)* routinemäßige Sitzung einer Bank; ~ **credit** Bankkredit; ~ **credit card** Kreditkarte; ~ **credit currency** nur teilweise gedecktes Papiergeld; ~ **credit work** Kreditbearbeitung bei einer Bank; ~ **crisis** Bankenkrise; ~ **currency** *(US)* Noten der amerikanischen Nationalbanken; ~ **debenture** zugunsten einer Bank ausgestellte Schuldverschreibung; ~ **debits** *(US)* Bankumsätze auf der Debetseite; ~ **debt** Bankschulden; **to subordinate** ~ **debts to trade debt** mit den Bankschulden hinter den Lieferantenschulden zurücktreten; ~ **deposit** Bankeinlage, Depositenguthaben; **daily** ~ **deposit** täglicher Bankauszug, Tagesauszug; ~ **deposit account** Guthabenkonto, Depositenkonto; ~**-deposit insurance** Depotversicherung; ~ **deposit interest** Zinsen auf ein Bankguthaben; ~ **deposit tax** *(US)* Depotsteuer; ~ **depositor** Bankkontoinhaber, Einleger; ~ **discount**[Bank]diskont; ~ **disclosure** *(Br.)* Offenlegungspflicht der Banken, Bankauskünfte über ein Kundenkonto; ~ **draft** Banktratte; ~ **earnings** Bankeinkünfte, -gewinne; ~ **economist** Bankbetriebswirt; ~ **economy** Bankbetriebs[wirtschafts]lehre; ~ **education** Bankausbildung; ~ **embezzlement** Bankunterschlagung; ~ **employee** Bankangestellter; ~**'s enquiry** *(Br.)* Bankanfrage; ~ **establishment** Bankinstitut; ~ **examination** *(US)* Bankrevision; ~ **examiner** *(US)* Bankrevisor; ~ **exchanges** *(US)* der Verrechnungs-

stelle eingereichte Schecks und Wechsel; ~ **experts** Bankfachleute; ~ **facilities** Bankfazilitäten; ~ **failure** Bankzusammenbruch; ~ **finance** Finanzierung durch die Bank; ~ **form** Bankformular; ~ **funds** Bankguthaben, von der Bank verwaltete Gelder; ~ **giro** Überweisung zu Lasten des Kreditkontos; ~ **giro credit slip** Lastschrifts-, Abbuchungsbeleg; ~ **group** Bankenkonzern, -konsortium, -gruppe; ~ **guarantee** Einlagengarantie, Depositenversicherung, *(customer)* Bankbürgschaft, Bürgschaft einer Bank; ~ **guarantor** Bankbürge; ~ **guaranty** *(customer, US)* Bankgarantie, Einlagengarantie, Depositenversicherung; ~ **holdings** Bankguthaben; ~ **holding company** Holdinggesellschaft im Eigentum einer Bank; ~ **holiday** *(Br.)* Bankfeiertag, gesetzlicher Feiertag; ~ **indebtedness** Bankschulden, -verschuldung; ~ **indorsement** Giro einer Bank; ~'s **inspector** Bankrevisor; ~ **insurance pool** Pleitenfonds; ~ **interest** Bankzinsen; ~ **interest paid** bezahlte Bankzinsen; ~ **interest received** erhaltene Bankzinsen; ~ **law** Bankrecht; ~ **ledger** Kontokorrentbuch einer Bank; ~ **lendings** Bankausleihungen; ~ **lendings abroad** ausländische Bankkredite; ~'s **letter box** Bankbriefkasten; ~ **liquidity** Liquidität einer Bank, Bankenliquidität; ~ **loan** Bankkredit, Anleihe einer Bank; **commercial ~ loan** Bankkredit mit 30 - 90 Tagen Laufzeit; **syndicated floating-rate ~ loan** konsortialiter gewährte zinsvariable Bankanleihe; ~ **loans and overdrafts** *(balance sheet, Br.)* Bankverbindlichkeiten; **to roll over ~ loans on a continuing basis** Bankkredite revolvierend einsetzen; ~ **loan demand** Nachfrage nach Bankkrediten; ~ **loan department** Kreditabteilung einer Bank; ~ **manager** Bankdirektor; ~ **management** Bankleitung, -vorstand; ~ **memorandum** Vereinbarung mit einer Bank; ~ **merger** Bankenfusion; ~ **messenger** Kassen-, Bankbote; ~ **minimum lending rate** Diskontsatz; ~ **money** *(banknotes and deposits, US)* Bankwährung, -valuta, Giralgeld; **to create further ~ money** *(US)* Kreditvolumen erhöhen; ~ **money order** Bankanweisung; ~ **nationalization** *(Br.)* Verstaatlichung der Banken; ~ **night** Kinovorstellung mit Lotterie und Preisverteilung; ~ **note** *(Br.)* Banknote, Kassenschein; ~ **notes in circulation** Banknotenumlauf; **to issue ~ notes** Banknoten in Umlauf setzen; **to withdraw ~ notes** Banknoten einziehen; ~**-note printing** Banknotendruck; ~'s **officer** Bankangestellter; ~ **official** [leitender] Bankbeamter; ~'s **opening hour** Schalteröffnung; **to curb private ~ operations** Banktätigkeit einschränken; ~ **overdraft** Überziehung des Bankkontos; ~ **paper** bankfähiges Papier, Bankwechsel, *(letters)* Bankpostpapier; ~ **parlance** Banksprache; ~ **payment advice** [Bank]überweisungsauftrag; ~ **place** Bankenplatz; ~ **portefeuille** Bankportefeuille, Effektenvermögen einer Bank; ~ **post** Briefpapier im Gewicht von 5 1/2 bis 10 engl. Pfund per Ries; ~ **post bill** *(Br.)* Solawechsel der Bank von England; ~ **post remittance** Postüberweisung im Auftrage einer Bank; ~'s **premises** bankeigenes Gebäude, Bankgrundstück; ~ **premises account** *(balance sheet)* Liegenschaftskonto; ~ **president** Vorstand einer Bank; ~ **rate** *(Br.)* Diskontsatz der Notenbank, Mindestausleihesatz der Notenbank, Bankdiskont; ~ **corporation rate** *(Br.)* Industriekreditsatz; **current ~ rate** *(Br.)* gültiger Bankdiskontsatz; **to increase the ~ rate** *(Br.)* Diskontsatz erhöhen; **to lower the ~ rate** *(Br.)* Diskontsatz senken; ~ **rate policy** *(Br.)* Diskontpolitik; ~ **receipt** Bankbeleg; ~ **receiver** Kassierer; ~ **reconciliation** Kontoabstimmung; ~ **reconciliation statement** Kontoabrechnung; ~ **records** Bankbelege; ~ **reference** Bankauskunft; ~ **reply** Bankantwort; ~ **report** Bankausweis, -bericht; ~ **reserves** Rücklagen einer Bank, Bankrücklagen; ~'s **resources** Aktiva einer Bank; ~ **return** *(Br.)* Bankausweis, *(US)* wöchentlicher Ausweis des New Yorker Clearinghauses und der Bank von England; ~ **return charges** Abschlußspesen; ~ **robber** Bankräuber; ~ **robbery** Banküberfall, -raub; ~ **robbery insurance** Versicherung gegen Banküberfall; ~ **secrecy** Bankgeheimnis; **to get around the ~ secrecy laws** zum Schutz des Bankgeheimnisses erlassene Bestimmungen umgehen; ~'s **security** Banksicherheit; ~ **shares** Bankwerte; ~ **shareholder** Bankaktionär; ~ **slip** Bankbeleg; ~ **shutdown** Bankenschließung; ~ **stamp** *(Br.)* Bankindossament, Giro einer Bank; **to speculate in ~ stocks** in Bankwerten spekulieren; ~ **statement** *(Br.)* Konto-, Bankauszug, -ausweis, *(balance sheet)* Bankbilanz, -ausweis; ~ **stock** Bankaktien; ~ **supervisory commission** Bankaufsichtsbehörde; ~ **teller** *(Br.)* [Bank]kassierer; ~ **transfer** Banküberweisung; ~ **transfer form** [Bank]überweisungsformular; ~ **trust** Bankkonzern; ~ **turnover** Bankumsatz; ~ **vault** Banktresor; ~**withdrawal** Bankabhebung, Abhebung vom Bankkonto.
bankable bankfähig, diskontierbar.
~ **bill** diskontierbarer Wechsel; ~ **paper** bankfähiges Papier; ~ **securities** bankfähige Sicherheiten.

bankbook Einzahlungs-, Einlagen-, Bankabrechnungsbuch, Kontobuch.
-banker Bankier, Bankverbindung, Zahlstelle;
cashing ~ einlösende Bank; **collecting ~** Inkassobank; **industrial ~** Industriebank; **issuing ~** Emissions-, Akkreditivbank; **merchant ~** Akzept-, Handelsbank; **merchant and accepting ~** Handels- und Akzeptbank; **originating ~** Konsortialführerin; **paying ~** [aus]zahlende Bank, Zahlstelle; **private ~** Privatbankier, -bankhaus;
to act as the ~ of the government für Bankgeschäfte des Staates zur Verfügung stehen; **to do business as a ~** Bankgeschäfte betreiben, Bankier sein.
banker's | **acceptance** Bankakzept; **prime ~ acceptance** *(US)* erstklassiges Bankakzept; ~ **acceptance credit** Akzeptkredit; ~ **advance** Bankkredit; ~ **association** *(Br.)* Bankiersvereinigung; ~ **balances** Bankeinlagen; ~ **bill** Bankakzept; ~ **blanket bond** Blankettversicherungsschein gegen Verluste aufgrund von Handlungen von Bankangestellten; ~ **books** Bankunterlagen; ~ **Books Evidence Act** *(Br.)* Gesetz über die Verwendung von Bankauskünften vor Gericht; ~ **card** Scheckkarte; ~ **check (cheque, Br.)** Bankscheck; ~ **commission** Bankprovision; ~ **correspondent** Bankverbindung; ~ **deposit rate** Zinssatz für Depositengelder; ~ **discount** Bankdiskont; ~ **draft** *(Br.)* Banktratte; ~ **duty of secrecy** Bankgeheimnis; ~ **exchange account** Wechselrechnung; ~ **functions** Aufgaben des Bankgeschäfts, Bankfunktionen; ~ **funds** von einer Bank verwaltete Mittel; ~ **guaranty** Bankgarantie; ~ **inquiry** Bankauskunft; ~ **lien** Zurückbehaltungsrecht der Banken, Bankenpfandrecht; ~ **note** Bankschein; ~ **order** *(Br.)* Zahlungs-, Überweisungsauftrag, Banküberweisung; **standing ~ order** Dauerauftrag an eine Bank, -überweisungsauftrag; ~ **payment** Zahlungsauftrag einer Bank; ~ **ratio** *(credit rating, US)* Verhältnis von Umlaufvermögen zu kurzfristigen Verbindlichkeiten; ~ **receipt** Depotschein; ~ **reference** Bankauskunft; ~ **rule** goldene Bankregel; ~ **ticket** *(bill of exchange)* Rückrechnung; ~ **transfer** Banküberweisung.
bankers' | **buying rate** Geldkurs; ~ **clearinghouse** *(Br.)* Bankenabrechnungsstelle; ~ **deposits** Bankeinlagen, -deposits; ~ **shares** *(US)* Aktien eines Investmenttrusts.
bankerese Bankfachsprache.
banking Bankwesen, -geschäft, -betrieb, -fach, Bankverkehr, Kreditgewerbe;
branch ~ Filialbanksystem; **chain ~** Bankgruppensystem, Filialbankwesen; **commercial ~** Depositen[bank]geschäft; **cooperative ~** genossenschaftliches Bankwesen, Genossenschaftswesen; **group ~** *(US)* Großbankwesen; **investment ~** Bankgeschäft in Anlagewerten, Effekten-, Emissionsgeschäft, Investitionsgeschäft; **large-scale ~** Großbankwesen; **private-sector ~** Privatbankenbereich; **syndicate ~** Konsortialgeschäft; **unit ~** *(Br.)* Einzelbankwesen;
~ **and public finance** Bank- und Finanzwesen;
~ *(a.)* bankmäßig, -technisch;
~ **accommodation** Bankfazilitäten; **to insure adequate ~ accommodations** ausreichende Bankfazilitäten zur Verfügung stellen; ~ **account** Bankkonto; **to have a ~ account with** Bankkonto bei ... haben; ~ **Act** *(Australia)* Bankgesetz; ~ **activity (activities)** Banktätigkeit; ~ **advance** Bankdarlehn, -kredit; ~ **affairs** Bankwesen; ~ **amalgamation** Bankenfusion; ~ **arrangement** Absprache mit der Bank; ~ **association** Bankiersvereinigung; ~ **business** Bankgeschäft, -fach, -wesen, -gewerbe; **to carry on ~ business** Bankgeschäft betreiben; **to carry on a bona fide ~ business** *(Br.)* staatlich genehmigtes Bankgeschäft betreiben; **to transact all types of ~ business** sämtliche Bankgeschäfte ausführen; ~ **capacity** Bankvolumen; ~ **centre** *(Br.)* Bankplatz; ~ **charges** Bankspesen, Provisionssätze der Banken; ~ **circles** Bankkreise; ~ **commission** Bankprovision; ~ **committee** Bankenausschuß, -enquête; ~ **communication** Bankverkehr; ~ **company (corporation, US)** Bankfirma, -gesellschaft, Aktienbank; ~ **concern** Bankunternehmen; ~ **conditions** Bankkonditionen; ~ **control** Bankenaufsicht; ~ **crisis** Bankkrise; ~ **custom** Bankusance; ~ **customer** Bankkunde; ~ **department** *(Bank of England)* Bankabteilung; ~ **employee** Bankangestellter; ~ **establishment** Bankunternehmen, Bankfirma, -anstalt; ~ **experience** Bankerfahrung; [complete] ~ **facilities** [alle] Bankgeschäfte; ~ **failure** Bankzusammenbruch; ~ **field** Bankfach; ~ **and Financial Dealings Act** *(US)* Bankgesetz; **usual ~ fringe benefits** für Bankangestellte übliche Zusatzvergütungen; ~ **function** Bankenfunktion, -aufgabe; **supplementary ~ functions** irreguläre Bankgeschäfte; ~ **hall** Schalterhalle; ~ **hours** Geschäfts-, Schalterstunden; **after ~ hours** nach Bank-, Kassenschluß; ~ **house** Bankge-

schäft, -haus, -anstalt; ~ **indebtedness** Bankschulden, -verschuldung; ~ **institution** Bankinstitut; ~ **interest** Bankanteil; ~ **interests** Bankkreise; **to have a sound general ~ knowledge** über solide Kenntnisse des gesamten Bankgeschäfts verfügen; ~ **law** Bankrecht; ~ **legislation** Bankengesetzgebung; **to be in the ~ line** im Bankfach tätig sein; ~ **machinery** Bankenapparat; ~ **matters** Bankwesen; ~ **office** Bankkontor; ~ **operation** Bankgeschäft, banktechnische Transaktion, Banktransaktion, -geschäft; ~ **organization** Bankenvereinigung; ~ **partnership** Bankgesellschaft, -firma; ~ **point of view** banktechnischer Standpunkt; ~ **policy** Bankpolitik; ~ **power** Umfang der zugelassenen Bankgeschäfte; ~ **practice** Bankpraxis; **to tidy up loose ~ practices** mit der Praktizierung unlauterer Bankmethoden Schluß machen; ~ **profession** Bankiersberuf; ~ **profit** Bankgewinn; **to be used for ~ purposes** bankgeschäftlich genutzt werden; ~ **regulations** staatliche Ordnung des Kreditwesens; ~ **regulator** Bankbehörde; ~ **reserves** Rücklagen einer Bank; ~ **rivals** Konkurrenzbanken; ~ **secrecy** Bankgeheimnis; ~ **secrecy law** Gesetz zur Wahrung des Bankgeheimnisses; ~ **sector** Bankensektor; ~ **statistics** bankstatistische Erhebungen; ~ **student** Banklehrling; ~ **subsidiary** Tochtergesellschaft einer Bank; ~ **supervision** Bankenaufsicht; ~ **support** Stützungsaktion durch Banken, Bankenintervention; ~ **syndicate** Bankenkonsortium; ~ **system** Banksystem, Bankapparat, -wesen; **free** ~ **system** (US) Bankenprivileg; ~ **technique** Bankwesen; ~ **theory** Kaufkrafttheorie des Geldes; ~ **trade** Bankgewerbe; ~ **transaction** Bankgeschäft, -transaktion; ~ **usage** Bankusance; ~ **world** Bankwelt.

bankroll (US) Bündel Banknoten;
~ (v.) finanzieren, Geldmittel bereitstellen;
to have a big ~ viel Geld zur Verfügung haben.

bankrupt, [adjudicated] Konkurs-, Gemeinschuldner, Insolvent, Bankrotteur, notorischer Schuldenmacher, Zahlungsunfähiger;
certificated (Br.) (discharged) ~ rehabilitierter Konkursschuldner; **fraudulent** ~ betrügerischer Bankrotteur; **involuntary** ~ Zwangsgemeinschuldner; **negligent** ~ fahrlässiger Konkursschuldner; **undischarged (uncertified,** Br.) ~ nicht entlasteter Gemeinschuldner; **voluntary** ~ Konkursschuldner aufgrund eigenen Antrags;
~ (a.) bankrott, im Konkurs, insolvent, zahlungsunfähig, pleite;
near ~ fast bankrott;
~ **of ideas** ideenarm;
~ (v.) bankrott machen, zum Konkurs treiben;
to adjudge (adjudicate) s. o. a ~ j. bankrott erklären, über j. den Konkurs verhängen, über jds. Vermögen das Konkursverfahren eröffnen; **to attach the incidents of a ~** Rechtswirkungen eines Konkurses beilegen; **to be ~** bankrott (im Konkurs) sein; **to be adjudged ~** für bankrott erklärt werden; **to become (go) ~** bankrott machen, in Konkurs geraten; **to declare o. s. ~** seinen Konkurs (Bankrott) anmelden; **to declare s. o. judicially to be a ~** über jds. Vermögen den Konkurs verhängen; **to discharge a ~** Konkursschuldner rehabilitieren; **to give up all one's claims upon the ~** auf alle Konkursansprüche verzichten; **to go ~** in Konkurs geraten (gehen), Konkurs (Bankrott) machen; **to make s. o. ~** j. zum Konkurs treiben; **to grant the ~ discharge** Konkursverfahren aufheben; **to liquidate the assets of a ~** Konkursmasse ausschütten; **to take the goods out of the order and disposition of the ~** Waren aus dem Vermögen des Konkursschuldners aussondern;
to liquidate a ~'s affairs Konkurssache abwickeln; **to carry on the ~'s business** Geschäft des Gemeinschuldners fortführen; **~'s certificate** Konkursaufhebungsbescheid, Rehabilitierungsbescheinigung; ~ **condition** Konkurszustand; **~'s creditor** Gemein-, Konkursgläubiger; ~ **customer** in Konkurs gegangener Kunde; **~'s debts** Schulden des Konkursschuldners; ~ **debtor** Konkursschuldner; ~ **estate** Konkurs-, Debitmasse; **to divide a ~'s estate** Konkursmasse ausschütten; ~ **law** Konkursrecht; **to be amenable to the ~ laws** konkursrechtlichen Bestimmungen unterliegen; ~ **member of a company** bankrotter Aktionär; ~ **merchant** Konkurs-, Gemeinschuldner; **~'s property** Konkursvermögen; ~ **stock** Restelager aus Konkursen, Konkurslager.

bankruptcy Bankrott, Konkurs[verfahren], Zahlungseinstellung, Insolvenz, Fallieren, Fallissement, Pleite, (fig.) Ruin, Bankrott, Schiffbruch;
verging on ~ am Rande des Bankrotts; **within measurable distance of** ~ nahe am (kurz vor dem) Bankrott;
fraudulent ~ betrügerischer Bankrott; **involuntary** ~ (US) von den Gläubigern beantragter Konkurs, Zwangskonkurs; **nation-**al ~ Staatsbankrott; **ordinary** ~ normales Konkursverfahren; **partnership** ~ Gesellschafterkonkurs; **reckless** ~ fahrlässiger Bankrott; **simple** ~ unverschuldeter (einfacher) Bankrott; **voluntary** ~ (US) vom Schuldner beantragter Konkurs; **wil(l)-full** ~ leichtsinniger Konkurs;
~ **of a deceased** ~ Nachlaßkonkurs; ~ **of a firm** Firmenbankrott; ~ **of a partnership** Gesellschafterkonkurs;
to be faced with ~ vor dem Konkurs stehen; **to be up against utter** ~ vom völligen Bankrott bedroht sein; **to drift towards** ~ auf den Konkurs zusteuern; **to file a petition in (declaration of)** ~ Antrag auf Konkurseröffnung stellen; **to force s. o. into** ~ j. zum Konkurs treiben; **to go into** ~ Konkurs machen; **to lodge a proof in** ~ Konkursforderung (Forderung zur Konkurstabelle) anmelden; **to proceed with the** ~ **of a debtor** Konkursverfahren über das Schuldnervermögen fortsetzen; **to throw s. o. in** ~ Konkursantrag gegen j. stellen; **to throw a debtor into** ~ Schuldner in den Konkurs treiben;
~ᵖ **Act** (Br.) Konkursordnung; **National** ~ᵖ **Act** (US) Konkursordnung; **to file a** ~ᵖ **Act petition** Konkursantrag stellen; ~ **action** Konkursverfahren; **to be thrown into a** ~ **action** in ein Konkursverfahren verwickelt sein; ~ **administration** Konkursverwaltung; ~ **assets** Konkursmasse; ~ **bond** Konkursverwalterkaution; ~ **case** Konkursfall; ~ **commissioner** Konkursrichter-, verwalter; ~ **costs** Konkurskosten, Kosten des Konkursverfahrens; ~ **court** Konkursgericht; **to act in place of the** ~ **court** an Stelle des Konkursgerichtes tätig werden; ~ **creditor** Konkursgläubiger; **to suffer from** ~ **disabilities** infolge eines Konkursverfahrens seine Geschäfte nicht wahrnehmen können; ~ **district** für Konkurssachen zuständiger Gerichtsbezirk, Bereich eines Konkursgerichts; ~ **estates account** (Bank of England) allgemeines Konkursverwaltungskonto; ~ **inhibition** konkursrechtliches Veräußerungsverbot, Veräußerungsverbot für den Gemeinschuldner, Konkursbeschlag; ~ **jurisdiction** konkursrechtliche Zuständigkeit; **to be subject to** ~ **jurisdiction** konkursrechtlichen Bestimmungen unterliegen; ~ **law** Konkursordnung, -recht, konkursrechtliche Bestimmungen; **to be liable to be proceeded against under the** ~ **law** konkursrechtlich belangt werden können; **to take the benefit of the** ~ **law** von den konkursrechtlichen Schutzbestimmungen profitieren; ~ **matters** Konkurssachen; ~ **notice** Konkursanmeldung; **to comply with a** ~ **notice** einem Konkurseröffnungsbeschluß nachkommen; **to serve a** ~ **notice on a debtor** Schuldner zur Zahlung unter Konkursandrohung auffordern; **to serve with a** ~ **notice** Konkurserklärung (Konkurseröffnungsbeschluß) zustellen; ~ **offence** Konkursdelikt; ~ **petition** Konkursantrag, -begehren, Antrag auf Konkurseröffnung; **to file a** ~ **petition** Konkursantrag stellen; ~ **proceedings** Konkursverfahren; **to apply for** ~ **proceedings** Antrag auf Eröffnung stellen; **to avoid** ~ **proceedings** Konkurs[verfahren] abwenden; **to initiate(institute)** ~ **proceedings against s. o.** Antrag auf Konkurseröffnung gegen j. stellen, Konkursverfahren einleiten (eröffnen); **to stop** ~ **proceedings** Konkursverfahren einstellen; **to terminate** ~ **proceedings** Konkurs aufheben; ~ **rate** Bankrottprozentsatz; **to be in** ~ **reorganization** im Vergleichsverfahren sein; **to take the** ~ **route** Konkursweg einschlagen; ~ **rules** Konkursbestimmungen; ~ **subject** Konkursgegenstand.

banner Fahne, (Br. advertising) Spann-, Werbespruchband, Streifenanzeige, (car) Stander, (at demonstrations) Transparent, Banner, (headline) Balkenüberschrift, Schlagzeile über die ganze Seite;
~ (v.) mit einer Schlagzeile über die ganze Seite veröffentlichen;
~ (a.) (US) hervorragend, führend;
carry a ~ Stander führen;
~ **cry** Wahlkampfslogan, -parole; ~ **headline** Balkenüberschrift; ~ **line** Schlagzeile über die ganze Seite; ~ **march** Protestmarsch; ~ **profit** einmaliger Gewinn; ~ **sales year** erfolgreiches Geschäftsjahr; ~**state** führender Staat; ~ **year for crops** hervorragendes Erntejahr.

banning | **of all steel import** totales Stahleinfuhrverbot;
~ **order** (South Africa) Beschränkung der persönlichen Freiheit.

banns | **of matrimony** Aufgebot;
to forbid the ~ gegen die Eheschließung Einspruch erheben; **to put up the** ~ Aufgebot bestellen.

banquet Festessen, Bankett;
~ **dinner** Galadinner; ~ **room** Festsaal.

banqueting hall Festsaal.

banquette erhöhter Fußweg, (US) Bürgersteig, Gehweg.

bantam shop (US) Kleinstladen.

baptism | of fire *(mil.)* Feuertaufe;
~ **register** Taufregister.

bar Bar, *(barriers)* Schranke, Hindernis, Barriere, Sperre, *(ingots)* Barren, *(barristers)* Anwaltsstand, Rechtsanwaltschaft, *(counter)* Theke, Getränkeausschank, Büfett, *(law court)* Gerichtshof, *(legal profession)* Anwaltsberuf, *(place of accused)* Platz des Angeklagten, *(plea)* peremptorische Einrede, Einwand, *(strip)* Riegel, Stange;
at the ~ in öffentlicher Gerichtsverhandlung; **at the ~ of public opinion** vor den Schranken der Öffentlichkeit; **behind ~s** *(fig.)* hinter Schloß und Riegel; **in ~s** ungemünzt;
colo(u)r ~ Rassenschranke; **legal ~** Rechtshindernis; **milk ~** Milchausschank; **quick lunch ~** Schnellimbißstube; **toll ~** Zollschranke; **utter (outer) ~** jüngere Anwälte;
~ **and bench** Richter und Anwälte; ~ **to marriage** Ehehindernis; ~ **to payment** Zahlungshindernis; ~ **of public opinion** Macht der öffentlichen Meinung; ~ **by statute of limitations** Ausschluß durch Verjährung;
~ *(v.)* verriegeln, sperren, hindern, *(law)* Rechtsweg ausschließen, *(ban)* verbieten, untersagen;
~ **in** einsperren; **s. o. from a competition** j. von einem Wettbewerb ausschließen; ~ **legal proceedings** Rechtsweg ausschließen; ~ **prescription** Verjährung ausschließen; ~ **a street** Straße absperren; ~ **s. o. from voting his stocks** j. an der Ausübung seines Aktienstimmrechts hindern;
to appear at the ~ vor Gericht auftreten; **to be admitted (come) to the ~** *(Br.)* als Anwalt zugelassen werden; **to be called within the ~** *(Br.)* zum Kronanwalt ernannt werden; **to be brought up for the ~** *(Br.)* zum Juristen erzogen werden; **to be placed behind prison bars ~s** eingesperrt werden; **to cross the ~** *(mar.)* in einen Hafen einlaufen; **to go behind ~s** Gefängnisstrafe antreten; **to go to the ~** *(Br.)* Anwalt werden; **to let down the ~s** alle Hemmungen fallen lassen, *(US)* Überwachung des Nachtlebens schleifen lassen; **to plead at the ~** plädieren; **to practise at the ~** als Anwalt tätig sein, Anwaltsberuf ausüben; **to read for the ~** Jura studieren; **to retire from the ~** anwaltliche Tätigkeit aufgeben; **to study for the ~** *(Br.)* sich für den Anwaltsberuf vorbereiten, sich des Studiums der Rechte befleißigen; **to try at the ~** öffentlich verhandeln; **to wind up behind ~s** sich im Gefängnis wiederfinden;
~ **association** *(US)* Anwaltsvereinigung; ~ **chart** *(statistics)* Balken-, Säulen-, Stabdiagramm; ~ **code** *(terminal)* Strichmarkierung; ~ **council** [Rechts]anwaltskammer; ~ **date** Ausschlußfrist; **to prepare for the ~ examination** [etwa] sich für das Assessor-Examen vorbereiten ~ **gold** Barrengold; ~ **parlo(u)r** Wirtsstube; ~ **room** Schankstube; ~ **silver** Barrensilber.

barbecue *(US)* Gartengrillfest.

barbed | comment scharfe Bemerkung; ~ **wire** Stacheldraht.

bare *(law)* bedingungslos;
~ **contract** einseitiger Vertrag, bedingungslose Abmachung; ~ **facts** nackte Tatsachen; **to earn a ~ living** nackten Lebensunterhalt verdienen; ~ **majority** einfache Mehrheit; ~ **necessaries of life** notdürftiger Unterhalt; ~ **nonsense** blanker Unsinn; ~ **treasury** leere Kasse; ~ **trustee** Fideikommißerbe.

barehanded mittellos.

bargain Handel, Geschäft, Abschluß, Kaufvertrag, *(assemblage of shops)* kleines Warenhaus, *(cheap purchase)* billiger Einkauf, Gelegenheitskauf, vorteilhafter Handel, Sonderangebot, Spottpreis, *(compact)* Abkommen, Übereinkunft, Abmachung, *(contract work)* im Stücklohn hergestellte Ware, *(stock exchange, Br.)* [Geschäfts]abschluß, Börsengeschäft;
into the ~ als Zugabe, gratis, obendrein, zusätzlich;
bad ~ unvorteilhafter Handel; **bona fide ~** ehrlicher Handel; **cash ~** Barabschluß; **catching ~** gewissenloses Wuchergeschäft; **chance ~** Gelegenheitskauf; **dead ~** Spottpreis; **~s done** *(stock exchange)* gehandelte Kurse; **excellent ~** äußerst preiswert; **fictitious ~** Scheingeschäft; **firm ~** *(stock exchange)* fester Abschluß; **good ~** vorteilhafter Kauf; **losing ~** schlechtes Geschäft, Verlustabschluß; **optional ~** Prämiengeschäft; **real ~** Okkasion; **time ~** Lieferungszeit-, Termingeschäft; **unconscionable ~** unsittliches Geschäft;
~ **for account** *(Br.)* Termingeschäft; ~ **for cash** Barabschluß; ~ **or contract in restraint of trade** zeitweiliges Berufs-, Wettbewerbsverbot, Konkurrenzverbot; ~ **and sale** Grundstückskaufvertrag;
~ *(v.)* feilschen, schachern, handeln, *(stipulate for)* vereinbaren, verhandeln, übereinkommen, abmachen;
~ **away** mit Verlust verkaufen, billig veräußern; ~ **away one's freedom** seine Freiheit verschachern; ~ **on a local basis** örtlich begrenzte Tarifverträge aushandeln; ~ **collectively** Tarifverhandlungen führen; ~ **over s. th.** um etw. feilschen;

to be a great gainer by a ~ an einem Geschäft groß verdienen; **to break a ~** Handel aufkündigen; **to close (conclude, drive) a ~** Geschäft abschließen; **to drive a hard ~** rücksichtslos seinen Vorteil wahren; **to drive a good ~** vorteilhaftes Geschäft zum Abschluß bringen; **to get s. th. as a ~** etw. billig einhandeln; **to get a th. dead ~** etw. spottbillig (zu einem Spottpreis) kaufen; **to give s. th. into the ~** etw. zugeben; **to make a ~** Kauf abschließen; **to make a good ~** gutes Geschäft machen; **to make the best of a bad ~** sich mit Humor aus der Affäre ziehen; **to rescind a ~** von einem Geschäft zurücktreten; **to seal a ~** Abschluß perfekt machen; **to stick to a ~** Vereinbarung einhalten; **to strike a ~** gutes Geschäft machen, handelseinig werden; **to throw s. th. into the ~** etw. zugeben, Zugabe gewähren;
~ **basement** Tiefgeschoß (Abteilung) mit Sonderangeboten, Ausverkaufsabteilung im Erdgeschoß; ~ **basement prices** Niedrigpreise, *(stock exchange)* gewinnbringende Anfangskurse; ~ **book** Schlußnotenregister; ~ **counter** Effektenschalter, *(warehouse, US)* Verkaufstisch für Sonderangebote; **to be on the ~ counter** *(stock exchange)* billig angeboten sein; ~ **day** Sondertag, *(stock exchange)* Abrechnungstag; ~ **hunter** Börsenspekulant; ~ **hunting** Jagd nach Gelegenheitskäufen, *(stock exchange)* Effektenspekulation; ~ **level** niedrigst kalkulierter Preis; ~ **money** Drauf-, An-, Handgeld; ~ **penny** Draufgeld; ~ **price** Vorzugs-, Gelegenheits-, Spott-, Ausverkaufspreis; ~ **sale** *(US)* Sonder-, Ausverkauf, Verkauf zu herabgesetzten Preisen, besonders preisgünstiges Warenangebot; ~ **sales advertising** *(US)* Ausverkaufsreklame, Werbung für Sonderangebote; ~ **tour** verbilligte Reise; ~ **tour fare** verbilligter Fahrpreis; ~ **work** in den Tarif einbezogene Arbeit, Kontrakt-, Tarifarbeit.

bargained, as ~ for wie verabredet.

bargainee Käufer, Abnehmer, Erwerber.

bargainer, bargainor Schacherer, Feilscher, *(negotiator)* Verhandler, *(vendor)* Verkäufer;
close ~ Preisdrücker; **collective ~** Tarifvertrags-, Tarifverhandlungspartner.

bargaining Kuhhandel, Handeln, Feilschen, *(collective agreement)* Tarifabschluß;
collective ~ Tarifverhandlungen; **company-wide ~** Tarifvertragsverhandlungen für den Gesamtbetrieb; **conference ~** Tarifkonferenz; **leapfrogging ~** Tarifverhandlungsmethode im überschlagenden Einsatz; **industry-wide ~** Manteltarifvertragsverhandlungen; **pressure ~** unter Streikdruckstehende Tarifverhandlungen; **single-plant ~** Einzeltarifvertrag, Betriebsvereinbarung; **site ~** Einzeltarifabschluß; **sole ~** ausschließliches Tarifverhandlungsrecht;
to leapfrog ~ Tarifverhandlungen im überschlagenden Einsatz führen;
~ **agency** Tarifverhandlungspartner; ~ **agenda** Verhandlungspunkte; ~ **agent** Tarifverhandlungsbevollmächtigter; **collective ~ agreement** Tarifvertrag; **contractual ~ agreement** ausgehandelte Tarifvertragsvereinbarung; **sole ~ agreement** Einzeltarifvertrag; **to be outside the ~ area** außerhalb des Verhandlungsspielraums liegen; **collective ~ association** Tarifverband; **to stay firmly in the ~ basement** *(prices)* sich weiterhin auf einem sehr niedrigen Niveau halten; ~ **body** Verhandlungsgremium; **to be in the ~ cards** im Verhandlungsspielraum liegen; ~ **chip** Verhandlungsobjekt; **collective ~ commission** Tarifkommission; ~ **counter** Verhandlungsinstrument; ~ **counts** Verhandlungspunkte; ~ **contract** Tarifforderung; ~ **disputes** Tarifstreitigkeiten; ~ **experience** Verhandlungserfahrung; ~ **give** ausgehandelte Konzession; ~ **group** Verhandlungsgruppe; **to break down ~ intransigence** Verhandlungsunlust überwinden; ~ **offer** Verhandlungsangebot; ~ **path** Kette von Angebot und Gegengebot; ~ **position** Verhandlungsposition; ~ **power** Verhandlungsstärke, -position, *(trade union)* Abschlußvollmacht; ~ **plant** ~ **problems** betriebliche Tarifprobleme; ~ **process** Tarifverhandlungsverfahren; **collective ~ provisions** Tarifvertragsbestimmungen; ~ **rights** Tarif[verhandlungs]rechte; ~ **room** Verhandlungsspielraum; ~ **round** Verhandlungsphase, -runde; ~ **session** Tarifsitzung; **national wages ~ structure** Manteltarifstruktur; **disciplined and ordered pay ~ system** diszipliniertes und geordnetes Tarifgehaltsverhandlungssystem; ~ **table** Verhandlungstisch; **to adopt post-tax ~ targets** Lohntarifziele den Steuererhöhungen anpassen; ~ **tariff** Verhandlungstarif; ~ **unit** Tarifgruppe, -vertragspartei.

barge Lastkahn, Schlepper, Schute, Leichter;
~ *(v.)* **in** *(fam.)* sich einmischen;
~ **operator** Leichterführer; **not to touch s. th. with a ~ pole** etw. nicht mal mit der Feuerzange anfassen; ~ **traffic** Schlepperverkehr.

bargee *(Br.)* Leichterführer;
  lucky ~ Glückskind.
bargeman Leichterführer.
bark *(v.)* *(US sl.)* marktschreierisch Kunden werben;
  ~ up the wrong tree falsche Spur verfolgen, auf der falschen Fährte (auf dem Holzweg) sein.
barkeeper Barbesitzer.
barker marktschreierischer Kundenwerber.
barmaid Schankkellnerin.
barman *(Br.)* Schankkellner.
barn Schuppen, Scheune.
barndoor Scheunentor;
  as big as a ~ nicht zu verfehlen.
barometer Barometer;
  ~ of public opinion Stimmungsmesser der öffentlichen Meinung;
  ~ reading Barometerablesung; **~ stocks** *(US)* Standardwerte.
baron *(Br.)* Baron, *(US)* Magnat;
  oil ~ Ölmagnat.
barony, of Fleet Street Pressezar.
barpost Schlagbaumpfosten.
barrable *(law)* aufhebbar.
barrack Baracke, Hütte, *(mansion)* Mietskaserne;
  ~s Kaserne;
  ~ *(v.)* in Baracken unterbringen, kasernieren, *(fam.)* anpöbeln;
  to confine to ~s *(mil.)* mit Arrest bestrafen; **to return to ~s** in die Kaserne einrücken;
  ~s duty *(mil.)* Innendienst; **~ flat** Barackenwohnung; **~s hospital** Militärkrankenhaus; **~ stores** *(Br.)* Unterkunftsgerät.
barrage Sperre, *(engineering)* Talsperre, *(mil.)* Sperrfeuer;
  air ~ Luftsperre;
  ~ of questions Schwall von Fragen;
  ~ *(v.)* *(fig.)* unter Beschluß nehmen, *(mil.)* Sperrfeuer schießen;
  ~ balloon Fesselballon.
barrator *(law)* bestechlicher Richter.
barratry Beschädigung der Ladung, *(law)* mutwilliges (schikanöses) Prozessieren.
barred ausgeschlossen;
  ~ by the statute of limitations verjährt;
  to be ~ at the end of the year am Jahresende verjähren; **to become ~** verjähren;
  ~ debt verjährte Schuld; **to perform a ~ obligation** verjährte Leistung erbringen.
barrel Faß, Tonne, *(US sl., candidate)* Bestechungsgeld;
  by ~s tonnen-, faßweise; **in ~s** in Gebinden;
  ~s Faßwaren;
  ~ of money Masse Geld;
  ~ cargo Faßladung; **~ house** *(US sl.)* Kneipe, Spelunke.
barren unfruchtbar, *(capital)* tot;
  ~ of issue ohne Nachkommenschaft;
  ~ land unfruchtbares Land; **~ money** totes Kapital.
barricade Straßensperre, Barrikade, Absperrung;
  ~ *(v.)* verbarrikadieren;
  to get on the ~s auf die Barrikaden steigen.
barrier Schranke, Barriere, Schutzgatter, *(customs)* Schlagbaum, *(fortress)* Grenzfestung, *(railway)* Stangengeländer, Brüstung, Sperre;
  barbed-wire ~ spanische Reiter; **constitutional ~s** von der Verfassung errichtete Schranken; **customs ~s** Zollschranken; **trade ~s, ~s of trade** Handelsschranken;
  ~ *(v.)* [off] absperren;
  to show one's ticket at the ~ seine Fahrkarte an der Sperre vorzeigen.
barring|of an action Klageverjährung; **~ of a claim** Anspruchsverjährung;
  ~ *(a.)* ausgenommen, abgesehen von;
  ~ accidents Unfall ausgenommen; **~ unforeseen developments** falls keine unvorhergesehenen Ereignisse eintreten; **~ errors** Irrtum vorbehalten.
barrister [-at-law] *(Br.)* plädierender Anwalt, *(US)* Anwalt, Prozeßanwalt;
  consulting ~ beratender Anwalt; **junior ~** Junior, -partner; **revising ~** Wahllistenprüfer; **vacation ~** Ferien-, Urlaubsvertreter; **woman ~** Rechtsanwältin;
  ~ appointed by the court Pflichtverteidiger;
  to appear on the roll of ~s im Anwaltsverzeichnis aufgeführt sein; **to brief a ~** Anwalt beauftragen (instruieren); **to disbar a ~** Rechtsanwalt aus der Anwaltschaft ausschließen.
barristership Advokatur, Advokatenstand.
barristress weiblicher Anwalt, Anwältin.

barroom Schankzimmer.
barrow Schubkarren;
  ~ boy Höker, *(fig.)* Schwarzhändlertyp.
barrowman *(Br.)* Höker, umherziehender Händler, Wandergewerbetreibender.
bartender Barmixer.
barter Tausch[geschäft], -handel, *(medium of exchange)* Tauschgegenstand, -mittel;
  ~ *(v.)* *(exchange)* ver-, ein-, austauschen, *(trade)*, Tauschhandel treiben, handeln;
  ~ away verschachern, verschleudern; **~ for** schachern, feilschen;
  to carry on ~ Tauschhandel treiben;
  ~ advertisement Tauschanzeige; **~ agreement (deal)** Tauschabkommen; **~ exchange (trade)** Tauschhandel, Kompensationsverkehr; **~ goods** Tauschwaren; **~ transaction** Kompensations-, Tauschgeschäft; **~ unit** Tauscheinheit.
barterable tauschfähig.
barterer Tauscher, Händler.
bartering Tauschgeschäft, -handel, *(payment in kind)* Bezahlung in Waren;
  international ~ zwischenstaatlicher Warenaustausch;
  ~ agreement Tauschhandelsabkommen; **~ goods** Tauschprodukte.
barton *(Br.)* Wirtschafts-, Pachthof.
baryta paper Barytpapier.
bascule bridge Klappbrücke.
base Basis, Grundlage, *(building)* Fundament, Grundmauer, *(el.)* Sockel, *(film)* Filmrohmaterial, *(fig.)* Basis, Fundament, *(mil.)* Stützpunkt, Etappe, rückwärtiges Armeegebiet, Versorgungs-, Operationsbasis, Reservoir, *(statistics)* Bezugs-, Grundwert, *(surveying)* Standlinie, *(street)* Packlage, *(taxation)* Steuerobjekt;
  off one's ~ *(US sl.)* völlig im Irrtum;
  air ~ Flugstützpunkt; **business ~** geschäftliche Basis; **foreign ~** ausländische Militärbasis; **naval ~** Marinestation, Flottenstützpunkt; **submarine ~** U-Bootstützpunkt;
  ~ of operation Operationsbasis, -linie, *(ship)* Einsatzhafen; **~ of supplies** Versorgungs-, Nachschubbasis;
  ~ *(a.)* (debased) unecht, falsch, *(inferior)* niedrigstehend, untergeordnet, *(of little value)* gering-, minderwertig;
  ~ *(v.)* gründen, stützen, basieren;
  ~ out *(marketing)* Widerstandslinie aufbauen; **~ taxation on the revenue** Einkommen zur Besteuerungsgrundlage nehmen;
  to be off ~ jeglicher Grundlage entbehren; **to take as a ~** fußen;
  ~ activity regionale Exportproduktion; **~ airfield** Aufmarschflugplatz; **~ bullion** Metall in Barrenform; **~ camp** Ausgangs-, Hauptlager; **~ coin** *(US)* Scheidemünze, *(Br.)* falsche Münze; **~ coinage** schlechte Münze; **~ company** Finanzierungsgesellschaft für Auslandtöchter; **~ court** Hinterhof, *(Br.)* niederes Gericht; **~ crude** Rohöl; **~ depot** *(mil.)* Hauptdepot; **~ fee** Grundgebühr; **~ gold** Gold von geringem Feingehalt; **~ hospital** Kriegslazarett; **~ lending rate** Mindestzinssatz; **~ level** Erosionsbasis; **~ line** *(advertising)* Schlußaussage, *(statistics)* Grundlinie, *(surveying)* Basislinie; **~ maintenance** *(mil.)* Parkinstandsetzung; **~ metal** unedles Metall; **~ metal goods** Eisen-, Blech- und Metallwaren; **~ motives** niedrige Beweggründe; **to form a ~ pattern** *(marketing)* Widerstandslinie aufbauen; **~ pay** Grundgehalt, *(guaranteed rate)* garantiertes Grundgehalt, Ecklohn; **~ period** *(statistics)* Zeitbasis, Ausgangszeitraum, Bezugsperiode, Basiszeitraum, -periode, *(US, excess profit)* Berechnungszeitraum; **~ price** Basis-, Einkaufs-, Grundpreis; **~ rate** Grundtarif, -gehalt, Grundtaxe, *(banking)* Überziehungskreditsatz; **guaranteed ~ rate** garantierter Mindestlohn; **~ rate of pay** Grundlohnsatz; **~ rate earnings** Grundlohnsatz; **~ salary** Grundgehalt; **~ service** *(mil.)* Bodendienst; **~ services** untergeordnete Dienste; **~ stock** eiserner Bestand, Grundvorrat; **~ stock method** Lagerbewertung zu Einkaufspreisen; **~ time** Normalarbeitszeit; **~ value** Basis-, Einstandswert; **~ wage rate** Grundlohn; **~ year** Basisjahr, *(statistics)* Vergleichsjahr.
based ansässig, *(mil.)* stationiert;
  ~ on anhand von;
  ~ cash auf Barzahlung berechnet;
  to be ~ beruhen, basieren; **to be ~ in A** in A stationiert sein; **to be ~ in a city** in einer Stadt heimisch werden; **to be ~ on mere suppositions** auf bloßen Annahmen beruhen.
basement Unterbau, Tiefparterre, Souterrain, Sockel-, Kellergeschoß;
  English ~ *(US)* Parterre[geschoß];
  ~ garage Tiefgarage; **~ shop (store, *US*)** Kellerladen[geschäft], *(department store)* Kellergeschoßabteilung.

basic grundlegend, grundsätzlich, fundamental;
~ **abatement** [Grund]freibetrag, Steuerfreibetrag; **to give** ~ **advice** einfache Auskünfte geben; ~ **agreement** Mantel-, Rahmenvertrag; ~ **allowance** Grundausstattung; ~ **amenities** soziale Grundausstattung; ~ **amount** Grundbetrag; ~ **balance of payments** Grundzahlungsbilanz; ~ **benefit** *(pension plan)* Sockelbetrag; ~ **compensation** Grundvergütung; ~ **concept** Grundkonzeption; ~ **concern** Grundanliegen; ~ **condition** Grundbegriff; ~ **contract** Grundvertrag; ~ **costs** Grundkosten ~ **course** Grundlehrgang; ~ **crops** *(US)* preisgestützte Landwirtschaftserzeugnisse; ~ **data** grundlegendes Material, statistisches Anfangsmaterial, *(time study)* Ausgangswerte; ~ **design flaws** grundlegende Konstruktionsfehler; ~ **dimensions** *(statistics)* Ausgangs-, Grundmaß; ~ **driving** *(mil.)* elementare Fahrschulung; ~ **expenditure** bleibende Unkosten; ~ **expenditure accounts** bleibende Aufwandskosten; ~ **facilities** Grundausstattung; ~ **fee** Grundgebühr, -betrag; ~ **flying training** fliegerische Grundausbildung; ~ **foods** Grundnahrungsmittel; ~ **formula** Grundformel; ~ **functions** grundsätzliche Aufgaben; ~ **hourly rate** Ecklohn; ~ **income** Grund-, Basiseinkommen; ~ **introduction** Grundeinführung; ~**s industry** Schlüssel-, Grundstoffindustrie; ~ **industry sector** Grundstoffbereich; ~ **inventory** Anfangsinventur; ~ **iron** Thomaseisen; ~ **items** Grundnahrungsmittel; ~**job factor points** Leistungsbewertungspunkte; ~ **material** Ausgangs-, Grundstoff; **industrial** ~ **materials** gewerbliche Grundstoffe; ~ **materials price** Grundstoff-, Basispreis; ~ **media concept** Grundkonzeption für den Mediaeinsatz; ~ **message** Hauptwerbegrundaussage; ~ **minimum limit of liability** Mindestgrenze für Haftungsschäden; ~ **national contract** Grundtarifvertrag; ~ **network** Hauptsendenetz einer Rundfunk-, Fernsehkette; ~ **objectives** *(establishment)* Leistungsziele; ~ **obligation** Grundverpflichtung; ~ **patent** grundlegendes Patent, Stammpatent; ~ **pay** Eck-, Grundlohn, -gehalt; ~ **pension** Grundrente; ~ **period** *(special drawing rights)* Zuteilungsperiode, *(taxation)* Veranlagungs-, Bemessungszeitraum; ~ **petrol** Benzinnormalzuteilung; ~ **piece rate** Akkord-, Stücklohn, unveränderter Stücklohnfaktor; ~ **planning** grundlegende Planung; ~ **points** *(job evaluation)* Ausgangswerte, -punkte; ~ **policy** grundsätzliche Richtlinien; **to share s. one's** ~ **position** jds. Grundeinstellung teilen; ~ **price** Basis-, Grundpreis; ~ **principles of the economy** Grundsätze der Wirtschaftsordnung; ~ **products** Grundprodukte; ~ **provisions** Grundnahrungsmittel; ~ **rate** *(advertising)* Anzeigengrundpreis, *(corporation tax, Br.)* einheitlicher Grundtarif, *(income tax)* Anfangssteuersatz, -tarif; ~ **rate of pay** Ecklohn[tarif]; ~ **rate of personal tax (income tax)** unterer Proportionalbereich der Einkommensteuertabelle; ~ **rate band of taxes** Anfangssteuersatz; ~ **rate settlement** Ecklohnregelung; ~ **ration** Grundzuteilung; ~ **reading** grundlegende Bücher; ~ **requirements** Grundvoraussetzungen; ~ **research** Grundlagenforschung; ~ **salary** Grundgehalt; ~ **scheme** Grundversorgungssystem; **to obtain** ~ **school-leaving qualification** seine Grundschulausbildung erfolgreich abgeschlossen haben; **in the** ~ **sectors** im Grundstoffbereich; ~ **size** genormte Größe, *(paper)* Mindeststärke; ~ **skills** Grundkenntnisse; ~ **standard cost** anfängliche Normalkosten; ~ **station** Hauptsendestelle; ~ **steel** Thomasstahl; ~ **stock** Grundstock; ~ **study** Grundstudium; ~ **table** Grundtabelle; ~ **training** Grundausbildung; ~ **training pattern** Ausbildungsstufen; ~ **unit** *(mil.)* Grundeinheit; ~ **value** Einheitswert eines Grundstücks; ~ **vocabulary** Basisvokabularschatz; ~ **wage** Grundlohn; ~ **wage rate** Grund-, Schicht-, Ecklohntarif; ~ **weight** *(paper)* Mindestgewicht; ~ **yield** risikofreier Ertrag.

basin *(canal)* Ausweichstelle, *(of a port)* Hafenbecken, Binnenhafen.

basing point *(long-distance rates)* Ausgangs-, Knotenpunkt;
~ **system** *(US)* Transportkostenberechnung vom Ausgangsort, Preisberechnungsverfahren auf einheitlicher Frachtbasis, Frachtausgangspunktsystem.

basing|rate Ausgangsfrachtsatz; ~ **tariff** einheitlicher Frachttarif, Streckentarif.

basis Basis, Grundlage, -stock, Fundament, *(essential)* Grund-, Hauptbestandteil, *(mil.)* Operationsbasis, *(securities)* effektiver Zinssatz eines Wertpapiers, Rendite;
on a 50/50 ~ auf paritätischer Basis; **on an equitable** ~ auf anteiliger Basis; **on a graduated** ~ auf abgestufter Basis; **on an international** ~ auf internationaler Grundlage; **on a nonpartisan** ~ auf unparteiischer Grundlage; **on a royalty** ~ gegen Zahlung einer Lizenzgebühr;
on the ~ **of facts** auf dem Boden der Tatsachen; **on a** ~ **of reciprocity** auf der Grundlage der Gegenseitigkeit;

adjusted ~ bereinigte Besteuerungsgrundlage; **annuity** ~ Rentenbasis; **armed-truce** ~ Waffenstillstandsgrundlage; **capital** ~ Kapitalbasis; **class** ~ Grundtarif; **cooperative** ~ genossenschaftliche Grundlage; **cost** ~ Bewertungsgrundlage; **gold** ~ Goldbasis; **gold-value** ~ Goldwertbasis; **insurance** ~ Versicherungsgrundlage; **legal** ~ Rechtsgrundlage; **negotiation** ~ Verhandlungsgrundlage; **profit and loss** ~ rein wirtschaftliche Grundlage; **rate** ~ Tarifgrundlage; **regional** ~ regionale Grundlage; **sound economic** ~ gesunde wirtschaftliche Grundlage;
~ **of accounting** Buchführungsmethode; ~ **of an agreement** Vertragsgrundlage; ~ **of allocation** Verteilungsschlüssel; ~ **of appointment** Bestellungsgrundlage; ~ **of assessment** steuerliche Bemessungs-, Berechnungsgrundlage; ~ **of calculation** Berechnungsgrundlage; ~ **of charge** *(bank)* Grundgebühr; ~ **of comparison** Verteilungsschlüssel, Vergleichsbasis, Vergleichsgrundlage; ~ **of compensation** Kompensationsgrundlage; ~ **of contract** Vertragsgrundlage; ~ **of discussion** Diskussionsgrundlage, -basis; ~ **of exchange** Umtauschverhältnis, Umrechnungssatz; ~ **of existence** Existenzgrundlage; ~ **of expansion** Expansionsbasis; ~ **for future development** Grundlage späterer Entwicklung; ~ **of integration** Integrationsbasis; ~ **for negotiations** Verhandlungsgrundlage; ~ **of prices** Grundlage der Preisberechnung; ~ **of rating** *(employees)* Beurteilungsgrundlage; ~ **for remuneration** Entschädigungsgrundlage; ~ **of revision** *(terms)* Revisionsgrundlage; ~ **of taxation** Besteuerungsgrundlage; ~ **of valuation** Bemessungs-, Bewertungsgrundlage;
to build up a business on a sound ~ Geschäft auf einer soliden Grundlage errichten; **to form the** ~ **of a patent** Patentgrundlage abgeben; **to have a** ~ **in fact** auf Tatsachen beruhen; **to operate on a nonprofit** ~ gemeinnützig arbeiten; **to serve as a** ~ als Grundlage dienen; **to spread its business** ~ Grundlage eines Unternehmens verbreitern; **to take as** ~ zugrunde legen; **to work on a cost-sharing** ~ auf der Basis der Kostenteilung zusammenarbeiten;
~ **obligation** Grundverpflichtung; ~ **rate** *(fire insurance)* Grundtarif, *(income tax)* Anfangssteuersatz; ~ **region** *(EC)* Basisregion.

basket Korb, *(statistics)* Warenkorb, *(mining)* Baggereimer;
made-in-USA ~ selbstgestricktes Nähkörbchen; **shopping** ~ Einkaufstasche; **waste-paper** ~ Papierkorb;
~ **of commodities** *(statistics)* Warenkorb; ~ **of available commodities** Wareneinkaufsangebot; ~ **of currencies** Währungskorb;
~ *(v.)* in den Papierkorb werfen;
to make up a ~ milde Gaben sammeln;
~ **cart** Einkaufswägelchen; ~ **case** Bein-, Armamputierter, *(fig.)* Torso; ~ **clause** *(US)* Generalklausel; ~ **dinner (lunch)** *(US)* Picknick; ~ **meeting** Picknickausflug.

bastard Bastard, uneheliches Kind;
special ~ nachträglich legitimiertes Kind; ~ **child** uneheliches Kind, Bastard; ~ **title** *(print.)* Schmutztitel; ~ **type** *(print.)* Bastardschrift.

bastardization *(US)* Unehelichkeitserklärung.

bastardize *(v.)* *(US)* für unehelich erklären.

bastardy *(US)* uneheliche Geburt;
~ **case** *(US)* Vaterschafts-, Alimentenprozeß; ~ **order** *(US)* Unterhaltsurteil; ~ **process** Unehelichkeitsverfahren.

bat Knüttel, Stock, *(mil.)* radargelenkte Gleitbombe, *(US sl.)* Kneiptour, Bierreise;
off one's own ~ ohne fremde Hilfe;
to go on a ~ *(US sl.)* Kneiptour machen; **to go to** ~ **for s. o.** für j. eintreten; **to have** ~**s in the belfry** einen Vogel haben; **to play off one's own** ~ auf eigenen Füßen stehen.

batch *(book trade)* Partie, *(group of persons)* Gruppe, *(processing)* gleichzeitig verarbeitete Papiermenge, Produktions-, Liefermenge;
attractive ~ Reizpartie;
~ **of extra benefits** Bündel von Sondervergünstigungen; ~ **of letters** Stoß Briefe; ~ **of prisoners** Trupp Gefangener;
~ **completion** *(book trade)* Partieergänzung; ~ **completion period** Partieergänzungszeitraum; ~ **processing** stapelweises Abarbeiten von Programmen, Schub-, Stapelverarbeitung; ~ **production** Serienproduktion; ~ **size** Serienumfang; ~ **system** System zur beschleunigten Prüfung von Eingängen am Kassenschalter.

bath Bad, *(bathroom)* Badezimmer;
~ **chair** Krankenstuhl; ~**s department** Bäderamt; ~ **paper** feines Briefpapier.

bathing establishment Badeanstalt.

bathroom, private *(hotel)* eigenes Bad.
baton *(Br.)* Gummiknüppel;
~ **in the knapsack** Marschallstab im Tornister;
to make a ~ charge mit dem Gummiknüppel vorgehen.
batter beschädigter Buchstabe;
~ *(v.)* beschädigen;
~ **down** zusammenschießen.
battered | letters *(print.)* lädierte (beschädigte) Buchstaben; ~
pavement abgetretenes Pflaster; ~ **veteran** altgedienter Soldat.
battery *(el.)* Batterie, *(intelligence test)* mehrfache Intelligenzprüfungen, *(law)* tätlicher Angriff, Tätlichkeit, Körperverletzung, *(mil.)* Batterie;
B ~ Anodenbatterie; **run-down ~** erschöpfte Batterie; **simple ~**
leichte Körperverletzung;
assault and ~ of a high and aggravated nature schwere
Körperverletzung;
to boost a ~ Batterie kurzzeitig stark laden;**to recharge a ~**
Batterie aufladen; **to run down a ~** Batterie erschöpfen; **to**
short-circuit a ~ Batterie kurzschließen;
~ **cell** Batterieelement; ~ **charger** Ladegerät; ~ **charging station**
Batterieladestelle; ~ **life** Lebensdauer einer Batterie; ~
operated batteriebetrieben; ~**-operated set** Batterieempfänger.
battle Kampfhandlung, Gefecht, Schlacht;
pitched ~ offene Feldschlacht;
~ **of export** Exportschlacht; ~ **of life** Lebenskampf; ~ **of retreat**
Rückzugsgefecht; ~ **of words** Wortgefecht;
to die in ~ kämpfend fallen; **to fight s. one's ~** jds. Sache
vertreten; **to fight one's own ~** sich allein durchschlagen; **to**
fight a losing ~ hoffnungslosen Kampf führen; **to run into ~**
Auseinandersetzungen haben;
~ **area** Gefechtsbereich; ~ **array** Schlachtordnung; ~ **clasp**
(mil.) Erinnerungsspange; ~ **cruiser** Schlachtkreuzer; ~ **dress**
Kampfanzug; ~ **fatigue** Kriegsneurose; ~ **field** Schlachtfeld; ~
fleet Schlachtflotte; ~ **lantern** Gefechtslaterne; ~ **order**
Schlachtordnung; ~ **plane** Front-, Schlachtflugzeug.
battleship Schlacht-, Linienschiff.
battue Razzia.
bawd Kupplerin.
bawdy house Bordell.
bay Bai, Bucht, *(airplane)* Zelle [im Flugzeugrumpf], *(fix)*
Klemme, Verlegenheit, verzweifelte Lage, *(railway)* Seitenbahnsteig, *(ship)* Schiffslazarett;
waving ~ Abschiedsbahnsteig;
~ **of masonry** Wandfach;
to carry off the ~s Lorbeeren ernten; **to hold (keep) at ~** in
Schach halten; **to stand at ~** zum Äußersten getrieben sein;
~ **window** Erkerfenster; ~ **work** Fachwerk.
bazaar Basar, Kaufhalle, *(fair for a charitable object)*
Wohltätigkeitsbasar;
~ **bargaining** Feilscherei.
bazooka Panzerbüchse-, faust.
beach Ufer, Strand;
sandy ~ Sandstrand;
~ *(v.)* **a ship** Schiff auf den Strand laufen lassen;
to be on the ~ *(sl.)* heruntergekommen sein; **to run on the ~** auf
den Strand laufen (auflaufen) lassen;
~ **area** Strandgebiet; ~ **drifting** Küstenversetzung; ~ **wagon**
(US) Kombiwagen.
beachcomber Strandgutjäger.
beachfront Küstenfront.
beachhead *(fig.)* ausbaufähige Anfangsposition, *(mil.)* Lande-,
Brückenkopf.
beaching a ship Stranden eines Schiffes.
beachman Strandarbeiter.
beachmaster *(mil.)* Landungsoffizier.
beacon Grenzmarkierungsmarke, *(aeronautics)* Funkfeuer,
-bake, *(fig.)* Fanal, *(mar.)* Leuchtfeuer, -turm, landfestes Seezeichen, *(pedesrtrian traffic Br.)* Verkehrszeichen für Fußgänger, Fußgänger-, Verkehrsampel;
flashing ~ *(Br.)* gelbes Blinklicht; **nondirectional ~** ungerichtetes Funkfeuer; **traffic ~** *(Br.)* Verkehrszeichen, -ampel;
~ *(v.)* mit Baken versehen;
~ **buoy** Bakentonne, Leuchtboje; ~ **course** Peilstrahl; ~ **light**
Leuchtfeuer.
beaconage Tonnen-, Bakengeld.
beaconing *(mar.)* Bebakung.
beaded tyre Wulstreifen.
beadle Gerichtsdiener, *(university)* Pedell.
beagle *(fig.)* Spürhund, Spion.
beam *(aeronautics)* Gleit-, Landungsstrahl, *(loudspeaker)* erfaßter Bereich;

off [the] ~ *(sl.)* auf dem Holzweg; **on the** ~ *(sl.)* auf Draht;
~ *(v.)* mit Richtstrahler senden, ausstrahlen, *(plane)* mit Funkleitstrahl führen;
~ **out a program(me)** Sendung ausstrahlen;
to be off the ~ völlig danebenliegen; **to come in on the** ~ auf dem
Richtstrahl anfliegen; **to fly the** ~ auf dem gefunkten Kurs
steuern; **to get on the** ~ *(radio sl.)* sich mikrophongerecht
hinstellen; **to stay on the** ~ auf Empfang bleiben;
~ **aerial (antenna)** Richtstrahler; **to be at one's ~ -ends** in einer
finanziellen Misere sein, auf dem letzten Loch pfeifen, pleite
sein; ~**-rider guidance** Funkleitstrahlsystem, Leitstrahlfeuerung; ~ **system** Leitstrahl-, Richtstrahlsystem; ~ **width** *(television)* Bündeldurchschnitt.
bean *(sl.)* Münze, Geldstück;
~**s** Moneten;
old ~ *(Br., sl.)* altes Haus;
to be full of ~s *(sl.)* lebenssprühend sein; **not to have a ~** keinen
roten Heller haben; **not to know one's ~s** *(US)* nicht die leiseste
Ahnung besitzen; **to spill the ~s** *(US sl.)* aus der Schule
plaudern;
~ **feast** Freudenfest.
bear *(fig.)* Tolpatsch, *(stock exchange)* Baissespekulant, Baissier,
Fixer;
~**s** *(US)* rückläufige Kurse;
~ *(v.)* tragen, führen, *(stock exchange)* fixen, auf Baisse
spekulieren;
~ **all before one** alles mit sich reißen; ~ **arms** waffenfähig sein; ~
arms against Krieg führen; ~ **an assertion** Behauptung bestätigen; ~ **away the palm** Sieg davontragen; ~ **away the prize** Preis
gewinnen; ~ **s.o. company** jem. Gesellschaft leisten; ~ **the costs**
Kosten bestreiten (tragen); ~ **the damage** für den Schaden
aufkommen; ~ **the date of** datiert sein vom; ~ **s. with dignity**
in difficult circumtances schwierige Lage mit Würde meistern;
~ **evidence** Zeugnis ablegen; ~ **the expenses** Kosten tragen; ~ **s.**
o. a hand jem. zur Hand gehen; ~ **inspection** sich sehen lassen
können; ~ **interest** Zinsen bringen; ~ **interest at ... per cent** sich
mit ...% verzinsen, mit ...% verzinslich sein; ~ **with the land**
(ship) auf Land zuhalten; ~ **to the left** links halten; ~ **a loss**
Verlust tragen; ~ **the market** Baisse herbeizuführen trachten; ~
in mind berücksichtigen; ~ **the name** Namen führen; ~ **an office**
Amt innehaben; ~ **out an assertion** Aussage (Behauptung)
bestätigen; ~ **out a statement** Erklärung bestätigen; ~ **a propor**
tion to in einem Verhältnis stehen; ~ **reference to** Bezug haben; ~
~ **the responsibility** Verantwortung tragen; ~ **sail** *(fig.)* erfolgreich sein; ~ **low sail** bescheiden auftreten; ~ **to sea** in See
stechen; ~ **a sense** Bedeutung haben; ~ **s. one's signature** mit
jds. Unterschrift versehen sein, jds. Unterschrift tragen; ~ **the**
stocks auf Baisse spekulieren, Kurse drücken; ~ **testimony**
Zeugnis ablegen; ~ **with s. o.** jem. geduldig zuhören; ~ **witness**
bezeugen, Zeugnis ablegen; ~ **false witness** falsches Zeugnis
ablegen;
to bring to ~ upon einwirken lassen; **to go a ~** *(Br.)* auf Baisse
spekulieren; **to raid the ~s** *(Br.)* sich in einer Baisse eindecken;
to sell a ~ *(Br.)* fixen, konterminieren;
~ *(a.)* *(market)* flau, lustlos, *(prices)* fallend;
~ **account** *(Br.)* Baisseposition, -engagement; **to take in a ~**
account *(Br.)* Baisseposition hereinnehmen; ~ **campaign**
Angriff der Baissepartei; ~ **clique** Baissepartei; ~ **covering**
Deckungskäufe der Baissepartei; ~ **garden** lärmende Versammlung; ~ **leader** Bärenführer, Reisebegleiter; ~ **market**
Baisse; ~ **operation** Baissespekulation; ~ **point** Baissemoment;
~ **pool** Vereinigung zu spekulativen Zwecken; ~ **position** Baisseposition; ~ **raid** Baissemanöver; ~**rumours** *(Br.)* Baissegerüchte; ~ **sale** *(Br.)* Baisseverkauf, Leerverkauf; ~ **seller** *(Br.)*
Baisse-, Leerverkäufer; ~ **speculation** Baissespekulationen; ~
transaction *(Br.)* Baissegeschäft.
bearable erträglich.
bearer Träger, *(bringer)* Überbringer, *(holder)* [Wechsel-,
Vollmachts-]inhaber, *(presenter of bill)* Vorzeiger, Präsentant, *(printing)* Druckleiste;
made out to ~ auf den Inhaber lautend; **payable to ~** an den
Überbringer zahlbar;
office ~ Amtsträger;
~ **of a bill** Wechselinhaber; ~ **of a cheque** *(Br.)* **(check, US)**
Scheckinhaber; ~ **of this letter** Überbringer dieses Briefes; ~
of a passport Paßinhaber; ~ **of the present** Überbringer des
Geschenks;
to issue (make out) to ~ auf den Inhaber ausstellen; **to turn into**
a ~ cheque *(Br.)* in einen Inhaberscheck umwandeln;
~ **bond** Inhaberobligation, -schuldverschreibung; ~ **certificate**
Inhaberzertifikat; ~ **cheque** *(Br.)* **(check, US)** Inhaberscheck; ~

clause Überbringerklausel; ~ **company** *(mil.)* Sanitätskompanie; ~ **debenture** Inhaberschuldverschreibung; ~'s **fee** Botenlohn; **in** ~ **form** auf den Überbringer lautend; ~ **instrument** Inhaberpapier; ~ **loan** Inhaberanleihe; ~ **policy** Inhaberpolice; ~ **scrip** Interimschein; ~ **securities** auf den Inhaber ausgestellte Wertpapiere, Inhaberpapiere; ~ **share** Inhaberaktie; ~ **stock** *(US)* Inhaberaktie; ~ **warrant** Anweisung auf den Inhaber.

beard *(letter)* Fleisch.

bearing *(conduct)* Benehmen, Verhalten, Betragen, *(influence)* Einfluß, *(nautical)* Orientierungszeichen, *(purport)* Bedeutung, Tragweite, *(radio)* Funkpeilung, *(tendency)* Orientierung, Tendenz;
~s Aspekte, Beziehungen, Sachverhalt;
true ~ *(fig.)* wahrer Sachverhalt;
~ *(a.)* auf Baisse spekulierend;
fixed interest ~ festverzinslich;
to bring s. o. to his ~ jem. den Kopf zurechtrücken; **to consider a matter in all its** ~s Sache von allen Seiten beleuchten; **to have a** ~ **on** im Zusammenhang stehen mit, von Bedeutung sein; **to have a strong** ~ **on** große Bedeutung haben für, enge Beziehungen haben mit; **to lose one's** ~s seine Orientierung verlieren, sich verirren; **to take one's** ~s orten, *(fig.)* sich orientieren;
~ **date of** datiert vom; ~ **4 per cent** 4prozentig; ~ **interest** verzinslich; ~ **no interest** unverzinslich;
~ **compass** Peilkompaß; ~ **direction** Peilrichtung.

bearish *(stock exchange)* baissetendenziös, auf Baisse gerichtet;
to be ~ **about unemployment** Arbeitslosenentwicklung negativ beurteilen;
~ **attitude** Baissehaltung; ~ **covering** Deckungskäufe der Kontermine; ~ **demonstration** *(Br.)* Baisseangriff; ~ **market** Baissemarkt; ~ **mood** Baissestimmung; ~ **operation** Baissespekulation, -manöver; ~ **sale** Blankoabgabe; ~ **speculation** Baissespekulation; ~ **tendency (tone)** Baissetendenz, -strömung.

bearishness Baissestimmung.

beast Tier, *(farming)* Vieh, *(fig.)* brutaler Mensch;
~ **of burden** Lasttier; ~ **of the chase** jagdbares Wild, Jagdwild; ~ **of a fellow** Bestie in Menschengestalt; ~s **of the plow** *(US)* plough, *Br.)* Pflugtiere.

beastliness Brutalität, *(coll.)* Scheußlichkeit.

beastly tierisch, viehisch, brutal;
~ **weather** Hundewetter.

beat Schlag, *(fig.)* [geistiger] Horizont, Gesichtskreis, *(patrol)* Streife, Runde, Rundgang, *(US, piece of news)* sensationelle Erstmeldung, Alleinmeldung, *(of policeman)* Revier, *(precinct)* Bezirk;
dead ~ *(Australia, sl.)* unsicherer Kunde;
~ *(v.)* *(price)* herabdrücken, *(US sl.)* beschummeln, reinlegen;
~ **the air** offene Türen einrennen; ~ **the band** *(sl.)* dem Faß den Boden ausschlagen; ~ **one's brains about** *(sl.)* sich über etw. den Kopf zerbrechen; ~ **about the bush** auf den Busch klopfen, sondieren; ~ **at the door** an die Tür klopfen; ~ **down** niederschlagen, *(seller)* herunter-, abhandeln; ~ **down a price** Preis drücken; ~ **the gun** *(US)* Aktien vor Börsenzulassung zum Verkauf anbieten; ~ **s. o. hands down** j. mit Leichtigkeit schlagen; ~ **the living hell out of s. o.** j. windelweich schlagen; ~ **hollow** vernichtend aufs Haupt schlagen; ~**it** *(US sl.)* abhauen, verduften; ~ **out a fire** Feuer austreten; ~ **a parley** klein beigeben; ~ **a proof** Korrekturbogen abziehen, Bürstenabzug machen; ~ **s. one's quarters** *(fig.)* j. überfallen; ~ **the record** Rekord brechen (schlagen); ~ **a retreat** *(fig.)* sich zurückziehen; ~ **s. o. into space** jem. im Weltraum zuvorkommen; ~ **up** zusammenschlagen, Rekruten *(mil.)* werben; ~ **one's way** *(US)* per Anhalter reisen;
to be off (out of) one's ~ außerhalb seines üblichen Wirkungskreises tätig werden; **to be on one's** ~ seine Runde machen; **to traverse one's** ~ seine *(US)* Runde machen;
[dead-] ~ *(a.)* *(Br.)* erschöpft, erschossen;
~ **-up** abgenutzt;
~ **frequency** Überlagerungsfrequenz; ~ **receiver** Überlagerungsempfänger; ~ **reception** Überlagerungsempfang.

beaten | track *(fig.)* üblicher Weg; **out off the** ~ **track** ungewöhnlich; ~ **zone** *(mil.)* bestrichener Raum.

beating | of the grounds Abschreiten der Gemeindegrenze;
to take a ~ strapaziöse Behandlung aushalten.

beatnik Nonkonformist, Bohemien.

beautician *(US)* Kosmetiker, Schönheitspfleger.

beauty *(coll.)* Prachtexemplar;
~ **aid** Schönheitspflegemittel; ~ **contest** Schönheitswettbewerb; ~ **farm** Schönheitspflegestätte; ~ **mark** attraktive Sehenswürdigkeit; ~ **shop (parlo(u)r)** Schönheitssalon; ~**queen** Schönheitskönigin; ~**spot** *(fig.)* Schönheitsfehler.

beck and call, to be at s. one's jem. auf den leisesten Wink gehorchen.

become *(v.)* werden, *(happen)* sich ereignen;
~ **due** fällig werden; ~ **effektive (operative)** in Kraft treten; ~ **extinct** *(firm)* erlöschen; ~ **final (valid)** rechtskräftig werden.

becoming schicklich, passend.

bed Bett, *(lodging)* Logis, Schlafstätte, Unterkunft, *(print.)* Zurichtung [der Druckform];
truckle ~ Ausziehbett, -liege;
~ **of concrete** Betonunterlage;
to be taken to ~ **with an illness** durch eine Krankheit ans Bett gefesselt sein; **to get out of** ~ **on the wrong side** mit dem linken Bein zuerst aufstehen;
~ **and board** Unterkunft und Verpflegung; ~ **and breakfast operation** *(Br.)* Verkauf und gleichzeitiger Rückkauf von Aktien; ~ **piece** *(bank notes)* Druckplatte; ~**-ridden** bettlägerig; ~**-sitting room** *(Br.)* Wohnschlafzimmer.

bedfellow Schlafkamerad;
to make strange ~s schlechte Gesellschaft darstellen.

bedrock *(fig.)* Grundlage, Fundament;
to get down to ~ der Sache auf den Grund gehen.

bedroom Schlafzimmer;
spare ~ Gästezimmer;
~ **community** *(US)* Wohnvorort.

bedside | manners, to have good *(doctor)* Patienten zu nehmen wissen; ~ **teaching** Unterricht am Krankenbett.

bedsitter Wohnschlafzimmer.

bee *(US)* Nachbarschaftshilfe;
to have a ~ **in one's bonnet** *(sl.)* einen Vogel haben;
~ **line** Luftlinie.

beef *(US sl.)* Meckerei, Nörgelei, Flausen im Kopf;
~ *(v.)* **about** *(fam.)* nörgeln, meckern, sich beschweren;
~ *(v.)* **up the industry** Industrie fördern; ~ **up a plant** *(sl.)* Betrieb Fett ansetzen lassen.

beep *(mil.)* kleiner Jeep, *(tel.)* Hinweissignal.

beer Bier;
bottled ~ Flaschenbier; **canned** ~ Bier in Dosen; **draught** ~ Bier vom Faß; **table** ~ helles Bier;
not all ~ **and skittles** *(Br.)* kein reines Vergnügen;
to think no small ~ **of o. s.** sich große Stücke einbilden;
~ **bottle** Bierflasche; ~ **brewer** Bierbrauer; ~ **cellar** Bierkeller; ~ **garden** Gartenlokal; ~ **glass** Bierglas; ~ **mat** Bierdeckel; ~ **mug** Bierkrug; ~ **money** *(Br.)* Trinkgeld; ~ **tax** Biersteuer.

beerhouse *(Br.)* Bierausschank, -lokal, -wirtschaft.

beetle boat *(Br.)* flaches Landungsboot.

befit *(v.)* sich schicken (geziemen).

befitting geziemend.

beg | for alms betteln; ~ **one's pardon** um Verzeihung bitten; ~ **the question** dem wahren Sachverhalt ausweichen.

begetting *(progeny)* Nachkommenschaft.

beggar Bedürftiger, Bettler;
~ **on horseback** Emporkömmling, Parvenue;
~**-my-neighbo(u)r policy** Leistungsbilanzüberschußpolitik.

beggary Bettlertum, Bettelei;
to reduce s. o. to ~ j. an den Bettelstab bringen.

begging Bettelei;
~**letter** Bettelbrief;
to go ~ betteln gehen.

begin *(v.)* beginnen, einleiten;
not to ~ **to do** nicht im Traum daran denken.

beginner Anlernling.

beginning Beginn, Anfang;
at the ~ **of April** Anfang April; **from the** ~ von Beginn (Anfang) an;
first ~s erste Ansätze;
~ **of the end** Anfang vom Ende; ~ **of the term** Semesterbeginn; ~ **investment** Gründungseinlage; ~ **point** Ausgangspunkt.

beguiler Betrüger.

behalf, on ~ **of** im Namen von, zugunsten;
for and on the ~ **of** für und im Auftrag von.

behave *(v.)* sich anständig benehmen.

behavio(u)r Verhalten, Einstellung, Betragen, Benehmen;
during good ~ *(judge)* auf Lebenszeit;
crowd ~ Massenverhalten; **good** ~ gute Führung, Wohlverhalten;
~ **of an animal** tierisches Verhalten; ~ **of the party** Parteiverhalten;
to be on one's best ~ sich von der besten Seite zeigen;
~ **control** Verhaltenskontrolle; ~ **document** Verhaltensdokumente; ~ **model** Verhaltensmodell; ~ **observation (research)** Verhaltensforschung; ~ **pattern** Verhaltensweise; ~ **psychol-**

ogy Verhaltenspsychologie; ~ **science** Verhaltenswissenschaft; ~ **space** Handlungsspielraum.

behavio(u)ral | adaptation Verhaltensanpassung; ~ **science** Verhaltensforschung; ~ **scientist** Verhaltensforscher; ~ **study** Verhaltensforschung; ~ **theory of a firm** verhaltensorientierte Unternehmenstheorie.

behavio(u)rist Verhaltensforscher.

behind hinterher, zurück, *(in arrears)* im Rückstand;
~ **the scenes** hinter den Kulissen;
to be ~ with one's payments mit seinen Zahlungen im Rückstand sein; **to be ~ with one's schedule** mit seinem Arbeitspensum im Rückstand sein; **to be ~ with one's work** mit seiner Arbeit im Rückstand sein; **to get left ~** Anschluß verlieren.

behindhand im Rückstand, *(badly off)* heruntergekommen, *(behind the times)* rückständig;
to be ~ with one's payments mit seinen Zahlungen im Rückstand sein; **to be ~ with one's rent** mit der Miete im Rückstand sein; **to be ~ with one's work** mit seiner Arbeit im Rückstand sein.

behoof Vorteil, Nutzen.

being Existenz, Wesen;
in ~ existent;
human ~ Mensch;
to call into ~ ins Leben rufen; **to come into ~** sich konstituieren.

beleaguer *(v.)* belagern;
to grow more ~d mehr und mehr in Schwierigkeiten kommen.

beleaguerer Belagerer.

beleagerment Belagerung.

belief Glaube, Überzeugung, Religion;
to the best of my knowledge and ~ nach bestem Wissen und Gewissen; **without ~ in its truth** *(prospectus)* ohne von der Wahrheit überzeugt zu sein.

believer in competition Verfechter des Wettbewerbsgedankens.

belittle *(v.)* verkleinern, herabsetzen, schwächen.

belittlement Herabsetzung, Schmälerung.

bell Klingel, Glocke, Schelle *(ship)* Schiffsglocke;
as sound as a ~ gesund wie ein Fisch; **with ~s on** aufgetakelt, in Gala; **diving ~** Taucherglocke; **to ~ the cat** mit dem Feuer spielen;
to bear the ~ ersten Platz einnehmen; **to carry away the ~** Preis davontragen; **to curse s. o. with ~, book and candle** j. mit Verwünschungen überhäufen; **to ring a ~** *(fam.)* Erinnerungen wecken; **to ring the ~** Nagel auf den Kopf, ins Schwarze treffen; ~ **ringing** Glockengeläut; ~ **tent** Gruppenzelt; ~ **transformer** Klingeltransformator.

bellboy *(US)* Page, Laufjunge.

bellhop *(US sl.)* Hotelpage.

bellicose kriegshetzerisch.

belligerence Kriegsführung.

belligerency Kriegszustand.

belligerent kriegführend, kriegerisch;
~ **occupation** kriegerische Besetzung; ~ **power** kriegsführende Macht; ~ **rights** Rechte eines kriegsführenden Staates.

belly | land *(v.)* Bauchlandung machen;
~ **landing** Bauchlandung.

bellyload Flugzeugladung.

bellytank Rumpfabwurfbehälter.

belong *(v.)* gehören, *(US)* Wohnrecht haben.

belongingness *(worker)* Zugehörigkeit.

belongings Habe, Habseligkeiten, Besitz, Sachen.
all one's ~ das ganze Vermögen, seine sieben Sachen; **personal ~** persönliche Habe.

below *(at foot of page)* untenstehend;
~ **the line** *(balance sheet)* unter dem Strich;
the court ~ das untere Gericht.

belt Streifen, Zone, *(geography)* Meerenge;
green ~ *(city)* Grüngürtel;
~ **of sharpness** *(photo)* Tiefenschärfebereich;
to have s. th. under one's ~ etw. vorzuweisen (aufzuweisen) haben; **to hit below the ~** unfair behandeln; **to pull one's ~ together** seinen Gürtel enger schnallen; **to tighten one's ~** another hole seinen Gürtel noch ein Loch enger schnallen;
~ **conveyor** Förderband; ~ **conveyor road** *(mining)* Förderbandstrecke; ~ **line** *(US)* Verkehrsgürtel; ~ **system of production** Produktion am laufenden Band; ~ **road** parallel verlaufende Straße; ~ **tightening** sparsames Wirtschaften.

bench Arbeitstisch, -bank, Werkbank, *(judge)* Richtersitz, *(judge taken collectively)* Richterschaft, Kollegium, *(parl.)* Abgeordnetenbank, -sitz, -platz;
on the ~ als Richter tätig;
the ~ Richterstand;

back ~es hintere Sitzreihe; **common law ~** *(Br.)* Gericht erster Instanz; **Front Opposition ~** *(Br.)* Oppositionsbank; **magistrate's ~** Richterbank; ~es **opposite** Oppositionsbänke; **Queen's ~** Oberhofgericht; **testing ~** Prüfstand; **Treasury ~** *(Br.)* Regierungsbank; **witness ~** Zeugenbank;
~ *(v.)* in ein Amt einsetzen, *(judge)* Richtersitz einnehmen;
to be elected to the ~ zum Richter ernannt werden; **to be on the ~es** dem Richterstand angehören; **to be raised to the ~es** *(Br.)* zum Richter ernannt werden; **to play to empty ~es** vor leeren Bänken spielen;
~ **show** Kleintierausstellung, -schau; ~ **warrant** richterlicher Haftbefehl.

benchers Werkbankarbeiter, *(Inn of Court, Br.)* älteres Mitglied.

bend Kurve;
the ~s *(fam.)* Luftdruckkrankheit;
to go on a ~ *(sl.)* auf eine Sauftour gehen.

benefaction Wohltätigkeit.

benefactor Wohltäter, *(donator)* Schenker.

benefice Pfründe;
to collate (appoint) to a ~ Pfründe verleihen.

beneficence Wohltätigkeit, *(settlement)* Schenkung, Stiftung.

beneficial vorteilhaft, nützlich, zuträglich, günstig, *(deriving a benefit)* nutznießend;
~ **to business** einträglich, vorteilhaft; ~ **to the health** gesundheitsfördernd;
~ **association** wohltätige Gesellschaft, Unterstützungsverein; ~ **enjoyment** Nießbrauchrecht; ~ **estate** Anwartschaftsrecht; **to obtain ~ experience in a profession** kostenlose Berufserfahrungen sammeln; ~ **improvements** Schönheitsreparaturen; ~ **interest** Nutznießung, Nießbrauch[recht], Begünstigtenrecht, *(certificate)* Begünstigungszertifikat, *(corporation)* Eigenkapital, *(insurance)* Versicherungsanspruch des Begünstigten; ~ **interest in possession** nutzungsberechtigter Besitz; ~ **occupant** Nießbrauchberechtigter; ~ **owner** materieller (wirtschaftlicher) Eigentümer, *(trust)* Treugeber; ~ **ownership** wirtschaftliches (materielles) Eigentum; ~ **property** Nießbrauch an einem Vermögen; ~ **service** kostenlose Nutznießung; ~ **society** Unterstützungsverein auf Gegenseitigkeit; ~ **use** Gebrauch nach Gutdünken.

beneficially | entitled aus eigenem Recht zustehend;
to be ~ interested materieller Rechtsinhaber sein.

beneficiary Begünstigter, *(insurance)* Versicherungsnehmer, Leistungsberechtigter, *(last will)* Vermächtnisnehmer, *(law)* Nießbraucher, Nutznießer, Nutzungsberechtigter, *(life annuity)* Forderungs-, Bezugsberechtigter, *(loan)* Kreditnehmer, -empfänger, *(postal service)* Empfänger einer Geldsendung, *(trust)* Bedachter, Berechtigter, Treuhandbegünstigter, Stipendiat;
authorized ~ Empfangsberechtigter; **donee ~** Drittbegünstigter, Begünstigter eines Vertrages zugunsten Dritter; **income ~** Einkommensbegünstigter; **primary ~** Hauptnutznießer, *(life annuitant)* Rentenempfänger; **rightful ~** Empfangsberechtigter, Begünstigter; **third-party ~** Begünstigter eines Vertrages zugunsten Dritter; **ultimate ~** wirklicher (eigentlicher) Begünstigter;
~ **under a guarantee** Garantiebegünstigter; ~ **in a provident fund** Bezugsberechtigter einer Versorgungsstiftung; ~ **of insurance** Versicherungsberechtigter, Begünstigter eines Versicherungsvertrages; ~ **of a letter of credit** Kreditbriefinhaber; ~ **under a settlement** Begünstigter einer Stiftung (Vermögensverwaltung); ~ **under a will** testamentarisch Bedachter;
~ **association** Unterstützungsverein; ~ **heir** Erbe mit Beschränkung auf das Nachlaßverzeichnis; ~ **owner** Nießbraucher; ~ **student** Stipendiat.

benefit *(advantage)* Vergünstigung, Vorteil, Wohltat, *(insurance)* Versicherungsleistung, *(social insurance)* Leistung, Rente, *(pecuniary aid)* Unterstützung, Beihilfe, Zuschuß, *(privilege)* Vorrecht, Privileg[ium], *(profit)* Nutzen, Gewinn, *(social security)* Unterstützung, *(theater)* Wohltätigkeitsveranstaltung, *(valuable consideration)* Vertragsinteresse;
for the ~ of zugunsten von; **for the public ~** im öffentlichen Interesse; **for the ~ of charity** für wohltätige Zwecke; **for the ~ of a company** zum Nutzen einer Gesellschaft; **for the ~ of a third party** zugunsten eines Dritten; **in pecuniary ~** in gewinnsüchtiger Absicht; **while drawing ~s** während des Bezuges von Leistungen;
~s *(factory)* Sozialeinrichtungen;
accident ~ Unfallentschädigung, -versicherungsleistung; **additional ~** Zusatzunterstützung; **basic ~** Grundleistung, Sockelbetrag; **comprehensive ~s** umfassende Sondervergünsti-

gungen; **death** ~ Sterbegeld, Hinterbliebenenrente; **definite** ~ festgesetzte Pensionszahlung; **disability (disablement,** *Br.*) ~ Versehrten-, Invalidenrente, *(insurance, US)* Erwerbsunfähigkeitsrente; **long-term disability** ~sRentenleistungen im Invaliditätsfall; **short-term disability** ~s Lohn- und Gehaltsfortzahlungen im Krankheitsfall; **dismemberment** ~ Rentenzahlung bei Gliederverlust; **drainage** ~ auf Meliorationen beruhender Wertzuwachs; **earnings-related** ~ lohnabhängige Arbeitslosenhilfe, Sozialversicherungsleistung; **extended** ~ *(unemployment insurance, Br.)* ins Ermessen gestellte weitere Arbeitslosenunterstützung; **extra** ~ Sondervergünstigung; **family** ~ Sozialzulage, Familienbeihilfe; **financial** ~ Vermögensvorteil; **flatrate** ~ *(social insurance)* Pauschalleistung; **forfeited** ~ in Fortfall gekommene Unterstützungsleistung; **fringe** ~ Sonder-, Nebenvergütung, zusätzliche Vergütung; *(director)* Aufwandsentschädigung, Gewinnbeteiligung, *(employee)* betriebliche Vergünstigungen, freiwillige Lohnneben-, Sozialleistungen; **funeral** ~ Sterbegeld; **general** ~ *(inprovements)* Wertzuwachs, *(real estate)* Meliorations-, Wertsteigerungs-, Nachbarschaftsgewinn; **hospital** ~ Krankenhauszuschuß; **immediate** ~ *(insurance)* sofortiger Versicherungsschutz; **industrial injury** ~ *(Br.)* Betriebsunfallrente, Rente im Fall einer Berufskrankheit; **insurance** ~ Versicherungsleistung; **invalidity** ~ Arbeitsunfähigkeitsrente; **layoff** ~ Entlassungsentschädigung, Abfindung; **legal** ~ Rechtsvorteil; **like** ~s entsprechende Vergünstigungen; **long-term** ~ erst in der Zukunft sich auswirkender Vorteil; **material** ~ erheblicher Vorteil; **maternity** ~ Wochengeld, -hilfe; **means-tested** ~ von einer Bedürftigkeitsprüfung abhängige Beihilfe, einer Bedürftigkeitsüberprüfung unterliegende Sozialzulage; **medical** ~s *(insurance)* ärztliche Leistungen; **minimum** ~ Mindestunterstützungssatz; **monthly retirement** ~ monatliche Altersrente; **national insurance dependency** ~s *(Br.)* Sozialzuschläge für Kinder; **noncontributory** ~s beitragsfreie Leistungen (Vergünstigungen); **old-age insurance** ~ *(US)* Altersrente; **out-of-work** ~ Arbeitslosenunterstützung; **package** ~ tarifliche Sondervergütung; **pecuniary** ~ materieller (finanzieller) Vorteil, Vermögensvorteil; **pension** ~ *(US)* Pensionszuwendung, Ruhegehalt; **personal** ~ persönlicher Vorteil; **post-employment** ~ Pensionszahlung; **preferential** ~ *(US)* Vorweg-, Vorausentnahme; **primary** ~ *(US)* Alters-, Grundrente; **promised** ~bedungene Leistung; **pro rata** ~ Anspruch in Höhe des Anteils; **public** ~ Gemeinwohl; **public assistance** ~s *(US)* Leistungen der Sozialversicherung; **recurring** ~s wiederkehrende Nutzungen; **retirement** ~ *(US)* Pensionsbezüge, Ruhegeld, Altersversorgung; **secondary** ~s zusätzliche Vergünstigungen; **severance** ~ Trennungsgeld, Abfindung, Abschlußzahlung bei Pensionierung; **sickness** ~ *(Br.)* Krankengeld, Leistungen im Krankheitsfall; **social security** ~s *(US)* Sozialversicherungsleistungen; **social welfare** ~ *(US)* [Fürsorgeleistungen aus der] Sozialhilfe; **special** ~ Enteignungsentschädigung; **standard** ~ Einheitsunterstützungssatz; **subsistence** ~Unterhaltsbeihilfe; **supplementary** ~ *(Br.)* Sozialhilfe, Fürsorgeunterstützung; **surgical** ~ Operationskostenzuschuß; **survivor's** ~ Witwen-, Waisenrente; **tax** ~ Steuererleichterung; **third-party** ~ Begünstigung Dritter; **training** ~ Ausbildungsbeihilfe; **unemployment** ~ *(Br.)* Arbeitslosenunterstützung, -geld; **unjustified** ~ ungerechtfertigte Bereicherung; **wagerelated** ~ lohnabhängige Unterstützungsleistung; **weekly** ~ Wochenunterstützung; **widow's** ~ Witwenrente, Hinterbliebenenbezüge; **withdrawal** ~ Abgangsregulierung [beim Versicherungsrückkauf];

~s **in cash** Barleistungen; ~ **of counsel** Recht auf Gestellung eines Pflichtverteidigers; **supplementary** ~s **for one's dependants** Sozialhilfe für den Lebensunterhalt von Familienangehörigen; ~ **of discussion** *(surety)* Einrede der Vorausklage; ~ **of division** Inanspruchnahme der Mitbürgen, *(law)* Einrede mehrerer vorhandener Bürgen, Ausgleichseinrede des Bürgen; ~ **of the doubt** *(law)* Rechtswohltat des Zweifels; ~ **of a good education** Vorteil einer guten Ausbildung; ~s **of inflation** Inflationsvorteile; ~ **of an invention** Erlös einer Erfindung; ~ **of inventory** *(heir)* Recht des Erben auf Inventareinrichtung, Recht auf Nachlaßbeschränkung; ~s **in kind** Sachbezüge, -leistungen; ~ **of the law** Rechtswohltat; ~ **from property** Vermögensrente;

~ *(v.)* begünstigen, zugutekommen, Nutzen bringen, nützen, vorteilhaft sein, *(taxation)* bevorzugt behandeln; ~ **by** Nutzen (Vorteil) ziehen, sich etw. zunutze machen, von etw. profitieren; ~ **by exchange** Kursgewinne mitnehmen; ~ **local industry** einheimische Industrie steuerlich begünstigen; ~ **the public interest (public welfare)** im öffentlichen Interesse liegen; ~ **under a will** testamentarisch (in einem Testament) bedacht sein;

to accept a ~ **under an instrument** Vorteile einer Urkunde in Anspruch nehmen; **to award supplementary** ~s **on a noncontributory basis** *(national insurance)* Sozialhilfe an beitragsfreie Angehörige gewähren; **to be eligible to a** ~ leistungsberechtigt sein; **to be entitled to** ~ Leistungsanspruch haben, rentenberechtigt sein; **to be in** ~ [Arbeitslosen]unterstützung beziehen; **to be out of** ~ *(unemployment)* ausgesteuert sein; **to be used for the** ~ **of the poor** für die Armen zur Verfügung gestellt werden; **to claim** ~ Unterstützungsansprüche stellen; **to confer** ~s **on s. o.** jem. Wohltaten erweisen; **to derive** ~ **from s. th.** Nutzen aus etw. ziehen, Vorteil von etw. haben; **to give s. o. the** ~ **of s. th.** j. in den Genuß einer Sache kommen lassen; **to give s. o. the** ~ **of the doubt** im Zweifelsfall zugunsten jds. entscheiden; **to provide** ~s **on competitive terms** konkurrenzfähiges Versorgungssystem einrichten; **to provide occupational** ~s **in addition to those provided by the state** betriebliche Zusatzrenten zur staatlichen Altersversorgung gewähren; **to reap** ~ **from s. th.** Nutzen aus etw. ziehen; **to take the** ~ **of an act** Schutzbestimmungen eines Gesetzes in Anspruch nehmen; **to take the** ~ **of the bankrupt law** von den konkursrechtlichen Schutzbestimmungen Gebrauch machen;

~ **association** *(Br.)* Wohltätigkeits-, Unterstützungsverein; ~ **building society** *(Br.)* Bausparkasse; ~ **certificate** Berechtigungsschein, schriftliches Zahlungsversprechen; ~ **change** Vergünstigungsverbesserungen; ~ **check** *(US)* Unterstützungsscheck; ~ **clause** Begünstigungsklausel; ~ **club** *(Br.)* Wohltätigkeitsverein; ~ **concert** Wohltätigkeitskonzert; ~ **cost analysis** Nutzen-, Kostenanalyse; ~ **cut** Unterstützungskürzung; ~s **formula** *(social security)* Rentenformel; ~ **fund** Unterstützungs-, Wohlfahrts-, Versicherungsfonds; ~ **limits** Rentenhöchstalter; **substantial** ~ **package** umfassendes Bündel von zusätzlichen Vergünstigungen; ~ **payments** Unterstützungszahlungen; ~ **pension** Ruhegehaltsbezüge, Ruhegeld; **defined** ~ **pension plan** Pensionskassensystem mit Rechtsanspruch; **target** ~ **pension plan** Pensionskassensystem ohne Rechtsanspruch; ~ **performance** Wohltätigkeitsveranstaltung; ~ **period** Unterstützungsperiode, -zeitraum; ~ **plan** Sozialzulagensystem, Vergünstigungswesen; ~ **program(me)** freiwillige Sozialzulagenwesen; **comprehensive** ~ **program(me)** umfassendes Sozialzulagewesen; **to come within a** ~ **range** in einen Vergünstigungsbereich fallen; ~ **rate** Unterstützungssatz; ~ **right** Anwartschaft[srecht]; **to have exhausted one's** ~ **rights** *(Br.)* ausgesteuert sein; ~ **society** *(Br.)* Wohltätigkeitsverein, Hilfskasse; **mutual** ~ **society** *(insurance, US)* Versicherungsverein auf Gegenseitigkeit; ~ **taxation** Verbrauchsprinzip der Besteuerung; ~ **year** *(national insurance)* Bezugsjahr.

Benelux Countries Beneluxländer.

benevolence Wohltätigkeit, Wohltat.

benevolent wohltätig, gemeinnützig; ~ **association** Wohltätigkeits-, Unterstützungsverein; ~ **contribution** Beitrag für gemeinnützige Zwecke; ~ **corporation** gemeinnützige Gesellschaft, (Körperschaft); ~ **fund** Versicherungs-, Unterstützungs-, Wohltätigkeitsfonds, Unterstützungskasse; ~ **institution** Hilfsverein, Unterstützungsverein, ~ **instrumentality** Wohltätigkeitsorganisation; ~ **neutrality** wohlwollende Neutralität; ~ **purposes** wohltätige Zwecke; ~ **society** *(Br.)* Wohltätigkeits-, Unterstützungsverein.

benign neglect Nichttätigkeit.

bent Zug, Neigung; ~ **of mind** Denkungsart.

bequeath *(v.)* [testamentarisch] vermachen, hinterlassen, vererben; ~ **a legacy** Vermächtnis aussetzen.

bequeathable hinterlassungsfähig.

bequeathal Vermächtnisaussetzung.

bequeather Erblasser, Testator.

bequest Vermächtnis, testamentarische Zuwendung, Legat; **charitable** ~ wohltätiges Vermächtnis; **conditional** ~ bedingtes Vermächtnis; **executory** ~ Vermächtnis einer Anwartschaft; **general** ~ Geldvermächtnis; **pious** ~ milde Stiftung; **residuary** ~ Vermächtnis des Reinnachlasses; **specific** ~ Einzel-, Sondervermächtnis; ~ *(v.)* im Erbwege stiften, vererben; **to make a** ~ Vermächtnis *(Legat)* aussetzen.

bereavement Verlust, Todesfall, Trauerfall.

Berne Convention Berner Konvention.

berserk, to go amoklaufen.

berth *(position, Br.)* Stelle, Stellung, *(ship)* Liege-, Ankerplatz, -grund, *(sleeper)* Schlafwagenplatz, *(sleeping place)* Kajütenbett, Koje; **on the** ~ *(marine transportation)* verladebereit;

anchoring ~ Ankerplatz; **customs** ~ Zollhandelsplatz; **discharging** ~ Löschplatz; **good** ~ (Br.) einträgliche Stelle; **loading** ~ Verladeplatz, -kai; **snug** ~ (Br.) einträglicher Posten;
~ (v.) am Kai festmachen, vor Anker gehen, (bed) Bettplatz zuteilen;
~ s. o. j. unterbringen; ~ **in the dock** docken;
to find a snug ~ (Br.) bequeme Stellung finden; **to give a wide** ~ (fig.) aus dem Wege gehen; **to have a good** ~ (Br.) gute Stelle haben; **to keep a good** ~ guten Abstand halten;**to load a ship on the** ~ Schiff mit Stückgut befrachten;
~ **cargo** Stückgutladung; ~ **deck** Zwischendeck; ~ **freighting** Stückgutfrachtgeschäft, Stückgutbefrachtung; ~ **rate** Stückguttarif; ~ **terms (ship)** Platzbedingungen.
berthage Kaigebühren, Hafen-, Ankergeld.
berthed, to be festgemacht (im Hafen) liegen;
to be ~ **amidships** in Schlafkojen mittschiffs untergebracht werden.
berther (US) Rangierer.
berthing Bettplatzverteilung.
beseech (v.) dringend bitten, ersuchen.
beseeming geziemend.
beset (v.) freien Zutritt behindern;
to be ~ **by s. th.** mit etw. konfrontiert werden.
besiege (v.) belagern, zernieren;
to be regularly ~**d by patients** von Patienten regelrecht überlaufen sein.
bespeak (v.) (table) vorausbestellen, (patent law).
bespoke | business Maßgeschäft; ~ **tailor** Maßschneider.
best, at im günstigsten Fall, (price) bestens, bestmöglich, billigst;
to be at one's ~ in Form sein; **to do one's level** ~ sein Bestmöglichstes tun; **to have the** ~ **of it** am besten dabei wegkommen; **to make the** ~ **of a bad business** das Beste aus einer verfahrenen Sache machen; **to make the** ~ **of one's opportunity** seine Chancen wahrnehmen; **to make the** ~ **of one's time** seine Zeit gut zu nutzen wissen; **to sell at** ~ **[possible rates]** bestens verkaufen; **to work with the** ~ es mit jedem aufnehmen können;
~ **buy** beste Qualität für geringsten Preis, vorteilhafter Einkauf; ~ **evidence** primärer Beweis; ~ **fit** (statistics) beste Anpassung; ~ **parts** (city) elegantes Viertel; ~ **quality** erste Sorte, feinste Qualität; ~ **quality paper** hochwertiges Papier; ~ **seller** Verkaufsschlager, (publishing) Bucherfolg; ~**-selling** am meisten verkauft.
bestow (v.) geben, schenken, verleihen;
~ **one's luggage** sein Gepäck verstauen; ~ **one's money wisely** sein Geld klug anlegen.
bestowal, bestowment Schenkung.
bet Wette, (stake) Wetteinsatz, gewetteter Betrag;
even ~ Wette mit gleichem Einsatz;
~ (v.) wetten [um], setzen, einsetzen;
~ **one's last dollar** (US sl.) seinen letzten Heller verwetten;
to accept a ~ Wette annehmen; **to be a fairly safe** ~ **for** ziemlich sicherer Kandidat sein; **to hedge against a** ~ sich gegen den Verlust einer Wette sichern; **to make (lay) a** ~ Wette anbieten (eingehen); **to take up a** ~ Wette annehmen; **to win a** ~ Wette gewinnen;
~ **reception** Wettannahme.
betray (v.) verraten, (maiden) verführen;
~ **a friend** Freund in der Not im Stich lassen; ~ **one's ignorance** seine Unkenntnis offenbar werden lassen; ~ **the secrets of a government** Staatsgeheimnisse enthüllen.
betrayal Verrat.
betrayer Verräter.
betrothal Verlobung.
betrothed Verlobter, Verlobte.
better Wetter, Wettender;
~**-off** bessergestellt;
to get the ~ **of s. o.** j. in den Sack stecken.
betterment Verbesserung, (house, land) Wertzuwachs, -steigerung, (land) Meliorationen;
~**s** (railroad company) Verbesserungen der Ladeanlagen;
~ **of loading facilities** Verbesserung der Ladeanlagen;
~ **levy** Wertzuwachsabgabe, (regional policy) Abschöpfung von Planungsgewinnen; ~ **tax** (Br.) Wertzuwachssteuer.
betting Wetten, Wettquote;
~ **book** Wettbuch; ~ **debts** Wettschulden; ~ **duties** Wettsteuern; ~ **house** Wettbüro; ~ **man** Gewohnheitswetter; ~ **office** Wettbüro, Wettannahme[stelle]; ~ **pool** Wettannahme; ~ **shop** Wettannahmestelle, -lokal; ~ **slip** Wettschein, -zettel; ~ **tax** Wettsteuer; ~ **transaction** (US) Buchmacherwette.
between decks Zwischendeck.
betweenmaid (Br.) Hausgehilfin, Zweitmädchen.

beverage Getränk, Erfrischung;
alcoholic ~**s** alkoholische Getränke; **nonalcoholic** ~**s** alkoholfreie Getränke;
~ **industries** Getränkeindustrie; ~ **tax** Getränkesteuer.
Beware! Vorsicht!
~ **of counterfeits** vor Nachahmungen wird gewarnt; ~ **of pickpockets** vor Taschendieben wird gewarnt; ~ **of traffic** Vorsicht, Ausfahrt!
biannual Halbjahreszeitschrift.
bias Befangenheit, Voreingenommenheit, Vorurteil, Parteilichkeit, (clothing) Schrägstreifen, (el.) Voltstärke, Gittervorspannung, (market research) subjektives Vorurteil, (test) unpräzise Stichprobe, Verzerrung, systematischer Fehler;
free from ~ vorurteilsfrei, unvoreingenommen; **on the** ~ diagonal;
personal ~ persönliches Vorurteil; **upward** ~ Verzerrung nach oben;
~ (v.) voreingenommen sein, beeinflussen;
~ **the opinion of the people** öffentliche Meinung beeinflussen.
biassed voreingenommen, unsachlich, tendenziös, parteiisch, (test) unzuverlässig;
to be ~ **in one's treatment of a subject** Thema einseitig behandeln;
~ **error** systematischer Fehler; ~ **estimate** verzerrter Schätzwert; ~ **question** Suggestivfrage.
bib, best ~ **and tucker** Sonntagsstaat.
bibliofilm Mikrofilm, Mikrat.
bibliography Buchbeschreibung, -nachweis.
biblioklept Büchermarder.
bibliologist Bücherkenner.
bibliomania Bücherleidenschaft.
bibliomaniac Büchernarr.
bibliophile Bücherliebhaber.
bibliothecary Bibliothekar.
bicameralism Zweikammersystem.
bicycle Fahrrad;
~ **stand** Fahrradstand; ~ **ticket** Fahrradkarte.
bicyclist Radfahrer.
bid [Lieferungs]angebot, Offerte, (at auction) Gebot, Steigern, (estimate) Kostenvoranschlag, (invitation, US) Einladung, (stock exchange) geboten, Geld;
at the best possible ~ bestens;
cash ~ Bargebot; **closing** ~ letztes Gebot; **competitive** ~ Konkurrenzangebot; **feigned** ~ Scheingebot; **firm** ~ festes Gebot; **first** ~ (at an auction) Erstgebot; **higher (further)** ~ Mehr-, Über-, höheres Gebot; **highest** ~ Höchstgebot; **last** ~ Höchst-, Meistgebot; **lowest** ~ geringstes Gebot, Mindestgebot; **maximum** ~ Meist-, Höchstgebot; **opening** ~ (auction) erstes Gebot; **performance** ~ Liefergarantie; **rigged (sham)** ~ Scheingebot; **straw** ~ (US) Scheingebot; **upset** ~ höheres Gebot zur Wiederaufnahme der Versteigerung, Anschlagsgebot; **winning** ~ (US) Zuschlagssubmission;
~ **and asked** (stock exchange) Geld und Brief; ~**s and offers** Kauf- und Verkaufsangebote, Käufe und Verkäufe; ~ **for bartering** Verhandlungsobjekt; ~ **in** Angebot von interessierter Seite, Selbststeigerung;
~ (v.) anbieten, (auction) bieten, Gebot abgeben, steigern, (tender) an einer Ausschreibung teilnehmen;
~ **against s. o.** j. überbieten; ~ **the banns** Aufgebot verkünden lassen; ~ **on a new bridge** Angebot für einen Brückenbau abgeben; ~ **s. o. to come in** j. hereinbitten; ~ **on government contracts** sich an staatlichen Ausschreibungen beteiligen; ~ **fair to succeed** wahrscheinlich Erfolg haben; ~ **for a house** auf ein Haus bieten; ~ **in** [im Eigentümerinteresse] überbieten, selbst ersteigern; ~ **off** sofortigen Zuschlag erhalten; ~ **over s. o.** höher bieten als ein anderer; ~ **a fair price** angemessenen Preis bieten; ~ **for safety** vorsichtig zu Werke gegen; ~ **for popular support** sich um die Volksgunst bemühen; ~ **up** steigern, überbieten, Preis in die Höhe treiben; ~ **up a stock 2 1/4 points to 178** Aktie um 2 1/4 Punkte auf 178 in die Höhe treiben; ~ **s. o. to a wedding** j. zur Hochzeit einladen;
to invite ~**s** (US) Auftrag ausschreiben; **to make a** ~ **for** sich bewerben um; **to make a bold** ~ **for s. th.** sich um etw. ernsthaft bemühen; **to make the first** ~ erstes Gebot abgeben; **to put** ~**s on the table** Angebote abgeben; **to raise one's** ~ sein Angebot erhöhen; **to retract (withdraw) a** ~ Angebot zurückziehen; **to solicit** ~**s** (US) ausschreiben, Ausschreibung vornehmen;
~ **bond** (US) Ausschreibungs-, Bietungsgarantie; ~ **competition** (US) Ausschreibungswettbewerb; ~**s evaluation** Offertenbewertung, -beurteilung; ~ **invitation** (US) Einladung, an Ausschreibungen teilzunehmen, Ausschreibung, Submission;

~ **price** gebotener Preis, *(stock exchange)* Geldkurs; ~ **protest** Ausschreibungsprotest; ~ **and asked quotations** Geld- und Briefkurse.

bidden guests geladene Gäste.

bidder Bietender, Bieter, Bewerber, Submittent, Ausschreibungsbeteiligter, Kauflustiger, -interessent;
base ~ Hauptbieter; **best** ~ Höchst-, Meistbietender; **by-**~ Scheinbieter; **competitive** ~ Gegenbieter; **last and highest** ~ Letztbietender, Ersteigerer; **lowest** ~ Mindestbietender; **mock (sham)** ~ Scheinbieter; **no** ~s keine Kaufinteressenten; **successful** ~ erfolgreicher Submittent, Auftragnehmer;
to allot (allocate) to the highest ~ dem Meistbietenden zuschlagen; **to sell to the highest** ~ dem Meistbietenden verkaufen.

bidding Gebot, Geheiß, *(auction)* Abgabe von Geboten, Bieten, *(invitation)* Abgabe von Angeboten, *(labo(u)r relations)* Arbeitsplatzausschreibung;
by-~ Hochtreiben durch Scheingebote; **competitive** ~ freie Ausschreibung; **dump** ~ Versteigerung mit verdecktem Mindestgebot; **first** ~ Erstgebot; **reserved** ~ beschränkte Versteigerung;
~ **of orders** Auftragsbeschaffung;
to lose out on a ~ bei einer Auftragszuteilung leer ausgehen;
~ **agreement** Angebotsausschließungsvertrag; ~ **period** Ausschreibungsfrist; ~ **price** Erstangebot; ~ **procedure** Vergabeverfahren; ~ **process** Ausschreibungsverfahren.

bidding most meistbietend.

bide *(v.)* **one's time** auf sein Chance warten.

biennial zweijährig.

big groß, stark, hoch;
to get too ~ **for one's boots** *(sl.)* größenwahnsinnig werden; **to stay very** ~ groß im Geschäft bleiben; **to talk** ~ große Reden führen;
~⌐**Board** *(US)* New Yorker Börse; ~ **boss** Vorgesetzter; ~ **break** große Chance; ~ **bud** *(US)* hohes Tier; ~**-bully** *(US coll.)* großkotzig; ~ **business** *(US)* Großbetrieb, -industrie, -unternehmen; **to act the** ~ **cheese** den dicken Wilhelm markieren, starken Mann spielen; ~ **city** Großstadt; ~ **city press** Großstadtpresse; ~ **earner** Großverdiener; ~ **finance** *(US)* Hochfinanz; ~⌐**Five** *(Br.)* die fünf Großbanken; ~ **game** Großwild, *(fig.)* hochgestecktes Ziel; ~ **head** Angeber, Großtuer; ~ **house** *(US sl.)* Kittchen, Kasten, Knast; **to have** ~ **ideas** große Rosinen im Kopf haben; ~ **income earner** Großverdiener; ~ **money** *(US)* Haufen Geld; ~ **name** großes Tier; ~ **producer** Großerzeuger; ~ **science** Forschung für Vorhaben im großen Stil; ~ **shot** *(photo)* Großaufnahme, *(US)* Bonze, hohes Tier; ~ **stick** politische Macht; ~ **talk** Angabe, Aufschneiderei; ~ **ticket** teurer Verkaufsartikel; ~ **ticket durables** teure Kapitalgüter; ~ **ticket items** hochwertige Erzeugnisse; ~ **time** *(US sl.)* herrliche Zeit, Hochzeit; ~**-time** *(sl.)* erstklassig, gewinnträchtig, sehr lukrativ; ~ **wheel** *(US)* einflußreiche Persönlichkeit.

bigamist Bigamist.

bigamous der Bigamie schuldig;
~ **marriage** Doppelehe, Bigamie.

bigamy Doppelehe, Bigamie.

bigwig *(sl.)* Bonze, hohes Tier, Würdenträger.

bigwiggedness *(sl.)* Bonzentum.

bilateral gegen-, zweiseitig, bilateral;
~ **contract** zweiseitiger (gegenseitiger) Vertrag; ~ **flow** gegenläufige Güter- und Geldströme; ~ **loan** zweiseitiger Kredit; ~ **monopoly** bilaterales Monopol; ~ **trade** bilateraler Handel; ~ **trade agreement** zweiseitiges Handelsabkommen; ~ **treaty** zweiseitiges Abkommen.

bilateralism Prinzip der Gegenseitigkeit, Bilateralismus.

bilge *(ship)* Kielraum.

bilingual zweisprachig.

bill *(US, abstract of account)* Kontoauszug, *(account)* Rechnung, Faktura, Nota, *(US, bank note)* Banknote, Geldschein, *(poster)* Anschlagbogen, Plakat, Affiche, Anschlag[zettel], *(bill of exchange)* Wechsel, Tratte, *(certificate)* Schein, Bescheinigung, Zettel, *(inventory)* Inventar, *(letter)* Brief, *(list)* Verzeichnis, Liste, Aufstellung, *(paper money)* Papiergeld, *(parl.)* Gesetzesvorlage, Gesetzentwurf, -antrag, *(plaintiff)* Klageschrift, Schriftsatz, *(receipt)* Quittung, *(statement of terms of contract)* Zusammenstellung der Vertragsbestimmungen;
when the ~ **matures** bei Ablauf des Wechsels;
acceptance ~ zum Akzept vorzulegender Wechsel, Tratte; **accepted** ~ Akzept; **accommodation** ~ Gefälligkeits-, Freundschafts-, Proformawechsel; **addressed** ~ Domizilwechsel; **administration** ~ *(US)* Regierungsvorlage; **advance** ~ Lombard-, Vorauswechsel; **after-date** ~ Datowechsel; **after-sight** ~

Nachsichtwechsel; **all-embracing** ~ umfassender Gesetzentwurf; **auction** ~ Auktionsliste; **antedated** ~ zurückdatierter Wechsel; **anticipated** ~ vor Verfallzeit eingelöster Wechsel; **approved** ~ einwandfreier Wechsel; **back** ~s unbezahlte Rechnungen; **backed** ~ avalierter Wechsel; **bank** ~ *(US)* Banknote; **bankable** ~ bankfähiger Wechsel; **blank** ~ Blankowechsel; **bogus** ~ Kellerwechsel, fingierter Wechsel; **bona-fide** ~ Wechsel über empfangene Ware; **branch** ~ Zahlstellenwechsel; **circulation** ~ umlaufender Wechsel; **clean** ~ *(ship)* positives Gesundheitsattest; **commercial** ~ Handels-, Warenwechsel; **continental** ~ *(Br.)* Festlandwechsel; **continuation** ~ Verlängerungswechsel, prolongierter Wechsel; **cotton** ~ Baumwollwechsel; **counterfeited** ~ gefälschter Wechsel; **country** ~ Inkasso-, Versandwechsel; **credit** ~ Kreditwechsel; **creditor's** ~ gerichtlich festgestellter Gläubigeranteil; **cross** ~ Gegenklage; **customer's** ~ Kundenwechsel; **dated** ~ Datowechsel; **deficiency** ~ *(Br.)* kurzfristige Regierungsanleihe der Bank von England; **demand** ~ Sichtwechsel; **discharged** ~ bezahlter Wechsel; **discount** ~ Diskontwechsel; **discountable** ~ diskontfähiger Wechsel; ~s **discounted** *(balance sheet)* Diskontwechsel, Diskonten; **dishono(u)red** ~ unbezahlter (protestierter, nicht honorierter) Wechsel; **documentary** ~ Dokumenttratte; **domestic** ~ Inlandwechsel; **domiciliary (domiciled)** ~ domizilierter Wechsel, Domizilwechsel; **wrongly drafted** ~ Wechsel mit unrichtigem Wortlaut; **drawn** ~ gezogener (ausgestellter) Wechsel; ~ **due** fälliger Wechsel; **eligible** ~ *(US)* landeszentralbankfähiger Wechsel; **exchequer** ~s *(Br.)* verzinsliche Schatzanweisungen, Schatzwechsel; **expired** ~ fälliger Wechsel; **fictitious** ~ *(Br.)* Schein-, Kellerwechsel; **finance** ~ langfristiger internationaler Wechsel, Finanzierungswechsel, *(parl.)* Finanzvorlage; **fine** ~ Primawechsel, erstklassiger Handelswechsel; **first-class** ~s Primardiskonten; **first-rate** *(Br.)* erstklassiger Wechsel; **fixed** ~ Datowechsel; **foreign** ~ ausländischer Wechsel, Auslandswechsel; **forged** ~ gefälschter Wechsel; **fortnightly** ~ *(Br.)* Mediowechsel; **foul** ~ *(ship)* negatives Gesundheitsattest; **freight** ~ Frachtbrief; **government** ~ *(parl.)* Regierungsvorlage; **grain** ~ Getreidewechsel; **guaranteed** ~ Bürgschafts-, Avalwechsel; **hand** ~ Schuldschein, *(bill of exchange)* eigener (trockener) Wechsel; ~s **held over** notleidende Wechsel; **hono(u)red** ~ eingelöster Wechsel; **house** ~ auf eigene Niederlassung gezogener Wechsel, trassierter eigener Wechsel; **inchoate** ~ *(Br.)* noch nicht vollständig ausgefüllter Wechsel; **indirect** ~ domizilierter Wechsel; **indorsed** ~ girierter (indosierter) Wechsel; **industrial** ~ Industrieakzept; **inland** ~ Inlandswechsel; **interim** ~ Interimswechsel; **investment** ~ *(US)* Anlagepapiere; **issued** ~ ausgestellter Wechsel; **labo(u)r reform** ~ Änderungsgesetz über das Gewerkschaftswesen; **local** ~ Platzwechsel; **long** ~ hohe Rechnung; **long[-dated]** ~ langfristiger Wechsel, Wechsel auf lange Sicht; **made** ~ *(Br.)* girierter Wechsel; **matured** ~ verfallener Wechsel; **memorandum** ~ Schuldwechsel, Kommissions-, Lieferschein; **mercantile** ~ Warenwechsel; **ministerial** ~ Regierungsvorlage; **money** ~ *(parl.)* Finanzvorlage; **one month's** ~ Monatswechsel; **navy** ~ Flottenvorlage; **negotiable** ~ börsenfähiger Wechsel, durch Indossament übertragbarer Wechsel; **negotiated** ~ weitergegebener Wechsel; **noneligible** ~ nicht [landes]zentralbankfähiger (diskontfähiger) Wechsel; **nonnegotiable** ~ unbegebbarer Wechsel, Rektawechsel; **nonparty** ~ von allen Parteien eingebrachter Gesetzentwurf; **nonvalue** ~ Gefälligkeitswechsel; **obligatory** ~ [notarielles] Schuldversprechen; **only** ~ Solawechsel; **order** ~ Orderwechsel; **ordinary** ~ normaler Wechsel; **original** ~ *(US)* Primawechsel, noch nicht girierter Wechsel; **out-of-town** ~ *(Br.)* Distanzwechsel; ~s **outstanding** *(balance sheet)* Wechselforderungen; **his outstanding** ~s seine Außenstände; ~ **overdue** überfällige Rechnung, *(bill of exchange)* abgelaufener Wechsel; **pawned** ~ sicherungsübereigneter Wechsel; ~s **payable** *(US, balance sheet)* Wechselverpflichtungen, -schulden, -obligo, Verbindlichkeiten aus Wechseln, Schuldscheinen und Akzepten; **payment** ~ zur Zahlung vorzulegender Wechsel; **penal** ~ Schuldurkunde mit Konventionalstrafe; **primary** ~ Primawechsel; **prime** ~ *(US)* erstklassiger Wechsel, erstklassige Diskonten; **private** ~ Kunden-, Handelswechsel; **private member's** ~ Initiativantrag eines Abgeordneten; **pro-forma** ~ Schein-, Kellerwechsel, fingierter Wechsel; ~ **protested** Protestwechsel; ~ **not provided for** ungedeckter Wechsel; **provisional** ~ Interimswechsel; **public** ~ *(Br.)* Regierungsvorlage; **query** ~ fauler Wechsel; **raised** ~ *(US)* durch Werterhöhung gefälschter Wechsel; **real** ~ echter Wechsel; **receipted** ~ quittierte Rechnung; ~s **receivable** *(US, balance sheet)* Besitzwechsel, Wechselbestand, Wechselforderungen, Debitoren, Kundenwechsel, Bestand an Wechseln, Schuld-

scheinen und Akzepten; **rediscountable** ~s zentralbankfähige Wechsel; **rediscounted** ~ weitergegebener Wechsel; ~ **rendered** vorgelegte Rechnung; **renewal** ~ Prolongations-, Verlängerungswechsel; ~s **retired** *(US)* vorzeitig eingelöste Wechsel; **returned** ~ Rück-, Retourenwechsel; **revised** ~ abgeändertes Gesetz; **sales** ~ *(US)* Warenwechsel; **sea** ~ Seewechsel; **second** ~ Sekundawechsel, zweite Wechselausfertigung; **security** ~ durch Effekten gesicherter Wechsel; **separate** ~ getrennte Rechnung; **shipping** ~ Konnossement, Frachtbrief, [Ver]ladeschein; **short** ~s Inkassowechsel; **short-dated (-sighted)** ~ kurzfristiger Wechsel, Wechsel auf kurze Sicht; **signed** ~ unterschriebener Wechsel; **sight** ~ Sichtwechsel; **single** ~ [notarielles] Schuldversprechen; **skeleton** ~ unausgefülltes Wechselformular; **sole** ~ nur in einer Ausfertigung ausgestellter Wechsel; **sterling** ~ in englischen Pfunden zahlbarer Wechsel; **strike** ~ *(Br.)* erpresserischer Gesetzesantrag; **subsisting** ~ in Kraft befindlicher Wechsel; **supplemental** ~ Zusatzantrag, *(lawyer)* erweiterter Schriftsatz; **swingeing** ~ *(fam.)* gepfefferte Rechnung; **tax** ~ *(US)* Steuerbescheid; **third-party** ~ Kundenwechsel; **three-month** ~ Dreimonatswechsel; **time** ~ Datowechsel; **touched** ~ *(ship)* negatives Gesundheitsattest; **town** ~ Platzwechsel; **trade** ~ Handels-, Kunden-, Warenwechsel; **transit** ~ Durchgangsschein; **treasury** ~ *(Br.)* unverzinslicher Schatzanweisung, kurzfristiger Schatzwechsel; **true** ~ *(criminal law)* begründete Anklageschrift, Eröffnung des Hauptverfahrens, Eröffnungsbeschluß; **unaccepted** ~ nicht akzeptierter Wechsel; **uncovered** ~ ungedeckter Wechsel; **undiscounted** ~ nicht diskontierter Wechsel; **unexpired** ~ noch nicht fälliger Wechsel; **unopposed** ~ Gesetzesvorlage ohne Gegenstimmen; **unpaid** ~ unbezahlter (nicht eingelöster) Wechsel, Rückwechsel; **unreceipted** ~ unquittierte Rechnung; **unstamped** ~ unverstempelter Wechsel; **value** ~ Konsignationswechsel; **wrongly worded** ~ Wechsel mit unrichtigem Wortlaut; **works council** ~ *(Br.)* Betriebsverfassungsgesetz; **worthless** ~ fauler Wechsel; ~s **and checks** Wechsel- und Scheckbestand; ~s **and money** *(stock exchange)* Brief und Geld;
~ **of acceptance** Akzept; ~ **out for acceptance** zur Annahme geschickter Wechsel; ~ **of admeasurement** Meßbrief; ~ **of adventure** Risikoerklärung [eines Schiffskapitäns]; ~ **of gross adventure** Bodmereivertrag; ~ **of amortization** Amortisations-, Tilgungsschein, Klageantrag; ~ **of attainder** parlamentarischer Strafbeschluß [wegen Hochverrats]; ~ **payable (made out) to bearer** Inhaberwechsel; ~ **of bottomry** Bodmereibrief; ~ **of carriage** [Bahn]frachtbrief; ~ **of certiorari** Revisionsantrag; ~ **in chancery** Antrag vor dem Kanzleigericht; ~ **of charges** *(US)* [Un]kosten-, Gebührenrechnung; ~s **in circulation** laufende Wechsel, Wechselumlauf; ~ **of clearance** Zollabfertigungsschein; ~ **for collection** Inkassowechsel; ~ **of commission** Provisionsrechnung; ~ **of complaint** Beschwerdeschrift; ~ **of conformity** Antrag auf Einleitung des Nachlaßkonkurses; ~ **of consignment** Frachtbrief; ~ **of conveyance** Speditionsrechnung; ~ **of costs** Spesen-, Gerichts-, Prozeßkostenrechnung, *(advocate)* Anwaltsgebühren-, Honorarrechnung, Liquidation; ~ **of taxed costs** Kostenfestsetzungsbescheid; ~ **of course of exchange** Kurszettel; ~ **of credit** Kreditbrief, Kreditkassen-, Darlehnskassenschein, *(US)* Schatzanweisung; ~ **in foreign currency** Auslandswechsel, ausländischer Wechsel, Wechsel in ausländischer Währung; ~ **of customs** Zollgebührenrechnung; ~ **on customers** Kundenwechsel; ~ **after date** Datowechsel; ~ **payable at fixed date after presentation** Zeitsichtwechsel; ~ **of debt** Schuldschein, -anerkenntnis; ~ **of delivery** Liefer-, Begleitschein, Ausfolgeschein; ~ **payable on demand** Wechsel auf Sicht, Sichtwechsel; ~ **on deposit** Depot-, Kost-, Pensionswechsel; ~ **of discount** Diskontnota; ~s **eligible for discount** Diskontmaterial; ~ **of discovery** Antrag auf Offenlegung und Urkundenvorlage; ~ **in distress** notleidender Wechsel; ~ **with documents attached** Wechsel mit anhängenden Papieren; ~ **drawn on s. o.** eigener (trockener) Wechsel; ~ **drawn after date** Datowechsel; ~ **drawn on goods sold** Handels-, Warenwechsel; ~ **to be encashed (for encashment)** Wechsel zum Inkasso; ~ **of emption** Kaufbrief, -kontrakt, -vertrag; ~ **of entry** *(Br.)* Zolldeklaration, -einfuhrschein, Einfuhrdeklaration, Importerklärung, Deklarationsschein; ~ **in equity** Antrag nach Billigkeitsrecht; ~ **of exception** Verfahrenseinrede.
bill of exchange Wechsel, Tratte;
  bankable ~ bankfähiger Wechsel; **blank** ~ Wechselblankett; **clean** ~ reiner Wechsel; **domestic** ~ Inlandswechsel; **first** ~ Primawechsel; **foreign** Auslandswechsel; **lost** ~ verlorengegangener Wechsel; **pawned** ~ sicherungsübereigneter Wechsel; **provisional** ~ Interimswechsel; **receipted** ~ quittierter Wechsel; **second** ~ Sekundawechsel; **sole** ~ Primawechsel;

~ **against documents** Wechsel gegen Dokumente.
bill | of exchequer *(Br.)* verzinsliche Schatzanweisung, Schatzwechsel; ~ **of expenditure** Ausgabenrechnung; ~ **of expenses** Liquidation, Spesen-, Kostenrechnung; ~ **of fare** Speisekarte, Menü; ~ **for foreclosure** Zwangsvollstreckungsantrag; ~ **of freight** Frachtbrief; ~ **on goods** Waren-, Handelswechsel; ~s **in hand** Wechselbestand, -portefeuille; ~ **of health** *(ship)* Gesundheitsattest; **foul** ~ **of health** negative Hafengesundheitsbescheinigung; **touched** ~ **of health** Gesundheitspaß mit Vermerk; ~ **for hotel** Hotelrechnung; ~ **of indemnity** *(parl.)* Amnestiebeschluß [für einen Minister]; ~ **of indictment** *(Br.)* Anklageschrift; ~ **of information** Strafverfolgungsantrag; ~ **at interim** Interimswechsel; ~ **of interpleader** Nebeninterventionsverfahren.
bill of lading Seefrachtbrief, Konnossement, *(US)* Frachtbrief, Ladeschein;
  air ~ *(US)* Luftfrachtbrief; **on-board** ~ Bordkonnossement; **clean** ~ echtes (reines) Konnossement, Konnossement ohne Vorbehalt; **consolidated** ~ Sammelkonnossement; **custody** ~ Lagerhalterkonnossement; **foul** ~ unreines Konnossement; **forwarder's** ~ Spediteurkonnossement; **government** ~ staatliches Konnossement; **grouped** ~ Sammelkonnossement; **inland-waterway** ~ Flußladeschein, -konnossement; **inward** ~ Import-, Einfuhrkonnossement; **marine** ~ Seekonnossement; **ocean** ~ Seekonnossement, -frachtbrief; **omnibus** ~ Sammelkonnossement; **order** ~ *(US)* Orderfrachtbrief; **order-notify** ~ Orderkonnossement; **outward** ~ Exportkonnossement; **railroad** ~ *(US)* Eisenbahnfrachtbrief; **received-for-shipment** ~ Übernahmekonnossement; **river** ~ Flußladeschein; **shipped** ~ Verschiffungs-, Bordkonnossement; **spent** ~ erloschener Frachtbrief; **straight** ~ *(US)* nicht begebbarer Namensfrachtbrief, nicht übertragbarer Ladeschein, auf den Namen ausgestelltes Konnossement, Namens-, Rektakonnossement; **through** ~ Durchfracht-, Durchkonnossement; **transshipment** ~ Umladekonnossement; **uniform** ~ Einheits-, Normalkonnossement; **uniform through export** ~ Durchgangskonnossement für das Ausland; **wharf** ~ Kaikonnossement;
~ **drawn in three copies** Konnossement in dreifacher Ausfertigung; ~ **to order** Orderkonnossement;
to make out a ~ Konnossement ausstellen;
~ **clause** Konnossementklausel; ~ **contract** Konnossementvertrag.
bill | on London Wechsel auf London; ~ **of materials** Stückliste; ~ **to mature** laufender (fällig werdender) Wechsel; ~s **about to mature** in Kürze fällige Wechsel; ~ **made out to order** auf Order lautender Wechsel; ~ **of mortality** Sterblichkeitstabelle, Totenliste; ~ **dishono(u)red by nonacceptance** nicht akzeptierter Wechsel; ~ **of oblivion** Amnestievorlage; ~ **at par** Pariwechsel; ~ **of parcels** spezifizierte Warenrechnung (Rechnungsaufstellung), Faktura; ~ **in Parliament** Parlamentsvorlage; ~ **of particulars** spezifizierte (detaillierte) Klageschrift, ergänzender Schriftsatz; ~ **payable to order** auf Order lautender Wechsel, Orderpapier; ~ **of peace** *(title)* Feststellungsklage; ~ **in pension** Kost-, Pensionswechsel; ~ **of permit** *(ship)* Passierschein; ~s **in portfolio** Wechselportefeuille, -bestand; ~ **of protest** Protesturkunde; ~ **noted for protest** protestierter Wechsel; ~ **of quantities** Baukostenvoranschlag, Mengen-, Leistungsverzeichnis; ~ **of receipts and expenditures** Einnahmen- und Ausgabenrechnung; ~ **of review** *(Br.)* Revisionsantrag [beim Oberhaus]; ~ **of revisor** Wiederaufnahmeantrag; ~ **of Rights** *(US)* Verfassungsurkunde; ~ **of sale** *(Br., letter of hypothecation)* Abtretungs-, Verpfändungsurkunde, Mobiliarschuld-, Pfandverschreibung, *(transfer of title)* Kaufvertrag, Verkaufsurkunde, -urkunde; **conditional** ~ **of sale** [etwa] Sicherungsübereignungsvertrag; **grand** ~ **of sale** Schiffsverkaufsurkunde; ~ **of sale by way of security** *(Br.)* Sicherungsübereignung durch schriftliche Erklärung; ~ **of security** Garantiewechsel; ~ **pledged as security for an advance** lombardierter Wechsel; ~s **in a set** Satz Wechsel, Wechsel in mehrfacher Ausfertigung; ~ **in full settlement** Ausgleichswechsel; ~ **at sight** Sichtwechsel; ~ **payable on sight** Sichtwechsel; **after sight** Nachsichtwechsel; ~ **of sight** schriftliche Warenbeschreibung, Eingangsdeklaration; ~ **of specie** Sortenzettel, Bordereau, Stückverzeichnis; ~ **of store** Wiedereinfuhrgenehmigung, -schein; ~ **of sufferance** *(Br.)* Erlaubnis zollfreier Warenausfuhr von Hafen zu Hafen, Zollpassierschein; ~ **of supply** Nachtragshaushaltsvorlage; ~ **in suspense** notleidender (uneingelöster) Wechsel; ~ **of taxes** *(US)* Steuerbescheid; ~ **of tonnage** Meßbrief; ~ **for a new trial** Antrag für Wiederaufnahme des Verfahrens; ~s **on us** *(balance sheet)* Abschnitte auf uns; ~ **[payable] at usance** Usowechsel; ~ **issued for value received in goods** Warenwechsel;

~ (v.) (announce) ankündigen, (invoice) berechnen, in Rechnung stellen, Rechnung ausschreiben, fakturieren, (poster) Zettel ankleben, durch Plakat bekanntmachen, plakatieren, anschlagen, reklamemäßig ankündigen, (register) in eine Liste eintragen, registrieren;

~ **goods** Waren in Rechnung stellen; ~ **s. o.** jem. eine Rechnung schicken; ~ **s. o. for his share of cost** jem. seinen Kostenanteil in Rechnung stellen;

to accept a ~ Wechsel akzeptieren; **to accept a** ~ **for collection** Wechsel zum Einzug hereinnehmen; **to act as surety for a** ~ Wechselbürgschaft übernehmen; **to advise a** ~ Wechsel avisieren; **to allow a** ~ **to lie on the table** Gesetzentwurf zurückstellen; **to amend a** ~ Gesetz (Gesetzesvorlage) abändern; **to answer a** ~ Wechsel honorieren; **to anticipate a** ~ Wechsel vor Fälligkeit einlösen; **to attend to the collection of a** ~ Inkasso eines Wechsels besorgen; **to back a** ~ Wechselbürgschaft leisten; **to block a** ~ **in a committee** Gesetzentwurf bei den Ausschußberatungen blockieren; **to bottle up a** ~ **in a committee** Gesetzentwurf in einem Ausschuß begraben; **to bring in a** ~ Gesetzesvorlage einbringen; **to bring a** ~ **to the floor** Gesetzesentwurf im Plenum einbringen; **to bring in a true** ~ Anklage für begründet erklären; **to buy up** ~**s** Wechsel aufkaufen; **to call up a** ~ **before a legislative body** Gesetzesantrag vor einer gesetzgebenden Körperschaft zur Debatte stellen; **to cancel a** ~ Wechsel durchstreichen; **to carry a** ~ Gesetzentwurf annehmen, Gesetz beschließen; **to cash a** ~ Wechsel einlösen (honorieren); **to cause a** ~ **to be noted** Wechsel protestieren lassen; **to charge s. th. on the** ~ etw. auf die Rechnung setzen; **to check a** ~ Rechnung prüfen; **to clear a** ~ Wechsel ziehen; **to closure a** ~ **in compartments** Gesetzentwurf stückweise erledigen; **to collect a** ~ Wechsel einziehen; **to commit a** ~ Gesetzentwurf einem Ausschuß überweisen; **to compute a** ~ Verfallstag eines Wechsels berechnen; **to debate a** ~ über ein Gesetz beraten; **to defeat a** ~ Gesetzentwurf ablehnen; **to deliver a** ~ Wechsel aus der Hand geben; **to discharge a** ~ Wechsel begleichen, einlösen; **to discount a** ~ Wechsel diskontieren; **to dishono(u)r a** ~ Wechselannahme verweigern; **to dispose of a** ~ Wechsel abgeben; **to do** ~**s** (Br.) Wechsel aufkaufen; **to domiciliate a** ~ Wechsel zahlbar stellen (domizilieren); **to draft a** ~ Gesetz ausarbeiten; **to draw a** ~ Wechsel ziehen (ausstellen), trassieren; **to draw** ~**s in sets of two** Wechsel in zwei Ausfertigungen ausstellen; **to draw up a** ~ Gesetzesvorlage ausarbeiten; **to draw a** ~ **of exchange in duplicate** Wechsel doppelt ausfertigen; **to drop a** ~ Gesetzentwurf ablehnen; **to encash a** ~ Einziehung eines Wechsels besorgen; **to endorse (indorse) a** ~ Wechsel mit Giro versehen (indossieren, girieren); **to endorse back a** ~ **of exchange** Wechsel zurückübertragen; **to engineer a** ~ **through Congress** (US) Gesetzentwurf durch den Kongreß bringen; **to enter a** ~ **short** Wechsel Eingang vorbehalten gutschreiben; **to enter protest of a** ~ Wechselprotest einlegen; **to extend a** ~ Wechsel prolongieren (verlängern); **to filibuster a** ~ (US) Gesetzentwurf verschleppen; **to fill a** ~ Gesetzesvorlage einbringen; **to fill the** ~ seinen Platz ausfüllen, den Anforderungen entsprechen; **to fill out a** ~ Wechselformular ausfüllen; **to find a true** ~ (US) Anklage für begründet erklären; **to foot a** ~ Zeche bezahlen; **to forge a** ~ Wechsel fälschen; **to furnish a** ~ **with surety** Wechsel mit Bürgschaft versehen; **to furnish a** ~ **with a stamp** Wechsel verstempeln, Wechselmarke aufkleben; **to get in** ~**s** ausstehende Rechnungen hereinbekommen; **to get s. one's** ~ **ready** Rechnung für j. fertig machen; **to give a** ~ Wechsel ausstellen (begeben); **to give currency to a** ~ Wechsel in Umlauf setzen; **to give a** ~ **on discount** Wechsel diskontieren lassen; **to give a firm a clean** ~ **of health** einer Firma korrektes Verhalten bescheinigen; **to give a** ~ **its second reading** zweite Lesung eines Gesetzentwurfes durchführen; **to go over (through one's)** ~**s** seine Rechnungen durchgehen; **to guarantee (guaranty) [due payment of] a** ~ Wechselbürgschaft leisten; **to have** ~**s** Schulden haben; **to have a** ~ **collected** Wechsel zum Inkasso geben; **to have a** ~ **noted** Wechselprotest aufnehmen lassen; **to have a** ~ **protested** Wechselprotest einlegen, Wechsel protestieren lassen; **to hold over a** ~ Wechsel prolongieren (verlängern); **to hono(u)r a** ~ Wechsel begleichen (einlösen, decken); **to hono(u)r a** ~ **at maturity** Wechsel bei Verfall einlösen; **to ignore a** ~ Anklage als unbegründet abweisen; **to inscribe across the face of a** ~ Vorderseite eines Wechsels girieren; **to inspect a** ~ Wechsel überprüfen; **to introduce a** ~ Gesetz[entwurf] einbringen; **to issue a** ~ Wechsel begeben; **to issue a** ~ **of exchange on s. o.** Wechsel auf j. ziehen; **to itemize a** ~ Rechnung spezifizieren; **to jam a** ~ **through Congress** (US) Gesetzesvorlage durchpeitschen; **to jettison a** ~ Gesetzentwurf fallen lassen; **to keep** ~**s afloat** Wechsel im Umlauf haben; **to keep a** ~ **in suspense** Wechsel Not leiden

lassen; **to kill a** ~ Gesetzentwurf ablehnen (zu Fall bringen); **to lay the** ~ **on the table** (US) Gesetzentwurf zurückstellen; **to leave a** ~ **unpaid (unprotected)** Wechsel nicht einlösen (honorieren); **to look favo(u)rably on a** ~ Gesetzentwurf befürworten; **to lose a** ~ Gesetzantrag nicht durchbringen; **to make out a** ~ Rechnung aufsetzen (erteilen, ausfertigen), (~ **of exchange**) Wechsel ziehen; **to make a** ~ **payable** Wechsel zahlbar stellen; **to make a** ~ **payable to order** Wechsel an Order stellen; **to make out a** ~ **payable thirty days** (d/d) laufenden Wechsel ausstellen; **to make out a** ~ **of lading** Konnossement ausstellen; **to meet a** ~ Rechnung begleichen, (~ **of exchange**) Wechsel einlösen (honorieren); **to meet a** ~ **with due hono(u)r** einer Tratte guten Empfang bereiten; **to negotiate a** ~ Wechsel begeben; **to note a** ~ Wechselprotest erheben; **to obstruct a** ~ Verabschiedung eines Gesetzentwurfes verhindern; **to offer a** ~ **for discount** Wechsel zum Diskont einreichen; **to oppose a** ~ **on the floor** Gesetzentwurf im Plenum bekämpfen; **to pass a** ~ Wechsel ziehen, Gesetz beschließen, Gesetz[entwurf] verabschieden; **to pass a** ~ **without a division** Gesetzentwurf ohne besondere Abstimmung verabschieden; **to pay a** ~ Wechsel einlösen; **to pay by means of a** ~ mittels Wechsel bezahlen; **to pay a** ~ **under protest** Wechsel unter Protesterhebung einlösen; **to pigeonhole a** ~ Gesetzesvorlage aufs tote Gleis schieben; **to pledge a** ~ **as security for a loan** Wechsel lombardieren; **to pocket a** ~ (US) Gesetzesvorlage nicht unterzeichnen; **to post** ~**s** Zettel anschlagen (ankleben); **to postdate a** ~ Wechsel vorausdatieren; **to present a** ~ Gesetzentwurf einreichen; **to present a** ~ **for acceptance** Wechsel zur Annahme (zum Akzept) vorlegen; **to present a** ~ **for payment** Wechsel zur Zahlung vorlegen; **to prolong a** ~ Wechsel verlängern (prolongieren); **to promote a** ~ **in parliament** Gesetzentwurf initiieren; **to protect a** ~ **at maturity** Wechsel bei Verfall einlösen; **to protest a** ~ **for nonpayment** Wechselprotest einlegen; **to protest a** ~ **for nonacceptance** Wechsel mangels Annahme protestieren; **to provide for a** ~ Deckung für einen Wechsel anschaffen; **to provide a** ~ **with acceptance** Tratte mit Akzept versehen; **to provide a** ~ **with guarantee (guaranty)** mit Wechselbürgschaft versehen; **to put a democratic stamp on a** ~ (US) einem Gesetzentwurf das Gütesiegel der Demokratischen Partei aufdrücken; **to railroad a** ~ **through Congress** (US) Gesetzesvorlage durchpeitschen; **to rattle a** ~ **through the house** (Br.) Gesetzesvorlage durchpeitschen; **to read a** ~ **for the third time** Gesetzvorlage in dritter Lesung behandeln; **to receipt a** ~ Rechnung quittieren; **to recommit a** ~ Gesetzentwurf an den Ausschuß zurückverweisen; **to redeem a** ~ Wechsel honorieren; **to rediscount a** ~ Wechsel rediskontieren; **to refer a** ~ **to a committee** Gesetzentwurf einem Ausschuß überweisen; **to refuse a** ~ Wechsel abweisen; **to reject a** ~ Wechsel zurückweisen, (parl.) Gesetzentwurf ablehnen (zurückweisen, nicht annehmen); **to remit a** ~ Wechsel einlösen; **to remit a** ~ **for collection** Wechsel zum Inkasso übersenden; **to renew a** ~ Wechsel prolongieren; **to report a** ~ (Br.) Gesetzentwurf wieder vorlegen; **to report a** ~ **with amendments** Gesetzesvorlage mit Änderungsvorschlägen dem Plenum vorlegen; **to represent a** ~ Wechsel erneut vorlegen; **to retain a** ~ **unsigned** Gesetzesvorlage nicht unterzeichnen; **to retire a** ~ Wechsel einlösen (honorieren); **to return a** ~ **accepted** Wechsel mit Akzept zurückschicken; **to return a** ~ **unpaid** Wechsel unbezahlt zurückgeben lassen (nicht honorieren); **to return an amount by a** ~ **of exchange** Betrag durch Wechsel übermachen; **to return a** ~ **to drawer** Wechsel retournieren; **to return a** ~ **protested** Wechsel unter Protest zurückgehen lassen; **to root out a** ~ **from under a pile of letters** Rechnung unter einem Stoß von Briefen hervorziehen; **to run up a** ~ große Rechnung machen, Rechnung anwachsen (anschreiben) lassen; **to rush a** ~ **through the house** Gesetzesvorlage durchpeitschen; **to send in one's** ~ seine Rechnung vorlegen; **to send a** ~ **up to the Upper House** (Br.) Gesetzentwurf dem Oberhaus vorlegen; **to set up** ~**s** Zettel ankleben; **to settle one's** ~ seine Rechnung begleichen; **to shelve a** ~ (Br.) Gesetzesvorlage aufs tote Gleis schieben (zurückstellen); **to sight a** ~ Wechsel mit Sicht versehen; **to sign a** ~ Wechsel unterschreiben; **to sign a** ~ **into law** einem Gesetz Rechtskraft verleihen; **to stick a** ~ **on a wall** Plakat ankleben; **to stop a** ~ Wechsel sperren; **to sue on a** ~ Wechselklage erheben; **to table a** ~ Gesetzentwurf einbringen, (US) Beratung eines Gesetzentwurfes vertagen; **to talk out a** ~ Gesetzentwurf bis zur Vertagung diskutieren; **to take a** ~ (US) Rechnung bezahlen; **to take up a** ~ Rechnung begleichen, (~ **of exchange**) Wechsel einlösen; **to take up a** ~ **under rebatement** (Br.) Wechsel vor Fälligkeit bezahlen; **to tender a** ~ **for discount** Wechsel zur Zahlung einreichen; **to throw out a** ~ Gesetzentwurf ablehnen; **to trade in** ~**s** Wechselreiterei betreiben; **to undertake to collect a** ~ Wechsel-

inkasso besorgen; **to undertake to discount a ~** Diskontierung eines Wechsels vornehmen; **to value a ~ upon** Wechsel ziehen auf; **to water down a ~** Gesetz verwässern; **to withdraw a ~** Wechsel zurückziehen (zurückrufen); **to write into a ~** in einen Gesetzentwurf aufnehmen (einarbeiten); **to write restrictions into a ~** Gesetzentwurf einschränken;
stick (post, US) no ~s! Plakatanschlag verboten!
~s account Wechselrechnung, -konto; **~s of Exchange Act** *(Br.)* Wechselordnung; **~ of Sale Act** *(Br.)* [etwa] Sicherungsübereignungsgesetz; **~ book** Wechselobligo, -buch; **~s for collection book** Buch (Liste) für Inkassowechsel; **~ broker** *(Br.)* Wechselmakler, *(exchange broker)* Geldwechsler, *(money broker)* Geldvermittler, -makler; **~ brokerage** *(Br.)* Akzeptgeschäft, Wechselgeschäft, -handel, -courtage; **~ case** *(Br.)* Wechselportefeuille, -bestand; **~ charges** Wechselspesen; **~-of-lading clause** Konnossementsklausel; **~ clerk** Angestellter der Wechselabteilung; **~ collector** Wechselinkassobüro; **~ commission** Wechselcourtage; **~ copying book** Wechselkopierbuch; **~ cover** Wechseldeckung; **~ credit** offener Wechselkredit; **~ creditor** Wechselgläubiger; **~ debt** Wechselverbindlichkeit, -schuld; **~ debtor** Wechselschuldner; **~ department** Wechselabteilung; **~ diary** Wechselobligo-, Verfallbuch; **~ discount** *(Br.)* Wechseldiskont; **~ discount rate** Wechseldiskontsatz; **~s discounted ledger (register, US)** Wechselverfallbuch; **~ discounter** Wechseldiskontierer, -makler; **~s discounting** Wechseldiskontierung, -geschäft; **~ file** Wechselregistratur, -archiv; **~ finance** Wechselfinanzierung; **~ forger** Wechselfälscher; **~ forgery** Wechselfälschung, *(bank notes)* Banknotenfälschung; **~ form** Wechselvordruck; **~ guaranty** Wechselbürgschaft; **~ heading** Titel einer Gesetzesvorlage; **~ jobber** *(Br.)* Wechselreiter; **~ jobbing** *(Br.)* Wechselspekulation; **~ ledger** *(~s discounted)* Wechselbuch, -obligo; **~ market** Diskontmarkt; **~s overdue account** Konto überfälliger Wechsel; **~s payable account** *(US)* Wechselkreditorenkonto; **~s payable book** *(US)* Wechselverfallbuch, -journal; **~ penal** Schuldurkunde mit Konventionalstrafe; **~ protest** Wechselprotest; **~ rate** Wechselkurs; **~s receivable account** *(US)* Wechseldebitorenkonto; **~s receivable book** *(US)* Wechseldebitorenbuch; **~s receivable journal** *(US)* Wechseldebitorenverfallbuch; **~ discounted register** *(US)* Wechselkopierbuch; **~ remittance** Wechselüberweisung; **~ stamp** Wechselstempel; **~ sticker** Zettel-, Plakatankleber, Anschläger; **~ sticking** Plakatanschlag; **~ surety** Wechselbürge; **~ transactions** Wechselgeschäft; **~ usury** Wechselwucher.
billboard *(US)* Anschlagtafel, -brett, -stelle, Werbeschild, Litfaßsäule, *(broadcasting)* Vorspann;
~ advertising *(US)* Plakatwerbung; **~ commercial** Fernsehwerbung in Plakatform; **~ hoarding** Anschlagstelle, -tafel, Litfaßsäule.
billed in Rechnung gestellt, berechnet;
~ cost Rechnungskosten [vor Abzug des Bardiskonts]; **~ order** angekündigte Kommissionsware; **~ weight** Rechnungsgewicht.
billet *(fig.)* Stellung, Posten, *(official requisition)* Quartierzettel, *(quarters)* Quartier, Truppen-, Ortsunterkunft;
a good ~ gute Stellung;
~ (v.) unterbringen, einquartieren, mit Einquartierung belegen; **to be ~ed upon s. o.** bei jem. im Quartier liegen.
billeting Zwangseinquartierung;
~ officer Quartiermacher; **~ paper** Quartierschein; **~ party** Quartiermacher.
billfold *(US)* Brief-, Geldscheintasche.
billhead Rechnungsvordruck.
billholder Wechselinhaber.
billholdings Wechselbestand, -portefeuille, Aktivwechsel.
billing Fakturieren, Rechnungsschreibung, -ausstellung, *(advertising)* Gesamtetat (Gesamtbudget, Umsatz) einer Werbeagentur, Etatsumme, *(bill sticking)* Zettelankleben;
line ~ *(railroad)* Gebührenverbuchung zwischen einzelnen Bahnhöfen; **memorandum ~** *(railroad, US)* Ausstellung eines Ersatzfrachtbriefes;
double ~ on travel expenses doppelte Reisespesenrechnung;
to get top ~ *(actor)* an erster Stelle genannt werden;
~ and guide book Fakturenhandbuch; **~ clerk** Fakturist; **~ date** *(US)* Rechnungs-, Fakturendatum; **~ department** *(US)* Rechnungs-, Fakturenabteilung; **~ error** *(US)* Fakturierungsfehler; **~ machine** Fakturiermaschine; **~ method** Fakturierungsmethode; **~ reference** *(railroad)* Warenbezeichnung.
billposter Plakat-, Zettelankleber.
billposting Bogenanschlag, Plakatanschlag, Plakatierung;
~ agency Plakatanschlaginstitut, Bogenanschlagsunternehmen; **~ order** Plakatierungsauftrag.
billy club *(US)* Gummiknüppel.

bimetallic bimetallisch.
bimetallism Doppelwährung, Bimetallismus.
bimetallist Anhänger der Doppelwährung, Bimetallist.
bimonthly alle zwei Monate, zweimonatlich.
bimotored zweimotorig.
binary | choice experiment binäres Auswahlexperiment; **~ flow chart** binäres Flußdiagramm.
binaural effect Raumtoneffekt.
binaurality Raumtonhören.
bind *(Br., sl.)* Plackerei, Quälerei;
~ (v.) (book) einbinden, *(oblige o. s.)* [sich] verpflichten;
~ o. s. Verbindlichkeit eingehen; **~ s. o. out as apprentice** j. in die Lehre geben; **~ a bargain** Handel abschließen; **~ two countries together** zwei Länder miteinander verbinden; **~ s. o. to pay a debt** *(sl.)* j. zur Begleichung seiner Schulden drankriegen; **~ a firm by signing the firm's name** Firma durch Zeichnung des Firmennamens verpflichten; **~ into** einheften; **~ o. s. under oath** sich eidlich verpflichten; **~ over** durch Bürgschaft verpflichten, *(on probation)* Bewährungsfrist geben; **~ one's principal** seinen Auftraggeber rechtlich verpflichten; **~ s. o. to secrecy** j. auf Geheimhaltung verpflichten.
binder *(cover)* Umschlag, Aktendeckel, *(insurance, US)* vorläufige Versicherungspolice, vorläufige Deckungszusage, *(newspaper)* Kreuzband, *(purchase of real estate)* Vorverkaufsvertrag;
spring-back ~ Ringmappe.
binding *(book cover)* Bucheinband, -decke, *(files)* Aktendeckel, Hefter, *(process of binding)* Buchbinderarbeiten;
adhesive ~ Klebeheftung; **flexible (limp) ~** flexibler Einband; **full fabric ~** Ganzgewebeeinband; **half fabric ~** Halbgewebeeinband; **imitation leather ~** Kunstledereinband; **leatherette ~** Kunstledereinband; **parchment ~** Pergamenteinband; **paste board ~** Pappeinband; **plastic ~** Plastikeinband; **rich ~** Luxuseinband;
~ in calf *(book)* Franzband; **~ over** *(witness)* Verpflichtungserklärung;
~ (a.) bindend, zwingend, verbindlich;
generally ~ allgemein verbindlich; **legally ~** rechtsverbindlich; **mutually ~** mit gegenseitiger Verbindlichkeit; **not ~** unverbindlich; **unilaterally ~** einseitig bindend;
~ on all creditors für alle Gläubiger rechtsverbindlich;
to be ~ upon s. o. rechtsverbindlich für j. sein; **to declare to be ~** für [rechts]verbindlich erklären; **to make it ~ on s. o. to do s. th.** j. verpflichten, etw. zu tun;
~ agreement bindende Abmachung, unwiderrufliches Abkommen; **~ authority** bindende Kraft; **~ commitment** bindende Verpflichtung; **~ contract for land** rechtsverbindlicher Grundstückskaufvertrag; **~ effect** bindende Wirkung; **~ force** bindende Kraft; **~ instruction** *(to jury)* verbindliche Rechtsbelehrung; **~ law** bindendes Gesetz; **not ~ offer** freibleibendes Angebot; **~ order** bindender Beschluß; **~ receipt (slip)** *(insurance)* Deckungszusage; **~ specifications** Einbandvorschriften.
binge *(sl.)* Bierreise, Sauftour;
to go on (have) a ~ auf eine Sauftour (Bierreise) gehen.
bingo Zahlen-, Glückslotto.
binominal distribution Häufigkeitsverteilung.
biographer Biograph.
biographical data Lebensdaten.
biography Biographie, Lebensbeschreibung.
biological | control biologische Schädlingsbekämpfung; **~ warfare** biologische Kriegsführung, Bazillenkrieg.
bipartisan | committee Zweiparteienausschuß; **~ foreign policy** von zwei Parteien unterstützte auswärtige Politik; **~ support** Unterstützung beider Parteien.
bipartite in doppelter Ausfertigung;
~ clearing zweiseitiges Zahlungsabkommen; **~ contract** zweiseitiger Vertrag; **~ system** *(US)* Zweiparteiensystem.
bird *(earth satellite)* Erdsatellit;
queer ~ komischer Kauz;
~ of passage Zugvogel, *(fig.)* unsteter Mensch;
to give an actor the ~ Schauspieler auspfeifen; **to give a union the ~ over a strike call** einem Streikaufruf der Gewerkschaft nicht Folge leisten; **to kill two ~s with one stone** zwei Fliegen mit einer Klappe schlagen;
a ~ in the hand is better than a ~ in the bush der Spatz in der Hand ist besser als die Taube auf dem Dach;
~s-and-bees-talk [Sexual]aufklärung; **~'s-eye view** Vogelperspektive.
birth Geburt, *(coming into life)* Entbindung, Niederkunft, *(origin)* Abstammung, Herkunft;
of illegitimate ~ unehelich [geboren];
humble ~ niedrige Abstammung;

~s, marriages and deaths Familiennachrichten; **~ of new ideas** Entstehung neuer Ideen;
to be British by ~ englische Staatsangehörigkeit seit Geburt besitzen; **to give ~ to** entstehen lassen, hervorbringen; **to notify (register) a ~** Geburt beim Standesamt melden; **~ certificate** Geburtsschein, -urkunde; **~ column** Geburtsanzeigen; **~ control** Geburtenkontrolle, -regelung, Familienplanung; **~ control aids** Empfängnisverhütungsmittel; **~-control pill** Empfängnisverhütungspille; **~ controller** Anhänger der Geburtenkontrolle; **~ date** Geburtsdatum; **~ hour** Geburtsstunde; **~ month** Geburtsmonat; **~ name** Geburtsname; **~ process** *(statistics)* Zugangsprozeß; **with a high ~ rate** geburtenstark; **with a low ~ rate** geburtenschwach; **crude ~ rate** nicht aufgegliederte Geburtenziffer; **falling ~ rate** Geburtsausfall; **to bring down the ~ rate** Geburtenrückgang erzielen; **~-rate decline** Geburtenrückgang; **~ registration** Geburtenregistrierung, Beurkundung von Geburten; **~ regulation** Geburtenregelung; **~ right** Erstgeburtsrecht; **~ year** Geburtsjahr.
birthday Geburtstag;
to give s. o. a ~ present jem. zum Geburtstag etw. schenken; **to be in one's ~ suit** im Adamskostüm sein.
birthland Geburtsland.
birthmark Geburtsmal.
birthplace Geburtsstadt, -haus.
biscuit, to take the dem Faß den Boden ausschlagen.
bissext Schalttag.
bissextile | day Schalttag; **~ year** Schaltjahr.
bit Stückchen, Bissen, Happen, *(broadcasting, film)* kleine Rolle, *(coin, Br.)* kleine Münze, *(coll.)* Weilchen, Augenblick, Kleinigkeit, *(data processing)* unauflösliche Informationsgrundeinheit, kleinste Darstellungseinheit, *(spare part)* Ersatzteil, *(tool)* Bohrer, Meißel;
not a ~ keine Spur, ganz und gar nicht; **~ by ~** sukzessive, nach und nach, Stück für Stück; **in ~s and pieces** stückweise; **the biter ~** der betrogene Betrüger; **my ~s and pieces** meine sieben Sachen;
to bite on the ~s sich etw. verkneifen; **to do one's ~** seine Pflicht erfüllen; **to draw ~** *(fig.)* Geschwindigkeit verlangsamen; **to eat every ~ of one's dinner** alles bis auf den letzten Krümel aufessen; **to give s. o. a ~ of one's mind** jem. gehörig Bescheid sagen; **to have a ~ of gumption** ein bißchen Grütze im Kopf haben; **to have saved a nice ~ of money** schönes Stück Geld gespart haben; **to pick up the ~s** Retter in der Not spielen; **to take the ~ between one's teeth** sich störrig zeigen;
~-player Komparse.
bitch *(sl.)* Beschwerde;
~ (v.) sich beschweren.
bite Bissen, Happen, *(etching)* Ätzen;
~ into exemptions Freibetragsbelastung; **~ of inflation** Inflationsbelastung;
~ (v.) beißen, stechen, *(etch)* ätzen;
~ the dust ins Gras beißen; **~ the hand that feeds one** seinen Wohltäter hintergehen; **~ off more than one can chew** sich zuviel zumuten; **~ off one's nose** sich ins eigene Fleisch schneiden; **to have a ~** Kleinigkeit essen; **to put the ~ on s. o.** *(US)* j. unter Druck setzen; **to put the tax ~ on** Steuerschraube anziehen; **to take a bigger ~ out of the economy** Konjunktur in zunehmendem Maße negativ beeinflussen.
biter bit betrogener Betrüger.
biweekly Halbmonatsschrift.
bizonal bizonal.
blab Klatschbase;
~ (v.) out a secret Geheimnis ausplaudern.
black Schwarzer, *(balance sheet, US coll.)* Gewinnzone, -bereich, *(mourning)* schwarze Kleidung, Trauerkleidung, *(trade-union term, Br., coll.)* Boykottware;
in the ~ *(US coll.)* zahlungsfähig, solvent, ohne Schulden; **in ~ and white** *(fig.)* schwarz auf weiß;
~s *(print)* Spieß;
~ (v.) schwärzen, *(boycott)* boykottieren, lahmlegen, bestreiken;
~ out verdunkeln, *(censorship)* unterdrücken, *(el.)* Stromzufuhr unterbrechen, *(jamming)* Rundfunkprogramm stören; **~ out the country** Strom im ganzen Land abschalten; **~ a shop** *(trade union)* der Gewerkschaft nicht genehmen Betrieb auf die schwarze Liste setzen; **~ supply** Versorgung unterbrechen; **to be in ~** Trauerkleidung tragen; **to be in the ~** *(US)* in der Gewinnzone (rentabel) sein; **to be back in the ~** *(US)* wieder mit Gewinn arbeiten, Gewinnschwelle wieder erreicht haben; **to bring back into the ~** *(US)* wieder in die Gewinnzone bringen; **to declare a hotel ~** Boykott über ein Hotel verhängen; **to have s.**

th. **down in ~ and white** etw. schwarz auf weiß nach Hause tragen; **to look ~ at s. o.** j. wütend (finster) ansehen; **to operate in the ~** *(US)* mit Gewinn arbeiten; **to say ~ in s. one's eye** j. herabsetzen, verächtlich machen; **to show up in ~ on the balance sheet** *(US)* sich auf der Aktivseite der Bilanz niederschlagen, Bilanzergebnis positiv gestalten;
~ (a.) schwarz, *(black marketing)* schwarz (ohne Marken) erhältlich, *(unlawful)* ungesetzlich;
~ as pitch pechschwarz;
~ and white advertising Schwarzweißanzeige; **to reduce the ~ area** Zivilisation vorantreiben; **~ belt** *(US)* Negerviertel; **~ book** Verzeichnis fauler Kunden; **to be in s. one's ~ books** bei jem. schlecht angeschrieben sein; **~ border** *(newspaper)* schwarzer Rand, Trauerrand; **~ bourse** Schwarzhandel [in Devisen]; **~-coated** *(Br.)* im Büro angestellt; **~-coated classes** *(Br.)* Büroangestellte; **~-coated proletariat** *(Br.)* Stehkragenproletariat; **~-coated worker** *(Br.)* Büroangestellter; **~ dog** *(coll.)* Katzenjammer, deprimierte Stimmung; **~ death** Pest; **~ exchange rate** Devisenkurs auf dem schwarzen Markt; **to get away with a ~ eye** mit einem blauen Auge davonkommen; **~ face** *(print.)* [halb]fette Schrift; **~ flag** Piratenflagge; **~ frame** schwarzer Rand, schwarze Umrandung; **~ gang** *(ship, sl.)* Maschinisten; **~ hands** schmutzige Hände; **~ hole** *(mil.)* strenger Arrest; **~ iron work** Schmiedearbeit; **~ letters** *(print.)* Fraktur, gotische Schrift; **~-letter day** Unglückstag; **~ level** *(television)* Austastpegel; **~ list** *(bankruptcy)* Insolventenliste, „Konkurse"; **~ list (v.)** auf die schwarze Liste setzen; **~ majority rule** schwarze Mehrheitsregierung; **~ man** *(US)* Schwarzer, Neger; **~ Maria** *(sl.)* Gefängniswagen, Grüne Minna; **~ mark for tardiness** schlechte Note für Verspätung.
black market Schwarzmarkt;
~ (v.) Schwarzhandel treiben;
to operate the ~ sich als Schwarzmarkthändler betätigen; **~ operations** Schwarzhandel[sgeschäft]; **~ operator** Schwarzhändler; **~ price** Schwarzmarktpreis.
black | marketeer Schwarzhändler; **~-marketeer (v.)** sich als Schwarzhändler betätigen; **~ marketing** Schwarzmarkthandel; **~ Monday** *(school)* erster Schultag; **~ print** Fettdruck; **~ rent** ungesetzliche Miete; **~ sheep** *(Br.)* Streikbrecher; **~ sheep of the family** *(Br.)* schwarzes Schaf der Familie; **~ side** Schattenseite; **~ snake** *(sl.)* Kohlenzug; **~ and tan** *(US)* Mulatte; **~ and tan bar** von Schwarzen und Weißen gemeinsam besuchte Bar; **~ tidings** schlechte Nachrichten; **in ~ and white** gedruckt, schriftlich; **~ widow** *(sl.)* unbeliebtes Mädchen; **~ words** unheilvoll klingende Worte.
blackbaiter *(sl.)* Sklavenhändler.
blackball Gegenstimme, schwarze Wahlkugel;
~ (v.) dagegen stimmen;
~ s. o. from a club jem. den Eintritt in einen Verein verwehren.
blackbirder *(sl.)* Sklavenhändler.
blackboard Wandtafel, *(school)* schwarze Tafel.
blacken *(v.) (fig.)* anschwärzen, verleumden.
blackface *(print.)* halbfette Schrift.
blacketeer *(US)* Schwarzhändler.
blackguard Schuft, Lumpenpack.
blacking schwarze Schuhwichse, *(censor)* Unterdrückung, Streichung;
to use the ~ technique *(trade union)* Politik der schwarzen Listen betreiben.
blacking out Verdunkelung;
~ material Verdunkelungsmaterial.
blackjack Piratenflagge, *(leather-covered club, US)* Totschläger.
blackleg *(strike, Br., sl.)* Streikbrecher, *(coll.)* Falschspieler, Gauner;
~ (v.) *(Br.)* gegen die Gewerkschaftssatzungen verstoßen; **~ work** *(Br.)* Streikarbeit.
blackleggery *(Br.)* gewerkschaftsfeindliches Verhalten, Streikbrechertum.
blacklist *(v.)* auf die schwarze Liste setzen;
~ a company from receiving government contracts Firma von der Beteiligung an Ausschreibungen der Regierung ausschließen; **to be ~ed** auf die schwarze Liste kommen.
blackmail Nötigung, Erpressung, Erpressergeld;
attempted ~ Erpressungsversuch; **literary ~** förmliche Erpressung;
~ (v.) erpressen, Erpressung begehen;
to level ~ Erpressungsversuch begehen; **~ racket** *(US)* Erpressertrick.
blackmailer Erpresser.
blackmailing Erpressung;
~ letter Erpresserbrief.

blackout, *(aeronautical)* Ausfall der Funkverbindungen, *(blockade)* Sperre, Blockierung, *(el.)* Stromsperre, *(mil.)* Verdunkelung, *(complete failure of memory)* Gedächtnisschwund;
intellectual ~ *(sl.)* geistige Blockade; **news ~** Nachrichtensperre;
trial ~ Verdunkelungsübung;
~ of consciousness Bewußtseinslücke;
to impose a ~ on information Nachrichtensperre verhängen;
~ time Verdunkelungszeit.
blacktop schwarze Straßendecke.
blackwash *(fig.)* Anschwärzung.
blame Schuld, Verantwortung, *(censure)* Tadel, Vorwurf;
~ for an accident Unfallschuld;
~ *(v.)* tadeln;
to be equally to ~ *(insurance)* zu gleichen Teilen schuldig sein; **to lay the ~ at s. one's door** jem. etw. in die Schuhe schieben; **to put the ~ upon s. o.** Schuld auf j. schieben.
blank *(blind window)* blindes Fenster, *(fig.)* hoffnungsloser Zustand, Nichts, Öde, *(lottery)* Niete, *(printed form)* Formular, Vordruck, Formblatt, Blankett, leeres Papier, *(~ space)* Lücke, leerer Raum, Zwischenraum, *(US)* unausgefülltes Formular;
in ~ blanko;
~s Leerdruck;
~ *(v.)* **out** *(print.)* gesperrt drucken;
~ *(a.) (form)* leer, *(form of bill)* unausgefertigt, *(unfilled space)* unbeschrieben, unbedruckt, unausgefüllt, unausgefertigt, blanko;
to accept in ~ blanko akzeptieren; **to amount to ~** *(assets)* gleich null sein; **to be a ~** *(stock exchange)* ohne Abschluß sein; **to draw a ~** Niete ziehen, *(fig.)* Fehlschlag erleiden; **to draw in ~** blanko trassieren; **to endorse in ~** blanko indossieren; **to fill in the ~** Blankoformular ausfüllen; **to leave a ~** frei (leer, unausgefüllt) lassen; **to leave a big ~ in s. one's life** große Lücke in jds. Leben hinterlassen; **to look ~** ganz verblüfft aussehen; **to make out in ~** blanko ausstellen; **to sign in ~** *(document)* blanko unterschreiben;
~ acceptance Blankoakzept, -annahme; **~ advance** Blankovorschuß; **~ audit** Blankoauftrag; **~ bill** Blankowechsel, Wechselblankett; **~ board** Schaufensterkarton; **~ bonds** *(Scot.)* Blankoobligationen; **~ book** Notizbuch; **~ certificate** Blankopapier; **~ check** *(US)* **(cheque,** *Br.)* Blankoscheck, Scheckformular; **to give s. o. a ~ check** jem. unbegrenzte Vollmachten erteilen; **~ cover** Briefumschlag ohne Adresse; **~ credit** Blankokredit, offener Kredit; **~ day** dienstfreier Tag; **~ endorsement** Blankoindossament; **~ engagement** Blankoauftrag; **~ face** verblüfftes Gesicht; **~ form** Blankoformular, Blankett; **~ idiot** *(sl.)* Vollidiot; **~ impossibility** absolute Unmöglichkeit; **~ leaf** Leerseite; **~ line** blinde Zeile; **~ material** Blind-, Füllmaterial; **~ page** leere (unbeschriebene, unbedruckte) Seite; **~ paper** Blankopapier; **~ policy** Policenformular, Blankopolice; **~ power of attorney** Blankovollmacht; **~ sheet of paper** weißes Blatt Papier; **~ signature** Blankounterschrift; **~ space** leerer (unbedruckter) Raum, Ausschluß; **~ transaction** Blankogeschäft; **~ transfer** Blankoübertragung, *(Br.)* Blankogiro, -indorsement; **~ vote** leerer Stimmzettel; **~ voting paper** leerer Stimmzettel.
blanket *(expense account)* pauschale Kostenangabe, *(fig.)* Decke, Hülle;
on the wrong side of the ~ außerehelich;
wet ~ *(fig.)* Miesmacher;
~ of clouds Wolkendecke; **~ of snow** Schneedecke;
~ *(v.)* **the entire market** ganzen Markt erfassen; **~ a rumo(u)r** Gerücht totschweigen (vertuschen);
~ *(a.) (US)* umfassend, gesamt, generell, global, allgemein gültig;
~ act Blankettgesetz; **~ ballot** Kandidatenliste aller Parteien; **~ bond** Blankoverpflichtung, *(mortgage)* sicherungsweise abgetretene Hypothek; **banker's ~ bond** Blankettversicherungsschein für Bankangestellte; **commercial ~ bond** *(US)* Blankettversicherungsschein für Versicherungsdelikte von Betriebsangehörigen; **~ clause** Generalklausel; **~ contract** *(broadcasting)* Gesamtabschluß; **~ injunction** generelles Verbot für bestimmte Streikaktionen; **~ instruction** umfassende Anweisung; **~ insurance** Kollektivversicherung; **~ mortgage** Gesamthypothek; **~ order** Blankoauftrag; **~ patent** umfassendes Patent; **~ policy** *(fire insurance)* Pauschalpolice; **~ position bond** *(US)* Blankettversicherungsschein; **~ price** Einheits-, Pauschalpreis; **~ prohibition** Globalverbot; **~ purchase order** Blanketteinkaufsauftrag; **~ rate** *(insurance, US)* Pauschaltarif, -satz, *(long distance traffic)* Sammeltarif; **~ sheet** Zeitung im Weltformat; **~ subsidy** generelle Zulage; **~ tariff supplement** Rahmenvertragsergänzung; **~ waybill** Kollektivfrachtbrief.
blanking paper Fondpapier.

blarny leere Redensarten, *(Irish)* verbindliche Sprache.
blasphemy Gotteslästerung.
blast, Sturm, *(fig.)* Fluch, verderblicher Einfluß, *(mining)* schlagende Wetter, *(tel., sl.)* [Telefon]anruf;
at full ~ *(coll.)* auf Hochtouren; **in ~** in Betrieb; **out of ~** außer Betrieb;
~ *(v.)* **s. one's reputation** j. um seinen guten Namen bringen;
to be going at full ~ in vollem Betrieb sein; **to give s. one a ~** *(sl.)* j. anrufen; **to sound a ~** Tusch blasen;
~ furnace Hochofen; **~ wall** Schutzwall.
blaster *(science fiction)* Strahler.
blatancy anmaßendes Benehmen.
blatant marktschreierisch.
blaze Feuerbann, Feuer, Lohe;
like ~s wie verrückt;
~ *(v.) (quotations)* in die Höhe schießen;
~ the news abroad Neuigkeit überall bekanntmachen; **~ a trail** *(fig.)* Weg bahnen;
to be in a ~ in Flammen stehen; **to go to ~s** zum Teufel gehen.
bleed *(advertising)* Anschnitt, angeschnittener Druck;
gutter ~ *(advertisement)* Innenanschnitt; **outside ~** Außenanschnitt;
~ *(v.)* [Seite] anschneiden, druckangeschnitten drucken;
~ for s. th. für etw. schwer bluten (blechen) müssen; **~ a country white** Land ausbluten lassen; **~ money from s. o.** Geld von jem. erpressen; **~ well** *(sl.)* Geld springen lassen;
~ *(a.)* druckangeschnitten;
~ advertisement angeschnittene Anzeige; **~ charge** Anschnittzuschlag; **~ difference** Beschnittzugabe; **~-off page** druckangeschnittene Seite; **~-page advertisement** angeschnittene Anzeige; **~ premium** Anschnittzuschlag.
blemish Makel, Schandfleck;
~ *(v.)* entstellen, verunstalten, *(fig.)* verleumden.
blend Mischung, *(alcohol)* Verschnitt;
~ *(v.)* **industrial experience with academic life** Industrieerfahrung mit dem Universitätsleben verbinden.
blended | fund *(Br.)* zur Versilberung bestimmter Nachlaß; **~ price** *(milk)* Durchschnittspreis.
blessings Glücksgüter;
to give its ~ absegnen.
blight Frostschaden, *(fig.)* schädlicher Einfluß.
blighted area heruntergekommenes Wohnviertel.
blighty *(leave)* Heimaturlaub;
~ wound Heimatschuß.
blimp *(airship)* Kleinluftschiff, *(cabin)* schalldichte Kabine, *(camera, US)* Schallschutzhaube, *(politics, Br.)* ultrakonservativer Reaktionär.
blind blind, *(fig.)* uneinsichtig, unbesonnen, *(Br., sl.)* blau, betrunken, *(letter addressed illegibly, sl.)* unleserlich addressierter Brief, *(pretext)* Bemäntelung, Vorwand, *(window)* Markise, Rouleau, Jalousie, Fenstervorhang;
roller ~ Rolljalousieladen; **short ~** Scheibengardine;
~ *(v.) (fig.)* verdunkeln, in den Schatten stellen, *(mil.)* bombenfest machen;
~ o. s. to facts sich den Tatsachen verschließen; **~ a trail** Spur verwischen;
to be struck ~ mit Blindheit geschlagen sein; **to fly ~** blindfliegen;
to lower the ~s Jalousien herunterlassen;
~ advertisement Blindanzeige; **~ alley** Sackgasse; **~-alley job** Beruf ohne Aufstiegsmöglichkeiten; **~ approach** Blindanflug; **~ area** Funkschatten, *(car)* toter Winkel; **~ baggage** *(deadhead, US sl.)* blinder Passagier; **~ baggage car** *(US)* Gepäckwagen ohne Durchgangstüren; **~ bargain** *(fam.)* Katze im Sack; **~ blocking** Blindprägung; **~ bombing** *(mil.)* Blindabwurf; **~ booking** *(film)* Blindbuchung; **~ calculator** blind schreibende Rechenmaschine; **~ car** Waggon ohne Plattform; **~ carbon copy** zusätzliche Kopie; **~ chance** blinder Zufall; **~ coal** Anthrazit; **~ copy** unleserliches Manuskript; **~ corner** unübersichtliche Straßenecke; **~ date** *(US)* Verabredung mit einem Unbekannten; **~ door** zugemauerte Tür; **~ drunk** *(sl.)* stockbesoffen; **~ entry** *(booking without voucher)* Blindbuchung, Pro-memoria-Buchung; **~ excuse** ungenügende Entschuldigung, faule Ausrede; **to turn a ~ eye on s. th.** bei etw. ein Auge zudrücken; **~ figure** undeutlich geschriebene Ziffer; **~ fixtures** geschlossene Ladenstelle; **~ flight** Blindflug; **~ flying** Blindfliegen, -flug, Instrumentenflug; **~ headline** ungeschickte Schlagzeile; **~ landing** Blindlandung; **~ landing system** Blindlandeeinrichtung; **~ letter** *(sl.)* schlecht adressierter (unbestellbarer) Brief; **~ lift** Jalousiezug; **~ man** Blinder; **~ man's dog** Blindenhund; **~ part** unbedruckter Teil; **~ person** Blinder; **~ print** Schimmel; **~ prod-**

uct test Anzeigenerinnerungstest; ~ **radio** *(US)* Hörfunk; ~ **shell** Blindgänger; ~ **side** *(fig.)* schwache Seite; ~ **space** *(print.)* Zwischenraum; ~ **spot** *(fig.)* schwache Stelle, *(radio)* Empfangsloch; ~ **staircase** Geheimtreppe; ~-**stamp** *(v.)* blindprägen; ~ **stamping** Prägedruck; ~ **tiger** *(US sl.)* illegaler Alkoholausschank; ~ **tooling** Blinddruck; ~ **traffic** Blindverkehr; ~ **turning** unübersichtliche Kurve; ~ **vein** blinde Erzader; ~ **waggon** unbeschrifteter Möbelwagen; ~ **window** Blendfenster.

blindness disability payments Invalidenrenten an Blinde.

blink Blinken, Schimmer;
on the ~ *(US sl.)* in untauglichem Zustand;
~ *(v.)* durch Lichtsignale mitteilen;
~ **the eyes** die Augen blenden, blinzeln;
~ **a fact** Tatsache leugnen; ~ **a question** einer Frage ausweichen;
to go on the ~ *(sl.)* reparaturbedürftig sein.

blinker Blinklicht, *(fig.)* Scheuklappen;
~**s** Schutzbrille;
~ *(v.)* *(fig.)* hinters Licht führen;
to put on the ~s *(fig.)* sich Scheuklappen aufsetzen;
~ **apparatus** Lichtsprech-, Blinkgerät; ~ **beacon** Blinkfeuer.

blinking nuisance dummer Unsinn.

blip *(radar)* Echozeichen, Leuchtfleck.

blister Brandblase, *(med.)* Zugpflaster.

blitz heftiger Luftangriff;
~ *(v.)* bombardieren;
~ **training** Schnellkurs.

blitzed areas zerbombte Gebiete.

blitzkrieg Blitzkrieg, *(fig.)* Überrumpelung.

blizzard Schneesturm.

bloc *(politics)* Block, Einheitsfront;
en ~ *(voting)* gesamt;
agricultural (**farm,** *US)* ~ grüne Front; **sterling** ~ Pfund-, Sterlingblock;
~ **grant** zur freien Verfügung gewährter Zuschuß; ~ **licence** *(patent)* Pauschallizenz.

block Block, *(advertising)* Sendereihe, *(blockade)* Hindernis, Absperrung, *(bookbinding)* Prägestempel, *(of buildings, US)* Häuser-, Geschäftsblock, Häuserkomplex, -viertel, Reihenhäuser, Straßenquadrat, *(business)* Anhäufung, *(exhibition)* Sockel, *(lot)* Partie, Paket, *(for notes)* Notizblock, *(parl.)* Obstruktion, Lahmlegung, *(print.)* Druckstock, -form, Klischee, *(railway)* Blockabschnitt, *(trade)* Wirtschaftsblock, *(traffic)* Verkehrsstockung;
in ~s in Bausch und Bogen; **on the ~** zur Versteigerung anstehend;
controlling ~ kontrollierendes Aktienpaket; **currency** ~ Währungsblock; **road** ~ Straßensperre; **traffic** ~ Verkehrshindernis, -stauung; **writing** ~ Schreibblock;
~ **of composition** Satzblock; ~ **of delegates** Delegiertengruppe; ~ **of flats** *(Br.)* Etagen-, Apartment-, Mehrfamilienhaus, Wohnblock; ~ **of houses** Häuserkomplex, -block; ~ **of offices** Bürohauskomplex; ~ **in a pipe** Rohrverstopfung; ~ **of securities** Effektenpaket; ~ **of shares** *(Br.)* (**stocks,** *US)* Aktienpaket; ~ **of surveys** Sammelvermessung; ~ **in the traffic** Verkehrsstauung, -störung; **large** ~ **of stock units** großes Aktienpaket;
~ *(v.)* *(obstruct)* hemmen, hindern, vereiteln, blockieren, verhindern, [ab]sperren, abriegeln, *(parl.)* durch Opposition verhindern;
~ **an account** Guthaben (Konto) sperren; ~ **a** (**the passage of a**) **bill** Beratung eines Gesetzentwurfes verhindern, Annahme eines Gesetzantrages blockieren; ~ **a credit balance** Guthaben sperren; ~ **in** Rohskizze machen, skribbeln; ~ **s. one's plans** jds. Pläne vereiteln; ~ **a special resolution** qualifizierten Mehrheitsbeschluß blockieren; ~ **traffic** Verkehr aufhalten (blockieren); ~ **the street to traffic** Straße sperren; ~ **up** absperren, blockieren; ~ **up a harbo(u)r** Hafensperre vornehmen;
to impose a ~ on Hindernis errichten; **to live five ~s from here** fünf Straßen weiter wohnen; **to market one's ~ of shares** (**stocks,** *US)* sein Aktienpaket auf den Markt bringen (verkaufen); **to tool a ~** Klischee nachschneiden;
~ **address** Blockadresse; ~ **advertisement** Klischeeanzeige; ~ **base** Klischeefuß; ~ **book** Blockbuch; ~ **booking** *(advertising)* Gesamtauftrag, *(motion picture)* Blockbuchung *(patent law)* Vergabe von Paketlizenzen; ~ **cabinet** Klischeeschrank; ~ **capitals** in Großbuchstaben schreiben; ~ **calendar** Abreißkalender; ~ **captain** Luftschutzwart; ~ **circuit** *(el.)* Sperrkreis; ~ **diagram** Säulendiagramm; ~ **floating** Wechselkursfreigabe; ~ **grant** *(Br.)* pauschaler Kommunalzuschuß, Zweckzuweisung; ~ **issue** Paketemission; ~ **letters** Druck-, Blockschrift, Druckbuchstaben; ~ **loading** Sammelvorladung; ~ **offer** *(investment trust)* Paketangebot; ~-**out** für Werbung gesperrte Sendezeit; ~

pavement *(US)* Steinpflaster, Pflasterdecke; ~ **policy** typisierter Versicherungsschein, Generalpolice; ~ **preservation** Klischeeaufbewahrung; ~ **printing** Handdruck; ~ **pull** Klischeeabzug; ~ **rate** *(electricity)* degressiv gestaffelter Tarif; ~-**to**-~ **rule** Festsetzung von Erschließungskosten entspr. den Grunderwerbskosten; ~ **signal** *(railway)* Blocksignal; ~ **slip** *(check book)* Kupon; ~ **station** *(railway)* Blockstelle; ~ **storage** Klischeeaufbewahrung; ~ **system** *(railway)* Blocksystem, *(US)* System zur beschleunigten Prüfung von Kasseneingängen; ~ **ticket** Sammelfahrschein; ~ **trade** *(stock market)* Pakethandel; **to negotiate prices on ~ trades** Paketzuschläge aushandeln; ~ **transaction in share parcels** Pakethandel; ~ **type** *(print.)* Blockschrift; ~ **vote** einheitliches Votum, Abstimmungsblock, Sammelstimme; ~ **white on block** Negativklischee; ~ **writing** Blockschrift.

blockade Blockierung, Stockung;
~ [**by sea**] Blockade, Schiffahrts-, Hafensperre, *(siege)* Belagerung, Zernierung;
close ~ scharf durchgeführte (strenge) Blockade; **economic** ~ Wirtschaftsblockade; **effective** ~ erfolgreiche (wirksame) Blockade; **hunger** ~ Hungerblockade; **long-distance** ~ Seesperre; **pacific** ~ Friedensblockade; **paper** ~ unwirksame Blockade; **public** ~ offizielle Blockade; **simple** ~ lokalisierte Blockade;
~ **of exchange** Devisensperre;
~ *(v.)* sperren, blockieren, *(mil.)* belagern, zernieren;
~ **a port** Blockade über einen Hafen verhängen;
to call off (**lift**) **a** ~ Blockade aufheben; **to notify a** ~ Blockade bekanntgeben; **to raise a** ~ Blockade aufheben; **to relax a** ~ Blockade lockern; **to render a** ~ **valid as against neutrals** auch gegen Neutrale wirksame Blockade durchführen; **to run the** ~ Blockade durchbrechen; **to tighten a** ~ Blockade verschärfen (verstärken);
~ **runner** Blockadebrecher; ~ **running** Blockadedurchbruch.

blockader Blockadeschiff.

blockading force Blockadestreitmacht.

blockbuster *(US)* Kassenschlager.

blocked gesperrt, blockiert;
to be ~ *(capital)* eingefroren sein;
~ **account** gesperrtes Konto, Sperrkonto; ~ **amount** Sperrbetrag; ~ **area** Sperrgebiet; ~ [**credit**] **balance** Sperrguthaben; ~ **credit** eingefrorener Kredit; ~ **currency** nicht frei konvertierbare und transferierbare Währung; ~ **deposit** Sperrdepot; ~ **foreign exchange** blockierte (eingefrorene) Devisen; ~ **funds** eingefrorene Gelder; ~ **letters** Blockschrift; ~-**out** für Werbesendungen gesperrt; ~ **property** eingefrorene (gesperrte) Vermögenswerte; ~ **road** Straße gesperrt; ~ **station** *(railway)* Blockstelle.

blockhouse Blockhouse, *(mil.)* Baracke.

blocking Sperrung, Sperre;
~ **of account** Kontensperre; ~ **a highway** Straßensperrung; ~ **of property** Vermögenssperre;
~ **arrangement** Stillhalteabkommen; ~ **mechanism** Sperrvorrichtung; ~ **minority** Sperrminorität; ~ **note** Sperrvermerk; ~ **patent** Sperrpatent; ~ **period** Sperrfrist; **to retain** ~ **powers in Parliament** Vetorechte im Parlament behalten.

blockmaker Klischeehersteller, -anstalt.

blockmaking Klischeeherstellung;
~ **charges** Klischeeherstellungskosten.

blockmaster Klischeehersteller.

blood Blut, *(relationship by descent)* Blutsverwandtschaft, Familie, Abstammung, Herkunft, Geschlecht;
allied by ~ blutsverwandt; **in cold** ~ kaltblütig; **near in** ~ nahe verwandt; **of the whole** ~ von den gleichen Eltern abstammend; **blue** ~ blaues Blut; **half** ~ Halbblut, halbblütige Geschwister; **one's own flesh and** ~ sein eigenes Fleisch und Blut; **whole** ~ vollblütig;
~ **and thunder** Mord und Totschlag;
to make bad ~ Unfrieden zwischen zwei Menschen stiften; **to make s. one's** ~ **boil** jds. Blut zum Sieden (Kochen) bringen; **to stir the** ~ böses Blut machen; **to sweat** ~ Blut und Wasser schwitzen;
~ **bank** Blutbank; ~ **bond** Blutsbande, verwandtschaftliche Beziehung; ~ **brother** Blutsbruder; ~ **cousin** Vetter ersten Grades; ~ **donation** Blutspende; ~ **donor** Blutspender; ~ **group** Blutgruppe; ~ **letting** Aderlaß, Selbstzerfleischung; ~-**and-thunder literature** Schundliteratur; ~ **money** Kopfgeld; ~ **poisoning** Blutvergiftung; ~ **pressure** Blutdruck; ~ **relation** Blutsverwandter; ~ **relationship** Blutsverwandtschaft; ~ **stream** Blutzirkulation; ~ **sucker** *(fig.)* Blutsauger; ~ **test** Blutprobe; ~ **transfusion** Bluttransfusion.

bloodguiltiness Blutschuld.

bloodhound Blut-, Schweiß-, Polizeihund.
bloodmobile fahrbare Blutspenderstelle.
bloodshed Blutvergießen.
bloodymindedness konstante Antihaltung.
bloom *(film)* Rückstrahlung, *(television)* Überstrahlung.
bloomer *(literature)* Stilblüte.
blossom Blüte[zeit].
blot Tintenklecks, *(erasure)* Rasur, *(fig.)* Makel, Schandfleck;
~ **on the character** Charakterfehler; ~ **on the escutcheon** Fleck auf der weißen Weste; ~ **on the landscape** Verunstaltung der Landschaft;
~ *(v.)* *(print.)* unsauber abziehen;
~ **one's copybook** *(coll.)* sich seine Chancen verscherzen, seinem guten Ruf Abbruch tun; ~ **out** aus-, durchstreichen;
~ **out the view** Sicht versperren.
blotted print durchgeschlagener Druck.
blotter Löscher, *(brokerage)* Orderbuch, Kladde, *(single-entry bookkeeping)* Tagebuch;
police ~ *(US)* polizeiliches Meldebuch;
~ **advertising** Löschblattreklame.
blotting|**pad** Schreibunterlage; ~ **paper** Löschpapier.
blow Schlag, Hieb, Stoß, *(brag, US sl.)* Prahlerei, Angabe, *(mar.)* steife Brise, starker Wind;
without striking a ~ kampflos;
finishing ~ Todesstoß;
~ **of fortune** Schicksalsschlag; ~ **of a fuse** Herausspringen einer Sicherung;
~ *(v.)* blasen, wehen, *(boast, US coll.)* prahlen, angeben, sich aufblasen, *(burst)* explodieren, *(clear off, sl.)* verduften, abhauen, türmen, *(fuse)* herausspringen, *(spend freely)* verschwenderisch ausgeben;
~ **o. s. to s. th.** *(US)* sich etw. leisten; ~ **one's brains out** sich eine Kugel durch den Kopf schießen; ~ **dust in s. one's eyes** jem. blauen Dunst vormachen; ~ **the gall about s. th.** *(fam.)* etw. verpfeifen; ~ **hot and cold** sein Mäntelchen nach dem Winde hängen; ~ **the lid off** *(sl.)* Skandal enthüllen; ~ **money** *(sl.)* Geld verpulvern; ~ **off steam** *(fig.)* sich abreagieren, seinem Herzen Luft machen; ~ **an oil well** Ölquelle durch Sprengung löschen; ~ **out** *(fuse)* herausspringen; ~ **out of its course** *(ship)* vom Kurs abgetrieben werden; ~ **over** *(scandal)* vergessen werden; ~ **one's top** *(sl.)* Wutanfall bekommen; ~ **one's own trumpet** sich beweihräuchern; ~ **up** als Riesenformat herausbringen, vergrößern, *(sl.)* sprengen, scheitern lassen; ~ **up a quarrel** Streit schüren; ~ **up way out of proportion** weit über Gebühr aufbauschen;
to come to ~**s** handgemein werden; **to go for a** ~ frische Luft schöpfen gehen;
~ **down** *(US, forestry)* Windbruch; ~ **job** *(airforce, sl.)* Düsenflugzeug; ~ **post** *(Br.)* Rohrpost.
blowback freiwillige Rückgabe von Diebesgut.
blowup photographische Vergrößerung, *(advertising)* zum Plakat vergrößerte Anzeige, Riesenformat, *(smash, US)* Zusammenbruch, Pleite, Bankrott.
bludgeon Knüppel, Totschläger.
~ *(v.)* niederknüppeln.
blue|**s** *(coll.)* melancholische Stimmung, Melancholie;
out of the ~ aus heiterem (blauem) Himmel, ganz plötzlich;
a true ~ Erzkonservativer, treuer Parteianhänger;
to appear (come) out of the ~ vom Himmel fallen, aus dem Nichts erscheinen; **to have the** ~**s** *(coll.)* in gedrückter Stimmung sein, Trübsal blasen;
~ *(a.)* bedrückt, niedergeschlagen, *(pol., Br.)* zuverlässig, konservativ;
~ *(v.)* **one's money** *(sl.)* mit dem Geld um sich schmeißen;
~ **airmail label** *(Br.)* Luftpostkleber; ~ **blood** Aristokrat, alter Adel; ~**-blooded** blaublütig; ~ **book** *(Br.)* Blaubuch, jährliche volkswirtschaftliche Gesamtrechnung, *(US)* Reiseführer für Autofahrer; ~ **button** *(London stock exchange)* autorisierter Maklergehilfe; ~ **chips** *(US, stock exchange)* erstklassige Effekten, Standard-, Spitzenwerte; ~**-collar people** *(US)* Fabrikarbeiter; ~**-collar reaction** *(US)* Reaktion der Arbeiterklasse; ~**-collar union** *(US)* Industriegewerkschaft; ~ **worker** *(US)* Fabrik-, Handarbeiter; ~ **devil** Säuferwahnsinn; **to have a** ~ **eye in the city** *(US)* an der Börse einen guten Namen haben; ~ **film** obszöner Film; ~ **funk** *(sl.)* Heidenangst; ~ **jacket** Blaujacke, Matrose; ~ **laws** *(US)* [puritanische] Sonntagsgesetze; ~ **light** *(mar.)* Blaufeuer; ~ **lookout** trübe Aussichten; ~ **man** *(policeman)* Blauer; ~ **Monday** *(US)* Alltag, Blauer Montag; ~ **moon** nie eintretendes Ereignis; **once in a** ~ **moon** äußerst selten; ~ **nose** *(US sl.)* hochnäsige (sittenstrenge) Person, Puritaner; ~ **notes** deckungsstockgesicherte Schuldurkunden; ~ **pencil** Blau-

stift; ~**-pencil** *(v.)* zensieren; ~ **period** schlechte Zeiten; ~ **peter** *(mar.)* Abfahrtssignalflagge; **the** ~ **Ribbon** das blaue Band; ~ **ribbon** *(first prize)* höchste Auszeichnung, *(teetotaller)* Abstinenzlerabzeichen; ~**-ribbon jury (panel)** besonders zusammengestellter Ausschuß; ~ **ribbon task force** hochdotierter Arbeitsstab; ~ **ribboner (ribbonist)** Mäßigkeitsapostel, Temperenzler; ~ **ruin** kompletter Reinfall; ~**-sky bargaining** unsinnige Forderungen im Rahmen eines Manteltarifvertrages; ~**-Sky Laws** *(US)* Gesetze gegen betrügerische Effektenemissionen; ~ **stocking** Blaustrumpf; ~**-streak** mit Blitzesschnelle; **to run like a** ~ **streak** *(US)* wie ein geölter Blitz laufen; **to talk a** ~ **streak** *(US)* wie ein Buch reden; ~ **ticket** *(mil., sl.)* schlichter Abschied.
bluebottle *(Br., sl.)* Blauer, Polizist.
blueprint Blau-, Lichtpause, Fotokopie, *(fig.)* Planung, Entwurf, Projektstudie;
~ **for action** Aktionsentwurf;
~ *(v.)* Lichtpause machen, *(fig.)* planen, detaillierten Entwurf ausarbeiten;
~ **apparatus** Lichtpausgerät; ~ **paper** Blau-, Lichtpauspapier; ~ **process** Lichtpausverfahren; ~ **stage** Entwurfsstadium.
blueprinter *(US)* Lichtpausgerät.
blueprinting paper Pauspapier.
bluff *(act of bluffing)* Einschüchterungsversuch, Bluff, Irreführung, *(cliff)* Steilküste, *(trick)* Reklame-, Propagandatrick;
blind man's ~ **of a fog** jede Sicht nehmender Nebel;
~ *(v.)* bluffen, Einschüchterungsversuch machen, einschüchtern, irreführen;
to call s. one's ~ j. auffordern seine Drohungen wahr zu machen.
blunder Mißgriff, Fehlgriff, Fehler, Schnitzer;
colossal ~ Riesenfehler; **serious** ~ grober Fehler;
~ **of the first magnitude** Fehler ersten Ranges;
~ *(v.)* Schnitzer machen, Bock schießen;
~ **out** mit etw. unbedacht herausplatzen; ~ **out an apology** Entschuldigung stammeln; ~ **through the dark** durchs Dunkle stolpern; ~ **work** Arbeit verfuschen;
to make a ~ *(fig.)* Bock schießen.
blur verwischte Stelle, Flecken, Klecks, *(fig.)* Makel, Schandfleck, *(printing)* unscharfer Druck;
~ **of light in the fog** Lichtklecks im Nebel; ~ **in one's memory** nebelhafte Erinnerung;
~ *(v.)* **out** auslöschen, tilgen; ~ **the view** Sicht versperren; ~ **the window of a car** Scheibe beschlagen lassen.
blurb Reklamestreifen, *(book reviews)* kurze Buchbesprechung, Waschzettel, Klappentext, Bauchbinde, *(television)* kurze Fernsehwerbung;
small ~ kurze Meldung;
~ **writer** Waschzettelverfasser.
blurred impression unscharfer Druck.
blurt *(v.)* **out a secret** Geheimnis ausquatschen.
blush, at the first auf den ersten Blick.
board *(billboard)* Anschlagtafel, *(board money)* Pension, Verpflegung, Beköstigung, Kostgeld, Unterhalt, *(directors of a company)* Vorstand, *(committee)* Ausschuß, Kommission, *(governmental department, Br.)* Ministerium, Ministerialabteilung, [Kollegial]behörde, Verwaltungsbehörde, Dienststelle, Amt, *(panel)* Gremium, Kollegium, *(piece of lumber)* Brett, Diele, *(radio, television)* Kontrollpult, *(ship)* Bord[wand], Deck, Schiffsseite, *(thick stiff sheet)* Karton, Pappe, *(US, stock exchange)* Börse;
above ~ einwandfrei; **bound in** ~**s** steif broschiert, kartoniert; **free on** ~ **(f. o. b.)** frei an Bord; **in** ~ binnenbords; **on** ~ an Bord; **on the** ~ *(stock exchange) (US)* börsenfähig; **on the** ~**s** auf der Bühne, *(Cambridge, Br.)* immatrikuliert;
administrative ~ Verwaltungsausschuß; **admission** ~ Zulassungsstelle; **advisory** ~ beratender Ausschuß, Beratungsausschuß; **arbitration** ~ *(US)* Schieds-, Schlichtungsausschuß; **Army** ~ *(Br.)* Militärverwaltung; **big** ~ *(stock exchange, US)* Kurstafel; **Big** ~ New Yorker Börse; **bulletin** ~ *(US)* Anschlagtafel, Schwarzes Brett; **Civil Aeronautics** ~ *(US)* Flugsicherungsbehörde; **conciliation** ~ Schlichtungsausschuß; **economic** ~ Wirtschaftsstelle; **examination (examining)** ~ Prüfungsstelle, -kommission; **executive** ~ geschäftsführender Ausschuß, *(company)* Vorstand; **festive** ~ Festtafel; **free** ~ Kostgeld; **full** ~ volle Pension; **group** ~ Konzernvorstand; **harbo(u)r** ~ Hafenbehörde; **local** ~ Gemeinderat; **management** ~ Vorstandsgremium; **managing** ~ Verwaltungsrat; **marketing** ~ Verteilerstelle; **mat** ~ Matrizenkarton; **medical** ~ Gesundheitsamt; **mining** ~ Bergamt; **municipal** ~ Gemeinderat, Magistrat; **notice** ~ Anschlagtafel; **original** ~ Gründerversammlung; **partial** ~ Halbpension; **pension** ~ Pensionsausschuß; **price adjustment** ~

(US) Preisbehörde; **rationing** ~ Bewirtschaftungsstelle; **revenue** ~ Finanzausschuß; **review** ~ *(US)* Prüfungsausschuß; **Sanitary** ~⍵ Gesundheitsbehörde; **selection** ~ Auswahlkommission; **shipping** ~ Schiffahrtsbehörde; **statutory** ~ gesetzlich vorgeschriebener Verwaltungsrat; **supervisory** ~ *(Br.)* Aufsichtsrat, Aufsichtsamt; **trade** ~ *(Br.)* Schlichtungsstelle für arbeitsrechtliche Streitfragen;

~ **and lodging (residence)** volle Pension, Kost und Logis, *(servant)* Unterkunft und Verpflegung; **free** ~ **and lodging** freie Station;

~⍵ **of the Admiralty** *(Br.)* Seekriegsleitung; ~⍵ **of Agriculture** *(Br.)* Landwirtschaftsministerium; ~ **of aldermen** *(US)* Stadtrat, -verordnetenversammlung; ~ **of arbitration** Schlichtungsausschuß; ~⍵ **of Audit** *(US)* Landesrechnungshof; ~ **of civil authority** *(US)* Ortsbehörde; ~ **of brokers** Maklersyndikat; ~⍵ **of Censors** Zensurbehörde; ~ **of a company (corporation,** *US)* Verwaltungsrat; ~ **of complaints** Beschwerdeausschuß; ~ **of conciliation** Schieds-, Schlichtungsamt; ~ **of control** Überwachungsstelle; ~ **of creditors** *(bankrupty)* Gläubigerausschuß; ~⍵ **of Customs** Zollbehörde; ~⍵ **of Customs and Excise** *(Br.)* Ministerialabteilung für Zölle und Verbrauchssteuern; ~ **of directors** Verwaltungsrat nach angelsächsischem Recht, *(acting board)* Firmenvorstand, *(newspaper)* Herausgebergremium; **local** ~ **of directors** Beirat; ~ **of discipline** Disziplinarausschuß; ~⍵ **of Economic Warfare** *(US)* Amt für Wirtschaftskrieg, -führung; ~⍵ **of Education** Unterrichtsministerium, *(US)* städtische Schulbehörde; ~ **of elections** Wahlausschuß, -komitee; ~ **of emigration** Auswanderungsamt; ~ **of examiners** Prüfungsausschuß, gremium; ~⍵ **of Exchequer** *(Br.)* Finanzministerium; ~ **of excise** *(US)* örtlicher Ausschuß für die Vergabe der Schankkonzession; **British** ~ **of film censors** Filmzensurbehörde; ~ **of equalization** *(US)* Behörde zur Vereinheitlichung örtlicher Steuersätze; ~ **of fire underwriters** [etwa] Brandkasse; ~⍵ **of Governors** Verwaltungs-, Aufsichtsrat, *(Federal Reserve System, US)* [etwa] Bundesbankdirektorium, *(International Monetary Fund)* Direktorium, *(school)* Schulaufsichtsbehörde; ~ **of guardians** Vormundschaftsrat, *(for the poor)* Fürsorgeausschuß; ~⍵ **of Health** Gesundheitsamt, Sanitätsbehörde; ~⍵ **of Inland Revenue** *(Br.)* Finanzbehörde; ~ **of inquiry** Untersuchungsausschuß, -kommission; ~ **of special inquiry** *(US, immigration)* Sonderausschuß in Einwanderungsfragen; ~ **of management** Vorstand, Direktorium; ~ **of managers** Vorstand; ~⍵ **of Mines** Oberbergamt; ~⍵ **of Narcotics and Dangerous Drinks** *(US)* Rauschgiftbehörde; ~⍵ **of Pardons** *(US)* Begnadigungsausschuß; ~ **of referees** Schiedsgerichtshof, *(income tax, Br.)* Sachverständigenbeirat für Steuerveranlagungen; ~ **of reference** Schiedskommission; ~⍵ **of Regents** *(US)* Kuratorium; ~ **of review** Überprüfungsausschuß, -stelle, *(real estate)* Beschwerdeausschuß in Grundstücksbewertungsfällen; ~s **of study** Fakultätsausschüsse; ~ **of supervisors** Spitzengremium, *(US)* kommunales Aufsichtsamt; ~ **of tax appeals** Oberfinanzgericht; ~ **of the town** Stadtschulamt; ~⍵ **of Trade** *(Br.)* Handelsministerium, *(US)* Handelskammer; ~ **of trustees** Beirat, Treuhänderausschuß, -rat, Kuratorium; ~ **made from wood pulp** Holzpappe; ~⍵ **of Works** *(Br.)* Amt für öffentliche Arbeiten, *(building)* Bauaufsichtsbehörde;

~ *(v.)* an Bord gehen, *(mil.)* entern, *(provide with meals)* ver-, beköstigen, in Pension haben, in Kost nehmen;

~ **with an aunt** bei einer Tante in Verpflegung sein; ~ **the gravy train** *(US)* Druckposten erhalten, *(shift expenses)* Ausgaben auf j. abwälzen; ~ **one's horse at a livery stable** sein Pferd in einem Mietstall einstellen; ~ **at a hotel** seine Mittagsmahlzeiten in einem Hotel einnehmen; ~ **in** in Pension (Kost) haben; ~ **out** auswärts essen; ~ **a plane** in ein Flugzeug einsteigen; ~ **a ship** an Bord gehen, *(mil.)* Schiff entern; ~ **a ship at B** sich in B einschiffen; ~ **students** an Studenten Zimmer vermieten; ~ **a train** in einen Zug einsteigen; ~ **up** mit Brettern verschalen; **to act above** ~ ganz offen handeln; **to appoint a** ~ Verwaltungsausschuß einsetzen; **to be on** ~ an Bord sein; **to be represented on the** ~ im Aufsichtsrat [vertreten] sein; **to elect to the** ~ in den Vorstand aufnehmen (berufen); **to go by the** ~ verloren (zugrunde) gehen; **to go (put) on** ~ an Bord gehen, sich einschiffen, in Schiff einsteigen; **to go to the** ~ unter den Tisch fallen; **to go on the** ~s Schauspieler werden, Theaterlaufbahn einschlagen; **to have one's** ~ **free** freie Kost haben, verpflegt werden; **to leave the** ~ aus dem Vorstand ausscheiden; **to provide full** ~ **and accommodation** Unterkunft und Verpflegung stellen; **to put on** ~ sich einschiffen; **to put out to** ~ in Pension geben; **to put up on the** ~ *(Br.)* ans schwarze Brett anschlagen; **to sell from** ~ frei von Bord verkaufen; **to remain on** ~ **ship** an Bord bleiben; **to serve at the pleasure of the** ~ an Vorstandsweisungen gebunden sein; **to**

ship on ~ an Bord verladen; **to sweep the** ~ ganzen Gewinn einstreichen, hundertprozentigen Sieg erringen; **to take goods on** ~ Waren an Bord nehmen; **to take full** ~ **and lodgings** mit voller Pension mieten; **to work for one's** ~ für Kost und Logis arbeiten;

~ **appointment** Berufung in den Vorstand, Vorstandsposition; ~ **approval** Vorstandsgenehmigung; ~ **candidate** Vorstandsanwärter; ~ **chairman** Vorstandsvorsitzender, -vorsitzer; ~ **charges** Verpflegungsgeld; ~ **company** Übernahmekonsortium; ~ **elections** Vorstands-, Aufsichtsratswahl; ~ **fence** *(US)* Latten-, Bretterzaun; **not within the compass of the** ~'s **jurisdiction** außerhalb des Einflusses des Vorstands; ~-**level** *(v.)* **industrial democracy** Mitbestimmung in wirtschaftlichen Fragen auf Vorstandsebene zulassen; ~ **lot** *(US, stock exchange)* handelsfähige Nominalgröße; ~ **majority** Vorstandsmehrheit; ~ **man** *(US)* Firmenmakler; ~ **meeting** Vorstands-, Präsidial-, Aufsichts-, Verwaltungsratssitzung; ~ **member** Präsidial-, Aufsichtsratsmitglied; **deputy** ~ **member** stellvertretendes Vorstandsmitglied; ~ **minutes** Vorstands-, Aufsichtsratsprotokoll; ~ **page** Kartonseite; ~ **receipt** Bordempfangsschein; ~ **residence** volle Pension; ~ **resolution** Vorstandsbeschluß; ~ **room** Sitzungsraum, *(stock exchange)* Börsensaal; ~-**room level** Vorstandsniveau; ~-**room quality** Vorstandsqualität; ~-**room row** Krach in der Vorstandsetage; ~ **of trade returns** *(Br.)* Wirtschaftsberichte des Handelsministeriums; ~ **seat** Vorstandssitz, Sitz im Aufsichtsrat; ~ **table** Verhandlungstisch; ~ **of Trade unit** Kilowattstunde; ~ **wages** *(servant)* Kostgeld; **to put on** ~ **wages** Kostgeld zahlen.

boardable zugänglich, *(ship)* enterbar.
boarded, to be ~ **up** mit Brettern vernagelt sein;
~-**out children** bei Pflegeeltern untergebrachte Kinder.
boarder Pensionär, Kostgänger, *(boarding school, Br.)* Internatsschüler, *(bookbinding)* Schmuckleiste;
day ~ Gast auf halbe Pension; **gentleman** ~ Pensionär, Rentner, Rentier;
to take in ~s Pensionäre annehmen.
boarding Beherbergung und Beköstigung, *(boards collectively)* Verschalung, *(mil.)* Entern;
~ **out** Auswärtsessen;
~ **card** Bordkarte; ~ **clerk** *(Br.)* Hafenzollbeamter; ~ **gate** Abgangsflugsteig; ~ **home** Internat; ~ **money** Kostgeld; ~ **officer** Hafen-, Zollbeamter; ~ **pass** Bordkarte; ~ **place** Internatsplatz; ~ **position** *(airplane)* Einsteigsposition; ~ **school** Internat; ~ **school costs** Internatskosten; ~ **ship** Hilfskreuzer.
boardinghouse Gasthaus, [Fremden]pension;
to keep a ~ Pension besitzen; **to live in a** ~ in einer Pension leben; ~ **guest** Pensionsgast; ~ **keeper** Pensionsbesitzer.
boardman *(stock exchange, US)* Firmenmakler.
boardwalk *(mil.)* Knüppeldamm, Trampelpfad, *(US)* Strandpromenade.
boat Boot, Schiff, Wasserfahrzeug;
cargo ~ Frachter, Frachtschiff; **compartment** ~ unsinkbares Boot; **flat-bottomed** ~ Landungsboot; **open** ~ Boot ohne Verdeck; **passenger** ~ Passagierschiff;
~ *(v.)* in einem Boot befördern;
to be (row) in the same ~ *(fig.)* im selben Boot sitzen, in der gleichen Lage sein; **to burn one's** ~s alle Brücken hinter sich abbrechen; **to launch a** ~ Boot aussetzen; **to put the** ~ **out** etw. riskieren; **to take to the** ~s in die Rettungsboote gehen;
~ **landing** *(US)* Anlegestelle; ~ **owner** Bootsbesitzer; ~ **proprietor** Booteigentümer; ~ **show** Bootsausstellung; ~ **train** Anschlußzug an Dampferlinie, Zug mit Dampferanschluß.
boatable schiffbar.
boatage Frachtgebühr.
boatel Bootsfahrerhotel.
boathouse Bootshaus.
boating Bootsfahren;
to go ~ Boot fahren;
~ **industry** Bootsindustrie.
boatload Schiffsladung.
bob *(Br., sl.)* Schilling;
~ *(v.)* **up** *(question)* hochkommen; ~ **up like a cork** sich nicht unterkriegen lassen;
to be tenpence to the ~ sich lausig fühlen.
bobby *(Br., coll.)* Schupo.
bodily körperlich, leiblich;
to rise ~ sich Mann für Mann erheben;
~ **harm (injury)** Körperverletzung; **great** ~ **harm (injury)** schwere Körperverletzung; ~ **heir** leiblicher Erbe; ~ **labo(u)r** körperliche Arbeit; ~ **member** [Körper]glied; ~ **search** Leibesuntersuchung; ~ **wants** leibliche Bedürfnisse.

body Körper, Leib, *(advertisement)* Haupttext, Haupt-, Kernbestandteil einer Anzeige, *(airplane)* Rumpf, *(association)* Vereinigung, *(of building)* Hauptgebäude, *(car)* Karosserie, *(collection)* Sammlung, *(corporation)* Körperschaft, Gesellschaft, *(corpse)* Leichnam, Leiche, *(main part)* Hauptteil, Organ, *(material)* Material, Stoff, Substanz, *(mil.)* Truppenverband, -körper, *(nexus)* Komplex, *(persons)* Gruppe, Gremium, Gesamtheit, *(print)* Schriftkegel, -grad, *(system)* System;
in a ~ geschlossen, insgesamt, gemeinsam;
administrative ~ Verwaltungsorgan, -gremium; **advisory ~** beratendes Organ, Beratungsgremium, -organ; **auxiliary ~** Hilfsorgan; **benefiting ~** begünstigende Stelle; **constituent ~** Wahlkörper, Wählerschaft; **controlling ~** Kontrollorgan; **corporate ~** juristische Person, [öffentlich-rechtliche] Körperschaft; **dead ~** Leiche, Leichnam; **deliberative ~** Beratungsausschuß; **diplomatic ~** diplomatisches Korps; **electoral ~** Wählerausschuß; **examining ~** Prüfungsausschuß; **executive ~** Exekutivorgan; **governing ~** leitendes Organ, Direktorium; **learned ~** gelehrte Versammlung; **legislative ~** gesetzgebende Körperschaft; **parent ~** Stammorgan; **permanent ~** ständiges Organ; **public ~** öffentliche Körperschaft; **self-governing ~** Selbstverwaltungskörper; **supervisory ~** Kontrollorgan; **undersealed ~** *(car)* Unterbodenschutz;
~ of an army Gros eines Heeres; **~ of clergy** Klerus; **main ~ of a book collection** Grundstock einer Büchersammlung; **~ of creditors** Gläubigergemeinschaft, -ausschuß; **general ~ of creditors** Gesamtheit der Gläubiger; **~ of curators** Kuratorium; **~ of delegates** Delegation, Delegiertengruppe; **~ of document** Gesamtinhalt einer Urkunde; **~ of electors** Wählerschaft, Wahlkörperschaft; **[strong] ~ of evidence** [umfangreiches] Beweismaterial, Beweiskomplex; **large ~ of facts** Fülle von Tatsachen; **~ of an instrument** Hauptteil einer Urkunde; **~ of public knowledge** Umfang dessen, was die Öffentlichkeit weiß; **~ of law** Gesetzgebungswerk, Hauptteil eines Gesetzes; **~ of a letter** eigentlicher Briefinhalt, Brieftext; **~ of men** Truppe; **large ~ of unemployed men** Massen von Arbeitslosen; **~ of merchants** Kaufmannschaft, -gilde; **strong ~ of police** starkes Polizeiaufgebot; **~ of regulations** Sammlung von Vorschriften; **~ of a river** Hauptstrom; **~ of a ship** Schiffsrumpf; **~ of a specification** Hauptinhalt einer Patentbeschreibung; **~ of a speech** Hauptteil einer Rede; **~ of teachers** Lehrerschaft, Schulkollegium; **~ of troops** Abteilung Soldaten; **scattered ~ of troops** versprengter Truppenteil; **~ of type** Schriftkegel; **~ of voters** Wählerschaft; **~ of workers** Arbeitskräfte;
~ (v.) verkörpern;
to act as a ~ als kollegiales Gremium (korporativ) handeln; **to do s. th. as a ~** etw. gemeinsam tun; **to resign in a ~** geschlossen demissionieren;
~ bag Schlafsack; **~ clothes** Leibwäsche; **~ colo(u)r drawing** Temperaentwurf; **~ copy** Haupttext; **to treat as a ~ corporate for tax purposes** steuerlich wie eine juristische Person behandeln; **~ execution** Taschenpfändung; **~ fount** Grundschrift; **~ matter** Text; **~ politic** Gebietskörperschaft; **~ servant** Leibdiener; **~ size** *(print.)* Kegel; **~ snatcher** Leichendieb; **~ snatching** Leichenraub; **~ style** Karosserieausführung; **~ type** *(print.)* Brotschrift.
bodyguard persönlicher Schutz, Leibwache, Leibwächter.
bodymaker Karosseriebauer.
bodymaking Karosseriebau;
~ plant Karosseriefirma.
bodywork Blockwagen, Karosserie.
bog (v.) down sich festfahren, *(firm)* zusammenbrechen;
to be ~ed down in steckenbleiben in.
bogus nachgemacht, falsch, gefälscht;
~ bank Schwindelbank; **~ bill** Kellerwechsel, *(US)* Falschgeld; **~ certificate** gefälschte Bescheinigung; **~ check** *(US)* gefälschter Scheck; **~ claim** erfundene Forderung; **~ company** Schwindelfirma; **~ concern** schwindelhafte Gründung; **~ firm** Schwindelfirma; **~ money** *(US)* Falschgeld, falsche Banknoten; **~ press** Fälscherwerkstatt; **~ signature** Gefälligkeitsunterschrift; **~ stock company** Schwindelgesellschaft; **~ title** falscher Titel; **~ trade in option** schwindelhafter Optionshandel; **~ transactions** Schein-, Schwindelgeschäft.
boil *(fig.)* heftige Bewegung;
in ~ in Wallung;
~ (v.) down *(fig.)* kondensieren; **~ down a story** Geschichte kürzen; **~ over** *(business cycle)* überschäumen.
boildown kurze Zusammenfassung.
boiler Dampfkessel, Heißwasserspeicher;
~ explosion Dampfkesselexplosion; **~ insurance** Dampfkesselversicherung; **~ plate** *(Br.)* Materndienstplatte.

boiling, the whole *(sl.)* gesamte Sippschaft;
to keep the pot ~ sein Leben fristen;
~-down technique *(note taking)* konzentrierte Darstellungsform; **~ point** Siedepunkt; **~ spring** heiße Quelle; **to be in ~ water** in Bedrängnis sein.
bold, as ~ as brass frech wie Oskar;
~ face *(print.)* fetter Satz, fette Schrift; **~-faced** *(print.)* halbfett gedruckt; **~ type** fette Schrift, Fettdruck, *(advertising)* Kernstück, Textblock.
bolster (v.) unterstützen, künstlich aufrechterhalten;
~ an industrial concern einem Industriekonzern finanzielle Polster verschaffen.
bolt Bolzen, *(bookbinding)* noch unaufgeschnittener Druckbogen, *(door)* Türriegel, Schieber, Verschluß, *(US, politics)* Verweigerung der Unterstützung des eigenen Kandidaten;
~ from the blue Blitz aus heiterem Himmel;
~ (v.) ver-, abriegeln, *(US, politics)* Parteibeschlüssen die Zustimmung versagen;
~ to the bran auf Herz und Nieren prüfen; **~ with the money** mit der Kasse durchgehen; **~ out** *(fig.)* genau untersuchen; **~ like a shot** wie der Blitz davonsausen;
to have shot one's last ~ sein ganzes Pulver verschossen haben;
to shoot the ~ Riegel vorschieben.
bolter Flüchtling, Rechtsbrecher.
bolthole Schlupfloch, Hintertürchen.
bomb Bombe, *(grenade)* Handgranate;
flying ~ fliegende Bombe; **razon ~** ferngesteuerte Bombe; **time ~** Zeitbombe;
~ (v.) mit Bomben belegen, bombardieren;
~ out ausbomben; **to pattern ~** mit einem Bombenteppich belegen;
~ attack Bombenanschlag; **~ bay** Bombenschacht; **~ carpet** Bombenteppich; **~ clearance** Bombenbeseitigung, -räumung; **~ damage** Bombenschaden; **~ disposal** Bombenräumung, Blindgängerbeseitigung; **~-disposal squad** Sprengkommando; **~ dropping** Bombenabwurf; **~ explosion** Bombenexplosion; **~ factory** Bombenfabrik; **~ load** Bombenladung; **~ outrage** Bombenanschlag, -attentat; **~ plane** Bombenflugzeug; **~ release** Bombenauslöser; **~ scare** Bombenalarm; **~ site** ausgebombtes Hausgrundstück; **~ splinter** Bombensplitter; **~ squad** Bombenentschärfungskommando; **~ threat** Bombendrohung; **~ thrower** Bombenabwerfer.
bombed out ausgebombt.
bomber Bombenflugzeug;
to intercept the enemy ~s feindlichen Bomberverband abfangen;
strategic ~ force strategische Bomberflotte; **~ group (wing, US)** Bombengeschwader.
bombing Bombardement, Bombenabwurf;
pattern ~ Bombenreihenwurf; **pinpoint ~** gezielter Bombenabwurf;
~ of target areas Flächenbombardement;
~ aeroplane Bombenflugzeug; **~ incident** Bombenanschlag; **~ raid** Bombenangriff.
bombproof shelter bombensicherer Unterstand.
bombshell, to come like a wie eine Bombe einschlagen.
bona fide gutgläubig, *(genuine)* echt, solide;
to act ~ gutgläubig (im guten Glauben) handeln;
~ acquisition gutgläubiger Erwerb; **~ bill** Wechsel über empfangene Ware; **~ business corporation** gutgläubige Handelsgesellschaft; **~ capital** aus verkäuflichen Waren bestehendes Kapital; **~ creditor** gutgläubiger Forderungsinhaber; **~ holder** *(commercial paper)* gutgläubiger Inhaber; **~ holder for value** *(bill of exchange)* wechselmäßig berechtigter Inhaber; **~ judgment creditor** gutgläubiger Vollstreckungsgläubiger; **~ mortgagor** in gutem Glauben handelnder Hypothekengläubiger; **~ offer** solides Angebot; **~ operation** Handeln im guten Glauben; **~ possessor** gutgläubiger (ehrlicher) Besitzer; **~ purchaser** gutgläubiger Erwerber; **~ residence** gewillkürter Wohnsitz; **~ third party** gutgläubiger Dritter; **~ transaction** gutgläubiger Erwerb.
bona fides *(lat.)* guter Glaube.
bonanza Glückstreffer, Fundgrube, Goldgrube, *(US)* unerwartet großer Gewinn;
business ~ hohe Gewinne abwerfendes Unternehmen;
to strike a ~ glücklichen Griff tun;
~ period of industrial development wirtschaftliche Blütezeit; **~ year** Erfolgsjahr.
bond *(agreement)* Übereinkommen, Abkommen, *(bonded warehouse, Br.)* Zollniederlage, -lager, *(debenture)* [öffentliche] Schuldverschreibung, festverzinsliches Wertpapier, Obligation, Anleihepapier, Pfandbrief, *(deed by which person binds*

himself) Schuldschein, [schriftliche] Verpflichtungserklärung, Haftungsversprechen, *(guaranty)* Bürgschafts[urkunde], Garantieschein, -erklärung, -verpflichtung, *(obligation)* Schuldschein, *(paper)* holzfreies Papier, *(surety)* Bürge, *(uniting tie)* Bündnis, Bund, Verbindung;

in ~ unter zollamtlichem Verschluß, zollamtlich verwahrt, unverzollt; **in** ~**s** in Fesseln; **out of** ~ verzollt, ab Zollager, vom versteuerten Lager; **out on** ~**s** *(criminal)* auf Kaution freigelassen; **under** ~ gegen Kaution;

~**s** Rentenwerte;

absolute ~ uneingeschränkter Schuldschein; **active** ~**s** *(Br.)* festverzinsliche Obligationen; **adjustment** ~**s** zu Sanierungszwecken ausgegebene (nur bei Gewinnerzielung verzinsliche) Schuldverschreibungen; **administrator's** ~ Kaution des Nachlaßverwalters; **Admiralty** ~ Seetransportschein; **annuity** ~**s** Rentenanleihe, -titel; **appeal** ~ Sicherheitsleistung bei Einreichung einer Berufung; **assumed** ~ übernommene Schuldverpflichtung [einer fusionierten Gesellschaft]; **attachment** ~ *(US)* [gerichtliche] Sicherheitsleistung; **authorized** ~**s** genehmigtes Anleihekapital; **average** ~ Havariebond; **baby** ~**s** *(US)* kleingestückelte Obligationen, Kleinobligationen, Wertpapiere mit geringem Nominalwert; **backed** ~**s** durch Pfandbestellung gesicherte Schuldverschreibungen; **bail** ~ anstelle einer Kaution abgegebene schriftliche Erklärung; **bearer** ~**s** auf den Inhaber lautende Obligationen, Inhaberschuldverschreibungen, -obligationen; **bid** ~ *(US)* Bietungsgarantie; **blanket position** ~ *(US)* Globalsicherungsschein gegen Verluste aus unerlaubten Handlungen im einzelnen festgelegter Angestellter; **bottomry** ~ Bodmereibrief, -vertrag; **business corporation** ~ *(US)* Industrieobligation; **callable** ~ kündbare Obligation (Schuldverschreibung); **called** ~**s** aufgerufene (ausgeloste) Obligationen; **cancelled** ~**s** getilgte Obligationen; **civil** ~**s** *(US)* Schuldverschreibungen der öffentlichen Hand; **class[ified]** ~**s** in verschiedenen Serien ausgegebene Schuldverschreibungen; **clean** ~**s** *(US)* Inhaberschuldverschreibungen ohne Giro (Einschränkung); **closed** ~ Schuldschein mit gleichbleibenden Bedingungen; **collateral mortgage** ~**s** durch Hypotheken gedeckte Schuldverschreibungen; **collateral trust** ~**s** durch Effektenlombard gesicherte Schuldverschreibungen (Obligationen); **colonial** ~**s** *(US)* Globalversicherungsschein gegen Versicherungsdelikte im einzelnen festgelegter Betriebsangehöriger; **conditional** ~ bedingter Schuldschein; **consol** ~**s** Ablösungsanleihe; **consolidated** ~**s** Ablösungsschuldverschreibungen; **consolidated mortgage** ~**s** durch Gesamthypothek gesicherte Schuldverschreibungen; **construction** ~ Kaution des Bauunternehmers; **continued** ~ *(US)* Obligation mit gleichbleibender Verzinsung; **contract** ~ Unternehmerkaution; **convertible** ~**s** *(US)* Wandelschuldverschreibungen; **corporate** ~**s** *(US)* Industrieobligationen, Schuldverschreibungen von Kapitalgesellschaften; **corporate mortgage** ~ *(US)* Hypothekenschuldverschreibungen [von Handelsgesellschaften; **corporation** ~**s** *(US)* Industrieobligationen; **county** ~**s** Kommunalobligationen; **coupon** ~**s** *(US)* Obligationen mit Zinsschein, Inhaberschuldverschreibungen mit Zinsschein, festverzinsliche Schuldverschreibungen; **court** ~ Sicherheitsleistung [bei Gericht]; **court of protection** ~ Vormundschaftsbestallung; **cumulative** ~ *(US)* Kaution bei Amtsantritt von Beamten in den USA; **currency** ~**s** *(US)* in gesetzlichen Zahlungsmitteln zahlbare Schuldverschreibungen; **customs** ~ *(Br.)* Zollkaution; **debenture** ~**s** *(US)* festverzinsliche Schuldverschreibungen; **debenture income** ~ *(Br.)* Obligationen (Schuldverschreibungen) ohne Zinsgarantie; **defaulted** ~**s** notleidende Obligationen; **defence** ~**s** Rüstungs-, Kriegsanleihe; **deferred** ~**s** *(US)* Obligationen mit aufgeschobener Verzinsung; **definit[iv]e** ~ endgültige Schuldverschreibung; **del credere** ~ *(Br.)* Garantieschein; **denominational** ~**s** in Stücken ausgegebene Obligationen; **development** ~**s** *(US)* zwecks Ausbau eines Unternehmens ausgegebene Obligationen, Meliorationsschuldverschreibungen; **disabled** ~**s** *(US)* ungültige Obligationen; **dividend** ~**s** *(US)* mit Dividendenberechtigung ausgestattete Obligationen; **divisional** ~ *(US)* hypothekarisch auf Teilstrecken gesicherte Eisenbahnanleihe; **dollar** ~ Dollarschuldverschreibung; **double** ~ bedingter Schuldschein; **drawn** ~**s** ausgeloste Schuldverschreibungen; **endorsed** ~ durch Wechsel verstärkte Obligation; **equipment** ~**s** *(US)* Schuldverschreibungen zur Finanzierung von Eisenbahnbedarf; **Exchequer** ~**s** *(Br.)* langfristige Schatzanweisungen; **export** ~ *(customs)* Ausfuhrkaution; **extended** ~**s** *(US)* prolongierte Schuldverschreibungen; **extension** ~ *(US)* später auch hypothekarisch gesicherte Eisenbahnobligation; **external** ~**s** in ausländischer Währung zahlbare Staatspapiere, Auslandsschuldverschreibungen; **farm loan** ~ landwirtschaftlicher

Pfandbrief; **fidelity** ~ Kaution gegen Veruntreuung; **fiduciary** ~ Kautionsverpflichtung; **first-lien collateral trust** ~ durch vorgehendes Pfandrecht an der hinterlegten Sicherheit gedeckter Pfandbrief; **first mortgage** ~ durch Ersthypothek gesicherte Schuldverschreibung; **floating-rate** ~**s** Obligationen mit Wechselkursfreigabe; **foreign** ~ ausländische Schuldverschreibung; **foreign DM** ~**s** DM-Auslandsanleihen; **foreign corporate** ~**s** *(US)* Obligationen ausländischer Gesellschafter; **forthcoming** ~ Sicherheitsleistung des Vollstreckungsschuldners; **free** ~ frei verfügbare (nicht als Sicherheit dienende) Obligation; **general mortgage** ~**s** durch Gesamthypothek gesicherte Schuldverschreibungen; **general obligation** ~**s** Kommunalobligationen; **gold** ~**s** Goldobligationen; **government** ~**s** *(US)* Staatsanleihen, -papiere, *(Br.)* staatliche Garantieverpflichtungen; **guarantee** ~ *(plant)* Garantieschein, Unternehmerkaution; **guaranteed** ~**s** mit Kapital- und Dividendengarantie ausgestattete Schuldverschreibungen; **guaranty** ~ Garantieschein; **heritable** ~ *(Scot.)* grundpfandmäßig gesicherte Obligation; **high-yield** ~**s** hochverzinsliche Obligationen; **improvement** ~**s** *(US)* zur Verbesserung öffentlicher Anlagen ausgegebene Obligationen; **income** ~**s** *(US)* Gewinnschuldverschreibungen, Gewinnobligationen, von Gewinnen in ihrer Verzinsung abhängige Obligationen; **indemnity** ~ *(US)* Garantieverpflichtung, Schadens-, Ausfallbürgschaft; **indeterminate** ~**s** *(US)* nach festgelegtem Termin kündbare Obligationen; **index-linked** ~ indexgekoppelte Obligation; **individual** ~ persönliche Schuldverpflichtung; **indorsed** ~ durch die Muttergesellschaft garantierte Obligation; **industrial [corporation]** ~**s** Industrieobligationen; **injunction** ~ Verpflichtung zur Sicherheitsleistung [vor Ergehen einer gerichtlichen Verfügung]; **instalment** ~**s** *(US)* in Raten rückzahlbare Obligationen, Amortisationsanleihe; **insular** ~**s** *(Br.)* Kolonialanleihe; **interchangeable** ~**s** auswechselbare Obligationen; **interest** ~**s** Gratisobligationen [an Stelle von Barverzinsung]; **interest-bearing** ~ zinstragende Obligation; **fixed interest** ~**s** festverzinsliche Obligationen; **interim** ~ kurzfristiger Schuldschein; **investment** ~**s** Anlagepapiere; **irredeemable** ~ unkündbare Obligation (Schuldverschreibung); **irrigation** ~**s** *(US)* Schuldverschreibungen zur Finanzierung von Bewässerungsprojekten; **joint** ~ Kollektivverpflichtung; **joint and several** ~ gesamtschuldnerische Verpflichtungserklärung; **judiciary** ~ Sicherheitsleistung [bei Gericht]; **land-grant** ~ *(US)* hypothekarisch gesicherte Eisenbahnobligation; **large** ~**s** Obligationen in Stückelung zu mehr als 1000 Dollar; **legal** ~**s** mündelsichere Schuldverschreibungen; **legal tender** ~ in gesetzlichen Zahlungsmitteln zahlbare Obligation; **liability** ~ absolut gültiger Unfallversicherungsschein; **liberty** ~**s** *(US)* Kriegsanleihe; **first lien** ~ erstrangig gesicherte Obligation; **junior lien** ~ durch im Range nachstehendes Pfandrecht gesicherte Schuldverschreibung; **prior lien** ~ durch Vorranghypothek gesicherte Obligation; **senior lien** ~**s** erstrangig gesicherte Pfandbriefe; **local** ~ *(Br.)* Kommunalschuldverschreibung, -obligation; **long-term** ~**s** Obligationen mit langer Laufzeit, langfristige Schuldverschreibungen; **lottery** ~ Auslosungsanleihe, Prämienlos; **lottery mortgage** ~ Prämienpfandbriefe; **maintenance** ~ *(US)* kaufmännischer Garantieschein; **master** ~ *(US)* Unternehmerkaution; **mortgage** ~ Grund-, Hypothekenpfandbrief; **first mortgage** ~**s** durch Ersthypothek gesicherte Schuldverschreibungen (Pfandbriefe); **mortgage-backed** ~ hypothekarisch besicherte Obligationen; **multiple-currency** ~**s** *(US)* in Währungen verschiedener Länder zahlbare Obligationen; **municipal** ~ *(US)* Kommunalschuldverschreibung; **naked** ~ einseitige Verpflichtung; **national development** ~**s** *(Br.)* 5%ige Staatsanleihe; **national war** ~ Kriegsanleihe; **negotiable** ~ Orderschuldverschreibung; **nonassented** ~**s** Obligationen, deren Besitzer der Unternehmenssanierung nicht zugestimmt haben; **new issue** ~ neue Obligation; **noncallable** ~ nicht vorzeitig kündbare Schuldverschreibung; **noninterest-bearing** ~**s** unverzinsliche Obligationen; **noninterest-bearing discount** ~ Obligation mit aufgeschobener (allmählich ansteigender) Zinszahlung; **nonnegotiable** ~ Namensschuldverschreibung; **obligatory** ~ festverzinsliche Schuldverschreibung; **official** ~ *(guardian, trustee)* Sicherheitsleistung; **official** ~ *(US)* öffentlich-rechtliche Ausfallbürgschaft; **option** ~ Aktienbezugsrechtsobligation; **optional** ~ jederzeit einlösbare Anleihe, Optionsanleihe; **order** ~**s** Orderschuldverschreibungen; **other** ~**s** *(balance sheet)* sonstige Verbindlichkeiten; **outstanding** ~**s** begebene Obligationen; **overlying** ~ durch nachstehende Hypothek gesicherte Schuldverschreibung; **own** ~**s** eigene Obligationen; **participating** ~ Schuldverschreibung mit Gewinnbeteiligung; **partial** ~ *(Br.)* Teilschuldschein, -schuldverschreibung; **passive** ~ zinslose Schuldverschreibung; ~**s payable** *(balance sheet)* fällige Obligationen, Obligationenschulden; **performance** ~ *(US)* Leistungsversprechen, Bietungsgarantie; **perpetual** ~s kündbare Anleihe; **plain** ~ ungesicherter Schuldschein; **position** ~ *(US)* Kautionsversicherungsschein zur Versicherung aller in einem Werk beschäftigter Angestellten; **post obit** ~ *(Br.)* beim Tode eines Dritten fälliger Schuldschein; **preference** ~ Prioritäts-, Vorzugsobligation; **preference income** ~s ertragsbedingte Prioritätsobligationen; **premium** ~ Prämienobligation; **premium savings** ~ Prämienbon; **premium treasury** ~ Prämienschatzanweisung; **pre-war** ~s *(US)* Schuldverschreibungen der USA vor 1917; **private** ~s Industrieschuldverschreibungen; **prize** ~ Auslosungsanleihe; **probate** ~ Kaution des Nachlaßverwalters; **profit-sharing** ~s Gewinnbeteiligungsobligationen; **provisional** ~ vorläufige Schuldverschreibung; **public** ~ Kaution eines Staatstreuhänders; **public** ~s öffentlich-rechtliche Obligationen, öffentliche Anleihepapiere, Staatsanleihe; **public utility** ~s Obligationen öffentlicher Versorgungsbetriebe, Versorgungswerte; **purchase-money** ~ Restkaufgeld; **quasi municipal** ~s *(US)* nicht vollwertige Kommunalobligationen; **ragged** ~s *(US)* Obligationen mit abgetrennten, noch nicht fälligen Kupons; **rail** ~ *(US)* Eisenbahnobligation; **railway** ~ *(Br.)* Eisenbahnobligation; **real-estate** ~s *(US)* Obligationen eines Immobilienfonds; **receiver's** ~ Verpflichtungsschein (Kaution) eines Treuhänders; **reciprocal** ~ gegenseitiger Verpflichtungsschein; **redeemable** ~s kündbare (auslosbare) Obligationen; **redeemed** ~ zur Rückzahlung aufgerufene Schuldverschreibung; **redelivery** ~ *(levy of execution)* Kautionsgestellung; **redemption** ~ neufundierte Obligation, Ablösungspfandbrief; **refunding** ~ Ablösungsschuldverschreibung; **refunding first mortgage** ~ *(US)* erststellig besicherte neufundierte Obligation; **registered** ~ *(Br.)* nicht übertragbare (auf den Namen lautende) Obligation, Namensobligation; **registered coupon** ~ Namensschuldverschreibung mit Inhaberkupons; **removal** ~ *(customs)* Zollfreigabeschein [für Verbringung in ein anderes Freilager], Umlagerungskaution; **renewal** ~ prolongierte Obligation, Ablösungsschuldverschreibung; **reorganization** ~ Sanierungsschuldverschreibung; **replevin** ~ Kaution im Vollstreckungsverfahren; **rescission** ~s Ersatzschuldverschreibungen; **respondentia** ~ Bodmereikredit auf Schiff und Ladung; **revenue** ~ *(US)* kurzfristige Staatsanleihe; **salvage** ~ Bergungsvertrag; **saving** ~ Sparbon; **savings** ~s *(US)* kleingestückelte Staatsobligationen; **schedule** ~ *(US)* betrieblicher Garantieversicherungsshhein anhand einer Personalaufstellung; **secured** ~ hypothekarisch abgesicherte (pfandgesicherte) Obligation; **security** ~ Garantieverpflichtung, Bürgschaftsschein, Kautionsurkunde; **semi-municipal** ~ *(US)* nicht vollwertige Kommunalobligation; **serial** ~s in Serien unterteilte Obligationen; **sewer** ~s Kommunalanleihen zur Kanalisationsfinanzierung; **short-term** ~s Obligationen mit kurzer Laufzeit; **similar** ~s gleichartige Obligationen; **simple** ~ hypothekarisch nicht besicherte Schuldverschreibung; **single** ~ persönlicher Verpflichtungsschein; **sinking-fund** ~s Schuldverschreibungen des Amortisationsfonds, Amortisationsobligationen; **small** ~ *(US)* Obligationen in Stückelung bis zu 500 Dollar; **special** ~ Sonderschuldverschreibung; **special assessments** ~ Anliegerbeiträge, Umlageverpflichtung; **stamped** ~ *(US)* durch besondere Vertragsbestimmungen gesicherte Obligation; **state** ~s *(US)* Staatsanleihen von Einzelstaaten, Staatsschuldverschreibungen; **Sterling** ~s in englischen Pfunden zahlbare Schuldverschreibungen; **straw** ~ wertloser Verpflichtungsschein; **supplementary** ~ Kautionsnachschuß; **surety** ~ *(US)* Verpflichtungs-, Garantieschein, Kautionsversicherung; **tax** ~ *(US)* Steuergutschein; **tax-anticipation** ~ *(Br.)* Steuergutschein; **tax-exempt** ~s ertragsteuerfreie Obligationen; **temporary** ~s vorläufige Obligationen; **term** ~s gleichzeitig fällig werdende Schuldverschreibungen; **terminal** ~s Eisenbahnobligationen, *(US)* staatliche Schuldverschreibungen an ausgediente Soldaten; **territorial** ~s Obligationen einer Gebietskörperschaft; **treasury** ~s *(US)* Kassen-, langfristige Schatzanweisungen, *(corporation, US)* firmeneigene Schuldverschreibungen; **trust** ~s Schuldverschreibungen über bevorrechtigte Forderungen; **trustee's** ~s *(US)* mündelsichere Papiere; **underlying** ~ *(US)* durch eine im Range vorgehende Hypothek gesicherte Schuldverschreibung, vorrangiger Pfandbrief; **unified** ~s *(US)* Konsols; **unissued** ~s noch nicht ausgegebene Schuldverschreibungen; **unpaid** ~s uneingelöste Obligationen; **unredeemable** ~s untilgbare Obligationen; **unsecured** ~ ungesicherter Schuldschein; **war** ~s Kriegsanleihe; **warehouse** ~ *(customs)* Zollverschlußschein; **water** ~s Obligationen kommunaler Wasserwerke;

~ **to (payable to) bearer** Inhaberobligation; ~s **purchased for**

cancellation zwecks Tilgung rückgekaufte Obligationen; ~ **for a deed** Auflassungsverpflichtungsschein; ~s **denominated in dollar** auf Dollar lautende Obligationen; ~ **of exchange** Wechselkontrakt; ~ **of indebtedness** Schuldschein; ~ **of indemnity** *(US)* Ausfallbürgschaft, Garantieverpflichtung; ~s **and other interests** *(balance sheet)* Beteiligungen und Wertpapiere; ~s **callable by lot** auslosbare Obligationen; ~ **and mortgage** Hypothekenpfandbrief; ~ **of necessity** Zwang der Notwendigkeit; ~s **under notice of redemption** zur Rückzahlung gekündigte Pfandbriefe; ~ **of obligation** Schuldschein, -verschreibung; ~ **with surety** Schuldverschreibung mit zusätzlicher Bürgschaftsurkunde; ~s **with attractive tax features** mit attraktiven Steuervorteilen ausgestattete Obligationen; ~ **for title** schuldrechtlicher Grundstückskaufvertag;

~ *(v.)* unter Zollverschluß nehmen (legen), *(assure payment of duties)* Zollkaution stellen, *(debenture)* Schuldverschreibung ausstellen, *(encumber)* Schuld konsolidieren, *(mortgage)* hypothekisieren, verpfänden;

~ **s. o.** Kaution für j. stellen lassen; ~ **goods** Ware in Zollverschluß legen; ~ **a road** Straße mit Kommunalobligationen finanzieren;

to be admitted in ~ unter Zollvormerkschein zugelassen werden; **to be in** ~ im Zollverschluß liegen; **to be under** ~s durch Verpflichtungen gebunden (vertraglich verpflichtet) sein; **to call in** ~s Obligationen kündigen; **to discharge a** ~ Schuldschein einlösen; **to enter into a** ~ Verpflichtung eingehen; **to enter a surety** ~ Garantieverpflichtung einzahlen; **to enter into a** ~ **with the customs authorities** Garantieverpflichtung gegenüber den Zollbehörden eingehen; **to file a** ~ Sicherheit bei Gericht stellen; **to float a** ~ Schuldverschreibung auf den Markt bringen; **to furnish a** ~ Kaution stellen; **to give a** ~ Verpflichtungsschein ausstellen; **to issue** ~s Pfandbriefe, Schuldverschreibungen (Obligationen) ausgeben; **to pay off** ~s Obligationen (Schuldverschreibungen) einlösen; **to place** ~s Pfandbriefe unterbringen; **to place under (put into)** ~ in Zollverschluß legen; **to post a** ~ Sicherheit hinterlegen, Kaution stellen; **to put out** ~s Schuldverschreibungen ausgeben; **to put up a** ~ Sicherheit stellen; **to put up a counter** ~ Gegensicherheit leisten; **to redeem** ~s Obligationen tilgen; **to redeem** ~s **by drawings** Pfandbriefe zur Rückzahlung auslosen; **to release from** ~ aus dem Zollverschluß nehmen; **to remain in** ~ unter Zollverschluß lagern; **to retire** ~s Schuldverschreibungen einlösen; **to sell two-year** ~s **on yield of 11%** Obligationen mit zweijähriger Laufzeit und einer 11%igen Rendite verkaufen; **to sign a** ~ Schuldschein ausstellen; **to subscribe** ~s Pfandbriefe zeichnen; **to take in** ~ unter Zollverschluß nehmen; **to take out of** ~ aus dem Zollverschluß nehmen, ausklarieren, verzollen;

~s **account** Aberdepot; ~ **amortization** Anleihetilgung, Tilgung von Schuldverschreibungen; ~ **amount** Anleihebetrag; ~ **analyst** Rentenfachmann; ~ **book** Obligationenbuch; ~ **broker** *(US)* Fondsmakler; ~ **capital** Anleihekapital; ~ **certificate** *(US)* Interimschein für eine Inhaberschuldverschreibung; ~ **circular** Prospekt über die Ausgabe von Obligationen; ~ **circulation** Pfandbriefumlauf; ~ **conversion** Anleihekonversion; ~ **coupon collection** Dividendeninkasso; ~ **creditor** Pfandbriefinhaber; ~ **crowd** *(US)* Fondshändler, -makler; ~ **debt** Pfandbriefschuld; ~ **debtor** Anleihe-, Obligationsschuldner; ~ **department** *(US)* Abteilung für festverzinsliche Werte; ~ **deposit** Rentendepot; ~ **discount** Pfandbriefagio; **to spread** ~ **discount over the years** das Disagio eines Pfandbriefs über die Jahre verteilen; ~ **dividends** Dividenden in Form eigener Obligationen; ~ **funds** *(investment company)* Rentenfonds; ~ **house** Pfandbriefinstitut; ~ **indebtedness** Anleiheverschuldung; ~ **indenture** Schuldverschreibungsurkunde; ~ **of fidelity insurance** Kautionsversicherung; ~ **interest** Obligationenzinsen; ~ **issue** Pfandbriefausgabe, Anleiheemission; **to float a** ~ **issue** Anleihe auflegen, Pfandbriefemission vornehmen; ~ **issue currency** Anleihewährung; ~ **management** Verwaltung des Obligationenvermögens; ~ **market** Anleihemarkt, Markt der festverzinslichen Werte, Pfandbriefmarkt; ~ **market investor** Kapitalgeber für den Pfandbriefmarkt; ~ **market yields** Erträge von Rentenpapieren, Rentenmarktrenditen; ~ **market weakness** Rentenmarktschwäche; ~ **note** Zollvermerkschein; **prize-winning** ~ **number** ausgeloste Prämiennummer; ~ **obligation** Anleiheschuld; ~ **paper** hochwertiges Briefpapier, *(notes)* Banknotenpapier; ~ **power** Vollmacht zur Übertragung von Schuldverschreibungen; ~ **premium** Pfandbriefagio; ~ **printing** Wertpapierdruck; ~ **purchase** Pfandbriefkauf; ~ **ratings** Qualitätsgruppierung festverzinslicher Effekten, Schätzungen des Nettowertes festverzinslicher Effekten; ~ **redemption** Tilgung von Obligationen; ~ **registrar** *(US)* Überwachungsstelle für Pfandbrief-, Obligationsausgabe; ~ **retirement** Kündigung von Obligationen; ~ **salesman** *(US)* Agent für Wertpapiere; ~ **sinking fund** Amortisationsfonds für Obligationen; ~ **store** Zollager; ~ **subscription receivables** *(US)* Debitoren aus Schuldverschreibungen; ~ **trading** Pfandbrief-, Obligationenhandel; ~ **trading department** Pfandbriefabteilung; ~ **trading officer** Händler in festverzinslichen Werten; ~ **underwriter** Anleihegarant; ~ **unit** Prämienzertifikat; ~ **value tables** Tabellen zur Berechnung des Nettoertrages von festverzinslichen Papieren; ~ **valuation** Wertberechnung einer Obligation; ~ **warrant** *(Br.)* Zollbegleitschein; ~ **washing** Umwandlung steuerpflichtiger Pfandbriefrenditen in steuerfreie Kapitalgewinne; ~ **yielding** Pfandbriefrendite.

bondage *(fig.)* Bindung, Zwang.

bonded *(under bond)* unter Zollverschluß [lagernd], unter zollamtlichem Verschluß, *(debted)* mit Schulden (Obligationen) belastet, *(pledged)* verpfändet, belastet, *(secured)* durch Schuldverschreibungen (Obligationen) gesichert, fundiert;
~ **to destination** Verzollung am Bestimmungsort;
to have goods ~ Waren unter Zollverschluß lagern;
~ **debt** fundierte Schuld, Obligations-, Anleiheschuld; **net** ~ **debt** *(municipal accounting)* Schuldscheinverschreibungen; ~ **factory** Fabrik zur Verarbeitung von Waren unter Zollverschluß; ~ **goods** zollpflichtige Waren, Waren unter Zollverschluß; ~ **indebtedness** *(US)* Anleiheschuldenlast; ~ **period** Zollagerfrist; ~ **port** Freihafen; ~ **shed** Zollschuppen; ~ **store** Zollspeicher, -lager; ~ **value** unverzollter Wert; ~ **vaults** Zollkeller; ~ **warehouse** privates Zollgutlager, Zollspeicher, Transitlager.

bonder Zolleinlagerer.

bondholder Obligationär, Obligationsinhaber, Pfandbriefinhaber, Wertpapierbesitzer.

bondholdings Pfandbriefbesitz.

bonding Zolleinlagerung;
~ **company** *(US)* Kautionsversicherungsgesellschaft; ~ **requirements** Verzollungsvorschriften; ~ **underwriter** Übernahmekonsortium für Obligationen (Pfandbriefe); ~ **warehouse** Lagerhaus für unverzollte Waren.

bondsman Frontpflichtiger, Leibeigener, *(surety)* Bürge.

bone *(blunder, US)* Schnitzer, grober Fehler, *(ship)* Skelett, *(US sl.)* Dollar;
~ **of contention** Streitgegenstand, Zankapfel;
~ *(v.)* **up** *(US sl.)* büffeln, ochsen;
to feel s. th. in one's ~s Vorahnung haben; **to have a** ~ **to pick with s. o.** mit jem. ein Hühnchen zu rupfen haben; **to make no** ~s **about it** nicht viel Federlesens machen; **to work one's fingers to the** ~ bis zur Erschöpfung (zum Umfallen) arbeiten;
~-**idle** stinkfaul; ~ **yard** *(US)* Schindanger, -grube.

boneshaker Knochenmühle.

bonnet *(Br., car)* Motorhaube.

bonfire Freudenfeuer;
to make a ~ **of s. th.** sich etw. vom Halse schaffen.

bonification Steuer-, Zollrückvergütung.

bonus *(compensation for a loan)* Kreditprovision, *(consideration for charter)* Konzessionsgebühr, *(douceur)* Bestechungsgeld, *(extra dividend)* Extra-, Superdividende, zusätzliche Dividende, [Dividenden]bonus, *(gratuity)* Gehaltsprämie, Tantieme, Sondervergütung, *(increase in salary)* Gehaltszulage, *(insurance, Br.)* Dividende, Gewinnanteil, *(automobile insurance, US)* Schadensfreiheitsrabatt, *(lump sum)* Pauschalvergütung, *(premium)* Prämie, Werbegeschenk, *(salesman)* Umsatztantieme, *(share of profits)* Gewinnbonus, -anteil, Gratifikation, *(subsidy to industry)* Subvention, *(sum given in addition)* Zugabe, Zuschlag, Bonus;
thrown in as a ~ als Extrabonbon;
anticipated ~ vorweggenommene Gewinnprämie; **capital** ~ Gratisaktie; **cash** ~ Gratifikation in bar, Bardividende; **Christmas** ~ Weihnachtsgratifikation; **cost-of-living** ~ Teuerungszulage; **deferred** ~ aufgeschobene Gewinnprämie; **dependency** ~ Kinderzulage; **end-of-tax-year** ~ [etwa] dreizehntes Gehalt; **executive** ~ Tantieme leitender Angestellter; **flat** ~ einheitliche Prämie, Pauschalprämie; **go-home** ~ Repatriierungsprämie; **group** ~ Gruppenprämie; **hazard** ~ Risikoprämie, Gefahrenzulage; **incentive** ~ Leistungszulage; **local** ~ Ortszulage; **no-claim** ~ *(Br.)* Prämie für unfallfreies Fahren; **noncontractual** ~ im Arbeitsvertrag nicht abgesicherte Gehaltsprämie; **nonproduction** ~ produktionsunabhängige Prämie (Zulage); **overtime** ~ Überstundenzulage; **performance-related** ~ leistungsbezogene Tantieme; **piece-rate** ~ Akkordprämie; **production** ~ *(US)* Leistungs-, Produktionsprämie; **profit-sharing** ~ Gewinnbeteiligungszulage; **regular attendance** ~ Prämie für regelmäßige

Einhaltung der Dienstzeit; **reversionary** ~ Summenzuwachs; **share** ~ *(Br.)* Gratisaktie; **special** ~ Sonderzulage; **step** ~ Stufenakkord, Leistungsprämie; **tax-free** ~ steuerfreie Prämie; **terminal** ~ Abschlußvergütung; **war** ~ Kriegszulage; **war veterans'** ~ Kriegsteilnehmerabfindung; **waste-reduction** ~ Prämie für verringerte Abfallproduktion;
~ **in cash** *(insurance)* ausgezahlter Gewinnanteil; ~ **fully equated to the levels of responsibility** dem Verantwortungsbereich voll entsprechende Tantieme; ~ **for special risk** Risikoprämie; ~ **on shares** Gratisaktie;
~ *(v.)* durch Prämien fördern, subventionieren;
to be entitled to a ~ tantiemenberechtigt sein; **to capture a nice** ~ **on foreign exchange** guten Devisenschnitt mitnehmen; **to declare a reversionary** ~ Summenzuwachs feststellen; **to go on a** ~ auf Prämienbasis arbeiten; **to link the minimum** ~ **to profitability** jährliche Mindestabschlußzahlung mit dem Gewinn koppeln; **to restore the compulsory annual** ~ **of one month's salary** 13. Gehaltszahlung zwangsweise wieder einführen;
~ **account** Prämienkonto; ~ **arrangement** Tantiemenvereinbarung; ~ **declaration** *(insurance)* Gewinnanteilsfestsetzung; ~ **distribution** Bonus-, Prämien-, Gewinnzuteilung; ~ **earnings** Prämieneinkommen; ~ **element** Prämienbestandteil; ~ **fund** Prämien-, Dividendenfonds; ~ **income** Tantiemeneinkünfte; ~ **issue** Tantiemen-, Prämiengewährung, *(company law)* Ausgabe von Gratisaktien; ~ **payment** Tantiemenvergütung; **accelerated** ~ **plan** beschleunigtes Prämiensystem; **nonpiecework** ~ **plan** kollektives Gruppenprämiensystem; ~ **reinforcement** Verwendung der Lebensversicherungsgewinnanteile zur Hypothekentilgung; ~ **reserve** Dividendenrücklage; ~ **scheme** Tantiemenregelung, *(insurance)* Gewinnplan; ~ **share** *(Br.)* **(stock,** *Br.)* Aufstockungs-, Genuß-, Gratisaktie; **flat** ~ **system** Pauschalprämiensystem, *(insurance)* Gewinnplan; **group** ~ **system** kollektives Gruppenprämiensystem; **task and** ~ **system** Prämienakkordsystem; **to work on a** ~ **system** auf Prämienbasis arbeiten; ~ **terms** Prämienbedingungen; ~ **transaction** Prämiengeschäft; ~ **trend** fortentwickeltes Tantiemenwesen; ~ **week** wohlfeile Woche.

bonussee Prämienempfänger.

booby Einfaltspinsel, Tölpel;
~ **hatch** *(Black Maria, sl.)* Grüne Minna, *(insane asylum, sl.)* Klappsmühle, *(prison, sl.)* Kasten, Kittchen, Knast; ~ **prize** Trostpreis; ~ **trap** *(fig.)* übler Streich; ~~-**trapped** mit einem Zeitzünder versehen.

boodle Falschgeld, *(politics)* Bestechungsgeld.

book Kassen-, Geschäftsbuch, *(membership)* Mitgliederverzeichnis, *(minutes)* Protokollbuch, *(ticket)* Block;
as shown by the ~s buchmäßig; **by the** ~ vorschriftsmäßig; **conformably to your** ~s mit Ihren Büchern übereinstimmend; **on balancing (closing) our** ~s beim Abschluß unserer Bücher; **in looking over the** ~s bei Durchsicht der Bücher; **without** ~s aus dem Gedächtnis;
account ~ Rechnungs-, Kontobuch; **account-current** ~ Kontogegenbuch; **bargain** ~ Schlußnotenregister; **bills payable** ~ *(US)* Wechseljournal-, verfallbuch; **bills receivable** ~ *(US)* Wechseldebitorenbuch; **bound** ~ gebundenes Buch; **case** ~ Entscheidungssammlung; **cash** ~ Kassenbuch; **check** *(US)* **(cheque,** *Br.)* ~ Scheckbuch; **claims** ~ Beschwerdebuch; **controversial** ~ umstrittenes Buch; **copying** ~ Kopierbuch; **debt** ~ *(Br.)* Schuldbuch; **desk** ~ Handbuch; **educational** ~ Schulbuch; **elevating** ~ erhebendes Buch; **exercise** ~ Schreibheft; **folio** ~ Buch im Folioformat; **forwarding** ~ Versandbuch; **gift** ~ Geschenkausgabe; **a great many** ~s große Menge Bücher; **hurt** ~ beschädigtes Buch; **inventory** ~ Bestands-, Inventarbuch; **invoice** ~ Einkaufsjournal; **law** ~ Rechtsbuch; **slovenly kept** ~s unordentlich geführte Bücher; **ledger** ~ Hauptbuch; **loose-leaf** ~ Buch in Loseblattform; **memorandum** ~ Memorial, Kladde; **military service** ~ Wehrpaß; **minute** ~ Protokoll, Notizbuch; **missing** ~ verlorengegangenes Buch; **open** ~ aufgeschlagenes Buch; **order** ~ Bestell-, Auftragsbuch; **out-[clearings]** ~ *(Br.)* Buch über die zur Verrechnung abgegebenen Schecks; **paperbound** ~ broschiertes Buch; **pay** ~ Soldbuch; **pocket** ~ Taschenbuch; **poll** ~ Wähler-, Wahlliste; **price-controlled** ~ preisgebundenes Buch; **printable** ~ druckfähiges Buch; **prize** ~ preisgekröntes Buch; **profound** ~ tiefgreifendes Buch; **published** ~s veröffentliche Werke; **rate** ~ Steuerrolle, *(advertising)* Preisliste; **ration** ~ Lebensmittelkarte; **recondite** ~ schwer verständliches Buch; **reference** ~ Nachschlagewerk; **request** ~ Beschwerdebuch; **rough cash** ~ Kassenkladde; **sales** ~ Warenverkaufsbuch; **savings bank** ~ Sparkassenbuch; **scrap** ~ Buch zum Einkleben von Zeitungsausschnitten; **signature** ~ Unterschriftenverzeichnis; **small** ~ Wehrpaß; **statute** ~ Gesetzessammlung; **statutory**

~s gesetzlich vorgeschriebene Rechnungsbücher; **sterling ~** wertvolles Buch; **stock ~** Lagerbuch, *(US)* Aktionärsregister; **store ~** Lager-, Bestandsbuch; **telephone ~** Telefonbuch; **transfer ~** Übertragungsregister; **untasted ~** noch nicht gelesenes Buch; **visitors' ~** Fremdenbuch; **warehouse ~** Lager-, Bestandsbuch; **waste ~** *(Br.)* Strazze, Kladde; **well-produced ~** gut ausgestattetes Buch; **White ~** *(pol.)* Weißbuch; **year ~** Jahrbuch; **~ of accounts** Konto-, Rechnungsbuch; **commercial ~s of account** kaufmännische Geschäftsbücher; **~ of adjournal** *(Scot.)* Strafgerichtsprotokolle; **~ of arrivals** Fremdenbuch; **~s of authority** Rechtsquellen; **~ in boards** Pappband; **~ of cargo** Frachtbuch; **~ of charges** Ausgabenbuch; **~ of commission** Auftrags-, Bestell-, Orderbuch; **~ of complaints** Beschwerdebuch; **~ of condolence** Kondolenzliste; **~s of Council and Session** Senats- und Sitzungsberichte; **~ or other debts** Außenstände und sonstige Forderungen; **~s in disorder** unordentlich geführte Bücher; **~ in the third edition** dritte Auflage; **~ of entries** Eingangsjournal, -buch; **~ as full of facts as an egg is full of meat** mit Tatsachen voll gestopftes Buch; **~ of final entry** Hauptbuch; **~ of original entry** Ursprungsjournal; **~ of [printed] forms** Formularsammlung; **~ difficult to get hold of** *(library)* stets ausgeliefertes Buch; **~ of invoices** Fakturenbuch; **~ loading** Frachtbuch; **~ of merchandise** Warenkontobuch; **~ of mileage tickets** Fahrscheinheft; **~ of plates** Bildband; **~ of rates** Zolltarif; **~s and records** Bücher und Geschäftspapiere; **~ to read** lesenswerte Bücher; **~ of receipts and expenditures** Einnahme- und Ausgabebuch; **~ of record** Register; **~s of reference** benutzte Literatur; **~ of remittances** Überweisungsbuch; **~ of sales** Verkaufsbuch, -journal; **~ of stamps** Markenheft, Freimarkenheftchen; **~s of a tax receiver** Steuerunterlagen des Finanzamtes; **~ of tickets** Fahrscheinheft; **~ of travel** Reisebeschreibung;

~ *(v.)* buchen, anschreiben, aufzeichnen, *(airplane)* Buchung aufgeben, *(enter in books)* [ver]buchen, *(passenger)* Fahrkarte kaufen (lösen), *(register)* eintragen, notieren; **~ for A** Fahrkarte nach A lösen; **~ ads** Anzeigen buchen; **~ in advance** im voraus bestellen, vorausbestellen, im Vorverkauf besorgen; **~ most of one's lucrative business through tax havens** lukrative Gewinne buchungstechnisch in Steueroasen anfallen lassen; **~ a long-distance call** Ferngespräch anmelden; **~ a personal call** Voranmeldung bestellen; **~ a contract for shipment** Lieferungsvertrag abschließen; **~ in conformity** gleichlautend buchen; **~ down** einschreiben; **~ s. o. for reckless driving** jem. wegen rücksichtslosen Fahrens einen Strafzettel verpassen; **~ freight** Frachtraum mieten; **~ for imports** sich Importe sichern; **~ an omitted item** Posten nachtragen; **~ an order** Auftrag annehmen (verbuchen); **~ one's passage** seine Schiffskarte (Flugkarte) bestellen; **~ a place** Platz belegen; **~ the return ticket** Rückfahrt belegen; **~ a room** Zimmer bestellen; **~ a seat** Karte im Vorverkauf lösen; **~ a seat on an aeroplane** Flugplatz bestellen; **~ seats for the theater over the telephone** Theaterkarten telefonisch bestellen; **~ a sleeper** Schlafwagenkarte lösen; **~ space** *(US coll.)* Anzeigenraum in Auftrag geben (buchen, belegen); **~ by telephone** telefonisch bestellen; **~ through [to ...]** durchbuchen; **~ a trunk call** *(Br.)* Ferngespräch anmelden; **to audit the ~s** Bücher prüfen (revidieren); **to autograph a ~** Buch mit einer Widmung versehen; **to balance the ~s** Bücher abschließen, Bilanz ziehen; **to be at one's ~s** über seinen Büchern sitzen; **to be deep in the ~s** hohe Schulden haben; **to be in s. one's bad ~s** bei jem. schlecht angeschrieben sein; **to be in the black ~** auf der schwarzen Liste stehen; **to be in s. one's good ~s** gute Nummer bei jem. haben; **to be on the ~s** als Mitglied eingetragen sein, *(balance sheet)* zu Buche stehen; **to be still on the ~s** noch gültig sein; **to be upon the ~s** eingetragenes Mitglied sein; **to begin a ~** Buch anlesen; **to bring to ~** verbuchen, *(fig.)* zur Rechenschaft ziehen; **to bring to ~s** in Büchern führen; **to canvass a territory for a ~** Buch in einem Bezirk im Subskriptionswege vertreiben; **to carry in ~s** verbuchen; **to catalog(ue) ~s** in ein Bücherverzeichnis aufnehmen; **to close the ~s** Bücher schließen; **to curl up with a good ~** es sich mit einem guten Buch bequem machen; **to cut a ~ open** Buch aufschneiden; **to disfigure a ~** Buch entstellen; **to displace a ~ in the library** Buch in der Bibliothek umstellen; **to enter in the ~s** buchen; **to expurgate a ~** bestimmte Buchstellen streichen; **to filch a ~ out of a library** Buch aus einer Bibliothek entwenden; **to foist a ~ on an author** Buch einem Autor zuschreiben; **to get in s. one's ~s** bei jem. Schulden machen; **to get a ~ ready for the press** Buch für den Druck fertigmachen; **to get into a ~** sich in ein Buch einlesen; **to get off the ~s** abbuchen; **to get one's ~s** seine Papiere erhalten, entlassen werden; **to go back on the ~s** auftragsmäßig wieder interessant werden; **to have finished a ~** mit einem Buch fertig

sein; **to have recourse on a ~** Buch konsultieren; **to have a new ~ on the stocks** neues Buch in Arbeit haben; **to have a ~ at hand** Buch greifbar haben; **to have a ~ printed** Buch in Druck geben; **to inspect the ~s** Bücher einsehen; **to interleave a ~** Buch mit weißem Papier durchschießen; **to keep the ~s** Bücher führen; **to keep ~s of account** ordnungsgemäße Buchführung haben; **to keep the ~s up to date** Bücher auf den neuesten Stand bringen; **to keep ~s by double entry** doppelte Buchführung haben; **to keep on the ~s as receivables** *(US)* buchmäßig weiterhin als Kundenforderungen behandeln; **to lay a ~ under contribution** Buch auswerten; **to lend [out] ~s** Bücher ausleihen; **to look up in a ~** in einem Buch nachsehen; **to list all one's ~** Bücherverzeichnis anlegen; **to make a ~** angenommene Wette eintragen; **to make up the ~s** Bücher abschließen; **to notice a ~** Buch anzeigen; **to obtain ~s to special order** nicht vorrätige Bücher auf Wunsch bestellen; **to open a ~** Buch aufschlagen; **to page through a ~** *(US)* in einem Buch herumblättern; **to post up the ~s** Geschäftsbücher übertragen; **to publish a ~** Buch veröffentlichen; **to put forth a new ~** neues Buch veröffentlichen; **to put a deal through one's ~** Geschäft buchungsmäßig erfassen; **to preserve ~s** Rechnungsbücher aufheben; **to read a ~ right through** Buch ganz lesen; **to read a book in the original** Buch im Urtext lesen; **to repeat without ~s** auswendig hersagen; **to review a ~** Buch rezensieren; **to revise a ~** Buch neu bearbeiten; **to run through a ~** Buch überfliegen; **to run into s. one's ~** bei jem. in Schulden geraten; **to shut a ~** Buch zuschlagen; **to shut the ~s** Unternehmen aufgeben; **to sort out the ~s** Bücher in einer Bibliothek überprüfen; **to start on a ~** Buch zu lesen anfangen; **to subscribe a ~** Buch im Subskriptionswege verkaufen; **not to suit s. one's ~** jem. nicht in den Kram passen; **to take one's name off the ~s** aus einer Gesellschaft austreten; **to throw the ~ at s. o.** j. aller nur möglichen Verbrechen beschuldigen; **to turn out ~s one after the other** Bücher am laufenden Band schreiben; **to undertake to publish a ~** Buch verlegen; **to write a ~** Buch schreiben;

~ account Kontokorrentkonto; **assigned ~ accounts** *(US)* abgetretene Buchforderungen; **~ agent** Verlagsvertreter, *(US)* Subskribentensammler; **to extinguish a ~ account** Buchschuld löschen; **~-back glueing** Rückenleimung; **~ backing** Bucheinbandrücken; **~ canvasser** Subskribentensammler; **~ car service** Bücherwagendienst; **~ card** *(library)* Ausleihkarte; **~ claim** Buchforderung; **~s close** Abschluß der Effektentransferbücher einer Gesellschaft; **~ cloth** Buchbinderleinwand; **~ club** Lesezirkel, Buchgemeinschaft; **~ collecting** Bücher sammeln; **~ collective transport** Büchersammelverkehr; **~ collector** Büchersammler; **~ composition** Werksatz; **~ cost** Buchwert; **~ cover** Buchdeckel, -umschlag; **~ credit** Buchkredit; **~ creditor** Buchgläubiger; **~ dealer** Buchhändler; **~ debt** Buchschuld; **~ debtor** Buchschuldner; **~ debts** Außenstände; **~ ends** Bücherstützen; **~ entry** Buchung; **~ equity** buchmäßig ausgewiesenes Kapital; **~ exhibition** Buchausstellung; **~ face** Buchschrift; **~ fair** Buch-, Büchermesse; **~ figures** *(bookkeeping)* Buchwerte; **open ~ credit** laufender Buchkredit; **in ~ form** in Buchstaben; **not published in ~ form** nicht als Buch erscheinen; **~ format** Buchformat; **~ hand** gestochene Schrift; **~ inventory** buchmäßiges Inventar; **~ inventory profit** Buchgewinn aufgrund veränderter Lagerbestandsbewertung; **~ jacket** Schutzumschlag, Buch-, Schutzhülle; **~ knowledge** Bücherwissen, Belesenheit, Buchgelehrsamkeit, Schulweisheit; **~ learning** Bücherwissen; **~ liability** *(carrier)* buchmäßige Haftung; **to be in the ~ line** im Buchhandel tätig sein; **~ list** Bücherliste; **~ loss** buchmäßiger Verlust; **~ market** Büchermarkt; **~ name** wissenschaftliche Bezeichnung; **~ notice** Buchankündigung, -anzeige; **~ number** Buchnummer; **~ order** Buchbestellung; **~ order form** Bücherbestellzettel; **~s open** Öffnung der Effektentransferbücher einer Gesellschaft; **~ packet** *(Br.)* Büchersendung; **~ paper** Buchpapier; **~ post** *(Br.)* Büchersendung, Beförderung als Drucksache; **to send by ~ post** *(Br.)* unter Kreuzband verschicken; **~ postage** *(Br.)* Drucksachengebühr; **~ printer** Buchdrucker; **~ printing** Buchdruck; **~ prize** Buchprämie; **~ profit** buchmäßiger Gewinn; **~ publisher** Verlagsbuchhändler; **~-purchases channels** Bezugswege für Bücher; **~ reference card** Buchlaufkarte; **~ review** Buchbesprechung, Kritik; **~ reviewer** [Bücher]rezensent, Buchkritiker; **~ sales agency** Buchverkaufsstelle; **~ sales point** Buchverkaufsstelle; **~ size** Buchformat; **~ slip** Bücherzettel; **~ stock** Lagerbestand an Büchern, Bücherbestand; **~ support** Bücherstütze; **~ surplus** buchmäßiger Überschuß; **~ table** Büchertisch; **~ token** *(Br.)* Büchergutschein; **~ trade** Buchhandel, -gewerbe; **mail-order ~ trade** Versandbuchhandel; **~ trade customer** Buchhandelskunde; **~ tray** Bücherbrett; **~ truck** Bücherwagen.

book value Bilanz-, Buch-, Nettowert eines Unternehmens; **at a ~ of** zu Buch stehend mit;

gross ~ Buchwert vor Abschreibungen; **net ~** Buchwert nach Vornahme von Abschreibungen;
  ~ of a company's resources Buchwert des Gesellschaftskapitals; **to be appreciably in excess of ~s** Buchwerte erheblich übersteigen; **to have a ~ of** zu Buch stehen mit; **to yield a profit over the ~** Buchwert übersteigenden Erlös erzielen; **to write down (up) the ~** Buchwert herabsetzen (heraufsetzen).

book wagon Bücherwagen.

bookable im Vorverkauf zu haben.

bookateria Buchhandel mit Selbstbedienung.

bookbinder Buchbinder.

bookbindery *(US)* Buchbinderei.

bookbinding Buchbinden.

bookboard Bücherbrett.

bookburning Bücherverbrennung.

bookcase Bücherregal, -gestell;
  revoling ~ drehbares Büchergestell.

bookdealer *(US)* Buchhändler.

booked besetzt, belegt, *(registered)* gebucht;
  as ~ overleaf wie umstehend;
  to be fully ~ ausverkauft sein; **to be heavily ~** voll besetzt sein; **to be ~ through 1981** bis Ende 1981 ausgebucht sein.

bookholder Lesepult.

booking Buchung, Bestellung, *(registration)* Eintragung, *(space)* Platzbelegung;
  advance ~ Vorverkauf, Vorausbestellung; **blind ~** *(film)* Blindbuchen; **freight ~** Belegen von Frachtraum; **heavy ~s** umfangreiche Vorbestellungen; **onto (onward) ~** *(airport)* Anschlußbuchung; **passage ~s** Belegung von Schiffsplätzen; **solid ~** feste Ausbuchung;
  ~ in advance Vorverkauf; **~ a call** *(US)* Gesprächsanmeldung; **to confirm a ~** Buchung bestätigen; **to make an early ~** rechtzeitig buchen; **to nail down one's ~** seine Buchung festmachen;
  ~ agency Tournee-Agentur; **~ clerk** *(Br.)* Schalterbeamter, Fahrkartenverkäufer; **~ fee** Vormerk-, Eintragungs-, Vorverkaufsgebühr; **~ item** Buchungsposten; **~ office** *(railway, Br.)* Fahrkartenschalter, -ausgabe, *(US, railroad)* Gepäckschalter; **~ operation** Buchungssatz; **~ operator** Fernamt; **~ order** Bestellzettel.

bookish | expression literarischer Ausdruck; **~ knowledge** Bücherweisheit; **~ person** Leseratte; **~ style** geschraubter Stil.

bookkeeper Buchhalter, Rechnungsführer;
  assistant ~ zweiter Buchhalter;
  to have been trained as a ~ als Buchhalter ausgebildet sein, buchhalterische Erfahrung haben.

bookkeeping Buchführung, -haltung;
  columnar ~ amerikanische Buchführung; **company ~** Geschäftsbuchführung; **conditional-purchase ~** *(booksellers)* Bedingtbuchhaltung; **double-entry (duplicate) ~** doppelte Buchführung; **electronic ~** elektronische Buchführung; **factory ~** Betriebsbuchhaltung; **mechanical ~** Maschinenbuchführung; **single-entry ~** einfache Buchführung; **tabular ~** amerikanische Buchführung;
  ~ by double (single) entry doppelte (einfache) Buchführung; **~ accountancy** Buchhaltungswesen; **~ costs** Buchführungskosten; **~ cycle** Buchungszyklus; **~ department** Buchhaltung; **~ entry** Buchungsposten; **~ error** Buchungsfehler; **to handle ~ functions** Buchungsarbeiten erledigen; **~ item** Buchungsposten; **~ loss** Buchverlust; **~ machine** Buchungsmaschine; **~ machine operator** Maschinenbuchhalter; **~ method** Buchungsverfahren; **~ rate** Verbuchungs-, Buchkurs; **~ records** Buchführungsbelege, Buchungsunterlagen; **~ supervisor** Buchhaltungschef, Chef der Buchhaltung[sabteilung]; **duplicated ~ system** Durchschreibebuchführung; **~ term** Buchhaltungsausdruck; **~-type entry** buchungsähnlicher Posten; **~ voucher** Buchhaltungsbeleg; **~ work** Buchführungsarbeit.

booklet Werbebroschüre, -faltblatt, Prospekt;
  free ~ kostenlose Broschüre.

bookmaker Bücherschreiber, *(racing)* Buchmacher;
  unlicensed ~ wilder Buchmacher.

bookmaking Kompilation eines Buches, *(racing)* Buchmacherei.

bookman Büchermensch.

bookmark[er] Lesezeichen.

bookmarking Kenntlichmachung in den Büchern;
  ~ of assigned accounts Kenntlichmachung abgetretener Forderungen.

bookmate Mitschüler, Studiengenosse, Schulkamerad.

bookmobile *(US)* Wanderbücherei.

bookplate Exlibris, *(library)* Buchzeichen.

bookrack Büchergestell.

bookrest Lesepult.

bookroom Bibliothek, Bücherzimmer, -stube.

bookseller Buchhändler;
  established ~ zugelassener Buchhändler;
  ~s' association Buchhändlervereinigung; **~ charter group** der Buchhändlervereinigung angeschlossene Buchhandlung; **~s' clearing company** Buchhändlerabrechnungsgemeinschaft; **~s' clearing and payment system** buchhändlerischer Abrechnungs- und Zahlungsverkehr; **retail ~ discount** Sortimenterrabatt; **~s' school of commerce** Buchhändlerschule; **~ trade delivery service** buchhändlerische Zustellungsdienste.

booksellerism Buchhändlertum.

bookselling Buchhandel;
  ~ trade Buchhändlergewerbe;
  departmental-store ~s Warenhausbuchhandel; **general ~s** Sortimentsbuchhandel; **intermediary ~** Zwischenbuchhandel; **retail ~** Sortimenter; **station ~s** Bahnhofsbuchhandel; **wholesale ~** Buchgroßhändler, Großbuchhandel; **wholesale antiquarian ~s** Großantiquariat.

bookshelf Bücherbord.

bookshop Buchladen, -handlung;
  pocket-edition ~ Taschenbuchladen; **retail ~** Sortimentsbuchhandlung.

bookstack Bücherregal, -gestell.

bookstall Buchhandlung, -laden, Zeitungskiosk, Zeitungs-, Bücherstand;
  ~ keeper Buchhändler.

bookstore *(US)* Buchhandlung, -laden.

bookwork Buchstudium, *(print.)* Werksatz.

bookworm Bücherwurm.

bookwright Bücherschreiber, Autor.

boom starke Nachfrage, Hausse, geschäftliche Blütezeit, wirtschaftlicher Aufschwung, [Hoch]konjunktur, Konjunkturaufschwung, *(US, bogus electioneering)* Stimmungs-, Wahlmache, Reklamerummel, *(film)* Galgen, *(mar.)* Baum, Ausleger, *(mil.)* Sperre, Sperrkette;
  backlog ~ Aufholkonjunktur; **big ~** Reklame; **building ~** Baukonjunktur; **consumer ~** Konsumgüterkonjunktur; **continuing ~** anhaltende Konjunktur; **cyclical ~** Hochkonjunktur, *(stock exchange)* konjunkturbedingte Hausse; **excess ~** überhitzte Konjunktur; **export ~** Exportkonjunktur; **internal ~** Inlandskonjunktur; **overdone ~** Überkonjunktur; **overheated ~** überhitzte Konjunktur; **prolonged ~** Hochkonjunktur, Zeit wirtschaftlicher Blüte; **shipbuilding ~** Konjunktur in der Schiffsbauindustrie; **specious ~** Scheinblüte, -konjunktur; **stock-market ~** Aktienhausse; **subsiding ~** abnehmende Haussebewegung, rückgängige Konjunktur; **wage-led ~** von Lohnerhöhungen angetriebene Konjunktur;
  ~-and-bust *(US coll.)* Zeit außergewöhnlichen Aufstiegs; **~ in capital investment** Investitionsgüterkonjunktur; **~ in equities** Aktienhausse; **~ of production goods** Produktionsgüterhochkonjunktur; **~ in the equity market** Kapitalmarktkonjunktur; **~ in the gilt-edged market** Hausse auf dem Markt für mündelsichere Anlagewerte; **~ in the property market** Immobilienhausse; **~ in real estate** Grundstückskonjunktur; **~ in stocks** Aktienhausse; **~ of a town** rapide Entwicklung einer Stadt;
  ~ *(v.)* *(advance with a rush)* hochkommen, aufwärtsstreben, rapiden Aufschwung nehmen, *(advertise)* Reklame machen, *(business)* konjunkturellen Auftrieb haben, *(electioneering)* Wahlpropaganda treiben, *(rise in value)* im Wert steigen; **~ the market** Kurse steigern; **~ after the war** nach dem Krieg groß ins Geschäft gekommen sein;
  to be on the dark side of the ~ im Konjunkturschatten liegen; **to curb the ~** Konjunktur zügeln, Hochkonjunktur bremsen; **to experience a ~** sich in einer Konjunkturphase befinden; **to overtake the ~** Konjunktur überhitzen; **to place a check on the ~** Konjunktur dämpfen;
  ~ boat *(mar.)* Deckboot; **~ city** aus dem Boden geschossene Stadt; **~ conditions** Haussebedingungen; **~ industry** aufblühendes Gewerbe; **~ market** Haussemarkt; **~ period** Konjunkturphase, *(stock market)* Haussephase; **~ price** Haussekurs; **~ profit** Konjunkturgewinn; **~ proportions** Konjunkturverhältnisziffern; **~ trend** konjunkturelle Aufwärtstendenz; **~ year** Konjunkturjahr; **~ years** Zeiten wirtschaftlicher Blüte.

boomer *(US)* Haussier, Spekulant.

booming *(a.)* Aufschwung nehmend, florierend;
  to be ~ im Aufschwung begriffen sein, Hochkonjunktur haben, *(book)* sich glänzend verkaufen, glänzend gehen; **to be ~ as a novelist** berühmter Schriftsteller sein;
  ~ business glänzend gehendes Geschäft; **~ demand** Nachfragekonjunktur; **~ economy** glänzende Konjunktur, Hochkonjunktur; **to keep up the ~ pace of capital investment** langfristige

Kapitalanlagen weiterhin bevorzugt vornehmen; **~ prices** *(stock exchange)* haussierende Kurse; **~ profits** glänzende Gewinne; **~ recovery** konjunkturelle Erholung; **~ year** Jahr wirtschaftlicher Blüte, Aufschwungsjahr.

boomlet vorübergehende Konjunktur, Kleinkonjunktur *(advertising)* Propaganda.

boomtime konjunkturelle Blütezeit, Hochkonjunktur;
~ level Hochkonjunkturniveau; **~ prices** Preise in hochkonjunkturellen Zeiten.

boomtown schnell aufstrebende Stadt.

boon Wohltat;
~ companion *(fellow)* Zechbruder.

boost *(US coll.)* Auftrieb, Preistreiberei, -steigerung, *(ballyhoo)* Reklame, *(promotion)* Nachhilfe, Förderung, Unterstützung;
~ to demand Nachfrageankurbelung; **~ to exports** Ausfuhr-, Exportförderung; **~ in pay** *(US sl.)* Gehaltserhöhung; **~ in taxes** Steueranstieg;
~ *(v.)* fördern, unterstützen;
~ s. th. für etw. Reklame machen, Werbetrommel für etw. rühren;
~ a battery Batterie kurzzeitig stark laden; **~ business** Wirtschaft ankurbeln; **~ a candidate** Kandidaten unterstützen; **~ a company into the black** Unternehmen in die Gewinnzone führen; **~ confidence** Selbstvertrauen stärken; **~earnings** Erträge ansteigen lassen; **~ the stagnant economy** Maßnahme zur konjunkturellen Belebung treffen; **~ s. o. into a position** j. protektionieren; **~ prices** Preise hinauftreiben; **~ sales** Umsatzsteigerung herbeiführen;
to give s. o. a ~ in business j. geschäftlich voranbringen.

booster Förderer, Fürsprecher, *(advertising)* Reklamemacher, *(el.)* Servomotor, *(prices)* Preistreiber, *(promotion)* moralische Unterstützung, *(railway)* Zusatzmaschine, *(rocketry)* Trägerrakete, *(technics)* Hilfsantrieb;
~ battery Zusatzbatterie; **~ gear** *(US)* Geländegang; **~ rocket** Startrakete; **~ shot** Wiederholungsimpfung; **~ station** Relaisstation.

boosting of exports Ausfuhrankurbelung.

boot Stiefel, *(Br., car)* Kofferraum, *(firing, sl.)* plötzliche Entlassung, Rausschmiß, *(mar., US)* Rekrut;
to ~ obendrein, zusätzlich;
Wellington ~s Gummistiefel;
~ *(v.)* **s. o.** *(sl.)* j. feuern;
~ out of office aus dem Amt vertreiben;
to bet one's ~s on s. th. *(sl.)* sich hundertprozentig auf etw. verlassen; **to die with one's ~s on** in den Sielen sterben, mitten aus der Arbeit weggerafft werden; **to get the ~** *(sl.)* gefeuert werden, fliegen; **to give s. o. the ~** *(sl.)* j. feuern (hinauswerfen); **to grow too big for one's ~s** größenwahnsinnig werden; **to put the ~ into s. o.** j. mit Füßen treten (miserabel behandeln); **to shake in one's ~s** vor Angst zittern.

bootblack *(US)* Stiefelputzer.

booth Verkaufs-, Schau-, Jahrmarktsbude, *(exhibition)* Messestand, *(film, radio)* schalldichte Zelle, *(tel., US)* Telefon-, Fernsprechzelle;
fund-raising ~ Sammelstelle für Geldspenden; **polling ~** Wahlzelle.

bootleg *(US)* geschmuggelte Spirituosen;
~ *(v.)* *(US)* illegal herstellen (schmuggeln);
~ wages *(US)* außertarifliche Löhne.

bootlegger *(US)* Alkoholschmuggler.

bootlegging *(US)* Alkoholschmuggel.

bootlick Kriecher, Speichellecker.

boots *(Br.)* Hausbursche, Hoteldiener.

booty Kriegsbeute, Plünderung, *(rich profit)* fetter Gewinn.

boozer *(Br., sl.)* Sauflokal, Kneipe.

border *(edge)* Rand, *(frontier)* Grenzgebiet, Staatslandesgrenze, *(print.)* Rand-, Zierleiste, Um-, Einrahmung, Einfassung;
national ~ Staatsgrenze;
~ *(v.)* **on** grenzen an;
to cross the ~ über die Grenze gehen; **to escape over the ~** über die Grenze entkommen; **to seal off the ~** Grenze hermetisch verschließen;
~ area Grenzgebiet; **~ clash** Grenzzwischenfall; **~ commission** Grenzkommission; **~ control** Grenzüberwachung; **~ country** Anliegerstaat; **~ crossing** Grenzübergang, -übertritt; **~ district** Grenzbezirk; **~ guards** [etwa] Bundesgrenzschutzangehörige, Grenzpolizei; **~ incident** Grenzzwischenfall; **~ lights** *(theater)* Soffittenlichter; **~ official** Grenzbeamter; **~ patrol** Grenzpolizei; **~ patrol official** Grenzschutzleiter; **~ point** *(US)* Grenzstation; **~ police post** Grenzpolizeistation; **~ population** Grenzbevölkerung; **~ revision** Grenzrevision; **~ rule** Randlinie;

~ service Grenzschutz; **~ state** Anliegerstaat; **~ station**, **-bahnhof**; **~ stone** Grenzstein; **~ territory** Grenzgebiet; **~ town** Grenzstadt; **~ traffic** Grenzverkehr; **~ treaty** Grenzabkommen; **~ troubles** Grenzschwierigkeiten; **~ violation** Grenzverletzung; **~ village** Grenzdorf; **~ war** Grenzkrieg; **~ warden** Grenzwache; **~ zone** Grenzzone.

bordereau Sortenzettel, Inhaltsvermerk.

borderer Anlieger, Anwohner, Grenzbewohner;
~ on the sea Küstenbewohner.

bordering angrenzend;
~ flight an der Rentabilitätsgrenze liegender Flug; **~ state** Anlieger-, Anrainer-, Grenz-, Randstaat.

borderland Grenzgebiet;
~ of science Grenzgebiet der Wissenschaft.

borderline Grenze, Grenzlinie, *(study)* Grenzgebiet;
~ case Grenzfall.

bored out of one's mind zu Tode gelangweilt.

born | alive lebend geboren; **foreign ~** im Ausland geboren;
~ out of wedlock unehelich;
true-~ american geborener Amerikaner; **~ businessman** geborener Geschäftsmann; **national ~ subject** *(Br.) (citizen, US)* Staatsangehöriger durch Geburt.

borne, to be ~ by zu Lasten von gehen; **to be ~ upon s. o.** jem. klarwerden.

borough *(Br.)* Gemeinde[bezirk], Stadtgemeinde, -bezirk, Marktflecken, *(parl.)* städtischer Wahlbezirk, *(US)* Stadtbezirk, Dorfgemeinde;
county ~ Kreis-, Bezirks-, Provinzialverband; **municipal ~** [etwa] kreisangehörige Stadt; **noncounty ~** *(Br.)* [etwa] kreisangehörige Stadt; **parliamentary ~** *(Br.)* städtischer Wahlkreis; **pocket ~** *(Br.)* vom Großgrundbesitzer beeinflußter Wahlkreis; **rotten ~** *(Br.)* verlassener Wahlkreis; **rural ~** Landkreis, ländlicher Bezirk;
~ council *(Br.)* Stadt-, Gemeinderat; **~ councillor** *(Br.)* Ratsherr, Stadtrat; **~ court** *(Br.)* Friedensgericht; **~-Englisch** *(Br.)* Vererbung auf den jüngsten Sohn; **~ fund** Gemeindekasse, Stadtsäckel; **~ holder** Bürgermeister; **~ master** *(Br.)* Bezirksbürgermeister; **~ rate** *(Br.)* Gemeindesteuer, -umlage, -abgabe; **~ session** *(Br.)* Sitzung der Friedensrichter; **~ town** Stadtgemeinde.

boroughhead *(Br.)* Bezirksbürgermeister.

borrow *(v.)* borgen, entnehmen, [ent]leihen;
~ heavily on a short-term basis sich kurzfristig erheblich verschulden; **~ at interest** gegen Zinsen leihen; **~ money** Darlehn (Kredit) aufnehmen; **~ money from s. o.** bei jem. eine Anleihe machen; **~ money on the security of an estate** Hypothek[arkredit] aufnehmen; **~ on mortgage from a long-term institutional lender** langfristiges Hypothekendarlehen bei einer Kapitalsammelstelle aufnehmen; **~ for the purchase of land** Grundstücksankauf finanzieren; **~ on a policy** Police beleihen; **~ at a substantial negative rate of interest** Darlehn zu erheblich verbilligten Zinssätzen aufnehmen; **~ on securities** Effekten lombardieren; **~ stock** Wertpapiere hereinnehmen; **~ trouble** *(US)* sich unnötig Sorgen machen; **~ up to the value of the property** Grundstück bis zu 100% seines Wertes beleihen; **~ the whole of the purchase price** Kredit für den gesamten Kaufpreis aufnehmen.

borrowable ausleihbar.

borrowed geborgt, geliehen;
~ capital Fremd-, Leih-, Kreditkapital; **~ funds** aufgenommene Gelder; **~ money** geliehenes Geld, Leihkapital, aufgenommenes Kapital, Leihkapital, -geld, Fremdmittel; **to live on ~ time** nicht mehr lange zu leben haben.

borrower Entlehner, Entleiher, *(loan)* Darlehns-, Kreditnehmer, Kreditkunde, Schuldner;
first-class ~ erste Adresse; **joint ~** Konsortialkreditnehmer; **personal ~** Privatkunde; **would-be ~** kreditsuchendes Unternehmen;
~ on bottomry Bodmereinnehmer, -schuldner;
to crowd out a private ~ from the capital market Unternehmen vom Kapitalmarkt verdrängen;
~'s bank Hausbank; **~'s note against ad rem security** dinglich gesicherter Schuldschein.

borrowing Leihen, Entlehnen, Borgen, *(loan)* aufgenommenes Geld, Darlehns-, Schuld-, Kreditaufnahme;
~s aufgenommene Schulden;
business ~ Geschäftskredit; **fixed-interest ~** Kreditaufnahme zu gleichbleibenden Zinssätzen; **foreign currency ~** Devisenkredit; **local authority ~** Kommunalkreditaufnahme; **long-term ~** langfristige Kreditaufnahme; **other ~s** *(balance sheet)* sonstige Fremdmittel; **public ~** Mittelaufnahme der öffentlichen Hand;

short-term ~ Ausleihungen im kurzfristigen Kreditgeschäft (am Geldmarkt); **temporary** ~ befristete Geldaufnahme; **treasury** ~ Steuergutscheinausgabe; **ultra vires** ~ Kreditaufnahme unter Zuwiderhandlung gegen die Satzung; **unauthorized** ~ nicht genehmigte Kreditaufnahme;

~ **on accounts receivable** *(US)* Kreditaufnahme durch Abtretung von Debitoren; ~ **by local authorities** Kreditaufnahme durch Kommunalbehörden; ~ **by a liquidator appointed by the court** Kreditaufnahme durch einen gerichtlich bestellten Liquidator; ~ **of money** Aufnahme von Geldern; ~ **by representative** Kreditaufnahme durch den Nachlaßverwalter; ~ **on collateral security** *(US)* Effektenlombardierung; ~ **ultra vires the company** satzungswidrige Kreditaufnahme;
to increase the ~**s at the bank** bei der Bank in erhöhtem Maße Kredit in Anspruch nehmen; **to ratify the** ~ **by resolution in general meeting** Kreditaufnahme durch einen Hauptversammlungsbeschluß genehmigen lassen;

~ **arrangements** Kreditvereinbarungen; ~ **authorization** *(director)* Kreditaufnahmebefugnis; ~ **capacity** Verschuldensmöglichkeit; ~ **corporation** Darlehensnehmerin; ~ **costs** Kreditkosten; ~ **country** kreditnehmendes Land, Schuldnerland; ~ **demand** Geldbedarf; ~ **expenses** Kreditkosten; ~ **facilities** Kreditmöglichkeiten; ~ **limit** Kreditaufnahmegrenze; ~ **member** *(building society, Br.)* zugeteilter Bausparer; ~ **needs** Kreditbedarf; ~ **peak** Periode höchster Kreditbeanspruchung; ~ **power** *(director)* Kreditaufnahmebefugnis; ~ **principle** Beleihungsgrundsätze; ~ **rate** Ausleihungssatz; ~ **rate of building societies** *(Br.)* Bauspardarlehnssatz; ~ **ratio** Kreditaufnahmekoeffizient; ~ **requirements** Kreditbedarf; **federal** ~ **requirements** *(US)* [etwa] Refinanzierungsmöglichkeiten durch die Landeszentralbank; ~ **reserve** Kreditreserve; ~ **resolution** Schuldenaufnahmebeschluß.

borstal | **institution** *(Br.)* Fürsorgeheim, Betreuungsverein für Jugendliche; ~ **training** Unterbringung in einem Fürsorgeheim.

bosom | **of the ocean** Tiefen des Ozeans; **in the** ~ **of one's family** im Schoße der Familie;
~ **friend** Busenfreund.

boss *(US coll.)* Betriebsleiter, Chef, Vorgesetzter, Direktor, *(leading personality)* tonangebender Mann, Macher, *(US sl., party politics)* Parteileiter, -führer, Bonze;
~ *(v.)* Chef sein, strenges Regiment führen, *(school, sl.)* verhauen;
~ **about** herumkommandieren; ~ **it** Meister sein, Laden schmeißen;
~ **the show** *(US sl.)* das entscheidende Wort sprechen, den Laden schmeißen;
to act the ~ Vorgesetzten herauskehren;
~ *(a.) (US sl.)* ausgezeichnet, erstklassig;
~ **rule** *(US)* Bonzentum; **to make a** ~ **shot** *(sl.)* durchfallen.

bossdom *(US)* Chefbereich, *(pol.)* Führerschaft, politische Kontrolle.

botel Motel für Bootsbesitzer.

both-to-blame *(law of insurance)* beiderseitiges Verschulden;
~ **collision clause** Klausel für beiderseitiges Verschulden.

bother Mühsal, Kummer, Sorge, Schererei;
~ *(v.)* belästigen, behelligen;
to have much ~ **in finding a house** nur unter großen Schwierigkeiten ein Haus finden können.

bottle Flasche;
drift ~ Flaschenpost;
~ *(v.)* auf Flaschen abfüllen (ziehen);
~ **up** auf Flaschen füllen, *(fig.)* unterdrücken, zurückhalten; ~ **up one's feelings** seine Gefühle unterdrücken; ~ **up inflationary forces** inflationäre Auswirkungen lediglich vorübergehend konterkarieren;
to be too fond of the ~ alkoholsüchtig sein; **to sell by the** ~ flaschenweise verkaufen;
~ **gas** Butangas; ~ **opener** Flaschenöffner; ~ **post** Flaschenpost; ~ **washer** Flaschenspülmaschine; ~ **washer** *(fig.)* Mädchen für alles.

bottleholder *(coll.)* Hintermann, Helfershelfer.

bottleneck enge Straße, Engpaß;
~ **in production** Engpaß in der Produktion; ~ **in supplies** Versorgungsengpaß;
to have reached a ~ in einen Engpaß geraten sein; **to run fast into** ~**s** schnell Engpässe sichtbar machen;
~ **inflation** sektorale Inflation.

bottom Grund, Boden, *(ship)* Schiffsboden, *(stock exchange)* Tiefpunkt, -stand, niedrigster Stand;
at ~ *(fig.)* billigst, im Grunde genommen; **at the** ~ unten; **at the** ~ **of the road** am Ende der Straße;

~ **dropped out** neuer Tiefstand; **foul** ~ *(ship)* fauler Boden; ~ **left** links unten;
~ **of the business** des Pudels Kern; ~ **of the market** Börsentiefstpunkt; ~ **of a page** Fuß einer Seite; ~ **of a recession** tiefster Rezessionspunkt; ~ **of the sea** Meeresboden, -grund;
~ *(v.)* **[out]** *(market)* Widerstandslinie aufbauen, Tiefststand überschreiten;
to be at the ~ zugrunde liegen, wahrer Grund für (Urheber von) etw. sein; **to be at the** ~ **of a business** hinter einer ganzen Sache stecken; **to be at the** ~ **of the table** Schlußbericht abgeben; **to be at the** ~ **of the tax pile** niedrigste Steuersätze zahlen; **to be embarked on the same** ~ gleiches Schicksal haben; **to come** ~ **of a list** ganz am Ende einer Liste stehen; **to get at the** ~ **of a matter** einer Sache auf den Grund kommen; **to go in british** ~ von englischen Schiffen transportiert werden; **to go to the** ~ ins Bodenlose fallen, *(ship)* versinken, absaufen; **to hit** ~ niedrigsten Stand erreichen; **to knock the** ~ **out of an argument** Argument zerpflücken; **to print notes at the** ~ **of a page** als Fußnoten drücken; **to reach (touch) the** ~ tiefsten Stand erreichen; **to seat at the** ~ **of a long table** am unteren Tafelrand platzieren; **to stand on one's own** ~ auf eigenen Füßen stehen, [wirtschaftlich] selbständig sein; **to touch the** ~ *(prices)* niedrigsten Stand erreichen; **the** ~ **has fallen out of the market** die Preise sind ins Bodenlose gesunken;
~ **cause** Grundursache; **to stake one's** ~ **dollar** *(US)* alles auf einmal riskieren; ~ **drawer** Aussteuer; ~ **facts** *(US)* Grundtatsachen; ~ **gear** *(car)* erster Gang; ~ **lands** *(US)* Schwemmland; ~ **price** äußerster Preis, Tiefstpreis, niedrigster Preis, *(stock exchange)* Tiefstkurs; ~**-of-the-line prices** Tiefstpreise; ~ **quality** schlechteste (niedrigste) Qualität; ~ **shelf** unterstes Regal.

bottoming *(road)* Packlage, Grundbau;
to be in the general ~ **area** sich konsolidieren, am unteren Wendepunkt sein; ~**-out pattern** Tiefstpunkt.

bottomry Bodmerei[geld], Schiffsverpfändung, -hypothek, Bodmereivertrag;
~ *(v.)* verbodmen, Schiff verpfänden;
to advance money on ~ Geld auf Bodmerei geben; **to borrow (raise, take) money on** ~ Geld auf Bodmerei leihen; **to lend money on** ~ Geld auf Bodmerei ausleihen;
~ **bond** Bodmereibrief, Schiffswechsel; ~ **bondholder** Bodmereigläubiger; ~ **debt** Bodmereischuld; ~ **insurance** Bodmereiversicherung; ~ **interest** Bodmereizinsen, -prämie; ~ **loan** Bodmereischuld, -geld; ~ **money** Bodmereidarlehn, -gelder.

bought gekauft;
~ **by auction** ersteigert; ~ **in bond** aus dem Zoll gekauft; ~ **for cash** gegen bar (Kasse) gekauft; ~ **on credit** auf Ziel gekauft;
~ **book (journal)** Einkaufsbuch; ~ **[and sold] note** *(Br., contract note)* Kaufnote, *(broker's memorandum)* Schlußschein.

boulevard Pracht-, Ringstraße, breite Allee, Boulevard;
~ **stop** *(US)* Straßenkreuzung mit Haltesignalen.

bounce Protzerei, *(US sl.)* Rausschmiß, plötzliche Entlassung;
~ *(v.) (US sl.)* an die Luft setzen, rausschmeißen, *(bill, fam.)* platzen.

bouncer Lügenmaul, Angeber, *(cheque)* ungedeckter Scheck, *(night club, US)* Rausschmeißer.

bound Schranke, Grenze, Limit;
out of ~**s** Betreten (Zutritt) verboten; **within narrow** ~**s** in engem Rahmen;
~ *(v.)* beschränken, in Schranken halten, begrenzen, limitieren; ~ **to** angrenzen an;
to be ~ **to fail** zum Scheitern verurteilt sein; **to be** ~ **by law** gesetzlich verpflichtet sein; **to be** ~ **by one's offer** an sein Angebot gebunden sein; **to be** ~ **over** durch Bürgschaft verpflichtet sein; **to be** ~ **up with s. o.** jem. eng verbunden sein; **to be** ~ **up in business** von seinen Geschäften völlig absorbiert werden; **to be** ~ **up in one's work** ganz in seiner Arbeit vertieft sein; **to be** ~ **up with the welfare of the community** vom allgemeinen Wohlstand abhängig sein; **to be within the** ~ **s of possibility** im Bereich des Möglichen liegen; **to be placed out of** ~ **for soldiers** *(Br.)* für Soldaten verboten sein; **to bring s. th. within** ~**s** etw. unter Kontrolle bringen; **to keep within the** ~**s of the law** sich auf den Boden des Gesetzes stellen; **to keep within the** ~**s of propriety** Anstand wahren, Anstandsregeln beherzigen; **to know no** ~**s** grenzenlos sein; **to place out of** ~**s** *(Br.)* zum Sperrgebiet erklären; **to take before the** ~ *(fig.)* zuvorkommen;
~ *(a.)* gebunden, broschiert, *(obliged)* verpflichtet, haftpflichtig;
duty-~ moralisch verpflichtet; **homeward** ~ auf der Rückreise; **jointly and severally** ~ gesamtschuldnerisch verpflichtet; **legally** ~ gesetzlich verpflichtet; **outward** ~ auf der Ausreise; **strike-**~ bestreikt;

~ **in boards** kartoniert; ~ **by contract** vertraglich gebunden; ~ **and determined** (*coll., US*) entschlossen; ~ **for** (*ship*) bestimmt nach; ~ **up** in Anspruch genommen;
~ **apprentice** vertraglich verpflichteter Lehrling Auszubildender; ~ **bailiff** Gerichtsvollzieher; ~ **insert** Beihefter, geheftete Beilage.

boundaries of municipality Gemeindegrenzen.

boundary Grenze, Begrenzung, Grenzlinie, Mark, (*marketing*) Reizschwelle, (*mil.*) Nahtstelle, (*mining*) Markscheide, (*technics*) Toleranzgrenze;
near the ~ an der Grenze;
artificial ~ künstliche Grenze; **natural (public)** ~ natürliche Grenze; **parochial** ~ Regionalgrenze; **private** ~ künstliche Grenze;
to adjust a ~ Grenze bereinigen; **to be beyond the** ~ **of human knowledge** jenseits menschlicher Erkenntnisse liegen; **to draw a** ~ Grenze abstecken; **to fix a** ~ Grenze ziehen; **to form a** ~ Grenze bilden;
~ **convention** Grenzabkommen; ~ **crossing** Grenzübergang, -überschreitung; ~ **customs** Grenzzoll; ~ **dispute** Grenzkonflikt, -streitigkeit; ~ **ditch** Grenzgraben; ~ **fence** Grenzzaun; ~ **lighting** (*aerodrome*) Randbefeuerung; ~ **line** Begrenzungs-, Grenzlinie; ~ **mark** Grenzmal; ~ **question** Grenzfrage, -problem; ~ **stone** Grenzstein; ~ **suit** Grenzstreitigkeit.

bounded tree Grenzbaum.

bounders (*US*) Grenzpunkte.

bounding angrenzend.

bounty (*benevolence*) Wohltätigkeit, Freigebigkeit, (*enlistment*) Handgeld, (*trade*) Subvention, Ausfuhr-, Einfuhrzuschuß, [Ausfuhr]prämie, Bonus;
child ~ Kinderzulage;
~ **on exportation** Ausfuhrprämie, -vergütung; ~ **on importation** Einfuhrprämie, -zuschuß; ~ **for manufacture** Herstellungsprämie;
to constitute unfair ~ Tatbestand der Exportsubventionierung erfüllen;
~ **certificate** Ausfuhrprämienschein; ~**-fed** subventioniert; ~ **feeding** Subventionswesen; ~ **lands** Schenkungsland.

bourgeois Spießbürger.

bourse Pariser Börse;
~º **valuation** Börsenbewertung.

boursiers [Pariser] Börsenmitglieder.

bout Arbeitsgang, Schicht;
drinking ~ Zechgelage;
to have a ~ **at** sich versuchsweise beschäftigen.

bow Verbeugung, Verneigung, (*ship*) Bug;
~ (*v.*) **to s. one's opinion** jem. zur Meinungsäußerung vorlegen; ~ **s. o. out** j. hinauskomplimentieren;
to draw the long ~ übertreiben, angeben; **to fire across the** ~ vor den Bug feuern; **to have more than one string to one's** ~ mehrere Eisen im Feuer haben;
~ **compass** Bogen-, Federzirkel.

bowdlerization Ausmerzung anstößiger Stellen.

bowdlerize (*v.*) anstößige Stellen ausmerzen.

bowing acquaintance flüchtige (oberflächliche) Bekanntschaft.

box (*advertisement*) Kästchen, Umrandung, (*small case*) Kasten, (*coll.*) Radio-, Fernsehgerät, Flimmerkiste, (*fig.*) Kasse, Fonds, (*luggage, Br.*) [großer] Reisekoffer, (*post office, US*) Post-, Schließfach, (*predicament*) Klemme, schwierige Lage, (*print.*) Kasten, Rahmen, Linieneinrahmung, (*theater*) Loge;
ambulance ~ Verbandskasten; **ballot** ~ Wahlkabine, -urne; **best defended** ~ (*mil.*) hervorragend verteidigte Stellung; **black-edged** ~ schwarz umrandeter Kasten; **call** ~ (*Br.*) Telefon-, Fernsprechzelle; **cash** ~ Geldkassette; **Christmas** ~ Weihnachtspäckchen; **electrical outlet** ~ Steckdose; **deed** ~ [Urkunden-] kassette; **insured** ~ (*post, Br.*) Wertpäckchen, -paket; **jury** ~ Geschworenenbank; **letter** ~ Briefkasten, Abholungsfach; **mail** ~ Postbriefkasten; **missionary** ~ Missionsbüchse; **money** ~ Sparbüchse, -schwein; **pillar** ~ Briefkasten; **plywood** ~ Sperrholzkiste; **post-office** ~ Postschließfach; **private** ~ Briefabholfach; **safe-deposit** ~ Schließ-, Stahl-, Bankfach, Safe; **telephone** ~ Telefonzelle; **tool** ~ Werkzeugkasten; **witness** ~ Zeugenstand; **wooden** ~ Holzkiste;
~ **on the right masthead** oberer Eckplatz der Titelseite; ~ **of matches** Schachtel Streichhölzer, Streichholzschachtel; ~ **of samples** Musterkasten; ~ **of tools** Werkzeugkasten;
~ (*v.*) (*Scot.*) bei Gericht einrenken;
~ **in** (*advertisement*) Text in Umrahmung stellen (umranden, einfassen); ~ **an article for sale** Ware für den Verkauf verpacken; ~ **up** in Schachteln verpacken; ~ **o. s. up** sich zurückziehen;

to be in the ~ im Zeugenstand sein; **to be one out of the** ~ zur Klicke gehören; **to be in the same** ~ in gleich übler Lage sein; **to be in the wrong** ~ auf dem Holzwege sein; **to clear a** ~ Briefkasten leeren;
~ **board** Kartonpapier; ~ **camera** (*photo*) Box, Kamera; ~ **drain** Abzugskanal; ~ **enamel paper** Hochglanzpapier; ~ **file** kastenförmiger Aktendeckel; ~ **head** (*print.*) umrandete Überschrift; ~ **letter** postlagernder Brief, Brief für das Postschließfach; ~ **lobby** Wandelgang; ~ **lunch** (*US*) Picknickkorb.

box number Chiffre[nummer], Kennziffer;
~ **advertisement** Chiffre-, Kennzifferanzeige.

box office Eintrittskasse, Vorverkaufsstelle, Kiosk, (*cinema*) Kinokasse, Kassenraum, (*fig., US*) Kassenerfolg;
~ **gross** Bruttokasseneinnahmen;
to fail at the ~ finanzieller Mißerfolg sein.

box-office Vorverkauf;
to be a great ~ **attraction** (*actor*) sehr hoch im Kurse sein, Kassenschlager sein; ~ **champ** Kassensieger; ~ **clerk** Kassierer; ~ **draw** (*US*) Kassenmagnet, -schlager; ~ **life** (*US*) Spieldauer; **insured** ~ **rate** (*Br.*) Wertpaketgebühr; ~ **receipts** Kasseneinnahmen; ~ **record** Kassenrekord; **to be a** ~ **success** (*US*) volle Kasse bringen, Kassenschlager sein; ~ **takings** Kasseneinnahmen.

box | rent (*US*) Schließfachmiete; ~ **room** Rumpelkammer; ~ **seat** (*theater*) Logensitz; ~ **shutter** klappbarer Fensterladen; ~ **sign** Leuchtkasten; ~ **sorting** Stimmabgabe in Kästchen; ~ **strapping** Stahlband für Verpackungskiste; ~ **ticket** Logenkarte; ~**-top offer** Prämie bei einer Verpackungsteileinsendung; ~ **truck** Kastenlieferwagen; ~ **wag(g)on** (*Br.*) gedeckter (geschlossener) Güterwagen, Fracht-, Güterwaggon, (*US*) Blockwagen, Lore.

boxcar (*US*) gedeckter (geschlossener) Güterwagen, (*US*) Fracht-, Güterwaggon.

boxed in Schachteln verpackt, (*books*) in Kassette;
~ **for export** in Seeverpackung;
~ **advertisement** umrandete Anzeige.

boxing Verpackungsmaterial, Schachteln, Kisten;
~ **in (up)** verpacken.

Boxing Day (*Br.*) zweiter Weihnachtsfeiertag.

boxkeeper (*theater*) Logenschließer.

boy, blue-eyed (fair-haired) Spitzenkandidat; **old** ~ ehemaliger Schüler; **white-haired** ~ hoffnungsvolle Nachwuchskraft, Protegé;
~ **next door** Nachbarsjunge;
to be past a ~ aus den Kinderschuhen heraus sein;
~ **sales** (*newspaper*) Einzelverkauf; ~º **Scouts** Pfadfinder.

boycott Boykott[verfahren], (*cartel law*) Sperre;
compound ~ zwangsweise ausgeübter mittelbarer Boykott; **negative** ~ Boykott durch Veröffentlichung einer schwarzen Liste; **positive** ~ durch besondere Anpreisung eigener Erzeugnisse durchgeführter Boykott; **primary** ~ unmittelbarer Boykott; **secondary** ~ mittelbarer Boykott;
~ **of finance** Finanzboykott; ~ **of lectures** Vorlesungsboykott;
~ (*v.*) boykottieren, in Verruf erklären;
to call off a ~ Boykott aufheben; **to put a shop under a** ~ Laden boykottieren;
~ **assistance** Boykottunterstützung; ~ **campaign** Boykottfeldzug; ~ **demands** Boykottforderungen; **to toe the central** ~ **line** sich der zentralgeleiteten Boykottpolitik anschließen; ~ **pressure** Boykottdruck.

boycottage Boykottanwendung.

boycotter Boykottdurchführer.

boycotting Boykottierung;
~ **of advertising media** Werbeboykott.

boycottism Boykottdurchführung.

bracery Geschworenenbeeinflussung.

bracket Gruppe, Schicht, (*architecture*) Konsole, Stützbalken, (*loan*) Tranche, (*demography*) demographisch definierte Bevölkerungsschicht, (*prop*) Schaufensterständer, (*print.*) Einschlußzeichen, (*statistics*) Kategorie, (*taxation*) Steuerklasse, Einkommensstufe, Rubrik;
in ~s in Klammern;
age ~ Altersstufe, -gruppe, -klasse; **income [tax]** ~ Einkommensteuerklasse, -gruppe; **middle income** ~s mittlere Einkommensteuerklassen; **round** ~s runde Klammern; **salary** ~ Besoldungsgruppe; **social** ~ Gesellschaftsschicht; **upper** ~ höhere Gesellschaftsschicht; **wage** ~ Lohnstufe;
~ (*v.*) einklammern, (*taxation*) in die gleiche Rubrik (Steuerklasse) einordnen;
~ **together at the top of the list** gemeinsam an die Spitze der Liste setzen; ~ **a word** Wort in Klammern einschließen;
to be in the higher income ~s zu den wohlhabenden Leuten zählen; **to be in low income** ~s geringes Einkommen haben.

braille Blindenschrift.
brain Gehirn, Verstand, Intelligenz, *(clever person)* Intelligenzbestie;
  electronic ~ Computer;
  to have s. th. on one's ~ sich ständig mit etw. befassen, Sache mit sich herumtragen, fixe Idee haben, nur Gedanken für eine Sache haben; **to have politics on the** ~ *(coll.)* politisch übermäßig interessiert sein; **to pick (suck) s. one's** ~**s** geistigen Diebstahl begehen; **to rack one's** ~ **about s. th.** sich über etw. den Kopf zerbrechen;
  ~ **capacity** Intelligenz; ~ **child** *(coll.)* geistiges Kind, Geistesprodukt, Gedankenblitz; **to sell a** ~ **child** *(coll.)* Gedankenblitz verkaufen; ~ **crack** Fimmel; ~ **damage** Gehirnschaden; ~ **drain** Abwanderung von Wissenschaftlern; ~ **gain** Zuwanderung wissenschaftlicher Führungskräfte; ~**-picking session** Meinungstest; ~ **power** Verstandeskräfte; ~ **storm** *(US)* plötzliche Erleuchtung, verrückter Einfall, hirnverbrannte Idee, Geistesblitz; ~**-storm** *(v.) (US)* gedanklich lösen; ~**storming** Ideenwirbel, -sitzung; ~ **sweat** *(coll.)* Gehirnschmalz; ~ **trust** *(US)* [politischer und wirtschaftlicher] Beratungsausschuß, Beraterstab, Gehirntrust, hochqualifizierte Expertengruppe, Expertenrat, wissenschaftlicher Beirat; ~ **truster** *(US)* Mitglied einer Fachberatergruppe, Unternehmensberater; ~ **wave** guter Einfall, Geistesblitz.
brainfag geistige Übermüdung (Erschöpfung).
brainsick geistesgestört.
brainsickness Geisteskrankheit, -gestörtheit.
brainwash *(v.)* Gehirnwäsche vornehmen.
brainwashing Gehirnwäsche.
brainwork geistige Arbeit, Geistestätigkeit, Kopfarbeit.
brainworker Geistesarbeiter;
  to be a ~ mit dem Kopf arbeiten.
brake Bremse, *(fig.)* Zügel, Einhalt;
  foot ~ Fußbremse;
  ~ *(v.)* bremsen;
  to act as a ~ **on s. one's activities** sich lähmend auf jds. Tätigkeitsdrang legen (auswirken); **to apply (operate) the** ~ Bremse anziehen (betätigen); **to jam on the** ~**s** mit voller Kraft bremsen, Vollbremsung durchführen; **to put a** ~ **on s. th.** einer Sache Einhalt gebieten; **to put on the** ~**s** *(car)* auf die Bremse treten, bremsen; **to shove on the** ~**s** kräftig auf die Bremse treten;
  ~ **fluid** Bremsflüssigkeit; ~**-fluid level** Bremsflüssigkeitspegel; ~ **horsepower** Bremsleistung; ~ **lever** Bremshebel; ~ **lights** Bremslicht; ~ **lining** Bremsbelag; ~ **parachute** Bremsfallschirm; ~ **pedal** Bremspedal, Bremse; ~ **shoe** Bremsbacke; ~ **van** *(railway, Br.)* Bremsabteil.
brakeload Bremsbelastung.
braking, dual doppeltes Bremssystem;
  ~ **power** Bremsleistung.
branch *(banking)* Neben-, Zweigstelle, Filiale, Depositenkasse, *(of business establishment)* Zweiggeschäft, -stelle, -niederlassung, Betriebsabteilung, Außen-, Nebenstelle, Filiale, Niederlasssung, *(part)* Unter-, Zweigabteilung, *(railway)* Zweigbahn, -linie, Nebenstrecke, *(society)* Zweigverein, *(subject of knowledge)* Fach, Zweig, Branche;
  account-holding ~ kontoführende Bankfiliale; **city** ~ Stadtfiliale, *(banking)* Stadtkasse; **local** ~ Zweigstelle, Filiale, *(party)* Ortsgruppe; **main** ~ Hauptfiliale, -niederlassung, Stammhaus; **manufacturing** ~ Fabrikationszweig; **overseas** ~ überseeische (ausländische) Niederlassung; **particular** ~ besonderes Gewerbe; **provincial** ~ *(bank)* Zweigniederlassung in der Provinz; **special** ~ Fach-, Sonderabteilung; **Special** ~⁹ *(Br.)* Staatssicherheitspolizei;
  provincial ~ **of an association** Landesgeschäftsstelle einer Vereinigung; ~ **of business** Geschäftszweig, -sparte, Spezialität; ~ **of a family** Seitenlinie einer Familie; ~ **of industry** Industrie-, Erwerbs-, Betriebs-, Handelszweig, Gewerbe[zweig]; **export-intensive** ~**es of industry** exportintensive Industriebereiche; ~ **of knowledge** Wissensgebiet; ~ **of production** Produktionszweig; ~ **of a river** Flußarm; ~ **of the sea** Meeresarm; ~ **of the service** *(mil.)* Truppengattung; ~ **of trade** Beruf-, Erwerbs-, Wirtschafts-, Gewerbezweig;
  ~ *(v.) (road)* sich gabeln;
  ~ **off** sich trennen, abzweigen; ~ **out** sich vergrößern; ~ **out into a dissertation** sich weitläufig über etw. verbreiten (auslassen); **to establish a new** ~ neue Filiale aufmachen; **to maintain** ~**es** Zweigstellen unterhalten; **to set up** ~**es** Filialgründungen vornehmen;
  ~ **account** Filialkonto; ~ **accounting** Filialbuchführung; ~ **activity** Filialtätigkeit, -geschäft; ~ **administration** Filialverwaltung; ~ **advice** Filialavis; ~ **balance sheet** Filialbilanz; ~ **bank**

Filialbank, Bankfiliale, Zweigbank; ~ **banking system (activities)** Filialbankensystem, -wesen; ~ **bill** Zahlstellenwechsel, Wechsel einer Bankfiliale; ~ **books** Filialgeschäftsbücher; ~ **building** Filialgebäude; ~ **business** Zweiggeschäft; ~ **establishment** Zweiggeschäft, -stelle, -niederlassung, -anstalt, Filiale; ~ **expenses** Filialaufwand, -unkosten; ~ **house** Zweigniederlassung, -unternehmen, Filiale; ~ **inventory** Filialinventar; ~ **investments** Investitionen bei Zweigunternehmen (im Filialbereich); ~ **line** *(railway)* Seiten-, Zweigbahn, Anschluß-, Nebenlinie, -bahn; ~**-line abandonment** Stillegung von Nebenlinien; ~ **manager** Direktor einer Niederlassung, Filialleiter, -vorsteher; ~ **meeting** Ortsverbandstreffen; ~ **network** Filialnetz; ~ **office** Zweigniederlassung, -stelle, Filialgeschäft, *(bank)* Depositenkasse; **to establish a** ~ **office** Filiale errichten; **to have 25** ~ **offices in operation** 25 Geschäftsstellen unterhalten; ~ **office tax** Filialsteuer; ~ **pilot** amtlich angestellter Lotse, geprüfter (lizensierter) Pilot; ~ **plant** Zweigbetrieb; ~ **post-office** Zweigpostamt, Postnebenstelle; ~ **premises** Filialbüro; ~ **procuration** Filialprokura; ~ **profit** Filialerträgnisse, -gewinne; ~ **railway** *(Br.)* (railroad, *US*) Zweigbahn; ~ **road** *(US)* Nebenstraße; ~ **school** *(mil.)* Truppenschule; ~ **shop** Filialgeschäft, -unternehmen; ~ **society** Zweigverein; ~ **statement** Filialbilanz; ~ **station** Zweigstation; ~ **store** *(US)* Zweiggeschäft; ~ **terminal line** Stichbahn; ~ **transactions** Filialabschlüsse.
branching Verzweigung, Verästelung;
  ~ **off** Abzweigung.
branchlet kleine Filiale.
brand *(fig.)* Makel, Schandfleck, *(kind of goods)* Sorte, Marke, Klasse, *(quality)* Qualität, *(trademark)* Schutzmarke, Güte-, Waren-, Fabrikzeichen, Markenerzeugnis, -artikel, -name;
  off-~ nicht markengebunden;
  fighting ~ Kampfmarke; **first-class** ~ erstklassiges Fabrikat; **house** ~ Firmenzeichen; **manufacturer's** ~ Fabrikmarke; **national** ~**s** *(US)* überall bekannte Qualitätserzeugnisse (Schutzmarken); **own** ~ Hausmarke; **private** ~ Markenbezeichnung einer Einzelhandelsgesellschaft; **top-selling** ~ Spitzenerzeugnis der Markenindustrie; **wildcat** ~ unerlaubtes Markenzeichen;
  ~ **of decentralization** Dezentralisierungsidee; ~ **of leadership** Führerschaftsimage; ~ **of showmanship** Art der Aufführung;
  ~ *(v.) (burn)* mit Brandzeichen versehen, Zeichen einbrennen, *(goods)* mit Warenzeichen (Firmenzeichen) versehen, zum Markenartikel entwickeln;
  ~ **on one's mind** seinem Gedächtnis unauslöschlich einprägen;
  ~ **acceptance** Anerkennung als Markenartikel; ~ **advertising** Marken[artikel]werbung; ~ **association** Markengemeinschaft; ~ **barometer** Markenbarometer, -index; ~ **choice** Markenwahl; ~ **comparison** Markenvergleich; ~ **competition** Marken[artikel-]wettbewerb; ~ **demand** Nachfrage nach einem Markenartikel; ~ **identity** Übereinstimmung mit dem Markenbild, Markenidentität; ~ **image** Markenbild, -symbol, Marken-, Werbestil, Markenvorstellung des Verbrauchers; ~ **label** Markenetikett; ~ **leader** Spitzenmarke; ~ **loyalty** Markentreue; ~ **management** Markenbetreuung; ~ **manager** Markenbetreuer, Produkt-Manager, Vertriebs-, Verkaufsleiter; ~ **name** Produkt-, Markenname; ~**-new** ganz neu, fabrik-, funkelnagelneu; ~ **policy** Markenpolitik; ~ **position** Bedeutung einer Marke im Konkurrenzumfeld, Markenbevorzugung; ~ **preference** Markenpräferenz, -vorliebe; ~ **price** Marken[artikel]-, Produkt-, Artikelpreis, Preis eines Markenerzeugnisses; ~ **recognition** Anerkennung als Markenartikel durch die Verbraucher, Markenwiedererkennung; ~ **supplier** Markenlieferant; ~ **trend survey** Markenindex.
branded mit einem Markenzeichen versehen;
  ~ **in one's memory** ins Gedächtnis eingegraben;
  ~ **article** Markenartikel; ~ **goods (commodities, merchandise, staple, US)** Markenartikel;
  to install ~ **goods** Markenartikel einbauen.
brass *(Br.)* Grab-, Gedenkplatte, *(dust, sl.)* Moos, Pinkepinke;
  top ~ *(US sl.)* hohes Tier;
  ~ **hat** *(mil., sl.)* hohes Tier; **not to care a** ~ **farthing** sich keinen roten Heller darum scheren; ~ **knuckles** Schlagring; **to part** ~ **rags with s. o.** sich mit jem. verkrachen; **to get down to** ~ **tacks** zum Wesentlichen (Kern der Sache) kommen.
brassage Münzgebühr.
brawl Schlägerei, Raufhandel;
  street ~ Straßenauflauf.
brawler Raufbold.
brawling *(Br.)* Ruhestörung.
breach Bruch Riß, Sprung, *(infringement)* Übertretung, Verstoß, Bruch, Verletzung, *(mil.)* Bresche, Einbruchstelle, Sturmlücke, *(waves)* Brecher, Brandung;

free from ~ and damages frei von Bruch und Beschädigung; **anticipatory** ~ angekündigte Vertragsverletzung, Erfüllungsverweigerung; **continuing** ~ fortgesetzte Vertragsverletzung; **constructive** ~ absichtliche Vertragsverletzung; **prison** ~ [Gefängnis]ausbruch; **social** ~ gesellschaftlicher Verstoß;
~ of arrestment Pfandbruch; **~ of close** widerrechtliches (unbefugtes) Betreten eines Grundstücks, Hausfriedensbruch; **~ of confidence** Verletzung der Geheimhaltungspflicht, Vertrauensbruch; **~ of contract (covenant)** Vertragsbruch, [positive] Vertragsverletzung, Nichterfüllung eines Vertrages; **fundamental ~ of contract** grundlegender Vertragsbruch; **~ of copyright** Urheberrechtsverletzung; **~ of discipline** Beeinträchtigung der Disziplin, Disziplinarvergehen; **~ of duty** Amtspflichtverletzung; **~ of legal duty** Verletzung einer Rechtspflicht; **~ of professional etiquette** standeswidriges Verhalten; **~ of faith** Vertrauensbruch; **~ of law** Gesetzesverletzung, Verletzung gesetzlicher Vorschriften; **~ of an oath** Eidbruch; **~ of order** Verstoß gegen die Geschäftsordnung; **~ of the peace** Störung der öffentlichen Ordnung, Landfriedensbruch; **~ of police regulations** Übertretung (Nichtbeachtung) von Polizeivorschriften; **~ of pound** Verstrickungs-, Pfandbruch; **~ of prison** Gefängnisausbruch, Ausbruch aus dem Gefängnis; **~ of privilege** Verstoß gegen die Privilegien einer Körperschaft, Immunitätsverletzung, *(discretionary power)* Zuständigkeitsüberschreitung; **~ of promise** Wortbruch, *(marriage)* Nichterfüllung eines Eheversprechens; **~ of the rules** Verstoß gegen die Regeln, Ordnungswidrigkeit; **~ of professional secrecy** Bruch des Berufsgeheimnisses, Verletzung des Berufsgeheimnisses; **~ of trust** Pflicht-, Vertrauensverletzung, Verletzung der Treuepflicht, treuwidrige Verfügung, Vertrauensbruch; **fraudulent ~ of trust** Untreue; **~ of warranty** Garantieverletzung, Verletzung der Gewährleistungspflicht, Gewährleistungsbruch, Verletzung einer vertraglichen Zusicherung;
~ (v.) (mil.) Bresche schlagen;
to commit a ~ of the partnership agreement Gesellschaftsvertrag verletzen; **to set up the ~** Vertragsverletzung feststellen; **to sue for ~ of contractual obligations** aus Vertragsbruch (wegen Nichterfüllung) klagen.

bread Brot, *(livelihood)* Lebensunterhalt;
in bad ~ in einem Schlamassel; **in good ~** in einer guten Stellung; **one's daily ~** sein täglich Brot;
~ buttered on both sides ungewöhnliches Glück; **~ and cheese** bescheidenes Mahl;
to earn one's ~ seinen Lebensunterhalt verdienen; **to eat the ~ of idleness** faules Leben führen; **to know where one's ~ is buttered** wissen, wo der Barthel den Most holt; **to sweat for one's ~** im Schweiß der Arbeit sein Brot verdienen; **to take the ~ out of s. one's mouth** j. brotlos machen;
~-alone costs of living einfachste Lebenshaltungskosten; **~ basket** Brotkorb; **~-board model** Testpackung; **~ coupon** Brotmarke; **~ line** Schlange Bedürftiger, *(fig.)* Existenzminimum; **to live below the ~ line** Existenzminimum nicht erreichen; **~ riot** Hungerrevolte; **~ shortage** Brotverknappung; **~ ticket** *(US)* Essensbon; **~ unit** *(ration card)* Brotmarke.
bread and butter *(fig.)* notwendiger Lebensunterhalt.
bread-and-butter materialistisch, prosaisch, *(juvenile, coll.)* kindisch, unreif;
~ business Hauptgeschäft; **~ education** nur auf den Broterwerb gerichtete Ausbildung; **~ economic issue** wirtschaftliche Tagesfragen, alltägliches Problem, Lebenshaltungsfrage; **~ face** Brotschrift; **~ letter** *(US)* Kutscherbrief; **~-minded** nüchtern, wirklichkeitsnah, materialistisch eingestellt; **~ program(me)** wirklichkeitsnahes Programm; **~ voter** prosaisch eingestellter Wähler.
breadearner, breadwinner Ernährer, Brotverdiener, Familienvater.
breadearning, breadwinning Broterwerb, Verdienen des Lebensunterhaltes.
break *(breakage)* Bruch, Bruchstelle, Lücke, *(collection for prisoner)* Sammlung, *(interruption)* Unterbrechung, *(labo(u)rer)* Arbeitspause, *(opening, US sl.)* Chance, glückliche Gelegenheit, *(print.)* Abschnitt, Ausgang, Spatium, *(prisoner)* Ausbruch, Fluchtversuch, *(radio program(me))* Sendeunterbrechung für Werbedurchsagen, *(free space)* Zwischenraum, Lücke, *(stock exchange, US)* Kurseinbruch, -sturz, *(typing)* Gedankenstrich;
during a ~ in school in einer Schulpause; **without a ~** in einer Schicht, ununterbrochen;
bad ~ *(coll.)* Fauxpas; **coffee ~** Kaffeepause; **even ~** *(coll.)* faire Chance; **lucky ~** glücklicher Zufall; **open ~** *(politics)* offener Bruch; **short ~** kleine Pause; **tea ~** Kaffee-, Teepause;

~ in one's course Richtungswechsel; **~ in the economic trend** Konjunkturumschwung; **~ of a journey** Reiseunterbrechung; **~ in one's life** Einschnitt im Leben; **an hour's ~ for lunch** einstündige Mittagspause; **~ in prices** Preissturz, -einbruch, Preisdurchbruch, *(stock exchange)* Kurseinbruch, Kurssturz; **~ in one's way of living** Änderung seiner Lebensgewohnheiten; **sharp ~ on the stock market** starker Kurseinbruch; **~ in the water mains** Wasserrohrbruch; **~ in the weather** plötzliche Wetteränderung; **~ from work** Arbeitsunterbrechung;
~ (v.) auf-, durchbrechen, verletzen, *(go bankrupt)* zusammenbrechen, bankrott machen, in Konkurs gehen, *(officer)* kassieren, *(stocks)* plötzlich im Kurs fallen, *(weather)* sich plötzlich ändern;
~ s. o. j. kleinkriegen; **~ adrift** sich losreißen, wegtreiben; **~ an agreement** Abmachung verletzen; **~ an appointment** Verabredung nicht einhalten; **~ an arbitration clause** *(court)* Schiedsgerichtsklausel aufheben; **~ away** durch-, abbrechen; **~ away from a party** Partei verlassen, aus einer Partei austreten; **~ the bank** [Spiel]bank sprengen; **~ a bargain** Handel aufkündigen; **~ the back of resistance** Widerstand brechen; **~ far below the previous low level** weit unter den letzten Tiefststand fallen; **~ the bonds** erlaubte Grenzen überschreiten; **~ bulk** mit Entladen (zu löschen) anfangen, umpacken; **~ camp** Zelt abbrechen; **~ into one's capital** sein Kapital angreifen; **~ a case** über ein Urteil beraten; **~ a code** entschlüsseln; **~ a contract** Vertragsverletzung begehen, vertragsbrüchig werden; **~ the current** Strom unterbrechen; **~ down** *(analyse, US)* aufgliedern, -schlüsseln, Analyse vornehmen, analysieren, *(candidate)* durchfallen, *(car)* ausfallen, Panne haben, *(classify)* klassifizieren, *(el.)* ausfallen, *(engine)* nicht mehr funktionieren, versagen, *(house)* niederreißen, abbrechen, *(mining)* hauen, *(negotiations)* scheitern, zusammenbrechen, *(orator)* aus dem Text kommen, steckenbleiben; **~ down the contribution of major divisions to sales and pretax earnings** *(US)* Anteil größerer Abteilungen am Umsatz und Ertrag aufschlüsseln; **~ down expenditure** *(US)* Unkosten aufschlüsseln; **~ down expenses** *(US)* Ausgaben aufgliedern; **~ down all opposition** j. Widerstand beseitigen (niederknüppeln, unterdrücken); **~ down from overwork** sich überarbeiten und zusammenbrechen; **~ down the enemy's resistance** feindlichen Widerstand brechen; **~ an engagement** Verlobung [auf]lösen; **~ and enter** einbrechen; **~ ground** *(fig.)* in Angriff nehmen, *(commence excavation)* mit den Ausschachtungsarbeiten beginnen; **~ new ground** Neuland erschließen; **~ o. s. of a habit** sich eine Unsitte abgewöhnen; **~ up one's household** seinen Haushalt auflösen; **~ the ice** *(fig.)* Unterhaltung anfangen; **~ in** einbrechen, *(land, Australia)* kultivieren; **~ in on a conversation** j. beim Reden unterbrechen; **~ in upon s. o.** jem. einen überraschenden Besuch abstatten; **~ into a five-pound note** Fünfpfundnote anreißen (wechseln); **~ into a house** in ein Haus einbrechen; **~ into the motion-picture industry** sich in der Filmindustrie beteiligen; **~ an item of news** *(US)* Nachricht veröffentlichen; **~ jail** aus dem Gefängnis ausbrechen; **~ one's journey** seine Reise unterbrechen; **~ the law** Gesetz verletzen; **~ open a letter** Brief aufreißen; **~ the line** *(editor)* umbrechen; **~ loose** ausbrechen; **~ a matter to s. o.** jem. etw. eröffnen, bei jem. etw. aufs Tapet bringen; **~ the neck of s. th.** das Schlimmste überstehen; **~ the news gently to s. o.** jem. etw. schonend beibringen; **~ a note** Geldschein wechseln; **~ one's oath** eidbrüchig (meineidig) werden; **~ through the obligations of a treaty** Vertragsbestimmungen nicht einhalten; **~ off a conversation** Gespräch abbrechen; **~ off an engagement** Verlobung [auf]lösen, sich entloben; **~ off for half an hour** halbstündige Pause machen; **~ off negotiations** Verhandlungen abbrechen; **~ an officer** Offizier entlassen; **~ open** aufbrechen, sprengen; **~ out** *(fire, illness, prisoner, war)* ausbrechen; **~ out into praise of s. o.** j. mit Lobsprüchen überschütten; **~ out a baggage room** Gepäckraum aufbrechen; **~ the peace** öffentliche Ruhe und Ordnung stören, Landfriedensbruch begehen; **~ prison** aus dem Gefängnis ausbrechen; **~ a record** Rekord brechen; **~ a rebellion** Aufruhr niederschlagen; **~ the rules** Regeln verletzen; **~ the Sabbath** Sonntagsruhe verletzen; **~ open a safe** Geldschrank (Safe) aufbrechen; **~ a seal** Siegel aufbrechen (erbrechen); **~ sharply** *(stock exchange)* starken Einbruch erleiden; **~ and enter a shop** Ladeneinbruch begehen; **~ a siege** Belagerung aufheben; **~ the stowage** mit dem Entladen beginnen; **~ a strike** Streik brechen; **~ through** durchbrechen, *(law)* übertreten; **~ through the obligations of a treaty** Vertragsbestimmungen nicht einhalten; **~ with old ties** alte Verbindungen lösen; **~ with tradition** mit der Tradition brechen; **~ up** entflechten, *(attack)* zerschlagen, *(make holidays)* Ferien machen, *(party)* auseinanderfallen, *(safe deposit)* aufbrechen, *(ship)* verschrotten, abwracken; **~ up the crowd** Menge

auseinandertreiben; ~ **up one's household** seinen Haushalt auflösen; ~ **up a meeting** Versammlung gewaltsam auflösen, ~ **up monopolies** Monopole auflösen; ~ **up without a motion being agreed on** sich trennen, ohne sich auf einen Antrag geeinigt zu haben; ~ **up a piece of work among several people** Arbeit auf mehrere Leute aufteilen; ~ **up a school** Schule [beim Ferienbeginn] schließen; ~ **up an old ship** Schiff verschrotten; ~ **up a train** Güterzug auflösen; ~ **a warranty** Garantieverpflichtung nicht einhalten; ~ **a will** Testament [durch gerichtliches Verfahren] anfechten (aufheben lassen); ~ **with s. o.** Verkehr mit jem. abbrechen; ~ **one's word** wortbrüchig werden;

to give s. o. a ~ *(coll.)* jem. eine Chance geben; **to hope for a** ~ **in the weather** auf eine Wetteränderung hoffen; **to make a** ~ Schicht (Pause) machen; **to make a bad** ~ *(US)* schlimmen Fehler machen; **to make a clean** ~ sich deutlich distanzieren; **to make a** ~ **for liberty** Fluchtversuch unternehmen; **to take a** ~ Pause einlegen.

break even *(US)* Geschäftsabschluß ohne Gewinn und Verlust; ~ *(v.)* plus minus null abschneiden, Gewinnschwelle (Rentabilitätsschwelle) erreichen, Verlust [noch] vermeiden, sich noch rentieren, kostendeckend arbeiten, *(fig.)* ungeschoren davonkommen;

~ **with s. o.** sich von jem. ohne Gewinn und Verlust trennen; ~ **on letters** *(post office)* bei der Briefbeförderung keine Verluste erleiden; ~ **analysis** Deckungsbeitragsrechnung; ~ **chart** Rentabilitätstabelle, Gewinnschwellendiagramm; ~ **date** Rentabilitätstermin, -zeitpunkt; ~ **day** *(stock exchange)* erfolgreicher Abschlußtag, Erfolgstag; ~ **figures** Rentabilitätsziffern; ~ **point** Kosten-, Gewinn-, Nutz-, Ertragsschwelle, Rentabilitätsschwelle, -grenze; ~ **rent** reine Miete, Ertragsmiete.

break-in period Einarbeitungszeit.

breakable zerbrechlich.

breakage Bruch[schaden], *(allowance)* Abzug (Entschädigung) für Bruchwaren, Refaktie;

free from ~ bruchfrei; **no risk for** ~ keine Gewähr für Bruch; ~ **in the water mains** Rohrbruch im Wasserleitungsnetz; **to allow for** ~ für Bruchschäden abziehen; **to pay for** ~s Bruchschaden ersetzen; ~ **clause** Bruchklausel.

breakaway | from a party Parteiaustritt; ~ **link** Ausklinkvorrichtung; ~ **movement** Abfallbewegung; ~ **union** Spaltengewerkschaft.

breakdown Auf-, Unterteilung, *(analysis, US)* Analyse, Aufschlüsselung, -gliederung, *(car)* Panne, *(classification)* Klassifizierung, *(el.)* Ausfall, *(engine)* Versagen, *(marriage)* Zerrüttung *(negotiations)* Scheitern, Zusammenbruch, *(of operation)* Betriebs-, Verkehrsstörung, Verkehrsstockung, *(service)* Stillstand, *(splitting up)* Aufspaltung, *(statistics)* Zer-, Aufgliederung;

complete ~ *(car)* Totalschaden; **irretrievable** ~ *(divorce proceedings, Br.)* unheilbare Zerrüttung; **job** ~ berufliche Aufschlüsselung; **nervous** ~ Nervenzusammenbruch; ~ **of a balance sheet** *(US)* Bilanzanalyse, -zergliederung; ~ **of a budget** Etataufschlüsselung; ~ **of costs** *(US)* Kostenaufgliederung, -aufschlüsselung; ~ **of expenses** Unkostenspezifizierung, Spesenaufgliederung; ~ **of global output figures** *(US)* Aufschlüsselung der gesamten Produktionszahlen; ~ **of a firm** Zusammenbruch einer Firma; ~ **of government** Zusammenbruch der öffentlichen Ordnung; ~ **according to income brackets** Gliederung nach Einkommensgruppen; ~ **of machinery** Maschinenausfall, -schaden; ~ **by occupations** *(US)* berufliche Aufgliederung, Aufschlüsselung nach Berufen; ~ **by percent** prozentuale Aufschlüsselung; ~ **of prices** Preisaufgliederung; ~ **of the railway** Zusammenbruch des Eisenbahnverkehrs;

to have a nervous ~ völlig durchdrehen;

~ **crane** Abschleppkran; ~ **gang** Unfallkolonne, -hilfsmannschaft, Hilfskolonne, -trupp, Abschleppmannschaft; ~ **lorry** Abschleppwagen; ~ **party** Abschleppkommando; ~ **service** Abschleppdienst, *(electricity)* Notdienst, *(tel.)* Störungsdienst; ~ **value** *(securities)* Substanzwert; ~ **van** *(Br.)* Abschleppwagen.

breaker *(law)* Übertreter, *(nautics)* Sturzsee, Brecher; ~s Brandung;

ice ~ Eisbrecher; **prison** ~ Ausbrecher; ~'**s yard** Autofriedhof.

breakfast room *(hotel)* Frühstückszimmer, -raum.

breaking Bruch, *(insolvency)* finanzieller Zusammenbruch; **prison** ~ Gefängnisausbruch;

~ **bulk** Teilverkauf, Löschen der Ladung, Beginn des Entladens; ~ **up cartels** Entkartellisierung; ~ **a case** *(lawcourt)* Erörterung eines Falles; ~ **a close** unbefugtes Betreten eines fremden

Grundstücks; ~ **of a contract** Vertragsverletzung; ~ **and entering** Einbruch; ~ **up of an establishment** Geschäftsaufgabe; ~ **up highways** Aufbrechen von Landstraßen; ~ **in** Eingewöhnung, *(land)* Kultivierung; ~ **jail** Gefängnisausbruch; ~ **of the law** Gesetzesverstoß; ~ **up a meeting** Beendigung (Schließung) einer Sitzung; ~ **off of negotiations** Abbruch der Verhandlungen; ~ **a quorum** Herbeiführung der Beschlußfähigkeit; ~ **the seals** Siegelbruch; ~ **of the sound barrier** Durchbrechen der Schallmauer; ~ **the stowage** Entstauungskosten; ~ **up of a train** Zugauflösung; ~ **up of work** Arbeitsaufteilung; ~~ **in difficulties** Anfangsschwierigkeiten; ~ **point** Festigkeitsgrenze, Bruchstelle; **to reach a** ~ **point** bis aufs Äußerste strapaziert sein.

breakneck speed halsbrecherisches Tempo.

breakthrough revolutionärer Erfolg, *(flying)* Durchbrechen der Schallmauer, Durchbruch; **armo(u)red** ~ *(mil.)* waffentechnischer Durchbruch; **to achieve a** ~ **in national political terms** politischen Durchbruch im ganzen Land erzielen.

breakup Aufbrechen, Zerbrechen, *(fig.)* Ruin, Niedergang, Verfall, *(mil.)* Entlassung, *(school)* Schulschluß, *(social gathering)* Aufbruch;

~ **of a meeting** Sprengung einer Versammlung; ~ **price** Abbruchpreis; ~ **value** Altmaterial-, Liquidations-, Schrott-, Ausschlachtungs-, Abbruchswert.

breakwater Hafendamm, Buhne, Wellenbrecher.

breast *(architecture)* Brüstung, Brandmauer, *(seat of consciousness)* Sitz der Gefühle, Gewissen;

~ **of the court** gerichtliches Ermessen; ~ **o. s. to s. th.** sich einer Sache mutig entgegenstellen; **to make a clean** ~ **of it** sich etw. von der Seele reden; ~ **wall** Futter-, Stützmauer.

breath Atem, *(fig.)* Hauch, Spur, leise Andeutung;

with his last ~ mit seinem letzten Atemzug; ~ **of a scandal** Andeutung eines Skandals; **not a** ~ **of suspicion** nicht der Schatten eines Verdachts; **to waste one's** ~ umsonst reden.

breathing | space Atempause; ~ **time** Atempause.

breeches, to wear the *(woman)* die Hosen anhaben; ~ **buoy** *(mar.)* Hosenboje.

breed Rasse, Art, Brut, Zucht; ~ **of horses** Gestüt; ~ *(v.)* züchten; ~ **s. o. as a scholar** j. für die Laufbahn eines Gelehrten erziehen.

breeder Brutreaktor, Brüter; **fast** ~ schneller Brüter; ~ **pile** Atombrüter; ~ **reactor** Brutreaktor; **fast** ~ **reactor** schneller Brüter.

breeding Bildung, Lebensart, Benimm, *(propagation of animals)* Züchten, Züchtung, Aufzucht; **bad** ~ schlechte Manieren; ~ **company** Züchtergenossenschaft; ~ **place** Brutstätte.

breeze Brise, *(fig.)* Lärm, Zank; **to kick up a** ~ Krach machen.

breve *(print.)* Kürzezeichen.

brevier *(print.)* Petitschrift.

breweries, brewery stocks *(US)* Brauereiwerte, -aktien.

brewing industry Brauereiwirtschaft.

bribable käuflich, bestechlich, der Bestechung zugänglich.

bribe Bestechungs-, Schmiergeld, Bestechungsgeschenk; ~ *(v.)* bestechen, kaufen; ~ **an official** Beamten bestechen; ~ **a witness** Zeugen bestechen; **to accept (take) a** ~ Bestechung[sgeld] annehmen, sich bestechen lassen; **to be above taking a** ~ unbestechlich sein.

bribegiver Bestecher.

briber Bestecher.

bribery Bestechung, Korruption;

open to ~ der Bestechung zugänglich, bestechlich; **attempted** ~ Bestechungsversuch; **commercial** ~ Angestelltenbestechung; **judicial** ~ Richterbestechung; ~ **and corruption** Bestechungsunwesen; ~ **of a creditor** Gläubigerbestechung; ~ **at elections** Wahlkorruption; ~ **of a juror** Geschworenenbestechung; ~ **of officials** Beamtenbestechung; **to accuse s. o. of** ~ j. der Korruption beschuldigen; **to be accused of attempted** ~ wegen Bestechungsversuchs angeklagt werden; **to practise** ~ bestechen; ~ **fund** Bestechungsfonds; ~ **revelations** Bestechungsenthüllungen; ~ **scandal** Bestechungsskandal.

bribetaker Bestochener.

bribetaking passive Bestechung.

bribing of witness Zeugenbestechung.

brick Ziegel, Baustein, *(Br., coll.)* Taktlosigkeit, *(first-rate good fellow, coll.)* Pfundskerl, famoser Kerl;
  refractory ~ feuerfester Ziegel;
  to be a regular ~ *(sl.)* famoser Kerl sein; **to be three ~s shy of a load** nicht alle beisammen haben; **to burn ~s** Ziegel brennen; **to drop a ~** *(Br., coll.)* ins Fettnäpfchen treten; **to have a ~ in one's hat** *(sl.)* unter Alkoholeinfluß stehen; **to make ~s without straw** Unmögliches versuchen;
  ~ wall Ziegelmauer; **to run one's head against a ~ wall** mit dem Kopf gegen die Wand rennen; **to see through a ~ wall** das Gras wachsen hören.
brickwork Backstein-, Ziegelrohbau.
bridal party Verlobungsfeier.
bridewell Besserungsanstalt.
bridge Brücke, *(advertising)* typographischer Effekt zur Führung des Lesers, *(radio)* musikalische Überleitung, *(ship)* Kommandobrücke;
  cantilever ~ Auslegerbrücke; **golden ~** goldene Brücke; **loading ~** Verladebrücke;
  ~ of boats Pontonbrücke; **~ over the line** Eisenbahnüberführung;
  ~ (v.) Brücke schlagen;
  ~ over a difficulty Schwierigkeit überbrücken; **~ a gap** überbrücken; **~ a gap in the market** Marktlücke schließen;
  not to cross one's ~s before one comes to them *(fam.)* sich nicht um ungelegte Eier kümmern; **to throw a ~** Brücke schlagen;
  ~ railing Brückengeländer; **~ toll** Brückengeld.
bridge-over Überbrückung;
  ~ advance Überbrückungsdarlehen; **~ facilities** Überbrückungsfazilitäten.
bridgebuilder Brückenbauer.
bridgebuilding Brückenbau.
bridgehead *(mil.)* Brückenkopf.
bridgemaster *(Br.)* Brückenwärter.
bridging|loan Überbrückungskredit; **~ transaction** Überbrückungsmaßnahme.
brief *(cab driver's licence)* Taxilizenz, -konzession, *(concise statement, Br.)* kurze Sachdarstellung, *(memorandum prepared by solictor, Br.)* kurze Darstellung eines Rechtsfalls für den Prozeßanwalt, Instruktion, Rechtsdarstellung, *(mil.)* Einsatzbesprechung, *(writ, US)* Schriftsatz;
  in ~ in kurzen Worten;
  counsel's ~ Mandat; **trial ~** *(US)* Verhandlungsschriftsatz; **watching ~** Beobachtungsauftrag [für einen Anwalt];
  ~ on appeal Berufungsausführungen, -begründung; **~ to counsel** schriftliche Instruktionen an den plädierenden Anwalt; **~ of title** Eigentumsnachweis, Übertragungsurkunde;
  ~ (v.) einweisen, unterrichten, beauftragen und informieren, instruieren, Instruktionen geben, *(mil.)* Lagebesprechung abhalten, *(summarize)* kurz zusammenfassen;
  ~ a case Dossier redigieren; **~ instructions to a barrister** Anwalt instruieren; **~ pleadings** Prozeßanwalt instruieren; **to be ~** sich kurz fassen; **to be ~ with s. o.** j. kurz abfertigen; **to deliver a ~ to a barrister** *(Br.)* Prozeßanwalt beauftragen; **to file a ~** *(US)* Schriftsatz einreichen; **to have plenty of ~s** vollbeschäftigter Anwalt sein; **to hold a ~** Sache vor Gericht vertreten; **to hold a ~ for s. o.** mit jds. Vertretung beauftragt sein, j. anwaltlich (als Anwalt) vertreten; **to hold a watching ~ for s. o.** jds. Interessen [bei Gericht] als Beobachter vertreten; **to present one's ~** seinen Fall vortragen; **to receive one's ~** *(pilot)* Fluganweisungen erhalten; **to submit a ~** *(US)* Schriftsatz einreichen; **to take a ~** Vertretung einer Sache vor Gericht übernehmen;
  ~ (a.) kurz[gefaßt], gedrängt, bündig, knapp;
  ~ account kurze Sachdarstellung; **~ address** kurze Ansprache; **~ bag (case)** Aktentasche, -mappe, Büchermappe; **~ paper** Kanzleipapier; **~ sojourn** vorübergehender Aufenthalt.
briefing Besprechung, Einweisung, Arbeitsanweisung, Unterrichtung, Instruktionsgebung, *(advertising)* Zusammenfassung für eine neue Werbeidee, *(mil., US)* Lage-, Einsatzbesprechung, *(pilot)* Flugberatung, *(pol.)* Kommuniqué;
  ~ of a lawyer Bestellung (Beauftragung) eines Anwalts;
  to have special ~s besonders eingewiesen sein;
  ~ conference *(advertising)* Instruktions-, Auftragsbesprechung; **~ meeting** Informationssitzung; **~ room** Besprechungs-, Lageraum; **~ tour** Informationsreise.
briefless ohne Instruktionen, *(lawyer)* ohne Klienten (Prozesse), unbeschäftigt.
briefly put kurz ausgedrückt.
brigade *(mil.)* Brigade;
  fire ~ *(Br.)* Feuerwehr;
  ~ of guards Leibgarde.

brigand Bandit, Straßenräuber.
brigandage Banditenwesen.
bright *(market)* freundlich;
  ~ as a new pin blitzblank;
  to be at best far from ~ im günstigsten Falle nicht sehr rosig sein; **~ prospects** glänzende Aussicht; **to see the ~ side of things** alles positiv (optimistisch) betrachten.
brightwork *(car)* blanke Teile.
brilliant|performance Glanzleistung; **~ speaker** glänzender Redner.
bring *(v.)* bringen, tragen, herbeischaffen.
bring *(v.)* **about** verursachen, in die Wege leiten, bewerkstelligen;
  ~ an accident Unfall verursachen; **~ an accusation** Anklage erheben; **~ an action against s. o.** Klage gegen j. erheben, Prozeß gegen j. anhängig machen, j. gerichtlich belangen; **~ a reconciliation** Versöhnung herbeiführen; **~ a resolution** Beschluß herbeiführen; **~ s. one's ruin** zu jds. Ruin führen.
bring *(v.)* **away** wegschaffen, -bringen.
bring *(v.)* **before** vorbringen;
  ~ the authority zur Anzeige bringen; **~ a case before the court** Klage anstrengen; **~ a dispute before the court** Streitigkeit vor Gericht bringen, Gericht mit einer Sache befassen; **~ s. o. before the magistrate** j. der Polizei vorführen; **~ a question before the public** Aufmerksamkeit der Öffentlichkeit auf etw. lenken.
bring *(v.)* **a charge** Strafanzeige erstatten, Anklage erheben.
bring *(v.)* **down** herabsetzen, ermäßigen, *(fig.)* [ins Unglück] stürzen;
  ~ s. o. j. stürzen;
  ~ a hostile aircraft feindliches Flugzeug abschießen; **~ a balance** Bilanz abschließen; **~ the government** Regierung stürzen; **~ the house** Zuhörerschaft zu stürmischem Beifall hinreißen; **~ a price** Preis herabsetzen; **~ the birth rate** Geburtenrückgang erzielen; **~ all resistance** allen Widerstand brechen.
bring *(v.)* **forth** ans Tageslicht bringen;
  ~ protests Proteste hervorrufen.
bring *(v.)* **forward** fördern, begünstigen, *(bookkeeping)* übertragen, auf neue Rechnung vortragen, *(move)* beantragen;
  ~ evidence Beweis erbringen; **~ at a meeting** auf die Tagesordnung einer Versammlung setzen lassen; **~ a pupil** Schüler fördern; **~ a witness** Zeugen herbeischaffen.
bring *(v.)* **home** überführen, überzeugend beweisen;
  ~ the bacon *(US coll.)* Preis davontragen.
bring *(v.)* **in** Geld eintragen, Gewinn einbringen (abwerfen), *(action)* Prozeß anhängig machen, *(film)* einspielen, *(import)* einführen, *(partner)* als Einlage einbringen, *(ship)* [als Prise] aufbringen;
  ~ 80,- DM a week wöchentlich 80 DM abwerfen; **~ a bill** Gesetzesantrag (Gesetzentwurf) einbringen; **~ a new fashion** neue Mode einführen; **~ goods** Waren einführen; **~ guilty** für schuldig erklären; **~ not guilty** freisprechen; **~ interest** Zinsen abwerfen; **~ a motion** Antrag einbringen; **~ quotations in a speech** Zitate bei einer Rede anbringen; **~ a verdict of guilty** schuldig sprechen; **~ a verdict of not guilty** auf Freispruch erkennen.
bring *(v.)* **into|the business** ins Geschäft einbringen; **~ court** vor Gericht bringen; **~ disrepute** in schlechten Ruf bringen; **~ fashion** in Mode bringen; **~ s. o. into trouble** j. in Schwierigkeiten bringen; **~ money into court** Geld bei Gericht hinterlegen; **~ a ship into dock** Schiff ins Dock bringen; **~ s. th. into hotchpot** aufs Erbteil anrechnen (in Anrechnung bringen).
bring *(v.)* **low** herunterwirtschaften.
bring *(v.)* **off** fortbringen, -schaffen;
  ~ the passengers and the crew Passagiere und Besatzung retten; **~ a difficult task** schwierige Aufgabe erfolgreich beenden.
bring *(v.)* **on|a bad cold** sich eine schwere Erkältung zuziehen; **~ the stage** auf die Bühne bringen; **~ a subject for discussion** Thema zur Diskussion stellen.
bring *(v.)* **out** *(girl)* in die Gesellschaft einführen, *(goods)* auf den Markt bringen, *(new issue)* plazieren, unterbringen, auflegen, *(publish)* herausbringen, -geben, veröffentlichen;
  ~ a book Buch herausbringen (veröffentlichen).
bring *(v.)* **over** zu seiner Meinung bekehren.
bring *(v.)* **pressure to bear on s. o.** Druck auf j. ausüben.
bring *(v.)* **round** *(coll.)* wieder auf die Beine bringen, *(win over)* herumkriegen, umstimmen.
bring *(v.)* **through a patient** Patienten durchbringen.
bring *(v.)* **to|account** berechnen, in Rechnung stellen; **~ s. o. to beggary** j. an den Bettelstab bringen; **~ book** zur Rechenschaft ziehen; **~ a close** zum Abschluß bringen; **~ a conversation round to one's favo(u)rite subject** Gespräch auf sein Lieblingsthema hinführen; **~ the hammer** zur Auktion bringen; **~ justice** verkla-

gen, gerichtlich belangen; ~ **light** ans Licht bringen, enthüllen; ~ **pass** zustandebringen; ~ **s. o. to his senses** j. zur Vernunft bringen.

bring *(v.)* **under rebels** Rebellen unterwerfen.

bring *(v.)* **up** *(call attention to)* wieder vorbringen, *(cite)* anführen, zitieren, *(prize)* aufbringen, *(rear)* groß-, aufziehen, *(troops)* heranführen;

~ **on Bill Hunter** [etwa] mit dem Struwelpeter erziehen; ~ **children** Kinder erziehen; ~ **a resolution at a meeting** Resolution in einer Versammlung einbringen; ~ **s. o. up before the court** j. vor Gericht bringen; ~ **to date** auf den neuesten Stand bringen.

bring-and-buy-bazaar Wohltätigkeitsbasar.

bringer Überbringer.

bringing | **an action** Klageerhebung; ~ **down** Herabsetzung; ~ **forward of a sum** Vortrag einer Summe; ~ **forward of a witness** Herbeischaffung eines Zeugen; ~ **in of a bill** Einbringung eines Gesetzzentwurfes; ~ **into hotchpot** Anrechnung aufs Erbteil, Erbausgleich; ~ **to light** Aufdeckung; ~ **money into court** gerichtliche Hinterlegung; ~**out** *(books)* Herausgabe, Veröffentlichung; ~ **up** Erziehung.

brink Rand, Kante;

to be on the ~ **of a crisis** kriseln; **to be on the** ~ **of the grave** am Rande des Grabes stehen; **to be on the** ~ **of ruin** kurz vor dem Zusammenbruch stehen; **to be on the** ~ **of war** am Rande eines Krieges stehen; **to bring back from the** ~ **of bankruptcy** gerade noch am Konkurs vorbeisteuern; **to come very close to the** ~ Krise gerade noch vermeiden; **to get a country on the** ~ **of war** Land an den Rand eines Krieges führen; **to go over the** ~ Abgrund überschreiten; **to walk on the** ~ *(pol.)* Krise durchstehen.

brinkman Krisenpolitiker.

brinkmanship *(mil.)* Krisenpolitik unter Eingehung außerordentlich hoher Risiken;

economic ~ Konjunktursteuerung unter Eingehung von Risiken.

brisk *(business)* lebhaft, flott;

~ *(v.)* **up** sich schnell erholen;

to go off ~**ly** reißenden Absatz finden; **to move** ~**ly ahead** rasch steigen;

~ **demand** lebhafte Nachfrage; ~ **market** lebhafte Börse; ~ **sale** glatter Absatz; ~ **trade** flotter Handel; ~ **state of trade** flotter Geschäftsgang.

briskness *(business)* Belebtheit;

~ **of trade** flotter Geschäftsgang.

Bristol | **board** glatter Karton; ~ **paper** Zeichenpapier.

British | **to the quick** durch und durch ein Engländer;

to be ~ **by birth** britischer Herkunft sein;

~ **Board of Film Censors** Britische Filmprüfstelle; ~ **Broadcasting Company** Britische Rundfunkgesellschaft; ~ **citizenship** britisches Bürgerrecht; ~ **Commonwealth of Nations** Staatenverband; ~ **Empire** Britisches Weltreich; ~ **Employers' Confederation** Spitzenverband der britischen Arbeitgeberverbände; ~ **Industries Fair** Britische Industriemesse; ~ **nationality** britische Staatsangehörigkeit; ~ **passport** britischer Paß; ~**protected person** britischer Staatsangehöriger; ~ **subject** britischer Untertan; **to cease to be a** ~ **subject** britische Staatsangehörigkeit verlieren; ~ **Tourist Authority** *(Br.)* Fremdenverkehrsamt; ~ **Travel and Holiday Association** Zentralorganisation für den Fremdenverkehr.

broach *(v.)* *(provisions)* anbrechen;

~ **a conversation** Gespräch anknüpfen; ~ **a question** Frage anschneiden; ~ **a subject** Thema zur Sprache (aufs Tapet) bringen.

broad breit, weit, ausgedehnt, *(language)* mit ausgeprägtem Dialekt, *(radio)* unscharf;

as ~ **as long** gehupft wie gesprungen;

~ **accent** starker Akzent; ~ **based** breit fundiert; ~ **gauge** *(railway)* Breitspur; ~ **hint** Wink mit dem Zaunpfahl; ~ **interpretation** weitgehende Auslegung; ~ **lands** ausgedehnte Ländereien; ~ **market** aufnahmefähiger Markt; ~**minded** liberal; ~**mindedness** liberale Einstellung; ~ **ocean** weiter Ozean; **in** ~ **outline** in großen Zügen; ~ **seal** Staatssiegel; ~ **views** weitherzige Ansichten.

broadband Breitband, großes Frequenzband.

broadcast Rundfunk[übertragung], -sendung, Radiosendung, *(program(me))* Rundfunkprogramm;

delayed ~ zurückgestellte Sendung; **news** ~ Nachrichtensendung; **outside** ~ Rundfunkreportage; **sponsored** ~ *(US)* Patronatssendung;

~ *(v.)* senden, durchgeben, durchsagen, durch Rundfunk verbreiten;

~ **Parliament permanently** alle Parlamentssitzungen im Rundfunk übertragen; ~ **on the shortwave band** auf Kurzwelle senden; ~ **the news** Nachrichten senden; ~ **a speech** Rede durch Rundfunk übertragen;

~ **account** Rundfunkbericht; ~ **address** Rundfunkansprache; ~ **advertising** [Rund]funk-, Radiowerbung, Werbefunk; ~ **announcement** Ankündigung im Rundfunk, Rundfunkansage, -durchsage; ~ **audience** [Rundfunk]hörerschaft; **outside** ~**s commentator** Rundfunkreporter; ~ **coverage** Rundfunkversorgung; ~ **day** Sendetag; ~ **division** Rundfunkabteilung; ~ **frequency** Rundfunkfrequenz; ~ **journalist** Rundfunkreporter; ~ **listener** Rundfunkhörer; ~ **media campaign** über den Rundfunk ausgestrahlte Werbekampagne; ~ **network** Sendergruppe; ~ **news** Rundfunknachrichten; ~ **production** *(advertising)* Werbesendung; ~ **program(me)** Rundfunkprogramm; ~ **publicity** Rundfunkwerbung; ~ **receiver** Rundfunk-, Radiogerät; ~ **receiving licence** Rundfunkgenehmigung; ~ **report** Rundfunkbericht; ~ **research** Höreranalyse, -forschung; ~ **revenue** Rundfunkeinnahmen; ~ **script** Rundfunkmanuskript; ~ **talk** Sendung, Rundfunkansprache.

broadcaster Rundfunksprecher, -kommentator, *(station)* Rundfunksender, -station.

broadcasting Rundfunk[übertragung], Radio;

road-traffic ~ Verkehrsfunk; **sound and television** ~ *(US)* Rundfunk und Fernsehen; **spot** ~ regionale Rundfunkreklame; **today's** ~ heutiges Rundfunkprogramm; **toll** ~ gebührenpflichtiger Rundfunk;

~ **of news** Nachrichtendurchsage;

~ **business** Rundfunkindustrie; ~ **cabin** Hörfunkkabine; ~ **Commission** Rundfunkverwaltungsrat; ~ **company** *(corporation)* Rundfunkgesellschaft; ~ **council** Rundfunkrat; ~ **equipment** Rundfunkgerät; ~ **front** Rundfunkgebiet; ~ **network** Rundfunk-, Sendergruppe; ~ **receiver** Rundfunkempfänger; ~ **rights** Senderechte; ~ **room** Senderaum; ~ **section** Rundfunkabteilung; ~ **station** [Rundfunk]sender, Rundfunkstation, -anstalt; **high-power** ~ **station** Großsender; ~ **team** Reportagemannschaft; **political** ~ **time** zugeteilte Rundfunkzeit für politische Sendungen; ~ **transmitter** Rundfunksender; ~ **wave** Rundfunkwelle.

broaden | *(v.)* **one's career as international banker** seinen Berufshorizont als internationaler Bankier ausweiten; ~ **one's horizon** seinen Gesichtskreis erweitern; ~ **its line of products** sein Produktionsprogramm ausweiten.

broadly tuned unscharf eingestellt.

Broadmoor patient *(Br.)* geisteskranker Krimineller.

broadsheet Plakat, einseitig bedruckter Prospekt, Flugblatt, -schrift, großformatige Drucksache.

broadside [großer] Faltprospekt, Werbeflugblatt, Schautafel, Demonstrationsblatt, Planobogen, *(critic)* Schimpfkanonade, *(ship)* Breitseite;

~ *(v.)* seitwärts rutschen;

~ **array** Richtantenne; ~ **size** Querformat.

broadway Hauptstraße.

brochure geheftete Druckschrift, Flugschrift, Broschüre, *(book trade)* Broschur;

provisional ~ Interimsbroschüre.

broiler *(agitator)* Unruhestifter, *(gridiron, US)* Grill.

broke *(sl.)* pleite, abgebrannt, blank, bankrott;

stone-~ *(sl.)* völlig pleite;

to go for ~ *(fam.)* alles auf eine Karte setzen.

broken kaputt, entzwei, zerbrochen, *(bankrupt)* bankrott, ruiniert, *(clouds)* durchbrochen, *(mil., US)* desertiert, degradiert, *(weather)* unbeständig;

~**down** altersschwach, funktionsunfähig, *(fig.)* heruntergekommen, abgewirtschaftet; ~ **down by** aufgeschlüsselt nach;

~ **account** *(Br.)* umsatzloses Konto; ~ **coal** Bruchkohle, Anthrazit; ~ **fortune** zerrüttete Vermögensverhältnisse; ~ **ground** unebener Boden; ~ **health** geschwächte Gesundheit; ~ **home** zerrüttete Familienverhältnisse; ~ **letter** Defektbuchstabe; ~ **money** Kleingeld; ~ **line** punktierte Linie; ~ **lot** *(US)* Effektenpaket unter 1000 Dollar Nominalwert; ~ **marriage** zerrüttete Ehe; ~ **number** Bruch; ~ **stone** Schotter, Split; ~ **time** Verlust an Zeit und Lohn, Verdienstausfall; ~ **week** angebrochene Woche.

broker [Börsen-, Waren-, Wechsel-, Handels]makler, *(agent)* Agent, *(go-between)* Mittelsmann, Vermittler, Zwischenhändler, *(dealer in sececondhand furniture, Br.)* Trödler, *(executioner)* Pfändungsbeamter;

arbitrage ~ Arbitrageur; **associate** ~ selbständiger Makler; **bank** ~ Bankagent; **bill** ~ Wechselmakler, *(money* ~*)* Geldvermittler; **bond** ~ Fondsmakler; **bullion** ~ Makler für den Handel mit ungemünztem Gold; **chartering** ~ Schiffs-, Frachtenmak-

ler; **commercial** ~ Handelsmakler; **commission** ~ *(US)* Provisionsmakler; **curb[stone]** ~ *(US)* Freiverkehrsmakler; **customs** ~ Zollagent; **discount** ~ Wechselmakler; **exchange** ~ Devisen-, Kurs-, Börsen-, Wechselmakler; **farm** ~ Makler für landwirtschaftlich genutzte Grundstücke; **floor** ~ *(US)* selbständiger Makler, Börsenmakler; **foreign** ~ Makler in Auslandswechseln; **freight** ~ Schiffs-, Frachtenmakler; **general line** ~ Makler auf Großmärkten; **hotel** ~ Hotelnachweis; **industrial** ~ Makler für gewerbliche Grundstücke; **inside** ~ *(Br.)* amtlich zugelassener Makler; **insurance** ~ Versicherungsagent, -makler; **intermediate** ~ Remissier, Zwischen-, Untermakler; **investment** ~ Makler für Anlagewerte, Finanzmakler, Makler für hochwertige Anlagepapiere; **land** ~ Immobilien-, Grundstücksmakler; **lease** ~ Pachtkommissionär; **listing** ~ hinzugezogener Makler; **marriage** ~ Heiratsvermittler; **mercantile** ~ Handelsmakler; **merchandise** ~ Handels-, Warenmakler; **money** ~ Geld-, Finanzmakler; **mortgage** ~ Hypothekenvermittler, -makler; **note** ~ *(US)* Makler für den Verkauf von Schuldscheinen, Wechselmakler; **odd-lot** ~ *(US)* Makler in kleinen Effektenabschnitten; **outside** ~ freier (nicht zur Börse zugelassener) Makler, Winkelmakler; **passage** ~ Auswanderungsagent; **personal loan** ~ Makler für (Vermittler von) Personalkrediten; **privilege** ~ *(US)* Spezialitätenmakler; **produce** ~ Waren-, Produktenmakler; **real-estate** ~ *(US)* Grundstücks-, Häuser-, Immobilienmakler; **securities** ~ Effektenmakler; **selling** ~ Verkaufsmakler; **ship** ~ Schiffs-, Frachtenmakler; **specialist** ~ *(US)* Spezialitätenmakler; **spot** ~ Platzmakler; **street** ~ *(US)* Freiverkehrs-, Winkelmakler; **sworn** ~ Kursmakler, vereidigter Makler; **unlicensed** ~ freier Makler;
to act as ~ als Makler fungieren, makeln; **to be a** ~ Maklergeschäfte betreiben; **to list with (place in the hands of) a real-estate** ~ einem Grundstücksmakler an die Hand geben;
~ **territory** Maklerbezirk.
broker's | **account** Maklerliquidation; ~ **award** Maklergutachten; ~ **board** Maklerstand; ~ **business** Börsenkommissionsgeschäft; ~ **charges** Maklergebühr; **to duck** ~ **charges** Maklergebühren sparen; ~ **commission** Maklerprovision, -gebühr, Courtage; ~ **confirmation** *(US)* Kommissionsnote; ~ **contract** Maklervertrag; ~ **failure** Maklerkonkurs; ~ **fee** Maklerprovision, Courtage; ~ **firm** Maklerfirma; ~ **loan** Maklerdarlehen; ~ **market** Propregeschäfte der Makler; ~ **memorandum (note)** Schlußnote, -schein, -zettel; ~ **order** Verschiffungsorder; ~ **return** Schiffszettel; ~ **row** Trödelmarkt; ~ **ticket** Börsenabrechnungszettel.
brokerage Maklergeschäft, *(commission)* Maklergebühr, -provision, Courtage;
banking ~ Bankprovision; **bill** ~ *(Br.)* Wechselcourtage; **buying** ~ Einkaufsprovision; **marriage** ~ Heiratsvermittlung[sbüro]; **outside** ~ freies Maklergeschäft; **selling** ~ Verkaufsprovision; **ship** ~ Schiffsmaklergeschäft; **shipping** ~ Schiffsmaklergeschäft;
~ **account** Courtagerechnung, -konto; ~ **board** Maklerausschuß; ~ **business** Maklergeschäft; ~ **charges** Maklergebühr; ~ **concern (firm, house, office)** Maklerfirma, -büro; ~ **contract** Maklervertrag; ~ **failure** Maklerbonus; ~ **fee** Maklergebühr; ~ **field** Maklerwesen; ~ **headquarters** Maklerzentrale; ~ **industry** Maklerstand; ~ **operation** Maklergeschäft; ~ **payment** Provisionsgewährung; ~ **practices** Maklerusancen; ~ **service** Maklertätigkeit.
broking Maklergeschäft;
outside ~ freie Maklertätigkeit;
~ **operations** Maklertätigkeit, -geschäft.
brothel öffentliches Haus, Bordell.
brother Bruder;
step ~ Stiefbruder;
~-**in-arms** Waffengefährte, Kriegskamerad; ~-**in-law** Schwager.
brotherhood Bruderschaft, *(US, railroad trade union)* Eisenbahnergewerkschaft.
brought gebracht, eingeleitet;
~ **to the attention** zur Kenntnis gebracht; ~ **out by our firm** in unserem Verlag erschienen; ~ **to trial** dem Gericht vorgeführt; ~ **up in business** kaufmännisch geschult;
~-**in capital** eingebrachtes Kapital; ~ **forward** Vortrag, Übertrag.
brown *(Br., sl.)* hereinlegen;
~ **paper** Packpapier; **in a** ~ **study** tief in Gedanken versunken.
brownout *(el., US)* Stromkürzung, -rationierung.
bruise Prellung, blaue Stelle.
bruit *(v.)* **it about** etw. überall herumerzählen.
bruited, to be ~ **about** im Umlauf sein.
brunch *(coll.)* ausgedehntes Frühstück.

brush Gebüsch, Strauchwerk, *(el.)* Stromabnehmer;
~ *(v.)* *(US sl.)* rausschmeißen, feuern;
~ **aside (away) difficulties** Schwierigkeiten übersehen; ~ **off** *(US sl.)* Entlassung, Hinauswurf.
brush *(v.)* **up** aufbessern;
~ **one's English** sein Englisch auffrischen.
brush-up *(language)* Auffrischung.
brutality Rohheit, Brutalität.
brute violence rohe Gewalt.
bubble *(fig.)* Seifenblase, *(advertising, film)* Sprechblase, *(Br., sl.)* [Gründungs]schwindel, Schwindelunternehmen, unsolides Unternehmen, *(motorcar, US)* Kleinstwagen;
~ *(v.)* **with ideas** voller Ideen stecken, über großen Ideenreichtum verfügen;
to prick the ~ Schwindel aufffliegen lassen;
~ **bath** Schaumbad; ~ **car** *(US)* Kleinstwagen, Kabinenroller; ~ **company** *(Br.)* Schwindelgesellschaft, Briefkastenfirma; ~ **scheme** Schwindelunternehmen.
buccaneer Freibeuter, Seeräuber.
buck *(dandy)* Geck, Stutzer, *(sl.)* Dollar;
~ *(v.)* opponieren, *(car)* sich ruckweise vorwärtsbewegen;
~ **s. one's authority** jds. Autorität in Frage stellen; ~ **the book clubs** gegen die Büchergemeinschaften zu Felde ziehen; ~ **for s. th.** *(US sl.)* etw. um jeden Preis haben wollen; ~ **the machine** *(sl.)* in Opposition treten; ~ **the recession** *(US)* sich mit allen Mitteln gegen die Rezession stemmen, Rezession nicht hochkommen lassen; ~ **up** sich aufrappeln; ~ **s. o. up** *(fam.)* j. aufmuntern (aufmöbeln);
to make quick ~**s** *(sl.)* schnell Geld verdienen, schnell zu Geld kommen; **to pass the** ~ *(US)* sich vor der Verantwortung drücken, jem. den schwarzen Peter zuschieben;
~ **passing** *(US sl.)* Abwälzen der Verantwortung; ~ **slip** interne Aktennotiz, innerbetriebliche Mitteilung.
bucked up by the news von den Nachrichten in Hochstimmung versetzt.
buckwagon *(US)* leichter Wagen.
bucket Eimer, Kübel;
by the ~ kübelweise;
~ *(v.)* **money** Geld scheffeln; ~ **orders** Winkelaufträge durchführen;
to kick the ~ *(sl.)* ins Gras beißen;
~ **seat** *(car, plane)* Klappsitz, Notsitz; ~ **shop** *(US)* Spielhölle, ominöse Kneipe, *(Br.)* Büro eines Freiverkehrsmaklers, *(US)* Winkelbörse; ~ **swindler** Schwindelmakler.
bucketeer *(US)* unreeller Börsenmakler.
bucketing *(US)* Betreiben unreeller Maklergeschäfte.
buckeye überladene Anzeige.
buckle *(v.)* | **down to work** mit der Arbeit ernsthaft anfangen; ~ **one's seat belt** Sicherheitsgurt anlegen.
buckram Steifleinen.
buckshot Streuladung.
buckstall Wildfalle.
budget Haushalt[splan], Staatshaushalt, Budget, Etat, Voranschlag, Vorausplanung, *(advertising)* Werbeetat, *(cost of living)* Lebenshaltungskosten, *(estimate of costs)* Kostenvorschau;
in accordance with the ~ dem Voranschlag entsprechend; **according to the** ~ etatmäßig; **not included in the** ~ außeretatsmäßig; **on a** ~ knapp dran; **provided in the** ~ in den Etat eingestellt, etatisiert;
administration expense ~ Verwaltungsetat; **adverse** ~ unausgeglichener Haushalt (Etat), Haushaltsdefizit; **advertising expense** ~ Werbeetat; **annual** ~ Jahreshaushalt[splan], -budget; **approved** ~ genehmigter Etat; **balanced** ~ ausgeglichener Haushalt; **business** ~ Geschäftsetat; **business-as-usual** ~ normaler Haushaltsplan; **capital expenditure** ~ Kapitalaufwandsvorschau, Investitionshaushalt; **cash** ~ *(US)* Kassenvoranschlag, Zahlungshaushalt; **city** ~ städtischer Haushaltsplan; **defence** ~ Haushalt des Verteidigungsministeriums; **department** ~ Abteilungsetat; **direct labo(u)r** ~ Arbeitskräftebedarf; **direct materials** ~ geschäftlicher Materialverbrauch; **double** ~ außerordentlicher Haushalt (Etat); **draft** ~ Haushalts-, Etatansatz; **easy** ~ leichtgewichtiger Etat; **expansionary** ~ ausgeweiteter Etat; **extraordinary** ~ außerordentlicher Haushalt; **financial** ~ Finanzhaushalt; **fixed** ~ für mehrere Jahre aufgestellter (festgelegter) Etat; **flexible** ~ beweglicher (elastischer) Etat; **forecast** ~ Konjunkturvorschau; **forward projection** ~ in die Zukunft projektierter Etatansatz; **give-away** ~ mit Wahlgeschenken belasteter Haushalt; **guideline** ~ Musteretat; **household** ~ *(fam.)* Familienbudget; **housewife's** ~ Hausfrauenetat; **local government** ~ Gemeindehaushalt, Kommunaletat; **master** ~ Gesamthaushaltsplan; **mechanical** ~ *(US)* aufgeschlüsselter Werbeetat;

minimum **weekly** ~ wöchentliches Existenzminimum; **municipal** ~ Gemeindehaushalt; **national** ~ Staatshaushalt; **operating** ~ Betriebsetat; **ordinary** ~ ordentlicher Etat; **overall** ~ Gesamtetat; **overall company** ~ Konzernetat; **overhead** ~ Gesamtetat; **performance** ~ Ist-Etat; **production** ~ Produktionsprogramm; **program(me)** ~ Solletat; **proposed** ~ Etats-, Haushaltsentwurf; **purchase** ~ Einkaufsetat; **sales (selling expense)** ~ Verkaufsetat; **separate** ~ Einzeletat; **shoestring** ~ unzureichender Etat; **sliding** ~ veränderlicher Etat; **state** ~ Staatshaushaltsplan; **static** ~ starrer Etat; **summary** ~ Gesamtetat; **supplementary** ~ Nachtragshaushalt, -etat, Haushaltsnachtrag; **supplies-approved** ~ beweglicher Etat; **tentative** ~ vorläufiger Etat; **tight** ~ knapper Etat; **time** ~ Zeiteinteilung; **total** ~ Haushaltsvolumen; **unbalanced** ~ unausgeglichener Etat; **variable** ~ den Produktionsschwankungen angepaßter Etat; **workmen's** ~ Arbeiterhaushalt;

~ **for acquiring art** Kunstetat; ~ **of inventions** Sack voll Erfindungen; ~ **of news** Fülle von Nachrichten; ~ **that shows a deficit** Verlustetat, -haushalt, Defizithaushalt;

~ **(v.) (US)** Haushaltsplan aufstellen, im Haushaltsplan unterbringen (vorsehen), *(fig.)* vorausplanen, *(wife)* mit dem Haushaltsgeld auskommen;

~ **for** in den Haushalt einstellen, im Budget (Etat) vorsehen, etatisieren; ~ **one's time** seine Zeit verplanen;

to approve the ~ Etats-, Haushaltsvoranschlag annehmen; **to balance the** ~ Etat (Haushalt) ausgleichen; **to balance an adverse** ~ Haushaltsdefizit ausgleichen; **to bite deeper into shoppers'** ~s größeres Loch in den Einkaufsetat reißen; **to break one's** ~ seinen Etat überschreiten; **to bury in a** ~ in einem Etat verstecken; **to debate on the** ~ Etat beraten, Haushaltsdebatte durchführen; **to draw up the** ~ Haushaltsplan (Etat) aufstellen; **to ease the stress on the** ~ angespannten Etat entlasten; **to enter an amount in the** ~ Posten etatisieren; **to exceed the** ~ Etat (Haushalt) überschreiten; **to fall within the** ~ haushaltsrechtlich genehmigt sein; **to fatten a** ~ Etat anreichern (auffüllen); **to fix the** ~ Etat festsetzen; **to fix an extreme limit for a** ~ Etats-, Haushaltshöchstgrenze festsetzen; **to have charge of a** ~ Etat verwalten; **to introduce the** ~ Haushaltsplan einbringen; **to keep to the** ~ Staatshaushalt (Budget) einhalten; **to keep an actual** ~ regelrechten Etat aufstellen und danach leben; **to keep the** ~ **in line** Etat ausgeglichen halten; **to live within one's** ~ seinen Etat nicht überziehen; **to make a** ~ Haushaltsplan (Etat) aufstellen; **to open the** ~ Haushaltsrede halten, Budget (Etat, Haushalt) vorlegen; **to pass the** ~ Etatsvorschlag annehmen; **to prepare the** ~ Haushaltsplan aufstellen; **to present the** ~ Haushaltsplan (Etat) vorlegen; **to prune a** ~ Etat beschneiden, Haushaltskürzungen vornehmen; **to put the** ~ **in the red** Haushaltsdefizit herbeiführen; **to rein back a** ~ Etatsansatz zurückführen; **to reject the whole** ~ **lock, stock and barrel** Gesamtetat mit allem Drum und Dran ablehnen; **to run the nation's** ~ für den Staatshaushalt verantwortlich sein; **to run a tight** ~ mit einem knappen Etat auskommen; **to scan a** ~ **for possible cutbacks** Etat auf Streichungsmöglichkeiten hin überprüfen; **to set the** ~ **on its feet again** Haushalt wieder ausgleichen; **to slash a** ~ Etat zusammenstreichen; **to throw out the whole** ~ Gesamtetat ablehnen; **to throw a** ~ **out of gear** ganzen Etat durcheinanderbringen; **to trim fat from one's** ~ übersetzten Etat (Haushalt) kürzen; **to trim government's own** ~s **to make room for private investments** Einsparungen im Staatshaushalt zugunsten privater Investitionen vornehmen; **to vote the** ~ Haushalt (Etat) genehmigen; **to work on a shoestring** ~ mit knappstem Etat auskommen müssen; **to wrench a** ~ **into final shape** Etatumfang endgültig festlegen;

~ **account** Konto laufender Zahlungen; ~ **accounting** Soll-, Plankostenrechnung; ~*9* **and Accounting Act (US)** Haushaltsgesetz; ~ **agency (US)** Haushaltsbehörde; ~ **allocation** Etatszuweisung; ~ **analyst** Haushalts-, Etatsfachmann, Haushaltsspezialist, -experte; ~ **appropriations** Ausgabenansätze; ~ **balancing** Etatsausgleich; ~ **bill (US)** Haushaltsvorlage; ~ **busting** Etatsausweitung; ~-**busting additions** ausweitende Etatsergänzungen; ~ **changes** Etatsänderungen; ~ **charge account** Kundenkonto mit festgelegter Kreditlinie; ~ **charge agreement** Einverständniserklärung bei Errichtung eines Kundenkreditkontos; ~ **commission (committee)** Haushalts-, Budgetausschuß; ~ **commissioner (EC)** Haushaltskommissar; ~ **control** Haushaltskontrolle; ~ **costs** Soll-, Plankosten; ~ **credit** Haushaltskredit; ~ **cut (cutting)** Etatkürzung, -abstrich; ~ **cutter** Etatkürzer; ~ **deadline** Haushaltsschlußtermin; ~ **debate** Beratung des Haushaltsplans, Etatsberatung; ~ **deficit** Defizit im Staatshaushalt, Haushaltsdefizit; **full employment** ~ **deficits** aus der Vollbeschäftigungspolitik entstandene Haushaltsdefizite; **to run a large** ~ **deficit** sich ein großes Haushaltsdefizit leisten;

department Haushaltsabteilung; ~ **difficulties** Etats-, Haushaltsschwierigkeiten; ~ **director** Leiter der Haushaltsabteilung; ~ **dissavings** Etatsmißbrauch; ~ **documents** Unterlagen für Festsetzung des Haushalts, Haushaltsvorlagen; ~ **equation** Haushaltsgleichung; ~ **equilibrium** Etats-, Haushaltsausgleich; ~ **estimates** Haushaltsvoranschlag, Etatansatz; **yearly** ~ **estimates** Jahresbudget; ~ **expenditure** Haushaltsausgaben; ~ **fare** *(aviation)* 21 Tage voraus gebuchter verbilligter Flugschein, im Vorverkauf erworbenes Flugticket; **to fall below** ~ **figures** Etatsansätze nicht erreichen; ~ **film** Werbefilmrolle; ~ **form** Haushaltsformular; ~ **funds** Etat-, Haushaltsmittel; **to apportion** ~ **funds** Haushaltsmittel zuteilen; ~ **grant** Annahme der Haushaltsvorlage, Haushaltsbewilligung, bewillige Haushaltsmittel; ~ **heading** Haushalts-, Etattitel; ~ **issue** Haushaltsdebatte; ~ **item** Haushalts-, Etattitel; ~ **keeper** Etatverwalter; ~ **keeping** Etatsverwaltung; ~ **law (US)** Haushaltsgesetz, -recht; **to hold the** ~ **line** festgesetzten Etat nicht überschreiten; ~ **maker** Aufsteller eines Etats; ~-**making agency** Haushaltsabteilung; ~ **man** Haushaltsspezialist; ~ **means** Haushaltsmittel; ~ **message** Haushaltsrede; ~ **mindedness** Etatsbewußtsein; ~ **needs** Etats-, Haushaltsbedürfnisse; ~ **office** Kämmerei; **Congressional** ~ **office (US)** [etwa] Haushaltsbehörde des Kongresses; ~ **ordinance** Haushaltssatzung; ~ **outlook** Etatsaussichten; ~ **payment** Teilzahlungskauf; ~ **period** Haushaltsperiode; ~ **price** billiger Preis; ~-**priced** preisgünstig, *(advertising)* realistisch kalkuliert; ~ **procedure** Verfahren bei der Aufstellung des Haushalts; ~ **program(me)** Haushaltsprogramm; ~ **proposal** Haushaltsvoranschlag; ~ **report** Haushaltsbericht; ~ **request** Haushaltsanforderung; **to prune** ~ **requests** Haushalts-, Etatsanforderungen beschneiden; ~ **resolution** Haushaltsverabschiedung; ~ **savings** Etatseinsparungen; ~ **session** Haushalts-, Etatsberatung; ~ **shift** Etatsveränderung; ~ **slash** Etatskürzung; ~ **slashings** Haushalts-, Etatsstreichungen; ~ **specialist** Haushaltsexperte; ~ **speech** Haushalts-, Etatsrede; ~ **squeeze** Etatsdruck; **week's** ~ **statement** wöchentlicher Haushaltsausweis; **unappropriated** ~ **surplus** Haushaltsüberschuß; ~ **system** Haushaltssystem; ~ **target** Etatsziel; ~ **taste** nicht verwöhnter Geschmack; ~ **trading** Etats-, Haushaltsberatung; ~ **troubles** Etatsschwierigkeiten; ~ **variance** Etatsabweichungen; ~ **work sheets** *(US)* Haushaltsvoranschlag; ~ **year** Etats-, Haushalts-, Budgetjahr.

budgetary Budget (Haushaltsplan, Etat) betreffend, haushaltsmäßig, -rechtlich, etatsmäßig;
extra-~ außerplan-, außeretatsmäßig, im Haushalt nicht vorgesehen;
~ **account** Haushaltsrechnung; ~ **accounting** Haushaltsrechnungsführung, Finanzplanung; ~ **agency** Haushaltsabteilung; ~ **allocation** Etatszuweisung; ~ **appropriations** Ansätze des Haushaltsplanes, bewilligte Haushaltsmittel, Haushaltsbewilligung; ~ **arrangement** Haushaltsvereinbarung; ~ **authority** Haushaltsbehörde; ~ **balance** Etatsausgleich; ~ **board (commission, committee)** Haushaltsausschuß; ~ **control** Etats-, Finanz-, Haushaltskontrolle; **industrial** ~ **control** finanzielle Betriebsplanung; ~ **costs** kostenmäßige Auswirkungen auf den Haushalt; ~ **deficit** Haushaltsdefizit; ~ **discipline** Haushaltsdisziplin; ~ **economies** Etatseinsparungen; ~ **estimate** Etats-, Haushaltsvoranschlag; ~ **expenditure** Haushaltsausgaben; **extra-**~ **expenditure** außeretatsmäßige Ausgaben; ~ **experience** Etatserfahrung; **medium-term** ~ **framework** mittelfristiges Haushaltssystem; ~ **funds** Haushaltsmittel; ~ **items** Etatsposten; ~ **means** Etats-, Haushaltsmittel; ~ **needs** Haushalts-, Etatbedürfnisse; ~ **negotiations** Etats-, Haushaltsberatungen; ~ **officer (US)** Haushaltsreferent; ~ **operations** Etatverschiebungen; ~ **period** Finanzperiode; **to hold domestic spending within the** ~ **plan** Inlandsausgaben im Etatsrahmen halten; **to change governments'** ~ **policies sharply from the expansionary to the restrictive** die bisher expansionsbedingte Etatspolitik auf einen scharf restriktiven Kurs umstellen; ~ **policy** Haushaltspolitik; ~ **practices** Budgetmaßnahmen; ~ **preparation** Etatsvorbereitung; ~ **procedure** Verfahren bei der Aufstellung des Haushalts; ~ **provisions** Bereitstellung von Etatsmitteln; ~ **question** Etats-, Haushaltsfrage; ~ **receipts** Finanzaufkommen; ~ **reform** Haushaltsreform; ~ **regulations** haushaltsrechtliche Bestimmungen; ~ **restraints** Etatsbeschränkungen; ~ **system** Haushaltssystem; ~ **target** Etatsziel; ~ **troubles** Etatsschwierigkeiten; ~ **year** Etats-, Finanz-, Haushaltsjahr.

budgeted im Haushalt (Etat) vorgesehen;
~ **expense plan** vorkalkulierter Prämienetat; ~ **level** geplanter Rahmen; ~ **production** Produktionsplanung.

budgeteer Haushaltsexperte, -spezialist.

budgeting Haushaltsaufstellung, Etatisierung, *(management)* Finanzplanung, Plankosten-, Planungsrechnung;

compulsory ~ Zwangsetatisierung; **cyclical** ~ antizyklische Haushaltspolitik, -ausgleich; **deficit** ~ Defizitfinanzierung, konjunkturbelebende Ausgaben der öffentlichen Hand; **long-range** ~ langfristige Haushaltspolitik; **surplus** ~ *(fiscal policy)* Überschußpolitik; **zero-base** ~ **approach** jeden Einzelposten grundsätzlich in Frage stellende Haushaltspolitik; ~ **method** Etatisierungsmethode; ~ **procedure** Etatisierungsverfahren.

buff *(US fam.)* Fan, Narr, begeisterter Anhänger.

buffer Puffer, *(data processing)* Pufferspeicher;
~ **financing** *(EC)* Ausgleichsvorratsfinanzierung; ~ **force** neutrale Truppen; ~ **state** Pufferstaat; ~ **stock** *(raw materials)* beweglich geführtes Lager, Reserve-, Vorratslager, *(EC)* Ausgleichsvorrat; ~ **zone** Puffergebiet, -zone.

buffet *(Br.)* Anrichte, Büffet, *(affliction)* Schicksalsschlag;
cold ~ kaltes Büffet; **pool-side** ~ Schwimmbadrestauration; ~ **car** *(US)* Speisewagen; ~ **snack** Imbiß im Selbstbedienungsspeisewagen; ~ **supper** warmes Büffet.

bug *(breakdown, US sl.)* technische Panne, *(burglar alarm, US)* Alarmanlage, *(joker in a piece of legislation)* hinterlistige Klausel, *(monitoring device, US)* Abhörvorrichtung, Wanze, *(trade unionism, US)* Gewerkschaftsmarke, *(US coll.)* Bazillus;
big ~ *(sl.)* Großkopfeter;
~s **in television** Fernsehstörung;
~ *(v.) (concealed microphone)* Abhörvorrichtung einbauen;
~ **out** *(airforce, sl.)* abhauen, Leine ziehen; ~ **a telephone** Telefonleitung abhören;
to put a ~ **in s. one's ear** *(US sl.)* jem. einen Floh ins Ohr setzen.

bugged *(US)* mit Abhörvorrichtungen versehen.

bugging *(US)* Einbau von Abhörvorrichtungen;
~ **case** Abhörvorfall; ~ **device** Abhörvorrichtung, -anlage; ~ **disclosure** Aufdeckung eines Abhörfalles; ~ **scandal** Abhörskandal.

build *(v.)* errichten, bauen, *(builder)* Baumeister sein, *(construct)* aufbauen, konstruieren;
~ **one's business in a country** sich in einem Land absatzmäßig verankern; ~ **castles in the air** Luftschlösser bauen; ~ **down to prices** zu niedrigsten Preisen bauen; ~ **on firm ground** auf festem Grund errichten; ~ **a house** Haus bauen (errichten); ~ **a locomotive** Lokomotive konstruieren; ~ **a railroad** *(US)* Eisenbahnlinie bauen; ~ **a road** Straße anlegen; ~ **a room in the attic** Dachgeschoß ausbauen.

build up aufbauen, aufstocken, *(mil.)* bereitstellen;
~ **s. o. j.** [politisch] aufbauen; ~ **by the addition of increments** wertmäßig durch kumulierte Zuwächse zunehmen; ~ **an area** Gelände ausbauen; ~ **a campaign** Wahlfeldzug vorbereiten; ~ **a case** Beweismaterial zusammentragen; ~ **a new connection** neue Verbindung herstellen; ~ **an empire** Reich gründen; ~ **an existence** sich eine Existenz aufbauen; ~ **an inventory** Lager aufstocken; ~ **a list** Liste zusammenstellen; ~ **a lot of loan demand** erheblichen Kreditbedarf auslösen; ~ **a reputation** sich einen Namen machen; ~ **reserves** Reserven ansammeln, Rücklagen bilden.

builder Baumeister, -unternehmer, *(clerk of the works)* Bauleiter, *(owner)* Bauherr, -träger;
house ~ Bauunternehmer; **racing car** ~ Rennwagenhersteller; ~ **of aircraft engines** Flugzeugmotorenhersteller;
~-**owner** Bauherr, -träger.

builder's | **account** Bauabrechnung; ~ **estimate** Baukostenvoranschlag; ~ **lock** Lagerschloß; ~ **manager** Bauleiter; ~ **price** Baukosten; ~ **project** Bauträgervorhaben; ~ **risk insurance** Baudiebstahls-, Bauhaftpflicht-, Bauunternehmerversicherung, Gefahrenzulage für Gebäudeversicherungen; ~ **risk policy** Baurisikopolice.

building Gebäude, Bauwerk, *(constructing)* Bauen, Errichten, *(staff)* Heranbildung;
~s *(balance sheet)* Geschäfts- und Wohngebäude;
additional ~ Anbau; **adjoining** ~ Nebengebäude; **ancient** ~ kulturhistorisches Baudenkmal; **bank** ~ Bankgebäude; **factory** ~ Fabrikgebäude; **farm** ~s Wirtschaftsgebäude; **freehold** ~ zinsfreies Gebäude; **high-rent** ~ hochverzinsliches Renditeobjekt; **high-rise** ~ Hochhaus; **industrial** ~ gewerblich genutztes Gebäude; **industrialized** ~s Fließbandbauten; **loft** ~ Speichergebäude; **main** ~ Hauptgebäude; **mortgaged** ~ hypothekarisch belastetes Hausgrundstück; **municipal** ~ städtisches Gebäude; **new** ~s Neubauten; **nonproductive** ~ nicht für die Produktion genutztes Gebäude; **nonqualifying** ~ nicht abschreibungsberechtigtes Gebäude; **occupied** ~ bewohntes Gebäude; **prefabricated** ~ Fertigbau; **private** ~ private Bautätigkeit; **public** ~ öffentliches Gebäude; **regular** ~ symmetrisches Gebäude; **side** ~ Anbau; **special purpose** ~s Zweckbauten; **standing empty** leerstehendes Gebäude; **wrecked** ~ abgerissenes Gebäude;

land and ~ *(balance sheet)* bebaute und unbebaute Grundstücke; ~ **under construction (in course of erection)** im Bau befindliches Haus; ~ **on contract** Auftragsbau; ~s **less depreciation** *(balance sheet)* Gebäude nach Abschreibungen; ~ **above ground** Hochbau; ~ **of a hospital** Krankenhauserrichtung; ~ **in good preservation** gut erhaltenes Gebäude; ~s **on real estate not owned by the company** Bauten auf fremden Grundstücken; ~ **or structure** Bauwerk; ~s **in use for the purpose of trade** gewerblich genutzte Gebäude; ~ **of a wall** Errichtung einer Mauer;
~ **is covered** das Gebäude ist versichert;
to assess a ~ Gebäude abschätzen, Einheitswert eines Gebäudes festsetzen; **to commence a** ~ mit dem Bau anfangen; **to erect a** ~ Gebäude errichten; **to give a quotation for** ~ **a garage** Baukostenvoranschlag für einen Garagenbau vorlegen; **to have the care of a** ~ Gebäude zu bewachen haben; **to invite tenders for a** ~ Gebäude im Submissionsweg ausschreiben; **to keep a** ~ **in repair** Gebäude unterhalten; **to modernize a** ~ Modernisierungsarbeiten an einem Gebäude durchführen; **to predetermine the costs of a** ~ Baukostenvoranschlag machen; **to put a freeze on** ~ Baustopp verfügen; **to rate a** ~ **for insurance purposes** Einheitswert eines Gebäudes für Versicherungszwecke schätzen lassen; **to reduce the assessment of a** ~ Einheitswert eines Gebäudes herabsetzen; **to restore a ruined** ~ Gebäude wiederherstellen; **to run up a** ~ Bau rasch errichten; **to scale a** ~ Gebäude maßstabsgerecht zeichnen; **to set too high a valuation on a** ~ Einheitswert eines Gebäudes zu hoch ansetzen; **to survey a** ~ Bauabnahme durchführen; **to survey a** ~ **for quantities** *(Br.)* Baukostenvoranschlag machen; **to take down a** ~ Gebäude abreißen;

~ **account** Gebäudekonto; ~ **activities** Bautätigkeit; ~ **advance** Baugeld-, Bauzwischenkredit; ~ **agreement loan** *(US)* Bauspardarlehen; ~ **alterations** Umbauten; ~ **application** Bauantrag; ~ **approach** Gebäudezugang; ~ **block** *(fig.)* Baustein; ~ **board** Bauausschuß; ~ **boom** Baukonjunktur; ~ **business** Bauwirtschaft; ~ **byelaw** *(Br.)* Generalbebauungsplan, Ortsstatut, örtliche Bauvorschriften (Bauordnung); ~ **capital** Baukapital, -gelder; ~ **case** Baustreitigkeit; **fallen** ~ **clause** Einsturzklausel; ~ **code** Bauordnung, [städtische] Bauvorschriften, Fluchtlinienplan; ~ **code violation** Zuwiderhandlung gegen baupolizeiliche Anordnungen; ~ **components** Bauelemente; ~ **construction** Gebäudeaufführung; ~ **constructor** Baumeister; ~ **consultant** Bausachverständiger; ~ **contract** Bauunternehmer, -vertrag; ~ **contracts in progress** in Ausführung befindliche Bauvorhaben; ~ **contractor** Bauunternehmer; ~ **contractors** Bauunternehmung; ~ **costs** Baupreise; ~ **development scheme** Bau-, Siedlungsprojekt; ~ **display** Gebäudedekoration; ~ **enterprise** Bauunternehmen; ~ **estate** Baugrundstück; ~ **estimate** Baukostenvoranschlag; ~ **expenses** Baukosten; **single-source** ~ **financing** Baufinanzierung aus einer Hand; ~ **foundation** Grundmauer; ~ **funds** Baugelder; ~ **ground** Bauplatz, -stelle; ~ **height** Gebäudehöhe; ~ **industries** Bauindustrie, -wesen; ~ **inspector** Baupolizei; ~ **issues** *(stock exchange)* Bauwerte, -aktien; ~ **labo(u)rer** Bauarbeiter; ~ **land** Bauland; ~-**land prices** Baulandpreise; ~ **law** Bauordnung, -recht; ~ **lease** *(Br.)* Erbbauvertrag; ~ **ledger** Gebäudehauptbuch; ~ **licence** Baugenehmigung; ~ **lien** Zurückbehaltungsrecht des Handwerkers; ~ **line** Bauflucht, Fluchtlinie; **to be in the** ~ **line** auf dem Bau arbeiten; ~ **loan** Baukredit, -darlehen; **home** ~ **and loan association** *(US)* Bausparkasse; ~ **loan agreement** *(US)* Bausparvertrag; ~ **loan contract** *(US)* Bausparvertrag; ~ **lot** *(US)* Baugrundstück, -parzelle; ~ **maintenance** Gebäudeunterhaltung; ~ **management** Gebäudeverwaltung; ~ **market** Baumarkt; ~ **material** Baubedarf; ~-**material merchant** Baumaterialienhändler; ~-**material producer** *(US)* Unternehmen des Baustoffsektors; ~-**material tax** Baumaterialenabgabe; ~ **operations** Bauvorhaben; ~ **operative** Bauarbeiter, -handwerker; ~ **order** Bauauftrag; ~ **outlay** Gebäudeausgaben, -unkosten; ~ **owner** Bauherr; ~ **pay** Bauarbeiterlöhne; ~ **permit** Bauerlaubnis, -genehmigung; ~ **plot** Baugrundstück, -parzelle; ~ **preservation order** Bauauflage; ~ **prices** Baupreise; ~ **program(me)** Bauprogramm; ~ **prohibition** Bauverbot; ~ **project** Bauvorhaben; **unfinished** ~ **projects** Bauüberhang; ~ **purpose** Bauvorhaben; ~ **quota** Baukontingent; **local** ~ **regulations** Bauvorschriften; ~ **restrictions** Baubeschränkungen; ~ **season** Bausaison; ~ **scheme** Bauprojekt; ~ **sector** Bausektor; ~ **share** Bauaktie; ~ **shed** Baubaracke, -bude; ~ **site** baureifes Land, Bauplatz, -stelle; **on the** ~ **site** am Bau; **large** ~ **site** Großbaustelle; **waste** ~ **sites** brachliegendes Bauland; ~ **slip** Baudock; ~ **slump** rückläufige Baukonjunktur; ~ **Societies Act** *(Br.)* Gesetz über Bausparkassen, Bausparkassengesetz; ~ **society** *(Br.)* Bausparkasse.

building-society | deposits *(Br.)* Bauspargelder, -einlagen, Bausparmittel; ~ **depositor** *(Br.)* Bausparer; ~ **funds** *(Br.)* Bausparmittel; ~ **guarantee** *(Br.)* Darlehnszusage einer Bausparkasse; ~ **interest** *(Br.)* Bausparzinsen; ~ **interest payable** fällige Bausparzinsen; ~ **interest received** *(Br.)* gezahlte Zinsen auf Bausparverträge; ~ **investor** *(Br.)* Bausparer; ~ **money** *(Br.)* Bausparsumme; ~ **mortgage** *(Br.)* Bausparhypothek; ~ **mortgage financing** *(Br.)* Hypothekenfinanzierung durch Bausparverträge; ~ **rates** *(Br.)* Bauspardarlehnssätze, Bausparkassenzinssätze; ~ **shares** *(Br.)* Anteile (Aktien) einer Bausparkasse.

building | spree Bauorgie; ~ **standards** Baurichtlinien; ~ **stocks** *(US)* Bauwerte, -aktien; ~ **strike** Bauarbeiterstreik; ~ **supplies** Baubedarf; ~ **survey** Gebäudebewertung, -schätzung; ~ **surveyor** Bausachverständiger, Gebäudeschätzer; ~ **tax** Bauabgabe; ~ **time** Bauzeit; ~ **trade** Bauindustrie, -fach, -gewerbe; ~-**trade operative (tradesman)** Bauhandwerker; ~ **trades pay** Löhne im Baugewerbe, Bauarbeiterlöhne; ~-**trade union** Bauarbeitergewerkschaft, [etwa] Gewerkschaft Bau, Steine, Erden; ~ **worker** Bauarbeiter; ~ **yard** Bauplatz.

buildup *(advertising)* Propaganda [für Einzelartikel], *(mil.)* Zusammenziehung von Kräften, Truppenansammlung, Bereitstellung, Aufmarsch, *(growth)* Anstieg, *(politics)* Persönlichkeitsaufbau;
arms ~ Waffenansammlung; **economic** ~ Wirtschaftsaufbau; ~ **of an account** Kontoaufstockung; ~ **of liquidity** Liquiditätsanstieg; ~ **of profits** Gewinnanstieg; ~ **of reserves** Rücklagenbildung; ~ **of stocks** Lageraufbau;
to give a ~ groß herausstellen; **to be given a great** ~ **in the press** in der Presse groß herausgebracht werden.

built gebaut, konstruiert;
solidly ~ dauerhaft gebaut.

built-in eingebaut;
~ **aerial** Einbauantenne; ~ **cupboard** fest eingebauter Schrank; ~ **department** Sonderabteilung; ~ **flexibility** *(economic policy)* eingebaute Flexibilität; ~ **maid service** *(US)* Übernahme von Aufgaben des Verbraucherhaushalts; ~ **obsolescence** geplanter Verschleiß; ~ **piece of furniture** eingebautes Möbelstück; ~ **stabilizers** antizyklisch wirkende Stabilisierungsmechanismen; ~ **technical progress** investitionsabhängiger technischer Fortschritt.

built-on angebaut.

built-up area bebautes Gebiet, *(traffic regulations)* geschlossene Ortschaft.

bulb Glühbirne;
to put forty-watt ~**s in** 40 Watt-Birnen einschrauben.

bulge *(mil.)* Frontausbuchtung, *(prices, US)* plötzliches, leichtes Anziehen der Effektenkurse, *(population)* geburtenstarke Jahrgänge, *(ship)* Schiffsboden;
~ **of applicants** zunehmende Zahl von Antragstellern; **postwar** ~ **in student numbers** Anwachsen der Studentenzahl seit Kriegsende;
to have a ~ **on s. o.** *(US sl.)* jem. gegenüber im Vorteil sein.

bulk Größe, Umfang, Menge, Masse, *(cargo)* unverpackte [Schiffs]ladung, *(stand)* Verkaufsstand;
by the *(Br.)* **(in,** *US)* ~ in Bausch und Bogen, im großen (ganzen), massenhaft, *(cargo)* lose, unverpackt;
breaking ~ Löschen der Ladung;
~ **of the army** Gros der Armee; ~ **of one's business** Hauptgeschäft, Geschäftsschwerpunkt; ~ **of a debt** Hauptteil einer Schuld; ~ **of export** Hauptausfuhr; ~ **of a fund** überwiegender Fondsanteil; ~ **of import** Haupteinfuhr; ~ **of population** Mehrzahl der Bevölkerung; ~ **of profit** Hauptgewinn; ~ **of one's property** Masse des Vermögens; ~ **of the votes cast** Gros der abgegebenen Stimmen;
~ *(v.)* umfangreich sein, *(weigh goods)* Gewicht feststellen, *(transport goods)* als Schüttgut verladen;
to break the ~ *(cargo)* Ladung brechen, zu löschen anfangen, in Bausch und Bogen (im ganzen) kaufen; **to get the** ~ **of one's income by way of commission** größeren Teil seines Einkommens im Provisionswege verdienen; **to load a vessel in** ~ Schiff mit Massengütern beladen; **to lose the** ~ **of one's goods** fast sein ganzes Vermögen verlieren; **to sell in** ~ in Bausch und Bogen verkaufen; **to sell s. th. without breaking** ~ ohne zu entladen verkaufen;
~ *(a.) (loose)* lose, unverpackt;
~ **article** Massenartikel, -gut; ~ **buyer** Großabnehmer; ~ **buying** Mengeneinkauf, Engrosbezug; ~ **cargo** Waggonladung, Schüttgut, -ladung, *(ship)* geschlossene Ladung, Bulkladung; ~ **carrier** Großraum-, Schüttguttransporter, -verfrachter, Massengutfrachter; ~ **commodity** Massengut, *(ship)* geschlossene Ladung; ~ **consignment** Massenlieferung; ~ **consumer** Großverbraucher; ~ **consumption** Massenverbrauch; ~ **fleet** Schüttgutflotte; ~ **franking** Barfreimachung; ~ **freight** Waggonfracht; ~ **goods** unverpackte (lose) Ware, Schüttgut, Sturzgüter; ~ **grain** loses Getreide; ~-**line costs** Grundkosten; ~ **mail** Postwurfsendung, Massendrucksachen; ~ **marking** Preisauszeichnung für eine ganze Warenpartie; ~ **materials** Schüttgut; ~ **mortgage** *(US)* Verpfändung ganzer Bestände; ~-**order price** Pauschalbezugspreis; ~ **printed matter** Massendrucksachen; ~ **production** Massenfertigung; ~ **purchase** Groß-, Mengeneinkauf; ~ **purchased** im Großeinkauf; ~ **purchasing** Groß-, Mengeneinkauf; ~ **rate** *(Br.)* Mengenrabatt; ~-**rate discount** Pauschalabschlag; ~ **sale** *(US)* Verkauf in Bausch und Bogen, Mengenumsatz, Massen-, Gesamtverkauf, Veräußerung des gesamten Vermögens; ~ **seat sales** Verkauf von Flugplätzen für Gruppenreisen; ~ **sample** Stückmuster; ~ **sampling** Stichprobenentnahme; ~ **shipment** Sturzgütersendung; ~ **storage** Großlager; ~ **store** *(Australia)* Warenhaus; ~ **supplier** Großlieferant; ~ **supply** Mengenlieferung; ~ **tariff** verbilligter Massenkauf; ~ **tour** Pauschalreise; ~ **transfer** *(enterprise, US)* Übertragung der beweglichen Sachwerte; ~ **transport** Massentransport; ~ **transportation** Massenverkehr.

bulkhead Stirnwand, *(ship)* Schott;
~ **deck** Schottendeck.

bulkiness Sperrigkeit.

bulky umfangreich, massig, sperrig;
~ **cargo** sperrige Ladung; ~ **goods** Sperrgut; ~ **paper** bauschiges Papier.

bull *(locomotive, US sl.)* Lokomotive, *(stock exchange)* Haussier, Haussespekulant, *(US sl., detective)* Polyp, Bulle, Kriminalbeamter;
~**s** *(US)* steigende Kurse;
~ **in a china shop** Elefant im Porzellanladen;
~ *(v.)* auf Hausse spekulieren, *(prices)* im Preis steigen;
~ **the market** auf Hausse kaufen, Preise hochtreiben, Kurse steigern;
to be all (feel) ~ *(market)* in Haussestimmung sein; **to give on a** ~ Haentausse position hereingeben; **to go a** ~ auf Hausse spekulieren; **to make a** ~ *(US)* groben Schnitzer begehen; **to run** ~ Haussier werden; **to take the** ~ **by the horns** *(fig.)* Stier bei den Hörnern packen;
~ *(a.)* steigend, haussetendenziös;
~ **account** *(Br.)* Hausseengagement; ~ **campaign** Kurstreiberei; ~ **clique** Haussepartei; ~**'s eye** Bullauge, *(film)* Blende; ~ **horn** *(navy)* Lautsprecheranlage; ~ **market** Börsenhausse, Haussemarkt; ~ **market's dotage** Haussemarktabschwächung; ~ **movement** Hausse[bewegung]; ~ **operation** Haussespekulation; ~ **pen** *(US sl.)* Beruhigungszelle; ~ **phase** Haupausse periode; ~ **point** *(coll.)* Vorzugsstellung, *(stock exchange)* Haussemoment; ~ **pool** Haussegruppe; ~ **position** Hausseposition; ~ **purchase** Kauf à la Hausse; ~ **ring** Stierkampfarena; ~ **run** Stierhetze; ~ **session** *(US)* Herrenabend; ~ **speculation** Haussespekulation; **on** ~ **support** aufgrund von Stützungskäufen der Haussepartei; ~-**at-a-gate tactics** heftige Angriffstaktik; ~ **transaction** Haussespekulation, -geschäft.

bulldog *(university, sl.)* Pedell;
~ **clip** Büroklammer; ~ **edition** *(US)* vordatierte Zeitung, inkomplette Provinzausgabe.

bulldoze *(v.)* terrorisieren, *(bulldozer)* planieren, *(fig.)* ins Bockshorn jagen.

bulldozer Planierraupe, Schuttramme, Großräumpflug.

bullet Gewehr-, Pistolenkugel, Geschoß, *(print.)* Blickfang, -punkt;
to bite on the ~ in den sauren Apfel beißen;
highspeed ~ **train** Blitzzug.

bulletproof schußsicher, kugelfest;
~ **jacket** kugelsichere Weste.

bulletin Nachrichtenblatt, Zeitschrift, *(broadcast report)* Wetterbericht, *(official report)* amtlicher Bericht, amtliche Zeitung, Tagesbericht, Bulletin, *(patient)* Krankenbericht;
news ~ Nachrichtendienst; **official** ~ offizieller Bericht; **painted** ~ gemaltes Außenplakat;
~ *(v.)* öffentlich bekanntmachen;
to issue a ~ Bulletin herausgeben;
~ **board** *(US)* Anschlagtafel, Schwarzes Brett.

bullfight Stierkampf.

bullion [Gold-, Silber]barren, ungemünztes Edelmetall [in Barren];
gold ~ Barrengold;
~**s abroad** *(balance sheet)* auswärtige Goldbestände; ~ **at the bank** Barvorräte der Bank; ~ **in transit** auf dem Transport befindliches Gold;

~ **board** gemalte Großfläche; ~ **broker** Edelmetallmakler; ~ **dealer** Edelmetallhändler; **gold** ~ **standard** Goldkernwährung; ~ **office** Ankaufstelle für ungemünztes Gold, Münzanstalt; ~ **point** Goldpunkt; ~ **reserve** Goldreserve; ~ **trade** Handel mit Edelmetallen; ~ **value** Gold- oder Silberwert einer geprägten Münze.

bullionism Theorie der reinen Metallwährung.

bullish steigend, haussetendenziös, haussierend;
   to be ~ in the long run auf lange Sicht auf eine Hausse setzen; **to continue ~** Haussebewegung fortsetzen; **to feel ~** haussieren; ~ **demonstration** Hausse[bewegung]; ~ **market** Haussemarkt; **to be in a ~ mood** haussieren; **to be hardly ~ news for a share price** sich kaum haussetendenziös auf einen Aktienkurs auswirken; ~ **performance** Haussebewegung; ~ **proclivities** steigende Tendenz; ~ **report** Haussenachricht; ~ **price rise** hausseartige Kurssteigerung; ~ **tendency (tone)** Haussestimmung, -tendenz.

bullishness Haussetendenz.

bully Flegel, *(protector of prostitute)* Zuhälter, *(mil.)* Kameradenschinder;
   ~ *(v.)* einschüchtern, tyrannisieren, drangsalieren;
   ~ *(a.) (US)* prima.

bulwark Bollwerk, Schutz, *(ship)* Schiffswand.

bum *(US sl.)* Stromer, Landstreicher, Schnorrer, *(spree)* Saufgelage;
   on the ~ auf der Walze;
   ~ **bailiff** *(Br.)* Büttel, Scherge.

bumbledom Wichtigtuerei, Beamtendünkel.

bumf *(paper)* Toilettenpapier, *(Br., sl.)* Papierkram, Wisch.

bump Stoß, *(airpocket)* Luftloch, *(fig., coll.)* Talent, Organ, Fähigkeit;
   ~ **of locality** Ortssinn;
   ~ *(v.) (car)* holpern, rumpeln;
   ~ **a car** Auto rammen, mit einem Auto zusammenstoßen; ~ **off** *(sl.)* kaltmachen, umbringen; ~ **into s. o. with a question** j. mit einer Frage überrumpeln; ~ **up prices** Preise heraufteiben; ~ **other workers** *(US)* anderen Arbeitern bei Entlassungen vorgehen.

bumper *(car)* Stoßstange, *(whopper, coll.)* Knüller;
   front ~ vordere Stoßstange;
   ~ *(a.)* ungewöhnlich groß;
   ~ **crop** *(fam.)* Rekordernte; ~ **present** üppiges Geschenk; ~ **sticker** Stoßstangenaufkleber.

bumpiness Böigkeit, *(road)* Holprigkeit.

bumping *(US)* Beibehaltung langjähriger Angestellter bei Entlassungen;
   ~ **bag** *(airplane)* Landungspuffer; ~ **post** Prellbock; ~ **right** *(US)* Recht auf Beibehaltung der Arbeitsplätze bei Entlassungen.

bumptious official aufgeblasener Beamter.

bumpy holprig, *(air)* böig.

bunce *(sl.)* Extragewinn.

bunch Bündel, Bund, *(group of persons)* Personengruppe;
   ~ **of keys** Schlüsselbund; ~ **of orders** Pack von Aufträgen, Auftragsbündel; ~ **of patterns** Schnittmusterkollektion.

bunched *(US, stock exchange)* fortlaufend notiert;
   ~ **costs** pauschal versteuerte Kosten; ~ **gains** sich steuerlich kräftig auswirkende Gewinnrealisierungen; ~ **income** für längeren Zeitraum in einem Steuerjahr anfallendes Einkommen.

bundle Bündel, Paket, Gebinde;
   in ~s bündelweise;
   ~ **of bank notes** Paket Geldscheine, Banknotenbündel; ~ **of files** Stoß Akten; ~ **of letters** Pack Briefe; ~ **of nerves** Nervenbündel; ~ **of notes** Banknotenbündel; ~ **of papers** Aktenbündel; ~ **of old rags** Lumpenbündel; ~ **of titled deeds** kompletter Satz von Eigentumsurkunden;
   ~ *(v.)* [zusammen]bündeln, einpacken;
   ~ **s. o. into a taxi** j. in ein Taxi verfrachten; ~ **up** einpacken; **to drop one's ~** *(Australia)* sich geschlagen geben; **to go a ~** hohe Wette eingehen; **to make up in ~s** in Bündeln packen; ~ **sale** Kopplungsverkauf.

bungalow eingeschossiges Haus, Bungalow;
   ~ **town** Bungalowsiedlung.

bunk Schlafkoje;
   to do a ~ *(fam.)* abhauen;
   ~ **inspection** *(mil.)* Stubenappell.

bunker *(mar.)* Kohlenbunker;
   ~ *(v.) (ship)* Kohle (Treibstoff) laden, bunkern;
   ~ **down for a long battle** sich für einen langen Kampf vorbereiten;
   to be ~ed *(fig.)* in Schwierigkeiten sein;
   ~ **coal** Bunkerkohle; ~ **rate in home ports** Bunkerpreise in Heimathäfen.

bunkhouse *(US)* Schlafbaracke, Arbeiterbaracke.

bunting *(US)* Fahnentuch, *(flags collectively)* Beflaggung;
   to put out ~ beflaggen.

buoy [Anker]boje, Bake, Seezeichen;
   life ~ Rettungsboje; **whistling ~** Heulboje;
   ~ *(v.)* Bojen auslegen;
   ~ **the bond market** Rentenmarkt inspirieren; ~ **off** ausbojen, durch Bojen kennzeichen; ~ **up the economic index** dem Konjunkturindex Auftrieb geben; ~ **a wreck** Schiffswrack markieren;
   to make fast to a ~ an einer Boje festmachen; **to pick up one's ~** an die Boje gehen; **to put down ~s** Bojen auslegen (verankern).

buoyage Betonnung, Markierung durch Bojen, Bojensystem.

buoyancy hydrostatischer Auftrieb, Tragvermögen, *(fig.)* Spannkraft, Lebensfreude, *(market)* Elastizität, Erholungsfähigkeit, *(taxes)* inflationsbedingter Anstieg;
   reserve ~ Auftriebsreserve.

buoyant *(market)* sehr fest, steigend;
   ~ **lift** statischer Auftrieb; ~ **market** feste Börse; ~ **performance** sehr feste Haltung.

burden Bürde, Last, Ladung, *(accounting)* Gemein-, Handlungsunkosten, *(obligatory expense)* unausweichliche Belastung, *(tonnage)* Tonnengehalt, Tragfähigkeit;
   absorbed ~ verrechnete Gemeinkosten; **departmental ~** auf die Abteilungen aufgeteilte Handlungsunkosten; **fiscal ~** steuerliche Abgaben (Lasten); **heavy ~** drückende Abgaben; **overabsorbed ~** Gemeinkostenüberdeckung; **real ~** *(Scot.)* Reallast, Grundstücksbelastung; **tax ~** Steuerlast, -belastung; **the white man's ~** Verantwortung der weißen Rasse; **underabsorbed ~** Gemeinkostenunterdeckung;
   ~ **of argument** Hauptpunkt einer Kontroverse; ~ **of costs** Kostenbelastung; ~ **of a covenant** mit dem Grundeigentum verbundene Pflichten; ~ **of debts** Schuldenlast; ~ **of debt service** Schuldendienstbelastung; ~ **of financing** Finanzierungslast; ~ **of interest** Zinslast; ~ **of proof** Beweislast; ~ **of taxation** Steuerlast; ~ **of travel** Reiseanstrengungen;
   ~ *(v.)* belasten, bepacken;
   ~ **s. o.** jem. zu Last fallen;
   ~ **the finances of the communities** Gemeindehaushaltungen belasten; ~ **with a mortgage** mit einer Hypothek belasten; ~ **with taxes** besteuern;
   to be a ~ to s. o. jem. zur Last fallen; **to be encumbered with the ~ of a lost war** mit der Hypothek eines verlorenen Krieges belastet sein; **to bear a ~** schwere Last tragen; **to become a ~ to** zur Last fallen; **to carry the ~ of American taxes** mit amerikanischen Steuerzahlungen belastet sein; **to cast the ~ of proof upon the plaintiff** dem Kläger die Beweislast auferlegen; ~ **one's memory with useless facts** sein Gedächtnis mit sinnlosen Einzelheiten belasten;
   to hold the affirmative ~ of proof beweispflichtig ein; **to impose a ~** aufbürden; **to shift the ~ of proof** Beweislast umkehren; **to throw off a ~** Last abschütteln;
   ~ **absorption rate** Gemeinkostenverrechnungssatz; ~ **adjustment** Unkostenaufteilung; ~ **base** Gemeinkostenverrechnungsbasis; ~ **center** Kostenstelle; **plant-wide ~ rate** Gemeinkostenzuschlag; ~ **sharing** *(NATO)* Lasten-, Kostenausgleich.

burdened | with debts schuldenbelastet; ~ **with taxation** steuerlich überlastet;
   ~ **estate** belastetes Grundstück.

burdensome contract lästiger Vertrag.

bureau Amts-, Geschäftszimmer, -stelle, Büro, *(chest of drawers)* Kommode, *(Br., desk)* Schreibtisch, -pult, *(government agency, US)* Dienststelle, *(US, insurance)* Verband;
   employment ~ Arbeits-, Stellennachweis, Stellenvermittlungsbüro; **information ~** Auskunfs-, Informationsbüro, Auskunftei; **marriage licence ~** *(US)* Standesamt; **technical ~** Konstruktionsbüro; **tourist ~** Fremdenverkehrsamt; **travel ~** Reisebüro; **typewriting ~** Schreibbüro; **weather ~** Wetteramt.

Bureau | of the Budget *(US)* Haushaltsabteilung des Schatzamtes der Vereinigten Staaten; ~ **of the Census** *(US)* Statistisches Bundesamt; ~ **de change** Wechselbüro; ~ **of Conciliation** Schlichtungsstelle; ~ **of Customs** *(US)* Zollamt; **National ~ of Economic Research** Statistisches Bundesamt; ~ **of Employment Security** *(US)* Sozialversicherungsbehörde; ~ **of Foreign and Domestic Commerce** *(US)* Innen- und Außenhandelsamt; ~ **of Internal Revenue** *(US)* Bundessteuerabteilung, -verwaltung; ~ **of Labor Statistics** *(US)* Statistisches Arbeitsamt; ~ **of Narcotics and Dangerous Drugs** *(US)* Rauschgiftbehörde; ~ **of Old-Age and Survivors Insurance** *(US)* Versicherungsaufsichtsamt; ~ **of Pensions** *(US)* Amt für Kriegswitwen und -waisen; ~ **of**

Public Roads *(US)* Straßenverkehrsamt; ~ **of Reclamation** *(US)* Behörde zur Finanzierung von Bewässerungsvorhaben; ~ **of State Security** staatlicher Sicherheitsdienst; ~ **of Standards** *(US)* [etwa] Physikalisch-Technische Bundesanstalt; ₂**chief** Bürochef; ₂ **company** Versicherungsverband; ₂ **de change facilities** Umtauschstelle für fremde Sorten; ₂ **rates** Verbandstarif.

bureaucracy bürokratisches Regierungssystem, Bürokratie; **overblown** ~ übermäßig aufgeblähter bürokratischer Apparat.

bureaucrat Bürokrat.

bureaucratic bürokratisch; ~ **behavio(u)r** bürokratisches Verhalten; **to make for** ~ **control** Büroorganisation im Griff haben; ~ **delay** bürokratische Verzögerung; ~ **expenditure** bürokratischer Aufwand; ~ **jargon** Beamtenjargon; ~ **mill** Mühlen der Bürokratie.

bureaucratism bürokratische Einstellung.

bureaucratist Bürokrat, Aktenmensch.

burgage Stadthaus.

burgee Haus-, Kontorflagge, Stander.

burgeon *(v.) (fig.)* ins Kraut schießen.

burgess *(Br.)* Abgeordneter, Ratsherr, Stadtrat; ~ **roll** Bürgerliste.

burgesship Wahl, Bürgerrecht.

burgh *(Scot.)* kreisfreie Stadt, Stadtgemeinde; **large** ~ *(Scot.)* Mittelstadt.

burglar Einbrecher; **cat** ~ Fassadenkletterer; ~ **alarm call** Alarmanlagenruf.

burglarious attempt Einbruchsversuch.

burglariously mit dem Vorsatz einzubrechen, mit Einbruchsabsicht.

burglarize *(v.) (US)* Einbruchdiebstahl begehen, einbrechen.

burglarproof einbruchsicher.

burglary [Einbruchs]diebstahl; **armed** ~ bewaffneter Einbruch; **attempted** ~ Einbruchsversuch; **to commit** ~ einbrechen, Einbruch begehen; ~ **attempt** Einbruchsversuch; ~ **[office] insurance** [gewerbliche] Einbruchsdiebstahlversicherung; ~ **policy** Einbruchsdiebstahlversicherungspolice.

burgle *(v.)* **a house** in ein Haus einbrechen.

burial Begräbnis, Beerdigung, Beisetzung, Leichenbegängnis; **Christian** ~ christliches Begräbnis; **solemn** ~ feierliches Begräbnis; **urn** ~ Urnenbeisetzung; ~ **at sea** Bestattung auf hoher See; ~ **case** Sarg; ~ **club** Sterbekasse; ~ **fund** Sterbekasse; ~ **ground** Begräbnisplatz, Friedhof; ~ **insurance** Sterbeversicherung; ~ **permit** *(US)* Begräbnisschein; ~ **place** Grabstätte, Begräbnisstätte; ~ **service** Trauerfeier; ~ **society** Sterbekasse; ~ **spot** Begräbnisplatz, Grabstätte; ~ **vault** Grabgewölbe; ~ **yard** Friedhof.

buried treasure vergrabener Schatz.

burk *(v.)* totschweigen.

burke *(v.)* ersticken, erwürgen, *(smother)* vertuschen, unterdrücken; ~ **a parliamentary question** parlamentarische Anfrage unter den Tisch fallen lassen.

burlesque Satire, Posse, *(US)* Varieté, Tingeltangel.

burn verbrannte Stelle, *(med.)* Brandwunde; **first-degree** ~ Verbrennung ersten Grades; ~ *(v.)* [ver]brennen; ~ **away** abbrennen; ~ **one's boats (bridges) behind one** alle Brücken hinter sich abbrechen; ~ **the candle at both ends** zu viel unternehmen, sich verausgaben (übernehmen), Raubbau mit seiner Gesundheit treiben; ~ **daylight** Tageslicht vergeuden, *(fig.)* Zeit verschwenden; ~ **down** abbrennen; ~ **off** abbrennen; ~ **one's fingers** *(fig.)* sich die Finger verbrennen; ~ **a hole in one's pocket** einem zwischen den Fingern zerrinnen; ~ **the midnight oil** sich in den Abendstunden fortbilden, Nachtarbeiter sein; ~ **o. s. out** seine Gesundheit ruinieren; ~ **in one's pocket** *(money)* ausgabefreudig sein; ~ **up** *(US sl.)* fuchsteufelswild machen; **to have money to** ~ *(US)* Geld wie Heu haben; ~ **mark** Brandnarbe.

burnout *(aerospace)* Brennschluß.

burnt offering Brandopfer.

bursar Schatzmeister, *(scholar, Scot.)* Stipendiat, *(university)* Quästor.

bursary *(Scot.)* Stipendium, *(Br.)* Schatzmeisteramt; ~ **holder** Stipendiat, Stipendiuminhaber.

burse Geldbörse, Säckel, *(scholarship, Scot.)* Stipendium.

burst Ausbruch, Explosion, *(tyre)* Panne, Reifenschaden; ~ **of applause** Beifallssturm; ~ **of a bomb** Bombenexplosion; ~ **of consumption** Konsumexplosion; ~ **of flame** Flammenausbruch; **strong** ~ **of growth** kräftiger Wachstumsanstieg; ~ **in the water main** Wasserrohrleitungsbruch; ~ *(v.)* **its banks** *(river)* über die Ufer treten; ~ **a door open** Tür aufbrechen; **to work in sudden** ~s stoßweise arbeiten; ~~**up** Pleite, Bankrott.

bury *(v.)* begraben, bestatten, beerdigen, beisetzen; ~ **o. s. in the country** sich aufs Land zurückziehen; ~ **the hatchet** *(fig.)* Kriegsbeil begraben; ~ **s. o. at sea** j. auf hoher See bestatten; ~ **o. s. in work** sich ganz in die Arbeit vertiefen.

burying ground (place) Friedhof, Grabstätte.

bus [Omni]bus, Autobus; **commuter** ~ im Pendelverkehr eingesetzter Omnibus; **double-decked (-decker)** ~ zweistöckiger Bus; **long-distance** ~ Fernverkehrsautobus; **rest-room equipped** ~ mit Liegemöglichkeiten ausgestatteter Bus; **roomy** ~ geräumiger Bus; **publicly run** ~ öffentlich betriebene Buslinie; **single-decked** ~ einstöckiger Bus; **electric trolley** ~ Obus; ~ *(v.)* mit dem Omnibus fahren (transportieren); **to be a fivepenny ride in the** ~ fünf Pence für den Bus kosten; **to go by (take a)** ~ mit dem Omnibus fahren; **to miss the** ~ *(sl.)* Gelegenheit (Chance) verpassen; **to put a** ~ **on the road** Omnibus in Betrieb nehmen; **to ride on a** ~ mit einem Omnibus fahren, Omnibus benutzen; **to take a** ~ **off the road** Omnibus aus dem Verkehr ziehen; ~ **advertising** Omnibuswerbung; ~ **area** Bushalteplatz; ~ **bar** *(el.)* Sammelschiene; ~ **boy** *(US sl.)* Pikkolo; ~ **company** Omnibusunternehmen; ~ **conductor** Omnibusschaffner; **to assess** ~ **connections efficiently** sich über die Busverbindungen vorher genauestens unterrichten; ~ **driver** Omnibusfahrer; ~ **fare** Omnibusfahrgeld; ~ **guide** Busfahrplan; ~ **lane** Sonderfahrbahn für Omnibusse, Bushaltelinie; **exclusive** ~ **lane** nur für Omnibusse befahrbare Straße; ~ **line** Omnibuslinie, -strecke; ~ **parking** Parkplatz für Omnibusse; ~ **pass** Omnibuszulassungskarte; ~ **passenger** Omnibusfahrgast, -benutzer; ~ **pool** *(US)* Busbahnhof; ~ **ride** [Omni]busfahrt; ~ **rider** Omnibusbenutzer; ~ **route** *(US)* Kraftfahr-, Omnibuslinie, -strecke; ~ **schedule** *(US)* Omnibusfahrplan; ~ **service** Omnibusverkehr; ~ **shelter** geschützte Bushaltestelle, Bushäuschen; ~ **station** Omnibusstation, -haltestelle; ~ **stop** Autobus-, Omnibushaltestelle; ~~**stop pillar** Haltestellensäule; ~ **terminal** Omnibusbahnhof; ~ **ticket** Omnibusfahrschein; ~ **timetable** Omnibusfahrplan; ~ **trip** Omnibusfahrt.

bush *(fig.)* Aushängeschild, *(inn)* Wirtshaus; **to beat about the** ~ wie die Katze um den heißen Brei herumgehen, um den heißen Brei herumreden; **to go** ~ *(fig.)* untertauchen.

bushel *(Br.)* Scheffel; **to hide one's light under a** ~ sein Licht unter den Scheffel stellen.

bushfighter Guerillakämpfer.

bushranger Wegelagerer, Strauchdieb.

business *(affair)* Angelegenheit, Sache, Geschäft, *(agenda)* Tagesordnung, *(audience)* Theaterpublikum, *(bargain)* Abschluß, Geschäft, *(total box-office receipts)* Gesamteinnahme, *(bustle)* Betriebsamkeit, *(calling)* Beruf, Geschäft, Beschäftigung, Gewerbe, Geschäftszweig, Tätigkeitsbereich, *(commercial house)* Geschäfts-, Handelsbetrieb, -unternehmen, Firma, Geschäft, *(customers)* Kundschaft, *(duty)* Aufgabe, Obliegenheit, Pflicht, *(entreaty)* Anliegen, *(shop)* [Laden]geschäft, Geschäftslokal, *(stock exchange)* Abschlüsse, *(trade)* Handel, Geschäftsleben, *(turnover)* Umsatz, *(workplace)* Arbeitsstätte, -platz; **anchored in** ~ in der Geschäftswelt verankert; **away on** ~ geschäftlich verreist; **before commencing** ~ vor Geschäftsbeginn; **held up by** ~ geschäftlich verhindert; **in** ~ im Geschäftsleben; **on** ~ geschäftlich, geschäftehalber, in Geschäftsangelegenheiten; **on the way to** ~ auf dem Wege zur Arbeit; **strictly for** ~ nur zu Geschäftszwecken; **within the ordinary course of** ~ im normalen Geschäftsverlauf; **doing** ~ *(US)* Unterhaltung eines Geschäftsbetriebes; ~ **done** *(stock exchange)* tatsächlich getätigte Börsenabschlüsse; **no** ~ **[done]** ohne Umsatz (Abschlüsse); **acceptance** ~ Akzeptgeschäft; **actual** ~ effektives Geschäft; **agency** ~ Agenturgeschäft; **banking** ~ Bankgewerbe; **big** ~ *(US)* führende Geschäftsleute, Großunternehmen, -industrie; **big-block** ~ *(stock exchange)* Pakethandel; **booming** ~ glänzend gehendes (glänzendes) Geschäft; **brisk** ~ lebhaftes Geschäft;

capital-oriented ~ kapitalintensives Unternehmen; **car-hire** ~ Mietwagengeschäft; **less-than-carload** ~ *(railroad)* Stückgutverkehr; **catering and take-out** ~ Speisenlieferung ins Haus; **chain-store** ~ Kettenladenunternehmen; **commercial** ~ Handelsbetrieb; **competing** ~ Konkurrenzgeschäft, -firma; **contango** ~ Prolongationsgeschäft; **contracting** ~ schrumpfendes Geschäft; **over-the-counter** ~ Tafelgeschäft; **current (daily)** ~ laufende Geschäfte; **departmentalized** ~ *(US)* dezentralisierter Betrieb; **dirty** ~ *(fig.)* sehr unangenehme Sache; **domestic** ~ Inlandsgeschäft; **dull** ~ mattes Geschäft; **existing** ~ schon bestehender Gewerbebetrieb; **extensive** ~ ausgedehnter Geschäftskreis; **family-owned** ~ Familienbetrieb; **fancy-goods** ~ Luxus-, Modewarengeschäft; **farming** ~ Landwirtschaftsbetrieb; **one's father's** ~ väterliches Geschäft; **fishy** ~ *(fig.)* faule Sache; **freight** ~ Spedition[sgeschäft]; **fresh** ~ neue Tagesordnung; **funny** ~ dunkles (zweideutiges) Geschäft; **general** ~ *(agenda)* Verschiedenes, *(insurance, Br.)* Sachversicherung; **going** ~ arbeitender Betrieb; **good** ~ große Umsätze; **hairdressing** ~ Friseurladen, -geschäft; **hard-nosed** ~ Geschäfte um jeden Preis; **high-level** ~ Hochkonjunktur; **high-risk** ~ Geschäftsbetrieb mit besonders hohem Risiko; **hole-and-corner** ~ anrüchiges Geschäft; **hotel** ~ Hoteliergewerbe; **import** ~ Importgeschäft; **incidental** ~ Zwischengeschäft; **incorporated** ~ Gesellschaftsunternehmen; **investment** ~ Anlagegeschäft; **joint** ~ Metageschäft; **land-office** ~ *(US coll.)* flott gehendes Geschäft, Bombengeschäft; **large-block trading** ~ *(stock exchange)* Pakethandel; **large-scale** ~ Großbetrieb; **law** ~ Rechtsangelegenheit; **long-term** ~ *(insurance, Br.)* Personenversicherung; **losing** ~ verlustbringendes Geschäft; **lucrative** ~ lukratives (einträgliches) Geschäft; **mail-order** ~ Versandhausgeschäft; **medium-sized** ~ mittelgroße Firma, Mittelbetrieb; **mercantile** ~ Handelsgeschäft; **new** ~ Neuabschlüsse; **nobody's** ~ außergewöhnliche Angelegenheit; **nonessential** ~ nicht unbedingt notwendige Arbeitsstelle; **odd** ~ Geschäft in kleinen Effektenabschnitten; **official** ~ Dienstsache; **one-line** ~ Spezialgeschäft; **one-man** ~ Einmannfirma; **option** ~ Terminhandel; **ordinary** ~ normaler Geschäftsgang, *(meetings)* übliche Tagesordnung; **any other** ~ *(agenda)* Verschiedenes, Sonstiges; ~ **overseas** Überseegeschäft; **parliamentary** ~ parlamentarische Angelegenheiten; **paying** ~ lohnendes (rentables) Geschäft; **not paying** ~ (~ **that does not pay)** unrentables Geschäft; **pending** ~ laufende Geschäfte; **picayune** ~ unbedeutendes Geschäft; **poor** ~ schlechtes Geschäft; **pressing** ~ dringendes Geschäft; **primary** ~ Hauptangelegenheit, wichtigste Aufgabe, wesentlichste Angelegenheit; **private** ~ Privatwirtschaft; **profitable** ~ nutzbringendes (gewinnbringendes, rentables) Geschäft; **public** ~ Unternehmen der öffentlichen Hand; **publishing** ~ Verlagsbuchhandel; **purchasing** ~ Einkaufstätigkeit; **railway express** ~ Expreßgutverkehr; **real-estate** ~ Immobiliengeschäft; **regular** ~ laufende Geschäfte; **remunerative** ~ lohnendes (einträgliches) Geschäft; **retail** ~ Einzelhandelsgeschäft; **risky** ~ gewagtes Geschäft; **rival** ~ Konkurrenzunternehmen; **roaring** ~ Bombengeschäft; **routine** ~ normale (laufende) Geschäftsangelegenheiten, *(fig.)* geistlose Beschäftigung; **safe** ~ sicheres Geschäft; **[early-]season** ~ [Vor]saisongeschäft; **[late-]season** ~ [Nach]saisongeschäft; **shady** ~ faules Geschäft, dunkles Gewerbe, zweifelhaftes Geschäft; **sham** ~ Scheingeschäft; **shipping** ~ *(US)* Transportgewerbe; **silly** ~ *(fig.)* dumme Sache; **slack** ~ ruhiges Geschäft; **slower** ~ Umsatzrückgang; **small** ~ *(US)* Mittel- und Kleinbetriebe, gewerblicher Mittelstand; **small infant** ~ *(US)* Kleinstbetrieb; **sound** ~ gesundes Unternehmen; **special** ~ *(company)* besondere Geschäftsvorfälle, *(meetings)* besondere Tagesordnungspunkte; **speculative** ~ Spekulationsgeschäft; **spot** ~ Platzgeschäft; **surety** ~ Kautionsversicherungsgeschäft; **total** ~ Gesamtumsatz; ~ **transacted** abgeschlossenes Geschäft, *(company meeting)* behandelte Tagesordnungspunkte; **unauthorized** ~ unbefugter Geschäftsabschluß; **unfinished** ~ *(agenda)* Unerledigtes; **union** ~ gewerkschaftliche Tätigkeit; **unofficial** ~ *(stock exchange, Br.)* Freiverkehr; **wearying** ~ aufreibende Angelegenheit; **well-established** ~ gut eingeführtes Geschäft; **well-situated** ~ Geschäft in guter Lage; **wholesale** ~ Großhandels-, Engrosgeschäft;

~ **of accepting bills** Akzeptgeschäft; ~ **on joint account** Konsortialgeschäft; ~ **for own account** Propre-, Eigengeschäft; ~ **of banking** Bankgeschäft; ~ **in used cars** Gebrauchtwagengeschäft; ~ **of the community** Gemeindeangelegenheit; ~ **done for the monthly clearance** Ultimogeschäft; ~ **with first-rate connections** Geschäft mit erstklassigem Kundenkreis; ~ **of distribution** Verteilergewerbe; ~ **in futures** Lieferungs-, Zeit-, Termingeschäft; ~ **of government** Regierungsaufgaben,

-geschäfte; ~ **of innkeepers** Gaststättengewerbe; ~ **of the instalment system** Abzahlungsgeschäft; ~ **of insurance** Versicherungsgeschäft; ~ **affected with a public interest** im öffentlichen Interesse liegendes Gewerbe; ~ **at issue** *(law court)* anstehende Sache; ~ **before the meeting** Tagesordnung; ~ **of merchandising** Warenhandel; ~ **of same nature** gleichartiger Geschäftsbetrieb; ~ **of similar nature** ähnlicher Geschäftsbetrieb; ~ **of peddling** Wandergewerbe; ~ **in question** betreffendes Geschäft; ~ **in securities** Effektenhandel; ~ **of spying** Spionagegeschäft; ~ **of the state** Staatsangelegenheiten; ~ **in the street** *(US)* nachbörsliche Geschäftsabschlüsse; ~ **transacted at large** im großen betriebenes Geschäft; ~ **to be transacted** vorgesehene Tagesordnung; ~ **of transportation** Transportgewerbe; ~ **before us** vorliegende Sache;

to accord permission to transact ~ Gewerbelizenz erteilen; **to affect** ~ Geschäft beeinträchtigen; **to attend to one's** ~ seinen Geschäften nachgehen; **to attend strictly to** ~ sich nur ums Geschäft kümmern; **to be about one's master's** ~ für seinen Dienstherrn tätig sein; **to be all** ~ nur Geschäftsmann sein, sich nur fürs Geschäft interessieren; **to be away on** ~ geschäftlich unterwegs sein; **to be at the bottom of a** ~ hinter der ganzen Sache stecken; **to be in** ~ in Betrieb sein, geschäftlich (kaufmännisch) tätig sein; **to be in** ~ **for o. s.** auf eigene Rechnung arbeiten; **to be connected in** ~ **with s. o.** mit jem. in Geschäftsverbindung stehen; **to be cut out for** ~ geborener Geschäftsmann sein; **to be detained by** ~ geschäftlich aufgehalten werden; **to be employed in a line of** ~ in einer Branche tätig sein; **to be engaged in** ~ sich geschäftlich betätigen, kaufmännisch tätig sein; **to be exact in** ~ im Geschäftsleben (in geschäftlichen Dingen) zuverlässig sein; **to be going to A on** ~ geschäftlich nach A fahren; **to be intent on one's** ~ sich nur um sein Geschäft kümmern; **to be liberal in** ~ im Geschäftsleben großzügig sein; **to be on** ~ beruflich zu tun haben; **to be out of** ~ sich zurückgezogen haben; **to be out of the whole** ~ sich nicht mehr im Geschäft auskennen; **to be s. one's own** ~ jds. eigene Angelegenheit sein; **to be sick of the whole** ~ den ganzen Kram satt haben; **to be used entirely for** ~ nur geschäftlich benutzt werden; **to be well versed in** ~ geschickter Geschäftsmann sein; **to be in** ~ **on one's own account** sein eigenes Geschäft haben (besitzen); **to be in a bad way of** ~ schlechtes Geschäft machen; **to be in a large way of** ~ bedeutendes Geschäft haben; **to boost** ~ Wirtschaft ankurbeln, Konjunktur anheizen; **to bring** ~ Kunden werben; **to bring a** ~ **to a successful conclusion** Geschäft zu einem erfolgreichen Abschluß bringen; **to build up a** ~ Geschäftsbetrieb aufbauen; **to build up a** ~ **on a sound basis** fundierte Geschäftsgründung vornehmen; **to carry on a** ~ Geschäft führen, Firma weiterführen; **to carry on the company's** ~ **so far as is necessary** Firmengeschäfte im erforderlichen Ausmaß einstweilig fortführen; **to carry on** ~ **on one's own account** Geschäft auf eigene Rechnung führen; **to carry on** ~ **in common with a view to profit** auf Gewinn ausgerichtetes Unternehmen gemeinsam betreiben; **to carry on the** ~ **of banking** Bankgeschäft betreiben; **to carry on the** ~ **of broker** Maklergeschäft betreiben; **to carry on a** ~ **on a large scale** Geschäfte in großem Maßstab betreiben; **to carry on a wholesale** ~ Großhandel betreiben; **to carry on a** ~ **in a small way** kleines Geschäft unterhalten; **to carry on the** ~ **under one's name** Geschäft unter seinem eigenen Namen führen; **to cease** ~ Geschäftsbetrieb einstellen; **to cease to carry on** ~ Geschäft nicht weiterführen; **to change one's line of** ~ Geschäftszweck ändern; **to come on** ~ in einer geschäftlichen Angelegenheit kommen; **to come to** ~ zur Sache kommen; **to commence** ~ Betrieb eröffnen; **to conclude a** ~ Geschäft abschließen; **to conduct a** ~ Geschäft führen; **to conduct law** ~ Prozesse führen; **to continue a deceased's** ~ Geschäft eines Verstorbenen fortführen; **to continue** ~ **on a cash basis** Verkäufe weiterhin als Kassageschäfte abwickeln; **to continue a** ~ **for one's own ends** Geschäft im eigenen Interesse fortführen; **to continue the** ~ **for the purpose of winding up** Geschäft bis zur Liquidation fortführen; **to deal with current** ~ laufende Geschäfte erledigen; **to deal with fresh** ~ in eine neue Tagesordnung eintreten; **to diversify away from a** ~ Geschäftssparte aufgeben; **to do** ~ geschäftlich tätig sein; **to do** ~ **as a banker** Bankier sein; **to do s. one's** ~ *(coll.)* jem. den Garaus machen; **to do big** ~ Großhandel betreiben; **to do good** ~ gute Geschäfte (Umsätze) machen; **to do** ~ **under the name of** unter dem Namen firmieren; **to do large** ~ **in ...** große Umsätze in ... tätigen; **to do a lively** ~ flotte Umsätze machen; **to do** ~ **with s. o.** Geschäftsbeziehungen mit jem. unterhalten; **to double** ~ Geschäftsvolumen (Umsatz) verdoppeln; **to drop out of a** ~ Geschäftszweig aufgeben; **to drum up** ~ Geschäft ankurbeln; **to embark upon a** ~ sich auf ein Geschäft einlassen; **to engage in a line of** ~ in einer Branche arbeiten; **to enliven** ~ Wirtschaft ankurbeln; **to enter private** ~ in die Wirtschaft gehen; **to entrust serious** ~ **to irresponsibles** wichtige Geschäftsangelegenheiten ungeeigneten Leuten übertragen; **to establish a** ~ Geschäft gründen; **to expand one's** ~ sein Geschäft erweitern (ausdehnen); **to face the collapse of one's** ~ vor dem geschäftlichen Zusammenbruch stehen; **to fail in** ~ bankrott machen; **to finance a** ~ Geschäft finanzieren; **to follow a** ~ einem Geschäft nachgehen; **to force s. o. out of** ~ j. aus dem Geschäft drängen; **to gain by one's** ~ bei seinem Geschäft verdienen; **to get** ~ Kundschaft erwerben; **to get down to** ~ zur Sache kommen; **to get to** ~ sich an die Arbeit machen; **to give s. o. sight into** ~ jem. geschäftlichen Einblick gewähren; **to give up one's** ~ sein Geschäft aufgeben; **to go about one's** ~ sich seinen Geschäften widmen; **to go about one's lawful** ~ einer geregelten Beschäftigung nachgehen; **to go into** ~ kaufmännischen Beruf ergreifen; **to go into** ~ **for o. s.** sich selbständig machen; **to go out of** ~ Geschäft aufgeben, aus einem Geschäft aussteigen; **to go out on** ~ *(sales agent)* auf [Vertreter-] tour gehen; **to grab** ~ Geschäfte wegnehmen; **to handle all sorts of** ~ Geschäfte aller Art erledigen; **to have** ~ **with s. o.** Geschäftsbeziehungen mit jem. haben; **to have a good run of** ~ gute Geschäfte machen; **to have no** ~ kein Recht haben; **to have no** ~ **to do s. th.** keinen Auftrag zu etw. haben; **to have a share in a** ~ Geschäftsanteil haben; **to have a small** ~ kleinen Handel betreiben; **to increase** ~ Umsatz steigern; **to introduce a private car into the** ~ Privatwagen ins Geschäft einbringen; **to invest money in a** ~ Geld in ein Geschäft stecken; **to keep in** ~ verdienen lassen; **to keep out of a** ~ sich aus einer Sache heraushalten; **to know one's** ~ sein Geschäft verstehen; **to know the** ~ **inside out** Geschäft von der Pike auf kennen; **to lose** ~ Geschäftsverluste erleiden, Kundschaft verlieren; **to make it one's** ~ etw. zu seiner Aufgabe machen; **to make over one's** ~ **to one's son** sein Geschäft auf den Sohn übertragen; **to manage the** ~ Geschäftsführer sein; **to mean** ~ *(fam.)* ernsthaft reflektieren (interessiert sein), es ernst meinen; **to mind one's own** ~ sich um seine eigenen Angelegenheiten kümmern; **to mix** ~ **with pleasure** das Angenehme mit dem Nützlichen verbinden; **to neglect one's** ~ seine Geschäfte vernachlässigen; **to open a** ~ Geschäft eröffnen; **to open a** ~ **on a large scale** Geschäft großzügig aufziehen; **to operate one's own** ~ eigenes Geschäft betreiben; **to place in a** ~ in einem Geschäft anlegen; **to play a part in a** ~ an einer Sache beteiligt sein; **to plough back in** ~ wieder im Geschäft anlegen; **to proceed to** ~ in die Tagesordnung eintreten; **to proceed to the next** ~ weiteren Punkt der Tagesordnung behandeln; **to proceed with the** ~ **of the day** Tagesordnung behandeln; **to pursue a line of** ~ einem Geschäftszweig (Gewerbe) nachgehen; **to put out of** ~ brotlos machen, *(firm)* aus dem Markt drängen; **to put through a** ~ Geschäft zu einem erfolgreichen Abschluß bringen; **to put a** ~ **back on its feet again** Geschäft wieder in die Höhe bringen; **to quit** ~ sich aus dem Geschäft[sleben] zurückziehen, sich zur Ruhe setzen; **to rate a** ~ Geschäft zu Kreditauskunftszwecken beurteilen; **to reckon a** ~ **generally as prosperous** Geschäftsbranche generell für gewinnträchtig halten; **to reduce a** ~ **one half** Geschäft um die Hälfte verkleinern; **to register a** ~ Gewerbe anmelden; **to remain active in** ~ im Geschäft tätig bleiben; **to remain in possession of a** ~ Geschäfte weiterführen dürfen; **to resume** ~ Geschäft wieder eröffnen, *(agenda)* wieder in die Tagesordnung eintreten; **to retire from** ~ sich aus dem Geschäft[sleben] zurückziehen; **to ride out a contraction of** ~ mit abnehmendem Geschäftsvolumen fertig werden; **to run a** ~ Gewerbe ausüben; **to secure a** ~ Geschäft zustande bringen; **to see s. o. on** ~ j. geschäftlich sprechen; **to sell out one's** ~ sein Geschäft verkaufen; **to sell out one's share of** ~ seinen Geschäftsanteil verkaufen; **to send s. o. about his** ~ j. kurz abfertigen; **to set a** ~ **on foot** Geschäft auf die Beine bringen; **to set up in** ~ **in competition** Konkurrenzbetrieb eröffnen; **to set up a** ~ **on a sound basis** fundierte Geschäftsgründung vornehmen; **to settle** ~ Geschäfte abwickeln (abschließen), Angelegenheit ins Reine bringen; **to settle down to** ~ sich ernstlich an die Arbeit machen; **to shirk one's** ~ seine Geschäfte vernachlässigen; **to squeeze out of** ~ aus dem Geschäft drängen; **to start a** ~ Geschäft errichten (gründen), in ein Geschäft einsteigen, sich etablieren; **to state one's** ~ **to the secretary** seine Wünsche der Sekretärin vortragen; **to stay in** ~ im Geschäft bleiben; **to stick to** ~ bei der Stange bleiben; **to stimulate** ~ Konjunktur intensivieren; **to succeed to a** ~ Geschäft übernehmen; **to take over a** ~ Firma übernehmen; **to talk about** ~ von Geschäften reden; **to train s. o. in** ~ j. für das Geschäft anlernen; **to transact** ~ geschäftlich tätig sein; **to transact** ~ **with s. o.** Geschäftsverbin-

dung mit jem. aufrechterhalten, geschäftliche Verbindungen mit jem. pflegen; **to transact any other ordinary** ~ übrige Tagesordnungspunkte erledigen; **to transfer a** ~ **from payment of invoices to open-account terms** vom Barzahlungs- zum Kontokorrentverkehr übergehen; **to travel on** ~ geschäftlich unterwegs sein, sich auf einer Geschäftsreise befinden; **to turn one's thoughts to** ~ **again** sich wieder seinen Geschäften zuwenden; **to use a garage only half for** ~ Garage nur teilweise gewerblich nutzen; **to wind up a** ~ Geschäft liquidieren; **to withdraw from** ~ sich vom Geschäft zurückziehen; **to work up a** ~ Betrieb zum Erfolg bringen, Geschäft hochbringen; **to write to new** ~ **next month** *(insurance)* im laufenden Monat keine Geschäfte mehr tätigen;

all ~ ganz sachlich;

~ **ability** kaufmännische Fähigkeiten, geschäftliche Leistungsfähigkeit; ~ **accomplishment** kaufmännische Fähigkeit; ~ **account** Geschäftskonto; ~ **action** Geschäftsvorgang; ~ **activity** Geschäftstätigkeit; ~ **acumen** Geschäftssinn, geschäftlicher Weitblick; ~ **address** Büroadresse, Firmenanschrift; ~ **administration** *(US)* Betriebswirtschaft[slehre]; ~ **administrator** Verwaltungsfachmann; ~ **advertisement** Geschäftsanzeige; ~ **advertiser** Wirtschaftswerbung betreibendes Unternehmen; ~ **advertising** Geschäftsreklame, Wirtschaftswerbung; ~ **affair** geschäftliche Angelegenheit; **routine** ~ **affairs** laufende Geschäftsangelegenheiten; ~ **agent** [Handels]vertreter, *(US, trade union)* Gewerkschaftsvertreter; ~ **agreement** Wirtschaftsabkommen; ~ **ailments** Krankheitserscheinungen eines Betriebes; ~ **aircraft (airplane)** Firmen-, Betriebsflugzeug; ~ **allowance** *(income tax)* Werbungskosten; ~ **analysis** Konjunkturanalyse; ~ **analyst** Konjunkturanalytiker; ~ **application** Antrag auf Erteilung einer Gewerbelizenz; ~ **appointment** geschäftliche Verabredung; ~ **area** Geschäftszone, -gebiet; ~ **arithmetic** kaufmännisches Rechnen; ~ **arrangement** geschäftliche Vereinbarung; ~ **assets** Geschäfts-, Betriebsvermögen; **to be a long-term** ~ **asset** zu den langfristigen Aktivposten eines Unternehmens zählen; ~ **associate** Geschäftsfreund; ~ **association** Geschäftsverbindung, *(trade association)* Wirtschaftsvereinigung; ~ **attitude** Geschäftsverhalten; ~ **auditing service** Buch- und Betriebsprüfung; ~ **background** wirtschaftlicher Hintergrund; ~ **bank** Geschäftsbank; ~ **barometer** Wirtschaftsbarometer; ~ **base** geschäftliche Basis; **to spread its** ~ **base** Grundlage seines Unternehmens verbreitern; ~ **basis** Geschäftsgrundlage; ~ **behavio(u)r** Benehmen im Betrieb; **conscious parallel** ~ **behavio(u)r** *(cartel law)* bewußt gleichlautendes Geschäftsverhalten; **better** ~ **bet** bessere Geschäftschancen; ~ **block** Geschäftsblock; ~ **bonanza** hohe Gewinne abwerfendes Geschäft; ~ **boom** Konjunktur[periode]; ~ **boosting program(me)** Konjunkturprogramm; ~ **borrower** gewerblicher Darlehnsnehmer; ~ **borrowing** gewerbliche Darlehnsaufnahme, Geschäftskredit; ~ **branch** Geschäftszweig, -sparte; ~ **bribery** Bestechung durch die Geschäftswelt (Wirtschaft); ~ **briefs** Kurznachrichten aus der Wirtschaft; ~ **budget** Geschäftsetat, Firmenbudget; **multiple storey** ~ **building** mehrstöckiges Bürogebäude; ~ **buying** Geschäftseinkäufe; ~ **call** Geschäftsbesuch, *(tel.)* Dienstgespräch; ~ **capacity** Geschäftsfähigkeit, -gewandtheit; ~ **capital** Firmen-, Gewerbe-, Betriebs-, Geschäftskapital; ~ **car** Firmen-, Geschäftswagen; ~ **card** Visiten-, Geschäftskarte; ~ **career** berufliche Laufbahn; ~ **cartel** Wirtschaftskartell; ~ **case** Geschäftsvorfall; ~ **casualties** Betriebskonkurse; ~ **center** *(US)* **(centre,** *Br.)* Wirtschafts-, Handels-, Geschäftszentrum; ~ **change** Konjunkturveränderung; ~ **changes** geschäftliche Veränderungen; ~ **circles** Wirtschaftskreise; ~ **cliché** geschäftsüblicher Ausdruck; ~ **client** Geschäftskunde; ~ **climate** Konjunkturklima; ~ **clothes** Berufskleidung; ~ **code** Geschäftskode; ~ **collapse** wirtschaftlicher Zusammenbruch; ~ **college** *(US)* Handelsakademie, -schule; ~ **columns** Geschäftsanzeigen; **to graduate from a** ~ **college** *(US)* [etwa] Kaufmannsprüfung bestehen; ~ **combination** Firmenzusammenschluß; **new** ~ **commission** Abschlußprovision; ~ **commitments** geschäftliche Verpflichtungen, Geschäftsverbindlichkeiten; ~ **committee** Firmenausschuß; ~ **communication** Geschäftsmitteilung; ~ **community** Geschäftswelt, Wirtschaftskreise, Geschäftszentrum; **to wind up a** ~ **company** Geschäft liquidieren; ~ **compulsion** geschäftliche Nötigung; ~ **concentration** Betriebskonzentration; ~ **concern** Geschäftsunternehmen, -betrieb; ~ **concerns** Geschäftsinteressen; ~ **concert** Geschäftsvereinbarung; ~ **conditions** Wirtschaftsverhältnisse; **general** ~ **conditions** allgemeines Wirtschaftsleben, Konjunkturbedingungen; ~ **conditions in the shipbuilding industry** Konjunktur in der Schiffsbauindustrie; ~ **conference** geschäftliche Besprechung; ~ **confidence** Vertrauen in die

Wirtschaftslage; ~ **confines** Grenzen des Geschäftslebens; ~ **connection** Geschäftsverbindung, *(business firm)* befreundete Firma; **very good ~ connections** lebhafte Geschäftsbeziehungen; **to establish ~ connections** Geschäftsbeziehungen anknüpfen; **to have ~ connections** Geschäftsverkehr haben; **to open new ~ connections** neue Geschäftsverbindungen anbahnen; **to open up ~ connections with a firm** in geschäftliche Beziehungen zu einer Firma treten; ~ **consultant** *(US)* Betriebsberater; ~ **contacts** geschäftliche Kontakte; **to make ~ contacts** Geschäftsverbindungen anknüpfen; ~ **contract** Wirtschaftsabkommen, -vertrag; ~ **contraction** Geschäftsrückgang; **[wartime] ~ control** [Kriegs]wirtschaftskontrolle; ~ **conversation** geschäftliche Besprechung; ~**cooperation committee** Kooperationsausschuß der Wirtschaft; ~ **corporation** *(US)* Handels-, Erwerbsgesellschaft, Geschäftsunternehmen, geschäftliches Unternehmen; ~ **Corporation Law** *(US)* Gesetz über die Errichtung von Handelsgesellschaften; ~ **correspondence** Handels-, Geschäftskorrespondenz; **to type ~ correspondence** Geschäftskorrespondenz erledigen; ~ **correspondent** Geschäftsfreund, Handelsverbindung; ~ **course** Handelskursus; ~ **creation** Geschäftsgründung; ~ **credit** Geschäfts-, Betriebskredit; ~ **credit relief** Steuervergünstigung für Betriebskredite; ~ **customer** Firmenkunde; ~ **customs** Geschäftsusancen; ~ **cycle** Konjunkturzyklus, -rhythmus, -phase, -ablauf, -verlauf, Wirtschaftskreislauf; **to buck the ~ cycle** *(US)* mit dem Konjunktureinbruch fertig werden; ~**-cycle adjustment** Konjunkturanpassung; ~**-cycle analysis** Konjunkturanalyse; ~**-cycle changes** zyklische Veränderungen; ~**-cycle indicator** Konjunkturindikator; ~**-cycle study** Konjunkturstudie; ~**-cycle terminology** Konjunkturterminologie; ~**-cycle turning** konjunktureller Wendepunkt; ~ **data** geschäftliche (betriebswirtschaftliche) Angaben; ~ **day** Werktag; ~ **dealings** Geschäftsabschlüsse; **to keep up ~ dealings** Geschäftsverbindungen unterhalten; ~ **debts** Geschäftsschulden; ~ **decision** geschäftliche Entscheidung; ~ **decline** Geschäftsrückgang; ~ **deductions** anerkannte Steuerabzugsbeträge; ~ **delegate** Gewerkschaftsvertreter; ~ **demand for credit** Kreditnachfrage der Wirtschaft; ~ **department** *(insurance company)* Akquisitionsabteilung; ~ **depression** Depression, Wirtschaftskrise, Flaute; ~ **development** Geschäftsentwicklung; ~ **development possibilities** geschäftliche Entwicklungsmöglichkeiten; ~ **dictionary** Wirtschaftswörterbuch; ~ **directory** Handelsadreßbuch; ~ **discretion** berufliche Schweigepflicht; ~ **district** Geschäftsgegend; ~ **doctor** Betriebsberater; ~ **documents** Geschäftsakten; ~ **downturn** Konjunkturrückgang; ~ **economics** *(Br.)* Geschäftspolitik, *(economic theory, Br.)* Betriebswirtschaftslehre; ~ **economist** *(US)* Betriebswirt; ~ **edge** Geschäftszweck; ~ **education** kaufmännische Ausbildung; ~ **effects** geschäftliche Auswirkungen; ~ **efficacy** positive geschäftliche Auswirkungen; ~ **end** *(coll.)* geschäftlicher Teil, Hauptteil; **ordinary ~ engagements** laufende kaufmännische Verpflichtungen; ~ **engineer** *(US)* selbständiger Betriebsberater; ~ **English** Handels-, Wirtschafts-, Kaufmannsenglisch; ~ **enterprise** gewerbliches Unternehmen, Wirtschafts-, Handelsunternehmen, Gewerbebetrieb; **large-scale ~ enterprise** Großbetrieb; ~ **entertaining expense allowance** Steuerfreibeträge für die Bewirtung von Geschäftsfreunden; ~ **entertainment** Bewirtung von Geschäftsfreunden; ~ **entity** Gewerbebetrieb; ~ **environment** sozialpolitische Einflußfaktoren; ~ **equipment** Büroausstattung; ~ **errand** Geschäftsbesorgung; ~ **establishment** Gewerbebetrieb; ~ **ethics** Geschäftsmoral; ~ **etiquette** geschäftliche Umgangsformen; ~ **evaluation** Firmenbewertung; ~ **executive** leitender Angestellter, betriebliche (kaufmännische) Führungskraft; ~ **executives** wirtschaftliche Führungskräfte; **top ~ executives** Spitzenkräfte der Wirtschaft; ~ **expansion** wirtschaftliche Expansion, Betriebsexpansion, *(economic cycle)* Konjunkturausweitung; ~ **expenses** Geschäftsunkosten, -spesen; ~ **experience** geschäftliche Erfahrung, Geschäftskenntnis, -erfahrung; **senior-level ~ experience** Geschäftserfahrungen im Bereich der leitenden Angestellten; ~ **experience at management level** geschäftliche Erfahrungen auf Vorstandsebene; ~ **failure** geschäftlicher Zusammenbruch, Zahlungseinstellung; ~ **family** Kaufmannsfamilie; ~ **fiasco** geschäftlicher Mißerfolg; ~ **finance** Unternehmensfinanzierung; ~ **financing** Unternehmens-, Geschäftsfinanzierung; ~ **firm** Handelsfirma; **enterprising ~ firm** unternehmerisch eingestellte Firma; **to level out ~ fluctuations** Konjunkturschwankungen ausgleichen; ~ **flight** Geschäftsflug; ~ **forecaster** Konjunkturprognostiker; ~ **forecast[ing]** Konjunkturprognose; ~ **forecasting service** Konjunkturvorschau; ~ **formation** Konjunkturentwicklung; ~ **fraud** betrügerisches Geschäftsge-

baren; ~ **friend** Geschäftsfreund, Korrespondent; ~ **friendship** Geschäftsfreundschaft; ~ **front** Geschäftswelt; ~ **fund** Betriebsfonds; ~ **future** zukünftige Konjunktur; ~ **gain** Geschäftsgewinn; ~ **gains** Einkünfte aus Gewerbebetrieb; ~ **game** Unternehmensplanspiel; ~ **gaming** Planspieldurchführung; ~ **getting** Akquisition; ~**-getting** akquirierend; ~ **getting department** *(insurance company)* Akquisitionsabteilung; ~ **gift** Werbegeschenk; ~ **gift-giving** Werbegeschenkverteilung; ~ **goods** Wirtschaftsgüter, Halbfabrikate; ~ **guest** Geschäftsfreund; ~ **hand** kaufmännische Handschrift; ~ **hazard** Unternehmerwagnis; ~ **hierarchy** Betriebshierarchie; ~ **history** Wirtschaftsgeschichte; ~ **hours** Geschäftszeit; **after ~ hours** nach Geschäftsschluß; **out of ~ hours** außerhalb der Geschäftsstunden (Geschäftszeit); ~ **house** Geschäftshaus, Firma; **sound ~ house** solide Firma; ~ **image** Firmenimage; ~ **improvement** konjettureller Auftrieb; ~ **income** Einkünfte aus Gewerbebetrieb, gewerbliche Einkünfte; ~ **incorporation** Firmenregistrierung; ~ **index** Handelsindex; ~ **indicator** Konjunkturbarometer, -indikator; **key ~ indicators** Hauptwirtschaftsdaten für die Konjunkturbeurteilung; ~ **inducement** Geschäftsanreiz; ~ **information** geschäftliche Informationen; ~ **institution** Wirtschaftsunternehmen; ~ **insurance** Betriebsversicherung; ~ **intelligence** Wirtschaftsnachrichten; ~ **interest** Geschäftsanteil, Einkünfte aus Gewerbebetrieb; ~ **interests** Geschäftsinteresse, geschäftlichen Interessen; ~ **interruption insurance** Betriebsstillstandsversicherung; ~ **inventory** Betriebsinventar; ~ **investment** Geschäfts-, betriebliche Investition; ~ **investment intentions** geplante Betriebsinvestitionen; ~ **invitee** Geschäftsbesuch; **ordinary ~ items** normale Tagesordnungspunkte; ~ **jet** Betriebsdüsenflugzeug; ~ **journalist** Wirtschaftsjournalist; ~ **journey** Geschäftsreise; ~ **judgment** Geschäftsbeurteilung; **reasonable ~ judgment** im Verkehr erforderliche Sorgfalt; ~ **knowledge** Geschäftskenntnis; ~ **law** Gewerberecht; ~ **leader** Wirtschaftsführer; ~ **leaders** führende Geschäftsleute; ~ **league** geschäftliche Vereinigung; ~ **lendings** Betriebs-, Geschäftskredite; ~ **letter** Geschäftsbrief; ~**-letter writing** Abfassen von Geschäftsbriefen; ~ **liabilities** Betriebs-, Geschäftsschulden; ~ **licence** Gewerbelizenz, -berechtigung, Geschäftserlaubnis; ~ **life** Wirtschaftsleben; ~ **life insurance** Partner-, Teilhaberversicherung; ~ **line** Wirtschaftszweig, Geschäftsbranche; ~ **links** geschäftliche Verbindungen; ~ **loan** Betriebs-, Geschäftskredit; ~ **location** geschäftliche Niederlassung, Geschäftssitz; ~ **looking** geschäftsmäßig aussehend; ~ **loss** Betriebs-, Geschäftsverlust; ~ **lunch[eon]** Arbeitsessen, geschäftliche Mittagsverabredung; ~ **machines** Büromaschinen; ~ **magnate** Großindustrieller; ~ **management** Betriebswirtschaft; ~ **manager** Betriebs-, Geschäftsführer, kaufmännischer Direktor, *(publishing business)* Verlagsleiter; ~ **manners** geschäftliche Umgangsformen; ~ **matter** geschäftliche Angelegenheit; ~ **measures** geschäftliche Dispositionen; ~ **meeting** geschäftliche Verabredung; ~ **method** Geschäftsmethode; ~ **mission** Geschäftsreise; ~ **morals** (morality) Geschäftsmoral; **to set a high standard of ~ morality** strenge Maßstäbe an die Geschäftsmoral anlegen; ~ **movement** Geschäftsleben; ~ **name** Firmen-, Geschäftsname, -bezeichnung; ~ **negotiations** geschäftliche Besprechungen, Verhandlungen; ~ **news** Wirtschaftsnachrichten; ~ **night** *(parl.)* Sitzungsabend; ~ **notice** Geschäftsmitteilungen, *(newspaper)* Bezugsbedingungen; ~ **obligations** Geschäftsverbindlichkeiten; ~ **observer** wirtschaftlicher Beobachter; ~ **occupation** kaufmännischer Beruf, gewerbliche Tätigkeit; ~ **office** Geschäftslokal; ~ **operation** Geschäftsbetrieb, -tätigkeit; ~ **opportunities** geschäftliche Möglichkeiten; ~ **organization** Geschäftsgründung; ~ **outfit** Geschäftsbetrieb; ~ **outlets** Wirtschaftsmärkte; ~ **outlook** Geschäftslage, -prognose, Wirtschaftsvorschau, *(business cycle)* Konjunkturaussichten; **to broaden one's ~ outlook** seine Wirtschaftskenntnisse vertiefen; ~ **owner** Geschäftsinhaber, -eigentümer; ~ **ownership** wirtschaftliches Eigentum; **sluggish ~ pace** lustlose Geschäftstätigkeit; ~ **package** *(airline)* Sondertarifangebot für Geschäftsreisende; ~ **page** Wirtschaftsteil einer Zeitung; ~ **paper** Wirtschafts-, Handelsblatt, *(trade acceptance)* Warenwechsel; ~ **part [of a town]** Geschäftszentrum; ~ **participation** Geschäftsbeteiligung; **to reshape ~ patterns** Modellformen in der Wirtschaft umgestalten; ~ **people** Geschäftsleute; ~ **performance** wirtschaftliche Leistungskraft; ~ **picture** Konjunkturbild; ~ **plan** Geschäftsvorhaben; ~ **planning** betriebliche Planung; **from a ~ point of view** geschäftlich betrachtet; ~ **policy** Geschäftsgebaren, Geschäftspolitik, -methoden; ~ **policy issues** geschäftspolitische Probleme; ~ **position** wirtschaftliche Stellung; ~ **practices** *(cartel law)* Geschäftsmethoden, -praktiken; **unfair ~ practices** unlautere Geschäftsmethoden; **deceptive ~ practices** *(US)* unlautere Machenschaften; **unethical ~practices** standeswidriges Geschäftsgebaren; **~ prediction** Konjunkturprognose; **~ premises** Geschäftsgrundstück, -lokal, Firmengebäude, Betriebsstätte; **~ press** Werbemitteilung; **~ principle** Geschäftsprinzip; **to retain one's ~ privacy** sein geschäftliches Interesse nicht sichtbar machen; **~ proceeds** Ertrag; **~ profit** Geschäftsgewinn; **~ profits** Einkünfte aus Gewerbebetrieb; **~ profit tax** Gewerbesteuer; **~ prognosis** Wirtschafts-, Konjunkturvorschau; **~ progress** Konjunkturanstieg; **to speed up one's ~ progress** sein berufliches Vorwärtskommen beschleunigen; **~ project** Geschäftsvorhaben, -projekt; **to show early ~ promise** früh vielversprechendes geschäftliches Talent zeigen; **~ promotion** wirtschaftliche Förderung; **~ property** *(asset)* Geschäfts-, Betriebsgrundstück, Geschäftsvermögen; **~ property appraisal** Taxe eines Geschäftsgrundstücks; **~ proportion** *(premises)* geschäftlich genutzter Teil; **~ proposition** geschäftlicher Vorschlag, Geschäftsvorschlag; **~ prospects** Konjunktur-, Geschäftsaussichten; **~ prosperity** Konjunkturauftrieb; **~ psychology** Betriebspsychologie; **~ publication** Wirtschaftsmagazin, geschäftliche Mitteilungen; **~ publications** Geschäftsmitteilungen; **~ purpose** Geschäftszweck, gewerblicher Zweck; **~ pursuit** geschäftliche Angelegenheit; **~ quarter** Geschäftsviertel, -gegend; **~ reactions** Reaktion der Geschäftswelt; **to justify a trip with good ~ reasons** Geschäftsreise mit zwingenden Gründen belegen; **~ recession** Geschäftsrückgang, Rezession; **~ record** Geschäftsbericht, -unterlagen, -bücher; **~ records** Geschäftsbücher, -unterlagen; **~ recovery** Wiedergesundung der Wirtschaft, Konjunkturbelebung; **~ reference** geschäftliche Empfehlung; **to escalate ~ regulation** Reglementierung der Wirtschaft eskalierend vorantreiben; **~ relations** Geschäftsverbindung, -beziehungen; **to be engaged in (have) ~ relations** in Geschäftsverbindung stehen; **~ relationship** Geschäftsverbindung; **~ reorganization** Firmensanierung; **~ reply card (envelope,** *US)* [bezahlte] Rückantwort, Freiumschlag; **~ reply mail** Werbeantwort; **~ reply service** Werbeantwortdienst; **~ report** Wirtschafts-, Geschäftsbericht; **~ reporter** Wirtschaftskorrespondent; **~ representatives** Repräsentanten der Wirtschaft; **~ reputation** geschäftliches Ansehen, Kredit; **~ research** Konjunkturforschung; **~ research institute** Konjunkturforschungsinstitut; **~ reserves** Betriebsreserven; **~ review** Wirtschaftszeitschrift; **~ revival** Geschäftsbelebung; **~ risk** Geschäftsrisiko; **~ round** Geschäftsreise, Tour; **~ roundup** Wirtschaftsumschau; **~ rules** *(US)* Geschäftsordnung; **~ savings** Abschreibungen plus nicht ausgeschüttete Gewinne; **~ savvy** Geschäftsverstand; **~ scale rate** Gewerbesteuersatz; **on the European ~ scene** im europäischen Wirtschaftsleben; **~ scheme** Geschäftsvorhaben; **~ school** Wirtschaftshochschule; **~ secret** Geschäftsgeheimnis; **~ section** Geschäftsgegend; **~ sector** Unternehmenssektor; **private ~ sector** private Wirtschaft; **~ seminar** Wirtschafts-, Betriebsseminar; **~ sense** Geschäftsklugheit, Erwerbssinn; **~ sense of all ~ men** allgemeine kaufmännische Anschauung; **to make ~ sense** sich geschäftlich auszahlen; **to make good ~ sense** kommerziell gesehen vernünftig sein; **~ setback** Konjunkturrückschlag; **~ share** Geschäftsanteil; **~ situation** Wirtschaftslage, -aussichten, konjunkturelle Situation; **unfavo(u)rable ~ situation** ungünstige Konjunktur; **~ situs** Sitz des Unternehmens, Geschäftssitz; **~ skill** Geschäftsgewandtheit; **~ slang** Geschäftssprache; **~ slowdown** verlangsamte Konjunkturbewegung; **domestic ~ slowdown** rückläufige Binnenkonjunktur; **~ slump** rückläufige Konjunktur, konjunkturelle Baissezeit; **~ solvency** Zahlungsfähigkeit; **~ sorrows** Geschäftssorgen; **~ spending** Investitionsaufwand; **~ spirit** Geschäftssinn; **~ stagnation** Geschäftsstockung; **~ standing** geschäftliches Ansehen, wirtschaftliche Position; **~ stationary** Geschäftsdrucksachen; **~ statistics** Betriebs-, Wirtschaftsstatistik; **~ street** Geschäftsstraße; **~ structure** Wirtschaftsstruktur; **~ struggle** Konkurrenzkampf; **~ study** kaufmännische Ausbildung; **~ style** Geschäftsverhalten; **~ success** Geschäftserfolg; **~ successor** Geschäftsnachfolger; **~ suit** Tages-, Geschäftsanzug, *(US)* guter dunkler Straßenanzug; **~ support** Unterstützung aus Wirtschaftskreisen; **~ switchboard** *(tel.)* Werkszentrale; **~ syndicate** Wirtschaftsvereinigung; **~ systems allied with entrepreneurial skill** unternehmerische Fähigkeiten voraussetzende Geschäftsbereiche; **~ tax** Gewerbesteuer; **~ taxation** Gewerbesteuer, -steuerwesen; **~ tempo** Konjunkturtempo; **~ tendencies** konjunkturelle Entwicklung; **~ tensions** geschäftliche Anstrengungen; **~ terminology** Wirtschaftsterminologie; **~ thinking** kaufmännische Denkweise; **~ ties** wirtschaftliche

Bindungen; **~ title** Berufsbezeichnung; **~ tour** Geschäftsreise; **~ town** Einkaufsstadt; **~ trade** Handelsverkehr; **~ trainee** kaufmännischer Lehrling, als Kaufmann Auszubildender; **~ training** kaufmännische Ausbildung; **~ training background** kaufmännischer Werdegang; **~ transaction** Geschäftsabschluß, vorfall, -gang; **to have ~ transactions with s. o.** mit jem. in Geschäftsverbindung stehen; **~ transfer** Geschäftsübertragung; **~ transfer agent** Nachweismakler; **~ travel** Geschäftsreise; **~ traveller** Geschäftsreisender; **~ trend** Geschäftsverlauf, -gang, *(economical cycle)* Konjunkturentwicklung; **regressive ~ trend** kontraktive Lageänderung, Konjunkturrückgang; **upward ~ trend** konjunkturelle Aufwärtsbewegung, Konjunkturaufstieg, -aufschwung; **~ trick** Geschäftstrick; **~ trip** Geschäfts-, Dienstreise; **~ truck** Betriebslastwagen; **~ trust** treuhänderisch geleitetes Unternehmen; **~ turning point** konjunktureller Wendepunkt; **~ tycoon** Großindustrieller; **~ undertaking** kaufmännisches Unternehmen, Geschäftsbetrieb; **~ upturn** Konjunkturaufschwung; **~ usage** Geschäfts-, Handelsgebrauch; **~ use** Betriebszweck; **~ user** gewerblicher Verbraucher; **~ venture** geschäftliches Unternehmen; **~ visa** Geschäftsvisum; **~ visitor** Geschäftsbesuch; **~ volume** Geschäftsvolumen; **~ ways** geschäftliche Möglichkeiten; **~ winner** geschäftlicher Erfolg; **~-wise** geschäftlich; **~ woman** Geschäftsfrau; **~ world** Geschäftswelt, -leben; **~ writing** Geschäftskorrespondenz, -verkehr.

business year Geschäftsjahr;
current ~ laufendes Geschäftsjahr; **last ~** abgelaufenes Geschäftsjahr; **natural ~** vom Kalenderjahr abweichendes Geschäftsjahr; **normal ~** normales Geschäftsjahr; **past ~** abgelaufenes Geschäftsjahr.

business zone Handelsgebiet, -zone.

businesslike geschäftsmäßig;
~ letter kühler (nüchterner) Geschäftsbrief; **to do in a ~ way** geschäftsmäßig erledigen.

businessman Kauf-, Geschäftsmann;
big ~ einflußreicher Geschäftsmann; **high-level ~** hochqualifizierter Geschäftsmann; **high-placed ~** wohldotierter Geschäftsmann; **prudent ~** umsichtiger Kaufmann; **shrewd ~** gewiegter Geschäftsmann; **serious ~** ordentlicher Kaufmann; **smart ~** gerissener Geschäftsmann;
~ in the news Wirtschaft im Tagesspiegel;
to be a keen ~ hinter seinem Geschäft her sein; **to be ~ all the time** sich nur für das Geschäft interessieren; **to make a successful ~** erfolgreichen Kaufmann abgeben; **to prove o. s. a good ~** sich als guter Geschäftsmann erweisen.

businessman's | bank Geschäftsbank; **~ lawyer** Wirtschaftsanwalt.

businessmen Geschäftsleute;
slow-to-invest ~ investitionsvorsichtige Wirtschaft; **small ~** kleine Geschäftsleute;
~ in the news Wirtschaftler im Tagesspiegel; **~ engaged in international trade** internationale Geschäftswelt;
to be nice to ~ wirtschaftsfreundlich sein.

businesswoman Geschäfts-, Kauffrau;
to be a good ~ geschäftüchtig sein.

busman Autobus-, Omnibusfahrer;
~'s holiday Berufsarbeit in der Freizeit.

bust Reinfall, *(bankruptcy)* Pleite, Bankrott, *(film)* Nah-, Großaufnahme;
agricultural ~ Zusammenbruch der Landwirtschaft;
~ (v.) bankrott machen, pleite gehen, *(demote)* degradieren;
~ (a.) (sl.) bankrott;
to go ~ Bankrott machen, pleite gehen.

buster *(sl.)* Prachtexemplar, *(huge success, sl.)* Riesenerfolg;
safe ~ Geldschrankknacker.

bustle Betrieb[samkeit], Geschäftigkeit, Übereifer.

bustler Wichtigtuer, Geschäftlhuber.

bustling betriebsam, geschäftig, übereifrig;
~ activity Hochbetrieb; **~ town** Stadt voller Leben.

busy beschäftigt, tätig, betriebsam, fleißig, *(intrudingly active)* aufdringlich, lästig, *(tel., US)* besetzt;
as ~ as a bee bienenfleißig;
~ (v.) o. s. about s. o. sich um j. bemühen; **~ o. s. with s. th.** sich mit etw. beschäftigen; **to be ~** voll beschäftigt sein mit;
[very] ~ day arbeitsreicher Tag; **~ hours** *(traffic)* Hauptverkehrszeit; **~ life** arbeitsreiches Leben; **~ period** verkehrsstarke Zeit; **~ season** Hauptsaison; **~ signal** *(tel., US)* Besetztzeichen; **~ street** belebte Straße.

busybody Geschäftlhuber.

busybodyish geschäftig, übereifrig.

busybodyness übertriebene Geschäftigkeit.

butcher Fleischer, Metzger, *(fig.)* Stümper, Pfuscher, *(slaughterer)* Mörder, Schlächter, Würger;

news ~ *(US sl.)* Zeitungsverkäufer;

~ *(v.)* niedermetzeln, abschlachten;

~ a job Arbeit verpfuschen.

butchery Schlächterei, Schlachtbank, *(fig.)* Blutbad, Metzelei.

butt Griff, *(cigarette)* Zigarettenstummel, *(fig.)* Zielscheibe.

butter mountain Butterberg.

butterfly *(fig.)* oberflächlicher Mensch;

to break a ~ on a wheel mit Kanonen auf Spatzen schießen.

button Klingelknopf, *(advertising)* Plastikplakette, *(auction, sl.)* Scheinkäufer, Lockvogel, *(computer)* Taste, *(road)* Rundkopfmarkierung;

not worth a ~ keinen Pfifferling wert;

not to care a ~ about s. th. sich den Teufel um etw. scheren; **to have lost a ~** spinnen, nicht ganz richtig im Oberstübchen sein; **to press the ~** automatisch in Betrieb nehmen; **to take s. o. by the ~** sich j. vorknöpfen;

~ boy Hotelpage, Liftboy.

buttoned up *(sl.)* sauber abgeschlossen.

buttonhole *(v.)* **s. o.** j. festnageln.

buttress *(arch.)* Widerlager, *(fig.)* Stütze;

~ *(v.)* **prices** Preise stützen.

butts and bounds Grundstücksgrenzen.

butty *(mining)* Akkordmeister.

buy Kauf, Kaufmöglichkeit, Geschäft;

good ~ guter Einkauf;

~ *(v.)* [an-, ab]kaufen, käuflich erwerben, *(auction, Br.)* ersteigern, erstehen, *(bribe)* bestechen, *(obtain)* beziehen, abnehmen.

buy *(v.)* **at | best** bestens einkaufen; **~ low figure (rate)** billig (wohlfeil) erwerben (kaufen); **~ goods at a sale** Waren auf einer Auktion erwerben; **~ a premium** über Pari kaufen; **~ retail** im kleinen einkaufen; **~ wholesale** zum Großhandelspreis (engros) kaufen.

buy *(v.)* **| back** zurückkaufen; **~ beforehand** vorkaufen.

buy *(v.)* **beyond one's means** über die zur Verfügung stehenden Geldmittel hinaus kaufen.

buy *(v.)* **by | auction** *(Br.)* ersteigern, bei einer Versteigerung erstehen, auf der Auktion erwerben; **~ the hundred pieces** hundertstückweise kaufen.

buy *(v.)* **for | the account** *(Br.)* auf Termin kaufen; **~ third account** auf fremde Rechnung kaufen; **~ cash** gegen bar (Kasse) kaufen; **~ ready money** bar bezahlen; **~ a rise auf Hausse** spekulieren; **~ settlement** *(Br.)* auf Lieferung (Termin) kaufen; **~ a mere song** spottbillig (fast umsonst, für einen Pappenstiel) kaufen; **~ speculative account** zu Spekulationszwecken kaufen.

buy *(v.)* **in** sich eindecken mit, *(auction)* selbst ersteigern, *(stock exchange)* Deckungskäufe vornehmen;

~ bulk im ganzen (engros) kaufen; **~ the lump** im ganzen (engros, im Großhandel) kaufen; **~ under the rule** sich zwangsweise eindecken.

buy *(v.)* **off** mit Geld abfinden;

~ a potential outside competitor möglichen Konkurrenten abfinden.

buy *(v.)* **on | contract** fest kaufen; **~ credit** auf Kredit (Borg, Pump) kaufen; **~ a fall** auf Baisse kaufen; **~ impulse** auf Grund plötzlicher Eingebung kaufen; **~ a scale** zu festen Preisen kaufen; **~ the sleeve** *(US)* auf Kredit (Borg, Pump) kaufen; **~ the instalment (deferred payment) system** *(US)* auf Abzahlung (Raten, Stottern) kaufen; **~ tick (trust)** auf Kredit (Borg, Pump) kaufen; **~ time** auf Kredit kaufen; **~ trial** auf Probe kaufen; **~ ex works terms** ab Fabrik kaufen.

buy *(v.)* **out** abkaufen, auskaufen;

~ the execution Pfändung verhindern; **~ a partner** seinen Partner auszahlen, Gesellschafter abfinden.

buy *(v.)* **over** bestechen;

~ one's head überbieten.

buy *(v.)* **to measure** nach Maß kaufen.

buy *(v.)* **up** aufkaufen;

~ s. one's stock jds. ganzen Vorrat abkaufen.

buy *(v.)* **| with a mortgage** mit Hilfe eines Hypothekendarlehns erwerben; **~ without soft finance** unter Verzicht auf entgegenkommende Finanzierungszusagen kaufen.

buy *(v.)* **| a borough** *(Br.)* Wahlstimmen kaufen; **~ bulk or packed goods** lose oder verpackt kaufen; **~ a bull** auf Hausse kaufen; **~ cheap** billig erwerben; **~ firm** fest kaufen; **~ first hand** direkt beziehen; **~ forward** auf Termin kaufen; **~ funds** Rentenwerte erwerben; **~ a house outright** Kaufpreis für ein Haus in bar hinterlegen; **~ some land** Grundbesitz erwerben; **~ a piece of land** Grundstück erwerben; **~ a place for the aged** sich in ein

Altersheim einkaufen; **~ only piecemeal** nur stückweise einkaufen; **~ in quantity** Großeinkauf tätigen; **~ ready-made** fertig (von der Stange) kaufen; **~ remnant (standby) space** Anzeigenleerraum belegen; **~ second-hand** antiquarisch kaufen; **~ and sell** Handel treiben; **~ a ticket** Fahrkarte lösen; **~ timber on the stump** Holz auf dem Stamm kaufen; **~ time** Zeit gewinnen; **~ unsight** unbesehen kaufen; **~ votes** Stimmen kaufen; **~ its way in by waiving repayment of state loans** Beteiligung durch Erlaß der Rückzahlung von Staatskrediten erwerben; **~ a witness** Zeugen bestechen;

~-American policy Kaufbindungspolitik; **~ order** Kaufauftrag; **~ signal** Kaufanreiz.

buyable käuflich.

buyback Rückkauf;

~ arrangement Rückkaufvereinbarung; **~ project** Rückkaufprojekt.

buyer [An]käufer, Abnehmer, Erwerber, Bezieher, *(buying agent)* Einkäufer, Einkaufskommissionär, *(would-be purchaser)* Reflektant, Kaufinteressent;

optional with the ~ nach Käufers Wahl;

~s Kundschaft, *(stock exchange)* Geld;

no ~s *(stock exchange)* Brief; **~s over** *(Br.)* Nachfrageüberhang, *(stock exchange)* mehr Geld als Brief;

more ~s than sellers *(market report)* mehr Geld als Brief;

~ of a spread Stellagenehmer;

let the ~ beware Risiko beim Käufer;

assistant ~ Hilfseinkäufer; **departmental ~** Warenhauseinkäufer; **seriously disposed ~** ernsthafter Reflektant; **economic ~** scharf kalkulierender Käufer; **fleet ~** Einkäufer von Firmenfahrzeugen; **forward ~** Termineinkäufer; **group ~s** Gemeinschaftseinkäufer; **home ~** privater Kunde; **industrial ~** Einkäufer für die Industrie; **intending ~** Kaufinteressent, Reflektant; **marginal ~** letztinteressierter Käufer; **no-resident ~** im Ausland ansässiger Einkäufer; **overseas ~** Käufer in Übersee; **potential ~** möglicher Käufer, Reflektant; **prospective ~** Kaufanwärter, Reflektant; **quantity ~** Grossist; **resident ~** ortsansässiger Käufer; **senior ~** erfahrener Einkäufer; **undisclosed ~** ungenannter Käufer; **up ~** Aufkäufer; **wholesale ~** Grossist; **willing ~** Kaufwilliger, -lustiger; **would-be ~** Kaufinteressent, Reflektant;

~ of a bill Wechselnehmer; **~ of clearance lines** Käufer beim Räumungsverkauf; **head ~ of the firm** Haupteinkäufer; **to be paid by the ~** zu Lasten des Käufers gehen; **to find no ~s** keinen Absatz finden;

~ category Käufergruppe.

buyer's | guide Katalog für Einkäufer; **~ contract good for the year** *(US)* das ganze Jahr gültiger Lieferungsvertrag; **~ duties** Verpflichtungen des Käufers; **~ list** Käuferliste, -verzeichnis; **~ market** Käufermarkt, vom Käufer beherrschter Markt; **~ monopoly** Käufermonopol; **~ obligations** Verpflichtungen des Käufers, Käuferpflichten; **~ option** *(Br.)* Kaufoption, Vorprämie; **~ option to double** *(Br.)* Nochgeschäft; **~ order** Kaufauftrag; **~ reaction** Reaktionen beim Käufer; **~ resistance** Kaufhemmung, Käuferwiderstand; **~ right of routing** Auswahlrecht der Frachtstrecke durch den Käufer.

buyer-up Aufkäufer.

buying An-, Einkauf, Kauf, Kaufen, Beschaffung, Bezug;

when ~ beim Kauf;

central ~ zentraler Einkauf; **cut-price ~** Einkauf zu Sonderpreisen; **direct ~** Direkteinkauf, -bezug; **impulse ~** plötzliches und unmotiviertes Kaufen; **instalment ~** Kauf auf Abzahlung; **space ~** *(US coll.)* Buchen (Belegen) von Anzeigenraum; **time ~** Belegen von Sendezeit;

~ back *(stocks)* Eindeckung; **~ in** *(securities)* [zwangsweise] Eindeckung; **~ outright** *(stocks)* Kassakauf; **~-up** Aufkauf;

~ on credit Kreditkauf; **~ on margin** *(stock exchange)* Effektendifferenzgeschäft; **~ an option** Optionserwerb; **~ out of a partner** Abfindung eines Gesellschafters; **~ under the rules** *(New York Stock Exchange)* Deckungskauf durch den Börsenvorstand [bei Leistungsverzug eines Börsenmitgliedes] **~ on a scale** sukzessiver Kauf von Wertpapieren zu verschiedenen Kursen; **~ and selling** Kauf und Verkauf; **giant scale ~ of securities** Erwerb von Anlagepapieren in großem Umfang; **~ of stocks** Aktienkäufe; **~ of votes** Stimmenkauf;

~ activity Einkaufstätigkeit; **~ agency** Einkaufsgesellschaft, -vertretung; **~ agent** Einkaufvertreter, Einkäufer; **~ area** Einzugsgebiet; **~ association** Einkaufsgenossenschaft; **~ behavio(u)r** Kauf-, Einkaufsverhalten; **~ binge** Kauforgie; **~ choice** Sortimentsbreite; **~ combine** Einkaufsverband; **~ commission** Einkaufsprovision; **~ committee** Einkaufskommission; **~ conditions** Kauf-, Einkaufsbedingungen; **~ considerations** Kaufüberlegungen; ~ **contract** Einkaufsvertrag; ~ **country** Käufer-land; ~ **decision** Kaufentschluß; **to make the** ~ **decision** über den Ankauf (Einkauf) entscheiden; ~ **and sales department** Einkaufs- und Verkaufsabteilung; ~ **desire** Kauflust; ~ **group** Einkaufsverband; ~ **habits** Kaufgewohnheiten [der Kund-schaft]; ~ **impulse** Kaufentschluß; ~ **incentive** Kaufanreiz; ~ **influence** Kaufeinflüsse; ~ **interest** Kaufinteresse; ~ **location** Einkaufsgegend; ~ **mission** Einkaufsdelegation; ~ **mood** Kauf-stimmung; ~ **motive** Kaufanlaß, Kaufmöglichkeit, -motiv; ~ **office** Einkaufsbüro; ~ **option** Kaufoption; ~ **order** Kaufauf-trag, *(stock exchange)* Käufe, Kaufabschlüsse; **to give a** ~ **order** zum Kauf aufgeben, Kaufauftrag erteilen; **to be firm (steady) on account of** ~ **orders** auf Käufe hin festliegen; ~ **organization** Einkaufsorganisation; **go-slow** ~ **pattern** zurückhaltendes Ein-kaufsverhalten; ~ **plan** Einkaufsprogramm; ~ **power** Kauf-kraft; **discretionary** ~ **power** frei verfügbare Kaufkraft; **excessive** ~ **power** überschüssige Kaufkraft; ~ **prejudice** Kauf-vorurteil; ~ **pressure** Kaufandrang; ~ **psychology** Einkaufspsy-chologie; ~ **public** Anlagepublikum; ~ **quota** Einkaufskon-tingent; ~ **rate** Geld-, Ankaufskurs; ~ **resistance** Kaufhem-mung, -zurückhaltung; ~ **resource** Bezugsquelle; **cooperative** ~ **society** Einkaufsgenossenschaft; ~ **spree** Einkaufstour, -bummel; ~ **trip** Einkaufstour; ~ **value** Kaufwert; ~ **wave** Käuferansturm.

buzz Summerzeichen;
~ *(v.)* anrufen, *(airplane)* in geringer Höhe überfliegen;
~ **word** Schimpfwort.

buzzer Summer.

buzzwig gewichtige Persönlichkeit.

by | -bidder Scheinbieter; ~-**bidding** Bieten zwecks Höhertreiben; ~-**business** Nebengeschäft; ~-**channel** Seitenkanal; ~-**election** *(Br.)* Ersatz-, Ergänzungs-, Nachwahl; ~-**election defeat** *(Br.)* Nachwahlniederlage; ~-**election losses** *(Br.)* Verlust bei Nach-wahlen; ~-**election standards** *(Br.)* Nachwahlmaßstäbe; **higher** ~-**election turnover** *(Br.)* höhere Nachwahlbeteiligung; ~-**end** Nebenzweck; ~-**interest** Sonder-, Privatinteresse; ~-**issue** Nebenfrage; ~-**lane** Seiten-, Nebenstraße; ~-**office** Nebenamt; ~-**pass** Ausweich-, Neben-, Umgehungsstraße; ~-**pass** *(v.)* **the traffic** Verkehr umgehen; ~-**place** Nebenplatz; ~-**product** Abfall-, Nebenprodukt; ~-**product recovery** Nebenproduktge-winnung; ~-**result** zusätzliches Ergebnis; ~-**room** Nebenraum; ~-**station** Ausweichbahnhof; ~-**term** *(Cambridge)* zusätzliches Semester; ~-**time** Freizeit; ~-**track** Nebengleis; ~-**work** Neben-beschäftigung, -beruf.

byelaws Statuten, Satzung [einer Aktiengesellschaft], *(imple-mentation)* Ausführungs, Durchführungsverordnung, *(local law, Br.)* Ortsstatut, Gemeindesatzung.

byname Spitzname.

byroad Seiten-, Anlieger-, Nebenstraße.

bystander Zuschauer;
~**s** Umstehende.

bystreet Nebenstraße.

byword stehende Redensart.

C

C *(US sl.)* Hundertdollarschein;
~° **print** farbiges Repro; ~**-ration** eiserne Ration (3500 Kalorien).
cab [Miet]wagen, Auto, Taxe, Taxi, Fiaker, Droschke, *(locomotive)* Führerstand, *(truck)* Fahrerhaus;
~ *(v.)* [it] *(fam.)* Taxi benutzen; ~ **it home** mit dem Taxi nach Hause fahren;
to call a ~ Taxe bestellen;
~ **company** Taxiverleih; ~ **driver** Taxifahrer; ~ **rank** Taxihaltestelle, Taxistand.
cabal Klüngel, Clique.
cabaret Kabarett, Kleinkunstbühne;
~ **show** Kabarettvorführung.
cabby *(Br.)* Taxichauffeur.
cabcart Mietwagen, Fiaker.
cabette Taxifahrerin.
cabin *(airplane)* Flugzeugkabine, Pilotensitz, *(airship)* Gondel, *(hut)* Bude, Hütte, *(railway, Br.)* Stellwerk[haus], *(ship)* Kabine, Kajüte;
deck ~ Touristenkabine; **second-class** ~ Kabine zweiter Klasse; **single first-class** ~ Einzelkabine in der ersten Klasse; **sleeping** ~ Schlafkoje;
~ *(v.)* **off** in Kabinen einteilen;
~ **attendant** Bordsteward; ~ **baggage** Hand-, Bordgepäck; ~ **boy** Kammersteward; ~ **class** *(ocean ship)* Kajüts-, Luxusklasse; ~ **cruiser** Kabinendampfer; ~ **department** *(ship)* Wirtschaftsabteilung; ~ **passenger** Kajütfahrgast, Kajütenpassagier, Passagier der Luxusklasse; ~ **staff** Flugstewardessen; ~ **trunk** Kabinenkoffer.
cabinet *(case)* Schrank, Schatulle, *(museum)* Vitrine, *(photo)* Fotoformat, *(pol.)* Kabinett, Regierung, Ministerium, *(room)* Beratungs-, Sitzungszimmer, *(secret room)* Geheimzimmer, *(study)* Privat-, Studierzimmer;
all-civilian ~ nur aus Zivilisten bestehende Regierung; **filing** ~ Aktenschrank; **shadow** ~ *(Br.)* Schattenkabinett, -regierung; **war** ~ Kriegskabinett;
to be slated for the ~ als Kabinettsmitglied vorgesehen sein; **to form a** ~ Regierung bilden; **to have a seat in the** ~ Sitz im Kabinett haben, Regierungsmitglied sein; **to leave the** ~ seinen Austritt aus der Regierung erklären; **to make changes in the** ~ Regierung umbilden; **to make up a** ~ Regierung bilden; **to pick the** ~ Kabinettliste zusammenstellen; **to quit the** ~ aus der Regierung austreten; **to reshuffle the** ~ Regierung umbilden; **to resign from the** ~ aus der Regierung austreten;
~ **action** Regierungshandlung, Kabinettsmaßnahme; ~ **advice** Kabinettsempfehlung; ~ **approval** Kabinettszustimmung; ~ **business** Tagesordnung einer Kabinettsitzung; ~ **colleague** Kabinettskollege; ~ **committee** Kabinettsausschuß; ~ **committee on energy** *(Br.)* Energieausschuß der Regierung; ~ **council** *(Br.)* Ministerrat, Sitzung des Ministerrats, Kabinettsitzung; ~ **councillor** Geheimrat, *(Br.)* Kabinettsmitglied; ~ **crisis** Regierungskrise; ~ **decision** Kabinettsbeschluß; ~ **edition** bibliophile Buchausgabe; **to control** ~ **facilities** über die Absendung von Depeschen entscheiden; ~ **government** Kabinettsregierung; ~ **job** Kabinetts-, Regierungsposten; **on** ~ **level** auf Regierungsebene; ~**-level energy department** Energiebehörde im Kabinettrang; ~ **meeting** Kabinettsitzung, Ministerrat; ~ **member** Kabinettsmitglied; ~ **minister** *(Br.)* Staats-, Kabinettsminister, Kabinetts-, Regierungsmitglied; ~ **office** Ministerposten, Kabinettsamt; ~ **office committee** [etwa] Kanzleramtsausschuß; **with** ~ **office coordination** unter Koordinierung durch das Kanzleramt; ~ **officer** Kabinetts-, Regierungsmitglied, Minister; ~ **post** Kabinettssitz; **to leak** ~ **proceedings** gezielte Indiskretionen über Ergebnisse von Kabinettsitzungen vornehmen; ~ **question** Kabinetts-, Vertrauensfrage; ~ **reshuffle** Kabinettsumbildung; ~ **rule** Kabinettsregierung; ~ **size** *(photo)* Kabinettsformat; ~ **system of government** Kabinettssystem; ~ **varnish** Möbelpolitur; ~ **wage** Bezüge der Regierung, Ministerbezüge; ~ **work** Möbeltischlerei, Kunsttischlerarbeit.
cabinetmaker Kunst-, Möbeltischler, *(pol.)* Ministermacher.
cabinetmaking Kunsttischlerei, *(pol.)* Regierungsbildung.
cable Kabel[depesche], *(el.)* [Leitungs]kabel, *(mar.)* Ankertau;
by ~ telegrafisch, per Kabel, auf dem Kabelwege;
armo(u)red ~ armiertes Kabel; **coaxial** ~ Sammel-, Einheitskabel; **submarine** ~ unterseeisches Kabel; **transatlantic** ~ transatlantisches Kabel, Seekabel;
~ *(v.)* kabeln, depeschieren, drahten;

~ **one's acceptance** Auftragsangebot telegrafisch bestätigen;
to lay a ~ Kabel auslegen; **to open a** ~ Kabel in Betrieb nehmen; **to send a** ~ Kabel schicken, kabeln;
~ **address** Kabel-, Telegrammadresse; ~ **advice** Drahtaviso; ~ **car** Kabine einer Drahtseilbahn; ~ **code** Telegrammcode; ~ **confirmation** Drahtbestätigung; ~ **connection** Kabelverbindung; ~ **expenses** Telegramm-, Kabelspesen; ~ **information** Kabel-, Drahtnachricht; ~ **laying** Kabelverlegung; ~ **message** Kabel, telegraphische Nachricht; ~ **network** Kabelnetz; ~ **order** Kabelauftrag, -überweisung; ~ **railway** Drahtseilbahn; ~ **rate** telegrafische Auszahlung, Kabel[auszahlungs]satz; **future** ~ **rate** Kabelsatz für Termingeschäfte; ~ **reply** Kabelantwort; ~ **report** Drahtbericht; ~ **steamer** Kabeldampfer; ~ **subscriber** Kabelfernsehteilnehmer; ~ **television** Kabelfernsehen; ~ **television operation** Kabelfernsehbetrieb; ~ **transfer** Drahtanweisung, Kabelüberweisung, -auszahlung, telegrafische Überweisung (Auszahlung, Geldanweisung).
cablegram Kabel, Überseetelegramm, Depesche.
cablese Telegrammstil.
cableway Drahtseilbahn.
cabling Kabeln, Telegrafieren.
cabman *(Br.)* Taxifahrer, -chauffeur.
caboodle *(sl.)* Sippschaft.
caboose [**car**] *(US)* Dienstwagen, *(ship)* Kombüse, Schiffsküche, *(US)* Dienstabteil.
cabotage Küstenschiffahrt, *(airline)* Inlandsfluglizenz.
cabstand Taxistand, -haltestelle.
ca'canny absichtliche Arbeitsverzögerung, *(factory)* künstliche Produktionseinschränkung;
~ *(v.)* *(production)* Fabrikation künstlich einschränken, *(parl.)* Obstruktion betreiben;
to adopt a ~ **policy** *(fam.)* Obstruktionspolitik betreiben; ~ **strike** absichtliche Produktionsverlangsamung.
ca'cannyism Obstruktionspolitik.
cache Versteck, Unterschlupf, Schlupfwinkel, *(exploration)* Proviant-, Lebensmittellager.
cachet Prestige, Ansehen.
cad Kasse gegen Dokumente.
cadaster Grund-, Flurbuch, Kataster.
cadastral katastermäßig;
~ **extract** Katasterauszug; ~ **map (plan)** Flurbereich, -karte, Katasterplankarte; ~ **number** Flur-, Katasternummer; ~ **survey** Katasteraufnahme.
cadastration Landvermessung, Katasteranlage.
cadastre Kataster, Grundbuch.
cadaver Kadaver, Leichnam.
caddie Laufbursche, Bote.
cadet Offiziersanwärter, Kadett;
~ **school** Kadettenanstalt; ~ **ship** Schulschiff.
cadge *(v.)* *(coll.)* schnorren, nassauern.
cadger Hausierer, Trödler, *(liver by trickery)* Nassauer, Schnorrer, Schmarotzer.
cadre Rahmen-, Stammorganisation, *(mil.)* Stamm, Kader.
caduciary right Heimfallrecht [des Staates].
café *(Br.)* Teestube.
cafeteria Restaurant mit Selbstbedienung, Selbstbedienungsrestaurant.
cage *(lift)* Kabine, Fahrkorb, *(mining)* Förderkorb, *(prison)* Gefängnis, Kerker, *(prisoners' camp)* Kriegsgefangenlager;
~ **of a staircase** Treppenhaus.
cagey *(fam.)* ausreichend.
cahoot *(US sl.)* Partnerschaft;
to be in ~ unter einer Decke stecken.
cajole *(v.)* herumkriegen.
cake | **of soap** Stück Seife;
to take the ~ dem Faß den Boden ausschlagen.
calaboose *(US sl.)* Loch, Kittchen.
calamity Unglück, Notlage, Desaster, Katastrophe;
~ **coverage** *(reinsurance)* Katastrophendeckung.
calculability Berechenbarkeit.
calculable berechenbar, *(reliable)* verläßlich.
calculate *(v.)* *(adapt)* planen, anpassen, *(ascertain beforehand)* berechnen, kalkulieren, *(perform calculation)* Berechnungen anstellen, *(compute)* berechnen, ausrechnen, ermessen, *(price)* kalkulieren, *(US, suppose)* annehmen, vermuten;
~ **closely** knapp kalkulieren; ~ **the costs of a journey** Reisekosten veranschlagen; ~ **the cost of setting** Satzpreis berechnen; ~

in dollars in Dollar rechnen; ~ **everything for effect** alles auf Effekt berechnen; ~ **on preferment** mit Beförderung rechnen; ~ **the selling price** Verkaufspreis kalkulieren; ~ **on a good trade** mit einem guten Abschluß rechnen.

calculated | at the rate of exchange ruling on ... berechnet nach dem Tageskurs vom ...;
~ **insult** absichtliche Beleidigung; ~ **price** Kalkulationspreis; ~ **risk** wohlabgewogenes Risiko.

calculating | of reserve Berechnung der Prämienreserve;
~ **machine** Rechenmaschine; ~ **rule** Rechenschieber.

calculation (computation) Be-, Er-, Ausrechnung, (estimate) Kostenvoranschlag, Kalkulation, (forecast) vorausschauende Berechnung;
according to my ~ nach meiner Berechnung (Rechnung); **after much** ~ nach sorgfältiger Überlegung; **at the lowest** ~ bei niedrigster Berechnung; **on a rough** ~ annähernd veranschlagt; **on a strictly commercial rate-of-return** ~ bei reinem Rentabilitätsdenken;
approximate ~ annähernde Schätzung; **complex** ~ komplizierte Berechnung; **conservative** ~ vorsichtige Berechnung; **exact** ~ genaue Berechnung, (business) knappe Kalkulation; **flat** ~ pauschale Berechnung; **higher rates** ~ Berechnung zu höheren Steuersätzen; **interim** ~ Zwischenkalkulation; **preliminary (previous)** ~ Voranschlag, Vorausberechnung, Vorkalkulation; **rough** ~ Überschlag, Voranschlag, **standard** ~ Normalkalkulation; **unit** ~ Einzelkalkulation; **wrong** ~ Fehlkalkulation;
~ **of benefit** Leistungsberechnung; ~ **of cost** Kostenkalkulation, Selbstkostenrechnung; ~ **of dividend** (trustee) Quotenberechnung; ~ **of earning power (productiveness, yield)** Rentabilitätsberechnung; ~ **of an error** Fehlerberechnung; ~ **of exchange** Devisen-, Wechselkursberechnung; ~ **of expenses** Berechnung der Kosten; ~ **of fees** Gebührenerrechnung; ~ **of freight** Frachtkalkulation, -berechnung; ~ **of the national income** Entstehungsrechnung des Sozialprodukts; ~ **of interest** Zins[be]rechnung; ~ **of premiums** Prämienberechnung; ~ **of probabilities** Wahrscheinlichkeitsrechnung; ~ **of profitability** Wirtschaftlichkeitsberechnung; ~ **of profits** Gewinnkalkulation, Rentabilitätsberechnung; ~ **of requirements** Bedarfsrechnung; ~ **of risk** Abschätzung des Risikos, Risikoabschätzung; ~ **of time** Fristenberechnung;
to be out in one's ~ sich verrechnet haben; **to include in one's** ~s einrechnen, einkalkulieren; **to make a** ~ Berechnung anstellen (vornehmen); **to throw out (upset) a** ~ Berechnung über den Haufen werfen;
~ **basis** Berechnungsgrundlage, Kalkulationsbasis; ~ **item** Kalkulationsfaktor.

calculative berechnend.

calculator Kalkulator, Berechner, (calculating machine) Rechenmaschine, -tafel, (set of tables) Berechnungstabelle[n].

calculatory kalkulatorisch.

calculus Kalkül.

calendar Kalender, (docket, US) Terminliste, -kalender, Prozeßregister, (parliament, US) Sitzungskalender, (register) Liste, Verzeichnis;
block ~ Abreißkalender; **follow-up** ~ Terminkalender; **perpetual** ~ hundertjähriger Kalender; **special** ~ Liste der anstehenden Termine, Verzeichnis der Sofortsachen; **tear-off** ~ Abreißkalender; **university** ~ (Br.) Hochschulordnung;
~ **of causes [in trial]** (US) Verhandlungs-, Terminkalender anstehender [Straf]sachen, Sitzungsliste; ~ **of special events** Liste anstehender Veranstaltungen; ~ **of prisoners** (Br.) Liste der Untersuchungsgefangenen;
~ (v.) in einen Kalender eintragen, registrieren;
to go on the ~ in die Tagesordnung aufgenommen werden; **to put a case on the** ~ (US) Verhandlungstermin in einer Sache ansetzen;
~ **call** (US) Aufruf einer Streitsache; ~ **day** Kalendertag; ~ **file** Wiedervorlagemappe; ~ **inspection** Terminüberprüfung; ~ **month** Kalendermonat; ~ **quarter** Kalendervierteljahr; ~ **year** Kalenderjahr.

calendarer Registrator.

calendered paper satiniertes Papier, Glanzpapier.

calf binding Lederband.

calibrate (v.) kalibrieren.

call Zuruf, (appointment) Berufung, Ruf, Ernennung, (bonds) Aufruf [zur Einziehung], Einlösungsaufforderung, (broker's note) Schlußnote, -schein, (calling) Berufung, Mission, (claim) Anspruch, Forderung, (data processing) Abruf, (demand) Nachfrage, (demand for unpaid capital) Nachzahlungsaufforderung [auf nicht eingezahlte Aktien], (fig.) Anziehungskraft,

Anlockung, (for funds) Zahlungsaufforderung, Abruf von Geldern, (option) Bezugs-, Kaufoption, (US, politics) Ausschußanweisung, (port) Anlaufen, (readiness) Abrufbereitschaft, (roll call) namentliche Abstimmung, (stock exchange, Br.) Differenz-, Zeitgeschäft, Prämiengeschäft auf Nehmen, (summons) Aufruf, Aufforderung, Befehl, Gebot, (summons to pay) Zahlungsaufforderung, (tel.) [Telefon]anruf, Telefongespräch, (university) Berufung, (visit) [kurzer] Besuch;
always on ~ in ständiger Bereitschaft, bereit, verfügbar; **at (on)** ~ auf Abruf (tägliche Kündigung, ohne Kündigung) rückzahlbar; **repayable at** ~ bei Vorzeigung rückzahlbar; **subject to** ~ täglich kündbar; **within** ~ in Rufweite;
application ~ erste Einzahlung [auf Aktien]; **bank** ~ Aufforderung zur Vorlage des Bankausweises; **business telephone** ~s Geschäftstelefonate; **collect** ~ (US) R-Gespräch; **conference** ~ (tel.) Sammelgespräch; **continental** ~ (Br.) Auslandsgespräch, Festlandsgespräch; **day-time** ~ (tel.) Tagesgespräch; **duty** ~ Höflichkeitsbesuch; **essential** ~ wichtiger Telefonanruf; **false** ~ Verwählen; **farewell** ~ Abschiedsbesuch; **first (second)** ~ (stock exchange) erste (zweite) Notierung; **fixed time** ~ (tel.) Festzeitgespräch; **foreign** ~ (tel.) Auslandsgespräch; **formal** ~ Anstandsbesuch; **further** ~ Nachschuß; **local** ~ (tel.) Ortsgespräch, -anruf; **long-distance telephone** ~ (US) Ferngespräch; **lost** ~ Verwählen; **morning** ~ kurzer Morgenbesuch; **night-time** ~ Nachtzeitgespräch; **manually operated** ~ handvermitteltes Gespräch; **off-peak** ~s Telefongespräche in der verbilligten Tarifzeit; **no** ~ **for** keine Veranlassung für; **official** ~ dienstliches Gespräch, offizieller Besuch, (tel.) Dienstgespräch; **outgoing** ~ (tel.) abgehendes Gespräch; **overseas** ~ Auslands-, Überseegespräch; **person-to-person** (US) (personal, Br.) ~ (tel.) [Gespräch mit] Voranmeldung; **personal** ~ persönlicher Besuch; **postman's** ~ Eintreffen der Post; **public** ~ (stock exchange) Kursfestsetzung im Zurufverfahren; **put and** ~ (US) Zeitkauf, Stellage; **reverse-charge** ~ (US) R-Gespräch; **roll** ~ Namensaufruf, -verlesung, (mil.) Appell; **second** ~ (stock exchange) zweite Notierung; **telephone** ~ Telefonanruf, -gespräch; **toll (trunk, Br.)** ~ Ferngespräch; **toll-free** ~ gebührenfreier Anruf; **transferred-charge** ~ (Br.) R-Gespräch; **urgent** ~ dringendes Gespräch;
~ **to arms** (mil.) Einberufung, Einziehung; ~ **to the Bar** (Br.) Zulassung zum Anwaltsberuf; ~ **for bids** öffentliche Ausschreibung; ~ **to a chair** Berufung auf einen Lehrstuhl; ~ **charged for** (tel.) gebührenpflichtiges Gespräch; ~ **for additional cover** Nachschußpflicht; ~ **on a customer** Kundenbesuch; ~ **for funds** Aufforderung zur Einzahlung; ~ **for help** Hilferuf; ~ **of the House** (parl.) Abstimmung durch Namensaufruf; ~ **of justice** Forderung der Gerechtigkeit; ~ **for redemption of a loan** Anleihekündigung, Aufforderung zur Rückzahlung; ~ **for margin** Nachzahlungsaufforderung für Aktionäre; ~ **of more** (Br.) Nachgeschäft; ~ **of names** Namensaufruf; ~ **to order** Eröffnung der Hauptversammlung, (parl.) Ordnungsruf; ~ **on the purse** (fam.) Attacke auf die Geldbörse; ~ **to quarters** (mil., US) Zapfenstreich; ~ **of a salesman** Vertreterbesuch; ~ **on shares** Aufforderung zur Einzahlung auf Aktien; ~ **of stocks** Zeitgeschäft; ~ **for supplies** Abruf von Versorgungsgütern; ~ **for tenders** (US) Ausschreibung, Submissionsaufforderung; ~ **on s. one's time** Inanspruchnahme von jds. Zeit; ~ **of troops** Truppenaushebung; ~ **of twice more** (Br.) Prämiengeschäft mit zweimal noch in Käufers Wahl;
~ (v.) (issue bonds) Schuldverschreibungen kündigen (aufrufen), (law court) aufrufen, (meeting) zusammen-, einberufen, anberaumen, (names) verlesen, (ships) anlegen, (tel.) anrufen, -telefonieren;
~ **about s. th.** wegen einer Sache vorsprechen; ~ **s. o. to account** von jem. Rechenschaft fordern; ~ **again** Besuch wiederholen; ~ **the control station of an airport** Flugplatzzentrale anfunken; ~ **to arms** einberufen, einbeziehen; ~ **attention to** Aufmerksamkeit richten auf; ~ **the banns** Aufgebot bestellen; ~ **to the Bar** (Br.) als Anwalt zulassen; ~ **bonds** Obligationen abrufen; ~ **s. o. to the chair** j. zum Vorsitzenden wählen; ~ **the calendar** (law court) Sache aufrufen; ~ **a case** Verhandlung festsetzen; ~ **another case** (court) andere Sache aufrufen; ~ **to the colo(u)rs** [zum Heeresdienst] einberufen, für den Wehrdienst erfassen; ~ **it a day** (coll., US) Feierabend machen; ~ **s. o. long-distance** Ferngespräch zu jem. anmelden; ~ **the docket** Sitzungsliste verlesen; ~ **an election** Wahl ausschreiben; ~ **a halt to** Einhalt gebieten; ~ **the jury** Geschworene (Schöffen) auslosen; ~ **a meeting of the creditors** Gläubigerversammlung einberufen; ~ **a meeting of shareholders (stockholders, US)** Hauptversammlung einberufen; ~ **to mind (memory)** sich ins Gedächtnis zurückrufen, sich erinnern; ~ **s. o. names** j. beleidigen; ~ **an**

option Prämiengeschäft eingehen; **~ to order** zur Ordnung rufen; **~ s. th. one's own** etw. sein eigen nennen; **~ a party** *(law court)* Partei aufrufen; **~ the plaintiff** Sache aufrufen; **~ for production of documents** Vorlage von Urkunden verlangen; **~ in question** bezweifeln, *(summon)* zum Verhör vorladen; **~ it quits** Feierabend machen, zu arbeiten aufhören; **~ when required** *(train)* nach Bedarf halten; **~ the roll** namentlich aufrufen, Namensliste verlesen; **~ a spade a spade** Kind beim Namen nennen; **~ at every station at the airport** *(train)* auf jeder Station halten; **~ the control station** *(aircraft)* Kontrollturm anfunken; **~ a strike** Streik ausrufen; **~ a taxi** Taxe bestellen; **~ a thing by its name** Sache beim richtigen Namen nennen; **~ s. o. as witness** j. als Zeugen laden (benennen).

call *(v.)* **aside** beiseitenehmen.

call *(v.)* **back** widerrufen, *(tel.)* zurückrufen, *(dipl.)* abberufen.

call *(v.)* **down** *(sl.)* abkanzeln, kritisieren.

call *(v.)* **for** verlangen, fordern;

~ the actor *(audience)* Schauspieler herausrufen; **~ letters** Briefe abholen; **~ a lot of money** viel Geld erfordern; **~ orders** Aufträge sammeln; **~ payment** zur Zahlung auffordern; **~ additional payment** Nachschußzahlung fordern; **~ prompt action** sofortiges Tätigwerden auslösen; **~ redemption** zur Kündigung aufrufen.

call *(v.)* **forth** auslösen, hervorrufen;

~ numerous protests zahlreiche Proteste hervorrufen.

call *(v.)* **in** kurz vorsprechen, *(debts)* [Forderung] einziehen, *(funds)* [Gelder] abrufen, [auf]kündigen, zur Nachzahlung auffordern, *(law)* außer Kraft setzen, *(loan, mortgage)* [Kredit, Hypothek] kündigen, *(retire from circulation)* außer Kurs setzen, einziehen;

~ on s. o. kurz bei jem. vorsprechen; **~ an army's outposts** Vorposten einziehen; **~ an expert** Sachverständigen zuziehen; **~ one's money** seine Gelder einziehen; **~ clipped money** schlechtes Geld außer Kurs setzen; **~ the police against demonstrators** Polizei gegen Demonstranten einsetzen; **~ s. th. in question** Sache beanstanden; **~ a specialist** Spezialisten zuziehen.

call *(v.)* **into being** ins Leben rufen.

call *(v.)* **off** abberufen;

~ the attention Aufmerksamkeit ablenken; **~ a boycott** Boykott aufheben; **~ a deal** Geschäft absagen; **~ an engagement** sich für Nichteinhaltung einer Zusage entschuldigen; **~ names from a list** Namen nach einer Liste ausrufen; **~ a strike** Streik abbrechen; **~ workers** Arbeitskräfte abziehen.

call *(v.)* **on** aufsuchen;

~ s. o. bei jem. [kurz] vorsprechen, jem. seine Aufwartung machen, j. besuchen, sich an j. wenden; **~ s. o. without an appointment** j. ohne vorherige Anmeldung aufsuchen; **~ a client** Kunden besuchen; **~ the Foreign Ministry** im Außenministerium vorsprechen; **~ s. o. to pay** j. zur Zahlung auffordern; **~ a place** kurzen Besuch abstatten.

call *(v.)* **out** aufrufen, *(trade union)* zum Streik aufrufen, *(troops)* ausheben;

~ s. o. j. zum Zweikampf herausfordern; **~ the lots** *(auction)* Lose ausrufen; **~ the fire brigade** Feuerwehr alarmieren; **~ the militia** Miliz einziehen; **~ s. one's name** j. ausrufen; **~ the state guard** Palastwache heraustreten lassen.

call *(v.)* **over** namentlich aufrufen, *(accounts)* ablesen, *(list of items)* verlesen;

~ s. o. over the coals jem. gehörig die Meinung sagen.

call *(v.)* **up** aufrufen, *(bill)* auf die Tagesordnung setzen, *(demand payment of)* einfordern, *(tel.)* antelefonieren, anrufen, ans Telefon rufen;

~ an account Konto kündigen; **~ an age group** Jahrgang aufrufen; **~ a bill before a legislative body** Parlamentsdebatte eines Gesetzentwurfes verlangen; **~ capital** zur Einzahlung von Kapital auffordern; **~ the image of a deceased friend** Bildnis eines verstorbenen Freundes heraufbeschwören; **~ troops** Truppen ausheben; **~ at will** nach Belieben abrufen.

call *(v.)* **upon** auffordern;

~ s. o. to give assistance j. um Unterstützung angehen; **~ to help** zur Hilfe heranziehen; **~ the insurance office for indemnity** von der Versicherung Entschädigung verlangen; **~ one's readers** sich an seine Leser wenden.

call, to accept a Telefongespräch annehmen; **to answer a ~** Telefongespräch abnehmen; **to be at the ~ of s. o.** jem. auf Abruf zur Verfügung stehen; **to be on ~** Bereitschaftsdienst haben; **to book a ~** Gespräch anmelden; **to cancel a ~** Gespräch abmelden; **to forward a ~** auf einen anderen Anschluß umstellen; **to give s. a ~** j. anrufen; **to give for the ~** Vorprämie kaufen; **to have a ~** to berufen werden; **to have the ~** sehr gefragt (begehrt) sein; **to have first ~ on s. th.** Vorrecht auf etw.

haben; **to make a ~ on s. o.** j. besuchen, jem. einen Besuch abstatten; **to make a ~ at the hospital** Krankenhausbesuch machen; **to make a ~~collect** *(US)* R-Gespräch führen; **to make a ~ at a port** Hafen anlaufen; **to make a ~ on shares** Einzahlung auf Aktien verlangen; **to make a fresh ~ on shares** neue Einzahlung auf Aktien ausschreiben; **to make a ~ on s. one's time** j. zeitlich in Anspruch nehmen; **to pay s. o. a ~** j. besuchen; **to pay for a ~** Ferngespräch bezahlen; **to pay a formal ~ on s. o.** jem. einen formellen Besuch abstatten; **to pay a ~ on shares** Einzahlungen auf Aktien leisten, eingeforderten Betrag auf Aktien einzahlen; **to place a long-distance ~** *(US)* Ferngespräch anmelden; **to put a ~ through** Ferngespräch herstellen (vermitteln); **to remain within ~** in Rufweite bleiben; **to return s. one's ~** jds. Besuch erwidern; **to screen a ~** Telefonanruf überprüfen; **to take all ~s** alle Anrufe entgegennehmen; **to take for the ~** Vorprämie verkaufen; **to transfer a ~** durchverbinden;

~~back *(interview)* Zweitinterview, *(salesman)* Wiederholungs-, nachfassender (zweiter) Vertreterbesuch, *(statistics)* Ansprechwiederholung; **~~back pay** Überstundenbezahlung; **~ bell** Tischglocke; **~ bird** Lockvogel; **~ board** *(railway, theater)* Aufruftafel, Anschlagbrett; **~ box** *(Br.)* Telefon-, Fernsprechzelle, Münzfernsprecher, Fernsprechkabine, -automat, -häuschen, *(US)* Postschließfach; **~ button** Klingelknopf; **~ car** Funktaxi; **to make a ~~collect** *(US)* R-Gespräch führen; **~ day** *(Br., barrister)* Zulassungstag; **~ deposits** Sichteinlagen, Tagesgeld; **~ feature** Einlösungsform; **~ forwarding** Weiterleitung eines Telefongesprächs; **~~in pay** garantierter Mindestlohn bei außertariflicher Arbeit; **~ letter** schriftliche Aufforderung zur Einzahlung auf Aktien, schriftliche Einzahlungsaufforderung; **~ letters** *(broadcasting)* Sendezeichen; **~ loan** *(Br.)* tägliches Geld, Tagesgeld, Geld auf tägliche Kündigung, Maklerdarlehen; **~ loan renewal rate** *(Br.)* Prolongationssatz für tägliches Geld; **~ market** Tagesgeldmarkt, Markt für tägliches Geld; **~ meeting** *(US)* Einberufung der Hauptversammlung; **~ money** *(Br.)* Tagesgeld, täglich fälliges Geld; **to mark down ~ money to 2 per cent** Tagesgeld um 2% herabsetzen; **~ money market** *(Br.)* Markt für tägliches Geld; **~ money rate** *(Br.)* Satz für tägliches Geld, Tagesgeldsatz; **~ number** *(library, US)* Bibliotheks-, Standort-, Buchnummer, *(tel.)* Anschluß-, Telefonnummer; **~ office** Fernsprechamt; **~ option** Kaufoption; **~~over** Namensaufruf; **to vote by ~~over** namentlich abstimmen; **~ pay** Anwesenheitsgeld; **~ prefix** *(tel.)* Vorwahlnummer; **~ premium** Vor-, Bezugsprämie; **~ premium transaction** Vorprämiengeschäft; **~ price** Vorprämienkurs; **~ protection** Kündigungsschutz; **~ rate** Satz für Tagesgeld, Tagesgeldsatz; **~ sign[al]** Rufzeichen; **~ slip** Vertreterbericht, *(US)* Bestelliste, *(library, US)* Bestellschein, Bücherbestellzettel, *(tel.)* Telefonzettel; **~ station** Telefonzentrale; **~ supper** *(Br., attorney)* Zulassungsdinner; **~ system** Telefonanlage; **~ ticket** *(shares)* Zahlungsaufforderungsschein; **~~up** *(mil.)* Einberufung, Einziehung.

callable jederzeit abrufbar, *(bonds)* kündbar, einziehbar;

~ by lot auslosbar; **~ bond** kündbares Wertpapier.

callboy [Hotel]page, *(ship)* Schiffsjunge.

called genannt, *(bonds)* zur Rückzahlung aufgerufen, *(capital)* gekündigt, *(securities)* eingefordert;

~ upon to pay zur Zahlung aufgefordert;

to be ~ for postlagernd; **to be ~ to the bar** als Anwalt zugelassen werden; **to be ~ within the bar** *(Br.)* zum Kronanwalt ernannt werden; **to be ~ for at station office** bahn[post]lagernd; **to be ~ away on business** geschäftlich abgerufen werden; **to be ~ up to** freigestellt werden; **to be ~ to the teaching profession** zum Lehramt berufen sein; **to be ~ up for military service** zur Ableistung der Wehrpflicht einberufen werden;

~~for article begehrter Artikel; **~ bond** außer Kurs gesetztes Wertpapier; **~~up capital** zur Einzahlung aufgefordertes Kapital.

caller Besucher, *(tel.)* Anrufer;

~'s letters postlagernde Briefe; **~'s register** Kondolenzbuch.

calligraphy Schönschrift.

calling *(mil.)* Einberufung, *(profession)* Beruf, Metier, Geschäft, Gewerbe, Stand, *(stockholders)* Ladung, *(summoning)* Aufforderung;

middle-class ~s bürgerliche Berufe; **public ~** öffentliche Ausübung eines Berufes;

~ to the Bar *(Br.)* Anwaltszulassung; **~~in of bank notes** Aufruf von Banknoten; **~ on customers** Kundenbesuch; **~ the docket** Aufruf der anstehenden Fälle; **~ an election** Wahlausschreibung; **~ of the House** *(parl., Br.)* Aufruf zur namentlichen Abstimmung; **~ of jury** Auslosung der Schöffen (Geschworenen); **due ~ of meeting** ordnungsgemäße Einberufung einer Versammlung; **~ of Parliament** Einberufung des Parlaments; **~ of the plaintiff** Aufruf des Klägers; **~ of the reserve** *(mil.)* Einberufung der Reserven; **~ of a roll** Namensverlesung; **~ to testify** Zeugenbenennung; **~ of witness** Zeugenaufruf.

calling in *(of money lent, securities)* Kündigung, Einziehung, Einforderung.

calling|off a deal Annullierung eines Geschäfts; **~ off a strike** Streikeinstellung; **~ out** *(mil.)* Einberufung.

calling|card *(US)* Visitenkarte; **~ clause** Anlaufklausel; **~ costs** Kontaktkosten; **~ day** Empfangstag, Jour; **~ hour** Sprechstunde; **~ round** Besuchstour.

calm *(stock exchange)* still, lustlos;
~ *(v.)* beruhigen, besänftigen.

calmative Beruhigungsmittel.

calming effect Beruhigungswirkung.

calorie|content Kaloriengehalt; **~-rich** kalorienreich.

calorific value Kalorienwert.

calumniate *(v.)* verleumden, üble Nachrede verbreiten.

calumniation Verleumdung, Ehrabschneidung.

calumniator Verleumder, Ehrabschneider.

calumnious report verleumderischer Bericht.

calumny Verleumdung, üble Nachrede, falsche Anschuldigung.

cambist Spezialist für ausländische Währungsarbitrage, Devisenhändler, *(book)* Umrechnungstabelle.

cambistry Wechselkunde.

camel ride, to take s. o. for a j. auf den Arm nehmen.

camelback *(car)* Runderneuerungsgummi.

camera Fotoapparat, Kamera, *(law court)* Richterzimmer, *(television)* Fernsehkamera;
in ~ unter Ausschluß der Öffentlichkeit; **off ~** außerhalb des Blickfelds der Öffentlichkeit;
film (movie) ~ Filmkamera; **hidden ~** versteckte Filmkamera; **to be heard in ~** unter Ausschluß der Öffentlichkeit stattfinden; **to hear a case in ~** für die Dauer der Verhandlung die Öffentlichkeit ausschließen; **to order a trial in ~** Öffentlichkeit ausschließen; **to sit in ~** geheime Beratung abhalten, *(court)* unter Ausschluß der Öffentlichkeit tagen (verhandeln); **to take evidence in ~** Beweisaufnahme unter Ausschluß der Öffentlichkeit vornehmen;
~ obscura Dunkelkammer; **~ reporting** *(television)* Direktübertragung, Livesendung; **~ safari** Fotosafari; **~ shot** Bildausschnitt, Kameraeinstellung, *(television)* Bildeinstellung; **~ speed** Bildfrequenz; **~ store** Fotogeschäft; **~ work** Kameraführung.

cameraman Kameramann, *(newspaper)* Bildberichterstatter, -reporter.

camouflage Maskierung, Täuschung, Irreführung, *(mil.)* Tarnung, Verschleierung;
~ *(v.)* verschleiern, vertuschen, *(mil.)* tarnen; **~ measures** Verschleierungsmaßnahmen.

camouflaged advertising Schleichwerbung.

camp Lager[platz], *(mil.)* Truppenübungsplatz, *(politics)* Lager, Partei, Anhänger, *(US)* Goldgräberkolonie, *(vacation)* Ferienlager;
concentration ~ Konzentrationslager; **detention ~** Anhaltelager; **holiday ~** Ferienlager; **internment ~** Internierungslager; **opposing ~** gegnerisches Lager; **prisoner-of-war ~** Kriegsgefangenenlager; **transit ~** Durchgangslager;
~ *(v.)* in einem Lager unterbringen, *(holidayer)* zelten, im Freien lagern;
~ out zelten, im Zeltlager wohnen; **~ on s. one's trail** *(US)* unablässig hinter jem. her sein;
to be in the same ~ einverständlich zusammenarbeiten; **to belong to different political ~s** verschiedenen politischen Richtungen angehören; **to break up a ~** Zelt abbrechen; **to close down a ~** Lager auflösen; **to establish one's ~** sein Lager aufschlagen; **to fall into an extreme ~** sich einer extremen Richtung anschließen; **to pitch a ~** Lager aufschlagen; **to send s. o. to a ~** j. in ein Lager einweisen; **to strike a ~** Lager abbrechen;
~ bed Feldbett; **~ chair** Klappstuhl; **~ commander** Lagerkommandant; **~ fire** Lagerfeuer; **~ follower** Schlachtenbummler, Marketender; **~ meeting** *(US)* Gottesdienst im Freien; **~ office** Lagerbüro.

campaign Werbekampagne, -feldzug, Sonderaktion, *(mil.)* Feldzug, *(pol.)* Wahlfeldzug;
advertising ~ Reklame-, Einführungs-, Werbefeldzug; **chickenfeed ~** mit kleinen Beiträgen finanzierter Wahlfeldzug; **cream ~** erfolgversprechender Werbefeldzug; **elaborate ~** großangelegte Werbekampagne; **electoral (election, electioneering) ~** Wahlfeldzug, -kampf; **introductory ~** Einführungskampagne, **-werbefeldzug; political ~** Wahlfeldzug, -kampf; **presidential ~** Wahlkampf für die Präsidentschaft; **press ~** Pressefeldzug; **public relations ~** Aufklärungsfeldzug; **publicity ~** Werbefeldzug, -aktion; **rousing ~** aufregender Wahlfeldzug; **sales ~** Verkaufsaktion, Absatzfeldzug; **smearing ~** Rufmord, Verleumdungsfeldzug; **whispering ~** Flüsterpropaganda;
~ of abuse Verleumdungsfeldzug; **~ to raise funds** Sammelaktion, finanzielle Hilfsaktion; **~ for members** Mitgliederwerbung; **~ for road safety** Feldzug für Verkehrssicherheit;
~ *(v.)* werben, *(mil.)* Feldzug mitmachen, *(politics)* Wahlpropaganda machen, *(US)* kandidieren;
~ against s. o. Wahlfeldzug gegen j. führen; **~ for the chancellorship** sich um das Kanzleramt bewerben;
to build up a ~ Wahlfeldzug vorbereiten; **to conduct a ~** Wahlfeldzug leiten; **to conduct a long-term ~** seine Politik langfristig ausrichten; **to launch a ~** Wahlfeldzug organisieren; **to lead a party into the election ~** Partei in den Wahlkampf führen; **to plan a ~** Wahlfeldzug vorbereiten; **to put an orator in requisition in a political ~** Redner in einem Wahlkampf einsetzen; **to wage a ~** Wahlkampf führen;
~ abuses unlautere Wahlkampfmethoden; **~ aid** Wahlkampfhilfe; **~ arguments** Wahlkampfargumente; **~ banner** Wahlkampftransparent; **~ basket** Wahlkampfgeschenkkorb; **~ button** *(US)* Parteiabzeichen für den Wahlkampf, Wahlkampfabzeichen; **~ chest** Wahlkampffonds, **-schatulle**; **~ coffer** Wahlkampfkasse; **~ committee** Wahlfeldzugsausschuß; **~ contribution** Wahlzuschuß; **political ~ contribution** Wahlkampfspende; **~ contributor** Wahlspender; **~ debate** Wahlfeldzugsdiskussion; **~ debts** Wahlkampfschulden; **~ documents** Wahlkampfschriften; **~ expenses** Wahlunkosten; **~ financing** Finanzierung eines Wahlfeldzugs, Wahlkampffinanzierung; **~ finances** Wahlgelder, Mittel für den Wahlkampf; **~ fund** Wahlfonds; **to divert ~ funds to one's personal use** Spendengelder für persönliche Zwecke verwenden; **~ gift** Wahlgeschenk; **~ manager** Wahlfeldzugleiter; **~ medal** *(mil.)* Erinnerungsmedaille; **~ money** Wahlkampfgelder; **~ organization** Wahlkampforganisation; **~ partner** Wahlkampfbeteiligter; **~ plan** Werbeplan; **~ platform** Wahl[kampf]programm; **~ pledge** Wahlkampfversprechen; **~ promise** Wahlversprechen; **~ series of sales letters** großangelegte Serie von Verkaufsbriefen; **~ spending** Wahlkampfausgaben; **~ start** Wahlkampfbeginn; **~ time** Wahlkampfzeiten; **~ trail** Wahlkampagne, Wahlreise; **~ train** Wahlsonderzug; **for political ~ use** für Wahlkampfzwecke.

campaigner *(mil.)* Kriegsteilnehmer;
old ~ Veteran.

campaigning, open rückhaltloser Wahlkampf;
to start ~ Wahlfeldzug beginnen.

camper Lagerteilnehmer, Zeltbewohner;
~ unit Campingwagen; **~ vehicle** Campingfahrzeug.

camping Zelten, Lagern, Camping;
~ equipment Zeltausstattung; **~ fees** Zeltplatzgebühren; **~ ground** Lager-, Zeltplatz; **~ holiday** Urlaub im Ferienlager; **~ place** Campingplatz; **~ site** Zeltplatz.

campship Lagerzuschuß.

campus Spiel-, Sportplatz, *(academic world)* Universitätsleben, akademische Welt, *(college ground)* Universitätsgelände, *(school)* Schulhof;
~ building Universitätsgebäude; **~ disorders** Universitäts-, Studentenunruhen; **~ generation** Studentengeneration; **~ leader** Studentenführer; **~ police** Universitätspolizei; **~ protest** Studentenproteste.

can Kanister, Sprühdose, *(Br.)* Blechkanne, *(garbage, US)* Mülleimer, Abfallkübel, -tonne, *(box of tin, US)* [Konserven]dose, -büchse, *(US sl., prison)* Gefängnis;
~ of worms *(US)* widerliche Angelegenheit;
~ *(v.)* *(US)* in Büchsen konservieren, eindosen, *(fire, US sl.)* rausschmeißen, feuern, *(record, coll.)* aufzeichnen, auf Band aufnehmen;
to carry the ~ *(fam.)* Kopf hinhalten müssen, Sündenbock abgeben; **to take the ~ back** *(fam.)* Verantwortung für etw. tragen;
~ industry *(US)* Konservenindustrie; **~ opener** *(US)* Büchsenöffner; **~ production** *(US)* Konservenproduktion; **~ worker** *(US)* Konservenarbeiter.

canal Kanal;
inter-oceanic ~ Seekanal; **locked ~** geschlossener Kanal;
~ for navigation Schiffahrtskanal;
~ *(v.)* kanalisieren;
to be linked with a ~ durch einen Kanal verbunden sein; **to build a ~** Kanal anlegen;

~ boat Kanalboot, Schleppkahn; **~ company** Kanalgesellschaft; **~ dues** Kanalgebühren; **~ lock** Kanalschleuse; **~ navigation** Kanalschiffahrt; **to preserve the ~'s neutrality** Neutralität des Kanals garantieren; **~ toll** Kanalabgabe, -gebühr; **~ traffic** Kanalverkehr; **~ treaty** Kanalabkommen; **~ worker** Kanalarbeiter; **~ zone** Kanalzone, -gebiet.

canalization Kanalisierung.

canalize *(v.)* kanalisieren, *(fig.)* in eine bestimmte Bahn lenken.

canapé belegtes Brot, belegter Toast.

canard irreführende Nachricht, Zeitungsente, Falschmeldung; **~ type aircraft** Entenflugzeug.

cancel Rückgängigmachung, Annullierung, *(print.)* Streichung, Korrektur; **~** *(v.)* durch-, ausstreichen, ungültig machen, *(annul)* annullieren, für ungültig (kraftlos) erklären, außer Kraft setzen, *(claim)* [Forderung] streichen, [Schuld] tilgen, niederschlagen, streichen, *(contract)* [Vertrag] aufheben (kündigen), *(countermand)* stornieren, abbestellen, sistieren, *(deface)* unkenntlich (unleserlich) machen, *(print.)* [aus]korrigieren, streichen, *(stamp)* entwerten, abstempeln; **~ an agreement** Vertrag aufheben; **~ one's booking** Platzbestellung rückgängig machen; **~ the charges** Kosten niederschlagen; **~ a check** *(US)* **(cheque, Br.)** Scheck stornieren; **~ a contract** Vertrag aufheben; **~ a debt** Schuld annullieren (erlassen); **~ each other** *(entries)* sich gegenseitig aufheben; **~ an entry (item)** Eintragung löschen, Posten streichen (austragen), Buchung stornieren; **~ figures** Zahlen ausstreichen; **~ a firm in the register of business names** Firma im Handelsregister löschen; **~ a garnishee order** Pfändungsbeschluß aufheben; **~ a guarantee** Garantiezusage aufheben (widerrufen); **~ a hearing** mündliche Verhandlung absetzen; **~ an indicator** *(car)* Richtungsanzeiger (Blinker) ausmachen; **~ an invitation** Einladung zurückziehen; **~ an item** Posten streichen; **~ a journey** Reise nicht stattfinden lassen; **~ a law** Gesetz aufheben; **~ a licence** Lizenz zurücknehmen; **~ a measure** Maßnahme rückgängig machen; **~ a mortgage** *(US)* Hypothek löschen; **an obligation** Engagement lösen; **~ an order** Auftrag rückgängig machen, abbestellen, Auftrag stornieren; **~ a paragraph** Absatz streichen; **~ postage stamps** Briefmarken entwerten; **~ a power of attorney** Vollmacht widerrufen; **~ a premium** Prämie stornieren; **~ a procuration** Prokura entziehen; **~ a registration** Eintragung löschen; **~ a trademark registration** Warenzeichen im Register löschen; **~ securities** verlorengegangene Wertpapiere für kraftlos erklären; **~ shares** Aktien kaduzieren; **~ special drawing rights** *(International Monetary Fund)* Sonderziehungsrechte aus dem Verkehr ziehen; **~ a vote** Wahl für ungültig erklären; **~ war debts** Kriegsschulden streichen (erlassen); **~ a will** Testament widerrufen.

cancellable aufhebbar, annullierbar.

cancellation Durch-, Ausstreichung, *(annulment)* Annullierung, Ungültigkeitserklärung, *(abolition)* Aufhebung, Abschaffung, Beseitigung, *(annulment)* Kraftloserklärung, *(countermanding)* Storno, Stornierung, Rückgängigmachung, Abbestellung, Sistierung, *(effacement)* Entwertung, *(insurance)* Policenverkürzung, *(stamps)* Entwertung; **subject to ~** kündbar; **contract ~** Vertrags[auf]kündigung; **short-term ~** kurzfristige Kündigung; **~ of charges** Kostenniederschlagung; **~ of a contract** Vertragsaufhebung, -kündigung, -rücktritt; **~ of a debt** Niederschlagung (Streichung) einer Schuld, Schuldenerlaß; **~ of a deed** Ungültigkeitserklärung einer Urkunde; **~ of an entry** Löschung (Stornierung) einer Eintragung, Storno; **~ of a firm in the register of business names** Löschung einer Firma im Handelsregister; **~ of a flasher (indicator)** Ausmachen eines Blinkers; **~ of a garnishee order** Aufhebung eines Pfändungsbeschlusses; **~ of a lease** Aufhebung eines Pachtvertrages; **~ of a licence** Lizenzrücknahme, -widerruf; **~ of a mortgage** *(US)* Hypothekenlöschung; **~ of an obligation** Lösung eines Engagements; **~ of an order** Auftragsstornierung, -stornierung; **~ of a paragraph** Streichung eines Absatzes; **~ of a premium** Prämienstornierung; **~ of a procuration** Prokuraentziehung; **~ of a registration** Annullierung einer Registereintragung, Registerlöschung; **~ of reserves** Rücklagenreduzierung; **~ of securities** Kraftloserklärung verlorengegangener Wertpapiere; **~ of unissued shares** Kaduzierung von Aktien, Aktienkaduzierung; **~ of stamps** Briefmarkenentwertung; **~ of trademark registrations** Löschung von Warenzeicheneintragungen; **~ of war debts** Kriegsschuldenstreichung; **~ of a will** Annullierung eines Testaments, Testamentswiderruf; **to apply for ~** *(trademark)* Löschung beantragen;

~ charge Annullierungsgebühr; **~ clause** Verfall-, Kündigungsklausel; **~ conditions** Kündigungsbestimmungen; **~ date** Kündigungstermin; **~ fee** Stornierungsgebühr; **~ mark** Entwertungsmarke, -stempel; **~ privilege** Kündigungsrecht; **~ proceedings** *(trademark law, US)* Löschungsverfahren; **~ rate** Stornierungssatz.

cancelled aufgehoben, storniert, annulliert; **until ~** bis auf Widerruf; **~ in error** irrtümlich annulliert; **to be ~** stornierbar, *(train)* fortfallen; **~ check** *(US)* **(cheque, Br.)** entwerteter (annullierter) Scheck; **~ at renewal** *(insurance)* gekündigt zwecks Aushandlung einer Folgeprämie; **~ stamps** entwertete Briefmarken.

canceller *(Br.)* Entwertungsstempel.

cancelling|**price** Abstandssumme; **~ stamp** Entwertungsstempel.

candid aufrichtig, ehrlich, redlich, offen; **to be perfectly ~** um ganz ehrlich zu sein; **~ account** ehrlicher Bericht; **~ camera** Kleinstbildkamera; **~ opinion** objektive Meinung; **~ photograph** Schnappschuß.

candidacy *(US)* Kandidatur.

candidate Kandidat, *(applicant)* [Berufs]anwärter, [Amts]bewerber, *(examinee)* Prüfungskandidat, Prüfling; **available ~** *(US)* Kandidat mit Erfolgsaussichten; **eligible ~** geeigneter Kandidat; **fusion ~** gemeinsamer Kandidat; **ideal ~** Bewerberideal; **labo(u)r ~** Kandidat der Arbeiterpartei; **nominative ~** vorgeschlagener Kandidat; **running ~** Gegenkandidat; **strong ~** aussichtsreicher (seriöser) Kandidat; **successful ~** gewählter Kandidat; **unopposed ~** einziger (alleiniger) Kandidat; **unsuccessful ~** durchgefallener Kandidat; **~ for devaluation** Abwertungskandidat, -anwärter; **~ for a post** Stellenbewerber; **~ for scholastic hono(u)rs** Doktorand; **~ for revaluation** Aufwertungsanwärter; **~ for the throne** *(Br.)* Thronprätendent; **~** *(v.)* sich bewerben, kandidieren; **to adopt a ~** *(Br.)* der Aufstellung eines Kandidaten zustimmen; **to ballot for a ~** *(US)* für einen Kandidaten stimmen; **to be a ~** unter den Kandidaten sein; **to agree to be a ~** Kandidatur annehmen; **to be a possible ~** als Bewerber in Betracht kommen; **to be on the short list of ~s** als Kandidat in der engeren Wahl stehen; **to boom a ~** Kandidaten kräftig unterstützen; **to defeat an opposing ~** Gegenkandidat schlagen; **to examine a ~** Kandidaten prüfen; **to groom a ~ for office** *(US)* Kandidaten lancieren; **to nominate a ~** Kandidaten aufstellen; **to pick the least deserving ~** ungeeignetsten Kandidaten auswählen; **to plump for a ~** alle Stimmen einem Kandidaten geben; **to propose (recommand) a ~** Kandidaten vorschlagen; **to put forward (up) a ~** Kandidaten aufstellen; **to question a ~** Kandidaten prüfen; **to run a ~** Kandidaten aufstellen; **to set up a ~** Kandidaten aufstellen; **to snow under a ~** Kandidaten mit großer Mehrheit schlagen; **to stand as ~** kandidieren, sich bewerben (als Kandidat aufstellen lassen); **to vote for the Labour ~** *(Br.)* sozialdemokratisch wählen.

candidateship, candidature *(Br.)* Kandidatur, Bewerbung, Anwartschaft; **to withdraw one's ~** seine Kandidatur zurückziehen.

candle Licht, *(el.)* Normalkerze; **not to be worth the ~** die Sache nicht der Mühe wert sein; **to burn the ~ at both ends** mehrere Dinge gleichzeitig tun, sich vollständig übernehmen; **to hold a ~ to** Vergleich mit etw. aushalten; **not fit to hold the ~ to s. o.** jem. nicht das Wasser reichen können; **~ end** *(fig.)* Krimskrams.

candlelight Kerzenlicht.

cando(u)r Aufrichtigkeit, *(impartiality)* Vorurteilslosigkeit, Offenheit.

candy store *(US)* Konditorei.

canister Kanister.

canned *(tinned, US)* konserviert, *(recorded)* auf Tonband aufgenommen, *(US)* mechanisch reproduziert; **~ beer** Bier in Dosen; **~ food** *(US)* Dosenkonserven; **~ goods** *(US)* Konserven; **~ music** Bandmusik; **~ speech** auf Band aufgenommene Rede.

canner *(US)* Konservenfabrikant.

cannery *(US)* Konservenfabrik.

cannibalism Kannibalismus; **to revert to ~** in den Kannibalismus zurückfallen.

cannibalization Ausschlachtung.

cannibalize *(v.)* [Betrieb, Kraftfahrzeug] ausschlachten.

canning *(US)* Konservenfabrikation.

cannon *(mil.)* Kanone;
  ~ **fodder** Kanonenfutter.
cannonade Artilleriefeuer.
canon Regel, Richtschnur, Vorschrift, *(fixed annual payment)* Erbzins;
  ~s **of conduct** Anstandsregeln; ~s **of construction** Auslegungsregeln; ~ **of descent (inheritance)** Erbfolge[ordnung]; ~s **of professional ethics** Standesregeln; ~s **of taxation** gesunde Besteuerungsprinzipien.
canopy Schutzdach;
  ~ **of clouds** geschlossene Wolkendecke;
  ~ **bed** Himmelbett.
cant *(fig.)* Kauderwelsch, *(jargon of thieves)* Gaunersprache, Jargon, *(occupational language)* Kunst-, Fachsprache;
  the same old ~ die alte Leier;
  ~ **term** Modewort.
canteen Kantine, *(buffet)* Erfrischungsstand, Büfett, *(mil.)* Feldküche, Kantine;
  industrial (works) ~ Betriebskantine;
  ~ **used exclusively for executives** nur für leitende Angestellte bestimmtes Kasino;
  to run a ~ Kantine unterhalten (betreiben);
  ~ **facilities** Kantineneinrichtungen; ~ **keeper** Kantinenwirt; ~ **manager** Kantinenleiter, -pächter; ~ **work** Kantinentätigkeit, -arbeit.
cantonal elections Kantonalwahlen.
cantonment *(mil.)* Ortsunterkunft.
canvas Zelt-, Packleinwand, *(truck)* Wagenplane;
  under ~ in Zelten.
canvass *(electioneering)* Wahl-, Propagandafeldzug, Stimmenwerbung, *(parl., scrutiny)* gründliche Untersuchung, Wahlprüfung, *(solicitation)* Auftrags-, Kundenwerbung, Werbefeldzug;
  broad ~ breit angelegte Erzählungsweise; **door-to-door** ~ Hausierertum;
  ~ **of votes** Wahlstimmenwerbung;
  ~ *(v.)* beeinflussen, *(advertisements)* Inserate sammeln (werben), *(customers)* [Kunden] besuchen, akquirieren, *(examine in detail)* gründlich prüfen, *(freshmen)* keilen, *(order)* [Aufträge] hereinholen, *(votes)* Wahlstimmen werben, Wahlbezirk bearbeiten;
  ~ **for s. o.** jds. Kandidatur unterstützen, Propaganda für j. machen;
  ~ **an area** Gebiet abklappern; ~ **for a candidate** Stimmenwerbung für einen Abgeordneten betreiben; ~ **for the conservative candidate** Stimmen für den konservativen Kandidaten werben; ~ **on** *(Br.)* **(in,** *US)* **behalf of charity** Geld für wohltätige Zwecke sammeln; ~ **a constituency** Wahlbezirk bearbeiten; ~ **a district for votes** in einem Wahlbezirk Stimmen werben; ~ **from door to door** hausieren gehen; ~ **an electorate** Wahlkreis bearbeiten; ~ **for a newspaper** Abonnenten für eine Zeitung werben; ~ **orders** Aufträge hereinholen; ~ **subscribers** Abonnenten werben; ~ **a territory for a subscription book** Buch in einem Bezirk im Subskriptionswege vertreiben; ~ **in a town** Stadt bereisen (bearbeiten); ~ **for votes** Wähler bearbeiten; ~ **the prospective votes in an election** Wahlaussichten untersuchen;
  to give s. o. the ~ j. entlassen; **to make a** ~ **of a constituency** Wahlreise durchführen.
canvasser *(advertisement, advertising)* Anzeigen-, Inseraten-, Annoncenwerber, *(US, returning officer)* Wahlstimmenprüfer, *(salesman)* Handlungsreisender, Handelsvertreter, *(subscriptions)* Akquisiteur, Abonnentensammler, -werber, *(votes)* Stimmenwerber;
  advertising (advertisement) ~ Inseraten-, Annoncenwerber; **book** ~ Subskribentensammler; **directory** ~ Adreßbuchsubskribentensammler; **freight** ~ Frachtenmakler; **insurance** ~ Versicherungsvertreter;
  No ~s, **no hawkers, no circulars!** Betteln und Hausieren verboten!
canvassing Beeinflussung, *(advertisements)* Sammlung von Inseraten, Annoncenakquisition, Annoncenwerbung, *(orders)* Akquirieren, Hereinholung von Aufträgen, *(US, return of votes)* Wahlstimmenprüfung, *(subscriptions)* Abonnentensammlung, -werbung, *(votes)* Stimmenwerbung, Wahlpropaganda;
  door-to-door ~ Hausierertum;
  ~ **of a constituency** Bearbeitung eines Wahlbezirks; ~ **of votes cast** Wahlstimmenuntersuchung;
  No ~ **allowed!** Hausieren verboten!
  ~ **campaign** Werbefeldzug, -aktion; ~ **department** Auftragsannahme-, Kundenwerbeabteilung.

cap|s Großbuchstaben, Versalien;
  full ~ Runderneuerung, Vulkanisierung;
  ~ **and gown** Universitätstracht;
  ~ *(v.)* vulkanisieren, runderneuern, *(university)* akademischen Grad verleihen;
  to set one's ~ **at s. o.** mit jem. anzubändeln suchen;
  ~ **paper** Packpapier; ~ **pistol** Spielzeugpistole.
capability [Leistungs]fähigkeit, *(legal capacity)* Rechtsfähigkeit;
  carrying ~ Ladungsfähigkeit; **counter-value** ~ *(mil.)* städtestrategische Schlagkraft; **counterforce** ~ *(mil.)* waffenstrategische Schlagkraft; **overkill** ~ *(mil.)* überschüssiges Vernichtungspotential; **strike-back** ~ *(mil.)* Vergeltungspotential;
  ~ **to contract** Vertragsfähigkeit; ~ **for being improved** Ameliorationsfähigkeit; ~ **to inherit** Erbfähigkeit.
capable *(able)* tüchtig, leistungsfähig, geeignet, tauglich, *(susceptible)* imstande;
  ~ **to act in law** geschäftsfähig; ~ **of attachment** pfändbar; ~ **to compete** wettbewerbs-, konkurrenzfähig; ~ **to contract (of contracting)** geschäfts-, vertragsfähig; ~ **of disposing** testierfähig; ~ **of improvement** verbesserungsfähig; ~ **of earning one's living** erwerbsfähig; ~ **of high production** hochleistungsfähig; ~ **of proof** beweisfähig; ~ **of personal property** vermögensfähig; ~ **of varying interpretations** verschieden auslegbar; ~ **of making a living** erwerbsfähig; ~ **of being registered** eintragungsfähig; ~ **of seating** *(theater)* mit einem Fassungsvermögen von; ~ **of sueing** aktiv legitimiert;
  to be ~ **of any crime** jedes Verbrechens fähig sein; **to be** ~ **of being sued** passiv legitimiert sein; **not to be** ~ **of translation** unübersetzbar sein.
capacitate *(v.)* ermächtigen, berechtigen, qualifizieren.
capacitated to act handlungsfähig.
capacity [Leistungs]fähigkeit, *(cubic content)* Fassungsvermögen, Kapazität, Rauminhalt, Größe, *(factory machine)* Leistungsfähigkeit, *(faculty)* Fähigkeit, Befähigung, Qualifikation, *(jurisdiction)* Zuständigkeit, *(legal competency)* Handlungs-, Geschäftsfähigkeit, *(maximum output)* Höchstleistung, *(position)* Stellung, Eigenschaft, *(ship)* Ladungs-, Tragfähigkeit, Tonnengehalt;
  of full legal ~ voll geschäftsfähig; **in the** ~ **as** in der Eigenschaft als; **in managerial** ~ in leitender Stellung; **in his ministerial** ~ in seiner Eigenschaft als Minister; **in an official** ~ in amtlicher Eigenschaft; **in supervisory** ~ in aufsichtsführender Stellung; **in an unofficial** ~ inoffiziell; **in their** ~ **of member** *(articles)* in ihrer Mitgliedereigenschaft;
  annual ~ Jahreskapazität; **banking** ~ Bankvolumen; **business** ~ Geschäftsfähigkeit; **carrying** ~ Belastungs-, Trag-, Ladungsfähigkeit; **contractual** ~ Vertrags-, Geschäftsfähigkeit; **disposing** ~ Testierfähigkeit; **earning** ~ Ertragsfähigkeit, Rentabilität; **excess** ~ Überkapazität; **fiduciary** ~ Treuhändereigenschaft; **financial** ~ finanzielle Leistungsfähigkeit; **floor weight** ~ Tragfähigkeit eines Stockwerks; **idle** ~ *(US)* ungenützte Kapazität; **industrial** ~ Industriekapazität; **legal** ~ Rechts-, Geschäftsfähigkeit; **limited** ~ beschränkte Geschäftsfähigkeit; **maximum** ~ Produktionsoptimum, -höchstleistung; **mental** ~ Zurechnungsfähigkeit; **full operating** ~ Leistungsfähigkeit bei voller Kapazitätsausnutzung; **physical** ~ körperliche Leistungsfähigkeit; **plant** ~ betriebliche Leistungsfähigkeit; **productive** ~ Produktions-, Leistungs-, Ertragsfähigkeit; **public** ~ *(municipal property)* Gemeinnützigkeit; **representative** ~ Vertretereigenschaft; **seating** ~ Fassungsvermögen, Sitzmöglichkeiten; **spare** ~ *(Br.)* freie (ungenützte) Kapazität; **spending** ~ Kaufkraft; **storage** ~ Lagerfähigkeit; **surplus** ~ Kapazitätsüberschuß; **taxable** ~ Steuerkraft, steuerliche Leistungsfähigkeit, Besteuerungsfähigkeit; **testamentary** ~ Testierfähigkeit; **total** ~ *(productive power)* Gesamtleistungsvermögen; **trustee** ~ Qualifikation zum Treuhänder, Treuhändereigenschaft; **unlimited** ~ unbeschränkte Geschäftsfähigkeit;
  ~ **to act** Geschäftsfähigkeit; ~ **to act as trustee** Treuhändereigenschaft; ~ **for advancement** Beförderungseignung; ~ **to borrow** Kreditaufnahmebefugnis; ~ **to charge security** Befugnis zur Gestellung von Sicherheiten; ~ **to compete** Wettbewerbsfähigkeit; ~ **to contract (of contracting)** Geschäfts-, Vertragsfähigkeit; ~ **to contract by bill** Wechselfähigkeit; ~ **to contract a loan** Kreditaufnahmebefugnis; ~ **to take delivery** Abnahmemöglichkeit; ~ **to develop** Entwicklungsfähigkeit; ~ **to earn rental return** Ertragswertsteigerung; ~ **for growth** Entwicklungsvermögen, Wachstumskapazität; ~ **to incur liability** Fähigkeit, Verbindlichkeiten einzugehen; ~ **to indorse** Girierfähigkeit; ~ **to marry** Heiratsfähigkeit; ~ **to pay** Zahlungsfähigkeit; ~ **to produce** Produktionsfähigkeit; ~ **of storage** Aufnahmefähigkeit von Lagerräumen; ~ **to sue** *(US)* Aktivle-

gitimation, Prozeßfähigkeit; ~ **to be sued** *(US)* Passivlegitimation, Prozeßfähigkeit; ~ **to make a will** Testierfähigkeit; ~ **to work** Arbeitsfähigkeit;

to act in one's individual ~ als Privatperson handeln; **to act in one's official** ~ amtlich tätig werden, in Ausübung seines Amtes handeln; **to act in one's** ~ **as guardian** in seiner Eigenschaft als Vormund tätig werden; **to be in** ~ rechtlich befugt sein; **to be within the** ~ **of young readers** auch für jugendliche Leser verständlich sein; **to be booked to** ~ *(advertising)* ganzen Anzeigenraum vergeben haben; **to be working to** ~ voll ausgelastet (beschäftigt) sein; **to bring to full** ~ auf Hochtouren bringen; **to cut back** ~ **by 50%** Kapazitäten um 50% verkleinern; **to employ to** ~ auslasten; **to have excellent business** ~ ausgezeichneter Geschäftsmann sein; **to have no** ~ **to act** handlungsunfähig sein, keine Handlungsbefugnis haben; **to operate close to (at near)** ~ Betriebskapazität beinahe (fast) voll ausnützen; **to work to** ~ Kapazität voll ausnützen (ausschöpfen); **to play to** ~ **audience** stets ein volles Haus haben; **large-~ car** Großraumfahrzeug; ~ **costs** Kosten bei voller Betriebsnutzung; ~ **crowd** *(theater)* ausverkauftes Parkett; ~ **cutbacks** Kapazitätsreduzierungen, -verringerung, -beschneidung; ~ **effect** Kapazitätseffekt; ~ **house** ausverkauftes Haus; ~ **output** Produktion bei voller Beschäftigung; ~ **problem** Kapazitätsproblem; ~ **requirements** Kapazitätserfordernisse; ~ **test** Eignungsprüfung; ~ **utilization** Kapazitätsausnutzung; ~ **utilization gap** Kapazitätsausnutzungslücke; ~ **variance** Leistungsabweichung; ~ **working** Kapazitätsauslastung.

cape Landspitze.

capias ad respondendum *(lat.)* Vorladung des Beklagten, Vorführungsbefehl.

capita, per nach Köpfen.

capital Kapital[ien], Stammvermögen, *(advantage)* Nutzen, Vorteil, *(balance sheet)* Kapitalanteil, *(chief city)* Hauptstadt, *(funds)* [Geld]mittel, *(letter)* Großbuchstabe, *(proprietorship)* Eigenkapital;

in ~s *(print.)* in Versalien gedruckt;

active ~ arbeitendes Kapital, Betriebs-, Umlaufkapital; **additional** ~ Zusatzkapital, neues Kapital; **advanced** ~ eingebrachtes Kapital, *(heir)* Erbvoraus; **ample** ~ reichliche Mittel; **artificial** ~ anderes Kapital als Grund und Boden; **authorized** ~ *(Br.)* genehmigtes (bewilligtes, registriertes) [Gesellschafts]kapital, Grund-, Stammkapital; **available** ~ flüssige Mittel, verfügbares Kapital; **average** ~ Durchschnittskapital; **bank's** ~ Kapital einer Bank; **bona-fide** ~ aus verkäuflichen Waren bestehendes Kapital; **borrowed** ~ fremdes Kapital, Fremdkapital, -mittel; ~ **brought in** eingebrachtes Kapital; **building** ~ Eigenmittel; **business** ~ Geschäfts-, Betriebskapital; **called-up** ~ eingefordertes Kapital; **circulating** ~ Umlaufkapital, -vermögen; **consumer's** ~ Konsumgüter; **additional contributed** ~ zusätzlich eingezahltes Grundkapital; **corporate** ~ *(US)* Kapital einer Aktiengesellschaft, Gesellschaftskapital; **dead** ~ unproduktives (brachliegendes, totes) Kapital; **debenture** ~ Erlös für begebene Obligationen, Obligationskapital; **declared** ~ deklariertes (angegebenes, festgesetztes, ausgewiesenes) Kapital; **deposit[ed]** ~ eingeschlossenes Kapital; **development** ~ Investitionskapital für Erweiterungsprojekte; **disengaged** ~ freies Kapital; **dry** ~ unverwässertes Gesellschaftskapital; ~ **due** Kapitalforderung; **employed** ~ arbeitendes Kapital; **engaged** ~ produktives Kapital; **equity** ~ Beteiligungs-, Eigenkapital; **equity share** ~ Stammkapital; **fictitious** ~ fiktives Kapital; **fixed** ~ Anlagevermögen, festliegendes (nicht realisierbares) Kapital, feste Kapitalanlage, *(permanent working capital)* betriebsnotwendiges Kapital; **floating** ~ Betriebs-, Umlaufkapital; **foreign** ~ ausländisches Kapital, Auslandsgelder; **free** ~ zinsfreies Kapital; **fresh** ~ neues Kapital; **frozen** ~ festliegendes Kapital; **fully paid** ~ voll eingezahltes Kapital; **granted** ~ genehmigtes Kapital; **high-geared** ~ hohes Eigenkapital; **idle** ~ unbeschäftigtes (totes, brachliegendes) Kapital; **immaterial** ~ geistiges (persönliches) Kapital; **impaired** ~ durch Verluste vermindertes Kapital; **industrial** ~ Industriekapital; **initial** ~ Anfangskapital; **initial circulating** ~ Anlaufkapital; **instrumental** ~ Produktionsgüter; **insured** ~ Versicherungskapital; **interest-bearing** ~ verzinsliches (werbendes) Kapital; **invested** ~ angelegtes (investiertes) Kapital, Kapitaleinlage, Einschuß, Einlage, Anfangseinlage, Anlage-, Investitions-, Einlagekapital, Anlagewerte; ~ **invested abroad** Auslandsinvestitionen; **investment** ~ Anlage-, Investitionskapital; **issued** ~ *(Br.)* effektiv ausgegebenes Kapital, zur Zeichnung aufgelegtes Grundkapital, Emissionskapital; **legal** ~ gesetzlich vorgeschriebenes Kapital; **liquid** ~ flüssige Mittel, Betriebs-, Umlaufkapital; **loan** ~ *(Br.)* Fremd-, Leih-, Anleihe-, Darlehnskapital; **locked-**

up ~ *(Br.)* festgelegtes (engagiertes) Kapital; **long-term funded** ~ langfristig angelegtes Kapital; **loose** ~ brachliegendes Kapital; **low-geared** ~ zu niedrig bemessenes Eigenkapital; ~ **lying idle** brachliegendes (totes) Kapital; **minimum** ~ Mindestkapital; **misappropriated** ~ fehlgeleitetes Kapital; **moneyed** ~ flüssiges Anlagekapital; **natural** ~ ursprüngliches Kapital; **net working** ~ arbeitendes Kapital; **nominal** ~ *(Br.)* Grund-, Gründungs-, Nominal-, Gesellschafts-, Stammkapital, *(US)* geringfügiges (nominelles) Kapital; **opening** ~ Anfangskapital; **ordinary** ~ *(corporation, US)* Stammkapital; **original** ~ Anfangs-, Gründungskapital; **out-of-date** ~ veraltete Anlagegüter; **outside** ~ Auslands-, Fremdkapital; **ownership (owned)** ~ Eigenkapital; **paid-in** ~ Einlagekapital; **paid-up** ~ voll eingezahltes Kapital, Kapitaleinschuß; **partly paid-up** ~ nicht voll eingezahltes Kapital; **permanent** ~ Anlagekapital; **private** ~ Privatvermögen; ~ **produced** aufgebrachtes Kapital; **producer's** ~ Produktionsgüter; **production (productive)** ~ arbeitendes Kapital, Produktionskapital; **property** ~ in Wertpapieren angelegtes Kapital; **put-in** ~ Einlage[kapital]; **quick** ~ werbendes (zinsbringendes) Kapital; **real** ~ effektiv benötigtes Kapital, *(real estate)* in Grundstücken angelegtes Kapital; **redeemed** ~ zurückgezahltes Kapital; **reduced** ~ herabgesetztes Kapital; **refugee** ~ Fluchtkapital; **registered** ~ genehmigtes Kapital, Nominalkapital; **requisite** ~ erforderliches Kapital, notwendiges Betriebsvermögen; **reserve** ~ bei der Liquidation ausschüttbare Rücklage, Reservekapital; **separate** ~ Privatvermögen; **share** ~ *(Br.)* Grund-, Aktienkapital; **shareholder's** ~ Aktienkapital; **shrinking** ~ schrumpfendes Kapital; **small** ~ geringes Kapital; **small ~s** *(print.)* Kapitälchen; **special** ~ Sondervermögen; **stated** ~ ausgewiesenes Geschäftskapital; **statutory** ~ satzungsmäßiges Gesellschaftskapital; **stock** ~ Grund-, Stammkapital; **subscribed** ~ gezeichnetes Kapital; **sunk** ~ amortisiertes Kapital; **tied-up** ~ festgelegtes Kapital; **total** ~ Gesamtkapital; **trade** ~ Betriebskapital, -kapital, Gewerbekapital, Geschäftsvermögen; **trade and financial** ~ Wirtschafts- und Finanzzentrum; **trading** ~ Betriebsvermögen, -mittel, Gewerbekapital; **unapplied** ~ totes Kapital; **uncalled** ~ noch nicht aufgerufenes Kapital, ausstehende Einlagen auf das Grundkapital; **unemployed (unused)** ~ totes (brachliegendes, freies) Kapital; **unissued** ~ nicht ausgegebenes Kapital; **unpaid** ~ noch nicht eingezahltes Kapital; **unproductive** ~ unproduktives (totes, brachliegendes) Kapital; **variable** ~ wechselndes Kapital; **venture** ~ Spekulations-, Risikokapital; **wage** ~ Lohnkapital; **withdrawable** ~ kündbares Kapital; **working** ~ Aktiv-, Betriebskapital, Betriebsmittel, Umlaufkapital; **short-time working** ~ kurzfristige Betriebsmittel; ~ **and Labo(u)r** Unternehmertum und Arbeiterschaft; ~ **of a company** *(Br.)* (corporation, US) Grundkapital einer Aktiengesellschaft; ~ **invested in real property** in Grundstücken angelegtes Vermögen; ~ **and reserves** *(balance sheet)* eigene Mittel, Eigenkapital; ~ **and surplus** *(US)* Kapital- und Gewinnrechnung; ~ **entitled to a dividend** dividendenberechtigtes Kapital; ~ **paid in property** Sacheinlage; ~ **of a partnership** Gesellschaftskapital; ~ **and surplus** *(US)* Kapital-, und Gewinnrechnung; ~ **to start with** Anfangskapital;

to accumulate ~ Kapital bilden; **to add to the** ~ dem Kapital zuschlagen; **to alienate** ~ Kapital abziehen; **to approve an increase of** ~ Kapitalerhöhung genehmigen; **to attract** ~ Kapital anlocken; **to be strapped for** ~ knappe (unzureichende) Kapitaldecke haben, kapitalknapp sein; **to be well provided with** ~ gute Kapitalausstattung haben; **to bring foreign** ~ **to a country** Auslandskapital anziehen; **to build up** ~ **abroad from untaxed income** im Ausland aus unversteuertem Einkommen Kapital bilden; **to call in** ~ Kapital kündigen; **to conscript** ~ Kapital der staatlichen Zwangswirtschaft unterwerfen; **to contribute** ~ Kapital einbringen (einschießen); **to convert into** ~ kapitalisieren, in Kapital umwandeln; **to derive** ~ **from** Nutzen ziehen aus; **to dispose of a large** ~ mit großen Kapitalbeträgen arbeiten; **to diversify one's** ~ sein Kapital in verschiedenen Gewerbesparten anlegen; **to eat up one's** ~ sein Kapital aufzehren; **to embark** ~ Kapital[ien] anlegen; **to enable** ~ **to build up at a faster rate** raschere Kapitalbildung ermöglichen; **to endow with** ~ mit Kapital ausstatten, Kapitalausstattung vornehmen; **to furnish** ~ Kapital zur Verfügung stellen; **to get new** ~ **through the equity security route** neues Kapital auf dem bewährten Wege der Aktienausgabe beschaffen; **to have a large** ~ **at hand** über ein großes Vermögen verfügen; **to have kept one's** ~ **intact** sein Kapital nicht angegriffen haben; **to have only limited** ~ **available** nur über begrenzte Kapitalmittel verfügen; **to increase the** ~ Kapitalerhöhung vornehmen, Kapital erhöhen; **to increase the amount of** ~ **contributed** Kapitaleinlage erhöhen; **to infuse fresh** ~ neues Kapital zuführen; **to introduce** ~ Kapital zuführen; **to invest** ~ Kapital anlegen (hineinstecken), Geld investieren; **to lack the requisite** ~ unzureichende Kapitaldecke haben; **to liberate** ~ Kapital freisetzen; **to live on (off) the** ~ vom Kapital (von der Substanz) leben; **to lock up** ~ *(Br.)* Kapital fest [an]legen; **to make** ~ **out of a case** Fall politisch ausschlachten; **to make** ~ **out of s. th.** Kapital aus etw. schlagen; **to make a call for** ~ Kapital zur Einzahlung aufrufen; **to make holes in (inroads on) one's** ~ sein Kapital angreifen; **to make party** ~ als Partei aus einer Sache Kapital schlagen; **to make propaganda** ~ Kapital aus etw. schlagen; **to make a big hole in one's** ~ gewaltig ins Geld gehen; **to mobilize** ~ Kapital flüssig machen; **to obtain** ~ **from the general public** Kapitalmarkt in Anspruch nehmen; **to pay** ~ Kapital einzahlen; **to pay a dividend out of the** ~ Dividende aus dem Kapital zahlen; **to procure** ~ Kapital beschaffen; **to provide with** ~ Kapital zur Verfügung stellen, mit Kapital ausstatten; **to raise** ~ Kapital aufbringen (aufnehmen); **to raise additional** ~ **for new plant facilities** neues Kapital zur Durchführung von Betriebserweiterungen aufnehmen; **to realize** ~ Kapital flüssigmachen; **to recall** ~ Kapital kündigen; **to reduce the share** ~ Kapitalherabsetzung vornehmen, Kapital zusammenlegen; **to repatriate** ~ Kapital wieder ausführen (aus dem Ausland zurückführen); **to subscribe** ~ Kapital zeichnen; **to take up new** ~ neues Kapital aufnehmen; **to tie one's** ~ sein Kapital fest anlegen; **to tie up** ~ *(US)* Kapital festlegen; **to touch** ~ Kapital angreifen; **to turn to private sources of** ~ Kapitalmarktpublikum in Anspruch nehmen; **to underwrite** ~ Kapital zeichnen; **to withdraw one's** ~ seine Einlage zurückziehen; **to write down** ~ Kapital herabsetzen; **to write one's name in** ~**s** seinen Namen in Großbuchstaben schreiben; **to write off** ~ Kapital abschreiben, Aktienkapital zusammenlegen, Kapitalzusammenlegung vornehmen;

~ **account** Kapitalkonto; **liberalized** ~ **account** liberalisiertes Kapitalkonto, *(enterprise)* Kapitalaufstellung; **to charge to** ~ **account** aufs Kapitalkonto übernehmen; ~ **accounting** Kapitalkontrolle; ~ **accretion** Kapitalzuwachs, -ansammlung; ~ **accumulation** Vermögens-, Kapitalbildung; ~ **adjustment** Berichtigung des Kapitals, Kapitalberichtigung; ~ **advancement** Erbvoraus in Form von Kapitalbeträgen; ~ **aid** Kapitalhilfe.

capital allowance *(Br.)* steuerlich zulässige Abschreibungen auf das Anlagevermögen, Anlagenabschreibung;
~ **carried forward** Abschreibungsvortrag; ~**s on furniture** *(Br.)* Abschreibungen auf Einrichtungsgegenstände;
to carry forward ~ Abschreibung auf Kapitalanlagegüter steuerlich vortragen;
~ᵃ **Act** *(Br.)* Anlagenabschreibungsgesetz; ~ **basis** Abschreibungsbasis; ~ **computation** *(Br.)* Abschreibungsberechnung.

capital|amount Kapitalhöhe, -betrag; ~ **appreciation** *(Br.)* Werterhöhung des Anlagevermögens, Anlagewertsteigerung, Vermögenszuwachs; ~ **appropriations** bereitgestellte Investitionsmittel, Kapitalverwendung, -einsatz; ~ **appropriation survey** Kapitaleinsatzübersicht; **short-term** ~ **areas** Gebiete für kurzfristige Kapitalanlagen; ~ **assets** Anlagevermögen, -kapital, festliegende Aktiva, fixe Anlagen, Kapitalanlagen, -vermögen; ~ **asset account** Kapitalanlagekonto; ~ **assistance** Kapitalhilfe; ~ **balance** Bilanzsaldo; ~ **base** Kapitalbasis; ~ **benefit** Kapitalgewinn; ~ **bonus** *(Br.)* Gratisaktie; ~ **boom** Investitionskonjunktur; ~ **borrowing** Kapitalaufnahme; ~ **budget** Investitionsplan, -haushalt; ~ **budgeting** Aufstellung von Investitionsplänen, Investitionsplanung; ~ **case** Kapitalverbrechen; ~ **change** Kapitalveränderung, -entwicklung; ~ **charge** aktivierungspflichtiger Kapitalaufwand, Kapitalkosten; ~ **city** Hauptstadt; ~ **clause** Satzungsbestimmung über die Kapitalstruktur einer Gesellschaft; ~ **coefficient** *(national income accountancy)* Kapitalkoeffizient; ~ **commitments** Kapitalverpflichtungen; ~ **connections** Kapitalverbindungen, -verflechtungen; ~ **conservation** Kapitalerhaltung; ~ **construction** Kapitalstruktur, -gefüge; ~ **consumption** Kapitalaufzehrung, -verzehr; ~ **contribution** Kapitaleinlage; ~ **cost** Kapitalaufwand; ~ **crime** Kapitalverbrechen; ~ **deepening** Steigerung der Kapitalintensität, Verbesserungsinvestitionen; ~ **demand** Kapitalbedarf; ~ **deposit** eingeschossenes Kapital; ~ **depreciation** Anlagewertminderung, Kapitalabschreibung, -entwertung, -verschleiß; ~ **depreciation account** Kapitalentwertungskonto; ~ **disbursements** Kapitalaufwendungen; ~ **distribution** Ausschüttung von Kapitalgewinnen; ~ **dividend** aus dem Kapital gezahlte Dividende; ~ **duty** Emissionssteuer; ~ **drain** Kapitalabfluß, -abwanderung, -abzug; ~ **element** *(annuity)* Kapitalanteil; ~ **endowment** Kapitalausstattung; ~ **equip-ment** Kapitalausstattung, -ausrüstung, -mittel, *(balance*

sheet) Anlagegüter; ~ **equipment cost** Kosten der Kapitalausstattung; ~ **error** grundlegender Irrtum; ~ **expansion** Kapitalausweitung.

capital expenditure[s] Investitionsausgaben, -aufwand, durchgeführte Investitionen, Kapitalaufwand, -verbrauch, -kosten, aktivierungspflichtiger Aufwand, Anlagekosten;
fixed ~ Kapitalaufwand für das Sachanlagevermögen; **initial** ~ Einrichtungs-, Anlagekosten;
to constitute ~ aktivierungspflichtig sein;
~ **account** Investitionsrechnung; ~ **activity** Investitionstätigkeit; ~ **appraisal** Anlagekostenschätzung; ~ **budget** Kapitalaufwandsvorschau; ~ **cutback** Investitionsdrosselung; ~ **evaluation** Kapitalaufwandsberechnung; ~ **program(me)** Investitionsprogramm; ~ **subject** Investitionsprojekt.

capital|export Kapitalausfuhr, -export; ~**-exporting country** Kapitalausfuhrland; ~ **flight** Kapitalflucht; ~ **flotation** Kapitalemission; ~ **flow** Kapitalwanderung, -strom, zufluß, -verlagerung; ~ **forecasting** Investitionsprognose; ~ **formation** Nettoanlageinvestition, Kapitalbildung; ~ **fund** Kapitalstock, Grund-, Stammkapital; **misappropriated** ~ **funds** Kapitalfehlleitung.

capital gain Veräußerungs-, Kapitalgewinn, Vermögensvorteil, *(stock exchange)* realisierter Kursgewinn;
chargeable ~**s** steuerpflichtige Kapitalgewinne; **net** ~ Kapitalreingewinn; **realized** ~ realisierter Kursgewinn;
~ **from sales** Veräußerungsgewinn.

capital gains Kapitalgewinne, Veräußerungsgewinne aus Vermögensgegenständen;
~ **and losses** Veränderungen im Anlagevermögen;
~ **account** Kapitalgewinnkonto; ~ **computation** Kapitalgewinnberechnung; ~ **distribution** *(stock exchange)* Ausschüttung realisierter Kursgewinne; ~ **levy** Kapitalzuwachssteuer, -gewinnabgabe; ~ **provision** *(income tax)* Bestimmungen über die steuerliche Behandlung von Kapitalgewinnen; ~ **tax** Spekulations-, Kapitalgewinn-, Kapitalzuwachssteuer; **short-term** ~ **tax** Steuer auf kurzfristige Kursgewinne; **to be liable to** ~ **tax** kapitalgewinnsteuerpflichtig sein; ~ **tax provisions** Kursgewinnsteuerbestimmungen; **to qualify for** ~ **treatment** der steuerlichen Behandlung als Kapitalgewinn unterworfen sein.

capital|gap Kapitallücke; ~ **gearing** festverzinslicher Kapitalanteil am Gesamtkapital; ~ **giver** Kapitalgeber.

capital goods Kapital-, Investitionsgüter, Produktionsmittel, -güter, Anlagewerte, -güter;
free ~**s** Kapitalgüter für mehrere Zwecke;
to replace ~ Investitionsgüter ersetzen;
~ **area** Investitions-, Kapitalgüterbereich; ~ **boom** Investitionsgüterkonjunktur; ~ **industries** Produktionsmittel-, Kapitalgüterindustrie, Investitionsgüterbereich; ~ **manufacturer** Investitionsgüterproduzent; ~ **outlay** Investitionsgüteraufwand; ~ **sector** Investitionsgüterbereich.

capital|grant Investitionszuschuß; ~ **growth** Kapitalzuwachs; ~ **heading** Haupttitel; ~ **impairment** Kapitalschmälerung; ~ **import** Kapitaleinfuhr; ~**-importing country** Kapitaleinflußland; ~ **improvement** Kapitalaufwand für weitere Ausbauten (technische Verbesserungen); ~ **improvement program(me)** *(community)* Kapitalanlageprogramm; ~ **income adjustment** Inflationsanpassung von Kapitaleinkünften; ~ **increase** Erhöhung des Kapitals, Kapitalzuwachs, -erhöhung, -aufstockung; ~ **increment** Kapitalzuwachs; ~ **indemnification** Kapitalabfindung; ~ **inflow** Kapitalzufluß; ~ **injection** Kapitalspritze; ~ **institution** Geldinstitut; ~**-intensive** kapitalintensiv; ~ **intention** Investitionsneigung; ~ **interest** Kapitalbeteiligung, -anteil; ~ **interest in a partnership** Anteil am Gesellschaftsvermögen; ~ **interrelation** Kapitalverflechtung.

capital investment Kapitalverwertung, Anlageinvestition, Investitionskapital, langfristig angelegtes Kapital, langfristige Kapitalanlage, Kapital-, Investitionsaufwand;
long-date (long-term) ~ langfristige Kapitalanlage;
~ **on inventories** Lagerinvestitionen;
to encourage ~ Investitionsvorhaben fördern; **to keep up the booming pace of** ~ bevorzugt weiterhin langfristige Kapitalanlagen vornehmen; **to remain gun-shy on** ~ investitionsunlustig bleiben; **to service its** ~ Kapitaldienst sicherstellen;
~ **goods industries** Kapitalgüterindustrie; ~ **plan** Investitionsprogramm; ~ **tax credits** Steuervergünstigungen für langfristige Kapitalanlagen.

capital|issue Kapitalemission; ~ **issue committee** Anleiheausschuß, Kapitalmarktlenkungsausschuß; ~ **issue restrictions** Emissionssperre; ~ **items charged against profits** über Gewinn- und Verlustkonto abgebuchte Kapitalbeträge; ~ **items disallowed for income-tax purposes** einkommensteuerlich nicht anerkannte Kapitalabschreibungen; ~ **letter** großer Buchstabe, Großbuchstabe; ~ **levy** Vermögensabgabe, -substanzsteuer; ~ **liability** Kapital-, langfristige Verbindlichkeit; ~ **link** Kapitalverflechtung; ~ **loss** Verminderung des Anlagevermögens, Kapitalverlust; **net ~ loss** Kapitalnettoverlust; ~ **loss provisions** *(income tax)* Bestimmungen über die steuerliche Behandlung von Kapitalverlusten; ~ **market** Kapitalmarkt; **to go to the ~ market** auf den Kapitalmarkt gehen; **to have access to the ~ market** Kapitalmarkt in Anspruch nehmen können; **to have little recourse to the ~ market** Kapitalmarkt nur geringfügig beanspruchen; ~ **market policy** Kapitalmarktpolitik; ~ **market rates** Kapitalmarktsätze; ~ **money** *(Br.)* Treuhandkapitalbeträge; ~ **movement** Kapitalverkehr, -bewegung, -umdisposition, -wanderung; **to be of a ~ nature** dem Kapital zuzurechnen sein; ~ **needs** Kapitalbedarf; ~ **offence** Kapitalverbrechen; ~ **outflow** Kapitalabflüsse; ~ **outlay** Kapitalaufwand; ~ **output ratio** *(national income accounting)* Kapitalkoeffizient; ~ **owner** Kapitalbesitzer, -eigner; ~ **ownership** *(balance sheet, US)* Eigenkapital; ~ **payment** Kapitalauszahlung; ~ **place of business** Hauptgeschäftssitz; ~ **planning** Kapitalanlagepolitik, planmäßige Kapitalanlage; ~ **pool** Investitions-, Kapitalfonds; ~**-poor** kapitalschwach; ~ **position** Kapitalstruktur; ~ **prize** Hauptgewinn; ~ **production** Bildung neuen Kapitals, Kapitalbildung; ~ **profit** Veräußerungsgewinn aus Investitionsgütern, Kapitalgewinn; ~ **program(me)** Investitionsprogramm; ~ **project** Investitionsprojekt, -vorhaben; **long-term ~ projects** langfristige Anlagevorhaben; ~ **property** Kapitalvermögen; ~ **punishment** Todesstrafe; ~ **raiser** Kapitalbeschaffer; ~ **raising** Kapitalaufbringung, -beschaffung.

capital rating *(US)* Beurteilung der Vermögenslage einer Kapitalgesellschaft, Kapitalbewertung, finanzielle Stellung; ~ **figures** Kapitalbewertungsziffern; ~ **result** Kapitalbewertungsergebnis.

capital│ratio Kapitalverhältnis; ~ **recapture (recovery) rate** Kapitalrückfluß; ~ **receipts** Kapitalerträge, -einkünfte; ~ **reconciciliation statement** *(Br.)* Ausweis über die Verwendung von Kapitalmitteln, Kapitalverwendungsnachweis; ~ **reconstruction** Kapitalumstrukturierung, -sanierung; ~ **recovery** Kapitaldeckung, *(debts)* Eingang abgeschriebener Forderungen; ~ **redemption** Kapitaltilgung; ~ **redemption insurance** Sparversicherung; ~ **redemption policy** Sparversicherungspolice; ~ **redemption reserve fund** Rücklage zum Rückkauf von Vorzugsaktien; ~ **reduction** Kapitalzusammenlegung, -herabsetzung; ~ **reduction plan** Kapitalherabsetzungsvorschlag; ~ **repayment** Kapitalzurückzahlung; ~ **requirement** Kapitalbedarf; ~ **reserve[s]** nicht steuerpflichtiger Kapitalgewinn, nicht ausschüttbare Rücklage, gesetzliche Rücklagen; ~ **resources** *(bank)* Eigenkapital; ~ **revenue** Kapitaleinkünfte; **net ~ rule** *(stock exchange, US)* Bestimmungen über das Nettokapitalverhältnis; ~ **safety (security)** Kapitalsicherheit, sichere Vermögenslage; ~ **sales** Kapitalumsatz; ~ **saturation** Kapitalsättigungspunkt; ~**-saving investments** kapitalsparende Investitionen; ~**-seeking investors** anlagesuchendes Publikum; ~ **sentence** Todesstrafe; ~ **share** Kapitalanteil; ~**'s share** volkswirtschaftliche Gewinnquote; ~ **ship** Schlacht-, Großkampfschiff; ~**-short** kapitalknapp; ~ **shortage** Kapitalknappheit, knappes Betriebskapital; ~ **speech** ausgezeichnete Rede; ~ **spending** Kapitalaufwand, -aufwendung, Investitionsaufwand, Kapitalgüterinvestitionen; ~ **spending boom** Investitionsgüterkonjunktur; ~ **spending survey** Investitionsübersicht; ~**-starved** kapitalarm.

capital stock *(US)* Aktien-, Grund-, Stammkapital, *(amount to be paid in)* Kapitaleinlage, eingebrachtes Kapital; **authorized ~** *(US)* genehmigtes Grundkapital; **cumulative preferred ~** *(US)* aus kumulativen Vorzugsaktien bestehendes Kapital; **issued ~** *(US)* effektiv ausgegebenes Aktienkapital, zur Zeichnung aufgelegtes Grundkapital; **minimum ~** *(US)* geringst zulässiges Grundkapital; **outstanding ~** *(US)* ausstehendes Aktienkapital; **~ not paid up** *(US)* nicht eingezahltes Aktienkapital; **preferred ~** *(US)* aus Vorzugsaktien bestehendes Kapital; **~ subscribed** *(US)* gezeichnetes Aktienkapital; **unissued ~** *(US)* nicht ausgegebenes Kapital;
to absorb ~ *(US)* Aktienkapital erwerben; **to divide the ~** *(US)* Aktienkapital zerlegen; **to increase the amount of ~ contributed** Kapitaleinlage erhöhen; **to raise the ~** Kapital erhöhen; **to reduce the ~** Aktienkapital zusammenlegen (herabsetzen);
~ **account** Kapitalkonto; ~ **exchange offer** Aktienumtauschangebot; ~ **law** *(Br.)* Anleihestockgesetz; ~ **tax** *(US)* Aktiensteuer.

capital│structure Kapitalstruktur, -zusammensetzung; **multiple ~ structure** *(Br.)* Ausstattung mit verschiedenen Aktien; ~ **structure ratio** Kapitalstrukturverhältnis; ~ **subsidy** Kapitalzuschuß; ~ **substance** Kapitalsubstanz; ~ **sum** Kapitalbetrag, -vermögen; ~ **sum insured** Versicherungssumme; **to return a ~ sum** Kapitalbetrag zurückzahlen; ~ **surplus** *(US)* in den Rücklagen steckendes zusätzliches Eigenkapital, Kapitalreserve; ~ **surplus account** *(US)* Kapitalzuwachskonto, Rücklagenkonto; ~ **surplus item** *(US)* Rücklageposten; ~ **tax** *(double taxation agreement)* Vermögenssteuer; ~ **transaction** Kapitaltransaktion, -bewegung, -leistung; ~ **transactions** Kapitalverkehr; ~ **transfer** Kapitaltransferierung, -übertragung; ~ **transfer tax** *(Br.)* Erbschafts- und Schenkungssteuer, Vermögensübertragungssteuer; ~ **trust** *(Br.)* Treuhandkapitalbeträge; ~ **turnover** Kapitalumschlag; ~ **turnover rate** Kapitalumschlagsverhältnis; **consumer ~~-type goods** verbrauchsnahe Investitionsgüter; ~ **valuation** Kapitalbewertung; ~ **value** Kapitalwert, festgesetztes Eigenkapital; ~ **venture** mit Risiko verbundenes Unternehmen; ~ **venturer** Risiko eingehender Unternehmer; ~ **widening** Erweiterungsinvestitionen; ~ **yield** Kapitalertrag; ~ **yields tax** *(Br.)* Kapitalertragssteuer.

capitalism Kapitalismus;
infant ~ Frühkapitalismus; **mature ~** Hochkapitalismus; **private ~** Privatkapitalismus; **senile ~** Spätkapitalismus; **state ~** Staatskapitalismus; **trade ~** *(Br.)* Wirtschaftskapitalismus.

capitalist [Groß]kapitalist;
~ **economy** kapitalistisches Wirtschaftssystem.

capitalistic kapitalistisch;
~ **enterprise** kapitalistisches Unternehmen; ~ **order** kapitalistische Wirtschaftsordnung; ~ **spirit** kapitalistische Einstellung; ~ **system** kapitalistisches System.

capitalization Kapitalisierung, Aktivierung, *(amount of bonds and stocks of a company)* Kapitalausstattung, Kapitalisierung [einer Gesellschaft], *(capital stock)* Grund-, Gesellschaftskapital, *(issuing watered stock)* Kapitalverwässerung;
insufficient ~ ungenügende Kapitalausstattung; **stock ~** Aktienkapital; **total ~** Gesamtkapitalausstattung;
~ **of a company** Kapitalausstattung einer Gesellschaft; ~ **of earnings** Ertragsaktivierung; ~ **of expenditure** Ausgabenübernahme auf Kapitalkonto; ~ **of interest** Hinzuschlagen der Zinsen zum Kapital; ~ **of land taxes** Grundsteuerkapitalisierung; ~ **of profits** Kapitalisierung von Gewinnen, Gewinnaktivierung;
~ **issue** Ausgabe von Gratisaktien bei Kapitalerhöhung; ~ **method** Kapitalisierungsmethode; ~ **result** Kapitalausstattungsergebnis; ~ **unit** Kapitalisierungsaufwand; **market value** Kapitalisierungsmarktwert.

capitalize *(Br.) (charge to capital account)* in Kapital umwandeln, auf Kapitalkonto übernehmen, aktivieren, Kapitalwert berechnen, kapitalisieren, *(become capitalist)* Kapitalist werden, *(provide with capital)* mit Kapital ausstatten, Kapitalausstattung vornehmen, *(writing)* mit großen Anfangsbuchstaben schreiben;
~ **an annuity** Rente kapitalisieren; ~ **the cost** Kostenaufwand aktivieren; ~ **on the errors of a rival firm** von den Fehlern der Konkurrenz profitieren; ~ **interest** Zinsen zum Kapital schlagen; ~ **on s. th.** sich auf etw. konzentrieren; ~ **on s. th. politically** aus einer Sache politisch Kapital schlagen; ~ **its reserves** Rücklagen in Kapital umwandeln; ~ **on a strike** von einem Streik profitieren.

capitalized, to be kapitalisiert werden;
~ **annuity** Kapitalrente; ~ **expenses** kapitalisierte (auf Kapitalkonto übernommene) Ausgaben; ~ **surplus** kapitalisierter Überschuß; ~ **value** kapitalisierter Wert, [Kapital]ertragswert.

capitation│fee Kopfbetrag, -gebühr; ~ **grant** nach Kopfzahlen gezahlter Zuschuß; ~ **tax** Kopfsteuer.

capites, per nach Kopfteilen.

capitulate *(v.)* kapitulieren.

capitulation *(mil.)* Kapitulation.

capricious disbelief *(witness)* mutwillige in Fragestellung einer Zeugenaussage.

capsule, space Raumsonde.

captain *(leading man)* führende Persönlichkeit, *(mining)* [Ober]steiger, *(police, US)* Polizeihauptmann, *(ship)* Kapitän, Kommandant;
~ **of industry** *(US)* Industrie-, Wirtschaftsführer, Großindustrieller; ~ **of the watch** *(ship)* Wachhabender; ~**'s entry** Zolldeklaration des Kapitäns; ~**'s manifest** Ladungsverzeichnis, -manifest; ~**'s patent** Schifferpatent für große Fahrt; ~**'s protest** Havarieattest, Seeprotest, Verklarung.

captation Erbschleicherei.

captator Erbschleicher.

caption *(advertising)* Textzeile, Bildtext, *(certification)* Beglaubigung, *(deed)* Einleitungsformel, Präambel, *(film)* Zwischentitel, *(heading)* Überschrift, Beschriftung, *(lawsuit)* Rubrum, Urteilskopf, *(newspaper, US)* kurzer Bildtext, Bildunterschrift, Legende, *(title)* Titel.

captious question verfängliche Frage.

captivate *(v.)* gefangennehmen, *(fig.)* bezaubern.

captive Gefangener;
~ *(a.)* gefangen, *(economics, US)* nur für den Eigenbedarf (nicht für den Markt) bestimmt;
~ **audience** unfreiwillige Zuhörerschaft; ~ **balloon** Fesselballon; ~ **insurance** Konzernversicherung; ~ **insurance company** konzern-, betriebseigene Versicherungsgesellschaft; ~ **market** monopolistischer Markt; ~ **mine** *(US)* eigengenutzte Bergwerksanlage; ~ **shop** *(US)* Betriebsladen, dem Betrieb gehöriges Geschäft.

captivity Kriegsgefangenschaft;
to return from ~ aus der Gefangenschaft heimkehren.

captor Erisennehmer, Gewahrsamsmacht.

capture Eroberung, *(mil.)* Gefangennahme, *(ship)* Prise;
~ **of a criminal** Festnahme eines Verbrechers; ~ **of a town** Einnahme einer Stadt;
~ *(v.)* gefangennehmen, erobern, erbeuten;
~ **attention** Aufmerksamkeit erregen; ~ **500 of the enemy** fünfhundert Gefangene machen; ~ **a fortress** Festung einnehmen; ~ **a prize** Preis gewinnen; ~ **a ship** Schiff aufbringen; ~ **a thief** Dieb ergreifen.

captured gefangengenommen;
to be ~ in Gefangenschaft geraten;
~ **property** Beute.

car *(airship)* Gondel, *(US, railroad carriage)* [Eisenbahn]waggon, Eisenbahnwagen, *(cart)* Wagen, *(film, US)* Aufnahmewagen, *(lift, US)* Fahrstuhl[kabine], *(motorcar)* Auto[mobil], [Kraft]wagen, Kraftfahrzeug, *(tramcar)* Straßenbahnwagen;
by ~ per Achse;
air-conditioned ~ klimatisierter Wagen; **antique** ~ Schnauferl; **armo(u)red** ~ Geldtransportwagen, Panzerfahrzeug; **baggage** ~ *(US)* Gepäckwagen; **cattle** ~ *(US)* Viehwagen; **café** ~ *(US)* Speisewagen; **closed** ~ *(US)* gedeckter (geschlossener) Güterwagen; **coal** ~ *(US)* Kohlenwaggon; **commuter** ~ *(US)* im Nahverkehr eingesetzter Waggon; **company** ~ firmeneigener Wagen; **container** ~ *(US)* Behälterwagen; **cruise** ~ Funkstreife; **defective** ~ *(US)* ausrangierter Waggon; **destination** ~ *(US)* Ortswagen; **dining** ~ *(US)* Speisewagen; **drawing-room** ~ *(US)* Salonwagen; **dumped** ~ herrenloses Auto; **economic (economy-sized)** ~ wirtschaftlicher Wagen; **electric** ~ Straßenbahnwagen; **executive-class** ~ Auto für gehobenere Ansprüche; **family** ~ Familienauto; **flat** ~ *(US)* Rungenwagen; **foreign** ~ *(US)* Waggon einer anderen Eisenbahngesellschaft; **four-passenger** ~ Viersitzer; **freight** ~ *(US)* Güterwagen, -waggon; **closed freight** ~ *(US)* geschlossener Güterwagen; **front-wheel-drive** ~ Wagen (Auto) mit Frontantrieb; **gas-guzzling** ~ Benzinfresser; **gondola** ~ *(US)* geschlossener Güterwagen; **grand prix** ~ Rennwagen der Formel 1; **~s handled** *(US)* insgesamt abgefertigte Waggons; **home** ~ eigener Waggon; **house** ~ gedeckter Güterwagen; **intermediate-sized** ~ Wagen der Mittelklasse; **invalid** ~ Auto für Körperbehinderte; **junk** ~ ausrangiertes Auto, Schrottauto; **lesser-priced** ~ billigeres Auto; **~s loaded** *(US)* insgesamt beladene Waggons; **licensed** ~ zugelassenes Auto; **low-milage** ~ wenig gefahrener Wagen; **low-priced** ~ billiges Auto; **lumber** ~ *(US)* Langholzwagen; **medium-powered** ~ mittelstarker Wagen; **motor** ~ *(Br.)* Kraftwagen, -fahrzeug, Auto; **motor rail** ~ *(US)* Draisine; **nonpolluting** ~ abgasfreies Auto; **off-line** ~ *(US)* außerhalb eingesetzter Waggon; **overhauled** ~ überholtes Auto; **owned** ~ *(carrier, US)* eigener Wagen; **package** ~ *(US)* Waggon für Schüttgutladungen; **passenger** ~ *(railroad, US)* Personenwagen; **parlor** ~ *(US)* Salonwagen; **piggyback flat** ~ *(US)* Flachwagen für den Huckepackverkehr; **platform** ~ *(US)* offener Güter-, Flachwagen, Waggon, Rungenwagen; **police** ~ Polizeiauto, Funkstreife; **popular-priced** ~ Volkswagen; **private** ~ Privatwagen, privates Kraftfahrzeug; **Pullman** ~ *(Br.)* Salonwagen, *(US)* Schlafwagen; **racing** ~ Rennwagen; **railway** ~ *(Br.)* Eisenbahnwagen, Waggon; **refrigerator** ~ *(US)* Kühlwagen; **rented** ~ Mietfahrzeug, -auto, -wagen; **restaurant** ~ *(US)* Speisewagen; **safety** ~ den Sicherheitsbestimmungen entsprechendes Auto; **secondhand** ~ Gebrauchtwagen; **self-drive** ~ selbstgefahrener Mietwagen; **serviceable** ~ *(US)* einsatzbereiter Waggon; **side-stanchion** ~ *(US)* Rungenwagen; **sleeping** ~ *(US)* Schlafwagen; **smoking** ~ *(US)* Raucher[wagen]; **souped-up** ~ *(US sl.)* frisiertes Auto;

squad ~ *(US)* Streifenwagen, Funkstreife; **subcompact** ~ Kleinstwagen; **tank** ~ Tankwagen; **train** ~ *(US)* Eisenbahnwagen; **tramway** ~ Straßenbahnwagen; **unserviceable** ~ *(US)* nicht einsatzfähiger Waggon; **used** ~ Gebrauchtwagen; **vintage** ~ Schnauferl;
~ **in distress** Pannenauto; **self-drive** ~**s for hire** Autovermietung für Selbstfahrer; **~s on line** *(railroad line, US)* gesamter Waggonpark; **used** ~ **with a small milage** wenig gefahrener Gebrauchtwagen; ~ **taken in part exchange** in Zahlung genommener Wagen; ~ **used partly during employment and partly privately** teils geschäftlich, teils privat genutztes Kraftfahrzeug; ~ **with new tyres** neu bereifter Wagen;
~ *(v.)* Auto fahren;
to back a ~ Auto rückwärts fahren (setzen); **to bring a** ~ **home to the finish** Wagen ins Ziel bringen; **to de-junk a** ~ Auto verschrotten; **to design a** ~ **with lower accident and repair-cost potential** unfallsicheres Kraftfahrzeug mit niedrigeren Reparaturkosteneigenschaften kreieren; **to drive a** ~ Kraftfahrzeug fahren, Auto steuern; **to drive one's own** ~ Autobesitzer sein, seinen eigenen Wagen fahren; **to furnish ~s** *(US)* Waggons stellen; **to get into a** ~ sich in einen Wagen setzen; **to give up one's** ~ sein Auto abschaffen; **to give the** ~ **a wash** Auto waschen; **to go by** ~ Auto fahren; **to hand s. o. out of a** ~ jem. aus dem Auto helfen; **to have a** ~ **of one's own** sein eigenes Auto fahren, Autobesitzer sein; **to hire a** ~ **by distance** Auto auf Kilometerbasis mieten; **to inspect a** ~ Autoinspektion durchführen; **to jack up a** ~ Auto aufbocken; **to keep one's** ~ **off the road** nicht mit dem Auto fahren; **to match new ~s on the market** neue Automodelle auf dem Markt einführen; **to nurse a** ~ **home** Wagen vorsichtig nach Hause fahren; **to operate a** ~ Auto fahren (lenken); **to order one's** ~ **round** seinen Wagen kommen lassen; **to pick up a** ~ Auto abschleppen; **to provide a** ~ Kraftfahrzeug zur Verfügung stellen; **to pull a** ~ **out of a skid** schleudernden Wagen abfangen; **to put the** ~ **away** Auto ab-, einstellen; **to put the luggage on top of the** ~ Gepäck auf dem Wagendach unterbringen; **to register a** ~ Auto anmelden; **to release a** ~ **for delivery** neues Automodell zum Verkauf freigeben; **to race one's** ~ **against a tree** mit dem Auto gegen einen Baum fahren; **to rent a** ~ Auto mieten; **to run a** ~ Auto unterhalten; **to run foul of a** ~ mit einem Auto zusammenstoßen; **to slip the** ~ **into the garage** Auto in die Garage schieben; **to smear the axle of a** ~ Auto abschmieren; **to soup (tune) up a** ~ Auto [für den Verkauf] frisieren; **to spot a freight** ~ *(US)* Güterwagen zur Entladestelle dirigieren; **to stuff a** ~ **with people** Auto überladen; **to supply ~s** *(US)* Waggons stellen; **to take a** ~ **out of storage** Wagen wieder in Betrieb nehmen; **to take over a** ~ Auto von der Fabrik übernehmen; **to take a ~'s number** Auto polizeilich (beim Verkehrsamt) anmelden; **to throw the** ~ **into gear** Gang einlegen; **to tow a broken** ~ Auto abschleppen; **to transfer a** ~ **from business to private use** Kraftfahrzeug zukünftig nur noch privat nutzen; **to travel by** ~ im Auto fahren; **to understand how to drive a** ~ sein Auto beherrschen; **to use a** ~ **for personal travel** Auto für Privatfahrten benutzen; **to use one's** ~ **sensibly** sein Auto mit Verstand benutzen;
all ~s parked at owners' risk Parken auf eigene Gefahr;
~ **accessories** Autozubehör; ~ **accessories firm** Autozulieferer; ~ **accident** Autounfall; ~ **air ferry service** Autoluftfährendienst; ~ **allowance** Autozuschuß; ~ **assembly** Automontage; ~ **assembly plant** Automontagewerk; ~ **association** Kraftfahrzeugverband; ~ **body** Karosserie; ~ **body firm** Karosseriebauer; ~ **boot** Kofferraum; ~ **brake** Wagenbremse; ~ **breaker** Besitzer eines Autofriedhofs, Autoausschlachter; ~ **building** *(US)* Waggonbau; ~ **bumper** Stoßstange; ~ **buying** Autokauf; ~ **card** Straßenbahn-, Omnibusplakat, Werbeplakat (Innenplakat) in öffentlichen Verkehrsmitteln; ~ **card advertising** Daueranschlag in Verkehrsmitteln; ~ **card rates** Anzeigentarif für Verkehrsmittelwerbung; **cut-price** ~ **center** Autozentrum mit Sonderpreisen; ~ **company** Autofirma; ~ **components** Autozubehör; ~ **components firm** Autozulieferungsbetrieb; ~ **components manufacturer** Autozulieferungsbetrieb; ~ **crash** Autozusammenstoß; ~ **dealer** Autohändler; **used-~ dealer** Gebrauchtwagenhändler; ~ **demurrage charges** *(US)* [Waggon]liegegelder; ~ **depot** *(US)* Waggondepot; ~ **door** Autotür; ~ **drive** Autofahrt; ~ **driver** Kraft-, Autofahrer; ~ **dump** Autofriedhof; ~ **equipment** *(US)* Waggonpark; ~ **exhaust** Kraftfahrzeugauspuff; ~ **expenses** Autounterhaltungskosten; ~ **factory** Autofabrik; ~ **ferry** Autofähre, *(airplane)* Autolufttransport; ~ **guarantee** Autogarantie; ~ **hire business** *(Br.)* Mietwagengeschäft; ~**-hire firm** *(Br.)* Autoverleih; ~**-hire service** *(Br.)* Mietwagenverleih; ~**-hiring organization** Autovermietung; ~

imports Autoeinfuhren; ~ **industry** Autoindustrie; ~ **insurance**
Auto-, Kraftfahrzeugversicherung; ~ **jack** Wagenheber; ~ **key**
Autoschlüssel; ~ **licence** Kraftfahrzeuglizenz, Autozulassung,
Zulassungspapiere, Kraftfahrzeugpapiere; **flat-rate ~ licence
fee** Kraftfahrzeugpauschalsteuer; ~ **line** Automodelle;
interest-free ~ loan zinsloser Autoanschaffungskredit; ~
maker Autofabrikant, -hersteller; ~ **manufacturing** Autoherstellung, -Automobilbau; ~ **market** Automarkt; **~-mile revenue** Unterhaltungsaufwand für ein Auto; ~ **milage** *(railroad
company, US)* Kilometergeld; ~ **number** Auto-, Wagennummer, *(railroad, US)* Waggonnummer; ~ **owner** Autobesitzer,
-eigentümer, Kraftfahrzeughalter; ~ **ownership** Autobesitz,
(US) gesamter Waggonbestand; ~ **park** Kraftfahrzeugbestand,
(Br.) Parkplatz; ~ **park with attendant** *(Br.)* bewachter Parkplatz; **~-park attendant** *(Br.)* Parkwächter; ~ **park-problem**
(Br.) Parkproblem; ~ **parts** Autoersatzteile; **to defer ~ payments** Aufschub für die Abzahlungsraten für das Auto erhalten; ~ **plant** Autofabrik; ~ **pool** Fahrgemeinschaft; ~
production Autoproduktion; ~ **purchase** Autokauf; ~ **radio**
Autoradio; **new ~ registrations** Neuzulassung von Kraftfahrzeugen; ~ **rental** Wagenmiete, Automietgebühr; **~-rental
agency (company)** Mietwagenvertretung, -verleih; **~-rental
costs** Miet-, Leihwagengebühr; **~-rental discount** Mietwagen-
verleihrabatt; **~-rental firm** Mietwagenfirma; **~-rental system**
Mietwagensystem; ~ **repairs** Autoreparatur; ~ **repair shop**
Autoreparaturwerkstatt; ~ **ride** Autofahrt; ~ **sales** Autover-
kaufszahlen; ~ **salesman** Autoverkäufer, -vertreter; ~ **seat**
Autositz; ~ **service** Wagenpflege, *(railroad, US)* Waggonliege-
geld; ~ **shed** Wagenschuppen; ~ **shopping** Einkäufe per Auto;
~ **shortage** *(US)* Waggonknappheit; ~ **sickness** Autokrankheit;
~-sleeper express *(US)* Ferienreisezug; ~ **standards** Standard-
modelle der Autoindustrie; ~ **starter** [Auto]anlasser; ~ **step**
Trittbrett; ~ **strike** Streik der Autobetriebe; ~ **supply** Autoangebot, *(US)* Waggongestellung; **junk-~ tax** Autoverschrottungs-,
Schrottbeseitigungsgebühr; ~ **theft**
Autodiebstahl; ~ **track** Autospur; ~ **trust** *(US)* Finanzierungsgesellschaft für Eisenbahnbedarf; ~ **trust certificate** *(US)* Zertifikat einer Gesellschaft für Eisenbahnfinanzierung; ~ **type**
Wagentyp; ~ **wash** Autowaschanlage; **~-wash service** Autowaschanstalt, Autoschnellwäscherei; ~ **wheel** Autorad; ~ **window** Autofenster; ~ **worker** Autoarbeiter.
caramelize *(v.) (sl.)* Abmachung bestätigen.
carat Karat.
caravan Karawane, *(Br.)* Wohnwagen[anhänger], *(motor car)*
Kombiwagen;
~ *(v.)* im Wohnwagen leben;
~ **of buses** Omnibuskarawane;
~ **leader** Karawanenführer; ~ **park** (site, *Br.*) Wohnwagen-
park, Campingplatz; ~ **route** Karawanenstraße; ~ **stand** fester
Wohnwagenplatz; ~ **test** willkürliche Verteilung von Warenproben, motorisiert durchgeführter Werbetest; ~ **trade**
Karawanenhandel; ~ **train** Karawanenzug.
caravaneer, caravanner Karawanenführer, *(car)* Wohnwagen-
besitzer.
caravanning Reisen im Wohnwagen.
caravansary Karawanserei.
carbon Kohlepapier, *(copy)* Durchschlag, Durchschrift, Kopie;
~ **bromide** photographischer Farbdruck; ~ **copy** Durchschlag;
to make a ~ copy durchschreiben, Durchschlag machen, Kopie
anfertigen; **~-copy order book** Durchschreibebestellbuch; ~
microphone Kohlemikrofon; ~ **paper** Pigment-, Kohlepapier;
~ **process** Pigmentdruckverfahren.
carbonized *(sl.)* im Rang erhöht, befördert.
carboy Korbflasche.
carbro photographischer Farbdruck.
carburettor Vergaser.
carcass Kadaver, Tierkörper.
card Karte, Billet, *(business)* Visiten-, Geschäftskarte, *(eccentric
person, coll.)* Kauz, Original, *(notice)* Mitteilung, Ankündigung, *(membership)* Mitgliedskarte, *(trade union)* Gewerkschaftsausweis;
on the ~s nicht unwahrscheinlich; **by the ~** präzise;
admission ~ Einlaß-, Eintrittskarte; **one's best ~** sein stärkstes
Argument; **business (calling) ~** Empfehlungs-, Geschäftskarte;
Christmas ~ Weihnachtskarte; **collective ~** gemeinsame Visitenkarte; **the correct ~** richtige Liste; **gratulation ~** Glückwunschkarte; **greetings ~** Glückwunschkarte; **identification ~**
Kennmarke, -karte, Ausweiskarte, Personalausweis; **identity
~** Personalausweis, Kennkarte; **index ~** Kartothek-, Karteikarte; **insurance ~** Versicherungskarte; **invitation ~** Einladungskarte; **knowing ~** schlauer Kerl, Fuchs; **letter ~**

Briefkarte; **membership ~** Mitgliedskarte; **New Year ~** Neujahrskarte; **postal ~** *(US)* Postkarte; **rate ~** *(US)* Anzeigenpreisliste, -tarif, Preistafel; **ration ~** Lebensmittelkarte; **a sure
~** eine sichere Sache; **visiting ~** *(Br.)* Visitenkarte; **voting ~**
Stimmkarte;
~ **of admission** Einlaßkarte; ~ **of the sea** Seekarte; ~ **of thanks**
Danksagungskarte;
~ *(v.)* auf Karten registrieren;
to ask for one's ~s um seine Entlassungspapiere bitten; **to get
one's ~s** entlassen werden; **to give s. o. his ~s** j. feuern; **to hand
one's ~ to s. o.** jem. seine Visitenkarte übergeben; **to have
another ~ to play** noch einen Pfeil im Köcher haben; **to have a ~
up one's sleeve** Geheimplan haben, etw. in petto haben; **to keep
one's ~s close to one's chest** Geheimniskrämer sein; **to leave
one's ~ on s. o.** seine Visitenkarte bei jem. abgeben; **to play
one's ~s badly** ungeschickt vorgehen; **to play a sure ~** erfolg-
versprechenden Plan verfolgen; **to play one's ~ well** geschickt
verhandeln; **to punch one's ~** *(factory)* Karte stechen; **to put
one's ~s on the table** seine Karten auf den Tisch legen; **to speak
by the ~** es sehr genau mit seinen Worten nehmen; **to throw up
one's ~s** das Spiel aufgeben;
~ **carrier, ~-carrying member** eingetragenes [Partei]mitglied; ~
case Visitenkartentäschchen; ~ **catalog(ue) (record)** Zettelkasten, -katalog, Kartei, Karthothek; ~ **file of terms** Fach-
wortkartei; ~ **file of writers** Einsenderkartei; ~ **holder**
Karteninhaber.
card-index Kartei, Kartothek;
current-order ~ Kartei der laufenden Bestellungen;
~ **of easy reference** leicht handhabbare Kartei; ~ **of suppliers**
Lieferantenkartei;
~ *(v.)* katalogisieren, Kartei anlegen, in Karteiform erfassen;
~ **cabinet** Karteischrank; ~ **file** Kartei; ~ **system** Karteikarten-
system, Hollerithverfahren; ~ **tray** Karteitrog.
card|-indexed in Karteiform; ~ **indexing** Anlage einer Kartei; ~
insertion Einlagekarten; ~ **punch** Lochkartenlocher; ~ **rack**
Kartenständer; ~ **rate** Anzeigentariff; ~ **rationing** Rationierung durch Karten; **punch-~ system** Lochkartensystem; ~ **table**
Kartentisch; ~ **trick** Kartenkunststück; ~ **vote** *(trade union)*
Abstimmung mit Delegiertenstimmen; ~ **voting** Abstimmen
mit Mehrfachstimmkarten (Delegiertenstimmkarten).
cardan shaft *(car)* Kardanwelle.
cardboard Pappe, Kartonpapier;
~ **box** Pappkarton; ~ **engineer** Packungsspezialist; ~ **fillers**
Kartoneinlagen.
carder Plakateur, Plakatanschläger.
cardinal Kardinal;
~ *(a.)* grundsätzlich, hauptsächlich;
~ **bishop** Kardinalbischof; **of ~ importance** von kardinaler
Bedeutung; ~ **number** Grundzahl; ~ **point** Kardinalpunkt; ~
principles Grundprinzipien.
cardinalship Kardinalswürde.
cardsharper Falschspieler.
care *(attention)* [Für]sorge, Betreuung, *(charge)* Obhut, Aufsicht, Pflege, Wartung, *(interest)* Anteilnahme, Interesse,
(legal ~) Sorgfalt;
in ~ unter Vormundschaft; **in good ~** in sicherer Obhut; **in the ~
of the police** unter polizeilicher Bedeckung; **needing ~** pflegebe-
dürftig; **with due [amount of] ~** mit gebührender Sorgfalt; **Take
~ (With ~)!** Vorsicht!
~ **of** *(c/o, Br.)* zu Händen (per Adresse) von;
child ~ Jugendpflege; **custodial ~** Pflegschaft; **due ~** angemessene Sorgfalt; **great (extraordinary) ~** erhöhte Sorgfaltspflicht;
increased ~ erhöhte Sorgfalt; **medical ~** ärztliche Betreuung;
ordinary (reasonable) ~ verkehrsübliche Sorgfaltspflicht;
slight ~ geringe Sorgfaltspflicht;
~ **of a car** Pflege eines Wagens; ~ **of children** Kinderbetreuung,
-fürsorge; **reasonable ~ and diligence** im Verkehr erforderliche
Sorgfalt; **reasonable ~ and skill** im Berufsleben erforderliche
Sorgfalt; ~ **of public money** Verwaltung öffentlicher Gelder; ~
of securities Effektenverwaltung; ~ **of the sick** Krankenpflege;
~ *(v.)* pflegen, sich kümmern;
~ **to do** Lust haben; ~ **for modern music** moderne Musik
schätzen; **not ~ a straw** sich nicht das geringste daraus machen;
to act with reasonable ~ and diligence mit der im Verkehr
erforderlichen Sorgfalt handeln; **to be under the ~ of a doctor**
unter ärztlicher Aufsicht stehen; **to be under the ~ of s. o.** von
jem. verwaltet werden; **to be free from ~** keine Sorgen haben; **to
be put into ~** in ein Fürsorgeheim kommen; **to be under ~ and
treatment** Patient einer Heil- und Pflegeanstalt sein; **to confide
s. th. to s. one's ~** jds. Sorge anvertrauen; **to consign to s. one's ~**
jds. Obhut anvertrauen; **to devote great ~ to s. th.** einer Sache

große Beachtung schenken; **to dissipate** ~ Sorgfalt außer acht lassen; **to exercise** ~ Sorgfalt anwenden; **to have a** ~ *(Br.)* vorsichtig sein; **to have the** ~ **of s. o.** für j. Sorge tragen; **to have** ~ **and oversight of s. o.** jem. als Pfleger zugeteilt sein; **to have the** ~ **of a building** Gebäude zu bewachen haben; **to observe** ~ Sorgfalt anwenden; **to place s. o. under** ~ **of a guardian** j. unter Vormundschaft stellen; **to place under the** ~ **of a probation officer** der Bewährungshilfe unterstellen; **to put o. s. under s. one's** ~ sich in jds. Obhut begeben; **to take** ~ Sorge tragen; **to take jolly good** ~ sich wohlweislich hüten; **to take** ~ **of children** auf Kinder aufpassen; **to take** ~ **of one's money** sein Geld zusammenhalten; **to take** ~ **of s. o.** j. versorgen (betreuen), sich um j. kümmern; **to take much** ~ sich große Mühe geben; **to trouble by the** ~ **of a large family** sich Sorgen um das Wohl einer großen Familie machen; **to use the** ~ **and caution of an ordinary man of business** Sorgfalt eines ordentlichen Kaufmanns anwenden; **to use** ~ **and skill in the exercise of one's duties** mit der Sorgfalt eines ordentlichen Kaufmanns handeln;

~ **committee** Wohltätigkeitsausschuß; ~**-label** *(garments)* Pflegehinweis; ~ **and protection order** Anordnung der Vormundschaft, Vormundschaftsbeschluß.

careenage Kielgeld.

career Laufbahn, Karriere, Werde-, Entwicklungsgang, Beruf; **at the height of one's** ~ auf dem Kulminationspunkt seiner Laufbahn; **in full** ~ im gestreckten Galopp; **academic** ~ akademische Laufbahn; **brilliant** ~ glänzende Laufbahn; **business** ~ beruflicher Werdegang; **candidate** ~ beruflicher Werdegang eines Bewerbers; **criminal** ~ Verbrecherlaufbahn; **House** ~ parlamentarische Laufbahn; **legal** ~ juristische Laufbahn; **previous** ~ bisherige Tätigkeit; **unblemished** ~ makellose Laufbahn; ~ **of resounding progress** erstaunliche Karriere; ~ *(a.) (US)* berufsmäßig; **to advance s. o. in his** ~ j. beruflich fördern, j. in seiner beruflichen Laufbahn fördern; **to be determinative of s. one's** ~ von entscheidendem Einfluß auf jds. Laufbahn sein; **to cap one's** ~ seine Laufbahn krönen; **to cut short a** ~ Laufbahn jäh beenden; **to be in mid-**~ seine Laufbahn noch nicht abgeschlossen haben; **to carve out a** ~ **for s. o.** j. lancieren; **to end one's** ~ seine Laufbahn beenden; **to enrich a** ~ Laufbahn wirkungsvoll beeinflussen; **to enter [upon] a** ~ Laufbahn einschlagen; **to envisage a** ~ **in research** Forschungstätigkeit anstreben; **to follow diplomacy as** ~ Berufsdiplomat werden; **to hew a** ~ **for o. s.** sich mühsam hocharbeiten; **to lay one's** ~ **on the line** seine Karriere aufs Spiel setzen; **to make a** ~ **for o. s.** Karriere machen; **to make a** ~ **out of a hobby** aus einer Liebhaberei einen Beruf machen; **to round off one's** ~ Höhepunkt seiner Laufbahn erreichen; **to spend one's entire** ~ **on the financial side** sich beruflich lediglich mit finanzwirtschaftlichen Fragen beschäftigen; **to take up as a** ~ als Beruf ergreifen; ~ **advancement** berufliche Förderung; ~ **ambassador** Berufsbotschafter; ~ **aspirations** Laufbahnbestrebungen; ~ **base** Laufbahngrundlage; ~**-building bureau** Berufsberatungsstelle; ~**-building centre** *(Br.)* **(center,** *US)* Berufsberatungszentrum; ~ **chances** berufliche Chancen, Berufschancen; ~ **choice** Berufswahl; ~ **civil servant** *(US)* Beamter auf Lebenszeit; **high-**~ **civil service** qualifiziertes Berufsbeamtentum; ~ **consul** Berufskonsul; ~ **costume** Berufskleidung; ~ **curve** Laufbahnkurve; ~ **comprehensive** ~ **details** detaillierter Lebenslauf; **to write with** ~ **details** beruflichen Werdegang mitteilen; ~ **development** berufliche Entwicklung; ~ **diplomat** Berufsdiplomat; ~ **enlargement** Ausweitung des beruflichen Wirkungskreises; ~ **experience** Berufserfahrung; ~ **guidance** Laufbahnlenkung; ~ **guide** Berufsleitfaden; ~ **history** beruflicher Werdegang; ~ **image** berufliches Image; ~ **interest** Berufsinteresse; ~ **man** *(US)* Berufsdiplomat; ~ **management** Laufbahnsteuerung; ~ **master** *(school, Br.)* Berufsberater; ~ **minister** Berufsgesandter; ~ **objectives** erstrebte Laufbahn; ~ **office** Berufsberatungszentrum; ~ **officer** Berufsberater; ~ **opportunity** Berufschance; ~ **pattern** Karrieremuster; ~ **pay** *(pension scheme)* auf das Durchschnittsgehalt abgestellte Rentenzahlung; ~ **planning** Berufsplanung; ~ **position** beruflich bedeutsame Stellung; ~ **potential** Berufsmöglichkeiten; ~ **professional** ausgebildeter Fachmann; ~ **progression** Laufbahnentwicklung, Ausbau der Laufbahnmöglichkeiten; ~ **prospects** Laufbahnaussichten, berufliche Möglichkeiten; ~ **seminar** Berufsseminar; ~ **service** Berufsbeamtentum; ~ **soldier** Berufssoldat; ~ **success** beruflicher Erfolg; **to be a good step** ~**-wise** sich karrieremäßig positiv auswirken; ~ **woman** berufstätige Frau.

careerist Karrieremacher.

careful sorgfältig, sorgsam, bedacht, besorgt, vorsichtig; **to be** ~ **enough** auf der Hut sein; **to be** ~ **about s. th.** sorgfältig mit etw. umgehen; **upon** ~ **consideration** nach sorgfältiger Überlegung; ~ **copy** saubere Abschrift; ~ **examination** sorgfältige Prüfung; ~ **workman** gewissenhafter Arbeiter.

carefulness Sorgfalt, Behutsamkeit.

careless sorglos, unbekümmert, unvorsichtig, fahrlässig; ~ **act** fahrlässige Handlung; ~ **driving** fahrlässiges (unachtsames) Fahren; ~ **job** schlampige Arbeit; ~ **remark** unüberlegte Bemerkung.

carelessness Nachlässigkeit, Liederlichkeit.

caret Einschaltzeichen.

caretaker *(of person)* Wärter, Pfleger, Amtsverwalter, *(house)* Hauswart, -meister, Kastellan, *(India)* Untermieter; **to run the country on a** ~ **basis for eight months** Land acht Monate als Übergangskabinett regieren; ~ **government** geschäftsführende Regierung, Übergangsregierung, -kabinett.

caretaking Betreuung, Pflege, Wartung.

carfare *(US)* Fahrpreis, -geld, Busgeld, *(small sum, coll.)* Pappenstil.

cargo [Schiffs]fracht, [Schiffs]ladung, Frachtgut; **without** ~ unbeladen; **air** ~ Luftfracht; **bulk** ~ Waggonladung, Schüttgut, Massengutladung; **bulky** ~ sperrige Ladung; **deck** ~ Deck-, Beiladung; **dry** ~ Trockenladung; **floating** ~ unterwegs befindliche (schwimmende) Ladung; **full** ~ volle Fracht; **general** ~ gemischte Ladung, Sammel-, Stückgutladung, Stückgüter; **homeward** ~ Rück-, Retourfracht; **inflammable** ~ feuergefährliche Ladung; **inward** ~ Herfracht; **joint** ~ Sammelladung; **light** ~ Leichtgut; **measurement** ~ sperrige Ladung, Sperrgut; **mixed** ~ gemischte Ladung, Sammelladung, Stückgut, -fracht, Stückgutladung; ~ **outward** abgehende Fracht, Hinfracht; **part** ~ Teilfracht; **return** ~ Rückfracht; ~ **saved** geborgene Ladung; **shifting** ~ lose Ladung; **short-landed** ~ bei Schiffsankunft festgestellte Fehlmenge; **substituted** ~ Ersatzladung; **undeclared** ~ nicht deklarierte Fracht; **valuable** ~ wertvolle Ladung; ~ *(v.) (coll.)* beladen; **to assort a** ~ Ladung zusammenstellen; **to carry** ~ Frachtgut befördern; **to close for** ~ Endtermin für die Frachtannahme festsetzen; **to discharge** ~ Ladung löschen, ausladen; **to embark** ~ Ladung einnehmen; **to enter a** ~ [Schiffs]ladung deklarieren; **to examine the** ~ Ladung überprüfen; **to get full** ~ Ladung vervollständigen; **to haul** ~ Schiffsladung befördern; **to have a lien upon a** ~ Frachtführerpfandrecht besitzen; **to jettison the** ~ Ladung über Bord werfen; **to land a** ~ Ladung löschen; **to take in** ~ einladen, Ladung einnehmen; **to take in the full complement of** ~ volle Ladung einnehmen; **to take a risk on a** ~ Ladung versichern; **to unload** ~ ausladen, Ladung löschen; ~ **agent** Frachtspediteur; ~ **aircraft (airplane)** Fracht-, Transportflugzeug; **hot** ~ **agreement** Zwangsabkommen mit Kunden eines bestreikten Betriebes; **hot** ~ **ban** Belieferungsverbot [für bestreikten Betrieb]; ~ **block** Ladeblock; ~ **boat** Frachtschiff, -dampfer; ~ **book** Lade-, Frachtbuch; ~ **carrier** Frachtschiff; ~ **[-carrying] capacity** Ladefähigkeit, -vermögen; ~ **carrying glider** Lastensegler; **institute** ~ **clause** zusätzliche Frachtdeckungsklausel; ~ **clerk** *(US)* Expedient; ~ **compartment** Ladesektor; ~ **automated** ~**-handling facility** automatische Gepäckbeförderungsanlage; ~ **flight** Frachtflug; ~ **hatch** Ladeluke; ~ **hold** Laderaum; ~ **insurance** Güterfrachtversicherung; ~ **lien** Frachtführerpfandrecht; ~ **liner** Linienfrachtschiff; ~ **liner shipping** Linienfrachtschiffsverkehr; ~ **list (manifest)** Frachtliste, Ladungsverzeichnis, -manifest; ~ **parachute** Lastenfallschirm; ~ **place** Laderaum; ~ **policy** Ladungs-, Fracht-, Güterversicherungspolice; ~ **port** [Lade]luke, Ladepforte; ~ **preference** Frachtvergünstigung; ~ **rates** Frachtsätze; ~ **revenue** Frachteinnahmen; ~ **sales executive** Frachtraumverkaufsleiter; ~ **section** Frachtabteil; ~ **service** Frachtdienst, -verkehr; **to fix** ~ **shares** Frachtanteile festlegen; ~ **sharing** Aufteilung des Frachtgeschäfts; ~ **ship** Frachtschiff; ~ **space** Fracht-, Laderaum; **surplus** ~ **space** freier Fracht-, Laderaum; ~ **stage** Ladegerüst; ~ **steamer** Last-, Frachtdampfer, -schiff; ~ **submarine** Unterseefrachter; ~ **tariff** Frachttarif; ~ **trailer** Lastschlepper; ~ **underwriter** Frachtenversicherer; ~ **vessel** Frachtschiff; **to divert a** ~ **vessel** Frachter umleiten; ~ **worker** Dock-, Hafenarbeiter.

cargoman Dockarbeiter.

carhop *(US)* Bedienung im Autorestaurant.

caricatural karikaturenartig.

caricature Karikatur; ~ *(v.)* Karikaturen zeichnen, karikieren.

caricaturist Karikaturzeichner.
caring committee Betreuungsausschuß.
carload *(US)* Minimum-, Waggon-, Massengut-, Wagenladung;
shipped in ~s *(US)* als Schüttgut, waggonweise, in Waggonladungen versandt;
mixed ~ *(US)* gemischte Warenladung, Stückgutladung, Stückgüter;
to handle a shipment as a ~ *(US)* Frachtsätze für Waggonladungen zur Anwendung bringen;
~ **amount** *(US)* Waggonladungsminimum; **less-than-**~ **business** *(US)* Stückgutverkehr; ~ **freight** *(US)* Waggonfracht; **less-than-**~ **delivery** *(US)* Stückgutlieferung; **less-than-**~ **freight** *(US)* Stückgut; **consolidated** ~ **freight** *(US)* gemeinsame Waggonladung, Sammel-, Stückgutladung; **mixed** ~ **freight** *(US)* Sammel-, Stückgutladung, Stückgüter; ~ **loadings** *(US)* Waggonsendungen; ~ **lot** *(US)* genormte Frachtlademenge, Wagen-, Waggonladung; **less-than-**~ **lot** *(US)* Stückgut; ~ **order** *(US)* Waggonauftrag; **less-than-**~ **order** *(US)* Stückgutauftrag; ~ **rate** *(US)* Waggonfrachtsatz, -rate, -ladungstarif; **less-than-**~**rate** *(US)* ermäßigter Frachttarif, Stückguttarif; **less-than-**~ **service** *(US)* Stückgutfrachtdienst; ~ **shipment** *(US)* Waggon-, Schüttgutladung; **minimum** ~ **weight** *(US)* Mindestgewicht für Waggonladungen.
carloading *(US)* Waggonsendung, -ladung, Schütt-, Massengut;
~s abgefertigte Waggons;
~ **company** *(US)* Frachtspediteur.
carlot *(US)* Waggon-, Güterwagenladung, genormte Frachtlademenge;
to ship in ~s *(US)* in Waggonladungen (als Schüttgut) versenden;
~ **rate** *(US)* Schüttgut-, Waggontarif; **mixed** ~ **rate** *(US)* Sammelladungstarif; ~ **shipment** *(US)* Massengut-, Waggonladung, Schüttgutsendung.
carmaker Autofabrikant, -hersteller.
carman Lastwagen-, Kraftfahrer, Chauffeur, *(US)* Omnibusfahrer, Straßenbahnführer.
Carnet Tir Zollbegleitscheinheft.
carnival Fasching, Karneval, *(travelling enterprise)* Wanderzirkus;
~ **licence** Narrenfreiheit; ~ **show** Karnevals-, Faschingsveranstaltung.
carpenter Zimmermann, Tischler, *(mar.)* Schiffszimmermann;
~ **scene** *(theatre)* Zwischenvorhang.
carpet Teppich, *(of bombs)* Bombenteppich;
red ~ *(welcome)* roter Teppich, großer Bahnhof;
~ *(v.)* zurechtweisen;
to be on the ~ zur Debatte stehen, auf dem Tapet sein; **to be put on the** ~ *(coll.)* zurechtgewiesen werden; **to lay out the red** ~ roten Teppich auslegen, großen Bahnhof veranstalten; **to push (sweep) under the** ~ unter den Teppich kehren;
~ *(a.)* aufgemacht;
~ **bombing** Teppichbombenwurf; ~ **knight** Salonlöwe; **to give s. o. a red**~ **reception** roten Teppich für j. auslegen, großen Bahnhof für j. veranstalten.
carpetbag Reisetasche;
~ *(a.)* schwindelhaft;
~ **government** Abenteuerregierung.
carpetbagger *(US)* politischer Abenteurer, Geschäftemacher, Pöstchenjäger, *(wildcat banker)* Winkelbankier.
carpeted, to find o. s. **courteously** sich einem großen Bahnhof gegenübersehen.
carpool *(US)* Fuhrpark, Fahrbereitschaft.
carport *(US)* Wagenunterstand, Unterstellmöglichkeit, Behelfsgarage, Autoschuppen, *(railway, Br.)* Personenwagen.
carriage *(business of carrying)* Fuhr-, Transportgeschäft, *(coach)* Wagen, *(cost of transport, Br.)* Abrollkosten, Transportkosten, -spesen, *(Beförderungs-, Frachtkosten, Fracht-, Roll-, Fuhrgeld, Fuhrlohn, *(management)* Leitung, Verwaltung, Durchführung, *(plane)* Fahrgestell, -werk, *(postage, Br.)* Paketporto, *(railway passenger car, Br.)* Eisenbahnwaggon, Personenwagen, *(transport)* Beförderung, Transport, *(typewriter)* Wagen;
by ~ per Achse;
~ **forward** *(Br.)* Frachtkosten per Nachnahme, Fracht bezahlt der Empfänger, Spesennachnahme, Transportkosten gehen zu Lasten des Empfängers, unfrankiert, unfrei; ~**free** frachtfrei, franko, frei Haus; ~ **inwards** Frachtspesen; ~ **paid** frachtfrei, franko; ~ **paid home** Transportkosten trägt der Absender; ~ **and duty prepaid** franko Fracht und Zoll;
additional ~ Frachtzu-, -aufschlag; **end** ~ *(Br.)* Schlußwaggon; **express** ~ *(Br.)* Eilzugwagen; **first-class** ~ *(Br.)* Personenwagen

erster Klasse; **hired** ~ Mietfuhre; **land** ~ Beförderung auf dem Landwege; **open** ~ *(Br.)* Rungenwagen; **port** ~ Hafenbahnfracht; **railway** ~ *(Br.)* [Eisenbahn]waggon, *(cost)* Eisenbahnfrachtkosten, *(transport)* [Eisenbahn]transport; **second-class** ~ *(Br.)* zweiter Klasse Wagen; **sleeping** ~ *(Br.)* Schlafwagen; **through** ~ *(Br.)* durchgehender Wagen, Kurswagen; **water** ~ Beförderung auf dem Wasserwege;
~ **by air** Lufttransport; ~ **of a bill** *(US)* Annahme (Durchbringung) eines Gesetzantrages; ~ **by canal** Kanalfracht; ~ **of goods** Gütertransport, Warenbeförderung, Verfrachtung, Frachtgeschäft, *(ocean freight)* Verladung; ~ **of goods by rail** Gütertransport per Bahn; ~ **for goods** *(Br.)* Gepäck-, Packwagen; ~ **on hire** Beförderung gegen Entgelt; ~ **by land** Landtransport; ~ **of letters** Beförderung von Briefen, Briefbeförderung; ~ **by mail** Beförderung mit der Post; ~ **of a motion** Annahme eines Antrags, Antragsannahme; ~ **of parcels** Paketbeförderung; ~ **by rail** Eisenbahntransport; ~ **by road** Straßentransport; ~ **by sea** Seetransport, Beförderung auf dem Seewege;
to charge for ~ Frachtkosten berechnen;
~ **account** Frachtkonto; ~ **body** Karosserie; ~ **builder** Wagenbauer; ~ **charges** Transport-, Frachtkosten; ~ **cradle** Gepäcknetz; ~ **drive** Zufahrtsweg; ~ **examiner** *(Br.)* Fahrkartenkontrolleur; ~ **expense** Fracht-, Transportkosten; ~ **lamp** Wagenlampe; ~ **operator** Fuhrmann; ~ **rates** Frachtsatz, -rate, Beförderungsgebührensätze; ~ **receipt** Ladeschein; ~ **return** *(Br.)* Waggonrücklauf; ~ **road** Kutsch-, Fahrweg; ~ **rotation period** Anschlagsdauer; ~ **top** Wagendach; ~ **trade** Luxusindustrie; ~**trade restaurant** Luxusrestaurant.
carriageable befahrbar, *(transportable)* transportfähig, transportierbar.
carriageway Fahrbahn, -weg;
dual (double) ~ doppelte Fahrbahn; **four-laned** ~ vierbahnige Fahrstraße.
carried, to be *(account)* auf Rechnung, *(bill)* angenommen werden, durchgehen;
to be ~ **away** *(audience)* begeistert mitgehen;
~ **forward** Vortrag; ~ **forward to new account** auf neue Rechnung vorgetragen; ~ **in stock** vorrätig.
carrier Fuhr-, Rollfuhr-, Transportunternehmer, Fuhrmann, -unternehmer, Beförderer, Verfrachter, Frachtführer, Spediteur, *(aircraft)* Luftfrachtführer, Lufttransportgesellschaft, *(bicycle)* Gepäckträger, *(communications)* Trägergesellschaft, *(el.)* Trägerstrom, -welle, *(grid, US)* Gepäckhalter, *(messenger)* Bote, Überbringer, *(print.)* Sammler, *(water transport)* Verfrachter, Verkehrsträger, *(warship)* Flugzeugträger;
~s Transportgesellschaft, Speditionsgeschäft, -firma;
air-cargo ~ Luftfrachtspediteur; **aircraft** ~ Flugzeugträger; **airline** ~ Lufttransportgesellschaft; **cargo** ~ Frachtschiff; **common** ~ [bahnamtlicher] Spediteur, gewerbsmäßiger Frachtführer, *(US)* öffentliches Verkehrsmittel, *(US, airline)* Luftverkehrslinie, *(US, transportation agency)* Transportgesellschaft, -unternehmen; **connecting** ~ Korrespondenzspediteur; **contract** ~ bahnamtlicher Rollfuhrunternehmer; **delivering** ~ Abrollspediteur; **destination** ~ Versand-, Hauptspediteur; **direct-working** ~ *(insurance)* Erst-, Rückversicherer; **domestic** ~ *(US)* Luftverkehrsgesellschaft; **freight** ~ Frachtflugzeug; **highway** ~ *(US)* Beförderungsgesellschaft; **industrial** ~ betriebliches Transportunternehmen; **initial** ~ Aufgabenspediteur; **inland** ~ Binnenfrachtführer; **intermediate** ~ Zwischenspediteur; **international** ~ internationale Fluggesellschaft; **issuing** ~ Hauptspediteur; **land** ~ Transportunternehmen; **long-haul** ~ Lufttransportgesellschaft für Langstreckenflüge; **mail** ~ *(US)* Briefträger; **marine** ~ Seefrachtführer; **motor-truck** ~ Lastwagentransportunternehmen; **nonorganization** ~ nicht verbandsangehörige Versicherungsgesellschaft; **nuclear** ~ atomangetriebener Flugzeugträger; **on-**~ übernehmender Spediteur (Reeder); **participating** ~ Teilhaberspedition; **pneumatic dispatch** ~ Rohrpostbüchse; **private** ~ Gelegenheitsspediteur; **professional** ~ gewerbsmäßiger Spediteur; **reinsured** ~ rückversicherte Gesellschaft; **scheduled** ~ *(US)* Linienfluggesellschaft; **specific commodity** ~ Spezialtransportunternehmen; **switching** ~ Platz-, Umschlagsspediteur; **supplemental** ~ Charterfluggesellschaft; **terminal** ~ Empfangsspediteur; **troop** ~ Truppentransporter; **water** ~ Fluß-, Seespediteur, Wasserfrachtführer;
common ~ **by air** Luftfrachtspediteur; ~ **by land** Frachtführer; **common** ~ **of passengers** *(US)* öffentliche Personenbeförderungsgesellschaft; ~ **by sea** Seefrachtführer, Verfrachter;
~ **and forwarding agent** Spediteur; ~**bag** Tragetüte; ~**based plane** Trägerflugzeug; ~ **borne aircraft** Decklande-, Trägerflugzeug; ~'s **business** Speditions-, Frachtfuhr-, Rollfuhrge-

schäft, Transportunternehmen; **motor ~'s business** Lastwagen-speditionsgeschäft; **~s' charges** Transportkosten; **~ competition** Transportunternehmerwettbewerb; **~ frequency** *(telecommunication)* Trägerfrequenz; **~'s liability** Transport-, Spediteurhaftung; **~ licence** Führerschein; **~'s lien** Spediteur-, Frachtführerpfandrecht; **~'s manifest** Frachtladungsverzeichnis; **~'s negligence** mangelnde Sorgfalt des Spediteurs; **~ pigeon** Brieftaube; **~'s receipt** Ladeschein, Spediteurbescheinigung; **~'s risk** der Spediteur trägt das volle Risiko; **~ shares** *(stock exchange)* Eisenbahnwerte; **~ telegraphy** Trägerfrequenztelegraphie; **~ telephony** Trägerfrequenztelefonie; **~ transmission** Trägerfrequenzübertragung; **common ~ transportation** *(US)* Beförderung durch öffentliche Verkehrsmittel.

carrot, the stick and the Zuckerbrot und Peitsche;
to hold out a ~ to s. o. j. mit einer Belohnung abwerben.

carry *(gun)* Schußweite, *(portage)* Trageplatz;
~ *(v.)* bringen, führen, tragen, *(appropriate money)* [Geld] verwalten, *(car)* Platz (Raum) bieten, *(figures)* übertragen, *(interest)* [Zinsen] tragen, *(letter)* überbringen, *(motion)* [Antrag] durchbringen, *(transfer entry)* übertragen, *(transport)* befördern, tranportieren, fahren;
~ arms Waffen tragen; **~ as asset[s]** aktivieren, auf der Aktivseite [einer Bilanz] aufführen; **~ one's audience with one** seine Anhörer in Begeisterung versetzen; **~ authority** Autorität genießen; **~ everthing before one** hundertprozentigen Erfolg verzeichnen; **~ a bill** Gesetz verabschieden; **~ in the books** in den Büchern führen (ausweisen); **~ book reviews** Bücherkritiken veröffentlichen; **~ cargo** Frachtgut befördern; **~ in a catalog(ue)** im Katalog aufführen; **~ coals to Newcastle** Eulen nach Athen tragen; **~ corn** Ernte einbringen; **~ costs** *(verdict)* zum Tragen der Kosten verpflichten; **~ a customer** Kunden anschreiben lassen; **~ the day** obsiegen, Oberhand gewinnen, Preis davontragen; **~ oil across the desert in pipelines** in Ölleitungen durch die Wüste befördern; **~ into effect** zur Durchführung bringen, in die Tat umsetzen; **~ an election** Wahl gewinnen, siegreich aus einer Wahl hervorgehen; **~ the farmers** *(US)* Landwirtschaft unterstützen; **~ a financial page** *(journal)* Wirtschaftsteil enthalten; **~ fire-arms** Handfeuerwaffen führen; **~ goods** Fracht befördern, *(US)* Artikel führen; **~ goods at published fare on set schedule** Gütertransport zu öffentlich festgelegten Tarifsätzen durchführen; **~ goods to the station** Güter zur Bahn befördern; **~ goods in stock** Waren auf Lager halten; **~ insurance** *(US)* Versicherung unterhalten, versichert sein; **~ an interest of 5%** mit 5% verzinslich sein, 5% Zinsen einbringen; **~ a law** Gesetz annehmen; **~ as liability (liabilities)** passivieren, als Passiva behandeln, auf der Passivseite [einer Bilanz] aufführen; **~ one's life in one's hands** Todesrisiko eingehen; **~ mail** Post befördern; **~ a member** für die Beiträge eines Mitglieds aufkommen; **~ modesty too far** zu bescheiden sein; **~ money about one** Geld bei sich haben; **~ a motion** Antrag durchbringen; **~ the news to everyone in the village** Nachricht überall hinausposaunen; **~ passengers for a consideration** Personenbeförderung gegen Entgelt übernehmen; **~ one's point** sein Ziel erreichen, sich mit seiner Ansicht durchsetzen; **~ the enemy's position** feindliche Stellung einnehmen; **~ an amount to reserve** Betrag den Rücklagen zuweisen; **~ to the reserve fund** dem Reservefonds zuführen; **~ at one's own risk** auf eigenes Risiko befördern; **~ securities** *(US)* Wertpapiere durchhalten; **~ securities at 9 per cent** Wertpapiere auf Kredit zu 9% verwahren; **~ silver** *(ore)* silberhaltig sein; **~ a state** *(US)* Wahlsieg in einem Einzelstaat davontragen; **~ goods in stock** Waren auf Lager halten; **~ heavy stocks** im Warenlager stark investiert haben; **~ a vote unanimously** Vorschlag einstimmig annehmen; **~ the war in the enemy's land** Krieg ins Feindesland tragen; **~ a weather forecast** Wetterbericht bringen; **~ weight** ins Gewicht fallen, von Bedeutung sein, Einfluß haben; **~ all the world before one** auf der ganzen Linie siegreich sein.

carry *(v.)* **away** wegtragen, fortschaffen, *(fig.)* mitnehmen, forttragen, verleiten, mit sich fortreißen.

carry *(v.)* **back** zurücktragen, -bringen;
~ o. s. to one's schooldays sich in die Schulzeit zurückversetzt fühlen.

carry *(v.)* **forward** *(bookkeeping)* vortragen, übertragen, *(stock exchange)* prolongieren;
~ the balance Saldo vortragen; **~ an item** Posten übertragen; **~ long-term losses** *(Br.)* Verluste längerfristig vortragen (mit späteren Gewinnen verrechnen); **~ to new account** auf neue Rechnung vortragen.

carry *(v.)* **into | effect** realisieren, zur Durchführung bringen; **~ execution** vollstrecken, zur Durchführung bringen; **~ port** in den Hafen bringen.

carry *(v.)* **off** fortschaffen, -tragen;
~ to prison ins Gefängnis abführen; **~ all the school prizes** alle Schulpreise gewinnen; **~ [it] well** eine Sache schmeißen.

carry *(v.)* **on** *(coll.)* sich auffällig benehmen, *(continue)* [Geschäft, Prozeß] fortführen, -setzen, weiterführen, -treiben;
~ with s. th. etw. weiter betreiben; **~ a business** Geschäft betreiben, geschäftlich (gewerblich) tätig sein; **~ a business under one's name** Geschäft unter seinem Namen fortführen; **~ commerce** Handel treiben; **~ a conversation** Gespräch fortsetzen (wiederaufnehmen); **~ a conversation in English** Gespräch in englischer Sprache führen; **~ at a loss** mit Verlust betreiben; **~ a suit against s. o.** Prozeß gegen j. führen; **~ a trade** Gewerbe betreiben; **~ with one's work** seine Arbeit fortsetzen.

carry *(v.)* **out** *(contract, measures)* ausführen, durchführen, verwirklichen, zum Abschluß bringen, tätigen, *(judgment)* vollstrecken, *(resolution)* ausführen;
~ a commission sich eines Auftrags entledigen; **~ official functions** öffentliche Aufgaben wahrnehmen; **~ the law** Gesetz zur Anwendung bringen; **~ payment** Zahlung leisten; **~ a procedure** Verfahrensmodus anwenden; **~ a product** *(bookkeeping)* Posten umbuchen; **~ one's promise** sein Versprechen einlösen; **~ the provisions of a will** Testament vollstrecken; **~ a reform** Reform durchführen; **~ within a given time** fristgemäß erledigen; **~ a work** Arbeit zu Ende führen.

carry *(v.)* **over** *(bookkeeping)* übertragen, Übertrag durchführen, *(stock exchange, Br.)* prolongieren, in Prolongation nehmen;
~ a balance Saldo vortragen; **~ stock** Effekten vortragen.

carry *(v.)* **through** aus-, durchführen;
~ an undertaking Unternehmen fortführen.

carry *(v.)* **up** *(bookkeeping)* vortragen, übertragen.

carry *(v.)* **with it** mit sich bringen, nach sich ziehen;
~ the right of six weeks annual leave Jahresurlaub von sechs Wochen beinhalten.

carry forward *(balance sheet, Br.)* Übertrag, Vortrag aus dem vorjährigen Rechnungsjahr;
tax-loss ~ Steuerverlustvortrag; **virtually unchanged ~** praktisch unveränderter Vortrag; **~ of excess allowance** Steuervortrag nicht ausgenutzter Abschreibungsmöglichkeiten.

carry-on | bag Reisetasche; **~ baggage** *(US)* Handgepäck.

carryall *(bag)* Einkaufs-, Reisetasche, *(car, US)* Kombiwagen, *(mil.)* Tragetasche.

carryback *(US)* *(balance sheet)* Verlustausgleich, -rücktrag;
~ adjustment Verlustausgleich; **~ period** Verlustrücktragszeitraum; **~ provisions** Verlustrücktragsbestimmungen.

carrying Beförderung, Transport, *(cost of ~)* Beförderungskosten;
during the ~ of his duties im Rahmen seiner Tätigkeit; **~ away** *(theft)* Wegschaffen; **~ of a bill** Gesetzannahme, Annahme einer Gesetzesvorlage; **~ express** Beförderung als Eilgut; **~ forward** *(bookkeeping)* Übertrag, Vortrag; **~ of an insurance** Aufrechterhaltung einer Versicherung; **~ on** Ausübung; **~ on business** Fortführung des Geschäfts; **~ on of a partnership business** Fortsetzung der Gesellschaftertätigkeit (des Gesellschafterverhältnisses); **~ out** Durch-, Ausführung; **~ out of agriculture, forestry or fishing operations** landwirtschaftlicher, Forst- oder Fischereibetrieb; **~ over** *(stock exchange, Br.)* glatte Prolongation; **~ agent** Spediteur; **~ business** Speditionsgeschäft, Transportunternehmen; **~ capacity** Lade-, Tragfähigkeit, Nutzlast; **~ charges** Betriebs-, Lagerkosten, *(building)* laufende Instandhaltungskosten, *(on inactive assets)* Unterhaltungskosten, *(stock exchange, Br.)* Maklerausführungsspesen, *(transport)* Speditions-, Transportkosten; **~ company** Spedition; **~ cost** Transport-, Beförderungskosten, *(administration)* Verwaltungskosten; **high ~ costs** *(inventory)* hohe Unterhaltungskosten; **~ day** *(Br.)* Report-, Prämien-Erklärungstag; **~ establishment** Speditionsgeschäft; **~ law** Ausführungsgesetz; **~s-on** Affäre; **scandalous ~s-on** skandalöse Geschichten; **~over business** *(Br.)* Prolongations-, Report-, Kostgeschäft; **~over day** *(Br.)* Report-, Erklärungstag; **~over rate** *(Br.)* Reportsatz, -kurs, Prolongationsgebühr, Kostgeld; **~ party** *(mil.)* Nachschubtrupp; **~ power** Tragkraft; **dual ~ road** Fernverkehrsstraße mit doppelter Fahrbahn; **~ trade** Fracht-, Transportgeschäft, Speditions-, Transportgewerbe, Güterverkehr, -spedition; **~ and forwarding trade** Speditions-, Transportgewerbe; **~ value** Buchwert; **~ van** Speditionswagen.

carryover *(Br.)* Report, Prolongation, *(crop)* Angebot aus der Vorjahresernte, [Ernte]überschuß, -übertrag, *(reserve)* Überbrückungsreserve, *(taxation, US)* Verlustvortrag;

~ **in the public mind** Nachhinken der öffentlichen Meinung;
~ **business** noch nicht erledigte Tagesordnungspunkte; ~ **funds** Etatüberschüsse; ~ **rate** *(Br.)* Reportsatz.
carshop *(US)* Eisenbahnausbesserungswerk.
carsick auto-, eisenbahnkrank.
cart Fuhrwerk, Karren;
  market ~ Marktkarren;
  ~ *(v.)* Karren anrollen;
  ~ **goods** Waren per Achse befördern; ~ **away the rubbish** Müll abfahren;
  to be in the ~ *(Br., sl.)* in der Klemme sein, in der Patsche sitzen;
  to put the ~ **before the horse** Pferd beim Schwanz aufzäumen;
  ~ **note** *(customs)* Benachrichtigung über Warenverlagerungen;
  ~ **road** Feld-, Waldweg.
cartage Rollgeld, Anfuhr-, Abroll-, Transportkosten, Fuhrlohn, Frachtgebühr, -spesen, -kosten, -geld, Zustellungsgebühren, *(short-distance carriage)* Nahtransport;
  regular ~ **company** Bahnspediteur; ~ **contractor** Rollfuhrunternehmer; ~ **limit** Zustellbezirk; ~ **note** Anfuhrrechnung; ~ **service** Rollfuhrdienst.
carte blanche Blankett, unbeschränkte Vollmacht, Blankovollmacht;
  ~ **order** Blankoauftrag.
carted goods Rollgut.
cartel Kartell[konvention], *(law of nations)* Abkommen über den Austausch von Kriegsgefangenen;
  compulsory ~ Zwangskartell; **conditions** ~ Konditionenkartell; **domestic** ~ Inlandskartell; **electoral** ~ Wahlabkommen; **export** ~ Ausfuhrkartell; **foreign** ~ Auslandskartell; **international** ~ internationales Kartell; **left-wing** ~ Linkskartell; **marketing** ~ Absatz-, Vertriebskartell; **market-price** ~ Preiskartell; **steel-pipe** ~ Stahlrohrkartell; **world** ~ Weltkartell;
  to break up a ~ Kartell auflösen; **to break up rules of a** ~ gegen Kartellvereinbarungen verstoßen; **to expand a** ~ Kartell vergrößern; **to join a** ~ einem Kartell beitreten; **to split the structure of a** ~ Kartell auflösen;
  ~ **activities** Kartelltätigkeit; ~ **agreement** Kartellvertrag, -vereinbarung; ~ **arrangement** Kartellvereinbarung; ~ **ban** Kartellverbot; ~ **bureau** Kartellausschuß; ~ **bureaucracy** Kartellbürokratie; ~ **combination in restraint of trade** Kartellorganisation; ~ **company** Kartellfirma; ~ **connections** kartellrechtliche Verbindungen, Kartellverbindungen; ~ **control** Kartellkontrolle; ~ **court** Kartellgericht; ~ **decree** Kartellverordnung; ~ **dispersal** Entkartellisierung; ~ **habits** Kartellusancen; ~ **interests** Kartellinteressen; ~**-like** kartellähnlich; ~**-like agreements** kartellähnliche Absprachen; ~ **matter** Kartellangelegenheit; ~ **negotiations** Kartellvereinbarungen; ~ **office** *(Br.)* Kartellbehörde; ~ **output** Produktionsleistung eines Kartells; ~ **pact** Kartellabkommen; ~ **participant** Kartellmitglied; ~ **participation** Kartellbeteiligung; **anti-**~ **people** Kartellgegner; **pro-**~ **people** Kartellanhänger; ~ **power** Kartellmacht; ~ **practices** Kartellisierungsmethoden; ~ **price** gebundener Preis, Kartellpreis **fixed** ~ **price** gebundener Preis, Kartellpreis; ~ **problems** Kartellfragen, -probleme; ~ **ramifications** Kartellisierungssystem; ~ **regulations** Kartellbestimmungen; ~ **relationship** Kartellbeziehungen; ~ **relinquishment** Kartellauflösung, -beseitigung; ~ **ship** Parlamentärschiff; ~ **termination** Kartellkündigung.
cartelising policy Kartellpolitik.
cartelism Kartellwesen.
cartelist Kartellanhänger.
cartelization Kartellisierung;
  compulsory ~ Zwangskartellisierung.
cartelize *(v.)* kartellisieren, zu einem Kartell zwingen.
cartelized product Kartellerzeugnis.
cartelizing policy Kartellpolitik.
cartelographer Kartellrechtsspezialist.
carter Fuhrmann, [Roll]fuhrunternehmer.
carting agent Rollfuhrunternehmer, -dienst.
cartload Fuder, Fuhre, Wagen-, Karrenladung;
  by ~**s** waggon-, wagenweise.
cartogram Kartogramm.
cartographer Kartograph.
cartographical kartographisch;
  ~ **distance** Kartenentfernung.
cartography Kartographie.
carton Schutzkarton;
  ~ **paper** Pigmentpapier.
cartonage Kartonage.
cartoon karikaturistische (humoristische) Zeichnung, Karikatur, *(design)* Musterzeichnung, *(film)* Zeichentrickfilm;

~ *(v.)* karikieren, als Karikatur zeichnen;
~ **film** Zeichentrickfilm; ~ **paper** Pigmentpapier.
cartoonist *(in newspapers)* Karikaturist, Pressezeichner;
  advertising ~ Werbezeichner.
cartridge Karton, *(film)* Filmpatrone, *(pickup of gramophone)* Tonabnehmer, *(tape recording, US)* Kassette;
  ball ~ scharfe Patrone; **film** ~ Filmkassette; **pre-recorded** ~ bespielte Kassette; **program(me)** ~ bespielte Kassette;
  ~ **movie for television** Kassettenfernsehfilm; ~ **paper** starkes Zeichenpapier; ~ **player** Kassettenspielgerät; ~ **television** Kassettenfernsehen; ~ **television program(me)** Kassettenfernsehprogramm; ~ **television rights** Kassettenfernsehrechte.
cartrivision Kassettenfernsehen;
  ~ **one-hour tape** Fernsehkassettenfilmband mit einstündiger Spieldauer.
carve *(v.)* schnitzen, meißeln.
carve *(v.)* **out** *(fig.)* Karriere machen;
  ~ **a career for o. s.** Karriere machen; ~ **a fortune** Vermögen machen; ~ **a large part of the market** sich einen großen Marktanteil sichern; ~ **an even greater share of a highly profitable yet competitive market** sich einen noch größeren hoch rentierlichen aber konkurrenzträchtigen Marktanteil sichern.
cascade *(v.)* *(letters)* massenhaft ankommen;
  ~ **bombing** Kaskadenbomben-, Markierungswurf; ~ **tax** kumulative Umsatzsteuer.
case Kiste, Behälter, Kasten, *(bookbinding)* Einbanddecke, *(~ at law)* Fall, Sache, Rechtssache, -fall, Streitsache, Rechtsstreit, -streitigkeit, Prozeß, *(illness)* Krankheitsfall, -zustand, *(patient, coll.)* Kranker, *(print.)* Setzkasten, *(windows)* Fensterfutter;
  as the ~ **may be** je nach Lage des Falles, je nach Sachlage; **in** ~ **of accident** im Falle eines Unfalls; **in** ~ **of an answer in the negative** im Verneinungsfalle; **in** ~ **of death** im Todesfall; **in** ~ **of doubt** im Zweifelsfall; **in** ~ **of emergency** im Notfall; **in** ~ **of fire** bei Brand; **in** ~ **of loss** im Schadensfall; **in** ~ **of need** im Notfall, notfalls; **in no** ~ keinesfalls; **in** ~ **of nondelivery** im Falle der Unzustellbarkeit; **in** ~ **of a fresh offence** im Wiederholungsfall; **in** ~ **of prevention** im Verhinderungsfall; **in** ~ **of war** im Kriegsfalle; **in no** ~ unter keiner Bedingung;
  affiliation ~ Vaterschaftsprozeß, Unterhaltssache; ~ **agreed-on** Einigung über den Sachverhalt im Prozeß, unstreitiger Sachverhalt; **airtight** ~ totsicherer Fall; **arbitral** ~ Schiedssache; **bankruptcy** ~ Konkurssache; **bolstered-up** ~ geschickt geführter Prozeß; **borderline** ~ Grenzfall; **certified** ~ dem Obergericht zur Entscheidung vorgelegte Sache; **cigarette** ~ Zigarettenetui; **civil** ~ Zivilprozeß, bürgerlicher Rechtsstreit; **commercial** ~ Handelssache; **concrete** ~ konkreter Fall; **copyright** ~ Urheberrechtsklage; **criminal** ~ Strafsache, -fall; **dismissed** ~ Verfahren eingestellt; **divorce** ~ Scheidungsprozeß, -sache; **dressing** ~ Reisenecessaire; **exceptional** ~ Ausnahmefall; **famous** ~**s** berühmte Rechtsfälle; **glass** ~ Schaukasten, Vitrine; **good** ~ aussichtsreiches Vorbringen; **hard** ~ schwerer Junge; **hardened** ~ hartgesottener Bursche; **in-between** ~ Grenzfall; **individual** ~ Einzelfall; **instant** ~ vorliegender Fall; **interesting** ~ interessanter Fall; **isolated** ~ vereinzelter Fall, Einzelfall; **jewel** ~ Schmucktruhe; **juvenile** ~ Jugendsache; **law** ~ Rechtsfall, Prozeßsache; **leading** ~ herrschende Meinung, Präzedenzfall; **legal** ~ Rechtssache, Rechtsangelegenheit; **lower** ~ Kleinbuchstabe; **main** ~ Hauptprozeß; **mental** ~ Fall von Geisteskrankheit; **new** ~**s** Neuerkrankungen; **packing** ~ Packkiste; **parallel** ~ Parallelfall; **particular** ~ Sonderfall; **paternity** ~ Vaterschaftsprozeß; **pending** ~ schwebender Prozeß; **petty** ~ Bagatellsache; **running-down** ~ Verkehrs[unfall]sache; **secondhand** ~ gebrauchte Kiste; **shut** ~ abgeschlossener Fall; **sealed** ~ verschlossener Behälter; ~ **stated** *(Br.)* vorgetragener Fall, Revisionsklage; **test** ~ Schulfall, Schul-, Musterbeispiel, *(law)* Grundsatzurteil, *(pol.)* Präzedenzfall; **tin-lined** ~ mit Blech ausgeschlagene Kiste; **upper** ~ Großbuchstabe; **urgent** ~ Dringlichkeitsfall;
  ~ **on appeal** Berufungssache; ~ **at bar** zur Entscheidung anstehende Sache, vorliegender Rechtsfall; ~**s and casks** Rollgut; ~**s on the cause list** zur Verhandlung anstehende Sachen; **clear** ~ **of cheating** einwandfreier Fall von Betrug; ~ **of conscience** Gewissensfrage; ~**s and controversies** Rechtsstreitigkeiten; ~ **before the court** zur Verhandlung anstehende Sache; ~ **difficult to deal with** schwieriger Fall; ~ **of for the defendant** für den Beklagten sprechender Sachverhalt; ~ **under dispute** Streitsache; ~ **of emergency** dringender Fall, Dringlichkeitssache; ~ **for exemption** Ausnahmefall; ~ **of fraud** Betrugsfall; ~ **of hardship** Härtefall; ~ **of first impression** völlig neuer Fall; **five** ~**s of influenza** fünf Grippefälle; ~ **at issue** strittiger Fall, Streitfrage;

~ of kidnapping Entführungsfall; ~ of (at) law Rechtsfrage; ~ for motion schriftliche Antragsbegründung; ~ of murder Mordfall; ~ of absolute necessity Fall absoluter Notwendigkeit; ~s paid and received *(banking)* Einzahlungen und Abhebungen; a ~ in point einschlägiges Beispiel, typischer Fall; ~ in precedent Präzedenzfall; ~ within the purview innerhalb der Zuständigkeit liegender Fall; ~ in question vorliegender (betreffender) Fall; ~ unprovided for by the rules in den Bestimmungen nicht vorgesehener Fall; ~s analogous to suretyship bürgschaftsähnliche Fälle; ~ of trespass Besitzstörungsklage; ~ of urgency Dringlichkeitssache;

~ *(v.)* in Kisten verpacken;

to arbitrate a ~ über eine Sache schiedsrichterlich verhandeln; to ask for a stated ~ auf Entscheidung antragen; to be counsel in a ~ Rechtssache führen; to call a ~ [at court] Sache aufrufen; to close a ~ Verhandlung schließen; to cognosce a ~ über eine Sache erkennen; to come down to ~s *(US)* zur Sache kommen; to deal with a ~ upon its merits zur Hauptsache verhandeln; to decide a ~ on its merits Fall allein aufgrund der ihm innewohnenden Umstände entscheiden; to dismiss a ~ Klage abweisen; to dispose of a ~ Fall erledigen; to docket the ~ of X vs. Y Sache X gegen Y ansetzen; to fail to make out one's ~ seine Klage nicht begründen können; to give a decision on a ~ Fall richterlich entscheiden; to give particulars of a ~ Klageanspruch substantieren; to give a ~ to the superior court Berufung zulassen; to handle a ~ Fall bearbeiten; to have a fair ~ for saying gute Argumente für etw. haben; to have a good ~ gute Prozeßaussichten haben; to have a strong ~ über starke Argumente verfügen, Recht auf seiner Seite haben; to have a ~ at law for damages Schadensersatzansprüche haben; to hear a ~ über eine Sache verhandeln; to lose one's ~ seinen Prozeß verlieren; to make out one's ~ seine Sache begründen (beweisen, Sache flüssig vortragen), Argumente vorbringen; to move into a ~ Fall aufgreifen; to open the ~ Verhandlung eröffnen; to plead a ~ Fall vortragen, Sache vertreten; to plead one's ~ well seine Sache gut vertreten; to proceed with a ~ über eine Sache verhandeln; to put a ~ to s. o. jem. einen Fall vortragen; to put a ~ in mothballs Fall einmotten; to put s. o. on a ~ j. mit einem Fall beauftragen; to put together a plausible ~ against s. o. ordnungsgemäßes Verfahren gegen j. eröffnen; to quote a ~ in point analogen Fall zitieren; to refer to the merits of a ~ sich zur Sache äußern; to remand a ~ Sache zurückverweisen; to remit a ~ Sache verweisen; to reopen a ~ Verfahren wiederaufnehmen; to rest one's ~ on equity seinen Fall auf Treu und Glauben abstellen; to return a ~ Verfahren wiederaufnehmen; to set down a ~ for hearing Termin zur mündlichen Verhandlung anberaumen; to sit in judgment on a ~ Sache verhandeln; to state a ~ Fall vortragen; to state one's ~ seinen Standpunkt vertreten; to stop a ~ Prozeß aussetzen; to submit the (a) ~ to the court Fall dem Gericht zur Entscheidung vorlegen, Fall dem Gericht vortragen; to submit a written statement of a ~ Fall schriftlich vortragen; to take a ~ to court Fall vor Gericht bringen; to take a concrete ~ konkreten Fall annehmen; to take one's ~ to the people sein Anliegen dem Volk unterbreiten; to throw a ~ back for remedy Fall zur Rechtsmittelhilfe zurückverweisen; to try a ~ Sache vor Gericht verhandeln; to win a ~ Prozeß gewinnen;

deviant-~ analysis Analyse abweichender Fälle; ~ binding fester Einband; ~ history Erfahrungsbericht, Personalakte, *(illness)* Krankengeschichte; ~ house *(sl.)* Bordell; ~ law auf früheren Entscheidungen beruhendes Recht, Präzedenzrecht; in accordance with prevailing ~ law in Übereinstimmung mit der Rechtsprechung; ~ lawyer erfahrener [Prozeß]anwalt; ~ load zu bearbeitende Fürsorgefälle; ~ method Fallmethode, *(sales policy)* praktisch ausgerichtete Verkäuferschulung; ~ overseer Faktor; ~ records Prozeßakten; ~ room Setzerei; ~ sheet Krankenblatt; ~ study Fallstudie, Fällestudium; ~ system Rechtsunterricht nach Präzedenzfällen.

casebook Entscheidungssammlung.

casement Fensterflügel.

casework, social Fürsorgetätigkeit, Sozialfürsorge, Einzelbetreuung, *(print.)* Handsatz.

caseworker Sozialfürsorger.

cash Bargeld, -zahlung, bares Geld, Barschaft, Barmittel, *(balance sheet)* flüssige Mittel, Kasse, Kassenbestand, *(bookkeeping)* Kassenkonto, *(stock exchange, US)* per Kasse; bought for ~ gegen Kasse gekauft; for prompt ~ gegen Barzahlung; for ~ only nur gegen Kasse (Barzahlung); in [ready] ~ [in] bar, in klingender Münze, gegen Barzahlung (Kasse); otherwise than for ~ nicht in bar; out of ~ ohne jedes Geld; payable in ~ in bar zu zahlen; short of ~ knapp bei Kasse; terms

strictly for ~ nur gegen Barzahlung; 3% for ~ 3% Skonto für Barzahlung; sold for ~ gegen bar verkauft; when in ~ nach Eingang;

counter ~ *(bank)* tägliche Kasse; ~ down in (gegen) bar, gegen Barzahlung; excess ~ Kassenüberschuß; foreign ~ Bardevisen; hard ~ klingende Münze, Hart-, Metallgeld; idle ~ brachliegende Barmittel; internal ~ eigene Barmittel; loose ~ Klein-, Münzgeld; net ~ Barzahlung, bar ohne Abzug, netto Kasse; operating ~ vorhandene Betriebsmittel; ~ paid in bar bezahlt; ~ paid and received Einzahlungen und Abhebungen; petty ~ Portokasse, kleine Kasse, *(small sums)* kleine Barposten; prompt ~ sofortige Barzahlung; proving ~ Kassensturz; ready ~ bares Geld, Bargeld; spot ~ bar ohne Abzug, sofortige Bezahlung, netto Kasse; ~ terms nur gegen Barzahlung, Barzahlung vorgesehen; total ~ received gesamte Bareinnahmen; treasury ~ Geld und sofort fällige Staatsbankguthaben; ~ withdrawn Barabhebung;

~ in advance netto Kasse im voraus; ~ in bank (at the bank, at bankers) *(balance sheet)* Bankguthaben, Guthaben bei Kreditinstituten; ~ at branches *(balance sheet)* Kassenbestand bei den Filialen; ~ in circulation Bargeldumlauf; ~ under the control of the court gerichtlich hinterlegtes Geld; ~ of conveyance Speditionskasse; ~ on current account laufendes Guthaben; ~ before delivery Kasse vor Lieferung; ~ on delivery Empfänger bezahlt, Barzahlung bei Lieferung, bar gegen Nachnahme; ~ less discount Barzahlung abzüglich Skonto; ~ against documents Kasse (Barzahlung) gegen Dokumente; ~ in (on) hand Bargeld, Barbestand, -vorrat, Geld-, Kassenbestand; ~ in house im Haus vorhandenes Bargeld; ~ at maturity zahlbar bei Fälligkeit; ~ with order Barzahlung bei Bestellung, zahlbar (Barzahlung) bei Auftragserteilung; ~ in settlement Barabdeckung; ~ to shareholders Barausschüttung an die Aktionäre; ~ on shipment zahlbar bei Verschiffung; short and overs *(US)* Kassenüberschüsse und Fehlbeträge; ~ in transit durchlaufende Gelder; ~ in vaults *(US)* Barbestand (Geldvorrat) einer Bank, Kassenbestand;

~ *(v.)* zu Geld machen, realisieren, *(collect)* einkassieren, einziehen;

~ bank notes Banknoten einlösen; ~ a bill Wechsel einlösen; ~ a check *(US)* (cheque, *Br.*) for s. o. Scheck für j. kassieren; ~ a check *(US)* (cheque, *Br.*) at a bank Scheck bei der Bank zur Einlösung vorlegen; ~ in *(salesman)* kassieren gegen, *(US)* bezahlen; ~ in on s. o. Geld bei jem. gewinnen; ~ in on s. th. Kapital aus etw. schlagen, sich an etw. gesundstoßen; ~ in on an idea Idee ausnützen, aus einer Idee Kapital schlagen; ~ in on one's profits seine Gewinne realisieren; ~ up Kasse[nsturz] machen;

to balance the ~ Kassensturz machen, Kasse abstimmen; to base on ~ auf Barzahlung berechnen; to be in charge of the ~ Kassenführung haben; to be in (out of) ~ (nicht) bei Kasse (Geld) sein; to be rolling in ~ im Geld schwimmen; to be short of ~ knapp bei Kasse sein; to be strapped for ~ völlig pleite sein; to buy for ~ gegen bar kaufen; to commit ~ near the bottom end Barmittel beim Börsentiefstpunkt einsetzen; to convert into ~ versilbern, zu Geld machen; to count up the ~ *(US)* Kasse abstimmen; to demand ~ on the barrelhead sofortige Barzahlung verlangen; to deposit a margin in ~ *(US)* Bareinschuß leisten; to draw ~ Bargeld abheben; to enter the ~ into the journal Kasse journalisieren; to find ~ Geldmittel bereitstellen; to free up bogged-down ~ Bargeldreserven freisetzen; to get a cheque *(Br.)* (check, *US*) ~ed at the bank Scheck bei der Bank eingelöst bekommen; to have ~ in hand Geld in der Kasse haben; to have no ~ on o. s. kein Geld bei sich haben; to have plenty of ~ [gut] bei Kasse sein; to keep ~ Kasse führen; to lock up one's ~ in one's trade sein Geld ins Geschäft stecken; to make off with the ~ mit der Kasse durchbrennen; to make remittance in ~ in bar übersenden; to make up the ~ Kasse[nsturz] machen; to meet ~ on delivery Nachnahme einlösen; to pay in ~ bar bezahlen; to pay ~ down bar bezahlen; to pay in hard ~ in gängiger Münze zahlen; to prove ~ Kassenprüfung vornehmen, Kassensturz machen; to pull in ~ Forderungen eintreiben; to purchase for ~ gegen bar kaufen; to put s. o. in ~ jem. Geld überweisen; to raise ~ Geld auftreiben; to reckon up the ~ Kasse machen; to run off with the ~ mit der Kasse durchbrennen; to run out of ~ sich verausgaben; to run short of ~ schwache Kassenbestände haben; to sell for ~ gegen Kasse (bar) verkaufen; to send ~ on delivery per Nachnahme schicken; to tally the ~ Kasse abstimmen; to tamper with the ~ sich an der Kasse vergreifen; to turn into ~ zu Geld machen, in bares Geld umsetzen, einlösen;

~ *(a.)* kassenmäßig;

~ **account** Kassa-, Kassenkonto, *(bank credit)* Bankguthaben; ~ **accountant** Kassenbuchhalter; ~ **accounting** Kassenbuchführung, -wesen; ~ **adjustment** Barregulierung; ~ **advance** Bar-, Kassenvorschuß, *(bank of issue)* Kassenkredit; ~ **allocation** Barausstattung; ~ **allowance** Barzuschuß, -vergütung; ~ **alternative** alternatives Barangebot; **with ~ alternative** in bar ausgezahlt; ~ **assets** Kassenbestand, -guthaben, Barbestände, -guthaben, -vermögen, -werte, *(balance sheet)* Kassenbestand und Bankguthaben; ~ **assets brought in** Barleistungen; ~ **assistance** bar ausgezahlte Unterstützung; ~ **audit[ing]** Kassenrevision, -prüfung, -aufnahme; ~ **auditor** Kassenrevisor; ~ **balance** Kassenbestand, -saldo, Geldbestand, -vorrat, Bestand an Geld, Barguthaben; **adverse ~ balance** Kassendefizit; ~ **balance theory** Kassenhaltungstheorie; **to maintain a ~ balance at a bank on a nonborrowing account** mit einer Bank nur kreditorisch arbeiten; ~ **bargain** Barabschluß; ~ **basis** *(accounting)* Buchführung der bar durchgeführten Geschäfte; ~ **benefit** *(life insurance)* Barvergütung, -dividende; **to be in ~-bind** auf Bargeld aus (versessen) sein; ~ **blotter** Kassenjournal; ~ **bonus** Barprämie, *(life insurance)* Barvergütung; ~ **budget** *(budgeting)* Kassenbudget, Kassenvorschau, Bedarfsrechnung; ~ **buildup** Baransammlung, Ansammlung von Bargeld; ~ **business** Kassa-, Bar-, Lokogeschäft; ~ **buying** *(stock exchange)* Kassakauf; ~ **capital** Barkapital, -vermögen; ~ **card** Bargeldkarte; ~**-card service** Bargeldkartensystem; ~ **carrier** *(US)* Rohrpostanlage für Geldtransport.

cash-and-carry *(US)* Verkauf gegen Barzahlung und ohne Kundendienst, Barverkauf [ohne Skontoabzug], Selbstabholung gegen Kasse;
~ *(a.)* nur gegen bar [und ohne Hauszustellung];
~ **clause** *(US)* Bestimmung über Barzahlung und Transport auf eigenen Schiffen; ~ **concern** Großhandelsunternehmen; ~ **store** *(US)* Barzahlungsgeschäft; ~ **system** *(US)* Barzahlungsverkaufssystem; ~ **wholesaler** Engros-Sortiment, Abholgroßhändler.

cash|ceilings amtlich festgelegte Ausgabenbegrenzung; ~ **check** Kassenprüfung; ~ **cheque** *(Br.)* Barscheck; ~ **clerk** Kassierer, Kassenverwalter, -wart; ~ **coiner** Dukatenesel; ~ **collateral** Barsicherheit; ~ **compensation** Barabfindung, Barvergütung; ~ **consignment** Sendung gegen Barzahlung; ~ **contract** Barzahlungsvertrag, Barvertrag, *(stock exchange)* Verkauf gegen Bargeld; ~ **control** Überwachung der Kassenbestände; ~ **cover** Bardeckung; ~ **credit** Bar-, Kontokorrentkredit; ~ **crop** *(US)* leicht verkäufliche Agrarerzeugnisse; ~ **customer** bar zahlender Kunde; ~ **day** Zahl-, Abrechnungstag; ~ **deficit** Fehlbetrag, Kassendefizit, -manko, -ausfall.

cash on delivery (C.O.D.) gegen (per) Nachnahme (Kasse), [zahl]bar bei Lieferung;
to meet ~ Nachnahme einlösen;
~ **consignment** Nachnahmesendung; ~ **fee** Nachnahmegebühr; ~ **package** *(US) (parcel, Br.)* (C.O.D. parcel) Nachnahmepaket; ~ **service** Postnachnahmedienst; ~ **shipment** Nachnahmesendung.

cash|demand Barmittelbedarf; ~ **department** Kasse, Kassenbüro, -verwaltung; ~ **deposit** Hinterlegung in bar, Barhinterlegung, -depot, -einlage; ~ **desk** [Zahl]stelle, -kasse, Kassenschalter; ~ **diary** Kassenkladde.

cash disbursement[s] ausgezahltes Geld, Kassenausgang, -auszahlungen, bare Ausgaben;
~ **book** Kassenausgangsbuch; ~ **journal** Kassenausgangsjournal; ~ **record** Kassenausgabebeleg.

cash discount Bar[zahlungs]rabatt, Bardiskont, [Kassa]skonto;
less 2% ~ 2% Rabatt (Skonto) bei Barzahlung;
~ **on sales** Rabatt bei Barzahlung;
to take ~ Skonto ausnutzen.

cash|dispenser Bargeldautomat; ~ **distribution** Barausschüttung; ~ **dividend** ausgeschüttete Dividende; ~ **donation** Bargeldspende, -geschenk; ~ **downpayment** Barzahlung; ~ **drain** Kassenanspannung; ~ **drawer** Kassenschublade; ~ **drawing** Barabhebung, Geldausgänge, -entnahme; ~ **earnings** Bareinnahmen, Kassengewinn; **gross ~ earnings** gesamter Bargewinn; ~ **entry** Kasseneintragung, -buchung; ~ **equity** Barkapital; ~ **expenditure** kassenmäßige Ausgaben, bare Ausgaben, Barausgaben, -auslagen; ~ **forecast** langfristige Gelddispositionen, Barmittelvorschau; **to be responsible for ~ forecasting** für die Gelddispositionen (Bereitstellung der erforderlichen Geldbeträge) verantwortlich zeichnen; ~ **funds** Barmittel, -bestände, *(temporary investment)* kurzfristige Zwischenanlage; **imprest ~ fund** Barvorschuß für die Portokasse; **to maintain ~ funds** *(public accounting)* Kassen unterhalten; ~**-fund flow** Barmittelzuschuß; **to approximate the ~ generation**

Näherungsrechnung der Kassenentwicklung vornehmen; ~ **gift** Bar-, Geldgeschenk; ~ **girl** Kassenmädchen; ~ **grants** Barzuschüsse; ~**-heavy** äußerst liquide, sehr flüssig; ~ **holdings** Bar-, Kassenbestand; ~**-holding charge** Bankgebühr für Kontoguthaben; **to lend to ~-hungry businessmen** an kreditbedürftige Kaufleute ausleihen; ~ **incentive** Barprämie; ~ **income** Bareinkommen; ~ **indemnity** Mankogeld, Fehlgeldentschädigung; ~ **inflow** Geldzugang; ~ **inflow on the pension side** Rentenbeitragseingänge; ~ **investment** investiertes Bargeld, Bareinlage; ~ **investor** Bargeldanleger; ~ **invoice** Barfaktur; ~ **item** Kassenposten, Bareingang, -einzahlung, Geldanlagen; ~ **journal** Kassenjournal; ~ **legacy** Barlegat; ~ **letter** Geldbrief; ~ **limits** Kreditbegrenzungen; ~ **limits in the public sector** Ausgabenbegrenzung im öffentlichen Bereich; ~ **limits on public spending** Beschränkungen der Ausgaben der öffentlichen Hände; **to produce ~ limits around budget time** Ausgabebeschränkungen bei der Etatsfeststellung festsetzen; **to set ~ limits on local authority spending** Höchstgrenzen für Kommunalausgaben festsetzen; ~ **line** *(US)* Kreditlinie; ~ **loan** Kassendarlehn; ~ **management** Gelddisposition, Kassenhaltung, *(banking)* Bündel internationaler Finanzdienstleistungen; ~ **management experience** Erfahrungen auf dem Gebiet der Gelddispositionen; **to tighten up the ~ management procedures throughout the world** Gelddispositionsmaßnahmen im ganzen Konzernbereich straffen; ~ **market** Kassenmarkt, *(stock exchange)* Kassamarkt; ~ **market value** Kassapreis; ~ **money** *(US)* bares Geld, Bargeld; ~ **mountain** Bargeldschwemme; ~ **note** Kassenanweisung *(banking, Br.)* [Aus]zahlungsanweisung; ~ **obligation** bare Verpflichtung; ~ **offer** Barangebot; ~ **office** Kassenraum, Kasse; ~**-on-invoice basis** Kassageschäft; ~ **operating statement** Barmittelergebnisrechnung; ~ **operation** Kassageschäft; ~ **order** *(bank)* Zahlungs-, Kassenanweisung, *(Br.)* Sichtwechsel, *(stock exchange)* Kassaorder; ~ **outlay** Baraufwand, -auslagen; ~ **outlet** Kassamarkt; ~ **overs** *(US)* Zuvielbeträge in der Kasse, Kassenüberschuß; ~ **pad** Kassenblock; ~ **payment** Geld-, Barzahlung, sofortige Zahlung, Kassaregulierung; ~ **payments** Kassenausgänge; **unrecorded ~ payment** unverbuchte Barzahlung; **to suspend ~ payment** Barzahlungen einstellen; ~ **payments book** Kassenausgangsbuch; ~ **payout** Barauszahlung; ~ **position** Bar-, Kassenposition, Kassenbestand, -status, Flüssigkeit, Liquidität, Liquiditätslage; **short-term ~ position** kurzfristige Liquidität; ~ **position ratio** Kassenstandskoeffizient; ~ **price** Preis bei Barzahlung, Bar[zahlungs]-, Effektivpreis, *(stock exchange)* Kassakurs, Kurs bei Barzahlung; ~ **prize** Geldpreis; ~ **problem** Liquiditätsproblem; ~ **proceeds** Kassenertrag, Barerlös, -ertrag; ~ **purchase** Barkauf, *(stock exchange)* Kassakauf; ~ **purchase offer** Bargebot; ~ **purchaser** Barkäufer; ~ **quotation** *(stock exchange)* Kassakurs; ~ **rate** *(cheque, Br.)* Scheckkurs; ~ **rates** *(stock exchange)* Kassakurs; ~ **ratio** *(banking)* Deckungs-, Liquiditätsgrad, -quote, Bargelddeckungsrate; ~ **realization** Versilberung; ~ **rebate** Barrabatt, Kassenrabatt; ~ **receipt** Kassenquittung; ~ **receipts** eingegangenes Geld, Bareingänge, -einnahmen, Kasseneingang, Veräußerungserträge; ~ **receipts book** Kasseneinnahmebuch; ~ **receipts journal** Kasseneingangsjournal; ~ **reconciliation** Kassenabstimmung; ~ **record** Kassenbeleg; ~ **reduction** Barabzug; ~ **refund** Barvergütung, Rückerstattung in bar; ~ **refund annuity** Kapitalrente; ~ **register** Kontroll-, Registrierkasse; **to operate a ~ register** Registrierkasse bedienen; ~ **remittance** Bargeldsendung, Barüberweisung; ~ **report** Kassenbericht; ~ **requirements** Geldbedarf, *(banking)* Mindestvorschriften über liquide Mittel; **public debtors' ~ requirements** Geldbedarf der öffentlich-rechtlichen Kreditnehmer; ~ **reserve** *(bank)* bare Reserve, Bargeldreserve, Bestand an Geld, Kassenreserve, *(investment fund)* Barmittel; **minimum ~ reserve** *(bank)* Barreserve, Mindestreserve; **operating ~ reserve** Betriebsmittelrücklage; ~ **resources** Kassenmittel, -reserve; ~ **and near ~ resources** liquide und fast liquide Eigenmittel; ~ **results** Kassenabschluß; ~**-rich** flüssig, liquide; ~ **safe** eiserner Geldschrank; ~**sale** Barverkauf, *(stock exchange)* Kassaverkauf, -geschäft; ~ **sales only** Verkauf nur gegen bar, Barverkauf; ~ **savings plan with bonus** prämienbegünstigtes Bausparen; ~ **security** Barsicherheit, -deckung; ~ **settlement** Barabrechnung, -ausgleich, -zahlung, Geld-, Kapital-, Barabfindung; ~**-settlement basis** Barabfindungsgrundlage; ~ **share-out** Barausschüttung, -verteilung; ~ **short** *(US)* Kassendefizit, -manko; ~ **situation** Kassenstand; ~ **squeeze** Liquiditätsdruck, -beengung; ~ **statement** Kassenausweis, -abschluß, -bericht, periodischer Kassen- und Bankbericht; ~ **store** *(US)* Barzahlungsgeschäft; **to husband meager** *(US)* **(meagre,** *Br.)* ~ **supplies** sorgsam mit knappen Liquiditätsmitteln umgehen; ~ **surplus** Kassenüberschuß; ~ **surrender value** *(life insurance)* Rückkaufswert; ~ **system** Barzahlungssystem; **on the ~ system** nur gegen bar; ~ **takings** Bareinnahmen; ~ **tenant** *(US)* Pächter [der seine Pacht in bar zu erlegen hat]; ~ **terms [of sale]** Barzahlungs-, Barpreisbedingungen, Zahlungsbedingungen bei Barzahlung; **in ~ terms** in Geld ausgedrückt; ~ **terms only** nur gegen Barzahlung; ~ **throwoff** Dividendenausschüttung zuzüglich Abschreibung, Bruttoertragsziffer; ~ **trades** *(stock exchange)* Barumsätze; ~ **transaction** Kassa-, Geld-, Bargeschäft; ~ **transactions** Bargeldverkehr, Kassenumsatz, -verkehr; ~ **turnover** Kassenumsatz; ~ **value** Barwert, -betrag, Kassafluß, *(policy)* Effektiv-, Geld-, Rückkauf-, Kapitalwert; **fair ~ value** Verkehrswert; ~**-value table** Kapitalwerttabelle; ~ **voucher** Kassenbeleg; ~ **withdrawal** Barabhebung.

cashable einziehbar.

cashbook Kassa-, Kassen-, Verkaufsbuch, Kassenstrazze; **counter ~** Kassengegenbuch; **petty ~** kleines Kassabuch; **rough ~** Kassenkladde; **subsidiary ~** Hilfskassenbuch; ~ **balance** Kassenbuchsaldo; ~ **bounty** Barprämie; ~ **entry** Kassenbucheintragung.

cashbox Geldschatulle, -kassette, *(shop)* Ladenkasse.

cashboy Kassenbote.

cashcard Barkreditkarte.

cashed, when nach Eingang [in der Kasse].

cashflow Kassenzufluß, *(balancing)* Dividendenausschüttung zuzüglich Abschreibung, Kapitalfluß aus Umsatz, Nettozugang an liquiden Mitteln, Bruttoertragsziffer, finanzielles Unternehmensergebnis; **negative ~** Überhang der Zahlungsausgänge; **retained ~** Anlagenabschreibungen und Rückstellungen für Pensionen; ~ **budget** Liquiditätsvorschau; ~ **control** Bruttoertragskontrolle; ~ **figures** Bruttoertragsziffern; ~ **forecast** Bruttoertragsvorschau; ~ **position** Bruttoertragslage; ~ **statement** Kapitalabschlußrechnung, Bruttoertragsanalyse.

cashier Kassierer, *(official)* Kassenführer, -disponent, -wart, Schalterbeamter, *(US)* Kassenvorsteher; **assistant ~** zweiter Kassierer, Kassengehilfe; **chief (head) ~** Hauptkassierer, Kassenverwalter, -leiter; **lady ~** Kassiererin; **paying ~** Auszahlungskassierer; **petty ~** Portokassenwart; **receiving ~** Einzahlungskassierer; **senior ~** Hauptbuchhalter; ~ **in charge of operations** Hauptkassierer; ~ *(v.) (mil.)* hinauswerfen, Abschied geben, unehrenhaft entlassen; **to act as ~** Kasse führen; **to be ~ed** *(mil.)* mit schlichtem Abschied entlassen werden.

cashier's | account Kassekonto, Kassenkonto; ~ **check** *(US)* Kassen-, Bankscheck; ~ **department** Kassenabteilung; ~ **desk** Kassenschalter, Zahlstelle; ~ **office** Zahlstelle, Kasse; ~ **receipt** Kassenquittung.

cashiered *(mil.)* hinausgeworfen, unehrenhaft entlassen.

cashiering, cashierment *(mil.)* schlichter Abschied, unehrenhafte Entlassung.

cashing Einziehung, [Ein]kassieren, Inkasso; ~ **of a check** *(US)* **(cheque,** *Br.*) Einlösung eines Schecks, Scheckeinlösung; **to undertake the ~ of a bill** Wechsel zum Inkasso übernehmen.

cashkeeper Kassierer.

cashkeeping Kassenführung.

cashless *(US)* bargeldlos; ~ **payment** *(US)* bargeldlose Zahlung.

cashlite Bußzahlung.

casing Verpackung.

casino [Spiel]kasino, Gesellschaftshaus; ~ **owner** Kasinobesitzer.

cask *(barrel)* großes Faß, Tonne, Gebinde, *(measure of capacity)* Rauminhaltsbezeichnung; **by the ~** faßweise; ~ **buoy** Tonnenboje.

casket Behälter, Kästchen, Schatulle, *(US)* Sarg.

cassation *(law)* Kassierung, Aufhebung, Ungültigkeitserklärung.

cassette Kästchen, *(photo, tape recording)* Kassette; **one-hour ~** Kassette mit einstündiger Laufzeit; ~ **player** Kassettenspielgerät; ~ **[tape] recorder** Kassettengerät.

cast *(adding of accounts)* Aufrechnung, Addition, *(computation)* Berechnung, *(film, theater)* Rollenbesetzung, -verteilung, *(kind)* Art, Gattung, *(print.)* Klischee; **all-star (star-studded) ~** Starbesetzung; ~ **of mind** Geistesrichtung; ~ **of parts** Rollenverteilung, -besetzung;

~ *(v.)* aufrechnen, addieren, zusammenrechnen, Saldo ziehen; ~ **accounts** zusammenrechnen; ~ **the balance** Saldo ziehen; ~ **one's bread upon the waters** sein Vermögen aufs Spiel setzen; ~ **the defendant** Beklagten Prozeß verlieren lassen; ~ **dust in s. one's eyes** jem. Sand in die Augen streuen; ~ **a gloom on the proceedings** Verfahren in seltsamem Licht erscheinen lassen; ~ **a horoscope** Horoskop aufstellen; ~ **interest** Zinsen ausrechnen; ~ **o. s. upon s. one's kindness** sich bittend an j. wenden; ~ **a new light on s. th.** Sache in ganz anderem Licht erscheinen lassen; ~ **lots** losen, Los entscheiden lassen; ~ **in one's lot with s. o.** jds. Schicksal teilen; ~ **a page** Seite klischieren; ~ **the parts in a play** Rollen in einem Stück verteilen; ~ **pearls before swine** Perlen vor die Säue werfen; ~ **into prison** ins Gefängnis werfen; ~ **a shadow on s. th.** Schatten auf etw. werfen; ~ **a slur upon s. one's reputation** jds. guten Ruf beeinträchtigen; ~ **a soldier** Soldaten entlassen; ~ **the first stone** *(fig.)* ersten Stein auf j. werfen; ~ **suspicion** Verdacht lenken; ~ **s. th. in s. one's teeth** j. einer Sache beschuldigen; ~ **one's vote** seine Stimme abgeben; **to be ~ as** Rolle zugewiesen bekommen; **to be ~ away** Schiffbruch erleiden; **to be ~ to pay the costs** zu den Kosten verurteilt sein; **to be ~ in damages** zum Schadensersatz verurteilt werden; **to be ~ down** niedergeschlagen sein; **to be ~ in a lawsuit** Prozeß verloren haben; **to take a ~** prägen.

cast *(v.)* **about for an excuse** nach einer Entschuldigung suchen.

cast *(v.)* **away** wegwerfen, *(fig.)* aufgeben, *(ship)* Schiff aufgeben.

cast *(v.)* **back** [Beschuldigung] zurückweisen.

cast *(v.)* **down** *(fig.)* demütigen; **to be ~** niedergeschlagen sein.

cast off Berechnung des Manuskriptumfangs; ~ *(v.) (copy)* Manuskriptteil berechnen, *(goods)* [Ware] ausmustern, -sondern.

cast *(v.)* **out** verbannen, verstoßen.

cast *(v.)* **up** *(reckon up)* ausrechnen; ~ **accounts** zusammenrechnen; ~ **amounts** aufrechnen; ~ **a column of figures** zusammenrechnen, -zählen, addieren; ~ **the total** Summe ziehen; ~ **the votes** Stimmen zählen.

cast *(v.)* **o. s. upon the mercy of the court** sich der Gnade des Gerichts anheimgeben.

cast | aside aufs Abstellgleis geschoben; ~ **goods** Ramschwaren; ~**-iron constitution** unverwüstliche Gesundheit; ~**-iron will** eiserner Wille; ~ **votes** abgegebene Stimmen.

castaway Schiffbrüchiger, *(outcast)* gesellschaftlich Geächteter; ~ *(a.)* schiffbrüchig, *(thrown away)* weggeworfen.

caste Kaste; **to lose one's ~** seine gesellschaftliche Stellung verlieren; ~ **system** Kastenwesen, -herrschaft.

castellan Schloßvogt, Kastellan.

castigate *(v.)* züchtigen, *(emend)* [Text] verbessern.

castigation Züchtigung, *(emendation)* Textverbesserung.

casting Aufrechnen, Zusammenrechnen; ~ **off** Umfangberechnung; ~ **[up] of figures** Addieren, Zusammenzählen; ~ *(a.)* ausschlaggebend; ~ **director** Rollenverteiler; ~ **directory** *(film company)* Rollenvermittlung; ~ **vote** ausschlaggebende Stimme; **to give the ~ vote** Abstimmung entscheiden.

castle Schloß, Gutshaus; ~ **in the air (Spain)** Luftschloß.

castle-builder Projektemacher, Phantast.

castoff *(print.)* abgesetztes Manuskript; ~ **clothes** abgelegte (ausrangierte) Kleidungsstücke.

casual Aushilfsarbeiter, -kraft, Gelegenheitsarbeiter, *(public aid)* vorübergehender Unterstützungsempfänger; ~**s** *(mil.)* Durchgangspersonal; ~ *(a.)* zufällig, gelegentlich, unregelmäßig; ~ **acquaintance** flüchtige Bekanntschaft; ~ **agent** Gelegenheitsagent; ~ **betting** gelegentliches Wetten; ~ **criminal** Gelegenheitsverbrecher; ~ **customer** Lauf-, Gelegenheitskunde; ~ **deficiency of revenue** unvorhergesehener Einnahmeausfall; ~ **deficit** *(budgeting)* unbeabsichtigtes Defizit; ~ **ejector** *(Br.)* fiktiver Räumungskläger; ~ **emolument** Nebeneinnahme; ~ **employee** Gelegenheitsarbeiter; ~ **employment** Gelegenheitsarbeit, gelegentliche Beschäftigung; ~ **event** Zufall; ~ **evidence** zufällig entstandenes Beweismittel; ~ **expenses** gelegentliche Ausgaben; ~ **homicide** schuldlose Tötung; ~ **income** Nebeneinkommen; ~ **insurance** Unfallhaftpflichtversicherung; ~ **labo(u)r** Gelegenheitsarbeit; ~ **labo(u)rer** Aushilfs-, Gelegenheitsarbeiter; ~ **loss** *(tax)* zufällig hervorgerufener besonderer Verlust; ~ **occupation** Gelegenheitsbeschäftigung; ~ **pauper** *(US)* Obdachloser, nicht ortsansässiger Fürsorgeempfänger; ~ **poor** *(Br.)* nicht ortsansässige Fürsorgebedürftige; ~ **profit**

Gelegenheitsgewinn; ~ **reader** Gelegenheitsleser; ~ **returns** Verlustliste; ~ **revenue** Nebeneinkünfte; ~ **sale** Gelegenheitsverkauf; ~ **ward** Asyl für Obdachlose, Obdachlosenasyl; ~ **work** Gelegenheitsarbeit; ~ **worker** nicht ständig Beschäftigter, Gelegenheitsarbeiter.

casualization Beschäftigung von Gelegenheitsarbeitern.

casualties *(mil.)* erlittene Verluste.

casualty Unfall[tod], Unglücksfall, Verunglückter, Verkehrsopfer, *(chance)* Zufall, *(inevitable accident)* unvermeidlicher Unfall, *(soldier or sailor killed)* Verunglückter;
to meet with a ~ Havarie erleiden;
~ **book** *(Lloyds)* Schiffsverlustliste; ~ **department** *(hospital)* Unfallabteilung, -station; ~ **insurance** *(US)* Unfallschadensversicherung; ~ **list** *(mil.)* Verlustliste; ~ **loss** Unfallschaden; ~ **premium** Unfallversicherungsprämie; ~ **sheet** *(Lloyds)* Verlustbenachrichtigung; ~ **ward** *(hospital)* Unfallstation.

cat | s and dogs *(stock exchange, US)* billige Spekulationspapiere;
to let the ~ out of the bag Katze aus dem Sack lassen, Geheimnis ausplaudern; to put the ~ among the pigeons Riesentumult hervorrufen; to see which way the ~ jumps sehen, wie der Hase läuft; to wait for the ~ to jump Entwicklung der Ereignisse abwarten;
~ **burglar** Fassadenkletterer; to lead a ~-and-dog life wie Katze und Hund leben; ~'s **eye** Katzenauge, Rückstrahler, *(roadway)* Markierungspfahl; to make a ~'s **paw** of s. o. willenloses Werkzeug aus jem. machen; ~-**sleep** Nickerchen; ~ **whisker** *(el.)* Detektornadel; the ~'s **whiskers** *(sl.)* haarscharf das Richtige.

catalog(ue) Katalog, Verzeichnis, Liste, *(price list)* Preisverzeichnis, *(prospectus)* Prospekt, *(university, US)* Hochschulordnung;
alphabetical ~ alphabetisches Verzeichnis; **author** ~ Autorenverzeichnis; **card** ~ Zettelkasten, -kartothek, -kartei; **classified** ~ nach Sachgebieten angeordneter Katalog; **descriptive** ~ ausführlicher Katalog; **dictionary** ~ alphabetischer Katalog; **fair** ~ Messekatalog; **library** ~ Bibliothekskatalog; **loose-leaf** ~ Katalog mit losen Seiten; **mail-order** ~ *(US)* Versandhauskatalog; **main** ~ Hauptkatalog; **museum** ~ Museumskatalog; **price** ~ Preisliste, -verzeichnis; ~ **raisonné** Stichwortverzeichnis; **subject** ~ Sachkatalog, Stichwortverzeichnis; **thematic** ~ thematisches Verzeichnis; **trade** ~ illustrierte Preisliste, Versandhauskatalog; **university** ~ *(US)* Hochschulordnung;
~ **of books** Bücherkatalog; ~ **of guidelines** Richtlinienkatalog; ~ **of merchandise** Warenkatalog; ~ **of sale** Auktionsliste, -katalog;
~ *(v.)* [im] Katalog (in ein Verzeichnis) aufnehmen, Katalog aufstellen, katalogisieren, in eine Liste eintragen, listenmäßig erfassen;
to carry in a ~ in einem Katalog anführen; to compile a ~ Katalog zusammenstellen; to delete in a ~ in einem Katalog streichen; to number the items in a ~ Katalogposten numerieren; to sell from one's ~ nur nach dem Katalog verkaufen; to skim through a ~ Katalog durchblättern; to work on a ~ Katalog zusammenstellen;
~ **sent free on request** auf Wunsch kostenlose Katalogzusendung;
~ **business** Versandhausgeschäft; ~ **company** Versandhausunternehmen; ~ **distribution plant** Versandhausbetrieb; in ~ **form** katalogmäßig angeordnet; ~ **goods** Versandhausartikel; ~ **house** Versandhaus; ~ **index** Inhaltsverzeichnis; ~ **number** Katalognummer; ~ **price** Katalog-, Listenpreis; ~ **sales** Verkauf nach Katalog, Versandhausumsatz; ~ **service** Versandhausdienst; ~ **store** *(US)* Versandhausgeschäft; ~ **wholesaler** Versandgroßhändler.

catalogued katalogisiert.

cataloguer Katalogbearbeiter.

cataloguing Katalogisierung.

cataloguize *(v.)* katalogisieren.

catapult *(aircraft)* Schleuderstarthilfe;
~ **start** *(airplane)* Schleuderstart.

catapulting Katapultieren.

catastrophe Katastrophe, Verhängnis, Schicksalsschlag;
~ **hazard** Katastrophenwagnis, -risiko; ~ **insurance** Krankenversicherung zur Abdeckung besonders hoher Risiken; ~ **limit** Risikobegrenzung bei Katastrophen; ~ **reinsurance** Katastrophenrückversicherung; ~ **reserve** außerordentliche Rücklage, Katastrophenrücklage; ~ **risk** Katastrophenwagnis, -risiko.

catastrophic loss Katastrophenschaden.

catch *(advantage)* ergriffene Gelegenheit, Gewinn, Vorteil, Fang, *(trick)* Falle, Kniff, Haken;
great ~ reiche Partie; **no** ~ schlechtes Geschäft;
~ *(v.)* fassen, fangen, *(criminal)* fassen, ergreifen;

~ **in the act** auf frischer Tat ergreifen; ~ **s. one's attention** jds. Aufmerksamkeit erregen; ~ **a disease** krank werden; ~ **fire** Feuer fangen; ~ **it** *(sl.)* sein Fett abkriegen; ~ **s. o. napping** j. überrumpeln; ~ **on** Schule machen, *(article)* populär werden, einschlagen, in Mode kommen, günstige Aufnahme (Anklang) finden; ~ **the post** Brief vor der Leerung des Briefkastens einwerfen; ~ **the speaker's eye** *(Br.)* das Wort erhalten; ~ **at a straw** nach einem Strohhalm greifen; ~ **a tartar** an den Falschen geraten; ~ **a train** den Zug erreichen; ~ **up with another car** Auto einholen; ~ **up with s. o.** jds. Vorsprung einholen; ~ **up a speaker** Redner unterbrechen;
to try to ~ **the chairman's eye** sich zum Wort melden.

catch | basin Auffangbecken; ~ **line** Schlagzeile, knallige Überschrift; ~ **phrase** Schlagwort, Werbespruch; ~ **pit** Klärgrube; ~ **question** Fangfrage; ~ **time charter** Zeitchartervertrag; ~ **title** Untertitel.

catchall *(US)* Allerwelts-, Tragetasche;
~ **bill** umfassender Gesetzesantrag.

catching | s *(deep-sea fishing)* Fang;
~ **air** zündende Melodie; ~ **bargain** Verkauf eines Anwartschaftsrechtes, *(inheritance)* Ablistung des Erbanteils; ~ **question** Fangfrage.

catchment Auffangbehälter, Reservoir;
~ **area** *(town)* Einzugsbereich, *(weather)* Einzugsgebiet; ~ **basin** Sammelbecken; ~ **board** Entwässerungsbehörde.

catchpenny wertlos, für den Kundenfang berechnet;
~ **article** Pfennig-, Schleuderartikel, Schundware; ~ **title** auf Kundenfang angelegtes Zitat.

catchpol Büttel, Gerichtsdiener.

catchword *(cue)* Blickfang-, Stichwort, *(dictionary)* Schlagwort, *(party life)* Parteiparole, *(printing)* Kolumnentitel;
~ **entry** Stichworteintragung; ~ **index** Schlagwortregister.

catchwork Bewässerungsanlage.

catechism, to put s. o. through his j. eingehend befragen.

categorical statement kategorische Behauptung.

categories | of investment Vermögensanlageklassen; ~ **of trade** Branchengruppen.

categorization Einstufung, Klassifizierung.

categorize *(v.)* kategorisieren, einstufen, klassifizieren.

category [Rang]klasse, Kategorie, Gruppe *(statistics)* Merkmalsklasse;
~ **of expenditure** Ausgabengruppe; ~ **of goods** Warengruppe; ~ **of occupation** Berufssparte; ~ **of persons** Personenkreis; ~ **of risks** *(insurance)* Gefahrenklasse; ~ **of ship** Schiffsklasse;
to come in (fall within) a ~ zu einer Kategorie gehören.

cater *(v.)* verpflegen, Lebensmittel liefern, *(for airliner)* fertige Menüs anliefern, *(furnish provisions)* Lebensmittel anschaffen (einkaufen);
~ **for** sorgen für; ~ **for the needs of customers** Kundenbedürfnisse befriedigen; ~ **for the small investor** Kleinanleger betreuen; ~ **for the masses** *(light program(me))* Programm für die breiten Massen ausstrahlen; ~ **for patients** Patienten behandeln; ~ **to a new public** Wünschen einer neuen Publikumsschicht entsprechen; ~ **to the public demand for the sensational** sich der Sensationslust der Öffentlichkeit beugen; ~ **for a situation** für eine Situation Vorsorge treffen; ~ **for all the special needs of a businessman** auf die Sonderwünsche eines Geschäftsmannes eingestellt sein; ~ **to (to, US) all taste** für jeden Geschmack etw. bringen; ~ **to low taste** *(tabloid newspaper)* sich auf das niedrige Niveau eines Massenpublikums einstellen; ~ **for public taste** dem öffentlichen Geschmack schmeicheln; ~ **for foreign tourists** Fremdenverkehr betreuen; ~ **cousin** weitläufiger Verwandter.

caterer *(provider of provisions)* [Lebensmittel]lieferant fertiger Speisen, Fertiggerichte-, Menülieferant, *(catering establishment)* Gaststättenbetrieb, Restaurateur, *(marine, Br.)* Einkäufer, Proviantmeister;
industrial ~ Menü-, Fertiggerichtelieferant; **industrial contract** ~ Vertragslieferant von Betriebskantinen.

catering Gaststättenwesen, gastronomische Betreuung;
business ~ gastronomische Betreuung der Geschäftswelt; **industrial** ~ Betriebskantinenwesen;
~ **for employees** Angestelltenverpflegung; ~ **for foreign visitors** Betreuung von Auslandsbesuchern;
~ **adviser** Werksküchenberater; **mobile** ~ **company** Gastronomielieferant; ~ **contractor** Vertragslieferant für Betriebskantinen; ~ **costs** Verpflegungskosten; ~ **department** Küchenverwaltung, *(plant)* Werksküche, Betriebskantine, Kasino[abteilung], *(shop)* Stadtküche; ~ **establishment** Gaststättenbetrieb, -einrichtung; ~ **facilities** Verpflegungsmöglichkeiten; ~ **field** Verpflegungssektor; ~ **firm** Gaststättenlieferant, *(film)*

Verleiher, Verleihfirma; ~ **industry** Gaststättengewerbe; **Hotel and** ~ **Industry Board** *(Br.)* Gewerbeausschuß für das Hotel- und Gaststättenwesen; ~ **market** Gaststättengewerbe; ~ **officer** Kasino-, Verpflegungsoffizier; ~ **service** *(airliners)* Kabinendienst, gastronomische Betreuung an Bord; ~ **system** *(plant)* Küchenverwaltung; ~ **trade** Gaststättengewerbe.

caterpillar Gleiskettenfahrzeug, Raupenschlepper;
~s **of society** Parasiten der Gesellschaft;
~ **drive** Gleiskettenantrieb; ~ **tractor** Raupenschlepper; ~ **truck** Raupenfahrzeug.

catholic tastes and interests weitgespannte und liberale Interessen.

cattle Vieh, Großvieh, Rinder;
~ **breeding** Rinderzucht; ~ **car** *(US)* Viehwagen; ~ **dealer** Viehhändler; ~ **drive** Viehtrieb; ~ **farmer** Viehzüchter; ~ **gate** *(Br.)* Weiderecht; ~ **lifting** Viehdiebstahl; ~ **loan company** Gesellschaft zur Finanzierung der Viehzucht; ~ **manifest** Viehfrachtliste; ~ **pass** Durchlauf für Weidevieh; ~ **range** Weideland; ~-**rearing** Viehzucht; ~ **show** Viehausstellung; ~ **stealing** Viehdiebstahl; ~ **trade** Viehhandel; ~ **trader** Viehhändler; ~ **train** Viehtransportzug.

cattleguard Viehschranke.

caucus *(local members of a party)* örtliche Parteileitung, *(meeting, US)* Parteiversammlung, -kongreß, -clique, -gremium, Wahl-, Programmversammlung;
labo(u)r ~ *(Australia)* Zusammenkunft von Gewerkschaftsvertretern;
~ *(v.)* Besprechung der Wahlliste (Wahlversammlung) abhalten;
~ **funds** Partei-, Wahlfonds.

causal kausal, ursächlich;
~ **condition** Kausalbedingung; ~ **connection** Kausalzusammenhang.

causality Kausalzusammenhang.

causation Verursachung, Ursächlichkeit;
~ **of inflation** Inflationsursache.

causative principle *(environmental safety)* Verursachungsprinzip.

cause Sache, Angelegenheit, Anliegen, *(law case)* Prozeß, Rechtsstreit, Fall, *(law of contract)* Vertragsgegenstand, *(reason)* Grund, Motiv, Ursache;
for ~ *(law of contract)* aus wichtigen Gründen; **without** ~ unentschuldigt; **without just** ~ ohne hinreichenden Grund; **on** ~ **shown** nach erfolgter Prüfung;
common ~ gemeinsame Sache, Zivilprozeß; **concurrent** ~ Zweitursache; **direct** ~ unmittelbare Ursache; **immediate** ~ unmittelbare Ursache; **instrumental** ~ mitwirkende Ursache; **invalidating** ~ Anfechtungsgrund; **just** ~ wichtiger Grund; **lawful** ~ gesetzlicher Grund; **living** ~s aktuelle Fragen; **matrimonial** ~s Ehesachen; **occasional** ~ auslösende Ursache; **pecuniary** ~ vermögensrechtliche Streitigkeit; ~ **pending** anhängige Sache, schwebender Prozeß; **petty** ~ Bagatellsache; **primary** ~ Grundursache; **probable** ~ hinreichender Grund, *(criminal)* hinreichender Verdacht; **proximate** ~ ursächlicher Zusammenhang, Kausalzusammenhang; **reasonable and probable** ~ triftiger Grund; ~ **shown** schlüssige Begründung; **testamentary** ~ Nachlaßsache;
~ **of accident** Unfallursache; ~ **of action** Klagegrund, -gegenstand, -anspruch; ~ **of appeal** angefochtene Entscheidung; ~ **to complain (for complaint)** Beschwerdegrund; ~ **of a valid contract** Klageanspruch aus einem gültigen Vertrag; ~ **beyond control** höhere Gewalt; ~ **of death** Todesursache; ~ **and effect** Ursache und Wirkung; ~ **of injury** Schadensursache; ~ **for leaving** Ausscheidungsgrund; ~ **for litigation** Prozeßstoff; **[proximate]** ~ **of loss** [unmittelbare] Schadensursache; ~ **for rescission** Anfechtungs-, Rücktrittsgrund; **underlying** ~ **of great social upheavals** Grundursache großer sozialer Umwälzungen; ~ **of the war** Kriegsursache, -grund;
~ *(v.)* bewirken, veranlassen, verursachen, Anlaß geben, herbeiführen;
~ **damage** Schaden verursachen (zufügen); ~ **a disturbance** Störung verursachen; ~ **a loss** Verlust zufügen; ~ **suit to be brought** mit dem Prozeß beginnen; ~ **s. o. trouble** jem. Schwierigkeiten bereiten;
to call a ~ Sache aufrufen; **to fight for one's** ~ für seine Sache eintreten; **to give** ~ **for complaint** Anlaß zur Klage (Beanstandungen, Beschwerde) geben; **to have** ~ **to complain** Beschwerdegrund haben; **to have good** ~ **for doing s. th.** völlig gerechtfertigt sein; **to have a** ~ **particularly at heart** besonderes Herzensanliegen haben; **to investigate the** ~ **of a railway accident** Ursachen eines Eisenbahnunglücks untersuchen; ~ **s. o. trouble** jem. Schwierigkeiten bereiten;

to make common ~ gemeinsame Sache machen; **to plead s. one's** ~ j. anwaltlich vertreten; **to show** ~ seine Gründe angeben; **to stay away without good** ~ nicht ausreichend entschuldigt fehlen; **to support a** ~ für eine Sache eintreten; **to take** ~ Prozeß aufnehmen; **to take up the** ~ **of the poor** sich der Armen annehmen; **to uphold a** ~ Sache vertreten;
~ **books** *(Br.)* Entscheidungssammlung; ~ **list** *(Br.)* Terminkalender, Prozeß-, Terminliste; ~ **obligation** Garantieverpflichtung.

causeway erhöhter Fußweg, [Straßen]damm.

caution Vorsicht, Warnung, *(police, Br.)* Verwarnung, *(prudence)* Vorsicht, *(real estate, Br.)* Vormerkung, Rangordnung, *(remarkable person, coll.)* Original, komisches Individium, *(right to appeal)* Rechtsmittelbelehrung, *(Scot., law)* Kaution, *(surety)* Bürge, Bürgschaft;
~, **concealed drive** Achtung, Ausfahrt!;
pre-weekend ~ *(stock market)* Zurückhaltung am Wochenende;
~ **over new investment** Zurückhaltung bei Neuanlagen;
~ *(v.)* warnen, verwarnen;
~ **the parties** Parteien belehren; ~ **a prisoner** Gefangenen verwarnen;
to lodge ~ **with the registrar** *(Br.)* Vormerkung eintragen lassen; **to show** ~ **in the placing of orders** knapp disponieren;
~ **juratory** *(Scot., law)* Kautionsstellung unter Eid; ~ **money** *(Br.)* [hinterlegte] Kautions-, Bürgschaftssumme, Bürgschaftshöhe, Garantiebetrag, -summe.

cautionary Sicherheit, *(Scot., law)* Bürgschaftsurkunde;
~ *(a.)* vorsorglich;
~ **card** *(block system)* Vorsichtsankündigung; ~ **judgment** vorbeugendes Unterlassungs-, Sicherheitsurteil; ~ **note** Vorsichtshinweis; ~ **signal** *(ship)* Warnsignal.

cautioner Vormerkungsbegünstigter, *(Scot.)* Bürge.

cautionry Bürgschaft.

cautious reserviert, vorsichtig, zurückhaltend.

cave *(politics, Br.)* Absonderung eines Parteiflügels.

caveat *(lat.)* Einspruch, Warnung, Vorbehalt, *(advice)* Vorausbenachrichtigung, *(land registry)* Vormerkung, *(patent law, US)* Patentanmeldung [mit dreimonatiger Einspruchsmöglichkeit], *(patent law, Br.)* Einspruch gegen Patenterneuerung;
~ **to will** Testamentsanfechtung;
~ *(v.)* Einspruch einlegen;
to put in a ~ Einspruch einlegen;
~ **emptor** Ausschluß der Gewährleistung, Gewährleistungs-, Mängelausschuß; ~ **venditor** Gewährleistung des Verkäufers; ~ **visitor** Sorgfaltspflicht der Reisenden.

caveator Einspruchskläger, Einspruchseinlegender, *(patent law, US)* Patentanmelder.

cavil *(v.)* überkritische Einwendungen vorbringen.

cease *(v.)* aufhören, ablassen, abstehen, *(firm)* erlöschen, *(payment)* fortfallen;
~ **to appear (be published)** Erscheinen einstellen; ~ **to do business** Geschäftsbetrieb einstellen; ~ **making bicycles** Fahrradproduktion einstellen; ~ **to exist** wegfallen, erlöschen, ablaufen; ~ **fire** Feindseligkeiten einstellen; ~ **to have force** außer Kraft treten; ~ **to hold office** aus dem Amt ausscheiden; ~ **payments** *(bank)* Zahlungen einstellen; ~ **to be valid** kraftlos werden; ~ **work** Arbeit einstellen;
~ **and desist order** *(US)* auf Unterlassung gerichtete einstweilige Verfügung, Unterlassungsanordnung, Wettbewerbsverbot; ~-**work instruction** Streikanordnung, -befehl.

ceasefire Einstellung der Feindseligkeiten, Feuereinstellung, Waffenruhe;
to preserve the ~ Waffenstillstandsabkommen einhalten;
~ **arrangements** Waffnstillstandsvereinbarung; ~ **conference** Waffenstillstandskonferenz; ~ **lines** Waffenstillstandslinien; ~ **resolution** Waffenstillstandsbeschluß; ~ **violation** Waffenstillstandsverletzung.

cede *(v.)* abtreten, überlassen, zedieren, *(insurance business)* auf den Rückversicherer übertragen.

cedent Zedent;
~ **state** abtretender Staat.

ceding office Erstversicherer.

ceiling Höchstbetrag, Höchstgrenze, *(export credit)* Plafond, *(performance)* Leistungsspitze, *(price)* gesetzlicher Höchstpreis, *(rent)* gesetzliche Höchstmiete, *(room)* Decke, *(salary)* Höchstgehalt;
absolute ~ *(plane)* Gipfelhöhe; **interest** ~ Höchstzinsen; **price** ~s Preisobergrenze, gesetzliche Höchstgrenze für Preise; **rent** ~ gesetzliche Höchstmiete; **service** ~ Grenzflughöhe; **wage** ~s festgesetzte Höchstlöhne;

~ **on earnings** Ertragsbegrenzung; ~ **of the economy** volkswirtschaftliche Kapazitätsgrenze; **defacto 5% ~ of gross domestic
product** praktische Höchstgrenze von 5% des Bruttosozialprodukts; ~**s on loans** *(lending business)* Kredithöchstsätze; ~ **of
profits** Gewinnbeschränkung, -begrenzung;
to hit the ~ *(coll.)* seine Beherrschung verlieren, an die Decke
(in die Luft) gehen; **to put a ~ on spending** Ausgabenhöchst-
grenze festsetzen;
~ **control** Plafondierung; ~ **figure** Höchstziffer; ~ **lamp**
Deckenlampe; ~ **panel** Deckenschild; ~**rate** Höchstsatz;**retail
~ price** Verbraucherhöchstpreis; ~ **wages** festgesetzte
Höchstlöhne.
ceilometer Wolkenhöhenmesser.
celebrate *(v.)* feiern, feierlich begehen;
~ **its centenary** hundertjähriges Jubiläum begehen; ~ **an event
with due ceremony** Ereignis festlich begehen; ~ **a feast** Fest
feiern; ~ **a marriage** Ehe eingehen (schließen).
celebration Fest, Feier[stunde];
bicentennial ~ Zweihundertjahrfeier; **focal ~** im Mittelpunkt
stehendes festliches Ereignis; ~ **of marriage** Eheschließung; ~
offer *(shop)* Eröffnungsangebot; ~ **treat** festliche Bewirtung.
celebrities Berühmtheiten.
celebrity status Berühmtheitsgrad.
celibacy Zölibat.
cell *(pol.)* [politische] Zelle, *(prison)* Gefängniszelle;
communist ~s in an industrial town kommunistische Zellen in
einer Industriestadt;
to set up ~s in a trade union Zellen in einer Gewerkschaft
bilden.
cellarage Kellergeschoß, -räume, *(rent)* Kellermiete.
cellophane tape Zellophan-, Filmklebestreifen.
cemetery Begräbnisort, Friedhof;
~° **Board** Friedhofsverwaltung; **to purchase a ~ plot in fast**
Grabstelle auf Dauer kaufen.
censor Zensor;
passed by the ~ von der Zensur freigegeben;
~ *(v.)* zensieren;
to pass the ~ von der Zensur durchgelassen werden;
must be submitted to the ~ zensurpflichtig.
censorable der Zensur unterworfen, zensurpflichtig.
censored | passage zensierte (von der Zensur gestrichene) Stelle;
to be ~ zensiert sein.
censorship Zensoramt, Zensur;
~ **of films** Filmzensur; ~ **of the mail** Post-, Briefzensur; ~ **of the
press** Pressezensur;
subject to ~ zensurpflichtig;
postal ~ Post-, Briefzensur; **strict ~** strenge Zensur;
to apply ~ der Zensur unterwerfen; **to lift ~** Zensur aufheben;
to tighten up the ~ Zensurbestimmungen verschärfen;
~ **regulations** Zensurbestimmungen; ~ **stamp** Zensurstempel.
censure Zensur, Tadel, Verweis, Rüge;
~ *(v.)* rügen, tadeln, Verweis erteilen;
to contain unfair ~s of a new book neues Buch einer unfairen
Rezension aussetzen; **to lay o. s. open to public ~** sich der
öffentlichen Kritik aussetzen; **to move a ~** Tadelsantrag stellen; **to pass a vote of ~ on the government** Mißtrauensantrag
gegen die Regierung annehmen;
~ **case** *(US)* Tadels-, Senatsverfahren; ~ **count** Tadelspunkt; ~
debate Tadelsdebatte; ~ **hearing** *(US)* Tadelsverfahren; ~
motion Mißtrauens-, Tadelsantrag; ~ **proceedings** Tadelsverfahren; ~ **resolution** Tadelsbeschluß, -votum; ~ **vote**
Tadelsvotum.
census Volkszählung, Gesamt-, Voll-, Totalerhebung, *(ground
rent)* Grundrente;
incomplete ~ *(statistics)* unvollständige Erhebung, Teilerhebung; **industrial ~** Betriebszählung; **traffic ~** Verkehrszählung;
world ~ Zählung der Weltbevölkerung;
~ **of business** Wirtschaftsstatistik, *(advertising)* Streuungserfassung; ~ **of distribution** Handels-
zählung, *(advertising)* Streuungserfassung; ~ **of housing** Woh-
nungszählung; ~ **of population** Volkszählung; ~ **of opinion**
Meinungsbefragung; ~ **of production** statistische Produktions-
erfassung, Industriezensus; ~ **of property** Vermögensabschät-
zung; ~ **of unemployment** Arbeitslosenzählung;
to take a ~ statistisch erfassen; **to take a ~ of the population**
Volkszählung vornehmen;
~° **Bureau** *(US)* Statistisches Bundesamt; ~ **data** statistisches
Material, Erhebungsangaben; ~ **distribution** Bevölkerungsda-
ten; ~ **employee** statistischer Angestellter; ~ **enumeration** statistische Erfassung; ~ **findings** Ergebnisse der Bevölkerungszählung; ~ **form** Erhebungsbogen; ~ **information** statistisch
erfaßte Einheit; ~ **moment** kritischer Moment; ~ **paper** Zähl-

bogen, -karte, Haushaltsfragebogen, -liste; ~ **procedure** Volkszählungsverfahren, statistisches Verfahren; ~ **questionnaire
(questionary,** *Br.)* statistischer Fragebogen; ~ **result** Volkszäh-
lungsergebnis; ~ **sheet** Volkszählungsbogen; ~ **statistics**
Bevölkerungsstatistik; ~ **table** Bevölkerungstabelle; ~ **taker**
Hilfsangestellter bei der Volkszählung; ~ **taking** Durchführung einer Volkszählung; ~ **tract** *(US)* zu statistischen
Zwecken herausgegriffenes Gebiet; ~ **year** Zensusjahr.
cent *(US)* Cent;
not worth a ~ keinen Heller (roten Marwedi) wert; **per ~**
Prozent;
three per ~s *(stock exchange)* dreiprozentige Wertpapiere.
cental [Getreide]zentner.
centenary Hundertjahrfeier.
center → **centre.**
centered, centred *(Br.)* auf Mitte gesetzt;
~ **on one's work** ganz auf seine Arbeit eingestellt.
central Zentrale, Zentralstelle, *(telephone, US)* Fernsprechamt,
-vermittlung;
~ *(a.)* *(house)* zentral [gelegen];
~ **administration** Zentral-, Hauptverwaltung; ~ **agencies** *(US)*
Zentralbehörden, -stellen; ~° **Arbitration Committee** *(Br.)* zentrale Schlichtungsstelle; ~ **area** *(aerodrome)* Flugsicherungs-,
kontrollbezirk; ~ **area shop** Geschäft im Stadtzentrum; ~ **association** Zentralverband; ~ **authority** Zentralbehörde; ~ **bank**
Zentral-, Notenbank; ~ **bank authority** Notenbankbehörde; ~
bank cooperation Zusammenarbeit der Notenbanken; **concerted ~ bank interventions** abgestimmte Notenbankinterventio-
nen; **to inject ~ bank money into the economy** der Wirtschaft
Zentralbankgeld zuführen; ~ **bank policy** Zentralbankpolitik,
Politik der Bundesnotenbank; ~ **banker** Zentralbank; ~ **banking governor** Notenbankpräsident; ~ **business district** Hauptgeschäftsgegend; ~ **buyer** Zentraleinkäufer; ~ **buying** zentraler
Einkauf; ~ **commission** Zentralkommission; ~ **committee** Zen-
tralkomitee, -ausschuß; ~ **entity** Kerngesellschaft; ~ **control
agency** Zentraleinkaufsbehörde; ~° **European Time** mitteleuropäische Zeit; ~ **core** Zentralpunkt; ~ **equipment bureau** Haupt-
beschaffungsstelle; ~ **executive body** Zentralorgan; ~ **executive
committee** Zentralausschuß; ~ **figures in a novel** Hauptfiguren
eines Romans; ~ **file** Zentralkartei; ~ **Germany** Mitteldeutsch-
land; ~ **governing body** Hauptverwaltungsorgan; ~ **government**
Zentralregierung; ~ **heating** Zentralheizung; ~ **idea** Kernge-
danke; ~° **Intelligence Agency** *(US)* Abwehr-, Geheimdienst; ~
issue Zentralthema, Kernpunkt; ~° **Land Charges Register** *(Br.)*
Hauptgrundbuchamt; ~ **line of railway** Hauptlinie; ~° **London
management** Hauptverwaltung; ~ **management** Hauptverwaltung; ~
market Hauptabsatzgebiet, Großmarkt; ~ **note-issuing bank**
zentrales Notenbankinstitut; ~ **office** Zentrale, Zentralstelle,
(court) Hauptgeschäftsstelle; ~ **office of information** Informa-
tionszentrale; ~ **organization** Zentralverband; ~ **planning** zentrale Planungstätigkeit, staatliche Wirtschaftsplanung; ~
power Zentralgewalt; ~ **railway station** *(Br.)* Hauptbahnhof;
~° **Register of the Department of Official Receivers** Gesamtkon-
kursliste; ~ **reservation** *(motorway)* Mittelstreifen; ~° **Reserve
Banks** *(US)* amerikanische Nationalbanken in New York und
Chicago; ~ **sector** *(mil.)* Mittelabschnitt; ~ **shopping district**
Hauptgeschäftsgegend; ~ **station** *(el.)* E-Werk, *(mar.)* Kommandostand, Bordzentrale; ~ **statistical office** *(Br.)* [etwa]
Statistisches Bundesamt; ~ **strip** Mittelstreifen; ~ **telephone
exchange** Zentrale; ~ **time** Normalzeit; ~ **traffic control** *(railway)* zentrale Verkehrssteuerung; ~ **valuation committee**
Steuerveranlagungsausschuß.
centralization Zentralisation.
centralize *(v.)* zentralisieren.
centralized | filing Zentralablage; ~ **purchase** zentraler (zentrali-
sierter) Einkauf.
centralizing tendency Zentralisierungstendenz.
centre *(Br.)* **center** *(US)* Zentralstelle, Zentrum, wichtiger Platz,
Mittelpunkt, *(bulk buying, US)* Großeinkaufsgebiet, *(city)*
Geschäftszentrum, Ausgangspunkt, *(fig.)* Herd, *(pol.)* Zentrum, Mitte, Zentrumspartei;
out of ~ außerhalb; **to the right of the ~** rechts von der Mitte;
amusement ~ Vergnügungsviertel; **art ~** Kunstzentrum; **banking ~** Hauptbankplatz, Bankenzentrum; **business (commercial) ~** Geschäftszentrum; **cost ~** Hauptkostenstelle; **distribution ~** *(mil.)* Ausgabezentrum; **financial ~** Finanzzentrum;
industrial ~ Industriezentrum; **manufacturing ~** Industriezentrum; **power ~** Machtkonzentration; **right ~** *(pol.)* rechte
Mitte; **shopping ~** Einkaufszentrum; **speech ~** sprachlicher
Mittelpunkt; **storm ~** Sturmzentrum; **training ~** Ausbildungszentrum; **youth ~** Jugendklub, -heim;

~ **of banking and international finance** internationales Bank- und Finanzzentrum; ~ **of commerce** Handelszentrum; **spiritual** ~ **of a country** geistiges Zentrum eines Landes; ~ **of a crisis** Krisenherd; ~ **of government** Regierungsviertel; ~ **of infection** Infektionsherd; ~ **of learning** Bildungszentrum; ~ **of page** Seitenmitte; ~ **of population** Bevölkerungszentrum; ~ **of power** Machtzentrum; ~ **of production** Produktionszentrum; ~ **for nuclear research** Atomforschungszentrum; ~ **of fashionable residence** vornehme Wohngegend; ~ **of the town** Stadtkern, -mitte, -zentrum; ~ **of trade** Wirtschaftszentrum;

~ (v.) in den Mittelpunkt stellen, konzentrieren, vereinigen auf, (technical) zentrieren;

~ **one's efforts** seine Bemühungen konzentrieren;

to be the ~ **of interests** im Mittelpunkt des Interesses stehen; **to be split down the** ~ völlig geteilter Meinung sein; **to move into the** ~ **of community affairs** am Gemeindeleben regen Anteil nehmen;

~ **base** Luftwaffenstützpunkt; ~-**left coalition** Mittelinkskoalition; ~ **light** Deckenlampe; ~ **party** Zentrumspartei; ~ **spread** (advertisement) doppelseitige Anzeige [in Heftmitte]; ~ **spread price** Preis für eine doppelseitige Anzeige in Heftmitte; ~ **strip** (motorway) Mittelstreifen.

centrepiece Mittelstück, Hauptpfeiler, (exhibition) Kernstück.

centrist Mann der Mitte, Gemäßigter.

cereal Getreide;

imported ~s Getreideeinfuhren;

~ **prices** Getreidepreis.

ceremonial Zeremoniell;

~ (v.) förmlich, protokollarisch;

~ **dress** protokollarisch vorgeschriebene Bekleidung; ~ **occasion** förmlicher Anlaß; ~ **opening of a congress** festliche Eröffnung einer Tagung; ~ **practice** Protokollverfahren; ~ **procedure** protokollarische Prozedur; ~ **rules** protokollarische Bestimmungen.

ceremonious, to be Umstände machen;

to take a ~ **leave** sich umständlich verabschieden.

ceremony Zeremonie, Feier[stunde];

high ~ bedeutender Staatsakt; **marriage** ~ Trauung; **silver anniversary** ~ Feier zum 25jährigen Bestehen;

to stand on ~ sehr formell sein.

certain gewiß, sicher, bestimmt, unbestreitbar, (reliable) zuverlässig, verläßlich;

almost ~ (statistics) fast sicher;

~ **to sell** mit sicheren Absatzmöglichkeiten;

to be ~ (facts) feststehen; **to make** ~ **of one's seats** vorgebuchte Plätze kontrollieren;

~ **day** bestimmter Tag; **to a** ~ **extent** bis zu einem gewissen Grad, gewissermaßen; ~ **price** durchschnittlicher Marktpreis; ~ **services** (lessor) der Höhe nach bestimmte Pachtleistungen.

certainty Klarheit, Gewißheit, Zuverlässigkeit, Sicherheit, sichere Tatsache;

~ **in a bill** Bestimmtheit beim Wechsel; ~ **of the subject matter** Bestimmtheit bei der Treuhandbestellung; ~ **of words** Bestimmtheit von Worten;

to describe with reasonable ~ mit genügender Bestimmtheit beschreiben.

certifiable (illness) anmeldepflichtig, sicher feststellbar.

certifiably insane (Br.) nachgewiesenermaßen geistesgestört.

certificate [amtliche] Bescheinigung, Bestätigung, Beglaubigung, Schein, Attest, (customs) Geleitzettel, (expert evidence) Gutachten, (policy) Transportpolice, (record) Beleg, Nachweis, Urkunde, (shipper) Befähigungsschein, (stock) Zertifikat, Anteilschein, (testimonial) Berechtigungsnachweis, -schein, [Prüfungs]zeugnis, Diplom, Testat;

attorney's ~ Urkunde über die Zulassung zur Anwaltschaft; **audit** ~ Prüfungsbescheinigung, -vermerk; **bankrupt's** ~ (Br.) Rehabilitierungsbescheinigung, Konkursaufhebungsbescheid; **bearer** ~ Inhaberzertifikat; **benefit** ~ Lebensversicherungspolice; **birth** ~ Geburtsschein, -urkunde; **blank** ~ Blankozertifikat; **bogus** ~ gefälschte Bescheinigung, gefälschtes Zeugnis; **builder's** ~ Beilbrief; **clearance** ~ Auseinandersetzungsschein, Unbedenklichkeitsbescheinigung, Zollerlaubnisschein; **clearinghouse** ~ (US) Anerkennungsurkunde im Bankenverkehr; **common stock** ~ Stammaktie; **consular** ~ Bescheinigung des Konsulats, Konsulatsbescheinigung; **coroner's death** ~ Totenschein; **customhouse** ~ Bescheinigung für zollfreie Wiederausfuhr; **death** ~ Totenschein, Sterbeurkunde; **doctor's** ~ ärztliches Attest; **duty-free entry** ~ Bescheinigung über abgabenfreie Verbringung ins Zollgebiet; **employment** ~ (US) Arbeitsbescheinigung; **face amount** ~ (investment trust) Nennwertzertifikat; **final architect's** ~ Bauabnahmeschein;

fractional ~ (Br.) Bruchteilsaktie; **furlough** ~ (US) Urlaubsschein; **gold** ~ (US) Goldzertifikat; **health** ~ Gesundheitspaß; **heir's** ~ (US) Erbschein; **identity** ~ Identitätsausweis; **import** ~ (customs) Unbedenklichkeitsbescheinigung, Einfuhrerlaubnis; **insurance** ~ Versicherungsschein; **interim** ~ Interims-, Zwischenschein; **investment** ~ Investmentanteil; **investment trust** ~ Anteilschein einer Kapitalanlagegesellschaft, Investmentzertifikat; **land** ~ (Br.) Grundbuchauszug; **leaving** ~ (Br.) Abschluß-, Abgangszeugnis, Arbeitsbescheinigung; **legal-aid** ~ (Br.) Bewilligung des Armenrechts, Armenrechtsbewilligung; **loan** ~ Darlehensurkunde; **marriage** ~ Eheschließungsurkunde, Trauschein; **master's** ~ Kapitänspatent; **medical** ~ ärztliches Attest; **motor-vehicle registration** ~ Kraftfahrzeugbrief; **notarial** (notarized) ~ Notariatsbescheinigung, **obligatory test** ~ Bescheinigung der technischen Überwachungsstelle; **organization** ~ (US) Gründungsurkunde, (bank) Konzessionsurkunde; **participation** ~ (US) Anteilsschein, Teilobligation; **practicing** ~ Anwaltsbescheinigung; **qualifying** ~ vorgeschriebene Bescheinigung, Tauglichkeitszeugnis; **registration** ~ Eintragungsbescheinigung, (alien) Aufenthaltsgenehmigung; **renewal** ~ Erneuerungsschein; **residence** ~ Aufenthaltsbestätigung; **school** ~ Schulzeugnis; **high-school** ~ (US) Zeugnis der mittleren Reife; **higher-school** ~ (Br.) Schul-, Abgangszeugnis, Abitur; **second** ~ (company) Gewerbeschein; **share** ~ (Br.) Aktienzertifikat, -urkunde; **silver** ~ (US) Silberzertifikat; **stock** ~ (US) Aktie, Aktienzertifikat; **tax-reserve** ~s (Br.) für Steuerrücklagen erworbene Wertpapiere mit steuerfreien Zinserträgen; **trading** ~ Gewerbeschein; **transit** ~ Durchreiseerlaubnis; **treasury** ~ (US) Schatzanweisung; **voting trust** ~ Stimmberechtigungsschein [zur treuhänderischen Übertragung des Aktienstimmrechts]; **warehouse** ~ (US) Lagerschein; **weight** ~ (railway) Wiegeschein, Gewichtsbescheinigung;

~ **of acknowledgement** mit Amtssiegel versehene Bescheinigung, Beglaubigungsvermerk; ~ **of airworthiness** Zulassungsbescheinigung eines Flugzeuges, Lufttauglichkeitszeugnis; ~ **of allotment** (US) Bezugsrechtsmitteilung, Zuteilungsanzeige, -benachrichtigung, -schein; ~ **of amendment** Notariatsvertrag über die Änderung eines Gesellschaftsvertrages; ~ **of analysis** Abnahmebescheinigung; ~ **of appointment** Bestallungs-, Ernennungsurkunde; ~ **of apprenticeship** Lehrbrief, Ausbildungs-, Lehr[lings]zeugnis; ~ **of approval** Genehmigungsbescheinigung; ~ **of assize** Wiederaufnahmegenehmigung; ~ **of authentication** Beglaubigungsschreiben; ~ **of authenticity** Echtheitsbescheinigung; ~ **of authority** Vollmachtsurkunde; ~ **of average** Havarieschein, -zertifikat; ~ **of baptism** Taufschein; ~ **[payable] to bearer** Inhaberpapier; ~ **of good behavio(u)r** Führungs-, Leumundszeugnis; ~ **of birth** Geburtsschein, -urkunde; ~ **of bonds** (Br.) Registrierungsbescheinigung; ~ **of character** Führungszeugnis; ~ **of charge** (Br.) [etwa] Grundschuldbrief; ~ **of citizenship** (US) Staatsangehörigkeitsausweis, -urkunde; ~ **of civil status** Personenstandsurkunde; ~ **of clearance inward** Einfuhrbescheinigung; ~ **of clearance outward** Export-, Ausfuhrbescheinigung; ~ **to commence business** Erlaubnisschein für den Geschäftsbeginn; ~ **of competency** Befähigungsnachweis; ~ **of good conduct** Leumunds-, Führungszeugnis; ~ **of public convenience and necessity** (common carrier, US) Befähigungsnachweis; ~ **of a copy** Beglaubigung einer Abschrift; ~ **of correction** (patent law) Änderungs-, Berichtigungsbescheid; ~ **for costs** (Br.) Kostenentscheidung; ~ **of the customhouse** Zollquittung; ~ **of damage** Schadensprotokoll, Bescheinigung über die Beschädigung an ausgeladenen Gütern; ~ **of death** Totenschein, Sterbeurkunde; ~ **of delivery** Auslieferungsbescheinigung, -schein; ~ **of deposit** (US) Depositen-, Einzahlungs-, Hinterlegungsschein [für Zeiteinlagen], Depositenquittung; **negotiable sterling** ~ **of deposit** (Br.) börsenfähige Bescheinigung über in Pfund hinterlegte Zeitdepositen; ~ **of discharge** (mil.) Entlassungsschein; ~ **of dissolution** Auflösungsbescheinigung; **general** ~ **of education** (Br., advanced level) Abitur[zeugnis], Reifeprüfung, -zeugnis; ~ **of secondary education** (Br.) Zeugnis der mittleren Reife; ~ **from last employer** Arbeitsbescheinigung; ~ **of employment** Beschäftigungsnachweis, Arbeitsbescheinigung, -zeugnis, -nachweis; ~ **of evidence** Verfahrenseinreden; ~ **of exemption** (company) Bescheinigung über Prospektbefreiung; ~ **to be final** vom Käufer anzuerkennendes Qualitätszeugnis; ~ **of fitness** Tauglichkeitsbescheinigung; ~ **of forfeiture** Nichtigkeitsbescheinigung; ~ **of funds** Hinterlegungsbescheinigung; ~ **of guarantee** Garantieschein; ~ **of health** Gesundheitsattest; ~ **of identity** Identitätsnachweis, Nämlichkeitszeugnis; ~ **of incorporation** (Br.) amtliche Registrierungsbescheinigung, Gründungsurkunde,

(US) Satzung; ~ **of indebtedness** Schuldschein, -anerkenntnis, *(US)* kurzfristige Schatzanweisung; ~ **of inspection** Abnahmebescheinigung, Beschaffenheits-, Prüfungszeugnis, Qualitätsabnahmeschein; ~ **of insurance** Versicherungsschein, -zertifikat; ~ **of interest** *(US)* Investmentzertifikat, Zertifikat einer Kapitalanlagegesellschaft; ~ **of inventory** Bestandsprüfungsbescheinigung; ~ **of lunacy** Einweisungsschein in eine Irrenanstalt; ~ **of marriage** Trauschein, Heiratsurkunde; ~ **of memory** Nachweis der Merkfähigkeit; ~ **of merit** *(mil.)* schriftliche Belobigung; ~ **of misfortune** *(bankrupt)* Bescheinigung unverschuldeten Mißgeschicks, Rehabilitierungsschein; ~ **of nationality** *(US)* Staatsangehörigkeitsausweis; ~ **of naturalization** Staatsangehörigkeitsurkunde, -ausweis, Einbürgerungsurkunde; ~ **of necessity** *(US)* Berechtigungsschein für verteidigungsbedingte schnelle Abschreibungsmöglichkeiten; ~ **of occupancy** genehmigter Bauplan; ~ **of organization** Gründungsurkunde; ~ **of origin** Ursprungszeugnis, Herkunftsbescheinigung; ~ **of participation** Investmentzertifikat, -anteil, Anteilschein; ~ **by a public officer** behördliche Bescheinigung; ~ **of ownership** Eigentumsurkunde; ~ **of pay and tax deducted** Gehaltsbescheinigung mit Angaben der Lohnsteuereinbehaltung; ~ **of pilot** Lotsenpatent; ~ **of posting** *(Br.)* Posteinlieferungsschein, Postquittung; ~ **of poverty** *(US)* Mittellosigkeits-, Armutszeugnis; ~ **of priority** Berechtigungsschein [für bevorzugte Lieferung, Dringlichkeitsbescheinigung; ~ **of proficiency** Befähigungsnachweis; ~ **of purchase** *(judicial sale)* Grunderwerbs-, Zuschlagsbescheinigung; ~ **of qualification** Befähigungsnachweis; ~ **of quality** Qualitätsbescheinigung; ~ **of receipt** Empfangsbescheinigung, Übernahmeschein, *(ship)* Verladeschein; ~ **of redemption** Tilgungsbescheinigung, -schein; ~ **of registration** Eintragungsbescheinigung, Registerausweis, *(alien)* Fremdenausweis, Meldeschein; ~ **of registry** Eintragungsbescheinigung, *(pol.)* Einbürgerungsurkunde, *(ship)* Flaggenattest, Schiffsregisterbrief; ~ **of renewal** Erneuerungsschein; ~ **of residence** Aufenthaltserlaubnis; ~ **of sale** *(foreclosure)* Zuschlagsbescheinigung; ~ **of service** Zustellungsurkunde, *(mil.)* Wehrpaß; ~ **of shipment** Lade-, Versandschein, Verschiffungsbescheinigung; ~ **of stock** *(US)* Kapitalanteilschein, Aktienzertifikat, -mantel, -sammelurkunde; ~ **of storage** Stauattest; ~ **of suretyship** *(Br.)* Garantieschein; ~ **of survey** Besichtigungsprotokoll, Vermessungsschein; **high-yielding** ~s **of tax deposit** hochverzinsliche Steuergutscheine; ~ **of title** *(US)* Eigentumsnachweis, [etwa] Grundbuchauszug; ~ **of tonnage** Meßbrief; ~ **of transfer** *(Br.)* [Effekten]lieferungsbescheinigung; ~ **in typewriting** Schreibmaschinenzeugnis; ~ **of vaccination** Impfzeugnis, -schein; ~ **of warranty** Garantieschein [des Verkäufers]; ~ **of weight** Gewichtsbescheinigung, -zeugnis;

~ *(v.)* bescheinigen, Bescheinigung (Zeugnis) ausstellen;

to buy in ~s **on a no-load basis** Investmentanteile ohne Provisionsaufschlag erwerben; **to furnish (hand) a** ~ Zeugnis (Attest) ausstellen; **to gain a** ~ Zeugnis bekommen; **to grant a** ~ Attest ausstellen; **to issue a** ~ Bescheinigung ausstellen; **to obtain a** ~ sich ein Zeugnis ausstellen lassen; **to produce a** ~ Zeugnis beibringen (vorbringen); **to provide a customer with a signed** ~ *(bank)* Zinsbescheinigung ausstellen; **to split a** ~ Investmentzertifikat stückeln; **to submit a** ~ **of good character** Leumundszeugnis vorlegen; **to suspend a shipper's** ~ einem Kapitän vorübergehend die Ausübung seines Berufs untersagen; **to take out a hunting** ~ Jagdschein lösen;

~ **buyer** *(US)* Investmentkäufer; ~ **capital** Kapital eines Investmentfonds; ~ **holder** *(US)* Anteilseigner, Zertifikatsinhaber; ~ **of deposit market** Börsengeldmarkt; **to have been educated to general** ~ **standards** *(Br.)* abgeschlossene höhere Schulbildung besitzen.

certificated amtlich zugelassen, *(Br.)* diplomiert;
~ **bankrupt** *(Br.)* rehabilitierter Gemein-, Konkursschuldner; ~ **engineer** Diplomingenieur; ~ **teacher** amtlich anerkannter Lehrer.

certification Bescheinigung, Schein, amtliche Beglaubigung, Bestätigung, Beurkundung, *(of a check, US)* Bestätigungs-, Gültigkeitsvermerk, Garantieerklärung, *(law)* Klageerwiderung, *(lunatic)* Entmündigung;
~ **of an agent** Anerkennung eines Vertreters; ~ **of an aircraft** Flugtauglichkeitszeugnis; ~ **of a check** *(US)* Scheckbestätigung; ~ **of a man's name** Identitätsurkunde; ~ **of signature** Unterschriftsbeglaubigung; ~ **of transfer** *(Br., shares)* Übertragungsbescheinigung; ~ **of union** Anerkennung einer Gewerkschaft [für Tarifverhandlungen];
~ **department** *(US)* Scheckkontrollabteilung; ~ **mark** Gütezeichen, Ursprungshinweis.

certificatory beglaubigend.
certified *(attested)* bescheinigt, *(authenticated)* beglaubigt, *(licensed)* amtlich zugelassen, diplomiert, *(med., Br.)* für unzurechnungsfähig erklärt, entmündigt;
~ **by a notary** notariell beglaubigt;
to be ~ **correct** *(accounts)* in Ordnung befunden werden;
~ **accountant** *(Br.)* öffentlich zugelassener Wirtschaftsprüfer; ~ **agriculturalist** Diplomlandwirt; ~ **broker** amtlich zugelassener Makler; ~ **carrier** Spediteur im Güterfernverkehr; ~ **check** *(US)* **(cheque, Br.)** [von einer Bank] bestätigter Scheck; ~ **copy** amtliche (notarielle) beglaubigte Abschrift; ~ **lunatic (insane)** entmündigter Geisteskranker; ~ **net sales** *(newspaper)* tatsächlich verkaufte Auflage; ~ **political economist** Diplomvolkswirt; ~ **public accountant** *(US)* beeidigter Wirtschaftsprüfer; ~ **financial statement** mit Prüfungsvermerk versehene Bilanz; ~ **transfer** *(Br.)* beglaubigte Abtretung; ~ **true copy** die Richtigkeit der Abschrift wird beglaubigt; ~ **union** *(US)* zu den Tarifverhandlungen bevollmächtigte Gewerkschaft.

certifier Aussteller einer Urkunde (Bescheinigung).
certify *(v.)* versichern, *(attest)* bescheinigen, bestätigen, attestieren, bezeugen, Zertifikat ausstellen, *(authenticate)* beglaubigen, beurkunden, *(judge)* höhere Anwaltskosten genehmigen;
~ **a check** *(US)* **(cheque, Br.)** Scheck [als gedeckt] bestätigen; ~ **s. one's character** sich Anständigkeit für jds. Anständigkeit verbürgen; ~ **s. one's insanity (s. o. a lunatic, as insane)** *(Br.)* j. wegen Geisteskrankheit entmündigen, j. amtlich für geisteskrank erklären;
this is to ~ hiermit wird beglaubigt.

certifying | a check *(US)* **(cheque, Br.)** Scheckbestätigung, Bestätigungsvermerk; ~ **of a document** amtliche Urkundenbeglaubigung; ~ **of a lunatic** *(Br.)* Entmündigung eines Geisteskranken;
~ **authority** bescheinigende Behörde; ~ **committee** Armenrechtsprüfungsausschuß; ~ **officer** Urkundsbeamter.

certiori *(lat.)* Revisionsverfahren;
~ **denied** *(US)* abgelehnter Revisionsantrag;
[writ of] ~ Aktenanforderung.

cessation Beendigung, Aufhören, Aussetzen, Einstellung, *(law)* Kassation, *(pause)* Stillstand;
~ **of agreement** Vertragsbeendigung; ~ **of arms** Waffenstillstand; ~ **of a branch** Einstellung eines Teilbetriebs; ~ **of a business** Stillegung eines Geschäftsbetriebs; ~ **of delivery** Liefereinstellung, Einstellung der Lieferung; ~ **of hostilities** Einstellung (Beendigung) der Feindseligkeiten (Kampfhandlungen); ~ **of imports** Einfuhrstopp; ~ **of membership** Erlöschen der Mitgliedschaft; ~ **of a publication** Eingehen einer Zeitschrift; ~ **of service** Beendigung des Dienstverhältnisses; ~ **of strike** Streikbeendigung; ~ **of trade** Einstellung des Geschäftsbetriebs; ~ **of work** Einstellung der Arbeit, Arbeitseinstellung, -niederlegung;
~ **provision** Stillegungsbestimmung.

cesser Aufhören, Ablauf, *(US)* Patentbeendigung.
cession Überlassung, Zession, [Rechts]abtretung, Verzicht, Zedierung, *(reinsurance business)* teilweise Wagnisabgabe, Rückversicherungsanteil;
~ **of administration** Übertragung der Verwaltungshoheit; ~ **of goods** *(debtor)* Vermögensübertragung; ~ **of a territory** Gebietsabtretung;
~ **number** *(reinsurance business)* Nummer des abgetretenen Wagnisses.

cessionary Rechtsnachfolger, Zessionar;
~ **bankrupt** zahlungsunfähiger Schuldner, der sein Vermögen übertragen hat.

cessor im Verzug befindlicher Schuldner.
cesspool Senk-, Sickergrube;
~ **clearing company** Senkgrubenabfuhr.

cestui | que trust Treuhandnehmer, -begünstigter, Nutznießer eines Stiftungsvermögens; ~ **que use** Begünstigter bei einer Grundstücksüberlassung, Nutzungsbegünstigter; ~ **que vie** Treuhandbegünstigter auf Lebenszeit eines Dritten.

chaff *(radar)* Stanniolstreifen, Radarstörfolie, *(trifle)* unbedeutende Angelegenheit;
to separate the ~ **from the wheat** Spreu vom Weizen scheiden.

chaffer Feilschen, Schacherei;
~ *(v.)* handeln, feilschen, schachern.

chafferer Schacherer.
chain Kette, *(advertising agency)* zusammenarbeitende Gruppe, *(branch)* Kettenunternehmen, Filialbetrieb, *(broadcasting)* Zusammenschluß von Sendern, *(car)* Schneekette;
~s Fesseln;
anchor ~ Ankerkette; **guard** ~ Sicherheitskette;
~ **of causation** Kausalzusammenhang; **complete** ~ **of sales ef-**

forts lückenlose Verkaufsanstrengungen; ~ **of events** Folge von Ereignissen, Verkettung von Umständen; ~ **of evidence** Beweiskette; ~ **of office** Amtskette; ~ **of shops** Filialbetrieb, Ladenkette; ~ **of succession** Verwandtenerbfolge; ~ **of title [of transference]** vollständiger Eigentumsnachweis [auf Grund von Urkunden];
~ *(v.)* **a prisoner** Gefangenen fesseln;
~ **banking** *(US)* Filialbankbetrieb; ~ **brand** *(US)* Eigenmarke eines Filialbetriebs; ~ **break** Werbeinblendung; ~ **bridge** Hängebrücke; ~ **broadcast** Ringsendung; ~ **discount** Abschlag vom Listenpreis, Stufenrabatt; ~ **drive** Kettenantrieb; ~ **drugstore** *(US)* Filialgeschäft; ~ **index** *(statistics)* verketteter Index; ~ **letter** Kettenbrief; ~ **organization** Einzelhandelskette; **to be ~-owned** Filialbetrieb sein; **~-reacting pile** Kernreaktor; ~ **reaction** Kettenreaktion; **to trigger a ~ reaction** Kettenreaktion auslösen; ~ **reactor** Kernreaktor; ~ **retailing organization** Einzelhandelskette; ~ **smoker** Kettenraucher.
chain store *(US)* Kettenladen, Filial-, Zweig-, Einheitspreisgeschäft;
~ **business** *(US)* Kettenladenunternehmen; ~ **tax** *(US)* Steuer auf Einheitspreisgeschäfte.
chain trade Kettenhandel.
chair Stuhl, Sessel, *(chairman)* Präsident, Vorsitzender, *(fig.)* Ehrensitz, *(judge)* Richterstuhl, *(magistrate)* Bürgermeisteramt, *(office of chairman)* Präsidium, Vorsitz, *(stool)* Rednerstuhl, *(university)* Lehrstuhl;
with A in the ~ unter dem Vorsitz von A, mit A als Vorsitzendem;
~! *(parl., Br.)* zur Ordnung!;
electrical ~ elektrischer Stuhl, Hinrichtungsplatz; **presidential ~** Präsidentenplatz; **professor's (professorial) ~** Lehrstuhl, Professur; **sedan ~** Autositz;
~ **of commerce** Professor für Handelswissenschaften; ~ **in economics** volkswirtschaftliche Professur; ~ **on the supervisory committee** Aufsichtsratsposten;
~ *(v.)* *(US)* als Vorsitzender fungieren, Vorsitz übernehmen, *(install)* auf einen Lehrstuhl berufen;
to accept a ~ Berufung annehmen; **to address the ~** sich an den Vorsitzenden wenden; **to appeal to the ~** Entscheidung des Vorsitzenden anrufen; **to assume the ~** Vorsitz übernehmen; **to be in the ~** Vorsitz führen, präsidieren; **to be moved into (voted in) the ~** zum Vorsitzenden gewählt werden; **to be offered a ~** auf einen Lehrstuhl berufen werden, Ruf erhalten; **to call to the ~** zum Vorsitzenden ernennen; **to establish a ~** Lehrstuhl errichten; **to fill a ~** Lehrstuhl besetzen; **to fill the [speaker's] ~** Vorsitz führen; **to fill a vacant ~** Lehrstuhl wiederbesetzen; **to found a new ~** neuen Lehrstuhl errichten; **to have passed the ~** schon Präsident gewesen sein; **to leave the ~** Sitzung aufheben; **to occupy the ~** Vorsitz führen, präsidieren, vorsitzen; **to offer a ~** auf einen Lehrstuhl berufen; **to pass the ~** Vorsitz abgeben; **to refuse a ~** Berufung ablehnen; **to second for the ~** für den Vorsitz abstellen; **to support the ~** sich der Meinung des Vorsitzenden anschließen; **to take the ~** Vorsitz (Präsidium) übernehmen, Präsidentenstuhl besteigen; **to take the ~ according to the rota** Vorsitz turnusmäßig übernehmen; **to vacate the ~** Sitzung aufheben;
~ **car** *(railroad, US)* Salonwagen, ~ **lift** Sessellift.
chairman Obmann, Vorsitzender, Präsident;
committee ~ Ausschußvorsitzender; **deputy ~** stellvertretender Vorsitzender; **honorary ~** Ehrenvorsitzender; **impartial ~** unparteiischer Vorsitzender; **party ~** Parteivorsitzender; **legally qualified ~** Vorsitzender mit Richterqualifikation;
~ **of the [supervisory] board** Verwaltungsratsvorsitzender; ~ **of a committee** Ausschußvorsitzender; ~ **of the executive board** Vorstandsvorsitzender; ~ **of the board of directors** Aufsichtsratsvorsitzender; ~ **of the board of management (managing board)** Vorstandsvorsitzender; ~ **of the Federal Reserve Board** *(US)* Bundesnotenbankpräsident; ~ **of a meeting** Versammlungsleiter; ~ **of the party** Parteivorsitzender; ~ **of the Post Office** *(Br.)* Präsident der Postverwaltung; ~ **by seniority** Alterspräsident; ~ **of the Stock Exchange Council** *(London)* Vorsitzender des Börsenvorstandes;
to act as ~ als Vorsitzender fungieren; **to be ~ of a meeting** Vorsitz auf einer Versammlung führen; **to elect s. o. ~** j. zum Vorsitzenden wählen; **to propose s. o. for ~** j. zum Vorsitzenden vorschlagen.
chairmanship Präsidentenamt, Präsidium, Leitung, Vorsitz;
under the ~ of unter dem Vorsitz von;
rotating ~ turnusmäßig wechselnder Vorsitz;
~ **of the supervisory committee** Aufsichtsratsvorsitz;
to be called to the ~ of zum Vorsitzenden bestellt werden.

chalet Landhaus.
chalk Kreide, Kalk, *(Br.)* angekreidete Schuld;
as different as ~ and cheese so verschieden wie Tag und Nacht; **colo(u)red ~** Bunt-, Farbstift;
~ *(v.)* *(record debits)* anschreiben, Kredit geben;
~ **up** rot im Kalender anstreichen; ~ **it up** Rechnung auflaufen lassen; ~ **up small monthly deficits** unbedeutende Monatsverluste rot im Kalender anstreichen.
challenge Herausforderung, *(dispute)* Bestreitung, Hinwendung, *(electioneering)* Anfechtung der Gültigkeit einer Stimme, *(exception taken to a juror)* Geschworenenablehnung, *(mil.)* Anruf durch den Wachposten;
general ~ grundsätzliche Ablehnung; **principal ~** Ablehnung wegen Befangenheit;
~ **for cause** Ablehnung unter Angabe eines bestimmten Grundes; ~ **to the favo(u)r** Ablehnung wegen Befangenheit; ~ **for a juror** Ablehnung eines Geschworenen; ~ **to the panel** *(Br.)* Gesamtablehnung der Geschworenen; ~ **to the poll** *(Br.)* Ablehnung einzelner Geschworener; ~ **of a witness** Ablehnung eines Zeugen;
~ *(v.)* herausfordern, *(contest)* anfechten, bestreiten, *(electioneering, US)* Einwendungen erheben;
~ **the accuracy of a statement** Richtigkeit einer Aussage anzweifeln; ~ **criticism** Kritik herausfordern; ~ **the competence** Zuständigkeit bestreiten; ~ **an election** Gültigkeit einer Wahl anfechten; ~ **a judge** Richter ablehnen; ~ **a juror** Geschworenen ablehnen; ~ **the legality of official actions** Rechtmäßigkeit amtlicher Maßnahmen nachprüfen lassen; ~ **s. one's rights** jds. Rechte bestreiten; ~ **s. one's succession** jds. Erbfolgerecht bestreiten; ~ **the validity** Gültigkeit bestreiten; ~ **the validity of a document** Echtheit einer Urkunde bestreiten; ~ **a vote** Gültigkeit einer Abstimmung anfechten; ~ **a witness** Zeugen ablehnen;
to accept a ~ Herausforderung annehmen, sich stellen; **to meet the ~** den Anforderungen gerecht werden; **to sound like a ~** wie eine Herausforderung klingen;
~ **cup** Wanderpreis.
challengeable anfechtbar.
challenger Herausforderer.
chamber Kammer, [Schlaf]zimmer, *(Exchequer, Br.)* Schatzamt, *(hall for meeting)* Sitzungssaal, *(parl.)* Kammer, Haus, *(solicitors, Br.)* Kanzlei, Anwaltsbüro;
in ~s in nichtöffentlicher Sitzung, unter Ausschluß der Öffentlichkeit;
~s *(Br.)* Junggesellenwohnung, *(business use, Br.)* Geschäftsräume, *(law court)* Richterzimmer, *(legislation)* Sitzungszimmer;
audience ~ Empfangszimmer; **barrister's ~s** *(Br.)* Anwaltskanzlei, -büro; **Lower ♀** Unterhaus; **Privy ♀** Geheimkabinett; **Upper ♀** Oberhaus; **widow's ~** *(London)* Dreißigster;
♀ of Accounts Rechnungskammer; **♀ of Agriculture** Landwirtschaftskammer; **♀ of Commerce** Handelskammer; **International ♀ of Commerce** Internationale Handelskammer; **♀ of Deputies** Abgeordnetenhaus; ~ **of horror** Gruselkabinett; ~ **of shipping** Schiffseigentümervereinigung;
~ *(v.)* Zimmer bereitstellen;
to hear a case in ~s Fall unter Ausschluß der Öffentlichkeit verhandeln; **to let ~s** *(Br.)* Zimmer vermieten; **to live in ~s** *(Br.)* möbliert (privat) wohnen; **to sit in ~s** unter Ausschluß der Öffentlichkeit verhandeln, als Einzelrichter tätig sein;
~ **arrest** Stubenarrest; ~ **barrister** nicht plädierender Anwalt; ~ **business** Tätigkeit als Einzelrichter; ~ **concert** Kammerkonzert; ~ **counsel** *(Br.)* beratender Anwalt, Rechtsberater; ~ **practice** *(Br.)* anwaltliche Tätigkeit außerhalb des Gerichts, beratende Praxis, Beratungspraxis; ~ **work** *(Br.)* Kanzleitätigkeit.
chamberlain Kammerherr, *(Scotl.)* Stadtkämmerer;
city ~ *(US)* Stadtkämmerer;
Lord Great ♀ of England Großkämmerer;
~'s department *(Scotland)* Finanzverwaltungsressort.
chambermaid *(hotel)* Stubenmädchen.
champagne breakfast Sektfrühstück.
champertous contract Anwaltsvereinbarung auf Erfolgshonorarbasis.
champerty *(US)* Erfolgsmandat.
champion Vertreter, Vorkämpfer, Verfechter;
~ **of free speech** Verfechter der Redefreiheit;
~ *(v.)* verfechten;
~ **the oppressed** sich der Sache der Unterdrückten annehmen; ~ **hoarder** Allessparer.
championship Meisterschaft.

chance Zufall, zufälliges Ereignis, Schicksal, Los, *(opportunity)* Chance, Möglichkeit, günstige Gelegenheit;
by a mere ~ durch reinen Zufall; **on the ~** angesichts der Möglichkeit;
last clear ~ *(accident insurance, US)* letzte Rettungschance; **not a dog's ~** nicht die geringste Chance; **lucky ~** glücklicher Zufall; **off ~** geringe Chance (Möglichkeit); **pure ~** glatter Zufall; **sporting ~** mit Risiko verbundene Chance;
~ of entry Beitrittsschance; **~ of a lifetime** einmalige Gewinnchance, Chance seines Lebens; **~ of profit** Gewinnchance; **slim ~ of success** geringe Erfolgschance; **~ in a thousand** einmalige Gelegenheit; **~ of winning** Gewinnchance;
~ (v.) geschehen, unerwartet eintreten, sich zufällig ereignen; **~ one's arm** *(coll.)* etw. riskieren; **~ it** es darauf ankommen lassen;
~ to be there zufällig anwesend sein;
to always have an eye to the main ~ immer nur aufs Geldverdienen aus sein; **to leave nothing to ~** nichts dem Zufall überlassen; **to miss one's ~** Gelegenheit versäumen, sich eine Chance entgehen lassen; **to pass up a ~** sich eine Chance entgehen lassen; **to stand a good ~** gute Aussichten haben; **to take one's ~** es darauf ankommen lassen; **not to take any ~s** kein Risiko eingehen; **to take close ~s** großes Risiko eingehen;
~ acquaintance Zufallsbekanntschaft; **~ bargain** Gelegenheitskauf; **~ child** uneheliches Kind; **~ customer** zufälliger Kunde, Laufkunde; **~ factor** *(statistics)* Zufallsmoment; **~ fluctuations** zufallsbedingte Schwankungen; **~ hit** Zufallstreffer; **~-medley** Raubhandel, Totschlag [aus Notwehr]; **~ meeting** zufälliges Zusammentreffen; **~ purchase** Gelegenheitskauf.
chancellery Staatskanzlei, Kanzleramt, *(diplomacy)* Gesandtschafts-, Konsulatskanzlei.
chancellor Kanzler, *(diplomacy)* Kanzleivorstand, *(university, US)* Rektor;
Lord ~ *(Br.)* Präsident des Oberhauses; **Vice-~** Vizekanzler; **~ of the Exchequer** *(Br.)* Finanzminister, Schatzkanzler; **~ of a university** Präsident einer Universität.
chancellorship Kanzleramt.
chancer *(v.)* nach Billigkeitsgrundsätzen schlichten.
chancery Kanzlei, Amt, *(administration of the court)* gerichtliche Verwaltung, *(court of equity, US)* Billigkeitsgericht, *(court of record)* Urkunden- und Registergericht, *(guardianship)* Vormundschaft, *(predicament)* hilflose Lage, Klemme;
in ~ unter gerichtlicher Verwaltung, bankrott, pleite;
to be in ~ in der Klemme sitzen;
~ court Kanzleigericht; **~ master** Rechtspfleger.
chandler Krämer, Händler;
ship ~ Schiffslieferant, Lieferant von Schiffsbedarf.
Chandler Act *(US)* Konkursordnung.
chandlery Kramladen.
change *(alteration)* Änderung, Abänderung, Veränderung, *(balance returned)* herausgegebenes Geld, Wechselgeld, *(clothes)* frische Wäsche, *(exchange)* Tausch, Austausch, *(legal right)* Übergang, *(small coin)* Scheidemünze, Kleingeld, *(stock exchange, Br.)* Börse, *(transfer of official)* Versetzung;
for a ~ zur Abwechslung; **on ~** *(Br.)* auf der Börse; **subject to ~ without notice** freibleibend;
~s ahead zukünftige Veränderungen; **basic ~** grundlegende Änderung; **business ~s** geschäftliche Veränderungen; **depreciation ~s** Änderung der Abschreibungsrichtlinien; **fractional ~s** geringfügige Veränderungen; **inventory ~s** Änderungen in der Lagerhaltung; **inventory valuation ~s** Änderungen in der Bestandsbewertung; **management ~s** Umbesetzungen im Vorstand; **organizational ~** organisatorische Veränderung; **peaceful ~** *(law of nations)* friedliche Veränderung; **small ~** Wechsel-, Kleingeld; **sudden ~** plötzlicher Umschwung; **verbal ~s** Änderung des Wortlauts; **violent ~** *(law of nations)* gewaltsame Veränderung; **zone ~** *(US)* Änderung des Flächennutzungsplanes;
~ of abode Wohnsitzwechsel, -veränderung; **~ of account** Kontoänderung; **~ in the economic activities** konjunktureller Wandel; **~ of address** Adressenänderung, Wohnungswechsel; **~ of air** Luftveränderung; **~s in allowances** *(income tax)* Freibetragsänderungen; **~s in fixed assets** Bewegung des Anlagevermögens, Anlagenveränderungen; **~ in the cabinet** Regierungswechsel; **~ of carriage** Wagenwechsel; **~ in climate** Klimaänderung; **~ of clothes** Umziehen; **~ in the coast line** Küstenversetzung; **~ in constitution** Verfassungsänderung, *(firm)* Satzungsänderung; **~ in demand** Umstrukturierung der Nachfrage; **proportionate ~ in demand** relative Nachfragemengenänderung; **~s in depreciation** Änderung der Abschreibungspolitik (Abschreibungsrichtlinien); **~ of design** Sujet-

wechsel; **~s in the direction of a firm** Veränderungen (Wechsel) im Vorstand; **~s in distribution** Wandel im Absatzweg; **~ of domicile** Wohnsitzverlegung; **~ of employer** Arbeitsplatzwechsel; **~ of employment** Wechsel des Arbeitsplatzes; **~s in exchange rates** Wechselkursveränderungen; **~s in the frontier line** Grenzveränderungen; **~ of goods** Güteraustausch; **~ of government** Regierungswechsel; **~ of hands** Besitzänderung, -wechsel; **~s in holding** Umstellungen im Wertpapierbesitz; **market ~s in interest** Änderung der Zinskonditionen; **~s in interest rates** Zinsänderung; **~ of job** Arbeitsplatzwechsel; **~ in leadership** Führungswechsel; **~s in a letter** Briefänderungen; **~ of life** kritisches Alter, Übergangsperiode, Klimakterium; **~ in the management** Führungswechsel; **~ in the membership of the board** Veränderungen (Umbesetzungen) im Vorstand; **~ of the ministry** Ministerwechsel; **~ of mood** Stimmungswechsel; **~ of name** Namenswechsel, -änderung; **~ of opinion** Meinungswechsel; **~ in the outlook** Umdenkungsprozess; **~ in ownership** Eigentums-, Besitzwechsel; **~ of parities** Paritätenänderung; **~ of parties** Parteiwechsel; **~ of partners** Gesellschafterwechsel; **~ in partnership** Veränderungen im Gesellschafterverhältnis; **~ of position** berufliche Veränderung, Stellungswechsel; **~s in prices** Preisveränderungen; **proportionate ~ in price** relative Preisänderung; **~ in process** Änderung des Produktionsverfahrens; **~ in the program(me)** Programmänderung, -wechsel; **~ in rates** Prämien-, Tarif-, Anzeigenpreisänderung; **~s in rates of taxes** Änderung der Steuersätze; **~ of regime** Regimewechsel; **~ of requirement** Nachfrage-, Bedarfswandel; **~ of residence** Aufenthaltswechsel, Wohnsitzveränderung; **~ in salary** Gehaltsänderung; **~ in salary scales** Lohntarifänderung; **~ of scene[ry]** *(fig.)* Ortsveränderung, Tapetenwechsel; **~ of the situation** Belegenheitswechsel; **~ of size** Formatänderung; **~ of solicitor** Anwaltswechsel; **~ of many sorts** mancherlei Veränderungen; **~s in the staff** Personalwechsel; **~ in style** Modeänderung; **~ in taste** Geschmackswandel; **~ of tax law** Steuerrechtsänderung; **~ of tendency** Stimmungswechsel; **~ of the tide** Gezeitenwechsel; **~ of title** Eigentumswechsel; **~ of trade name** Firmenänderung; **~ of use** Nutzungs-, Gebrauchsänderung; **~s in the valuation** Bewertungsänderungen; **~ in the value of money** Geldwertveränderung; **~ in the par values** Paritätenänderung; **~ of venue** Änderung des Gerichtsstandes; **~s in volume** Mengenänderung; **~ of voyage** Änderung des Reiseweges; **~ of the weather** Wetteränderung; **abrupt ~ of the weather** Wettersturz;
~ (v.) *(alter)* [ver]ändern, *(el.)* umschalten, transformieren, *(exchange)* aus-, umtauschen, *(money)* ein-, umwechseln;
~ about *(prices)* schwanken; **~ from amber to green** *(traffic lights)* von Gelb auf Grün umschalten; **~ a bed** Bett frisch beziehen; **~ one's conditions** sich verheiraten; **~ for the better** sich vorteilhaft verändern; **~ foreign currency** ausländisches Geld umwechseln; **~ for dinner** sich zum Abendessen umkleiden; **~ down** *(gear)* in einen niedrigeren Gang herunterschalten; **~ for** *(railway)* umsteigen; **~ front** sich auf die andere Seite schlagen, Frontwechsel vornehmen; **~ gear** *(car)* in einen anderen Gang schalten; **~ hands** in andere (fremde) Hände übergehen; **~ hands at ...** *(stock exchange)* gehandelt werden zu ..., umgesetzt werden mit ...; **~ one's lodgings** umziehen; **~ one's mind** seine Ansicht (Meinung) ändern, sich anders besinnen; **~ one's note** zurückstecken; **~ oil** Öl erneuern (wechseln); **~ one's opinion** seine Meinung ändern; **~ over** *(industry)* umstellen; **~ a partnership to a corporation** Offene Handelsgesellschaft in eine Aktiengesellschaft umwandeln; **~ places with another** Plätze tauschen; **~ one's position** seine Stellung wechseln; **~ one's profession** umsatteln, anderen Beruf ergreifen; **~ sides** *(politics)* umfallen; **~ one's skin** sein Verhalten ändern; **~ the subject** Thema wechseln; **~ trains** umsteigen; **~ one's tune** bescheidener werden; **~ up** *(gear)* heraufschalten;
to find a great ~ in s. o. j. sehr verändert finden; **to get ~** Geld herausbekommen; **to give ~ (for)** Geld herausgeben [auf]; **to give the wrong ~ to a customer** einem Kunden falsch herausgeben; **to measure the ~ in prices** Preisveränderungen erfassen; **to point to a ~** auf veränderlich zeigen; **to ring the ~s** Thema von allen Seiten beleuchten, *(sl.)* j. beim Geldwechseln übers Ohr hauen; **to undergo a ~** Änderung erfahren;
~ report Veränderungsmeldung.
change-over Umwälzung, *(el.)* Umschaltung;
~ costs Umstellungskosten; **~ employment** Übergangsbeschäftigung; **~ production** vorübergehende Produktion; **~ station** Relaisstation.
changeable veränderlich, abänderungsfähig;
~ of mind wankelmütig.
changeling untergeschobenes Kind, Wechselbalg.

changing | of gears Schalten der Gänge; **~ of the guard** Wachablösung;
~ sides *(pol.)* Schwankung;
~ room Umkleidezimmer.

channel Flußbett, schiffbarer Wasserweg, Kanal, Fahrrinne, *(band of frequencies)* Frequenzband, Kanal, *(fig.)* Kanal, Bahn, Weg;
sent into the ordinary ~s of trade *(patent law)* ordnungsgemäß in den Verkehr gebracht; **through diplomatic ~s** auf diplomatischem Wege; **through official (authorized) ~s** auf dem Dienstweg, auf offiziellem Weg; **through the usual ~s** auf dem üblichen Weg;
administrative ~ Verwaltungsweg; **commercial ~** Handelsweg; **main ~** Hauptschiffahrtsweg; **natural ~** *(river)* Hauptbett; **navigable ~** Fahrrinne; **radio telephone ~** Funksprechkanal;
~ of collection Einziehungsweg; **~s of commerce** Handelsweg; **~ of communication** Nachrichtenweg; **~ of distribution** Absatzweg; **~s of information** Informationsmöglichkeiten; **~s and outlets** Vertriebskanäle; **~s of supply** Versorgungswege; **~s of trade** Handelswege;
~ *(v.)* durch einen Kanal befördern, *(fig.)* zuführen;
~ all one's energies into s. th. all seine Energie auf etw. Bestimmtes konzentrieren; **~ one's interests** seine Interessen in eine Richtung lenken; **~ money into social expenditure** Geldströme in den Sozialausgabenetat einschleusen; **~ refugees into a camp** Flüchtlinge in ein Lager einschleusen;
to cross the ~ über den Kanal fahren; **to direct a matter into other ~s** Angelegenheit in andere Bahnen lenken; **to go through the proper ~s** Dienstweg benützen, Amtsweg einhalten; **to go through the usual ~s** durch alle Instanzen gehen; **to have secret ~s of information** Geheiminformationen haben; **to ignore ~s** Instanzenweg überspringen (nicht einhalten);
~ freight Kanalfracht; **~ markings** Fahrwasserbezeichnung; **cross-~ steamer** Kanaldampfer; **~ tunnel** Kanaltunnel.

channelize *(v.)* kanalisieren;
~ traffic Verkehr steuern.

channelling of scarce materials Steuerung von Engpaßwaren.

chaos Chaos, Durcheinander, Wirrwarr;
financial ~ Finanzwirrwarr.

chapbook Volksbuch.

chaperon Anstandsdame, -wauwau.

chapman *(Br.)* Höker, Hausierer.

chapter *(bill)* Gesetzesartikel, *(book)* Kapitel, Abschnitt *(student organization)* Ortsgruppe;
to the end of the ~ bis ans Ende;
introductory ~ einführendes Kapitel;
~ of accidents Unfallserie; **dark ~ of our history** trauriges Kapitel unserer Geschichte; **new ~ in one's life** neuer Lebensabschnitt; **~ and verse** genaue Beweise;
~ *(v.)* in Kapitel einteilen;
to arrange in ~s in Kapitel aufgliedern;
~ house *(US, fraternity)* Klubhaus.

char, chare *(Br., coll.)* Gelegenheitsarbeit;
~ *(v.)* als Reinemachefrau arbeiten, beschäftigen.

charabanc *(Br.)* Touristenbus, Ausflugsautobus.

character Charakter[stärke], Wesen, Wesensmerkmal, Gesinnung, *(key)* Chiffre, Geheimzeichen, *(letter)* Buchstabe, Kenn-, Schriftzeichen, *(person)* Persönlichkeit, *(quality)* Eigenschaft, *(reputation)* Ruf, Leumund, *(status)* Stellung, Dienstrang, *(testimonial)* Arbeitszeugnis, *(theater)* Rolle;
in ~ mit dem Wesen übereinstimmend; **in his ~ as ambassador** in seiner Eigenschaft (Stellung) als Botschafter; **in large ~s** in großen Buchstaben; **of good moral ~** charakterlich einwandfrei; **of strong ~** charakterfest; **out of ~** wesensfremd;
fine ~ anständiger Charakter; **generic ~** Gattungsmerkmal; **intellectual ~** geistige Begabung; **personal ~** Auskunft zur Person; **public ~** in der Öffentlichkeit bekannte Persönlichkeit; **quasi-trust ~** konzernähnlicher Charakter; **strange ~s** sonderbare Schriftzüge, merkwürdige Leute; **written ~** Zeugnis;
~ of business Geschäftstyp; **~ of a contract** Wesen eines Vertrages; **two ~s strongly opposed** zwei grundverschiedene Charaktere; **~s taken from life** aus dem Leben genommene Chraktere; **~s in a novel** Romanfiguren;
to assume s. one's ~ unter jds. Namen handeln; **to be quite a ~** ein Original sein; **to bear a good ~** guten Ruf besitzen; **to deliver a certificate of good ~** gutes Führungszeugnis vorlegen; **to estimate a ~** Charakter beurteilen, Charakterbeurteilung vornehmen; **to form the ~** Charakter bilden; **to give a servant a good ~** einer Hausangestellten ein gutes Zeugnis ausstellen; **to have the ~ of a place hunter** im Rufe eines Strebers stehen; **to have gained the ~ of a miser** als Geizhals verschrieen sein; **to**
have the ~ of reserves *(funds)* Rücklagencharakter haben; **to know s. one's ~** jds. Handschrift kennen; **to mould a ~** Charakter bilden; **to run down s. one's ~** j. in einen üblen Ruf bringen; **to take away s. one's ~** jem. den guten Ruf nehmen, Rufmord an jem. begehen;
~ actor Charakterdarsteller; **~ analysis** Charakteranalyse; **~ assassination** Rufmord; **~ building** Charakterbildung; **~-building** charakterbildend; **~ count** *(manuscript, Br.)* Berechnung des Satzumfangs, Umfangsberechnung; **~ definition** *(computer)* Zeichenwiedergabe; **~ evidence** Leumundsbeweis; **~ reference** Dienstleistungszeugnis, persönliche Referenzen; **~ spacing** *(terminal)* Dikteneingabe.

characteristic Kennzeichen, Merkmal;
personal ~s persönliche Eigenschaften;
~ sign wesentliches Merkmal.

characterization Charakteristik, Charakterisierung, Kennzeichnung, Kenntlichmachung.

characterize *(v.)* charakterisieren, schildern, kennzeichnen.

charactery Zeichenschrift.

charcoal drawing Kohlezeichnung.

charge *(accusation)* Bezichtigung, Beschuldigung, [Straf]anzeige, Anklage[punkt], *(bishop)* Hirtenbrief, *(bookkeeping)* Belastung, *(care)* Aufsicht, Gewahrsam, Obhut, Sorge, Verwaltung, *(commission)* Anweisung, Auftrag, Verantwortung, Vorschrift, *(criminal law)* Anklage[schrift], *(fee)* Gebühr, Taxe, Eintrittsgeld, *(financial burden)* Belastung, finanzielle Last, Schuld, *(to jurors)* Rechtsbelehrung, *(load)* Last, Belastung, Fracht, *(mil.)* Angriff, Ansturm, Attacke, *(obligation)* Verpflichtung, *(office)* Amt, Stelle, Verantwortlichkeit, *(person entrusted to the care)* Pflegebefohlener, Pflegling, Schützling, Mündel, *(price)* geforderter Preis, Forderung, Kosten, *(on property)* [Vermögens]belastung, Grundpfandrecht, Pfandbestellung, *(thing entrusted to the care)* anvertrautes Gut, Pfandeigentum, Depositum, *(will)* Auflage;
at a ~ of für eine Gebühr von; **at a moderate ~** wohlfeil, billig; **at his own ~** auf seine Kosten; **at a small ~** für eine geringe Gebühr; **at the ~ of** zum Preise von; **free of ~** unentgeltlich, gratis, kostenfrei, -los, gebührenfrei, lasten-, spesenfrei; *(delivery)* frei Haus, *(postage)* franko; **in ~** diensthabend; **in ~ of** in Vertretung, im Auftrag, in der Obhut von; **no ~** *(bill of exchange)* ohne Kosten; **no ~ is made for packing** Verpackung wird nicht berechnet;
account-carrying ~ *(bank)* Verwaltungsgebühr, Kontospesen; **additional ~** Zusatzgebühr, Preis-, Gebührenzuschlag, Mehrbelastung; **annuity ~** Rentenschuld; **balancing ~** Steuerbelastung für zu hoch vorgenommene Abschreibungen; **basic ~** Grundgebühr; **broker's ~** Maklergebühr; **capital ~** Kapitalaufwand; **carrier's ~** Transportkosten; **carrying ~** *(US, storage)* Verwaltungsgebühr; **collective ~** Gesamthypothek; **consular ~** Konsulargebühr; **counter ~** Widerklage; **customary ~** gewöhnlicher (üblicher) Preis; **deferred ~** passiver Rechnungsabgrenzungsposten, Berichtigungsposten; **direct ~** unmittelbare Belastung; **excessive ~** überhöhte Gebühr, Überforderung; **fiscal ~** Steuerlast; **fixed ~** konkretisierte dingliche (feste) Belastung; **floating ~** offene Gesamtbelastung, Global-, Generalverpfändung, Höchstbetragshypothek; **forwarding ~** Abfertigungsgebühr; **general ~** *(to jurors)* allgemeine Rechtsbelehrung; **general equitable ~** formloses Grundpfandrecht; **hit-and-run~** Anklage wegen Fahrerflucht; **inclusive ~** Gesamtgebühr; **Inland Revenue ~** Pfandrecht des Finanzamtes für Erbschaftssteuern; **land ~** Grundstücksbelastung, Grundschuld, Reallast; **registered land ~** *(Br.)* [etwa] Buchgrundschuld; **unregistered land ~** *(Br.)* [etwa] Briefgrundschuld; **~ levied on** Umlage; **limited owner's ~** *(Br.)* gesetzliche Sicherungshypothek des Nießbrauchers, Nießbrauchbelastung; **maintenance ~** *(banking)* monatliche Bankspesen; **money ~** finanzielle Belastung, *(mortgaging)* Hypothekenbelastung; **mortgage ~** hypothekarische Belastung; **omnibus ~** *(building society)* Globalpfandbestellung; **limited owner's ~** gesetzliche Sicherungshypothek des Nießbrauchers für bezahlte Erbschaftssteuer; **pending ~** schwebende Anklage; **prior ~** Vorbelastung, -last; **public ~** Sozialhilfe-, Fürsorgeempfänger; **reconsignment ~** Rücksendungsgebühr; **redeemable ~** rückzahlbare Belastung; **registered ~** *(Br.)* eingetragene Reallast; **registrable ~** eintragungsfähige Belastung; **rent ~** Verpfändung von Mieteinkünften; **reserve ~** *(postage)* Gebühr bezahlt Empfänger; **service ~** *(agency)* Dienstleistungs-, Bearbeitungsgebühr, *(unit trust, Br.)* Verwaltungskosten, -gebühr; **specific ~** konkretisierte dingliche Belastung; **subsequent ~** *(Br.)* Nachbelastung, nachrangige Grundstücksbelastung; **supplementary ~** Mehrbelastung, Zuschlag, Nachforderung; **taxation**

Steuerbelastung; **transfer ~** *(railroad)* Umladegebühr; **unit ~** Gebühr pro Einheit; **user ~** Benutzungsgebühr, -kosten; **usual ~** übliche Gebühr;

no ~ for admission Eintritt frei; **~ for admittance** Eintrittsgebühr; **normal ~ paid to agent for letting** übliche Wohnungsmaklergebühr; **~ on book debts** Verpfändung der Buchforderungen (Außenstände); **tariff ~ on calls** Fernsprechgebühr; **~ on calls made but not paid** Verpfändung noch nicht geleisteter Nachzahlungsforderungen; **~ of corruption** Korruptionsanklage; **~ for delivery** Zustellgebühr; **no ~ for delivery** frei ins Haus; **~ for depreciation** Abschreibungskosten; **~ for diverting mail to a new address** Nachsendegebühr; **~ to duty** Steuerbelastung, -schuld; **~ to enter heir** *(Scot.)* Aufforderung zum Erbschaftsantritt; **~ of espionage** Spionageanschuldigung; **~ to estate duty** Erbschaftssteuerveranlagung, -belastung, -schuld; **~ of extortion** Anklage wegen Bestechung; **~ for fixing** Anbringungskosten; **~ on goodwill** Verpfändung des Firmenwertes; **~ of an indictment** Anklagepunkt; **~s on income** Einkommensbelastungen; **~ of invasion** Invasionsbeschuldigung; **~ on land** Grundstückslast; **~ on a life policy** Verpfändung einer Lebensversicherungspolice; **~ for overdraft** Überziehungsprovision; **~ on a patent** Patentverpfändung; **~ on property** Eigentumsbelastung; **~ not proven** *(Scot.)* Freispruch mangels Beweises; **~ for rent** Verpfändung von Mieteinkünften; **~ on uncalled share capital** Verpfändung von Ansprüchen auf Kapitaleinzahlung, Verpfändung restlicher Kapitaleinzahlungsansprüche; **~ on a ship** Schiffsbelastung, -pfandrecht; **~ for transmitting money** Überweisungsgebühr; **~ by way of legal mortgage** *(Br.)* Grundpfandrecht, Hypothekisierung, Hypothekenbelastung;

~ *(v.) (accuse)* beschuldigen, anklagen, *(costs)* erheben, *(debit)* anlasten, belasten, in Rechnung setzen, debitieren, abrechnen, ansetzen, anschreiben, *(entrust with)* beauftragen, *(fix price)* berechnen, ansetzen, fordern, *(subject to financial burden)* belasten mit, Zahlungsverpflichtungen auferlegen;

~ an account Konto belasten; **~ [against] s. one's account** debitieren, jem. in Rechnung stellen, j. belasten; **~ [an account] with all the expenses** [Konto] mit sämtlichen Unkosten belasten; **~ s. o. with an amount** j. mit einer Summe belasten; **~ an amount to s. one's account** jds. Konto mit einem Betrag belasten; **~ back** zurückbelasten; **~ s. th. on the bill** etw. auf die Rechnung setzen; **~ the carriage of the parcel in advance** Paketnachnahme vornehmen; **~ commission** Provision berechnen; **~ s. o. with a commission** jem. einen Auftrag erteilen; **~ corporation tax** Körperschaftssteuer erheben; **~ cost directly to the department** Kosten unmittelbar auf die Abteilung verrechnen; **~ customers for holding cash in their tills** Kreditkunden mit einer Gebühr belasten; **~ a day** pro Tag berechnen; **~ for delcredere** Delkredere berechnen; **~ duty** Steuer verlangen, besteuern; **~ s. o. with neglecting his duty** j. einer Pflichtverletzung bezichtigen; **~ no entrance fee** keine Eintrittsgebühr erheben; **~ the expense to s. o.** jem. die Spesen anlasten; **~ an expense on (to) an account** Unkosten über ein Konto buchen; **~ an expense to the public debt** Kosten der Staatskasse übernehmen; **~ a fee** Honorar liquidieren, Gebühr erheben; **~ forward** nachnehmen; **~ freight** Frachtkosten berechnen; **~ by the hour** stundenweise berechnen; **~ interest** Zinsen berechnen (belasten); **~ the jury** *(judge)* Geschworene belehren, den Geschworenen Richtlinien geben; **~ one's land** seinen Grundbesitz belasten; **~ one's memory** sein Gedächtnis mit belasten; **~ s. o. with murder** j. unter die Anklage des Mordes stellen; **~ s. o. with negligence** j. der Nachlässigkeit bezichtigen; **~ off** [uneinbringliche Forderung] abschreiben, abbuchen, absetzen; **~ the postage to the customer** dem Kunden Porto belasten; **~ s. o. a price for s. th.** jem. einen Preis für etw. in Rechnung setzen; **~ the old price** früheren Preis berechnen; **~ property to estate duty** Nachlaß zu Erbschaftssteuerzwecken veranlagen; **~ property as security** Grundstück zu Sicherheitszwecken belasten; **~ purchases to an account** Besorgungen anschreiben lassen; **~ s. o. a sum** jem. einen Betrag berechnen; **~ a sum to the debit** Betrag zu Lasten eines Kontos vortragen; **~ s. o. with a task** j. mit einer Aufgabe betrauen; **~ s. o. with theft** j. des Diebstahls beschuldigen;

to acquit s. o. of a ~ j. von einer Anklage freisprechen; **to answer a ~** sich wegen einer Anklage verantworten; **to answer a ~** sich gegen eine Anklage verteidigen; **to be free from any ~** lastenfrei sein; **to be in s. one's ~** in jds. Obhut sein; **to be in ~ of a business** mit der Leitung eines Geschäfts betraut sein; **to be in ~ of the cash** Kassenführung haben; **to be in ~ of a class** Klassenaufsicht führen; **to be in complete ~ of doing** absolute Handlungsfreiheit haben; **to be in ~ of an office** einem Amt

vorstehen; **to be on ~ of ...** wegen ... angeklagt sein; **to be booked on ~ of ...** *(fam.)* wegen ... angezeigt werden; **to be delivered on board free of ~** frei an Bord zu liefern; **to be in ~** amtieren; **to be within the ~ of corporation tax** der Körperschaftssteuer unterliegen; **to become a ~ upon the parish** der Gemeinde zur Last fallen; **to become a ~ on the public** der Öffentlichkeit zur Last fallen; **to be under a ~** unter Anklage stehen; **to be under ~ of s. o.** jds. Aufsicht unterstehen; **to bring a ~ against s. o.** Beschuldigung gegen j. vorbringen, Strafanzeige gegen j. erstatten; **to commit to the ~ of s. o.** jem. anvertrauen, in jds. Obhut übergeben; **to create a ~** *(Br.)* Hypothek (Grundschuld) bestellen; **to defray the ~[s]** Kosten tragen; **to dismiss a ~** Anzeige zurückziehen; **to dismiss a ~ of indictment** Eröffnung des Hauptverfahrens ablehnen; **to drop a ~** Anklage fallenlassen; **to face a ~ of resisting arrest** Klage wegen Widerstands gegen die Staatsgewalt zu erwarten haben; **to face a ~ of corruption** einer Korruptionsanklage entgegensehen; **to file a criminal ~ against s. o.** Anzeige gegen j. erstatten; **to give in ~ of s. o.** jem. anvertrauen (übergeben), jem. in Verwahrung geben; **to give s. o. in ~** j.in polizeilichen Gewahrsam geben, j. der Polizei übergeben; **to give s. o. the ~ of s. th.** jem. mit der Aufsicht über etw. betrauen; **to give s. o. strict ~** jem. ausdrückliche Weisungen erteilen; **to go free of ~** kostenlos sein; **to have the ~ of s. th.** für etw. zuständig sein, Aufsicht über etw. haben; **to have a ~ on** Pfandrecht haben; **to have in ~** in Verwahrung haben; **to have ~ of a child** Kind zu beaufsichtigen haben; **to have ~ or conduct of a ship** Kommandogewalt über ein Schiff ausüben; **to lay a ~ on s. th.** Gebühr für etw. erheben; **to lay s. th. to s. one's ~** Anklage gegen j. erheben; **to leave s. th. in s. one's ~** etw. jds. Obhut anvertrauen; **to look after the welfare of one's ~** für das Wohlergehen seiner Pflegebefohlenen sorgen; **to make a ~** Gebühr berechnen; **to make an additional ~** nachberechnen, -belasten; **to make a ~ stick** Beschuldigung beweisen; **to meet a ~** sich der Anklage stellen; **to meet a ~ with a stiff denial** Anklage glatt ablehnen; **to minimize the ~ of duty** Steuerbelastung so niedrig wie möglich halten; **to perform the duties of one's ~** Pflichten seines Amtes nachkommen; **to plead no contest to a single ~** gegen einen Einzelpunkt einer Anklage keinen Widerspruch einlegen; **to prefer a ~** Anklage erheben; **to put s. o. in ~ of s. th.** j. mit der Aufsicht betrauen; **to put s. o. in temporary ~** j. vorübergehend als Betriebsleiter einsetzen; **to purge o. s. against a ~** sich gegen eine Anklage behaupten; **to reduce a murder ~ to aggravated assault** anstatt auf Mord nur noch auf schwere Körperverletzung plädieren; **to reject a ~** Beschuldigung zurückweisen; **to retaliate ~ on the accuser** Beschuldigung auf den Kläger zurückfallen lassen; **to support a ~** Last auf sich nehmen; **to sustain a ~** einer Anklage stattgeben; **to take s. o. in ~** j. festnehmen; **to take ~ of a body** Leiche beschlagnahmen; **to take ~ of s. one's property** jds. Vermögen verwalten; **to take ~ of s. th.** Aufsicht über (Leitung von) etw. übernehmen; **to take ~ of valuable articles** Wertgegenstände verwahren; **to throw out a ~** Anklage fallenlassen.

charge account *(US)* Kunden-, Anschreibungskonto, laufendes Konto;

budget ~ mit bestimmtem Kreditlimit ausgestattetes Kundenkonto;

~ application form Antragsformular für Eröffnung eines Kundenkreditkontos; **~ payment** Regulierung eines Anschreibungskontos; **~ terms** Bedingungen für Kundenkonten.

charge|agreement Einverständniserklärung mit den Bedingungen des Kundenkreditkontos; **~ book** Gebührenverzeichnis; **advice duration and ~ call** *(tel.)* Gebührenansage; **~ card** Kundenkreditkarte; **~ carrier** Ladungsträger; **~ certificate** *(Br., land register)* Belastungsnachweis, Grundpfandrechtsbescheinigung; **~ customer** Teilzahlungs-, Kreditkunde, Kunde [der anschreiben läßt]; **~ form** Verpfändungsformular; **~ hand** Vorarbeiter; **~ indicator** *(tel.)* Gebührenmelder; **~-off** Abschreibung, Absetzung, Abbuchung; **~ purchase** Kreditkauf; **~s register** *(Br.)* Lasten-, Hypothekenregister, [etwa] Abteilung III des Grundbuchs; **~ sale** Kreditverkauf; **~ sheet** *(Br.)* Polizeiregister, Haftliste, -ersuchen; **~ ticket** *(US)* Belastungsformular.

charges *(accessory expenses)* Spesen, Gebühren, *(costs)* [Un]kosten, Kosten und Auslagen, *(customs)* Belastungen, *(solicitor, Br.)* Anwaltsgebühren;

all ~ paid gebühren-, kostenfrei; **adding ~** einschließlich der Spesen; **by adding your ~** zuzüglich ihrer Spesen; **after deduction of ~** nach Abrechnung der Spesen; **all ~ included** unter Inbegriff sämtlicher Spesen; **~ deducted** abzüglich der Kosten; **clear of ~** kostenfrei; **free of all ~** spesenfrei; **liable to ~** ge-

bührenpflichtig; **no** ~ **for delivery** frei Haus geliefert;
accrued ~ aufgelaufene (entstandene) Kosten; **accumulated** ~ aufgelaufene Kosten; **additional** ~ Neben-, Mehrkosten, *(postage)* Nachporto, Gebührenzuschlag; **advanced** ~ *(railway)* Kostenvorschuß; **advertising** ~ Anzeigen-, Insertionsgebühren, Anzeigen-, Annoncentarif; **airline** ~ Flugpreise; **arbitration** ~ Schiedsgebühren; **auction** ~ Versteigerungsgebühren; **average** ~ Havariegelder; **back** ~ Nachforderungen, Retour-, Rückspesen, *(banking)* Abschlußgebühr; **bank** ~ Bankspesen; **bill** ~ Wechselspesen; **board** ~ Verpflegungsgeld; **brokerage** ~ Maklergebühren, -kosten; **business** ~ Geschäftsspesen; **capital** ~ [aktivierungspflichtiger] Kapitalaufwand; **carrying** ~ *(US, for commodities)* Verwaltungsgebühren, *(maintenance)* Betriebskosten, *(stocks)* Makler[ausführungs]-spesen; **collect-on-delivery** ~ Nachnahmespesen; **collecting** ~ Einzugsgebühren, Inkassospesen; **dead** ~ Gemeinkosten, Betriebsunkosten; ~ **deducted** abzüglich der Kosten; **deferred** ~ [to expense] *(balance sheet)* transitorische Posten, vorausbezahlte Aufwendungen; **demurrage** ~ Liegegebühren; **depreciation** ~ Abschreibungskosten; **per diem** ~ Tagesspesen; **discount** ~ Diskontspesen; **establishment** ~ Generalunkosten; **excessive interest** ~ wucherische Zinsforderungen; **extra** ~ [Sonder]zuschlag, Aufschlag, Sonderkosten, Nachforderung; **financing** ~ Finanzierungskosten; **fiscal** ~ Steuerlasten; **fixed** ~ feste Kosten, wiederkehrende Spesen, Fest-, Fixkosten; ~ **forward[ed]** *(Br.)* per Nachnahme, unter Nachnahme der Spesen, Spesennachnahme; **forwarding** ~ Versandspesen, Speditionsgebühren; **freight** ~ Frachtkosten; **hotel** ~ Zimmertarif; **insurance** ~ Versicherungskosten; **interest** ~ Zinsbelastung, -last; **labo(u)r** ~ Lohnkostenanteil; **landing** ~ Löschungsgebühren; **law** ~ Gerichtsgebühren, Prozeßkosten; **legal** ~ *(Br.)* Anwaltsgebühren; ~ **levied** erhobene Gebühren; **loading** ~ Verladegebühren, Verladungskosten; **maintenance** ~ Unterhaltungsaufwand, Instandhaltung-, Erhaltungs-, Wartungskosten; **management** ~ Verwaltungskosten, *(investment trust)* Verwaltungsgebühr; **moderate** ~ zivile Preise; **normal service** ~ *(banking)* übliche Bankspesen; **notarial** ~ Notariatsgebühren; **ocean** ~ Verschiffungskosten; **other** ~ *(balance sheet)* sonstige Verbindlichkeiten; **outward** ~ *(ship)* Ausreisekosten; **overabsorbed** ~ zu hoch angesetzte Gemeinkosten; **overhead** ~ Generalunkosten; **overriding** ~ nicht erstattungsfähige Anwaltskosten; **packing** ~ Verpackungskosten; **petty** ~ kleine Spesen; **port** ~ Hafengebühren; **postal** ~ Portokosten, Postgebühren; **protest** ~ *(bill of exchange)* Protestspesen, -kosten; **public utility** ~ Gebühren der öffentlichen Versorgungsbetriebe; **rail** ~ *(US)* Eisenbahnfrachtkosten; **revenue** ~ über Unkostenkonto abzubuchender Kapitalaufwand; **running (standing)** ~ laufende Unkosten; **salvage** ~ Bergungskosten; **service and activity** ~ Bankspesen; **shipping** ~ *(US)* Verladegebühren, Transport-, Versandkosten; **social** ~ Soziallasten; **special** ~ besondere Kosten; **storage (storing)** ~ Lagerungsgebühr, Lagerkosten; **subsequent** ~ Nachkosten; **switching** ~ *(railway)* Kosten für das Rangieren; **telephone** ~ Telefongebühren; **total** ~ Gesamtforderung; **transit** ~ Transit-, Durchgangsgebühren; **transport[action]** ~ Versendungs-, Beförderungs-, Transportkosten; **travelling** ~ Reisespesen, -kosten; **underabsorbed** ~ zu niedrig angesetzte Gemeinkosten; **unsupported** ~ unbegründete Beschuldigungen; **usual** ~ übliche Unkosten; **warehouse** ~ Lagerkosten, -geld; **working** ~ Betriebskosten;
~ **paid in advance** Kostenvorschuß; **normal** ~ **paid to agent for letting** übliche Wohnungsmaklergebühr; ~ **to be collected** Spesen-, Nachnahmegebühren; ~ **to be deducted** abzugsfähige Unkosten (Spesen); ~ **on capital** Kapitalbelastungen, -verpfändung; ~ **to capital** aktivierungspflichtiger Kapitalaufwand; ~ **of carriage** Fracht-, Fuhrlohn, Beförderungs-, Transportkosten; ~ **of debenture** Rückzollschuldgebühren; ~ **for delivery** Zustellgebühr, -kosten; ~ **on an estate** Nachlaßkosten; ~ **for freight** Frachtkosten; ~ **falling on a legatee** mit einem Legat verbundene Belastungen; ~ **of merchandise** Handlungsunkosten; ~ **and mortgages** Grundpfandrechte und sonstige Grundstückslasten; ~ **for postal service** Postgebühren; ~ **for recovering** Erhebungskosten; ~ **for reloading (transshipment)** Umladegebühren; ~ **for storage** Lagerkosten; ~ **for taxation** steuerliche Belastungen; ~ **for unloading** Ab-, Auslade-kosten, Kosten des Löschens;
to be burdened with ~ **for depreciation** mit Abschreibungskosten belastet sein; **to be exempt from** ~ gebührenfrei sein, Gebührenfreiheit genießen; **to involve additional** ~ mit zusätzlichen Kosten verbunden sein; **to levy** ~ Gebühren erheben; **to put o. s. to** ~ sich in Unkosten stürzen;
on ~ **collect basis** *(IATA)* gegen Nachnahme des Flugpreises.

chargé d'affaires *(dipl.)* Geschäftsträger.
chargeability Zurechen-, Anrechenbarkeit.
chargeable belast-, anrechenbar, zu belasten mit, *(taxable)* der Besteuerung unterliegend, besteuerbar;
~ **to** zu Lasten von; ~ **to the parish** zu Lasten der Gemeinde; ~ **with** verantwortlich für;
to be ~ **against income** mit dem Einkommen verrechnet werden; **to be** ~ **with negligence** fahrlässig gehandelt haben; **to be** ~ **with theft** wegen Diebstahls angeklagt werden; **to be** ~ **to tax** steuerpflichtig sein; **to become** ~ **to the parish** der Gemeinde zur Last fallen;
~ **accounting period** *(Br.)* Veranlagungszeitraum; ~ **amount** anrechnungspflichtiger Betrag; ~ **income** steuerpflichtiges Einkommen; ~ **offence** gerichtlich zu belangendes Vergehen; ~ **profit** steuerbarer Gewinn; ~ **time** *(tel.)* Gebührenminuten; ~ **weight** frachtpflichtiges Gewicht.
chargee *(Land Registration Act, Br.)* Hypothekengläubiger.
charging Auf-, Anrechnung, Belastung, *(taxation)* Besteuerung; ~ **of estate duty** *(Br.)* Erbschaftssteuerfestsetzung; ~ **what the traffic will bear** differenziertes Frachtberechnungssystem;
~ **clause** *(trustee)* Honorar-, Vergütungsklausel; ~ **lien** Zurückbehaltungsrecht, Sicherungspfandrecht; ~ **order** *(Br.)* dinglicher Arrest, Beschlagnahmeverfügung, [gerichtliches] Veräußerungsverbot, *(company)* Pfändungsbeschluß über Gesellschaftsanteile; ~ **period** *(bank)* Abrechnungszeitraum.
charitable wohltätig, mildtätig, karitativ, gemeinnützig;
~ **or benevolent** karitativ oder wohltätig; ~ **or deserving** karitativ oder förderungswürdig; ~ **and philanthropic** karitativ und menschenfreundlich;
to hold to be ~ Gemeinnützigkeit zuerkennen;
~ **bequest** wohltätiges Vermächtnis; **for** ~ **causes** für wohltätige Zwecke; ~ **construction** freundliche Auslegung; ~ **contract** Schenkungsvertrag; ~ **contribution** *(income tax return)* Beiträge für wohltätige Zwecke (zu wohltätigen Stiftungen), wohltätige Spende; ~ **corporation** gemeinnützige Vereinigung; ~ **disposition** Schenkung, Spende; ~ **educational institution** Stiftsschule, schulgeldfreie Anstalt; ~ **endowment** Wohltätigkeitseinrichtung; ~ **enterprise** wohltätiges Unternehmen; ~ **establishment** Wohltätigkeitsanstalt, -einrichtung; ~ **foundation** milde (wohltätige) Stiftung; ~ **gift** karitative Schenkung; ~ **hospital** Samariterkrankenhaus; ~ **institution** Wohltätigkeitsanstalt, -einrichtung, gemeinnützige Einrichtung, Versorgungsanstalt, karitative Einrichtung, wohltätige Stiftung; ~ **nature of a gift** Gemeinnützigkeit einer Zuwendung; **for a** ~ **object** für wohltätige Zwecke; ~ **organization** karitativer Verband, Hilfswerk, Wohltätigkeitsverein, Wohlfahrtsorganisation; ~ **purposes** karitative (mild-, wohltätige) Zwecke; ~ **relief** Fürsorgeunterstützung; ~ **school** Stiftsschule, schulgeldfreie Anstalt; ~ **society** Wohltätigkeitsverein; ~ **subscription** Spende für wohltätige Zwecke; ~ **trust** wohltätige Stiftung; ~ **undertaking** Fürsorgeunternehmen; ~ **use** wohltätiger Zweck, Wohltätigkeitszweck; ~ **view** nachsichtige Beurteilung.
charities gemeinnützige Körperschaften;
to leave all one's money to ~ sein ganzes Vermögen für wohltätige Zwecke bestimmen;
~ᵍ **Act** *(Br.)* Gesetz über die Errichtung gemeinnütziger Stiftungen.
charity Mild-, Wohltätigkeit, Gemeinnützigkeit, *(alms)* milde Gabe, Almosen, *(charitable trust)* wohltätige Stiftung, *(institution)* Pflegeheim, *(public provision for care)* Wohlfahrtspflege;
for ~ zu wohltätigen (mildtätigen) Zwecken;
foreign ~ Stiftungsvermögen im Ausland; **large** ~ hochherzige Mildtätigkeit; **misdirected** ~ falsch angewandte Wohltätigkeit; **private** ~ private Mildtätigkeit; **public** ~ öffentliche Wohlfahrt, Fürsorge; **pure** ~ gebührenfreie gemeinnützige Einrichtung;
to be reduced to ~ auf Almosen angewiesen sein, der Fürsorge anheimfallen; **to contribute to a work of** ~ Wohltätigkeitsbeitrag leisten; **to dispense** ~ milde Gaben (Almosen) verteilen; **to do works of** ~ sich karitativ betätigen; **to judge other people with** ~ seine Mitmenschen nachsichtig beurteilen; **to leave one's money to** ~ sein Vermögen für wohltätige Zwecke bestimmen; **to live on** ~ von Almosen leben, Wohlfahrtsempfänger sein; **to practise** ~ **towards s. o.** Nachsicht jem. gegenüber üben; **to subscribe to** ~ für wohltätige Zwecke spenden; **to subscribe liberally to** ~ auf dem Wohltätigkeitsgebiet beispielhaft sein;
~ **ball** Wohltätigkeitsball; ~ **bazaar** Wohltätigkeitsbasar; ~ **bill** Gesetz für Wohlfahrtszwecke; ~ **child** von der Fürsorge betreutes Kind, Waisenkind; ~ **collection** Sammlung zu wohltätigen Zwecken; ~ **commission** Wohltätigkeitsausschuß; ~ᵍ **Commissioner** Stiftungsaufsichtsamt; ~ **estate** Stiftungsver-

mögen; ~ **fund** Wohltätigkeitsfonds, Unterstützungskasse; ~ **house** Pflegeheim; ~ **market** Wohltätigkeitstransfer einer Volkswirtschaft; ~ **organization** Wohltätigkeitsorganisation; ~⁹ **Organization Society** Wohltätigkeitsverein; ~ **performance** Wohltätigkeitsveranstaltung; ~ **school** Waisenschule; ~ **stamp** Wohltätigkeitsmarke; ~ **trustee** Stiftungstreuhänder; ~ **work** Sozialarbeit, Wohlfahrtspflege; ~ **worker** Wohlfahrtspfleger, Sozialfürsorger.

charleton Kurpfuscher, Quacksalber, Scharlatan; ~ *(a.)* marktschreierisch.

charlatanry Kurpfuscherei, Quacksalbertum.

charm price optischer Preis, Blickfangpreis.

charnel house Leichenhaus.

chart Karte, *(US)* graphische Darstellung, *(marine map)* Seekarte, *(in tabular form)* Tabelle, Berechnungstafel, Schaubild, Diagramm;
  admiralty ~ Admiralitätskarte; **calculation** ~ Berechnungstafel; **equal-area** ~ flächengetreue Karte; **genealogical** ~ genealogische Tabelle; **ocean** ~ Seekarte; **organizational** ~ Organisationsplan; **weather** ~ Wetterkarte;
  ~ **of accounts** Kontenplan; ~ **of the organization** Organisationsschema;
  ~ *(v.)* auf einer Karte einzeichnen;
  ~ **a course** Kurs abstecken, einem Kurs folgen; ~ **a course of action** Aktionsplan entwerfen.

charter *(chartering)* Chartern, Mieten, Befrachten, Befrachtung, *(US, of corporation)* Satzung [einer Aktiengesellschaft], *(pol.)* Verfassung[surkunde], Charter, *(privilege)* [Bank]konzession, Privileg, *(instrument in writing)* Gründungs-, Konzessions-, Stiftungsurkunde;
  advance booking ~ Vorausbuchungscharter; **bank** ~ Bankenprivileg; **blank** ~ Freibrief; **Constitutional** ~⁹ Verfassungsurkunde; **corporation** ~ Gründungsurkunde; **dead-weight** ~ Faulfracht; **federal** ~ *(US)* Bankkonzession; **head** ~ Hauptfrachtvertrag; **inclusive tour** ~ Chartergenehmigung für Touristenpauschalreisen; **round-trip** ~ Charter für Hin- und Rückreise; **Royal** ~⁹ königliche Verleihungsurkunde; **state** ~ *(US)* Bankkonzession; **time** ~ Zeitcharter, Charter auf Zeit;
  ~ **of a borough** Gemeindesatzung; ~ **for a general cargo** Verfrachtung auf Stückgüter; ~ **of incorporation** Gründungs-, Gesellschafts-, Körperschaftsurkunde, Innungsbrief, Stiftungsurkunde; ~ **by the lump** Verfrachtung eines Schiffes im ganzen; ~ **by progress** *(Scot., law)* Verlängerungsurkunde für eine Konzession; ~⁹ **of the United Nations** Statut der Vereinten Nationen;
  ~ *(v.)* chartern, mieten, verfrachten, heuern, *(let)* befrachten, vermieten, verchartern;
  ~ **a bank** Bankkonzession erteilen; ~ **a car** Auto mieten; ~ **a ship by the bulk** Schiff für Massenbefrachtung chartern; ~ **by the lump** im ganzen verfrachten; ~ **a route** Fluglinie abstecken; **to go on** ~s Charterflugzeug benutzen; **to grant a** ~ Privilegien (Konzession) gewähren, konzessionieren; **to operate** ~s Charterflüge durchführen; **to take on** ~ chartern, mieten;
  aircraft ~ **agreement** Luftchartervertrag; ~ **airline** Chartergesellschaft; ~ **amendment** Satzungsänderung; ~ **booking** *(airplane)* Buchung auf einer Chartermaschine; ~ **capacity** Charterkapazität; ~ **carrier** Charter[flug]gesellschaft; ~ **fare** Charterflugschein; ~ **fee** *(bank)* Konzessionsgebühr; ~ **flight** Charterflug; ~ **hire** Chartermietgebühr; ~ **land** freie Liegenschaften; ~ **load** Freigut; ~ **master** *(Br.)* Grubenpächter; ~ **member** Gründungsmitglied; ~ **money** Stamm-, Schiffs-, Flugzeugmiete; ~ **operation** Chartergeschäft; ~ **operator** Chartergesellschaft, -unternehmen; ~ **passenger** Fluggast einer Chartergesellschaft; ~ **plane** Charterflugzeug; ~ **powers** Konzessionsumfang; ~ **price** Charterpreis; ~ **provisions** Satzungsbestimmungen; ~ **rates** Befrachtungstarif, Chartersatz; ~ **requirement** Satzungserfordernis; ~ **traffic** Verkehr von Chartermaschinen.

charterable befrachtbar.

charterage *(mar.)* Befrachtung, Charter.

chartered befrachtet, gechartert, *(licensed)* verbrieft, konzessioniert, zugelassen, *(granted)* berechtigt, privilegiert, diplomiert;
  ~ **accountant** *(Br.)* beeidigter (geprüfter) Bücherrevisor, Wirtschaftsprüfer; ~ **aircraft** Chartermaschine, -flugzeug; **to travel in a** ~ **aircraft** Charterflugzeug benutzen; ~ **bank** *(Br.)* privilegierte (konzessionierte) Bank; ~ **company** *(Br.)* **(corporation)** privilegierte Gesellschaft; ~ **exemption** *(Br.)* zugestandene Steuerfreiheit; ~ **freight** Fracht laut Charter; ~⁹ **Institute of Patent Agents** *(Br.)* Patentanwaltskammer; ~ **patent agent** *(Br.)* zugelassener Patentanwalt; ~ **rights** verbriefte Rechte; ~ **ship** gechartertes Schiff; ~ **time** Konzessionszeit.

charterer Befrachter;
  owner and ~ Ver- und Befrachter.

chartering Befrachtung, Charterung, Chartern, Mieten;
  ~ **of ships** Charterschiffahrt;
  ~ **broker** Befrachtungs-, Schiffsmakler; ~ **business** Charter-, Frachtgeschäft.

charterparty Chartervertrag, -partie, Befrachtungs-, Frachtvertrag.

charterhouse *(ship)* Kartenhaus.

chartroom Navigationsraum, Kartenzimmer.

charwoman Aufwarte-, Putzfrau, Raumpflegerin.

chase Jagd, Verfolgung, *(Br.)* Jagdrevier, -gelände, *(law)* Jagdrecht, *(print.)* Formrahmen;
  wild-goose ~ fruchtloses Unterfangen;
  ~ **for money** Jagd nach dem Geld;
  ~ *(v.)* jagen, verfolgen;
  to have ~d **s. o. for weeks** *(letter)* immer wieder nachgesandt worden sein.

chaser *(plane)* Jagdflugzeug, *(submarine)* U-Bootjäger.

chassis *(motor)* Fahrgestell, Chassis.

chasten *(v.)* züchtigen, strafen.

chattel | s Hab und Gut, bewegliches Vermögen (Eigentum), Fahrnis, Mobilien;
  personal ~s zum persönlichen Gebrauch bestimmtes Vermögen, zum persönlichen Gebrauch bestimmte Gegenstände; **real** unbewegliche Habe, Rechte an einem Grundstück; **[goods and]** ~ bewegliches Eigentum, Mobiliar; **land and** ~s *(balance sheet)* Grundvermögen und bewegliche Sachen, Liegenschaften, Mobiliar;
  ~ **interest** Rechte aus beweglichen Sachen; ~ **mortgage** Fahrnishypothek, [etwa] Sicherungsübereignung; ~ **mortgage note** Pfandschein; ~ **mortgagee** *(US)* Pfandgläubiger, Sicherungsnehmer; ~ **mortgagor** Sicherungs-, Pfandgeber; ~ **paper** *(US)* Verkehrspapier; **to invest 5% of their assets in** ~ **paper** 5% des Anlagevermögens in Beleihungen beweglichen Vermögens investieren.

chatterbox Plappermaul, Plauderer, *(sl.)* Sprechanlage.

chaud-medley Tötung im Affekt.

chauffeur Chauffeur, Fahrer;
  to act as ~ chauffieren.

chauvinism übertriebener Patriotismus, Chauvinismus.

chauvinist Chauvinist.

cheap *(price)* billig, verbilligt, niedrig, preiswert, günstig, wohlfeil, *(of inferior value)* von geringerem Wert, gering;
  dirt ~ *(sl.)* außerordentlich billig;
  to buy s. th. ~ etw. billig erwerben; **to buy s. th. on the** ~ etw. zu herabgesetzten Preisen erwerben; **to feel** ~ **about** ganz verdattert sein; **to get** ~ billig erstehen; **to get off** ~ *(sl.)* mit einem blauen Augen davonkommen; **to hold s. th.** ~ etw. geringschätzen; **to make o. s.** ~ sich schäbig aufführen; **to sell dirt-**~ verschleudern, zu Schleuderpreisen verkaufen;
  exceptionally ~ **article** spottbilliger Gegenstand; ~ **conduct** schäbiges Benehmen; ~ **fare** ermäßigter Fahrpreis; ~ **fares market** *(airlines)* Markt für verbilligte Flüge; ~-**fare passenger** Benutzer verbilligter Flugscheine; ~ **finery** kitschiger Schmuck; ~ **flattery** unaufrichtige Schmeicheleien; ~ **Jack** billiger Jakob; ~ **money** billiges Geld, billige Geldsätze; ~ **money policy** Politik des billigen Geldes, Niedrigzinspolitik; ~ **pennyworth** *(Br.)* billiger Einkauf; ~ **quality** minderwertige Qualität; **to travel by the** ~est **route** billigste Fahrstrecke benutzen; ~ **seats** Plätze zu volkstümlichen Preisen; ~ **skate** *(US sl.)* Knicker, Geizkragen; ~ **ticket** Fahrkarte zu zurückgesetzten Preisen; ~ **trip** Ausflug zu verbilligten Preisen.

cheapen *(v.)* *(become cheaper)* billiger werden, im Preis sinken, *(lower the price)* verbilligen, Preis herabsetzen, *(make low)* geringschätzig machen;
  ~ **o. s.** sich kümmerlich aufführen.

cheapening Verbilligung;
  ~ **of interest rates** Zinsverbilligung; ~ **of money** Geldverbilligung, Verbilligung der Geldsätze.

cheapie *(US)* billiger Laden.

cheapness Billigkeit, niedriger Preis, *(small value)* Geringwertigkeit.

cheat Betrug, Betrügerei, Mogelei, Täuschung, Vorspiegelung falscher Tatsachen;
  ~ *(v.)* betrügen, übervorteilen;
  ~ **at cards** falsch spielen; ~ **the customs** Zoll beschummeln; ~ **in an examination** ein Examen pfuschen; ~ **justice** sich der gerechten Strafe entziehen; ~ **s. o. out of his money** j. um sein Geld bemogeln.

cheater Betrüger, Schwindler.

check Hemmnis, Hindernis, *(baggage, US)* [Gepäck]aufbewahrungsschein, *(cheque, US)* Scheck, *(chip)* Präsenzmarke, *(cloakroom, US)* Garderobenmarke, *(control)* Aufsicht, Kontrolle, Nach-, Überprüfung, *(curbing)* Dämpfung, *(slip, US)* Kassenzettel, -schein, Rechnungszettel, *(ticket)* Schein, *(token of identification, US)* Kontrollmarke, -schein, *(voucher)* Bon, Gutschein, Koupon;
ante-dated ~ *(US)* vordatierter Scheck; **bad ~** ungedeckter Scheck; **baggage** *(US)* **(cloakroom,** *Br.)* **~** Gepäckaufbewahrungsschein; **cashier's ~** *(US)* Bank-, Kassenscheck, Scheck auf sich selbst; **certified ~** *(US)* von einer Bank bestätigter Scheck; **clearing-house check** *(US)* Verrechnungsscheck; **cold ~** *(US)* gefälschter Scheck; **counter ~** *(US)* Kassenscheck, Quittungsformular für Barabhebungen; **customer's ~** *(US)* Kundenscheck; **delivery ~** *(railroad, US)* Gepäckempfangsschein; **dividend ~** Dividendenschein, -scheck; **dollar ~** auf Dollar lautender Scheck; **luggage ~** *(Br.)* Gepäckschein; **marked ~** *(US)* gekennzeichneter Scheck; **nonnegotiable ~** *(US)* auf den Namen lautender Scheck; **on-the-spot ~** erste Augenscheinnahme; **overdue ~** *(US)* verspätet vorgelegter Scheck; **own ~** *(US)* eigener Scheck; **pass-out ~** *(Br.)* Kontermarke, Kontrollschein [im Theater]; **post ~** Kontrolle nach Erscheinen; **postal ~** Postscheck; **raised ~** *(US)* durch Erhöhung des Betrages gefälschter Scheck; **rate ~** Überprüfung von Frachtrechnungen; **redemption ~** *(US)* Verrechnungsscheck für Ausgleichsbeträge; **rubber ~** *(US)* ungedeckter Scheck; **sales ~** *(US)* Kassenzettel; **snap ~** Stichprobe, stichprobenartige Überprüfung; **spot ~** Stichprobe, Prüfung an Ort und Stelle; **storage ~** *(railroad)* Lagerschein; **third-party ~** *(US)* Fremdscheck; **time [-keeping] ~** Kontrollmarke; **travel(l)er's ~** Reisescheck; **undated ~** *(US)* undatierter Scheck; **voucher ~** *(US)* Verrechnungsscheck;
~ cashed over the counter *(US)* am Schalter eingelöster Scheck; **~s paid in for collection** *(US)* zum Einzug hereingegebene Schecks; **~ on delivery** Abnahmekontrolle; **~ for deposit only** *(US)* Verrechnungsscheck; **~ on the operation** *(US)* Arbeitskontrolle;
~ *(v.) (accounts)* justizieren, *(collate)* kollationieren, Abschriften vergleichen, *(examine)* überprüfen, nachprüfen, revidieren, kontrollieren, *(US, railroad)* zur Beförderung als Reisegepäck übernehmen, *(stop)* lahmlegen, aufhalten, bremsen, hemmen, hindern, *(tick off)* abhaken;
~ against vergleichend nachprüfen; **~ in** sich anmelden (registrieren), *(airport)* sich bei der Flugabfertigung melden, *(employee)* Kontrolluhr stechen, Karte stempeln; **~ in with a hotel** *(US)* sich [bei einem Hotel] anmelden; **~ off** nachprüfen, kontrollieren, [nach Durchsicht] abzeichnen, an-, abstreichen; **~ off goods** Bestandsaufnahme machen; **~ [off] names on a list** Namen auf einer Liste abhaken; **~ out** *(Br.)* Karte [nach Arbeitsbeendigung abstempeln, *(US)* aus einem Hotel ausziehen, Hotel nach Rechnungsbegleichung verlassen, *(US, cash)* Geld mittels Scheck abheben; **~ out luggage** *(Br.)* Gepäck abholen; **~ up** nachprüfen, kontrollieren; **~ up [on] information** Auskunft nachprüfen; **~ up on a matter** Angelegenheit überprüfen;
~ one's baggage *(US)* sein Gepäck aufgeben; **~ a bill** Rechnung prüfen; **~ the books** Bestandsaufnahme machen, *(auditing)* Bücher revidieren; **~ a copy with the original** Abschrift mit dem Original vergleichen; **~ the enemy's advance** feindlichen Vormarsch stoppen; **~ an entry** Posten abhaken; **~ s. one's extravagant spending** jds. hemmungsloser Ausgabenwirtschaft ein Ende bereiten; **~ figures** Zahlen vergleichen (nachrechnen); **~ investments** Subventionen bremsen; **~ production** Produktion drosseln; **~ quality** Qualität prüfen; **~ s. one's statements** jds. Behauptungen nachprüfen; **~ a trunk** *(US)* Koffer aufgeben; **to cash (hand, pass) in one's ~s** seine Spielmarken beim Kassierer einreichen; **to certify a ~** *(US)* Scheck bestätigen; **to clear a ~** *(US)* Scheck verrechnen; **to give s. o. a blank ~** *(fig.)* jem. freie Hand lassen; **to keep in ~** in Schach (an der Kandare) halten, etw. unter Kontrolle haben; **to keep a ~ on one's temper** sein Temperament zügeln; **to mark a ~** *(US)* Scheck bestätigen; **to pay in a ~ for collection** Scheck zum Einzug einreichen; **to put a ~ on production** Produktion drosseln (abbremsen);
~ account *(US)* Kontrollkonto, Gegenrechnung; **~ alteration and forgery insurance** *(US)* Scheckversicherung; **~ card** *(US)* Scheckkarte; **~ clerk** *(US)* Arbeitszeitkontrolleur; **fake ~ customer** *(US)* Scheckfälscher; **~ exchange** *(coll.)* Sichtwechsel; **~ figure** Kontrollziffer; **~ guarantee card** *(US)* Euroscheckkarte; **~-in** *(airport)* Abfertigung; **~-in counter** *(airpost)* Abfertigungsschalter; **~-in desk** [Flug]abfertigungsschalter; **~-in time** *(airport)* rechtzeitige Meldung am Abfertigungsschalter;

Vergleichs-, Abfertigungszeit; **no ~-in time** *(airport)* kein Meldeschluß; **~ interview** Kontrollinterview; **~ key** *(Br.)* Hausschlüssel; **~ list** alphabetische Liste, Prüf-, Vergleichsliste, Kontrolliste, *(list of voters, US)* Wählerliste; **~ lock** Sicherheitsschloß; **~ mark** Kontrollzeichen, -vermerk; **~ money** *(US)* Giral-, Buchgeld; **~ number** Kontrollnummer; **~ register** Ausgabenkontrollbogen; **~ sample** Probemuster; **~ slip** Kassenzettel; **~ stamp** Wechselstempel; **~ system** *(US)* Girowesen, -system; **~ taker** Kontrolleur, *(theater)* Kontrollmarkenabnehmer; **~ test** Gegenversuch; **~ valve** Drosselklappe, Absperrventil; **~ weighter** Gewichtskontrolleur; **~ weighing** Nachwiegen.
checkable kontrollierbar, nachprüfbar.
checkbook *(US)* Scheckbuch, -heft, *(Br.)* Kontrollbuch;
~ money *(US)* Giralgeld.
checked by geprüft von.
checker Aufsichtsbeamter, Überprüfer, *(account)* [Rechnungs]-kontrolleur, *(pattern)* Karomuster;
cargo ~ Ladungsprüfer.
checking Kontrolle, [Nach]prüfung, Nachrechnung, *(advertising)* Streuprüfung, *(curbing)* Dämpfung, Drosselung, *(inventory)* Inventurkontrolle;
spot ~ stichprobenartige Überprüfung;
~ of accounts Bücherrevision, Rechnungsprüfung; **~ of baggage** *(US)* Gepäckaufgabe; **~ of books** Abstimmung der Bücher; **~ of coverage** *(insurance)* Überprüfung der Gültigkeit einer Police; **~ of credits** Kreditkontrolle; **~ of investment activities** Investitionsdrosselung; **~ of quality** Qualitätsprüfung; **~ of the weight** Gewichtskontrolle;
~ account *(US)* Scheckkonto, Girokonto, Gegen-, Kontrollrechnung; **~ clerk** Gegenbuchhalter; **~ copy** Belegexemplar; **~ credit** Prüfung der Kreditunterlagen; **~ deposits** *(US)* Sichteinlagen; **~ device** Prüfvorrichtung, Kontrollvorrichtung; **~ form** Kontrollzettel, -abschnitt; **~ operation** Prüfung.
checkman *(Br.)* Fahrkartenkontrolleur.
checkmate Schachmatt;
~ *(v.)* schachmatt setzen.
checkoff *(US)* Lohnabzug von Gewerkschaftsbeiträgen durch den Betrieb, *(company store)* Abzüge für Kantinenverbrauch;
~ agreement Tarifvereinbarung über Lohnabzüge durch den Betrieb; **~ sheet** Überprüfungsbogen; **~ system** *(US)* Lohnabzugsverfahren.
checkout | clerk Kontrollangestellter; **~ counter** Abfertigungsschalter.
checkover Nachprüfung, *(medicine)* Generaluntersuchung.
checkpoint Grenzkontroll-, Übergangsstelle, Orientierungs-, Kontrollpunkt, -station, Durchlaßposten.
checkroll Liste der Bediensteten.
checkroom *(US)* Gepäckaufbewahrung, -raum, Aufbewahrungsraum, *(wardrobe)* Kleiderablage, Garderobe;
~ fee Aufbewahrungsgebühr; **~ woman** Garderobenfrau, Garderobiere.
checkup Kontrolle, Überprüfung;
general ~ *(US)* gründliche (eingehende) ärztliche Untersuchung;
~ of the cash Kassenrevision.
checkweigher *(Br.)* Gewichtskontrolleur.
cheer Hochruf, Aufheiterung, Ermunterung;
~ *(v.)* mit Hoch-, Bravo-, oder Hurrarufen begrüßen.
cheerful *(market)* freundlich, lebhaft, etw. fester.
cheese Käse;
big ~ *(sl.)* hohes Tier;
~ cutter *(film)* Klangreflektor, Neger; **~ paring** Knauserei, Knickerei; **~-paring economies** übertriebene Sparsamkeit.
cheesed off, to be es satt haben, restlos bedient sein.
chemical | agent *(mil.)* Kampfstoff; **~ engineering** Industriechemie; **~ industry** chemische Industrie; **~ issues** *(stock exchange)* chemische Werte, Chemiewerte; **~ warfare** chemischer Krieg; **~ warfare officer** ABC-Abwehroffizier; **~ works** chemische Fabrik.
chemicals *(stock exchange)* Chemiewerte.
chemist *(Br.)* Apotheker, Drogist;
dispensing ~ geprüfter Apotheker;
~'s shop *(Br.)* Apotheke, Drogerie.
cheque *(Br.)* **(check,** *US)* Scheck;
paid by ~ durch Bankanweisung bezahlt;
advised ~ avisierter Scheck; **bad ~** ungedeckter Scheck; **bank ~** Kassenscheck; **banker's ~** Bankscheck; **bearer ~** Inhaberscheck; **blank ~** Scheckformular, Blankoscheck; **blocked ~** gesperrter Scheck; **bogus ~** gefälschter Scheck; **cancelled ~** entwerteter (annullierter) Scheck; **cash ~** Barscheck; **cleared ~**

abgerechneter Scheck; **crossed ~** *(Br.)* gekreuzter Scheck, Verrechnungsscheck; **~ dated ahead** vordatierter Scheck; **defective ~** fehlerhafter Scheck; **dishono(u)red ~** nicht eingelöster Scheck; **dud ~** ungedeckter Scheck; **endorsed ~** girierter Scheck; **flash ~** ungedeckter Scheck; **foreign ~** Auslandsscheck; **forged ~** gefälschter Scheck; **guaranteed ~** beglaubigter Scheck; **inchoate ~** *(Br.)* nicht fertig ausgefüllter Scheck; **initialled ~** *(banking)* auf Echtheit der Unterschrift geprüfter Scheck; **invalid ~** unvollständiger Scheck; **kite ~** ungedeckter Scheck, Scheck ohne Deckung; **limited ~** *(Br.)* limitierter Scheck; **lost ~** abhandengekommener Scheck; **marked ~** *(Br.)* bestätigter (gekennzeichneter) Scheck; **memorandum ~** als Sicherheit ausgestellter Scheck; **metropolitan ~** *(Br.)* Scheck auf Großlondon; **mutilated ~** beschädigter Scheck; **negotiable ~** girierfähiger Scheck; **nonnegotiable ~** Rekta-, Verrechnungsscheck; **open ~** Inhaber-, Barscheck; **order ~** Orderscheck; **out-of-town ~** *(Br.)* auswärtiger Scheck; **outstanding ~** noch nicht eingelöster Scheck; **overdue ~** verfallener Scheck; **paid ~** eingelöster Scheck; **pay ~** Gehaltsscheck; **personal ~** von einem Nichtkaufmann ausgestellter Scheck; **post-dated ~** nachdatierter Scheck; **postal ~** Postscheck; **protested ~** protestierter Scheck; **returned ~** retournierter (unbezahlter) Scheck, Rückscheck; **stale ~** verjährter Scheck; **stopped ~** gesperrter Scheck; **town ~** *(Br.)* Platzscheck, Scheck auf die Londoner City; **travel(l)er's ~** Reisescheck; **treasurer's ~** Bankscheck; **unbacked ~** nicht indossierter Scheck; **unclaimed ~** nicht in Anspruch genommener Scheck; **uncleared ~** uneingelöster Scheck, noch nicht abgerechneter Scheck; **uncovered ~** ungedeckter Scheck; **uncrossed ~** nicht firmierter Scheck, Kassen-, Barscheck; **unendorsed ~** nicht girierter Scheck; **unlimited ~** *(Br.)* der Höhe nach unbegrenzter Scheck; **unpaid ~** nicht eingelöster Scheck; **worthless ~** ungedeckter Scheck;
~ only for account *(Br.)* Verrechnungsscheck; **~ to bearer** Inhaberscheck, auf den Überbringer lautender Scheck; **~s in process of collection** zum Einzug gesandte Schecks; **~ without cover** ungedeckter Scheck; **~ irregularly endorsed** nicht ordnungsgemäß girierter Scheck; **~s in hand** Scheckbestand; **~ without sufficient funds** ungedeckter Scheck; **~ to order** Orderscheck; **~ not to order** Rektascheck; **~ lost in the post** auf dem Postwege abhandengekommener Scheck; **~ without provision** ungedeckter Scheck; **~ with receipt form attached** *(Br.)* Scheck mit angehefteter Quittung; **~ in full settlement of a claim** zum Ausgleich eines Anspruchs begebener Scheck;
to accept a ~ Scheck annehmen; **to alter a ~** Scheck fälschen; **to bounce a ~** Scheck platzen lassen; **to cash (collect) a ~** Scheck einlösen, zur Einlösung vorlegen; **to credit a ~ as cash before clearance** Scheck vor Einreichung gutschreiben; **to cross a ~** *(Br.)* Verrechnungsscheck ausstellen; **to date a ~ ahead** Scheck vorausdatieren; **to deposit a ~** Scheck zur Gutschrift einreichen; **to dishono(u)r a ~** Scheck nicht einlösen (zurückweisen); **to draw a ~** Scheck ausstellen; **to enclose a ~ in settlement** zum Rechnungsausgleich einen Scheck beifügen; **to endorse a ~** Scheck girieren; **to forge a ~** Scheck fälschen; **to get the ~ cashed at the bank** Scheck bei der Bank einlösen; **to issue bad ~s** ungedeckte Schecks ausgeben, Scheckbetrug begehen; **to issue a ~ against an account** Scheck auf ein Guthaben ziehen; **to kite a ~** *(US)* Scheckbetrag fälschen; **to lodge a ~ with a bank for collection** Scheck einer Bank zum Einzug übergeben; **to make out a ~** Scheck ausstellen (ausschreiben); **to mark a ~** *(Br.)* Scheck bestätigen; **to obliterate the writing of a ~** Scheck durch Streichungen ungültig machen; **to offer a ~ in payment** Scheckzahlung anbieten; **to pass a ~ through the clearinghouse** Scheck im Clearing verrechnen; **to pay a ~** Scheck honorieren; **to pay by ~** mit Scheck bezahlen; **to present a ~ for certification** Scheck zur Bestätigung vorlegen; **to present a ~ through the clearing** Verrechnungsscheck einreichen; **to present a ~ for payment** Scheck zur Zahlung vorlegen; **to raise a ~** Scheck höher beziffern, Scheckziffern in betrügerischer Absicht erhöhen; **to refer a ~ to the drawer** Scheck an den Aussteller zurückgeben; **to reject a ~** Scheck zurückweisen; **to remit by ~** mit einem Scheck bezahlen; **to send a ~ in settlement** Scheck zum Ausgleich übersenden; **to stop a ~** Scheck sperren; **to tear a ~ out of the book** Scheck vom Scheckheft abtrennen; **to trace a ~** Scheck verfolgen; **to value ~s on London** Schecks auf London ausstellen; **to write out a ~** Scheck ausschreiben;
~ account Giro-, Scheckkonto, Scheckrechnung; **~ account depositor** Giro-, Scheckkontoinhaber; **~ Act** *(Br.)* Scheckgesetz; **~ alteration** Scheckfälschung; **~ alteration and forgery insurance** Scheckversicherung; **~ bank** *(Br.)* Girobank; **~ book** Scheckbuch, -heft; **to make an application for a ~ book** Scheckbuch anfordern; **~ and bill transactions** Scheck- und Wechsel-

verkehr; **~ card** Scheckkarte; **~ card holder** Scheckkarteninhaber; **~ cashing** Einlösung eines Schecks, Scheckinkasso; **~ cheats** Scheckbetrügereien; **~ clearance** Scheckabrechnung; **~ clearing-system** Scheckverrechnungssystem; **~ collection** *(Br.)* Inkasso von Schecks, Scheckinkasso, -einzug; **~ collection charges** *(Br.)* Scheckinkassospesen; **~ currency** Giralgeld; **~ department** Giroabteilung; **~ forger** Scheckfälscher; **~ forgery** Scheckfälschung; **~ form** *(Br.)* Scheckformular; **~ combined and receipt form** kombiniertes Scheck- und Quittungsformular; **~ fraud** Scheckbetrug; **~ protection device** Scheckschutzvorrichtung; **~ rate** Scheckkurs; **~ rate with insurance** Scheckversicherungssatz; **~ register** Scheckliste; **~ stamp** Scheckstempel; **~ stub** Scheckleiste; **~ transactions** Scheckverkehr; **~ trickster** Scheckbetrüger; **~ writing** Scheckausstellung.
chequelet *(Br.)* Quittungsheft [einer Bank].
chequered carrer wechselvolle Laufbahn.
cherish *(v.)* **an idea** an einer Idee festhalten.
cherry on the cake das Pünktchen auf dem I.
cherrystone *(fig.)* wertlose Sache.
chest Geldkasse, *(jewelry)* Kassette;
 university ~ Universitätskasse;
 ~ of drawers Kommode;
 to get s. th. off one's ~ sich etw. von der Seele reden.
chestnut *(coll.)* abgestandener Witz, olle Kamelle;
 to pull the ~s out of the fire die Kastanien aus dem Feuer holen.
chic *(coll.)* Eleganz, Schick;
 ~ (a.) schick, elegant, geschmackvoll;
 to become ~ für schick gehalten werden.
chicane Schikane, *(subterfuge)* Rechtskniff, -verdrehung;
 ~ (v.) schikanieren, *(litigation)* verdrehen, Rechtskniffe anwenden.
chicanery Schikane, Rechtsverdrehungen.
chicken Hühnchen;
 to count one's ~s before they are hatched das Fell des Bären verkaufen, bevor er erlegt ist;
 ~ stake *(Br.)* kleiner Einsatz.
chickenfeed Hühnerfutter, *(sl.)* geringer Lohn, Pfennigbeträge, *(intelligence service)* Lockmittelinformation;
 ~ campaign mit kleinen Beträgen finanzierter Wahlfeldzug.
chief *(head)* Leiter, Vorsteher, *(US mil.)* Inspizient, *(principal)* Vorsteher, Besitzer, Hauptinhaber, *(superior)* Vorgesetzter, Chef;
 copy ~ Cheftexter; **department ~** Abteilungschef; **senior ~** Seniorchef;
 ~ of a branch Dezernent; **~ of a department** Abteilungschef, -leiter; **~ of police** *(US)* Polizeipräsident; **~ of Protocol** Protokollchef; **~ of staff** Generalstabschef; **~ of state** Staatschef, -oberhaupt;
 to report daily to one's ~ seinem Vorgesetzten täglich Bericht erstatten;
 ~ (a.) oberster, erster, höchster, hauptsächlich;
 ~ accountant Ober-, Hauptbuchhalter; **~ agency** Generalvertretung; **~ agent** Generalvertreter; **~ assistant** Hauptmitarbeiter; **~ attraction** Hauptanziehungspunkt, -attraktion; **~ cashier** Hauptkassierer; **~ challenge** Hauptanliegen; **~ clerk** Bürovorsteher, -chef, Kanzleivorsteher, *(bookkeeping)* erster Buchhalter, Disponent, *(official)* Amtmann; **~ commissioner** Polizeidirektor; **~ constable** *(Br.)* Polizeipräsident, -chef; **~ creditor** Hauptgläubiger; **~ culprit** Hauptschuldiger; **~ designer** Chefkonstrukteur; **~ editor** Hauptschriftleiter; **~ engineer** Chefingenieur, technischer Betriebsleiter, *(ship)* erster Maschinist; **~ Examiner** Examens-, Prüfungsleiter; **~ executive [officer]** Vorstandsmitglied, *(local government)* [etwa] Hauptverwaltungsbeamter; **~ financial officer** *(Br.)* Kämmerer; **~ group** Hauptgruppe; **~ ingredient** Hauptbestandteil; **~ inspector** Oberaufseher; **~ Inspector of Taxes** *(Br.)* [etwa] Oberfinanzpräsident; **~ judge** *(US)* Gerichtspräsident; **~ justice** Gerichtspräsident; **~ labo(u)r** Hauptarbeit; **~ land registrar** *(Br.)* Leiter des Grundbuchamtes; **~ magistrate** Ortsvorsteher, Chef der Verwaltung, Verwaltungschef; **~ management** Oberleitung; **~ manager** Hauptgeschäftsführer; **~ general manager** Generaldirektor; **~ market** Hauptabsatzmarkt; **~ meal** Hauptmahlzeit; **~ negotiator** Hauptunterhändler; **~ news** wichtigste Nachrichten; **~ occupation** Hauptbeschäftigung, -beruf; **~ office** Hauptbüro; **~ officer** leitender Beamter, Amtsleiter; **~ operator** [Telefon]zentrale; **~ partner** Seniorchef; **~ point** Hauptpunkt; **~ problem** Hauptproblem; **~ product** Hauptprodukt; **~ purpose in life** Hauptlebenszweck; **~ purser** Oberzahlmeister; **~ rent** *(Br.)* Miet-, Pachtzins; **~ rival** Hauptkonkurrent; **~ town [of a country]** Landeshauptstadt; **~ value** *(customs)* Höchstwert; **~ witness** Kronzeuge.

child Kind, Nachkomme, Abkömmling, *(infant)* Säugling;
from a ~ von Kindheit an;
adopted ~ angenommenes Kind, Adoptivkind; **bastard (illegit-**
imate) ~ uneheliches Kind; **charity ~** Waisenkind; **college-age**
~ Kind auf der Universität; **evacuee ~** evakuiertes Kind; **foster**
~ Pflegekind; **handicapped ~** behindertes Kind; **illegitimate ~**
uneheliches Kind; **incapable ~** unmündiges Kind; **legitimate ~**
eheliches Kind; **maladjusted ~** schwer erziehbares Kind;
natural ~ uneheliches Kind; **neglected ~** verwahrlostes Kind;
new-born ~ neugeborenes Kind; **nurse ~** Pflegekind; **only ~**
Einzelkind; **orphan ~** Waisenkind; **posthumo(u)s ~** nachgebo-
renes Kind; **precocious ~** frühreifes Kind; **preschool ~** noch
nicht schulpflichtiges Kind; **qualifying ~** *(child benefit)* kinder-
geldberechtigtes Kind; **spoilt ~** verzogenes Kind; **educationally**
subnormal ~ unterdurchschnittlich ausgebildetes Kind; **un-**
adopted ~ elternloses Kind; **unmanageable ~** schwieriges Kind;
wayward ~ moralisch gefährdetes Kind;
~ receiving full-time education at a university Kind in der
Universitätsausbildung; **~ under guardianship (in tutelage)**
unter Vormundschaft stehendes Kind, Mündel; **~ born in wed-**
lock eheliches Kind; **~ born out of wedlock** uneheliches Kind;
to abandon a new-born ~ Kind aussetzen; **to abdicate a ~** Kind
enterben; **to adopt a ~** Kind annehmen (adoptieren); **to affili-**
ate a ~ upon a putative father jem. die Vaterschaft eines unehelichen Kindes zuschieben; **to kidnap a ~** Kind entführen; **to put**
a ~ out to nurse Kind in Pflege geben; **to substitute a ~** Kindesunterschiebung begehen; **to withdraw a ~ from school** Kind von
der Schule nehmen;
~ allowance *(Br.)* Steuerfreibetrag für Kinder, *(US)* Kindergeld; **cash ~ benefit** *(Br.)* bar ausgezahltes Kindergeld; **tax-free**
~ benefit *(Br.)* steuerfreies Kindergeld; **~ benefit system** *(Br.)*
Kindergeldsystem; **~ bounty** *(US)* Kinderzulage, -schlag; **~**
care Jugendpflege; **~ dependency allowance** *(Br.)* Freibetrag
für unterstützte Familienangehörige; **~ destruction** Kindestö-
tung; **~ development** Kindeserziehung; **~ evacuation scheme**
Kinderlandverschickung; **~ exemption** *(US)* Kinderfreibetrag,
Steuerfreibetrag für Kinder; **~ genius** Wunderkind; **~ guidance**
Kinderfürsorge; **~ guidance center** Jugendgesundheitsdienst;
~ guidance clinic Kinderberatungsstelle; **~ health visitor**
Gesundheitspfleger; **~'s insurance benefit** *(social insurance,*
US) Waisenzusatzrente; **~ labo(u)r** Kinderarbeit; **~ labor laws**
(US) Kinderschutzgesetzgebung; **~ neglect** Kindervernachläs-
sigung; **~ placing** Verbringung eines Kindes zu Pflegeeltern;
~'s play *(fig.)* kinderleichte Sache, Kinderspiel; **~ prodigy**
Wunderkind; **~ rearing** Kinderaufzucht; **~ relief** *(Br.)* Kinderermäßigung, Steuerfreibetrag für Kinder; **~ stealing** Kindes-
raub; **~ tax allowance** *(Br.)* Steuerfreibetrag für Kinder,
Kinderfreibetrag; **~ tax allowance income limit** *(Br.)* Kinder-
freibeträge ausschließende Privateinkünfte des Kindes; **~ wel-**
fare Jugendfürsorge, -schutz; **~ welfare legislation** Jugend-
fürsorgegesetzgebung; **~ welfare worker** Jugendpfleger.
childbirth Niederkunft, Entbindung, Geburt;
~ allowance Wochenhilfe; **~ care** Säuglingspflege.
childhood Kindesalter, Kindheit;
to emerge from ~ Kinderschuhe ablegen;
early ~ education Kindesfrüherziehung; **~ memories** Kindheitserinnerungen.
childminding Kinderbeaufsichtigung.
children, autistic verhaltensgestörte Kinder; **preschool-age ~**
noch nicht schulpflichtige Kinder;
~ and young persons Kinder und Jugendliche;
to give the ~ a treat Kinderfest veranstalten; **to have no ~**
kinderlos sein; **to have ~ underfoot** Kinder am Rockzipfel
hängen haben; **to leave one's ~ in utter neglect** seine Kinder
völlig unversorgt zurücklassen; **to settle one's ~** seine Kinder
sicherstellen (versorgen);
~ and Young Persons Act *(Br.)* Jugendschutzgesetz.
children's allowance *(Br.)* Kinderzuschläge, *(US)* Kindergeld,
(US) Steuerfreibetrag für Kinder; **~ book** Kinderbuch; **~ court**
Jugendgericht; **~ department** *(stores)* Kinderabteilung; **~**
endowment insurance Aussteuerversicherung; **~'s home** Kin-
derheim; **~ hour** *(radio)* Kinderstunde; **~ labo(u)r** Kinderarbeit; **~ magazine** Kinderzeitschrift; **~ officer** *(Br.)* Jugend-
amtsleiter; **~'s party** Kinderfest; **~'s storybook** Kinderbuch;
~'s ward *(hospital)* Kinderstation.
chill Schauer, Kältegefühl, Frösteln;
~s and fevers Schüttelfrost;
to catch a ~ sich erkälten (eine Erkältung zuziehen);
~ reception kühler (frostiger) Empfang.
chilled cargo Kühlgut.
chilling a sale verabredetes niedriges Bieten.

chime *(v.)* **in** sich ins Gespräch mischen;
~ with s. o. jem. nach dem Munde reden.
chimney stack Fabrikschornstein.
chin, to keep one's ~ up Ohren steif halten.
Chinatown Chinesenviertel.
chink *(sl.)* Pinkepinke;
~ *(v.)* mit Geld klimpern.
chip Splitter, Span, *(game)* Spielmarke;
as dry as a ~ abgestanden, uninteressant;
~ *(v.)* s. o. *(coll.)* j. piesacken (hänseln);
~ in *(US)* mit Geld einspringen;
to be a ~ of the same old block aus dem gleichen Holz geschnitzt
sein; **to have plenty of ~** *(US sl.)* Zaster haben; **to have a ~ on**
one's shoulder streitbar wie ein Zinshahn (sehr aggressiv) sein;
when the ~s are down wenn die Würfel gefallen sind.
chirograph Urkundenschluß.
chit Bon, Gutschein, *(memo, Br.)* kurze Notiz.
chit-chat Bürotratsch.
choice Wahl, Belieben, *(assortment)* [Aus]wahl, Sortiment, *(the*
pick) Auslese, Elite;
free ~ freie Wahl; **wide ~** große Auswahl;
wide ~ of candidates viele Bewerber; **~ of career (life)** Berufswahl; **~ of employment (job)** Berufsentscheidung, -wahl; **~ of**
language gewählte Sprache; **free ~ of physician** freie Arztwahl;
free ~ of profession freie Berufswahl; **~ of program(me)** Pro-
grammwahl; **~ of our troops** unsere Kerntruppe; **~ of type**
Schriftwahl;
to guarantee the poor a free ~ among all the medical services
available den Armen freie Wahl ärztlicher Leistungen garantieren; **to have no ~** keine Wahl haben; **to have the best ~**
vollkommene Auswahl haben; **to leave to s. one's ~** es jem.
freistellen; **to make one's ~** seine Wahl treffen; **to make a**
careful ~ sorgfältig auswählen; **to make a good ~** gut wählen; **to**
make a wrong ~ Fehlgriff tun; **to take pretty much one's ~** sich
ganz in Ruhe aussuchen;
~ *(a.)* vorzüglich, [aus]erlesen, *(of picked quality)* von ausgesuchter Qualität;
~ article[s] (goods) ausgesuchte Ware, Qualitätsware; **~ bind-**
ing Prachteinband; **~ brand** vorzügliche Sorte; **~ commodities**
vorzügliche Waren; **~ quality** ausgesuchte (erste) Qualität.
choicest quality erlesene Qualität; **~ selection** reichhaltigste
Auswahl.
choke Starterklappe;
~ *(v.)* **off access** Zugang drosseln; **~ off a discussion** Diskussion
nicht aufkommen lassen;
~ throttle Starterklappe.
choose *(v.)* aussuchen, Auswahl treffen, optieren;
~ s. o. for their leader j. zum Anführer wählen.
choosy, to be wählerisch sein.
chop *(brand)* Marke, Sorte, *(China trade)* amtlich gestempeltes
Dokument, *(of meat)* Schnitzel;
first ~ erster Güte; **grand ~** *(China trade)* Zollschein,
Einfuhrbewilligung;
~s and changes Wechselfälle;
~ *(v.)* **and change** unentschlossen sein; **~ into a conversation**
sich in ein Gespräch einmischen; **~ prices** Preise stark
herabsetzen;
to be due for the ~ *(coll.)* auf der Entlassungsliste stehen; **to get**
the ~ *(fam.)* fristlos entlassen werden.
chophouse billiges Restaurant.
chopping and changing ewiges Hin und Her.
chord Saite, *(fig.)* Ton, Gemütsbewegung;
to seem to strike a ~ einem irgendwie bekannt vorkommen; **to**
strike a responsive ~ among the audience Ton treffen, der beim
Publikum ankommt; **to touch the right ~** richtige Saite
anschlagen.
chore *(uneasy job)* unangenehme Aufgabe, *(US)* Gelegenheits-
Hausarbeit;
~ *(v.)* *(US)* Hausarbeit erledigen.
chose Gegenstand, Sache, Objekt, Fahrnis, *(law)* Rechtsobjekt;
local ~ ortsfeste Sache; **~ transportable (transitory)** bewegliche
Sache;
~ in action Forderungs-, Immaterialgüterrecht, unkörperli-
cher Rechtsgegenstand, obligatorisches Forderungsrecht.
Christian burial kirchliche Beerdigung; **~ name** Ruf-, Vorname.
Christmas Weihnachten;
Father ~ *(Br.)* Weihnachtsmann;
~ bells Weihnachtsglocken; **~ bonus (gratuity)** Weihnachts-
geld, -gratifikation; **~ box** *(Br.)* Weihnachtsgeschenk; **~ card**
Weihnachtskarte; **~ carol** Weihnachtslied; **~ day** Weihnachts-
tag; **~ draw** Weihnachtslotterie; **~ expenses** Weihnachtsaus-

gaben; ~ **gift** Weihnachtsgeschenk; ~ **gift list** Weihnachtsgeschenkliste; ~ **package** Weihnachtspaket; ~ **party** Weihnachtsfeier; ~ **present** Weihnachtsgeschenk; ~ **shopping** Weihnachtseinkäufe, -markt; ~ **time** Weihnachtszeit; ~ **tree** Weihnachtsbaum.

chronic illness chronische Krankheit.

chronicle Chronik, Bericht;
~ (v.) auf-, verzeichnen.

chronicler Chronist.

chronological zeitlich geordnet, chronologisch;
~ **table** Zeittafel.

chronology chronologische Anordnung.

chronometer Zeitmesser.

chuck (Br., sl.) Entlassung, Hinauswurf, Feuern, (meal, US sl.) Mahlzeit;
~ (v.) **away** verplempern; ~ **a drunken man out of a pub** Betrunkenen aus dem Lokal herausschmeißen; ~ **one's money around** mit seinem Geld herumschmeißen; ~ **out** auf die Straße setzen, herausschmeißen; ~ **up** (sl.) seine Stellung an den Nagel hängen; ~ **up the sponge** Flinte ins Korn werfen;
to give s. o. the ~ (Br.) j. feuern (entlassen);
~ **wagon** (US sl.) Proviant-, Picknickwagen.

chucker-out (sl.) Rausschmeißer.

chum enger Freund, (US, room-mate) Zimmergenosse;
new ~ (Australia) Neueinwanderer.

chunk Batzen, große Portion, (market research) nicht repräsentativer Personenkreis;
large ~ erhebliche Summe;
large ~ **of money** großer Geldbrocken; ~ **of votes** hoher Stimmenanteil;
~ **sampling** planlose Stichprobenauswahl, (statistics) Raffprobe.

church, within the pale of the im Schoße der Kirche;
national ~ Staatskirche;
to sever from the ~ aus der Kirche austreten;
~ **assembly** (Br.) Kirchenversammlung; ~ **attendance** Kirchenbesuch; ~ **authorities** Kirchenbehörde; ~ **ceremony** kirchliche Feier; ~ **committee** Kirchenausschuß; ~ **council** Kirchenvorstand; ~ **fair** Kirmes; ~ **festival** kirchlicher Feiertag; ~ **lands** geistliche Besitztümer, Kirchenländereien; ~ **membership** Kirchenzugehörigkeit, Gemeindezugehörigkeit; ~ **property** Kirchenvermögen; ~ **rates** (Br.) Kirchensteuern; ~ **register** Kirchenregister, Kirchenbuch; ~ **ring** Trauring; **to be** ~-**run** von der Kirche betrieben werden; ~ **tax** (US) Kirchensteuer; ~ **warden** (Br.) Kirchenvorstand -steher.

churchmen Geistlichkeit.

churchyard Totenacker, Friedhof.

chute Müllschlucker.

cif Kosten, Versicherung, Fracht;
~ **agent** Exportvertreter mit Sitz im Käuferland; ~ **landed** cif-Klausel incl. Abladekosten; ~ **price** cif-Preis.

cigar lighter Zigarettenanzünder.

cine-|camera Filmkamera; ~ **film** Kamerafilm; ~ **matinee** Filmmatinee; ~ **projector** Filmprojektor.

cinema (Br.) Kino, Lichtspieltheater;
to go to the ~ ins Kino gehen; **to own a** ~ Kinobesitzer sein;
~ **addict** Filmfanatiker; ~ **advertising** (Br.) Kino-, Diapositivwerbung; ~ **attendance** Kinobesuch; ~ **audience** Kinopublikum; ~ **business** Filmgeschäft; ~ **goer** Kinobesucher; ~ **goers** Filmpublikum; ~ **industry** Filmindustrie, -wesen; ~ **operator** Filmvorführer; ~ **organ** Kinoorgel; ~ **palace** Filmtheater, Kinopalast; ~ **performance** Film-, Kinovorstellung; ~ **program(me)** Film-, Kinovorstellung; ~ **proprietor** Kinobesitzer; ~ **rights** Filmrechte; ~ **screen** Filmleinwand; ~ **show** Filmvorführung; ~ **slide** (Br.) Diapositiv; ~ **theater** (US) (theatre, Br.) Filmtheater.

cinemactor Filmstar.

cinematic filmisch;
~ **device** filmischer Kunstgriff.

cinematize (v.) verfilmen, Film drehen.

cinematograph (Br.) Filmvorführapparat.

cinematographer Kameramann.

cinerarium Urnenfriedhof.

cipher (code) Geheimschrift, Chiffre, (fig.) Null, unbedeutende Person, (figure) Ziffer, Zahl, (initials) Namenszeichen, (secret writing) Chiffre, Codewort, Geheimschrift, (zero) Null;
in ~ chiffriert, verschlüsselt;
~ (v.) (put into secret writing) chiffrieren, verschlüsseln;
~ **out a sum** Betrag kalkulieren; ~ **telegrams by hand** Telegramme ohne Schlüsselmaschine verschlüsseln;
to write a message in ~ Nachricht chiffrieren;

~ **breaking** Entschlüsselung; ~ **clerk** Ent-, Verschlüsseler; ~ **code** Chiffrier-, Codeschlüssel, Telegrammcode; ~ **dispatch** verschlüsseltes Telegramm; ~ **documents** Verschlüsselungsunterlagen; ~ **group** Schlüsselgruppe; ~ **key** Code-, Chiffreschlüssel; ~ **office** Chiffrierstelle; ~ **officer** Schlüsseloffizier; ~ **room** Code-, Verschlüsselungsraum; ~ **telegram** verschlüsseltes Telegramm, Chiffretelegramm; ~ **text** verschlüsselter Text, Schlüsseltext.

ciphered message chiffrierte (verschlüsselte) Meldung.

ciphering Chiffrierung, Verschlüsselung;
~ **service** Chiffrier-, Verschlüsselungsabteilung.

circle Kreis, (circus) Arena, Zirkusmanege, (society) Gesellschaftskreis, Zirkel, (sphere of influence) Wirkungsgebiet, -kreis, Einflußsphäre, (theater) Rang;
in a ~ ohne Unterbrechung; **in business** ~s in Geschäftskreisen; **in financial** ~s in der Finanzwelt; **in Foreign Office** ~s in Kreisen des Auswärtigen Amtes;
commercial ~s Kreise der Wirtschaft; **dress** ~ (theater) erster Rang, Balkon; **elite** ~ ausgewählter Kreis; **governmental** ~s Regierungskreise; **political** ~s politische Kreise; **specialist** ~s Fachwelt; **theatrical** ~ Theatergemeinde; **upper** ~ (theater) zweiter Rang, Galerie; **vicious** ~ Teufelskreis;
~ **of acquaintance** Bekanntenkreis; ~ **of customers** Kundenkreis; ~ **of friends** Freundeskreis; ~ **of latitude** Breitenkreis; ~ **of longitude** Längenkreis; ~ **of readers** Leserkreis;
~ (v.) (mil.) einschließen, umzingeln;
~ **s. th. cautiously** an etw. vorsichtig herangehen; ~ **over the landing field** über dem Flugplatz kreisen; ~ **round** zirkulieren; **to argue in a** ~ bei der Diskussion nicht weiterkommen; **to go on** ~ auf Rundreise gehen; **to move in the leading** ~s in den führenden Kreisen verkehren; **to square the** ~ unmögliches Wirklichkeit werden lassen;
~ **chart** Kreisschaubild; ~ **line** (underground, Br.) Ringlinie.

circled figure Klammerzahl.

circuit (airplane) Rundflug, (area) Gebiet, (assizes) Gerichtsbezirk, (circular tour) Rundreise, regelmäßiger Besuch, (county, Br.) Amtsbezirk, (el.) Leitung, Stromkreis, Schaltschema, (postman) Bestellgang, (theater) Theaterring;
in ~ (tel.) angeschlossen;
closed ~ Betriebsfernsehen; **integrated** ~ integrierter Schaltkreis; **make-and-break-**~ Unterbrecherstromkreis;
~ **of the city** Rundfahrt durch die Stadt, Stadtrundfahrt;
~ (v.) zirkulieren, kreisen;
to do a ~ (airplane) Platzrunde fliegen; **to go on** ~ (Br.) in verschiedenen Bezirken Gericht abhalten; **to make a** ~ Runde zahlen; **to put in** ~ (tel.) anschließen; **to travel over a regular** ~ (theatrical company) feste Gastspielvorführungen geben;
~ **breaker** (el.) Stromkreisunterbrecher; ~-**busy signal** Besetztzeichen; ~ **court** (US) ordentliches Gericht; ~ **court of appeal** (US) Berufungs-, Beschwerdegericht; ~ **diagram** (tel.) Schaltschema.

circuitous way weitschweifige Art.

circuitry Schaltkreis;
~ **drawings** Schaltschema.

circuity of action Umständlichkeit eines Verfahrens, Prozeßverzögerung.

circular Zirkular, Rundschreiben, Umlauf-, Laufzettel, (advertisement) Prospekt;
Court ~ (Br.) Hofnachrichten;
to issue a ~ Rundschreiben verschicken;
~ (a.) kreisförmig, (periodical) regelmäßig wiederkehrend;
~ **chart** Kreisdiagramm; ~ **cheque** (Br.) Reisescheck; ~ **flow of the economy** Wirtschaftskreislauf; ~ **flow of goods** Güterkreislauf; ~ **flow of money** Geldkreislauf; ~ **letter** Rundschreiben, Laufzettel, Umlaufschreiben, Briefdrucksache; ~ **letter of credit** Reisekreditbrief; ~ **note** Prospekt, Rund-, Umlaufschreiben, Zirkular, (banking) Reisekreditbrief, (dipl.) Zirkularnote; ~ **offer** Prospektangebot; ~ **order** Runderlaß, Umlauf; ~ **road** Umgehungs-, Ringstraße, -bahn; ~ **staircase** Wendeltreppe; ~ **ticket** Fahrscheinheft; ~ **tour (trip)** Rundreise, -fahrt; ~ **traffic** Kreisverkehr.

circularization Prospektversand.

circularize (v.) Rundschreiben versenden, (advertisement) Prospekte verschicken.

circulate (v.) in Umlauf sein, umlaufen, zirkulieren, (money) umlaufen, kursieren, (put in circulation) in Umlauf setzen, ausstreuen;
~ **bills** Wechsel girieren; ~ **a letter** Brief in Umlauf setzen; ~ **false news** falsche Nachrichten verbreiten; ~ **freely (slowly)** (money) hohe (niedrige) Umlaufgeschwindigkeit haben; ~ **reports** Meldungen verbreiten.

circulating umlaufend, im Umlauf [befindlich];
~ **assets** Umlaufvermögen; ~ **bank notes** [Bank]notenumlauf; ~ **capital** Betriebs-, Umlaufkapital; ~ **library** Wanderbücherei; ~ **magazine** Lesezirkel; ~ **medium** Tausch-, Zahlungsmittel; ~ **notes** Notenumlauf; ~ **value** *(bank notes)* Umlaufwert.

circulation Umlauf, Verkehr, *(distribution)* Verbreitung, Absatz, *(legal tender)* umlaufende Zahlungsmittel, *(newspaper)* Auflage, Auflagenhöhe;
in ~ in Umlauf, kursierend; **out of** ~ außer Kurs [gesetzt]; **active** ~ Notenumlauf; **average** ~ *(newspaper)* Durchschnittsauflage; **bond** ~ Pfandbriefumlauf; **city-zone** ~ Ortsverbreitung; **daily** ~ Tagesauflage; **delivered** ~ ausgelieferte Auflage; **forced** ~ Zwangskurs; **guaranteed minimum** ~ garantierte Mindestauflage; **monetary** ~ Geldumlauf; **net paid** ~ tatsächlich abgesetzte Auflage; **reader** ~ Gesamtleserzahl; **wide** ~ hohe Auflage;
~ **of the air** *(mining)* Bewetterung; ~ **of bank notes** [Bank]notenumlauf; ~ **of bills** Wechselumlauf; ~ **among businessmen** in der Geschäftswelt abgesetzte Auflage; ~ **of capital** Kapitalverkehr; ~ **of goods** Güterumlauf; ~ **of money** Geldumlauf; ~ **of news** Verbreitung von Nachrichten; ~ **of notes and coins** Bargeldumlauf; ~ **of securities** Wertpapierumlauf;
to be in ~ umlaufen, in Umlauf sein, kursieren; **to be out of** ~ nicht mehr im Umlauf sein; **to disappear from** ~ außer Umlauf kommen; **to put a coinage in** ~ Münzen in Verkehr bringen; **to put false money in** ~ Falschgeld in den Verkehr bringen; **to recall (withdraw) from** ~ außer Umlauf (Kurs) setzen, aus dem Verkehr ziehen, *(book)* einziehen, zurückziehen; **to set in** ~ in Umlauf setzen; **to withdraw a book from** ~ Buch aus dem Verkehr ziehen;
~ **analysis** Verbreitungs-, Leser-, Auflagenanalyse; ~ **area** Verbreitungsgebiet; ~ **base** Auflagenhöhe; **current** ~ **base** augenblickliche Grundauflage; ~ **bonus** Überschreitung einer garantierten Auflage, Auflagenbonus; ~ **breakdown** Auflagenverteilung; ~ **compromise** Auflagenangleichung; ~ **control** Auflagenkontrolle; ~ **density** Verbreitungsdichte; ~ **figure** Auflagenziffer; ~ **growth** Auflagenanstieg; ~ **manager** *(newspaper)* Vertriebsleiter; **mass** ~ **newspaper** Massenblatt; ~ **method** Auflagenmethode; ~ **privilege** Banknotenprivileg; ~ **pump** Umwälzpumpe; ~ **rates** Auflagenziffer; ~ **rate base** auflagenbedingte Anzeigenpreisliste; ~ **statement** *(US)* Schatzamtsbericht über den Notenumlauf; ~ **tax** *(US)* Geldverkehrssteuer.

circumduction *(Scot.)* Ausschlußfrist für schriftliches Klagevorbringen.

circumferential expressway Umgehungsstraße.

circumnavigate *(v.)* umschiffen.

circumscribe *(v.)* umschreiben, definieren;
~ **one's interests** seinen Interessenkreis begrenzen.

circumscription Begrenzung, Umschreibung, *(coin)* Umschrift, Beschriftung.

circumstance Umstand;
pomp and ~ zeremonielle Notwendigkeiten; **unfortunate** ~ unglücklicher Umstand.

circumstances *(formalities)* Zeremoniell, Formalitäten, Förmlichkeiten, *(financial condition)* finanzielle Verhältnisse, Vermögensverhältnisse, *(surrounding facts)* Umstände, Sachlage, -verhalt, Tatumstand;
in the ~ nach Lage der Dinge; **in the appropriate** ~ gegebenenfalls; **in easy** ~ gut situiert; **in flourishing** ~ in glänzenden Verhältnissen; **in no** ~ auf keinen Fall, keineswegs; ~ **permitting** unter Umständen; **under these** ~ unter diesen Verhältnissen; **without** ~ ohne Aufwand;
aggravating ~ erschwerende Umstände; **attendant** ~ Begleitumstände; **bad (reduced)** *(financial standing)* schlechte Vermögensverhältnisse; **decayed** ~ zerrüttete Verhältnisse; **easy (flourishing, good)** ~ günstige (gute) Vermögensverhältnisse; **exceptional** ~ außergewöhnliche Umstände; **extenuating** ~ mildernde Umstände; **favo(u)rable** ~ gute Verhältnisse; **indigent** ~ ärmliche Verhältnisse; **intervening** ~ eingetretene Hindernisse; **narrow** ~ beschränkte Verhältnisse; **pecuniary** ~ Vermögensverhältnisse; ~ **permitting** soweit es die Umstände zulassen; **pinched** ~ beschränkte Verhältnisse; **reduced** ~ schlechte Vermögensverhältnisse; **straightened** ~ beschränkte Vermögensverhältnisse; **surrounding** ~ Begleitumstände; **unforeseen** ~ unvorhergesehene Hindernisse; **my worldly** ~ meine finanziellen Verhältnisse; **wretched** ~ kümmerliche Verhältnisse;
~ **of the case** Umstände des Einzelfalles; ~ **of a family** Familienverhältnisse;
to accommodate o. s. to ~ den Umständen Rechnung tragen; **to adapt o. s. to** ~ sich den Verhältnissen anpassen; **to be in good** ~

in guten Verhältnissen leben; **to be no** ~ **to s. th.** *(US)* keinen Vergleich mit etw. aushalten; **to be ruled by** ~ sich von den Umständen leiten lassen; **to be in straitened** ~ in dürftigen Verhältnissen leben; **to live in narrow** ~ in ärmlichen Verhältnissen leben.

circumstanced, well in guten Verhältnissen.

circumstantial umständlich, eingehend, Nebenumstände;
~ **account** detaillierter Bericht; ~ **case** Indizienurteil; ~ **evidence** Indizienbeweis ~ **prosperity** wirtschaftlicher Wohlstand.

circumstantiate *(v.)* aufgrund von Begleitumständen (durch Indizien) beweisen.

circumstantiation Beweisführung aufgrund von Begleitumständen.

circumvent *(v.)* vereiteln, umgehen;
~ **a law** Gesetz umgehen; ~ **a patent** Patent umgehen; ~ **a town** Stadt umgehen.

circumvention Umgehung, Vereitelung, Hinterschiebung;
~ **of the law** Gesetzesumgehung, Rechtsbeugung; ~ **of a patent** Patentumgehung.

circus Zirkus[arena], Manege, *(Br.)* runder Platz;
~ **show** Zirkusvorstellung.

cistern [Wasser]tank.

citable zitierbar, anführbar.

citation Zitat, *(mil.)* ehrenvolle Erwähnung, *(summons)* Streitverkündigung, Vorladung;
~ **of authorities** Anführung höchstrichterlicher Entscheidungen; ~ **of a decision** Anführen (Zitierung) einer Gerichtsentscheidung;
to serve a ~ **upon s. o.** jem. eine Ladung zustellen.

citatory, letters schriftliche Vorladung.

cite *(v.)* *(quote)* anführen, zitieren, *(summons)* vorladen;
~ **s. th.** sich auf etw. berufen; ~ **an authority** sich auf eine Vorentscheidung berufen; ~ **s. o. before the court** j. vor Gericht laden.

citied stadtähnlich.

citizen Bürger, *(inhabitant)* Einwohner, *(subject)* Landesangehöriger, Staatsbürger, -angehöriger, *(US)* Zivilist;
average ~ Durchschnittbürger; **fellow** ~ Mitbürger; **free** ~ freier Bürger; **last-advantage** ~ am schlechtesten gestellter Bürger; **natural (native born,** *US***)** Staatsangehöriger durch Geburt; **naturalized** ~ *(US)* naturalisierter [eingebürgerter] Amerikaner; **nonresident** ~ *(US)* Staatsbürger mit Wohnsitz im Ausland; **orderly** ~ friedlicher Bürger; **resident** ~ *(US)* Staatsbürger mit Wohnsitz in den USA; **voting and tax-paying** ~ Vollbürger;
~ **of honor** *(US)* Ehrenbürger; ~ **of the United States** amerikanischer Staatsbürger; ~ **of the world** Weltbürger;
~**s' action group** Bürgerrechtsgemeinschaft, -initiative; ~**'s Advice Bureau** *(Br.)* Sozialhilfeberatungsstelle; ~**'s band** *(US)* Verkehrswelle; ~ **band radio communication** *(US)* Verbindung über die Verkehrswelle; ~ **group** Bürgergruppe; ~ **iniative** Bürgerrechtsinitiative; **environment-conscious** ~ **initiative group** umweltbewußte Bürgerrechtsgruppe (Bürgerrechtsgemeinschaft); ~ **rights** *(US)* Landes-, Bürgerrechte.

citizenry Bürgerschaft.

citizenship [Staats]bürgerrecht, *(nationality)* Staatsangehörigkeit, -bürgerschaft;
dual ~ doppelte Staatsbürgerschaft; **state** ~ *(US)* Staatsangehörigkeit eines Einzelstaates; **United States** ~ amerikanische Staatsangehörigkeit;
~ **by birth** Staatsangehörigkeit durch Geburt;
to acquire ~ Staatsangehörigkeit erwerben; **to be admitted to** ~ *(US)* eingebürgert werden; **to deprive of** ~ expatriieren, Staatsangehörigkeit aberkennen; **to renounce** ~ Staatsangehörigkeit aufgeben; **to retain one's** ~ seine Staatsangehörigkeit behalten.

citizenize, to einbürgern, Staatsangehörigkeit verleihen.

City, the *(Br.)* Innenstadt;
Federal ~ *(US)* Bundeshauptstadt.

city [Groß]stadt, *(center)* Stadtmitte, Innenstadt, Geschäftsgegend, *(London)* Altstadt, *(municipal corporation, US)* Stadtgemeinde;
blitzed ~ bombardierte Stadt; **boom** ~ aus dem Boden geschossene Stadt; **central** ~ Kleinstadt; **crowded** ~ dichtbevölkerte Stadt; **dead** ~ tote Innenstadt; **free** ~ freie Stadt; **ghost** ~ *(US)* verlassene Stadt; **medium-sized** ~ mittelgroße Stadt; **open** ~ *(mil.)* offene Stadt;
to be in the ~ Geschäftsmann sein; **to be free of a** ~ Bürgerrechte besitzen; **to found a new** ~ neue Stadt gründen;
~ **arms** Stadtwappen; ~ **article** *(Br.)* Börsenbericht; ~ **attorney** *(US)* Stadtsyndikus; ~ **authorities** Stadtverwaltung, -behörden; ~ **boardroom** Vorstandsetage; ~ **bonds** Stadtanleihe; ~

branch Stadtkasse, Stadtfiliale; **~-bred** in der Stadt aufgewachsen; ~ **budget** städtischer Haushaltsplan; ~ **by(e)-law** Ortsstatut; ~ **cabinet** Stadtverwaltung; ~ **center** Stadtzentrum, Innenstadt, Stadtmitte; ~ **capital market committee** zentraler Kapitalmarktausschuß; ~ **chamberlain** *(US)* Stadtkämmerer; ~ **clerk** *(US)* Stadtsyndikus; ~ **collections** Stadtinkassi; ~ **collection department** Abteilung für Stadtinkassi; ~ **commission** städtischer Ausschuß; ~ **commissioner** *(US)* Stadtratsmitglied, Abteilungsleiter in der Stadtverwaltung; ~ **companies** *(City of London)* Gilden und Zünfte; ~ **concessionaire** städtischer Konzessionär; ~ **core** Stadtkern; [30 member] ~ **council** *(US)* dreißigköpfiger Gemeinde-, Stadtrat; **to chair the ~ council** *(US)* im Stadtrat sitzen; ~ **councilman** *(US)* Stadtverordneter, Ratsherr; ~ **court** *(US)* Stadtgericht; ~ **crest** Stadtwappen; ~ **customer** Stadtkunde; ~ **desk** *(newspaper)* Lokalredaktion; ~ **dweller** Stadtbewohner; ~ **disobedience** Steuerstreik; ~ **edition** Stadtausgabe; ~ **editor** *(Br.)* Redakteur des Börsenteils, *(US)* Lokalredakteur; ~ **election** Gemeindewahlen; ~ **employee** *(US)* städtischer Angestellter; **at ~ expenses** auf Kosten der Stadt; ~ **fathers** Stadtrat, -väter; ~ **federation** *(US, trade union)* Ortskartell; ~ **freedom** Gerechtsame einer Stadt, Bürgerrecht; ~ **gas** Stadtgas; ~ **government** Stadtverwaltung; ~ **guide** Städteführer; ~ **hall** Magistratsgebäude, Stadthalle, Rathaus, Bürgermeisterei; ~ **hospital** städtisches Krankenhaus; ~ **institutions** städtische Einrichtungen; ~ **items** *(US)* Schecks (Wechsel) auf die Stadt, in der sie zum Inkasso eingereicht sind; ~ **levy** städtische Umlage; ~ **limits** Stadtgrenzen; ~ **look** großstädtisches Aussehen; ~ **man** *(Br.)* Finanz-, Geschäftsmann, *(bank)* Bankangestellter; ~ **manager** *(US)* Stadtdirektor, Amtsbürgermeister; ~ **manager plan** *(US)* Amtsbürgermeistersystem; **~'s managing director** *(US)* Stadtdirektor; ~ **news** *(Br.)* Börsennachrichten; ~ **office** Stadtbüro, *(newspaper)* Lokalredaktion; ~ **ordinance** *(US)* Gemeindesatzung; ~ **park** Stadtpark; ~ **plan** Stadtplan; ~ **planner** Stadtplaner; ~ **planning** Städtebau, -planung; ~ **police** Gemeindepolizei; **big ~ press** Großstadtpresse; ~ **price** Großhandelspreis, *(stock exchange)* Börsennotierung; ~ **property (real estate)** städtischer Grundbesitz, städtisches Eigentum; ~ **recorder** Magistratsdirektor; ~ **region** Startregion, -gebiet; ~ **regulation** städtische Verordnung; ~ **salesman** Stadtreisender; ~ **services** städtische Dienstleistungen; ~ **state** autonomer Stadtstaat; ~ **taxes** städtische Abgaben; ~ **tax collector** *(US)* Stadtkämmerei; ~ **traffic** großstädtischer Verkehr; ~ **traffic planner** Stadtverkehrsplaner; ~ **transport** *(Br.)* **(transportation,** *US)* städtische Verkehrsmittel; ~ **treasurer** Stadtkämmerer; ~ **ward** *(Br.)* städtischer Wahlbezirk; ~ **warrant** Zahlungsanweisung des Stadtkämmerers; ~ **zone** *(US)* Stadtgebiet.

cityfolk *(US)* Stadtbewohner, Städter.

cityscape Stadtform.

civic [staats]bürgerlich, *(pertaining to a city)* städtisch; ~ **authorities** Gemeinde, Stadtverwaltung, städtische Behörden; ~ **center** *(US)* **(centre,** *Br.***)** Behördenviertel; ~ **culture** Bürgerkultur; ~ **duties** Bürgerpflichten; ~ **enterprise** Kommunalbetrieb; ~ **government** Stadtverwaltung; ~ **headliners** prominente Bürger; ~ **life** Leben in der Stadt; ~ **obligations** staatsbürgerliche Pflichten; ~ **problems** städtische Probleme; ~ **reception** Empfang durch die Stadtverwaltung; **to deprive of ~ rights** [staats]bürgerliche Ehrenrechte aberkennen.

civics *(US)* Gemeinschafts-, Staatsbürgerkunde.

civies Zivilklamotten.

civil bürgerlich, privat-, zivilrechtlich; ~ **action** bürgerliche Rechtsstreitigkeit, zivilrechtliche Klage, Zivilprozeß; ~ **administration** Zivilverwaltung; **~ Aeronautics Administration** Verwaltungsbehörde für die Verkehrsluftfahrt; **~ Aeronautics Board** *(US)* Bundesamt für die Verkehrsluftfahrt, Flugsicherungsbehörde; ~ **affairs** Verwaltungsangelegenheiten; **~ Aid Certificate** *(Br.)* Armenrechtszeugnis; ~ **air guard** *(Br.)* Luftschutzbund; ~ **authorities** Zivilbehörden; ~ **aviation** Verkehrsluftfahrt; **~ Aviation Act** *(Br.)* Luftfahrzeuggesetz; ~ **aviation agreement** Verkehrsluftfahrtabkommen; **International ~ Aviation Organization** *(ICAO)* Internationale Verkehrsluftfahrtorganisation; ~ **bonds** *(US)* Schuldverschreibungen der öffentlichen Hand; ~ **case** Zivilrechtsfall, bürgerliche Rechtsstreitigkeit; **~ Code** Bürgerliches Gesetzbuch; ~ **commotion** Aufruhr, Landfriedensbruch, innere Unruhen, Bürgerkrieg; ~ **commotion clause** Aufruhrklausel; ~ **commotion insurance** Aufruhrversicherung; ~ **contract** Ehevertrag; ~ **corporation** Gesellschaft des bürgerlichen Rechts; ~ **damages** *(US)* Ersatz des Drittschadens; ~ **damages act (bill, law)** Recht des Schadensersatzes, Schadensersatzrecht; **~ death** *(US)* Rechtstod; ~ **debt** Beschwerdesumme; **~ Defence** *(US)* Zivilvertei-

digung, Luftschutz, ziviler Bevölkerungsschutz; **~ Defence Corps** Luftschutzorganisation; **~ Defence Office** Amt für Zivilschutz, Luftschutzbehörde; ~ **disobedience** bürgerlicher Ungehorsam, passiver Widerstand, *(nonpayment of taxes)* Steuerstreik; ~ **dispute** bürgerliche Rechtsstreitigkeit; ~ **district** Verwaltungsbezirk; ~ **duties** Bürgerpflichten; ~ **economy** städtischer Haushalt; ~ **employment** bürgerlicher Beruf; ~ **enforcement proceedings** *(US, price control)* Zwangsverfahren; ~ **engineer** Bauingenieur; ~ **engineering** Tiefbau; ~ **enterprise** städtisches (gemeinnütziges) Unternehmen; ~ **establishment** Beamtenschaft; ~ **government** Zivilverwaltung; ~ **justice** Zivilgerichtsbarkeit; ~ **law** römisches Privatrecht, bürgerliches Recht, Zivilrecht; **~-law** bürgerlich-, zivilrechtlich; ~ **league** *(US)* Bürgervereinigung; ~ **liability** zivilrechtliche Haftung; **~ Liberties Union** *(US)* Gesellschaft zum Schutz der Bürgerrechte, Rechtsschutzgesellschaft; ~ **liberty** bürgerliche Freiheit; ~ **life** bürgerliches Leben (Laufbahn); **~ List** *(Br.)* Zivilliste; ~ **loan** *(US)* öffentliche Anleihe; ~ **marriage** standesamtliche Trauung, Ziviltrauung; ~ **nuisance** Besitzstörung; ~ **obligation** schuldrechtliche Verpflichtung; ~ **office** Zivilbehörde; ~ **officer** *(US)* Staatsbeamter; ~ **pension** Beamtenpension; **~ Practice Act** *(US)* Zivilprozeßordnung; ~ **procedure** Zivilprozeß; ~ **proceedings** zivilrechtliches Verfahren, Zivilprozeß; ~ **process** gerichtliche Verfügung; ~ **registration** Beurkundung des Personenstandes; ~ **remedy** Rechtsbehelf in Zivilsachen; ~ **responsibility** zivilrechtliche Haftung, Passivelegitimation; ~ **rights** staatsbürgerliche Rechte, Grundrechte; **~ Rights Association** Bürgerrechtsbewegung; ~ **rights program(me)** Bürgerrechtsprogramm; ~ **salvage** Bergung.

civil servant Berufs-, Zivil-, Staatsbeamter, Beamter im höheren (öffentlichen) [Staats]dienst; **career** *(US)* **(established,** *Br.***)** ~ Beamter auf Lebenszeit, planmäßiger Beamter, Berufsbeamter, Planstelleninhaber; **retired ~** Beamter im Ruhestand; **to become a ~** in den Staatsdienst übernommen werden.

civil service Staats-, Verwaltungsdienst, Zivilverwaltung, Beamtenapparat, Berufsbeamtentum, *(career)* Beamtenlaufbahn; **classified ~** *(US)* Berufsbeamtentum; **to be on ~** im Staatsdienst (als Beamter) angestellt sein; **to enter the ~** Beamtenlaufbahn einschlagen; **National ~ Act** *(US)* Beamtengesetz; ~ **bureaucracy** Beamtenbürokratie; ~ **cut** Einsparungen bei der öffentlichen Verwaltung; ~ **examination** Staatsexamen; ~ **grades** Beamtenrangstufen; ~ **job** Beamtenposition; ~ **pay** Beamtengehalt; ~ **pay agreement** *(Br.)* Beamtengehälterabkommen; ~ **pay bargaining** Tarifverhandlungen über die Festsetzung von Beamtengehältern; ~ **pay research unit** *(Br.)* Untersuchungsausschuß zur Anpassung von Beamtengehältern; ~ **reform** Beamtenreform; ~ **relationship** Beamtenverhältnis; ~ **system** Berufsbeamtentum; ~ **union** *(Br.)* Beamtengewerkschaft.

civil | side *(law court)* zivilrechtliche Abteilung; ~ **society** bürgerliche Gesellschaft; ~ **status** Personenstand; ~ **stock** Schuldverschreibungen der öffentlichen Hand; ~ **suit** zivilrechtliches Verfahren, Zivilprozeß, -verfahren; ~ **suit for damages** Klage auf Schadenersatz, Schadenersatzklage; ~ **township** Unterbezirk; ~ **wrongs** unerlaubte Handlungen; ~ **year** bürgerliches Jahr, Kalenderjahr.

civilian Zivilperson, Zivilist, Bürger; ~ *(a.)* zivil, bürgerlich; **to vacate the ~s from the city** Zivilbevölkerung aus der Stadt evakuieren; **~ Conservation Corps** Naturschutzbehörde; ~ **detainee** Zivilinternierter; ~ **dress** Zivilkleidung; **in ~ life** im Zivilleben; ~ **needs** Bedürfnisse des zivilen Sektors; ~ **population** Zivilbevölkerung; ~ **requirements** Zivilbedarf; **to go back to ~ rule** verfassungsmäßigen Zustand wiederherstellen.

civilianize *(v.)* Garnisonsstadt aufheben.

civility Höflichkeit, Lebensart, Bildung; **in ~** höflicherweise.

civilizable bildungsfähig.

civilization Kultur, Zivilisation; **western ~** abendländische Kultur.

civilize *(v.)* der Zivilisation zugänglich machen.

civilized zivilisiert, gebildet, kultiviert, höflich; ~ **country** Kulturstaat.

civilizer Kulturträger.

civism Bürgertugend.

civvies *(Br.)* Zivilklamotten.

civvy Zivilist; **in ~ street** *(Br.)* im Zivilleben.

claim Klageanspruch, *(advertising)* Werbeanspruch, -behauptung, *(insurance)* Versicherungsanspruch, *(mining)* Mutung, Schürfeinheit, *(pretension)* Behauptung, *(purchase)* Beanstandung, [Mängel]rüge, Reklamation, *(title)* [Rechts]anspruch, Forderung, Anrecht, *(US)* Staatsland;
accessory ~ Nebenforderung, -anspruch; **accrued** ~ entstandener (eingetretener) Schadensanspruch; **acknowledged** ~ anerkannte Forderung; **additional** ~ Hilfsantrag; **adverse** ~ *(pledged thing)* entgegenstehender Anspruch, Gegenanspruch, Interventionsanspruch; **allowed** ~ anerkannte Forderung; **alternative** ~ wahlweiser Anspruch; **allowable** ~ zulässige Forderung; **anterior** ~ älterer Anspruch, ältere Forderung; **assigned** ~ abgetretene Forderung; **bad** ~ zweifelhafte Forderung, schlecht begründeter Anspruch; **bogus** ~ fingierte Forderung; **book** ~ Buchforderung; **compensation** ~ Entschädigungsanspruch; **conflicting** ~ *(patent)* entgegenstehender Anspruch; **contingent** ~ bedingte Forderung, Eventualanspruch; **continual** ~ stets erneuerte Forderung; **contractual** ~ Vertragsanspruch; **creditor** ~ Gläubigerforderung; **cross** ~ Gegenforderung, -anspruch; **damages** ~ Schadensersatzanspruch; **unconcealed damages** ~ Schadenersatzanspruch wegen offensichtlicher Beschädigung; **death** ~ Anspruch aus einer Sterbeversicherung; **debt** ~ schuldrechtlicher Anspruch; **deferred** ~ nachrangige Konkursforderung; **disablement** ~ Anspruch auf Invalidenrente; **disputed** ~ strittige Forderung; **dormant** ~ nicht durchgesetzte Forderung; **doubtful** ~ hinsichtlich des Rechtsanspruchs zweifelhafte Forderung; **enforceable** ~ einklagbarer Anspruch, vollstreckbare Forderung; **equalization** ~ Ausgleichsforderung; **equitable** ~ billigkeitsrechtlicher Anspruch; **exaggerated** ~s übertriebene Forderungen; **existing** ~ gesetzlicher Anspruch; **extinct** ~ erloschene Forderung; **false** ~ unberechtigter (betrügerischer) Anspruch; **first** ~ erster Anspruch, Vorhand; **forfeited** ~ verfallener Anspruch; **fraudulent** ~ Versicherungsbetrug; **freight** ~ Frachtforderung; **frivolous** ~ leichtfertig erhobene Forderung; **generic** ~ Gattungsanspruch; **good** ~ vollgültiger Anspruch; **hypothecary** ~ Hypothekenforderung; **independent** ~ *(patent law)* Nebenanspruch; **indirect** ~ Schadensersatzforderung für mittelbar zugefügten Schaden; **insurance** ~ Versicherungsanspruch; **interfering** ~s *(patent)* kollidierende (widerstreitende) Ansprüche; **irrecoverable** ~ uneinbringliche Forderung; **know-loss** ~ Schadensersatzanspruch wegen unbestrittenen Frachtverlustes; **lawful** ~ gesetzlicher (berechtigter) Anspruch; **legal** ~ rechtmäßiger Anspruch, Rechtsanspruch; **legitimate** ~ begründete Forderung; **liability** ~ Schadensersatzklage; **litigious** ~ strittige Forderung; **main** ~ Hauptanspruch; **maritime** ~ seerechtlicher Anspruch; **minimum** ~ Mindestanspruch; **mining** ~ Mutungsrecht; **moderate** ~s mäßige Ansprüche; **mortgage** ~ Hypothekenforderung; **mutual** ~s gegenseitige Forderungen; **nonprovable** ~ nicht nachweisbare Konkursforderung; **noncontingent** ~ unbedingte Forderung; **omnibus** ~ *(patent law)* zusammenfassender Patentanspruch; **outlawed** ~ *(US)* verjährte Forderung, verjährter Anspruch; **overcharge** ~ Überforderung; **partnership** ~ Gesellschaftsanspruch; **patent** ~ Patentanspruch; **pay** ~ Gehaltsanspruch, -forderung; **pecuniary** ~ Geldforderung, Zahlungsanspruch; **pensions** ~ Pensions-, Versorgungs-, Ruhegehaltsanspruch; **preference (preferential, priority)** ~ bevorrechtigte Forderung, Vorzugsanspruch, *(bankruptcy)* Aussonderungsrecht, abgesonderte Befriedigung; **pretended** ~ angebliche Forderung; **prior** ~ vorgehender (älterer) Anspruch; **provable** ~ anmeldefähige Konkursforderung; **proved** ~ anerkannte Konkursforderung; **recoverable** ~ einklagbare (eintreibbare) Forderung; **restitution** ~ Wiedergutmachungs-, Restitutionsanspruch; **rightful** ~ berechtigter Anspruch; **salary** ~ Gehaltsforderung; **secured** ~ gesicherte Konkursforderung; **sound** ~ begründeter Anspruch; **statute-barred** ~ verjährte Forderung; **subsequent** ~ spätere Reklamation; **substantiated** ~ begründeter Anspruch; **supplemental** ~ Nachforderung; **tax** ~ Steuerforderung; **territorial** ~ Gebietsanspruch; **third-party** ~s Ansprüche Dritter; **tort** ~ Schadensersatzanspruch aus unerlaubter Handlung; **total** ~ Gesamtforderung; **unforceable** ~ nicht einklagbarer Anspruch, nicht beitreibbare Forderung; **unfounded** ~ unberechtigte Forderung; **unlimited** ~ ziffernmäßig nicht begrenzte Forderung; **unsecured** ~ ungesicherte Forderung, *(bankruptcy)* Masseanspruch; **unsettled reported** ~s noch nicht regulierte Schadensfälle; **unsubstantiated** ~ nicht nachgewiesene Forderung; **valid** ~ begründeter Anspruch; **more valid** ~s nähere Ansprüche; **wage** ~s Lohnforderungen;
~ **for abatement** Steuererlaßantrag; ~ **under an act** gesetzlicher Anspruch; ~ **of (to) alimony** Unterhaltsanspruch [der geschie-

denen Ehefrau], Alimentenforderung; ~ **provable in bankruptcy** Konkursforderung; ~ **barred by the Statute of Limitations** verjährter Anspruch, verjährte Forderung; ~ **for benefit** Unterstützungsanspruch; ~ **arising from a bill** Wechselforderung; ~ **to capital allowance** Inanspruchnahme von Abschreibungen; ~ **of cognizance or conusance** Hauptintervention; ~ **to compensation (for damages)** Entschädigungs-, Schadenersatzanspruch; ~ **under consideration** vorliegende Klage; ~ **for conversion** Herausgabeanspruch; ~ **to copyright** Urheberrechtsanspruch; ~s **on credit institutions** Forderungen gegen Kreditinstitute; ~ **for damages** Antrag auf Schadensersatz; ~ **for damages observed** Schadenersatzanspruch für festgestellte Schäden; ~ **for delay in transit** Ersatzanspruch für Transportverzögerung; ~ **and delivery** Herausgabeanspruch; ~ **against the estate** Masseanspruch, Nachlaßforderung; ~ **of exemption** *(US)* Aussonderungsanspruch; ~ **for shorter hours** Forderung nach Arbeitszeitverkürzung; ~ **for indemnity** Schadensersatzanspruch; ~ **of inheritance** *(US)* Erb[schafts]anspruch; ~ **founded on a written instrument** vertraglich begründete Forderung; ~ **to leadership** Führungsanspruch; ~ **liquidated by litigation** Prozeßforderung; ~ **for loss or damages** Schadenersatz, Entschädigungsanspruch; ~ **for maintenance** Unterhaltungsanspruch; ~ **met by the art** durch den Stand der Technik neuheitsschädlich getroffener Anspruch; ~ **for money** Geldforderung; ~ **on mortgage** hypothekarische Forderung; ~ **for national assistance** *(Br.)* Sozialhilfeanspruch; ~ **of financial non-support** *(students, US)* Nachweis nichterfolgter elterlicher Unterstützung; ~ **of ownership, right and title** Herausgabe-, Eigentumsklage, Klage auf Herausgabe des Eigentums; ~ **for a patent** Patentanspruch; ~ **entitled to priority** bevorrechtigte Forderung, Prioritätsanspruch; ~ **for tax refund** Steuerrückerstattungsanspruch; ~ **ad rem** dinglicher Anspruch; ~ **for rent** Mietforderung; ~ **to remuneration** Honoraranspruch; ~ **to repayment** *(overpaid taxes)* Erstattungsanspruch; ~ **for replacement** Wiederbeschaffungsanspruch; ~ **in return** Gegenforderung; **prior** ~ **to satisfaction** *(bankruptcy)* Anspruch auf bevorrechtigte Befriedigung; ~ **by suit** Klageanspruch; ~ **for taxes** Steuerforderung; ~ **to title** Besitzanspruch; ~ **founded in tort** Schadensersatzanspruch aus unerlaubter Handlung; ~s **in winding up** Liquidationsforderungen;
~ *(v.)* beanspruchen, [ein]fordern, *(witness)* behaupten;
~ **s. th.** etw. für sich in Anspruch nehmen; ~ **s. th. from s. o.** Forderung gegen j. geltend machen; ~ **acquaintance with s. o.** j. zu kennen behaupten; ~ **an allowance** *(Br.)* Steuerfreibetrag in Anspruch nehmen; ~ **back** zurückfordern; ~ **s. th. back from s. o.** Rückforderungsanspruch gegen j. geltend machen; ~ **benefits** Unterstützungsansprüche stellen; ~ **compensation for a loss** Schadenersatz beanspruchen; ~ **damages** Schadensersatzansprüche stellen, Schadenersatz beanspruchen; ~ **descent from s. o.** seine Abstammung auf j. zurückführen; ~ **one's due** seine Rechte geltend machen; ~ **against a negligent motorist** Versicherungsansprüche gegen einen fahrlässigen Autofahrer erheben; ~ **priority** Vorrang beanspruchen; ~ **a privilege** Vorrecht beanspruchen; ~ **repayment** Erstattung beantragen, Erstattungsanspruch geltend machen; ~ **one's right** sein Recht fordern; ~ **the right to do s. th.** Recht für sich in Anspruch nehmen; ~ **subsequently** nachfordern; ~ **tax relief** Steuervergünstigungen in Anspruch nehmen; ~ **a title** Eigentum beanspruchen;
~ **to be an expert** sich als Sachverständiger aufspielen; ~ **to be the rightful heir** Erbansprüche geltend machen;
to abandon a ~ Anspruch fallen lassen; **to adjust a** ~ Versicherungsanspruch regulieren; **to admit a** ~ Forderung (Anspruch) anerkennen (zulassen), Reklamation erkennen; **to admit a** ~ **on its merits** Anspruch dem Grunde nach anerkennen; **to advance a** ~ Anspruch erheben (geltend machen); **to advance a** ~ **for indemnification** Schadenersatzklage einreichen; **to allow a** ~ einem Anspruch stattgeben; **to allow s. one's** ~ **without a question** jds. Forderung widerstandslos anerkennen; **to answer a** ~ Anspruch befriedigen; **to assert a** ~ Anspruch geltend machen; **to assign a** ~ Forderung abtreten; **to buy up a** ~ **for cash** Anspruch in bar abfinden; **to collect a** ~ Forderung eintreiben; **to constitute a** ~ Anspruch begründen; **to contest a** ~ Forderung (Anspruch) bestreiten; **to defend a** ~ Anspruch bestreiten; **to demur to a** ~ Forderung beanstanden; **to disallow a** ~ Forderung zurückweisen; **to enforce a** ~ Anspruch durchsetzen, Forderung gerichtlich geltend machen; **to enter a** ~ Forderung einreichen; **to establish a** ~ Anspruch feststellen; **to establish one's** ~ seinen Anspruch als berechtigt nachweisen; **to establish a** ~ **for relief of tax** Steuervergünstigungsanspruch begründen; **to exaggerate one's** ~s übertriebene Forderungen stellen; **to file a** ~ Anspruch anmelden; **to file a** ~ **in court** Forderung einkla-

gen; **to file a proof for a** ~ Anspruchsberechtigung nachweisen; **to find for the plaintiff as** ~**ed** Klageantrag stattgeben; **to give notice of a** ~ Schaden anmelden; **to give up all** ~**s** auf alle Ansprüche verzichten; **to handle** ~**s** Schadensfälle bearbeiten; **to have a** ~ anspruchsberechtigt sein; **to have no** ~ **whatsoever on s. o.** überhaupt keine Ansprüche gegen j. haben; **to impugn a** ~ Forderung bestreiten; **to jump a** ~ sich einen Anspruch anmaßen; **to keep up a** ~ Anspruch aufrechterhalten; **to lay** ~ **to** beanspruchen, Anspruch erheben auf, Forderung einreichen (erheben); **to limit time to make proof of one's** ~**s** Frist zur Forderungsanmeldung setzen; **to litigate a** ~ Forderung einklagen; **to lodge a** ~ Forderung erheben, Anspruch geltend machen; **to lodge a** ~ **for compensation** Schadenersatz verlangen; **to lodge with s. o. a** ~ **for $ 5000** jem. eine Forderung über 5000 Dollar vorlegen; **to make a** ~ Forderung einreichen, rügen; **to make a** ~ **for damages** Schadensersatz beantragen; **to make good one's** ~ Gültigkeit seiner Forderung beweisen; **to make a** ~ **in respect of a defect** Mängelrüge vorbringen; **to make a** ~ **for separate assessment** getrennte Einkommensbesteuerung beantragen; **to mark out a** ~ Grundstück abstecken; **to maverick a** ~ *(US)* Anspruch mit unseriösen Mitteln sichern; **to meet the** ~**s of one's creditors** seine Gläubiger befriedigen; **to meet an insurance** ~ **in full** Versicherungsansprüche voll abdecken; **to moderate one's** ~**s** seine Forderungen herunterschrauben, seine Ansprüche mäßigen; **to override s. one's** ~**s** sich über jds. Ansprüche hinwegsetzen; **to own a** ~ **against s. o.** *(US)* obligatorischen Anspruch gegen j. haben; **to pay a** ~ Forderung befriedigen; **to peg out a** ~ Mutung abstecken; **to place a** ~ Schadensersatz beanspruchen; **to prefer a** ~ Anspruch erheben; **to prefer a** ~ **against s. o.** Forderung gegen j. geltend machen; **to prejudice one's** ~ seinem Anspruch Abbruch tun; **to press a** ~ auf einer Forderung bestehen; **to prosecute a** ~ Forderung einklagen; **to prove a** ~ [Konkurs]forderung nachweisen (anmelden); **to put forward a** ~ Anspruch erheben (geltend machen); **to put in a** ~ Anspruch geltend machen, *(after an accident)* Ansprüche gegen die Versicherungsgesellschaft erheben; **to put in a** ~ **for damages** Schadenersatz beanspruchen; **to put in a** ~ **for a grant** Zuschuß bei der Regierung beantragen; **to put a** ~ **in issue** Forderung bestreiten; **to quit a** ~ auf einen Anspruch verzichten; **to raise a** ~ Anspruch erheben (geltend machen); **to raise a** ~ **in ordinary proceedings** Anspruch im ordentlichen Gerichtsverfahren geltend machen; **to recognize a** ~ Anspruch anerkennen; **to reduce a** ~ Forderung reduzieren (nachlassen); **to reject a** ~ Anspruch (Reklamation) zurückweisen; **to relinquish a** ~ von einer Forderung Abstand nehmen, sich eines Anspruchs begeben; **to remise a** ~ sich eines Anspruchs begeben; **to remit a** ~ Forderung nachlassen (erlassen); **to renounce a** ~ von einer Forderung absehen, auf eine Forderung verzichten; **to resist a** ~ Anspruch bestreiten; **to run down a** ~ Forderung ablehnen; **to satisfy a** ~ Anspruch (Forderung) befriedigen; **to segregate a** ~ *(US)* Mutungsanspruch aufteilen; **to set a** ~ **aside** Klage abweisen; **to set off** ~**s** gegenseitige Forderungen verrechnen (ausgleichen); **to set up a** ~ **for s. th.** Forderung (Anspruch) auf etw. erheben; **to settle a** ~ Forderung regulieren; **to stake off a mining** ~ Mutungsrecht abstecken; **to substantiate a** ~ Klage (Anspruch) näher begründen; **to support one's** ~ Gültigkeit seiner Forderung beweisen; **to sustain a** ~ Anspruch aufrecht erhalten; **to sustain s. o. in his** ~ jds. Anspruch anerkennen; **to transfer a** ~ **upon s. o.** Forderung auf j. übertragen; **to turn down a** ~ Forderung zurückweisen; **to vindicate a** ~ Anspruch erheben; **to waive a** ~ auf einen Anspruch verzichten; **to withdraw one's** ~ von seinen Forderungen abgehen; **to write off a doubtful** ~ *(Br.)* zweifelhafte Forderung abschreiben;

~ **adjuster** *(insurance)* Regulierungsbeauftragter, Schadensregulierer; ~ **administration** *(insurance)* Bearbeitung von Versicherungsansprüchen; ~ **agent** Schadensregulierer; ~**s agreement** *(insurers)* Schadenregelungsvereinbarung; ~ **assessment** Bewertung eines Anspruchs; ~ **blank** *(US)* Anspruchsformular; ~ **bond** *(enforcement proceedings)* Sicherheitsleistung des Beklagten; ~ **book** Beschwerdebuch; ~ **check** Forderungsnachweis, *(US)* Fahrzeugpapiere; **Mixed** ~**s Commission** *(German property)* gemischte Schiedskommission; ~ **costs** *(insurance)* Regulierungskosten; ~ **debtor** Anspruchsschuldner; ~ **department** Reklamationsabteilung; **no-**~ **discount entitlement** *(Br.)* Anspruch auf Schadensfreiheitsrabatt; ~ **expense** *(insurance)* Rückstellung für noch nicht regulierte Schadensfälle; ~ **form** Anspruchs-, Antrags-, Schadensformular; **previous** ~**-free years** schadensfreie Versicherungsjahre; ~ **holder** Konzessions-, Lizenzinhaber, *(mining)* Mutungsinhaber; ~ **inspector** *(insurance company)* Schadensregulierer, Versicherungsin-

spektor; **professional** ~**s investigator** freiberuflicher Schadensfeststeller; ~ **jumper** *(mining)* Usurpator eines fremden Grubenanteils; ~ **jumping** vorweggenommene Schürfrechte; ~ **letter** Beschwerdeschreiben; ~**s management** Bearbeitung von Versicherungsansprüchen; **disputed** ~**s office** *(insurance company)* Rechtsabteilung; ~ **papers** Anspruchsunterlagen; ~ **payment** *(insurance)* Anspruchsregulierung, Schadensbegleichung; ~ **prevention** *(accident insurance)* Verhinderung der Entstehung von Schadenersatzansprüchen; ~ **procedure** Verfahren zur Regelung von Versicherungsansprüchen; **complete** ~**s ratio** *(insurance)* gesamter Schadenswert im Verhältnis zum Prämienaufkommen; **bad** ~**s record** *(motor insurance)* Schadenshäufigkeit; ~ **reserves** *(insurance company)* Schadensreserven; ~ **results** *(insurance)* Schadensergebnisse; ~**s service provided** Dienstleistungen bei der Abwicklung von Versicherungsansprüchen; ~ **settlement** *(insurance)* Schadens-, Anspruchsregulierung, Regelung eines Versicherungsfalles; **full-time** ~**s staff** ganztägig beschäftigtes Regulierungspersonal; ~ **tracer** Ersuchen um Feststellung der Gültigkeit eines Anspruchs.

claimable zu fordern, einklag-, beanspruchbar.

claimant Anspruch-, Antragsteller, Anspruchs-, Forderungsberechtigter, Kläger, *(bill of exchange)* Regreßnehmer, *(complainant)* Beschwerdeführer, *(law of inheritance)* Erbanwärter, *(insurance)* Geschädigter, *(patent law)* Anmelder, *(plaintiff)* Kläger;

rightful ~ Anspruchsberechtigter;

~ **for a patent** Patentberechtigter; ~ **to the throne** Thronanwärter, -bewerber.

claiming back Herausgabe-, Restitutionsanspruch.

clair, en unchiffriert.

clamo(u)r Lärm, Getöse, Tumult;

~ *(v.)* **s. o. down** j. niederschreien.

clamp | on wage increases Lohnbremse;

~ *(v.)* **a ban on newspapers** Zensurvorschriften für Zeitungen erlassen; ~ **ceilings on prices** Höchstpreise festsetzen; ~ **down** Druck ausüben, *(administration)* schärfer überwachen; ~ **down on credit** Kreditbremse zur Anwendung bringen; ~ **down on liquidity** Liquiditätsbestimmungen verschärfen; ~ **limits on spending** Ausgabenbeschränkungen anordnen.

clampdown schärfere Überwachung;

~ **on credit** Kreditbeschränkung; ~ **on money** verschärfte geldmarkttechnische Maßnahmen.

clan Stamm, Clan, *(clique)* Clique, Partei, Sippschaft.

clandestine heimlich, verstohlen;

~ **marriage** heimliche Eheschließung; ~ **meeting** heimliche Zusammenkunft, Geheimversammlung; ~ **pact** Geheimabkommen; ~ **printing** Geheimdruckerei; ~ **tract** verbotene Flugschrift; ~ **trade** unerlaubter Handel, Schleichhandel; ~ **trader** Schleichhändler; ~ **transmitter** Geheimsender.

clang colo(u)r Klangfarbe.

clanger unpassende Bemerkung;

to drop a ~ ins Fettnäpfchen treten.

clap Klatschen;

~ **of thunder** Donnerschlag;

~ *(v.)* applaudieren, klatschen;

~ **handcuffs on s. o.** jem. Handschellen anlegen; ~ **import duties on** mit Einfuhrzoll belegen; ~ **s. o. in prison** j. ins Gefängnis werfen; ~ **s. o. on the shoulder** j. auf die Schulter klopfen; ~ **up** ins Gefängnis werfen.

claptrap Reklame, Anpreisung;

~ **journalism** Revolver-, Boulevardjournalismus.

clarification Klärung, Klarstellung;

~ **plant** Kläranlage.

clarify *(v.)* klarstellen, klären.

clash Konflikt, Widerstreit, Reibung, *(car)* Zusammenstoß, Kollision;

by ~ **of hands** durch Handschlag;

~ **of arms** bewaffneter Zusammenstoß; ~ **of interests** Interessenkollision; ~ **of opinions** Meinungsverschiedenheit; **violent** ~**es with the police** heftige Zusammenstöße mit der Polizei; ~ **of powers** Kompetenzstreitigkeit;

~ *(v.)* aneinandergeraten, *(interest)* widerstreiten, sich kreuzen, kollidieren, *(statements)* unvereinbar sein.

clashing | interests widerstreitende Interessen; ~ **opinions** widerstreitende Meinungen.

class Art, [Wert]klasse, Schicht, Gruppe, Gattung, Rangstufe, Kategorie, *(lecture)* Kurs[us], Lehrgang, Vorlesung, *(mil.)* Rekrutenjahrgang, *(quality)* ausgezeichnete Qualität, Grad, Güteklasse, Sorte, *(railway)* Wagenklasse, *(rank)* soziale Stellung, Stand, gesellschaftlicher Rang, *(rating of ship)* Schiffs-

klasse, *(school, US)* Jahrgang, *(society)* Gesellschaftsklasse, Schicht, Kaste, *(university, US)* [Studenten]jahrgang;
the ~es die oberen Zehntausend;
administrative ~ *(Br.)* höherer Dienst; **the educated** ~es die Gebildeten, gebildete Schichten; **evening** ~es Abendkurse, Fortbildungskurse; **executive** ~ gehobener Dienst; **first** ~ *(railway)* erste Klasse; **the higher** ~es die oberen Schichten; **industrial** ~ Berufsschulklasse; **labo(u)ring** ~es Arbeiterbevölkerung, Werktätige; **leisured** ~es begüterte Klassen; **the lower** ~es das niedere Volk, die unteren Volksschichten; **middle** ~ Mittelstand; **moneyed** ~es besitzende Klassen; **overcrowded** ~ überfüllte Schulklasse; **professional** ~es Angehörige freier Berufe; **proprietary** ~es besitzende Klassen; **ruling** ~es herrschende Klassen; **salaried** ~ Gehaltsempfänger; **second** ~ *(railway)* zweite Klasse; **technical (vocational)** ~ Berufsschulklasse; **trading** ~ Gewerbestand, Geschäftsleute; **the upper** ~es Oberschicht; **middle-upper** ~ gehobene Mittelschicht; **working** ~ Arbeiterstand, -schaft;
the ~es and the masses die Besitzenden und das Proletariat;
~ **of 1981** Jahrgang 1981; ~ **of beneficiaries** Kreis der Begünstigten; ~ **of business** Geschäftszweig, *(insurance)* Versicherungssparte; **my** ~ **of business** meine Kundschaft; ~ **of claims** Anspruchsgruppe; ~ **of consumers** Verbraucherschicht; ~es **of contract** Vertragstypen; ~es **of contributions** Beitragsklassen; ~ **of credit** Kreditart; ~es **of creditors** Gläubigergruppen; ~ **of debtors** Schuldnergruppe; ~ **of entrepreneurs** Unternehmerschicht; **taxable** ~ **of goods** steuerpflichtige Warengattung; **best** ~ **of hotel** erstklassiges Hotel; ~ **of income** Einkommensart; ~es **of insurance** Versicherungsarten; ~ **of literature** Literaturgattung; ~es **of persons** Personengruppen; ~ **of population** Bevölkerungsschicht; ~es **of revenue** Einkunftsarten; ~ **of risk** *(insurance)* Gefahrenklasse; ~ **of securities** Wertpapiergattung; ~ **of shares** Aktiengattung, -kategorie; ~es **of shareholders** Aktionärskategorien; ~ **of stock** *(US)* Aktienkategorie, -gattung; ~ **of vehicle** Kraftfahrzeugklasse;
~ *(v.)* einstufen, klassifizieren, in Gruppen (Klassen) einordnen, -gruppieren;
to arrange in ~es klassifizieren; **to attend** ~es Kurse besuchen; **to be in charge of a** ~ Klassenaufsicht führen; **to be in the same** ~ **with s. th.** mit etw. gleichwertig sein; **not to be in the same** ~ **with s. o.** an j. nicht heranreichen; **to be at the top of one's** ~ Klassenbester (Erster) sein; **to belong to a** ~ zu einer Gruppe (Klasse) gehören; **to go up into a higher** ~ Klassenziel erreichen; **to head one's** ~ Klassenerster sein; **to hold** ~es **for discussions** *(school)* Diskussionsgruppen einrichten; **to put back into a lower** ~ *(school)* zurückversetzen; **to stay down in a** ~ [Schul]klasse wiederholen; **to travel second** ~ zweiter Klasse reisen;
~ *(a.)* zu einer Gesellschaftsschicht gehörig;
first-~ prima, erstklassig; **high-**~ von erstklassiger Qualität; **second-**~ zweitklassig, -rangig;
~ **action** *(law court)* Gemeinschaftsklage, Sammelprozeß; **to file a** ~ **action motion** gemeinsamen Klageantrag einreichen; ~ **affiliation** Klassenzugehörigkeit; ~ **barriers** Klassenschranken; ~ **basis** Grundtarif; ~ **bonds** in Serien ausgegebene Schuldverschreibungen; **first-**~ **cabin** Kabine in der ersten Klasse; ~ **captain** *(school)* Klassensprecher; ~ A **charges** *(land registry)* [etwa] Belastungen in Abteilung I; ~ **conflict** Klassenkampf; ~-**conscious** klassenbewußt; ~ **consciousness** Klassenbewußtsein; ~ I **contributor** *(Br.)* normalbeschäftigter Sozialversicherungspflichtiger; ~ A **deductions** *(US)* Werbungskosten; ~ B **deductions** *(US)* Sonderausgaben; ~-**destructive** klassendiskriminierend; ~ **difference (distinction)** Klassenunterschied; ~ **enemy** Klassenfeind; ~ **exercises** *(school)* Klassenübungen, -aufsatz; ~ **feeling** Klassenbewußtsein; ~ **fellow** Klassenkamerad, Mitschüler; ~ **gift** Schenkung an einen bestimmten Personenkreis; **high-**~ **goods** erstklassige Erzeugnisse; ~ **hatred** Klassenhaß; ~ **interest** Klasseninteresse; ~ **interval** Klassenbreite, *(statistics)* Klassengröße; ~ **legislation** Klassengesetzgebung; **not to appear in the** ~ **list** in der Prüfung durchfallen; ~ **load** *(school)* Klassenstärke; ~ **lottery** Klassenlotterie; **first-**~ **matter** Briefpost; **second-**~ **matter** Drucksachen; ~ **meeting** Klassentreffen; ~ **meeting of shareholders** gruppenweise stattfindende Aktionärsversammlung; ~ **index of patents** Verzeichnis der Patentklassen; ~ **number** *(library)* Bibliotheksnummer; **second-**~ **passenger** Reisender zweiter Klasse; **working-**~ **population** die arbeitenden Klassen, Arbeiterbevölkerung, Werktätige; ~ **prefect** *(school)* Klassensprecher; ~ **prejudice** Standes-, Klassenvorurteil; ~ **price** Preis für gehobene Schichten; ~ **privileges** Klassenvorrechte; ~ **publication** exklusive Veröffentlichung; ~ **rate** Grundgehalt, -tarif, *(insurance)*

Tarifprämie, *(common carrier)* Sonder-, Gruppentarif; ~ **rating** *(railway)* Tarifeinstufung; ~ **register** Klassenbuch; ~ **restaurant** vornehmes Restaurant; ~ **rights** Aktionärsrechte der gleichen Aktiengattung; **first-**~ **road** *(US)* Straße erster Ordnung; ~ **size** Klassengröße; ~ **solidarity** Klassensolidarität; ~ **struggle** Klassenkampf; ~ **tariff** Tariftabelle; ~ **teacher** Klassenlehrer; **first-**~ **ticket** Fahrkarte erster Klasse; ~ **war[fare]** Klassenkampf; ~-**warfare ideas** Klassenkampfempfinden.
classbook *(US)* Klassenbuch.
classed, to be *(Br.)* Universitätsprüfung bestehen;
~ A *(ship)* zur A-Klasse gehörend;
~ **catalog(ue)** nach Sachgebieten geordneter Katalog.
classic erstklassig, ausgezeichnet, *(in accordance with a coherent system)* den anerkannten Richtlinien entsprechend, *(classical)* klassisch;
~ **author** Klassiker; ~ **clothes** konventionelle Kleidung; ~ **event** historisches Ereignis; ~ **example** klassisches Beispiel.
classical klassisch, humanistisch;
~ **architecture** klassischer Baustil; ~ **economics** klassische Schule; ~ **education** humanistische Bildung.
classifiable klassifizierbar.
classification An-, Rangordnung, Eingruppierung, Klassifizierung, Klassifikation, Aufschlüsselung, *(insurance)* Einteilung in Gefahrenklassen, *(salaries)* [Gehalts]einstufung;
fixed asset ~ Bezeichnung der Anlagegegenstände; **freight** ~ Frachttarif; **functional** ~ Aufgliederung nach Sachgebieten; **job (occupational)** ~ Berufszugehörigkeit; **International Patent** ~ internationale Patentklassifikation; **security** ~ *(US)* Geheimhaltungseinstufung;
~ **of accounts** Aufgliederung der Konten, Kontengliederung; ~ **of diplomatic agents** Rangordnung der diplomatischen Vertreter; ~ **of cars** *(railway)* Einteilung der Waggons nach Klassen; ~ **in customs tariffs** Gliederung der Waren nach Zolltarifen; ~ **of documents** Beschriftung von Urkunden; ~ **of entries** Buchungsaufgliederung; ~ **of evidence** Beweisklassifizierung; ~ **of expenses** Kostenaufgliederung; ~ **of goods** Warenklasseneinteilung; ~ **of insurance** Einteilung in Gefahrenklassen; ~ **of patents** Patentklassifizierung; ~ **of profits** Gewinnklassifizierung; ~ **of properties** Vermögensschichtung; ~ **of risks** Risikoeinstufung, Einteilung in Gefahrenklassen; ~ **of ships** Schiffsklassifizierung;
to make ~s Einstufungen vornehmen;
~ **Act** *(US)* Besoldungsordnung; ~ **card** Verwendungskarte; ~ **certificate** *(ship)* Klassifikationsattest; ~ **change** *(salaries)* Gruppenveränderung; **demotional (ingrade)** ~ **change** niedrigere Einstufung ohne Lohnkürzung; ~ **committee** Einstufungsausschuß; ~ **plan** Stellenplan; ~ **rating** Tarifeinstufung; ~ **record** Verwendungskarte; ~ **register** Schiffsklassenregister; ~ **society** *(marine insurance)* Klassifizierungsgesellschaft; ~ **system** Klassifizierungssystem; ~ **schedule** Einstufungstabelle; ~ **sheet** Beurteilungsblatt; ~ **statistics** Klassifikationszahlen; ~ **switching** *(railway car)* Zugauflösung nach Wagenklassen; ~ **territory** *(railway)* Tarifanwendungsgebiet; ~ **track** *(railway)* Verschiebegleis; ~ **yard** *(railway)* Verschiebebahnhof.
classificatory klassenbildend.
classified klassifiziert, nach Klassen eingeteilt, *(mil.)* im Sicherheitsinteresse geheimhalten;
~ **ads** *(US)* rubrizierte Anzeigen, Kleinanzeigen; ~ **ad department** *(US)* Kleinanzeigenabteilung; ~ **advertisements** kleine Anzeigen; ~ **announcements** Kleinanzeigen; ~ **bonds** in Serien ausgegebene (abgestufte) Schuldverschreibungen; ~ **civil service** *(US)* Berufsbeamtentum; ~ **column** Kleinanzeigenrubrik; ~ **directory** Branchenadreßbuch; ~ **files** nach Sachgebieten abgelegte Akten; ~ **index** Sachgruppenindex; ~ **information** *(US)* Geheiminformation, Verschlußsache; ~ **list of supplies** Bezugsquellennachweis; ~ **material** *(US)* Geheimpapiere; ~ **matter** *(mil., US)* Verschlußsache; ~ **report** *(US)* Geheimbericht; ~ **road** *(Br.)* Landstraße erster Ordnung; ~ **service** *(US)* gehobener Dienst; ~ **stock** *(US)* Vorrangaktie; ~ **tax** Klassensteuer; ~ **trial balance** nach Gruppen geordnete Probebilanz.
classify *(v.)* einstufen, klassifizieren, nach Klassen einteilen, kategorisieren, einordnen, -gruppieren, rangieren, *(customs)* tarifieren, *(mil.)* mit Geheimhaltungsstufe versehen;
~ **books by subjects** Bücher nach Sachgebieten einordnen; ~ **officers in nine grades** Beamte in neun Klassen einteilen; ~ **a road** *(Br.)* zur Landstraße erster Ordnung erheben; ~ **under a tariff item** unter eine Tarifposition einreihen.
classless klassenlos.
classmate Klassenkamerad, Mitschüler.
classroom Klassenzimmer, -raum;
~ **instruction** Berufsschulunterricht; ~ **time** Seminarzeit.

classwork *(US)* Klassenarbeit.

classy *(sl.)* Klasse, erstklassig, pfundig.

clause Klausel, [besondere] Bedingung, Bestimmung, *(paragraph)* Absatz, Paragraph, *(reservation)* Zusatz, Vorbehalt; **abandonment** ~ Abandonklausel; **acceleration** ~ Verfall-, Fälligkeitsklausel; **additional** ~ Zusatzbestimmung; **admitted-value** ~ Klausel Wert erkannt; **agreed-amount** ~ *(insurance)* Versicherungspolice unter Ausschluß des Selbstbehalts; **arbitration** ~ Schiedsgerichtsklausel; **attestation** ~ Beglaubigungsvermerk, -formel; **[general] average** ~ Havarieklausel; **bailee** ~ Gewahrsamsklausel; **basket** ~ *(US)* Generalklause; **benefit** ~ *(insurance)* Begünstigungsklausel; **bill-of-lading** ~ Konnossementklausel; **blanket** ~ Generalklausel; **both-to-blame collision** ~ Kollisionsklausel für beiderseitiges Verschulden; **cancellation** ~ Kündigungs-, Rücktrittsklausel; **cash-and-carry** ~ *(US)* Bestimmung über Barzahlung und Transport auf eigenen Schiffen; **codicillary** ~ *(last will)* Nachtragsbestimmung; **co-insurance** ~ Selbstbehaltsklausel; **collision** ~ Kollisionsschadenklausel; **comminatory** ~ *(will)* Erbausschußklausel; **commodity** ~ *(US)* Eigentumsvorbehaltsklausel; **competitive** ~ Konkurrenzklausel; **conditional** ~ auflösende Bestimmung; **conscience** ~ Gewissensklausel; **contractual** ~ Vertragsklausel; **convertibility** ~ Konversions-, Umwandlungsklausel; **craft** ~ Leichterklausel; **currency** ~ Währungsklausel; **customary** ~ ortsübliche Klausel, Usancebestimmung; **defeasance** ~ Verwirkungsklausel; **latent defect** ~ Klausel über Haftung für versteckte Mängel; **depreciation** ~ Entwertungsklausel; **derogatory** ~ Abweichungsklausel; **determinative** ~ Aufhebungsklausel; **devaluation** ~ Abwertungsklausel; **deviation** ~ Wegeabweichungsklausel; **discretionary** ~ Kannvorschrift; **dispositive** ~ Verfügungsklausel; **dragnet** ~ *(tariff law)* Generalklausel; **earthquake** ~ Erdbebenklausel; **emergency** ~ Dringlichkeits-, Notklausel; **enacting** ~ Einführungsformel; **escalator** ~ Not-, Gleitklausel; **escape** ~ *(law of contract)* Sicherheits-, Rücktrittsklausel, *(international agreement)* Ausweichklausel, *(tariff commission, US)* Konzessions-, Rücknahmeklausel, *(trade union)* Austrittsklausel; **exemption** ~ *(Br.)* Ausnahme-, Freistellungsklausel; **fair wage** ~ Klausel zur Sicherstellung der Zahlung ausreichender Löhne; **final** ~ Schlußbestimmung; **first refusal** ~ *(US)* Vorkaufsklausel; **forfeiture** ~ Verwirkungs-, Verfallklausel; **fraudulent** ~ in arglistiger Absicht eingefügte Klausel; **free-of-capture and seizure** ~ Kriegsausschlußklausel; **full interest admitted** ~ Versicherungsinteresse anerkannt; **general** ~ Generalklausel; **gold** ~ Goldklausel; **hand-written** ~ handschriftlich eingefügte Klausel; **hardship** ~ Härteklausel; **hedge** ~ *(US)* Vorbehaltsklausel; **incontestable** ~ Unanfechtbarkeitsklausel; **inserted** ~ eingefügte Bestimmung; **institute cargo** ~es *(Br.)* Klauseln für Seewarenversicherung, zusätzliche Frachtdeckungsklauseln; **insurance** ~ Versicherungsklausel; **interpretation** ~ Auslegungsbestimmung; **iron-safe** ~ *(fire insurance)* Panzerschrankklausel; **ironclad** ~ unumgehbare Klausel; **jurisdictional** ~ Gerichtsstandsklausel; **let-out** ~ Ausweich-, Umgehungsklausel; **lightning** ~ Blitzschlagklausel; **loss payable** ~ Schadenersatzklausel; **memorandum** ~ *(marine insurance)* Freizeichnungsklausel; **most-favo(u)red-nation** ~ Meistbegünstigungsklausel; **national treatment** ~ Inlandsbehandlungsklausel; **negligence** ~ Freizeichnungsklausel für Fahrlässigkeit; **nonliability** ~ Haftungsausschlußbestimmung; **objects** ~ *(company)* Zweckbestimmungs-, Gewerbezweckklausel; **omnibus** ~ General-, Sammelklausel; **onerous** ~ lästige Bedingung; **optional** ~ Options-, Alternativ-, Fakultativklausel; **order** ~ Orderklausel; **overreaching** ~ Weitergeltungsklausel; **overriding** ~ Aufhebungsklausel; **participation** ~ Allbeteiligungsklausel; **penal** ~ Strafbestimmung; **policy proof of interest** ~ Versicherungsinteresse anerkannt; ~ **potestative** Rücktrittsklausel; **printed** ~ vorgedruckte Klausel; **prolongation** ~ Verlängerungsklausel; **protective** ~ Schutzbestimmung; **reciprocity** ~ Gegenseitigkeitsklausel; **reduced rate average** ~ Selbstbeteiligungsklausel bei verringerter Prämienzahlung; **relieving** ~ Entlastungsklausel; **renewal** ~ automatische Verlängerungsklausel; **repeating** ~ Aufhebungsklausel; **rescinding** ~ Aufhebungsklausel, -bestimmung; ~ **reserving errors** Irrtumsvorbehalt; ~ **reserving price** Preisvorbehaltsklausel; **restraint** ~ Wettbewerbsverbot; **restrictive** ~es einschränkende Bestimmungen, Modalitäten; **restriction** ~s Modalitäten, einschränkende Bestimmungen; **rise and fall** ~ Gleit-, Anpassungsklausel; **safety** ~ *(life insurance)* Nachschußklausel bei Versicherungsvereinen auf Gegenseitigkeit; **saving** ~ Ausnahmebestimmung, Vorbehaltsklausel; **secret** ~ Geheimbestimmung; **separability** ~ Teilgültigkeitsklausel; **shifting** ~

Ersatzvermächtnisklausel; **clear space** ~ Freiraumklausel; **free space** ~ Freiraumklausel; **special** ~s Sonderabreden; **standard average** ~ Unterversicherungsklausel; **standard warehouse-to-warehouse** ~ übliche Haus-zu-Hausklausel, Transportversicherungsklausel; **strike** ~ Streikklausel; **subordinate** ~ Nebensatz; **subrogation** ~ Rechtseintrittsklausel; **sue and labo(u)r** ~ *(insurance)* Selbstbehaltsklausel, *(mar.)* *(Br.)* Klausel über Schadensabwendung und Schadensminderung; **suicide** ~ *(life insurance)* Selbstmordklausel; **superimposed** ~ Zusatzklausel; **termination** ~ Bestimmung über die Vertragsdauer; **testamentary** ~ Testamentsbestimmung, -klausel; **theft** ~ Diebstahlklausel; **three-fourth loss** ~ Dreiviertelverlustklausel; **transshipment** ~ Transitklausel; **tying** ~ Preisbindungsklausel, *(antitrust law, US)* Kopplungsklausel; **understood** ~ selbstverständliche Bestimmung; **valuation** ~ Wertklausel; **admitted value** ~ Klausel Wert anerkannt; **violating law** ~ Haftungsausschluß bei Tod infolge Teilnahme an rechtswidrigen Unternehmungen; **war** ~ Kriegsklausel; **war-risk** ~ Kriegsrisikoklausel; **warranty** ~ Gewährleistungsklausel; ~ **by** ~ Punkt um Punkt; ~ **of accession** Beitrittsklausel; ~ **of accrual** Anwachsungsklausel; ~s **in a contract** Vertragsklauseln; ~ **of denunciation** *(international law)* Kündigungsklausel; ~ **stipulating jurisdiction** Gerichtsstandsklausel; ~s **of a law** Gesetzesbestimmungen; ~es **in a memorandum** Satzungsbestimmungen; ~ **not to order** Rektaklausel; ~ **of preemption** Vorkaufsklausel; ~s **governing a sale** Verkaufs-, Veräußerungsbedingungen, -bestimmungen; ~ **which cannot be upheld** unhaltbare Bestimmung; ~ **of warranty** Garantieklausel; ~ **of a will** Bestimmung eines Testaments; **to adhere strictly to a** ~ sich unnachgiebig an eine Bestimmung halten; **to come within the scope of (be covered by) a** ~ unter eine Bestimmung fallen; **to guard by** ~s verklausulieren, mit Klauseln absichern; **to have a** ~ **inserted** Klausel aufnehmen lassen; **to insert (put) a** ~ **into a contract** einem Vertrag eine Klausel beifügen; **to make a** ~ **void** Bestimmung annullieren; **to mortgage o. s. to a** ~ sich einer Bestimmung unterwerfen.

claustrophobia Platzangst.

clausula Urteilstenor.

clean einwandfrei, *(faultless)* fehlerfrei, schuldlos, *(impartial)* unbefangen, unparteiisch, *(piece of paper)* unbeschrieben, leer, *(precious stone)* makellos, rein; ~ *(v.)* säubern, reinigen; **to dry-**~ chemisch reinigen; ~ **down** gründlich reinigen; ~ **out** saubermachen; ~ **out a harbo(u)r** Hafen ausbaggern; ~ **house** *(US sl.)* reinen Tisch machen; ~ **s. o. out** *(sl.)* j. ausnehmen (schröpfen); ~ **from the shelves** Regal ausräumen; ~ **up** entrümpeln, *(fig.)* bereinigen, *(sl.)* absahnen, sich gesundstoßen; ~ **up a balance sheet** Bilanz bereinigen; ~ **up its own backyard** seinen eigenen Hinterhof in Ordnung bringen; ~ **up a city** mit der Korruption in einer Stadt aufräumen, Korruptionssumpf einer Stadt beseitigen; **to be** ~ keine Vorbehalte aufweisen; **to come** ~ *(sl.)* mit der vollen Wahrheit herausrücken, beichten, singen; **to go** ~ **off one's head** völlig durchdrehen; **to keep the party** ~ keine anstößigen Witze erzählen; ~ **acceptance** bedingungsloses (vorbehaltloses, unbeschränktes) Akzept; ~ **advertisement** einwandfreie (saubere) Werbung; ~ **air** saubere Luft; ~ **bill** Wechsel ohne Dokumentensicherung, *(bill of lading)* echtes Konnossement [ohne Einschränkungen (Giro, Vorbehalt)]; ~ **bill of health** einwandfreier Gesundheitspaß; ~ **bill of lading** reines (echtes) Konnossement [ohne Einschränkungen (Vorbehalt)]; ~ **bond** *(US)* Inhaberobligation ohne Giro (Einschränkungen); **to make a** ~ **breast of it** jem. reinen Wein einschenken; ~ **conscience** reines Gewissen; ~ **copy** Reinschrift; **to make a** ~ **copy** ins reine schreiben; ~ **credit** nicht dokumentarisch gesicherter Trassierungskredit; ~ **dollar** echter (unverfälschter) Dollar; ~ **draft** Tratte ohne Dokumente; ~ **evidence** widerspruchloses Beweismaterial; ~-**fingered** ehrlich; ~ **gold** reines Gold; ~ **hands** redliches Verhalten; **to come with** ~ **hands** reine Weste haben; ~-**handed** schuldlos, unbestochen; ~ **impression** Reindruck; ~-**lived** mit einwandfreiem Lebenswandel (sauberer Weste); ~ **living** geregeltes Leben; ~ **paper** sauberes Papier; ~ **patent** einwandfreies Patent; ~ **payment** Bezahlung gegen offene Rechnung; ~ [**printer's**] **proof** korrigierter Text, Reinabzug, Revisionsbogen, fehlerloser Korrekturbogen; ~ **receipt** vorbehaltlose Empfangsbestätigung; ~ **record** einwandfreie Vergangenheit; **to have a** ~ **record** nicht vorbestraft sein; ~ **sheet of paper** neues Blatt Papier; **to put some** ~ **sheets on a bed** Bett frisch beziehen; **to make a** ~ **sweep** in Bausch und Bogen verkaufen; ~ **ticket** Wahlzettel ohne Abänderungen; ~ **water** sauberes Wasser.

cleaned | out *(coll.)* pleite;
to be ~ out of s. th. völlig ausverkauft sein; **to have a suit ~** Anzug reinigen lassen.
cleaner *(charwoman, US)* Reinemache-, Putzfrau, *(machine)* Reinigungsmaschine.
cleaners Reinigungsanstalt;
window ~ Fensterputzer;
to send to the ~ zur Reinigung schicken, reinigen lassen; **to take s. o. to the ~** *(sl.)* j. total ausnehmen.
cleaning Reinigung, Reinemachen;
dry ~ chemische Reinigung; **heavy ~** Großreinemachen; **~ of streets** Straßenreinigung;
~ company Reinigungsanstalt; **~ woman** Putz-, Reinemachefrau.
cleanse *(v.)* reinigen, säubern.
cleansing department Straßenreinigungsbehörde.
cleanup Säuberung, Entgiftung, Reinigung, *(workshop)* Aufräumen des Arbeitsplatzes, *(US sl.)* Reibach;
environment ~ Säuberung der Stadtrandgebiete;
~ period Aufräumzeit.
clear deutlich, klar, bestimmt, übersichtlich, verständlich, *(cargo)* unbefrachtet, leer, ohne Ladung, *(claim)* unanfechtbar, *(free)* frei, offen, *(free from blame)* schuldlos, *(net)* netto, ohne Abzug, *(road)* offen, frei, *(unencumbered)* unbelastet, schuldenfrei;
all ~ *(signal)* Entwarnung; **as ~ as mud** *(fam.)* klar wie Kloßbrühe; **in ~** im Klartext;
~ of charges spesenfrei; **~ after debts paid** nach Abzug der Schulden; **~ of the enemy** feindfrei; **~ from faults** fehlerfrei; **~ from guilt** schuldlos; **~ of income tax** nach Abzug der Einkommensteuer; **~ of any suspicion** von jedem Verdacht befreit;
~ *(v.) (check)* kompensieren, im Verrechnungsverkehr abrechnen, *(computer)* löschen, *(debt)* bezahlen, begleichen, abführen, [Schulden] abtragen, glattstellen, *(declare innocent)* für einwandfrei befinden, rehabilitieren, entlasten, freisprechen, *(empty)* ausleeren, -räumen, *(gain)* Reingewinn erzielen, netto verdienen, *(pay dues)* ausklarieren, Zollformalitäten erledigen;
~ o. s. sich entlasten (rechtfertigen); **~ an account** Rechnung bezahlen; **~ for action** *(mil.)* gefechtsklar machen; **~ the air** klare Verhältnisse schaffen; **~ the balance** Saldo ausgleichen; **~ a bill** Wechsel einlösen; **~ a business** Geschäft ins reine bringen; **~ a canal from obstruction** Kanal räumen; **~ 15 per cent** *(sl.)* 15 Prozent Reingewinn erzielen; **~ o. s. of a charge** seine Unschuld nachweisen; **~ a check** *(US)* **(cheque,** *Br.)* Scheck verrechnen; **~ the coast** sich von der Küste fernhalten; **~ one's conscience** sein Gewissen entlasten; **~ the courtroom** Gerichtssaal räumen lassen; **~ o. s. of a crime** sich vom Verdacht eines Verbrechens reinigen; **~ s. o. of debt** jds. Schulden bezahlen; **~ the decks for action** Schiff zum Gefecht klarmachen; **~ one's desk** seinen Schreibtisch aufräumen; **~ the docket** anstehende Gerichtsfälle erledigen; **~ an estate** Besitz entschulden; **~ an examination paper** *(Br.)* alle Prüfungsfragen beantworten; **not to ~ one's expenses** nicht einmal die Unkosten decken; **~ a field of mines** Minen räumen; **~ goods** Waren verkaufen; **goods out of bond** Waren ausklarieren (verzollen); **~ goods at the customhouse** Waren verzollen; **~ the ground** Landstück urbar machen; **~ insanitary areas** Elendsgebiete beseitigen; **by instal(l)ments** in Raten abzahlen; **~ one's luggage through the customs** *(Br.)* sein Gepäck zollamtlich abfertigen lassen; **~ s. one's mind** jem. etw. klarmachen; **~ a mortgage** Hypothek tilgen; **~ a number** Landeerlaubnis (Sendeerlaubnis) erteilen; **~ an obstacle** Hindernis überwinden; **~ a port** aus dem Hafen auslaufen; **~ a profit** Reingewinn erzielen; **~ one's property of debts** seinen Grundbesitz von Belastungen frei machen; **~ one's quarantine** Quarantäne machen; **~ a room** Zimmer räumen; **~ a ship for action** Schiff gefechtsklar machen; **a ship of her cargo** Schiff entladen, Ladung löschen; **~ a shop** ausverkaufen; **~ slums** Elendsgebiete sanieren; **~ snow from the street** Schnee von der Straße räumen; **~ s. one's stock** jem. den ganzen Vorrat abkaufen; **~ old stock** Lager räumen; **~ the streets** Straßen säubern; **~ a thousand £ a year** netto 1000,- Pfund jährlich verdienen; **~ a title** Anspruch als berechtigt nachweisen.
clear away beseitigen, weg-, fortschaffen;
~ the debris from a town Stadt entrümpeln; **~ difficulties** Schwierigkeiten ausräumen.
clear *(v.)* **in (inwards)** *(ship)* einklarieren.
clear *(v.)* **off** wegbringen, fortschaffen, *(debt)* abtragen, bezahlen, tilgen, *(goods)* abstoßen, ausverkaufen;
~ arrears of work Rückstände aufarbeiten.

clear *(v.)* **out** Lager ausverkaufen, *(ship)* ausklarieren;
~ s. o. jem. sein letztes Geld kosten;
~ of the country Land verlassen, auswandern.
clear *(v.)* **up** aufräumen, in Ordnung bringen;
~ one's desk seinen Schreibtisch aufräumen; **~ a matter** Angelegenheit klären.
clear, to be ~ of s. o. j. bezahlt haben; **to be ~ about s. th.** sich über etw. klar sein; **to be ~ of s. th.** etw. überwunden haben; **to be ~ of suspicion** nicht mehr verdächtigt werden; **to get ~ of debt** seine Schulden bezahlen; **to get ~ of s. th.** etw. loswerden; **to keep ~ of s. th.** sich von etw. fernhalten; **to make one's meaning ~** seine Ansicht unmißverständlich zum Ausdruck bringen;
to give a ~ account genaue Darstellung geben; **~ amount** Nettobetrag; **~ and present danger** unmittelbar bevorstehende Gefahr; **~ annuity** steuerfreie Rente; **~ bills** bezahlte Rechnungen; **~ business day** Bankschaltertag; **~ case of fraud** glatter Schwindel (Betrugsfall); **~-channel station** Großsender; **the ~ contrary** das genaue Gegenteil; **~-cut** glasklar; **three ~ days** *(notice)* drei volle Tage; **~ estate** unbelastetes Grundstück; **~ evidence** einwandfreier Beweis; **~ and convincing evidence** überzeugender Beweis; **~ gain** Rein-, Nettogewinn; **to write a ~ hand** deutlich (saubere Handschrift) schreiben; **~ head** heller Kopf; **~-headed** scharfsinnig; **~ income** Nettoeinkommen; **~ judgment** gesundes Urteil; **~ loss** Nettoverlust; **~ majority** absolute Majorität (Mehrheit); **~ market price** angemessener Tagespreis; **~ market value** *(inheritance tax)* echter Verkehrswert; **~ ten minutes** volle zehn Minuten; **~ profit** Nettoeinkommen, Reinertrag; **~ and convincing proof** einwandfreier und klarer Beweis; **~ residue** reiner Nachlaß, Nachlaßrest; **~ road** freie Fahrt; **a ~ spot in a cloudy sky** *(fig.)* ein Lichtblick; **~ swing** *(US)* gute Gelegenheit; **~ title** unangreifbares Eigentum, unbestrittenes Recht, *(US, mining)* regelrechte Mutung; **~ annual value** Nettojahresertragswert, Jahresreingewinn; **~ water** offenes Fahrwasser.
clearance Aufräumungsarbeiten, *(airplane)* Abfertigung, Freigabe, *(bridge)* lichte Höhe, *(car)* Bodenfreiheit, *(cheque)* Ver-, Abrechnung, *(certificate of clearing)* Zollschein, *(city)* Sanierung, *(customs)* zollamtliche Abfertigung, Zollabfertigung, -erledigung, Verzollung, *(debts)* Zahlung, Begleichung, Tilgung, *(disencumbering)* Freimachen von grundbuchlichen Belastungen, *(dues)* Klarierungsgelder, *(of letter box)* Briefkastenleerung, *(mil.)* Freigabeerklärung, *(person)* Unbedenklichkeitserklärung, *(ship)* Klarierung, Auslaufgenehmigung, *(space)* Zwischenraum, *(of stock)* Lagerräumung, *(woods)* Abholzung, Lichtung;
customs ~ Zollabfertigung; **~ inwards** Ein[gangs]deklaration; **~ outwards** Aus[gangsde]klaration;
~ through the customs Zollabfertigung, Verzollung; **~ of goods** zollamtliche Abfertigung; **~ of goods from warehouse** Warenverzollung im Zollager; **~ of payments** Zahlungsausgleich;
to effect customs ~ Zollabfertigung vornehmen; **to have a favo(u)rable ~ over the road** *(car)* auf der Straße gut liegen, gute Straßenlage haben;
~ area *(Br.)* Sanierungs-, Abbruchgebiet; **~ card** *(employee, US)* Arbeitsbescheinigung, Dienstzeugnis; **~ certificate** Unbedenklichkeitsbescheinigung, *(ship)* Seebrief, *(customs)* Zollbescheinigung, Abfertigungsschein, Ausklarierungsschein; **~ charges** zollamtliche Abfertigungsgebühren, Zollabfertigungsgebühren; **~ chit** Laufzettel; **~ fee** [Zoll]abfertigungsgebühr; **~ item** Abrechnungsposten; **~ light** *(airplane)* seitliches Begrenzungslicht; **~ loan** Maklerdarlehn; **~ order** *(Br.)* Räumungsurteil; **~ papers** *(Br.)* Zoll-, Verzollungspapiere; **~ price** Ausverkaufspreis; **~ sale** Räumungsverkauf, [freiwilliger] Aus-, Inventur-, Totalausverkauf; **~ space** *(motor)* Verdichtungsraum.
cleared verzollt, *(sold out)* ausverkauft;
~ and customs duty paid verzollt und Zoll bezahlt;
~ goods verzollte Waren.
clearing *(agriculture)* urbar gemachtes Land, *(banking)* Ver-, Abrechnung, Abrechnungsverfahren, -verkehr, Giroverkehr, *(from charge)* Entlastung, Rechtfertigung, *(compensation)* Kompensation, *(customs)* Verzollung, *(removal)* Räumung, *(ship)* Ausklarierung, Auslaufen, *(woods)* Rodung, Ausholzung;
~s Verrechnungssumme, -masse;
bank ~s Bankabrechnung; **country ~** Abrechnung der Regionalbanken; **general ~** allgemeiner Giroverkehr, bargeldloser Zahlungsverkehr; **heavy ~** starker Giroverkehr; **interbank ~s** Lokalumschreibung; **international ~s** internationaler Verrechnungsverkehr; **local ~s** Ortsabrechnung; **town ~** *(Br.)* Giroverkehr innerhalb von Großlondon;

~ **of an account** Kontoglattstellung; ~ **of goods** *(liquidation)* [Total]ausverkauf; ~ **of slums** Sanierung von Elendsgebieten; **periodic ~ in accordance with tax regulations** periodische Sammelabrechnung im Sinne des Steuerrechtes;

~ **account** Verrechnungs-, Clearingkonto; ~ **advances** Clearing-, Verrechnungsvorschüsse; ~ **agent** Abnahmespediteur; ~ **agreement** Clearing-, Verrechnungsabkommen; ~ **area** Verrechnungsraum; ~ **asset** Verrechnungs-, Clearingguthaben; **bilateral ~ agreement (arrangement)** zweiseitiges Verrechnungsabkommen; ~ **balance** Verrechnungssaldo, -spitze; ~ **bank** *(Br.)* Giro-, Abrechnungsbank, dem Abrechnungsverkehr (Giroverkehr) angeschlossene Bank; ~ **bank customers** Girokundschaft; ~ **bill** Klarierungsbrief; ~ **business** Verrechnungs-, Abrechnungsverkehr; ~ **certificate** Auseinandersetzungszeugnis, *(customs)* Zollabfertigungsschein; ~ **cheque** *(Br.)* Verrechnungsscheck; ~ **claims** Clearing-, Verrechnungsforderungen; ~ **company** *(mil.)* Sanitätskompanie; ~ **country** am Verrechnungsabkommen beteiligtes Land, Verrechnungsland; ~ **currency** Verrechnungswährung; ~ **debt** Verrechnungs-, Clearingschuld; **--bank deposits** Giroeinlagen; ~ **department** Giroabteilung; ~ **form** Abrechnungsformular; ~ **hospital** *(Br.)* Feldlazarett; ~ **item** Abrechnungsposten; ~ **office** Konversionskasse; ~ **operation** Verrechnungs-, Abrechnungsverfahren; ~ **rate** Verrechnungskurs; ~ **ratio** Verrechnungsschlüssel; ~ **sheet** *(stock exchange)* Abrechnungsbogen; ~ **station** *(US)* Hauptverbandsplatz; ~ **system** Abrechnungs-, Clearingsystem, Abrechnungs-, Giroverkehr; ~ **transactions** Spitzengeschäfte, Verrechnungsgeschäft, -verkehr; ~ **transfer** Spitzenausgleich; ~ **unit** Verrechnungseinheit; ~ **voucher** *(Bank of England)* Verrechnungs-, Abrechnungsbeleg; ~ **works** Aufräumungsarbeiten.

clearinghouse Girostelle, Abrechnungs-, Girozentrale, Ausgleichskasse, Abrechnungsbörse, Clearinghaus;

~ **agent** Abrechnungsbank, Mitglied einer Clearingringvereinigung, die mit Nichtmitgliedern im Abrechnungsverkehr steht; ~ **association** Giroverband, Clearing[haus]vereinigung; ~ **balance** Gesamtbetrag der täglichen Debet- und Kreditsalden einer Girozentrale; ~ **bank return** [wöchentlicher] Ausweis (Wochenausweis) einer Girozentrale; ~ **business** Abrechnungsverkehr; ~ **certificate** Anerkennungsurkunde im Bankenverkehr; ~ **check** *(US)* **(cheque,** *Br.)* Clearinghaus-, Giro-, Verrechnungsscheck; ~ **exchange rates** Inkassotarif der dem Abrechnungsverkehr angeschlossenen Banken; ~ **facilities** Abrechnungserleichterungen; ~ **proof** Tagesausweis einer Verrechnungsstelle; ~ **settlement** Ausgleich des nach erfolgter Abrechnung im Verrechnungsverfahren verbleibenden Salden; ~ **statement** Wochenausweis einer Abrechnungsvereinigung (Girostelle); ~ **stock** im Clearingverkehr abgerechnete Aktie; ~ **system** Girosystem.

clearway *(Br.)* Halteverbotsstraße.

cleavage *(pol.)* Zersplitterung.

clemency Nachsicht, Milde, Gnade;

to show ~ begnadigen;

to refuse a ~ plea Gnadengesuch ablehnen.

clergy Geistlichkeit, Klerus.

clergyman Geistlicher, Priester;

beneficied ~ Pfründenbesitzer.

clerical kanzleimäßig;

~ **assistant** Bürohilfe, -hilfskraft; ~ **costs** Bürounkosten; ~ **equipment** *(US)* Bürobedarf, -einrichtung; ~ **error** Schreibfehler; ~ **force** Büropersonal, Schreibkräfte; ~ **misprision** Justizfehler; ~ **mistake** Schreibfehler; ~ **occupation** Bürobeschäftigung; ~ **officer** Büroangestellter; ~ **operations** Büroarbeit; ~ **position** Bürotätigkeit; ~ **procedure** Sekretariatssystem; ~ **records** Bürounterlagen; ~ **routine** Büroerfahrung; ~ **service** Bürodienst, -tätigkeit; ~ **staff** Büropersonal, Schreibkräfte; ~ **work** Schreib-, Büroarbeit; ~ **work measurement** Ermittlung der Büroarbeitszeit; ~ **worker** Büroangestellter; **-ℓ and Administrative Workers' Union** *(Br.)* [etwa] Angestelltengewerkschaft.

clericalism *(pol.)* Klerikalismus.

clerk *(Br.)* juristischer Angestellter, *(employee)* Büroangestellter, kaufmännischer Angestellter, Kontorist, *(office)* Sachbearbeiter, *(secretary)* Schreiber, Schriftführer, Kanzlist, Sekretär, *(US, shop assistant)* Handlungsgehilfe, Verkäufer, *(municipal officer)* Stadtsyndikus, *(officer in charge of records)* Urkundsbeamter;

the ~ *(urban and rural district, Br.)* Gemeindedirektor;

articled ~ Anwaltsgehilfe, Rechtspraktikant; **authorized ~** für Börsengeschäfte bevollmächtigter Angestellter; **bank ~** Bank-

angestellter; **barrister's ~** Bürovorsteher; **booking ~** Schalterbeamter; **bookkeeping ~** Buchhalter; **chief ~** Bürovorsteher, -chef; **city ~** *(Br.)* städtischer Beamter; **collecting ~** Inkassokommis; **confidential ~** [etwa] Prokurist; **conveyancing ~** Notariatsgehilfe; **copying ~** Expedient; **correspondence ~** Korrespondent; **counsel's ~** *(Br.)* Bürovorsteher; **entering ~** Buchhalter; **estimating ~** Kalkulator; **forwarding ~** Expedient; **government ~** Regierungsbeamter; **head ~** Bürovorsteher, -vorstand; **inferior ~** untergeordneter Angestellter; **junior ~** zweiter Buchhalter; **lady ~** Kontoristin; **managing ~** Disponent, Geschäftsführer, Prokurist, *(lawyer's office, Br.)* Bürovorsteher; **office ~** Büroangestellter; **parish ~** Gemeindesekretär; **polling ~** Wahlbeisitzer; **post-office ~** Postbeamter; **recording ~** Protokollführer; **salaried ~** Büroangestellter, -kraft; **senior ~** Hauptbuchhalter, *(lawyer's office)* Bürovorsteher; **shipping ~** Expedient, Leiter der Versandabteilung, *(US)* Spediteur; **signing ~** Zeichnungsberechtigter, [etwa] Handlungsbevollmächtigter; **solicitor's ~** *(Br.)* Kanzleikraft; **specialized ~** Fachkraft [im Büro]; **telegraph ~** Telegrafenbeamter; **time ~** Zeitkontrolleur; **town ~** *(Br.)* Stadtdirektor, *(US)* Stadtsyndikus; **travel(l)ing ~** Geschäftsreisender; **treasury ~** Finanzbeamter; **unsalaried ~** Volontär;

-ℓ of the Assembly *(US)* Parlamentssekretär; **-ℓ of Assize** *(Br.)* Gerichtsbeamter; ~ **of the Board of Works** Bauaufseher; ~ **to the council** Stadtsyndikus; ~ **of court** *(Br.)* Berichterstatter, Urkundsbeamter, Protokollführer, Gesschäftsstellenleiter, Justizsekretär; ~ **of the House of Commons** Verwaltungsdirektor des Unterhauses; ~ **of the market** Marktaufseher; ~ **of the treasury** Finanzbeamter; ~ **of the weather office** Wetteramtssprecher; ~ **of works** *(Br.)* Bauaufsicht, -leiter;

~ *(v.)* als Büroangestellter (Handlungsgehilfe) arbeiten, *(US)* als Verkäufer arbeiten;

~**'s fee** Schreibgebühr.

clerkship Schreiberstelle, Buchhalterposten.

clever, to be too ~ by half viel zu schlau sein.

cleverness, to prove one's seine Intelligenz beweisen.

clew *(US)* Leitfaden.

cliché *(Br.)* Druckstock, Klischee, *(fig.)* Gemeinplatz, abgedroschene Phrase;

~ **manufacturer** Klischeeanstalt; ~**-ridden** stereotyp.

clicker *(Br., sl.)* Anreißer, Kundenfänger.

cliency Klienten, Klientele.

client *(customer)* Kunde, Auftraggeber, *(factoring)* Anschlußfirma, *(of lawyer)* Mandant, Klient, *(of physician)* Patient, *(purchaser)* Abnehmer, *(stock market)* Auftraggeber, Besteller;

high-income ~ gut verdienender Klient; **industrial ~** Kunde aus der Industrie, industrieller Auftraggeber; **potential ~** potentieller Mandant; **solvent ~** zahlungsfähiger Mandant;

to accommodate a ~ einem Kunden einen Dienst erweisen; **to advise a ~** Mandanten beraten; **to alienate s. one's ~ from s. o.** jem. die Kundschaft abjagen;

~ **account** *(Br.)* Anderkonto; **solicitor's ~ account** *(Br.)* Anwaltsanderkonto; ~ **company** Kundenfirma, Kundin; ~ **contact** Kundenkontakte; ~ **list** Mandanten-, Kundenliste; ~ **money** Kundengelder; **to hold a ~'s money** *(Br.)* Anderkonto verwalten; ~ **relations** Kundenbeziehungen.

clientele Kundschaft, Klientele, Kundenkreis, *(of professional men)* Praxis, Mandantenstamm;

agricultural ~ ländliche Verbraucherschaft; **upper-income ~** gutverdienende Kundschaft.

cliff Abhang, Klippe, Felswand;

~ **dweller** *(US sl.)* Bewohner einer Mietskaserne; ~ **hanger** *(sl.)* aufregender Fortsetzungsroman, *(radio, sl.)* aufregende Fortsetzungssendung; ~ **hanger election** *(sl.)* aufregende Wahl.

climate Klima, *(company)* Betriebsklima, *(fig.)* Klima, Atmosphäre;

bracing ~ Reizklima; **business ~** Konjunkturklima; **favo(u)rable political ~** politische Konjunktur; **high-level ~** Höhenklima; **rank ~** üppiges Klima; **relaxing ~** Schonklima; **salubrious ~** gesundes Klima; **soft (warm) ~** mildes Klima; ~ **for investment** Anlagenklima; ~ **of opinions** allgemeine Lebenseinstellung; ~ **of professionalism** Berufsklima;

to be seasoned to a ~ an ein Klima gewöhnt sein;

~ **change** Klimaveränderung; **automatic ~ control** automatische Klimasteuerung, Klimaanlage.

climatic conditions Klimaverhältnisse.

climatologist Klimatologe.

climax Höhepunkt, Gipfel;

~ *(v.)* Höhepunkt erreichen;

to near the ~ sich dem Höhepunkt zu bewegen.

climb Aufstieg, Kletterpartie;
speedy ~ rasanter Aufstieg;
~ *(v.)* **down** *(fig.)* klein beigeben, Rückzieher machen, von seinem hohen Roß herunterkommen; ~ **out of** sich herausarbeiten aus; ~ **out of touch with reality** Boden der Wirklichkeit verlassen; ~ **to the top jobs** Spitzenstellungen erreichen.

climb-down Rückzug, Rückzieher.

climber Bergsteiger, *(coll.)* gesellschaftlicher Streber.

clinch Entscheidung, endgültige Regelung;
~ *(v.)* entscheiden, endgültig regeln;
~ **an argument** jeden Zweifel beseitigen, zwingend argumentieren.

clincher entscheidendes Argument;
the ~ absoluter Knüller;
~ **tyre** Wulstreifen.

cling *(v.) (fig.)* anhänglich sein;
~ **to s. th.** einer Sache anhaften; ~ **to the coast** *(ship)* von der Küste nicht freikommen; ~ **to the hope of being rescued** sich Hoffnungen auf eine Rettung machen; ~ **to s. o. like ivy** sich wie eine Klette an j. hängen; ~ **to an opinion** an einer Meinung festhalten; ~ **to one's possessions** an seinem Besitz hängen; ~ **to the side of the mind** im Unterbewußtsein haften bleiben.

clinic Krankenhaus, Klinik, *(customers)* Beratung und Aufklärung, *(US, seminar)* Fachseminar;
mobile ~ fahrbare Klinik; **privately owned** ~ Privatkrankenhaus, -klinik.

clinical | death klinischer Tod; ~ **picture** Krankheitsbild.

clinicar fahrbare Klinik.

clink *(sl.)* Knast, Kasten.

clip Heft-, Papierklammer, *(excerpt from film)* Einblendung anderer Filmaufnahmen, *(US)* schnelle Gangart;
~ *(v.)* schneiden, abtrennen, *(newspaper items)* ausschneiden;
~ **s. one's car** *(sl.)* j. anfahren; ~ **out of a newspaper** aus der Zeitung ausschneiden; ~ **papers together** Papiere zusammenheften; ~ **a ticket** Fahrkarte lochen; ~ **s. one's wings** jem. die Flügel beschneiden (stutzen);
~ **sheet** Klappentext, Waschzettel.

clipboard Manuskripthalter.

clipper Schnelldampfer, *(airplane)* Verkehrsflugzeug, *(sl.)* tolle Sache;
newspaper ~ Ausschnittsbüro, -dienst.

clippie Straßenbahn-, Busschaffner.

clipping *(of coupons)* Abtrennung, *(newspaper)* Zeitungsausschnitt;
~ **bureau** *(US)* Korrespondenz-, Ausschneidebüro; ~ **service** *(US)* Zeitungsausschnittdienst.

cloak *(fig.)* Bemäntelung, Deckmantel;
under the ~ unter dem Vorwand;
~ *(v.)* verschleiern, bemänteln;
to use patriotism as ~ **for violence** Gewalttätigkeiten mit Vaterlandsliebe bemänteln.

cloakroom Garderobenablage, *(railway)* Gepäck[aufbewahrungs]raum;
ladies' ~ *(Br.)* Damentoilette;
to leave one's luggage at the ~ *(Br.)* sein Gepäck aufbewahren lassen; **to leave one's things in the** ~ seine Garderobe abgeben;
~ **attendant** Garderobenfrau, *(railway)* Gepäckaufbewahrungsbeamter; ~ **facilities** Ankleideräume; ~ **fee** Aufbewahrungsgebühr; ~ **ticket** Gepäckaufbewahrungsschein.

clock [Stand, Turm, Wand]uhr, *(machine)* Kontrolluhr, *(taxi)* Fahrpreisanzeiger;
like one o' ~ wie verrückt;
speaking ~ telefonische Zeitansage; **time** ~ Kontroll-, Stechuhr;
~ *(v.)* Arbeitszeit registrieren;
~ **in** Arbeitsbeginn registrieren, zum Dienst antreten, stempeln; ~ **out** Arbeitsschluß registrieren;
to punch the ~ *(US)* zum Dienst antreten, Arbeitsbeginn registrieren; **to put the** ~ **back** Uhr zurückstellen, *(fig.)* reaktionäre Maßnahmen ergreifen;
~ **card** Stechkarte; ~ **hours** *(time study)* Ist-Zeit; ~ **stamp** *(US)* Eingangsstempel.

clockwise im Uhrzeigersinn.

clockwork, like wie geölt (am Schnürchen);
~ **railway** Spielzeugeisenbahn.

clodhopper Hinterwäldler.

clog Hemmnis, Hindernis;
~ **on the equity of redemption** *(Br.)* Behinderung des Pfandauslösungsrechtes;
~ *(v.)* Pfandauslösung behindern, Ablösungsrecht ausschließen;

~ **one's memory with useless facts** sein Gedächtnis mit sinnlosen Einzelheiten belasten; ~ **the redemption** *(Br.)* Pfandauslösung durch Vereinbarung ausschließen.

close *(accounting)* Abschluß, *(last element of advertising)* Anzeigenschluß, abschließender Kaufappell, *(conclusion)* Schluß, Ende, *(plot of land)* abgeschlossener Grundbesitz;
at the ~ **of the financial period** am Schluß der Rechnungsperiode; **at the** ~ **of the year** am Jahresende; **towards the** ~ **of the century** am Ausgang des Jahrhunderts;
books ~ Abschluß der Effektentransferbücher einer Gesellschaft; **complementary** ~ Schlußformel;
~**-down** Betriebsstillegung; ~**-up** eingehende Untersuchung, *(film, photo)* Großaufnahme;
~ **of argument** Schluß der Beweisführung; ~ **of the case** Beendigung des Klagevortrages; ~ **of exchange** Börsenschluß; ~ **of a meeting** Sitzungsschluß; ~ **of navigation** Schiffahrtssperre; ~ **of pleadings** Beendigung der Einreichung von Klagesätzen; ~ **of the term** Semesterschluß; ~ **of the year** Jahresschluß;
~ *(v.)* schließen, beenden, *(account, debate)* [ab]schließen, *(mortgage, US coll.)* für verfallen erklären, *(source of income)* versiegen;
~ **with s. o.** mit jem. einverstanden sein; ~ **at 185 1/2 against 185** *(stock exchange)* mit 185 1/2 gegen 185 schließen; ~ **an account** Konto abschließen; ~ **a bankruptcy** Konkursverfahren einstellen; ~ **a bargain** Geschäft abschließen; ~ **the books** Bücher abschließen; ~ **a case** Beweisaufnahme schließen; ~ **a chapter** Kapitel abschließen; ~ **a contract** Vertrag abschließen; ~ **the court** Verhandlung schließen; ~ **a deal** Abschluß tätigen; ~ **dearer** *(stock exchange)* bei Börsenschluß höher notieren; ~ **a debate (discussion)** Debatte (Aussprache) schließen (beenden); ~ **its doors for reasons of economy** Betrieb aufgrund von Sparsamkeitsmaßnahmen schließen; ~ **down** *(factory)* Betrieb schließen (stillegen), *(stop work)* Schicht machen; ~ **down a branch office** Filiale eingehen lassen; ~ **down a factory because of lack of orders** Fabrik wegen Auftragsmangels stillegen; ~ **down for holidays** Betriebsferien machen; ~ **down temporarily** Betrieb vorübergehend einstellen; ~ **firm** *(stock exchange)* fest schließen; ~ **a gap** Lücke schließen; ~ **higher in active trading** in gängigen Aktien höhere Schlußkurse erzielen; ~ **in** einfrieden, -einschließen; ~ **in on s. o.** j. von allen Seiten bedrängen; ~ **with the land** *(ship)* sich dem Land nähern; ~ **a line** *(railway)* Betrieb auf einer Strecke einstellen; ~ **upon measures** sich über zu ergreifende Maßnahmen (Maßregeln) einigen; ~ **a meeting** Sitzung schließen (beenden); ~ **for heavy motor traffic** für Lastwagenverkehr sperren; ~ **off** Rechnung abschließen; ~ **off to the public** dem öffentlichen Zugang verschließen; ~ **with an offer** Anerbieten annehmen; ~ **out** *(US)* Ausverkauf durchführen; ~ **the proceedings** Verfahren einstellen; ~ **with a better result** mit einem besseren Ergebnis abschließen; ~ **the rights** urheberrechtlich geschütztes Material für Werbezwecke erwerben; ~ **a road** Straße sperren; ~ **a submission list** Subskriptionsliste schließen; ~ **temporarily** Betrieb vorübergehend einstellen (schließen); ~ **up** Reihen schließen, *(print.)* [Satz] anschließen, kompresser setzen; ~ **2-up** *(stock exchange)* bei Börsenschluß 2 Shilling höher stehen; ~ **up shop** Geschäft schließen; ~ **a year in the red** Jahr mit Verlust abschließen, Verlustabschluß tätigen;
to be drawing to a ~ vor dem Abschluß stehen; **to bring a letter to a** ~ Brief abschließen; **to draw to a** ~ zum Ende kommen, sich dem Ende zuneigen; **to keep o. s.** ~ sich abseits halten; **to keep** ~ **for a time** zeitweilig untertauchen; **to live** ~ sparsam leben; **to write an effective** ~ eindrucksvollen Briefabschluß finden;
~ *(a.)* ab-, eingeschlossen, *(capital)* knapp, *(confined)* streng bewacht, *(exclusive)* nicht öffentlich, exklusiv, *(narrow)* eng, begrenzt, *(retired)* zurückgezogen, *(stock exchange)* Schluß fest;
~ **to the market** marktnahe; ~ **set** kompreß;
~ **air support** Nahunterstützung durch Flugzeuge, Nahkampfunterstützung; ~ **argument** lückenloser Beweis; ~ **attack** Nahangriff; ~ **attention** gespannte Aufmerksamkeit; ~ **betting** gleiche Chancen; ~ **blockade** scharf durchgeführte (strenge) Blockade; ~ **call** knappes Entkommen, Beinahe-Unfall; ~ **check** genaue Überprüfung; ~ **column** *(mil.)* geschlossene Marschkolonne; ~ **combat** *(mil.)* Nahkampf; ~ **company** *(Br.)* Gesellschaft mit beschränktem Mitgliederkreis, [etwa] Familiengesellschaft; ~ **confinement** strenge Haft; ~ **copy** wortgetreue Kopie; ~ **corporation** *(US)* [etwa] Gesellschaft mit beschränkter Haftung; ~ **correspondence** vertraulicher Briefwechsel; ~ **customer** verschlossener Mensch; ~ **debate** eifrige Diskussion; ~**-down** Betriebsstillegung; ~ **election** knappes Wahlergebnis; ~ **escape** knappes Entkommen; ~ **friend** enger

Freund; ~ **hand** *(fig.)* Knicker; ~ **interval** *(mil.)* Tuchfühlung; ~ **investigation** eingehende (gründliche) Untersuchung; ~ **jail execution** Strafvollzug im Zuchthaus; ~-**knit combination** *(US)* Zusammenschluß; ~ **money** *(capital market)* teures Geld; ~ **observer** scharfer Beobachter; **to advance in** ~ **order** geschlossen vorgehen; ~ **port** Binnenhafen; ~ **price** scharf kalkulierter Preis; ~ **prisoner** streng bewachter Gefangener; **in** ~ **proximity** in nächster Nähe; **to live in** ~ **quarters** eng zusammengepfercht wohnen; ~ **ranks** dichte Reihen; ~ **reasoning** bündige (lücken-lose) Beweisführung; ~ **relations** nahe (enge) Verwandte; ~ **scholarship** *(Br.)* nur an bestimmte Kandidaten verteiltes Stipendium; ~ **season** Schonzeit; ~ **shave** Kahlrasur; *(coll.)* knappes Entkommen; **to have a** ~ **shave** mit knapper Not davonkommen; **to make a** ~ **study of s. th.** etw. eingehend studieren; ~ **style** knapper Stil; ~ **touch** *(mil.)* Tuchfühlung; ~ **translation** wortgetreue Übersetzung; ~-**up** *(motion picture)* Groß-, Nahaufnahme; ~ **vote** knappes Wahlergebnis; ~ **work** anhaltende Arbeit[en].

closed geschlossen;
road ~ Straße gesperrt; **temporarily** ~ vorübergehend geschlossen;
~ **for a half-holiday** am Nachmittag geschlossen; ~ **down for lack of orders** wegen Auftragsmangels geschlossen; ~ **on one side** *(road)* halbseitig gesperrt; ~ **for the summer** im Sommer geschlossen; ~ **today** heute Betriebsruhe; ~ **for heavy motor traffic** für Lastwagen gesperrt; ~ **for vehicles** für Fahrzeuge gesperrt;
to be ~ **by the statute of limitations** *(expenses)* steuerlich endgültig anerkannt sein; **to have** ~ **for the summer** im Sommer geschlossen sein;
~ **account** abgeschlossenes Konto, *(fig.)* endgültig abgeschlossene Angelegenheit; ~ **area** Sperrgebiet; ~ **book** *(fig.)* Buch mit sieben Siegeln; ~ **circuit** Ruhestromkreis, *(television)* Kabelfernsehsystem für bestimmte Teilnehmer; ~-**circuit current** Ruhestrom; ~-**circuit system** internes Fernsehnetz; ~-**circuit telecast** *(television)* betriebliche Fernsehsendung, Betriebsfernsehen; ~ **column** *(mil.)* aufgeschlossene Marschkolonne; ~ **court** unter Ausschluß der Öffentlichkeit; **to sit in** ~ **court** unter Ausschluß der Öffentlichkeit tagen; ~ **door** *(traffic policy)* Tarifbegünstigung; **to sit behind** ~ **doors** geheime Beratung abhalten; ~ **economy** Volkswirtschaft ohne Außenhandel.

closed-end | account *(depreciation method)* geschlossener Bestand; ~ **investment company** *(US)* Kapitalanlagegesellschaft mit geschlossenem Anlagefonds; ~ **fund** *(US)* Investmentfonds mit begrenzter Emissionshöhe; ~ **mortgage** von der Höhe der Forderung auf dem Umfang des belasteten Grundstücks unabhängige Hypothek; ~ **question** Frage mit vorgegebenen Antwortmöglichkeiten.

closed | freight car geschlossener Güterwagen; ~ **indent** Warenbestellung eines bestimmten Markenerzeugnisses; ~ **issue** *(capital market)* unveränderliche Anleihe; ~-**mindedness** Dogmatismus; ~ **mortgage** *(coll., US)* nicht aufstockungsfähige Hypothek, dem Betrag nach unveränderliche Hypothek; ~ **professions** gesperrte Berufszweige; ~ **sea** *(international law)* zum Hoheitsgebiet gehörige Gewässer; ~ **season** *(hunting)* Schonzeit; ~ **session** nichtöffentliche Sitzung, Sitzung unter Ausschluß der Öffentlichkeit; **to order the case to be heard in** ~ **session** Öffentlichkeit ausschließen; **to hear a case in** ~ **session** unter Ausschluß der Öffentlichkeit verhandeln; ~ **shop** gewerkschaftspflichtiger Betrieb; ~-**shop agreement** Gewerkschaftsmonopolabkommen, Gewerkschaftszugehörigkeit voraussetzender Arbeitsvertrag; ~ **union** Gewerkschaft mit Mitgliedersperre.

closely | spaced kompreß;
to go ~ **into a matter** sich eingehend mit einer Sache beschäftigen; **to translate** ~ genau übersetzen.

closeness Genauigkeit, *(parsimony)* Knickrigkeit, Geiz;
~ **in estimation** Präzision einer Schätzung; ~ **to life** Lebensnähe; ~ **of relationship** Nähe der Verwandtschaft; ~ **of a translation** Genauigkeit einer Übersetzung; ~ **of a vote** annähernde Stimmengleichheit, geringe Stimmendifferenz.

closeout *(US, clearance sale)* Teilausverkauf, *(dismissal)* Entlassung;
storage ~ Lagerraum;
~ **sale** Ausverkauf wegen Geschäftsaufgabe, Räumungsverkauf.

closer Beschließer;
to be much ~ **to s. o.** jem. näher stehen.

closet Arbeitszimmer, Kabinett, Privatraum, *(US)* Abstellkammer;
water ~ Toilette;

~ *(a.)* privat, geheim, vertraulich;
~ *(v.)* einschließen, sicher verwahren;
to be ~**ed with s. o.** mit jem. eine vertrauliche Unterredung haben.

closing *(advertising)* Anzeigenschluß, *(account)* [Ab]schluß, *(broadcasting)* Werbefunkschluß, *(contract)* Abschlußverhandlung, *(shutting)* Schließung, Stillegung, *(termination)* Beendigung;
on ~ **our books** bei Abschluß unserer Bücher; **owing to the** ~ **of business** wegen Geschäftsaufgabe;
earlier ~ früherer Ladenschluß; **fiscal** ~ Rechnungsabschluß; **half-day** ~ *(Br.)* früher Ladenschluß; **real estate** ~ Abschlußformalitäten beim Grundstückskauf; **Saturday** ~ geschäftsfreier Sonnabend; **steady** ~ *(stock exchange)* fester Schluß; **Sunday** ~ Sonntagsruhe;
~ **an account** Rechnungsabschluß; ~ **of bankruptcy proceedings** Einstellung des Konkursverfahrens; ~ **of the books** Bücherabschluß; ~ **for cargo** Verladeschluß; ~ **of contract** Vertragsabschluß; ~ **of a deal** Geschäftsabschluß; ~ **of the exchange** Börsenschluß; ~ **down of a factory** Betriebsstillegung; ~ **of the frontier** Grenzschließung; ~ **of the polls** Beendigung des Wahlvorgangs; ~ **of a port** Hafensperre, -schließung; ~ **in the red** *(US coll.)* Verlustabschluß; ~ **of a road** Straßenabsperrung; ~ **the sale** Verkaufsabschluß; ~ **of a speculative position** *(stock exchange)* Glattstellung; ~ **of the stock exchange** Börsenschluß; ~ **of subscription** Zeichnungsschluß; ~ **of title** *(law, US)* Auflassung; ~ **of transfer** Schließung der Aktienumschreibebücher [vor der Generalversammlung];
to be ~ **down** schließen, zumachen, *(plant holiday)* geschlossen Ferien machen; **to bring the** ~ **of the gold window to private people** Goldverkäufe an die private Kundschaft einstellen;
~ **address** Schlußplädoyer; ~ **agent** Abschlußagent; ~ **agreement** *(US)* schriftliche Abschlußvereinbarung; ~ **bid** Höchstgebot, letztes Gebot; ~ **ceremony** Schlußfeier; ~ **date** *(advertising)* Anzeigenschluß, *(bank account)* Abschlußtag, *(loan)* Abschlußtermin, *(tender)* Ausschreibungsschluß; ~ **date (day) for application** letzter Anmeldetag, Anmeldefrist, letzter Bewerbungstermin; **early** ~ **day** geschäftsfreier Nachmittag, Nachmittagsschluß der Geschäfte; **late** ~ **day** Spätschließungstag; ~ **days of the year** letzte Tage des Jahres; ~ **department** *(real estate business)* Abschlußabteilung; ~-**down sale** *(US)* Räumungsschlußverkauf; ~ **entry** Abschlußbuchung; ~ **fees** Abschlußgebühren; ~ **hour** *(advertising)* Anzeigenschluß, *(shop)* Geschäftsschluß, Ladenschlußzeit; **official** ~ **hours** Geschäftsschluß, Dienstschluß; ~ **inventory** Schlußbestand, -inventur; ~ **item** Abschlußposten; ~-**out sale** Räumungsschlußverkauf; ~ **paragraph** Schlußabsatz; ~ **price** *(stock exchange)* Schlußkurs; ~ **quotation** Börsenschlußkurs, Schlußnotierung; ~ **rate** *(foreign exchange)* Schlußkurs; ~ **remarks** Schlußbemerkungen; ~ **scene** *(theater)* Schlußszene; ~ **session** Abschlußsitzung, Schlußsitzung; ~ **speech** Abschlußansprache; ~ **statement** Endabrechnung, Abschlußabrechnung; ~ **stock** Schlußbestand; ~ **time** Laden-, Geschäftsschluß, Feierabend, *(bank)* Schalterschluß, *(restaurant)* Polizeistunde; ~ **trial balance** bereinigte Probebilanz; ~ **words** Schlußworte; ~ **year** letztes Jahr.

closure Schließung, *(parl.)* Schluß der Debatte;
kangaroo ~ Abkürzung der Debatte auf bestimmte Punkte;
~ **for cargo** Verladeschluß; ~ **of a debate** Schluß einer Diskussion, Abschließen einer Debatte; ~ **of the frontier** Abriegelung der Grenze; ~ **of an antique plant** Stillegung (Schließung) eines veralteten Betriebs;
~ *(v.) (Br.)* Debatte zum Abschluß bringen, Diskussion schließen, Wort entziehen;
~ **a bill by compartments** Gesetzesvorlage stückweise erledigen; ~ **the debate** Debatte zum Abschluß bringen;
to apply the ~ **of a debate** Debatte schließen; **to demand the** ~ **of the debate** Antrag auf Schluß der Debatte stellen; **to move the** ~ *(parl.)* Schluß der Debatte beantragen.

cloth Tuch, Stoff, *(book)* Leinwand, Leinen;
bound in ~ in Leinen;
~ **binding** Leinenband; ~ **board** Leinwanddecke; ~ **sausage** Polsterrolle.

clothe *(v.)* **with powers** mit Vollmachten ausstatten.

clothes Kleider, Kleidung;
in plain ~ in Zivil;
castoff ~ ausrangierte Kleidungsstücke; **classic** ~ konventionelle Kleidung; **off-the-peg** ~ fertige Kleider, Fertigkleidung; **old** ~ abgetragene Kleider; **proper** ~ korrekte Kleidung; **ready-made (store)** ~ fertige Kleider;
~ **proper to such an occasion** für ein derartiges Ereignis korrekte Kleidung;

to be still in one's swaddling ~ *(fig.)* noch in den Anfängen stecken;

~ **drier** Wäschetrockner; ~ **horse** Wäsche-, Trockengestell; ~ **line** Wäscheleine; ~ **peg (pin)** Wäscheklammer; ~ **press** Kleiderschrank; ~ **rack (tree)** Kleiderständer.

clothing Bekleidungsgegenstände, Kleidung;

~ **allowance** Kleidergeld, -zulage; ~ **book** Kleiderkarte; ~ **coupon** Textilpunkt, Kleiderkartenabschnitt; ~ **industry** Bekleidungsindustrie; ~ **manufacture** Bekleidungsgewerbe; ~ **ration book** Kleiderkarte; ~ **store** *(US)* [Herren]bekleidungsgeschäft.

cloture *(US)* Schluß der Debatte;

to move ~ Antrag auf Schluß der Debatte stellen.

cloud Wolke, Bewölkung, *(dark spot)* Fehler, dunkler Fleck [im Edelstein];

in the ~**s** in Gedanken vertieft; **no** ~**s** wolkenfrei; **under a** ~ unter dem Schatten eines Verdachts, *(in disgrace)* in Ungnade; ~ **of dust** Staubwolke; ~ **on title** *(US)* Rechtsmangel; ~**s of war** Kriegswolken;

~ *(v.)* **s. one's mind** jds. Gemüt verdunkeln;
to be in the ~**s** in höheren Regionen schweben; **to be floating on the** ~**s** sich wie im siebenten Himmel fühlen; **to cast a** ~ **on s. th.** Schatten auf etw. werfen;

~ **bank** Wolkenbank; ~ **base** Wolkenzentrum; ~ **burst** Wolkenbruch; ~ **cover** Wolkendecke; ♀ **-Cuckoo-Land** Wolkenkuckuckheim; ~ **map** Wolkenkarte; ~ **top** Wolkenobergrenze.

clouding of consciousness Bewußtseinstrübung.

cloudland Wolkenkuckucksheim.

clouter *(sl.)* Autodieb.

clover, to be in im Wohlstand leben.

cloverleaf *(highway)* Kleeblatt[konstruktion].

club Klub, Verein, geschlossene Gesellschaft;

benefit ~ Unterstützungs-, Hilfsverein; **flagship** ~ führender Verein; **incorporated (registered)** ~ eingetragener (rechtsfähiger) Verein; **select** ~ exklusiver Klub; **service** ~ gemeinnütziger Verein; **unincorporated members'** ~ nicht rechtsfähiger Verein; **workman's** ~ Arbeiterverein;

~ *(v.)* sich zu einem Verein zusammenschließen;
~ **efforts** sich gemeinsam bemühen; ~ **together** [für gemeinsame Zwecke] zusammensteuern, -legen;
to enrol as a member of a ~ als Vereinsmitglied aufnehmen; **to get into a** ~ einem Verein beitreten, Vereinsmitglied werden; **to join the** ~ **of the handouts** zum Almosenempfänger werden; **to suspend a member of a** ~ Vereinsmitglied vorübergehend ausschließen;

~ **account** Vereinskonto; ~ **activities** Vereinstätigkeit; ~ **book** Mitgliederliste; ~ **building** Klubhaus, Vereinsgebäude; ~ **car** *(railroad, US)* Salonwagen; ~ **chit** abgezeichneter Ausgabenbeleg, Bon; ~ **due (fee)** Vereinsbeitrag; ~ **employees** Klubpersonal; ~ **etiquette** Klub-, Vereinszeremoniell; ~ **facilities** Klubeinrichtungen; ~ **fund** Vereinsvermögen; ~ **manager** Vereins-, Klubsekretär; ~ **membership** Klub-, Vereinsmitgliedschaft; ~ **money** Klub-, Vereinsbeitrag; ~ **night** Klubabend; ~ **officer** Vereinsfunktionär; ~ **premises** Klub-, Vereinsgrundstück; ~ **rules** Vereinssatzung; ~ **staff** Klubpersonal; ~ **subscription** Vereins-, Klub-, Mitgliedsbeitrag.

clubbiness *(fig.)* innere Verbundenheit.

clubbing offer *(US, advertising)* Anzeigenrabatt beim Belegen mehrerer Zeitschriften.

clubfellow Klub-, Vereinsmitglied.

clubhouse Klub-, Vereinshaus.

clubland *(London)* Klubviertel.

clublaw Vereinsrecht, *(lynch law)* Faustrecht, Lynchjustiz.

clubmate Klub-, Vereinsmitglied.

clubmobile Kantinenfahrzeug.

clubroom Vereins-, Klubzimmer.

clue Anhaltspunkt, Spur, Fingerzeig, *(novel)* Leitfaden, *(riddle)* Schlüssel, Lösungshilfe;

~**s given below** untenstehende Anhaltspunkte;
to find a ~ auf die Spur kommen; **to have no** ~ *(coll.)* keinen Schimmer haben; **to offer a** ~ **for an explanation** Anhaltspunkt für eine Erklärung abgeben.

clumsy | style schwerfälliger Stil; ~ **workman** ungeschickter Arbeiter.

cluster *(parachute)* Mehrfachfallschirm, *(persons)* Haufen, Menge, Anhäufung, Schwarm;

~ **of islands** Inselgruppe; ~ **of spectators** Zuschauermenge;
~ *(v.)* **around** herumstehen; ~ **around the 20 per cent mark** sich fast einheitlich um die 20% Grenze bewegen;
~ **sampling** *(statistics)* Klumpenauswahlverfahren.

clustering analysis Sammel-, Gruppenanalyse.

clutch [Schalt]kupplung, Kupplungshebel, *(fig.)* Umklammerung;

the ~**es of the moneylenders** die gierigen Hände der Geldverleiher; ~ **at popularity** Popularitätshascherei;
~ *(v.)* kuppeln;
~ **at a straw** nach einem Strohhalm greifen;
to fall into s. one's ~**es** jem. in die Hände fallen; **to let in the** ~ Kupplung einschalten; **to stay out of the** ~**es of major distributors** *(film business)* sich dem Würgegriff des Filmverleihgeschäfts entziehen;

~ **disk** Kupplungsscheibe; ~ **facing (lining)** Kupplungsbelag; ~ **pedal** Kupplungspedal; ~ **plate** Kupplungsscheibe.

clutter Durcheinander, Wirrwarr.

co-author Mitverfasser.

co-director Vorstandskollege.

co-driver Beifahrer.

co-star *(v.)* gemeinsam auftreten.

coach Kutsche, [Reise]omnibus, Autobus, *(body of car)* Karosserie, *(railway carriage, Br.)* Eisenbahnwagen, *(training)* Repetitor, Einpauker, *(US, sedan)* Limousine;

air-conditioned ~ klimatisierter Reiseomnibus; **motor** ~ Omnibus für Fernfahrer; **slow** ~ *(fig.)* Umstandskrämer; **state** ~ Staatskutsche;
~**-and-four** Vierspänner;
~ *(v.)* als Einpauker (Repetitor) tätig sein, einpauken, trainieren, Nachhilfeunterricht geben;
~ **s. o. for an examination** j. auf eine Prüfung vorbereiten;
to go to a ~ Nachhilfeunterricht nehmen; **to travel by** ~ Reiseomnibus benutzen;

~ **box** Kutschersitz; ~ **class** *(US)* Touristenklasse; ~ **driver** Kutscher; ~ **fare** Omnibusfahrschein; ~ **horse** Kutschpferd; ~ **house** Wagenschuppen, Remise; ~ **party** Reisegesellschaft; ~ **station** Omnibusbahnhof; ~ **tour** Omnibusreise; ~ **yard** *(Br.)* Verschiebebahnhof für Personenwagen.

coachbuilder Karosseriebauer.

coachbuilding Karosseriebau.

coacher Einpauker, Repetitor.

coaching Einpauken, Repetitortätigkeit, Nachhilfeunterricht, -stunden, Privatunterricht;

~ **fee** Stundengeld; ~ **traffic** *(railway, Br.)* Personenverkehr.

coachman Kutscher.

coachwork Karosseriearbeit.

coaction Zusammenwirken.

coadjutant Beistand.

coadjutor Gehilfe, Mitarbeiter, Assistent.

coadministration gemeinsame Verwaltung.

coadministrator Mitdirektor.

coadventure gemeinsame Spekulation.

coal Kohle;

anthracite ~ Anthrazitkohle; **cob** ~ Nußkohle **house** ~ Hausbrandkohle; **coking** ~ Kokskohle; **lean** ~ arme (magere) Kohle; **live** ~**s** glühende Kohlen; **pit** ~ Steinkohle;
~ *(v.)* Kohlen einnehmen;
to call s. o. over the ~**s** jem. die Hölle heiß machen; **to carry** ~**s to Newcastle** Eulen nach Athen tragen; **to haul s. o. over the** ~**s** jem. eins aufs Dach geben, jem. aufs Dach steigen; **to heap** ~**s of fire on s. one's head** glühende Kohlen auf jds. Haupt sammeln; **to lay in** ~ sich mit Kohlen eindecken; **to pile more** ~ **on** Kohlen nachlegen; **to recover byproducts from** ~ Kohlenreprodukte gewinnen;

~ **area** Kohlenrevier; **to develop a** ~ **area** Kohlenschätze eines Gebiets erschließen; ~ **bank** *(US)* Kohlenlager, -halde, -flöz; ~ **bed** Kohlenflöz; ~ **board** *(Br.)* Kohlenbehörde; ~ **bunker** Kohlenbunker; ~ **car** *(US, railroad)* Kohlenwagen; ~ **and Steel Community** Montanunion; ~ **consumption** Kohlenverbrauch; ~ **contractor** Kohlenlieferant; ~ **control** Kohlebewirtschaftung; ~**'s cost advantages** Kostenvorteile bei der Verwendung von Kohle; ~ **crisis** Kohlenkrise; **not to expect** ~ **demands from the utilities** nicht mit größeren Kohlenanforderungen von den Versorgungsbetrieben rechnen; ~ **deposit** Kohlenvorkommen; ~ **depot** Kohlenlager; ~ **export** Kohlenausfuhr; **to be at the** ~ **face** vor Ort sein; ~ **factor** *(Br.)* Kohlenhändler; ~ **famine** Kohlenmangel; ~ **field** Kohlenrevier, -distrikt; **to work a** ~ **field** Kohlenfeld ausbeuten; ~**-fired** kohlenbeheizt; ~ **gas** Kohlengas; ~ **glut** Kohlenüberhang; ~ **hawker** Kohlenhändler; ~ **heaver** Kohlenträger; ~ **industry** Kohlenindustrie; ~ **and steel industry** Montanindustrie; ~ **levy** Kohlenabgabe; ~ **merchant** Kohlenhändler; ~ **mine** Kohlenzeche, -bergwerk; ~ **miner** Gruben-, Bergarbeiter, Kumpel; ~ **mines nationalization** *(Br.)* Bergbausozialisierung; ~ **mining** Kohlenbergbau; ~**-mining district** Kohlenrevier; ~**-mining industry** Kohlenbergbau; ~

operator Zecheneigentümer; ~ **output** Kohlenförderung; ~ **output per man per day** tägliche Kohlenförderung pro Kopf; ~ **owner** Zechenbesitzer; ~ **pinch** kritische Kohlensituation; ~ **producer** Zechenproduzent; ~-**production area** Kohlenrevier; ~ **reserves** Kohlenvorrat; ~ **sales office** Kohlenverkaufsbüro; ~ **scuttle** Kohleneimer; ~ **shed** Kohlenschuppen; ~ **ship** Kohlenschiff; ~ **shovel** Kohlenschaufel; ~ **shuttle** Kohlenschütte; ~ **stockpile** Kohlenhalde, ~ **supply** Kohlenlieferungen, -versorgung; ~ **supplier** Kohlenlieferant; ~ **tip** Kohlenabladeplatz, -halde; ~ **train** Kohlenzug; ~ **transport** Kohlentransport; **hard-~ unit** Steinkohleneinheit; ~ **use** Kohlenverbrauch; ~ **user** Kohlenverbraucher, -abnehmer; ~ **wharf** Kohlenhafen; ~ **yard** Kohlenlager.

coalhouse Kohlenschuppen.

coalesce (v.) sich vereinigen, zusammenwachsen.

coalescence Vereinigung, Verbindung.

coaling Kohlenübernahme;
~ **ship** Bekohlungsschiff; ~ **station** (mar.) Kohlenhafen, Bunkerstation.

coalition Vereinigung, Zusammenschluß, (pol.) Koalition;
centre-right ~ Mitte-Rechtskoalition; **government** ~ Regierungskoalition; **grand** ~ große Koalition; **left-wing** ~ Linkskoalition; **right-wing** ~ Rechtskoalition;
~ **in fighting** Koalitionskämpfe; ~ **in power** Regierungskoalition;
to disrupt a ~ Koalition sprengen; **to enter into a** ~ Koalition eingehen; **to form a** ~ Koalition bilden; **to keep a** ~ **in office** Koalitionsregierung im Amt bestätigen; **to patchwork a** ~ Koalitionsregierung zusammenschustern; **to prise open the** ~ Koalitionsregierung auseinanderbrechen; **to reshuffle a** ~ Koalitionsregierung umbilden; **to work out a** ~ Koalitionsregierung zustande bringen;
~ **agreement** Koalitionsvereinbarung; ~ **cabinet (government)** Koalitionsregierung; ~ **committee** Koalitionsausschuß; ~ **goal** Koalitionsziel; **center-left** ~ **government** Mitte-Linkskoalitionsregierung; ~ **formation** Koalitionsbildung; ~ **group** technische Fraktion; ~ **minister** Koalitionsminister; ~ **partner** Koalitionspartner; ~ **party** Koalitionspartei; ~ **problem** Koalitionsfrage, -problem; ~ **rule** Koalitionsregierung; ~ **talks** Koalitionsgespräche.

coalitioner Koalitionsanhänger.

coalitionist Koalitionsanhänger.

coalize (v.) koalieren, Koalition eingehen.

coalpit Kohlengrube.

coapplicant Mitantragsteller.

coarse (not fine) grob, (inferior in quality) gering[wertig];
~ **screen** (television) grober Raster, Grobraster.

coassignee Mitzessionar.

coast Küste, Meeresufer;
~ **preyed upon by pirates** von Piraten heimgesuchte Küste;
~ (v.) Küstenschiffahrt betreiben; ~ **along slowly** langsam an der Küste entlangfahren; ~ **one's way out of a loss** aus einem Kostental (Verlusttal) heraussteuern;
to clear the ~ sich von der Küste fernhalten; **to range (run down) the** ~ an der Küste entlangfahren;
the ~ **is clear** (fig.) die Luft ist rein;
~ **area** Küstengebiet; ~ **blockade** Küstenblockade; ~ **guard** (Br.) Küstenpolizei, -wache; ☲ **Guard** (US) Küstenwach-, Küstenrettungsdienst; ~-**guard cutter** Küstenwachschiff, -boot, Zollkutter, -schiff; ~-**guard station** Küstenwachstation; ~ **light** Leuchtfeuer; ~ **patrol** Küstenwache; ~ **pilot** Küstenlotse; ~ **station** (radio) Küstenstation; ~ **survey** Küstenvermessung; ~ **trade** Küstenhandel; ~ **waiter** (Br.) Zollbeamter im Küstenhandel; ~ **waters** Küstengewässer.

coast-to-coast (US) alle Sender umfassend;
~ **network** Gemeinschaftssendung; ~ **radio speech** Rundfunkansprache über alle Sender.

coastal | **aircraft** Küstenflugzeug; ~ **area** Küstengebiet; ~ **city** Küstenstadt; ~ **defence** Küstenverteidigung; ~ **fishery** Küstenfischerei; ~ **navigation** Küstenschiffahrt; ~ **shipping** Küstenschiffahrt; ~ **state** Küstenstaat; ~ **steamer** Küstendampfer; **inter-~ traffic** (US) großer Küstenverkehr; ~ **waters** Küstengewässer.

coaster Küstenfahrer, -fahrzeug, -dampfer, (amusement park) Berg-und Talbahn, (person) Uferbewohner;
~ **brake** (bicycle) Rücktrittbremse.

coastguardman Angehöriger des Küstenwachdienstes.

coasting Küstenschiffahrt;
~ **cargo** Küstenfracht; ~ **pilot** Küstenlotse; ~ **steamer** Küstendampfer.

coasting trade Küstenhandel;
to be in the ~ Küstenschiffahrt betreiben.

coasting | **trader** Küstendampfer; ~ **vessel** Küstenwachschiff.

coastline Küstenlinie, -strich.

coastman Küstenbewohner.

coastwise trade Küstenhandel, -schiffahrt.

coat | **of arms** Wappen; **national** ~ **of arms** Staatswappen; ~ **of paint** Farbenstrich;
to cut one's ~ **according to one's cloth** sich nach der Decke strecken; **to turn one's** ~ seinen Mantel nach dem Winde hängen;
~ **armour** (Br.) Familienwappen.

coated paper mattes Kunstdruckpapier.

coax (v.) **a secret out of s. o.** Geheimnis aus jem. herauslocken.

coaxer Überredungskünstler.

cobbled mit Kopfsteinen gepflastert.

Cobdenism Freihandelslehre, Manchestertum.

cobelligerency Kriegsbeteiligung.

cobelligerent mitkriegführender Staat.

cobeneficiary Mitbegünstigter.

cobweb Schlinge, Intrige;
~s **of the law** Tücken (Fallstricke) des Gesetzes.

cock (gas, water) [Gas-, Wasser]hahn, (leader) Anführer;
~ **on his own dunghill** (coll.) Haustyrann; ~ **of the walk (roost)** Hahn im Korbe;
to go off half ~ (fig.) überstürzt handeln; **to knock into a** ~ed **hat** (sl.) total fertigmachen, zu Brei schlagen; **to live like a fighting** ~ wie die Made im Speck leben;
~-**and-bull story** Ammenmärchen, Lügengeschichte, Jägerlatein.

cocket (Br.) Zollpassierschein, (seal) Zollsiegel;
~ (v.) zollamtlich versiegeln.

cockpit (airplane) Führerraum, Pilotensitz, (fig.) Kampfplatz, Arena.

cocksure totsicher.

cocktail Cocktail, (upstart, Br.) Emporkömmling, Parvenüe;
~ **of ads** (US) Anzeigenfriedhof, -plantage;
~ (v.) Cocktail geben.

cockup (print.) Initiale.

cocontractor Mitunternehmer.

cocreditor Solidargläubiger.

code Code, Geheimschrift, Chiffre, Chiffrierschlüssel, (law) Gesetzbuch, Gesetzessammlung, Kodifizierung, Kodex, (mar., mil.) Signalbuch, (system of principles) Vorschriftensammlung;
in ~ verschlüsselt;
cable ~ Telegrammkode; **cipher** ~ Zahlenkode; **criminal** ~ Strafgesetzbuch; **five-unit (letter)** ~ Fünferalphabet; **highway** ~ (Br.) Straßenverkehrsordnung; **International Seamen's** ☲ Seemannsordnung; **Judicial** ☲ (US) Sammlung von gerichtlichen Verfahrensbestimmungen; **medical** ~ ärztliche Standesordnung; **moral** ~ Sittenkodex; **high moral** ~ hohe moralische Grundsätze; **Morse** ~ Morsealphabet; **naval** ~ Signalbuch; **penal** ~ Strafgesetzbuch; **post** ~ (Br.) Postleitzahlsystem; **probate** ~ Nachlaßordnung; **International Signal** ☲ Flaggensignalsystem; **social** ~ Gesellschaftsordnung; **tax** ~ Abgabenordnung; **telegraphic** ~ Telegrammcode; **Uniform Commercial** ☲ (US) vereinheitlichtes Handelsrecht; **United States** ☲ Gesetzessammlung von Bundesgesetzen; **zip** ~ (US) Postleitzahl;
~ **against bribery** Verhaltenscode zur Bekämpfung des Bestechenswesens; ~ **of conduct** Verhaltensgrundsätze, Pflichten-, Verhaltenskodex; ~ **of ethics** Standesordnung; ~ **of hono(u)r** Ehrenkodex; ~ **of hospitality** ungeschriebene Gesetze der Gastfreundlichkeit; **social** ~ **of good manners** gesellschaftliche Verhaltensweise; ~ **of signals** Flaggensignalsystem; ~ **of standards** Richtlinien;
~ (v.) (advertising) mit Kennziffer versehen, (message) verschlüsseln, chiffrieren;
~ **documents** Belege kontieren; ~ **a telegram** Telegramm chiffrieren;
to break a ~ Chiffretext entschlüsseln; **to write a dispatch (a message) in** ~ Code benutzen, Nachricht verschlüsseln; **to live up to the** ~ sich nach ungeschriebenen Gesetzen richten;
~ **address** Codeadresse, Chiffreanschrift; ~ **centre** (Br.) (center, US) Schlüsselzentrale, Chiffrierstelle, (postal system) mit Abkürzungen versehener Postbezirk; ~ **clerk** Verschlüßler, Chiffrierbeamter; ~ **date** Datumsangabe; ~ **figure** Schlüsselzahl; ~ **group** Schlüsselgruppe; ~ **key** Chiffrierschlüssel; ~ **language** Geheimsprache; ~ **letter** Kennbuchstabe; ~ **letters** Rufzeichen; ~ **message** verschlüsselte Nachricht; ~ **name** Deckname; ~ **number** Kennziffer, Chiffrezahl, (post) Postleit-

zahl; ~ **selector** *(tel.)* Netzgruppenwähler; ~ **sheet** Schlüsselkatalog, -blatt; ~ **signal** Peil-, Funkrufzeichen; ~ **system** Schlüsselverfahren; ~ **switch** *(tel.)* Amtsnamenwähler; ~ **table** Tarntafel; ~ **telegram** Chiffretelegramm; ~ **time** Aufgabezeit; ~ **word** Deck-, Kenn-, Codewort.

codebook Codebuch.

codebtor Mitschuldner.

coded|letter chiffrierter (verschlüsselter) Brief; ~ **message** verschlüsselte Meldung.

codefendant Mitbeklagter.

codesheet Kodierung, Code-, Schlüsselplan.

codetermine *(v.)* paritätisch mitbestimmen.

codetermination paritätische Mitbestimmung.

codex Kodex, altes Manuskript.

codicil Testamentsanhang, -zusatz, -nachtrag.

codicillary als [Testaments]nachtrag.

codification Kodifizierung.

codify *(v.)* kodifizieren.

coding *(advertising)* Kennziffernanbringung, *(of a message)* Abfassen in Codesprache, Verschlüsselung, Chiffrierung, *(data processing)* Verschlüsseln [von Daten];
built-in dealers' ~ eingebaute Händlerkodierung;
~ **verification** Codekontrolle.

coeditor Mitherausgeber.

coeducation Gemeinschaftserziehung;
~ **school** Gemeinschaftsschule.

coefficient Koeffizient, Faktor;
~ **of acceleration** Beschleunigungsfaktor; ~ **of determination** *(statistics)* Bestimmtheitskoeffizient; ~ **of equivalence** *(EC)* Ausgleichskoeffizient; ~ **of wages** Lohnfaktor.

coemption Aufkauf.

coemptor Aufkäufer.

coequal Standesgenosse;
~ *(a.)* gleichrangig, -gestellt.

coerce *(v.)* zwingen, nötigen.

coercion Zwang, Nötigung, *(pol.)* Zwangsregulierung;
~ **of witness** Zeugennötigung;
to act under ~ unter Zwang handeln; **to employ means of** ~ Zwangsmaßnahmen anwenden; **to pay money under** ~ zwangsweise zahlen.

coercionist Anhänger der Zwangswirtschaft.

coercive|measures Zwangsmaßnahmen; ~ **methods** Zwangsmethoden; ~ **reasons** zwingende Gründe.

coestate Miteigentum.

coexecutor Mittestamentsvollstrecker.

coexist *(v.)* nebeneinander bestehen, koexistieren.

coexistence Koexistenz, friedliches Zusammenleben;
peaceful ~ friedliche Koexistenz.

coffee|break *(US)* Kaffeepause; ~ **exchange** Kaffeebörse; ~ **house** Café; ~ **mill** Kaffeemühle; ~ **room (shop,** *US)* *(hotel)* Frühstückszimmer, -raum; ~ **stall** Kaffeebude; ~ **tavern** alkoholfreies Restaurant; **to be in the** ~ **trade** in der Kaffeebranche sein; ~ **vendor** Kaffeebudenbesitzer; ~ **vending machine** Kaffeeautomat.

coffer Kasten, Kiste, Truhe;
~**s** Schatzkammer;
~**s of a bank** Depoteinrichtungen einer Bank; ~**s of the state** Staatsschatz.

cofferdam *(mar.)* Kofferdamm.

coffered ceiling Kassettendecke.

coffin Sarg;
to drive a nail into s. one's ~ Nagel für jds. Sarg sein.

cofounder Mitbegründer.

cogency zwingende Kraft, Stichhaltigkeit, Triftigkeit.

cogent zwingend, überzeugend, triftig, stichhaltig;
~ **reasons** dringende (zwingende) Gründe.

cognate Blutsverwandter;
~ *(a.)* blutsverwandt;
~ **inventions** verwandte Erfindungen; ~ **language** verwandte Sprache.

cognation Verwandtschaft;
natural ~ Blutsverwandtschaft.

cognition Erkennungsvermögen.

cognizable vor ein Gericht gehörig, gerichtlich verfolgbar;
to be ~ **by the court** zur Zuständigkeit des Gerichts gehören.

cognizance Kenntnisnahme, *(judicial hearing)* Verhandlung, *(law court)* Gerichtsbarkeit, gerichtliche Zuständigkeit, Kompetenz, *(defensive plea, Br.)* Klageanerkennung;
judicial ~ Gerichtskundigkeit;
to be beyond s. one's ~ außerhalb jds. Zuständigkeit liegen; **to go beyond s. one's** ~ nicht in jds. Kompetenz fallen; **to come**

under the ~ **of s. o.** zu jds. Zuständigkeit gehören; **to fall under the** ~ **of a court** zur Zuständigkeit eines Gerichts gehören; **to have** ~ zuständig sein; **to take** ~ **of s. th.** amtlich Notiz (Kenntnis) von etw. nehmen; **to take special** ~ **of s. th.** etw. genau untersuchen.

cognizant *(law)* kompetent, zuständig.

cognomen Familien-, Zu-, Beiname.

cognosce *(v.)* **a case** über eine Sache erkennen, Sache entscheiden.

cognovit Schuldanerkenntnis;
~ **clause** *(US)* Unterwerfungsklausel; ~ **note** *(US)* Schuldanerkenntnis mit Unterwerfungsklausel, schriftliches Schuldanerkenntnis.

coguarantor Mitbürge.

coguardian Gegen-, Mitvormund.

coguardianship gemeinsame Vormundschaft.

cogwheel railway Zahnradbahn.

cohabit *(v.)* zusammenleben, in wilder Ehe leben.

cohabitant Mitbewohner.

cohabitation Zusammenwohnen;
~ **in state of adultery** Konkubinat, wilde Ehe.

cohabiter Mitbewohner.

coheir Miterbe.

coherence logischer Zusammenhang;
~ **of speech** Klarheit der Rede.

coherent logisch zusammenhängend;
~ **plan** einheitlicher Plan.

coheritage Miterbschaft, gemeinsame Erbschaft.

cohost *(v.)* dem Gastgeber assistieren.

coil *(el.)* Spule;
~ *(v.)* **[up]** aufrollen;
~ **antenna** Spiralantenne; ~ **stamps** Briefmarken in perforierten Bögen.

coin Münze, Geldstück, *(coined money)* gemünztes Geld, *(hard money)* Hartgeld;
in gold ~ **of the US** in Goldwährung der USA;
bad ~ falsches Geldstück; **base** ~ *(Br.)* Falschgeld, *(US)* Scheidemünze; **battered** ~ beschädigtes Geldstück; **common** ~ gängige Münze; **counterfeit** ~ Falschgeld; **current** ~ gangbare Münze; **debased** ~ Metallgeld; **defaced** ~ abgenützte Münze; **detrited** ~ abgegriffene Münze; **divisional** ~ Scheidemünze; **false** ~ Falschgeld; **foreign** ~**s** ausländische Geldsorten; **gold** ~ Goldstück; **home** ~ inländische Münze; **legal** ~ gesetzliches Zahlungsmittel; **light** ~ *(US)* untergewichtige Münze; **minor** ~ *(US)* Scheidemünze; **ready** ~ bares Geld; **silver** ~ Silbermünze; **small** ~ Kleingeld, Scheidemünze; **spurious** ~ Falschgeld; **standard** ~ Münze mit gesetzlich vorgeschriebenem Feingehalt; **token** ~ Scheidemünze; **undebased** ~ vollwertige Münze; **wornout** ~ abgegriffene Münze;
~**s in circulation** Münzumlauf; **current** ~ **of the realm** *(Br.)* gängige Landeswährung;
~ *(v.)* münzen, prägen, *(fig.)* zu Geld machen;
~ **again** umprägen; ~ **money** Geld prägen (scheffeln); ~ **base money** Falschmünzerei betreiben; ~ **below the standard** geringwertig ausprägen; ~ **new words** neue Wörter bilden;
to adjust a ~ einer Münze das richtige Gewicht geben; **to call in** ~**s** Geld einziehen; **to counterfeit** ~ Münzen fälschen, Münzfälschung begehen; **to debase** ~**s** Münzen verringern; **to get off false** ~ Falschgeld unterbringen; **to mint** ~**s** Münzen schlagen; **to pass the** ~ Geld in Verkehr bringen; **to pay s. o. back in his own** ~ jem. mit gleicher Münze heimzahlen; **to rate a** ~ Münze taxieren; **to retire** ~**s from circulation** Münzen aus dem Verkehr ziehen; **to strike** ~**s** Münzen schlagen; **to test a** ~ **for weight** Münzgewicht überprüfen; **to unload a bad** ~ **on s. o.** jem. eine falsche Münze andrehen;
~ **box** *(US)* Münzfernsprecher; ~ **changer** Geldwechsler; ~ **collection** Münzsammlung; ~**-operated machine** Münzautomat; ~ **slot** Münzeinwurf; ~ **stamper** Prägestempel; ~ **weight** Münzgewicht.

coinage *(coins)* geprägtes Geld, Münzen, Hartgeld, *(cost of coinage)* Präge-, Münzkosten, *(stamping)* Münzprägung, *(system of coins)* Münzsystem;
debased ~ Münzverschlechterung; **decimal** ~ Dezimalwährung; **new** ~ Neuprägung;
to appreciate the ~ Münzwert erhöhen; **to pay s. o. back in his own** ~ jem. mit gleicher Münze heimzahlen; **to put a** ~ **in circulation** Münzen in Verkehr bringen;
~ **Act** *(Br.)* Münzgesetz; ~ **offence** Münzvergehen, -verbrechen; ~ **ratio** *(US)* gesetzlich festgelegtes Gewichtsverhältnis der Gold- und Silbermünzen.

coincide *(v.)* sich zeitlich decken.

coincidence Zufall, Zusammentreffen;
   ~ **of wants** Bedürfniskoinzidenz.
coincidental Koinzidenzmethode, *(broadcasting)* Telefonbefragung.
coined|brand name Phantasiemarkenname; ~ **word** erfundenes Wort, Kunstwort.
coiner *(counterfeiter of coins, Br.)* Falschmünzer, *(one who coins)* Münzer.
coinhabitant Mitbewohner.
coinheritance Miterbschaft, gemeinsame Erbschaft.
coining Geldprägen, Geldprägung;
   false ~ Falschmünzerei;
   ~ **of money** Geldprägung;
   to be simply ~ **money** *(Br.)* Geld wie Heu (Mist) verdienen, Geld scheffeln;
   ~ **value** Münzwert.
coinsurance Mitversicherung, Selbstbehalt bei Unterdeckung;
   ~ **clause** Mitversicherungs-, Selbstbehaltsklausel.
coinsure *(v.)* mit-, rückversichern.
coinsured mitversichert, mit Selbstbeteiligung.
coinsurer Rückversicherer.
cointerested mitbeteiligt.
coinventor Miterfinder.
cojuror Eideshelfer.
coke Koks, *(snow)* Kokain;
   ~ **breeze** Abfallkoks; ~ **oven** Koksofen.
cold Kälte, *(illness)* Erkältung;
   to be left out in the ~ leer ausgehen, kaltgestellt werden;
   ~ **check** *(US sl.)* gefälschter Scheck; ~ **comfort** magerer Trost; ~ **facts** nackte Tatsachen; **to have** ~ **feet** *(fig.)* kalte Füße bekommen; ~ **front** Kaltluftfront; ~ **harbo(u)r** Schutzhütte; ~ **news** bedrückende Nachrichten; ~-**pig** *(v.)* *(sl.)* kalte Dusche verabfolgen; ~ **reason** nüchterner Verstand; ~ **reception** frostiger Empfang; ~ **shoulder** *(fig.)* kalte Schulter; **to give the** ~ **shoulders to s.o.** jem. die kalte Schulter zeigen; ~ **snap** plötzlicher Kälteeinbruch; ~ **spectator** teilnahmsloser Zuschauer; ~ **steel** blanke Waffe; ~ **storage** Kühlhauslagerung; **to put into** ~ **storage** *(fig.)* auf die lange Bank schieben; ~-**storage room** Kühlraum; ~-**storage ship** Kühlschiff; ~-**storage training** *(US)* vorsorgliche Ausbildung leitender Angestellter; ~ **type** Fotosatz; ~ **war** *(pol.)* kalter Krieg; ~ **warrior** *(pol.)* kalter Krieger; **to throw** ~ **water on a plan** der Begeisterung einen Dämpfer aufsetzen; ~ **wave** Kältewelle; ~ **welcome** kühler Empfang.
coldstore *(v.)* *(US)* im Kühlhaus lagern.
colegatee Mitvermächtnisnehmer.
colessee Mitpächter.
coliquidator Mitliquidator.
collaborate *(v.)* zusammen-, mitarbeiten, *(pol.)* kollaborieren, Feind in hochverräterischer Weise unterstützen;
   ~ **in a work** sich an einem Werk beteiligen.
collaboration Zusammenarbeit, -wirken, *(on a book)* Beteiligung, Mitwirkung, *(pol.)* Kollaboration;
   quiet ~ geheimes Zusammenwirken;
   ~ **deal** Vereinbarung über betriebliche Zusammenarbeit.
collaborator Mitarbeiter, *(pol.)* Kollaborateur.
collage Collage.
collapse Zusammenbruch, Fehlschlag, *(building)* Einsturz, *(med.)* Kollaps;
   business ~ wirtschaftlicher Zusammenbruch; **financial** ~ finanzieller Zusammenbruch; **world price** ~ Zusammenbruch der Weltmarktpreise;
   ~ **of a bank** Bankkrach; ~ **of a building** Gebäudeeinsturz; ~ **of an enterprise** Zusammenbruch eines Unternehmens; ~ **of the government** Regierungssturz; ~ **of the market** Börsenkrach; ~ **of a minister** Sturz eines Ministers; ~ **of prices** Preiszusammenbruch, -sturz, *(stock exchange)* Kurssturz; ~ **of the whipping system** Zusammenbruch des Fraktionszwanges;
   ~ *(v.)* einfallen, -stürzen, *(price)* zusammenbrechen, *(state)* zerfallen;
   ~ **like a house of cards** wie ein Kartenhaus zusammenstürzen;
   to face the ~ **of one's business** vor dem geschäftlichen Zusammenbruch stehen; **to reach near-**~ *(traffic)* beinahe zusammenbrechen.
collapsible|boat Faltboot; ~ **carton** Faltschachtel; ~ **corporation** *(income tax)* aus Steuergründen vorübergehend gegründete Gesellschaft; ~ **roof** Rollverdeck.
collar, *(pearls)* Kollier, *(for orders)* Ordenskette;
   ~ *(v.)* *(coll.)* sich aneignen, erwischen; ~ **a thief** Dieb beim Kragen nehmen;
   to wear no man's ~ kein Parteigänger sein; **to work against the** ~ *(fig.)* schwere Arbeit verrichten;

~ **work** *(fig.)* anstrengende Arbeit; **white-**~ **worker** *(US)* [Büro]angestellter.
collate *(v.)* [Schriftstücke] vergleichen, kollationieren.
collated telegram verglichenes Telegramm.
collateral *(kinsman, US)* Verwandter in der Seitenlinie, *(property pledged)* Sicherungsgegenstand, Pfand, *(security)* Deckung, [Darlehns]sicherheit, Besicherung;
   acceptable as ~ beleihbar, lombardfähig;
   additional ~ zusätzliche Sicherheiten; **bank (banking)** ~ bankübliche Sicherheiten, Banksicherheit; **commodity** ~ Warensicherheit; **industrial** ~ *(US)* Sicherheit durch Hinterlegung von Industrieaktien; **joint** ~ *(US)* gemeinsame Sicherheit; **mixed** ~ Lombardsicherung durch Hinterlegung verschiedener Effekten; **regular** ~ *(US)* Sicherheit durch Hinterlegung handelsüblicher Effekten; **stock-exchange** ~ *(US)* Sicherheit in Form an der New Yorker Börse gehandelter Effekten;
   to be eligible as ~ lombardfähig sein; **to be ineligible to serve as** ~ *(US)* als Lombardunterlage nicht gewertet werden; **to borrow on** ~ **[on securities]** Darlehn gegen Lombardierung von Wertpapieren aufnehmen; **to commute** ~ zur Besicherung gegebene Effekten auswechseln; **to furnish** ~ zusätzliche Sicherheit leisten; **to give** ~ Sicherheit leisten; **to lend (loan) on** ~ abgesicherten Kredit (Lombardkredit) gewähren, lombardieren; **to pledge as** ~ zu Besicherungszwecken verwenden; **to post additional** ~ Lombardsicherheiten erhöhen; **to serve as** ~ als [Lombard]deckung dienen; **to substitute different** ~ Lombardsicherheiten auswechseln;
   ~ *(a.)* zusätzlich, *(relative)* in der Seitenlinie verwandt, *(subordinate)* untergeordnet, nebensächlich, *(subsidiary)* akzessorisch;
   ~ **acceptance** Interventions-, Notakzept; ~ **advance** Lombardkredit; ~ **advantage** Nebenvorteile; ~ **agreement** Nebenabkommen, -abrede, *(bank)* Sicherungsvereinbarung, Lombardvertrag; ~ **ancestors** Verwandte in der aufsteigenden Seitenlinie; ~ **assurance** *(conveyancing)* zusätzlich gewährte Sicherheit; ~ **attack** Urteilsanfechtung im Nebenverfahren; ~ **bail** Mitbürgschaft; ~ **bill** *(US)* Lombardwechsel; ~ **circumstances** Begleit-, Nebenumstände; ~ **claim** Lombardforderung; ~ **clause** Nebenbestimmung; ~ **contract** Nebenvertrag; ~ **credit** abgesicherter (gedeckter) Kredit, *(securities)* Lombardkredit; ~ **damage** Nebenschaden; ~ **debt** Lombardschuld; ~ **degree of kindred** Seitenverwandtschaft; ~ **deposit** *(US)* Lombarddepot, Lombardbestände; ~ **descent** Abstammung von einer Nebenlinie; ~ **endorsement** Gefälligkeitsgiro; ~ **estoppel** inzident getroffene Gerichtsentscheidung; ~ **evidence** unterstützendes Beweismaterial; ~ **facts** unstreitige Tatsachen; ~ **fund** Sicherheitsfonds; ~ **government** Nebenregierung; ~ **guaranty** Gesamtbürgschaft; ~ **inheritance tax** Erbschaftssteuer für aus einer Seitenlinie stammenden Nachlaß; **by** ~ **hand** auf indirektem Wege; ~ **heir** aus der Seitenlinie stammender Erbe; ~ **holdings** *(US)* Lombardbestände; ~ **inheritance** Erbschaft von der Seitenlinie; ~ **insurance** zusätzliche Versicherung; ~ **issue** Nebenfrage; ~ **kinsman** Verwandter in der Seitenlinie; ~ **loan** Lombardkredit, -darlehn; ~ **loan agreement** Lombardvertrag; ~ **loan business** Lombardgeschäft; ~ **mortgage bonds** hypothekarisch gesicherte Schuldverschreibungen; ~ **negligence** positive Vertragsverletzung; ~ **note** *(US)* durch Verpfändung von Sicherheiten gedeckter Schuldschein; ~ **performance** Nebenleistung; ~ **position** Sicherheits-, Pfandposition; ~ **proceedings** Nebenverfahren; ~ **promise** akzessorisches Versprechen, Bürgschaftsversprechen; ~ **proof** Nebenbeweis; ~ **relation** Verwandter in der Seitenlinie; ~ **securities** lombardfähige Wertpapiere, Lombardsicherheit; ~ **security** [durch Verpfändung geleistete] zusätzliche Sicherheit (Deckung), Lombarddeckung, Sicherheitsleistung; **to apply shares as** ~ **security** *(US)* Aktien als Kreditunterlage verwenden; **to give** ~ **security** doppelte Sicherheit leisten; **to serve as** ~ **security** als Lombarddeckung fungieren; ~ **transactions** Nebengeschäfte; ~ **trust bonds** *(US)* durch Effektenlombard gesicherte Obligationen; ~ **trust certificate** *(US)* Treuhand-, Investmentzertifikat; ~ **trust indenture** Lombardvertrag; ~ **trustee share** *(US)* Anteilschein einer Kapitalanlagegesellschaft; ~ **undertaking** formlose zusätzliche Verpflichtung; ~ **value** Beleihungs-, Lombard[ierungs]wert; ~ **warranty** weitere (zusätzliche) Sicherheit.
collaterally related in der Seitenlinie verwandt.
collaterate *(v.)* Schuld durch Pfandbestellung besichern, *(US)* Verpfändung von Wertpapieren vornehmen, lombardieren.
collation Textvergleichung, *(bookkeeping)* Kollation, Vergleichung, Kollationierung, *(hotchpot)* Ausgleich unter Miterben, Ausgleichspflicht, *(telegram)* Verifizierung durch Wiederholung.

collator Ausgleichspflichtiger.
colleague Kollege, Mitarbeiter, Berufskamerad;
  cabinet ~ Kabinettskollege; **closest** ~ engster Mitarbeiter;
  ~ **family** Partnerschaftsfamilie.
col leagueship Kollegialität.
collect | of the day *(church)* Tageskollekte;
  ~ *(v.) (accumulate)* [an]sammeln, *(cheques)* einziehen, einlösen, einsammeln, einkassieren, *(come together)* sich einfinden, zusammenkommen, *(money)* erheben, vereinnahmen, *(taxes)* erheben, einziehen;
  ~ **a bill** Rechnungsbetrag kassieren; ~ **a bill when due** Wechsel bei Fälligkeit einlösen; ~ **a check** *(US)* *(cheque, Br.)* Scheck kassieren (einlösen, einziehen); ~ **a claim** Forderung eintreiben; ~ **contributions** Geldbeträge einsammeln; ~ **curios** Antiquitäten sammeln; ~ **outstanding debts** Außenstände einziehen; ~ **dividends** Dividenden beheben; ~ **evidence** Beweismaterial zusammentragen; ~ **the goods** Waren abnehmen; ~ **information** Erkundigungen einziehen; ~ **the letters** Briefkasten leeren; ~ **the luggage** *(Br.)* Gepäck [in der Wohnung] abholen; ~ **money due** Außenstände einziehen; ~ **the money for the newspaper once a month** Zeitungsgeld monatlich kassieren; ~ **on a note** Wechsel zur Zahlung vorlegen (einlösen); ~ **orders** Aufträge sammeln; ~ **for the poor** für die Armen sammeln; ~ **rents** Mieten einziehen; ~ **stamps** Briefmarken sammeln; ~ **taxes** Steuern eintreiben; ~ **one's thoughts** sich sammeln;
  ~ *(a.) (US)* gegen Nachnahme;
  ~ **call** *(tel., US)* R-Gespräch; ~ **shipment** Frachtnachnahme.
collect on delivery (C. O. D.) Zahlung gegen (per) Nachnahme, zahlbar bei Lieferung;
  to send a package ~ Paket gegen Nachnahme schicken;
  ~ **fee** Nachnahmegebühr; ~ **parcel (package)** Nachnahmepaket.
collected gesammelt, *(fig.)* gefaßt, gesammelt.
collectible *(cheque)* kassierbar, eintreib-, einlösbar, *(coupon)* fällig, *(money)* einziehbar, beitreibbar.
collecting *(bills of exchange)* Einziehung, Einzug, Inkasso, *(tax)* Beitreibung;
  ~ **of bills of exchange** Wechselinkasso; ~ **information** Nachrichtenbeschaffung; ~ **of luggage** *(Br.)* Gepäckabholung;
  debt-~ agency Inkassostelle, -büro; ~ **agent** Inkassovertreter, -beauftragter; ~ **bank (banker, US)** Inkassobank, Zahlstelle; ~ **box** Sammelbüchse; ~ **business** Inkasso[geschäft]; ~ **card** Sammlerausweis; ~ **charges** Einzugs-, Inkassospesen; ~ **clerk** Kassenbote; ~ **commission** Inkasso-, Einziehungsprovision; ~ **point** *(US)* Sammelstelle, -lager; ~ **point for captured goods** *(US)* Beutesammelstelle; ~ **rates** Inkassotarif; ~ **service** *(luggage)* Abholstelle; ~ **society** *(Br.)* gemeinnütziger Verein; ~ **station** Sammelplatz; ~ **vehicle** Zubringerfahrzeug; ~ **zone** Sammelgebiet.
collection *(bill, debts)* Inkasso, Einziehung, Einzug, *(church)* Kollekte, *(collecting of money)* [Geld]sammlung, *(letters)* Briefkastenleerung, *(luggage)* Abholung, *(set)* Kollektion, *(sum collected)* Spende, Almosensammlung, *(taxes)* Beitreibung, Einziehung, *(university, Br.)* Zwischen-, Semesterprüfung, *(works of art)* Sammlung;
  after ~ *(letterbox)* nach der Leerung; **for** ~ zur Einziehung, zum Inkasso; **ready for** ~ abholbereit;
  inward ~**s** Inlandsinkassi; **par** ~ Inkasso zum Pariwert; **slow** ~**s** schleppend eingehende Inkassobeträge; **stamp** ~ Briefmarkensammlung; **tax** ~ Steuererhebung, -einziehung, -eingänge;
  ~ **in aid of an undertaking** zweckbestimmte Geldsammlung; ~**s due from banks** *(balance sheet)* Inkassoforderungen an Banken; ~ **of bills** Wechselinkasso; ~ **of charges** Spesennachnahme, Gebührenerhebung; ~ **of checks (cheques, Br.)** Scheckeinzug, -inkasso; **par** ~ **of cheques** *(Br.)* Inkasso von Wechseln zum Pariwert ohne Spesenabzug; ~ **of a claim** Forderungseinziehung, Einzug einer Forderung; ~ **by customer** Selbstabholung; ~ **of debts** Eintreibung von Forderungen, Forderungseinziehung; ~ **and delivery** Abhol- und Zustelldienst; ~ **on delivery** *(US)* Zahlung gegen Nachnahme; ~ **of documents** Dokumenteninkasso; ~ **of draft** Tratteninkasso; ~ **of publisher's enclosure** Abholung von Verlegerbeischüssen; ~ **of illegal fees** übermäßige Gebührenerhebung; ~ **of freight charges** Frachteninkasso; ~**s by hand** *(US)* Boteninkassi; ~ **of income tax** Einkommensteuererhebung; ~ **of information** Nachrichtenbeschaffung; ~ **of legal costs** Justizbeitreibung; ~ **of letters (mail)** Postabholung, Briefkastenleerung; ~ **of luggage** *(Br.)* Gepäckabholung; ~ **of money** Geldeinziehung; ~ **of news** Einholung von Nachrichten; ~ **of notes** Notizensammlung; ~ **of paintings** Gemäldesammlung; ~ **of patterns** Muster-

kollektion; ~ **of premiums** Beitrags-, Prämieneinziehung; ~ **for charitable purposes** Sammlung für wohltätige Zwecke; ~ **of quotations** Zitatensammlung; ~ **of refuse** Müllabfuhr; ~ **of rents** Mietinkasso; ~ **of rubbish** Ansammlung von Gerümpel; ~ **of samples** Musterkollektion; ~ **at source** Quellenbesteuerung; ~ **of postage stamps** Briefmarkensammlung; ~ **of statistics** statistische Erhebungen; ~ **of taxes** Steuererhebung;
  to attend to the ~ **of a bill** Wechselinkasso besorgen; **to await** ~ abholbereit sein; **to be ready for** ~ zur Abholung bereitliegen; **to effect** ~**s** Inkassi besorgen; **to entrust a bank with the** ~ einer Bank Inkassoauftrag erteilen; **to make a** ~ Kollekte veranstalten; **to make a** ~ **of samples** Muster zusammenstellen; **to present for** ~ zum Inkasso vorzeigen; **to raise for** ~ sammeln, Sammlung veranstalten; **to receive for** ~ zum Inkasso übernehmen; **to remit for** ~ zur Einziehung übersenden; **to speed up** ~ **of debts** Schulden beschleunigt beitreiben; **to speed up the** ~ **of estate taxes** Einziehung von Erbschaftssteuern beschleunigen; **to take up a** ~ mit dem Klingelbeutel herumgehen; **to undertake the** ~ **of a firm** Inkassi eines Unternehmens übernehmen;
  ~ **account** Inkassokonto; ~ **activities** Inkassotätigkeit; ~ **advice** Inkassoaviso; ~ **agency (agent)** Inkassobüro, -stelle; **house** ~ **agency** eigene Inkassogesellschaft; ~ **area** Zoll- und Steuerbezirk; ~ **bank[er]** Inkassobank; ~ **box** Sammelbüchse; ~ **business** Inkassogeschäft; ~ **card** Inkassokarteikarte; ~ **charges** Inkasso-, Einzugsspesen; ~ **check** *(US)* *(cheque, Br.)* Inkassoscheck; ~ **clerk** Inkassobeamter; ~ **commission** Inkassokommission, -provision, -gebühr; ~ **correspondence** Inkassokorrespondenz; ~ **costs** Einzugskosten, -spesen; ~ **department** Inkassoabteilung; ~ **devices** Inkassoeinrichtungen; ~ **district** Steuererhebungsbezirk; ~ **efforts** Inkassoanstrengungen; ~ **expense(s)** Einziehungskosten, Inkassospesen, -aufwand; ~ **fee** Inkassogebühr; ~ **form** Inkassoformular; ~ **item** Inkassoabschnitt, -wechsel; ~ **ledger** Inkassowechselkonto; ~ **letter** *(US)* Mahnschreiben, Inkassobrief; ~ **manager** Inkassobearbeiter; ~ **methods** Inkassomethoden; ~ **number** Inkassonummer; ~ **order** Inkasso-, Einzugsauftrag; ~ **order form** Postauftragsformular; **average** ~ **period** Durchschnittsdauer eines eingeräumten Kredits; ~ **policy** Inkassopolitik; ~ **proceedings (procedure)** Einziehungs-, Beitreibungsverfahren; ~ **proceeds** Inkassogegenwert; ~ **rate** Hebesatz, Zahlungsrate; ~ **round** Haussammlung; ~ **service** Inkassodienst; ~ **sequence** Mahnbriefserie; ~ **system** Einzugsverfahren, Inkassosystem; ~ **technique** Inkassoverfahren; ~ **teller** Schalterbeamter für den Inkassoverkehr; ~ **trouble** Einziehungsschwierigkeiten; ~ **window** Einziehungsschalter; ~ **work** Inkassogeschäft.
collective Gemeinschaft, Gruppe, *(gr.)* Sammelwort, *(pol.)* Produktionsgemeinschaft, Kollektiv;
  ~ *(a.)* gemeinsam, gemeinschaftlich, kollektiv;
  ~ **account** Sammelkonto; ~ **agreement** Gesamtvereinbarung, *(bargaining)* Tarifvertrag, -vereinbarung, Kollektivvertrag; ~ **agreement provisions** Tarifvertragsbestimmungen; ~ **bargainer** Tarifverhandlungs-, Vertragspartner.
collective bargaining gemeinsame Verhandlungen, Tarifverhandlungen, Kollektivverhandlungen;
  to be recognized by an employer for the ~ **of wages and conditions** als Verhandlungspartner zur Aushandlung von Tariflöhnen und -arbeitsbedingungen vom Arbeitgeber anerkannt sein;
  ~ **advertising sign** Sammelplakat; ~ **agent** Tarifbevollmächtigter; ~ **agreement** Kollektiv-, Tarifvereinbarung; ~ **association** Tarifvereinigung; ~ **commission** Tarifkommission; ~ **consignment** Sammelladung; ~ **contract** Tarifvertrag; ~ **pack** *(book trade)* Sammelballen; ~ **remittance** Sammelüberweisung; **to rally a party round the free** ~ **standard** Partei auf eine Politik der Nichteinmischung in Verhandlungen der Tarifpartner festlegen; **to worship before the free** ~ **totem pole** freier Tarifvereinbarungen zwischen den Sozialpartnern anbeten; ~ **undertaking** *(book trade)* Sammelrevers.
collective | behavio(u)r Gesamtverhalten; ~ **bargainor** Tarifverhandlungspartner; ~ **bill of lading** Sammelkonnossement; ~ **body** Kollektiv; ~ **call** *(tel.)* Sammelrufzeichen, Konferenzgespräch; ~ **card** gemeinsame Visitenkarte; ~ **charge** Gesamtgrundschuld; ~ **consignment** Sammelladung; ~ **contract** Tarifvertrag; **to make** ~ **contracts mandatory** obligatorische Kollektivverträge einführen; ~ **contract termination** *(US)* Tarifkündigung; ~ **culpability** *(pol.)* Kollektivschuld; ~ **deed** Sammelurkunde; ~ **deposit** Sammeldepot; ~ **economy** Kollektivwirtschaft; ~ **enforcement** gemeinsame Durchsetzung; ~ **executive** Ausführungskollektiv; ~ **expenditure** Sammelaufwendung; ~ **farm** Kolchose, landwirtschaftliche Produktionsgenossenschaft; ~ **farming** kollektive Bewirtschaftung; ~

formula Sammel-, Kollektivformel; ~ **goods** öffentliche Einrichtungen, Kollektiv-, Gemeineigentum, Gemeinschaftsgüter; ~ **guaranty** Kollektivgarantie; ~ **insurance** Gruppenversicherung; ~ **interest** Gesamt-, Kollektivinteresse; ~ **labo(u)r agreement** ganzen Industriezweig umfassendes Tarifabkommen, Kollektivabkommen, -vertrag; **to make ~ labo(u)r agreements mandatory** obligatorische Kollektivverträge eingehen; ~ **leadership** kollektive Führung, Führungskollektiv; ~ **liability** *(international law)* Kollektivhaftung; ~ **mark** Güte-, Verbandszeichen, Kollektivmarke; **to take ~ measures** Kollektivmaßnahmen ergreifen; ~ **mortgage** Gesamthypothek; ~ **name** Sammelbegriff; ~ **note** *(dipl.)* Kollektivnote; ~ **number** *(tel.)* Sammelanschluß, -nummer; ~ **organization** Kollektiveinrichtung; ~ **overhaul** Gesamtüberholung; ~ **ownership** gemeinsamer Besitz, Gemeinschaftseigentum, Kollektivbesitz, -eigentum; ~ **passport** Sammelpaß; ~ **permit** Sammelausweis; ~ **petition** gemeinsam eingebrachtes Gesuch; ~ **power** Gesamtvollmacht; ~ **punishment** Kollektivstrafe; ~ **recreation** gemeinsame Erholung; ~ **representative** Tarifvertragspartner; **⁰ Reserve Unit** kollektive Reserveeinheit; ~ **responsibility** Haftungsgemeinschaft; ~ **security** *(pol.)* kollektive Sicherheit; ~ **self-defence** *(law of nations)* kollektive Selbstverteidigung; ~ **shipment** Sammelladung; ~ **shopping** Gemeinschaftseinkauf; ~ **show** Sammelschau; ~ **ticket** Sammelfahrschein; ~ **title** Sammelbezeichnung; ~ **transport** Sammeltransport; ~ **treaty** Kollektivvertrag; ~ **visa** Sammelvisum; ~ **wage agreement** Lohntarif-, Kollektivvertrag.
collectively als Gesamtheit;
  to bargain ~ Tarifverhandlungen führen.
collectivism Kollektivismus.
collectivist Anhänger des Kollektivismus.
collectivistic kollektivistisch.
collectivity Kollektiv-, Gesamteigentum.
collectivization Kollektivierung.
collectivize *(v.)* kollektivieren.
collector Sammler, *(customs)* Zolleinnehmer, *(debts)* Inkassobeamter, -bearbeiter, -reisender, *(meter reading)* Stromableser, *(taxes)* Steuereinnehmer, Vollziehungsbeamter;
  art ~ Kunstsammler; **debt ~** Inkassobeauftragter, -mandatar; **district ~** *(US)* örtlich zuständiger Finanzbeamter; **rent ~** Mieteinnehmer; **stamp ~** Briefmarkensammler; **tax ~** *(Br.)* Steuereinzieher, -einnehmer; **ticket ~** Fahrkartenabnehmer; ~ **of antiques** Antiquitätensammler; ~ **of coins** Münzsammler; ~ **of the customs** Zolleinnehmer; ~ **of customs and excise** *(Br.)* Zollamt; ~ **of decedents' estate** Nachlaßpfleger; ~ **of a port** Hafeneinnehmer; ~ **of internal revenues** *(US)* Finanzamtsleiter; ~ **of taxes** *(Br.)* Steuereinnehmer; ~**'s item** Sammlerstück, -objekt.
collectorship Sammeltätigkeit, *(taxation)* Steuereinnahmestelle;
college *(Br.)* College, Universität, Hochschule, Akademie;
  agricultural ~ landwirtschaftliche Hochschule; **business ~** Wirtschaftshochschule; **commercial ~** Handels[hoch]schule; **electoral ~** Wählerkollegium; **engineering ~** technische Hochschule; **private venture ~** private Unterrichtsanstalt; **teachers' ~** Lehrerbildungsanstalt; **training ~** *(Br.)* Hochschule für Lehrerbildung;
  ~ **of further education** Fortbildungsschule; **to expel from ~** von der Universität verweisen; **to go to ~** Universität besuchen, studieren; **to have been to ~** Hochschulbildung haben;
  ~**-age son** Sohn in der Universitätsausbildung; ~**-boy** Student; ~**-bred** auf der Universität gewesen; ~ **course** Hochschullehrgang; ~ **degree** *(US)* Universitätsgrad; ~ **dropout** Versager auf der Universität; ~ **education** akademische Bildung, Universitätsstudium, -ausbildung; ~ **entrance examination** Universitätsaufnahmeprüfung; ~ **fees** Collegegebühren; ~ **graduate** Akademiker; ~ **man** Student, Akademiker; ~ **professor** Universitätsprofessor; ~ **town** Universitätsstadt; ~**-trained** mit akademischer Bildung; **to be ~-trained** Universität besucht haben; ~ **training** Universitätsausbildung; ~ **tuition** Collegegelder; ~ **widow** *(US)* Studentenliebchen; ~ **year** akademisches Jahr; ~ **years** Universitätsjahre, -zeit; ~ **youths** *(US)* Oberschüler.
collegian *(Br., sl.)* Gefängnisinsasse.
collegiate | dictionary Schulwörterbuch; ~ **school** *(Br.)* höhere Schule.
collide *(v.)* zusammenstoßen, kollidieren;
  ~ **head on with** frontal zusammenstoßen; ~ **with s. one's interests** Interessenkollision mit jem. haben.
colliding interests kollidierende Interessen.
collier *(miner)* Bergmann, *(ship)* Kohlenschiff.

colliery Kohlenbergwerk, Zeche;
  ~ **company** Bergwerksgesellschaft.
collision Zusammenstoß, Kollision, *(car)* Karambolage;
  head-on ~ Frontalzusammenstoß; **railway ~** Zug-, Eisenbahnzusammenstoß; **rear-end ~** Auffahrunfall;
  ~ **and damages** Schadensersatzklage wegen Schiffszusammenstoß; ~ **of interests** Interessenkonflikt, -kollision; ~ **of persons** Konfrontation mit Dritten; ~ **at sea** Schiffszusammenstoß, -unfall; ~ **of trains** Zug-, Eisenbahnzusammenstoß; ~ **between two vessels** Schiffskollision;
  to come into ~ zusammenstoßen, kollidieren; **to come into ~ with s. one's interests** mit jds. Interessen zusammenstoßen; **to find o. s. in ~ with the forces of the law** mit den Vertretern des Gesetzes in Konflikt geraten;
  ~ **clause** *(ship)* Zusammenstoß-, Kollisionsklausel; **both-to-blame ~ clause** Kollisionsklausel für beiderseitiges Verschulden; ~ **course** *(fig.)* *(ship)* Kollisionskurs; ~ **damage** Kollisionsschaden; ~ **damage responsibility** Eigenhaftung, Selbstbehalt; ~ **damage waiver** Haftungsausschluß bei der Haftpflichtversicherung; ~ **insurance** *(US)* Kaskoversicherung; **full coverage ~ insurance** hundertprozentige (vollgedeckte) Kaskoversicherung.
collocation *(debt payment)* Reihenfolge.
collocutor Gesprächspartner.
colloquial gesprächsweise, mündlich;
  ~ **expression** Ausdruck der Umgangssprache; ~ **language** Umgangssprache.
colloquium Kolloquium, *(libel action)* Sachvortrag.
collotype Lichtdruck.
collude *(v.)* in geheimem Einverständnis handeln.
collusion heimliches Einverständnis, geheime Absprache, unerlaubte Verabredung, Verdunkelungsmanöver;
  ~ **of facts** Verdunkelung des Sachverhalts;
  to act in ~ with s. o. im geheimen Einverständnis mit jem. handeln.
collusive abgekartet, abgesprochen, heimlich verabredet, sittenwidrig herbeigeführt;
  ~ **action** abgekartetes Vorgehen; ~ **agreement** heimliche Absprache; ~ **bidding** manipulierte Angebotsabgabe; ~ **price (tender)** vorher abgesprochenes Angebot; ~ **tendering** Ausschreibungsabsprache.
colon Doppelpunkt.
colonels, the Militärjunker.
colonial Kolonist, Bewohner einer Kolonie, kolonial, aus den Kolonien stammend;
  ~**s** *(stock exchange)* Kolonialpapiere;
  quasi-~ *(a.)* kolonialähnlich;
  ~ **bank** *(Br.)* Kolonialbank; ~ **bill** Kolonialwechsel; ~ **bond** Kolonialanleihe; ~ **civil servant** Kolonialbeamter; **⁰ and Development Corporation** *(Br.)* Finanzierungsinstitut zur Förderung der wirtschaftlichen Entwicklung der Kolonien; ~ **empire** Kolonialreich; ~ **era** Kolonialzeit; ~ **goods** Kolonialwaren; ~ **government** Kolonialregierung; ~ **market** *(Br., stock exchange)* Markt für Kolonialwerte, Überseemarkt; ~ **merchant** Kolonialwarenhändler; ~ **minister** Kolonialminister; **⁰ Office** *(Br.)* Kolonialministerium; ~ **people** Kolonialvolk; ~ **policy** Kolonialpolitik; ~ **possession** Kolonie, Kolonialbesitz; ~ **power** Kolonialmacht; ~ **preference** *(Br.)* Vorzugszölle zwischen England und seinen Kolonien; ~ **produce** Kolonialprodukte, -waren; ~ **securities (stocks)** *(Br.)* Kolonialpapiere; ~ **territory** Kolonialgebiet; ~ **trade** Kolonialhandel; ~ **war** Kolonialkrieg; ~ **wares** Kolonialwaren.
colonialism Kolonialsystem, -politik.
colonialistic kolonialistisch.
colonist Kolonist.
colonization Besiedlung, Kolonisation, Kolonisierung, *(US, electioneering)* vorübergehende Wähleransiedlung.
colonize *(v.)* besiedeln, kolonisieren;
  ~ **labo(u)rers** Arbeiterkolonie gründen.
colonizer Siedler, *(state)* Kolonialmacht.
colonade Vorbau.
colony Kolonie, Niederlassung, Ansiedlung;
  convict ~ Sträflingskolonie; **Crown ⁰** *(Br.)* Kronkolonie; **industrial ~** Industrieansiedlung; **infant ~** junge Kolonie; **labo(u)r ~** Arbeitersiedlung; **mandated ~** Kolonialmandat; **penal ~** Strafkolonie;
  ~ **of artists** Künstlerkolonie;
  to establish a ~ Kolonie gründen; **to raise a ~ to the status of a substantive nation** einer Kolonie die Unabhängigkeit gewähren.
colophon Impressum.

colo(u)r Farbe, Färbung, *(character)* Gesinnung, Charakter, *(US, law)* auf den ersten Anschein hin glaubhaftes Recht, *(pretence)* Vorwand, Deckmantel, *(mil., US)* tägliche Flaggenparade, *(print.)* Druckerschwärze, Druckfarbe, *(semblance)* Anschein, *(shade)* Schein, Spur;

off ~ unwohl, deprimiert; **under false ~s** unter falscher Flagge; **under ~ of law** mit dem Anschein des Rechts; **under ~ of one's office** unter Mißbrauch seiner amtlichen Stellung; **with the ~s** im Heer dienend; **without ~ of right** ohne das geringste Recht; **~s** *(regiment)* Fahne, Flagge;

local ~ *(novel)* Lokalkolorit; **oil ~s** Ölfarben; **political ~** politische Gesinnung; **water ~s** Wasserfarben;

~ of authority scheinbare Vertretungsmacht; **political ~ of a journal** politische Tendenz einer Zeitung; **~ of law** Mäntelchen (Anschein) des Rechts; **~ of office** Amtsanmaßung; **~ of title** angeblicher Eigentumsanspruch, Rechtsschein;

to attack an opponent under ~ of patriotism seinen Gegner unter dem Deckmantel der Vaterlandsliebe angreifen; **to be called to the ~s** zu den Fahnen einberufen werden, Gestellungsbefehl erhalten; **to be off ~** sich lausig fühlen; **to cast false ~s on s. th.** falsches Licht auf etw. werfen; **to come off with flying ~s** glänzenden Sieg erringen; **to desert one's ~s** desertieren; **to display one's ~s** Flagge hissen (zeigen); **to get one's ~** sein Mitgliedsabzeichen erhalten; **to give a false ~ to news** Nachrichten sinnverfälschend aufmachen; **to have ~ of title to s. th.** scheinbaren Eigentumsanspruch haben; **to hold possession under ~s of title** aufgrund behaupteten Rechtstitels das Besitzrecht ausüben; **to join the ~s** einberufen werden; **to lend ~ to a story** Geschichte glaubwürdig erscheinen lassen; **to lower one's ~** *(fig.)* seine Flagge streichen; **to nail one's ~s to the mast** nicht kapitulieren; **to nail one's ~s to the mast of free trade** überzeugter Anhänger der Freihandelslehre sein; **to sail under false ~s** unter falscher Flagge segeln, *(fig.)* seine wahren Gefühle verbergen; **not to see the ~ of s. one's money** von jem. keinen Pfennig Geld bekommen; **to see s. th. in its true ~** Realitäten anerkennen; **to serve with the ~s** Militärdienst ableisten; **to show the ~s** Flagge hissen; **to show one's true ~** sein wahres Gesicht zeigen; **to stick to one's ~s** an seiner Meinung festhalten; **to troop the ~s** Fahnenparade abnehmen; **to want some ~** kränklich aussehen;

~ ad *(US coll.)* mehrfarbige Anzeige, Farbanzeige; **~ bar** Rassendiskriminierung; **~-blind** farbenblind; **~ blindness** Farbenblindheit; **~ block** *(Br.)* Farbklischee; **~ cast** Farbfernsehsendung; **~ chart** Farbskala; **~ composition** Farbkomposition; **~ distortion** Farbabweichung; **~ effect** Farbeffekt; **~ engraving** *(US)* Farbklischee; **~ film** Farbfilm; **~ filter** *(photo)* Farbfilter; **keyed automatic ~ gain control** *(television set)* automatisch justierte Kontrolle der Farbeinstellung; **~ gradation** Farbtönung, -schattierung; **~ guard** *(mil.)* Fahnenabordnung; **~ line** Rassenschranke; **water-~ pencil** Farbstift; **~ photo** Farbaufnahme, -foto; **~ photography** Farbfotografie; **~-picture tube** Röhre für Farbfernseher; **consumer ~ preference** Farbenbevorzugung des Konsumenten; **~ prejudice** Rassenvorurteil; **~ print** Farbdruck, -abzug; **~ printing** Mehrfarben-, Buntdruck; **~ problem** Rassenfrage, Negerproblem; **~ proof** Farbandruck; **~ receiver** Farbfernseher; **~ scheme** Farbenzusammenstellung; **~ sergeant** dienstältester Unteroffizier; **~ separation** Farbentrennung; **~ service** Wehrdienst; **~ set** Farbfernsehgerät; **~ set boom** Konjunktur in Farbfernsehgeräten; **~ slide** Farbdiapositiv; **~ supplement** Farbbeilage; **~ television** Farbfernsehen; **~-television broadcasting** Farbfernsehsendung; **~-television sales** Umsätze in Farbfernsehgeräten; **~-television set** Farbfernsehgerät, -fernseher; **~ unit** Farbanzeige; **~ videotape player** Wiedergabegerät für Farbfernsehfilme.

colo(u)rable glaubwürdig, angeblich, anscheinend, plausibel, glaubhaft, *(fictitious)* vorgeblich, fingiert;

~ alteration *(patent law)* scheinbare Patentabänderung [zu Umgehungszwecken], Patentumgehung; **~ cause** Glaubhaftmachung; **~ claim** plausibler Anspruch, *(bankruptcy)* aussonderungsberechtigte Forderung, Aussonderungsanspruch; **~ imitation** täuschend ähnliche Nachahmung, *(trademark law)* geringfügige Veränderung; **~ invocation of jurisdiction** glaubhafte Zuständigkeitsbegründung; **~ pleading** Einwendungen mittels Gegenvorbringen; **~ title** unzureichender Eigentumsanspruch; **~ transaction** Scheingeschäft.

colo(u)red farbig, *(fig.)* gefärbt, beschönigt, koloriert;

~ cartridge Farbmine; **~ impression** Farbdruck; **~ labo(u)r** farbige Arbeitskräfte; **~ news** gefärbte Nachrichten; **~ paper** getöntes Papier, Buntpapier; **~ pencil** Farbstift; **~ people** Farbige; **~ plate** Farbenkunstdruck; **~ report** gefärbter Bericht; **highly ~ tale** übertriebene Geschichte.

colo(u)rful | report farbiger Bericht; **~ style of writing** farbige Schreibe.

colo(u)ring Farbgebung, Kolorit;
~ agent Farbzusatz.

colo(u)rless farblos, nichtssagend, *(neutral)* unparteiisch, neutral;

to lead a ~ existence uninteressantes Leben führen; **~ style** farbloser Stil.

colt Fohlen, *(Br., lawcourt)* junger Anwalt.

column *(of figures)* senkrechte Reihe, Zahlenkolonne, *(file)* Zug, Reihe, *(mil.)* Kolonne, *(mar.)* in Kiellinie fahrende Schiffe, *(newspaper)* Rubrik, Spalte, Kolumne, *(print.)* Schriftblock, Satzspalte, *(US, special department)* Unterhaltungsteil, Feuilletonabteilung;

printed in double ~ zweispaltig gedruckt;

adjoining ~ nebenstehende Spalte; **advertisement (advertising) ~s** Anzeigenteil; **auxiliary ~** *(bookkeeping)* Hilfsspalte; **financial ~s** Handels-, Wirtschaftsteil; **fifth ~** *(pol.)* fünfte Kolonne; **flying ~** fliegende Kolonne; **lonely hearts ~** Ratgeber, Seufzerspalte; **obituary ~** Spalte für Todesanzeigen; **preceding ~** Vorspalte;

~ of figures Zahlenreihe, -kolonne; **~ of local news** Lokalspalte; **~ of motor vehicles** Kraftwagenkolonne; **~ of type** Druckspalte;

to add up a long ~ of figures lange Zahlenkolonne zusammenzählen; **to arrange in ~s** rubrizieren; **to devote a ~ to book criticism** für Bücherrezensionen zur Verfügung stellen; **to drive in a ~** in Kolonne fahren; **to pull out of a ~** aus einer Kolonne ausscheren;

~ depth Spaltenhöhe; **~ heading** Spaltenüberschrift; **~ height** Spaltenhöhe; **~ inch** Spaltenmaß; **~ length** Spaltenlänge; **~ line** Spaltenlinie; **~ measure** Spaltenbreite, -maß; **~ millimeter price** Millimeterpreis; **~ width** Spaltenbreite.

columnar spaltenweise, in Spalten;

~ [system of] bookkeeping amerikanische Buchführung; **~ sheet** Kolonnenbogen; **~ total** Seitengesamtbetrag.

columnist *(US)* Kolumnist, Feuilletonist, Leitartikler.

coma, to lapse into a in anhaltende Bewußtlosigkeit versinken.

comaker *(bill of exchange)* Mitaussteller, -unterzeichner.

comanagement Mitbestimmung[srecht].

comb *(v.)* | **the whole city** ganze Stadt durchsuchen; **~ a department** Abteilung zwecks Einsparung gründlich durchforsten; **~ out government departments** überschüssige Regierungsstellen durchkämmen.

combat *(mil.)* Gefecht, Kampfeinsatz, Kampfhandlung;

aerial ~ Luftkampf; **close ~** Nahkampf; **single ~** Zweikampf; **~ aircraft** Kampfflugzeug; **~ area** Kampfgebiet; **~ branch** Kampfeinheit; **~ car** *(US)* Kampfwagen; **~ command** Kampfgruppenstab; **~ efficiency** Kampfwert; **~ exercise** Gefechtsübung; **~ fatigue** Kriegsneurose; **~ group** Kampfgruppe; **~ helicopter** Kampfhubschrauber; **~ job** Kampfeinsatz; **~ order** Gefechtsbefehl; **~ patrol** Stoßtrupp; **~ practice** Kampferfahrung; **~ readiness** Gefechtsbereitschaft; **~ service** Gefechtseinsatz; **~ team** Kampfgruppe; **~ training** Gefechtsausbildung; **~ troops** Kampfeinheiten; **~ unit** Kampfverband; **~ zone** *(US)* Gefechtsbereich, Kampfgebiet, -feld.

combatant Angehöriger der Kampftruppen, Kriegsteilnehmer; **~** *(a.)* kampfbereit.

comb[ing]-out *(mobilization of manpower, Br., sl.)* Musterung der bisher Unabkömmlichen, Auskämmungsprozeß [zur Freimachung von Arbeitskräften].

combination Verbindung, Vereinigung, Kombination, *(alliance)* Zusammenschluß, Bündnis, *(cartel)* Ring, Kartell, *(of groups)* Trust, Konzern, Interessengemeinschaft, Pool, *(lock)* Ziffern-, Buchstabenkombinationsschloß, *(motor cycle)* Motorrad mit Beiwagen, *(patent law)* patentfähige Zusammenstellung;

business ~ Geschäftszusammenschluß; **close ~s** *(US)* Zusammenschlüsse auf kapitalistischer Basis; **commercial ~** Handelsvereinigung; **contract ~s** *(cartel law, US)* lockere (kartellähnliche) Zusammenschlüsse; **corporate ~** Konzernzusammenschluß; **horizontal ~** horizontaler Konzern; **loose ~s** *(cartel law, US)* lockere Vereinbarungen; **price ~** Preiskartell; **production ~** Produktionskartell; **unlawful ~** ungesetzlicher Zusammenschluß;

~ of circumstances Zusammentreffen von Umständen; **~ of a court** Zusammensetzung eines Gerichts; **~ of offices** Ämtervereinigung; **~ of powers** Personenvereinigung; **~ in restraint of trade** wettbewerbsbeschränkender Zusammenschluß, Wettbewerbskartell; **~ used to open a safe** Safekombination; **~ of workmen** Arbeitervereinigung;

to enter into ~ with s. o. Interessengemeinschaft mit jem. eingehen; **to support a college by a ~ of income from endorsements and fees from students** Kollege mittels Stiftungsbeträgen und Studentengebühren unterstützen;
~ **car** *(railroad, US)* Mehrzweckwaggon; ~ **lock** Kombinations-, Vexier-, Geheimschloß; ~ **milage and rate prorate** *(US)* kombinierter Frachttarif; ~ **movement** Konzernentwicklung; ~ **offer** Kopplungsangebot; ~ **plate** kombinierte Ätzung; ~ **rate** *(advertising)* kombinierter Anzeigenpreis, Kombinationstarif, *(railway)* Durchfrachtsatz, -tarif; ~ **room** *(university, Br.)* Gemeinschaftsraum; ~ **run** Sammeldruck; ~ **sale** Kopplungsverkauf; ~ **sheet** Sammelbogen; ~ **tariff** kombinierter Tarif.
combine [Unternehmer]zusammenschluß, Trust, Konzern, Pool, *(agriculture)* Mähdrescher, *(community of interests)* Interessengemeinschaft, *(politics)* politische Interessengemeinschaft, *(union)* Verband, Ring, Zusammenschluß;
buying (purchasing) ~ Einkaufsverband, Abnehmerkartell; **horizontal** ~ horizontales Kartell; **interlocking** ~ Konzernverflechtung; **trading** ~ Handelskonzern; **wheat** ~ Weizenkartell; ~ **of producers** Erzeugerverband;
~ *(v.)* fusionieren, zusammenschließen, -stellen, vereinigen, *(i./tr.)* sich vereinigen (zusammenschließen);
~ **business with pleasure** das Angenehme mit dem Nützlichen verbinden; ~ **one's efforts** gemeinsame Anstrengungen machen; ~ **two electoral lists** zwei Wahllisten miteinander verbinden; ~ **with a majority** in der Majorität aufgehen; ~ **buying** Gemeinschaftseinkauf; ~ **price** Verbandspreis.
combined gemeinsam, gemeinschaftlich;
~ **action** gemeinsames Vorgehen; ~ **aerial** Gemeinschaftsantenne; ~ **arms** *(mil.)* Truppenverband; ~ **attack** zusammengefaßter Angriff; ~ **board** gemischter Ausschuß; ⌕ **Certificate of Value and Origin** *(Br.)* kombiniertes Wert- und Ursprungszeugnis; ⌕ **Coal Control Group** deutsche Kohlenbergbauleitung; ~ **depreciation and upkeep method** kombinierte Abschreibungs- und Erhaltungsmethode; ~ **edition** *(magazine)* Kombinationsausgabe; ~ **edition discount** Kombinationsrabatt; ~ **efforts** gemeinsame Bemühungen; ~ **annual fee** pauschale Jahresgebühr; ~ **endowment and whole life insurance** gemischte Lebensversicherung auf den Erlebens- und Todesfall; ~ **financial statement** Konzernbilanz; ~ **income** *(married couple)* gemeinsames Einkommen; ~ **issues** Doppelnummer; ~ **operations** kombinierte militärische Aktionen; ~ **rail and road ticket** Anschlußfahrkarte; ~ **rate** Kombinationstarif, -preis; ~ **tube and bus journey** Fahrt auf U-Bahn und Bus; ~ **work** Gemeinschaftsarbeit.
combustibles feuergefährliche Güter.
combustion engine *(Br.)* **(motor, US)** Verbrennungsmotor.
come *(v.)* ankommen;
~ **of age** volljährig werden; ~ **clean** *(sl.)* mit der Wahrheit herausrücken; ~ **in negative colo(u)rs** negative Resultate zeitigen; ~ **a cropper** ruiniert sein, reinfallen; ~ **expensive** teuer sein; ~ **of a good family** aus einer guten Familie stammen; ~ **rather high** *(costs)* sich recht hoch stellen; ~ **it** *(coll.)* erreichen, schaffen; ~ **it a bit strong** erheblich übertreiben; ~ **true** sich verwirklichen.
come *(v.)* **about** passieren, sich ereignen.
come *(v.)* **abroad** ins Ausland gehen.
come *(v.)* **across** zufällig treffen;
~ **with** *(sl.)* blechen (berappen) müssen; ~ **s. th. in a curio shop** etw. in einem Antiquitätenladen auftreiben; ~ **a treasure** auf einen Schatz stoßen.
come *(v.)* **again** zurückkehren, *(sl.)* zusätzlichen Betrag berappen müssen.
come *(v.)* **along** *(coll.)* gut vorankommen.
come *(v.)* **at** | **a true knowledge of o. s.** sich selbst erkennen; ~ **a true picture** sich ein klares Bild machen.
come *(v.)* **away clearly** sich leicht lösen.
come *(v.)* **back** ins Gedächtnis zurückkehren, *(physical activity)* seine frühere Kondition zurückgewinnen;
~ **a changed man** sich völlig verändert haben.
come *(v.)* **before** | **a conciliation court** einem Schlichtungsausschuß vorliegen; ~ **the judge** vor den Richter kommen; ~ **the United Nations Assembly next week** bei der nächsten Sitzung der Vereinten Nationen zur Sprache kommen.
come *(v.)* **between** Entfremdung verursachen.
come *(v.)* **by** erwerben, gewinnen, *(inherit)* zu etw. kommen, erben; ~ **one's death tragically** auf tragische Weise ums Leben kommen; ~ **money** zu Geld kommen.
come *(v.)* **down** abgewiesen werden, *(airplane)* herunterkommen, landen, *(fall sick, coll.)* erkranken an, *(lose social position)* an Ansehen verlieren, *(pay down, coll.)* anzahlen, *(prices)* fallen;

~ **to begging** an den Bettelstab gelangen; ~ **to s. one's favo(u)rite charity** jem. wie üblich etw. für die von ihm bevorzugten Wohltätigkeitszwecke zur Verfügung stellen; ~ **handsomely** sich freigebig (als anständig) erweisen; ~ **a peg or two** mit seinen Ansprüchen zurückstecken, ganz klein und häßlich werden; ~ **step by step** schrittweise abgebaut werden; ~ **on s. o. like a ton of bricks** *(coll.)* j. gehörig herunterputzen; ~ **in the world** bessere Tage erlebt haben.
come *(v.)* **forward** an die Öffentlichkeit treten;
~ **as a candidate** sich als Kandidat vorstellen; ~ **as surety** sich als Bürge anbieten.
come *(v.)* **home** Wirkung zeitigen, einschlagen;
~ **to roost** *(faults)* sich jetzt rächen.
come *(v.)* **in** *(arrive)* ankommen, einlaufen, sich einstellen, eintreten, *(fashion)* in Mode kommen, *(fall heir)* erben, *(goods)* eintreffen, *(money, order, tax)* eingehen, *(partner)* eintreten, *(pol.)* an die Macht (ans Ruder) kommen, *(royalty)* fließen, *(train)* einfahren, einlaufen;
~ **crowds in** Scharen herbeiströmen; ~ **for a fortune** Erbschaft machen, Vermögen erben; ~ **handy** zustatten kommen; ~ **for a lot of trouble** sich eine Menge Scherereien zuziehen; ~ **a share** sich beteiligen wollen; ~ **well** *(money)* gut hereinkommen.
come *(v.)* **into** eintreten, *(become heir)* beerben;
~ **business in** ein Geschäft eintreten; ~ **demand** gesucht sein; ~ **fashion** Mode werden; ~ **force (operation) [on the date of publication]** [mit dem Tage der Veröffentlichung] in Kraft treten; ~ **a fortune** Vermögen erben; ~ **money** plötzlich zu Geld kommen; ~ **one's own** erhalten, was einem zusteht; ~ **possession** in den Besitz gelangen; ~ **power** *(party)* Regierung übernehmen; ~ **property** Vermögen erben (erwerben), zu Vermögen gelangen; ~ **bad times** schlechte Zeiten erleben; ~ **vogue** Schule machen, sich durchsetzen.
come *(v.)* **off** entstammen, *(events)* stattfinden, *(get free)* entkommen, *(play)* abgesetzt werden, *(ship)* abkommen;
~ **badly in a will** bei einer Erbschaft benachteiligt werden; ~ **best** am besten abschneiden; ~ **at ten o'clock** seinen Dienst um 10 Uhr beenden; ~ **very fine** *(weather)* sehr gut werden; ~ **with flying colo(u)rs** Sieg davontragen; ~ **the gold standard** Goldwährung aufgeben; ~ **one's perch (high horse)** von seinem hohen Roß heruntersteigen; ~ **the production line** Fließband verlassen, in Massen angefertigt werden; ~ **all right** sich programmgemäß entwickeln; ~ **well** günstig abschneiden.
come *(v.)* **on** *(cold)* im Anzug sein, *(in film)* auftreten, *(television)* auf dem Bildschirm erscheinen, *(train)* ankommen, *(to the university)* zur Universität kommen;
~ **again** *(theater)* wieder aufgeführt werden; ~ **like gangbusters** wie das Donnerwetter daherkommen; ~ **flashy** *(US sl.)* auffallend gekleidet sein; ~ **strike** in den Streik treten; ~ **strong** stark zunehmen; ~ **surprisingly** erstaunlich vorankommen; ~ **for trial** vor die Kammer (zur Verhandlung) kommen; ~ **next week** nächste Woche stattfinden.
come *(v.)* **out** *(article)* [mit einem Artikel] herauskommen, *(become known)* bekannt werden, *(book, newspaper)* erscheinen, herauskommen, *(make one's debut)* in die Gesellschaft eingeführt werden, *(Br.)* am Hofe vorgestellt werden, *(prisoner, Br.)* aus der Haft vorgeführt werden, *(strike)* streiken, in Ausstand treten, Arbeiten einstellen;
~ **against s. th.** gegen etw. agitieren; ~ **against a tariff** sich gegen ein Tarifabkommen aussprechen; ~ **in one's true colo(u)rs** sein wahres Gesicht zeigen; ~ **of s. th. with flying colo(u)rs** aus einer Sache siegreich hervorgehen; ~ **of date** veralten, aus der Mode kommen; ~ **at the little end of the horn** *(coll.)* schlecht wegkommen; ~ **into the open** *(fig.)* seine Karten aufdecken; ~ **with an extraordinary story** mit einer außergewöhnlichen Geschichte herausrücken; ~ **on strike** Arbeit einstellen, streiken; ~ **top** *(university)* Bester werden; **to always ~ well** photogen sein.
come *(v.)* **over** *(pol.)* Parteiwechsel vornehmen, übertreten;
~ **faint** Schwächeanfall bekommen.
come *(v.)* **round** *(agent)* vorbeikommen, vorsprechen, *(circuitous road)* Umweg fahren, *(recover from an illness, coll.)* sich erholen, *(term)* fällig werden;
~ **to s. one's way of thinking** sich im Endeffekt jds. Meinung anschließen.
come *(v.)* **through** *(candidate, US)* durchkommen, bestehen, Erfolg haben, *(letters)* durchdrücken, -schlagen, *(telephone call)* durchkommen;
~ **a serious illness** schwere Krankheit überstehen; ~ **into the results** sich auf das Betriebsergebnis auswirken.
come *(v.)* **to** sich belaufen auf, ausmachen, *(inherit)* erben, Erbschaft machen, *(recover)* Bewußtsein wiedererlangen;

~ **s. o. for advice** Rat von jem. haben wollen; ~ **anchor** *(fig.)* zur Ruhe kommen; ~ **an arrangement** Abkommen treffen, zu einer Einigung gelangen; ~ **a decision** Entscheidung treffen; ~ **$ 100** sich auf 100 Dollar belaufen; ~ **a great deal of money** eine dicke Stange Geld kosten; ~ **double the estimate** sich auf das Doppelte des Voranschlags belaufen; ~ **an end (close)** ablaufen; ~ **to grief** Unfall haben, zu Schaden kommen; ~ **hand** eingehen; ~ **a head** sich zuspitzen; ~ **light** enthüllt werden; ~ **much** Erfolg haben; **never** ~ **much** es nicht weit bringen; ~ **nothing** sich zerschlagen; ~ **preferment** befördert werden; ~ **close quarters** in ein Handgemenge geraten; ~ **the scratch** *(fig.)* Probe bestehen; ~ **one's senses** *(fig.)* wieder auf den Boden der Wirklichkeit zurückkehren; ~ **a standstill** zum Stillstand kommen; ~ **terms** sich einigen (vergleichen, verständigen); ~ **the same thing** auf das Gleiche hinauskommen; ~ **an understanding** zu einer Verständigung gelangen; ~ **a vote** zur Abstimmung kommen; ~ **years of discretion** volljährig werden.

come *(v.)* **under** unter eine Bestimmung fallen;
~ **the cognizance of ...** zur Zuständigkeit von ... gehören; ~ **a separate heading** unter eine besondere Rubrik fallen; ~ **s. one's influence** unter jds. Einfluß geraten; ~ **office charges** zu den Bürounkosten gehören.

come *(v.)* **up** *(lottery number)* herauskommen, *(question)* auftauchen, aufgeworfen werden, zur Sprache kommen, *(to the university, Br.)* zur Universität kommen, Universität beziehen, *(in use)* in Mode kommen, aufkommen;
~ **before the court** dem Gericht zur Entscheidung vorgelegt werden; ~ **for discussion** Besprechungsthema abgeben; ~ **to the mark (to scratch)** den Erwartungen entsprechen; ~ **to town** *(Br.)* nach London kommen; ~ **to the university** zur Universität gehen; ~ **with** zur Sprache bringen, aufwerfen, vorbringen.

come *(v.)* **upon** | **s. o. for alimony** Unterhaltszahlungen von jem. verlangen; ~ **s. o. for damages** j. wegen Schadenersatzes belangen; ~ **the parish** der Gemeinde zu Last fallen; ~ **hidden treasure** verborgenen Schatz finden; ~ **s. o. for a sum** Betrag von jem. fordern.

come *(v.)* **with** *(money)* bezahlen.

come *(v.)* **within** | **s. one's duties** zu jds. Aufgabenbereich gehören;
~ **the scope of the law** unter die Bestimmungen eines Gesetzes fallen; ~ **the terms of a contract** unter die vertraglichen Bestimmungen fallen.

come-at-able *(coll.)* erreichbar, zugänglich.

come-off *(coll.)* Ausflucht, Vorwand.

come-on *(US sl.)* Köder, Kaufanreiz, Lockmittel.

comeback *(pol.)* Rück-, Wiederkehr, Rehabilitierung, Comeback, Wiederauftauchen, *(cause for complaint, US sl.)* Beschwerdegrund;
~ **in prices** Kurs-, Preiserholung;
to have a ~ **against s. o.** Regreßanspruch gegen j. haben; **to make one's** ~ *(party)* sich erneut durchsetzen, wieder zur Macht kommen; **to make a strong** ~ wieder stark im Kommen sein;
~ **vehicle** Rückkehrmöglichkeit.

comedown Niedergang, Abstieg, Reinfall.

comedy komische Situation, *(theater)* Lustspiel, Komödie;
light ~ Schwank;
~ **program(me)** Unterhaltungsprogramm.

comer Ankömmling, *(applicant)* Bewerber;
first ~ Zuerstkommender;
to be a ~ *(US sl.)* kommender Mann sein.

comfort Bequemlichkeit, Komfort, *(bedquilt, US)* Steppdecke;
cold ~ magerer Trost; **homely** ~ wohnliche Umgebung; **every modern** ~ aller Komfort;
to derive ~ **from s. th.** aus etw. Trost schöpfen; **to draw little** ~ **from** sich kaum damit trösten können; **to give the enemy aid and** ~ dem Feinde Vorschub leisten; **to live in** ~ komfortabel leben, behagliches Leben führen; **to receive a few grains of** ~ nur kümmerlichen Komfort erhalten;
~ **ride** bequeme Reisemöglichkeit; ~ **standard** bequemer Lebensstandard; **public** ~ **station** *(US)* öffentliche Bedürfnisanstalt.

comfortable behaglich, bequem, wohnlich;
to be ~ gut sitzen;
to live in ~ **circumstances** im Wohlstand leben; ~ **income** gutes Einkommen; ~ **independence** finanzielle Unabhängigkeit; ~ **maintenance** standesgemäßer Unterhalt.

comfortably, to be ~ **housed** bequem wohnen; **to be** ~ **off** zu den wohlhabenden Leuten zählen; **to live** ~ angenehmes Leben führen.

comic | **opera** Operette; ~ **paper** Witzblatt; ~ **strip** humoristische Bildergeschichte; ~ **writer** Lustspieldichter.

coming Ankunft, *(event)* Eintritt;
~ **of age** Erreichung der Volljährigkeit, Mündigwerden; ~ **of voting age** Wahlmündigkeit; ~ **in of goods** Wareneingang; ~ **into force** Inkrafttreten; ~ **into an inheritance** Übernahme einer Erbschaft; ~ **out of a book** Erscheinen eines Buches; ~ **together of firms** Firmenzusammenschluß;
~ *(a.)* kommend, zukünftig;
~ **fashion** kommende Mode; ~ **man** *(politics)* vielversprechender Politiker.

comity entgegenkommendes Respekt;
on principles of ~ aus Gründen der Höflichkeit;
judicial ~ Anerkennung ausländischer Gerichtsentscheidungen;
~ **of nations** gutes Einvernehmen der Nationen.

command Kommando, Befehl, Anordnung, *(Br.)* königliche Einladung, *(dominion)* Macht, Herrschaft, *(mil.)* Kommando-[gewalt, -bereich], Befehl, Befehlsbereich;
at ~ dienstbereit, *(mil.)* einsatzbereit, *(on order)* auf Bestellung; **higher** ~ *(Br.)* höhere Führung; **naval** ~ Flottenkommando; **supreme** ~ oberste Heeresleitung, Oberkommando;
sufficient ~ **of English** ausreichende englische Sprachkenntnisse; ~ **of goods** Warenanforderung; ~ **of a language** Beherrschung einer Sprache; ~ **of the world market** Beherrschung des Weltmarktes;
~ *(v.)* befehlen, kommandieren;
~ **the entrance of a valley** *(fort)* beherrschende Stellung über einen Talzugang haben; ~ **$ 1000 in an emergency** im Notfall über 1000 Dollar verfügen; ~ **both harbo(u)r and city** *(fleet)* sowohl den Hafen als die Stadt beherrschen; ~ **the market** Markt beherrschen; ~ **one's passions** seine Leidenschaften zügeln; ~ **a high price** hoch im Preis sein; ~ **s. one's services** über jds. Dienste verfügen; ~ **the service of many officials** Disziplinargewalt über viele Beamte ausüben; ~ **great sums of money** über große Geldbeträge disponieren können; ~ **sympathy** Mitleid verdienen; ~ **a fine view** herrliche Aussicht gewähren;
to be in ~ Kommando führen; **to have a** ~ **of several languages** mehrere Sprachen beherrschen; **to have** ~ **over one's temper** über Selbstbeherrschung verfügen; **to put under s. one's** ~ jem. unterstellen.
~ **car** Kübelwagen; ~ **economy** Kommandowirtschaft; ~ **paper** *(Br.)* Regierungsvorlage; ~ **performance** Pflichtveranstaltung, hochoffizielle Angelegenheit, *(theater)* Privatvorstellung; ~ **post** Befehlsstand, -einheit; ~ **planning system** Befehlswirtschaft.

commandant [Platz]kommandant, Befehlshaber.

commandeer *(v.)* *(compel for military service)* zum Wehrdienst pressen, *(seize for military purposes)* requirieren, *(take arbitrarily, coll.)* organisieren.

commander Kommandant;
~ **in chief** Oberbefehlshaber; ~ **of the guard** Wachhabender.

commanding befehlend, beherrschend, dominierend, *(mil.)* kommandierend, befehlshabend;
~ **general** kommandierender General; ~ **height** beherrschende Höhe, *(fig.)* Kommandobrücke; ~ **officer** Kommandant.

commanditaire Kommanditist.

commandment gerichtliche Anordnung.

commando Kommandounternehmen;
~ **raid** Kommandoüberfall; ~ **squad** [etwa] Sondereinheit des Bundesgrenzschutzes.

commarchio Grundstücksgrenze.

commemoration Gedenkfeier;
~ **day** Stiftungsfest.

commemorative | **issue** Gedenk-, Sonderausgabe; ~ **postmark** Sonderstempel.

commence *(v.)* einleiten, anfangen, beginnen, *(university, Br.)* promovieren;
~ **an action (suit, US) against s. o.** gegen j. prozessieren, Prozeß gegen j. anstrengen; ~ **business** Geschäftsbetrieb beginnen.

commencement Anfang, Beginn, *(university)* Abschlußfeier;
~ **of an action** Klageerhebung; ~ **of a bankruptcy** Konkursbeginn; ~ **of building** Baubeginn; ~ **of business** Geschäftsbeginn, -eröffnung; ~ **of a career** Beginn einer Laufbahn; ~ **of an insurance** Versicherungsbeginn; ~ **of a liquidation** Liquidationsbeginn; ~ **of a lease** Pachtbeginn; ~ **of proceedings** Verfahrensbeginn, Rechtshängigkeit; ~ **of prosecution** Anklageerhebung; ~ **of a sentence** Strafbeginn; ~ **of war** Kriegsbeginn; ~ **of the winding up** Liquidationsbeginn; ~ **of work** Arbeitsaufnahme; ~ **of a year** Jahresanfang;
~ **provisions** Steuerbestimmungen über den Beginn eines Gewerbebetriebs.

commencing|employment Beschäftigungsbeginn; ~ **salary** Anfangsgehalt.
commend (v.) empfehlen, lobend erwähnen;
  ~ **s. th. to one's care** jem. etw. anvertrauen; ~ **s. o. upon his good manners** jds. gutes Benehmen lobend hervorheben; ~ **a man to his employer** jem. für seinen Arbeitgeber eine Empfehlung mitgeben; ~ **itself to the public** sich von allein in der Öffentlichkeit durchsetzen; ~ **one's wares** seine Ware anpreisen.
commendam, to hold in Pfründe verwalten.
commendation Empfehlung.
commendatory letter Empfehlungsbrief.
commensurate angemessen, entsprechend.
comment Bemerkung, Erklärung, Stellungnahme, Kommentar, Meinungsäußerung, Werturteil;
  ~**s** Ausführungen;
  fair ~ sachliche Kritik; **garbled** ~ entstellter Kommentar; **no** ~ keine Erklärung, kein Kommentar;
  ~ (v.) Anmerkungen machen, kommentieren;
  ~ **on a text** Text mit Anmerkungen versehen;
  to cause a good deal of ~ ziemliches Gerede auslösen; **to decline to** ~ Kommentar ablehnen; **to give rise to much** ~ viel von sich reden machen; **to make one's** ~ **upon s. th.** mit Anmerkungen versehen, etw. kommentieren; **to receive much negative** ~ starke Kritik erfahren; **to refrain from** ~**s** sich jedes Kommentars enthalten.
commentarial erläuternd, kommentierend.
commentary Kommentar, Erläuterung, (annotation) Anmerkung, Aktennotiz, -vermerk, (broadcasting) Hörbericht;
  legal ~ juristischer Kommentar; **press** ~ Pressekommentar; **radio** ~ Rundfunkkommentar; **running** ~ Rundfunkreportage; ~ **on the political situation** Bericht zur Lage, politischer Kommentar;
  to make a ~ **on a text** Text mit Erläuterungen versehen (kommentieren); **to write a** ~ Kommentar verfassen.
commentation of a text Erklärung eines Textes, Textauslegung, -kommentierung.
commentator Kommentator, (radio) Funkberichterstatter, Rundfunkkommentator;
  ~ **on politics** politischer Kommentator.
commerce [Handels]verkehr, Warenverkehr, [Außen]handel;
  active ~ lebhafter Handelsverkehr, (mercantile shipping on own ships) Außenhandel mit eigenen Schiffen; **agricultural** ~ Handel mit landwirtschaftlichen Erzeugnissen; **domestic** ~ (US) Binnenhandel; **export** ~ Außenhandel; **extensive** ~ ausgedehnter Handel; **foreign** ~ Außenhandel, Export; **internal** ~ (US) inner-, zwischenstaatlicher Handelsverkehr; **international** ~ Welthandel; **interstate (intrastate)** ~ (US) zwischenstaatlicher Handel, Binnenhandel; **maritime** ~ Handelsschiffahrt; **neutral** ~ Handelsverkehr neutraler Staaten; **overseas** ~ Überseehandel; **passive** ~ Außenhandel mit fremden Schiffen; **peacetime** ~ Friedenswirtschaft; **transmarine** ~ überseeischer Handel; **waterborne** ~ Handel auf dem Wasserwege; **world** ~ Welthandel;
  ~ **and industry** Handel und Gewerbe; ~ **with foreign nations** (US) Außenhandelsbeziehungen eigener mit fremden Staatsangehörigen; ~ **among the states** (US) Wirtschaftsverkehr zwischen den einzelnen Bundesstaaten, Binnenhandel, zwischenstaatlicher Handel;
  to carry on ~ **with** Handel treiben; **to introduce goods into the** ~ **of another country** Waren auf den Markt eines anderen Landes verbringen;
  ~ **clause** (US, constitution) Handelsvertragsvollmacht.
Commerce Department (US) Handels-, Wirtschaftsministerium;
  ~ **experts** Sachverständige des Wirtschaftsministeriums; ~ **figures** Ziffern des Wirtschaftsministeriums; ~ **Report** Bericht des Handelsministeriums (Wirtschaftsministeriums).
commerce|destroyer Handelszerstörer, Kaperschiff; ~ **destroying** Handelskrieg, (sales agent) Tour; **to go out** ~ **destroying** (sales agent) auf Tour gehen.
commercial (broadcasting, television) Patronatssendung, Werbesendung, -funk, -spot, Fernsehspot, (traveller, Br., coll.) Handelsreisender, Vertreter;
  integrated ~ eingeblendete Werbesendung;
  ~ (a.) geschäftlich, kaufmännisch, für den Handel bestimmt, handeltreibend, gewerblich, kommerziell, geschäftlich, (economic) wirtschaftlich, (having financial profit) auf Gewinn abgestellt, merkantil eingestellt, (large-scale) in großen Mengen erzeugt;
  ~ **acceptance credit** Warenremboerskredit; ~ **activities** gewerbliche Betätigung; **to be engaged in** ~ **activities** einer kaufmännischen Betätigung nachgehen; ~ **advantage** Han-

delsvorteil; ~ **adventurer** Spekulant; ~ **advertising** Wirtschaftswerbung; ~ **advice** Handels-, Wirtschaftsbericht; ~ **age** konsumfreudiges Zeitalter; ~ **agency** Handelsvertretung, (US) [Kredit]auskunftei; ~ **agency referee book** (US) Nachschlagewerk einer Auskunftei; ~ **agent** (US) Handelsvertreter; ~ **agreement** Handelsabkommen; ~ **air transportation** Güterflugverkehr; ~ **aircraft** Verkehrsflugzeug; ~ **airline** Verkehrsluftfahrt; ~ **airliner** Linienflugzeug; ~ **airport** Verkehrsflughafen; ~ **alcohol** Sprit; ~ **alliance** Handelsvertrag; ~ **announcements** (broadcasting) geschäftliche Mitteilungen; ~ **applicant** gewerblicher Antragsteller; ~ **appointment** kaufmännische Beschäftigung; ~ **apprentice** [Handels]lehrling; ~ **arbitration** wirtschaftliche Schiedsgerichtsbarkeit, Schiedsgerichtswesen der Wirtschaft, Handelsschiedsgerichtsbarkeit; ~ **arithmetic** kaufmännisches Rechnen; ~ **art** Gebrauchs-, Werbegraphik; ~ **art company** graphischer Betrieb; ~ **articles** Handelsartikel; ~ **artist** Werbe-, Gebrauchsgraphiker; ~ **association** Wirtschaftsvereinigung; ~ **attaché** Handelsattaché; ~ **automobile** Nutzfahrzeug; ~ **aviation** Verkehrs-, Handelsluftfahrt; ~ **bank** Handelsbank, Rembourskreditinstitut; ~ **banking** Rembourskreditgeschäft, Geschäftsbankwesen; ~ **bar** (US) Gold- oder Silberbarren; ~ **bill** Handelswechsel; ~ **bookkeeping** kaufmännische Buchführung; ~ **books** Geschäftsbücher; ~ **borrowing** Geschäftskredite; ~ **broadcasting** Werbefunk; ~ **broker** Produktenmakler; ~ **building** gewerblich genutztes Gebäude; ~ **business** Handelsunternehmen; **to be engaged in a** ~ **business** Handelsgeschäft betreiben; ~ **car** Nutzfahrzeug, Geschäfts-, Lieferwagen; ~ **cause** handelsrichterliche Sache, Handelssache; ~ **center** Handelszentrum, Handelsmittelpunkt, Wirtschaftszentrum; ~ **circles** Kaufmannskreise; **in** ~ **circles** in kaufmännischen Kreisen; ~ **clause** (US) Handelsklausel; ~ **college** Handelshochschule, -akademie; ~ **commitments** Warenverbindlichkeiten; ~ **communications** geschäftliche Mitteilungen; ~ **concern** Handelsunternehmen, -firma; ~ **construction** gewerbliche Bautätigkeit; ~ **contract** Handelsvertrag; ~ **convention** Handelsabkommen; ~ **corporation** Handelsgesellschaft; ~ **correspondence** Handelskorrespondenz; ~ **correspondence course** Handelskorrespondenzkursus; ~ **cost** Handlungsunkosten; **at their** ~ **cost** die Unkosten deckend; ~ **counsellor** Handelsattaché; ~ **course** kaufmännischer Lehrgang, Handelskursus; ~ **court** [etwa] Kammer für Handelssachen; ~ **credit** Handelskredit, Waren-, Bank-, Rembourskredit, (credit rating) geschäftlicher Kredit; ~ **credit company** Finanzierungsgesellschaft, Gesellschaft zur Finanzierung von Warenkrediten; ~ **credit department** Rembourabteilung; ~ **credit documents** Warenkreditunterlagen; ~ **credit guarantee** Warenkreditbürgschaft; ~ **credit information** Kreditauskunft; ~ **crisis** Wirtschaftskrise; ~ **dealings** Handelsgeschäfte; ~ **debt** Warenschuld; ~ **delegate** Vertreter der Wirtschaft; ~ **development** wirtschaftliche Entwicklung; ~ **dictionary** Wirtschaftswörterbuch, Wörterbuch der Handelssprache; ~ **directory** Branchenadreßbuch; ~ **discount** Skonto; ~ **discounts (discount notes)** Diskonten; ~ **domicile** Sitz der gewerblichen Niederlassung; ~ **draft** Handelswechsel; ~ **education** kaufmännische Ausbildung, Handelsschulausbildung; ~ **effects** Effekten; ~ **efficiency** (machine) Nutzeffekt, ~ **engineer** Wirtschaftsingenieur; ~ **engineering** Warentechnik; ~ **English** Wirtschaftsenglisch; ~ **enterprise** gewerbliches Unternehmen, Geschäfts-, Handelsunternehmen; ~ **establishment** Handelsunternehmen; **medium-sized** ~ **establishment** Unternehmen des gewerblichen Mittelstandes; ~ **examination** Abschlußexamen an der Handelsschule; ~ **exhibition** Wirtschaftsmesse; ~ **factory** Handelsniederlassung; ~ **failure** Zahlungseinstellung, Konkurs, Bankrott; ~ **farmer** über den Eigenbedarf hinaus produzierender Landwirt; ~ **fertilizer** Handelsdünger; ~ **field** Handelsgebiet; ~ **finance company** Finanzierungsgesellschaft; ~ **firm** Geschäftshaus, Handelsfirma; ~ **fleet** Handelsflotte; ~ **flight** geschäftsbedingte Flugreise; ~ **frustration** Einwendung höherer Gewalt; ~ **gazette** Handelsblatt, Börsenzeitung; ~ **geography** Wirtschaftsgeographie; **to have** ~ **glamo(u)r** für die Geschäftswelt sehr verlockend sein; ~ **grouping** Wirtschaftsblock; ~ **hono(u)r** Kaufmannsehre; ~ **hotel** Durchgangshotel; ~ **house** Handelsfirma; ~ **insolvency** Zahlungsunfähigkeit; ~ **instrument** Handelspapier; ~ **insurance** Vertrauensschaden-, Garantieversicherung; ~ **intelligence department** (Board of Trade) Auskunftsabteilung; ~ **interests** kaufmännische Interessen, Wirtschaftsinteressen; ~ **items** Geschäftsdrucksachen; ~ **jargon** geschraubter Geschäftsstil; ~ **jet aircraft** Düsenverkehrsflugzeug; ~ **land** gewerblich genutztes Grundstück, Geschäftsgrundstück; ~ **law** Handels-, Wirtschaftsrecht; ~ **league**

Handelsunion; ~ **lease** Mietvertrag über gewerblich genutzte Räume; ~ **leg-up** wirtschaftliche Hilfe; ~ **legislation** Handelsgesetzgebung; ~ **lendings** Geschäftskredite; ~ **letter** Geschäftsbrief; ~ **letter of credit** Handelskreditbrief, Akkreditiv, Warenkreditbrief; ~ **line** kaufmännisches Fach; ~ **lines** Wirtschafts-, Geschäftszweige; ~ **list** Sitzungsliste der Kammer für Handelssachen; ~ **loading** raumsparende Verladung; ~ **loan** Warenkredit; ~ **location** Handelsniederlassung; ~ **magazine** Wirtschaftszeitschrift; ~ **man** Geschäftsmann, *(US)* Geschäftsreisender; ~ **mark** Warenbezeichnung; ~ **men** Kaufmannschaft, Geschäftswelt; ~ **minute** *(broadcasting, television)* Werbeminute; ~ **morality** Geschäfts-, Wirtschaftsmoral; ~ **motoring and road transport** gewerbsmäßiger Kraftfahrzeugverkehr; ~ **nation** Handelsvolk; ~ **negotiations** Handelsbesprechungen; ~ **news** Handels-, Wirtschaftsnachrichten; ~ **newspaper** Wirtschaftszeitung, Börsenblatt; ~ **note** handelsübliches Papierformat; ~ **occupation** Handelsstand; ~ **operation** Handelsgeschäft, Geschäftsabschluß; ~ **operator** gewerbliches Unternehmen; ~ **order** geschäftlicher Auftrag; ~ **overflight** Überfliegung mit Handelsflugzeugen; ~ **paper** kurzfristiges Handelspapier, Handels-, Warenwechsel; ~ **papers** *(post)* Geschäftspapiere, Handelskorrespondenz; ~ **paper house** *(US)* Wechselmaklerfirma; ~ **paper market** Diskont-, Schuldscheinmarkt; ~ **paper rates** *(US)* Sätze für Handelswechsel; ~ **parity** *(US)* Handelsparität; ~ **partnership** Handelsgesellschaft; ~ **photo** Werbefoto; ~ **pitch** Auktionsstand; ~ **plane** Verkehrsflugzeug; ~ **policy** Handels-, Wirtschaftspolitik; *(insurance)* Ausschließlichkeitspolice für Berufstätige; ~ **policy devices** handelspolitische Praktiken; ~ **position** Handelsposition; ~ **practice** Handelsbrauch; **to be consistent with sound ~ practice** im kaufmännischen Leben üblich sein; ~ **practice of the bookselling trade** Handelsbräuche des Buchhandels; ~ **price** im freien Kräftespiel entstandener Preis; ~ **profession** Kaufmannstand; ~ **profit** Geschäftsgewinn; ~ **program(me)** *(broadcasting)* Werbefunksendung; ~ **prominence** wirtschaftliche Bedeutung; ~ **property** Geschäftsgebäude, -grundstück; ~ **prospects** Geschäftsaussichten; ~ **puff** Warenanpreisung; ~ **purpose** wirtschaftliche Bedeutung; **for ~ purposes** zu gewerblichen Zwecken; ~ **pursuits** Geschäftsbetrieb; ~ **radio** private Rundfunkanstalt, Werbefunk; ~ **railroad** *(US)* gewerbliche Eisenbahnlinie; ~ **rate of exchange** *(US)* Devisen-, Wechselkurs; ~ **real-estate investment** Investitionen in Geschäftsgrundstücken; ~ **relationship** Geschäfts-, Handelsbeziehungen; ~ **report** Wirtschafts-, Handelsbericht; ~ **representative** Wirtschaftsvertreter; ~ **research** Wirtschaftsforschung; ~ **revolution** wirtschaftliche Umwälzung; ~ **right** Recht auf Handel; ~ **rip-offs** reißerische Verkaufspraktiken; ~ **risk** Geschäftsrisiko, Unternehmerwagnis; ~ **room** *(hotel, Br.)* Besprechungs-, Konferenzzimmer; ~ **sale** Warenverkauf; ~ **sale rooms** Verkaufsräume von Produktenbörsen; ~ **sample** Warenmuster; **on a ~ scale** gewerbsmäßig; ~ **scene** kommerzielles Fernsehen; ~ **school** Handelsschule; ~ **school examination** Kaufmannsgehilfenprüfung; ~ **science** Wirtschaftswissenschaften; ~ **secretary** Handelsattaché; ~ **section** *(consulate)* Handelsabteilung; ~ **service** *(airline)* regulärer Liniendienst; **in ~ service** im regelmäßigen Einsatz; ~ **services** gewerbliche Leistungen, Handelstätigkeit; ~ **shipment** *(US)* Warenversand; ~ **shipping** Handelsschiffahrt; ~ **signs** handelsübliche Abkürzungen; ~ **size** marktfähige (gängige) Größe; ~ **spirit** Geschäftssinn; ~ **sponsoring of program(me)s** privatwirtschaftliche Finanzierung von Rundfunkprogrammen; ~ **spot** Werbedurchsage, -film; ~ **standardization** Warennormung; ~ **standards of solvency** übliche Liquiditätsfordernisse; ~ **station** privat betriebener Sender; ~ **stationery** Geschäftsdrucksachen; ~ **statistics** Handelsstatistik; ~ **storage** Warenlagerung; ~ **street** Geschäftsstraße; ~ **studio** Werbeatelier; ~ **subject** kaufmännisches Thema; ~ **success** kaufmännischer Erfolg; ~ **supplement** *(newspaper)* Handelsbeilage, -teil; ~ **survey** Marktanalyse; ~ **teacher** Gewerbe-, Handelslehrer; ~ **television** Werbefernsehen; ~ **television franchise** Werbefernsehlizenz; ~ **television licence** Werbefernsehlizenz; ~ **television station** Werbefernsehstation; ~ **tenant** gewerblicher Mieter; ~ **term** Handelsausdruck, -bezeichnung; ~ **terms** Lieferklauseln; ~ **theory** *(economics)* Werttheorie; ~ **timber** Nutzholz; ~ **town** Handelsstadt; ~ **trainee** Handlungslehrling, als Kaufmann Auszubildender; ~ **transaction** Geschäftsabschluß; ~ **transport aircraft** Verkehrsflugzeug; ~ **traveller** Handlungsreisender, Vertreter [im Außendienst]; ~ **treaty** Handelsvertrag, Wirtschaftsabkommen; ~ **trucking company** Kraftwagenspedition; ~ **undertaking** kaufmännisches Unternehmen, *(advertising)* Werbeunternehmen; ~ **use** gewerbliche Nutzung; ~ **value** Handels-,

Marktwert; ~ **variety** Handelssorte; ~ **vehicle** Nutzfahrzeug; ~ **warehouse** Warenspeicher; ~ **wares** Handelsware; ~ **work** Akzidenzdrucksachen; ~ **world** Kaufmannschaft, Geschäftswelt; ~ **writing** Schriftsprache des Kaufmanns.

commercialese Geschäftsstil.

commercialism Geschäftssinn.

commercialization Kommerzialisierung.

commercialize *(v.)* kommerziell auswerten (verwerten), in den Handel bringen, marktfähig machen.

commercialized merkantil.

commercially in kommerzieller Weise, geschäftlich.

commination Strafandrohung.

comminatory strafandrohend.

commingle *(v.)* *(law of contract)* sich vermischen.

commingled goods vermischt gelagerte Waren.

comminglement Vermischung.

commissar Volkskommissar.

commissarial kommissarisch.

commissariat Kommissariat, *(mil.)* Verpflegungswesen, Intendantur, *(pol.)* Volkskommissariat;
~**magazine** Verpflegungsamt.

commissaries *(US)* Proviant.

commissary Kommissar, Beauftragter, *(mil.)* Verpflegungsausgabe, -stelle, Kantine, *(Br., university)* Universitätsrichter.

commission *(agent's remuneration)* Kommission[sgebühr], [Makler]gebühr, *(authority)* Vollmacht, *(bailment)* unentgeltliche Verwahrung, *(bankruptcy)* Bonifikation, *(brokerage)* Courtage, *(charge)* [Geschäfts]auftrag, Geschäftsbesorgung, Kommission, Bestellung, Mandat, *(committee)* Ausschuß, *(consul)* Ernennungsschreiben, *(department head)* Verkaufsprovision, *(duty)* übertragene Pflicht, *(entrusting of authority)* Auftrag, Beauftragung, Bevollmächtigung, *(law court, US)* gerichtliches Ersuchen, *(mil.)* Offizierstelle, -patent, *(office)* Amt, Funktion, *(official)* Bestallungsurkunde, *(patent)* Patent, *(perpetration)* Begehung, Verübung, *(ship)* Indienststellung;

deducting your ~ unter Abzug Ihrer Provision; **free of ~** provisionsfrei; **in ~** in amtlicher Stellung (dienstlicher Vertretung), *(in order)* in gebrauchsfähigem Zustand, funktionierend; **in ~ with ...** in Kommission bei ...; **liable (subject) to ~** gegen eine Provision, provisionspflichtig; **on (by way of)** im Auftrag, bevollmächtigt; **sold on ~** auf Kommissionsbasis verkauft;

3 per cent ~ 3% Provision;

accepting ~ Akzeptprovision; **accrued ~** Provisionsforderung, Provisionsanspruch; **additional ~** Zusatzprovision; **address ~** Provision des Befrachters; **agent's (agency) ~** Vertreterprovision; **allocation ~** Zuteilungsausschuß; **arbitration ~** Schlichtungsausschuß; **auctioneer's ~** Auktionskosten; **auditing ~** Revisions-, Prüfungsausschuß; **banking ~** Bankprovision, -spesen; **border ~** Grenzkommission; **broker's ~** Maklerprovision; **buying ~** Einkaufskommission, -provision; **charity ~** Wohltätigkeitsausschuß; **city ~** städtischer Ausschuß; **complaints ~** Beschwerdeausschuß; **control ~** Überwachungsausschuß; **counterbalance ~** Stornogebühr; **delcredere ~** Delkredereprovision; **drawing ~** Ausstellerprovision; **electoral ~** Parlamentsausschuß zur Untersuchung einer Wahl; **exchange ~** Wechselprovision; **Federal Trade ℀** *(US)* Ausschuß zur Bekämpfung des unlauteren Wettbewerbs; **final ~** Abschlußprovision; **flat 3% ~** dreiprozentige Pauschalprovision; **gross ~** Bruttoprovision; **governing ~** Kontrollausschuß; **guarantee ~** Aval-, Delkredereprovision; **illicit ~** unerlaubte Vergütung; **informal ~** informeller Ausschuß; **insurance ~** Versicherungsprovision; **joint ~** gemischter Ausschuß; **mediation ~** Vermittlungsausschuß; **monetary ~** Währungskommission; **net ~** Nettoprovision; **new business ~** Abschlußprovision; **paid ~** Provisionsaufwendungen; **overdraft ~** Überziehungsprovision; **overriding ~** Abschlußprovision des Generalvertreters; **parliamentary ~** parlamentarischer Ausschuß, Parlamentsausschuß; **permanent ~** ständige Kommission; **reasonable ~** angemessene Provision; **~s received** Provisionserträge; **renewal ~** Verlängerungs-, Prolongationsprovision; **~s rogatory** *(Br.)* Rechtshilfeersuchen; **Royal ℀** *(Br.)* königliche Enquete, Untersuchungsausschuß; **sales ~** Abschlußprovision; **secret ~** verbotene Sonderkommission, Schmiergeld; **seller's (selling) ~** Verkaufs-, Umsatzprovision; **six months ~** Semesterprovision; **small ~s** kleine Besorgungen; **special ~** Sonderausschuß, -kommission; **split ~** Provisionsgebühr für Durchführung eines Aktiensplits; **standstill ~** Stillhalteausschuß; **straight ~** vorbehaltlos gezahlte Provision; **tax ~** Steuerausschuß; **turnover ~** Umsatzprovision; **underwriting ~** Abschlußprovision, Provision aus Konsortialbeteiligungen, Bonifikation; **valuation ~**

Bewertungsausschuß; **vigilance ~** *(US)* Überwachungsausschuß; **world economic ~** Weltwirtschaftskommission;
~ for acceptance Akzeptprovision; **~ of an act of bankruptcy** Konkursvergehen; **~ to agents** Vertreterprovisionen; **~ of anticipation** *(Br.)* Vollmacht zur vorzeitigen Steuereinziehung; **~ of appeal** [zeitweise eingesetztes] Berufungsgericht; **~ of appraisement** Bewertungsausschuß, -kommission; **~ of appraisement and sale** Verkaufs- und Bewertungskommission; **~ charged by the bank** von der Bank in Ansatz gebrachte Provision; **~ of bankruptcy** Untersuchungsausschuß für Konkursfälle; **~ to buy** Einkaufsermächtigung; **~ to codify** Formulierungsausschuß; **~ for collecting** Einzugs-, Inkassoprovision; **~ on contangoes** Reportprovision; **~ of control** Überwachungsausschuß; **~ of a crime** Begehen eines Verbrechens; **~ to take depositions** Rechtshilfeersuchen für Zeugenaussagen; **~ for domicil[iat]ing** Domizilprovision; ⚘ **of the European Communities** Kommission der Europäischen Gemeinschaften; **~ to examine witnesses** *(US)* Ausschuß zur Einvernahme ausländischer Zeugen, Rechtshilfeersuchen; **~ on guarantee** Avalprovision; **~ of inquiry** Untersuchungskommission, -ausschuß; **~ of lunacy** Entmündigungsausschuß; ⚘ **on Narcotic Drugs** Suchtstoffkommission; **~ of an offence** Begehung einer Übertretung; **~ on options** Optionsprovision; **~ on overdraft** Überziehungsprovision; **~ paid on sales** Verkaufsprovision; **~ of partition** Teilungsausschuß; **~ of the peace** *(Br.)* Friedensrichteramt; **~ of rebellion** Androhung der Beugestrafe; **~ on industrial relations** *(Br.)* Untersuchungsausschuß zu Fragen der Arbeitnehmerpolitik; **~ of review** Revisionsbehörde; ⚘ **on Human Rights** Menschenrechtskommission; **~ on sales effected** Kommissions-, Umsatzprovision; **~ to salesman** Vertreterprovision; **~ of a ship** Indienststellung eines Schiffes; **~ of the stock exchange** Börsenzulassungsausschuß; **~ on taxation** Steuerausschuß; **~ of a theft** Begehung eines Diebstahls; **~ of unlivery** Ausschuß zur Untersuchung einer Schiffsladung;
~ *(v.)* beauftragen, bevollmächtigen, ermächtigen, *(appoint)* zu einem Amt ernennen, abordnen, *(mil.)* zum Offizier ernennen, Offizierspatent verleihen, *(for piece of work)* in Auftrag geben, bestellen, beordern, *(ship)* in Dienst stellen;
~ one's bank to pay one's taxes seine Bank mit der rechtzeitigen Bezahlung seiner Steuern beauftragen; **~ s. o. to buy s. th.** j. mit dem Einkauf von etw. beauftragen;
to accord a ~ Provision gewähren; **to appoint a ~** Ausschuß einsetzen; **to appoint s. o. as buyer on ~** j. auf Provisionsbasis anstellen; **to be in ~** kommissarisch verwaltet werden; **to be in the ~** *(Br.)* Friedensrichter sein; **to be in ~ all the year** *(car)* das ganze Jahr in Betrieb sein; **to be entitled to a ~** Provisionsanspruch haben; **to be on the ~** Ausschuß-, Kommissionsmitglied sein; **to be out of ~** *(elevator)* nicht funktionieren; **to be subject to a ~** provisionspflichtig sein; **to buy and sell on ~** Provisionsgeschäfte machen; **to carry out a ~** Geschäftsbesorgung (Auftrag) erledigen; **to charge ~** Provision berechnen; **to discharge a ~** Auftrag ausführen; **to draw a ~** Provision bekommen; **to establish a ~** Ausschuß einsetzen; **to entrust s. o. with a ~** jem. einen Auftrag erteilen; **to execute a ~** Kommission erledigen; **to form a ~ for the purpose of investigation** Untersuchungskommission bilden; **to form part of a ~** einem Ausschuß angehören; **to give s. o. a ~** jem. einen Auftrag erteilen; **to have earned one's ~** provisionsberechtigt sein, berechtigte Provisionsansprüche haben; **to have two or three small ~s for s. o.** einige kleine Besorgungen für j. zu erledigen haben; **to head a ~** Ausschuß leiten, Ausschußvorsitzender sein; **to hold a ~** *(mil.)* Offiziersstelle innehaben; **to hold an office in ~** Amt kommissarisch ausüben; **to lay one's case before a ~** seinen Fall einem Ausschuß vorlegen; **to make a ~** Kommission kassieren; **to obtain a ~** *(mil.)* zum Offizier befördert werden; **to open a ~** Ausschußtätigkeit beginnen; **to put an office into ~** Funktionen auf einen Ausschuß übertragen; **to put into ~** provisorisch verwalten, *(ship)* in Dienst stellen; **to put out of ~** außer Betrieb setzen, *(ship)* außer Dienst stellen; **to receive a ~** Provision bekommen; **to receive one's ~** *(mil.)* Offizier werden; **to resign one's ~** *(officer)* seinen Abschied nehmen; **to return a ~** Provision zurückvergüten; **to save on ~** Provision sparen; **to sell goods on ~** auf Provisionsbasis arbeiten, Kommissionsgeschäfte machen; **to send on ~** kommissionsweise überlassen; **to set up a ~** Ausschuß einsetzen, Kommission bilden; **to sit on a ~** Ausschußmitglied sein, einem Ausschuß angehören; **to take goods on ~** Waren in Kommission nehmen; **to trade on ~** Kommissionsgeschäfte abschließen;
~ account Provisionskonto, -rechnung; **~ agency** Agentur, Kommissionsgeschäft; **~ agent** Provisionsvertreter, Kommis-

sionär; **general ~ agent** Generalvertreter; **straight ~ arrangement** üblicher Provisionsvertrag; **~ basis** Provisionsgrundlage; **on a ~ basis** kommissionsweise; **to be paid (operate) on a ~ basis** als Provisionsvertreter (auf Provisionsgrundlage) arbeiten; **to execute orders in listed securities on a ~ basis** Effektengeschäfte auf Provisionsbasis durchführen; **to supply on a ~ basis** Kommissionslieferung vornehmen; **to take on a ~ basis** in Kommission übernehmen; **~ book** Bestell-, Auftrags-, Orderbuch; **~ broker** *(US)* Börsenkommissionsfirma; **~ brokerage** *(securities)* Maklerprovision; **~ business** Kommissionsgeschäft, Maklerei; **~ buyer** Einkaufskommissionär; **~ chairman** Ausschußvorsitzender; **~ charge** Provision[sgebühr], *(broker)* Courtage[satz]; **~ cost** Provisionshöhe; **~ day** *(law court, Br.)* Eröffnungstag; **~ dealings** Geschäfte auf Kommissionsbasis; **~ earnings** Provisionseinnahmen, -einkünfte; **~ fees** Provisionsgebühren; **~ government** *(city)* Ausschußregierung; **~ house** *(US)* Maklerfirma; **~ income** Provisionseinkünfte; **~ insurance** Versicherung gegen entgangene Provisionseinnahmen; **~ investigations** Ausschußuntersuchungen; **~ man** Kommissionär, Abschlußagent; **half ~ man** *(Br.)* Vermittlungsagent; **~ manager** Amtsbürgermeister; **~ manager plan** Amtsbürgermeistersystem; **~ manufacture** Auftragsbetrieb; **~ marketing** Kommissionshandel; **~ member** Ausschußmitglied; **~ merchant** Kommissionär, Kommissionsfirma, -geschäft, -haus, Provisions-, Handelsagent; **~ note** Provisionsrechnung, -aufstellung, -gutschrift; **~ plan** Provisionsschema, Provisionsrechnungssystem; **~'s proceedings** Ausschußverhandlungen; **to publish the ~'s proceedings** Ausschußprotokoll veröffentlichen; **~ projection** Ausschußprognose; **~ proposal** Ausschußvorschlag; **~ publisher** Kommissionsverlag; **~ rate** Provisions-, Kommissionssatz, *(stock exchange, US)* Courtage, Maklergebühr; **~ rebate** *(stockbroker)* Provisionsnachlaß; **~ revenues** Provisionseinkünfte; **~ ruling** Ausschußentscheidung; **~ sales** provisionspflichtige Umsätze; **~ schedule** Provisionstabelle; **~ selling** Verkauf auf Provisionsbasis; **~ slip** Provisionsbeleg; **~ splitting** Provisionsteilung; **~-starved** provisionshungrig, -gierig; **~ statement** Provisionsabrechnung; **~ system** Provisionswesen; **~ vacancy** unbesetzte Ausschußstelle.
commissionable provisionspflichtig;
~ media provisionsfähige Werbemittel.
commissionaire *(Br.)* Dienstmann, Bote, *(hotel)* Türhüter.
commissional bevollmächtigt, beauftragt, betraut;
~ appointment Ausschußernennung; **~ business** Auftragsgeschäft.
commissioned bevollmächtigt, beauftragt, betraut, *(mil.)* im Offiziersrang, *(ship)* in Dienst gestellt;
to be ~ to do den Auftrag haben;
~ officer Offizier.
commissioner Beauftragter, Bevollmächtigter, *(bookmaker, sl.)* Buchmacher, *(of an estate, Scot.)* Gutsverwalter, *(committee member)* Kommissions-, Ausschußmitglied, *(government)* Behördenleiter, *(judge)* beauftragter Richter, *(mil.)* Unterhändler;
~s Regierungskommission, Aufsichtsbehörde;
bankruptcy ~ beauftragter Konkursrichter; **Civil Service ~** *(Br.)* Leiter der Prüfungskommission für Beamtenanwärter; **competition ~** *(EC)* Kommissar für Wettbewerbsfragen; **county ~** *(US)* Friedensrichter; **development ~** *(EC)* Kommissar für Entwicklungsländer; **farm ~** *(EC)* Landwirtschaftskommissar; **general ~** Sonderbeauftragter, *(US)* obere Finanzbehörde, Finanzgericht; **government ~** Regierungs-, Staatsbeauftragter; **High ⚘** Hochkommissar; **industry ~** *(EC)* Wirtschaftskommissar; **police ~** *(US)* Polizeipräsident; **royal ~** *(Br.)* Staatsbeauftragter, Mitglied einer Untersuchungskommission; **shipping ~** *(US)* Seemannsamtsleiter; **special ~** *(Br.)* Richter in Steuersachen; **wreck ~** Strandvogt;
⚘ **of Audits** *(Br.)* [etwa] Bundesrechnungshof, Rechnungsprüfungsamt; **~ of banking** *(US)* Bankenkommissar; **~ of bankruptcy** beauftragter Konkursrichter; **~ for matrimonial causes** Einzelrichter in Ehesachen; ⚘ **of Customs** *(US)* Oberste Zollverwaltung; ⚘ **of Customs and Excise** *(Br.)* Ministerialabteilung für Zölle und Verbrauchssteuern, Finanzverwaltung; **~ of deeds** *(US)* Urkundsperson; **~ of highways** Straßenbauamt; ⚘ **of Immigration** *(US)* Einwanderungskommissar; ⚘ **of Inland Revenue** *(Br.)* Bundesfinanzbehörde; ⚘ **of Internal Revenue** *(US)* Bundesfinanzamt; ⚘ **of Patents** *(US)* Präsident des Patentamtes; ⚘ **of Metropolitan Police** *(London)* Polizeipräsident; ⚘ **of Sewers** *(Br.)* Wasser- und Kanalbauamt; ⚘ **of Supply** Grundsteuerausschuß; ⚘ **of Taxation** Steuerabteilung; **~ for women's affairs** Beauftragte für Frauenfragen.
commissionership Kommissionstätigkeit.

commit *(v.)* *(entrust)* anvertrauen, betrauen, übertragen, überliefern, überlassen, *(oblige)* verpflichten, Verpflichtung eingehen, verbindlich machen, *(order)* in Auftrag geben, bestellen, *(perpetrate)* begehen, verüben;

~ o. s. sich binden (engagieren), sich eine Blöße geben (komprommittieren); ~ o. s. to s. th. sich auf etw. festlegen, sich verleiten lassen;

~ an act of bankruptcy Konkursvergehen begehen; ~ an act of misconduct sich danebenbenehmen; ~ into administration Nachlaßverwaltung anordnen; ~ a bill Gesetzesvorlage an einen Ausschuß überweisen; ~ to s. one's care jds. Fürsorge übergeben; ~ to the charge of s. o. jds. Obhut übergeben; ~ a debtor Schuldnervermögen verwalten lassen; ~ a felony Verbrechen begehen, verbrechen; ~ murder Mordtat begehen, zum Mörder werden; ~ a number of frauds sich zahlreiche Betrügereien zuschulden kommen lassen; ~ a fund to the care of trustees Vermögensmasse Treuhändern anvertrauen; ~ s. o. to jail (prison) j. einsperren (ins Gefängnis einliefern); ~ to memory sich einprägen, auswendig lernen; ~ o. s. to a method sich auf eine Methode festlegen; ~ o. s. on easing money sich für Geldmarkterleichterungen einsetzen; ~ an offence Straftat begehen; ~ to paper zu Papier bringen; ~ a prisoner for trial Verhafteten zwecks Aburteilung dem Gericht übergeben (in Untersuchungshaft nehmen); ~ in trust zu treuen Händen übergeben; ~ suicide Selbstmord begehen; ~ s. th. to writing etw. zu Papier bringen (niederschreiben).

committed *(earnings)* zweckgebunden.

commitment Verbindlichkeit, [finanzielle] Verpflichtung, *(act of committing)* Übertragung, -antwortung, *(commission)* Auftrag, *(consignment)* Überweisung, *(stock exchange, US)* Engagement, Kauf-, Verkaufsverpflichtung;

given the made ~s angesichts der eingegangenen Verpflichtungen; without any ~ ganz unverbindlich;

advance ~ Kreditzusage; binding ~ bindende Verpflichtung; contractual ~s vertragliche Verpflichtungen; foreign ~s außenpolitische Verpflichtungen; foreign-exchange ~s Devisenengagements; fortnightly ~s Mediofälligkeiten; percentage ~ prozentuales Engagement; personal ~ persönliches Engagement; purchase ~ Bonifikation;

~ of a bill Überweisung eines Gesetzentwurfs; ~ of employees Engagement der Belegschaft; ~s arising from endorsements Indossamentverbindlichkeiten; ~s for future delivery *(US)* Terminengagements; ~ to a mental institution *(US)* Anstaltsunterbringung; ~ to prison Einlieferung ins Gefängnis, Einweisungsanordnung; a party's ~ to tariff reduction parteiliche Festlegung auf Zollsenkungen;

to enter into a ~ Engagement eingehen; to have various ~s verschiedene [finanzielle] Verpflichtungen haben; to lighten the ~s Engagements lösen; to make a ~ Abschluß tätigen; to make corporate ~ Betriebsverpflichtungen eingehen; to meet one's ~s seinen Verpflichtungen nachkommen; to fail to meet one's ~s seinen Verpflichtungen nicht nachkommen; to shorten ~s Aufträge zurückziehen; to undertake a ~ Verpflichtung eingehen;

~ appropriations *(EC)* Bereitstellung von Beträgen für eingegangene Verpflichtungen; ~ commission Bereitstellungsprovision; ~ credit Bereitstellungskredit; ~ interest Bereitstellungszinsen.

committal *(act of committing)* Übertragung, -antwortung, *(funeral)* Begräbnis, *(offender)* Einweisung, *(parl.)* Überweisung an einen Ausschuß, *(stock exchange)* Engagement;

~ for debts Schuldhaft; ~ of a judgment debtor Inhaftierung eines Vollstreckungsschuldners; ~ to prison Einlieferung in die Haftanstalt; ~ for trial Versetzung in den Anklagezustand, Anordnung der Untersuchungshaft;

~ order persönlicher Arrestbefehl, Überstellungsbeschluß; ~ service Grabrede.

committed *(politics)* gebunden, festgelegt, engagiert;

~ in the presence of an officer von der Polizei ins Gefängnis gebracht;

to be ~ to sich festgelegt haben auf.

committee Ausschuß, Kommission, Gremium, Komitee, *(guardian, Br.)* Amtsvormund, Kurator;

on the ~ im Ausschuß;

ad-hoc ~ Sonderausschuß; adjustment ~ Schlichtungsausschuß; administrative ~ Verwaltungsausschuß; advisory ~ Gutachterkommission; agenda ~ Tagesordnungsausschuß; agricultural ~ Agrarausschuß, -kommission; appeal ~ Berufungsausschuß; appraisement ~ Bewertungsausschuß; arbitration ~ Vermittlungs-, Schlichtungs-, Schiedsausschuß; assessment ~ Veranlagungsausschuß; auditing ~ Rechnungsprü-

fungsausschuß; budget ~ Haushaltsausschuß; cabinet ~ Kabinettsausschuß; central ~ Zentralausschuß; conciliation ~ Vergleichsausschuß; conference ~ *(US)* Vermittlungs-, Beratungsausschuß; control ~ Kontrollausschuß; consultative ~ beratender Vorstand, Beratungsausschuß; coordinating ~ Koordinierungsausschuß; credentials ~ Vollmachtenprüfungsausschuß; decision-making ~ beschließender Ausschuß; defence ~ Verteidigungsausschuß; departmental ~ ministerieller Ausschuß; district ~ Kreis-, Bezirksausschuß, *(US)* Bezirksverwaltungsstelle, *(politics)* Parteiausschuß; drafting ~ Redaktionsausschuß; Economic and Finance ~ *(UNO)* Wirtschafts- und Finanzausschuß; election ~ Wahlausschuß; employee stock purchase ~ Betriebsausschuß für den Erwerb betriebseigener Aktien; establishment ~ *(local government, Br.)* Personalausschuß; executive ~ geschäftsführender Ausschuß, Vollzugs-, Aktions-, Exekutivausschuß; expert ~ Sachverständigengremium; fact-finding ~ Ermittlungs-, Untersuchungsausschuß; factory ~ Betriebsrat; finance ~ Finanzausschuß; foreign affairs ~ Ausschuß für auswärtige Angelegenheiten; Foreign Relations ~ auswärtiger (außenpolitischer) Ausschuß; four-power ~ Viermächteausschuß; general ~ allgemeiner Ausschuß; general purpose ~ Richtlinienausschuß; governmental ~ Regierungsausschuß; grievance ~ Beschwerdeausschuß; house ~ *(club)* Klubhauskomitee; hybrid ~ gemischter Ausschuß; interagency ~ interministerieller Ausschuß; interdepartmental ~ interministerieller Ausschuß; interparliamentary ~ interparlamentarischer Ausschuß; intersessional ~ *(parl.)* Ferienausschuß; interstate ~ *(US)* zwischenstaatlicher Ausschuß; investigating ~ Untersuchungsausschuß; joint ~ gemeinsamer Ausschuß, *(parl., Br.)* gemischter (paritätischer) Ausschuß; joint apprentice ~ Betriebsausbildungsausschuß; judicial ~ Rechtsausschuß; kitchen ~ Verpflegungsausschuß; learned ~ Expertengremium; legal ~ Rechtsausschuß; liaison ~ Verbindungsausschuß; main ~ Hauptausschuß; management advisory ~ Vorstandsberaterausschuß; managing ~ geschäftsführender Ausschuß; mediation ~ Vermittlungsausschuß; membership ~ Aufnahmeausschuß; mixed ~ gemischter Ausschuß; monetary ~ Währungsausschuß; national ~ Landesgruppe; negotiating ~ Verhandlungsausschuß; organizing ~ Organisations-, Geschäftsordnungsausschuß; parliamentary ~ parlamentarischer Ausschuß; permanent ~ ständiger Ausschuß; planning ~ Planungsausschuß; policy ~ Ausschuß zur Festlegung der Geschäftspolitik; preparatory ~ vorbereitender Ausschuß; Presidential ~ Präsidentalausschuß, *(EC)* Ausschuß des Präsidenten; price-control ~ Preisüberwachungsausschuß; procedural ~ Verfahrensausschuß; provisional ~ vorübergehend eingesetzter Ausschuß; prudential ~ beratender Ausschuß; Public Accounts ~ *(parl., Br.)* Rechnungsprüfungsausschuß; public-welfare ~ Wohlfahrts-, Sozialhilfeausschuß; resolution ~ Resolutionsausschuß; rules ~ *(US)* Geschäftsordnungsausschuß; secret ~ *(Br.)* Sonderausschuß; security ~ Sicherheitsausschuß; select ~ *(Br.)* engerer Ausschuß, Untersuchungs-, Sonderausschuß; senate ~ Senatsausschuß; sessional ~ *(parl.)* ständiger Ausschuß; shop ~ *(Br.)* Betriebsrat; sifting ~ Tagesordnungsausschuß; special ~ Sonderausschuß; standing orders ~ *(parl.)* Geschäftsordnungsausschuß; statistical ~ statistischer Ausschuß; statutory ~ gesetzlich vorgeschriebener Ausschuß; steering ~ Lenkungsausschuß; stock-exchange ~ *(Br.)* Börsenkommission, -vorstand; strike ~ Streikausschuß; subordinate ~ nachgeordneter Ausschuß; subsidiary ~ Hilfs-, Nebenausschuß; supervisory ~ Kontroll-, Überwachungsausschuß; tax ~ Steuerausschuß; technical ~ Fachausschuß; temporary ~ vorläufiger Ausschuß; trade ~ *(US)* Handelsausschuß; trade-union ~ Gewerkschaftsausschuß; watch ~ *(local government, Br.)* polizeilicher Überwachungsausschuß; workers' ~ Arbeiterausschuß; working ~ Arbeitsausschuß; works ~ Betriebsrat;

~ on Admission *(US)* Zulassungsausschuß; ~ of award Vergabeausschuß; ~ of commercial men Handelsausschuß; ~ of conference *(US)* Vermittlungsausschuß; ~ of creditors Gläubigerbeirat; ~ for development aid Entwicklungsausschuß; ~ of experts Sachverständigenbeirat; ~ of hono(u)r Ehrenkomitee; ~ of the whole House als Ausschuß zusammengetretenes Plenum, Plenarausschuß; ~ of inland transport Binnenverkehrsausschuß; ~ of inquiry Untersuchungsausschuß; ~ of inspection *(Br., bankruptcy)* Gläubigerausschuß; ~ for the Journals *(Br.)* Protokollprüfungsausschuß; ~ in lunacy Amtsvormund; ~ for management Verwaltungsrat; ~ for merchandise traffic Frachtenausschuß; ~ of one Einerausschuß; ~ for Privileges *(Br.)* Privilegienausschuß [des Oberhauses]; ~ for General Purposes *(Br.)* Börsenvorstand der Londoner Börse; ~ on rules in the

House (*Br.*) Geschäftsordnungsausschuß; ² **for Scientific and Industrial Research** (*Br.*) Forschungsamt; ~ **on social questions** Sozialausschuß; ² **of the Stock Exchange** (*Br.*) Börsenvorstand; ~ **on stock list** (*US*) Börsenzulassungsstelle; ² **of Supply** (*Br.*) Haushaltszuschuß; ~ **of three** Dreierausschuß; ² **of Ways and Means** (*Br.*) Steuerbewilligungs-, Haushaltsausschuß; ~ **in a winding up** (*Br.*) Gläubigerausschuß bei einer Liquidation; **to appoint a** ~ Ausschuß einsetzen (konstituieren); **to appoint to a** ~ in einen Ausschuß berufen; **to attend upon a** ~ einem Ausschuß zur Verfügung stehen; **to be on a** ~ einem Ausschuß angehören, in einem Ausschuß sitzen; **to be elected in a** ~ in einen Ausschuß gewählt werden; **to belong to a** ~ zu einem Ausschuß gehören; **to call a ~ of the whole house** (*Br.*) Zusammentreten des Hauses zu einer Kommission beantragen; **to cease to form part of a** ~ aus einem Ausschuß ausscheiden; **to constitute a** ~ Ausschuß konstituieren; **to establish a** ~ Ausschuß einsetzen; **to form a** ~ Ausschuß gründen; **to go into** ~s in Sonderausschüssen beraten; **to name a** ~ Ausschuß einsetzen; **to pass a measure through a** ~ Ausschußresolution herbeiführen; **to put a ~ into working shape** einem Ausschuß die Möglichkeit zur Arbeitsaufnahme verschaffen; **to put a** ~ **out of business** Ausschuß auflösen; **to refer a question to a** ~ Frage an einen Ausschuß verweisen; **to resolve itself into a** ~ sich als Ausschuß konstituieren; **to serve on a** ~ Ausschußarbeit leisten, in einem Ausschuß sitzen; **to set up a ~ on the following lines** Ausschuß nach folgenden Grundsätzen zusammensetzen; **to set up a ~ of inquiry** Untersuchungsausschuß einsetzen; **to sit on a** ~ einem Ausschuß angehören; **to throw off a** ~ aus einem Ausschuß ausschließen;

~ **appointment** Ausschußernennung; ~ **arrangement** Ausschußvereinbarung; ~ **assignment** Ausschußbesetzung; ~ **attention** Interesse des Ausschusses, Ausschußinteresse; ~ **chairman** Ausschußvorsitzender; ~ **chairmanship** Ausschußvorsitz; ~ **colleague** Ausschußkollege; ~ **consultations** Ausschußberatungen; ~ **council** Ausschußberater; ~ **cuttings** Kürzungsvorschläge eines Ausschußes; ~ **debate** Ausschußdiskussion; ~ **determination** Ausschußbeschluß; ~ **discussions** Ausschußberatungen; ~ **files** Ausschußakten; ~ **hearings** Ausschußuntersuchungen, -vernehmungen; ~ **meeting** Ausschußsitzung; **to attend a** ~ **meeting** an einer Ausschußsitzung teilnehmen; ~ **member** Ausschußmitglied; ~'**s proposal** Ausschußvorschlag, -empfehlung; ~'**s recommendations** Ausschußempfehlungen; ~ **record** Ausschußprotokoll; ~ **report** Kommissionsbericht; ~ **room** Beratungszimmer; ~ **ruling** Ausschußentscheidung; ~ **staff** Ausschußpersonal; ~ **stage** Ausschußstadium, Beratungsstadium einer Gesetzesvorlage; **to be in the** ~ **stage** dem Ausschuß vorliegen; ~ **system** (*Br.*) Ausschußverwaltung; **to sweep away secrecy from** ~ **votes** mit den geheimen Ausschußabstimmungen aufräumen.

committeeman (*US*) Ausschußmitglied.
committeeship Ausschußzugehörigkeit.
committer Auftraggeber.
committing magistrate Untersuchungsrichter.
committitur Haftanordnung.
commixture (*civil law*) Vermengung, Vermischung.
commodate (*law*) freiwilliges Darlehn.
commodities Waren, Artikel, Gebrauchsgüter;
agricultural ~ landwirtschaftliche Erzeugnisse; **basic** ~ Rohstoffe; **bulk** ~ Massengüter; **choice** ~ vorzügliche Ware; **export** ~ Exportwaren, Ausfuhrgüter; **graded** ~ sortierte Waren; **high-priced** ~ Waren mit hohen Verkaufspreisen; **household** ~ Haushaltswaren, -gegenstände; **import** ~ Einfuhrwaren; **inland** ~ einheimische Waren; **manufactured** ~ Industrieerzeugnisse; **marketable** ~ absatzfähige Waren; **nonbasic** ~ (*US*) landwirtschaftliche Erzeugnisse [die keiner Produktionssteuerung bedürfen]; **perishable** ~ verderbliche Waren; **price-maintained** ~ preisstabile Waren; **primary** ~ Rohstoffe; **rationed** (*scarce*) ~ Mangelware, bewirtschaftete Waren; **representative** ~ vertretbare Sachen, Fungibilien; **standardized** ~ genormte Waren (Güter); **staple** ~ Stapelware, -gut; **stockpiled** ~ eingelagerte Waren; **taxable** ~ steuerpflichtige Waren (Artikel); **well-known** ~ gut eingeführte Artikel;
~ [**not**] **under control** [nicht] bewirtschaftete Waren;
to own ~ Warenlager besitzen;
~ **clause** (*US*) Verbot der Beförderung spediteureigener Güter; ~ **indicator** Warenbarometer.
commodious (*apartment*) geräumig.
commodity [Handels]ware, [Gebrauchs]artikel, Erzeugnis, Gut, (*convenience*) Annehmlichkeit, (*stock exchange*) per Termin gehandelte Rohstoffe;
dead ~ unverkäufliche Waren; **import** ~ Einfuhrware;

~ **advance** Warenbevorschussung; ~ **agreement** Warenabkommen; ~ **aid** projektgebundene Hilfe; ~ **boom** Warenkonjunktur, Warenpreishausse; ~ **cargo** Warenladung; ~ **carry scheme** Vortrag auf Warentermingeschäfte; ~ **classification** Warenverzeichnis; ~ **clause** (*US*) Eigentumsverbotsklausel [im Speditionsgeschäft]; ~ **code** Warenverzeichnis; ~ **collateral** Warenlombard; ~ **commission** Warenbörsenausschuß; ~ **competition** Warenkonkurrenz, -wettbewerb; ~ **consumption** Warenverbrauch; ~ **contract** Warenabschluß; ~ **coverage** Bedarfsdeckung; ~ **credit** Warenkredit; ~ **credit corporation** (*US*) Preisstützungsbehörde für die Landwirtschaft; ~ **dealer** Warenhändler; ~ **dividend** (*US*) Sachdividende; ~ **dollar** (*US*) Warendollar; ~ **economics** Warenkunde; ~ **exchange** Warenbörse; ² **Exchange Act** (*US*) Gesetz über die Errichtung von Warenbörsen; ² **Exchange Authority** (*US*) Überwachungsbehörde für die Warenbörse; ~ **Exchange Inc.** (*COMEX*) Metallbörse; ~ **exports** Rohstoffexporte; ~ **futures** Warentermingeschäft; ~ **future trader** Warenterminhändler; ² **Futures Trading Commission** (*CFTC, US*) Kontrollbehörde für die Warenterminbörsen; ~ **grade** [Waren]sorte; ~ **income** Einkünfte aus Warenlieferungen; ~ **industry** Grundstoffindustrie; ~ **loan** Warenkredit; ~ **market** Waren-, Produktenbörse; ~ **marketing** Warenabsatz; ~ **money** (*US*) Indexwährung; ~ **paper** (*US*) Dokumententratte; ~ **pattern** Waren-, Güterstruktur; **wholesale** ~ **price** Großhandelspreis; ~ **price** Rohstoff-, Warenpreis; ~ **price boomlet** Kleinkonjunktur in Warenpreisen; ~ **price forecasting** Warenpreis-, Rohstoffpreisprognose; ~ **price movements** Rohstoffpreisbewegungen; ~ **rate** Einzeltarif, (*airline*) Vorzugstarif, Vorzugssatz im Luftfrachtverkehr, (*US*) Diskontsatz für Dokumententratten; ~ **sales** Warenumsatz; ~ **specialization** Warenspezialisierung; ~ **standard** Naturalgeld; ~ **tariff** Warentarif; ~ **terms of trade** Warenaustauschverhältnis; ~ **trading** Rohstoff-, Warenhandel; ~ **theory of money** Geldwerttheorie; ~ **value** Waren-, Sachwert.

commodore Lotsenkommando, (*leading vessel in a convoy*) Leitschiff.
common gemeinsames Benutzungsrecht, Mitbenutzungsrecht, (*pasture*) Allmende, Gemeindeland, -wiese, -acker, -gut, (*right of* ~) Dienstbarkeit;
in ~ gemeinsam, in gemeinschaftlichem Besitz, (*heirs*) in ungeteilter Gemeinschaft; **out of the** ~ ungewöhnlich;
~s (*US*) öffentlicher Park; **the** ~s der dritte Stand, das einfache Volk;
~ **of digging** Schürfrecht; ~ **of estovers** Brennholzgerechtigkeit; ~ **or garden** (*fam.*) Feld-, Wald- oder Wiesen-; ~ **of pasture** Weidegerechtigkeit; ~ **of piscary** Fischereigerechtigkeit; ~ **of turbary** Torfstechgerechtigkeit;
~ (*a.*) [allgemein] üblich, geläufig, gewöhnlich, gebräuchlich, alltäglich, (*inferior*) geringwertig, niedrig, (*public*) öffentlich, allgemein, (*shared*) gemeinsam, gemeinschaftlich;
to act in ~ **with s. o.** gemeinsame Sache mit jem. machen; **to be on short** ~s nicht genug zu essen haben; **to have interests in** ~ gemeinsame Interessen haben; **to have nothing in** ~ **with s. o.** keinerlei gemeinsame Interessen haben; **to hold in** ~ gemeinsam besitzen, Gesamteigentümer sein; **to put one's funds in** ~ gemeinsame Kasse machen;
~ **accent** gewöhnlicher Akzent; ~ **advantage** allgemeiner Nutzen; ² **Agricultural Fund** (*EC*) Gemeinsamer Agrarfonds; ² **Agriculture Policy** (*CAP*) Agrarpolitik der Europäischen Gemeinschaften; ~ **apartment** gemeinsames Gastzimmer; ~ **appearance** angenommene Prozeßeinlassung eines Säumigen; ~ **appendant** dinglich gesichertes Weiderecht; ~ **appurtenant** gemeinsames Weiderecht; ² **Assembly** (*ECU*) gemeinsame Versammlung; ~ **assumpsit** Schadenersatzklage aus vertragsähnlichem Verhältnis; ~ **assurance** (*Br.*) Beweisdokument über Besitzwechsel; ~ **average** einfache Havarie; ~ **bail** Bürgschaft für Erscheinen vor Gericht; ~ **bar** Einrede [gegen Besitzstörungsklage], Rechtseinwand; ~ **barrator** Prozeßanstifter; ~ **calamity** (*life insurance*) gleichzeitige Todesvermutung; ~ **capital stock** (*US*) Stammkapital.

common carrier (*US*) Spediteur, gewerbsmäßiger Frachtführer, Transportunternehmer, (*US*) öffentliches Verkehrsmittel, Verkehrsunternehmen, (*airline, US*) Luftverkehrslinie;
~ **by air** Luftfrachtspediteur; ~ **of goods for hire** Lohnfrachtführer;
~ **principle** Grundsatz der gemeinwirtschaftlichen Verkehrsbedienung.
common|cause (*law*) Zivilverfahren, -prozeß; **to make** ~ **cause** gemeinsame Sache machen; ~ **coin** gängige Münze; ~ **consent** einhellige Meinung; ~ **council** (*US*) Gemeinde-, Stadtrat; ~

council chamber Sitzungszimmer des Stadtrats; ~ **councilman** Gemeinderatsmitglied, Stadtrat; ~ **counts** übliche Klagebegründungsformeln; ~ **crier** öffentlicher Ausrufer; ~ **criminal** Gewohnheitsverbrecher; ~ **danger** (average) gemeinsame Gefahr; ~ **debtor** Gemeinschuldner; ~ **decency** natürlicher Anstand; ~ **denominator** gemeinsamer Nenner; ~ **design** (criminal law) gemeinsamer Vorsatz; ~ **domestic life** gemeinsame Haushaltsführung; ~ **drunkard** Gewohnheitstrinker; ~ **employment** gemeinsame Beschäftigung; ~ **enterprise** Gemeinschaftsbetrieb; ~ **event** alltägliches Ereignis; ~ **expense** (freight and passenger service) gemeinsam anfallende Kosten; ~ **expression** geläufiger Ausdruck, alltägliche Redensart; ~ **feeling** allgemeines Volksempfinden; ~ **fields** Allmende, Gemeindeland; ~ **foolscap** Konzeptpapier; ~ **form** (mil.) ordentliches Verfahren; ~ **fund** Gemeinschaftskasse, gemeinsame Kasse; ~ **fund costs** (Br.) Prozeßkosten; ~ **goal** gemeinsames Ziel; **for the ~ good** im Interesse der Allgemeinheit; ~ **grave** Massengrab; ~ **ground** Gemeindeland, Allmende, (fig.) gemeinsame Grundlage; **to be on ~ ground** auf gleichen Voraussetzungen fußen, gleiche Wellenlänge haben; ~ **hall** Gemeindesaal, Aula, Rathaus; ~ **hazard** (fire insurance) allgemeine Feuersgefahr; **the ~ herd** die breite Masse; ~ **household** häusliche Gemeinschaft; ~ **humanity doctrine** (carrier) Versorgungspflicht; ~ **informer** Spitzel, Denunziant; ~ **interest** Interessen der Allgemeinheit; ~ **knowledge** Allgemeinwissen, -gut; **to be ~ knowledge among bankers** in Bankkreisen allgemein bekannt sein; ~ **labo(u)r** ungelernte Arbeit, Handarbeit, (Sunday laws) normale Geschäftstätigkeit; ~ **labo(u)r rates** Tariflöhne für ungelernte Arbeiter; ~ **labo(u)rer** ungelernter Arbeiter; ~ **land** Gemeindeland, Allmende; ~ **law** bürgerliches Recht, Zivilrecht, (unwritten law) Gewohnheitsrecht; ~**-law** gewohnheitsrechtlich; ~**-law action** Zivilprozeß, bürgerliche Rechtsstreitigkeit; ~**-law agreement** (Road Traffic Act, Br.) Ausschluß der Schadensausgleichspflicht; ~**-law lien** Zurückbehaltungsrecht; ~**-law marriage** eheähnliches Zusammenleben; ~**-law mortgage** vertragliches Grundpfandrecht, Verkehrshypothek; ~**-law procedure** Zivilprozeßverfahren; ~ **lawyer** auf Zivilrecht spezialisierter Anwalt; ~ **liquor dealer** rückfälliger Schnapshändler; ~ **lodging house** Obdachlosenasyl; ~ **make of goods** minderwertiges Fabrikat; ~ **manners** ordinäres Benehmen;

Common Market Gemeinsamer Markt;
to join the ~ dem gemeinsamen Markt beitreten;
~ **Community** Europäische Wirtschaftsgemeinschaft; ~ **countries** Mitglieder des Gemeinsamen Marktes; ~ **formation** Gründung des Gemeinsamen Marktes; ~ **membership** Zugehörigkeit zum Gemeinsamen Markt; ~ **organization** Marktordnungen der EG; ~ **territory** europäische Wirtschaftsregion; ~ **Treaty** Montanunionsvertrag.

common|marketeer Befürworter des gemeinsamen Marktes; ~ **name (noun)** Gattungsname; ~ **nuisance** öffentliches Ärgernis; ~ **opinion** allgemeine (öffentliche) Meinung; ~ **owners** Miteigentümer; ~ **ownership** Eigentum nach Bruchteilen; ~ **parts of a building** allgemein zugängliche Gebäudeteile; **the ~ people** die einfachen Leute, das gemeine Volk; ~ **peril** (average) gemeinsame Gefahr; ~ **phrases** abgedroschene Phrasen; ~ **pleas** für bürgerliche Rechtsstreitigkeiten zuständiges (ordentliches erstinstanzliches) Gericht; ~ **point** (carrier) gemeinsamer Tarifausgangspunkt; ~ **price** üblicher Preis; ~ **property** Gemeingut; ~ **purse** gemeinsame Kasse; ~ **repute** allgemeine Ansicht; ~ **right** Gemein-, Mitbenutzungsrecht; ~ **room** Versammlungs-, Gemeinschaftsraum, (school) Lehrerzimmer; **the ~ run** die Allgemeinheit; ~ **school** (US) Volksschule; ~ **seal** (Br.) Firmensiegel, (local government) Dienstsiegel; ~ **seller** gewerbsmäßiger Verkäufer; ~ **sense** gesunder Menschenverstand, Wirklichkeitssinn; **down-to-earth ~ sense** praktischer Menschenverstand; **to make doing a thing basic ~ sense** vernünftig erscheinen lassen; ~ **sergeant** (Br.) Urkundsbeamter; ~ **service** gemeinsames Arbeitsverhältnis; ~ **share** (Br.) Stammaktie, -anteil; ~ **soil** Gemeindeland; ~ **status** (Br.) Commonwealth-Staatsangehörigkeit; ~ **stock** (US) Stammaktie; ~ **stock account** (US) Stammkapitalkonto; ~ **stock funds** (US) Aktien eines nur aus Aktien bestehenden Investmentfonds; ~ **stockholder** (US) Stammaktionär; ~ **suit** Zivilprozeß, -verfahren, bürgerliche Rechtsstreitigkeit; ~ **supplies** gemeinschaftliche Versorgungsgüter; ~ **talk** Stadtgespräch; ~ **thief** Gewohnheitsdieb; ~ **trust** gemeinsame Treuhandverwaltung; ~ **use** (antitrust law, US) Gemeingebrauch; ~ **victualler** Gastwirt; ~ **way** Gemeindeweg; ~ **weal (welfare)** Gemeinwohl, -wesen; ~ **year** Normaljahr.

commonable in gemeinsamem Besitz, (pasture) zur Gemeindeweide zugelassen.

commonage gemeinsames Nutzungsrecht, (pasture) Weidegerechtigkeit.

commonalty Allgemeinheit, einfache Bürger.

commoner (Br.) Bürgerlicher, (common ground) Nutzungsberechtigter, (House of Commons) Unterhausmitglied;
to be a ~ von bürgerlicher Abkunft sein.

commonplace Gemeinplatz, Platitüde, Binsenwahrheit;
to talk ~s über nebensächliche Dinge sprechen;
~ **(a.)** alltäglich, abgedroschen;
~ **kind of man** Durchschnittsbürger.

commonwealth Gemeinwesen, Staat, Volk, Nation, bürgerliche Gesellschaft, (Br.) Commonwealth;
~ **of learning** Gelehrtenwelt; ~ **of letters** literarische Welt; ~ **of Nations** Gemeinschaft der Nationen.

Commonwealth|citizen (Br.) Staatsangehöriger des Commonwealth; ~ **preferences** Vorzugszölle für Länder des Commonwealth.

commorancy Aufenthalt.

commotion Aufruhr, Aufstand, Tumult;
civil ~ innere Unruhen, Bürgerkrieg.

communal kommunal, gemeindlich, (owned in common) in gemeinsamem Besitz;
~ **bonds** Kommunalobligationen; ~ **disturbances** Volksunruhen; ~ **elector** Kommunal-, Gemeindewähler; ~ **estate** (law) Gütergemeinschaft; **to bring one's property into the ~ estate** sein Eigentum in die Gütergemeinschaft einbringen; ~ **farm** Gemeindeland; ~ **forest** Gemeindewald; ~ **institutions** Gemeindeeinrichtungen; ~ **intercourse** Nachbarschaftsverkehr; ~ **kitchen** Volks-, Gemeinschaftsküche; ~ **land** Gemeindeland; ~ **life** Gemeindeleben; ~ **organization** Gemeinde, Kommunaleinrichtung; ~ **sense** Gemeinschaftsgefühl; ~ **toilet** Bedürfnisanstalt; ~ **trading (undertaking)** Kommunal-, Gemeindebetrieb.

communalism Selbstverwaltungsprinzip.

communality (statistics) Gemeinsamkeitsgrad.

communalization Eingemeindung, Kommunalisierung.

communalize (v.) eingemeinden, kommunalisieren.

communicable disease ansteckende Krankheit.

communicate in Verbindung (im Verkehr) stehen, (make known) mitteilen, benachrichtigen, übermitteln;
~ **(v.) s. th. to s. o.** jem. etw. übermitteln, j. von etw. benachrichtigen; ~ **with s. o.** sich mit jem. in Verbindung setzen;
~ **a disease** Krankheit übertragen; ~ **a document to s. o.** j. mittels einer Urkunde in Kenntnis setzen; ~ **an illness** Krankheit übertragen; ~ **one's intention** seinen Willen kundtun; ~ **by letter** brieflich verkehren; ~ **regularly with s. o.** mit jem. laufend in Verbindung stehen.

communicating|door Verbindungstür; ~ **rooms** (hotel) nebeneinander liegende Zimmer.

communication Gedanken-, Meinungsaustausch, Informationsfluß, Einwirkungsmöglichkeit, (connection) Verbindung, (information) Mitteilung, Benachrichtigung, Information, (line of ~) Verkehrsverbindung, -weg, (masonry) Sitzung, (mil.) Verbindungs-, Nachschubwege;
~**s** Verbindungswege, Verkehrswesen, (telecommunications) Fernmeldeverbindungen;
banking ~ Bankverkehr; **commercial ~s** geschäftliche Mitteilungen; **confidential ~s** vertrauliche Mitteilungen; **direct ~** direkte Verbindung, direkter Verkehr; **external ~** Auslandsnachrichten; **government ~s** Regierungsmitteilungen; **internal ~s** Inlandsmitteilungen; **long-line ~** Fernverbindung; **postal ~** postalische Verbindung, Postverbindung; **press ~s** Pressenachrichten, -mitteilungen; **private ~s** Privatkorrespondenz; **privileged ~** nur für den Anwalt bestimmte Information, Berufsgeheimnis, (law of libel and slander) Äußerungen in Wahrnehmung berechtigter Interessen, (parl.) Äußerungen im Rahmen der parlamentarischen Immunität; **telegraphic ~** Telegraphenverkehr; **telephone ~** telephonische Mitteilung; **through ~** direkter Verkehr; **wireless ~** Rundfunknachricht; **written ~** schriftliche Benachrichtigung;
~ **of acceptance** Annahmeübermittlung; ~ **of intention** Willenskundgebung; ~ **from the President** (US) Botschaft des Präsidenten; ~ **by rail** Eisenbahnverbindung; ~ **to the customer** Kundenbenachrichtigung; ~ **of disease** Krankheitsverbreitung, Übertragung einer Krankheit; ~ **of an error** Irrtumsanzeige; ~ **of offer** Übermittlung eines Angebots;
to be in ~ with s. o. Korrespondenz mit jem. führen, in Korrespondenz mit jem. stehen; **to break off all ~ with s. o.** alle Beziehungen (jeden Verkehr) mit jem. abbrechen; **to get into (effect) ~ with s. o.** mit jem. in Verbindung treten; **to issue a ~** Verlautbarung veröffentlichen;

$\stackrel{\circ}{\sim}$ **Agency** *(US)* Informationsstelle; ~ **band** *(radio)* Frequenzband; ~s **behavio(u)r** Gemeinschaftsverhalten; ~ **center** *(mil.)* Nachrichtenzentrum, Fernmeldestelle; ~ **company** Verkehrsgesellschaft; ~ **cord** *(railway)* Notbremse; ~ **cost** Übermittlungskosten; ~ **engineer** Fernmeldeingenieur; ~ **engineering** Fernmeldetechnik; ~ **equipment** Fernmeldeausstattung; ~ **facilities** Fernmeldeeinrichtungen; ~ **gap** Informationslücke; ~s **industry** Fernmeldeindustrie; ~ **line** Verbindungslinie; ~s **link** Verbindungsglied; ~ **market** Kommunikationsmarkt; ~ **media** Werbeträger, -medien, Kommunikationsmittel; **computer-controlled electronic** ~ **network** computergesteuertes elektronisches Fernmeldenetz; ~ **research** Kommunikationsforschung; ~ **room** *(man of war)* Kommandostand; ~ **satellite** Nachrichtensatellit; ~ **service** Nachrichtenwesen, -dienst, -system; ~ **snarl** Verkehrswirrwarr; ~s **system** Verkehrssystem, -netz, Verteilungssystem, *(tel.)* Nachrichtenwesen; **to set up a** ~ **system** terroristische Vereinigung gründen; ~ **trench** *(mil.)* Verbindungsgraben; ~ **zone** *(mil.)* Etappe, Etappengebiet, rückwärtiges Armeegebiet.

communicational exchange Nachrichtenaustausch.

communicator Übermittler, *(Br.)* Notbremse;
  to be a first-class ~ **face-to-face and on paper** sich sowohl mündlich wie auch schriftlich überzeugend verständlich machen können.

communion gemeinsamer Besitz, *(religion)* Glaubensgemeinschaft;
  ~ **of goods** [eheliche] Gütergemeinschaft.

communiqué amtliche Verlautbarung, Regierungserklärung, Kommuniqué;
  formal ~ offizielles Kommuniqué;
  to issue a ~ Verlautbarung veröffentlichen.

communism Kommunismus.

communist Kommunist;
  ~ **party** kommunistische Partei.

community Gemeinwesen, Gemeinde, *(common ownership)* gemeinsamer Besitz, Kollektiv, *(EC)* Gemeinschaft, *(married couple, US)* eheliche Gütergemeinschaft, Errungenschaftsgemeinschaft, *(neighbo(u)rhood)* Nachbarschaft, *(public)* Öffentlichkeit, Volk, Publikum, Allgemeinheit;
  Atlantic $\stackrel{\circ}{\sim}$ Atlantische Gemeinschaft; **conventional** ~ vertraglich vereinbarte (eheliche) Gütergemeinschaft; **conjugal** ~ eheliche Gemeinschaft; **European Coal and Steel** $\stackrel{\circ}{\sim}$ Europäische Gemeinschaft für Kohle und Stahl; **legal** ~ gesetzliche Gütergemeinschaft; **international** ~ Völkergemeinschaft; **rural** ~ ländliche Gemeinde, Landgemeinde; **scientific** ~ wissenschaftliche Fachgemeinschaft; **urban** ~ Stadtgemeinde; **village** ~ Dorfgemeinschaft;
  ~ **of goods** Gütergemeinschaft; ~ **of heirs** *(US)* Erbengemeinschaft; ~ **of ideas** Ideengemeinschaft; ~ **of [rights and] interests** [Rechts- und] Interessengemeinschaft; ~ **of monks** Mönchsorden; ~ **of profits** Gewinngemeinschaft; ~ **of religion** Religionsgemeinschaft; $\stackrel{\circ}{\sim}$ **of the Six** Sechsergemeinschaft;
  to be harmful to the ~ für die Allgemeinheit abträglich sein; **to make requisitions upon a** ~ einer Gemeinschaft Requisitionen auferlegen;
  ~ **account** Gemeinschaftskonto; ~ **action** Gemeinschaftsmaßnahmen; ~ **affairs** Gemeindeangelegenheiten; ~ **aid** *(EC)* Gemeinschaftshilfe; ~ **antenna** *(radio)* Gemeinschaftsantenne; ~ **association** Bürgergemeinschaft; ~ **budget** *(EC)* Gemeinschaftsetat, Etat der Europäischen Gemeinschaft; ~ **bulletin board** Gemeindeaushang, -tafel; ~ **care** Gemeindefürsorge; ~ **centre** Gemeindezentrum, Nachbarschaftsheim, Dorfgemeinschaftshaus, *(Br.)* Volksbildungsheim; ~ **chest** *(US)* Wohlfahrtsfonds; ~ **company** Dachgesellschaft; ~-**conscious** gemeinschaftsbewußt; ~ **consciousness** Gemeinschaftsgefühl, -bewußtsein; ~ **council** Gemeindevorstand; ~ **debt** *(married couple)* gemeinschaftliche Schuld; ~ **development** Gemeindeentwicklung; ~ **district** Gemeindebezirk; ~ **estate** Gemeinschaftseigentum; ~ **expenses** *(EC)* Gemeinschaftsausgaben; ~ **facilities** Kommunalanlagen; ~ **fund** gemeinsamer Fonds; ~ **group** Gruppengemeinschaft, Bürgergemeinschaft; ~ **hospital** Kommunalkrankenhaus; ~ **house** Mehrfamilienhaus, *(US)* Gemeindezentrum; ~ **institution** *(EC)* Gemeinschaftsorgan; ~ **land** Kommunalgrundstück; ~ **Land Act** *(Br.)* Baulandbeschaffungsgesetz; ~ **land scheme** *(Br.)* kommunaler Baulandbeschaffungsplan; **at** ~ **level** *(EC)* auf Gemeinschaftsebene; ~ **market** Markt der Europäischen Gemeinschaften; ~ **market organization** Marktordnung der Europäischen Gemeinschaften; ~ **organ** Gemeinschaftsorgan; ~ **planning** Gemeinschaftsplanung; ~ **ports** Häfen der Europäischen Gemeinschaft; ~ **preferences** *(EC)* Gemeinschaftspräferenzen; ~ **procedure** *(EC)*

Gemeinschaftsverfahren; ~ **project** Gemeinschaftsprojekt, -vorhaben; ~ **property** *(married couple, US)* [gesetzliche] Güter, Errungenschaftsgemeinschaft; ~ **quota** *(EC)* Gemeinschaftskontingent; ~ **recreation** Gemeinschaftserholung; ~ **relations** *(EC)* Gemeinschaftbeziehungen; ~ **responsibilities** Teilnahme (Interesse) am Gemeinschaftsleben; ~ **service** *(penal system)* Gemeinschaftsdienst; ~ **support** Kommunalhilfe; ~ **tariff quotas** *(EC)* Gemeinschaftszollkontingente; ~ **transit documents** Transitpapiere der Europäischen Gemeinschaft; ~ **trust** *(US)* städtische Treuhandgesellschaft zur Verwaltung öffentlicher Stiftungen; ~ **worker** Sozialpfleger; ~ **works** Gemeinschaftsunternehmungen.

communization Sozialisierung, Vergesellschaftung.

communize *(v.)* sozialisieren, vergesellschaften.

commutable umwandelbar, austauschbar, *(penalty)* durch Geld ablösbar.

commutation *(buying-off)* Ablösung, *(change)* Umwandlung, *(interchange)* Austausch, Auswechslung, *(money paid by way of ~)* Ablösungssumme, *(punishment)* Ablösung, Strafänderung, -milderung, *(US, travel)l)ing on a commutation ticket)* Benutzung einer Dauerkarte, regelmäßige Benutzung öffentlicher Verkehrsmittel, Pendelverkehr;
  ~ **of an annuity** Rentenablösung; ~ **of copyright** Ablösung eines Verlagsrechts; ~ **of a death sentence to life imprisonment** Umwandlung einer Todesstrafe in lebenslängliches Zuchthaus; ~ **of a rent** Mietablösung; ~ **of a right of user** Ablösung einer Dienstbarkeit; ~ **of a sentence** Strafumwandlung, -ermäßigung; ~ **of taxes** pauschalierte vorzeitige Steuerzahlung, Steuerablösung;
  ~ **column** *(life insurance)* Kommutationswertspalte; ~ **debt** Ablösungsschuld; ~ **fare** *(US)* Abonnementsfahrpreis; ~ **home** *(Br.)* Fürsorgeinternat; ~ **link** Verbindungsglied; ~ **rates** *(US)* Zeitkartentarif; ~ **tables** Umrechnungstabelle; ~ **ticket** *(US)* Bezirks-, Netz-, Zeit-, Abonnementsfahr-, Dauerkarte; ~ **traffic** Zeitkarten-, Pendelverkehr.

commutative auswechselbar, vertauschbar;
  ~ **contract** wechselseitiger Vertrag; ~ **justice** solide Verkehrsgrundsätze.

commute *(v.)* *(buy off)* [Lasten]ablösen, *(change payment)* umwandeln, *(communication ticket, US)* hin- und herfahren, pendeln, Dauerfahrkarte (Netzkarte) benutzen, *(instalment system)* einmalige Zahlung leisten, *(interchange)* um-, austauschen, *(pay in gross)* durch Kapitalzahlung abfinden, *(punishment)* verwandeln;
  ~ **an annuity into a lump sum** Rente durch Pauschalzahlung ablösen; ~ **a death sentence** Todesstrafe umwandeln; ~ **freight charges** Frachtkosten bezahlen; ~ **to work** mit einer Zeitkarte zur Arbeit fahren.

commuter *(Br.)* Vorortbewohner, *(US, railroad ticket)* Monats-, Dauer-, Netz-, Zeitkarteninhaber, Berufsverkehrsteilnehmer, Pendler;
  weekly ~ *(US)* Wochenpendler;
  ~ **aircraft** *(US)* im Pendelverkehr eingesetztes Flugzeug; ~ **airline** *(US)* Nahverkehrsgesellschaft; ~ **airlines** *(US)* Flugzeugnahverkehr; ~ **airliner** *(US)* Nahverkehrsflugzeug; ~ **area** *(US)* Nahverkehrsbezirk, -gebiet; ~ **belt** Einzugsbereich; ~ **bus** *(US)* für den Pendelverkehr eingesetzter Omnibus; ~ **car** *(US)* Nahverkehrswagen; ~ **crisis** *(US)* Krise des Berufsverkehrs; ~ **fare** *(US)* Monats-, Dauer-, Netz-, Zeitkarte; ~ **flow** *(US)* Pendlerstrom; ~ **line** *(US)* Pendlerstrecke, Nahverkehrslinie; ~ **lines** *(US)* Nahverkehrsnetz; ~ **miles travelled** *(US)* von Zeitkarteninhabern gefahrene Bahnkilometer; ~ **rail service** *(US)* Berufsverkehrseinrichtungen der Bahn; ~ **railroad** *(US)* Nahverkehrsbahn; ~ **schedule** *(US)* Pendlerfahrplan; ~ **service** *(US)* Nahverkehrs-, Pendelbetrieb; **local** ~ **station** *(US)* Nahverkehrsbahnhof; ~ **suburban area** *(US)* Nahverkehrsgebiet; ~ **traffic** *(US)* Berufs-, Pendlerverkehr; ~ **train** *(US)* Vorort-, Pendler-, Nah-, Berufsverkehrszug; ~ **trip** *(US)* Reise im Pendlerverkehr; ~ **zone** *(US)* Nahzone, Pendelgebiet, Pendlereinzugsbereich.

commuting *(US)* Nah-, Berufsverkehr, Pendeln;
  coast-to-coast ~ *(US)* Pendelverkehr von einem Ende des Kontinents zum anderen;
  ~ **business** *(US)* Pendlerverkehr; ~ **costs** *(US)* tägliche Fahrtkosten; ~ **distance** *(US)* Pendelentfernung; ~ **executive** *(US)* täglich pendelnder leitender Angestellter; ~ **motorist** *(US)* Autopendler; ~ **ordeal** *(US)* tägliches Abenteuer im Berufsverkehr; **rush hours** ~ **trip** *(US)* Pendelverkehr in Spitzenverkehrszeiten.

compact Vertrag, Abkommen, Pakt;
  by general ~ laut allgemeiner Übereinkunft;

~ **between states** Staatsvertrag;
~ *(v.)* Übereinkommen treffen;
~ *(a.)* dicht gedrängt;
~ **car** *(US)* Kompakt-, Kleinwagen; ~ **estate** abgerundeter Besitz; ~ **model** Kompaktmodell.

Companies, associated verbundene Unternehmen; **interrelated ~** verschachtelte Gesellschaften;
to consolidate ~ Firmen zusammenschließen; **to have holdings in several ~** an verschiedenen Gesellschaften beteiligt sein;
~ **Act** *(Br.)* [etwa] Aktiengesetz; ⌀ **promotor** Gründer von Gesellschaften, Finanzierungsvermittler; ⌀ **Registry (Registration Office)** Gesellschafts-, Firmenregister; ~ **winding-up rules** *(Br.)* Vorschriften über die Gesellschaftsliquidation.

companion Begleiter, Genosse, *(manual)* Handbuch, Leitfaden, *(partner)* Teilhaber, Compagnon, *(ship)* Kajütstreppe;
boon ~ Zechbruder; **life ~** Lebensgefährte;
~ **at arms** Waffengefährte; ~**s in distress** Leidensgenossen; ~**s in misfortune** Schicksalsgenossen; ~**s on a journey** Mitreisende; ~ **guide** Begleitkatalog; ~ **piece** Seiten-, Gegenstück, Pendant; ~ **provision** Zusatzbestimmung, ~ **volume** Begleitband.

companionship Zusammenleben, Zusammensein, *(print.)* Arbeitskolonne, -gruppe, *(social life)* geselliges Beisammensein;
to provide ~ Gesellschaft leisten.

company [Handels]gesellschaft, Firma, Unternehmen, Betrieb, *(being together)* Begleitung, Gesellschaft, *(guild, Br.)* Gilde, Genossenschaft, *(mil.)* Kompanie, *(ship)* Besatzung, Mannschaft, *(society)* Geselligkeit, gesellschaftliches Leben, Umgang, Verkehr, *(theater)* Wandertruppe;
in the corporate name of a ~ in Vollmacht für eine Gesellschaft;
absorbing ~ *(merger)* aufnehmende Gesellschaft; **accepting ~** *(insurance)* Rückversicherer; **affiliated ~** Tochter-, Beteiligungs-, Konzerngesellschaft; **alien ~** auswärtige Gesellschaft; **associated ~** *(Br.)* geschäftlich verbundenes Unternehmen; **auditing ~** Wirtschaftsprüfungs-, Revisions-, Treuhandgesellschaft; **banking ~** Bankinstitut; **benefit ~** *(Br.)* Unterstützungsverein; **bogus ~** Briefkastenfirma, Schwindelgesellschaft; **broadcasting ~** Rundfunkgesellschaft; **bubble ~** *(Br.)* Schwindelgesellschaft; **cattle loan ~** Gesellschaft zur Finanzierung der Viehzucht; **ceding ~** *(insurance law)* Erstversicherer; **chartered ~** *(Br.)* konzessionierte (privilegierte) Handelsgesellschaft; **claimant ~** *(group relief)* Gewinnabführungsbeträge entgegennehmende Gesellschaft, Verlustausgleich beantragende Gesellschaft; **client ~** Kundin; **close ~** *(Br.)* [etwa] Familiengesellschaft; **closed-end investment ~** *(US)* Investmentgesellschaft mit beschränkter Emissionsmöglichkeit; **commercial credit ~** Gesellschaft zur Finanzierung von Warenkrediten, Finanzierungsgesellschaft; **consolidated ~** konsolidierte Gesellschaft, Konzerngesellschaft; **constituent ~** Gründergesellschaft; **consumer goods ~** Unternehmen der Konsumgüterindustrie; **controlled ~** beherrschtes Unternehmen; **controlling ~** herrschende Gesellschaft, Dachgesellschaft; **corresponding ~** befreundete Gesellschaft; **debtor ~** Schuldnerin; **defective ~** fehlerhaft entstandene Gesellschaft; **defunct ~** stillgelegte Gesellschaft; **dispossessed ~** enteignete Gesellschaft; **dissolved ~** liquidierte (abgewickelte) Gesellschaft; **diversified ~** Gesellschaft mit breitgestreutem Produktionsprogramm; **little diversified ~** ziemlich einseitige Produktionsgesellschaft; **dock ~** Dockgesellschaft; **family-held ~** Familienunternehmen; **financial ~** *(Br.)* Finanzierungsgesellschaft; **newly formed ~** neu entstandene Gesellschaft; **forward-looking ~** fortschrittliches Unternehmen; **forwarding ~** Transport-, Speditionsgesellschaft; **gas ~** städtisches Gaswerk; **government ~** staatliche Gesellschaft; **guarantee ~** Kautionsversicherungsgesellschaft; **holding ~** Beteiligungs-, Holding-, Dachgesellschaft; **incorporated ~** *(Br.)* handelsgerichtlich eingetragene (rechtsfähige) Gesellschaft, *(US)* Aktiengesellschaft; **industrial ~** Industrieunternehmen; **insurance ~** Versicherungsgesellschaft; **interrelated ~** Schachtelunternehmen; **investment ~** Kapitalanlagegesellschaft; **issuing ~** emittierende Gesellschaft; **joint-stock ~** *(Br.)* Aktiengesellschaft, *(US)* [etwa] Kommanditgesellschaft auf Aktien; **lessor ~** verpachtete Gesellschaft, Verpächterin; **life assurance ~** *(Br.)* Lebensversicherungsgesellschaft; **limited [liability] ~** *(Br.)* [etwa] Gesellschaft mit beschränkter Haftung; ~ **limited by guarantee** *(Br.)* Gesellschaft mit beschränkter Nachschußpflicht; ~ **limited by shares** *(Br.)* [Oberbegriff der britischen] Kapital-, Aktiengesellschaft; **managing ~** Betriebsgesellschaft; **manufacturing ~** Fabrikationsgesellschaft, Herstellungsbetrieb; **marginal ~** an der Grenze der Rentabilität liegende Gesellschaft; **merger ~** fusionierte Gesellschaft; **mining ~** Bergbaugesellschaft; **multimarket ~** Unternehmen mit breit gestreuten Absatzmärkten; **multiprod-**

uct ~ Unternehmen mit breitgestreutem Produktionsprogramm; **mutual insurance ~** Versicherungsverein auf Gegenseitigkeit; **nationalized ~** *(Br.)* verstaatlichte Gesellschaft; **nonconsolidated ~** nicht konsolidierte Gesellschaft; **nonoperating ~** verpachtete Gesellschaft; **nonprofit [-making] ~** gemeinnützige Gesellschaft; **nonprospectus ~** durch Simultangründung entstandene Gesellschaft; **one-man ~** *(US)* Einmanngesellschaft; **operating ~** Betriebsgesellschaft; **original ~** Gründergesellschaft; **overdiversified ~** Unternehmen mit überproportionalem Fertigungsprogramm; **oversea ~** Übersee-, Auslandsgesellschaft; **parent ~** Dach-, Muttergesellschaft, Stammhaus; **participating ~** beteiligte Gesellschaft; **private ~ [with limited liability]** *(Br.)* auf höchstens 50 Mitglieder beschränkte Aktiengesellschaft, Personengesellschaft; **exempt private ~** *(Br.)* [früher] Familiengesellschaft; **private limited ~** *(Br.)* [etwa] Gesellschaft mit beschränkter Haftung; **privately-held ~** privatwirtschaftlich betriebenes Unternehmen; **proprietary ~** kontrollierende Gesellschaft; **prospectus ~** Gesellschaft mit Börsenprospekt, *(Br.)* Gründergesellschaft; **public ~** öffentlich-rechtliche Gesellschaft; **public limited ~** *(Br.)* [etwa] Aktiengesellschaft; **public service ~** Dienstleistungsunternehmen; **public-utility ~** öffentlicher Versorgungsbetrieb; **publishing ~** Verlagsunternehmen; **quasi-public ~** Gesellschaft mit öffentlich-rechtlichen Befugnissen, gemischtwirtschaftliches Unternehmen; **railway ~** Eisenbahngesellschaft; **real-estate ~** Grundstücks-, Terrain-, Immobiliengesellschaft; **registered ~** *(Br.)* [handelsgerichtlich] eingetragene Gesellschaft (Firma); **related ~** Schwesterfirma; **reorganized ~** sanierte Gesellschaft; **resultant ~** neu entstandene Gesellschaft; **road ~** *(theater, US)* Wandertruppe; **safe ~** Gesellschaft zur Aufbewahrung von Wertgegenständen; **select ~** ausgewählter Kreis, auserlesene Gesellschaft; **ship's ~** Schiffsmannschaft, Besatzung; **shipping ~** Reederei; **standing ~** fortbestehende Gesellschaft; **state-run ~** Staatsbetrieb, -unternehmen; **statutory ~** *(Br.)* [privat betriebenes] Versorgungsunternehmen; **general steam navigation (steamship) ~** allgemeine Dampfschiffahrtsgesellschaft; **stock ~** *(US)* Aktiengesellschaft; **subsidiary ~** Organ-, Schachtel-, Tochter-, Konzerngesellschaft; **surrendering ~** gewinnabführende Gesellschaft, *(group relief)* Gesellschaft, bei der ein Verlust entstanden ist; **surviving ~** übernehmende Gesellschaft; **theatrical ~** Theatergemeinschaft, -truppe; **trading ~** Handelsgesellschaft; **transferee ~** übernehmende Gesellschaft; **transferor ~** übertragende Gesellschaft; **transit ~** Verkehrsunternehmen; **transport ~** *(Br.)* Transport-, Speditionsgesellschaft; **transportation ~** *(US)* Speditionsfirma; **public transportation ~** *(US)* öffentliches Verkehrsunternehmen; **trucking ~** Speditionsbetrieb; **trust ~** Treuhandgesellschaft; **unincorporated ~** nicht rechtsfähige Gesellschaft, Personalgesellschaft; **unlimited ~** *(Br.)* Kapitalgesellschaft mit unbeschränkter Haftung; **unquoted ~** an der Börse nicht notiertes Unternehmen; **unregistered ~** *(Br.)* nicht rechtsfähige Gesellschaft, Personalgesellschaft; **vendor ~** *(merger)* veräußernde (einbringende) Gesellschaft; **well-managed ~** gut geleitete Gesellschaft; **wound-up ~** aufgelöste Gesellschaft; **direct-writing ~** Rückversicherungsgesellschaft; ~ **dominating the market** marktbeherrschendes Unternehmen; ~ **limited by shares** *(Br.)* Aktien-, Kapitalgesellschaft; ~ **of merchants** Handelsgesellschaft; ~ **of players** Schauspielertruppe; ~ **of the police** Bereitschaft der Schutzpolizei;
to administer a ~ from red to black *(US coll.)* Betrieb aus den roten Zahlen herausführen; **to be in bad ~** sich in schlechter Gesellschaft befinden; **to be fond of ~** Geselligkeit lieben, gesellig sein; **to bear s. one's ~** jem. Gesellschaft leisten; **to convert into a ~** in eine Gesellschaft umwandeln; **to dissolve a business ~** Gesellschaft liquidieren (auflösen); **to enter a ~** in eine Gesellschaft als Teilhaber eintreten; **to establish a ~** Gesellschaft errichten; **to expect ~** Gäste erwarten; **to float (form, found, Br.) a ~** Gesellschaft gründen; **to force a ~ into a chapter 10 proceeding** *(US)* Gesellschaftskonkursverfahren einleiten; **to form into a ~** in eine Gesellschaft umwandeln; **to have an interest in a ~** an einer Gesellschaft beteiligt sein; **to incorporate a ~** Gesellschaft handelsgerichtlich eintragen; **to keep ~** Umgang haben, verkehren; **to liquidate a ~** Gesellschaft liquidieren; **to part ~ with s. o.** sich von jem. trennen; **to pick one's ~** auf seinen Umgang achten; **to promote a ~** Gesellschaft gründen; **to put a private ~ on the road to a public stock offering** Aktieneinführung einer privaten Kapitalgesellschaft vorbereiten; **to put a ~ in the black** *(US coll.)* Rendite bei einem Unternehmen erzielen; **to register a ~** Firma handelsgerichtlich eintragen lassen; **to reorganize a ~** Firma sanieren; **to set up (start) a ~** Gesellschaft gründen; **to subscribe for shares in a**

~ Gesellschaftsanteile übernehmen; **to take a ~ off the books** Firma im Handelsregister löschen; **to take over a ~** Gesellschaft übernehmen; **to turn a firm into a joint stock ~** Firma in eine Aktiengesellschaft umwandeln; **to wind up a ~** Gesellschaft auflösen (liquidieren);

~ **account** Gesellschafts-, Firmenkonto; ~ **accounts** Betriebsbuchhaltung; ~ **accountant** Betriebsbuchhalter; ~ **address** Firmenanschrift; ~ **agreement** Gesellschaftsvertrag; ~ **anniversary** Betriebsjubiläum; ~ **archive** Firmen-, Betriebsarchiv; ~ **assessment** *(US)* Firmenveranlagung; ~ **auditor** Betriebsrevisor; ~'s **balance sheet** Firmenbilanz; ~'s **bank** Hausbank; ~'s **bankruptcy** Firmenbankrott; ~ **banquet** Betriebsbankett; ~-**wide bargaining** Tarifvertragsverhandlungen für das Gesamtunternehmen; ~ **benefit** betriebliche Sozialbeihilfe; ~ **bonus plan** Betriebsprämienwesen; ~ **bookkeeping** Firmenbuchhaltung; **to expand ~ business** Geschäftsbetrieb ausweiten; ~ **buying** Firmenerwerb; ~ **cafeteria** Betriebskasino; ~'s **capital** Firmenkapital; ~ **car** firmeneigener Wagen; ~-**car tax rules** Steuerbestimmungen für betriebseigene Fahrzeuge; ~ **celebration** Betriebsfest; ~ **check** Firmenscheck; ~ **colony** Betriebssiedlung; ~ **comments** *(Br.)* Hauptversammlungsberichte; ~ **contribution** Firmen-, Betriebszuschuß; ~ **council** *(US)* paritätischer Betriebsrat; ~ **creditor** Firmengläubiger; ~ **customer** Kundin, Firmenkunde; ~'s **debt** Gesellschafts-, Firmenschuld; ~'s **default** Zahlungsunfähigkeit einer Gesellschaft; ~ **dining-room** Betriebskasino; ~ **diversifications** Produktionsausweitung eines Unternehmens; ~ **dwelling** Betriebs-, Dienst-, Werkswohnung; ~ **earnings** Betriebseinnahmen, -erträge; ~ **employee** Firmenangestellter; ~ **family allowance** betriebliche Familienbeihilfe; ~ **files** Firmenakten; ~ **finance** Firmenfinanzwesen; ~ **financial statement** Firmenstatus; ~'s **financial year** Gesellschafts-, Firmenjahr; ~ **flat** Dienst-, Betriebswohnung; ~ **form** Betriebsformular; ~ **fund** Betriebsfonds, Gesellschaftskapital; **executives' ~ group protection** Gruppenversicherung für leitende Angestellte; ~'s **guarantee** Firmengarantie; ~ **head** Firmeninhaber; ~ **history** Firmengeschichte; ~ **hotel suite** betriebseigene Hotelsuite; ~ **house** Werkswohnung; ~ **housing** Unterbringung in Werkswohnungen; ~ **identification card** Firmen-, Betriebsausweis; ~ **labo(u)r policies** Betriebspolitik; ~ **law** *(Br.)* [etwa] Aktienrecht; ~ **law directives** *(EC)* Aktienrechtsdirektiven; ~ **lawyer** Firmenanwalt, -syndikus; ~ **liabilities** Geschäfts-, Firmenschulden; ~ **magazine** Werkszeitung; ~ **man** Betriebsangehöriger; ~ **management** Firmenleitung; **to be on one's ~ manners** seine besten Manieren zur Schau stellen; ~ **material** *(carrier)* Betriebsmaterialien; ~ **meeting** *(Br.)* Gesellschafterversammlung; ~ **meeting column** *(Br.)* Hauptversammlungsspalte; ~'s **name** Firmenname; ~ **note** Firmenwechsel; ~'s **object** Gesellschaftszweck; ~ **obligations** Firmenverbindlichkeiten; ~ **official** Firmenangehöriger; ~ **oldtimer** langjähriges Belegschaftsmitglied; ~ **owner** Firmeneigentümer; ~ **ownership** Firmeneigentum; ~ **[-financed] pension** Betriebspension; ~ **pension scheme** betriebliche Altersversorgung; ~ **pensioner** Firmenpensionär; ~ **personnel** Betriebspersonal; ~ **president** Firmenchef; ~ **plane** Firmenflugzeug; ~ **planner** Betriebsplaner; ~ **plant** Werksanlage; ~ **physician** Werksarzt; ~ **policy** Unternehmenspolitik; ~ **premises** Betriebsgebäude, -grundstück; ~ **profit** Gesellschaftsgewinn; ~ **progress** Entwicklung eines Unternehmens; ~ **promoter** Firmengründer; ~ **promotion** Firmengründung; ~ **property** Firmen-, Betriebsvermögen; ~ **prospectus** Subskriptionsanzeige einer neuen Gesellschaft, Gesellschaftsprospekt; ~ **publication** Werks-, Betriebszeitung; ~ **radio commercial** betriebliche Werbedurchsage; ~ **rating** Firmenveranlagung; ~ **reconstruction** *(Br.)* Firmensanierung, Sanierungsumgründung; ~ **recruiter** Firmenanwerber; ~'s **registered office** Firmensitz; ~ **reimbursement** Firmenvergütung; ~ **release** Firmenmitteilung; ~ **reorganization** Sanierung einer Firma, Sanierungsumgründung; ~ **resolution** Gesellschaftsbeschluß; **a ~'s resources** Gesellschaftskapital; ~ **result** Geschäfts-, Betriebsergebnis; **at ~'s risk** auf Gefahr der Gesellschaft; ~ **ruling** Betriebsanweisung; ~ **sales** Unternehmensabsatz, Firmenumsatz; ~ **savings system** betriebliche Sparförderung, Werkssparen; ~ **secretary** oberster Verwaltungsbeamter [eines Unternehmens]; ~ **seniority** *(Br.)* Betriebszugehörigkeitsdauer; ~ **servant** Betriebsangehöriger, Firmenangestellter; **service equipment** *(railway)* Bahnausstattungsgegenstände; ~ **size** Betriebs-, Firmen-, Unternehmensgröße; ~ **spokesman** Firmensprecher; ~ **sports grounds** Betriebssportplatz; ~ **staff** Werksangehörige; ~ **statement** Firmenbilanz; ~ **stationery** Firmenbriefbogen; ~ **stock** Firmenaktien; ~ **store** *(US)* betriebseigenes [Laden]geschäft, Kantine; ~ **strategy** langfristige

Firmen-, Werks-, Betriebspolitik; ~ **supplier** Firmenlieferant; ~'s **surplus** Betriebsgewinn; ~ **task** unternehmerische Aufgabe; ~ **tax** *(Br.)* Körperschaftssteuer; ~ **taxation** Körperschaftsbesteuerung; ~ **time** betriebliche Arbeitszeit; **in ~ time** während der Betriebszeit; **to hold a meeting in ~ time** Versammlung während der Arbeitszeit abhalten; ~ **togetherness** betriebliches Zusammensein; ~ **town** *(US)* Firmen-, Werkssiedlung; ~ **tradition** Firmentradition; ~ **union** *(US)* Betriebsgewerkschaft, gelbe Gewerkschaft; ~-**wide bargaining** Tarifvertragsverhandlungen für das Gesamtunternehmen; ~'s **financial year** Gesellschaftsjahr.

comparability Vergleichbarkeit.
comparable vergleichbar, entsprechend;
~ **figures** Vergleichszahlen; ~ **period** Vergleichszeitraum; ~ **rate** Vergleichstarif.
comparative vergleichend, *(relative)* verhältnismäßig, relativ;
~ **advantage** vergleichsweise Ausgangsstellung; ~ **advertising** vergleichende Werbung; ~ **balance sheet** Vergleichsbilanz; ~ **bullion content** *(Br.)* festes Wechselpari; **to live in ~ comfort** bequemes Leben führen; ~ **costs** komparative Kosten, vergleichsweise Unkostensituation; ~ **figures** Vergleichszahlen, -ziffern; ~ **government** vergleichende Regierungslehre; ~ **income statement** Gewinn- und Verlustrechnung mit Vergleichszahlen aus dem Vorjahr; ~ **interpretion** vergleichende Auslegung; ~ **jurisprudence** vergleichende Rechtswissenschaft, Rechtsvergleich; ~ **literature** vergleichende Literaturwissenschaft; ~ **negligence** *(US)* Mitverschulden; ~ **rectitude** Schuldabwägen; ~ **rate schedule** Tarifvergleichstabelle; ~ **statement** vergleichende Aufstellung; ~ **story** vergleichende Werbeaussage; ~ **term** relativer Begriff; ~ **value** Vergleichswert.
compare *(v.)* vergleichen, vergleichend gegenüberstellen, *(collate)* kollationieren;
~ **the books** Bücher vergleichen; ~ **a copy with the original** Abschrift mit dem Original vergleichen; ~ **two documents** Urkunden kollationieren; ~ **notes** Meinungen austauschen.
compared with in Vergleich mit, im Vergleich zu;
~ **the year before** im Vorjahresvergleich.
comparing prices Preisvergleich.
comparison Vergleich, Kollationierung;
by ~ vergleichsweise;
~s *(US)* periodische Kontrollaufstellungen [zwischen Maklern und Banken];
inter-factory ~ zwischenbetrieblicher Vergleich; **juridical ~** Rechtsvergleich;
~ **of costs** Kostenvergleich; ~ **of documents** Urkundenvergleich; ~ **of handwriting** Handschriftenprüfung; ~ **of road and rail costs** Kostenvergleich zwischen Straße und Schiene; ~ **of yields** Ertragsvergleich;
to stand a ~ Vergleich aushalten;
~ **level** Vergleichsstandard; ~ **shopping** zu Kontrollzwecken vorgenommener Einkauf bei der Konkurrenz; ~ **slip** *(US)* Kontrollbeleg [des Maklers]; ~ **table** vergleichende Übersicht.
compartment *(agenda, Br.)* Abschnitt der Tagesordnung, *(railway)* [Wagen]abteil, Coupé, *(section)* Abteilung, Sektion, *(ship)* Schott;
first-class ~ Erste-Klasse-Abteil; **pressurized ~** Druckluftkabine; **sleeping ~** Schlafwagenabteil; **smoking ~** Raucherabteil; **watertight ~**s wasserdichte Schotten;
~ **for dispatch** *(post)* Verteil- und Abgangsfach;
~ **boat** unsinkbares Boot; ~ **car** Schlafwagen; ~ **panel** Abteilplakat; ~ **train** Schlafwagenzug.
compartmentalize *(v.)* in Abteilungen aufteilen;
to be ~d *(fig.)* nur in Klischees denken können.
compass Kompaß, *(circle)* Umkreis, Umfang;
~ *(v.)* im Schilde führen;
to be beyond s. one's ~ über jds. Horizont gehen;
~ **error** Fehlweisung, Kompaßfehler.
compassion Mitgefühl, -leid.
compassionate humanitär;
~ **allowance** Unterhaltszahlung an die geschiedene Ehefrau, Notunterhalt; ~ **leave** *(Br.)* Sonderurlaub, Urlaub aus familiären Gründen.
compatibility Vereinbarkeit, *(television)* Verwendbarkeit für Farbwie Schwarzweißsendungen.
compatible miteinander vereinbar.
compatriot Landsmann.
compatriotism Landsmannschaft.
compear *(v.) (Scot.)* vor Gericht erscheinen (vertreten sein).
compearance *(Scot.)* Erscheinen (Vertretensein) vor Gericht.
compeer Standesgenosse.
to have no ~s nicht Seinesgleichen haben.

compel *(v.)* zwingen, nötigen;
~ **payment** Zahlung erzwingen.
compellable witness aussagepflichtiger Zeuge.
compellability of witness Aussagezwang für einen Zeugen.
compendium Kompendium, Grund, Leitfaden, Handbuch;
~ **of law** Gesetzessammlung.
compensable aufrechenbar, ersetzbar, ausgleichbar;
~ **death** *(Workmen's Compensation Act, US)* schadenersatzpflichtiger Unfalltod; ~ **injury** *(US)* ersatzpflichtiger Betriebsunfall, entschädigungspflichtige Betriebsverletzung.
compensate *(v.)* erstatten, vergüten, entgelten, entlohnen, *(counterbalance)* ausgleichen, kompensieren, *(indemnify)* entschädigen, schadlos halten, *(make amends)* ersetzen, Ersatz leisten;
~ **s. o. for a loss** j. für einen Verlust entschädigen; ~ **each other** sich gegenseitig aufheben; ~ **s. o. for his broken time** jem. seinen Verdienstausfall ersetzen; ~ **a workman for his injuries** einem Arbeiter Schadenersatz für einen Betriebsunfall leisten.
compensating | adjustment Entschädigungsausgleich; ~ **balance** Kontokorrent-, Mindestguthaben; ~ **error** *(bookkeeping)* Gegenfehler, *(statistics)* ausgleichsfähiger Fehler; ~ **gear** Differentialgetriebe; ~ **item** Ausgleichsposten; ~ **tax** Ausgleichssteuer.
compensation *(amends)* [Schaden]ersatz, *(counterbalance)* Ausgleich[ung], Kompensation, *(US, customs)* Ausgleichszoll, *(indemnification)* Entgelt, Abstandsgeld, Entschädigung, [Schadens]abfindung, *(offset)* Gegenrechnung, *(reimbursement)* Rückerstattung, *(salary, US)* Lohn, Gehalt, Vergütung, *(workmen, US)* Unfallentschädigung, Geldrente;
by way of ~ als Ersatz (Entschädigung) für;
above-average ~ überdurchschnittliche Vergütung; **additional** ~ besondere Entschädigung; **advance** ~ Schadensbevorschussung; ~ **agreed upon** vertraglich vereinbarte Entschädigung; **annual** ~ Abfindung in Form eines Jahresgehalts; **basic** ~ Haupteinkünfte; **cash** ~ Barvergütung, -abfindung; **deferred** ~ hinausgeschobene Abfindung; **dismissal** ~ Abfindung; **equivalent** ~ Wertersatz; **executive** ~ Vergütung für leitende Angestellte; **fair and reasonable** ~ angemessene Vergütung; **financial** ~ finanzielle Entschädigung; **gross** ~ Bruttoverdienst; **legal** ~ gesetzlich zustehende Entschädigung; **money (pecuniary)** ~ Abfindungssumme; ~ **payable** geschuldete Entschädigung; **scanty** ~ dürftige Entschädigung; **sickness** ~ Krankengeld; **total** ~ Bruttovergütung, -entgelt; **workman's** ~ *(US)* betriebliche Unfallentschädigung, Betriebsunfallschutz; **year-end** ~ Jahresabschlußvergütung;
~ **in cash** Barabfindung; ~ **for damage** Schadenersatz; ~ **for expropriation** Enteignungsentschädigung; ~ **for improvements** Ersatz für werterhöhende Aufwendungen; ~ **for industrial diseases** Schadenersatz für Betriebskrankheiten; ~ **proportional to the injuries** den Verletzungen entsprechende Entschädigung; ~ **for law of office** Entschädigung für den Verlust eines Vorstandspostens (Verwaltungsratpostens); ~ **for loss of amenities** Schadenersatz für Verschlechterung der Wohngegend; ~ **for loss of office** Abfindungsentschädigung; ~ **irrespective of negligence** fahrlässigkeitsunabhängiger Schadenersatz; ~ **by operation of law** gesetzlich vorgesehene Ausgleichsmöglichkeit; ~ **for outlay [incurred]** Kostenerstattung; ~ **to dispossessed owners** Enteignungsentschädigung; ~ **for pain and suffering** *(US)* Schmerzensgeld; ~ **by reconvention** Entschädigung im Wege der Widerklage; ~ **for use** Nutzungsentgelt; ~ **over and above the contractual wages** übertarifliche Vergütung;
to accept ~ sich abfinden lassen; **to assess** ~ Entschädigung festsetzen; **to award** ~ Schadensersatz (Entschädigung) zuerkennen; **to be entitled to** ~ Abfindungsansprüche haben; **to claim as (demand)** ~ Schadensersatz verlangen; **to disallow** ~ keine Entschädigung gewähren; **to pay** ~ Vergütung (Entschädigung) gewähren; **to set the** ~ *(US)* Gehaltsfestsetzung vornehmen; **to settle the amount of** ~ Entschädigung vereinbaren; **to turn over a** ~ Ersatz herausgeben;
~ **account** Ausgleichskonto; **Workmen's ~ Act** *(US)* Arbeiterunfallversicherungsgesetz; ~ **agreement** *(international law)* Schadensersatzvereinbarung, Kompensationsabkommen; ~ **award** im Schiedsverfahren festgesetzte Entschädigung; ~ **benefit** Unfall-, Betriebsschadensrente; ~ **business** Kompensationsgeschäft; ~ **claim** Entschädigungs-, Schadensersatzanspruch; ~ **costs** Schadensersatzaufwand; ~ **deal** Kompensationsgeschäft; ~ **demand** Vergütungsanspruch; ~ **device** *(US)* Gehalts-, Vergütungsmöglichkeit; ~ **expert** *(US)* Gehälterfachmann, -experte; ~ **field** *(US)* Vergütungs-, Gehaltswesen; ~ **formula** Entschädigungsformel; ~ **fund** Ausgleichsfonds; ~ **history** Aufstellung über früher gezahlte Vergütungen;

Gehaltsentwicklung; ~ **insurance** *(US)* Arbeiterunfallversicherung; ~ **insurance premium** Arbeiterunfallversicherungsprämie; ~ **law** Arbeiterunfallversicherungsgesetz; ~ **money** Entschädigungsbetrag; ~ **office** Kriegsschäden-, Kompensationsamt; ~ **package** *(US)* Gesamtvergütung; ~ **payments** Entschädigungs-, Abfindungszahlung, Schadensersatzleistung; ~ **period** *(workmen)* Entschädigungszeit; **deferred** ~ **plan** *(US)* zeitlich verlagerte Gewinnvergütungen; **overall** ~ **program** *(US)* umfassendes Programm zusätzlicher Vergünstigungen; ~ **provisions** Entschädigungsbestimmungen; ~ **scheme** Ausgleichsplan, -regelungs, Kompensationsschema; ~ **stock** Abfindungsbetrag.
compensational als Ausgleich (Kompensation).
compensative entschädigend, ausgleichend, vergütend.
compensatory ausgleichend, entschädigend;
~ **adjustment** Ausgleichsregelung; **money** ~ **amount** geldwerter Ausgleichsbetrag; ~ **balance** *(banking)* Ausgleichskonto; ~ **charge** Ausgleichsabgabe; ~ **concession** Ausgleichszugeständnis; ~ **damages** *(US)* Schadensersatz[leistung], Ersatz des tatsächlichen Schadens; ~ **dumping** Preisdifferenzierung multinationaler Firmen; ~ **duty** Ausgleichszoll; ~ **finance** antizyklische Finanzpolitik; ~ **financing of export fluctuations** *(International Monetary Fund)* Ausgleichsfinanzierung von Ausfuhrschwankungen; ~ **financing facility** Ausgleichsfinanzierungsmöglichkeiten; ~ **fiscal policy** antizyklische Konjunkturpolitik; ~ **interest** Staffel-, Zinseszinsen; ~ **item** Ausgleichsposten; ~ **measures** Ausgleichsmaßnahmen; ~ **payment** Ausgleich-, Entschädigungs-, Abfindungszahlung; ~ **price** *(EC)* Ausgleichspreis; ~ **principle of taxation** Steuerausgleichsprinzip; ~ **spending** Defizitwirtschaft; ~ **tax** Ausgleichssteuer; ~ **time off** Ausgleichsurlaub für Überstunden.
compère *(Br.)* Konferencier, Ansager;
~ *(v.)* ansagen.
compete *(v.)* im Wettbewerb stehen, konkurrieren;
[un]able to ~ konkurrenz[un]fähig;
~ **with s. o.** mit jem. in Wettbewerb treten; ~ **with each other** sich [gegenseitig] Konkurrenz machen; ~ **against other countries** mit anderen Ländern konkurrieren; ~ **head on** im Wettbewerb Kopf an Kopf liegen; ~ **for a job** sich um einen Posten bewerben; ~ **with a price** mit einem Preis konkurrieren; ~ **for a prize** an einem Preisausschreiben teilnehmen; ~ **for a scholarship** sich um ein Stipendium bemühen.
competence *(ability)* Fähigkeit, Befähigung, *(authority)* Kompetenz, [Amts]befugnis, Zuständigkeit, *(legal capacity)* Geschäftsfähigkeit, *(court)* Zuständigkeits-, Geltungsbereich, *(in office)* Aufgaben-, Zuständigkeits-, Dienstbereich, *(qualification)* Tauglichkeit, Qualifikation, *(subsistence)* genügendes Auskommen, Fortkommen;
administrative ~ Verwaltungstalent; **exclusive** ~ ausschließliche Zuständigkeit; **general** ~ Allzuständigkeit; **limited (restricted)** ~ bedingte Geschäftsfähigkeit; **technical** ~ fachliches Können;
~ **to contract** Vertragsfähigkeit; ~ **to dispose of property** Verfügungs-, Dispositionsfähigkeit; ~ **to give evidence** Zeugnisfähigkeit; ~ **in marketing** umfassende Kenntnisse des Absatzwesens;
to be within (without) the ~ **of a court** innerhalb (außerhalb) der Zuständigkeit eines Gerichts liegen; **to disclaim** ~ sich für unzuständig erklären; **to enjoy a** ~ sein [gutes] Auskommen haben; **to exceed one's** ~ seine Zuständigkeit überschreiten; **to fall within the** ~ **of s. o.** zu jds. Zuständigkeit gehören; **to have a** ~ sein Auskommen (zu leben) haben; **to have a bare** ~ gerade genug zum Leben haben; **to have a** ~ **of learning** hinlängliche Kenntnisse haben; **to lie within s. one's** ~ in jds. Zuständigkeit liegen.
competency genügendes Auskommen;
small ~ kleine Rente;
to enjoy a ~ sein Auskommen haben.
competent kompetent, befugt, fachkundig, zuständig, berechtigt, *(adequate)* ausreichend, angemessen, *(fit)* fähig, befähigt, *(testator)* zurechnungsfähig;
not ~ nicht zuständig, unzuständig;
[legally] ~ **to contract** vertrags-, geschäftsfähig; ~ **to dispose** verfügungsberechtigt; ~ **to dispose by will** testierfähig; ~ **to give evidence** zeugnisfähig; ~ **to make a decision** beschlußfähig; ~ **to inherit** erbfähig;
to be mentally ~ zurechnungsfähig sein; **to consider o. s.** ~ sich für berechtigt halten; **to declare o. s. to be** ~ sich für zuständig erklären; **not to be** ~ **to dispose of property** [etwa] nicht befreiter Vorerbe sein; **not to be** ~ **to speak on a matter** zu einem Thema keine Erklärungen abgeben dürfen;

~ authority zuständige Behörde; **~ court** zuständiges Gericht; **~ evidence** zulässiges Beweismaterial; **~ judge** zuständiger Richter, *(expert)* Sachverständiger; **~ knowledge to speak English** ausreichende englische Sprachkenntnisse; **~ parties** Vertragsparteien; **~ person** Sachverständiger; **in ~ quarters** in unterrichteten Kreisen; **~ supply of provisions** ausreichende Versorgung; **~ teacher** geeigneter Lehrer; **~ witness** *(will)* den gesetzlichen Vorschriften Genüge leistender Zeuge.

competing im Wettbewerb, konkurrierend;
not ~ außer Konkurrenz;
~ brands Konkurrenzmarken; **~ business** Konkurrenzgeschäft; **~ corporation** Konkurrenzgesellschaft; **~ firm** Konkurrenzfirma; **~ merchandise** Konkurrenzware; **~ offer** Konkurrenzangebot; **~ producer** Konkurrenzfirma, -betrieb; **~ product** Konkurrenzerzeugnis; **~ outfit** Konkurrenzbetrieb, -firma.

competition Konkurrenz[kampf], Wettbewerb, *(broadcasting)* von verschiedenen Sendern gleichzeitig ausgestrahlte Werbeeinblendung, *(prize contest)* Preisausschreiben;
able to meet ~ konkurrenz-, wettbewerbsfähig; **out of (without) ~** außer Konkurrenz, konkurrenzlos;
active ~ lebhafte Konkurrenz; **administered ~** regulierter Wettbewerb; **atomistic ~** vollständiger Wettbewerb; **brand ~** Konkurrenz der Markenartikel; **commodity ~** Warenkonkurrenz; **cooperative ~** gemeinsamer Wettbewerb; **cutthroat ~** existenzgefährdender Wettbewerb, Schmutzkonkurrenz; **destructive ~** wirtschaftlich unsinniger Wettbewerb, ruinöse Konkurrenz; **fair ~** ehrlicher (lauterer) Wettbewerb; **free ~** Freiheit des Wettbewerbs; **heightened ~** gesteigerter Wettbewerb; **imperfect ~** *(US)* unvollkommener (ungleicher) Wettbewerb; **industry ~** Warenkonkurrenz; **intensified ~** verstärkter Wettbewerb; **keen ~** scharfe Konkurrenz; **knocking ~** herabsetzende Werbung; **knockout ~** Ausscheidungswettkampf; **low-price ~** Unterbietung mittels niedriger Preise; **mean ~** unlauterer Wettbewerb, Schmutzkonkurrenz; **monopolistic ~** Wettbewerb zwischen monopolisierten Unternehmen, monopolistischer Wettbewerb; **nonprice ~** außerpreislicher Wettbewerb; **open ~** freier Wettbewerb; **perfect ~** *(US)* vollkommener Wettbewerb; **potential ~** Konkurrenzmöglichkeit; **prize ~** Preisausschreiben; **pure ~** *(US)* vollkommene Konkurrenz; **retail ~** Einzelhandelswettbewerb; **ruinous ~** ruinöser Wettbewerb; **severe ~** scharfer Wettbewerb; **strong ~** starke Konkurrenz; **weak ~** schwache Konkurrenz; **workable ~** *(US)* funktionsfähiger Wettbewerb;
~ from abroad Auslandskonkurrenz; **~ in armaments** Wettrüsten; **trade ~ between countries** internationaler Wettbewerb; **unfair ~ in trade** unlauterer Wettbewerb; **~ in weapons** Rüstungswettlauf;
to be in ~ with s. o. mit jem. in Konkurrenz stehen, mit jem. konkurrieren; **to be afraid of ~** Konkurrenz fürchten; **to be defying all ~** im Wettbewerb nicht zu schlagen sein; **to be entered in a ~** zum Wettbewerb angemeldet sein; **to be exposed to severe ~** scharfer Konkurrenz ausgesetzt sein; **to be up against stiff ~** von scharfem Wettbewerb bedrängt werden; **to check ~** der Konkurrenz Einhalt gebieten; **to contend with ~** gegen eine Konkurrenz aufkommen müssen; **to curb foreign ~** Auslandskonkurrenz eindämmen; **to defy ~** der Konkurrenz die Spitze bieten; **to defy all ~** im Wettbewerb nicht zu schlagen sein; **to distort ~** Wettbewerb verzerren; **to drop out of a ~** aus einem Wettbewerb ausscheiden; **to eliminate ~** Wettbewerb ausschalten; **to engage in unfair ~** unlauteren Wettbewerb betreiben; **to enter into ~** in Konkurrenz (Wettbewerb) treten; **to face world ~ for export markets** auf dem Exportmarkt konkurrenzfähig bleiben; **to go in for a ~** sich an einem Preisausschreiben beteiligen; **to meet ~** der Konkurrenz die Stirn bieten; **to protect domestic products from foreign ~ by trade barriers** Inlandserzeugnisse durch Zollschranken vor der Auslandskonkurrenz schützen; **to pry open to ~** Wettbewerbsvoraussetzungen schaffen; **to put up for ~** Wettbewerb ausschreiben; **to restrain (restrict) ~** Wettbewerb beschränken; **to set up a business in ~** Konkurrenzbetrieb eröffnen; **to sustain ~** es mit der Konkurrenz aufnehmen können; **to take part in a ~** sich an einem Wettbewerb beteiligen; **to throw open a job to ~** Position ausschreiben;
~ clause Wettbewerbsklausel; **~ department** Wettbewerbsabteilung, *(EC)* Wettbewerbsbehörde; **~ law** *(US)* Wettbewerbsgesetz; **~ point** Konkurrenzpunkt; **~ policy** Wettbewerbspolitik; **~ reasons** Wettbewerbs-, Konkurrenzgründe; **~ rules** Wettbewerbsrichtlinien, -regeln; **~ site** Wettkampfstätte.

competitive konkurrenzfähig, wettbewerbsfähig, auf Wettbewerb eingestellt;
~ ability Wettbewerbsfähigkeit; **~ acts (activity)** Wettbewerbs-

tätigkeit; **~ advantage** Vorteil vor der Konkurrenz; **~ advertising** *(US)* aggressive Werbung, Konkurrenzwerbung; **~ article** Konkurrenzerzeugnis, -artikel; **~ assault** Konkurrenzangriff; **~ atmosphere** Wettbewerbssituation; **on a ~ basis** auf der Grundlage des Wettbewerbs; **~ bid** Konkurrenz-, Gegenangebot; **~ bidding** Submissionsverfahren; **~ boost** Wettbewerbsanreiz; **~ brand** Konkurrenzerzeugnis; **~ business world** Wettbewerbswirtschaft; **~ capacity** Wettbewerbsfähigkeit; **~ civil service examination** Aufnahmeprüfung in den höheren Verwaltungsdienst; **~ clause** Konkurrenzklausel; **~ climate** Wettbewerbsklima; **~ conditions** Konkurrenzverhältnisse; **under fully ~ conditions** unter Bedingungen des freien Wettbewerbs; **~ copy** aggressiver Werbetext, herabsetzende (aggressive) Werbung; **~ demand** Zusatznachfrage; **~ determination of prices** Preisbildung im freien Wettbewerb; **~ devaluation** zur Exportsteigerung vorgenommene Abwertung; **~ disadvantage** Wettbewerbsnachteil; **~-distorting** wettbewerbsverzerrend; **~ distortions** Wettbewerbsverzerrungen; **~ economy** Wettbewerbswirtschaft; **~ edge** Schärfe des Konkurrenzkampfes; **~ element** Wettbewerbselement; **~ enterprise** Konkurrenzbetrieb; **~ examination** Aufnahme-, Zulassungsprüfung; **~ exhibition** Leistungsschau; **~ firm** Konkurrenzfirma; **~ gain** Konjunkturgewinn; **~ imbalance** ungleiche Konkurrenzlage, Wettbewerbsverzerrung; **~ industries** Konkurrenzgewerbe; **~ limitations** Wettbewerbseinschränkungen; **~ line** Konkurrenzerzeugnis; **~ market** Wettbewerbs-, Konkurrenzmarkt; **to hold one's own in ~ markets** sich gegen die Konkurrenz im Markt durchsetzen; **~ material** Konkurrenzfabrikat; **unfair ~ methods** unlautere Geschäftsmethoden; **~ mood** Wettbewerbsstimmung; **~ moves** Wettbewerbsmaßnahmen; **to demonstrate one's ~ muscles** seine Wettbewerbsstärke demonstrieren; **~ point** *(transportation)* von zwei Eisenbahnlinien angefahrener Ort; **~ policy** Wettbewerbspolitik; **~ position** Wettbewerbsstellung, Konkurrenzfähigkeit; **~ power** Konkurrenzfähigkeit; **~ practices** Wettbewerbstätigkeit; **~ pressure** Konkurrenzdruck; **~ price** wettbewerbsfähiger Preis, Konkurrenz-, Kampfpreis; **~ problem** Konkurrenz-, Wettbewerbsproblem; **~ product** Konkurrenzerzeugnis, -artikel; **~ quotation** Konkurrenzangebot; **~ rate** Konkurrenztarif; **~ reaction** Reaktion der Konkurrenz; **~ reasons** Konkurrenzgründe; **~ requirements** Wettbewerbserfordernisse; **~ restraint** Wettbewerbsbeschränkung; **~ restrictions** Wettbewerbsbeschränkungen; **~ selection** Konkurrenzauslese; **~ situation** Wettbewerbs-, Konkurrenzlage; **~ society** Wettbewerbsgesellschaft; **~ spirit** Konkurrenzeinstellung, -gesinnung; **~ strategy** Wettbewerbsstrategie; **~ strength** Wettbewerbsfähigkeit, -stärke; **~ struggle** Konkurrenzkampf; **~ system** Wettbewerbssystem; **~ tariff** *(railway)* Konkurrenztarifvertrag; **~ tendering** Ausschreibung; **~ threat** Konkurrenzdrohung; **~ thrust** Konkurrenzkampf; **~ traffic** Konkurrenzverkehr; **~ unit** Wettbewerbseinheit; **~ wage** von der Konkurrenz gezahlte Löhne, Wettbewerbslohn; **~ zeal** Wettbewerbseifer, eifrige Konkurrenztätigkeit.

competitor [Mit]bewerber, *(firm)* Konkurrenzfirma, -betrieb, Konkurrent, *(prize)* Wett-, Preisbewerber, Kandidat;
cut-price ~ preisdrückender Konkurrent; **cutthroat ~** Wettbewerber mit unlauteren Geschäftsmethoden;
my ~s in trade meine Konkurrenz;
to be ahead of one's ~s konkurrenzlos dastehen; **to be one jump ahead of one's ~s** der Konkurrenz immer um eine Nasenlänge voraus sein; **to catch up with the ~s** mit der Konkurrenz gleichziehen; **to drive a ~ out of business** Konkurrenzfirma vom Markt verdrängen; **to forestall a ~** der Konkurrenz zuvorkommen; **to get the jump on one's (lead all) ~s** gesamte Konkurrenz überflügeln; **to put ~s out of business** Konkurrenz aus dem Markt verdrängen; **to undercut a ~** Konkurrenten unterbieten; **~ firm** Konkurrenzfirma; **~'s goods** Konkurrenzerzeugnisse; **~'s price** Konkurrenzpreis.

competitiveness Wettbewerbs-, Konkurrenzfähigkeit;
nonprice ~ Wettbewerbsfähigkeit auf allen vom Preis unabhängigen Gebieten.

competitorship Wettbewerberschaft.

compilation Sammlung, Zusammenstellung, Kompilation, *(book)* Sammelwerk;
~ of a dictionary Zusammenstellung (Bearbeitung) eines Wörterbuches.

compile *(v.)* zusammenstellen, -tragen, kompilieren;
~ a catalog(ue) Katalog zusammenstellen; **~ a dictionary** Wörterbuch verfassen; **~ a list** Liste aufstellen.

compiled statutes Sammlung von Gesetzen und Verordnungen.

compiler Kompilator, *(data processing)* Übersetzungsprogramm, *(dictionary)* Bearbeiter, Verfasser.

complain *(v.)* [about] sich beschweren [über], reklamieren;
 to have reason to ~ Grund zur Klage haben.
complainant Kläger, Beschwerdeführer.
complaining party Beschwerdeführerin, Klägerin.
complaint Beanstandung, [Dienstaufsichts]beschwerde, *(economics)* Reklamation, Mängelrüge, *(illness)* Beschwerde, Krankheit, *(insurance)* Schadensanzeige, *(first pleading, US)* erster Sachvortrag, *(statement of claim)* Klageschrift;
 in case of ~ bei Beanstandungen; **on** ~ **of** auf Beschwerde von; ~s **if any** eventuelle Beschwerden; **cross** ~ Widerklage; **formal** ~ formelle Beschwerde; **heart** ~ Herzbeschwerden; **legitimate** ~ berechtigte Reklamation; **third-party** ~ *(US)* Streitverkündung;
 ~ **concerning quality** Qualitätsrüge; ~ **from a customer** Kundenbeschwerde;
 to adjust ~s Beschwerden abhelfen; **to bring one's** ~s **to attention** Beschwerden vorbringen; **to bring a** ~ **to s. one's notice** Beanstandungen bei jem. geltend machen; **to consider a** ~ Mängelrüge berücksichtigen; **to disallow a** ~ Beschwerde ablehnen; **to dismiss a** ~ Berufung (Beschwerde) zurückweisen; **to file a** ~ Klage[schrift] (Beschwerde) einreichen; **to file a** ~ **against s. o.** Beschwerde über j. erheben; **to have cause for** ~ Grund zur Beschwerde haben; **to have no cause (ground) for** ~ keinen Beschwerdegrund haben; **to lodge a** ~ **with s. o.** sich beschwerdeführend an j. wenden; **to lodge a** ~ **against one's neighbour** sich über seinen Nachbarn beschweren; **to look into a** ~ sich mit einer Beschwerde befassen; **to make a** ~ Mängelrüge erheben; **to make a** ~ **against s. o.** sich über j. beschweren, Beschwerde über j. vorbringen; **to make a** ~ **about** Beschwerdeweg einschlagen; **to remove a cause of** ~ einer Beschwerde abhelfen;
 ~s **department** Beschwerde-, Reklamationsabteilung; ~ **letter** Reklamations-, Beschwerdebrief; ~s **office** Beschwerdeinstanz, -abteilung, -stelle; ~s **panel** Beschwerdeausschuß; ~s **procedure** Reklamations-, Beschwerdeverfahren.
complaisance Zuvorkommenheit, Entgegenkommen, Gefälligkeit.
complaisant willfährig, gefällig, entgegen-, zuvorkommend.
complement Ergänzung, Vervollständigung, Vervollkommnung;
 full ~ vollständige Besatzung; **ship's** ~ Schiffsbesatzung;
 ~ *(v.)* ergänzen, vervollständigen, komplettieren.
complementary ergänzend, komplementär;
 to be ~ sich ergänzen;
 ~ **demand** komplementäre Güternachfrage; ~ **goods** Komplementärgüter; ~ **insurance** Zusatzversicherung; ~ **line** verwandtes Sortiment; ~ **needs** Komplementärbedürfnisse; ~ **rules** Ergänzungsvorschriften; ~ **statement** ergänzende Ausführungen.
complete vollständig, vollzählig, vollkommen, komplett, ganz;
 ~ **in itself** *(legislative act)* nicht ergänzungsbedürftig;
 ~ *(v.)* ergänzen, fertigstellen, vervollständigen, komplettieren, *(bring to a close)* abschließen, abwickeln, beendigen, erledigen, *(fill up)* ausfüllen;
 ~ **a call** [telefonische] Verbindung herstellen; ~ **one's collection** seine Sammlung ergänzen; ~ **a contract** Vertrag erfüllen; ~ **a crew** Mannschaftsbestand auffüllen; ~ **one's education** seine Erziehung abschließen; ~ **a form** Formular ausfüllen; ~ **payment** Abschlußzahlung leisten; ~ **with provisions** mit Vorräten versehen; ~ **a questionnaire (questionary,** *Br.)* Fragebogen ausfüllen; ~ **a return of income** Einkommensteuererklärung abgeben; ~ **one's sentence** Strafe verbüßen; ~ **a task** Aufgabe erfüllen;
 to give a ~ **account** detaillierten Bericht geben; ~ **audit** zum Jahresschluß durchgeführte Prüfung, Jahresrevision; ~ **block** *(Br.)* Vollklischee; **to have** ~ **charge of a business** Geschäft vollständig allein leiten; ~ **copy** vollständige Abschrift; ~ **determination of cause** rechtskräftige Prozeßentscheidung; ~ **edition** Gesamtausgabe, -auflage; ~ **knowledge** umfassende Kenntnisse; ~ **and permanent loss of the right arm** Dauerverlust des rechten Armes; ~ **outfit** komplette Ausstattung; ~ **patent** endgültiges Patent; ~ **payment** Abschlußzahlung; ~ **plate** *(US)* Vollklischee; ~ **specification** *(patent law)* endgültige Beschreibung; ~ **success** voller Erfolg; ~ **voucher copy** vollständiges Belegexemplar, komplette Belegnummer; ~ **works** sämtliche Werke.
completed vollendet, fertiggestellt;
 ~ **audit** Jahresrevision; ~ **execution** durchgeführte Vollstreckung; ~ **offence** vollendetes Verbrechen; ~ **oil well** fertiggestellte Bohranlagen; ~ **transaction** abgeschlossenes Geschäft.

completion Vollendung, Beendigung, Ergänzung *(filling out)* Ausfüllung, *(fulfilment)* Erfüllung, Durchführung, *(subsequent delivery)* Nachlieferung, *(transfer of land)* Abschlußformalitäten;
 near ~ kurz vor dem Abschluß; **in process of** ~ in der Verarbeitung begriffen; **on** ~ **of contract** nach Vertragserfüllung;
 ~ **of an attempt** Vollendung eines Versuchs; ~ **of a collection** Vervollständigung einer Sammlung; ~ **of a contract** Vertragserfüllung; ~ **of education** Abschluß der Ausbildung; ~ **of form** Formularausfüllung; ~ **of sale and purchase** *(Br.)* Erfüllung des Kaufvertrages; ~ **of sentence** Verbüßung einer Strafe, Strafverbüßung; ~ **of service** Beendigung eines Dienstverhältnisses; ~ **of transaction** Geschäftsabschluß, -beendigung; ~ **of work** Beendigung einer Arbeit, Arbeitsbeendigung;
 ~ **date** Fertigstellungstermin; ~ **rate** Vollständigkeitssatz.
complex Komplex, Inbegriff, Gesamtheit;
 inferiority ~ Minderwertigkeitskomplex;
 to work off a ~ Komplex abreagieren;
 ~ *(a.)* zusammengesetzt, *(fig.)* kompliziert, schwierig, verzwickt;
 ~ **system of government** kompliziertes Regierungssystem; ~ **trust** *(income tax)* wohltätige Stiftung; ~ **word** zusammengesetztes Wort.
complexion *(fig.)* Aussehen, Charakter;
 to put a fresh ~ **on s. th.** einer Sache einen neuen Anstrich verleihen.
complexity Kompliziertheit, Schwierigkeit.
compliance *(assent)* Einwilligung, *(complaisance)* Willfährigkeit, Zuvor-, Entgegenkommen, *(observation)* Befolgung, Einhaltung;
 in ~ **with your instructions** gemäß Ihrer Anordnungen;
 ~ **with a clause in a contract** Erfüllung einer Vertragsklausel; ~ **with a condition** Erfüllung einer Bedingung; ~ **with the law** Beachtung des Gesetzes; ~ **with legal formalities** Einhaltung der gesetzlichen Formalitäten;
 to act in ~ **with one's orders** auftragsgemäß handeln; **to be sure of s. one's** ~ jds. Einwilligung sicher sein; **to refuse** ~ **with a court order** sich einem Gerichtsbeschluß widersetzen.
compliant willfährig, gefällig, nachgiebig, entgegenkommend.
complicacy Kompliziertheit, Schwierigkeit.
complication Komplikation, Erschwerung.
complicity Mitschuld, Mittäterschaft, Teilnahme.
compliment Kompliment, Empfehlung, Höflichkeitsbezeigung;
 with ~s zur gefälligen Kenntnisnahme; **with** ~s **of the author** im Auftrage des Verfassers; **without any** ~s ohne Umstände;
 my respectful ~s hochachtungsvoll;
 ~s **of the season** Weihnachts-, Neujahrsglückwünsche;
 to be fishing for ~s auf Komplimente aus sein; **to pay one's** ~s **to s. o.** jem. ein Kompliment machen, jem. einen Höflichkeitsbesuch abstatten; **to return a** ~ Gegenkompliment machen; ~ **slip** höfliche Begleitnotiz.
complimentary höflich, *(given free)* gratis;
 ~ **account** Werbungskonto; ~ **close** Höflichkeitsschlußformel; ~ **closure** Schlußformeln; ~ **copy** Freiexemplar, *(magazine)* Werbenummer, -exemplar, *(author)* Frei-, Autorenexemplar; ~ **dinner** Bankett, Festessen; ~ **list** Freiexemplarliste; ~ **prefixes (suffixes)** Höflichkeitsfloskeln, Schlußformeln; ~ **reference** lobende Bezugnahme; ~ **seat** Ehrenplatz; ~ **subscription** kostenloses Abbonnement; ~ **ticket** Ehren-, Freikarte.
complot Verschwörung, Komplott.
comply *(v.) (act in accordance)* nachkommen, willfahren, erfüllen, darauf eingehen, einwilligen, sich einlassen (auf);
 ~ **with a clause in a contract** sich an eine Vertragsbestimmung halten, Vertragsbestimmung erfüllen; ~ **with conditions** Bedingungen erfüllen; ~ **with instructions** Anordnungen nachkommen; ~ **with a law** Gesetz befolgen; ~ **with one's principal's instructions** den Weisungen seines Auftraggebers Folge leisten; ~ **with regulations** Ausführungsbestimmungen befolgen; ~ **with a request** einem Gesuch stattgeben; ~ **with the strict requirements** den strengen Vorschriften Genüge leisten; ~ **with the rules** sich den Vorschriften fügen, sich den Verfahrensregeln unterwerfen; ~ **with the terms** den Bedingungen entsprechen; ~ **with a time limit** Frist einhalten; ~ **with a wish** einem Wunsch nachkommen.
component Bestandteil, *(building)* Bauelement;
 civilian ~ ziviles Gefolge; **primary** ~ Grundbestandteil;
 ~ **maker** Zubehörfertiger; ~ **part** wesentlicher (konstituierender) Bestandteil; ~ **sentence** Teilaussage; ~ **supplier** Zulieferer, Zulieferungsbetrieb.
comport | *(v.)* **o. s. with dignity** sich würdevoll benehmen; **not** ~ **with a high position** einer hohen Stellung unwürdig sein.

compos mentis *(lat.)* bei klarem Verstand.
compose *(v.)* bilden, formen, *(arrange)* beilegen, [Schriftstück] abfassen, aufsetzen, ausarbeiten, *(print.)* [ab]setzen, *(put together)* zusammensetzen;
~ **o. s.** sich sammeln; ~ **one's affairs** seine Geschäfte ordnen; ~ **with one's creditors** mit seinen Gläubigern einen Vergleich abschließen; ~ **one's differences** Streitigkeiten beilegen; ~ **a line** *(print.)* Zeile setzen; ~ **a scheme** Plan ausarbeiten; ~ **a sentence** Satz bilden; ~ **in slips** in Spalten setzen; ~ **a speech** Rede verfassen.
composed gefaßt, gesetzt, gelassen.
composer Verfasser, Autor, Schriftsteller, *(music)* Komponist.
composing *(print.)* Schriftsetzerei, -satz, Satz;
~ **area** Satzbreite; ~ **frame** Schriftkasten; ~ **machine** Setzmaschine; ~ **room** Setzerei; **part-time** ~ **room staff** teilzeitbeschäftigte Metteure und Setzer.
composite Zusammenfassung [mehrerer Pläne];
~ *(a.)* zusammengesetzt, gemischt;
~ **advertisement** Kollektivanzeige, rubrizierte Anzeige; ~ **carriage** *(railway)* gemischter Eisenbahnwagen; ~ **demand** zusammengesetzte Nachfrage; ~ **flow** private und öffentliche Entwicklungshilfe; ~ **index number** Generalindex; ~ **life method of depreciation** Gruppenabschreibung; ~ **line** *(el.)* Simultanleitung; ~ **number** zusammengesetzte Zahl; ~ **photography** Fotomontage; ~ **plate** zusammengesetztes Klischee; ~ **rate** Durchschnittsteuersatz; ~ **rates of depreciation** allgemeine Abschreibungssätze; ~ **school** *(Canada)* Berufsschule; ~ **work** *(copyright)* Gemeinschaftsarbeit.
composition Übereinkunft, Abkommen, *(cliché)* Klischeemontage, *(combination)* Zusammensetzung, *(compromise)* Kompromiß, Vergleich, Verständigung, *(creation)* Geisteswerk, *(documents)* Abfassen, Aufsetzen, Entwerfen [von Schriftstücken], *(gr.)* Satzkonstruktion, *(print.)* Setzen, [Schrift]satz, *(school, US)* Arbeit, Schulaufsatz, *(sum paid to compound)* Vergleichs-, Abfindungssumme *(lump-sum settlement)* Ablösungs-, Pauschalsumme, Pauschalierung, *(talents)* geistige Beschaffenheit, Anlage;
amicable ~ gütliche Abmachung (Regelung, Übereinkunft); **forced** ~ Zwangsvergleich; **free** ~ *(school)* Aufsatz; **hand** ~ *(print.)* mit der Hand gesetzter Schriftsatz, Handsatz; **justified** ~ ausgeschlossener Satz; **machine** ~ Maschinensatz; ~ **offered** Vergleichsangebot; **out-of-court** ~ außergerichtlicher Vergleich; **own** ~ *(music)* eigene Komposition; **rationalized** ~ rationelle Satzherstellung; **special** ~ Sondervereinbarung; **unjustified** ~ Flattersatz;
~ **in bankruptcy** *(within the bankruptcy law)* Konkurs-, Gläubiger-, Liquidations-, Zwangsvergleich; ~ **of the Cabinet** Zusammensetzung der Regierung; ~ **of a court** Zusammensetzung eines Gerichts; ~ **with creditors** Gläubigervergleich; ~ **by deed of arrangement** *(Br.)* außergerichtlicher Gläubigervergleich; ~ **for stamp duty** Stempelsteuerpauschalierung; ~ **studded with errors** von Fehlern strotzender Aufsatz; ~ **of a letter** Aufbau eines Briefes; ~ **of a matter** *(patent law)* Stoffverbindung; ~ **of ten shillings in the pound** *(Br.)* fünfzigprozentige Steuerbefreiung; ~ **of the soil** Bodenzusammensetzung;
to come to a ~ Vergleich abschließen; **to do a** ~ Aufsatz schreiben; **to effect a** ~ Vergleich abschließen; **to enter into a** ~ **with s. o.** in Verhandlungen mit jem. eintreten; **to make a** ~ vergleichsweise Regelung treffen; **to make a** ~ **with one's creditors** sich mit seinen Gläubigern akkordieren; **to pay for the** ~ Satzkosten bezahlen; **to reject a** ~ Vergleichsangebot ausschlagen; **to set aside a** ~ Vergleich aufheben;
~ **acceptance form** Vergleichszustimmungsformular; ~ **agreement** Vergleichsvertrag, -vereinbarung; ~ **board** *(print.)* Satzbrett; ~ **case** Vergleichsfall; ~ **cost** *(print.)* Satzkosten; ~ **deed** Vergleichsurkunde, -vereinbarung; ~ **metal** Legierung; ~ **order** Anordnung eines Zwangsvergleiches; ~ **pattern** *(print.)* Satzanweisung, -muster; ~ **payment** Abfindungszahlung; ~ **proceedings** Vergleichsverfahren; ~ **settlement** Vergleichsregelung, -abkommen; ~ **tax** pauschalierte Steuer.
compositor Schriftsetzer, Metteur.
composure Gelassenheit, Gemütsruhe.
compotation Zechgelage.
compound Zusammensetzung, Mischung, *(fenced enclosure)* Diplomatenghetto, *(goldminers, South Africa)* Zwangslager, *(mil.)* Truppen-, Internierungslager, *(word)* zusammengesetztes Wort;
prison ~ Gefangenenlager;
~ *(v.)* zusammensetzen, vermischen, *(debt)* [Schuld] ablösen (tilgen), *(settle in bulk)* pauschalieren, *(settle by mutual concession)* in Güte regeln, durch Vergleich erledigen, Vergleich

abschließen (eingehen), gegen Entschädigung beilegen, *(come to terms)* sich einigen (vergleichen);
~ **with one's creditors** Arrangement mit seinen Gläubigern treffen; ~ **a debt** Schuld abtragen; ~ **a felony** Verbrecher wegen erhaltener Entschädigung nicht verfolgen, Verbrecher aus Eigennutz begünstigen; ~ **one's interest quarterly** Zinsen vierteljährlich bezahlen; ~ **for a tax** Steuerpauschale zahlen;
~ *(a.)* zusammengesetzt;
~ **amount** Zinseszinsbetrag; ~ **arbitration** Mehrfacharbitrage, Arbitrage über mehrere Zwischenplätze; ~ **arrangement** *(el.)* Verbundwirtschaft; ~ **calculation (computation) of interests** Zinseszinsrechnung; ~ **discount** [um Zinsen] vermehrtes Kapital; ~ **duty** gemischter Wertzoll; ~ **entry** Sammelbuchung; ~ **householders** *(Br.)* Mieter, der seine Wassergeldgebühr in die Mietzahlung einschließt; ~ **interest** Staffel-, Zinseszinsen; ~ **item** Sammelposten; ~ **journal entry** Sammelbuchung; ~ **machinery** Aggregat; ~ **option** Doppelprämiengeschäft; ~ **policy** Generalpolice; ~ **rate** Zinseszinssatz; ~ **settlements** zusammengefaßte Vermögensverwaltungen; ~ **word** zusammengesetztes Wort.
compound interest Staffel-, Zinseszinsen;
at ~ auf Zinseszins;
~ **formula** Zinseszinsformel; ~ **method of depreciation** Zinseszinsabschreibungsmethode.
compound | journal entry zusammengefaßte (-gesetzte) Journalbuchung, -eintragung; ~ **larceny** schwerer Diebstahl; ~ **locomotive** Verbundlokomotive; ~ **option** Doppelprämiengeschäft; ~ **policy** Generalpolice; ~ **present value** zinstragendes Kapital.
compoundable ablösbar, abfindbar.
compounded settlement pauschale Abgeltung.
compounder Ersatzleistender, *(US)* Vergleichschließender, -schuldner.
compounding | of claims vergleichsweise Forderungsbefriedigung; ~ **with one's creditors** Gesamtvergleich mit seinen Gläubigern; ~ **a felony** eigennützige Nichtanklage eines Verbrechens; ~ **of rates** Kommunalabgabenablösung, Steuerablösung.
comprehend *(v.)* verstehen, begreifen, einsetzen, erfassen, *(include)* einschließen, umfassen, enthalten.
comprehensible begreiflich, verständlich;
to be ~ **only to specialists** nur von Fachleuten verstanden werden.
comprehension Fassungs-, Begriffsvermögen, Verständnis;
to be beyond one's ~ über jds. Horizont gehen; **to be quick of** ~ schnell auffassen.
comprehensive detailliertes Layout, *(school, Br.)* Gesamt-, Einheitsschule;
~ *(a.)* umfassend, weit, allgemein;
~ **plus collision** *(US, insurance)* Vollkasko; ~ **coverage** *(insurance, US)* Teilkasko; ~ **development** *(Br.)* Altstadtsanierung; ~ **development area** *(Br.)* [etwa] Altstadtsanierungsgebiet; ~ **examination** Intelligenzprüfung, -test; ~ **faculty** Fassungsvermögen; ~ **high-ticket family policy** hochwertige Familienpauschalversicherung; ~ **insurance** *(car, Br.)* kombinierte Haftpflicht- und Kaskoversicherung; ~ **insurance policy** *(Br.)* Kaskoversicherungspolice; ~ **knowledge** umfassende Kenntnisse; ~ **law** umfassendes Gesetz; ~ **layout** detailliertes Layout; ~ **liability and property damage insurance** *(US)* Haft- und Diebstahlsversicherung; ~ **offer** umfassendes Angebot; ~ **program(me)** umfassendes Programm; ~ **report** eingehender Bericht; ~ **secondary education** Gesamtschulausbildung; ~ **school** *(Br.)* Einheits-, Gesamtschule; ~ **term** Sammelbegriff; ~ **university** *(Br.)* Gesamthochschule; ~ **word** vielsagendes Wort.
comprehensiveness Begriffsvermögen.
comprehensivize *(v.)* *(Br.)* Gesamt-, Einheitsschule einrichten.
comprint Rauhdruck.
comprise *(v.)* einschließen, umfassen, einbeziehen, einbegreifen;
~ **in an account** einrechnen.
comprised zusammengesetzt.
compromise Kompromiß[lösung], Kompromißvorschlag, gegenseitiges Zugeständnis, Nachgeben, Konzession, *(arrangement)* außergerichtlicher Vergleich, vergleichsweise Regelung, Abfindungsvertrag;
by way of a ~ im Vergleichswege;
suggested ~ Kompromißvorschlag;
~ **arrived at by the parties** von den Parteien erzielter Vergleich; **a** ~ **of sorts** eine Art Kompromiß;
~ *(v.)* Kompromiß schließen, schlichten, vergleichen; ~ **with s. o.** sich mit jem. vergleichen; ~ **a claim** Anspruch im Wege des Vergleichs befriedigen; ~ **a dispute** Streit vergleichsweise beilegen;

to agree to a ~ einer vergleichsweisen Regelung zustimmen; **to allow** ~ Spielraum für Kompromißbereitschaft lassen; **to arrive at a ~ with s. o.** sich mit jem. vergleichen, Vergleichsregelung mit jem. treffen; **to effect a ~ with s. o.** Vergleichsregelung mit jem. treffen;

~ **agreement** Kompromißvereinbarung; ~ **bill** Kompromißgesetz; ~ **candidate** Kompromißkandidat; ~ **formula** Kompromißformel; ~ **package** Kompromißangebot; ~ **payment** Abfindungszahlung; ~ **plan** Kompromißplan; ~ **position** Kompromißhaltung.

comptroller *(public officer)* Rechnungs-, Kostenprüfer, Revisor, *(US)* Bilanzprüfer, höherer Revisionsbeamter;
ℂ **General** *(US)* Präsident des Bundesrechnungshofs; **state** ~ Präsident des Rechnungshofes;
~ **of accounts** Rechnungsprüfer, Revisor; ~ **in bankruptcy** *(Br.)* Aufsichtsamtsleiter für Konkursverwalter; ~ **of the Currency** *(US)* Währungskommissar; ~ **of the customs** Hafenzollamt; ℂ **and Auditor-General** *(Br.)* Präsident des Rechnungshofs; ℂ **General** *(US)* Präsident des Bundesrechnungshofs; ℂ **General of Patents, Designs and Trademarks** *(Br.)* Präsident des Patentamtes.

compulsion Nötigung, Zwang, Druck, *(psychopathology)* Trieb; **under** ~ zwangsweise, gezwungen, unter Druck;
~ **for disclosure** Offenlegungspflicht; ~ **of labo(u)r** Zwangsbewirtschaftung der Arbeitskräfte;
to be under ~ to do s. th. etw. unter Zwang tun; **to pay under** ~ auf Drohungen hin zahlen; **to sign a treaty of peace under** ~ Friedensvertrag unter Druck abschließen.

compulsorily retired zwangspensioniert.

compulsoriness zwingender Charakter.

compulsory obligatorisch, verbindlich, vorgeschrieben, zwangsweise, zwingend;
~ **administration** Zwangsverwaltung; ~ **administration order** Zwangsverwaltungsbeschluß; ~ **arbitration** Zwangsschlichtung; ~ **area** *(Br.) (land register)* eintragungspflichtiges Gebiet; ~ **bankruptcy** Zwangsabwicklung, -liquidation; ~ **budgeting** Zwangsetatisierung; ~ **checkoff** *(US)* zwangsweise Einhaltung von Gewerkschaftsbeiträgen durch den Arbeitgeber; ~ **clauses** zwingende Bestimmungen; ~ **collection** Zwangsbeitreibung; ~ **connection** *(water supply)* Anschlußzwang; ~ **contribution** Zwangs-, Pflichtbeitrag, Zwangsabgabe; ~ **conversion** Zwangskonversion; ~ **delay** *(strike, US)* gesetzliche Überlegungspflicht; ~ **delivery** Zwangsabgabe; ~ **deposit scheme** Zwangssparen; ~ **education** allgemeine Schulpflicht; ~ **incorporation** Zwangseintragung; ~ **insurance** Zwangs-, Pflichtversicherung; ~ℂ **Insurance Act** *(Br.)* Pflichtversicherungsgesetz; ~ **insurance against third-party risks** Unfallhaftpflichtversicherung; ~ **labo(u)r** Arbeitsverpflichtung, Zwangsarbeit; ~ **land purchase** Grundstücksenteignung; ~ **landing** Pflichtlandung; ~ **levy** Zwangsabgabe, Zwangsgeld; ~ **licence** Zwangslizenz; ~ **liquidation** Zwangsvergleich, -liquidation; ~ **listing** *(real estate)* Maklerkartell; ~ **loan** Zwangsanleihe; ~ **means** Zwangsmittel; ~ **measures** Zwangsmaßnahmen; ~ **medical examination** Pflichtuntersuchung; ~ **member** Pflichtmitglied; ~ **membership** Zwangsbeitritt; ~ **military service** allgemeine Wehrpflicht, Militärdienstpflicht; ~ **nonsuit** Klageabweisung wegen Unschlüssigkeit; ~ **organization** Organisationszwang; ~ **payment** erzwungene Zahlung; ~ **pilotage** Lotsenzwang; ~ **powers** Erzwingungsrecht; ~ **prepayment** Frankierungszwang; ~ **process** *(witness)* Zwangsvorführung; ~ **realization** Zwangsglattstellung; ~ **registration** Eintragungs-, Anmeldezwang; ~ **retirement on a pension** Zwangspensionierung; ~ **sale (purchase)** *(Br.)* Zwangsverkauf, Enteignung; ~ **school age** schulpflichtiges Alter, Pflichtschulalter; ~ **school attendance** Schulzwang; ~ **service** Zwangsdienst, -leistung, Dienstzwang; ~ **settlement** Zwangsvergleich; ~ **subject** Pflichtfach; ~ **surrender** *(Scot.)* Zwangsverkauf, Enteignung; ~ **syndicate** Zwangs-, Pflichtkartell; ~ **union membership** erzwungene Gewerkschaftszugehörigkeit; ~ **usage** Benutzungszwang; ~ **winding-up** Zwangsliquidation.

compunction Gewissensbisse.

compurgation Schuldlossprechung.

computability Berechenbarkeit.

computable berechenbar.

computation *(data processing)* Verschlüsseln, Übertragen auf Lochkarten, *(estimate)* Schätzung, Kalkulation, Überschlag, *(reckoning)* Er-, Berechnung;
at a rough ~ bei vorläufiger Schätzung;
income-tax ~ Einkommensteuerberechnung; **lowest** ~ niedrigster Kostenanschlag; **domestic return-on-capital** ~ Berechnung der Inlandskapitalrendite;

~ **of account** Kontenabrechnung; ~ **of the capital allowance** *(Br.)* Berechnung der Abschreibungsbeträge auf das Anlagevermögen; ~ **of a charge** Berechnung einer Belastung; ~ **of costs** Kostenanschlag, Berechnung der Kosten; ~ **of exchange** Wechselkursberechnung; ~ **of income** Einkommensberechnung; ~ **of interest** Zins[be]rechnung; ~ **of period** Fristberechnung; ~ **of profits** Gewinnermittlung; ~ **of share value** Berechnung des Aktienwertes; ~ **of time (term)** Fristen-, Zeitberechnung;
to make a ~ of s. th. Kalkulation von etw. vornehmen, etw. berechnen (kalkulieren);
~ **table** Berechnungstafel.

computational error Rechen-, Berechnungsfehler.

compute *(v.)* er-, be-, ausrechnen, *(estimate)* Überschlag machen, kalkulieren, überschlagen;
~ **a bill** Verfall[stag] eines Wechsels ausrechnen; ~ **the capital allowance** *(Br.)* Abschreibungsbeträge auf das Anlagevermögen berechnen; ~ **the income for assessment at higher rates** Einkommen für die Steuerveranlagung mit höheren Sätzen veranschlagen; ~ **interest** Zinsen ausrechnen; ~ **one's losses at £ 100** seine Verluste auf 100 £ schätzen; ~ **a period** Frist berechnen; ~ **a profit** Gewinn einkalkulieren; ~ **a sum** Summe zusammenrechnen.

computed tare Durchschnittstara.

computer Computer, Elektronenrechner;
electronic ~ Elektronengehirn, -rechner;
to dial a ~ Computer anwählen; **to initialize a** ~ Computer erstmalig in Betrieb nehmen; **to send by ~ over a telephone line** mittels Computer telefonisch übertragen;
~ **age** Computerzeitalter; ~ **application** Computereinsatz; ~ **assembled forecast** Computervorschau; ~ **auditing** Computerrevision; ~ **centre** Rechenzentrum; ~-**controlled** computergesteuert; ~ **double talk** Computermischmasch; ~ **engineer** Computeringenieur; ~ **equipments** Datenverarbeitungsgeräte; ~ **hookup** zusammengeschaltetes Computernetz; ~ **industry** Computerindustrie; ~ **installation** Computereinrichtung; ~ **language** Computersprache; ~ **lingo** Computerkauderwelsch; **world-wide ~ linkup** weltweiter Computerverbund; ~ **market** Computermarkt; ~ **network** Computerverbundnetz; ~ **output** Computerergebnis; ~ **programming** Computerprogrammierung; ~ **reservation network** computergesteuertes Buchungssystem; ~ **science** Informatik; ~ **service** Computerwesen; ~ **service fee** Computerbenutzungsgebühr; ~ **terms** Computerausdrücke; ~ **training** Computerausbildung; ~ **training center** *(US)* **(centre,** *Br.)* Computerausbildungszentrum; ~ **use** Computerbenutzung; ~ **user** Computerbenutzer.

computerize *(v.)* auf Datenverarbeitung umstellen.

computerized mit Computern ausgestattet.

computerized | composition Computersatz; ~ **forecast** Computervorhersage; ~ **layout** Computerlayout.

computing | center Rechen-, Computerzentrum; ~ **machine** Rechenmaschine; ~ **service** Datenverarbeitungszentrum; ~ **services industry** Datenverarbeitungsindustrie.

comrade-in-arms Waffengefährte.

con, pro and Für und Wider.

con man Schwindler, Hochstapler.

conceal *(v.)* verbergen, verheimlichen, verstecken, *(balance sheet)* verschleiern, *(mil.)* geheimhalten, verschleiern, tarnen;
~ **foreign assets** ausländische Vermögenswerte verheimlichen; ~ **one's financial condition** seine Vermögensverhältnisse verschleiern; ~ **evidence** Beweismaterial unterdrücken; ~ **a fugitive** einem Flüchtling Unterschlupf gewähren; ~ **the true state of affairs** wahre Sachlage verschleiern.

concealed | assets verschleierte Vermögenswerte, stille Reserven, schwarze Bestände; ~ **loss** unbemerkt gebliebener Verlust.

concealing | property Vermögensverschleierung; ~ **theft** Diebstahlsunterdrückung.

concealment *(balance sheet)* Verheimlichung, Geheimhaltung, Verschleierung, *(insurance law)* Anzeigepflichtverletzung, *(mil.)* Tarnung;
active (fraudulent) ~ arglistiges Verschweigen; **deliberate** ~ absichtliches Verschweigen; **material** ~ Verschweigen wesentlicher Tatsachen (Umstände);
~ **of assets** Vermögensverschleierung; ~ **of birth** Unterlassung der Geburtsanmeldung; ~ **of documents** Urkundenunterdrückung; ~ **of evidence** Unterdrückung von Beweismaterial; ~ **of a fugitive** Unterschlupfgewährung für einen Flüchtigen; ~ **of material facts** Tatsachenunterdrückung; ~ **of profits** Gewinnverschleierung;
to stay in ~ sich versteckt halten.

concede *(v.)* zugestehen, zugeben, bewilligen, einräumen, *(electioneering, US)* Wahlsieg überlassen, Niederlage zugeben;

~ an advantage to s. o. jem. einen Vorteil einräumen; **~ a favo(u)r** Vergünstigung gewähren; **~ a point** in einem Punkt nachgeben; **~ a privilege** Vorrecht einräumen; **~ the right to cross land** Wegerecht einräumen; **~ territory** Landstück abtreten.

conceded facts zugestandene Tatsachen.

conceit Dünkel, Selbstgefälligkeit, Einbildung, *(idea)* Idee, Einfall.

conceive *(v.)* begreifen, verstehen, *(become pregnant)* schwanger werden.

conceived as follows wie folgt abgefaßt.

concentrate konzentrierte Nahrung;
~ *(v.)* konzentrieren, zusammenziehen;
~ in cities sich in Städten ansammeln (konzentrieren); **~ on the mines operating most economically** sich auf die kostengünstigsten Zechen konzentrieren; **~ on two points** sich auf zwei Punkte konzentrieren; **~ troops** Truppen aufmarschieren lassen (konzentrieren, zusammenziehen).

concentrated | fire konzentriertes Feuer; **~ food** konzentrierte Nahrungsmittel.

concentration Ansammlung, Konzentration, Konzentrierung, Zusammenballung, *(statistics)* Ballung;
economic ~ Konzentrationsprozeß der Wirtschaft; **large urban ~s** große Zusammenballungen in den Städten; **market ~** Absatzkonzentration;
~ of capital Kapitalkonzentration; **~ of economic power** Konzentration wirtschaftlicher Macht; **~ of industries** industrielle Zusammenballung; **~ of investments** Anlagenkonzentration; **~ of ownership** Kapital-, Eigentumskonzentration; **~ of power** Machtzusammenballung; **~ of troops** Truppenkonzentration, -aufmarsch, -ansammlung, -zusammenziehung;
to require great ~ große Konzentrationskraft abverlangen.

concept Begriff, Auffassung, Konzept;
~ of breakdown *(divorce proceedings)* Zerrüttungsprinzip;
~ formation Begriffsbildung.

conception Vorstellung, Begriff, *(advertising)* Grundlagenausarbeitung, *(idea)* Konzeption, Idee, Geistesschöpfung;
anti-free market ~ marktfeindliche Konzeption; **general legal ~s** allgemeine Rechtsbegriffe;
high ~ of one's duties hohe Pflichtauffassung;
to have a clear ~ feste Vorstellung haben;
~ control Empfängnisverhütung.

concern *(enterprise)* Betrieb, Handelsgeschäft, [industrielles] Unternehmen, Firma, Geschäft, Konzern, *(interest)* Interesse, Anteil, Sorge, *(matter)* Angelegenheit, Sache, Belang, Aufgabe;
banking ~ Bankenkonzern; **big ~** Großbetrieb; **borrowing ~** kreditaufnehmendes Unternehmen, Kreditnehmerin; **business ~** Geschäftsunternehmen; **commercial ~** [Handels]firma, Geschäftsbetrieb; **controlled ~** abhängiges (beherrschtes) Unternehmen; **financial ~s** Finanzangelegenheiten; **first ~** noch im Besitz der Gründerfamilie befindliches Unternehmen; **flourishing ~** blühendes Unternehmen; **going ~** in Betrieb befindliches Unternehmen, bestehendes Handelsgeschäft; **industrial (manufacturing) ~** gewerbliches Unternehmen, Industrieunternehmen; **large ~** Großunternehmen; **paying ~** rentables Geschäft; **pretty ~** nette Geschichte; **primary ~** Hauptsorge; **private ~** Privatangelegenheit; **small ~s** Lappalien; **trading ~** Wirtschafts-, Handelsunternehmen; **whole ~** Gesamtunternehmen; **the whole ~** der ganze Krempel;
private ~ of a family Familienangelegenheit;
~ *(v.) (be interested)* beschäftigen, interessieren, *(relate to)* betreffen, angehen;
~ o. s. with s. th. sich für etw. interessieren; **~ s. o.** j. angehen; **~ o. s. about s. o.** sich um j. bemühen;
to be of immediate ~ to s. o. j. unmittelbar angehen; **to be a matter of** Anlaß zur Beunruhigung geben; **to have a ~ in a business** Geschäftsanteil besitzen; **to have no ~ in a matter** mit einer Sache nichts zu tun haben; **to make a ~ going** Geschäft hochbringen; **to manage the ~** Geschäftsleitung haben; **to meddle in s. one's ~s** sich in jds. Angelegenheiten einmischen; **to purchase an enterprise as a going ~** Unternehmen mit sämtlichen Aktiven und Passiven übernehmen; **to show no ~ at all** überhaupt kein Interesse zeigen; **to show ~ for an invalid** an einem Gebrechlichen Anteil nehmen; **to sink all one's money in the ~** sein ganzes Geld ins Geschäft stecken;
to whom it may ~ wen es angeht.

concerned beteiligt, interessiert;
~ about beunruhigt; **~ or interested** direkt oder indirekt beteiligt;
to be ~ betroffen (beteiligt) sein; **to be ~ about s. one's health**

sich um jds. Gesundheitszustand Sorgen machen; **to be ~ in a plot** in eine Verschwörung verwickelt sein; **to be ~ for s. one's safety** um jds. Sicherheit besorgt sein;
~ parties Beteiligte.

concerning betreffs, bezüglich, hinsichtlich.

concernment Belang, Bedeutung.

concert Konzert, *(agreement)* Einverständnis, *(dipl.)* Abkommen über gemeinsames Vorgehen;
in ~ with in Einvernehmen mit;
~ of Europe (of the Great Powers) Konzert der Großmächte;
~ *(v.) (devise)* ausdenken, planen, *(plan together)* zusammenarbeiten, gemeinsam planen;
to act in ~ with s. o. mit jem. zusammenwirken;
~ goer Konzertbesucher; **~ hall** Konzerthalle; **~ presentation** Konzertaufführung; **~ room** Konzertraum, -halle.

concerted gemeinsam geplant, gemeinschaftlich;
~ action gemeinschaftliche Aktion, *(economic policy)* konzertierte Aktion; **~ attack** geschlossener Angriff; **to act with no ~ plan** ohne festen Plan handeln; **~ practices** *(cartel)* aufeinander abgestimmtes Verhalten.

concertina folding Leporellofalzung.

concertmaster Konzertmeister, erster Geiger.

concession Vergünstigung, Bewilligung, Zugeständnis, Entgegenkommen, Genehmigung, Konzession, *(customs)* Zollzugeständnis, *(piece of land)* überlassenes Stück Land, *(privilege)* Verleihung, Konzession, *(settlement)* Niederlassung, *(stock exchange)* [Kurs]abschwächung, *(US)* Gewerbeerlaubnis, -genehmigung, Lizenz;
by mutual ~ bei gegenseitigen Zugeständnissen;
extrastatutory ~ außergesetzliche Steuererleichterung; **international ~** internationale Niederlassung; **mining ~** Abbaurecht, Bergbaukonzession; **oil ~** Erdölkonzession; **preliminary ~** *(US)* Vorkonzession; **price ~** Preiskonzession, -zugeständnis **railway ~** *(Br.)* Eisenbahnkonzession; **reciprocal ~s** beiderseitige Zugeständnisse; **snack-bar ~** Imbißstube; **tariff ~** Zugeständnis auf einem Zollgebiet, Tarifzugeständnis; **tax ~** steuerliches Zugeständnis; **wage ~s** Lohnzugeständnisse;
wide-reaching ~s weitreichende Zugeständnisse;
~s on depreciation Abschreibungsvergünstigungen; **~ at a fair** Messekonzession; **~ of land** Landkonzession; **~ of a licence** Einräumung einer Lizenz; **~ of a mine** Bergwerkskonzession; **to apply for a ~** um eine Konzession einkommen; **to give ~s in return** Gegenkonzessionen machen; **to grant a ~** Konzession verleihen, Lizenz vergeben; **to make ~s** Zugeständnisse (Konzessionen) machen; **to make a ~ of a right to s. o.** jem. ein Recht zugestehen; **to withdraw a ~** Konzession entziehen (zurücknehmen); **to withhold a ~** *(customs)* Zugeständnis aussetzen;
~ basis Konzessionsgrundlage; **to let out on a ~ basis** im Konzessionswege vergeben; **~ fee** Konzessionsgebühr; **basic acquisition fee** einmalige Gebühr zur Erlangung einer Konzession, einmalige Konzessionsgebühr; **~ revenue** Konzessionseinkünfte; **~ stand** Verkaufsbude, Kiosk.

concessionaire Konzessionär, Konzessionsinhaber.

concessionary Konzessionsinhaber;
~ right Konzessionsrecht;
~ *(a.)* konzessioniert, im Konzessionswege, lizenziert, bewilligt.

concierge Hausmeister[sfrau], Pförtner[in], Portier.

conciliate *(v.)* beschwichtigen, versöhnen.

conciliation Schlichtung, Versöhnung, Sühneverfahren, Ausgleich;
industrial ~ Schlichtungswesen in der Wirtschaft;
~ Act Schiedsordnung; **~ board** Schlichtungsstelle; **~ commissioner** ständiger Schlichter; **~ committee** Schlichtungsausschuß; **~ court** Sühnegericht, Schiedskommission, Schlichtungsausschuß; **~ facilities** Schlichtungseinrichtungen; **~ hearing** Sühnetermin; **~ procedure** Sühne-, Vergleichs-, Vermittlungsverfahren; **~ scheme** Vergleichsvereinbarung; **~ services** Schlichtungstätigkeit.

conciliator Schlichter, Vermittler;
government ~ staatlicher Schlichter.

conciliatory | gestures Versöhnungsgesten; **~ proceedings** Sühne-, Güteverfahren; **~ proposal** Sühne-, Schlichtungs-, Vermittlungsvorschlag, Vorschlag zur Güte.

concise kurz, knapp, abgekürzt;
~ style prägnanter Stil.

conclave Konklave, Geheimsitzung;
to sit in ~ geheime Sitzung (Geheimbesprechung) abhalten.

conclude *(v.)* beenden, beschließen, *(bargain, sale)* abschließen;
~ an agreement Vertrag abschließen; **~ to the country** *(common law pleading)* Verfahren vor das Schwurgericht bringen; **~ a**

lecture Vorlesung schließen; ~ **a letter** Brief [ab]schließen; ~ **peace** Frieden schließen; ~ **by saying ...** mit den Worten schließen ...; ~ **a speech** Vortrag beenden; ~ **a treaty** Abkommen abschließen.

concluded, to be Schluß folgt.

concluding abschließend;
~ **lines** Schlußsätze; ~ **provisions** Schlußbestimmungen; ~ **section** Schlußabschnitt; ~ **sentence** Schlußsatz; ~ **words** Schlußworte.

conclusion *(concluding part)* Schlußbestimmungen, *(decision)* Beschluß, *(estoppel)* [prozeßentscheidende] Einrede, [peremptorischer] Einwand, *(logic)* Schlußfolgerung, *(obligation)* bindende Verpflichtung, *(pleading)* Schlußantrag, *(termination)* [Ab]schluß, Ausgang, Ende;
at the ~ of his speech am Ende seiner Rede (Schluß seiner Ansprache); **in ~** abschließend;
false ~ Trug-, Fehlschluß;
~ **arrived at** gefaßte Beschlüsse; **legal ~** Rechtsfolgerung;
~ **of an agreement** Abschluß eines Vertrages, Vertragsabschluß; ~ **of a bargain** Geschäftsabschluß; ~ **of a book** Ende eines Buches; ~ **of fact** Tatsachenfeststellung; ~ **of law** rechtliche Schlußfolgerung, Rechtsfolgerung; ~ **of an insurance contract** Abschluß eines Versicherungsvertrages; ~ **of peace** Abschließen eines Friedensvertrages, Friedensschluß; ~ **of session** Schluß einer Sitzungsperiode;
to arrive at the ~ zu der Überzeugung (dem Schluß) gelangen; **to bring a business to a successful ~** Geschäft zu einem erfolgreichen Abschluß bringen; **to draw ~s** Schlußfolgerungen ziehen; **to jump at (rush into) a ~** voreilige Schlüsse ziehen; **to reach a ~** zu einer Entscheidung kommen; **to try ~s** *(Br.)* sich zu messen versuchen.

conclusive entscheidend, beweiskräftig, schlüssig, *(final)* endgültig, abschließend;
~ **argument** durchgreifendes Argument; ~ **evidence (proof)** zwingender (unwiderleglicher, schlüssiger) Beweis; ~ **force** Beweiskraft; **to lack ~ force** keine Beweiskraft haben; ~ **presumption** *(law)* unwiderlegliche [Rechts]vermutung.

conclusiveness Beweiskraft, Schlüssigkeit.

concoct | *(v.)* **an excuse** sich eine Ausrede ausdenken; ~ **a plan** Plan ausbrüten (aushecken).

concoction *(plan)* Ausbrüten, Aushecken;
to be a ~ from beginning to end von A - Z erfunden sein.

concomitance Gleichzeitigkeit, gleichzeitiges Vorhandensein.

concomitant | **s of old age** Alterserscheinungen;
~ **circumstances** Begleitumstände.

concord Übereinstimmung, Einmütigkeit, Einigkeit, Einklang.

concordance, in ~ with in Übereinstimmung mit.

concordant übereinstimmend, einhellig;
~ **depositions** sich deckende (übereinstimmende) Zeugenaussagen.

concordat Konkordat.

concourse Zusammentreffen, *(gathering)* [Menschen]auflauf, Menschengewühl, *(law)* Klagenhäufung, *(railroad station, US)* Bahnhofshalle, *(road, US)* Fahrweg;
unforeseen ~ of circumstances unvorhergesehenes Zusammentreffen von Umständen.

concrete Beton, Zement;
high-quality ~ hochwertiger Beton; **prestressed ~** Spannbeton;
reinforced ~ armierter Beton;
~ *(v.)* betonieren, *(fig.)* konkretisieren;
~ *(a.)* greifbar, gegenständlich, konkret;
~ **block** Betonstein; ~ **case** konkreter Fall, Einzelfall; ~ **construction** Betonbau; ~ **mixer** Betonmischmaschine; ~ **pavement** Betonpflaster; ~ **pile** Betonpfeiler; ~ **platform** Betonplattform; ~ **quality** bestimmte Qualität; ~ **steel** Stahlbeton; ~ **wall** Betonmauer.

concretize *(v.)* konkretisieren.

concubinage wilde Ehe, Konkubinat.

concur *(v.)* zusammentreffen, *(agree)* übereinstimmen, *(law of bankruptcy)* gemeinsam vorgehen;
~ **with a proposal** einem Vorschlag beistimmen; ~ **on questions of foreign policy** in der Außenpolitik konform gehen; ~ **with the speaker** dem Redner beipflichten; ~ **with s. o in thinking** jds. Ansicht beistimmen.

concurator Gegen-, Mitvormund.

concurrence *(meeting of minds)* Übereinstimmung, Einverständnis, Zusammentreffen, *(coincidence)* zeitliches Zusammentreffen, *(law)* Konflikt, Kollision;
~ **of jurisdiction** wahlweise Zuständigkeit, Kompetenzstreit[igkeit], -konflikt; ~ **of opinion** einhellige Meinung;
to act in ~ gemeinschaftlich vorgehen.

concurrent gleichlaufend, -seitig, nebeneinanderbestehend, *(law)* gleichberechtigt, kollidierend, konkurrierend;
~ **cause** Mitursache; ~ **claims** konkurrierende Ansprüche; ~ **conditions** gegenseitige [Vertrags]verpflichtungen, Zug um Zug zu erfüllende Bedingungen; ~ **fire insurance** gleichzeitige Feuerversicherung des gleichen Objekts bei mehreren Gesellschaften; ~ **interests** nebeneinander bestehende (kollidierende) Rechte; ~ **jurisdiction** wahlweise (konkurrierende) Zuständigkeit; ~ **lease** gleichzeitig abgeschlossene Pacht; ~ **liens** *(maritime insurance)* gleichrangige Zurückbehaltungsrechte; ~ **negligence** mitwirkendes Verschulden; ~ **powers** konkurrierende Gewalten; ~ **resolution** *(parl.)* gleichlautender Beschluß; ~ **sentence** Urteil über Delikte in Idealkonkurrenz; ~ **views of several experts** übereinstimmende Sachverständigengutachten; ~ **writ** Zweitanfertigung einer Klage.

concuss *(v.)* durch Drohungen erzwingen.

concussion Stoß, *(law, Scot.)* Nötigung, räuberische Erpressung;
~ **of the brain** Gehirnerschütterung.

condemn *(v.)* *(declare guilty)* verurteilen, *(building)* für gebrauchsunfähig erklären, *(disapprove)* mißbilligen, tadeln, verdammen, *(goods)* beschlagnahmen, konfiszieren, einziehen, *(land, US)* enteignen, *(patient)* aufgeben, *(ship)* für seeuntüchtig erklären;
~ **the defendant in costs** Beklagten zur Zahlung der Prozeßkosten verurteilen; ~ **to death** zum Tode verurteilen; ~ **s. o. on slight evidence** j. aufgrund geringen Indizienmaterials verurteilen; ~ **land for a railway** Grundstück für Eisenbahnzwecke enteignen; ~ **as a lawful prize** für gute Prise erklären, mit Beschlag belegen; ~ **a murderer to life imprisonment** Mörder zu lebenslanger Haftstrafe verurteilen; ~ **to pay a fine** zu einer Geldstrafe verurteilen; ~ **private property** Privatgrundstück enteignen; ~ **defective provisions** schlecht gewordene Lebensmittel konfiszieren; ~ **a ship** Schiff für seeuntüchtig erklären; ~ **slum dwellings** verfallene Häuser für unbewohnbar erklären; ~ **stores** Vorratslager beschlagnahmen; ~ **as unfit for human consumption** für die menschliche Ernährung als ungeeignet erklären; ~ **as untrustworthy** als unglaubwürdig verwerfen; ~ **a captured vessel** aufgebrachtes Schiff und Ladegut prisengerichtlich einziehen; ~ **to five years hard labo(u)r** zu fünf Jahren Zuchthaus verurteilen.

condemnation Ab-, Verurteilung, *(admiralty law)* prisengerichtliche Einziehung, *(building)* Unbrauchbarkeitserklärung, *(goods)* Beschlagnahme, Einziehung, Konfiskation, Konfiszierung, *(land, US)* [Zwangs]enteignung, *(ship)* Seeuntauglichkeitserklärung;
to incur s. one's ~ sich jds. Tadel zuziehen;
~ **award** *(US)* Enteignungsbeschluß; ~ **money** *(US)* Entschädigungsbetrag; ~ **proceedings** *(real estate, US)* Enteignungsverfahren.

condemned beschlagnahmt, konfisziert, *(land, US)* enteignet, *(prize)* für gute Prise erklärt, *(ship)* seeuntüchtig, abbruchreif;
~ **to pay** zur Zahlung verurteilt;
~ **property** enteignetes Grundstück.

condensed kurz gefaßt, abgekürzt, *(print.)* kompreß;
~ **balance sheet** kondensierte Bilanz, Bilanzauszug; ~ **milk** kondensierte Milch; ~ **type** schmale (schmallaufende) Schrift, Schmalschrift.

condescence *(Scot. law)* Klagebegründung.

condign *(v.)* *(punishment)* angemessen.

condition Bedingung, Auflage, *(social standing)* Vermögenslage, gesellschaftliche Stellung, *(shop)* Klima, *(state)* Beschaffenheit, Zustand, Lage, Verfassung, *(status)* Familien-, Personenstand, *(stipulation)* Bedingung, Klausel, Abmachung, Vereinbarung, Übereinkommen;
at moderate ~s billigst gestellt; **in ~** in guter Verfassung; **in a dilapidated ~** *(building)* in heruntergekommenem Zustand; **in flying ~** startbereit; **in good ~** gut erhalten; **in perfect ~** in einwandfreiem Zustand; **in a rundown ~** *(business)* in heruntergekommenem Zustand; **in a trying ~** in mißlicher Lage; **in working ~** betriebsfähig; **in good working ~** in gutem und betriebsfähigem Zustand; **on ~** *(goods)* in Kommission; **on ~ that** unter der Bedingung, daß; **on easy (onerous) ~s** zu leichten (schweren) Bedingungen; **on equal (same, changed) ~s** zu unveränderten Bedingungen; **out of ~** in schlechter Verfassung, nicht in Kondition, *(goods)* in schlechtem Zustand; **subject to one ~** unter einer Bedingung; **under favo(u)rable ~s** zu günstigen Bedingungen; **under existing (normal) ~s** unter normalen Bedingungen (Verhältnissen);
additional ~s Zusatz-, Nebenbedingungen; **affirmative ~** ausdrücklich zugesicherte Bedingung; **~s agreed upon** angenommene Bedingungen; **basic ~** Grundbedingung; **business ~s**

Geschäftsbedingungen; **buying** ~s Kaufbedingungen; **casual** ~ Zufallsbedingung; **certain** ~s bestimmte Bedingungen; **collateral** ~ Nebenbedingung; **competitive** ~s Konkurrenzbedingungen; **compulsory** ~ zwingend vorgeschriebene Bedingung; **concurrent** ~s Zug um Zug zu erfüllende Bedingungen; **consistent** ~ konforme Bedingung; **contingent** ~ ungewisse Bedingung; **deliverable** ~ lieferfähiger Zustand; **delivery** ~s Lieferbedingungen; **dependent** ~ Abhängigkeitsverhältnis; **disjunctive** ~ wahlweise zu erfüllende Bedingung; **dissolving** ~ auflösende Bedingung; **distressed** ~ Notlage; **economic** ~ Wirtschaftslage; **essential** ~ notwendige Bedingung; **explicit** ~ ausdrückliche Bedingung; **express** ~ ausdrückliche Bestimmung; **faultless** ~ fehlerloser Zustand; **less favo(u)rable** ~s erschwerte Bedingungen; **financial** ~ Finanzlage; **fixed** ~s festgesetzte Bedingungen; **fundamental** ~ Grundbedingung; **apparent good** ~ offensichtlich guter Zustand; **housing** ~s Wohnungsverhältnisse; **illegal** ~ rechtlich unzulässige Bedingung; **implied** ~s stillschweigende (selbstverständliche) Bedingungen; **impossible** ~ unmögliche Bedingung; **independent** ~ selbständige Bedingung; **inherent** ~ am Grundstück haftende Bedingung; **insurance** ~s Versicherungsbedingungen; **laid-down** ~ festgelegte Bedingung; **lawful** ~ rechtlich zulässige Bedingung; **living** ~s Lebensverhältnisse, -bedingungen; **local** ~s örtliche Verhältnisse; **main** ~ Haupt-, Grundbedingung **market** ~s Marktlage, Konjunktur, Absatzverhältnisse; **mixed** ~ gemischte Bedingung; **modifying** ~s einschränkende Bestimmungen; **mutual** ~ Zug um Zug zu erfüllende Bedingung; **negative** ~ ausdrücklich zugesichertes Unterlassen, Unterlassungsverpflichtung; **normal working** ~s *(machine)* übliche Betriebsbedingungen; **operating** ~s Betriebsverhältnisse; **payment** ~s Zahlungsbedingungen; **perfect** ~ *(goods)* einwandfreier Zustand; **positive** ~ positive Bedingung; **possible** ~ mögliche Bedingung; **potestative** ~ Potestativbedingung; **precedent** ~ aufschiebende Bedingung; **printed** ~s vorgedruckte Bedingungen; **qualifying** ~s einschränkende Bedingungen; **repugnant** ~ mit einem Vertrag unvereinbare Bedingung; **resolutive** ~ auflösende Bedingung; **resolutory** ~ auflösende Bedingung, Resolutivbedingung; **restrictive** ~ Unterlassungsverpflichtung; **sales** ~s Verkaufsbedingungen; **onerous selling** ~s erschwerte Absatzverhältnisse; **single** ~ Einzelbedingung; **sound** ~ unbeschädigter Zustand; **special** ~ Sonderbestimmung; **spot** ~s Bedingungen bei Barzahlung; **statutory** ~ gesetzliche Voraussetzung; **strained** ~s gespannte Lage; **stringent** ~ strenge Bedingung; **subsequent** ~ nachher zu erfüllende Bedingung, auflösende Bedingung; **sufficient** ~ ausreichende Bedingung; **suspensory** ~ aufschiebende Bedingung; **testing** ~s Prüfungsbedingungen; **trading** ~s Geschäftsbedingungen; **unfulfilled** ~ unerfüllte Bedingung; **unlawful** ~ ungesetzliche (unzulässige) Bedingung; **working** ~s Arbeitsbedingungen;

~s **of acceptance** Annahmebedingungen; ~ **laid down in an agreement** Vertragsbestimmung; ~s **against alienation** Veräußerungsverbot; ~ **of appointment** Anstellungsbedingungen; ~s **of apprenticeship** Bestimmungen des Ausbildungsvertrages; ~s **of approval** Genehmigungsbestimmungen; ~s **of avoidance** Anfechtungs-, Rücktrittsbedingungen; ~s **of a bank** Bankkonditionen; ~s **in the capital market** Kapitalmarktsituation; ~s **of carriage** Beförderungsbedingungen; **[general]** ~s **of contract** [allgemeine] Vertragsbestimmungen; ~s **set forth in a contract** vertraglich festgelegte Bedingungen; ~s **which are contrary to public policy** gegen das öffentliche Interesse gerichtete Bedingungen; ~s **in a deed** ausdrücklich festgelegte Bedingungen; ~s **of delivery** Lieferbedingungen; ~ **of employment** Beschäftigungsverhältnisse; ~ **of entitlement** Berechtigungsbestimmungen; ~s **of entry** Einreisebedingungen; ~s **of goods** ausgezeichnete Beschaffenheit von Waren; ~ **of grant** Zuschußbedingung; ~ **of one's health** Gesundheitszustand; ~s **of labo(u)r** Arbeitsbedingungen; ~s **precedent to liability** Haftpflichtvoraussetzungen; ~ **in life** Lebensstellung, -stand; ~s **of membership** Beitrittsbedingungen; ~s **for patentability** Patentvoraussetzungen; ~s **precedent to the policy** Vorbedingungen für die Policengültigkeit; ~s **in restraint of marriage** Heiratsbeschränkungen; ~ **of a road** Straßenbeschaffenheit; ~s **of sale** Liefer-, Verkaufsbedingungen; ~s **of service** Dienstleistungsverhältnisse; ~s **of subscription** Abonnementsbedingungen; ~ **of success** Erfolgsbedingung; ~s **of supply** Versorgungsbedingungen; ~ **of a vehicle** Zustand eines Fahrzeugs; ~ **of visibility** Sichtbedingungen; ~s **of the workers** Lage der Arbeiter;

~ *(v.)* bedingen, zur Bedingung machen, *(stipulate)* [Vertragsbestimmungen] ausbedingen, *(test)* Beschaffenheit von Waren prüfen, *(university, US)* Nachprüfung auferlegen;

~ **for o. s.** sich ausbedingen; ~ **[up]on** abhängig machen von; **to agree upon certain** ~s bestimmte Bedingungen annehmen; **to answer a** ~ Bedingung erfüllen; **to be in fair** ~ in ziemlich guter Verfassung; **to be out of** ~ nicht konditioniert sein; **to be in a poor** ~ schlecht erhalten sein; **to be subject to a** ~ **as to the price** einer Preisbindung unterliegen, preisgebunden sein; **not to be in a** ~ **to travel** nicht reisefähig sein; **to change one's** ~s sich verheiraten; **to comply with the** ~s Bedingungen (Voraussetzungen) erfüllen; **to impose** ~s **on s. o.** jem. Bedingungen auferlegen; **to lay down** ~s Bedingungen festlegen; **to make s. th. a** ~ sich ausbedingen; **to make one's** ~s seine Bedingungen stellen; **to meet a** ~ Bedingung erfüllen; **to obtain favo(u)rable** ~s vorteilhafte Bedingungen erhalten; **to set up a** ~ Bedingung stellen; **to settle** ~s Bedingungen festlegen; **to settle certain** ~s sich auf bestimmte Bedingungen einigen; **to work off one's** ~s *(university, US)* seine Nachprüfung absolvieren; **to work under difficult** ~s unter schwierigen Bedingungen arbeiten.

conditional bedingt, ausbedungen, abhängig, freibleibend, vertragsgemäß;
highly ~ sehr durch die Umstände bedingt;
~ **acceptance** bedingte Annahme, Annahme unter Vorbehalt, *(bill of exchange)* bedingte [Wechsel]annahme, Annahme unter Vorbehalt; ~ **agreement** an Bedingungen geknüpftes Abkommen; ~ **appearance** bedingte Klageeinlassung; ~ **bequest** bedingtes Legat; ~ **clause** auflösende Bestimmung; ~ **contract** bedingter Vertrag; ~ **delivery** bedingte Urkundenbegebung; ~ **device** Vermächtnis mit Auflage; ~ **estate** bedingtes Eigentum; ~ **fee** Fideikommiß; ~ **indorsement** beschränktes Giro; ~ **judgment** bedingtes Urteil; ~ **lease** bedingter Pachtvertrag; ~ **legacy** Vorerbschaft; ~ **obligation** bedingte Verpflichtung; ~ **offer** freibleibendes Angebot; ~ **order** freibleibender Auftrag; ~ **pardon** bedingter Straferlaß; ~ **probability** *(statistics)* bedingte Wahrscheinlichkeit; ~ **purchase** bedingter Erwerb; ~ **rate** Frachttarif mit ausgeschlossenem Risiko; ~ **sales agreement contract** *(US)* Kauf[vertrag] unter Eigentumsvorbehalt, Ratenzahlungskauf; ~ **vendor** Vorbehaltsverkäufer.

conditioned bedingt, be-, eingeschränkt, abhängig;
well ~ in gutem Zustand.

condolence Beileid[sbezeugung];
to offer s. o. one's ~ jem. sein Beileid aussprechen;
~ **card** Beileidsbezeugung, -karte.

condominium Mitbesitz, -eigentum, *(apartment, US)* Eigentumswohnung, *(joint sovereignty)* gemeinsame Mandatsverwaltung;
~ **apartment** *(US)* Eigentumswohnung; ~ **building** *(US)* Appartmenthaus; ~ **office building** *(US)* Stockwerkseigentumsbürogebäude; ~ **residence** *(US)* Eigentumswohnung; ~ **principle of ownership** *(US)* Stockwerkseigentumssystem; ~ **residence** *(US)* Eigentumswohnung.

condonation *(divorce)* Verzeihung.
condone *(v.) (divorce offence)* verzeihen.
conduce *(v.)* förderlich sein;
~ **to the success of an enterprise** zum Erfolg eines Unternehmens beitragen.
conducive dienlich, förderlich.
conduct *(behavio(u)r)* Betragen, Benehmen, Verhalten, Wesen, dienstliche Führung, *(management)* Leitung, Verwaltung;
by ~ durch schlüssiges Verhalten;
bad ~ schlechtes Benehmen; **cheap** ~ schäbiges Benehmen; **disorderly** ~ ordnungswidriges Verhalten, Erregung öffentlichen Ärgernisses; **good** ~ Wohlverhalten, *(convict)* gute Führung; **improper** ~ ungehöriges Benehmen; **irreproachable** ~ untadeliges Verhalten; **market** ~ Verhalten auf dem Markt; **outrageous** ~ unerhörtes Verhalten; **professional** ~ standesgemäßes Verhalten; **right** ~ ordnungsmäßiges Verhalten; **safe** ~ freies Geleit; **unbecoming** ~ ungebührliches Betragen;
~ **of affairs** Leitung der Geschäfte; ~ **of one's own affairs** Durchführung (Erledigung) eigener Angelegenheiten; ~ **discreditable to a barrister (unbefitting a solicitor, Br.)** standeswidriges Verhalten eines Anwalts; ~ **of a board meeting** Leitung einer Vorstandssitzung; ~ **of business** Amtsführung, -ausübung; **proper** ~ **of business** ordnungsmäßige Geschäftsführung, -leitung; ~ **of a case** Prozeßführung; ~ **of a meeting** Leitung einer Hauptversammlung; ~ **of negotiations** Verhandlungsführung; **editorial** ~ **of a newspaper** Redaktion einer Tageszeitung; ~ **in office** Amtsführung; ~ **of operations** Betriebsführung; ~ **of parties** Parteiverhalten; ~ **of a poll** Veranstaltung einer Meinungsumfrage; ~ **of state** Staatsverwaltung; **inconsistent** ~ **with the standards** mit berufsethischen Grundsätzen unvereinbares Verhalten; ~ **inconsistent with the**

standard the house is entitled to expect from its members *(parl., Br.)* Verhalten das dem nicht entspricht, was das Parlament von seinen Mitgliedern erwarten darf; ~ **unbecoming an officer and gentleman** standes- und ehrenrühriges Betragen; ~ **unbefitting a solicitor** *(Br.)* standeswidriges Verhalten; ~ **of war** Kriegsführung;

~ *(v.) (manage)* anordnen, führen, verwalten, leiten, *(behave)* sich verhalten (benehmen, betragen);

~ **a business** Geschäft betreiben; ~ **one's business affairs** seine geschäftlichen Angelegenheiten erledigen; ~ **a campaign** Wahlfeldzug leiten; ~ **one's own case** *(law court)* sich selbst [vor Gericht] vertreten; ~ **the correspondence** Korrespondenz führen; ~ **s. o. to the door** j. zur Tür geleiten; ~ **an investigation** Untersuchung leiten; ~ **a lawsuit** Prozeß führen; ~ **o. s. in a proper manner** sich ordnungsgemäß benehmen; ~ **negotiations** Verhandlungen leiten (führen); ~ **a test** Versuch durchführen; ~ **the visitors through the museum** Museumsbesucher führen; ~ **o. s. well** sich richtig benehmen;

to be under ~ **of s. o.** unter jds. Leitung stehen; **to enjoin a** ~ **on s. o.** jem. sein Verhalten vorschreiben; **to uphold a** ~ Verhalten billigen;

~ **book** Führungsbuch; ~ **money** *(Br.)* Zeugengebühr, *(travel(l)ing expenses)* Reisegeld; **good** ~ **prize** *(school)* Preis für gutes Benehmen; ~ **sheet** *(mil.)* Strafbuchauszug.

conducted | **money** *(travel(l)ing expenses)* Reisegeld; ~ **tour** Gesellschaftsreise.

conducting | **law business** *(US)* Prozeßführung; ~ **wire** Leitungsdraht.

conductor [Geschäfts]leiter, Direktor, *(orchestra)* Dirigent, Kapellmeister, *(public conveyance, US)* [Omnibus]schaffner, Zugführer, Straßenbahnführer;

~ **of an expedition** Expeditionsleiter;

~ **rail** *(railway)* Leitschiene.

confabulation Plauderei.

confection Konfektionsartikel;

~ *(v.)* konfektionieren.

confectioner Konditor.

confectionery Süßigkeiten, Konditorware, Konditorei.

confederacy Staatenbund, Konföderation, *(criminal law)* Komplott, Verschwörung.

confederal government Bundesregierung.

confederate Verbündeter, Alliierter, Bundesgenosse;

~ *(v.)* sich verbünden, verbinden.

confederated states *(US)* Gliedstaaten.

confederation *(business)* Dachverband, Bündnis;

~ **of British Industries** Bundesverband der britischen Industrie; ~ **of states** Staatenbund;

to engage in a ~ Bündnis eingehen.

confer *(v.) (converse)* sich besprechen, verhandeln, Unterredung haben, *(grant)* verleihen, gewähren, übertragen;

~ **authority on s. o.** j. bevollmächtigen; ~ **with** Rücksprache nehmen (besprechen) mit; ~ **a benefit on s. o.** jem. eine Vergünstigung zukommen lassen; ~ **a contract** Auftrag erteilen; ~ **with one's counsel** *(Br.)* sich mit seinem Anwalt besprechen; ~ **a degree on s. o.** jem. einen akademischen Grad verleihen; ~ **a favo(u)r on s. o.** jem. eine Gefälligkeit (Gunst) erweisen; ~ **a jurisdiction on a court** Zuständigkeit eines Gerichtes begründen; ~ **procuration** Prokura erteilen; ~ **a reward on s. o.** jem. eine Belohnung gewähren.

conferee *(US)* Besprechungs-, Konferenzteilnehmer.

conference Beratung, Besprechung, *(association of firms)* Absprache über eine gemeinsame Politik, *(conversation)* Unterredung, *(with lawyer)* Anwaltsbesprechung, *(meeting)* Tagung, Konferenz, Sitzung, Besprechung, *(pol.)* Verhandlung zwischen Ausschüssen gesetzgebender Körperschaften, *(shipowner)* Frachtenausschuß;

outside a ~ am Rande einer Konferenz;

annual ~ Jahrestagung; **business** ~ geschäftliche Besprechung; **closed-door** ~ Konferenz hinter verschlossenen Türen; **disarmament** ~ Abrüstungskonferenz; **economic** ~ Wirtschaftskonferenz; **formal** ~ formelle Konferenz; **forthcoming** ~ bevorstehende Konferenz; **industrial** ~ Handelsbesprechungen; **informal** ~ informelles Treffen; **interdepartmental** ~ Abteilungsleiterbesprechung; **intraorganizational** ~ Konferenzschaltung; **maritime** ~ Schiffahrtskonferenz; **monetary** ~ Währungskonferenz; **news** ~ Pressekonferenz; **peace** ~ Friedenskonferenz; **press** ~ Pressekonferenz; **round-table** ~ Konferenz am runden Tisch; **shipping** ~ Schiffahrtskonferenz; **top-level (summit)** ~ Gipfelkonferenz; **three-power** ~ Dreimächtekonferenz; **trade** ~ Handelskonferenz, Wirtschaftsbesprechungen; **world economic** ~ Weltwirtschaftskonferenz;

~ **of a committee** Ausschußsitzung; ~ **of a degree** Verleihung eines akademischen Grades; ~ **of delegates** Delegiertenkonferenz; ~ **of foreign ministers** Außenministerkonferenz; ~ **via picturephone** Bildtelefonkonferenzschaltung; ~ **on sea law** Seerechtskonferenz; ~ **of the editorial staff** Redaktionskonferenz; **to be in** ~ Besprechung haben, Besprechungen führen; **to be in** ~ **with one's colleagues** sich mit seinen Mitarbeitern besprechen; **to call (convene, convoke) a** ~ Konferenz einberufen; **to hold a** ~ sich besprechen, Beratung abhalten; **to preside at a** ~ Konferenz leiten; **to take part in a** ~ an einer Besprechung teilnehmen; **to sit in a** ~ *(US)* an einer Konferenz teilnehmen, Konferenzteilnehmer sein;

~ **agenda** Tagesordnung einer Konferenz; ~ **bargaining** Tarifkonferenz; ~ **business** Tagungsordnung einer Sitzung (Tagung); ~ **call** *(v.)* Sammel-, Konferenzgespräch; ~ **call hook-up** Sammelgesprächsschaltung; ~ **center** *(US)* **(centre,** *Br.)* Konferenzzentrum; ~ **chamber** Konferenzsaal; ~ **committee** *(US)* Beratungsausschuß; ~ **delegate** Tagungs-, Sitzungs-, Konferenzteilnehmer; ~ **diplomacy** Konferenzdiplomatie; ~ **facilities** Konferenzanlagen; ~ **fee** Beratungsgebühr; ~ **hall** Konferenzsaal; ~ **handbook** Tagungsprogramm, -heft; ~ **interpreter** Konferenzdolmetscher; ~ **leader** Tagungs-, Sitzungsleiter; ~ **member** Tagungs-, Konferenzmitglied; ~ **negotiations** Konferenzverhandlungen; ~ **paper** Tagungsbericht; ~ **phone** Konferenzgespräch; ~ **plan** Tagungsprogramm; ~ **platform** Konferenzebene, -forum; ~ **proceedings** Konferenzablauf; ~ **program(me)** Tagungsprogramm; ~ **rates** Konferenzfrachten; ~ **recommendations** Konferenzempfehlungen; ~ **report** Tagungsbericht; ~ **room** Konferenz-, Besprechungszimmer; ~ **selling** Verkaufsaktion im Vorführungsraum; ~ **table** Verhandlungstisch; ~ **telephone call** Konferenzgespräch; ~ **terms** *(shipowners)* Konferenzbedingungen; ~ **ticket** Tagungsausweis.

conferencier *(entertainer)* Konferencier, *(leading member)* wichtiges Konferenzmitglied.

conferment | **of a degree** Verleihung eines akademischen Grades; ~ **of a title** Titelverleihung.

conferrable verleihbar.

conferring of contract Auftragserteilung.

confess *(v.)* gestehen, eingestehen, *(law)* förmlich anerkennen;

~ **a crime** Verbrechen gestehen, Geständnis ablegen; ~ **a debt** Schuld anerkennen; ~ **fully** vollständiges Geständnis ablegen; ~ **o. s. guilty** Geständnis ablegen, geständig sein, seine Schuld eingestehen; ~ **a judgment** Urteil anerkennen; **to refuse to** ~ kein Geständnis ablegen.

confession Zugeständnis, Eingeständnis, *(criminal law)* Geständnis, *(religion)* Bekenntnis, Konfession, Glaubensgemeinschaft;

on his own ~ auf Grund seines eigenen Geständnisses;

extorted ~ erpreßtes Geständnis; **extra-judicial** ~ außergerichtliches Geständnis; **implied** ~ mittelbares Geständnis; **judicial** ~ gerichtliches Geständnis; **naked** ~ bloßes Geständnis; **simple** ~ formelles Geständnis; **voluntary** ~ freiwilliges Geständnis;

~ **and avoidance** Einrede [ohne Klageleugnung]; ~ **of defence** Klagerücknahme aus Rechtshängigkeitsgründen; ~ **of faith** Glaubensbekenntnis; ~ **of guilt** Schuldbekenntnis; ~ **of judgment** *(US)* Anerkenntnis des Beklagten; ~ **of signature** Anerkenntnis der Unterschrift;

to extort a ~ Geständnis erzwingen (abpressen); **to make a full** ~ umfassendes Geständnis ablegen; **to retract a** ~ Geständnis widerrufen.

confessional konfessionell;

~ **arithmetic** Konfessionsproporz; ~ **equality** Proporz der Bekenntnisse; ~ **school** Konfessionsschule.

confide *(v.)* anvertrauen, zu treuen Händen übergeben;

~ **s. th. to s. one's care** etw. jds. Fürsorge anvertrauen.

confidence *(information)* vertrauliche Mitteilung, *(trust)* Vertrauen, Sicherheit;

in ~ vertraulich;

creditor ~ Vertrauen des Gläubigers; **customer** ~ Vertrauen der Kundschaft; **entire** ~ volles Vertrauen; **implicit** ~ blindes Vertrauen; **investor** ~ Vertrauen des Anlagepublikums; **personal** ~ persönliches Vertrauensverhältnis; **public** ~ Vertrauen in der Öffentlichkeit; **shaken** ~ erschüttertes Vertrauen;

~**s communicated during their marriage** während der Ehe übermittelte vertrauliche Kenntnisse;

to admit s. o. into one's ~ j. in Vertrauen ziehen, jem. sein Vertrauen schenken; **to ask for a vote of** ~ *(parl.)* Vertrauensfrage stellen; **to be in the** ~ **of s. o.** jds. Vertrauensmann sein, jds. Vertrauen genießen; **to deserve s. one's** ~ jds. Vertrauen

rechtfertigen; **to force one's way into s. one's ~** sich in jds. Vertrauen drängen; **to have s. one's complete ~** jds. unbedingtes Vertrauen besitzen (haben); **to have ~ in newspaper reports** Zeitungsberichten Glauben schenken; **to justify s. one's ~** jds. Vertrauen rechtfertigen; **to lose the ~ of the people** öffentliches Vertrauen verlieren; **to place ~ in s. o.** Vertrauen in j. setzen; **to preserve strict ~** volle Diskretion wahren; **to tell s. o. s. th. in strict ~** jem. etw. unter dem Siegel der Verschwiegenheit mitteilen; **to restore ~ in the currency** Vertrauen in die Währung wiederherstellen; **to shake the ~** Vertrauen erschüttern; **to take s. o. into one's ~** j. ins Vertrauen ziehen; **to treat in strictest ~** streng vertraulich behandeln; **to worm o. s. into s. one's ~** sich in jds. Vertrauen einschleichen;
~ coefficient statistische Sicherheit; **~ debate** *(parl.)* Vertrauensdebatte; **~ figure** *(forecasting)* Vertrauensgrad; **~ game** Schwindelmethode, Bauernfängerei; **~ man** Bauernfänger, *(US)* gewerbsmäßiger Börsenschwindler; **~ trick** *(Br.)* Bauernfängerei; **~ trickster** Betrüger, Bauernfänger; **~ vote** *(parl.)* Vertrauensvotum; **to pass a vote of ~** *(parl.)* Vertrauen aussprechen, Vertrauensvotum gewähren.
confident Vertrauensmann;
~ *(a.)* sicher, zuversichtlich;
~ of victory siegessicher;
~ person *(Scot.)* Geschäftsteilhaber.
confidential vertraulich;
private and ~ streng vertraulich; **strictly ~** streng vertraulich; **to become too ~ with strangers** Dritten gegenüber zu vertrauensselig sein;
~ agent Vertrauensmann, -person; **~ books** Geheimsachen; **~ clerk** Privatsekretär; **~ communication** vertrauliche Mitteilung; **to have a ~ conversation** Gespräch unter vier Augen haben; **~ creditor** geheimer Kreditgeber; **~ data** vertrauliche Angaben; **~ discount** Vertrauensrabatt; **~ documents** Geheimakten; **~ information** vertrauliche Kenntnisse; **~ letter** vertraulicher Brief; **~ matter** Vertrauenssache; **to be of a ~ nature** vertraulichen Charakter haben; **~ person** Vertrauensperson; **~ place (post)** Vertrauensposten, -stellung; **~ relationship** Vertrauensverhältnis; **~ report** vertraulicher Bericht, Privatinformation, *(personnel file)* Beurteilung; **~ secretary** Privatsekretär[in]; **~ talk** privates (vertrauliches) Gespräch, Gespräch unter vier Augen.
confidentially vertraulich, unter dem Siegel der Verschwiegenheit;
to treat ~ vertraulich behandeln.
confidentiality Vertraulichkeit;
~ gap Geheimhaltungslücke, Loch.
confinable einschränkbar.
confine Grenze, Grenzgebiet, Bezirk, *(fig.)* Rand, Schwelle;
on the ~s of death an der Schwelle des Todes;
utmost ~s of space äußerste Grenzen des Weltraums;
~ *(v.)* begrenzen, beschränken, *(restraint)* Bewegungsfreiheit einschränken, *(shut up)* einsperren, einkerkern;
~ o. s. sich beschränken;
~ s. one's authority within certain limits jds. Vollmachten auf ein bestimmtes Gebiet beschränken; **~ o. s. to facts** sich lediglich an Tatsachen halten; **~ o. s. to one's house** sich in sein Haus zurückziehen; **~ one's remarks to specific points** sich nur zu bestimmten Punkten äußern; **~ one's studies to one subject** sich in seinem Studium auf ein Gebiet beschränken; **~ o. s. to the subject** sich auf sein Thema beschränken.
confined begrenzt, beschränkt, *(woman)* kurz vor der Geburt;
~ in an asylum im Irrenhaus; **~ to barracks** *(mil.)* unter Ausgangssperre; **~ by dikes** eingedämmt; **~ as a patient** in stationärer Behandlung;
to be ~ to bed bettlägerig sein; **to be ~ to the house by illness** wegen Krankheit nicht ausgehen können.
confinement Beschränkung, Einengung, *(imprisonment)* Einkerkerung, Arrest, Haft, Inhaftierung, *(accouchement)* Niederkunft, Entbindung;
close ~ strenge Haft; **solitary ~** Einzelhaft;
~ in an asylum Unterbringung in einer Heilanstalt, Anstaltsverbringung; **~ to barracks** Kasernenarrest; **~ to quarters** Stubenarrest;
to attend a ~ *(doctor)* einer Niederkunft beiwohnen; **to keep s. o. ~ in** j. in strenger Haft halten; **to place under ~** in Haft nehmen;
~ grant Entbindungsbeihilfe.
confirm *(v.)* befestigen, bestärken, *(corroborate)* bekräftigen, bestätigen, *(ratify)* ratifizieren, *(religion)* konfirmieren, firmen, einsegnen;
~ an agreement Übereinkommen bestätigen; **~ an appointment**

Ernennung bestätigen; **~ full contents** vollinhaltlich bestätigen; **~ by letter** brieflich bestätigen; **~ by oath** eidlich erhärten; **~ an order** Auftrag bestätigen; **~ a report** Bericht bestätigen; **~ a rumo(u)r** Gerücht bestätigen; **~ a telephone message by letter** Telefongespräch brieflich bestätigen; **~ a suspicion** Verdacht bestätigen; **~ s. o. in a title** jds. Eigentumsrecht bestätigen; **~ a treaty** Abkommen ratifizieren; **~ one's words** Richtigkeit einer Aussage bestätigen; **~ in writing** schriftlich bescheinigen.
confirmable bestätigungsfähig, ratifizierbar.
confirmation [Gegen]bestätigung, Bestätigung[sschreiben], *(auditing)* Testat, *(conveyance)* Auflassung, *(corroboration)* Bekräftigung, Erhärtung, *(religion)* Konfirmation;
in ~ of our conversation in Bestätigung unseres Gesprächs;
bank ~ Bestätigung eines Bankauszugs; **negative ~** negatives Testat, eingeschränkter Bestätigungsvermerk; **positive ~** positives Testat, vorbehaltloser Bestätigungsvermerk; **verbatim ~** *(telegram)* Wort-für-Wort-Bestätigung;
~ of an appointment Bestätigung einer Anstellung; **~ of an arrangement** Vergleichsbestätigung; **~ of balance** Kontokorrentbestätigung; **~ of a booking** Buchungs-, Auftragsbestätigung; **~ by a court of justice** gerichtliche Bestätigung; **~ of executor** Bestätigung des Testamentvollstreckers; **~ of a grant** Bestätigung einer Konzession; **~ of indorsement** Girobestätigung; **~ of a judgment** Aufrechterhaltung eines Urteils; **~ of news** Bestätigung von Nachrichten; **~ of an order** Auftragsbestätigung; **~ of a rumo(u)r** Bestätigung eines Gerüchtes; **~ of sale** gerichtlich bestätigter Zwangsverkauf; **~ of a signature** Unterschriftsbeglaubigung; **~ of a telephone offer** Bestätigung eines fernmündlich gemachten Angebots; **~ in writing** schriftliche Bestätigung;
~ blank Bestätigungsformular; **~ deed** Bestätigungsurkunde; **~ note** Bestätigungsschreiben; **~ slip** Ausführungsanzeige.
confirmative bestätigend, bekräftigend.
confirmatorily in bestätigendem Sinne.
confirmatory | letter Bestätigungsschreiben; **~ note** *(common carrier, US)* Auftragsbestätigung, Übernahmebescheinigung.
confirmed bestätigt, bestärkt, *(illness)* chronisch;
to be ~ Bestätigung finden;
~ bachelor eingefleischter Junggeselle; **~ credit** Kreditbestätigung; **~ irrevocable credit** bestätigtes unwiderrufliches Akkreditiv; **~ drunkard** Gewohnheitstrinker; **~ habits** eingewurzelte Gewohnheiten; **to be a ~ invalid** immerfort krank sein; **~ sceptic** ewiger Skeptiker.
confirmee Konfirmand.
confirming | my letter in Bestätigung meines Briefes; **~ our telephone conversation** in Bestätigung unseres Telefongespräches; **~ house** *(Br.)* Zahlungsgarant für Auslandsaufträge.
confirmor Zeuge, Bestätigender.
confiscable einziehbar, konfiszierbar, beschlagnahmefähig.
confiscate *(v.)* beschlagnahmen, einziehen, kassieren, konfiszieren;
~ goods Waren beschlagnahmen; **~ contraband goods** Schmuggelwaren mit Beschlag belegen.
confiscated unter Beschlagnahme, beschlagnahmt, eingezogen;
to be ~ beschlagnahmt sein;
~ by the customs authorities vom Zoll eingezogen.
confiscation Beschlagnahme, Verfallserklärung, Einziehung, Konfiszierung;
not to be liable to ~ beschlagnahmefrei sein;
~ loss Beschlagnahmeverlust; **~ order** Beschlagnahmeverfügung.
confiscatory wie eine Beschlagnahme wirkend;
~ rates kostenmäßig nicht gedeckte Tarifsätze; **~ taxes** ruinöse Steuern.
conflagration Feuersbrunst, Flächenbrand;
~ area *(fire insurance)* Großbrandbereich.
conflict Konflikt, Widerspruch, *(antagonism)* Widerstreit, Kontroverse;
armed ~ bewaffnete Auseinandersetzung; **industrial (labo(u)r) ~** Arbeitskampf, -konflikt, Lohnstreitigkeit; **racial ~** Rassenkampf; **wordy ~** wortreiche Kontroverse (Auseinandersetzung);
~ of conscience Gewissenskonflikt; **long-drawn-out ~ between employers and workers** langanhaltende Auseinandersetzung zwischen Arbeitgebern und -nehmern; **~ of evidence** widersprechendes Beweismaterial, Widersprüche in den Zeugenaussagen; **~ of interest** Interessenkonflikt, -kollision; **~ of jurisdiction** Kompetenzkonflikt, Zuständigkeitsstreit; **~ of laws** Kollisionsrecht;
~ *(v.)* in Widerspruch stehen;
~ with a claim *(patent law)* mit einem Anspruch kollidieren;

to bring interests into ~ Interessenkollision hervorrufen; **to come into** ~ **with s. o.** mit jem. in Widerstreit geraten; **to have a** ~ **with great difficulties** mit großen Schwierigkeiten fertigwerden müssen; **to put a** ~ **into perspective** Auseinandersetzung in die richtige Perspektive rücken;
~ **situation** Konfliktsituation.

conflicting | claim *(patent law)* entgegenstehender (kollidierender) Anspruch; ~ **evidence** widersprechende Zeugenaussagen; ~ **interests** entgegenstehende (kollidierende) Interessen; ~ **jurisdiction** Kompetenzkonflikt; ~ **statements** sich widersprechende Angaben; ~ **views** entgegengesetzte Meinungen.

confluence Menschenauflauf.

conform *(v.)* entsprechen, anpassen, *(be a conformist, Br.)* der Staatskirche angehören;
~ **o. s.** sich anpassen;
~ **with an arrangement** einem Abkommen (einer Vereinbarung) entsprechen; ~ **with circumstances** sich den Umständen anpassen; **not to** ~ **to a clause** Vertragsbestimmung nicht einhalten; ~ **to a clause** mit einer Vertragsbestimmung übereinstimmen; ~ **to fashion** der Mode entsprechen; ~ **to the law** sich dem Gesetz unterwerfen; ~ **to orders** Instruktionen befolgen; ~ **with provisions** in Übereinstimmung mit den Bestimmungen handeln; ~ **to international standards** der zwischenstaatlichen Übung entsprechen; ~ **to the usages of society** sich den gesetzlichen Konventionen fügen;
~ *(a.)* übereinstimmend, konform;
~ **copy** gleichlautende Abschrift.

conformable gleichlautend, übereinstimmend, konform;
~ **to your advice** konform Ihrer Aufgabe; ~ **to your books** mit Ihren Büchern übereinstimmend; ~ **to custom** usancemäßig; ~ **to instructions** laut Anweisung; ~ **to law** gesetzlich; ~ **to your wishes** Ihren Wünschen entsprechend.

conformance Übereinstimmung.

conformation Unterwürfigkeit, Fügsamkeit.

conformed copy *(US)* gleichlautende Abschrift.

conformist Konformist.

conformity Übereinstimmung, Gleichförmigkeit;
in ~ **with** gleichlautend, in Übereinstimmung mit; **in** ~ **with your orders** gemäß Ihrem Auftrag; **in** ~ **with the receipts** nach Maßgabe der Eingänge; **in** ~ **with the regulations** den Bestimmungen gemäß;
~ **in dividend politics** gleichbleibende Dividendenpolitik; ~ **to fashion** neueste Mode;
to act in ~ **with the contract** einem Vertrag gemäß handeln; **to be in** ~ **with the market** marktgerecht sein; **to enter in** ~ gleichlautend buchen.

confound *(v.)* durcheinanderbringen, verwirren;
~ **means with ends** Mittel und Zwecke verwechseln.

confraternity *(occupation)* Berufsgenossenschaft, *(religion)* Sekte.

confrere Genosse, Kollege.

confront *(v.)* gegenüberliegen, *(face hostily)* feindlich entgegentreten, Stirn bieten;
~ **difficulties** Schwierigkeiten gegenüberstehen; ~ **s. o. with a lie** j. Lügen strafen; ~ **two witnesses** zwei Zeugen einander gegenüberstellen (konfrontieren).

confrontation *(witnesses)* Gegenüberstellung, Konfrontation;
~ **situation** Konfrontationslage.

confuse *(v.)* verwechseln, verwirren;
~ **accounts** Konten durcheinanderbringen; ~ **dates** Daten verwechseln.

confusion *(escheat)* Heimfall, *(intermixture)* Vermischung, Vermengung, *(merging of rights)* Verschmelzung;
~ **of battle** Schlachtgetümmel; ~ **of boundaries** Grenzverwirrung; ~ **of debts** Untergang von Forderungen, Konfusion; ~ **of goods** Gütervermengung, Warenvermischung; ~ **of names** Namenverwechslung; ~ **of rights** *(US)* Vereinigung von Gläubiger und Schuldner in einer Position, Fusion; ~ **of terms** Wortverwechslung; ~ **of trademarks** Verwechslung von Warenzeichen, Warenzeichenverwechslung.

confutable widerlegbar.

confutation Widerlegung.

confute *(v.)* widerlegen.

congenial gleichartig, geistesverwandt;
to be ~ **to s. o.** jem. zusagen (passen);
~ **manners** gewinnendes Wesen; ~ **relationship** kollegiales Verhältnis.

congenital defect angeborener Defekt.

congest *(v.)* blockieren, verstopfen, überfüllen;
~ **the market** Markt überschwemmen; ~ **the traffic** Verkehr behindern, Verkehrsstau herbeiführen.

congested übervölkert;
~ **with traffic** vom Verkehr verstopft;
to become ~ **towards evening** Abends am meisten verstopft sein;
~ **area** dichtbesiedeltes (übervölkertes) Gebiet, Ballungsgebiet; ~ **state of the goods traffic** Stockung im Güterverkehr; ~ **streets** verstopfte Straßen.

congestion Ansammlung, Andrang, Stauung, Stau;
air ~ Verstopfung der Luftwege; **traffic** ~ Verkehrsstockung, -stauung, Stau;
~ **of the brain** Blutandrang zum Gehirn; ~ **of population** Überbevölkerung; ~ **of traffic** Verkehrsstockung;
~ **charge** *(shipping)* Frachtzuschlag [bei Güterstau]; ~ **point (spot)** Verkehrsstauung; ~ **problems** Wartezeitprobleme; ~ **surcharge** Zuschlag wegen Überfüllung des Hafens.

conglomerate Zusammenballung, Anhäufung, Konglomerat, *(industrial concern, US)* Konzern[gruppe], Misch-, Großkonzern, Industriezusammenballung;
~ *(v.)* zusammenballen;
~ *(a.)* zusammengewürfelt;
~ **bid** Konzernangebot; ~ **merger** Konzernfusion; **to see an out in the** ~ **route** Ausweg in weiteren Konzernzusammenschlüssen sehen; **to take the** ~ **route to growth** im Wege des Zukaufs zu einem Konzern heranwachsen; ~ **stocks** Konzernaktien; ~ **target** Konzernziel.

conglomeration of assets Anhäufung von Vermögenswerten.

congratulate *(v.)* **s. o.** jem. seine Glückwünsche aussprechen.

congratulation Glückwunsch;
~ **card** Gratulations-, Glückwunschkarte;
to receive ~**s** Glückwünsche entgegennehmen.

congratulatory | address Glückwunschansprache; ~ **letter** Glückwunschschreiben; ~ **message** Glückwunschadresse; ~ **speech** Glückwunschansprache; ~ **telegram** Glückwunschtelegramm.

congregate *(v.)* sich versammeln, zusammenkommen;
~ *(a.)* kollektiv.

congregation Versammlung, *(Oxford)* Senatsversammlung.

congress Tagung, Begegnung, Zusammenkunft, Kongreß, Versammlung;
~ *(US)* Kongreß, gesetzgebende Versammlung;
medical ~ Ärztekongreß; **world** ~ Weltkongreß;
~ **of Industrial Organization (C.I.O.)** Industriegewerkschaftsverband;
to attend a ~ an einem Kongreß teilnehmen; **to hold a** ~ Kongreß (Tagung) abhalten; **to sit in** ~ *(US)* Kongreßabgeordneter sein; **to vacate one's seat in** ~ **by resignation** *(US)* seinen Kongreßsitz aufgeben und sich zurückziehen;
~ **center** Kongreßzentrum; ~ **hall** Kongreßhalle; ~ **member** Kongreßteilnehmer; ~ **party** *(India)* Kongreßpartei.

congressional Tagungen betreffend;
to win ~ **acceptance** Zustimmung des Kongresses herbeiführen; ~ **committee** *(US)* Parlaments-, Kongreßausschuß; ~ **debate** *(US)* Kongreßdebatte; ~ **district** *(US)* Wahlbezirk; ~ **elections** *(US)* Kongreßwahlen; ~ **inquiry** *(US)* Kongreßuntersuchung; ~ **investigation** *(US)* Kongreßuntersuchung; ~ **liaison** *(US)* Verbindung zum Kongreß; ~ **medal** *(US)* Verdienstmedaille; ~ **opposition** Widerstand des Kongresses; ~ **outlines** *(US)* vom Kongreß erlassene Richtlinien; ~ **ratification** *(US)* Ratifizierung durch den Kongreß; ~ **recess** *(US)* Kongreßferien, Parlamentsferien; ~ **record** *(US)* Parlamentsprotokoll; ~ **report** *(US)* Sitzungsbericht des Kongresses; ~ **seat** *(US)* Parlamentssitz; ~ **sentiment** Stimmung im Kongreß; ~ **vote** *(US)* Kongreßabstimmung.

congressionalist Mitglied einer Kongreßpartei.

congressman *(US)* Kongreßmitglied, -abgeordneter.

congruence Übereinstimmung.

congruent übereinstimmend.

conical buoy Kegel-, Spitzboje.

conjectural mutmaßlich.

conjecture Vermutung, Annahme;
reduced to ~**s** auf Vermutungen angewiesen.

conjoint verbunden, vereinigt, gemeinsam;
~ **minister** Ministerkollege.

conjointly gemeinschaftlich;
to act ~ gemeinsam handeln; **to inherit** ~ miterben, zusammen erben.

conjoints Eheleute.

conjugal ehelich;
~ **community** eheliche Gemeinschaft; ~ **consortium** Ehegemeinschaft, eheliche Lebensgemeinschaft; ~ **duty** eheliche Pflicht; ~ **life** Eheleben; ~ **relation** eheliches Verhältnis; ~ **rights** eheliche Rechte.

conjunct vereinigt, verbunden, *(law)* beteiligt, mitbetroffen;
~ **attempt** gemeinsam unternommener Versuch; ~ **person** der Mittäterschaft Verdächtigter.
conjunction Verbindung, Vereinigung;
unusual ~ **of events** ungewöhnliches Zusammentreffen von Ereignissen.
conjunctive denial globales Bestreiten.
conjuncture Zusammentreffen ungünstiger Ereignisse, Krise.
conjuration *(solemn appeal)* feierlicher Appell, *(conjuring trick)* Zaubertrick, Kunststück.
conjure *(v.)* beschwören, auflehnen.
conk *(v.)* out *(motor, sl.)* streiken, absterben.
connate angeboren.
connect *(v.)* verbinden, verknüpfen, *(v./intr.)* im Zusammenhang stehen;
~ **ideas** Ideen assoziieren; ~ **o. s. as a partner with a house** in eine Firma als Teilhaber eintreten; ~ **two telephone subscribers** zwei Fernsprechteilnehmer miteinander verbinden; ~ **with a train** Zuganschluß haben.
connected verbunden, zusammenhängend;
closely ~ eng liiert;
~ **by marriage** verschwägert; ~ **in parallell** parallel geschaltet; ~ **by telephone** mit Telefonanschluß;
to be ~ **with an affair** in eine Angelegenheit verwickelt sein; to be influentially ~ gute Beziehungen haben; to be intimately ~ in enger Beziehung stehen; to be well ~ über gute Verbindungen (Beziehungen) verfügen; to become ~ in verwandtschaftliche Beziehungen treten;
~ **expenses** notwendige Aufgaben; ~ **load** Gesamtbelastung.
connecting|carrier Anschlußreederei; ~ **cord** *(US)* Anschlußschnur; ~ **line** Nebenlinie; ~ **line accounting** gemeinsames Frachtenrechnungswesen; ~ **link** Verbindungslinie; ~ **plug** *(el.)* Stecker; ~ **train** Anschlußzug.
connection (connexion, *Br.*) Anschluß, *(airplane)* Anschluß, *(body of customers)* Kundschaft, Klientele, *(el.)* Verbindung, Anschluß, Schaltung, *(friends)* Bekanntenkreis, *(line of communication)* Verbindung, Anschluß, *(relation)* Verwandtschaft, *(religious society)* Religionsgemeinschaft, Sekte, *(supplier of narcotics, US sl.)* Rauschgifthändler, *(tel.)* Anschluß, Verbindung;
broken ~ unterbrochenes Telefongespräch; business ~ Geschäftsverbindung; cable ~ Kabelverbindung; far-reaching ~s weitreichende Beziehungen; financial ~ kapitalmäßige Bindung; first-rate ~s erstklassiger Kundenkreis; foreign ~s auswärtige Beziehungen; high-echelon ~s Verbindungen auf höchster Ebene; hot-water ~s Heißwasseranlage; plane ~ Anschlußflug; political ~s politische Beziehungen; proximate ~ unmittelbarer Kausalzusammenhang; telephone ~ Telefonverbindung; through ~ durchgehende Verbindung; train ~ Zugverbindung, Bahnanschluß; trunk ~ Fernverbindung; wide ~ ausgedehnte Kundschaft; widespread ~s ausgedehnte Beziehungen; wrong ~ *(tel.)* falsche Telefonverbindung, Fehlverbindung;
~ **by air** Flugverbindung; ~ **between Church and State** Verbindung zwischen Kirche und Staat; ~ **to the mains** Anschluß an das Stromnetz; ~ **by marriage** Schwägerschaft; ~ **of mine** Verwandte[r] von mir; ~ **by sea** Schiffsverbindung; ~ **of long standing** langjährige Geschäftsverbindung; ~ **of a new telephone** Herstellung eines Telefonanschlusses;
to break off ~s Beziehungen abbrechen; to build up a new ~ neue Geschäftsverbindung herstellen; to catch one's ~ seinen Anschluß erreichen; to dispose over wide ~s über gute Beziehungen verfügen; to enter into ~ with s. o. mit jem. in Verbindung treten; to get a ~ [Telefon]anschluß erhalten; to have ~s abroad Auslandsbeziehungen haben; to have good ~s gute Beziehungen haben; to make one's ~ *(US)* seinen Anschluß erreichen; to miss one's ~ seinen Anschluß versäumen; to open up a business ~ with a firm Geschäftsbeziehungen mit einer Firma aufnehmen; to run in ~ with *(train)* Anschluß haben; to work up a ~ sich einen Kundenstamm schaffen;
~ **plug** Verbindungsstecker.
connector *(el.)* Stecker, *(fig.)* Bindeglied, *(waggon)* Kupplung;
matching ~ passender Stecker.
connivance stillschweigende Genehmigung, wissentliches Gewährenlassen, *(corrupt assent)* Begünstigung, geheimes Einverständnis, Vorschubleistung;
done with the ~ of im strafbaren Einverständnis mit.
connive *(v.)* *(law)* stillschweigend Vorschub leisten, im geheimen Einverständnis stehen;
~ **at s. one's escape** jds. Flucht stillschweigend dulden; ~ **at a fraud** einem Betrug im Geheimen zustimmen.

connoisseur Sachkenner, Kunstsachverständiger;
~ **of power** erfahrener Machtinhaber.
connotation Nebenbedeutung.
connubial ehelich.
connubiality Ehestand.
conquer *(v.)* erobern, einnehmen;
~ **one's independence** seine Unabhängigkeit erringen; ~ **territory from s. o.** jem. Land abgewinnen;
to stoop to ~ sein Ziel durch Zugeständnisse zu erreichen suchen.
conquest Eroberung, Unterwerfung, Unterjochung, *(Scot. law)* Gütererwerbung;
to make a ~ of s. o. j. für sich gewinnen.
consanguineous blutsverwandt.
consanguinity Blutsverwandtschaft;
collateral ~ Verwandtschaft in der Seitenlinie; lineal ~ Verwandtschaft in gerader Linie.
conscience Gewissen, *(law)* Rechtsempfinden;
against good ~ gegen das Rechtsempfinden gerichtet; on grounds of ~ aus Gewissensgründen; upon my ~ auf mein Wort;
clear ~ gutes Gewissen; wide ~ elastisches Gewissen;
to clear one's ~ sein Gewissen entlasten; to have s. th. on one's ~ starke Unruhe über etw. empfinden; to have a guilty ~ schlechtes Gewissen haben; to make s. th. a matter of ~ Gewissensfrage aus etw. machen; to salve one's ~ sein Gewissen beruhigen;
~ **clause** Gewissensklausel; ~ **fund** *(US)* Steuersünderfonds; ~ **money** *(Br.)* anonyme Steuernachzahlung, Reuegeld; ~-**proof** abgebrüht; **for** ~ **sake** aus Gewissensgründen; ~-**smitten** von Gewissensbissen geplagt.
conscientious gewissenhaft;
~ **objection** Kriegsdienstverweigerung; ~ **objector** Kriegsdienstverweigerer, *(Br.)* Impfgegner; ~ **scruples** Gewissensbisse, -skrupel; ~ **worker** pflichtbewußter Arbeiter.
conscious bei Bewußtsein;
~ **of Europe** europabewußt;
to be ~ **of s. th.** von einer Sache überzeugt sein; to look ~ betreten aussehen;
~ **level** Bewußtseinsschwelle; ~ **liar** bewußter Lügner; ~ **parallelism of action** *(cartel law, US)* bewußt gleichartiges Verhalten.
consciousness Bewußtseins[zustand];
class ~ Klassenbewußtsein;
moral ~ **of a nation** ethisches Empfinden eines Volkes;
to recover ~ Bewußtsein wiedererlangen.
conscribe *(v.)* *(mil.)* einziehen, einberufen, zwangsweise ausheben.
conscript Einberufener, Wehr[dienst]pflichtiger, ausgehobener Rekrut;
~ **exempted provisionally** vorübergehend Zurückgestellter, UK Gestellter;
~ *(v.)* *(labo(u)r)* dienstverpflichten, *(mil.)* [zum Militärdienst] einberufen;
~ **capital** Kapital der staatlichen Zwangswirtschaft unterwerfen; ~ **reserves** Reserven einberufen;
~ *(a.)* zwangsweise verpflichtet, *(mil.)* einberufen, eingezogen;
~ **fathers** Mitglieder einer gesetzgebundenen Körperschaft; ~ **labo(u)r** zwangsverpflichtete Arbeitskräfte; ~ **soldiers** einberufene Soldaten.
conscriptee *(US)* Wehrpflichtiger.
conscription Einberufung, Truppen-, Zwangsaushebung;
general ~ allgemeine Wehrpflicht; industrial ~ Arbeits[zwangs]verpflichtung; universal ~ allgemeine Wehrpflicht;
~ **of labo(u)r** Dienstverpflichtung; ~ **of wealth** verschärfte Besteuerung größerer Vermögen, Vermögensbesteuerung, -abgabe;
~ **order** Einberufungsbefehl.
conscriptive system Wehrdienstwesen.
consecrate *(religion)* weihen, einsegnen;
~ *(v.)* **one's life to an idea** sein Leben einer Idee widmen.
consecration Priesterweihe.
consecution Aufeinanderfolge;
~s **of events** Serie von Ereignissen.
consecutive aufeinanderfolgend, fortlaufend;
on five ~ **days** an fünf Tagen hintereinander; ~ **narrative** zusammenhängende Erzählung; ~ **quotation** variable Notierung; ~ **sentence** Urteil über Delikte in Realkonkurrenz; ~ **symptoms** *(med.)* Folgeerscheinungen.
consecutively, to quote fortlaufend notieren;
~ **numbered** fortlaufend numeriert.

consensual contract obligatorischer Vertrag, Konsensualvertrag.
consensus übereinstimmende Meinung, Übereinstimmung;
~ **ad idem** *(lat.)* Willensübereinstimmung; ~ **of opinion** vorherrschende Ansicht, übereinstimmende Meinung.
consent Zustimmung, Einverständnis, Einwilligung;
by common ~ einverständlich, mit allseitiger Zustimmung; **by mutual** ~ in gegenseitigem Einverständnis; **requiring** ~ zustimmungsbedürftig; **with** ~ einvernehmlich, mit Zustimmung; **with one** ~ einstimmig, einmütig; **without our** ~ ohne unsere Genehmigung;
express ~ ausdrückliche Zustimmung; **implied** ~ stillschweigendes Einverständnis; **parental** ~ elterliche Einwilligung; **prior** ~ vorherige Zustimmung; **oral** ~ mündliche Zustimmung; **recording** ~ Eintragungsbewilligung; **reluctant** ~ notgedrungene Zustimmung; **written** ~ schriftliche Bestätigung, schriftliches Einverständnis;
~ **out of court** außergerichtliche Einigung; ~ **of creditors** Gläubigerzustimmung; ~ **to marriage** Heiratserlaubnis; ~ **of members** Mitgliederzustimmung; ~ **to a request** Antragsgenehmigung; ~ **without reserve** vorbehaltlose Zustimmung;
~ *(v.)* einwilligen, einverstanden sein, sich einverstanden erklären, Zustimmung geben, zustimmen, genehmigen, gutheißen, billigen;
~ **to s. th. being done** seine Zustimmung zu etw. geben; ~ **to a proposal** einem Vorschlag zustimmen; ~ **to being president** Präsidentenwahl annehmen; ~ **to a reduction of price** in eine Preisherabsetzung einwilligen;
to be chosen by general ~ einstimmig gewählt werden; **to give one's** ~ seine Zustimmung geben, seine Einwilligung erteilen; **to give a ready** ~ sofort seine Zustimmung geben; **to obtain s. one's** ~ jds. Einwilligung erhalten; **to require** ~ zustimmungsbedürftig sein; **to refuse** ~ **to the marriage** Heiratseinwilligung versagen; **to settle by** ~ durch Vergleich erledigen; **to sign** ~ seine Zustimmung zu erkennen geben; **to withdraw one's** ~ seine Zustimmung widerrufen;
silence gives ~ Schweigen bedeutet Zustimmung;
~ **decree (judgment)** zustimmender Beschluß, Anerkenntnisurteil, *(antitrust law, US)* Vergleich zwischen klagender Regierung und beklagter Privatpartei, Prozeßvergleich; ~ **election** *(trade union)* Einigung über eine Betriebsratswahl; ~ **rule** gerichtliches Räumungsanerkenntnis; ~ **stock** dividendenberechtigtes Stammaktien.
consentaneous einstimmig, mit allgemeiner Zustimmung.
consequence Auswirkung, Folge, Folgeerscheinung, Konsequenz, Resultat, *(importance)* Bedeutung, Wichtigkeit, *(social importance)* Einfluß, Ansehen;
bad ~s schlimme Folgen; **legal** ~s Rechtsfolgen; **serious** ~s schwerwiegende Folgen; **world-wide** ~s globale Auswirkungen;
~ **of dismissal** Entlassungsfolgen; ~s **of a war** Folgen eines Krieges, Kriegsfolgen;
to abide by the ~s Folgen auf sich nehmen; **to be followed by** ~s Konsequenzen haben; **to be a man of** ~ bedeutender (einflußreicher) Mann sein, **to be of no** ~ nichts auf sich haben; **to bear the** ~s Folgen auf sich nehmen; **to take the** ~s die Folgen tragen.
consequent Folge[erscheinung], Folgerung;
~ *(a.)* folgerichtig, konsequent.
consequential logisch folgend, folgerichtig;
~ **costs** Folgekosten eines Schadens; ~ **damage** mittelbarer Schaden, Folgeschaden; ~ **damages** Schadensersatz für entgangenen Gewinn; ~ **effects of an action** Rückwirkungen einer Klage; ~ **loss** mittelbarer Schaden, Folgeschaden; ~ **loss insurance** Folgeschadenversicherung.
conservable konservierbar.
conservancy Forsterhaltung, *(board of conservators, Br.)* Kontrollbehörde über Forste, Häfen und Schiffahrt, Flußkommission;
Thames ~ Board *(Br.)* Strom- und Hafengericht.
conservation Erhaltung, Bewahrung, Konservierung, *(forest)* Naturschutzgebiet;
food ~ Lebensmittelkonservierung;
~ **of assets** Erhaltung von Vermögenswerten; ~ **of social order** Bewahrung der Gesellschaftsordnung;
~**-minded** umweltschutzbewußt; ~ **zone** Fischereischutzzone.
conservationist Umweltschützer.
conservatism Konservatismus, konservative Grundsätze.
Conservative Konservierungsmittel, *(Br.)* Konservativer, Tory;
~ *(a.)* mäßig, vorsichtig, *(politics)* konservativ, der konservativen Partei angehörend;
to be ~ konservativ eingestellt sein;

~ **estimate** vorsichtige Berechnung (Schätzung); ~ **investment** vorsichtige Kapitalanlage; ~ **Party** *(Br.)* konservative Partei; ~ **practice** *(balance sheet)* Realisationsprinzip; ~ **wing** konservativer Flügel.
conservator Aufsichtsbeamter, *(banking, US)* Bankenkommissar, *(guardian, US)* Amtsvormund, Kurator, *(museum)* Museumsdirektor, Konservator;
~ **of rivers** *(Br.)* Flußbehörde, -bauamt.
conservatory *(Br.)* Treib-, Gewächshaus, Wintergarten;
~ *(a.)* konservierend, *(Br.)* strompolizeilich.
conserve Konserve, Eingemachtes, *(confection)* Konfekt;
~ *(v.)* *(fruit)* konservieren, einmachen;
~ **one's health** seine Gesundheit festigen.
consider *(v.)* erwägen, in Erwägung ziehen, Betrachtungen anstellen, bedenken, in Betracht ziehen;
~ **an appointment** Anstellung ins Auge fassen; ~ **buying a car** Ankauf eines Wagens in Erwägung ziehen; ~ **the details of a proposal** auf einen Vorschlag näher eingehen; ~ **the expense** Kosten berücksichtigen; ~ **the feelings of other people** auf die Gefühle anderer Rücksicht nehmen; ~ **an offer** Angebot in Erwägung ziehen; ~ **s. o. trustworthy to the extent of $ 10.000** j. bis zu einer Höhe von 10.000 Dollar für kreditwürdig halten.
considerable beträchtlich, namhaft, erheblich;
~ **amount** große Summe; ~ **damage** beträchtlicher Schaden; ~ **expenses** erhebliche Unkosten; ~ **income** gutes Einkommen.
consideration *(bill of exchange)* Valuta, *(compensation)* Entschädigung, *(of contract)* [Gegen]leistung, Vergütung, Entgelt, *(equivalent)* Gegenwert, -leistung, Äquivalent, *(meditation)* Überlegung, Erwägung, Würdigung, *(premium)* Prämie, *(regard)* Rücksichtnahme, *(judicial ruling)* richterliche Entscheidung;
after careful ~ nach reiflicher Überlegung; **for a valuable** ~ gegen Entgelt; **in** ~ in Anbetracht, mit Rücksicht auf; **upon** ~ nach Prüfung; **without** ~ unentgeltlich;
active ~s ernsthafte Überlegungen; **adequate** ~ gleichwertige (angemessene) Gegenleistung, Entgelt; ~ **bargained for** vereinbarte Gegenleistung; **concurrent** ~ gleichzeitige Gegenleistung; **continuing** ~ dauernde Gegenleistung; ~ **due** fällige Gegenleistung; **equitable** ~ aus Billigkeitsgründen zuerkannte Gegenleistung; **executed** ~ bewirkte Gegenleistung; **executory** ~ noch zu bewirkende (zukünftige) Gegenleistung; **express** ~ ausdrücklich festgelegte Gegenleistung; **fair** ~ angemessene Gegenleistung; **fixed** ~ feste Gegenleistung; **further** ~ nochmalige Verhandlung; **good** ~ ausreichende Gegenleistung, moralisch bedingte Gegenleistung; **gratuitous** ~ unentgeltliches Leistungsversprechen; **illegal** ~ ungesetzliche (unerlaubte) Gegenleistung; **immoral** ~ sittenwidrige Gegenleistung; **impossible** ~ unmögliche Leistung; **legal** ~ rechtlich zulässige Gegenleistung; **meritorious** ~ auf einer Anstandspflicht beruhende Gegenleistung; **money (pecuniary)** ~ dem Geldwert entsprechende Gegenleistung; **moral** ~ moralische Verpflichtung; **nominal** ~ symbolische Gegenleistung; **past** ~ Vorleistung; **sufficient** ~ ausreichende Gegenleistung, hinreichender Gegenwert; **tax** ~s steuerliche Überlegungen; **vague** ~ unbestimmte Gegenleistung; **valuable** ~ geldwerte Gegenwert, angemessene (geldwerte) Gegenleistung, Vertragsinteresse; **antecedent valuable** ~ abschätzbare im voraus gewährte Gegenleistung;
~ **of evidence** Beweiswürdigung; ~ **for a bill of exchange** Gegenwert für einen Wechsel; ~ **of a debt** Rechtsgrund einer Forderung; ~s **of liquidity** Liquiditätsüberlegungen, -erwägungen;
to be in ~ geprüft (erwogen) werden; **to be left (ruled out) of** ~ außer Betracht bleiben; **to be under** ~ in Beratung sein; **to be still under** ~ noch beraten werden; **to come into** ~ in Betracht kommen; **to do s. th. for a** ~ etw. gegen eine Vergütung tun; **to do anything for a** ~ gegen Bezahlung zu allen Schandtaten bereit sein; **to give** ~ **for a bill** Valuta für einen Wechsel anschaffen; **to give due** ~ notwendige Aufmerksamkeit schenken, gebührende Rücksicht nehmen; **to give a matter careful** ~ Angelegenheit sorgfältig überlegen; **to leave s. th. out of** ~ etw. außer Betracht lassen; **to take into** ~ berücksichtigen, in Betracht (Erwägung) ziehen; **to take a request into favo(u)rable** ~ Gesuch in wohlwollende Erwägung ziehen;
~ **clause** Entgeltsklausel; ~ **money** Gegenwert in Geld, Entschädigung, *(shares, Br.)* Effektenstempel.
considered, all things alles eingerechnet (wohlberechnet);
to be ~ Berücksichtigung finden.
considering in Anbetracht von, im Hinblick auf, *(preamble)* von der Erwägung geleitet;
~ **it** Rücksicht auf; ~ **that ...** in Anbetracht, daß ...; ~ **all circumstances** in Anbetracht aller Umstände.

consign *(v.)* übergeben, behändigen, *(deposit in bank)* [in die Bank] einzahlen, hinterlegen, *(entrust)* anvertrauen, *(transfer)* übertragen, überweisen, *(transmit)* [Waren] über-, zusenden, ausliefern, verfrachten, verschicken, konsignieren, in Kommission geben;
~ **to s. one's care** jds. Obhut anvertrauen; ~ **by rail** per Bahn schicken; ~ **a room to s. one's use** Raum für j. vorsehen; ~ **to writing** schriftlich aufsetzen.

consignatary *(Br.)* Verwahrer, Depositar.

consignation *(depositing, Scot.)* Hinterlegung, Deponierung, *(transmitting)* Übersendung, Überweisung, Zusendung;
to ship goods to the ~ of s. o. Waren an j. zum Versand bringen.

consignatory Mitunterzeichner.

consigned | goods Konsignations-, Kommissionsware; ~ **money** anvertrautes Geld, Depositengelder.

consignee *(addressee)* [Waren]empfänger, Adressat, Auftragnehmer, *(commission merchant)* Kommissionär;
duty for ~'s account Zoll geht zu Lasten des Empfängers.

consigner *(Scot. law)* Hinterleger.

consignment *(assigning)* Übertragung, *(commission)* Kommission, Kommissionsauftrag, Konsignation[sgeschäft], *(delivery)* Verabfolgung, Übergabe, *(depositing)* Hinterlegung, Deponierung, *(escrow agreement)* Hinterlegungsvertrag, *(goods consigned)* [Waren]sendung, Auslieferung, Kommissionssendung, -ware, *(shipping)* Ver-, Übersendung, Versand, Zustellung, Spedition, Verfrachtung;
on ~ kommissionsweise; **on checking the ~** bei Durchsicht der Sendung; **shipping on ~** auf eigene Rechnung versandt;
collective ~ Sammelladung; **gold ~** Goldtransport; **mixed ~** Sammelladung; **retail ~** Einzelsendung; **small ~s** Stückgut;
~ **on approval** Auswahl-, Ansichtssendung; ~ **of books** Büchersendung; ~ **of goods** Warenpartie; ~ **by goods train** *(Br.)* Frachtgut[sendung]; ~ **for inspection** Ansichtssendung; ~ **of merchandise** Warensendung; ~ **in part** Teilsendung, -versand; ~ **in specie** Barsendung; ~ **of valuables** Wertsendung;
to hold a ~ covered as from today Warensendung ab heute versichert haben; **to make out a ~** Frachtbrief ausstellen; **to send on ~** in Kommission geben; **to send a ~ by passenger train** Warensendung per Eilgut schicken; **to take goods on ~** Waren in Kommission nehmen;
~ **account** Kommissionskonto; ~ **agent** Kommissionär; **to supply on a ~ basis** Kommissionslieferungen vornehmen; ~ **book** Kommissionswarenbuch; ~ **contract** Kommissionsvertrag; ~ **goods** Kommissionswaren; ~ **invoice** Kommissionsrechnung, Konsignationsfaktura; ~ **marketing** Vertrieb auf dem Kommissionswege; ~ **note** Versandanzeige, Warenbegleit-, Ladeschein, Frachtbrief; **as per ~ note of ...** *(Br.)* laut Ladeschein vom ...; ~ **sale** Konsignations-, Kommissionsverkauf; ~ **stock (store)** Konsignations-, Kommissionslager.

consignor *(assignor)* Übertragender, Zedent, *(freighter)* Verfrachter, Verlader, Aufgeber, *(sender)* Ver-, Über-, Absender;
~'s **merchandise** Kommissionsware.

consist *(v.)* sich zusammensetzen, bestehen;
~ **mainly of shares** im wesentlichen aus Aktien bestehen.

consistency Folgerichtigkeit, Vereinbarkeit, *(fig.)* Haltbarkeit, Beständigkeit, *(opinion poll)* Widerspruchsfreiheit [der Befragten].

consistent im Einklang mit, vereinbar, übereinstimmend;
~ **with the law** mit den Gesetzen vereinbar;
not to be ~ with im Widerspruch stehen; **to be ~ with sound commercial practice** im ordentlichen kaufmännischen Leben üblich sein;
~ **business policy** Stetigkeit in der Geschäftsführung; ~ **friend of the working classes** konsequenter Freund der arbeitenden Bevölkerung; ~ **method** einheitliche Methode; ~ **practice** ständige Rechtssprechung.

consistory Ratsversammlung.

consociate Genosse, Teilhaber.

consolation prize Trostpreis.

consolatory letter Kondolenzbrief.

console *(radio, television)* Truhe.

consolidate *(v.)* *(combine)* vereinigen, zusammenziehen, *(debts)* konsolidieren, fundieren, *(mortgages)* zusammenschreiben, Gesamthypothek bilden, *(shares)* [Aktien] zusammenlegen;
~ **actions** Klagen miteinander verbinden; ~ **banks** Banken fusionieren; ~ **two bills** zwei Gesetze zusammenfassen; ~ **business companies** Firmen zusammenschließen (verschmelzen); ~ **one's influence** seinen Einfluß verstärken; ~ **mortgages** Gesamthypothek bilden; ~ **one's position** seine Stellung festigen; ~ **proceedings** Verfahren vereinigen, Prozesse verbinden; ~ **shipments** *(US)* Sammelladungen zusammenstellen; ~ **the subsidia-**ry's **financial statement with one's own** Tochtergesellschaft in die Gewinn- und Verlustrechnung mit einbeziehen (bilanzmäßig konsolidieren); ~ **troops** Truppen zusammenziehen.

consolidated vereinigt, fundiert, *(balance sheet)* konsolidiert, *(fig.)* gefestigt, gestärkt;
~ **accounts** konsolidierter Konzernabschluß; ~ **Act** *(Br.)* Haushaltsgesetz; ~ **annuities** fundierte Staatsleihe, Staatsrente; ~ **balance sheet** konsolidierter Konzernabschluß, Gemeinschafts-, Konzernbilanz; ~ **bonds** *(US)* durch Gesamthypothek besicherte Schuldverschreibungen; ~ **charges** *(parl., Br.)* Dauerbewilligungen; ~ **company (corporation)** Konzerngesellschaft; ~ **debt** konsolidierte (fundierte) Schuld; ~ **delivery system** gemeinsames Auslieferungssystem; ~ **earnings statement** *(US)* Nachweis über den Reingewinn; ~ **engine** *(US)* schwere Güterzuglokomotive; ~ **financial statement** Konzernbilanz, konsolidierte Bilanz; ~ **fund** *(Br.)* konsolidierter Staatsfonds, Britische Staatskasse; ~ **fund services** *(Br.)* Staatsschuldendienst; ~ **group** Konzern[gruppe]; ~ **income** konsolidierte Betriebseinnahmen; ~ **loan** fundierte Anleihe; ~ **measures** Konsolidierungsmaßnahmen; ~ **mortgage** *(US)* Gesamthypothek; ~ **first mortgage bonds** *(US)* gesicherte Schuldverschreibungen; ~ **profit and loss account** konsolidierte Gewinn- und Verlustrechnung; ~ **report** zusammengefaßter Bericht; ~ **revenue fund** *(Br.)* aus Staatspapieren bestehender Sonderfonds in selbständigen Kolonien; ~ **sales** Konzern-, Gruppenumsatz; ~ **school** durch Zusammenlegungen entstandene Schule; ~ **shipment** *(Br.)* Sammelladung; ~ **[financial] statement** Konzernbilanz, konsolidierte Bilanz; ~ **income statement** *(US)* konsolidierte Gewinn- und Verlustrechnung; ~ **profit and loss statement** konsolidierte Gewinn- und Verlustrechnung; ~ **stocks** *(Br.)* fundierte (konsolidierte) Papiere; ~ **subsidiaries** [bilanzmäßig] konsolidierte Tochtergesellschaften; ~ **surplus** Konzernüberschuß; ~ **earned surplus** *(US)* Konzernrücklage; ~ **tax returns** *(corporation, US)* konsolidierte Steuererklärung.

consolidating financial statement Konsolidierungsbogen.

consolidation *(loan)* Konsolidierung, *(market)* [Be]festigung, *(merger)* Zusammenlegung, Fusion[ierung];
corporate ~ *(US)* Fusion von Aktiengesellschaften; **political ~** politische Konsolidierung;
~ **of actions** Klagenhäufung, Klagen-, Prozeßverbindung; ~ **of banks** Bankenfusion; ~ **of benefits** Pfründenvereinigung; ~ **of corporations** *(US)* Fusion von Aktiengesellschaften; ~ **of firms** Firmenverschmelzung; ~ **of funds** Kapitalkonsolidierung; ~ **of indebtedness** Schuldenkonsolidierung; ~ **of the market** Befestigung des Marktes; ~ **of mortgages** Zusammenschreibung von Hypotheken, Bildung einer Gesamthypothek; ~ **of the national debt** Konsolidierung der Staatsschuld; ~ **of patents** Patentzusammenfassung; ~ **of one's position** Festigung seiner Stellung; ~ **of railway lines** Fusion von Eisenbahngesellschaften; ~ **of shares** Zusammenlegung des Aktienkapitals;
~ **balance sheet** Fusionsbilanz; ~ **excess** Fusionsgewinn; ~ **expenditure** Fusionskosten; ~ **locomotive** *(US)* schwere Güterzuglokomotive; ~ **measures** Konsolidierungsmaßnahmen; ~ **policy** *(balance sheet)* Anwendung der konsolidierten Bilanzmethode; ~ **profit** Fusionsgewinn; ~ **reserve** Konsolidierungsrücklage; ~ **rule** Anordnung der Klageverbindung; ~ **sale** Gemeinschaftsverkauf.

consols *(Br.)* fundierte Staatsanleihe, Staatsrenten;
to consist of ~ aus Staatspapieren bestehen;
~ **certificate** *(Br.)* Staatsanleiheschein; ~ **market** *(Br.)* Markt für Staatsanleihen.

consonance Übereinstimmung;
~ **of opinions** Meinungsgleichheit.

consonant übereinstimmend, vereinbar.

consort Gatte, Gattin, *(ship)* im Geleitzug fahrendes Schiff;
prince ~ Prinzgemahl;
~ *(v.)* umgehen (verkehren) mit; ~ **with criminals** verbrecherischen Umgang haben; ~ **with one's equals** mit Seinesgleichen verkehren.

consortial konsortial.

consortium Konsortium, Syndikat, Gruppe, *(conjugal fellowship)* eheliche Gemeinschaft;
aid ~ Hilfskonsortium;
~ **of banks** Finanz-, Bankenkonsortium; ~ **of companies** Firmenkonsortium, -syndikat;
to head a ~ Konsortialführung haben;
~ **aid** Konsortialhilfe; ~ **partner** Konsortialmitglied.

consortship *(maritime insurance)* Genossenschaftsvereinbarung.

conspectus Abriß, Resümee, Zusammenfassung, Zusammenschau.

conspicuous deutlich, sichtbar, ins Auge fallend, auffällig;
to be ~ by one's absence durch Abwesenheit glänzen; **to make o. s. ~** Aufmerksamkeit auf sich ziehen; **to render o. s. ~** sich hervortun;
~ consumption Prestigekonsum; **to put in a ~ place** an gut sichtbarer Stelle aufhängen; **~ service** hervorragende Dienste.

conspiracy Verschwörung, Komplott, Konspiration;
civil ~ Verabredung zu unerlaubter Handlung; **criminal ~** Verabredung zu einer strafbaren Handlung; **intra-enterprise ~** *(US)* unzulässige Absprache zwischen Konzernchefs;
~ to overthrow the government Verschwörung zum Sturz der Regierung; **~ of silence** Verschwörung des Schweigens;
to be roped into a ~ in eine Verschwörung verwickelt sein; **to discover a ~** Verschwörung aufdecken; **to form a ~** Verschwörung anzetteln.

conspirator Verschwörer, Konspirator, Komplotteilnehmer;
fellow ~ Mitverschwörer.

conspire *(v.)* sich verabreden (verschwören), sich zu strafbarem Tun verabreden, Komplott schmieden;
~ against the government Komplott gegen die Regierung anzetteln (schmieden); **~ to ruin s. o.** sich zu jds. finanziellem Ruin zusammentun.

constable *(Br.)* Schutzmann, Polizist, Polizeibeamter, *(US)* Justizbeamter mit polizeilichen Aufgaben;
chief ~ *(Br.)* Polizeipräsident; **county ~** Gemeindepolizist, Gendarm; **petty ~** *(Br.)* örtlicher Polizeichef; **police ~** Polizeibeamter, Polizist; **special ~** Hilfspolizist; **traffic ~** Verkehrspolizist;
~ of a castle Kastellan;
to authorize a ~ to enter and search the premises Hausdurchsuchungsbefehl für die Polizei ausstellen; **to overrun (outrun) the ~** sich verschulden, sich in Schulden stürzen, über seine Verhältnisse leben.

constablewick örtlicher Polizeibezirk.

constabulary Schutz-, Polizeitruppe, Gendarmerie;
county ~ Gendarmerie.

constancy *(fig.)* Standhaftigkeit, Treue, Unerschütterlichkeit.

constant gleichbleibend, konstant, unveränderlich, *(fig.)* unerschütterlich, verläßlich, treu;
to be ~ to one's friends seinen Freunden die Treue halten; **to be ~ in one's devotion to scientific studies** sich mit beharrlicher Hingabe seinen wissenschaftlichen Aufgaben widmen;
~ capital konstantes Kapital; **~ change** stetiger Wechsel; **~ costs** feste (gleichbleibende, konstante) Kosten; **~ prices** konstante Preise; **~ production** kontinuierliche Produktion; **~ rain** anhaltender Regen; **~ returns to scale** konstante Skalenerträge.

constat *(official)* Aktenvermerk, -notiz.

constellation Konstellation, *(splendid assemblage)* glänzende Versammlung.

consternate *(v.)* verwirren, verblüffen, konsternieren.

consternation Bestürzung.

constituency Wählerschaft, Wahlkreis, *(body of customers, coll.)* Kundenkreis, Kundschaft, *(readership)* Leserkreis, *(subscribers)* Abonnentenkreis;
agricultural ~ ländlicher Wahlkreis; **marginal ~** Wahlkreis mit knapper Mehrheit;
to get in for a ~ sich um einen Wahlkreis bewerben; **to nurse one's ~** sich um seinen Wahlkreis kümmern; **to represent (sit for) a ~** Wahlbezirk vertreten; **to stand for a ~** sich als Kandidat aufstellen lassen;
~ area Wahlbezirk; **~ association** Wählervereinigung; **~ duties** Wahlkreisverpflichtungen; **~ organization** Wahlkreisapparat; **~ parties** im Wahlkreis vertretene Parteien; **~ revision** Wahlkreisrevision, Wahlkreisänderung; **~ work** Wahlkreisarbeit.

constituent *(component part)* Bestandteil, Komponente, *(authorizing person)* Auftraggeber, Vollmachtgeber, Aussteller, *(pol.)* Wähler, Wahlberechtigter;
~ *(a.)* verfassunggebend, konstituierend, *(having powers to elect)* wählend, wahlberechtigt;
~ assembly verfassunggebende Versammlung, Nationalversammlung; **~ body** Wahlkörper, Wählerschaft; **~ company** Gründer-, Tochter-, Konzerngesellschaft; **~ fact** Tatbestandsmerkmal; **~ parts** Bestandteile; **~ population** wahlberechtigte Bevölkerung; **~ power** verfassunggebende Gewalt; **~ states** Gliedstaaten; **~ territories** zugehörige Gebiete; **~ territory of a customs unit** Zollunionsteilnehmerland.

constitute *(v.) (appoint)* beauftragen, bestellen, *(empower)* bevollmächtigen, *(establish)* ernennen, einsetzen, festsetzen, begründen, errichten, *(make up)* ausmachen, bilden, *(parl.)* konstituieren;

~ a committee Ausschuß einsetzen (bilden); **~ completely** rechtsgeschäftlich begründen; **~ s. one's entire estate** jds. ganzen Besitz ausmachen; **~ s. o. one's heir** *(US)* j. zu seinem Erben einsetzen; **~ an indenture a valid, binding and legal agreement** Vereinbarung rechtsgültig gestalten; **~ s. o. a judge** j. als Richter einsetzen; **~ o. s. a judge of conduct** sich als Sittenrichter aufspielen; **~ a leading case** Präzedenzfall bilden; **~ a precedent** Präzedenzfall abgeben; **~ o. s. a party** Partei bilden; **~ a public danger** gemeingefährlich sein; **~ a quorum** Beschlußfähigkeit ergeben, beschlußfähig sein; **~ a tribunal** Gerichtshof einsetzen.

constituted authorities eingesetzte Behörden.

constituting a public danger gemeingefährlich.

constitution [Staats]verfassung, [Staats]grundgesetz, *(appointment)* Ernennung, Bestellung, Beauftragung, *(company)* Satzung, *(physical condition)* Konstitution, *(establishment)* Bildung, Errichtung, *(structure)* Bau, Struktur, Zusammensetzung;
in good ~ in guter Verfassung;
draft ~ Verfassungsentwurf; **economic ~** Wirtschaftsverfassung; **Federal ~** *(US)* Bundesverfassung; **rigid ~** starre (festgelegte) Verfassung; **state ~** Staatsverfassung; **unwritten ~** ungeschriebene Verfassung; **weak ~** schwache Konstitution; **workable ~** brauchbare Verfassung;
~ of a committee Zusammensetzung (Einsetzung) eines Ausschusses; **~ of a court** Bestellung eines Gerichtshofes; **~ of a firm** Firmensatzung; **~ of a quorum** Herstellung der Beschlußfähigkeit;
to abrogate the ~ Verfassung aufheben; **to adopt a ~** Verfassung annehmen; **to amend a ~** Verfassung ändern; **to come within the framework of a ~** unter Verfassungsbestimmungen fallen; **to entrench in a ~** verfassungsrechtlich schützen; **to give a country a ~** einem Land eine Verfassung geben; **to infringe the ~** Verfassungsbruch begehen; **to overthrow a ~** Verfassung aufheben;
~ committee Verfassungsausschuß.

constitutional gesetzes-, verfassungsmäßig, -treu, konstitutionell;
to find s. th. ~ etw. für verfassungskonform halten; **to go for (take) a ~** *(coll.)* Verdauungsspaziergang machen;
~ amendment *(US)* Zusatzartikel zur Verfassung, Verfassungsänderung; **~ basis** verfassungsmäßige Grundlage; **~ charter** Verfassungsurkunde; **~ changes** Verfassungsänderung; **~ committee (convention)** Verfassungsausschuß; **~ complaint** Verfassungsbeschwerde; **~ convention** verfassungsgebende Versammlung, Nationalversammlung; **~ court** Verfassungsgericht, *(US)* ordentliches Bundesgericht; **~ crisis** Verfassungskrise; **~ democracy** Verfassungsdemokratie; **~ expert** Fachmann auf dem Gebiet des Verfassungsrechts; **~ formula** Verfassungsvorschrift; **~ framework** Verfassungssystem; **~ government** konstitutionelle Staatsform, verfassungsmäßige Regierung; **on ~ grounds** auf Grund verfassungsrechtlicher Bedenken; **~ guarantee** in die Verfassung eingebaute Garantien; **~ issue** Verfassungsproblem; **~ law** Verfassungs-, Grundgesetz, Verfassungsrecht; **~ liberty** von der Verfassung gewährleistete Freiheit; **~ limitations** verfassungsrechtliche Beschränkungen; **~ means** verfassungsgemäße Mittel; **~ monarchy** konstitutionelle Monarchie; **~ order** verfassungsmäßige Ordnung; **~ power** verfassungsmäßige Gewalt; **~ principle** Verfassungsgrundsatz; **~ provision** Verfassungsbestimmung; **~ reality** Verfassungswirklichkeit; **~ referendum** in der Verfassung vorgesehene Volksbefragung; **~ reform** Verfassungsreform; **~ right** verfassungsmäßig garantiertes Recht, Grundrecht; **to give a ~ rubberstamp** verfassungsmäßig absegnen; **~ rules** vom Parlament kontrollierter Herrscher; **~ solution** verfassungsmäßig durchführbare Lösung; **~ state** Rechtsstaat; **~ statement** verfassungsrechtliche Auslegung; **~ system** Verfassungssystem; **~ weakness** konstitutionelle Schwäche.

constitutionalism Konstitutionalismus, verfassungsmäßige Regierungsform.

constitutionalist Anhänger der konstitutionellen Regierungsform, Verfassungsanhänger, -rechtler.

constitutionality Verfassungsmäßigkeit.

constitutionalize *(v.)* konstitutionell machen.

constitutionally, to be ~ appointed nach den Verfassungsbestimmungen ernannt werden; **to be ~ barred from seeking a third term as governor** aus verfassungsrechtlichen Gründen nicht ein drittes Mal für den Gouverneursposten kandidieren können.

constitutive gesetzgebend, konstituierend, konstitutiv;
~ effect rechterzeugende Wirkung.

constrain *(v.)* zwingen, nötigen.
constrained gezwungen, unnatürlich;
~ **manner** geziertes Wesen.
constraint Zwang, Zwangslage, Nötigung, *(fig.)* Verlegenheit, Befangenheit, Zurückhaltung;
under ~ gezwungen, zwangsweise;
to act under ~ unter Druck (in einer Zwangslage) handeln; **to put s. o. under** ~ j. unter Druck setzen; **to show** ~ **in s. one's presence** sich in jds. Gegenwart betont zurückhalten; **to speak with** ~ zurückhaltend sprechen.
constricted outlook beschränkte Sicht, beengter Gesichtskreis.
construct *(v.)* bauen, konstruieren, entwerfen;
~ **an aircraft** Flugzeug konstruieren; ~ **a building** Gebäude errichten; ~ **a factory** Fabrik bauen; ~ **a theory** Theorie ausarbeiten.
construction Gebilde, *(act of constructing)* Bau, Errichtung, Aufführung, Konstruktion, *(building)* Gebäude, Bauwerk, Baulichkeit, Anlage, *(grammar)* Satzbau, *(interpretation)* Deutung, Auslegung, *(method of building)* Bauweise;
under ~ im Bau [befindlich];
artificial ~ gekünstelte Auslegung; **building** ~ Gebäudeerrichtung; **conventional** ~ konventionelle Bauweise; **equitable** ~ großzügige Auslegung; **extensive** ~ weite Auslegung; **factory** ~ Bau von Fabriken; **faulty** ~ Fehlkonstruktion; **housing** ~ Wohnungsbau; **judicial** ~ rechtliche Auslegung; **liberal** ~ weite Auslegung; **modern** ~ moderne Konstruktion; **narrow** ~ enge Auslegung; **private residential** ~ freifinanzierter Wohnungsbau; **public** ~ öffentliche Bautätigkeit, öffentlich geförderter Wohnungsbau; **residential** ~ Wohnungsbau[wesen]; **road** ~ Straßenbau; **skeleton building** ~ Stahlgerüstkonstruktion; **strict** ~ enge Auslegung;
~ **of a building** Errichtung eines Gebäudes, Gebäudeerrichtung; ~ **of a contract** Vertragsauslegung; ~ **of documents** Urkundeninterpretation; ~ **under licence** Nachbau; ~**s in progress** im Bau befindliche Anlagen, Anlagen im Bau; ~ **of new roads** Neubau von Straßen, Straßenneubau; ~ **of a sentence** Urteilsauslegung; ~ **of a vessel** Schiffsbau; ~ **of a will** Testamentsauslegung;
to be of very solid ~ sehr solide gebaut sein; **to be still under** ~ noch im Bau sein; **to put another** ~ **on s. one's words** jds. Worte ganz anders auslegen; **to put a wrong** ~ **on s. one's action** jds. Handlungsweise falsch auslegen;
~ **account** Baukonto, -rechnung; ~ **activity** Bautätigkeit; ~ **agreement** *(bargaining)* Tarifabkommen der Bauindustrie; ~ **amount** Baukonto; ~ **authority** Baufachmann; ~ **bond** Kaution eines Bauunternehmers; ~ **camp** Bauarbeiterlager; ~ **car** Materialwagen; ~ **code** Bauverordnung; ~ **company** Baufirma; ~ **contract** öffentlicher Bauauftrag; ~ **contract award** Bauvergabe, -auftragserteilung; ~ **costs** Baukosten; ~ **cost index** Baukostenindex; ~ **department** Bauabteilung; ~ **earnings** Einnahmen der Bauwirtschaft; ~ **employment** Beschäftigung in der Bauindustrie; ~ **engineer** Bauingenieur; ~ **engineering** Bauwesen, -technik; ~ **equipment** Baugerät; ~ **financing** Baufinanzierung; ~ **industry** Bauwirtschaft, -industrie, -gewerbe; **to zero in on the** ~ **industry** mit der Bauindustrie den Anfang machen; ~ **job** Bautätigkeit; ~ **loan** Baudarlehen; ~ **machine** Baumaschine; ~ **machines industry** Baumaschinenindustrie; ~ **market** Baumarkt; ~ **material** Baumaterial; ~ **mortgage** Bauhypothek; ~ **pay** Bauarbeiterlöhne; ~ **prices** Baupreise, -kosten; **correctly costed** ~ **program(me)** sorgfältig kalkuliertes Bauprogramm; ~ **project** Anlage-, Bauprojekt; **public** ~ **project** öffentliches Bauvorhaben; **to keep the** ~ **sector afloat** Bauwirtschaft gerade noch aufrechterhalten; ~**s services** Leistungsangebot auf dem Bausektor; ~ **set** Baukosten; ~ **site** Baugelände; ~ **spending** Investitionen auf dem Bausektor; ~ **strike** Bauarbeiterstreik; **modern** ~ **techniques** moderne Bauverfahren; ~ **time** Bauzeit; ~ **train** Baumaterialienzug; ~ **volume** Bauvolumen; ~ **wages** Bauarbeiterlöhne; ~ **wage increase** Anstieg der Bauarbeiterlöhne; ~ **work** Bauarbeiten; ~ **work stoppage** Einstellung der Bautätigkeit; ~ **worker** Bauarbeiter; ~ **yard** Baugelände.
constructional bau-, konstruktionstechnisch;
~ **defect** *(machine)* Konstruktionsfehler; ~ **engineer** Maschinenbauingenieur; ~ **engineering** Maschinenbau; ~ **features** Konstruktionsmerkmale; ~ **iron** Moniereisen; ~ **steel** Baustahl; ~ **trade** Baugewerbe.
constructive baulich, *(law)* präsumtiv, hypothetisch, angenommen, fingiert;
to be ~ **at a meeting** sich bei einer Sitzung konstruktiv verhalten;
~ **abandonment** mittelbare Besitzaufgabe; ~ **assent** aus dem Verhalten zu entnehmende Zustimmung; ~ **authority**

Anscheinsvollmacht; ~ **breaking into a house** einbruchsähnliche Tatbestände; ~ **conversion** imaginäres Zubehör; ~ **crime** strapazierter Verbrechenstatbestand; **to claim** ~ **damages** Ersatz des mittelbaren Schadens verlangen; ~ **delivery** mittelbare Besitzverschaffung; **to constitute** ~ **delivery** mittelbaren Besitz verschaffen; ~ **eviction** *(law)* faktische Exmittierung; ~ **features** Konstruktionsmerkmale; ~ **form** Baustil, -form; ~ **fraud** Unterschlagung, Untreue, *(law of contract)* sittenwidriges Geschäft; ~ **injury** fingierter Schaden; ~ **[total] loss** *(marine insurance)* fingierter Totalverlust; ~ **malice** vermutete böse Absicht; ~ **milage** *(US)* Reisegeldpauschale für Kongreßmitglieder; ~ **murder** Mord kraft gesetzlicher Fiktion; ~ **notice** fahrlässige Unkenntnis, zurechenbare Kenntnis; ~ **ownership** wirtschaftlicher Besitz; ~ **possession** fingierter (gesetzlich vermuteter, mittelbarer) Besitz; ~ **receipt of income** *(taxation)* als im Vorjahr zugeflossen behandeltes Einkommen; ~ **seizure** Beschlagnahme durch Veräußerung; ~ **side of the market** *(US)* Haussepartei; ~ **suggestion** konstruktiver Vorschlag; ~ **taking** Aneignung für eigene Zwecke, Absicht der rechtswidrigen Zueignung; ~ **trade** Baugewerbe; ~ **treason** als Hochverrat geltende Verschwörung; ~ **trust** fingiertes Treuhandeigentum; ~ **wilfulness** bewußt in Kauf genommene Leichtfertigkeit; ~ **work** Kunstbauten.
constructor Erbauer, Konstrukteur.
construe *(v.)* auslegen, deuten;
~ **a clause extensively** Bestimmung weit auslegen; ~ **a foreign language into English** ausländische Sprache ins Englische übersetzen; ~ **a law** Gesetz auslegen; ~ **restrictively** eng auslegen; **an unskil(l)fully drawn will** unsachgemäßes Testament auslegen; ~ **wrongly** falsch auslegen.
consuetude Gewohnheit, Brauch.
consuetudinary gewohnheitsmäßig;
~ **law** *(US)* Gewohnheitsrecht.
consul Konsul;
career ~ Berufskonsul; ~ **general** Generalkonsul; **honorary** ~ Wahl-, Honorarkonsul; **trading** ~ Wahlkonsul; **vice** ~ Vizekonsul;
~ **of career** Berufskonsul;
to recognize a ~ Konsul formell anerkennen.
consulage Konsulatsgebühren.
consular konsularisch;
~ **affairs** Konsulatsangelegenheiten; ~ **agency** konsularische Vertretung; ~ **agent** Konsularvertreter; ~ **appointment** konsularische Ernennung; ~ **archives** Konsulatsbehörde; ~ **assignment** konsularisches Aufgabengebiet; ~ **authority** Konsulatsbehörde; ~ **certificate** Konsulatsbescheinigung; ~ **convention** Konsularabkommen, -vertrag; ~ **corps** konsularisches Korps; ~ **court** Konsulatsgericht; ~ **deal** Konsularabkommen; ~ **department** Konsulatsabteilung; ~ **district** Konsulatsbezirk; ~ **documents** Konsulatspapiere, -fakturen; ~ **employee** Konsulatsangehöriger; ~ **fees** Konsulatsgebühren; ~ **flag** Konsulatsflagge; ~ **functions** konsulare Aufgaben, Konsulatsfunktionen; **to prepare a** ~ **invoice** Konsulatsfaktura ausstellen; **to get the** ~ **invoices legalized** Konsulatsfakturen beglaubigen lassen; ~ **jurisdiction** Konsulargerichtsbarkeit; ~ **office** Konsulat; ~ **officer** Konsulatsbeamter; ~ **post** Konsulatsposten; ~ **power** konsularische Gewalt; ~ **program(me)** Konsulatsprogramm; ~ **protection** konsularischer Schutz; ~ **rank** konsularischer Rang; ~ **receipts** Konsulatseinnahmen; ~ **regulations** Konsulatsvorschriften; ~ **relations** konsularische Beziehungen; ~ **report** Konsulatsbericht; ~ **representative** konsularischer Vertreter; ~ **revenues** Konsulatseinnahmen; ~ **salary** Gehalt eines Konsuls; ~ **seal** Konsulatssiegel; ~ **section** Konsulatsabteilung; ~ **service** konsularischer Dienst, Konsulatsdienst; ~ **status** Konsularstatus; ~ **system** Konsulatssystem; ~ **title** konsularischer Titel; ~ **transactions** konsularische Amtshandlungen; ~ **treaty** Konsularabkommen; ~ **visa** Sichtvermerk.
consulate Konsulat;
~ **general** Generalkonsulat.
consult *(v.)* *(call in as adviser)* [als Berater] zuziehen, *(consider)* in Erwägung ziehen, berücksichtigen, im Auge haben, *(seek advice from)* zu Rate ziehen, sich beraten lassen, um Rat fragen, konsultieren;
~ **with** Rücksprache nehmen mit;
~ **one's own advantage** seinen eigenen Vorteil bedenken; ~ **a barrister** Anwalt zuziehen; ~ **books** in Büchern nachschlagen; ~ **s. one's convenience** jem. so wenig Ungelegenheiten wie möglich machen; ~ **a dictionary** in einem Wörterbuch nachschlagen; ~ **a doctor** Arzt aufsuchen (konsultieren); ~ **documents** Urkunden einsehen; ~ **official documents** Akten

einsehen; ~ **an expert** Sachverständigen zu Rate ziehen; ~ **one's own interests** an sich selbst denken, auf seinen Vorteil bedacht sein; ~ **one's lawyer** sich mit einem Anwalt beraten (besprechen); ~ **the relevant literature** einschlägige Literatur heranziehen; ~ **a map** Karte studieren; ~ **about a matter** Beratung über einen Fall abhalten; ~ **one's notes** seine Notizen heranziehen; ~ **records** Akten beiziehen; ~ **one's watch** nach der Uhr sehen; ~ **with one's fellow workers** sich mit seinen Mitarbeitern absprechen (beraten).

consultancy Beratungstätigkeit;
engineering ~ technischer Beratungsdienst; **management** ~ Beratung des Vorstands;
~ **agreement** Beratungsvertrag; ~ **division** Beratungsabteilung; ~ **fees** Beratungsgebühren; ~ **organization** Beratungsfirma; ~ **services** Beratungstätigkeit, -dienst.

consultant [ständiger] Gutachter, [technischer] Berater;
actuarial ~ versicherungsstatistische Autorität; **economic** ~ Wirtschaftsberater; **industrial** ~ Industrieberater; **labo(u)r relations** ~ Berater in Gewerkschaftsfragen; **political** ~ politischer Berater; **public relations** ~ Berater in Fragen der Öffentlichkeitsarbeit; **tax** ~ Steuerberater;
~ **on business policy** Berater der Geschäftsleitung; ~ **to industry** Industrieberater;
to be retained for three years as ~ dreijährigen Beratungsvertrag bekommen;
~ **economist** Wirtschaftsberater; ~ **engineer** beratender Ingenieur; ~ **fees** Beratungsgebühren; ~ **field** Beratungswesen; ~ **member** beratendes Mitglied; ~ **service** Beratungsdienst; **inhouse** ~ **unit** betriebliche Beratergruppe.

consultary response gutachtliche Äußerung eines Gerichts.

consultation Rücksprache, Beratung, Konsultation, Fühlungnahme;
after ~ **with my colleagues** nach Rücksprache mit meinen Mitarbeitern; **on** ~ **with** im Benehmen mit;
legal ~ juristische Beratung;
~ **of books** Benutzung von Büchern; ~ **of a dictionary** Nachschlagen im Wörterbuch; ~ **of documents** Einsichtnahme in Urkunden; ~**s on cabinet level** Konsultationen (Beratungen) auf Regierungsebene;
to ask ~ **of s. o.** j. um seinen Rat bitten; **to enter into** ~**s** mit den Beratungen beginnen; **to hold a** ~ Beratung abhalten; **to hold** ~ **with s. o.** sich mit jem. ins Benehmen setzen;
~ **committee** Beratungsausschuß; ~ **fees** Beratungskosten, -gebühren.

consultative (a.) beratend;
⌐ **Assembly of the Council of Europe** Beratende Versammlung des Europarates; **in** ~ **capacity** in beratender Eigenschaft; ~ **committee** beratender Ausschuß; ~ **group** Beratergremium; ~ **pact** Konsultativpakt; ~ **powers** Beratungsbefugnisse; ~ **supervision** (management) in Form der Beratung ausgeübte Aufsicht.

consulting, after ~ **with** nach Rücksprache mit; **upon** ~ **our records** bei Durchsicht unserer Bücher;
-- (a.) beratend;
~ **agreement** Beratungsvertrag; ~ **barrister** (Br.) beratender (plädierender) Anwalt; ~ **days** Sprechtage; ~ **engineer** beratender Ingenieur, technischer Berater; ~ **engineering firm** Industrieberatung; ~ **fee** Beratungsgebühr; ~ **field** Beratungsgebiet, -wesen; ~ **firm** Beratungsfirma; ~ **hour** [ärztliche] Sprechstunde; ~ **organization** Unternehmensberatung, Beratungsfirma; **to farm out to a** ~ **organization** an eine Beratungsfirma gegen Sonderhonorar vergeben; ~ **outfit** Beratungsagentur; ~ **room** Sprechzimmer; ~ **service** Beratungsdienst.

consumable verbrauchbar, konsumierbar;
~ **goods** Verbrauchswaren, -güter.

consume (v.) verbrauchen, konsumieren, aufbrauchen, (waste) verschwenden;
~ **away with grief** an Kummer dahinsiechen; ~ **one's fortune** Vermögen durchbringen; ~ **a lot of oil** (car) viel Öl verbrauchen, starken Ölverbrauch haben.

consumed, to be vergriffen sein;
~ **quantity** Verbrauchsmenge.

consumer Verbraucher, Konsument, Abnehmer, Kunde;
average ~ Durchschnittsverbraucher; **bulk** ~ Großverbraucher; **domestic** ~ Inlandsverbraucher; **final** ~ End-, Letztverbraucher; **high-income** ~ potenter Kunde; **household** ~ Haushaltsverbraucher; **industrial** ~ gewerblicher Verbraucher (Abnehmer); **large-scale** ~ Großverbraucher; **manufacturing** ~ gewerblicher Verbraucher; **principle** ~ Hauptverbraucher; **prospective** ~ potentieller Kunde; **ultimate** ~ End-, Letztverbraucher;

procedures and ~**s** Produzenten und Konsumenten;
~ **of electricity** Stromabnehmer, -verbraucher;
to let ~**s in on the shopping tips** der Verbraucherschaft Einblick in die Kaufneigungen geben; **to pass increased labo(u)r costs on to** ~**s** Lohnkostenerhöhung auf die Verbraucher abwälzen;
~**s' ability to buy** Konsumentenkaufkraft; ~ **acceptance** Konsum-, Kaufbereitschaft, Aufnahmebereitschaft; ~ **activist** Verbraucherrepräsentant; ~ **advertisement (advertising)** Kunden-, Endverbraucherwerbung; ~ **advertiser** Endverbraucherwerbung betreibendes Unternehmen; ~ **advisory council** (Br.) Verbraucherausschuß; ~ **advisory service** Verbraucherberatungsdienst; ~ **advocate** Verbraucheranwalt; ~ **affluence** Verbraucherüberschuß; ~ **assembly** Verbrauchertagung; ~ **association** Verbraucherverband; ~ **attitude** Einstellung des Verbrauchers; ~ **behavio(u)r** Konsum-, Verbraucherverhalten; ~ **behavio(u)r probing** Studie über das Verbraucherverhalten; ~ **board** Verbraucherkomitee; ~ **boom** Konsum-, Verbrauchsgüterkonjunktur; ~ **boycott** Verbraucherboykott; ~ **buying** Verbrauchsnachfrage; ~ **buying habit** Verbrauchergewohnheiten; ~ **buying survey** Verbraucherumfrage; ~**s' capital** Konsumvermögen; ~ **capital-type goods** verbrauchsnahe Investitionsgüter; ~ **caution** Zurückhaltung auf der Verbraucherseite; ~ **center** Verbraucherzentrum; ~**'s choice** Verbraucherwahl; ~ **clampdown** Verbrauchskontrolle; ~ **colo(u)r preference** Farbenbevorzugung durch die Verbraucherschaft; ~ **complaints** Verbraucherbeschwerden; ~ **confidence** Zuversicht der Verbraucherschaft; ~**-conscious** verbraucherbewußt, -freundlich; ~ **consciousness** Verbraucherbewußtsein, -freundlichkeit; ~ **contest** Kundenwettbewerb; ~ **cooperation** Genossenschaftswesen; ~ **cooperative** Konsumgenossenschaft; ~ **cooperative store** Konsum[laden]; ~ **counselling** Kunden-, Verbraucherberatung.

consumer credit Verbraucher-, Konsumenten-, Kundenkredit;
~ **advertising** Konsumentenkreditwerbung; ~ **agency** Abzahlungs-, Finanzierungs-, Warenkreditgesellschaft; ~ **control** Konsumptivkreditlenkung; ~ **industry** Konsumptivkreditwirtschaft; ~ **restrictions** Konsumtivkreditbeschränkungen.

consumer|crusade Verbraucherfeldzug; ~ **decision** Verbraucherentscheidung; ~ **demand** Verbrauchernachfrage; ~ **deposit** Kundenguthaben; ~ **desire** Verbraucherwunsch; ~ **dissatisfaction** Unzufriedenheit der Verbraucherschaft; ~ **durables** langlebige Gebrauchs-, Konsumgüter; ~ **economics** Verbraucherwirtschaft; ~ **education** Verbrauchererziehung; ~ **enterprise** Konsumbetrieb; ~ **expenditure** Verbraucheraufwand, gesamtwirtschaftliche Konsumausgaben; ~ **expenditure study** Untersuchung über die Verbraucherausgaben; ~ **finance company** (US) Teilzahlungsbank; ~ **financing** Konsumentenfinanzierung.

consumer|['s] goods Konsum-, Verbrauchsgüter;
industrial ~ gewerbliche Verbrauchsgüter; **long-life** ~ langlebige Konsumgüter; **low unit-priced** ~ billige Einheitspreiskonsumgüter; **nondurable** ~ kurzlebige Verbrauchsgüter; **perishable** ~ kurzlebige Konsum-, Verbrauchsgüter;
~ **advertising** Konsumwerbung; ~ **boom** Konsumgüterkonjunktur; ~ **company** Unternehmen der Konsumgüterindustrie; ~ **industry** Bedarfs-, Konsumgüterindustrie; ~ **leasing** Konsumgüterleasing; ~ **sector** Konsum-, Verbrauchsgüterbereich, -sektor.

consumer|group Konsumenten-, Verbrauchergruppe; ~ **guidance** Verbraucheraufklärung; ~ **habits** Verbrauchergewohnheiten, Konsumverhalten; ~ **hard goods** langlebige Konsumgüter; ~ **income** Verbrauchereinkommen; ~ **industry** Konsumgüterindustrie; ~ **information** Verbraucherinformationen; ~ **inquiry** Verbraucherbefragung; ~ **insistence** Markentreue; ~ **instalment debts** Verschuldung auf der Verbraucherseite; ~ **instal(l)ment credit (loan)** Kunden-, Abzahlungskredit; ~ **interest** Verbraucherinteresse; ~ **interview** Verbraucherinterview; ~ **investigation** Untersuchung des Verbrauchermarktes; ~ **item** Gebrauchs-, Konsumartikel; ~ **jury test** Wirkungsprüfung durch ausgewählte Verbraucher; ~ **level** Verbraucherstufe; ~ **loan company** (US) Finanzierungsgesellschaft für Kleinkredite; ~ **loan rates** Abzahlungskreditsätze; ~ **magazine** Verbraucherzeitschrift; ~ **mail panel** postalische Verbraucherbefragung; ~ **market** Konsum-, Verbrauchsgütermarkt; ~ **market analysis** Analyse des Verbrauchermarktes; ~ **member** Mitglied einer Verbrauchergenossenschaft; ~**-minded** verbraucherfreundlich; ~ **motivation** Verbrauchermotivierung; ~ **movement** Verbraucherbewegung; ~ **nation** Verbraucherland; ~ **need** Verbraucherbedürfnis; **daily** ~ **needs** täglicher Konsumbedarf; ~ **nondurables** kurzlebige Verbrauchsgüter; ~ **optimism** Verbraucheroptimismus; ~ **organization** Verbraucherorganisation, -verband; **~orientated** konsumbewußt, -orientiert; **~ orientation** Konsumorientierung; **~ panel** repräsentative Verbrauchergruppe; **~'s actual car buying performance** Verbraucheraufwendungen für Autoanschaffungen; **~'s preference** Bevorzugung durch den Verbraucher; **~ price** Konsumenten-, Verbraucherpreis; **ultimate ~ price** Endverbraucherpreis; **~ price index** Verbraucherpreis-, Lebenshaltungsindex; **~ problem** Verbraucherproblem; **~ products** Konsumgüter, Verbrauchererzeugnisse; **~ promotion** Verkaufsförderung beim Endverbraucher; **~ prosperity** Verbraucherkonjunktur; **~ protection** Verbraucherschutz; **~ protection act** Verbraucherschutzgesetz; **~ protection committee** Verbraucherausschuß; **~ protection advisory committee** Beratungsausschuß für Verbrauchschutzfragen; **~ protection legislation** Gesetzgebung zum Schutz der Verbraucher; **~ protection office** Verbraucherschutzstelle; **~ psychology** Verbraucherpsychologie; **~ publication** Publikumszeitschrift; **~ purchasing** Verbrauchsnachfrage; **~ purchasing behavio(u)r** Kaufverhalten des Konsumenten; **~ purchasing motives** Kaufmotive des Konsumenten; **~ purchasing power** Konsumentenkaufkraft; **~ quantity** Verbrauchsmenge; **~s' rent** Konsumentenrente; **~ research** Kunden-, Verbraucheranalyse, Verbraucherbefragung, Konsumforschung; **~ resistance** Käuferunlust, Zurückhaltung der Verbraucher; **~s' risk** Verbraucherrisiko; **~'s role** Stellung des Verbrauchers; **~ sales** Kundenverkäufe; **~ sample** Verbraucherstichprobe; **~ sentiment** Verbraucheransichten; **~ service** Kundendienst; **~ share** Verbraucheranteil; **~ side** Verbraucherseite; **~ society** *(Br.)* Konsumgenossenschaft; **~ sovereignty** Konsumentensouveränität, Verbrauchermacht; **~ spending** Konsum-, Verbrauchsaufwendung, -aufwand, konsumptive Ausgaben; **~ spending slowdown** abnehmende Kauflust der Verbraucherschaft; **~ spending spree** Ausgabenfreudigkeit der Verbraucherschaft; **~s' strike** Verbraucherstreik; **~ studies** Untersuchungen des Verbrauchermarktes; **~ subsidiary** Konsumgütergesellschaft; **~'s surplus** Konsumenten-, Verbraucherrechte; **~ survey** Verbraucherumfrage, Verbraucher-, Konsumentenbefragung; **~'s taste** Kundengeschmack; **~ test** Warentest; **~ traffic** Kundenverkehr; **~s' union** Konsumentenverband; **~ unit** Verbrauchereinheit; **~ wants** Kunden-, Verbraucherwünsche; **~s' wealth** Wohlstand der Verbraucher.

consumerism Verbraucherherrschaft.
consumerite Vertreter der Verbraucherschaft.
consuming | area Verbrauchsgebiet; **~ country** Bedarfsland; **~ habits** Verbrauchergewohnheiten; **~ industry** Verbrauchsindustrie; **~ market** Verbrauchsmarkt; **~ public** Verbraucherschaft; **~ region** Verbrauchsgebiet; **~ state** Verbraucherstaat; **~ unit** Verbrauchseinheit.
consummate *(v.)* **| a marriage** Ehe vollziehen; **~ a sale** Verkauf abschließen;
~ *(a.)* vollendet, vollständig;
with ~ art mit künstlerischer Vollendung; **to be a ~ master of one's craft** sein Handwerk restlos beherrschen; **~ scoundrel** abgefeimter Gauner.
consummation Vollendung, Erfüllung;
~ of one's ambition Erfüllung seines Ehrgeizes; **~ of a deal** Geschäftsabschluß; **~ of a life's work** Abschluß einer Lebensarbeit; **~ of a marriage** Vollziehung der Ehe.
consumption Verbrauch, Verzehr, Konsum, Konsum, Konsumierung, Bedarf, Absatz, *(waste)* Verschwendung;
for ~ on the premises zum Verzehr an Ort und Stelle; **unfit for human ~** für die menschliche Ernährung ungeeignet;
additional ~ Mehrverbrauch; **annual ~** Jahresverbrauch; **conspicuous ~** demonstrativer Konsum, Geltungskonsum; **daily ~** Tagesverbrauch; **decreased ~** Verbrauchsrückgang; **domestic ~** Inlandsverbrauch, -bedarf; **everyday ~** täglicher Bedarf; **excess ~** übermäßiger Verbrauch, Mehrverbrauch; **final ~** unproduktiver Verbrauch, Endverbrauch; **fuel ~** Kraftstoff-, Benzinverbrauch; **government ~** staatlicher Bedarf; **high-mass ~** Massenkonsum; **home ~** Inlands-, Eigenverbrauch; **increased ~** Konsum-, Verbrauchssteigerung; **industrial ~** gewerblicher Verbrauch; **internal ~** Inlands-, Selbstverbrauch; **local ~** Platzbedarf; **low oil ~** *(car)* geringer Ölverbrauch; **nominal ~** Verbrauchssoll; **normal ~** üblicher Verbrauch; **overall ~** Gesamtverbrauch; **peacetime ~** Friedensbedarf; **per capita ~** pro-Kopf-Verbrauch; **personal ~** privater Verbrauch, Eigenverbrauch; **power ~** Stromverbrauch; **private ~** Eigen-, Selbstverbrauch; **productive ~** produktiver Verbrauch; **seasonal ~** Saisonbedarf; **total ~** Gesamtverbrauch; **unproductive ~** unproduktiver Verbrauch;

~ of beer Bierverbrauch, -konsum; **~ in bulk** Massenverbrauch; **~ of costs** Kostenverzehr; **total ~ of current** Gesamtstromverbrauch; **~ of electricity** Stromverbrauch; **~ of a fortune** Vermögensverschleuderung; **~ of material** Materialverbrauch; **~ on the spot** Platzkonsum; **~ in use** Substanzverzehr;
to enter goods for ~ Waren zum freien Verzehr einführen; **to gallop to high ~** hohe Verbrauchszahlen erreichen; **to increase ~** Verbrauch steigern; **to keep personal ~ down** privaten Verbrauch einschränken; **to maintain high ~** Verbrauchskonjunktur aufrechterhalten; **to reduce ~** Verbrauch einschränken; **to withdraw goods from warehouse for ~** Waren aus dem Zollager zum freien Verkauf offerieren;
~ area Konsum-, Verbrauchsgebiet; **~ capacity** Konsumkraft, Kaufkraft einer Verbraucherschicht; **~ capital** Konsumgüter; **~ control** Verbrauchslenkung; **~ credit** Konsumenten-, Konsumtivkredit; **~ differential** unterschiedlicher Verbrauch; **~ economy** Verbrauchswirtschaft; **free ~ entry** freie Einfuhr zum sofortigen persönlichen Verzehr bestimmter Waren; **~ excess** Mehrverbrauch; **~ expenditure** Konsumaufwand, Ausgaben für den Lebensunterhalt; **~ figures** Verbrauchsziffern; **~ function** Konsumfunktion; **~ gain** Konsumzuwachs; **~ goods** Konsum-, Verbrauchsgüter; **~ goods industry** Bedarfs-, Verbrauchsgüterindustrie; **~ line** Verbrauchskurve; **~ loan** Konsumenten-, Verbraucherkredit; **~ market** Verbrauchermarkt; **public ~ monopoly** staatliches Verbrauchermonopol; **~ patterns** Verbrauchsgewohnheiten; **~ prospect** Konsumvorschau; **~ ratio** Konsumquote; **~ record** Verbrauchsrekord; **~ shifts** Verbrauchsumschichtungen; **~ standard** Verbrauchseinheit; **~ tax** Verbrauchsabgabe, -steuer; **~ test** Benzinverbrauchstest; **~ trend** Verbrauchsrichtung, -trend; **~ unit** Verbrauchseinheit; **~ value** Verbrauchswert; **~ voucher** Bedarfsdeckungsschein.
consumptive | demand Konsumentenbedarf; **~ power** Verbrauchs-, Konsumkraft.
contact Berührung, Beziehung, Verbindung, Fühlung[nahme], Kontakt, *(el.)* Anschluß, Kontakt, *(med.)* Kontaktperson, Ansteckungsverdächtiger, *(mil.)* Feindberührung;
business ~s geschäftliche Kontakte; **close ~** enger Kontakt; **established ~s** hergestellte Verbindungen; **face-to-face ~** persönlicher Kontakt; **initial ~** erste Kontaktaufnahme; **personal ~** persönliche Kontaktaufnahme;
~ with other cargo Berührung mit anderen Ladungen; **~ with the enemy** Feindberührung;
~ *(v.)* in Verbindung setzen mit, Fühlung nehmen, Kontakt (Verbindung) aufnehmen, kontaktieren, geschäftliche Beziehungen aufnehmen;
~ s. o. by mail mit jem. brieflich in Verbindung treten;
to be in ~ with s. o. mit jem. in Fühlungnahme sein; **to be in close ~ with s. o.** enge Fühlung mit jem. haben; **to break ~** *(el.)* Stromkreis unterbrechen; **to enter into ~ with s. o.** mit jem. in Verbindung treten; **to establish (make) ~s** Verbindungen anknüpfen (herstellen), Fühlung (Verbindung) aufnehmen; **to make ~** *(el.)* Strom einschalten; **to make personal ~s** persönliche Fühlung nehmen; **to make useful social ~s** sich gute Beziehungen verschaffen;
~ breaker *(el.)* Stromunterbrecher, -ausschalter; **~ flight** Flug mit Bodensicht; **~ interview** Kontakt-, Kurzinterview; **~ lens** Kontaktschale; **~ man** Kontakt-, Verbindungsmann, Kontaktperson, Behördenvermittler; **~ mail panel** postalische Verbraucherbefragung; **~ mine** *(mil.)* Tretmine; **~ point** Kontaktstelle; **~ print** *(photo)* Kontaktstreifen.
contacting Kontaktieren.
contactual survey Kontaktumfrage.
contagion Ansteckung, ansteckende Krankheit, Seuche, Verseuchung, *(fig.)* ansteckender Einfluß.
contagious *(disease)* direkt übertragbar, ansteckend, *(example)* ansprechend;
~ disease ansteckende Krankheit, Seuche; **~ matter** Krankheitsstoff.
contain *(v.)* enthalten, fassen, *(forces, mil.)* binden, *(pol.)* eindämmen;
~ s. one's enthusiasm jds. Begeisterung bremsen.
container [Versand]behälter, Kanister;
food ~ Lebensmittelbehälter; **freight ~** Frachtbehälter; **heavily shielded ~** strahlungssicherer Behälter; **shipping ~** Versandbehälter; **small ~** Kleinbehälter;
to handle ~s Großbehälter verladen;
~ berth Behälteranlegestelle; **~ car** Behälterwagen; **~ car service** Behälterverkehr; **~ facilities** Behälteranlagen, -einrichtungen; **~ lot** *(carrier)* Behälterpartien; **~ operation** Behälterbetrieb; **~ premium** mehrfach verwendbarer Warenbehälter; **~**

service Behälterverkehr; ~ **ship** Behälterschiff; ~ **shipment** Behälterfrachtversand, -verkehr; ~ **terminal** Behälterbahnhof; ~ **traffic** Behälterverkehr; ~ **train** Behälterzug.

containerization Behälterisierung.

containerize *(v.)* in Behältern transportieren (verpacken).

containing action *(mil.)* Bindung von Feindkräften, Befriedungsaktion.

containment Eindämmungspolitik.

contaminate *(v.)* verunreinigen, verschmutzen, [radioaktiv] verseuchen, infizieren.

contamination Verunreinigung, Verschmutzung, [radioaktive] Verseuchung, Infizierung;
~ **of rivers** Verseuchung der Flüsse; ~ **of the water supply** Verseuchung der Wasserversorgung.

contango *(Br., stock trade)* Report[prämie], Prolongationsgebühr, Kursaufschlag, Aufgeld, Kostgeschäft;
~ *(v.) (Br.)* Reportgeschäfte machen;
~ **business** *(Br.)* Report-, Kost-, Prolongationsgeschäft; ~ **day** *(Br.)* Reporttag; ~ **money** *(Br.)* Prolongationskosten; ~ **rate** *(Br.)* Prolongationsgebühr.

contemplate *(v.)* Absicht haben, erwägen, vorhaben;
~ **a state of war** für den Kriegsfall vorgesehen sein; ~ **a visit** Besuch ins Auge fassen.

contemplation Erwägung, Vorhaben, *(law)* Vorsatz, rechtsgeschäftliche Absicht;
in ~ **of death** *(estate tax)* im Hinblick auf den Todesfall;
~ **of bankruptcy** Konkursvorsatz; ~ **of insolvency** vorsätzliche Herbeiführung der Zahlungsunfähigkeit;
to have a new novel in ~ Gedanken über einen neuen Roman anstellen.

contemplative life beschauliches Leben.

contemporaneous gleichzeitig, *(in the same period)* zeitgenössisch;
~ **performance** Erfüllung Zug um Zug.

contemporary Zeit-, Altersgenosse;
~ *(a.)* zeitgenössisch, gleichaltrig;
~ **events** Gegenwartsgeschehen; ~ **record of events** zeitgenössischer Bericht; ~ **style** zeitgenössischer Stil.

contemporize *(v.)* zeitlich zusammenfallen.

contempt Ver-, Mißachtung, Geringschätzung, *(disgrace)* Schmach, Schande;
in ~ **of all rules and regulations** in Mißachtung aller Konventionen;
constructive ~ Nichtbefolgung einer rechtlichen Anordnung;
criminal ~ Störung der Rechtspflege; ~ **of court** Mißachtung des Gerichts, Ungebühr vor Gericht, *(nonappearance)* absichtliches Nichterscheinen; ~ **of congress** *(US)* Mißachtung der Parlamentshoheit; ~ **of death** Todesverachtung;
to be in ~ sich einer Ungebühr schuldig gemacht haben; **to be exposed to public** ~ allgemeiner Mißachtung ausgesetzt sein; **to cite for** ~ **of court** wegen Mißachtung des Gerichts vorladen; **to fall into** ~ in Ungnade geraten; **to feel** ~ **for s. o.** j. verachten; ~ **charge** Anklage wegen Mißachtung des Gerichts.

contemptible conduct nichtswürdiges Verhalten.

contend *(v.)* streiten, kämpfen, ringen, *(complete)* wetteifern, sich bewerben, *(plead)* vorbringen, bestreiten;
~ **with difficulties** mit Schwierigkeiten zu kämpfen haben; ~ **in friendly rivalry** in friedlichem Wettstreit stehen; ~ **with a robber for one's life** mit einem Räuber um sein Leben kämpfen.

contender, serious ernsthafter Bewerber;
~ **for a franchise** Lizenzbewerber.

contending entgegen-, gegenüberstehend;
~ **for a prize** Preiswettbewerb;
~ **claims** widerstreitende Ansprüche; ~ **parties** streitende Parteien.

content *(amount of material in substance)* Gehalt, *(capacity)* Rauminhalt, Umfang, Volumen, Fassungsvermögen, *(parl., Br.)* Zustimmung, Jastimme, Stimme dafür, *(satisfaction)* Zufriedenheit, Befriedigung;
not ~ *(House of Lords, Br.)* dagegen; ~ **received** bezahlt erhalten; ~ **unknown** Inhalt unbekannt;
~**s** Inhalt, Inhaltsverzeichnis;
gold ~ Goldgehalt; **principle** ~ Hauptinhalt;
~ **of a letter** Briefinhalt; ~ **of a room** Zimmerausmaße;
~ *(a.)* zufrieden, *(pol., Br.)* einverstanden;
to approve of the ~ **of an article** einem Zeitungsartikel zustimmen; **to declare o. s.** ~ einverstanden sein, *(pol., Br.)* mit Ja stimmen; **to live in peace and** ~ friedliches Dasein führen;
~ **analysis** *(speech)* Inhaltsanalyse; ~**s heading** Rubrik.

contention Vorbringen, Argument, Behauptung, *(controversy)* Kontroverse, Meinungsstreit, Wortgefecht.

contentious streitig, strittig, kontradiktorisch;
~ **business** streitige Zivilsache; ~ **clause in a treaty** umstrittene Vertragsklausel; ~ **issue** Streitfrage, -punkt; ~ **jurisdiction** streitige Gerichtsbarkeit; ~ **matters of legislation** strittige Gesetzesmaterie; ~ **point** Streitpunkt; ~ **possession** strittiges Besitzrecht; ~ **procedure** *(dipl.)* Verfahren zur Regelung eines Streitfalles.

contest *(competition)* [Verbraucher]wettbewerb, Preisausschreiben, *(dispute)* Bestreiten, *(electioneering) (Br.)* Wahlkampf, *(matter in a dispute)* Disput, Streitfall, Rechtsstreit;
electoral ~ *(Br.)* Wahlkampf;
~ *(v.)* anfechten, bestreiten, *(compete)* an einem Wettbewerb teilnehmen;
~ **for a borough** *(Br.)* für einen Wahlkreis kandidieren; ~ **a claim** Anspruch bestreiten; ~ **an election** Wahlergebnis anfechten; ~ **every inch of ground** jeden Zentimeter des Bodens verteidigen; ~ **for a prize** sich an einem Wettbewerb beteiligen; ~ **s. one's right** jds. Recht streitig machen; ~ **a seat in Parliament** sich um einen Parlamentssitz bewerben, für das Parlament kandidieren; ~ **a statement** Behauptung bestreiten; ~ **a will** Testament anfechten;
to enter the ~ Kampf aufnehmen; **to run a** ~ Wettstreit veranstalten.

contestability of marriage Eheanfechtbarkeit.

contestable anfechtbar, bestreitbar, strittig.

contestant Anfechtender, streitende Partei, *(parl.)* Kandidat, *(participator in contest)* Wettbewerbsteilnehmer, Wettbewerber, Konkurrent;
~ **of election returns** Wahlanfechter; ~ **in legal proceedings** Prozeßteilnehmer.

contestation Auseinandersetzung, Kontroverse;
in ~ strittig, umstritten.

contested umstritten, streitig, strittig;
~ **election** bestrittenes Wahlergebnis, angefochtene Wahl.

contestee Beklagter, *(candidate, US)* umstrittener Kandidat.

contester Wettbewerber.

context Redeverbindung, Zusammenhang, Kontext;
in this ~ in diesem Zusammenhang; **unless the** ~ **otherwise requires** sofern sich aus dem Zusammenhang nichts anderes ergibt;
to guess the meaning from the ~ Inhalt aus dem Wortzusammenhang entnehmen; **to put s. th. into** ~ etw. in der richtigen Perspektive sehen; **to take words out of** ~ Worte aus dem Zusammenhang reißen.

contextual nach dem textlichen Zusammenhang;
~ **quotation** wörtliches Zitat.

contiguity Angrenzen, Nähe, Nachbarschaft.

contiguous angrenzend, anstoßend, benachbart;
~ **and compact** *(school district)* angrenzend und zusammenhängend;
to be ~ angrenzen;
~ **association** Nachbarverein; ~ **plots of land** zusammenhängende Grundstücke; ~ **zone** Kontinuitätsgrenze.

continence Mäßigkeit, Enthaltsamkeit.

continent festes Land, Festland, Erdteil, Kontinent;
self-contained ~ autarker Kontinent;
to travel on the ~ *(Br.)* Europareise machen.

continental festländisch, kontinental, das Festland betreffend, *(Br.)* fremd, nicht englisch;
~ **bills** *(Br.)* Wechsel auf Plätze des europäischen Kontinents; ~ **bourse** *(Br.)* Festlandsbörse; ~ **breakfast** *(Br.)* einfaches Frühstück; ~ **call** *(Br.)* Auslandsgespräch; ~ **climate** Binnenklima; ~ **high** Festlandshoch; ~ **interior** Inneres eines Kontinents; ~ **orders** *(Br.)* Aufträge vom Festland; ~ **port** *(Br.)* Kontinentalhafen; ~ **power** Landmacht; ~ **press** *(Br.)* Festlandspresse; ~ **shelf** Festlandssockel, Kontinentalplateau; ~ **tour** *(Br.)* Europareise; ~ **trade** *(Br.)* Europahandel.

contingencies unvorhergesehene Ausgaben, Nebenausgaben, *(balance sheet)* Eventualverbindlichkeiten, Rückstellungen für noch nicht feststehende Risiken;
~ **of war** Auf und Ab des Krieges;
to allow (provide) for ~ für unvorhergesehene Ausgaben zurückstellen; **to be prepared for all** ~ auf alle Eventualitäten (auf alles) vorbereitet sein; **to depend on** ~ von Zufällen abhängen;
~ **account** Rückstellungskonto für unvorhergesehene Verpflichtungen; ~ **reserve** Reservefonds, Notrücklage.

contingency ungewisses (zufälliges, unvorhergesehenes) Ereignis, Eventualität, Eventualfall;
in case of a ~ falls unvorhergesehene Umstände eintreten sollten;

life ~ von der Lebensdauer abhängiges Risiko;
~ **with double aspect** subsidiäres Heimfallrecht;
~ **fund** außerordentlicher Rücklagenfonds, außerordentliche Reserven, Notrücklage, Eventual-, Garantiefonds; ~ **insurance** Versicherung gegen besondere Risiken; ~ **plan** Krisen-, Notstandsplan, Notfallplanung; ~ **planning** militärisch-politische Notstandsplanung; ~ **reserve** Sicherheitsrücklage, Delkredererückstellung, Rückstellungen für Eventualverbindlichkeiten; ~ **risk** versichertes Risiko; ~ **table** Kontingenztafel, Frequenzverteilungssystem.

contingent [Pflicht]anteil, [Beteiligungs]quote, Kontingent, *(mil.)* Truppenkontingent;
annual ~ Jahreskontingent;
to fix a ~ kontingentieren;
~ *(a.)* möglich, eventuell, ungewiß, zufallsbedingt;
~ **account** *(Br.)* außerordentlicher Reservefonds, Delkrederekonto; ~ **advantage** möglicher Vorteil; ~ **annuity** Rente mit unbestimmter Laufzeit; ~ **asset** potentieller Aktivposten; ~ **beneficiary** *(insurance)* bedingt Begünstigter; ~ **charges (cost)** Eventualkosten; ~ **claim** Eventualforderung, -anspruch; ~ **condition** [vom Zufall abhängige] ungewisse Bedingung; ~ **duty** Ausgleichszoll; **still** ~ **second edition** noch fragliche zweite Ausgabe; ~ **estate** Erbanwartschaft; ~ **expenses** unerwartete (unvorhergesehene) Ausgaben; ~ **fee** *(US)* Erfolgshonorar; ~ **fee contract** *(US)* Erfolgshonorarvereinbarung; ~ **fund** *(US)* außerordentlicher Rücklagenfonds, Delkredererereserve; ~ **interest** Anwartschaftsrecht; ~ **interest in personal property** nicht übertragbares Anwartschaftsrecht; ~ **legacy** Vermächtnis unter Auflage; ~ **liability** Eventualverpflichtung; ~ **liabilities of endorsements on bills discounted** *(balance sheet)* Giroverbindlichkeiten; ~ **liabilities in respect of acceptances** Verpflichtungen aus geleisteten Akzepten; ~ **order** gekoppelter Auftrag; ~ **profit** noch nicht realisierbarer Gewinn; ~ **property** Reservekapital; ~ **receivables** *(US)* ungewisse Forderungen; ~ **remainder** bedingtes Anwartschaftsrecht; ~ **reserve** Rückstellung für unvorhergesehene Ausgaben; ~ **right** Anwartschaftsrecht; ~ **use** potentieller Nießbrauch.

contingently, to be ~ **indebted** aus Giroverbindlichkeiten schulden; **to be** ~ **liable** bedingt haften.

continuable prolongationsfähig, prolongierbar.

continual kontinuierlich, stetig, fortwährend, unaufhörlich;
~ **claims** stets erneuerte Forderung; ~ **complaints** fortgesetzte Beschwerden; ~ **rain** Dauerregen.

continuance Fortbestand, Dauer, Stetigkeit, Beständigkeit, Bleiben, *(adjournment, US)* Vertagung, Aufschub, Aussetzung;
during the ~ **of the war** während der Kriegsdauer; **for a** ~ auf die Dauer;
~ **of a contract** Vertragsdauer; ~ **of a business firm** Fortbestand einer Firma; ~ **in office** Verbleiben im Amt; ~ **of a partnership** Fortsetzung eines Gesellschaftsverhältnisses; ~ **in a place** Aufenthalt an einem Ort; ~ **of the proceedings** Vertagung des Verfahrens; ~ **of prosperity** anhaltende Konjunktur; ~ **of fine weather** anhaltend schönes Wetter, Schönwetterperiode;
to prevent further satisfactory ~ **of the relationship** *(dismissal)* [etwa] Fortsetzung des Arbeitsverhältnisses nicht zumutbar erscheinen lassen;
~ **rate** Zugehörigkeitsdauer.

continuation Fortdauer, Fortbestand, Fortsetzung, Fort-, Weiterführung, *(extension)* Erweiterung, Verlängerung, *(library)* Fortsetzungswerk, *(Br., stock exchange)* Prolongation[sgeschäft], Report-, Kostgeschäft;
fortnightly ~ *(Br.)* Medioprolongation;
~ **of a business** Weiterführung eines Geschäfts; ~ **of a railroad** *(US)* Ausbau einer Eisenbahnlinie; ~ **of a story** Fortsetzung einer Geschichte; ~ **of study** Fortsetzung des Studiums; ~ **of use** *(patent)* Weiterbenutzung;
to give (take) in ~ in Report geben (nehmen);
~ **bill** *(Br.)* Prolongationswechsel; ~ **business** *(Br.)* Prolongations-, Report-, Kostgeschäft; ~ **class** Fortbildungsklasse, Aufbauklasse, -schule; ~ **clause** *(marine insurance, Br.)* Verlängerungs-, Prolongationsklausel; ~ **course** Fortbildungslehrgang, -kursus; ~ **day** *(Br.)* Reporttag; ~ **education** berufliche Fortbildung; ~ **policy** Erneuerungspolice; ~ **rate** *(Br.)* Reportgebühr, -satz, Prolongationsgebühr; ~ **school** Mittel-, Fortbildungsschule; ~ **schooling** weiterführender Unterricht, Fortbildung; ~ **sheet** Fortsetzungsblatt; ~ **teaching** Aufbauschulunterricht; ~ **training** berufliche Fortbildung.

continuative education Fortbildungswesen.

continue *(v.)* fortdauern, *(adjourn, US)* vertagen, *(keep up)* fortführen, -setzen, *(remain in existence)* weiterbestehen, *(Br., stock exchange)* in Prolongation (Report) nehmen;

~ **a business** Geschäft fortführen; ~ **a case** mündliche Verhandlung wiederaufnehmen; ~ **in demand** fortlaufend gefragt sein; **to still** ~ **in weak health** weiterhin gesundheitlich geschwächt sein; ~ **high** *(prices)* hohen Stand behaupten; ~ **one's journey** seine Reise fortsetzen; ~ **a judge in his post** Richter auf seinem Posten belassen; ~ **negotiations** Verhandlungen fortführen; ~ **in office** im Amt [ver]bleiben; ~ **at (in) a place** an einem Ort bleiben; ~ **relations with s. o.** Beziehungen mit jem. aufrechterhalten; ~ **at school for another year** Schule ein weiteres Jahr besuchen; ~ **one's study** sein Studium fortsetzen.

continued fortgesetzt, anhaltend, nachhaltig, kontinuierlich, *(serial)* in Fortsetzungen erscheinend;
favo(u)rably ~ *(advertising)* ununterbrochen günstig aufgenommen;
to be ~ **[in our next]** *(newspaper)* Fortsetzung folgt; **to be** ~ **in office** im Amt erneut bestätigt werden; ~ **in next column** Fortsetzung siehe nächste Spalte; ~ **favo(u)rable** *(advertising)* ununterbrochen günstig aufgenommen;
~ **account** Übertrag; ~ **bonds** *(US)* prolongierte Obligationen; ~ **existence** Fortbestand; ~ **interest** fortbestehendes Interesse; ~ **story** Fortsetzungsgeschichte; ~ **use** *(patent)* Weiterbenutzung; ~ **voyage** Weiterreise.

continuing andauernd, fortgesetzt;
~ **account** Kontokorrentkonto; ~ **agreement** *(US)* Kontokorrentvertrag mit gleichbleibend gestellten Sicherheiten; ~ **appropriation** nicht verbrauchte Etatsanteile; ~ **boom** anhaltende Konjunktur; ~ **consideration** andauernde Gegenleistung; ~ **conspiracy** auf Dauer angelegte Verschwörertätigkeit; ~ **covenant** Dauerverpflichtung; ~ **crisis** Anhalten der Krise; ~ **damages** fortlaufende Schadensersatzzahlungen; ~ **guarantee** *(US)* Kreditbürgschaft, Dauergarantie; ~ **member** Dauermitglied; ~ **nuisance** anhaltende Belästigung (Besitzstörung); ~ **offence** fortgesetztes Verbrechen, Fortsetzungsdelikt; ~ **policy** sich automatisch erneuernder Versicherungsvertrag.

continuity Stetigkeit, Kontinuität, ununterbrochener Kausalzusammenhang, *(broadcasting)* verbindender Text, Zwischenansage, *(film)* Drehbuch, *(market)* Stetigkeit, *(manuscript)* Manuskript, *(theater)* Rollenbuch;
~ **in advertising** fortlaufender Werbeeinsatz; ~ **of employment** Beschäftigungskontinuität; ~ **of operation** durchgehender Betrieb; ~ **of question** Fragenfolge in einer Erhebung; ~ **of service** stetige Betriebszugehörigkeit; ~ **of state** Fortbestand des Staates;
to break the ~ Zusammenhang unterbrechen;
~ **girl** Skriptgirl; ~ **panel** Streifenanzeige; ~ **premium** Zugabenwerbung in Sammelform; ~ **writer** Drehbuchautor.

continuous laufend, kontinuierlich, fortgesetzt, fortdauernd, ununterbrochen;
~ **adverse use** fortgesetzte bestrittene Nutzung; ~ **audit** laufende Revisionsarbeiten; ~ **borrower** *(banking)* Dauerkunde; ~ **borrowing** Dauerkredit; ~ **caster** Stranggußanlage; ~ **casting** Stranggießen; ~ **casting process** Stranggußverfahren; ~ **chore** Dauerarbeit; ~ **crime** unter mehrere Gerichtszuständigkeiten fallendes Verbrechen; ~ **current** *(el.)* Gleichstrom; ~ **easement** dauernde Grunddienstbarkeit; ~ **employment** Dauerbeschäftigung; ~ **form** Endlosformular; ~ **industry** sämtliche Phasen durchführender Industriebetrieb; ~ **injury** immer wieder auftauchende Verletzung; ~ **inventory** permanente Bestandsaufnahme; ~ **investigation** Reihen-, Indexuntersuchung; ~ **manufacturing** Serienfertigung; ~ **mill** kontinuierliche Walzenstraße; ~ **operations** durchgehende Arbeitszeit, Dauerbetrieb; ~ **performance** *(cinema)* Nonstop-, Dauervorstellung; ~ **possession** Dauerbesitz; ~ **printing** Endlosdruck; ~ **process** durcharbeitender Betrieb; ~ **rating** *(electricity)* Dauerleistung, *(machine)* Dauerbelastung; ~ **record** fortlaufend geführte Akte; ~ **studies** nicht unterbrochenes Studium; ~ **succession of visitors** ununterbrochene Besuchererfolge; ~ **tape** Endloslochstreifen; ~ **tone** Halbtonwirkung.

contort *(v.)* **a word out of its ordinary meaning** Wortbedeutung verzerren.

conto(u)r Profil;
~ **line** Höhenlinie, Isokurve; ~ **map** Höhenlinienkarte.

contra Gegenposten;
per ~ als Gegenforderung (Gegenleistung);
the pros and ~s das Für und Wider;
to settle a debt per ~ mit einer Summe aufrechnen;
~ *(a.)* gegen, wider, abweichend;
~ **bonos mores** gegen die guten Sitten;
~ **account** Gegen-, Wertberichtigungskonto; ~ **asset** *(balance sheet)* Gegenposten; ~ **entry** *(Br.)* Gegenbuchung, Storno[buchung]; ~ **item** Kontraposition.

contraband Konter-, Schmuggel-, Bannware;

absolute ~ absolute Konterbande; **conditional** ~ bedingte (relative) Konterbande; **occasional** ~ gelegentliche Konterbande; ~ **by analogy** Konterbande gleichgestellte Transporte; ~ **of war** Kriegskonterbande;

~ **(v.)** schmuggeln;

to be seized as ~ als Konterbande beschlagnahmt werden; **to run** ~ Schmuggel (Schleichhandel) betreiben;

~ **articles (goods)** verbotene Waren, Konterbande, Bann-, Schmuggelwaren; ~ **baggage** (US) verkehrswidrig als Gepäck deklarierte Waren; ~ **trade** Schmuggel; ~ **vessel** Schmugglerschiff.

contrabandism Schleichhandel, Schmuggel.

contrabandist Schmuggler, Schleichhändler.

contraception methods (measures) Geburtenbeschränkungsmaßnahmen.

contraceptive Verhütungsmittel.

contract Vertrag, Kontrakt, Vereinbarung, *(agreement for performance of work)* Auftrag, Verdingung, Submission, Ausschreibung, *(agreement for supply of goods)* Lieferungsvertrag, *(deal)* Abschluß, *(deed)* Vertragsurkunde, *(piecework, US)* Akkord, *(railway, dial.)* Zeitkarte;

according to (as may be required by) ~ vertragsgemäß; **as provided in the** ~ wie vertraglich vereinbart, laut Vertrag; **at the time of making the** ~ zur Zeit des Vertragsabschlusses; **bound by** ~ vertraglich verpflichtet; **by** ~ *(US)* vertraglich; **by private** ~ freihändig, unter der Hand; **contrary to the terms of the** ~ vertragswidrig; **during the life of a** ~ während der Vertragsdauer; **in** ~ im Akkord; **in making the** ~ beim [Ver]kauf[s]abschluß; **liable under** ~ vertraglich verpflichtet; **looking to a future** ~ mit Aussicht auf einen zukünftigen Vertragsabschluß; **stipulated by (under)** ~ vertraglich [vereinbart]; **subject to** ~ gültig nur bei Vertragsabschluß; **subject to formal** ~ vorbehaltlich eines noch abzuschließenden Vertrages; **subject to the terms of a** ~ vorbehaltlich der Vertragsbestimmungen; **true to the** ~ vertragstreu; **under** ~ im Vertragsverhältnis mit; **when the ~ was effected** bei Wirksamwerden des Vertrages;

accessory ~ akzessorische Verpflichtung, akzessorischer Vertrag, Zusatz, Nebenvertrag; **accident insurance** ~ Unfallversicherungsvertrag; **administrative** ~ Verwaltungsabkommen; **agency** ~ Agenturvertrag; **exclusive agency** ~ Ausschließlichkeitsvertrag; **aleatory** ~ Risikovertrag, Spielvertrag; **annuity** ~ [Leib]rentenvertrag; **apprenticeship** ~ Ausbildungs-, Lehrlingsvertrag; **army** ~ Heeresauftrag; **bare** ~ schlichter Vertrag; **basic** ~ Rahmen-, Grundvertrag; **bilateral** ~ zweiseitiger Vertrag; **binding** ~ rechtsverbindlicher Vertrag; **broker's** ~ *(stock exchange)* Schlußnote, -schein; **brokerage** ~ Maklervertrag; **building** ~ Bau[unternehmer]vertrag; **burdensome** ~ lästig gewordener Vertrag; **certain** ~ Vertrag über bestimmte Leistungen; **charitable** Schenkungsvertrag; **close-shop** ~ *(US)* Gewerkschaftszugehörigkeit voraussetzender Arbeitsvertrag; **collateral** ~ Nebenvertrag; **collective bargaining** ~ Tarifvertrag; **commutative** ~ zweiseitig verpflichtender (wechselseitiger) Vertrag; **conditional** ~ bedingter Vertrag; **conditional sales** ~ Kaufvertrag unter Eigentumsvorbehalt; **consensual** ~ obligatorischer Vertrag, Konsensualvertrag; **construction** ~s öffentliche Bauaufträge; **constructive** ~ gesetzliches Schuldverhältnis; **continuing** ~ laufender Vertrag; **cost-of-living escalator** ~ mit Preisgleitklausel ausgestatteter Vertrag; **cost-plus** ~ *(US)* Werklieferungsvertrag; **cost-plus a fixed-fee** ~ *(US)* Vertrag mit Preisfestsetzung nach den Kosten zuzüglich Verrechnung fester Zuschläge (einer Leistungsprämie); **defective** ~ fehlerhafter Vertrag; **delivery** ~ Liefer[ungs]vertrag; **dependent** ~ unselbständiger Vertrag; **development** ~ Vertrag über Entwicklungsvorhaben; **divisible** ~ Vertrag auf teilbare Leistung, teilbarer Vertrag; **draft** ~ Vertragsentwurf; **employment** ~ Arbeitsvertrag; **entire** ~ Vertrag auf unteilbare Leistung, **estate** ~ Grundstückskaufvertrag; **exclusive-dealing** ~ Ausschließlichkeitsvertrag; **executed** ~ erfüllter (wirksamer) Vertrag; **executory** ~ schwebender (noch nicht erfüllter, obligatorischer) Vertrag; **existing** ~ bestehender Vertrag; **express** ~ ausdrücklich geschlossener Vertrag; **fair and reasonable** ~ angemessener Vertrag; **family** ~ Familienabkommen; **feigned** ~ Scheinvertrag; **a few** ~s einige Geschäftsabschlüsse; **fictitious** ~ fingierter Vertrag, Scheinvertrag; **fiduciary** ~ Treuhandvertrag; **final** ~ endgültiger Vertrag; **fixed-price** ~ Festpreisvertrag; **fixed price-incentive fee** ~ Festpreisvertrag mit Leistungszuschlägen; **fixed-price** ~ **with provision for redetermination of price** *(US)* Festpreisauftrag mit Neufestsetzung des Preises; **straight fixed-price** ~ Festpreisvertrag, Auftrag zu regulärem Festpreis; **formal** ~ formbedürftiger Vertrag;

freight ~ vertraglich vereinbarte Fracht; **fresh** ~ neuer Vertrag; **frustrated** ~ objektiv unmöglich gewordener Vertrag; **future** ~ *(stock exchange, US)* Liefer[ungs]vertrag; **gambling** ~ Spielvertrag; **gaming** ~ Wettvertrag; **government** ~ Staatsauftrag; **gratuitous** ~ Vertrag über eine unentgeltliche Leistung, unentgeltlicher Vertrag; **guarantee** ~ Garantievertrag; **hazardous** ~ ungewisser Vertrag, Risikovertrag; **hire purchase** ~ *(Br.)* Teil-, Raten-, Abzahlungsvertrag; **horizontal** ~ horizontaler Vertrag; **illegal** ~ unerlaubter (widerrechtlicher) Vertrag; **immoral** ~ unmoralischer Vertrag; **impaired** ~ verletzter Vertrag; **implied** ~ stillschweigender (konkludent abgeschlossener) Vertrag; **indemnity** ~ Garantievertrag; **independent** ~ Vertrag über selbständige Leistungen; **individual** ~ Einzelvertrag; **indivisible** ~ unteilbarer Vertrag; **infants'** ~s Verträge Minderjähriger; **informal** ~ formfreier Vertrag; **instal(l)ment** ~ Abzahlungs-, Ratenzahlungsvertrag, -geschäft, Lieferungsvertrag; **insurance** ~ Versicherungsvertrag; **invalid** ~ ungültiger Vertrag; **joint** ~ gemeinschaftlicher Vertrag, Gesamtvertrag; **labo(u)r** ~ Dienst-, Arbeitsvertrag; **large** ~ Großabschluß; **lease** ~ Miet-, Pachtvertrag; **legally binding** ~ rechtgültiger (rechtsverbindlicher) Vertrag; **leonine** ~ leoninischer Vertrag; **licensing** ~ Lizenzvertrag; **life** ~ Vertrag auf Lebenszeit; **life-insurance** ~ Lebensversicherungsvertrag; **loan** ~ Darlehnsvertrag; **main** ~ Grundvertrag; **marine** ~ Seebeförderungsvertrag; **marriage** ~ Ehevertrag; **master** ~ einheitlicher Arbeitsvertrag; **mixed** ~ gemischter Vertrag, Vertrag mit ungleichen Leistungen; **six-month** ~ halbjähriger Vertrag, Halbjahresvertrag; **multiple delivery** ~ Vertrag über mehrere Lieferungen; **mutual** ~ gegenseitige Übereinkunft, gegenseitiger Vertrag; **naked** ~ unverbindlicher Vertrag; **nude** ~ einseitiger (unentgeltlicher) Vertrag; **one-sided** ~ einseitiger Vertrag; **onerous** ~ entgeltlicher Vertrag; **open** ~ Grundsatzvereinbarung; **open-end** ~ unbefristeter Lieferungsvertrag; **option** ~ Vertrag über den Abschluß eines Prämiengeschäftes; **oral** ~ mündlicher Vertrag; **original** ~ Hauptvertrag; **partnership** ~ Gesellschaftsvertrag; **passenger** ~ Personenbeförderungsvertrag; **personal** ~ höchstpersönlicher (individueller) Vertrag; **pignorative** ~ Pfandvertrag; **pooling** ~ Kartellabkommen; **pre-** ~ Vorvertrag; **pre-incorporation** ~s Verträge vor Gesellschaftseintragung; **preliminary** ~ Vorvertrag; **principal** ~ Hauptvertrag; **procedural** ~ Prozeßweg nicht ausschließender Vertrag; **proper** ~ ordnungsgemäßer Vertrag; **prototype** ~ Mustervertrag; **provisional** ~ vorläufiger Vertrag; **public** ~s öffentliche Aufträge; **publishing** ~ Verlagsvertrag; **purchase** ~ Kaufvertrag; **quasi** ~ vertragsähnliches Verhältnis, kaufähnlicher Vertrag; **real** ~ dinglicher Vertrag; **reciprocal** ~ *(Br.)* gegenseitiger Vertrag; **running** ~ laufender Vertrag; **sales** ~ Kaufvertrag; **sealed** ~ notarieller Vertrag; **separable** ~ vom Hauptvertrag unabhängiger Nebenvertrag; **service** ~ Dienst[leistungs]vertrag; **several** ~ Einzelvertrag; **sham** ~ Scheinvertrag; **shipping** ~ Transport-, Frachtvertrag; **simple** ~ formfreier (einfacher) Vertrag; **simulated** ~ Scheinvertrag; **social** ~ Sozialabkommen; **specialty** ~ formbedürftiger (gesiegelter) Vertrag; **standard** ~ Mustervertrag; **standing** ~ fester (laufender) Vertrag; **substituted** ~ Ersatzvertrag; **supply** ~ Lieferungsvertrag; **synallagmatic** ~ gegenseitiger (zweiseitiger) Vertrag; **testamentary** ~ Erbvertrag; **third-party beneficiary** ~ Vertrag zugunsten Dritter; **triangular** ~s dreiseitige Verträge; **turnkey** ~ schlüsselfertiger Bauvertrag; **tying** ~ Exklusivvertrag; **uncompleted** ~s *(balance sheet)* noch nicht abgeschlossene (unfertige) Vertragsleistungen; **unconscionable** ~ mit Treu und Glauben unvereinbarer Vertrag; **underlying** ~ zugrundeliegender Vertrag; **underwriting** ~ Konsortialvertrag; **unenforceable** ~ nicht einklagbarer Vertrag; **unfulfilled** ~ noch nicht erfüllter Vertrag; **unilateral** ~ einseitiger (einseitig bindender) Vertrag; **unprofitable** ~ unrentabler Vertrag; **unreasonable** ~ unzumutbarer Vertrag; **unsealed** ~ formfreier Vertrag; **usurious** ~ wucherischer Vertrag; **valid** ~ rechtsgültiger Vertrag; **verbal** ~ mündlicher Vertrag; **voidable** ~ anfechtbarer Vertrag; **wage** ~ Spiel-, Wettvertrag; **written** ~ schriftlicher Vertrag; **two years'** ~ Zweijahresvertrag;

~ **that can be upheld** gültig bleibender Vertrag;

~ **of affreightment** Charter-, Fracht-, Befrachtungsvertrag; ~ **of agency** Auftragsverhältnis, Vertretungs-, Vertretervertrag; ~ **in respect of alimony** Unterhaltsvertrag; ~ **of annuity** [Leib]rentenvertrag; ~ **of apprenticeship** Ausbildungs-, Lehr[lings]vertrag; ~ **of arbitration** Schiedsvertrag; ~ **of bailment** Hinterlegung[svertrag]; ~ **for benefit of third party (in consideration of another)** Vertrag zugunsten Dritter; ~ **of benevolence** einseitig begünstigender Vertrag; ~ **of borrowing** Darlehnsvertrag; ~ **to build** Bauauftrag, -vertrag; ~ **of carriage** Speditionsvertrag; ~ of copartnery Teilhaber-, Gesellschaftsvertrag; ~ by deed förmlicher Vertrag; ~ for [future] delivery Liefer[ungs]-vertrag; ~ for the delivery of goods Warenlieferungsvertrag; ~ of employment Arbeits-, Dienstvertrag; ~ as an entity Vertrag in seiner Gesamtheit; ~ drawn up in due form ordnungsgemäß errichteter Vertrag; ~ for futures (US) Lieferungs-, Terminvertrag; ~s with a gold clause Goldklauselverträge; ~ of guaranty Bürgschaftsvertrag; ~ under hand (Br.) schriftlicher Vertrag; ~ of hire Miet-, Pachtvertrag; ~ of hire purchase Abzahlungs-, Ratenzahlungsvertrag; ~ for a holiday Urlaubsvertrag; ~ void because of illegality ungesetzlicher und deshalb nichtiger Vertrag; ~ tainted with immorality sittenwidriger Vertrag; ~ of indemnity Haftungsfreistellungs-, Garantievertrag; ~ of insurance Versicherungsvertrag; ~ for labo(u)r and materials Werklieferungsvertrag; ~ enforceable at law einklagbare Vertragsverpflichtung; ~ of lease Miet-, Pachtvertrag; ~ of loan for use Leihvertrag; ~ of (to) manufacture Werkvertrag; ~ of marine insurance Seetransportversicherungsvertrag; ~ for necessaries Vertrag zur Sicherstellung des notwendigen Lebensunterhaltes, Vertrag über Gegenstände des notwendigen Lebensbedarfs; ~ lacking mutuality Vertrag mit nichtverbürgter Gegenseitigkeit; ~ of partnership Teilhaber-, Gesellschaftsvertrag; ~ of pledge Verpfändungsvertrag; ~ of premises Mietvertrag; ~ prohibited by statute gesetzlich verbotener Vertrag; ~ concerning the leaving of property by will Erbschaftsvertrag; ~ offending public policy gegen die guten Sitten verstoßender Vertrag; ~ for public works Submissionsvertrag; ~ of purchase Kaufvertrag; ~ of recharter Unterfrachtvertrag; ~ of record gerichtlich protokollierte Vereinbarung; ~ in restraint of trade Konkurrenzvertrag, Kartellvereinbarung, Wettbewerbsbeschränkungsvertrag; ~ to defraud the revenue Vertrag zu Zwecken der Steuerhinterziehung, Steuerhinterziehungsvertrag; ~ for sale Kaufvertrag; executory ~ for sale obligatorischer Kaufvertrag; ~ for the sale of goods Kaufvertrag über bewegliche Sachen; ~ for the sale of land (Br.) (real estate, US) Grundstückskaufvertrag; special ~ under seal gesiegelter Vertrag; ~ to sell (US) Kaufvertrag über bewegliche Sachen; ~ to sell for future delivery Kaufvertrag über zukünftige Lieferungen; ~ for services Geschäftsbesorgungsvertrag; ~ of personal service persönlicher Dienstleistungsvertrag, Geschäftsbesorgungsvertrag; ~ of speciality notarieller Vertrag; ~ for subscription Zeichnungsvertrag; ~ rendered void by statute aufgrund Gesetzes ungültiger Vertrag; ~ of suretyship Bürgschaftsvertrag ohne Einrede der Vorausklage; ~ by tender Submission, Ausschreibung; ~ of training Ausbildungsvertrag; ~ of warranty Garantieversprechen; ~ for work and labo(u)r (service) Werkvertrag; ~ for work and materials Werklieferungsvertrag; ~ for public works Ausschreibung öffentlicher Arbeiten; ~ in writing schriftlicher Vertrag; ~ good for one year Jahresvertrag, das ganze Jahr gültiger Liefervertrag;

~ (v.) Geschäft[svertrag] abschließen (eingehen), sich vertraglich verpflichten, kontrahieren, (abstract) Auszug machen, zusammenstreichen, (bargain) vertraglich übernehmen;

~ o. s. for s. th. sich vertraglich zu etw. verpflichten; ~ an alliance with another country Bündnis mit einem anderen Land eingehen; ~ a bargain Handel abschließen; ~ to build a bridge Brückenbauauftrag annehmen; ~ on one's own credit auf eigene Rechnung kontrahieren; ~ debts Schulden machen; ~ with a firm einer Firma einen Auftrag erteilen; ~ bad habits schlechte Gewohnheiten annehmen; ~ an illness sich eine Krankheit zuziehen; ~ in (labo(u)r party, Br.) sich zur Bezahlung von Parteibeiträgen verpflichten; ~ liabilities Verpflichtungen eingehen; ~ a loan Anleihe (Kredit) aufnehmen; ~ a marriage Ehe eingehen; ~ out sich freizeichnen, vertraglich ausschließen, (National Insurance, Br.) sich nicht an der Sozialversicherung beteiligen, (subcontract) Unterauftrag vergeben; ~ o. s. out of an obligation sich einer Verpflichtung durch einen Vertragsabschluß entziehen; ~ out of payment of a levy sich an einer Umlage nicht beteiligen; ~ into the state pension scheme betriebliche Altersversorgung jetzt in die staatliche Versorgung einbeziehen; ~ out of the state pension scheme aus der staatlichen Altersversorgung ausscheiden; ~ a publicity campaign Werbefeldzug durchführen; ~ to supply a factory Liefervertrag mit einer Fabrik abschließen; ~ with s. o. for s. th. Werkvertrag mit jem. abschließen; ~ for work Arbeit im Werkvertrag übernehmen; to adopt (assume) a ~ Vertrag annehmen; to affirm a ~ Vertrag bestätigen; to annul (avoid) a ~ Vertrag aufheben; to approbate a ~ Vertrag genehmigen; to assent to a ~ einem Vertrag zustimmen; to avoid a ~ Vertrag aufheben; to avow a ~ Vertrag anerkennen; to award a ~ Zuschlag erteilen; to be awarded a

juicy government ~ fetten Regierungsauftrag erhalten; to be bound by a ~ vertraglich verpflichtet sein; to be of essence for a ~ von wesentlicher Bedeutung für einen Vertrag sein; to be provided for in a ~ vertraglich vorgesehen sein; to be under ~ to s. o. im Dienstverhältnis zu jem. stehen; to be in the running for a ~ sich um einen Auftrag bemühen; to bind o. s. by ~ sich vertraglich verpflichten; to break a ~ vertragsbrüchig werden, Vertragsverletzung begehen; to buy on ~ fest kaufen; to cancel a ~ Vertrag aufheben; to carry out a ~ Vertrag erfüllen; to come under a ~ unter einen Vertrag fallen; to complete (conclude) a ~ Vertrag abschließen; to comply with the clauses of a ~ sich an die Vertragsbestimmungen halten; to confer the ~ Zuschlag erteilen; to consider the ~ void Vertrag als nichtig betrachten (behandeln); to count on a ~ als Vertragsfolge darstellen; to determine a ~ Vertrag beendigen; to disaffirm a ~ Vertrag nicht bestätigen; to disaffirm an invalid ~ ungültigen Vertrag anfechten; to discharge a ~ Vertrag beenden; to dissolve a ~ Vertrag kündigen; to draft a ~ Vertrag entwerfen (aufsetzen); to draw up a ~ Vertrag ausfertigen; to draw up a ~ for signature Vertrag unterschriftsreif vorlegen; to embody a clause in a ~ Klausel in einen Vertrag einfügen; to enforce payment of a ~ Vertragsleistung erzwingen; to enter [into] a ~ Vertrag abschließen (eingehen); to enter a ~ under a misapprehension Mißverständnisse beim Vertragsabschluß haben; to enter a reservation in respect of a ~ Vertragsvorbehalt aufnehmen; to establish privity of ~ Vertragsverhältnis herstellen; to execute a ~ Vertrag erfüllen; to fall within the scope of (under) a ~ unter einen Vertrag fallen; to form a ~ Vertrag zustande bringen; to fulfil a ~ Vertrag erfüllen; to get a ~ für eine Leistung den Zuschlag erhalten; to get behind with the performance of a ~ mit den Vertragsleistungen in Verzug kommen; to give out by ~ in Submission vergeben; to go on with a ~ Vertragsverhältnis fortsetzen; to hono(u)r a ~ Vertrag einhalten; to impair the obligations of a ~ Vertragsverpflichtungen abschwächen; to insert a clause into a ~ einem Vertrag eine Klausel beifügen; to interpret a ~ Vertrag auslegen; to invalidate a ~ Vertrag für nichtig erklären (annullieren); to keep a ~ alive Vertrag aufrechterhalten; to land a ~ Vertragsabschluß erzielen; to let out a work by ~ (US) Arbeit im Akkord vergeben; to live up to the letter of a ~ Vertrag bis zum letzten I-Tüpfelchen erfüllen; to make a ~ Vertrag abschließen (eingehen); to make a ~ binding Rechtsgültigkeit eines Vertrages herbeiführen; to make a ~ under duress zu einem Vertrag gezwungen werden, Vertrag unter Druck abschließen; to make a ~ for supply of coal Kohlenlieferungsvertrag abschließen; to negotiate a ~ in exhausting detail Vertrag bis in die kleinsten Einzelheiten aushandeln; to obtain the ~ Zuschlag erhalten; to perform a ~ Vertrag erfüllen; to place a ~ Durchführung eines Auftrags vergeben; to prepare a ~ Vertrag aufsetzen; to prolong a ~ Vertrag verlängern; to put a clause into a ~ einem Vertrag eine Klausel beifügen; to put hedges in a ~ Vertrag verklausulieren; to put some work out to ~ Werkvertrag über etw. abschließen; to put some work up to ~ Arbeit im Submissionswege vergeben; to ratify a ~ Vertrag ratifizieren; to read through a ~ Vertrag genau durchlesen; to recede from a ~ von einem Vertrag zurücktreten; to renegotiate a ~ Vertrag neu aufsetzen; to renew a ~ Vertrag erneuern; to reprobate a ~ Vertrag aufheben; to repudiate a ~ during infancy Vertragserfüllung wegen Minderjährigkeit ablehnen; to rescind a ~ by mutual consent Vertrag in gegenseitigem Einverständnis aufheben; to revoke a ~ Vertrag kündigen; to satisfy a ~ Vertrag erfüllen; to secure a ~ für eine Lieferung den Zuschlag erhalten; to set aside a ~ Vertrag aufheben; to set forth conditions in a ~ Vertragsbestimmungen festlegen; to set up a breach of ~ sich auf Vertragsbruch berufen; to sever a ~ Vertrag auflösen; to sign a ~ Vertrag unterzeichnen; to snag a ~ sich einen Auftrag sichern; to submit a ~ all cut and dried unterschriftsreifen Vertrag vorlegen; to sue on a ~ aus einem Vertrag klagen; to supersede by a new ~ durch einen neuen Vertrag ersetzen; to take in ~ (US) in Akkord nehmen; to tender for a ~ sich um einen im Submissionsweg zu vergebenden Auftrag bewerben; to terminate a ~ Dienstvertrag lösen; to terminate a ~ for cause Vertrag aus wichtigem Grunde kündigen; to treat a ~ as repudiated von einem Vertrag zurücktreten; to undertake by ~ (US) auf Akkord übernehmen; to vary the terms of a ~ Vertragsbestimmungen abändern; to violate a ~ Vertragsverletzung begehen; to vitiate a ~ Vertrag ungültig machen (für nichtig erklären); to void a ~ Vertrag ungültig machen (umstoßen); to withdraw from a ~ vom Vertrag zurücktreten; to word a ~ Vertrag formulieren; to write a ~ Vertrag aufsetzen;

~ authorization *(government accounting)* Vollmacht zur Auftragsvergabe auch außerhalb des Etatsjahrs; **~ award** Auftragserteilung, -vergabe, Vergabe öffentlicher Aufträge; **~-awarding procedure** Vergabeverfahren; **~ bargaining demands** Tarifforderungen; **~ bidder** Ausschreibungsteilnehmer; **~ bond** Unternehmerkaution; **~ book** Schlußscheinbuch; **~ breaker** Vertragsbrüchiger, vertragsbrüchige Partei; **~ breaking** vertragsbrüchig; **~ cancellation** Vertragskündigung, -aufhebung; **~ carrier** Vertragsspediteur; **~ carrier permit** Speditionslizenz; **industrial ~ caterer** Vertragslieferant von Betriebskantinen; **~ change** Vertragsänderung; **~ claim** Vertragsanspruch; **~ clause** Vertragsbestimmung, -klausel; **~ combination** *(US)* Unternehmenszusammenschluß; **~ creditor** Vertragsgläubiger; **~ date** vertraglich vorgesehener Termin; **~ debt** vertraglich geschuldete Leistung; **simple ~ debt** Vertragsanspruch; **~ debtor** Vertragsschuldner; **~ department** *(department store)* Engrosabteilung; **not to be of the ~ description** *(goods)* den Vertragsbedingungen nicht entsprechen; **~ execution** Vertragsdurchführung; **~ freight** ermäßigte Fracht; **~ gains** Vertragsvorteile; **~ goal** Vertragsziel; **~ goods** Vertragsgegenstand, -ware; **~ grade** vertraglich vereinbarte Sorte; **~ hours** vertragliche Arbeitszeit; **~ improvements** vertragliche Verbesserungen; **~ insurance** Vertragsversicherung; **~ journal** Submissionsanzeiger; **~ labo(u)r** vertraglich übernommene Arbeit; **~ law** Schuldrecht; **~ market** *(US)* Terminmarkt; **~ negotiations** *(US)* Tarifverhandlungen; **~ note** *(Br.)* Auftragsbestätigung, -schein, Ausführungsanzeige, *(stock exchange)* Abschlußnote, Schlußnote, -schein, Vertragsstempel; **~ obligation** Vertragspflicht, vertragliche Verpflichtung; **severable ~ obligation** von anderen unabhängige Vertragsverpflichtung; **to meet one's ~ obligations** seinen vertraglichen Verpflichtungen nachkommen; **~ package** *(bargaining)* Tarifpaket; **~ pattern** Vertragsmuster; **~ period** vertragliche Laufzeit, Vertragszeit, -dauer; **~-placing authority** öffentlicher Auftraggeber; **~ price** vertraglich vereinbarter Preis, Übernahme-, Submissions-, Liefer-, Vertragspreis; **~ processing** *(Br.)* Lohnveredelung; **~ proposal** Vertragsvorschlag; **~ provisions** Vertragsbestimmungen; **~ rate** Vertragsquote; **at the ~ rate** zum Vertragspreis; **~ rejection** Vertragsablehnung; **~ renewal** Vertragserneuerung, -verlängerung; **~ rent** vertraglich ausbedungene Pacht (Miete); **~ service system** *(Br.)* Vertrauensarztsystem; **~ settlement** Vertragsregelung; **~ sheet** Börsenumsatzliste, Abrechnungsblatt des Börsenmaklers; **~ shop** *(US)* Akkordbetrieb; **similar ~ situation** gleichgelagerte Vertragssituation; **~ stamp** Schlußnotenstempel; **~ strike** Streik zur Durchsetzung von Tarifforderungen; **~ supplies** Vertragsmenge; **~ system** *(US)* Vergebung von Arbeiten im Akkord; **~ system of wage payment** *(US)* Akkordsystem; **~ talks** Vertragsverhandlungen; **~ termination** Tarifkündigung; **~ terms** Vertragsbedingungen; **to fail to complete within ~ time** mit den [Vertrags]leistungen in Verzug kommen; **~ trade (trading)** *(stock exchange)* Termingeschäft; **~ type** Vertragstyp; **~ value** Vertragswert; **~ vehicle** angemietetes Fahrzeug; **~ violation** Vertragsverletzung; **~ wage payment** *(US)* Akkordlohnzahlung; **~ work** *(US)* im Stücklohn geleistete Arbeit, Akkordarbeit; **~ year** Anzeigen-, Insertions-, Abschlußjahr.

contractant Kontrahent, vertragschließender Teil, Vertragsschließender.

contracted space *(advertising)* Platzvorschrift.

contractible undercarriage *(aircraft)* einziehbares Fahrgestell.

contracting [for work] Gedinge-, Akkordwesen;
~-in *(international arbitration)* ausdrückliche Vereinbarung der Zulassung des ordentlichen Rechtsweges; **~-out** ausdrücklicher Ausschuß des ordentlichen Rechtsweges; **~ into the state pension scheme** Beteiligung am staatlichen Altersversorgungswerk;
~ (a.) vertragschließend;
~ governments vertragsschließende Regierungen; **~ officer** Vergabebeamter; **~-out clause** *(law of nations)* Freizeichnungsklausel; **~ parties (partners)** vertragsschließende Parteien, Kontrahenten, Vertragspartner; **high ~ parties** hohe Vertragsschließende; **~ policy** Vergabepolitik; **~ price** Lieferungspreis; **~ state** Vertragsstaat.

contraction Schrumpfung, *(abbreviation)* Abkürzung, Verkürzung, Kurzwort, *(illness)* Zuziehung;
~ of the currency Einschränkung des Notenumlaufs; **~ of debts** Kontrahierung von Schulden, Schuldenaufnahme; **~ in demand** Nachfrageschrumpfung, schrumpfende Nachfrage; **~ of credit issues** Kreditbeschränkung; **~ of liquidity** Liquiditätsschrumpfung; **~ of marriage** Eheschließung; **~ in production** Produktionseinschränkung.

contractive tendencies Abschwächungstendenzen.
contractor *(employer)* Unternehmer, *(mining)* Hauptgedingenehmer, Grubenpächter, *(party to a bargain)* Vertragsschließender, Vertragspartei, Kontrahent, *(supplier)* Auftragnehmer, [Submissions]lieferant, Lieferer;
~ advertisement ~ Werbeunternehmen, -agentur; **army ~** Heereslieferant; **builder and ~, building ~** Bauunternehmer; **carting ~** Rollfuhrunternehmer; **catering ~** Vertragslieferant von Betriebskantinen; **coal ~** Kohlenlieferant; **haulage ~** Beförderungsunternehmer; **independent ~** unabhängiger Unternehmer, Übernehmer eines Werkvertrages; **joint ~** Mitkontrahent; **labo(u)r ~** Arbeitsvermittlungsstelle; **main ~** Hauptlieferant, Generalunternehmen; **prime ~** Hauptlieferant; **road ~** Straßenbauunternehmer; **road transport ~** Transportunternehmer; **timber ~** Holzlieferant;
~ to the government (Crown, Br.) Staatslieferant, Übernehmer von Staatsaufträgen;
~'s all risk policy Pauschalversicherungspolice für Bauunternehmer; **~ association** Unternehmerverband; **~'s estimate** Baukostenvoranschlag, *(awards)* Submissionsangebot; **~'s liability** Unternehmerhaftpflicht; **to drive on ~ performance** höhere Leistungen von den Lieferanten fordern.

contractual vertraglich, vertragsmäßig, auf Vertrag gegründet; **quasi-~** vertragsähnlich;
~ agreement vertragliche Vereinbarung; **~ arrangement** vertragliche Vereinbarung; **~ autonomy** Vertragsautonomie; **~ capacity** Vertragsfähigkeit; **~ cartel** Verdingungskartell; **~ claim** vertraglich begründeter Anspruch; **~ clause** Vertragsklausel; **~ commitments** vertragliche Verpflichtungen; **~ document** Vertragsurkunde; **~ due date** vereinbarter Zahlungstermin; **~ duties** Vertragspflichten, *(customs)* Vertragszölle; **~ fidelity** Vertragstreue; **~ force** vertragliche Auswirkung; **~ liability** Vertragshaftung; **~ liberty** Vertragsfreiheit; **~ obligation** Vertragsverpflichtung, vertragliche Verpflichtung; **~ period** Vertragsdauer; **~ position** vertragliche Position; **~ power** Abschlußvollmacht; **~ problem** Vertragsproblem; **~ promise** Vertragszusage; **~ provisions** Vertragsbestimmungen; **~ rate** Vertragsquote; **~ regime** *(US)* vertragliches Güterrecht; **~ relations** vertragliche Beziehungen, Vertragsbeziehungen; **quasi-~ relationship** vertragsähnliches Verhältnis; **~ right to redeem** vertragliches Auslösungsrecht; **~ saving** [etwa] Sparen über vermögensbildende Leistungen, Betriebssparen; **~ share** Vertragsanteil; **~ stipulation** Vertragsvereinbarung; **~ tenancy** vertraglich vereinbartes Mietsverhältnis; **~ term** Vertragsbedingung, -begriff; **~ treaty** *(law of nations)* rechtsgeschäftlicher Vertrag; **~ undertaking** Vertragszusage; **~ wages** *(US)* Tarif-, Akkordlohn; **~ year** Insertions-, Abschlußjahr.

contracyclical *(a.)* antizyklisch.
contradict *(v.)* Widerspruch erheben, widersprechen;
~ a statement einer Behauptung widersprechen.
contradiction Unvereinbarkeit, Widerspruch;
~ in terms innerer Widerspruch;
to be in ~ im Widerspruch stehen.
contradictional widersprechend, unvereinbar;
~ statements sich widersprechende Erklärungen.
contradictiousness Widerspruchsgeist.
contradictory *(law)* streitig.
contrahent Vertragspartner, Kontrahent;
~ (a.) vertragsschließend.
contrariety Widersprüchlichkeit, Unvereinbarkeit;
~ of interest Interessensgegensatz.
contrainjection *(airplane)* Treibstoffeinspritzung.
contrary Gegenteil;
failing proof to the ~ bis zum Beweis des Gegenteils;
~ (a.) gegensätzlich, entgegengesetzt, im Gegenteil, konträr, *(weather)* ungünstig;
~ to the evidence im Widerspruch zum Beweisergebnis; **~ to one's knowledge** wider besseres Wissen; **~ to the law** gesetzwidrig; **~ to regulations** vorschriftswidrig;
to act ~ to instructions seinen Anweisungen zuwiderhandeln; **to be ~ to expectations** den Erwartungen nicht entsprechen; **to be ~ to the purpose** dem Zweck zuwiderlaufen; **to be ~ to the rule** gegen die Regeln verstoßen; **to prove the ~** Gegenbeweis führen;
~ report widersprechender Bericht.
contrast Kontrast, Gegensatz, *(television)* Bildkontrast;
~ (v.) kontrastieren, sich abheben, abstechen;
~ strongly with one's own opinion mit seiner eigenen Meinung in starkem Gegensatz stehen; **~ imported goods with the domestic product** Importware mit einheimischen Erzeugnissen vergleichen;

to be a great ~ to one's brother von seinem Bruder grundverschieden sein.

contravene *(v.)* zuwiderhandeln, übertreten, verletzen, im Widerspruch stehen, *(heir of entail, Scot.)* Fideikommißbestimmungen verletzen;
~ **a law** Gesetz verletzen, gegen ein Gesetz verstoßen; ~ **s. one's plans** jds. Pläne vereiteln; ~ **the first principles of equity** einfachste Grundsätze der Billigkeit verletzen; ~ **the regulations** den Bestimmungen zuwiderhandeln; ~ **a statement** einem Dementi entgegentreten.

contravener Übertreter.

contravention *(law)* [Gesetzes]übertretung, Polizeistrafen unterliegendes Delikt, Zuwiderhandlung, Verstoß;
in ~ unter Verletzung von; **in** ~ **of the rules** gegen die Vorschriften;
~ **of the law** Gesetzesübertretung;
to act in ~ **of a right** unter Verletzung eines Rechts handeln.

contribute *(v.)* zuwenden, beitragen, Beitrag leisten, beisteuern, mitwirken, erwirtschaften, *(money)* zu-, nach-, einschießen, *(newspaper)* schriftliche Beiträge liefern, einsenden;
liable to ~ beitragspflichtig;
~ **to the advancement of science** zur Förderung der Wissenschaften beitragen; ~ **an article to a commemorative volume** Artikel zu einer Festschrift beisteuern; ~ **capital** Kapital einbringen, Einlage vornehmen; ~ **cash** Bareinlage leisten; ~ **towards the costs** sich an den Kosten beteiligen; ~ **to the Red Cross** dem Roten Kreuz eine Spende zukommen lassen; ~ **to the government's downfall** zum Sturz der Regierung beitragen; ~ **equally towards the losses sustained by a firm** Geschäftsverluste zu gleichen Teilen tragen; ~ **equally to the pleasure of the evenings** gleichmäßig zur abendlichen Entspannung beitragen; ~ **to the expenses** Unkostenbeitrag leisten; ~ **food and clothing for the refugees** Verpflegung und Bekleidung für die Flüchtlinge spenden; ~ **new information on a scientific problem** neue Erkenntnisse zur Lösung eines wissenschaftlichen Problems beisteuern; ~ **to a newspaper (newspaper articles)** Artikel für eine Zeitung schreiben, Zeitungsartikel beisteuern; ~ **to a present** sich an einem Geschenk beteiligen; ~ **one's services** mitarbeiten, seine Arbeitskraft einbringen; ~ **one's share** seinen Anteil beitragen (Beitrag leisten); ~ **to the success** zu dem Erfolg beitragen; ~ **a sum of money** Geldbetrag stiften, beisteuern; ~ **to a work of charity** Wohltätigkeitsbeitrag leisten.

contributed capital eingezahltes Grundkapital.

contributing | box Beitragsfonds; ~ **editor** Korrespondent, freier Mitarbeiter; ~ **member** zahlendes Mitglied; ~ **values** umlagenpflichtige (beitragspflichtige) Vermögenswerte.

contribution *(article)* wissenschaftlicher Beitrag, *(bankruptcy)* Masseverteilung, *(capital)* Gesellschaftseinlage, Einlagekapital, *(compulsory payment)* Zwangsbeitrag, *(donation)* Zuwendung, Spende, *(insurance)* Schadensbeteiligung, *(fire insurance)* umgelegter Schadensanteil, Ausgleichszahlung, *(joint liability)* Quote, *(limited partner)* [Gesellschafter]einlage, *(membership due)* Beitrag, *(mining)* Zubuße [zu einem Kux], *(share)* Prämieneinzahlung, *(subscription)* [Geld]spende, *(war tax)* Kontribution, Kriegssteuer, -auflage;
liable to ~ beitragspflichtig;
additional ~ Zusatz-, Nachschußleistung; **average** ~ Havariebeitrag; **capital** ~ Kapitalaufbringung, -einbringung, Einlage; **charitable** ~ Beitrag zu wohltätigen Zwecken, Spende; **compulsory** ~ Pflicht-, Zwangsbeitrag; ~ **credited** *(national insurance)* angerechneter Sozialversicherungsbeitrag; ~**s still due** noch fällige Beiträge; **employee's** ~ *(social insurance)* Arbeitnehmeranteil; **employer's** ~ *(social insurance)* Arbeitgeberanteil; **financial** ~ finanzieller Zuschuß; **flat-rate** ~ pauschaler Beitragssatz, *(social insurance)* Einheitsbeitrag; **graded** ~ gestaffelter Beitragssatz; **graduated** ~ gestaffelte Beitragsleistung, gestaffelter [Sozialversicherungs]beitrag; **increased** ~ Beitragserhöhung; **initial** ~ Stammeinlage; **lost** ~ verlorener Zuschuß; **minimum** ~ Mindestbeitrag; **monthly** ~ *(saving)* monatliche Sparrate (Sparleistung); **national insurance** ~ *(Br.)* Sozialversicherungsbeitrag; **once-for-all special** ~ *(Br.)* einmalige Vermögensabgabe; **periodical** ~ laufender Beitrag; **political** ~ Förderbeitrag; **prorata** ~ anteilsmäßiger Beitrag; ~**s received** Beitragsaufkommen; **social** ~s soziale Abgaben (Beitragsleistungen); **social security** ~ *(US)* Sozialversicherungsbeitrag; **special** ~ Sonderbeitrag, -abgabe; **state** ~s staatliche Zuwendungen; **substantial** ~ wesentlicher Beitrag; **tax-deductible** ~ steuerabzugsfähige Spende; **unasked (voluntary)** ~ freiwillige Spende (Zuwendung); **voluntary war** ~ Kriegsabgabe;
~ **of alms** Almosenbeitrag; ~**s in arrears** Beitragsrückstände; ~ **to general average** Verlustbeteiligung bei gemeinschaftlicher

Havarie; ~ **to capital** Kapitalaufbringung, -einbringung, -einzahlung; ~ **in cash** Bareinlage; ~ **to charity** wohltätige Spende; ~ **to a church** Kirchgeld; ~ **to the expenses** Unkostenbeitrag; ~**s received by the life insurance companies** Beitragseinnahmen der Lebensversicherungsgesellschaften; ~ **in kind** Naturalleistung, Sacheinlage; ~ **to a magazine** Zeitschriftenbeitrag; ~ **to a paper** wissenschaftlicher Beitrag; ~ **of each party in a marriage settlement** Ehegattenanteil in einem Heiratsvertrag; ~**s to a pension trust** *(balance sheet)* Beiträge zur Altersversorgung; ~ **to periodicals** Beiträge für Zeitschriften; ~ **for political purposes** politischer Spendenbeitrag; ~ **for the poor** Spende für die Armen; ~ **pro rata** Anteil, Quote; ~**s to the relief fund** Spenden an den Unterstützungsfonds; **allowable** ~ **for superannuation benefits** steuerlich anerkannter (abzugsfähiger) Pensionskassenbeitrag; ~**s to a trust scheme** Beiträge für eine Pensionskasse; ~**s which came in** eingegangene Spenden; **to accept** ~**s in any size** Spenden in jeder Höhe entgegennehmen; **to adjust one's** ~**s in line with the general index of retail prices** seine Sparleistungen dem Einzelhandelspreisindex anpassen (inflationsmäßig absichern); **to adjust** ~**s in line with any change in prices** monatliche Sparleistungen der Preisinflation anpassen; **to assess the** ~ Beitragshöhe festlegen; **to be in arrears with the payment of one's** ~ mit seiner Beitragsleistung im Rückstand sein; **to be entitled to a** ~ Ausgleichsansprüche haben; **to be liable up to their** ~**s** *(limited partners)* in Höhe ihrer Kommanditeinlage haften; **to be supported by voluntary** ~**s** durch freiwillige Spenden unterhalten werden; **to collect** ~**s** Beiträge einsammeln; **to credit with a** ~ *(national insurance)* Versicherungsbeitrag anrechnen; **to impose a** ~ Beitrag durch Umlage erheben; **to lay a country under** ~ einem Land eine Kontribution auferlegen, Land brandschatzen; **to lay one's friends under** ~ *(Br.)* seine Freunde um finanzielle Unterstützung angehen; **to levy a** ~ Kontribution auferlegen; **to make a** ~ Beitrag leisten; **to make** ~**s towards the cost of maintenance** Zuschuß zu den Unterhaltskosten leisten; **to make** ~**s to the pension trust** Beitrag zur Pensionskasse leisten; **to make sixty regular monthly** ~**s over five years** fünfjährigen Sparvertrag mit sechzig Monatsraten abschließen; **to obtain** ~ *(cosurety)* Ausgleichansprüche erhalten; **to pay one's** ~ seinen Beitrag leisten (zahlen); **to pay** ~**s into the scheme** Beiträge in die Sozialversicherung einzahlen;
~ **box** Beitragsfonds; ~ **card** *(Br.)* Sozialversicherungskarte; ~ **clause** *(fire insurance)* Umlegungsbestimmung; ~ **conditions** Beitragsbestimmungen, -bedingungen; **to be subject to** ~ **conditions** von Beitragszahlungen abhängig sein; ~ **deduction scheme** Einzug der Gewerkschaftsbeiträge durch den Arbeitgeber; ~ **dues** *(US)* Beitragsleistung; ~ **margin** Deckungsbeitrag; ~ **period** Beitragsabschnitt; ~ **plan** *(life insurance)* Gewinnbeteiligungssystem; ~ **rate** Beitragssatz; ~ **record** *(social insurance)* anrechnungsfähige Beitragszeit; ~ **refund** Beitragserstattung; ~ **rights** *(law of insurance)* Ausgleichsansprüche; ~ **scale** Beitragsstaffel; ~ **table** Beitragstabelle; ~ **week** *(national insurance)* Beitragswoche; ~ **year** *(national insurance)* sozialversicherungspflichtiges Jahr, Beitragsjahr.

contributive beisteuernd, mitwirkend.

contributor Spender, Beitragsleistender, -pflichtiger, Leistungspflichtiger, *(newspaper)* Mitarbeiter;
big-business ~ Spendenstrom aus der Großindustrie; **employee** ~ *(national insurance)* versicherungspflichtiger Arbeitnehmer; ~ **of capital** Kapitaleinleger, -aufbringer; **regular** ~ **to a newspaper** ständiger Mitarbeiter einer Zeitung.

contributory beitragspflichtiges Mitglied, Beitragspflichtiger, -leistender, *(contributing factor)* fördernder Umstand, *(shareholder, Br.)* solidarisch haftender Aktionär, Nachschußpflichtiger;
~ *(a.)* mitwirkend, beitragend, beitragspflichtig, *(liable member, Br.)* nachzahlungspflichtig;
~ **basis** Beitragsbemessungsgrundlage; ~ **causes** mitverursachende Umstände, mitwirkende Ursachen; ~ **fund** Beitragsfonds; ~ **infringement** *(patent law)* Beteiligung an einer Patentverletzung; ~ **member** beitragspflichtiges Mitglied; ~ **mortgage** für mehrere Gläubiger bestellte Hypothek; ~ **negligence** konkurrierendes Verschulden; ~ **pension** beitragspflichtige Pension (Rente); ~ **pension scheme** beitragspflichtige Pensionskassensystem; ~ **plan** beitragspflichtiges Pensionssystem; ~ **scheme** Beitragsverfahren; ~ **scheme of insurance** Umlageverfahren einer Versicherung; ~ **value** *(average)* beitragspflichtiger Wert; ~ **general value** *(average)* beitragspflichtiger Wert zur großen Havarie.

contrition Reuegefühl.

contrivable erdenkbar, durchführbar.

contrivance Vorrichtung, Einrichtung, Apparat, *(invention)* Erfindung, *(scheme)* Plan, Bewerkstelligung;
to escape by the ~ of one's friends mit Hilfe seiner Freunde entkommen.

contrive *(v.)* **with prices rising every month** seinen Haushalt trotz jeden Monat steigender Preise bewerkstelligen.

control Macht, Verfügungsgewalt, -macht, Kontrolle, Herrschaft, Beherrschung, Einfluß, *(airplane)* Steuerung, Leitwerk, *(command)* Leitung, Ordnung, *(decisive influence)* ausschlaggebender Einfluß[bereich], *(economic planning)* Bewirtschaftung, Zwangswirtschaft, *(el.)* Regulierung, Regelung, *(management)* Leistung, *(restraint)* Beschränkung, *(supervision)* Aufsicht, Kontrolle, Steuerung;
in ~ aufsichtsführend; **out of ~** außer Kontrolle geraten; **under ~ *(person)*** entmündigt; **under parental ~** unter elterlicher Gewalt; **under various ~** unter wechselnder Leitung; **without ~** uneingeschränkt, unbeaufsichtigt, frei;
accounting ~ Überwachung der Buchführung; **air ~s** Flugüberwachungsgeräte; **air traffic ~** Luftraumüberwachung; **birth ~** Geburtenbeschränkung, -regelung; **border ~** Grenzkontrolle; **budgetary ~** Haushaltskontrolle, -überwachung; **coding ~** Überwachung der Verschlüsselungstätigkeit; **commodity ~** Warenbewirtschaftung; **credit ~** Kreditaufsicht; **creditor ~** Gläubigeraufsicht; **currency ~** Devisenbewirtschaftung; **economic ~** Wirtschaftslenkung, Zwangswirtschaft; **entire ~** absolute Kontrolle; **exchange ~** Devisenbewirtschaftung; **export ~** Ausfuhrkontrolle; **financial ~** finanzielle Überwachungstätigkeit; **foreign exchange ~** Devisenbewirtschaftung, -kontrolle, -zwangswirtschaft; **frontier ~** Grenzüberwachung; **governmental ~** Staatsaufsicht, Wirtschaftslenkung; **housing ~** Bewirtschaftung des Wohnungsmarktes, Wohnungszwangswirtschaft; **import ~** Einfuhrkontrolle; **industrial ~** Kontrolle der Wirtschaft; **internal ~** betriebseigene Überwachung; **international ~** internationale Verfügungsgewalt (Kontrolle); **inventory ~** Vorratsbewirtschaftung, Bestands-, Lagerkontrolle; **investment ~** Investitionslenkung; **joint ~** gemeinsame Verfügungsmacht; **marketing ~** Absatz-, Vertriebssteuerung; **monopolistic ~** monopolistische Beherrschung; **operational ~** *(mil.)* operative Leitung; **overhead ~** zentrale Kontrolle; **parental ~** elterliche Aufsicht (Gewalt); **passport ~** Paßkontrolle; **price ~** Preiskontrolle, -überwachung; **administrative price ~** staatliche Preisüberwachung; **production ~** Produktionslenkung; **property ~** Vermögenskontrolle; **quality ~** statistische Güteüberwachung; **quantitative ~** Mengenkontrolle; **rent ~** *(Br.)* Mietpreisbindung, Mieterschutz; **sanitary ~** sanitäre Überwachung, Aufsichtstätigkeit der Gesundheitsbehörde; **sovereign ~** souveräne Verfügungsgewalt; **speed ~** Geschwindigkeitskontrolle; **standby ~** für bestimmte Zwecke gesetzlich vorgesehene Staatsaufsicht; **state ~** staatliche Aufsicht, Staatsaufsicht; **statistical quality ~** statistische Güteüberwachung; **strict ~** strenge Kontrolle; **supervisory ~** Überwachungssystem; **traffic ~** Verkehrskontrolle; **wartime ~** Kriegsbewirtschaftung;
~ of an advance Kreditüberwachung; **~ of the air** Luftraumbeherrschung; **social ~ of business** Staatsinterventionismus; **~ of capital** Kapitallenkung; **~ of costs** Kostenkontrolle; **~ over several departments** Leitung mehrerer Abteilungen; **~ of drink** Alkoholverbot; **~ of foreign exchange** Devisenbewirtschaftung; **~ of exports** staatliche Exportregelung; **statutory ~ of incomes** staatliche Einkommensregelung; **~ of investment** Investitionskontrolle, -lenkung; **~ of lettings** *(Br.)* Mieterschutz; **~ of the market** Absatzlenkung; **quality ~ of materials** Materialkontrolle; **~ of monopolies** Monopolkontrolle; **~ of a motor car** Herrschaft über ein Fahrzeug; **~ of newspapers** Überwachung der Presse; **~ of operations** Betriebsüberwachung; **~ in ownership interests** ausschlaggebender Kapitalanteil; **~ of production** Produktionskontrolle, -überwachung; **~ of profits** Gewinnbeschränkung; **~ of purchasing power** Kaufkraftlenkung; **~ of rent** *(Br.)* Mietpreisbindung, Mieterschutz; **~ and reporting** *(mil.)* Fliegerleit- und Flugmeldedienst; **~ of the seas** Seeherrschaft; **~ of traffic** Verkehrsregelung, -lenkung, -steuerung -kontrolle; **~ by the treasury** *(Br.)* Aufsicht des Schatzamtes; **~ of a wireless set** Lautstärkeregelung eines Rundfunkgeräts;
~ *(v.)* leiten, lenken, regeln, *(check)* kontrollieren, überwachen, [über]prüfen, *(dominate)* beherrschen, Gewalt haben, ausschlaggebenden Einfluß ausüben, *(economize)* unter Zwangswirtschaft stellen, bewirtschaften, *(el.)* regeln, regulieren, *(manage)* leiten, lenken, steuern, *(supervise)* überwachen, beaufsichtigen, Aufsicht führen;
~ o. s. sich beherrschen; **~ the accounts** Konten überwachen

(überprüfen); **~ a company by holding a majority of the shares** Unternehmen durch Aktienmehrheit kontrollieren (beherrschen); **~ the economic life of a region** Wirtschaftsleben einer Gegend entscheidend beeinflussen; **~ expenditure** Unkosten niedrig halten; **~ housing** Wohnungsmarkt bewirtschaften; **~ a preponderant part of the market** entscheidenden Marktanteil besitzen; **~ the rise in the cost of living** der Steigerung der Lebenshaltungskosten Einhalt gebieten; **~ one's temper** sein Temperament zügeln; **~ traffic** Verkehr regeln (bewältigen); **~ an undertaking** Unternehmen leiten;
to abolish the ~ of imports Einfuhrkontrollbestimmungen aufheben; **to assume the ~** Leitung übernehmen; **to be beyond s. one's ~** außerhalb jds. Einflußbereich liegen; **to be in ~ of s. th.** Leitung von etw. innehaben; **to be under ~** unter Kontrolle stehen, beaufsichtigt werden; **to be under ~ of customs officers** der Zollaufsicht unterliegen; **to break loose from all ~** alle Dämme brechen; **to dismantle wartime ~s** kriegsbedingte Wirtschaftsbeschränkungen abbauen; **to exercise ~** Kontrolle ausüben; **to exercise supervisory ~s** Aufsichtstätigkeit ausüben; **to get beyond s. one's ~** jem. über den Kopf wachsen; **to gain ~ of the government** an die Macht kommen; **to get flood waters under ~** Überschwemmung in den Griff bekommen; **to have ~ of a department** Abteilung leiten; **to have a situation under ~** Herr der Lage sein; **to have ~ of an undertaking** an der Spitze eines Unternehmens stehen; **to keep under ~** im Zaum halten; **to leave no one clearly in ~** keine regierungsfähige Mehrheit ermöglichen; **to lift a ~** Bewirtschaftungsmaßnahme aufheben; **to lose ~ of o. s.** Selbstbeherrschung verlieren; **to lose ~ of an aircraft** Gewalt über ein Flugzeug verlieren; **to lose ~ of one's car** Gewalt über sein Auto verlieren; **to pass into the ~ of s. o.** in den Besitz von jem. übergehen; **to place under ~** unter Vormundschaft stellen, entmündigen; **to put under government ~** staatlich bewirtschaften lassen; **to remove ~s** Restriktionen abbauen; **to speak without ~** rückhaltlos sprechen; **to take ~ of the railways** Eisenbahnen verstaatlichen; **to wield omnipotent ~** unumschränkt herrschen;
~ account Hauptbuchsammel-, Kontrollkonto; **~ board** Aufsichtsamt; **~ budget** beweglicher Etat; **~ car** *(airship)* Führergondel; **~ card** Kontrollkarte; **~ center** *(US)* (centre, *Br.*) Überwachungszentrum; **~ chart** *(statistics)* Darstellung der Bevölkerungsdichte; **~ clock** Kontrolluhr; **~ column** *(airplane)* Steuerknüppel; **~ commission** Kontrolkommission, Aufsichtsamt; **~ engineering** Maßnahmen zur laufenden Fertigungskontrolle; **~ experiment** Vergleichsexperiment, Gegen-, Kontrollversuch; **~ group** *(inquiry)* Kontrollgruppe; **~ limit** *(statistics)* Prüfungs-, Kontrollgrenze; **~ methods** Kontrollmethoden; **~ office** Bewirtschaftungs-, Überwachungsstelle; **~ officer** Aufsichtsbeamter, -führender; **♀ of Borrowing Order** *(Br.)* Kommunalkreditordnung; **~ organization** Kontrollorganisation; **~ panel** Bedienungspult; **gas ~ pedal** *(car)* Gaspedal; **~ purposes** Kontrollzwecke; **~ relay** Steuer-, Kontrollrelais; **~ room** zentraler Kommandoraum, Zentrale, *(film)* Regieraum; **~ signal** Steuerungs-, Verkehrszeichen; **~ stick** *(airplane, coll.)* Steuerknüppel; **~ switch** Kontrollhalter; **~ system** Überwachungs-, Bewirtschaftungssystem, **~ team** Untersuchungskommission; **~ test** Gegenprobe; **~ ticket** Kontrollschein; **~ tower** Flugsicherungs-, Kontrollturm; **~ unit** *(data processing)* Steuerwerk; **~ vessel** Überwachungsschiff; **~ zone** *(traffic)* Nahverkehrsbezirk.

controllable nachprüfbar, kontrollierbar.

controlled kontrolliert, überwacht, *(administered)* gelenkt, bewirtschaftet, gesteuert, *(airplane)* ferngesteuert, *(price)* preisgestoppt;
government-~ unter Staatsaufsicht;
to be ~ by foreign interests vom Ausland kontrolliert werden, ausländischem Einfluß unterliegen;
~ area Kontrollgebiet; **~ circulation** *(US)* Freiexemplarliste; **~ company** abhängige Gesellschaft, beherrschtes Unternehmen; **~ crossing** Verkehrsregelung an einer Kreuzung; **~ currency** bewirtschaftete Devisen; **~ disarmament** überwachte Abrüstung; **~ distribution** Absatzlenkung; **~ economy** gelenkte Wirtschaft, Planwirtschaft; **~ exports** Exportlenkung; **~ finance** Finanzkontrolle; **~ house** *(Br.)* der Mieterschutzgesetzgebung unterliegendes Haus; **~ price** amtlich festgesetzter [Stopp]preis, gebundener Preis; **~ recognition formula** Methode der Werbeerfolgskontrolle; **~ response** *(mil.)* abgestufte Vergeltung; **~ rocket** gesteuerte Rakete; **~ sample** *(statistics)* gelenkte Stichprobe, charakteristische Marktuntersuchung; **~ sampling** repräsentative Auswahl, Stichprobenauswahl nach statistischen Gesichtspunkten, statistisches Auswahlverfahren für Marktforschungszwecke.

controller Leiter, Aufseher, Lenker, Kontrolleur, Aufsichtsbeamter, Nachprüfer, *(auditor)* staatlicher Rechnungsprüfer, Revisor, *(US)* Leiter des Rechnungswesens, Verantwortlicher für die betriebliche Informationswirtschaft, Kontroller, *(el.)* Regler;
  corporate ~ Revisionsbeamter;
  ~ of accounts Rechnungsrevisor; **≗ and Auditor General** *(Br.)* Präsident des Rechnungshofes; **~ of the currency** *(US)* [etwa] Bankenkommissar; **~ of investments** Koordinator des Investitionsbereiches; **~ of materials** Materialverwalter.
controllership Aufseheramt, Kontrolleurstelle.
controlling *(US)* Informationswirtschaft;
  ~ of traffic Verkehrsregelung;
  ~ (a.) überwachend, maßgebend;
  to be ~ ausschlaggebend sein;
  ~ account Gegenrechnung, *(US)* Kontrollbuch; **~ agreement** Beherrschungsvertrag; **~ authority** Aufsichtsbehörde; **~ body** Aufsichtsorgan; **~ company** beherrschende Gesellschaft, Holding-, Dachgesellschaft; **~ interest** ausschlaggebender Kapitalanteil, Mehrheitsbeteiligung, Kapitalmehrheit; **~ power** beherrschende Stellung; **~ [stock] interest** ausschlaggebender Kapitalanteil; **to acquire a ~ interest in a concern** Kapitalmehrheit (Sperrminorität) in einem Unternehmen erwerben; **~ shareholder** *(Br.)* **(stockholder,** *US)* Aktienmajoritätsbesitzer.
controversial strittig, streitig, umstritten, kontrovers, polemisch;
  ~ book umstrittenes Buch; **~ opinion** bestrittene Ansicht; **~ subject** Streitfrage; **~ speech** umstrittene Rede.
controversialist Polemiker.
controversialize *(v.)* polemisieren.
controversy Streitfrage, Disput, Meinungsverschiedenheit, Kontroverse, Polemik, *(law)* Rechtsstreit, -sache, Prozeß;
  beyond (without) ~ unzweifelhaft, fraglos, unstrittig;
  press ~ Pressepolemik;
  to carry on a ~ with s. o. Meinungsverschiedenheit mit jem. haben; **to enter into a ~** polemisieren.
controvert *(v.)* diskutieren, debattieren, *(claim)* bestreiten;
  ~ a statement Richtigkeit einer Behauptung bestreiten.
controverter Polemiker.
contumacious aufsässig, widerspenstig, *(law court)* trotz Ladung nicht erscheinen.
contumaciousness, contumacy *(law court)* absichtliches Nichterscheinen vor Gericht;
  to condemn for ~ in Abwesenheit verurteilen.
conurbation Gruppengroßstadt;
  ~ area Ballungsgebiet.
convalesce *(v.)* genesen, gesund werden.
convalescence Genesung, Rekonvaleszenz.
convalescent Genesender, Rekonvaleszent;
  ~ home (hospital) Rekonvaleszentenheim, Genesungsheim, Sanatorium.
convector heater Raumheizgerät, Heizstrahler.
convenable geeignet.
convenances Anstandsformen, Konventionalität.
convene *(v.) (assemble)* zusammentreten, sich versammeln, *(cite)* amtlich vorladen, *(convoke)* einberufen;
  ~ an assembly Versammlung einberufen; **~ s. o. before a court** j. vor Gericht laden (verklagen); **~ a meeting** Versammlung (Tagung) einberufen; **~ properly** satzungsgemäß einberufen.
convener Einberufer, *(Scotland)* Rats-, Ausschußvorsitzender.
convenience Belieben, Praktikabilität, *(easiness)* Bequemlichkeit, Komfort, *(lavatory, Br.)* Wasserklosett, WC, *(lodging)* Zweckmäßigkeit;
  as a matter of ~ aus Zweckmäßigkeitsgründen; **for accounting ~** zur Erleichterung der Buchhaltung; **at one's ~** gelegentlich; **at your earliest ~** bei erster Gelegenheit, sobald als möglich; **for accounting ~** zur Erleichterung der Buchhaltung; **with all ~** mit allem Zubehör; **with all modern ~s** mit allem (dem allerneuesten) Komfort;
  built for ~ bequem zu bewirtschaften;
  in-flight ~ Bequemlichkeit während des Fluges; **public ~** öffentliche Bedürfnisanstalt;
  to have all modern ~ über den neuesten Komfort verfügen; **to make a ~ of s. o.** j. ausnutzen; **to pay at ~** gelegentlich bezahlen; **to plan a house for ~** ganz auf Zweckmäßigkeit abgestelltes Haus entwerfen; **to suit one's ~** ganz nach eigenem Belieben handeln;
  ~ goods Güter des täglichen Bedarfs, Bedarfsdeckungs-, Verbrauchsgüter; **~store** Bedarfsartikelgeschäft.
convenient passend, geeignet, bequem, zweckdienlich, opportun, günstig;

to be ~ bequem zu erreichen;
  ~-sized handlich; **at a ~ time** zu einer genehmen Zeit; **~ tool** geeignetes Werkzeug.
conveniently near the bus stop ganz in der Nähe der Omnibushaltestelle.
convening of meetings Einberufung von Versammlungen.
convention Übereinkommen, -kunft, Abmachung, *(common consent)* gemeinsame Zustimmung, allgemeine Übereinstimmung, *(custom)* [stillschweigende] Gewohnheit (Gepflogenheit), Anstandsregeln, *(dipl.)* Kollektiv-, Staatsvertrag, Konvention, *(meeting)* Zusammenkunft, Versammlung, Tagung, *(mil.)* Militärkonvention, *(pol.)* gesetzgebende Versammlung, *(political party, US)* Parteikonvent, -tag, -kongreß, Delegierten-, Wahlmännerversammlung, *(summoning of meeting)* Einberufung;
  ~s anerkannter Brauch;
  annual ~ Jahresversammlung; **commercial ~** Handelsabkommen; **constitutional ~** verfassungsgebende Nationalversammlung; **copyright ~** Urheberrechtsabkommen; **cultural ~** Kulturabkommen; **international ~** zwischenstaatliche Vereinbarung; **joint ~** *(US)* gemeinsame Sitzung von Kongreß und Senat; **judicial ~** Vereinbarung aufgrund einer Gerichtsanordnung; **Geneva ≗** Genfer Konvention; **leonine ~** leoninischer Vertrag; **national ~** Nationalkonvent; **nominating ~** Wählerversammlung; **sales ~** Vertreterbesprechung; **social ~s** gesellschaftliche Konventionen; **state-wide ~** Kongreß auf Bundesebene; **straits ~** Meerengenabkommen; **universal ~** Weltabkommen; **Universal Postal ≗** Weltpostvertrag;
  ~ for the avoidance of double taxation Doppelbesteuerungsabkommen; **~ of navigation** Schiffahrtsabkommen;
  to accede to a ~ einer Konvention beitreten; **to open a ~ for signature** Abkommen zur Unterzeichnung auflegen;
  ~ application Verbandsanmeldung; **~ business** Tagungswesen; **~ center** *(US)* **(centre,** *Br.)* Kongreß-, Tagungszentrum; **~ country** Signatarmacht; **~ date** Datum der Verbandspriorität; **~ facilities** Tagungseinrichtungen; **~ hall** Versammlungshalle; **~ money** gemeinsame Währung; **~ priority** Verbandspriorität; **~ resort** Tagungsort; **~ tariff** Vertragstarif; **~ trip** Tagungsausflug.
conventional herkömmlich, üblich, gewohnheitsrechtlich, konventionell, *(stipulated)* vertragsgemäß, vertraglich vereinbart;
  ~ community vertragliche Gütergemeinschaft; **~ design** gängige Sorte; **to have only ~ designs in stock** nur gängige Sorten auf Lager haben; **~ estate** vertragliches Herrschaftsrecht; **~ forces** *(mil.)* konventionelle Streitkräfte; **~ greeting** übliche Begrüßung; **~ heir** *(US)* Vertragserbe; **~ interest** vereinbarter Zinssatz; **~ rate of interest** üblicher Zinssatz; **~ lien** Vertragspfand; **~ mortgage** vertragliches Grundpfandrecht; **~ necessities** Güter des gehobenen Bedarfs; **~ power station** herkömmliches Elektrizitätswerk; **~ proprieties** gesellschaftliche Konventionen; **~ remarks** übliche Bemerkungen; **~ style** Gesprächsstil; **~ tariff** vereinbarter Zolltarif; **~ tariff system** Zolltarifvereinbarung; **~ trustee** behördlich bestellter Verwalter (Treuhänder); **~ type** *(motorcar)* Standardausführung; **~ war** konventioneller Krieg; **to escalate a ~ war into nuclear warfare** konventionellen Krieg in einen Atomkrieg eskalieren lassen; **~ weapons** konventionelle Waffen.
conventionality Schablonenhaftigkeit, Üblichkeit.
conventionary vertragsmäßig.
conventioneer *(US)* Versammlungsmitglied, Tagungsteilnehmer.
converge *(v.)* **on the capital** *(army)* auf dem Anmarsch auf die Hauptstadt sein.
convergence of streets Zusammenlaufen von Straßen.
conversable gesprächig, mitteilsam;
  ~ evening geselliger Abend.
conversance Vertrautheit.
conversant bewandert, vertraut;
  ~ with finance in finanziellen Dingen erfahren;
  to be ~ with s. th. mit etw. vertraut sein.
conversation Gespräch, Unterredung, Unterhaltung, Konversation, *(social interchange)* gesellschaftlicher Umgang, Verkehr;
  by way of ~ gesprächsweise;
  casual ~ Alltagsgespräche; **criminal ~** Ehebruch; **inanimate ~** langweilige Unterhaltung; **private ~** persönliche (vertrauliche) Unterredung; **snappy ~** angeregtes Gespräch; **spirited ~** angeregte Unterhaltung;
  television ~ with the press fernsehübertragenes Pressegespräch; **~ by telephone** Telefongespräch;
  to carry on a ~ Gespräch fortsetzen (wieder aufnehmen); **to conduct a ~** Gespräch führen; **to engage s. o. in a ~** j. in ein Gespräch verwickeln; **to engross a ~** Gesprächsführung an sich

reißen, Gesprächsrunde beherrschen; **to enter into a ~** Gespräch mit jem. anknüpfen; **to lead the ~ round to the political situation** Gespräch auf die politische Lage bringen; **to linger in ~** ausgedehntes Gespräch führen; **to monopolize a ~** Gesprächsführung an sich reißen, Gesprächsrunde beherrschen; **to start a ~** Gespräch eröffnen; **to sustain a ~ for hours** stundenlange Gespräche führen; **to work the ~ round to s. th.** Gespräch auf etw. lenken;

~ **piece** Gesprächsgegenstand, -knochen.

conversational gesprächig;

~ **English** Umgangsenglisch; **to take the ~ lead** Gesprächsführung an sich reißen, Gesprächsrunde beherrschen; ~ **power** Unterhaltungsgabe; ~ **style** Gesprächsstil; ~ **voice** Konversationston.

conversationalist gewandter Gesprächspartner, guter Gesellschafter.

converse Gegenteil, Umkehrung, *(familiar discourse)* zwangloses Gespräch, vertrauliche Unterhaltung;

~ *(v.)* vertrautes Gespräch führen;

~ **with books** sich intensiv mit Büchern beschäftigen.

conversion *(unauthorized assumption)* widerrechtliche Aneignung, *(character)* geistige (charakterliche) Wandlung, *(commutation)* Umwandlung, *(enterprise)*, Umstellung, *(of debentures)* Umtausch, Einlösung, Konversion, Konvertierung, *(politics)* Meinungswechsel, Übertritt, *(process of converting)* Umänderung, Umarbeitung, *(reduction of foreign exchange)* Umrechnung, Umwechslung, *(religion)* Glaubenswechsel, Bekehrung, *(shares)* Zusammenlegung, *(wrongful appropriation)* widerrechtliche Aneignung (Verwendung), Besitzentziehung;

suitable for ~ *(house)* leicht umzubauen, umbaufähig; **compulsory ~** Zwangskonversion; **constructive ~** Eigentumserwerb durch Verarbeitung; **direct ~** unmittelbare Aneignung; **equitable ~** Versilberung, Verwertung; **fraudulent ~** Unterschlagung, Veruntreuung; **house ~** Hausumbau; **loan ~** Anleiheumwandlung, -konversion;

~ **of 5 per cents into 4 per cents** Umtausch von 5 prozentigen in 4 prozentige Wertpapiere; ~ **of bank notes** Noteneinlösung; ~ **of coins** Umschmelzung von Münzen; ~ **into a company** Vergesellschaftung; ~ **of corporations** Umwandlung von Kapitalgesellschaften; ~ **of debts** Schuldumwandlung; ~ **in equity** Umwandlung von Grundeigentum in bewegliches Eigentum, Vermögensumwandlung; ~ **into flats** Umbau in Appartementwohnungen; ~ **into a nontaxable form** Umwandlung in eine steuerfreie Anlage; ~ **of funds to one's own use** Unterschlagung von Geldern; ~ **from gas and oil to coal** Umstellung von Gas und Erdöl auf Kohle; ~ **of landed property into cash** Realisierung (Versilberung) von Grundbesitz; ~ **of a loan** Anleiheumwandlung; ~ **of notes into gold** Umwechslung von Banknoten in Gold; ~ **of production** Produktionsumstellung; ~ **of realty into property** Umwandlung von unbeweglichem in bewegliches Vermögen; ~ **of rooms to office use** Zweckentfremdung einer Wohnung; ~ **of shares into stock** Umwandlung voll einbezahlter Kapitalanteilsrechte in Aktien; ~ **of merchant ships into war ships** Umbau von Handels- zu Kriegsschiffen; ~ **of stocks** Änderung der Aktienstückelung; ~ **to one's own use** Unterschlagung;

to be guilty of ~ sich der Unterschlagung schuldig machen; **to hold s. o. liable for ~** j. der Unterschlagung bezichtigen; **to suffer ~** Wandlungsklage erheben; **to sue for ~** Wandlungsklage erheben; **to undergo ~** modernisiert werden;

~ **account** Umstellungsrechnung, -konto; ~ **amount** Umstellungsbetrag; ~ **balance** Umstellungs-, Konversionsguthaben; ~ **center** *(US)* **(centre, Br.)** Einbauzentrum; ~ **chart** Umrechnungstabelle; ~ **cost** Verarbeitungskosten; ~ **factor** Umrechnungsfaktor; ~ **feature** Konversionsklausel; ~ **key** Umrechnungsschlüssel; ~ **loan** Konversions-, Umschuldungsanleihe; ~ **offer** Konversionsangebot; ~ **office** Konversionskasse, Umtauschstelle; ~ **period** Umtauschfrist; ~ **price** Umrechnungskurs; ~ **privilege** Konversions-, Umwandlungsrecht, *(group term life insurance)* Umwandlungsrecht in eine individuelle Dauerlebensversicherung; ~ **provisions** Konversionsbestimmungen; ~ **rate** Umrechnungssatz, -kurs; ~ **scheme** Umtauschaktion; ~ **sheet** Umstellungsrechnung; ~ **table** Konversions-, Umrechnungstabelle; ~ **training** Umschulung.

convert *(religion)* Übergetretener;

~ *(v.)* *(building)* strukturell verändern, umbauen, *(cash)* realisieren, versilbern, *(change money)* um-, einwechseln, *(currency)* umrechnen, *(debentures)* umtauschen, umwandeln, konvertieren, zusammenlegen, *(el.)* umformen, transformieren, *(pol.)* zum Übertritt in eine andere Partei veranlassen,

(assume possession) sich Eigentum unberechtigt aneignen, *(religion)* konvertieren, bekehren, *(turn into)* umwandeln;

~ **into capital** kapitalisieren, in Kapital umwandeln; ~ **into cash (money)** zu Geld machen, realisieren; ~ **s. o. to Christianity** j. zum Christentum bekehren; ~ **into a public company** vergesellschaften, in eine Aktien-, Publikumsgesellschaft umwandeln; ~ **a factory** Fabrikbetrieb umstellen; ~ **into nontaxable form** steuerfrei anlegen; ~ **funds to another purpose** Vermögensmasse anderweitig anlegen; ~ **funds to one's own use** fremdes Geld für sich verwenden; ~ **s. th. in one's head** etw. im Kopf umrechnen; ~ **into finished products** zu Fertigwaren verarbeiten; ~ **a loan** Anleihe umwandeln; ~ **pounds into francs** Pfunde in Franken umtauschen; ~ **one's realty into personalty** seinen Grundbesitz realisieren; ~ **from rights in land to rights in money** Grundstücksrechte in Geldansprüche umwandeln; ~ **a room to office use** Zimmer zweckentfremden; ~ **shares** Aktien zusammenlegen; ~ **fully paid shares into stock** voll eingezahlte Kapitalanteilsrechte in Aktien umwandeln; ~ **to one's own use** unrechtmäßig für sich verwenden.

converted umgerechnet;

~ **cruiser** Hilfskreuzer; ~ **flats** in Teilwohnungen umgebaute große Wohnung; ~ **mews** umgebaute Ställe.

converter *(US)* Verschlüsselungsgerät.

convertibility Umwandelbarkeit, Konvertierbarkeit;

external ~ freie Konvertierbarkeit; **full ~** Vollkonvertierbarkeit; **restricted ~** beschränkte Konvertierbarkeit;

~ **into cash** Flüssigmachung, Versilberung; ~ **of currency** Währungskonvertibilität; ~ **for nonresidents** Ausländerkonvertierbarkeit; ~ **of sterling** Pfundkonvertibilität;

to restore ~ by easy stages Konvertibilität in Etappen wiederherstellen;

~ **agreement** Konversionsabkommen; ~ **clause** Konvertierbarkeitsklausel.

convertible *(US)* Kabriolett;

~ *(a.) (car)* mit aufklappbarem Dach, *(debentures)* umwandelbar, konvertierbar, *(paper money)* umwechsel-, einlösbar, *(realizable)* umsetz-, verwert-, realisierbar, *(reducible)* umrechenbar;

readily ~ into cash sofort realisierbar;

~ **aircraft** Verwandlungsflugzeug; ~ **assets** realisierbare Vermögenswerte; ~ **bonds** Wandelschuldverschreibungen; ~ **bond issue** Optionsanleihe; **freely ~ currency** frei konvertierbare Währung; ~ **debentures** Wandelschuldverschreibungen; ~ **financing** Finanzierung durch Ausgabe von Wandelschuldverschreibungen; ~ **loan stock** konvertierbarer Anleihestock; ~ **money** einlösbares Papiergeld; ~ **paper currency** konvertierbares Papiergeld; ~ **preferred stock** Vorzugsaktie mit Umtauschrecht; ~ **prohibition** Verarbeitungsverbot; ~ **securities** handelbare Wertpapiere; ~ **stock** umtauschfähige Aktie.

converting | permit Verarbeitungsgenehmigung; ~ **prohibition** Verarbeitungsverbot; ~ **restriction** Verarbeitungsbeschränkung.

convertiplane Verwandlungsflugzeug.

convey *(v.) (impart)* vermitteln, mitteilen, übermitteln, *(surrender)* [Grundstück] auflassen, *(transfer)* abtreten, übertragen, übereignen, zedieren, *(transmit)* übermitteln, übersenden, *(transport)* befördern, transportieren, versenden, spedieren;

~ **away** zedieren, abtreten; ~ **electricity** Elektrizität leiten; ~ **goods in transit** Waren im Durchgangsverkehr abfertigen; ~ **greetings by letter** Grüße schriftlich übermitteln; ~ **information** Informationen zukommen lassen; ~ **by land** auf dem Landwege befördern; ~ **land to a purchaser** Grundstück an einen Käufer auflassen; ~ **an author's meaning** Auffassung eines Autors wiedergeben; ~ **both passengers and goods** Personen und Fracht befördern; ~ **one's sincere wishes** seine herzlichen Wünsche übermitteln; ~ **to the station in a bus** in einem Bus zum Bahnhof befördern; ~ **by water** verschiffen.

conveyable *(law)* übertragbar, abtretbar, *(transportable)* transportierbar, beförderungsfähig.

conveyance *(el.)* Leitung, *(instrument of transfer)* Auflassungs-, Übertragungsurkunde, *(surrender)* Auflassung, Umschreibung, Liegenschaftsübertragung, *(transfer)* Übereignung, Abtretung, Zession, *(transmission)* Übermittlung, -sendung, *(transporting)* Beförderung, Spedition, Über-, Versendung, Transport, *(vehicle)* Fahrzeug, Fuhrwerk, Wagen, Vehikel, Fahrgelegenheit, Transport-, Beförderungsmittel;

absolute ~ Übereignung frei von allen Rechten; **compulsory ~** Beförderungszwang; **conditional ~** bedingte Übereignung; **fraudulent ~** Gläubigerbenachteiligung, Vollstreckungsvereitelung; **mesne ~** Übereignung durch eine Mittelsperson; **ordinary ~** außergerichtliche Auflassung; **open-air ~** *(el.)*

Freileitung; **primary** ~ Auflassung; **public** ~ öffentliches Beförderungsmittel; **re**~ Rückabtretung; **secondary** ~ Nachübereignung zusätzlicher Rechte; **submarine** ~ *(el.)* Unterwasserleitung; **voluntary** ~ unentgeltliche Eigentumsübertragung;
~ **by air** Lufttransport; ~ **by aircraft** Lufttransport; ~ **in bulk** Massenbeförderung; ~ **to defraud a creditor** Vollstreckungsvereitelung; ~ **of goods** Gütertransport; ~ **of land** Grundstücksübertragung; ~ **by land** Landtransport; ~ **of land** Eigentumsübertragung eines Grundstücks; ~ **in mass** Massenbeförderung; ~ **in pais** Übertragung an Ort und Stelle; ~ **of passengers** Personenbeförderung; ~ **of a patent** Patentübertragung; ~ **of property** Vermögens-, Eigentumsübertragung; ~ **by rail** Eisenbahntransport; ~ **of real estate** [Grundstücks]auflassung; ~ **of real property** Grundstücksveräußerung, Auflassung; ~ **by record** Grundstücksübertragung durch staatlichen Hoheitsakt; ~ **with (without) registration** *(Br.)* Grundstücksübertragung mit (ohne) gleichzeitiger Grundbucheintragung; ~ **by sea** Beförderung auf dem Wasserweg; ~ **of sound** Schallübertragung; ~ **of title** Rechtsübertragung; ~ **to trustee for benefit of creditors generally** Vermögensübertragung auf den Treuhänder zugunsten aller Gläubiger; ~ **by water** Wassertransport;
to draft a ~ Übertragungsurkunde aufsetzen;
~ **tax** Beförderungssteuer.
conveyancer Spezialanwalt für Grundstücksfragen, Notar.
conveyancing Ausfertigung von Abtretungsurkunden, *(transfer of title)* Eigentumsübertragung;
⚖ **Act** *(Br.)* Auflassungsgesetz; ~ **cost (fee)** Notariatsgebühren für die Auflassung; ~ **lawyer** Notar; ~ **matter** Grundstücksangelegenheiten.
conveyer, conveyor Beförderer, Frachtführer, *(assigner)* Abtreter, Zedent, *(bringer)* Überbringer, *(plant)* Fließband, *(mechanical apparatus)* Förderanlage, -gerät, Transporteinrichtung, *(mining)* Förderschranke, Schnecke, Becherwerk;
~ **assembly line** Fließbandmontage; ~ **band (belt)** Fließ-, Montage-, Förderband; **coal** ~ **belt** Kohlentransportband; **to stand at a** ~ **belt** am Fließband arbeiten; ~-**belt city** Fließbandstraßenstadt; ~-**belt production** Fließbandarbeit; ~-**belt system** Fließbandprinzip; ~ **bucket** Förderkübel; ~ **line production** Fließbandfertigung; ~ **principle** Fließbandsystem; **belt** ~ **road** Förderbandstrecke; ~ **system** Fertigungsstraße; ~ **track** Förderband; **box-type** ~ **system** Kastenförderungsanlage; ~-**type elevator** Paternoster.
conveying | of information Weitergabe von Informationen; ~ **capacity** Förderleistung; ~ **plant** Förderanlage; ~ **speed** Fördergeschwindigkeit; ~ **spiral** Transportschnecke.
convict überführter Verbrecher, Verurteilter, Sträfling, Straftäter, Strafgefangener, Zuchthäusler;
~ *(v.)* überführen, für schuldig erklären;
~ **o. s.** sich selbst belasten; ~ **s. o. of an error** jem. einen Irrtum nachweisen; ~ **s. o. of murder** j. des Mordes überführen;
~ **colony** Sträflingskolonie; ~ **establishment** Strafanstalt; ~ **goods** im Zuchthaus hergestellte Waren; ~ **labo(u)r** Sträflings-, Zuchthausarbeit; ~ **prison** *(Br.)* Zuchthaus.
convicted, previously einschlägig vorbestraft.
conviction Meinung, Überzeugung, *(criminal)* Schuldigsprechung, Verurteilung, Überführung;
on ~ nach strafrichterlicher Aburteilung;
first ~ erste Verurteilung; **former** ~ frühere Verurteilung, Vorstrafe; **political** ~ politische Überzeugung; **previous** ~ einschlägige Vorstrafe; **religious** ~ religiöse Überzeugung; **summary** ~ Verurteilung durch den Einzelrichter, Verurteilung im Schnellverfahren;
~ **of the accused** Verurteilung des Angeklagten;
to act up to one's ~ aus innerster Überzeugung handeln; **to be open to** ~ sich überzeugen (mit sich reden) lassen; **to be prosecuted to** ~ rechtskräftig verurteilt werden; **not to carry much** ~ nicht sehr überzeugend klingen; **to have a** ~ **previous for ...** wegen ... einschlägig vorbestraft sein; **to have no** ~s nicht vorbestraft sein; **to live up to one's** ~ seiner Überzeugung gemäß handeln; **to quash a** ~ Schuldspruch aufheben; **to uphold a** ~ Strafurteil bestätigen.
convincing | argument schlagender Beweis; ~ **proof** überzeugender (schlagender) Beweis.
convocation [Ein]berufung, *(meeting)* Versammlung.
convocator Einberufer, Versammlungsteilnehmer.
convoke *(v.)* **| a meeting** Sitzung einberufen; ~ **Parliament** Parlament einberufen.
convoy *(protection)* Schutz, Bedeckung, Begleitung, Eskorte, *(ship)* Schiffs-, Schutzgeleit, Konvoi, Geleitschutz, Geleitzug, *(vehicles)* Kraftwagen-, Fahrzeugkolonne;

~ **of prisoners** Gefangenentransport; ~ **of trucks** Lastwagenkolonne;
~ *(v.)* eskortieren, schützend geleiten;
~ **prisoners** Gefangene transportieren; ~ **ships** Schiffe im Konvoi begleiten; ~ **a merchant ship by a destroyer** Handelsschiff im Schutzgeleit eines Zerstörers fahren lassen; ~ **troop ships across the Atlantic** Truppentransporte im Geleitzug über den Ozean eskortieren; ~ **a supply column** einer Nachschubkolonne Geleit geben;
to attack a ~ **by submarines** Konvoi mit Unterseebooten angreifen; **to block a** ~ Konvoi festhalten; **to sail under** ~ im Geleitzug fahren;
~ **ship** Geleitzugschiff, -fahrzeug.
cook Koch, Köchin;
~ *(v.)* [ab]kochen, zubereiten, *(reactor)* radioaktiv machen;
~ **a balance sheet** Bilanz frisieren (verschleiern); ~ **with radar** *(sl.)* sehr erfolgreich sein; ~ **s. one's goose** *(sl.)* jem. den Garaus machen; ~ **up** zusammenbrauen; ~ **up a story** Geschichte erfinden;
~ **general** *(Br.)* Mädchen für alles.
cooked accounts frisierte Bücher.
cookie-pusher Gesellschaftsmensch, Salonlöwe.
cooking | of accounts Bücher-, Kontofälschung; ~ **of a balance sheet** Bilanzverschleierung, -frisur; ~ **of evidence** Beweisfälschung.
cookout *(US)* Gartengrillfest.
cool *(fig.)* kühl, beherrscht;
~ **as a cucumber** die Ruhe selbst, kalt wie eine Hundeschnauze; ~ *(v.)* **down** abkühlen, *(coll.)* sich beruhigen (abregen), seine Ruhe wieder finden; ~ **it** besonnen bleiben; ~ **off** *(economy, inflation)* sich abkühlen;
~ **one's coppers** seinen Durst stillen; ~ **s. one's enthusiasm** auf jds. Begeisterung abkühlend wirken; ~ **one's heels** sich die Beine in den Leib stehen;
to be ~ **towards s. o.** sich jem. gegenüber sehr reserviert verhalten; **to keep one's** ~ seine Ruhe bewahren; **to let s. o.** ~ **his heels** j. lange warten lassen; **to lose one's** ~ *(sl.)* seine Beherrschung verlieren;
~ **behavio(u)r** kaltes (kaltschnäuziges) Verhalten; ~ **chamber** Kühlraum; ~ **customer** geriebener Kunde; **to keep a** ~ **head** ganz besonnen bleiben; **a** ~ **thousand pounds** *(fam.)* glatte tausend Pfund; ~ **reception** kühler Empfang; ~ **store** Gefrierfach.
cooler Kühlraum, -schrank, *(sl.)* Kittchen, Knast;
wine ~ Weinkühler.
coolhouse Kühlhaus.
coolie Kuli, Tagelöhner;
~ **labo(u)r** Kuliarbeit.
cooling Abkühlung;
air ~ Luftkühlung;
~ **of the economy** Konjunkturabkühlung;
~ **installation** *(railway)* Kühleinrichtung; ~ **tank** Kühlschrank; ~ **water** *(car)* Kühlwasser.
cooling-off | inflation Inflationsabkühlung; ~ **period** *(strike law)* Abkühlungszeit; ~ **relations** Abkühlung der Beziehungen; ~ **treaty** *(law of nations)* Abkühlungsvertrag.
cooling time *(labo(u)r law)* Abkühlungszeit.
coöp *(coll.)* Konsum;
~ **advertising** Gemeinschaftswerbung; ~ **work** Gemeinschaftsarbeit.
cooper Küfer, *(Br.)* Weinverkäufer.
cooperate *(v.)* kooperieren, *(economics)* geschäftlich zusammenarbeiten;
~ **with friends in starting a social club** mit Freunden gemeinsam einen geselligen Verein aufziehen; ~ **to the success of s. th.** zum Erfolg von etw. beitragen.
cooperation Zusammenarbeit, Zusammenwirken, Beteiligung, Mitarbeit, Mitwirkung, Beteiligung, *(economic association)* Vereinigung zu einer Genossenschaft, genossenschaftlicher Zusammenschluß, *(factory, Br.)* betriebliche Kooperation, *(patent law)* Erfindergemeinschaft;
in ~ **with the management** in Kooperation mit der Betriebsleitung;
consumer ~ Verbrauchergenossenschaft; **economic** ~ wirtschaftliche Zusammenarbeit; **employee** ~ Zusammenarbeit mit der Belegschaft; **fiscal** ~ Zusammenarbeit in Steuersachen; **marketing** ~ Absatzgenossenschaft; **monetary** ~ Zusammenarbeit auf dem Währungsgebiet; **producers'** ~ landwirtschaftliche Absatzgenossenschaft; **union-management** ~ Zusammenarbeit der Gewerkschaften mit der Unternehmerschaft;
~ **between banks** Bankenkooperation;

to enlist s. one's ~ jds. Mitarbeit gewinnen; **to intensify economic ~** wirtschaftliche Zusammenarbeit vertiefen;

~ agreement Kooperationsvereinbarung; **~ apartments** genossenschaftlich errichtete Wohnungen; **~ movement** Genossenschaftsbewegung.

cooperationist Genossenschaftler, Genossenschaftsmitglied.

cooperative Genossenschaft, Gemeinschaft;

agriculture ~ landwirtschaftliche Absatzgenossenschaft; **building ~** Baugenossenschaft, -sparkasse; **consumers' ~** Konsumgenossenschaft; **credit ~** Kredit-, Darlehnsverein; **farm[ers'] ~** (US) landwirtschaftliche Absatzgenossenschaft; **marketing ~** Absatzgenossenschaft; **producers' ~** landwirtschaftliche Absatzgenossenschaft; **wholesale ~** Einkaufsgenossenschaft;

~ (a.) genossenschaftlich, (operating jointly) zusammenarbeitend, mitarbeitend, -wirkend, kooperativ;

to feel ~ sich zur Zusammenarbeit bereitfinden;

~ advertising (Br.) Gemeinschaftswerbung; **~ advertising program(me)** Gemeinschaftswerbesendung; **International ≗ Alliance** Internationaler Genossenschaftsverbund; **~ analysis of broadcasting ratings** Popularitätsanalyse von Rundfunkprogrammen; **~ apartment houses** (US) Siedlungshäuser; **~ association** (US) [Wirtschafts-, Erwerbs]genossenschaft; **~ marketing association** Absatzgenossenschaft; **~ purchasing association** Bezugsgenossenschaft; **~ sales (selling) association** Einkaufs-, Verkaufsgenossenschaft; **~ association for production** Produktionsgenossenschaft; **~ bank** genossenschaftliches Kreditinstitut, Genossenschaftbank; **~ banking** genossenschaftliches Kreditwesen; **~ banking society** Genossenschaftsbank; **~ basis** genossenschaftliche Grundlage; **~ building** auf genossenschaftlicher Basis gebautes Mehrparteienhaus; **~ building society** (Br.) Bausparkasse; **~ buying** gemeinsamer Warenbezug; **~ buying association** Einkaufsgenossenschaft; **~ buying office** Zentralbezugsgenossenschaft; **~ competition** gemeinsamer Wettbewerb; **~ credit association (union)** Kreditgenossenschaft; **~ delivery** gemeinschaftlicher Zustellungsdienst; **~ distribution** gemeinschaftlicher Absatz, Gemeinschaftsvertrieb; **~ education** mit praktischer Ausbildung gekoppeltes Studium; **~ enterprise** Genossenschaftsunternehmen; **~ farming** genossenschaftlicher Ein- und Verkauf der Landwirte; **~ health plan** gemeinsames Gesundheitsprogramm verschiedener Unternehmer; **~ housing** genossenschaftlicher Wohnungsbau; **~ insurance** genossenschaftliches Versicherungswesen; **~ marketing** genossenschaftliches Absatz-, Vertriebswesen; **~ marketing association** Vertriebs-, Absatzgenossenschaft; **~ member** Genossenschaftsmitglied; **~ movement** Genossenschaftsbewegung; **~ organization** genossenschaftliche Organisation; **to change a firm to ~ ownership** Unternehmen in eine Genossenschaft umwandeln; **~ plan** Studium mit zwischenzeitlicher praktischer Ausbildung; **~ purchasing** betrieblicher Warenbezug zu verbilligten Preisen, Gemeinschaftseinkauf; **~ retail shop** (Br.) Konsum[geschäft], Konsumladen; **~ retail society** Konsumgenossenschaft des Einzelhandels; **~ retail store** Konsum[geschäft]; **~ sales (selling)** Gemeinschafts-, Genossenschaftsverkauf; **~ sales (selling) organization** Verkaufsgenossenschaft; **~ shop** (Br.) Konsum[geschäft], Konsumladen; **~ industrial society** (Br.) Erwerbs- und Wirtschaftsgenossenschaft; **~ retail society** (Br.) Konsumgenossenschaft; **~ purchasing society** (Br.) [Konsum]genossenschaft, Erwerbs- und Wirtschaftsgenossenschaft, Konsum[verein]; **~ wholesale society** genossenschaftliche Großhändlervereinigung, Großeinkaufsgesellschaft; **~ spirit** genossenschaftliches Denken; **~ stock** Genossenschaftskapital; **~ trading system** Genossenschaftswesen; **≗ Union** (Br.) Genossenschaftsverband; **~ venture** Gemeinschaftsunternehmen; **~ warehouse society** [Groß]einkaufsgenossenschaft.

cooperatively genossenschaftlich organisiert.

cooperator Mitarbeiter, (society) Konsumvereinsmitglied.

coopt (v.) hinzuwählen, kooptieren.

cooptation Zuwahl, Kooptation.

cooptative hinzugewählt.

coopted member nachgewähltes (kooptiertes) Mitglied.

cooptee Kooptierter, hinzugewähltes Mitglied.

coordinate Gleichgestellter;

~ (a.) gleich-, beigeordnet, gleichrangig, koordiniert, (school) nach Geschlechtern getrennt;

~ (v.) koordinieren, gleichordnen, -schalten, -stellen, aufeinander abstimmen;

~ authority gleichgeordnete Dienststelle; **~ clause** (gr.) beigeordneter Satz; **~ court** gleichgeordnetes Gericht; **~ jurisdiction** in gleichem Rang stehende Gerichtsbarkeit; **~ system** Koordinatensystem.

coordinated | advertising gemeinsame Werbestrategie; **~ policy** einheitliche (koordinierte) Politik.

coordinating | body (committee) Koordinierungsausschuß; **~ office** Koordinierungsbüro, -stelle; **~ taxation** (EC) Steueranpassung.

coordination Koordinierung, Gleichordnung, -stellung, -schaltung;

administrative ~ Koordinierung auf dem Verwaltungsgebiet; **~ of transport** Transportkoordinierung, Koordinierung des Transportwesens; **~ of transportation** (US) Transportkoordinierung;

to lack ~ nicht genügend koordiniert sein;

~ allowance (US) [über mehrere Wochen ausgedehnte] Ausgleichszahlungen bei Entlassungen; **~ committee** Koordinierungsausschuß; **~ decision** Koordinierungsbefugnis; **~ functions** Koordinationsaufgaben; **~ line** (mil.) Nahtstelle; **~ procedure** Koordinationsverfahren.

coordinator Koordinator.

coowner Miteigentümer, -inhaber.

coownership Miteigentum;

~ of ships Mit-, Partenreederei.

cop (sl.) Polyp;

a fair ~ Erwischtwerden auf frischer Tat;

~ on the beat Streifenpolizei, Verkehrsstreife;

~ (v.) it Prügel bekommen; **~ out** ungeschoren davonkommen; **~-out** faule Ausrede.

coparcenary (Br.) Miterbschaft, (joint heirship) gemeinsam geerbter Grundbesitz, Gesamthandseigentum, Eigentum zur gesamten Hand;

coparcener (joint heir) [dinglicher] Miterbe, (joint owner) Eigentümer zur gesamten Hand;

to be ~ anteilsberechtigt sein.

coparceny gleicher Erbschaftsanteil;

to hold an estate in ~ gemeinsam Grundbesitz geerbt haben.

copartner Mitinhaber, -besitzer, Partner, Sozius, Teilhaber;

~ in a ship Mitreeder.

copartnership Teilhaberschaft, Mitbesitz, (company) Sozietät, Handelsgenossenschaft, Gesellschaft, (ships) Parten-, Mitreederei;

contributory ~ Teilhaberschaft durch Erwerb von Aktien; **labo(u)r ~** Arbeitergewinnbeteiligung, Gewinnbeteiligung der Arbeitnehmer;

~ of labo(u)r Gewinnbeteiligung der Arbeitnehmer;

to go into ~ with s. o. als Teilhaber bei jem. eintreten.

copartnery Teilhabervertrag.

copassenger Mitreisender.

copatentee Patentmitinhaber.

cope (v.) **with** es aufnehmen mit, fertig werden, bewältigen;

~ the growing amount of work immer noch zunehmenden Arbeitsanfall bewältigen; **~ difficulties** mit Schwierigkeiten fertig werden; **~ a situation** sich einer Situation gewachsen zeigen; **~ a task** einer Aufgabe gewachsen sein; **~ the traffic** Verkehr bewältigen können.

copied out abschriftlich.

copier (apparatus) Kopierapparat, (person) Kopist, (plagiarist) Plagiator;

~ business Kopierapparateindustrie.

copies | still in hand noch vorhandene Exemplare;

to make three carbon ~ of a letter Brief mit drei Durchschlägen schreiben; **to run off ~** Abschriften herstellen.

copilot Kopilot, zweiter Flugzeugführer.

copious umfassend, vollständig;

~ supply reichlicher Vorrat.

coplaintiff Nebenkläger.

copper (coin) Kupfermünze;

~s (stock exchange) Kupferaktien, -werte;

a few ~s ein paar Pfifferlinge;

not to care a ~ (US) keinen roten Heller dafür geben;

~ block (Br.) Kupferklischee; **~ coin** Kupfergeld, -münze; **~ engraving** Kupferstich, -ätzung; **~ exporter** Kupferausfuhrland; **~ gravure** Kupfertiefdruck; **~ issues** Kupferwerte, -aktien; **~ market** Markt für Kupferwerte; **~ money** Kupfergeld; **~ plate** Kupferplatte; **~ plate printing** Kupfertiefdruck; **~ wire** Kupferdraht.

coproduce (v.) zusammen herstellen.

coproduction Koproduktion;

~ agreement Koproduktionsvertrag.

copy Durchschlag, Abschrift, Niederschrift, Kopie, Duplikat, [Neu]ausfertigung, (advertisement) Werbung, Reklame-, Anzeigentext, Reproduktionsvorlage, (book) Exemplar, (document) Ausfertigung, (imitation) Nachbildung, Nachahmung, *(leasehold, Br.)* Pachtgut, *(manuscript)* Satz-, Druckvorlage, druckfertiges Manuskript, *(material for a story)* Stoff für einen Bericht, *(model)* Muster, Modell, Exemplar, *(painting)* Nachahmung, Reproduktion, *(transcript)* Instrument, Urkunde; **as per the enclosed ~** laut beigefügter Abschrift; **by way of ~** abschriftlich; **for ~ conform** für gleichlautende Abschrift; **in a single ~** in einer Abschrift;

advance ~ Vorabdruck; **attested ~** beglaubigte Abschrift; **first authentic ~** erste vollstreckbare Ausfertigung; **autograph ~** eigenhändige Abschrift; **bulky ~** Exemplar in Großformat; **carbon ~** Durchschlag; **blind carbon ~** zusätzliche Kopie; **checking ~** Belegexemplar; **certified ~** beglaubigte Abschrift; **certified true ~** für die Richtigkeit der Abschrift; **clean ~** Reinschrift; **close ~** wortgetreue Abschrift; **complimentary ~** Werbenummer; **conformed ~** *(US)* gleichlautende Kopie (Abschrift); **dead ~** *(print.)* abgesetztes Manuskript; **defective ~** Mängelexemplar; **diplomatic ~** mit dem Original genau übereinstimmende Abschrift; **dirty ~** unübersichtliches Manuskript; **disparaging ~** *(advertising)* herabsetzende (aggressive) Werbung; **educational ~** *(advertising)* erzieherische Werbung; **exact ~** gleichlautende Abschrift; **examined ~** beglaubigte (mit dem Original verglichene) Abschrift; **exemplified ~** beglaubigte Abschrift, Ausfertigung; **fair ~** saubere Abschrift, Reinschrift; **file ~** Aktendurchschlag; **foul ~** Entwurf, Konzept; **free ~** Freiexemplar; **fresh ~** Neuausfertigung; **full ~** vollständige Abschrift; **hardback ~** gebundenes Buch; **identical ~** gleichlautende Abschrift; **institutional ~** Original; **new ~** neues Exemplar; **notarized ~** notariell beglaubigte Abschrift; **office ~** beglaubigte (amtliche) Abschrift; **photostatic ~** Fotokopie; **pirate ~** Raubdruck; **poor ~** Exemplar verminderter Qualität; **press ~** Presseexemplar; **presentation ~** Gratisexemplar; **reason-why ~** *(advertising)* Überzeugungsreklame; **review ~** Rezensions-, Besprechungsexemplar; **rough ~** [Roh]entwurf, Konzept; **secondhand ~** antiquarisches Exemplar; **sample ~** Probeexemplar; **specimen ~** Probe-, Ansichts-, Beleg-, Gratisexemplar; **surplus ~** überschüssiger Durchschlag; **third ~** Drittabschrift; **true ~** wortgetreue (gleichlautende) Abschrift; **true and attested ~** wortgetreue und beglaubigte Abschrift; **voucher ~** Belegexemplar;

~ of application Antragskopie; **~ of bill** Wechselabschrift, -kopie; **~ of birth certificate** Zweitschrift des Geburtsscheins; **~ in facsimile** Faksimileabschrift; **~ on file** Archivexemplar; **~ of guarantee** Garantiedurchschlag; **~ of invoice** Rechnungsdurchschlag, -kopie; **certified ~ of invoice** beglaubigte Rechnungskopie; **~ of petition** Antragskopie; **~ for private use** Handexemplar, Vorabdruck; **~ sent gratis for publicity** Besprechungsexemplar;

~ (v.) nachbilden, reproduzieren, Kopie anfertigen, kopieren, abschreiben, *(photography)* Abzug machen, abziehen; **~ during an examination** in einem Examen pfuschen; **~ fair** ins reine schreiben; **~ a letter out fair** saubere Abschrift eines Briefes anfertigen; **~ music** Noten schreiben; **~ notes** Buchexzerpte machen; **~ out** abschreiben, ins reine schreiben, kopieren, Kopie anfertigen; **~ a passage from a book** Buchstelle abschreiben; **~ s. one's good points** sich jds. Pluspunkte anzueignen suchen;

to attach a ~ in Abschrift beifügen; **to attest a ~ of record** Abschrift beglaubigen; **to cast up ~** Manuskript berechnen; **to certify a ~** Abschrift beglaubigen; **to deliver a ~** Ausfertigung erteilen; **to furnish a ~** Abschrift erteilen; **to have a print-ready ~** druckfertigen Anzeigentext bereithalten; **to have a ~ of one's own** Durchschlag erhalten haben; **to hold ~** Korrekturen lesen; **to make good ~** Sensationsnachricht abgeben (darstellen); **to make a ~ of a deed** Zweitausfertigung einer Urkunde anfertigen; **to make (write) a fair ~ of a letter** Reinschrift von einem Brief anfertigen; **to mark a ~** Korrekturen auf einem Manuskript anbringen; **to read over a ~** Abschrift vergleichen; **to review a ~** Manuskript durchsehen; **to send a ~ of the balance sheet** Bilanzduplikat einreichen; **to take a ~** Abschrift nehmen; **to wait for more ~** *(printers)* weiteres Satzmanuskript benötigen;

~ appeal Attraktivität der Anzeigenaussage; **~ approach** Textaufhänger, Anzeigenthema; **~ block** Notizblock; **~ body** Hauptbestandteil einer Anzeige; **~ book maxims** Gemeinplätze; **~ boy** Redaktionsbote; **~ casting** Umfangschätzung, Textauszählen; **~ chief** Cheftexter; **~ date** Einsendetermin, Anzeigenschluß, -termin, *(broadcasting)* Werbefunkschluß; **deadline** *(US)* Redaktions-, Anzeigenschluß, -termin; **~ deed** Zinsbrief; **~ department** *(advertising)* Textabteilung; **~ desk** *(US)* Redaktionstisch; **~-edit** *(v.)* Umbruch machen; **~ editing** Umbruch; **~ editor** *(US)* Umbruchredakteur; **~-fit** *(v.)* einspie-

geln; **~ fitting** Spiegeln, Einspiegeln; **~ invoice** Rechnungskopie; **~ money** Schriftsteller-, Autorenhonorar; **~ paper** Durchschlagpapier; **~ platform** Gestaltungsgrundlage, Ideenprogramm eines Werbefeldzuges, Werbeplattform; **~ point** Werbeargument im Text; **~ preparation** Manuskriptvorbereitung; **~ print** Reproduktion; **~ proof** Korrekturabzug; **~ purchaser** Verlagsbuchhändler; **~ research** Textanalyse; **~ slip** Schreibvorlage; **~ styling** Manuskriptbearbeitung; **~ supervisor** Cheftexter; **~ test** Umfrageforschung; **~ testing** *(advertising)* Testen der Werbewirkung, Anzeigenuntersuchung, *(print.)* Textprüfung; **~ typing** Manuskriptabschreiben.

copyable kopierfähig.
copybook Schreibheft [mit Vorlage], *(penmanship)* Briefkopierbuch;
   to blot one's ~ *(Br., coll.)* seine Chancen verscherzen;
   ~ (a.) abgedroschen, alltäglich;
   ~ maxims Gemeinplätze.
copycat *(Br., coll.)* Vervielfältigungsapparat.
copygraph Hektographiergerät;
   ~ (v.) hektographieren.
copyhold *(Br.)* Lehnsgut, Lehen, Erbpacht.
copyholder *(copyreader)* Korrekturenleser, Korrektorengehilfe, *(law, Br.)* Erbpächter, *(typesetter)* Manuskripthalter.
copyholding Korrekturenlesen.
copying *(v.)* Kopieanfertigung, Abschriftnahme, Abschreiben;
   ~ apparatus Vervielfältigungsapparat; **~ clerk** Abschreiber, Kopist, Expedient; **~ cost** Kopierunkosten; **~ equipment** Kopiergerät; **~ fee** Abschreibgebühr; **~ ink** Kopiertinte; **~ machine** Kopiermaschine, -gerät, -apparat; **~ paper** Durchschlagpapier; **~ pencil** Tintenstift; **~ press** Kopierpresse; **~ process** Kopierverfahren; **~ ribbon** Farbband.
copyist Abschreiber, *(plagiarist)* Nachdrucker, Plagiator.
copyman *(US)* Hilfsredakteur.
copyrapid Blitzkopieren.
copyreader Korrekturleser, *(US)* Umbruchredakteur.
copyright Alleinnutzungs-, Abdrucks-, Vertriebs-, Urheber-, Verlagsrecht, geistiges (literarisches) Eigentum;
   out of ~ urheberrechtlich nicht mehr geschützt, Verlagsrecht erloschen;
   ad-interim ~ vorläufiger Urheberschutz; **international ~** zwischenstaatliches Urheberrecht; **lapsed ~** erloschenes Urheberrecht; **literary ~** Urheberrecht an literarischen Werken; **~ out** Verlagsrecht erloschen; **reserved** Nachdruck verboten; **subsisting ~** noch bestehendes Urheberrecht;
   ~ in designs *(Br.)* Musterschutz; **~ entered at Stationer's Hall** alle Rechte vorbehalten; **~ of original works** *(Br.)* Urheberrecht an ursprünglichen Werken;
   ~ (v.) urheberrechtlich schützen, Verlagsrecht übernehmen; **to cancel a ~** Schutzvermerk für ungültig erklären; **to commute a ~** Verlagsrechte ablösen; **to file an application for registration of ~** Urheberschutz (Verlagsrechte) beantragen; **to infringe a ~** Urheberrecht verletzen; **to own a ~** Verlagsrecht besitzen; **to renew a ~** Verlagsrecht erneuern, Urheberrecht verlängern;
   ~ (a.) verlags-, urheberrechtlich;
   ~ act Urheberrechtsgesetz; **~ case** Klage wegen Verletzung des Urheberrechts; **Universal ~ Convention** Welturheberrechtsabkommen; **~ deal** Urheberrechtsvereinbarung; **~ edition** verlagsrechtlich geschützte Ausgabe; **~ fees** Urheberrechtsgebühren; **~ holder** Urheberrechtsinhaber; **~ infringement** Urheberrechtsverletzung; **~ law** Urheberrecht; **~ notice** Urheberrechts-, Nachdruckvermerk, *(patent law)* Patentanmeldung; **~ office** *(US)* Urheberrechtsbehörde; **~ period** Schutzfrist; **~ procedure** Urheberrechtsverfahren; **~ protection** Schutz des Urheberrechts; **~ registration** *(US)* Registrierung des Urheberrechtes.
copyrightable urheberschutzfähig, urheberrechtsfähig;
   ~ material für Urheberschutz aufgenommene Werke.
copyrighted verlagsrechtlich geschützt;
   ~ in all situations alle Rechte vorbehalten;
   to be ~ urheberrechtlichem Schutz unterliegen;
   ~ production urheberrechtlich geschützte Produktion; **~ publication** urheberrechtlich (verlagsrechtlich) geschützte Veröffentlichung; **~ work** urheberrechtlich geschütztes Werk.
copywriter [Reklame]textschreiber, [Werbe]texter, -schriftsteller, Anzeigentexter.
copywriting Abfassung eines Reklametextes, Werbetexterstellung.
coracialist Rassenanhänger.
coram|judice *(lat.)* vor einem ordnungsgemäß besetzten Gericht; **~ non judice** vor einem unzuständigen Gericht.
corbel Balkenträger, Konsole.

cord Schnur, Band, Bindfaden, *(bookbinding)* Schnur, Bund, *(el.)* Litze, Leitungsschnur, *(fig.)* Fessel, *(measure)* Klafter;
~ *(v.)* ver-, zuschnüren, festbinden.
corded ladder Strickleiter.
cordon Abriegelung, Absperrung, [Ab]sperrkette, *(ribbon)* Ordensband;
sanitary ~ sanitäre Absperrung;
~ **of forts** Festungsgürtel; ~ **of police** Polizeikordon;
~ *(v.)* [off] absperren;
~ **bleu** *(fig.)* hoher Würdenträger, hochgestellte Persönlichkeit.
cordoned off by the police polizeilich abgesperrt.
core Herz, Kern, Mark, *(cable)* Seele, Leiter;
to the ~ zutiefst, bis ins Innerste;
city ~ Stadtkern; **hard** ~ *(unemployment)* Restbestand [der Arbeitslosigkeit];
~ **of the earth** Erdkern; **hard** ~ **of relatively stable earnings** sichere Ertragsgrundlage; ~ **of a party** Kern einer Partei;
to be English to the ~ urenglische Eigenschaften verkörpern; **to get to the** ~ **of a subject** auf den Urgrund eines Themas stoßen;
to touch s. o. to the ~ j. an seiner empfindlichsten Stelle treffen;
~ **area** Kerngebiet; ~ **form** *(staggering)* Blockzeit.
corkscrew *(v.)* | **one's way through the crowd** sich durch die Menge schlängeln; ~ **the truth out of s. o.** jem. die Wahrheit aus der Nase ziehen.
corn Getreide, Korn, *(Br.)* Weizen, *(US)* Mais, *(melodrama, sl.)* Schnulze, Schmachtfetzen;
to acknowledge the ~ *(US)* sich geschlagen geben; **to tread (trample) on s. one's** ~**s** jem. auf die Hühnerauge treten, jem. auf die Seele herumtrampeln;
~ **broker** Getreidemakler; ~ **chandler** *(Br.)* Saathändler; ~ **exchange** *(US)* Getreidebörse; ~ **factor** *(Br.)* Getreidehändler;
~ **growing** Getreideanbau; ~ **market** Getreidemarkt; ~ **production** Getreideerzeugung, -produktion; ~ **tax** Getreidezoll.
corner Straßenecke, *(book)* Eckenverstärkung, *(position of difficulty)* Verlegenheit, Klemme, *(ring)* Aufkäufergruppe, [Spekulations]ring, Schwänze, *(sl.)* Beuteanteil;
done in a ~ hintenherum erledigt; **round the** ~ gleich um die Ecke, ganz nahe;
street ~ Straßenecke;
~ *(v.)* *(buy up)* aufkaufen, hohe Preise aufzwingen;
~ **the market** Waren zu Spekulationszwecken aufkaufen; ~ **a witness** Zeugen verwirren (in die Enge treiben);
to back s. o. into a ~ j. in die Ecke drängen; **to be in a tight** ~ in der Klemme sitzen; **to come from all** ~**s** von allen Ecken und Enden kommen; **to cut** ~**s** *(fig.)* etw. Unkorrektes tun, unorthodox vorgehen; **to cut off a** ~ Abkürzung nehmen; **to drive s. o. into a** ~ j. in die Enge treiben; **to have turned the** ~ über den Berg (das Schlimmste hinweg) sein; **to live round the** ~ ganz in der Nähe wohnen; **to look at s. o. from the** ~ **of one's eye** j. kritisch von der Seite ansehen; **to make a** ~ **in wheat** ganzes Weizenangebot aufkaufen; **to push into a** ~ in die Enge treiben; **to stand one's** ~ *(sl.)* seinen Teil dazu beitragen; **to take a** ~ Kurve nehmen; **to turn the** ~ kritische Situation meistern, *(US)* Umschwung verzeichnen;
~ **boy** Rowdy; ~ **bullet** *(advertising)* Firmeneindruck; ~ **card** Briefkopf in der oberen rechten Ecke; ~ **grocery** *(US)* Eckladen; ~ **house** Eckhaus; ~ **influence** *(land)* wertsteigernder Faktor; ~ **man** Eckensteher, *(Br.)* Aufkäufer; ~ **room** Eckzimmer; ~ **shop** Eckladen; ~ **stone** Grund-, Eckstein; ~ **stone of success** Grundlage des Erfolgs; **to lay the** ~ **stone** Grundstein legen; ~ **table** Ecktisch; **hole-and-**~ **transactions** geheime Machenschaften; ~ **window** Eckfenster.
cornerer *(Br.)* Aufkäufer.
cornet Fahnenjunker.
cornfield Korn-, Getreidefeld.
cornland *(US)* Getreideland.
cornloft Getreidespeicher.
corny *(US sl.)* kitschig, schmalzig.
corollary Folgeerscheinung;
~ **of indemnity** Schadensersatzfolge.
coronation Krönung, Krönungsfeier;
~ **ceremony** Krönungsfeierlichkeiten; ~ **oath** Krönungseid; ~ **procession** Krönungszug.
coroner Leichenbeschauer und Untersuchungsrichter;
~**'s court** Geschworenengericht; ~**'s inquest** amtliche Totenschau; ~**'s jury** Leichenschaukommission.
cornet *(ice-cream cone)* Hörnchen.
corporal *(mil.)* Unteroffizier;
~ *(a.)* körperlich, leiblich, physisch;
~ **possession** persönlicher Besitz; ~ **punishment** Prügelstrafe.

corporate vereinigt, verbunden, *(company)* inkorporiert, korporativ, körperschaftlich, gesellschaftlich, zu einer juristischen Person gehörend;
~ **act** Gesellschaftshandlung; ~ **acquisition** Firmenanschaffung; ~ **action** zustimmungspflichtige Gesellschaftertätigkeit, *(law court)* Klage einer Aktiengesellschaft; **to take** ~ **action** gemeinsam handeln; ~ **advertising** Firmenwerbung; ~ **agent** *(US)* Firmenvertreter; ~ **aircraft** Firmenflugzeug; ~ **air travel** betrieblicher Flugverkehr; ~ **amalgamation** Gesellschaftsfusion; ~ **analysis** Firmenbewertung; ~ **articles** *(US)* Gründungsurkunde, Satzung; ~ **assets** *(US)* Gesellschaftsvermögen, Firmeneigentum, Vermögen einer Aktiengesellschaft; ~ **authority** *(Br.)* Gemeindebehörde, Stadtrat; ~ **banking** *(US)* Aktienbankwesen; ~ **bankruptcy** *(US)* Firmenkonkurs; ~ **boardrooms** Vorstandsetage; **body** ~ Körperschaft, juristische Person des öffentlichen Rechts, Personengesamtheit, korporative Vereinigung; **bonded** *(insurance)* Sammeldepot; ~ **bonds** *(US)* Industrieobligationen, Schuldverschreibungen von Aktiengesellschaften, industrielle Schuldverschreibungen; ~ **bond market** *(US)* Markt für Industrieanleihen; ~ **books** *(US)* Geschäftsbücher einer Aktiengesellschaft; ~ **borrower** kreditaufnehmende Firma; ~ **bribery** Bestechung durch die Wirtschaft; ~ **bureaucracy** *(US)* Wirtschaftsbürokratie; ~ **business** *(US)* Firmen-, Gesellschaftsangelegenheit; ~ **bylaws** *(US)* Gesellschaftsstatuten; ~ **cash** bare Betriebsmittel; **to raise** ~ **cash** notwendige Betriebsmittel aufbringen; ~ **charter** *(US)* Gründungsurkunde; ~ **client** *(US)* Firmenkunde; **to make** ~ **commitments** *(US)* betriebliche Verpflichtungen eingehen; ~ **consolidation** *(US)* Fusion von Aktiengesellschaften; ~ **creditor** *(US)* Firmen-, Gesellschaftsgläubiger; ~ **customer** *(US)* Firmenkunde; ~ **depreciation** *(US)* Firmenabschreibung; ~ **deterioration** Firmenverfall; ~ **development** *(US)* Firmen-, Gesellschaftsentwicklung; ~ **director** *(US)* Vorstandsmitglied; ~ **disaster** *(US)* Betriebsunglück; ~ **earnings** *(US)* Gewinnsituation eines Unternehmens; ~ **election** *(US)* Vorstandswahl; ~ **elite** Firmenelite; ~ **equity** *(US)* Firmenvermögen nach Abzug aller Verbindlichkeiten; ~ **estate** *(US)* Firmen-, Gesellschaftsvermögen; ~ **enterprise** *(US)* Körperschaft des Privatrechts; ~ **etiquette** *(US)* Betriebsknigge; ~ **executive** *(US)* leitender Angestellter; ~ **exigencies** *(US)* Betriebsbedürfnisse; ~ **existence** Bestehen der Gesellschaft; ~ **expenditure** *(US)* Firmenaufwand, -unkosten; ~ **family** *(US)* Betriebsfamilie; ~ **fiduciary** Treuhandgesellschaft; ~ **finances** *(US)* Betriebs-, Firmenfinanzen; ~ **financial counseling** *(US)* finanzielle Beratung der gewerblichen Wirtschaft; ~ **form** Gesellschaftsform; ~ **franchise** Rechtsfähigkeit einer Körperschaft; ~ **funds** Gesellschafts-, Firmenmittel; ~ **growth** *(US)* Unternehmenswachstum; ~ **head** *(US)* Unternehmensleiter; ~ **headquarters** *(US)* Firmenhauptquartier, Zentrale; ~ **identity** einheitliches Erscheinungsbild eines Unternehmens; ~ **image** *(US)* Leit-, Vorstellungsbild eines Unternehmens in der Öffentlichkeit, Firmenimage; ~ **income** *(US)* Gesellschafts-, Körperschaftseinkommen, Einkommen einer Aktiengesellschaft; ~ **income tax** *(US)* Körperschaftssteuer; ~ **income tax exemption** *(US)* Körperschaftssteuerfreibetrag; ~ **income tax return** *(US)* Körperschaftssteuererklärung; ~ **investment** *(US)* Firmeninvestition; ~ **issue** *(US)* Emission einer Aktiengesellschaft; ~ **jet** *(US)* betriebseigenes Düsenflugzeug; ~ **law** [Gesellschafts]satzung; ~ **legal person** Rechtsfähigkeit einer Körperschaft; ~ **liability** *(US)* Firmen-, Gesellschaftshaftung, Haftung einer Aktiengesellschaft; ~ **limit** Stadt-, Gemeindegrenze; ~ **liquidity** *(US)* Firmenliquidität, Liquidität eines Unternehmens; ~ **losses** *(US)* Firmenverluste, Verluste einer Gesellschaft; ~ **management** *(US)* Firmen-, Gesellschaftsleitung, -führung, Geschäftsleitung einer Aktiengesellschaft; ~ **meeting** *(US)* Gesellschafterversammlung; ~ **member** Vollmitglied einer Körperschaft; ~ **merger** Gesellschaftsfusion, Zusammenschluß von Gesellschaften; ~ **minutes** *(US)* Aufsichtsrats-, Sitzungsprotokoll; ~ **mortgage** *(US)* dingliche Belastung eines Gesellschaftsvermögens; **to map** ~ **move** *(US)* Betriebsverlagerung vorbereiten; ~ **name** Firmen-, Gesellschaftsname; **to sue in its** ~ **name** unter dem handelsgerichtlichen Namen klagen; ~ **net worth** Eigenkapital [einer Gesellschaft]; ~ **network** *(US)* Firmennetz; ~ **objective** *(US)* Gesellschaftszweck, -ziel, Geschäftszweck einer Gesellschaft; ~ **officer** *(US)* Vorstandsmitglied; ~ **ownership** Firmen-, Gesellschaftseigentum; ~ **parlance** Betriebsjargon; **to deviate from the** ~ **pattern** *(US)* vom Betriebsüblichen abweichen; ~ **planning** *(US)* langfristige Unternehmensplanung, unternehmerische Gesamtplanung; ~ **policy** *(US)* Geschäfts-, Unternehmenspolitik; ~ **powers** Satzungsbefugnisse einer juristischen Person, Gesellschaftsbefugnisse;

profit *(US)* Firmen-, Unternehmens-, Gesellschaftsgewinn; ~ **promotion** *(US)* betriebliche Förderung; ~ **property** *(US)* Firmen-, Gesellschaftsvermögen, Firmeneigentum, Körperschaftseigentum, *(Br.)* Gemeindevermögen; ~ **proprietorship** *(US)* Reinvermögen einer Aktiengesellschaft; ~ **purpose** *(US)* Gesellschaftszweck, *(Br.)* Gemeindeaufgaben; ~ **pyramid** Betriebspyramide; ~ **reorganization** *(US)* Gesellschafts-, Firmensanierung, Firmenreorganisation; ~ **report** *(US)* Gesellschaftsbericht; ~ **requirements** Firmenerfordernisse; ~ **resolution** *(US)* Gesellschafts-, Vorstandsbeschluß; ~ **responsibility** Gesamtverantwortung; ~ **rights** Rechte einer juristischen Person; ~ **seal** *(US)* Gesellschafts-, Firmensiegel; ~ **shares** (stock, US) Anteilsrechte an einer Gesellschaft; ~ **secretary** Direktionsassistent[in]; ~ **sickness** *(US)* Firmenmängel; ~ **signature** *(US)* Firmenunterschrift; ~ **spending** *(US)* Firmenaufwendungen; ~ **statement** *(US)* Bilanz einer Aktiengesellschaft, Gesellschaftsbilanz, Jahresabschluß; ~ **stock** *(US)* Aktien; ~ **strategy** *(US)* Unternehmensstrategie; ~ **structure** *(US)* Betriebs-, Verwaltungsaufbau, Gesellschaftsform; ~ **success** *(US)* Unternehmenserfolg; ~ **suretyship** Bürgschaftsleistung einer Aktiengesellschaft; ~ **surplus** *(US)* Firmenreingewinn, Gesellschaftsreingewinn; ~ **tax** *(Br.)* Körperschaftssteuer; ~ **tax cut** *(Br.)* Körperschaftssteuerherabsetzung; ~ **tax privilege** *(Br.)* Körperschaftssteuervergünstigung; ~ **tax rate** *(Br.)* Körperschaftssteuersatz; ~ **taxation** *(Br.)* Körperschaftsbesteuerung, Besteuerung von Körperschaften; ~ **town** kreisfreie Stadt; ~ **treasurer** *(US)* Finanzvorstand; ~ **trust** *(US coll.)* Aktienkonzern; ~ **trustee** mit einer Nachlaßverwaltung beauftragtes Kreditinstitut; **to pierce the** ~ **veil** *(US)* Einzelgesellschafter persönlich haftbar machen; ~ **vigo(u)r** Stärke einer Gesellschaft (eines Unternehmens).

corporation Korporation, juristische Person, Körperschaft, *(area governed by a municipal corporation)* Stadtgebiet, *(city, Br.)* Stadtbehörde, -gemeinde, -verwaltung, Körperschaft, Anstalt, *(registered company, Br.)* [eingetragene] Gesellschaft, Handelsgesellschaft, *(guild, Br.)* Innung, Zunft, Gilde, *(US, joint stock company)* Kapital-, Aktiengesellschaft, *(municipal enterprise, US)* Kommunalbetrieb, *(incorporated society, Br.)* eingetragener Verein, *(statute of a city)* Gemeindeverfassung; **affiliated** ~ *(US)* Organ-, Konzern-, Zweiggesellschaft, angegliederte Gesellschaft; **Agricultural Credit** ⱽ *(US)* landwirtschaftliche Kreditbank; **airline** ~ Luftverkehrsgesellschaft; **alien** ~ *(US)* ausländische Gesellschaft; **banking** ~ *(US)* Aktienbank; **broadcasting** ~ Rundfunkanstalt; **business** ~ *(US)* Kapitalgesellschaft; **chartered** ~ eingetragene (konzessionierte) zugelassene Gesellschaft; **close** ~ *(US)* Gesellschaft mit begrenztem Gesellschafterkreis, Familiengesellschaft; **collapsible** ~ *(US)* aus Steuergründen vorübergehend gegründete Gesellschaft; **commercial** ~ Kapital-, Handelsgesellschaft; **competing** ~ Konkurrenzunternehmen, -firma, -gesellschaft; **complete** ~ mit allen Rechten ausgestattete Gesellschaft; **consolidated** ~ Konzerngesellschaft, fusionierte Aktiengesellschaft; **debtor** ~ Schuldnerin; **development** ~ *(city)* Entwicklungsgesellschaft; **dissolved** ~ aufgelöste Gesellschaft; **diversified** ~ Gesellschaft mit breitgestreutem Produktionsprogramm, breitgefächertes Unternehmen; **domestic** ~ *(US)* inländische Körperschaft (Kapitalgesellschaft); **dummy** ~ vorgeschobene Gesellschaft, Stroh-, Scheingesellschaft; **eleemosynary** ~ gemeinnützige, wohltätige Stiftung; **employee-owned** ~ Unternehmen im Eigentum der Arbeitnehmer; **financial** ~**s** *(US)* Banken und Versicherungen; **fly-by-night** ~ unsicheres Unternehmen; **foreign** ~ *(US)* ausländische Gesellschaft; **government** ~ *(US)* staatliche Aktiengesellschaft; **higher-grade** ~ höher eingestuftes Unternehmen; **industrial** ~ *(US)* Industrieunternehmen; **joint stock** ~ *(US)* Aktien-, Kapitalgesellschaft; **limited-dividend** ~ Gesellschaft mit Dividendenbeschränkung; **local** ~ *(US)* Gebietskörperschaft; **membership** ~ *(US)* eingetragener Verein; **migratory** ~ nach Satzungserfordernissen eines anderen Staates errichtete Gesellschaft; **mining** ~ *(US)* Bergbaugesellschaft; **moneyed** ~ Bank-, Versicherungsgesellschaft; **multidivision** ~ geographisch aufgegliederte Gesellschaft; **municipal** ~ *(US)* Stadtgemeinde, Gebietskörperschaft, *(Br.)* Gemeinde-, Kommunalverband, Stadtbehörde; **nonprofit** ~ *(US)* gemeinnütziges Unternehmen; **nonresident foreign** ~ *(US)* nichtansässige ausländische Gesellschaft; **nonstock** ~ *(US)* nicht auf Gewinn gerichtete Gesellschaft mit beschränkter Haftung; **nontrading** ~ gemeinnützige Körperschaft; **open** ~ Gesellschaft mit Vorstandswahl in der Hauptversammlung; **parent** ~ Mutter-, Dachgesellschaft; **private** ~ *(US)* privatrechtliche Gesellschaft, Körperschaft des Privatrechts; **private stock** ~ *(Br.)*

private Aktiengesellschaft; **professional** ~ Berufsgenossenschaft; **public** ~ *(US)* öffentlich-rechtliche Gesellschaft, Körperschaft, Körperschaft des öffentlichen Rechts, Wirtschaftsunternehmen der öffentlichen Hand; **public service** ~ *(US)* Dienstleistungsbetrieb; **public utility** ~ öffentlicher Versorgungsbetrieb; **publicly-owned** ~ *(US)* Publikumsgesellschaft; **quasi** ~ *(US)* Selbstverwaltungsorganisation; **quasi-public** ~ *(US)* gemischtwirtschaftliches Unternehmen, gemischter Versorgungsbetrieb, Regiebetrieb; **real estate** ~ *(US)* Grundstücks-, Immobiliengesellschaft; **registered** ~ *(US)* eingetragene Gesellschaft; **reorganized** ~ sanierte Gesellschaft; **seasonal** ~ Saisongesellschaft; ~ **sole** *(Br.)* Einmanngesellschaft; **state** ~ staatliche Gesellschaft; **statutory** ~ Körperschaft des öffentlichen Rechts; **stock** ~ *(US)* Aktiengesellschaft [nach amerikanischem Recht]; **subsidiary** ~ Organgesellschaft; **trading** ~ kaufmännisches Unternehmen, Handels-, Erwerbsgesellschaft, *(marketing)* Absatz-, Vertriebsgesellschaft; **tramp** ~ Briefkastenfirma; **unlimited** ~ *(US)* Gesellschaft des bürgerlichen Rechts; **wholly-owned** ~ Gesellschaft im ausschließlichen Schachtelbesitz;
~ **de facto** *(US)* fehlerhaft errichtete Aktiengesellschaft; ~ **de jure** *(US)* rechtswirksam errichtete (ordnungsgemäß gegründete) [Aktien]gesellschaft; ~ **dominating the market** marktbeherrschendes Unternehmen; ~ **of traders** Kaufmannsgilde, Handelsinnung; ~ **acting as trustee** treuhänderisch tätige Gesellschaft;
to organize a ~ Gesellschaft gründen;
~ **accounting** Rechnungswesen einer Aktiengesellschaft; **industrial** ~ **bonds** *(US)* Industrieobligationen; ~ **books** Gesellschaftsbücher; ~ **bylaws** Ausführungsbestimmungen zur Satzung; ~ **capital** *(US)* Gesellschaftskapital, Kapital einer [Aktien]gesellschaft; ~ **charter** *(US)* Gründungsurkunde; ~ **council** *(US)* Syndikus, Justiziar; ~ **debts** *(US)* Gesellschaftsschulden, Schulden einer Aktiengesellschaft; ~ **duty** *(Br.)* Erbschaftssteuerabgabe; ~ **earnings** Gesellschaftsgewinn; ~ **entrance tax** Register-, Gründungssteuer; ~ **executive** *(US)* leitender Angestellter; ~ **finance** *(US)* Firmenfinanzen, Finanzierung von Aktiengesellschaften; ~ **income return** *(US)* Körperschaftssteuererklärung; ~ **income tax** *(US)* Körperschaftssteuer; ~ **law** *(US)* Aktienrecht, -gesetz; ~ **lawyer** auf Gesellschaftsrecht spezialisierter Anwalt; ~ **licence** Gesellschaftskonzession; ~ **loan** *(Br.)* Kommunalanleihe; ~ **meeting** Gesellschafterversammlung; ~ **minutes** Vorstandsprotokoll, Gesellschaftsbericht; ~ **official** [leitender] Angestellter einer Aktiengesellschaft; ~ **paper** *(US)* begebbares Papier einer Aktiengesellschaft; ~ **president** Vorstandsvorsitzender; ~ **property** *(US)* Firmen-, Gesellschaftsvermögen, *(Br.)* Gemeindevermögen; ~ **rate** *(US)* Körperschaftssteuersatz; ~ **report** *(US)* Rechenschaftsbericht auf einer Generalversammlung; ~ **reporting** Berichterstattung der Aktiengesellschaften; ~ **stock** *(Br.)* Kommunalwerte, -obligationen; ~ **story** Sonderberichterstattung über eine Aktiengesellschaft; ~ **tax** *(US)* Körperschaftssteuer; ⱽ **Taxation Act** *(US)* Gesetz über die Besteuerung von Aktiengesellschaften; ~ **tramway** städtische Straßenbahn.

corporation tax Körperschaftssteuer;
advance ~ Körperschaftssteuervorauszahlung; ~ **due** fälliger Körperschaftssteuerbetrag; **mainstream** ~ Körperschaftssteuerrestzahlung, gegen Vorschüsse verrechnete Körperschaftssteuer;
~ **overprovided in previous years** zuviel gezahlte Körperschaftssteuer;
to have no application under ~ für die Körperschaftssteuerfestsetzung nicht anwendbar sein;
~ **computation** Körperschaftssteuerberechnung; ~ **legislation** Körperschaftssteuergesetzgebung; ~ **liability** Körperschaftssteuerschuld; ~ **rate** Körperschaftssteuersatz; ~ **scheme (system)** Körperschaftssteuersystem.

corporative korporativ, körperschaftlich, genossenschaftlich;
~ **investor** investierende Kapitalgesellschaft; ~ **state** Ständestaat.

corporator Gesellschafts-, Gründungsmitglied.

corporeal greifbar, physisch, materiell, körperlich;
~ **hereditament** vererbliche Gegenstände; ~ **property** körperliche Gegenstände, greifbare Vermögenswerte.

corps Truppe;
army ~ Armeekorps; **diplomatic** ~ Diplomatisches Korps; **Royal Army Medical** ⱽ *(Br.)* Sanitätskorps, -truppe;
ⱽ **of Engineers** Pioniertruppe;
~ **area** Korpsbereich.

corpse Leiche, Leichnam;
~ *(v.)* *(theater, sl.)* verpatzen.

corpsman Sanitäter.

corpus Körper, Leib, *(body of law)* Gesetzsammlung, *(fund)* Stammkapital;
~ **delicti** Beweisstück.

corral *(v.)* mit Beschlag belegen, sich etw. aneignen.

correct *(v.)* [Eintragungen] berichtigen, richtigstellen, verbessern, abändern, korrigieren, *(account)* bereinigen, *(photo)* entzerren, *(punish)* strafen, tadeln, züchtigen, *(school)* nachsehen;
~ **o. s.** sich [in der Rede] verbessern;
~ **an account** Rechnung durch Nachrechnen berichtigen; ~ **an amount** Rechnungsbetrag berichtigen; ~ **a manuscript** Manuskript korrigieren; ~ **a mistake** Fehler verbessern; ~ **a proof (the press)** Korrektur lesen; ~ **a statement** Erklärung berichtigen;
to proof-~ Korrekturen besorgen;
~ *(a.)* einwandfrei, vorschriftsmäßig, korrekt, fehlerfrei, richtig;
to calculate ~ **to five decimal places** auf fünf Stellen genau berechnen; **to find** ~ für richtig befinden;
~ **answer** richtige Antwort; ~ **attest** für die Richtigkeit; ~ **behavio(u)r** ordnungsgemäßes Verhalten; ~ **calculation** sorgfältige Kalkulation; ~ **description** genaue Beschreibung; ~ **dress** korrekter Anzug; ~ **statement** genaue Erklärung; ~ **style** richtiger Stil; ~ **time** genaue Zeit.

corrected policy berichtigte Versicherungspolice.

correcting and adjusting entry Berichtigungsbuchung.

correction Berichtigung, Richtigstellung, Verbesserung, *(account)* Bereinigung, *(print.)* Fehlerverbesserung, Korrektur, *(punishment)* Zurechtweisung, Tadel, Züchtigung, Besserungsmaßnahmen;
subject to ~s Irrtum vorbehalten, ohne Gewähr; **under** ~ bei der Korrektur;
end ~s *(statistics)* Korrekturen der Extremwerte; **proofreader's** ~s Korrekturzeichen;
~ **of an account** Kontoberichtigung; ~ **of an examination paper** Korrektur einer Examensarbeit; ~ **of exercises** Durchsicht von Schulheften; ~ **of a mistake** Fehlerbeseitigung; ~ **of the press** Fahnenkorrektur, Druckberichtigung; ~ **of a proofsheet** Korrekturenlesen, Druckfahnenverbesserungen; ~s **in red ink** Korrektureintragungen in roter Tinte; ~ **of a river** Flußregulierung; ~ **of school children's work** Korrektur von Schularbeiten; ~s **for type** Korrekturangaben;
to make the first (rough) ~ Vorkorrektur lesen; **to publish a** ~ Berichtigung (Richtigstellung) veröffentlichen; **to speak under** ~ Irrtumsvorbehalt machen;
~ **fluid** Korrekturlack; ~ **mark** Korrekturzeichen; ~ **notice** Berichtigungsmitteilung, *(carrier business)* Berichtigung einer Frachtrechnung.

correctional institution Besserungsanstalt, *(US)* Militärstrafanstalt.

correctitude Korrektheit;
to behave with utmost ~ sich vollkommen korrekt verhalten, sich äußerster Korrektheit befleißigen.

corrective *(med.)* Besserungsmittel;
~ *(a.)* korrektiv, richtigstellend;
~ **action** Abhilfemaßnahmen; ~ **affidavit** berichtigte Erbschaftssteuererklärung; ~ **justice** ausgleichende Gerechtigkeit; ~ **measures** Abhilfemaßnahmen; ~ **training** *(Br.)* vorbeugende Verwahrung vorbestrafter Jugendlicher.

correctness Korrektheit, Richtigkeit.

corrector of the press Korrektor, Korrekturenleser.

correlate *(v.)* in Wechselwirkung bringen, in Wechselbeziehung stehen;
~ **the dates** Termine aufeinander abstimmen; ~ **the office hours** Amtstunden aneinander angleichen.

correlation table Häufigkeitstabelle.

correlative aufeinander abgestimmt.

correspond *(v.) (business)* in Geschäftsbeziehungen stehen, *(communicate)* korrespondieren, im Briefwechsel stehen, Briefe wechseln, *(be in harmony)* entsprechen, übereinstimmen;
~ **with s. o.** mit jem. im Briefwechsel (in brieflicher Verbindung) stehen; ~ **to the description** *(goods)* mit der Beschreibung übereinstimmen; ~ **on a matter** über etw. korrespondieren (einen Briefwechsel führen); ~ **to s. one's needs** jds. Bedürfnissen entsprechen; ~ **to sample** dem Muster entsprechen; ~ **to the spirit of a treaty** dem Geist eines Vertrages entsprechen; **not to** ~ **to modern traffic** Anforderungen des modernen Verkehrs nicht gewachsen sein.

correspondence brieflicher Verkehr, Briefverkehr, -wechsel, Schriftwechsel, Korrespondenz, *(business relation)* Geschäftsverbindung, *(journalist)* Beiträge;

banker's ~ Korrespondenzbank; close ~ vertrauter Briefwechsel; commercial ~ Handelskorrespondenz; foreign ~ Auslandskorrespondenz; government ~ Briefwechsel mit Behörden; outstanding ~ Briefschulden; postal ~ Briefpostsendungen; time-stamped ~ mit Einzelstempel versehene Korrespondenz;
~ **between cause and effect** Kausalzusammenhang; ~ **with description** *(goods)* Übereinstimmung mit der Beschreibung; ~ **elect for Berlin** für Berlin vorgesehener Korrespondent;
~ **that has passed between us** miteinander geführte Korrespondenz;
to attend to one's ~ Korrespondenz erledigen; **to be in** ~ miteinander korrespondieren; **to break off** ~ Verbindung abbrechen; **to carry on a** ~ Briefwechsel (briefliche Beziehungen) unterhalten; **to commence a** ~ in Verbindung treten; **to cut off one's** ~ **with s. o.** seine Korrespondenz mit jem. abbrechen; **to discontinue (drop a)** ~ Korrespondenz einstellen; **to go through one's** ~ eingegangene Post durchsehen; **to hold a** ~ freundliche Beziehungen pflegen; **to keep up a secret** ~ geheimen Briefwechsel führen; **to open a** ~ Briefwechsel einleiten; **to resume with** ~ Korrespondenz wieder aufnehmen; **to stand in** ~ in dauernder Korrespondenz stehen;
~ **classes** Fernunterricht; ~ **clerk** Korrespondent; ~ **college** Fernlehranstalt; ~ **column** Leserbriefspalte; ~ **course** Fernunterricht, -lehrgang, -studium, Korrespondenzkurs; ~ **course student** Fernstudent; ~ **school** Fernunterrichtsschule, -lehrinstitut; ~ **study** Fernunterricht; ~ **supply** Schreibmaterialien; ~ **ticket** Umsteigefahrschein.

correspondent Briefpartner, *(US, banking)* Korrespondenzbank, *(business friend)* Geschäftsfreund, *(employee)* Korrespondent, Angestellter, *(informant)* Gewährsmann, *(newspaper)* [Zeitungs]berichterstatter;
from our ~ eigener Bericht;
banking ~ Bankverbindung; **business** ~ Handelskorrespondent; **domestic (home)** ~ Inlandskorrespondent; **foreign** ~ auswärtiger Berichterstatter, Auslandskorrespondent; **newspaper** ~ Zeitungsberichterstatter; **out-of-town** ~ *(bank)* Korrespondenzbank; **overseas** ~ überseeischer Korrespondent; **special** ~ Sonderberichterstatter; „Times" ~ **in Bonn** Vertreter der „Times" in Bonn; **war** ~ Kriegsberichterstatter;
to act as ~ als Berichterstatter tätig sein; **to be a bad** ~ selten Briefe schreiben; **to entrust a matter to one's** ~ eigenen Korrespondenten mit etw. beauftragen;
~ *(a.)* übereinstimmend, entsprechend;
~ **bank** Korrespondenzbank; ~ **forwarder** Korrespondenzspediteur.

corresponding im Briefwechsel stehend, korrespondierend;
~ **to the original** mit dem Original übereinstimmend;
~ **entry** gleichlautende Buchung; ~ **factor** Korrespondenzfaktor; ~ **member** korrespondierendes Mitglied; ~ **period** Vergleichszeitraum; ~ **secretary** Korrespondent[in].

corridor Korridor, Gang, Flur, *(train)* Gang;
air ~ Luftkorridor;
~ **carriage (coach)** Durchgangswagen; ~ **panel** Gangschild; ~ **train** Durchgangszug, D-Zug.

corrigenda *(book)* Druckfehlerverzeichnis.

corrigendum Druckfehler.

corroborate *(v.)* bekräftigen, erhärten;
~ **s. o. in his statements** jds. Aussagen bestätigen.

corroborating evidence zusätzliches Beweismaterial.

corroboration Bestätigung, Bekräftigung, Erhärtung;
~ **of a statement** Bestätigung einer Aussage.

corrugated | cardboard Wellpappe; ~ **iron** Wellblech; ~ **road** zerfurchte (aufgerissene) Straße.

corrupt bestechlich, unredlich, korrupt, *(immoral)* verworfen, verdorben;
~ *(v.)* bestechen, kaufen;
~ **the electorate** Wählerschaft korrumpieren;
~ **administration** korrupte Verwaltung; ~ **air** schlechte Luft; ~ **intent** wucherischer Vorsatz, wucherische Absicht; ~ **judge** käuflicher Richter; ~ **passage** Fehlerstelle; ~ **practices** Durchstechereien, Bestechungsmanöver, [Wahl]bestechung, Bestechlichkeit; ~ **Practices Act** *(US)* Gesetz zur Verhinderung von Wahlvergehen; ~ **press** käufliche Presse; **for a** ~ **purpose** in sittenwidriger Weise; ~ **text** Text voller Fehler, verderbter Text.

corruptible bestechlich, der Bestechung zugänglich, käuflich;
~ **government officials** bestechliche Staatsbeamte.

corruptibility Bestechlichkeit, Käuflichkeit.

corruption Bestechung, Bestechlichkeit, Korruption, *(body)* Verfall;
electoral ~ Wahlbestechung, -beeinflussung; **general** ~ allge-

meine Bestechung; **judicial ~** Richterbestechung; **unblushing ~** schamlose Bestechung;
bribery and ~ Durchstechereien;
~ of a language Entartung einer Sprache; **~ in public life** Korruption der Öffentlichkeit; **~ of style** Stilbruch; **~ of a text** Textentstellung; **~ of a witness** Zeugenbestechung;
to be proof against ~ gegen Bestechung gefeit sein;
~ allegation Korruptionsvorbringen; **to jail on a ~ charge** wegen Bestechung zu einer Gefängnisstrafe verurteilen.

corvette Korvette, U-Boot-Begleitschiff.

cosignatory Mitunterzeichner;
~ powers Konsignatarmächte.

cosmetic treatment Schönheitspflege.

cosmetician Kosmetiker.

cosmic *(mil.)* geheime Kommandosache;
~ (a.) kosmisch, weltumfassend.

cosmopolis Weltstadt.

cosmopolitan | atmosphere Weltstadtatmosphäre; **~ city** Weltstadt; **~ outlook** kosmopolitischer Weitblick.

cosmopolite Kosmopolit, Weltbürger.

cosmopolitism Weltbürgertum.

cosmos Kosmos, Weltall, Universum.

cosponsorship Beteiligung an einer Werbesendung.

cost [Un]kosten, Geschäftskosten, Spesen, Auslagen, Aufwand, Kostenbetrag, *(balance sheet)* Anschaffungspreis, *(law court, Br.)* Gerichtskosten, *(loss)* Verlust, Nachteil, Schaden, *(price)* Preis;
all ~s included unter Einschluß sämtlicher Kosten; **at ~** zum Selbstkostenpreis, zum Erwerbswert, *(investment fund)* auf Anschaffungsbasis, *(stock exchange)* zu Ankaufskursen, zum Ankaufspreis; **at the ~ of s. o.** auf jds. Kosten; **at all ~s** um jeden Preis; **at common ~** auf gemeinsame Rechnung; **at great ~** mit großen Kosten verbunden; **at less than ~** unter Einkaufspreis; **at little (small) ~** billig; **at my ~** auf meine Kosten; **at one's own ~** auf eigene Kosten; **awarding the ~s** unter Auferlegung der Kosten; **exclusive of ~s** ausschließlich der Kosten; **free of ~** kostenlos, umsonst, gratis; **from the standpoint of ~s** vom Kostenstandpunkt aus; **in deference to the ~s** mit Rücksicht auf die Kosten; **on payment of ~** unter Tragung (Auferlegung) der Kosten; **to my ~** auf meine Kosten; **with ~** kostenpflichtig, unter Auferlegung der Kosten; **without ~** kostenlos, umsonst, gratis; **without regard to ~** ohne Rücksicht auf die Kosten, wobei das Geld keine Rolle spielt;
accident ~s Unfallkosten; **accounting ~s** Kosten der Buchführung, Buchhaltungsaufwand; **accrued ~s** aufgelaufene (entstandene) Kosten; **actual ~** effektive Herstellungs-, Selbst-, Gestehungskosten; **added ~s** zusätzliche Kosten; **additional ~s** Mehrkosten; **adjusted ~s** auf den Tageswert umgerechnete Kosten; **administrative ~s** *(US)* Verwaltungskosten; **advancement ~s** Kosten für weitere Ausbildung; **advertising ~** Werbekosten; **agency ~** Agenturunkosten; **~s agreed on** vereinbarte Spesen (Kosten); **amortized ~s** Kosten nach Abschreibung, Kosten zum Buchwert; **annual report ~s** Kosten der Herstellung des Jahresberichts; **~s arising from it** daraus entstehende Kosten; **assembly ~s** Montagekosten; **assessment ~s** Veranlagungskosten; **asset ~s** Kosten des Anlagevermögens; **assured ~s** feststehende Unkosten; **~s attendant on** daraus erwachsende Kosten; **automobile-operating (maintenance) ~s** Kosten der Unterhaltung eines Kraftfahrzeugs; **average ~** Durchschnittsaufwand, -preis, -kosten; **balance-of-payments ~** Zahlungsbilanzaufwand; **basic ~** Grundkosten; **billed ~** Rechnungskosten, Kosten vor Abzug des Bardiskonts; **bunched ~s** pauschalierte Kosten; **capacity ~s** Kosten bei voller Betriebsausnutzung; **per capita ~s** Kosten (Ausgaben) pro Kopf der Bevölkerung; **capital ~** Kapitalaufwand; **capitalized ~s** auf Kapitalkonto übernommene (kapitalisierte) Kosten; **common ~s** Gemeinkosten; **common fund ~s** *(Br.)* Prozeßkosten; **comparative ~s** vergleichsweise Unkostensituation; **compensation ~s** Schadensbetrag; **composite ~s** verbundene Kosten; **constant ~s** gleichbleibende (konstante) Kosten; **controllable ~s** wechselnde Kosten; **per-copy ~s** Kosten pro Exemplar; **court ~s** Gerichtskosten; **current ~** augenblicklicher Kostenaufwand, Kostenaufwand zu Marktpreisen; **debt-service ~s** Schuldentilgungsaufwand; **decreasing ~s** abnehmende (fallende) Kosten; **deductible donation ~s** steuerabzugsfähiger Schenkungsaufwand; **defendant's ~s** Kosten des Beklagten; **delivery ~s** Zustellungskosten; **demolition ~s** Abbruchkosten; **departmental ~s** Abteilungskosten; **depleted ~s** Kostenrückstand nach Abzug der Substanzverringerung; **depreciation ~s** Abnutzungsaufwand; **development ~s** Entwicklungskosten; **direct ~** leistungsabhängige Kosten, Einzelkosten; **distribution**

~s Vertriebs-, Absatzkosten; **dives ~s** *(US sl.)* Kostenvorschuß [für den Anwalt]; **double ~s** Kosten zum anderthalbfachen Satz; **enormous ~s** unerschwingliche Kosten; **escapable ~s** vermeidbare Kosten; **estimated ~s** geschätzte Kosten, Kostenaufwand, Unkostenschätzung; **excess ~s** Mehraufwand, Mehrkosten, -ausgaben; **excessive ~s** übermäßige Kosten, Kostenüberhöhung; **expansion ~** Erweiterungskosten; **expired ~** abgeschriebener Kostenanteil; **exploitation ~s** Ausbeutungskosten; **factory ~** Fabrikpreis; **factory overhead ~s** allgemeine Betriebsunkosten; **final ~s** *(law court)* gesamte Prozeßkosten; **financing ~s** Finanzierungskosten; **first ~** Gestehungskosten, Selbstkostenpreis, Anschaffungskosten, *(purchase price)* Einkaufspreis; **fixed ~** feststehende (feste, fixe) Kosten; **fuel ~s** Heizungskosten; **future ~s** zukünftig anfallende Kosten; **general ~s** Gemeinkosten, Selbst-, Generalunkosten; **hauling ~s** *(railway)* Zustellungsgebühren; **health care ~s** Kosten der Gesundheitsvorsorge; **heating ~s** Heizungskosten; **heavy ~s** beträchtliche Unkosten; **high first ~** hohe Anfangskosten; **holding ~s** Lagerhaltungskosten; **hospital ~s** Krankenhauskosten; **idle capacity ~** Kostenaufwand für ungenutzte Kapazität; **imputed ~s** kalkulierte Kosten; **increasing ~s** zunehmender Kostenanteil; **incremental ~s** nahe der Rentabilität liegende Kosten; **~s incurred** aufgelaufene (entstandene) Kosten; **indirect ~** Gemein-, Generalunkosten, mittelbare Kosten; **inflation ~s** Kosteninflation; **initial ~** Anlagekosten; **intangible ~s** Kosten für immaterielle Werte; **interest ~** Passivzinsen; **interlocutory ~s** während des Verfahrens anfallende Gebühren, Kosten im Zwischenverfahren; **intermediate ~s** Zwischenkosten; **invoice ~** Einkaufspreis; **involved ~s** erwachsene Spesen; **itemized ~s** Einzelkosten; **land ~** Grundstückspreis; **landed ~** Löschungskosten, *(customs)* Preis bei der Anlieferung, Anlieferungskosten; **law ~s** Kosten der Rechtsverfolgung, Prozeßkosten; **legal ~s** Prozeß-, Verfahrenskosten, Gerichtskosten; **legitimate ~s** rechtlich zulässige Kosten; **living ~s** Lebenshaltungskosten; **manufacturing ~s** Herstellungs-, Produktionskosten; **marginal ~s** Grenzkosten, an der Grenze der Wirtschaftlichkeit liegender Aufwand; **marketing ~s** Kosten des Vertriebs, Vertriebskosten; **medical ~s** Arztkosten; **minimum ~** Mindestkosten; **net ~** Nettopreis, -kosten; **noncash ~s** nicht in bar anfallende Unkosten; **~s occurring** daraus erwachsende Kosten; **operating ~** Betriebskosten, Kosten der Betriebsführung; **automobile operating ~s** Kraftfahrzeugunterhaltungskosten; **general operating ~s** Betriebsgemeinkosten; **household operating ~s** Kosten der Haushaltsführung; **office-operating ~s** allgemeine Geschäftsunkosten; **operational ~s** Betriebskosten; **opportunity ~** alternative Kosten; **organization ~s** Gründungskosten, -aufwand; **original ~** *(outlay for assets)* Anschaffungs-, Erwerbskosten, Ankaufswert, *(public utility accounting)* Herstellungs-, Gründungsaufwand; **out-of-pocket ~s** Barauslagen, -aufwendungen, variable Kosten; **overhead ~s** Fertigungsgemeinkosten; **packaging ~s** Verpackungskosten; **partial ~** Kostenanteil; **party-and-party ~** notwendig gewordene (erstattungsfähige) Anwaltskosten; **pension-plan benefit ~s** Kosten einer Altersversorgung; **plant construction ~s** Kosten für Betriebsbauten; **post-mortem ~s** nachkalkulierte Kosten; **predetermined ~** vorkalkulierte Kosten; **prime ~** Selbst-, Gestehungskosten, *(purchase price)* Einkaufspreis, Anschaffungswert, -kosten; **processing ~s** Verarbeitungs-, Fabrikationskosten; **production ~s** Gestehungskosten, Produktionsaufwand, -kosten; **progressive ~s** progressive Kosten; **prohibitive ~s** untragbare Kosten; **prospective ~s** voraussichtliche Kosten; **purchase-related ~s** mit der Anschaffung verbundene Unkosten; **purchasing ~s** Warenbeschaffungskosten; **real ~s** Grundkosten; **~s receivable** *(US)* Kostenforderungen; **recoverable ~s** beitreibbare Kosten, Kostenrückstand; **recovering ~s** laufende Geschäftsunkosten; **regressive ~s** degressive Kosten; **related ~s** notwendige Kosten; **relevant ~s** entscheidungsrelevante Kosten; **renewal ~s** Erneuerungskosten; **reorganization ~s** Sanierungskosten; **replacement ~s** Wiederbeschaffungskosten; **~s reserved** Kostenentscheidung vorbehalten; **residual ~s** Restkosten, Kostenrückstand; **resulting ~s** Folgekosten; **rising ~s** steigende Kosten; **runaway ~** schnellen Steigerungen unterworfene Kosten; **running ~s** laufende [Geschäfts]unkosten; **salvage ~** *(insurance)* Bergungskosten; **scheduled ~s** vorkalkulierte Kosten; **selling ~s** Vertriebs-, Verkaufskosten; **service ~** abschreibungsfähige Kosten; **shutdown ~s** Kosten der Betriebseinstellung (Betriebsstillegung); **skyrocketing (soaring) ~s** steil ansteigende (steil in die Höhe schießende) Kosten; **social ~** Soziallasten; **solicitor's ~s** *(Br.)* Anwaltsgebühren; **special ~s** spezifizierte Kosten; **specific ~s** Einzelkosten; **standard** ~ vorkalkulierte (konstante) Kosten, Plan-, Einheits-, Richt-, Normal-, Standardkosten; **basic standard** ~ Grundstandardkosten; **standby** ~s feste (fixe) Kosten; **starting-load** ~s Kosten vor Anlauf der Fertigung; **stock-issue** ~s Emissionskosten; **sunk** ~s einmalige (nicht relevante) Produktionskosten; **supervisory** ~s Betriebsüberwachungskosten; **supplemental** ~s Preisaufschlag, -zuschlag; **supplementary** ~s Fertigungsgemeinkosten; **surveying** ~s Vermessungskosten; **talent** ~ *(broadcasting)* Produktionskosten; **target** ~s vorkalkulierte Kosten; **after-tax** ~ Kostenaufwand nach Steuerbegleichung; **taxable** ~s *(law court)* erstattungsfähige Prozeßkosten; **terminal** ~ End-, Grenzkosten; **total** ~ Gesamtkosten; **total production** ~s Gesamtproduktionskosten; **traceable** ~s direkte Kosten; **transit** ~s durchlaufende Kosten, Transitkosten; **transportation inland** ~s Kosten des Antransportes; **treble** ~s Kosten zum zweieinhalbfachen Satz; **trucking** ~s Speditions-, Straßentransportkosten; **turnover** ~s allgemeine Betriebsunkosten; **uncontrollable** ~s von der Kostenstelle nicht beeinflußbare Kosten; **uneconomic** ~s laufende Unkosten; **unit** ~s Stückkosten; **average unit** ~s Durchschnittskosten per Einheit; **low per-unit** ~s niedrige Stückkosten; **standard unit** ~s Normalkosten per Einheit; **untaxable** ~s *(law court)* noch nicht festgesetzte (nicht erstattungsfähige) Kosten; **unavoidable** ~s feste Kosten; **user** ~ Benutzungsgebühr; **variable** ~ ungewisse (variable) Kosten; **average variable** ~s proportionale variable Kosten; **volume** ~ fixe Kosten, Engroskosten; **workroom** ~s Werkstattkosten; ~ **written off** abgeschriebener Kostenanteil;

~, **insurance and freight (cif)** Kosten, Versicherung und Fracht; ~s **necessarily incurred in the conduct of a business** bei der Geschäftsführung notwendigerweise entstehende Ausgaben; ~ **of an action** Prozeßkosten; ~ **of acquisition** Anschaffungspreis, -kosten; ~s **of adjudication** Kosten des Konkursverfahrens; ~s **of administration** Verwaltungskosten; ~s **for advertising** Werbungsunkosten; ~ **of appeal** Berufungskosten; ~ **of appraisal** Schätzungskosten; ~ **of arbitration** Schiedsgerichtskosten; ~s **of resisting the bankruptcy proceedings** bei der Konkursabwehr entstandene Kosten; ~ **of borrowing** Kreditbeschaffungskosten; ~ **of building** Baukosten; ~ **of capital** durchschnittliche Kapitalkosten; ~ **of a car** Anschaffungskosten eines Kraftfahrzeugs; ~ **of carriage** Bahnfracht, Beförderungskosten, Frachtgebühren; ~ **in carrying business** laufende Unkosten; ~ **of carrying real estate** [Grundstücks]unterhaltungskosten; ~ **of checking operations** Überprüfungskosten; ~ **of collection** Inkasso-, Einzugsspesen; ~ **of construction** Errichtungskosten, Bau-, Entwicklungs-, Konstruktionskosten; ~s **of unbilled contracts** unverrechnete Auftragskosten; ~ **of credit** Kreditkosten; ~ **of going to court** Kosten einer Gerichtsverhandlung; ~s **of customs clearance** Zollabfertigungskosten; ~s **of the day** pro Tag entstehende Verhandlungskosten; ~ **of delivery** Liefer-, Versandkosten; ~ **of depreciation** Abschreibungsaufwand, -kosten; ~s **of development** Entwicklungskosten; ~s **of distribution** Vertriebs-, Versandkosten; ~ **of dividends** *(insurance company)* Gewinnbeteiligungskosten; ~ **of drainage** Kanalisationskosten; **rising** ~s **of energy** steigende Energiekosten; ~ **of enrolment** Immatrikulationsgebühr; ~ **of entertainment** Repräsentationskosten; ~ **of business entertainment** Bewirtungskosten für Geschäftsfreunde; ~ **of entry** Eintrittspreis; ~ **of equipment** Installations-, Ausstattungskosten; ~ **of erection** Aufstellungs-, Montage-, Installationskosten; ~ **of exchange** Umtauschspesen-, kosten; ~ **of execution** Zwangsvollstreckungskosten; ~s **and expenses** Kosten und Auslagen; ~ **of exploration** Forschungsaufwand; ~ **of financing** Finanzierungskosten; ~s **for flying** Flugunkosten; ~ **and freight** alle Frachtkosten bis zum Ankunftshafen vom Verkäufer bezahlt; ~s **of goods manufactured** Fabrikations-, Herstellungs-, Produktionskosten; ~ **of goods purchased** Einstandspreis der Waren; ~s **of goods and services** Preis für Güter und Dienstleistungen; ~ **of goods sold** Kosten der gesamten Warenlieferung, *(US)* Kostennachweis für hergestellte und verkaufte Waren; ~ **of illness** Krankheitskosten; ~s **of implementation** Durchführungskosten; ~s **of improvements** Meliorationskosten, Verbesserungs-, Verschönerungsaufwand; ~s **of increase** festgesetzte erstattungsfähige Kosten; ~ **of the insert** Beilagenpreis; ~s **of issue** Kosten des Rechtsstreits; ~ **of installation** Anlagekosten; ~ **of insurance** Versicherungskosten; ~ **per item** Stückkosten; ~ **of labo(u)r** Lohnaufwand, -kosten, Löhne und Gehälter; **rising** ~s **of land** steigende Grunderwerbskosten; ~ **to launch** Startkosten; ~ **of levy** Pfändungskosten; ~ **per line** Zeilenpreis; ~s **of liquidation** Liquidationskosten; ~s **of litigation** Prozeßkosten.

cost of living Unterhalts-, Lebenshaltungskosten; **advanced (increased)** ~ erhöhte Lebenshaltungskosten; **to slow down the rising** ~ gestiegene Lebenshaltungskosten (Teuerung) abbremsen; **built-in** ~ **adjuster** automatischer Lebenshaltungskostenausgleichfaktor; ~ **adjustment** Lohnangleichung an die Lebenshaltungskosten; ~ **adjustment formula** Lebenshaltungskostenausgleichformel; ~ **allowance** Lebenshaltungszuschuß, Teuerungszuschlag; **high** ~ **bonus** Teuerungszulage; ~ **clause** Lebenshaltungskostenklausel; ² **Council** *(US)* Lebenshaltungskostenbehörde; ~ **escalator** Lebenshaltungsgleitklausel; ~ **escalator adjustment** automatische Lohnangleichung an die gestiegenen Lebenshaltungskosten; **full** ~ **escalator plan** System mit vollwirksamer Preisgleitklausel für Lebenshaltungskosten; **high** ~ **grants** Überteuerungszuschüsse; ~ **increase** Lebenshaltungskostenanstieg; ~ **index** Lebens[haltungs]kostenindex; **high** ~ **region** teures Pflaster, teure Wohngegend; ~ **rise** Anstieg der Lebenshaltungskosten.

cost | of maintenance Unterhalts-, Instandhaltungskosten; ~ **of management** Verwaltungs-, Bewirtschaftungskosten; ~ **of manufacture (making)** Fabrikations-, Herstellungs-, Produktionskosten, Herstellungspreis; ~ **of marketing** Absatz-, Vertriebskosten; ~ **of material** Materialkosten, -aufwand; ~ **of materials including changes in inventories** *(balance sheet)* Aufwendungen nach Verrechnung mit Bestandsveränderungen; ~ **of raw materials** Rohstoffbeschaffungskosten; ~ **of membership** Mitgliedschaftskosten; ~ **of money** Geldeinstands-, Geldbeschaffungskosten; ~ **of motoring** Autounterhaltungskosten; ~ **of operation** Betriebs[un]kosten; ~ **of organizing a corporation** Gründungskosten; ~s **of packing** Verpackungskosten; ~s **of paper** Papierkosten; ~s **as between party and party** erstattungsfähige Kosten eines Rechtsstreites; ~ **of a patent** Patentunkosten; ~ **of patent right** Patenterwerbskosten; ~s **payable out of the estate** Massekosten; ~ **of petrol** Benzinkosten; ~ **of plant addition** Betriebserweiterungskosten; ~ **of a prescription** Rezeptkosten; ~ **of preserving and administrating the bankrupt's estate** Kosten des Konkursverfahrens; ~s **of printing** Druckkosten; ~s **of poor prisoners' defence** Kosten der Pflichtverteidigung; ~ **of proceedings** Verfahrenskosten; ~ **of production** Produktionspreis, -kosten, *(publisher)* Herstellungskosten; **running** ~s **of a project** Kosten einer Projektdurchführung; ~s **of promotion** Gründungskosten; ~ **of protest** *(bill of exchange)* Wechselprotestkosten; ~ **of purchase** Anschaffungskosten; ~ **of raw materials** Aufwendungen für Rohstoffe; ~s **of realization** Verwertungs-, Versilberungskosten; ~s **of references** Fürsorgekosten; ~ **of relocation** Repatriierungskosten; ~ **of repairs** Reparatur-, Instandsetzungskosten; ~ **of repair work carried out by outside contractors** Fremdreparaturen; ~ **to replace (of replacement, replacing)** Wiederbeschaffungswert, -kosten, Auswechslungskosten; ~ **per reply** Kostenanteil pro Anfrage; ~ **of roadbuilding** Straßenbaukosten; ~ **of sales** Absatz-, Vertriebskosten, Verkaufsunkosten; ~ **of salvage** Bergungskosten; ~s **of samples** Musterkosten; ~ **on a higher scale** höhere Gebührensätze; ~ **of securities** ausmachender Effektenwert; ~ **of social security** Sozialversicherungskosten, -aufwand; ~ **of domestic services** Aufwand für eine Hausangestellte; ~ **of servicing** Dienstleistungs-, Wartungskosten; ~ **of a share** Aktienwert; ~ **of site** Grunderwerbskosten; ~ **due to a solicitor** *(Br.)* Anwaltskosten; ~ **of the stock** Aktienkaufpreis; ~ **of storage** Lagerkosten; ~ **of breaking the stowage** Verstauungs-, Entstauungskosten; ~ **of a structure** Kosten der Gebäudeerrichtung; ~ **of suing** Prozeßkosten; ~s **to be taxed** festzusetzende Kosten; ~ **per thousand** Tausenderpreis; ~ **of time** *(broadcasting, television)* Werbeaufwand pro Minute; ~ **of tombstone** Grabsteinkosten; ~s **of transfer** Übertragungskosten, Transfergebühr bei Aktienverkäufen; ~ **of transportation** Transport-, Beförderungskosten; ~ **of travel between home and work** Kosten für Fahrten zwischen Wohnung und Betrieb; ~ **of treatment** Behandlungskosten; ~ **of type** Satzkosten; ~s **of umpirage** Kosten des Schiedsgerichtsverfahrens; ~ **per unit** Stückkosten; ~ **of upkeep** Unterhaltungs-, Wartungskosten; ~ **of war** Kriegskosten; ~s **to be borne by ...** Kosten gehen zu Lasten von ...;

~ **(v.)** kosten, zu stehen kommen, *(calculate prime cost)* Selbstkosten einer Ware veranschlagen, Preis kalkulieren; ~ **an unholy amount of money** heilloses Stück Geld kosten; ~ **article** Selbstkostenpreis einer Ware feststellen; ~ **a good deal [of money]** viel Geld kosten; ~ **dearly** viel kosten; ~ **s. o. dearly** j. teuer zu stehen kommen; ~ **the earth** kleines Vermögen kosten; ~ **easily a thousand pounds** glatte tausend Pfund kosten; ~ **no end of money** jede Menge Geld kosten; ~ **a job**

Kostenaufwand berechnen, Kostenberechnung vornehmen; ~ a lot an den Beutel gehen; ~ **a matter of $ 100** etwa 100 Dollar kosten; ~ **money** sehr teuer sein; ~ **a mint of money** viel Geld verschlingen; ~ **a packet of money** Haufen Geld kosten; ~ **s. o. his neck** jem. an den Kragen gehen; ~ **peanuts** nur Pfifferlinge kosten; ~ **much time** viel Zeit erfordern; ~ **DM 3000 a year to run a car** 3000 DM jährlich für die Unterhaltung eines Autos aufbringen müssen;

to allocate to bear the ~s Kosten auferlegen; **to allow ~s** Kostenrechnung anerkennen; **to amortize ~s over a period of three years** Unkosten über drei Jahre verteilen; **to apportion the ~s** Kosten aufteilen (umlegen); **to ascertain the ~s** Kosten ermitteln; **to award ~s** Kosten auferlegen; **to award ~s against s. o.** j. kostenpflichtig verurteilen; **to be condemned in (ordered to pay the) ~s** zu den Kosten verurteilt werden, Kosten auferlegt bekommen; **to be sentenced to bear the ~s** kostenfällig verurteilt werden; **to bear the ~ of an undertaking** Kosten eines Unternehmens übernehmen; **to build a house without regard to ~** beim Hausbau überhaupt nicht sparen; **to calculate the ~s** Kosten berechnen; **to calculate the ~ of setting** Satzpreis berechnen; **to cancel the ~s** Kosten niederschlagen; **to carry ~s** Kostenfolgen haben, Kosten nach sich ziehen, *(law judgment)* über die Kosten entscheiden; **to charge ~s directly to the department** Kosten unmittelbar auf jede Abteilung verrechnen; **to control ~s** Kosten in den Griff bekommen; **to count the ~** *(fig.)* sich die Folgen vorher überlegen; **to cover the ~** zur Kostendeckung; **to cover production ~s** Kostendeckung sicherstellen; **to cut ~s** Kosten reduzieren; **to cut back on ~s** Kosteneinsparung vornehmen; **to cut ~s throughout a company** ganzen Betrieb kostenmäßig durchforsten; **to deduct the ~s** Kosten steuerlich absetzen; **to dismiss with ~s** kostenpflichtig abweisen; **to divide the ~s between the parties** Kosten gegeneinander aufheben; **to figure up the ~s** Kosten berechnen; **to fix the ~s** Kosten festsetzen; **to hold down on ~s** geringen Kostenaufwand haben, Kosten niedrig halten; **to hold the line on ~s** Kostenniveau halten; **to itemize ~s** Kosten aufgliedern; **to keep down the ~s** Kosten möglichst niedrig halten; **to keep ~s in line** Kosten niedrig halten; **to keep track of ~s** Kosten nachgehen; **to live at s. one's ~s** zu seinem Schaden erfahren; **to live at s. one's ~s** auf jds. Kosten leben; **to make a showing on ~** sich kostenmäßig auswirken; **to meet the ~s** Kosten bestreiten; **to order to bear the ~s** Kosten auferlegen; **to pass ~s on** Unkosten abwälzen; **to pass on rising ~s without becoming uncompetitive** gestiegene Kosten ohne Verschlechterung der Wettbewerbssituation weitergeben (weiterbelasten); **to pay the ~ incurred** entstandene Kosten übernehmen; **to pay for the ~ of keeping a car on the road** Unterhaltskosten eines Autos tragen; **to pick up the entire ~ of a pension plan** Gesamtkosten der Pensionsregelung übernehmen; **to pile up the ~s** Rechnung hochschrauben; **to reckon the probable ~** sich die voraussichtlich entstehenden Kosten ausrechnen; **to reckon the ~ of an undertaking** Kostenaufwand eines Unternehmens kalkulieren; **to reduce ~s** Unkosten senken (verringern); **to review ~s** Kostenrechnung überprüfen; **to run one's ~s through the roof** Kosten nicht mehr verkraften können; **to save 30% on ~s versus competitors** Kostenersparnis von 30% gegenüber der Konkurrenz erzielen; **to sell at ~** zum Einkaufspreis verkaufen; **to slash ~s** Unkosten drastisch reduzieren; **to spare no ~** keine Kosten scheuen; **to spread the ~s** Kosten verteilen; **to stand at ~ ... at** mit einem Herstellungswert von ... zu Buche stehen; **to supply at a small extra ~** mit einem kleinen Aufschlag liefern; **to tax ~** *(law court)* Anwaltskosten festsetzen, Kosten nachprüfen.

cost | **absorption** Kostenwertberichtigung, -übernahme; ~ **account** Kostenanschlag, *(expense account)* Unkostenkonto; ~ **account** *(v.)* Kosten kalkulieren; ~ **accountancy** Betriebskalkulation; ~ **accountancy method** Kostenrechnung; ~ **accountant** [Betriebs]kalkulator, Kostenrechner, -fachmann; ~ **accounting** Kostenrechnung, [Betriebs]kalkulation, Berechnung des Selbstkostenpreises, betriebliches Rechnungswesen, [Selbst]kostenberechnung, -kalkulation, *(bookkeeping)* Kostenbuchhaltung; **current ~ accounting** Betriebskalkulation zu Marktpreisen; **distributive ~ accounting** Zuschlagskalkulation; ~ **accounting department** Kalkulationsabteilung; ~ **accounting system** Kostenrechnungsverfahren, -system; ~ **accruing** Kostenanfall; ~ **adjustment** Kostenanpassung, -angleichung; ~ **advantage** Kostenvorteil; ~ **allocation** Kostenaufteilung, -umlage, -umlegung; ~ **analysis** Kostenanalyse; ~ **analyst** Kostenanalytiker, -fachmann; ~ **approach** Kostenmethode; ~ **assignment** Kostenaufteilung; ~ **averaging** Durchschnittskostenmethode, *(stock exchange)* Kostenausgleich; ~ **basis of accounting** Bewertungsgrundlage [der Rentabilitätsberech-

nung], Kostengrundlage; ~ **benefit** Kostenvorteil; ~ **benefit analysis** Analyse der Kostenvorteile, Kostennutzenanalyse; **to use a ~ benefit approach** Kostenvorteil methodisch untersuchen; ~ **benefit trade-off** Abwägung der Kostenvorteile; ~ **bond** *(at court)* Sicherheitsleistung; ~ **book** Kalkulationsbuch, *(law)* Gebührenverzeichnis, *(mining)* Kuxbuch, *(raw materials)* Einkaufspreisliste; ~ **book company** *(Br.)* bergrechtliche Gewerkschaft; ~ **book principle** *(mining)* Einnahmen-Ausgaben-Rückführungssystem; ~ **bookkeeping** Kostenbuchhaltung; ~ **boost** plötzlicher Kostenanstieg; ~ **bracket** Kostengruppe; ~ **breakdown** Kostenaufschlüsselung, -aufgliederung; ~ **budget** Kostenplan; ~ **card** Kostenbeleg; **job-order ~ card** Kostenrechnungskarte; ~ **center** Kostenstelle, -abteilung; ~ **accounting centre** *(Br.)* Kostenstellenrechnung; ~ **changes** Kostenveränderungen; ~ **chart** Kostentabelle; ~ **clerk** Kostenrechner, Betriebskalkulator; ~ **comparison** Kostenvergleich; ~-**conscious** kostenbewußt; ~ **conciousness** Kostenverantwortung, -bewußtsein; ~ **control** Kostenkontrolle, -überwachung, -lenkung; ~-**control account** Kostengegenkonto; ~-**control program(me)** Kostenüberwachungsprogramm; ~ **curve** Kostenkurve; ~ **cuts** Kostenabbau; ~ **cutter** Sparkommissar, Kosteneinsparer; ~ **cutting** Ausgabenbeschränkung, Kostenabbau, -senkung, -einsparung; ~-**cutting** kostensparend; **to prevent ~ cutting at the budget rate** etatsmäßig vorgesehene Kürzungssätze verhindern; ~-**cutting drive** Einsparungsfeldzug, Sparprogramm; ~ **cutting program(me)** Kostensenkungsprogramm; ~ **data** Kostenunterlagen, -angaben; ~ **department** Kalkulationsabteilung; ~ **difference** Kostenunterschied; ~ **disadvantage** Kostennachteil; ~ **distribution** Kostenumlage, -zurechnung, -verteilung, -aufteilung; ~ **effect** Kostenwirkung; ~-**effective** kostenintensiv, -wirksam, mit hohen Kosten verbunden; ~ **effectiveness** Effizienz des Mitteleinsatzes, höchste Kostenrentabilität; ~ **element** Kostenbestandteil, -elemente; ~ **estimate** Kostenvoranschlag, -schätzung; ~ **factor** Kostenfaktor; ~ **finding** Kostenkalkulation, -festsetzung, -bestimmung, -erfassung; ~ **finding division** Kalkulationsabteilung; ~ **fraction** Kostenanteil, -bruchteil; ~-**free** frei von allen Kosten, umsonst, kostenfrei, -los; ~ **function** Kostenfunktion; ~ **guidance** Kostenlenkung; ~ **hurricane** Kostensturm; ~ **increase** Kostensteigerung; ~ **increase factor** Kostensteigerungsfaktor; **to absorb part of the ~ increase** Kostenerhöhungen teilweise auffangen; ~ **inflation** Kosteninflation; ~ **issue** Kostenfrage, -punkt; ~ **item** Unkostenposten; ~ **keeper** Kostenrechner, Betriebskalkulator; ~ **keeping** Kostenbuchhaltung, *(accountancy)* Betriebs-, Kostenkalkulation; ~ **ladder** Kostenleiter; ~ **ledger** Hilfskonto für Kostenberichtigungen; ~ **limit** Kostenbegrenzung; ~ **line** Kostenkurve; ~ **location accounting** *(US)* Kostenstellenrechnung; ~ **method** Kostenberechnungsmethode; **job ~ method** Kostenrechnungsprinzip, -art, -methode; ~ **or market whichever is lower method** *(balance sheet, US)* Niederstwertprinzip; **specific order ~ method** Kostenrechnungssystem für auftragsweise Fertigung; ~ **method of valuation** *(inventory taking)* Bewertung zum Rechnungswert, Zeitwertprinzip; ~ **orientation** Kostenorientation; ~-**orientated** kostenorientiert; ~ **overrun** Überschreitung der angesetzten Kostenlinie, Kostenüberschreitung, -verteuerung; ~ **pass-alongs** Kostenabwälzung; ~ **picture** Kostenbild.

cost-plus *(US)* Lohnaufwand plus Material und Unternehmergewinn, Selbstkosten plus prozentualer Aufschlag, Kosten zuzüglich Verdienstspanne, Gestehungskosten plus Gewinnspanne;

~ **contract** *(US)* Werklieferungsvertrag; ~ **a fixed fee contract** Vertrag mit Preisfestsetzung nach den Kosten zuzüglich Verrechnung fester Zuschläge; ~ **incentive fee contract** Vertrag mit Preisfestsetzung nach den Kosten zuzüglich Leistungsprämien; ~ **pricing** Preiskalkulation durch Gewinnzuschlag auf Herstellungskosten; ~ **principle** Lohnaufwandprinzip.

cost | **point** Kostenpunkt; ~ **prediction** Kostenvorschau; ~ **pressure** Kostendruck.

cost price Kosten-, Wareneinstandspreis, Selbstkosten[preis], Gestehungskosten, Herstellungskosten, Einkaufs-, Einstands-, Fabrikpreis;

at ~ zum Ankaufswert (Selbstkostenpreis);

to express ~s in average price for the year which is the base Kostenpreise in Durchschnittspreisen des Vergleichsjahres ausdrücken; **to let s. o. have s. th. at ~** jem. etw. zum Selbstkostenpreis berechnen; **to sell below (under) ~** unter dem Herstellungswert (Selbstkostenpreis) verkaufen; ~ **squeeze** Kostenpreisschere, Druck der Herstellungskosten.

cost | **principle** Kostenprinzip; ~ **problem** Kostenfrage, -problem; ~ **process chart** Tabelle über die Herstellungskosten; ~ **push**

Kostensteigerung; ~-**push inflation** kostentreibende Inflation, Kosteninflation; **lowest ~ range** niedrigster Kostensatz; ~ **rate** Unkostenanteil; ~s **receivable** *(US)* Kostenforderungen; ~ **record** Kostenbeleg, Spesenzettel; ~ **recovery** Deckung der Kosten, Kostenabschreibung, -wertberichtigung, Ausgaben-, Kostendeckung; ~ **recovery for tax purposes** steuerbedingte Kostenverteilung; ~ **reduction** Kostensenkung, -abbau, Unkostenverringerung; ~ **reduction program(me)** Kostensenkungsplan; **to fall victim to a ~-reduction program(me)** Opfer eines Sparprogramms werden, einem Sparprogramm zum Opfer fallen, von Einsparungsmaßnahmen betroffen werden; ~ **reimbursable contract** Vertrag auf der Basis zu erstattender Selbstkosten; ~ **rent** *(Br.)* Kostenmiete; ~-**rent society** *(Br.)* Baugesellschaft zur Herstellung von Häusern mit Kostenmiete; ~ **report** Unkostenbericht; ~ **saving** Kostenersparnis, -einsparung; ~-**saving** kostensparend; ~ **schedule** Kostentabelle; ~-**of-service principle** Kostendeckungsprinzip, Äquivalenzprinzip; ~ **sharing** Kostenbeteiligung, -teilung; ~ **sheet** Kostenblatt, -anschlag, -aufstellung, -abrechnung; **manufacturing ~ sheet** Betriebsabrechnung; ~ **side** Kostenseite; ~ **squeeze** Kostendruck; ~ **standard** Kalkulationsnorm; ~ **statement** Kostenaufstellung; ~ **studies** Kostenuntersuchungen; ~ **structure** Gliederung der Kosten, Kostengefüge, -struktur; ~ **survey** Kostenübersicht; ~ **system** Rentabilitätsberechnung, Kostenrechnungssystem, [Selbst]kostenrechnung; **estimating ~ system** Kostenrechnungsverfahren mit vorausgeschätzten Kosten; **normal ~ system** Normalkostenrechnung; **standard ~ system** Kostenindex-, Einheitspreissystem; **to install a ~ system** Kostenrechnungssystem einführen; ~ **target** Kostenplanziel; ~ **trend** Kostenentwicklung; ~ **unit** Kosteneinheit, -träger; ~ **unit accounting** Kostenträgerrechnung; ~ **value** Herstellungs-, Anschaffungs-, Einkaufs-, Kosten-, Erwerbswert; ~ **variation** Kostenabweichung; ~ **voucher** Kostenbeleg; ~ **voucher inventory** Beleginventur.

costean *(v.) (Br.)* schürfen.

costermonger *(Br.)* Straßenhändler, Höker; ~'s **trade** Hökerhandel.

costing Berechnung des Selbstkostenpreises, Preisberechnung, [Selbst]kosten-, Rentabilitätsberechnung, Kostenkalkulation, -berechnung, -rechnungssystem, -verfahren; **absorption ~** Kostenaufteilungsverfahren; **direct (marginal, Br.) ~** Grenzplanungs-, Grenzplankostenrechnung, Kostenspezifikationsverfahren; **job-order (process) ~** Kostenrechnungssystem für auftragsweise Fertigung; **responsibility ~** verantwortlich aufgeteilte Kostenkalkulation; ~ **department** Kalkulationsabteilung; ~ **unit** Kosteneinheit, -träger.

costless *(a.)* kostenlos.

costliness Kostspieligkeit.

costly kostbar, kostspielig, teuer.

costume Kostüm; ~ **ball** Kostümfest; ~ **designer** Couturier; ~ **film** Ausstattungsfilm; ~ **jewel[le]ry** Modeschmuck; ~ **piece** *(theater)* Ausstattungs-, Kostümstück.

costumier Kostümverleih[er].

cosurety Mitbürge.

cosuretyship Mitbürgschaft.

cot Hütte, Kate, Schuppen, Stall, *(hospital)* Krankenbett, *(mil.)* Feldbett; ~ **case** Bettlägriger.

cote Stall, Verschlag, Schuppen; **dove ~** Taubenschlag.

cotenancy gemeinsame Pachtung, Mitpacht.

cotenant Mitpächter.

coterie erlesener Kreis, exklusiver Zirkel; **literary ~** literarischer Zirkel, Lesekreis.

cotrustee Mit-, Gegentreuhänder.

cottage *(country house, US)* Landhaus, Villa, Sommersitz, *(country labo(u)rer, Br.)* Werks-, Arbeiterwohnung, Landarbeiterhütte, *(dwelling)* Hütte, Kate, Bauernhaus; **farm labo(u)rers' ~** Landarbeiterwohnung; **weekend ~** Wochenendhaus; ~ **allotment** *(Br.)* Schrebergarten; ~ **industry** Heimarbeit, -industrie; ~ **period** Zeitalter der Hausindustrie; ~ **system** *(Br.)* betriebliches Eigenheimsystem.

cottager Häusler, Kätner, *(Br.)* Gutsarbeiter, Landarbeiter, *(US)* Villenbesitzer.

cotter Kleinbauer.

cottier *(Br.)* Pachthäusler, *(cotter)* Kleinbauer; ~ **system** *(Ireland)* Pachtvergabe im Wege öffentlichen Aufgebots; ~ **tenancy** *(Scotland)* Kleinpachtvertrag.

cotton Baumwolle; ~ *(v.)* übereinstimmen, harmonieren, gut auskommen; ~ **on** *(fam.)* kapieren; ~ **on to s. th.** sich mit etw. befreunden; ~ **belt** Baumwollzone; ~ **bill** Baumwollwechsel; ~ **exchange** Baumwollbörse; ~ **goods** Baumwollartikel; ~ **market** Baumwollmarkt; ~ **mill** Baumwollspinnerei; ~ **printer** Kattundrucker; ~ **wool** Rohbaumwolle, Watte.

couch Sofa, Chaiselongue, Couch, Liegebett; ~ *(v.)* formulieren, ausdrücken, abfassen; ~ **a reply in insolent terms** Antwort unverschämt formulieren; ~ **in writing** Gesuch schriftlich abfassen; ~ **in a popular style** gemeinverständlich abfassen; ~ **a demand in certain terms** Forderung in bestimmte Redewendungen kleiden.

couchette *(railway)* Liegewagenplatz.

cough *(v.)* **up** *(US sl.)* blechen, seinen Beutel ziehen.

coulisse *(stock exchange, theatre)* Kulisse.

coulissier Kulisser.

council Rat[sversammlung], Ratssitzung, beratende Versammlung, *(advisory body)* [Staats-, Kron]rat, *(deliberation)* Beratung, *(ecclesiastical)* Konzil, *(law)* Senat, *(town)* Behörde, *(university)* Fakultäts-, Senatssitzung; **advisory ~** beratender Ausschuß, Beirat; **borough ~** *(New Zealand)* Gemeinderat, -ausschuß; **cabinet ~** *(US)* Kabinettsitzung; **city ~** *(US)* Stadt-, Gemeinderat; **common ~** *(London)* Stadtrat; **company ~** *(US)* paritätischer Betriebsrat; **county ~** *(Br.)* Kreisausschuß, -tag, Grafschaftsrat; **district ~** Bezirksausschuß; **economic ~** Wirtschaftsrat, -ausschuß; **Economic and Social ≈** Wirtschafts- und Sozialausschuß; **executive ~** Vollzugsausschuß; **factory ~** *(Br.)* Betriebsrat; **family ~** Familienrat; **local ~** Gemeinde-, Stadtrat, örtlicher Verwaltungskörper; **management ~** Direktorium eines Industrieunternehmens; **municipal ~** Gemeinde-, Stadtrat, Magistrat; **parish ~** Gemeinderat; **Privy ≈** *(Br.)* Geheimer Staatsrat; **security ~** *(United Nations)* Sicherheitsrat; **select ~** *(US)* Stadtratsausschuß; **shop ~** *(Br.)* Betriebsrat; **town ~** Stadt-, Gemeinderat; **Trusteeship ≈** *(UN)* Treuhänderrat; **works ~** Betriebsrat; **≈ of Mutual Economic Aid** *(COMECON)* Rat für gegenseitige Wirtschaftshilfe; ~ **of economic advisers** *(US)* wirtschaftlicher (wissenschaftlicher) Beirat, Wirtschaftsbeirat; ~ **of the bar** Vorstand der Rechtsanwaltschaft, Kammervorstand; **≈ of Better Business Bureaus** Gesellschaft zur Bekämpfung unlauteren Wettbewerbs; **≈ of Conciliation** *(Br.)* Schlichtungsausschuß; **≈ of Elders** Ältestenrat; ~ **on environmental quality** Ausschuß für Fragen des Umweltschutzes, *(US)* Umweltverbesserungsbehörde; **≈ of Europe** Europarat; **≈ of European Municipalities** Rat der europäischen Gemeinden; **≈ of Industrial Designs** *(Br.)* Formgebungsausschuß; **≈ of Ministers** *(EC)* Ministerrat der Europäischen Gemeinschaften; **≈ of Foreign Ministers** Außenministerrat; **≈ of National Defence** *(US)* Verteidigungsrat; ~ **of physicians** Ärztekollegium; **≈ of Scientific and Industrial Research** *(Br.)* Forschungsrat; **≈ of State** *(US)* Staatsrat; ~ **to the stock exchange** *(London)* Börsenzulassungsausschuß, -vorstand, -aufsichtsbehörde; ~ **on wage and price stability** *(Br.)* Stabilitätsrat; ~ **of war** Kriegsrat; **to call a ~** Ratssitzung anberaumen; **to chair the city ~** Stadtratsvorsitzender sein; **to hold ~** Ratsversammlung abhalten; **to meet in ~** Ratsversammlung abhalten; **to summon a ~** Ratsmitglieder zusammenrufen; **works ~ bill** *(Br.)* Betriebsverfassungsgesetz; ~ **board** Ratsversammlung, Stadtratssitzung, *(table)* Ratstisch, grüner Tisch; ~ **chamber** Sitzungssaal, Ratszimmer; ~ **decision** Ratsentscheidung, Beiratsbeschluß; ~ **dwelling** *(Br.)* mit Mitteln des sozialen Wohnungsbaus finanziertes Haus; ~ **estate** Siedlung; ~ **flat** *(Br.)* Sozialwohnung; ~ **hall** Stadthalle; ~ **home** *(Br.)* Sozialwohnung; ~ **house** *(Br.)* von der Stadt vermietete Wohnung, Sozialwohnung; ~ **house building** *(Br.)* Errichtung von Wohnungen mit Mitteln des sozialen Wohnungsbaus; ~ **house tenant** *(Br.)* Sozialmieter; ~ **housing** *(Br.)* sozialer Wohnungsbau; ~ **landlord** *(Br.)* Vermieter einer Sozialwohnung; ~ **manager** Stadtdirektor; ~ **meeting** Ratsversammlung, -treffen, Magistrats-, Stadtratssitzung, *(company)* Beiratssitzung; **EEC ≈ presidency** Präsidentenamt im Rat der Europäischen Gemeinschaft; **to hold the ~ presidency** *(EEC)* Präsidentschaft im Europäischen Ministerrat stellen; ~ **recommendation** Ratsempfehlung; ~ **resolution** Rats-, Gemeindebeschluß; ~ **room** [Stadt]ratszimmer; ~ **school** Gemeinde-, Kreisschule; ~ **sources said** aus Ratskreisen verlautet; ~ **staff** Beraterstab; ~ **tenancy** *(Br.)* Sozialmiete; ~ **table** Ratstisch; ~ **tenant** *(Br.)* Sozialmieter; ~ **vacancy** freigewordener Ratssitz.

councillor, councilor *(US)* Rats-, Magistratsmitglied, Stadtrat, Ratsherr, *(advisor of sovereign)* vortragender Rat;

county ~ Kreisausschuß, Grafschaftsrat; **Privy** ≗ *(Br.)* Mitglied des geheimen Staatsrates; **town** ~ *(Br.)* Stadtverordneter, Gemeinderat, Gemeinderatsmitglied, Ratsherr;
~ **person** Kreisausschußmitglied.

councilman *(US)* Stadtverordneter, Gemeinderatsmitglied, Ratsmitglied, -herr.

councillorship Ratsherrenwürde.

counsel *(advice)* Rat[schlag], *(adviser)* Berater, Ratgeber, *(legal adviser, Br.)* Prozeßbeistand, -berater, -vertreter, Sachwalter, plädierender Anwalt, *(consultation, US)* Beratung, *(deliberation)* Beratung, Beratschlagung, Verhandlung, *(plan)* Vorhaben, Vorsatz, Absicht, Plan;
assigned ~ Offizialverteidiger; **chamber** ~ *(Br.)* beratender Anwalt; **conveyancing** ~ *(Br.)* Fachanwalt für Grundstücksrecht; **corporation** ~ *(US)* Justiziar, [Konzern]syndikus; **defence** ~ Strafverteidiger; **defending** ~ *(Br.)* Strafverteidiger; **free** ~ kostenlose Beratung; **general** ~ *(Br.)* mit der ständigen Vertretung beauftragter Anwalt; **junior** ~ *(Br.)* Assessor; **leading** ~ *(Br.)* bedeutender Anwalt; **of** ~ Prozeßbevollmächtigter einer Sozietät; **opposing** ~ *(Br.)* gegnerischer Anwalt, Gegenanwalt; **plaintiff's** ~ *(Br.)* klägerischer Anwalt; **prosecuting** ~ Staatsanwalt; **Queen's** ~ *(Br.)* Kronanwalt, Justizrat;
~ **in chambers** *(Br.)* beratender Anwalt; ≗ **for the Crown** *(Br.)* öffentlicher Ankläger; ~ **for the defence** Prozeßbevollmächtigter für die beklagte Partei, Strafverteidiger; **a** ~ **of perfection** *(coll.)* schwer zu erreichendes Ideal; ~ **for the plaintiff** *(Br.)* klägerischer Anwalt; ~ **for the prosecution** Anklagevertreter, Staatsanwalt;
~ *(v.)* raten, Rat geben;
~ **to the contrary** Gegenteil raten; ~ **and procure** Beihilfe leisten; ~ **about-to-be-booted executives** kurz vor der Entlassung stehende leitende Angestellte beraten; ~ **an early start** zu einem frühen Aufbruch raten;
to act as ~ **for s. o.** *(Br.)* anwaltschaftlich vertreten, für j. als Anwalt auftreten, j. juristisch beraten; **to ask** ~ **of s. o.** j. um Rat fragen; **to be** ~ **in a case** *(Br.)* Rechtssache führen (vertreten); **to be heard by** ~ *(Br.)* seine Sache durch einen Anwalt vortragen lassen; **to be of** ~ **with** gleiche Pläne haben; **to be represented by** ~ *(Br.)* anwaltschaftlich (durch einen Anwalt) vertreten sein; **to brief a** ~ *(Br.)* zum Anwalt bestellen, Anwalt mit einer Sache beauftragen; **to confer with one's** ~ *(Br.)* sich mit seinem Anwalt beraten; **to designate a** ~ **for the defence** *(Br.)* Strafverteidiger bestellen; **to employ a** ~ *(Br.)* Anwalt zuziehen; **to give [good]** ~ [guten] Rat[schlag] erteilen; **to have able** ~ *(defendant)* guten Verteidiger haben; **to hear** ~ **on both sides** *(Br.)* Prozeßbevollmächtigte beider Parteien plädieren lassen; **to hire legal** ~ sich rechtlichen Rat holen; **to hold** ~ **with s. o.** sich mit j. beraten; **to hold one's** ~ sich mit seiner Meinung zurückhalten; **to hold** ~ **with one's own heart** mit sich zu Rate gehen; **to keep** ~ verschwiegen sein; **to keep one's** ~ sich in Stillschweigen hüllen, seine Meinung für sich behalten; **to retain a** ~ *(Br.)* Anwalt zwecks Dauerberatung engagieren; **to retain as special** ~ *(Br.)* als Sonderberater engagieren; **to take** ~ beratschlagen; **to take** ~ **with s. o.** sich mit jem. beraten, j. zu Rate ziehen; **to take** ~'**s opinion** Anwalt befragen; **to take** ~ **of one's pillow** etw. überschlafen; **to take** ~ **together** sich miteinander beraten, gemeinsam beratschlagen.

counsel | '**s brief** *(Br.)* Mandatserteilung, Prozeßauftrag; ~'**s fees** *(Br.)* Anwaltsgebühren; ~ **keeper** verschwiegener Mensch, Bewahrer eines Geheimnisses; ~ **keeping** verschwiegen; ~'**s opinion** *(Br.)* Anwalts-, Rechtsgutachten; ~'**s signature** anwaltschaftliche Unterschrift; ~'**s speech** *(Br.)* Plädoyer.

counsellee Beratender.

counsel(l)ing Beratungsdienst;
employee ~ Beratung in Personalfragen; **retirement** ~ Beratung in Pensionsfragen, Pensionärsberatung;
~ **of employees** Angestelltenberatung;
financial ~ **firm** Beratungsfirma für finanzielle Aufgabengebiete; ~ **service** Beratungdienst; ~ **specialist** Fachberater; ~ **work** Beratungstätigkeit.

counsel(l)or Berater, Ratgeber, *(US)* beratender Anwalt, juristischer Berater, Rechtsanwalt, Rechtsberater;
authorized ~ zugelassener Anwalt; **diplomatic** ~ *(Br.)* Botschaftsrat;
~ **of embassy** *(Br.)* Botschaftsrat 1. Klasse; ~ **at law** *(US)* Rechtsanwalt, -beistand; ~ **of legation** *(Br.)* Gesandtschaftsrat, vortragender Legationsrat.

count *(counting)* Zählung, *(esteem)* Wertschätzung, *(indictment)* [An]klagepunkt, *(pleading)* Klagegrund, -begründung, *(reckoning)* Rechnung, *(sum total)* Gesamtsumme, Endzahl;
common (general) ~ zusammengefaßte Klagegründe; **money** ~s

Klagebegründungsformeln bei Zahlungsklagen; **omnibus** ~ umfassende Klagebegründung; **special** ~ substantiierte Klagebegründung;
~ **of indictment** Anklagepunkt; ~ **and reckoning** *(Scot. law)* Zwangsvergleichsverfahren;
~ *(v.)* *(add)* zusammenzählen, *(debit)* in Rechnung stellen (bringen), belasten, *(be of importance)* zählen, ins Gewicht fallen, von Bedeutung sein, *(include)* mit-, an-, einrechnen, *(plead)* plädieren, vortragen, *(reckon)* rechnen, *(tell money)* [Geld] zählen;
~ **on s. o.** sich auf j. verlassen, mit jem. rechnen; ~ **again** [Geld] nachzählen; ~ **s. th. against s. o.** jem. etw. zur Last legen; ~ **back** zurückrechnen; ~ **one's chickens before they're hatched** Rechnung ohne den Wirt machen, den Tag vor dem Abend loben; ~ **on contract** als Vertragsfolge darstellen; ~ **the costs** Kosten kalkulieren (berechnen), *(fig.)* Folgen bedenken; ~ **down** Startzählung durchführen; ~ **down money** Geld aufzählen; ~ **on one's fingers** an den Fingern abzählen; ~ **o. s. fortunate** sich glücklich schätzen; ~ **s. o. among one's best friends** j. zu seinen besten Freunden zählen; ~ **it one's glory** sich als Verdienst anrechnen; ~ **heads** *(coll.)* Zahl der Anwesenden feststellen; ~ **upon s. one's help** mit jds. Hilfe rechnen; ~ **without one's host** Rechnung ohne den Wirt machen; ~ **the house** *(parl.)* Zahl der Anwesenden (Beschlußfähigkeit) feststellen; ~ **in** *(US sl.)* durch Schwindel bei der Stimmenzählung zum Wahlsieger erklären; ~ **s. o. in** j. als zugehörig betrachten; ~ **kin with s. o.** *(Scot.)* mit jem. verwandt sein; ~ **for little** nicht sehr hilfreich sein; ~ **money before s. o.** jem. Geld vorzählen; ~ **out** *(Br., pol.)* Gesetzantrag durch Vertagung zunichte machen, Unterhaus vertagen, *(US sl.)* durch schwindelhafte Stimmenzählung durchfallen lassen; ~ **out the house** *(Br.)* Beschlußunfähigkeit feststellen; ~ **over** durchrechnen, -zählen; ~ **the daily receipts** Kasse machen; ~ **as success** als Erfolg buchen; ~ **towards** anrechnen auf; ~ **up** *(US)* zusammenzählen, Kasse machen; ~ **upon an increase in one's salary** auf Gehaltserhöhung hoffen; ~ **upon a statute** auf eine gesetzliche Bestimmung Bezug nehmen; ~ **the votes** Stimmen auszählen; ~ **wrong** sich verzählen (verrechnen);
to be found guilty on all ~s in allen Anklagepunkten für schuldig befunden werden; **to be out of all** ~ völlig unberechenbar sein; **to call a** ~ Stimmenauszählung verlangen; **to declare a** ~ **out** Beschlußfähigkeit durch Stimmenzählung feststellen lassen; **to have lost** ~ **of one's books** über die Anzahl seiner Bücher den Überblick verloren haben; **to keep** ~ richtig zählen; **to leave out of** ~ unberücksichtigt lassen; **to lose** ~ sich verzählen; **to take not much** ~ **of what people say** auf das Gerede der Leute wenig geben;
~~-**out** *(parl., Br.)* Feststellung der Beschlußunfähigkeit, Unterhausvertagung.

countable berechenbar, zählbar.

countdown Auszählung, *(rocket launching)* Schlußprüfung, Startzählung.

countenance Gesichtsausdruck, Miene, *(support)* [moralische] Unterstützung, Gunstbezeigung;
out of ~ völlig verwirrt;
~ *(v.)* begünstigen, Vorschub leisten;
to keep one's ~ Haltung bewahren; **to lend** ~ **to s. o.** jem. Unterstützung angedeihen lassen; **to lend** ~ **to a report** einem Bericht Glaubwürdigkeit verleihen; **to put a good** ~ **on the matter** gute Miene zum bösen Spiel machen; **to put (starve) s. o. out of** ~ j. aus der Fassung bringen.

countenancer Gönner, Unterstützer.

counter Schalter, *(bar)* Getränkeausschank, Bar, Theke, *(imitation coin)* [Spiel]marke, Rechenpfennig, Jeton, *(luggage)* Gepäckannahme, -ausgabe, *(meter)* Zähler, Zählwerk, Rechner, *(print.)* Bunze, *(shop)* Ladentisch, Zählbrett, Zahltisch, Kasse, *(sl.)* Mammon, *(stock exchange)* Schranke, *(window)* Bankschalter;
over the ~ am Schalter, an der Kasse, *(US, securities)* im Freiverkehr, freihändig verkauft; **payable over the** ~ am Schalter zahlbar; **sold over the** ~ Verkauf gegen bar; **under the** ~ ungesetzlich, unter dem Ladentisch;
~ *(v.)* entgegenwirken, Gegenschlag tun;
~ **blandly** selbstsicher mit einer Gegenfrage antworten; ~ **a proposal with one of one's own** mit einem Gegenvorschlag antworten;
to be behind the ~ hinter dem Ladentisch stehen, verkaufen; **to hand across (in at) the** ~ [Post] am Schalter abgeben (aufgeben); **to run** ~ **to a plan** Plan durchkreuzen; **to sell over the** ~ *(US)* [Effekten] freihändig verkaufen; **to take the** ~ Laden besorgen;

~ **account** Gegenkonto, Kontrollregister, -verzeichnis; ~ **accusation** Gegenbeschuldigung; ~ **action** *(pol.)* Gegenaktion; ~ **advertising** Abwehrwerbung; ~ **advice** gegenteiliger Rat; ~ **appeal** Anschlußberufung; ~ **argument** Gegenargument; ~ **assurance** Gegen-, Rückversicherung; **over-the-~ business** *(US)* außerbörslicher Verkehr, Freiverkehr, Schaltergeschäft; ~ **card** [Theken]aufsteller, Preisschild; ~ **cash** tägliche Kasse; ~ **check** *(US)* Blankobank-, Kassenscheck; ~ **clerk** Kassierer, Schalterbeamter; ~ **demonstration** Gegendemonstration; ~ **display** Ladentischauslage, Auslagenwerbung [auf dem Ladentisch], *(bar)* Thekenaufsteller; ~ **display container** Verkaufsständer, stummer Verkäufer auf der Theke; ~ **evidence** Gegenbeweis; ~**feasance** Geldfälschung; ~ **hand** Aushilfe; ~ **item** Gegenposten; **over-the-~ market** *(US)* Freiverkehr, Telefonhandel; ~ **memorial** *(UNO)* Klagebeantwortung; ~ **note** *(dipl.)* Gegennote; ~ **notice** *(law)* Gegenanordnung; ~ **publicity** Abwehrwerbung; ~ **question** Gegenfrage; **over-the-~ reports** *(unlisted securities, US)* Kursblatt; ~ **requirements** Zahlungsaufforderungen am Kassenschalter; ~ **rolls** doppelte Akten, Aktenduplikat; **under-the-~ sales** ungesetzlicher Ladenverkauf, Verkäufe unter dem Ladentisch; ~ **service** Schalterdienst; **over-the-~ trading** *(US)* Schalterverkehr, freihändiger Effektenverkauf; ~ **valuation** Gegengutachten.

counteraccusation Gegenbeschuldigung.
counteract *(v.)* zuwiderhandeln;
~ **an influence** Einfluß bekämpfen.
counteracting forces Gegenkräfte.
counteraction Gegenmaßnahme, Entgegenwirken, Durchkreuzung, Hintertreibung, *(neutralization)* Neutralisierung, *(pol.)* Gegenaktion.
counteraffidavit gegenteilige eidesstattliche Erklärung.
counterappeal Anschlußberufung.
counterargument Gegenargument.
counterassurance *(Br.)* Rückversicherung.
counterattack Gegenangriff.
counterbail Nachbürge.
counterbalance *(account)* Gegensaldo, *(counterpoise)* Gegengewicht;
~ *(v.)* *(account)* aufwiegen, kompensieren, [durch Gegenrechnung] ausgleichen, aufheben, entgegenhalten.
counterbalanced by saldiert durch.
counterbid Gegengebot.
counterbill Gegenwechsel.
counterblast *(fig.)* kräftige Entgegnung.
counterblockade Gegenblockade;
~ *(v.)* Gegenblockade verhängen.
counterblow Gegenschlag.
counterbond Rückbürgschaft, Gegenverpflichtung, -verschreibung.
countercharge Gegenbeschuldigung, Wider-, Gegenklage.
countercheck Hindernis;
to be a ~ to s. th. einer Sache im Wege stehen.
counterclaim Gegenforderung, -anspruch, Widerklage;
~ **for damages** Schadensersatzforderungen im Wege der Gegenklage;
~ *(v.)* Gegenforderung erheben, Gegenansprüche stellen (geltend machen);
to plead a ~ Widerklage erheben.
counterclaimant Widerkläger.
counterclockwise entgegengesetzt zum Uhrzeiger.
countercurrent Gegenströmung.
countercyclical *(a.)* antizyklisch;
~ **compensatory government policy** antizyklische Konjunkturpoltik, Konjunkturtherapie; ~ **investment fund** zur Konjunktursteuerung gebildeter Investmentfonds; ~ **measures** konjunkturdämpfende Maßnahmen; ~ **monetary policy** monetäre Konjunkturpolitik; **to play its ~ role** sich wie üblich antizyklisch verhalten.
counterdeclaration Gegenerklärung.
counterdeed *(secret writing)* geheimer Widerruf, geheime notarielle Erklärung gegensätzlichen Inhalts.
counterdemand Gegenforderung.
counterdemonstration Gegendemonstration, -kundgebung.
counterdeterrence *(mil.)* Gegenabschreckung.
counterdraw *(v.)* gegenseitig aufeinander ziehen.
countereffect Gegenwirkung.
counterinquiry Gegenuntersuchung.
counterentry Gegenposten, Gegen-, Stornobuchung;
to make a ~ gegenbuchen.
counterespionage Gegenspionage, Abwehr;
~ **office** Abwehrstelle; ~ **service** Abwehrdienst.

counterevidence Gegenbeweis.
counterfeit Fälschung, Nachahmung, Falsifikat, *(copy)* unberechtigter Nachdruck, *(imposter)* Betrüger, Hochstapler, *(spurious note)* falsche Banknote;
~**s** Falschgeld;
~ *(v.)* fälschen, nachmachen, *(imitate)* nachahmen, *(reprint)* nachdrucken, [unberechtigt] nachahmen;
~ **coins** falschmünzen, Falschmünzerei treiben; ~ **death** sich tot stellen; ~ **money** Falschgeld anfertigen; ~ **poverty** Armut vortäuschen; ~ **a signature** Unterschrift fälschen;
~ *(a.)* falsch, unecht, gefälscht, nachgemacht, untergeschoben, *(print.)* nachgedruckt;
~ **bill of exchange** falscher (gefälschter) Wechsel; ~ **book (copy)** Nachdruck; ~ **coins** Falschgeld; ~ **jewels** unechter Schmuck; ~ **money** Falschgeld; **to pass ~ money** Falschgeld in Umlauf setzen; **to put off a ~ note** Falschgeld loswerden; ~ **presentment** Falschdarstellung; ~ **reprint** unberechtigter Nachdruck; ~ **ring** Fälscherzentrale, Falschmünzerbande.
counterfeited nachgemacht, gefälscht;
~ **bill of exchange** gefälschter (falscher) Wechsel; ~ **impression** Nachdruck.
counterfeiter Falschmünzer, [Urkunden]fälscher;
~ **of banknotes** Banknotenfälscher.
counterfeiting [Münz]fälschung, Falschmünzerei, Banknotenfälschung;
~ **of money** Geldfälschung;
~ **ring** Falschmünzerbande, Fälscherzentrale.
counterfoil Kontrollabschnitt, -blatt, *(coupon)* Kupon, Zinsschein, *(luggage)* Gepäckzettel, -schein, *(talon)* Abschnitt, Talon;
~ **of a check** *(US)* **(cheque, Br.)** Scheckabschnitt;
~ **book** Talonbuch, Abreißblock; ~ **waybill** Frachtbriefdoppel.
counterforce Abschreckungsstreitkräfte.
countergirl Ladenmädchen, Verkäuferin.
Counterinflation|Act *(Br.)* Gesetz zur Bekämpfung der Inflation; ~ **policy** Antiinflationspolitik.
counterinflationary *(a.)* antiinflationär.
counterinquiry Rückfrage.
counterinsurance Rückversicherung.
counterinsurgence Aufstandsbekämpfung.
counterintelligence Abschirmdienst, Spionageabwehr, Gegenspionage;
~ **Corps** *(US)* Spionageabwehrdienst.
counterjumper *(coll.)* Ladendiener, -schwengel.
counterletter Rückübertragungsverpflichtung.
counterman Verkäufer, *(restaurant)* Servierer.
countermand Absage, Widerruf, Annullierung, Storno, Stornierung, Abbestellung;
~ **of payments** Zahlungswiderruf, Storno; ~ **of payment of a cheque** *(Br.)* **(check, US)** Scheckstornierung; ~ **of a will** Testamentswiderruf;
~ *(v.)* widerrufen, wieder absagen, aufheben, rückgängig machen, *(order for goods)* abbestellen, [Auftrag] zurücknehmen, -ziehen, annullieren, stornieren;
~ **an order** Auftrag stornieren (annullieren); ~ **payment** *(cheque)* Zahlungsauftrag stornieren; ~ **by wire** abtelegraphieren; ~ **a will** Testament widerrufen.
countermandate Gegenauftrag.
countermanded, until bis auf Widerruf; **unless ~** mangels gegenteiliger Nachricht;
~ **payment** Zahlung gesperrt.
countermanding Abbestellung, Zurückziehung;
~ **of orders given** Stornierung erteilter Aufträge.
countermarch Rückmarsch, *(fig.)* völliges Umdenken.
countermark Kontrollzeichen, Gegenzeichen, Kontrollstempel, *(minting)* Stempelzeichen;
~ *(v.)* mit Gegenzeichen versehen.
countermine *(fig., mil.)* Gegenmine;
~ *(v.)* *(fig.)* unterminieren, durch einen Gegenanschlag vereiteln, *(mil.)* Gegenmine vertreiben, konterminieren.
countermotion *(parl.)* Gegenantrag.
countermove Gegenzug.
countermovement Gegenbewegung.
counternote *(dipl.)* Antwortnote.
counternotice Gegenanordnung, *(tenant)* Gegenkündigung;
to serve an appropriate ~ zu einer Mietkündigung ordnungsgemäß Stellung nehmen.
counterobligation Gegenverpflichtung.
counteroffensive *(mil.)* Gegenoffensive;
to make a ~ public relations campaign Gegenkampagne auf dem PR-Gebiet aufziehen.

counteroffer Gegengebot, -offerte.

counterorder Gegenorder, -auftrag, Abbestellung, Stornierung, *(mil.)* Gegenbefehl;
~ *(v.)* abbestellen, stornieren, absagen.

counterpart Kopie, Gegenstück, *(duplicate)* Duplikat, Zweitschrift, weitere Ausfertigung, Doppel, gleichlautende Abschrift, *(money, US)* Gegenwertmittel, *(opposite number)* Kollege;
~ **account** *(US)* Gegenwertkonto; ~ **fund** *(US)* Gegenwertmittel, -fonds; ~ **writ** Doppel einer Klageverfügung.

counterpetition Gegenantrag;
~ *(v.)* Gegenantrag stellen (einbringen).

counterpetitioner Gegenantragsteller.

counterplea *(US)* Gegeneinwand, Widerklage, Replik.

counterplead dagegen anführen, Gegeneinwand erheben.

counterplot Gegenschlag.

counterpoise Gegengewicht;
~ *(v.)* ausgleichen, kompensieren.

counterpreparation rechtzeitige Gegenmaßnahme.

counterpressure Gegendruck.

counterproof *(print.)* Gegenabdruck.

counterpropaganda Gegenpropaganda.

counterproposal neuer Antrag, Gegenvorschlag.

counterprove *(v.)* Gegenabdruck machen.

counterquestion Gegenfrage.

counterreckoning Gegenrechnung.

counterremittance Gegendeckung, -rimesse.

counterrevolution Konter-, Gegenrevolution.

counterrevolutionary, counterrevolutionist Konterrevolutionär.

countersabotage Sabotageabwehr.

countersale Gegenverkauf.

counterseal Gegensiegel.

countersecure *(v.)* zusätzliche Sicherheit gewähren, rückbürgen.

countersecurity Gegen-, Rückbürgschaft, *(person)* Rückbürge.

counterside Gegenseite.

countersign Beglaubigungsvermerk, Gegenzeichnung, Mitunterschrift, Gegenzeichnen, *(mil.)* Lösungswort, Parole;
~ *(v.)* gegenzeichnen, *(fig.)* bestätigen, sanktionieren.

countersignature Gegenzeichnung, -unterschrift, zweite Unterschrift, *(approval)* Genehmigung.

countersigner Gegenzeichner.

counterspy Abwehroffizier, Agent.

counterstamp zusätzlicher Genehmigungsstempel.

counterstatement Gegendarstellung, -erklärung, -behauptung, Gegenaufstellung.

counterstatute Gegenverordnung.

counterstipulation Gegenbedingung.

counterstock Talon.

countersuit Widerklage, Gegenklage.

countersurety *(US)* Gegen-, Rückbürgschaft.

countertally Talon.

countertendency Gegenbestrebung, -tendenz.

counterterrorist policy Terroristenbekämpfungspolitik.

counterterroristic policy Terroristenbekämpfungsmaßnahmen.

countertheory entgegengesetzte Theorie.

countertrend Gegentendenz.

countertype entgegengesetzter Typ.

countervail *(v.)* ausgleichen.

countervailing ausgleichend;
~ **charge** Ausgleichsabgabe; ~ **credit** Gegenakkreditiv; ~ **duty** Ausgleichs-, Kompensationszoll, Umsatzausgleichssteuer; ~ **excise duty** Einfuhrabgabe; ~ **measure** Gegenmaßregel; ~ **power** *(US)* gegengewichtige Marktmacht, Abwehrkartell.

countervalue Gegenwert.

counterview entgegengesetzte Ansicht, Gegenansicht.

countervote *(v.)* nieder-, überstimmen.

counterweigh *(v.)* Gegengewicht bilden, ausgleichen, kompensieren.

counterweight Gegengewicht.

counterwitness Gegenzeuge.

counterwork Gegenoperation, *(book)* Gegenwerk.

counties, home *(Br.)* London am nächsten gelegene Grafschaften;
~ **of cities** *(Scotland)* [etwa] kreisfreie Großstädte.

counting Rechnen, Zählen, Zählung;
not ~ **the children** Kinder nicht mitgerechnet;
second ~ Nachzählung;
~ **out** Auszählung;
~ **of votes** Stimmenzählung;
~ **board** Zählbrett; ~ **machine** Rechenmaschine; ~ **room** Buchhaltungsabteilung.

countinghouse *(Br.)* Kontor, Büro, Buchhaltungsabteilung.

countries, middle-income Länder mit mittlerer Finanzierungskraft; **nonsnake** ~ nicht der Währungsschlange angehörende Staaten; **third-world** ~ Länder der dritten Welt;
~ **of Communist obedience** unter kommunistischer Herrschaft stehende Länder.

countrified ländlich, *(fig.)* bäuerlich, ungeschliffen.

country Land, Staat, Heimat-, Geburts-, Vaterland, *(law)* Geschworene, Jury, *(people)* Bevölkerung, Einwohner, Volk, Nation, *(place of abode)* bleibender Wohnsitz, *(public opinion)* Öffentlichkeit, *(region)* Gegend, Gebiet, Landstrich;
from all over the ~ aus dem ganzen Lande; **in the** ~ auf dem Lande; **throughout the** ~ durch das ganze Land, im ganzen Lande, überregional; **up** ~ landeinwärts; **within the** ~ im Inland;

advanced ~ Industrienation; **advanced industrial** ~ hochentwickeltes Industrieland; **agricultural** ~ Agrarstaat; **attending** ~ Teilnehmerland; **border (bordering)** ~ Anliegerstaat; **broken** ~ schwieriges Gelände; **civilized** ~ Kulturstaat; **clearing** ~ am Verrechnungsabkommen beteiligtes Land; **communist-ruled** ~ kommunistisch beherrschtes Land; **consuming** ~ Verbraucherland; **exchange-controlling** ~ Land mit Devisenbewirtschaftung; **export** ~ Ausfuhrland; **flat** ~ Flachland; **food-short** ~ unter Nahrungsmittelmangel leidender Staat; **free-currency** ~ nicht devisenbewirtschaftetes Land; **gold-producing** ~ Goldland; **God's own** ~ Vereinigte Staaten von Nordamerika; **hard-currency** ~ Land mit harter Währung, Hartwährungsland; **high-developed** ~ hoch industrialisiertes Land; **less-developed** ~ Entwicklungsland; **importing** ~ Einfuhrland; **industrial** ~ Industriestaat; **landlocked** ~ Land ohne Zugang zum Meer, Binnenstaat; **member** ~ Mitgliedsstaat; **mother** ~ Mutterland; **native** ~ Heimatstaat, Geburtsland; **neighbo(u)ring** ~ Nachbarland, Anliegerstaat; **nonclearing** ~ Land ohne Verrechnungsabkommen; **nonmember** ~ Nichtmitgliedsstaat; **nonunion** ~ *(Br.)* nicht dem Weltpostverein angehörendes Land; **open** ~ freies Gelände; **parent** ~ Vaterland; **payments-surplus** ~ Land mit Handelsbilanzüberschüssen; **producing** ~ Herkunftsland; **raw-material producing** ~ Rohstoffland; **recipient** ~ Empfängerland; **red-clay** ~ *(fig.)* wenig ertragreiches Land; **right-wing** ~ nach Rechts tendierender Staat; **settled** ~ besiedeltes Land; **shipping** ~ Herkunftsland; **short-of-exchange** ~ devisenschwaches Land; **soft-currency** ~ währungsschwaches Land; **strong-currency** ~ währungsstarkes Land; **third-world** ~ Staat der dritten Welt; **transit** ~ Durchgangs-, Durchfuhrland; **underdeveloped** ~ unterentwickeltes Land, Entwicklungsland; **unknown** ~ *(fig.)* unbekanntes Gebiet; **war-worn** ~ kriegzerstörtes Land;
~ **of one's adoption** zweites Vaterland, Wahlheimat; ~ **of one's birth** Geburts-, Heimatland; ~ **whence he came** *(deportation)* Wohnsitzland; ~ **based on a free and social order** auf freiheitlicher Gesellschaftsordnung beruhender Staat; ~ **of consignment (destination)** Bestimmungsland; ~ **of delivery** Lieferland; ~ **of domicile** Belegenheitsland; ~ **of exportation** Ausfuhrland; ~ **of importation** Einfuhrland; **a** ~ **and its inhabitants** Land und Leute; ~ **of nationality** Heimatstaat; ~ **of origin** Quellenstaat, Ursprungsland; ~ **importing agricultural products** Agrarimportland; ~ **of purchase** Einkaufs-, Einfuhrland; ~ **of established residence** Wohnsitzland, -staat; ~ **of sale** Verkaufsland; ~ **of shipment** Verschiffungs-, Absenderland; ~ **with a high (low) monetary standard** valutastarkes (valutaschwaches) Land;
to appeal to the ~ *(Br.)* Neuwahlen ausschreiben; **to be banished from a** ~ aus einem Land gewiesen werden; **to die for one's** ~ für sein Vaterland fallen; **to dwell in the** ~ auf dem Lande wohnen; **to explore a** ~ Land erforschen; **to flee (fly) the** ~ landesflüchtig werden; **to go to the** ~ *(parl., Br.)* Neuwahlen ausschreiben; **to go down into the** ~ in die Provinz (aufs Land) gehen; **to go up** ~ sich ins Landesinnere begeben; **to invade a** ~ in ein Land einfallen; **to leave the** ~ **for good** außer Landes gehen, auswandern; **to live in the** ~ auf dem Lande leben; **to move into the** ~ aufs Land umziehen; **to originate from the** ~ vom Lande stammen; **to prohibit s. o. from leaving the** ~ jem. die Ausreise verweigern; **to put a** ~ **economically on its feet again** Land wirtschaftlich sanieren (wieder auf die Beine bringen); **to represent a** ~ Belange eines Landes vertreten; **to return to one's own** ~ in sein Heimatland zurückkehren; **to rule over a** ~ über ein Volk herrschen; **to run the** ~ landesflüchtig werden; **to travel over a** ~ Land bereisen;
~ **bank** *(Br.)* Regionalbank; ~ **banker** *(Br.)* Regionalbankier; ~ **bill** *(Br.)* Regionalwechsel; ~ **box** *(Br.)* kleines Landhaus; ~ **branch** Provinzfiliale; ~ **bumpkin** Bauerntölpel; ~ **cheque** *(Br.)* Regionalbankscheck; ~ **clearing** *(Br.)* Regionalclearing,

Abrechnung der Regionalbanken; ~ **club** *(US)* Sport- und Gesellschaftsklub; ~ **collections** Inkasso auf Regionalbanken; ~ **cousin** Vetter vom Lande; ~ **district** *(Br.)* Landbezirk; ~ **doctor** Landarzt; ~ **estate** Landbesitz, landwirtschaftliches Grundstück; ~ **gentleman** Landedelmann; ~ **group** Ländergruppe; ~ **home** Landsitz; ~ **house** Landhaus, Villa; ~ **house chat-in** zwangloses Wochenendgespräch; ~ **lane** Landstraße, -weg; ~ **life** Leben auf dem Lande, Landleben, ländliches Leben; ~ **note** *(Br.)* Regionalwechsel; ~ **park** *(Br.)* förderungswürdiges Erholungsgebiet; ~ **party** Bauernpartei; ~ **people** Landbevölkerung; ~ **retreat** Landsitz; ~ **risks** Länderrisiken; ~ **road** Landstraße; ~ **seat** [größerer] Landbesitz; ~ **setting** ländliche Umgebung; ~ **share** *(International Monetary Fund)* Länderanteil; ~ **shipper** Inlandsspediteur; ~ **site** Landsitz; ~ **store** *(US)* Einzelhandelsgeschäft für die landwirtschaftliche Bevölkerung, Gemischtwaren-, Dorfladen; ~ **town** *(Br.)* Provinzstadt; ~ **trade** Binnenhandel; ~**wide** im ganzen Land, überregional; ~ **worker** Landarbeiter.
countryman Dorf-, Landbewohner;
   fellow ~ Landsmann.
countryside Landschaft, -strich;
   to be deeply buried in the ~ ungestört auf dem Lande wohnen;
   ⚲ **Commission** *(Br.)* Landschaftsschutzamt.
county *(Br.)* Grafschaft, *(US)* Verwaltungsbezirk, Kreis;
   administrative ~ *(Br.)* Verwaltungsbezirk, [etwa] Landkreis, kreisfreie Stadt; **registration** ~ Meldebezirk;
   ⚲ **of London** Großlondon;
   ~ **affairs** Kommunal-, Selbstverwaltungsangelegenheiten; ~ **agent** landwirtschaftlicher Berater; ~ **association** *(territorial army, Br.)* Wehrbezirk; ~ **attorney** *(US)* Staatsanwalt, öffentlicher Kläger; ~ **board of equalization** Bezirksausschuß für Steuerausgleichsfragen; ~ **bonds** Provinzial-, Kommunalobligationen; ~ **borough** *(Br.)* kreisfreie Stadt, Bezirks-, Kreisstadt; ~ **business** Kommunalangelegenheit; ~ **clerk** *(US)* Geschäftsstellenleiter; ~ **college** *(Br.)* Fortbildungs-, Berufsschule; ~ **commissioner** Bezirksvorsteher, *(US)* Friedensrichter; ~ **constabulary** Gemeindepolizist; ~ **corporate** *(Br.)* kreisfreie Stadt, Bezirks-, Kreisstadt; ~ **council** *(Br.)* Kreisrat, -ausschuß, Bezirkstag, -rat, Gemeinderat, Grafschaftsrat; **council register** *(Br.)* Geschäftsregister; ~ **councillor** *(Br.)* Kreisrat; ~ **court** *(Br.)* Amtsgericht, Gericht erster Instanz, *(US)* Kreisgericht; ~ **district** Gemeindebezirk; ~ **fair** Großmarkt; ~ **family** *(Br.)* Adelsfamilie; ~ **farm** *(US, local)* armer Bauernhof; ~ **farm bureau** landwirtschaftliche Beratungsstelle; ~ **fund** Kommunalvermögen; ~ **general fund** kommunale Haushaltsmittel; ~ **government** Kreis-, Gemeindeverwaltung; ~ **hospital** Kreiskrankenhaus; ~ **house** *(US)* Armenhaus; ~ **jail** *(US)* Kreis-, Gemeindegefängnis; ~ **library** Bezirksbibliothek, *(legal library)* Rechtsbibliothek; ~ **manager** *(US)* oberster Verwaltungsbeamter; ~ **member** Vertreter des flachen Landes; ~ **office** *(US)* Bezirks-, Kreisamt; ~ **officer** *(US)* Kreis-, Kommunalbeamter; ~ **police** Gendarmerie; ~ **powers** kommunale Befugnisse; ~ **property** Kreis-, Kommunalvermögen; **for** ~ **purposes** für kommunale Zwecke; ~ **rate** *(Br.)* Kommunal-, Kreis-, Gemeinde-, Bezirksumlage; ~ **seat** *(US)* Kreisstadt; ~ **sessions** *(Br.)* quartalsweise stattfindende Strafgerichtstermine; ~ **town** *(Br.)* kreisfreie Stadt, Kreisstadt, Kreis[haupt]stadt; ~ **treasurer** *(Br.)* Grafschaftskämmerer, Kreiskämmerer; ~ **treasury** Kommunal-, Kreisvermögen; ~ **warrant** kommunale Auszahlungsanweisung, Kommunalschuldschein.
coup *(pol.)* Staats-, Gewaltstreich;
   ~ **d'état** Staatsstreich; ~ **de grâce** Gnadenstoß; ~ **de main** *(mil.)* Handstreich;
   to pull off a ~ Coup landen.
coupé Coupé, zweitürige Limousine, *(railway, Br.)* Halbabteil.
couple [Ehe]paar, *(connection)* Verbindung, Bindeglied, *(el.)* Elektrodenpaar;
   in ~**s** paarweise;
   courting ~ Tanzpaar; **married** ~ Ehepaar;
   married ~ **without encumberment** Ehepaar ohne Verpflichtungen; **extra** ~ **of job opportunities** Nebenarbeiten, um Geld dazu zu verdienen;
   ~ *(v.)* koppeln, *(coll.)* verheiraten, *(el.)* zusammenschalten;
   ~ **two railway coaches** zwei Waggons aneinander koppeln;
   to hunt (run) in ~**s** *(fig.)* stets im gegenseitigen Einverständnis handeln.
coupled rate gekoppelter Tarif.
coupler | plug Gerätestecker; ~ **socket** Gerätesteckdose.
coupling Kupplung, *(el.)* Anschlußstück, *(railway coaches)* Zusammenkoppeln;

automatic ~ *(railway)* selbsttätige Kupplung, *(car)* automatische Kupplung; **disk** ~ Scheibenkupplung; **fluid** ~ hydraulische Kupplung;
   ~ **chain** Kupplungskette; ~ **disk** Kupplungsscheibe; ~ **rod** Kuppelstange.
coupon *(advertising)* Einsendeabschnitt, *(counterfoil)* Kontrollabschnitt, *(dividend warrant)* Gewinnanteilschein, *(interest warrant)* Zinsschein, Kupon, *(Br., pol., sl.)* Zustimmung des Parteiführers [zu einer Kandidatur], *(ration ticket, Br.)* [Lebensmittel]kartenabschnitt, Marke, *(theater)* Abonnementskarte, *(ticket)* Gutschein, Kassenzettel, Bon, Berechtigungsschein, Kupon;
   ex ~ (~ **off**) ohne Koupon; **on** ~ (**with** ~, *US*) auf Marken (Karten);
   clothing ~ Kleiderkartenabschnitt, Textilpunkt; **current** ~ laufender Kupon; **detached** ~ abgetrennter Kupon; **dividend** ~ Dividendenschein; **food** ~ Lebensmittelkartenabschnittt; **free-gift** ~ Gutschein; **interest** ~ Zinsschein, -kupon; **international reply** ~ internationaler Antwortschein; **matured** ~ noch nicht zur Zahlung eingereichter Kupon; **maturing** ~ fällig werdender Kupon; **outstanding** ~**s** notleidende Kupons; **ration** ~ Lebensmittelmarkenabschnitt; **return** ~ Kupon in Form einer Bestellkarte;
   ~ **in arrears** rückständiger Kupon;
   to cash a ~ Bezugsschein einlösen; **to deposit** ~**s** Kupons hereingeben; **to detach** ~**s** Kupons abtrennen; **to recover the** ~ Kuponabschlag einbringen; **to spend (surrender)** ~**s** Marken abgeben;
   ~ **bond** *(US)* Inhaberschuldverschreibung, -obligation [mit Zinsschein]; ~ **book** Kuponkonto; ~ **candidate** *(parl.)* empfohlener Kandidat; ~ **check** *(US)* Kuponscheck; ~ **clipper** *(US)* Kuponschneider; ~ **collection department** Inkassoabteilung für Zinsscheine; ~ **collection teller** *(US)* Kuponkassierer; ~**free** marken-, bezugsscheinfrei; ~ **goods** markenpflichtige Waren; ~ **holder** Kuponinhaber; ~ **ledger** Kuponkonto; ~ **majority** Mehrheit parteitreuer Abgeordneter; ~**-paying department** Kuponkasse; ~ **payments account** *(US)* Kuponkonto; ~ **credit** ~ **plan** Gutscheinsystem; ~ **rate** Zinssatz für festverzinsliche Wertpapiere; ~ **redemption** Gutscheineinlösung; ~ **scheme** Werbeaktion mit beigefügten Kupons; ~ **service** Kuponeinlösung; ~ **sheet** Kupon-, Zinsscheinbogen; **ex** ~ **sheet** ohne Dividendenbogen; ~ **tax** Kuponsteuer; ~ **teller** Kuponkassierer.
couponed auf Marken, markenpflichtig.
courage Mut, Tapferkeit;
   to have the ~ **of one's conviction** Zivilcourage haben; **to pluck up** ~ Mut fassen; **to take one's** ~ **in both hands** all seinen Mut zusammennehmen.
courier Kurier, Eilbote, *(attendant)* Reisebegleiter;
   ~ *(v.)* als Kurier unterwegs sein;
   ~ **handling** Behandlung als Kuriersache; ~ **route** Kurierweg; ~ **service** Kurierwesen, -dienst.
course *(aircraft)* Flugrichtung, *(behavio(u)r)* Benehmen, Betragen, Verhaltensweise, *(body of law)* [Rechts]sammlung, *(career)* Laufbahn, Karriere, *(journey)* Gang, Fahrt, Reise, *(of lectures)* Lehrgang, Kursus, *(meal)* Gericht, Gang, *(med.)* Kur, *(mining)* Ader, stehendes Flöz, *(progress)* [Ver]lauf, Ablauf, Fortschritt, Verfahren, *(ship)* Kurs, Fahrtrichtung, *(stock exchange)* Wechselkurs, [Kurs]notierung, *(tendency)* Marktlage, Tendenz, *(turn)* Turnus, regelmäßiger Wechsel, *(university)* Vorlesungszyklus, *(way)* Richtung, Weg;
   in the ~ **of** im Verlauf; **in** ~ **of construction** im Bau [begriffen]; **in the** ~ **of the conversation** gesprächsweise; **in** ~ **of execution** in der Durchführung begriffen; **in due** ~ zur rechten Zeit, rechtzeitig; **in due** ~ auf dem ordentlichen Rechtsweg; **in the** ~ **of my life** im Verlauf meines Lebens; **in the** ~ **of liquidation** während der Liquidation; **in the ordinary** ~ **of things** üblicherweise; **in the** ~ **of a year** binnen Jahresfrist, im Laufe eines Jahres;
   basic ~ Grundausbildungskursus; **civil** ~ römisches Recht; **evil** ~**s** üble Gewohnheiten; **extension** ~ Volkshochschulkursus; **first** ~ erster Gang; **forced** ~ Zwangskurs; **four-meal** ~ Mahlzeit mit vier Gängen; **full-credit** ~ vollständiger Kursus; **high-school** ~ Mittelschullehrgang; **in-company** ~ innerbetrieblicher Ausbildungskursus; **middle-school** ~ Mittelschulbildung; **new** ~ *(pol.)* Neuorientierung; **non-credit** ~ kostenloser Kursus; **out-of-company** ~ außerbetrieblicher Kursus; **refresher** ~ Wiederholungs-, Auffrischungskursus; **tortuous** ~ gewundener Pfad; **total immersion** ~ Intensivsprachkursus; **training** ~ Übungs-, Ausbildungslehrgang; **full year's** ~ ganzjähriger Lehrgang;

~ of action Handlungsweise; ~ of affairs Geschäftsgang; [ordinary, regular] ~ of business üblicher Geschäftsgang, -ablauf; ~ of conduct Verhaltensweise; ~ of disease Krankheitsverlauf; ~ of education Lehrplan; ~ of employment normaler Arbeits-, Geschäftsablauf; ~ of events Lauf der Ereignisse, Hergang; ~ of exchange (Br.) Wechselkurs[zettel]; forced ~ of exchange (Br.) Zwangskurs; ~ of instruction in accounting Buchprüferlehrgang; ~ of justice Lauf der Gerechtigkeit; ~ of law Rechtsgang, -verfahren; ~ of lectures Vortragszyklus, Vorlesungsverzeichnis, -reihe, Zyklus von Vorlesungen; ~ of life Lebenslauf, -weg; regular ~ of manufacture normaler Produktionsablauf; ~ of nature natürlicher Lauf der Dinge; uncomplicated ~ of an operation glatter Verlauf einer Operation; ~ of ore Erzgang; ~ of river Flußverlauf; autonomous ~ of study selbständige Arbeitsweise, Studienlehrgang; ~ of trade [Markt]tendenz, Geschäftsgang; normal ~ of trade üblicher Geschäftsablauf, [Markt]tendenz; ~ of training Ausbildungskurs; ~ of a vessel Schiffskurs; ~ of the voyage übliche Route; ~ (v.) Kurs einschlagen (verfolgen); ~ through s. th. Sache flüchtig durchgehen;

to act in the ordinary ~ of one's business im Rahmen der üblichen Geschäftsbedingungen handeln; to adopt a new ~ neuen Kurs einschlagen; to alter the ~ Kurs ändern; to alter one's ~ umschalten; to attend a ~ Vorlesung hören, an einem Kurs teilnehmen; to be in ~ of construction im Bau sein; to be off her ~ (ship) vom Kurs abgekommen sein; to be on a ~ abkommandiert sein; to be blown off ~ vom Kurs abkommen; to chart one's ~ seinen Kurs festlegen; to choose the safest ~ auf Nummer sicher gehen; to detach for a ~ zu einem Lehrgang abstellen, abkommandieren; to enrol(l) for a ~ Vorlesung belegen; to follow one's own old ~ seinen bisherigen Lebenswandel fortsetzen; to get off ~ vom Kurs abkommen; to give a ~ of lectures Reihe von Vorträgen (Vortragszyklus) halten; to go through a ~ Kursus durchlaufen; to hold a ~ Vorlesung halten; to hold one's ~ seinen Kurs halten, beharrlich seinen Weg verfolgen; to impede the ~ of justice in den Gang der Rechtspflege eingreifen; to keep to one's ~ beharrlich seinen Weg verfolgen; to keep a middle ~ (pol.) mittlere Linie einhalten; to let matters take their ~ die Dinge sich entwickeln lassen; to plot the ~ Kurs abstecken; to prevent the ~ of justice Recht verdrehen; to pursue a realistic ~ realistischen Kurs einschlagen; to pursue one's steady ~ seinen Kurs unbeirrt verfolgen; to run its ~ seinen Verlauf nehmen; to set ~ for the open sea Kurs auf das offene Meer nehmen; to sign up for a ~ sich zu einem Kursus anmelden; to stay on the ~ Kurs einhalten; to steer the ~ Kurs steuern; to take a ~ Kurs belegen, an einem Kurs teilnehmen; to take one's own ~ seinen eigenen Weg gehen, nach eigenem Ermessen handeln; to take part in a ~ for advanced students an einem Kursus für Fortgeschrittene teilnehmen; to try another ~ andere Methode anwenden (versuchen); to undergo a ~ of treatment sich einer Kur unterziehen; to write s. o. in due ~ jem. zu gegebener Zeit schreiben;

five-~ dinner Dinner mit fünf Gängen; ~ material Kursusmaterial; ~ work Kursustätigkeit.

court Gericht, (hall) Gerichtssaal, (of law) Gericht[shof], -behörde, (residence) Residenz, Regierung, (retinue) Hofstaat, (sitting of court) Gerichtssitzung, (open space) Hof[raum], Vorplatz;

at the discretion of the ~ nach richterlichem Ermessen; before a full ~ vor versammeltem Gericht; by order of the ~ auf Grund richterlicher Verfügung, von Gerichts wegen; in ~ vor Gericht; out of ~ ohne gerichtliche Mitwirkung, außergerichtlich, (fig.) ohne jede Chance, indiskutabel; pending before the ~ vor Gericht anhängig;

~ above höhere Instanz, Obergericht; administrative ~ Verwaltungsgericht; ambulatory ~ fliegendes Gericht; appellate ~ zweitinstanzliches Gericht, Berufungsgericht; bankruptcy ~ Konkursgericht; ~ below untergeordnetes Gericht, Vorinstanz; cartel ~ Kartellgericht; children's ~ Jugendgericht; circuit ~ (US) erstinstanzliches (ordentliches) Gericht; civil ~ (US) Gericht für bürgerliche Rechtsstreitigkeiten, Gericht erster Instanz, Amtsgericht; commercial ~ Kammer für Handelssachen; conciliation ~ Gütestelle; regularly constituted ~ ordnungsgemäß besetztes Gericht; constitutional ~ Verfassungsgericht; coroner's ~ Untersuchungsgericht; county ~ (Br.) Gericht erster Instanz, Grafschaftsgericht, (US) Kreisgericht; criminal ~ (Br.) Strafkammer; Customs ☨ (US) Bundeszollgericht; disciplinary ~ Dienststrafkammer; district ~ (US) Bezirksgericht; divided ~ Mehrheitsentscheidung; Federal ☨ (US) Bundesgericht; forest ~ Forstgericht; full ~ voll besetztes Gericht, Kammersitzung, Plenum; General ☨ (US) Gesetzge-

bende Versammlung; higher ~ Berufungsinstanz; industrial ~ [for trade disputes] (Br.) Schiedsgericht für Arbeitssachen; industrial arbitrational ~ [for trade disputes] (Br.) Gewerbegericht; inferior ~ Gericht erster Instanz, Gericht mit sachlich beschränkter Zuständigkeit; international ~ internationales Gericht; Justice ☨ (Br.) Stadtgericht; juvenile ~ (US) Jugendgericht; labor ~ (US) Arbeitsgericht; law ~ Gericht[shof], ordentliches Gericht; The Law ☨ Justizpalast; local ~ (Br.) örtliches (einzelstaatliches) Gericht, (US) erstinstanzliches Gericht; lower ~ Vorinstanz, nachgeordnetes Gericht; Magistrates ~ (Br.) (Magistrate's, US) ☨ Schnellgericht; maritime ~ Seeamt; martial ~ Militärgericht, Kriegs-, Standgericht; metropolitan ~ (London) [etwa] Amtsgericht; municipal ~ (US) Stadtgericht; naval ~ Seeamt; open ~ tagendes Gericht, öffentliche Gerichtsverhandlung; ordinary ~ ordentliches Gericht; orphans ~ (New Jersey, Pennsylvania, Maryland, Delaware) Vormundschafts- und Nachlaßgericht; parish ~ (Louisiana) Nachlaßgericht; police ~ (US) Polizei-, Schnellgericht; prefect's ~ (New Mexiko) Nachlaßgericht; prize ~ Prisengericht; probate ~ (US) Nachlaßgericht; provisional ~ (US) Sondergericht der Besatzungsmacht; remand ~ Haftprüfungskammer; Restrictive Practices ☨ (Br.) Kartellgericht; reviewing ~ Rechtsmittelinstanz; small debts ~ Bagatellgericht; special ~ Sondergericht; summary ~ martial Standgericht; superior ~ [etwa] Landgericht, (US) oberstes einzelstaatliches Gericht; supreme ~ (US) Oberster Gerichtshof; surrogate's ~ Vormundschafts- und Nachlaßgericht; tax ~ Finanzgericht, -hof; territorial ~s (US) Gerichte im Territorium der USA; trial ~ erstinstanzliches Gericht;

High ☨ of Admiralty Seeamt, -gerichtshof, Prisengericht; ~ of aldermen (Br.) Stadtverordnetenversammlung; [circuit] ~ of appeal letztinstanzliches Berufungs-, Beschwerdegericht, Revisions-, Kammergericht, Kassationshof; ~ of arbitration Schiedsgericht[shof]; ~ of arbitration of the chamber of commerce (New York) kaufmännisches Schiedsgericht; ~ of assistance Gemeinde-, Kirchenrat; ~ of assizes Schwurgericht; ~ of attachments Forstgericht; ~ sitting in banc Plenarsitzung; ~ of bankruptcy Konkursgericht; ~ of chancery Kanzleigericht; ~ of claims (US) Gericht zur Entscheidung über Ansprüche gegen die öffentliche Hand; ☨ of Claims (US) Bundesgericht für Entschädigungsansprüche; ~ of common council Londoner Stadtrat; ☨ of Common Pleas (US) Landgericht; ~ of commissioners of sewers Aufsichtsamt für Einhaltung von Abwässerungsbestimmungen; ~ of conciliation Schlichtungsausschuß, Schiedsamt; ~ of construction zur Auslegung eines Testaments zuständiges Gericht; ~ of Customs Appeals (US) Gericht für Berufungen in Zollsachen; ☨ of Customs and Patent Appeal Beschwerdeinstanz in Zoll- und Patentangelegenheiten; ~ of directors geschäftsführender Ausschuß, Direktorenversammlung; ☨ for Divorce and Matrimonial Causes Ehescheidungsgericht; ~ of domestic relations Vormundschaftsgericht; ☨ of Equity Billigkeitsgericht für Zivilklagen; ☨ of Errors Berufungs-, Revisionsgericht; Supreme ☨ of Errors (Connecticut) Kassationsgerichtshof; ~ for the correction of errors Appellations-, Revisionsgericht; ☨ of Criminal Appeal (Br.) Berufungsgericht in Strafsachen; ☨ of Exchequer (Br.) Finanzhof, -gericht; ~ of hono(u)r Ehrengericht, (Br.) Disziplinargerichtshof; ☨ of Hustings (London) Stadtgericht; ~ of inquiry (mil.) Untersuchungskommission, Militärgericht; ~ of the first instance Gericht erster Instanz, erstinstanzliches Gericht; ☨ of International Commercial Arbitration Internationaler Handelsgerichtshof; ☨ of St. James (Br.) Britische Regierung; Supreme ☨ of Judicature (Br.) Oberster Gerichtshof; ~ of competent jurisdiction zuständiges Gericht; ~ of limited jurisdiction Gericht mit beschränkter Zuständigkeit; summary ~ of jurisdiction Schnellgericht; ~ of justice Gericht[shof], Untersuchungsgericht, ordentliches Gericht, zuständige Gerichtsbehörde; Permanent ☨ of International Justice Ständiger Internationaler Gerichtshof, Weltgerichtshof, (European Community) Gerichtshof der Europäischen Gemeinschaften; High ☨ of Justice Berufungsgericht; ~ of law ordentliches Gericht; ☨ of Justice Seat (Br.) oberstes Forstgericht; ☨ of Justiciary (Scot.) Revisionsgericht für Strafsachen; ☨ of Ordinary (US) Nachlaßgericht; ☨ of Oyer and Terminer (Br.) für Hoch- und Landesverratsfälle zuständiges Gericht; ~ of patents appeal Berufungsinstanz in patentrechtlichen Streitigkeiten; ~ of probate Nachlaßgericht; ☨ of Protection (Br.) Gerichtsabteilung zur Vermögensverwaltung Geisteskranker, [etwa] Vormundschaftsgericht; ~s of record ordentliche Gerichte; ~ of referees (Br.) Gericht für Streitigkeiten bei der Arbeitslosenunterstützung; ~ of requests (Br.) unteres

Gericht; ~ **of last resort** letztinstanzliches Gericht; ~ **of review** *(bankruptcy matters)* Berufungsgericht; **European ♀ of Human Rights** Europäischer Gerichtshof für Menschenrechte; ♀ **of Session** *(Scot., law)* Obergericht, Oberstes Gericht für Zivilsachen; ♀ **of General Session** *(US)* erstinstanzliches Gericht für Strafsachen; ♀ **of Quarter Sessions** *(Br.)* Gericht für Strafsachen; ♀ **of Survey** *(Br.)* Beschwerdeinstanz für Eigentümer seeuntüchtig erklärter Schiffe; ~ **available at all times** ständig tagendes Gericht; ~ **of trade** Gewerbegericht; **Supreme ♀ of the United States** Oberstes Bundesgericht der Vereinigten Staaten; **competent** ~ **of the vendor** für den Lieferanten zuständiges Gericht; ~ **of ward** Vormundschaftsgericht;

~ *(v.)* **disaster** mit dem Feuer spielen; ~ **s. one's favo(u)r** um jds. Gunst buhlen;

to appear in (before a) ~ vor Gericht erscheinen; **to apply to the** ~ **for permission to borrow** *(receiver)* beim Gericht Kreditaufnahme beantragen; **to arrange a case out of** ~ Sache außergerichtlich beilegen; **to assign a day for a hearing in** ~ Gerichtstermin ansetzen; **to attend personally in** ~ persönlich vor Gericht erscheinen; **to be put (ruled) out of** ~ mit der Klage abgewiesen werden; **to be received at** ~ bei Hof empfangen werden; **to be presented at** ~ bei Hof vorgestellt werden; **to be responsible to the** ~ dem Gericht Rechnung zu legen haben; **to bring into** ~ als Beweis beibringen; **to bring s. o. into** ~ j. verklagen; **to bring a matter before the** ~ Gericht mit einer Sache befassen; **to bring up before the** ~ dem Richter vorführen; **to cite s. o. before the** ~ j. vor Gericht laden (zitieren); **to come before the** ~ vor [den Schranken des] Gericht[s] erscheinen; **to come within the jurisdiction of a** ~ unter die Zuständigkeit eines Gerichts fallen; **to complain in a** ~ **of law** als Kläger auftreten; **to convene s. o. before the** ~ j. vor Gericht laden (zitieren); **to declare a** ~ **in session** [Gerichts]sitzung eröffnen; **to establish in** ~ gerichtlich feststellen; **to fight s. o. through the** ~**s** Sache mit jem. gerichtlich austragen, gegen j. durch alle Instanzen prozessieren; **to give evidence on s. one's behalf in a law** ~ für j. vor Gericht aussagen; **to go before the** ~ klagen, Gerichtsweg beschreiten, vor Gericht gehen, gerichtliche Entscheidung herbeiführen; **to have the** ~ **cleared** Gerichtssaal räumen lassen; **to have a friend at** ~ einflußreiche Beziehungen haben, einflußreichen Fürsprecher haben; **to have a sequel in** ~ gerichtliches Nachspiel haben; **to hold** ~ Gerichtssitzung (Gerichtsverhandlung) abhalten; **to hold a** ~ Hof halten; **to hold for the** ~ für das Gericht verwahren; **to introduce at** ~ bei Hofe vorstellen; **to invoke the aid of a** ~ Gericht anrufen; **to land in** ~ sich vor Gericht wiederfinden; **to lay a matter before the** ~ Gericht mit einer Sache befassen; **to lose a case in** ~ Prozeß verlieren; **to open the** ~ Gerichtssitzung eröffnen; **to order the** ~ **to be cleared** Gerichtssaal räumen lassen; **to pay into** ~ bei Gericht einzahlen; **to perpetrate a fraud on the** ~ Gericht irreführen; **to put into** ~ verklagen; **to remit to a lower** ~ an das untere Gericht zurückverweisen; **to report to the** ~ dem Gericht einen Fall als Berichterstatter vortragen; **to represent o. s. in** ~ sich selbst vor Gericht vertreten; **to resort to** ~ Gericht anrufen; **to rule out of** ~ Klage abweisen; **to set up a** ~ Gericht einsetzen; **to settle a case out of** ~ Sache außergerichtlich beilegen; **to sit in** ~ Gerichtssitzung abhalten; **to submit to the** ~ **for decision** dem Gericht zur Entscheidung vorlegen; **to surrender o. s. to the** ~ sich dem Gericht stellen; **to take s. o. to** ~ gerichtlich gegen j. vorgehen; **to take a country to** ~ **for breaking community rules** Land wegen Verletzung der Gemeinschaftsrichtlinien vor Gericht bringen; **to vest in the** ~**s** den Gerichten obliegen;

~ **action** gerichtliches Vorgehen, gerichtliche Maßnahmen; ~ **approval** Genehmigung des Gerichts; **to seek** ~ **attention** Aufmerksamkeit des Gerichts zu erregen suchen; ~ **ball** Hofball; ~ **ban** gerichtliche Auflage; ~ **baron** *(Br.)* Gutsgericht; **to lose a** ~ **battle** Prozeß verlieren; ~ **calendar** Hofalmanach; ~ **case** Rechtssache, -fall, Prozeß; **to drop a** ~ **case** Klage fallen lassen; ~ **circular** *(Br.)* Hofnachrichten; ~ **costs** Gerichts-, Prozeßkosten; ~ **day** Gerichtstag; ~ **decree** Gerichtsbeschluß; ~ **decision** Gerichtsentscheidung; ~ **declaration** gerichtliche Feststellung; ~ **dress** Talar, richterliche Amtskleidung; ~ **etiquette** Hofzeremoniell; ~ **fashion** Hoftracht; ~ **fees** *(Br.)* Gerichtsgebühren, -kosten; **to win a** ~ **fight** gerichtliche Auseinandersetzung gewinnen; ~ **guard** Justizwachtmeister; ~ **guide** Hofalmanach; ~ **hand** Kanzleischrift; ~ **hearing** Anhörung durch das Gericht, Gerichtsverhandlung; ~ **injunction** gerichtliche Verfügung, gerichtliches Verbot; ~ **interpretation** gerichtliche Auslegung; ~ **interpreter** Gerichtsdolmetscher; ~ **issue** Prozeßfall; ~ **lady** Hofdame; ~ **lands** *(Br.)* Allodialgüter; ~ **litigation** Rechtsstreit, gerichtliche Auseinandersetzung; ~ **lodge** Herrenhaus; ~ **mar-**

tial Stand-, Kriegsgericht; ~~**martial** *(v.)* vor ein Kriegsgericht stellen; ~ **mourning** Hoftrauer; ~ **official** Justizbeamter, Gerichtsperson; ~ **order** gerichtliche Verfügung, Gerichtsbeschluß; ~ **order for the maintenance of children** Unterhaltsurteil; **to fail to comply with a** ~ **order** Anordnungen des Gerichts zuwiderhandeln; **to sue for a** ~ **order** gerichtliche Entscheidung beantragen; ~ **papers** Gerichtsakten; ~ **order payments** Zahlungen aufgrund einer gerichtlichen Verfügung; ~ **personnel** Justizbeamte; ~ **practice** Praxis des Gerichts, Gerichtsordnung, -verfügung; **supreme** ~ **practice** höchstrichterliche Rechtsprechung; ~ **proceedings** Gerichtsverhandlung, gerichtliches Verfahren; ~ **procedure** Gerichtsverfahren; ~ **promises** leere Versprechungen; ~ **records** Gerichtsakten; ~ **registrar** Urkundsbeamter der Geschäftsstelle, Protokollführer; ~ **reports** *(US)* Berichterstattung über Gerichtsfälle; ~ **rolls** Gerichtsprotokoll, -akten; ~ **room** Gerichtssaal; ~ **rules** Verfahrensvorschriften; ~ **ruling** Gerichtsbeschluß; ~ **ruling favo(u)rable to industry** wirtschaftsfreundliche Gerichtsentscheidung; **to defy an adverse** ~ **ruling** sich über eine gegenteilige Gerichtsentscheidung hinwegsetzen; ~ **settlement** gerichtlicher Vergleich; ~ **suit** Gerichtsverfahren; **to bring fresh** ~ **suits** neue Prozeßverfahren in Gang bringen; ~ **stage** Gerichtsstadium; ~ **trial** Gerichtsverfahren.

courtesy Höflichkeit, Verbindlichkeit, *(business)* Entgegenkommen, Gefälligkeit, *(present)* kleines Geschenk, Aufmerksamkeit, *(widower)* Nutznießung [am Grundbesitz];

by ~ **of** mit freundlicher Genehmigung;

common ~ *(coll.)* anständiges Benehmen;

~ **of the port** *(US)* Befreiung von der Zollrevision des Gepäcks; ~ **of the road** Verkehrsrücksicht;

to be in ~ **bound to do s. th.** anstandshalber (moralisch) zu etw. verpflichtet sein; **to hold upon** ~ im Wege der Vergünstigung durch einen Dritten besitzen; **to live with s. o. by** ~ aus Gefälligkeit bei jem. wohnen dürfen;

~ **call** Höflichkeitsbesuch; ~ **card** Gutschein; ~ **lie** Notlüge; ~ **light** *(car)* türabhängige Innenbeleuchtung; ~ **patrol** Verkehrsstreife; ~ **title** ehrenhalber verliehener Titel, Ehrentitel; ~ **visit** Höflichkeitsbesuch.

courthouse Gerichtsgebäude, *(US local)* Provinzstadt.

courtyard Hof[raum], Hinterhof.

cousin, full leiblicher Vetter;

~ **in the first remove** Vetter ersten Grades; ~ **twice removed** Vetter zweiten Grades;

to be a first ~ **with** *(fig.)* eng verwandt sein.

cousinhood Vetterschaft, Verwandtschaft.

covenant *(agreement)* Vereinbarung, Abmachung, Zusicherung, *(charter)* Statut, Satzung, *(clause)* Vertragsklausel, *(document)* [schriftlicher] Vertrag, Vertragsurkunde, Kontrakt;

affirmative ~ Verpflichtung zu zukünftigen Leistungen; **collateral** ~ Nebenabkommen; **continuing** ~ Dauerverpflichtung; **declaratory** ~ deklaratorischer Vertrag; **dependent** ~ abhängige Verpflichtung; **executed** ~ erfüllter Vertrag; **executory** ~ schwebender Vertrag; **express** ~ ausdrückliche Verpflichtung; **general** ~ schuldrechtliche Verpflichtung; **implied** ~ stillschweigend enthaltene Verpflichtung; **independent** ~ abstrakte Verpflichtung; **inherent** ~ wesentliche Vertragspflicht; **mutual** ~ gegenseitiger Vertrag; **negative** ~ Unterlassungsverpflichtung; **obligatory** ~ schuldrechtlicher Vertrag; **particular** ~ besondere Abmachungen; **personal** ~ schuldrechtlicher Vertrag, einseitig verpflichtender Vertrag; **positive** ~ unbeschränktes Nutzungsrecht; **principal** ~ Hauptpflicht, -verpflichtung; **qualified** ~ beschränktes Nutzungsrecht; **restrictive** ~ Nutzungsbeschränkung; **special (separate)** ~ Sondervereinbarung; **transition** ~ Übergangsvertrag; **usual** ~ übliche Rechtsmängelgewährleistung;

~ **not to compete** Wettbewerbsabkommen; ~ **to convey** Auffassungsvereinbarung; ~ **against encumbrances** *(banking)* Negativverpflichtung; ~ **in gross** schuldrechtliche Nebenverpflichtung; ~ **to insure** Vertragspflicht aus Aufrechterhaltung einer Versicherung; ~ **of marriage** Heiratsvertrag, Ehevertrag; ~ **to give a portion** Pflichtteilvereinbarung; ~ **of nonclaim** *(real estate)* Klageverzichtserklärung; ~**s held to touch and concern the land** Vereinbarungen mit dinglicher Wirkung; ♀ **of the League of Nations** Völkerbundspakt; ~ **to renew** Option für eine Vertragsverlängerung; ~ **in restraint of trade** wettbewerbsbeschränkende Vereinbarung, Konkurrenzklausel; ~**s running with the land** [etwa] Belastungen in Abteilung 2 des Grundbuchs; ~ **not to sue** Schiedsgerichts-, Klageverzichtsvereinbarung; ~ **for title** Rechtsmängelgewährleistung; ♀ **of the United Nations** Satzung der Vereinten Nationen; ~ **of warranty** *(lease)* Rechtsmängelgarantie;

~ (v.) sich verpflichten, Vertrag schließen, [vertraglich] vereinbaren;

to enter into a ~ sich vertraglich verpflichten;

~ **breaker** Vetragsbrecher; **~-breaking** vertragsbrüchig; **full** ~ **deed** *(US)* Grundstücksübertragungsurkunde.

covenanted vertraglich verpflichtet;

~ **benefit** *(insurance)* vertraglich (vertragsmäßig) zustehender Versicherungsgewinn, *(Br., unemployment insurance)* auf Beitragszahlungen beruhende Arbeitslosenunterstützung.

covenantee Begünstigter eines Vertrages, Vertragsberechtigter.

covenantor Verpflichteter, Kontrahent, Vertragspartei.

coventrate, coventrize *(v.)* durch Bomben völlig zerstören, ausradieren.

cover Umhüllung, Hülle, Emballage, *(advertising)* Anzeigenraum auf dem Umschlag, *(backing of notes)* Geld-, Notendeckung, *(book)* Buchdeckel, Umschlagdeckel, *(envelope)* [Brief]umschlag, Kuvert, *(of a firm)* [Firmen]mantel, *(insurance)* Deckung, Versicherungsschutz, *(meal)* Gedeck, Kouvert, *(mil.)* Schutz, *(~ page)* Umschlags- und Titelseite, *(philately)* Ganzsache, *(pretext)* Deckmantel, Vorwand, *(security)* Abschirmung, Sicherheit, Deckung, Bürgschaft, *(shelter)* Obdach, *(tyres)* Reifendecke;

for want of ~ mangels Deckung; **in loose** ~ broschiert; ~ **into** *(US)* in die Staatskasse eingezahlt; **under** ~ unter Kreuzband, beiliegend, eingeschlossen, eingeschlagen, *(fig.)* geheim, versteckt, verborgen; **under** ~ **of** unter der Adresse von; **under separate** ~ in besonderem Umschlag, mit getrennter Post; **under this** ~ beigeschlossen, in der Anlage; **used as** ~ zur Deckung verwendet; **without** ~ ungedeckt, ohne Deckung;

accidental ~ *(mil.)* natürliche Deckung; **additional** ~ weitere (zusätzliche) Deckung, Deckungszuschuß, Nachschußzahlung; ~ **afloat** Deckung angeschafft; **air** ~ *(mil.)* Luftsicherung; **back** ~ Rückseite; **book** ~ Schutzumschlag; **cash** ~ Barsicherheit; **duplicated** ~ doppelter Versicherungsschutz; **dust** ~ *(book)* Schutzumschlag; **fighter** ~ *(mil.)* Jagdfliegerschutz; **front** ~ vordere Umschlagseite; **full** ~ volle Deckung; **gold** ~ *(currency)* Golddeckung; **inside** ~ innere (vierte) Umschlagseite; **metallic** ~ *(currency)* Metalldeckung; **protection** ~ Schutzumschlag; **provisional** ~ vorläufige Deckungszusage; **requisite** ~ genügende (hinreichende) Deckung; **slipover** ~ *(book)* Schutzhülle;

heat-retaining ~**s for swimming pools** wärmebindende Schwimmbadabdeckungen;

~ *(v.) (comprehend)* beinhalten, enthalten, behandeln, umfassen, *(by insurance)* decken, *(letter)* enthalten, *(protect)* decken, *(reimburse)* ausgleichen, *(report, US)* Bericht erstatten, berichten, als Berichterstatter arbeiten, erfassen, abdecken, *(take care)* betreuen;

~ **o. s.** sich eindecken, sich [für eine Zahlung] erholen; ~ **a wide area** sich sehr weit ausdehnen; ~ **the balance of £ 100 into** ... Saldo von 100 Pfund übertragen auf ...; ~ **a bill** Deckung für einen Wechsel anschaffen; **barely** ~ **the cost** kaum die Kosten decken; ~ **a country by car** Land mit dem Auto befahren; ~ **debts** Schulden abdecken; ~ **a deficit** Defizit abdecken (tilgen); ~ **a distance** Strecke zurücklegen; ~ **the election** über die Wahlen berichten; ~ **the expenses** Auslagen bestreiten, Kosten decken; **to** ~ **our expenses** zur Deckung unserer Unkosten; ~ **o. s. with glory** sich mit Ruhm bedecken; ~ **an insurance** Versicherung decken; ~ **the landing of the invading army** den Invasionstruppen Feuerschutz gewähren; ~ **a letter to s. o.** Brief an j. adressieren; ~ **liabilities** Verpflichtungen nachkommen; ~ **over a loan** Anleihe überzeichnen; ~ **all losses** alle Verluste abdecken; ~ **a meeting of shareholders** über eine Hauptversammlung berichten; ~ **ten miles at high speed** 15 km mit großer Geschwindigkeit fahren; ~ **money into the treasury** *(US)* Geld beim Schatzamt abliefern, Geld aufs Finanzamt überweisen; ~ **the needs of a journey** für seine Reisebedürfnisse ausreichen; ~ **the rate** Kurs sichern; ~ **in the unemployment relief** in die Arbeitslosenfürsorge einbeziehen; ~ **the requirements** Bedarf decken; ~ **the retreat** Rückzug decken; ~ **s. o. with a revolver** j. mit einem Revolver in Schach halten; ~ **a route** Strecke befahren; ~ **United Nations sessions** über die Sitzungen der UNO berichten; ~ **short sales** Fixgeschäfte abdecken; ~ **the whole subject** ganzes Thema abhandeln; ~ **a territory** *(salesman)* Gebiet betreuen, Bezirk bearbeiten; ~ **up** vertuschen;

to call for additional ~ Nachschuß einfordern; **to furnish s. o. with** ~ jem. Deckung anschaffen; **to lodge stock as** ~ Aktien als Deckung hinterlegen; **to make provision for** ~ **of a bill of exchange** Deckung für einen Wechsel anschaffen; **to operate without** ~ ungedeckte Transaktionen vornehmen; **to provide**

with ~ Deckung (Schutz) gewähren; **to put under** ~ Deckung verschaffen; **to read a book from** ~ **to** ~ Buch von A bis Z (ganz) lesen; **to run off one's** ~ Kautionssumme einbüßen; **to serve as a** ~ als Deckung dienen; **to take** ~ Deckung suchen;

~ **address** Deckadresse; ~ **afloat (in transit)** Deckung angeschafft; ~ **charge** *(restaurant)* Couvert, Gedeck; ~ **design** Umschlagszeichnung, Titelbild; ~ **folder** eingelegter Prospekt; ~ **girl** Photomodell auf der Titelseite, Titelbildschönheit; ~ **letter** Begleitbrief; ~ **name** Deck-, Tarnname; ~ **note** *(Br.)* vorläufige Deckungszusage, Zwischenbescheinigung über eine abgeschlossene Versicherung, Deckungszusage; ~ **organization** Deck-, Tarnorganisation; ~ **page** Titel-, Umschlagseite; ~ **paper** Umschlagkarton, -papier; ~ **picture** Umschlagbild; ~ **plate** Abdeckplatte; ~ **price** Einzelexemplarpreis; ~ **purchases** Deckungskäufe; ~ **ratio** *(bank notes)* Deckungsverhältnis, Deckungsquote; **to lose one's** ~ **spot** namentliche Titelseitenerwähnung verlieren; ~ **stock** schweres Faser-, Umschlagpapier; ~ **story** Titelgeschichte; ~ **subject** Umschlagbild; **~-up** Vertuschung.

coverage *(advertising)* Streubreite, -abdeckung, -dichte, Streuung, Reichweite, *(agreement)* Geltungsbereich, *(assets to meet liabilities)* zur Deckung vorhandene Mittel, *(inclusion)* Erfassung, Einbeziehung, *(insurance, US)* Versicherungsschutz, -umfang, Deckung, *(market reached)* Reichweite, Verbreitung, *(news reporting)* Berichterstattung, *(public relations)* Betreuung, *(radio, television)* Deckungsbereich, Reichweite, *(statistics)* erfaßter Bereich (Personenkreis), Reichweite;

asset ~ Deckung durch Aktiva; **automatic** ~ automatische Deckung; **business insurance** ~ Deckungsumfang für den Betrieb abgeschlossener Versicherungen; **commercial** ~ Versicherungsschutz im gewerblichen Bereich; **company** ~ betriebliches Anwendungsgebiet; **comprehensive** ~ Teilkaskoversicherung; **election** ~ Berichterstattung über die Wahlen; **extended** ~ *(fire insurance)* zusätzlicher Versicherungsschutz; **full** ~ volle Deckung; **live television** ~ direkte Fernsehübertragung; **medical payments** ~ Insassenunfallversicherung; **overlapping** ~ sich überschneidender Geltungsbereich; **restricted** ~ eingeschränkte Versicherung; **road service** ~ Pannendienstversicherung; **spot** ~ unmittelbare Berichterstattung, Direktsendung; **standard warehouse-to-warehouse** ~ *(carrier)* Versicherungsschutz im Rahmen der Haus-zu-Haus-Klausel; **suburban** ~ Berichterstattung über Vorstadtereignisse; **term-life** ~ Risikolebensversicherungsschutz; **twenty per cent gold** ~ zwanzigprozentige Golddeckung;

television ~ **of the election campaign** Fernsehberichterstattung über den Wahlkampf; ~ **by unemployment relief** Einbeziehung in die Arbeitslosenfürsorge;

to have ~ *(US)* versichert sein; **to join in the** ~ Deckung gemeinsam übernehmen; **to withdraw** ~ keinen Versicherungsschutz gewähren;

~ **contract** Versicherungsvertrag; ~ **cost** *(advertising)* Streuungskosten; ~ **requirements** Deckungserfordernisse.

covered gedeckt, geschützt;

~ **by contract** vertraglich abgesichert; ~ **by shipping documents** durch Verschiffungspapiere gedeckt; ~ **into the treasury** *(US)* in die Staatskasse eingezahlt;

to be ~ Deckung in Händen haben, *(issue)* überzeichnet sein, *(insurance)* versichert sein; **to be** ~ **by advances** durch Vorschüsse gedeckt sein; **to be** ~ **with advertisements** mit Reklame übersät sein; **to be** ~ **by the amount insured** voll durch die Versicherung gedeckt sein; **to be** ~ **by a survey** von einer Untersuchung erfaßt werden; **to be held** ~ gedeckt sein;

~ **area** *(Br.)* überdachter Vorplatz, *(mil.)* Schußbereich, vom Feuer bestrichener Raum; ~ **industries** in die Arbeitslosenfürsorge miteinbezogene Industrien; ~ **job** *(US)* pflichtversicherte (sozialversicherte) Tätigkeit; ~ **period** Berichtszeit; ~ **sector** Verbreitungsgebiet; ~ **waggon** *(Br.)* geschlossener Güterwagen, *(US)* Planwagen.

covering Hülle, Mantel, Futteral, *(screen)* Schutz, Deckung, *(stock exchange)* Deckungskauf;

~ **a loss** Verlustdeckung; ~ **a risk** Deckung eines Risikos; ~ **agreement** Mantelvertrag; ~ **claim** Deckungsforderung; ~ **deed** Deckungsschein, Treuhandurkunde; ~ **entry** falsche Buchung; ~ **force** Sicherungstruppen; ~ **form** Versicherungsformular; ~ **funds** Deckungsmittel; ~ **letter** Begleitschreiben; **to send a** ~ **letter** Begleitschreiben beigeben; ~ **note** *(fire insurance)* Deckungszusage; ~ **order** Deckungsauftrag; ~ **party** *(mil.)* Begleitkommando; ~ **position** *(mil.)* Aufnahmestellung; ~ **purchase** Deckungskauf; ~ **warrant** *(government accounting)* Deckungsverfügung, Einzahlungsanordnung.

coverside Jagdrevier, -gebiet.

covert Obdach, Versteck, Unterschlupf, Schlupfwinkel;
  feme ~ verheiratete Frau;
  ~ behavio(u)r *(psychology)* verborgenes Verhalten; **~ coat** Staubmantel.
coverture Familienstand der Ehefrau;
  under ~ in ehemännlicher Gewalt.
covetous geldgierig.
covin geheimes Einverständnis.
covision gemeinschaftliche Fernsehempfangsanlage.
cow *(v.)* **into obedience** durch Einschüchterung zum Gehorsam zwingen.
cowcatcher *(locomotive)* Bahnräumer, *(US sl.)* kurze Werbebotschaft [in einer Werbesendung], Vorspann.
coworker Mitarbeiter.
coy schüchtern, spröde, affektiert;
  ~ of speech wortkarg.
cozen *(v.)* prellen, betrügen;
  ~ s. th. out of s. o. jem etw. abschmeicheln.
cozy behaglich, gemütlich, bequem;
  to be ~ with s. o. mit jem. auf vertrautem Fuße stehen.
crab Querulant, Miesmacher;
  to turn out ~s *(sl.)* schiefgehen, mißlingen.
crabbed unleserlich.
crack Krach, Knall, *(chance, coll.)* Gelegenheit, Chance;
  ~ of doom Donner des Jüngsten Gerichts; **~ of a pistol** Pistolenschuß, -knall;
  ~ (a.) prima, erstklassig;
  ~ (v.) a bottle of wine einer Weinflasche den Hals brechen; **~ a crib** in ein Haus einbrechen; **~ down** *(US coll.)* disziplinarisch vorgehen, *(police, US)* Razzia durchführen; **~ down on s. o.** bei jem. energisch durchgreifen, j. unter die Fuchtel nehmen; **~ a safe** Geldschrank knacken; **~ up** marktschreierisch anpreisen, *(airplane)* abstürzen, Bruch machen, völlig durchdrehen, *(nervous breakdown)* Nervenzusammenbruch haben;
  to fall between the ~s of responsibility an den Nahtstellen von Verantwortungsbereichen auftreten;
  to be ~ed pleite sein; **to have a ~ at** Versuch unternehmen; **to paper over the ~s** Risse verkleben;
  ~ antiguerilla unit Eliteeinheit zur Bekämpfung von Terroristen; **~ regiment** Elitetruppe; **~ unit** Kerntruppe.
crackajack Prachtkerl, Kanone.
crackbrain Spinner, Verrückter.
crackbrained, to be einen Vogel haben;
  ~ scheme verrückter Plan.
crackdown *(US sl.)* Maßregelung;
  ~ on strikes Streikbekämpfung; **~ on tax evasion** durchgreifende Maßnahmen gegen Steuerhinterziehungen.
cracker *(sl.)* Kladderadatsch, *(firework)* Frosch, Schwärmer.
crackman Geldschrankknacker.
crackup *(airplane)* Bruchlandung, schwerer Flugzeugunfall, *(sl.)* seelischer Zusammenbruch.
cradle Wiege, *(fig.)* Anfangsstadium;
  from the ~ von Jugend an; **from ~ to grave** von der Wiege bis zur Bahre; **in the ~** in den ersten Anfängen;
  ~ of western culture Wiege der westlichen Zivilisation,
  ~ (v.) the telephone receiver Telefonhörer auflegen;
  to rock a ~ *(fig.)* Familienleben pflegen.
craft Beruf, Gewerbe, *(aircraft)* Flugzeug, *(handicraft)* Handwerk, *(ship)* Fahrzeug, *(trickery)* Kniffe, Tricks;
  by ~ durch List;
  customs ~ Zollboot; **fire-fighting ~** Feuerlöschboot; **frontier control ~** Zollkutter des Küstenschutzes; **inland waterway ~** Binnenwasserfahrzeug; **pilot ~** Lotsenboot; **police ~** Polizeiboot; **water ~** Wasserfahrzeug;
  to be one of the ~ Mann vom Fach sein; **to learn a ~** Handwerk erlernen; **to see one's frail ~ through to calmer economic waters** sein gebrechliches Staatsschiff in ruhige Konjunkturgewässer steuern;
  ~ clause Leichterklausel; **~ guild** Handwerksinnung, Zunft; **~(s) shop** Kunsthandlung; **~ show** Kunstgewerbeschau; **~ union** *(US)* Fachgewerkschaft; **amalgamated ~ union** vereinigte Fachgewerkschaft; **~ worker** Facharbeiter.
craftsman Handwerker, Gewerbetreibender, *(artisan)* Künstler;
  skilled ~ Facharbeiter;
  ~'s establishment Handwerksbetrieb; **~-made** in Handarbeit hergestellt.
craftsmanship Handwerkerstand.
craftsmaster Handwerksmeister.
cram Gewühl, Gedrängel, *(coaching)* Einpauken;
  ~ (v.) vollstopfen, an-, überfüllen, *(coach)* pauken, büffeln, ochsen;

~ a candidate Prüfling einpauken; **~ an essay with quotations** Ausarbeitung mit Zitaten spicken; **~ a lesson** Lektion pauken; **~ papers into a drawer** Papiere in eine Schublade stopfen; **~ up a subject** sich ein Thema einpauken;
  ~ course *(fam.)* Blitzkursus, -lektion; **~ shop** Presse.
crammed | with people mit Menschen überfüllt; **~ with quotations** mit Zitaten gespickt.
crammer [Ein]pauker, Repetitor.
cramming Paukerei;
  ~ establishment Presse.
cramming course Nachhilfekursus.
cramp Krampf, *(fig.)* Verkrampfung;
  writer's ~ Schreibkrampf;
  ~ (v.) s. one's progress jds. Vorankommen behindern; **~ s. one's style** jds. Entfaltungsmöglichkeiten beschneiden, jem. die Flügel stutzen.
cramped verkrampft, *(handwriting)* schwer zu lesen;
  ~ for space räumlich beengt;
  to be ~ for room an Platzmangel leiden, zusammengepfercht sein;
  ~ discomfort qualvolle Enge.
cranage Krangebühren, -geld.
crane, derrick Montagekran; **highspeed ~** Hochleistungs-, Schnellkran; **hoisting ~** Hebekran; **travelling ~** Laufkran;
  ~ driver Kranführer; **~ dues** Krangeld, -gebühren; **~ jib** Kranausleger; **~ truck** Kranwagen.
crank Kurbel, *(caprice)* fixe Idee, Manie, *(twist in speech)* Wortspiel, -verdrehung;
  ~ (v.) up Motor anwerfen, *(fig.)* ankurbeln; **~ up production** Produktion ankurbeln.
cranked up vorbereitet, startbereit.
cranking up of production Produktionsankurbelung.
crash Karambolage, Kollision, Zusammenstoß, *(airplane)* Bruchlandung, Absturz, *(banking)* Bankkrach, *(stock exchange)* Zusammenbruch, Krach;
  aircraft ~ Flugzeugabsturz; **fatal ~** Absturz mit Todesfällen; **railway ~** Eisenbahnunglück; **stock-market ~** Zusammenbruch des Aktienmarktes;
  ~ (v.) zusammenbrechen, *(airplane)* Bruchlandung machen, abstürzen, *(business)* pleite gehen, *(car)* karambolieren, kollidieren;
  ~ an aircraft Absturz eines Flugzeugs verursachen; **~ the amber** bei Gelb über die Kreuzung fahren; **~ the gate** Einlaß schinden; **~ a meeting** *(US)* sich in eine Versammlung einschmuggeln; **~ a party** *(coll.)* uneingeladen erscheinen; **~ television** Fernsehempfänger ohne Gebühr benutzen;
  ~ barrier Leitplanke; **~ boat** *(US)* Rettungsboot; **~ course** Schnellkurs; **~ diet** Blitzdiät; **~ dive** *(submarine)* Schnelltauchen; **~ finish** Papier mit Leinenstruktur; **~ halt** *(vehicle)* plötzliches Anhalten; **~ helmet** Sturzhelm; **~ job** Sofortauftrag; **~-land** *(v.)* Bruchlandung machen, abstürzen; **~ landing** Bruchlandung; **to make a ~ landing** bruchlanden; **~ language course** Intensivsprachkursus; **~ pad** Stoßdämpfer, *(sl.)* Notquartier; **~ program(me)** Blitz-, Sofort-, Notprogramm; **~ safety precautions** Unfallschutzmaßnahmen; **~ truck (wagon)** *(US)* Rettungsfahrzeug.
crate Lattenkiste, Verschlag, *(sl.)* [Flugzeug]kiste.
crater [Bomben]krater.
crawfish *(US sl.)* Ausreißer, Drückeberger.
crawl *(v.)* kriechen, schleichen, *(fig)* sich dahinschleppen, *(traffic)* kriechen;
  ~ to s. o. jem. hinten hineinkriechen;
  to be reduced to a ~ *(traffic)* nur noch dahinkriechen; **to go at a ~** sehr gemächlich gehen, langsam dahinschleichen; **to make s. one's flesh** jem. eine Gänsehaut einjagen.
crawler *(lazy person)* Faulpelz, *(servile person)* Kriecher, Speichellecker;
  ~ lane *(motorway)* Kriechspur; **~ tractor** Raupenschlepper.
crawling | in traffic verkehrsbedingtes Dahinschleichen;
  ~ floating *(exchange rates)* Stufenflexibilität; **~ peg** periodisch korrigierter Wechselkurs, stufenweise Wechselkursänderung.
crayon Zeichenstift;
  in ~ in Pastell.
crave *(v.)* **for mercy** um Gnade flehen.
craven Feigling, Memme.
craze Fimmel, fixe Idee, Manie, *(insanity)* Wahn, Geistesstörung;
  latest ~ letzter Modeschrei;
  modern ~ of holiday camps modebedingter Ferienlagerfimmel.
crazy *(dilapidated)* baufällig;
  ~ quilt Flickendecke.

cream Rahm, Sahne, *(cosmetics)* Creme, Salbe, *(substance used for polishing)* Politur, *(fig.)* Creme, Blüte, Auslese, Elite;
furniture ~ Möbelpolitur;
~ **of society** Spitzen der Gesellschaft, obere Zehntausend; ~ **of a story** Pointe einer Geschichte;
~ *(v.)* **away (off) profits** Gewinne abschöpfen; ~ **off traffic** Verkehr aufnehmen;
~ **campaign** Werbefeldzug im erfolgversprechendsten Gebiet;
~ **plan** *(advertising)* Ansprache der Zielgruppen.
creamery Molkerei, Milchladen.
crease *(paper)* Eselsohr.
creaser *(bookbinding)* Rückenstempel.
create *(v.)* schaffen, gründen, ins Leben rufen, *(fashion, theater)* kreieren;
~ **capital goods** Kapitalgüter schaffen; ~ **a charter** Satzung geben; ~ **a corporation** *(US)* Gesellschaft gründen; ~ **a demand** Bedarf hervorrufen; ~ **a disturbance** Auflauf verursachen; ~ **an Earl** in den Grafenstand erheben; ~ **a fashion** Mode einführen; ~ **a favo(u)rable public opinion** günstige Aufnahme in der Öffentlichkeit erzielen; ~ **a fee simple** Lehen gewähren; ~ **new forms of life** neue Lebensformen hervorrufen; ~ **a bad impression** schlechten Eindruck hinterlassen; ~ **an industry** Industriezweig ins Leben rufen; ~ **interests** Ansprüche begründen; ~ **new jobs** neue Arbeitsplätze beschaffen; ~ **legal relations** Rechtsbeziehungen herstellen; ~ **liability** Haftung begründen; ~ **money** Geld schöpfen; ~ **a mortgage** Hypothek bestellen; ~ **a scandal** Skandal auslösen; ~ **social unrest** soziale Unruhen hervorrufen; ~ **a trust** Treuhandverhältnis begründen; ~ **a new want** neues Bedürfnis erwecken.
creation Schaffung, Gründung, *(Br.)* Erneuerung, *(fashion, theater)* Kreierung, Kreation, *(thing created)* Werk, Schöpfung;
latest ~s *(fashion)* neueste Modeschöpfungen;
~ **of an agency** Begründung eines Vertreterverhältnisses; ~ **of bank credit (deposits)** Kredit-, Giralgeldschöpfung; ~ **of a charge** Grundschuldbestellung; ~ **of currency** Geldschöpfung; ~ **of dwellings** Errichtung von Wohnungen; ~ **of interests** Anspruchbegründung; ~ **of new jobs** Schaffung neuer Arbeitsplätze, Arbeitsplatzbeschaffung; ~ **of two additional judges** Ernennung zweier weiterer Richter; ~ **of liability** Haftungsentstehung; ~ **of licence** Begründung eines Nutzungsrechtes; ~ **of means of payments** Giralgeld-, Zahlungsmittelschöpfung; ~ **of money** Geldschöpfung; ~ **of a mortgage** Hypothekenbestellung; ~ **of mortgages over ships** Schiffshypothekenbestellung; ~ **of an obligation** Begründung eines Schuldverhältnisses; ~ **of Peers** Ernennung von Lords; ~ **of reserves** Rücklagenbildung, Bildung von Rücklagen; ~ **of new resources** Erschließung neuer Hilfsquellen; ~ **of a trust** Treuhanderrichtung, Errichtung einer Stiftung; ~ **of a trust by will** testamentarische Treuhanderrichtung; ~ **of social unrest** Hervorrufung sozialer Unruhen; ~ **of value** Wertschöpfung; ~ **of a new want** Erweckung eines neuen Bedürfnisses; ~ **of work** Arbeitsbeschaffung;
to cost like all ~ *(coll.)* Heidengeld kosten.
creative schöpferisch, gestaltlich, gestaltend, kreativ;
to be ~ of suspicion Verdacht erregen;
~ **artist** Gestalter; ~ **copy** außergewöhnlicher Werbetext; ~ **copy and art work** Anzeigengestaltung; ~ **director** künstlerischer Leiter einer Werbeagentur; ~ **mind** schöpferischer Geist; ~ **power** Schöpferkraft; ~ **thought** kreatives Denken, schöpferische Denkweise; ~ **work** Gestaltung[sarbeit]; ~ **writing** Schriftstellertätigkeit.
creativeness, creativity schöpferische Kraft, Produktivität.
creator Schöpfer, Urheber;
~ **of wealth** Vermögensbegründer.
creature Geschöpf, Werkzeug, Günstling, *(animal, US)* Haustier;
~ **of circumstances** Opfer der Verhältnisse; **mere ~ of a dictator** willenloses Werkzeug eines Diktators; ~ **of the government** Regierungsspitzel; ~ **of habit** Gewohnheitstier; ~ **of impulse** Gefühlsmensch;
~ **comforts** materielle Annehmlichkeiten.
creche *(Br.)* Kinderkrippe, -hort, Kleinkinderbewahranstalt.
credence Glaubwürdigkeit;
to give ~ to gossip dem Gerede Glauben schenken.
credentialled mit Vollmachten ausgestattet.
credentials *(certificate)* Zeugnis, *(diplomacy)* Beglaubigungsschreiben, *(reference)* Empfehlungsschreiben, Referenzen;
to bear highest ~ erstklassige (prima) Referenzen haben; **to present one's ~s** sein Beglaubigungsschreiben überreichen; **to verify the ~ of a delegate** Vollmachten eines Delegierten überprüfen;
~ **committee** Vollmachtenprüfungsausschuß.

credibility Glaubwürdigkeit;
~ **of a witness** Glaubhaftigkeit eines Zeugen;
to establish one's ~ Glaubwürdigkeit erringen;
~ **gap** Mangel an Glaubwürdigkeit, Vertrauensschwund; ~ **test** Analyse der Glaubwürdigkeit.
credible *(witness)* glaubhaft, glaubwürdig;
~ **person** verläßliche Person.
credibly informed glaubhaft unterrichtet.
credit Kredit, Darlehn, *(broadcasting, film)* Einzelaufführung [eines Schauspielers], *(credit side of account)* Haben, Entlastung, *(income tax, US)* abzugsfähiger Betrag, Anrechnung, Freibetrag, *(published information)* Quellenhinweis, -angabe, *(letter of credit)* Akkreditiv, Kreditbrief, *(Br., pol.)* Vorgriff auf das Budget, Haushaltsvorgriff, *(reputation for solvency)* [kaufmännischer] Kredit, Kreditwürdigkeit, Bonität, *(repute)* guter Ruf, Ansehen, Verdienst, *(school certificate, university, US)* Anrechnungspunkt, Abgangszeugnis, *(sum placed at disposal)* Guthaben, Gutschrift, Habensaldo, *(trustworthiness)* Glaubwürdigkeit, Zuverlässigkeit;
at three months' ~ Ziel gegen drei Monate; **by raising a ~** auf dem Kreditwege; **for short ~** auf kurzen Termin; **for using ~** zur Inanspruchnahme des Kredits; **of the highest ~** in höchstem Ansehen; **to s. one's ~** zu jds. Gunsten; **to the ~ of my account** zugunsten meines Kontos; **unworthy of ~** unglaubwürdig; **upon (on) ~** Kredit, Zeit, Ziel); **without ~** kreditlos; **worthy of ~** kreditwürdig;
acceptance ~ Akzeptkredit; **additional ~** Zusatzkredit; **agricultural ~** landwirtschaftlicher Kredit, Agrarkredit; **agricultural short-term ~** *(Br.)* kurzfristiger Agrarkredit; **anticipatory ~** *(Br.)* Versandbereitstellungskredit, Akkreditivvorschuß; **armament ~** *(Br.)* Rüstungskredit; **auxiliary ~** Unterakkreditiv; **back-to-back ~** *(US)* Gegenakkreditiv; **bank ~** Bankkredit; **blank ~** Blankokredit; **book ~** Buchkredit; **clean ~** nicht dokumentarisch gesicherter Trassierungskredit; **collateral ~** *(US)* gedeckter (gesicherter) Kredit, Lombardkredit; **commercial ~** Bank-, Warenkredit, Bankrembours; **confirmed ~** *(Br.)* bestätigter Kredit; **consumer ~** Abzahlungskredit; **short-term consumer ~** kurzfristiger Kundenkredit; **counter ~** Unterakkreditiv; **countervailing ~** Gegenakkreditiv; **covered ~** besicherter Kredit; **creative ~** schöpferischer Kredit; **declined ~** abgelehnter Kredit[antrag]; **deferred ~s [to income]** *(US)* transitorische Passiva; **deferred-payment ~** *(US)* Teil-, Raten-, Abzahlungskredit; **divisible ~** teilbares Akkreditiv; **document ~** Kreditbrief mit Dokumenten; **documentary ~** Rembours-, Dokumentenkredit; **dollar ~** Dollarkredit; **domestic ~** *(US)* Einfuhr-, Importkredit; **draft ~** Rembourskredit; **earned-income ~** *(US)* Steuerfreibetrag für Einkünfte aus gewerblicher Tätigkeit; **easier ~** billigerer Kredit; **erroneous ~s** irrige Gutschriften; **established ~** festbegründeter Ruf; **exchange ~** Devisenkredit; **export ~** Ausfuhr-, Exportkredit; **extended ~** prolongierter Kredit; **first-rate ~** erstrangiger Kredit; **fixed-interest ~** Festsatzkredit; **foreign ~** Auslandskredit; **fresh ~** neu aufgenommener Kredit; **frozen ~** eingefrorener Kredit; **global ~** Rahmenkredit; **government ~** Staatskredit; **government-backed ~** staatsverbürgter Kredit; **guaranteed ~** bestätigter Kredit; **hire-purchase ~** *(Br.)* Teil-, Raten-, Abzahlungskredit; **holdover ~** Überbrückungskredit; **impaired ~** beeinträchtigter Ruf; **import ~** Einfuhr-, Importkredit; **industrial ~** Industriekredit; **instalment ~** Ab-, Raten-, Teilzahlungskredit; **interim ~** Zwischen-, Überbrückungskredit; **intermediate ~** Zwischenkredit; **investment ~** Anlagekredit; **irrevocable ~** unkündbares Akkreditiv; **joint ~** Konsortialkredit; **land ~** Grundstückskredit; **limited ~** begrenzter Kredit; **local ~** örtlicher Kredit, Platzkredit; **long[-term] ~** langfristiger Kredit; **low-interest ~** Kredit zu niedrigem Zinssatz; **medium-term commercial ~** mittelfristiger Warenkredit; **mercantile ~** Warenkredit; **a month's ~** monatlicher (monatlich eingeräumter) Kredit; **municipal ~** Kommunalkredit; **mutual ~s** gegenseitige Gutschriften; **~ needed** Kreditbedarf; **negotiable ~** begebbares Akkreditiv; **offset ~** Verrechnungskredit; **open ~** offener (ungedeckter) Kredit, Blankokredit, Kontokorrentkredit, *(Br.)* nicht dokumentarisch gesicherter Trassierungskredit; **open-book ~** laufender Buchkredit; **operational ~** Betriebsmittelkredit; **overdrawn ~** überzogener Kredit; **overnight ~** *(banking)* Tagesgeld; **packing ~** *(Br.)* Akkreditivvorschuß, Versandbereitstellungskredit; **paper ~** offener Wechselkredit; **permanent ~** Dauerakkreditiv; **personal ~** Personalkredit; **poor ~** schwacher Kredit; **private ~** Personalkredit; **producer's ~** Produzentenkredit; **production ~** Produktionskredit; **public ~** öffentliches Ansehen; **pump-priming ~** Förderungskredit; **real-estate ~** Immobiliar-, Grundstückskredit; **reconstruction ~** Wiederaufbaukredit;

recoverable ~ widerrufliches Akkreditiv; **rediscount** ~ Rediskontkredit; **refinanceable** ~ refinanzierbarer Kredit; **reserve bank** ~ *(US)* [etwa] Kassenkredit bei der Landeszentralbank; **retail** ~ Konsumptivkredit; **retail book** ~ Kundenkredit des Kaufmanns; **revocable** ~ widerrufliches Akkreditiv; **revolving** ~ revolvierender (sich automatisch erneuernder, wiederauflebender) Kredit; **roll-over** ~ kurzfristig finanzierter langfristiger Kredit; **secondary** ~ *(US)* Gegenakkreditiv; **secured** ~ besicherter Kredit; **short-term** ~ kurzfristiger Kredit, *(suppliers)* Lieferantenkredit; **small** ~ schwacher Kredit; **social** ~ Sozialkredit; **stand-by** ~ Bereitschaftskredit, Kredit-, Darlehnszusage; **standing** ~ laufender Kredit; **starting** ~ Anlaufkredit; **stopgap** ~ Überbrückungskredit; **storage** ~ Kredit auf eingelagerte Waren; **store** ~ *(US)* kurzfristiger Kundenkredit, Anschreibenlassen beim Kaufmann; **straight** ~ normales Akkreditiv; **supplementary** ~ Ergänzungskredit; **supplier's** ~ Lieferantenkredit; **syndicated** ~ von einem Konsortium gewährter Kredit, Konsortialkredit; **tax** ~ *(US)* Steuergutschrift, -freibetrag, -vergünstigung; **temporary** ~ Zwischenkredit; **thirty days'** ~ dreißig Tage Ziel; **three months'** ~ drei Monate Ziel (dato); **tied** ~ projektgebundener Kredit; **tight** ~ restriktive Kreditwirtschaft; **total** ~ **extended** Kreditvolumen insgesamt; **trade** ~ Lieferantenkredit; **transferable** ~ *(US)* teilbares Akkreditiv; **transmitted** ~ durchgeleiteter Kredit; **uncovered** ~ ungedeckter Kredit; **unconfirmed** ~ *(Br.)* widerruflicher (unbestätigter, offener) Kredit, unbestätigtes Akkreditiv; **unimpaired** ~ ungeschmälerter Ruf; **unlimited** ~ unbegrenzter Kredit; **unsecured** ~ ungedeckter Kredit; **untied** ~ projektfreier Kredit; **unused** ~ nicht benötigter (nicht in Anspruch genommener) Kredit; **used** ~ in Anspruch genommener Kredit; **wholesale** ~ Großhandelskredit; **working capital** ~ Betriebsmittelkredit;
~ **in current account** Kredit in laufender Rechnung, Kontokorrentkredit; ~ **on joint account** Metakredit; ~ **in the invisible balance** Leistungsbilanzguthaben; ~ **at the bank** Bankguthaben; ~ **with a savings bank** Sparkassenguthaben; ~ **in blank** Blankokredit; ~s **falling into the budget** haushaltsrechtlich genehmigte Kredite; ~ **on call** kündbarer Kredit; ~ **against collateral** *(US)* Kredit gegen Sicherheiten; ~ **and debit** Soll und Haben; ~ **for dependents** *(US)* Steuerfreibeträge für Familienangehörige; ~ **to one's family** Pluspunkt (Aushängeschild) für seine Familie; ~ **on real estate** Immobilien-, Realkredit; ~ **to be carried forward to profit and loss account** auf Gewinn- und Verlustkonto vorzutragender Kreditsaldo; ~ **of the firm** Geschäftskredit; ~ **given flat** zinslos gewährter Kredit; ~ **on goods** Warenkredit; ~ **by way of guarantee** Avalkredit; ~s **for imports** Importkredite; ~ **granted for improvement** Meliorationskredit; ~ **within the limit of** ... Kredit bis zur Höhe von ...; ~ **on mortgage** hypothekarisch gesicherter Kredit; ~ **on landed property** Immobiliarkredit; ~ **with a savings bank** Sparkassenguthaben; ~ **against securities** Lombardkredit; ~ **granted by suppliers** Lieferantenkredit; ~ **in use** in Anspruch genommener Kredit;
~ *(v.)* im Haben buchen, *(enter sum on credit side of account)* gutschreiben, *(grant credit)* kreditieren, [auf] Kredit geben, [ver]borgen, [ver]leihen;
~ **an account** Konto erkennen, einem Konto gutschreiben; ~ **in account** Rechnung kreditieren; ~ **by balance** per Saldo gutschreiben; ~ **£ 10 to a customer** einem Kunden 10 Pfund gutschreiben; ~ **a bad debt** faule Schuld streichen; ~ **an employee on the company books with shares of stock** einem Angestelltenkonto Unternehmensaktien gutschreiben; ~ **the proceeds to an account** Gegenwert einem Konto gutschreiben; ~ **a story** einer Geschichte Glaubwürdigkeit beimessen; ~ **s. o. with s. th.** jem. etw. zuschreiben; ~ **s. o. with three hours** *(university, US)* jem. für einen Kursus drei Punkte anrechnen; ~ **s. o. with a sum** jem. einen Betrag gutschreiben, j. für einen Kredit entlasten; ~ **taxes** *(double taxation)* Steuern anrechnen;
to add to s. one's ~ jds. Ansehen steigern; **to affect the** ~ Kredit erschüttern; **to allow a** ~ Kredit bewilligen; **to allow a** ~ **not beyond a certain figure** Kredit nur in einem beschränkten Rahmen gewähren; **to appear in s. one's** ~ jem. gutgeschrieben werden; **to apply for a** ~ Kreditgesuch einreichen; **to ask for larger** ~s höhere Kredite in Anspruch nehmen; **to be in** ~ **at the bank** Bankkredit haben; **to be out of (without)** ~ keinen Kredit haben; **to be sufficiently in** ~ ausreichenden Habensaldo aufweisen; **to be a** ~ **to one's school** seiner Schule alle Ehre machen; **to be in high** ~ **with one's colleagues** von seinen Kollegen voll respektiert werden; **to be to the** ~ **of the party in power** auf das Konto der Regierungspartei gehen; **to buy on** ~ auf Kredit (Borg, Rechnung) kaufen; **to call in a** ~ Kredit kündi-

gen; **to cancel a** ~ Akkreditiv annullieren; **to carry an article to s. one's** ~ j. für einen Posten erkennen; **to carry no** ~ *(course)* nicht angerechnet werden; **to check a** ~ Kredit prüfen; **to clamp down on** ~s Kreditbremse zur Anwendung bringen; **to confirm a** ~ Akkreditiv bestätigen; **to contract** ~ Kreditmittel (Kreditmöglichkeiten) einschränken; **to create** ~ Kredit schöpfen; **to curtail** ~s Kredite verkürzen; **to deal in** ~s Kredite gewähren (vergeben); **to deserve** ~ Anerkennung verdienen; **to eat up a** ~ Kredit aufbrauchen; **to enjoy unlimited** ~ unbegrenzten Kredit genießen; **to enjoy** ~ **to the extent of a certain amount with s. o.** jem. für eine bestimmte Summe gut sein; **to enter a sum to s. one's** ~ jds. Konto einen Betrag gutschreiben; **to establish a** ~ Akkreditiv erstellen; **to establish a** ~ **with s. o.** Kredit bei jem. eröffnen; **to exceed a** ~ Kreditlinie überschreiten; **to expand** ~ Kreditmöglichkeit erweitern; **to extend a** ~ Kreditverlängerung gewähren; **to forfeit one's** ~ seinen Kredit verlieren; **to furnish with** ~ Kredit verschaffen (gewähren); **to give** ~ Kredit geben; **to give s. o.** ~ **for s. th.** jem. etw. hoch anrechnen; **to give s. o.** ~ **for hundred pounds** jem. einen Kredit in Höhe von hundert Pfund geben (gewähren) **to give** ~ **to a report** einem Bericht Glauben schenken; **to give s. o. a bank** ~ jem. einen Bankkredit einräumen; **to give very short** ~ nur sehr kurzfristigen Kredit gewähren; **to go among the** ~s auf der Habenseite zu verbuchen sein; **to go into** ~ kreditorisch werden, ins Haben kommen; **to grant a** ~ Kredit bewilligen (einräumen); **to grant a** ~ **by overdraft** Überziehungskredit gewähren; **to have great** ~ **with s. o.** großen Einfluß bei jem. haben; **to have** ~ **with a bank** über Kreditfazilitäten bei einer Bank verfügen; **to increase a** ~ Kredit erhöhen; **to lay up** ~s Kredit einfrieren lassen; **to lend** ~ **to the earlier reports** frühere Berichte anscheinend bestätigen; **to liberalize** ~ Kreditbedingungen erleichtern; **to lose one's** ~ **with the public** öffentliche Glaubwürdigkeit verlieren; **to make** ~ **available** Kreditmittel bereitstellen; **to make** ~ **easier** Krediterleichterungen einführen; **to obtain** ~ **at a bank** Bankkredit eingeräumt erhalten; **to obtain** ~ **by false pretences** Kreditbetrug begehen; **to obtain** ~ **by fraud** sich Kredit erschleichen, Kreditbetrug begehen; **to open a** ~ Kreditlinie eröffnen; **to outrun one's** ~ seinen Kredit überziehen; **to overdraw a** ~ Kredit überziehen; **to pass (place) an article to s. one's** ~ jem. für einen Posten erkennen; **to pass to the** ~ Gutschrift erteilen; **to pay in a sum to s. one's** ~ Betrag auf jds. Konto einzahlen; **to place an amount to s. one's** ~ jem. einen Betrag gutschreiben; **to place the proceeds to the** ~ **of an account** Gegenwert einem Konto gutschreiben; **to pledge one's husband's** ~ auf Kredit des Mannes einkaufen; **to pledge the husband's** ~ **for necessaries** [etwa] Schlüsselgewalt ausüben; **to provide with** ~ Kredit verschaffen; **to pump up** ~ Kreditapparat auf Schwung bringen; **to put a sum to s. one's** ~ jds. Konto einen Betrag gutschreiben; **to raise** ~ Kredit aufnehmen; **to receive upon** ~ auf Kredit erhalten; **to reduce a** ~ Kredit einschränken; **to reestablish a firm's** ~ Kredit eines Unternehmens wiederherstellen; **to reflect** ~ **on s. o.** jem. zur Ehre gereichen; **to refuse further** ~ weitere Kreditwünsche abschlägig bescheiden; **to repay a** ~ Kredit zurückzahlen (abdecken); **to respond for a** ~ für einen Kredit einstehen; **to restrict a** ~ Kredit einschränken; **to scale** ~s Kredite nach ihrer Größenordnung aufführen; **to sell on** ~ auf Kredit verkaufen, kreditieren; **to strain one's** ~ seinen Kredit überziehen (überschreiten); **to stretch** ~ Kredit überziehen; **to take a** ~ Kredit in Anspruch nehmen; **to take** ~ **for s. th. to o. s.** sich etw. als Verdienst anrechnen; **to take a course for five** ~s *(US)* Lehrgang mit fünf Anrechnungspunkten belegen; **to tap new sources of** ~ neue Kreditquellen erschließen; **to tighten** ~s Kreditschraube anziehen; **to undermine** ~ Kredit untergraben; **to use a** ~ Kredit in Anspruch nehmen; **to vote** ~s **in instal(l)ments** Kredit sukzessive bewilligen; **to withdraw a** ~ Kreditangebot zurückziehen; **to withhold a** ~ Kreditgesuch abschlägig bescheiden, keinen Kredit gewähren;
~ **abuse** Kreditmißbrauch; ~ **accommodation** Kreditgewährung, -fazilität.
credit account kreditorisch geführtes Konto, *(store)* Anschreibkonto;
to close a ~ kreditorisch geführtes Konto kündigen; **to open a** ~ **with s. o.** sich Kredit einräumen lassen; **to open a** ~ **in s. one's favo(u)r** Kredit zu jds. Gunsten eröffnen.
credit | advice Gutschriftsanzeige, -aufgabe; **to send a** ~ **advice** Gutschriftsanzeige erteilen; ~ **agency** Kreditvermittlungsbüro, *(~ bureau)* Kreditauskunftei; ~ **agency report** Kreditauskunft; ~ **agreement** Kreditabkommen, -vereinbarung; **standby** ~ **agreement** für Investitionszwecke im voraus vereinbarte langfristige Kreditzusage; ~ **allocation** Kreditkontingentierung; ~ **analysis** Kreditprüfung; ~ **analyst** Kreditfachmann,

-prüfer; ~ **applicant** Kreditantragsteller; ~ **application** Kreditgesuch, -antrag; ~ **application form** Kreditantragsformular; ~ **approval** Kreditzusage, -genehmigung; ~ **arrangement** Kreditabkommen, -vereinbarung; ~ **association** Kreditgenossenschaft; ~ **authorization** Kreditgenehmigung.

credit balance Guthaben, Haben-, Aktivsaldo, Habenposten, *(balance of payments)* aktive Zahlungsbilanz;
~ **maintained** unterhaltenes Guthaben; **your** ~ Saldo zu Ihren Gunsten;
~ **with other banks** *(balance sheet)* Nostroguthaben; ~ **to be carried forward on profit and loss account** auf Gewinn- und Verlustkonto vorzutragender Kreditsaldo.

credit| bank *(Br.)* Kreditanstalt, -bank, -institut; ~ **bank balance** Bankguthaben, Guthabensaldo; ~ **basis** monetäre Basis; ~ **bill** Kreditwechsel; ~ **blotter** *(stock exchange)* Gutschriftskladde; ~ **brake** Kreditbremse, -restriktion; ~ **bureau** Kreditauskunftei; **retail** ~ **bureau** Einzelhandelskreditauskunftei; ~ **business** Kreditgewerbe; ~ **buying** Kreditkauf; ~ **candidate** Kreditsucher; ~ **capacity** Kreditfähigkeit; ~ **card** Kreditkarte; ~ **card charges** Kreditkartengebühr; ~ **card holder** Kreditkartenbesitzer, -inhaber; ~ **card network** Kreditkartennetz; ~ **card organizer** Kreditkartenausgabestelle; ~ **card service** Kreditkartensystem; ~ **checking** Überprüfung der Kreditfähigkeit, Bonitäts-, Kreditprüfung; ~ **checking service** Bonitätsprüfungssystem; ~ **circulation** Papiergeldumlauf; ~ **Clearing House** *(US)* Vermittlungsstelle für Kreditauskünfte; ~ **column** *(newspaper)* Anerkennungsspalte; ~ **commitment** Kreditengagement; ~ **committee** Kreditausschuß; ~ **conditions** Kreditbedingungen; ~ **contraction** Kreditbeschränkung; ~ **control** staatliche Kreditregulierung, Kreditüberwachung; ~ **control authority** Kreditüberwachungsstelle; ~ **cooperative** Kreditgenossenschaft; **agricultural** ~ **cooperative** landwirtschaftliche Kreditbank; ~ **corporation** Darlehnsgesellschaft; ~ **cost** Kreditkosten; ~ **coupon plan** bargeldloses Verkaufssystem; ~ **crisis** Kreditkrise; ~ **crunch** Kreditverknappung; ~ **crunches** Kreditzügel; ~ **currency** Buch-, Giralgeld; ~ **customer** Kreditkunde; ~ **dealings** Geschäftsabschlüsse mit Kreditgewährung; ~ **decision** Kreditentschluß; ~ **deflation** Kreditdeflation; ~ **demand** Kreditbedarf; ~ **department** Darlehnsabteilung; ~ **devices** Krediteinrichtungen; ~ **economy** Kreditwirtschaft; ~ **element** Kreditfaktor; ~ **enquiry** *(Br.)* Anfrage über die Kreditfähigkeit, Auskunft; ~ **enquiry agency** Kreditauskunftei; ~ **entry** Habenbuchung, Gutschrift; ~ **expansion** Kreditausweitung; ~ **expense** Kreditkosten; ~ **expert** Bank-, Kreditfachmann; ~ **extension** Kreditausweitung, -expansion; ~ **facilities** Kreditfazilitäten, -apparat; **to grant a firm** ~ **facilities** einer Firma Kreditfazilitäten zur Verfügung stellen; ~ **field** Kreditgewerbe; ~ **files** Kreditunterlagen, -registratur; ~ **folder** Kreditakte; ~ **foncier** Bodenkreditbank; ~ **form** *(US)* Kreditvordruck; ~ **granting** Krediteinräumung; ~ **grantor** Kreditgeber; ~ **guarantee** Kreditbürgschaft; ~ **guarantee package** ganzes Bündel kreditverbürgender Maßnahmen; ~ **hour** *(US)* anrechenbare Vorlesungsstunde; ~ **inflation** inflationistische Kreditausdehnung, übermäßige Kreditausweitung; ~ **information** Kreditauskunft; ~ **information department** Kreditinformationsabteilung; ~ **inquiry** *(US)* Bitte um Kreditauskunft; ~ **institution** Kreditinstitut; **publicly owned** ~ **institution** öffentlichrechtliches Kreditinstitut; ~ **instruction** Akkreditivauftrag; ~ **instrument** Kreditinstrumentarium, Finanzierungsmittel; ~ **insurance** Kreditversicherung; ~ **insurance policy** Kreditversicherungspolice; ~ **insurer** Kreditversicherungsgesellschaft; ~ **interchange** gegenseitige Kreditauskunft; ~ **interchange bureau** *(US)* Austauschstelle über Kreditinformationen; ~ **interest** Habenzinsen; ~ **investigation** Kreditwürdigkeitsprüfung; ~ **investigator** Kreditprüfer; ~ **invisible balance** positive Leistungsbilanz; ~ **item** Guthabenposten, Gutschrift; ~ **letter** Kreditbrief; ~ **limit** *(Br.)* Kreditgrenze, -linie, -rahmen, -marge; **to place a** ~ **limit on an account** *(Br.)* Kreditlinie für ein Konto festsetzen; **to run over the** ~ **limit** *(Br.)* eingeräumten Kredit überziehen.

credit line *(US)* Kreditrahmen, Kreditlinie, -marge, Höhe eines Kredits;
unused ~ *(US)* nicht ausgenutzte Kreditlinie;
to apply for a ~ *(US)* Kreditantrag stellen; **to establish a** ~ *(US)* Kreditlinie für ein Konto festsetzen; **to increase a** ~ *(US)* Kredit[linie] erhöhen; **to open a** ~ *(US)* Kreditlinie eröffnen; **to run a** ~ *(US)* Kreditlinie offenhalten; **to run over the** ~ *(US)* Kreditlinie überschreiten.

credit| list Liste der kreditfähigen Kunden; ~ **loss** Kreditausfall; ~ **machinery** Kreditmechanismus; ~ **man** *(US)* Kreditbearbeiter; ~ **management** Kreditverwaltung; ~ **manager** Leiter der Kreditabteilung; ~ **margin** Kreditmarge; ~ **market** Kreditmarkt; **to draw heavily on the** ~ **market** Kreditmärkte heftig in Anspruch nehmen; ~ **mechanism** Kreditmechanismus; ~ **memorandum** *(US)* Gutschrift[anzeige], -zettel, Einzahlungsbeleg; ~ **mobilier** Effektenkreditanstalt; ~ **money** Buch-, Giralgeld; ~ **multiplier** Giralgeldschöpfungsmultiplikator; ~ **needs** Kreditbedürfnisse, -ansprüche; ~ **note** Gutschrift[anzeige], -mitteilung; ~ **offer** Kreditangebot; ~ **operations** Kreditgeschäft; **inflated** ~ **operations** Überspannung des Kredits; ~ **operative** Kreditgenossenschaft; ~ **order** Kreditauftrag; ~ **organization** *(US)* Kreditorganisation; ~ **package** gebündeltes Kreditangebot; **to arrange for a** ~ **package** umfassendes Kreditangebot sicherstellen; ~ **period** Laufzeit eines Kredits; ~ **policy** Kreditpolitik; **restrictive** ~ **policy** restriktive Kreditpolitik; ~ **policy measures** kreditpolitische Maßnahmen; ~ **portfolio** Kreditportefeuille; ~ **position** Kreditwürdigkeit; ~ **poverty** unzureichendes Kreditangebot; ~ **principles** Kreditgrundsätze; ~ **private account** privates Kreditkonto; ~ **purchase** Kreditkauf; ~ **rate** Habenzinssatz; ~ **rating** *(US)* Kreditunterlagenprüfung, Einschätzung der Kreditwürdigkeit, Bonitätsbeurteilung, -prüfung; **to give s. o. a high** ~ **rating for competence** *(US)* jem. erfolgreichen Befähigungsnachweis zuerkennen; ~ **rating book** *(US)* Kreditwürdigkeitsliste; ~ **ratio** *(US)* Verhältnis von Eigen- zu Fremdkapital; ~ **rationing** *(US)* Kreditrationierung, -beschränkung; ~ **report** Kreditauskunft, -information; ~ **report on file** Dossierinformation; ~ **reporting agency** Handels-, Kreditauskunftei; ~ **request** Kreditgesuch; ~ **requirements** Kreditbedarf, -bedürfnis; ~ **reserve** nicht in Anspruch genommener Kreditteil; ~ **resources** Kreditquellen, -mittel, -möglichkeiten; ~ **restraint** Kreditrestriktion, -bremse; ~ **restriction** Kreditdrosselung, -beschränkung, -restriktion; ~ **returns account** Aufgabe einer Gutschriftsstornierung; ~ **risk** Kreditrisiko; **to appraise a** ~ **risk** Kreditrisiko abschätzen; **to assume the** ~ **risk** Kreditrisiko (Delkredere) übernehmen; ~ **risk insurance** Kreditrisikoversicherung; ~ **robbery** Kreditbetrug; ~ **rules** Kreditrichtlinien; ~ **sale** Kreditverkauf, Verkauf auf Kreditbasis; ~ **sales on open accounts** Kreditverkäufe in offener Rechnung; ~ **sale agreement** *(Br.)* Abzahlungs-, Ratenzahlungsvertrag [für fünf und mehr Raten]; ~ **service charge** Kreditgebühr; ~ **service organization** Kreditauskunftsverband; **general** ~ **shares** Finanzaktien; ~ **shipment** kreditierte Warensendung; ~ **shopping** Kreditkäufe; ~ **side** Habenseite; **to be on the** ~ **side** Guthaben haben; ~ **situation** kreditpolitische Situation; ~ **slip** *(Br.)* Einzahlungsbeleg, Bon, Gutschein; ~ **society** *(Br.)* Darlehnsverein; ~ **solvency** Bonität; ~ **squeeze** Kreditverknappung, -restriktion, -schraube; ~ **standing (status)** Kreditfähigkeit, -würdigkeit, -status, kaufmännischer Ruf, Bonität; ~ **standards** Kreditnormen, -richtlinien; **to shade** ~ **standards** Kreditaufnahme erleichtern; ~ **statement** Kreditauskunft; ~ **strain** Kreditanspannung; ~ **stretching** langfristige Kreditgewährung; ~ **stringency** Kreditknappheit; ~ **structure** Kreditgefüge, -struktur; ~ **suggestion** Kreditvorschlag; ~ **supply** Kreditbeschaffung, -versorgung; ~ **surplus** Aktivüberschuß; ~ **system** Kreditwesen; **to open the** ~ **tap** Kredithahn aufdrehen; ~ **terms** Kreditbedingungen; **to buy on** ~ **terms** im Kreditwege erwerben; **to grant** ~ **terms to s. o.** jem. Waren auf Kredit liefern; ~ **ticket** *(banking system)* Gutschriftsbeleg; ~ **tightness** Kreditverknappung; ~ **transactions** Kreditgeschäftsverkehr; **open-market** ~ **transactions** Transaktionen der offenen Marktpolitik; ~ **transfer** bargeldlose Überweisung, Überweisung zu Lasten des Kreditkontos; ~ **union** Kreditgarantiegemeinschaft, *(cooperative organization, US)* Kreditgenossenschaft, *(people's bank)* Volksbank; ~ **use** Kreditinanspruchnahme; ~ **volume** Kreditvolumen; ~ **vote** Krediteinräumung; **to pass a** ~ **vote** Kreditgesuch bewilligen; ~ **voucher** Einzahlungsbeleg; ~ **work** Kreditbearbeitung; ~ **worthiness** Kreditwürdigkeit; ~-**worthy** kreditwürdig; ~ **year** Jahr der Laufzeit eines Kredits.

creditability Kreditfähigkeit, Vertrauenswürdigkeit.

creditable kreditfähig, solide, zuverlässig;
~ **attempt** ehrenwerter Versuch.

credited, to be kreditiert sein;
~ **to s. one's account** jds. Konto gutgeschrieben;
~ **amounts** kreditierte Beträge.

crediting Gutschrift, Kreditierung;
~ **of interest** Zinsgutschrift.

creditor Gläubiger, Kreditor, Forderungsberechtigter, *(credit side)* Habenseite;
for the purpose of paying the ~**s** zur Befriedigung der Gläubiger;
~**s** *(balance sheet)* Kreditoren, Verbindlichkeiten;

antecedent ~ Gläubiger einer vor [verschleiernder] Vermögensübertragung entstandenen Forderung; **assenting ~s** zustimmender Gläubiger; **attaching ~** pfändender Gläubiger, Pfändungsgläubiger, Arrest-, Vollstreckungsgläubiger; **bankruptcy ~** Konkursgläubiger; **bill ~** Wechselgläubiger; **bond ~** Pfandbriefgläubiger; **book ~** buchmäßig festgestellter Gläubiger; **catholic ~** erstklassig (dinglich) gesicherter Gläubiger; **certificate ~** *(municipal accounting)* Schuldscheininhaber; **confidential ~** zu vertrauensseliger Kreditgeber; **corporate ~** *(US)* Gesellschaftsgläubiger; **debtor and ~** Debet und Kredit; **deferred ~** *(bankruptcy)* den gewöhnlichen Konkursgläubigern nachstehender Gläubiger; **dissatisfied ~** unbefriedigt gebliebener Gläubiger; **dissenting ~** nicht zustimmender Gläubiger; **domestic ~** inländischer Gläubiger; **double[-secured] ~** doppelt gesicherter Gläubiger; **executing (execution) ~** Vollstreckung betreibender (pfändender) Gläubiger, Vollstreckungsgläubiger; **executor ~** Nachlaßgläubiger mit dem Recht der Nachlaßverwaltung; **existing ~** hypothekarisch gesicherter Gläubiger; **fellow ~** Mitgläubiger; **foreign ~** Auslandsgläubiger; **general ~** einfacher Konkursgläubiger, Massegläubiger; **individual ~** persönlicher Gläubiger [eines Gesellschafters]; **joint ~** Gesamtgläubiger; **judgment ~** Vollstreckungsgläubiger; **junior ~** nachrangiger Gläubiger; **lien ~** Pfandgläubiger; **mercantile ~** berufsmäßiger Geldverleiher; **mortgage ~** hypothekarisch gesicherter Gläubiger, Hypothekeninhaber; **nonassenting ~** [einem Vergleich] nicht zustimmender Gläubiger; **nonprivileged ~** Massegläubiger; **ordinary ~** Massegläubiger; **paid-off ~s** abgefundene Gläubiger; **partnership ~** Firmen-, Gesellschaftsgläubiger; **petitioning ~** antragstellender Gläubiger; **preferential** *(Br.)* **(preferred, US) ~** (bevorrechtigter) [Konkurs]gläubiger, Vorzugsgläubiger; **principle ~** Hauptgläubiger; **private ~** Privatgläubiger; **privileged ~** bevorrechtigter (priviligierter) Konkursgläubiger; **~ ranking equally** gleichrangiger Gläubiger; **secondary ~** nachstehender Gläubiger; **secured ~** *(US)* absonderungsberechtigter (dinglich gesicherter) Gläubiger; **fully (partly) secured ~** voll (teilweise) gesicherter [Konkurs]gläubiger; **simple contract ~** nicht bevorrechtigter (gewöhnlicher) Gläubiger; **single ~** einfach gesicherter Gläubiger; **specialty ~** Gläubiger einer verbrieften Schuld **subsequent ~** nachrangiger Gläubiger; **sundry ~s** diverse Gläubiger, verschiedene Kreditoren; **trade ~s** Warengläubiger, Lieferanten, *(account current)* Gläubiger aus Kontokorrentgeschäften; **unprotected ~** nicht bevorrechtigter Gläubiger; **unsecured ~** einfacher Konkursgläubiger; **urgent ~** drängender Gläubiger; **warrant ~** *(municipal accounting)* Schuldscheininhaber;

~ of a bankrupt's estate Massegläubiger; **~ with a colo(u)rable claim** aussonderungsberechtigter Gläubiger; **~s who rank equally (with equality of rights)** gleichrangige Gläubiger; **~ of a ~** Gläubiger eines Konkursgläubigers; **~ of an estate** Nachlaßgläubiger; **~s of a firm (partnership)** Firmen-, Gesellschaftsgläubiger; **~ at large** einfacher Konkursgläubiger, Massegläubiger; **~ expected to rank** voraussichtlicher Gläubiger; **~ of real-estate securities** Grundpfandgläubiger; **~ in trust** Treugeber;

to arrange with one's ~s sich mit seinen Gläubigern auseinandersetzen; **to arrange with one's ~s for an extension of time** sich mit seinen Gläubigern wegen eines Zahlungsaufschubs verständigen; **to be a ~ on the bank books** Bankkonto haben; **to be protected from its ~s by court decree** gerichtlich angeordneten Gläubigerschutz genießen; **to be liable to be proceeded against by one's ~s** von seinen Gläubigern verklagt werden können; **to come to terms with one's ~s** mit seinen Gläubigern einen Vergleich schließen; **to compound (compose) with ~s** mit Gläubigern einen Vergleich schließen, sich mit Gläubigern vergleichen; **to defeat one's ~s** seine Gläubiger hintergehen; **to delay ~s** Gläubiger hinhalten, Gläubigerbehinderung betreiben; **to discharge a ~** Gläubiger befriedigen; **to enter into the rights of a ~** Gläubigerrechte erhalten; **to evade one's ~s** sich seinen Gläubigern entziehen; **to favo(u)r a ~** Gläubiger begünstigen; **to feed one's ~s with empty promises** seine Gläubiger mit leeren Versprechungen hinhalten; **to hinder ~s** Gläubigern den Zugriff verwehren; **to marshal ~s** Rangordnung der Gläubiger feststellen; **to meet the claims of one's ~s** Gläubiger befriedigen; **to pay one's ~s in full** seine Gläubiger voll auszahlen; **to pay off one's ~s** seine Gläubiger abfinden; **to prefer one ~ over one's others** einzelnen Gläubiger bevorzugen; **to put off ~s** Gläubiger vertrösten; **to put off a ~ with an instalment** Gläubiger mit einer Ratenzahlung beruhigen; **to run away from one's ~s** sich seinen Gläubigern durch die Flucht entziehen; **to settle with one's ~s** seine Gläubiger abfinden;

~ account Kreditorenkonto; **~'s assent** Gläubigerzustimmung; **~ bank** Gläubigerbank; **[third party] ~ beneficiary** Begünstigter eines Vertrages zugunsten Dritter; **~'s bill** *(bankruptcy)* Klage auf abgesonderte Befriedigung; **~ claim** Gläubigerforderung, -anspruch, -interesse; **~ confidence** Vertrauen der Gläubiger; **~ control** Überwachung durch die Gläubiger; **~s committee** Gläubigerausschuß; **~ country** Gläubigerland; **~ debtor relation** Gläubiger-Schuldner-Verhältnis; **~s' figure** Aktivwert; **~ interest** Gläubigerrecht, -interesse; **~ interest rate** Habenzinsen; **~s' ledger** Kreditorenbuch; **~ limit** *(International Monetary Fund)* Limit für die Gläubigerländer; **~ management** Gläubigerverwaltung [eines bankrotten Geschäftes]; **~s' meeting** Gläubigerversammlung; **~ nation** Land mit einem Zahlungsbilanzüberschuß; **~s' petition** von den Gläubigern gestellter Konkursantrag; **~ position** Gläubigerposition, -stellung; **~s' representation** Gläubigervertreter; **~'s right** Gläubigerrecht; **~s' voting right** Stimmberechtigung der Gläubiger.

creditress Gläubigerin.

credulous leichtgläubig.

credulity Leichtgläubigkeit.

creed Glaubensbekenntnis, -erklärung.

creek *(Br.)* kleine schmale Bucht, kleiner Hafen, *(US)* Nebenfluß.

creep Gruseln, Gänsehaut, *(close opening)* Kriechöffnung, Durchlaß;
~ *(v.) (prices)* langsam steigen, *(tyres)* rutschen;
~ in *(mistake)* unterlaufen; **~ into s. one's favo(u)r** sich bei jem. einschmeicheln; **~ up** *(speedometer)* steigen;
to give s. o. the ~s j. schaudern lassen, j. eiskalt überlaufen; **to make s. one's flesh ~** jem. eine Gänsehaut einjagen.

creeper *(penny-a-liner, sl.)* Zeilenschinder, *(person)* Schleicher, Kriecher.

creeping | barrage *(mil.)* Feuerwalze; **~ current** *(el.)* Kriechstrom; **~ inflation** schleichende Inflation; **~ sensation** Gänsehaut, gruseliges Gefühl; **~ sickness** schleichende Krankheit.

creepy story gruselige Geschichte.

cremate *(v.)* einäschern.

cremation Einäscherung, Feuerbestattung;
~ cemetary Urnenfriedhof; **~ certificate** *(documents)* Vernichtungsverhandlung.

crematorium, cremetory *(US)* Krematorium, Einäscherungshalle, Feuerbestattungsanstalt.

crêpe paper Kreppapier.

crest Wappen;
at the ~ of the wave *(fig.)* zum günstigsten Zeitpunkt;
family ~ Familienwappen.

crestfallen niedergeschlagen.

cretin Schwachsinniger, Kretin.

crew Mannschaft, Belegschaft, *(airship, ship)* Besatzung, *(mob)* Haufen, Bande, Pöbel;
air ~ Flugzeugbesatzung; **ground ~** Bodenpersonal; **gunner's ~** Geschützmannschaft; **scratch ~** wildzusammengewürfelte Mannschaft; **train ~** *(US)* Zugpersonal; **wild ~** ungezügelte Mannschaft;
all the ~ of jobbers and swindlers ganze Baggage von Schiebern und Schwindlern; **~ of labo(u)rers** Arbeitermannschaft; **~ of a lorry** LKW-Besatzung; **~ of a train** *(US)* Zugpersonal; **to pay off the ~** *(ship)* Besatzung abmustern;
~'s accommodation Mannschaftsraum; **~ captain** Mannschaftsführer, -kapitän; **~ chief** Flugkapitän; **~ cut** militärischer Haarschnitt, Bürstenhaarschnitt; **~ compartment** Besatzungskabine; **~ list** Mannschaftsliste, Musterrolle; **~ member** Besatzungsmitglied; **~ size** Kopfzahl der Besatzung.

crewman Besatzungsmitglied.

crib *(baby)* Krippe, *(hut)* Hütte, Kate, *(Br, school)* Klatsche, Eselsbrücke, *(seaside resort)* Ferienhaus, *(speakeasy, US)* Spelunke;
~ *(v.) (school, Br.)* abschreiben, mogeln, spicken;
to crack a ~ in ein Geschäft einbrechen;
~ house (joint) *(US)* Spelunke.

cribbler *(Br.)* Mogler.

crier Ausrufer;
common ~ öffentlicher Versteigerer; **town ~** Stadtausrufer.

crime Verbrechen, strafbare Handlung, Straftat, Delikt, *(coll.)* Jammer, *(gross violation of human law)* Missetat, Übeltat, Freveltat;
accomplished ~ vollendetes Verbrechen; **atrocious ~** Greueltat; **attempted ~** Versuch einer strafbaren Handlung; **capital ~** Kapitalverbrechen; **common law ~** absolut strafbare Handlung; **constructive ~** auf Analogie beruhender Strafbestand; **continuing ~** Dauerstraftat; **high ~** schweres Vergehen; **political ~** Staatsverbrechen;

~ against humanity Verbrechen gegen die Menschlichkeit, Humanitätsverbrechen; **~ against the other** Ehegattenstraftat; **inchoate ~** nichtvollendete Straftat; **infamous ~** ehrenrührige Straftat; **penitentiary ~** zuchthauswürdiges Verbrechen; **quasi ~** Ordnungswidrigkeit; **statutory ~** gesetzlich nominierte Straftat; **ugly ~** gemeines (abscheuliches) Verbrechen; **unfathomed ~** unaufgeklärtes Verbrechen; **violent ~** Gewaltverbrechen;
~ of violence Gewaltverbrechen;
to be implicated in a ~ in ein Verbrechen verwickelt sein; **to be linked by ~** Umgang mit Verbrechern haben; **to be old in ~** abgefeimter Verbrecher sein; **to class as ~** als Verbrechen einstufen; **to commit a serious ~** schweres Verbrechen begehen; **to confess a ~** Verbrechen gestehen; **to detect a ~** Verbrechen aufdecken; **to have been convicted of previous ~s** einschlägig vorbestraft sein, Vorstrafen haben; **to impute a ~ on s. o.** jem. ein Verbrechen anlasten; **to instigate s. o. to a ~** j. zu einem Verbrechen anstiften; **to pay the penalty of a ~** Verbrechen sühnen; **to perpetrate a ~** Verbrechen verüben; **to slur a ~** Verbrechen vertuschen;
~ detection Verbrechensaufspürung, Verbrechensaufklärung; **~ fiction** Detektiv-, Kriminalroman; **~ legislation** Strafgesetzgebung; **~ play** Kriminalstück; **~ prevention** Verbrechensverhütung; **~-prone** verbrecherisch veranlagt; **~ rate** Verbrechensprozentsatz, -ziffer, Kriminalitätsziffer; **~ reporter** Gerichtsreporter; **~ sheet** *(mil.)* Vorstrafenregister; **~ writer** Kriminalschriftsteller.
criminal Verbrecher, Rechtsbrecher;
dangerous ~ gemeingefährlicher Verbrecher; **habitual ~** Gewohnheits-, Berufsverbrecher; **hardened ~** verstockter Verbrecher; **loose ~** auf freiem Fuß befindlicher Verbrecher; **~ under sentence of death** zum Tode verurteilter Verbrecher;
to make a ~ appear in court Verbrecher vorführen; **to be labelled a ~** zum Verbrecher gestempelt werden; **to land a ~** Verbrecher schnappen; **to nail down a ~** Verbrecher zur Strecke bringen; **to run down a ~** Verbrecher in die Enge treiben; **to spot a ~** Verbrecher aufspüren; **to surrender a ~ to the police** Verbrecher der Polizei übergeben; **to trail a ~** Verbrecher verfolgen; **to try a ~ for murder** Verbrecher wegen Mordes verhören;
~ *(a.)* verbrecherisch, strafbar, kriminell;
~ act strafbare Handlung, Straftat; **~ action** öffentliche Anklage, Strafverfahren; **~ appeal** Berufung in Strafsachen; **~ assault and battery** gewaltsame Körperverletzung; **~ career** Verbrecherlaufbahn; **~ case** Kriminalfall, Strafsache; **~ charge** Anklage, Beschuldigung, [Straf]anzeige; **~ code** Strafgesetzbuch; **~ complaint** Strafanzeige; **~ conduct** strafbares Verhalten; **~ conspiracy** Verabredung zu einer strafbaren Handlung; **~ conversation** außereheliche Verkehr, Ehebruch; **~ court** Strafkammer, -gericht; **~ discretion** Strafmündigkeit; **~ disposition** kriminelle Veranlagung; **~ gross negligence** strafbare grobe Fahrlässigkeit; **~ information** Strafanzeige; **~ injuries compensation** *(Br.)* Entschädigung für Opfer von Gewaltverbrechen; **~ insanity** Strafmündigkeit; **~ intent** verbrecherische Absicht, strafrechtlicher Vorsatz; **~ investigation** kriminalistische (strafrechtliche) Untersuchung, Erkennungsdienst; **~ investigation department** *(Br.)* Kriminalpolizei; **~ jurisdiction** Strafgerichtsbarkeit; **~ justice** Strafgerichtsbarkeit, Strafrecht; **~ law** Strafrecht; **to become amenable to ~ law** strafmündig werden; **♀ Law Act** *(Br.)* Strafrechtsgesetz; **♀ Law Amendment Act** Strafänderungsgesetz; **~ lawyer** Strafverteidiger; **~ leanings** verbrecherische Anlage; **~ letters** *(Scot.)* Einleitung eines Strafverfahrens; **~ liability** strafrechtliche Verantwortlichkeit, Zurechnungsfähigkeit, Strafmündigkeit; **~ libel** strafbare Beleidigung; **~ mischief** Unruhestiftung; **~ misconduct** strafwürdiges Fehlverhalten; **~ motive** Motiv eines Verbrechens; **~ negligence** strafbare Fahrlässigkeit; **~ offence** strafbare Handlung, Straftat; **~ offender** Straftäter; **~ organization** Verbrecherorganisation; **~ procedure** Strafverfahren, -prozeß; **~ proceedings** Strafprozeß; **to institute (take) ~ proceedings** Strafverfahren einleiten; **~ process** Vorladung des Angeschuldigten, Strafprozeß; **~ prosecution** Strafverfolgung; **~ record** Vorstrafenverzeichnis, Strafregister; **no ~ record** nicht vorbestraft; **to have a ~ record** vorbestraft sein; **~ responsibility** Strafmündigkeit, Zurechnungsfähigkeit; **to stiffen ~ sentences** härtere Strafurteile erlassen; **~ statistics** Kriminal-, Verbrechensstatistik; **~ suit** Strafverfahren; **~ syndicalism** *(US)* ungesetzliche Zusammenschlüsse; **~ trial** Strafverfahren.
criminalism kriminelle Veranlagung, Kriminalität.
criminalistics Kriminalistik.
criminality Kriminalität.
criminate *(v.)* anklagen, beschuldigen.

crimination Anklage, Beschuldigung.
criminology Kriminalwissenschaft.
crimp *(mar., sl.)* Werber, Seelenverkäufer, *(US sl.)* Behinderung;
to put a ~ in prices *(US sl.)* Preise durcheinander bringen.
cringe Speichelleckerei, Unterwürfigkeit, kriecherische Höflichkeit.
cringe *(v.)* kriecherisch, schmeicheln;
~ before a policeman einem Polizisten kriecherisch begegnen.
crinkled paper Kreppapier.
cripple Krüppel, *(plane, ship)* aktionsunfähig machen;
war ~ Kriegsversehrter;
~ *(v.)* zum Krüppel machen, *(fig.)* schwächen, lahmlegen, paralysieren;
~ industry Industrie paralysieren.
crippled verkrüppelt;
~ by its losses *(army)* infolge von Verlusten aktionsunfähig; **~ by lack of money** durch Geldmangel lahmgelegt; **~ ship** aktionsunfähiges Schiff.
crisis Krise, *(theatre)* Wendepunkt, Höhepunkt;
cabinet ~ Regierungskrise; **commercial (economic) ~** Wirtschaftskrise; **commuter ~** Krise des Berufsverkehrs; **continuing ~** andauernde Krise, Dauerkrise; **final ~** endgültiger Zusammenbruch; **financial ~** finanzielle Krise, Finanzkrise; **monetary ~** Währungskrise;
~ of confidence Vertrauenskrise; **~ of leadership** Führungskrise; **~ in the money market** Geldmarktkrise;
to be on the brink of a ~ kriseln; **to draw to a ~** Krisenpunkt erreichen; **to ease the ~** Krise beseitigen; **to get over a ~** Krise überwinden; **to go through a ~** Krise durchmachen; **to have passed the ~** über den Berg sein; **to meet the ~** Krise überwinden; **to pass through a ~** Krise durchlaufen;
potential ~-breeding elements potentielle Krisenherde; **~ centre** Krisenzentrum; **~-conscious** krisenbewußt; **feeling ~** Krisenstimmung; **~ fund** Krisenfonds; **~ industries** von der Krise befallene Industriezweige; **~ management** Krisensteuerung, -kontrolle, Unternehmungsführung unter Krisenbedingungen; **~ money** Fluchtgeld; **~-prone** krisenanfällig; **~-proof** krisenfest; **~-ridden industries** von der Krise betroffene Industriezweige; **~ situation** Krisensituation; **~ solution** Krisenlösung; **~ staff** Krisenstab; **~ stage** Krisenstadium, kritisches Stadium.
crisp *(behavio(u)r)* flott, *(style)* lebendig, klar;
~ air frische Luft; **~ answer** schlagfertige Antwort.
criterion Tatbestands-, Unterscheidungsmerkmal, Kriterium, Kennzeichen;
poor ~ schwacher Bewertungsmaßstab;
to be the ~ maßgebend sein.
critic Kritiker, Rezensent;
art ~ Kunstkritiker; **literary ~** Bruchrezensent.
critical kritisch, abwägend, krisenhaft, *(patient)* gefährlich krank;
to be ~ of a th. etw. an einer Sache auszusetzen haben;
to win ~ acclaim Beifall der Kritiker finden; **~ altitude** *(airplane)* kritische Höhe, Volldruckhöhe; **~ attitude** kritische Einstellung; **~ audience** anspruchsvolle Zuhörerschaft; **~ circumstances** kritische Umstände; **~ date** maßgeblicher Zeitpunkt; **to write a ~ examination** Kritik schreiben; **to look on everything with a ~ eye** an allem und jedem Kritik üben; **~ position** kitzlige Lage; **~ opinions on art and literature** kritische Meinungsäußerungen in Kunst- und literarischen Fragen; **~ remark** kritische Bemerkung; **~ speed** *(airplane)* Durchsackgeschwindigkeit; **~ treatise** kritische Abhandlung; **~ velocity ratio** Machsche Zahl.
criticism kritische Abhandlung, Kritik, *(book)* Rezension, Besprechung;
open to ~ anfechtbar; **sensitive to ~** kritikempfindlich;
adverse ~ abfällige Kritik; **constructive ~** konstruktive Kritik; **discriminating ~** scharfe Kritik; **historical ~** Quellenkritik; **loud ~** heftige Kritik; **negative ~** unfruchtbare Kritik; **sane ~** vernünftige Kritik; **scathing (slashing) ~** vernichtende Kritik; **textual ~** Textkritik; **venomous ~** tödliche Kritik;
to be beyond ~ über alle Kritik erhaben sein; **to invite (ask for) ~** zur Kritik herausfordern; **to lay o. s. open to ~** sich der Kritik aussetzen; **to make a ~** Kritik üben; **to receive unfavo(u)rable ~** schlechte Kritiken bekommen.
critique Rezension, Kritik, kritische Besprechung (Abhandlung).
critizable kritisierbar, anfechtbar.
critizise *(v.)* zensieren, kritisieren;
~ s. one's work jds. Arbeit kritisieren.
croak Miesmacher, Unke;
~ *(v.)* Unglück prophezeien, unken.

crock *(coll.)* Wrack, *(motor car)* alte Kutsche (Kiste);
  old ~ *(fam.)* völlige Ruine;
  ~ *(v.)* up arbeitsunfähig machen.
crocodile tears Krokodiltränen.
crockery Gebrauchsgeschirr, Steingut.
croft *(Br.)* kleines Pachtgut.
crofter *(Br.)* Kleinbauer, Kätner.
cronk *(sl.)* unsolide.
crony alter Bekannter;
  old ~ Busenfreund.
crook Schwindler, Gauner;
  on the ~ hintenherum, betrügerisch.
crooked schwindelhaft;
  ~ **stick** Krückstock; ~ **ways** krumme Wege.
croon song Schnulze, Schmachfetzen.
crooner Schlagersänger.
crop [Getreide]ernte, Getreide auf dem Halm, *(cultivation)*
  Bebauung, Kultivierung, *(mining)* Ausgehendes;
  under ~ angebaut;
  away (off) -going ~ Ernte auf dem Halm; **bad** ~ schlechte
  Ernte; **forward** ~ frühe Ernte; **grain** ~ *(Br.)* Getreideernte;
  heavy ~ reiche (hervorragende) Ernte; **main** ~ erste Ernte; **poor**
  ~ schlechte Ernte; **short** ~ Mißernte; **standing** ~ *(law)* Früchte
  (Ernte) auf dem Halm; **thriving** ~ gut stehende Ernte;
  ~ **ruined by hail** verhagelte Ernte; ~ **of mistakes** Haufen Fehler;
  ~ **of questions** Fülle von Fragen;
  ~ *(v.)* Ernte tragen, *(cultivate)* bebauen, *(paper, photo)*
  beschneiden;
  ~ **out** *(mining)* zutage treten; ~ **heavily** reichen Ertrag bringen;
  ~ **up** *(difficulties)* sich einstellen, eintreten; ~ **up in the course of**
  a conversation im Verlauf des Gesprächs auftauchen;
  to be under ~ *(land)* kultiviert sein; **to get the** ~**s in** Ernte bergen
  (einbringen); **to produce heavy** ~**s** reiche Ernte einbringen; **to**
  sell the ~ **standing** Ernte auf dem Halm verkaufen;
  ~ **damage** Ernteschaden; ~ **density** Bestandsdichte; ~ **duster**
  Schädlingsbekämpfungsflugzeug; ~ **dusting** Ernteberieselung
  zur Insektenbekämpfung; ~ **estimate** Ernteschätzung; ~ **fail-**
  ure Mißernte; ~ **forecast** Erntevorschau; ~ **growing** Getreideanbau; ~ **insurance** Ernteversicherung; ~ **loan** Erntefinanzierungskredit; ~ **prospects** Ernteaussichten; ~ **shortage**
  knappe Ernte; ~ **year** Erntejahr; ~ **yield** Ernteertrag.
cropper *(failure)* Fehlschlag, Mißerfolg, *(US)* Pächter;
  share ~ Landarbeiter auf Naturallohnbasis;
  to come a ~ *(coll.)* ruiniert sein, reinfallen, sich blamieren.
cropping *(reproduction)* Bildausschnittsbestimmung.
croquis Skizze, *(mil.)* Kroki.
cross Kreuz, Merkzeichen, *(conflict)* Auseinandersetzung,
  Unannehmlichkeit, *(crosspoint)* Kreuzung[sstelle], *(suffering)*
  Leiden, Schicksal, *(swindle)* Gaunerei, Schwindel;
  on the ~ *(sl.)* auf unredliche Weise;
  Red ⚹ Rotes Kreuz; **Distinguished Service** ⚹ *(Br.)* Verdienst-
  kreuz;
  ~ *(v.)* *(bill of exchange)* querschreiben, *(race)* vermischen, *(sl.)*
  betrügen, *(street)* kreuzen;
  ~ **160** *(stock exchange)* Kurs von 160 überschreiten; ~ **the**
  Atlantic Atlantik überqueren; ~ **the border** Grenze überschreiten; ~ **the channel** über den Kanal fahren; ~ **the floor of the**
  house *(parl., Br.)* zur Gegenpartei übergehen; ~ **s. one's hand**
  with a piece of money jem. ein Trinkgeld geben, j. schmieren;
  ~ **at an intersection** Straßenkreuzung überqueren; ~ **the line into**
  illegality sich illegaler Methoden bedienen; ~ **one's mind** einem
  durch den Kopf gehen; ~ **not negotiable** *(check)* Übertragbarkeit eines Schecks ausschließen; ~ **out** ausstreichen; ~ **s. one's**
  path jem. in die Quere kommen; ~ **s. one's plans** jds. Pläne
  durchkreuzen; ~ **in the post** *(letters)* sich kreuzen; ~ **a river**
  Fluß überqueren; ~ **the street** Straße überqueren; ~ **a train**
  Anschluß haben; ~ **swords with s. o.** *(fig.)* sich mit jem. herum-
  streiten; ~ **one's t's and dot one's i's** äußerst pingelig sein;
  to bear one's ~ sein Kreuz auf sich nehmen, sein Schicksal
  tragen; **to make one's** ~ mit einem Kreuz unterschreiben; **to**
  mark with a ~ ankreuzen; **to mark a place on a map with a** ~
  Stelle auf der Karte mit einem Kreuz kennzeichnen; **to put a** ~
  against certain items gewisse Posten mit einem Kreuz
  kennzeichnen;
  ~ *(a.)* widersprüchlich, *(awkward)* widerwärtig, *(coll.)* ärgerlich, mürrisch;
  criss-~ kreuz und quer; **as** ~ **as two sticks** *(coll.)* sehr verärgert;
  ~ **acceptance (accommodation, Br.)** Wechselreiterei; ~ **account**
  (Br.) Rikambiorechnung; ~ **action** Gegen-, Widerklage; ~
  addition Queraddition; ~ **appeal** Anschlußberufung; ~**-appeal**
  (v.) Anschlußberufung einlegen; ~ **beam (girder)** Querträger; ~

bench *(parl.)* Bank der unabhängigen Abgeordneten; ~**-bench**
  (Br.) parteilos, unabhängig; ~ **bencher** *(Br.)* Unabhängiger,
  Parteiloser; ~ **bill** *(bill of exchange, Br.)* Rück-, Gegenwechsel;
  ~**-border traffic** kleiner Grenzverkehr; ~ **breeding** Rassenkreu-
  zung; ~**-channel service** Schiffsverkehr zwischen England und
  dem Festland; ~**-channel steamer** Kanaldampfer; ~**-channel**
  transport operator Kanalfährenunternehmer; ~**-check** *(v.)*
  genauestens überprüfen (kontrollieren); ~**-claim** *(v.)* Gegenanspruch, -forderung geltend machen; ~ **complaint** Widerklage;
  ~**-country** querfeldein, ins Blaue, *(car)* geländegängig; ~**-**
  country flight Überlandflug; ~**-country mobility** Geländegän-
  gigkeit; ~**-country telegraph line** Überlandleitung; ~**-country**
  vehicle geländegängiges Fahrzeug; ~**-default clause** *(syndicat-*
  ed loans) sich überall auswirkende Verzugsklausel; ~ **demand**
  Gegenforderung; ~ **elasticity of demand** Kreuzelastizität der
  Nachfrage; **to make** ~ **entries** Gegenbuchungen vornehmen; ~
  entry Storno-, Umbuchung; ~**-errors** Ausschlußrevision; ~
  examination Kreuzverhör; ~**-examine** *(v.)* einem Kreuzverhör
  unterwerfen; ~ **exchange** *(Br.)* Wechselarbitrage über drei oder
  mehr Plätze; ~ **fire** *(fig.)* Kreuzfeuer von Fragen, *(tel.)* Störge-
  räusch; ~**-fire of criticism** Kreuzfeuer der Kritik; ~ **firing** *(stock*
  exchange, Br.) Wechselreiterei; ~ **guarantee** wechselseitige
  Bürgschaft; ~ **heading** Zwischenüberschrift; ~ **holdings of**
  shares wechselseitiger Aktienbesitz; ~ **index** zusätzliches Inhaltsverzeichnis; ~ **investment** Kapitalbewegungen zwischen
  Industrieländern; ~ **liability** *(ship)* gegenseitige Haftung; ~**-**
  license *(v.)* Gegenlizenz ausstellen; ~ **licenser** Lizenzaustausch;
  ~ **licensing** Lizenzaustausch; ~ **licensing of patents** Patentaustausch; ~ **motion** Gegenantrag; ~ **order** *(stock exchange)*
  Kompensationsorder; ~ **ownership** wechselseitige Kapitalverflechtung; ~ **petition** Gegenantrag; ~ **picketing** doppelte
  Streikpostenaufstellung durch zwei Gewerkschaften; ~ **prod-**
  uct set Mengenprodukt; ~ **purposes** gegensätzliche Ziele; **to be**
  at ~ **purposes** sich gegenseitig mißverstehen; ~ **question** Kreuzverhör; ~**-question** *(v.)* ins Kreuzfeuer nehmen; ~ **rate** *(cur-*
  rency) Kreuz-, Querkurs, Umtauschsatz, -verhältnis; ~**-refer**
  (v.) verweisen; ~ **reference** Kreuz-, Querverweis; ~ **sale** *(bro-*
  ker) unzulässiger Selbsteintritt; ~ **section** Kreuzweg, *(sta-*
  tistics) repräsentativer Durchschnitt; **industrial** ~ **section**
  wirtschaftlicher Querschnitt; ~ **section of the consumers** Ver-
  braucherquerschnitt, Querschnitt durch die Verbraucherschaft; ~ **section of electors** repräsentativer Wählerdurch-
  schnitt; ~ **section of the people** Bevölkerungsdurchschnitt; ~
  section paper kariertes Papier; ~**-sectional analysis** Kreuzaus-
  wertung; ~ **size** Querformat; ~ **street** Querstraße; ~ **study**
  Querschnittuntersuchung; ~ **subsidization** *(common carrier)*
  Gewinnausgleich; ~**-sue** *(v.)* Gegenklage anstrengen, Widerklage erheben; ~ **suit** *(US)* Widerklage; ~ **tabulation** vergleichende Klassifizierung; ~ **talk** *(tel.)* Nebensprechen, *(Br.)*
  Austausch von Bemerkungen quer durch den Sitzungssaal;
  ~**-town route** Durchgangsstraße; ~ **trade** *(US)* Börsenkompen-
  sationsgeschäft; ~ **traffic** Gegenverkehr; ~ **voting** Abstimmung mit der Gegenpartei; ~ **wind** Gegenwind; ~ **word**
  wütendes Wort.
crossbar Latte.
crosscurrent Gegenströmung.
crosscut Abkürzungsweg.
crossed durchgekreuzt, durchgestrichen;
  ~ **generally** *(cheque)* ohne Angabe einer bestimmten Bank; ~
  specially nur an eine Bank zahlbar;
  to keep one's fingers ~ die Daumen drücken;
  ~ **cheque** *(Br.)* Verrechnungsscheck, gekreuzter Scheck; ~
  threads Fadenkreuz.
crosshead Überschrift über die ganze Breite.
crossing Kreuzen, Kreuzung, *(cheque, Br.)* Querschreiben, Verrechnungsvermerk, *(crosswalk)* Fußgängerüberweg, *(passing)*
  Überquerung, *(ship)* Überfahrt;
  account payee ~ *(Br.)* Verrechnungsvermerk nur zur Gutschrift des Empfängers; **boundary** ~ Grenzübergang; **channel** ~
  [Kanal]überfahrt; **controlled** ~ geregelte Kreuzung; **general** ~
  (cheque, Br.) allgemeiner Verrechnungsvermerk; **grade** *(US)*
  (level, Br.) ~ schienengleiche Überführung, schienengleicher
  Bahnübergang; **not negotiable** ~ Kreuzung nur zur Verrechnung, Nichtübertragsbarkeitsvermerk; ~ **patch** *(coll.)* Brumm-
  bär; **pedestrian** ~ Fußgängerüberweg; **rough** ~ stürmische
  Überfahrt; **signal-controlled** ~ Verkehrsampelkreuzung; **spe-**
  cial ~ besondere Scheckkreuzung; **street** ~ Straßenkreuzung;
  underground ~ Tunnelüberung;
  ~ **of the frontier** Grenzübergang; ~ **with gates** beschrankter
  Bahnübergang; ~ **the line** Äquatortaufe; ~ **off (out)** Aus-,
  Durchstreichung; ~ **the road** Straßenüberquerung;

to have a smooth ~ gute Überfahrt haben;
~ **gate** Bahnschranke; ~ **keeper** Schrankenwärter; ~ **light** Ampel; ~ **point** Übergangsstelle.
crossover Straßenübergang, Kreuzung, *(changeover)* Umsteigeplatz.
crosspoint *(Br.)* Schienenkreuzung.
crossroad Seiten-, Querstraße;
at the ~s am Kreuzweg seines Lebens; **free of ~s** kreuzungsfrei; ~s [Straßen]kreuzung, *(fig.)* Scheideweg;
~ *(a.) (US)* ländlich, kleinstädtisch;
to come to the ~s am Scheideweg stehen;
~ **grocery** *(US)* kleiner Lebensmittelladen.
crosstie *(Br.)* Eisenbahnschwelle.
crosstalk *(v.) (tel.)* übersprechen.
crosswalk Fußgängerüberweg, Straßenübergang.
crosswind *(airplane)* Seitenwind.
crosswire, to go schief gehen.
crossword | paper Kreuzworträtselzeitung; ~ **puzzle** Kreuzworträtsel.
croupier Bankhalter.
crow *(US)* Neger;
as the ~ flies im Vogelflug, in der Luftlinie;
white ~ *(fig.)* weißer Rabe, Seltenheit;
~ *(v.)* **over an unsuccessful rival** über einen erfolglosen Konkurrenten triumphieren;
to eat ~ *(US)* bittere Pille schlucken müssen; **to have a ~ to pluck with s. o.** mit jem. ein Hühnchen zu rupfen haben; **to pluck a ~** leeres Stroh dreschen;
~ **flight** Luftlinie; **in a ~ line** in der Luftlinie; **~'s nest** *(mar.)* Krähennest, Ausguck.
crowd Volksauflauf, Zulauf, [Menschen]menge, *(US sl.)* Haufen, Gruppe, Gesellschaft;
in ~s in Massen;
jolly ~ lustige Gesellschaft;
~ of books Büchermenge; **~s of people** Menschenmassen; **the whole ~ of shareholders** alle Aktionäre; **~ of eager shoppers** kauflustige Menge; **~ of witnesses** Unmenge von Zeugen;
~ *(v.)* **out** Zeitungsartikel wegen Platzmangels nicht bringen; ~ **a debtor** Schuldner bedrängen; ~ **forward** nach vorn drängen; ~ **in an hour** in einer Stunde unterbringen; ~ **out of the capital market** Kapitalmarkt überbeanspruchen, private Kreditnehmer aus dem Kapitalmarkt verdrängen; ~ **a matter** *(US)* Sache pressieren; ~ **the mourners** *(sl., US)* es ungebührlich eilig haben; ~ **a room with furniture** Zimmer mit Möbeln überladen; ~ **round s. o.** sich um j. drängen;
to be one of the ~ zur Clique gehören; **to follow the ~** sich der Mehrheit anschließen; **to get into a ~** ins Gedränge geraten; **to pull in the ~s** Massenpublikum anziehen; **to push (wriggle) one's way through the ~** sich durch eine Menschenmenge drängen;
would pass in a ~ geht gerade noch so hin;
~ **behaviou(u)r** Massenverhalten; ~ **control** Beherrschung der Masse; ~ **panic** Massenpanik; ~ **pleasers** erfolgreiche Massenartikel; ~ **psychology** Massenpsychologie; ~ **shot** Massenaufnahme; ~ **suggestion** Massensuggestion.
crowded belebt, dicht gedrängt, *(street)* verkehrsreich;
~ **to capacity** bis auf den letzten Platz gefüllt; ~ **to overflowing** zum Bersten voll; ~ **with people** vollgestopft mit Menschen; ~ **with traffic** verkehrsreich;
to be ~ for time sehr beschäftigt sein; **to be ~ with** wimmeln von;
~-out article wegen Platzmangels zurückgestellter Zeitungsartikel; ~ **audience** überfüllter Zuhörerraum; ~ **bus** vollgestopfter Bus; ~ **city** dichtbevölkerte Stadt; ~ **hours** Hauptverkehrszeit; ~ **party** zahlreich besuchte Abendgesellschaft; ~ **profession** überfüllter Berufszweig; ~ **state** Überfüllung; ~ **streets** überfüllte Straßen.
crowding out of the capital market Überbeanspruchung des Kapitalmarktes, Verdrängung privater Kreditnehmer aus dem Kapitalmarkt.
crown Krone, Thron, *(Br.)* Staat, Fiskus, *(Br.)* Souverän, *(coin)* Krone, *(splendour)* Krönung;
half a ~ halbe Krone;
~ **of one's labo(u)rs** die Krönung seiner Arbeit;
~ *(v.)* krönen;
~ **all** erfolgreich abschließen, Krone aufsetzen, um das Unglück vollzumachen; ~ **a feast** Höhepunkt einer festlichen Veranstaltung darstellen;
to be annexed to the ~ *(Br.)* der Krone anheimhalten; **to come to the ~** Thron besteigen;
~ **agent** *(Br.)* Kronanwalt für Zivilsachen; ~ **appointment** Berufung durch den Sovereign; ~ **assessor** *(Br.)* Schätzer des

Finanzamtes, Steuerschätzer; ~ **cases** *(Br.)* Strafsachen; ~ **colony** *(Br.)* Kronkolonie; ~ **court** *(Br.)* Geschworenengericht; ~ **debts** *(Br.)* Forderungen der Krone; ~ **estate** Krongut, -land; ~ **jewels** Reichskleinodien; ~ **land** *(Br.)* staatliche Domäne, Staatsdomäne; ~ **Land Commissioner** *(Br.)* Domänenverwaltung; ~ **law** *(Br.)* Strafrecht; ~ **lawyer** *(Br.)* Kronjurist; ~ **official** *(Br.)* Staatsbeamter; ~ **office** *(King's Bench, Br.)* Staatsanwaltschaft; ~ **paper** *(Br.)* Liste der anstehenden Strafsachen, Strafterminliste; ~ **prince** Kronprinz; ~ **property** *(Br.)* fiskalisches Eigentum; ~ **solicitor** *(Br.)* Staatsanwalt; ~ **subject** britischer Staatsangehöriger; ~ **user** *(Br.)* Benutzung durch den Staat.
crowned with success von Erfolg gekrönt.
crowner Krönung, Vollendung, *(bar)* Aufstecker, *(Scot. law)* Leichenbeschauer.
crowning Krönung, glorreiche Vollendung;
~ **event of the evening** Krönung des Abends.
crucial entscheidend, kritisch;
~ **date** Stichtag; ~ **debate** entscheidende Debatte; ~ **issue** Kernproblem; ~ **movement** kritischer Augenblick; ~ **period** kritische Zeit; ~ **point** entscheidender Punkt; **to come to the ~ point** zum Kern einer Sache kommen; ~ **question** Kernfrage; ~ **test** Feuerprobe; ~ **vote** Kampfabstimmung.
crude Rohprodukt;
~ *(a.)* unverarbeitet, roh, *(fig.)* primitiv, ungeschliffen, taktlos, *(fruit)* unreif, roh;
~ **birth rate** nicht aufgegliederte Geburtenziffer; ~ **facts** nackte (ungeschminkte) Tatsachen; ~ **ideas** unausgegorene Ideen; ~ **life of an uncivilized country** primitive Lebensweise eines unzivilisierten Landes; ~ **log cabin in the mountains** einfach zusammengeschlagene Berghütte; ~ **materials** Rohmaterial; ~ **manners** ungeschliffene (ungehobelte) Manieren; ~ **metal** Rohmetall; ~ **oil** Roh-, Erdöl; ~ **rate** *(unemployment)* saisonal nicht bereinigter Arbeitslosenprozentsatz; ~ **scheme** schlampig ausgearbeitetes Verfahren; ~ **sugar** Rohzucker; ~ **trade** nicht bereinigte Außenhandelsziffern.
crudity *(fig.)* Taktlosigkeit, Geschmacklosigkeit.
cruel grausam, unmenschlich, entsetzlich;
~ **disposition** Hang zur Grausamkeit; ~ **punishment** harte (grausame) Bestrafung; ~ **war** unbarmherziger (grausamer) Krieg.
cruelty Mißhandlungen, Quälerei;
mental ~ *(law, US)* seelische Grausamkeit;
~ **to animals** Tierquälerei; ~ **to children** Kindesmißhandlungen.
cruise Vergnügungsreise, Kreuzfahrt;
round-the-world ~ Weltreise; **training ~** Kreuzfahrt;
~ *(v.)* Kreuzfahrt machen, Vergnügungsreise zur See unternehmen, *(airplane)* mit Reisegeschwindigkeit fliegen, *(taxi)* nach Kundschaft Ausschau halten;
to go on a ~ Kreuzfahrt (Vergnügungsfahrt) unternehmen;
~ **car** *(US)* Funkstreife; ~ **ship** Vergnügungsdampfer; ~ **speed** *(airplane)* Dauerreisegeschwindigkeit; ~ **train** Rundreisezug.
cruiser *(mil.)* Kreuzer, *(pleasure trip)* Vergnügungsdampfer, *(person, US)* Vergnügungsreisender, *(police car, US)* Streifenwagen, Verkehrsstreife, *(streetwalker, sl.)* Strichmädchen;
armed merchant ~ Hilfskreuzer; **armo(u)red ~** schwerer Kreuzer; **battle ~** Schlachtkreuzer; **cabin ~** Kabinendampfer; **protected ~** leichter Kreuzer;
~ **tank** schwerer Panzer.
cruiseway Schiffahrtsroute für Vergnügungsreisen.
cruising *(taxi)* Umschau nach Fahrgästen;
~ *(a.)* auf Fahrgastsuche;
~ **altitude** Normalflughöhe; ~ **market** Kreuzfahrtgeschäft; ~ **range** Aktionsradius; ~ **speed** *(airplane, car)* Dauer-, Reisegeschwindigkeit; ~ **speed** *(mar.)* Marschgeschwindigkeit.
crumb Krume, Krümel, Brosame;
to a ~ bis aufs I-Tüpfelchen;
a few ~s of information spärliche Informationen.
crumble feiner Schutt;
~ *(v.)* abbröckeln, Kursrückgang erleiden;
~ **into dust** zu Staub zerfallen; ~ **up an estate** Gut parzellieren;
~ **to pieces** in Stücke zerfallen.
crumbling of prices Abbröckeln der Kurse.
crumple *(v.) (material)* schrumpfig werden;
~ **up** *(paper)* zusammenknüllen.
crunch Krise, Konfrontation;
to come to the ~ in eine Krisensituation geraten.
crusade Kreuzzug;
free collective bargaining ~ Feldzug für Tarifvertragsfreiheit;
~ *(v.)* Kreuzzug durchführen.

crush Strudel, dichtes Gewühl, Gedrängel, *(sl.)* Flirt, Schwarm, *(social event)* überfüllte Veranstaltung;
~ at the gate Ansturm am Eingang;
~ *(v.)* *(fig.)* zerschmettern, vernichten;
~ into the front seats sich in die vordersten Sitze drängen; **~ out a cigarette** Zigarette ausdrücken; **~ out the juice from oranges** Orangensaft auspressen; **~ one's way through the ~** sich rücksichtslos durch die Menge drängen;
~ barrier Absperrungsgitter; **~ room** *(theater)* Foyer.
crushed | to death zu Tode getrampelt; **~ by taxation** von Steuern bedrückt.
crusher Zerkleinerungsmaschine, Bruchwerk, *(sl.)* Polyp.
crushing prima, toll;
~ defeat überwältigende Niederlage.
crust Kruste;
thin ~ of ice dünne Eiskruste.
crusted over with ice mit einer Eiskruste bedeckt.
crutch Krücke, *(fig.)* Krücke, Stütze, Hilfe;
to go on ~es auf Krücken gehen.
cry Schrei, [Aus]ruf, Zuruf, *(applause)* Beifallsruf, *(slogan)* Schlagwort, *(street monger)* Ausrufen;
within ~ in Rufweite;
all the ~ *(US)* der letzte Schrei, die neueste Mode; **far (long) ~** langer Weg; **the popular ~** die Stimme des Volkes; **war ~** Kriegsgeschrei;
~ for help Hilferuf; **much ~ for little wool** viel Lärm um Nichts, viel Geschrei und wenig dahinter;
~ down niederschreien, -brüllen; **~ down s. o.** j. herabsetzen; **~** *(v.)* **halves** Halbpart verlangen; **~ over spilt milk** *(coll.)* sinnloses Bedauern äußern; **~ for the moon** nach den Sternen greifen; **~ the news all over the town** Neuigkeit in der ganzen Stadt verbreiten; **~ off at the last moment** im letzten Augenblick absagen; **~ out** laut verkünden, *(fig.)* sich heftig beklagen; **~ out against s. th.** etw. heftig verdammen; **~ quarter** um Gnade bitten; **~ quits** alles wieder in Ordnung ansehen; **~ stinking fish** das eigene Nest beschmutzen; **~ up** in den Himmel heben, gewaltige Reklame machen; **~ wolf** blinden Alarm schlagen;
to follow in the ~ mit den Wölfen heulen.
crying himmelschreiend;
for ~ out loud zum Aus-der-Haut-Fahren;
~ for the moon Sucht nach den Sternen;
~ injustice schreiende Ungerechtigkeit; **~ need** dringende Notwendigkeit; **to supply the ~ wants of a people** dringendste Bedürfnisse eines Volkes befriedigen.
cryptanalysis Geheimschriftanalyse.
cryptocommunist verkappter (getarnter) Kommunist.
cryptograph Geheimschrift, Schlüssel, Code.
cryptographer Ent-, Verschlüsseler.
cryptographic keys Verschlüsselungsunterlagen.
cryptophony Sprachverschlüsselung, verschlüsselter Sprechverkehr.
cryptography Schlüsselwesen.
cryptogram in Geheimschrift geschrieben.
cryptomechanism Schlüsselmaschine.
crystal Kristall[glas], Glaswaren;
as clear as ~ glasklar; **~ control** Quarzsteuerung; **~ detector** Detektor; **~ Palast** Glaspalast; **~ set** Detektorempfänger.
crystallization Kristallisation, *(debt)* Konkretisierung.
crystallize *(v.)* sich kristallisieren, feste Form annehmen, *(debt)* sich konkretisieren;
~ into a definite plan sich zu einem festen Plan entwickeln.
cub Küken, *(airplane)* Leichtflugzeug;
unlicked ~ grüner Bengel;
~ reporter *(Br.)* unerfahrener Reporter.
cube Würfel;
~ *(v.)* **a number** Zahl zur dritten Potenz erheben.
cubic | capacity Volumen, *(car)* Hubraum; **~ content** Rauminhalt; **~ measure** Raummaß; **~ meter** *(US)* (**metre**, *Br.*) Festmeter.
cubicle Einzelzelle.
cuckoo | in the nest Kuckucksei, Fremdkörper;
a bit ~ ein bißchen plemplem.
cudgel Knüttel, Knüppel;
~ *(v.)* **one's brains** sich den Kopf zerbrechen;
to take up the ~ in den Kampf eingreifen; **to take up the ~s for s. o.** für j. Partei ergreifen.
cudgelling Tracht Prügel.
cue Fingerzeig, Wink, *(attitude of mind)* Stimmung, Laune, *(for film editor)* Hinweis, *(part to perform)* Rolle, Aufgabe;
~ *(v.)* einweisen;

not to be in the ~ for reading zum Lesen keine Lust haben; **to miss one's ~** sein Stichwort verpassen; **to take one's ~ from s. o.** sich j. zur Richtschnur nehmen;
~ card *(broadcasting)* Spickzettel; **~ sheet** vergleichende Klassifizierung.
cuff Manschette;
off the ~ ohne Manuskript, frei;
to speak off the ~ *(US)* aus dem Stegreif sprechen.
cuffo *(show business, sl.)* umsonst.
cull drittklassiges Holz, Ausschußware;
~ *(v.)* auslesen, auswählen;
~ extracts from the best authors ausgewählte Auszüge der besten Autoren veröffentlichen; **~ one's words** seine Worte sorgfältig wählen.
cully Kumpan.
culminant auf dem Gipfelpunkt, kulminierend.
culminate *(v.)* kulminieren, *(career)* Höhepunkt erreichen;
~ in bankruptcy schließlich zum Konkurs führen.
culmination Gipfel, Höhepunkt;
to reach the ~ of one's career Höhepunkt seiner Laufbahn erreichen.
culminating point Gipfel-, Höhepunkt, Kulmination.
culpable schuldhaft, straffällig;
to hold s. o. ~ j. für schuldig halten;
~ homicide Totschlag; **~ ignorance** schuldhafte Unkenntnis; **~ negligence** strafbare Fahrlässigkeit.
culprit Täter, Schuldiger, Beschuldigter, Angeklagter;
to discover the ~ Täter feststellen.
cult Kult[gemeinschaft], *(fig.)* Idol;
~ of personality Persönlichkeits-, Personenkult.
cultivable bestellbar, kultivierbar, zivilisierbar.
cultivate *(v.)* kultivieren, *(civilize)* zivilisieren, *(refine)* veredeln, verfeinern, *(soil)* bearbeiten, bestellen;
~ s. one's acquaintance jds. Bekanntschaft pflegen; **~ one's land in a good and husbandlike manner** seinen Boden im Rahmen einer ordnungsgemäßen Bewirtschaftung bestellen; **~ good manners** sich guter Manieren befleißigen; **~ the market** Marktpflege betreiben.
cultivated kultiviert, zivilisiert;
~ area Anbaugebiet, -fläche, Kulturfläche.
cultivating the market Marktpflege.
cultivation Kultivierung, *(culture)* Kultur, feine Bildung, *(soil)* Ackerbestellung;
under ~ angebaut;
extensive ~ extensive Bodenbewirtschaftung;
~ of cereals Getreideanbau; **~ of a friendship** Pflege einer Freundschaft; **~ of the soil** Bodenbearbeitung;
to allow land to go out of ~ Land verfallen lassen; **to bring land into ~** Land in Kultur nehmen; **to go out of ~** nicht mehr angebaut werden; **to restrict ~** Anbaubeschränkungen erlassen;
~ methods Anbaumethoden.
cultivator Landwirt.
cultural kulturell, in kultureller Hinsicht;
~ activities kulturelle Ereignisse; **~ affairs division** Kulturabteilung; **~ agreement** Kulturabkommen; **~ attaché** Kulturattaché; **~ capital** Kulturzentrum; **~ center** *(US)* (**centre**, *Br.*) Kulturzentrum; **~ convention** Kulturabkommen; **~ diplomacy** Kulturpolitik im Ausland; **~ editor** Redakteur des kulturellen Teils; **~ exchanges** Kulturaustausch; **~ facilities** kulturelle Einrichtungen; **~ hall** Veranstaltungsraum; **~ imperialism** Kulturimperialismus; **~ institute** Kulturinstitut; **~ landscape** Kulturlandschaft; **~ lag** Bildungslücke; **~ level** Bildungsstand; **~ life** kulturelles Leben; **~ matter** Kulturfragen; **~ mobility** kulturelle Mobilität; **~ program(me)** Kulturprogramm; **~ property** Kulturgüter; **~ revolution** *(China)* Kulturrevolution; **~ variety** Kulturrasse; **~ wilderness** Bildungsnotstand.
culture *(refinery)* Veredelung, Verfeinerung.
culture Kultur, Kultiviertheit, Bildung, *(agriculture)* Bewirtschaftung, Bestellung, Bebauung, Ackerbau, *(biol.)* Züchtung;
alien ~ wesensfremde Kultur; **beauty ~** Schönheitspflege; **established ~** überlieferte Kultur; **pearl ~** Perlenzucht; **wide ~** Allgemeinbildung;
~ of trees Baumzucht;
~ area Kulturraum, -gebiet, -landschaft; **~ center** *(US)* (**centre**, *Br.*) Kulturzentrum; **~ critic** Kulturkritiker; **~ epoch** Kulturepoche; **~ factor** Kulturfaktor; **~ lag** Zurückbleiben eines Kulturzweiges; **~ minister** Kultusminister; **~ pattern** Kulturform; **~ pearl** Zuchtperle; **~ period** Kulturepoche; **~ sequences** kulturelle Folgewirkungen; **~ stage** Kulturstufe; **~ trait** Kulturmerkmal; **~ world** Kulturumwelt.

cultured kultiviert;
  to be ~ Kultur haben;
  highly ~ man hochkultivierter Mann; **~ pearl** Zuchtperle.
culturist Kulturbeflissener;
  physical ~ Freizeitgestalter.
culvert Abzugskanal.
cum|dividend mit (einschließlich) Dividende; **~ drawing** inklusive Ziehung; **~ new** mit Bezugsrecht auf junge Aktien; **~ rights** mit Bezugsrecht (Optionsrecht).
cumulate (v.) [sich] anhäufen, (law) kumulieren, Klagen vereinigen.
cumulation Anhäufung, (law) Klagenvereinigung.
cumulative zusätzlich, kumulativ, anhäufend;
  ~ argumentation zusammenfassende Beweisführung; **~ audience** erfaßte Gesamthörerzahl; **~ dividend** Dividende auf kumulative Vorzugsaktien; **~ effect** gesteigerte (kumulative) Wirkung; **~ evidence** Beibringung massierter Beweise; **~ figures** Kumulationswerte; **~ fund** (Br.) thesaurierender Fonds; **~ legacy** Zusatzvermächtnis; **~ multistage system** (taxation) Mehrphasensystem; **~ offence** in Realkonkurrenz begangene Straftat; **~ participating preference shares** (Br.) kumulative, mit einer besonderen Dividendenberechtigung ausgestattete Vorzugsaktien, kumulative Prioritäten; **~ preference shares (stocks,** US) kumulative Vorzugsaktien; **~ preferred capital stock** (US) aus kumulativen Vorzugsaktien bestehendes Kapital; **~ punishment** Straferhöhung beim Rückfalltäter; **~ remedy** zusätzlicher Rechtsbehelf; **~ table** Summentabelle; **~ tax table** Steuerergänzungstabelle; **~ sentence** Gesamtstrafe; **~ stocks** (US) kumulative Aktien; **~ votes** kumulierte Stimmen; **~ voting** (US) Stimmenhäufung, kumulative Stimmenabgabe.
cunning Schlauheit, Verschmitztheit;
  ~ (a.) verschlagen, gerissen, durchtrieben.
cup Becher, (revelry) Trink-, Zechgelage, Zecherei;
  in one's ~s betrunken;
  challenge ~ Wanderpokal;
  my ~ of tea meine Kragenweite; **hardly everyone's ~ of tea** kaum nach jedermanns Geschmack;
  not to be s. o.'s ~ of tea (Br., coll.) j. nichts angehen; **to be s. one's ~ of tea** genau das Richtige für j. sein.
cupboard unit Anbauschrank.
cupidity Habgier, Geldgier.
curable defect heilbarer Mangel.
curative heilend;
  ~ act Fehler beseitigende Handlung; **~ effect** Heilwirkung.
curator Verwalter, (museum) Kurator;
  ~ absentis (US) Abwesenheitspfleger; **~ ad hoc** für einen bestimmten Fall bestellter Vormund; **~ for an absent person** Abwesenheitspfleger; **~ bonis** Pfleger, Verwalter, (Scot.) Vormund eines Minderjährigen; **~ of an estate** (US) Nachlaßpfleger; **~ ad litem** Prozeßpfleger.
curatorial vormundschaftlich.
curatorship Vormundschaftsamt, Pflegschaft, Sorgerecht.
curatory Kuratorium.
curb Bordstein, Gehweg, (stock exchange, US) Nach-, Freibörse, -verkehr, (restraint) Eindämmung, Drosselung, Bremsen, Zügelung;
  on the ~ (US) nach-, außerbörslich, im Freiverkehr;
  monetary ~s Drosselung des Geldangebots;
  ~ on consumption Konsumdrosselung; **~ on dividend rises** Dividendenstopp; **~ of exports** Ausfuhrbeschränkung; **~ on import** Einfuhrdrosselung;
  ~ (v.) bremsen, eindämmen, drosseln, (business cycle) dämpfen, zügeln, bremsen, (fig.) an die Kandare legen;
  ~ private banking operations private Banktätigkeit einschränken; **~ the boom** Konjunktur zügeln; **~ domestic demand** Inlandsnachfrage dämpfen; **~ expenditure** Ausgaben drosseln; **~ foreign competition** ausländische Konkurrenz eindämmen; **~ inflation** Inflation zügeln; **~ the money supply** zurückhaltende Geldversorgungspolitik betreiben; **~ production** Produktion drosseln; **~ wages** Löhne drosseln;
  to impose ~s on credit Kreditbeschränkungen verfügen;
  ~ broker (US) Freiverkehrsmakler; **~ exchange** (US) Freiverkehrsbörse, -kulisse; **New York ⌖ Exchange** New Yorker Freiverkehrsbörse; **~ key** Schnelltaste; **~ market** (US) Freiverkehr[smarkt]; **~ [market] price** (US) Freiverkehrskurs; **~ roof** Mansardendach; **~ service** (US) Bedienung im Auto; **~-service restaurant** (US) Autorestaurant; **~ stocks** (US) im Freiverkehr (Telefonverkehr) gehandelte Werte, Freiverkehrswerte.
curbing Dämpfung, Eindämmung, Drosselung, Zügelung;
  ~ of the boom Dämpfung der Konjunktur, Konjunkturzügelung, -dämpfung; **~ of inflation** Eindämmung der Inflation.

curbstone Rand-, Bordstein, Bordschwelle;
  ~ broker (US) Freiverkehrsmakler.
curbstoner (stock exchange, US coll.) Freiverkehrsmakler.
cure Kur, Heilverfahren, -behandling, (proceedings) Heilung;
  under ~ in Behandlung;
  ~ of addiction Entziehungskur; **~ by verdict** Verfahrensmangelheilung im Urteilswege;
  ~ (v.) sich einer Kur unterziehen;
  ~ an addict Entziehungskur bei jem. durchführen; **~ a default** Verzug wiedergutmachen, Rechtsmangel heilen; **~ a defect** Mangel heilen; **~ social discontent by making war abroad** von sozialen Mißständen durch einen auswärtigen Krieg ablenken; **~ s. o. of an idea** j. von einer Idee abbringen; **~ s. o. of an illness** j. von einer Krankheit heilen; **~ poverty** der Armut steuern;
  to be past ~ unheilbar krank sein; **to undergo a ~** Kur gebrauchen;
  ~-all Allheilmittel; **~ guest** Kurgast.
curfew (mil.) Ausgehverbot, Ausgangsbeschränkung, (police) Sperr-, Polizeistunde;
  to lift the ~ Ausgehverbot (Sperrstunde) aufheben;
  ~ order Polizeistundenverordnung.
curia Kurie.
curio Antiquität, Rarität, Kuriosität;
  to collect ~s Antiquitäten sammeln; **to hunt ~s** Antiquitätenläden abgrasen;
  ~ dealer Antiquitätenhändler, Antiquar; **~ hunter** Antiquitätensammler; **~ hunting** Sammeln von Antiquitäten; **to go ~ hunting** Antiquitätenbummel machen; **~ shop** Antiquitätengeschäft.
curiosities Antiquitäten.
curiosity Neugier, Wißbegierde;
  ~ shop Raritäten-, Antiquitätenladen; **~ value** Seltenheitswert.
curious (coll.) komisch, wunderlich, (literature) pornographisch, obzön;
  ~ discrimination strenge Unterscheidung; **~ investigation** genaue Untersuchung.
currencies, EEC Währungen der Europäischen Gemeinschaft;
  to weld their ~ into a tight bloc ihre Währungen zu einem festen Block zusammenschweißen.
currency (general acceptance) allgemeine Gültigkeit, Geltung, Geltungsbereich, Gebräuchlichkeit, Gangbarkeit, (rate of exchange) amtlicher Kurs, (circulation of money) [Geld]umlauf, [Geld]zirkulation, umlaufendes Geld, (legal tender) Zahlungsmittel, Kurantgeld, (standard) Währung, Valuta, (time of circulation) [Um]laufzeit, (validity of money) Gültigkeit;
  in the legal ~ of the country in der Landeswährung; **payable in ~** in Devisen zahlbar;
  adjustable ~ elastische Währung; **asset ~** (US) nur durch Aktiva der Emissionsbank gedeckte Währung; **automatic ~** elastische Währung; **auxiliary ~** Ersatzgeld, Geldsurrogat; **blocked ~** nicht frei konvertierbare Währung; **continental ~** (Br.) Festlandswährung; **controlled ~** Währungskontrolle, staatlich gelenkte Währung; **credit ~** Buch-, Giralgeld; **debased ~** minderwertiges Geld; **deposit ~** (US) bargeldloses Zahlungsmittel; **depreciated ~** abgewertete Währung; **devalued ~** abgewertete Währung; **divisional ~** Klein-, Wechselgeld; **domestic ~** Landes-, Binnenwährung; **double ~** Doppelwährung; **normally drawable ~** (International Monetary Fund) für Ziehungen normalerweise geeignete Währung; **elastic ~** elastische Währung; **emergency ~** Notgeld; **flexible ~** flexible (elastische, regulierte) Währung; **forced ~** Zwangswährung; **foreign ~** ausländische Währung, Devisen-, Fremdwährung, ausländische (fremde) Valuta, Devisen; **fractional ~** (US) Kleingeld; **free ~** frei konvertierbare Währung; **gold ~** Goldwährung; **gold and silver ~** Doppel-, Gold- und Silberwährung; **hard ~** gesunde (harte) Währung; **home ~** inländische Währung; **internal ~** Inlands-, Binnenwährung; **investment ~** (Br.) für Investitionen zur Verfügung stehende Devisenbeträge; **lawful ~ [of a country]** Landeswährung; **legal [tender] ~** gesetzliche (gesetzlich anerkannte) Währung; **local ~** Landeswährung; **managed ~** staatlich regulierte (gesteuerte) Währung, [behördlich] manipulierte Währung; **metropolitan ~** Hauptwährung; **metallic ~** gemünztes Geld, Metallwährung; **national ~** Landeswährung; **note ~** Papierwährung; **overvalued ~** überbewertete Währung; **paper ~** Papiergeld; **property ~** (Br.) durch Verkauf eines außerhalb des Sterlingblocks gelegenen Grundstücks vereinnahmte Devisen; **reserve ~** Reservewährung; **silver ~** Silberwährung; **soft ~** weiche (schwache) Währung; **sound ~** gesunde Währung, sichere Valuta; **stabilized ~** stabilisierte Währung; **stable ~** feste (stabile) Währung; **standard ~** Einheitswährung;

~ of bank notes Banknotenumlauf, Geldzirkulation; **~ of a bill** Laufzeit eines Wechsels; **~ of a contract** Vertragswährung; **~ with multiple exchange rates** Währung mit verschiedenen Wechselkursen; **~ backed by gold** Währung mit Golddeckung; **~ of a lease** Laufzeit eines Pachtverhältnisses; **~ of money** Geldumlauf, -zirkulation;
to debauch the ~ Währung korrumpieren; **to deface the ~** Währung entwerten; **to soon gain ~** bald allgemein bekannt sein; **to give ~ to a bill** Wechsel in Umlauf setzen; **to have general ~** *(report)* weite Verbreitung gefunden haben; **to have short ~** bald aus der Mode sein; **to restore the ~** Währung sanieren; **to restore confidence in the ~** Vertrauen in die Währung wiederherstellen; **to revalue a ~** Währung aufwerten;
~ account Valuta-, [Fremd]währungskonto; **~ accounting** Währungsbuchhaltung; **~ adjustment** Währungsangleichung; **~ agreement** Devisen-, Währungsabkommen; **~ allowance** Devisenzuteilung; **~ appreciation** [Währungs]aufwertung, Wechselkursaufwertung; **~ appreciation against the dollar** Höherbewertung einer Währung gegenüber dem Dollar; **~ arbitrage** Devisenarbitrage; **~ area** Währungsgebiet; **~ assets** Devisenguthaben; **foreign ~ balance** Währungsguthaben; **~ and Bank Notes Act** *(Br.)* Zahlungsmittelgesetz, Notenbankgesetz; **~ bill** *(Br.)* Fremdwährungs-, Valuta-, Devisenwechsel; **~ bloc** Währungsblock; **~ bonds** Valutaobligationen, Fremdwährungsschuldverschreibungen; **~ change-over** Währungsumstellung, -änderung; **~ circulation** Wert der umlaufenden Noten; **~ claim** Valutaforderung; **~ clause** Effektiv-, Valuta-, Währungsklausel; **~ conditions** Währungsverhältnisse; **~ control** Devisenbewirtschaftung, -kontrolle; **~ conversion** Währungsumstellung; **electronic ~ converter** elektronisches Kursumrechnungsgerät; **[free] ~ country** [nicht] devisenbewirtschaftetes Land; **hard-~ country** Land mit stabiler Währung, valutastarkes Land; **soft-~ country** Land mit unstabiler Währung, valutaschwaches Land; **foreign ~ credit** Kredit in fremder Währung, Fremdwährungskredit; **~ crisis** Währungskrise; **~ dealer** Devisenhändler; **~ dealing** Devisengeschäfte, -verkehr; **~ declaration** Devisenerklärung; **~ demands** Devisenanforderungen; **holiday ~ demands** Anforderungen für Ferien- und Reisegelder; **~ depreciation** Geldentwertung; **~ devaluation** Währungsabwertung; **~ disparities** Währungsdisparitäten; **~ doctrine** *(US)* Golddeckungsprinzip; **~ draft** Valutawechsel; **~ dumping** Valutadumping; **~ economist** Währungsfachmann; **~ evasion** Währungsflucht; **~ exchange** Devisenbörse, Wechselstube; **~ exchange shortage** Devisenknappheit; **~ exchange standard** Devisenwährung; **~ expansion** Währungsausweitung; **~ exposure management** Verwaltung von Fremdwährungsguthaben; **~ float** Politik freigegebener Wechselkurse; **~ flow** Devisenstrom, -verlagerung; **~ fluctuations** Schwankungen des Wechselkurses, Valutaschwankungen; **~ form** Devisenformular; **~ fund** Währungsfonds; **~ gain** Währungsgewinn; **~ gyration** Währungsunsicherheit; **~ hoarding** Geldhortung; **~ holdings** Devisenbestände; **~ instability** unstabile Währung; **~ law** Währungsgesetz; **~ leakage** Valutaverlust; **~ liabilities** Devisen-, Valutaverbindlichkeiten; **~ loan** Fremdwährungsanleihe; **~ loss** Währungs-, Valuta-, Devisenverlust; **~ manipulation** Währungsmanipulation, Devisenschiebung; **~ market** Devisenbörse, -markt; **~ movements** Geldbewegungen; **~ notes** *(Br.)* englische Schatzscheine [im ersten Weltkrieg]; **~ offence** Devisenvergehen; **~ operator** Währungsspekulant; **~ option** Devisenposition; **~ paper** Banknotenpapier; **~ payment** Valutazahlung; **~ policy** Währungspolitik; **~ position** Devisensituation; **~ principle** Golddeckungsprinzip; **~ problem** Währungsproblem; **~ profiteer (racketeer)** Devisenschieber; **~ racket** Devisenschiebung; **~ rates** *(Br.)* per Pfund notierte Devisenkurse; **~ reform** Währungsreform, -umstellung; **~ regulation** Valutaregulierung, Devisenbestimmung, -vorschrift; **~ reserve** Devisen-, Währungsreserve; **~ revaluation** Aufwertung einer Währung; **~ restrictions** Devisenbeschränkungen; **~ risk** Währungsrisiko; **~ shortage** Valutaknappheit; **to help s. o. with the ~ side** jem. Hilfe bei währungspolitischen Fragen angedeihen lassen; **~ slide** Abrutschen der Währung; **~ smuggling** Devisenschmuggel; **~ snake** Währungsschlange; **~ speculation** Valuta-, Währungsspekulation; **~ speculator** Währungsspekulant; **~ stability** Währungsstabilität; **~ stabilization** Stabilisierung der Wechselkurse; **~ stabilization fund** Währungsstabilisierungsfonds; **~ supply** Zahlungsmittelversorgung; **~ swap** Devisenswap; **~ system** Währungssystem; **~ theory** Geldtheorie; **~ trade** Devisenhandel; **~ transaction** Valutaabschluß, -geschäft; **~ transfer** Devisentransfer; **~ trouble** Währungsschwierigkeiten; **~ unit** Zahlungsmitteleinheit; **~ value** Devisenwert; **~ windfall** unerwarteter Währungsschnitt.

current Strom, Strömung, *(el.)* Strom;
continuous (direct) ~ Gleichstrom;
cold ~ of air kalter Luftzug; **~ of high frequency** Hochfrequenzstrom; **~s of trade** Handelsströme;
~ (a.) *(circulating)* zirkulierend, umlaufend, kursierend, *(frequent)* häufig, *(negotiable)* kurs-, verkehrsfähig, *(present)* gegenwärtig aktuell, augenblicklich, laufend, *(salable)* [markt]gängig, leicht verkäuflich, *(usual)* gang und gäbe, kurant, *(valid)* gültig, gangbar;
~ on exchange börsengängig;
to be ~ sich gut verkaufen, *(money)* kursieren; **to be no longer ~** nicht mehr gültig sein; **to break the ~** Stromzufuhr unterbrechen; **to furnish a factory with ~** elektrischen Strom in eine Fabrik legen; **to influence the ~ of thought** allgemeine Denkweise beeinflussen; **to pass for ~** als gültig angenommen werden.

current account laufendes (offenes, tägliches) Konto, laufende Rechnung, *(US)* Giro-, Kontokorrentkonto, Sichteinlage, *(balance of payment)* Leistungsbilanz;
credit ~ kreditorisch geführtes Kontokorrentkonto;
to have a ~ in laufender Rechnung stehen;
~ advance Kontokorrentkredit; **~ balance** Kontokorrentguthaben; **~ business** Kontokorrentgeschäft, -verkehr; **~ credit** Kontokorrentkredit; **~ customer** Kontokorrentkunde; **~ deficit** *(balance of payment)* Leistungsbilanzdefizit; **~ deposits** Sicht-, Kontokorrenteinlagen; **~ deposits and other accounts** *(bank balance sheet)* Einlagen auf gebührenfreie Rechnung und sonstige Gläubiger; **~ ledger** Kontokorrentbuch; **~ money** *(US)* Giralgeld; **~ operations** Kontokorrenttransaktionen; **~ receivables** *(US)* Kontokorrentforderungen; **~ register** Kontrollbuch für ein Kontokorrentbuch; **~ surplus** *(balance of payments)* Leistungsbilanzüberschuß; **~ user** Kontokorrentkunde.

current | advertising gegenwärtig laufende Werbekampagne; **~ affairs** Tagesereignisse, -politik; **~ articles** gängige Ware (Produkte); **~ assets** *(balance sheet)* kurzfristiges Umlaufvermögen, kurzfristige Vermögenswerte; **~ asset item** Posten des Umlaufvermögens; **~ balance** derzeitiger Saldo, Kontokorrentguthaben, *(balance of payments)* Leistungsbilanz; **~ breaker** *(el.)* Stromunterbrecher; **~ budget** Voretat; **~ business** laufende Geschäfte; **~ capital** Umsatz-, Betriebskapital; **~ catalog(ue)** derzeit gültiger Verkaufskatalog; **~ circuit** *(el.)* Stromkreis; **~ coin** gängige Münze; **~ consumption** *(el.)* Stromverbrauch; **~ cost** Tageskosten, Kostenaufwand zu Marktpreisen; **~ cost profit after deducting taxation payable** Gewinn bei Kalkulation zu Marktpreisen nach Abzug fälliger Steuern; **~ coupon** laufender Kupon; **~ demand** laufende (kontinuierliche) Nachfrage; **~ deposits** Kontokorrenteinlagen; **~ deposits and other accounts** *(balance sheet)* Einlagen auf gebührenfreie Rechnungen und sonstige Gläubiger; **~ events** Tagesereignisse; **~ exchange** Tageskurs; **~ expenditure** Betriebskosten innerhalb eines bestimmten Zeitraumes; **~ expenses** laufende Unkosten; **~ fashion** augenblicklich herrschende Mode; **~ funds** liquide Mittel, Umlaufmittel, Umlaufvermögen einschließlich kurzfristiger Anlagewerte; **~ goods** Verbrauchsgüter; **~ handwriting** flüssige Handschrift; **~ income** im Rechnungsabschnitt anfallendes Einkommen; **~ intensity** *(el.)* Stromstärke; **~ interest** laufende Zinsen; **~ investment** vorübergehende Anlagen; **~ issue of a magazine** neueste Zeitschriftennummer; **~ liabilities** *(balance sheet)* kurzfristiges Fremdkapital, innerhalb eines Jahres zu tilgende Verbindlichkeiten; **~ maintenance** Unterhaltungsaufwand; **at ~ market price** zum Tageskurs; **~ market value** Zeit-, Tages-, Marktwert; **~ maturity** innerhalb eines Jahres fällige Verbindlichkeit; **~ meter** *(el.)* Stromzähler; **~ money** Landeswährung; **~ month** laufender Monat; **~ number** letzte Ausgabe [einer Zeitschrift]; **~ obligations** laufende Verbindlichkeiten; **~ operating concept of net income** laufendes Verbuchungsverfahren des Nettowertes; **~ operating expenses** laufende Betriebsunkosten; **~ opinion** weit verbreitete Meinung; **~ outlay cost** augenblicklicher Kostenaufwand; **to sell for ~ payment** gegen bar verkaufen; **~ portion of long-term debt** im nächsten Jahr rückzahlbarer Anteil langfristiger Schulden; **~ position** *(banking)* Flüssigkeits-, Liquiditätsstatus; **~ price** Tages-, Marktpreis, *(stock exchange)* Tageskurs; **at the ~ price** zum Tageskurs; **~ quality** gängige Qualität; **~ quotation** Tageskurs; **~ rate** Tageskurs; **~ rate of exchange for sight drafts on London** Tageskurs für Sichtwechsel auf London; **~ rate of wages** jeweils gültige Löhne, gültiger Lohntarif; **~ [position] ratio** Liquiditätsverhältnis; **~ receipts** Umlaufvermögen; **~ receivables** *(US)* Umlaufvermögen; **~ revenue** im Rechnungsjahr anfallende

Einkünfte; ~ **supply** *(el.)* Stromversorgung; ~ **taxes** Steuerschulden; ~ **tax year** laufendes Steuerjahr; ~ **transactions** laufende Geschäfte (Umsätze); ~ **transfer** laufende Transferzahlungen; **to be in** ~ **use** allgemein gebräuchlich sein; ~ **value** gegenwärtiger Marktwert, Zeit-, Tageswert; ~ **wages** in einem bestimmten Zeitabschnitt anfallende Löhne; ~ **year** Rechnungsjahr; ~ **yield** Umlaufrendite, *(securities)* Effektivverzinsung.

curriculum *(lat.)* Studien-, Ausbildungs-, Lehrplan;
~ **vitae** Lebenslauf;
to draw up a ~ **vitae** Lebenslauf aufsetzen; **to lay a** ~ Lehrplan festlegen.

curse Fluch, Verwünschung, *(religion)* Exkommunikation;
not worth a tinker's ~ keinen Pfifferling wert;
~ *(v.)* verfluchen, verdammen.

cursive kursiv;
~ **script** Schreibschrift; ~ **type** Kursivdruck.

cursor Lichtpunkt, Blinker.

cursory flüchtig, oberflächlich;
~ **inspection** oberflächliche Untersuchung.

curtail *(v.)* schmälern, abkürzen, [ver]kürzen, *(expenses)* verkürzen, beschneiden, einschränken, drosseln;
~ **an allowance of money** [Geld]zuwendung kürzen; ~ **an essay** Aufsatz kürzer fassen; ~ **one's expenses** seine Ausgaben einschränken; ~ **one's holidays** einen Teil seiner Ferien streichen; ~ **a lecture** Vorlesung vorzeitig abbrechen; ~ **s. o. of his privileges** jds. Vorrechte beschränken; ~ **production** Produktion drosseln; ~ **s. one's rights** j. in seinen Rechten schmälern; ~ **a speech** Rede abkürzen; ~ **wages** Löhne herabsetzen.

curtailed beeinträchtigt, geschmälert;
to be ~ **in one's rights** seine Rechte geschmälert sehen;
~ **expectation of life** verkürzte Lebenserwartung; ~ **inspection** abgebrochene Prüfung; ~ **word** Kurzwort.

curtailing of production Produktionsbeschränkung, -drosselung.

curtailment Schmälerung, Be-, Einschränkung, Drosselung;
~ **of expenses** Beschneiden von Ausgaben; ~ **of one's holiday** Urlaubsabkürzung; ~ **of powers** Vollmachtsbeschränkung; ~ **of production** Produktionsbeschränkung, -drosselung; ~ **of service** Einschränkung des Zugverkehrs.

curtain Vorhang, Gardine, *(fig.)* Schleier;
behind the ~ hinter den Kulissen;
classification ~ *(Br.)* Geheimhaltungsbestimmungen; **fireproof** ~ *(theater)* eiserner Vorhang; **iron** ~ *(pol.)* Eiserner Vorhang; **red-tape** ~ wiehernder Amtsschimmel; **safety** ~ *(theater)* eiserner Vorhang; **silken** ~ *(Br.)* Nachrichtenzensur; **spring** ~ Rouleau; **uranium** ~ Nichtzulassung britischer Atomwissenschaftler zu US-Projekten;
~ **of fire** *(mil.)* Feuervorhang; ~ **of mist** Nebelwand; ~ **of troops** Truppenschleier;
~ *(v.)* mit Vorhängen versehen, *(fig.)* verschleiern, verbergen, verhüllen;
~ **off part of a room** Teil eines Zimmers abteilen;
to draw the ~**s** Vorhänge vorziehen; **to draw a** ~ **over s. th.** *(fig.)* etw. mit dem Mantel der christlichen Nächstenliebe bedecken; **to face the final** ~ vor seinem Ende stehen; **to lift the** ~ Schleier lüften; **to ring down the** ~ **on a scene** Mantel des Vergessens über einen Vorgang breiten; **to take one's last** ~ *(theater)* zum letzten Mal auftreten;
~ **call** *(theater)* Hervorruf; ~ **lecture** Gardinenpredigt; ~ **lifter** *(theatre)* kurzes Vorspiel, Einakter; ~ **raiser** Vorbericht; ~ **roller** Rouleau; ~ **wall** nichttragende Außenwand; ~ **walling** Aluminiumbauweise mit Wandverkleidungselementen.

curtate verkürzt, reduziert.

curtesy [of England] *(US)* Nießbrauch, Nutznießung [des überlebenden Ehemannes am Grundbesitz].

curtilage umschlossener Hofraum.

curve *(statistics)* Schaulinie, Kurve;
cost ~ Kostenkurve;
~**s** runde Klammern;
banked ~ überhöhte Kurve; **upward** ~ Aufwärtskurve;
~ **in a road** Straßenkurve;
to be on a rising ~ sich in einer ansteigenden Kurve befinden; **to round a** ~ Kurve ausfahren; **to take** ~**s at a high speed** zu schnell in den Kurven fahren;
~ **chart** Liniendiagramm.

cushion Polster, Kissen, Puffer, *(advertising)* Sicherheitsfaktor, *(broadcasting, television)* Füller, Puffersendung, *(car)* Stoßdämpfer;
air ~ Luftkissen; **leather** ~ Lederkissen;
~ **of air** Luftkissen; ~ **of moss** Mooskissen; ~ **of orders** Auftragspolster; ~ **of stock** Aktienvorrat, -polster;

~ *(v.)* polstern, *(fig.)* ab-, auffangen, dämpfen;
~ **complaints** Beschwerden unterdrücken; ~ **the decline** Kurssturz auf-, abfangen; ~ **the downswing** konjunkturelle Talfahrt auffangen; ~ **fluctuations** Schwankungen auffangen; ~ **inflationary factors** inflatorische Ausstrahlungen auffangen; ~ **losses** Verluste auffangen;
to fall back on a broad ~ **of diversification** zu einer wohlgepolsterten Produktionsbreite Zuflucht nehmen;
~ **factor** Dämpfungsfaktor; ~ **rider** Luftkissenfahrzeug; ~ **tyre** Hochelastik-, Halbluftreifen.

cushioned seat Polstersitz.

cuss Verwünschung;
not worth a ~ keinen Pfifferling wert;
not to care a ~ einem völlig schnuppe sein.

custodee Pflegling, Schutzbefohlener.

custodial vormundschaftlich;
~ **care** Pflegschaft; ~ **sentence** Haftstrafe; ~ **service** Treuhänder-, Betreuungstätigkeit.

custodiam *(Br.)* dreijähriges Kronlehn.

custodian Hausmeister, *(bank)* verwahrende Bank, *(guardian, US)* Vormund, *(trustee)* amtlicher Verwahrer, Treuhänder;
Alien Property ⚖ *(US)* Treuhänder für Feindvermögen; **lawful** ~ gesetzlicher Vormund; **legal** ~ amtliche Verwahrungsstelle, gesetzliche Hinterlegungsstelle;
~ **of property** Vermögensverwalter; ⚖ **of Enemy Property** *(Br.)* Treuhänder für Feindvermögen;
to appoint a ~ Treuhänder einsetzen; **to serve as** ~ Treuhänderfunktionen wahrnehmen;
~ **account** *(investment trust)* Treuhandkonto, Depotkonto; ~ **agreement** Depotvertrag; ~ **bank** *(investment trust)* Depotbank; ~**'s contract** Treuhändervertrag; ~ **office** Treuhandstelle; ~ **warehouse** *(US)* Konsignationslager.

custodianship *(guardianship, US)* Vormundschaft, *(securities)* Effektenverwaltung, Depotgeschäft;
~ **account** *(US)* Depot[konto]; ~ **department** *(US)* Effekten-, Depotabteilung; ~ **fee** *(US)* Depotgebühr; ~ **receipt** *(US)* Depotschein.

custody Obhut, Schutz, Aufsicht, *(bank, Br.)* Verwahrung, Aufbewahrung, Depot, *(confinement)* Untersuchungshaft;
entitled to ~ sorgeberechtigt; **in** ~ in Haft; **in safe** ~ im Gewahrsam; **remanded in** ~ in Untersuchungshaft;
official ~ amtliche Verwahrung; **police** ~ Polizeigewahrsam; **probationary** ~ zur Bewährung ausgesetzte Haftstrafe; **protective** ~ Schutzhaft; **safe** ~ Aufbewahrung, Verwahrung, *(Br.)* Depot;
~ **of the children** Sorge[recht] für die Kinder; ~ **held for joint depositors** Verwahrstücke für gemeinsame Hinterleger, Sammeldepot; ~ **held for sole depositor** Einzeldepot; ~ **held for executor** Depotverwahrung für einen Testamentsvollstrecker; ~ **of the law** öffentliche Hinterlegung; ~ **held in joint names** Sammeldepot; ~ **held for a partnership** Gesellschafts-, Firmendepot; ~ **of property** Vermögensverwaltung; ~ **of securities** *(Br.)* Aufbewahrung von Wertpapieren; ~ **held for trustee** Treuhänderdepot;
to apply for ~ Sorgerecht beantragen; **to be in** ~ **of a guardian** unter Vormundschaft (Kuratel) stehen; **to be awarded** ~ **of the children** Sorgerecht für die Kinder zugesprochen erhalten; **to be held in** ~ sich in Untersuchungshaft befinden; **to be remanded in** ~ in Untersuchungshaft bleiben; **to deliver the goods into** ~ **of the carrier** Ware dem Spediteur übergeben; **to deliver goods into the personal** ~ **of an innkeeper** Sachen dem Gastwirt zur Aufbewahrung übergeben; **to detain in** ~ in Untersuchungshaft halten; **to discharge from** ~ aus der Haft entlassen; **to entrust to the** ~ **of s. o.** in jds. Verwahrung geben; **to give into** ~ in Verwahrung geben; **to give s. o. into** ~ j. der Polizei übergeben; **to give a child in** ~ **of an aunt** Kind einer Tante anvertrauen; **to have (hold) in** ~ verwahren, in Verwahrung haben, *(accused)* in Haft halten; **to keep in** ~ **until trial** in Untersuchungshaft nehmen, Untersuchungshaft anordnen; **to keep in safe** ~ *(Br.)* aufbewahren; **to leave one's jewellery in safe** ~ *(Br.)* seinen Schmuck im Tresor lassen; **to leave a sum of money in s. one's** ~ jem. Geld zur Aufbewahrung geben; **to make allowances for** ~ Untersuchungshaft anrechnen; **to obtain** ~ **of a child** zum Vormund eines Kindes bestellt werden; **to place securities in safe** ~ *(Br.)* Wertpapiere ins Depot legen; **to remain in the** ~ **of the father** sorgerechtlich beim Vater bleiben; **to remand s. o. in** ~ j. in Vorbeugungshaft nehmen; **to take into** ~ in Verwahrung (Gewahrsam) nehmen, *(prisoner)* inhaftieren, verhaften; **to take into** ~ **on suspicion of financial impropriety** wegen des Verdachts finanzieller Unregelmäßigkeiten verhaften;

~ bill of lading Lagerhalterkonnossement; **safe-~ business** *(Br.)* Depotgeschäft; **safe-~ charges** *(Br.)* Depotgebühren; **safe-~ department** *(Br.)* Depotabteilung; **safe-~ receipt** *(Br.)* Depotschein; **safe-~ fee** *(Br.)* Depot-, Aufbewahrungsgebühr; **safe-~ item** *(Br.)* Depot-, Verwahrstück; **~ procedure** Sorgerechtsverfahren.

custom *(customers)* Kundschaft, Kunden[kreis], Klientel, *(due)* Abgabe, Gebühr, Auflage, *(habitual buying)* Kaufgewohnheit, *(usage)* Gewohnheit[srecht], fester Brauch, Sitte, Herkommen, Gepflogenheit, Usance;
according to ~ nach der Verkehrssitte, usancemäßig; **by ~** üblicherweise; **in accordance with local ~** ortsüblich; **with a good ~** mit guter Kundschaft;
established ~ Sitten und Gebräuche; **general ~** Verkehrssitte, Landesbrauch, -sitte; **large ~** großer Kundenkreis; **legal ~** *(US)* Gewohnheitsrecht; **local ~** örtliche Gepflogenheit; **maritime ~** Seemannsbrauch; **particular ~** Ortsgebrauch; **social ~s** gesellschaftliche Gepflogenheiten; **special ~** Orts-, Platzgebrauch; **strong ~s** tief eingewurzelte Sitten; **time-hono(u)red ~** althergebrachter Brauch;
~ of bookselling Buchhändlergepflogenheiten; **~ of the country** Landesbrauch, -sitten und Gebräuche, Verkehrssitte; **~ of the locality** Ortsgebrauch; **~s of London** Londoner Ortsgebrauch; **~ of merchant** kaufmännisches Gewohnheitsrecht, Kaufmannsbrauch, Handelsbrauch, -recht; **~ at the port** Hafenusancen, -brauch; **~ of the Realm** *(Br.)* Landesbrauch; **~ of the trade** Handelsbrauch, Usance; **~ and usage** Sitte; **~ and usage of war** Kriegsbrauch;
~ *(v.)* mit Kundschaft versorgen, *(duty)* verzollen;
to build up ~ Kundschaft bekommen; **to draw ~** Kunden anziehen; **to entice away the ~ of s. o.** jem. die Kundschaft wegnehmen; **to have s. one's ~** j. zu seinen Kunden zählen; **to have a good ~** viel Zuspruch (großen Zulauf) haben; **to have little ~** wenig Kundschaft haben; **to lose all one's ~** seine gesamte Kundschaft verlieren; **to retain an old ~** alten Brauch beibehalten; **to withdraw one's ~ from a shop** in einem Laden in Zukunft nicht mehr einkaufen;
~ *(a.) (US)* auf Bestellung angefertigt, bestellt;
~ body *(car)* Spezialkarosserie; **~-built** *(US)* einzeln angefertigt, bestellt; **~ car** Spezial-, Sonderanfertigung; **~ clothes** *(US)* Maßanzüge; **~ department** *(US)* Maßabteilung; **~ design** auf Bestellung angefertigtes Muster; **~-made** auf Bestellung angefertigt, nach Maß gemacht, bestellt; **~ order** Auftragsfertigung; **~ tailor** *(US)* Maßschneider; **~-tailored suit** *(US)* Maßanzug; **~ work** *(US)* Maßarbeit.

customs *(duty)* Steuer, Zoll, *(administration)* Zollbehörden, -verwaltung, -wesen, -amt;
internal ~ binnenländische Zölle; **~ inwards** Einfuhrzoll; **~ outwards** Ausfuhrzoll;
~ and excise duties Zölle und Steuern;
to clear through the ~ zollamtlich abfertigen, Zollformalitäten erledigen, verzollen, klarieren; **to get s. th. through the ~** etw. durch den Zoll schmuggeln; **to get one's luggage** *(Br.)* **(baggage, US) through the ~** sein Gepäck zollamtlich abfertigen lassen; **to pass through the ~** Zoll passieren; **to pay the ~** Zoll bezahlen; **to pre-clear ~** Zollformalitäten vorweg erledigen;
~ act Zollverordnung; **~ agent** Zollagent; **~ area** Zollgebiet, -inland; **~ authorities** Zollverwaltung; **~ barrier** Zollschranke; **~ berth** Zoll-, Landeplatz; **~ bill of entry** Zolleingangsdeklaration; **~ bond** *(Br.)* Zollkaution; **~ broker** Zollmakler; **~ certificate** zollamtliche Bescheinigung, Zollbescheinigung, -abfertigungsschein; **~ charges** Zollgebühren; **~ classification** [Zoll]tarifierung; **~ clearance** zollamtliche Abfertigung; **to effect ~ clearance** zollamtlich (beim Zoll) abfertigen lassen, Zollabfertigung veranlassen, Zollabfertigung vornehmen lassen; **to enter for ~ clearance** Zollabfertigungsantrag stellen; **~ clearance fee** Zollabfertigungsgebühr; **~ clearing house** Zollabfertigungsstelle; **~ collection district** Zollgrenzbezirk; **~ convention** Zollabkommen; **~ court** *(US)* Zollgericht; **~ craft** Zollboot; **~ custody** Zollgewahrsam; **~ debenture** Zollrückschein; **~ declaration** *(parcel)* Zolldeklarierung, -erklärung, -inhaltserklärung; **~ declaration form** Zollabfertigungsformular; **~ declaration and receiving office** Zollabfertigungsstelle; **~ department** Zollabteilung; **~ desk** Zollschalter; **~ district** Zollgebiet, -bezirk; **~ documentation (documents)** Zoll[abfertigungs]papiere; **~ drawback** *(reexportation)* Zollrückvergütung; **~ and excise duties** *(Br.)* Zölle und Gebrauchssteuern; **~ duties of a fiscal nature** Finanzzölle; **to eliminate ~ duties** Zölle beseitigen; **to introduce ~ duties** Zölle einführen; **to levy ~s duties** Zölle erheben; **to reduce the ~s duties** Zollsätze herabsetzen; **~ duty** [Waren]zoll, Zollabgabe, -gebühr; **to evade**

~ duty Zollhinterziehung begehen; **~ duty reduction** Zollsenkung; **~ enclave** Zollanschlußgebiet; **~ enforcement** Durchführung der Zollvorschriften; **~ entry** Zolldeklaration, -erklärung; **to pass a ~ entry** Zollerklärung abgeben; **~ examination** zollamtliche Untersuchung, Zollrevision, -abfertigung, -kontrolle; **~ expediter** Zollspediteur; **~ facilities** Zollerleichterungen; **~ figures** Zolleinnahmezahlen; **~ floor** Zollhalle; **~ formalities** Zollformalitäten; **to attend to the ~ formalities** Zollformalitäten erledigen; **~-free zone** Zollausschlußgebiet; **~ guard** *(US)* Zollbeamter; **~ hall** Zollhalle; **~ import certificate** zollamtliche Einfuhrbestätigung; **~ inspection** Zollrevision, -abfertigung, -kontrolle, Grenzkontrolle; **~ inspector** Zollaufseher, -inspektor; **~ invoice** Zollfaktura; **~ jurisdiction** Zollhoheit; **~ letter** Zollbenachrichtigung; **~ matter** Zollsache; **~ note** Zollvermerksein; **~ offence** Zollvergehen; **~ office** Grenzzollamt; **~ office en route** Zolldurchgangsstelle; **~ official (officer)** Zollbeamter; **~ officials** Zollpersonal; **to be under control of ~ officers** der Zollaufsicht unterliegen; **~ overseer** Zollaufseher; **international ~ pass** Zollpassierschein, Carnet; **~ passbook** Zollbegleitschein; **~ penalty** Zollstrafe; **~ penny** Rückzoll; **~ people** Zollpersonal; **~ permission** zollamtliche Erlaubnis; **~ permit** Zollerlaubnis, -freigabe, Zollabfertigungsschein; **~ policy** Zollpolitik; **~ post** Zollgrenzstelle, Zollstation; **~ procedure** Zollverfahren; **~ rebate** *(US)* Zollrückvergütung; **~ receipts** Zollschein, -quittung, -einnahmen; **across-the-board ~ reduction** lineare Zollsenkung; **~ regime** Zollsystem, -tarif, -verzeichnis; **~ regulations** zollamtliche Bestimmungen, Zollbestimmungen, -verordnung; **~ revenue** Zolleinnahmen; **~ seal** Zollverschluß, -plombe; **~ service** Zolldienst; **to be in the ~ service** Zollbeamter (im Zolldienst) sein; **~ shed** Zollschuppen; **~ sovereignty** Zollhoheit; **~ specification** *(Br.)* Zollausfuhrerklärung, -einfuhrerklärung; **~ station** Zollstation, -stelle, -bahnhof; **subordinate ~ station** untere Zollbehörde; **~ store** Zollspeicher; **~ tare** Zollgewicht, -tara; **~ tariff** Zolltarif, -register, -verzeichnis; **~ territory** Zollanwendungsgebiet; **~ treatment** zollrechtliche Behandlung; **~ union** Zollunion, -anschluß; **to enter into a ~ union** einer Zollunion beitreten; **to institute a ~ union** Zollunion bilden; **~ valuation** Zollbewertung, -abschätzung; **~ valuation procedure** Zollabschätzungsverfahren; **~ value** Zollwert; **~ violation** Zollvergehen, -zuwiderhandlung; **~ visa** Zollvermerk; **~ warehouse** Zollspeicher, -niederlage; **~ warrant** Zollauslieferungsschein; **~ waterguard service** *(Br.)* Küstenzolldienst; **~ weight** Zollgewicht; **~ yard** Zollhof, -schuppen.

customable gebühren-, abgabe-, zollpflichtig.

customary üblich, gebräuchlich, gewohnheits-, usancemäßig;
paying freight as ~ in gewöhnlicher Fracht;
~ in a place ortsüblich; **~ in trade** handelsüblich;
~ clause handelsübliche (ortsübliche) Klausel; **~ dispatch** handelsübliche Sorgfalt bei der Versendung; **~ freehold** Erbpachtrecht; **~ gifts** übliche Geschenke; **~ law** Gewohnheitsrecht; **~ international law** internationales Gewohnheitsrecht; **~ interpretation** übliche Auslegung; **~ investigation** Zollfahndungsdienst; **~ rate of interest** landesübliche Zinsen; **~ risks** handelsübliche Risiken; **~ services** *(tenant)* althergebrachte Dienstleistungen; **~ tare** übliche Tara; **~ tenant** Erbpachtbesitzer.

customer [Geschäfts]kunde, Debitor, *(client)* Mandant, Klient, *(factoring)* Drittschuldner, *(purchaser)* Abnehmer, Käufer, Auftraggeber, Besteller, *(restaurant)* Besucher, Gast, Kunde, *(strike breaker)* Streikbrecher;
against the interests of ~s kundenfeindlich;
~s Kundenkreis, -stamm, Kundschaft, Klientele, Abnehmer;
accidental (casual) ~ Laufkunde; **all his ~s** sein gesamter Kundenkreis; **average ~** Durchschnittskunde; **bad ~** fauler Kunde; **big ~** Großkunde; **cash ~** Barzahlungskunde; **chance ~** gelegentlicher Kunde, Laufkunde; **charge-account ~** Kreditkunde; **city ~** Stadtkunde; **cool ~** geriebener Kunde; **corporate ~** Firmenkundschaft; **credit ~** Kreditkunde; **defaulting ~** nichtzahlender (säumiger) Kunde; **delinquent ~** säumiger Kunde, Kunde mit Zahlungsrückständen; **economy-minded ~** sparsamer Kunde; **faithful ~** treuer Kunde; **foreign ~** Auslandskunde; **home-town ~** Kunde im Stadtgebiet; **industrial ~** gewerblicher Abnehmer; **key ~** wichtigster Kunde; **local ~** täglicher Kunde; **lower-income ~s** Kundschaft mit niedrigerem Einkommen; **loyal ~** zuverlässiger Kunde; **main ~** Hauptkunde; **negligent ~** säumiger Zahler; **out-of-town ~** auswärtiger Kunde; **potential ~** möglicher Käufer (Kunde); **price-finicky ~** preisempfindlicher Kunde; **prospective ~** möglicher (potentieller) Kunde; **queer ~** merkwürdiger Kauz; **registered ~** in die Kundenkartei aufgenommener (eingetragener) Kunde; **regu-**

lar (standing, steady) ~ regelmäßiger Gast, Stammkunde; **rum ~** gefährlicher Kunde; **steady ~s** feste Kundschaft, Stammkundschaft; **stray (street) ~** gelegentlicher Kunde, Laufkunde; **ugly ~** übler Kunde;
~ who has come from abroad auswärtiger Kunde; **~ of a bank** Bankkunde; **~s defecting to other markets** Kundenabwanderung auf andere Märkte; **~ of long standing** langjähriger Kunde;
to acquire ~ Kunden (Kundschaft) gewinnen, Kunden akquirieren (werben); **to aim at the needs of ~s** auf die Kundenwünsche abstellen; **to alienate ~s** Kunden ausspannen; **to approach a ~** an einen Kunden herantreten; **to attend a ~** Kunden bedienen; **to attract ~s** Kunden anlocken; **to bring ~s** Kunden zuführen; **to canvass ~** Kundschaft besuchen, Kunden werben; **to carry a ~** Kunden anschreiben lassen; **to charge the postage to the ~** Porto dem Kunden anlasten; **to draw (entice) away ~s** Kundschaft abspenstig machen; **to draw ~s into the store** Kunden (Kundschaft) anlocken; **to drum up ~** Kunden werben (akquirieren); **to forward goods to a ~** Kunden beliefern; **to get new ~s** neue Kundschaft bekommen; **to high-pressure ~** Kunden bearbeiten; **to introduce ~s** Kunden zuführen; **to keep in with a ~** (fam.) Kunden pflegen; **to lose one's ~s** seine Kundschaft verlieren; **to make advances to ~s** Kunden bevorschussen; **to pass a tax on to the ~** Steuer auf den Kunden abwälzen; **to recommend ~s** Kunden überweisen; **to regard a ~ as lost** Kunden als verloren abschreiben; **to restructure one's whole approach to ~s** Kundenwerbung auf eine völlig neue Basis stellen; **to retain ~s** Kundschaft erhalten; **to serve ~s** Kunden (Kundschaft) bedienen; **to serve the last ~** letzten Kunden abfertigen; **to tout ~** Kunden zutreiben;
~'s acceptance Kundenwechsel; **~ account** Kunden-, Abnehmerkonto; **~ advisory group** Kundenberatungsgruppe; **~ agent** Exportgroßhändler; **~ allowance** Kundenrabatt, Kaufpreisnachlaß; **~ balance** Kundenguthaben; **average ~ balance in year** durchschnittlicher Saldenstand der Kundschaft; **~'s book** Gegenrechnungsbuch; **~'s card** Kundenkarteikarte; **~ charge** üblicher Preis; **~'s check (US) (cheque, Br.)** Kundenscheck; **~ company** Kundenbetrieb; **~ complaint** Kundenbeschwerde, Reklamation, Mängelrüge; **~ confidence** Vertrauen der Kundschaft; **~ contest** Kundenwettbewerb; **~ counsellor** Kundenberater; **~ country** Abnehmerland; **~'s credit account** Kundenkreditkonto; **~'s credit balance** Kundenguthaben; **to put ~ demands first** Kundenwünschen Vorrang einräumen; **~ deposits** Kundeneinlagen; **~-directed** kundenbewußt; **~'s grievance** Kundenbeschwerde; **~ group** Käufer-, Kundengruppe; **~ information campaign** Aufklärungsfeldzug für die Kundschaft; **~ interest** Verbraucher-, Kundeninteresse; **~'s investments** Kundeneffekten; **~'s ledger** Kundenbuch; **~'s ledger account** Kundenkonto; **~'s ledger sheet** Kundenkontrollblatt; **~s' liabilities due to documentary and commercial credits** (balance sheet) Verpflichtungen der Kundschaft aus dokumentarischen Krediten und Remboursktrediten; **~s' liability on account of acceptances** (balance sheet) Wechselobligo aus den Akzeptverbindlichkeiten der Kundschaft, Kundenakzepte; **~s' liabilities for acceptances and guarantees** Verpflichtungen der Kundschaft aus Wechsel- und Garantieverbindlichkeiten; **~s' limit** Kundenkreditlinie; **~ list** Kundenkartei; **~s' loan** Kundenkredit; **~ loyalty** Kundentreue; **~'s man** Kundensachbearbeiter, (securities) Effektenberater; **~'s mandate** Kundenauftrag; **~s' money** Kundengelder; **~'s name** Kundenname; **to cater for the ~ needs** Kundenbedürfnisse befriedigen; **~s' notes** Kundenwechsel; **~ number** Kundennummer; **~'s obligations** Kundenverpflichtungen, -verbindlichkeiten; **~'s order** Kundenauftrag; **for ~ orientation** zur Unterrichtung der Kundschaft; **~ ownership** (US) Aktienbesitz der Abnehmerschaft von Versorgungsbetrieben; **~'s portfolio** Kundenportefeuille; **~'s position at the bank** Kundenbeurteilung durch die Bank; **~ prejudice** Käufervorurteil; **~'s purchase** Kundeneinkaufsbetrag; **~ recommendation** Kundenempfehlung; **~ register** Kundenliste; **~ relations** Kundeninformationsdienst; **~ relationship** Kundenverhältnis; **~s' reputation** Kundenansehen; **~ requirements** Kundenbedürfnisse; **~ resistance** Widerstände der Kundschaft; **~ returns** Warenrückgabe von Kunden; **~s' room** Kundenberatungszimmer; **~ sales** Kundenumsätze; **~ satisfaction** Zufriedenstellung eines Kunden; **~s' security department** (banking) Depotabteilung; **~ service** Kundendienst; **~s' sight deposits** täglich fällige Kundeneinlagen, Sichteinlagen; **~'s signature** Kundenunterschrift; **~'s statement** Kontoauszug; **~s' term deposits** Kundentermineinlagen; **~'s trade** Kundenbetrieb; **~ traffic** Kundenverkehr; **~'s undertaking** Kundenverpflichtung; **~ wants** Kundenwünsche.

customhouse Zollamt, -haus, -abfertigungsstelle;
to clear the ~ Zoll entrichten; **to enter at the ~** beim Zoll angeben, Zolldeklaration abgeben; **to enter out at the ~** (ship) Zollkontrolle passieren;
~ agent (broker) Zollmakler, -agent; **~ bond** Zoll-, Steuerschein; **~ broker** Zollagent, -makler; **~ charges** Zollspesen, -gebühren, -abgaben; **~ clearance (entry)** Zolldeklaration, -erklärung; **~ duty** Zollabgabe; **~ fees** Zollgebühren; **~ officer** Zollbeamter; **~ officials** Zollpersonal, -verwaltung; **~ permit** Zollabfertigungsschein; **~ receipt** Zollquittung; **~ regulations** Zollordnung; **~ seal** Zollsiegel, -plombe, -verschluß; **to remove the ~ seal** Zollplombe abnehmen; **~ searcher** Durchsuchungsbeamter des Zolls.
customize (v.) auf Bestellung (nach Maß) anfertigen.
cut (block) Klischee, Druckstock, (capital) [Kapital]herabsetzung, (film) Schneiden, Film-, Tonschnitt, (forest) abgeholzte Waldlichtung, (interest) Zinskupon, (newspaper) Zeitungsausschnitt, (reduction) [Preis]ermäßigung, -abbau, Kürzung, Reduktion, Beschneidung, Streichung, Schnitt, Herabsetzung, (road) Wegeabkürzung, (share, sl., US) Anteil, (student, coll.) Schwänzen, Blaumachen, (television) Einschneiden ohne Blendung, (text) Kürzung;
of the latest ~ nach der neuesten Mode;
aerospace ~ Kürzungen im Raumfahrtprogramm; **aid ~** Kürzung ausländischer Hilfsprogramme; **big ~** starke Ermäßigung; **committee ~** Kürzungsvorschläge eines Ausschußes; **expenditure ~** Ausgabenbeschneidung; **power ~** Stromeinsparung; **price ~** Preisreduktion, -herabsetzung, -abbau; **quick ~** Schnellstop; **salary ~** Gehaltskürzung; **short ~** Abkürzungsweg; **tax ~** Steuerherabsetzung; **wage ~** Lohnkürzung, -abbau; **~ in the budget** Etatskürzung; **~ of a coat** Schnitt eines Rockes; **~ in consumption** Verbrauchsrückgang, Konsumeinschränkung; **~ in the exemption** Freibetragskürzung; **~ in expenditure** Ausgabenkürzung; **~ in export** Export-, Ausfuhrrückgang; **~s in a film** herausgeschnittene Filmstellen; **~s in government expenditure** Kürzungen der Staatsausgaben; **~s in income tax** Einkommensteuersenkungen; **~ in interest rates** Zinssenkung; **~ of s. one's jib** äußeres Erscheinungsbild; **~ in minimum lending rate** (Br.) Herabsetzung des Mindestdiskontsatzes; **~ in the minimum reserve requirements** Mindestreservensenkung; **~s in overtime** zurückgehende (Abbau der) Überstundenzeit; **~ in pay** Lohnabzug; **~ in prices** Preisherabsetzung; **~ in production** Produktionsdrosselung; **~ in railway fares** Ermäßigung der Eisenbahnfahrpreise; **~ in rates** Gebührensenkung, Tarifabbau; **~ in rations** Rationenkürzung; **~ in rents** Mieterabsetzung, -senkung; **~ in salary** Gehaltskürzung; **~ in strength** Herabsetzung der Truppenstärke; **~ in wages** Lohnabbau;
~ (v.) kürzen, Abstriche (Kürzungen) vornehmen, beschneiden, (bookkeeping) [Verlust] abbuchen, abschreiben, (engrave) gravieren, (prices) herabsetzen, abbauen, reduzieren, (US sl.) Gewinn teilen, (school, university, sl.) schwänzen, blau machen;
~ an article by half Artikel um die Hälfte kürzen; **~ a book [open]** Buch aufschneiden; **~ business** Geschäft aufgeben; **~ a caper** Luftsprung machen, sich auffallend benehmen; **~ a claim** Anspruch reduzieren; **~ coal** Kohlen hauen; **~ one's coat according to one's cloth** sich nach der Decke strecken; **~ one's comb** (coll.) seine Ansprüche zurückstecken; **~ all connections with s. o.** mit jem. nichts mehr zu tun haben wollen, Beziehungen mit jem. abbrechen; **~ a corner** Kurve schneiden; **~ corners** (fig.) unorthodox vorgehen; **~ corners in legal procedure** (coll.) Gerichtsverfahren unkonventionell abwickeln; **~ a dash** bedeutende Rolle spielen; **~ s. o. dead** j. nicht beachten (vollständig isolieren); **~ s. o. dead in the street** auf der Straße über j. völlig hinwegsehen; **~ the discount rate** Diskont[satz] herabsetzen; **~ the enemy to pieces** Feind vernichtend schlagen; **~ one's expenses** seine Ausgaben reduzieren; **~ one's eye** (sl.) Lunte riechen; **~ it fat** prominent werden; **~ a feather** (coll.) sich verdächtig machen; **~ a poor figure** armselige Rolle spielen, jämmerliche Figur abgeben; **~ a film** Film schneiden; **~ it fine** knapp berechnen, genauestens kalkulieren, es gerade noch schaffen; **~ the ground from under s. one's feet** jem. das Wasser abgraben, jds. Argumente vorwegnehmen; **~ the gun** (sl.) Motor drosseln; **~ by half** auf die Hälfte herabsetzen; **~ s. o. to the heart** jem. in der Seele weh tun; **~ no ice** ohne Wirkung bleiben; **~ an inventory** Lager abbauen; **~ a lecture** Vorlesung schwänzen; **~ loose** sich gehen lassen, Hemmungen fallen lassen, (escape from prison) ausbrechen; **~ o. s. loose from one's family** trotz seiner Familie völlig unabhängig leben; **~ one's losses** seine Verluste abschreiben (abbuchen); **~ a melon** (US) außerordentliche Dividende ver-

teilen; ~ **the price** Preis herabsetzen; ~ **prices** empfohlene Listenpreise unterbieten; ~ **production** Produktion drosseln; ~ **s. o. to the quick** j. sehr kränken; ~ **rates** Gebühren senken, Tarif herabsetzen; ~ **the rations** Rationen kürzen; ~ **a record** Schallplatte bespielen, *(Br.)* Rekord brechen; ~ **the rediscount rate** *(US)* Diskontsatz herabsetzen; ~ **and run** *(coll.)* sich schnellstens aus dem Staube machen; ~ **s. one's salary** jds. Gehalt herabsetzen; ~ **a scene** *(theater)* Streichungen in einem Auftritt vornehmen; ~ **a shine** prominent werden, bedeutende Rolle spielen; ~ **s. o. short** j. unterbrechen, jem. das Wort abschneiden; ~ **short a career** Laufbahn plötzlich beenden; ~ **a speech short** Rede abkürzen; ~ **speed** Geschwindigkeit drosseln (herabsetzen); ~ **a splash** bedeutende Rolle spielen, prominent sein; ~ **one's stick** *(mar., sl.)* abhauen, desertieren; ~ **taxes** Steuern senken; ~ **one's teeth on it** etw. mit der Muttermilch einsaugen; ~ **a tooth** *(coll.)* kapieren; ~ **one's throat** Ast absägen, auf dem man sitzt; ~ **and try** mit Kombinationsgabe und Risikoinkaufnahme vorgehen; ~ **one's way** sich einen Weg bahnen; ~ **both ways** für und wider einer Sache besprechen; ~ **one's wisdom teeth** durch Erfahrungen klug werden.

cut *(v.)* **at all one's hopes** seine ganzen Hoffnungen zunichte machen.

cut *(v.)* **away** sich davonmachen.

cut back *(v.)* einschränken, *(film, novel)* zurückblenden; ~ **speed** Geschwindigkeit drosseln.

cut down *(v.)* *(manuscript)* zusammenstreichen, *(reduce)* herabsetzen, reduzieren, kürzen, *(retrench)* einschränken; ~ **an article** Zeitungsartikel zusammenstreichen; ~ **s. one's allowances** jds. Spesen herabsetzen; ~ **on costs** zur Kostensenkung beitragen; ~ **the drug bill** Arzneimittelkosten senken; ~ **expenses** Ausgaben einschränken; ~ **on one's foreign purchasing** seine Auslandskäufe einschränken; ~ **on a lot** sich in vielen Dingen einschränken; ~ **prices** Preise herabsetzen (abbauen); ~ **the price of an article** Warenpreis ermäßigen (reduzieren); ~ **s. one's profits** jds. Gewinnbeteiligung vermindern; ~ **s. one's salary** Gehaltskürzung bei jem. vornehmen; ~ **to size** auf die richtigen Dimensionen zurückführen; ~ **s. o. down to size** *(US sl.)* jem. gehörig die Meinung sagen.

cut in *(v.)* *(conversation)* unterbrechen, *(el., engine)* einschalten, *(traffic)* sich [unvorschriftsmäßig] einfädeln; ~ **s. o. in the spoils** *(sl.)* j. an der Beute beteiligen; ~ **titles in a motion picture** Film und Text versehen.

cut off *(v.)* Zufuhr abschneiden, *(coupon)* abtrennen, *(heir)* enterben, *(tel.)* trennen, unterbrechen; ~ **a son's allowance** dem Sohn den Wechsel sperren; ~ **the argument** Weiterbesprechung einer Sache abbrechen; ~ **one's correspondence with s. o.** Korrespondenz mit jem. abbrechen; ~ **a debate** Debatte abkürzen; ~ **the enemy's retreat** dem Feind den Rückzug abschneiden; ~ **an entail** Fideikommiß aufheben; ~ **s. o. from an estate** j. enterben; ~ **the gas** Gas abdrehen; ~ **one's life by accident** sein Leben durch einen Unfall verlieren; ~ **the negotiations** Verhandlungen abbrechen; ~ **post, water and electricity services** *(strikers)* Post-, Wasser- und Elektrizitätsversorgung unterbrechen; ~ **a sample** Muster abschneiden; ~ **s. o. off with a shilling** j. vollständig enterben; ~ **supplies** Zufuhr abschneiden; ~ **the water at the main** Haupthahn abstellen (abdrehen); ~ **a yard of cloth from the roll** Kleiderkupon vom Tuchballen abschneiden.

cut out *(v.)* *(switch off)* aus-, abschalten; ~ **superfluous details** überflüssige Einzelheiten weglassen; ~ **s. o. of his fortune** j. um sein Vermögen bringen; ~ **the middlemen** Vermittler ausschalten; ~ **a picture out of a newspaper** Bild aus der Zeitung ausschneiden; ~ **the small traders** kleine Geschäftsleute vom Markt verdrängen; ~ **West** *(fam.)* sich nach dem Westen absetzen; ~ **work for s. o.** jem. ein tüchtiges Stück Arbeit zuteilen.

cut over *(v.)* ausforsten.

cut through *(v.)* Abkürzungsweg einschlagen.

cut under *(v.)* unter dem Marktpreis verkaufen; ~ **a competitor in trade** Konkurrenten im Handel unterbieten.

cut up *(v.)* *(US sl.)* aus dem Häuschen sein; ~ **a book** Buch abwertend kritisieren; ~ **the enemy's forces** feindliche Streitkräfte vernichten; ~ **for sale** ausschlachten; ~ **well** *(sl.)* reich sterben, großes Vermögen hinterlassen.

cut, to be a ~ above s. o. [**else**] ein gutes Stück über jem. stehen; **to be quite a different ~** aus völlig anderem Holz geschnitzt sein; **to be ~ out for a job** für eine Aufgabe wie geschaffen sein; **to give s. o. the ~ direct** j. in auffälliger Weise schneiden; **to have one's work ~ for one** mit der gestellten Aufgabe fertig werden; **not to like the ~ of s. one's jib** *(sl.)* j. äußerst unsympathisch finden, j. nicht riechen können; **to make ~s in** Abstriche

(Kürzungen) vornehmen, beschneiden; **to make ~s in an article** Kürzungen in einem Artikel vornehmen, Artikel kürzen; **to make one's second ~** zum zweiten Mal Heu machen; **to make painful ~s in welfare** erhebliche Kürzungen bei den Sozialleistungen vornehmen; **to take a short ~** Abkürzungsweg einschlagen;

~ *(a.)* ermäßigt, erniedrigt, herabgesetzt;

~-**and-come again** Hülle und Fülle; ~ **and dried** längst entschieden; ~-**and-dried affair** abgekartete Sache; ~-**in advertisement** an mehrere Seiten Text angeschlossenes Inserat, *(local advertising)* lokale Werbeeinschaltung; ~ **flowers** Schnittblumen; ~-**off rule** Trennlinie; ~-**out letters** gestanzte Buchstaben; ~ **price** ermäßigter (reduzierter) Spezial-, Sonderpreis; ~-**price** heruntergesetzt, billig; ~-**price car buying** Autokauf zu Sonderpreisen; ~-**price competitor** preisunterbietende Konkurrenz; ~-**price shop** Diskontgeschäft; ~ **rate** *(US)* herabgesetzter (äußerster) Preis.

cut-rate *(US)* ermäßigt, herabgesetzt, äußerst kalkuliert; ~ **fare** stark verbilligte Fahrkarte; ~ **price** schärfstens kalkulierter Preis, Kampf-, Schleuder-, Unterbietungs-, Reklame-, Werbepreis.

cutback *(film)* Rückblende, Wiederholung, *(laying-off of workers)* Arbeitskräfteabbau, *(US)* Reduzierung, Kürzung, Abbau, Abstrich, Einschränkung;
expenditure-account ~ Beschneidung des Spesenetats; ~ **in capital spending** Kürzung von Investitionsvorhaben; ~ **in investments** Abbau der Investitionstätigkeit; ~ **in orders** Auftragskürzung; ~ **in prices** Preisrücknahme, -abbau; ~ **of production** Produktionsdrosselung; ~ **in staff** Verkleinerung der Belegschaft;
~ **target** Kürzungssoll.

cutoff Wegabkürzung, *(accounting)* Einstellung des Buchungsverkehrs für Revisionszwecke, *(industry, US)* Einstellung bestimmter Fertigungszweige;
~ **of foreign aid** Einstellung der Auslandshilfe;
~ **date** Inventurtermin; ~ **point** Trennungsstrich; ~ **rule** *(newspaper)* Trennlinie [zum Anzeigenteil]; ~ **statement** Zwischenbilanz.

cutout Ausschnitt, Ausstanzstück, Schablone, *(car)* Auspuffklappe, *(el.)* Kurzschluß, *(film)* herausgeschnittene Szene.

cutter, revenue Zollwachschiff, -kutter.

cutthroat Halsabschneider, Meuchelmörder, Gewaltverbrecher;
~ *(a.)* mörderisch, halsabschneiderisch, ruinös;
~ **competition** Schmutzkonkurrenz, halsabschneiderische Konkurrenz, mörderischer Wettbewerb; ~ **competitor** Konkurrenzfirma mit unanständigen Geschäftsmethoden; ~ **price** Schleuder-, Kampfpreis, mörderischer (ruinöser) Preis.

cutting Ausschnitt, Ausschnitt, *(of plant)* Steckling, Setzling, *(prices)* Unterbieten, Herabsetzung, Preisdrückerei, Konkurrenzunterbietung;
~**s** *(film)* Filmabfälle;
newspaper (press) ~ Zeitungsausschnitt; ~ **off** Abtrennung; ~ **away wreck** Kappen von Wrackteilen; ~ **back of production** Produktionskürzung; ~ **down** Herabsetzung, Kürzung; ~ **down the expenses** Abstrich von Unkosten; ~ **in** *(traffic)* [unvorschriftsmäßige] Einfädelung; ~ **of inventory** Lagerabbau; ~ **the melon** *(US coll.)* Ausschüttung einer außerordentlichen Dividende; ~ **from a newspaper** Zeitungsausschnitt; ~ **of prices** Preisabbau, -herabsetzung, -reduzierung; ~ **of rations** Rationenkürzung; ~ **of wages** Lohnkürzung, -herabsetzung; **to prevent cost** ~ **of the budget rate** etatsmäßig vorgesehene Kürzungssätze verhindern;
~ **remark** beißende Bemerkung; ~ **room** *(film)* Schneideraum; ~ **trade** Schleudergeschäft; ~ **tradesman** Preisdrücker.

cy-près doctrine *(law of inheritance)* möglichst wohlwollende Auslegung des Erblasserwillens.

cybernetics Kybernetik.

cycle Zyklus, Kreislauf, Folge, Serie, *(engine)* Motortakt;
business (economic) ~ Konjunkturzyklus, -rhythmus, -verlauf, -ablauf; **down-**~ Konjunkturrückgang; **up-**~ konjunkturelle Aufwärtsbewegung;
~ **of economy** Konjunkturzyklus; ~ **in productivity** Produktivitätszyklus;
business ~ **analysis** Konjunkturanalyse; ~ **billing** über den Monat verteilte Rechnungsaufstellung; ~ **car** Kleinwagen, Kabinenroller; ~ **dealer** Fahrradhändler; ~ **depot** Fahrradaufbewahrung; ~-**induced** konjunkturbedingt; ~ **issue dates** periodisch wiederkehrende Erscheinungstermine; ~ **path** Radfahrweg; ~ **rider** *(fig.)* Konjunktursteurer; ~ **track** Fahrradweg; ~ **trade** Fahrradgeschäft; ~ **trailer** Fahrradanhänger; **business-turning point** konjunktureller Wendepunkt.

cyclical zyklisch, konjunkturrhythmisch, konjunkturell;
~ **analysis** Konjunkturanalyse; ~ **boom** konjunkturelle Wirtschaftsblüte, Hochkonjunktur, Hausse; ~ **budgeting** [anti]zyklische Wirtschaftspolitik, konjunkturell ausgerichtete Haushaltspolitik; **highly** ~ **business** stark konjunkturbedingtes Geschäft; ~ **considerations** konjunkturpolitische Überlegungen; ~ **contraction of general business activity** zyklische Konjunkturschrumpfung; ~ **course** Konjunkturverlauf; ~ **decline** konjunktureller Rückgang, Konjunkturschwäche, -rückgang; ~ **depression** Tiefkonjunktur; ~ **downswing** konjunktureller Einbruch, Konjunkturabschwung; ~ **downswing phase** Phase konjunktureller Talfahrt; ~ **downturn** konjunktureller Abschwung, Konjunkturabschwung; ~ **factor** konjunktureller Faktor; ~ **fall** Konjunkturrückgang, -sturz; ~ **fall in steel demand** konjunkturbedingter Nachfragerückgang in Stahl; ~ **field** Konjunkturgebiet; ~ **fluctuations [in business]** konjunkturelle Schwankungen, Konjunkturschwankungen; ~ **improvement** konjunkturelle Besserung; ~ **improvement in productivity** konjunkturbedingte Produktivitätssteigerung; ~ **industries** stark konjunkturabhängige (-empfindliche) Industriezweige; ~ **influence** Konjunktureinflüsse; ~ **irregularity** konjunkturelle Schwankungen; ~ **maladjustment** konjunkturelle Fehlanpassung; ~ **movement** zyklischer Konjunkturverlauf, Konjunkturbewegung; ~ **pattern** Konjunkturschema; ~ **policy** Konjunkturpolitik; **to be in line with** ~ **policy** als konjunkturgerecht anzusehen sein; ~ **price increase** konjunkturbedingter Preisanstieg; ~ **prospects** Konjunkturaussichten; **for** ~ **reasons** aus konjunkturpolitischen Gründen, konjunkturbedingt; ~ **recovery** Wiederanziehen der Konjunktur, Konjunkturanstieg, -belebung, -erholung; ~ **rise in price** konjunkturbedingter Preisauftrieb; ~ **situation** konjunkturpolitische Lage; ~ **strains** konjunkturelle Anstrengungen; ~ **swing** *(US)* Konjunkturumschwung, -wende; ~ **tendencies** konjunkturelle Tendenzen; **past** ~ **time pattern** Modelle aus früheren Konjunkturperioden; ~ **trend** Konjunkturverlauf, -tendenz, -änderung, -entwicklung, -verlauf, konjunkturelle Entwicklung; ~ **turnaround** konjunkturelle Tendenzwende; ~ **unemployment** konjunkturell bedingte Arbeitslosigkeit; ~ **upsurge** konjunktureller Auftrieb; ~ **upswing** konjunktureller Aufschwung; **to strengthen the** ~ **upswing** Konjunkturaufschwung intensivieren; ~ **uptrend** Konjunkturauftrieb; ~ **upward movement** konjunkturelle Aufwärtsbewegung.

cyclically│induced konjunkturbedingt; ~ **undesirable** konjunkturpolitisch unerwünscht;
to contract ~ zyklischen Kontraktionen unterworfen sein.

cyclist Radfahrer.

cyclone Wirbelsturm.

cyclorama *(US)* Rundgemälde.

cylinder *(engine)* Zylinder, *(print.)* Rotationswalze;
~ **print** Walzdruck.

D

dab *(expert, coll.)* Experte, Könner, *(printing)* Farbballen, *(sl.)* Fingerabdruck;
  ~ *(v.)* etching abklatschen, klischieren;
  to be a ~ at s. th. sich auf eine Sache verstehen.

dabble *(v.)* sich oberflächlich beschäftigen, pfuschen;
  ~ **in (at) law** in der Juristerei dilettieren; ~ **in politics** politisieren; ~ **in speculative concerns** sich auf gewagte Geschäfte einlassen; ~ **on the stock exchange** [ein bißchen, mit kleinsten Gewinnen] an der Börse spekulieren; ~ **in writing** nebenbei schriftstellern.

dabbler Amateur, Dilettant, Pfuscher, *(stock exchange)* Börsendilettant, kleiner Spekulant;
  ~ **in politics** politischer Kannegießer, Stammtischpolitiker.

dabster *(Br., dial.)* Experte, Könner, Meister, *(dabbler, coll.)* Stümper, Pfuscher, Dilettant.

dactylogram Fingerabdruck.

dagger Dolch, *(fig.)* Kriegsfuß, *(print.)* Kreuzzeichen;
  to be at ~s drawn auf Kriegsfuß stehen; **to speak ~s** verletzende Worte sprechen.

dailies, leading führende Tageszeitungen.

daily Tageszeitung, täglich erscheinende Zeitung, *(insurance agent)* Tagesbericht, *(servant, Br.)* Tagesmädchen;
  ~ *(a.)* werktäglich, täglich, *(fig.)* tagtäglich, ständig;
  to appear ~ täglich erscheinen;
  ~ **allowance** Tagesspesen, Tagegeld, Verpflegungsentschädigung; ~ **balance** Tagesbestand, *(account)* täglicher Saldo; **average ~ balance** *(interest computation)* Durchschnittstagessaldo; ~ **balance book** Tagesabschlußbuch; **one's ~ bread** sein tägliches Brot; ~ **breader** *(Br.)* Pendler, Zeitkarteninhaber; ~ **Bullion Return** *(Br.)* Tagesausweis der Bank von England über ihre Goldbestände; ~ **capacity** [maschinelle] Tagesleistung; ~ **cash settlement** *(motor carrier agent)* Tagesabrechnung; ~ **consumer needs** täglicher Konsumbedarf; ~ **consumption** Tagesverbrauch; ~ **dozen** Routinearbeit, *(coll.)* morgendliche Freiübungen, tägliche Gymnastik; ~ **earnings** Tagesverdienst; ~ **emplanement** täglicher Flugzeugverkehr; ~ **experience** alltägliche Erfahrung; ~ **extra pay** Tageszulage; ~ **fee** Tagegeld; ~ **interest** Tageszinsen; ~ **loadings** Tagesversand; ~ **loading list** Tagesversandmeldung; ~ **loan** *(money, Br.)* Tagesgeld; ~ **mail** Tagespost; ~ **[news]paper** Tageszeitung; ~ **newspaper press** Tagespresse; ~ **occupation** übliche Beschäftigung; ~ **output** Tagesproduktion, -leistung; ~ **pay** Tagesentlohnung; ~ **payroll** tägliche Lohnauszahlung; ~ **performance report** täglicher Arbeitsbericht; ~ **press** Tagespresse; ~ **price per sheet** Bogentagespreis; ~ **prints** *(US)* Tageszeitungen; ~ **produce** Tagesleistung, -produktion; ~ **quotation** Tagesnotierung, -kurs; ~ **rate** *(banking)* Tagessatz, *(rent-a-car)* Tagesgrundpreis, Tageslohnsatz; ~ **ration** Tagesration, -satz, -bedarf; ~ **receipts** tägliche Einkünfte, Tageseinnahme; ~ **report** Tagesbericht; ~ **returns** Tagesumsatz; **the ~ round** der tägliche Trott; ~ **routine** Tagesablauf, Alltagsbeschäftigung, Dienstbetrieb; ~ **sales** Tagesumsatz, -einnahme; ~ **schedule** Tagesprogramm; ~ **servant** Tageshilfe, Lohndiener; ~ **shipment** *(US)* Tagesversand; ~ **shopping** täglicher Einkauf; **to do one's ~ stint** sein Tagespensum erledigen; ~ **takings** Tageseinnahmen; ~ **task** Tagewerk; ~ **telegraphic quotation** tägliche Kursdepesche; ~ **turnover** Tagesumsatz; ~ **wages** Tagelohnsatz, -verdienst; ~ **wage rate** Tageslohnsatz.

dainty köstlich, erlesen, exquisit;
  to be ~ about one's food Ansprüche an sein Essen stellen, verwöhnt sein.

dairy Molkerei;
  ~ **cattle** Milchvieh; ~ **farm** Meierei, Molkerei; ~ **farming** Molkerei-, Milchwirtschaft; ~ **husbandry** Milchwirtschaft; ~ **industry** Milchwirtschaft; ~ **lunch** *(US coll.)* Milchbar; ~ **produce** Molkereierzeugnisse; ~ **products** Molkerei, Meiereierzeugnisse.

dairyman Melker, Schweizer, *(seller)* Milchmann, -händler.

daisy *(sl.)* Perle, Prachtstück.

dam [Stau]damm, Deich, Talsperre;
  ~ *(v.)* eindämmen, stauen;
  ~ **up one's feelings** seine Emotionen zügeln; ~ **up s. one's eloquence** jds. Beredsamkeit Einhalt gebieten.

damn, not to give a sich nichts daraus machen.

damage Schaden, Beschädigung, Nachteil, Beeinträchtigung, *(loss)* Verlust, Einbuße, *(sl.)* Zeche, Rechnung;
  ~s [gerichtlich anerkannter] Schadensersatz[anspruch], Scha-

densbetrag, Entschädigung, Entschädigungssumme, Schadloshaltung;
  held (liable) for (liable to pay, respond in) ~s schadenersatzpflichtig, zum Schadenersatz verpflichtet;
  accidental collision ~ durch einen Autounfall entstandener Schaden; **actual ~** tatsächlicher (tatsächlich entstandener) Schaden; **actual ~s** angemessener Schadenersatz; **added ~s** erlittenen Schaden übersteigender Ersatzanspruch, Buße; **ascertained ~** festgestellter Schaden; **affirmative ~** geltendgemachter Schadensersatz; **airraid ~** Bombenschaden; **awarded ~s** zuerkannter Schadenersatz; **cattle ~** durch Vieh angerichteter Schaden; **civil ~s** *(US)* zivilrechtlicher Schadensersatzanspruch gegen Personen [durch deren Alkoholausschank Dritte Schaden anrichten]; **compensatory ~s** Ersatz des tatsächlichen Schadens, Ausgleichsentschädigung; **consequential ~** mittelbarer Schaden, Folgeschaden; **consequential ~s** Schadensersatz für entgangenen Gewinn; **contemptuous ~s** formaler Schadenersatz; **contingent ~s** *(US)* bedingt zuerkannter Schadensersatzanspruch; **continuing ~s** fortlaufende Schadensersatzzahlungen; **criminal ~** schwere Sachbeschädigung, verbrecherische Schadenszufügung; **direct ~** unmittelbarer Schaden; **direct ~s** Ersatz des unmittelbaren Schadens; **discretionary ~** im Ermessenswege zuerkannter Schadenersatz; **~ done** verursachter Schaden; **excessive ~s** überhöhte Schadensersatzleistungen; **exemplary ~s** verschärfter Schadensersatz, Bußgeld; **fair ~s** angemessener Schadensersatz; **extensive ~** beträchtlicher Schaden; **fee ~s** *(real estate)* Ersatz des Substanzschadens; **field ~** Flurschaden; **general ~s** *(national insurance)* Ersatz der üblichen Schäden, nicht in Geld feststellbarer Schaden; **indirect ~** mittelbarer Schaden; **intervening ~s** durch Verzögerung der Zuerkennung entstehender Schadenersatz; **irreparable ~s** Ersatz für nicht wiedergutzumachenden Schaden; **known ~** *(carrier)* festgestellter Schaden; **land ~s** Enteignungsentschädigung; **liquidated ~s** vertraglich festgesetzte (vereinbarte, vorausgeschätzte) Schadenssumme, vertraglich anerkannten Schadensersatzanspruch, Vertrag-, Konventionalstrafe; **malicious ~** vorsätzliche Sachbeschädigung; **material ~** materieller Schaden, Sachschaden, Schaden wirtschaftlicher Art; **minimal ~** Bagatellschaden; **necessary ~s** Ersatz aller Schadensfolgen; **negligible ~** unbedeutender Schaden; **nominal ~** nomineller (geringfügiger, unbedeutender) Schaden; **nominal ~s** aus Rechtsgründen zuerkannter Schadensersatz, der Form halber festgesetzte geringe Schadensersatzleistung; **observed ~** festgestellter Schaden; **pecuniary ~s** Schadensersatz in Geld; **permanent ~s** *(real property)* anerkannte Schadenshaftung; **personal ~** Personenschaden; **presumptive ~s** Bußgeld, Konventionalstrafe; **prospective ~s** Ersatz des unmittelbaren Schadens; **proved ~** festgestellter Schadensersatzanspruch; **proximate ~** unmittelbarer Schaden; **punitive ~s** *(US)* Bußgeld, Buße; **remote ~** indirekter (nicht voraussehbarer) Schaden; **resulting ~** entstandener Schaden; **retributive ~s** *(US)* verschärfter Schadensersatz; **serious ~** *(mar.)* schwere Havarie; **ship ~** Havarie, Seeschaden; **slight ~** leichte Beschädigung; **small ~** geringfügige Schäden; **special ~** Schaden im Einzelfall, konkreter Schaden; **special ~s** Schadensersatz für Folgeschaden, *(national insurance)* besonders nachzuweisender zusätzlicher Schadensersatzanspruch; **speculative ~** vorausberechenbarer Schaden; **speculative ~s** für Folgeschäden vorsorglich festgesetzter Schadensersatz; **substantial ~s** Schadensersatz für tatsächlich eingetretene Schäden, Schadenersatz in beträchtlicher Höhe; **~ suffered** erlittener Schaden; **~s sustained** entstandene Ersatzansprüche; **temporary ~s** Ersatz für zeitweise erlittenen Schaden; **unaccrued ~** noch nicht eingetretener Schaden; **unliquidated ~s** der Höhe nach nicht festgestellter Schadensbetrag, unbezifferte Schadensforderung; **war ~** Kriegsschäden; **water ~** Wasserschaden; **wilful ~** absichtliche Beschädigung;
  ~ **resulting from an accident** Unfallfolgen; ~s **for breach of contract** Schadensersatz wegen Vertragsverletzung; ~ **to a car** Autobeschädigung, -schaden; ~ **to cargo** Schäden der Ladung; ~ **chargeable to you** von Ihnen zu vertretender Schaden; ~ **to credit** Kreditschädigung; ~s **for deceit** Schadenersatz wegen arglistiger Täuschung; ~ **by intrinsic defects** Schaden durch inneren Verderb; ~s **for delay in finishing** Schadensersatz wegen verspäteter Fertigstellung; ~s **for wrongful dismissal** Schadensersatz wegen widerrechtlicher Kündigung; ~ **to a factory** Fabrikbeschädigung; ~ **[caused] by fire** Brand-, Feuer-

schaden; **partial ~ to goods** Teilschaden; **~s at large** Pauschalentschädigung; **~s at law** gesetzlicher Schadensersatzanspruch; **~ by lightning** Blitzschaden; **~ through loss of use** Nutzungsschaden; **~ to machinery** Maschinenschaden; **~s for nonacceptance** Schadenersatz wegen Annahmeverweigerung; **~s for nondelivery** Schadenersatz wegen ausgebliebener Lieferung; **~s for nonfulfil(l)ment** Schadenersatz wegen Nichterfüllung; **~s for pain and suffering** *(Br.)* Schmerzensgeld; **~ to person** Körperverletzung; **~ to property** Sachbeschädigung, -schaden, Vermögensschaden; **~ to reputation** Ruf-, Kreditschädigung; **~ by sea** Seeschaden, Havarie; **~ by a storm** Windbruch, Sturmschäden; **unliquidated ~s for tort** unbezifferter Schadensersatz wegen unerlaubter Handlung; **~s for the tort of deceit or fraud** Schadensersatz für Täuschungs-, oder Betrugsdelikte; **~ in transit** Transportschaden; **~ caused by water** Wasserschaden; **~ by sea water** Seeschaden, Havarie;

~ *(v. t.)* schaden, [be]schädigen, Schaden zufügen, *(infringe)* beeinträchtigen, benachteiligen, *(injure)* verletzen, *(v. i.) (lose in value)* Schaden nehmen, an Wert verlieren;

to ascertain ~s Schaden feststellen (aufnehmen); **to assess the ~** Schaden ermitteln (abschätzen); **to assess the ~s** Schadenersatz der Höhe nach feststellen; **to award ~s** auf Schadenersatz erkennen, zur Leistung von Schadenersatz verurteilen; **to be answerable for ~s** Schaden zu vertreten haben, schadenersatzpflichtig sein; **to be awarded ~s** Anspruch auf Schadenersatz erhalten; **to be awarded entitlement in ~s** Anspruch auf Schadenersatz erhalten; **to be cast in ~s** zum Schadenersatz verurteilt werden; **to be liable in (responsible for) ~s** für einen Schaden haften, schadenersatzpflichtig sein; **to bear the ~** Schaden tragen; **to bring an action for ~s against s. o.** j. auf Schadenersatz verklagen; **to cause ~** Schaden zufügen (anrichten), schaden, beschädigen; **to claim as ~s** Entschädigung fordern (beanspruchen); **to do s. one's cause irreparable ~** jds. Sache unersetzlichen Schaden zufügen; **to claim constructive ~s** Ersatz des mittelbaren Schadens verlangen; **to claim ~s for breach of contract** Schadenersatz wegen Vertragsbruchs verlangen; **to claim ~s for loss of expectation of life** Schadenersatz für geringere Lebenserwartung verlangen; **to collect ~s** Schadenersatz verlangen; **to come upon s. o. for ~s** j. wegen Schadenersatzes belangen; **to disallow ~s** Schadenersatz verweigern; **to do ~ to one's reputation** seinem Ruf schaden; **to estimate the ~** Schaden abschätzen (aufnehmen, ermitteln); **to inflict ~** Schaden zufügen; **to lay ~s** Schadenersatz berechnen (feststellen); **to make good the ~ done to s. o.** jem. seinen Schaden ersetzen; **to mitigate one's ~** seinen Schaden mildern; **to obtain ~s** entschädigt werden; **to obtain ~s in tort** Schadenersatz wegen unerlaubter Handlung erlangen; **to offer an equivalent for ~ done** gleichwertigen Schadensersatz anbieten; **to order ~s** zur Schadenersatzleistung verurteilen; **to pay for (respond in, *US*) ~s** Schadenersatz leisten; **to prove the ~ to one's credit** Kreditschädigung nachweisen; **to recover ~s** Schadenersatz erhalten; **to repair the ~** Schaden beheben; **to seek 2 million in ~s** zwei Millionen Dollar Schadenersatz einklagen; **to sound in ~s** Schadenersatzanspruch begründen; **to sue for ~s** auf Entschädigung klagen; **to sue for ~s at large** Grundsatzurteil beantragen; **to sue for ~s by way of recovery** Schadenersatz auf dem Regreßwege verlangen; **to suffer ~** Schaden erleiden (nehmen), *(ship)* Havarie machen; **to suffer permanent ~** Dauerschaden davontragen; **to sustain ~** Schaden erleiden, geschädigt werden; **to value ~** Schaden abschätzen;

~s claim Schadenersatzanspruch; **faisant (feasant)** Schadenszufüger; **cattle ~ feasant** durch Vieh angerichteter Schaden; **~s law** Schadenersatzrecht; **~ report** Schadensbericht, -aufstellung; **~s suit** Schadenersatzprozeß, -klage; **~ survey** *(average)* Havariegutachten.

damageable leicht zu beschädigen.

damaged beschädigt, schadhaft, defekt, *(spoiled)* verdorben; **badly ~** schwer beschädigt; **slightly ~** leicht beschädigt; **seriously ~** schwer beschädigt; **~ by fire** feuerbeschädigt; **~ by sea water** durch Seewasser beschädigt; **~ in transit** auf dem Transport beschädigt; **~ condition** schlechte Beschaffenheit, beschädigter Zustand; **~ goods** Ausschuß[ware], *(cargo)* Havarieware; **in a ~ state** in schlechtem Zustand; **at a ~ valuation** zu herabgesetzten [Tax]preisen.

damager Schadenzufüger.

damaging admission nachteiliges Zugeständnis.

dame Matrone, alte Dame, *(school)* Vorsteherin, Direktorin; **~ school** *(Br.)* Privatschule für Mädchen.

damn Fluch, *(sl.)* Deut, Pfifferling; **~** *(v.)* verurteilen, ablehnen, verwerfen;

~ a book Buch einhellig ablehnen; **~ a play** Stück durchfallen lassen; **not to care a ~** sich einen Dreck um etw. kümmern; **not to be worth a ~** keinen Pfifferling wert sein.

damnable weather miserables Wetter.

damnation Verdammung, Ablehnung.

damnification Schädigung, Beeinträchtigung.

damnify *(v.)* [be]schädigen, Schaden zufügen.

damning evidence erdrückendes Beweismaterial.

damnum *(lat.)* Verlust, Schaden.

damp Feuchtigkeit, *(fig.)* Entmutigung, Dämpfer, *(mining)* Gruben-, Schlagwetter; **~** *(v.) (fig.)* dämpfen, bremsen; **~ down import demands** Einfuhrbedürfnissen nicht voll entsprechen; **~ s. one's spirit** jds. Begeisterung dämpfen; **to cast a ~ over the holidays** Schatten auf die Ferientage werfen; **~ start** Starthilfe bei Feuchtigkeit.

dampen *(v.)* dämpfen, drosseln; **~ inflation** Inflation zügeln.

dampening of business spending Dämpfung (Drosselung) der Investitionstätigkeit; **~ of demand** Nachfragedämpfung; **~ down of inflation** Inflationsdrosselung; **~ of output** Produktionsdrosselung; **~ of rates of growth** Abschwächung der Wachstumsraten.

damper Schieber, *(cash register, US sl.)* Registrierkasse, *(fig.)* Dämpfer; **to cast a ~ on** entmutigen.

dance Tanz; **~** *(v.)* **attendance upon s. o.** bei jem. antichambrieren; **~ to s. one's tune** nach jds. Pfeife tanzen; **~ another tune** sich den veränderten Verhältnissen anpassen; **~ after s. one's whistle** nach jds. Pfeife tanzen; **to lead s. o. a pretty ~** j. ganz schön an der Nase herumführen; **~ band (orchestra)** Tanzorchester, -kapelle.

dancing hall *(US)* öffentliches Tanzlokal; **~ master** Tanzlehrer; **~ partner** Tanzpartner; **~ room** Tanzlokal, -boden; **~ saloon** *(US)* öffentliches Tanzlokal; **~ school** Tanzschule.

dandy note *(Br.)* Zollfreigabeschein.

danger Gefahr, Gefährdung, Risiko, *(railway)* Haltesignal, -zeichen; **in ~ of death** in Todesgefahr; **in the presence of ~** angesichts der Gefahr; **apparent ~** unmittelbare (augenscheinliche) Gefahr; **common ~** gemeinsame Gefahr; **constant ~** dauernde Gefahr; **extreme ~** äußerste Gefahr; **imminent ~** unmittelbare Gefahr; **public ~** Gefahr für die Öffentlichkeit; **~ of bankruptcy** Konkursgefahr; **~ of breakage** Bruchgefahr; **~ of collapsing** Einsturzgefahr; **~ of prejudicing the course of justice** Verdunkelungsgefahr; **~ of inflation** Inflationsgefahr; **immediate ~ to life** unmittelbare Lebensgefahr, Leibesgefahr; **~ to life and limb** Gemeingefahr; **~s of navigation** Gefahren der Seefahrt, Schiffahrtsrisiko; **~ to peace** Friedensbedrohung; **~s of the river** Flußrisiko; **~s of the road** *(bill of lading)* Gefahr des schlechten Straßenzustands; **~s of the sea** Seegefahr, -risiko; **~s to national security** Gefahr für die Staatssicherheit; **~ to shipping** Gefahrenquelle für die Schiffahrt; **~s incident to travel** reiseübliche Gefahren; **~ of war** Kriegsgefahr; **to be in mortal ~** in Todesgefahr schweben; **to be out of ~** außer Gefahr sein; **to incur ~** sich Gefahren aussetzen; **to wash in all ~s** allen Gefahren standhalten; **~, building unsafe!** Vorsicht, Baustelle, Einsturzgefahr!; **~ area** Gefahrenzone; **~ bonus** Gefahrenzulage; **to be on the ~ list** lebensgefährlich erkrankt sein; **~ money** Gefahrenzulage, -geld; **~ point** Gefahrenpunkt; **~ position** *(railway)* Gefahrensignal; **~ signal** Gefahrsignal; **to have the effect of a ~ signal** Signalwirkung ausüben; **~ spot** Gefahrenpunkt, -stelle; **~ warning** Gefahrenmeldung; **~ zone** Gefahrenzone, *(mar.)* Warngebiet, *(pol.)* Krisengebiet, *(mil.)* Sperrzone, -gebiet; **~-zone bonus** Gefahrenzulage.

dangerous gefährlich, unsicher, riskant, bedenklich; **~ to health** gesundheitsschädlich; **~ per se** von Natur aus gefährlich; **to be ~ for the public** Gefahr für die öffentliche Sicherheit darstellen, gemeingefährlich sein; **~ articles** Gefahrgüter; **~ cargo** gefährliche Ladung; **~ driving** Verkehrsgefährdung; **~ goods** gefährliches Transportgut; **to be on ~ ground** *(coll.)* sich auf gefährlichem Boden bewegen (befinden); **~ occurrence** gefährliches Ereignis; **~ place** Gefahrenstelle; **~ premises** gefährliche Betriebe; **~ state** Gefährdungszustand; **~ trades** gefährliche Gewerbe.

dangle *(v.)* | **bright prospects before s. o.** jem. eine glänzende Zukunft vorgaukeln; ~ **round s. o.** um jem. herumscharwenzeln, jem. nicht vom Leibe gehen.

dangler Schürzenjäger, *(advertisement)* Deckenhänger, Mobile.

darbies Handschellen.

dark Dunkelheit, *(fig.)* Ungewißheit;
~ *(a.)* unklar, dunkel, kompliziert, *(obscure)* unverständlich;
~ **for a month** *(theater)* einen Monat lang geschlossen;
to be in the ~ im Dunkeln tappen; **to be kept in the** ~ im Ungewissen gehalten werden; **to be quite in the** ~ **about s. th.** gar nichts über etw. wissen; **to keep s. th.** ~ Geheimnis bewahren; **to keep s. o. in the** ~ j. im Ungewissen lassen;
~ **ages** Mittelalter; ⚲ **Continent** Schwarzer Kontinent, Afrika; ~ **curtain material** Verdunkelungsmaterial; **to habo(u)r** ~ **designs** dunkle Absichten hegen; ~ **dungeon** finsteres Verlieẞ; ~ **future** freudlose Zukunft; ~ **glasses** Sonnenbrille; ~ **horse** Außenseiter, unbeschriebenes Blatt, unbekannte Größe, *(pol.)* Überraschungskandidat, wenig bekannter Kandidat; ~ **lantern** Blendlaterne; ~ **room** *(photo)* Dunkelkammer; ~ **side of things** Schattenseite der Dinge; **to look on the** ~ **side of things** alles immer nur pessimistisch betrachten; ~ **secret** dunkles Geheimnis; ~ **slide** *(photo)* Kassette.

darken *(v.)* verdunkeln;
not ~ **s. one's door** jds. Schwelle nicht betreten.

darkened room verdunkeltes Zimmer.

darkness Dunkelheit, *(fig.)* Ungewißheit, Unklarheit;
under cover of ~ unter dem Schutz der Dunkelheit.

darkroom *(photo)* Dunkelkammer;
~ **equipment** Dunkelkammerausrüstung.

dash Schuß, Anflug, *(sudden rush)* stürmischer Anlauf, Vorstoß, Schwung, Elan, *(stroke of the pen)* Federstrich, *(telegraphy)* Morsestrich;
~ **at the enemy** Sturm auf den Feind;
~ *(v.)* **out one's brains** sich den Kopf zerbrechen; ~ **off an essay** Aufsatz herunterschreiben; ~ **to pieces** in Stücke schlagen; ~ **wine with water** Wein mit Wasser vermischen;
to cut a ~ gute Figur machen; **to make a** ~ **at the enemy** auf den Feind losstürmen; **to make a** ~ **for freedom** Vorstoß für die Freiheit unternehmen; **to show a** ~ **of improvement** leichte Besserungstendenz erkennen lassen;
~ **control-knob** Kontrollknopfregelung auf dem Armaturenbrett; ~ **light** Armaturenbrettbeleuchtung.

dashboard *(car)* Armaturen-, Instrumentenbrett;
anti-impact ~ stoßgedämpftes Amaturenbrett;
~ **display** Armaturenanzeiger; ~ **light** Armaturenbeleuchtung.

data Einzelheiten, Angaben, Unterlagen, Zahlen-, Ziffernmaterial, *(statistics)* Beobachtungsmaterial;
brief ~ kurze Angaben; **business** ~ Betriebsangaben; **fundamental** ~ grundlegende Tatsachen; **general** ~ allgemeine Angaben; **integrated** ~ zusammengefaßte Daten; **personal** ~ Personalien, Angaben zur Person; **statistical** ~ statistisches Material;
~ **of production** Produktionsziffern; ~ **of sales** Verkaufsziffern, Umsatzzahlen; **personal** ~ **and testimonial** Bewerbungsunterlagen;
to bring ~ **to internationally comparable standards** Zahlenmaterial in einer international vergleichbaren Weise aufbereiten; **to collect** ~ Daten erfassen; **to furnish** ~ Informationen beschaffen; **to process** ~ Daten verarbeiten; **to register** ~ **with s. o.** jem. Angaben vorlegen;
~ **bank** Datenbank; ~ **caption** Daten-, Texterfassung; ~ **case** *(airplane)* Vorschriftenfach; ~ **cell** Magnetstreifen; ~ **collection** Text-, Datenerfassung; ~ **communication** Datenübermittlung; ~ **computer** Rechengerät; ~ **gathering** Daten-, Texterfassung; ~-**gathering process** Datenspeicherungsverfahren; ~ **handling** Datenverarbeitung; ~-**handling** datenverarbeitend; ~-**handling capacity** Datenverarbeitungskapazität; ~ **logger** Dauerspeicher; **same-day priority** ~ **post door-to-door service** Zustellung von Vorrangpost am gleichen Tag; ~ **processing** Materialaufbereitung; ~ **processing center** Rechenzentrum; ~ **processing equipment** Einrichtungen für Datenverarbeitung; ~ **processing facilities** Datenverarbeitungsanlagen; ~ **processing machine** Rechenanlage; ~-**manager** Leiter der Datenverarbeitung; ~-**processing plan** Datenverarbeitungsschema; ~ **record** Datensatz, -stapel; ~ **retrieval** Datenrückgewinnung; ~ **set** Datenverarbeitungsgerät; ~ **sheet** statistische Tabelle; ~ **storage** Datenspeicherung; ~ **storage process** Informationsspeicherverfahren; ~ **transmission** Datenübertragung; **electronic** ~ **transmission process** elektronisches Informationsübermittlungsverfahren; ~ **transmission system** Datenübertragungssystem; ~ **transmitter** Datenübermittler.

date [Ausfertigungs]datum, Datum und Ortsangabe, *(appointment, coll.)* Verabredung, Stelldichein, Rendezvouz, *(assigned length of time)* Frist, *(bill of exchange)* Ausstellungstag, *(coin)* Herstellungsjahr, *(fixed day)* Termin, Zeitangabe, -punkt, *(period)* Epoche, Zeitraum;
after ~ nach dato; **as per** ~ bis zum heutigen Tage; **at an early** ~ in nicht zu langer Zeit; **at the earliest** ~ so früh wie möglich; **at a long** ~ auf lange Sicht; **at the usual** ~ Ziel wie gewöhnlich; **from this** ~ nach dato; **in order of** ~ datumsmäßig; **of recent** ~ neueren Datums, modern; **of the same** ~ gleichen Datums, vom gleichen Tag, gleichzeitig; **out of** ~ veraltet, überholt, *(check)* Einlösungsfrist abgelaufen; **prior to** ~ vordatiert; **three months after** ~ **to** ~ bis auf den heutigen Tag; **under this** ~ unter heutigem Datum; **under** ~ **of the 1st inst.** vom 1. des Monats datiert; **up to** ~ aktuell, zeitgemäß, modern; **without** ~ undatiert, ohne Zeitangabe (Datumsangabe), *(à jour)* bis dato, auf dem laufenden;
appointed ~ Stichtag, festgesetzter Termin; **average** ~ mittlerer Termin; **[average] due** ~ [durchschnittlicher] Verfalltag [eines Wechsels], Fälligkeitstermin; **calendar** ~ Kalendertag; **cancellation** ~ *(contract)* Kündigungstermin; **closing** ~ Schlußtermin, *(advertising)* Anzeigenschluß, *(tender)* Ausschreibungsschluß; **code** ~ *(food)* Datumsangabe; **commencing** ~ Anfangstermin; **contract** ~ Vertragsdatum; **crucial** ~ Stichtag; **due** ~ verstrichener Termin, Fälligkeitsdatum; **effective** ~ Zeitpunkt des Inkrafttretens; **earliest** ~ **available** frühester Antrittstermin; **earliest practicable** ~ frühestmöglicher Zeitpunkt; **expiration (expiry)** ~ Ablauftermin; **false** ~ gefälschtes Datum; **filing** ~ Einreichungstermin; **final** ~ *(for payment)* äußerster Termin, Ausschlußfrist, Endtermin; **fixed** ~ Stichtag; **focal** ~ [bei einer Durchschnittsberechnung] angenommenes Datum; **incomplete** ~ *(bill of exchange)* Datum unvollständig; **interest** ~ Zinstermin; **key** ~ Stichtag; **long** ~ langes Ziel; **mailing** ~ Versandtermin; **next preceding** ~ letztvorhergehender Termin; **no** ~ *(book)* ohne Angabe einer Jahreszahl; **order** ~ Auftragsdatum; **postal** ~ Datum des Poststempels; **priority** ~ Prioritätsdatum; **purchase** ~ Anschaffungstag; **redemption** ~ Rückzahlungs-, Tilgungstermin; **shipping** ~ Verschiffungstag, *(US)* Versandtermin; **short** ~ kurzes Ziel, kurze Frist; **sold** ~ Verkaufsdatum; **specified** ~ bestimmter Zeitpunkt; **starting** ~ Anfangstermin; **succeeding** ~ nächstfolgender Termin; **target** ~ letzter Termin, Stichtag; **value** ~ *(bookkeeping)* Wertstellungstermin, *(cheque)* Eingangsdatum; **wrong** ~ irrtümliches (falsches) Datum;
~ **of acquisition** Erwerbsdatum, Anschaffungstag; ~ **of adjudication** Konkurseröffnungstermin; **closing** ~ **of application** Bewerbungstermin, Anmeldefrist; ~ **of appointment** Ernennungstag; ~ **of taking up appointment** Antrittstermin; ~ **of arrival** Ankunftstag; ~ **of assessment** Veranlagungstag; ~ **of a bill** Fälligkeit eines Wechsels; ~ **of bill of lading** Konnossementsdatum; ~ **of birth** Geburtsdatum; ~ **of commencement** Anfangstag; ~ **of completion** Fertigstellungstermin; ~ **of completion of a mandate** Mandatsbeendigung; ~ **of death** Todestag; ~ **of declaration** *(dividends)* Erklärungstag; ~ **of delivery** [Ab]liefer[ungs]termin; ~ **of discount** Diskonttag; ~ **of dismissal** Entlassungstag; ~ **of dispatch** Zeitpunkt der Lieferung, Datum des Versands, Versandtermin; ~ **of disposal** Veräußerungstermin; ~ **of dissolution** Auflösungstermin; ~ **of distribution** Verteilungstermin; ~ **of execution of a document** Ausfertigungsdatum einer Urkunde; ~ **of expiry** Verfalltag; ~ **of expiration (expiry)** Verfalltag; ~ **of filing** Antragsdatum; ~ **of grant** Erteilungstermin; ~ **of hearing** *(liquidation)* Anhörungstermin; ~ **of impression** Druckjahr; ~ **of independence** Unabhängigkeitstag; ~ **of injury** Unfalltag; ~ **of inscription** Eintragungstermin, -tag; ~ **of insertion** Anzeigentermin; ~ **of invoice** Rechnungsdatum; ~ **of issue** Ausgabe-, Ausstellungsdatum, *(loan)* Emissionstag, -termin; ~ **of leaving** Ausscheidungstermin; ~ **of a letter** Briefdatum; ~ **of mailing** Absendetag; ~ **of marriage** Hochzeitsdatum; ~ **of maturity** Einlösungstermin, Fälligkeits-, Verfalltag; ~ **of a mortgage** Entstehungszeitpunkt einer Hypothek; ~ **of order** Auftragsdatum; ~ **of origin** Entstehungsdatum; ~ **of patent** Einreichungstermin; ~ **of payment** Aus-, Einzahlungstermin; ~ **of policy** Versicherungstermin; ~ **as per postmark** Datum des Poststempels; ~ **of publication** Veröffentlichungsdatum; ~ **of purchase** Anschaffungstag; ~ **of receipt** Eingangs-, Empfangsdatum; ~ **of a receiving order** Datum des Konkurseröffnungsbeschlusses; ~ **of redemption** Einlösungstermin, -frist, Rückzahlungs-, Tilgungstermin; ~ **of registration** Eintragungsdatum; ~ **of shipment** *(US)* Absendetag, Versandtermin, Verschiffungstag; ~ *(v.)* Datum festsetzen (bestimmen), [Urkunde] datieren;

~ **in advance** vorausdatieren; ~ **ahead** *(cheque)* vordatieren; ~ **back** zurückdatieren; ~ **forward** vordatieren; ~ **from** stammen aus; ~ **a letter** Brief datieren (mit Datum versehen); ~ **tickets** Fahrkarten datieren; ~ **to** zurückgehen auf; ~ **from the war** auf den Krieg zurückzuführen sein, aus dem Krieg stammen; ~ **s. th. by years** berechnen; ~ nach Jahren berechnen;
to agree on a ~ Termin für die Zahlung vereinbaren; **to appoint a** ~ Termin festsetzen; **to be out of** ~ nicht mehr auf dem laufenden sein, *(fashion)* aus der Mode sein; **to be up to** ~ **with one's work** mit seiner Arbeit auf dem laufenden sein; **to bear** ~ **of** datiert sein von; **to bring a list up to** ~ Liste auf den neuesten Stand bringen; **to fill in the** ~ Datum einsetzen; **to fix a** ~ Termin festsetzen; **to fix on a** ~ sich über einen Termin einigen; **to go out of** ~ veralten; **to have a** ~ *(coll.)* Verabredung haben; **to keep for a later** ~ für einen späteren Zeitpunkt aufheben; **to keep up to** ~ auf dem laufenden halten; **to keep the books up to** ~ Bücher à jour halten; **to make a** ~ *(US)* sich verabreden, Verabredung treffen; **to make out a bill payable thirty days** ~ laufenden Wechsel ausstellen; **to postpone a** ~ Termin verlegen; **to set (settle) a** ~ Termin (Datum) festsetzen;
~ **available** möglicher Arbeitsbeginn; ~ **basis** Ausgangsdatum; ~ **block** Termin-, Abreißkalender; ~ **book** Tagebuch; ~ **box** Datumanzeiger; ~**cancel** *(v.)* mit dem Datumsstempel entwerten; ~ **line** Datumsgrenze, *(newspaper)* Datumszeile; ~ **plan** Terminplan; ~ **schedule** Datenschema; ~ **stamp** Eingangs-, Datum-, Tages-, Poststempel; ~**stamp** *(v.)* mit einem Datumsstempel versehen.
dated datiert, *(old)* veraltet, überholt;
~ **as of ...** datiert vom ...; ~ **from London** aus London datiert; **desperately** ~ hoffnungslos veraltet; **long-**~ langfristig; **short** ~ kurzfristig;
to be ~ **up** *(US)* alle Abende vergeben haben;
~ **earned surplus** Geschäftsgewinn ab Sanierung; ~ **papers** innerhalb eines bestimmten Zeitraums rückzahlbare Papiere.
dateless undatiert, ohne Datum.
datemark Jahresstempel.
dater Tages-, Datumsstempel.
dating Datieren, Datierung, *(extension of credit)* Fristverlängerung;
seasonal ~ *(US)* Zahlungsfrist bei Auftragsplazierung und Zahlungsregulierung vor der Saison;
~ **back** Rückdatierung; ~ **forward** Vorausdatierung.
dation of an office Verleihung eines Amtes.
dative *(law)* widerruflich, absetzbar;
decree ~ *(trustee)* Ernennungsurkunde;
~ **tutelage** übertragene Vormundschaft.
datum Unter-, Grundlage, gegebene Tatsache, Prämisse, Voraussetzung;
~ **line** Grund-, Standlinie; ~ **point** Ausgangspunkt; ~ **quantity** Referenzmenge.
daub [Roh]putz, Rauhputz;
~ *(v.)* beschmutzen, beschmieren, *(disguise)* übertünchen, bemänteln;
~ **plaster on a wall** Wand verputzen.
daughter-in-law Schwiegertochter.
dawdle *(v.)* herumbummeln;
~ **away one's time** seine Zeit verbummeln; ~ **over one's work** Zeit bei der Arbeit vertrödeln.
dawn Tagesanbruch;
~ **of a new era** Anbruch einer neuen Zeit.
day Tag, *(~ agreed upon)* Termin, *(journey)* Tagesreise, *(at-home)* Besuchs-, Empfangstag;
all ~ **[long]** den ganzen Tag, ganztägig; **before** ~ vor Tagesanbruch; **by** ~ bei Tageslicht; **by the** ~ *(labo(u)rer)* im Tagelohn; **for one** ~ **in court** pro Verhandlungstag; **in hono(u)r of the** ~ zur Feier des Tages; **in [the]** ~**s to come** in kommenden Zeiten; **in his school** ~s in seiner Schulzeit; **on the appointed** ~ fristgerecht; **on a given** ~ an einem bestimmten Tag; **per** ~ täglich; **to the end of one's** ~s bis ans Lebensende;
account ~ *(stock exchange)* Zahltag; **appearance** ~ Gerichtstermin; **appointed** ~ Termin, Stichtag; **auction** ~ Auktionstermin; **artificial** ~ Tageszeit; **better** ~s bessere Tage (Zeit); **bill** ~ *(US)* Tag der Einbringung von Gesetzesanträgen; **blank** ~ dienstfreier Tag; **business** ~ Geschäftstag; **cash** ~ Abrechnungs-, Zahltag; **clear** ~s volle Tage; ~ **certain** festes Datum, Termin; **civil** ~ Kalendertag; **contango** ~ Reporttag; **court** ~ Gerichtstag; **eagle** ~ *(mil., sl.)* Löhnungstag; **field** ~ ereignisreicher Tag; **fixed** ~ bestimmter Tag, Termin; **free** ~ freier Tag; **8 h (eight-hour)** ~ Achtstundentag; **general election** ~ Wahltag, -termin; **intercalary** ~ Schalttag; **judicial** ~ Gerichts-, Sitzungstag; **labor** ~ *(US)* Arbeiterfeiertag; **law** ~ Verfalltag; **lawful** ~

Werk-, Arbeits-, Sitzungstag; **lay** ~s Liegetage; **leap** ~ Schalttag; **legal** ~ Gerichtstag; **natural** ~ Kalendertag; **nonbusiness** ~ *(Br.)* Bankfeiertag, kein Geschäftstag; **nonjudicial** ~ sitzungsfreier (gerichtsfreier) Tag; **odd** ~ Schalttag; ~ **off** freier Tag, Ruhetag; **open** ~ freier Tag; **quarter** ~ Quartalstag; **red-letter** ~ denkwürdiger Tag, Feiertag; **return** ~ Tag des persönlichen Erscheinens vor Gericht; **three** ~s **running** drei Tage nacheinander; **settling** ~ *(stock exchange)* Zahltag, Abrechnungs-, Stichtag; **term** ~ festgesetzter Tag; **trading** ~ Börsentag; **undergraduate** ~s Studentenzeit; **working** ~ Arbeitstag;
~ **of account** *(stock exchange)* Abrechnungs-, Zahltag; ~ **of appearance** Verhandlungstermin; ~s **in banc** *(law court)* Sitzungstage; ~ **of birth** Geburtstag; ~ **in court** Verhandlungstag, *(US)* rechtliches Gehör; ~s **of creation** Entstehungszeit; ~ **of death** Todestag; ~ **of delivery** Liefer[ungs]tag, -termin; ~s **of demurrage** Überliegezeit, Extraliegetage; **fine** ~ **for ducks** *(coll.)* regnerischer Tag; ~ **for election** Datum der Wahl; ~ **of entry** Einklarierungs-, Einschiffungstag; **the** ~ **after the fair** zu spät um eine Chance zu nutzen; ~s **of glory** glanzvolle Zeiten; ~s **of grace** geduldete Verzugs-, Respekttage, *(insurance)* Nachfrist; ~ **of hearing** Gerichtstermin; ~ **of issue** *(securities)* Ausgabetag; ~ **of Judgment** Tag des Jüngsten Gerichts; ~ **of maturity** Verfalltag, Zahlungstermin; ~ **of nomination** Beförderungs-, Ernennungstag; ~ **of obligation** gesetzlicher Feiertag; ~ **of payment** Fälligkeits-, *(wages)* Zahltag; ~ **of presentation** Vorlegungstag; ~ **of reckoning** Tag des Jüngsten Gerichts; ~ **of respite** Nachsichttag; ~ **of rest** Ruhetag; ~ **of service** Zustellungstag; ~ **of settlement** Verrechnungs-, Liquidationstag; ~ **of sickness** Krankheitstag; ~s **after sight** Tage nach Sicht; ~ **of supply** *(mil.)* Tagesration [einer militärischen Einheit]; ~ **fixed for trial** Verhandlungstermin; ~s **of paid vacation** bezahlte Urlaubs-, Ferientage; **closing** ~s **of the year** letzte Tage des Jahres;
to adjourn a case for three ~s Verhandlung für drei Tage aussetzen; **to agree upon a** ~ Tag (Termin) festsetzen (bestimmen, vereinbaren); **to appoint a** ~ Termin festlegen (anberaumen); **to appoint a** ~ **to meet again** sich für einen anderen Tag bescheiden; **to arrange to take a** ~ **off** sich einen Tag freinehmen; **to call it a** ~ *(coll.)* Feierabend (für heute Schluß) machen; **to carry the** ~ Sieg davontragen; **to charge a** ~ pro Tag verlangen; **to end one's** ~s seine Tage beschließen; **to fall on evil** ~s Pech haben; **to fix a** ~ **for the hearing** Termin anberaumen; **to give s. o. a** ~ **off** jem. einen Tag frei geben; **to have had one's** ~ sich überlebt haben; **to hire by the** ~ tageweise beschäftigen; **to keep one's** ~ pünktlich sein; **to know the time of the** ~ wissen, was es geschlagen hat; **to meander through a listless** ~ *(stock exchange)* lustlosen Tag hinter sich bringen; **to name a** ~ Tag bestimmen (festsetzen); **to name the** ~ Neuwahlentermin bekanntgeben; **to put aside for a rainy** ~ Notgroschen zurücklegen; **to run** ~ **and night** Tag und Nacht verkehren; **to take a** ~ **off** sich einen Tag freigeben lassen (freinehmen); **to work all** ~ **long** den ganzen Tag über arbeiten; **to work by the** ~ im Tagelohn arbeiten; **to work** ~ **and night** Tag und Nacht arbeiten;
~ **attendance** Tagesbesuch; ~ **bed** Ruhebett, Sofa; ~ **bill** Tageswechsel; ~ **boarder** Gast mit Teilpension; ~ **boy** *(Br.)* Tagesschüler, Fahrschüler; ~ **car (coach, US)** Personenwagen; ~ **care** Tagesbetreuung; ~ **care center** *(US)* **(centre, Br.)** Tageskindergarten, Kindertagesstätte; ~~**care enrolment** Anmeldung zum Tagesheim für Kleinkinder; ~ **continuation school** Berufsschule; **10** ~s **date** zehn Tage nach dato.
day-to-day | **business** laufende Geschäfte; ~ **loan** *(Br.)* täglich fälliges Maklerdarlehen; ~ **money** täglich fälliges Geld, Tagesgeld; ~ **option** *(Br.)* bis zum nächsten Tag 14.45 Uhr laufendes Prämiengeschäft; ~ **policy** Tagespolitik; ~ **position** täglicher Kontostand.
day | **editor** Tagesredakteur; ~ **flight** Tagesflug; ~ **guest** Tagesgast; ~ **hour** Tagesstunde; ~**'s journey** Tagesreise; ~ **labo(u)r** Tagesarbeit, Tagewerk; ~ **labo(u)rer** Tagelöhner; ~ **letter** *(US)* Brieftelegramm; ~ **loan** *(stock exchange, US)* Maklerdarlehn; ~ **nurse** Tagesschwester; ~ **nursery** Kinderkrippe, Kindertagesheim, -stätte; ~ **off** freier Tag, Ruhe-, Ausgehtag; ~ **option** *(Br.)* Prämiengeschäft bis zum nächsten Tag; ~ **order** *(US)* Tagesauftrag; ~**'s output** Tagesleistung [einer Fabrik]; ~**'s pay** Tageslohn; ~ **pupil** externer Schüler; ~ **rate** Tageslohn, -satz; ~**'s rate** *(stock exchange)* Tagessatz, -kurs; ~ **rates system** Tagelohnsystem; ~**'s receipts** Tageseinnahme; ~ **release** Freistellung zur beruflichen Fortbildung; ~~**release course** eintägiger Bildungskurs, Berufsschulkursus; ~ **scholar** Fahr-, Tagesschüler; ~ **school** Tagesschule; ~ **servant** Tageshilfe; ~ **shift (turn)** Tagesschicht; ~ **supply** Tagesvorrat; **to check the** ~**'s takings** Tageseinnahmen nachprüfen; ~ **task** Tagewerk; ~

ticket Rückfahrkarte mit eintägiger Gültigkeit; **a ~'s wage** Tagelohn; **~ waiter** Tageskellner; ⚲ **Wireless Bulletin** *(US)* Presseagentur.

daybook Journal, Memorial, Tagebuch, Kladde;
to enter in the ~ in das Journal eintragen.

daybreak Tagesanbruch.

daydream Wachtraum, Träumerei, Phantasiegebilde, Luftschloß;
~ *(v.)* Wachträume haben.

daydreamer Träumer.

daylight Morgengrauen, Abenddämmerung, *(fig.)* Klarheit, Erleuchtung, *(photo)* Tageslicht;
before ~ vor dem Morgengrauen; **in broad ~** am hellichten Tag; **~** *(v.)* *(US)* Nebenberuf während der eigentlichen Arbeitszeit ausüben;
to beat the ~ out of s. o. j. mörderisch verdreschen; **to let ~ into s. th.** etw. der Öffentlichkeit zugänglich machen; **to see ~ at last** endlich einen Hoffnungsschimmer sehen;
~ lamp Tageslichtlampe; **~ loading factor** Tageslichtfaktor; **~ loading magazine** Tageslichtkassette; **~ saving** Ausnutzung des Tageslichtes, Zeitvorverlegung; ⚲ **-Saving Act** *(Br.)* Gesetz zur Einführung der Sommerzeit; **~ time** Sommerzeit.

dayman Tagelöhner.

dayroom Aufenthalts-, Tagesraum.

daytime Tageszeit;
~s im Laufe des Tages.

daywork Zeitlohn-, Schichtarbeit, Arbeit im Tageslohn.

dayworker Schichtarbeiter.

daze Benommenheit;
to be in a ~ benommen sein.

dazzle Leuchten, Glanz;
~ of light Lichtflut;
~ *(v.)* *(fig.)* Bewunderung erregen, blenden, verwirren;
~ lamp Blendlampe; **~ paint** *(mar.)* Tarnbemalung.

dazzler *(sl.)* Blender, Angeber.

dazzling diamonds glitzernde Diamanten.

de-facto | government de-fakto Regierung; **~ recognition** vorläufige Anerkennung.

de-icing fluid Enteisungsflüssigkeit.

de-junk *(v.)* **autos** Autos verschrotten.

dead *(dullness)* Geschäftslosigkeit, -stille;
at (in) the ~ of night mitten in der Nacht;
~ *(a.)* tot, gestorben, *(building)* unbewohnt, *(civil death)* bürgerlich tot, *(dull)* flau, still, stockend, umsatz-, geschäftslos, *(el.)* stromlos, *(exhausted, coll.)* völlig erledigt, todmüde, restlos fertig, *(idle)* unproduktiv, stillgelegt, *(volcano)* erloschen;
as ~ as a doornail mausetot; **~-beat** fertig, erledigt, abgehetzt, todmüde; **~ poor** ganz arm; **stone ~** völlig erledigt; **~-tired** todmüde;
~ to advice taub für Ratschläge; **as ~ as mutton** mausetot; **~ from the neck up** saudämlich;
~ *(v.)* **a letter** Brief als unzustellbar erklären;
to be ~ against it entschieden dagegen sein; **to declare s. o. legally ~** für tot (verschollen) erklären; **to lie ~ upon one's hands** brachliegen; **to shoot ~** erschießen;
~ account *(Br.)* totes (unbewegtes, umsatzloses) Konto; **~ air** *(radio, sl.)* Sendepause, Funkstille; **~ animal** Tierkörper; **~ article** Ladenhüter; **~ assets** unproduktive [Kapital]anlagen; **~ bargain** spottbilliger Preis, Spottpreis; **~ beat** *(US sl.)* unsicherer Kunde, Nassauer, Schnorrer; **~ body** Leichnam, Leiche; **~ book** Ablage nicht mehr verwendeter Funksendungen; **~ calm** Flaute; **~ capital** brachliegendes (totes) Kapital; **~ city** tote Stadt; **~ certainty** absolute Gewißheit; **~ charges** Gemeinkosten; **~ commodity** Ladenhüter, unverkäufliche Ware; **~ duck** völlig wertloser Mensch; **to be a ~ duck** zum Scheitern verurteilt sein; **~ end** Sackgasse; **to come to a ~ end** in eine Sackgasse geraten sein; **~-end job** Position ohne Aufstiegschancen; **~-end kill** jugendlicher Verbrecher; **~-end street** *(US)* Sackgasse; **~ failure** Fiasko; **~ file** abgelegte Akte; **~ floor** Blindboden; **~ forms** leere Formalitäten; **~ freight** Leer-, Ballast-, Fehl-, Faulfracht; **~ gilding** matte Vergoldung; **~ hand** *(mortmain)* tote Hand; **~ horse** vorausbezahlte Arbeit; **~ hours** umsatzschwache Geschäftszeit; **~ job** *(print.)* Werk im Stehsatz; **~ language** tote Sprache; **~ last** weitabgeschlagen an letzter Stelle liegen; **~ law** ungültiges Gesetz; **~ letter** unbestellbarer (unzustellbarer) Brief, *(law)* außer Kraft getretene Verordnung; **to become a ~ letter** außer Gebrauch kommen; **~-letter office** Büro für unbestellbare Sendungen; **to help s. o. at a ~ lift** jem. in einer schweren Lage beistehen; **~ load** totes Gewicht, Eigengewicht, Belastung ohne Nutzgewicht, Totlast; **~ loan** *(Br.)* kurzfristig verlängertes Darlehn; **~ lock** Riegelschloß; **~**

loss reiner Verlust, Totalverlust; **~ lying** brachliegend; **~ man's part** *(Br.)* Nachlaßrest für den Nachlaßverwalter; **to step into a ~ man's shoes** jds. Erbschaft antreten; **~-man control** Notsteuervorrichtung; **~ march** Totenmarsch; **~ market** flauer Markt; **~ matter** *(print.)* abgesetztes Manuskript, Ablegesatz; **~ metal** Blindmaterial; **~ money** brachliegendes Geld, totes Kapital; **~ number** unbenutzte Nummer; **to be ~ nuts about s. th.** auf etw. ganz versessen sein; **~ office** Beerdigungsgottesdienst; **~ pan** *(US sl.)* Ölgötze; **~ parcel post** Postamt für unbestellte Pakete; **~'s part** *(Br.)* frei verfügbarer Nachlaß; **~ person** Toter; **a ~-and-alive place** gottverlassenes Nest; **~ plates** nicht mehr benutzte Klischees; **~ pledge** Faustpfand; **~ rail** Hilfsschiene; **~ reckoning** *(ship)* Besteck; **~ rent** fester Pachtzins, *(mining, Br.)* Bergregal-, Mindestpacht, Minimalpacht bei einer Bergwerksverpachtung; **~ room** schalldichter Raum; **~ sale** flauer Absatz; **~ season** tote Saison, ruhige Jahreszeit, Sauregurkenzeit; **~ security** *(Br.)* wertlose (nicht realisierbare) Sicherheit; **at a ~ set** festgefahren; **to make a ~ set upon s. o.** j. verbissen angreifen; **~ silence** Totenstille; **~ soil** unfruchtbarer Boden; **~ space** toter Winkel; **~ spot** *(retail shop)* ungünstiger Platz; **~-stick landing** Landung mit abgestelltem Motor; **~ stock** *(book shop)* unverkaufte Exemplare, *(capital)* totes Kapital, *(farming)* totes Inventar, *(unsalable goods)* Partieware, unverkäufliche Waren (Bestände); **~ stop** völliger Stillstand; **to come to a ~ stop** schlagartig aufhören (stehenbleiben); **~ street** Sackgasse; **~ time** betrieblich bedingte Verlustzeit, Lohnausfall, *(atomics)* Sperrzeit, *(labo(u)r relations)* bezahlte Freizeit; **~ time of the year** geschäftslose Zeit, Flautezeit, stille Saison; **~ track** totes Gleis; **~ use** zukünftiges Nießbrauchrecht; **~ waggon** *(US)* Totenwagen; **~ wall** freistehende Mauer; **~ water** stehendes Wasser; **~ weight** Leer-, Betriebs-, Eigengewicht, *(national debt, Br.)* ungedeckter Teil der Staatsschuld; **to be a ~ weight on the business** *(fam.)* Belastung für das Geschäft sein; **~-weight capacity** Bruttoladefähigkeit; **~-weight debt** *(Br.)* ungedeckter Teil der Staatsschuld; **~-weight tonnage** Gesamtzuladungsgewicht, Leertonnage; **~ wire** stromloser Leiter; **~ work** vorbereitende Arbeit; **to be ~ wrong** völlig falsch liegen; **~ zone** *(radio)* tote Zone.

deadborn totgeboren;
~ child Totgeburt.

deadening Schalldämpfung.

deadfall Falle.

deadhead totes (unentschiednenes) Rennen, *(bus)* Leerbus, *(nonpaying guest)* umsonst wohnender Gast, *(US)* Freikarteninhaber, *(passenger)* blinder Passagier, *(wire)* gebührenfreies Telegramm;
~ *(v.)* Freifahrtschein (freien Zutritt) haben, *(taxi driver)* Leerfuhre haben;
to peddle a ~ Umsonstgeschäft machen;
~ agency untätige Regierungsstelle; **~ transportation** Beförderung von Freikarteninhabern.

deadheading Transport von Arbeitskräften;
~ pay Wegegeld.

deadhouse Leichenhalle, -schauhaus.

deadline *(US)* Fristablauf, Stichtag, letzter [Ablieferungs]termin, *(advertising)* Anzeigenschluß, *(print.)* äußerste Frist, Redaktionsschluß;
publisher's ~ *(US)* Anzeigenschluß;
~ for application *(US)* Anmeldeschluß; **~ for tenders** Ausschreibungsfrist;
to meet the ~ *(US)* Frist einhalten;
~ date Stichtag; **~ misser** *(US)* Terminverpatzer; **~ vehicle** in Reparatur befindliches Fahrzeug.

deadlock völliger Stillstand, Stockung, Patt;
~ *(v.)* zum völligen Stillstand bringen;
to be at a ~ stocken, ins Stocken geraten sein; **to break ~s** verfahrene Situation bereinigen, Stockung bei Verhandlungen überwinden; **to come to a ~** sich völlig festfahren, an einen toten Punkt gelangen; **to overcome a ~** toten Punkt überwinden; **to reach a ~** in eine Sackgasse geraten; **to rest in ~** auf einen toten Punkt angelangt (festgefahren) sein.

deadlocked | council paralysierter Stadtrat; **~ negotiations** festgefahrene Verhandlungen.

deadly tödlich, totbringend;
~ enemy Todfeind; **~ weapon** tödliche Waffe.

deadness Geschäftslosigkeit, *(stock exchange)* Flaute.

deadpan expression undurchdringlicher Gesichtsausdruck, Pokergesicht.

deadpay betrügerisch weiterbezogener Sold.

deadwood Plunder, Gerümpel, *(unsalable stock)* Ladenhüter, *(useless persons)* Spreu, nutzlose Glieder [einer Organisation];

to clean out the ~ morsches Holz herausschneiden, *(fig.)* effektiv nicht mehr benötigte Arbeitskräfte entlassen; **to possess the ~** *(US sl.)* im Vorteil sein.

deaerate *(v.)* entlüften.

deaerator Entlüftungsanlage.

deaf | as an adder (a doorpost) stocktaub; **~ and dumb** taubstumm; **~-aid** Hörgerät; **to turn a ~ ear to entreaties** Bitten laufend überhören.

deaf-and-dumb | alphabet Taubstummenalphabet; **~ language** Taubstummensprache.

deal *(advertising)* Gratisangebot, *(bargain)* Handel, abgeschlossenes Geschäft, Abschluß, Transaktion, Abmachung, -kommen, *(clandestine arrangement)* [politischer] Kuhhandel, *(coll.)* Handlungsweise, Verfahren, Politik, *(special offer)* besonderes Angebot, *(quantity)* Menge, Teil, Portion;
big ~ dickes Geschäft; **cash ~** Barverkauf; **fair ~** *(US)* Grundsatz der liberalen Wirtschaftspolitik; **forward ~** Abschluß auf künftige Lieferung, Zeitgeschäft; **good ~** gute Sache, gutes Geschäft; **ministerial ~s** ministerielle Absprachen; **New ~** *(US)* sozialpolitisches Reformprogramm, neue Politik; **rough ~** unfaire Behandlung; **square ~** ehrliche Abmachung, faires Geschäft;
~ on joint account Beteiligungs-, Metagegeschäft; **good ~ of money** viel Geld; **~ between parties** Parteiabsprache, parteipolitischer Kuhhandel; **~ on the stock exchange** Börsencoup; **great ~ of influence** großer Einfluß; **great ~ of money** viel Geld; **great ~ of traffic on the road** starker [Straßen]verkehr;
~ *(v.)* handeln, Handel treiben, Geschäfte machen, Geschäftsverkehr haben, *(occupy)* sich befassen, sich beschäftigen, in Geschäftsverbindung stehen, Geschäftsverkehr haben, *(act as intermediary)* vermitteln;
~ in an article Artikel führen; **~ badly by s. o.** j. schlecht behandeln; **~ in credits** Kredite vergeben; **~ with a culprit** Angeklagten aburteilen; **~ with unforeseen difficulties** mit unvorhergesehenen Schwierigkeiten fertigwerden; **~ directly with the senior corporate officers** unmittelbar mit den leitenden Firmenangestellten verhandeln; **~ fairly with s. o.** sich fair gegenüber jem. verhalten; **~ in goods of all kinds** Krämerladen führen; **~ at arm's length** seine Geschäfte freizügig betreiben; **~ at arm's length with s. o.** j. sehr distanziert behandeln, mit jem. nur auf rein geschäftlicher Basis verhandeln; **~ at length about** sich in längeren Auslassungen ergehen, längere Ausführungen machen; **~ in a line** in einer Branche tätig sein; **~ with a party leader** mit einem Parteiführer Geheimvereinbarungen treffen; **~ only in small lots** nur kleine Mengen verkaufen; **~ in money** sich mit Geldsachen beschäftigen, Geldhändler sein; **~ in options** Optionsgeschäfte machen; **~ in politics** sich mit Politik befassen; **~ in rights** Bezugsrechte handeln; **~ at s. one's shop** bei jem. kaufen; **~ strictly by the rules** sich streng nach den Vorschriften richten.

deal *(v.)* **out** ver-, zuteilen;
~ alms Almosen verteilen; **~ gifts** Geschenke verteilen; **~ justice** Recht sprechen; **~ provisions** Provisionen zuschustern.

deal *(v.)* **with | s. o.** mit jem. in Geschäftsverbindung stehen, mit jem. verkehren;
~ an application Gesuch erledigen; **~ a case** Prozeß verhandeln; **~ a difficulty** mit einer Schwierigkeit fertig werden; **~ a grievance** einer Beschwerde abhelfen; **~ a messenger** Boten abfertigen; **~ an order** Auftrag (Bestellung) ausführen; **~ a piece of business** Angelegenheit erledigen; **~ a problem** sich mit einem Problem auseinandersetzen; **~ a subject** sich mit einem Gegenstand befassen.

deal, to be a good ~ too zealous übereifrig sein; **to call off a ~** Geschäft absagen; **to do (negotiate) a ~** *(stock exchange)* Schluß vermitteln, Abschluß tätigen; **to get in on a good ~** gutes Geschäft machen; **to give s. o. a fair ~** j. anständig behandeln; **to have a good ~ to do** alle Hände voll zu tun haben; **to have a great ~ of trouble with s. o.** mit jem. einen schweren Stand haben; **to have spent a good ~ of trouble over a work** viel Ärger mit einer Arbeit gehabt haben; **to make a ~** Abkommen treffen; **to make a ~ with s. o.** mit jem. einen Abschluß machen; **to make a little ~ in stocks as a feeler** Markt mit kleinen Börsenumsätzen abtasten, versuchsweise ein bißchen spekulieren; **to spend a good ~ of money** eine Menge Geld ausgeben; **to think a great ~ of s. o.** große Stücke auf j. halten;
to be able to see through a ~ board durch eine Bretterwand sehen können; **~ clincher** entscheidender Faktor beim Vertragsabschluß; **~ proneness** Bereitschaft zur Abnahme von Sonderangeboten.

dealer Händler, Kaufmann, *(distributing agent)* Vertreter, *(go-between)* Vermittler, *(retailer, US)* Verteiler, [Wieder]verkäufer, Fachgeschäft, Einzelhändler, *(stock exchange)* Wertpapier-, Effektenhändler, Makler, *(supplier)* Lieferant;
~s Geschäftsleute, Fachhandel;
antique ~ Antiquitätenhändler; **authorized ~** Vertragshändler; **auto[mobile] ~** Autohändler; **cattle ~** Viehhändler; **exempted ~** freier Börsenmakler [einer Kapitalsammelstelle]; **franchised ~** zugelassener Händler; **free ~** *(law)* Handels-, Kauf[manns]-frau; **general ~** Gemischtwarenhändler; **heavy ~** Händler mit bedeutenden Umsätzen; **independent ~** selbständiger Kaufmann; **itinerant ~** Hausierer; **local ~** Platzvertreter; **money ~** Geldwechsler, Devisenhändler; **motorcar ~** Autohändler; **odd-lot ~** *(US)* Händler in kleinen Effektenabschnitten; **petty ~** unbedeutender Händler; **plain ~** aufrichtiger Mensch; **real-estate ~** Grundstücks-, Immobilienmakler; **recognized ~** Vertragshändler; **resident ~** alteingesessener Kaufmann; **retail ~** Detail-, Einzelhändler; **secondhand ~** Altwarenhändler; **securities ~** Effektenhändler; **small ~** Krämer; **stamp ~** Briefmarkenhändler; **wardrobe ~** Kleiderhändler; **wholesale ~** Großhändler;
~ in antiquities Antiquitätenhändler; **~ in used cars** Gebrauchtwagenhändler; **~ in foreign exchange** Devisenhändler; **~ in fancy goods** Modewarengeschäft; **~ in gasoline** Treibstoffhändler; **~ in job goods** Partiewarenhändler; **~ in motor vehicles** Kraftfahrzeughändler; **~ in produce** Produktenhändler; **~ in rags** Lumpenhändler; **~ in secondhand books** Antiquar; **~ in securities (stocks)** Effektenhändler; **~ in unlisted securities** Freiverkehrsmakler;
to withhold supplies of goods from a ~ Händler nicht mehr beliefern;
~'s abatement Händlerrabatt; **~ acceptance** Abnahme durch Wiederverkäufer; **~ aids** Verkaufshilfe für Händler, Werbematerial; **~ aid advertising** werbliche Unterstützung des Händlers, Werbemittel als Verkaufshilfe; **~ allowance** Händlerrabatt; **~'s brand** Händlermarke; **~ broadside** Werbeflugblatt; **~'s buyer** Wiederverkäufer; **~ contest** Händlerwettbewerb; **to sell below ~ costs** unter dem normalen Handelspreis verkaufen; **~ control** Händlerkontrolle, -überwachung; **~'s discount** Einzelhändlerrabatt; **~ display** Auslagenmaterial für Händler; **~ force** Händlergefolgschaft; **to refill its ~ forecourts** Vormachtstellung als Händler wiedergewinnen; **~ franchise** Exklusiv-, Alleinverkaufsrecht; **~ help** Reklamebeigabe; **~ imprint** eingedruckter Bezugsquellennachweis, eingedruckte Händleranschrift; **~ incentive context** Händlerwettbewerb; **~ interview** Händlerinterview; **~ inventory** Einzelhändlerlager; **~ markup** kaufmännische Verdienstspanne; **~ merchandising plan** Händlerwerbung; **~ network** Händlernetz; **~ organization** Händlerorganisation, -vereinigung; **~ outlet** Händlerorganisation; **~ premium offer** Zugabenangebot für Händler; **~'s price** Wiederverkaufspreis; **~'s rebate** Händlerrabatt; **~ research** Händleranalyse, -befragung; **~ show** Fachmesse; **~ showroom** Ausstellungsraum eines Händlers; **~ stock** Handelslager; **~ survey** Einzelhandelserhebung, Händlerbefragung; **~ talk** Verkaufsgespräch.

dealership rights Konzessionsrechte.

dealing Handlungsweise, Verhalten, Geschäftsgebaren, *(bargain)* Geschäft, Handel, Abschluß, *(business intercourse)* Umgang, [Geschäfts]verkehr, Geschäftsgebaren;
~s Umsätze, Geschäftsumsatz, Transaktionen, *(relations)* Umgang, Verkehr, Verbindungen, Beziehungen;
continuous ~s *(banking)* laufende Geschäftsverbindung; **exclusive ~s** Ausschließlichkeitsvereinbarungen; **fair ~** korrektes Geschäftsgebaren; **few ~s** mäßige Börsenumsätze; **foreign-exchange ~s** Devisenhandel; **important ~s** bedeutende [Börsen]umsätze; **inter-office ~s** *(securities)* Telefonverkehr; **lively ~s** lebhafter Geschäftsverkehr; **money ~s** Geldgeschäfte; **no ~s** ohne Umsatz; **ordinary ~s** gewöhnliche Zahlungsbedingungen; **rights ~** Bezugsrechtshandel; **square ~** anständiges Geschäftsgebaren; **underhand ~** Schiebung;
~ for the account *(Br.)* Termin-, Zeitgeschäft; **~s for the account** Geschäfte auf laufende Rechnung; **~ for cash** Kassageschäft; **~ with a complaint** Beschwerdeerledigung; **~s in foreign exchange** Devisenhandel; **~ for a fall** Baissespekulation; **~s in options** Optionsgeschäft; **~ out** Ver-, Austeilen; **~s prior to the date of a receiving order** Geschäftsverkehr vor Konkurseröffnung; **~ in real estate** Immobilienhandel; **~ for a rise** Haussespekulation; **~ for the settlement** *(Br.)* Termingeschäfte; **~ in stocks** *(Br.)* Effektenhandel, -geschäft; **~s as per usage** Usancenhandel; **~s in wool** Wollhandel;
to be punctual in one's ~s Liefer- und Zahlungsbedingungen einhalten; **to cease ~s** Handelsbeziehungen einstellen; **to have ~s with s. o.** mit jem. in Geschäftsbeziehungen stehen;

~costs Börsen-, Maklergebühren; **~ rates** Abschlußsätze; **~ room** Wechselstube.

dean Vorsitzender, Präsident, *(dipl.)* Doyen, *(university)* Dekan; **~ of Faculty** *(Scot.)* Präsident der Anwaltskammer; **≗ of Guild Court** *(Scotland)* Bauaufsichtsamt.

deanship Amt des Doyens.

dear teuer, hoch im Preis, kostspielig; **to cost ~** teuer zu stehen kommen; **to get ~[er]** teurer werden, sich verteuern; **~-bought** zu überhöhten Preisen eingekauft; **~ money** teures Geld, Geldknappheit.

dearness teurer Preis, Teuerung, *(expensiveness)* Kostspieligkeit; **artificial ~** künstliche Teuerung; **~ allowance** *(pay)* Teuerungszulage.

dearth Mangel, Verknappung.

death Tod, Todesfall, Ableben, Sterben; **as sure as ~** bombensicher; **in contemplation of ~** angesichts des Todes; **at the point of ~** an der Schwelle des Todes; **at the time of ~** im Zeitpunkt des Todes; **dressed up to ~** aufgetakelt; **in the event of ~** im Todesfalle; **until ~** bis ans Lebensende; **accidental ~** Unfalltod; **actual ~** *(insurance)* eingetretene Todesfälle; **apparent ~** Scheintod; **civil ~** bürgerlicher Tod, Rechtstod; **expected ~** *(insurance)* angenommene Todesfälle; **instantaneous ~** sofortiger Tod; **natural ~** natürlicher Tod; **presumptive ~** Todesvermutung; **simultaneous ~** *(US)* gleichzeitiger Tod; **violent ~** gewaltsamer Tod; **~ by exposure** Tod durch Erfrieren; **~ by misadventure** Tod durch Unglücksfall, Unfalltod; **~ through external, violent and accidental means** Tod durch gewaltsame äußere Einwirkung; **to be ~ on s. th.** *(sl.)* etw. aus dem Effeff verstehen; **to be the ~ of s. o.** *(coll.)* jds. Sargnagel sein; **to be sick to ~** etw. nicht mehr ausstehen können; **to court ~** Tod suchen; **to die a natural ~** eines natürlichen Todes sterben; **to do to ~** zu Tode reiten; **to escape ~ by a narrow margin** mit knapper Not dem Tode entgehen; **to flog o. s. to ~** sich zu Tode arbeiten; **to go one's ~** alles riskieren; **to lie under a sentence of ~** zum Tode verurteilt sein; **to meet ~ calmly** dem Tode ruhig entgegensehen; **to notify a ~** Todesfall anzeigen; **to punish a crime with ~** Verbrechen mit dem Tode bestrafen; **to put s. o. to ~** j. umbringen; **to rush into a certain ~** in den sicheren Tod rennen; **to snatch s. o. from the jaws of ~** j. dem Tod entreißen; **~ agony** Todeskampf; **~ announcement** Todesanzeige; **~ bell** Sterbeglöckchen, Totenglocke; **~ benefit** Unterstützungszahlung im Todesfall, Hinterbliebenenversorgung, Sterbegeld; **~ benefit protection** Sterbegeldvorsorge; **~ camp** Todeslager; **~ certificate** Totenschein, Sterbeurkunde; **~ chair** *(US)* elektrischer Stuhl; **~ chamber** Sterbezimmer; **~ claim** Anspruch aus einer Sterbeversicherung; **~ cup** Giftbecher; **~ debts** Begräbnisschulden; **to be at ~'s door** an der Schwelle des Todes stehen; **~ duty** *(Br.)* Nachlaß-, Erbschaftssteuer; **~ grant** *(Br.)* Sterbebeihilfe; **~ march** Todesmarsch; **~ mask** Totenmaske; **~ notice** Todesanzeige; **~ penalty** *(US)* Todesstrafe; **~ place** Todesort; **crude ~ rate** nicht aufgegliederte Sterblichkeitsziffer; **natal ~ rate** Geburtensterblichkeitsziffer; **~ rattle** Todesröcheln; **~ ray** Todesstrahl; **~ registration** Beurkundung eines Sterbefalles; **~ roll** Unfalliste, *(mil.)* Verlustliste; **~ row** Todeszellen; **~ sentence** Todesstrafe, Todesurteil; **~ strip** Todesstreifen; **~ tax** *(US)* Erbschaftssteuer; **~ toll** Todesziffer; **~ trap** Todesfalle.

death warrant Todesurteil, Hinrichtungsbefehl; **to sign the ~ of an enterprise** *(fam.)* einem Unternehmen den Todesstoß versetzen.

deathbed Sterbebett, Totenbett; **~ bequest** Schenkung auf dem Totenbett; **~ confession** Geständnis auf dem Sterbebett; **~ deed** Erklärung auf dem Sterbebett.

deathblow Todesstoß, *(fig.)* tödlicher Schlag, Todesstoß.

deathday Todestag.

deathly stillness Totenstille.

deathman Henker.

deathtrap Todesfalle.

deathwatch Totenwache.

debacle *(government)* Zusammenbruch, *(stock exchange)* Katastrophe, Zusammenbruch.

debar *(v.)* ausschließen; **~ persons who have been convicted of crime from voting at elections** Vorbestraften das Wahlrecht entziehen; **~ s. o. from a right** j. eines Vorrechts berauben.

debark *(v.)* ausschiffen, landen, löschen.

debarkation Ausschiffung, Landung, Löschung.

debarment Ausschließung, Ausschluß.

---

debarred | from commerce vom Handel abgeschnitten; **to be ~ from succeeding (inheriting)** von der Erbschaft ausgeschlossen sein.

debase *(v.)* im Wert verringern, entwerten, verschlechtern, *(coins)* Münzen verfälschen, verschlechtern; **~ the currency** Währung verschlechtern.

debasement Verringerung, Verschlechterung; **~ of coin[age]** Münz-, Währungsverschlechterung.

debatable strittig, streitig, diskutabel, bestreitbar; **~ ground** strittiges Grenzgebiet, *(fig.)* Zankapfel; **~ land** umstrittenes Gebiet.

debate Debatte, Diskussion, Verhandlung; **after much ~** nach endlosen Diskussionen; **beyond ~** unbestreitbar; **~s** gerichtliche Verhandlungen, *(parl.)* öffentliche Verhandlungen; **budget ~** Haushaltsdebatte; **crucial ~** entscheidende Debatte; **economic ~** Wirtschafts-, Konjunkturdebatte; **full-dress ~** große Aussprache [im Plenum], Plenarsitzung; **heated ~** hitzige (heftige) Debatte; **narrow ~** begrenzter Diskussionskreis; **open ~** öffentliche Debatte; **protracted ~** langwierige Debatte; **televised ~** fernsehübertragene Diskussion; **warm ~** heftige (hitzige) Debatte; **zealous ~** eifrige Diskussion; **~ on the budget** Haushaltsdebatte; **~ on home affairs** innenpolitische Debatte; **~** *(v.)* diskutieren, erörtern, debattieren, *(deliberate)* beraten, beratschlagen, verhandeln; **~ an account** Rechnung anfechten; **~ a bill** über einen Gesetzesentwurf beraten; **~ across the floor** mit der Regierungspartei debattieren; **~ a subject** Thema erörtern; **~ the tariff question** über Zollfragen diskutieren; **to be in ~** über etw. verhandeln; **to be down for ~** zur Diskussion (Beratung) anstehen; **to close a ~** Debatte beenden (schließen); **to commence a ~** in eine Aussprache eintreten; **to gag a ~** *(Br.)* Debatte abwürgen; **to open a ~** Diskussion eröffnen; **to prevent a ~** Debatte abwürgen; **to renew a ~** Debatte wiederaufnehmen; **to resume the ~** Diskussion wieder aufnehmen; **to start a ~** Debatte (Diskussion) in Gang bringen; **to submit a question to the ~** Frage zur Diskussion stellen; **to take a hand in the ~** sich an der Diskussion beteiligen, an einer Aussprache teilnehmen, in die Debatte eingreifen; **to wind up the ~** Diskussion schließen.

debater Redner, Diskussionsteilnehmer; **perennial ~** Dauerredner.

debating | point Streitpunkt, -gegenstand; **~ society** Debattierklub; **~ time** Redezeit.

debauch Ausschweifung, Orgie; **~** *(v.)* korrumpieren, *(v/t)* verkommen.

debenture *(acknowledgement of debt)* Schuldanerkenntnis, -schein, *(bond)* Obligation, [ungesicherte] Schuldverschreibung, *(Br.)* Pfandbrief, *(drawback)* Rückzoll-, Zollrückgabeschein, *(promissory note)* Schuldschein; **bearer ~** Inhaberschuldverschreibung, -obligation; **convertible ~s** Wandelschuldverschreibungen; **customs ~** Zollrückgabeschein; **documented ~** verbriefte Schuld; **entire ~** gesamte Schuldsumme; **first ~s** Prioritäten; **floating ~** Höchstbetragsschuldverschreibung; **fractional ~s** kleingestückelte Schuldverschreibungen, Teilschuldverschreibungen; **guaranteed ~s** verbürgte Schuldverschreibungen; **income ~s** *(Br.)* gewinnabhängige verzinsliche Schuldverschreibungen, Gewinnschuldverschreibungen; **irredeemable ~s** unkündbare Obligationen; **already issued ~s** bereits begebene Schuldverschreibungen; **long-term ~s** langfristige Schuldverschreibungen; **mortgage ~** *(Br.)* hypothekarisch gesicherte Schuldverschreibung, [Hypotheken]pfandbrief; **naked ~** *(Br.)* ungesicherte Schuldverschreibung; **parliamentary ~s** Gewinnschuldverschreibungen; **partial ~** Teilschuldverschreibung; **participating ~** Gewinnobligation, -schuldverschreibung; **perpetual ~s** unkündbare Schuldverschreibungen; **railway ~** *(Br.)* Eisenbahnobligation; **redeemable ~** rückkaufbare (kündbare) Obligation; **redeemed ~** wiedereingelöste Schuldurkunde; **registered ~** Namensschuldverschreibung, -obligation; **second ~s** Prioritäten zweiten Ranges; **secured ~** hypothekarisch gesicherte Schuldverschreibung; **short-term ~s** kurzfristige Schuldverschreibungen; **simple ~s** hypothekarisch nicht gesicherte Schuldverschreibungen; **single ~** Einzelschuldverschreibung; **unissued ~s** noch nicht ausgegebene Schuldverschreibungen; **unsecured ~** ungesicherte Schuldverschreibung; **~ payable to bearer** Inhaberschuldverschreibung; **~ secured by a charge** dinglich gesicherte Schuldverschreibung; **to convert ~s into shares** Schuldverschreibungen in Aktien umwandeln; **to discharge** ~s Schuldverschreibungen ablösen; **to issue** ~s Schuldverschreibungen in Verkehr bringen; **to reissue** ~s Obligation neu emittieren, Schuldverschreibungen erneut ausgeben;

~ **bond** *(Br.)* festverzinsliche Schuldverschreibung, Obligation, *(Br.)* Pfandbrief, *(customs)* Rückzollschein; ~ **book** Rückzollbuch; ~ **capital** Erlös für begebene Obligationen, Anleihekapital; ~ **certificate** Zollrückgabeschein; ~ **conditions** Ausgabebedingungen; ~ **creditor** Schuldscheinberechtigter, Obligationär; ~ **form** Schuldurkunde[formular]; ~ **goods** Rückzollgüter; ~ **holder** *(Br.)* Schuldverschreibungsinhaber, Obligationär, *(Br.)* Pfandbriefinhaber; ~ **income bond** Schuldverschreibung ohne Zinsgarantie; ~ **interest price** bezahlte Schuldscheinzinsen; ~ **issue** Emission von Schuldverschreibungen, Obligationsausgabe; ~ **stock** *(US)* Vorzugsaktie, *(Br.)* [meist hypothekarisch gesicherte] Obligation, Schuldverschreibung, *(bonded debt)* Anleiheschuld, Schuldverschreibungskapital; ~ **trust deed** *(Br.)* auf einen Treuhänder übertragene Sicherheit, Schuldurkunde eines Treuhänders.

debentured durch Schuldschein gesichert, *(drawback)* rückzollberechtigt;

~ **goods** Waren unter Zollverschluß, Rückzollgüter.

debility Schwäche, Kraftlosigkeit, Hinfälligkeit;

general ~ allgemeiner Erschöpfungszustand; **nervous** ~ Nervenschwäche.

debit Debet[posten], Schuldposten, -saldo, Soll, *(entry on debit side)* Kontobelastung, Lastschrift, *(industrial insurance)* Inkassoeinzugsgebiet, *(left-hand side of account)* Soll-, Debetseite;

to the ~ **of** zu Lasten von;

annual ~ jährlicher Fehlbetrag; **bank** ~ Sollbuchung einer Bank; **unadjusted** ~s *(railroad accounts)* transitorische Posten; **your** ~ Saldo zu Ihren Lasten;

~ **and credit** Soll und Haben;

~ *(v.)* in Rechnung stellen, an-, belasten, debitieren, im Soll buchen;

~ **an account** auf Rechnung schreiben, Konto belasten; ~ **interest on a loan account to an active current account** laufendes Kontokorrentkonto mit den Zinsen des Kreditkontos belasten; ~ **a purchaser (customer) with [for the amount of] goods sold** Käufer (Kunden) für verkaufte Waren belasten;

to be at s. one's ~ bei jem. belastet sein; **to carry a sum to s. one's** ~ jds. Konto mit einem Betrag belasten; **to initiate** ~s **for payment of premiums** Versicherungsprämien im Abbuchungsverfahren bezahlen lassen; **to leave a balance to one's** ~ Debetsaldo stehenlassen; **to pass to s. one's** ~ j. debitieren (belasten); **to pass an amount to the** ~ **of an account** Konto mit einem Betrag belasten; **to place a sum to s. one's** ~ jds. Konto mit einem Betrag belasten;

~ **account** debitorisch geführtes Konto, Debet-, Debitorenkonto; ~ **advice** Belastungsaufgabe, -anzeige, Lastschrift; **executor's** ~ **account** debitorisch geführtes Testamentvollstreckerkonto; ~ **advice** Belastungsaufgabe, -anzeige, Lastschrift; ~ **balance** Sollbuchung, Soll-, Verlust-, Debetsaldo, *(balance of payments)* passive Zahlungsbilanz; **your** ~ **balance** Saldo zu Ihren Lasten; **to show a** ~ **balance** Debetsaldo aufweisen; **to wipe off a** ~ **balance** Debetsaldo (Forderung) abbuchen; ~ **column** Soll-, Debetspalte; ~ **element** Debetfaktor; ~ **entry** Sollbuchung, Lastschrift; ~ **interest** Sollzinsen; ~ **interest rate** Sollzinssatz; ~ **item** Passiv-, Sollposten; ~ **memorandum** *(US)* Belastungsanzeige, Lastschrift; ~ **note** Lastschriftanzeige; ~ **products** *(Br.)* Sollzinszahlen, -nummern; ~ **raiser** Kreditnehmer zu Schuldtilgungszwecken; ~ **rate** Sollzinssatz; ~ **ticket** Belastungsformular.

debit side Debet-, Sollseite;

to be on the ~ im Soll (Debet) stehen; **to carry (enter) to the** ~ im Soll buchen; **to enter s. th. to the** ~ **of an account** Konto mit etw. belasten, etw. im Debet eines Kontos eintragen, im Soll buchen.

debit|slip Lastschrifts-, Abbuchungsbeleg, Belastungszettel; ~ **ticket** Belastungsanweisung, -formular; ~ **trade balance** negative Handelsbilanz; ~ **voucher** Debet-, Lastschriftbeleg.

debitable belastbar.

debiting Lastschrift;

direct ~ **system** Lastschrift-, Rechnungseinzugs-, Abbuchungsverfahren.

debitor Schuldner.

deblock *(v.)* entsperren, freigeben;

~ **frozen accounts** eingefrorene Guthaben freigeben.

deblocking Freigabe, Entsperrung.

debrief *(v.) (mil.)* Einsatzerfolg analysieren.

debriefing *(mil.)* Einsatzbesprechung, -analyse.

debris Trümmer, Bauschutt.

debt [Geld]schuld, Verschuldung, Forderung, *(debit account)* Schuldposten, *(fig.)* Pflicht, Verpflichtung;

free from ~ schuldenfrei; **in** ~ in den roten Zahlen; **deep[ly involved]** in ~ überschuldet, schuldenbelastet; **over head and heels in** ~ hoffnungslos verschuldet; **in payment of a** ~ zur Begleichung einer Schuld; **owing to** ~s schuldenhalber;

~s *(balance sheet, Br.)* Verbindlichkeiten, Debitoren, Außenstände, Passiva;

~s **abroad** Auslandsschulden; **absolute** ~ unbedingt zu zahlende Schuld; **accumulative** ~s aufgelaufene Schulden; **active** ~s verzinsliche Forderungen, Außenstände, Schuldforderungen; ~s **active and passive** Aktiva und Passiva; **ancestral** ~ Erblasserschuld; **antecedent** ~ frühere Schuld; **assigned** ~ abgetretene Forderung; **bad** ~s *(US)* zweifelhafte (dubiose) Forderungen, Dubiosen, uneinbringliche Außenstände (Forderungen), faule Schulden; **bad** ~s **collected** eingegangene, schon abgeschriebene Forderungen; **barred** ~ verjährte Forderung; **blocked** ~ gesperrte (blockierte) Forderung; **bonded** ~ *(US)* Anleiheschuld; **book** ~ buchmäßige Forderung, Buchforderung, Außenstände; ~ **certain** unbedingt zu zahlende Schuld; **civil** ~ obligatorische Schuld; **collateral** ~ Lombardschuld; **commercial** ~ Warenschuld; **company** ~s Firmenschulden; **consolidated** ~ konsolidierte Schuld; **contingent** ~ bedingte (eventuell zu zahlende) Forderung; **contract** ~ vertraglich geschuldete Leistung; ~s **contracted** Verschuldung; **corporation** ~s *(US)* Firmenschulden; **current** ~s *(US)* laufende Schulden; **deadweight** ~ *(Br.)* nicht durch Vermögenswerte gedeckter Teil der Staatsschuld; **deferred** ~s nachrangige [Konkurs]forderungen; **disputed** ~s bestrittene Forderungen; **doubtful** ~s *(Br.)* Dubiosen, zweifelhafte Außenstände (Forderungen); ~s **due** fällige Schulden (Forderungen); **entire** ~ gesamte Schuldsumme, Gesamtschuld; **existing** ~ fällige Schuld; **external** ~s Auslandverschuldung; **financial** ~s Geldschulden, laufende Verpflichtungen; **floating** ~ kurzfristige (unfundierte) Staatsschuld; **foreign** ~s Auslandsschulden; **frozen** ~s eingefrorene Forderungen, Stillhalteschulden; **fraudulent** ~ durch betrügerische Machenschaften entstandene Forderungen; **funded** ~ Anleiheschuld; **future** ~ noch nicht fällige Schuld, zukünftige Forderung; **gambling** ~ Spielschuld; **garnished** ~ gepfändete Forderung; **good** ~s sichere Außenstände; **government** ~ Staatsschuld, öffentliche Schuld; **gross** ~ *(US)* gesamte Schuldsumme, Gesamtschuld; **heavy** ~s drückende (erhebliche) Schulden, große Schuldenlast; **heavy-weighing** ~ drückende Schuld; **hypothecary** ~ durch Grundpfandrecht gesicherte Forderung; **increased** ~s Schuldenerhöhung; ~s **incurred** eingegangene Verbindlichkeiten; **individual** ~s *(partner)* persönliche Schulden; **insolvable** ~s unbezahlbare Schulden; **instalment** ~s in Raten zu tilgende Schulden; **interest-bearing** ~ verzinsliche Forderung; **internal** ~ innere Schuld, Inlandsverschuldung; **irrecoverable** ~s uneinbringliche Schulden, verlorene Außenstände; **joint and several** ~ Gesamtschuld; **judgment** ~ Vollstreckungsforderung, vollstreckbare (ausgeklagte, im Feststellungsverfahren anerkannte) Forderung; **just** ~ rechtsgültige (vollgültige) Schuld; **legal** ~ einklagbare Forderung; **liquid** ~ sofort fällige Forderung; **liquidated** ~ bezahlte Schuld; **local** ~s Schulden von Gebietskörperschaften; **long-term** ~ *(balance sheet)* langfristige Verschuldung; **money** ~ Geldschuld; **mortgage** ~ Hypothekenforderung; **municipal** ~s Kommunalverbindlichkeiten, -schulden; **mutual** ~s gegenseitige Forderungen; **National** ~ Staatsschuld; **net bonded** ~ *(municipality)* Schuldscheinverpflichtungen; **nonbusiness** ~s nicht zum Gewerbebetrieb gehörige Schulden; **nonpreferential** ~ Masseforderung; **nonprovable** ~ unbegründete Forderung; **ordinary** ~s nicht bevorrechtigte Forderungen, Masseschulden; **oppressive** ~ drückende Schuld; **other** ~s *(balance sheet)* sonstige Verbindlichkeiten; **outstanding** ~s offene Verbindlichkeiten; ~ **owed by us** *(balance sheet)* Firmenschulden; ~ **owed to us** *(balance sheet)* Firmenforderungen; ~ **owing** fällige Schuld; ~s **owing and accruing** gegenwärtige und künftige Forderungen; ~ **paid** getilgte Forderung; **paid-up** ~ abgetragene Schuld; **partnership** ~s Firmen-, Gesellschaftsschulden; **passive** ~s unverzinsliche Schulden; **permanent** ~ fundierte Schuld; **perpetual** ~ unablösliche Schuld; **petty** ~s Bagatellschulden; **post-retirement** ~s nach dem Ausscheiden eines Gesellschafters entstandene Schulden; **pre-existing** ~s schon bestehende Schulden; **preferential (preferred,** *US)* ~s bevorzugt zu befriedigende (bevorrechtigte) Konkursforderungen, vor der Masseverteilung zu begleichende Schulden; **prescriptive** ~ verjährte Schuld; **pressing** ~s drückende Schulden; **prestabilization** ~s Schulden vor der Währungsreform; **private** ~s *(partner)* persönliche Schulden; **privileged** ~ bevorrechtigte Konkursforderung; **provable** ~ *(bankruptcy)* anmeldbare (anmeldungsfähige) Forderung; **not provable** ~ unbegründete Konkursforderung; **proved** ~ nachgewiesene Forderung, *(bankruptcy)* anerkannte (festgestellte) Konkursforderung; **public** ~ *(US)* Staatsschuld, öffentliche Schuld; **pure** ~ fällige Forderung; ~s **receivable** *(US)* Außenstände; ~s **recoverable** [beitreibbare] Außenstände; ~s **recovered** [nachträglich] eingetriebene Schulden; **registered** ~ Schuldbuchforderung; **remaining** ~s übrigbleibende Schulden, Restschuld; **reproductive** ~ *(Br.)* durch Vermögenswerte gedeckter Teil der Staatsschuld; **running** ~s laufende Verschuldung; **run-up** ~s aufgelaufene Schulden; **secured** ~ gesicherte (sichergestellte) [Konkurs]forderung; **separate** ~s *(partner)* Privatschulden; **shorter-term** ~ mittelfristige Verschuldung; **simple contract** ~ vertraglich geschuldete Leistung; **simulated** ~ erdichtete Forderung; **small** ~ Bagatellschuld; **solvent** ~ jederzeit realisierbare Forderung; **specialty** ~ verbriefte Forderung; **staggering** ~s bedenkliche (riesige) Schulden; **stale** ~ verjährte Schuld; **statute-barred** ~ verjährte Forderung; **subordinated** ~ im Range nachgehende Forderung; **surviving** ~ restliche Schuld; **total** ~ gesamte Schuldsumme; **trade** ~s Geschäfts-, Lieferantenschulden; **uncertain** ~s unsichere Außenstände; **uncollected** ~s *(bank balance)* Forderungen an Kunden; **uncrossed** ~ ungetilgte Schuld; **unfunded** ~ nicht fundierte Staatsschuld; **unified** ~ konsolidierte Schuld; **unliquidated** ~ der Höhe nach unbestimmte Schuld; **unsecured** ~s ungedeckte Schulden; **vast** ~s haushohe Schulden; **war** ~s Kriegsschulden; **whole** ~ Gesamtschuld; ~s **written off** abgeschriebene Außenstände;

~ **founded on open account** Kontokorrentschuld; ~s **in arrears** Schuldenrückstand; ~ **barred by the Statute of Limitations** verjährte Forderung (Schuld); ~s **provable in bankruptcy** im Konkursfall anmeldefähige Forderungen; ~ **proved in proceedings of bankruptcy** festgestellte Konkursforderung; ~ **founded on a bill** Wechselschuld; ~s **of a business enterprise** Geschäftsschulden; ~ **by special contract** notariell verbriefte Forderung; ~ **founded on contract** vertraglich begründete Forderung; ~ **by simple contract** nicht verbriefte Vertragsforderung; ~s **contracted before bankruptcy** vor Konkurseröffnung eingegangene Schulden; ~s **owed under court orders** gerichtlich feststehende Schulden; ~ **secured by a document** verbriefte Schuld; ~s **of the estate** Nachlaßschulden; ~s **of the firm** Firmenschulden; ~ **founded on merchantable goods** Forderung aufgrund von Warenverbindlichkeiten; ~ **of gratitude** Dankesschuld; ~ **of hono(u)r** Ehren-, Spielschuld; ~ **contracted during infancy** als Minderjähriger eingegangene Schuld; ~ **evidenced by a judgment** im Feststellungsverfahren anerkannte Forderung; ~ **at law** einklagbare Forderung; ~ **dead in law** nicht einklagbare Forderung; ~s **having priority** bevorrechtigte (vorrangige) Forderungen; ~s **on mesne process** im Nebenprozeß eingeklagte Forderungen; ~ **due to recognizance** Kautionsschuld; ~ **of record** gerichtlich festgestellte Forderung; ~s **incurred before (after) retirement** vor (nach) dem Ausscheiden entstandene Gesellschaftsschulden; ~s **covered by a security** dinglich gesicherte Forderung; ~s **on specialty** verbriefte Forderungen; ~ **of old standing** schon lange bestehende Schuld; ~s **written of as bad** ~s **for tax purposes** steuerlich anerkannte Dubiosen;

to acknowledge a ~ Schuld anerkennen; **to admit** a ~ Schuld anerkennen; **to answer** a ~ Schuld bezahlen; **to answer for** a ~ sich für eine Schuld verbürgen; **to appropriate** a ~ Zweckbestimmung von Zahlungen festlegen; **to assign** a ~ Forderung abtreten; **to assume** ~s Schulden übernehmen; **to attach** a ~ Forderung pfänden; **to bar** a ~ **by the Statute of Limitations** Verjährungseinwand gegen eine Forderung erheben; **to be in** ~ Schulden haben, verschuldet sein; **to be deep in** ~ hohe Schulden haben; **to be head over heels (up to the ears) in** ~ *(fam.)* bis über die Ohren in Schulden stecken; **to be heavily overextended with** ~ in höchstem Maße verschuldet sein; **to be in** ~ **to everybody** überall Schulden haben; **to be involved in** ~ in Schulden verwickelt sein; **to be liable for one's wife's** ~s für die Schulden der Ehefrau aufkommen müssen; **to be out of** ~ schuldenfrei sein; **to call in** ~s Schulden eintreiben; **to cancel** a ~ Schuld erlassen; **to charge off** a ~ uneinbringliche Forderung abschreiben; **to claim** a ~ Schuld einfordern; **to claim one's** ~s **from s. o.** Schuldner anmahnen; **to cognize** a ~ Schuld anerkennen; **to collect outstanding** ~s Außenstände hereinholen; **to compound** a ~ Schuld abtragen; **to contract** ~s Schulden eingehen (machen); **to cover** ~s Schulden abdecken; **to credit bad** ~s

faule Schulden streichen; **to die deeply in** ~ tief verschuldet sterben; **to discharge** a ~ Schuld begleichen; **to encumber o. s. with** ~s sich mit Schulden belasten; **to evade payment of one's** ~s sich um die Bezahlung seiner Schulden herumdrücken; **to expand the floating** ~ kurzfristige Verschuldung vergrößern; **to fall into** ~ in Schulden geraten; **to free o. s. from** ~s sich schuldenfrei machen, seine Schuld bezahlen (begleichen); **to fund** a ~ Schuld konsolidieren; **to gather in** ~s Schulden kassieren; **to get clear of** ~ seine Schulden bezahlen; **to get into** ~ sich verschulden; **to get out of** ~ seine Schulden loswerden; **to go into** ~ **at a record clip** sich ungewöhnlich verschulden; **to guarantee** a ~ sich für eine Schuld verbürgen; **to hold s. o. liable for the whole** ~ j. für die ganze Schuld haftbar machen; **to involve o. s. in** ~s sich mit Schulden belasten; **to incur** ~s Schulden machen (eingehen); **to keep out of** ~ sich schuldenfrei halten; **to leave nothing but** ~s nicht als Schulden hinterlassen; **to liquidate** a ~ Schuld bezahlen; **to lodge a proof of** ~ **with the official receiver** Forderung beim Konkursverwalter anmelden; **to make due allowance for doubtful** *(Br.)* **(bad**, *US)* ~s Rückstellungen für dubiose Forderungen vornehmen; **to meet one's** ~s seine Schulden bezahlen (begleichen); **to outlaw** a ~ Forderung verjähren lassen; **to owe** ~s Schuldenlast tragen; **to pay its** ~s **down the line** alle Schulden begleichen; **to pay [off]** a ~ Schuld tilgen (abbezahlen); **to pile up** ~s Schulden anwachsen lassen; **to plunge into** ~s sich in Schulden stürzen; **to prove** a ~ *(bankruptcy)* Konkursforderung nachweisen; **to recover** ~s Schulden eintreiben; **to recover outstanding** ~s ausstehende Schulden einkassieren; **to redeem** ~s Schulden tilgen; **to reduce** ~s Schulden abbauen; **to release from** a ~ Schuld erlassen; **to renounce** a ~ Schuld nicht anerkennen; **to report** a ~ Forderung anmelden; **to run into** ~ sich verschulden; **to satisfy** a ~ Schuld bezahlen; **to score up** ~s Schulden machen; **to settle one's** ~s seine Schulden bezahlen (begleichen), sich mit seinen Gläubigern arrangieren; **to sink** a ~ Schuld abtragen; **to stand security for** a ~ Schuld verbürgen; **to sue for** a ~ Forderung einklagen; **to summon s. o. for** ~ j. auf Bezahlung seiner Schulden verklagen; **to take on** ~s sich verschulden; **to waive** a ~ Schuld erlassen; **to wipe off** ~s Schulden annullieren; **to work off** a ~ Schuld abarbeiten; **to write off bad** *(US)* **(doubtful**, *Br.)* ~s zweifelhafte Schulden abschreiben;

bad ~s **collected account** *(US)* Konto für nachträglich eingegangene Dubiosen; ~ **administration** Schuldenverwaltung; ~ **balance** Debetsaldo; ~ **balance carried forward** Verlustvortrag; ~ **book** Verfallsbuch; ~ **claims** schuldrechtliche Ansprüche; ~ **collecting** Schuldeneintreibung; ~-**collecting agency (business)** Inkassobüro; ~-**collecting department** Inkassoabteilung; ~-**collecting work** Inkassotätigkeit; ~ **collection** Schuldeneintreibung; ~ **collector** Inkassobeauftragter; ~ **conference** Schuldenkonferenz; ~ **consolidation** Konsolidierung von Schulden; ~ **conversion** Schuldenumwandlung, -ablösung, Anleihekonversion, *(securities)* Wertpapierumtausch; ~ **coverage** Schuldendeckung; ~ **discount** Kreditdisagio; ~ **equity ratio** Verschuldensgrad, Verbindlichkeiten zu Eigenkapitalverhältnis; ~ **expansion** Schuldenzunahme; ~ **financing** Finanzierung mittels Forderungsabtretung, Fremdfinanzierung; ~ **funding** Schuldenkonsolidierung, Umschuldung; ~ **instrument** *(securities)* Schuldurkunde, Schuldtitel; **short-term** ~ **instrument** kurzfristiger Schuldtitel; ~ **issue** Schuldaufnahme; ~ **ledger** Schuldbuch; ~ **limit** *(municipal accounting)* Verschuldungsgrenze; ~ **liquidation** Schuldentilgung; ~ **management** Schuldenverwaltung; ~ **margin** *(municipal accounting)* Verschuldungsspielraum; ~ **monetization** Erhöhung des Zahlungsmittelumlaufs; ~s **profit levy** Kreditgewinnabgabe; ~ **pyramid** Schuldenpyramide; ~ **raiser** Kreditnehmer zum Zweck der Schuldtilgung; ~ **ratio** Verschuldungsgrad, Verschuldungskoeffizient; ~ **readjustment** Schuldenregulierung; ~ **receivable** *(US)* Forderungen, Außenstände; ~ **redemption** Schuldentilgung; ~ **redemption reserve** Schuldentilgungsrücklage; ~ **reduction** Schuldenabbau; ~ **refunding** Umschuldung; **National** ~ **Register** Staatsschuldbuch; ~ **register claims** Schuldbuchforderungen; ~ **relief** Schuldenerlaß; **bad** ~s **reserve** *(US)* Rückstellung für Dubiosen; **tax-free bad-** ~ **reserve level allowed to banks** *(US)* steuerfrei gebildete Reservengrenze für die Rückstellung ungewisser Bankschulden; ~ **retirement** Schuldenabbau; ~ **securities** Schuldpapiere; ~ **service** Schuldentilgungsdienst; ~ **to meet** ~ **service charges** Belastungen des Schuldentilgungsdienstes erfüllen; ~ **service costs** Schuldentilgungsaufwand; ~ **servicing** Schuldentilgungsdienst; ~ **servicing burden** Schuldentilgungslast; ~ **situation** Schuldensituation.

debtee Gläubiger.

debtless schuldenfrei, ohne Schulden.
debtor Verpflichteter, Schuldner, Debitor, *(debit side)* Debet-[seite], Soll-, Passivseite, *(of creditor)* Darlehens-, Kreditnehmer;
~s *(balance sheet)* Forderungen, Debitoren;
absconding ~ unbekannt verzogener (flüchtiger) Schuldner; **attached** ~ gepfändeter Schuldner; **bad** ~ schlechter (zahlungsunfähiger) Schuldner; **bill** ~ Wechselschuldner; **bond** ~ *(Br.)* Obligations-, Pfandbriefschuldner; **book** ~ Buchschuldner; **common** ~ *(Scot.)* Gemeinschuldner; **defaulting** ~ säumiger Schuldner; **dubious** ~ schlechter (unsicherer) Schuldner; **embarrassed** ~ in Schwierigkeiten befindlicher Schuldner; **execution** ~ Vollstreckungsgläubiger; **general** ~ Gesamtschuldner; **insolvent** ~ zahlungsunfähiger Schuldner; **joint** ~s gemeinsame Schuldner, Mit-, Solidar-, Gesamthandschuldner; **judgment** ~ Vollstreckungsschuldner; **mortgage** ~ Hypothekenschuldner; **poor** ~ zahlungsunfähiger Schuldner; **primary** ~ selbstschuldnerisch Haftender; **principal** ~ Hauptschuldner; **public** ~ öffentlichrechtlicher Kreditnehmer; **secondary** ~ sekundär haftender Schuldner; **sole** ~ Einzel-, Alleinschuldner; **solvent** ~ solventer Schuldner; **sundry** ~s *(balance sheet)* verschiedene Debitoren, Außenstände; **tardy** ~ *(US)* säumiger Schuldner; **tax** ~ Steuerschuldner;
~ **in account current** Kontokorrentschuldner; ~ **in arrears** säumiger Schuldner; ~ **of a bank** Bankschuldner; ~ **by endorsement** Giroschuldner; ~ **to a loan** Darlehnsschuldner; ~ **on mortgage** Hypothekenschuldner;
to allow a ~ **time to pay** einem Schuldner Zahlungsfrist gewähren; **to crowd a** ~ Schuldner bedrängen; **to discuss a** ~ Schuldner ausklagen; **to distrain upon a** ~ gegen einen Schuldner zwangsvollstrecken; **to inquire into the assets of a** ~ Schuldner auspfänden; **to serve upon a** ~ dem Schuldner zustellen; **to summon a** ~ Schuldner vor Gericht laden;
~ **account** Debetkonto; ~'s **acknowledgment** Schuldanerkenntnis; ~'s **assets** Konkursmasse; ~ **balance** Debet-, Sollsaldo; ~ **bank** *(US)* einem Clearinghaus verschuldete Bank; ~ **company (corporation,** *US)* Schuldnerin; ~ **country** Schuldnerland; ~'s **creditor relation** Schuldner-Gläubigerverhältnis; ~'s **declaration** Insolvenzerklärung; ~'s **duty** Schuldnerverpflichtung; ~'s **figure** Passivwert; ~ **group** Schuldnergruppe; ~ **interest rates** Sollzinsen; ~ **nation** Schuldnerland; **poor** ~'s **oath** Offenbarungseid; ~'s **petition** Konkurseröffnungsantrag des Gemeinschuldners; ~'s **property** Schuldnervermögen, Konkursmasse; **creditor-**~ **relation** Gläubiger-Schuldnerverhältnis; ~ **side** Debet-, Schuldner-, Sollseite; ~'s **summons** gerichtliche Zahlungsaufforderung; ~ **warrant** Besserungsschein.
debug *(v.)* Fehler beseitigen, *(clandestine microphone)* Wanzen ausbauen.
debugging *(punch card system)* Programmberichtigung.
debunk *(v.)* s. o. jem. seinen Nimbus nehmen, j. entglorifizieren.
debunker Enthüller, Entlarver.
debunking *(sl.)* Entglorifizierung.
debureaucratization Entbürokratisierung.
debus *(v.)* aus einem Bus aussteigen.
début *(girl)* Einführung in die Gesellschaft, *(theater)* erster Auftritt, Debüt;
to make one's ~ zum erstenmal auftreten.
debutante Debütant.
decade Dekade, Jahrzehnt;
~ **of development** Entwicklungsjahrzehnt.
decadence Niedergang, Verfall, Dekadenz.
decalcomania Abziehplakat, -bild.
decamp *(v.)* *(mil.)* heimlich abmarschieren, *(fig.)* sich aus dem Staube machen.
decampment *(fig.)* heimlicher Abzug.
decapitate enthaupten, *(US coll.)* [aus politischen Gründen] absägen, plötzlich entlassen.
decapitation Enthauptung, *(US)* Absägen, plötzliche Entlassung.
decartelization [Konzern]entflechtung, Entkartellisierung;
~ **agency** Kartellentflechtungsbehörde; ~ **branch** Entflechtungsabteilung; ~ **law** Entflechtungs-, Entkartellisierungsgesetz; ~ **plan (program(me))** Entflechtungsplan, -programm.
decartelize *(v.)* entflechten, entkartellisieren.
decasualization Auskämmung ungelernter Arbeiter.
decay *(building)* Baufälligkeit, Verfall, Niedergang, Ruin, *(geol.)* Verwitterung, *(goods)* Verderb, Fäulnis, Zersetzung;
senile ~ Altersschwäche;
~ **of intellectual power** Nachlassen der Verstandeskräfte;
~ *(v.)* verfallen, in Verfall geraten, zugrunde gehen, *(goods)* verderben;

to be in ~ *(house)* verfallen (baufällig) sein; **to die of** ~ an Altersschwäche sterben; **to fall into** ~ *(custom)* außer Gewohnheit kommen, *(house)* verfallen, in Verfall geraten.
decayed | **with age** altersschwach;
~ **circumstances** zerrüttete Vermögensverhältnisse.
decease Ableben, Sterbefall, Hinscheiden, Tod;
~ *(v.)* [ver]sterben;
~ **without heir** ohne Nachkommen sterben.
deceased | **estate** Nachlaß, Erbschaft; ~ **person** Verstorbener, Erblasser.
decedent *(US)* Verstorbener;
~'s **estate** *(US)* Nachlaß; ~ **estate law** *(New York)* Erbrecht.
deceit Hinterlist, Falschheit, Tücke, Ränke, *(law)* Täuschung, betrügerische Handlung, Betrug, Betrügerei;
attempted ~ Täuschungsversuch; **intentional** ~ Täuschungsabsicht; **wilful** ~ arglistige Täuschung;
to be incapable of ~ keiner Falschheit fähig sein; **to be liable to** ~ arglistige Täuschung begehen; **to practice** ~ Betrug begehen, betrügen.
deceitful arglistig, hinterlistig, betrügerisch;
~ **plea** Scheinvorbringen, Prozeßbetrug.
deceivable leicht zu täuschen.
deceive *(v.)* betrügen, betrügerisch handeln, hintergehen, täuschen;
~ **o. s.** sich täuschen (einer Täuschung hingeben); ~ **o. s. with a fond hope** sich trügerischen Hoffnungen hingeben;
to be ~**d in s. o.** sein Vertrauen in j. getäuscht sehen.
deceiver Betrüger, Schwindler;
arch ~ Erzbetrüger.
decelerate *(v.)* Geschwindigkeit verlangsamen.
deceleration Geschwindigkeitsabnahme.
decennial Zehnjahresfeier.
decency Anstand, Schicklichkeit;
for ~'s **sake** anstandshalber;
to preserve ~ Anstand wahren.
decent schicklich, moralisch, einwandfrei;
~ **behavio(u)r** anständiges Benehmen; **to live in** ~ **conditions** in ordentlichen Verhältnissen leben; ~ **fellow** *(coll.)* netter Kerl; ~ **fortune** ganz ordentliches Vermögen; ~ **language** gesittete Sprache; ~**-sized house** Haus in vernünftigen Größenabmessungen.
decentralization Dezentralisierung, Dezentralisation, Auflockerung, Entflechtung;
~ **in banking** Bankendezentralisation, -entflechtung; ~ **of federal government departments** Dezentralisation von Bundesbehörden;
~ **committee** Dezentralisierungsausschuß; ~ **program(me)** Dezentralisierungsplan.
decentralize *(v.)* entflechten, auflockern, dezentralisieren.
decentralizing dezentralistisch.
deception Täuschungshandlung, Irreführung, Irrtumserregung, Betrug;
to practise ~ **on the public** Öffentlichkeit hintergehen.
deceptive täuschend, irreführend;
~ **advertising** täuschende (betrügerische, irreführende) Reklame; ~ **mark** irreführendes Warenzeichen.
decibel Phonstärke;
to establish maximum noise level for airplanes of between 102 and 108 ~s Höchstwerte von 102 bis 108 Phon für Flugzeuge zulassen;
10-~ **reduction** Geräuschverringerung um 10 Phon.
decide *(v.)* entschließen, entscheiden, bestimmen, Entscheidung treffen, Beschluß (Entschluß) fassen, *(court)* für Recht erkennen, *(date)* festsetzen, *(law of nations)* Empfehlungen beschließen;
~ **upon s. th.** sich für etw. entscheiden; ~ **a battle** Erfolg einer Schlacht bestimmen; ~ **a case** in einer Sache entscheiden; ~ **upon a day** Termin festsetzen; ~ **against a holiday** sich nicht zu einer Ferienreise entschließen; ~ **by a majority of votes** mit Stimmenmehrheit beschließen; ~ **on the merits of each particular case** von Fall zu Fall entscheiden; ~ **against the plaintiff** Urteil zu Ungunsten des Klägers fällen; ~ **for (in favo(u)r of) the plaintiff** Urteil zugunsten des Klägers fällen; ~ **upon a method of work** sich für eine Arbeitsmethode entscheiden; ~ **upon a necessary purchase** notwendige Anschaffungen beschließen; ~ **the point** über die Zuständigkeitsfrage entscheiden; ~ **a point of law** Rechtsfrage entscheiden; ~ **unanimously** einstimmig beschließen.
decided entschieden, eindeutig;
to be quite ~ **about s. th.** ziemlich fest entschlossen zu etw. sein;
~ **difference** entschiedener Unterschied; ~ **opinion** feste

Ansicht; ~ **refusal** eindeutige Absage; ~ **step forward** unzweifelhafter Fortschritt; **to have a ~ superiority over s. o.** jem. entschieden überlegen sein.

decile Zehntelstelle.

decimal Dezimalstelle;
~**s** *(red numbers)* [Zins]nummern;
~ *(a.)* dezimal;
~ **account** Dezimalrechnung; ~ **coinage** Dezimalwährung; ~ **currency** Dezimalwährung; ⚖ **Currency Act** *(Br.)* Gesetz zur Einführung der Dezimalwährung; ~ **figure** Kommastelle; ~ **fraction** Dezimalbruch; ~ **place** Dezimalstelle; ~ **system** Dezimalsystem.

decipher *(v.)* entziffern, -schlüsseln, dechiffrieren.

decipherable entzifferbar.

decipherment Entzifferung, Entschlüsselung, Dechiffrierung.

decision Entscheid[ung], Entschluß, Stellungnahme, *(arbitration)* Schiedsspruch, *(law court)* [richterliche] Entscheidung, Beschluß, Urteil;
in accordance with the committee's ~ laut Beschluß des Ausschusses; **pending a ~ of the court** solange die richterliche Entscheidung aussteht;
appealed ~ angefochtene Entscheidung; **alternative** ~ Alternativentscheidung; **arbitration board** ~ Schiedsspruch; **armchair** ~ Entscheidung am grünen Tisch; ~ **complained of** angefochtene Entscheidung; **court** ~ gerichtliche Entscheidung, Gerichtsbeschluß, -entscheidung; **discretionary** ~ Ermessensentscheidung; **final** ~ endgültiger Bescheid, *(court)* Endurteil, rechtskräftige Entscheidung; **interlocutory** ~ Zwischenentscheidung; **irrevocable** ~ unwiderrufliche Entscheidung; **judicial** ~ Gerichtsentscheidung, -urteil, Richterspruch, richterliche Entscheidung; **leading** ~ grundsätzliche Entscheidung, Präzedenzfall; **legal** ~ gerichtlicher Entscheid, Urteil; **majority** ~ Mehrheitsbeschluß; **preliminary** ~ Vor[ab]entscheidung; **previous** ~ frühere Entscheidung; **provisional** ~ vorläufiger Bescheid, Vorbescheid, -entscheidung; **reasoned** ~ mit Gründen versehene Entscheidung; **top-level management** ~ auf höchster Ebene getroffene Entscheidung; **ultimate** ~ endgültige Entscheidung;
~ **ex aequo et bono** Ermessensentscheidung; ~ **set aside** [durch Rechtsmittelinstanz] aufgehobene Entscheidung; ~ **of character** Charakterfestigkeit; ~ **of a court** gerichtliche Entscheidung, Gerichtsentscheidung; ~ **of highly political importance** hochpolitische Entscheidung; ~**s of the judge** richterliche Entscheidungen; ~ **of the majority** Mehrheitsbeschluß; ~ **on merits** Urteil dem Grunde nach, Sachentscheidung; ~ **to retire** Pensionsentschluß; ~ **to spend** Investitionsentschluß; ~ **of a suit** Entscheidung eines Rechtsstreites; ~ **of the Supreme Court** höchstrichterliche Entscheidung;
to abide by a ~ sich an eine Entscheidung halten; **to adjourn a** ~ Entscheidung aussetzen; **to appeal against a** ~ [Gerichts]entscheidung anfechten; **to approve a** ~ Urteil bestätigen; **to arrive at a** ~ zu einer Entscheidung kommen; **to be closely involved with** ~**s** entscheidendes Mitspracherecht haben; **to bring about a** ~ Entscheidung herbeiführen; **to come to a** ~ sich entschließen; **to endorse a** ~ Entscheidung billigen; **to face a difficult** ~ vor einer schweren Entscheidung stehen; **to force a** ~ Entscheidung mit Gewalt herbeiführen; **to give a** ~ **on a case** Fall richterlich entscheiden; **to give a** ~ **in s. one's favo(u)r** zu jds. Gunsten entscheiden; **to hold a** ~ **over** Entscheidung zurückstellen; **to lack** ~ unentschlossen sein; **to make a** ~ **on s. th.** in einer Sache befinden; **to make a final** ~ endgültige Entscheidung treffen; **to make quick** ~**s on loans and overdrafts** rasche Entscheidungen bei der Kreditgewährung oder der Einräumung von Überziehungskrediten treffen; **to overrule a** ~ Entscheidung umstoßen; **to overrule a** ~ **of the lower court** Entscheidung der unteren Instanz abändern; **to pass a** ~ Entscheidung fällen; **to postpone a** ~ Entschluß vertagen; **to press for a** ~ auf eine Entscheidung drängen; **to reach a** ~ Entscheidung (Entschluß) fassen; **to refer for** ~ zur Entscheidung vorlegen; **to rescind a** ~ Beschluß für nichtig erklären, Entscheidung aufheben; **to reserve one's** ~ sich die Entscheidung vorbehalten; **to revise a** ~ von einem Entschluß abgehen, Entscheidung abändern; **to submit to a** ~ sich mit einer Entscheidung abfinden; **to take a** ~ Entscheidung treffen; **to uphold a** ~ Gerichtsurteil in zweiter Instanz bestätigen;
~ **maker** Entscheidungsträger; ~ **making** Beschlußfassung, Entscheidungsfindung; ~**-making powers** Mitbestimmungsrechte; ~**-making process** Entscheidungsprozeß; ~**-making unit** Entscheidungsinstanz; ~ **model** Entscheidungsmodell; ~ **problem** Entscheidungsproblem; ~ **space** *(statistics)* Entscheidungsraum; ~ **team** entscheidendes Gremium.

decisive entscheidend, maßgebend, ausschlaggebend;
to be ~ for s. one's career jds. Laufbahn entscheidend bestimmen;
~ **battle** Entscheidungskampf, -schlacht; ~ **oath** Parteieid; ~ **proof** schlüssiger (ausschlaggebender) Beweis; ~ **tone** entschlossener Ton; ~ **vote** ausschlaggebende Stimme.

decisory oath Parteieid.

deck Deck, *(airplane)* Tragfläche, *(cage)* Plattform, *(story)* Stockwerk, *(waggon, US)* Dach;
on ~ auf Deck, *(US coll.)* auf dem Posten, bereit;
lower ~ Zwischendeck; **the lower** ~ *(Br., coll.)* Maate und Matrosen, Mannschaftsgrade; **main** ~ Vorderdeck; **middle** ~ Mitteldeck; **top** ~ *(bus)* oberstes Stockwerk; **upper** ~ *(bus)* oberes Stockwerk;
~ *(v.)* **up** auf dem Deck aufstapeln;
to clear the ~**s** Schiff gefechtsklar machen; **to ship on** ~ auf Deck verladen; **to walk on the** ~ auf dem Deck auf und abgehen;
single ~ **bus** einstöckiger Omnibus; ~ **cabin** Touristenkabine; ~ **cargo** Decklast, -güter; ~ **chair** Liegestuhl; ~ **class** Touristenklasse; ~ **flooring** Decksbelag; ~ **hand** gewöhnlicher Matrose; ~ **lander** Decklandeflugzeug; ~ **log** Logbuch; ~ **passage** Deckspassage; ~ **passenger** Reisender der Touristenklasse; **the lower** ~ **ratings** die Mannschaftsgrade.

deckle Büttenrand;
~ **edge paper** Büttenpapier.

deckload Decksladung.

declaim *(v.)* Rede halten.

declamation öffentlicher Vortrag, öffentliche Ansprache.

declarant Erklärender, Abgeber einer Erklärung, *(US)* Anwärter auf die Staatsbürgerschaft.

declaration offizielle Erklärung, *(attorney)* Anklagerede, *(bankruptcy)* Anmeldung, *(of court)* Entscheidung einer Rechtsfrage, *(customs)* Zolldeklaration, -erklärung, *(insurance)* Angabe des Versicherungswertes, *(plaintiff's statement, US)* Klageschrift, Schriftsatz, *(prisoner, Scot.)* Aussage vor dem Untersuchungsrichter, *(proclamation)* Manifest, Proklamation, *(proposal)* Verlobungsantrag, *(statement)* Erklärung, Aussage, *(witness, US)* Versicherung an Eides Statt;
binding ~ bindende Erklärung; **customs** ~ Zollerklärung; **dying** ~ Aussage auf dem Sterbebett; **explicit** ~ formelle Erklärung; **export** ~ *(US)* Ausfuhrdeklaration; **false** ~ falsche Angabe; **import** ~ *(US)* Einfuhrerklärung; **income-tax** ~ *(Br.)* Einkommensteuererklärung; ~ **inwards** *(Br.)* Zolleinfuhrerklärung; **judicial** ~ Parteivorbringen; ~ **outwards** *(Br.)* Zollausfuhrerklärung, Ausklarierung; **palliative** ~ abschwächende Erklärung; **self-serving** ~ Abgabe einer Erklärung im eigenen Interesse, Schutzbehauptung; **solemn** ~ feierliche Erklärung; **statutory** ~ *(Br.)* eidesstattliche Erklärung; **sworn** ~ Aussage unter Eid; **unilateral** ~ einseitige Erklärung; **vesting** ~ *(trustee)* Übertragungserklärung;
~ **of accession** Beitrittserklärung; ~ **of alienage** *(Br.)* Aufgabe der Staatsangehörigkeit; **statutory** ~ **of assent** formlose Zustimmungserklärung; ~ **of assignment** Abtretungserklärung; ~ **of bankruptcy** Konkurserklärung, -anmeldung; ~ **of blockade** Blockadeerklärung; ~ **of charge** Feststellung des Rechtes auf abgesonderte Befriedigung; ~ **in chief** Hauptbegründung einer Klage; ~ **of contents** Zolldeklaration, Inhaltsangabe; ~ **of death** Todeserklärung; ~ **of default** Erklärung des Börsenvorstands [über nicht eingehaltene Verpflichtungen]; ~ **of dividends** Dividendenfestlegung, -ausschüttung, *(bankruptcy proceedings)* Quotenverteilung; ~ **as to election expense** *(parliament)* Erklärung über die Wahlangaben; ~ **of enrolment** Beitrittserklärung; ~ **by the government** Regierungserklärung; ~ **of guarantee** Bürgschaftserklärung; ~ **of guaranty** Bürgschafterklärung; ~ **of homestead** *(US)* Feststellung der Heimstätteneigenschaft eines Grundstücks; ~ **of inability to pay one's debts** Zahlungsunfähigkeitserklärung; ~ **of income** Einkommensteuererklärung; ⚖ **of Independance** *(US)* Unabhängigkeitserklärung; ~ **of insolvency** Insolvenzerklärung, Vergleichsanmeldung; ~ **of intention** Willenserklärung, *(law of nations)* Grundsatzerklärung, *(US)* Naturalisationserklärung; ~ **against interest** selbstbelastende Erklärung; ~ **of interest** Absichtserklärung; ~ **of interim dividends** Ausschüttung von Zwischendividenden; ~ **of legitimacy** Legitimation; **public** ~ **of financial interests** Offenlegung finanzieller Beteiligungen; ~ **of membership** Beitrittserklärung; ~ **in lieu of oath** *(Br.)* Versicherung an Eides Statt, eidesstattliche Erklärung; ~ **on oath** eidliche Erklärung; ~ **of an opinion** Meinungsäußerung; ~ **of options** Prämienerklärung; ⚖ **of Paris** Pariser Seerechtsdeklaration; ~ **of patents nullified** Nichtigkeitserklärung von Paten-

ten; ~ **of policy** Grundsatzerklärung, Absichtserklärung; ~ **of the poll** Bekanntmachung des Wahlergebnisses; ~ **of principal** Offenlegung des Auftraggebers, *(pol.)* Grundsatzerklärung; ~ **of property** Vermögenserklärung, -anmeldung; ~ **of rights** Katalog der Grundrechte; ~ **of plaintiff's rights** Feststellungsurteil zugunsten des Klägers; ~ **of shipment** Versandbestätigung; ~ **of solvency** *(Br.)* Solvenzerklärung bei Gesellschaftsauflösung; ~ **of trust (use)** schriftliche Begründung eines Treuhandverhältnisses; ~ **of value** Wertanzeige, -angabe; ~ **above the value** zu hohe Wertangabe; ~ **of export value** Exportwerterklärung; ~ **of the value received** Angabe des Versicherungswertes; ~ **of war** Kriegserklärung; ~ **of weight** Gewichtsangabe;

to **file a statutory** ~ eidesstattliche Erklärung abgeben; **to file a** ~ **of bankruptcy** Konkursantrag stellen, Konkursanmeldung vornehmen; **to give (make) a** ~ Erklärung abgeben, seine Waren deklarieren; **to give a written** ~ Revers ausstellen; **to make a** ~ *(customs)* Waren deklarieren; **to make one's** ~ seine Klageschrift einreichen; **to make a solemn** ~ feierliche Erklärung abgeben; **to take note of a** ~ von einer Erklärung Kenntnis nehmen;

~ **form** Begleitadresse, *(marine insurance)* Wertangabeformular.

declarator *(Scot. law)* Eigentumsfeststellungsklage;
~ **of trust** Feststellungsklage auf Vorliegen eines Treuhandsverhältnisses.

declaratory feststellend, erklärend, deklaratorisch, *(law)* interpretierend;
to be ~ feststellen;
~ **action** Feststellungsklage; **to seek** ~ **action** Feststellungsklage erheben; ~ **clause** Erläuterungsbestimmung; ~ **decree** Feststellungsbeschluß; ~ **judgment** Feststellungsurteil; ~ **law** erläuterndes Gesetz; ~ **part of a judgment** Urteilsbegründung; ~ **part of a law** materielle Gesetzesvorschriften; ~ **statement** deklaratorische Erklärung; ~ **statute** Berufungsgesetz.

declare *(v.)* erklären, aussagen, Erklärung abgeben, feststellen, anmelden, formell bekanntgeben, *(customs)* [zollamtlich] deklarieren, zur Verzollung anmelden, *(to a tax inspector)* seine Einkommenssteuererklärung abgeben, *(institue legal proceedings)* Klage einbringen, klagen, *(propose)* Verlobungsantrag machen, *(before witness)* [vor Zeugen] feierlich erklären;

~ o. s. seine Meinung kundtun; ~ **an action admissible** Zulässigkeit einer Klage feststellen, Klage für zulässig erklären; ~ **s. o. to be of age** j. für volljährig erklären; ~ **o. s. a bankrupt** sich für zahlungsunfähig erklären, seinen Konkurs anmelden; ~ **a bargain off** sich von einem Geschäft zurückziehen; ~ **s. o. legally dead** j. für tot erklären; ~ **a dividend** Dividende verteilen (ausschütten, festsetzen), *(trustee)* Abschlagsquote verteilen; ~ **a dividend in stock of the corporation** Gratisaktien gewähren, Dividende in Form eigener Aktien ausschütten; ~ **due für** fällig erklären; ~ **an election void** Wahl für nichtig erklären; ~ **an engagement off** Verlobung [auf]lösen; ~ **s. o. at the exchange** j. öffentlich für bankrott erklären; ~ **o. s. guilty** sich schuldig bekennen; ~ **o. s. an heir** sich als Erben benennen (zum Erben erklären); ~ **one's income** seine Einkommensteuererklärung abgeben; ~ **o. s. to be innocent** sich für unschuldig erklären, seine Unschuld beteuern; ~ **one's insolvency** sich für zahlungsunfähig erklären; ~ **one's interests** *(board member)* seine persönlichen Beteiligungen offenlegen; ~ **s. o. a lunatic** j. für geisteskrank erklären; ~ **null and void** für [null und] nichtig erklären; ~ **on oath** unter Eid erklären (aussagen); ~ **off** zurücktreten, absagen; ~ **open** für eröffnet erklären, eröffnen; ~ **one's opinion** seine Meinung äußern; ~ **an option** *(stock exchange)* Prämie erklären; ~ **a paper signed by o. s.** die Unterschrift anerkennen; ~ **a lawful prize** für gute Prise erklären; ~ **property** Vermögen anmelden; ~ **the results of the poll** Abstimmungsergebnis veröffentlichen, Wahlergebnis bekanntgeben; ~ **a right** Feststellungsurteil ergehen lassen; ~ **for public sale** zum Verkauf anbieten; ~ **a state of siege** Belagerungszustand verhängen; ~ **a state of war** Kriegszustand erklären; ~ **a strike** Streik proklamieren (ausrufen); ~ **o. s. the successor** sich zum Nachfolger erklären; ~ **a trust** Treuhandverhältnis begründen; ~ **the value** Wert [bei der Verzollung] angeben; ~ **war on (against) a country** einem Land den Krieg erklären; ~ **one's willingness** sich bereit erklären; ~ **before witness** in Zeugengegenwart erklären;

to have s. th. to ~ etw. zu verzollen haben;

declared *(customs)* zollamtlich erklärt, deklariert, *(judgment)* verkündet;
to be ~ **a fool** für verrückt erklärt werden;

~ **abstention** angegebene Stimmenthaltung; ~ **capital** festgesetztes Kapital; **wrongfully** ~ **cargo** falsch deklarierte Ladung; ~ **dividend** ausgeschüttete Dividende; ~ **[valuation] rate** Werttarif; ~ **valuation** Wertangabe.

déclassé sozial abgesunken.

declassification *(mil., US)* Aufhebung von Geheimhaltungsbestimmungen (Geheimhaltungsstufen), Freigabe von Geheimmaterial;
~ **procedure** Verfahren zur Freigabe von Geheimmaterial.

declassified *(mil., US)* freigegeben.

declassify *(v.)* *(US)* Geheimhaltungsbestimmungen (Geheimhaltungsstufen) aufheben, Geheimmaterial freigeben.

declination höfliche Ablehnung, *(judge, Scot.)* Ablehnung wegen Befangenheit, *(Scot. law)* Richterablehnung.

declinatory | **exception** Einwand gegen die Zuständigkeit; ~ **plea** Ablehnungserklärung.

decline *(business cycle)* Abschwächung, Abschwung, Abnahme, *(deterioration)* Niedergang, Verfall, Verschlechterung, Rückläufigkeit, *(falling off)* Senkung, Abhang, *(med.)* Verfall, Siechtum, *(nation)* Abstieg, Niedergang, *(prices)* Fallen, Sinken, Sturz, Rückgang, Rückwärtsbewegung, Absinken, *(stock exchange)* Kursrückgang, -abschlag, Baisse;

brisk ~ starker Kursverfall; **business** ~ Rezession; **general** ~ allgemeiner Geschäftsrückgang; **marked** ~ ausgeprägter Rückgang; **price** ~ Sinken der Preise, *(stock exchange)* Kursrückgang; **slight** ~ geringe Abschwächung; **stock-market** ~ Rückgang der Aktienkurse (Börsenkurse); **sudden** ~ plötzliche Baisse;

~ **in economic activity** rückläufige Konjunkturbewegung; **sharp** ~ **in economic activity** Konjunktureinbruch; ~ **of the birth rate** Geburtenrückgang; ~ **in business** Geschäftsrückgang, Schrumpfung des Geschäftsvolumens; ~ **in consumption** Verbrauchsrückgang; ~ **in demand** Nachfragerückgang, -einbruch; ~ **in earnings** Ertragsrückgang, -minderung; ~ **in exports** Ausfuhrrückgang; ~ **in income** Einkommensrückgang; ~ **in industry** rückläufige Bewegung der industriellen Fertigung; ~ **in investments** nachlassende Investitionstätigkeit; ~ **in jobs** rückläufiges Angebot an Arbeitsplätzen; ~ **of life** Lebensabend; ~ **in manpower** Absinken der Belegschaftsziffern; ~ **in mortality** Sterblichkeitsrückgang; ~ **in oil purchases** rückläufige Ölbezüge; ~ **in orders** Auftragsrückgang; ~ **in prices** Preissenkung, Preissturz, *(stock exchange)* Nachgeben der Kurse, Kursrückgang, -rückschlag; ~ **in production** Produktionsrückgang, Absinken der Leistungsfähigkeit; ~ **in prosperity** Konjunkturrückgang; ~ **in quotation** Baisse; ~ **in revenue** Einnahmerückgang; ~ **in sales** Absatzrückgang, Umsatzrückgang; ~ **of the saving boom** rückläufige Sparkonjunktur; ~ **in stock prices (of the stock market)** allgemeiner Kursrückgang; ~ **of strength** Kräfterückgang, Abnahme der Kräfte; ~ **in unemployment** abnehmende Arbeitslosenzahlen, rückläufige Arbeitslosigkeit; ~ **in value** Wertminderung; ~ **in the value of money** Geldentwertung;

~ *(v.)* *(bend aside)* abfallen, abschüssig sein, *(decrease)* abnehmen, zurückgehen, geringer werden, *(deteriorate)* sich verschlechtern, *(health)* verfallen, seine Kräfte verlieren, *(price)* fallen, weichen, sinken, heruntergehen, *(refuse)* Absage erteilen, absagen, *(shun consent)* [höflich ablehnen, nicht zustimmen, *(stock exchange)* Rückgang erfahren, nachgeben;

~ **acceptance** Annahme verweigern; ~ **in economic usefulness** sich verschleißen; ~ **an invitation** Einladung absagen; ~ **an offer** Angebot ablehnen; ~ **an order** Auftrag ablehnen; ~ **rapidly** schnell sinken; ~ **the responsibility** *(insurance)* Haftpflicht ablehnen; ~ **slightly** *(quotations)* geringfügig nachgeben; ~ **with thanks** dankend ablehnen;

to be on the ~ *(prices)* zur Neige gehen, im Absinken (Fallen) begriffen sein; **to experience a** ~ Kursrückgang erfahren; **to sell at a** ~ mit einem Abschlag verkaufen; **to suffer a** ~ Rückgang erleiden;

~ **guarantee** Garantie gegen Preisrückgang; ~ **list** *(insurance)* Verzeichnis der abzulehnenden Risiken.

declining | **an order** Auftragsablehnung;
~ *(a.)* *(prices, market)* rückgängig, schwindend, zurückgehend, nachgiebig, sinkend, fallend;
to be ~ **daily** *(business)* Tag um Tag zurückgehen;
~ **age** vorgerücktes Alter; ~ **balance depreciation** degressive Abschreibung; ~ **balance method of depreciation** degressive Abschreibungsmethode; ~ **birth rate** rückläufige Geburtenrate; ~ **market** nachlassende (nachgebende) Kurse; ~ **prices** nachgebende Kurse; ~ **stocks** fallende Aktien; **to show a** ~ **tendency** sich abschwächen; ~ **years** vorgerücktes Alter, Lebensabend.

declutch *(v.)* auskuppeln.

declutching Auskuppeln.

decode *(v.)* [Funkspruch] entziffern, entschlüsseln, dechiffrieren.

decoded in Klartext.

decoder Entschlüsseler.

decoding Entzifferung, -schlüsselung.

decolonization *(US)* Beendigung der Kolonialregierung.

decolonize *(v.) (US)* entkolonialisieren.

decompose *(v.)* sich zusetzen (auflösen).

decompression chamber Druckausgleichskammer.

deconcentrate *(v.)* entflechten.

deconcentration [Konzern]entflechtung;
~ **law** Entflechtungsgesetz; ~ **plan** Entflechtungsplan; ~ **program(me)** Entflechtungsprogramm.

deconsolidated accounts nichtkonsolidierter Abschluß.

decontaminate *(v.)* entgiften, entseuchen.

decontamination Entgiftung, Entseuchung.

decontrol Freigabe, Aufhebung, Abbau der Zwangswirtschaft (Planwirtschaft);
price ~ Freigabe der Preise, Aufhebung (Abbau) der Preiskontrollbestimmungen;
~ **of imports** Einfuhrliberalisierung; ~ **of rents** Mietfreigabe, Aufhebung des Mieterschutzes;
~ *(v.)* Zwangswirtschaft abbauen, freigeben, liberalisieren, aus der Bewirtschaftung herausnehmen;
~ **prices** Preiskontrolle aufheben, Preisüberwachungsvorschriften abbauen; ~ **rents** Mieten freigeben;
~ **provisions** *(Rent Act, Br.)* aufgehobene Mieterschutzbestimmungen.

decontrolled nicht mehr bewirtschaftet, frei, liberalisiert.

decor Dekorierung, *(theatre)* Ausstattung.

decorate *(v.)* dekorieren, *(give mark of distinction)* auszeichnen;
~ **a house** Schönheitsreparaturen durchführen.

decorating paper Dekorationspapier.

decoration Verzierung, Dekorierung, *(mark of hono(u)r)* [Dienst]auszeichnung, Ehrenzeichen, Orden;
Christmas ~s Weihnachtsschmuck;
to award a ~ Auszeichnung verleihen.

decorator Dekorateur.
window ~ Schaufensterdekorateur.

decorum Etikette, Anstandsregeln;
to go with proper ~ im würdigen Rahmen ablaufen; **to maintain one's ~** das Dekorum wahren.

decorous schicklich, geziemend.

decoy *(fig.)* Lockvogel, Köder, *(mar.)* U-Bootfalle, *(mil.)* Falle, Lockobjekt, Scheinanlage;
~ *(v.)* ködern, *(v/tr.)* in die Falle gehen;
~ **across the frontier** über die Grenze locken;
~ **airport** Scheinflugplatz; ~ **duck** *(fig.)* Lockvogel; ~ **letter** Köderbrief; ~ **ship** U-Bootfalle.

decrease *(decline)* Abnahme, Abnehmen, *(diminution)* [Ver]minderung, Verringerung, Kürzung, Rückgang, Reduzierung;
on the ~ im Abnehmen begriffen, rückläufig;
~ **in capital** Kapitalverminderung; ~ **in consumption** Verbrauchsrückgang; ~ **in demand** Nachfragerückgang; ~ **in imports** Einfuhrrückgang; ~ **in liquidity** Liquiditätsrückgang, -abnahme; ~ **in population** Bevölkerungsrückgang, -abnahme; ~ **of pressure** Luftdruckabnahme; **considerable ~ in prices** beträchtlicher Kurs-, Preisrückgang; ~ **of receipts** Mindererlös; ~ **in risks** *(insurance)* Gefahrenminderung; ~ **in sales** Absatz-, Umsatzschrumpfung; ~ **in share prices** Rückgang der Aktienkurse; ~ **in speed** Herabsetzung der Geschwindigkeit; ~ **in staff** Personalabbau, -verringerung; ~ **of stocks** Abnahme der Bestände; ~ **in temperature** Temperaturabnahme, -rückgang; ~ **in traffic** Verkehrsrückgang, -abnahme; ~ **in turnover** Umsatzrückgang; ~ **in unemployment** Verringerung der Arbeitslosigkeit; ~ **in value** Wertverringerung, -minderung;
~ *(v.) (diminish)* abnehmen, geringer werden, sich vermindern, *(quotations)* zurückgehen, schwächer liegen (werden), fallen;
to be on the ~ rückläufig (im Abnehmen) sein.

decreasing abnehmend, in der Abnahme begriffen;
~ **costs** abnehmende Unkosten; ~ **returns** rückläufige Erträge.

decree An-, Verordnung, [amtlicher] Erlaß, Vorschrift, Verfügung, Bestimmung, Gesetz, Dekret, *(court)* Gerichtsbeschluß, Entscheid, Urteil;
by ~ auf dem Verordnungswege;
the above ~ die oben zitierte Verordnung; ~ **absolute** Endurteil, rechtskräftiges Urteil, rechtskräftiger Beschluß, *(nullity)* Scheidungsurteil; ~ **arbitral** *(Scot.)* Schiedsspruch, Schiedsgerichtsentscheidung; **consent ~** Anerkenntnisurteil, Prozeßver-

gleich; **court ~** Gerichtsbeschluß; ~ **dative** Testamentsvollstreckerbestellung; **declaratory ~** Feststellungsurteil; **deficiency ~** Feststellung der Hypothekenrestschuld; **emergency ~** Not[stands]verordnung; **executory ~** Vollstreckungstitel; **final ~** rechtskräftiges Urteil, Endurteil; **interlocutory ~** Zwischenurteil, -verfügung; **judicial ~** richterliche Verfügung; ~ **nisi** *(Br.)* bedingtes (vorläufiges) Scheidungsurteil; **provisional ~** vorläufiges Urteil;
~ **in absence** *(Scot.)* Versäumnisurteil; ~ **of adjudication** Konkurseröffnungsbeschluß; ~ **of annulment** Aufhebungsbeschluß; ~ **in bankruptcy** Konkurseröffnungsbeschluß; ~ **pro confesso** Versäumnisurteil; ~ **of constitution** Feststellungsurteil; ~ **of court [of justice]** Gerichtsbeschluß; ~ **of dissolution** Auflösungsbeschluß; ~ **of divorce** Scheidungsurteil; ~ **of distribution** Beschluß über die Nachlaßverteilung; ~ **of forthcoming** *(Scot.)* Pfändungs- und Überweisungsbeschluß; ~ **of insolvency** Eröffnung des Vergleichsverfahrens, *(estate)* Nachlaßkonkurseröffnung; ~ **of strict foreclosure** Zwangsvollstreckungsanordnung; ~ **of locality** örtlicher Verteilungsbeschluß; ~ **of nullity** [Ehe]nichtigkeitsurteil; ~ **of registration** Vollstreckbarkeitsbeschluß;
~ *(v.)* verordnen, dekretieren, Dekret erlassen, verfügen, gerichtlich anordnen, entscheiden;
to annul a ~ Beschluß aufheben; **to bring a ~ into operation** Verordnung anwenden (zur Anwendung bringen); **to enter a ~** Gerichtsbeschluß erlassen; **to execute a ~** Beschluß ausfertigen; **to issue a ~** Verordnung erlassen; **to issue a formal ~** Beschluß ergehen lassen; **to pass a ~** Verordnung erlassen, verordnen; **to recall a ~** Verordnung zurückziehen; **to rescind (reserve) a ~** Beschluß aufheben; **to rule by ~** mit Notverordnungen regieren; **to sign a ~ of adjudication** Konkurseröffnungsbeschluß erlassen; **to stop the execution of a ~** Durchführung einer Verordnung aussetzen; **to submit a ~ to s. o. for signature** Verordnung jem. zur Unterschrift vorlegen;
~ **law** Notverordnung.

decreeable dekretierbar.

decrement, double *(insurance)* Ausscheidetafel mit zwei Ausscheideursachen;
equal ~ of life *(insurance)* gleichmäßiger Abgang von versicherten Leben;
~ **table** *(life insurance)* Mortalitätstafel.

decrepit altersschwach, hinfällig;
~ **old age** Altersschwäche.

decrepitude Altersschwäche, Gebrechlichkeit;
~ **of age** Altersschwäche.

decretal order einstweilige Anordnung.

decry *(v.)* herabsetzen, verächtlich machen, *(coins)* für zahlungsungültig erklären.

decryptment *(US)* Entschlüsselung.

decurrent rent nachschüssige Rente.

decursive *(interest)* nachschüssig.

dedicate *(v.)* einweihen, widmen, zuschreiben, *(public use, coll.)* zum öffentlichen Gebrauch bestimmen, der Öffentlichkeit zugänglich machen, feierlich eröffnen;
~ **a book** Buch widmen; ~ **a day for pleasure** ganzen Tag ausspannen; ~ **a highway** Straße dem öffentlichen Verkehr übergeben; ~ **one's life** sein Leben widmen (weihen); ~ **one's pen to truth** schriftstellerisch für die Wahrheit eintreten; ~ **to the public** *(copyright, US)* zugunsten der Allgemeinheit verzichten; ~ **certain tax revenues to a hospital** Steuereinnahmen für ein Krankenhaus zweckbestimmen.

dedicated engagiert.

dedication *(book)* Zueignung, Widmung, *(inauguration)* Einweihung, *(real estate)* Überlassung zum allgemeinen Gebrauch;
common-law ~ gewohnheitsrechtliche Widmung;
~ **of a highway** Straßenfreigabe, Verkehrsübergabe; ~ **of land for public use** Überlassung von Land zum öffentlichen Gebrauch; ~ **to the public** *(copyright, US)* Verzicht zugunsten der Allgemeinheit, Gemeinfreierklärung des Schutzrechtes; ~ **of tax revenues** Zweckbestimmung von Steuereinnahmen;
to write a ~ in a book Widmung in ein Buch schreiben;
~ **ceremonies** *(US)* Einweihungsfeierlichkeiten; ~ **day** Kirchweih.

dedicator Zueigner.

deduce *(v.)* schlußfolgern, logisch ableiten;
~ **one's descent from** seine Abstammung herleiten.

deduct *(v.)* absetzen, abrechnen, abziehen, in Abzug bringen, kürzen;
~ **cost** Kosten absetzen; ~ **the cost for transportation from the profit** Transportkosten vom Gewinn in Abzug bringen; ~ **the discount** Skonto abziehen; ~ **one's expenses** seine Unkosten

abziehen (abrechnen); ~ **an item** Posten [ab]streichen; ~ **income tax at the standard rate from the payment** Steuer zum Normalsatz in Abzug bringen; ~ **an item from an account** Rechnungsposten abziehen; ~ **a sum** Betrag in Abzug bringen; ~ **from the tax** von der Steuer absetzen; ~ **a tax at source** Steuer an der Quelle einbehalten; ~ **5% from the wage** 5% vom Lohn einbehalten.

deducted (a.) abzüglich;
charges ~ nach Abzug der Kosten; **tax** ~ nach Abzug der Steuern;
to be ~ **from a sum** von einer Summe abgehen.

deductible absetzbar, abziehbar, abzugsfähig;
tax-~ steuerabzugsfähig;
~ **from income tax** einkommensteuerabzugsfähig;
to be fully ~ **current expenses** voll abzugsfähige laufende Ausgaben darstellen; **to be** ~ **for federal income-tax purposes** (US) bei der Einkommensteuererklärung abzugsfähig sein;
~ **average** (insurance) Selbstbehalt; ~ **clause** (insurance) Selbstbehaltsklausel; **DM 300,-** ~ **comprehensive insurance** Fahrzeugversicherung mit 300,- DM Selbstbehalt; ~ **provision** (insurance) Selbstbehaltsbestimmung, -klausel.

deducting unter Abzug, abzüglich, ab;
after ~ **your charges** nach Abzug Ihrer Spesen.

deduction Abrechnung, Absetzung, Abzug, Abstrich, Kürzung, (income tax) abzugsfähiger Betrag, Steuerabzüge, Absetzungsbeträge von der Steuer, (rebate) Abschlag, Nachlaß, Rabatt, (reserve) Rückstellung, (withholding) Einbehaltung;
admitted as ~ steuerabzugsfähig; **all** ~**s made** nach Abzug aller Spesen; **free of** ~**s** frei von Abzügen; **subject to a** ~ mit einem Rabatt von; **subject to** ~ **of** unter Abzug, mit einem Rabatt von; **without** ~ unverkürzt, ohne Abzug (Rückstellung);
~**s** Abgänge, (income tax) anerkannte Steuerabzugsbeträge; **allowable** ~**s** steuerlich zulässige Absetzungen, steuerlich anerkannte Abzüge, steuerabzugsfähige Aufwendungen; **fixed** ~**s** feststehende Lohnabzüge; **flat-rate** ~**s** Pauschalabsetzungen; **income-tax** ~ Einkommensteuerabzug, neutraler Aufwand; **income-tax** ~**s** (balance sheet) Erlösschmälerungen; **itemized** ~**s** (taxation) aufgegliederte Abzugsbeträge; **marital** ~ (gift and estate tax) Freibetrag für die Ehefrau; **office-at-home** ~ Steuerabzug für das Büro im eigenen Haus; **payroll** ~ Lohnsteuerabzug; **permitted** ~**s** (labo(u)r law) gesetzlich zugelassene Lohnabzüge; **previous** ~ Vorabzug; **prior-period** ~**s** Vorjahresabzüge, steuerabzugsfähige Beträge in früheren Bilanzen; **special** ~ Steuerabzüge für Sonderausgaben; **standard** ~ (US) pauschaler Freibetrag, abzugsfähiger Pausch[al]betrag; **minimum standard** ~ (US) feststehender Mindestfreibetrag; **statutory** ~**s** gesetzlich feststehende Abzüge; **travel and entertainment expense** ~**s** steuerlich absetzbare Beträge für die Bewirtung von Geschäftsfreunden; **variable** ~**s** schwankende Lohnabzüge;
coding ~**s from allowances** in die Lohnsteuertabelle eingearbeitete Freibetragsabzüge; ~ **of a claim** Herleitung eines Anspruchs; ~ **for special clothing** steuerlich anerkannte Abzüge für Berufskleidung; ~ **for depletion** Absetzung für Substanzverringerung; ~ **for depreciation** Absetzung für Abnutzung; **allowable** ~ **for estate duty** (Br.) zulässige Erbschaftssteuerabzüge; ~ **for exemption** (US) zulässiger Steuerabzug; ~ **for expenses** (Br.) Abzug für Geschäftsauslagen; ~**s allowed for gifts to charity** Steuerfreibeträge für karitative Zuwendungen; ~ **from gross income** Abzug für Betriebsausgaben; ~ **of input tax** Vorsteuerabzug; ~ **of losses against two following years** zweijähriger Verlustvortrag; ~ **new for old** (marine insurance) Anrechnung des Altwertes; ~ **from pay** Gehaltsabzüge, Lohnabzüge; **automatic** ~ **from pay** automatische Abbuchung vom Lohnkonto; ~**s from pay for insurance and pension** Lohnabzüge für Versicherungsprämien und Pensionsbeiträge; ~ **from the price** Preisnachlaß, Rabatt; ~ **from salary** Gehaltsabzug; ~ **of a sum from a quota** Quotenkürzung um einen Betrag; ~ **of superannuation contributions** Einbehaltung von Beiträgen zur Pensionskasse; ~ **for tax** Steuereinbehaltung, -abzug, Rückstellung für Steuern; ~ **of tax at source** Steuerabzug an der Quelle, Quellensteuerabzug; ~ **from a national savings bank direct transfer account** (Br.) automatische Abbuchung von einem Postsparkassenkonto; ~ **from wages** Einbehaltung vom Lohn, Lohnabzüge; ~**s from working capital** Betriebskapitalschmälerung; ~ **from the yearly rent** Nachlaß von der Jahresmiete;
to be allowable ~**s for tax purposes** steuerlich abzugsfähig sein; **to claim the cost of rent of premises as a** ~ Kosten der Büromiete steuerlich absetzen; **to draw one's** ~ seine Schlußfolgerungen ziehen; **to itemize one's** ~**s** Steuerabzüge detailliert

aufführen; **to make a previous** ~ **of 5%** vorweg 5% abziehen; **to qualify for special** ~ (Br.) sonderausgabenberechtigt sein; ~ **card** Lohnsteuerkarte; ~ **limit** Freibetragsgrenze.

deductive method deduktive Methode.

deed Tat, Werk, Handlung, Ausführung, (document) Urkunde, Dokument, Schriftstück, förmlicher Vertrag, Instrument, (instrument of conveyance, US) Grundstücksübertragungs-, Zessionsurkunde;
by ~ in förmlicher Weise; **in word and** ~ in Wort und Tat; **liable under a** ~ vertraglich verpflichtet;
blank ~ Grundstückskaufvertragsformular; **composition** ~ (Br.) Abfindungs-, Vergleichsvertrag, Gläubigervergleich; **enrolled** ~ gerichtlich hinterlegte Urkunde; **gift** ~ Schenkungsurkunde; **gratuitous** ~ unentgeltlicher Vertrag; **indented** ~ wechselseitig bindender Vertrag; **leasehold** ~ Pacht-, Mietertrag; **mortgage** ~ Verpfändungsurkunde, (real estate) Hypothekenbrief, -urkunde; **notarial** ~ Notariatsakt, -urkunde; **private** ~ privatschriftliche Urkunde; **purchase** ~ Kaufvertrag, -urkunde; **quitclaim** ~ (US) Zessionsurkunde; **title** ~ Eigentums-, Besitz-, Erwerbsurkunde, (real estate) Grundstückskaufvertrag; **transfer** ~ Übertragung, Zessionsurkunde, Begebungsvertrag, (real estate) Auflassungsurkunde; **trust** ~ Treuhandvertrag; **vesting** ~ Übertragungs-, Bestallungsurkunde; **warranty** ~ Garantieversprechen, -urkunde, -vertrag, Gewährleistungsvertrag;
~ **of abdication** Abdankungsurkunde; ~ **of accession** Zustimmung der Gläubiger zu einem Schuldenregelungsplan; ~ **of accessory** Beitrittsurkunde; ~ **of amalgamation** Fusionsvertrag; ~ **of apprenticeship** Ausbildungs-, Lehrlingsvertrag; ~ **of arrangement** (Br.) beurkundeter außergerichtlicher Vergleich, Vergleichsurkunde, -vertrag; ~ **of assignation (assignment)** Zessions-, Abtretungsurkunde; ~ **of assumption** Treuhandübernahmevertrag; ~ **of bargain and sale** Kaufvertrag über ein Grundstück; ~ **for the benefit of creditors** zugunsten der Gläubiger abgeschlossener Vertrag; ~ **of composition** Vergleichsurkunde, -vertrag; ~ **of conveyance** Übertragungs-, Abtretungs-, Auflassungsurkunde; ~ **of covenant** Nebenverpflichtungen; ~**s of covenant in favo(u)r of charities** für wohltätige Zwecke eingegangene Verpflichtungen; ~ **of discharge** Erklärung über die Beendigung eines Treuhandverhältnisses; ~ **of donation** Schenkungsvertrag; ~ **in fee** Grundstücksauflassungsurkunde; ~ **of inspectorship** Vereinbarung über die Fortführung des Geschäfts nach der Liquidation des Schuldnervermögens unter Aufsicht eines Gläubigerausschusses; ~ **of ownership** Besitz-, Eigentumsurkunde; ~ **of partition** schriftliche Teilungsvereinbarung; ~ **of partnership** Gesellschaftsvertrag, -statuten; ~ **of postponement** Rangrücktrittserklärung; ~ **of property** Vermögensübertragung; ~ **of protest** Protesturkunde; ~ **of real estate** Grundstücksvertrag; ~ **of release** löschungsfähige Quittung; ~ **of renunciation** Verzichtsurkunde; ~ **of sale** Kaufvertrag; ~ **of separation** (Br.) Trennungsvereinbarung; ~ **of settlement** Vergleich, Abfindungsvertrag, (corporation) Stiftungs-, Gründungsurkunde; ~ **executed by a solicitor** öffentliche Urkunde; ~ **of suretyship** Bürgschaftsschein; ~ **of transfer** Zessionsurkunde; ~ **of trust** (US) (commonlaw mortgage) Hypothekenbestellungsurkunde, Sicherungsübereignung; ~ **of variation** Abänderungsurkunde;
~ (v.) urkundlich übertragen;
~ **one's estate** sein Vermögen übertragen;
to be rewarded for one's good ~**s** für seine guten Werke belohnt werden; **to do a good** ~ **every day** jeden Tag eine gute Tat tun; **to draw up a** ~ Urkunde aufsetzen; **to execute a** ~ aus einer Urkunde vollstrecken; **to frustrate a** ~ Urkunde ungültig machen; **to make a** ~ förmlichen Vertrag abschließen; **to register a** ~ Urkunde vom Notar aufnehmen lassen; **to seal a** ~ Urkunde siegeln; **to string up to a** ~ zu einer Tat ermuntern; ⩰ **of Arrangement Act** (Br.) [etwa] Vergleichsordnung; ~ **box** Urkundenkassette; ~ **poll** einseitige Rechtserklärung, einseitiger (einseitig verpflichtender) Vertrag; ~ **registration** (US) [etwa] Grundbucheintragung; ~**s registry** (Ireland) Grundbuchamt.

deem (v.) glauben, meinen, halten;
~ **it one's duty** es für seine Pflicht halten; ~ **fit and proper** für richtig und schicklich halten; ~ **s. th. a pleasure** etw. als Vergnügen betrachten; ~ **it right to do so** es für richtig halten; ~ **well of s. th.** gute Meinung von etw. haben.

deep Tiefe, (firmament) Firmament;
in the ~ **of winter** mitten im tiefsten Winter;
ocean ~ Tiefe des Ozeans;
~**s of knowledge** unendliches Wissen; ~ **of space** Unendlichkeit des Weltalls;

~ *(a.)* tief, *(fig.)* reiflich, sorgfältig;

~ **in peace** im tiefen Frieden; ~ **in thoughts** in Gedanken versunken; ~ **in the woods** im tiefen Wald;

to be ~ in one's book in seinem Buch ganz versunken sein; **to be ~ in debt** hohe Schulden haben; **to be too ~ for s. o.** für j. zu hoch sein; **to have drunk ~ of the pleasures of life** Leben in vollen Zügen genossen haben; **to study ~ into the night** bis nach Mitternacht arbeiten;

~ **card** *(sl.)* durchtriebener Bursche; ~ **designs** dunkle Absichten; ~ **disappointment** schwere Enttäuschung; ~ **draught** Tiefgang; **~-drawing** *(ship)* tiefgehend; **to go off at (in) the ~ end** *(US)* sich unüberlegt auf etw. einlassen; ~ **enemy** radikaler Feind; **~etching** Tiefätzung; ~ **freeze** Tiefkühlschrank, *(economics)* Lohn- und Preisstop; ~ **gratitude** innige Dankbarkeit; **to listen with ~ interest** konzentriert zuhören; **~-lying causes** schwerwiegende Gründe; ~ **motive** verborgener Beweggrund; **a ~ one** *(sl.)* ein ganz Durchtriebener; ~ **poverty** größte Armut; **~-read** sehr belesen; **~-rooted** tief eingewurzelt; **~-rooted dislike** eingefleischte Abneigung; ~ **sea** Tiefsee, Hochsee; **~-sea diver** Tiefseetaucher; **~-sea fishing** Hochseefischerei; **~-sea lead** Tiefenlot; **~-sea research** Tiefseeforschung; **~-seated** fest verwurzelt; ~ **sleep** Tiefschlaf; ~ **study** eingehendes Studium; ~ **therapy** *(med.)* Tiefenbehandlung; ~ **thinker** scharfsinniger Denker; **in ~ waters** in Schwierigkeiten (Verlegenheit); **to be in ~ waters** *(fig.)* das Wasser bis zum Hals stehen haben; ~ **wrong** schweres Unrecht.

deepen *(v.)* tiefer legen, vertiefen, *(mining)* abteufen.

deepfreeze *(v.)* tieffrieren.

deeply sorgfältig, gründlich;

to go ~ into s. th. gründlich in etw. einsteigen; ~ **devised** reiflich überlegt; **to be ~ indebted** schwer verschuldet sein; ~ **offended** tief beleidigt.

deepwaterman Hochseeschiff.

deface *(v.)* *(make illegible)* unleserlich (unkenntlich) machen, ausstreichen, *(spoil the appearance)* verunstalten, entstellen;

~ **a bond** Verpflichtung annullieren; ~ **the coinage** Währung verschlechtern; ~ **a stamp** [Brief]marke entwerten.

defaced unleserlich gemacht;

~ **coin** abgenutzte Münze; ~ **stamp** entwertete Briefmarke.

defacement Unkenntlichmachung, Ausstreichung, Auslöschung, Unleserlichmachen, *(injury to outward appearance)* Verunstaltung, Entstellung, *(stamp)* Entwertung;

~ **of bank note** Geldscheinentwertung.

defacer, defacing stamp Entwertungsstempel.

defalcate *(v.)* unterschlagen, veruntreuen, Veruntreuung begehen.

defalcation Unterschlagung, Veruntreuung [öffentlicher Gelder], veruntreuter Betrag, Unterschlagungssumme;

to make up ~s to the extent of $ 10.000 zehntausend Dollar unterschlagen, Veruntreuung in Höhe von zehntausend Dollar begehen.

defalcator Veruntreuer.

defamation Verleumdung, Verunglimpfung, Ehrverletzung, üble Nachrede, Diffamierung;

~ **of character** Ehrabschneidung; ~ **of a competitor's reputation** Rufschädigung (Anschwärzung) der Konkurrenz; ~ **process** Verleumdungsprozeß.

defamatory verleumderisch, defamierend;

~ **per se** Formalbeleidigung; ~ **action** Verleumdungsklage; ~ **imputation** Verleumdung, verläumderische Beschuldigung; ~ **letter** Schmähbrief; ~ **matter** beleidigendes (ehrenrühriges, verleumderisches) Material; ~ **statement** beleidigende Äußerung, diffamierende Behauptung, Rufschädigung; ~ **words** beleidigende Worte.

defame *(v.)* verleumden, diffamieren, verunglimpfen.

default *(contract)* Vertragsverletzung, Verschulden, *(of duty)* [Pflicht]versäumnis, *(failure to perform)* [Zahlungs]verzug, Nichterfüllung (Nichteinhaltung) einer Verbindlichkeit, *(nonappearance)* Nichterscheinen [vor Gericht], Ausbleiben, *(suspension of payments)* Zahlungsunfähigkeit, -einstellung, Insolvenz;

by ~ im Versäumnisverfahren; **in ~** säumig; **in ~ of** mangels, in Ermangelung von; **in the event of ~** im Verzugsfall; **in ~ of evidence** mangels Beweises; **in ~ whereof** widrigenfalls; **on (upon) ~ of payment** mangels Zahlung, bei Nichtzahlung, bei Verzug;

tenant's ~ Verzug des Mieters, Mietverzug; **wilful ~** vorsätzliche Unterlassung;

~ **of the acceptor** verweigerte Wechselannahme; ~ **of appearance** Terminversäumnis; ~ **of defence** Vernachlässigung der Prozeßführung; ~ **in delivery** Lieferverzug; ~ **in an engagement**

Nichterfüllung einer Verbindlichkeit; ~ **of heirs (issue)** Erbenlosigkeit, Heimfallrecht; ~ **of interest** Zinsverzug; ~ **in paying** Zahlungsverzug; ~ **of payment** Zahlungsverzug; ~ **of a term** Fristversäumnis;

~ *(v.)* *(enter a ~ against)* wegen Nichterscheinens verurteilen, *(be in delay)* in Verzug geraten, [Raten]zahlungen nicht einhalten, *(fail to appear)* [vor Gericht] nicht erscheinen, *(fail to perform)* seinen Verpflichtungen nicht nachkommen, nicht erfüllen, *(become insolvent)* zahlungsunfähig werden, *(trustee)* keine Rechenschaft geben können;

~ **on a debt** Schuld nicht bezahlen; ~ **a dividend** Dividende ausfallen lassen; ~ **in one's mortgage payment** mit der Verzinsung und Amortisation seiner Hypothek in Verzug geraten; ~ **in paying a note** mit der Zahlung eines Wechsels in Verzug geraten; ~ **in payment** mit den Zahlungen in Verzug kommen (geraten); ~ **in the repayment of principal** Kapital nicht zurückzahlen können;

to be in ~ im Verzug sein; **to be in ~ of acceptance** im Annahmeverzug sein; **to be in ~ with one's obligations** mit seinen Verpflichtungen im Rückstand sein; **to be sentenced by ~** in Abwesenheit verurteilt werden; **to cure a ~** Verzug wiedergutmachen; **to declare the defendant in ~** Versäumnisurteil gegen den Beklagten erlassen; **to deliver judgment by ~** Versäumnisurteil erlassen; **to enter a ~ against s. o.** Versäumnisurteil gegen j. erlassen; **to hold s. o. in ~** j. in Verzug setzen; **to lose a case by ~** Prozeß durch Versäumnisurteil verlieren; **to make ~** seinen Verbindlichkeiten nicht nachkommen, in Zahlungsverzug kommen, *(fail to appear)* vor Gericht nicht erscheinen; **to make ~ in the payment of interest** mit den Zinszahlungen im Verzug sein; **to put in ~** in Verzug setzen; **to suffer ~** Versäumnisurteil gegen sich ergehen lassen; **to win a case by ~** Prozeß durch ein Versäumnisurteil gewinnen;

~ **action** *(Br.)* Mahnverfahren; ~ **authority** säumige Behörde; ~ **fee** Säumnisgebühr; ~ **fine** Verspätungszuschlag; ~ **interest** Verzugszinsen; **to exercise ~ power** *(local government, Br.)* Ersatzvornahmen anordnen; ~ **procedure** Versäumnisverfahren; ~ **summons** *(Br.)* Mahnverfahren, *(summons to pay)* Vorladung bei Zahlungsverzug.

defaulted | bonds *(US)* notleidende (nicht mehr bediente) Obligationen; ~ **mortgage** verfallene Hypothek.

defaulter säumiger Zahler (Schuldner), *(defaulting party)* säumige Partei, nicht Erschienener, *(insolvent debtor, Br.)* zahlungsunfähiger Schuldner, Insolvent, Bankrotteur, *(mil., Br.)* Delinquent, *(misappropriation)* Veruntreuer;

declared ~ *(London)* zahlungsunfähiges Börsenmitglied; ~ **of property entrusted** Unterschlager anvertrauter Gelder; ~ **book** *(mil.)* Schuldverzeichnis; ~ **sheet** *(mil.)* Strafbuchauszug.

defaulting *(nonappearance)* Ausbleiben im Termin, Nichterscheinen, *(nonperformance)* Nichterfüllung;

~ *(a.)* säumig, im Verzug, *(law court)* ausgeblieben, *(stock exchange, Br.)* zahlungsunfähig;

~ **debtor** zahlungsunfähiger Schuldner; ~ **party** im Verzug befindliche Partei; ~ **tenant** Mietschuldner.

defeasance Annullierung, Aufhebung, Ungültigkeits-, Nichtigkeitserklärung;

~ **clause** Heimfall-, Verwirkungsklausel.

defeasanced anfechtbar, aufhebbar, umstoßbar.

defeasibility Anfechtbarkeit, Aufhebbarkeit.

defeasible auflösend bedingt, anfechtbar, annullierbar.

defeat *(law)* Ungültigkeitserklärung, Annullierung, *(mil.)* Niederlage;

crushing ~ vernichtende Niederlage; **voting ~** Abstimmungsniederlage;

~ **of a motion** Überstimmen (Ablehnung) eines Antrags, Antragsablehnung; ~ **of a plan** Vereitelung eines Plans; ~ **at the polls** Wahlniederlage;

~ *(v.)* *(law)* für [null und] nichtig (ungültig) erklären, annullieren, aufheben, *(politics)* schlagen, Niederlage bereiten;

~ **a bill** Gesetzentwurf ablehnen; ~ **an opposing candidate** Gegenkandidaten schlagen; ~ **a claim** Anspruch zu Fall bringen; ~ **one's creditors** seine Gläubiger benachteiligen, Befriedigung der Gläubiger vereiteln (verzögern); ~ **the ends of justice** der Gerechtigkeit den Todesstoß versetzen; ~ **s. o. of his hopes** jds. Hoffnungen zunichte machen; ~ **a motion** Antrag ablehnen; ~ **s. o. of his plans** jds. Pläne durchkreuzen; ~ **the provisions of a will** Testamentsbestimmungen anfechten; ~ **a right** Recht entziehen; ~ **by vote** überstimmen;

to meet with a ~ at the polls Wahlniederlage erleiden; **to suffer ~** Niederlage hinnehmen müssen;

to be ~ed unterliegen, verlieren.

defeated party unterlegene Partei.
defeating of creditors Gläubigerbenachteiligung.
defeatism Defätismus.
defeatist Defätist, Miesmacher.
defect Mangel, Manko, Fehler, Defekt, schadhafte Stelle;
free from ~s fehlerfrei, mangelfrei;
apparent ~ äußerlich erkennbarer (augenscheinlicher) Mangel; **formal ~** Formfehler; **intrinsic ~** innerer Mangel; **invisible ~** unsichtbarer Mangel; **latent (hidden) ~** versteckter (verborgener) Mangel [beim Kauf] (Defekt); **inherent ~** innewohnender Mangel; **manufacturing ~** Fabrikationsfehler; **mental ~** Störung der Geistestätigkeit, geistiger Defekt; **minor ~s** kleinere Mängel; **obvious ~** offenkundiger (offener) Mangel; **patent ~** offensichtlicher Mangel; **physical ~** körperlicher Defekt, Gebrechen; **redhibitory ~** *(US)* Gewährleistungs-, Wandlungsfehler; **structural ~** Konstruktionsfehler;
~ of authority Vollmachtsfehler; **~ in character** Charakterfehler; **~ of construction** fehlerhafte Konstruktion, Konstruktionsfehler; **~ by deterioration** Abnutzungsfehler; **~ of design** Gestaltungsmangel; **~ of eyesight** Augenfehler; **~ of form** Formfehler; **~ in highway** schlechter Straßenzustand; **~ in insulation** mangelnde Isolierung; **~ of judgment** mangelnde Urteilskraft; **~ in machinery** Maschinenfehler; **~ of memory** Gedächtnisschwäche; **~ of quality** nicht ausreichende Qualität, Sachmangel; **~ of substance** materiellrechtlicher Fehler, wesentlicher Vertragsfehler; **~s in a system of education** Unvollkommenheiten eines Erziehungssystems; **~ of title** Rechtsmangel; **~ due to workmanship** Fertigungsfehler;
~ (v.) in ein anderes Land desertieren;
to be liable for ~s für Mängel haften, der Mängelhaftung unterliegen; **to cure the ~** Mangel heilen; **to make a claim in respect of a ~** Mängelrüge vorbringen; **to notify a ~** Mängelrüge geltend machen; **to remedy ~s** Mängel beseitigen; **to reveal a ~** Fehler offenlegen; **to supply a ~** Fehler beseitigen; **to warn of ~s** auf Fehler aufmerksam machen;
latent ~ clause Garantieklausel für versteckte Mängel.
defection Abfall, Pflichtvergessenheit, Treubruch, *(pol.)* Umfall, Übertritt, Parteiwechsel;
~ of contract Vertragsverletzung.
defective *(Br.)* Geisteskranker, -schwacher;
~ (a.) *(faulty)* beschädigt, defekt, fehler-, mangel-, schadhaft, *(incomplete)* unvollständig, unvollkommen, unzulänglich;
mentally ~ geistesschwach;
~ in moral sense moralisch angekränkelt; **~ in workmanship** qualitätsmäßig nicht ausreichend;
~ article Fehlfabrikat; **~ brakes** unzulängliche Bremsen; **~ car** *(railway)* ausrangierter Waggon; **~ child** anormales Kind; **~ company** fehlerhaft errichtete Gesellschaft; **~ compliance** mangelhafte Erfüllung; **~ condition of the goods** mangelhafter Warenzustand; **~ contract** fehlerhafter Vertrag; **~ currency** fehlerhafte Münzen; **~ material** Materialfehler; **~ memory** schlechtes Gedächtnis; **~ packing** unzureichend (fehlerhafte) Verpackung; **~ sheet** Defektbogen; **~ thing** mangelhafte Sache; **~ title** mit Mängeln behaftetes Recht, Rechtsmangel; **~ unit** fehlerhaftes Stück.
defectiveness Schadhaftigkeit, Mangelhaftigkeit, *(incompleteness)* Unzulänglichkeit;
mental ~ Geisteskrankheit, -schwäche.
defector Überläufer.
defence *(Br.)* **defense** *(US)* *(accused party)* beklagte Partei, *(defendant's answer)* Einlassung, Verteidigungsvorbringen, Bestreitung der Klage, Klagebeantwortung, *(law)* Einwendung, Einrede, *(mil.)* Schutz, Verteidigung, Abwehr;
by way of ~ einredeweise; **in his own ~** zu seiner Rechtfertigung; **in ~ of life** aus (in) Notwehr;
~s *(mil.)* Verteidigungsanlagen, -werk, *(Scot.)* Klagebeantwortung;
affirmative ~ Gegenvorbringen; **air ~** Fliegerabwehr, Luft[raum]verteidigung; **active air ~** Fliegerabwehr; **passive air ~** Luftschutz; **antiaircraft ~** Flug-, Luftabwehr; **antimissile ~** Raketenabwehranlagen; **Civil ℒ** *(US)* Luftschutz; **coastal ~** Küstenverteidigung; **complete ~** prozeßhindernde Einrede; **dilatory ~** aufschiebende Einrede; **equitable ~** Einrede des nichterfüllten Vertrages; **forward ~** Vorwärtsverteidigung; **frivolous ~** Verschleppungseinwand; **good ~** begründete Einwendung; **inadmissible ~** unzulässiges Vorbringen; **legal ~** rechtlich zulässiges Vorbringen; **meritorious ~** materiellrechtliches Vorbringen; **national ~** Landesverteidigung; **original ~** ursprüngliche Einrede; **partial ~** Vorbringen gegen Teile der Klage; **peremptory ~** peremptorische Einrede, restloses Bestreiten; **personal ~** persönlicher

Einwand, *(negotiable instruments)* auf bestimmte Wechselinhaber beschränkte Einwendungen; **pretermitted ~** verspätetes Gegenvorbringen; **real ~** *(negotiable instrument)* Ausstellungseinwand; **self-~** Notwehr; **sham ~** unbegründetes Gegenvorbringen; **state of the art ~** Einwand des seinerzeitigen Stands der Technik;
~ of action Klageeinlassung; **~ in bar** prozeßhindernde Einrede; **~ by counsel** Verteidigung durch einen Anwalt; **~ in depth** *(mil.)* Tiefenverteidigung; **~ for dismissal** [etwa] prozeßhindernde Einrede; **~ against enemies** Schutz vor feindlichen Angriffen; **~ of equitable estoppel** Einrede der Unzulässigkeit des Rechtsweges; **~ of privilege** Rechtfertigungsgrund; **~ of set-off** Aufrechnungseinwand; **~ of truth** *(US)* Wahrheitsbeweis; **~ of usury** Wuchereinwand;
to abandon the ~ Verteidigung niederlegen; **to address the jury in one's own ~** sich selbst vor Gericht verteidigen; **to amend the ~** neue Verteidigungsmittel vortragen; **to assume the ~** [Straf]verteidigung übernehmen; **to bar a ~** Einrede abschneiden; **to be briefed for the ~** mit der Verteidigung beauftragt werden; **to bring forward a ~** Einrede geltend machen; **to conduct the ~ of s. o.** j. verteidigen; **to conduct one's own ~** sich selbst [vor Gericht] vertreten; **to deliver a ~** Klagebeantwortung einreichen; **to deliver a counterclaim with the ~** bei der Klagebeantwortung Gegenansprüche geltend machen; **to designate a counsel for the ~** Strafverteidiger bestellen; **to fight in ~ of one's country** sein Land verteidigen; **to plead in one's ~** zu seiner Verteidigung anführen; **to put up a clever ~** sich geschickt verteidigen; **to rebut a ~** Gegenvorbringen widerlegen; **to reserve one's ~** sich seine Beweisanträge vorbehalten; **to set up a ~** Einrede vorbringen; **to state s. th. in one's ~** etw. zu seiner Verteidigung vorbringen (geltend machen); **to take ~** Einspruch erheben;
ℒ of the Realm Act *(Br.)* Kriegsnotstandsgesetz; **~ activities** Durchführung von Rüstungsaufträgen; **~ agency** *(US)* Verteidigungsbehörde; **~ area** für Neutrale gesperrtes Seegebiet, Verteidigungsgebiet; **~ attaché** Militärattaché; **~ award** Rüstungsauftragsvergabe; **~ bill** Rüstungsvorlage; **~ bonds** Rüstungs-, Kriegsanleihe; **~ budget** Verteidigungsetat; **~ certificate** *(Br.)* Armenrechtsbescheinigung; **~ concept** Verteidigungskonzeption; **~ contract** Rüstungsauftrag; **to bid on ~ contracts** sich an Rüstungsausschreibungen beteiligen; **~ contracting procedure** Verfahren bei der Vergabe von Verteidigungsaufträgen; **~ contractor** Rüstungsbetrieb; **~ contribution** Wehrbeitrag; **~ costs** Verteidigungslasten; **~-included costs** Verteidigungsfolgekosten; **ℒ Council** Verteidigungsrat; **~ counsel** Strafverteidiger; **~ cut** Kürzung des Verteidigungsetats; **ℒ Department** *(US)* Verteidigungsministerium; **~ early warning line** Radarfrühwarnkette; **~ economy** Wehrwirtschaft; **~ expenditure** Verteidigungsausgaben; **~ factory** Rüstungsbetrieb; **coastal ~ force** leichte Marineeinheiten vor der Küste; **~-induced costs** Folgekosten bei Verteidigungsanlagen; **~ land** militärisch genütztes Gelände; **~ lawyer** Strafverteidiger; **~ layoffs** Entlassungen im Rüstungssektor; **~ line** Widerstandslinie; **~ loan** Rüstungsanleihe; **~ loan bond** Kriegs-, Rüstungsanleihe; **~ matter** Verteidigungsfragen; **ℒ Minister** Verteidigungsminister; **ℒ Ministry** Verteidigungsministerium; **~ order** Verteidigungs-, Rüstungsauftrag; **~ pact** Verteidigungsbündnis; **~ payroll** Gehaltsliste von Rüstungsbetrieben; **~ plant** Rüstungsbetrieb; **~ plant worker** Rüstungsarbeiter; **~ procurement** Beschaffungswesen; **~ production** Rüstungs-, Kriegsproduktion; **to use its ~ production lines** für die Ausführung von Rüstungsaufträgen benutzen; **~ profit** Rüstungsgewinn; **~ purchases** Rüstungskäufe; **~ purposes** Verteidigungszwecke; **~ research** Forschungsaufgaben auf dem Verteidigungssektor; **ℒ Secretary** *(US)* Verteidigungsminister; **~ spending** Verteidigungsausgaben; **~ supplier** Rüstungszulieferungsbetrieb; **~ test** *(mil.)* Probemobilmachung; **~ treaty** Verteidigungspakt; **~ war** Abwehrkrieg; **~ witness** Zeuge der Verteidigung; **overall negotiated ~ work** insgesamt abgeschlossene Verteidigungsaufträge.
defenceless schutz-, wehr-, hilflos.
defend *(v.)* schützen, verteidigen, *(accused)* verteidigen, *(law)* sich auf eine Klage einlassen, sich verteidigen, bestreiten;
~ o. s. sich verantworten; **~ s. o.** *(law court)* für j. als Verteidiger auftreten, j. verteidigen; **~ an action** sich auf eine Klage einlassen, Klagebehauptungen bestreiten; **~ one's case** [Klage]anspruch bestreiten; **~ one's country** sein Vaterland verteidigen; **~ the course of the administration** Verwaltungsmaßnahmen in Schutz nehmen; **~ in court of law** als Beklagter auftreten; **~ by their guardians appointed for that purpose** Klage mit Hilfe eines Prozeßvormundes entgegennehmen; **~ one's**

life sich verteidigen; ~ **a suit** Klagebehauptungen bestreiten, Prozeß als Beklagter führen;
to **appear to** ~ als Verteidiger auftreten.
defendant Beklagter, beklagte Partei, *(US)* Angeklagter;
~ **added** nachträglich mitverklagte Partei; **counterclaiming** ~ Widerkläger; **plaintiff and** ~ Kläger und Beklagter; **principal** ~ Hauptbeklagter;
~ **in court of appeal** Berufungsbeklagter; ~ **in errror** Revisionsbeklagter;
to **appear for the** ~ als Prozeßbevollmächtigter für die beklagte Partei auftreten; to **be** ~ **in an action for damages** auf Schadenersatz verklagt sein;
~**'s answer** Klagebeantwortung; ~ **company (corporation)** beklagte Gesellschaft, Beklagte.
defended geschützt, verteidigt;
to **be** ~ **by counsel** von einem Anwalt verteidigt werden;
~ **judgment** kontradiktorisches Urteil.
defender *(Scot.)* Verteidiger, Anwalt;
public ~ *(US)* Pflichtverteidiger.
defense *(US)* → **defence.**
defensible verteidigungsfähig.
defensive *(mil.)* Verteidigung, Abwehr, Defensive;
to **be (stand) on the** ~ sich in der Defensive befinden; to **put s. o. on the** ~ j. in die Defensive treiben;
~ *(a.)* defensiv;
~ **allegation** Verteidigungsvorbringen, Beweisantritt; ~ **alliance** Defensivbündnis; ~ **issues** Rüstungswerte; ~ **measures** Verteidigungsmaßnahmen; ~ **portion** *(investment trust, US)* risikoschwächerer Teil [der Effektenanlage]; ~ **position** Abwehr-, Verteidigungsstellung; ~ **post** Widerstandsnest; ~ **site** Verteidigungsstellung; ~ **strike** Abwehrstreik; ~ **war** Abwehrkrieg; ~ **weapon** Defensivwaffe; ~ **zone** Verteidigungszone.
defer *(v.)* ver-, auf-, hinausschieben, zurückstellen, verzögern, vertagen, *(balance sheet)* als Rechnungsabgrenzung behandeln, *(law court)* verweisen, *(mil., US)* [vom Wehrdienst] zurück-, freistellen;
~ **s. th. to a later date** etw. auf später verschieben; ~ **making a decision** Entscheidung zurückstellen; ~ **one's departure for a week** seine Abreise um eine Woche verschieben; ~ **a duty** Steuerzahlungstermin hinausschieben; ~ **to one's elders** sich den Wünschen der älteren Familienmitglieder fügen; ~ **a judgment** Urteilsverkündung aussetzen; ~ **until further notice** bis auf weiteres verschieben; ~ **to s. one's opinion** jem. anheimstellen; ~ **payment** Zahlung aufschieben; ~ **a sentence** Urteilsverkündung aussetzen; ~ **sine die** auf unbestimmte Zeit verschieben.
deference Achtung, Ehrerbietung, Rücksichtnahme;
in ~ **to** aus Achtung vor; **out of** ~ **to** aus Rücksicht auf; **with all due** ~ mit allem gehörigen Respekt;
blind ~ **to authorities** Behördenfrommheit; ~ **of the law** Achtung vor dem Gesetz;
to **show** ~ **to a judge** einem Richter Respekt bezeugen.
deferment Vertagung, Aufschiebung, Aufschub;
occupational ~ *(mil., US)* berufsbedingte Zurückstellung, berufliche Unabkömmlichkeit;
~ **from military service** *(US)* Zurückstellung vom Militärdienst;
to **apply for** ~ **of a hearing** Terminvertagung beantragen.
deferrable *(mil.)* Zurück-, UK-Gestellter;
~ *(a.)* aufschiebbar, *(mil.)* zurückstellbar.
deferral Vertagung, Aufschiebung, Aufschub, *(accounting method)* Rechnungsabgrenzung, transitorische Abgrenzung;
~ **of investment program(me)s** zurückgestellte Investitionsvorhaben.
deferred hinausgeschoben, ausgesetzt, vertagt, der Zukunft vorbehalten, zurückgewiesen, *(mil., US)* zurückgestellt, unabkömmlich;
~ **accounts** Zwischenkonten, Konten zwecks späterer Gutschriften; ~ **accounts receivable** *(US)* noch nicht fällige Forderungen; ~ **airfreight** in Leerzeiten beförderte Luftfracht; ~ **[life] annuity** aufgeschobene [Leib]rente, in der Zukunft fällige Rente, Anwartschaftsrente, hinausgeschobene Annuität; ~ **asset** zeitweilig nicht einlösbarer Aktivposten, *(balance sheet)* transitorischer, noch nicht fälliger Posten; ~ **bonds** *(Br.)* Obligationen mit ansteigender Zinszahlung; ~ **call on shares** aufgeschobene Aktieneinzahlung; ~ **charge [to expense]** vorausgezahlte Aufwendungen, *(balance sheet, US)* transitorische Posten, Posten der Rechnungsabgrenzung; ~ **charges and prepaid expenses** *(US)* Rechnungsabgrenzungsposten; ~ **claim** befristete Forderung; ~ **credits to income** *(balance sheet, US)*

transitorische Passiva, passive Rechnungsabgrenzungen; ~ **creditors** nachrangige Konkursgläubiger; ~ **debit** transitorischer Posten; ~ **debt** nachrangige Konkursforderung; ~ **delivery** *(stock exchange)* Lieferungsaufschub; ~ **demand** zurückgestellter Bedarf, Konsumverzicht; ~ **dividends** Dividenden mit aufgeschobener Fälligkeit; ~ **entry** ausgesetzter Buchungsposten; ~ **expenses** *(US)* transitorische Aktiva, transitorische Posten; ~ **fund** aufgeschobene Staatsschuld; ~ **income** *(US)* im voraus eingegangene Beträge, transitorische Passiva, Rechnungsabgrenzungsposten; ~ **item** *(US)* transitorischer Posten, Übergangs-, Rechnungsabgrenzungsposten; ~ **liability** *(accounting, US)* gestundete Schuld, passivierte Einnahme; ~ **life annuity** Anwartschaft auf eine Leibrente; ~ **maintenance (repairs)** aufgeschobene Reparaturkosten; ~ **national taxes on income** zurückgestellte Einkommensteuerzahlungen; ~ **pay** Lohneinbehaltung; ~ **payment** *(US)* Stundung des Kaufpreises, Ratenzahlung; ~ **payment sale** *(US)* Abzahlungsgeschäft; ~ **payment system** *(US)* Ratenzahlungsverkauf; to **buy on the** ~ **payment system** *(US)* auf Ratenzahlung (Abschlagszahlung) kaufen; to **sell s. th. on the** ~ **payment system** *(US)* auf Abzahlung verkaufen; ~ **premium** nachträglich zahlbare Prämie; ~ **profit** vorweggenommener Gewinn; ~ **rate** verbilligter Tarif für Brieftelegramme; ~ **rebate** kumulativer Rabatt für wiederkehrende Käufe, nachträglicher Umsatzbonus; ~ **revenue** *(US)* antizipatorische Passiva, im voraus eingegangene Erträge; ~ **savings** Ratensparen, steuerbegünstigtes Sparen; ~ **savings plan** steuerbegünstigtes Sparen; ~ **sentence** ausgesetzte Urteilsverkündung; ~ **service contracts** *(balance sheet)* bereits abgerechnete Dienstleistungsverträge; ~ **shares** *(Br.)* Nachzugsaktien; ~ **ordinary shares** Nachzugsaktien; ~ **share ownership** Nachzugsaktienbesitz, steuerbegünstigter Aktienbesitz; ~ **stock** *(US)* Nachzugsaktien; ~ **taxes** *(balance sheet)* zurückgestellte Steuerzahlungen; ~ **[rate] telegram** Brieftelegramm; ~ **wage** Lohneinbehaltung.
deferring relay *(el.)* Zeitrelais.
defiance Widerstand, Herausforderung;
to **act in** ~ **of the law** Gesetzesbestimmungen bewußt mißachten; to **act in** ~ **of orders** Anordnungen zuwiderhandeln; to **bid** ~ **to a policeman** Widerstand gegen die Staatsgewalt leisten; to **bid** ~ **to common sense** dem gesunden Menschenverstand Hohn sprechen; to **live in open** ~ **with s. o.** in offener Feindschaft mit jem. leben.
deficiency *(short balance)* Unterbilanz, *(defect)* Fehler, Mangel, *(deficit)* Manko, Fehlbetrag, fehlende Summe, *(inadequacy)* Unzulänglichkeit, Mangelhaftigkeit, *(production)* Ausfall, *(taxation)* Steuerfreibetrag;
from ~ **of means** aus Mangel an Mitteln;
total estimated ~ geschätzter Gesamtverlust; **mental** ~ Störung der Geistestätigkeit, Geistesschwäche; **physical** ~ körperlicher Defekt, Gebrechen;
~ **of assets** Vermögensdefizit; **estimated** ~ **from realization of assets** geschätzter Liquidationsverlust; ~ **of blood** Blutarmut; ~ **of capital** Kapitalmangel; ~ **of the coin** Münzverschlechterung; ~ **to unsecured creditors** *(balance sheet)* Verlustbeiträge ungesicherter Gläubiger; ~ **of demand** fehlende Nachfrage; ~ **of food** Unterernährung; ~ **of houses** Bedarf an Wohnhäusern; ~ **in infrastructure** Infrastrukturbedarf; ~ **to owners** *(balance sheet)* Kapitalverpflichtungen; ~ **in proceeds (receipts)** Mindereinnahmen; ~ **of a ship's cargo** Seeschaden; ~ **in stock** [Lager]fehlbestand; ~ **in title** Rechtsmangel; ~ **in weight** Fehlgewicht, Gewichtsmanko;
to **make good (up for) a** ~ Defizit decken, fehlende Summe ergänzen; to **supply the** ~ Defizit ausgleichen;
~ **account** *(bankruptcy proceedings)* Aufstellung der Verlustquellen; ~ **advances** *(Br.)* Vorschüsse der Bank von England, Kassenvorschüsse; ~ **appropriations** *(US)* Nachtragsbewilligung; ~ **assessment** Mankoberechnung; ~ **bill** *(US)* Nachtragsetat; ~ **bills** *(Bank of England)* kurzfristige Anleihen; ~ **contribution** Verlustbeitrag; ~ **disease** Mangelkrankheit; ~ **fund** *(US)* Nachtrags-, Notetat; ~ **goods** Mangelware; ~ **guarantee** Ausfallbürgschaft; ~ **judgment** *(US)* Ausfallurteil; ~ **letter** Steuermahnschreiben; ~ **payments** Ausgleichszahlungen an Landwirte, Agrarpreissubventionen; ~ **report** *(mil.)* Verlustmeldung; ~ **reserves** Rückstellungen für Mindereinnahmen; ~ **statement** *(US)* Verlustbilanz, -überschuß.
deficient fehlend, *(defective)* fehlerhaft, mangelhaft;
mental ~ Geistesschwacher;
~ *(a.)* *(defective)* fehlerhaft, mangelhaft, *(inadequate)* unzulänglich, unzureichend;
mentally ~ geistesschwach, schwachsinnig, unzurechnungsfähig;

to be mentally ~ geistigen Defekt haben; **to be ~ in means** nicht genügend Mittel haben; **to be ~ in weight** kein volles Gewicht haben;
~ **amount** Fehlbetrag; ~ **delivery** fehlerhafte Lieferung, Mankolieferung; ~ **estate** unergiebiger Grund und Boden.

deficit Defizit, Ausfall, Verlust, Fehl-, Minusbetrag, Manko, fehlende Summe, *(deficiency in receipts)* Mindereinnahme, *(short balance)* Unterbilanz, Passivsaldo;
showing a ~ verlustausweisend (-aufweisend);
balance-of-payments ~ Zahlungsbilanzdefizit; **budget[ary]** ~ Fehlbetrag im Staatshaushalt, Haushaltsdefizit; **cash** ~ Kassenmanko, -defizit; **casual** ~ unbeabsichtigtes Defizit; **current account** ~ negative Leistungsbilanz; **export** ~ Außenhandelsdefizit; **external** ~ Passivsaldo der Zahlungsbilanz; **fiscal** ~ Haushaltsdefizit, Fehlbetrag im Staatshaushalt; **foreign-trade** ~ Außenhandelsdefizit; **government's** ~ Staatsdefizit; **operating** ~ Betriebsverlust; **public sector** ~ Defizit der öffentlichen Hände; **revenue** ~ Steuerdefizit, -ausfall; **tax** ~ Steuerausfall, -defizit; **trade** ~ Handelsbilanzdefizit, Passivsaldo im Außenhandel;
~ **in the balance of trade** Passivsaldo der Handelsbilanz; ~ **in the budget** Haushaltsdefizit; ~ **on current account** negative Leistungsbilanz; ~ **in the financial accounts** Finanzdefizit; ~ **in expense fund** Kassendefizit; ~ **in the nonmerchandising field** Defizit auf anderem als dem Warengebiet; ~ **in revenues** Steuerausfall; ~ **without spending** Defizit durch Steuersatzsenkung; ~ **in taxes** Steuerdefizit, -ausfall, Minderaufkommen; ~ **on trade and services** Passivsaldo im Waren- und Dienstleistungsverkehr;
to close with a ~ mit einem Fehlbetrag abschließen; **to cover a** ~ Ausfall decken, Defizit abdecken; **to make good a** ~ Defizit (Verlust) decken (ausgleichen); **to meet a** ~ Fehlbetrag ausgleichen; **to show a** ~ mit einem Defizit abschließen, Verlust (Fehlbetrag, Defizit) aufweisen; **to settle a** ~ Defizit ausgleichen; **to slip into** ~ ins Defizit (in rote Zahlen) geraten; **to show a** ~ mit einem Defizit abschließen, Verlust aufweisen; **to work out heavy** ~s mit schweren Verlusten arbeiten;
~ **account** Verlustkonto; ~ **area** wirtschaftliches Verlustgebiet; ~ **balance** *(balance of payments)* negative Zahlungsbilanz; ~ **balance of international payments** internationales Zahlungsbilanzdefizit; ~ **countries** Defizitländer; ~ **financing** Defizitwirtschaft; ~ **guarantee** Ausfallbürgschaft; ~ **margin** Verlustspanne; ~ **nation** devisenschwaches Land; ~ **projection** Defizitvorschlag; ~ **spending** *(US)* Defizitfinanzierung, öffentliche Verschuldung durch Anleiheaufnahme.

defile *(v.)* beschmutzen, beflecken, besudeln, *(file off)* vorbeimarschieren, defilieren;
~ **a sacred place** Heiligtum schänden.

define *(v.) (mark by limits)* abgrenzen, umgrenzen, genaue Grenzen angeben, *(word)* definieren;
~ **one's attitude** Stellung nehmen; ~ **itself against the background** sich scharf vom Hintergrund abheben; ~ **boundaries** Grenzen festlegen; ~ **duties** Pflichtenkreis festlegen; ~ **a common policy** gemeinsame Politik festlegen; ~ **one's position** feste Position beziehen; ~ **s. one's powers** jds. Vollmacht abgrenzen; ~ **the powers of a court** Vollmachten eines Gerichts genau festlegen; ~ **property** Eigentum kennzeichnen.

definite bestimmt, deutlich, genau [festgelegt];
reasonably ~ hinreichend bestimmt;
to become ~ Rechtskraft erlangen;
~ **and certain amount** Betrag in bestimmter Höhe; ~ **answer** präzise Antwort; ~ **benefit plan** Pensionssystem mit feststehenden Lohnprozentsätzen; ~ **order** fester Auftrag, *(court)* rechtskräftiger Beschluß; **no** ~ **frontier** nicht genau festgelegte Grenze; **to give s. o.** ~ **information as to one's intentions** j. über seine Absichten in keiner Weise im Unklaren lassen; ~ **invention** fertige Erfindung; ~ **period** Frist; **for a** ~ **period** für eine bestimmte Zeit; ~ **statement of policy** präzise Grundsatzerklärung; ~ **rights** genau umschriebene (festgelegte) Rechte; ~ **sale** abgeschlossener Verkauf; ~ **statement** genaue Angabe; ~ **sum** bestimmter Betrag; **to come to a** ~ **understanding** zu einer endgültigen Vereinbarung gelangen.

definition Begriffsbestimmung, Definition, Erklärung, Erläuterung, *(radio)* Trennschärfe, *(television)* Bildschärfe;
absolute ~ zwingende Begriffsbestimmung; **working** ~ Arbeitsdefinition, Definition als Diskussionsgrundlage.

definitive *(final)* abschließend, endgültig, definitiv;
~ **answer** endgültige (definitive) Antwort; ~ **bond** Schuldverschreibungsurkunde; ~ **edition** endgültige Ausgabe; ~ **judgment** endgültiges (eindeutiges) Urteil, *(law court)* Endurteil; ~ **offer** festes Angebot; ~ **sentence** Endurteil.

deflate *(v.)* Luft ablassen, *(fig.)* klein und häßlich werden;
~ **a currency** Zahlungsmittelumlauf einschränken, Deflation durchführen, Deflationspolitik betreiben; ~ **its way out of its balance of payments difficulties** seiner Zahlungsbilanzschwierigkeiten mittels deflationistischer Maßnahmen Herr werden; ~ **the reputation** Ruf schmälern.

deflated tyre Reifen mit ungenügendem Druck.

deflation Deflation, *(advertising)* Eliminierung irrtümlicher Antworten, *(geol.)* Winderosion;
~ **of credit** Kreditrestriktion;
~ **gap** deflatorische Lücke; ~ **policy** Deflationspolitik.

deflationary deflationistisch;
~ **crisis** Deflationskrise; ~ **factors** deflationistische Faktoren; ~ **gap** Deflationslücke; ~ **influence** deflationistische Einflüsse; ~ **measures** deflationäre Maßnahmen; ~ **movement** Deflationsbewegung; ~ **period** Deflationszeit; ~ **policy** deflatorische Währungspolitik, Deflationspolitik; ~ **process** Deflationsprozeß; ~ **program(me)** Deflationsprogramm; ~ **tendency** deflationistische Tendenz.

deflationist Deflationsanhänger.

deflator Preisbereinigungsfaktor.

deflect *(v.) (radar)* ablenken;
~ **a stream** Strom ableiten.

deflection *(radar)* Ablenkung;
~ **of trade** Verkehrsverlagerung.

deforce *(v.)* s. th. from s. o. jem. etw. widerrechtlich vorenthalten.

deforcement widerrechtliche Vorenthaltung, *(land)* verbotene Eigenmacht, *(Scot.)* Widerstand gegen Vollstreckungsbeamte.

deforest *(v.)* abholzen, Kahlschlag vornehmen, roden.

deforestation Abholzung, Kahlschlag, Rodung.

deform *(v.)* verunstalten, entstellen.

deformation Verunstaltung, Entstellung, Mißbildung.

deformity Mißbildung;
congenital ~ Geburtsfehler.

defraud Übervorteilung, Unterschlagung, Hinterziehung;
~ *(v.)* hintergehen, betrügen, unterschlagen;
~ **an author of his royalties by ignoring copyright** Autor unter Mißachtung der Urheberrechte um seine Tantieme bringen; ~ **the authorities** Finanzamt betrügen; ~ **a creditor** Gläubiger betrügen (hintergehen); ~ **the customs** Zoll hinterziehen; ~ **the revenue** Steuerhinterziehung begehen, Steuern hinterziehen.

defraudation Übervorteilung, Betrug, Unterschlagung, Hinterziehung;
~ **of the customs** Zollhinterziehung; ~ **of the revenue** Steuerhinterziehung.

defrauded purchaser betrogener Käufer.

defrauder *(customs)* Zollhinterzieher.

defrauding secured creditors *(US)* Benachteiligung (Hintergehung) bevorrechtigter Gläubiger.

defray *(v.) (expenses)* bestreiten, tragen;
~ **the cost of s. th.** Kosten von etw. tragen; ~ **the expenses** Unkosten bestreiten; ~ **s. one's expenses** jds. Spesen bestreiten, j. freihalten; ~ **the expenses of a trip** Kosten einer Reise übernehmen.

defrayable bestreitbar;
to be ~ **by the town** *(municipal accounting)* von der Stadt getragen werden.

defrayal Bestreitung (Bezahlung) der Kosten.

defreeze *(v.)* tiefgekühlte Lebensmittel auftauen.

defrost *(v.) (foreign exchange)* Sperrmaßnahmen aufheben.

defroster Enteisungsanlage.

defunct ehemalig, außer Betrieb, geschlossen, *(dead)* verstorben;
~ **company** aufgelöste (im Handelsregister gelöschte) Gesellschaft; ~ **paper** eingegangene Zeitung.

defuse *(v.)* a bomb Bombe entschärfen.

defy *(v.)* | **every attack** *(fortress)* jedem Angriff Trotz bieten; ~ **every climate** *(constitution)* jedem Klima gewachsen sein; ~ **competition** keine Konkurrenz aufkommen lassen; ~ **description** nicht zu beschreiben sein; ~ **the law** sich dem Gesetz widersetzen; ~ **one's superiors** seinen Vorgesetzten den Respekt versagen.

degenerate *(v.)* entarten, degenerieren.

degeneration Entartung, Degeneration.

degradation Rangaberkennung, *(demotion)* niedrigere Tarifeinstufung, *(disgrace)* Erniedrigung, Entwürdigung, Entstehung, *(mil.)* Degradation, Degradierung, Rangverlust;
to live in (a life of) ~ in unwürdigen Verhältnissen leben.

degrade *(v.) (demote)* in eine niedrigere Tarifgruppe einstufen, *(bring shame upon)* erniedrigen, entehren, entwürdigen, *(Cambridge University)* Examen um ein Jahr verschieben.

degraded degradiert.
degrading entehrend, entwürdigend;
  to speak ~ly geringschätzig sprechen;
  ~ affair erniedriegende Affäre, ehrenrührige Angelegenheit.
degree Grad, Rang, Klasse, *(unit of measurement)* Grad, Ausmaß, Maßstab, *(blood relation)* Verwandtschaftsgrad, *(criminal law, US)* Grad, *(step)* Stufe, Schritt, *(university)* akademische Würde, akademischer Grad, Diplom;
  by ~s stufenweise, Schritt für Schritt; **by slow ~s** ganz allmählich; **to a [high] ~** in hohem Maße; **to some ~** einigermaßen;
  academic akademischer Grad; **bachelor's ~** Bakkalaureat; **forbidden ~s** verbotene Verwandtschaftsgrade; **high ~** hoher Rang; **honorary ~** ehrenhalber verliehener akademischer Grad; **Masonic ⚶** Freimaurergrad; **ordinary (pass) ~** gewöhnlicher Universitätsgrad; **prohibited ~** verbotener Verwandtschaftsgrad; **third ~** *(police)* unzulässige Gewaltanwendung, dritter Grad; **university ~** akademischer Grad;
  ~ of care Umfang der Sorgfaltspflicht; **~ of comparison** Vergleichsmaßstab; **~ of consanguinity** Verwandtschaftsgrad; **~ of disablement (disability)** Arbeitsunfähigkeits-, Invaliditätsgrad; **~ of discretion** Ermessensausmaß; **~ of doctor** Doktorwürde; **~ of doctor of literature** Doktorgrad der Literaturwissenschaften; **eight ~s of frost** acht Grad Kälte; **~ with first hono(u)rs** Prädikatsexamen; **~ of humidity** Luftfeuchtigkeitsgrad; **~ of independence** Unabhängigkeitsgrad; **~ of latitude** *(geol.)* Breitengrad; **~ of liquidity** Liquiditätsgrad, *(savings)* Flüssigkeitsgrad; **high ~ of liquidity** starke Liquiditätsposition; **~ of longitude** *(geol.)* Längengrad; **~ of quality** Qualitätsgrad; **military ~ of rank** militärische Rangstufe; **~ of relationship** Verwandtschaftsgrad; **~ of risk** Gefahrenumfang; **~ of saturation** Sättigungsgrad; **~ of self-sufficiency** Selbstversorgungsgrad; **~ of urgency** Dringlichkeitsstufe; **~ of utility** Grenznutzen;
  ~ *(v.)* akademischen Grad verleihen;
  to advance by ~s schrittweise vorankommen; **not to be in the slightest ~ interested** überhaupt nicht interessiert sein; **to be scrupulous to a ~** ein bißchen zu pingelig sein; **to confer a ~** akademischen Grad verleihen (zuerkennen); **to freeze at 32 ~s** bei Null Grad frieren; **to go up for a ~** ins Doktorexamen steigen; **to have some ~ of ownership by US capital** amerikanische Kapitalbeteiligung aufweisen; **to have reached a high ~ of excellence** höchsten Ansprüchen genügen; **to have received one's ~ in Oxford** in Oxford promoviert haben; **to hold a ~** akademischen Grad besitzen; **to insult s. o. to the last ~** j. zutiefst beleidigen; **to put a prisoner through the third ~** Gefangenen einem Folterverhör unterwerfen; **to register 15 ~s centigrade** 15 Grad Celsius anzeigen; **to serve in a minor ~** untergeordnete Dienste verrichten; **to study for a ~** akademischen Abschluß anstreben; **to take one's ~** promovieren;
  ~ conferring Promotionsverleihung; **~ day** Promotionstag; **~ demanding** nur für Akademiker; **~ examination** Promotionsexamen; **~ fee** Promotionsgebühr; **~ granting** Doktorverleihung; **~-granting university** Universität mit dem Recht der Promovierung; **~-level qualification** Promotionsvoraussetzung.
degression *(taxation)* Degression, progressive Abnahme.
degressive absteigend, degressiv;
  ~ depreciation degressive Abschreibung; **~ tax** degressive Steuer; **~ taxation** degressive Besteuerung.
dehort *(v.)* abraten.
dehydrated vegetables Trockengemüse.
deice *(v.)* enteisen.
deicer Enteisungsanlage.
de-industrialize *(v.)* entindustrialisieren.
del credere *(Br.)* Delkredere[haftung], Bürgschaft;
  to charge for ~ Delkredere berechnen; **to stand ~** Bürgschaft leisten, Delkredere übernehmen;
  ~ account Delkrederekonto; **~ agency** Delkrederevertretung; **~ agent** Delkredereagent, Garantievertreter; **~ agreement** Delkrederevereinbarung, Garantievereinbarung; **to act on a ~ basis** Delkredererisiko übernehmen; **~ bond** Garantie-, Gewährschein [im Kommissionsgeschäft]; **~ commission** Delkredereprovision; **~ reserve** Delkredererückstellung; **~ responsibility** Delkrederehaftung.
delate *(v.) (Scot.)* denunzieren.
delation *(Scot.)* Anzeige, Denunziation.
delay *(loss of time)* Zeitverlust, *(postponement)* Verzögerung, Verzug, *(respite)* Stundung, Aufschub, Verschiebung, Frist[verlängerung];
  without ~ ohne Aufschub, unverzüglich; **without undue ~** ohne schuldhaftes Zögern;
  creditor's ~ Gläubigerverzug; **debtor's ~** Schuldnerverzug;

government-caused ~s vom Staat zu vertretende Verzögerung; **an hour's ~** Frist von einer Stunde; **the law's ~s** gesetzliche Frist; **short ~** kurze Frist; **unavoidable ~** unvermeidbarer Aufschub;
  ~ of creditors Gläubigerbenachteiligung; **~ in delivery** verspätete Ablieferung, Lieferverzug, -verzögerung; **~ in dispatch** verzögerter Versand; **~ in loading** Ladeverzögerung; **~ in giving notice** Benachrichtigungsverzug; **~s in execution of order** Auftragsverzögerung; **~ in paying rent** verzögerte Mietzahlung; **~ in payment** Stundung, Fristgewährung, Zahlungsverzug; **~ in presentment** verzögerte Vorlegung; **~ of the proceedings** Prozeßverschleppung; **~ in settlement of long-term orders** Verzögerung nicht abgerechneter Fertigungsaufträge; **~ by strike** streikbedingte Verzögerung; **~ in transit** Transportverzögerung;
  ~s are dangerous Gefahr im Verzug;
  ~ *(v.)* verzögern, verschieben, hemmen;
  ~ creditors Gläubiger hinhalten; **~ one's departure** seine Abfahrt verschieben; **~ payment** im Zahlungsverzug sein; **~ the proceedings** Prozeß verschleppen; **~ traffic** Verkehr aufhalten; **to admit of no ~** keinen Aufschub erlauben (dulden); **to bear no ~** keinen Aufschub dulden; **to grant a ~** Fristverlängerung zugestehen; **to grant a ~ for payment** Fristverlängerung zugestehen, Zahlung stunden; **to hold in ~** in Verzug setzen; **to leave without ~** sofort aufbrechen; **to obtain a ~ of payment** Zahlungsaufschub erreichen; **to permit of no ~** keine Verzögerung zulassen; **to plead postal ~** sich auf verspätete Zustellung berufen; **to suffer ~** Verzögerung erleiden; **to use ~** aufschieben; **to write without ~** unverzüglich schreiben;
  ~ action Verzögerung; **~ allowance** Vergütung für nicht verschuldeten Arbeitsausfall; **~ time** betrieblich bedingte Verlustzeit.
delayable aufschiebbar.
delayed, to be sich hinausschieben, Verzögerung erleiden; **not to be ~** unaufschiebbar sein;
  ~ action verspätetes Handeln; **~-action bomb** Zeitbombe, Bombe mit Zeitzünder; **~-action device** *(photo)* Selbstauslöser; **~-action fuse** Verzögerungszünder; **~ delivery** Lieferverzug; **~ delivery bond** Lieferkaution; **~ ignition** Spätzündung; **~ payment** verspätete Zahlung; **~ performance** verspätete Erfüllung; **~ train** aufgehaltener Zug.
delayer Verzögerungsgrund.
delaying | action *(mil.)* hinhaltendes Gefecht; **~ effects** aufschiebende Wirkung; **~ tactics** Hinhaltungs-, Verzögerungstaktik.
delectation Vergnügen, Ergötzen;
  to be suitable for the ~ of half-educated people der Ergötzung Halbgebildeter dienen.
delegable delegierbar.
delegacy Abordnung, Delegation, *(act of delegating)* Delegierung.
delegate *(deputy)* Delegierter, Abgeordneter, Abgesandter, Deputierter, Volksvertreter, *(representative)* Bevollmächtigter;
  the ~s der Vorstand;
  walking ~ *(trade union)* Funktionär auf Besuchsreise;
  ~ *(v.)* abordnen, delegieren, *(authorize)* bevollmächtigen, *(assign a debtor)* Schuldforderung abtreten;
  ~ s. o. as ambassador j. als Botschafter entsenden; **~ authority to s. o.** jem. Untervollmacht erteilen; **~ power** Vollmacht erteilen; **~ responsibility** Verantwortlichkeiten delegieren; **~ rights to a deputy** Rechte auf einen Bevollmächtigten übertragen;
  ~ *(a.)* delegiert, beauftragt, abgeordnet;
  ~ vote Abgeordnetenstimme.
delegated übertragen, abgeordnet;
  ~ jurisdiction übertragene Gerichtsbarkeit; **~ legislation** abgeleitete Normsetzung, delegierte Gesetzgebung.
delegation *(of authority)* [Vollmachts]übertragung, Bevollmächtigung, *(body of delegates)* Abordnung, Delegation, Deputation, *(of debt)* Schuldübernahme;
  high-powered ~ mit allen Vollmachten ausgestattete Abordnung; **imperfect ~** nicht befreiende Schuldübernahme; **peace ~** Friedensdelegation; **perfect ~** befreiende Schuldübernahme; **Suez Canal ~s** Suez-Kanal-Aktien; **trade ~** Handelsabordnung; **workers' ~** Arbeiterabordnung;
  ~ of authority Vollmachtsübertragung; **~ of duty** Delegierung von Pflichten; **~ of powers** Übertragung von Befugnissen, Vollmachtsübertragung; **~ of legislative powers** Übertragung der Gesetzgebungsgewalt; **the ~ from Texas** die Abgeordneten von Texas;
  to head a ~ Delegation leiten.
delegatory bevollmächtigt, abgeordnet, delegiert.

delete *(v.)* ausradieren, löschen;
~ from the agenda von der Tagesordnung absetzen; **~ an entry** Eintragung löschen; **~ a nation** Volk ausrotten.

deleted by the censor von der Zensur gestrichen;
~ matter *(print.)* Streichsatz; **~ record** im Katalog nicht mehr aufgeführte Grammophonplatte; **~ word** *(computer)* gelöschtes Wort.

deletion Löschung, Streichung, *(balance sheet)* Abgang;
~s due to the censor Zensurstellen, -lücke; **~ of a nation** Ausrottung eines Volkes.

deliberalization Entliberalisierung.

deliberalize *(v.)* entliberalisieren, von der Liberalisierungsliste streichen.

deleterious ingredients gesundheitsgefährdende Bestandteile.

deliberate wohlüberlegt, bedachtsam, *(on purpose)* vorsätzlich;
~ *(v.)* überlegen, erwägen, nachdenken, beraten, beratschlagen, konferieren;
~ with o. s. mit sich zu Rate gehen; **~ a proposition** über einen Vorschlag beratschlagen; **~ upon a question** über eine Frage beraten;
to retire to ~ sich zur Beratung zurückziehen;
~ attack *(mil.)* Angriff nach Bereitstellung; **~ insult** beabsichtigte Beleidigung; **~ judgment** abgewogenes Urteil; **~ lie** vorsätzliche Lüge; **~ misrepresentation** bewußt falsche Darstellung; **~ misstatement of facts** arglistige Täuschung; **~ plan** wohl überlegter Plan; **~ policy** gezielte Politik; **~ trenches** sorgfältig angelegte Schützengräber.

deliberation Überlegung, Erwägung, Beratung;
after long ~s nach sorgfältigen (reiflichen) Überlegungen;
~s Verhandlungsprotokoll;
to bring under ~ zur Diskussion (Beratung) stellen; **to come under ~** zur Beratung kommen; **to enter into a ~** in eine Beratung eintreten.

deliberative beratend, sorgsam abwägend;
~ assembly beratende Versammlung; **~ body** beratende Körperschaft; **~ function** beratende Funktion; **~ voice** beratende Stimme.

delicacy Feingefühl, Takt, *(health)* Zartheit, zarte Gesundheit;
to be of great ~ *(political situation)* äußerst heikel sein.

delicate zart, zerbrechlich, schwächlich, *(fig.)* heikel, kitzlig, delikat, bedenklich;
to be at their most ~ sich im heikelsten Stadium befinden;
~ air herrliche Luft; **~ bloom** *(fig.)* Mimose; **to be in a ~ condition** in anderen Umständen sein; **to tread on ~ ground** *(coll.)* sehr delikate Fragen behandeln; **to be of ~ health** von zarter Gesundheit sein; **~ manners** vornehme Manieren; **~ surgical operation** kritische Operation; **~ question** heikle (delikate) Frage; **~ situation** delikate (heikle) Situation; **~ workmanship** auserwählte Arbeit.

delicately, to put it um es vornehm auszudrücken.

delicatessen Feinkost, Delikatessen.

delict Delikt, unerlaubte Handlung, Vergehen.

delight Vergnügen;
to be a sheer ~ wahre Augenweide sein.

delimit *(v.)* Grenze festsetzen, be-, abgrenzen.

delimitation Grenzziehung, -festlegung.

delimitize *(v.)* von Beschränkungen befreien.

delinquency Verfehlung, Pflichtvergessenheit, *(offence)* Vergehen, Kriminalität;
juvenile ~ Jugendkriminalität; **international ~** völkerrechtliches Unrecht; **tax ~** *(US)* verspätete Steuerzahlung, Steuerrückstand;
~ amount *(US)* Steuerrückstand.

delinquent [Misse]täter, Delinquent, Straffälliger;
child (juvenile) ~ jugendlicher Täter;
~ *(a.)* säumig, pflichtvergessen, *(tax)* rückständig, säumig;
to be ~ in payment mit der Zahlung im Rückstand sein;
~ customer säumiger Kunde, Kunde mit Zahlungsrückständen; **~ list** Liste der Steuerschuldner; **~ magistrate** pflichtvergessener Beamter; **~ minor** jugendlicher Straffälliger; **~ special assessments** *(US)* rückständige Umlagen; **~ tax** *(US)* rückständige Steuer, Steuerrückstand; **~ tax due** *(income tax)* Säumniszuschlag.

delirious irreredend, phantasierend;
to be ~ with fever Fieberphantasien haben.

delirium tremens Säuferwahnsinn.

deliver *(v.)* *(goods)* [ab]liefern, ausliefern, andienen, *(hand over)* einliefern, abgeben, aushändigen, *(liberate)* befreien, *(make delivery)* zustellen, übergeben, -mitteln, *(pronounce)* verkünden, aussprechen;
~ o. s. sich stellen;

~ o. s. against a bill sich gegen einen Gesetzesantrag aussprechen; **~ a blow in the cause of freedom** der Freiheit eine Gasse bahnen; **~ s. o. from captivity** j. aus der Gefangenschaft befreien; **~ s. th. into s. one's charge** jem. etw. zu getreuen Händen übergeben; **~ a copy** Abschrift erteilen; **~ a counter-claim** Gegenforderung geltend machen; **~ a course of lectures** Vorlesung[sreihe] halten; **~ s. o. from death** j. vom Tode retten; **~ a deed** Urkunde aushändigen; **~ a document** Urkunde begeben; **~ free door** frei Haus liefern (ausfolgen); **~ in duplicate** doppelt ausfertigen; **~ over an estate to one's son** seinen Besitz auf seinen Sohn übertragen; **~ a fortress to the enemy** Festung dem Feind übergeben; **~ goods** Waren [aus]liefern; **~ goods to s. one's address** jem. Waren ins Haus bringen; **~ the goods on board** Waren an Bord bringen; **~ goods on sale or return** Waren in Kommission geben; **~ the goods alongside the ship** Waren an der Längsseite Schiff liefern; **~ in** zur Kenntnisnahme vorlegen; **~ into s. one's hands** jem. eigenhändig übergeben; **~ a long harangue** sich in Tiraden ergehen; **~ s. th. at s. one's house** jem. etw. frei Haus liefern; **~ an instrument** Papier begeben; **~ a judgment** Urteil verkünden (fällen); **~ judgment by default** Versäumnisurteil erlassen; **~ a letter** Brief zustellen (austragen); **~ luggage** Gepäck zustellen; **~ the mail** Post zustellen (austragen); **~ a message** Botschaft (Bestellung) ausrichten, bestellen, Nachricht überbringen; **~ o. s. of an opinion** seine Meinung kundtun; **~ an oration** Ansprache halten; **~ into orbit** in die Umlaufbahn befördern; **~ over** übergeben; **~ over to execution** dem Exekutionkommando überstellen; **~ in payment** in Zahlung geben; **~ possession** Besitz verschaffen; **~ to posterity** der Nachwelt überliefern; **~ over one's property to one's son** sein Vermögen auf seinen Sohn übertragen; **~ parcels** Pakete zustellen; **~ on schedule** rechtzeitig abliefern; **~ specification of goods** Warenaufstellung zusenden; **~ a speech** Rede halten (steigen lassen); **~ from stock immediately** sofort vom Lager liefern; **~ subsequently** nachliefern; **~ a telegram** Telegramm zustellen; **~ a telegram over the telephone** Telegramm telefonisch durchsagen (zusprechen); **~ within the specified time (the time stipulated)** Lieferfrist einhalten, fristgerecht liefern; **~ in trust** in Verwahrung geben, hinterlegen, anvertrauen; **~ up** aushändigen, -folgen; **~ up a fortress to the enemy** Festung dem Feind übergeben; **~ up stolen goods** Diebesgut abliefern.

deliverable liefer-, bestellbar;
~ free on board frei an Bord zu liefern;
~ condition (state) lieferfähiger Zustand.

deliverance Lieferung, Übergabe, *(Scot. law)* Spruch der Geschworenen;
~s of a judge richterliche Äußerungen; **~ of judgment** Urteilsfällung; **~ of an opinion** Meinungsäußerung;
to wage ~ Bürgschaft für pünktliche Lieferung übernehmen.

delivered [aus]geliefert;
~ at ... franko ab ..., Erfüllungsort ...; **~ on board** frei Bord; **~ customs cleared** verzollt geliefert; **~ at docks** im Dock abgeliefert; **~ in execution** *(land)* von der Vollstreckung erfaßt; **~ free** frei Haus; **~ free of charge** kostenlose Lieferung, franko; **~ free Berlin (destination)** franko Berlin (Bestimmungsort); **~ free at residence** Lieferung frei Haus; **~ free at station** Lieferung franko Bahnhof; **~ by hand** durch Boten abgegeben; **~ here** frei ab hier; **~ on site** Lieferung frei Baustelle; **~ in store** frei Warenhaus;
when ~ nach erfolgter Lieferung;
to be ~ on board free of charge frei an Bord zu liefern; **to be ~ of a child** entbunden werden; **to be ~ at three days notice** in drei Tagen lieferfähig sein; **to be ~ in five days** fünf Tage Lieferzeit haben; **to be ~ free railway station** frei Bahnstation geliefert werden;
~ price Lieferpreis; **~ weight** ausgeliefertes Gewicht, Auslieferungsgewicht.

deliverer Lieferant, *(letter)* Zusteller.

deliveries Eingänge;
unsolicited ~ *(book trade)* unverlangte Sendungen;
~ accounting wertmäßige Abrechnung.

delivering | of possession Besitzverschaffung;
~ charges Lieferspesen, -kosten; **~ carrier** Auslieferer, Abholspediteur.

delivery *(childbirth)* Endbindung, Niederkunft, *(criminal)* Auslieferung, *(of goods)* Anfuhr, Ein-, Ab-, Auslieferung, Lieferung, Ausfolgung, Zusendung, *(handing over)* Überbringung, Übergabe, Aus-, Einhändigung, Abgabe, Herausgabe, *(mail)* Austragung, Zustellung, *(placing in legal possession)* Besitzeinweisung, *(speech)* Vortragsweise, -art, *(transfer)* Übergabe, -tragung;

against ~ of gegen Auslieferung von; **at the time of** ~ im Zeitpunkt der Lieferung; **by special** ~ *(US)* durch Eilboten; **cash** *(Br.)* **(collect,** *US***) on** ~ **(C.O.D.)** Zahlung gegen Nachnahme, zahlbar bei Lieferung, *(stocks)* gegen Kasse; **for immediate** ~ sofort zu liefern; **for short** ~ kurzfristig lieferbar; **in proof of** ~ zum Nachweis der Lieferung; **on** ~ gegen Aushändigung, bei Lieferung; **free on** ~ frei gegen Lieferschein; **payable on** ~ bei Lieferung fällig, zahlbar bei Lieferung; **pending** ~ bis zur Ablieferung; **ready for** ~ lieferbar, versandfertig; **spot** ~ am Platz verfügbar;

accomplished ~ Erfüllung; **actual** ~ *(law)* unmittelbare Besitzverschaffung; **additional** ~ Nachlieferung; **authorized** ~ ordnungsgemäße Übergabe; **bad** ~ mangelhafte (nicht vertragsgemäße) Lieferung, *(stock exchange)* nicht lieferbar; **completed** ~ Auslieferung; **conditional** ~ bedingte Begebung; **constructive** ~ mittelbare Besitzverschaffung (Übergabe); **cooperative** ~ gemeinschaftlicher Zustellungsdienst; **10-day** ~ zehntägige Lieferfrist; **deferred** ~ *(stock exchange)* aufgeschobene Lieferung, Lieferverzögerung; **deficient** ~ fehlerhafte Lieferung; **delayed** ~ verspätete Lieferung, Lieferverzug; **door** ~ *(US)* Hauszustellung; **door-to-door pickup and** ~ *(carrier)* Zustellung von Haus zu Haus; **due** ~ ordnungsgemäße Zustellung; **early-morning** ~ Frühzustellung; **express** ~ *(Br.)* Eilzustellung, Zustellung durch Eilboten; **forward** ~ *(stock exchange)* spätere Lieferung; **first** ~ *(cheque)* Erstbegebung; **free** ~ portofreie Zustellung, Zustellung frei Haus; **freight** ~ Frachtzustellung; **future** ~ *(stock exchange)* Terminlieferung; **general** ~ *(US)* postlagernd, Abholung am Schalter; **good** ~ *(stock exchange)* bestimmungsgemäße Ablieferung, lieferbar; **immediate** ~ sofortige Lieferung; **improper** ~ unsachgemäße Übergabe; **individually owned** ~ eigener Zustellungsdienst; **internal** ~ innerbetriebliche Lieferung; **late** ~ verspätete Ablieferung; **less-than-carload** ~ Stückgutlieferung; **mail** ~ Postzustellung; **manual** ~ tatsächliche Übergabe; **overnight** ~ *(railway)* Zustellungsdienst innerhalb von 24 Stunden; **parcel** ~ Paketzustellung; **part** ~ Teillieferung; **partial** ~ Teillieferung; **postal** ~ Briefzustellung, -ausgabe, Zustellung durch die Post; **priority** ~ Vorzugsbelieferung; **prompt** ~ sofortige Lieferung; **railway** ~ Eisenbahnzustellung; **road and rail** ~ Lieferung per LKW oder mit der Bahn; **rural** ~ Landpostzustellung; **rural free** ~ freier Landzustellungsdienst; **same-day** ~ Lieferung am gleichen Tage; **second** ~ Übergabe zunächst hinterlegter Urkunden; **special** ~ *(US)* durch Eilboten, Eilzustellung; **spot** ~ *(stock exchange)* prompte (sofortige) Lieferung; **subsequent** ~ Nachlieferung; **successive** ~ Sukzessivlieferung; **symbolical** ~ *(law)* fiktive (fingierte) Übergabe, mittelbare Besitzverschaffung; **taking** ~ Abnahme; **trial** ~ Probelieferung; **valid** ~ gültige Übergabe; **war** ~ Kriegslieferung; **wrongful** ~ Lieferstörung;

~ **to addressee** Zustellung an den Empfänger; ~ **by air** Luftpostzustellung; ~ **in arrears** rückständige Lieferung; ~ **of a bill of exchange** Wechselbegebung; ~ **at call** Lieferung auf Abruf; ~ **of a captive** Gefangenenbefreiung; ~ **of coin** Sorteneinlieferung; ~ **of certified copies** Ausfertigung beglaubigter Abschriften; ~ **of a deed** Aushändigung einer Urkunde, Urkundenaushändigung, -zustellung; ~ **of defence** Einreichung der Klagebeantwortung; ~ **in escrow** *(US)* Übergabe [einer Urkunde] zu treuen Händen an einen Dritten; ~ **of a fortress** Festungsübergabe; ~ **of fuel** Brennstoffzufuhr; ~ **of goods** Warenlieferung; ~ **of goods into the custody of the railway** Übergabe der Ware an die Eisenbahn; ~ **of the goods alongside the ship** Warenlieferung Längsseite Schiff; ~ **of hostages** Geiselstellung, Gestellung von Geiseln; ~ **by instalments** Lieferung in Raten, Teil-, Sukzessivlieferung; ~ **of a judgment** Urteilsverkündung; ~ **of letters** Briefzustellung; ~ **of luggage** *(Br.)* Gepäckausgabe; ~ **of the mail** Postzustellung; ~ **of a message** Übermittlung einer Botschaft; ~ **by mistake** versehentliche Lieferung; ~ **of mortgage** Hypothekenbestellung; ~ **of opinion** Abgabe einer Meinung, Meinungsäußerung; ~ **of possession** Besitzverschaffung; ~ **from the quay** Lieferung ab Kai; ~ **by rail** Bahnversand, Anlieferung (Auslieferung) auf der Schiene; ~ **as required** Lieferung nach Abruf; ~ **free at residence** Lieferung frei Haus; ~ **by road** Anlieferung per LKW; ~ **by sea or inland waterway** Anlieferung auf dem See- oder Binnenwasserweg; ~ **of securities** Ausfolgung gestellter Sicherheiten; ~ **shipside** Anlieferung an Schiffsseite; ~ **of a speech** Vortrag einer Rede; ~ **of stocks** Aushändigung (Lieferung) von Wertpapieren; ~ **of substitute** Ersatzlieferung; ~ **of a telegram** Telegrammzustellung; ~ **alongside the vessel** Längsseitlieferung; ~ **of a writ** gerichtliche Zustellung; **to accept** ~ Lieferung entgegennehmen; **to ask for** ~ **of other goods** Ersatzlieferung verlangen; **to assure** ~ Lieferung sicher-

stellen; **to be bad** ~ nicht jederzeit handelbar sein; **to be late in** ~ im Lieferverzug sein; **to be not yet available for** ~ noch nicht lieferbar sein; **to buy forward (for future,** *US***)** ~ *(stock exchange)* auf Lieferung kaufen; **to come by the first** ~ mit der Frühpost zugestellt werden; **to constitute a good** ~ *(securities)* jederzeit handelbar sein; **to effect (execute)** ~ Lieferung vornehmen; **to guarantee prompt** ~ **of goods** für prompte Lieferung einstehen; **to have a good** ~ gut vortragen können; **to make** ~ **on a cash basis** Lieferungen gegen Barzahlung vornehmen; **to pay on** ~ bei Lieferung bezahlen; **to promise** ~ **within one week from receiving order** achttägige Lieferzusage nach Auftragseingang geben; **to prove** ~ Zustellung nachweisen; **to refuse** ~ Herausgabe verweigern; **to refuse to accept (take)** ~ **of goods** Warenannahme verweigern; **to require** ~ **within four weeks order** Lieferung vier Wochen nach Auftragserteilung erwarten; **to sell for future** ~ auf zukünftige Lieferung (Abruf) verkaufen; **to sell for spot** ~ loco verkaufen; **to sell on** ~ auf Lieferung verkaufen; **to speed up** ~ schnell liefern; **to stop** ~ Lieferung einstellen; **to take** ~ Lieferung abnehmen; **to have been put on notice to take** ~ im Annahmeverzug sein; **to take** ~ **of goods** Ware abnehmen; **to take** ~ **of stocks** Wertpapierlieferung entgegennehmen; **to take orders for future** ~ Warenbestellungen entgegennehmen; **not to take** ~ **in due time** sich im Annahmeverzug befinden; **to warrant punctual** ~ pünktliche Lieferung garantieren;

~**-acceptance period** Abnahmefrist; ~ **area** *(post)* Zustellgebiet; ~ **bond** Kaution zur Freigabe beschlagnahmter Waren; ~ **bonus** Auslieferungsprämie; ~ **book** Auslieferungs-, Lieferbuch; ~ **boy** Botenjunge, Laufbursche; ~ **car** Lieferwagen; ~ **cart** Lieferwagen; ~ **charge** Auslieferungsgebühr, -kosten, Zustellgebühr; ~ **clause** [Aus]lieferungsklausel; ~ **company** Paketzustellungsgesellschaft; **[long-term]** ~ **conditions** [langfristige] Lieferbedingungen; ~ **contract** Liefer[ungs]vertrag; ~ **cost** Versand-, Zustellungskosten; **[scheduled]** ~ **date** [festgesetzter] Liefertermin (Zeitpunkt der Lieferung), Ablieferfrist, -termin; **to be very specific on** ~ **dates** Liefertermine unbedingt einhalten; ~ **day** *(Br.)* Liefertag; ~ **delay** Lieferverzögerung; ~ **department** Auslieferungs-, Versandabteilung; ~ **dock** Lieferdock; ~ **equipment** Fuhrpark [für Kundendienst]; ~ **equipment account** Fahrzeugkonto; ~ **expenses** Versand-, Zustellungskosten; ~ **failures** Lieferschwierigkeiten; ~ **fee** *(post)* Zustellungsgebühr; **to subcontract the** ~ **function to professional carriers** Auslieferungsaufgaben auf das Speditionsgewerbe übertragen; ~ **girl** Laufmädchen; **to report immediately any** ~ **holdup** Lieferhindernis sofort melden; ~ **instructions** Liefervorschriften; ~ **item** Liefergegenstand; ~ **lag** Lieferverzögerung, -verzug; ~ **licence** Liefergenehmigung; ~ **lorry** Lieferwagen; ~ **note** Bordereau, Lieferschein, Auslieferungszettel; ~ **obligation** Ablieferungspflicht; ~ **office** Abgabestelle, *(Br.)* zuständiges Postamt; ~ **operation** Zustelldienst; ~ **order** Lieferschein, -auftrag, *(warehouse)* Anweisung zur Auslieferung von Lagergut, Lagerschein; ~ **output** Förderleistung; ~ **period** Lieferzeit, -frist; **lengthening** ~ **periods** länger werdende Lieferfristen; ~ **pipe** Druckrohr; ~ **place** Erfüllungsort; ~ **point** Ablieferungsplatz; ~ **port** Auslieferungshafen; ~ **power** Liefermöglichkeit; ~ **price** Lieferpreis; ~ **problems** Lieferschwierigkeiten; ~ **quota** Ablieferungskontingent; ~ **receipt** Übergabebescheinigung, Warenempfangsschein; ~ **room** *(hospital)* Kreißsaal; ~ **route** Zustellungsweg [der Post]; ~ **schedule** Lieferplan; ~ **service** Zustelldienst; **high-speed** ~ **service** Eilbotenzustellung; **parcel** ~ **service** Paketzustelldienst; **pickup and** ~ **service** Abhol- und Zustellungsdienst; **special** ~ **service** *(US)* Eilbotensendung; ~ **service to retail bookseller agents** Zustelldienst an Sortimenter-Kommittenten; **to settle on a scheduled weekly** ~ **service** vereinbarungsgemäß wöchentlich nur einmal zustellen; ~ **slip** Begleit-, Lieferschein, -beleg, Auslieferungszettel; ~ **station** *(US, public library)* Bücherabgabestelle; ~ **supervision** Wareneingangsüberwachung; ~ **system** Zustellungswesen, -dienst; **consolidated** ~ **system** *(US)* gemeinsamer Zustellungsdienst mehrerer Firmen; ~ **terms** Lieferbedingungen; ~ **ticket** Lieferschein, Auslieferungsschein, -bescheinigung, *(stock exchange)* Lieferungsanzeige; ~ **time** Lieferzeit; ~ **tricycle** Geschäftsdreirad; ~ **truck** *(US)* Lieferwagen; ~**-truck account** Fuhrparkkonto; ~ **up** Ausfolgung, -händigung; ~ **van** *(Br.)* Lieferwagen; ~ **verification** Wareneingangsbescheinigung; ~ **volume** Fördermenge; ~ **wagon** *(US)* Lieferwagen; ~ **weight** ausgehendes Gewicht; ~**-wise** was die Lieferung anbetrifft.

deliveryman Lieferbote, Lieferant, Austräger, Auslieferungsfahrer.

delta wing Deltaflügel.

delude (v.) täuschen, betrügen, irreführen, hintergehen;
~ o. s. with false hopes sich Illusionen (Selbsttäuschungen) hingeben.

deluge Überschwemmung;
~ of claims Flut von Forderungen; ~ of crimes Hochflut von Verbrechen.

deluged with letters mit Briefen überschwemmt.

delusion (law) Täuschung, Irreführung;
under the ~ in dem Wahn;
insane ~ Zwangsvorstellung; mental ~ Sinnestäuschung;
~s of grandeur Größenwahn;
to labo(u)r under a ~ unter dem Einfluß eines Irrtums handeln.

delusive irreführend.

demagog(ue) Volksaufwiegler, Demagoge.

demand (call for commodities) Nachfrage, Bedarf, (claim) [Rechts]anspruch, Schuldforderung, (el.) Stromverbrauch, (request) [An]forderung, Erfordernis, Verlangen, Ersuchen, Begehren;
in [great] ~ [sehr] gefragt, gesucht, beliebt; not in ~ ohne Nachfrage; on ~ bei Vorkommen (Vorlage), (bill of exchange) auf Verlangen (Aufforderung); payable on ~ (bill of exchange) zahlbar auf Verlangen, bei Sicht fällig;
accumulated ~ Bedarfsballung, -massierung; active ~ lebhafte Nachfrage; adaptable ~ elastische Nachfrage; additional ~ Nachforderung, Mehrbedarf; anticipated ~ voraussichtlicher Bedarf; backlog ~ Nachholbedarf, Bedarfsreserve; bank-loan ~ Nachfrage nach (Bedarf an) Bankkrediten; booming ~ Nachfragekonjunktur; brand ~ Nachfrage nach einem Markenartikel; brisk ~ lebhafte (starke) Nachfrage; capital ~ Kapitalbedarf; composite ~ zusammengesetzte Nachfrage; compulsory ~ (against vendor) Intervention des wahren Eigentümers; considerable ~ bedeutende Nachfrage; cross ~ Gegenforderung, (law court) Widerklage; decreasing ~ Nachfragerückgang; deferred ~ aufgeschobener (zurückgestellter) Bedarf; derived ~ mittelbar entstandener Bedarf; domestic ~ Inlandsnachfrage; effective ~ tatsächliche Nachfrage; effectual ~ durch vorhandenes Bargeld gedeckte Nachfrage; elastic ~ elastischer Bedarf; excessive ~ Überforderung, -bedarf; exorbitant ~ unmäßige Forderung; freshly expanding ~ sich lebhaft entwickelnde Nachfrage; external (foreign) ~ Auslandsnachfrage; great ~ starke (große) Nachfrage; growing ~ ständig wachsende Nachfrage; holiday currency ~s Anforderungen für Ferien- und Reisegelder; home ~ Inlandsbedarf; huge ~ ungeheure Nachfrage; immediate ~ plötzlich auftretende Nachfrage; improved ~ Bedarfserhöhung; increased ~ Bedarfszunahme, gesteigerter Bedarf; [constantly] increasing ~ [ständig] steigende Nachfrage; inelastic ~ unelastischer (starrer) Bedarf; insignificant ~ unbedeutende Nachfrage; internal ~ Binnennachfrage; keen ~ starke (hektische) Nachfrage; labo(u)r ~ Arbeitskräftebedarf; legal ~ berechtigte Forderung, Rechtsanspruch; liquidated ~ festgestellte Forderung, Zahlungsanspruch; little ~ geringe Nachfrage; lively ~ lebhafte Nachfrage; market ~ Marktbedürfnisse; midyear ~s Anforderungen zum Halbjahresultimo; minimum ~ Mindestbedarf; money ~ Geldforderung; overall economic ~ gesamtwirtschaftliche Nachfrage; pecuniary ~ Geldforderung; pent-up ~ (US) Nachfragestau, aufgestauter Bedarf, Nachholbedarf; persistent ~ hartnäckige Forderung; personal ~ Zahlungsaufforderung; pressing ~ Nachfragesog; potential ~ möglicher (potentieller) Bedarf; primary ~ vordringlicher Bedarf; reasonable ~ billige Forderung; reduced ~ Minderbedarf; replacement ~ Nachholbedarf; rush ~ plötzlich auftretende Nachfrage; seasonal ~ saisonbedingte Nachfrage; schedule ~ gesamter volkswirtschaftlicher Bedarf; slack ~ spärliche (schwache) Nachfrage; sluggish ~ träge Nachfrage; stale ~ (US) fast verjährte Forderung; steady ~ beständige (andauernde) Nachfrage; strong ~ lebhafte (starke) Nachfrage; total ~ Gesamtbedarf; unliquidated ~ der Höhe nach unbestimmte Forderung; unreasonable ~ übertriebene (unmäßige) Forderung; vague ~ unklare Forderung; wage (workers') ~s Lohnforderungen; world ~ Weltbedarf; yearly ~s Anforderungen zum Jahresultimo;
supply and ~ Angebot und Nachfrage;
~ for advances Kreditbedarf; ~s for amendment Abänderungswünsche; ~ for assignment Übertragungsanspruch; ~ backed by the power and desire to buy durch Kaufkraft und Kaufbereitschaft gestützte Nachfrage; reasonable public ~ for a bank ausreichendes, öffentliches Bedürfnis auf Erteilung einer Bankkonzession; ~ for borrowing Darlehnsbedarf; ~ for [long-term investment] capital [langfristiger] Kapitalbedarf; ~ for compensation Schadensersatzforderung; private ~ for credit

Nachfrage nach Personalkrediten; ~ for delivery Lieferverlangen, -nachfrage; ~ for every description Nachfrage nach allen Qualitäten; ~ for electricity Elektrizitätsbedarf; ~ for energy Energienachfrage; ~s on an estate Forderungen gegen einen Nachlaß; ~ for funds Kapitalbedarf; ~ of one's job Arbeitsanfall; ~ for labo(u)r Arbeitskräftebedarf; ~s of labo(u)r Gewerkschaftsforderungen; ~ for loans Kreditbedarf; ~ for luxuries Nachfrage nach Gütern des gehobenen Bedarfs; ~s for the minister to resign Rücktrittsaufforderungen an den Minister; ~ for money Geldbedarf; ~ for new mortgages Hypothekenbedarf; ~ for oil Ölbedarf; ~ for payment Zahlungsaufforderung, Mahnbescheid; ~ for a poll Abstimmungsersuchen, (company meeting) Antrag auf schriftliche Abstimmung nach Kapitalanteilen; ~ for the rent Mietforderung; ~ for repayment Rückzahlungsaufforderung; heavy ~s on the staff starke Inanspruchnahme der Mitarbeiter; ~ upon s. one's time Inanspruchnahme (Beanspruchung) von jds. Zeit; great ~ for typists großer Bedarf an Stenotypistinnen; ~ in writing schriftliche Aufforderung;
~ (v.) verlangen, beanspruchen, in Anspruch nehmen, [er]fordern;
~ in addition zusätzlich verlangen; ~ an immediate answer sofort beantwortet werden müssen; ~ back zurückfordern, -verlangen; ~ s. one's business (gatekeeper) jds. Besuchsgrund erfragen; ~ damages Schadenersatz verlangen; [as] extra nachfordern, zusätzlich fordern; ~ payment of a debt Bezahlung einer Schuld verlangen; ~ surrender zur Übergabe auffordern;
to abate one's ~s Rückzieher machen; to address a ~ Antrag einbringen; to be in brisk ~ lebhaft begehrt werden; to be in great (much in) ~ sehr begehrt (gefragt) sein, hoch im Kurse stehen; to be in little ~ schlecht gehen; to create a ~ Bedarf hervorrufen (schaffen); to curb ~ Nachfrage dämpfen; to declare a ~ admissible Antrag für zulässig erklären; to drop a ~ Forderung fallen lassen; to give in to ~s Forderungen gegenüber nachgeben; to have many ~s on one's time [zeitlich] sehr besetzt sein; to make ~s on railway lines Eisenbahnverkehr belasten; to make great ~s on s. o. hohe Anforderungen an j. stellen; to make no great ~ s on s. o. wenig von jem. verlangen; to meet the ~ Bedarf befriedigen (decken); to meet the increasing ~ steigenden Bedarf decken; to meet the ~s of road safety der Verkehrssicherheit genügen; to outstrip (outpace) the ~ Bedarf übersteigen; to pay on ~ auf Verlangen (bei Vorzeigung) zahlen; to persist in a ~ auf einer Forderung beharren; to put down one's ~s in writing seine Forderungen schriftlich vorbringen; to put out its own ~ for long-term capital langfristiges Kapitalbedürfnis sichtbar machen; to recede from one's ~s seine Forderungen aufgeben; to reject ~s Forderungen entgegentreten; to satisfy the ~ Bedarf decken, Nachfrage befriedigen; to stand on one's ~ auf seiner Forderung bestehen; to supply the ~ Nachfrage befriedigen;
~ analysis Nachfrage-, Bedarfsanalyse; ~ bill (US) Sichtwechsel; ~ certificate of deposits (US) bei Sicht ausfolgbare Einzahlungsbescheinigung einer Bank; ~ creation Nachfrage-, Bedarfsschöpfung; ~ curve Nachfragekurve; ~ deposits fällige Soforteinlage, Sichteinlage, laufendes Konto, Kontokorrentkonto, tägliches (täglich fälliges) Geld; ~ draft (US) Sichtwechsel; ~ effect Nachfragewirkung, -effekt; ~-increasing effects nachfragesteigernde Wirkungen; ~ function Nachfragefunktion; ~-induced nachfragebedingt; ~ instrument (US) Sichtpapier; ~ lag Angebotsverzögerung; ~ loan (money) (US) tägliches Geld, Tagesgeld; ~ management Nachfragesteuerung; restrictive ~ management policies zurückhaltende Politik bei der Nachfragesteuerung; ~ meter (el.) [Strom]zähler; ~ note Sichtwechsel, (rates) Zahlungsaufforderung, Mahnschreiben, (Br.) Steuerbescheid; ~ paper Sichtwechsel; excessive ~ pressure überhöhter Nachfragedruck; ~ price (stock exchange) Geldkurs; ~ pull Nachfragesog; ~-pull inflation nachfragebedingte Inflation, Nachfragesoginflation; ~-pull measures nachfragesteigernde Maßnahmen; ~ quotation (stock exchange) Geldnotiz; ~ rate (el.) Höchstverbrauchertarif, (foreign exchange) Sichtkurs, Geldkurs; ~ savings deposits sofort fällige Spareinlagen; ~ schedule Bedarfsliste, listenmäßige Darstellung der Nachfrageentwicklung; ~ shift Nachfrageverschiebung; ~ sterling Sichtwechsel auf London; ~ trend Bedarfsentwicklung.

demandable einklagbar.

demandant Forderer, (US) Kläger, Antragsteller.

demander Gläubiger, (customer) Käufer, Kunde.

demandress Klägerin.

demarcate (v.) abgrenzen.

demarcation Gebietsabgrenzung, Grenzziehung, -festlegung, Demarkation,*(trade unions)* strenge Abgrenzung der Berufsgruppen;
~ **line** Demarkationslinie; ~ **problems in industry** gewerkschaftliche Abgrenzungsprobleme.

démarche *(dipl.)* Demarche, diplomatischer Schritt.

demean *(v.)* o. s. sich würdelos benehmen (erniedrigen).

demeano(u)r Verhalten, Auftreten, Gebahren, Benehmen, Betragen.

demented schwachsinnig, geistesgestört.

dementi Dementi, Richtigstellung.

dementia Schwachsinn, Wahnsinn;
precocious ~ Jugendirresein; **senile** ~ Altersschwachsinn.

demerge *(v.)* entfusionieren.

demerger Entfusionierung.

demerit tadelnswertes Verhalten, unwürdiges Benehmen;
~ **mark** *(school)* Minuspunkt.

demesne freier Grundbesitz, Eigenbesitz, Grundeigentum, *(manor place)* Landsitz, Gut, vom Grundstücksbesitzer selbst verwaltete Ländereien, *(province)* Sonder-, Arbeitsgebiet, Domäne;
~ **of the crown** *(Br.)* Krongut, -domäne, Staatsdomäne; ~ **of the state** Staatseigentum, staatliche Domäne, Domänenland;
to hold in ~ Grundeigentum besitzen;
~ **lands of the Crown** *(Br.)* eigengenutztes Land.

demilitarization Entmilitarisierung, Überführung in die Zivilverwaltung.

demilitarize *(v.)* entmilitarisieren.

demilitarized zone entmilitarisierte Zone.

demimonde Halbwelt.

demisable übertragbar.

demise Ableben, Tod, Hinscheiden, *(law)* Verpachtung, *(by will)* Vermachung;
~ **and redemise** Pacht- und Rückverpachtung; ~ **of the crown** Thronfolge;
~ *(v.)* *(convey)* [Grundstück] übertragen, *(lend on lease)* [Grundstück] verpachten;
~ **by will** Grundbesitz testamentarisch vermachen.

demised premises Miet-, Pachtgrundstück.

demission Rücktritt, Abdankung, Demission.

demist *(v.)* **the windscreen** Windschutzscheibe belüften.

demister *(car)* Scheibenbelüfter.

demit *(v.)* **an office** Amt niederlegen, demissionieren.

demob *(coll., Br.)* Demobilmachung;
~ **suit** Entlassungsanzug.

demobilization Demobilmachung, Auflösung einer Armee;
~ **centre** *(Br.)* **(center,** *US)* Entlassungsstelle.

demobilize *(v.)* demobilisieren, [aus dem Wehrdienst] entlassen;
~ **an army** Armee auflösen.

democracy Demokratie;
absolute (pure) ~ unmittelbare Demokratie; **industrial** ~ Wirtschaftsdemokratie; **parliamentary** ~ parlamentarische Demokratie; **participatory** ~ Demokratie mit aktiver Beteiligung der Staatsbürger; **people's** ~ Volksherrschaft; **representative** ~ repräsentative Demokratie;
to live uncomfortably with ~ sich nur schwer mit der Demokratie abfinden können.

democrat Demokrat, *(US)* demokratisches Parteimitglied.

democratic demokratisch;
~ **dictatorship** autoritäre Demokratie; ~ **government** demokratische Regierungsform; ~ **party** *(US)* demokratische Partei; ~ **process** Demokratisierung[sprozeß]; **to choose the** ~ **road** sich für die Demokratie entscheiden; **to play the** ~ **rules** demokratische Spielregeln einhalten; ~ **system** demokratisches Regierungssystem.

democratization Demokratisierung.

democratize *(v.)* demokratisieren.

demodisc Demoband.

demographer Bevölkerungspolitiker.

demographic[al] bevölkerungsstatistisch;
~ **characteristics** demographische Merkmale; ~ **measures** bevölkerungspolitische Maßnahmen; ~ **situation** Bevölkerungslage; ~ **statistics** Bevölkerungsstatistik; ~ **structure** demographische Struktur, Bevölkerungsstruktur; ~ **trend** Bevölkerungstrend, -entwicklung.

demography Bevölkerungswissenschaft, -statistik.

demolish *(v.)* abbrechen, abreißen, niederreißen, demolieren.

demolition *(building)* Abbruch[arbeit], Niederreißung, Zerstörung, Demolierung, *(annulment)* Ungültigkeitserklärung, *(fortress)* Schleifung;
due for ~ abbruchreif;

~ **bomb** *(mil.)* Sprengbombe; ~ **charge** *(mil.)* Sprengsatz, geballte Ladung; ~ **company** Abbruchbetrieb, -gesellschaft; ~ **contractor** Abbruchunternehmer; ~ **cost** Aufräumungs-, Abbruchkosten; ~ **cost insurance** Versicherung gegen Abbruchkosten; ~ **engineer** Abbruchspezialist; ~ **firm** Abbruchbetrieb, -gesellschaft; ~ **order** *(Br.)* Abbruchanordnung; ~ **party** Sprengkommando; ~ **permit** Abbruchbewilligung; ~ **site** Abbruchstelle; ~ **team** Sabotagekommando; **to sell at** ~ **value** auf Abbruch verkaufen; ~ **works** Abbrucharbeiten.

demolitionist radikaler Umstürzler.

demon Dämon, Besessener, *(go, Br., coll.)* Schwung, Tempo, *(person of great energy)* Teufelskerl;
to be a ~ **for work** *(coll.)* unermüdlicher Arbeiter (arbeitswütig, arbeitsbesessen) sein;
~ **driver** hervorragender Autofahrer.

demonetization Außerkurssetzung, Entwertung.

demonetize *(v.)* [Münzen] einziehen, *(withdraw from circulation)* außer Kurs setzen, entwerten.

demonstrability Beweisbarkeit.

demonstrable nachweisbar.

demonstrably false statement nachweislich falsche Erklärung.

demonstrate *(v.)* nachweisen, beweisen, *(make a demonstration)* Demonstration durchführen, demonstrieren, öffentliche Kundgebung veranstalten, *(mil.)* Demonstration durchführen, *(show publicly)* vorführen;
~ **a car** Auto vorführen; ~ **against the rising costs of living** gegen die gestiegenen Lebenshaltungskosten demonstrieren.

demonstration *(argumentation)* Beweis[führung], *(car)* öffentliche Vorführung, *(mil.)* Schein-, Ablenkungsmanöver, *(proof)* Beweisführung, Manifestation, öffentliche Kundgebung, Demonstration, *(expression)* Äußerung, Bekundung, Manifestation, *(stock exchange)* Börsenmanöver;
at a ~ auf einer Kundgebung;
bearish ~ *(Br.)* Baissebewegung, -angriff, **bullish** ~ *(Br.)* Haussebewegung; **false** ~ unrichtige Erklärung; **military** ~ militärische Demonstration; **practical** ~ praktische Vorführung; **student** ~ Studentendemonstration;
~ **of a new car** Vorführung eines neuen Wagens; ~ **of defect** Mängelanzeige; ~ **by discontented workmen** Demonstration unzufriedener Arbeiter; ~ **of the fleet** Flottendemonstration;
to be accompanied by ~**s of public sympathy** unter lebhafter Beteiligung der Bevölkerung stattfinden; **to disperse** ~**s** Demonstrationen auflösen; **to make a** ~ Demonstration veranstalten, demonstrieren; **to seek for a** ~ **of s. one's guilt** nach einem Beweis für jds. Schuld forschen; **to take part in a** ~ Demonstration veranstalten, an einer Demonstration teilnehmen;
~ **area** Vorführgebiet; ~ **car** Vorführwagen; ~ **class** Modellklasse; ~ **farm** Musterfarm; ~ **flight** Probeflug; ~ **material** *(school)* Anschauungsmaterial; ~ **model** Vorführungsmodell; ~ **plot** Vorführungsgelände; ~ **purpose** Vorführungszweck; ~ **school** Musterschule.

demonstrational film Werbeinstruktionsfilm.

demonstrative überzeugend, ausdrucksvoll, auffällig,
~ **cordiality** demonstrative Herzlichkeit; ~ **evidence** Augenscheinsbeweis; ~ **force** Beweiskraft; ~ **legacy** beschränktes Gattungsvermächtnis.

demonstrator Teilnehmer an einer Demonstration, Demonstrant, *(car)* Vorführmodell, *(exhibitor)* Vorführer, *(one who proves)* Beweisführer, Erklärer;
to disperse ~**s by the police** Demonstranten durch polizeiliche Maßnahmen zerstreuen; **to take** ~**s into custody** Demonstranten festnehmen;
~ **machine** Vorführungsmaschine.

demoralization Demoralisierung, Sittenverderbnis.

demoralize *(v.)* zermürben, entmutigen, demoralisieren;
~ **an army** Disziplin einer Armee untergraben.

demoralized market äußerst gedrückter Markt.

demoralizing effect demoralisierende Wirkung.

demote *(v.)* *(employee)* tariflich niedriger einstufen, zurückstufen, *(mil.)* degradieren, *(school, US)* in eine niedere Klasse zurückversetzen;
~ **to the rank below** in den nächstniederen Rang versetzen.

demothball *(mil.)* entmotten, einsatzbereit machen.

demotion *(US, employee)* niedrigere Tarifeinstufung, *(mil.)* Degradierung, Degradation, Dienstgradherabsetzung.

demotional niedriger werdend;
~ **classification change** niedrigere Tarifeinstufung, Einstufung in eine niedrigere Lohngruppe; ~ **salary decrease** mit niedrigerer Einstufung verbundene Gehaltskürzung.

demount *(v.) (stamp)* ablösen, *(wheel)* abmontieren.
demountable abmontierbar.
demur Einwand, Einwendung, Einrede, Widerspruch;
~ *(v.)* Bedenken äußern, *(law)* Einwendungen (Einrede, Rechtseinwand) erheben, einwenden, Forderung beanstanden;
~ **to a demand** einer Forderung widersprechen; ~ **at working on Sundays** Sonntagsarbeit verweigern;
to make no ~ keinen Einwand erheben.
demurrable nicht schlüssig.
demurrage *(banking, Br.)* Spesen für Noteneinlösung, *(railway)* [Wagen]standgeld, *(ship)* Überliegegeld, -zeit, Wartezeit, Verzugskosten, *(storage, coll.)* Lagergeld, -gebühren;
to allow on ~ überliegen lassen; **to be on** ~ Liegezeit überschritten haben;
~ **charges** Liegegebühren, [Wagen]standgeld; ~ **clause** Verzugs-, Überliegegeldklausel; ~ **contract** Liegegeldvereinbarung; ~ **rate** Liegegeldsatz.
demurrant Einwände erhebende Partei, Einsprucherhebender.
demurrer [Rechts]einwand, Einwendung;
general ~ prozeßhindernde Einrede, Prozeßeinwand, Rüge der Unschlüssigkeit; **speaking** ~ Rüge mangelnder Schlüssigkeit, Einrede neuen Beweismaterials; **special** ~ auf Formfehler gestützter Einwand, prozessuale Einwendung;
~ **to action** prozeßhindernde Einrede; ~ **to evidence** *(US)* Einwand der fehlenden Beweiserheblichkeit, Beweiseinrede; ~ **to interrogatories** *(witness)* Beanstandung der Fragestellung; ~ **at law** Rechtseinwand;
to interpose a ~ Einwendungen erheben;
~ **book** Prozeßakte.
den Höhle, Versteck, *(fam.)* Arbeitszimmer, Bude;
gambling ~ Spielhölle; **the lion's** ~ Höhle des Löwen; **opium** ~ Opiumhöhle;
~ **of robbers** Räuberhöhle; ~ **of thieves** Mördergrube; ~ **of vice** Lasterhöhle.
denationalization Entstaatlichung, Reprivatisierung, Überführung in die Privatwirtschaft.
denationalize *(v.)* entstaatlichen, reprivatisieren, in die Privatwirtschaft überführen, *(deprive of nationality)* Nationalität entziehen;
~ **partially** teilprivatisieren.
denaturalization Denaturalisierung, Wiederausbürgerung, Aberkennung der Staatsbürgerschaft, Ausbürgerung.
denaturalize *(v.)* denaturalisieren, Einbürgerung zurücknehmen, ausbürgern, Staatsangehörigkeit aberkennen.
denaturalized ausgebürgert;
to become ~ Staatsangehörigkeit verlieren.
denature *(v.)* ungenießbar machen.
denial Verneinung, *(of claims)* Bestreiten, *(dementi)* Dementi, *(negative reply)* abschlägige Antwort, Absage, Verweigerung, Ablehnung;
flat (formal) ~ glatte Ablehnung, formelles Dementi; **general** ~ Bestreiten des gesamten Klagevorbringens; **official** ~ amtliches Dementi; **self** ~ Selbstverleugnung; **softened** ~ abgeschwächtes Dementi; **specific** ~ Bestreiten einzelner Klagebehauptungen; **unqualified** ~ uneingeschränktes Dementi;
~ **of application** Antragsablehnung; **repeated** ~**s of a charge** wiederholtes Leugnen eines Angeklagten; ~ **of hearing** verweigerte Anhörung; ~ **of justice** Rechtsverweigerung, Vorenthaltung eines rechtsstaatlichen Verfahrens; ~ **of a request for help** Ablehnung eines Hilfesuchens; ~ **of responsibilty** Ablehnung von Verantwortung;
to accept the ~ **of s. th.** sich das Bestreiten einer Sache gefallen lassen; **to give a formal** ~ **to a statement** Behauptung formell dementieren, Dementi abgeben; **to issue a** ~ Dementi herausgeben; **to meet with a** ~ abschlägige Antwort erhalten; **to take no** ~ sich nicht abweisen lassen.
denied on the law aus rechtlichen Gründen abgewiesen.
denigrate *(v.)* anschwärzen, verunglimpfen.
denigration Verunglimpfung, Anschwärzung.
denization *(Br.)* Einbürgerung ohne politische Rechte.
denizen *(Br.)* teilweise eingebürgerter Ausländer, *(US)* eingebürgerter Ausländer, Person mit Wohnsitz in den USA;
~ *(v.)* teilweise einbürgern.
denominate *(v.)* bezeichnen, benennen;
~ **s. th. a crime** etw. als Verbrechen bezeichnen.
denomination *(class)* Klasse, Kategorie, *(designation)* Benennung, Bezeichnung, *(division)* Nenner, *(money)* Sorte, Nennwert, Wertbezeichnung, *(religion)* Konfession, religiöses Bekenntnis, Sekte, *(shares)* Stückelung, *(weight)* Gewichtseinheit;

in ~**s of** in Stücken (in der Stückelung) von; **of low** ~ kleingestückelt;
small ~**s** kleine Stückelungen, Banknoten mit kleinem Nennwert; **temporary** ~ vorläufige Stückelung;
~**s of goods** Warenbezeichnung; ~ **of a loan** Anleihestückelung; ~ **of shares (stocks, US)** Aktienstückelung;
to issue in ~**s of $ 10.000** in Stücken von 10.000 Dollar ausgeben;
large ~ **deposit** Großeinlage.
denominational konfessionell;
~ **organisation** konfessionell gebundene Organisation; ~ **school** Konfessionsschule; ~ **value** Nennwert.
denominationalism Konfessions-, Proporzpolitik.
denominationalize *(v.)* konfessionell aufspalten, konfessionalisieren.
denominator Nenner;
common ~ gemeinsamer Wertmesser, Generalnenner.
denouement Enthüllung, *(drama)* Lösung des Knotens.
denounce *(v.)* kündigen, *(censure)* öffentlich rügen, bloßstellen, brandmarken, *(criminal)* anzeigen, Strafanzeige erstatten, denunzieren;
~ **one's accomplices** seine Mittäter denunzieren; ~ **s. o. to the authorities** j. bei den Behörden anzeigen; ~ **s. o. as an imposter** Schwindler bloßstellen; ~ **a trade pact with 3 months notice** Handelsvertrag mit dreimonatiger Frist kündigen; ~ **s. o. as a spy** j. der Spionage beschuldigen; ~ **a treaty** Staatsvertrag aufkündigen; ~ **s. o. as an upstart** j. als Emporkömmling behandeln.
denouncement öffentliche Rüge, Bloßstellung, Brandmarkung, *(indictment)* Anzeige, Denunziation, *(treaty)* Kündigung;
~ **of a new work** *(US)* Unterlassungsverfügung gegen Neubauerrichtung.
denouncer Anzeigender, Denunziant.
dense dicht, *(fig.)* beschränkt, schwerfällig, verbohrt, *(photo)* gut belichtet;
too ~ überbelichtet;
~ **crowd** dichte Menschenmenge; ~ **fog** dichter Nebel; ~ **forest** undurchdringlicher Wald; ~ **ignorance** hoffnungslose Dummheit, Borniertheit; ~**minded** beschränkt, verbohrt; ~ **population** Bevölkerungsdichte; ~ **smoke** dichte Rauchwolke; ~ **texture** dichtes Gewebe.
densely | populated region dichtbevölkerte Gegend; ~ **crowded streets** Straßen voll von Menschen.
density Dichte, *(fig.)* Beschränktheit, Verbohrtheit, *(photo)* Schwärzung;
social ~ soziale Dichte; ~ **of circulation** Streudichte von Werbemedien; ~ **of development** Bebauungsdichte; ~ **of distribution of firms** Wirtschafts-, Betriebsdichte; ~ **of the fog** Nebeldichte, dichter Nebel; ~ **of a forest** Undurchdringlichkeit eines Waldes; ~ **of freight** beförderte Gütermenge; ~ **of passengers** Verkehrsdichte; ~ **of population** Bevölkerungsdichte; ~ **of traffic** Verkehrsdichte.
dent Beule, Delle;
~ **in earnings** Ertragseinbuße; ~ **in one's pride** Schlag gegen jds. Stolz;
~ *(v.)* **one's motor-car in a collision** sich beim Zusammenstoß eine Beule an seinem Auto holen;
to make a ~ **in one's fortune** *(fam.)* sein Vermögen angreifen; **to put a big** ~ **in the economy** Konjunkturkurve einbeulen.
dental | surgeon Zahnarzt; ~ **treatment** zahnärztliche Behandlung.
denuclearization Kernwaffenverbot.
denude *(v.)* entblößen, berauben.
denuded by his creditors of every penny he had von seinen Gläubigern um den letzten Pfennig gebracht.
denunciation Anzeige bei einer Behörde, *(treaty)* Kündigung;
subject to ~ kündbar;
~ **of the armistice** Kündigung des Waffenstillstands; ~ **of a traitor** Bloßstellung eines Verräters; ~ **of vengeance** Rachedrohungen.
denunciator Denunziant.
denunciating denunzierend.
denutrition Nahrungsentzug.
deny *(v.)* ab-, verleugnen, in Abrede stellen, verneinen, *(refuse)* verweigern, abschlagen;
~ **o. s.** Selbstverleugnung üben; ~ **s. one admission** jem. die Aufnahme versagen; ~ **admittance** Zutritt verwehren; ~ **an agreement** Vertrag nicht anerkennen; ~ **an assertion** Behauptung bestreiten; ~ **a charge** Beschuldigung leugnen; ~ **o. s. for one's children** zugunsten seiner Kinder verzichten; ~ **any knowledge of a plan** jegliche Kenntnis von einem Plan ab-

streiten; ~ **the invention level** *(patent law)* Erfindungshöhe bestreiten; ~ **liability** Haftung ablehnen; ~ **a motion** *(court)* Antrag abweisen; ~ **o. s. nothing** sich nichts abgehen lassen; ~ **a request** Gesuch ablehnen; ~ **one's signature** Rechtsgültigkeit seiner Unterschrift bestreiten; ~ **a statement** Erklärung dementieren, Behauptung bestreiten; ~ **that s. o. has any talent** jem. jegliche Begabung absprechen; ~ **s. th. to be true** etw. dementieren; ~ **visitors** Besucher abweisen.

deobligate *(v.)* *(governmental accounting)* Haushaltstitel auflösen.

deobligation *(governmental accounting)* Auflösung von Haushaltstiteln.

depart *(v.)* fortgehen, abreisen, -fahren, *(in pleading)* Klageabweichung vornehmen, vom Klagegegenstand abweichen, Klagebegründung ändern, *(ship)* gehen, *(train)* abgehen, abfahren;
~ **from** abweichen von, etw. aufgeben; ~ **from a custom** von einer Gewohnheit abgehen; ~ **from old customs** alte Bräuche aufgeben; ~ **from one's duty** seine Pflicht vernachlässigen, sich seiner Pflicht entziehen; ~ **from life** aus dem Leben scheiden; ~ **from one's plan** seinen Plan ändern; ~ **from one's reserve** aus seiner Reserve heraustreten; ~ **from one's subject** vom Thema abweichen.

departed Heimgegangener, Verstorbener;
~ *(a.)* tot, gestorben.

department *(administrative district)* Verwaltungsgebiet, *(governmental agency)* Dienst-, Geschäfts-, Regierungsstelle, *(branch of business)* Branche, Geschäftszweig, *(field)* Fach-, Arbeitsgebiet, Geschäftskreis, -zweig, *(ministry, US)* Ministerium, *(mil.)* Bereich, *(office)* Abteilung, Ressort, Dezernat, Referat, *(plant)* Betriebsabteilung, *(section)* Zweig;
accounting ~ Buchhaltung; **actuarial** ~ Abteilung für Versicherungsstatistik; **Agricultural** ≗ *(US)* Landwirtschaftsministerium; **appointments** ~ Personalabteilung; **banking** ~ Bankenabteilung; **bond** ~ *(US)* Abteilung für festverzinsliche Wertpapiere; **claim** ~ *(insurance company)* Schadensabteilung; **Commerce** ≗ *(US)* Wirtschaftsministerium; **commercial development** ~ Abteilung für Vertriebsplanung und Verkaufsförderung; **criminal investigation** ~ *(Br.)* Erkennungsdienst, Kriminalpolizei; **economic-policy** ~ wirtschaftspolitische Abteilung; **Education** ≗ *(Br.)* Erziehungsministerium; **engineering** ~ technische Abteilung; **built-in export** ~ eingegliederte Exportabteilung; **external** ~ Außenabteilung; **health** ~ Gesundheitsamt; **filing** ~ Registratur; **finance** ~ Finanzabteilung; **fire** ~ *(US)* Feuerwehr; **foreign** ~ Auslandsabteilung; **government** ~ *(Br.)* Ministerialabteilung, Ministerium; **initiating** ~ federführende Abteilung; **inspection** ~ *(life insurance)* Untersuchungsabteilung; **Interior** ≗ *(US)* Innenministerium; **[capital] issue** ~ Emissionsabteilung; **law (legal)** ~ Rechtsabteilung; **men's clothing** ~ Abteilung für Herrenbekleidung; **Navy** ≗ *(US)* Marineministerium; **operating** ~ Betriebsabteilung; **patent** ~ Patentabteilung; **payroll** ~ Lohnbüro; **personnel** ~ Personalabteilung; **Post Office** ≗ *(US)* Postministerium; **production** ~ Produktionsabteilung; **proper** ~ zuständige Dienststelle; **purchasing** ~ Einkaufsabteilung; **records** ~ Erkennungsdienst; **Revenue** ≗ *(Br.)* Finanzverwaltung; **sales** ~ Verkaufsabteilung; **sanitation** ~ Abteilung für sanitäre Einrichtungen; **shipping** ~ Versandabteilung; **State** ≗ *(US)* Ministerium des Äußeren, Auswärtiges Amt; **statistical** ~ statistische Abteilung; **technical** ~ Betriebsabteilung; **transit** ~ *(US)* Abteilung für Inkassi auswärtiger Plätze; **trust** ~ Abteilung für Vermögensverwaltungen, Treuhandabteilung; **watertight** ~ *(ship)* wasserdichte Abteilung;
≗ **of Agriculture** *(Ireland, US)* Landwirtschaftsministerium; ≗ **of the Air Force** *(US)* Luftwaffenministerium; ≗ **of the Army** *(US)* Heeresministerium; ≗ **of Commerce** *(US)* Handels-, Wirtschaftsministerium; ≗ **of National Defence** *(Canada)* Verteidigungsministerium; ≗ **of Defense** *(US)* Verteidigungsministerium; ≗ **of Economic Affairs** *(Br.)* Wirtschaftsministerium; ≗ **of Education** *(Br.)* Ministerium für Unterricht und Wissenschaft, Erziehungsministerium; ≗ **of Employment** *(Br.)* Arbeitsministerium; ≗ **of Energy** Energieministerium; ≗ **of Environment** *(Br.)* Ministerium für Umweltfragen; ≗ **of Environmental Conservation** *(US)* Ministerium für die Erhaltung der natürlichen Umwelt; ≗ **of Fish and Game** Fisch- und Wildbehörde; ≗ **of German** *(university)* deutschsprachige Abteilung; ≗ **of Health, Education and Welfare** *(US)* Gesundheits-, Erziehungs- und Wohlfahrtsministerium; ≗ **of Health and Social Security** *(Br.)* Gesundheits- und Sozialministerium; **surgical** ~ **of a hospital** chirurgische Abteilung eines Krankenhauses, Chirurgie; ≗ **of Industry** Industrieministerium; ≗ **of the**

Interior *(Canada, US)* Innenministerium; ≗ **of Justice** *(US)* Justizministerium; ≗ **of Labor** *(US)* Arbeitsministerium; ~ **of modern languages** neusprachliche Abteilung; ~ **of liberal arts** *(US)* philosophische Fakultät; ~ **of licensing affairs** Konzessionsabteilung; ≗ **for National Savings** *(Br.)* Postsparkassenbehörde; ≗ **of the Navy** *(US)* Marineministerium; ≗ **of Revenues** Finanzverwaltung; ≗ **of Social Security** *(Br.)* Sozialministerium; ≗ **of State** *(US)* Auswärtiges Amt, Außenministerium, Ministerium des Äußeren; ≗ **of Trade and Industry** *(Br.)* Handels- und Industrieministerium; ≗ **of Transport** *(Br.)* Verkehrsministerium; ≗ **of Transportation** *(US)* Verkehrsministerium; ≗ **of the Treasury** *(US)* Finanzministerium, Schatzamt; ~ **of war** *(US)* Kriegsministerium;
to comb out a ~ Regierungsstelle zwecks Einsparung gründlich durchforsten; **to solve a problem between the ~s concerned** Fragenkreis zusammen mit den zuständigen Abteilungen lösen;
~ **budget** Ministeriumsetat; ~ **head** *(US)* Abteilungsvorstand, -leiter, -chef, Dezernent, Minister; **assistant** ~ **head** stellvertretender Abteilungschef; ~ **hospital** Lazarett, Militärkrankenhaus; ~ **manager** Abteilungsleiter; ~ **official** Ministerialbeamter; ~ **store** *(US)* Warenhaus; ~ **store branch** *(US)* Warenhausfiliale; **~-store chain** *(US)* Warenhauskette; ~ **store group** *(US)* Warenhauskonzern; **~-store licence** *(US)* Gewerbelizenz für ein Warenhaus; **~-store sales** *(US)* Warenhausumsätze; **~-store shares** *(US)* Warenhausaktien; ~ **trial** *(US)* Disziplinarverfahren.

departmental abteilungsweise, *(state)* ministeriell;
~ **accounting** dezentralisiertes Rechnungswesen; ~ **administration** Ministerialverwaltung; ~ **budget** Abteilungsetat; ~ **burden** Stellengemeinkosten; ~ **buyer** Einkäufer [für ein Warenhaus]; ~ **charges** Einzelkosten einer Abteilung; ~ **chief** Abteilungsvorstand, -chef; ~ **classification** Aufgliederung nach Abteilungen; ~ **committee** interministerieller Ausschuß; ~ **duties** Abteilungsaufgaben; ~ **earnings** Einkünfte einer Behörde; ~ **function** Abteilungsaufgabe; ~ **gift** Abteilungsgeschenk; ~ **head** Abteilungsleiter, -chef; ~ **library** Abteilungsbibliothek; ~ **manager** Abteilungsleiter; ~ **markup** Branchenhandelsspanne; ~ **minister** Fach-, Ressortminister; ~ **officials** *(US)* Ministerialbeamte; ~ **order** *(US)* Ministerialerlaß; ~ **overheads** abteilungsweise aufgeschlüsselte Handlungsunkosten; ~ **personnel** Abteilungsangehörige, -personal; ~ **profit** abteilungsweise aufgeschlüsselter Gewinn; ~ **ranking** Berufswertung nach Abteilungen; ~ **record** Abteilungsbericht; ~ **regulations** ministerielle Ausführungsbestimmungen; ~ **spending** *(government)* Ministeriumsetat; ~ **store** *(Br.)* Warenhaus; **~-store bookselling** Warenhausbuchhandel.

departmentalization Dezentralisation, betriebliche Aufgliederung, Aufgliederung in Abteilungen.

departmentalize *(v.)* dezentralisieren, nach Betriebsabteilungen aufgliedern.

departure Weggang, Aufbruch, Ab-, Ausreise, *(airplane)* Abflug, *(abandonment)* Abweichung, Abwendung, Aufgeben, Aufgabe, *(mil.)* Abmarsch, Ausmarsch, Abrücken, *(train)* Abgang, Ab-, Ausfahrt;
maximum ~ höchstzulässige Normabweichung; **new** ~ Neuorientierung; **scheduled** ~ *(US)* [fahr]planmäßige Abfahrt;
~ **from an old custom** Aufgabe eines alten Brauches; ~ **from discipline** Bruch der Disziplin; ~ **from the law** Rechtsbeugung; **new** ~ **in physics** neue physikalische Entdeckung; ~ **from a principle** Abgang von einem Grundsatz, Aufgabe eines Prinzips; ~ **of trains** Zugabgänge, Abfahrt;
to accelerate one's ~ seine Abreise beschleunigen (vorverlegen); **to notify one's** ~ sich abmelden; **to take a** ~ *(mar.)* Schiffsort bei der Abfahrt bestimmen; **to take one's** ~ fortgehen, abreisen; **to take a new** ~ neues Verfahren anwenden;
~ **line** Abfahrtsgleis; ~ **lounge** Abflughalle; ~ **platform** Abgangs-, Abfahrtsbahnsteig; ~ **point** Abgangsort; ~ **station** Versand-, Abgangsbahnhof; ~ **time** *(airplane)* Abflugzeit; ~ **track** Ausfahrtsgleis.

depeculation Amtsunterschlagung.

depend *(v.)* abhängig (angewiesen) sein, abhängen, *(law suit)* noch unentschieden sein, schweben, in der Schwebe sein;
~ **on s. o.** sich auf j. verlassen; ~ **from the ceiling** an der Decke hängen; ~ **on circumstances** von den Umständen abhängen; ~ **on one's father** von seinem Vater finanziell abhängig sein; ~ **on foreign supplies** auf ausländische Lieferungen angewiesen sein; ~ **on a permission** genehmigungspflichtig sein, von einer Erlaubnis abhängen; ~ **on one's pen for a living** seinen Lebensunterhalt als Schriftsteller verdienen; ~ **on supply and demand** von Angebot und Nachfrage abhängen;

to have nothing to ~ upon kein Vermögen (nichts zum Leben) haben.

dependability Verläßlichkeit.

dependable zuverlässig, verläßlich.

dependant [Familien]angehöriger, Abhängiger, *(income tax)* Unterhaltsberechtigter;
surviving ~s Hinterbliebene;
~'s benefit *(Br.)* Hinterbliebenenrente; **~ relative** Familienangehöriger; **~ relative allowance** *(Br.)* Steuerfreibetrag für erwerbsunfähige Familienangehörige.

dependence *(body of dependants)* abhängige Familienangehörige, Abhängigkeit, Angewiesensein, *(law)* Ausstehen, Schwebe[zustand], *(reliance)* Vertrauen, Verlaß;
in ~ *(law suit)* noch unentschieden, in der Schwebe;
~ of the crop upon the weather Wetterabhängigkeit der Ernte; **~ on exports** Exportabhängigkeit; **~ upon one's parents** finanzielle Abhängigkeit von seinen Eltern; **~ on foreign trade** Exportabhängigkeit;
to end one's ~ upon one's parents sich von seinen Eltern finanziell unabhängig machen; **to live in ~** in Abhängigkeit leben; **to place ~ on s. one's word** Vertrauen in jds. Worte setzen.

dependencies Nebengebäude, *(assets likely to accrue, Br.)* voraussichtliche Einnahmen, Zuwächse;
~ of an estate angrenzende Ländereien.

dependency Abhängigkeit, *(annex to hotel)* Nebengebäude, Dependenz, *(pol.)* abhängiges Gebiet, Schutzgebiet, Protektorat;
total ~ vollständige Abhängigkeit;
~ of an estate Grundstückzubehör;
~ allowance Kinderbeihilfe; **~ benefit** *(Br.)* Leistung an Unterhaltsberechtigte; **~ bonus** Kinderzulage; **~ exemption** *(US)* Steuerfreibetrag für Familienangehörige; **~ need** Abhängigkeitsbedürfnis.

dependent unselbständig, abhängig, *(law)* noch nicht entschieden, in der Schwebe;
~ upon friends auf die Hilfe (Unterstützung) von Freunden angewiesen; **~ upon success** erfolgsbetont, -abhängig;
to be ~ on alms auf Unterstützung angewiesen sein; **to be financially ~ on s. o.** finanziell von jem. abhängig sein; **to be ~ on one's son's earnings** auf die Unterstützung seines Sohnes angewiesen sein;
in a ~ capacity unselbständig; **~ child** unversorgtes Kind; **~ condition** Abhängigkeitsverhältnis; **~ contract** abhängiger Vertrag; **~ covenant** abhängige Verpflichtung; **~ personal service** *(double taxation agreement)* unselbständige Arbeit; **~ promise** von vertraglich ausbedungenen Vorleistungen abhängiges Versprechen; **~ relationship** Abhängigkeitsverhältnis; **~ relative revocation** Auslegungsgrundsätze bei Testamentsnachträgen; **~ state** Vasallenstaat; **~ territory** Schutzgebiet.

depict *(v.)* schildern, anschaulich ausstellen.

depiction anschauliche Darstellung, Schilderung.

deplane *(v.)* [Flugzeug] entladen.

deplano widerspruchslos, *(law)* außergerichtlich.

deplaning *(airplane)* Entladung.

depletable *(accounting)* dem Substanzverkehr unterworfen.

deplete *(v.) (stores)* erschöpfen, ausbeuten, *(taxation)* abschreiben;
~ a garrison of troops Garnison von Truppen entblößen; **~ the treasury** Staatskasse erschöpfen.

depleted | cost Kostenrückstand nach Abzug der Substanzverringerung; **~ gas-bag** leere Gasflasche.

depletion *(assets)* substantielle Abnutzung, Substanzverringerung, -verlust, -verzehr, *(stores)* Erschöpfung, Ausbeutung, *(US, taxation)* Abschreibung;
accrued ~ entstandene Substanzverringerung;
~ of an army Ausblutung einer Armee; **~ of capital** Kapitalentblößung; **~ of inventories** Lagerabbau; **~ of resources** Erschöpfung der natürlichen Hilfsquellen;
to slow the down ~ of resources Substanzvernichtung von Bodenschätzen verlangsamen;
~ allowance (charges, expenses) Abschreibung für Substanzverringerung.

deplorable accident bedauernswerter Unfall.

deploy *(v.) (mil.)* sich entfalten, Gefechtsformation einnehmen, bereitstellen, *(nuclear weapon)* stationieren;
~ labo(u)r Arbeitskräfte einsetzen.

deployment *(mil.)* Entfaltung, Bereitstellung, *(nuclear weapon)* Stationierung;
~ in depth *(mil.)* Tiefengliederung; **~ of labo(u)r** Arbeitskräfteeinsatz;
rapid ~ force strategische Eingreifreserve.

depoliticization Entpolitisierung.

depoliticize *(v.)* entpolitisieren.

depone *(v.) (Scot.)* schriftliche Aussage unter Eid machen.

deponent Abgeber einer eidesstattlichen Erklärung, Aussagender.

depopulate *(v.)* entvölkern, aussiedeln, veröden.

depopulation Entvölkerung, Aussiedlung.

deport *(v.)* deportieren, verschicken, verschleppen, zwangsverschicken, *(aliens)* Ausländer ausweisen (abschieben);
~ o. s. with dignity Würde zur Schau stellen, würdig auftreten.

deportation Zwangsverschickung, Verschleppung, Deportation, *(alien)* Landesverweisung, Ausweisung, Abschiebung;
mass ~ Massendeportierung;
~ of an undesirable alien Abschiebung eines unerwünschten Ausländers;
~ order Ausweisungsbeschluß.

deportee Deportierter, Ausgewiesener, Abgeschobener.

deportment Benehmen, Betragen, Umgangsformen, Haltung.

deposable absetzbar.

deposal Absetzung.

depose *(v.)* aussagen, Aussage machen, zu Protokoll geben, *(monarchy)* absetzen, entthronen, *(say under oath)* eidlich bezeugen, unter Eid aussagen;
~ from office eines Amtes entsetzen, absetzen.

deposer [vereidigter] Zeuge.

deposit *(in bank)* eingezahltes Geld, Bankeinlage, [Geld]einlage, Bankeinlage, Einzahlung, *(first instalment)* Anzahlung, *(forfeit money)* Angeld, Hand-, Draufgeld, *(geology)* Lagerstätte, *(giving in trust)* Hinterlegung[svertrag], Deponierung, Depot, Aufbewahrung, Verwahrung, Verwahrungsvertrag, *(insurance company)* Hinterlegungssumme, Depot, Kaution, *(money lodged)* Gelddepot, *(pledge)* [Unter]pfand, *(storing)* Einlagerung;
for ~s only nur zur Sicherheit, nur für Depotzwecke; **kept on ~** im Depot verwahrt, depotverwahrt; **on ~** in Verwahrung, als Depot; **subject to the ~ of collateral security consisting of first-rate stocks** *(US)* gegen Hinterlegung erstklassiger Aktien; **~s** Einlagenbestand, *(Br.)* Spareinlagen, *(securities)* Lombardbestände;
authorized ~ Ermächtigungsdepot; **bank ~** Bankeinlage, Depositenguthaben, Giralgeld; **bankers' ~s** Bankeinlagen; **blocked ~** gesperrtes Depot; **call ~s** jederzeit abrufbare Einlagen, Sichteinlagen; **cash ~** Geldhinterlegung, Bardepot; **clearing-bank ~s** Giroeinlagen; **collective ~** Sammeldepot; **commercial ~** Firmendepot; **conventional ~** vertraglich vereinbarte Hinterlegung; **current ~** Kontokorrenteinlage, täglich fälliges Guthaben, *(bank balance)* Einlagen auf gebührenfreier Rechnung; **demand ~s** *(US)* laufende Konten, Einlagen auf Sicht, Sichteinlagen, täglich fällige (kurzfristige) Einlagen, täglich fälliges Geld; **adjusted demand ~s** *(Br.)* abgewickelte (ausgeglichene) Tagesgelder; **demand ~ subject to check** *(US)* per Scheck verfügbare Einlagen; **derivative ~** Lombarddepot; **fixed [-term] ~s** Termin-, Fest-, Kündigungsgeld, Einlage mit fester Laufzeit, Einlage auf Depositenkonto; **foreign ~s** Guthaben im Ausland; **frozen ~** *(US)* gesperrtes Depot; **general ~** Depot unter Streifband, Sammelverwahrung; **government ~s** Guthaben staatlicher Stellen; **gratuitous ~** unentgeltliche Verwahrung; **individual ~s** nicht von Banken unterhaltene Guthaben; **interbank ~s** gegenseitige Bankguthaben; **intercompany ~s** *(balance sheet)* Buchforderung gegen andere; **interest-bearing ~** verzinsliche Bankeinlage; **involuntary ~** gesetzliches Verwahrungsverhältnis; **irregular ~** Summenverwahrung; **joint ~** gemeinschaftlich (oder einzeln) verfügbares Depot; **judicial ~** gerichtlich angeordnete Verwahrung; **long-term ~** langfristige Einlage, Depositen mit Kündigungsfrist, Termineinlagen; **major ~** Hauptlagerstätte; **naked ~** unentgeltlicher Verwahrungsvertrag; **necessary ~** durch Geschäftsführung ohne Auftrag notwendiges Verwahrungsverhältnis; **omnibus ~** Sammeldepot; **open ~** offenes Depot; **other ~s** Privatdepositen; **packed ~** verschlossenes Depot; **pension ~s** Einzahlungen in die Pensionskasse; **primary ~s** *(US)* durch effektive Einlagen geschaffene Depositen, effektive Einlagen; **private ~** privates Guthaben; **public ~s** Guthaben der öffentlichen Hand, *(Br.)* Guthaben der Bank von England; **quasi ~** verwahrungsähnliches Verhältnis; **regular ~** Einzelverwahrung, Depot; **safe ~** Aufbewahrung in Stahlkammern, Tresor, Stahlkammer; **savings ~** Spareinlage; **savings-bank ~** Sparkassenguthaben; **securities ~** Wertpapier-, Effektendepot; **short-term ~** kurzfristige Einlage; **sight ~s** Sichteinlagen; **special ~** *(US)* Einzelverwahrung, -depot, *(banking, Br.)* Mindestreserven; **stock ~** Effektendepot; **three-months ~** Dreimonatsgeld; **thrift**

~ *(US)* Sparguthaben; **time** ~ *(US)* Festgeld, langfristige Einlage, Kündigungsgeld, mit Kündigungsfrist angelegtes Geld, befristete Depositengelder, Termingelder; **total ~s** Gesamteinzahlungen; **trust** ~ Treuhänder-, Anderdepot; **unclaimed ~s** nicht in Anspruch genommene Depositen; **uninsured** ~ unversicherte Einlage; **unrecorded ~s** nicht belegte Einzahlungen; **vault** ~ verschlossenes Depot; **voluntary** ~ vereinbarte Hinterlegung;

~ **at call** *(Br.)* Sichteinlage; ~ **in a bank** Bank-, Depositenguthaben, Bankdepot; **~s with the central bank** bei der Zentralnotenbank unterhaltene Guthaben; **special ~s with the Bank of England** [etwa] vorgeschriebene Mindestreserven; ~ **of bills** Wechseldepot; **~s with building societies** Bausparguthaben; ~ **at call** *(Br.)* Sichteinlage; **~s for collection** Depositen zur Einziehung; ~ **subject to contract** bei Nichtabschluß des Kaufvertrages rückzahlbare Anzahlung; **~s on current account** Kontokorrent-, Sichteinlagen, täglich fällige Einlagen, Giroeinlagen; **~s by customers** *(balance sheet)* Guthaben auf Kontokorrentkonto, fremde Gelder, Fremdgelder; **~s on deposit account** Festgeldeinlagen, langfristige Einlagen; **~s and drawings** Einzahlungen und Abhebungen; ~ **of gold** Goldlager, -vorkommen; ~ **of the land certificate** *(Br.)* Hinterlegung des Grundschuldbriefes; ~ **on lease** Depot zu vermieten; ~ **of money** Gelddepot, -hinterlegung; **~s with maturity of six months** Einlagen mit sechsmonatlicher Laufzeit; **~s at long notice** langfristige Einlagen; ~ **at seven days' notice** mit siebentägiger Kündigung fällige Einlagen; **~s at short notice** kurzfristige Einlagen, Kündigungsgelder, Einlagen mit Kündigungsfrist, Termineinlagen, kurzfristige Depositen; ~ **for a fixed period** Einlage auf feste Kündigung, Depositeneinlage; ~ **at post office** Postscheckguthaben; ~ **of proxies** Hinterlegung von Stimmrechtsermächtigungen; ~ **in a savings account (bank)** Spareinlage; ~ **of securities** Wertpapierdeponierung, Effektendepot; ~ **of shares** Aktienhinterlegung; **~s with suppliers** geleistete Anzahlungen; ~ **of title deeds** Hinterlegung von Besitzurkunden, Eigentumsurkunden; **~s in transit** Durchlaufposten, transitorische Guthaben; ~ **with a trustee savings bank** Sparkassenguthaben;

~ *(v.) (goods)* deponieren, hinterlegen, in Verwahrung (ins Depot) geben, *(money)* einzahlen, Einzahlung leisten; ~ **an amount** Betrag hinterlegen; ~ **articles for safe custody** Gegenstände ins Depot einliefern; ~ **with the Bank of England** [etwa] Mindestreserven bei der Bundesnotenbank unterhalten; ~ **s. th. with s. o.** jem. etw. zu verwahren (zur Verwahrung) geben; ~ **documents with a bank** einer Bank Urkunden zur Aufbewahrung übergeben; ~ **in court** bei Gericht hinterlegen; ~ **the duty [repayable]** Zollgarantie leisten; ~ **duty copies of a book** Pflichtexemplare bei den Bibliotheken abliefern; ~ **irrevocably** unwiderruflich hinterlegen; ~ **money with s. o.** Geld bei jem. hinterlegen; ~ **money with a bank** Geld bei einer Bank deponieren; ~ **papers with one's lawyer** Urkunden seinem Anwalt übergeben; ~ **in the post office** zur Post geben; ~ **a quarter of the price of the house** Viertel des Hauswertes anzahlen; ~ **securities** Wertpapiere hinterlegen; ~ **as underlying security** zur Sicherheit hinterlegen; ~ **securities for safe custody** *(Br.)* **(custodianship,** *US)* Wertpapiere ins Depot einliefern; ~ **a will** Testament hinterlegen;

to accept ~s Einlagen entgegennehmen; **to fix a ~ for 30 days notice** Guthaben auf einen Monat fest anlegen; **to increase the special ~s with the Bank of England** Mindestreserven erhöhen; **to leave a ~** Betrag für etw. deponieren (hinterlegen); **to leave DM 100,- as ~** 100,- DM anzahlen; **to maintain ~s with the reserve bank in a special account** *(US)* Mindestreserven unterhalten; **to make a ~** *(US)* Pfand hinterlegen, *(banking, Br.)* Einlage machen, Einzahlung leisten, *(US)* Anzahlung leisten, anzahlen; **to make special ~s with the Bank of England** Mindestreserven bei der Bank von England erhöhen; **to pay a ~** *(Br.)* Anzahlung (Einzahlung) leisten, anzahlen, *(guarantee)* Kaution leisten (stellen); **to pay an amount as ~** *(Br.)* Anzahlung leisten, Betrag anzahlen; **to pay a ~ on goods** Anzahlung für eine Lieferung leisten; **to place s. th. on ~** etw. ins Depot geben; **to place securities into a ~** *(US)* Wertpapiere ins Depot einliefern; **to release special ~s** Mindestreservevorschriften lockern; **to restore their special ~s with the Bank of England** [etwa] Mindestreserve bei der Bundesnotenbank wiederauffüllen; **to take ~s from the general public** öffentliche Einlagen entgegennehmen; **to take title to the ~** Eigentumsrecht an einem Depot erwerben;

~ **account** *(US)* Einlagenkonto, Guthaben[konto], Depositenkonto, festangelegtes Geld, Festgeldkonto, Termineinlagen, *(savings account, Br.)* Sparkonto, *(bailment)* Hinterlegungskonto; **ordinary** ~ **account with the National Savings Bank** *(Br.)* Sparkassenbuchkonto; **to have a** ~ **account with the Federal Reserve Bank** *(US)* Mindestreserven bei der Landeszentralbank unterhalten; ~ **administration** *(pension plan)* Verwaltung des Fondsvermögens; ~ **administration pension** Gruppenrentenversicherungssystem; ~ **balance** Guthabensaldo, -konto; ~ **bank** Giro-, Depositenkonto; ~ **banking** Depositengeschäft; ~ **book** *(National Savings Bank, Br.)* Postsparbuch; **safe** ~ **box** Schließfach; ~ **business** Depotgeschäft, *(loan bank)* Lombardgeschäft; ~ **capital** Einlagekapital; ~ **certificate** Hinterlegungsschein, Festgeldbescheinigung, -quittung, Depositenschein; ~ **company** Stahlfachverwahrungsgesellschaft, *(Br., investment company)* Depotbank, Hinterlegungsstelle; ~ **copy** Belegexemplar für öffentliche Bibliotheken; ~ **currency** *(US coll.)* Giral-, Buchgeld, bargeldlose Zahlungsmittel; ~ **department (division)** Depositenabteilung; ~ **function** *(banking)* Passivgeschäft; ~ **growth** Depositenzunahme; ~ **holdings** Depotbestand; ~ **insurance** Depotversicherung; ~ **items** Depositenposten; ~ **ledger** *(Br.)* Depotbuch; ~ **liabilities** Kontokorrentverpflichtungen; ~ **line** durchschnittlicher Kreditsaldo; ~ **list** *(US)* Effektenverzeichnis, Depotverzeichnis, *(checks)* Fälligkeitsliste für Schecks; ~ **money** Depositen[gelder], Giral-, Buchgeld; ~ **passbook** *(Br.)* Sparkassenbuch; ~ **policy** Einlagenpolitik; ~ **premium company** Gegenseitigkeitsverein mit gleich hohen Prämiensätzen; ~ **rate** Habenzinssatz, Depositenzinsen; **special** ~**s ratio** *(Br.)* Mindestreservesatz; ~ **receipt** Hinterlegungs-, Eingangsquittung, Einzahlungsbeleg, Depotquittung, -schein; ~ **records** Depotunterlagen; ~ **register** *(Br.)* Register über alle für Einzahlungen auf Depositenkonten ausgegebene Quittungen; **special** ~**s requirements** *(Br.)* Mindestreservebestimmungen; ~ **slip** *(US)* Einzahlungsquittung, -beleg, -schein, Depotschein, -bescheinigung, -quittung; ~ **society** *(Br.)* Sparergenossenschaft, Depositenkasse; **special** ~**s system** *(Br.)* Mindestreservesystem; **bank** ~ **tax** *(US)* Depotsteuer; ~ **ticket** *(US)* Einzahlungsbeleg, -schein; ~ **warrant** Depotschein, Hinterlegungsschein.

depositary Hinterlegungsstelle, *(bailee)* Verwahrer; **authorized** ~ *(US)* Devisenbank, -händler; **limited** ~ *(US)* Depotbank mit Beschränkungen bei der Depotannahme; ~ **bank** Depotbank, verwahrende Bank; ~ **certificate** Einzahlungs-, Hinterlegungsbeleg; ~ **state** Verwahrerstaat.

depositation Hinterlegung, Deponierung.

deposited|bill Depotwechsel; ~ **funds** Depositen[kapital]; ~ **share** *(Br.)* **(stock,** *US)* hinterlegte Aktie.

depositee Verwahrer.

depositing, on ~ **of** gegen Hinterlegung von; ~ **of baggage** *(US)* **(luggage,** *Br.)* Gepäckabgabe; ~ **of coupons** Hereingabe von Kupons; ~ **of documents** Urkundenhinterlegung; ~ **business** Depotgeschäft.

deposition *(bailment)* Hinterlegung[svertrag], Aufbewahrung, *(evidence)* beglaubigte schriftliche Zeugenaussage, *(monarch)* Entthronisierung, Absetzung, *(on oath)* eidliche Zeugenaussage, *(official)* Amtsenthebung, Absetzung; ~ **de bene esse** Verlesung einer schriftlichen Zeugenaussage im Gericht; **to make a** ~ Aussage machen; **to make a** ~ **on oath** Aussage eidlich erhärten; **to place a** ~ **on the court records** Zeugenaussage zu Protokoll nehmen; **to take ~s** eidliche Aussagen zu Protokoll nehmen.

depositor Hinterleger, Einzahler, Einleger, Einlagerer, Konto-, Depositeninhaber; **checking-account** ~ Kontokorrentkunde; **savings-bank** ~ Spareinleger, Sparbuchbesitzer; ~ **of a bank** Bankkunde; ~**'s book** Einlagebuch; ~**'s custody** Effekten-, Wertpapierdepot; ~**'s ledger** Depositenkonto.

depository Aufbewahrungs-, Verwahrungsort, Hinterlegungsstelle, Niederlage, Depot, *(bank, US)* Hinterlegungsstelle für Staatsgelder, öffentliches Geldinstitut, *(depositary)* Verwahrer, *(furniture)* [Möbel]speicher, *(goods)* Lagerhaus, Stapelplatz, Magazin, *(records)* Registratur; **authorized** ~ *(Br.)* staatlich anerkannte Hinterlegungsstelle, Hinterlegungsstelle für Devisenwerte; **night** ~ Nachttresor; ~ **for goods** Warenniederlage, Lagerhaus; ~ **for records** Registratur, Archiv; ~ **bank** *(US)* öffentliches Geldinstitut; ~ **bond** Depotgarantie; ~ **institution** *(US)* öffentliches Geldinstitut; ᴼ **Institutions Deregulation and Monetary Control Act** *(US)* Gesetz über den freien Wettbewerb zwischen Banken, Sparkassen und Kreditgenossenschaften; ~ **stores** Warendepot.

depot Aufbewahrungsort, -raum, *(railroad station, US)* Bahnhof, *(stores)* Lager[haus], -platz, Magazin, Speicher, Niederlage;
advance ~ *(mil.)* vorgeschobenes Versorgungs-, Verpflegungslager; **base ~** *(mil.)* Etappenlager; **branch ~** *(mil.)* Nebenlager; **coal ~** Kohlenniederlage; **freight ~** *(US)* Güterbahnhof; **fuel-oil ~** Treibstoff-, Kraftstofflager; **furniture ~** [Möbel]speicher, -magazin; **general ~** *(mil.)* Nachschublager; **goods ~** *(US)* Güterbahnhof; **grain ~** Getreidelager; **intermediate ~** *(mil.)* Zwischenlager; **shunting ~** Auswahllager; **storage ~** Lagerhaus; **timber ~** Holzlager; **tramway ~** Straßenbahndepot;
~ for spares Ersatzteillager;
~ bookstore Depotbuchhandlung; **~ extra discount** *(book trade)* Depotrabattzuschlag; **~ grounds** *(US)* Bahnhofsgelände; **~ institution** Geldinstitut; **~ ship** Versorgungsschiff; **~ waggon** *(US)* kleiner Gepäckkarren.

depravation Entartung, Sittenlosigkeit, Verworrenheit;
~ of morals Verfall der Moral.

deprave *(v.)* demoralisieren;
~ the coinage Währung verschlechtern.

depravity Verderbtheit, Verdorbenheit, Verworfenheit.

deprecate *(v.)* ablehnen, mißbilligen, verwerfen;
~ a scheme gegen ein Vorhaben sein.

deprecation Mißbilligung.

depreciable abschreibungsfähig, -pflichtig, abschreibbar;
~ amount Abschreibungsbetrag; **~ asset life** abschreibungsfähige Nutzungsdauer; **~ cost** abschreibbare Kosten, Abschreibungskosten; **~ property** *(US)* abschreibungsfähige Vermögenswerte; **~ value** Abschreibungsgrundwert.

depreciate *(v.)* geringschätzen, verachten, heruntersetzen, heruntermachen, *(currency)* ab-, entwerten, devaluieren, *(decline)* im Wert (Preis) sinken (fallen), *(reduce in price, value)* im Preis (Wert) herabsetzen, *(underrate)* unterschätzen, -bewerten, *(write off)* abschreiben;
~ fixed assets Anlagevermögen abschreiben; **~ faster** *(balancing)* schneller abschreiben; **~ a machine by 15 per cent** 15% des Maschinenwerts abschreiben; **~ a new machine over a shorter period** neugekaufte Maschine beschleunigt abschreiben; **~ the pound** Pfund abwerten; **~ for tax purposes** steuerlich anerkannte Abschreibungen vornehmen; **~ in value** im Preis fallen.

depreciated | cost Restbuchwert; **~ currency** notleidende Währung; **~ value** Abschreibungsrestwert;
to be fully (partly) ~ ganz (teilweise) abgeschrieben sein.

depreciating currency sich entwertende Währung.

depreciation Wertminderung, -verlust, Entwertung, *(foreign exchange)* Kursrückgang, -verlust, *(~ procedure)* Abschreibungsverfahren, *(provision for ~ in balance sheet)* Abschreibung[srückstellung], *(reduction in price)* Preisherabsetzung, *(underrating)* Unterbewertung, *(writing off)* Abschreibung;
liable to ~ abschreibungsfähig;
accelerated ~ [steuerbegünstigte] beschleunigte (vorzeitige) Abschreibung; **accrued ~** Wertminderungsrückstellung; **accumulated ~** Wertberichtigung für Abnutzung; **annual ~** *(Br.)* jährliche Abschreibung auf das Anlagevermögen; **balance-sheet ~** bilanzmäßig anerkannte Abschreibungen; **capital ~** Kapitalentwertung, -verzehr; **declining-balance ~** degressive Abschreibung; **deducted ~** Wertminderungsabschlag; **excessive ~** übermäßige Abschreibung; **extraordinary ~** Sonderabschreibung; **faster capital goods ~** schnellere Abschreibungsmöglichkeit für Anlagegüter; **fixed ~** feststehender Abschreibungssatz; **functional ~s** Abschreibungen auf Rationalisierungsinvestitionen; **historic ~** angefallene Abschreibungsbeträge; **maximum ~** höchstmöglicher Abschreibungssatz; **normal (ordinary) ~** Normalabschreibung; **physical ~** aufgrund natürlicher Abnutzung erforderliche Abschreibung, Gebrauchsabschreibung, tatsächliche Entwertung; **rapid ~** Schnellabschreibung; **real-estate ~** Grundstücksabschreibung; **special ~** Sonderabschreibung; **straight-line ~** lineare Abschreibung; **tax ~** steuerlich anerkannte Abschreibung; **theoretical ~** buchmäßige Abschreibung; **trade-weighted average ~** *(currency agreement)* durchschnittlicher Kursverlust gewichtet nach dem Handelsvolumen; **value ~** Wertverminderung, -verlust;
~ for age altersbedingte Abschreibung; **~ on fixed assets** Abschreibungen auf das Anlagevermögen, Anlagenabschreibung; **~ on tangible assets** Abschreibungen auf Sachanlagen; **~ of buildings** [Abschreibung für] Gebäudeabnutzung, Gebäudeabschreibung; **~ of capital** Kapitalverzehr, -entwertung; **~ of coin** Devalvation; **~ of currency** Abwertung der Währung, Geldentwertung; **~ of industrial equipment** Abschreibung auf Betriebsanlagen, Anlagenabschreibung; **~ on investments** Abschreibungen auf das Anlagevermögen (auf Beteiligungen); **~ on land** Grundstücksabschreibung; **~ of machinery** Abschreibungen auf den Maschinenpark; **~ of money** Geldwertminderung; **~ on office furniture and equipment** Abschreibung auf die Betriebs- und Geschäftsausstattung; **~ according to plan** ordentliche Abschreibungen; **~ on plant** Abschreibung der Betriebsanlagen; **~ of premises** Grundstücksabschreibung; **~ of property owned** Grundstücksabschreibung; **~ on replacement value** Abschreibung vom Wiederbeschaffungswert; **~ in value** Wertverringerungsverlust; **~ for wear and tear** *(Br.)* Abschreibung für Abnutzung, Gebrauchsabschreibung;
to accelerate ~ steuerbegünstigt vorzeitig abschreiben; **to allocate ~** Abschreibungen zeitlich verteilen; **to allocate total ~ to replace plant and other assets** alle Abschreibungsvergünstigungen zur Erneuerung des Anlagenparks einsetzen; **to allow for ~** für Abschreibungen zurückstellen; **to allow for ~ of office furniture** für Büroeinrichtungen abschreiben; **to be vulnerable to ~** auf Abschreibungsmöglichkeiten stark reagieren; **to charge ~s** Abschreibungen vornehmen, Abschreibungsbeträge absetzen; **to charge ~ of equipment onto costs** Abschreibungen auf die Preise abwälzen; **to earn one's ~** seine Abschreibungen verdienen; **to interrupt ~** Abschreibung aussetzen; **to loosen rules on ~** Abschreibungsmodalitäten lockern; **to mark down 10 per cent for ~** 10% abschreiben; **to spread one's ~ over several years** seine Abschreibungen steuerlich über mehrere Jahre verteilen; **to suffer a ~** Wertminderung erfahren; **to take the maximum ~ allowable for tax purposes** höchste steuerlich zugelassene Abschreibungssätze in Anspruch nehmen;
~ account Konto Abschreibungen, Abschreibungskonto; **accrued ~ account** Abschreibungsrücklagenkonto; **capital ~ account** Kapitalentwertungskonto; **~ accounting** Abschreibungsbuchung, systematisch durchgeführtes Abschreibungsverfahren; **~ accruals** entstandene Abschreibung; **~ adjustment** Abschreibungsausgleich; **~ allowance** Abschreibungsmöglichkeit, -betrag, Entwertungsrücklage; **~ base (basis)** Abschreibungsobjekt; **~ benefit** Abschreibungsvorteil; **~ breaks** *(US)* Abschreibungsvergünstigungen; **~ changes** Änderungen in den Abschreibungsrichtlinien; **~ charge** Abschreibungssatz, -betrag; **~ charges** Abschreibungsbetrag, -kosten; **to compute the annual ~ charge** jährlichen Abschreibungssatz berechnen; **~ clause** Entwertungsklausel; **~ date** Abschreibungsstichtag; **~ expense** Abschreibungsaufwand; **~ expense computation** Abschreibungsberechnung; **~ date** Abschreibungsstichtag; **~ facilities** Abschreibungserleichterungen; **~ factors** Abschreibungsfaktoren; **~ formula** Abschreibungsformel; **~ fund** Rücklage für Abschreibungen; **real-estate ~ fund** Grundbesitzentwertungsfonds; **~ guidelines** Abschreibungsrichtlinien; **~ method** Abschreibungsmethode; **combined ~ and upkeep method** Abschreibungs- und Erhaltungsmethode; **~ period** Abschreibungszeitraum; **~ policies** Abschreibungspolitik; **~ practice** Abschreibungspraxis; **~ procedure** Abschreibungsverfahren; **~ provisions** steuerliche Abschreibungsregeln; **~ rate** Abschreibungssatz, -quote, Entwertungssatz; **~ reform** Reform der Abschreibungsrichtlinien; **~ reserve** Rückstellung für Abschreibungen, Wertminderungsrücklage; **~ reserve account** Konto für Abschreibungsrücklagen; **~ rules** Abschreibungsrichtlinien; **~ schedule** Abschreibungssystem; **~ tax policy** steuerliche Abschreibungspolitik; **~ unit** Bewertungsgruppe;
declining balance method of ~ degressive Abschreibungsmethode; **fixed percentage method of ~** gleichmäßige Abschreibungsmethode vom Buchwert; **[in]direct method of ~** [in]direkte Abschreibungsmethode; **output method of calculating ~** *(US)* Abschreibungsmethode nach Gewinn und Rentabilität, auf dem Umfang der Anlagenausnutzung beruhende Abschreibungsmethode; **reducing-fraction method of calculating ~** *(US)* Abschreibungsmethode vom Anschaffungswert mit fallenden Quoten; **service output ~ method** Abschreibungsmethode auf der Basis der erbrachten Leistungen; **sinking-fund method of calculating ~** *(US)* Abschreibungsmethode mit steigenden Quoten; **straight-line method of calculating ~** *(US)* Abschreibungsmethode mit gleichmäßigen Quoten; **time-method of calculating ~** *(US)* Abschreibungsmethode nach Quoten.

depreciatory geringschätzig, verächtlich.

depredation Raubzug, Überfall.

depress *(v.)* *(cast gloom upon)* entmutigen, deprimieren, [Stimmung] drücken, *(performance)* mindern, abschwächen, *(price)* [herab]drücken, herabsetzen, senken, vermindern, *(trade)* niederdrücken, abflauen lassen;

~ **the market** Kurse drücken; ~ **news** Nachrichten unterdrücken; ~ **the pedal** Gaspedal durchdrücken.

depressed *(market)* flau, gedrückt, abgeschirmt, matt, mißgestimmt, *(price)* herabgesetzt, gesenkt, ermäßigt;
financially ~ finanziell schlecht gestellt;
to be ~ *(market)* darniederliegen, gedrückt (abgeschwächt) sein; **to be easily** ~ leicht gedrückter Stimmung (depressiv veranlagt) sein;
~ **area** *(Br.)* Notstandsgebiet; **semi-permanently** ~ **area** nahezu ständiges Notstandsgebiet; **~-area aid** *(Br.)* Notstandshilfe; ~ **classes** *(Br.)* Parias, unterdrückte Bevölkerungsschichten; ~ **industries** von der Krise betroffene Gewerbezweige; ~ **roadway** eingesunkene Straße; ~ **spirits** gedrückte Stimmung; ~ **state** *(stock exchange)* gedrückte Stimmung.

depressing news deprimierende (niederziehende) Nachrichten.

depression *(prices)* Fallen, Sinken, [Preis]senkung, *(spirits)* Niedergeschlagenheit Depression, Bedrücktheit, *(stock exchange)* Abschwächung, Baisse, *(trade)* Depression, Gedrücktsein, tiefe Wirtschaftskrise, Flaute, Geschäftsstille, Tiefstand, Konjunkturtief, *(weather)* Tief[druckgebiet], Zyklon;
business ~ Wirtschaftskrise; **cyclical** ~ Konjunkturtief; **economic** ~ Wirtschaftskrise; **great (world-wide)** ~ Weltwirtschaftskrise; **nervous** ~ nervöse Depression;
~ **in agriculture** Landwirtschaftskrise; ~ **of the market** Preisdruck, Baissestimmung; **full** ~ **of the pedal** Durchdrücken des Gaspedals; ~ **of prices** Kurs-, Preiseinbruch; ~ **in a road** Straßensenkung; ~ **of trade** Darniederliegen des Handels, Wirtschaftsrückgang;
to be deep in ~ von den Auswirkungen der Wirtschaftskrise besonders betroffen sein; **to commit suicide during a fit of** ~ sich in einem Schwermutsanfall das Leben nehmen; **to find s. o. in a state of deep** ~ j. völlig niedergedrückt antreffen; **to hide from the enemy in a slight** ~ sich vor dem Feind in einer flachen Mulde verbergen; **to show a** ~ Konjunkturrückgang erfahren;
~ **era** *(US)* Depressions-, Krisenzeit; ~ **level** Konjunkturtief; ~ **low** Konjunkturmulde; **pre-~ model** Vorkrisenmodell; ~ **period** Depressionsphase; **~-proof** krisensicher; ~ **time** Depressionsphase, rückläufige Konjunkturphase; ~ **year** schlechtes Geschäftsjahr.

deprivation *(bereaving)* Beraubung, Entziehung, Entzug, *(depositing)* Enthebung, Aberkennung, *(loss)* empfindlicher Verlust;
~ **of benefice** *(Br.)* Amtsenthebung eines Geistlichen; ~ **of citizenship** Aberkennung der Staatsbürgerschaft, Ausbürgerung; ~ **of health** Beeinträchtigung der Gesundheit; ~ **of office** Amtsenthebung; ~ **of a pension** Aberkennung des Ruhegehaltes; ~ **of civil rights** Aberkennung der bürgerlichen Ehrenrechte; ~ **of constitutional rights** *(US)* Entziehung verfassungsmäßig zustehender Rechte.

deprive *(v.)* entziehen, berauben, *(dispossess)* Besitz entziehen;
~ **s. o. of his citizenship** jem. die Staatsangehörigkeit aberkennen, j. ausbürgern; ~ **s. o. of his eyesight** j. seines Augenlichts berauben; ~ **s. o. of food** jem. Nahrungsmittel vorenthalten; ~ **s. o. of his office** j. seines Amtes entheben; ~ **s. o. of his pension** jem. das Ruhegehalt aberkennen; ~ **s. o. of a week's pay** jem. seinen Wochenlohn vorenthalten; ~ **of power** entmachten; ~ **of a right** entrechten; ~ **of civil rights** Ehrenrechte aberkennen.

deprived children elternlose Kinder.

deproletarianization Entproletarisierung.

depth Tiefe, *(feeling)* Tiefe, Intensivität;
from the ~ **of misery** aus tiefstem Elend; **in the** ~ **of despair** in der größten Verzweiflung; **in the** ~ **of one's heart** im tiefsten Herzen; **in the** ~ **of night** mitten in der Nacht; **in the** ~ **of winter** im tiefsten Winter;
~ **of column** *(advertising)* Spaltenhöhe, *(mil.)* Marschtiefe; ~ **of the country** Landesinnere; ~ **of focus** *(photo)* Tiefenschärfe; ~ **of page** Satzhöhe; ~ **of thought** *(book)* Gedankentiefe;
to add ~ **to one's career experiences** seine beruflichen Erfahrungen vertiefen; **to be beyond s. one's** ~ über jds. Begriffsvermögen gehen; **to be within one's** ~ Boden unter den Füßen (Grund) haben; **to get out of one's** ~ Boden unter den Füßen verlieren;
~ **charge** Wasserbombe; ~ **finder** Tiefenlot, -sonde; ~ **interview** Tiefeninterview; ~ **psychologist** Tiefenpsychologe; ~ **psychology** Tiefenpsychologie.

depurge *(v.)* *(party life)* in Gnaden wieder aufnehmen.

deputation Deputation, Abordnung, Abgesandte;
to send a ~ **to confer with s. o.** Abordnung zu Verhandlungen mit jem. entsenden.

depute *(v.)* abordnen, mit Vollmacht entsenden, delegieren;
~ **s. o. to do s. th.** j. zu etw. bevollmächtigen.

deputize *(v.)* abordnen, delegieren, Stellvertreter sein;
~ **for s. o.** als jds. Vertreter fungieren; ~ **for the department head** Abteilungsleiter vertreten.

deputy *(Australia, Canada)* Geschäftsträger, *(boardinghouse manager, Br.)* Pensionsvorsteher[in], *(coal mine, Br.)* Grubenbeauftragter, *(M.P.)* Abgeordneter, Parlamentsmitglied, Deputierter, Delegierter, *(proxy)* Beauftragter, Bevollmächtiger, Stellvertreter;
acting as ~ in Vertretung; **by** ~ in Stellvertretung;
ambassador's ~ Botschafter-Stellvertreter; **former** ~ ehemaliger Abgeordneter; **general** ~ ständiger Vertreter; **retiring** ~ bisheriger Abgeordneter; **special** ~ Sonderbevollmächtigter, **-beauftragter**, *(sheriff, US)* Hilfspolizist; **unattached** ~ parteiloser Abgeordneter;
to act as ~ als Stellvertreter auftreten (fungieren); **to find a** ~ sich vertreten lassen; **to make s. o. one's** ~ j. zu seinem Vertreter bestimmen, j. mit seiner Vertretung beauftragen;
~ *(a.)* stellvertretend;
~ **chairman** stellvertretender Vorsitzender, Vizepräsident; ~ **consul** Vizekonsul; ~ **governor** Vizegouverneur; ~ **judge** Hilfsrichter; ~ **lecturer** Hilfslehrer; ~ **manager** stellvertretender Geschäftsführer; ~ **mayor** zweiter Bürgermeister; ♁ **Foreign Minister** Außenministerstellvertreter; ~ **registrar** stellvertretender Standesbeamter; ~ **secretary** stellvertretender Staatssekretär; ~ **sheriff** stellvertretender Polizeipräsident.

deputyship Stellvertretung.

deraign *(v.)* Anspruch beweisen.

derail *(v.)* entgleisen;
~ **a plan** Plan zum Scheitern bringen.

derailment Entgleisung.

derange *(v.)* durcheinander bringen, verwirren, *(machine)* derangieren, *(render insane)* geistig zerrütten, wahnsinnig machen;
~ **s. o.** geistige Störung bei jem. veranlassen; ~ **the health** Gesundheit beeinträchtigen; ~ **plans for a holiday** Ferienpläne durcheinanderbringen.

deranged, mentally geistesgestört;
to be ~ [**in one's mental faculties**] geistig gestört (geistesgestört) sein; **to become** ~ *(machine)* in Unordnung sein, nicht funktionieren.

derangement Durcheinander, Wirrwarr, *(insanity)* Geistesgestörtheit, -störung, -zerrüttung;
mental ~ geistige Umnachtung; **nervous** ~ Nervenzerrüttung; **temporary mental** ~ vorübergehende Störung der Geistestätigkeit;
~ **of mind** Geistesstörung; ~ **of trade** Störung (Unterbrechung) des Handelsverkehrs.

derate *(v.)* **of local taxes** *(Br.)* landwirtschaftlich genutzte Grundstücke von den Gemeindesteuern befreien.

derating of local taxes *(Br.)* Befreiung von Gemeindesteuern, Grundsteuererleichterung, -befreiung;
~ **Act** *(Br.)* Gesetz über die Befreiung von Gemeindeabgaben; ~ **system** Steuerbefreiungsverfahren.

deration *(v.)* Rationierung aufheben.

derationed goods freigegebene (nicht mehr bewirtschaftete) Waren.

derationing Aufhebung der Zwangsbewirtschaftung.

deregister *(v.)* im Handelsregister löschen.

deregistration Löschung im Handelsregister.

deregulate *(v.)* einschränkende Bestimmungen aufheben.

deregulation Aufhebung einschränkender Bestimmungen;
to eye ~ **route** Abschaffung einschränkender Bestimmungen ins Auge fassen.

deregulationize *(v.)* einschränkende Bestimmungen aufheben.

derelict herrenloses Gut, *(ship)* [treibendes] Wrack, *(tract of land)* trockengelegtes Land;
~s Wrackteile;
~ *(a.)* *(abandoned)* herrenlos, aufgegeben, *(house)* verlassen, baufällig, *(unfaithful, US)* nachlässig, untreu;
~ **to duty** *(US)* pflichtvergessen;
to be ~ **of (in) one's duty** *(US)* seine Pflichten vernachlässigen;
~ **children** verwahrloste Kinder; ~ **land** Industrieödland; ~ **ship** aufgegebenes Schiff, Wrack.

dereliction *(neglect by wilful abandonment)* schuldhafte Vernachlässigung, *(utter forsaking)* Besitz-, Eigentumsaufgabe;
~ **of duty** Pflicht-, Dienstvernachlässigung, Pflichtversäumnis.

derequisition *(Br.)* Rückkehr zur Zivilverwaltung, Aufhebung der Beschlagnahme, *(housing)* Aufhebung der Wohnungszwangswirtschsft;
~ *(v.)* Beschlagnahme aufheben, *(housing)* Wohnraumbewirtschaftung aufheben, Wohnraum freigeben.

derestrict *(v.)* Einschränkungsmaßnahmen aufheben;
~ **a road** Geschwindigkeitsbeschränkungen für eine Straße aufheben.

derestricted | area unbegrenzte Geschwindigkeitszone; ~ **road** keiner Geschwindigkeitsbegrenzung unterliegende Straße.

derestriction Lockerung von Einschränkungsmaßnahmen, *(speed limit)* Aufhebung der Geschwindigkeitsbeschränkung;
~s **of traffic** Verkehrserleichterungen;
~ **sign** Schild zur Aufhebung der Geschwindigkeitsbegrenzung.

derestrictive measures Lockerungsmaßnahmen.

deride *(v.)* s. **one's efforts** sich über jds. Anstrengungen mockieren.

derision Gespött;
to become an object of ~ zum Gegenstand des Gespötts werden; **to bring s. o. into** ~ j. zur Zielscheibe seines Spottes machen.

derisive offer lächerliches Angebot.

derisory | offer nicht ernst gemeintes Angebot; ~ **remark** unwichtige Bemerkung.

derivation Abstammung, Herkunft;
to study the ~ **of words** etymologische Bedeutung von Wörtern studieren.

derivable erreichbar.

derivative abgeleitet, nicht originär, sekundär;
~ **acquisition** abgeleiteter (nicht originärer) Erwerb; ~ **action** *(US)* Aktionärsklage für die Gesellschaft, Prozeßstandschaft; ~ **conveyance** zusätzliche Grundstücksbeurkundung; ~ **deposit** sekundäres Giralgeld; ~ **title** nicht originärer Rechtstitel; ~ **word** abgeleitetes Wort.

derive *(v.)* herstammen, seinen Ursprung haben, *(sl.)* ableiten, abzweigen, *(ling.)* ableiten;
~ **benefit from s. th.** Vorteil (Nutzen) aus etw. ziehen; ~ **an idea from an author** einem Autor eine Idee stehlen; ~ **income from an investment** Rendite erzielen, Kapitaleinkünfte beziehen; ~ **great pleasure from one's studies** seinem Studium mit Freude obliegen; ~ **profit** Nutzen ziehen; ~ **a title** Recht herleiten; ~ **a word from the Greek** Wort aus dem Griechischen ableiten.

derived | circuit *(el.)* Nebenschlußstromkreis; ~ **demand** mittelbar entstandener Bedarf, abgeleitete Nachfrage; ~ **income** abgeleitetes Einkommen;
to be ~ **from Latin** aus dem Lateinischen stammen.

derogate *(v.)* zum Nachteil gereichen, abträglich sein, Abbruch tun, beeinträchtigen, schmälern;
~ **from o. s.** sich zu seinem Nachteil verändern; ~ **from one's dignity** seiner Würde Abbruch tun; ~ **from a right** Rechtsanspruch verlieren.

derogation Beeinträchtigung, Herabwürdigung, Nachteil, Abbruch, Schmälerung;
in ~ **of** in Abweichung von; **without** ~ **from dignity** ohne Beeinträchtigung der Würde;
~ **of a law** Teilaufhebung eines Gesetzes; ~ **from a privilege** Beeinträchtigung eines Vorrechtes;
to be a ~ **to s. th.** einer Sache Abbruch tun.

derogative abträglich, nachteilig, schmälernd.

derogatory nachteilig, beeinträchtigend, abträglich, schmälernd;
~ **to o. s.** seiner unwürdig;
to be ~ beeinträchtigen, schaden, abträglich sein; **to do s. th.** ~ **to one's position** seine eigene Stellung erschüttern;
~ **clause** *(last will)* Abänderungsklausel; ~ **remarks** abträgliche Bemerkungen.

derrick Ladebaum;
~ **car** Kranwagen; ~ **crane** Montagekran.

derrickman Kranführer.

deruralization Verstädterung.

deruralize *(v.)* verstädtern.

descant Bemerkung, Kommentar;
~ *(v.)* **upon a subject** sich langatmig über ein Thema verbreiten.

descend *(v.)* *(be derived)* abstammen, *(pass by inheritance)* durch Erbschaft zufallen, im Erbwege übergehen, *(go down)* herab-, heruntersteigen, sinken, sich senken, *(parachute)* mit dem Fallschirm abspringen, *(plane)* niedergehen, landen, *(river)* abwärtsfahren;
~ **to details (particulars)** zu Einzelheiten übergehen; ~ **to more recent events** auf neuere Ereignisse zu sprechen kommen; ~ **from father to son** vom Vater auf den Sohn übergehen; ~ **from a noble family** aus adliger Familie stammen; ~ **to fraud** sich zum Betrug hergeben, sich eines Betruges schuldig machen; ~ **to s. one's level** sich jds. Niveau anpassen; ~ **into a mine** in eine Grube einfahren; ~ **steeply** *(road)* stark fallen, sich stark senken; ~ **upon a defenceless village** unbefestigtes Dorf angreifen.

descendance Abstammung, Herkunft.

descendant Leibeserbe, Ab-, Nachkomme, Abkömmling;
lineal ~ direkter Abkömmling;
to leave no ~s ohne Nachkommenschaft sterben.

descender *(print.)* Unterlänge.

descendible vererbbar.

descent *(airplane, balloon)* Niedergehen, *(derivation)* Abstammung, Herkunft, *(issue)* Deszendenz, *(family tree)* Stammbaum, *(incursion)* Angriff, Einfall, Überfall, *(downward course)* Niedergang, Abstieg, Verfall, *(law)* Zufallen durch Erbschaft, Vererbung, Übergang im Erbwege, *(parachute)* Fallschirmabsprung, *(temperature)* Fallen;
of legitimate ~ von ehelicher Abstammung; **of noble** ~ von vornehmer Abstammung, von adliger Abkunft;
collateral ~ Abstammung in der Seitenlinie, Seitenabstammung; **gradual** ~ gemächliche Senke; **lineal** ~ Abstammung in gerader Linie;
~ **upon the enemy** feindlicher Einfall, Invasion;
to claim ~ **from s. o.** seine Abstammung auf j. zurückführen; **to make numerous** ~s zahlreiche Angriffe durchführen; **to take land by** ~ Grundbesitz erben; **to trace one's** ~ **back to** seine Abstammung (Stammbaum) zurückverfolgen.

describable beschreibbar.

describe *(v.)* bezeichnen, beschreiben, schildern;
~ **s. o. as really clever** j. für außergewöhnlich gescheit halten; ~ **o. s. as a doctor** sich als Arzt bezeichnen.

description Beschreibung, Schilderung, Darstellung, *(of s. o.)* Personenbeschreibung, Signalement, *(sort)* Qualität, Sorte, Art, Gattung;
by ~ laut Beschreibung; **of every** ~ von jeder Art (Sorte), in jeder Qualität; **of the same** ~ gleichartig; **of the worst** ~ von der schlimmsten Sorte;
~s *(Br., stock exchange)* Wertpapiere;
better ~ feinere Waren; **current** ~s gangbare Sorten; **detailed** ~ nähere (genaue) Bezeichnung, Einzelbeschreibung; **faithful** ~ genaue Beschreibung; **full** ~ ausführliche Beschreibung; **home** ~s *(Br., stock exchange)* heimische Werte; **job** ~ Arbeits-, Stellen-, Tätigkeitsbeschreibung; **leading** ~s *(Br.)* führende Werte; **particular** ~ ausführliche Beschreibung; **patent** ~ Patentbeschreibung; **prior public printed** ~ *(patent law)* Vorveröffentlichung; **specified** ~ genaue Beschreibung; **speculative** ~s *(Br.)* Spekulationspapiere; **technical** ~s technische Darstellungen; **thumbnail** ~ ungefähre Beschreibung;
~ **of account** Kontobezeichnung; ~ **of commodities** Warenbeschreibung, -bezeichnung; ~ **of contents** Beschreibung des Inhalts, Inhaltsbeschreibung; ~ **of goods** Warenbezeichnung; ~ **of land** Grundstücksbeschreibung; ~ **of securities** Effektengattung;
to answer to ~ mit der Personalbeschreibung übereinstimmen; **to circulate the** ~ **of a criminal** Verbrechersignalement veröffentlichen; **to correspond with the** ~ der Beschreibung entsprechen, mit der Beschreibung übereinstimmen; **to give a** ~ beschreiben; **to take the** ~ **of s. o.** jds. Signalement aufnehmen.

descriptive beschreibend, erläuternd, darstellend;
~ **catalog(ue)** beschreibender Katalog; ~ **labelling** übliche Etikettierung; ~ **narration** anschauliche Erzählung; ~ **signalement** *(US)* Personenbeschreibung; ~ **financial statement** erläuterte Finanzübersicht.

descry *(v.)* ausfindig machen.

deseasonalized item saisonbereinigte Größe.

desecrate *(v.)* entweihen, profanieren.

desecration Entweihung, Profanierung;
~ **of a grave** Grabschändung.

desegregate *(v.)* Rassentrennung (Rassenschranken) aufheben.

desegregation Aufhebung der Rassentrennung (Rassenschranken).

desequestration Aufhebung der Zwangsverwaltung.

desequestrate *(v.)* Zwangsverwaltung aufheben.

desert Wüste, Einöde, Ödland, *(merit)* Wert, Verdienst;
backward ~s rückständige Wüstengebiete;
~ *(v.)* verlassen, im Stich lassen, aufgeben, *(mil.)* überlaufen, desertieren;
~ **arguments of persuasion** Überredungskünste fallen lassen; ~ **the colo(u)rs** fahnenflüchtig werden; ~ **the diet** *(Scot. law)* Anklagepunkt aufgeben; ~ **one's duty** vom Dienst desertieren; ~ **one's party** von seiner Partei abfallen; ~ **one's wife without cause** Ehefrau böswillig verlassen;
to be judged according to one's ~s nach seinem Verdienst eingeschätzt werden; **to be punished according to one's** ~(s) gerechte Strafe erhalten; **to be rewarded according to one's** ~s entsprechend belohnt werden; **to deal with s. o. according to his**

~s j. gerecht behandeln; **to get one's** ~ seinen wohlverdienten Lohn bekommen; **to give each a place according to his** ~s jeden entsprechend seinem Rang plazieren;
~ *(a.)* verlassen, unbewohnt;
~ **areas** Wüstengebiete; ~ **caravan** Wüstenkarawane; ~ **fringe** Wüstenrandgebiet; ~ **island** unbewohnte Insel; ~ **land** Wüstengebiet; ~ **rat** alter Wüstenfuchs; ~ **reclamation** Rückgewinnung von Wüstengebieten; ~ **tribe** Wüstenvolk, -stamm.

deserted unbewohnt, *(street)* verlassen;
~ **hut** verlassene Hütte; ~ **premises** verlassenes Anwesen; ~ **region** unbewohntes Gebiet.

deserter Überläufer, Fahnenflüchtiger, Deserteur, *(fig.)* Abtrünniger, *(sailor)* bordflüchtiger Seemann.

desertification Versteppung.

deserting fahnenflüchtig.

desertion Verlassen, *(dereliction of duty)* Pflichtvergessenheit, *(fig.)* Abtrünnigwerden, *(mil.)* Fahnenflucht, Desertion, *(of wife)* böswilliges Verlassen der Ehefrau;
constructive ~ ehewidriges Verhalten; **obstinate** ~ unberechtigtes Getrenntleben;
~ **of one's party** Abfall von seiner Partei.

deserve *(v.)* verdienen, würdig sein;
~ **well of one's country** sich um sein Land verdient gemacht haben; ~ **our help** unserer Hilfe würdig sein; ~ **ill of s. o.** j. einen schlechten Dienst erweisen; ~ **good pay** gute Bezahlung verdienen; ~ **punishment** Strafe verdienen; ~ **to be sent to prison** Gefängnisstrafe verdient haben.

deservedly wohlverdientermaßen.

deserving verdienstvoll, verdient, würdig;
to be ~ **of s. th.** einer Sache wert (würdig) sein;
~ **cause** gute Sache.

design *(act)* graphische (industrielle) Form[gebung], Gestaltung, Design, *(construction)* Ausführung, Konstruktion[szeichnung], *(pattern)* Anordnung, Muster, Modell, *(plan)* Plan, Absicht, Projekt, Vorhaben, *(sketch)* Entwurf, Skizze, Anlage, *(statistics)* Versuchsanordnung;
by ~ absichtlich;
conventional ~ gängiges Muster; **custom** ~ auf Bestellung angefertigtes Muster; **factorial** ~ betrieblicher Versuchsplan; **faulty** ~ *(machine)* fehlerhafte Konstruktion, Fehlkonstruktion, Konstruktionsfehler; **industrial** ~ gewerbliche Formgebung, gewerbliches Muster; **our latest** ~s unsere letzten Modelle; **improvement on 1981** ~ verbessertes Modell von 1981; **ornamental** ~ Ziermuster; **registered** ~ eingetragenes Geschmacksmuster;
~s **for a dress** Entwürfe für ein Kleid; ~ **for a revolution** Revolutionsplan;
~ *(v.) (contrive)* planen, *(draw)* zeichnen, skizzieren, entwerfen, *(intend)* beabsichtigen, vorhaben;
~ **s. o. for the bar** j. zum Juristen ausersehen; ~ **a book in binding** Bucheinband entwerfen; ~ **a building** Plan eines Hauses entwerfen; ~ **a dress** Kleid entwerfen; ~ **a plane** Flugzeug konstruieren;
to be poor in ~ architektonisch schlecht gegliedert sein; **to have** ~s böse Absichten haben; **to have** ~s **on s. one's money** es auf jds. Geld abgesehen haben; **to open one's** ~s seine Absichten mitteilen; **to work up** ~s Entwürfe ausarbeiten;
♂ **Act** *(Br.)* Geschmacksmustergesetz; ~ **book** Musterbuch; ~ **engineer** Konstrukteur; ~ **paper** Karopapier; ~ **patent** *(US)* geschütztes Geschmacksmuster; ~ **requirements** charakteristische Mustereigenschaften; ~ **work** Entwicklungsarbeit.

designate *(v.) (appoint to office)* benennen, bestimmen, designieren, *(describe as)* bezeichnen, markieren, kennzeichnen, *(identify by name)* betiteln, bezeichnen;
~ **boundaries** Grenzen festlegen; ~ **a counsel for the defence** Verteidiger bestellen; ~ **an heir** Erben bestimmen; ~ **an officer for a command** einem Offizier ein Kommando übertragen; ~ **the persons to be arrested** Personenkreis der Arrestanten festlegen; ~ **s. o. as (for) one's successor** j. zum Nachfolger ausersehen (designieren);
~ *(a.)* vorgesehen, ausersehen, designiert.

designated, duly ordnungsgemäß bestellt;
~ **time** bestimmte Zeit.

designation Bezeichnung, *(nomination)* Bestimmung, Ernennung, Position;
~ **of abode** Wohnsitzbestimmung; ~ **of s. one's duty** Pflichtenfestlegung; ~ **of an invention** Titel einer Erfindung; ~ **to a post** Benennung für einen Posten, Benennung für eine Position; ~ **of a successor** Bestimmung (Ernennung) eines Nachfolgers;
to be known under several ~s verschiedene Bezeichnungen tragen.

designed absichtlich, vorsätzlich;
~ **for s. one's good** zu jds. Besten bestimmt; ~ **as a children's playroom** als Kinderzimmer entworfen;
~ **speed** vertraglich ausbedungene Geschwindigkeit.

designee *(US)* Beauftragter.

designer technischer Zeichner, Entwerfer, Formgestalter, Gebrauchsgraphiker, *(fig.)* Ränkeschmied;
costume (dress) ~ Modeschöpfer, -zeichner; **industrial** ~ Formgestalter, industrieller Formgeber; **pattern** ~ Modellzeichner; ~ **of patterns** Formgestalter, Musterzeichner.

designing Formgestaltung;
~ **department** Konstruktionsbüro.

desirable property *(house agent)* schönes Anwesen.

desire Wunsch, Bedürfnis, Anliegen, Begehren, Verlangen;
at the ~ **of the manager** auf Ersuchen des Hauses; **in accordance with your** ~ wunschgemäß, wie gewünscht;
~ **to buy** Kaufinteresse; **a country's** ~ **for friendly relations** Wunsch eines Landes auf gutnachbarliche Beziehungen; ~ **for knowledge** Wissensdrang.

desist *(v.)* aufhören;
to cease and ~ unterlassen; ~ **to prosecute** von der Verfolgung Abstand nehmen.

desk Pult, Schreibtisch, *(Br.)* Schalter, *(clerical performance)* Büro-, Kanzleiarbeit, *(counter)* Ladentisch, *(literary profession)* Schriftstellerei, literarische Beschäftigung (Betätigung), *(governmental section)* Abteilung, Ressort, *(US, journalism)* Umbruchredaktion, *(person officiating, coll.)* Mann hinterm Schreibtisch, Rezeption;
flat-top ~ Schreibtisch mit flachem Aufbau; **loan** ~ *(library)* Buchausgabe; **pay** ~ Kassenschalter, Kasse; **reading** ~ Lesepult; **reception** ~ *(hotel)* Empfangsschalter, -chef, Empfang; **roll-top** ~ Schreibtisch mit Rollvorrichtung;
pay at the ~! an der Kasse zu zahlen;
to be chained to one's ~ an den Schreibtisch gefesselt sein; **to lie at the** ~ ausliegen;
~ **appointments** Schreibtischgarnitur; ~ **audit** Buchprüfung auf Grund mitgenommener Belege; ~ **book** Handbuch; ~-**bound** an den Schreibtisch gefesselt; ~ **calendar** Terminkalender; ~ **clerk** *(US)* Hotelportier; ~ **copy** Gratisexemplar; ~ **editor** Chef vom Dienst; ~-**bound executive** Schreibtischarbeiter, -stratege; ~ **job** *(in war)* Druckposten; ~ **jobber** Grossist ohne eigenes Lager (mit Streckengeschäft); ~ **knife** Radiermesser; ~ **lamp** **(light)** Schreibtischlampe; ~ **man** *(US)* Redaktionsmitglied; ~ **number** Kontrollziffer; ~ **officer** zuständiger Sachbearbeiter; ~ **pad** Schreibtischunterlage; ~ **research** sekundärstatistische Auswertung; ~ **room** Platz für einen Schreibtisch; ~ **sergeant** *(US)* wachhabender Polizist; ~ **set** Schreibzeug; ~-**side interview** Exklusivinterview; ~-**top calculator** Tischrechner; ~-**top terminal** Börsenkurswiedergabegerät; ~ **tray** Briefkorb; ~ **work** Schreibtisch-, Büroarbeit.

desolate *(region)* unbewohnt, verlassen;
~ *(v.)* verwüsten, verheeren, entvölkern.

desolated ausgeplündert.

desolation Verwüstung, Verheerung;
~s **caused by war** Kriegsverwüstungen;
the ~s **of the times** die Trostlosigkeit der Gegenwart.

despacheur *(maritime law)* Havariesachverständiger.

despair Verzweiflung;
~ *(v.)* **of mankind** an der Menschheit verzweifeln;
to drive s. o. to ~ j. zur Verzweiflung treiben.

despatch *(dipl.)* Gesandtschaftsbericht.

desperate | act Verzweiflungsakt; ~ **criminal** Gewaltverbrecher; ~ **debt** uneinbringliche Forderung.

desperation Verzweiflung, Hoffnungslosigkeit.

despoil *(v.)* berauben, plündern.

despoiler Plünderer, Räuber.

despoliation Plünderung, *(landscape)* Zersiedlung.

despondent | note *(stock market)* schwache Tendenz; ~ **prisoner** verzweifelter Gefangener.

despot Tyrann, Autokrat, Despot, Gewaltherrscher.

despotic tyrannisch, despotisch;
~ **act** Willkürhandlung.

despotism Willkürherrschaft, Gewaltherrschaft, Tyrannei, Despotie.

dessert Nachtisch, Dessert.

destination Reiseziel, Bestimmungsort, Adresse, *(airplane)* Flugziel, *(purpose)* Zweckbestimmung, *(Scot.)* Ersatzeinsetzung, *(succession of heirs)* Erbfolge;
final ~ endgültiger Bestimmungsort, Zielort; **hostile** ~ feindliche Bestimmung [von Konterbande]; **single** ~ Begrenzung auf eine Fluglinie;

~ **of goods sold** Absatzrichtung;
to arrive at (reach) one's ~ sein Reiseziel erreichen, am Bestimmungsort ankommen;
~ **charges** *(car)* Überführungskosten; ~ **station** Bestimmungsbahnhof.
destine *(v.)* bestimmen, vorsehen;
~ **money to build a house** Geld für einen Hausbau vorsehen.
destined from birth for the army seit Geburt für eine militärische Laufbahn vorgesehen;
to be ~ **to the gallows** für den Galgen bestimmt sein.
destiny Schicksal, Los, Geschick;
to meet one's ~ vom Schicksal ereilt werden.
destitute Hilfloser, -bedürftiger;
~ *(a.)* verarmt;
~ **of all means** aller Mittel beraubt; ~ **of all power** völlig machtlos; ~ **of common sense** bar jedes gesunden Menschenverstands;
to be left ~ völlig mittellos zurückbleiben; **to be** ~ **of merit** jeder Grundlage entbehren; **to be** ~ **of sympathy** keines Mitleids fähig sein;
~ **or necessitous circumstances** Unterhaltsbedürftigkeit.
destitution Armut, Elend, Not, Mittellosigkeit;
reduced to ~ völlig verarmt;
~ **and misery** Not und Elend;
to be in utter ~ großen Mangel leiden;
~ **wage** Hungerlohn.
destocking Lagerabbau durch Auftragskürzung.
destroy *(v.)* *(insurance)* vernichten, demolieren;
~ **a building** Gebäude niederreißen; ~ **the discipline of troops** Truppen demoralisieren; ~ **a document** Urkunde beseitigen; ~ **a legislative function** Funktion des Gesetzgebers abschaffen; ~ **s. one's powers of resistance** jds. Widerstandskräfte aufzehren; ~ **a work of art** Kunstwerk vernichten (zerstören).
destroyed by flames den Flammen zum Opfer gefallen.
destroyer *(navy)* Zerstörer;
~ **escort** *(US)* Geleitzerstörer.
destruction Zerstörung, Vernichtung, Ausrottung, Verwüstung, Verheerung;
malicious ~ vorsätzliche Sachbeschädigung; **partial** ~ *(of goods)* Teiluntergang; **record** ~ Aktenvernichtung; **root-and-branch** ~ totale Zerstörung; **wanton** ~ rücksichtslose Zerstörung;
~ **of documents** Urkundenbeseitigung; ~ **caused by the fire** durch das Feuer angerichtete Zerstörung; ~ **of goods** *(law)* Untergang von Sachen; ~ **of money** Geldvernichtung; ~ **of reputation** Rufschädigung; ~ **of the subject matter of contract** Untergang des Vertragsgegenstands; ~ **of a town by an earthquake** Zerstörung einer Stadt durch ein Erdbeben;
to rush to one's own ~ seiner Vernichtung entgegengehen.
destructionist Zerstörungswütiger, Umstürzler, Revolutionär.
destructive schädlich, verheerend, *(fig.)* verderblich, destruktiv;
~ **of health** gesundheitsschädlich;
~ **competition** wirtschaftlich unsinniger Wettbewerb; ~ **criticism** vernichtende Kritik; ~ **effect** verheerende Wirkung; ~ **insects and pests** Schädlinge; ~ **storm** verheerender Sturm.
destructor Müllverbrennungsanlage.
desuetude Ungebräuchlichkeit;
~ **of a law** Unwirksamwerden eines Gesetzes;
to fall into ~ außer Gebrauch kommen.
desultory unmethodisch, planlos, ziellos;
~ **conversation** unzusammenhängendes Gerede; ~ **reading** planloses Lesen; ~ **remark** nicht zum Thema gehörige Bemerkung.
detach *(v.)* [ab]trennen, -schneiden, absondern, ablösen, *(mil.)* abstellen, -kommandieren;
~ **a cable** Kabel losmachen; ~ **a coach from a train** Waggon abkuppeln; ~ **coupons due** verfallene Zinsscheine ablösen; ~ **for a course** zu einem Lehrgang abkommandieren; ~ **a key from a key-ring** Schlüssel von einem Schlüsselbund losmachen; ~ **a ship from a fleet** Schiff aus einem Flottenverband herauslösen; ~ **a state from a confederation** Staat von einem Staatenbund abtrennen; ~ **o. s. from the world** sich von der Welt zurückziehen.
detached abgetrennt, abgesondert, *(house)* einzelstehend, *(fig.)* unvoreingenommen, unparteiisch, objektiv, *(mil.)* abkommandiert, -gestellt;
to be ~ *(house)* freistehen, *(soldier)* abgestellt sein;
~ **coupons** getrennte Kupons; ~ **house** freistehendes Haus; ~ **parcels of goods** gesonderte Warenpartien; ~ **party** abgestellter Truppenteil; **to take a** ~ **view of events** Ereignisse mit Gelassenheit aufnehmen.

detaching of coupons Kouponabtrennung.
detachment Absonderung, Trennung, Loslösung, *(fig.)* Unparteilichkeit, Objektivität, Uninteressiertheit, *(mil.)* Abstellung, Abkommandierung, Sonderkommando;
~ **essential to a historian** für einen Historiker unabdingbare Objektivität; ~ **of the United States from European Affairs** Gleichgültigkeit der USA an Fragen der europäischen Politik.
detail Einzelheit, Detail, *(US, particularized account)* genaue Beschreibung (Darstellung), *(US, body of persons)* Arbeitsgruppe, *(detailed treatment)* ausführliche Behandlung, *(television)* Bildausschnitt, *(written list of services, Br.)* Tagesbefehl;
in ~ im einzelnen, detailliert, Punkt für Punkt; **full ~s obtainable from ...** genaue Auskunft erteilt ...; **with full ~s** detailliert, im einzelnen;
~**s** nähere Umstände;
fashion ~s modische Einzelheiten; **financial ~s** Einzelheiten über die finanziellen Abmachungen; **full** ~ genaue Einzelheiten; **media** ~ alle Einzelheiten eines Werbemittels; **minor ~s** unbedeutendeeinzelheiten;
~**s of a business contract** Einzelbestimmungen eines Wirtschaftsabkommens; **a few ~s of the evening program(me)** einige Hinweise auf das Abendprogramm;
~ *(v.)* ausführlich beschreiben, einzeln aufführen, detaillieren, substantiieren, *(mil.)* abstellen, -kommandieren;
~ **s. o. for a duty** jem. einen bestimmten Aufgabenkreis zuweisen; ~ **s. o. for a particular service** j. zu einer Arbeit einteilen; ~ **a story of the shipwreck** Schiffbruch in allen Einzelheiten schildern;
to be a stickler for ~s sich um jede Einzelheit kümmern; **to cut out superfluous ~s** überschüssige Einzelheiten weglassen; **to do s. th. with minute** ~ Punkt für Punkt erledigen; **to enter into the smallest ~s** auf die kleinsten Kleinigkeiten eingehen; **to get lost in the ~s** sich in Einzelheiten verlieren; **to give exact ~s** genaue Details angeben; **to give full ~s** nähere Einzelheiten anführen; **to go into ~s** ins einzelne gehen, alle Umstände darlegen; **to go too deeply into ~s** sich in Einzelheiten verlieren; **to leave out the ~s** Einzelheiten weglassen; **to pass over the ~s** Einzelheiten übergehen; **to relegate ~s to foot notes** Einzelheiten in Fußnoten unterbringen; **to reproduce a ~ of a printing** Bildausschnitt reproduzieren;
~ **account** Einzelkonto; ~ **drawing** Einzelzeichnung; ~ **paper** Durchzeichenpapier; ~ **work** Detailarbeit.
detailed ausführlich, eingehend, detailliert;
~ **account** spezifizierte Rechnung; ~ **audit** ins einzelne gehende Revision; ~ **description** Schilderung in allen Einzelheiten, Detailschilderung; ~ **drawing** Detailzeichnung; ~ **information** detaillierte Auskunft; ~ **negotiations** Einzelbesprechungen; ~ **statement** detaillierte Aufstellung, Detailbericht; **to make a** ~ **statement** detaillierte Aufstellung machen; ~ **survey** genaue Vermessung.
detailing *(advertising business)* Propagandistenwerbung.
detailman *(US)* Ärztebesucher.
detain *(v.)* auf-, zurückhalten, warten lassen, nicht weglassen, *(police)* zurückbehalten, in Haft behalten, gefangenhalten, festnehmen, internieren;
~ **compulsory** in eine Heilanstalt einweisen; ~ **in custody** in Untersuchungshaft behalten; ~ **goods** Waren zurückbehalten (anhalten); ~ **a pupil** Schüler nachsitzen lassen; ~ **wages** Lohn einbehalten;
to be ~ed in office by business geschäftlich aufgehalten werden; **to be ~ed by work** beruflich verhindert sein.
detained in Haft, inhaftiert, interniert;
~ **by accident** durch einen Unfall aufgehalten; ~ **in business** geschäftlich verhindert; ~ **in captivity** in Gefangenschaft, als Gefangener festgehalten; ~ **by ice** vom Eise eingeschlossen; ~ **for interrogation** zu Verhörzwecken festgehalten; ~ **for trial** in Untersuchungshaft;
to be compulsorily ~ **under the Mental Health Act** zwangsweise in eine Nervenheilanstalt eingewiesen sein; **to be** ~ **in office by unexpected callers** durch unangemeldete Besucher im Büro aufgehalten werden; **to be** ~ **in port** im Hafen festgehalten werden; **to be** ~ **by work** beruflich verhindert sein.
detainee [politischer] Häftling, Untersuchungshäftling, Internierter;
civilian ~ Zivilinternierter.
detainer Vorenthaltung, *(detention in custody)* Haftbefehl, verlängerte Haftanordnung;
forcible ~ Besitzstörung, widerrechtliche Zurückhaltung von Grundbesitz; **lawful** ~ rechtmäßiger Freiheitsentzug; **unlawful** ~ widerrechtliche Vorenthaltung; **unlawful forcible** ~ Rechtsberaubung.

detaining power Gewahrsamsmacht.

detainment Zurückhaltung, *(marine insurance)* Beschlagnahme.

detect *(v.)* entdecken, ausfindig machen, aufdecken, *(detective)* als Detektiv tätig sein;

~ **s. o. in the act** j. auf frischer Tat entdecken; ~ **a crime** Verbrechen aufdecken; ~ **an escape of gas** Gasaustritt feststellen; ~ **several mistakes** mehrere Fehler nachweisen; ~ **a ray of hope** Hoffnungsschimmer ausfindig machen.

detectaphone *(tel.)* Abhörgerät.

detection Entdeckung, Aufdeckung, Ermittlung, Entlarvung;

~ **of crime** Aufdeckung eines Verbrechens; ~ **of a fraud** Aufdeckung eines Betruges; ~ **of a thief** Entlarvung eines Diebes; **to escape** ~ der Entdeckung entgehen;

~ **method** *(research)* Ermittlungsverfahren; ~ **rate** Aufklärungsprozentsatz.

detective Kriminalist, Kriminalbeamter, Geheimpolizist, Detektiv;

private ~ Privatdetektiv;

~ **agency** Detektei; ~ **bureau of the police force** Kriminalpolizei; ~ **fiction** Kriminal-, Detektivroman; ~ **film** Kriminalfilm; ~ **force** Kriminalpolizei; ~ **inspector** Kriminalinspektor; ~ **novel** Krimi[nalroman]; ~ **novelist** Kriminalschriftsteller; ~ **officer** Detektiv; ~ **police** Kriminalpolizei; ~ **story** Detektivgeschichte, Kriminalroman.

détente Entspannung.

detention *(detainment)* Zurückhaltung, *(police)* Festnahme, *(state of being detained)* Haft, Gefangenhaltung, *(mil.)* Arrest, *(school)* Nachsitzenlassen, Jugendarrest, *(seizure)* Beschlagnahme;

compulsory ~ zwangsweise Unterbringung; **preventive** ~ *(Br.)* Sicherungsverwahrung, Vorbeugehaft; **unlawful** ~ ungesetzliche Haft, Freiheitsberaubung;

~ **of goods** Warenbeschlagnahme; ~ **on a journey** unfreiwilliger Aufenthalt während einer Reise; ~ **of the mail by bad weather** wetterbedingte verspätete Postzustellung; ~ **on bread-and-water diet** *(mil.)* strenger Arrest; ~ **in hospital** zwangsweiser Krankenhausaufenthalt; ~ **in jail** Inhaftierung; ~ **of a motorist by a traffic officer** Anhalten eines Kraftfahrers durch einen Verkehrspolizist; ~ **by police** Polizeihaft; ~ **in a reformatory** Einweisung in eine Erziehungsanstalt, Unterbringung in einem Jugendgefängnis; ~ **upon remand** vorbeugende Haft; ~ **of a ship** Zurückhaltung eines Schiffes; ~ **pending trial** Untersuchungshaft; ~ **of wages** Einbehaltung von Löhnen, Lohneinbehaltung;

to give a boy ~ Jungen nachsitzen lassen; **to order the** ~ **of a ship** Beschlagnahme eines Schiffes anordnen;

~ **allowance** *(mil.)* Tagegeld; ~ **barracks** Militärgefängnis; ~ **camp** Anhalte-, Internierungs-, Konzentrationslager; ~ **centre** *(Br.)* **(center, US, home)** Besserungsanstalt, Jugendstrafanstalt; ~ **charges** Beschlagnahmekosten; ~ **hospital** geschlossene Anstalt; ~ **order** Haftbefehl.

deter | *(v.)* **potential buyers** potentielle Käufer abschrecken; ~ **war** Krieg durch Abschreckung verhindern.

detergents Haushaltsreinigungsmittel.

deteriorate *(v.)* sich verschlechtern (nachteilig verändern), *(become depreciated)* an Wert verlieren, Wertminderung erfahren, *(goods)* verderben, *(morals)* entarten, verfallen, in Verfall geraten, *(trade)* zurückgehen;

~ **markedly** sich merklich verschlechtern; ~ **the public morals** öffentliche Moral verderben;

to be liable to ~ **in value** einer Wertminderung ausgesetzt sein.

deterioration *(depreciation)* Wertminderung, *(goods)* Verderb, *(growing worse)* Verschlechterung, Verfall, *(impairment)* Entartung, Degenerierung, *(wear and tear)* Verschleiß;

inherent ~ innerer Verderb, leichte Verderblichkeit;

~ **of currency** Geld-, Währungsverschlechterung; ~ **in morals** moralischer Verfall, Sittenverfall, Entartung der Sitten; ~ **of the financial position** Vermögensverschlechterung; ~ **in prices** Preisverfall; ~ **of professionalism** schwindende Berufsethik; ~ **of purchasing value of money** Verschlechterung der Kaufkraft; ~ **in quality** Qualitätsverschlechterung; ~ **in relations** Verschlechterung der Beziehungen; ~ **of the trade balance** Verschlechterung der Handelsbilanz; ~ **of the weather** Wetterverschlechterung.

determent Abschreckung[smittel].

determinable bestimmbar, festsetzbar, *(law)* auflösbar, befristet, zeitlich begrenzt;

~ **amount** bestimmbarer Betrag; ~ **contract** kündbarer Vertrag; ~ **fee** befristete Gebühr; ~ **freehold** eigentumsähnliche beschränkte Nutzung; ~ **life interest** bedingtes Eigentumsrecht an einem Grundstück.

determinate bestimmt, festgelegt, festgesetzt, *(definitive)* endgültig, *(resolute)* entschlossen, resolut, fest entschieden;

~ **answer** endgültige Antwort; ~ **decree** vorher festgelegter Beschluß; ~ **fine** Geldstrafe in bestimmter Höhe; ~ **obligation** im einzelnen festgelegte Verpflichtung, Speziesschuld; ~ **order of precedence** festgelegte Rangordnung.

determinatedness Entschlossenheit.

determination Bestimmung, Festsetzung, Entscheidung, *(delimitation)* Grenzziehung, Abgrenzung, *(determinatedness)* Entschlossenheit, Zielstrebigkeit, Entschlußkraft, *(judicial decision)* Entscheidung, Entschluß, *(end of tenancy)* Ablauf, Ende, Beendigung, *(resolution)* Beschluß, Resolution;

employment ~ Beendigung eines Arbeits-, Dienstverhältnisses; **final** ~ endgültige Entscheidung; **quantity** ~ Mengenbestimmung; **retail-price** ~ Bestimmung (Festsetzung) des Einzelhandelspreises; **self-**~ Selbstbestimmung;

~ **of an agreement** *(cartel)* Aufhebung einer Kartellabsprache; ~ **to build** Bauabsicht; ~ **of compensation** Schadensfestsetzung; ~ **of conditions** Festsetzung von Bedingungen; ~ **to conquer** Eroberungsdrang; ~ **of a contract** Vertragsablauf; ~ **of cost** Kostenfestsetzung; ~ **of a court** Gerichtsentscheidung; ~ **of a date** Bestimmung eines Zeitpunktes; ~ **of earning power** Prüfung der Ertragsfähigkeit; ~ **of employment** Beendigung eines Dienst-, Arbeitsverhältnisses; ~ **of frontier** Festlegung einer Grenze, Grenzfestsetzung; ~ **of a lease** Beendigung eines Nutzungsrechtes, Pachtablauf; ~ **of national income** Nachfrageabhängigkeit des Volkseinkommens; ~ **of the meaning of a word** Bestimmung einer Wortbedeutung; ~ **of penalty** Strafzumessung; ~ **of price** Preisbestimmung, -festsetzung; **competitive** ~ **of prices** Preisbestimmung durch die Konkurrenz; ~ **of profits** *(double taxation agreement)* Gewinnvermittlung; ~ **of quotas** Kontingentfestsetzung; ~ **between right and wrong** Unterscheidung zwischen Recht und Unrecht; ~ **of a speech** Ende (Beendigung) einer Rede; ~ **of a tax** Steuerfestsetzung; ~ **of tenancy** Beendigung des Mietverhältnisses, Mietbeendigung; ~ **of traffic** Verkehrsermittlung; ~ **of will** Widerruf einer Nutzungserlaubnis;

to carry out a plan with ~ Plan entschlossen durchführen; **to come to a** ~ Entschluß fassen, zu einer Entscheidung gelangen; **to shake s. one's** ~ j. in seinem Entschluß wankend machen;

~ **clause** Bestimmung über die Vertragsdauer, *(guarantor)* Ablaufklausel.

determinative bestimmend, entscheidend;

~ **of s. one's career** von entscheidendem Einfluß auf jds. Laufbahn;

~ **clause** Aufhebungsklausel.

determine *(v.)* *(decide)* entscheiden, sich entscheiden, Entschluß fassen, zu einem Entschluß kommen, *(fix)* feststellen, -setzen, bestimmen, ermitteln, *(fix boundaries)* Grenze festlegen, *(terminate)* sein Ende finden, beenden, ablaufen;

to hear and ~ *(judge)* nach Anhörung entscheiden;

~ **an agreement** Abkommen beenden; ~ **s. one's career** jds. Laufbahn entscheidend beeinflussen; ~ **a cause** *(court)* Sache entscheiden; ~ **s. one's character** jds. Charakter entscheidend beeinflussen; ~ **a contract** Vertrag beendigen; ~ **a date for a meeting** Sitzungstermin festlegen; ~ **s. o. against further delay** j. gegen weitere Verschiebung beeinflussen; ~ **s. one's fate** jds. Schicksal entscheiden; ~ **an income** Einkommen ermitteln; ~ **a meeting place** Treffpunkt bestimmen; ~ **a price** Preis festlegen (festsetzen); ~ **profits** Gewinne ermitteln; ~ **where one is going to spend a holiday** sich über den diesjährigen Ferienort schlüssig werden.

determined festgelegt, entschieden, *(settled)* festgelegt, entschieden;

to be ~ **by the amount of the market** *(price)* vom Marktvolumen bestimmt werden; **to be** ~ **to know** unbedingt wissen wollen; **to be more** ~ **than ever** mehr denn je entschlossen sein; **to be** ~ **to start early** früh aufbrechen wollen.

deterrence Abschreckung, Abschreckungsmittel;

counter ~ Gegenabschreckung; **graduated** ~ abgestufte Abschreckung.

deterrent Abschreckungsstreitmacht, -mittel, -waffe;

graduated ~ abgestufte Abschreckung;

to act as a ~ **against crime** der Verbrechensverhütung (als Abschreckungsmittel) dienen;

~ **effect** abschreckende Wirkung, Abschreckungswirkung; ~ **power** Abschreckungspotential; ~ **sentence** abschreckende Strafe.

dethronement Absetzung, Entthronung.

detinue [widerrechtliche] Zurückbehaltung, Besitzvorenthaltung.

detonation Detonation, Explosion.
detonate *(v.)* detonieren, explodieren.
detonator Sprengkapsel, *(fog signal)* Knallkapsel.
detour Abstecher, *(road, US)* [Verkehrs]umleitung, Umweg;
~ *(v.) (US)* Umweg machen;
~ **the traffic** *(US)* Verkehr umleiten;
to make a ~ Umweg machen;
~ **ticket** Umsteigefahrschein.
detract *(v.)* entziehen, wegnehmen, *(divert)* ablenken, zerstreuen;
~ **attention** Aufmerksamkeit ablenken; ~ **much from s. one's pleasure** jds. Vergnügen entscheidend beeinträchtigen; ~ **from s. one's reputation** jds. Ruf schaden.
detraction Verunglimpfung, Rufschädigung, Beeinträchtigung, Herabsetzung;
~ **from s. one's merits** Verdienstschmälerung, Schmälerung von jds. Verdienst.
detractive verleumderisch, verunglimpfend.
detractor Miesmacher, Lästerzunge, *(calumniator)* Verleumder, Rufschädiger.
detrain *(v.)* Zug verlassen.
detriment Schaden, Nachteil, Beeinträchtigung, *(Br., university)* Abnutzungsgebühr;
to the ~ **of** zum Nachteil (Schaden) von; **without** ~ **to our interests** ohne Beeinträchtigung unserer Belange;
~ **already incurred** bereits eingetretener Schaden; **legal** ~ Rechtsnachteil;
to know nothing to s. one's ~ nichts Nachteiliges über j. wissen.
detrimental nachteilig, verlustbringend;
~ **to our interests** unseren Interessen abträglich;
to be ~ **to s. one's interests** jds. Interessen Abbruch tun; **to work long hours to the** ~ **of one's health** zum Nachteil seiner Gesundheit zu lange arbeiten.
detrited coin abgegriffene Münze.
detritus Geröll, Schutt;
loose ~ **of lost traditions** *(coll.)* kümmerliche Überbleibsel verlorengegangener Tradition.
deuce *(sl.)* Pech;
~ **to pay** Haufen Schwierigkeiten; **a** ~ **of a row** ein Höllenlärm; **to have the** ~ **to pay** sich eine schöne Suppe eingebrockt haben; **to play the** ~ **with s. o.** Schindluder mit jem. treiben.
devalorization Abwertung;
~ **profit** Abwertungsgewinn; ~ **rate** Abwertungssatz.
devalorize *(v.)* abwerten.
devaluate *(v.)* abwerten, devaluieren.
devaluation [Währungs]abwertung, Abwertung durch Paritätsveränderung, Entwertung;
~ **of money** Geldentwertung; ~ **of the dollar** Dollarabwertung; ~ **of the pound** Pfundabwertung;
~ **clause** Abwertungsklausel; ~ **measures** Abwertungsmaßnahmen; ~ **policy** Abwertungspolitik.
devalue *(v.)* abwerten.
devastate *(v.)* zerstören, verwüsten, verheeren.
devastated by fire vom Feuer zerstört.
devastating verheerend, *(fig.)* niederschmetternd.
develop *(v.)* entwickeln, entfalten, fördern, *(building ground)* erschließen, *(mil.)* Angriff eröffnen, *(mine)* aufschließen, *(photo)* entwickeln, *(relations)* ausbauen, fördern, *(natural resources)* nutzbar machen;
~ **building lots** *(land)* Bauland erschließen; ~ **a coal area** Kohlenschätze eines Gebietes erschließen; ~ **a country** Land erschließen; ~ **a district** Gebiet erschließen; ~ **some new facts** einige neue Tatsachen zu Tage bringen; ~ **a film** Film entwickeln; ~ **gradually** allmählich Gestalt annehmen; ~ **an illness** sich eine Krankheit zuziehen; ~ **in an author's mind** im Kopf eines Autors Gestalt annehmen; ~ **statistical information** statistisches Material aufbereiten; ~ **a strong organization** leistungsfähigen Verband aufbauen; ~ **into one of the greatest ports** sich zu einem der größten Häfen mausern; ~ **one's plans to an audience** seine Pläne dem Publikum vortragen; ~ **an enemy's position** feindliche Stellung ausspähen; ~ **s. one's powers** jds. Fähigkeiten zur Entfaltung bringen; ~ **a property** Grundstück baulich erschließen; ~ **natural resources** Bodenschätze nutzbar machen; ~ **weakness** *(market)* schwach werden;
to let things ~ sich die Dinge entwickeln lassen.
developable entwicklungsfähig, erschließbar, *(film)* entwickelbar;
~ **position** ausbaufähige Stellung.
developed entwickelt, *(building ground)* baureif;
highly ~ **countries** hoch industrialisierte Länder; **less** ~ **countries** Entwicklungsländer; ~ **tract of land** erschlossenes Gelände.

developer Bauunternehmer, Grundstückserschließer, *(photo)* Entwickler;
slow ~ *(child)* Spätentwickler.
developing | of prints Herstellung von Abzügen;
~ **area** Entwicklungsgebiet; ~ **bath** *(photo)* Entwicklungsbad; ~ **countries (world)** Entwicklungsländer; ~ **dish** *(photo)* Entwicklungsschale; ~ **paper** Abzugspapier; ~ **room** Entwicklungsraum; ~ **tank** *(photo)* Entwicklerbottich; ~ **time** *(photo)* Entwicklungszeit.
development Ausbau, Förderung, *(building, Br.)* Bauvorhaben, -ausführung, *(land)* Erschließung, *(mining)* Aufschließung, *(photo)* Entwicklung, *(real estate)* erschlossenes Gelände, *(natural resources)* Nutzbarmachung;
in process of ~ in der Entwicklung begriffen; **ripe for** ~ baureif; **career** ~ berufliche Entwicklung; **civic** ~ Stadterschließung; **commercial** ~ Verkaufsförderung; **community** ~ Förderung zurückgebliebener Gemeindegrundstücke; **economic** ~ wirtschaftliche Erschließung; **housing** ~ Wohnsiedlung; **industrial** ~ industrielle Erschließung; **interim** ~ zwischenzeitliche Entwicklung; **land** ~ Erschließung von Baugelände; **long-term** ~ langfristige Entwicklung; **politico-economic** ~s wirtschaftspolitische Entwicklungen; **railway** ~ Eisenbahnausbau; **regional** ~ Strukturverbesserung; **residential** ~ Entwicklung zur Wohngegend; **ribbon** ~ *(Br.)* Stadtrandsiedlung; **scientific** ~s wissenschaftliche Errungenschaften; **tariff** ~ zollpolitische Entwicklung; **urban** ~ städtebauliche Entwicklung;
~ **of building ground** Erschließung von Baugelände, Baulanderschließung; ~ **of commercial business** Erschließung von Geschäftsgrundstücken; ~ **of business tendencies** konjunkturelle Entwicklung; ~ **of deposits** Entwicklung der Einlagen; ~ **of photographic films** Entwicklung photographischer Filme; **latest** ~**s in foreign policy** neuestes Stadium der auswärtigen Politik; ~ **of foreign trade** Außenhandelsentwicklung; ~ **of housing** Entwicklung des Wohnungsbaus; ~ **of land** Baulanderschließung; ~ **of prices** Preisentwicklung; ~ **of reserves** Rücklagenentwicklung; ~ **of supervisors** Weiterbildung von Führungskräften; ~ **in technology** technologische Entwicklung; ~ **of a trade area** Aufschließung eines Marktes; ~ **of traffic** Verkehrszunahme, -entwicklung;
to authorize ~ *(Br.)* Baubewilligung erteilen; **to await further** ~s weitere Entwicklung abwarten;
~ **account** Entwicklungsunkostenkonto; ~ **agency** Grundstückserschließungsgesellschaft; **new-town** ~ **agency** Planungsbehörde für neue Städte; ~**-aid** Entwicklungshilfe; ~**-aid man** Entwicklungshelfer; ~ **area** *(Br.)* Entwicklungs-, Notstands-, Fördergebiet, *(land)* Bau-, Siedlungsgelände, *(town planning, Br.)* Ortsplanungsgebiet; ~ **assistance** Entwicklungshilfe; **International** ~ **Association** *(IDA)* internationale Entwicklungsorganisation; ~ **banks** Entwicklungsbanken; **Inter-American** ~ **Bank** Entwicklungsbank für die lateinamerikanischen Länder; ~ **Board** *(Br.)* Entwicklungsbehörde für Zonenrandgebiete; ~ **bonds** *(US)* zwecks Ausbau eines Unternehmens ausgegebene Obligationen; ~ **budget** Entwicklungsetat; **industrial** ~ **certificate** industrielle Erschließungsgenehmigung; ~ **charges** Entwicklungskosten, -ausgaben, *(town and country planning)* Erschließungsgebühr, Baulandabgabe; ~ **Commissioners** Entwicklungsbehörde; ~ **company** Erschließungsgesellschaft; **industrial** ~ **company** Industrieförderungsgesellschaft; ~ **committee** Entwicklungsausschuß; ~ **concern** *(US)* Terraingesellschaft; ~ **contract** Vertrag zum Entwicklungsvorhaben; ~ **corporation** *(US)* Baulandförderungsgesellschaft; ~ **costs** Entwicklungskosten; **property** ~ **costs** Aufschließungskosten; ~ **countries** Entwicklungsländer; **commercial** ~ **department** Abteilung Vertriebsplanung und Verkaufsförderung; ~ **district** *(Br.)* Gebiet mit hoher Arbeitslosigkeit, Fördergebiet; ~ **engineer** Entwicklungstechniker; -ingenieur; ~ **expenditure** Erschließungsaufwand, *(mineral deposits, US)* Ausbaukosten, -aufwand; ~ **expenses** Entwicklungskosten, *(land)* Erschließungskosten; **initial** ~ **expenses** *(production)* Anlaufkosten; ~ **expert** Entwicklungsfachmann; ~ **freeze** Veränderungssperre; ~ **fund** Entwicklungsfonds; **fund for overseas territories** Entwicklungsfonds für die überseeischen Gebiete; ~ **gain** Erschließungsgewinn; **regional** ~ **grant** *(Br.)* Investitionszuschuß [in Fördergebieten]; ~ **land** Erschließungsgelände, -grundstück, Bauerwartungsland; ~ **land market** Markt für Bauerwartungsland; ~ **land tax** *(Br.)* Baulanderschließungsabgabe, Bauerwartungslandabgabe; ~ **level** Entwicklungsniveau; ~ **loan** Entwicklungsanleihe, -kredit, -darlehn; ~ **loan fund** Entwicklungsanleihenfonds; ~ **office** Touristenförderungsbüro; ~ **operation** Entwicklungsvorhaben; ~ **organization** Entwicklungseinrichtung; ~ **plan**

Bauleit-, Erschließungs-, Bebauungsplan, *(land)* Baulanderschließungsprojekt, *(zoning)* Flächennutzungsplan; ~ **planning** Planung der Entwicklung, Entwicklungsplanung, *(building)* Bauleitplanung; ~ **planning economist** Entwicklungsplaner; ~ **policy** wirtschaftliches Entwicklungsprogramm; ~ **policy conception** entwicklungspolitische Konzeption; **business ~ possibilities** geschäftliche Entwicklungsmöglichkeiten; ~ **potentialities** Entwicklungsmöglichkeiten; ~ **priorities** Entwicklungsprioritäten, -vorrechte; ~ **problem** Entwicklungsproblem; ~ **program(me)** Fortbildungsprogramm; ~ **project** Entwicklungsvorhaben; ~ **scheme** Ausbauplan, Entwicklungsvorhaben; ~ **service** Fortbildungseinrichtungen; ~ **site** Erschließungsgelände; ~ **stage** Gründungsstadium; ~ **team** Entwicklungsgruppe; ~ **time** Entwicklungszeit; ~ **value inherent in the land** Wert als Bauerwartungsland, Grundstückswert durch Ortserschließung, durch Baulanderschließung gestiegener Grundstückswert, Erschließungswert; ~ **work** Entwicklungsarbeiten.

developmental entwicklungsmäßig, -freudig;
~ **age** Entwicklungsalter; ~ **aid work** Entwicklungshilfe; ~ **marketeer** aufgeschlossener Absatzfachmann; ~ **requirements** Entwicklungsbedürfnisse; ~ **sweep** Entwicklungsskala.

devest *(v.) (law)* Ansprüche aufheben (für ungültig erklären), *(v./i.)* verlorengehen;
~ **o. s. of one's rights** sich selbst seiner Rechte begeben.

deviate *(v.)* | **from a course** vom Kurs abweichen; ~ **from one's duty** seine Pflicht vernachlässigen; ~ **from instructions** von Weisungen abweichen; ~ **from justice** das Recht beugen; ~ **from a principle** von einem Grundsatz abgehen; ~ **from the main subject** vom eigentlichen Thema abkommen.

deviation *(insurance)* Risikoveränderung, *(patent law)* Gebrauchsmuster, *(pol.)* Abweichlertum, *(ship)* Kursabweichung, *(master and servant)* selbständiges Handeln, *(statistics)* Zufallsabweichung;
mean ~ *(statistics)* durchschnittliche Abweichung; **permissible** ~ zulässige Abweichung; **primary** ~ primäre Abweichung; **standard** ~ mittlere quadratische Abweichung, *(statistics)* Standardabweichung; ~ **of actual cost** Istkostenabweichung; ~ **from the course** Kursabweichung; ~ **from the party line** Abweichung von der Parteilinie; ~ **of quality** Qualitätsabweichung; ~ **from the rules** Abgehen von den Regeln, Regelabweichung; ~ **from the voyage** Abweichung von der Reiseroute;
~ **clause** *(international goods traffic)* Toleranz-, Wegabweichungsklausel.

deviationist *(pol.)* Abweichler, Abtrünniger;
right-wing ~ Rechtsabweichler.

device *(contrivance)* Vorrichtung, Gerät, Apparat, *(design)* Muster, *(motto)* Devise, Wahlspruch, *(plan)* Plan, Entwurf, Zeichnung, *(trick)* Kunstgriff, Trick, Schlich, List, Manöver;
by ~ **or descent** auf Grund testamentarischer oder gesetzlicher Erbfolge; **left to one's own** ~**s** sich selbst überlassen;
collection ~ **s** Inkassoeinrichtungen; **fail-safe** ~ Sicherheitsvorrichtung; **fraudulent** ~ Schwindelunternehmen; **ingenious** ~ sinnreiche Vorrichtung; **mechanical** ~**s** mechanische Vorrichtungen; **modern technical** ~**s** Errungenschaften der modernen Technik; **national** ~ Hoheitszeichen; **nuclear** ~ Atombombe; **procedural** ~ Verfahrenstrick; **safety** ~ Sicherheitsvorrichtung;
~ **for loading and unloading** Hilfsmittel zum Beladen und Entladen; ~ **for protection of checks** *(US)* (cheques, Br.) Scheckschutzvorrichtung; ~ **to put the police off the scent** Trick zur Ablenkung der Polizei;
~ **patent** Vorrichtungspatent.

devil Teufel, Dämon, *(attorney, Br.)* Anwaltsvertreter, -assessor, Hilfsanwalt, *(coll.)* Teufelskerl, *(literary hack)* literarischer Tagelöhner, *(papermaking)* Reißwolf, *(pep, coll.)* Schneid, Draufgängertum;
between the ~ and the deep blue sea in der Klemme, in einem Dilemma (einer verzweifelten Lage), zwischen zwei Feuern; **like the** ~ wie der Teufel, wild;
blue ~ Auswirkungen des Säuferwahnsinns; **poor** ~ armer Schlucker; **printer's** ~ Druckfehlerteufel;
the ~ and all *(coll.)* alles nur Erdenkbare; ~ **a bit** nicht die Spur; **a** ~ **of a business** eine teuflische Sache; ~ **of a fellow** Teufelskerl; **the ~ of it** das Vertrackte an der Sache; ~ **of a job** Heidenarbeit; ~ **of a mess** Mordsdurcheinander; **the** ~ **to pay** heiße Suppe zum Auslöffeln, ernste Sorgen; **a** ~ **in petticoats** eine Furie, ein Teufelsweib; ~ **among the tailors** Hexensabbat, großes Durcheinander;

~ *(v.)* untergeordnete Arbeit leisten, *(journalist)* als Lohnschreiber arbeiten, *(junior counsel)* als Anwaltsgehilfe tätig sein, als Hilfsanwalt fungieren, Terminvertretungen übernehmen;
~ **a colleague** Anwaltskollegen vertreten;
to be the ~ **incarnate** wahrer Dämon sein; **to be working like the** ~ wie ein Besessener arbeiten; **to give the** ~ **his due** jedem das Seine geben; **to go to the** ~ *(sl.)* vor die Hunde gehen; **to have the** ~ **of a time** teuflische Zeit haben; **to play the** ~ **with s. o.** Schindluder (Teufelsspiel) mit jem. treiben; **to play the** ~ **with one's health** seine Gesundheit ruinieren; **to raise the** ~ **about it** Höllenlärm schlagen; **to raise the** ~ **in s. o.** *(coll.)* jds. Leidenschaften entfachen; **to send s. o. to the** ~ j. zum Teufel schicken; **to talk of the** ~ **and he is sure to appear** man soll den Teufel nicht an die Wand malen; **to whip the** ~ **round the stump** durch List und Tücke ans Ziel gelangen;
the ~ **take the hindmost** den Letzten beißen die Hunde; **talk of the** ~ **and his horns will appear** man soll nicht vom Teufel sprechen, wenn man vom Teufel spricht ist er nicht weit;
the ~**'s advocate** Advocatus diaboli; ~ **box** *(coll.)* Elektronengehirn; ~ **dodger** Scheinheiliger, Betbruder; ~ **may-care** verantwortungslos.

devilish teuflisch;
to be in a ~ **hurry** es fürchterlich eilig haben; ~ **plot** widerwärtige Intrige.

devilment Schurkenstreich.

devilry Teufelei, teuflisches Treiben, Teufelsbande.

devious abwegig, irrig;
~ **path** Umweg; **to take a** ~ **route to avoid busy streets** verkehrsreichen Straßen auf einem Umweg ausweichen; **to get rich by** ~ **ways** auf recht ungewöhnliche Weise reich werden.

devisable vererblich, testierbar.

devisal Vermachen, Hinterlassen.

devise *(legacy)* Legat, Vermächtnis [von Grundbesitz], *(will)* Testament[sbestimmung], Verfügung von Todes wegen, letztwillige Verfügung;
conditional ~ bedingte letztwillige Verfügung; **contingent** ~ bedingtes Vermächtnis; **executory** ~ aufschiebend bedingtes Vermächtnis; **general** ~ Vermächtnis bezüglich des gesamten Grundbesitzes; **lapsed** ~ nicht wirksam gewordene letztwillige Verfügung; **residuary** ~ Verfügung über den restlichen Grundbesitz; **special** ~ Vermächtnis bezüglich einzelner Grundstücke; **specific** ~ Grundstücksvermächtnis;
~ *(v.) (contrive)* erfinden, planen, *(land)* Grundbesitz vermachen, letztwillig verfügen;
~ **some good plan** sich einen guten Plan ausdenken; ~ **a scheme for making money** Dukatenesel erfinden; ~ **ways and means** Mittel und Wege finden; ~ **by will** testamentarisch vermachen; **to take land by** ~ Grundbesitz erben.

devisee testamentarischer Erbe, Testamentserbe, *(legacy)* Vermächtnisnehmer;
residuary ~ Haupterbe von Grundbesitz [nach Abzug der Nachlaßverbindlichkeiten].

devising letztwillige Verfügung.

deviser Erfinder.

devisor Erblasser [von Grundbesitz], Testator.

devoirs Höflichkeitsbezeigungen;
to pay one's ~ **to s. o.** jem. seine Aufwartung machen.

devolution Entwicklung, Ablauf, Abrollen, *(inheritance)* Heimfall, Erbfolge, Zufallen durch Erbschaft, *(parl.)* Verweisung an einen Ausschuß, *(passing to successor)* Rechtsübergang, -nachfolge;
~ **of authority** Übergang von Verwaltungsbefugnissen; ~ **of the Crown** Thronfolge; ~ **upon death** (of inheritance, *US*) Erbanfall, Eigentumsübergang von Todeswegen; ~ **of power** Vollmachtsdelegierung; ~ **of property** Eigentumsübertragung, Vermögensübergang; ~ **of title** Eigentumsübergang;
~ **bill** *(Br.)* Gesetz zur Übertragung von Amtsgewalt; ~ **debate** *(Br.)* Debatte über die Einführung regionaler Selbstverwaltung; ~ **plan** *(Scot.)* Selbstverwaltungsplan; ~ **policy** Übergangspolitik.

devolve *(v.)* übergehen, übertragen [werden], *(inheritance)* anheimfallen;
~ **duties upon s. o.** Funktionen auf j. übertragen; ~ **upon the heir** auf den Erben übergehen; ~ **powers upon s. o.** Vollmachten auf j. übertragen; ~ **property upon s. o.** Vermögen auf j. übertragen; ~ **responsibility on s. o.** Verantwortung auf j. abwälzen; ~ **upon s. o.** jem. im Erbwege anfallen; ~ **upon the vice-president** auf den Vizepräsidenten übergehen; ~ **work on a subordinate** Arbeit an einen Untergebenen abgeben.

devolvement Heimfall.

devote *(v.)* weihen, widmen;
  ~ o. s. **anew to business** sich erneut ganz dem Geschäft widmen;
  ~ o. s. **to charity** sich der Wohltätigkeit verschreiben; ~ **a
  column to book criticism** [Zeitungs]spalte für Bücherrezensionen zur Verfügung stellen; ~ **one's time to s. o.** jem. seine Zeit
  widmen.
devoted treu ergeben, aufopfernd;
  ~ **to industry** *(district)* rein industriell genutzt;
  to be ~ to one's children in der Betreuung der Kinder aufgehen;
  to be ~ to book critics für Bücherrezensionen vorgesehen sein;
  to be wholly ~ to a cause sich völlig für eine Sache aufopfern;
  ~ **subjects** treu ergebene Untertanen.
devotedly│attached völlig hingegeben; **to be ~ attached to tradition** ganz in alten Traditionen aufgehen; **to serve one's master ~**
  seinem Herrn in hingebungsvoller Treue dienen.
devotee begeisterter Anhänger, glühender Verehrer;
  ~ **of sport** Sportfanatiker;
  to be surrounded by his ~s von seinen Anhängern umringt sein.
devotion Ergebenheit, Anhänglichkeit;
  ~ **to duty** Pflichtergebenheit; ~ **of a mother to her children**
  Aufopferung einer Mutter für ihre Kinder; ~ **to work** Hingabe
  an die Arbeit.
devotional book Erbauungsbuch.
devotionalist Frömmler.
devour *(v.) (fig.)* verschlingen, gierig in sich aufnehmen;
  ~ **a new detective novel** neuen Kriminalroman sofort
  verschlingen.
devout gottesfürchtig, streng religiös;
  ~ **supporter** aufrichtiger Befürworter; ~ **wishes for your success**
  herzliche Erfolgswünsche.
dexterity comes by experience Übung macht den Meister.
diabetes Zuckerkrankheit.
diabetic diet Diabetikerkost.
diagnose diagnostizieren.
diagnosis Diagnose.
diagram graphische Darstellung, Schaubild, Tabelle, Schema,
  Berechnungstafel, Diagramm;
  ~ *(v.)* graphisch darstellen.
dial *(clock)* Ziffernblatt, *(radio set)* Skala, Skalenscheibe, *(tel.)*
  Wähl-, Nummernscheibe;
  ~ *(v.) (broadcast)* Sender einstellen, *(tel.)* [auf der Nummern-
  scheibe] wählen;
  ~ **a computer** Rechenanlage anwählen; ~ **all day** ganzen Tag
  telefonieren; ~ **a wrong number** falsch[e Nummer] wählen; ~
  the police station Überfallkommando anrufen;
  ~-**a-bus** Busruf; ~-**an-expert service** telefonisch erreichbare
  Fachauskunftsstelle; **direct ~ number** Durchwahlnummer; ~
  system Selbstwählbetrieb, -verkehr; ~ **telephone** Selbstwählfernsprecher; ~ **telephone system** Selbstwählsystem, -betrieb,
  -verkehr; ~ **tone** Summer, Amts-, Freizeichen; **delayed ~ tone**
  Besetztzeichen.
dialect Mundart, Dialekt;
  ~ **atlas** Sprachenatlas.
dialler, magic automatischer Telefonwähler.
dial(l)ing Anwählen;
  direct ~ Durchwahl; **direct distance ~** *(US)* Fernwahl; **intercity
  ~** Selbstwählfernverkehr; **international subscriber (direct) ~**
  internationaler Selbstwählverkehr; **long-distance ~** Fern[lei-
  tungs]wahl; **toll-line ~** *(US)* Selbstwählfernverkehr; **trunk ~**
  (Br.) Fernwahl; **subscriber-trunk ~** *(Br.)* Selbstwählfernverkehr;
  ~ **apparatus** Selbstwählfernsprecher, Selbstwähler; **direct ~
  system** Durchwahlsystem; **direct inward-~ system** Selbstwählverkehr; ~ **tone** Freizeichen.
dialogue *(pol.)* Zwiegespräch.
diaphone Selbstwähler.
diamond Diamant;
  rough ~ unbearbeiteter Diamant, ungeschliffener Edelstein,
  (fig.) weiches Herz in rauher Schale;
  ~ **cut ~** Wurst wider Wurst, List gegen List;
  ~ **field** Diamantenfeld; ~ **necklace** Brillantenhalsband; ~ **pencil** Glaserdiamant; ~ **ring** Brillantring; ~ **wedding** diamantene
  Hochzeit.
diaphram *(camera)* Blende, *(tel.)* Membrane;
  ~ **opening** Blendenöffnung; ~ **shutter** Blendverschluß.
diapositive Diapositiv.
diarist Tagebuchschreiber.
diarize *(v.)* Tagebuch führen, im Tagebuch eintragen.
diary Tagebuch, *(journal)* Journal, *(tickler)* Verfallbuch,
  Vormerk-, Terminkalender;
  bill ~ Wechselverfallbuch.

to keep a ~ Tagebuch führen;
  ~ **fever** eintägiges Fieber; ~ **method** *(broadcasting)* Hörer-
  befragungsmethode.
dibs *(sl.)* Zaster, Moneten, Draht.
dica *(print.)* Cicero.
dice Würfel;
  loaded ~ falscher Würfel;
  ~ *(v.)* **away a fortune** Vermögen durchbringen;
  to play ~ würfeln.
dicebox Knobel-, Würfelbecher.
dichotomous question Ja-Nein-, Alternativfrage.
dick *(sl.)* Schnüffler, Detektiv.
dicker *(US)* Schacher, Tauschhandel;
  ~ *(v.) (US)* Tauschgeschäfte machen.
dickey *(car)* Rück-, Notsitz;
  ~ **box** Fahrersitz.
dictate Gebot, Befehl, Diktat;
  the ~s of conscience das Gebot des Gewissens;
  ~ *(v.)* vorschreiben, diktieren;
  ~ **a letter** Brief diktieren; ~ **a line of action** das weitere Vorgehen genauestens bestimmen; ~ **terms to s. o.** jem. Bedingungen
  auferlegen; ~ **terms to a defeated enemy** einem geschlagenen
  Feind Friedensbedingungen diktieren.
dictated peace Diktatfrieden.
dictating machine, dictaphone *(Br.)* Diktiergerät, -maschine,
  Diktaphon.
dictation Diktat[schreiben], diktierter Text;
  to be tired of s. one's constant ~s jds. dauernde Befehlshaberei
  satt haben; **to take ~** Diktat aufnehmen; **to transcribe ~** Diktat
  auf die Schreibmaschine übertragen; **to write at (from) s. one's
  ~** nach jds. Diktat schreiben, von jem. ein Diktat aufnehmen.
dictator Diktator, Gewaltherrscher, unumschränkter Machthaber;
  ~ **on a small scale** Diktator in der Westentasche;
  to be ~s of dress and fashion Modezaren sein.
dictatorial diktatorisch, absolut, unumschränkt;
  near-~ diktaturähnlich;
  ~ **rule** Diktatorherrschaft.
dictatorship Diktatur;
  military ~ Militärdiktatur;
  ~ **of the proletariat** Diktatur des Proletariats;
  to revert to ~ zur Diktatur zurückkehren.
diction Vortrag, Diktion, Stil, *(US)* korrekte Aussprache.
dictionary Wörterbuch, Lexikon;
  business ~ Wirtschaftswörterbuch; **computerized ~** elektronisches Wörterbuch; **legal ~** Rechtswörterbuch; **pocket ~**
  Taschenwörterbuch; **pronouncing ~** Aussprachewörterbuch;
  subject (technical) ~ Fach-, Spezialwörterbuch; **walking ~**
  (coll.) wandelndes Wörterbuch;
  ~ **of occupational titles** Berufsverzeichnis;
  to have swallowed a ~ sich schwer verständlich ausdrücken; **to
  include a word in a ~** Wort ins Lexikon aufnehmen;
  ~ **catalog(ue)** alphabetisches Bücherverzeichnis; ~ **definition**
  Wörterbuchdefinition; ~ **maker** Lexikograph; ~ **making**
  Abfassung eines Wörterbuches; ~ **slip** Wörterbuchzettel; ~
  work Wörterbuchtätigkeit.
dictograph Abhörgerät.
dictum Ausspruch, *(law)* richterliche Meinung, *(current saying)*
  Maxime, geflügeltes Wort;
  obiter ~ nebenbei geäußerte Bemerkung; **simplex ~** bloße
  Meinungsäußerung.
diddle *(v.)* **s. o.** *(fam.)* j. übers Ohr hauen.
die Würfel, *(stamp)* Präge-, Münzstempel, Matrize;
  sine ~ *(lat.)* ohne Anberaumung eines neuen Termins; **upon the
  ~** auf dem Spiel [stehend];
  ~ *(v.)* sterben, umkommen, *(engine)* stehenbleiben, absterben,
  (fig.) Todesängste ausstehen;
  ~ **of old age** an Altersschwäche sterben; ~ **in one's bed** eines
  natürlichen Todes sterben; ~ **a beggar** als Bettler sterben; ~ **in
  one's boots** mitten im Leben weggerafft werden; ~ **for one's
  country** für sein Vaterland fallen; ~ **by violent death (by violence)** eines gewaltsamen Todes sterben; ~ **deeply in debt** tief
  verschuldet sterben; ~ **in common disaster** gemeinsam umkommen; ~ **in the last ditch** bis zum letzten Atemzug kämpfen; ~
  down *(fire)* erlöschen; ~ **dunghill** feige sterben; ~ **like flies** wie
  die Fliegen sterben; ~ **game** kämpfend sterben; ~ **by one's own
  hand** Selbstmord begehen; ~ **in harness** in Ausübung seines
  Berufes (in den Sielen) sterben; ~ **of hunger** Hungers sterben,
  verhungern; ~ **of an illness** infolge (an) einer Krankheit sterben; ~ **intestate** ohne ein Testament zu hinterlassen sterben; ~
  leaving issue Nachkommen hinterlassen; ~ **with laughter** sich

totlachen; ~ **a martyr** Märtyrertod erleiden; ~ **a natural death** eines natürlichen Todes sterben; ~ **out** aussterben; ~ **poor** in Armut sterben; ~ **simultaneously** gleichzeitig versterben; ~ **to the world** der Welt den Rücken kehren; ~ **from a wound** einer Verwundung erliegen;

~**-cut** ausgestanztes Markenemblem; ~**-cut stamping** Reliefdruck.

diehard hartnäckiger Reaktionär, sturer Anhänger.

diem, per *(lat.)* pro Tag, täglich; **post** ~ nach dem Fälligkeitstag; **per** ~ **pay** Tagegeld.

dies | non *(lat.)* kein Geschäftstag, geschäftsfreier Tag, *(law court)* gerichtsfreier Tag;

~ **ad quem** Endtermin, Fristende; ~ **a quo** Fristbeginn.

diesel electric locomotive Diesellokomotive.

diet Parlament, *(Germany)* Landtag, *(hearing)* Vernehmungstermin, *(for meals)* Diät, Schonkost, *(sitting in court)* Gerichtssitzung;

low ~ magere Kost; **strict** ~ strenge Diät;

~ *(v.)* Diät halten;

to be put upon a ~ auf Krankenkost gesetzt sein; **to go on a** ~ sich einer Diätkur unterziehen; **to offer a full** ~ **of national and international coverage** über nationale wie internationale Ereignisse gleichmäßig und detailliert berichten; **to take a** ~ Diät leben; **to vary one's** ~ Diätänderung vornehmen;

to be a ~ **faddist** mit einer strengen Diät leben; ~ **kitchen** Diätküche; ~ **restrictions** Diätvorschriften; ~ **sheet** Diätzettel.

dietary Diätvorschrift, -zettel;

~ **rules** Diätvorschriften.

dieting Schlankheitskur.

differ *(v.)* abweichen, sich unterscheiden, verschieden sein, *(disagree)* verschiedener Meinung sein, differieren, sich nicht einig sein, *(opinion)* auseinandergehen, *(testimony)* nicht übereinstimmen, widersprüchlich sein;

~ **with s. o.** mit jem. verschiedener Meinung sein; ~ **widely in their tastes** völlig verschiedene Geschmäcker haben;

to agree to ~ sich nicht mehr darüber streiten, daß man verschiedener Meinung ist.

difference Unterschied, Unterscheidung, Verschiedenheit, *(in amount)* Differenz, Unterschiedsbetrag, *(criterion)* Kennzeichen, Unterscheidungsmerkmal, *(disagreement)* Unstimmigkeit, Uneinigkeit, Differenz, Streit, *(math.)* Differenz, Rest, *(produce exchange)* Qualitätsunterschied, *(stock exchange)* Kursdifferenz;

minute ~ feiner Unterschied; **negligible** ~ geringfügiger Unterschied; **price** ~ Preisunterschied, -differenz, *(stock exchange)* Kursdifferenz;

~ **in age** Altersunterschied; ~ **submissible to arbitration** schiedsgerichtsfähige Meinungsverschiedenheit; ~ **in costs of production** unterschiedliche Produktionskosten; ~ **of exchange** Kursdifferenz; ~ **in level** Niveauunterschied; ~ **of opinion** Meinungsverschiedenheit; ~ **between cash and settlement price** *(stock exchange)* Differenz zwischen Kassa- und Terminkurs; ~ **in prices** Preisunterschied, -differenz; ~ **in price levels** unterschiedliches Preisniveau; ~ **in rates** Kursunterschied, *(freight)* Frachtsatzunterschied; ~ **in temperature** Temperaturunterschied; ~ **in treatment** unterschiedliche Behandlung; ~ **in weight** Gewichtsunterschied;

~ *(v.)* Unterschied machen, differenzieren;

to adjust a ~ Differenz richtigstellen; **to make all the** ~ Sache ganz anders aussehen lassen; **to make a great deal of** ~ von ziemlicher Bedeutung sein; **to make not much** ~ ziemlich unwichtig sein; **not to make two straws'** ~ *(coll.)* völlig bedeutungslos sein; **to make up a** ~ Streit schlichten; **to pay the** ~ Differenz herauszahlen; **to settle one's** ~**s** seine Meinungsverschiedenheiten beilegen; **to sink one's** ~**s** seine Meinungsverschiedenheiten begraben; **to speculate for** ~**s** Differenzgeschäfte machen; **to split the** ~ strittigen Preisunterschied (sich in die Differenz) teilen;

~ **limen (threshold)** Unterschiedsschwelle.

different verschieden[artig], abweichend;

to feel a ~ **man** sich ganz anders als früher fühlen; **to wear a** ~ **suit every day** jeden Tag etw. anderes anziehen.

differential Unterschiedsmerkmal, *(advertising)* Tarifunterschied, *(difference in prices)* Kursgefälle, *(difference in rates)* Frachtdifferenz, *(difference in wages)* Lohngefälle, *(fare)* Fahrpreisdifferenz, *(motor vehicle)* Differential;

freight ~ Frachtunterschied; **inter-industry** ~ industrielles Lohngefälle, Wirtschaftsgefälle; **inter-plant** ~ betriebliches Lohngefälle; **interest** ~ Zinsgefälle; **liquidity** ~ Liquiditätsgefälle; **price** ~ Preisgefälle; **wage** ~ Lohnunterschied, -gefälle; **regional wage and salary** ~ regionales Lohngefälle;

~ *(a.)* besonders, charakteristisch, unterschiedlich, gestaffelt; ~ **calculus** Differentialrechnung; ~ **costing** Grenzkostenlehre; ~ **coupling** Diffentialkupplung; ~ **duty** Vorzugs-, Differentialzoll; ~ **equation** Differentialgleichung; ~ **feature** Unterscheidungsmerkmal; ~ **gear** Differentialgetriebe; ~ **line** *(traffic)* Linie mit Vorzugstarif; ~ **piece-rate system** Differential-, Stücklohnverfahren; ~ **price** Preisstaffel, -spanne, gestaffelter Preis, Staffelpreis; ~ **price system** Preisdifferenzierung, Tarifstaffel; ~ **quotient** Differentialquotient; ~ **rate** Ausnahmefrachtsatz, -tarif; ~ **tariff** Differential, Staffeltarif, *(common carrier)* Ausnahmetarif, *(customs)* Differentialzoll; ~ **wage** Staffellohn.

differentiate *(v.)* Unterschied machen, [sich] unterscheiden, differenzieren, *(wages)* staffeln.

differentiation Unterscheidung, Differenzierung;

~ **of labo(u)r** Arbeitsteilung.

difficult | of access schwer zugänglich; ~ **to get** schwer zu beschaffen; ~ **to grasp** schwer verständlich; **to be placed in** ~ **circumstances** sich in einer schwierigen Lage wiederfinden; ~ **language** schwer zu erlernende Sprache; **to be a** ~ **man to get on with** schwer zu behandelnder Mensch sein; ~ **task** schweres Stück Arbeit.

difficulties Schwierigkeiten, finanzielle Bedrängnis;

further ~ neue Schwierigkeiten; **initial** ~ Anlaufschwierigkeiten; **pecuniary** ~ finanzielle Schwierigkeiten, Zahlungsschwierigkeiten;

~ **of organization** Organisationsschwierigkeiten; ~ **of supply** Versorgungsschwierigkeiten;

to be confronted with ~ vor Schwierigkeiten stehen; **to be in financial** ~ Schulden haben, in mißlicher finanzieller Lage sein; **to deal with unforeseen** ~ mit unvorhergesehenen Schwierigkeiten fertig werden; **to encounter** ~ in [finanzielle] Schwierigkeiten geraten; **to have** ~ **in making both ends meet** sich nur mit Mühe über Wasser halten können; **to meet with** ~ auf Schwierigkeiten stoßen; **to remove** ~ Schwierigkeiten beheben; **to run up against** ~ plötzlich Schwierigkeiten bekommen; **to tide over one's** ~ seiner Schwierigkeiten Herr werden.

difficulty Schwierigkeit, schwierige Sache, Mühe, Problem;

~ **in the money market** Geldmarktklemme.

dig Graben, *(push)* Stoß, Puff, *(cutting remark)* sarkastische Bemerkung, *(student, US sl.)* Büffler, Streber;

~**s** *(Br., sl.)* Studentenbude;

~ **in the side** Rippenstoß;

~ *(v.)* *(Br., sl.)* Bude haben, hausen;

~ **away** *(coll.)* büffeln, ochsen; ~ **o. s. in** *(mil.)* sich eingraben, *(fig.)* seine Position verstärken, feste Stellung beziehen; ~ **for information** Informationen zu erlangen suchen; ~ **out** *(fig.)* ans Tageslicht bringen, aufdecken; ~ **a pit** Fallgrube ausheben, *(fig.)* Falle stellen; ~ **deep into one's pocket** tief in die Tasche greifen; ~ **the staff out from under the paperwork mountain** Belegschaft von der Last des bürokratischen Papierkrams befreien; ~ **up** *(fig.)* ans Tageslicht bringen, aufdecken, *(US sl.)* Geld ergattern (herausrücken); ~ **up the hatchet (tomahawk)** das Kriegsbeil ausgraben;

to give s. o. a ~ *(fig.)* jem. eins verpassen (auswischen); **to have a slight** ~ **at s. o.** j. leicht sarkastisch behandeln; **to have a** ~ **at Spanish** es einmal mit der spanischen Sprache versuchen.

digest Fall-, Gesetzessammlung, *(abstract)* Zusammenfassung, Abriß, Auszug;

~ **of the week's news** Zusammenstellung der Neuigkeiten einer Woche, Wochenüberblick;

~ *(v.)* *(classify)* klassifizieren, kodifizieren, *(fig.)* innerlich verarbeiten, in sich aufnehmen;

~ **an insult** *(coll.)* Beleidigung herunterschlucken; ~ **what one reads** seinen Lesestoff verdauen.

digestion Verdauung, *(fig.)* innerliche Verarbeitung.

digging Graben, *(region, US)* Bergbaubezirk.

diggings *(Br., coll.)* Bude, Behausung, Quartier;

to live in ~ *(Br.)* eigene Bude besitzen.

digit Ziffer, Dezimalstelle;

~ **display** *(computer)* Zahlenfeld.

digital | calculator Digitalrechner; ~ **watch** Digitaluhr.

dignified old lady würdige alte Dame.

dignify *(v.)* ehren, auszeichnen;

~ **a small collection of books by calling it a library** kleine Büchersammlung euphemistisch mit Bibliothek bezeichnen.

dignitary Würdenträger.

dignity Würde, hoher Rang, *(newspaper)* Niveau;

the whole ~ **of the country** alle Würdenträger des Landes; ~ **of labo(u)r** Idol der Arbeit; ~ **of man** Menschenwürde; ~ **of soul** Seelengröße;

to be beneath s. one's ~ unter jds. Würde sein; **to reach the ~ of treason** an Verrat grenzen; **to stand [up] on one's ~** sehr formell sein, sich nichts vergeben.

digress *(v.)* abweichen, abschweifen;
~ **from the main subject** vom Hauptthema abkommen.

digression Abschweifung, Abweichung.

dijudication Ver-, Aburteilung.

dike Deich, Damm, Hinderniswall, *(fig.)* Bollwerk;
~ *(v.)* eindämmen.

diker Deicharbeiter.

dilapidate *(v.)* einreißen, zerstören;
~ **a building** Haus verfallen lassen; ~ **a fortune** Vermögen vergeuden.

dilapidated baufällig, verfallen, abbruchreif, verwahrlost;
~ **abode** verkommenes Quartier; ~ **looking car** dringend reparaturbedürftiges Auto; ~ **fortune** verschleudertes Vermögen; ~ **old house** verfallenes altes Haus.

dilapidation Verfall, *(building)* Baufälligkeit, *(lease)* bei der Pachtbeendigung notwendige Reparaturen;
~s Baubeschädigungen;
to be responsible for all ~s *(outgoing tenant)* für alle Reparaturen aufzukommen haben.

dilate *(v.)* sich ausdehnen;
~ **upon a subject** Thema detaillierter behandeln.

dilatoriness Saumseligkeit, Zögern.

dilatory säumig, saumselig, *(law)* aufschiebend, verzögernd, hinhaltend, dilatorisch;
~ **in undertaking business** nicht geschäftüchtig;
~ **defence** hinhaltendes Taktieren, *(law court)* aufschiebender (dilatorischer) Einwand; ~ **methods** Verschleppungsmethoden; ~ **motion** Verzögerungsantrag; ~ **payer** säumiger Zahler; ~ **payment** langsame Bezahlung; ~ **plea** dilatorische (prozeßhindernde) Einrede; ~ **policy** dilatorische Behandlung, Verzögerungspolitik, -taktik.

dilemma Verlegenheit, Klemme, Dilemma;
moral ~ Gewissensnot;
to be in a ~ in der Klemme sitzen; **to pose a ~** Verlegenheit verursachen.

dilettante Amateur, Dilettant, Laie, Nichtfachmann, *(dabbler)* Stümper, Pfuscher.

dilettantish dilettantisch, stümperhaft.

dilettantism Dilettantismus.

diligence Eifer, Fleiß, *(law)* Sorgfalt, Sorgfaltspflicht, *(Scot. law)* Zwangsvollstreckung;
with all ~ mit der erforderlichen (gehörigen) Sorgfalt;
due ~ sorgsame Erfüllung, im Verkehr erforderliche Sorgfalt; **extraordinary ~** außergewöhnlich hohe Sorgfaltspflicht; **great (high) ~** erhöhte Sorgfaltspflicht; **low ~** geringe Sorgfalt; **necessary ~** erforderliche Sorgfalt; **ordinary ~** verkehrsübliche Sorgfaltspflicht; **reasonable ~** zumutbare Sorgfalt; **reasonable care and ~** im Verkehr erforderliche Sorgfalt; **special ~** von einem Fachmann erwartete Sorgfaltspflicht;
~ **exercised in regard to any and all of one's affairs** Sorgfalt wie in eigenen Angelegenheiten; ~ **usual in ordinary business** im gewöhnlichen Verkehr erforderliche Sorgfalt;
to act with reasonable care and ~ mit der im Verkehr erforderlichen Sorgfalt handeln; **to bestow great ~** große Sorgfalt anwenden; **to do one's (give, use) ~** erforderliche Sorgfalt anwenden; **to employ (exercise) ~** Sorgfalt anwenden; **to exercise the required degree of skill and ~** die im Verkehr erforderliche Sorgfalt anwenden.

diligent arbeitsam;
to be ~ in one's business fleißig seinen Geschäften nachgehen.

dilute *(v.)* verdünnen, *(stocks)* verwässern, *(weaken)* schwächen;
~ **the equity with stock dividends** Nettoanteil mit der Ausgabe von Gratisaktien verwässern; ~ **labo(u)r** ungelernte Arbeiter einstellen; ~ **time** Zeit vergeuden; ~ **wine with water** Wein mit Wasser mischen.

dilutee ungelernter Arbeiter.

dilution Verdünnung, Verwässerung;
~ **of labo(u)r** Einstellung ungelernter Arbeiter; ~ **of stocks** Aktienverwässerung; ~ **of time** Zeitvergeudung, -verschwendung.

dim halbdunkel, verschwommen, *(fig.)* schwer von Begriff;
~ *(v.)* **the headlights** Fernlicht abblenden; ~ **out** abblenden; ~ **the sight** Sicht trüben;
to get ~ *(eyesight)* nachlassen;
~ **forebodings** düstere Vorahnungen; ~ **outlines of buildings** verschwommene Gebäudekonturen; ~ **recollections of childhood** schwache Erinnerungen an die Kindheit; **to take a ~ view of s. th.** etw. mit Skepsis betrachten.

dim-out teilweise Verdunkelung;
cultural ~ Drosselung der kulturellen Betätigung.

dime Zehncentstück;
~s Geld, Gewinn;
to be a dozen a ~ *(US)* spottbillig sein, nachgeworfen bekommen;
~ **museum** *(US)* Kuriositätenmuseum; ~ **novel** *(US)* Groschen-, Schund-, Hintertreppenroman; ~ **store** *(US)* Niedrig-, Einheitspreisgeschäft; ~**-store product** *(US)* Niedrig-, Einheitspreiserzeugnis.

dimension Ausdehnung, Dimension;
~s Größenverhältnisse, Umfang, Raummaß, Format;
~**s of a room** Ausmaße eines Zimmers;
~ *(v.)* abmessen, dimensionieren;
to take the ~s of a room Zimmer ausmessen.

dimensional dimensional;
three-~ film dreidimensionaler Film.

diminish *(v.)* *(become less)* abnehmen, geringer werden, sich verringern (vermindern), *(put down)* herabsetzen, *(reduce)* [Ausgaben] einschränken, ermäßigen;
~ **the value of an evidence** Aussage stark entwerten; ~ **the country's wealth** Reichtum eines Landes reduzieren; ~ **in value** Wertverlust erleiden.

diminishable reduzierbar.

diminished *(business)* zurückgegangen;
~ **proceeds** Minndererlös; ~ **responsibility** verminderte Zurechnungsfähigkeit; ~ **return** Ertragsrückgang.

diminishing | food supplies schwächer werdende Nahrungsmittelversorgung; ~ **productivity** Produktivitätsrückgang; ~ **returns** abnehmender Ertrag, Ertragsrückgang; ~ **utility** Grenznutzen; ~ **value** abnehmender Wert.

diminution Verminderung, Reduzierung, Abnahme, *(in a record sent up)* Auslassung, Unvollständigkeit;
~ **of capital goods** Kapitalgüterverringerung; ~ **of expense** Kostenverringerung; ~ **of a price** Preisreduzierung; ~ **of profits** Gewinnschrumpfung; ~ **of taxes** Steuerherabsetzung, -milderung; ~ **in value** Wertminderung; ~ **in weight** Gewichtsminderung;
to hope for a small ~ of taxes auf kleine Steuererleichterungen hoffen; **to show a considerable ~ of profits** beträchtlichen Ertragsrückgang aufweisen.

dimmed abgeblendet;
~ **by the deeds of his son** von den Leistungen seines Sohnes in den Schatten gestellt;
~ **light** abgeblendetes Licht.

dimmer *(car)* Abblendvorrichtung, *(theater)* Bühnenlichtregulator.

dimming of lights Scheinwerferabblendung.

din Lärm, Getöse, *(fig.)* Durcheinander, Wirrwarr;
~ *(v.)* **s. th. into s. o.** jem. etw. einhämmern; ~ **into s. one's ears the importance of hard work** jem. die Notwendigkeit harter Arbeit vorpredigen;
to make so much ~ derartigen Krach machen.

dine | *(v.)* out auswärts essen; ~ **out on a story** Geschichte immer wieder zum Besten geben; ~ **with Lord Humphrey** am Hungertuch nagen.

diner Abendgast, *(dining car, US)* Speisewagen;
roadside ~ Straßenrestaurant;
to take off the ~ *(US)* Speisewagen abhängen.

dingbat *(sl.)* Moneten.

dingdong *(a.)* ernsthaft;
to get to work ~ mit Eifer an die Arbeit gehen;
~ **struggle** wechselvoller Kampf.

dinghy Beiboot, *(airplane)* Schlauchboot.

dining | alcove Eßecke; ~ **car** Speisewagen; ~**-car worker** Speisewagenangestellter; ~ **chair** Eßzimmerstuhl; ~ **hall** Speisesaal; ~ **recess** Eßecke; ~ **room** Speisesaal; **private ~ room** Vorstandskasino; ~ **saloon** *(ship)* Speiseraum.

dinner [Fest]essen, Diner;
candlelight ~ Kerzendinner; **slap-up ~** vorzügliches Essen;
to give a ~ Abendessen geben;
~ **bell** Tischglocke; ~ **bucket** *(US)* Essensträger; ~ **card** Tischkarte; ~ **clothes** Abendanzug; ~ **dress** kleines Abendkleid; ~ **jacket** Smoking; ~ **pail** *(US)* Essensträger; ~ **party** Abendgesellschaft; ~ **speech** *(US)* Tischrede; ~ **set (service)** Tafelgeschirr; ~ **table** fahrbarer Serviertisch.

diocese Sprengel, Diözese.

dip Eintauchen, *(business cycle)* Geschäftrückgang, [Wirtschafts]flaute, *(mining law)* Tiefgang, *(US sl., pick-pocket)* Taschendiebstahl, *(downward slope)* Bodensenke;
daily ~ tägliches Bad; **staining ~** Farblösung;

~ **in business** Konjunkturmulde; ~ **in a curve** Knick in einer Kurve; ~ **of the horizon** Depressionswinkel; ~ **in prices** Preisverfall; ~ **in the road** Senkung der Straße;

~ *(v.)* ein-, untertauchen, *(business cycle)* zurückgehen, *(cause trouble, coll.)* in Schwierigkeiten verwickeln, *(pilfer, sl.)* Taschendiebstahl begehen, beklauen, *(stock exchange)* [ab]-sinken;

~ **into a book** Blick in ein Buch werfen; ~ **the flag** Flagge dippen; ~ **the headlights** Scheinwerfer abblenden; ~ **below the horizon** *(sun)* hinter dem Horizont versinken; ~ **into one's purse** seine Geldbörse zücken; ~ **sharply** *(road)* sich scharf senken;

to have a ~ into an author sich flüchtig mit einem Autor beschäftigen; **to have a ~ into a book** flüchtigen Blick in ein Buch werfen.

diploma Diplom, Ernennungsurkunde, Abgangs-, Prüfungszeugnis, *(official document)* amtliches Schriftstück, Urkunde; **high-school ~** *(US)* Abschlußzeugnis an der Oberschule; **teachers' ~** Lehramtsbefähigung;

~ **in architecture** Architektendiplom; ~ **in business administration** betriebswirtschaftlicher Abschluß;

~ *(v.)* mit einem Zeugnis versehen, Diplom verleihen;

to confer (furnish with) a ~ Diplom zuerkennen;

~ **holder** Diplominhaber; ~ **piece** Gesellenstück.

diplomacy Diplomatie, *(fig.)* diplomatisches Vorgehen, politischer Takt;

conference ~ Konferenzdiplomatie; **dollar ~** *(US)* Dollarpolitik; **open-mouth ~** Politik der unverblümten Sprache; **peacemaking ~** Friedendiplomatie; **secret ~** Geheimdiplomatie; **step-by-step ~** Politik der kleinen Schritte;

~ **by conferences** Konferenzdiplomatie;

to attain one's end by ~ auf diplomatischem Wege an sein Ziel gelangen; **to use a little ~ (act with) ~** diplomatisch vorgehen.

diplomat Diplomat, Gesandter;

career ~ Berufsdiplomat; **professional ~** Berufsdiplomat; **resident ~** akkreditierter Diplomat; **skilled ~** gewandter Diplomat;

to be a good ~ diplomatisch sein;

~**'s dwelling** Diplomatenwohnsitz.

diplomatic diplomatisch, *(fig.)* diplomatisch, taktvoll, geschickt, klug;

to be ~ in dealing with people seine Mitmenschen zu behandeln (nehmen) wissen;

~ **accreditation** Akkreditierung; ~ **action** diplomatischer Schritt, diplomatische Tätigkeit; ~ **activity** diplomatische Aktivität; ~ **agency** Auslanddienststelle, diplomatische Vertretung; ~ **agent** diplomatischer Vertreter; **to appoint a ~ agent** diplomatischen Vertreter ernennen; ~ **answer** diplomatische Antwort; ~ **asylum** diplomatisches Asyl; ~ **bag** Kurierpost; ~ **body (corps)** diplomatisches Korps; **formal ~ break** Abbruch der diplomatischen Beziehungen; ~ **career** diplomatische Laufbahn; ~ **channels** diplomatische Kanäle; **through ~ channels** auf dem üblichen diplomatischen Wege; **in ~ communications** im diplomatischen Verkehr; ~ **copy** mit dem Original genau übereinstimmende Abschrift; ~ **courier** diplomatischer Kurier; ~ **customs** diplomatische Gebräuche; **to enjoy ~ immunities** diplomatische Immunität genießen; ~ **intercourse** diplomatischer Verkehr; ~ **language** Diplomatensprache; **at ~ level** auf diplomatischer Ebene; ~ **life** Diplomatenleben; ~ **management** diplomatische (taktvolle) Regelung (Erledigung); ~ **methods** diplomatisches Verfahren; ~ **mission** diplomatische Vertretung; **to put a number of ~ noses out of joint** alteingebürgerte diplomatische Gepflogenheiten mißachten; ~ **observer** diplomatischer Beobachter; ~ **passport** Diplomatenpaß; ~ **personnel** diplomatische Bedienstete; ~ **post** Diplomatenposten; ~ **pouch** Diplomatengepäck, Kuriergepäck; ~ **privilege** diplomatische Immunität, Exterritorialität; **to be entitled to ~ privileges** diplomatische Vorrechte genießen; ~ **profession** Diplomatenberuf; ~ **protection** diplomatischer Schutz; ~ **quarter** Diplomatenviertel; **in ~ quarters** in diplomatischen Kreisen; ~ **recognition** diplomatische Anerkennung; **to exchange ~ recognition** sich gegenseitig diplomatisch anerkennen; **to enter into (establish) ~ relations** diplomatische Beziehungen aufnehmen; **to reestablish (resume) ~ relations** diplomatische Beziehungen wiederherstellen; **to suspend ~ relations** diplomatische Beziehungen unterbrechen; ~ **representation** diplomatische Vertretung, Auslandsvertretung; **to recall a ~ representative** diplomatischen Vertreter abberufen; ~ **round** Alltagsleben eines Diplomaten; **to be in the ~ service** Diplomat (Beamter des Auswärtigen Amtes) sein; **to enter the ~ service** in das Auswärtige Amt (den diplomatischen Dienst) eintreten; ~ **soundings** diplomatische Sondierung.

diplomatist Diplomat.

diplomatize *(v.)* diplomatisch vorgehen.

dipped *(headlight)* abgeblendet.

dipper Baggereimer; *(thief, fam.)* Taschendieb;

~ **dredger** Schaufelbagger; ~ **switch** Abblendschalter.

dipping | light Abblendlicht; ~ **rod** Wünschelrute.

dipstick Meßstab.

dire äußerst;

~ **necessity** dringende Notwendigkeit; ~ **poverty** größte Armut; ~ **sisters** Furien; **to be in ~ want** sich in großer Not befinden.

direct direkt, gerade, unmittelbar, persönlich, *(descent)* direkt, in gerader Linie;

~ *(v.)* richten, lenken, *(address)* [Brief] adressieren, *(control)* beaufsichtigen, beherrschen, leiten, steuern, dirigieren, *(film)* Regie führen, *(manage)* [Betrieb] leiten, führen, lenken, *(last will)* bestimmen, *(order)* anordnen, anweisen, verfügen, bestimmen, gebieten, befehlen, *(workers)* einsetzen, einschleusen;

~ **an advance to be made** Vorrücken befehlen; ~ **the aerial towards a station** Funkantenne auf einen Sender einstellen; ~ **s. one's attention to s. th.** jds. Aufmerksamkeit auf etw. lenken; ~ **a counsel** Anwalt zurechtweisen; ~ **goods to s. o.** jem. Waren unmittelbar zuschicken; ~ **jurors** Geschworenen Rechtsbelehrung erteilen; ~ **a letter to s. o.** Brief an j. richten; ~ **a letter to s. one's business address** Brief an jds. Büroadresse schicken; ~ **measures against s. o.** Maßnahmen gegen j. ergreifen; ~ **a parcel correctly** Paket ordnungsgemäß beschriften; ~ **s. o. to the station** jem. den Weg zum Bahnhof zeigen; ~ **one's steps towards home** seine Schritte nach Hause lenken; ~ **s. o. wrongly** jem. eine falsche Auskunft geben; ~ **a work** Arbeit leiten; ~ **the workmen** Arbeitskräfte beaufsichtigen;

to dispatch goods ~ to s. o. jem. Waren unmittelbar zuschicken;

to go ~ *(train)* durchgehen;

~ **action** Direktaktion; ~**-action advertising** auf spontane Kaufreaktion abgestellte Werbung; ~ **advertising** Konsumenten-, Direktwerbung; ~ **answer** klare Antwort; **to make a ~ answer to the charges brought against o. s.** sich ganz offen (freimütig) zu den vorgebrachten Beschuldigungen äußern; ~ **attack against judgment** Urteilsanfechtung; ~ **buying** Direkteinkauf, -bezug; ~ **cause** unmittelbare Ursache; ~ **charge** unmittelbare Belastung; ~ **collection** direktes Inkasso; ~ **commerce** Direkthandel; ~ **commercial** unmittelbare Werbesendung; ~ **communication** direkte Verbindung; ~ **competition** *(railroad)* Wettbewerb zweier Eisenbahnlinien; **to be in ~ contact with s. o.** unmittelbaren Kontakt mit jem. haben; **in ~ contradiction** im offenen Gegensatz; **the ~ contrary** das direkte Gegenteil; ~ **cost** direkte Kosten, Selbstkosten, Einzelkosten; ~ **costing** *(US)* Teil-, Grenz[plan]kostenrechnung; ~ **current** *(el.)* Gleichstrom; ~**-to-customer selling** Direktverkauf an den Kunden; ~ **damage** unmittelbarer Schaden; ~ **debit** automatische Abbuchung, Direktabbuchung; ~ **debiting** *(banking)* Abbuchungs-, Lastschriftverfahren, Abbuchungsgenehmigung; ~ **debiting service** Abbuchungs-, Rechnungseinzugs-, Lastschriftverfahren; ~ **descendant** direkter Nachkomme; **to be a ~ descendant of s. o.** unmittelbar von jem. abstammen, jds. direkter Nachkomme sein; ~ **discourse** direkte Rede; ~**-dial telephone** Durchwahlapparat; ~**-dial telephone with bathroom extension** Durchwahlapparat mit Badezimmeranschluß; ~ **dialling** *(tel.)* Durchwahl; **international ~ dialling** internationaler Selbstwählverkehr; ~ **distribution** Produzentenhandel; ~ **endorsement** *(US)* Vollgiro; ~ **evidence** Beweis aufgrund eigener Wahrnehmung, *(law)* unmittelbarer Beweis; ~ **examination** *(law court, US)* Zeugenvernehmung durch Zeugen der anderen Partei; ~ **exchange** *(foreign exchange)* Mengenkurs, -notierung, fester Umrechnungskurs; ~ **expenses** direkte (feste) Kosten; ~ **departmental expenses** unmittelbar bei einer Abteilung anfallende Verwaltungskosten; ~ **financing** Direktkredit der Wirtschaft; ~ **flight** Direktflug; ~ **goods account** eigenes Materialkonto; ~ **government** Volksbefragung; ~ **hit** *(mil.)* Volltreffer; ~ **indorsement** *(US)* Vollgiro; ~**-injected engine** Einspritzmotor; ~ **injection** *(fuel)* Benzineinspritzung; ~ **insurance** Erst-, Direktversicherung; ~ **insurer** Erstversicherer; ~ **interest** unmittelbares Interesse; ~ **investments** Direktinvestitionen; ~ **labo(u)r** unmittelbar geleistete Arbeitszeit; ~ **labo(u)r cost** Fertigungslöhne, Fertigungslohnkosten; ~ **labo(u)r hour** Fertigungslohnstunde; ~ **liability** *(US)* unbestrittene und unbedingte Verbindlichkeit; ~ **line** *(descent)* direkte Linie, *(tel.)* Direktleitung; ~ **loss** *(insurance)* versicherter (unmittelbarer) Schaden; ~ **loss by fire** unmittelbarer Feuerschaden; ~**-mail advertising (shot)** Direktwerbung durch die Post, Postversandwerbung, -streuung, -wurfsendung; ~-**mail literature** Reklamematerial für Postwurfsendungen, Postwurfprospekt; ~-**mail marketing** Verkaufsmethode zur Beschaffung postalischer Aufträge; ~-**mail media** direkte Werbemittel; ~-**mail method** postalische Befragung; ~-**mail promotion** Direktwerbung durch die Post; ~-**mail selling** Verkauf durch Postversand, Versandhandel; ~-**mail solicitation** Postversandwerbung; ~ **marketing** Direktabsatz, individuelle Absatzpolitik; ~-**marketing manufacturer** Fabrikhandel; ~ **material** Fertigungs-, Produktionsmaterial; ~-**material costs** unmittelbarer Materialaufwand; ~ **method** (language) direkte Methode, Intensivmethode; ~ **obligation** unbestrittene Verpflichtung; ~ **payment** endgültige Zahlung; ~ **placement** Direktplazierung; ~ **port** vorbestimmter Hafen; ~ **premium** Zugabe; ~ **primary** (US) Vorwahl; ~ **process** Direktaufnahme; ~ **purchase** Beziehungskauf; ~ **rates** (Br.) in Pence notierte Devisenkurse; ~ **ray** Bodenstrahl; ~-**reporting agency system** (insurance) unmittelbares Unterstellungsverhältnis; ~ **responsibility** persönliche Verantwortung; ~ **route** kürzeste Route; ~ **sale** Direktverkauf, -absatz, -vertrieb, Verkauf ohne Zwischenhändler; ~ **sale to the public** (stock exchange) freihändiger Verkauf; ~ **scanning** (television) punktförmige Abtastung; ~ **selling** Direktverkauf, -absatz; ~ **selling costs** unmittelbare Verkaufskosten; ~ **shipment** Direktversand; ~ **speech** (ling.) direkte Rede; ~ **take-off** Senkrechtstart; ~ **tax** direkte (nicht abwälzbare) Steuer; ~ **taxation** direkte Besteuerung; ~ **train** durchgehender Zug; ~ **vision finder** (photo) Direktsucher; ~ **vote** direkte (unmittelbare) Wahl; ~ **voting** Direktwahl; ~ **wages** unmittelbare (direkte) Lohnkosten; **to have a** ~ **way of speaking** ganz ungeniert sprechen; ~-**writing company** (carrier) Rückversicherungsgesellschaft.

directed, as laut Verfügung, nach Vorschrift;
~ **economy** gelenkte Wirtschaft, Planwirtschaft.

directedness, other Außenleitung.

direction Richtung, (address) Adresse, Aufschrift, Beschriftung, Anschrift, (board) Vorstand, Direktion, Direktorium, (capital control) Bewirtschaftung, (film, theater) Spielleitung, Regie, (instruction) [An]weisung, Belehrung, Unterweisung, Richtschnur, Direktive, (jurors, Br.) Rechtsbelehrung, (equity law, US) Anrede des Gerichts in einer Klageschrift, (managing) Leitung, Lenkung, Geschäftsführung, (order) Verfügung, Anordnung, Anweisung, Vorschrift, Auftrag, (region) Gegend, Richtung, (traffic) Fahrtrichtung;
according to ~s nach Anweisung, laut Verfügung, weisungsgemäß; **from all** ~s von allen Seiten; **by** ~ **of** auf Veranlassung (Weisung) von; **subject to** ~s weisungsgebunden; **under the** ~ **of** unter der Leitung von;
~s (master, Br.) prozeßleitende Bestimmung;
insufficient ~s ungenaue Adressenangabe; **stage direction** Bühnenanweisung;
~ **of approach** Anflugrichtung; ~ **of a company** Leitung einer Gesellschaft; ~s **to the constables** Anweisungen an die Polizei; ~ **of consumption** Verbrauchslenkung; ~s **for correctors** Korrekturvorschriften; **new** ~ **in education** neue Richtung im Erziehungswesen; ~ **of labo(u)r** Arbeits[einsatz]lenkung; ~s **on a parcel** Paketbeschriftung; ~ **of the traffic** Verkehrsregelung; ~ **of the treasury** Weisung des Finanzministeriums; ~s **for use** Gebrauchsanweisung, -vorschrift;
to act according to ~s weisungsgemäß handeln; **to assume the** ~ **of an enterprise** Leitung eines Unternehmens übernehmen; **to fly in a northerly** ~ in eine nördliche Richtung (nach Norden) fliegen; **to follow** ~s Weisungen folgen (nachkommen); **to give** ~s Anweisungen geben, dirigieren; **to give** ~ **to servants** Dienstpersonal einweisen; **to give s. o. full** ~s jem. genaueste Instruktionen geben; **to go by the** ~s sich nach erteilten Anweisungen richten; **to have a good sense of** ~ guten Ortssinn haben; **to lose one's sense of** ~ seinen Orientierungssinn verlieren; **to scatter in all** ~s nach allen Richtungen davonlaufen; **to take the** ~ **of affairs** (coll.) Sache in die Hand nehmen; **to work under s. one's** ~s nach jds. Anweisungen arbeiten;
~ **card** (luggage) Gepäckzettel; ~ **finder** Peilempfänger, Funkpeiler; ~ **finding** Funkpeilung; ~ **indicator** (car) Richtungsweiser, Blinker; ~-**finding aerial** Richt-, Rahmenantenne, (airplane) Kursanzeiger; ~ **line** (print.) Normzeile; ~ **order** (labo(u)r exchange) arbeitsamtliche Zuweisung; ~ **post** Wegweiser; ~ **sign** Hinweisschild, Verkehrszeichen; ~ **word** (print.) Merkwort, Kustos.

directional | antenna (aerial) Richtantenne, -strahler; ~ **filter** Bandfilter; ~ **gyro** (airplane) Richtkreisel; ~ **message** Richtfunksendung; ~ **radio** Peil-, Richtfunk; ~ **sign** Hinweiszeichen; ~ **transmitter** Peil-, Richtfunksender.

directive Direktive, Weisung, Richtlinie, Verfügung;
treasury ~s (Br.) [etwa] geldpolitische Maßnahmen des Schatzamtes;
~ **rule** Verhaltungsregel;
~ (a.) richtungsgebend, -weisend, lenkend;
~s **of a political party** Parteidirektiven.

director Direktor, Vorsteher, Leiter, Geschäftsführer, (on the board) Aufsichtsratsmitglied, (broadcasting) Aufnahme-, Sendeleiter, Programmdirektor, (manager) Vorstandsmitglied, (mil.) Kommandogerät, (mus.) Dirigent, (teacher) Lehrer, Ratgeber, (theater, film, US) Spielleiter, Regisseur;
acting ~ (Br.) geschäftsführendes Vorstandsmitglied, geschäftsführender Direktor; **alternate** ~ turnusmäßig zuständiger Direktor; **assistant** ~ stellvertretender Direktor; **associate** ~ stellvertretender Direktor; **corporate** ~ (US) Vorstands-, Aufsichtsratsmitglied; ~ **designate** in Aussicht genommener Direktor; **executive** ~ (International Monetary Fund) geschäftsführender Direktor, Vorstandsmitglied; **executive** ~s Direktorium; ~ **general** Generaldirektor; **individual** ~ Einzelvorstand; **inside** ~ (US) Vorstandsmitglied; **interested** ~ privat interessiertes Vorstandsmitglied; **junior** ~ Juniorchef; **labo(u)r-relations** ~ Arbeitsdirektor; **managing** ~ geschäftsführendes Vorstandsmitglied; **operating** ~ [Eisenbahn]betriebsleiter; **ordinary** ~ einfaches Vorstandsmitglied; **permanent** ~s Dauervorstand; **retiring** ~ ausscheidender Direktor, ausscheidendes Vorstandsmitglied; **service** ~ hauptamtlich tätiges Verwaltungsratsmitglied; **sole** ~ Einzelvorstand, Alleinvorstand; **technical** ~ technischer Direktor;
~ **of advertising** Werbeleiter; ~ **of the budget** (US) Leiter der Haushaltsabteilung; ⌕ **of Census** (US) Präsident des Statistischen Bundesamt; ~ **of chorus** Chorleiter; ~ **of education** (Br.) Schulamtsleiter; ~ **of finance** Finanzchef; ⌕-**General of Fair Trading** (Br.) Kartellamtsleiter; ~ **of labo(u)r affairs** (relations) Arbeitsdirektor; ⌕ **of the Mint** (US) Präsident des Münzamtes; ~ **of music** Orchesterdirigent; ⌕ **of the Office of Management and Budget** (US) Budgetdirektor; ~ **of operations** Einsatz-, Projektleiter; ~ **of production** Produktionsleiter; ~ **of public prosecution** (US) öffentlicher Ankläger, (Br.) Generalstaatsanwalt; ~ **general of railroads** (US) [Bundes]bahnpräsident; ~ **of research** Forschungsleiter; ~ **of sales** Verkaufsleiter, -chef; ~ **of savings** (Br.) Postsparkassenamt; ~ **of studies** Akademiedirektor; **to act as** ~ Vorstandsmitglied sein; **to act as a** ~ **of a limited company** Geschäftsführer einer GmbH sein; **to appoint an over-age** ~ pensionsreifes Vorstandsmitglied bestellen; **to make s. o. a** ~ j. zum Direktor machen (ernennen);
~'s **act** Vorstandshandlung; ~'s **emoluments** Vorstandsbezüge, Bezüge des Verwaltungsrats; ~s' **examination** Revision durch den Vorstand; ~s' **expenses** Vorstandsspesen; ~s' **fees** Aufsichtsratssitzungsgelder, Verwaltungsratsvergütung, (management) Vorstandsbezüge, Direktorenhonorar; ~s' **guarantee** Vorstandsbürgschaft; ~'s **interests** Vorstandsbeteiligungen; ~ **meeting** Vorstands-, Aufsichtsratssitzung; ~'s **office** Direktion; ~s' **pension** Vorstandspension; ~s' **powers** Vorstandsbefugnisse; ~'s **percentage of profit** Vorstandstantieme; ~s' **remuneration** Aufsichtsratsvergütung, (management) Vorstandsbezüge, -vergütungen; ~s' **report** Vorstandsbericht.

directorate (board of directors) Direktorium, Direktion, Geschäftsleitung, (office of director) Aufsichtsrat-, Direktorenposten;
interlocking ~ Schachtelaufsichtsrat;
~ **analysis** Analyse des Vorstands.

directorial leitend, direktorial;
~ (film) Regietätigkeit.

directorship Verwaltungsratsposten, (management) Direktorenstelle, Vorstandssitz, -posten, (theater) Intendanz;
overlapping ~ Schachtelaufsichtsrat.

directory (collection of rules) Vorschriftensammlung, Richtschnur, Leitfaden, (list of inhabitants) Adreßbuch, Einwohnerverzeichnis, (trade) Branchen-, Firmenverzeichnis;
business ~ Handelsadreßbuch; **classified** (mercantile, trade) ~ Branchenadreßbuch; **postal** ~ Postamtsadreßbuch; **telephone** ~ Telefonbuch;
~ **of enquiries** (tel.) Auskunft; ~ **of hotels** Hotelanzeiger; ~ **of industries** (railroad) Firmenverzeichnis im Bereich einer Eisenbahnlinie; ~ **of post offices** Postamtsadreßbuch; ~ **of suppliers** Bezugsquellennachweis;
~ (a.) leitend, richtungsgebend;
~ **calls** (surveying) angenäherte Angaben; ~ **canvasser** Adreßbuchakquisiteur; ~ **inquiries** [Telefon]auskunft; ~s **statute** Sollvorschrift; ~ **trust** nach bestimmten Richtlinien zu verwaltender Fonds.

dirigible Luftschiff;
~ *(a.)* lenkbar.
dirigism Dirigismus.
dirigistic dirigistisch.
diriment aufhebend, annullierend;
~ **impediment** trennendes Ehehindernis.
dirt Schmutz, Dreck, *(loose earth)* Erdreich, lockere Erde, *(obscene words)* unflätige Reden, *(rubbish)* Plunder, Schund;
hard ~ Schutt; **soft** ~ Müll, Kehrricht;
to do s. o. ~ *(US sl.)* j. in gemeiner Weise hereinlegen; **to fling ~ at** s. o. **(s. one's reputation)** j. verleumden, Verleumdungen über j. verbreiten; **to have to eat** ~ sich demütigen lassen müssen; **to throw money about like** ~ mit Geld nur so um sich werfen; **to treat** s. o. **like** ~ j. wie Dreck behandeln;
~**-cheap** zu einem Spottpreis, spottbillig; ~ **farmer** *(US coll.)* selbständiger Landwirt; ~ **road** *(US coll.)* unbefestigte Straße; ~ **track** Aschenbahn; ~ **waggon** *(US)* Müllwagen.
dirty schmutzig, dreckig, *(fig.)* gemein;
to do the ~ **on** s. o. *(Br.)* j. gemein behandeln;
~ **business** schmutziges Geschäft; ~ **end of the stick** unangenehmer Teil einer Aufgabe; **to wash one's** ~ **linen in public** *(fig.)* öffentlich seine schmutzige Wäsche waschen; ~ **lot** Lumpenpack; ~ **money** *(Br.)* Schmutzzulage; ~ **proof** *(print.)* unleserlicher Abzug; **to play** s. o. **a** ~ **trick** *(Br.)* j. gemein behandeln; ~ **weather** Sauwetter; **to scribble** ~ **words on W. C. walls** Wände einer Bedürfnisanstalt mit unanständigen Wörtern beschmieren; ~ **work** niedrige Arbeit, Dreckarbeit, *(fig.)* Mord und Totschlag.
disability Unvermögen, Unfähigkeit, Invalidität, Berufs-, Erwerbs-, Dienst-, Arbeitsunfähigkeit, *(legal incapacity)* Geschäftsunfähigkeit, *(mil.)* Kampfunfähigkeit;
absolute ~ absolutes Unvermögen; **canonical** ~ kirchliches Ehehindernis; **civil** ~ Ehehindernis; **general** ~ *(law)* Geschäftsunfähigkeit; **legal** ~ Rechtsunfähigkeit; **partial** ~ Arbeitsunfähigkeit, Teilinvalidität; **permanent** ~ Vollinvalidität; **physical** ~ Erwerbs-, Arbeitsunfähigkeit, Körperbeschädigung; **sickness** ~ auf Krankheit beruhende Erwerbsunfähigkeit; **special** ~ *(law)* beschränkte Geschäftsfähigkeit; **temporary** ~ zeitweilige (vorübergehende) Invalidität (Arbeitsunfähigkeit); **total** ~ vollständige Erwerbsunfähigkeit, Vollinvalidität;
~ **for legal action** Geschäfts-, Prozeßunfähigkeit; ~ **incurred in the line of duty** Wehrdienstbeschädigung; ~ **of a lunatic** Geschäftsunfähigkeit eines Geisteskranken; ~ **for service** Dienst-, Erwerbsunfähigkeit; ~ **to sue** Prozeßunfähigkeit;
to be under ~ geschäftsunfähig sein; **to be under a special** ~ *(infant)* beschränkt geschäftsfähig sein; **to cease to be under** ~ geschäftsfähig werden; **to lie under** ~ geschäftsunfähig sein;
~ **allowance** Erwerbsunfähigkeitsentschädigung; ~ **benefit** Invalidenunterstützung, -rente, Versehrtenrente; **exceptionally severe** ~ **benefit** *(Br.)* Versehrtenrente bei Schwerstbeschädigung; **long-term** ~ **benefits** Rentenleistungen im Invaliditätsfall; **short-term** ~ **benefits** Lohn- und Gehaltsfortzahlung im Krankheitsfall; ~ **clause** *(insurance)* Invaliditätsklausel; ~ **freeze** *(social security)* Einfrieren der Unfallversicherungsprämien; ~ **fund** *(Br.)* Invaliditätsfonds; ~ **insurance** Arbeiterrenten-, Unfall-, Invaliditätsversicherung; ~ **insurance benefit** *(US)* Erwerbsunfähigkeits-, Invalidenrente; **tax-free** ~ **payments** steuerfrei erhaltene Invalidenzahlungen; ~ **pension** Erwerbsunfähigkeitsrente; ~ **rate** *(Br.)* Invaliditätsgrad.
disable *(v.)* *(cripple)* verkrüppeln, *(impair in worth)* im Wert beeinträchtigen, entwerten, *(labo(u)rer)* untauglich (erwerbsunfähig) machen, *(v./i.)* *(law)* für geschäftsunfähig erklären, entmündigen, *(mil.)* [wehr]dienst-, kampfunfähig machen;
~ **an estate** Gut verwirtschaften; ~ s. o. **from inheriting real estate** j. vom Grunderwerb im Erbschaftswege ausschließen; ~ **a ship** Schiff außer Dienst stellen.
disabled *(pl.)* Invaliden, Erwerbsunfähige;
~ *(a.)* körperlich behindert, invalide, berufs-, dienstuntauglich, [dauernd] unfähig, arbeits-, erwerbsunfähig, *(legally incompetent)* geschäftsunfähig, *(mil.)* untauglich, dienstunfähig, kriegsversehrt, *(out of work)* betriebsunfähig, außer Betrieb, *(ship)* manövrierunfähig, seeuntüchtig;
partially ~ erwerbsbeschränkt; **seriously** ~ schwerbeschädigt; **war-**~, ~ **in the war** kriegsbeschädigt;
to be permanently ~ dauernd erwerbsunfähig sein; **to become** ~ arbeitsunfähig werden;
~ **bonds** *(Br.)* ungültige Obligationen; ~ **ex-serviceman** Kriegsbeschädigter, -versehrter; ~ **people** Körperbehinderte; ~ **person** Erwerbsunfähiger, Körperbeschädigter, Invalide; ~ **soldier** Kriegsbeschädigter, -versehrter; ~ **worker** Invalide.

disablement Arbeits-, Berufs-, Erwerbsunfähigkeit, Schwerbeschädigteneigenschaft, Invalidität, *(incapacity)* Behinderung, Geschäftsunfähigkeit, *(mil.)* Kampfunfähigkeit, *(ship)* Manövrierunfähigkeit, Seeuntüchtigkeit;
partial ~ Teilinvalidität; **permanent** ~ Erwerbsunfähigkeit; **temporary** ~ vorübergehende Erwerbs-, Arbeitsunfähigkeit; **total** ~ Vollinvalidität;
~ **annuity** Invaliditäts-, Versehrten-, Invalidenrente; ~ **benefit** *(Br.)* Invaliden-, Versehrtenrente; ~ **claim** Anspruch auf Invalidenunterstützung; ~ **gratuity** *(Br.)* Invalidenrente bei Beschädigungen unter 20%; ~ **insurance** *(Br.)* Arbeiterrenten-, Invaliden-, Invaliditätsversicherung; ~ **pay** Auszahlung der Versehrtenrente; ~ **pension** Invaliden-, Versehrtenrente; ~ **relief** Invalidenfürsorge; ~ **resettlement** Wiedereingliederung von Körpergeschädigten; ~ **resettlement officer** Rentensachbearbeiter für Umschulungsfälle.
disabling injury zur Erwerbsunfähigkeit führender Betriebsunfall.
disabuse *(v.)* eines Besseren belehren;
~ s. o. **of silly prejudices** jem. seine törichten Vorurteile nehmen.
disaccord Nichtübereinstimmung, Mißverständnis.
disaccustom *(v.)* s. o. **to** s. th. jem. etw. abgewöhnen.
disadvantage Nachteil, Verlust, Schaden, *(unfavo(u)rable condition)* ungünstige Lage;
~**s of bankruptcy** Konkursnachteile; ~ **of localization** Belegenheitsnachteile;
to labo(u)r under a ~ unter ungünstigen Bedingungen arbeiten; **to put** s. o. **at a** ~ **when attending international conferences** j. bei internationalen Konferenzen benachteiligen; **to sell at a** ~ mit Verlust verkaufen; **to take** s. o. **at a** ~ jds. ungünstige Lage zu seinem Vorteil ausnutzen.
disadvantaged benachteiligt.
disadvantageous nachteilig, unvorteilhaft, schädlich, ungünstig;
in a ~ **position** in einer unvorteilhaften Lage.
disadvantageousness Nachteiligkeit, Schädlichkeit.
disaffect *(v.)* verstimmen.
disaffection *(pol.)* Unzufriedenheit, Verstimmung.
disaffiliation Nichtzugehörigkeit.
disaffirm *(v.)* *(contract)* nicht bestätigen, *(judgment)* aufheben.
disafforest *(v.)* abforsten, abholzen.
disafforestation Entwaldung, Abholzung.
disagio Abschlag, Disagio.
disagree *(v.)* nicht einverstanden sein, *(account)* nicht übereinstimmen, *(climate)* nicht bekommen, *(witnesses)* im Widerspruch miteinander stehen, einander widersprechen;
~ **with** s. o. anderer Meinung als j. sein, Differenzen mit jem. haben; ~ **violently with** s. th. bei einer Sache entschieden anderer Meinung sein.
disagreeable|accident ekliger Unfall; ~ **weather** scheußliches Wetter.
disagreement Meinungsverschiedenheit, Umstimmigkeit, Differenz, *(real property law)* Ausschlagung.
disallow *(v.)* *(disapprove)* nicht anerkennen, zurückweisen, nicht zugeben (gestatten);
~ **an account** Rechnung als unrichtig zurückweisen; ~ **a charge** Anklageerhebung ablehnen; ~ **a claim** *(judge)* Anspruch abweisen; ~ **compensation** Schadenersatz nicht anerkennen.
disallowance Ablehnung, Zurückweisung, Mißbilligung, Nichtanerkennung, *(auditor)* Entlastungsverweigerung;
~ **of a charge** Ablehnung der Anklageerhebung; ~ **of a claim** Abweisung eines Anspruches; ~ **of costs** Ablehnung von Kosten; ~ **of disbursement** Ausgabenstreichung; ~ **of a plea** Zurückweisung einer Einrede.
disappear *(v.)* verschwinden, *(custom)* verlorengehen;
~ **from circulation** außer Umlauf kommen.
disappearing bed Klappbett.
disappointment Enttäuschung, *(plan)* Vereitelung.
disapprobation Mißbilligung.
disappropriate *(v.)* *(spiritual corporation)* enteignen.
disappropriation *(spiritual corporation)* Enteignung.
disapproval Mißbilligung, Mißfallen, Tadel;
to swing round into clear ~ sich klar und deutlich dagegen aussprechen.
disapprove *(v.)* nicht einverstanden sein, mißbilligen;
~ **of** s. one's **action** jds. Handlungsweise nicht billigen können; ~ **of an objection** Einspruch verwerfen.
disarm *(v.)* entwaffnen, abrüsten, *(fig.)* freundlich stimmen, besänftigen;
~ **criticism** der Kritik den Wind aus den Segeln nehmen; ~ s. o. **of his rifle** jem. das Gewehr wegnehmen.

disarmament Abrüstung, Entwaffnung;
  controlled ~ kontrollierte Abrüstung; **universal** ~ allgemeine Abrüstung;
  ~ **commission** Abrüstungskommission; ~ **conference** Abrüstungskonferenz; ~ **pact** Abrüstungsvertrag; ~ **talks** Abrüstungsverhandlungen.

disarmer Abrüstungsanhänger, -befürworter.

disarming Entwaffnung.

disarrange (v.) durcheinanderbringen, verwirren;
  ~ **s. one's plans** jds. Pläne durcheinander bringen.

disarray Durcheinander, (clothes) schlampige Kleidung.

disassemble (v.) auseinandernehmen, demontieren.

disassembly Demontage.

disassociation Spaltung.

disaster Unglück, Unglücksfall, Mißgeschick, Katastrophe;
  financial ~ finanzielle Katastrophe; **public** ~ nationale Katastrophe; **railway** ~ Eisenbahnkatastrophe, -unglück;
  ~ **at sea** Seeunfall;
  to be on the verge of ~ am Rande einer Katastrophe stehen; ~ **area** Katastrophengebiet; **to design (declare) a major** ~ **area** zum Katastrophengebiet erklären; **common** ~ **clause** (law) gleichzeitige Todesvermutung; ~ **committee** Katastrophenausschuß; ~ **control** Katastrophenbekämpfung; ~ **forecasting** Katastrophenvorschau; ~ **prevention council** Katastrophenschutz; ~**-prone area** katastrophengefährdetes Gebiet; ~ **relief** Katastrophenhilfe; ~ **signal** Katastrophenanzeichen; ~ **situation** Katastrophenfall; ~**-struck** katastrophengeschädigt; ~ **unit** Katastropheneinsatzverband.

disastrous|flood katastrophale Überschwemmung, Überschwemmungskatastrophe; ~ **policy** Katastrophenpolitik; ~ **year** Katastrophenjahr.

disavow (v.) leugnen, in Abrede stellen, (unauthorized act) nicht anerkennen, nicht genehmigen;
  ~ **a share in a plot** seine Teilnahme an einer Verschwörung ableugnen.

disavowal Nichtanerkennung, Widerruf, Dementi;
  ~ **of a child** Verleugnung eines Kindes.

disband (v.)|**an army** Truppen entlassen; ~ **a commission** Ausschuß auflösen.

disbandment (mil.) Auflösung, Truppenentlassung.

disbar (v.) **a barrister** (Br.) Anwalt aus der Anwaltschaft ausschließen (von der Anwaltsliste streichen).

disbarment (Br.) Ausschluß aus der Anwaltschaft;
  ~ **order** Verbot der Praxisausübung.

disbench (v.) (Br.) aus dem Anwaltsvorstand ausstoßen.

disburden (v.) von einer Bürde befreien, entlasten;
  ~ **one's mind** sein Herz ausschütten; ~ **one's mind to a friend** sich einem Freund eröffnen; ~ **one's heart of a secret** Geheimnis loswerden.

disbursable auszahlbar.

disburse (v.) [Geld] auszahlen, auslegen, ausgeben;
  ~ **s. one's full and entire part** jem. seinen Anteil voll auszahlen; ~ **revenues** Einnahmen verwenden.

disbursement [Aus]bezahlung, (money expended) Ausgabe, Auslage;
  ~s Aufwendungen;
  capital ~s Kapitalaufwendungen; **cash** ~s Dividendenausschüttungen; **dividend** ~s Dividendenausschüttungen; **heavy** ~s umfangreiche Auszahlungen; **social** ~s soziale Aufwendungen;
  ~s **to client's debit** Auslagen zu Lasten des Kunden; ~ **in money** Leistung in Geld; ~ **of revenues** Einnahmenverwendung;
  to recover one's ~s seine Auslagen zurückvergütet erhalten; **to refund the** ~s Auslagen zurückerstatten;
  ~ **account** Auslagenaufstellung; **cash** ~ **records** Aufzeichnungen über den Kassenausgang; ~ **voucher** Ausgaben-, Auszahlungsbeleg, Zahlungsanweisung.

disburser Auszahler, Ausgeber.

disbursing|account Auszahlungskonto; ~ **agent** Auszahlungsbeauftragter; ~ **officer** (US) Kassierer für Auszahlungen, (mil.) Zahlmeister; ~ **order** Auszahlungsanweisung, -verfügung.

disc Schall-, Grammophonplatte;
  parking ~ Parkscheibe;
  ~ **brakes** Scheibenbremsen; ~ **clutch** Scheibenkupplung; ~ **drum braking system** Scheibenbremssystem; ~ **jockey** Schallplattenansager, Rundfunkunterhalter; ~ **jockeying** Schallplattenansage, Rundfunkunterhaltung; ~ **parking** Parkscheibensystem.

discard Ausrangieren;
  into the ~ zu den Akten;
  ~ (v.) ausrangieren, als unbrauchbar ablegen;

~ **assets** Anlagen außer Betrieb setzen; ~ **old beliefs** frühere Ansichten über Bord werfen; ~ **old friends** alte Freunde fallen lassen; ~ **an old suit** alten Anzug ausrangieren; ~ **the unnecessary** Unwesentliches weglassen;
  to throw into the ~ zu den Akten (beiseite) legen.

discarded|assets stillgelegte Anlagen; ~ **coat** abgelegter (ausrangierter) Rock; ~ **property** weggeworfener Gegenstand.

discardment (asset) Außerbetriebsetzung.

discern (v.) wahrnehmen, unterscheiden;
  ~ **good and evil** zwischen Gut und Böse unterscheiden können; ~ **the truth** Wahrheit erkennen.

discernment Unterscheidungsvermögen, Urteilskraft, Einsicht.

discharge (acquittal) Freispruch, (crew) Abmusterung, (criminal) Entlassungsverfügung, (criminal law) Haftentlassung, Entlassungsanordnung, (dismissal) Verabschiedung, Entlassung, (injunction) Aufhebung, (freeing from obligation) Befreiung, Entbindung, (mil.) Abschied, (from office) Dienstenthebung, -entlassung, Amtsenthebung, (payment of debt) Tilgung, Abgeltung, Bezahlung, Begleichung, (performance of obligation) Erfüllung, Ausführung, Verrichtung, Erledigung, Leistung, (receipt) Quittung, (release) Entlastung, (unloading) Aus-, Entladen, Löschung;
  in ~ **of** zur Begleichung von; **in the** ~ **of his duty** in Erfüllung seiner Pflicht, bei Ausübung seines Dienstes; **in** ~ **of official duty** in amtlichem Auftrag; **in full** ~ zum vollen Ausgleich; **to our** ~ zu unserer Entlastung;
  absolute ~ (accused) voller Freispruch, bedingungslose Entlastung, (bankruptcy) vollständige Entlastung; **conditional** ~ (accused) bedingter Freispruch, bedingte Entlastung; **constructive** ~ vom Angestellten erzwungene Kündigung; **dishono(u)rable** ~ (mil.) unehrenhafte Entlassung, Entfernung aus dem Heer; **free** ~ freies Löschen; **final** ~ Schlußbescheinigung; **free** ~ freies Löschen; **full** ~ (bankrupt) endgültige Entlastung; **override** Ausladung über Schiffsseite; **prompt** ~ sofortige Erfüllung; **unjust** ~ unberechtigte Entlassung;
  ~ **of the accused** Einstellung des Verfahrens gegen den Angeklagten; ~ **by agreement** einverständliche Vertragsbeendigung; ~ **without allowance** Entlassung und Abstellung zur Reserve; ~ **from the army** Entlassung aus dem Heer; ~ **of a bankrupt (in bankruptcy)** Entlastung (Rehabilitierung) eines Gemeinschuldners; ~ **of a bill** Tilgung (Erlöschen) einer Wechselverbindlichkeit; ~ **of business** Geschäftsbesorgung; ~ **of cargo** Löschen der Ladung; ~ **for cause** begründete Entlassung; ~ **for a just cause** berechtigte Kündigung; ~ **without cause** grundlose Entlassung; ~ **of contract** Vertragsbeendigung, -erfüllung; ~ **from custody** Haftentlassung; ~ **of a debtor** Entlastung des Gemeinschuldners; ~ **of debts** Entrichtung von Schulden, Schuldentilgung; ~ **from draft** Freistellung vom Wehrdienst; ~ **of duties** Dienstausübung, Aufgabenwahrnehmung, Ausübung von Amtspflichten; ~ **of duty** Pflichterfüllung; ~ **of the defendant** Entlastung des Beklagten; ~ **of an employee** Entlassung eines Angestellten; ~ **of (from) an engagement** Enthebung von einer Verpflichtung; ~ **by frustration** Vertragsbeendigung infolge objektiver Unmöglichkeit; ~ **in full** vollständige Quittung; ~ **from hospital** Entlassung aus dem Krankenhaus, Krankenhausentlassung; ~ **of a jury** Entlassung der Geschworenen; ~ **of liabilities** Tilgung (Begleichung) von Verbindlichkeiten; ~ **of a mortgage** Hypothekentilgung, -löschung; ~ **of an obligation** Erlöschen eines Schuldverhältnisses, Erfüllung von Verpflichtungen; ~ **from office** Amts-, Dienstenthebung; ~ **from parole** (prisoner) endgültige Entlassung; ~ **by performance** Leistungserfüllung; ~ **from prison** Entlassung aus dem Gefängnis; ~ **of a receiving order** Aufhebung eines Konkurseröffnungsbeschlusses; ~ **of seamen** Abmusterung von Seeleuten; ~ **of tax** Steuerbefreiung; ~ **for unfitness** (mil.) Entlassung wegen mangelnder Tauglichkeit; ~ **of a worker** Entlassung eines Arbeiters;
  ~ (v.) (dismiss) entlassen, abbauen, (library) in der Kartei streichen, (from office) entheben, (pay) entrichten, tilgen, abgelten, abtragen, bezahlen, (perform obligation) Pflicht tun, erfüllen, ausführen, (release) entlasten, (seaman) abmustern, (unload) aus-, entladen, löschen;
  ~ **an account** Konto ausgleichen; ~ **the accused** Angeklagten außer Verfolgung setzen; ~ **the accused on every count** Angeklagten in allen Punkten freisprechen; ~ **afloat** Schiff muß schwimmend löschen; ~ **a bankrupt** Gemeinschuldner entlasten, Konkursschuldner rehabilitieren; ~ **a bill** Wechsel einlösen; ~ **a bond** Schuldschein einlösen; ~ **from all calls due** von weiteren Einzahlungsverpflichtungen freistellen; ~ **a cargo** entladen, Ladung löschen; ~ **for a just cause** aus berechtigten Gründen entlassen; ~ **a contract** Vertrag beenden; ~ **a court**

order Gerichtsbeschluß (gerichtliche Anordnung) aufheben; ~
a creditor Gläubiger befriedigen; ~ **the crew** Mannschaft entlassen (abmustern); ~ **a debt** Schuld begleichen (tilgen); ~ **the
directors from responsibilities** Vorstand entlasten; ~ **one's
duties** seine Aufgaben wahrnehmen; ~ **an employee** Angestellten entlassen; ~ **an encumbrance** Grundstücksbelastung löschen; ~ **an errand** Botengang erledigen; ~ **an injunction**
einstweilige Verfügung aufheben; ~ **one's liabilities** seine
Schulden bezahlen, seinen Verpflichtungen (Verbindlichkeiten) nachkommen; ~ **one's liabilities in full** seine Schulden voll
bezahlen; ~ **from liabilities** von der Haftpflicht befreien; ~ **s. o.
on licence** j. bedingt entlassen; ~ **the members of the jury**
Geschworene entlassen; ~ **a merchant vessel** Handelsschiff
entladen; ~ **a mortgage** Hypothek löschen; ~ **s. o. of his oath** j.
seines Eides entbinden; ~ **s. o. from an obligation** j. aus einer
Verpflichtung entlassen; ~ **an obligation** Verpflichtung erfüllen; ~ **an order of the court** Gerichtsbeschluß aufheben; ~
passengers *(vehicle)* Reisende absetzen; ~ **a patient from a
hospital as cured** Patienten als geheilt aus einem Krankenhaus
entlassen; ~ **from performance** von der Verpflichtung zur Leistung befreien; ~ **any proceedings in court** Verfahren einstellen;
~ **process of execution** Zwangsvollstreckung einstellen; ~ **a
servant for being dishonest** Hausangestellten wegen Unredlichkeit entlassen; ~ **a surety** Bürgen freistellen; ~ **a trustee** Treuhänder entlasten; ~ **a workman** Arbeiter entlassen; ~ **a writ**
Handelsbeschluß aufheben;
to apply to the court for an order of ~ Aufhebung des Konkursverfahrens beantragen; **to be faithful in the** ~ **of one's duties**
seine Pflichten getreulich erfüllen; **to get one's** ~ *(bankrupt)*
Entlastung als Konkursschuldner erhalten; **to grant a** ~ Entlastung erteilen; **to grant the bankrupt's** ~ Konkursverfahren
aufheben; **to grant a** ~ **[un]conditionally** [un]eingeschränkte
Entlastung erteilen; **to take one's** ~ *(mil.)* sich entlassen lassen;
~ **book** Seefahrtsbuch; ~ **case** Entlassungsfall; ~ **certificate**
(mil.) Entlassungsschein; ~ **note** *(navy)* Ausschiffungsbefehl; ~
papers Entlassungspapiere; ~ **petition** Ablehnungsantrag; ~
pipe Ablaßrohr; ~ **ticket** *(mil.)* Entlassungsschein.
dischargeable entlassungsfähig, *(payable)* zahlbar, fällig.
discharged *(bill)* eingelöst, *(from employment)* abgebaut,
entlassen;
until ~ **in full** bis zur Schuldentilgung; ~ **and acquitted** bezahlt
und quittiert, *(accused)* freigesprochen;
to be ~ **from the forces** als Soldat entlassen werden; **to be** ~ **on
the ground of insufficient evidence** aus Mangel an Beweisen freigesprochen werden; **to be** ~ **from liability** von der Haftung befreit werden;
~ **bankrupt** entlasteter (rehabilitierter) Gemein-, Konkursschuldner; ~ **battery** entladene Batterie; ~ **bill** bezahlter Wechsel; ~ **debt** getilgte Schuld; ~ **prisoner aid** Gefangenenfürsorge.
dischargee *(mil.)* Entlassener.
discharger Entlader, *(apparatus)* Entladevorrichtung.
discharging | an encumbrance Löschung einer Grundstücksbela-
stung; ~ **a trustee** Treuhänderentlastung;
~ **berth** Entladestelle; ~ **expenses** Entlade-, Löschkosten, Ent-
ladegebühren; ~ **fees** Löschungsgebühren; ~ **gear** Entladevorrichtung; ~ **permit** Löscherlaubnis; ~ **place** Löschplatz,
Entladestelle.
disciple Schüler.
disciplinable strafbar;
~ **offence** Disziplinarvergehen, -fall.
disciplinal erzieherisch, schulend.
disciplinarian Disziplinarvorgesetzter;
to be a poor ~ Laschheit einreißen lassen; **to be a strict** ~
gestrenger Zuchtmeister sein.
disciplinarily auf dem Disziplinarwege.
disciplinary disziplinarisch;
~ **action** Disziplinarmaßnahmen; ~ **authority** Disziplinarbehörde; ~ **barracks** *(mil.)* Militärstrafanstalt; ~ **case** Diszipli-
narfall; ~ **committee** *(Bar Council, Br.)* Ehrengericht; ~ **court**
Disziplinar-, Dienststrafkammer; ~ **fine** Ordnungs-, Disziplinarstrafe; ~ **jurisdiction** Disziplinargerichtsbarkeit; ~ **measures** Disziplinarmaßnahmen; **to take** ~ **measures** Disziplinarmaßnahmen ergreifen; ~ **offence** Dienstvergehen; ~ **policy**
Disziplinarpolitik; ~ **power** Disziplinarbefugnis, -gewalt; ~
proceedings (procedure) Dienststraf-, Disziplinarverfahren; ~
punishment Disziplinarstrafe; **to award a** ~ **punishment** Disziplinarstrafe verhängen; **to inflict** ~ **punishment on s. o.** j. disziplinarisch belangen; **to transfer for** ~ **reasons** strafversetzen; ~
regulations Dienststraf-, Disziplinarordnung; ~ **scourge** Disziplinarstrafe; ~ **transfer** Strafversetzung; ~ **trial** Disziplinarverfahren.

discipline Disziplin, Zucht, *(body of law)* Kodex von Vorschriften, *(punishment)* Bestrafung, Strafe, Züchtigung, *(subject of
teaching)* Unterrichtsfach, Wissenszweig, Disziplin;
industrial ~ Betriebsdisziplin; **military** ~ Mannszucht, Drill;
party ~ Parteidisziplin; **school** ~ Schuldisziplin;
~ **in a company** Betriebsdisziplin; ~ **of the mind** Geisteswissen-
schaft;
~ *(v.)* disziplinieren, an Disziplin gewöhnen, *(mil.)* drillen;
~ **o. s.** Selbstzucht üben, sich an Selbstdisziplin gewöhnen; ~
badly behaved children ungezogene Kinder disziplinieren;
to keep under ~ in Zucht halten; **to maintain** ~ für Aufrechterhaltung der Disziplin sorgen; **to show perfect** ~ sich sehr diszipliniert verhalten;
~ **entry** *(railroad, US)* schriftlicher Verweis.
disclaim *(v.)* ausschlagen, Verzicht leisten, verzichten, nicht
anerkennen, *(defendant)* Klage leugnen;
~ **s. th.** etw. dementieren;
~ **allowance** von Abschreibungsmöglichkeiten keinen Gebrauch machen; ~ **authorship** Urheberschaft ablehnen; ~ **by
deed a power** Vollmacht urkundlich ausschlagen; ~ **an estate**
Erbschaft ausschlagen; ~ **all intention of doing s. th.** jegliche
Absichten für ein Vorhaben in Abrede stellen; ~ **liability** *(insurance)* Deckung ablehnen; ~ **liability for a loss** Schadensersatzpflicht ablehnen; ~ **an office** Amt ausschlagen; ~ **property
of a bankrupt** Vermögen des Konkursschuldners nicht zur
Masse heranziehen; ~ **onerous property** *(receiver)* auf unwirtschaftliche Vermögensteile verzichten; ~ **responsibility for
s. th.** Verantwortung für etw. ablehnen; ~ **a right** auf ein
Recht (einen Anspruch) verzichten; ~ **one's right to income**
auf zustehende Einkünfte verzichten.
disclaimant Verzichtender.
disclaimed property verlassenes Grundstück.
disclaimer *(law)* Gegenerklärung, öffentlicher Widerruf, Dementi, *(law of inheritance)* Erbausschlagung, -verzicht, *(liquidation)* Verzicht des Liquidators, *(patent law)* Patentberichtigung, *(in pleading)* vollständige Klageleugnung, *(renunciation)* Verzichtleistung, -erklärung, *(person renouncing)* Verzichtender, *(trustee)* Niederlegung eines Treuhänderamtes;
~ **of allowance** Nichtinanspruchnahme von Abschreibungsmöglichkeiten; ~ **of authorship** Ablehnung der Urheberschaft;
~ **of contract** Vertragsverzicht; ~ **of an estate** Erbschaftsausschlagung, Erbverzicht; ~ **of liability** Haftungsausschluß; ~ **of
onerous property by liquidator** Verzichtserklärung des Abwicklers auf Verwertung unrentabler Vermögensgegenstände; ~ **of
responsibility** Obligoverzicht; ~ **of a right** Rechtsverzicht;
to file a ~ Verzichtserklärung abgeben; **to issue a** ~ Dementi
herausgeben; **to send a** ~ **to the press** der Presse ein Dementi
zugehen lassen;
~ **clause** Verzichtsklausel, *(documentary letter of credit)*
Freizeichnungsklausel.
disclamation Nichtanerkennung.
disclose *(v.)* aufzeigen, offenbaren, -legen, aufdecken, enthüllen,
ans Licht bringen, *(insurance)* [Versicherungsfall] anzeigen;
~ **s. th. to s. o.** jem. etw. eröffnen, jem. eine Eröffnung machen;
~ **confidence** vertrauliche Mitteilungen preisgeben; ~ **one's
designs** seine Absichten zu erkennen geben; ~ **documents**
Urkunden offenlegen; ~ **all material facts** alle rechtserheblichen Tatsachen offenlegen; ~ **confidential information** unerlaubtes Informationsmaterial zugänglich machen; ~ **classified
information to an unauthorized person** Verschlußsachen unberechtigten Personen zugänglich machen; ~ **one's interest**
(director) seine Beteiligungen zu erkennen geben; ~ **an invention** *(patent law)* Erfindung offenbaren; ~ **great learning** *(book)*
großes Wissen zeigen; ~ **material inadequacy in the reserve**
Unangemessenheit der Rücklagen beanstanden; ~ **the name of
the principal** Auftraggeber benennen; ~ **one's point of view**
seine Ansicht kundtun; ~ **research and development costs** Bilanzangaben über Forschungs- und Entwicklungsaufwand
machen; ~ **a secret** Geheimnis preisgeben (verraten); ~ **secret
transactions** vertrauliche Geschäftsabschlüsse offenlegen; ~
skilfully concealed thefts sorgfältig verborgene Betrügereien
ans Tageslicht bringen.
disclosed reserves offene Reserven.
disclosure Enthüllung, Aufdeckung, Eröffnung, Offenbarung,
Bekanntgabe, *(balance sheet)* Offenlegung detaillierter Angaben in Fußnoten im Revisionsbericht, *(corporation)* Publizität,
(patent law) Patentbeschreibung;
bank ~ Offenlegungspflicht für Banken; **compulsory** ~ gesetzlich vorgeschriebene Offenlegungspflicht; **corporate** ~ Bilanz-
publizität von Aktiengesellschaften; **mandatory** ~ obligatorische Offenbarungspflicht;

~ **by an agent** Offenlegung durch den Versicherungsvertreter;
~ **of a fraud** Aufdeckung eines Betruges; ~ **of information** Offenlegung einer Informationsquelle; ~ **of classified information to an unauthorized person** Überlassung von Verschlußsachen an Unberechtigte; ~ **of confidential information** Preisgabe vertraulicher Informationen; ~ **of interest** *(director)* Mitteilung über seine Eigeninteressen (Selbstbeteiligung); ~ **of an invention** *(patent law)* Offenbarung einer Erfindung; ~ **of all material facts** Offenlegung aller rechtserheblichen Tatsachen; ~ **of the name of the principal** Benennung (Offenlegung) des Auftraggebers; ~ **of research and development costs** Bilanzangaben über Forschungs- und Entwicklungskosten; ~ **of a secret** Preisgabe eines Geheimnisses; ~ **of vote** Preisgabe des Wahlgeheimnisses;
to be privileged from ~ nicht der Offenlegungspflicht unterliegen;
~ **provisions** Offenlegungsbestimmungen; ~ **requirements** Publizitätserfordernisse; ~ **threshold** Offenlegungsschwelle.
discography Schallplattenverzeichnis.
discomfit *(v.) (plan)* durchkreuzen;
~ **s. o.** j. aus der Fassung bringen; ~ **plans** Pläne durchkreuzen.
discomfiture *(mil.)* Niederlage, Schlappe, *(plan)* Vereitelung, Durchkreuzung.
discomfort Unannehmlichkeit;
~**s endured by explorers in the Arctic** von Polarforschern ausgehaltene Beschwernisse.
discommode *(v.)* Unannehmlichkeiten verursachen.
discommon *(v.)* Gemeindeland der allgemeinen Nutzung entziehen.
discompose *(v.)* aus der Fassung bringen.
discomposure Fassungslosigkeit.
disconcert *(v.)* aus der Fassung bringen;
~ **s. one's plans** jds. Pläne durchkreuzen (zunichtemachen).
disconcerted bestürzt;
not easily ~ nicht leicht aus der Fassung zu bringen.
disconformity Unstimmigkeit.
disconnect *(el.)* unterbrechen, aus-, abschalten;
~ *(v.)* **service** Lieferungen einstellen; ~ **a telephone line** Telefonleitung unterbrechen.
disconnecting|key Trenntaste; ~ **switch** Trennschalter.
disconnection *(el.)* Unterbrechung, Abschaltung, Trennung;
~ **of service** Einstellung der Lieferung; ~ **of telephone lines** Unterbrechung des Telefonverkehrs.
discontent Unzufriedenheit.
discontinuance *(interruption)* Unterbrechung, Aufhebung, Nichtfortsetzung, *(newspaper)* Abbestellung, *(public works)* Einstellung, *(stopping)* Eingehen, Aufhören, Abbruch, Beendigung, *(suit)* Absetzung eines Prozesses, [Prozeß]aussetzung, *(zoning ordinance)* Verstoß;
~ **of action** Klagerücknahme; ~ **of a bus line** Einstellung (Aufgabe) einer Omnibuslinie; ~ **of a business** Geschäftseinstellung, -aufgabe; ~ **of a conversation** Abbruch eines Gesprächs, Gesprächsbeendigung; ~ **of an estate** Aufhebung eines Fideikommiß; ~ **of payments** Fortfall von Zahlungen; ~ **of a public performance** Abbruch einer öffentlichen Vorstellung; ~ **of proceedings** Einstellung des Verfahrens; ~ **of prosecution** Einstellung eines Strafverfahrens; ~ **of subscription** Abbestellung eines Abonnements; ~ **of a suit** *(US)* Klagerücknahme; ~ **of travel** Einstellung des Reiseverkehrs.
discontinue *(v.) (break off)* unterbrechen, einstellen, aufhören, *(subscription)* abbestellen;
~ **an action** Klage fallenlassen (zurücknehmen); ~ **a bus line** Omnibuslinie aufheben (einstellen); ~ **a business** Geschäft aufgeben; ~ **a connection** Verbindung lösen; ~ **a correspondence** Korrespondenz einstellen; ~ **an estate** Fideikommiß aufheben; ~ **a habit** von einer Gewohnheit abgehen; ~ **a lawsuit** Prozeß einstellen; ~ **the manufacture** Herstellung einstellen; ~ **the membership** Mitgliedschaft aufheben; ~ **a newspaper** Zeitung abbestellen; ~ **a public performance** öffentliche Vorstellung abbrechen; ~ **the proceedings** Verfahren einstellen; ~ **a public performance** öffentliche Vorstellung abbrechen; ~ **publication** Erscheinen einstellen; ~ **a right** Recht aufgeben; ~ **one's subscription** seine Beitragsleistungen einstellen; ~ **a subscription to charity** Spendenzahlungen beenden; ~ **a suit** *(US)* Klage zurücknehmen; ~ **one's visits** seine Besuche einstellen.
discontinued, to be *(newspaper)* Erscheinen einstellen, *(payment)* fortfallen, in Fortfall kommen;
~ **business** eingestellter Geschäftsbetrieb.
discontinuing order Aussetzungsbeschluß.
discord Meinungsverschiedenheit;
to be at ~ **with s. o.** im Widerspruch zu jem. stehen.

discount *(bill of exchange)* Diskont, Zinsabzug, *(deduction)* Abzug, Abstrich, *(depreciation in value)* Wertminderung, *(disagio)* Disagio, *(discounting)* Diskontierung, *(insurance)* Prämiennachlaß, -rabatt, Beitragsermäßigung, *(for prompt payment)* Skonto, *(rate of ~)* Diskontsatz, *(rebate)* Rabatt, Preisnachlaß, -abschlag, Rabattrechnung, *(shop, US)* Einzelhandelsladen mit Rabattsystem, *(stock exchange)* Disagio, *(trading in futures)* Kursabschlag, Deport;
at a ~ mit Rabatt (Skonto), *(issue of a loan)* unter Pari; **deducting** ~ abzüglich Skonto; **less** ~ ab[züglich] Diskont (Skonto); **cash less** ~ bar ohne Abzug; **subject to** ~ rabattfähig; ~**s** Diskonten, Diskontwechsel;
abnormal ~ außergewöhnlicher Preisnachlaß; **additional** ~ Sonderrabatt; **adjusted** ~ gestaffelter Rabatt, Staffelskonto; **anticipation** ~ *(US)* Nachlaß für vorfristige Zahlung; **arithmetical** ~ offenes Disagio; **bank** ~ Bankdiskont; **bill** ~ Wechseldiskont; **bond** ~ Pfandbriefagio; **cash** ~ Barzahlungs-, Kassaskonto; **commercial** ~ diskontierter Warenwechsel; **compound** ~ Diskont auf Zinseszins; **confidential** ~ Vertrauensrabatt; **dealer's** ~ Händlerrabatt; **debt** ~ Kreditdisagio; **deferred** ~ *(US)* von der Gesamtabnahme abhängiger Rabatt; ~ **earned** Diskonterlös, -erträge, Skontoerträge, *(retail accounting)* Händlerrabatt; **combined edition** ~ *(advertising)* Vorzugspreis (Rabatt) für Belegung mehrerer Regionalausgaben desselben Blattes; **employee** ~ Angestelltenrabatt; **extra** ~ Sonderrabatt; **frequency** ~ *(advertising)* Rabatt bei Serienbelegung, Serienrabatt; **functional** ~ Funktionsrabatt; ~ **granted** Kundenskonti; ~**s lost** nicht in Anspruch genommene Skonti, Skontoverlust; **market** ~ *(Br.)* Privatdiskont; **mass** ~ Mengenrabatt; **missed** ~ Skontoverlust; **no** ~ feste Preise; ~**s outstanding** *(Br.)* Wechselobligo; **patronage** ~ Rabatt für Stammkunden, Treuerabatt; ~**s payable** *(balance sheet, US)* Diskontverbindlichkeiten; **quantity** ~ Ermäßigung bei Mengenabnahme, Mengenrabatt; **retail** ~ Einzelhändlerrabatt; **retained** ~ einbehaltene Skonti; **simple** ~ einfacher Diskont; **sliding-[scale]** ~ Rabatt-, Nachlaßstaffel; **special** ~ Sonderrabatt; **stock** ~ Effektenagio; **time** ~ Bardiskont; **trade** ~ Rabatt für Wiederverkäufer, Händlerrabatt; **true** ~ *(loan)* offenes Disagio; **unamortized debt** ~ Pfandbriefdisagio, Disagiogewinn; **volume** ~ Mengenrabatt; ~ **of a bill** Wechseldiskont; ~ **for cash** Barzahlungsskonto, [Kassa]skonto, Barzahlungsrabatt; **five per cent** ~ **for cash** bei Barzahlung 5% Rabatt; ~ **for customers** Kundenrabatt; ~ **allowed to dealer** Händlerrabatt; ~ **on forward dollars** Disagio auf Termindollars; ~ **for prepayment** Vorausskonto; ~ **for quantities** Mengenrabatt; **cash** ~ **on sales** Skonto bei Barzahlung; ~ **on treasury bills** Schatzwechselagio;
~ *(v.)* abrechnen, abziehen, Rabatt gewähren, Abzug vornehmen, *(act beforehand)* vorwegnehmen, *(bill of exchange)* diskontieren, *(depreciate in value)* beeinträchtigen, im Wert herabsetzen;
~ **a bill for early payment** Skonto für vorzeitige Rechnungsbegleichung abziehen; ~ **one's enjoyment of a book by reading its advance review** Lesegenuß eines Buches durch Lesen der Besprechungen vorwegnehmen; ~ **an expected inheritance** Erbschaftserwartung vorwegnehmen; ~ **the market** Marktentwicklungen im voraus berücksichtigen; ~ **negotiable papers** begebbare Wertpapiere diskontieren; ~ **news** *(stock exchange)* Nachrichten bei der Kursfestsetzung berücksichtigen; ~ **s. one's story** jds. Geschichte nur teilweise glauben;
to accept bills for ~ Wechsel zum Diskont hereinnehmen; **to allow** ~ Ermäßigung (Rabatt) gewähren, Skonto einräumen; **to allow 2 per cent** ~ **for cash** 2 Prozent Kassaskonto gewähren; **to allow the usual** ~ übliche Rabattsätze gewähren; **to allow a** ~ **of 5% with orders of 100** bei Bezug von 100 Stück 5% Rabatt gewähren; **to be at a** ~ unter Pari stehen; **to be entitled to a 50 per cent** ~ **on purchases** Rabattanspruch von 50% haben; **to be subject to 4%** ~ 4% Rabatt genießen; **to buy at a** ~ mit Disagio kaufen; **to buy at a market** ~ mit Rabatt kaufen; **to cut the** ~ Diskontsatz herabsetzen; **to deduct the** ~ Rabatt (Skonto) abziehen; **to give a bill on** ~ Wechsel diskontieren lassen; **to give** ~ **on non-net books** Preisnachlässe auf nichtpreisgebundene Bücher einräumen; **to increase (raise) the** ~ Diskontsatz heraufsetzen (erhöhen); **to lodge a note in a bank for** ~ Wechsel von einer Bank diskontieren lassen; **to lower (mark down the)** ~ Diskont[satz] herabsetzen; **to open at a slight** ~ *(stock exchange)* leicht abgeschwächt eröffnen; **to present for** ~ zum Diskont vorlegen; **to reduce the** ~ Diskont[satz] herabsetzen; **to sell at a** ~ mit Verlust (Disagio) verkaufen, *(v. i.)* unter Pari stehen; **to sell at a market** ~ mit Rabatt verkaufen; **to spread bond** ~ **over the years** Pfandbriefdisagio über die Jahre verteilen; **to take cash** ~**s** Skonto ausnutzen; **to take on** ~ diskontieren;

~ **account** Disagiokonto; **with 2 1/2% ~ allowance for settlement within one month** 2 1/2% Skonto bei Rechnungsbegleichung innerhalb eines Monats; ~ **bank** Diskontbank; ~ **basis** Diskontbasis; ~ **bills** Diskontwechsel, Diskonten; ~ **bookseller** Sortimentsbuchhändler; ~ **broker** Diskont-, Wechselmakler; ~ **business** Diskontgeschäft; ~ **charges** Diskontspesen; ~ **company (corporation,** *US*) Kundenfinanzierungsbank, Diskontgesellschaft; ~ **credit** Rabattgutschrift, *(banking)* Diskontkredit; ~ **days** Diskonttage; ~ **deduction** Skontoabzug; ~ **department** Wechselabteilung; ~ **department store** *(US)* Billigladen, Einkaufszentrum; ~ **expenses** *(US)* Wechselspesen; ~ **holdings** *(US)* Wechselbestand, Diskontportefeuille; ~ **house** *(Br.)* Diskont-, Wechselbank, *(retailing, US)* Einkaufszentrum, Billigladen, Einzelhandelsbetrieb mit Sonderrabatt; ~ **ledger** Wechselbuch, -obligo; ~ **limit** Diskontgrenze; ~ **liquidation** Wechselabrechnung; ~ **market** *(Br.)* Wechsel-, Diskontmarkt, Markt für kurzfristige Wertpapiere; ~ **note** Diskontabrechnung, -gutschrift; ~ **office** Diskontkasse; ~ **outlet** Rabattladen; ~ **period** Diskontierungszeitraum; ~ **piracy** Skontoschinderei; ~ **policy** Diskontpolitik; ~ **practices** Rabattmethoden; ~ **price** Rabattpreis; ~ **promise** Diskontzusage; ~ **quotation** Disagionotierung; ~ **rate** Barrabatt, Diskontsatz, Bankrate, -diskontsatz; **to increase (raise) the ~ rate** Diskontsatz heraufsetzen; **to lower the ~ rate** Diskontsatz herabsetzen (senken); **to mark down the ~ rate** Diskontsenkung vornehmen; ~ **rate change** Diskontänderung; ~ **rate rise** Diskonterhöhung; ~ **register** Wechselkopierbuch; ~ **request** Skontoersuchen; ~ **selling** Verkäufe im Diskontladen; ~ **shop (store)** *(US)* Einzelhandelsladen mit Rabattsystem, Einkaufszentrum; ~ **sum** Skonto-, Rabattbetrag; ~ **terms** Skonto-, Rabattbedingungen; ~ **ticket** Rabattmarke; ~ **trading** Diskontgeschäft; ~ **transactions** Diskont-, Wechselgeschäfte; ~ **turnover** Diskontumsatz; **to borrow freely at the ~ window** *(US)* unbeschränkte Rediskontfazilitäten in Anspruch nehmen.

discountability Diskontierbarkeit, -fähigkeit.

discountable diskontierbar, diskontfähig.

discounted diskontiert; **to be ~** diskontiert werden; **to get a bill ~** Wechsel diskontieren lassen; ~ **bills** Diskonten, Diskontverbindlichkeiten; ~ **cashflow method** Barwertrechnung; ~ **value** Diskontwert.

discounter Besitzer eines Rabattgeschäfts; **limited-range ~** Einkaufszentrum mit begrenztem Warenangebot.

discounting Diskontieren, Diskontgeschäft, Abzinsung; ~ **of bills (notes)** Wechseldiskontierung; ~ **of earnings** Gewinnvorwegnahme; ~ **for mortality** *(pension plan)* Inansatzbringen von Sterbefällen; ~ **the news** *(stock exchange)* Nachrichteneinschätzung; ~ **for severance** *(pension plan)* Einkalkulierung eventueller Entlassungen.

discourage *(v.)* abschrecken, entmutigen.

discouragement Abschreckung.

discourse Vorlesung, Ansprache, *(conversation)* Unterhaltung, Gespräch; ~ *(v.)* Ansicht darlegen; **to hold a ~ with s. o.** sich mit jem. unterhalten.

discourser Vortragender, Redner, Sprecher.

discover *(v.)* entdecken, ausfindig machen, ermitteln, *(international law)* entdecken; ~ **one's assets** *(bankrupt)* seine Vermögensverhältnisse offenbaren (darlegen); ~ **the cause for an illness** Krankheitsursache entdecken; ~ **a good chauffeur** *(coll.)* guten Chauffeur auftreiben; ~ **some error or mistake in a return of income** Fehler oder Irrtümer bei der Einkommensteuerveranlagung feststellen; ~ **a secret to one's friends** seinen Freunden ein Geheimnis enthüllen; **to suddenly ~ that it was too late to catch the train** plötzlich feststellen, daß es für den Zug zu spät war; **liability to ~** Auskunftspflicht.

discoverer Entdecker.

discovert unverheiratete Frau, Witwe; ~ *(a.)* unverheiratet, ledig.

discovery Ent-, Aufdeckung, Enthüllung, *(insurance)* Versicherungsanzeige, *(making known)* Offenlegung, Auskunftserteilung, *(mining)* Auffindung von Bodenschätzen, *(patent law)* gebrauchsmusterfähige Erfindung; **liable to ~** vorlagepflichtig; **technical ~** technische Erfindung; ~ **of one's assets** *(bankrupt)* Darlegung (Offenbarung) seiner Vermögensverhältnisse; ~ **of documents** Aufklärungspflicht, Bekanntgabe prozeßwichtiger Urkunden; ~ **of facts** Tatsachenenthüllung; ~ **and inspection** Vorlagezwang zwecks Augenscheinseinnahme; ~ **upon oath** *(Br.)* Bekanntgabe von Urkunden an die Gegenpartei; ~ **of property** *(bankruptcy proceedings)* Offenlegung des Schuldnervermögens; ~ **of stolen goods** Auffinden gestohlener Sachen; **to give ~ to documents** Urkundeninhalt bekanntgeben; **to make ~** Tatsachen mitteilen; **to make ~ of documents** Urkundenvorlage anordnen; **to make a ~ of the whole plot** gesamte Verschwörung aufdecken; ~ **claim** Mutungsanspruch; ~ **period** *(insurance)* Anzeigespielraum für Verluste; ~ **vein** Haupterzader.

discredit Mißkredit, schlechter Ruf, Verruf; ~ **to one's family** Schande für die ganze Familie; ~ *(v.)* diskreditieren, in Mißkredit (Verruf) bringen; ~ **s. one's evidence** Richtigkeit von jds. Aussage bestreiten; ~ **the evidence of a witness** Zeugenaussagen keine Bedeutung beimessen; ~ **s. o. with the public** j. seine öffentliche Glaubwürdigkeit verlieren lassen; **to bring into ~** in Mißkredit (Verruf) bringen; **to make ~ upon o. s.** sich in Mißkredit bringen; **to bring ~ to s. one's authority** jds. Autorität erschüttern; **to fall into ~** in Verruf geraten; **to throw serious ~ on the newspaper accounts** Zeitungsberichte in äußerst zweifelhaften Ruf erscheinen lassen; **to throw ~ upon a statement** Behauptung in Zweifel ziehen.

discreditable ehrenrührig, schimpflich; ~ **acquaintances** anrüchige Bekanntschaften; **conduct ~ for a barrister** standeswidriges Verhalten für einen Anwalt; ~ **profession** schimpfliches Gewerbe; ~ **report** schlechter Ruf.

discreet diskret, taktvoll, verschwiegen; **to be an absolutely ~ person** so verschwiegen sein wie das Grab; **to maintain a ~ silence** mit Stillschweigen übersehen, diskret Schweigen bewahren.

discrepancies *(broadcasting)* in letzter Minute vorgenommene Manuskriptänderung.

discrepancy Abweichung, Unstimmigkeit, Diskrepanz; ~ **between two accounts** Kontenunstimmigkeit; ~ **in amounts** *(cheque)* Differenz zwischen Zahl und Wort; ~ **in the deposition of a witness** Widerspruch in einer Zeugenaussage; ~ **in weight** Gewichtsabweichung; **to have a ~ in one's account** Differenz in seiner Rechnung haben.

discrepant verschieden, abweichend, nicht übereinstimmend, diskrepant; ~ **accounts** einander widersprechende Berichte.

discrete getrennt, für sich alleinstehend.

discretion *(criminal law)* Strafmündigkeit, *(discreetness)* Diskretion, Verschwiegenheit, Takt, *(liberty of deciding)* Gutdünken, Ermessen, Ermessensfrage, Verfügungs-, Entscheidungsfreiheit, *(prudence)* Umsicht, Klugheit; **at ([up]on) ~** nach Gutdünken (Belieben); **at one's [own] ~** nach seinem Belieben [eigenem Ermessen]; **within the ~ of the court** im freien Ermessen des Gerichts; **absolute ~** freies Ermessen; **administrative ~** Ermessen der Verwaltungsbehörde; **large ~** großer Ermessensspielraum; **sound judicial ~** vernünftiger Gebrauch der richterlichen Ermessensfreiheit; **professional ~** berufliche Schweigepflicht, Berufsgeheimnis; ~ **of a court** Ermessen des Gerichts; ~ **of the directors** Vorstandsermessen; ~ **of a judge** richterliches Ermessen; **to abuse one's ~** sein Ermessen mißbrauchen; **to act with ~** mit Umsicht handeln; **to be left to one's own ~** sich selbst überlassen sein; **to be at s. one's ~** jds. Ermessen anheimgestellt sein; **to be left to the ~ of the court** dem richterlichen Ermessen überlassen bleiben; **to be vested with ~** nach freiem Ermessen entscheiden können; **to come to years of ~** strafmündig werden; **to confide in s. one's ~** sich auf jds. Verschwiegenheit verlassen; **to have full ~ to act** volle Handlungsfreiheit haben; **to leave s. th. to s. one's ~** im Ermessen stellen, jem. freie Hand lassen; **to surrender at ~** sich auf Gnade und Ungnade übergeben; **to use one's ~** von seinem Ermessensrecht Gebrauch machen.

discretionary beliebig, willkürlich, dem Gutdünken überlassen, dem Ermessen anheimgegeben, nach billigem Ermessen; ~ **account** *(US)* Guthaben zur freien Verfügung bei einem Effektenmakler; ~ **action** Ermessenshandlung; ~ **beneficiary** im Ermessenswege Begünstigter; ~ **buying power** frei verfügbare Kaufkraft; ~ **clause** Kannvorschrift; ~ **damages** im Ermessenswege zuerkannter Schadensersatz, Ermessensschaden; ~ **income** frei verfügbares Einkommen; ~ **jurisdiction** Befugnis zu Ermessensentscheidungen; ~ **market power** *(big business)* Preisbestimmungsposition; ~ **matter** Ermessenssache; ~ **order** *(stock exchange)* Vertrauensorder; **extra ~ payment** besondere Ermessenszahlung; ~ **power** Ermessensbefugnis; **to exceed**

one's ~ **powers** seinen Ermessensspielraum mißbrauchen (überschreiten); **to give s. o.** ~ **powers** jem. unumschränkte Vollmacht erteilen; ~ **priorities** Prioritäten mit Ermessenspielraum; ~ **provision** Kannbestimmung; ~ **remedy** Ermessensbehelf; ~ **stabilizer** wirtschaftspolitische Sofortmaßnahmen; ~ **spending** Ausgaben zur freien Verfügung; ~ **settlement trust** (*Br.*) nach freiem Ermessen gehandhabte Vermögensverwaltung; ~ **time** absolute Freizeit; ~ **trust** Investmentgesellschaft mit breitgestreutem Aktienportefeuille; ~ **wants** elastischer Bedarf.

discriminate (*v.*) unterschiedlich (nachteilig) behandeln, diskriminieren, zurücksetzen;
~ **against other candidates** gegen andere Bewerber zurücksetzen; ~ **in favo(u)r of s. o.** j. bevorzugt behandeln; ~ **between persons** Personen unterschiedlich behandeln; ~ **racially** Rassendiskriminierung begehen.

discriminating unterscheidend, auseinanderhaltend;
~ **criticism** scharfe Kritik; ~ **duty** Differentialzoll; ~ **monopoly** Monopolmißbrauch; ~ **prices** unterschiedliche Preise; ~ **purchaser** umsichtiger Käufer; ~ **rate** Prohibitivsatz; ~ **tariff** diskriminierender Zoll; ~ **taste in literature** feine literarische Geschmacksunterschiede; ~ **treatment** diskriminierende (unterschiedliche) Behandlung.

discrimination (*acute discernment*) Urteilskraft, Scharfblick, Unterscheidungsvermögen, (*constitutional law*) Verletzung des Gleichberechtigungsprinzips, (*surety*) Einwand der Vorausklage, (*unequal treatment*) unterschiedliche Behandlung, Vorzugsbehandlung, Diskriminierung, Zurücksetzung, Benachteiligung;
built-in ~ (*taxation*) in das Steuersystem eingebaute Diskriminierung; **job** ~ Benachteiligung im Arbeitsleben; **racial** ~ Rassendiskriminierung; **tax** ~ unterschiedliche Steuerbehandlung, Steuerdiskriminierung;
~ **against** Schlechterstellung; ~ **in favo(u)r of s. o.** Begünstigung (Bevorzugung) einer Person; ~ **in favo(u)r of nonunion men** Bevorzugung von Nichtgewerkschaftsmitgliedern; ~ **against goods from foreign countries** Diskriminierung (Benachteiligung) ausländischer Erzeugnisse; ~ **in customs duties** Zolldiskriminierung; ~ **of a party in interest** Diskriminierung einer Prozeßpartei; ~ **in prices** Preisdifferenzierung, -spaltung; ~ **in rates** Tarifdifferenzierung;
to eliminate the ~s Handelsbeschränkungen aufheben.

discriminative diskriminierend, unterschiedlich, charakteristisch, (*discriminatory*) diskriminierend;
~ **duties** unterschiedliche Aufgabengebiete; ~ **features** Unterscheidungsmerkmale; ~ **treatment** diskriminierende Behandlung.

discriminatory unterscheidend, unterschiedlich, benachteiligend;
~ **action** diskriminierende Handlungsweise; ~ **conduct** diskriminierendes Verhalten; ~ **duty** Prohibitivzoll; ~ **prices** diskriminierende Preisgestaltung; ~ **rates** Prohibitivsätze; ~ **retaliation** diskriminierende Vergeltungsmaßnahmen; ~ **taxation** steuerliche Vorzugsbehandlung; ~ **treatment** diskriminierende Behandlung.

discrown (*fig.*) der Würde berauben.

discursive Thema wechselnd, abschweifend.

discuss (*v.*) besprechen, diskutieren, (*law*) Hauptschuldner ausklagen;
~ **in advance** vorberaten, -besprechen; ~ **a bottle** (*hum.*) Flasche Wein kosten; ~ **at some length** ausführlich besprechen; ~ **a matter** über eine Sache beraten; ~ **a matter in detail** Angelegenheit in allen Einzelheiten erörtern; ~ **a point** (*parl.*) Punkt erledigen; ~ **point for point** Punkt für Punkt durchgehen; ~ **a question thoroughly** Frage eingehend diskutieren; ~ **the situation** die Lage besprechen; ~ **outside subjects** alle Fragengebiete berühren;
to invite to ~ zur Diskussion stellen.

discussant (*US*) Diskussionsteilnehmer.

discussible diskutabel, diskutierbar.

discussion Besprechung, Diskussion, Debatte, Erörterung, Meinungsaustausch, Verhandlung, (*civil law*) Ausklagung eines Hauptschuldners, (*Scot. law*) Rangordnung der Nachlaßgläubiger;
after much ~ nach längeren Erörterungen (Verhandlungen); **under** ~ zur Diskussion stehend;
animated ~ bewegte Diskussion; **face-to-face** ~ Gespräch unter vier Augen; **at home** ~s zu Hause geführte Gespräche; **learned** ~ gelehrtes Gespräch; **lively** ~ bewegte Diskussion; **open** ~ Debatte; **preliminary** ~ Vorberatung, -besprechung; **thorough** ~ gründliche Diskussion; **political** ~ **of the day** politische Tagesfragen;

to be still under ~ noch nicht erledigt sein, noch beraten werden; **to begin (open, start) the** ~ Diskussion eröffnen; **to close the** ~ Debatte (Diskussion) schließen; **to come up for** ~ zur Diskussion gestellt werden, zur Sprache kommen; **to declare the** ~ **closed** (*Erörterung*) für beendet erklären, Diskussion schließen; **to enter [into] a** ~ in eine Diskussion eintreten; **to hold** ~s verhandeln; **to join the** ~ sich in die Diskussion einschalten; **to keep up a** ~ Diskussion in Gang halten; **to need** ~ einer Diskussion bedürfen; **to open a** ~ zur Diskussion stellen, Debatte eröffnen; **to participate in a** ~ an einer Diskussion teilnehmen; **to reanimate the** ~ Diskussion wieder in Gang bringen; **to schedule for** ~ für die Diskussion vorgehen; **to spend an hour over the** ~ **of a bottle of port** eine Stunde bei einer Flasche Portwein zusammensitzen; **to widen into a general** ~ sich zu einer Generaldebatte ausweiten;
~ **circle** Diskussionskreis; ~ **group** Diskussionsgruppe; ~ **program(me)** Diskussionsprogramm; ~ **session** Diskussionskreis; ~ **stage** Diskussionsstadium.

disdain Geringschätzung, Verachtung;
~ (*v.*) verachten, geringschätzen;
~ **an offer of help** es unter seiner Würde halten, ein Hilfsangebot anzunehmen.

disease Krankheit, Leiden;
contagious ~ ansteckende Krankheit, Seuche; **hereditary** ~ Erbkrankheit; **industrial (vocational)** ~ Berufskrankheit; **mental** ~ Geisteskrankheit; **notifiable** ~s meldepflichtige Krankheiten;
to contract a ~ sich eine Krankheit zuziehen;
~-**breeding occupation** Berufskrankheiten hervorrufende Beschäftigung.

diseased krank, erkrankt;
~ **in body and mind** krank an Körper und Seele.

diseconomies of scale Kostenprogression.

diseconomy Unproportionalität der Kosten.

disembark (*v.*) landen, aussteigen, (*v. i.*) ausschiffen.

disembarkation Ausschiffung, Landung.

disembodied technical progress vom Kapitaleinsatz unabhängiger technischer Fortschritt.

disemplane (*v.*) Flugzeug verlassen.

disencumber (*v.*) | **an estate** Grundstück entschulden; ~ **o. s. of a load** sich von einer Last befreien.

disencumbrance Entschuldung, Entlastung.

disenfranchise (*v.*) Wahlrecht nehmen, (*licence*) Konzession entziehen.

disengage (*v.*) entbinden, (*decartelize*) entflechten, (*fiancé*) sich entloben, (*free from obligations*) [sich von Verbindlichkeiten] befreien, (*mil.*) sich absetzen;
~ **the clutch** auskuppeln.

disengaged (*unoccupied*) unbesetzt, unbeschäftigt, (*tel.*) nicht besetzt, frei.

disengagement (*decartelization*) Entflechtung, (*pol.*) Auseinanderrücken der Machtblöcke;
military ~ Abbau des militärischen Potentials;
~ **of troops** Truppenentflechtung;
~ **agreement** Entflechtungsabkommen.

disentail Befreiung von einer festgelegten Erbfolge;
~ (*v.*) von einer festgelegten Erbfolge befreien;
~ **an estate** Fideikommiß auflösen.

disentailing | **assurance, to execute a** ~ Aufhebung erbrechtlicher Bindungen durchführen; ~ **deed** Fideikommiß-Aufhebungsvertrag.

disentailment Fideikommißauflösung.

disentangle (*v.*) entwirren, entflechten;
~ **traffic** Verkehr entwirren.

disentanglement Entflechtung;
~ **of traffic** Verkehrsentwirrung.

disenthronement Entthronung.

disentitle (*v.*) eines Rechtsanspruchs berauben.

disentomb (*v.*) exhumieren.

disentombment Exhumierung.

disequilibrium (*currency*) Gleichgewichtsstörung, Störung des Gleichgewichts, Ungleichgewicht;
~ **in the balance of payments** unausgeglichene Zahlungsbilanz, Zahlungsbilanzungleichgewicht.

disestablish (*v.*) **the Church** Kirche und Staat trennen.

disestablishment of the Church Trennung von Kirche und Staat.

disfavo(u)r Ungnade, Ungunst, Mißbilligung;
in my ~ zu meinen Ungunsten;
to fall into ~ in Ungnade fallen; **to incure s. one's** ~ sich jds. Ungnade zuziehen; **to look upon s. th. with** ~ etw. mit Mißfallen betrachten.

disfigure *(v.)* verunstalten, entstellen.
disfigured by advertisement durch Reklame verschandelt.
disfigurement Verschandelung, Verunstaltung, körperliche Entstellung.
disforest *(v.)* abholzen.
disfranchise *(v.)* Wahlrecht (Stimmrecht) entziehen;
~ **to be ~d** Stimmrecht (Wahlrecht) verlieren.
disfranchisement Wahlrechtsentziehung.
disgrace Ehrlosigkeit, *(loss of favo(u)r)* Ungnade, Ungunst;
~ **to the city authorities** Schandfleck für die Stadt;
~ *(v.)* entehren, schänden;
~ **s. o. j.** in Ungnade entlassen; ~ **the family name** seiner Familie Schande bereiten, Familiennamen entehren;
to be a ~ to a party Schandfleck für eine Partei sein; **to be in ~ with s. o.** bei jem. in Ungnade stehen; **to bring ~ on one's family** seiner Familie zur Unehre gereichen; **to have fallen into ~ with one's companions** Achtung seiner Freunde verloren haben.
disgraceful schändlich, schimpflich, ehrenrührig;
to be an action ~ for all concerned für alle Beteiligten gerade kein Ruhmesblatt sein.
disguise Verkleidung, Vermummung, *(act of concealing)* Irreführung, Täuschung, *(actor)* Maske;
under the ~ unter dem Vorwand;
~ *(v.)* verschleiern, bemänteln, verbergen;
~ **the facts** Tatsachen verschleiern; ~ **one's handwriting** seine Handschrift verstellen; ~ **one's plans** seine Pläne verbergen; ~ **one's worries beneath a cheerful appearance** seine Sorgen hinter betont fröhlichem Auftreten verbergen;
to make no ~ of one's feelings seine Gefühle nicht verbergen; **to strip s. o. of his ~** jem. die Maske vom Gesicht reißen.
disguised, to write a letter in a ~ hand Brief mit verstellter Handschrift schreiben.
disgust Abscheu, Widerwille, Ekel.
dish Schüssel, Platte, *(meal)* Gericht, Speise, *(space)* Radarspiegel, Parabolreflektor;
not my ~ nicht mein Fall;
the ~es Geschirr;
cold ~ kaltes Gericht; **meat ~** Fleischplatte; **standing ~** *(fig.)* ewige Leier;
~ **that is off** *(restaurant)* ausgegangenes Gericht;
~ *(v.) (shelve, sl.)* erledigen, kaltstellen;
~ **one's hopes of being elected** seine Hoffnungen auf eine Wiederwahl zunichte machen; ~ **out** Speisen austeilen, *(fig.)* auftischen, erzählen; ~ **out one's opponents** *(coll.)* seine Gegner ausmanövrieren; ~ **up** mundgerecht darbieten; ~ **up the usual arguments** die üblichen Argumente vorbringen (servieren); ~ **up the contents of a book in another form** Buchinhalt neuverbrämt vorbringen; ~ **up the dinner** das Essen auftragen, servieren; ~ **up some excuse or other** *(coll.)* irgendeine Entschuldigung auftischen; ~ **up well-known facts in a new form** wohlbekannte Tatsachen lediglich neuformuliert vorbringen; ~ **up the same subject in every shape** gleiches Thema von allen Seiten beleuchten;
to wash up the ~es Geschirr abwaschen;
~ **cloth** Spüllappen; **~-warmer** Warmhalteplatte.
disherison Enterbung.
dishoard *(v.)* neu investieren.
dishoarding *(money)* Neuinvestition.
dishonest unreell, unredlich;
~ **business** unreelles Geschäft; **to engage in a ~ lawsuit** sich in einen üblen Rechtsstreit einlassen.
dishonesty Unredlichkeit, Untreue, Betrug.
dishono(u)r Unehre, Schmach, Schande, *(refusal to accept)* Akzeptverweigerung, *(refusal to pay)* Nichthonorierung, -einlösung;
~ **to the nation** Schande für die Nation; ~ **by nonacceptance** *(bill of exchange)* Nichtannahme; ~ **for nonpayment** Nichtbezahlung eines Wechsels;
~ *(v.) (refuse to accept)* nicht akzeptieren, Annahme verweigern, *(refuse to pay)* nicht honorieren (einlösen);
~ **a bill** Annahme eines Wechsels verweigern, Wechsel Not leiden lassen; ~ **a check** *(US)* **(cheque, Br.)** Scheck zurückgehen lassen; ~ **a draft by nonacceptance** Annahme eines Wechsels verweigern; ~ **one's promise** Versprechen nicht einhalten; ~ **one's word** sein Wort brechen;
to be a ~ to one's regiment sein Regiment in Verruf bringen; **to bring ~ on one's family** seiner Familie zur Unehre gereichen; **to show ~ to a draft** Tratte nicht akzeptieren.
dishono(u)rable unredlich, unehrenhaft, ehrenrührig, schändlich;
~ **discharge** *(mil.)* Entlassung wegen Wehrunwürdigkeit.

dishono(u)red *(mil.)* in Unehren verabschiedet;
~ **bill** notleidender Wechsel; ~ **check** *(US)* **(cheque, Br.)** nicht eingelöster Scheck.
dishoused wohnungslos.
dishwasher Tellerwäscher, *(machine)* Geschirrspülautomat.
dishwater Abwasch-, Spülwasser, *(tea, coffee)* dünne Brühe.
disillusion Enttäuschung, Ernüchterung.
disimprison *(v.)* auf freien Fuß setzen.
disincarcerate *(v.)* aus der Haft entlassen.
disincentive arbeitshemmender Faktor, fehlender Anreiz, Anreizblockierung, *(fiscal policy)* Abschreckungsmittel;
~ **to business** negative Konjunktureinwirkung; ~ **to members of the managerial classes** keinerlei Anreiz für die Unternehmerschaft; ~ **to work** fehlender Arbeitsanreiz;
~ *(a.)* hemmend, hindernd;
~ **to investment** investitionshemmend; ~ **to work** arbeitshemmend;
to be ~ to saving sich hemmend auf die Spartätigkeit auswirken;
~ **effects of taxation** abschreckende steuerliche Auswirkungen.
disinclination Abneigung;
~ **to buy** Kauflust; ~ **to meet people** ungeselliges Wesen; ~ **to work** Arbeitsunlust, -abneigung;
to show a ~ to books an Büchern kein Interesse haben.
disinclined abgeneigt;
~ **to buy** kaufunlustig.
disincorporate *(v.)* Verein auflösen.
disincorporation Vereinsauflösung.
disinflation Inflationsabbau durch gezielte Maßnahmen.
disinherit *(v.)* enterben.
disinheritance *(US)* Enterbung.
disintegrate *(v.)* zersetzen, auflösen, disintegrieren, *(party)* auseinanderfallen.
disintegration Zersetzung, *(party)* Auseinanderfallen;
~ **of nucleus** Kernzerfall.
disinter *(v.)* exhumieren.
disinterest Uneigennützigkeit, Interesselosigkeit, *(disadvantage)* Nachteil;
to the ~ of the public unter Benachteiligung öffentlicher Interessen;
~ *(v.)* **o. s.** seine Gleichgültigkeit bekunden; ~ **o. s. in a question** an einer Frage nicht interessiert sein.
disinterested uneigennützig, selbstlos;
not altogether ~ von persönlichen Gefühlen nicht völlig frei; ~ **witness** neutraler (objektiver) Zeuge.
disinterestedness Selbstlosigkeit.
disintermediation Bruttoverlust an Einlagegeldern.
disinterment Exhumierung.
disinvestment *(US)* Zurückziehung von Anlagekapital, *(diminution of capital goods)* Produktionseinschränkung, *(reduction of inventories)* Lagerabbau;
~ **abroad** Realisierung ausländischer Vermögenswerte.
disjointed *(speech)* unzusammenhängend.
disjunctive|allegation Haupt- und Hilfsvorbringen; ~ **term** Alternativbedingung.
disk [Signal]scheibe, *(US) (gramophone)* Grammophon-, Schallplatte, *(tel.)* Wähl-, Nummernscheibe;
call indicator ~ *(telephone exchange)* Nummernanzeiger; **calling** ~ *(telephone exchange)* Anrufklappe; **gramophone** ~ Grammophonplatte; **identity (identification)** ~ *(mil.)* Erkennungsmarke; **recording** ~ Zählscheibe;
~ *(v.) (US)* auf Schallplatten aufnehmen;
~ **jockey** Schallplattenansager, Rundfunkunterhalter; ~ **jockeying** Rundfunkunterhaltung, Schallplattenansage; ~ **signal** *(railway)* Scheibensignal; ~ **system** Schallplattenmethode; ~ **wheel** Scheibenrad.
dislocate *(v.) (factory)* verlagern;
~ **the traffic** Verkehr durcheinanderbringen; ~ **workers** Arbeitskräfte umsetzen.
dislocation *(disorder)* störender Wechsel in den Lebensgewohnheiten, *(factory)* Verlagerung, *(mil.)* Truppenbewegung, -verschiebung;
~ **of bread supplies** Störung der Brotversorgung; ~ **of the currency** Währungsverfall; ~ **of trade** Nichtfunktionieren des Handels; ~ **of traffic** Verkehrsdurcheinander, Verkehrsverlagerung; ~ **of workers** Umsetzung von Arbeitskräften.
dislodge *(v.)* ausquartieren, *(mil.)* verdrängen, vertreiben, *(officeholder)* vertreiben;
~ **the enemy from a position** Feind aus einer Stellung vertreiben.
dislodgment Ausquartierung, *(mil.)* Vertreibung.

disloyal treulos, nicht loyal, unloyal, illoyal.
disloyalty Illoyalität, Treulosigkeit.
dismantle (v.) (equipment) [Betriebseinrichtungen] demontieren, aus-, abbauen, abreißen, (wreck) abwracken;
~ **an agency** Behörde (Dienststelle) auflösen; ~ **an engine** Motor auseinandernehmen; ~ **exchange control** Devisenbewirtschaftung aufheben; ~ **a fortress** Festung schleifen; ~ **a house** Haus abreißen; ~ **a roof** Haus abdecken; ~ **a ship** Schiff abtakeln; ~ **trade barriers** Handelsschranken abbauen.
dismantlement Aus-, Abbau, Demontage, Abbruch, (ship) Abtakelung, (wreck) Abwracken;
~ **of an agency** Behördenauflösung.
dismantling Demontage, Abbau;
industrial ~ Industriedemontage;
~ **of trade barriers** Abbau von Handelsschranken;
~ **cost** Abbruchkosten; ~ **list** Demontageliste; ~ **operations** Demontagearbeiten; ~ **program(me)** Demontageprogramm.
dismember (v.) (country) zerstückeln, (deprive of membership) der Mitgliedschaftsrechte berauben, aus einem Verein ausschließen;
~ **a territory** Staatsgebiet aufteilen.
dismemberment Gliederverlust, (country) Zerstückelung, (removal from membership) Vereinsausschluß;
~ **of a territory** Aufteilung eines Staatsgebiets; ~ **benefit** Versehrtenunterstützung bei Gliederverlust; ~ **schedule** Gliedertaxe.
dismiss (v.) weg-, fortschicken, (get rid of) abtun, ablegen, aus seinen Gedanken verbannen, (official) [aus dem Dienst] entlassen, verabschieden, [Beamte] abbauen, (wife) verstoßen;
~ **the accused** Angeklagten freisprechen; ~ **an action** Klage abweisen; ~ **s. one's appeal** jds. Berufung zurückweisen (verwerfen); ~ **a case [with costs]** Klage [kostenpflichtig] abweisen; ~ **a case for want of prosecution** Klage wegen Prozeßverschleppung abweisen; ~ **a charge** Verfahren einstellen; ~ **the charge [on indictment]** Eröffnung des Hauptverfahrens ablehnen; ~ **a class** Schulklasse aus dem Unterricht entlassen; ~ **a clerk** Buchhalter entlassen; ~ **a complaint** Beschwerde zurückweisen; ~ **with costs** kostenpflichtig abweisen; ~ **the crew** Schiffsvolk abdanken; ~ **any personal feeling** sich von persönlichen Gefühlen völlig freimachen; ~ **immediately** fristlos kündigen; ~ **without justification** unberechtigt entlassen; ~ **a meeting** Versammlung auflösen; ~ **without notice** fristlos entlassen (kündigen); ~ **an officer from the service for neglect of duty** Offizier wegen Pflichtversäumnis entlassen; ~ **an official** Beamten aus dem Dienst entfernen; ~ **an official for unsatisfactory conduct** Beamten wegen schlechter Führung entlassen; ~ **a petition** Behandlung eines Gesuchs ablehnen; ~ **a petition in bankruptcy** Eröffnung des Konkursverfahrens ablehnen; ~ **s. o. from his post** j. seines Amtes entheben; ~ **for redundancy** als nicht mehr benötigte Arbeitskraft entlassen; ~ **a servant** Dienstboten entlassen; ~ **a servant without notice** Hausangestellten fristlos kündigen; ~ **s. o. speedily** j. schleunigst abfertigen; ~ **a subject** Thema fallenlassen; ~ **summarily** fristlos entlassen; ~ **a tariff issue with a brief reference** sich mit einer Tarifauseinandersetzung nach kurzer Stellungnahme nicht mehr beschäftigen; ~ **all thoughts of revenge** alle Rachegedanken verbannen; ~ **an employee unfairly** (Br.) Angestellten sozial ungerechtfertigt kündigen; ~ **for want of sufficient ground** als unbegründet zurückweisen.
dismissal [Dienst]entlassung, Enthebung, Entsetzung, Verabschiedung [von Beamten], (wife) Verstoßung;
~ **agreed** Klageabweisung mit Zustimmung der Partei; **instant** ~ sofortige Entlassung; **mass** ~s Massenentlassungen; **summary** ~ fristlose (sofortige) Entlassung; **top-level** ~ Entlassung von Spitzenkräften; **unfair** ~ (Br.) sozial ungerechtfertigte Kündigung; **unlawful** ~ wiederrechtliche fristlose Entlassung; ~ **of an action** Klageabweisung; ~ **of appeal** Zurückweisung (Verwerfung) der Berufung; ~ **of a criminal case** Einstellung des Strafverfahrens; ~ **with costs** kostenpflichtige Zurückweisung; ~ **on grounds of redundancy** Entlassung wegen nicht mehr benötigter Arbeitskräfte; ~ **for misconduct** Entlassung wegen ungehörigen Verhaltens; ~ **with notice** befristete Kündigung; ~ **without notice** fristlose Entlassung, (lease) nicht fristgemäße Kündigung; ~ **from a post** Amtsenthebung, -entsetzung; ~ **without prejudice** Klageabweisendes Urteil ohne Sachentscheidung; ~ **of proceedings** Klagerücknahme; ~ **for exceptional reasons** außerordentliche Kündigung; ~ **from service** Dienstenthebung;
to claim unfair ~ Einwand einer sozial ungerechtfertigten Kündigung erheben; **to justify summary** ~ zur fristlosen Kündigung aus wichtigem Grund berechtigt sein;

~ **compensation** Abstandsgeld, Entlassungsentschädigung, -ausgleich, -gehalt; ~ **notice** Kündigung[smitteilung]; **to issue** ~ **notice** Kündigungsbenachrichtigung zustellen; ~ **pay** Entlassungsgeld; ~ **payment** Entlassungsabfindung, -geld; ~ **procedure** Entlassungsverfahren; ~ **wage** Entlassungsgehalt, -zahlung, Abstandsgeld.
dismissed entlassen, ausgeschieden, (judgment) abgewiesen;
~ **for want of equity** mit der Klage abgewiesen;
to be (get) ~ entlassen werden; **to be** ~ **[from] the service** (mil.) seine Entlassung erhalten; **to be** ~ **from one's suit** mit seiner Klage abgewiesen werden; **to be** ~ **for being dishonest** wegen Unredlichkeit entlassen werden.
dismissible absetzbar, widerruflich.
dismission Entlassung, (from office) Amtsenthebung;
~ **of a jury** Entlassung der Geschworenen; ~ **of troops** Entlassung von Truppen.
dismortgage (v.) Hypothek ablösen.
dismount Abmontieren, Demontage;
~ (v.) abmontieren, (jewel(e)ry) aus der Fassung nehmen;
~ **from a bicycle** vom Fahrrad absteigen.
disnaturalization Wiederausbürgerung.
disnaturalize (v.) wieder ausbürgern.
disobedience Ungehorsam, Gehorsamsverweigerung;
civil ~ bürgerlicher Ungehorsam, (nonpayment of taxes) Steuerstreik;
~ **to orders** Nichtbefolgung von Anweisungen.
disobedient ungehorsam, widerspenstig;
to be ~ **to the law** Gesetze nicht befolgen.
disobey (v.) nicht befolgen, verlegen, übertreten;
~ **the law** Gesetz nicht befolgen.
disoblige (v.) kränken, unhöflich begegnen.
disobliging unhöflich, ungefällig.
disoccupation Unbeschäftigtsein.
disorder Verwirrung, Durcheinander, Unordnung, (breach of public order) Ordnungswidrigkeit, öffentliche Ruhestörung, Tumult, Krawall, Aufruhr;
mental ~ Geistesstörung; **nervous** ~ nervöse Störung; ~ **of the digestive system** Magenverstimmung, Verdauungsstörungen; ~s **of the mind** geistige Störungen;
~ (v.) durcheinanderbringen, Störungen hervorrufen;
to deal with the ~s **in the capital** Aufruhr in der Hauptstadt niederwerfen; **to fall in** ~ (convoy) auseinanderbrechen; **to retreat in** ~ sich ungeordnet zurückziehen; **to stir up** ~ Unruhe stiften; **to throw into** ~ durcheinanderbringen, in Aufruhr versetzen.
disordered zerrüttet, geisteskrank;
mentally ~ **person** Geisteskranker.
disorderliness unbotmäßiges Verhalten;
~ **in a public place** Erregung öffentlichen Ärgernisses.
disorderly unbotmäßig, aufrührerisch, (law) Ärgernis erregend, ordnungswidrig;
to be ~ **in a bar** sich in einer Bar ungehörig aufführen;
~ **behavio(u)r** unbotmäßiges Verhalten; ~ **conduct** ordnungswidriges Verhalten, grober Unfug; ~ **crowd** aufrührerische Massen; ~ **desk** nicht aufgeräumter Schreibtisch; ~ **house** Bordell; **to lead a** ~ **life** liederliches Leben führen; ~ **mob** Pöbel; ~ **person** Ruhestörer, Erreger öffentlichen Ärgernisses; ~ **rabble of a former crack regiment** zügelloser Haufen eines ehemaligen Eliteregiments; ~ **room** nicht aufgeräumtes Zimmer.
disorganization Desorganisation.
disorganize (v.) durcheinanderbringen, desorganisieren.
disorganized by the fog wegen des Nebels völlig aus den Fugen.
disorientate (v.) seine Orientierung verlieren.
disown (v.) ablehnen, verleugnen;
~ **a child** Kind verleugnen (verstoßen); ~ **an heir** Erben nicht anerkennen; ~ **one's signature** seine Unterschrift nicht anerkennen.
disownment of a child Verstoßung eines Kindes.
disparage (v.) schmälern, verunglimpfen, (competitive goods) herabsetzen;
~ **in a profession** beruflich herabsetzen; ~ **everything** alles in den Dreck ziehen.
disparagement Herabsetzung, Schmälerung, Verruf, Verunglimpfung, Verächtlichmachung;
without ~ **to you** ohne Ihnen zu nahe treten zu wollen;
trade ~ Verleumdung im Geschäftsverkehr, Anschwärzung der Konkurrenz;
~ **of a competitor** Anschwärzung der Konkurrenz; ~ **of goods** Verunglimpfung von Konkurrenzerzeugnissen;
to refer to s. o. in terms of ~ in herabsetzender Weise von jem. sprechen.

disparaging verächtlich, herabsetzend, geringschätzig;
~ **competition** herabsetzende Werbung; ~ **copy** herabsetzender Werbetext, herabsetzende (aggressive) Werbung; ~ **statement** herabsetzende Behauptung.

disparagingly, to speak sich herabsetzend äußern, herabsetzende Bemerkungen machen.

disparities in the newspaper accounts of the accident Unvereinbarkeiten von Zeitungsberichten über einen Unfall.

disparity Verschiedenheit, Ungleichheit, Unvereinbarkeit, Disparität;
~ **of age** Altersunterschied; ~ **in position** Verschiedenheit der Stellungen; ~ **in price** Preisunterschied.

dispark *(v.)* der Öffentlichkeit zugänglich machen.

dispassionate unparteiisch.

dispatch *(Br.)* [amtlicher] Kriegsbericht, *(conveying agency)* Spedition, Versandunternehmen, -betrieb, *(dismissal)* Entlassung, *(killing)* Tötung, *(prompt settlement)* schnelle Erledigung (Durchführung), Eile, Promptheit, *(sending)* Absendung, Beförderung, Auslieferung, Versand, [Waren]abfertigung, *(wire)* Nachricht, Depesche, Telegramm;
ready for ~ versandfähig, -bereit; **with** ~ sofort, eiligst, prompt; **with the utmost** ~ mit tunlichster Beschleunigung;
~**es** *(newspaper)* Nachrichten;
customary ~ *(port)* hafenüblicher (prompter) Versand; **happy** ~ Harakiri; **original** ~ ursprüngliche Meldung; **outgoing** ~ abgehender Bericht; **pneumatic** ~ Rohrpost[einrichtung]; **speedy** ~ Eilabfertigung;
~ **on approval** Ansichtsversand; ~ **of business** Geschäftserledigung; ~ **of current business** Erledigung eiliger Sachen; ~ **of goods** Warenversand, Güterversand, Versandabwicklung; ~ **of fast goods** Eilgutabfertigung; ~ **of luggage** *(Br.)* Gepäckabfertigung; ~ **of mail** Postabfertigung; ~ **of a matter** Erledigung einer Angelegenheit; ~ **of a petition** schnelle Erledigung eines Gesuches; ~ **by rail** Bahnversand; ~ **of telegrams** Telegrammaufgabe; ~ **of troops** Truppenentsendung;
~ **discharging only** Eilgeld nur im Löschhafen; ~ **half demurrage** Eilgeld in Höhe des halben Liegegeldes; ~ **loading only** Eilgeld nur im Ladehafen; ~ **half demurrage all time saved** Eilgeld in Höhe des halben Liegegeldes; ~ **half demurrage working time saved** Eilgeld in Höhe des halben Liegegeldes für die gesparte Arbeitszeit;
~ *(v.)* abschicken, -senden, expedieren, befördern, aufliefern, fortschicken, *(mil.)* in Marsch setzen, *(kill)* ins Jenseits befördern, töten, *(settle promptly)* rasch erledigen;
~ **a business** Geschäft erledigen; ~ **current business** Eilsachen sofort erledigen; ~ **a convoy** Konvoi auf den Weg bringen; **to soon** ~ **one's dinner** sein Essen rasch vertilgen; ~ **goods direct to s. o.** jem. Waren unmittelbar zuschicken; ~ **goods to their destination** Waren an ihren Bestimmungsort dirigieren; ~ **a letter** Brief absenden; ~ **the mail** Post abfertigen; ~ **a condemned man** Verurteilten hinrichten; ~ **a messenger** Boten entsenden; ~ **a telegram** Telegramm befördern (aufgeben); ~ **a train** Zug ablassen;
to be mentioned in ~**es** *(soldier)* ehrenhaft im Heeresbericht erwähnt werden; **to be** ~**ed** zum Versand gelangen; **to hurry up the** ~ **of a telegram** Telegramm beschleunigt aufgeben; **to receive** ~**es from all parts of the world** Zeitungsnachrichten aus aller Herren Länder erhalten; **to work with the greatest possible** ~ mit größtmöglicher Beschleunigung arbeiten;
~ **agency** Depeschen-, Telegrafenbüro; ~ **bag** *(US)* Kuriertasche; ~ **boat** Depeschenboot, Aviso; ~ **book** Abfertigungsbuch; ~ **box** Depeschentasche, Kurier-, Diplomatengepäck; ~ **carrier** Kurier; ~ **case** Aktenmappe; ~ **charges** Versandkosten, -spesen; ~ **clerk** Expedient, Abfertiger, Abfertigungsangestellter; ~ **computer** Digitalrechenanlage; ~ **department** Versandabteilung; ~ **earnings** Entladegewinn [bei sofortiger Löschung]; ~ **expenses** Versandkosten; ~ **goods** *(Br.)* Eilfracht, -gut; ~ **instructions** Versand-, Abfertigungs-, Beförderungsvorschriften; ~ **money** *(Br.)* Vergütung für schnelles Entladen, Eilgeld, Beschleunigungsgebühr; ~ **note** *(Br.)* Verladeschein, Versandanzeige, -schein, Begleitadresse, -zettel, Frachtzettel, Paketkarte, Postbegleitschein; ~ **office** Abfertigungsstelle; ~ **order** Versand-, Speditionsauftrag; ~ **point** Aufgabebahnhof, Versandort; ~ **regulations** Versand-, Abfertigungsvorschriften; ~ **reliability** zuverlässige Abfertigung; ~ **rider** *(mil.)* Meldefahrer; ~ **riding** *(mil.)* Meldefahrt; ~ **service** Expedition, Versandabteilung; ~ **station** Versandstation, -bahnhof; ~ **table** Abfertigungstisch; ~ **tube** Versandrolle; ~ **vessel** Depeschenboot, Aviso.

dispatched goods Versandwaren.

dispatcher Expedient, Absender, *(production, US)* Produktionskontrolleur, *(of train, US)* Fahrdienstleiter;
train ~ *(US)* Fahrdienstleiter;
good ~ **of business** flinker Arbeiter.

dispatching Abfertigung, Expedition, Versand;
~ **clerk** Expedient, Abfertiger; ~ **office** Abfertigungsstelle, Expedition, *(post-office)* Abgangspostamt; ~ **station** Abgangs-, Versandbahnhof.

dispauper *(v.)* *(US)* Armenrecht entziehen.

dispel *(v.)* | **boredom** Langeweile vertreiben; ~ **doubts** Zweifel verbannen; ~ **the fog** Nebel auflösen.

dispensary Apotheke, *(mil.)* Krankenrevier.

dispensation Aus-, Ver-, Zuteilung, *(management)* Verwaltung, *(suspension of a rule of law)* Nichtanwendung, Ausnahmebewilligung;
marriage ~ Befreiung von einem Ehehindernis, Ehedispens; ~ **of charity** Almosenverteilung; ~ **of food** Nahrungsmittelverteilung; ~ **of justice** Rechtsanwendung; **happy** ~ **of nature** glückliche Veranlagung; ~ **of Providence** Fügung der Vorsehung, göttliche Fügung;
to give a ~ *(inspector of taxes)* Steuerbefreiung gewähren.

dispense *(club)* Ausschank, Bar;
~ *(v.)* aus-, ver-, zuteilen, *(law)* Ausnahmegenehmigung erteilen, *(med.)* auf Rezept abgeben;
~ **s. o. from s. th.** j. von etw. entbinden;
~ **alms** Almosen vergeben; ~ **with the calling of witnesses** auf das Erscheinen von Zeugen verzichten; ~ **charity** für wohltätige Zwecke spenden; ~ **with the doctor's services** auf ärztliche Betreuung verzichten; ~ **s. o. from an examination** jem. eine Prüfung erlassen; ~ **one's favo(u)r to s. o.** jem. seine Gunst zuwenden; ~ **with formalities** auf Förmlichkeiten verzichten; ~ **food** Nahrungsmittel verteilen; ~ **with hand labo(u)r** ohne Handarbeiter auskommen; ~ **justice** Gesetze anwenden, Recht sprechen; ~ **with a law** Gesetz nicht anwenden; ~ **s. o. from the necessity of earning his living** j. der Notwendigkeit entheben, sich seinen Lebensunterhalt verdienen zu müssen; ~ **with an oath** auf Vereidigung verzichten; ~ **a prescription** Arzneimittel verabreichen (zurechtmachen); ~ **with a promise** nicht auf Einhaltung eines Versprechens bestehen; ~ **rations** Rationen ausgeben; ~ **with the signature of a witness** auf die eidesstattliche Erklärung eines Zeugen verzichten.

dispenser Apotheker, Arzneimittelhersteller, *(bar)* stummer Verkäufer.

dispeople *(v.)* entvölkern.

dispersal Streuung, Verbreitung, Verteilung, *(airplane)* getrennte Abstellung;
~ **of assets** Anlagenstreuung; ~ **of industrial facilities** aufgelockerte Ansiedlung industrieller Fertigungsbetriebe; ~ **of ownership** Eigentumsstreuung; ~ **of stock ownership** Aktienstreuung; ~ **of troops** Zersplitterung von Truppen, Truppenzersplitterung;
to order the ~ **of an assembly** Auflösung einer Versammlung anordnen;
~ **point** getrennter Abstellplatz.

disperse *(v.)* auflockern, sich verlieren, sich zerstreuen, auseinandergehen;
~ **aircraft** Flugzeuge getrennt abstellen; ~ **at ten o'clock** um 10 Uhr aufbrechen; ~ **the crowd** Menge auseinandertreiben; ~ **the fog** Nebel auflösen; ~ **a meeting** Versammlung auflösen; ~ **news** Nachrichten verbreiten.

dispersed | **in width** *(mil.)* in Fliegermarschbreite;
~ **airport** aufgelockert angelegter Flugplatz; ~ **formation** *(mil.)* aufgelockerte Formation.

dispersion *(advertising)* Streuung von Werbemitteln;
regional ~ regionale Streuung;
~ **of the fog** Nebelauflösung; ~ **of goods** Güterverteilung; ~ **of industry** industrielle Auflockerung; **wide** ~ **of ownership** breite Eigentumsstreuung; ~ **of profits** Gewinnverteilung;
~ **area** *(advertising campaign)* Streubereich.

displace *(v.)* verlagern, verlegen, *(deport)* deportieren, verschleppen, *(remove)* versetzen, absetzen, *(ship)* verdrängen;
~ **s. o. in s. one's affection** Platz eines anderen in jds. Zuneigung einnehmen; ~ **a book in the library** Buch in der Bibliothek umstellen; ~ **a government official** Staatsbeamten ablösen; ~ **human labo(u)r by machinery** menschliche Arbeitskraft durch Maschinen ersetzen; ~ **volunteers by a professional army** Freiwillige durch Berufssoldaten ersetzen.

displaced verschleppt, vertrieben, deportiert;
forcibly ~ zwangsverschickt;
~ **person** Flüchtling, Ausgewiesener, Vertriebener, Zwangsverschleppter; ~ **shares** nicht notierte Aktien.

displacement Versetzung, *(exilement)* Verschleppung, *(factory)* Verlagerung, *(ship)* Tonnengehalt, Tonnage, Wasserverdrängung;
light ~ Leertonnage; **load** ~ Ladetonnage;
~ **of funds** anderweitige Kapitalverwendung; ~ **of human labo(u)r by machinery** Ersatz menschlicher Arbeitskraft durch Maschinen, Arbeitsplatzvernichtung, Freisetzungen; ~ **of population** Bevölkerungsverschiebung;
~ **ton** Verdrängungstonne; ~ **tonnage** Verdrängungstonnage.

display Pomp, Prunk, *(data processing)* Schirmbild-, Datensichtgerät, *(goods)* [Schaufenster]auslage, Werbeschau, Ausstellung, *(information)* Informationsdarstellung, *(print.)* Hervorhebung, Auszeichnung, hervorgehobene Textstelle, *(types)* große Schrifttypen;
on [permanent] ~ [dauernd] ausgestellt;
air ~ Flugschau; **counter** ~ Ladentischauslage; **fashion** ~ Modeschau; **firework** ~ Feuerwerkveranstaltung; **industrial** ~ Auslage (Schau) industrieller Erzeugnisse, Industrieschau; **interior** ~ Auslage innerhalb des Ladens; **mass** ~ Massenauslage; **official** ~ offizieller Empfang, Repräsentation; **point-of-purchase** ~ Herkunftsortschau; **pyramid** ~ Auslage in Pyramidenform; **seasonal** ~ Saisonauslage; **window** ~ Schaufensterauslage, Dekorationsfenster;
~ **of fireworks** Feuerwerksveranstaltung; ~ **of the flag** Flaggenentfaltung; ~**s of friendship** Freundschaftsbezeugungen; ~ **of power** Machtentfaltung; ~ **in the shopwindow** Schaufensterauslage;
~ *(v.)* prunken, protzen, *(goods)* zeigen, zur Ansicht vorlegen, auslegen, ausstellen, aushängen, dekorieren, *(print.)* hervorheben;
~ **activity** Aktivität zeigen; ~ **the flag** Flagge zeigen; ~ **goods in the window** Waren im Schaufenster ausstellen; ~ **one's ignorance** seine Unwissenheit erkennen lassen (zur Schau stellen); ~ **a notice** Anschlag machen; ~ **for sale** zum Verkauf ausstellen, dekorieren; ~ **no signs of emotion** keine Gefühlserregung erkennen lassen; ~ **text matter** Text auszeichnen;
to be fond of ~ gern groß in Erscheinung treten; **to be on public** ~ öffentlich ausgestellt sein; **to have a horror of** ~ ganz gegen Repräsentationspflichten eingestellt sein; **to make a great** ~ großen Prunk entfalten; **to make a** ~ **of one's knowledge** mit seinem Wissen protzen; **to make a great** ~ **of sorrow** seinen Schmerz ganz offen zeigen; **to make a** ~ **of wealth** seinen Reichtum öffentlich zeigen; **to set up the** ~ Auslage herrichten;
~ **advertisement** Großanzeige; ~ **advertising** Schlagzeilenwerbung; ~ **aids** Verkaufshilfen; ~ **board** Schautafel; ~ **box** Schaukarton, Ausstellungsschachtel; ~ **builder** Schaufensterdekorateur; ~ **cabinet** Vitrine; ~ **card** Dekorationskarte; ~ **case** Vitrine, Schau-, Auslagekasten; ~ **colo(u)r** Dekorationsfarbe; ~ **compositor** *(print.)* Akzidenzsetzer; ~ **contractor** Ausstellungsunternehmen; ~ **equipment** Auslagenmaterial; ~ **figure** Schaufensterpuppe; ~ **hand** *(print.)* Akzidenzsetzer, *(fireworks)* Feuerwerker; ~ **kiosks** Werbebauten; ~ **letters** Großbuchstaben; ~ **line** Auszeichnungszeile; ~ **man** Schauwerbegestalter; **window-~ material** Dekorationsmaterial; ~ **package** Schaupackung; ~ **poster** Aushangsplakat; ~ **room** Ausstellungsraum; ~ **screen** Bildschirm; ~ **selector** Bildwähler; ~ **sign** Dekorationsetikett; ~ **stand** Auslagestand, Dekorationsgestell, Vitrine; ~ **type** *(print.)* Auszeichnungs-, Titelschrift; ~ **types** Übergrößen; ~**-type advertisement** besonders gestaltete Anzeige; ~ **unit** *(el.)* Darstellungseinheit; ~ **window** Dekorations-, Auslagefenster; ~ **work** Dekorationsarbeiten, Schaufensterdekoration, Auslagengestaltung.

displayed *(print.)* auffallend gedruckt;
goods ~ Ausstellungsware.

displayer Packungsgestalter.

disposable verfügbar, disponibel, *(thrown away after use)* wegwerfbar;
~ **capital** zur Verfügung stehendes Kapital, *(general meeting)* verfügbares Eigenkapital; ~ **goods** disponible (sofort verfügbare) Ware, Wegwerfgüter; ~ **income** *(social accounting, US)* Nettoeinkommen [nach Steuerabzug], frei verfügbares Einkommen nach Steuern; ~ **portion of property** testierfähiger [frei verfügbarer] Vermögensanteil [des Erblassers]; ~ **[budget] surplus** *(budgetary accounting)* frei verfügbarer Überschuß.

disposables Wegwerf-, Einweggüter.

disposal *(arrangement)* Anordnung, *(control)* Verfügung[srecht], *(sale)* Absatz, Verkauf, Veräußerung, *(settlement)* Erledigung, *(transfer)* Besitzwechsel, Übergabe;
at one's ~ verfügbar; **at your** ~ zu Ihrer Verfügung; **for** ~ zum Verkauf;

~ **of an asset** Anlagenveräußerung, Vermögensverfügung; ~ **of books** Beseitigung der Buchungsunterlagen; ~ **of business affairs** Erledigung geschäftlicher Angelegenheiten (von Geschäftsvorgängen); ~ **of a daughter in marriage** Verheiratung einer Tochter; ~ **of a difficulty** Beseitigung einer Schwierigkeit; ~ **of an estate by sale** Gutsverkauf; ~ **of land** Veräußerung von Grundbesitz; ~ **of all material resources** Verfügung über sämtliche Rohstoffquellen; ~ **of money by will** Geldvermächtnis; ~ **of motion** Antragserledigung; ~ **of patent rights** Veräußerung von Patentrechten; ~ **of a piece of business** Erledigung einer geschäftlichen Angelegenheit; ~ **of property** Vermögensverfügung; ~ **of a question** Erledigung einer Frage; ~ **of household refuse (rubbish)** Müllabfuhr; ~ **of troops** Truppenverwendung;
to be at s. one's ~ jem. zur Verfügung stehen; **to have large capital at one's** ~ große Kapitalbeträge zur Verfügung haben; **to have money at one's** ~ Geld zur Verfügung haben, über Geldbeträge disponieren können; **to have entire** ~ **of an estate** über ein Vermögen frei verfügen können; **to hold (place) at s. one's** ~ zu jds. Verfügung halten (stellen); **to put one's purse at s. one's** ~ jem. [finanziell] zur Verfügung stehen;
~ **instructions** Verkaufsanweisung; ~ **items** *(book trade)* Disponenden; ~ **price** Verkaufspreis; ~ **proceeds** Veräußerungserlös; ~ **request** Verwertungsantrag; **bomb-~ squad** Bombenräumkommando; ~ **tax** Abfallbeseitigungsgebühr; ~ **unit** Abfallbeseitigungsanlage; ~ **value** Verkaufserlös.

dispose *(v.)* anordnen, einrichten, *(get rid of)* loswerden, sich vom Hals schaffen, *(incline the mind)* bewegen, veranlassen, geneigt machen, *(make disposal)* Verfügung treffen, verfügen über, anordnen, disponieren, Bestimmung treffen, lenken, *(sell)* verkaufen, abgeben, absetzen, veräußern, unterbringen, losschlagen, abschaffen, *(settle)* [endgültig] erledigen, *(make use)* anwenden, verwenden, brauchen;
~ **of s. o.** j. unschädlich machen; ~ **s. o. to accept a position** j. zur Annahme einer Stellung veranlassen; ~ **of an affair** Sache erledigen; ~ **of an amendment** Gesetzesänderung verfügen; ~ **of a body** Leiche exhumieren; ~ **of s. o. in a couple of articles** j. in einer Artikelserie fertigmachen; ~ **of one's business** sein Geschäft verkaufen; ~ **of a large capital** mit großem Kapital arbeiten; ~ **of a case** Fall erledigen; ~ **of s. one's fate** über jds. Schicksal entscheiden; ~ **of one's fortune in charity** sein ganzes Vermögen für wohltätige Zwecke bestimmen; ~ **of goods** Waren absetzen; ~ **of an issue** Anleihe begeben; ~ **of land** Grundstück veräußern; ~ **by lots** verlosen; ~ **of the morning's mail (post,** *Br.)* Frühpost bearbeiten; ~ **of one's opponents** seine Widersacher ins Gefängnis werfen; ~ **of a paper** *(examination)* alle Fragen beantworten; ~ **of one's possessions** seines Besitzes entsagen; ~ **of a question** Frage erledigen; ~ **of rubbish** Müll beseitigen; ~ **of one's time** über seine Zeit verfügen (frei bestimmen); ~ **of by will** letztwillig verfügen.

disposed eingestellt, gesinnt, gestimmt, gelaunt;
~ **of** veräußert, abgegeben, verkauft;
easily ~ leicht verkäuflich; **not** ~ *(loan)* unbegeben; **well** ~ **to s. o.** freundlich für j. eingestellt;
to be ~ disponiert sein; **to be** ~ **of by agreement** gütlich geregelt werden; **to be ill** ~ **towards** kritisch eingestellt sein gegen; **to be well** ~ **to the Cabinet** regierungsfreundlich eingestellt sein; **to feel** ~ geneigt sein; **to have** ~ **of an affair** Angelegenheit erledigt haben; **to have** ~ **of all arguments** alle Argumente widerlegt haben.

disposer Verkäufer, Veräußerer.

disposing | of property Vermögensdisposition;
~ **capacity (mind, US)** Verfügungsberechtigung, Testierfähigkeit;
to be of sound and ~ **mind** *(US)* testierfähig sein.

disposition *(arrangement)* Einteilung, Verteilung, Anlage, Aufstellung, Anordnung, *(bestowal)* Verfügung, Disposition, Verleihung, *(character)* Charakteranlage, *(clause)* Bestimmung, Klausel, *(control)* freie Verfügung[smacht], Disposition, *(mood)* [Börsen]stimmung, *(sale)* Verkauf, Veräußerung, *(talent)* Anlage, *(transfer)* Übergabe, Aushändigung, Übertragung[surkunde];
~**s** Vorkehrungen, Vorbereitungen, Dispositionen;
criminal ~ kriminelle Veranlagung; **final** ~ endgültige Erledigung; **outright** ~ unbeschränkte Verfügungsmacht; **testamentary** ~ Verfügung von Todes wegen, letztwillige Verfügung; **voluntary** ~ rechtsgeschäftliche Verfügung;
~ **of appointment** Verfügungsbefugnis zur Einstellung von Arbeitskräften, Einstellungsbefugnis; ~ **to buy** Kauflust, -bereitschaft; ~ **of funds** Mittelverwendung; ~ **of furniture in a room** Anordnung der Möbel in einem Zimmer; ~ **of rooms in a**

building Zimmeraufteilung in einem Gebäude, Raumanordnung; ~s of the statute Gesetzesbestimmungen; ~ of shipping Einsatz der Schiffahrt; ~ by testament Übertragung durch letztwillige Verfügung; ~ of troops Truppeneinsatz, -aufstellung; ~ inter vivos Verfügung unter Lebenden; ~ of deferred income tax Auflösung von Einkommenssteuerrückstellungen; ~ of net income Verwendung des Reinerlöses (Reingewinns); voluntary ~ of land unentgeltliche Grundstücksübertragung; general ~ to leave early allgemeine Aufbruchsstimmung; ~ of profits Gewinnverwendung; ~ of property Vermögensdisposition, -verfügung, Eigentumsverfügung; ~ of decedent's property Nachlaßverfügung; ~ of reserves Rücklagen-, Reservenauflösung; ~ by will Verfügung von Todes wegen, testamentarische Verfügung;

to have a cheerful ~ freundliches Gemüt haben; to have a natural ~ to catch cold sich leicht Erkältungen zuziehen; to have a ~ to take offence leicht übelnehmen; to have the ~ of property verfügungsberechtigt sein; to make a ~ of Verfügung treffen; to make one's ~s seine Vorkehrungen treffen; to place at s. one's ~ jem. zur Verfügung stellen.

dispositive|clause (Scot. law) Verfügungsklausel; ~ **facts** rechtsbegründende Tatsachen.

dispossess (v.) Räumungsverfahren durchführen, (expropriate) Besitz entziehen, enteignen;
~ **of property** aus dem Besitz vertreiben; ~ **a tenant** Räumungsbefehl gegen einen Mieter durchführen;
~ **proceedings** Räumungsklage; ~ **warrant** Räumungsbefehl.

dispossession Besitzentziehung, (ejection) zwangsweise Entfernung, Räumung.

disproportion Mißverhältnis, Unproportionalität;
~ **in age** Altersunterschied; ~ **of supply and demand** Mißverhältnis zwischen Angebot und Nachfrage.

disproportionate unverhältnismäßig, nicht im Verhältnis stehend, unproportioniert;
to give a ~ **amount of one's time to reading** überdimensionale Zeit auf das Lesen verwenden.

disprove (v.) Gegenteil beweisen, widerlegen.

disputable unerwiesen, strittig, streitig;
~ **presumption** widerlegbare Vermutung.

disputant Rechthaber.

disputation Disputation.

dispute mündliche Auseinandersetzung, Kontroverse, Wortstreit, Disput, Auseinandersetzung, Debatte;
beyond (without) ~ unzweifelhaft, unstreitig, außerhalb jeder Diskussion stehend; **in** ~ umstritten, strittig;
collective ~ Tarifauseinandersetzung; **frontier** ~ Grenzstreitigkeit; **labo(u)r** ~ arbeitsrechtliche Auseinandersetzung, Arbeitskonflikt; **religious** ~s religiöse Auseinandersetzungen; **trade** ~ Auseinandersetzung mit den Gewerkschaften, Arbeitsstreitigkeit; **wage** ~ Lohnstreitigkeit;
~s **under a contract** Meinungsverschiedenheit über die Auslegung einzelner Vertragsbestimmungen; ~ **at law** Rechtsstreit; ~ **over pay** Lohnstreitigkeiten; ~ **over a point of law** Auseinandersetzung über eine Rechtsfrage;
~ (v.) diskutieren, erörtern, debattieren, (contract) anfechten, bestreiten;
~ **an advance of the enemy** einer Landung des Feindes Widerstand entgegensetzen; ~ **a claim** Rechtsanspruch bestreiten; ~ **a decision** Entscheidung angreifen; ~ **an election result** Wahlergebnis anfechten; ~ **every inch of the ground** um jeden Fußbreit des Bodens kämpfen; ~ **the possession with s. o.** jem. den Besitz streitig machen; ~ **the possession of the ground** Besitzverhältnisse bestreiten; ~ **a statement** Behauptung bestreiten; ~ **s. one's title** jds. Eigentumsrechte bestreiten; ~ **the validity of a document** Echtheit einer Urkunde bestreiten; ~ **the victory to s. o.** jem. den Sieg streitig machen; ~ **a will** Testament anfechten, Gültigkeit eines Testaments bestreiten;
to be in ~ strittig sein; **to be based on how much is in the** ~ sich nach dem jeweiligen Streitwert richten; **to settle a** ~ **by arbitration** Streit durch Schiedsspruch erledigen; **to settle a** ~ **by negotiation** Streitfall auf dem Verhandlungswege beilegen;
~s **procedure** Verfahren zur Regelung arbeitsrechtlicher Streitigkeiten, Verfahren zur Beilegung von Tarifstreitigkeiten.

disputed|claims office (insurance) Rechtsabteilung; ~ **election** angefochtene Wahl; ~ **point** Streitpunkt, -objekt; ~ **title** bestrittenes Eigentumsrecht.

disqualification Ausschließungsgrund, Disqualifizierung, (incompetence) Unfähigkeit, Untauglichkeit, Unvermögen, Disqualifikation, (driving licence, Br.) Führerscheinentzug, (judge, US) Befangenheit, (for office) Unfähigkeit [zur Bekleidung eines Amtes], Untauglichkeitserklärung;

~s **of a bankrupt** Rechtsverluste eines Konkursschuldners; ~ **from benefit** Rentenausschließungsgrund; ~ **of a director** Vorstandsenthebung; ~ **of a judge** (US) Ausschluß vom Richteramt [wegen Befangenheit]; ~ **of licence** (Br.) Führerscheinentzug; ~ **of a person for office** Unfähigkeit zur Bekleidung öffentlicher Ämter; ~ **from being a witness** Zeugnisunfähigkeit;
to be a ~ **for public office** für die Übernahme eines öffentlichen Amtes disqualifizieren; **to operate as a** ~ **to a member to sit and vote in the House of Commons** (Br.) jem. die Unterhausfähigkeit nehmen; **to remove the** ~ **on a driving licence** (Br.) eingezogenen Führerschein zurückgeben.

disqualified|by age wegen Altersschwäche untauglich; ~ **for making a will** testierunfähig;
to be ~ **from taking part in the Olympic games** von der Teilnahme an der Olympiade ausgeschlossen werden.

disqualify (v.) (deprive of right) zur Ausübung eines Rechts unfähig machen, (incapacitate) ausschließen, disqualifizieren, unfähig (untauglich) machen (erklären);
~ **o. s.** (judge) sich für befangen erklären; ~ **from benefit** Leistungsanspruch ausschließen; ~ **from a contest** von einem Wettbewerb ausschließen; ~ **from driving** (Br.) Führerschein entziehen; ~ **a driving licence** (Br.) Führerschein einziehen; ~ **a judge** Richter von der Ausübung des Richteramtes ausschließen; ~ **s. o. for military service** für den Militärdienst untauglich (wehruntüchtig) machen, für wehruntauglich erklären; ~ **s. o. from holding office** j. zur Bekleidung eines Amtes als unfähig erklären; ~ **s. o. for a profession** j. für einen Beruf als ungeeignet erscheinen lassen; ~ **from making a will** testierunfähig machen; ~ **s. o. as (of being a) witness** jem. die Zeugenqualifikation nehmen, j. zeugnisunfähig machen.

disquiet Unruhe, Beunruhigung, Besorgnis;
to cause considerable ~ **in some capitals** in verschiedenen Hauptstädten erhebliche Besorgnisse auslösen.

disquieting news beunruhigende Nachrichten.

disquisition Rede, Abhandlung.

disrate (v.) (maritime law) degradieren, (ship) ausrangieren.

disregard Mißachtung, Geringschätzung;
~ **of the law** Nichtbefolgung des Gesetzes;
~ (v.) außer Acht lassen;
~ **s. one's objections to a proposal** jds. Widerstände gegen einen Vorschlag ignorieren; ~ **a warning** Warnung in den Wind schlagen.

disrepair Reparaturbedürftigkeit, (building) Baufälligkeit, (business life) schlechter Zustand;
to be in ~ dringend reparaturbedürftig sein; **to fall into** ~ in Verfall geraten, baufällig werden, zusammenstürzen.

disreputability schlechter Ruf.

disreputable übel beleumundet, verrufen;
~ **bar** anrüchige Kneipe; **to lead a** ~ **life** unsittlichen Lebenswandel führen; ~-**looking** verboten aussehend.

disrepute Mißkredit, (bad reputation) schlechter Ruf;
~ (v.) **s. o.** j. in üblen Ruf bringen;
to be in ~ in Mißkredit stehen; **to bring into** ~ in Verruf bringen.

disrespect Respektlosigkeit, Unerbietigkeit;
to treat s. o. with ~ j. respektlos behandeln.

disrespectfully, to speak respektlose Reden führen.

disroot (v.) (fig.) entwurzeln.

disrupt (v.) zertrümmern, zerbrechen;
~ **a coalition** Koalition sprengen; ~ **a family** Familie auseinanderreißen; ~ **communications** Verbindungen unterbrechen; ~ **a market** Markt spalten.

disruption Zerschlagung, Spaltung, Trennung;
industrial ~ Zerschlagung von Industriebetrieben;
~ **of business activities** Unterbrechung der Geschäftstätigkeit; ~ **of a coalition** Sprengung einer Koalition; ~ **of an empire** Zusammenbruch eines Reiches; ~ **of a family** Auseinanderreißen einer Familie; ~ **of government** Auseinanderfallen der Regierung; ~ **in the market** Marktspaltung.

diss (v.) (Br., print.) Satz ablegen.

dissatisfaction Unzufriedenheit, Nichtbewilligung, -genehmigung.

dissatisfied with one's salary mit seiner Gehaltsregelung nicht zufrieden.

dissaving Über-die-Verhältnisse-leben.

dissect (v.) zergliedern, genau analysieren, (accounts) aufgliedern, (med.) sezieren.

dissection Zergliederung, genaue Analyse, (med.) Sektion;
judicial ~ gerichtlich angeordnete Obduktion;
~ **of accounts** Kontenaufgliederung.

dissector tube Bildzerlegerröhre.

disseize *(v.)* of an estate widerrechtlich von einem Grundstück vertreiben.

disseizee Enteigneter.

disseizin widerrechtliche Besitzentsetzung.

dissemble *(v.)* verbergen, verhehlen;
~ **one's emotions** seine Gefühle verbergen, sich nichts anmerken lassen.

dissembler Heuchler, Simulant.

disseminate *(v.)* verbreiten, ausstreuen;
~ **ideas** Ideen verbreiten; ~ **a program(me)** Programm auflockern.

dissemination Ausstreuung, Verbreitung;
~ **of news** Nachrichtenstreuung; ~ **of program(me)s** Programmauflockerung; ~ **of a false report** Verbreitung einer Falschmeldung; ~ **of a rumo(u)r** Verbreitung eines Gerüchts.

dissension Meinungsverschiedenheit;
~s **between rival groups in politics** Meinungsverschiedenheiten zwischen politischen Gruppen.

dissent Meinungsverschiedenheit, *(majority decision)* Ansicht der Minderheit;
with no (without) ~ einstimmig;
~ *(v.)* verschiedener Ansicht sein, nicht übereinstimmen;
~ **from an agreement** einer Vereinbarung nicht zustimmen; ~ **from s. one's opinion** abweichende Meinung haben (vertreten); **strongly** ~ **from what the last speaker said** sich in keiner Weise den Ausführungen des Vorredners anschließen können;
to express strong ~ ganz entschieden eine gegenteilige Ansicht vertreten.

dissenter Sektenmitglied, Andersdenkender, Nonkonformist.

dissentient Andersdenkender, abweichende Stimme, Gegenstimme.

dissentient, dissenting *(corporation law)* opponierender Aktionär;
~ *(a.)* abweichend, nicht übereinstimmend;
~ **creditor** einem Vergleich nicht zustimmender Gläubiger; ~ **minority** überstimmte Minderheit; ~ **opinion** *(law court, US)* Minderheitsvotum; ~ **shareholder** Minderheitsaktionär; ~ **voice** Gegenstimme; **to be resolved (pass) with one** ~ **voice** mit allen gegen eine Stimme angenommen werden; **with one** ~ **vote** mit einer Gegenstimme.

dissert *(v.)* Vortrag halten, Abhandlung schreiben.

dissertation Dissertation, Doktorarbeit, Promotionsschrift;
to deliver a ~ **upon a subject** über etw. dissertieren, seine Doktorarbeit über ein Thema schreiben; **to do a** ~ Dissertation schreiben.

dissertator Vortragender, Verfasser einer Dissertation.

disserve *(v.)* schlechten Dienst erweisen.

disservice schlechter Dienst, Nachteil;
to do s. o. a ~ jem. einen schlechten Dienst erweisen.

dissident Andersdenkender, Dissident, *(pol.)* Abweichler.

dissimilar ungleichartig;
~ **tastes** verschiedene Geschmacksrichtungen.

dissipate *(v.)* zerstreuen, verscheuchen, vertreiben;
~ **clouds** Wolken auflösen; ~ **doubts** Zweifel zerstreuen; ~ **one's efforts** seine Anstrengungen verzetteln; ~ **one's fortune** seinen Besitz durchbringen;
to fall into ~ **ways** sich Ausschweifungen hingeben.

dissipated life zügelloses Leben.

dissipation *(diversion)* Zerstreuung, Zügellosigkeit, Ausschweifungen, *(cloud, fog)* Auflösung, *(waste)* Verschwendung, Vergeudung;
~ **of one's fortune** Verschleuderung seines Vermögens;
to allow o. s. a little ~ sich ein wenig Zerstreuung leisten.

dissociable unvereinbar, unverträglich, unsozial.

dissociality unsoziales Verhalten, Egoismus.

dissociate *(v.)* o. s. sich distanzieren (lossagen);
~ **s. o. from his position** j. unabhängig von seiner Stellung bewerten; ~ **o. s. from a question** an einem Problem nicht interessiert sein, sich an einer Frage uninteressiert zeigen.

dissociated personality gespaltene Persönlichkeit.

dissociation Lossagung, Distanzierung, *(psychology)* Bewußtseinsspaltung;
~ **of personality** Persönlichkeitsspaltung.

dissoluble *(marriage)* auflösbar.

dissolute liederlich, ausschweifend;
~ **conduct** zügelloses Verhalten; **to lead a** ~ **life** ausschweifendes Leben führen.

dissolution Aufhebung, Trennung, *(cartels)* Entflechtung, *(of firm)* Auflösung, Löschung, Liquidation;
compulsory ~ Zwangsauflösung; **de facto** ~ Aufgabe der Geschäftstätigkeit;

~ **of an assembly** Aufhebung einer Versammlung, *(antitrust law, US)* Entflechtung; ~ **of a contract** Vertragsaufhebung, -annullierung; ~ **of a corporation** Auflösung (Liquidation) einer Gesellschaft; ~, **divestiture and divorcement** *(antitrust law, US)* Entflechtungsmaßnahmen; ~ **of a marriage** Eheauflösung, -scheidung, Ehenichtigkeitserklärung; ~ **of Parliament** *(Br.)* Parlamentsauflösung; ~ **of a partnership** Auflösung eines Gesellschaftsverhältnisses (einer Handelsgesellschaft), Firmenauflösung; ~ **of a treaty** Vertragsaufhebung;
~ **order** *(company law)* Liquidationsbeschluß; ~ **sale** Liquidationsverkauf.

dissolvable auflösbar.

dissolve *(film)* Überblendung;
(v.) auflösen, aufheben, beenden, ungültig erklären, liquidieren, *(film)* überblenden, *(antitrust law, US)* entflechten, *(parl.)* sich auflösen;
~ **an assembly** Versammlung auflösen; ~ **a business partnership** Gesellschaft liquidieren; ~ **a contract** Vertrag aufheben; ~ **an injunction** einstweilige Verfügung aufheben; ~ **a marriage** Ehe aufheben (für ungültig erklären); ~ **a meeting** Sitzung schließen; ~ **Parliament** *(Br.)* Parlament auflösen.

dissolving shutter *(photo)* Überblendverschluß.

dissuade *(v.)* abraten, abbringen;
~ **a friend from marrying on a small salary** Freund von der Eheschließung bei geringen Bezügen abraten.

distance Entfernung, Abstand, Distanz, Strecke, *(fig.)* Reserve, Zurückhaltung, Distanz, *(time)* zeitlicher Abstand;
airline ~ Entfernung in der Luftlinie, Luftentfernung; ~ **covered** zurückgelegte Strecke, Fahrstrecke; **long** ~ *(tel., US)* Fernamt; **overall stopping** ~ Bremsweg; **short** ~ geringe Entfernung;
~ **on a map** Kartenentfernung; **some** ~ **to the school** ziemlich langer Schulweg; ~ **of time** Zeitabschnitt;
long-~ *(v.) (US)* Ferngespräch führen;
to be a great ~ **off** weitab liegen; **to be no** ~ **at all** nahe gelegen sein, keine Entfernung darstellen; **to be within [easy] walking** ~ zu Fuß [bequem] zu erreichen sein; **to call s. o. long-**~ *(US)* Ferngespräch zu jem. anmelden; **to cover a** ~ **in stages** Strecke in Etappen zurücklegen; **to hire a car by** ~ Auto auf Kilometerabrechnung mieten; **to judge a** ~ Entfernung abschätzen; **to keep one's** ~ Distanz halten, sich zurückhalten; **to keep s. o. at a** ~ j. auf Distanz halten; **to keep one's** ~ **from the radical left** Distanz zu den Linksradikalen bewahren; **to live within easy** ~ **of one's work** in unmittelbarer Nähe seines Arbeitsplatzes wohnen; **to look back over a** ~ **of fifty years** Zeitraum von fünfzig Jahren überblicken; **to mark off a** ~ **on the map** Entfernung auf einer Karte abstecken;
long-~ **call** *(tel., US)* Ferngespräch; **long-**~ **flight** Weitstreckenflug; ~ **freight** Distanzfracht; ~ **light** *(car)* Fernlicht; ~ **marker** Kilometerschild; **long-**~ **mover** Fernspediteur; **long-**~ **operator** *(tel., US)* Fernanmeldung; ~ **rate** Differenzfrachtsatz, *(car)* Kilometersatz; ~ **reconnaissance** *(mil.)* Fernaufklärung; ~ **scale** Entfernungsskala; ~ **shot** *(photo)* Fernaufnahme; ~ **tariff** Kilometertarif; **long-**~ **traffic** *(tel., US)* Fernverkehr; **long-**~ **train** Fern-, Schnellzug, D-Zug; **long-**~ **transport** Ferntransport, -verkehr; **short-**~ **transport** Nahbeförderung, Nahtransport, -verkehr.

distant entfernt, *(faint)* schwach, unbedeutend, *(location)* abgelegen, *(reserved)* distanziert, reserviert, kühl, zurückhaltend;
to be ~ **to s. o.** j. kühl (distanziert, reserviert) behandeln; **to be three miles** ~ **from the station** fünf Kilometer vom Bahnhof entfernt liegen;
~ **action** Fernwirkung; ~ **cousin** entfernter Vetter; ~ **early warning** Frühwarnung; ~ **early warning line** Frühwarnanlage; **in the** ~ **future** in der fernen Zukunft; ~ **goal** Fernziel; ~ **likeness** entfernte Ähnlichkeit; ~ **look** abwesender Blick; ~ **reading instrument** Fernanzeigegerät; ~ **recollection** schwache Erinnerung; ~ **reconnaisance** *(mil.)* Fernaufklärung; ~ **recording** Fernregistrierung; ~ **relation** weitläufiger Verwandter; ~ **resemblance** schwache Ähnlichkeit; ~ **signal** *(railway)* Vorsignal; ~ **view** Fernblick.

disguise *(v.)* **one's distaste** sein Mißfallen verbergen.

distemper Unruhe, Aufruhr.

distinct verschieden, getrennt, abgesondert;
~ **memory** deutliche Erinnerung; ~ **order** genauer Auftrag; ~ **pronunciation** deutliche Aussprache; ~ **refusal** glatte Ablehnung.

distinction Unterschied, Rang, *(decoration)* Auszeichnung, Ehrenzeichen, *(distinguishing mark)* Unterscheidungsmerkmal, Kennzeichen, *(hono(u)r)* Ruf, Ruhm, *(quality)* Erstklassigkeit, hervorragende Qualität;

with ~ *(school)* mit Auszeichnung; **without ~ of persons** ohne Ansehen der Person; **without ~ of race** ohne Unterschied der Rasse;

academic ~s akademische Auszeichnungen (Ehrungen); **class ~** Klassenunterschied;

~ without a difference spitzfindige Unterscheidung; **~ of rank** Rangunterschied;

to confer a ~ upon the retiring prime minister dem zurücktretenden Premier eine Auszeichnung verleihen; **to draw a ~** Unterschied machen; **to have great ~ of manner** hervorragende Manieren haben; **to make a clear ~** scharfe Grenze ziehen; **to receive a ~** Auszeichnung erhalten; **to win ~ in public life** sich im öffentlichen Leben auszeichnen.

distinctive *(trademark law)* unterscheidungsmäßig, kennzeichnend, charakteristisch;

~ badge Rangabzeichen; **~ feature** Unterscheidungsmerkmal; **~ flag** Schutzflagge; **~ mark** *(trademark)* spezifisches Warenzeichen; **~ name** Markenname; **~ number** *(car)* bestimmte Nummer.

distinguish *(v.)* unterscheiden, auseinanderhalten, *(make discernible)* kennzeichnen, charakterisieren;

~ o. s. sich auszeichnen; **~ between cases apparently similar** anscheinend ähnliche Fälle auseinanderhalten; **~ s. o. in a crowd** j. in einer Menschenmenge ausmachen; **~ o. s. in an examination** Prüfung mit Auszeichnung bestehen.

distinguished hervorragend, ausgezeichnet;

to be ~ as an economist hervorragender Volkswirtschaftler sein; **to have a ~ career in the diplomatic service** glänzende Laufbahn als Diplomat zurückgelegt haben; **~ colleague** verehrter Kollege; ⚔ **Conduct Medal** *(Br.)* Kriegsverdienstmedaille; ⚔ **Service Order** Kriegsverdienstkreuz.

distinguishing mark Kennzeichen, Unterscheidungsmerkmal.

distort *(v.)* verdrehen, entstellen, *(tel.)* verzerren;

~ competition Wettbewerb verzerren; **~ the meaning of a text** Sinn eines Textes entstellen.

distorted verzerrt, entstellt;

~ cost verzerrte Kosten; **~ newspaper accounts** verzerrte Zeitungsberichte.

distortion Wortverdrehung, *(tel.)* Verzerrung;

~ of competition Wettbewerbsverzerrung; **~ of facts** Tatsachenverdrehung; **~ of results** Verzerrung bei Ergebnissen; **~ of a text** Textverdrehung.

distract *(v.)* ablenken;

~ the mind Aufmerksamkeit ablenken.

distracted between hope and fear zwischen Hoffnung und Angst hin-und hergerissen.

distraction Ablenkung, Unterhaltung, Erholung, Zerstreuung;

to drive s. o. to ~ with silly questions j. mit törichten Fragen reinweg verrückt machen; **to find a wholesome ~ by reading** sich bei seiner Lektüre angenehm zerstreuen.

distrain *(v.)* pfänden, Pfändung ausbringen, exekutieren, mit Beschlag belegen, beschlagnahmen, *(take as pledge)* sicherheitshalber zurückbehalten;

~ chattels for nonpayment of rent Pfändung in das bewegliche Vermögen wegen nicht bezahlter Pacht betreiben; **~ upon s. o.** sich schadlos an jem. halten; **~ upon s. one's belongings** jds. Eigentum pfänden, jds. Pfändung betreiben; **~ upon a debtor** sich aus dem Pfandobjekt eines Schuldners befriedigen; **~ upon s. one's furniture for rent** jds. Möbel wegen rückständiger Miete pfänden.

distrainable pfändbar, der Zwangsvollstreckung unterworfen.

distrained goods gepfändete Waren.

distrainee Vollstreckungs-, Pfändungsschuldner, Gepfändeter.

distrainer, distraining party Pfand-, Pfändungsgläubiger.

distraint Beschlagnahme, Pfändung, dinglicher Arrest, Zwangsvollstreckung;

~ of property Vermögensbeschlagnahme;

to be subject to ~ der Zwangsvollstreckung unterliegen; **to levy a ~** Pfändung (Zwangsvollstreckung) betreiben; **to sue for a ~** Pfändung beantragen.

distress Beschlagnahme, Pfändung, Zwangsvollstreckung, *(distressed state)* Erschöpfung, *(object seized)* gepfändeter Gegenstand, Pfand, *(seizure)* Beschlagnahme, Pfändung, Zwangsvollstreckung, *(ship)* Seenot, *(state of danger)* Gefahr, Bedrängnis, gefährliche Lage, *(taxation)* Steuerpfändung, *(want)* Notlage, Notstand, Bedürftigkeit;

in ~ *(ship)* in Seenot; **privileged from ~** unpfändbar, pfändungsfrei;

economic ~ wirtschaftliche Notlage; **~ infinite** unbeschränkte Beschlagnahme; **mental ~** seelischer Schaden; **second ~** Anschlußpfändung; **simulated ~** *(ship)* vorgetäuschte Notlage;

~ and danger *(ship)* Not und Gefahr; **~ for nonpayment of rent** Pfändung wegen rückständiger Miete;

~ *(v.)* *(cause anguish)* mit Sorge erfüllen, beunruhigen, *(distrain)* beschlagnahmen, mit Beschlag belegen, pfänden, in Bedrängnis (Gefahr) bringen;

~ o. s. sich beunruhigen; **~ on s. o.** gegen j. zwangsvollstrecken; **to be in ~** Mangel leiden, in bedrängter Lage sein; **to be in great ~** sich in großer Notlage befinden; **to be subject to ~** pfändbar sein; **to become filled with ~** in Angst geraten; **to go out to a ship in ~** einem in Seenot geratenen Schiff zu Hilfe eilen; **to levy (put in) a ~ on s. th.** etw. mit Beschlag belegen, aufgrund gerichtlicher Verfügung beschlagnahmen, Pfändung vornehmen (ausbringen), Zwangsvollstreckung betreiben; **to put in in ~** *(ship)* in Not einlaufen; **to relieve ~ among the poor** Armut lindern;

~ call Hilferuf, *(ship)* Notsignal, SOS; **~-call wavelength** Notrufwelle, -frequenz; **~ committee** Hilfskomitee; **~ damage feasant** Pfändung wegen Viehschaden; **~ flag** Notflagge; **~ light** Notfeuer; **~ merchandise** notleidende Waren; **~ message** Hilferuf; **~ rocket** Notrakete; **~ sale (selling)** Not-, Pfandverkauf, Zwangsversteigerung; **~ signal** Gefahr-, Not-, Hilfesignal, *(ship)* SOS; **to fly a ~ signal** Notsignal setzen; **~ warrant** Vollstreckungsbefehl, Arrestanordnung, Pfändungsbeschluß; **~ work** Notstandsarbeiten.

distressed notleidend, in Not, *(seized)* gepfändet;

~ area *(Br.)* Gebiet mit hoher Arbeitslosigkeit, Elends-, Notstandsgebiet; **~ condition** Notlage; **~ person** Notleidender.

distributable ausschüttungs-, verteilungsfähig, verteilbar;

~ profit zur Ausschüttung kommender Gewinn; **~ property** für die Gläubiger zur Verfügung stehendes Vermögen.

distributary channel zusätzlicher Kanal, Seitenkanal.

distribute *(v.)* aus-, auf-, verteilen, zur Verteilung bringen, ausschütten, *(advertising)* streuen, verbreiten, *(allocate)* zuteilen, *(mail)* zustellen, austragen, *(sell)* vertreiben, absetzen, *(troops)* gliedern;

~ alms Almosen gewähren; **~ the assets** *(partners)* sich auseinandersetzen; **~ an additional (supplementary) dividend** zusätzliche Dividende ausschütten; **~ equally** gleichmäßig aufteilen, *(stock)* repartieren; **~ an estate** Erbauseinandersetzung durchführen, Nachlaß verteilen; **~ a film** Film verleihen; **~ justice** Recht sprechen, Gerechtigkeit handhaben; **~ the letters into wrong boxes** *(print.)* falsch ablegen; **~ by lots** auslosen; **~ manure over a field** Feld düngen; **~ parcels all over the town** Pakete in der ganzen Stadt austragen; **~ the proceeds** Erlös (Gewinn) verteilen; **~ pro rata** anteilig aufteilen; **~ in a fixed ratio** aufschlüsseln; **~ trading profits** Börsengewinne ausschütten; **~ the type** *(print.)* ablegen.

distributed, widely weit verbreitet;

~ lag periodenübergreifender Verzögerungseffekt; **~ profits** ausgeschüttete Gewinne.

distributee *(US)* gesetzlicher Erbe, Teilnehmer an der Nachlaßverwaltung, Nachlaßberechtigter.

distributing | agency Vertriebsgesellschaft; **~ agent** Gebietsvertreter, Großhandelsvertreter; **~ box** *(el.)* Verteilerdose; **~ enterprise** Vertriebsgesellschaft, -unternehmen; **~ mains** *(el.)* Verteileranlage; **post-~ office** Verteilerpostamt; **~ organization** Verteilerorganisation; **~ syndicate** *(US)* Emissionskonsortium, Konsortialführerin, Verleihungskartell; **~ trade** Verteilergewerbe, Absatzwirtschaft.

distribution *(advertising)* Streuung, *(apportionment)* Auf-, Ein-, Zu-, Verteilung, Ausschüttung, *(arrangement)* Einteilung, systematische Anordnung, *(coverage)* Verbreitung, *(donation)* Gabe, Zuteilung, Spende, *(marketing)* Absatz und Vertrieb, *(mil.)* Gliederung, *(political economy)* Güterverteilung, Verteilung des Volkseinkommens, *(post office)* Postverteilung, *(print.)* Ablegen des Schriftsatzes;

capital ~ *(investment company)* Ausschüttung von Kapitalgewinnen; **charitable ~** milde Gabe, Spende; **dual ~** *(US)* zweigleisiges Vertriebssystem; **exclusive ~** ausschließlicher Absatzweg; **final ~** End-, Schlußverteilung; **income ~** Einkommensverteilung; **[non]qualifying ~** *(Br.)* [nicht] zur Körperschaftsvorauszahlung verpflichtende Dividendenausschüttung; **own vehicle ~** Vertrieb mittels eigenem Fahrzeugparks; **percentage ~** prozentuale Verteilung; **preliminary ~** Abschlagszahlung; **prize ~** Preisverteilung; **prorata ~** anteilige Ausschüttung; **secondary ~** nachbörslicher Wertpapierhandel, Pakethandel; **selective ~** Verteilung durch einen ausgewählten Händlerkreis; **tax-free ~** steuerfreie Dividendenausschüttung;

~ of assets of a bankrupt's estate Schluß-, Masseverteilung; **~ of business** *(law court)* Geschäftsverteilung; **~ of circulars** Prospektverteilung; **~ of costs** Kostenumlage; **~ of credit** Kredit-

lenkung; ~ **among the creditors** Aufteilung unter den Gläubigern; ~ **of crops** Fruchtwechsel; ~ **of current** Stromverteilung; ~ **in depth** *(mil.)* Tiefengliederung; ~**of a deceased's estate** Erbauseinandersetzung, Erb-, Nachlaßverteilung; ~ **of dividends** Dividendenausschüttung, -verteilung; ~ **of a film** Filmverleih; ~**of the net gain** Verteilung des Reingewinns; ~ **of goods** Güter-, Warenverteilung; ~ **of income** Einkommensverteilung, -streuung, *(investment trust)* Ertragsausschüttung; ~ **of industry** Streuung industrieller Fertigungsstätten; ~ **of justice** Handhabung der Gerechtigkeit, Rechtsprechung; ~ **of labo(u)r** Arbeitsaufteilung; ~ **of labo(u)r according to occupation** Erwerbspersonen nach Wirtschaftsbetrieben und Stellung im Beruf; ~ **of land** Landverteilung; ~ **of losses** Verlustaufteilung; **free ~ by mail** per Post versandte Freiexemplare; ~ **of money in charity** Spende zu wohltätigen Zwecken; ~ **of a newspaper** Zeitungsvertrieb; ~ **and partition** *(US)* Nachlaßverteilung; ~ **of partnership loss** Verlustaufteilung; ~ **of partnership profit** Aufteilung des Gesellschaftergewinns; ~ **of pay** Soldauszahlung; ~ **on a percentage basis** prozentuale Aufteilung; ~ **of population** Bevölkerungsgliederung; ~ **of powers** Gewalteinteilung; ~ **of prizes** Preis-, Prämienverteilung; ~ **of production** Produktionsgliederung; ~ **of proceeds (profits)** Ausschüttung von Gewinnen, Gewinnverteilung, -ausschüttung, Reingewinnverwendung; **proposed ~ of profit** Gewinnverteilungsvorschlag; ~ **of property** Vermögensaufteilung, -verteilung; ~ **of publications** Pressevertrieb; ~ **of responsibilities** Zuständigkeitsverteilung; ~ **of risk** Gefahrenverteilung; ~ **of surplus** Reingewinnverwendung; ~ **of trading profits** Ausschüttung von Börsengewinnen; ~ **of a trust fund** Ausschüttungen aus einem Treuhandvermögen; ~ **of wealth** Vermögens-, Güterverteilung, Verteilung des Volkseinkommens;
to have a very wide ~ überall vorkommen; **to make a ~ of 8%** Gewinnanteil von 8% ausschütten;
~ **advantage** Vertriebsvorteil; ~ **agency** Verteilungsstelle; ~ **agreement** Vertriebsabsprache, Absatzabkommen, Vertriebsvereinbarung; ~ **area** Absatzgebiet; ~ **board** *(el.)* Schalttafel; ~ **box** *(el.)* Verteilerkasten; ~ **cartel** Absatz-, Vertriebskartell; ~ **center** *(US)* **(centre,** *Br.)* Absatzzentrum; ~ **channel** Absatz-, Vertriebs-, Handelsweg; ~ **classification** Beschränkung des Verteilerkreises; ~ **costs** Verkaufs-, Vertriebs-, Absatzkosten; ~ **cost analysis** Vertriebskostenanalyse, -untersuchung; ~ **curve** Verteilungs-, Absatzkurve; ~ **date** Ausschüttungstermin; ~ **department** Vertriebsabteilung; ~ **equipment** Vertriebseinrichtungen; ~ **expense** Absatzkosten, Vertriebsunkosten; ~ **form** Ausschüttungsformular; ~ **indices** Vertriebs-, Absatzkennzahlen; ~ **key** Verteilerschlüssel; ~ **list** Verteilerliste; ~ **map** *(el.)* Schaltplan; ~ **manager** Vertriebsleiter, Leiter der Vertriebsabteilung; ~ **method** Vertriebs-, Absatzmethode; ~ **network** Verteilernetz; **large-scale ~ operation** großräumiges Vertriebsgebiet; ~ **opportunities** Vertriebsmöglichkeiten, -wege; ~ **outlets** Vertriebsgebiet; ~ **plan** Vertriebsprogramm, -plan; ~ **ratio** Verteilungsschlüssel; ~ **service** Vertriebstätigkeit; ~ **statistics** Verkaufsstatistik; ~ **system** Vertriebs-, Absatz-, Verteiler-, Verteilungssystem; **growing ~ task** wachsende Vertriebsaufgaben; ~ **warehouse** Auslieferungslager.
distributional adjustment Verteilungsanpassung.
distributive ver-, austeilend;
~ **cost accounting** Zuschlagskalkulation; ~ **enterprise** Vertriebsgesellschaft; ~ **facilities** Verteilungsapparat, Absatzeinrichtungen; ~ **finding of the issue** Quotenurteil; ~ **justice** ausgleichende Gerechtigkeit; ~ **machinery** Vertriebsapparat; ~ **salesmen** Vertriebsfachleute; ~ **share** *(US)* gesetzliches Erbteil, Pflichtteil; ~ **state** Verteilerstaat; ~ **system** Verteilungssystem; ~ **trade** Verteilergewerbe, Absatzwirtschaft.
distributor Verteiler, Auslieferer, Händler, Wiederverkäufer, Vertriebsorganisation, *(agent)* Bezirksvertreter, Eigenhändler, Generalvertreter, *(film)* Filmverleih[er];
sole ~ alleiniger Versand, Alleinvertrieb; **wholesale ~** Großhändler;
to be sole ~ alleinvertriebsberechtigt sein;
~ **agreement** Händlervereinbarung; ~ **audit** Warenbestandsprüfung; ~ **cable** Zündkabel; ~ **discount** Händler-, Wiederverkäuferrabatt; ~ **shaft** Verteilerwelle; ~ **trade** Verteilergewerbe.
distributorship Vertreterbereich.
distributory road Verteiler[straße].
district [Verwaltungs]bezirk, Kreis[amt], Distrikt, *(city)* Stadtviertel, *(fig.)* Arbeitsgebiet, *(region)* Gegend, Rayon, Gebiet, *(tract of land)* Landstrich;
by ~s bezirksweise;
administrative ~ Amts-, Verwaltungsbezirk; **purely agricul-**

-tural ~ rein landwirtschaftliche Gegend; **central shopping (business) ~** Hauptgeschäftsgegend; **city ~** städtischer Bezirk, Stadtbezirk; **civil ~** Verwaltungsbezirk; **coastal ~** Küstenbezirk; **congressional ~** *(US)* Wahlbezirk eines Kandidaten für das Repräsentantenhaus; **constituency ~** Wahlkreis; **county ~** *(Br.)* Land-, Gemeindebezirk; **federal ~** *(US)* Regierungssitz; **economic ~** Wirtschaftsbezirk; **electoral (election) ~** Wahlbezirk; **highway ~** Straßenbezirk; **judicial ~** *(US)* Gerichtsbezirk; **lake ~** Seengebiet; **local ~** Gemeinderat; **low-rent ~** Niedrigmietengegend; **magisterial ~** Verwaltungsbezirk; **militia ~** Landwehrbezirk; **municipal ~** Kommunalbezirk; **polling ~** Wahlbezirk; **postal ~** Zustellbezirk; **receiving ~** Aufnahmegebiet; **high-rent residential ~** teure Wohngegend; **rural ~** ländlicher Bezirk; **school ~** Schulbezirk; **senatorial ~** *(US)* Senatsbezirk; **town ~** Stadtbezirk; **urban ~** *(Br.)* [etwa] kreisangehörige Stadt;
~ **devoted to industry** reiner Industriebezirk; ~ **free from labo(u)r troubles** von Arbeiterunruhen verschontes Gebiet; ~ *(v.)* in Bezirke einteilen;
to scour the whole ~ ganze Gegend nach etw. abklappern; **to work a ~** Bezirk bearbeiten (bereisen);
~ **agent** Bezirksvertreter; ~ **agreement** Ortstarif; ~ **asylum** Obdachlosenheim; ~ **attorney** *(US)* Staats-, Amtsanwalt; ~ **auditor** Bezirksrevisor; ~ **authorities** Bezirksverwaltung, -behörde; ~ **Federal Reserve Bank** *(US)* [etwa] Landeszentralbank; ~ **center** *(US)* **(centre,** *Br.)* Gemeindezentrum; ~ **clerk** *(court)* Geschäftsstellenleiter; ~ **collector** *(US)* örtlich zuständiger Finanzbeamter; ~ **command** *(Br.)* Militärbereich; ~ **committee** Kreis-, Bezirksausschuß, *(US)* Bezirksverwaltung, *(pol.)* Parteiausschuß; ~ **constable** *(US)* Bezirksamtmann; ~ **convention** Bezirkstagung; ~ **council** *(Br.)* Stadt-, Gemeinderat; ~ **court** *(US)* Amts-, Bezirks-, Kreisgericht; ~ **general hospital** Bezirkskrankenhaus; ~ **heating** Fernheizung; ~ **inspector** Bezirksinspektor; ~ **jobber** *(stock exchange, US)* Bezirksagent; ~ **judge** *(US)* Amts-, Bezirks-, Kreisrichter; ~ **line** Bezirksgrenze; ~ **manager** Bezirksleiter; ~ **nurse** Gemeindeschwester; ~ **office** Bezirksagentur einer Bank, *(post)* Bezirkspostamt; ~**organizer** *(trade union, Br.)* Bezirksbeauftragter; ~ **railway** Vorort-, Kreisbahn; **metropolitan and ~ railway** *(London)* Stadt- und Vorortbahn; ~ **rate** Kreisumlage; ~ **registry** *(Br.)* Filialkanzlei; ~ **probate registry** Bezirksgeschäftsstelle des Nachlaßgerichts; ~ **sales** Bezirksumsatz; ~ **salesman** Bezirksvertreter; ~ **school** *(US)* Kreisschule; ~ **seat** Bezirksmandat; ~ **signalman** Oberzugleitung; ~ **supervisor** Bezirksaufsichtsbeamter; ~ **surveyor** Bezirksaufsichtsbeamter; ~ **valuer** *(US)* Nachlaßschätzer; ~ **visitor** *(Br.)* Pfarramtsgehilfe, Wohlfahrtspfleger[in].
distringas *(Br.)* Pfändungsbefehl.
distrust Mißtrauen, Argwohn;
to have a ~ of foreigners Ausländern gegenüber mißtrauisch sein.
distrustful mißtrauisch, argwöhnisch;
to be ~ of o. s. kein Selbstvertrauen haben; **to be ~ of one's own capabilities** sich nichts zutrauen; **to be ~ of s. one's motives** jds. Motiven nicht trauen.
disturb *(v.)* beunruhigen, belästigen, stören, *(el.)* stören;
~ **a ceremony** Feierlichkeit stören; ~ **s. one's calculations** jds. Berechnungen über den Haufen werfen; ~ **the classes** *(school)* Unterricht stören; ~ **s. one's lawful enjoyment** j. in seinem Besitz stören; ~ **s. one's lawful enjoyment of a right** j. im Genuß seines Rechtes stören; ~ **the papers on a desk** Papiere auf einem Schreibtisch durcheinanderbringen; ~ **the peace** öffentliche Ruhe und Ordnung stören; ~ **traffic** Verkehr behindern.
disturbance Beeinträchtigung, Behinderung, Belästigung, störender Eingriff, *(psych.)* seelische Erregung;
atmospheric ~s atmosphärische Störungen; **political ~s** politische Unruhen;
~ **of broadcast reception** gestörter Rundfunkempfang; ~ **of s. o. in the lawful enjoyment of his right** Behinderung im Genuß eines Rechtes, Rechtsbehinderung; ~ **of franchise** Beeinträchtigung einer Konzession; ~ **of the peace** Störung der öffentlichen Ruhe und Ordnung, Aufruhr, Tumult; ~ **of circulation** Kreislaufstörung; ~ **of common** unberechtigte Allmendenutzung; ~ **of development** Entwicklungsstörung; ~ **of possession** Besitzstörung; ~ **of repose** Störung der Nachtruhe; ~ **of right of way** Behinderung eines Wegerechtes; ~ **of a tenant** Mieterbelästigung; ~ **of trade** störende Eingriffe in die Handelsbeziehungen; ~ **of the traffic** Verkehrsbehinderung; ~ **of public or religious worship** Beeinträchtigung der ungehinderten Religionsausübung, Gottesdienststörung;
to create (raise) a ~ Aufruhr anstiften;
~ **allowance** Umstellungsentschädigung.

disturbed [seelisch] erregt, gestört;
~ **area** Erdbebengebiet; ~ **market** *(stock exchange)* lebhafte (bewegte) Börse.
disturber Störer;
~ **of the peace** Unruhestifter, Ruhestörer, Friedensbrecher.
disturbing news beunruhigende Nachrichten.
disunion *(pol.)* Zersplitterung, Spaltung, Trennung.
disunionism Spaltungsbewegung.
disunite *(v.)* trennen, spalten.
disunited *(party)* zersplittert.
disuse Nichtgebrauch, -benutzung, -verwendung;
to fall into ~ außer Gebrauch kommen.
disused ungebräuchlich, veraltet.
disutility Nutzlosigkeit, Lästigkeit, negativer Nutzen;
marginal ~ Grenzproduktivität.
disvestiture, disvestment Konzentrationsminderung durch Abstoßen einzelner Betriebe (unrentabler Betriebseinheiten).
ditch Drainier-, Straßen-, Wassergraben, Flußbett;
drainage Abwässerungsgraben;
~ *(v.)* Gräben ziehen, durch Abzugsgräben entwässern, *(airplane)* zur Bruchlandung führen, *(train, US)* entgleisen;
~ **a car** Auto in den Straßengraben fahren; ~ **one's plane** Notlandung auf dem Wasser machen;
to be in the last ~ in größter Not sein; **to die in the last** ~ kümmerlich verrecken;
to be ~**ed** im Straßengraben landen, *(train, US)* entgleisen;
last ~ **defence** letzte Verteidigungslinie; ~ **water** schales stehendes Wasser; **as clear as** ~ **water** völlig undurchsichtig; **dull as** ~ **water** stinklangweilig.
ditching Meliorationsarbeiten.
divan Chaiselongue, Liegesofa;
~ **bed** ausziehbares Bett.
dive Kellerlokal, Spelunke, Kaschemme, *(airplane)* Sturzflug, *(Br.)* Unterführung, *(mar.)* Unterwassertauchfahrt;
~ *(v.)* *(airplane)* Sturzflug machen, *(submarine)* tauchen, auf Tauchstation gehen;
to nose-~ Sturzflug machen;
~ **down on the enemy** sich auf den Feind stürzen; ~ **for pearls** nach Perlen tauchen; ~ **into one's pocket** in die Tasche langen;
~ **into the streets** im Straßengewühl untertauchen; ~ **into a subject** sich in ein Thema vertiefen;
~ **bar** Kellerbar; ~ **bomber** Sturzbomber, -kampfflugzeug; ~ **cost** *(Br.)* Armenrechtskosten.
diver Taucher, *(Br., sl.)* Taschendieb.
diverge *(v.)* verschiedener Meinung sein, voneinander abweichen, divergieren;
~ **from the beaten track** von der Norm abweichen.
divergence Auseinandergehen, Divergenz;
~ **of opinion** Meinungsverschiedenheit; ~ **between two results** Divergenz zweier Ergebnisse.
divergent auseinandergehend;
~ **testimonies** widersprechende Aussagen.
diverse ungleich, verschieden, andersartig, *(multiform)* vielförmig, mannigfaltig;
~ **citizenship** *(US)* verschiedene Staatsangehörigkeit.
diversification Verschiedenartigkeit, Diversifizierung, Diversifikation, *(dispersion of investments)* Anlagenstreuung, verteilte Anlagen, *(investment trust, US)* Effektenauswahl, *(variation of products)* Auffächerung des Produktionsprogramms;
bank ~ Aufgabenausweitung des Bankgeschäftes; **broad** ~ breites Produktionsprogramm; **legitimate** ~ berechtigte Ausweitung des Aufgabenbereichs; **product** ~ reichhaltiges (weitgestreutes) Produktionsprogramm;
~ **away from military and into civilian aircraft** Verlagerung des Schwerpunkts von der militärischen auf zivile Luftfahrt; ~ **into nonbanking financial areas** Ausdehnung der Tätigkeit auf bankfremde Finanzgebiete; ~ **into other energy sources** Ausbreitung in andere Energiebereiche; ~ **into manufacturing** Ausweitung (Auffächerung) des Produktionsprogramms; ~ **of product lines** Auffächerung des Warensortiments; ~ **of products** Reichhaltigkeit (Vielseitigkeit) des Produktionsprogramms, Erweiterung der Produktenpalette, Produktdifferenzierung; ~ **of risk** Risikoverteilung, -streuung, Gefahrenverteilung; ~ **of shareholding** Streuung des Aktienbesitzes;
to force some outfits into ~ einzelne Betriebe zur Anlagenstreuung zwingen; **to grow rapidly through** ~ rasch ein breitgestreutes Investitionsprogramm anstreben; **to owe one's performance to** ~ seinen Erfolg einem breitgefächerten Produktionsprogramm verdanken; **to spend heavily on both geographical and product** ~ große Investitionen zur Anlagenstreuung sowohl geographisch wie auf dem Produktionsgebiet vornehmen;

~ **area** verändertes (aufgefächertes) Produktionsgebiet; **to jump on the** ~ **bandwaggon** der allgemeinen Tendenz breitgestreuter Produktionsprogramme folgen; ~ **efforts** Produktions-, Ausweitungsanstrengungen; ~ **merger** durch Fusionen entstandener Mischkonzern; ~ **move** Anstrengungen zur Ausweitung des Produktionsprogramms; **to spur broad** ~ **moves in certain industries** in bestimmten Wirtschaftsgebieten zu einer beschleunigten Ausweitung der Produktionsprogramme beitragen; ~ **policy** Politik der Risikoverteilung, (Anlagenstreuung); ~ **possibilities** Möglichkeiten der Produktionsauffächerung; ~ **problem** Problem der Anlagenstreuung; ~ **process** Ausweitungsprozeß; ~ **program(me)** weitgestreutes Produktionsprogramm; ~ **record** erfolgreich durchgeführte Produktionsausweitung; ~ **strategy** Politik der von langer Hand vorbereiteten Anlagenstreuung.
diversified abwechslungsreich, mannigfaltig, *(capital)* verteilt angelegt, verschieden gelagert, risikomäßig gestreut, *(production program(me))* aufgefächert;
little ~ **company** ziemlich einseitig ausgerichtete Produktionsgesellschaft; ~ **concern** Unternehmen mit breitgestreutem Produktionsprogramm; ~ **producer** Hersteller mit breitem Produktionsprogramm.
diversify *(v.)* abwechslungsreich gestalten, variieren, *(capital)* Risikostreuung betreiben, verteilt (risikomäßig gestreut) anlegen, *(corporation)* Produktionsprogramm auffächern, Anlagenstreuung vornehmen;
~ **into air travel** sich dem Lufttransportgeschäft zuwenden; ~ **into outside banking** seine Tätigkeit auf bankfremde Geschäfte ausdehnen; ~ **away from a business** Geschäftssparte aufgeben; ~ **one's capital** sein Vermögen in verschiedenen Sparten (risikomäßig gestreut) anlegen; ~ **into complementary fields** ähnliche Sortimentsgruppen dazunehmen; ~ **into the nonbanking fields** alle Arten des Finanzierungsgeschäfts betreiben; ~ **into foods** in die Nahrungsmittelindustrie eindringen; ~ **into commercial markets** sich dem kommerziellen Sektor intensiver zuwenden; ~ **one's investments** sein Geld mit verteiltem Risiko anlegen; ~ **one's product lines** sein Warensortiment auffächern (ausweiten); ~ **out of aerospace industry into manufacturing** einseitig auf Bedürfnisse der Raumfahrtindustrie abgestelltes Produktionsprogramm auffächern; ~ **out of large-scale urban industries into small-scale units and village industries** städtische Großunternehmen zugunsten von Kleinbetrieben und ländlichen Fertigungseinheiten aufgeben; ~ **production** Produktionsprogramm auffächern.
diversifying Anlagen-, Produktionsstreuung;
to make some ~ **of pension funds mandatory** Teilstreuung des Vermögens eines Pensionsfonds zur Auflage machen.
diversion Zerstreuung, Unterhaltung, Ablenkung, Zeitvertreib, *(change of route, Br.)* Umleitung;
favo(u)rite ~**s** bevorzugte Freizeitbeschäftigung; **indoor** ~**s** Gesellschaftsspiele; **outdoor** ~**s** Belustigungen im Freien; **traffic** ~ *(change of route, Br.)* Verkehrsumleitung;
~ **of commission** Aufteilung der Provisionsgebühren; ~ **of a fund** Zweckentfremdung eines Fonds; ~ **of manpower** Arbeitskräfteverteilung; ~ **of the mind from business** Ablenkung von geschäftlichen Interessen; ~ **of production** Produktionsverlagerung; ~ **of a stream** Flußumleitung; ~ **of traffic** *(Br.)* Verkehrsumleitung; ~**s of youth** jugendlicher Zeitvertrieb;
to create (make) a ~ Täuschungsangriff durchführen; **to seek** ~ nach einem Zeitvertreib Ausschau halten;
~ **order** *(law of nations)* Kursanweisung.
diversionism *(communism)* Abweichung, Sabotage.
diversity Vielfältigkeit, Verschiedenartigkeit;
~ **of citizenship** *(US)* Verschiedenheit der Staatsangehörigkeit; ~ **of investment** Anlagenstreuung; ~ **of opinions** Breite der geäußerten Ansichten;
to manage increased ~ der Führung einer immer breiter gefächerten Unternehmensgruppe gerecht werden.
divert *(v.)* ablenken, abzweigen, *(Br.)* umleiten, *(recreate)* zerstreuen, unterhalten;
~ **o. s.** sich ablenken; ~ **s. one's attention** jds. Aufmerksamkeit ablenken; ~ **a bus route** *(Br.)* Omnibuslinie verlegen; ~ **the conversation** dem Gespräch eine andere Richtung geben; ~ **the course of a river** Fluß umleiten; ~ **a fund** Fonds zweckentfremden; ~ **production** Produktionsschwerpunkt verlagern; ~ **all receipts into one's bank account** alle Einnahmen zu seinem Bankkonto dirigieren; ~ **a sum for charity** Betrag für wohltätige Zwecke abzweigen; ~ **trade from a country** Handelsströme eines Landes umleiten; ~ **traffic** *(Br.)* Verkehr umleiten; ~ **to one's personal use** für sich persönlich (für eigene Zwecke) verwenden (abzweigen).

diverted abgelenkt;
~ **funds** zweckentfremdete Mittel; ~ **traffic** *(Br.)* umgeleiteter Verkehr.

diverting attack *(mil.)* Entlastungsangriff.

divest *(v.)* | s. o. of s. th. jem. den Besitz entziehen; ~ **o. s. of one's authority** seine Vollmacht zurückgeben; ~ **o. s. of an office** von einem Amt zurücktreten; ~ **an official of power and authority** Beamten seiner Stellung entheben; ~ **s. o. of his property** j. seines Eigentums berauben; ~ **o. s. of a right** auf ein Recht verzichten.

divestible aufhebbar.

divestiture Besitzentziehung, *(antitrust law, US)* Entflechtung.

divestment Besitzentziehung.

divide *(v.)* trennen, teilen, *(country)* teilen, spalten, *(distribute)* verteilen, *(mathematics)* dividieren, *(parl.)* im Hammelsprung abstimmen;
~ **9 per cent** 9% Dividende ausschütten; ~ **a book into chapters** Buch in Kapitel einteilen; ~ **the costs between the parties** Kosten gegeneinander aufheben; ~ **up a country** Land aufteilen; ~ **a bankrupt's estate** Konkursmasse ausschütten; ~ **the House** *(parl., Br.)* namentlich (im Hammelsprung) abstimmen lassen; **to propose to ~ the house on a question** Frage zur Abstimmung stellen; ~ **the meeting** Meinungen der Sitzungsteilnehmer auseinandergehen lassen; ~ **money equally** Geld gleichmäßig verteilen; ~ **the profits** Gewinn verteilen, Gewinnverteilung vornehmen; ~ **one's property amongst one's heirs** sein Vermögen unter seine Erben aufteilen; ~ **one's time between work and play** Arbeit und Vergnügen gleichmäßig verteilen; ~ **a town in wards** Stadt in Bezirke einteilen; ~ **up the work** Arbeit aufteilen.

divided *(dividend)* ausgeschüttet, *(stock exchange)* geteilt, nicht einheitlich;
to be ~ on a question in einer Frage geteilter Meinung sein; ~ **opinions** geteilte Ansichten.

dividend Dividende, Gewinnanteil, *(bankruptcy)* [Konkurs]quote, Rate;
cum ~ *(Br.)* mit (einschließlich) Dividende, samt Kupon; **ex ~** *(Br.)* ohne (exklusive) Dividende; ~ **off** *(US)* ohne Dividende; ~ **on** *(US)* einschließlich Dividende;
accrued ~ aufgelaufene Dividende; **accumulated (accumulation) ~s** aufgelaufene Dividenden; **additional ~** Zusatzdividende; **annual ~** Jahresdividende; **bond ~** Dividende in Form eigener Obligationen; **cash ~** Bardividende; **collected ~s** abgehobene Dividenden; **~s not yet collected** noch nicht abgehobene Dividenden; **commodity ~** *(US)* Sachdividende; **consent ~** beim Aktionär versteuerte Dividende; **contingent ~** unvorhergesehene Dividende; **cumulative ~** zusätzliche Dividende, Zusatzdividende, Dividende auf kumulative Vorzugsaktien; **declared ~** erklärte (ausgeschüttete) Dividende; **deferred ~** Dividende mit aufgeschobener Fälligkeit; **distributed ~** ausgeschüttete Dividende; **due ~** fällige Dividende; **extraordinary ~** außerordentliche Dividende; **final ~** Schlußdividende, *(bankruptcy)* Schlußquote; **first ~** *(bankruptcy)* Abschlagsquote; **fixed ~** Festdividende, garantierte Dividende; **foreign ~** ausländische Dividende; **gross ~** Bruttodividende; **guaranteed ~** garantierte Dividende; **initial ~** Anfangsdividende; **interim ~** Zwischen-, Abschlagsdividende; **Irish ~** *(fam.)* Besteuerung; **last year's ~** Vorjahrsdividende; **life insurance ~** Prämie; **limited ~** limitierte Dividende; **liquidation ~** Schlußdividende, Liquidationsquote, -anteil; **mandated ~s** mit Inkassoauftrag abgehobene Dividenden; **maturity ~** *(life insurance)* fällige Prämienbeteiligung; **mid-year ~** Halbjahresdividende; **mortuary ~** *(life insurance)* Todesfallprämie; **national ~** Nationaleinkommen; **net ~** *(Br.)* Dividende abzüglich Steuer; **noncumulative ~** gewöhnliche Dividende; **optional ~** Gratisaktie mit Wahlrecht der Barabfindung; **ordinary ~** Stammdividende; **paid-out ~** ausgeschüttete Dividende; **passed ~** ausgefallene Dividende; **~s payable** fällige Dividende, Dividendenansprüche; **pending ~** noch ausstehende Dividende; **post-mortem ~** *(life insurance)* Todesfallprämie; **preferential ~** Vorzugsdividende; **preferred ~** Vorzugsdividende; **preferred fixed ~** Vorzugsdividende mit fester Verzinsung; **property ~** Dividende in Form von Gratisaktien anderer Aktiengesellschaften; ~ **proposed** vorgeschlagene Dividende; **quarterly ~** Vierteljahresdividende; **regular ~** an festen Terminen zahlbare (normale) Dividende; **retained ~** einbehaltene Dividende; **reversionary ~** rückständiger Gewinnanteil; **scrip ~** *(US)* Berechtigungsschein für spätere Dividendenleistung; **semiannual ~** Halbjahresdividende; **sham ~** fiktive Dividende, Scheindividende; **special ~** außerordentliche Dividende; **special settlement ~** *(life insurance)* Gewinn-, Prämienbeteiligung;

stable ~ gleichbleibende Dividende; **statutory ~** satzungsmäßige Dividende; **stock ~** *(US)* Gratisaktie, Dividende in Form von Aktien; **super (surplus) ~** *(US)* außerordentliche Dividende, Superdividende, Bonus; **taxable ~** steuerpflichtige Dividende; **total ~** Gesamtdividende; **unauthorized ~** unzulässige Dividende; **uncalled (unclaimed) ~** nicht behobene Dividende; **uniform ~** Einheitsdividende; **unpaid ~** noch nicht ausgezahlte Dividende;
~ **on account** Zwischen-, Interims-, Abschlagsdividende; **~s in arrear** Dividendenrückstände; ~ **of a bankrupt's estate** Konkursquote, -dividende; ~ **paid out of the capital** aus dem Kapital gezahlte Dividende; **possible ~ to unsecured creditors** voraussichtliche Quote ungesicherter Konkursgläubiger; ~ **at interim** Abschlagsdividende; ~ **payable in kind** Dividende in Form von Gratisaktien anderer Gesellschaften, Sachdividende; ~ **in liquidation** Liquidationsanteil, -rate;
to allow one's ~ to accumulate seine Dividenden sich ansammeln lassen; **to be eligible for the ~ received exclusion provided by the Internal Revenue Code** *(Br.)* das von der Steuergesetzgebung vorgesehene Schachtelprivileg genießen; **to be entitled to a ~** dividendenberechtigt sein; **to collect a ~** Dividende abheben; **to cut its ~** Dividende herabsetzen; **to declare a ~** Dividende festsetzen (verteilen, ausschütten); **to declare a stock ~ (~ in stock of the corporation)** *(US)* Gratisaktien ausgeben; **to default a ~** Dividende ausfallen lassen; **to distribute a ~** Dividende ausschütten; **to distribute an additional (supplementary) ~** zusätzliche Dividende ausschütten; **to distribute a higher ~** höhere Dividendenausschüttung vornehmen; **to guarantee a ~** Dividende garantieren; **to have paid 10% ~ last year** im letzten Jahr 10% Dividende gezahlt haben; **to omit (pass, US) a ~** Dividende ausfallen lassen, Geschäftsjahr ohne Dividendenausschüttung abschließen; **to pay a ~ out of capital** Dividende aus dem Kapital zahlen; **to produce ~s** *(fig.)* sich auszahlen; **to propose (recommend) a ~** Dividende vorschlagen; **to raise the ~** Dividende erhöhen; **to rank for ~** *(Br.)* dividendenberechtigt sein; **to rank for July ~** *(Br.)* schon im Juli an der Dividendenausschüttung teilnehmen; **to yield a ~** Dividende abwerfen; **to yield 14 per cent ~** 14% Dividende bringen;
~ **account** Dividendenkonto; ~ **accumulation** Dividendenansammlung; ~ **addition** *(life insurance)* zusätzliche Gewinnbeteiligung; ~ **announcement** Dividendenerklärung; ~ **arrears** Dividendenrückstände; ~ **balance** Restdividende; ~ **bonds** *(US)* mit Dividendenberechtigung ausgestattete Obligationen; ~ **book** Aktionärverzeichnis [zur Dividendenauszahlung]; ~ **check** *(US)* **(cheque,** *Br.)* Dividendenscheck; ~ **continuity** Dividendenkontinuität; ~ **coupon** Gewinnanteil-, Dividendenschein, Kupon; ~ **curb** Dividendenkürzung; ~ **cutting** Dividendenkürzung; ~ **date of record** Dividendenschluß; ~ **day** Dividendentermin; ~ **declaration** Dividendenerklärung; ~ **disbursement** Dividendenausschüttung; ~ **disbursing agent** Dividendenauszahlungsstelle; ~ **distribution** Dividendenverteilung, -ausschüttung; ~ **equalization account** Dividendenausgleichskonto; ~ **equalization reserve** Dividendenausgleichsrücklage; **~freedom** *(Br.)* Befreiung von der Dividendenbegrenzungsvorschrift; ~ **fund** Dividendenfonds; ~ **guarantee** Dividendengarantie; ~ **income** Dividendeneinkommen, -einnahme; ~ **increase** Dividendenerhöhung; ~ **limitation** Dividendenbeschränkung; **statutory ~ limitations** gesetzliche Dividendenbegrenzungen; ~ **list** Dividendenverzeichnis; ~ **mandate** *(Br.)* Dividendenüberweisungsauftrag; ~ **omission** Dividendenausfall; ~ **payers** *(US)* Dividendenpapiere; **~-paying ability** Dividendenfähigkeit; **~-paying securities** börsengängige Dividendenwerte; **~-paying stock** Dividendenpapier; ~ **payment (payout,** *US)* Dividendenausschüttung; **total ~ payment** Dividendensumme; ~ **period** Dividendenzeitraum; ~ **policy** Dividendenpolitik; ~ **provision** Dividendenrücklage; ~ **rate** Dividendensatz; ~ **receiver** Dividendenempfänger; ~ **recommendation** Dividendenvorschlag; ~ **record** Aufstellung über bisher gezahlte Dividenden; ~ **reduction (remission)** Dividendenkürzung, -herabsetzung; ~ **register** Dividendenverzeichnis; ~ **reinvestment** wiederangelegte Dividendenausschüttungen; ~ **remittance** Dividendentransfer; ~ **repatriation** Dividendentransfer; ~ **requirements** Dividendenerfordernisse; ~ **reserve fund** Dividendenrücklage; ~ **restrictions** Dividendenbeschränkungen, -begrenzung; ~ **rights** Dividendenberechtigung; **to rank in ~ rights** dividendenberechtigt sein; **to rank first in ~ rights** dividendenbevorrechtigt sein; ~ **share** Gewinnanteil; ~ **statement** Dividendenerklärung; ~ **tax** Dividendenabgabe, -steuer; ~ **taxation** Dividendenbesteuerung; **pending ~ timetable** Dividendenerwartungstabelle;

~ **top** (Br.) oberer Abschnitt eines Dividendenscheines; ~ **warrant** Dividendenabschnitt, Dividenden-, Gewinnanteilschein, Kupon; ~ **yield** Dividendenrendite, Effektenrendite; ~ **yield basis** Dividendenrenditegrundlage; ~ **yield ratio** Dividendenrenditeverhältnis.

divider card Trennkarton.

dividers Stechzirkel.

dividing | line (road) Trennlinie; ~ **rule** Trenn-, Spaltenlinie; ~ **value** Scheidewert.

diving Tauchen;
~ **bell** Tauchglocke; ~ **board** Sprungbrett; ~ **dress** Tauchanzug; ~ **equipment** Tauchausrüstung; ~ **helmet** Taucherhelm; ~ **suit** Taucheranzug.

divisibility of a patent Aufspaltbarkeit des Patentrechts.

divisible teilbar;
~ **contract** teilbarer Vertrag; ~ **obligation** Teilobligation; ~ **performance** teilbare Leistung; ~ **surplus** verteilbarer Überschuß.

divisibility Teilbarkeit.

division Teilung, Auf-, Verteilung, (administration, US) ministerielle Abteilung, (administrative district) Verwaltungsbezirk, (counting of votes) Stimmenzählung, (dividing) [Ein]teilung, (country) Teilung, Spaltung, (dividing line) Grenze, Trennlinie, (electoral district, Br.) Wahlkreis, -bezirk, (industry) Fachgruppe, Sparte, Geschäftszweig, (law court) Kammer, Senat, (mil.) Division, (officials, Br.) Beamtenkategorie, (parl., Br.) namentliche Abstimmung, Hammelsprung, (print.) Trennungszeichen, (railroad, US) Eisenbahnstrecke, (ward, Br.) Gefängnisabteilung;
on ~ bei der Abstimmung;
Antitrust ⍾ (US) Kartellbehörde; **equal** ~ Stimmengleichheit; **finance** ~ Finanzabteilung; **the first, second, third** ~ gestaffelte Haftverschärfungsstrafen; **geographical** ~ geographische Gliederung; **industrial** ~ Gewerbe-, Industriezweig; **payroll** ~ Lohnabteilung, -büro; **production** ~ Produktionsabteilung; **professional** ~ fachliche Gliederung; **quarterly session** ~ (Br.) Kreisgericht; **snap** ~ überraschende Abstimmung; **tie** ~ unentschiedene Abstimmung;
~ **of a bankrupt's estate** Ausschüttung der Konkursmasse, Konkursausschüttung; ~ **of a city** Stadteinteilung; ~ **of a conglomerate** Konzernbetrieb; ~ **of disbursement** (treasury) Auszahlungsabteilung; ~ **of employment** Arbeitsteilung; ~ **of an estate** Nachlaßteilung; ~ **of labo(u)r** Arbeitsteilung; ~ **of land** Grundstücksteilung; ~ **of markets** Abgrenzung der Verkaufsgebiete, Aufteilung von Absatzmärkten, Markt-, Absatzaufteilung; ~ **of money** Geldverteilung, -aufteilung; ~ **of opinion** Meinungsverschiedenheit; ~ **of powers** Gewaltenteilung; ~ **of profits** Gewinnausschüttung, -verteilung; ~ **of quotas** Quotenaufteilung; ~ **of rates** (carrier) Gebührenteilung; **second** ~ **of the civil service** (Br.) mittlere Beamtenposition, -stellung, -laufbahn; ~ **into shares** Stückelung; ~ **of territory** Gebietsteilung;
to bring ~ **into a family** Streit in eine Familie tragen; **to challenge a** ~ Abstimmung provozieren; **to come to a** ~ abstimmen, zur Abstimmung gelangen; **to go into** ~ zur Abstimmung schreiten; **to pass a bill without a** ~ Gesetzantrag ohne besondere Abstimmung verabschieden; **to press a** ~ auf eine Abstimmung drängen; **to stir up** ~s **in a nation** feindliche Gruppen in einer Nation ins Leben rufen, Spaltung einer Nation herbeiführen;
~ **bell** Abstimmungsglocke, -zeichen; ~ **heading** Untertitel; ~ **lobby** Abstimmung im Hammelsprung; ~ **manager** (US) Abteilungsleiter; ~ **mark** Teilstrich, Teilungsmarke; ~ **president** (US) Abteilungspräsident; ~ **sales manager** Bezirksverkaufsleiter; ~ **sign** Teilungszeichen.

divisional | administration (Br.) (local government) Bezirksaußenstelle; ~ **application** (patent law) Anmeldung für den ausgeschiedenen Teil; ~ **artillery** Divisionsartillerie; ~ **bond** auf einer Teilstrecke hypothekarisch gesicherte Eisenbahnobligation; ~ **chairman** Zonenpräsident; ~ **coin** Scheidemünze; ~ **court** Bezirksgericht; ~ **head** Abteilungsleiter; ~ **headquarters** (mil., Br.) Divisionshauptquartier; ~ **examination** Verwaltungsexamen; ~ **line** Trennungslinie; ~ **manager** Bezirksleiter; ~ **meeting** (US) Abteilungsbesprechung; ~ **officer** (trade union, Br.) Gebietsbeauftragter; ~ **wall** Trennwand.

divorce Ehescheidung, -auslösung;
absolute ~ Eheauflösung; **foreign** ~ ausländisches Scheidungsurteil; **limited** ~ Trennung von Tisch und Bett, gerichtlich angeordnetes Getrenntleben;
~ **by mutual consent** (Br.) [Ehe]scheidung im gegenseitigen Einverständnis; ~ **on grounds of guilt** Ehescheidung wegen Verschuldens; ~ **of a marriage** Ehescheidung;
~ (v.) sich scheiden lassen;
~ **Church from State** Kirche vom Staat trennen; ~ **one's husband** sich von seinem Ehemann scheiden lassen; ~ **a word from its context** Wort aus dem Zusammenhang reißen;
to get (obtain) a ~ Scheidungsurteil erwirken, Scheidung erlangen, sich scheiden lassen, geschieden werden; **to grant a** ~ auf Scheidung erkennen; **to petition for** ~ auf Ehescheidung klagen; **to seek a** ~ sich scheiden lassen; **to sue for a** ~ Ehescheidung beantragen, Scheidungsklage einreichen;
~ **case** Ehe-, Scheidungssache; ~ **court** Scheidungsgericht; ~ **decree** [Ehe]scheidungsurteil; ~ **judge** Scheidungsrichter; ~ **law** Ehescheidungsrecht; ~ **law reform** Ehescheidungsreform; ~ **petition** Scheidungsantrag, -klage; ~ **proceedings** Ehescheidungsverfahren; **to start (take)** ~ **proceedings** Ehescheidung[sklage] einleiten; ~ **rate** Scheidungsprozentsatz; ~ **suit** Ehescheidungssache, Scheidungsprozeß.

divorced geschieden;
~ **parties** geschiedene Ehegatten.

divorcee Geschiedene[r].

divorcement Scheidung, (US) Entflechtung.

divorcer Scheidungskläger, (US) Scheidungsgrund.

divulgate (v.) enthüllen, öffentlich bekanntmachen.

divulgation Bekanntmachung, Enthüllung;
~ **of a rumo(u)r** Verbreitung eines Gerüchtes.

divulge (v.) verbreiten, in Umlauf setzen, enthüllen;
~ **information** Information weitergeben; ~ **a plot** Verschwörung enthüllen; ~ **the state of an account** Kontostand preisgeben.

do (Br.) Feier, Festlichkeit, (go, Australia, sl.) Erfolg, Treffer, (raid) Überfall, (take-in) Gaunertrick, Schwindel;
fair ~ anständige Behandlung; **family** ~ Familienfeier; **poor** ~ (hotel) schlechte Bedienung;
~**'s and** ~ **nots of a society** gesellschaftlich Erlaubtes und Verbotenes; **all talk and no** ~ nichts als Geschwätz;
~ (v.) tun, machen, (buy up, Br.) Wechsel aufkaufen, (carry out) ausführen, (effect) bewirken, (perform) leisten, (work) verrichten;
a ~ **from the start** von Anfang an nichts als Betrug;
~ **s. o. an article at ...** jem. einen Artikel für ... ablassen; ~ **badly** schlechte Geschäfte machen; ~ **s. o. badly** j. schwer reinlegen; ~ **bills** (Br.) Wechsel aufkaufen; ~ **business** Geschäfte abwickeln; ~ **one's business for s. o.** (coll.) j. finanziell erledigen; ~ **a commission** Auftrag ausführen; ~ **a country in a fortnight** Land in zwei Wochen besichtigen; ~ **civil engineering at the University** Tiefbau an der Universität studieren; ~ **a lot of correspondence** Menge Briefe erledigen; ~ **brilliantly at an examination** Examen glänzend bestehen; ~ **s. o. a favo(u)r** jem. einen Gefallen erweisen; ~ **the fictions in a magazine** Romane in einer Zeitschrift rezensieren; ~ **s. o. the hono(u)r** jem. die Ehre erweisen; ~ **the innocent** den Unschuldigen spielen; ~ **the interpreter** Dolmetscher abgeben (machen); ~ **justice to s. o.** jem. Gerechtigkeit widerfahren lassen; ~ **one's lessons** seine Schulaufgaben machen (erledigen); ~ **a hundred miles** (car) Spitzengeschwindigkeit von 160 Km erreichen; ~ **one's military service** seinen Wehrdienst ableisten; ~ **the needful** das Erforderliche veranlassen; ~ **odd jobs** allerlei Arbeiten (Gelegenheitsarbeiten) verrichten; ~ **s. o. out of a job** j. um seine Stellung bringen; ~ **very nicely** finanziell gut wegkommen; ~ **a picture gallery** Betrieb einer Gemäldegalerie absolvieren; ~ **the polite** (fam.) sich von seiner höflichsten Seite zeigen; ~ **s. o. all right** jem. gut passen; ~ **a translation** Übersetzung anfertigen; ~ **a good turn to s. o.** j. einen guten Dienst erweisen; ~ **up** (dwelling) instandsetzen, (wrap up) [Waren] einpacken; ~ **well** vorwärtskommen, Erfolg haben, (make money) viel Geld verdienen; ~ **o. s. well** (fam.) es sich gut gehen lassen; ~ **well by s. o.** j. gut behandeln; ~ **contrastingly well** sich auffallend wohltuend unterscheiden; ~ **without the services of a secretary** sich ohne Sekretärin behelfen; ~ **wonders** Wunder bewirken; ~ **ten years** zehn Jahre absitzen;
~ **away** abschaffen, weglassen; ~ **away with s. o.** j. beseitigen; ~ **away with a department** Abteilung auflösen; ~ **down** (Br., coll.) hereinlegen, übers Ohr hauen; ~ **for s. o.** jem. den Haushalt führen; ~ **for an office** sich gut für ein Büro eignen; ~ **in** betrügen, begaunern, übers Ohr hauen; ~ **s. o. in** (sl.) j. um die Ecke bringen; ~ **into English** ins Englische übersetzen; ~ **out** (room, coll.) säubern, reinigen, aufräumen; ~ **s. o. out of his money** j. um sein Geld betrügen; ~ **over again** nochmals bearbeiten, überarbeiten; ~ **up** (repair) instandsetzen, (US sl.) zugrunderichten, ruinieren, (wrap up) einpacken; ~ **o. s. up** sich zurechtmachen, Toilette machen; ~ **up brown** (sl.) ausnehmen,

reinlegen; **to can ~ with a good night's sleep** längeren Nacht-schlaf dringend benötigen; **~ without** verzichten, entbehren, sich behelfen;

to build a summer house for s. th. to ~ Gartenhaus bauen, um etw. zu tun zu haben; **to have just enough to ~ on** gerade sein Auskommen haben; **to have nothing to ~ with a matter** mit einer Sache nichts zu tun haben; **to take part in a ~** *(fam.)* an einem großen Empfang teilnehmen.

do|-all Faktotum; **~-gooder** Wohlmeinender, Weltverbesserer; **~-it-yourself** Selbstmachen, Basteltätigkeit; **~-it-yourselfism** Selbsthilfemethode; **~-nothing** Faulenzer, Faulpelz, Nichtstuer; **~-nothingness** Untätigkeit, Nichtstuerei.

dock Dock, Kai, Schiffswerft, *(artificial basin)* Hafenbecken, *(landing pier)* Landungs-, Anlageplatz, Pier, *(railroad, US)* Laderampe, *(siding, Br.)* Abstellgleis, *(wage cut)* Lohnkürzung, *(warehouse)* Lager-, Packhof;

delivered at ~ ins Dock abgeliefert; **in ~** *(car)* in Reparatur; **~s** Dock, Hafenanlagen;

dry (graving) ~ Trockendock; **floating (flooding) ~** Schwimmdock; **loading ~** Ladedock, Landungs-, Verladeplatz; **naval ~s** Marinewerft; **offshore ~** einseitiges Dock; **tide ~** Dockschleuse; **unloading ~** Entladedock; **wet ~** Schwimmdock;

~ (v.) (go into dock) ins Dock gehen, docken, am Kai festmachen, *(make less)* entziehen, einbehalten, kürzen;

~ the entail Erbfolge aufheben; **~ s. o. out of his pension** jem. die Pension aberkennen; **~ the soldiers of part of their rations** den Soldaten die Rationen kürzen; **~ a space vehicle** Raumschiff ankoppeln; **~ a train** Zug aufs Abstellgleis bringen; **~ £ 20 off s. one's wages** jem. zwanzig Pfund vom Lohn abziehen; **~ a workman's wages** Arbeitslohn kürzen;

to be in the ~ auf der Anklagebank sitzen, im Anklagezustand sein; **to be in dry ~** *(fam.)* arbeitslos sein; **to go into ~** docken, ins Dock gehen, *(person)* sich einer Krankenhausbehandlung unterziehen; **to go into dry ~** ins Trockendock gehen; **to leave ~** aus dem Dock gehen; **to put a ship in ~** Schiff ins Dock bringen; **to stand in the ~** auf der Anklagebank sitzen; **to take a ship into ~** Schiff eindocken; **to take a ship out of ~** Schiff aus dem Dock bringen;

~ authorities Hafenbehörde; **~s Board** *(Br.)* Hafenamt; **~ brief** *(Br.)* kostenlos übernommener Verteidigungsauftrag, Bestallung eines Armenanwalts, Anwaltsauftrag; **~ charges (dues)** Dockgebühren, Hafengeld; **~ company** Lagerhausgesellschaft; **~ crew** Entlademannschaft; **~ duty** Dockgeld; **~ facilities** Dockanlagen; **~ gate** Dock-, Hafenschleuse; **~ inspector** Dockmeister, Ablader; **~ labo(u)rer** Dock-, Hafenarbeiter, Ablader; **~ labo(u)rer strike** Dockarbeiterstreik; **~ landing account** *(Br., port authority)* Frachtgutmeldeformular; **~ light** Hafenfeuer; **~ owner** Lagerhausbesitzer; **~ port** Dockhafen; **~ receipt** *(Br.)* Dockempfangs-, Lagerschein, *(US)* Interimsschein über die erfolgte Anlieferung von Gütern zur Verschiffung, Kaiannahme-, Ablieferungsschein, Kaiquittung; **~ rent** Docklagermiete; **dry ~ repair** Trockendockreparatur; **~ siding** Kaianschluß; **~ stocks** *(Br.)* Wertpapiere von Lagerhausgesellschaften; **~ strike** Hafenarbeiterstreik; **~ warehouse** Lagerhof, Packhof; **~ warrant** *(Br.)* Docklagerschein; **~ worker** Dock-, Hafenarbeiter.

dockage Dockgebühren, *(wages, US)* Lohnabzug.

docked, to have one's salary Gehaltskürzung erfahren.

docker *(Br.)* Schauermann, Hafen-, Dockarbeiter, Ablader, *(advocate)* Strafverteidigung.

docket *(agenda, US)* Tagesordnung, *(calendar in cases, US)* Liste zu behandelnder Sachen, Terminkalender bei Gericht, Prozeßliste, *(customhouse warrant, Br.)* Zollquittung, Passierzettel, *(delivery order, Br.)* Lieferschein, -bewilligung, Bestellschein, *(index)* Inhaltsverzeichnis, *(label)* Waren[adreß]zettel, Etikett, *(list)* Liste, Verzeichnis, *(list of judgments)* Urteilsregister, *(patent office)* Patentamtbeglaubigung, -angabe, *(purchasing permit, Br.)* Einkaufsgenehmigung, Kaufbewilligung, *(record of proceedings)* [Prozeß]protokoll, *(register of papers)* Verzeichnis der Aktenstücke eines Prozesses;

on the ~ *(fam.)* in Bearbeitung;

appearance ~ Gerichtstagebuch; **bar ~** inoffizielle Prozeßliste; **execution ~** Pfändungsliste; **judgment ~** Urteilsregister; **trial ~** *(US)* Verhandlungsliste; **wages ~** Lohnliste;

~ (v.) (attach label) mit Etikett versehen, etikettieren, beschriften, *(certify)* beglaubigen, *(endorse)* in ein Verzeichnis eintragen, *(enter into the docket book)* in die Prozeßliste eintragen, *(extract)* Auszug machen, ausziehen, *(extract proceedings)* Prozeßauszug anfertigen;

~ a case Termin ansetzen; **~ the case of X vs Y** die Sache X gegen Y ansetzen; **~ goods** Waren etikettieren;

to clear the ~ *(US)* anhängige Gerichtsfälle erledigen; **to strike a ~** Konkurs anmelden;

~ book (list) Prozeßliste; **~ fee** Prozeßgebühr.

docketing Eintragung.

docking *(space ship)* Ankoppelung, Kopplungsmanöver;

~ of pay *(US)* Lohnabzug;

~ area Dockgebiet; **~ facilities** Dockanlagen.

dockland Hafenviertel.

dockmaster Hafenmeister, -kommissar.

docksman Dockarbeiter.

dockside Dockwand.

dockyard [Schiffs]werft.

doctor Arzt, Doktor, *(tribe)* Medizinmann;

panel ~ Kassenarzt;

~ in attendance behandelnder Arzt; **ᴅ of Civil Law** Doktor der Rechte; **ᴅ of Civil and Common Law** Doktor beider Rechte; **ᴅ of Engineering Science** Doktor der Ingenieurwissenschaften; **ᴅ of Medicine** Doktor der Medizin; **ᴅ of Philosophy** Doktor der Philosophie;

~ (v.) (university) Doktorwürde verleihen, promovieren, *(cook)* frisieren, zurechtmachen;

~ accounts Bücher fälschen; **~ a balance sheet** Bilanz frisieren; **~ election results** Wahlergebnis verfälschen; **~ a sick man** Kranken behandeln;

to consult a ~ Arzt zu Rate ziehen; **to license a ~** einem Arzt die Zulassung erteilen; **to run to a ~** sich an einen Arzt wenden; **~'s bill** Arztrechnung, Liquidation; **~'s call** Arztbesuch, Visite; **~'s certificate** ärztliche Bescheinigung, Attest; **~'s degree** Doktorwürde, -grad; **to take one's ~'s degree** sein Doktorexamen (seinen Doktor) machen, promovieren; **~'s fee** Arzthonorar; **to get a ~'s mandate** Auftrag erhalten, den Retter des Vaterlandes abzugeben; **~'s visit** Arztbesuch, Visite.

doctoral hood Doktorhut.

doctorate Doktorgrad, -titel, -würde;

to receive one's ~ from Harvard seinen Doktor auf der Harvard Universität machen.

doctored tomcat kastrierter Kater.

doctorize *(v.)* seinen Doktor machen, doktorieren, promovieren.

doctorship Doktortitel, -würde.

doctrinaire Prinzipienreiter, Doktrinär.

doctrine Lehrmeinung, Lehre, Doktrin;

party ~ Parteiprogramm;

~ of conversion Doktrin der Umwandlung von Grundvermögen in Geld; **~ of equivalency** *(patent law)* Äquivalenzlehre; **~ of frustration of adventure** Lehre von der Vertragsgrundlage; **~ of strict liability** Grundsatz der Gefährdungshaftung; **~ of reputed ownership** Lehre von der Eigentumsvermutung; **~ of prescription** Lehre von der Verjährung; **~ of relation back** Lehre von der rückwirkenden Kraft; **~ of class struggle** Klassenkampfdoktrin; **~ of ultra wires** Lehre von der Überschreitung der Satzungsbefugnisse; **~ of unfair trade** Verbot der Warenursprungsfälschung.

document Beweis-, Beleg-, [amtliches] Schriftstück, Urkunde, Dokument, Akte[nstück], Unterlage;

in the above ~ in besagtem Schreiben; **founded on (supported by) ~s** urkundlich belegt;

~s Verlade-, Schiffsunterlagen, Verschiffungspapiere;

accompanying ~ Begleitpapier; **ancient ~s** über dreißig Jahre alte Urkunden; **ancillary ~** zusätzliche Urkunde; **authentic ~** echte Urkunde; **authoritative ~** maßgebliche Urkunde; **average ~s** *(marine insurance)* Schadensunterlagen; **clean ~** uneingeschränkte Urkunde; **commercial ~s** geschäftliche Unterlagen, Geschäftspapiere; **confidential ~** vertrauliche Schriftstücke; **confirmed ~** *(US)* beglaubigte Abschrift; **customs ~** Zolldokumente, -papiere; **duplicate ~s** Dokumente in zweifacher Ausfertigung; **evidentiary ~** beweiserhebliche Urkunde; **export ~s** Export-, Ausfuhrpapiere; **fabricated (forged) ~** gefälschte Urkunde; **foreign-trade ~s** Außenhandelspapiere; **forwarding ~s** Frachtpapiere, -dokumente; **impounded ~** beschlagnahmte Urkunde; **incriminating ~s** belastende Beweisstücke, Belastungsmaterial; **individual ~** Einzelurkunde; **irregular ~** unvollständige Urkunde; **judicial ~s** Prozeßakten; **notarial ~** Notariatsurkunde; **official ~** öffentlichen Glauben genießende Urkunde, amtliches Dokument, amtliches Schriftstück; **priority ~s** Prioritätsbelege; **private ~** Privaturkunde; **privileged ~** vertrauliche Urkunde; **public ~** amtliche Veröffentlichung (Urkunde), öffentlichrechtliche Urkunde; **~s required** beizubringende Unterlagen; **secret ~** Geheimdokument; **shipping ~s** Verschiffungs-, Frachtpapiere, Verladedokumente; **supporting ~s** Unterlagen, Nebenurkunden, Belege, ergänzende Dokumente;

~s against acceptance Dokumente gegen Akzept; ~s for application *(patent law)* Anmeldeunterlagen; ~s pertaining to the case in court Prozeßakten; ~ of charge Verpfändungsurkunde; ~s in default (sufferance) notleidende Papiere; ~s to be destroyed zur Vernichtung bestimmte Urkunden; ~ under hand nicht gesiegelte Urkunde; ~ drawn up before a lawyer notarielle Urkunde; ~s for the meeting Tagungsunterlagen; ~ drawn up before a notary notarielle Urkunde; ~ that is not in [legal] order ungültige Urkunde; ~s against payment Auslieferung der Verladepapiere (Schiffspapiere) gegen Bezahlung, Kasse gegen Dokumente; ~s joined to a report einem Bericht beigegebene Unterlagen; ~s of shipment Verladepapiere; ~s in support Belegstücke, ergänzende Dokumente, Nebenurkunden; ~s of a tender Ausschreibungsunterlagen; ~ of title Traditionspapier, Eigentums-, Besitztitel, Besitzurkunde; ~ of title to goods Traditionspapier unbeweglicher Sachen, Besitztitel, -urkunde; ~ of title to land Eigentumsnachweis für ein Grundstück;
~ *(v.) (furnish with necessary papers)* mit den notwendigen (amtlichen) Papieren versehen, *(prove by documents)* urkundlich (dokumentarisch) belegen, *(shipping)* mit den Verladepapieren versehen;
~ one's claim seinen Anspruch urkundlich belegen; ~ a ship Schiff mit amtlichen Papieren ausstatten; ~ a traveller Reisenden mit den erforderlichen Ausweisen versehen;
to affix a seal to a ~ Urkunde siegeln; to affix one's signature to a ~ Urkunde unterfertigen; to alter a ~ Urkunde abändern; to annex a ~ to a report Bericht einer Urkunde beifügen; to append a ~ to a dossier Urkunde einem Exposé beifügen; to call for production of ~s Vorlage von Urkunden verlangen; to compare two ~s Urkunden kollationieren; to defeat a ~ Urkunde für ungültig erklären; to deliver a ~ Urkunde abgeben; to dispute (challenge) the validity of a ~ Echtheit einer Urkunde bestreiten; to draw up a ~ Urkunde aufsetzen; to earmark a ~ Urkunde mit einem Kennzeichen versehen; to endorse a ~ auf der Rückseite einer Urkunde vermerken; to evidence a ~ urkundlich belegen; to execute a ~ Dokument abfassen, Urkunde unterfertigen; to fabricate (falsify) a ~ Urkunde fälschen; to file a ~ Urkunde zu den Akten legen; to hoist a spurious ~ on s. o. jem. eine falsche Urkunde aufschwatzen; to forge a ~ Urkunde verfälschen; to furnish ~s Unterlagen beibringen; to have a ~ authenticated Urkunde beglaubigen lassen; to have a ~ witnessed Urkunde in Zeugengegenwart legalisieren lassen; to impound a ~ Urkunde in gerichtliche Verwahrung nehmen; to inspect a ~ Urkunde einsehen; to list a ~ Urkunde aufführen; to lodge a ~ Urkunde hinterlegen; to make out a ~ in duplicate Urkunde doppelt ausfertigen; to mislay a ~ Urkunde verlegen; to place ~s on deposit with a bank Urkunden bei einer Bank aufbewahren lassen; to place a ~ on record Urkunde zu den Akten legen; to preserve ~s Akten aufbewahren; to produce a ~ Urkunde vorlegen; to produce ~s in support [of an allegation] beweisstützende Urkunden vorlegen; to prove by ~s dokumentieren, urkundlich (dokumentarisch) nachweisen (belegen); to put in a ~ in a law case Urkunde in einen Prozeß einführen; to refer to a ~ as proof Urkunde zum Beweis heranziehen; to route ~s Urkunden auf dem Amtsweg weiterleiten; to settle a ~ Urkunde in rechtsgültige Form bringen; to stamp one's approval on a ~ einer Urkunde durch Siegelung Rechtskraft verleihen; to subscribe to a ~ Urkunde unterschreiben; to support by ~s urkundlich belegen; to suppress a ~ Urkunde unterdrücken; to tamper with a ~ Inhalt einer Urkunde verfälschen; to tender ~s Dokumente vorlegen; to withhold a ~ Urkunde nicht herausgeben;
~ bill Dokumententratte; ~ bills Versandpapiere; ~ center *(US)* (centre, *Br.*) Dokumentationszentrum; ~ credit Dokumentenkredit; ~s tax Urkundensteuer.
documentalist Urkundenbearbeiter.
documentarist Produzent von Dokumentarfilmen.
documentary *(book)* Dokumentarbericht, *(film)* Dokumentar-, Kulturfilm, *(radio, television)* Dokumentarsendung;
~ *(a.)* urkundlich, durch Urkunden belegt, dokumentarisch; to have ~ authority Beweiskraft haben; ~ bill (draft) Dokumententratte, Tratte mit Dokumenten; ~ credit Dokumentenakkreditiv; ~ credit operations Dokumentenakkreditivgeschäft; ~ letter of credit Dokumentenakkreditiv; ~ evidence beweiserhebliche Urkunde, Urkundenbeweis, dokumentarischer Beweis; to give ~ evidence urkundlich beweisen (belegen); ~ file Urkundensammlung; ~ film Dokumentar-, Kulturfilm; ~ film of topical interest gegenwartsnaher Dokumentarfilm; ~ material Urkundenmaterial; ~ picture Dokumentaraufnahme; ~ proof Urkundenbeweis, urkundliches Beweismaterial; ~ ref-

erence Dokumentennachweis; ~ report Dokumentarbericht; ~ stamp Stempel-, Steuermarke.
documentation Glaubhaftmachung durch Unterlagen;
~ of cost Kostennachweis; ~ of imports Einfuhrbeglaubigung; ~ for a meeting Sitzungsunterlagen; ~ center *(US)* (centre, *Br.*) Dokumentationszentrum.
documented urkundlich belegt;
~ credit Dokumentarkredit.
dodge Kniff, Schlich, Trick, Kunstgriff;
on the ~ hintenherum;
~ *(v.)* Winkelzüge machen, sich [um die Arbeit] herumdrücken;
~ along entlangtrotten; ~ the column sich vom Dienst drücken; ~ the law Gesetz (gesetzliche Bestimmungen) umgehen; ~ military service sich um den Militärdienst drücken, sich dem Militärdienst entziehen; ~ a question sich um die Beantwortung einer Frage herumdrücken; ~ a tax Steuer umgehen; ~ traffic dem Verkehr ausweichen;
to be up to all ~s alle Tricks kennen; to be up to a ~ or two es faustdick hinter den Ohren haben.
dodger Drückeberger, *(US, Australia)* Handzettel, Reklameprospekt;
tax ~ Steuerhinterzieher; work ~ Arbeitsscheuer.
dodging, artful geschickte Ausweichtaktik;
~ *(a.)* arbeitsscheu.
dodo [geistig] Zurückgebliebener, *(airforce, sl.)* Flugnovize.
doer Ausführender, Handelnder, *(cheater, sl.)* Betrüger, Schwindler, *(Scot. law)* Bevollmächtigter, *(theater)* Darsteller.
dog [Jagd]hund, *(ostentatious style)* Getue, Gehabe, *(promissory note, US)* Schuldschein, *(sportive fellow, coll.)* Kerl, Bursche;
ambulance ~ *(mil.)* Sanitätshund; house ~ Haushund; lame (lazy) ~ lahme Ente; lucky ~ Glückspilz; message-carrying ~ *(mil.)* Meldehund; sly ~ schlauer Fuchs;
~ in the manger Neidhammel;
~ *(v.)* mit Hunden hetzen, *(fig.)* beharrlich auf den Fersen bleiben;
~ s. one's footsteps jem. auf dem Fuße folgen; ~ a suspected thief Diebesverdächtigen beschatten;
to be top ~ das Sagen haben, Boß sein; to drive to the ~s ruinieren, kaputtmachen; to feel as sick as a ~ sich hundeelend fühlen; to follow s. o. like a ~ jem. wie ein Hündchen folgen; to give a ~ a bad name [and hang him] jem. etw. anhängen; to go to the ~s vor die Hunde gehen; to help a lame ~ over a stile jem. in der Not beistehen; j. aus einer schwierigen Lage befreien; to keep a ~ and bark o. s. Arbeit seiner Angestellten verrichten; to let sleeping ~s lie alte Geschichten auf sich beruhen lassen; to put on the ~ sich großtun, prahlen, sich brüsten; to take a hair of the ~ that bit you seinen Kater in Alkohol ersaufen; to throw to the ~s als wertlos ansehen und wegwerfen; to throw discretion to the ~s auf die ganze Geheimnistuerei pfeifen;
~ blanket Hundedecke; ~ box *(Br.)* Hundeabteil; ~ catcher Hundefänger, *(pol.)* unbedeutendes Amt; not even a ~s chance nicht die geringste Chance; ~-cheap spottbillig; ~-days Hundstage; to have one's ~ days miserable Zeit durchmachen; to die a ~'s death eines jämmerlichen Todes sterben; ~-'s ear *(in a book)* Eselsohr; ~'s-ear *(v.)* Eselsohren machen; ~ fancier Hundeliebhaber; ~-hungry hungrig wie ein Wolf; ~ iron Krampe, Klammer; ~-Latin Küchenlatein; ~ lead Hundeleine; ~ licence Genehmigung zum Halten eines Hundes; ~ licence fee *(Br.)* Hundesteuer; to lead a ~'s life Hundeleben führen; to lead s. o. a ~'s life j. wie einen Hund behandeln, jem. das Leben zur Hölle machen; ~-like devotion hündische Ergebenheit; ~ owner Hundebesitzer; ~-poor bettelarm; ~ show Hundeausstellung; ~-sick hundeelend; ~ tag Hundemarke, *(US sl.)* Erkennungsmarke; ~ tax *(US)* Hundesteuer; ~ tent *(mil., US sl.)* Feldzelt; ~-tired abgehetzt, todmüde.
dogface *(mil., US sl.)* Rekrut, Landser.
dogfight Handgemenge, *(mil.)* Panzernahkampf, heftiger Luftkampf.
dogged by misfortune vom Unglück verfolgt.
dogger *(mar.)* Doggerboot.
doggo mäuschenstill.
doghouse Hundehütte, *(fig.)* elende Bude, elende Drecksbude, Hundeloch;
in the ~ *(fig.)* in Ungnade [gefallen].
dogma Lehrmeinung, Dogma.
dogmatic[al] dogmatisch, doktrinär, autoritär, anmaßend.
dogmatism Dogmatismus.
dogmatize *(v.)* dogmatische Behauptungen aufstellen.
dogsbody *(sl.)* Packesel, Kuli, Aushilfskraft.
dogwatch *(mar.)* Hunds-, Spaltwache, Plattfuß.

doing Tun, Handeln, *(sl.)* gesellschaftliches Leben;
> **nothing** ~ ausgeschlossen, nichts zu machen; **nothing** ~ **under a thousand dollars** unter tausend Dollars fasse ich die Sache nicht an; **there is nothing** ~ der Markt ist praktisch tot; **there is very little** ~ die Geschäfte gehen schlecht;
> ~**s in the Balkans** Ereignisse auf dem Balkan; ~ **one's business** *(US)* Ausübung eines Geschäftsbetriebes;
> **to be** ~ **well** gut vorankommen.

doldrums windstille Zone;
> **in the** ~ *(fig.)* in mieser Stimmung, deprimiert, in einer Flaute;
> **to be locked in the** ~ richtige Flaute durchstehen müssen.

dole *(alms)* Almosen, Spende, *(Br., coll.)* Erwerbs-, Arbeitslosenunterstützung, -geld;
> ~ *(v.)* Almosen verteilen;
> ~ **out** in kleinen Rationen austeilen; ~ **out 10% plus increases across the board** über 10% hinausgehende Lohnerhöhung zugestehen;
> **to be on (draw) the** ~ *(Br.)* Arbeitslosenunterstützung (Arbeitslosengeld) beziehen, stempeln gehen; **to be entitled to the** ~ *(Br.)* zur Arbeitslosenunterstützung berechtigt sein; **to collect one's** ~ *(Br.)* seine Arbeitslosenunterstützung kassieren; **to go on the** ~ *(Br.)* sich zur Erwerbslosenunterstützung melden;
> ~ **drawer** *(Br.)* Arbeitslosenunterstützungsempfänger, Stempelbruder; ~ **meadow** Gemeindewiese; ~ **queue** *(Br.)* Arbeitslosenschlange.

doll Puppe, *(sl.)* hübsche aber dumme Pute;
> ~ *(v.)* **o. s. up** *(coll.)* sich aufdonnern; ~ **up a car** Auto frisieren.

dollar Dollar;
> **clean** ~ echter Dollar; **investment** ~**s** *(Br.)* Dollarbeträge zum Ankauf von Überseebeteiligungen durch britische Staatsangehörige;
> **to calculate in** ~**s** in Dollars rechnen;
> ~ **acceptance** Dollarakzept; ~ **amount** Dollarbetrag; ~ **area** Dollarraum, -block; ~**-a-year-man** *(US)* ehrenamtlich für die Regierung Tätiger, Eindollarmann; ~ **balance** Dollarguthaben; ~ **bonds** Dollarbonds, -titel; ~ **check** Dollarscheck; ~ **country** zum Dollarblock gehöriges Land; ~ **credit** Dollarkredit; ~ **debentures** Dollarobligationen; ~ **deficit** Dollardefizit, Dollardevisen; ~ **deposits** Dollarguthaben; ~ **depreciation** Dollarabwertung; ~ **diplomacy** Dollarpolitik; ~ **drain** Dollarabfluß; ~ **drawings** Dollarabzug, -abzüge; ~ **drive** Ausfuhrförderung in den Dollarraum; ~ **earner** Dollarverdiener; ~ **exchange** auf Dollar lautendes Akzept; **to steer gently towards** ~ **finance** vorsichtig zur Dollarfinanzierung überreden; ~ **flight** Dollarflucht; ~ **foreign bonds** Dollaranleihe; ~ **gain** Dollargewinn; ~ **gap** Dollarlücke; ~ **holdings** Dollarbestände; ~ **hunt** Dollarjagd; ~ **imperialism** Dollarherrschaft; ~ **income** Dollareinkommen; ~ **king** Dollarkönig; ~ **loan** Dollaranleihe; ~ **outflow** Dollarabfluß; ~ **premium** *(Br.)* Förderungsprämie für Ausfuhren in den Dollarraum; ~ **quotation** Dollarnotiz; ~ **rate** Dollarkurs; **dwindling** ~ **resources** schwindende Dollarreserven; ~ **rescue** Dollarrettung; ~ **scrips** *(US)* Besatzungsgeld; ~ **shortage** Dollarknappheit; ~ **store** *(US)* Einheitspreisgeschäft; ~ **stringency** Dollarknappheit; ~ **support** Stützung des Dollars; ~ **surplus** Dollarüberschuß; **to protect the** ~ **value of business transactions by asking for future payments in terms of the price of gold** Dollarwert von Geschäftsabschlüssen durch Vereinbarungen zukünftiger Kaufpreisbelegungen zu Goldpreisbedingungen sichern.

dollop *(coll.)* Masse, Menge;
> **to draw another** ~ **of government cash** weitere Barbeträge der Regierung in Anspruch nehmen.

dolly *(film)* fahrbarer Kameratisch, Kamerawagen, -fahrgestell;
> ~ **camera** fahrbare Filmkamera.

domain Bezirk, Feld, Aufgabengebiet, *(landed estate)* freies Grundeigentum, *(sovereignty)* Kron-, Staatsgut, Domäne, *(sphere of action)* Herrschaftsbereich;
> **in the** ~ **of science** im Bereich der Wissenschaft;
> **direct** ~ Domänenbesitz; **economic** ~ Wirtschaftsraum; **eminent** ~ staatliche Oberhoheit; **national** ~ Staatsvermögen; **public** ~ *(US)* Staatseigentum; **state** ~ Staatseigentum; **to be in the public** ~ *(patent, US)* urheberrechtlich nicht mehr geschützt sein, allgemein zugänglich sein; **to come into s. one's** ~ in jds. Aufgabengebiet fallen.

domestic Hausangestellte[r];
> ~**s** Landesprodukte, inländische Erzeugnisse;
> ~ *(a.)* *(home)* häuslich, heimisch, *(inland)* inländisch, innerstaatlich, einheimisch, binnenwirtschaftlich, *(pol.)* innenpolitisch;
> ~ **activity** Binnenkonjunktur; ~ **affairs** häusliche (innere, innenpolitische) Angelegenheiten; ~ **agency** Stellenvermitt-

lung; ~ **agreement** Familienabkommen; ~ **airfare** Inlandsflugpreis; ~ **allowance** *(US)* Prämie für die Drosselung landwirtschaftlicher Produkte; ~ **animal** Haustier; ~ **appliance** Haushaltsgerät; ~ **arbitration agreement** inländischer Schiedsvertrag; ~ **article** Inlandserzeugnis; ~ **bill** Inlandswechsel; ~ **building** Wohnhaus; ~ **business** Inlandsgeschäft; ~ **business slowdown** rückläufige Binnenkonjunktur; ~ **capacity** Inlandskapazität; ~ **capital** Inlandskapital; ~ **car** Inlandswagen; ~ **cartel** Inlandskartell; ~ **commerce** Binnenhandel; ~ **consumption** Inlandsverbrauch, Binnenkonsum; ~ **corporation** *(US)* inländische Kapitalgesellschaft; ~ **correspondent** Inlandskorrespondent; ~ **court** innerstaatliches Gericht; ~ **currency** Landeswährung; ~ **customer** Inlandskunde; ~ **demand** Binnenbedarf, -nachfrage, Inlandsnachfrage; **to bring** ~ **demand up to target** für den Inlandsbedarf angesetzte Planziffern erreichen; ~ **difficulties** innenpolitische Schwierigkeiten; ~ **duties** häuslicher Pflichtenkreis; ~ **economy** Hauswirtschaft, -haltskunde; ~ **equilibrium** binnenwirtschaftliches Gleichgewicht; ~ **exchange** *(US)* Inlandswechsel; **in the** ~ **field** innenpolitisch; ~ **financing** Inlandsfinanzierung; ~ **help** Haushaltshilfe; ~ **goods** einheimische Wirtschaftsgüter; ~ **income** inländische Einkünfte; ~ **industry** Heim-, Hausindustrie, inländische Industrie; ~ **investments** Inlandsinvestitionen; ~ **issues** innenpolitische Fragen; ~ **jurisdiction** *(law of nations)* innerstaatliche Zuständigkeit; ~ **law** innerstaatliches Recht; ~ **legislation** innerstaatliche Gesetzgebung; ~ **liabilities** Inlandsverbindlichkeiten; ~ **life** häusliche Gemeinschaft, Familienleben; ~ **liquidity** Inlandsliquidität; ~ **loan** Industrieanleihe; ~ **mail** *(US)* Inlandspost; ~ **manufacture** Landesfabrikat; ~ **market** Binnen-, Inlandsmarkt; ~ **measures** binnenwirtschaftliche Maßnahmen; ~ **needs** Haushaltsbedarf, *(inland needs)* Inlandsbedarf, -bedürfnisse; ~ **news** Inlandsnachrichten; ~ **order** Inlandsauftrag; ~ **ordering** Inlandsaufträge; ~ **parcel** Inlandspaket; ~ **payment** Inlandszahlung; ~ **policy** *(insurance business)* verbundene Hausratsversicherung; ~ **policy staff** *(US)* innenpolitisches Beratergremium; ~ **postage** Inlandsporto; ~ **postal money order** *(Br.)* Inlandspostanweisung; ~ **postal service** *(Br.)* Inlandspostverkehr; ~ **price** Inlandspreis; ~ **problems** innenpolitische Probleme; ~ **proceedings** Verfahren in familienrechtlichen Angelegenheiten; ~ **producer** Inlandserzeuger; ~ **product** Inlandsprodukt; ~ **production** Inlandsproduktion; ~ **purposes** häusliche Zwecke; ~ **quarrels** innenpolitische Auseinandersetzungen; ~ **rates** *(post, Br.)* Inlandspostgebühren; ~ **recession** Inlandsrezession; ~ **relations** Familienbeziehungen; ~ **relations law** *(US)* Familienrecht; ~ **remedies** innerstaatliche Rechtshilfe; ~ **route** Inlandsstrecke; ~ **safety** innere Sicherheit; ~ **sales** Inlandsabsatz; ~ **scene** Familienszene; ~ **science** Hauswirtschaftslehre; ~ **science college** Haushaltsschule; ~ **servant** Hausangestellte[r], Raumpflegerin; ~ **service** Raumpflege, *(post)* Inlandsdienst; ~ **shelter** eigener Luftschutzkeller; ~ **staff** Hauspersonal; ~ **state of business** Binnenkonjunktur; ~ **struggle** innenpolitische Auseinandersetzungen; ~ **system** Heimindustrie; ~ **telegram** *(Br.)* Inlandstelegramm; ~ **trade** Binnenhandel; ~ **traveller's letter of credit** *(US)* Inlandsreisekreditbrief; ~ **trouble** häuslicher Ärger; ~ **trunk route** inländische Hauptfluglinie; ~ **turnover** Inlandsumsatz; **for** ~ **use** für den Eigenbedarf; ~ **value** Inlandswert; ~ **violence** Hausfriedensbruch; ~ **warfare** Bürgerkrieg; ~ **workers** inländische Arbeitskräfte; ~ **workshop** Heimarbeitsbetrieb.

domesticate *(v.)* *(naturalize)* naturalisieren, einbürgern, an häusliches Leben gewöhnen, zu Haustieren machen;
> ~ **a foreign custom** ausländische Sitte einbürgern; ~ **a word** Fremdwort in die Landessprache aufnehmen.

domestication Gewöhnung an häusliches Leben, *(naturalization)* Einbürgerung.

domicile *(bill of exchange)* Zahlungsadresse, -ort, Zahlstelle, Domizil[ort], *(dwelling)* Wohnung, *(residence)* [Wohn]sitz, Aufenthalts-, Wohnort;
> **commercial** ~ Wohnsitz der gewerblichen Niederlassung; **de facto** ~ faktischer Wohnsitz; **derived** ~ abgeleiteter Wohnsitz; **domestic** ~ örtlicher Wohnsitz; **elected** ~ gewillkürter Wohnsitz; **foreign** ~ Auslandswohnsitz; **legal** ~ gesetzlicher Wohnsitz, Gerichtsstand; **matrimonial** ~ gemeinsamer ehelicher Wohnsitz; **municipal** ~ Wohnsitz in einer Gemeinde; **natural** ~ Geburtswohnsitz; **necessary** ~ gesetzlich vorgeschriebener Wohnsitz; **quasi-national** ~ erforderlicher Daueraufenthalt;
> ~ **of choice** gewillkürter Wohnsitz; ~ **of a corporation** Sitz der gewerblichen Niederlassung; ~ **of dependence** *(Br.)* abgeleiteter Wohnsitz; ~ **by operation of law** gesetzlicher Wohnsitz; ~ **of origin** *(contract)* Erfüllungsort; ~ **of succession** Nachlaßwohnsitz;

~ *(v.) (bill of exchange)* domizilieren, zahlbar stellen, *(settle)* Wohnsitz begründen (haben), sich niederlassen (ansässig machen);
to abandon one's ~ seinen Wohnsitz aufgeben; **to be governed by the law of** ~ nach dem Recht des Wohnsitzes beurteilt werden; **to change one's** ~ seinen Wohnsitz verlegen; **to elect** ~ **at a place** Wohnsitz begründen; **to establish a** ~ Wohnsitz begründen; **to take up one's** ~ sich niederlassen.
domiciled wohnhaft, eingesessen, beheimatet, ansässig;
~ **in** mit Wohnsitz in; **not** ~ ohne Domizilangabe;
to be ~ **abroad** im Ausland ansässig sein;
~ **acceptance** Domizilakzept; ~ **bill** Domizilwechsel.
domiciliary den Wohnsitz betreffend;
~ **administration** Nachlaßverwaltung am Wohnsitz des Erblassers; ~ **permit** Aufenthaltserlaubnis; ~ **right** Hausrecht; ~ **visit** [polizeiliche] Haussuchung.
domiciliate *(v.) (bill)* domizilieren, zahlbar stellen.
domiciliated bill Domizilwechsel.
domiciliation Zahlbarstellung, Domizilangabe;
~ **provision** Domizilgebühr.
dominance [Vor]herrschaft, Macht, Einfluß.
dominant herrschend, dominierend;
~ **estate** herrschendes Grundstück; ~ **factor** entscheidender Faktor; ~ **leader** Führerpersönlichkeit; ~ **partner in a business** ausschlaggebender Geschäftspartner; ~ **position** beherrschende (dominierende) Position (Stellung); ~ **tenement** *(law)* herrschendes Grundstück.
dominate *(v.)* beherrschen, starken Einfluß ausüben, dominieren;
~ **the market** Markt beherrschen; ~ **numerically** zahlenmäßig beherrschen; ~ **[over] others by force of character** dominierende Stellung innehaben; ~ **over people** über ein Volk herrschen; ~ **the town** *(fortress)* Stadt beherrschen, dominierende Lage über eine Stadt einnehmen.
domination Beherrschen, Vorherrschen;
foreign ~ Fremdherrschaft;
~ **of the market** Marktbeherrschung; ~ **of program(me) ownership** Beherrschung der Programmzeiten; ~ **of the world** Weltherrschaft.
domineer *(v.)* tyrannisieren, despotisch herrschen.
domineering character despotischer Charakter.
dominical rest Sonntagsruhe.
dominion Macht, Herrschaft, Regierungsgewalt, *(territory)* Herrschaftsgebiet, Hoheitsrecht, -gebiet, Dominium;
to be under s. one's ~ in jds. Herrschaftsbereich leben.
domino *(masquerade costume)* Domino;
~! Schluß! Aus!;
~ **effect** *(pol.)* Dominowirkung, -effekt; ~ **theory** *(pol.)* Dominotheorie.
donate *(v.)* Schenkung machen, schenken, stiften.
donated | stock unentgeltlich zur Verfügung gestellte Aktien, *(US)* zurückgegebene Gründeraktien; ~ **surplus** *(US)* Portefeuille eigener Aktien.
donation unentgeltliche Zuwendung, Schenkung, [Geld]spende, Stiftung, *(blood)* Blutspende, *(deed of)* Schenkungsurkunde, *(capital stock)* Aktienschenkung;
by way of ~ schenkungsweise;
charitable ~ mildtätige Stiftung; **gratuitous** ~ unentgeltliche Schenkung; **onerous** ~ mit einer Auflage verbundene Schenkung; **political** ~ Spende für politische Zwecke; **remunerative** ~ Schenkung in Anerkennung geleisteter Dienste;
covenanted ~**s to charity** verbriefte Spenden für wohltätige Zwecke; ~ **mortis causa** Schenkung von Todes wegen; ~ **to the Red Cross** Spende für das Rote Kreuz; ~**s to the fund of refugees** Zuwendungen an den Flüchtlingsfonds; ~ **in kind** Sachspende; ~ **of real estate** Grundstücksschenkung; ~ **inter vivos** Schenkung unter Lebenden;
to make a ~ **of s. th. to s. o.** jem. etw. zum Geschenk machen; **to revoke a** ~ Schenkung widerrufen; **to solicit** ~**s** um Spenden bitten;
deductible ~ **costs** abzugsfähiger Schenkungsaufwand; ~ **lands** Landschenkung.
donator Schenker, Spender.
donatory *(Br.)* Schenkungsempfänger.
done geschehen, ausgefertigt, *(paid)* bezahlt, *(stock exchange)* gehandelt;
~ **brown** *(coll.)* völlig über den Löffel barbiert; ~ **in duplicate** in zweifacher Ausfertigung; ~ **out of one's money** um sein Geld betrogen; ~ **up** *(coll.)* erschöpft, kaputt; ~ **with** *(coll.)* erledigt;
to feel absolutely ~ **in** sich total betrogen fühlen; **to have** ~ **with politics** von der Politik die Nase voll haben.

donee Schenkungsempfänger, Beschenkter, *(appointor)* Vollmachtnehmer, -ausübender;
~ **country** Empfängerland.
donkey Esel, *(fig.)* Dummkopf;
~ **boiler** Hilfskessel; ~**'s breakfast** Strohsack; **for** ~**'s years** *(Br., fam.)* seit einer Ewigkeit.
donkeywork Kuli-, Routinearbeit.
donor Geber, Schenker, Stifter, Spender, *(med.)* Blutspender, *(party conferring power)* Treugeber, Vollmachtgeber;
blood ~ Blutspender;
~ **country** Geberland;
~ **of a power of appointment** Vollmachtgeber.
doodle Gekritzel.
doom Schicksal, Los, *(fig.)* Gerichtstag;
~ *(v.)* **to death** zum Tode verurteilen;
to send s. o. to his ~ j. in den Tod schicken; **to spell the** ~ Todesurteil bedeuten;
~ **prophet** Weltuntergangsprophet.
doomsday jüngstes Gericht;
to put off s. th. till ~ etw. bis zum St. Nimmerleinstag verschieben;
~ **machine** *(Kahn)* Weltuntergangsmaschine.
door Tür, *(mar.)* Luke;
at death's ~ an der Schwelle des Todes; **from** ~ **to** ~ von Haus zu Haus; **next** ~ nebenan, *(fig.)* beinahe, fast; **out of** ~**s** draußen, außerhalb; **packed to the** ~**s** voll besetzt; **within** ~**s** im Hause;
back ~ Hintertür; **communicating** ~ Verbindungstür; **entrance (front)** ~ Eingangstür; **fire** ~ feuerfeste Tür; **street** ~ Haustür; **three** ~**s away** drei Häuser weiter, gleich nebenan; ~ **to success** Erfolgsleiter;
to answer the ~ Tür öffnen; **to bang the** ~ **on s. th.** etw. unmöglich machen; **to be next** ~ **to a miracle** an ein Wunder grenzen; **to close the** ~**s** *(banking)* Schalter schließen, Zahlungen einstellen; **to close the** ~ **upon any discussion** jede weitere Diskussion unmöglich machen; **to close the** ~ **against an agreement upon disarmament** sich gegen ein Abrüstungsabkommen aussprechen; **to force an open** ~ offene Türen einrennen; **to keep within** ~**s** zu Hause bleiben; **to lay s. th. at s. one's** ~ jem. die Verantwortung für etw. zuschieben; **to lay a charge at s. one's** ~ jem. die Schuld in die Schuhe schieben; **to lay a crime at s. one else's** ~ einem Dritten ein Verbrechen anlasten; **to open a** ~ **to abuses** dem Mißbrauch Tür und Tor öffnen; **to open a** ~ **to agreements on international affairs** Politik der offenen Tür betreiben; **to open a** ~ **to a settlement** Vergleich ermöglichen; **to pay for articles at the** ~ Waren bei [der] Lieferung bezahlen; **to show s. o. the** ~ j. hinausweisen; **to take one's meals out of** ~**s** außerhalb speisen; **to turn s. o. from the** ~ j. von der Schwelle weisen;
~ **bell** Türglocke, -klingel; ~ **chain** Sicherheitskette; ~ **key** Hausschlüssel; ~ **key child** Schlüsselkind; ~ **lock** Türschloß; ~ **mat** Abtreter; ~ **money** Eintritts-, Einlaßgeld, Eintrittsgebühr; ~ **panel** *(car)* Türverkleidung; ~ **spring** automatischer Türschließer.
door-to-door | market Hausverkauf; ~ **pickup and delivery** *(carrier)* Zustellung von Haus zu Haus; ~ **salesman (seller)** Hausierer, Vertreter, Direktverkäufer; ~ **selling** Direkt-, Hausverkauf, Verkauf durch Vertreter; ~ **service** bahnamtlicher Rollfuhrdienst; ~ **transport** Beförderung von Haus zu Haus.
doorkeeper, doorman *(US)* Pförtner, Hausmeister, Portier.
doorplate Türschild.
doorstep | salesman Hausierer, Wandergewerbetreibender; ~ **trading** Hausierhandel, Wandergewerbe.
doorway Türeingang.
dope *(addict, US sl.)* Rauschgiftsüchtiger, *(advertising)* Waschzettel, *(narcotic, sl.)* Rauschgift, Droge;
inside ~ *(sl.)* vertrauliche [Presse]information;
~ *(v.)* Aufputschmittel geben, *(take drugs)* Rauschgift nehmen, *(petrol)* mit einem Zusatzmittel versehen;
~ **s. o.** *(fig, US sl.)* j. übers Ohr hauen; ~ **out** ausfindig machen; ~ **out a plan** Plan ausarbeiten;
~ **addict (fiend)** Rauschgiftsüchtiger; ~ **merchant (pedlar, seller)** Rauschgifthändler; ~ **peddling (running, selling)** Rauschgifthandel; ~ **ring** Rauschgiftbande; ~ **smuggling** Rauschgiftschmuggel.
doper Rauschgifthändler.
dormant schlummernd, Geheim, *(idle)* ungebraucht, unbenutzt, brachliegend, tot, *(inactive)* still;
to lie ~ *(interest)* unverzinslich sein, sich nicht verzinsen, *(nonappearance)* [vor Gericht] nicht erscheinen, Termin versäumen;

~ **account** umsatzloses Konto; ~ **balance** ungenutzter Saldo; ~ **capital** totes Kapital; ~ **claim** noch unentschiedener Anspruch, nicht durchgesetzte Forderung; ~ **disease** noch nicht ausgebrochene Krankheit; ~ **execution** zurückgestellter Pfändungsauftrag; ~ **facilities** entwicklungsfähige Anlagen; ~ **funds** unverzinsliche Gelder; ~ **judgment** verjährtes Urteil; ~ **law** unanwendbar gewordenes Gesetz; ~ **money** totes Kapital; ~ **partner** stiller Teilhaber; ~ **partnership** stille Gesellschaft; ~ **stock** Ladenhüter; ~ **title** ruhender Rechtsanspruch; ~ **warrant** Blankovollmacht.

dormer window Gaube, Mansardenfenster.

dormitory *(US)* Studentenheim, Wohnheim, *(Br.)* Schlafsaal; ~ **suburb (town)** *(US)* Wohnvorort, Schlafstadt.

dos-a-dos accreditif *(US)* Gegenakkreditiv.

dosage Dosierung, Dose.

dose Dosis, Portion, kleine Menge, *(fig.)* bittere Pille; lethal ~ tödliche Dosierung; ~ *(v.)* dosieren, Dosis verschreiben, *(take one's medicine)* Medizin nehmen, Arznei schlucken; **to give s. o. a ~ of flattery** jem. die Schmeicheleien in Dosen verabreichen.

dosimeter Meßgerät für Strahlenschäden.

doss house *(sl.)* Obdachlosenasyl.

dossier Akten[heft], urkundliche Unterlagen, *(information)* Personalakte, Dossier.

dossman *(Br., sl.)* Herbergsvater.

dot Pünktchen, Tüpfelchen, *(dowry)* Mitgift, *(Morse code)* Punkt; **on the ~** *(coll.)* auf die Sekunde; **to a ~** bis aufs I-Tüpfelchen; **correct to a ~** äußerst penibel; ~ *(v.)* punktieren; ~ **an area** sich dicht an dicht in einem Gebiet befinden; ~ **articles of account** Rechnungsposten abstreichen; ~ **and carry one** äußerst methodisch vorgehen, ein Steinchen zum anderen fügen; ~ **down** rasch notieren; ~ **and go one** *(fig.)* auf Krücken gehen, *(coll.)* stoßweise vorankommen; ~ **the i's and cross the t's** peinlich genau (äußerst pingelig) sein; **to arrive on the ~** auf die Sekunde pünktlich kommen; **to pay on the ~** auf den Tisch des Hauses zahlen.

dotage Altersschwäche, Senilität; **to be in one's ~** senil sein.

dotal eingebracht; ~ **property** Mitgift.

dotation *(dowry)* Aussteuer, *(endowment)* Dotierung, Stiftung.

dotted punktiert; ~ **about** verstreut; ~ **with cottages** mit Landhäusern übersät; ~ **frame** punktierter Rand; ~ **line** gestrichelte (punktierte) Linie, Punktlinie; **to sign on the ~ line** *(fig.)* kritiklos unterschreiben.

dotty schwankend, unsicher; **to be ~ on one's legs** auf schwachen Beinen stehen.

double Doppel, Dublette, *(copy)* Kopie, Abschrift, *(duplicate)* Duplikat, *(counterpart)* Doppelgänger, *(film)* Double, *(horse racing)* Doppelwette, *(mil.)* Laufschritt; ~ *(v.)* verdoppeln, *(print.)* doppelt setzen; ~ **one's income** sein Einkommen verdoppeln; ~ **a part** Rolle mit übernehmen; ~ **one's stake** seinen Einsatz verdoppeln; ~ **a sum** Summe verdoppeln; ~ **itself in time** sich mit der Zeit verdoppeln; ~ **up** zusammenfalten, kniffen; ~ **up with pain** sich vor Schmerzen krümmen; **to give s. o. the ~** jem. durch die Lappen gehen; **to pay ~ the value** doppelten Wert bezahlen; **to play ~ or quits** alles riskieren; ~ *(a.)* doppelt, zweifach; ~ **accident benefit** *(Br.)* **(indemnity, US)** doppelte Leistung bei Unfalltod; ~ **account system** doppelte Buchführung; ~ **act** *(entertainers)* Doppelvorführung; ~ **agent** Doppelagent; ~ **the amount** doppelter Betrag; ~ **assessment** Doppelveranlagung; ~ **back pay** um das Doppelte erhöhter Lohnrückstand; ~ **bed** Doppelbett; ~-**bedded** zweibettig; ~ **bedroom** Zweibettzimmer; ~ **beer** Bock-, Starkbier; ~-**bill** *(v.)* doppelte Spesen in Rechnung stellen; ~-**billing technique** System der doppelten Rechnungsausstellung; ~ **bond** *(Scot. law)* Schuldurkunde mit festgelegter Vertragsstrafe; ~ **bottom** doppelter Boden, *(coll.)* Preissturz, *(US, stock exchange)* äußerster Tiefstand; ~ **budget** außerordentlicher Haushalt; ~ **card** *(US)* Postkarte mit Rückantwort; ~-**check** *(v.)* doppelt überprüfen; ~ **claim** Doppelanspruch; ~-**coated paper** zweifach gestrichenes Kunstdruckpapier; ~ **column** Spalte; ~-**column type area** zweispaltiger Satz; ~ **costs** Kosten zum anderthalbfachen Satz; ~ **creditor** doppelt gesicherter Gläubiger; ~ **cropping** Doppelwirtschaft;

~-**cross** *(v.)* betrügen, täuschen, hintergehen; ~ **damages** doppelt zuerkannter Schadensersatz; ~ **dealer** Betrüger, Achselträger; ~ **dealing** Doppelzüngigkeit, Übers-Ohr-Hauen; ~-**decked** *(bus)* zweistöckig; ~-**decker** *(bus)* zweistöckiger Bus; ~-**declining balance depreciation** geometrisch degressive Abschreibung; ~-**declutch** *(v.)* zweimal kuppeln; ~ **door** Doppeltür; ~-**Dutch** Kauderwelsch, böhmische Dörfer; **to talk ~ Dutch** dummen Unsinn reden; ~-**dyed villain** Erzgauner; ~-**edged** *(fig.)* zweischneidig; ~ **earner** Doppelverdiener; ~ **entry** Doppeleintrag; ~-**entry bookkeeping** doppelte Buchführung; ~ **exposure** Doppelbelichtung; ~-**faced** unaufrichtig; ~ **feature program(me)** Programm mit zwei Hauptfilmen; **to be well into ~ figures** gut und gern zweistellige Zahlen erreichen; ~-**fronted sign** doppelseitige Tafel; **to play a ~ game** Doppelspiel treiben; ~ **glazing** Doppelverglasung; ~-**headed train** Zug mit zwei Lokomotiven; ~ **house** Doppelhaus; ~ **indemnity** *(insurance, US)* doppelte Versicherungssumme bei Unfalltod; ~ **indemnity clause** *(US)* Doppelversicherungs-, Unfallzusatzversicherungsklausel; ~ **insurance** Doppelversicherung; ~ **issue** Doppelheft; ~ **jeopardy** zweimalige Anklage wegen des gleichen Vergehens; ~ **journey** Hin- und Rückfahrt; ~-**leaded** doppelt durchschossen; ~ **letter** Brief mit doppeltem Porto; ~ **liability** Nachschußpflicht [in gleicher Höhe], *(US, bank stock)* doppelte Haftung von Bankaktionären; **to lead a ~ life** Doppelleben führen; ~ **line** zweigleisige Bahn; ~-**name paper** *(US)* Wechsel mit zwei Unterschriften; ~ **option** Stellagegeschäft, Doppelprämie; ~ **page** Doppelseite; ~-**page spread** doppelseitige (zweiseitige) Anzeige; ~-**park** *(v.)* neben einem abgestellten Wagen parken; ~ **patenting** Doppelpatentierung; ~ **pay** Doppelverdienst; ~ **pleading** maßgebende Anspruchsbegründung; ~ **postcard** Antwortkarte; ~ **price** *(stock exchange)* An- und Verkaufskurs; ~ **rate** *(advertisement)* doppelter Preis; **on ~ receipt** gegen doppelten Schein; ~ **room** Doppelzimmer; ~ **sampling** zweistufiges Stichprobenverfahren; ~ **security** zweifache Sicherheit; **to perform a ~ service** zweierlei Zwecken dienen; ~ **shift** Doppelschicht; ~-**spaced** *(typewriter)* weitzeilig; ~ **spread** zweiseitige Anzeige; ~ **standard** Doppelwährung, Bimetallismus, *(fig.)* zweierlei Maßstab, doppelter Moralkodex; ~-**storied (-storeyed,** *Br.)* zweistöckig; ~-**system sound recording** getrennte Bild- und Tonaufnahme; ~ **take** *(fig.)* Spätzündung; ~ **talk** zweideutige Redeweise; **to claim ~-tax relief** *(Br.)* Vergünstigungen aus dem Doppelbesteuerungsabkommen in Anspruch nehmen; ~-**tax rule** versteuerte Einnahmen auf schon versteuerte Umsätze; ~ **taxation** Doppelbesteuerung; ~-**taxation agreement** Doppelbesteuerungsabkommen; ~-**taxation loopholes** Lücken im Doppelbesteuerungsabkommen; ~-**taxation relief** *(Br.)* steuerliche Anrechnung im Ausland gezahlter Steuern; ~ **time** Lohnzuschlag [für Nacht-, Feiertagsarbeit]; ~ **track** Doppelgleis; ~-**track[ed]** doppel-, zweigleisig, -spurig; ~ **value** *(landlord and tenant, Br.)* doppelte Nutzungsentschädigung bei Räumungsverzug; ~ **waste** *(tenant bound to repair)* doppelte Substanzverringerung; ~ **wedding** Doppelhochzeit; ~ **will** Berliner Testament.

doublet *(print.)* Dublette, *(radio)* Dipolantenne.

doubling Verdopplung, *(trick)* Fluch, Kniff, Trick, Winkelzug; ~ **of sales** *(turnover)* Umsatzverdoppelung.

doubt Zweifel, Bedenken, Besorgnis; reasonable ~ berechtigter Zweifel; ~ *(v.)* **s. one's abilities** jds. Fähigkeiten bezweifeln; ~ **the truth of a report** Wahrheit eines Berichtes anzweifeln; **to give s. o. the benefit of the ~** j. im Zweifelsfall für unschuldig erklären; **to have some ~s left** noch Bedenken hegen; **to leave s. o. in no ~ about s. th.** j. über etw. nicht im Unklaren lassen; **to dispel ~s** Zweifel beseitigen; **to make no ~** keinen Zweifel hegen, sicher sein; **to raise ~s** Bedenken erregen.

doubtful zweifelhaft, bedenklich, dubios, unsicher; ~ **accounts** dubiose Forderungen, Dubiose, ~ **character** fragwürdiger Charakter; ~ **claim** rechtlich unsicherer Anspruch; ~ **debts, notes and accounts** *(Br.)* dubiose Forderungen; ~ **debts provision** Rückstellung für Dubiosen; ~ **neighbo(u)rhood** anrüchige Nachbarschaft; ~ **title** zweifelhafter Rechtstitel.

dough *(sl., US)* Draht, Zaster, Pinkepinke, Moneten.

doughboy *(US)* Landser.

doughnut tire *(US sl.)* großer Ballonreifen.

dove *(pol.)* Taube; ~**s** *(pol.)* Friedenspartei; ~ **of peace** Friedenstaube; ~ **wing** Anhänger friedlicher Politik.

dovecote Taubenschlag; **to flutter the ~** Spießbürger erschrecken.

dovetail *(v.)* **with s. one's policy** sich nahtlos jds. Politik anpassen.
Dow Jones-Index *(US)* Aktienindex.
dowager *(Br.)* Witwe.
dower *(US)* Nießbrauchrecht der Witwe, Witwenteil, Witwenleibgedinge, Wittumsrecht;
~ **by custom** Witwennießbrauch nach Ortsgebrauch;
~ *(v.) (daughter)* Mitgift aussetzen, *(widow)* Leibgedinge aussetzen;
~ **a daughter** Tochter ausstatten;
~ **interest** Witwenanteil.
dowerless ohne Mitgift.
down Abwärtsbewegung, *(grudge)* Groll, *(low state)* unangenehmer Zustand;
~ *(a.)* nach unten, abwärts, *(Br.)* nicht in London, *(condition of humility)* in elenden Verhältnissen lebend, heruntergekommen, *(into the city, US)* nach dem Geschäftsviertel zu, *(goods)* wenig gefragt, *(journalism)* im Druck, zum Druck gegeben, *(low)* in bescheidenen Verhältnissen, in geringer Stellung, *(prices)* heruntergegangen, gefallen, niedrig, billiger, *(directed to the terminal)* zur Endstation hin, *(tyres)* platt, *(river)* flußabwärts, *(train, Br.)* von London abfahrend, *(university, Br.)* nicht an der Universität;
cash ~ *(money)* gegen bar, bar auf den Tisch; **nothing** ~ keine Anzahlung; **put** ~ [im Testament] bedacht; **written** ~ verzeichnet, gebucht;
~ **in the country** auf dem Lande, in der Provinz; ~ **to date** zeitgemäß modern; ~**-to-earth** ernüchternd; ~ **to the ground** *(coll.)* perfekt, ganz und gar; ~ **to the last man** bis zum letzten Mann; ~**-the-line** auf der ganzen Linie, rückhaltlos, vorbehaltlos; ~ **in the mouth** niedergedrückt, -geschlagen, deprimiert; ~**-and-out** geld- und arbeitslos; ~ **with pneumonia** durch eine Lungenentzündung außer Gefecht gesetzt; ~ **a stream** stromabwärts; ~ **to our times** bis auf die Gegenwart;
~ *(v.)* **a plane** Flugzeug landen; ~ **tools** *(Br.)* Arbeit niederlegen, streiken;
to be ~ [im Preise] heruntergegangen sein, *(river)* wieder normale Wasserhöhe haben, *(shares)* niedrig stehen, *(telephone lines)* gestört sein; **to be** ~ **for £ 100** hundert Pfund schulden; **to be** ~ **on s. o.** über j. herfallen, j. auf dem Kieker haben; **to be** ~ **5 degrees** um fünf Punkte gefallen sein; **to be** ~ **in the dumps** *(fam.)* Trübsal blasen; **to be** ~ **with flu** wegen Grippe das Bett hüten müssen; **to be** ~ **on s. o. like a hammer** j. wie ein Verrückter angreifen; **to be** ~ **at the heel** völlig abgerissen sein; **to be** ~ **in the hips** sich lausig fühlen; **to be** ~ **for Monday** für Montag angesetzt sein; **to be** ~ **and out** auf dem letzten Loch pfeifen; **to be** ~ **for the third reading** zur dritten Lesung anstehen; **to be** ~ **on one's uppers** *(fam.)* in bedrängter Lage sein; **to bring** ~ **an aeroplane** Flugzeug abschießen; **to bring** ~ **the prices** Preissenkung bewirken; **to bring** ~ **s. one's pride** jds. Stolz demütigen; **to close** ~ **a factory because of steel shortage** Fabrik wegen Stahlmangels stillegen; **to come** ~ **on s. o.** sich j. richtig vornehmen; **to come** ~ **to earth** in die Wirklichkeit zurückkehren; **to come** ~ **on one's luck** Pech gehabt haben; **to come** ~ **from Oxford** Abschlußexamen in Oxford ablegen; **to come** ~ **in the world** sozial absinken; **to feel** ~ **in spirits** deprimiert sein; **to get** ~ **from a bus** aus einem Bus aussteigen; **to get** ~ **to work** sich an die Arbeit machen; **to go** ~ *(Br.)* London verlassen, *(prices)* weichen, heruntergehen, wohlfeiler werden, *(ship)* untergehen, sinken, *(story)* geglaubt werden, *(student, Br.)* in die Ferien gehen, *(touch on)* erfolgreich sein; **to go** ~ **to the country** *(Br.)* aufs Land fahren; **to haul** ~ **a flag** Flagge einziehen; **to have a** ~ **on s. o.** j. nicht leiden können; **to have heard nothing** ~ **to date** bis heute nichts gehört haben; **to have s. o.** ~ **in one's will for $ 10.000** jem. in seinem Testament 10.000,- Dollar vermachen; **to have come** ~ **in the world** bessere Tage gesehen haben; **to hiss** ~ auszischen; **to hunt s. o.** ~ j. stellen; **to lay** ~ **one's arms** Waffen niederlegen; **to let a ship go** ~ **the wind** Schiff seinem Schicksal überlassen; **to mark [the prices of] goods** ~ Waren billiger notieren; **to offer** ~ unterbieten; **to pay** ~ sofort bezahlen; **to put s. one's name** ~ **for £ 1** jem. als wohltätigen Spender für 1 Pfund in eine Liste eintragen; **to see s. o.** ~ **for a speech** j. als Redner aufgeführt sehen; **to send s. o.** ~ *(Br.)* j. relegieren; **to settle** ~ **to work** sich an die Arbeit machen; **to shoot** ~ **an aeroplane** Flugzeug abschießen; **to take** ~ zu Papier bringen; **to take** ~ **a letter** Brief stenografisch aufnehmen; **to write** ~ niederschreiben;
~ **cycle** rückläufiger Konjunkturzyklus; ~**-to-earth** wirklichkeitsbezogen; ~**-faced** mit Sorgenfalten; ~ **lead** Antennenzuführung; ~ **line** *(US)* im Stadtzentrum fahrende Linie; ~ **money** Bargeld; ~**-and-outer** restlos Gebrochener; ~ **payment** *(Br.)* Bar-, Sofortzahlung, *(US, instalment)* Anzahlung[sbetrag]; **to**

make a ~ **payment** *(US)* anzahlen, Anzahlung leisten; ~ **payment requirements** *(US)* Anzahlungsbedingungen; ~ **period** *(factory)* Stilliegen; ~ **platform** *(London)* Bahnsteig für abgehende Züge, *(US)* Bahnsteig für ins Stadtzentrum fahrende Züge; ~ **time** *(factory, US)* betrieblich bedingte Verlustzeit; ~**-tools strike** *(Br.)* Arbeitsniederlegung; ~ **train** *(Br.)* Provinzzug, *(US)* stadteinwärts fahrender Zug; ~ **trip** *(US sl.)* Reise.
downcome plötzlicher Abstieg, Niedergang, Sturz.
downdrag Niedergang.
downfall Ruin, Niedergang, *(pol.)* Untergang, Sturz, Fall;
~ **of a fortress** Fall einer Festung.
downgrade *(fig.)* Niedergang, *(road)* Gefälle;
on the ~ auf dem absteigenden Ast;
~ *(v.)* in eine niedrigere Tarifgruppe einstufen, *(classify)* Geheimhaltungsstufe herabsetzen, *(mil.)* degradieren;
~ **s. o.** jem. eine Niederlage beibringen;
to be on the ~ *(business)* schlecht gehen, heruntergekommen sein, *(price)* fallen, sinken.
downgrading niedrigere Tarifeinstellung, *(classification)* Herabsetzung der Geheimhaltungsstufe, *(mil.)* Degradierung;
~ **of property** niedrigere Vermögenseinstufung.
downhill abwärts;
to go ~ *(fig.)* immer tiefer fallen.
Downing Street Regierung;
to take into ~ *(Br.)* ins Kabinett nehmen.
downing tools Arbeitsniederlegung.
downpay *(US)* Anzahlung.
downpipe Abflußrohr.
downpoint Herabsetzung der Punktzahl;
~ *(v.) (rationing)* Punktzahl herabsetzen.
downpour Platzregen.
downright offen, geradeheraus, *(absolute)* hundertprozentig;
to refuse ~ glatt ablehnen;
~ **language** unzweideutige Sprache; ~ **nonsense** glatter (kompletter) Unsinn; ~ **lie** glatte Lüge; ~ **no** kategorisches Nein; ~ **truth** reine Wahrheit.
downshift *(gear)* Herunterschalten;
~ **in rates** Tarifsenkung;
~ *(v.) (gear)* herunterschalten.
downside | block auf die Kurse drückendes Aktienpaket; ~ **potential** Abschwächungstendenzen; ~ **risk** Verlustrisiko.
downslope, to be on a sich in einer Abwärtsbewegung befinden.
downstage im Vordergrund der Bühne.
downstairs ein Stockwerk tiefer, im Souterrain;
~ **merger** Fusion der Mutter- mit der Tochtergesellschaft; ~ **room** unteres Zimmer.
downstream strom-, flußabwärts;
~ **industries** nachgelagerte Industrien; ~ **investment** Investitionen in nachgelagerte Produktionen, Wiederanlage [von Ölgeldern]; ~ **operations** Transaktionen zur Wiederanlage von Ölgeldern.
downswing, cyclical Konjunkturabschwung;
to be on a ~ *(sales)* Umsatz-, Absatzrückgang aufweisen.
downtime *(US)* betrieblich bedingte Verlustzeit, *(computer)* Ausfallzeit.
downtown *(US)* Alt-, Innenstadt, Stadtmitte, Geschäftszentrum, -viertel;
~ *(a.)* im Geschäftsviertel gelegen, in der Innenstadt;
to go ~ in die Stadt gehen;
~ **area** Geschäftsgegend; ~ **district** Geschäftsgegend; ~ **hotel** im Stadtzentrum (zentral) gelegenes Hotel; ~ **office** Stadtbüro; ~ **ticket office** zentral gelegenes Reisebüro; ~ **property** zentral gelegenes Grundstück; ~ **sales** Gesamtumsatz der im Stadtzentrum gelegenen Geschäfte; ~ **store** in der Hauptgeschäftsgegend gelegenes Geschäft; ~ **traffic** Verkehr im Stadtzentrum.
downtrend Abwärtsbewegung, Konjunkturrückgang;
~ **of business** Konjunkturrückgang; ~ **in economic activity** konjunkturelle Talfahrt; ~ **of exports** Exportabschwächung; ~ **in interest rates** rückwärtige Entwicklung des Zinsgefälles; ~ **in new orders** Auftragsrückgang.
downturn *(business activity)* Abwärtsbewegung, Geschäftsrückgang, Flaute, Konjunkturabschwächung;
abrupt ~ plötzliches Nachlassen der Konjunktur; **business (economic)** ~ rückläufige Konjunkturbewegung, konjunkturelle Abwärtsbewegung;
~ **in manufacturing** Produktionsrückgang; ~ **in the market** rückläufige Marktbewegung; ~ **in prices** rückläufige Preisentwicklung.
downward abwärts, *(economy)* rückgängig, rückläufig, *(fig.)* abwärts, bergab, zugrunde;

to be ~ rückläufig sein; **to look** ~ im Preis sinken;
~ **business trend** Abschwächung der Konjunktur; ~ **movement** Rückgang, Abwärtsbewegung, rückläufige Bewegung, rückgängige Tendenz; ~ **movement of prices** rückläufige Preisbewegung (Kursentwicklung); **to end in a** ~ **note** in einer Abwärtsbewegung ausklingen; ~ **phase** rückläufige Konjunkturphase, Abschwungphase; **to be on the** ~ **path** sich im Niedergang befinden, seinem Ruin zustreben; **to exert cumulative** ~ **pressure on economic activity** sich in kumulierender Weise negativ auf die Konjunkturentwicklung auswirken; ~ **swing** Konjunkturabschwung; ~ **tendency** Baisse, fallende (rückgängige) Tendenz; ~ **tendency in interest rates** Zinssenkungstendenz; ~ **trend** rückläufige Tendenz, Konjunkturabschwächung, -rückgang; ~ **trend in subscription** Abonnentenschwund; **to show a** ~ **trend of economic activity** konjunkturelle Abschwächungen erfahren.

downwash Abwind.
downway *(law of nations)* Talweg, *(shipping)* tiefste Schiffsrinne.
downwind Fallwind;
~ **landing** Rückenwindlandung.
dowry Aussteuer, Ausstattung, Mitgift;
to bring as a ~ als Mitgift einbringen; **to provide a girl with a** ~ Mädchen ausstatten;
~ **hunter** Mitgiftjäger; ~ **insurance** Aussteuerversicherung.
doyen Doyen.
doze *(v.)* dösen, schlummern;
~ **away the time** Zeit verträumen; ~ **off** eindösen.
dozen, by the dutzendweise;
baker's (printer's) ~ dreizehn Stück; **a round** ~ volles Dutzend;
~s **and** ~s **of times** dutzendmal;
to sell articles in sets of a ~ Waren nach dem Dutzend verkaufen; **to talk nineteen to the** ~ *(Br.)* das Blaue vom Himmel herunterschwätzen.
drab Bagatellbetrag, *(dullness)* Farblosigkeit, Eintönigkeit;
~ *(a.)* monoton, trübsinnig;
~ **earnings** geringfügige Erträgnisse; **to lead a** ~ **existence** jämmerliches Dasein führen; **to be on the** ~ **side** schlecht verdienen.
draconian measures drakonische Maßnahmen.
draft *(allowance)* Gutgewicht, *(on bank)* [Zahlungs]anweisung, *(bill of exchange)* Tratte, [trassierter] Wechsel, Handelswechsel, *(delegation)* Abordnung, *(drafted person)* Aufgebotener, Wehrdienstpflichtiger, *(draught)* Tiefgang, *(drawing of bill)* Ziehung, *(drawing of money)* Geldabhebung, *(mil., US)* Rekrutierung, Musterung, Einberufung, Zwangsaushebung, *(rough copy)* Fassung, Anlage, Entwurf, Konzept, *(selection)* Auswahl, *(sketch)* Zeichnung, Skizze;
addressed ~ angezeigte Tratte; **alternative** ~ Gegenentwurf; **amended** ~ abgeänderter Entwurf; **arrival** ~ Tratte mit beigefügten Verschiffungsdokumenten; **bank[er's]** ~ Bankscheck, -tratte, -wechsel; **clean** ~ Tratte ohne Dokumente; **demand** ~ Sichtwechsel; **documentary** ~ Dokumententratte; **first** ~ Konzept, erster Entwurf; **fixed** ~ Tratte ohne Respekttage; **house** ~ trassiert eigener Wechsel; **interest-bearing** ~ Tratte mit Zinsvermerk; **nonadvised** ~ nichtangezeigte Tratte; **preliminary** ~ Vorentwurf; ~s **receivable** *(balance sheet, US)* Debitoren aus Wechselforderungen; **presentation** ~ Sichtwechsel; **reimbursement** ~ Rembourswechsel; **rough** ~ Vorentwurf; **sight** ~ Sichttratte; **three months'** ~ Dreimonatstratte; **time** ~ Zeit-, Nachsichtwechsel; **universal** ~ allgemeine Wehrpflicht;
~ **for a parliamentary bill** Gesetzentwurf; **rough** ~ **of a contract** Vertragsentwurf; ~ **after date** nach dato zahlbar gestellter Wechsel; ~s **and cheques in hand** *(Br., balance sheet)* Wechsel- und Scheckbestand; ~ **of a letter** Entwurf eines Briefes, Briefentwurf; ~ **of a resolution** Entschließungsentwurf; **serious** ~ **on national resources** bedenkliche Beanspruchung des Staatsvermögens; ~ **[payable] at sight** Sichttratte, -wechsel; ~ **for a speech** Entwurf für eine Rede, Redeentwurf;
~ *(v.)* [Schriftstück] aufsetzen, entwerfen, verfassen, konzipieren, formulieren, *(detach troops)* abkommandieren, abstellen, detachieren, *(US mil.)* einziehen, zum Heeresdienst einberufen, zwangsausheben;
~ **an age group** *(mil., US)* Jahrgang einziehen; ~ **a [parliamentary] bill** Gesetzentwurf ausarbeiten; ~ **as enlisted man** *(US)* zur Bundeswehr einziehen; ~ **in a new management** neue Geschäftsleitung einsetzen; ~ **s. o. as vice-presidential candidate** j. zur Wahl als Vizepräsident vorschlagen;
to advise a ~ Tratte ankündigen (avisieren); **to give a** ~ **due protection** Tratte akzeptieren; **to have a quick** ~ reißend abgehen; **to have a** ~ **protested for nonpayment** Tratte mangels Zahlung protestieren; **to hono(u)r a** ~ Wechsel einlösen; **to hono(u)r a** ~ **on sight** Tratte bei Vorzeigung honorieren; **to**

make a ~ Entwurf anfertigen; **to make a** ~ **on s. o.** Wechsel auf j. ziehen; **to make a** ~ **on one's account** von seinem Konto abheben, Kontoabhebung vornehmen; **to make a** ~ **on s. one's friendship** jds. Freundschaft in Anspruch nehmen; **to make a** ~ **on one's means** seine Mittel einsetzen; **to make out a** ~ Tratte ausstellen; **to make a rough** ~ flüchtig entwerfen; **to meet one's** ~s seine Akzepte einlösen; **to negotiate a** ~ Tratte begeben; **to present a** ~ **for acceptance** Wechsel zur Annahme vorlegen; **to show dishono(u)r to a** ~ Tratte nicht akzeptieren;
~ *(a.)* *(mil., US)* zum Wehrdienst eingezogen;
~ **act** *(US)* Wehrpflicht-, Rekrutierungsgesetz; ~ **agenda** Tagesordnungsentwurf; ~ **agreement** Vertrags-, Abkommensentwurf; ~ **allowance** Gutgewicht; ~ **articles** Mustersatzung; ~ **bill** Gesetzentwurf; ~ **board** *(mil., US)* Musterungskommission; ~ **book** *(Br.)* Wechsel[kopier]buch; ~ **call** *(mil., US)* Einberufung; ~ **card** *(US)* Einziehungsbescheid; ~ **collection** Wechselinkasso; ~ **committee** Redaktionsausschuß; ~ **contract** Vertragsentwurf; ~ **convention** Abkommensentwurf; ~ **credit** Rembourskredit; ~ **deferment** *(US)* Rückstellung [von der militärischen Dienstpflicht]; ~ **deferment rules** *(US)* Rückstellungsrichtlinien; ~ **economy** gelenkte Wirtschaft, Planwirtschaft; ~ **evader (dodger)** *(mil., US)* Drückeberger, Wehrdienst-, Dienstpflichtverweigerer; ~**-exempt** *(US)* vom Wehrdienst befreit; ~ **form** Entwurfsform; ~ **law** Gesetzentwurf, *(mil., US)* Einberufungsgesetz; ~ **leave** *(US)* Wehrurlaub; ~ **legislation** vorgesehene Gesetzgebung; ~ **letter** Briefentwurf; ~ **order** *(US)* Einberufungsbefehl; ~ **paper** mittelfeines Konzeptpapier; ~ **proposal** Vorschlagsentwurf; ~ **record** *(US)* Rekrutierungsliste; ~ **register** Wechselverzeichnis; ~ **report** Berichtsentwurf; ~ **resistance** *(US)* Wehrdienstverweigerung; ~ **resister** *(US)* Wehrdienstverweigerer; **to submit a** ~ **resolution** Entschließungsentwurf vorlegen; ~ **scheme of a railway** Eisenbahnprojekt; ~ **statement** Entwurf einer Erklärung; ~ **statute** Gesetzentwurf; ~ **treaty** Vertragsentwurf.
drafted *(mil., US)* eingezogen, rekrutiert.
draftee *(US)* Einberufener, Rekrutierter, Wehrdienstpflichtiger, Eingezogener.
drafter Verfasser, Aussteller, *(tel.)* Auftraggeber eines Fernspruchs.
drafting Textabfassung, Fassung, Formulierung;
~ **of a bill** Wechselausfertigung; ~ **of a section** Formulierung eines Absatzes;
~ **committee** Entwurfsausschuß; ~ **office** ausfertigende Stelle, Konstruktionsbüro; ~ **paper** Zeichenpapier; ~ **rooms** *(US)* Konstruktionsbüro.
draftsman, draughtsman *(Br.)* Ab-, Verfasser, Gestalter, Aussteller, *(building line)* Konstruktions-, Bauzeichner, *(marine engineering)* Konstrukteur.
draftsmanship Formulierungskunst, Abfassung, Ausstellung.
drag Hemmschuh, Hindernis, Belastung, *(influence, US)* Einfluß, Protektion, *(motor car, sl.)* Auto, *(proceedings)* schleppendes Verfahren, *(tel.)* Telegrammverzögerung;
~ **on recovery** konjunkturelle Bremse;
~ *(v.)* schlecht (flau) gehen, *(time)* dahinschleichen;
~ **its anchor** *(ship)* vor Anker treiben; ~ **one's brains** sich den Kopf zerbrechen; ~ **one's feet** absichtlich verzögern, Angelegenheit hinauszögern, sich Zeit lassen; ~ **by head and shoulders** an den Haaren herbeiziehen; ~ **s. o. into s. th.** j. in etw. hineinziehen; ~ **on** sich hinschleppen, *(conversation)* sich dahinschleppen, *(lawsuit)* hinziehen; ~ **on a miserable (wretched) existence** jämmerliches Dasein führen; ~ **behind the orchestra** hinter dem Orchester herhinken; ~ **out an affair** Angelegenheit hinziehen; ~ **s. o. out of bed** j. aus dem Bett schmeißen; ~ **a prisoner out of his hiding place** Sträfling aus seinem Versteck hervorholen; ~ **out the negotiating process** Verhandlungsablauf hinziehen; ~ **a river for a missing child** Fluß nach einem verlorenen Kind absuchen; ~ **a subject in** Thema mit Gewalt zur Sprache bringen; ~ **the truth out of s. o.** Wahrheit aus jem. herauspressen; ~ **up a child** *(coll.)* Kind recht und schlecht erziehen; ~ **up towards the end of term** zum Semesterschluß langweilig werden;
to be a ~ **on s. o. all one's life** sein ganzes Leben lang für j. eine Belastung sein; **to let a matter** ~ Sache treiben lassen;
~ **anchor (sheet)** Treibanker; ~ **clause** *(tariff law)* Sammelklausel; ~ **race** *(sl.)* Autowettfahrt; ~ **rope** Abschleppseil.
dragging *(business)* schleppend, flau.
dragline *(aeroplane)* Schlepp-, Leitseil.
dragnet Schleppnetz, *(police)* Fangnetz;
~ **clause** Sammelklausel; ~ **technique** Schleppnetzfahndung.
dragon Drache, *(fig.)* Anstandswauwau;
~'s **teeth** *(mil.)* Panzersperre, Höckerhindernis.

drain starke Inanspruchnahme, Belastung, *(channel)* Abzugskanal, Entwässerungsgraben, *(money)* Abzüge, [Geld]abfluß, *(street)* Gosse, Straßenrinne;
down the ~ *(fig.)* zum Fenster hinaus;
~s Kanalisation;
brain ~ Abwanderung von Wissenschaftlern; **foreign ~** Kapitalabwanderung;
~ of bullion (gold, *Br.)* Goldabfluß; **strong ~ on the dollar holdings** starker Sog auf die Dollarbestände; **~ on our gold reserves** Abfluß unserer Goldreserven; **~ on liquidity** Liquiditätsanspannung; **~ of money** Geldabzug, -abfluß; **great ~ on the purse** schwere finanzielle Belastung; **~ on the resources** Inanspruchnahme von Hilfsquellen; **great ~ on the country's resources** große Belastung der Staatsfinanzen; **~ of specie** Bargeldabzug; **~ on the strength** Kräftebeanspruchung;
~ *(v.)* entwässern, trockenlegen, dränieren, *(fig.)* aufbrauchen, erschöpfen, *(building)* ans Kanalnetz anschließen;
~ away ablaufen, [Geld] abziehen; **~ the water away** Wasser ableiten; **~ an area** Gebiet entwässern; **~ a country** Land völlig ausplündern; **~ upon a country's resources** Land nach und nach seiner Hilfsquellen berauben; **~ s. one's purse** jds. Geldbeutel leeren; **~ away the specie of a country** Bargeld eines Landes aus dem Verkehr ziehen; **~ a country of its wealth** Wohlstand eines Landes erschöpfen, Land aussaugen; **~ s. o. dry** j. bis auf den letzten Tropfen auspressen;
to be on the ~ an die Kanalisation angeschlossen sein; **to be a ~ on s. one's purse** jds. Geldbeutel in Anspruch nehmen; **to go down the ~** in die Binsen gehen, sich in Luft auflösen, *(go bankrupt)* pleite gehen; **to throw money down the ~** Geld zum Fenster hinauswerfen;
~ cock Abfluß-, Entwässerungshahn; **~ pipe** Abflußrohr; **~pipe trousers** Nietenhosen; **~ pit** Gesenk; **~ valve** Abflußventil.
drainage *(system)* Kanalisationssystem, Entwässerung, Austrocknung, Trockenlegung, Dränage, Melioration;
~ area *(US)* Flußgebiet, Einzugsgebiet; **~ basin** Flußeinzugsgebiet; **~ benefit** Meliorationswertzuwachs; **~ canal** Sammelgraben; **~ district** Dränagebehörde, Meliorationsbezirk; **~ pit** Sickerloch; **~ pump** Lenzpumpe; **~ rate** Entwässerungsgebühr; **~ shaft** Entwässerungsschacht; **~ system** Entwässerungsanlage, Dränagesystem; **~ tube** Leckleitung; **~ tunnel** Entwässerungsschacht; **~ well** Entwässerungsbrunnen.
drained, to have ~ o. s. dry *(writer)* sich ausgeschrieben haben.
drainer Kanalisationsarbeiter.
draining | well Senkgrube;
to be ~ away langsam dem Ende zugehen.
drainpipe Abflußrohr.
drama Schauspiel, Drama, *(dramatic affairs)* dramatisches (erregendes) Geschehen;
~ of prewar vintage Vorkriegsdrama;
~ group Laienspielgruppe.
dramatic dramatisch, spannend, bühnengerecht;
~ changes in the international situation dramatische Veränderungen in der Weltlage; **~ critic** Theaterkritiker; **~ criticism** Theaterkritik; **~ effect** dramatische Wirkung; **~ performance** Aufführung eines Dramas; **~ rights** Bühnenrechte.
dramatis personae *(theater)* Personenverzeichnis.
dramatist Dramatiker, Bühnenschriftsteller.
dramatization of a novel Bühnenbearbeitung eines Romans.
dramatize *(v.)* für die Bühne bearbeiten, *(fig.)* dramatisieren.
dramaturgical bühnenwirksam.
drape *(v.)* drapieren, ausschmücken;
~ with flags mit Fahnen schmücken.
draper Textilkaufmann, Tuch-, Stoffhändler;
~'s shop Textilladen, -geschäft.
drapery Drapieren, *(textile fabric)* Textilien, *(textile trade, Br.)* Stoff-, Textilhandel, *(US)* Vorhangstoffe, Vorhänge;
~ business Textilhandel; **~ shop** Textilgeschäft, -laden.
drastic durchgreifend, rigoros, drastisch;
~ measures to cure inflation drastische (rigorose) Maßnahmen zur Inflationsbekämpfung.
draught Fischzug, -fang, *(current of air)* Luftzug, *(ship)* Tiefgang;
at a ~ auf einen Zug;
~ of beer Schluck Bier;
to feel the ~ *(Br., sl.)* in arger Bedrängnis sein;
~ animal Zugtier; **~ beer** Bier vom Faß, Faßbier.
draughtsman Ab-, Verfasser, Aussteller, *(building line)* Bauzeichner.
draw *(attraction)* Zug-, Anziehungskraft, Schlager, Zugartikel, *(drawn money)* abgehobener Betrag, *(feeler)* verfängliche Bemerkung, Fangfrage, *(lottery)* Ver-, Auslosung, Ziehung, *(theater)* Ziehen;

big ~ große Attraktion; **box-office ~** *(US)* Kassenschlager, -magnet; **Christmas ~** Weihnachtslotterie; **great ~** Kassenschlager; **this month's ~** Auslosung dieses Monats; **real ~** Anziehungspunkt;
~ on reserves Anspannung der Reserven;
~ *(v.)* *(attract)* anziehen, anlocken, *(interest, profit)* ziehen, *(make out)* ausstellen, trassieren, *(money)* abheben, *(make picture)* zeichnen, *(salary)* beziehen, erhalten, *(ship)* Tiefgang haben.
draw *(v.)* **against s. o.** auf j. ziehen.
draw *(v.)* **aside** beiseitenehmen.
draw away *(v.)* **customers** Kunden abspenstig machen.
draw back *(v.)* sich zurückziehen, Rückvergütung erhalten, *(bill)* zurücktrassieren, *(duty)* als Rückzoll bekommen;
~ by lot *(bonds)* ver-, auslosen.
draw down *(v.)* **the blinds** Jalousien herablassen.
draw in *(v.)* *(days)* kürzer werden;
~ a bill Wechsel einlösen; **~ one's expenditure** sich in seinen Ausgaben einschränken; **~ one's horns** bescheidener leben; **~ a loan** Kredit kündigen.
draw into *(v.)* **the station** *(train)* in die Station einfahren; **~ s. o. into talk** j. ins Gespräch ziehen; **~ s. o. into purchase by flattery** j. durch Schmeicheleien zum Kauf verführen; **~ s. o. into a conspiracy** j. in eine Verschwörung verwickeln.
draw off *(v.)* *(print.)* Druckbogen abziehen, *(troops)* ab-, zurückziehen.
draw on *(v.)* *(obtain by applying)* heranziehen, *(cause)* verursachen, veranlassen, *(refer)* Bezug nehmen auf, *(war)* heranziehen, im Anzug sein;
~ s. o. Wechsel auf j. ziehen, jem. eine Zahlungsaufforderung zukommen lassen, *(fig.)* jds. Hilfsmittel in Anspruch nehmen; **~ disaster** Unglück herbeiführen; **~ each other (mutually)** gegenseitig aufeinander ziehen; **~ one's imagination** seine Phantasie spielen lassen; **~ s. o. for money** j. um Geld angehen; **~ one's capital** sein Kapital angreifen; **~ the International Monetary Fund** auf den Internationalen Währungsfonds ziehen; **~ the reserves** Reserven angreifen; **~ one's savings** auf seine Ersparnisse zurückgreifen.
draw out *(v.)* herauslocken;
~ of an account von einem Konto abheben; **~ money from the bank** Geld von der Bank abheben; **~ a scheme** Plan ausarbeiten; **~ of the station promptly** pünktlich abfahren.
draw together *(v.)* zusammenziehen.
draw up *(v.)* [schriftlich] abfassen, in richtiger Form ausfertigen, aufsetzen, konzipieren, *(mil.)* sich formieren, Truppen aufmarschieren lassen;
~ with s. o. j. einholen; **~ a balance sheet** Bilanz aufstellen; **~ a budget** Etat aufstellen; **~ a contract** Vertrag aufsetzen (ausfertigen); **~ a document** Urkunde ausstellen; **~ an estimate** Kostenvoranschlag machen; **~ an itinerary** Reiseroute aufstellen; **~ minutes** Protokoll aufnehmen; **~ a petition** Gesuch aufsetzen; **~ a policy** Versicherungspolice ausfertigen; **~ the program(me)** Programm aufstellen; **~ proposals** Vorschläge ausarbeiten; **~ a scheme** Plan entwerfen; **~ a statement of account** Kontoauszug anfertigen; **~ at the station entrance** beim Bahnhofseingang vorfahren; **~ a will** Testament errichten.
draw upon *(v.)* | **s. o.** sich bei jem. erholen; **~ one's memory** sein Gedächtnis bemühen; **~ one's reserves** auf seine Reserven zurückgreifen; **~ ruin upon o. s.** seinen eigenen Ruin herbeiführen; **~ one's savings** seine Ersparnisse angreifen.
draw *(v.)* | **an account (a balance)** Rechnung (Bilanz) aufstellen; **~ the exact amount** per netto Appoint ziehen; **~ long applause** langanhaltenden Beifall hervorrufen; **~ applause from the audience** einem Publikum Beifall abringen; **~ per appoint** per Saldo kassieren (Appoint ziehen); **~ s. one's attention to o. s.** jds. Aufmerksamkeit auf sich ziehen; **~ large audiences** große Zuhörerschaft anlocken; **~ a bill of exchange on s. o.** sich einen Wechsel von einem Konto auszahlen lassen; **~ a blank** Niete ziehen, Reinfall erleben; **~ blasts from s. o.** in jds. Schußlinie geraten; **~ bonds** Obligationen auslosen; **~ a bye** Freilos ziehen; **~ a check** *(US)* (**cheque,** *Br.)* Scheck ausstellen; **~ a check** *(US)* (**cheque,** *Br.)* **upon an account** Scheck auf ein Konto ziehen; **~ to a close** sich dem Ende nähern, zu Ende gehen; **~ a commission on a transaction** Provision aus einem Geschäft beziehen; **~ a comparison** Vergleich ziehen; **~ conclusions** Schlußfolgerungen (Schlüsse) ziehen; **~ consolation in s. th.** Trost in etw. finden; **~ the curtain on outlays** Ausgabeposten verschwinden lassen; **~ customers into the store** Kunden anziehen; **~ at long (short) date** Wechsel auf lange (kurze) Zeit ziehen; **~ a deed** Urkunde ausfertigen; **~ deep** *(ship)* großen

Tiefgang haben; ~ **a document from one's wallet** der Brieftasche ein Schriftstück entnehmen; ~ **the dole** *(Br.)* Arbeitslosenunterstützung beziehen; ~ **to an end** dem Ende zugehen; ~ **the enemy's fire** feindliches Feuer auf sich ziehen; ~ **it fine** auf jede Kleinigkeit achten, es ganz genau nehmen; ~ **food** *(mil.)* Essen fassen; ~ **on s. one's generosity** jds. Großzügigkeit ausnutzen; ~ **to a head** *(fig.)* Krisenpunkt erreichen; ~ **heavily on the credit market** Kreditmärkte stark in Anspruch nehmen; ~ **a regular income** regelmäßige Einkünfte beziehen; ~ **interest** Zinsen abwerfen; ~ **before the judge** vor Gericht bringen; ~ **the line at s. th.** bei etw. nicht mehr mitmachen; ~ **the longbow** *(coll.)* gewaltig angeben, tüchtig aufschneiden; ~ **lots** losen; ~ **it mild** *(coll.)* bei der Wahrheit bleiben; ~ **money** Geld entnehmen; ~ **on s. o. for money** j. um Geld angehen; ~ **the moral from s. th.** Lehre aus etw. ziehen; ~ **at par** Wechsel al pari trassieren; ~ **a parallel** Parallele ziehen; ~ **a picture of s. o.** j. zeichnen, Zeichnung von jem. anfertigen; ~ **a good price** guten Preis erzielen; ~ **a prize in a lottery** in der Lotterie gewinnen; ~ **the profits** Gewinne entnehmen; ~ **rations** Verpflegung empfangen; ~ **rein** *(fig.)* Zügel anziehen; ~ **no reply from s. o.** keine Antwort von jem. herausbekommen; ~ **a salary** Gehalt beziehen; ~ **samples** Muster nehmen; ~ **to scale** maßstabsgerecht zeichnen; ~ **a sheet** *(print.)* Druckbogen abziehen; ~ **on sight** Sichtwechsel ziehen; ~ **a streak** seine Künste übertreiben; ~ **one's supplies from abroad** sich im Ausland eindecken; ~ **one's sword against s. o.** gegen j. zu Felde ziehen; ~ **the winner** Gewinnlos ziehen; **to be a big** ~ starke Anziehungskraft ausüben; **to be eligible for inclusion in the** ~ an der Auslosung teilnehmen; **to be a great** ~ **at political meetings** zugkräftiger Redner auf politischen Versammlungen sein; **to be quick on the** ~ schnell mit dem Revolver bei der Hand sein; **to end in a** ~ unentschieden ausgehen; ~**-in** *(road)* Bucht; ~ **leaf** *(table)* Ansatzstück; ~**-leaf table** ausziehbarer Tisch.

drawback Nachteil, Hindernis, Schattenseite, *(money remitted)* Rückvergütung, -erstattung, *(refund of duty)* Export-, Zollrückvergütung, -erstattung, Ausfuhrvergütung, Rückzoll, Prämie, *(refund of taxes)* Steuerrückvergütung;
~ **application** Rückerstattungsantrag; ~ **slip** Verrechnungsbeleg; ~ **system** *(department store)* [bargeldloses] Verrechnungssystem, bargeldloser Verkehr.

drawbridge Zugbrücke.

drawee *(bill)* [Wechsel]bezogener, bezogene Firma, Trassat, Übernehmer, Akzeptant;
alternative ~ Alternativbezogener;
~ **in case of need** Notadressat;
~ **bank[er]** bezogene Bank.

drawer Aussteller, Trassant, Ordergeber, Entnehmer;
~ **dead** Aussteller verstorben; **fellow** ~ Mitaussteller; **secret** ~ Geheimfach;
~ **of a bill** Wechselaussteller; ~ **of a document** [Urkunden]aussteller;
~**'s account** Konto des Ausstellers; ~**'s domicile** Ausstellungsort; ~**'s signature** Unterschrift des Ausstellers; ~**'s verification** Bestätigung durch den Aussteller.

drawgate Schleusentor.

drawing *(bill of exchange)* Ziehen, Ausstellen, Trassieren, *(of bonds)* Auslosen, *(cashing)* Ab-, Erhebung, Geldabhebung, *(design)* Zeichnung, Skizze, *(lottery)* Ver-, Auslosung, Ziehung, *(sketch)* [Bau]entwurf;
cum ~ incl. Ziehung; **in** ~ richtig gezeichnet, *(fig.)* zusammen passend; **redeemable by** ~ auslosbar;
~**s** Abhebungen, Entnahmen, *(International Monetary Fund)* Schuldaufnahme, Mittelbeanspruchung, *(revenue)* Einnahmen, Tageslosung;
annual ~ jährliche Verlosung; **cash** ~**s** Geldausgänge; **current** ~ *(bonds)* nächste Auslosung; **dollar** ~**s** Dollarabzüge, -abhebungen; **personal** ~**s** Privatentnahmen; **serial** ~**s** Serienziehung;
~ **on s. o.** Ziehung auf j.; ~ **on an account** Entnahme, Abdisposition, Disposition über ein (Abhebung von einem) Konto; ~**s on account current** Kontokorrentabhebungen; ~ **apart** Beiseitenehmen; ~ **back** Rückzug; ~ **of a cheque** Scheckausstellung; ~ **of lots** Auslosung; ~ **by partners** Gesellschafterentnahmen; ~ **of a patent** Patentzeichnung; ~ **of prizes** Gewinnziehung; ~ **for redemption** Auslosung; ~ **on free reserves** Entnahme aus freien Rücklagen; ~ **and redrawing** Wechselreiterei; ~ **of salary** Bezug von Gehalt; ~ **up** Ausfertigung, Abfassung, Formulierung;
~ **account** Girokonto, offenes (laufendes) Konto, *(agent)* Spesen-, Vorschußkonto, *(personal account)* Konto für Privatentnahmen, Entnahmekonto; ~ **authorization** *(export trade)*

Negoziierungskredit, Ermächtigung, Dokumententratte auf den Käufer zu ziehen; ~ **block** Zeichenblock; ~ **board** Reißbrett; **back to the** ~ **board** ins Konstruktionsbüro zurück; **to be still on the** ~ **board** noch im Planungsstadium sein; **to take ten years from the** ~ **board to construction and into operation** zehn Jahre für den Weg vom Konstruktionsbüro über die Ausführung zur Inbetriebnahme benötigen; ~ **card** *(US)* Zugnummer, zugkräftiges Stück; ~ **certificate** Auslosungsschein; ~ **commission** Trassierungsprovision; ~ **copy** Zeichenvorlage; ~ **credit** Dispositions-, Trassierungskredit; ~ **date** Auslosungstermin; ~ **day** Ziehungstag; ~ **ink** Ausziehtusche; ~ **instrument** Zeichengerät; ~ **list** Ziehungsliste; ~ **office** *(Br.)* Konstruktionsbüro; ~ **pad** Zeichenblock; ~ **paper** Zeichenpapier; ~ **pen** Reißfeder; ~ **pencil** Zeichenstift; ~ **pin** Reißzwecke; ~ **rate** *(bills)* Verkaufssatz, -kurs, Briefkurs; ~ **right** Auslosungsrecht, *(on fund)* Verfügungsrecht, Abhebungsbefugnis, *(International Monetary Fund)* Ziehungsrechte; ~ **room** Salon, Wohnzimmer, *(reception, Br.)* formeller Empfang, *(railroad, US)* Salon, Privatabteil; ~ **room on a level with the garden** ebenerdiges Wohnzimmer; **to hold a** ~ **room** Empfang geben; ~**-room play** *(theater)* Gesellschaftsstück; ~ **set** Zirkelkasten.

drawn *(bank)* bezogen;
artificially ~ in Juristendeutsch aufgesetzt; **duly** ~ ordnungsgemäß ausgestellt;
~ **against uncollected funds** Deckung erst bei Zahlungseingang; ~ **by lots** ausgelost;
to be ~ verlost werden; **not to be** ~ *(lottery)* nicht herauskommen; **to feel** ~ **to s. o.** sich zu jem. hingezogen fühlen; **to live at daggers** ~ **with s. o.** auf gespanntem Fuß mit jem. leben;
~ **battle** unentschiedene Schlacht; ~ **bonds** ausgeloste Obligationen (Schuldverschreibungen); ~ **number** *(lottery)* [Gewinn]los; **long** ~**-out discussion** übermäßig ausgeweitete Diskussion; ~**-out story** nicht endenwollende Geschichte.

dray Bierwagen;
~ *(v.)* als Rollkutscher tätig sein.

drayage *(US)* Rollgeld;
~ **company** Speditionsgesellschaft.

drayman Bier-, Rollkutscher.

dream, wish (pipe, US) Wunschtraum;
~ *(v.)* **away one's time** seine Zeit verträumen.

dreamland Traumland.

dreamworld Traumwelt.

dreamy recollection verschwommene (vage) Erinnerung.

dredge *(v.)* ausbaggern;
~ **away** mit dem Bagger wegräumen.

dredger Bagger.

dredging operations Baggerarbeiten.

dregs of mankind Abschaum der Menschheit.

drenched to the skin bis auf die Haut durchnäßt.

dress Anzug, Kleidung, Toilette, *(mil.)* Anzug, Uniform;
in full ~ im Gesellschaftsanzug;
ball ~ Ballrobe; **battle** ~ Kampfanzug; **evening** ~ Abendanzug; **everyday** ~ Alltagskleid; **full** ~ Gesellschafts-, Galaanzug; **travelling** ~ Reiseanzug;
~ *(v.)* *(ore)* aufbereiten, *(theater)* kostümieren, *(type founding)* zurichten;
~ **badly** sich miserabel (geschmacklos) anziehen; ~ **s. o. down** j. anschnauzen; ~ **the house** Theater durch Freikartenausgabe füllen; ~ **a room** Zimmer putzen (säubern, herrichten); ~ **a salad** Salat anmachen; ~ **ships** Toppflaggen hissen; ~ **a shop-window** Schaufenster dekorieren, Auslage herrichten; ~ **for supper** sich zum Abendessen umziehen; ~ **up** sich in Gala werfen, sich aufdonnern; ~ **up the year-end books** Jahresabschlußbilanz verschönern;
~ **affair** Galaveranstaltung; ~ **allowance** Kleiderzuschuß; ~ **box** *(theater)* Proszeniumsloge; ~ **circle** *(theater)* erster Rang; ~ **clothes** Gesellschaftsanzug; ~ **coat** Frack; ~ **designer** Modezeichner; ~ **hire** Kostümverleih; ~ **parade** Modeschau; ~ **regulations** Anzugs-, Kleiderordnung; ~ **rehearsal** *(theater)* Kostümprobe; ~ **shop** Konfektionsgeschäft; ~ **suit** Frackanzug.

dressed | plainly bürgerlich gekleidet;
~ **like a dog's dinner** nach der neuesten Mode gekleidet; ~ **fit to kill** bunt herausgeputzt, aufgetakelt; ~ **up to the nines** aufgedonnert, aufgetakelt, pikfein, in Schale geschmissen;
all ~ **up and nowhere to go** *(fam.)* bestellt und nicht abgeholt;
to be ~ **up to kill** sich unmöglich angezogen haben.

dresser Schaufensterdekorateur, *(attendant)* Ankleidefrau, Friseuse, *(cupboard, Br.)* Anrichte, Geschirrschrank, *(furniture, US)* Frisierkommode, Toilettentisch, *(theatre)* Kostümier, *(techn.)* Aufbereiter, Appretierer, *(type)* Zurichter.

dressing Bekleidung, *(print.)* Zurichtung;
window ~ Schaufensterdekoration;
to give s. o. a ~ down jem. tüchtig den Kopf waschen;
~ case Reisenecessaire; **~ jacket** Frisiermantel; **~ parade** *(mil.)* Parade in Galauniform; **~ pattern** Schnittmuster; **~ rehearsal** *(theater)* Kostüm-, Generalprobe; **~ room** Umkleideraum, *(theater)* Künstlergarderobe; **~ suit** Abend-, Frackanzug; **~ uniform** *(mil.)* großer Dienstanzug.
dressmaker Modeschöpfer.
dressman Vorführmann.
drift Kursversetzung, *(customers)* Abwanderung, *(inactivity)* Treibenlassen, tatenloses Warten, Untätigkeit, *(influence)* bestimmender Einfluß, *(mining)* Strecke, Stollen, *(radio set)* Schwankungen, *(tendency)* Strömung, Richtung, Tendenz;
in the ~ *(mining)* vor Ort;
snow ~ Schneeverwehung; **wage ~** Lohnrichtung, -drift;
general ~ of the political affairs generelle Entwicklung der politischen Lage; **~ of labo(u)r into the towns** Abwanderung ländlicher Arbeitskräfte in die Städte; **~ from the land** Landflucht; **~ towards the right** Rechtstendenz; **~ of trade** Geschäftsverlagerung, Kundenabwanderung;
~ *(v.)* *(customers)* abwandern, *(road)* verwehen;
~ towards bankruptcy auf den Konkurs zusteuern; **~ down** *(prices)* abbröckeln;
to get the ~ of an argument Gedankengang eines Arguments verstehen; **to let s. th. ~** Dinge treiben lassen;
~ anchor Treibanker; **~ avalanche** Staublawine; **~ bottle** Flaschenpost; **~ ice** Treibeis; **~ mining** Stollen-, Streckenbetrieb.
driftage Treibgut, angeschwemmtes Gut.
drifter Treibnetzfischdampfer, *(fig.)* zielloser Mensch.
drifting sand Treib-, Flugsand.
driftway Viehweg.
driftwood Treibholz.
drill *(fig.)* methodische Ausbildung, *(machine)* Bohrgerät, -maschine, *(mil.)* Drill, Exerzieren;
~ *(v.)* methodisch ausbilden, *(mil.)* exerzieren;
~ French grammar französische Grammatik pauken.
drilled-in eingepaukt.
driller Bohrmaschine, -gerät, *(coach)* Einpauker, *(mil.)* Ausbilder.
drilling | rights Bohr-, Schürfrechte; **~ ship** Bohrschiff.
drink [alkoholisches] Getränk;
~s extra Getränke nicht einbegriffen;
ice ~ eisgekühltes Getränk; **soft (temperance) ~** alkoholfreies Getränk;
food and ~ Speisen und Getränke; **~ of water** Schluck Wasser;
~ *(v.)* trinken, alkoholische Getränke zu sich nehmen;
~ to the bride auf die Braut anstoßen; **~ deep** starker Trinker sein; **~ more than is good for one** mehr trinken als man verträgt; **~ in a story** Geschichte gierig in sich aufnehmen; **~ s. o. under the table** j. unter den Tisch trinken;
to be on the ~ *(coll.)* dem Trunke frönen; **to be under the influence of ~** unter Alkoholeinfluß stehen;
~ dispenser Getränkeautomat; **~s industry** Getränkeindustrie; **~ money** Trinkgeld.
drinker Trinker, Zecher, Trunkenbold, Säufer.
drinking Zecherei, Trinkgelage;
under-age ~ Jugendalkoholismus; **~ bout** Zechgelage, Bierreise, Sauftour; **~ fountain** Trinkbrunnen; **~ habits** Trinkgewohnheiten; **~ house** Trinkstube; **~ kiosk** Getränkeausschank; **~ water** Trinkwasser.
drip coffee *(US)* Filterkaffee.
drive *(advertising campaign)* Werbefeldzug, -aktion, -anstrengungen, verstärkter Werbeeinsatz, *(approach)* An-, Auffahrt, *(hunting)* Treibjagd, *(hurried dispatch of business)* Hochdruckbetrieb, auf Hochtouren laufender Betrieb, *(organized effort, US)* Aktion, Vorstoß, *(into garage)* Garageneinfahrt, *(go)* Antriebskraft, Energie, Schwung, Tempo, *(mil.)* Vorstoß, kraftvolle Offensive, *(money collection, US)* Geldsammlung, Sammelaktion, *(motive)* Beweggrund, Motiv, *(motoring)* Autospazierfahrt, Ausflug, *(park)* Fahrweg, *(path in the wood)* Schneise, *(US, sale under price)* Schleuderverkauf, Verkauf unter Preis, *(sociology)* Antrieb, *(US, stock exchange)* Baisseangriff, *(tendency)* Tendenz, Richtung, Strömung, Neigung, *(wisecrack, US)* witzige Bemerkung, Stichelei;
all-wheel ~ Geländeantrieb; **~ back** Rückfahrt; **chain ~** Kettenantrieb; **export ~** Exportförderung; **front ~** Vorderantrieb; **great ~** große Anstrengung; **an hour's ~ away** eine Fahrstunde entfernt; **membership ~** Mitgliederwerbung; **right-hand ~** *(car)* Rechtssteuerung; **sales ~** Absatzsteigerung, -anstrengung, verstärkter Werbeeinsatz; **trial ~** Probefahrt;

15 minutes ~ from the airport 15 Autominuten vom Flugplatz; **~ of business** geschäftiges Treiben; **~ and initiative** Energie und Unternehmungsgeist; **~ to raise money for the blind** Sammelaktion zugunsten der Blinden;
~ *(v.)* Fahrzeug lenken, steuern, [be]fahren, mit dem Auto fahren, *(mining)* Stollen vortreiben;
~ accident-free unfallfrei fahren; **~ all before one** jeden Widerstand überwinden; **~ along at 60 miles an hour** mit 100 Stunden Kilometern fahren; **~ at** *(coll.)* hinzielen auf; **~ away** wegfahren; **~ away at one's work** *(fam.)* wie ein Kümmeltürke arbeiten; **~ back** zurückfahren; **~ from the back-seat** *(fig.)* aus dem Hintergrund operieren; **~ a good bargain** Geschäft zu einem vorteilhaften Abschluß bringen; **~ a hard bargain** kompromißlos verhandeln; **~ on one's master's business** im Geschäftsinteresse fahren; **~ a car** Auto lenken (fahren); **~ one's car** seinen eigenen Wagen fahren; **~ with caution** vorsichtig fahren; **~ s. o. into a corner** j. in die Enge treiben; **~ s. o. to death** j. in den Tod hetzen; **~ down into the country** aufs Land hinausfahren; **~ the enemy out of their positions** Feind aus seinen Stellungen vertreiben; **~ right up to the front door** vor dem Haupteingang vorfahren; **~ home** klarmachen, zu Bewußtsein bringen; **~ on the horn** nicht von der Hupe heruntersteigen; **~ into** einfahren; **~ like mad** *(coll.)* wie ein Verrückter fahren; **~ by the map** nach Karte fahren; **~ s. th. to the last minute** etw. bis zur letzten Minute hinausschieben; **~ the nail home** Angelegenheit endgültig erledigen; **~ s. o. neurotic** j. zu einem Nervenzusammenbruch treiben; **~ on** weiterfahren, *(fig.)* eifrig betreiben; **~ out** aus-, spazieren fahren; **~ out the composition** Satz strecken; **~ over s. o.** j. überfahren; **~ one's point home** seinen Standpunkt begründen; **~ to the public danger** öffentliche Sicherheit beim Autofahren gefährden; **~ recklessly** rücksichtslos fahren; **~ s. o. to resign** j. zum Rücktritt zwingen; **~ on the right of the road** rechts fahren; **~ on the wrong side of the road** auf der falschen Straßenseite fahren; **~ s. o. round the bend** *(fam.)* j. um den Verstand bringen; **~ s. o. out of his senses** j. um den Verstand bringen; **~ a ship upon the rocks** Schiff auf die Felsen schleudern; **~ side by side** nebeneinander fahren; **~ into a skid** gegensteuern; **~ slowly** langsam fahren; **~ stakes** sich häuslich niederlassen; **~ s. o. to the station** j. zum Bahnhof fahren; **~ through** durchfahren; **~ a trade** Gewerbe ausüben; **~ a roaring trade** glänzende Geschäfte machen; **~ a tunnel** Tunnel bohren; **~ up to s. one's house** bei jem. vorfahren; **~ up a hill in second gear** Steigung im zweiten Gang nehmen; **~ up the prices** Preise in die Höhe treiben; **~ at walking speed** Schritt fahren; **~ the wrong way in a one-way street** Einbahnstraße in falscher Richtung befahren; **~ while disqualified** trotz eingezogenen Führerscheins fahren; **~ while intoxicated** in betrunkenem Zustand fahren; **~ while uninsured** ohne gültige Haftpflichtversicherung fahren; **~ without a licence** ohne Führerschein fahren; **~ without lights** ohne Licht fahren; **~ one's workmen too hard** seine Arbeitskräfte übermäßig ausnutzen;
to be lacking in ~ Initiative vermissen lassen; **to go for a ~** Autofahrt machen; **to launch (start) a ~** Aktion starten; **to launch a fund raising ~** Sammelaktion starten; **to make a great ~ to raise $ 5.000** große Sammelaktion für 5.000 Dollar unternehmen; **to take s. o. for a ~** j. [im Auto] mitnehmen, *(fig.)* j. hereinlegen.
drive-in *(coll.)* Restaurant mit Kundenbedienung im Fahrzeug, Autokino, *(banking)* Autoschalter;
~ establishment Laden für Einkäufe vom Auto aus; **~ restaurant** Autorestaurant, -rasthaus; **~ store** *(US)* Ladengeschäft mit besonderem Bedienungsfenster; **~ window** *(US)* Autoschalter.
drive | -off Abfahrtsrampe; **~-on** Zufahrtsrampe; **~-yourself** selbstgefahrener Mietwagen.
drivel Gefasel, Geschwätz;
~ *(v.)* plappern, faseln.
driven out of one's course vom Kurs abgekommen, abgetrieben.
driver Fahrer, Fahrzeugführer, *(overseer, coll.)* Antreiber, Schinder;
bus ~ Busfahrer; **hit-and-run ~** flüchtiger Fahrer; **high-risk ~** hohes Risiko darstellender Autofahrer; **learner-~** Fahrschüler; **public service vehicle ~** Führer eines öffentlichen Verkehrsfahrzeugs; **safe ~** zuverlässiger Fahrer; **taxi ~** Taxichauffeur, -fahrer;
~ of a truck Lastwagenfahrer;
to be a hit-and-run ~ Fahrerflucht begehen;
~'s cab Führerhaus, -stand; **truck-~ helper** Beifahrer; **~'s license** *(US)* (licence, *Br.*) Führerschein; **to endorse a ~'s license** *(US)* (licence, *Br.*) Eintragung auf dem Führerschein machen; **to suspend the ~'s licence** *(US)* Führerschein entziehen; **~'s**

licence *(Br.)* **(license,** *US)* **bureau** Führerscheinausgabestelle; **~'s seat** Fahrersitz; **to be in the ~'s seat** *(fig., US)* stärkere Stellung haben; **~'s test** *(US)* Fahrprüfung.

driveway Fahrbahn, *(US, approach)* Auffahrt, *(into garage)* Garageneinfahrt;
  private ~ Privateinfahrt.

driving Fahren, *(mining)* Streckenbetrieb;
  ~ abroad Auslandsfahrten; **accident-free ~** unfallfreies Fahren; **careless ~** leichtfertige Fahrweise; **dangerous ~** Verkehrsgefährdung; **furious ~** Rasen; **hit-and-run ~** Fahrerflucht; **motorway ~** *(Br.)* Fahren auf der Autobahn; **reckless ~** rücksichtslose Fahrweise, Raserei; **safe ~** Fahrsicherheit; **smooth ~** angenehmes Fahren;
  ~ while asleep Einschlafen am Steuer; **~ carelessly** leichtfertige Fahrweise; **~ in a column (convoy)** Kolonnenfahrt; **~ under the influence of drink** *(Br.)* **(alcohol,** *US)* Autofahren unter Alkoholeinfluß, Trunkenheit am Steuer, Fahren in betrunkenem Zustand; **~ while disqualified** Fahren trotz eingezogenen Führerscheins; **~ while intoxicated** *(US)* Trunkenheit am Steuer, Fahren in betrunkenem Zustand; **~ without licence** *(Br.)* Fahren ohne Führerschein; **~ without lights** Fahren ohne Licht; **~ while uninsured** Fahren ohne Haftpflichtversicherung;
  to be charged with dangerous ~ wegen Verkehrsgefährdung angeklagt werden; **to be good at ~** gut fahren können, ein guter Fahrer sein; **to book s. o. for reckless ~** jem. wegen rücksichtslosen Fahrens einen Strafzettel verpassen; **to disqualify from ~** Führerschein (Fahrerlaubnis) entziehen; **to have a conviction for dangerous ~** Verkehrsvorstrafe haben;
  ~ age Führerscheinalter; **~ ban** *(Br.)* Fahrverbot, Führerscheinentzug; **~ belt** Treibriemen; **~ disqualification** Führerscheinentzug; **~ force** treibende Kraft, Antriebskraft; **to be the ~ force behind the scenes** hinter einem Unternehmen stecken, treibende Kraft des Ganzen sein; **~ gear** Getriebe; **~ habits** Fahrpraktiken; **to constitute a ~ hazard** Gefahr beim Autofahren darstellen; **~ instruction** Fahrunterricht; **~ instructor** Fahrlehrer; **~ lessons** Fahrstunden, -unterricht; **to take ~ lessons** Fahrunterricht nehmen; **~ licence** *(Br.)* Führerschein, Fahrerlaubnis; **to be disqualified from holding a ~ licence** *(Br.)* Führerschein entzogen bekommen; **to endorse a ~ licence** *(Br.)* Eintragung auf dem Führerschein machen; **to forfeit one's ~ licence** *(Br.)* Führerschein entzogen bekommen; **to suspend a ~ licence** *(Br.)* Führerschein vorübergehend abnehmen; **to take out a ~ licence** *(Br.)* Führerschein bekommen; **to withdraw a ~ licence** *(Br.)* Führerschein entziehen; **~ mirror** Rückspiegel; **~ offence** Verkehrsübertretung, -vergehen; **~ order** Fahrtauftrag; **~ performance** fahrerische Leistung, Fahrkünste; **international ~ permit** internationaler Führerschein; **~ pleasure** Freude am Fahren; **accident-free ~ record** unfallfreies Fahren; **~ regulations** Fahrvorschriften; **~ school** Fahrschule; **~-school instruction** Fahrschulunterricht; **~-school customer** Fahrschüler; **~ seat** Fahrersitz; **to be in the ~ seat** *(fig.)* Verantwortung tragen; **~ sensation** Fahrgefühl; **~ techniques** Fahrtechnik; **~ test** Fahrprüfung; **to pass one's ~ test** *(Br.)* seinen Führerschein machen, Fahrprüfung bestehen; **~ wheel** Steuerrad.

drizzle feiner Sprühregen, Nieselregen;
  ~ (v.) nieseln;
  ~ over s. o. sich negativ über j. äußern.

drone *(aeronautics)* unbemanntes (ferngesteuertes) Flugzeug, *(monotonous tone)* Brummen, Summen, Dröhnen, *(sluggard)* Schmarotzer, Nichtstuer, Drohne;
  the parson's endless ~ das endlose Geleier des Pfarrers;
  ~ of an engine Dröhnen des Motors;
  ~ (v.) faulenzen;
  ~ one's life away sein Leben im Müßiggang verbringen;
  to hear the noise of a city subdued to a ~ abgeschwächtes Großstadtgeräusch hören.

droop *(v.)* erschöpft zusammensinken, umfallen, *(fig.)* sich sinken (Kopf hängen) lassen, *(prices)* fallen, abflauen, abbröckeln.

drooping *(prices)* abbröckelnd, abflauend;
  to stand like a ~ lily *(coll.)* völlig geknickt dastehen; **to revive the ~ spirits of a party** die erschlafften Lebensgeister einer Partei wieder beleben.

drop Tröpfchen, *(el.)* Abfall, *(fig.)* Kleinigkeit, Quentchen, *(inclination)* steiler Abhang, plötzliche Senkung, starkes Gefälle, *(prices)* Sturz, plötzliches Fallen, Sinken, Rückgang, *(social decline)* gesellschaftlicher Abstieg, *(stock exchange)* Einbruch, Baisse;
  at the ~ of a hat *(US coll.)* beim geringsten Anlaß, bei jeder passenden und unpassenden Gelegenheit; **by ~s** tröpfchenweise, in kleinen Portionen;

air ~ Absetzen von Fallschirmspringern; **price ~** Kursrückgang, -schlag;
  ~ in the bucket Tropfen auf den heißen Stein; **~ in consumption** Konsumrückgang; **~ in the customs duty** Verkürzung der Zollsätze; **~ in demand** Nachfragerückgang; **~ in earnings** Ertragsrückgang; **sharp ~ in export orders** scharfer Ausfuhrrückgang; **~ in investments** Investitionsschwund; **~ in market rates** Verbilligung der Geldmarktsätze; **a ~ in the ocean** Tropfen auf den heißen Stein; **~ in prices** Kurs-, Preisrückgang; **~ in prices of stock** Kursrückgang; **~ in production** Produktionsrückgang; **~ in profits** Gewinnrückgang; **~ in sales** Rückgang in Verkäufen, Abschwächung des Umsatzes, Umsatzrückgang; **~ in share prices** Kursrückgang, Sinken der Aktienkurse; **~ in stocks** Lagerrückgang, -abbau; **~ in takings** Einnahmenrückgang; **sudden ~ of temperature** plötzlicher Temperaturrückgang, -sturz; **~ in turnover** Umsatzrückgang; **~ in unemployment** Arbeitslosenrückgang; **~ in value** Wertabfall; **~ in voltage** Spannungsabfall;
  ~ (v.) *(correspondence)* einschlafen, *(prices)* fallen, sinken, zurückgehen, *(US, university)* relegieren, ausschließen;
  ~ across s. o. zufällig auf j. stoßen;

drop *(v.)* **behind** zurückbleiben;
  ~ to the rear ins Hintertreffen geraten.

drop *(v.)* **in** *(call)* kurz vorbeikommen, hereinschauen, *(orders)* eingehen, einlaufen;
  ~ on s. o. bei jem. kurz vorsprechen, jem. einen kurzen Besuch abstatten; **~ for a moment** für einen Augenblick hereinschauen.

drop *(v.)* **into** | **a fortune** unerwartet zu einem Vermögen gelangen; **~ the habit** sich langsam abgewöhnen; **~ oil into s. th.** Öl auf etw. gießen; **~ on a party** in eine Gesellschaft hineinschneien.

drop *(v.)* **off** *(customers)* wegbleiben, *(el.)* abfallen;
  ~ from last year hinter dem letzten Jahr zurückbleiben.

drop *(v.)* **on to a secret** auf ein Geheimnis stoßen.

drop *(v.)* **out** ausfallen;
  ~ of s. th. sich aus einer Sache zurückziehen, nicht mehr mitmachen; **~ of a contest** aus einem Wettbewerb ausscheiden; **an employee ~** Angestellten aussteuern; **~ of the management arrangement of 60 days' notice** sich mit einer zweimonatigen Kündigung aus einer Vereinbarung über die Vorstandsbesetzung zurückziehen; **~ of the race for subscribers** aus dem Wettlauf für neue Subskribenten ausscheiden; **~ of things entirely** sich gänzlich zurückziehen.

drop *(v.)* **through** durchfallen.

drop *(v.)* **upon** | **s. o.** j. zufällig treffen; **~ s. o. like a ton of bricks** auf j. wie ein Geier herabstoßen.

drop *(v.)* | **s. o.** mit jem. alle Beziehungen abbrechen, *(with the car)* j. absetzen; **~ s. one's acquaintance** j. fallen lassen; **~ an action** Klage zurücknehmen (fallenlassen); **~ foreign aid** Auslandshilfe einstellen; **~ the anchor** ankern, vor Anker gehen; **~ a brick** *(coll., Br.)* ins Fettnäpfchen treten; **~ the charge** Einstellung des Verfahrens veranlassen, Ermittlungsverfahren einstellen; **~ correspondence** Korrespondenz (Briefwechsel) einstellen; **~ court proceedings** Gerichtsverfahren einstellen; **~ s. o. at his door** jem. zu Hause absetzen; **~ all operational duties** sich völlig aus der Geschäftsführung zurückziehen; **~ a hint** jem. einen Hinweis geben; **~ s. th. like a hot chestnut (potato)** etw. wie eine heiße Kartoffel fallen lassen; **~ a letter** *(printer)* Buchstaben zu setzen vergessen; **~ a letter into the postbox (pillar box,** *Br.)* Brief einwerfen, Brief in den Briefkasten einwerfen; **~ s. o. a line** jem. ein paar Zeilen schreiben; **~ a lot of money on a deal** bei einem Geschäft viel Geld einbüßen; **~ a matter** Sache ruhen lassen; **~ a meagre 5/8** nur um knapp 5/8 fallen; **~ a member from the roll** j. von der Mitgliederliste streichen; **~ money** *(sl.)* Geld loswerden; **~ s. o. for nonpayment of dues** j. wegen Nichtbezahlung seiner Mitgliederbeiträge ausschließen; **~ by parachute** mit dem Fallschirm abwerfen; **~ parachutists** Luftlandetruppen absetzen; **~ a passenger** Fahrgast (Mitfahrer) absetzen; **~ a patent** Patent fallen lassen; **~ the pilot** *(fig.)* Piloten absetzen, wichtige Persönlichkeit entlassen; **~ two points** um zwei Punkte fallen; **~ a policy** Versicherungspolice kündigen; **~ in quality** Qualitätsrückgang erfahren; **~ to the rear** ins Hintertreffen geraten; **~ a remark** beiläufige Bemerkung machen; **~ shifts** Feierschichten einlegen; **~ a subject** Thema fallenlassen, Sache zu den Akten legen; **~ a word in s. one's ear** jem. etw. zuflüstern; **~ one's work** seine Arbeit niederlegen;
  to be ready to ~ zum Umfallen müde; **to drink to the last ~** *(fig.)* bis zur Neige leeren; **to get the ~ on s. o.** *(US coll.)* jds. ungünstige Lage ausnutzen; **to have a ~ in one's eye** *(coll.)*

einen sitzen haben; **to have taken a ~ too much** einen über den Durst getrunken haben, leicht betrunken sein; **to suffer a dramatic ~ in public support** im Ansehen der Öffentlichkeit einen dramatischen Rückschlag erleiden; **to take a ~ now and then** sich gelegentlich ein Gläschen zu Gemüte führen; **to work till one ~s** bis zum Umfallen arbeiten;

~ bomb Fliegerbombe; **~ bottom** *(railway carriage)* Bodenklappe; **~ box** *(US)* Briefkasten; **~ compartment** Versenktisch; **~ curtain** *(theater)* Pausenvorhang; **~ letter** *(US)* Ortsbrief; **~ letter box** toter Briefkasten; **~ message** *(mil.)* Abwurfmeldung; **lower inter-~ mileage** geringer Kilometeranteil einzelner Frachtstücke; **~ pit** Arbeitsgrube; **~ point** Abwurfstelle; **~ scene** *(theater)* dramatische Schlußszene; **~ seat** Klappsitz; **~ shipment** Direktverkauf durch Grossisten ohne eigenes Lager; **~ shipment delivery** Streckengutlieferung; **~ shipment wholesaler (shipper)** Großhändler mit Streckengeschäft, Grossist ohne eigenes Lager, auftragsvermittelnder Großhändler, *(US)* Aufträge einsammelnder Makler; **~ sound** Wetter-, Fallsonde; **~ table** Klapptisch; **~ tank** Abwurftank; **~ zone** *(parachuters)* Absprunggelände.

drophead Versenkvorrichtung;
~ coupé geschlossener Wagen mit versenkbarem Verdeck.

dropoff | in enrolments Immatrikulationsrückgang; **~ en-route** *(waggon)* Abhängung unterwegs; **~ in profits** Gewinnrückgang; **~ in tourists** Rückgang des Touristenstromes;
~ charge *(car renting)* Abstellgebühr, Rückführungskosten.

dropped, to be unter den Tisch fallen, *(payments)* in Fortfall kommen, aufhören; **to have ~** *(prices)* gefallen sein.

dropout *(coll.)* Versager, Niete.

dropper Falschgeldverteiler.

dropping | of prices Abflauen der Kurse; **~ of trade barriers** Aufhebung von Handelsschranken;
~ field Absprunggelände; **~ ground** Holzzwischenlagerplatz; **~ point** Abwurfstelle; **~ zone** *(parachuters)* Absprunggelände.

dross Abfall, wertloses Zeug, Schlacke;
~ (a.) wertlos, vergänglich.

drought Dürre, Trockenperiode;
~-stricken von der Trockenheit schwer betroffen; **~ tide** Dürrezeit.

drove getriebene Herde, *(fig.)* Herde, Menge, *(narrow drain, Br.)* schmaler Ent-, Bewässerungsgraben;
~ of tourists Touristenstrom.

drover Viehhändler.

drown *(v.)* ertrinken;
to be ~ed *(vote)* untergehen.

drowned man Ertrunkener.

drowning man Ertrinkender.

drowse *(v.)* dahindösen, geistig abstumpfen.

drub *(v.) s. th. into s. o.* jem. etw. einhämmern.

drudge Packesel, Kuli, Roboter;
~ (v.) at dictionary making sich mit der Lexikonherstellung abplagen;
to be the ~ Aschenputtel sein.

drudgery Schinderei, Abplacken

drug Droge, Arzneimittel, *(narcotics)* Rauschgift;
~s Apothekerwaren;
dangerous ~ Rauschgifte; **stupefying ~** Betäubungsmittel; **~ on the market** unverkäufliche (schlecht verkäufliche) Ware, Ladenhüter;
~ (v.) mit Drogen betäuben, Drogen verschreiben, *(coll.)* Rauschgift nehmen;
to administer ~s Narkotika verabreichen; **to be a ~ on the market** sich schwer verkaufen, Ladenhüter sein;
~ abuse Drogenmißbrauch; **~ addict** Rauschgiftsüchtiger; **~ addiction** Rauschgiftsucht; **~ authority** Rauschgiftdezernat; **~ dealer** Rauschgifthändler; **~ education** Drogenaufklärung; **~ fiend** Rauschgiftsüchtiger; **~ habit** Drogen-, Rauschgiftsucht; **~ investigator** Rauschgiftermittler; **~ offence** Rauschgiftverfahren; **~ pedlar** Rauschgifthändler; **~ pusher** Rauschgifthändler; **~ traffic** Rauschgifthandel, -verkehr; **~ trafficker** Drogen-, Rauschgifthändler; **~ trafficking offence** Vergehen gegen den Rauschgifthandel.

druggist Drogist, Pharmazeut, *(Scot., US)* Apotheker.

drugless ohne Arznei.

drugstore *(US)* Apotheke, Drogerie, Ausschank;
~ owner *(US)* Apothekenbesitzer.

drum Trommel, zylindrischer Behälter, *(sl.)* Renntip;
with ~s beating mit klingendem Spiel;
~ (v.) (US) [Kunden] werben, Werbetrommel rühren; **~ s. th. into s. o. (s. one's head)** jem. etw. eintrichtern; **~ out of the party** aus der Partei ausstoßen; **~ up** zusammentrommeln;

~ up business Geschäft ankurbeln, *(fam.)* Reklametrommel rühren; **~ up customers** *(US)* Kunden [an]werben; **~ up a lesson** Lektion einpauken; **~ up a new majority** knappe Mehrheit zustandebringen;
to beat (thump) the ~ auffällige Werbung betreiben;
~ wheel Kabeltrommel.

drumfire *(fig.)* Trommelfeuer.

drumhead court martial Standgericht.

drummer Trommler, Schlagzeuger, *(commercial traveller, US)* Handlungsreisender, Vertreter, *(tout)* Kundenfänger;
~ floater Reisegepäckversicherung [für Handlungsreisende].

drunk Zechgelage, Sauferei, *(drunken person, sl.)* Betrunkener;
~ (a.) betrunken;
beastly ~ stinkbesoffen; **three parts ~** *(fam.)* ganz schön betrunken; **~ with joy** freudetrunken; **~ as a lord (to the light, sl.)** besinnungslos betrunken, sternhagelvoll.

drunkard Trinker, Säufer;
habitual ~ Gewohnheitstrinker, Alkoholiker.

drunken person Betrunkener.

drunkenness Trunkenheit;
habitual ~ Alkoholismus.

drunkometer *(sl.)* Gerät zur Messung des Alkoholspiegels.

dry *(prohibitionist)* Alkoholgegner;
~ (v.) austrocknen, verdunsten;
~ out *(addict)* Entziehungskur machen; **~ up** ver-, austrocknen, *(labo(u)r reserves)* versiegen, *(orders)* aufhören, ausbleiben;
to go ~ *(US coll.)* Alkoholverbot einführen; **keep ~!** vor Feuchtigkeit schützen!; **to turn the whole country ~** das ganze Land trockenlegen, Alkoholverbot für das ganze Land aussprechen;
~ (a.) trocken, niederschlagsarm, dürr, ausgedorrt, *(without alcohol, sl.)* alkoholfeindlich, unter Alkoholverbot, *(mil.)* ohne scharfe Munition, *(plain)* schmucklos, nüchtern, ungeschminkt, nackt, *(without feeling)* kühl, gleichgültig, teilnahmslos;
~ as a bone knochentrocken; **as ~ as dust** stinklangweilig;
~ battery Trockenbatterie; **~ book** langweiliges Buch; **~ bridge** *(US)* Bahn-, Straßenüberführung; **~ capital** unverwässertes Gesellschaftskapital; **~ cargo container** Trockenfrachtbehälter; **~-clean** *(v.)* chemisch reinigen; **~ cleaners** chemische Reinigungsanstalt; **~ climate** trockenes Klima; **~ dock** Trockendock; **~-dock** *(v.)* ins Trockendock bringen; **with ~ eyes** ungerührt; **~ exchange** fingiertes Tauschgeschäft; **~ facts** ungeschminkte Tatsachen; **~ farm** Trockenfarm; **~ fountain pen** leerer Füllfederhalter; **~ goods** *(US)* Textilwaren, Textilien; **~ goods business** *(US)* Textilgeschäft; **~-goods store** *(US)* Textilgeschäft; **~ humo(u)r** trockener Humor; **~ ice** Trockeneis; **~ law** *(US)* Prohibitionsgesetz; **~ lecture** uninteressante Vorlesung; **~ milk** Trockenmilch; **~ money** Bargeld, bares Geld; **~ mortgage** [etwa] Grundschuld; **~ nurse** Kinder-, Säuglingsschwester; **~-out** *(addict)* Entziehungskur; **~ posting** Naßklebeverfahren; **~ provisions** feste Nahrungsmittel; **~ rent** Naturalzins; **~ rot** Trockenfäule; **~ trust** abstraktes Treuhandverhältnis; **~ walling** Trockenmauer; **~ war** unblutiger Krieg; **~ weight** Trockengewicht; **~ wit** trockener Witz; **~ work** langweilige Arbeit.

drying | up of labo(u)r reserves Versiegen des Arbeitskräftereservoir;
~ chamber Trockenkammer; **~ machine** Wäschetrockner.

dryland Dürregebiet.

dual zweifach, doppelt;
~ carriageway *(Br.)* Fernverkehrsstraße mit Parallelbahnen; **~ citizenship** doppelte Staatsbürgerschaft; **~ consciousness** gespaltene Persönlichkeit; **~ control** *(airplane)* Zweifachsteuerung; **~ distribution** *(US)* zweigleisiges Vertriebssystem; **~ gold price** gespaltener Goldpreis; **~ mandate** Doppelmandat; **~ membership** Doppelmitgliedschaft; **~ nationality** doppelte Staatsangehörigkeit; **~ ownership** Doppeleigentum; **~ pay system** *(transportation)* Lohnrechnungsverfahren mit zwei Möglichkeiten; **~ personality** gespaltene Persönlichkeit; **~ pricing** Doppelpreissystem; **~ purpose** einem doppelten Zweck dienend; **~ tyres** Zwillingsbereifung; **~-use package** wiederverwendbare [Ver]packung, Mehrwegpackung.

duality of ownership doppeltes Eigentum.

dub *(v.)* synchronisieren;
~-in Toneinblendung.

dubbing Synchronisierung.

dubious zweifelhaft, ungewiß, unsicher, dubiös;
~ answer zweideutige Antwort; **~ character** undurchsichtiger Charakter; **~ company** in schlechtem Ruf stehende (unseriöse) Gesellschaft; **~ compliment** zweifelhaftes Kompliment; **~**

hono(u)r zweifelhafte Ehre; ~ **paper** Papier von zweifelhaftem Wert; ~ **stocks** schlechte Papiere; ~ **undertaking** unsicheres Unternehmen.

duck *(chap, US, sl.)* Bursche, Kerl, *(darling)* Schätzchen, *(fabric)* Packleinwand, *(mil.)* Amphibienfahrzeug;
like a ~ **in a thunderstorm** *(coll.)* völlig verstört; **like water off a** ~'s **back** ohne die geringste Wirkung;
lame ~ lahme Ente, Invalide, *(US)* bankrotter Spekulant; **sitting** ~ leicht zu erlegende Beute;
~ *(v.) (US)* sich drücken, *(airplane)* unterfliegen; ~ **out** *(US sl.)* verduften, sich verdünnisieren; ~ **a payment** Zahlungsverpflichtung nicht einhalten;
to play ~**s and drakes with one's life** sein Leben leichtsinnig aufs Spiel setzen; **to play ~s and drakes with one's money** mit seinem Geld nur so um sich schmeißen; **to take to s. th. like a ~ to water** völlig natürlich auf etw. reagieren;
~'s **egg** Niete; ~ **soup** *(US sl.)* kinderleichte Sache; **in two shakes of a** ~'s **tail** gleich, sofort.

ducking Schiffstaufe.

duct Schriftzug.

ductile *(fig.)* fügsam, lenkbar.

dud *(banknote, sl.)* falsche Banknote, Fälschung, *(dropout)* Versager, Niete, *(shell)* Blindgänger;
~s Krempel, Klamotten, Siebensachen;
~ *(a.)* nachgemacht;
~ **check** *(US) (cheque, Br.)* ungedeckter Scheck; ~ **note** gefälschte Banknote; ~ **ranch** *(US)* Touristenranch; ~ **stock** unverkäufliche Waren.

due *(charge)* Gebühr, angemessen, richtig, vorschriftsmäßig, pflichtgemäß, *(course)* schuldig, zustehend, geschuldet, *(debt)* Verpflichtung, Schuld, *(membership)* Beitrag, *(right)* Anspruch, *(share)* [zukommender] Anteil, gebührender Lohn;
~ *(a.)* gebührend, geziemend, *(course)* genau, *(mature)* fällig, [sofort] zahlbar, *(owing)* schuldig, zustehend, geschuldet;
before [falling] ~ vor Verfall; **not yet** ~ noch nicht fällig; **past** ~ überfällig; **until** ~ bis zur Verfallzeit; **when** ~ bei Verfall, zur Verfallzeit;
~ **at call** täglich fällig;
amount ~ Schuldbetrag, fälliger Betrag; **balance** ~ Debetsaldo; **fees** ~ fällige Gebühren; **growing** ~ fällig werdend; **interest** ~ angefallene (fällige) Zinsen; **long past** ~ längst überfällig; **mails** ~ ausgebliebene Post; **rent** ~ fällige Miete; **salary** ~ fälliges Gehalt; **tax** ~ Steuersoll; **wages** ~ fälliger Lohn;
~ **from affiliates** *(balance sheet)* Forderungen an Konzernunternehmen; ~ **from banks** *(balance sheet)* Guthaben bei [anderen] Banken, Nostroguthaben; ~ **to banks** *(balance sheet)* Bankschulden, Nostroverpflichtungen; **debts** ~ **to us** Passivschulden; **debts** ~ **and owing** Aktiva und Passiva; ~ **from other funds** *(governmental accounting)* Guthaben bei anderen Etatstiteln; ~ **to other funds** *(governmental accounting)* Verpflichtungen bei anderen Etatstiteln;
to be ~ geschuldet werden, zustehen, fällig sein, *(mail)* ausgeblieben sein, *(train)* ankommen; **to be** ~ **to arrive** planmäßig ankommen sollen; **to be** ~ **to careless driving** auf leichtsinnige Fahrweise zurückzuführen sein; **to be** ~ **to retire** Altersgrenze erreicht haben; **to be** ~ **to s. o.** jem. zuzuschreiben sein, jem. gebühren; **to become (fall)** ~ zahlbar [fällig] werden, verfallen; **to claim one's** ~ verlangen, was einem zusteht; **to declare** ~ für fällig erklären; **to fall** ~ **next month** nächsten Monat fällig werden; **to get one's** ~ nach Verdienst behandelt werden; **to give the devil his** ~ jedem das Seine geben lassen; **to pay when** ~ pünktlich zahlen; **to take up a draft when** ~ Wechsel bei Fälligkeit einlösen;
~ **bill** *(US)* Promesse; **with** ~ **care** mit gehöriger Sorgfalt; ~ **and reasonable care** im Verkehr erforderliche Sorgfalt; **to be received with** ~ **ceremonies** mit dem zustehenden Protokoll empfangen werden; ~ **compensation** volle Entschädigung; **after** ~ **consideration** nach sorgfältiger (reiflicher) Überlegung; **in** ~ **course** zur rechten Zeit, fristgemäß, -gerecht; ~-**course holder** gutgläubiger Inhaber; ~ **course of law** rechtmäßiges Verfahren; ~ **date (day)** Fälligkeit, Fälligkeitsdatum, -termin, Verfalltag; **to fix a** ~ **date** fällig stellen; ~ **diligence** gehörige Sorgfalt; **in** ~ **form of law** in rechtsgültiger Form, formgerecht; **hono(u)r** bereitwillige Annahme; ~ **influence** erlaubte Beeinflussung; **to take all** ~ **measures** notwendige Vorkehrungen treffen; ~ **and proper notice** ordnungsgemäße Benachrichtigung, fristgerechte Kündigung; **to take** ~ **notice** gehörige Vormerkung nehmen; ~ **payment** rechtzeitige (fristgemäße) Zahlung; ~ **process of law** ordnungsgemäßes Verfahren; ~ **proof** *(insurance law)* ausreichender Nachweis; ~ **protection** bereitwillige Annahme; ~

regard gehörige Rücksicht; ~ **reward** angemessene Belohnung; ~ **service** ordnungsgemäße Zustellung; **in** ~ **time** fristgemäß, -gerecht, termingerecht; **to give s. o.** ~ **warning** jem. fristgemäß kündigen.

dues *(club)* [Vereins]beitrag, *(duties)* Abgaben, *(fees)* Gebühren, *(toll)* Zoll;
dock ~ Dockgebühren; **ferry** ~ Fährgeld; **fiscal** ~ fiskalische Gebühren; **fixed** ~ feste Gebühren; **harbo(u)r** ~ Hafengebühren; **market** ~ Stand-, Marktgebühren, -abgaben; **membership** ~ Mitgliedsbeitrag; **periodic** ~ *(US)* laufende Beiträge; **pier** ~ Anlegegebühren; **port** ~ Hafenabgaben; **public** ~ Abgaben; **town** ~ Gemeindeabgaben; **union** ~ Gewerkschaftsbeiträge; **variable** ~ veränderliche Gebühren;
~ **paid in advance** vor Fälligkeit gezahlte Schulden;
to collect ~ Beiträge erheben; **to levy** ~ Gebühren erheben; **to pay one's** ~ seinen Anteil (Beitrag) zahlen, seinen Verpflichtungen nachkommen, *(US sl.)* seine Erfahrungen machen;
~ **checkoff** automatische Beitragseinbehaltung; ~ **increase** Beitragserhöhung; ~ **payer** Gebührenzahler; ~ **shop** gewerkschaftspflichtiger Betrieb; ~ **tax** *(US)* Mitgliedschaftssteuer.

duel Duell, Zweikampf;
students' ~ Mensur;
to fight a ~ sich duellieren.

duenna Anstandsdame.

duffel bag *(mil.)* Kleider-, Seesack.

duffer *(peddler)* Hausierer, *(sl.)* Ramschware, Schund, Talmi, *(stupid person, Br., coll.)* Stümper, Pfuscher.

dug-in job Bombenstellung.

dugout *(mil.)* Unterstand, *(Br., sl.)* reaktivierter Offizier.

dull *(goods)* nicht verlangt (gefragt), schwer verkäuflich, *(mirror)* blind, *(person)* stumpfsinnig, schwer von Begriff, beschränkt, *(season)* still, geschäftslos, *(trade)* flau, lustlos, matt;
~ **as ditchwater** mordslangweilig; ~ **of sale** wenig begehrt; ~ **owing mainly to lack of support** in erster Linie mangels Interesse lustlos;
~ *(v.)* sich abschwächen, *(fig.)* abstumpfen;
to be ~ **of comprehension** schwer von Begriff sein; **to find work deadly** ~ Arbeit stupide finden; **to turn** ~ flau werden;
~ **book** uninteressantes Buch; ~ **business** mattes Geschäft; **thoroughly** ~ **evening** total verlorener Abend; **deadly** ~ **hole** trostloses Nest; ~ **market** lustlose Börse; ~ **occupation** langweiliger Beruf; ~ **performer** *(stock exchange)* schlechtgehendes Papier; ~ **prospects** trostlose Aussichten; ~ **sale** schleppender Absatz; ~ **season** tote Saison; ~ **style** trockener (langweiliger) Stil; ~ **time of business** Geschäftsstille; ~ **little town** langweilige Kleinstadt.

dullness *(stock exchange)* Börsenflaute, *(trade)* Flaute, Geschäftslosigkeit, -stille, Lustlosigkeit, Stagnation;
~ **in the stock market** flaue Stimmung auf dem Aktienmarkt.

duly *(properly)* ordnungsgemäß, gebührend, vorschriftsmäßig, richtig, gehörig, *(punctually)* pünktlich, *(in due time)* zur rechten Zeit, rechtzeitig;
~ **appointed** ordnungsgemäß bestellt; ~ **authorized** mit gehöriger Vollmacht versehen; ~ **completed** formgerecht abgeschlossen; ~ **determined by notice to quit** ordnungsgemäß gekündigt; ~ **drawn** ordnungsgemäß ausgestellt; ~ **received** richtig erhalten; ~ **signed** ordnungsgemäß unterschrieben.

dumb stumm, sprachlos;
~ **bidding** Versteigern mit verstecktem Mindestgebot; ~-**waiter** drehbarer Abstelltisch, *(US)* Speiseaufzug.

dumdum bullet Dumdumgeschoß.

dummy *(book)* Blindband, -muster, Probeband, *(counterfeit)* Attrappe, *(crash test)* Unfallpuppe, *(man of straw)* Strohmann, *(model)* [Ausstellungs]muster, *(sham package)* Leer-, Schaupackung, Leeraufmachung, Aufmachungsmuster, *(shop window)* Schaufensterpuppe, *(theater)* Statist, *(traffic tower, US sl.)* Verkehrsturm;
~ *(a.)* nachgemacht, unecht, *(sham)* vorgeschoben, fingiert;
to stand there like a stuffed ~ wie ein Ölgötze dastehen;
~ **activity** Scheintätigkeit; ~ **advertisement** fingierte Annonce; ~ **agency** Scheinvertretung; ~ **branch** Scheinfiliale; ~ **car** Draisine; ~ **charge** *(mil.)* Platzpatrone; ~ **concern** Scheinunternehmen; ~ **corporation** *(US)* vorgeschobene Gesellschaft, Stroh-, Scheingesellschaft, Briefkastenfirma; ~ **director** Proformadirektor; ~ **editor** Sitzredakteur; ~ **grenade** *(mil.)* Übungshandgranate; ~ **gun** Revolverattrappe; ~ **investor** Scheinanleger; ~ **package** Schaupackung, Attrappe; ~ **run** Probelauf; ~ **salesman** stummer Verkäufer; ~ **tank** Tankattrappe; ~ **tender** Scheinangebot; ~ **transaction** Scheingeschäft; ~ **treatment** *(statistics)* fiktive Behandlung; ~ **warhead** blinder Gefechtskopf; ~ **works** Scheinanlage.

dump dumpfer Fall, Plumps, *(car, US)* Müllabfuhr, Depot, Lagerplatz, Speicher, *(device for dumping)* Kippvorrichtung, *(dumping)* Ab-, Entladen, *(dumping ground)* Müll-, Schuttabdeplatz, Schutthalde, Kippe, *(mining)* Halde, *(money, sl.)* Heller, *(railway car)* Kippwagen, *(shabby house, sl.)* Spelunke, Absteige, *(Br., thick piece)* Klumpen, Brocken;
ammunition ~ Munitionslager, trash ~ *(US)* Müllkippe;
~ *(v.)* abladen, auskippen, *(mil.)* stapeln, lagern, *(rubbish)* Müll abladen, *(stock exchange)* Effektenpakete billig abstoßen, *(export trade)* Ware in großer Menge billig auf den Markt bringen, ins Ausland zu Schleuderpreisen verkaufen, Dumping betreiben;
~ **coal** *(US)* Kohle auf Halde schütten; ~ **goods on a foreign market** Waren im Ausland billig auf den Markt werfen; ~ **overboard** über Bord werfen;
to be in the ~s niedergeschlagen sein, *(stocks)* billig zu haben sein; **not to care a ~** *(coll.)* sich einen Dreck um etw. kümmern;
~ **body** Kippeinrichtung; ~ **car** Müllwagen; ~ **heap** Schutthaufen, -halde; ~ **pile** Schutthaufen; ~ **truck** *(US)* Kippwagen; ~ **wagon** *(US)* Müllwagen, -abfuhr.
dumpage *(US)* Abladerecht.
dumpcart Kippwagen.
dumped goods Dumpingwaren.
dumper *(truck)* Kippwagen.
dumping Deponie, Schutt-, Müllabladen, *(export trade)* Warenausfuhr zu Schleuderpreisen, Schleuderausfuhr, *(price)* Unterbietung des Konkurrenzpreises, Preisunterbietung, Dumping;
fly ~ wilde Deponie; **foreign exchange ~** Valutadumping; **hidden ~** verschleiertes Dumping; **price ~** Preisunterbietung;
~ **car** Müllwagen, -abfuhr; ~ **cart** Kippwagen; ~ **charge** Müllkippengebühr, *(export trade)* Dumpingverfahren, Anklage wegen Verstoßes gegen die Dumpingbestimmungen; ~ **complaint** Dumpingklage; ~ **device** Abladevorrichtung; ~ **duties** Ausgleichzoll gegen Schleuderausfuhren; ~ **ground** *(mining)* Haldengelände, *(US, rubbish)* Müll-, Schuttabladeplatz; ~ **place** Schuttablageplatz; ~ **practices** Dumpingpraktiken; ~ **truck (waggon)** Kippwagen, Müllfahrzeug.
dun *(creditor)* Forderer, drängender Gläubiger, *(demand for payment)* Zahlungsaufforderung, *(dunner)* Schuldeneintreiber;
~ *(v.)* mahnen, drängen, j. drängend zur Zahlung auffordern;
to be ~ed by one's creditors von seinen Gläubigern gedrängt werden.
dune Düne;
~ **buggy** Strandauto.
dung Mist, Dung;
~ **cart** Mistkarren.
dungeon Verlies, Kerker;
~ *(v.)* **up** einkerkern.
dunghill Misthaufen, *(fig.)* schmutzige Wohnung, Loch.
dunnage *(personal effects)* persönliches Gepäck, *(railway)* Staumaterial, *(ship)* Schiffsgarnierung, *(wood)* Stammholz;
~ **allowance** *(railway)* tariffreie Beförderung von Staumaterial.
dunner drängender Gläubiger, Schuldeintreiber.
dunning | **letter** Mahnbrief, dringende Zahlungsaufforderung; ~ **screw** Mahnung, Zahlungsaufforderung.
duopoly Marktkontrolle durch zwei Firmen.
duostroller *(US)* Zwillingskinderwagen.
dupable vertrauensselig, einfältig.
dupe Angeführter, Betrogener, *(coll.)* Filmkopie;
~**s** zusätzliche Werbematerialkopien;
to be ~d Opfer einer Täuschung sein.
duper Bauernfänger.
dupery Bauernfängerei, Übertölpelung.
duplex | **apartment** *(US)* **(flat, Br.)** Wohnung mit Zimmern in verschiedenen Stockwerken; ~ **house** *(US)* Zweifamilienhaus; ~ **telegraphy** Gegensprechtelegrafie; ~ **telephony** Gegensprechverkehr.
duplicate *(second copy)* Doppel, Duplikat, gleichlautende Abschrift, Gleichschrift, Zweit-, Neu-, zweite Ausfertigung, *(discharge of bankrupt)* Entlastungszeugnis für Gemeinschuldner, *(second of exchange)* Sekunda-, Duplikatwechsel, Wechselduplikat, *(pawnbroker's ticket)* Pfandschein, *(replacement of document)* Ersatzurkunde;
in ~ in doppelter Ausfertigung, doppelt ausgefertigt;
~ **of exchange** Wechselduplikat; ~ **of invoice** Rechnungsdoppel; ~ **of waybill** Frachtbriefdoppel;
~ *(v.)* Duplikat anfertigen, kopieren, vervielfältigen; ~ **with another** *(accounts)* miteinander übereinstimmen; ~ **keys for the front door** Ersatzschlüssel für die Eingangstür anfertigen lassen;

to draw a bill of exchange in ~ Wechsel doppelt ausfertigen; **to make out s. th. in ~** Duplikat von etw. anfertigen, etw. doppelt ausfertigen;
~ **bill** Wechselduplikat; ~ **receipted bills** quittierte Rechnungen in doppelter Ausfertigung; ~ **block** Duplikatätzung; ~ **bookkeeping** doppelte Buchführung; ~ **check** *(US)* **(cheque,** Br.**)** Scheckduplikat; ~ **consignment note** Frachtbriefduplikat; ~ **copy** Zweitschrift; ~ **deposit slip** Einzahlungsbelegdurchschlag; ~ **document** Zweitausfertigung; ~ **invoice** Rechnungsdoppel; ~ **key** Nachschlüssel; ~ **parts** Ersatzteile; ~ **receipt** Quittungsduplikat; ~ **sample** *(statistics)* Wiederholungsstichprobe; ~ **taxation** Doppelbesteuerung; ~ **waybill** Frachtbriefduplikat; ~ **will** in zwei Urschriften errichtetes Testament.
duplicating | **book** Kopierbuch; ~ **machine** Vervielfältigungsapparat; ~ **paper** Saugpostpapier.
duplication Vervielfältigung, *(copy)* Kopie, Abschrift, Duplikat, *(double entry)* doppelte Buchung.
duplicator Kopier-, Vervielfältigungsapparat.
duplicity Duplizität, *(deceit)* Doppelzüngigkeit, *(law court)* gleichzeitige Verhandlung mehrerer Rechtssachen.
durability Lebensdauer, *(stability)* Wiederstandsfähigkeit.
durable haltbar, dauerhaft, beständig, *(stable)* widerstandsfähig;
~**s**, ~ **goods** langlebige Gebrauchsgüter (Wirtschaftsgüter), dauerhafte Konsumgüter.
duration Dauer, Laufzeit;
for the ~ für die Dauer einer Vereinbarung; **for the ~ of the war** während des Krieges, auf Kriegsdauer; **of short ~** kurzfristig; **mean ~** mittlere Laufzeit;
~ **of appointment** Amtsdauer; ~ **of benefits** Unterstützungszeitraum; ~ **of a bill** Laufzeit eines Wechsels; ~ **of a call** *(tel.)* Gesprächsdauer; ~ **of copyright** Schutzfrist; ~ **of flight** Flugdauer; ~ **of lease** Pachtdauer; ~ **of life** *(insurance)* Lebensdauer; ~ **of offer** Gültigkeit einer Offerte; ~ **of patent** Gültigkeit eines Patents; ~ **of a policy** Laufzeit einer Police; ~ **of rent** Mietzeit; ~ **of sunshine** Sonnenscheindauer; ~ **of transit** Transitdauer; ~ **of validity** Geltungs-, Gültigkeitsdauer;
to pick up a ~ job Dauerberuf finden.
duress *(compulsion)* Nötigung, Zwang, *(restraint of liberty)* Freiheitsberaubung, Einkerkerung;
under ~ unter Druck, durch Nötigung gezwungen;
mental ~ psychischer Zwang; **physical ~** Nötigung durch körperliche Gewalt; **political ~** politische Erpressung;
~ **of goods** widerrechtliche Besitzergreifung; ~ **of imprisonment** Freiheitsberaubung;
to act under ~ unter widerrechtlichem Zwang handeln; **to be under ~** gefangengehalten werden; **to make a contract under ~** zu einem Vertrag gezwungen werden.
dusk | **of the evening** Abenddämmerung;
~ **hour** Dämmerstunde.
dust Staub, *(Br.)* *(earthy remains)* sterbliche Hülle, Leichnam, *(refuse ready for collection, Br.)* Kehrricht, abfuhrbereiter Müll, *(sl.)* Moos, Zaster, Pinke-Pinke, *(turmoil)* Wirbel, Aufregung;
humiliated to the ~ bis ins letzte gedemütigt;
~ *(v.)* abwischen, -stauben, *(v/i)* staubig machen (werden);
~ **s. one's jacket** jem. eine Tracht Prügel verabreichen;
to bite the ~ ins Gras beißen, im Felde fallen; **to drag in the ~** in den Schmutz ziehen; **to kick up (raise)** ~ viel Staub aufwirbeln; **to shake the ~ off one's feet** *(fig.)* entrüstet weggehen; **to take s. one's ~** *(US coll.)* von jem. überholt werden; **to throw ~ in s. one's eyes** jem. Sand in die Augen streuen;
~ **bowl** Staubloch; ~ **box** *(Br.)* Mülleimer, -kasten, -tonne; ~ **cart** *(Br.)* Müll[abfuhr]wagen, Müllabfuhr; ~ **coat** Staubmantel; ~ **content** Staubgehalt; ~ **cover** *(book)* Schutzumschlag, *(typewriter)* Schreibmaschinenhülle; ~ **devil** Windhose; ~ **hole** Müll-, Abfallgrube; ~ **jacket** Schutzumschlag; ~ **pan** Kehrrichtschaufel; ~ **removal** Entstaubung; ~ **shoot** Müllschlucker; **to have a ~-up with s. o.** *(coll.)* Auseinandersetzung mit jem. haben; ~ **wrapper** *(book)* Schutzumschlag.
dustbin *(Br.)* Mülleimer, -tonne.
dustcloth Staubtuch.
dustman *(Br.)* Müllfahrer, -abfuhr.
dusty, not so *(fam.)* gar nicht so übel.
Dutch *(US sl.)* unten durch, schlecht angeschrieben;
double ~ Kauderwelsch;
to beat the ~ mit dem Teufel fertig werden; **to be all ~ to s. o.** jem. wie böhmische Dörfer vorkommen; **to go ~** getrennte Kasse (Rechnung) machen; **to talk [double] ~** Kauderwelsch reden;
~ **auction** Versteigerung mit laufend erniedrigtem Ausbietungspreis; ~ **courage** *(coll.)* angetrunkener Mut; ~ **treat**

getrennte Kasse; **to talk to s. o. like a ~ uncle** j. gehörig zurechtweisen, jem. gehörig die Meinung sagen.

dutiability Zollpflichtigkeit.

dutiable zoll-, steuer-, gebühren-, abgabenpflichtig;
~ **goods** zollpflichtige Waren; ~ **value** Zollwert.

duties Aufgabenbereich;
customs ~ Zölle; **fiduciary** ~ Pflichten eines Treuhänders; **fiscal** ~ staatliche Abgaben; **honorary** ~ ehrenamtliche Aufgaben; **onerous** ~ schwere Pflichten; **rostered** ~ nach dem Dienstplan anfallende Aufgaben;
~ **of an agent** Vertreterbefugnisse; ~ **of a director** Vorstandsaufgaben; ~ **of a job** Aufgabengebiet; ~ **of a soldier** soldatische Aufgaben (Pflichten); ~ **on spirits** Alkoholsteuern;
to acquaint s. o. with his ~ j. in seinen Aufgabenkreis einführen; **to allocate** ~ Pflichtenkreis zuweisen; **to attend to one's** ~ seinen Pflichten obliegen; **to discharge** ~ Aufgaben wahrnehmen; **to enter upon new** ~ neuen Aufgabenbereich übernehmen; **to impose new** ~ neue Zollbestimmungen erlassen; **to introduce customs** ~ Zölle einführen; **to pay the** ~ **of a vessel** Schiff beim Zollamt deklarieren; **to pursue one's** ~ seine Aufgaben erledigen; **to refund** ~ Zölle vergüten; **to take up one's** ~ Stelle antreten; **to transfer** ~ **upon** Aufgaben übertragen.

duty *(customs)* Zoll[gebühren], Eingangsabgabe, *(fee)* Gebühr, Taxe, Auflage, *(impost)* [Verbrauchs]abgabe, [Verbrauchs]steuer, *(machine)* Nutzleistung, *(obligation)* Verbindlichkeit, Verpflichtung, Pflicht, Obliegenheit, Schuld, Schuldigkeit, *(reference)* Höflichkeitsbezeigung, -geste, *(service)* Dienst[pflicht], Aufgabe;
comformable to one's ~ pflichtgemäß; **exempt from (free of)** ~ *(customs)* zollfrei, *(fees)* gebühren-, spesenfrei, *(tax)* steuer-, abgabenfrei; **in** ~ **bound** von Rechts wegen, moralisch verpflichtet; **in the course of** ~ dienstlich; **liable (subject) to** ~ *(customs)* zollpflichtig, verzollbar, *(tax)* steuerpflichtig; **off** ~ dienstfrei, außerdienstlich; ~ **off** unversteuert, unverzollt; **on** ~ im Dienst, diensttuend; ~ **paid** versteuert, *(customs)* verzollt, nach Verzollung; **no** ~ **paid** unversteuert, *(customs)* unverzollt; ~ **unpaid** unverzollt; **when available to assume** ~ frühestmöglicher Diensteintritt;
account ~ *(Br.)* Nachlaßsteuer [für bewegliche Sachen]; **additional** ~ *(customs)* Zollaufschlag, Zuschlagzoll, *(tax)* Steuerzuschlag; **agricultural** ~ Agrarzoll; **basic** ~ Ausgangszollsatz; ~ **chargeable** zu erhebender Zoll; **civic** ~ staatsbürgerliche Pflicht, Bürgerpflicht; **commercial** *(Br.)* **(compensation, compensative, countervailing,** US**)** ~ Ausgleichszoll; **compound** ~ kombinierter Zoll, Mischzoll; **conjugal** ~ eheliche Pflicht; **conventional** ~ Vertragszollsatz; **customs** ~ Zoll; **customhouse** ~ Zollabgabe; **death** ~ *(Br.)* Nachlaß-, Erbschaftssteuer; **differential (discriminating)** ~ Staffel-, Vorzugs-, Differentialzoll; **dumping** ~ Ausgleichszoll für Schleuderausfuhr; **estate** ~ *(Br.)* Erbschafts-, Nachlaßsteuer; **excess** ~ überzahlte Steuer; **excise** ~ Warensteuer [für Inlandwaren], Verbrauchssteuer, -abgabe; **export** ~ Ausfuhr-, Ausgangszoll; **extra** ~ Steuerzuschlag; **import** ~ Einfuhrabgabe, -zoll; **indirect** ~ indirekte Steuer; **inhabited house** ~ *(Br.)* Wohngebäudesteuer; **judicial** ~ Rechtspflicht; **legacy** ~ *(Br.)* Vermächtnissteuer; **legal** ~ Rechtspflicht; **long** ~ Rück-, Nettozoll; **mineral rights** ~ *(Br.)* Bergregalabgabe; **mixed** ~ gemischter Wertzoll; **overpaid** ~ überzahlte Steuer; **penal** ~ Strafzoll; **preferential** ~ Vorzugszoll; **prohibitive** ~ Schutzzoll; **protective** ~ Schutzzoll; **railway passengers** ~ *(Br.)* Beförderungssteuer; **reciprocal** ~ gegenseitige Leistung; **retaliatory** ~ Retorsions-, Vergeltungs-, Kampfzoll; **revenue** ~ fiskalische Gebühr; **reversion value** ~ Heimfallsteuer; ~ **saved** gesparte Steuer; **short** ~ Zoll mit Rabatt; **special** ~ Sonderaufgabe; **specific** ~ Mengen-, Stückzoll; **stamp** ~ Stempelsteuer, -gebühr, -abgabe; **succession** ~ *(Br.)* Erbschaftssteuer für unbewegliches Vermögen; **tariff** ~ Zolltarif; **tonnage** ~ Tonnenzoll; **transit** ~ Durchgangszoll; **unascertained** ~ Pauschalzoll; **undeveloped land** ~ *(Br.)* Bauplatzabgabe; **uniform** ~ Einheitszoll; **ad valorem** ~ Wertzoll;
~ **to accept goods** Warenabnahmeverpflichtung; ~ **to account** Rechnungs[legungs]pflicht; ~ **of anchorage** Anker-, Hafengeld; ~ **of arbitration** Schiedsrichteramt; ~ **per article** Stückzoll; **common** ~ **of care** allgemeine Sorgfaltspflicht; ~ **charged by the weight** Gewichtszoll; ~ **on checks** *(US)* **(cheques,** *Br.*) Schecksteuer; ~ **payable on death** Erbschaftssteuer; ~ **to deliver** Lieferverpflichtung; ~ **of diligence** Sorgfaltspflicht; ~ **to disclose (of disclosure)** Anzeige-, Offenbarungspflicht; ~ **of entry** Eingangs-, Einfuhrabgabe; ~ **on export** Ausfuhrabgabe; **general** ~ **of fidelity** allgemeine Treupflicht; ~ **on importation** Einfuhrzoll; ~ **on increment value** Wertzuwachssteuer; ~ **not to disclose confidential information** Verschwiegenheitspflicht; ~ **on inheri-**

tance Erbschaftssteuer; ~ **payable on instalments** in Raten zahlbare Steuer; **statutory** ~ **to insure** gesetzliche Versicherungspflicht; ~ **on manufactures** Industriewarenzoll; ~ **on matches** Zündwarensteuer; ~ **to register** Registrierungspflicht; ~ **to report** Anzeigepflicht; ~ **of secrecy** Verschwiegenheits-, Geheimhaltungspflicht; ~ **of supervision** Überwachungspflicht; ~ **to furnish support** *(US)* Unterhaltspflicht; ~ **to pass good title** Eigentumsverschaffungspflicht; ~ **of tonnage** Tonnengeld; ~ **charged by weight** Gewichtszoll;
to acquit o. s. of a ~ sich einer Verpflichtung entledigen; **to assign a** ~ **to s. o.** jem. einen Aufgabenbereich zuweisen; **to be derelict in one's** ~ *(US)* Pflicht vernachlässigen; **to be exempt from** ~ zollfrei sein; **to be off** ~ freihaben, außer Dienst sein; **to be on** ~ Dienst haben; **to be s. one's** ~ zu jds. Obliegenheiten gehören, jem. als Pflicht obliegen; **to be slack in one's** ~ seine Pflichten vernachlässigen; **to be subject to** ~ dem Zoll unterliegen, zollpflichtig sein; **to be under** ~ verpflichtet sein; **to be under a legal** ~ **to account** rechnungspflichtig sein; **to collect** ~ Zoll erheben; **to depart (deviate) from one's** ~ seine Pflicht vernachlässigen; **to deposit the** ~ **repayable** Zollgarantie leisten; **to detail s. o. for a** ~ jem. einen bestimmten Aufgabenkreis zuweisen; **to discharge one's** ~ seine Pflicht erfüllen, seinen Pflichten nachkommen; **to do** ~ **for s. o.** jds. Dienst versehen; **to eliminate customs** ~ Zoll beseitigen; **to enter upon one's** ~ seinen Dienst antreten, seine Tätigkeit aufnehmen; **to esteem it a** ~ als seine Pflicht ansehen; **to fail in one's** ~ seine Pflicht vernachlässigen; **to fall short in one's** ~ seine Pflicht nicht hinlänglich erfüllen; **to fulfil one's** ~ seine Pflicht erfüllen; **to go off** ~ Dienst beenden; **to go on** ~ *(soldier)* Wache schieben; **to go through free of** ~ zollfrei passieren; **to import free of** ~ zollfrei einführen; **to impose** ~ besteuern, mit Steuern belegen; **to lay a** ~ **[up]on s. th.** Zoll (Steuern) auf etw. legen; **to levy** ~ Zoll erheben; **to pay** ~ **on** versteuern, *(customs)* verzollen, Zoll bezahlen (entrichten); **to perform one's** ~ seine Pflicht tun; **to remit** ~ Zoll erlassen; **to repeal a** ~ Zoll aufheben; **to report for** ~ sich zum Dienst melden; **to shirk** ~ sich seiner Pflicht (einer Verpflichtung) entziehen; **to take the** ~ **off goods** Waren von der Zollpflicht ausnehmen; **to take up one's** ~ seinen Aufgabenbereich übernehmen; **to take up** ~ **as early as possible** seinen Dienst baldmöglichst antreten;
to benefit from a ~ **advantage** tarifmäßig profitieren; ~**-bound** gesetzlich (moralisch) verpflichtet; ~ **call** Pflicht-, Höflichkeitsbesuch; ~ **change** Tarifänderung; ~ **computation** Zoll-, Steuerberechnung; ~ **copy** Pflichtexemplar; ~ **drawback** Zollerstattung, -rückvergütung; ~**-free** abgabe-, steuer-, zollfrei; **to import s. th.** ~**-free** etw. zollfrei einführen; ~**-free articles** zollfreie Waren; ~**-free entry certificate** Bescheinigung über abgabefreies Verbringen in das Zollgebiet; ~**-free raw material** zollfreie Rohstoffe; ~**-free return** zollfreie Wiedereinfuhr; ~**-free shop** zollfreier Laden; ~**-free shopping** Einkauf zollfreier Gegenstände; ~ **mark** Zollstempel; ~ **officer** Offizier vom Dienst; ~**-paid entry** Zolleinfuhrerklärung; ~**-paid sale** Verkauf nach Verzollung; ~ **pay** Prämiengeld; ~ **roster** *(mil.)* Dienstplan, -einteilung; ~ **stamp** Stempelmarke; ~ **station** Dienstsitz; ~ **team** diensttuender Stab; ~ **threshold** Steuerschwelle; ~ **train** Dienstzug.

dux *(Br.)* Klassenerster.

dwarf Zwerg;
~ *(a.)* *(fig.)* verkümmern (verkrüppeln) lassen.

dwell *(v.)* sich aufhalten, wohnen, hausen, *(remain)* verbleiben, verweilen;
~ **in the country** auf dem Lande wohnen; ~ **at greater length on a subject** Thema weiter ausführen (ausführlich behandeln); ~ **upon a subject** bei einem Thema verweilen; ~ **in s. one's memory** in jds. Gedächtnis haften; ~ **in a place** an einem Ort wohnen; ~ **upon s. th.** über etw. nachdenken; ~ **too much upon one's past** sich zu sehr mit seiner Vergangenheit beschäftigen, zu stark in seiner Vergangenheit leben;
to let one's glance ~ **on s. o.** j. prüfend ansehen.

dweller Bewohner;
city (town) ~ Stadtbewohner; **out-**~ Vorstadtbewohner.

dwelling Wohnung, Aufenthalt, Behausung, *(housing unit)* Wohnungseinheit;
above-average ~ überdurchschnittliche Wohnung; **crowded** ~ überbelegte Wohnung; **furnished** ~ möblierte Wohnung; **industrial** ~ Werkswohnung; **multiple** ~ Mietsgebäude, -haus, -kaserne; **multiple-family** ~ Mehrfamilienhaus; **official** ~ Dienstwohnung; **overcrowded** ~s überbelegte Wohnungen; **owner-occupied** ~ *(Br.)* Eigenheim; **principal** ~ Hauptwohnung; **private** ~ Privatwohnung; **privately financed** ~ frei finanzierte Wohnung; **separate** ~ abgeschlossene Wohnung; **single-**

(one-) family ~ Einfamilienwohnung; **small** ~ Kleinwohnung; **substandard** ~ Elendsquartier; **tenanted** ~ Mietwohnung; **uncontrolled (unrestricted)** ~ freier (nicht bewirtschafteter) Wohnraum;
to remove ~s **from control** *(Br.)* Wohnungen aus der Mieterschutzgesetzgebung herausnehmen; **to take up one's** ~ sich niederlassen, seinen Wohnsitz aufschlagen;
~ *(a.)* wohnhaft;
~ **accommodation** Wohnmöglichkeit; ~ **appraisal** Wohngrundstücksschätzung; ~ **house** Wohngebäude, -haus; ~ **place** Wohnort, -sitz, dauernder Aufenthaltsort; ~ **unit** Wohnungseinheit; **lower-price (low-rental)** ~ **unit** billiges Mietshaus; **single-family** ~ **unit** Einfamilienwohnungseinheit.
dwindle *(v.)* *(prices)* sinken, fallen, schwinden, abnehmen;
~ **away** dahinschwinden, *(political party)* schrumpfen; ~ **down** zusammenschrumpfen; ~ **by waste** *(estate)* durch Verschwendung zusammenschrumpfen.
dwindling Abnahme, Schwinden, *(prices)* Fallen, Sinken;
~ **of stocks** Lagerschrumpfung;
~ *(a.)* sinkend, fallend, schwindend, schrumpfend;
~ **assets** Kapitalschwund, Schwund des Eigenkapitals, Vermögensabfall; ~ **production** Produktionsabnahme; ~ **sales** Absatzschrumpfung.

dye Farbe, Farbstoff;
of the deepest ~ *(fig.)* von der übelsten Sorte;
~ *(v.)* färben;
~ **in the grain (wool)** waschecht färben;
~ **stuff** Farbstoff; ~ **transfer** Farbfotodiapositiv, Farbfotoabzug; ~ **works** Färberei.
dyed in the wool *(fig.)* in der Wolle gefärbt.
dyeing Färbereigewerbe.
dyer Färber.
dying sterbend;
~ **without issue** Erbenlosigkeit;
~ **declaration** Erklärung auf dem Sterbebett; ~ **man** Sterbender; ~ **words** letzte Worte, Sterbeworte; ~ **year** zuendegehendes Jahr.
dynamic | advertising schwungvolle Werbung; ~ **company** dynamisches Unternehmen; ~ **peg** stufenweise Wechselkursänderung.
dynamite, political politisches Dynamit;
~ *(v.)* sprengen, in die Luft jagen.
dynamiter Sprengstoffattentäter.
dynamiting [Dynamit]sprengung.
dynast Dynast, Herrscher.
dynasty Herrschergeschlecht, -haus, Dynastie.

E

E *(Lloyds, Br.)* unterste Klasse, *(US)* hervorragende Leistung.

each, 10 £ 10 Pfund das Stück.

eager begierig, erpicht;
~ **to buy** kauflustig, -willig; ~ **for fame** auf Ruhm erpicht; ~ **about one's progress** karrieresüchtig;
to be ~ **for knowledge** wißbegierig sein; **to be** ~ **for news** ungeduldig auf Nachrichten warten; **to be** ~ **for praise** lobeshungrig sein, nach Lob dürsten; **to be less than** ~ **to do** nicht gerade begeistert sein.

eagerness | **to buy** Kauflust; ~ **to succeed** Erfolgssucht, -streben.

eagle day *(mil., sl.)* Löhnungstag.

ear Gehör, *(newspaper)* Titelbox;
to be all ~s ganz Ohr sein; **to be by the** ~s *(coll.)* sich in den Haaren liegen; **to be up to the** ~s **in debt** bis zum Hals in Schulden stecken; **to be up to the** ~ **in work** mit Arbeit überladen sein; **to be over head and** ~s **in debt** bis zum Hals verschuldet sein; **to bring s. th. about one's** ~s sich etw. einbrocken; **to bring a storm about one's** ~s Proteststurm hervorrufen; **to close one's** ~s **to the truth** seine Augen vor der Wahrheit verschließen; **to come to s. one's** ~s jem. zu Ohren kommen; **to fall on deaf** ~s auf taube Ohren stoßen; **to give one's** ~s **for it** sein Leben dafür geben; **to go in one** ~ **and out of the other** beim einen Ohr herein- und beim anderen herausgehen; **to have s. one's** ~ jederzeit Zugang bei jem. haben; **to have everyone about one's** ~s die ganze Welt auf dem Hals haben; **to have one's** ~s **to the ground** dem Lauf der Ereignisse aufmerksam folgen; **to have the** ~ **of the house** *(parl.)* das Wort haben; **to keep one's** ~s **open for scandals** Skandalgeschichten mit dem größten Vergnügen hören; **to lend an** ~ **to s. o.** jem. Gehör schenken; **to listen with all one's** ~s gespannt zuhören; **to listen with one's third** ~ im Unterbewußtsein zuhören; **to prick up one's** ~s die Ohren spitzen; **to send s. away with a flea in his** ~ jem. gehörig den Kopf waschen; **to turn a deaf** ~ **on s. th.** taube Ohren für etw. haben; **to turn a sympathetic** ~ **to s. one's request** jds. Vorbringen äußerst freundlich aufnehmen; **to win s. one's** ~ jds. Aufmerksamkeit erregen;
~ **bashing** Seelenmassage, Maßhalteappell; ~ **plugs** Ohrenstöpsel; ~ **specialist** Ohrenfacharzt.

Earl Marshal *(Br.)* Oberzeremonienmeister.

earliest, at your ~ **convenience** so bald wie möglich; **at the** ~ **possible date** zum frühest möglichen Zeitpunkt.

early frühzeitig, *(in time)* rechtzeitig;
~ **in the list** am Anfang der Liste;
to arrive ~ **for a meeting** früh zu einer Versammlung kommen; ~ **answer** baldige Antwort; ~ **bird** Frühaufsteher; ~**-bird issue** *(US)* vordatierte Zeitung, Frühausgabe; ~**-bird price** Werbe-, Einführungspreis; ~ **capitalism** Frühkapitalismus; ~**-childhood education** Kinderfrüherziehung; ~ **closing** früher Geschäfts-, Ladenschluß; ~ **closing act** *(Br.)* Ladenschlußgesetz; ~**-closing day** früher Arbeitsschluß, *(shop)* nachmittags geschlossen; ~ **door** *(theater)* Einlaß 1/2 Stunde vor der Vorstellung; ~ **general election** vorgezogene Parlamentswahlen; **the** ~ **hours** Stunden nach Mitternacht; ~ **mist** *(fig.)* Anfangsstadium; ~**-morning delivery** Frühzustellung; ~**-morning edition** Morgenausgabe; **to take an** ~ **opportunity to do s. th.** erstbeste Gelegenheit wahrnehmen, etw. zu erledigen; **in the** ~ **part of the century** am Anfang des Jahrhunderts; ~ **price** Einführungspreis; ~ **retirement** vorzeitige Pensionierung; ~ **returns** schneller Umsatz; ~ **riser** Frühaufsteher; ~ **spring** Frühlingsbeginn; **to detect at an** ~ **stage** frühzeitig entdecken; ~ **vegetables** Frühgemüse; ~ **warning** *(mil.)* Vorwarnung, Früh-, Voralarm; ~ **warning** airborn Frühwarngerät; **to provide for** ~ **warning of air attack** Frühwarnsystem gegen Luftangriffe installieren; ~ **warning aeroplane** im Frühwarnsystem eingesetztes Flugzeug; ~**-warning line** Frühwarnanlage; ~ **warning satellite** Frühwarnsatellit; ~**-warning signal** Frühwarnsignal; ~**-warning station** Frühwarnstation; ~**-warning system** Vor-, Frühwarnsystem.

earmark Eigentumszeichen, Identitäts-, Kennzeichen, Unterscheidungsmerkmal;
under ~ gekennzeichnet;
~ *(v.)* kennzeichnen, *(finance)* bestimmen, vorsehen, bereit-, zurückstellen, [für Geldlieferungen] zurücklegen;
~ **for o. s.** für sich selbst reservieren;
~ **a check** Scheck sperren; ~ **a document** Urkunde mit einem Kennzeichen versehen; ~ **funds** Beträge für etw. bereitstellen;
~ **funds for a purpose** Beträge zweckbestimmen; ~ **goods for**

export Güter für den Export bestimmen; ~ **for a key position** für eine Schlüsselstellung vormerken (ausersehen); ~ **securities** Wertpapiere zur Verfügung halten; ~ **a sum of money for research** bestimmten Geldbetrag für Forschungszwecke zur Verfügung stellen;
~ **rule** *(money in a bank)* Vermischungstheorie.

earmarked zurück-, bereitgestellt, *(account)* gesperrt, *(banking, coll.)* für eine ausländische Bank reserviert, *(tax)* zweckgebunden;
to hold gold ~ **for foreign account** Gold für ausländische Rechnung im Depot halten;
~ **account** zweckgebundenes Konto; ~ **asset** zweckgebundener Vermögensteil (Vermögenswert); ~ **balance at bank** zweckgebundenes Bankguthaben; ~ **funds** zweckbestimmte (bereitgestellte) Mittel; ~ **gold** Goldreserve bei ausländischen Bankinstituten.

earmarking | **of funds** Bereitstellung (Zweckbestimmung) von Geldern; ~ **of gold** Goldreserve bei ausländischen Bankinstituten; ~ **of taxes** Zweckbindung von Steuererträgen; ~ **transactions** Bereitstellungsmaßnahmen.

earn *(v.)* erwerben, gewinnen, einnehmen, *(wages)* verdienen, als Lohn erhalten;
able to ~ arbeits-, erwerbsfähig;
~ **one's bread and butter** sich seinen Lebensunterhalt selbst verdienen; ~ **sixty dollars a day** täglich sechzig Dollar verdienen; ~ **a character for audacity** in den Ruf der Kühnheit gelangen; ~ **enough to live on** auskömmliches Gehalt haben; ~ **interest** Zinsen bringen; ~ **one's living** seinen Lebensunterhalt verdienen; ~ **one's living by writing** seinen Lebensunterhalt als Schriftsteller verdienen; ~ **a good living** gut verdienen; ~ **in the open market** *(rent)* im freien Markt erzielen; ~ **a packet of money** Bombengehalt kassieren; ~ **a reputation for generosity** als großzügig gelten; ~ **s. o. respect** jem. Respekt eintragen; ~ **a good salary** schönes Gehalt haben.

earned verdient, *(interest)* angesammelt, angefallen;
hard-~ sauer verdient;
~ **freight** angefallene (verdiente) Transportkosten; ~ **hours** Lohnstunden; ~ **income** *(Br.)* Einkünfte aus selbständiger Arbeit (Erwerbstätigkeit), Einkünfte aus gewerblicher Tätigkeit; **to tax** ~ **income more leniently** Arbeitseinkommen milder besteuern; ~ **income allowance** *(Br.)* Freibetrag für Einkünfte aus freiberuflicher Tätigkeit; ~ **income category** Art der Erwerbseinkünfte; ~ **income credit** *(US)* Steuervergünstigung für Einkünfte aus Gewerbstätigkeit; ~ **income relief** *(Br.)* Steuervergünstigung (Freibetrag) für Berufstätige; ~ **income tax** *(US)* Gewerbeertragssteuer; **hard-**~ **money** schwer verdientes Geld; ~ **premium** Prämieneinnahme; ~ **rate** *(railroad)* tatsächlich abgerechneter Tarif; **well-**~ **rest** wohlverdiente Ruhe; ~ **surplus** *(balance sheet, US)* den Rücklagen zugewiesener (thesaurierter) Gewinn, [etwa] gesetzliche Rücklagen; **to reconcile one's** ~ **surplus** *(US)* Wertberichtigung bei den gesetzlichen Rücklagen vornehmen; ~ **unappropriated surplus** *(US)* nicht verteilter Reingewinn, Gewinnvortrag, ~**-surplus account** *(US)* Rücklagenkonto.

earner Erwerbstätiger, Verdiener;
double ~ Doppelverdiener; **middle-income** ~s mittlere Einkommensschicht; **profitable** ~ Gewinnfaktor; **salary** ~ Gehaltsempfänger; **wage** ~ unselbständiger Arbeitnehmer, Lohnempfänger, Erwerbsperson;
~ **of foreign exchange** Devisenbringer.

earnest Ernst, *(money)* Drauf-, Handgeld, *(token)* Vorgeschmack, Probe;
in good ~ in vollem Ernst;
~ **of one's good intentions** Pfand für seine guten Absichten;
to give an ~ **of one's talent** Kostprobe seiner Fähigkeiten geben; **to set to work in** ~ sich ernsthaft an die Arbeit machen;
~ *(a.)* ernsthaft, gewissenhaft, eifrig;
~ **money** Draufgabe, -geld, Auf-, An-, Handgeld; ~ **prayer** inbrünstiges Gebet; ~ **request** dringendes Gesuch; ~ **worker** harter Arbeiter.

earning [Geld]verdienen, Erwerb;
~ **advancement** Einkommensanstieg; ~ **assets** ertragbringende (werbende) Aktiva, *(Federal Reserve Bank, US)* gewinnbringende [Kapital]anlage; ~ **capacity** Ertragsfähigkeit, Rentabilität, *(worker)* Erwerbsfähigkeit; **decreased** ~ **capacity** verminderte Erwerbsfähigkeit; ~**-capacity standard** normale Ertragskraft; ~**-capacity value** Ertragswert; ~ **gains** Erträge,

Gewinne; ~ **power** Erwerbsfähigkeit, -kraft, *(business)* Ertragsfähigkeit, -kraft, Rentabilität; **to even out fluctuations in ~ power** Ertragsschwankungen ausgleichen (auffangen); **to run into more ~ troubles next year** im nächsten Geschäftsjahr nur mit Mühe gewinnträchtig werden können; ~ **value** Ertragswert.

earnings *(income)* Einkommen, Einkünfte, Bezüge, *(profit)* Gewinn, Ertrag, Erlös, *(salary)* Gehalt, *(wages)* Verdienst, Arbeitslohn;

accumulated ~ *(balance sheet, US)* Gewinnvortrag, freie Rücklage; **actual ~** tatsächlicher Verdienst; **after-tax ~** Erträge (Gewinn) nach [Abzug von] Steuern; **airline ~** Erträgnisse einer Fluggesellschaft; **annual ~** Jahresverdienst; **appropriated ~** *(US)* den Rücklagen zugewiesene Gewinne; **average ~** Durchschnittseinkommen, -verdienst; **commission ~** Provisionseinnahmen, -künfte; **company (corporation, US)** ~ Gesellschaftsgewinn, -einkünfte, Firmenertrag; **current ~** laufender Gewinn; **daily ~** Tagesverdienst; **distributable ~** ausschüttungsfähige Gewinne (Erträge); **drab ~** geringfügige Erträge; **foreign ~** *(company)* Erlöse von Auslandstöchtern; **full-time ~** Gesamtverdienst; **future ~** zukünftige Erträge; **gross ~** Bruttoeinnahmen, -verdienst; **guaranteed ~** garantierter Verdienst; **hard-currency ~** Deviseneinnahmen aus Hartwährungsländern, Einnahmen in harter Währung; **hourly ~** Stundenlohn; **average hourly ~** Stundendurchschnittslohn; **incidental ~** Nebenverdienst; **increased ~** Ertragssteigerung; **individual ~** Pro-Kopf Einkommen; **industrial ~** gewerbliche Einkünfte, Einkünfte aus Gewerbebetrieb; **net ~** Reingewinn, -verdienst, Nettoverdienst, -einkommen, -gewinn, -erträge; **normal ~** Normalverdienst; **operating ~** Betriebserträgnisse; **all other ~** alle übrigen Einkünfte; **overseas ~** Einkünfte aus dem Überseegeschäft; **past ~** früherer Gewinn; **personal ~** Einkünfte aus freiberuflicher Tätigkeit; **~ ploughed (plowed, US) back** nicht entnommener (wieder angelegter) Gewinn; **potential ~** geschätzte Verdienstmöglichkeiten; **pretax ~** Gewinn vor Steuern; **professional ~** Einkünfte aus freiberuflicher Tätigkeit; **real ~** Reallohn, -einkommen; **reckonable ~** *(national insurance)* anrechnungsfähige Einkünfte; **record ~** Rekordgewinne; **reinvested ~** wiederangelegte Erträge, Wiederanlagebeträge; **reported net ~** ausgewiesener Reingewinn; **retained ~** *(US)* einbehaltene Erträge (Gewinne), Gewinnvortrag, thesaurierter (nicht ausgeschütteter, im Geschäft wieder angelegter) Gewinn; **shipping ~** Einkünfte aus dem Schiffsverkehr; **spare-time ~** nebenberufliche Einkünfte; **spendable ~** ausgezahltes Gehalt; **surplus ~** *(US)* nicht verteilter Gewinn, Gewinnüberschuß; **taxable ~** zu versteuernder Gewinn; **unremitted ~** nicht überwiesene Erträge; **year's net ~** Jahresüberschuß;

joint taxable ~ of husband and wife gemeinsame steuerpflichtige eheliche Einkünfte; **~ on investment abroad** Erträge aus auswärtigen Investitionsvorhaben; **~ in kind** Naturalerträge, Sachvergütungen; **~ on management** Unternehmerlohn; **~ on services** Ertrag aus dem Dienstleistungsgeschäft; **~ per share** Aktienrendite, -ertrag, Gewinnentwicklung je Aktie; **~ per stock unit** Erlös per Lagereinheit; **~ before tax** Gewinn vor Steuern;

to boost ~ Erträge ansteigen lassen; **to deal with wife's ~ entirely separately for tax purposes** Erwerbseinkommen der Ehefrau aus Steuergründen getrennt veranlagen; **to generate additional ~ through investments in special undervalued situations** Ertragschancen durch Investitionen auf bisher vernachlässigten Gebieten verbessern; **to have a wife's ~ treated separately** Einkünfte der Ehefrau steuerlich getrennt veranlagen lassen; **to live on immoral ~** von der Zuhälterei leben; **to plough back ~** Gewinn nicht entnehmen; **to send ~ into a dive** Erlössituation rapide verschlechtern; **to show ~ by mere bookkeeping devices** Erträge lediglich buchungstechnisch erzielen;

retained ~ account *(US)* Gewinnvortragskonto; **~-and-cost approach** Verteilungsansatz der Volkseinkommensberechnung; ~ **base** Ertragslage, Ertragsposition; ~ **comparison** Gewinn-, Ertragsvergleich; ~ **cover** Erlösdeckung; ~ **coverage** *(brokerage)* Ertragsdeckung; ~ **curve** Ertragskurve; ~ **dip** Ertragsrückgang; ~ **distortion** verzerrtes Ertragsbild; ~ **drop** Ertragsrückgang; ~ **expectations** Ertragserwartungen; ~ **estimate** Gewinn-, Ertragsvorschau; ~ **figures** Ertragszahlen; ~ **gains** Ertragszunahme; ~ **growth** Ertrags-, Gewinnsteigerung, -zuwachs, Ertragszunahme; ~ **growth expectation** Ertragszunahmeaussichten; ~ **guidelines** Lohnleitlinien; ~ **improvement** Rentabilitäts-, Ertragsverbesserungen; ~ **increase** Ertragssteigerung; **to indicate the maximum ~ increase compatible with growth and stable prices** Orientierungsdaten für die Tarifpart-

ner setzen; ~ **index** Einkommensindex, Gehältersindex; ~ **inflation** Ertragsinflation; ~ **ladder** Ertragsleiter; ~ **level** Gehaltsniveau; **price-~ multiple** Kurs- und Ertragsmultiplikator; ~ **opportunities** Ertragschancen; ~ **performance** Ertragskraft, -leistung; ~ **picture** Erlösbild; ~ **pinch** Erlösverknappung; **to maintain its good ~ position** weiterhin gute Erträge erwirtschaften; ~ **potential (power)** Ertragskraft, -lage, -position; ~ **progress** progressive Ertragsentwicklung; ~ **projection (prospects)** Ertragsaussichten; ~ **quality** Ertragsfähigkeit; ~ **record** *(employee)* Einkommensentwicklung; ~ **recovery** Ertragsaufbesserung; **~-related** lohn-, gehaltsabhängig; **~-related insurance scheme** lohngekoppeltes Versicherungssystem; **~-related part of the state pension** bruttolohnbezogener Altersversorgungsanteil; **~-related supplement** verdienstbezogener Zuschlag; **~-to-sales ratio** Kurs-, Ertragsverhältnis; **corporate ~ report** *(US)* Gesellschaftsbericht, Gewinn- und Verlustaufstellung, Gewinnausweis, Ertragsrechnung; ~ **rise** Ertrags-, Gehälteranstieg; **net ~ rule** Nettoertragswertberechnung; ~ **slide** Ertragsrückgang; ~ **squeeze** Erlösdruck; ~ **stability** gleichbleibende Ertragslage; ~ **stabilization** Ertragsstabilisierung; ~ **statement** Gewinn- und Verlustrechnung, Gewinnausweis, Ertragsrechnung; **unappropriated ~ surplus** *(US)* Gewinnrücklage; ~ **target** Ertragsplanziel; **accumulated ~ tax** *(US)* Steuer für nicht ausgeschüttete Gewinne, Steuer auf Gewinnvortrag; ~ **trend** Ertrags-, Einkommenstendenz; ~ **yield** Ertragsergebnis; **~-yield basis** Kurs-, Gewinnrendite.

earphone Kopfhörer.

earpiece *(tel.)* Hörmuschel, *(newspaper)* Kastensatz am Zeitungskopf.

earplug Geräuschunterdrücker.

earth Erde, Erdball, -kugel, *(continent)* Festland, *(el.)* Erde, Erdverbindung, *(ground)* Boden;

down to ~ nüchtern, prosaisch, unromantisch;

~ (v.) (el.) erden;

to come back to ~ wieder auf den Boden der Wirklichkeit zurückkehren; **to cost the ~** ein Heidengeld kosten; **to drop to ~** landen; **to escape from ~** Erdanziehungskraft überwinden; **to look like nothing on ~** schlecht aussehen; **to move heaven and ~** Himmel und Hölle in Bewegung setzen; **to run to ~** endlich auftreiben (aufstöbern);

to dive back into the ~'s atmosphere in die Erdatmosphäre eintauchen; ~ **cable** Erdkabel; **~-closet** Latrine; ~ **connection** *(el.)* Erdung; ~ **current** *(el.)* Erdstrom; ~ **satellite** Erdsatellit; ~ **tremor** Erdstoß; ~ **wave** Bodenwelle.

earthly *(coll.)* menschenmöglich, denkbar;

to have no ~ chance nicht die geringste Chance haben; **no ~ doubt** nicht der geringste Zweifel; ~ **goods** Glücksgüter; ~ **joys** weltliche Vergnügungen; ~ **possessions** irdische Güter; **no ~ reason** kein erdenkbarer Grund; **no ~ use** nicht zu gebrauchen, peinlich nutzlos.

earthmoving machinery Bulldozer.

earthquake Erdbeben, *(fig.)* Umwälzung, Unruhe;

to be thrown down by an ~ von einem Erdbeben zerstört sein; ~ **activity** Erdbebentätigkeit; ~ **area** vom Erdbeben betroffenes Gebiet; ~ **clause** *(insurance)* Erdbebenklausel; ~ **disaster** Erdbebenkatastrophe; ~ **hazard** Erdbebenrisiko; ~ **insurance** Erdbebenversicherung; **~-proof** erdbebensicher; ~ **relief** Erdbebenhilfe; ~ **shock** Erdbebenstoß; ~ **victim** Erdbebenopfer.

earthwork *(road)* Unterbau;

~s Erdarbeiten, Erd-, Bodenbewegungen, Erdwall.

earwitness Ohrenzeuge.

ease Annehmlichkeit, Zwanglosigkeit, Ungezwungenheit, *(relaxation)* Entspannung, Entlastung, Bequemlichkeit, *(tranquillity)* Ausgeglichenheit, Leichtigkeit, Unbefangenheit;

at ~ zwanglos, ruhig, ausgeglichen; **with ~** mühelos, mit Leichtigkeit;

a fractional ~ Kursabschwächung um einen Bruchteil; **pecuniary ~** finanzielle Erleichterungen;

~ in credit Erleichterungen der kreditpolitischen Situation; **~ of enforcement** erleichterte Vollstreckungsmöglichkeit; **~ of manners** Ungeniertheit, ungezwungenes Benehmen; **~ of mind** Seelenruhe; **~ of money** Geldflüssigkeit; **~ in money rates** Erleichterung (Entspannung) am Geldmarkt, liquiditätsmäßige Entlastung der Banken; **~ from pain** Schmerzerleichterung; **~ of realization** erleichterte Versilberung; **~ of transport** gute Verkehrsmöglichkeiten;

~ (v.) erleichtern, beruhigen, entspannen, Entspannung verschaffen, entlasten, auflockern, *(stock prices)* nachgeben, abbröckeln, fallen;

~ o. s. of a burden sich von einer Belastung befreien; **~ the congestion in a street** Verkehrsstau beseitigen; **~ one's con-**

science sein Gewissen entlasten; ~ **credit controls** kreditpolitische Erleichterungen gewähren; ~ **the crisis** Krise beseitigen; ~ **a fraction** *(prices)* etw. abbröckeln; ~ **down** Geschwindigkeit (Fahrt) vermindern; ~ **a car down to thirty miles** nur noch mit einer Geschwindigkeit von fünfzig Stundenkilometern fahren; ~ **down interest rates** Zinssätze weiter senken; ~ **in gradually** allmählich einlullen; ~ **s. o. in his work** j. langsam einarbeiten; ~ **s. o. into a job** jem. eine Stellung besorgen; ~ **nontariff barriers to foreign suppliers** nicht zollbedingte Einfuhrbestimmungen für auswärtige Lieferanten lockern; ~ **off** abschwächen, *(prices)* nachlassen, -geben, fallen, sinken, abbröckeln, *(situation)* sich entspannen; ~ **out of office** aus dem Amt verdrängen; ~ **pressure** Druck vermindern; ~ **seasonality pressure** für Druckausgleich saisonaler Schwankungen sorgen; ~ **s. o. of his purse** j. um seinen Geldbeutel erleichtern; ~ **the economic situation** Konjunktur entspannen; ~ **tension** Lage entspannen; ~ **the traffic** Verkehr entlasten; ~ **up** leichter werden, *(money)* billiger werden; ~ **s. o. in his work** j. langsam einarbeiten;
to be at ~ with s. o. ungezwungen mit jem. verkehren; **to continue one's run toward ~ in money rates** Tendenz in der Politik der Geldmarkterleichterungen fortsetzen; **to feel at ~** sich wie zu Hause fühlen; **to give s. o. ~** jem. Erleichterungen verschaffen; **to live at ~** in guten Verhältnissen (ohne Sorgen) leben; **to live a life of ~** sorgenloses Leben führen; **to put s. o. at his ~** jem. die Befangenheit nehmen; **to set s. one's mind at ~** j. von seiner Unruhe befreien, j. beruhigen; **to take one's ~** es sich bequem machen; **to write at ~** ganz gelöst schreiben.

eased off a fraction *(stock market)* etw. abgeschwächt.

easement Erleichterung, *(law)* Grunddienstbarkeit, Realservitut; **affirmative ~** positive Grunddienstbarkeit; **apparent ~** Grunddienstbarkeit, die keines Nachweises bedarf; ~ **appurtenant** subjektiv dingliche Grunddienstbarkeit; **continuous ~** ununterbrochen ausgeübte Dienstbarkeit; **discontinuing ~** im Einzelfall ausgeübte Dienstbarkeit; **equitable ~** dienstbarkeitsähnliche Verpflichtung; **negative ~** negative Grunddienstbarkeit; **nonapparent ~** nachweispflichtige Grunddienstbarkeit; **quasi ~** der Grunddienstbarkeit ähnliches Recht;
~ **of access** Zutritts-, Notweg-, Wegerecht; ~ **in gross** beschränkt persönliche Dienstbarkeit; ~ **of light** nachbarliches Verbot der Lichtrechtbeschränkung; ~ **of necessity** Dienstbarkeit als Notrecht; ~ **of way** Wegerecht;
to commute a right of user of an ~ Dienstbarkeit ablösen; **to grant an ~** Grunddienstbarkeit einräumen.

easer *(fig.)* Stütze.

easier *(stock exchange)* leichter, niedriger;
to be ~ schwächer liegen; **to become ~** abflauen; **to become a little ~** *(situation)* sich entspannen; **to make it ~ on s.o.** Druck von jem. nehmen; **to make credit ~** Krediterleichterungen gewähren;
to have an ~ day *(money market)* leichter sein; ~ **money** leichteres (billigeres) Geld; **to reflect ~ money circumstances** sich auf erleichterte Geldmarktbedingungen einstellen.

easiness Ungeniertheit, Ungezwungenheit;
~ **of belief** Leichtgläubigkeit; ~ **of the capital market** Auflockerung des Kapitalmarktes; ~ **on the money market** Geldmarktflüssigkeit.

easing Erleichterung;
~ **off** *(stock exchange)* Fallen, Sinken, Nachgeben; ~ **of the capital market** Kapitalmarktentspannung, Auflockerung des Kapitalmarktes, Erleichterungen für den Kapitalmarkt; ~ **of controls** Abbau von Kontrollfunktionen; ~ **[up] in credit** Krediterleichterungen, -lockerung, kreditpolitische Erleichterungen, Erleichterungen für das Kreditgeschäft; ~ **of cyclical conditions** konjunkturelle Auflockerung, Konjunkturentspannung; ~ **of the flow of patents** erleichterte Patentverwertungsmöglichkeiten; ~ **up on foreign investments** Erleichterungen bei Auslandsinvestitionen; ~ **of monetary policy** geldmarkttechnische Erleichterungen, Liquiditätsverbesserungen für den Bankenapparat; ~ **in money rates** Erleichterungen am Geldmarkt; ~ **of restrictions** Lockerung von Beschränkungen; ~ **of short-term rates** Entspannung am Markt für kurzfristige Geldmarktpapiere; ~ **of the tension** Entspannung der Lage; ~ **of trade curbs** Milderung von Handelsbeschränkungen;
to commit o. s. on ~ money sich für Geldmarkterleichterungen einsetzen; **to contribute to the ~ of the political situation** zur Entspannung der politischen Lage beitragen;
~ **of admission requirements** erleichterte Zulassungsbedingungen; ~ **share prices** abbröckelnde Aktienkurse.

East Osten, Orient;
~ **West[ern] trade** Ost-West-Handel.

Easter | Fair Ostermesse; ~ **holidays** Osterferien.

eastern östlich, morgenländisch, orientalisch;
♀ **Bloc** Ostblock; ~ **countries** Orient; ♀ **European Time** osteuropäische Zeit; ~ **question** orientalische Frage; ~ **route** östlicher Kurs; ♀ **Seaboard** Atlantikküste.

easy leicht, mühelos, *(commodity)* wenig gefragt, *(compliant)* kulant, *(market)* ruhig, weichend, flau, lustlos, *(money)* flüssig, billig;
free and ~ ohne Formalitäten; **as ~ as shelling peas** kinderleicht;
~ **of access** leicht zugänglich; ~ **of digestion** leicht verdaulich; ~ **in one's mind** sorglos, unbeschwert; ~ **to reach** bequem zu erreichen; ~ **to understand** leicht verständlich; ~ **to use** bequem zu handhaben;
to be ~ zu allem bereit sein, alles mitmachen, *(market)* ruhig liegen; **to be ~ to get on with** nicht schwer zu nehmen sein; **to be ~ in one's mind** ruhiges Gemüt haben; **to go ~** es sich leicht machen, *(proceed with caution)* vorsichtig vorgehen; **to go ~ with s. o.** j. mit leichter Hand regieren; **to go ~ on a subject** *(US)* Thema nur antippen; **to make o. s. ~** es sich bequem machen; **to take an ~** Ruhepause einschieben; **to take it ~** es nicht so genau nehmen; **take it ~** beruhige dich;
~**-care** *(clothes)* pflegeleicht; ~ **carriage** ungezwungene Haltung; ~ **chair** [bequemer] Sessel; ~ **circumstances** Wohlhabenheit; **in ~ circumstances** wohlhabend; **to live in ~ circumstances** in guten Verhältnissen leben; ~**-clean** einfach zu reinigen; **to be an ~ finish** *(money market)* am Schluß leicht sein; ~ **game** leichtes Spiel; ~**-going** bequem, gemächlich, *(fig.)* unbeschwert; ~**-going chap** gutmütiger Kerl; **to lead an ~ life** bequemes Leben führen; ~**-mannered** gesellschaftlich gewandt; ~ **mark** *(coll.)* leichte Beute; ~ **market** flüssiger Geldmarkt, Markt mit großem Geld-, Warenangebot, *(stock exchange)* freundliche Börse; ~ **money market** *(US)* Bankenliquidität, Geldmarktflüssigkeit; ~ **meat** leichte Beute; ~ **money** billiges (leicht verdientes) Geld; ~ **money policy** *(US)* Politik des billigen Geldes; ~ **money rates** leichte Geldmarktsätze; **by ~ payment** unter Zahlungserleichterung; ~ **person to get on with** verträglicher Mensch, leicht zu nehmender Zeitgenosse; ~ **profit** müheloser Gewinn; **to travel by ~ stages** in bequemen Etappen reisen; **within ~ reach of the station** vom Bahnhof bequem zu erreichen, bahnhofsnahe; ~ **street** *(coll.)* angenehme Verhältnisse; **to put s. o. on ~ street** jem. das Leben erleichtern; ~ **style** flüssiger Stil; ~ **terms** günstige Geschäftsbedingungen; **on ~ terms** zu günstigen Bedingungen; ~ **terms of payment** günstige Zahlungsbedingungen; **to come in an ~ third** bequem den dritten Platz belegen; **to have an ~ time** bequemes Dasein fristen; ~ **victory** müheloser Sieg.

eat *(v.)* essen, speisen, verzehren;
~ **away the coastline** *(sea)* Küstenlinie anfressen; ~ **à la carte** nach der Karte essen; ~ **crow** *(fig.)* eine Kröte schlucken; ~ **one's dinner** *(terms) (Br.)* Jura studieren; ~ **dirt** sich demütigen lassen; ~ **one's head off** *(coll.)* wie ein Scheunendrescher fressen; ~ **one's heart out** *(coll.)* sich vor Gram verzehren; ~ **high on the hog** mit dem großen Löffel essen; ~ **humble pie** unter demütigenden Bedingungen ausharren, zu Kreuze kriechen; ~ **a small helping of humble pie** ein bißchen zu Kreuze kriechen; ~ **out** auswärts essen; ~ **out of s. one's hand** jem. aus der Hand fressen; ~ **s. o. out of house and home** jem. den letzten Brotkrumen wegfressen (die Haare vom Kopf fressen); ~ **one's salt** Gastfreundschaft in Anspruch nehmen; ~ **up** absorbieren, *(sl.)* etw. schlucken, kritiklos hinnehmen; ~ **up one's capital** sein Kapital aufzehren; ~ **up a distance** *(car)* Kilometer fressen; ~ **up savings** Ersparnisse aufbrauchen; ~ **up a third of the annual budget** ein Drittel des Jahresetats verschlingen; ~ **up all s. one's time** jem. seine ganze Zeit stehlen; ~ **well** guten Appetit haben; ~ **one's words** zu Kreuze kriechen.

eaten | up with curiosity vor Neugierde platzen;
to be ~ out außerhalb des Hauses eingenommen werden.

eatery Gaststätte.

eating Speise, Nahrung;
~ **facilities** Eßmöglichkeiten; ~ **house** Gasthaus, Speiselokal; ~ **housekeeper** Gasthausbesitzer; ~ **place** Mittagstisch.

eaves Dachtraufe.

eavesdrop *(v.)* belauschen.

eavesdropper Lauscher.

eavesdropping *(criminal law, Br.)* verbotenes Lauschen.

ebb Ebbe *(fig.)* Neige, Tiefstand;
~ **and flow** Ebbe und Flut;
~ *(v.)* abnehmen, weniger werden;
to be on the ~ *(fam.)* an Einfluß verloren haben; **to be at a low ~** heruntergekommen sein.

echelon *(attack)* Welle, *(aviation)* Staffelflug, -formation, *(mil.)* staffelförmige Aufstellung, *(range of command)* Befehlsebene, *(rank)* Stufe, Rang;
in ~ staffelförmig aufgestellt;
higher ~s Führungsspitzen, *(mil.)* höhere Chargen; **lower** ~s niedrigere Ränge; **reserve** ~s Reserveeinheit;
~ *(v.)* staffelförmig anordnen, staffeln;
to be in the lower ~s zu den unwichtigeren Leuten gehören; **to fly in** ~ im Staffelflug fliegen;
middle-~ staff member zur mittleren Führungsschicht gehöriges Belegschaftsmitglied.
echo Echo, *(fig.)* Anklang, Widerhall, Resonanz, *(radar)* Schattenbild, *(repeater)* Nachbeter, Nachahmer, *(tel.)* Echo, *(television)* Geisterbild;
~ *(v.)* [Ton] zurückwerfen;
~ **the views** der gleichen Ansicht sein; ~ **every word of his leader** alle Worte seines Führers nachbeten;
~ **sounder** Echolot mit Ultraschall; ~ **sounding** *(mar.)* Echolotung.
echolocation Echolotung.
eclipse Finsternis, *(fig.)* Verdüsterung;
partial ~ partielle Finsternis;
~ *(v.)* verfinstern, *(fig.)* in den Schatten stellen;
to go into temporary ~ vorläufig in den Hintergrund treten; **to suffer an** ~ Ruhm einbüßen.
ecological ökologisch, umweltfreundlich;
~ **disaster** Umweltkatastrophe; ~ **fallacy** Gruppenfallschluß; ~ **pressure** Belastung des Naturhaushaltes; ~ **relationship** Umweltbeziehung.
ecologist Ökologe.
ecology Ökologie, Umweltfreundlichkeit.
econometric ökonometrisch.
econometrician Ökonometriker.
econometrics Ökonometrie.
economic *(of economics)* [national]ökonomisch, [volks]wirtschaftlich, wirtschaftswissenschaftlich, *(paying expenses)* wirtschaftlich, rentabel, *(pertaining to a household)* hauswirtschaftlich;
~ **accounting** volkswirtschaftliches Rechnungswesen; ~ **actions** wirtschaftspolitische Maßnahmen; ~ **activity** konjunkturelle Aktivität, *(trade cycle)* konjunkturelle Belebung; **to overheat the** ~ **activity** Konjunktur überhitzen; **to pep up (stimulate)** ~ **activity** Konjunktur intensivieren, Wirtschaft ankurbeln; ~ **adjustment** Wirtschaftsausgleich; ~ **advantage** wirtschaftlicher Vorteil; ~ **adviser** Wirtschaftsberater; ~ **agency** Wirtschaftsdienststelle, -behörde; ~ **agreement** Wirtschaftsabkommen, Handelsabkommen; ~ **aid** Wirtschaftshilfe; ~ **aims** Wirtschaftsziele; ~ **analysis** Wirtschaftsanalyse; ~ **angle** wirtschaftlicher Gesichtspunkt; ~ **application** praktische Anwendung; ~ **appraisal** Wirtschaftlichkeitsberechnung; ~ **area** Wirtschaftsgebiet, -raum; ~ **aspects** wirtschaftliche Gesichtspunkte, *(general outlook)* Konjunkturaussichten; ~ **aspects of traffic** verkehrswirtschaftliche Fragen; ~ **assets** Wirtschaftsgüter; ~ **assimilation (attachment)** wirtschaftliche Angliederung; ~ **assistance** Wirtschaftshilfe; ~ **atmosphere** Konjunkturatmosphäre; ~ **autarchy** Autarkie, wirtschaftliche Unabhängigkeit; ~ **balance** Handelsbilanz; ~ **base ratio** regionaler Exportbasiskoeffizient; **sound** ~ **basis** gesunde wirtschaftliche Grundlage; ~ **battle** Konjunkturschlacht; ~ **behavio(u)r** ökonomisches Verhalten; ~ **bloc** Wirtschaftsblock; ~ **blockade** Wirtschaftsblockade; ~ **boom** Konjunkturaufschwung; ~ **boycott** Konjunkturboykott; **to ease the** ~ **brakes** Konjunkturbremse zurückhaltend anwenden; ~ **brinkmanship** Konjunktursteuerung unter Inkaufnahme von Risiken; ~ **business** wirtschaftliches Aufgabengebiet; ~ **buyer** rechnender (sorgfältig kalkulierender) Käufer; ~ **challenge** wirtschaftliche Herausforderung; ~ **change** Strukturwandlung, konjunkturelle Veränderung; ~ **chaos** wirtschaftliches Chaos, Wirtschaftschaos; ~ **circulation** Wirtschaftskreislauf; ~ **clauses** Handelsbestimmungen; ~ **climate** Konjunkturklima; ~ **club** *(US)* Industrie-, Wirtschaftsklub; ~ **comeback** Rückkehr in den Kreis der Wirtschaftsmärkte; ~ **commentary** Wirtschaftskommentar; ~ **commentator** Wirtschaftskommentator; ~ **commission** Wirtschaftsausschuß; ≗ **Commission for Europe** *(ECE)* Wirtschaftskommission der Vereinten Nationen für Europa, Europäische Wirtschaftskommission; ≗ **Commission for Latin America** *(ECLA)* Wirtschaftskommission für Lateinamerika; ≗ **and Social Committee** *(Common Market)* Wirtschafts- und Sozialausschuß; ~ **concentration** Konzentration der Wirtschaft; ~ **conditions** Wirtschaftslage, Erwerbsverhältnisse, Konjunktur; **sound** ~ **conditions** gesunde Wirt-

schaftsverhältnisse; **to improve the** ~ **conditions** Konjunktur beleben; **international** ~ **conference** internationale Wirtschaftskonferenz; ~ **conflict** ökonomischer Konflikt; ~ **consultancy** Wirtschaftsberatungsfirma; ~ **consultant** Wirtschaftsberater; ~ **continuity** kontinuierliche Wirtschaftspolitik; ~ **control** Wirtschaftskontrolle; **to suit** ~ **conveniences** wirtschaftlichen Zweckmäßigkeitserwägungen entsprechen; ~ **cooperation** wirtschaftliche Zusammenarbeit; ≗ **Cooperation Administration** *(ECA)* Verwaltung für europäische wirtschaftliche Zusammenarbeit; **to intensify** ~ **cooperation** wirtschaftliche Zusammenarbeit vertiefen; ~ **correspondent** Handels-, Wirtschaftskorrespondent; ~ **cost** laufende Unkosten; ≗ **and Social Council** Wirtschafts- und Sozialrat; ~ **course** Konjunkturaussichten, -verlauf; ~ **crime** Wirtschaftsverbrechen; ~ **crisis** Wirtschaftskrise; ~ **cycle** Konjunkturzyklus, -verlauf; ~ **data** wirtschaftliche Angaben, Konjunkturdaten; ~ **debate** Konjunkturdebatte; ~ **decisions** wirtschaftspolitische Entscheidungen; ~ **decline** wirtschaftlicher Niedergang, Konjunkturrückgang; ~ **depression** Wirtschaftskrise, wirtschaftliche Depression; ~ **determinism** wirtschaftliche Zwangsläufigkeit; ~ **development** wirtschaftliche Entwicklung, wirtschaftliche (konjunkturelle) Erschließung; ~ **development committees** *(Br.)* Ausschüsse für wirtschaftliche Entwicklungsfragen; ~ **dip** rückläufige Konjunktur, Konjunkturrückschlag, -einbruch; ~ **disaster** Wirtschaftskatastrophe; ~ **distress** wirtschaftliche Notlage, wirtschaftlicher Notstand; ~ **district** Industriegegend; ~ **doctrine** Wirtschaftsdoktrin; ~ **domain** Wirtschaftsraum; ~ **domination** wirtschaftliche Vorherrschaft; ~ **downswing** rückläufige Konjunkturphase; ~ **downturn** wirtschaftlicher Niedergang, Konjunkturrückgang; ~ **dynasty** Wirtschaftsdynastie; ~ **editor** Wirtschaftsredakteur; ~ **efficiency** wirtschaftliche Leistungsfähigkeit, Wirtschaftlichkeit; ~ **emergency plan** Notstandsprogramm für die Wirtschaft; ~ **entity** wirtschaftliche Einheit; ~ **equilibrium** wirtschaftliches Gleichgewicht; ~ **espionage** Wirtschaftsspionage; ~ **evaluation** wirtschaftliche Aufwertung; ~ **expansion** wirtschaftliche Ausdehnung, Wirtschaftsausbau; ~ **expansion program(me)** Wirtschaftsprogramm; ~ **expert** Wirtschaftssachverständiger; ~ **factors** Konjunktur-, Wirtschaftsfaktoren; ~ **federation** wirtschaftliche Vereinigung; ~ **field** wirtschaftliches Gebiet; ~ **fluctuations** Konjunkturschwankungen; ~ **forces** wirtschaftliche Kräfte; ~ **forecast** Konjunkturvorhersage, -vorschau; ~ **forecaster** Konjunkturbeobachter; ~ **forum** Wirtschaftsforum; ~ **freedom** Gewerbefreiheit; ~ **friction** wirtschaftlicher Reibungskoeffizient; ~ **front** Wirtschaftskreise; ~ **function** Geschäftätigkeit, Aufgabenbereich in der Wirtschaft; ~ **fusion** wirtschaftlicher Zusammenschluß; ~ **geography** Wirtschaftsgeographie; ~ **geology** praktische Geologie; ~ **gloom** wirtschaftliche Misere; ~ **goods** Wirtschaftsgüter; ~ **grasp** wirtschaftlich vertretbare Möglichkeit; ~ **group** Wirtschaftsgruppe; ~ **growth** Wirtschaftswachstum, Steigerung des Sozialprodukts; ~ **growth march** wirtschaftlicher Wachstumsprozeß; ~ **growth rate** Wachstumsrate der Volkswirtschaft; ~ **handicap** wirtschaftliche Belastung; ~ **harmonies** Prinzipien der sozialen Anpassung; ~ **history** Wirtschaftsgeschichte; ~ **horizon** Konjunkturhorizont; **to lighten the** ~ **horizon** Konjunkturhorizont aufhellen; ~ **ills** Konjunkturkrankheiten; ~ **imbalance** fehlendes konjunkturelles Gleichgewicht; ~ **imperialism** Wirtschaftsimperialismus; ~ **impetus** konjunkturelle Impulse, Konjunkturaufschwung; ~ **implications** konjunkturelle Auswirkungen; ~ **indicator** Konjunkturanzeichen, -indikator, -barometer; ~ **indicators** statistische Schlüsselwerte für die Wirtschaft; ~ **independence** wirtschaftliche Unabhängigkeit, Autarkie; ~ **influences** Wirtschafts-, Konjunkturbeeinflussung; ~ **information** Konjunkturdaten; ~ **institutions** wirtschaftliche Institutionen; ~ **integration** wirtschaftliche Integrierung; ~ **intercourse** Handels-, Wirtschaftsverkehr; ~ **interest** *(ownership of business)* Kapitalanteil; ~ **interests** wirtschaftliche Belange; ~ **isolationism** Wirtschaftsisolationismus; ~ **issue** Wirtschaftsfrage; **bread-and-butter** ~ **issues** wirtschaftliche Tagesfragen; ~ **journal** Wirtschaftszeitung; ~ **journalist** Wirtschaftsjournalist; ~ **laggard** wirtschaftlich Zurückgebliebener; **to pump into the leak** ~ **landscape** in die ausgedörrte Konjunkturlandschaft hineinpumpen; ~ **law** ökonomisches Gesetz; ~ **laws** Wirtschaftsgesetzgebung; ~ **leader** Wirtschaftsführer; ~ **leadership** Wirtschaftsführung; ~ **liberalism** Wirtschaftsliberalismus; ~ **life** Wirtschaftsleben, *(asset)* wirtschaftliche Lebens-, Nutzungsdauer; **to control the** ~ **life of a region** Wirtschaftsleben einer Gegend entscheidend beeinflussen; ~ **loss** Schaden wirtschaftlicher Art; ~ **lot size** wirtschaftliche Losgröße, rationelle Stückzahl; ~ **management** *(econom-*

ics) Konjunktursteuerung; ~ **manager** Konjunktursteuerer; ~ **manipulation** staatliche Wirtschaftslenkung; in ~ **matters** auf wirtschaftlichem Gebiet; **general ~ matters** allgemeine volkswirtschaftliche Fragen; ~ **maturity** volkswirtschaftlicher Reifezustand; ~ **measures** konjunkturpolitische Maßnahmen; ~ **method** ökonomische Methode; ~ **miracle** Wirtschaftswunder; ~ **mismanagement** Mißwirtschaft; ~ **mobilization** Mobilmachung der [Volks]wirtschaft; ~ **motives** ökonomische Beweggründe; ~ **nationalism** Autarkiestreben; ~ **news** Nachrichten aus dem Wirtschaftsleben; ~ **news agency** Wirtschaftspressedienst; ~ **offensive** Wirtschaftsoffensive; ~ **operation** wirtschaftlicher (rentabler) Betrieb, Wirtschaftlichkeit; ~ **order** Wirtschaftsordnung; ~ **order quantity** wirtschaftliche Auftragsgröße; **bright ~ outlook** gute Konjunkturaussichten; ~ **overheating** Konjunkturüberhitzung; ~ **overlord** Wirtschaftszar; ~ **package** Konjunkturankurbelungspaket; ~ **panel** Wirtschaftsausschuß; ~ **peace** Wirtschaftsfrieden; ~ **penetration** wirtschaftliche Durchdringung; ~ **performance** wirtschaftliches Leistungsvermögen, Entwicklung der Volkswirtschaft, Konjunkturleistung; ~ **period** Wirtschafts-, Konjunkturperiode; ~ **phenomenon** wirtschaftliche Erscheinungsform; ~ **picture** Konjunktur-, Wirtschaftsbild, Wirtschaftslage; **fifth ~ plan** Fünfjahresplan; ~ **planning** Wirtschaftsplanung, volkswirtschaftliche Planung; **central ~ planning** administrative Wirtschaftslenkung; ~ **planning board** *(Br.)* Planungsbehörde; ~ **planning council** *(Br.)* Wirtschaftsrat; ~ **planning regions** *(Br.)* volkswirtschaftliche Planungsgebiete, Strukturverbesserungsbezirke; ~ **plight** schwierige Wirtschaftslage.

economic policy Konjunktur-, Wirtschaftspolitik, wirtschaftliche Erwägungen;
~ **and social policy** Wirtschafts- und Sozialpolitik;
~ **activism** konjunkturpolitischer Aktivismus; ~ **agenda** konjunkturpolitische Tagesordnung; ~ **debate** Konjunkturdebatte; ~ **decisions** wirtschaftspolitische Entscheidungen; ~ **goal** konjunkturpolitisches Ziel; ~ **measures** Konjunkturmaßnahmen; ~ **official** konjunkturpolitischer Mitarbeiter; ~ **problems** wirtschaftspolitische Probleme; ~ **team** Beratungsgremium für konjunkturpolitische Fragen; ~ **tools** konjunkturpolitisches Instrumentarium.

economic|policymaker Wirtschafts-, Konjunkturpolitiker; ~ **potential** Wirtschaftspotential; ~ **power** wirtschaftliche Machtstellung; **sufficient ~ power** *(antitrust law)* hinreichende wirtschaftliche Marktmacht; ~ **preeminence** wirtschaftliche Vorrangstellung; ~ **pressure** wirtschaftlicher Druck; ~ **pressures** Geldsorgen; **to exert ~ pressure** wirtschaftlichen Druck ausüben; ~ **principles** ökonomisches Prinzip, Wirtschaftlichkeitsprinzip; ~ **priorities** Handelsvorrechte; ~ **privileges** wirtschaftliche Privilegien (Vorrechte); ~ **problems** wirtschaftspolitische Probleme; ~ **process** Wirtschaftsablauf, volkswirtschaftliche Entwicklung; ~ **profit** Grenzkostenergebnis; ~ **program(me)** Wirtschafts-, Konjunkturprogramm; ~ **progress** wirtschaftlicher Fortschritt; ~ **project** Wirtschaftsprojekt; ~ **prospects** Konjunktur-, Entwicklungsaussichten; ~ **pundit** Konjunkturberater; ~ **quantities** ökonomische Größen; ~ **questions** Wirtschaftsfragen; ~ **realism** Wirtschaftsrealismus; ~ **reality** wirtschaftliche Realitäten; ~ **rebounds** Wiederaufschwung der Wirtschaft, Konjunkturaufschwung; ~ **recession** wirtschaftliche Rezession, Rezession [der Wirtschaft]; ~ **reconstruction** Wiederaufbau der Wirtschaft; ~ **recovery** Wirtschafts-, Konjunkturbelebung, Wirtschaftsaufschwung, konjunkturelle Belebung; ~ **reform** Wirtschaftsreform; ~ **regime** Wirtschaftssystem; ~ **region** Wirtschaftsraum; ~ **regulator** Konjunkturregulativ; ~ **rehabilitation** wirtschaftlicher Wiederaufbau; ~ **relations** Wirtschaftsbeziehungen; ~ **relationship(s)** wirtschaftlicher Zusammenhang; ~ **rent** *(Ricardo)* Grundrente, *(landlord)* Kosten[vergleichs]miete; ~ **reorganization** Konjunktur-, Wirtschaftsankurbelung; ~ **report** Konjunktur-, Wirtschaftsbericht, *(White Paper, Br.)* Nationalbudget; ~ **reprisals** wirtschaftliche Repressalien; ~ **research** Konjunktur-, Wirtschaftsforschung; ~ **research division** Konjunkturforschungsabteilung; ~ **research institute (organization)** Konjunktur-, Wirtschaftsforschungsinstitut; ~ **researcher** Konjunkturforscher; ~ **resemblance** Wirtschaftsähnlichkeit; ~ **resources** *(country)* Wirtschaftskraft; ~ **review** Wirtschaftsmagazin; ~ **revival** Konjunkturbelebung; ~ **rights** wirtschaftliche Rechte; ~ **ruin** wirtschaftlicher Ruin; ~ **sabotage** Wirtschaftssabotage; ~ **sanctions** wirtschaftliche Sanktionen; ~ **science** *(US)* Wirtschaftswissenschaft, Volkswirtschaftslehre; ~ **self-sufficiency** wirtschaftliche Autarkie; ~ **setup of a country** *(US)* Wirtschaftsstruktur eines Landes; ~

shrinkage Abnehmen der wirtschaftlichen Kapazität; ~ **situation** wirtschaftspolitische Lage, Konjunktur-, Wirtschaftslage; **to ease the ~ situation** Konjunkturentspannung herbeiführen; ~ **slack period** konjunkturelle Flautezeit; ~ **slackening** Konjunkturflaute, Nachlassen der (nachlassende) Konjunktur; ~ **slowdown** Abschwächung der Konjunktur, Konjunkturabschwächung, -verlangsamung; ~ **slump** rückläufige Konjunktur; **in the ~ sphere** im Bereich der Wirtschaft; ~ **stability** Wirtschaftsstabilität; ~ **stabilization** Stabilisierung der Konjunktur; ~ **stagnation** wirtschaftliche (konjunkturelle) Stagnation; ~ **statistics** Wirtschaftsstatistik, Konjunkturstatistik; ~ **stimulation** Konjunkturanreiz, -ankurbelung; ~ **stimulus** Konjunkturanreiz; ~ **strategy** langfristige Konjunkturpolitik; ~ **strength** Wirtschaftskraft; ~ **structure** Wirtschaftsstruktur; ~ **struggle** Konkurrenzkampf; ~ **study** Rentabilitätsuntersuchung, Konjunkturstudie; ~ **subject** Wirtschaftsfrage; ~ **summit** Gipfelkonferenz für Wirtschaftsfragen, Wirtschaftsgipfel; ~ **summitry** wirtschaftliche Gipfeldiplomatie; ~ **superiority** wirtschaftliche Überlegenheit; ~ **supremacy** wirtschaftliche Übermacht; ~ **support** Wirtschaftshilfe; ~ **survey** Wirtschaftsbericht, ⌐ **Survey** *(Br.)* Nationalbudget; ~ **system** Wirtschaftssystem, -ordnung; **free ~ system** freiheitliche Wirtschaftsordnung; ~ **tailspin** Konjunktursturz; ~ **talks** Wirtschaftsgespräche; ~ **temperature** konjunkturelles Klima, Konjunkturklima; ~ **term** Wirtschaftsausdruck; ~ **terminology** Wirtschaftssprache, -terminologie; ~ **territory** Wirtschafts-, Industriegebiet; ~ **theorist** Wirtschaftstheoretiker; ~ **theory** Volkswirtschaftstheorie; ~ **thinking (thought)** Wirtschaftsdenken; ~ **throttle** Konjunkturdrosselung; ~ **trend** Wirtschaftstendenz, konjunktureller Entwicklungsverlauf, Konjunkturverlauf, -entwicklung, -trend; ~ **trough** Konjunkturtief, -mulde, Wellental der Konjunktur; ~ **turn** konjunktureller Wendepunkt; ~ **turnaround** Konjunkturwende; ~ **uncertainty** konjunkturelle Unsicherheit; ~ **union** Wirtschaftsunion; ~ **unit (unity)** Wirtschaftseinheit; **single ~ unit** einheitliches Wirtschaftsgebilde; ~ **upswing** Konjunkturanstieg; ~ **upturn** wirtschaftlicher Wiederanstieg; Konjunkturanstieg, -belebung; ~ **use** Nutzungsdauer; ~ **value** wirtschaftlicher Wert; ~ **vitality** wirtschaftliche Leistungsfähigkeit; ~ **wants** Anforderungen der Volkswirtschaft; ~ **war[fare]** Wirtschaftskrieg[führung]; **to stir up the ~ waters** Konjunkturklima stören; ~ **welfare** materielles Wohlergehen; ~ **whole** wirtschaftliche Einheit; ~ **woes** Wirtschaftskalamität; ~ **worth** wirtschaftlicher Wert; ~ **wrench** Wirtschaftskrise; ~ **writing** Abfassung von Wirtschaftsbeiträgen.

economical [volks]wirtschaftlich, *(thrifty)* sparsam [im Gebrauch], ökonomisch, haushälterisch;
politico-~ wirtschaftspolitisch;
to be ~ sparsam umgehen; **to be ~ of time** Zeit sparen;
~ **administration** sparsame Verwaltung; ~ **car** im Verbrauch sparsames Auto; ~ **operation** wirtschaftlicher (rentabler) Betrieb; ~ **realities** wirtschaftliche Gegebenheiten; ~ **society** Wirtschaftsgesellschaft; ~ **speed** *(ship)* Nutzungsgeschwindigkeit; **to be of low ~ strength** nicht krisenfest sein.

economically|-beleaguered wirtschaftlich bedrängt; ~ **speaking** vom wirtschaftlichen Standpunkt aus.

economics [Volks]wirtschaft, *(science, Br.)* Volkswirtschaftslehre, Wirtschaftswissenschaft, Nationalökonomie;
applied ~ angewandte Volkswirtschaftslehre; **business ~** *(Br.)* Betriebswirtschaft; **capitalistic ~** kapitalistisches Wirtschaftssystem; **consumer ~** Verbraucherwirtschaft; **home ~** *(US)* Hauswirtschaftslehre; **international ~** Weltwirtschaft; **pure ~** allgemeine Volkswirtschaftslehre; **rural ~** Landwirtschaft; **social ~** Sozialwissenschaft; **stop-go ~** antizyklisch gesteuerte Volkswirtschaft; **world ~** Weltwirtschaft;
~ **of control** interventionistische Marktwirtschaft; ~ **of a country** Wirtschaftssystem eines Landes; ~ **of distribution** Verteilerwirtschaft; ~ **of industrial organization** sektorale Konjunkturpolitik; ~ **of production** Produktionswirtschaft; ~ **of publishing** Verlagsgeschäft; ~ **of road and rail transport** Verkehrswirtschaft;
to be taught ~ Wirtschaftswissenschaften hören;
~ **bookshop** Fachbuchhandlung für Wirtschaftsliteratur; ~ **degree** volkswirtschaftliches Diplom; ~ **graduate** [etwa] Doktor der Volkswirtschaft; ~ **portfolio** Wirtschaftsressort; ~ **unit** Volkswirtschaftsabteilung.

economies Ersparnisse, Sparmaßnahmen, Abstriche;
financial ~ finanzielle Einsparungen; **major ~** größere Einsparungen; **managerial ~** verwaltungsmäßige Einsparungen; **risk-bearing ~** Einsparungen durch erhöhte Übernahme eigenen Risikos; **technical ~** technische Einsparungen;

~ in administration Verwaltungseinsparungen; **~ of scale** Kostenersparnisse (Kostendegression) durch optimale Betriebsvergrößerung;

to look into ~ sparsam wirtschaften; **to make ~** Einsparungen vornehmen; **to reap ~ of scale** Profite durch optimale Auftragsgrößenordnungen erzielen.

economist, [political] [Volks]wirtschaftler, Volkswirt, Wirtschaftswissenschaftler, [National]ökonom;

academic ~ Volkswirt mit akademischem Abschluß; **business ~** Betriebswirt; **rural ~** Agrarwirtschaftler, Agronom;

~-lawyer Wirtschaftsanwalt; **~'s terminology** nationalökonomische Terminologie.

economization sparsame Wirtschaft, Sparsamkeit.

economize (v.) (practise economy) sparsam wirtschaften (umgehen), [zusammen]sparen, durch Einsparungen herauswirtschaften, einsparen, sparsam leben, überflüssige Ausgabe (Kosten) vermeiden, Abstriche machen, sich einschränken, (use sparingly) sparsam anwenden, haushalten;

~ on light and fuel unnötige Licht- und Heizungskosten vermeiden.

economizer Sparer, haushälterischer Mensch.

economy (economics) [Volks]wirtschaft, Wirtschaftslehre, Nationalökonomie, (system of rules) organisches System, Organisation, Aufbau, Anordnung, (economic trend) Konjunktur, (thrift) Sparsamkeit, Ökonomie, Ersparnis, Wirtschaftlichkeit, Ausnutzung, [Kosten]einsparung;

for ~'s sake aus Ersparnisgründen;

agrarian ~ Agrarwirtschaft; **barter ~** Tausch-, Naturalwirtschaft; **booming ~** glänzende Konjunktur; **branch-factory ~** von Filialgründungen abhängige Wirtschaftlichkeit; **capitalist ~** kapitalistische Wirtschaft; **collective ~** Kollektivwirtschaft; **competitive ~** Wettbewerbs-, Konkurrenzwirtschaft; **highly competitive ~** intensive Wettbewerbswirtschaft; **controlled ~** gelenkte Wirtschaft, Plan-, Zwangswirtschaft; **declining ~** rezessive Konjunktur; **defence ~** Wehrwirtschaft; **depressed ~** Wirtschaftsflaute; **directed ~** gelenkte Wirtschaft; **domestic ~** Hauswirtschaft, Haushaltskunst; **draft ~** Plan-, gelenkte Wirtschaft; **enterprise ~** (US) Unternehmerwirtschaft; **extensive ~** extensive Wirtschaft; **external ~** Außenwirtschaft; **faltering ~** abklingende Konjunktur; **financial ~** Finanzwirtschaft; **flat ~** Konjunkturflaute; **free-enterprise (market) ~** freie Marktwirtschaft; **guided ~** gesteuerte Wirtschaft; **home ~** Binnenwirtschaft; **industrial ~** gewerbliche Wirtschaft; **integrated ~** integrierte Wirtschaft; **intensive ~** intensive Wirtschaft; **internal ~** Binnenwirtschaft, (plant) innerbetriebliche Rationalisierung; **isolated ~** Einzelwirtschaft; **labo(u)r-tight ~** angespannte Arbeitslage; **laissez-faire ~** freie Marktwirtschaft; **managed ~** Planwirtschaft; **mixed ~** gemischte Wirtschaftsform; **money ~** Geldwirtschaft; **national ~** Volkswirtschaft, Nationalökonomie; **no-growth ~** Nullwachstumswirtschaft; **oil-based ~** ölabhängige Wirtschaft; **overall ~** Gesamtwirtschaft; **over-exuberant ~** überschäumende Konjunktur; **peacetime ~** Friedenswirtschaft; **planned ~** [staatliche] Plan-, Zwangswirtschaft, staatlicher Dirigismus, konzertierte Wirtschaft; **political ~** Volkswirtschaftslehre, Wirtschaftswissenschaft, Nationalökonomie; **applied political ~** Staatswirtschaft[slehre]; **price-controlled ~** preisüberwachte Wirtschaft; **private ~** Privatwirtschaft; **regimented ~** reglementierte Wirtschaft; **rigid ~** strengste Sparsamkeit; **self-contained ~** autarke Volkswirtschaft; **~ slowing ~** Konjunkturabschwächung; **social ~** Nationalökonomie, Volkswirtschaftslehre; **social market ~** soziale Marktwirtschaft; **totalitarian ~** Zwangswirtschaft; **uncontrolled ~** freie Wirtschaft; **undermanned ~** unterbesetzte Wirtschaft; **unorganized ~** gewerkschaftsfreie Wirtschaft; **wartime ~** Kriegswirtschaft; **world-wide ~** Weltwirtschaft;

~ of abundance Überschußwirtschaft; **~ run by parliamentary committee government** von parlamentarischen Ausschüssen gesteuerte Wirtschaft; **~ in fuel consumption** (car) geringer Benzinverbrauch; **~ of labo(u)r** Arbeitsersparnis; **~ in operation** Wirtschaftlichkeit in der Betriebsführung; **~ in process of integration** sich integrierende Wirtschaft; **~ in raw materials** Rohstoffersparnis; **~ of scarcity** Sparsamkeitswirtschaft; **~ of space** Raumersparnis; **~ in spending** Ausgabenwirtschaft; **~ of time** Zeitersparnis; **~ as a whole** gesamte Wirtschaft;

to affect the ~ Konjunktur beeinflussen; **to come to grips with the ~** Konjunktur in den Griff bekommen; **to cool the ~** Konjunkturabkühlung herbeiführen; **to cool off an overheated ~** überhitzte Konjunktur abkühlen; **to disturb the ~ of Europe** europäisches Wirtschaftssystem durcheinanderbringen; **to get the ~ back on the tracks** Konjunktur wieder zum Anlauf bringen; **to give the ~ a shot in the arm** (US) der Wirtschaft eine

Konjunkturspritze geben; **to give the ~ a push** Konjunkturanstoß geben; **to handle the ~** Konjunktur steuern (im Griff haben), Konjunktursteuerung beherrschen; **to have a grip on the ~** Konjunktur in den Griff bekommen; **to heat up the ~** Konjunktur anheizen; **to hold the ~ back** Konjunktur zügeln; **to keep the ~ in high gear** Wirtschaft auf Hochtouren laufen lassen; **to keep the ~ jogging along by another little fix** Konjunktur mit einem weiteren kleinen Trick am Leben erhalten; **to keep the ~ running at a high level** hohes Konjunkturniveau aufrechterhalten; **to keep the ~ on the straight and narrow** Konjunktur im Zaum halten; **to keep the ~ ticking over** Konjunktur gerade noch in Schwung halten; **to keep the ~ on a stable upward** gleichmäßige Aufwärtsbewegung der Wirtschaft herbeiführen; **to make o. s. a great factor in the ~** in der Wirtschaft eine große Rolle spielen; **to manage the ~** Konjunktur steuern; **to move the ~ toward full employment** Vollbeschäftigungszustand in der Wirtschaft herbeiführen; **to overheat the ~** Konjunktur überhitzen; **to pep up the ~** Wirtschaft ankurbeln; **to place great strains on the ~** Wirtschaft großen Belastungen aussetzen; **to practise ~** sparsam wirtschaften, sparen; **to push the ~ further towards a slump** sich weiter dem Konjunkturzusammenbruch nähern; **to put the ~ on a richer monetary diet** Wirtschaft geldflüssiger machen, für wirtschaftspolitische Liquidität sorgen; **to ride the ~ at full gallop** Konjunktur auf höchstes Tempo bringen; **to run the ~ at a high level of job-creating demand** Konjunktursteuerung mit dem Ziel steigender Nachfrage nach Arbeitsplätzen vornehmen; **to rush the ~ back to full employment levels** Vollbeschäftigungszustand sofort wiederherstellen, sofort wieder durchstarten; **to slow down the ~** Konjunktur verlangsamen; **to stabilize the ~** stabile Konjunkturpolitik betreiben; **to switch its ~** Wirtschaft umstellen; **to take enough of the pep out of the ~** ausreichende konjunkturelle Bremsen betätigen; **to turn the ~ around** Konjunktur ankurbeln; **to turn the ~ back up again** Konjunktur wieder ankurbeln; **to under-pin the ~** Konjunktur stützen;

~ cabin Touristenabteil; **~ campaign** Sparfeldzug; **~ car** Kraftfahrzeug der Mittelklasse; **~ carburettor** Sparvergaser; **~ class** (airplane) Touristenklasse; **~-class passenger** Fluggast in der Touristenklasse; **~-class travel** Flug in der Touristenklasse; **~ drive** Sparfeldzug; **~ excursion** Gesellschaftsreise in der Touristenklasse; **~ fare** Touristenflugschein, -karte; **~ market** Absatzgebiet für billige Artikel; **~ measures** Einschränkungs-, Sparmaßnahmen; **~ menu** Touristenmenü; **~ ministry** Wirtschaftsministerium; **~ model** billiges Modell, Sparmodell; **~ pack** Sparpaket; **~ plane** Touristenflugzeug; **~-priced** vergleichsweise preisgünstig, zu niedrigem Preis angeboten; **~-of-effort principle** Wirtschaftlichkeitsprinzip; **~ room** Aufenthaltsraum für durchreisende Touristen; **scheduled ~ round trip** (US) Touristenrundreise in einer Linienmaschine; **~ run** (car) sparsamer Verbrauch, (test) Wirtschaftlichkeitsprüfung; **~ seat** Touristenflugschein; **~ size** Verbraucherpackung; **~-sized** (US) in Großpackung; **~-sized car** wirtschaftlicher Wagen; **~ wave** Sparwelle.

ecosystem Naturhaushalt.

edge Rand, Grenze, (fig.) Schärfe, Spitze;

on ~ ungeduldig; **~ on** im Begriff zu, kurz vor; **over the ~** verrückt; **with gilt ~s** (book) mit Goldschnitt;

sole ~ over (fam.) alleiniger Vorteil über; **clear ~ over other candidates** klarer Vorsprung vor anderen Bewerbern; **~ of a forest** Waldrand; **fine ~ of interest** besonderes Engagement;

~ (v.) **away** (ship) abhalten; **~ down** (prices) schwächer tendieren, nachgeben; **~ s. o. out of a job** j. aus einer Stellung verdrängen; **~ the road** Fahrbahn begrenzen; **~ up** (prices) langsam anziehen; **~ one's way into a job** sich in eine Stellung hineindrängen; **~ one's way through the crowd** sich durch eine Menschenmenge schieben; **~ a word in** ein Wort einschieben; **to be all on ~** aufs Äußerste gespannt sein; **to give s. o. the ~** jem. eine [Gewinn]chance geben; **to give s. o. the rough ~ of one's tongue** bissige Bemerkungen über j. machen, jem. Beleidigungen an den Kopf werfen; **to give an ~ to one's style** in beißendem Stil schreiben; **to have an ~ on** (US sl.) betrunken sein; **to have the ~ on (over s. o.)** (sl.) jem. gegenüber im Vorteil sein, jem. überlegen sein; **to have one's nerves on ~** mit seinen Nerven am Ende sein; **not to put too fine an ~ upon it** kein Blatt vor den Mund nehmen, frei von der Leber reden; **to set s. one's teeth on ~** j. kribbelig machen; **to skirt the ~ of poverty** am Rande der Armut leben; **to take the ~ off an argument** einem Argument seine Schärfe nehmen; **to take the ~ off pleasures** Vergnügungen ihren Reiz nehmen;

~ tool (fig.) gefährliche Maßnahme; **to play with ~ tools** mit dem Feuer spielen.

edgelining Fahrbahnrandbegrenzungslinie.

edict Edikt, Verordnung.

edifice Gebäude, Bau, *(fig.)* Gefüge;
~ **of one's hope** Gespinst von Hoffnung.

edit *(v.) (book, newspaper)* herausgeben, als Herausgeber fungieren, *(revise)* redigieren, druckfertig machen;
~ **books for use in schools** Schulbücher herausgeben; ~ **a collection of letters** Briefsammlung veröffentlichen; ~ **a motion picture** Film zur Veröffentlichung fertigmachen; ~ **news for the public** Nachrichten für die Öffentlichkeit aufmachen; ~ **a newspaper** Zeitung redigieren (als Herausgeber leiten).

edictal citation *(Scot. law)* öffentliche Ladung.

edited by herausgegeben (unter Leitung) von.

editing Herausgabe, Redaktion;
~ **job** *(work)* Herausgebertätigkeit; ~ **terminal** Korrekturterminal; ~ **typewriter** Textverarbeitungsanlage; ~ **work** Redaktions-, Herausgebertätigkeit.

edition Ausgabe, Veröffentlichung, *(newspaper)* Nummer, *(total)* Auflage;
abridged ~ gekürzte Ausgabe; **cheap** ~ billige Ausgabe, Volksausgabe; **city** ~ *(newspaper)* Stadtausgabe; **complete** ~ vollständige Ausgabe; **copyright** ~ berechtigte [Buch]ausgabe; **corrected** ~ verbesserte Auflage; **damaged** ~ beschädigtes Werk; **definitive** ~ unveränderte Auflage, Ausgabe letzter Hand; **double-column** ~ zweispaltig gedruckte Ausgabe; **enlarged** ~ erweiterte Auflage; **erroneous** ~ fehlerhaftes Werk; **first** ~ Original-, Erstauflage; **folio** ~ Ausgabe im Folioformat; **late** ~ Abendausgabe; **latest** ~ Nachtausgabe; **library** ~ Bibliotheksausgabe; **limited** ~ beschränkte Auflage; **local** ~ Bezirksausgabe; **morning** ~ Morgenausgabe; **new** ~ Neuauflage, -ausgabe; **one-volume** ~ einbändige Ausgabe; **original** ~ Originalausgabe; **pirated** ~ unberechtigt nachgedruckte Ausgabe, unerlaubter Nachdruck, Raubdruck; **pocket** ~ Taschenausgabe; **pony** ~ Ausgabe in Miniform; **popular** ~ Volksausgabe; **revised** ~ [neu]bearbeitete (überarbeitete) Auflage; **revised and improved** ~ durchgesehene und verbesserte Auflage; **single-volume** ~ einbändige Ausgabe; **special** ~ Sonderausgabe, *(newspaper)* Extrablatt; **splendid** ~ Prachtausgabe; **Sunday** ~ Sonntagsausgabe; **teacher** ~ Ausgabe nur für Lehrer; **unabridged** ~ ungekürzte Ausgabe; **weekly** ~ Wochenausgabe; **screen** ~ Filmfassung;
~ **de luxe** Pracht-, Luxusausgabe;
to have reached (run up to) an 8th ~ acht Auflagen erzielt (erlebt) haben.

editor Herausgeber, Schriftleiter, Redakteur, *(broadcasting)* Programmleiter, *(chief)* Chefredakteur, *(editorial writer)* Leitartikler, *(publishing house, US)* Lektor;
~s Schriftleitung, Redaktion[sstab];
art ~ Bild- und Umbruchredakteur; **assistant** ~ Redaktionsassistent, Hilfsredakteur; **city** ~ *(Br.)* Redakteur des Wirtschaftsteils, *(US)* Lokalredakteur; **dramatic** ~ Theaterreszensent; **financial** ~ *(US)* Redakteur des Wirtschaftsteils, Wirtschaftsredakteur; **full-time** ~ festangestellter Redakteur; **joint** ~s Herausgebergremium; **the learned** ~ der gelehrte Verfasser; **legal** ~ juristischer Redakteur; **managing** ~ Hauptschriftleiter, Chefredakteur; **news** ~ Chef vom Dienst; **prison** ~ Sitzredakteur; **publicity** ~ für den Anzeigenteil verantwortlicher Redakteur; **sub-** ~ zweiter Redakteur, Hilfsredakteur; **woman** ~ Herausgeberin;
~ **in chief** verantwortlicher Herausgeber, Hauptschriftleiter, *(US)* Chefredakteur; ~ **of a dictionary** Wörterbuchverfasser; ~ **publisher** Besitzer und Herausgeber;
letter to the ~ Eingesandt;
~-**proprietor** Eigentümer und Herausgeber; ~'s **office** Redaktionsbüro.

editorial redaktioneller Artikel, Leitartikel;
front-page ~ Leitartikel auf der ersten Seite;
to run an ~ Leitartikel veröffentlichen;
~ *(a.)* redaktionell;
~ **advertisement** redaktionell aufgemachte (gestaltete) Anzeige; ~ **advertising** redaktionelle Werbung; ~ **article** Leitartikel; ~ **assistance** redaktionelle Unterstützung; ~ **board (bureau)** Redaktionsbüro; ~ **close (closing)** Redaktionsschluß; ~ **column** Leitartikel; ~ **comment** redaktioneller Kommentar; ~ **complaining** redaktionelle Beschwerde; ~ **conduct of a newspaper** Redaktion einer Zeitung; ~ **conference** Redaktionskonferenz; ~ **content** redaktioneller Inhalt; ~ **copy** redaktioneller Text; ~ **department** Redaktion[sbüro, -abteilung], Schriftleitung; ~ **duties** redaktioneller Aufgabenbereich; ~ **freedom** redaktionelle Freiheiten; ~ **leader** Leitartikel; ~ **management** Redaktion, Schriftleitung; ~ **matter** redaktioneller Text (Teil);

~ **network** weitverzweigtes Redaktionsnetz; ~ **objective** Redaktionsziel; ~ **office** Redaktionsbüro, Schriftleitung; ~ **opinion** redaktionelle Meinungsäußerung; ~ **outline** Redaktionsentwurf; ~ **page** Leitartikelseite; ~ **part** redaktioneller Teil; ~ **policies** redaktionelle Tendenz, Redaktionspolitik; ~ **preparation** redaktionelle Aufbreitung (Aufmachung); ~ **publicity** redaktionell aufgemachte Werbung; ~ **revision** redaktionelle Durchsicht; ~ **rooms** Redaktionsräume; ~ **section** redaktioneller Teil; ~ **space** redaktioneller Teil [einer Zeitung]; ~ **staff** Redaktionsstab, Schriftleitung; **to hire** ~ **talents** redaktionellen Nachwuchs anwerben; ~ **unit** Redaktionsstab; ~ **view** Meinung der Schriftleitung; ~ **work** Herausgeber-, Redaktionstätigkeit, -arbeit; ~ **worker** Redaktionsmitarbeiter; ~ **writer** Leitartikler.

editorialist Leitartikler.

editorialize *(v.) (US)* im Leitartikel (redaktionell) Stellung nehmen, *(write editorials)* Leitartikel schreiben.

editorialized advertisement redaktionell aufgemachte Werbung.

editorializing redaktionelle Stellungnahme.

editorship redaktionelle Leitung, Redaktion;
under the ~ **of** unter der Redaktion von.

editress Herausgeberin.

educate *(v.)* erziehen, unterrichten;
~ **one's son for the bar** seinen Sohn zum Juristen ausbilden lassen.

educated gebildet;
to be well ~ gute Erziehung genossen haben, gebildet sein; **to be** ~ **at home** Privatunterricht gehabt haben; **to be entirely self-**~ Autodidakt sein; **to be only half** ~ nur eine Grundausbildung genossen haben;
~ **diction** kultivierte Sprache; ~ **guess** auf Erfahrung beruhende Annahme; ~ **man** gebildeter Mensch; ~ **people** gebildetes Publikum.

education Ausbildung, Erziehung, Bildungsgang, *(science of teaching)* Bildungs-, Schulwesen;
adult ~ Erwachsenenbildung; **agricultural** ~ landwirtschaftliches Fachschulwesen; **allround** ~ umfassende Bildung; **bread-and-butter** ~ nur auf den Broterwerb ausgerichtete Ausbildung; **business** ~ Handelsschulbildung; **central-school** ~ höhere Schulbildung; **classical** ~ humanistische Bildung; **co-**~ gemeinsame Erziehung von Knaben und Mädchen; **college** ~ akademische Bildung, Hochschulbildung, Universitätsausbildung; **commercial** ~ kaufmännische Ausbildung; **compulsory** ~ Schulpflicht, -zwang; **continued** ~ Fortbildung; **elementary** ~ Volksschulbildung; **free** ~ kostenlose Ausbildung; **further** ~ Weiterbildung, *(Br.)* Fortbildungsunterricht; **general grammar-school** ~ Gymnasialausbildung; **good general (liberal)** ~ gute Allgemeinbildung; **grammar-school** ~ Gymnasialausbildung; **higher** ~ Hochschulbildung; **high-school** ~ *(US)* Gymnasialausbildung; **home** ~ Privaterziehung; **industrial** ~ Betriebsausbildung; **job-oriented** ~ berufsbezogene Ausbildung; **legal** ~ juristische Vorbildung; **many-sided** ~ vielseitige Ausbildung; **non-state** ~ Privatschulausbildung; **preschool** ~ vorschulische Erziehung; **primary** ~ *(Br.)* Grund-, Volksschulausbildung; **professional** ~ Berufsausbildung; **public** ~ öffentliches Schulwesen; **recurrent** ~ Ausbildung und Praxis im periodischen Wechsel; **secondary** ~ zweiter Bildungsgang; **slap-up** ~ *(sl.)* erstklassige Ausbildung; **slum back-street** ~ asoziale Hinterhofeinflüsse auf die Erziehung; **technical** ~ Fachausbildung; **tertiary** ~ Hochschulbildung; **thorough** ~ gründliche Ausbildung; **university** ~ Hochschulbildung; **vocational** ~ Berufsschulausbildung;
~ **for the bar** juristische Ausbildung; ~ **for commerce** Handelsschulbildung;
to complete one's ~ seine Erziehung (Ausbildung) abschließen; **to continue one's** ~ sich fortbilden; **to finance s. one's** ~ jds. Studium finanzieren; **to give s. o. a political** ~ j. politisch schulen; **to go on to higher** ~ studieren wollen; **to have had a good** ~ gute Erziehung genossen haben; **to have a thorough** ~ gründliche Ausbildung erhalten; **to have a wide** ~ sich vielseitig gebildet haben; **to obtain one's** ~ **at Oxford** Universität in Oxford besuchen;
♀ **Act** *(Br.)* Berufsausbildungsgesetz; ~ **allowance** Erziehungsbeihilfe, Ausbildungszuschuß; ~ **authority** Erziehungsbehörde; ~ **committee** Schulausschuß; **adult** ~ **course** [etwa] Volkshochschule; ~ **expenditure** Aufwand für das Erziehungswesen; ~ **department** *(Br.)* Erziehungs-, Wissenschaftsministerium; ~ **grant** Erziehungsbeihilfe, Ausbildungszuschuß; ♀ **Minister** Kultusminister; **aid-to-**~ **program(me)** Ausbildungszuschußprogramm; ~ **and training scheme** Ausbildungsprogramm; ~ **secretary** *(Br.)* Erziehungsminister.

educational erzieherisch, pädagogisch;

~ Act *(US)* Berufsausbildungsgesetz; ~ **advertising** belehrende Werbung, Aufklärungsreklame; ~ **age** Erziehungsalter; ~ **aid** Erziehungsbeihilfe; ~ **aim** bildungspolitisches Ziel; ~ **allowance** Ausbildungszuschuß, Erziehungsbeihilfe; ~ **appliance** Lehrmittel; low ~ **attainment** niedriger Bildungsstand; ~ **background** [Aus]bildungsgang; ~ **body** Erziehungsgremium; ~ **book** Schul-, Lehrbuch; ~ **book company** Schulbuchverlag; ~ **broadcasting** Schulfunk; ~ **center** Bildungsstätte, -zentrum; ~ **endowment** Ausbildungsbeihilfe; ~ **endowment insurance** *(Br.)* Ausbildungsversicherung; ~ **establishment** Lehr-, Erziehungsanstalt, Bildungsstätte; ~ **facilities** Bildungsmöglichkeiten; ~ **film** Lehrfilm; ~ **grant** Ausbildungsbeihilfe; ~ **headphone** Kopfhörer für Unterrichtszwecke; ~ **institution** Lehranstalt, Bildungseinrichtung; ~ **level** Bildungsniveau, -stand; ~ **magazine** bildende (belehrende) Zeitschrift; ~ **material privilege** Lehrmittelfreiheit; ~ **matters** Erziehungswesen; ~ **opportunities** Bildungschancen; ~ **panel** Erziehungs-, Ausbildungsausschuß; ~ **piece** Informationsartikel; untapped ~ **potential** Begabtenreserve; ~ **priority area** Bildungsnotstandsgebiet; ~ **provisions** Bildungsvorkehrungen; ~ **publisher** Schulbuchverlag; to have high ~ **qualifications** hohen Ausbildungsgrad nachweisen; ~ **requirements** Bildungsvoraussetzungen; ~ **services** Bildungseinrichtungen; ~ **sociology** Sozialpädagogik; ~ **system** Erziehungssystem, -wesen, Schulwesen; ~ **tariff** Erziehungszoll; ~ **television** Bildungsfernsehen; ~ **training scheme** Ausbildungsprogramm; special ~ **treatment** Sondererziehung; general ~ **value** allgemeiner Bildungswert; ~ **work** Bildungsarbeit.

educationalist Erzieher, Erziehungswissenschaftler.

educator Erzieher, Pädagoge, *(appliance)* Bildungsmittel.

efface *(v.)* löschen, ausstreichen, auslöschen, tilgen;

~ o. s. sich zurückhalten (im Hintergrund halten);

~ **unpleasant memories of the past** unliebsame Begebenheiten der Vergangenheit aus dem Gedächtnis tilgen.

effaceable auslöschbar.

effacement Löschung, Ausstreichung, Tilgung;

self-~ persönliche Zurückhaltung.

effect *(law)* Kraft, Gültigkeit, Geltung, *(machine)* [Nutz]leistung, *(purport)* Sinn, Inhalt, *(result)* Wirkung, Auswirkungen, Effekt, Konsequenz, Ergebnis;

calculated for ~ auf Effekt berechnet; in ~ in Wirklichkeit, tatsächlich; of no ~ wirkungslos, fruchtlos, vergeblich; to the ~ that des Inhalts, daß; with ~ from mit Wirkung vom; without (of no) ~ unwirksam;

binding ~ bindende Wirkung; collateral ~ Nebenwirkung; constitutive ~ rechtserzeugende Wirkung; cumulative ~ kumulierende Wirkung; delaying ~ aufschiebende Wirkung; detrimental ~ nachteilige Wirkungen; general ~ Gesamtwirkung; legal ~ Rechtswirkung, -wirksamkeit; mechanical (useful) ~ Nutzleistung; retrospective ~ *(law)* rückwirkende Kraft; stage ~ Bühnenwirksamkeit; suspensory ~ aufschiebende Wirkung; telling ~ durchschlagende Wirkung; total (whole) ~ Gesamtleistung;

~ of a contract Vertrags[aus]wirkung; ~s of depression Depressionsauswirkungen; ~ of evidence Beweiskraft; habitude ~ of an abuse Gewohnheitsmißbrauch; ~ of inflation Inflationsauswirkung; ~s of an injury Folgewirkungen einer Verletzung; ~ of our labo(u)r Ergebnis unserer Bemühungen; disastrous ~s on liquidity katastrophale Liquiditätsauswirkungen; ~ of [giving] notice Benachrichtigungswirkung, Kündigungswirkung; ~ of registration Eintragungs-, Registrierungswirkung; ~s of risk Risikoauswirkungen; retrospective ~ of a statute rückwirkende Kraft eines Gesetzes; ~ of a tax Steuerauswirkung; ~ of war Kriegsauswirkung, -folge;

~ *(v.)* bewirken, zustandebringen, aus-, herbei-, durchführen, tätigen, zur Ausführung bringen, bewerkstelligen;

~ **collection for a firm** Inkassodienst für eine Firma leisten; ~ **a compromise** sich verständigen, zu einer Verständigung gelangen; ~ **a corresponding entry** gleichlautende Buchung vornehmen; ~ **a cure** Kur erfolgreich abschließen; ~ **customs clearance** sich zollamtlich abfertigen lassen; ~ **exchange deals on London** Abschlüsse auf London tätigen; ~ **improvements** Ameliorationen vornehmen; ~ **an insurance policy** Versicherungspolice abschließen; ~ **an order** Auftrag ausführen; ~ **payment** Zahlung leisten (bewirken); ~ **a policy** Police ausfertigen, Versicherung abschließen; ~ **one's purpose** sein Ziel (seinen Zweck) erreichen; ~ **a retreat in good order** *(mil.)* sich geordnet zurückziehen; ~ **a sale** Verkauf abschließen (tätigen); ~ **a settlement between two parties** Vergleich zustande bringen; ~ **foreign exchange transactions** Abschlüsse in Devisen tätigen;

~ **a transfer in the books** Umbuchung (Übertrag) in den Büchern vornehmen;

to be still in ~ noch Geltung haben; to bring (carry) into ~ zur Ausführung bringen; to cease to have ~ unwirksam werden; to come into ~ in Kraft treten, wirksam sein; to deprive of ~ außer Kraft setzen; to feel the ~s of an illness Nachwirkungen einer Krankheit spüren; to give ~ to s. th. einer Sache Nachdruck verleihen; to give ~ to a law einem Gesetz Rechtskraft verleihen; to have the desired ~ gewünschte Wirkung zeitigen; to have a great ~ on s. o. j. günstig beeinflussen; to have ~ on the market Markt beeinflussen, Auswirkungen auf den Markt zeitigen; to have no ~ on the balance sheet bilanzneutral sein; to offset the ~s Wirkungen ausgleichen; to produce an ~ Wirkung ausüben; to put into ~ in die Tat umsetzen; to remain in ~ wirksam bleiben; to suffer from the ~s of the hot weather Hitzeauswirkungen spüren; to take ~ seine Wirkung tun, *(law)* wirksam werden, Geltung haben; to take ~ on January 1st am 1. Januar in Kraft treten; to write a letter to the ~ Brief des Inhalts schreiben.

effects *(at bank)* Bankguthaben, *(cash)* Barbestand, -vorräte, Kassenbestand, *(movables)* Mobilien, bewegliches Eigentum, *(property)* Effekten, Vermögensstücke, Aktiva, Vermögenswerte, Habseligkeiten, Sachbesitz, Habe;

no ~ *(cheque)* kein Guthaben, keine Deckung; ~ not cleared *(Br.)* noch nicht verrechnete Abschnitte; personal ~ Gegenstände des persönlichen Gebrauchs, persönliche Gebrauchsgegenstände (Habe); real and personal ~ *(last will)* gesamter Nachlaß;

to seize s. one's personal ~ jds. persönliches Gepäck beschlagnahmen, *(innkeeper)* Zurückbehaltungsrecht des Gastwirts ausüben.

effected, to be zustande kommen, zur Ausführung kommen.

effective *(finance)* gemünztes Geld, Bargeld, *(mil., effective strength)* Effektiv-, Iststärke, *(soldier)* ausgebildeter Soldat;

~ *(a.)* wirklich, effektiv, vorhanden, rechtsgültig, einsatzbereit, diensttauglich, kampffähig, *(striking)* effektvoll, eindrucksvoll;

~ **in advertising** werbewirksam; ~ **immediately** mit sofortiger Wirkung; ~ **as of July 1st** mit Wirkung vom 1. Juli;

to be ~ gelten; to become ~ Gültigkeit erlangen, in Kraft treten; to cease to be ~ unwirksam werden, außer Kraft treten;

~ **blockade** wirkungsvolle Blockade; ~ **capital** Betriebskapital; ~ **conversion** echte Konversion; ~ **date** [Zeitpunkt des] Inkrafttreten[s], Stichtag; ~ **demand** wirksame (effektive) Gesamtnachfrage; ~ **force** Effektivkraft; ~ **instrument** gültige Urkunde; ~ **interest yield** effektive Verzinsung, Effektivverzinsung; ~ **market** effektiver Markt; ~ **money** umlaufendes Geld, Bargeld; ~ **output** Nutzleistung; ~ **pay rate** tatsächliches Gehalt; ~ **punishment** wirksame Bestrafung; ~ **range** *(mil.)* wirksame Schußweite; ~ **rate** *(finance)* effektiver Zinssatz; ~ **selling** zum Abschluß führende Verkaufstätigkeit; ~ **speech** erfolgreiche Rede; ~ **strength** *(mil.)* Istbestand, Ist-, Effektivstärke; ~ **troops** einsatzbereite Truppen; ~ **unit** fehlerfreies Stück; ~ **value** *(el.)* effektiver (tatsächlicher) Wert, Effektivwert.

effectiveness Wirksamkeit, Leistungsstand, -fähigkeit;

advertising ~ Werbewirkung;

to lift ~ Schlagkraft erhöhen.

effectual wirksam, *(valid)* [rechts]gültig, in Kraft, bindend;

~ **demand** durch vorhandenes Bargeld gedeckte Nachfrage; ~ **punishment** wirkungsvolle Strafe; to take ~ steps wirksame Schritte ergreifen.

effectuate verwirklichen, bewerkstelligen.

efficacious tätig, energisch, *(effective)* wirksam, wirkungsvoll.

efficiency *(capacity)* Leistungsfähigkeit, Leistungsstand, Tüchtigkeit, *(effectiveness)* Leistung[skraft], Wirtschaftlichkeit, *(engine)* Kapazität, Nutzeffekt, Wirkungsgrad;

business ~ Leistungsfähigkeit eines Geschäfts; commercial ~ Wirtschaftlichkeit; economic ~ wirtschaftliche Leistungsfähigkeit; hill-climbing ~ *(car)* Steigungsfähigkeit; hourly ~ [menschliche] Stundenleistung; increased ~ Leistungssteigerung, Mehrleistung; industrial ~ wirtschaftliche Leistungsfähigkeit; job ~ berufliche Leistungsfähigkeit; management ~ Leistungsfähigkeit des Vorstands; marginal ~ Grenznutzen; marketing ~ Leistungsfähigkeit des Absatzapparates; mean ~ Durchschnittsleistung; occupational ~ Berufstüchtigkeit; operating (plant) ~ betriebliche Leistungsfähigkeit, Betriebsleistung; productive ~ Produktionsfähigkeit;

fighting ~ of a fleet Kampfkraft einer Flotte; ~ of a law Wirksamkeit eines Gesetzes; ~ per unit Einzelwirkungsgrad; ~ in one's work berufliche Tüchtigkeit;

~ **apartment** Zimmer mit Dusche und Kochnische; ~ **audit** *(nationalized industry, Br.)* Leistungsüberprüfung, Wirtschaftlichkeits-, Rationalisierungsprüfung; ~ **bar** *(salary)* leistungsabhängige Gehaltshöchstgrenze; ~ **bonus** Leistungszulage; ~ **bonus plan** Leistungslohnsystem; ~ **contest** Leistungswettbewerb; ~ **department** Leistungskontrollabteilung; **high-~ engine** Hochleistungsmotor; ~ **engineer** *(US)* Rationalisierungsfachmann; ~ **engineering** *(US)* Rationalisierungsstudium; ~ **expert** *(US)* Sachverständiger in Fragen der Leistungskontrolle; ~ **factor** Leistungsfaktor,-bewertung, Gütegrad; ~ **level** Leistungsgrad; ~ **premium** Leistungsprämie; ~ **rating** Leistungsbewertung, -schätzung, -beurteilung; ~ **ratio** Wirksamkeitsverhältnis; ~ **record** *(personnel files)* Leistungsangaben; ~ **report** *(US)* *(mil.)* Personalbeurteilung, Leistungsbericht; ~ **survey** *(factory)* Leistungskontrolle; ~ **term** Wirkungsgrad; ~ **test** *(machine)* Leistungsprüfung; ~ **unit** Leistungseinheit, -maßstab; **labo(u)r ~ variance** Leistungsabweichung; ~ **wages** Leistungslohn; ~ **wage plan formula** Leistungslohnformel.

efficient gut funktionierend, leistungsfähig, wirtschaftlich, *(producing effect)* wirksam;
to be ~ **in one's work** leistungsfähig sein;
~ **intervening cause** unterbrochener Kausalzusammenhang; ~ **machinery** leistungsfähige Maschinen; ~ **secretary** tüchtige Sekretärin; ~ **staff of teachers** leistungsfähiges Lehrergremium; ~ **state** *(ship)* fahrbereiter Zustand; ~ **system** gut funktionierendes System; ~ **working** Funktionieren.

effluent *(sanitary engineering)* Abwässer;
~ **drain** Abwässerkanal.

efflux Fristablauf;
~ **of funds** Mittelabflüsse; ~ **of gold** Goldabfluß, -abwanderung; ~ **of liquidity** Liquiditätsabfluß.

effluxion of time Zeitablauf.

effort Bemühung, Mühe, Anstrengung, Vorkehrung, Bestreben, Bestrebung, Arbeitsaufwand, *(coll.)* Leistung;
all-out ~ enorme Anstrengungen; **combined ~s** vereinte Anstrengungen; **development ~s** Entwicklungsvorhaben; **directing ~** Regieanstrengung; **fruitless ~s** ergebnislose Bemühungen; **mass ~** massierte Anstrengungen; **research ~** Forschungstätigkeit; **simple ~s** geringe Anstrengungen; **superhuman ~s** übermenschliche Anstrengungen; **unlucky ~s** fruchtlose Bemühungen; **voluntary ~s** freiwillige Spenden; **war ~(s)** Kriegsanstrengungen; **wasted ~** verlorene Mühe;
~s of negotiation Verhandlungsversuche; **~s to rationalize** Rationalisierungsanstrengungen;
to combine one's ~s gemeinsame Anstrengungen machen; **to make an ~** sich anstrengen; **to make every ~ to get a job** sich mit allen Mitteln um eine Stellung bemühen; **to redouble one's ~s** seine Bemühungen verdoppeln; **to relax one's ~s in** seinen Bemühungen nachlassen; **to renew one's ~s** erneute Anstrengungen machen; **to spare no ~** keine Mühe scheuen;
~ **limitation** Leistungsbegrenzung.

effusive | compliments überschwengliche Komplimente;
to be ~ **in one's thanks** sich überströmend bedanken.

egalitarian gleichmacherisch.

egalitarianism Gleichmacherei.

egg Ei, *(mil., sl.)* Wasser-, Fliegerbombe;
as full as an ~ vollgepropft; **as sure as ~s** so sicher wie das Amen in der Kirche; **in the ~** *(fig.)* im Anfangsstadium; **bad ~** faule Sache (Angelegenheit), Nichtsnutz; **nest ~** Sparpfennig, -groschen; **old ~** *(fam.)* alter Knabe;
~ *(v.)* **s. o. on** j. antreiben;
to put all one's ~s in one basket alles auf eine Karte setzen; **to kill a plot in the ~** Verschwörung im Anfangstadium zunichtemachen; **to prove a bad ~** gescheitert sein; **to teach one's grandmother to suck ~s** einer Henne das Eierlegen beibringen wollen;
~ **coal** Nußkohle.

eggbeater *(sl.)* Hubschrauber.

egghead *(US)* Intellektueller, Studierter, Eierkopf.

eggheadish *(US)* intellektuell.

ego Persönlichkeit, Selbst;
to play the ~ game seinen Standpunkt durchsetzen; ~ **massage** Persönlichkeitsmassage.

egotism Selbstüberhebung, Geltungsbedürfnis.

egotist geltungsbedürftiger Mensch.

egress *(real estate)* Zugang, Zutritt.

eight, to be behind the in einer schwierigen Lage sein; **to have one over the ~** *(fam.)* zu tief ins Glas geschaut haben;
~-hour [working] day Achtstunden[arbeits]tag; ~ **stocks** *(US)* in kleinen Posten gehandelte Aktien.

eighth of page *(advertising)* Achtelseite.

eject *(v.)* *(from office)* entsetzen, entheben, *(from property)* heraussetzen, zwangsräumen, Zwangsräumung durchführen;
~ **an agitator from a meeting** Zwischenrufer aus dem Saal entfernen lassen; ~ **a tenant** Zwangsräumung gegen einen Mieter durchführen, Mieter zur Räumung zwingen.

ejection zwangsweise Entfernung, Räumung, Vertreibung, *(aeronautics)* Schleudersitzvorrichtung;
~ **from an office** Entfernung aus dem Amt, Amtsentsetzung; ~ **seat** *(plane)* Katapult-, Schleudersitz; **to sue for ~** auf Räumung klagen.

ejectment Besitzentsetzung, Räumung;
equitable ~ *(Louisiana)* Räumungsklage; **justice ~** Räumungsverfahren.

ejector Kläger im Räumungsprozeß;
~ **seat** Katapult-, Schleudersitz.

eke *(v.)* **out** mühsam erarbeiten, herausschinden;
~ **a scanty living** sich kümmerlich durchschlagen.

el *(US coll.)* Hochbahn.

elaborate *(v.)* aufstellen, entwickeln, ausarbeiten, ausführlich behandeln;
~ **one's proposal** sich ausführlich über seinen Vorschlag verbreiten; ~ **a theory** Theorie aufstellen;
~ *(a.)* sorgfältig [ausgearbeitet];
~ **design** kunstvolles Muster; ~ **dinner** ausgedehntes Dinner; **to make an ~ study** bis ins Einzelne gehende Untersuchung durchführen.

elaboration [sorgfältige] Ausarbeitung;
~ **of a plan** Ausführung eines Planes; ~ **of a theory** Aufstellung einer Theorie.

elapse *(v.)* ablaufen, verstreichen, verfliegen.

elastic elastisch, anpassungsfähig, dehnbar, geschmeidig;
~ **conscience** weites Gewissen; ~ **currency** elastische Währung; ~ **demand** elastische Nachfrage; ~ **money** elastische Währung; ~ **rules** elastische Bestimmungen; ~ **supply** elastisches Angebot.

elasticity | of demand Nachfrage-, Bedarfselastizität; **cross ~ of demand** Kreuzelastizität; ~ **of the market** Elastizität des Marktes; ~ **of production** Produktionselastizität; **overall ~ of supply** Angebotselastizität;
to lose one's ~ of mind seine geistige Spannkraft verlieren.

elbow Ell[en]bogen, *(pipe, road)* Knie, Knick;
at one's ~ ganz nahe; **out at ~s** abgetragen, *(fig.)* auf den Hund gekommen;
~ *(v.)* *(road)* scharfe Krümmung machen; ~ **one's way through the crowd** sich rücksichtslos durch die Menge drängen;
to be up to the ~s in work alle Hände voll zu tun haben; **to raise one's ~** *(coll.)* einen trinken;
~ **board** Fensterbrett; ~ **grease** Schufterei; **to put a bit of ~ grease in it** *(coll.)* sich kräftig ins Zeug legen; ~ **room** *(fig.)* Ellenbogenfreiheit, Spielraum.

elder Senior;
~ **officer** rangälterer Offizier; ~ **statesman** erfahrener (hochgeachteter) Staatsmann; ~ **title** besserer Rechtstitel.

elect *(v.)* [aus]wählen, *(decide)* sich entscheiden (entschließen), *(vote)* Wahlrecht ausüben;
~ **a new board** Neuwahl des Aufsichtsrates vornehmen; ~ **a chairman** zum Vorsitzenden wählen; ~ **one's domicile** seinen Wohnsitz begründen; ~ **s. o. to be a member** j. ins Abgeordnetenhaus wählen; ~ **s. o. from among the members present** j. aus einem gegebenen Gremium (Kreis der Mitglieder) wählen; ~ **to an office** für ein Amt wählen; ~ **s. o. to be president (to the presidency)** j. zum Präsidenten wählen; ~ **from (amongst) themselves** aus ihrer Mitte wählen; ~ **for a term of four years** auf vier Jahre wählen;
~ **to become a lawyer** sich zur Anwaltslaufbahn entschließen;
~ *(a.)* gewählt, designiert.

elected gewählt;
to be ~ into Parliament ins Parlament gewählt werden; **to be ~ for a term of two years** für die Dauer von zwei Jahren gewählt werden;
~ **official** Wahlbeamter.

election Wahl, Wählen, *(debtor)* Wahlrecht, *(shareholder)* Option, *(taxation schedule)* Veranlagungswahlrecht;
with an eye on the ~s im Hinblick auf die Wahlen;
board ~ Wahlen zum Aufsichtsrat; **by-~** Nachwahl; **cantonal ~s** Kantonalwahlen; **cliffhanger ~** aufregende Wahl; **desperately close-run ~** Kopf-an-Kopf Rennen bei einer Wahl; **congressional ~s** Kongreßwahlen; **contested** *(US)* **(disputed) ~** angefochtenes Wahlergebnis, angefochtene Wahl; **closely contested ~** umstrittene Wahl; **direct ~** direkte Wahl; **free ~s** freie Wahlen; **general ~s** *(Br.)* allgemeine Wahlen, Parlamentswahl;

indirect ~ indirekte Wahl; **local ~s** *(Br.)* Gemeindewahl; ~ **made** *(taxpayer)* ausgeübtes Wahlrecht; **mid-term ~** Zwischenwahl; **municipal ~** *(US)* Gemeinde-, Kommunalwahl; **new ~** Neuwahl; **off year ~s** Zwischenwahlen; **parliamentary ~s** Wahlen zum Parlament, Parlamentswahlen; **presidential ~s** Präsidentschaftwahlen; **primary ~** *(US)* Vorwahl, Wahlmännerversammlung; **provincial ~s** Provinzwahlen; **quiet ~s** ruhiger Wahlverlauf; **re-~** Wiederwahl; **regular ~** übliche (regelmäßige) Wahl; **senatorial ~s** Senatswahlen; **squeak-through ~** knapp gewonnene Wahlen; **special ~** Nachwahl; **state ~s** Landtagswahlen; **uncontested ~** Wahl ohne Gegenkandidaten; **widow's ~** *(last will)* Wahlrecht der Witwe;
~ **of directors** Vorstandswahl; ~ **of the directors' committee** Aufsichtsratswahl; ~ **made** *(taxpayer)* ausgeübtes Wahlrecht; ~ **by an absolute majority** absolute Mehrheitswahl; **~s in the offing** anstehende (bevorstehende) Wahlen; ~ **of a president** Präsidentenwahl; ~ **by direct universal suffrage** allgemeine [unmittelbare] Wahlen;
to be defeated at an ~ in einem Wahlkampf unterliegen; **to be eligible for ~** wahlfähig sein; **to be neck and neck in an ~** bei einer Wahl Kopf an Kopf liegen; **to call for an early ~** vorgezogene Parlamentswahlen abhalten; **to call a general ~** allgemeine Wahlen ansetzen; **to call a new ~** Neuwahlen ansetzen, Wahlen ausschreiben; **to carry an ~** siegreich aus einer Wahl hervorgehen; **to challenge an ~** Wahl anfechten; **to contest an ~** Wahl[ergebnis] anfechten; **to cover the ~s** über die Wahlen berichten; **to declare an ~ void** Wahl für ungültig erklären; **to gerrymander an ~** *(US)* Wahlschiebung begehen; **to hold an ~** Wahl durchführen, Wahl abhalten; **to hold simultaneous ~ on state and national level** gleichzeitig auf Bundes- und Landesebene Wahlen abhalten; **to hold ~s under international supervision** Wahlen unter internationaler Aufsicht abhalten; **to influence the ~s** Wahlen beeinflussen; **to invalidate an ~** Wahl für ungültig erklären; **to poll as much as 25% in an ~** 25% bei einer Wahl erzielen; **to put in for an ~** als Kandidat auftreten; **to put up for [an] ~** als Kandidaten vorschlagen **to qualify for an ~** den Wahlvoraussetzungen Genüge leisten; **to rig an ~** Wahlschiebungen begehen; **to run in an ~** bei einer Wahl kandidierender Wahlkandidat sein; **to spring a surprise ~** überraschend Neuwahlen ansetzen; **to stand for [an] ~** für eine Wahl kandidieren; **to sway the ~s** Wahlen beeinflussen; **to turn an ~** Wahlausgang entscheidend beeinflussen; **to void an irregular ~** vorschriftswidrige Wahl für ungültig erklären; **to win an ~ with a narrow margin** Wahl knapp gewinnen; **to work for s. one's ~** jds. Wahl betreiben;
~ **address** Wahlaufruf; ~ **agent** Wahlkampfbeauftragter; ~ **alliance** Wahlbündnis; ~ **auditor** Wahlprüfer; ~ **battle** Wahlschlacht; ~ **battle cry** Wahlkampfslogan; ~ **board** Kreiswahlausschuß; ~ **campaign** Wahlkampf, -feldzug, -kampagne; **to lead a party into the ~ campaign** Partei in den Wahlkampf führen; ~ **campaign costs** Wahlkampfkosten; ~ **campaign promise** Wahlversprechen; ~ **commission** Wahlprüfungskommission; ~ **commissioner** *(US)* Wahlprüfer; ~ **committee** Wahlausschuß, -komitee, *(parl.)* Wahlprüfungsausschuß; ~ **contest** *(US)* Wahlanfechtung, -einspruch, -protest; ~ **costs** Wahlaufwand, -unkosten; ~ **cry** Wahlschlager, Wahlslogan; ~ **day** Wahltag; **to register on ~ day itself** sich erst am Wahltag als Wähler registrieren lassen; ~ **defeat** Wahlniederlage; ~ **dinner** zur Finanzierung des Wahlkampfes gegebenes Essen; ~ **district** *(US)* Wahlkreis, -bezirk; ~ **dower** Pflichtteil der Witwe; **to beat the ~ drums** Wahltrommel schlagen, Wahlpropaganda betreiben; ~ **effects** Auswirkungen einer Wahl; **on ~ eve** am Vorabend der Wahl; **to be free of ~ eve** nicht dem Druck der öffentlichen Meinung am Vorabend der Wahl ausgesetzt sein; **~-eve radio appeal** Rundfunkansprache am Tag vor der Wahl; ~ **expenses** Wahlkampfkosten; ~ **fight** Wahlkampf; ~ **forecasting** Wahlprognose; ~ **fund** Wahlkampffonds; ~ **hour** Wahltermin; ~ **issue** Wahlkampfthema, Wahlthema; ~ **judge** Mitglied des Wahlprüfungsausschusses; ~ **law** Wahlgesetz; ~ **manifesto** Wahlmanifest, -proklamation; ~ **meeting** Wahl-, Wählerversammlung; ~ **period** Wahlzeit; ~ **petition** *(Br.)* Wahlanfechtung, -einspruch; ~ **placard (poster)** Wahlplakat; ~ **plan** Wahlprogramm; ~ **plank** Wahlversprechen; ~ **pledge** Wahlversprechen; ~ **precinct** *(US)* Wahlkreis, -bezirk; ~ **process** Wahlvorgang; ~ **program(me)** Wahlprogramm; ~ **promise** Wahlversprechen; ~ **prospects** Wahlansichten; ~ **push** Wahlkampftrubel; ~ **quotient** Wahlquotient; ~ **recess** Wahlferien; ~ **results (returns)** amtliches Wahlergebnis, -resultat, -protokoll, -akten; **to canvass ~ returns** Wahlergebnis überprüfen; **to manipulate ~ returns** Wahlergebnis manipulieren; ~ **speaker** Wahlredner; ~ **speech** Wahlrede; ~ **stunt** Wahlschlager ~

time Wahlzeit; ~ **trigger** Wahlauslösungsmoment; **left-wing ~ victory** Wahlsieg der linken Wähler; ~ **year** Wahljahr.
electioneer *(v.)* Wahlstimmen sammeln, Wahlfeldzug (Wahlkampf) durchführen, Wahlpropaganda treiben, Wahlreden halten, Wähler bearbeiten.
electioneerer Wahlagent, -agitator, -taktiker, Stimmenwerber.
electioneering Wahlagitation, -propaganda, -umtriebe;
~ **agent** Wahlagent; ~ **campaign** Wahlfeldzug; ~ **franchise** Wahlrecht; ~ **manoeuvre (practices)** Wahlmanöver, -mache, -umtriebe; ~ **program(me)** Wahlprogramm; ~ **propaganda** Wahlpropaganda; ~ **sweetener** Wahlbonbons; ~ **tour** Wahlreise.
elective *(US)* fakultatives Studium, Wahlfach;
~ *(a.)* durch Wahl bestimmt, *(facultative)* wahlfrei, fakultativ, *(exerting power of choice)* wahlberechtigt;
~ **act** Wahlakt; ~ **assembly** Wahlversammlung; ~ **body** Wahlkörperschaft; ~ **campaign** *(US)* Wahlkampf; ~ **chances** Wahlaussichten, -chancen; ~ **committee** Wahlvorstand; ~ **consul** Wahlkonsul; ~ **course** Auswahllehrgang; ~ **franchise** *(US)* Wahlrecht; ~ **judiciary** gewählte Richter; ~ **monarchy** Wahlmonarchie; ~ **office** im Wege der Wahl besetztes Amt, Wahlamt; ~ **process** Wahlvorgang; ~ **study** Wahlstudium; ~ **subject** Wahlfach; ~ **system** Wahlsystem.
electiveness Wahlvermögen.
elector Wähler, *(US)* Wahlmann;
communal ~ Gemeindewähler; **registered qualified ~** *(US)* Wahlberechtigter, eingetragener Wähler;
to be registered as ~ in den Wahllisten eingetragen sein.
electoral | address Wahlrede; ~ **alliance** Wahlbündnis; ~ **ally** Wahlbündnispartner; ~ **apathy** Wahlmüdigkeit; ~ **area** Wahlbezirk; ~ **arrangement** Wahlabmachung, -abkommen; ~ **blessing** Wahlgeschenk; ~ **body** Wahlorgan; ~ **campaign** Wahlfeldzug; ~ **cartel** Wahlabkommen; ~ **chances** *(US)* Wahlaussichten; ~ **clientele** Wählerstamm; ~ **college** *(US)* Wähler-, Wahlkollegium, Wahlmännerausschuß; ~ **commission (committee)** Wahlausschuß, -vorstand, -komitee; ~ **concerns** Wahlinteressen; ~ **contest** Wahlkampf; ~ **corruption** Wahlbestechung, -beeinflussung; ~ **counts** *(US)* Wahlmännerstimmen; ~ **defeat** Wahlniederlage; **to bring some ~ dividends** sich bei der Wahl in etwa auszahlen; ~ **division (district, US)** Wahlbezirk, -kreis; ~ **duty** Wahlpflicht; ~ **following** Wählergefolgschaft; **to play the ~ hand for s. o.** jem. bei der Wahl behilflich sein; ~ **list (register)** Wähler-, Wahlliste; **to combine two ~ lists** zwei Wahllisten miteinander verbinden; **to recount (scrutinize) an ~ list** Wählerliste nachprüfen; ~ **pact** Wahlbündnis, -abkommen; ~ **participation** Wahlbeteiligung; ~ **performance** Wahlerfolg; ~ **politics** wahlpolitische Maßnahmen; ~ **practices** Wahlpraktiken, -machenschaften; ~ **process** Wahlvorgang; ~ **procedure** Wahlverfahren; ~ **prospects** Wahlaussichten; ~ **quota** Wahlkontingent; ~ **quotient** Wahlquotient; ~ **reform** Wahlreform; ~ **reform society** Wahlreformgesellschaft; ~ **register** Wahl-, Wählerliste, -verzeichnis; ~ **showdown** Wahlauseinandersetzung; ~ **strategist** Wahlstratege; ~ **support** Wählerunterstützung; ~ **system** Wahlsystem; **gerrymandered ~ system** willkürliches Wahlkreissystem; ~ **triumph** Wahlsieg; ~ **troubles** Wahlsorgen; ~ **victory** Wahlsieg; ~ **vote** Wahlstimme; ~ **vote certificate** Wahlschein.
electorally significant von Bedeutung für die Wahlen.
electorate Stimmenberechtigter, *(pl.)* Wählerschaft, *(district)* Wahlkreis, -bezirk;
to canvass an ~ Wahlbezirk bearbeiten; **to corrupt the ~** Wählerschaft korrumpieren;
~'s response Reaktion der Wähler.
electric *(coll.)* Elektrische [Straßenbahn];
~ *(a.)* elektrisch;
~ **automobile** Elektromobil; ~ **bulb** Glühbirne; ~ **cable** Elektrizitätsleitung; ~ **cart** Elektrowagen; ~ **chair** *(US)* elektrischer Stuhl, *(fig.)* Hinrichtung auf dem elektrischen Stuhl; ~ **company** E-Werk; ~ **current** elektrischer Strom; ~ **eye** Fotozelle; ~ **goods fair** Elektromesse; ~ **fence** elektrisch geladener Drahtzaun; ~ **field** elektronisches Feld; ~ **heater** elektrischer Heizofen; ~ **light** elektrisches Licht; ~ **light switch** Lichtschalter; ~ **locomotive** elektrische Lokomotive, Elektrolok; ~ **meter** Elektrizitätszähler; ~ **motor** Elektromotor; ~ **motorcar** Draisine; ~ **plant** Elektroanlage; ~ **power company** Elektrizitätsgesellschaft; ~ **power consumption** Stromverbrauch; ~ **power supply** Stromversorgung; ~ **railway** elektrische Eisenbahn; ~ **shock** elektrischer Schlag; ~ **signs (spectaculars, US)** bewegliche Lichtwerbung; ~ **sign advertising** Licht-, Leuchtreklame, Leuchtwerbung; ~ **torch** elektrische Taschenlampe; ~ **typewriter** elektrische Schreibmaschine; ~ **utility** Elektrizitätsunternehmen.

electricals Elektrizitätsaktien, -werte.
electrical | appliances elektrische Geräte; ~ **appliance manufacturer** Elektrogerätehersteller; ~ **circuit** Stromkreis; ~ **engineer** Elektrotechniker; ~ **engineering** Elektrotechnik; ~–**engineering industry** elektrotechnische Industrie; ~ **fitter** Elektromonteur; ~ **goods** elektrische Geräte; ~ **industries** Elektrotechnik; ~ **issues** Elektrizitätswerte, -aktien; ~ **outfitter** Elektrohändler, -geschäft; ~ **sign** Lichtreklame; ~ **transcription** Tonübertragung, -bandaufnahme.
electrician Elektrotechniker, -installateur.
electricity, to generate Elektrizität erzeugen;
~ **Act** *(Br.)* Elektrizitätswirtschaftsgesetz; ~ **bill** Stromrechnung; ~ **board** Elektrizitätsgesellschaft; ~ **consumption** Stromverbrauch; ~ **cut** Stromsperre; ~ **generation** Strom-, Elektrizitätserzeugung; ~ **grid** Elektrizitätsverbundnetz; ~ **industry** Elektrizitätsindustrie; ~ **meter reader** Stromableser; ~ **policy** Energiepolitik; ~ **rate** *(Br.)* Stromtarif; ~ **sales** Elektrizitätsverbrauch; ~ **shares** Elektrowerte; ~ **supply** Elektrizitätsversorgung; ~–**supply industry** Elektrizitätsversorgungswirtschaft; ~–**supply undertaking** Elektrizitätsversorgungsbetrieb; ~ **tariff** *(US)* Stromtarif; ~ **works** Elektrizitätswerk.
electrification Elektrifizierung.
electrified elektrifiziert;
~ **obstacle** Starkstromsperre.
electrify *(v.)* *(railway)* elektrifizieren;
~ **an audience** Publikum von den Sitzen reißen.
electrocute *(v.)* durch elektrischen Strom töten.
electrocution tödlicher Unfall durch elektrischen Strom.
electronic | accounting Elektronenbuchführung; ~ **battlefield** Computerschlachtfeld; ~ **brain** Elektronengehirn; ~ **calculator** Elektronenrechner; ~ **computer** elektronische Rechenmaschine; ~ **data processing** elektronische Datenverarbeitung; ~ **flash** Elektronenblitz; ~ **ignition system** Transistorzündung; ~**s industry** Elektronenindustrie; ~ **war** Computerkrieg.
electrotechnics Elektroindustrie, Funkmeßwesen.
electrotype Galvano, Kupferklischeé;
~ *(v.)* galvanisch klischieren.
eleemosynary wohltätig, karitativ;
~ **corporation** milde Stiftung; ~ **gifts** milde Gaben.
elegit, [writ of] Vollstreckungsbefehl;
~ **creditor** Vollstreckungsgläubiger.
element *(building industry)* Bauelement, [Grund]bestandteil, Faktor, *(el.)* Element, *(mil.)* Truppenkörper, -einheit, -teil, *(plane)* Rotte, *(natural sphere)* Sphäre, gewohnte Umgebung, *(science)* Anfangsgründe, Grundlagen, *(trace)* Körnchen, Fünkchen;
~**s** wesentliche Punkte, *(knowledge)* Vorkenntnisse;
the ~s Naturgewalten, Wetterverhältnisse;
essential ~s wesentliche (regelmäßige) Bestandteile (Erfordernisse); **nonessential ~s** unwesentliche (fakultative) Bestandteile (Erfordernisse); **personal ~** der humanitäre Aspekt; ~**s of a contract** Vertragsbestandteile; ~**s of costs** Kostenbestandteile; **important ~s in a good government** wichtige Grundbestandteile erfolgreicher Staatskunst; ~**s of insurance** Versicherungsaspekte; ~ **of an offence** Tatbestandsmerkmal einer Gesetzesverletzung; ~ **of truth** ein Körnchen Wahrheit; ~ **of uncertainty** Unsicherheitsfaktor;
to be in one's ~ sich in seinem Element fühlen; **to be exposed to the fury of the ~s** den Gewalten des Sturmes ausgesetzt sein; **to be in one's ~ when taking part in a political debate** sich bei politischen Gesprächsthemen richtig wohl fühlen; **to be out of one's ~** sich unbehaglich fühlen; **to be well grounded in the ~s** gute Vorkenntnisse haben.
elemental elementar, urgewaltig;
~ **fury of a storm** Elementargewalt eines Sturms; ~ **particle** Elementarteilchen.
elemental breakdown Zerlegung eines Arbeitsvorgangs.
elementary grundlegend, elementar;
~ **education** Grund-, Volksschulbildung; ~ **family** *(sociology)* Kleinfamilie; ~ **instruction** Grundschulausbildung; ~ **knowledge** Elementarkenntnisse; ~ **school** Volks-, Grundschule; ~ **student** *(US)* Volksschüler; ~ **unit** *(statistics)* kleinste Untersuchungseinheit.
elephant, white kostspieliger unnützer Besitz.
elevate *(v.)* | **a commoner to the nobility** Bürger in den Adelsstand erheben; ~ **s. o. to a higher rank** j. im Rang erhöhen; ~ **one's voice** lauter sprechen.
elevated erhaben, vornehm;
to be slightly ~ *(coll.)* angeheitert sein;
~ **antenna** Hochantenne; ~ **personage** hochgestellte Persönlichkeit; ~ **position** gehobene Stellung; ~ **railway** Hochbahn.

elevating | book erhebendes Buch; ~ **charge** *(railway)* Speichergebühren; ~ **service** *(carrier)* Beförderung von und zum Speicher.
elevation Erhöhung, Anhöhe, *(of ground)* Bodenerhöhung, Anhöhe, *(height above sea level)* Meereshöhe, *(preferment)* Standes-, Rangerhöhung, Beförderung, *(refinement)* Veredelung, Verfeinerung, Aval;
~ **of the mind** Erhabenheit des Geistes; ~ **to nobility** Erhebung in den Adelsstand; ~ **in rank** Rangerhöhung; ~ **to a throne** Thronbesteigung.
elevator *(US)* Fahrstuhl, Aufzug, Lift, *(agriculture, US)* Getreidespeicher, Silo, *(plane)* Höhensteuerruder;
electric ~ elektrischer Aufzug; **passenger ~** Personenaufzug;
~ **car** *(US)* Fahrstuhlkabine; ~ **company** Aufzugs-, Fahrstuhlgesellschaft; ~ **conductor** *(US)* Fahrstuhlführer; ~ **man** (**operator**, *US*) Fahrstuhlführer; ~ **public liability insurance** *(US)* Aufzugsversicherung; ~ **receipt** Lagerschein [eines Getreidespeichers]; ~ **shaft** *(US)* Aufzugsschacht; ~ **signal** *(US)* Fahrstuhlrufanlage; ~ **starter** *(US)* Fahrstuhldruckknopf.
eleven | s leichter Vormittagsimbiß;
~**th-hour change in the program(me)** Programmänderung in der letzten Minute; ~**th-hour panic** Torschlußpanik; ~–**plus examination** *(Br.)* Aufnahmeprüfung in die höhere Schule.
eligibility *(fitness to be elected, US)* Wählbarkeit, passives Wahlrecht, *(for job)* Befähigung, Eignung, Qualifikation;
~ **for admission** Erfüllung der Aufnahmebedingungen; ~ **for appointment** Anstellungsvoraussetzungen; ~ **for benefit** Leistungsberechtigung; ~ **for discount** (**rediscount**, *US*) Diskontfähigkeit; ~ **for naturalization** Einbürgerungsfähigkeit; ~ **for office** Einstellungsfähigkeit; ~ **for registration** Registrierfähigkeit; ~ **for relief** Fürsorgeberechtigung; ~ **to serve as collateral** *(US)* Lombard-, Deckungsfähigkeit; ~ **for vacation** Urlaubsanspruch; ~ **of voting** Wahlberechtigung;
~ **committee** Zulassungsausschuß; ~ **requirements** Berechtigungserfordernisse; ~ **rule** *(Bank of England)* Rediskontrichtlinien.
eligible akzeptable Partie, geeignet, passend, den Vorbedingungen entsprechend, *(banking)* bank-, diskontfähig, diskontierbar, *(desirable)* angenehm, wünschenswert, akzeptabel, *(job)* befähigt, qualifiziert, *(qualified to be chosen)* wählbar, passiv, wahlfähig;
~ **for benefit** leistungsberechtigt; ~ **for [re]discount** [re]diskontfähig; ~ **for election** passiv wahlberechtigt; ~ **for membership** mitgliedschaftsfähig; ~ **for an occupation** beruflich geeignet; ~ **for a pension** pensionsberechtigt; ~ **for a post** anstellungsberechtigt, für einen Posten qualifiziert; ~ **for promotion** beförderungswürdig; ~ **for reelection** wiederwählbar; ~ **for registration** eintragungsfähig; ~ **for relief** fürsorge-, unterstützungsberechtigt; ~ **to serve as collateral** *(US)* deckungs-, lombardfähig, beleihbar; ~ **for vacation** urlaubsberechtigt;
to be ~ for s. th. Anspruch (Anrecht) auf etw. haben; **to be ~ for admission** Zulassungsbedingungen erfüllen; **to be ~ for income-tax relief** Einkommensteuererleichterungen nach sich ziehen; **to be ~ for the dividend received exclusion provided by the Internal Revenue Code** das von der Steuergesetzgebung vorgesehene Schachtelprinzip genießen; **to be ~ for membership in a society** Eintrittsvoraussetzungen für eine Vereinsmitgliedschaft erfüllen; **to be ~ to be paid** zur Rückzahlung anstehen; **to be ~ for promotion** zur Beförderung anstehen; **to be ~ for registration** registrierungspflichtig sein; **to be ~ for release on parole** für eine bedingte Entlassung in Frage kommen; **to be ~ for state savings premiums** prämienbegünstigt sparen können; **to be ~ for a Tariff Commission recommendation of mandatory relief** zeitweise zu zollpolitischen Vergünstigungen berechtigt sein; **to be ~ to vote** im wahlfähigen Alter sein; **to become ~ for company pension** am Betriebspensionsplan teilnehmen können;
~ **bill of exchange** *(Br.)* diskontfähiger Wechsel; ~ **candidate** geeigneter Kandidat; ~ **investment** *(US)* mündelsichere Anlage; ~ **liabilities** diskontfähige Verbindlichkeiten, zentralbankfähige Depositen; ~ **deposit liabilities** landeszentralbankfähige Verbindlichkeiten auf Einlagekonten; ~ **paper** *(US)* diskont- und lombardfähiges Papier; ~ **young man** gute Partie; ~ **vote** wahlberechtigte Stimme.
eliminate *(v.)* ausschließen, -schalten, -scheiden, -sondern, eliminieren, beseitigen;
~ **an account** *(US)* Konto auflösen; ~ **competition** Konkurrenz ausschalten; ~ **personal considerations** persönliche Überlegungen außer Acht lassen (zurückstellen); ~ **customs barriers** Zollschranken abbauen; ~ **unprofitable lines** unrentable Eisenbahnstrecken stillegen; ~ **the middleman** Zwischenhandel

ausschalten; ~ **unprofitable operations** unrentable Produktionsgebiete aufgeben; ~ **a possibility** Möglichkeit ausschließen; ~ **quotas** Quoten beseitigen; ~ **risk** Risiko ausschalten; ~ **slang words from an essay** Slangausdrücke aus einem Aufsatz entfernen; ~ **wholesalers** Großhandel umgehen.

elimination Ausmerzung, Ausschaltung, Eliminierung, Beseitigung;
~ **of an account** (US) Kontoauflösung; ~ **of competition** Ausschaltung der Konkurrenz; ~ **of personal considerations** Außerachtlassung (Zurückstellung) von persönlichen Überlegungen; ~ **of customs barriers** Abbau der Zollschranken; ~ **of an error** Fehlerbeseitigung; ~ **of unprofitable lines** Stillegung unrentabler Eisenbahnstrecken; ~ **of the middleman** Ausschaltung des Zwischenhandels; ~ **of unprofitable operations** Aufgabe unrentabler Produktionsgebiete; ~ **of quotas** Quotenbeseitigung; ~ **of risk** Ausschaltung von Risiken; ~ **of wholesalers** Umgehung des Großhandels;
~ **contest** Ausscheidungskampf; ~ **ledger** Hilfsbuch für Erstellung der Konzernbilanz.

eliminator (el.) Sperrkreis;
shock ~ (car) Stoßdämpfer.

elite Elite, Auslese, Blüte, (mil.) Elitetruppe, (typewriter) Kleinschreibmaschinentype;
~ **circle** ausgewählter Kreis; ~ **society** Spitzen der Gesellschaft; ~ **status** Elitestatus.

elocution Vortrag, Vortragsstil, -kunst, (ironical) schwülstiges Gerede.

elocutionist Vortragskünstler.

elope (v.) **with a lover** mit einem Liebhaber durchbrennen.

elopement Entlaufen.

eloper Ausreißer.

eloquence Beredsamkeit, Redegabe, Eloquenz.

eloquent redegewandt;
~ **address** fließende Rede.

elucidate (v.) **a passage** Passage erläutern.

elucidation Erläuterung, Aufstellung.

elude (v.) (law) umgehen, (obligation) sich entziehen;
~ **observation** nicht bemerkt werden; ~ **payment** sich einer Zahlung entziehen; ~ **s. one's understanding** sich jds. Verständnis entziehen; ~ **the vigilance of one's guardians** seinen Bewachern entkommen.

elusion Ausweichen, Umgehung;
~ **of a law** Gesetzesumgehung.

elusive memory unzuverlässiges Gedächtnis.

emancipate (v.) selbständig (unabhängig) machen, sozial gleichstellen, emanzipieren.

emancipated emanzipiert.

emancipation Gleichberechtigung, bürgerliche Gleichstellung, Befreiung, Emanzipation, (enfranchisement of minor) Volljährigkeitserklärung;
express ~ Selbständigmachen mit eigener Wohnung; **partial** ~ vorzeitige partielle Volljährigkeitserklärung;
~ **from the authority of one's parents** Volljährigkeitserklärung; ~ **of women** Frauenemanzipation;
~ **movement** Emanzipationsbewegung.

emancipator Befreier.

embank (v.) eindeichen, eindämmen.

embankment Eindeichung, Eindämmung, (road) Damm, gemauerte Uferstraße;
~**s** Uferbauten.

embargo (blocking of harbo(u)r) Hafensperre, Blockade, (news) Nachrichtensperre, (suspension of commerce) Handelsverbot, Ausfuhrsperre, Embargo, (temporary sequestration) vorübergehende Beschlagnahme;
arms ~ Waffenembargo, Ausfuhrverbot für Waffen; **broken** ~ unterlaufene Nachrichtensperre; **civil** ~ Embargo auf eigene Schiffe; **outright economic** ~ vollständige Sperre des Wirtschaftsverkehrs; **exchange** ~ Devisensperre; **gold** ~ Goldausfuhrverbot; **hostile** ~ völkerrechtliches Embargo, Embargo gegen feindliche Schiffe; **loan** ~ Kreditsperre;
~ **on foreign exchange** Devisensperre; ~ **on exports** Ausfuhrsperre, -embargo, -verbot; ~ **on gold** Goldembargo, -ausfuhrverbot; ~ **on imports** Einfuhrstopp, -embargo; ~ **on shipping** Schiffahrtssperre; ~ **on frontier trade** Grenzsperre;
~ (v.) Blockade (Embargo) verhängen, Handelsverkehr sperren, beschlagnahmen;
to be under an ~ beschlagnahmt (mit Embargo belegt) sein; **to impose an** ~ Embargo verhängen; **to lay** ~ **on** Beschlag legen auf, beschlagnahmen, Blockade durchführen, Embargo verhängen; **to lay an** ~ **on free speech** Redefreiheit beschränken; **to lift the** ~ Beschlagnahme aufheben; **to put an** ~ **on** Embargobe-

stimmungen erlassen; **to put an** ~ **on all public rejoicings** (fam.) alle öffentlichen Lustbarkeiten verbieten; **to raise the** ~ **of a ship** Beschlagnahme eines Schiffes aufheben; **to slap an** ~ **on Embargo** auferlegen; **to take off an** ~ (ship) Beschlagnahme aufheben;
~ **Act** Embargogesetz; ~ **debate** Embargodebatte; ~ **issue** Embargofrage; ~ **list** Embargoliste; ~ **policy** Embargopolitik; ~ **recommendations** Embargoempfehlungen.

embark (v.) (engage in enterprise) hineinziehen, verwickeln, (go on board) sich einschiffen, an Bord gehen, (invest) Geld anlegen, (plane) Flugzeug besteigen;
~ **[up]on** (engage in scheme) sich einlassen;
~ **on a business** Geschäft eröffnen; ~ **again upon a business** sich erneut in ein Geschäft einlassen; ~ **on a new business undertaking** sich an einem neugegründeten Unternehmen beteiligen; ~ **capital in trade** sein Geld unternehmerisch arbeiten lassen; ~ **on a career** sich einem Beruf verschreiben; ~ **passengers and cargo** Passagiere und Ladung aufnehmen; ~ **in a project** sich in eine Spekulation einlassen; ~ **upon a quarrel with s. o.** sich in einen Streit mit jem. verwickeln; ~ **troops** Truppen verladen.

embarkation Verladung, Einschiffung, (passenger) Reiseantritt;
~ **card** (airport) Abflugkarte; ~ **officer** Verladebeamter.

embarked an Bord.

embarkment Einschiffung.

embarrass (v.) komplizieren, erschweren, (involve in financial difficulties) in [Geld]verlegenheit bringen;
~ **s. o. with parcels** j. mit seinen Paketen belästigen; ~ **s. o. with indiscreet questions** j. durch indiskrete Fragen in Verlegenheit setzen.

embarrassed in Verlegenheit, peinlich berührt, (complicated) verwickelt, kompliziert, (financially) in Verlegenheit, in Geldverlegenheit, in Zahlungsschwierigkeiten [befindlich];
~ **by debts** verschuldet;
to be ~ **by a bank failure** von einem Bankzusammenbruch betroffen sein; **to be** ~ **by lack of money** in Geldverlegenheit sein; **to become** ~ (in a speech) sich verheddern;
~ **business** zerrüttete Verhältnisse; **to be in** ~ **circumstances** in Geldverlegenheit sein; ~ **estate** überschuldeter Besitz.

embarrassment finanzielle Bedrängnis, Zahlungsschwierigkeit, Geldverlegenheit, (uneasiness of mind) Verlegenheit, Verwirrung, peinliche Angelegenheit;
financial ~ schlechte Finanzlage; **pecuniary** ~ Geldklemme, -verlegenheit;
to be in pecuniary ~ in Geldverlegenheit sein; **to plunge into political** ~ in politische Schwierigkeiten (eine unangenehme politische Lage) bringen.

embassy Botschaft[sgebäude], Gesandtschaftsgebäude, (body of persons) Botschaftspersonal, diplomatische Vertreter, (function) Botschafteramt, -würde;
on an ~ in diplomatischer Mission;
to close an ~ Botschaft aufheben; **to create (establish) an** ~ Botschaft errichten; **to send s. o. on an** ~ j. in diplomatischer Mission entsenden;
~ **attaché** Botschaftsattaché; ~ **building** Botschaftsgebäude; ~ **car** Botschaftsfahrzeug, -wagen; ~ **car park** Botschaftsparkplatz; ~ **counsellor** Botschaftsrat; ~ **grounds** Botschaftsgelände; ~ **official** Botschaftsangehöriger; ~ **spokesman** Botschaftssprecher, Sprecher der Botschaft; ~ **staff** Botschaftspersonal.

embattle (v.) **a city** Stadt zur Festung ausbauen.

embattled (fig.) unter Beschuß.

embed (v.) **in one's memory** seinem Gedächtnis einprägen.

embedded fest eingefügt;
~ **in one's memory** tief ins Gedächtnis eingegraben.

embellish (v.) **a story** Geschichte ausschmücken.

embezzle (v.) sich an anvertrautem Geld vergreifen, unterschlagen, veruntreuen, Untreue begehen;
~ **the funds of a ward** sich an Mündelgeldern vergreifen; ~ **a large sum** Unterschlagungen begehen, große Summe Geld veruntreuen; ~ **trust funds** Depots unterschlagen.

embezzlement Unterschlagung, Veruntreuung, Defraudation;
~ **of bank funds** Unterschlagung von Bankgeldern; ~ **of trust money** Depotunterschlagung.

embezzler Veruntreuer.

emblem Symbol, Emblem, Sinnbild;
~ **of peace** Friedensemblem.

emblements Früchte auf dem Halm.

embodiment Verkörperung, Personifikation, Inkarnation, (formulation) Abfassung, Formulierung, (insertion) Einfügung.

embody (v.) verkörpern, personifizieren, (principles in law) konkrete Form geben;

~ **a clause in a contract** Klausel in einen Vertrag einfügen; ~ **new features** neue Konstruktionselemente beinhalten; ~ **one's ideas in a speech** seinen Ideen in einer Ansprache konkrete Form geben; ~ **terms in an agreement** Bestimmungen in eine Vereinbarung aufnehmen; ~ **a treaty in a law** Vertrag gesetzlich verankern.

emboss *(v.)* prägen.

embossed geprägt;
~ **note-paper** geprägtes Briefpapier; ~ **stamp** Präge-, Trockenstempel.

embossing Prägedruck.

embrace *(v.)* umfassen, beinhalten, *(receive readily)* bereitwillig annehmen;
~ **all the cases in a single formula** alle Fälle in einer einzigen Formel zusammenfassen; ~ **s. one's cause** sich jds. Angelegenheit zu eigen machen; ~ **four departments** vier Abteilungen umfassen; ~ **jurors** Geschworene bestechen; ~ **an offer** Angebot annehmen; ~ **an opportunity** von einer sich bietenden Gelegenheit Gebrauch machen; ~ **a situation** Situation voll erfassen.

embracer Bestecher.

embracery Bestechungsversuch;
~ **of jurors** Geschworenenbestechung.

embroider *(v.)* **a story** Bericht ausschmücken.

embroiled | **in a war** in einen Krieg verwickelt;
to be ~ with s. o. in einen Streit mit jem. verwickelt sein.

embroilment Verwicklung.

embryo Leibesfrucht.

embus *(v.) (mil.)* auf Kraftfahrzeuge verladen.

embusqué *(mil.)* Drückeberger.

emcee *(US sl.)* Ansager, Konferenzier.

emcy Zeremonienmeister.

emend *(v.)* abändern, verbessern, berichtigen;
~ **a passage in a book** Passage in einem Buch abändern; ~ **a text** Text kritisch durchsehen.

emendate *(v.)* verbessern, berichtigen.

emendation Verbesserung, Berichtigung;
~ **of a text** Textdurchsicht, Textverbesserung;
to make ~s in a corrupt text Fehler in einem fehlerhaften Manuskript beseitigen.

emendator Textverbesserer, Korrektor.

emendatory textverbessernd.

emerge *(v.)* auftauchen, zutage treten, zum Vorschein kommen, auftauchen, *(become apparent)* sich herausstellen (entwickeln), *(state)* entstehen;
~ **with small advances** *(stock exchange)* mit kleinen Kursaufbesserungen schließen; ~ **into a strong position from the elections** gestärkt aus den Wahlen hervorgehen; ~ **from poverty** sich hocharbeiten; ~ **unscathed** unangefochten bleiben.

emergence Auftauchen, Hervor-, Emporkommen, Sichtbarwerden, *(state)* Entstehung.

emergencies, in in dringenden Fällen;
to provide for ~ für einen Notfall Vorsorge treffen.

emergency Notlage, -fall, -stand, *(service)* Not-, Behelfsdienst;
in case of ~ notfalls; **under cover of ~** durch das Notstandsgesetz gedeckt;
national ~ nationaler Notstand, Staatsnotstand; **wartime ~** kriegsbedingter Notstand;
to be confronted by an ~ mit einer Gefahrensituation konfrontiert werden; **to be ready for every ~** für jeden Notfall vorbereitet sein; **to be used only in an ~** nur im Notfall benutzt werden dürfen; **to command $ 5.000 in an ~** im Notfall über 5.000 Dollar verfügen; **to dismantle the ~** Notstandsgesetzgebung abbauen; **to meet an ~** einem Notfall abhelfen; **to provide for ~** gegen Notfälle Vorsorge treffen; **to rise to the ~** sich einer Notlage voll gewachsen zeigen;
~ **actions** Notstandsmaßnahmen; ~ **action notification** Notstandswarnung, -ankündigung; ~ **address** Notadressat; ~ **administration** Notstandsverwaltung; ~ **aid** Soforthilfe; ~ **aid program(me)** Notstands-, Soforthilfeprogramm; ~ **alert** Katastrophenalarm; ~ **amortization** beschleunigte Abschreibung; ~ **assignment** Sondereinsatz; ~ **authoritarian rule** Notstandsregierung; ~ **barrack** Notbaracke; ~ **bed** Notbett; ~**-bed service** Bereitstellung von Notbetten; ~ **board** Notstandsbüro, -gremium, -kommission; ~ **brake** Notbremse; ~ **braking situation** plötzliches Bremsmanöver; ~ **bridge** Befehls-, Notbrücke; ~ **budget** Notetat; ~ **cabinet meeting (session)** Sitzung des Notstandskabinetts; ~ **call** *(tel.)* dringendes Gespräch, Notruf; ~ **car** Hilfswagen; ~ **charge** *(transportation)* Zusatztarif in Notstandsfällen; ~ **clause** Dringlichkeits-, Not-, Gefahrenklausel; ~ **coalition** Not-

standsregierung; ~ **committee** Hilfskomitee; **national ~ council** zentrale Notstandsbehörde; ~ **currency** Notgeld; ~ **current** Notstrom; ~ **decree** Notverordnung; ~ **department** Hilfsdienst; ~ **door (exit)** Notausgang; ~ **drought assistance** staatliche Unterstützung bei durch Dürre verursachten Notfällen; ~ **edition** Befehlsausgabe; ~ **enactment** Notverordnung; ~ **facilities** *(US)* Sachanlagen der Rüstungsindustrie; ~ **fund** Notstands-, Reserve-, Hilfsfonds; ~ **hands** Reservekräfte; ~ **handle** Notbremse; ~ **hospital** Rettungsstation; ~ **import duties** Krisenabgaben auf Einfuhren; ~ **instructions** Anweisungen für Notfälle; ~ **job** Aushilfsstellung; ~ **landing** Notlandung; **to make an ~ landing** Notlandung vornehmen; ~**-landing field (ground)** Behelfs-, Hilfslandeplatz; ~ **legislation** Notstandsgesetze; ~ **light** Notbeleuchtung; ~ **loan** Notstandsdarlehn; ~ **loss** Elementarschaden; ~ **man** *(tram)* Reservefahrer; ~ **means** für Notfälle bereitgestellte Beträge; ~ **measures** Hilfs-, Not[stands]maßnahmen, außerordentliche Maßnahmen, Notverordnungen, Ausnahmegesetzgebung; ~ **money** Notgeld; ~ **needs** Notbedarf; ~ **number** Notrufnummer, Telefonnotruf; ~**-operating center** Ausweichbetrieb; ~ **operation** sofortige Operation; ~ **period** Dauer des Notstands; ~ **powers** Notstandsermächtigung; **to assume ~ powers** Notstandsmaßnahmen verhängen; ⁀ **Powers Act** *(Br.)* Notstandsgesetz; ~ **protection for threatened industries** Notstandsmaßnahmen für bedrohte Industriezweige; ~ **provisions** Notstandsbestimmungen; ~ **purpose** Ausnahmefall; ~ **rate** Notstandtarif; ~ **ration** eiserne Ration; ~ **regime** Notstandsregierung, Notstandsherrschaft; ~ **relief service** Notstandsdienst; ~ **repairs** unbedingt notwendige Reparaturen; **to slap ~ restrictions on some items** *(EEC)* in Krisenzeiten einzelne Positionen mit Einfuhrbeschränkungen belegen; ⁀ **Revenue Act** *(US)* Notstandsgesetz; ~ **roadside telephone** Notrufanlage; ~ **room** Notaufnahmezimmer, Unfallklinik; ~ **routing system** Umleitungssystem bei Verkehrsstauungen; ~ **rule** Notstandsregierung, Regierung mittels Notverordnungen; ~ **sale** Notverkauf; ~ **service** Behelfs-, Bereitschaftsdienst; ~ **session** Notstandssitzung; ~ **set** Ersatz-, Hilfsanlage; ~ **snack** kleiner Imbiß in Notfällen; ~ **squad** Bereitschaftspolizei; ~ **staff** Krisenstab; ~ **stairs** Notausgang, -treppe; ~ **state** Notstand; **to take ~ steps** Notmaßnahmen ergreifen; ~ **stocks** Krisenbestände; ~ **supply** Notvorrat; ~ **support** Unterstützung in Notfällen; ~ **tax** Notstandsabgabe, Krisensteuer; ~**-traffic signal** Warnblinkanlage; ~ **train** Hilfszug; ~ **treatment** ärztliche Versorgung von Verkehrsopfern; ~ **vehicle** Hilfsfahrzeug; ~ **visit** Urlaub in einer dringenden Familienangelegenheit; ~ **wage** für Notstandsarbeiten gezahlte Löhne; ~ **[relief] work** Notstandsarbeit.

emergent danger unmittelbar bevorstehende Gefahr.

emerging | **continent** aufstrebender Kontinent; ~ **countries** neu entstandene Staaten.

emeritus *(lat.)* im Ruhestand, emeritiert.

emigrant Auswanderer, Emigrant;
~ **agent** Auswanderungsvermittler; ~ **labo(u)rer** eingewanderter Arbeiter; ~**s' remittances** Auswanderungsüberweisungen; ~ **ship** Auswandererschiff; ~ **traffic** Auswandererverkehr.

emigrate *(v.)* auswandern, in die Emigration gehen, emigrieren.

emigration Auswanderung, Emigration, Emigrantentum;
~ **of capital** Kapitalabwanderung;
~ **agent** Auswanderungsberater; ~ **figures** Auswanderungszahlen; ~ **issue** Auswanderungsproblem; ~ **office** Auswanderungsbüro, -behörde; **chief ~ officer** Leiter der Auswanderungsbehörde; ~ **tax** Auswanderungssteuer.

emigree Emigrant, Auswanderer.

Emily Post *(US)* Tante Emma.

eminence Bodenerhebung, Anhöhe, *(elevated position)* hoher Rang, hohe Stellung;
to have the ~ of Vorrang haben; **to rise to ~** zu Rang und Würden gelangen; **to win ~ as a scientist** als hervorragender Wissenschaftler anerkannt sein.

eminent hervorragend, berühmt, eminent, ausgezeichnet;
~ **domain** *(US)* Enteignung; **to take land by ~ domain** *(US)* Enteignungsverfahren durchführen; ~ **domain proceedings** *(US)* Enteignungsverfahren; ~ **services** ungewöhnliche Dienste; ~ **statesman** hervorragender Staatsmann; ~ **success** außergewöhnlicher Erfolg.

emissary Abgesandter [mit Geheimauftrag], Emissär, Bote.

emission Ausstrahlung, *(issue)* Ausgabe, Emission, Inumlaufsetzung;
above-par ~ Überpari-Emission;
~ **of banknotes** Banknotenausgabe; ~ **of a bill of credit** Kreditbriefausstellung;
~ **standards** Immissionsauflagen.

emit *(v.) (banknotes)* ausgeben, in Umlauf setzen;
~ **a bill of credit** Kreditbrief ausstellen; ~ **an order** Verfügung (Anordnung) erlassen.

emitter Aussteller, Emittent.

emolument Nutzen, Gewinn, *(compensation)* Vergütung;
~**s** Einkommen, [Amts]einkünfte, Aufwandsentschädigung, Nebeneinkünfte, -einnahmen;
casual ~**s** Gelegenheitseinnahmen; **taxable** ~**s** steuerpflichtige Einkünfte;
~**s of a chairman** Bezüge des Aufsichtsratsvorsitzenden; ~**s of office or employment** Dienstbezüge oder Arbeitseinkommen; ~**s of a member of Parliament** Diäten; ~**s subject to tax** steuerpflichtige Einkünfte.

emotion Gefühlsregung, -bewegung, Erregung;
to appeal to s. one's ~s an jds. Gefühl appellieren.

emotional|act Affekthandlung; ~ **disturbances** emotional bedingte Erregungszustände; ~ **sales argument** an das Gefühl appellierendes (emotionales) Verkaufsargument; ~ **traits** *(marketing)* Affektivität.

emotionalism Gefühlsduselei.

empanel *(v.)* in eine Liste eintragen;
~ **a juror** Geschworenen in die Schöffenliste eintragen, als Schöffe erfassen.

emperor Kaiser.

emphasis Schwergewicht, Bedeutung, *(phonetics)* Ton, Akzent, Unterstreichung, Betonung;
with ~ mit Nachdruck, nachdrücklich;
to lay ~ on s. th. einer Sache Gewicht beimessen; **to lay special ~ on language study** dem Sprachunterricht besondere Bedeutung zumessen; **to place ~ on s. th.** Nachdruck auf etw. legen; ~ **opinion** deutlich zum Ausdruck gebrachte Meinung.

emphasize *(v.)* hervorheben, Nachdruck legen auf;
~ **the importance of careful driving** Notwendigkeit vorsichtigen Fahrens unterstreichen; ~ **in one's speech** in seiner Rede hervorheben.

empire Reich, Imperium;
industrial ~ Wirtschaftsimperium.

Empire products Waren aus den Ländern des British Commonwealth.

empirical study empirische Studie.

emplane *(v.)* in ein Flugzeug steigen (verladen).

emplead *(v.)* anklagen.

employ Beschäftigung[sverhältnis], Stellung, Dienst;
in ~ beschäftigt; **in the ~ of** im Dienst von, angestellt (beschäftigt) bei; **out of ~** stellungs-, erwerbs-, arbeitslos;
~ *(v.) (engage)* anstellen, [Angestellte] beschäftigen, arbeiten lassen, [Arbeiter] einstellen, unter Vertrag nehmen, *(use)* an-, verwenden, gebrauchen;
~ **s. o.** j. in Nahrung setzen; ~ **to advantage** vorteilhaft anwenden; ~ **an agent** Vertreter einsetzen; ~ **an expert accountant** Buchsachverständigen zuziehen; ~ **on full-time basis** ganztägig beschäftigen; ~ **all one's energies in s. th.** einer Sache seine ganze Kraft widmen; ~ **fully** voll beschäftigen; ~ **a man to look after the garden** j. mit Gartenarbeiten beschäftigen; ~ **s. o. as secretary** j. als Sekretär[in] beschäftigen; ~ **one's spare time** sich seine Freizeit einteilen, sich in seiner Freizeit beschäftigen; ~ **s. o. temporarely** j. kurzfristig beschäftigen;
to be ~ in s. one's ~ bei jem. beschäftigt (angestellt) sein, in jds. Diensten stehen; **to enter the ~ of** Dienst antreten; **to take in one's ~** in seinen Dienst nehmen.

employability Arbeitsfähigkeit.

employable ver-, anwendbar, verwendungsfähig, *(person)* arbeitsfähig.

employed beschäftigt, angestellt, berufstätig;
gainfully ~ gegen Entgelt beschäftigt, erwerbstätig; **permanently ~** fest angestellt; **self-~** selbständig;
~ **on full time (a full-time basis)** ganztägig beschäftigt, vollbeschäftigt;
to be ~ angestellt (beschäftigt) sein, Arbeit haben, in Arbeit stehen; **to be ~ as** Verwendung finden als; **to be ~ in a bank** Bankangestellter sein, bei einer Bank arbeiten; **to be continuously ~** in einem ständigen Beschäftigungsverhältnis stehen; **to be ~ at a lower status** mit niedrigeren Arbeiten beschäftigt werden;
~ **capital** produktives (arbeitendes) Kapital; ~ **inventor** angestellter Erfinder; ~ **person** Beschäftigter, Arbeitnehmer; **self-~ person** selbständiger Erwerbstätiger.

employee *(Br.)* **employe** *(US)* Beschäftigter, Angestellter, Arbeitnehmer, Dienstverpflichteter, Lohn-, Gehaltsempfänger, Betriebsangehöriger, Bediensteter;
~**s** Personal, Angestellte, Belegschaft;

additional ~ zusätzliche Arbeitskräfte; **black-coated** ~ *(Br.)* höherer Büroangestellter; **borrowed** ~ ausgeliehene (abgestellte) Arbeitskraft; **census** ~ statistischer Angestellter; **city** ~ städtischer Angestellter; **conscripted** ~ Dienstverpflichteter; **covered** ~ versicherter Angestellter; **eligible** ~ bezugsberechtigter Angestellter; **executive** ~ leitender Angestellter; **full-time** ~ ganztägig beschäftigter Angestellter; **government** ~ Angestellter des öffentlichen Dienstes, *(US)* Staatsbediensteter, Beamter; **high-salaried** ~ hochbezahlter Angestellter; **hotel and catering** ~**s** Personal des Hotel- und Gaststättengewerbes; **hourly** ~ auf Stundenlohnbasis Beschäftigter, Stundenarbeiter; **loaned** ~ abgestellter Angestellter; **long-service** ~ langjähriger Angestellter; **managerial** ~ leitender Angestellter; **nonunion** ~ nicht gewerkschaftlich organisierter Angestellter; **operating** ~**s** *(railway)* Betriebspersonal; **part-time** ~ halbtägig beschäftigter Angestellter; **permanent** ~ Festangestellter; **profit-sharing** ~ gewinnbeteiligter Arbeitnehmer; **prounion** ~ gewerkschaftsfreundlich eingestellter Angestellter; **public-sector** ~**s** Angestellte der öffentlichen Hand; **redundant** ~ überschüssige Arbeitskraft; **relocated** ~ in die Zentrale zurückversetzter Angestellter; **salaried** ~ Gehaltsempfänger; **short-term** ~ Kurzarbeiter; **state** ~ Angestellter im öffentlichen Dienst; **substandard** ~ untertariflich bezahlter Arbeiter; **superannuated** ~ pensionsfähiger Angestellter; **supervisory** ~ Angestellter mit Aufsichtsfunktionen; **top-caliber** ~ hochqualifizierter Angestellter; **turnover-prone** ~ unsteter (fluktuierender) Arbeitnehmer; **white-collar** ~ *(US)* höherer [Büro]angestellter; **woman** ~ Angestellte;
~**s of municipal governments** Kommunalangestellte; ~**s on temporary loan** Leihkräfte, -arbeiter; ~ **outside a pension scheme** an der Pensionskasse nicht beteiligter Arbeitnehmer;
to be a permanent ~ fest angestellt sein; **to give an ~ the amount of notice to which he is entitled** die einem Angestellten zustehende Kündigungsschutzfrist einhalten; **to give an ~ warning** Angestellten kündigen; **to leave ~s no worse off after tax** Arbeitnehmereinkünfte für zusätzliche Steuerzahlungen ausgleichen; **to lend an** ~ **to s. o.** Angestellten zu jem. abstellen; **to move an** ~ Angestellten versetzen; **to pay off an** ~ Angestellten auszahlen; **to report an** ~ **for misconduct** Angestellten zur disziplinarischen Bestrafung melden; **to restore an** ~ **to his old place** einem Angestellten seine alte Stellung wiedergeben; **to rid o. s. of an** ~ Angestellten loswerden; **to take on a new** ~ j. neu einstellen; **to transfer** ~**s** Arbeitskräfte umsetzen; **to unionize** ~**s** Arbeitnehmer zum Eintritt in die Gewerkschaft veranlassen;
~ **appraisal** *(US)* Angestelltenbeurteilung; ~ **appraisal program(me)** *(US)* Beurteilungsprogramm für Angestellte; ~**s' association** Arbeitnehmerverband; ~ **attitude** Arbeitnehmereinstellung; ~**-attitude measurement** Betriebsklimauntersuchung; ~**-attitude survey** Betriebsumfrage; ~ **benefit** vom Arbeitnehmer bezahlter Sozialversicherungsanteil; ~ **benefit paid by company** *(national insurance)* Arbeitgeberanteil; ~**-benefit association** betrieblicher Versicherungsverein auf Gegenseitigkeit; ~**-benefit plan (system)** *(US)* betriebliches Sozialzulagenwesen; ~**-benefit and service division** Sozialabteilung; ~**-benefit trust** betrieblicher Sozialfonds, Sozialkapital; ~**'s bonus** Angestelltentantieme; ~ **compensation** Arbeitnehmervergütung; ~ **Compensation Act** *(US)* Unfallentschädigungsgesetz für Staatsangestellte; ~**'s contribution** *(national insurance)* Arbeitnehmeranteil; ~ **cooperation** Zusammenarbeit von Betrieb und Belegschaft; ~**s' council** Betriebsrat; ~ **counselling** Angestelltenberatung; ~ **discount** Rabatt für Werks-, Ladenangestellte; ~ **election** Betriebswahl; ~**-employer relations** Arbeitgeber-Arbeitnehmerverhältnis; ~ **food service** Betriebskantineneinrichtung; ~ **grievances** Beschwerden der Angestellten; ~ **handbook** Betriebshandbuch; ~ **home** Werkswohnung; ~**'s invention** Arbeitnehmererfindung; ~**s' layoff** Personal-, Belegschaftsabbau; ~ **loyalty** Betriebsloyalität; ~ **morale** Betriebs-, Arbeitsmoral; ~ **motivation** *(US)* arbeitsfördernder Faktor; ~**s' newsletter** Nachrichten für die Belegschaft; ~ **organization** Arbeitnehmerorganisation; **to be ~-owned** in Arbeitnehmerhand sein; ~ **ownership** Arbeitnehmereigentum; ~**s' panel** Arbeitnehmerbeisitzerliste; ~ **participation in industry** Gewinnbeteiligung der Arbeitnehmer; ~ **party** von den Angestellten finanzierte Veranstaltung; ~ **pension** Angestelltenrente; ~ **profit sharing** Gewinnbeteiligung der Arbeitnehmer; ~ **publication** Betriebszeitung; ~ **rating** Angestellteneinstufung; ~ **rating chart** betriebliches Beurteilungsblatt eines Angestellten; ~ **relations** innerbetriebliche Beziehungen; ~**s' annual report** für die Belegschaft zusammengestellter Jahresbericht; ~**s' representation** Arbeit-

nehmer-, Betriebsvertretung; ~ **representative** Arbeitnehmervertreter; ~ **requirements** Personalbedürfnisse; ~ **retirement** Angestelltenpensionierung; ≗ **Retirement Security Act** *(US)* Pensionssicherungsgesetz; ~'s **right** Arbeitnehmerrechte; ~-**right committee** Ausschuß zur Wahrung von Arbeitnehmerrechten; ~ **roster** Stellenbesetzungsplan; ~ **security** Sicherung des Arbeitsplatzes; ~ **services** freiwillige Sozialleistungen; ~ **shares** Belegschaftsaktien; ~-**share offer** Belegschaftsaktienangebot; ~-**share ownership** *(Br.)* Beteiligung der Belegschaft am Aktienkapital; ~s' **shares plan** System der Ausgabe von Belegschaftsaktien; ~ **status** Angestelltenverhältnis; ~ **stock** *(US)* an die Belegschaft ausgegebene Aktien, Belegschaftsaktie; ~-**stock bonus** *(US)* aus Gratisaktien bestehender Pensionsfonds; ~-**stock ownership** *(US)* Beteiligung der Belegschaft am Aktienkapital; ~-**stock ownership plan** *(E.S.O.P., US)* Kapitalübernahmeplan für Arbeitnehmer, Belegschaftsaktiensystem; ~ **stock-purchase committee** *(US)* Belegschaftsaktienausschuß; ~ **suggestion system** betriebliches Vorschlagwesen; ~ **test** betriebliche Eignungsprüfung; ~ **theft** Betriebsdiebstahl; ~ **training** innerbetriebliche Ausbildung; ~ **turnover** Angestelltenfluktuation; ~'s **withholding exemption** Lohnsteuerfreibetrag; ~'s **withholding exemption certificate** Lohnsteuerfreibetragsformular.

employer *(commission)* Auftraggeber, *(head of business)* Unternehmer, Arbeitgeber, Prinzipal, Dienst-, Lehrherr; ~s Arbeitgeber-, Unternehmerschaft;
current ~ augenblicklicher Arbeitgeber; **ex** ~ früherer Arbeitgeber; **most recent** ~ letzter Arbeitgeber;
~ **and his agent** Auftraggeber und Auftragnehmer; ~s **and employed** Arbeitgeber und Arbeitnehmer; ~ **of labo(u)r** Arbeitgeber, Auftraggeber;
to accrue to the ~ dem Arbeitgeber zufallen; **to ask one's** ~ **for a rise** *(US)* seinen Dienstherrn um Gehaltserhöhung ansprechen; **to be a large** ~ viele Leute beschäftigen; **to give notice to one's** ~ seinem Arbeitgeber kündigen;
~s' **association** Unternehmer-, Arbeitgeberverband; ~ **class** Unternehmerschicht; **British** ≗ s **Confederation** Dachverband Britischer Unternehmer; ~ **contribution** *(national insurance)* Arbeitgeberanteil; ~s' **domination** Vorherrschaft der Arbeitgeber; ~s' **fund** Unternehmerfonds; ~ **group** Arbeitgebergruppe; ~ **health welfare** betriebliche Gesundheitspflege; ~'s **liability** Unfallhaftpflicht des Arbeitgebers, Betriebs-, Arbeitgeberhaftpflicht; ≗ s **Liability Act** *(US)* Betriebshaftpflichtgesetz; ≗ s' **Liability Assurance Corporation** *(Br.)* Betriebshaftpflichtversicherungsgesellschaft; ~'s **liability insurance** Betriebshaftpflichtversicherung; ~'s **liability policy** Betriebshaftpflichtpolice; ~s' **national insurance contribution** *(Br.)* Arbeitgeberanteil an der Sozialversicherung, Sozialversicherungsbeitrag des Arbeitgebers; ~s' **organization** Arbeitgeberverband; ~-**owned** im Eigentum des Arbeitgebers; ~s' **panel** Arbeitgeberbeisitzerliste; **on the** ~s' **premises** in Arbeitgeberbetrieben; ~ **representative** Arbeitgebervertreter.

employing class Unternehmerklasse.

employment *(occupation)* Beschäftigung, Tätigkeit, Geschäft, Beruf, *(situation)* unselbständige Arbeit, Stelle, [An]stellung, Beschäftigungs-, Angestellten-, Dienst-, Arbeitsverhältnis, *(use)* Gebrauch, An-, Verwendung, *(utilization)* Verwertung;
in course of one's ~ in der Arbeitszeit; **in public** ~ im öffentlichen Dienst; **on** ~ werktätig; **outside the scope of** ~ außerhalb des Beschäftigungsverhältnisses; **[thrown] out of** ~ stellen-, arbeits-, beschäftigungslos;
additional ~ zusätzliche Beschäftigungsmöglichkeit; **basic** ~ Erwerbstätigkeit mit überregionaler Bedeutung; **casual** ~ gelegentliche Beschäftigung, Gelegenheitsarbeit; **common** ~ gemeinsames Beschäftigungsverhältnis; **compulsory** ~ Beschäftigungszwang; **constant** ~ Dauerbeschäftigung; **construction** ~ Beschäftigung in der Bauindustrie; **continuous** ~ Dauerbeschäftigung, ständiges Beschäftigungsverhältnis; **contracted-out** ~ nicht pflichtversichertes Beschäftigungsverhältnis; **efficient** ~ rationelle Ausnutzung; **contributor's** ~ *(national insurance)* versicherungspflichtiges Beschäftigungsverhältnis; **excepted** ~ *(Br.)* nicht sozialversicherungspflichtiges Beschäftigungsverhältnis; **exclusive** ~ einzige Beschäftigung; **factory** ~ Beschäftigung in der Industrie; **fluctuating** ~ stetiger Arbeitsplatzwechsel; **full** ~ Vollbeschäftigung; **full-time** ~ hauptamtliche (ganztägige) Beschäftigung, Ganztagsbeschäftigung; **gainful** ~ Erwerbstätigkeit; **guaranteed** ~ garantierter Jahreslohn; **hazardous** ~ gefährlicher Beruf; **insurable** ~ *(Br.)* sozialversicherungspflichtiges Beschäftigungsverhältnis; **irregular** ~ unregelmäßige Beschäftigung; **labo(u)r** ~ Arbeitseinsatz; **manufacturing** ~ Beschäftigung im industriellen Bereich; **maximum** ~ Beschäftigungsoptimum; **night** ~ Nachtarbeit; **nonbasic** ~ Erwerbstätigkeit mit regionaler Bedeutung; **on-site** ~ Beschäftigung auf der Baustelle; **overall** ~ Gesamtheit aller Beschäftigten; **overfull** ~ Übervollbeschäftigung; **part-time** ~ verkürzte Arbeitszeit, Teilzeitbeschäftigung, Halbtagsbeschäftigung, stundenweise Beschäftigung, Kurzarbeit; **payroll** ~ unselbständige Tätigkeit; **pensionable** ~ ruhegehaltsfähiges Dienstverhältnis; **private** ~ privates Arbeitsverhältnis; **probationary** ~ Probeanstellung, -beschäftigung; **professional** ~ berufliche Tätigkeit; **profitable** ~ einträgliche Beschäftigung; **prospective** ~ zukunftsträchtige Beschäftigung; **public** ~ Staatsdienst; **reduced** ~ verringerte Beschäftigungsmöglichkeit; **regular** ~ feste Anstellung; **rural** ~ Beschäftigung in der Landwirtschaft; **seasonal** ~ saisonabhängige Beschäftigung; **sedentary** ~ sitzende Beschäftigung; **self-** ~ selbständige Tätigkeit; **service** ~ Beschäftigung in der Dienstleistungsindustrie; **side-line** ~ Nebenbeschäftigung; **state** ~ Beschäftigung im Staatsdienst; **suitable** ~ zusagende (angemessene) Beschäftigung, passende Stellung; **underground** ~ illegale Beschäftigung; **unstable** ~ ungleichmäßige Beschäftigung; **wage-earning** ~ unselbständige Beschäftigung; **wanted** *(newspaper)* Stellengesuche; **wife's** ~ Beschäftigungsverhältnis der Ehefrau; **year-long** ~ durchgängige Jahresbeschäftigung; **youth** ~ Beschäftigung von Jugendlichen;
~ **of apprentices** Einstellung von Lehrlingen; ~ **of a local bank** Einschaltung einer Bank am Platze; ~ **worldly** ~ **or business** *(Sunday Laws)* unerlaubte Geschäftstätigkeit; ~ **of capital** Kapitalanlage; ~ **of a casual nature** gelegentliche Beschäftigung; ~ **of children** Kinderarbeit; ~ **of a counsel** Zuziehung eines Anwalts; ~ **of force** Gewaltanwendung; ~ **of funds** Mittel-, Kapitalverwendung; ~ **of labo(u)r** Arbeitskräfteeinsatz; ~ **of elderly people** Beschäftigung älterer Arbeitnehmer; ~ **of a solicitor** *(Br.)* Inanspruchnahme (Zuziehung) eines Anwalts; ~ **of troops** Einsatz von Truppen, Truppenverwendung;
to arise out and in the course of ~ *(injury)* aus dem Beschäftigungsverhältnis herrühren; **to be in** ~ in Stellung (beschäftigt, angestellt) sein; **to be in full** ~ vollbeschäftigt sein; **to be out of** ~ arbeitslos (erwerbslos) sein; **to be thrown out of** ~ arbeits-, beschäftigungslos werden, seine Stellung verlieren; **to change one's** ~ seinen Arbeitsplatz wechseln; **to ensure full** ~ Vollbeschäftigung sicherstellen; **to find** ~ unterkommen, Beschäftigung finden; **to find** ~ **for s. o.** j. unterbringen, j. in den Arbeitsprozeß eingliedern; **to find** ~ **with a firm** bei einer Firma ankommen; **to give** ~ Arbeit geben, beschäftigen; **to give s. o.** ~ j. in sein Geschäft einstellen; **to grow to a full-time** ~ sich zur Ganztagsarbeit, -beschäftigung entwickeln; **to have to be prepared to accept** ~ **of a different kind** auch bereit sein müssen, eine berufsfremde Tätigkeit auszuüben; **to obtain** ~ Arbeit erhalten; **to preserve** ~ Beschäftigungslage sichern; **to procure** ~ **for s. o.** jem. Arbeit verschaffen; **to provide** ~ Arbeit beschaffen; **to provide local** ~ ortsgebundene Arbeitsplätze bereitstellen; **to re-enter an** ~ Stellung wiederannehmen; **to seek** ~ Arbeit suchen; **to take** ~ Beschäftigungsverhältnis eingehen; **to take on** ~ Arbeit aufnehmen; **to terminate** ~ Beschäftigungsverhältnis beenden; **to terminate s. one's** ~ jem. kündigen; **to throw out of** ~ entlassen;
≗ **Act** *(US)* Gesetz zur Aufrechterhaltung der Vollbeschäftigung; ~ **agency** Stellen-, Anstellungs-, Arbeitsvermittlungsbüro; ~ **agent** Stellenvermittler; ~ **agreement** Dienstvertrag; ~ **applicant** Arbeitsuchender, Stellenbewerber; ~ **application** Bewerbungsantrag; ~ **application blank** Bewerbungsformular; ~ **bureau** *(Br.)* Arbeits-, Beschäftigungs-, Stellennachweis, Stellenvermittlungsbüro; **juvenile** ~ **bureau** *(Br.)* Berufsberatungsstelle; ~ **category** Beschäftigungskategorie, -art; ~ **certificate** *(US)* Arbeitsbescheinigung; ~ **center** Beschäftigungszentrum; ~ **conditions** Beschäftigungsbedingungen; **minimal** ~ **content** Mindestauswirkung auf die Beschäftigungslage; **existing** ~ **contract** *(US)* Dienstverhältnis; **to terminate an** ~ **contract without notice** *(US)* Dienstverhältnis fristlos kündigen; ~ **costs** personelle Unkosten; **hourly** ~ **costs** Stundenlohnkosten; ~-**creating** Arbeitsplätze bewirkend; ~ **data** Beschäftigungszahlen; ~ **date** Beschäftigungszeit; ~ **decline** Beschäftigungsrückgang; ~ **density** Beschäftigungsdichte; ~ **department** Arbeitsministerium; ~ **exchange** *(Br.)* staatlicher Arbeits-, Stellennachweis, Arbeitsvermittlung[sbüro]; ~ **figures** Beschäftigungszahlen, -ziffern; ~ **fluctuations** Beschäftigungsschwankungen; **life-time** ~ **guarantee** lebenslängliche Beschäftigungszusage; ~ **history** beruflicher Werdegang, frühere Arbeitstätigkeit; ~ **income** berufliches Einkommen; ~ **interview** persönliche Vorstellung; ~ **manager** Personalchef; ~ **market** Arbeits-, Stellenmarkt; ~ **office** Einstellungsbüro; **public** ~

office *(US)* staatlicher Arbeitsnachweis; **youth ~ officer** *(Br.)* Arbeitsdienstführer; **~ office report** *(US)* Arbeitsamtnachweis; **~ opportunity** Beschäftigungsmöglichkeit; **~ papers** Arbeitspapiere; **~ pattern** Beschäftigungsstruktur; **~ period** Anstellungs-, Beschäftigungszeit; **~ picture** Beschäftigungsstand; **~ policies** Arbeitsmarktpolitik; **~ possibilities** Beschäftigungsmöglichkeiten; **~ possibilities picture** Übersicht über die Beschäftigungsmöglichkeiten, Beschäftigungsüberblick, -übersicht; **to cut the ~ potential** Beschäftigungsmöglichkeiten beschneiden; **~ procedure** Arbeits-, Beschäftigungsnachweis [für eine Einzelperson]; **~ program(me)** Arbeitsbeschaffungsprogramm; **ꟼ Protection Act** *(Br.)* Gesetz zum Schutz von Arbeitnehmerrechten; **ꟼ Production Act** *(Br.)* Arbeitsschutzgesetz; **~ rate** Beschäftigungsprozentsatz; **~ records** *(US)* Arbeits-, Beschäftigungsnachweis [für eine Einzelperson], Arbeitspapiere; **~ retirement income** Ruhegehaltsbezüge von Gehaltsempfängern; **ꟼ Retirement Income Security Act** *(ERISA, US)* Gesetz zur Sicherung von Ruhegehaltsbezügen von Angestellten; **~ right** Beschäftigungsanspruch, Recht auf Arbeit; **~ service** Stellenvermittlung; **youth ~ service** *(Br.)* Arbeitsdienst; **~ spread** Arbeitsstreckung; **~ stability** stabile Arbeitsmarktlage; **~ stabilization** Beruhigung des Arbeitsmarktes; **~ standard** Beschäftigungsgrad; **~ statement** *(corporation)* Verlautbarung über die Entwicklung der Belegschaftssituation; **~ statistics** Beschäftigungsnachweis; **~ subsidy** staatlicher Beschäftigungszuschuß; **temporary ~ subsidy** *(Br.)* Staatszuschüsse für Teilzeitbeschäftigte; **selective ~ tax** *(Br.)* Lohnsummensteuer; **~ termination** Beendigung des Beschäftigungsverhältnisses; **~ test** [betriebliche] Eignungsprüfung; **~ trend** Beschäftigungsentwicklung; **~ volume** Beschäftigungsvolumen; **~ work** unselbständige Tätigkeit.

emporium Handelsstadt, -zentrum.

empower *(v.)* bevollmächtigen, Vollmacht erteilen, ermächtigen, berechtigen, Genehmigung erteilen;
~ s. o. to operate on an account jem. Kontovollmacht erteilen.

empowered befugt, ermächtigt;
to be ~ bevollmächtigt sein.

empowerment Bevollmächtigung, Ermächtigung.

empties gebrauchte Verpackung, leere Fässer, Leergut;
~ returned Leergut zurück;
~ are not taken back Leergut wird nicht zurückgenommen.

emptiness *(fig.)* Hohlheit, Leere;
to feel an ~ geistige Leere empfinden.

emptor Käufer.

empty Leergut, -material, *(car)* Leerwagen;
~ *(a.) (destitute)* leer, nichtssagend, eitel, inhaltslos, *(house)* leer[stehend], unbewohnt, verlassen, *(ship, vehicle)* leer, unbefrachtet, ohne Ladung, unbeladen;
returned ~ leer zurück;
~ of joy bar jeder Freude; **~ of meaning** bedeutungslos; **~** *(v.)* **a house** Haus räumen; **~ itself into the sea** ins Meer münden; **s. one's shop** jem. seinen ganzen Bestand abkaufen; **to be ~ of s. th.** einer Sache entbehren; **to stand ~** freistehen, leerstehen;
to come ~-handed mit leeren Händen kommen; **to come home ~-handed** unverrichteter Sache heimkehren; **~ pleasure** nichtssagende Vergnügungen; **~ promises** leere Versprechungen; **~ return running** Rücklauf von Leergut; **~ ship** unbeladenes Schiff; **on an ~ stomach** auf nüchternen Magen; **~ talk** leeres Gerede; **~ taxi** freies Taxi; **~ threats** leere Drohungen; **~ wag(g)on** Leerwagen; **~ weight** *(airplane)* Eigen-, Leergewicht; **~ wine** Wein ohne Bukett (Blume); **to pay s. o. in ~ words** j. mit nichtssagenden Worten abspeisen.

enable *(v.)* befähigen, *(authorize)* berechtigen, ermächtigen, Vollmacht geben;
~ a company to resume normal bus service einer Verkehrsgesellschaft die Wiederaufnahme des regulären Omnibusverkehrs gestatten; **~ s. o. to retire** jem. die frühzeitige Pensionierung ermöglichen.

enabling act (statute) *(US)* Ermächtigungsgesetz.

enact *(v.)* gesetzlich verfügen, Gesetzeskraft verleihen, *(theater)* inszenieren, aufführen;
~ a law Gesetz (gesetzliche Verfügung) erlassen;
be it further ~ed that wird folgendes Gesetz beschlossen.

enacting clause Gesetzesformel.

enactment Verordnung, Erlaß, *(enacting)* Erlaß eines Gesetzes, *(theater)* Darstellung [einer Rolle];
by legislative ~ durch einen Akt zur Gesetzgebung;
~s repeated aufgehobene Rechtsvorschriften;
~ as to evidence Beweisvorschrift; **~ of law** Verabschiedung eines Gesetzes.

enactor Gesetzgeber, *(theater)* Darsteller.

enamel plate (sign) Emailleschild.

enamel(l)ed paper Kunstdruckpapier.

encamp *(v.)* Lager aufschlagen (beziehen).

encampment [Flüchtlings]lager.

encash *(v.) (Br.)* [Wechsel] in bar einlösen, einziehen, kassieren.

encashable *(Br.)* einkassierbar.

encashment *(Br.)* Einkassierung, Inkasso;
~ of debts Schuldeneinziehung; **~ of post cheques** Postscheckeinlösung**to effect ~** Inkasso besorgen;
~ charges Einzugsspesen; **~ credit** Branchenüberziehungskredit; **~ order** Inkassomandat, -auftrag.

encipher *(v.)* chiffrieren, verschlüsseln.

encircle *(v.)* umzingeln, *(mil.)* einkesseln.

encircled by enemy forces von feindlichen Kräften eingekesselt.

encirclement Einkesselung, Einschluß, *(pol.)* Einkreisung.

enclave Enklave, Einschlußgebiet.

enclavement of a territory Einschluß eines Gebiets.

enclose *(v.) (subjoin)* [Brief] beifügen, beilegen;
~ a cheque *(Br.)* Scheck beifügen; **~ common land** Gemeindeeigentum privatisieren; **~ in parenthesis** einklammern, in Klammern setzen; **~ a receipt with a letter** Quittung in einen Brief einlegen; **~ with a wall** mit einer Mauer umgeben.

enclosed anbei, einliegend, in der Anlage, beigeschlossen;
~ ground bebaute (kultivierte) Fläche; **~ space** umbauter Raum;
~ please find beiliegend erhalten Sie.

enclosing a check unter Beifügung eines Schecks.

enclosure Ein-, Beilage, Beipack, Briefbeilage, Anlage, *(advertising)* Warenbeilage, *(bookseller)* Beischuß, *(land)* eingefriedetes Grundstück, Einfriedigung;
~ of common land Privatisierung von Gemeindegrundstücken.

encode *(v.)* verschlüsseln, chiffrieren.

encodement Verschlüsselung, verschlüsselter Text.

encore *(theater)* Zugabe, Dakaporuf;
~ *(v.)* um eine Zugabe bitten.

encounter *(mil.)* Zusammenstoß, Gefecht;
~ *(v.)* zusammenstoßen.

encourage *(v.)* fördern, unterstützen, *(criminal law)* anstiften;
~ s. o. in his studies jds. Studien fördern; **~ an enterprise** Unternehmen fördern; **~ imports** Einfuhren begünstigen; **~ production** Produktionssteigerung hervorrufen.

encouragement Förderung, Unterstützung, Begünstigung, *(criminal)* Anstiftung;
~ of the arts Förderung der schönen Künste; **~ of emigration** Förderung der Auswanderung; **~ of imports** Einfuhrbegünstigung; **~ of industry** Industrieförderung.

encroach *(v.)* beeinträchtigen, schmälern, eingreifen, übergreifen, *(trespass)* unberechtigt eindringen, im Besitz stören;
~ upon übergreifen auf, Eingriff machen in; **~ upon one's capital** sein Kapital angreifen; **~ upon s. one's functions** jds. Befugnisse eingreifen; **~ upon one's kindness** jds. Güte mißbrauchen; **~ upon the land** *(sea)* auf Land vordringen; **~ [up]on s. one's land** in jds. Besitzrecht eingreifen; **~ upon s. one's prerogatives** jds. Vorrechte angreifen; **~ upon s. one's rights** jds. Rechte beeinträchtigen (antasten); **~ upon s. one's time** jds. Zeit über Gebühr beanspruchen.

encroachment Übergriff, Eingriff, Beeinträchtigung, *(fixture)* Überbau, *(illness)* allmähliches Fortschreiten;
~ of access Zugangsbehinderung; **~ upon one's capital** Kapitalschmälerung; **~ of jobs** Arbeitsbehinderung; **~ upon s. one's rights** Eingriff in jds. Rechte; **~s made by the sea upon land** Vordringen der See aufs Festland.

encumber *(v.)* dinglich belasten;
~ o. s. with unnecessary luggage überflüssiges Gepäck mitnehmen; **~ a mind with useless learning** Gehirn mit nutzlosem Wissen belasten; **~ with a mortgage** mit einer Hypothek belasten; **~ one's real property** Grundpfandrecht auf seinem Grundbesitz bestellen; **~ a room with useless furniture** Zimmer mit unnötigen Möbeln vollstellen.

encumbered [mit Schulden] belastet, überschuldet, verschuldet;
to be ~ with debts völlig verschuldet sein; **to be ~ with a large family** durch eine große Familie an seiner vollen Entfaltung gehindert sein; **to be ~ with a mortgage** hypothekarisch belastet sein;
~ estate [hypothekarisch] belasteter Grundbesitz.

encumbering goods Sperrgut.

encumbrance Belastung, Behinderung, *(claim on real estate)* [Grundstücks]belastung, Hypothekenschulden;
free from ~s schulden-, lastenfrei, entschuldet; **without [family] ~** ohne Anhang;

to be an ~ on s. o. Belastung für j. darstellen; **to carry prior ~s** vorbelastet sein, Vorlasten haben; **to free an estate of ~s** Grundstück entschulden.

encumbrancer Pfandgläubiger, *(mortgager)* Hypothekengläubiger;
junior ~ nachstehender Hypothekengläubiger.

encyclop(a)edia Konversationslexikon.

end *(aim)* Absicht, Zweck, Ziel, Ende, Beendigung;
at a loose ~ ohne regelmäßige Beschäftigung; **at the ~ of the century** beim Ausgang des Jahrhunderts; **for one's own ~** zum eigenen Nutzen; **from one ~ to the other** vom Anfang bis zum Ende; **from beginning to ~** von A bis Z; **in the ~** schließlich; **in order to ~ the matter** um zu einem Ende zu kommen; **on ~** ununterbrochen, hintereinander; **to the ~ of the chapter** bis zum bitteren Ende; **to no ~** vergebens; **to the ~ of time** bis zum Ende aller Tage; **without ~** fortwährend, immer und ewig;
advertising ~ Reklamezweck; **candle ~s** Kerzenstummel; **cigarette ~** Kippe; **private ~s** Privatinteressen, -zwecke;
~ of an adventure Schluß eines Abenteuers; **no ~ of applause** nicht enden wollender Beifall; **no ~ of a fool** *(sl.)* Vollidiot; **~ in itself** Selbstzweck; **~ of a letter** Briefschluß; **~ of a line** Zeilenausgang; **the long ~ of the market** *(Br.)* Teilmarkt für Papiere mit einer Laufzeit über fünf Jahre; **the short ~ of the market** *(Br.)* Teilmarkt für kürzerfristige Papiere; **~ of a meeting** Sitzungsschluß; **~ of the month** Ultimo; **~ of the ration book area** Ende der Lebensmittelkartenzeit; **~ of a series** Auftragsbeendigung; **~ of a term** Fristablauf; **~ to violence** Beendigung der Gewalttaten; **~ of the war** Kriegsende; **~ of will** Testamentsschluß; **~ of the year** Jahresultimo;
~ (v.) enden, zu Ende bringen, aufhören, abschließen, *(put to death)* umbringen, vernichten, töten;
~ a break *(print.)* letzte Zeile mit Spatien füllen; **~ one's days in peace** friedlichen Lebensabend haben; **~ in a draw** unentschieden ausgehen; **~ in failure** Mißerfolg sein, mißglücken; **~ in nothing** in Rauch aufgehen, im Sande verlaufen, verpuffen; **~ one's quarrel** seinen Streit begraben; **~ off one's speech** seine Rede abschließen; **~ in smoke** im Sande verlaufen, in Rauch aufgehen, verpuffen; **~ up by marrying** j. schließlich (letzten Endes) heiraten; **~ up in prison** sich im Gefängnis wiederfinden; **~ up that way** darauf hinauslaufen; **~ one's days in a workhouse** Lebensabend im Armenhaus verbringen;
to attain (gain) one's ~ sein Ziel erreichen; **to be the ~ of s. o.** jds. Karriere beenden; **to be at an ~** mit seinen Mitteln (Kräften) am Ende sein; **to be no ~ of a benefit** Heidenarbeit sein; **to be at the receiving ~ of s. th.** einer Sache wehrlos ausgesetzt sein; **to be at the ~ of one's petrol** kein Benzin mehr haben; **to be at the ~ of one's resources** seine Mittel aufgebraucht haben; **to be at the ~ of one's tether** seine Geduld erschöpft haben; **to be at one's wits ~** mit seinem Latein am Ende sein; **to begin at the the wrong ~** am falschen Ende anfangen; **to bring war to an ~** Krieg beenden; **to collide ~ on** *(ship)* rückwärts (am Heck) zusammenstoßen; **to come to the ~ of one's tether** mit seinen Künsten (seinem Latein) am Ende sein; **to cost s. o. no ~ of money** j. eine gewaltige Geldsumme kosten; **to come to a bad ~** schlimmes Ende finden, böses Ende nehmen; **to come in at the tail ~** als letzter durchs Ziel gehen; **to come to an untimely ~** schon früh versterben; **to draw to an ~** sich dem Ende nähern; **to fight to the bitter ~** bis zum bitteren Ende standhalten; **to follow s. o. to the ~s of the earth** jem. bis ans Ende der Welt folgen; **to get the dirty ~ of the stick** den Kürzeren ziehen; **to get hold of the wrong ~ of the stick** Sache in den falschen Hals bekommen; **to go off the deep ~** sich unüberlegt auf etw. einlassen, seine Haut zu Markte tragen; **to have s. th. at one's fingers' ~s** etw. wie am Schnürchen können (im Griff haben); **to have no ~ of fun** *(coll.)* Mordsspaß haben; **to have trouble without ~** nicht enden wollende Schwierigkeiten haben; **to have the right ~ of the stick** *(fam.)* schließlich der Gewinner sein; **to keep one's ~ up** *(Br.)* seinen Mann stehen, bis zum Schluß durchhalten; **to make both ~s meet** mit seinem Einkommen knapp auskommen, gerade genug zum Leben haben, sich nach der Decke strecken; **to meet no ~ of interesting people** jede Menge (eine Fülle) interessanter Leute kennenlernen; **to put an ~ to s. th.** einer Sache Einhalt gebieten, Schluß mit etw. machen; **to serve some private ~s** privaten Zwecken dienen; **to start at the wrong ~** am falschem Ende anfangen; **to think no ~ of o. s.** sich für sehr bedeutend halten;
~ abutment *(bridge)* Landpfeiler; **~-of-the-year adjustment** Rechnungsabgrenzung zum Jahresultimo; **~ carriage** *(railway)* letzter Wagen, Schlußwaggon; **~-cleared zone** *(aerodrome)* hindernisfreie Zone; **~ corrections** *(statistics)* Korrekturen der Extremwerte; **~-on course** praxisbezogener Ausbil-

dungsgang; **~-of-month figures** Monatsendstände; **~ gate** *(truck)* Ladeklappe; **~ house of a street** letztes Haus einer Straße; **~ item** Endprodukt; **~ money** Reservefonds; **~-of-month influences** Ultimoeinflüsse; **~-of-month settlement loan** Ultimogeld; **~-of-month terms** Ultimobedingungen; **~ paper** *(bookbinding)* Vorsatzpapier, Innenspiegel, Schutzblatt; **~-processing plant** Weiterverarbeitungsbetrieb; **~ product** Endprodukt, Grenzprodukt, Fertigware; **~-of-season sale** Saisonschlußverkauf; **~ sleeve** *(cable)* Endverschluß; **~-use certificate** Endverbraucherzeugnis; **~-year pressure** Jahresultimobeanspruchung.

endanger *(v.)* gefährden, in Gefahr bringen;
~ a country öffentliche Sicherheit gefährden; **~ the maintenance of public order** Aufrechterhaltung der öffentlichen Sicherheit gefährden; **~ an undertaking** Unternehmen gefährden.

endangerment Gefährdung.

endeavo(u)r Bestreben, Bestrebung, Bemühung, Anstrengung;
~ to please one's wife Bemühungen seine Frau zufriedenzustellen;
~ (v.) sich anstrengen (bemühen), streben nach;
to make every ~ alles Erdenkliche versuchen; **to use one's best ~s** sich voll einsetzen.

ended *(fiscal year)* abgelaufen;
~ or determined durch Zeitablauf oder Kündigung beendet.

ending Beendigung, Abschluß, *(letter)* Schlußform;
~ a tenancy Pachtbeendigung;
~ date Schlußtermin.

endless ununterbrochen, unaufhörlich;
~ belt endloses Band; **~ chain** Paternoster; **~ discussions** endlose Diskussionen; **~ resources** unerschöpfliche Mittel; **~ space** unendlicher Weltraum; **to be an ~ talker** ohne Punkt und Komma reden; **~ task** nicht enden wollende Arbeit.

endorsable durch Indossament übertragbar, girierbar, indossierbar;
~ instrument Orderpapier.

endorse *(v.)* vermerken, *(bill)* durch Indossament begeben, indossieren, girieren, begeben, mit Giro versehen, *(confirm)* bestätigen, bekräftigen;
~ s. one's action jds. Handlungsweise zustimmen; **~ a bill of exchange** Wechsel indossieren (durch Indossament übertragen); **~ back a bill of exchange** Wechsel durch Indossament zurückübertragen; **~ in blank** blanko indossieren; **~ a candidate** Kandidaten unterstützen; **~ a decision** Entscheidung billigen; **~ s. th. on a document** etw. auf der Rückseite einer Urkunde vermerken; **~ in full** voll girieren; **~ generally** blanko girieren; **~ a motorist's driving licence** *(Br.)* Strafe auf dem Führerschein vermerken; **~ an opinion** sich einer Ansicht anschließen; **~ over** übertragen, zedieren; **~ specially** an eine bestimmte Person (voll) indossieren; **~ the terms of a settlement** Vertragsbedingungen gutheißen; **~ s. one's views** sich jds. Entscheidung anschließen.

endorsed mit Giro versehen, giriert;
~ in blank blanko giriert;
~ bond durch Wechsel verstärkte Obligation.

endorsee Girat, Indossat[ar], Wechselübernehmer;
~ of a check *(US)* *(cheque, Br.)* Scheckinhaber.

endorsement Giro, Indossament, *(confirmation)* Zustimmung, Bestätigung, Genehmigung, Billigung, *(insurance)* [Versicherungs]nachtrag, Zusatz[klausel], *(political backing)* politische Unterstützung, *(writing on back of document)* rückseitiger Vermerk;
transferable by ~ indossabel, girierbar;
accommodation ~ Gefälligkeitsindossament; **blank ~** Blankoindossament, -giro; **conditional ~** beschränktes Indossament; **fiduciary ~** fiduziarisches Indossament; **forged ~** Girofälschung; **general ~** Vollindossament; **irregular ~** in der Form abweichendes Indossament; **partial ~** Teilindossament; **post ~** Nachindossament; **qualified (restrictive) ~** beschränktes Giro (Indossament), Rektagiro, -indossament; **special ~** Vollgiro, -indossament;
~ made out to bearer Inhaberindossament; **~ in blank** Blankoindossament, -giro; **~ on a document** Vermerk auf einer Urkunde; **~ of a driving** *(Br.)* *(driver's, US)* licence Strafvermerk auf dem Führerschein, Führerscheineintragung, Eintragung auf dem Führerschein; **~ in full** Vollgiro; **~ of an opinion** Bekräftigung einer Ansicht; **~ on insurance policy** Versicherungs-, Policennachtrag, -vermerk; **~ in procuration** Prokuraindossament; **~ supra protest** Indossament nach Protest; **~ without recourse** Giro ohne Verbindlichkeit; **~ of a writ** abgekürzte Klagebegründung;

to place an ~ indossieren, girieren; **to transfer by ~** durch Giro übertragen;
~ book *(insurance company)* Nachtragsbuch; **~ liabilities** Indossamentenverbindlichkeiten; **~ provision** Giroprovision.
endorser Girant, Indossant, Begebender, *(guarantor of bill)* Aval-, Wechselbürge;
accommodation ~ Girant aus Gefälligkeit; **preceding (previous, prior) ~** Vor[der]mann; **qualified ~** Girant ohne Verbindlichkeit; **subsequent ~** Nachmann, Hintermann, nachfolgender Indossant, späterer Girant;
~'s liability Wechselverpflichtung, Regreßpflicht.
endow *(v.)* dotieren, ausstatten, *(dower)* Witwenteil einräumen, *(furnish with money)* stiften, gründen, subventionieren;
~ a bed in hospital Krankenhausbett stiften; **~ with capital** mit Kapital ausstatten; **~ a fund** Fonds dotieren; **~ a prince with an ap(p)anage** Fürsten abfinden; **~ a professorship** Professur gründen.
endowed ausgestattet, dotiert;
to be ~ by nature with great talents hervorragend begabt sein;
to be ~ with ample financial means finanziell reichlich ausgestattet sein;
~ charity milde [wohltätige] Stiftung; **richly ~ foundation** reich dotierte Stiftung; **~ institution** Stiftung; **~ school** Stifterschule.
endowment Stiftung, Pfründe, Dotation, *(of dower)* Ausstattung, Aussteuer, *(gift)* Anlage, Begabung, Talent;
~s Stiftungsgelder, -fonds;
charitable ~ mildtätige Stiftung; **genetic ~** Erbmasse; **natural ~s** natürliche Begabung;
~ with capital Kapitalausstattung;
[pure] ~ assurance *(Br.)* Versicherung auf den Erlebensfall, Aussteuer-, Versorgungs-, Erlebensversicherung; **~ assurance scheme** *(Br.)* Aussteuerversicherungsplan; **with profits ~ basis** *(insurance)* mit Gewinnbeteiligung; **to post an ~ bond** Versicherungsbürgschaft hinterlegen; **~ contract** Versicherungsvertrag zur Sicherstellung der Ausbildung; **~ fund** Mittel einer Stiftung, Stiftungsvermögen, -gelder; **~ insurance** *(US)* Versicherung auf den Erlebensfall, Aussteuerversicherung; **~ period** Erlebenszeit; **~ policy** Lebensversicherungspolice.
endproduct Endprodukt, Grenzprodukt, -erzeugnis.
endue *(v.)* **s. o. with an office** j. mit einem Amt bekleiden.
endurance Ausdauer, *(airplane)* Maximalflugzeit;
beyond (past) ~ unerträglich;
to come to the end of one's ~ am Ende seiner Belastbarkeit anlangen; **to have great powers of ~** über große Widerstandskräfte verfügen;
~ flight Dauerflug; **~ limit** *(material)* Ermüdungsgrenze; **~ strength** Widerstandsfähigkeit; **~ test** Zuverlässigkeitsprobe.
endure *(v.)* aushalten, ertragen, durchmachen;
~ misfortune Unglück ertragen.
enduring dauernd, beständig;
~ peace dauerhafter Frieden.
enemy Feind, Gegner, Gegenspieler, Widersacher, *(hostile forces)* Feindstaat, -kräfte;
clear of the ~ feindfrei;
alien ~ Angehöriger eines Feindstaates, feindlicher Ausländer; **declared ~** entschiedener Gegner; **public ~** *(US)* Volksfeind; **sworn ~** Todfeind;
~ of the people Staats-, Volksfeind;
to abandon a position to the ~ Stellung dem Feind überlassen; **to aid and comfort the ~** Feindbegünstigung begehen; **to be one's own ~ (nobody's ~ but one's own)** sich selbst im Wege stehen; **to be an ~ of discipline** disziplinfeindlich sein; **to drive the ~ out of the country** Feind aus dem Lande vertreiben; **to fall into the hands of the ~** in Feindesgewalt fallen; **to feel for the ~** Feindfühlung nehmen; **to go over to the ~** zum Gegner übergehen (überlaufen), ins feindliche Lager übergehen; **to make an ~ of s. o.** sich j. zum Feind machen; **to range o. s. with the ~** mit dem Feind halten; **to soften an ~** Gegner zermürben;
~ action Kriegs-, Feindeinwirkung; **~ aircraft** Feindflugzeug; **~ alien** feindlicher Ausländer; **~ camp** gegnerisches Lager; **~-controlled property** vom Feind beschlagnahmtes Vermögen; **~ country** feindliches Ausland, Feindesland; **~ flag** feindliche Flagge; **~ fleet** feindliche Flotte; **~ forces** Feindkräfte; **~ government** feindliche Regierung; **~ incursion** *(plane)* Feindeinflug; **~ line** feindliche Front; **~ movements** Feindbewegungen; **~ number one** Hauptfeind; **~ property** Feindvermögen; **~ propaganda** Feindpropaganda; **~-occupied territory** Feindgebiet; **~ ship** feindliches Schiff; **~ troops** feindliche Truppen; **~ world** feindliche Umwelt.
energetic tätig, energisch, tatkräftig, voll Tatendrang;
~ gap Energielücke.

energy Energie, Tatkraft, Kraftaufwand, *(el.)* Energie;
electrical ~ elektrische Energie;
to be full of ~ voller Tatkraft sein; **to lack ~** keine Energie haben, kraftlos sein; **to throw all one's ~ into a task** sich mit ganzem Nachdruck auf eine Aufgabe konzentrieren;
~ area Energiesektor; **~ bill** Energiegesetzvorlage; **~ business** Energiewirtschaft; **~ committee** Energieausschuß; **~ conservation** Einschränkung des Energieverbrauchs, Energieeinsparung; **~ conservation measures** Maßnahmen zur Energieeinsparung; **~ conservation program(me)** Energiesparprogramm; **~ consumption** Energieverbrauch; **to reduce ~ consumption** Energieverbrauch einschränken, Energie sparen; **~ crisis** Energiekrise; **~ economy** Energiewirtschaft; **~ equivalent** Steinkohleneinheit; **~ export** Energieexport; **~ field** Energiewesen, -gebiet; **~ output** Energieproduktion; **~ overseer** Energieberater; **~ package** Bündel energiepolitischer Maßnahmen; **~ policy** Energiepolitik; **~ potential** Energiepotential; **~ production** Energieproduktion; **~ resources** Energiequellen; **~ savings** Einsparungen auf dem Energiesektor; **~-saving potential** Energieeinsparungsmöglichkeiten; **~-saving program(me)** Programm für Energieeinsparung; **⩎ Secretary** *(Br.)* Staatssekretär im Energieministerium, Energieminister; **~ sector** Energiebereich; **~ shortage** Energieknappheit; **~ source** Energiequelle; **electrical ~ supply** Energieversorgung; **~ supply company** Energieversorgungsgesellschaft.
enface *(v.)* aufdrücken;
~ a draft with the words ... auf die Vorderseite des Wechsels die Worte ... setzen.
enfaced paper *(Br.)* Schuldschein der indischen Regierung.
enfacement Aufschrift, Aufdruck, Vermerk, *(bill of exchange)* Wechselvermerk auf der Vorderseite.
enfeoffment Belehnung.
enforce *(v.)* erzwingen, durchsetzen, durchführen, geltendmachen, *(compel observance of)* vollziehen, vollstrecken, zur Geltung bringen;
~ the blockade Blockade durchführen; **~ one's claims by suit** seine Ansprüche gerichtlich geltend machen; **~ a contract** Vertragsleistung erzwingen, aus einem Vertrag klagen; **~ a course of action upon s. o.** Aktionen gegen j. durchführen; **~ a demand** Forderung durchsetzen; **~ discipline** für Disziplin sorgen; **~ a judgment by execution** Urteil vollstrecken lassen, Vollstreckung eines Urteils betreiben; **~ a law** einem Gesetz Geltung verschaffen, Gesetz durchführen; **~ a lien upon s. one's property** Pfandverwertung vornehmen; **~ a monopoly** Monopol ausüben; **~ an order** gerichtliche Entscheidung vollstrecken; **~ payment by legal proceedings** Zahlung gerichtlich beitreiben; **~ one's rights** seine Rechte gerichtlich durchsetzen; **~ [respect of] a rule** Einhaltung einer Bestimmung erzwingen; **~ one's will upon s. o.** jem. seinen Willen aufzwingen.
enforceability Erzwingbarkeit, Einklagbarkeit.
enforceable *(executory)* einklagbar, vollstreckbar, [rechtlich] betreibbar;
provisionally ~ vorläufig vollstreckbar;
~ by legal proceedings vor Gericht durchsetzbar;
to be ~ at law einklagbar sein.
enforced | judgment vollstreckter Titel; **~ liquidation** Zwangsvergleich; **~ sale** Zwangsverkauf.
enforcement Geltendmachung, Durchsetzung, Vollstreckung, Vollziehung;
law ~ Anwendung eines Gesetzes, Gesetzesvollzug;
~ of foreign awards Durchsetzung ausländischer Schiedssprüche; **~ of a claim** Geltendmachung einer Forderung; **~ through a court** gerichtliche Durchsetzung; **~ of conditions** Durchsetzung von Bedingungen; **~ of a judgment** Zwangs-, Urteilsvollstreckung; **strict ~ of a new law** strenge Anwendung eines neuen Gesetzes; **~ of a lien** Pfandverwertung; **~ of monopoly** Monopolausübung; **~ of an order** Vollstreckung einer gerichtlichen Verfügung; **collective ~ of resale prices** Preisbindung der zweiten Hand; **~ of a right** Durchsetzung eines Rechtsanspruchs; **~ of supports** *(US)* Vollstreckung von Unterhaltsansprüchen; **~ by writ** Zwangsvollstreckung;
~ action *(law of nations)* Zwangsaktion, -maßnahme; **~ agency** Vollstreckungs-, Durchführungsorgan, -behörde; **~ measures** Zwangsmaßnahmen; **~ officer** Vollstreckungsbeamter; **~ order** Vollstreckungsbefehl, -klausel; **~ proceedings** *(foreign judgment)* Vollstreckungsverfahren; **~ provisions** Durchführungsbestimmungen.
enforcing authority Vollzugsbehörde.
enfranchise *(v.)* Wahlrecht (Bürgerrecht) verleihen;
~ s. o. j. zur Wahl zulassen; **~ a city** einer Stadt politische Rechte gewähren.

enfranchised stimmberechtigt;
 to be ~ Wahlrecht erhalten.
enfranchisement Wahlrechtsverleihung, Verleihung des Bürgerrechtes;
 ~ of leaseholds *(Br.)* Pachtlandbefreiung.
engage *(v.) (bind by contract)* verpflichten, *(book)* [Platz] bestellen, belegen, *(employ)* einstellen, anstellen, beschäftigen, engagieren, in Dienst (unter Vertrag) nehmen, *(mar.)* anheuern, *(mil.)* angreifen, *(pledge o. s.)* sich verpflichten (binden);
 ~ o. s. sich verloben; **~ o. s. to s. o.** bei jem. in Dienst treten; **~ actively** sich aktiv betätigen; **~ in an activity** Tätigkeit aufnehmen; **~ in business** Geschäftsmann werden; **~ the clutch** Kupplung einlassen; **~ s. o. in [a] conversation** j. in ein Gespräch verwickeln (ziehen); **~ o. s. for dinner** sich zum Abendessen verabreden, Abendeinladung annehmen; **~ in discussion** sich an der Diskussion beteiligen; **~ the freight** Fracht bedingen; **~ a gear** Gang einlegen (einschalten); **~ in** sich beschäftigen (befassen) mit, sich einlassen auf; **~ an interpreter** [als] Dolmetscher engagieren; **~ a lawyer** Rechtsanwalt beauftragen; **~ in a line of business** in einer Branche tätig werden; **~ the line for 20 minutes** Telefon zwanzig Minuten blockieren; **~ in negotiations** in Verhandlungen eintreten; **~ to manage a business** sich für die Geschäftsführung zur Verfügung stellen; **~ the master** *(ship)* Schiffer anstellen; **~ men** Leute anheuern; **~ in politics** sich auf die Politik werfen; **~ o. s. to provide capital** sich zur Bereitstellung des Kapitals verpflichten; **~ rooms at a hotel** Zimmer in einem Hotel bestellen; **~ seamen** Seeleute anmustern (anheuern); **~ o. s. for the season** sich für die Saison verpflichten; **~ seats at the theater** Theaterplätze reservieren; **~ s. o. as secretary** j. als Sekretär[in] engagieren; **~ a servant again** Hausangestellte wieder einstellen; **~ the services of a lawyer** Dienste eines Anwalts in Anspruch nehmen; **~ a stateroom** Prominentensuite bestellen; **~ a taxi** sich ein Taxi nehmen; **~ in a wide variety of lending activities** gesamten Fächer des Darlehnsgeschäfts zur Verfügung stellen; **~ for three years** [sich] für drei Jahre verpflichten.
engaged *(betrothed)* verlobt, *(booked)* belegt, besetzt, *(bound)* verpflichtet, versagt, *(employed)* beschäftigt, *(table)* reserviert;
 ~! Nummer besetzt!;
 ~ in aviation *(insurance)* während des Fluges, in der Luft; **~ in commerce** als Kaufmann tätig; **~ in employment** in Ausübung einer Arbeitnehmertätigkeit;
 to be ~ in business geschäftlich tätig sein; **to be fully ~** voll ausgebucht sein; **to be ~ in politics** sich mit Politik befassen; **to be ~ on the preparations for departure** mit den Abreisevorbereitungen beschäftigt sein; **to be ~ in writing a novel** an einem Roman arbeiten (sitzen);
 ~ couple Brautleute, Verlobte; **~ signal (tone)** Besetztzeichen.
engagement *(appointment)* Verabredung, *(betrothal)* Verlobung, *(contract)* Abmachung, *(employment)* Stellung, Stelle, Ein-, Anstellung, Beschäftigung, Engagement, *(mil.)* Gefecht, Kampfhandlung, Feindberührung, *(obligation)* Verpflichtung, Verbindlichkeit, *(railway)* betriebliche Belastung, *(theater)* Engagement;
 owing to previous ~ aufgrund vorheriger Verabredung (Verpflichtungen); **without ~** freibleibend, ohne Gewähr, unverbindlich;
 ~s Zahlungsverpflichtungen;
 bear ~s *(stock exchange)* Engagements der Baissepartei; **blank ~** Blankoauftrag; **bull ~s** Engagements der Haussepartei; **current ~s** laufende Verpflichtungen; **foreign ~** Auslandsengagement; **fresh ~** Neueinstellung; **implied ~** stillschweigende Verpflichtung; **mutual ~s** gegenseitige Bindungen; **obligatory ~** bindende Verpflichtung; **public ~s** Verpflichtungen der Öffentlichkeit gegenüber; **social ~s** gesellschaftliche Verpflichtungen;
 ~ of the first gear Einschaltung des ersten Ganges; **~ of seamen** Anmusterung von Seeleuten;
 to be under an ~ to s. o. jem. gegenüber vertraglich verpflichtet sein; **to break an ~** Vereinbarung nicht einhalten; **to break off an ~** Geschäft rückgängig machen; **to bring about an ~** *(mil.)* Gefecht herbeiführen; **to carry out one's ~s** seinen Verbindlichkeiten nachkommen; **to enter into an ~** Verabredung treffen; **to have an ~ for the evening** abends verabredet (besetzt) sein; **to have found a lucrative ~** gut bezahlten Posten gefunden haben; **to have numerous ~s for next week** vollbesetzten Terminkalender haben; **to have a previous ~** anderweitig versagt sein; **to keep one's ~s** seine Verpflichtungen einhalten; **to liquidate an ~** Position lösen; **to meet one's ~s** seinen Verbindlichkeiten nachkommen, seine Schulden bezahlen; **to withdraw from one's ~s** sich seinen Verpflichtungen entziehen;

~ announcement Verlobungsanzeige; **~ book** Terminkalender, Merkbuch; **~ celebration** Verlobungsfeier; **~ ring** Verlobungsring.
engaging einnehmend, anziehend, fesselnd;
 to have an ~ manner verbindliches Wesen haben.
engine Maschine, Motor, *(railway)* Lokomotive;
 cut-off ~ abgestellter Motor; **dead ~** ausgefallener Motor; **fire ~** Feuerspritze; **junketed ~** frisierter Motor; **light ~** alleinfahrende Lokomotive; **noisy ~** lautgehender Motor; **oil ~** Ölmotor; **pumping ~** Pumpe; **ramjet ~** Staustrahltriebwerk; **second ~** Hilfslokomotive; **standing ~** stillstehende Lokomotive; **steam ~** Dampfmaschine; **special tuned ~** frisierter Motor; **two-stroke ~** Zweitaktmotor; **turbojet ~** Turbostrahltriebwerk;
 to harm the ~ sich nachteilig auf den Motor auswirken; **to kill (stall) the ~** Motor abwürgen; **to set an ~ going** Maschine (Motor) in Gang bringen; **to soup up an ~** *(US sl.)* Motor frisieren; **to start the ~** Motor anlassen;
 ~ block Motorblock; **~ bonnet** *(Br.)* Motorhaube; **~ breakdown** Motorstörung, -panne; **~ builder** Maschinenbauer; **~ building** Maschinenbau; **~ capacity** Motorleistung; **~ car** Maschinengondel; **~ combat battalion** *(mil.)* leichtes Pionierbatallion; **~ company** *(US)* Löschzug; **~-driven** maschinell betrieben; **~ driver** Maschinist, *(railway)* Lokomotivführer; **~ fitter** Maschinenschlosser; **~ house** Maschinenhaus; **~ life** Lebensdauer eines Motors; **~ oil** Maschinenöl; **~ output** Maschinenleistung; **~ park** *(mil.)* Pionierpark; **~ room** Maschinensaal, *(ship)* Maschinenanlage; **~ set** Maschinensatz; **~ shaft** Motorwelle; **~ shed** Lokomotivschuppen; **~ tender** Lokomotivanhänger; **~ trouble** Maschinenschaden, Motorpanne, -defekt; **~ works** Maschinenfabrik; **~ worker** Arbeiter in einer Maschinenfabrik; **~ yard** Lokomotivhof.
engineer Ingenieur, Techniker, *(efficient manager)* geschickter Unternehmer, Organisator, *(mil.)* Pionier, *(railroad, US)* Lokomotivführer;
 administrative ~ Verwaltungsingenieur; **agricultural ~** Agraringenieur; **bridge and road ~** Brücken- und Straßenbauingenieur; **business ~** *(US)* selbständiger Betriebsberater; **chief ~** technischer Betriebsleiter; **civil ~** Tiefbauingenieur; **construction ~** Maschinenbauingenieur; **consultant (consulting) ~** beratender Ingenieur; **electric-lighting ~** Beleuchtungstechniker; **electrical ~** Elektroingenieur; **erecting ~** Konstrukteur; **industrial (operation, production, plant) ~** Betriebsingenieur; **managing ~** technischer Leiter; **mechanical ~** Maschinenbauer; **mining ~** Bergbauingenieur; **naval ~** Schiffsingenieur; **project ~** Entwurfsingenieur, ausführender Ingenieur; **salesman ~** technischer Verkäufer, Vertriebsingenieur; **sanitary ~** Ingenieur für Sanitäranlagen; **superintendent ~** Fabrikationsleiter, Betriebsingenieur; **water-power ~** Wasserwirtschaftsingenieur;
 chief ~ in charge of production Produktionsleiter; **chief ~ of the plot** Haupt der Verschwörung; **chief ~ of a ship** Schiffsingenieur;
 ~ *(v.)* als Ingenieur tätig sein, *(construct)* [Straßen] bauen, anlegen, *(fig.)* steuern, deichseln, bewerkstelligen;
 ~ a bill through Congress Gesetzentwurf durch den Kongreß bringen; **~ a party** Leiter einer Reisegesellschaft (Reiseleiter) sein; **~ a plan** deichseln; **~ a plot** Verschwörung anzetteln, Kopf einer Verschwörung sein; **~ a project** Projekt durchführen; **~ a resolution** Resolution durchbringen; **~ a scheme** Coup landen;
 ~'s department [etwa] Baudezernat; **~ manager** Wirtschaftsingenieur.
engineering Ingenieurwissenschaft, Technik, Maschinenbau, *(fig.)* Tricks, Intrigenspiel, Manipulation, *(mil.)* Pionierwesen;
 administrative ~ Verwaltungstechnik; **aeronautical ~** Flugzeugbau; **automobile (automotive, US) ~** Kraftfahrzeugbau; **chemical ~** Industriechemie; **civil ~** Tiefbau; **commercial ~** Warentechnik; **constructional ~** Maschinenbau; **design ~** Anlagenkonstruktion; **electrical ~** Elektrotechnik; **highway ~** Straßenbau; **industrial ~** Fertigungssteuerung, Betriebstechnik; **irrigation ~** Bewässerungstechnik; **light ~** feinmechanische Industrie; **major ~** großer technischer Aufwand; **management ~** *(US)* Betriebstechnik; **marine ~** Schiffsmaschinenbau; **mechanical ~** Maschinenbau; **mining ~** Bergbau; **municipal ~** Erstellung kommunaler Anlagen; **process ~** Verfahrenstechnik; **production ~** Fertigungstechnik; **project ~** Abwicklungstechnik; **railway ~** Eisenbahnbau; **sanitary ~** Bau sanitärer Anlagen;
 ~ *(a.)* technisch;
 ~ charges Konstruktionskosten; **~ college** technische Hochschule; **~ contract** Tiefbauauftrag; **~ department** technisches

Büro; ~ **design** Konstruktionsentwurf; ~ **development** technische Entwicklung; ~ **facilities** technische Einrichtungen; ~ **fair** technische Messe; ~ **feat** bedeutende technische Leistung; ~ **firm** Konstruktionsfirma; ~ **force** technischer Stab; ~ **industry** Maschinenindustrie; ~ **journal** technische Zeitschrift; ~ **operations** Tiefbauarbeiten; ~ **release** technische Freigabe; ~ **school** Maschinenbauschule; ~ **science** Ingenieurwissenschaft; ~ **shop** Konstruktionsfirma; ~ **specialist** Fachingenieur; ~ **staff** technischer Stab; ~ **standards** technische Normvorschriften; ~ **works** Maschinenfabrik; ~ **worker** Tiefbauarbeiter.

enginehouse Lokomotivschuppen, *(fire brigade)* Spritzenhaus.

engineman Maschinenwärter.

English, Queen's korrektes Englisch;
  in plain ~ unverblümt;
  ~ **basement** *(US)* hohes Kellergeschoß; ~ **bond** *(masonry)* Blockverband; ~ **finish** matt satiniertes Druckpapier; ~ **speaking nations** englischsprechende Völker.

Englishman, true-born richtiger Engländer.

engrave *(v.)* [ein]gravieren, ätzen.

engraver Graveur;
  ~ **on copper** Kupferstecher;
  ~**'s proof** *(US)* Klischeeabzug.

engraving Gravur, Gravierarbeit, Klischee[herstellung], *(block)* Klischee;
  full-tone ~ Volltonätzung; **half-tone ~** Halbtonätzung;
  ~ **in copper** Kupfergravur, -ätzung;
  ~ **establishment** Gravieranstalt; ~ **plate** Druckplatte; ~ **process** Ätzverfahren.

engross *(v.)* ins Reine schreiben, in Reinschrift erstellen, ausfertigen, *(monopolize)* Markt monopolisieren;
  ~ **s. one's whole attention** jds. volle Aufmerksamkeit beanspruchen; ~ **the conversation** Unterhaltung an sich reißen, Gesprächsrunde beherrschen; ~ **a document** Urkunde aufsetzen; ~ **s. one's time** jds. Zeit in Anspruch nehmen.

engrossed in Anspruch genommen, usurpiert, *(market)* monopolisiert;
  to be ~ in one's work ganz in seiner Arbeit versunken sein;
  ~ **bill** gedruckte Parlamentsvorlage.

engrosser Verfasser einer Urkunde, Urkundsbeamter, *(monopolist)* Monopolist.

engrossing Großeinkauf;
  ~ **hand** Kanzleischrift.

engrossment Abschreiben von Urkunden, Reinschrift, Urkundenausfertigung, *(monopoly)* Monopolisierung.

enhance *(v.)* ausweiten, wertvoller werden, *(prices)* in die Höhe treiben;
  ~ **in price** im Preis steigen; ~ **the prices of goods** Warenpreise erhöhen; ~ **the value of land** Grundstückswerte steigen lassen.

enhancement Steigerung, Erhöhung, Ausweitung, Verteuerung;
  ~ **in prices** Preissteigerung; ~ **in value** Wertsteigerung.

enjoin *(v.)* *(direct)* anweisen, vorschreiben, *(prohibit by judicial order)* gerichtlich untersagen;
  ~ **a conduct upon s. o.** jem. sein Verhalten vorschreiben; ~ **a duty on s. o.** jem. eine Pflicht auferlegen; ~ **on s. o. the necessity for economy** jem. Sparsamkeit vorschreiben; ~ **silence** Stillschweigen auferlegen.

enjoy *(v.)* sich erfreuen, genießen, nutznießen;
  ~ **o. s.** sich gut amüsieren; ~ **a break from work for half an hour** sich eine halbstündige Arbeitspause genehmigen; ~ **credit** Kredit genießen; ~ **a fortune** vermögend sein; ~ **good health** sich guter Gesundheit erfreuen; ~ **one's holiday** seine Ferien genießen; ~ **income** Einkünfte zur Verfügung haben; ~ **a privilege** bevorrechtigt sein; ~ **a good reputation** guten Ruf haben; ~ **one's responsibility** Verantwortungsfreude zeigen; ~ **a right** Recht genießen.

enjoyment Genuß, Nutzung, *(law)* Rechtsausübung;
  adverse ~ Grunddienstbarkeitsausübung; **quiet ~** ungestörter Besitz;
  ~ **of a good income** Verfügung über ein gutes Einkommen; ~ **of land** Grundstücksnutzung; ~ **of property** Besitz-, Eigentumsausübung; ~ **of a right** Ausübung eines Nutzungsrechtes; ~ **of work** Arbeitsfreude;
  to allow the lessee quiet ~ dem Pächter ungestörten Pachtgenuß gestatten; **to be in ~ of good health** sich eines guten Gesundheitszustandes erfreuen; **to live only for ~** nur dem Vergnügen leben.

enlarge *(v.)* ausweiten, ausdehnen, erweitern, vergrößern, verbreitern;
  ~ **the area of operations** Aktionsbereich ausdehnen; ~ **the local area of operations** örtlichen Geschäftsbereich ausweiten; ~ **bail** Sicherheitsleistung (Kaution) erhöhen; ~ **one's business** seinen Betrieb (sein Geschäft) vergrößern (ausdehnen); ~ **one's circle of acquaintances** seinen Bekanntenkreis erweitern; ~ **one's fortune** sein Vermögen vermehren; ~ **one's house** sein Haus vergrößern; ~ **the scope of an invention** Umfang einer Erfindung erweitern; ~ **one's knowledge** seine Kenntnisse erweitern; ~ **the mind** Gesichtskreis erweitern; ~ **the payment of a bill** Wechsel prolongieren; ~ **a photograph** Fotografie vergrößern; ~ **one's possessions** seine Besitzungen vergrößern; ~ **one's premises** anbauen, ausbauen; ~ **proportionally** proportional vergrößern; ~ **a recognizance** Schuldscheinsumme erhöhen; ~ **upon a subject** sich über etw. verbreiten; ~ **one's view** seinen Gesichtskreis erweitern; ~ **one's vocabulary** seinen Wortschatz bereichern; ~ **well** *(photo)* sich gut vergrößern lassen.

enlarged erweitert, vermehrt;
  ~ **acceptance** *(bill)* bedingte Annahme; ~ **committee** erweiterter Ausschuß; ~ **copy** Vergrößerung; ~ **edition** erweiterte Ausgabe; ~ **and revised edition** vermehrte und verbesserte Auflage; ~ **negative** Negativvergrößerung.

enlargement Ausweitung, Vergrößerung, Erweiterung, *(photo)* vergrößerte Aufnahme, Vergrößerung, *(print.)* Vergrößerung;
  ~**s** *(building)* Erweiterungsbauten, Anbau;
  ~ **to a building** Anbau; ~ **of business** Geschäftsausdehnung; ~ **of capacity** Kapazitätserweiterung; ~ **of the mind** Erweiterung des Gesichtskreises.

enlarger Vergrößerungsapparat.

enlarging statute Erweiterungsgesetz.

enlighten *(v.)* aufklären;
  ~ **s. o. on a subject** j. mit einem Thema näher vertraut machen.

enlightened aufgeklärt, vorurteilsfrei.

enlightenment Aufklärung;
  to work for the ~ of mankind sich für die Aufklärung der Menschen einsetzen.

enlist *(v./i.)* *(engage for service)* anstellen, einstellen, engagieren, *(expert)* heranziehen, *(mil.)* zum Heeresdienst einberufen, *(v./t.)* sich stellen;
  ~ **the aid of the court** Hilfe des Gerichts in Anspruch nehmen; ~ **in the army** Soldat werden; ~ **for the army in a war** sich freiwillig zum Kriegsdienst melden; ~ **s. o. for a good cause** j. für eine gute Sache gewinnen; ~ **s. o. in an enterprise** j. für ein Geschäft interessieren; ~ **s. one's help for the Red Cross** sich jds. Mitarbeit für das Rote Kreuz versichern; ~ **public interest in a matter** Öffentlichkeit für etw. interessieren; ~ **a mechanic** Mechaniker einstellen; ~ **photography for educational purposes** sich der Photographie als Bildungsmittel bedienen; ~ **a recruit** Rekruten einziehen; ~ **the service of s. o.** sich jds. Dienste versichern, j. zur Unterstützung heranziehen; ~ **soldiers** Soldaten werben; ~ **s. o. in support of a cause** j. für eine Sache gewinnen; ~ **as a volunteer** als Freiwilligen einstellen, *(v./i.)* sich als Freiwilligen werben lassen.

enlisted | in the army rekrutiert, [ein]gezogen;
  ~ **grade** *(US)* Unteroffiziers-, Mannschaftsdienstgrad; ~ **man** *(US)* Einberufener, Gezogener, Soldat; ~ **men** *(US)* Unteroffiziere und Mannschaften; ~ **specialist** *(US)* Dienstverpflichteter, Wehrersatzsoldat.

enlistee *(US)* Gezogener, Einberufener.

enlistment *(engagement)* Anwerbung, Einstellung, Engagierung, *(mil.)* Rekrutierung, Anwerbung, *(written document)* Anwerbezettel;
  Foreign Ƥ Act *(Br.)* Rekrutierungsgesetz für Ausländer; ~ **allowance** *(US)* Treueprämie; ~ **order** *(US)* Stellungsbefehl.

enliven *(v.)* beleben, ankurbeln, aufpulvern;
  ~ **business** Konjunktur ankurbeln; ~ **a discussion** Diskussion beleben; ~ **a party** geselliges Beisammensein in Schwung bringen.

enlivening | of business Geschäftsbelebung, Konjunkturankurbelung; ~ **strains of music** aufpulvernde Musikfetzen.

ennoble *(v.)* nobilitieren, in den Adelsstand erheben.

ennoblement Erhebung in den Adelsstand, Nobilitierung.

enough genügend, genug, ausreichend;
  safe ~ durchaus sicher; ~ **and to spare** mehr als genug, übergenug;
  to have ~ to live on auskömmliche Existenz (genug zu leben) haben.

enounce *(v.)* bekanntmachen.

enquiry → inquiry.

enrich *(v.)* anreichern, bereichern, *(supply with ornament)* ausschmücken, reich verzieren;
  ~ **one's mind** geistiger Gewinn sein; ~ **o. s. from public office** sich öffentlich bereichern.

enriched, to be ~ by a legacy durch ein Vermächtnis profitieren;
  ~ **pile** angereicherter Meiler.

enrichment Bereicherung, *(agric.)* Anreicherung, *(building)* Ausschmückung, Verzierung;
  unjust ~ ungerechtfertigte Bereicherung.

enrol(l) *(v.) (mil.)* ausheben, rekrutieren, mustern, *(register in a list)* Namen in einer Liste eintragen, [als Mitglied] eintragen, registrieren, verzeichnen, *(register on rolls of court)* gerichtlich registrieren, *(make fair copy, US)* Reinschrift herstellen, *(seaman)* anmustern, anheuern, *(university)* in die Matrikel eintragen, sich immatrikulieren, Semester belegen;
  ~ o. s. sich einschreiben; ~ **for a course of lectures** Vorlesung (Kolleg) belegen; ~ **a law** Gesetz registrieren; ~ **s. o. as a member of a society** j. als Vereinsmitglied aufnehmen; ~ **men in the army** Rekruten ausheben; ~ **o. s. in a society** einer Gesellschaft als Mitglied beitreten; ~ **as subscriber** sich in eine Subskribentenliste eintragen; ~ **workers** Arbeitskräfte einstellen.

enrolled | bill formgerecht erlassenes Gesetz; ~ **law agent** *(Scot. law)* zugelassener Rechtsbeistand; ~ **member** *(pol.)* eingetragenes Mitglied; ~ **tonnage** *(US)* eingetragene Tonnage.

enrollee Kursusteilnehmer, *(applicant)* Antragsteller.

enrolling officer Musterungsoffizier.

enrol(l)ment Anmeldung, Einschreibung, Eintragung, *(mil.)* Anwerbung, Rekrutierung, Konskription, *(recording officially)* [amtliche] Registrierung, *(school)* Einschulung, *(seaman)* Anmusterung, *(society)* Beitrittserklärung, *(university, US)* Immatrikulation, Semesterbelegung;
  ~ **of vessels** *(US)* Schiffsregistrierung, -eintragung; ~ **fee** Einschreibegebühr; ~ **office** Registratur; ~ **rate** Prozentsatz eines voll in der Ausbildung befindlichen Jahrgangs; ~ **records** Anmeldungsunterlagen.

ensemble Gesamtwirkung, *(theater)* Ensemble.

ensign Abzeichen, *(flag)* [Schiffs]flagge, Nationalflagge, *(US mil.)* Fahnenjunker;
  ~ **hoisted union down** Notflagge; **red** ~ *(Br.)* Flagge der Handelsmarine; **white** ~ *(Br.)* Kriegsflagge;
  ~**s of authority** Machtsymbole;
  to dip one's ~ Fahne senken.

ensilage Silo-, Grünfutter.

ensnare *(v.)* verstricken, umgarnen.

ensnarled in a plot in ein Komplott (eine Verschwörung) verstrickt.

ensue *(v.) (from)* sich ergeben [aus];
  ~ **from a misunderstanding** aus einem Mißverständnis entstehen.

ensuing consequences sich ergebende Folgen.

ensure *(v.)* gewährleisten, garantieren, Erfolg verbürgen;
  ~ **s. o. enough to live on** jds. Lebensunterhalt sicherstellen; ~ **s. o. a good post** jem. eine gute Stellung versprechen; ~ **the smooth settlement of a business** für glatte Erledigung einer Angelegenheit sorgen.

entail Erb-, Stamm-, Familiengut, Majorat, Fideikommiß, nicht frei vererbliches Grundstück, *(in office)* vorherbestimmte Nachfolgeordnung;
  quasi ~ fideikommißähnliche Bestimmung;
  ~ *(v.)* zur Folge haben, *(law)* Grundbesitz in Fideikommiß umwandeln, als Fideikommiß vererben;
  ~ **upon s. o.** jem. auferlegen; ~ **an estate on s. o.** Gut auf j. als Fideikommiß vererben; ~ **great expenses** große Ausgaben verursachen (zur Folge haben);
  to bar *(dock)* **an** ~ Erblehn veräußern; **to break the** ~ Fideikommiß auflösen, Unveräußerlichkeit eines Erblehns aufheben; **to cut off the** ~ Erbfolge aufheben; **to found an** ~ Fideikommiß konstruieren, Majorat errichten (stiften).

entailed | estate Familiengut, Majorat, Fideikommiß; ~ **interest** erbmäßig festgelegter Besitz; ~ **property** unveräußerlicher Grundbesitz.

entailment Fideikommißerrichtung.

entangle *(v.)* verwickeln, in Verlegenheit bringen;
  ~ **o. s. in s. th.** sich in eine Sache verwickeln; ~ **o. s. with moneylenders** sich mit Geldleihern einlassen.

entangled verwickelt, umgarnt, in Verlegenheit;
  ~ **in a shady business** in ein anrüchiges Geschäft verwickelt;
  to become ~ in kompromittierende Beziehungen geraten.

entanglement Verwicklung, Verstrickung;
  barbed-wire ~ Drahtverhau; **external** ~**s** außenpolitische Verwicklungen;
  to have an ~ **with a woman** Liaison unterhalten; **to unravel an** ~ Verwirrung lösen.

entente Entente, Bündnis.

enter *(v.) (become a party)* eingehen, kontrahieren, unterzeichnen, *(book)* eintragen, [Posten] aufführen, [ver]buchen, *(copyright)* Verlagsrecht wahren, *(customs)* deklarieren, *(data*

processing) eingeben, tasten, *(law, US)* Rechtsansprüche geltend machen, *(mil.)* einrücken, *(place to account)* in Rechnung stellen, *(register)* eintragen, registrieren, *(ship)* anmelden, einklarieren;
  ~ **an action against s. o.** Klage gegen j. erheben; ~ **into an agreement** Vertrag [ab]schließen (eingehen); ~ **into a binding agreement** bindende Verpflichtung eingehen; ~ **into an alliance** Bündnis eingehen, sich liieren; ~ **[up] an amount in the expenditure** Betrag als Ausgabe verbuchen; ~ **an appearance** sich [auf eine Klage] einlassen; ~ **the army** Soldat werden; ~ **an arrangement** auf einen Vergleich eingehen; ~ **into a bargain** Geschäft (Handel) abschließen; ~ **battle** Schlacht beginnen; ~ **a bill short** Wechsel Eingang vorbehalten gutschreiben; ~ **into a bond** Schuldverschreibung ausstellen; ~ **in the books** in die Bücher eintragen; ~ **a book in a catalog(ue)** Buch katalogisieren; ~ **a book at Stationers' Company** *(Br.)* Buch gegen unerlaubten Nachdruck registrieren lassen; ~ **into business** ins Geschäftsleben treten; ~ **into business relations** neue Geschäftsverbindungen anknüpfen; ~ **into s. one's calculations** von jem. schon einkalkuliert sein; ~ **upon a career** Laufbahn einschlagen; ~ **upon a new career** Berufswechsel vornehmen; ~ **a cargo** Schiffsladung deklarieren; ~ **a caveat** Einspruch einlegen; ~ **into the channels of distribution** *(customs)* in den freien Verkehr überführen; ~ **a child as a pupil** Schüler anmelden; ~ **a city** *(mil.)* in eine Stadt einrücken (eindringen); ~ **a college** in ein College eintreten; ~ **into competition** in Wettbewerb treten; ~ **in conformity** gleichlautend buchen; ~ **for consumption** Abfertigung zum freien Verkehr beantragen; ~ **into a contract** Vertrag schließen; ~ **into a conversation** sich an einer Unterhaltung beteiligen; ~ **a country** einreisen, Land betreten; ~ **a country illegally** sich in ein Land einschmuggeln; ~ **on the credit side** im Haben buchen; ~ **to the credit of s. o.** jem. gutschreiben; ~ **goods at the customhouse** beim Zoll angeben, zollamtlich deklarieren; ~ **to the debit of s. o.** jem. in Rechnung stellen; ~ **in the debit side** ins Soll buchen; ~ **a deed** Vertrag registrieren lassen; ~ **a deposition on the record** Zeugenaussage ins Protokoll aufnehmen; ~ **into details** sich mit den Einzelheiten beschäftigen; ~ **a document into the record** Urkunde zu den Prozeßakten einreichen; ~ **upon one's duties** seinen Dienst antreten; ~ **upon new duties** neuen Aufgabenbereich übernehmen; ~ **into engagements** Verbindlichkeiten (Verpflichtungen) eingehen; ~ **o. s. for an examination** sich zur Teilnahme an einer Prüfung [an]melden; ~ **into s. one's feelings** mit jem. sympathisieren; ~ **goods** Waren zur Verzollung deklarieren; ~ **goods for consumption** Waren zum freien Verkehr einführen; ~ **a harbo(u)r** in einen Hafen einlaufen; ~ **a hospital** Krankenhaus aufsuchen; ~ **upon an inheritance** *(US)* Erbschaft antreten; ~ **inwards** Fracht eines Schiffes bei der Einfahrt zollamtlich anmelden; ~ **an item in the ledger** Posten ins Hauptbuch eintragen (verbuchen); ~ **a judgment** Urteil erlassen (fällen); ~ **land** *(US)* sich als Grundstückserwerber eintragen lassen; ~ **public life** in der Öffentlichkeit bekannt werden; ~ **into an official list** amtlich registrieren; ~ **a ministry** Ministerium übernehmen; ~ **into the minutes** in ein Protokoll aufnehmen; ~ **one's name** sich einzeichnen (eintragen); ~ **one's name on a list** seinen Namen in eine Liste eintragen; ~ **one's name in the visitors' book** seinen Namen ins Gästebuch schreiben, Anmeldeformular ausfüllen; ~ **the navy** zur Marine gehen; ~ **into negotiations with s. o.** in Verhandlungen mit jem. eintreten; ~ **in one's notebook** in sein Notizbuch eintragen, notieren; ~ **into particulars** auf Einzelheiten eingehen; ~ **into pecuniary obligations** finanzielle Verpflichtungen übernehmen; ~ **upon an office** Amt antreten; ~ **an order** Verfügung erlassen; ~ **s. one's order** jds. Auftrag buchen; ~ **outwards** Fracht eines Schiffes bei der Ausfahrt anmelden; ~ **into a partnership** sich assoziieren, Gesellschaftsverhältnis eingehen, als Teilhaber eintreten; ~ **upon a new phase** in ein neues Stadium treten; ~ **a plea** Einrede erheben; ~ **the port** in den Hafen einlaufen; ~ **a profession** Beruf ergreifen; ~ **the legal profession** Jurist werden; ~ **upon a property** Erbschaft antreten; ~ **a proposal** Vorschlag einreichen (einbringen); ~ **protest** formell Protest erheben, Verwahrung einlegen; ~ **into one's own recognizance** persönlich die Garantie für etw. übernehmen; ~ **on the record** ins Protokoll aufnehmen; ~ **an estate at the Register of Deeds Office** Grundstück im Grundbuchamt eintragen; ~ **into relations** Beziehungen aufnehmen (anknüpfen); ~ **into the rights of a creditor** Gläubigerstellung erhalten; ~ **a room** Zimmer betreten; ~ **satisfaction** Hypothek im Grundbuch löschen lassen; ~ **a boy at a school** Jungen auf die Warteliste einer Schule setzen lassen; ~ **a seaman on the ship's books** Seemann anheuern; ~ **into s. one's service** in jds. Dienste eintreten; ~ **a**

ship inwards Einfuhrzoll für ein Schiff deklarieren; ~ **short** zu wenig deklarieren; ~ **a society** einer Gesellschaft beitreten; ~ **a student at a university** Studenten immatrikulieren; ~ **a suit** einer Prozeßpartei beitreten; ~ **upon another term of office** neue Amtsperiode beginnen; ~ **the territory** Hoheitsgebiet betreten; ~ **a train** in einen Zug einsteigen; ~ **into a treaty of peace** sich an einem Friedensvertrag beteiligen; ~ **a tunnel** in einen Tunnel einfahren; ~ **a university** Universität beziehen; ~ **up** *(bookkeeping)* Posten aufnotieren, [Buchungen] vervollständigen; ~ **upon** *(office)* Stellung antreten; ~ **the war** in den Krieg eintreten; ~ **a writ** Vorladung anordnen.

enterable eintragungs-, buchungsfähig.

entering Eintritt, *(registration)* Einschreibung, Eintragung, [Ver]buchung, Registrierung, *(student)* Zulassung, Immatrikulation;

~ **an agreement (a contract)** Eingehen eines Vertrages, Vertragsabschluß; ~ **of appearance** Klageeinlassung; ~ **upon a career** Beginn einer Laufbahn; ~ **of a country into the war** Kriegseintritt eines Landes; ~ **upon one's duties** Diensteintritt; ~ **a judgment** Urteilsregistrierung; ~ **and leaving the country** Ein- und Ausreise; ~ **office** Amtsantritt; ~ **upon service** Dienstantritt; ~ **short** Gutschrift „Eingang vorbehalten"; ~ **the station** Einfahrt in den Bahnhof; ~ **up** Eintragung, [Ver]buchung; ~ **clerk** Buchhalter.

enterprise *(business)* Unternehmen, -nehmung, Geschäft, [Gewerbe]betrieb, *(spirit of ~)* Unternehmungsgeist, *(venture)* Spekulation, Wagnis, Unternehmen;

agricultural ~ landwirtschaftlicher Betrieb; **business** ~ geschäftliches (gewerbliches) Unternehmen, Geschäftsunternehmung, -betrieb, Handels-, Gewerbebetrieb; **commercial** ~ Handelsbetrieb, -unternehmen; **wholesale commercial** ~ Großhandelsfirma; **communal** ~ Kommunal-, Gemeindebetrieb; **cooperative** ~ genossenschaftlicher Betrieb, Genossenschaftsunternehmen; **corporate** ~ Unternehmen der gewerblichen Wirtschaft, Kapitalgesellschaft; **corporative** ~ genossenschaftliche Unternehmung, Genossenschaftsunternehmen; **domestic** ~ Inlandsunternehmen; **family-owned** ~ Familienbetrieb; **financial** ~ Finanzierungsinstitut; **foreign** ~ ausländisches Unternehmen; **free** ~ freies Unternehmertum; **government [-owned]** ~ Betrieb der öffentlichen Hand, Regie-, Staatsbetrieb, Staatsunternehmen; **heavy-industrial** ~ Unternehmen der Schwerindustrie; **high-cost** ~ kapitalintensives Unternehmen; **individual** ~ Einzelfirma; **industrial** ~ Industrieunternehmen, gewerblicher Betrieb, Gewerbebetrieb; **joint** ~ Zusammenschluß zu einem gemeinsamen Zweck, Gemeinschaftsunternehmen; **large[scale]** ~ Großbetrieb; **manufacturing** ~ Herstellungs-, Fertigungs-, Gewerbe-, Fabrikationsbetrieb; **medium-sized established privately owned** ~ anerkannter mittelgroßer Privatbetrieb; **mixed** ~ gemischtwirtschaftliches Unternehmen; **monopolistic** ~ Monopolunternehmen; **municipal** ~ städtisches Unternehmen, Kommunal-, Gemeindebetrieb; **nationalized** ~ verstaatlichtes Unternehmen; **nonagricultural** ~ nicht landwirtschaftlicher Betrieb; **nonprofit** ~ gemeinnütziger Betrieb, gemeinnütziges Unternehmen; **private (privately owned)** ~ Privatwirtschaft, -unternehmen, -betrieb; **productive** ~ ertragreiches Unternehmen; **profitable** ~ einträglicher Betrieb, gewinnbringendes Unternehmen; **promising** ~ vielversprechendes Unternehmen; **prosperous** ~ erfolgreiches Unternehmen, gutgehender Betrieb; **publicly-owned** ~ gemeinwirtschaftliches Unternehmen, Unternehmen der öffentlichen Hand; **public-service** ~ *(US)* gemeinnütziger Betrieb; **semi-public** ~ gemischtwirtschaftliches Unternehmen; **single** ~ Einzelunternehmen; **solid** ~ solides Geschäft; **speculative** ~ gewagte (riskante) Unternehmung, Spekulationsfirma, -geschäft; **state** ~ staatlicher Betrieb, Regiebetrieb, Betrieb der öffentlichen Hand; **subsidiary** ~ Tochtergesellschaft; **trading** ~ Unternehmen der gewerblichen Wirtschaft, Handelsunternehmen; **unincorporated** ~ nicht registriertes Gewerbe; **wildcat** ~ riskantes Unternehmen, Schwindelunternehmen;

to accrue to an ~ einem Unternehmen zufließen; **to be a man of great** ~ sehr unternehmerisch eingestellt sein; **to carry on an** ~ Unternehmen betreiben; **to have large sums in an** ~ große Beträge in einem Unternehmen investiert haben; **to invest one's money in a business** ~ sich an einem Unternehmen beteiligen; **to launch an** ~ neues Unternehmen starten; **to milk an** ~ Unternehmen ausbeuten; **to participate financially in an** ~ sich an einem Unternehmen finanziell beteiligen; **to prefer private** ~ **to government control** der Privatwirtschaft vor der Zwangswirtschaft den Vorzug geben;

~ **accounting** Firmenbuchführung; ~ **affiliation** Unternehmensverflechtung; ~ **cost** Selbstkosten; **free-** ~ **economy** freie

Unternehmerwirtschaft; **free-** ~ **industry** freies Unternehmertum; ~ **liability** Unternehmenshaftung; **free-** ~ **system** freie Marktwirtschaft (Unternehmerwirtschaft); ~ **value** Firmenwert.

enterprising wagemutig, unternehmungslustig, unternehmend, unternehmerisch;

~ **business firm** unternehmerisch eingestellte Firma; ~ **personality** unternehmerisch eingestellte Persönlichkeit.

entertain *(v.)* unterhalten, ergötzen, *(receive)* Gäste haben, gastlich aufnehmen, Gastfreundschaft üben, gastliches Haus führen, bewirten;

~ **o. s.** sich unterhalten (amüsieren); ~ **an action** Klage für zuständig erklären; ~ **business connections** Geschäftsbeziehungen unterhalten; ~ **company** Gäste haben; ~ **customers** Kunden bewirten; ~ **a great deal** Geselligkeit pflegen, großes Haus führen; ~ **doubts** Zweifel hegen; ~ **a high esteem for s. o.** j. hoch verehren; ~ **a kindly feeling for s. o.** jem. freundschaftliche Gefühle entgegenbringen; ~ **friends to dinner** Freunde zum Abendessen eingeladen haben; ~ **guests over the weekend** am Wochenende Logierbesuch haben; ~ **an idea** sich mit einem Gedanken tragen; ~ **hostile intentions regarding s. o.** feindlich gegenüber jem. eingestellt sein; ~ **an offer** Angebot in Betracht ziehen; ~ **a proposal** Vorschlag in Erwägung ziehen; ~ **a risk** Risiko übernehmen; ~ **charitable sentiments** Wohltätigkeitsüberlegungen anstellen.

entertainer Gastgeber, Wirt, *(artist)* Unterhaltungskünstler, Unterhalter.

entertaining | an overseas customer Bewirtung eines Geschäftsfreundes aus Übersee;

~ **expenses** Bewirtungskosten; ~ **pursuit** unterhaltsame Freizeitbeschäftigung.

entertainment Unterhaltung, Vergnügung, *(hospitable provision)* Gastfreundschaft, gastliche Aufnahme, Bewirtung, gesellschaftliche Veranstaltung, Repräsentation, *(performance)* Aufführung, Vorstellung, Unterhaltungsstück;

business ~ Bewirtung von Geschäftsfreunden;

~ **of customers** Kundenbewirtung;

~ **advertising** Werbung der Vergnügungsbranche; ~ **allowance** Aufwandentschädigung; ~ **committee** Vergnügungsausschuß; ~ **complex** Unterhaltungszentrum; ~ **duty** *(Br.)* Vergnügungssteuer; ~ **expenses** Bewirtungsspesen, Aufwandsentschädigung; ~ **field** Vergnügungsindustrie; ~ **film** Unterhaltungsfilm; ~ **industry** Vergnügungsindustrie, -branche; ~ **president** Leiter der Unterhaltungsabteilung; ~ **schedule** Unterhaltungsprogramm; ~ **show** Unterhaltungsprogramm; ~ **spot** Unterhaltungslokal, Vergnügungsetablissement; ~ **tax** Lustbarkeits-, Vergnügungssteuer; ~ **world** Vergnügungsindustrie, -wesen.

enthrone *(v.)* inthronisieren.

enthronement Inthronisierung, Thronbesteigung.

enthusiasm | for work Arbeitslust, -freude;

to radiate ~ Begeisterung hervorrufen.

enthusiast for (about) politics politisch Interessierter.

enthusiastic welcome Ovation.

entice *(v.)* anlocken, verlocken, verleihen;

~ **away customers** Kunden von jem. abziehen (abspenstig machen, abwerben); ~ **s. o. from his duty** jem. von der Arbeit ablenken;

~ **servants** Angestellte abwerben.

enticement [Kunden]anlockung, *(servants)* Abwerbung;

~ **of employees** *(Br.)* Abwerbung von Arbeitskräften.

entire *(philat.)* Ganzsache;

~ *(a.)* ganz, vollkommen, -zählig, -ständig, komplett, uneingeschränkt, *(law)* ungeteilt;

to reproduce an article ~ Artikel vollständig abdrucken;

~ **amount** voller Betrag; ~ **animal** lebendes Tier; ~ **affection** aufrichtige Zuneigung; ~ **balance of my estate** mein Restvermögen; ~ **benefit** alleinige Vergünstigung; ~ **confidence** volles Vertrauen; ~ **contract** ungeteilter Vertrag; ~ **control** absolute Kontrolle; ~ **day** Kalendertag; ~ **income** Gesamteinkommen; ~ **interest** Gesamtanteil; ~ **loss of sight** vollständiger Verlust des Sehvermögens; **to be** ~ **master of one's property** völlig frei über sein Vermögen verfügen können; ~ **need** Gesamtbedarf; ~ **population** Gesamtbevölkerung; ~ **proceeds** Gesamtertrag; ~ **structure** Bauwerk als Ganzes; ~ **tenancy** Pachtung in einer Hand; ~ **use** alleinige Verfügung, alleinige Nutzung, Nutzung.

entirely without understanding geschäftsunfähig.

entireties, to have land by gemeinsamen [ungeteilten] Grundbesitz mit jem. haben.

entirety Gesamtheit, Ungeteiltheit;

~ **of contract** *(fire insurance)* Vertragseinheit; ~ **of estate** Gesamtbesitz;

to examine a question in its ~ Frage in ihrem ganzen Zusammenhang prüfen; **to relate a story in its** ~ Geschichte vollständig wiedergeben.

entitle *(v.)* berechtigen, Anspruch geben, *(give name)* betiteln, benennen, mit einem Titel anreden;
~ **the holder to purchase** Inhaber zum Bezug berechtigen.

entitled betitelt, *(authorized)* berechtigt, ermächtigt;
not ~ nicht berechtigt, unberechtigt; **party** ~ Berechtigter; ~ **to act** handlungsfähig; ~ **to alimony** *(wife)* unterhaltsberechtigt; ~ **to asylum** asylberechtigt; ~ **to attend** teilnahmeberechtigt; ~ **to benefit** unterstützungsberechtigt; ~ **to capital allowance** *(Br.)* abschreibungsberechtigt; ~ **to a claim** forderungsberechtigt; ~ **to damages** zum Schadenersatz berechtigt; ~ **to develop** erschließungsfähig; ~ **to dispose** verfügungsberechtigt; ~ **to a dividend** dividendenberechtigt; ~ **to draw** bezugsberechtigt; ~ **to inherit** erbberechtigt; ~ **to maintenance** *(child)* unterhaltsberechtigt; ~ **to a pension** pensionsberechtigt, ruhegehaltsfähig; ~ **to sign** zeichnungs-, unterschriftsberechtigt; ~ **to sue** aktiv legitimiert; ~ **to vote** wahlberechtigt;
to be ~ to s. th. [Rechts]anspruch (Anrecht) auf etw. haben; **to be ~ to do s. th.** berechtigt (qualifiziert) sein für etw; **to be ~ to draw a pension** zum Bezug einer Pension berechtigt (pensionsberechtigt) sein; **to be ~ to a redundancy payment** soziale Abfindungsansprüche haben; **to be ~ to rescission** anfechtungsberechtigt sein; **to be ~ to speak and to vote** volles Stimmrecht haben.

entitlement Berechtigung, Betitelung;
family passage and baggage ~ Anspruch auf Erstattung der Kosten für die Anreise der Familienmitglieder und das Gepäck;
~ **to benefit** Unterstützungsberechtigung; ~ **to commutation** Ablösungsrecht, -berechtigung; ~ **to holidays** Urlaubsanspruch.

entity Wesen, Gebilde, *(agency)* Dienststelle, Organisation, Behörde;
economic ~ wirtschaftliche Einheit; **legal** ~ Rechtspersönlichkeit, -träger; **politico-economic** ~ wirtschaftpolitische Einheit; **smooth[ly] running** ~ reibungslos laufender Betrieb; ~ **accounting** Konzernbuchführung.

entomb *(v.)* begraben, beerdigen.

entombment Begräbnis, Beerdigung.

entonrage Umgebung, Begleitung.

entrain *(v.)* Truppen verladen.

entrainer Truppenverlader.

entraining *(air)* Einströmen, *(mil.)* Truppenverladung.

entrainment Truppenverladung.

entrance Eintritt, Eintreten, *(admission fee)* Eintrittsgebühr, Eingang, Zugang, *(door, gateway)* Einfahrt, Haustür, Tor, *(harbo(u)r)* Hafeneinfahrt, *(liberty to enter)* Eintrittserlaubnis, -recht, Zulassung, Zutritt, Zugang, *(theater)* Auftritt;
at one's ~ **upon office** beim Amtsantritt;
backstair ~ Hintertreppeneingang; **carriage** ~ Einfahrt; **front** ~ Vordereingang; **main** ~ Haupteingang; **no** ~! Eintritt verboten!, Betreten verboten!; **private** ~ Separateingang; **secret** ~ geheimer Zugang; **side** ~ Nebeneingang;
~ **by air** Einflug; **no** ~ **except on business** Unbefugten ist der Eintritt verboten; ~ **to a cave** Zugang zu einer Höhle; ~ **into college** Eintritt ins College; ~ **upon one's duties** Dienstantritt; ~ **to the harbo(u)r** Hafeneinfahrt; ~ **upon an inheritance** *(US)* Erbschaftsantritt; ~ **upon ministerial office** Antritt (Übernahme) eines Kabinettspostens; ~ **of a ship into a port** Einlaufen eines Schiffes in den Hafen; ~ **to a school** Schuleintritt;
to force one's ~ **into a house** sich gewaltsam Eingang in ein Haus verschaffen; **to have free** ~ freien Eintritt haben; **to make one's** ~ eintreten; **to pay one's** ~ sein Eintrittsgeld (seine Aufnahmegebühr) [be]zahlen; **to use the back** ~ Hintereingang benutzen;
~ **buoy** Einfahrtsboje; ~ **certificate** Aufnahmebescheinigung; ~ **complex** Eingangskomplex; ~ **door** Eingangstür; ~ **duty** Einfuhr-, Eingangszoll; ~ **examination** Aufnahmeprüfung; **to pass the** ~ **examination** Aufnahmeprüfung bestehen; ~ **fee** Eintrittspreis, Zulassungs-, Aufnahmegebühr; ~ **hall** Eingangshalle, Flur; ~ **lock** Einfahrtsschleuse; ~ **money** Eintrittsgeld; ~ **rate** Anfangslohn; ~ **region** Einzugsgebiet; ~ **requirements** Eintritts-, Zulassungs-, Aufnahmevoraussetzungen; ~ **stake** Startgeld; ~ **visa** Einreisevisum; ~ **zone** Einflugzone.

entrancement Verzückung, Bezauberung.

entrant Bewerber, Teilnehmer;
new ~**s onto the labo(u)r market** neu in den Arbeitsprozeß eintretende Kräfte.

entrap *(v.)* **into buying s. th.** zum Kauf von etw. verführen; ~ **into contradicting o. s.** sich in Widersprüche verwickeln; ~ **a criminal** Verbrecher zu einer strafbaren Handlung provozieren.

entrapment *(criminal law)* Provozierung zu einer strafbaren Handlung.

entreat *(v.)* dringend bitten, ersuchen;
~ **a favo(u)r of s. o.** Vergünstigung von jem. erbitten; ~ **s. one's indulgence** j. um Nachsicht bitten; ~ **s. o. to show mercy** j. um Gnade anflehen.

entreaty dringende Bitte, Ersuchen.

entrée Ein-, Zutritt, *(France)* Zwischengericht, *(US)* Hauptgericht;
to have the ~ **of a house** Zutritt zu einem Haus haben.

entrench *(v.)* | **o. s.** sich verbarrikadieren; ~ **in a constitution** verfassungsrechtlich schützen; ~ **upon s. one's rights** jds. Rechte schmälern.

entrenched fest etabliert;
to be solidly ~ *(custom)* fest verankert sein;
~ **clauses** eingearbeitete Schutzklauseln.

entrenchment Einbau verfassungsrechtlicher Schutzklauseln, *(encroachment)* Schmälerung, *(mil.)* Verschanzung, Schanzarbeiten.

entrepôt Waren-, Zollniederlage, Lager-, Stapelplatz, Transitlager, Speicher,*(commercial center)* Handelszentrum;
~ **trade** Wiederausfuhrhandel.

entrepreneur Unternehmer, *(theater)* freier Produzent;
independent ~ unabhängiger Unternehmer; **individual** ~ Einzelunternehmer; **private** ~ Privatunternehmer; **trendy** ~ modebewußter Unternehmer;
~ **functions** unternehmerische Funktionen.

entrepreneurial unternehmerisch;
~ **ability** unternehmerische Eigenschaften; ~ **activity** Unternehmertätigkeit; ~ **association** Unternehmerverband; ~ **business venture** unternehmerisches Risiko; ~ **capacity** Unternehmereigenschaften; ~ **class** Unternehmertum, -klasse; ~ **company** Unternehmerbetrieb; **proven** ~ **flair in planning, negotiating and managing new business** unternehmerisches Geschick bei der Planung, Aushandlung und Durchführung von Neuabschlüssen; ~ **function** Unternehmerfunktion; ~ **group** Unternehmergruppe; ~ **income** Bruttoeinkommen aus Unternehmertätigkeit, Unternehmereinkommen; ~ **instinct** unternehmerische Begabung; ~ **management** Unternehmertum, Betriebsführung durch den Eigentümer; ~ **organization** Unternehmerorganisation; ~ **problem** Führungsproblem; ~ **profit** Unternehmergewinn; ~ **qualities** Unternehmereigenschaften; ~ **risk** Unternehmerrisiko; ~ **skill** Unternehmereigenschaft; ~ **spirit** Unternehmungsgeist; **to be gifted with** ~ **spirit** unternehmerisch veranlagt sein; ~ **system** Unternehmerwirtschaft.

entrepreneurship *(US)* Unternehmerschaft, -tum.

entresol Zwischengeschoß.

entruck *(v.)* *(mil.)* auf Lastkraftwagen verladen.

entrust *(v.)* anvertrauen;
~ **the care of s. th. to s. o.** jem. etw. zu treuen Händen überlassen; ~ **a matter to one's correspondent** Angelegenheit seinem Geschäftsfreund übertragen; ~ **an employee with executive functions** Angestellten mit Führungsaufgaben betrauen; ~ **s. o. with the sale** jem. den Verkauf übertragen; ~ **s. o. with a sum** jem. einen Geldbetrag anvertrauen; ~ **s. o. with a task** j. mit einer Aufgabe betrauen.

entry *(coming into possession)* Besitzergreifung, -antritt, *(criminal)* Einbruch, *(customs)* [Zoll]deklaration, -anmeldung, Einklarierung, *(dictionary)* Stichwort, Eintrag, *(door)* Eingangstür, *(entrance)* Eintritt, Einzug, Einfahrt, *(entrance hall)* Flur, Vestibül, Vorhalle, Vorsaal, *(into the harbo(u)r)* Einlaufen, *(item)* Eintrag, Vermerk, *(item in accounts)* [Buchungs]posten, gebuchter Posten, Buchung, Rechnungsposten, *(mil.)* Einrücken, *(mining)* Hauptförderstrecke, *(money)* Eingang von Geldern, *(recording)* [Protokoll]eintragung, Vormerkung, *(river)* Flußmündung, *(sport)* Meldung, *(theater)* Auftritt;
as per ~ laut Eingang; **upon** ~ nach Eingang;
actual ~ tatsächliche Inbesitznahme; **adjusting (adjustment)** [**journal**] ~ Berichtigungsbuchung; **author** ~ Autoreneintrag; **bookkeeping** ~ Buchung; **bookkeeping-type** ~ buchungsähnlicher Posten; **catchword** ~ Stichwortaufführung; **closing** ~ abschließende Buchung; **compound** ~ Sammelbuchung; **correcting** ~ Berichtigungsbuchung; **corresponding** ~ entsprechende Buchung; **counter** ~ Gegenbuchung; **credit** ~ Kreditposten, Gutschrift; **cross** ~ Storno-, Umbuchung; **customhouse** ~ Zolldeklaration, -erklärung; **debit** ~ Debetposten, Lastschrift; **dictionary** ~ Wörterbucheintragung; **double**

~ doppelte Buchführung; **erroneous** ~ irrtümliche Buchung; **false** ~ falscher Eintrag; **forcible** ~ verbotenes Eindringen, Eigenmacht; **fraudulent** ~ Falschbuchung; **homestead** ~ *(US)* Registrierung eines Siedlungsanspruchs; **illegal** ~ ungesetzmäßige Einreise; **intervening** ~ Zwischeneintragung; ~ **inwards** Einfuhrdeklaration; **no** ~ verbotener Eingang, *(form)* Fehlanzeige; **open** ~ Inbesitznahme vor Zeugen; **opening** ~ Eröffnungsbuchung; **original** ~ Grundbuchung; ~ **outwards** Zollausgangserklärung, Ausfuhrdeklaration; **periodic** ~ periodische Eintragung; **post** ~ späterer Eintrag; **preemption** ~ Eintragung eines Vorkaufsrechtes; **prime** ~ *(customs)* vorläufige Zolldeklaration; **reversing** ~ Stornobuchung; **short** ~ Unterdeklaration; **single** ~ einfache Buchführung; **subject** ~ Stichworteintragung; **subsequent** ~ nachträgliche Buchung; **supplementary** ~ Nachtragsbuchung; **suspense** ~ transitorische (vorläufige) Buchung; **title** ~ Titelaufführung; **transfer** ~ Übertragungsvermerk; **unauthorized** ~ Unbefugten ist der Eintritt verboten; **unlawful** ~ *(of estate)* unrechtmäßige Inbesitznahme; **winning** ~ *(newspaper competition)* richtige Lösung; **wrong** ~ falsche (unrichtige) Buchung, Falschbuchung; ~ **of appearance** Protokollierung der Einlassung des Beklagten;~ **under bond** Einfuhr unter Zollvormerkschein; **forcible** ~ **of a building** Hausfriedensbruch; ~ **of cause for trial** Beantragung eines Verhandlungstermins; ~ **into the Common Market** Beitritt zum Gemeinsamen Markt; ~ **in conformity** gleichlautende Buchung; ~ **of a country into world politics** Erscheinen eines Landes auf der weltpolitischen Bühne; ~ **for consumption** Abfertigungsantrag zum freien Verkehr; ~ **in regular course of business** Routinebuchung einer Geschäftstransaktion; ~ **at the customhouse** Zolldeklaration, -erklärung; ~ **and departure of a vessel** Ein- und Auslaufen eines Schiffes; ~ **into a diary** Tagebucheintragung; ~ **into a dictionary** Wörterbucheintragung; ~ **into effect** *(of ordinances)* Inkrafttreten; ~ **into the forces** [etwa] Eintritt in die Bundeswehr; ~ **of goods** Wareneinfuhr; ~ **for duty-free goods** Deklaration für zollfreie Waren; ~ **for home use** Zolldeklaration für den Eigenverbrauch; ~ **of judgment** Gerichtsprotokoll; ~ **for marriage in speech** Herausgabeanspruch wegen nichteingehaltenen Heiratsversprechens; ~ **in the minute book** Protokollierung, Protokollaufnahme; ~ **into the minutes** Aufnahme in das Protokoll; ~ **of the month** Monatsanfang; ~ **upon office** Amtsantritt; ~ **in the passbook** Sparbucheintragung; ~ **made in (on) the register** *(Br.)* Register-, Grundbucheintragung; ~ **on the roll** Parteierklärung vor Gericht; ~ **of satisfaction** *(mortgage)* Löschungsvermerk; ~ **into service** Dienstantritt; ~ **closed to traffic** gesperrt für Fahrzeuge aller Art; ~ **for home use** Einfuhrdeklaration für Inlandsverbrauch; ~ **into the war** Kriegseintritt; ~ **for warehousing** Transiterklärung, Einlagerungsschein [für Zollspeicher]; **to adjust an** ~ Buchung berichtigen (abändern); **to alter an** ~ Buchung abändern; **to cancel an** ~ Posten streichen, Eintragung löschen; **to carry over an** ~ Posten übertragen; **to check an** ~ Posten abstreichen; **to effect an** ~ Buchung vornehmen; **to make an** ~ eintragen, [ver]buchen; **to make an** ~ **against s. o.** j. belasten; **to make a false (wrong)** ~ irrtümlich buchen; **to make an official** amtlich registrieren; **to make an** ~ **of goods** Waren beim Zoll deklarieren; **to make one's** ~ *(theater)* auftreten; **to make a supplementary** ~ nachträgliche Buchung vornehmen; **to make an** ~ **in the register** ins Register eintragen; **to make a triumphal** ~ **into a town** wie ein Triumphator in eine Stadt einziehen; **to make an** ~ **of a transaction** Vorgang (Geschäftstransaktion) verbuchen; **to pass an** ~ **in conformity** gleichlautend buchen; **to post each** ~ **singly** jeden Posten einzeln übertragen; **to reciprocate an** ~ **on the books** gleichlautend buchen; **to rectify an** ~ Buchung abändern; **to reverse an** ~ rückbuchen, Buchung stornieren; **to strike out a wrong** ~ falsche Buchung streichen; **to tick off an** ~ Posten abstreichen; ~ **age** Eintrittsalter; ~ **bond** Zollkaution; ~ **book** Eintragungsbuch; **(double) single** ~ **bookkeeping** (doppelte) einfache Buchführung; ~ **card** Eintrittskarte; ~ **charge** Buchungsgebühr; ~ **clerk** *(mercantile house)* Buchhalter; ~ **door** Eingangs-, Haustür; ~ **fee** *(sport)* Nenngebühr, -geld, -schein; ~ **form** *(contest)* Anmeldeformular, -schein ~ **hall** Vorsaal, Halle; ~ **inwards** Einfuhrdeklaration; ~ **job** Anfangsstellung; ~ **keyboard** Eingabetastatur; ~ **list** Melde-, Teilnehmerliste; ~ **money** Eintrittsgeld; ~ **negotiations** Beitrittsverhandlungen; ~ **outwards** Ausfuhrdeklaration; ~ **permit** Einreiseerlaubnis, -genehmigung; ~ **and registry permit** Zuzugsgenehmigung; ~ **point** Eintrittsdatum; ~ **talks** Beitrittsverhandlungen; ~ **tax** Passagesteuer; ~ **visa** Einreisevisum; ~ **word** *(library)* Stichwort.
entryman *(US)* Ansiedler.
entryway Zugang, Zufahrt.

enumerate *(v.)* *(count)* zählen, *(name on by one)* [einzeln] aufzählen;
~ **items** Posten spezifizieren.
enumerated | catalog(ue) Zuständigkeitskatalog; ~ **powers** *(US)* gesetzlich festgelegte Machtbefugnisse.
enumerating the population Bevölkerungszählung.
enumeration *(counting)* Zählung, *(detailed mention)* [Einzel]aufzählung;
~ **process** Volkszählungsverfahren.
enumerator Zähler.
enunciate *(v.)* **one's words clearly** seine Worte klar formulieren.
enure *(v.)* *(act)* in Kraft treten, gelten.
envelop *(v.)* einwickeln, *(mil.)* umfassen.
envelope Briefumschlag, -hülle, -kuvert, Kuvert, *(airship)* Ballonhülle;
adhesive ~ gummierter Briefumschlag; **close-lined** ~ Leinenumschlag; **commercial** ~ Geschäftsumschlag; **embossed** ~ Briefumschlag mit aufgedruckter Briefmarke; **pay** ~ Lohntüte; **penalty** ~ *(US)* Briefumschlag frei durch Ablösung; **postage** ~ abgestempelter Briefumschlag; **sealed** ~ versiegelter Umschlag; **self-addressed** ~ addressierter Rückumschlag, Freiumschlag; **stamped** ~ frankierter Briefumschlag, Freiumschlag; **unsealed** ~ offener Briefumschlag; **window** ~ Fenster[brief]umschlag;
~**s to match** passende Kuverts;
~ *(v.)* *(letter)* kuvertieren, mit einem Umschlag versehen, in einen Briefumschlag legen;
to stick down an ~ Kuvert verschließen (zukleben);
~ **addresser** Adressiermaschine; ~ **addressing** Adressieren von Briefumschlägen; **pay** ~ **advertising** Lohntütenwerbung; ~ **addressing agency** Briefversandunternehmer; ~ **corner card** Absenderangabe [beim Geschäftsbriefumschlag]; ~ **file** Karton für Briefumschläge; ~ **moistener** Anfeuchter; ~ **opener** Brieföffner; ~ **sealer** Petschaft, Briefverschlußmaschine; ~ **stuffer** Briefbeileger, Postwurfsendung.
enveloping | attack *(mil.)* Umfassungsangriff; ~ **machine** Kuvertiermaschine.
envelopment *(mil.)* Umfassungsangriff, -manöver.
environed with forests von Wald umgeben.
environment Umgebung, äußere Lebensbedingungen, Beziehungsfeld, [wirtschaftliche] Umwelt, Umwelterscheinungen;
home ~ häusliche Umgebung; **hostile** ~ feindliche Umwelt; **moral** ~ Milieu; **natural** ~ natürliche Umwelt; **physical** ~ gegenständliche Umwelt; **social** ~ soziale Umwelt;
to adjust o. s. to one's ~ sich seiner Umgebung anpassen; **to be kind to the** ~ umweltfreundlich sein;
~ **area** Umwelt-, Stadtrandgebiet; ~ **chamber** Klimakammer; ~**-conscious** umweltbewußt; ~ **control** Umweltkontrolle; ~ **damage** Beeinträchtigung der Umwelt; **heredity-versus-debate** Diskusion über die Bedeutung von Erbanlagen und Umwelt; ~ **demonstration** Umweltdemonstration; ♀ **Department** Umweltbehörde; ~ **forecast** Umweltprognose; ~ **man** Fachmann für Umweltfragen; ~ **minister** Minister für Umweltfragen; ~ **planning** Umweltplanung, -gestaltung; ~ **pollution** Umweltverschmutzung; ~ **problems** Umweltschutzprobleme; ~ **science** Umweltwissenschaft; ♀ **Secretary** *(Br.)* Minister für Umweltfragen; ~ **thinking** Umweltdenken.
environmental umweltbedingt, umgebend;
~ **agency** Behörde für Umweltschutzfragen; ~ **approval** Zustimmung der Umweltschutzbehörde; ~ **area** Umweltgebiet, -zone, Stadtrandgebiet; ~ **aspects** Umweltauswirkungen; ~ **changes** Umweltveränderungen; ~ **cleanup** Säuberung des Stadtrandgebietes; ~ **conditions** Umweltbedingungen; ~ **control** Umweltkontrolle; ~ **damage** Umweltschäden; ~ **defense** *(US)* (defence, *Br.*) ~ **fund** Umweltschutzfonds; ~ **department** Umweltbehörde, -schutzabteilung; ~ **derogation** Verschlechterung der Umweltbedingungen; ~ **effect** *(factors)* Umwelteinflüsse; ~ **goal** räumliches Entwicklungsziel; **on** ~ **grounds** aus umweltbedingten Gründen; ~ **health commission** Umweltkommission; ~ **impact** Umweltbeeinflussung; ~ **influences** Umwelteinflüsse; ~ **issue** Umweltfrage; ~ **law** Umweltschutzrecht; ~ **legislation** Umweltschutzgesetzgebung; ~ **market** Markt für Umweltgestaltung; ~ **office** Umweltamt, -behörde; ~ **officer** Beauftragter für den Umweltschutz, Beamter des Umweltschutzes; ~ **panel** Umweltausschuß; ~ **penalty** Bußgeld für Umweltverschmutzungen; ~ **planning** Umweltplanung; ♀ **Policy Act** *(US)* Umweltschutzgesetz; ~ **politics** Umweltpolitik; ~ **pollution** Umweltverschmutzung; ~ **problem** Umweltproblem; ~ **program(me)** Umweltschutzprogramm; ~ **protection** Umweltschutz; ~ **protection law** Umweltschutzgesetz; ~ **psychology** umweltbedingte Psychologie; ~ **question** Umweltproblem;

~ **regulations** Umweltschutzanordnungen; ~ **restrictions** einschränkende Bestimmungen aus Umweltschutzgründen; ~ **rules** Umweltschutzbestimmungen; ~ **safety** Umweltschutz; ~ **services** *(Br.)* Aufwendungen für Umweltschutzaufgaben; ~ **standards** Umweltnormen; ~ **study** Umweltstudie; ~ **thinking** Umweltdenken; ~ **vote** Stimmen der Umweltschützer.

environmentalist Umweltschützer, -fachmann;
~ **movement** Umweltschutzbewegung; ~ **pressure** Druck der Umweltschützer.

environmentally, to get ~ **adjusted** Umweltbedingungen aufrechterhalten.

environs, in the ~ **of** im Großraum von; ~ **of a town** Umgebung (Großraum) einer Stadt.

envisage *(v.)* in Aussicht nehmen.

envoy Sendbote, diplomatischer Vertreter, Gesandter;
extraordinary ~ außerordentlicher Gesandter; ~ **extraordinary and minister plenipotentiary** außerordentlicher und bevollmächtigter Minister.

epidemic seuchenartig;
~ **disease** Epidemie, Seuche.

epigraph Denkspruch, Motto.

epilog(ue) Nachwort, Epilog.

epoch Abschnitt, Zeitabschnitt.

equal Standesgenosse;
~ **in age** Altersgenosse;
~ *(a.)* gleichmäßig, -berechtigt, paritätisch, *(tranquil)* gleichmütig, gleichförmig, ruhig;
~ **to cash** so gut wie bares Geld; ~ **to one's merit** jds. Verdienst entsprechend; ~ **in points** punktgleich; ~ **in size** gleich groß; ~ **in strength** von gleicher Stärke;
to be the ~ **of s. o.** jem. ebenbürtig sein; **to be** ~ **to anything** zu allem entschlossen sein; **to be** ~ **to any emergency** in jeder Notsituation seinen Mann stehen; **to be** ~ **to s. one's expectations** jds. Erwartungen entsprechen; **to be** ~ **to a glass of wine** einem Glas Wein nicht abgeneigt sein; **to be** ~ **to an occasion** sich einer Situation gewachsen zeigen; **to be** ~ **to a task** einer Aufgabe gewachsen sein; **to be no longer** ~ **to the strain of business** den geschäftlichen Anstrengungen nicht mehr länger gewachsen sein; **not to feel** ~ **to receiving visitors** vor Gästeempfängen einen Horror haben; **to find one's** ~ *(coll.)* ebenbürtigen Gegner finden; **to have risen above one's** ~s über die anderen herausgewachsen sein; **to treat s. o. as an** ~ j. als Gleichberechtigten behandeln;
~ **angle map** winkelgetreue Karte; **of** ~ **area** *(map)* flächengetreu; ~ **benefit** gleichmäßige Begünstigung; **of** ~ **birth** ebenbürtig; ~ **degree** gleicher Verwandtschaftsgrad; ~ **distribution of taxes** Steuergleichheit; **to speak English and French with** ~ **ease** Englisch genauso beherrschen wie Französisch; **to be on** ~ **footing with s. o.** jem. gleichrangig sein; ~ **justice under the law** Gleichheit vor dem Gesetz; ~ **mind** Gleichmut; ⚯ **Opportunity Program** *(US, universities)* Chancengleichheitsprogramm; ~ **partners** Gesellschafter mit gleichen Geschäftsanteilen; **in** ~ **parts** zu gleichen Teilen; ~ **pay for** ~ **work** gleicher Lohn für gleiche Leistung; ⚯ **Pay Act** *(Br.)* Lohngleichheitsgesetz; ~ **protection of the law** *(US)* Gleichheit vor dem Gesetz; ~ **rank** Gleichrang; ~ **rights** gleiche Rechte; ~ **rights of men and women** Gleichberechtigung von Mann und Frau; **to fight for** ~ **rights** für die Gleichberechtigung kämpfen; **to have** ~ **rights** gleichberechtigt sein; **to contribute** ~ **shares to the expenses** gleichmäßig zu den Unkosten beitragen; **to go** ~ **shares** gleichen Anteil haben; ~ **standard** Gleichwertigkeit; **of** ~ **standing** gleichstehend; ~ **status** Gleichberechtigung; ~ **sum of money** gleichhoher Geldbetrag; ~ **and uniform taxation** einheitliche Besteuerung; **on** ~ **terms** zu gleichen Bedingungen, gleichberechtigt; ~ **treatment** Gleichbehandlung, -stellung; ~ **value** Gleichwertigkeit.

equality Gleichmäßigkeit, -wertigkeit, -berechtigung, Parität;
in case of ~ **in points** bei gleicher Punktzahl; **on a footing of** ~ auf der Grundlage der Gleichberechtigung;
~ **of armaments** Rüstungsgleichheit; ~ **of freight rates** Frachtenausgleich; ~ **before the law** Gleichheit vor dem Gesetz; ~ **under public law** staatsrechtliche Gleichstellung; ~ **of opportunity** Chancengleichheit; ~ **of pay** Lohngleichheit, gleiche Entlohnung; ~ **of ranks of creditors** Ranggleichheit von Gläubigern; ~ **of rights** gleicher Rang, Ranggleichheit, Gleichberechtigung; ~ **in size** Größengleichheit; ~ **of status** politische Gleichberechtigung; ~ **of treatment** Gleichbehandlung; ~ **of votes** Stimmengleichheit; ~ **in wages** Lohngleichheit;
to be on an ~ **with s. o.** auf gleicher Stufe mit jem. stehen; **to treat s. o. on a footing of** ~ mit jem. wie mit Seinesgleichen verkehren;

~ **clause** *(US)* Verfassungsgrundsatz der Gleichberechtigung; ~ **money** gleichwertiger Geldbetrag.

equalization Ausgleich, Gleichstellung, Angleichung, *(rates)* Frachtenausgleich, *(el.)* Entzerrung;
~ **of assessments** Angleichung der Einheitswerte; ~ **of supplies** Bedarfsausgleich;
~ **account** zu Ausgleichszwecken über das ganze Jahr verteilte Reparaturkosten, *(Exchequer, Br.)* Interventionsfonds; ~ **benefit** Ausgleichsleistung; ~ **board** Ausgleichsstelle; ~ **claim** Ausgleichsanspruch; ~ **debt** Ausgleichsschuld; ~ **fee** Ausgleichsumlage, -abgabe; ~ **fund** Ausgleichsfonds; **Exchequer** ⚯ **Grant** *(Br.)* staatliche Ausgleichszuweisung; ~ **levy** Ausgleichsabgabe; ~ **office** Ausgleichskasse; ~ **pay** Teuerungszulage; ~ **payments** Ausgleichszahlungen; ~ **period** Ausgleichsfrist, -zeitraum; ~ **point** Ausgleichspunkt; ~ **price** Ausgleichskurs; ~ **rate** Ausgleichsquote; ~ **reserve** Ausgleichsrücklage; ~ **sum** Ausgleichssumme, -betrag; ~ **tax** Ausgleichsfolgesteuer.

equalize *(v.)* ausgleichen, gleichstellen, *(el.)* entzerren;
~ **accounts** Konten ausgleichen; ~ **incomes** Einkommen angleichen; ~ **wages** Löhne angleichen.

equalizing | **assessment of taxes** Steuerausgleich; ~ **dividend** Ausgleichsdividende; ~ **gear** *(car)* Ausgleichsgetriebe; ~ **process** Ausgleichsverfahren; ~ **rate** Ausgleichstarif.

equally | **divided** Stimmengleichheit; ~-**ranking** gleichrangig, -berechtigt;
to contribute ~ **to the expense** sich an den Kosten gleichmäßig beteiligen; **to rank** ~ *(creditors)* gleichberechtigt sein, gleichen Rang haben;
~ **ranking creditors** gleichrangige Gläubiger.

equanimity, to bear with ~ mit Gleichmut ertragen.

equate *(v.)* ausgleichen *(treat as equivalent)* auf die gleiche Stufe stellen, gleichsetzen;
~ **the expenses with the income** Ausgaben dem Einkommen anpassen.

equated | **abstract of account** Staffelauszug; ~ **calculation of interest** Staffelzinsrechnung; ~ **interest** Staffelzinsen.

equator Äquator.

equation Ausgleich[ung], *(mathematics)* Gleichung;
personal ~ persönliche Beobachtungsfehler;
~ **of currency** Währungsausgleich; ~ **of supply and demand** Gleichgewicht (Gesetz) von Angebot und Nachfrage; ~ **of exchange** Währungsausgleich; ~ **of interest** Zinsstaffel; ~ **of payments** Feststellung des mittleren Zahlungstermins; ~ **of prices** Preisausgleich; ~ **of taxes** Steuerausgleich;

equilibrium Gleichgewicht;
political ~ politisches Gleichgewicht;
~ **of the balance of payments** Zahlungsbilanzgleichgewicht; ~ **of an industry** Marktgleichgewicht; ~ **of prices** Preisgleichgewicht; ~ **of supply and demand** Ausgleich von Angebot und Nachfrage;
~ **level** Gleichgewichtszustand; ~ **price** Gleichgewichtspreis, Wettbewerbspreis; ~ **theory** statische Preistheorie, Gleichgewichtstheorie.

equip *(v.)* ausrüsten, ausstatten, einrichten;
~ **o. s. with s. th.** sich etw. anschaffen (zulegen); ~ **a ship** Schiff ausrüsten; ~ **a shop with tools** Betrieb installieren; ~ **a works with new plant** in einer Fabrik neue Maschinen installieren.

equipage *(mil.)* Ausrüstungsgegenstände, Kriegsgerät.

equipment Betriebs-, Geschäftseinrichtung, Ausstattung, Ausrüstung, *(fig.)* geistiges Rüstzeug, *(machine)* Apparatur, Gerät, Maschinenanlage, -park, *(mil.)* Ausstattung, Kriegsgerät, *(rolling stock)* rollendes Material, Wagenpark, *(tools)* Arbeitsgerät, Ausrüstungsgüter, -gegenstände, Gerätschaften;
bridge ~ Brückengerät; **camping** ~ Camping-, Lagerausrüstung; **capital** ~ Kapitalausrüstung, -ausstattung; **delivery** ~ Wagenpark; **energy-saving** ~ energiesparende Geschäftsausstattung; **factory** ~ Betriebseinrichtung, -ausstattung; **farm** ~ landwirtschaftliche Maschinen; **field** ~ *(mil.)* feldmarschmäßige Ausrüstung; **furniture and** ~ *(balance sheet)* Geschäftsausstattung, Maschinen und Einrichtungen; **idle** ~ nicht ausgenutzte Betriebsanlagen; **laboratory** ~ Laborausstattung; **machinery and** ~ *(balance sheet)* Maschinen- und Betriebsausrüstung; **major** ~ Großgerät; **mechanical** ~ Maschinenanlage; **modern** ~ moderne Anlagen; **national capital** ~ volkswirtschaftliches Gesamtvermögen; **office** ~ Büroeinrichtung, -ausstattung; **optional** ~ *(car)* Zusatzausstattung; **production** ~ Produktions-, Betriebseinrichtung; **radar** ~ Radarausrüstung, -einrichtung; **rented** ~ gemietete Ausrüstung; **replacement** ~ Ersatzausstattung; **skin-diving** ~ Sporttaucherausrüstung; **special** ~ Sonderausstattung; **store** ~ Geschäftsausrüstung; **tool** ~ Werkzeugausstattung; **transport** ~ Verkehrseinrichtung;

electrical ~ of a motor car Elektroausstattung eines Autos; ~ of a ship Schiffsausrüstung; ~ for a voyage Reiseausrüstung; to be classified as ~ zur Ausrüstung (Ausstattung) gerechnet werden; to replace worn-out ~ abgenutzte Anlagen ersetzen; ~ account Ausrüstungskonto, Maschinenerneuerungskonto; delivery ~ account Fahrzeugkonto; ~ analysis (product engineering) Maschinenbelegungsplan; ~ bonds (US) Schuldverschreibungen zur Finanzierung für Eisenbahnbedarf; ~ breakdown Zusammenbruch einer Produktionsanlage; ~ builder Ausstatter; ~ curtailment Drosselung der Betriebsausstattung; ~ depot (mil.) Zeugamt; ~ goods Ausrüstungsgegenstände, -güter; ~ investment Investitionen für die Betriebseinrichtungen; ~ lease Maschinenmiete; ~ leasing Ausrüstungsvermietung; ~ note (US) Schuldverschreibung zur Deckung rollenden Materials; ~ operation costs Betriebskosten für Fahrzeuge und Maschinen; ~ purchase Erwerb von Ausrüstungsgegenständen; ~ record Verzeichnis der Einrichtungsgegenstände; ~ rent Gerätemiete; ~ replacement Ersatz von Betriebseinrichtungen; ~ standardization Vereinheitlichung der Ausrüstung; ~ trust (US) Finanzierungsgesellschaft für Eisenbahnbedarf; ~ trust agreement (US) Vereinbarung über die Verpfändung von Eisenbahnmaterial; ~ trust certificates (US) durch Verpfändung von Eisenbahnmaterial gesicherte Schuldverschreibungen.

equitable billig, gerecht, (law) billigkeitsrechtlich;
~ action Klage im Equityverfahren; ~ apportionment Aufteilung im Innenverhältnis; ~ assets gepfändetes Vermögen; ~ assignee Forderungszessionar; ~ assignment [etwa] stille Abtretung, formlose Forderungsabtretung; general ~ charge formloses Grundpfandrecht, Pfandbestellung ohne Sicherungsübereignung; ~ claim rechtmäßiger Anspruch, berechtigte Forderung; ~ conversion Vermögensumwandlung; ~ defence persönliche Einwendung; ~ easement formlose Dienstbarkeit, dienstbarkeitsähnliche Verpflichtung; ~ ejectment Räumungsklage; ~ election Wahlrecht; ~ estate (US) sachenrechtsähnliches Recht an Immobilien; ~ estoppel Einrede der Unzulässigkeit einer Rechtsausübung; ~ execution Zwangsverwaltereinsetzung; ~ garnishment Offenbarungsverfahren; ~ interest Begünstigtenrecht, Anwartschaftsrecht, billigkeitsrechtlicher Anspruch, Rückübereignungsanspruch des Sicherungsgebers; ~ interests (balance sheet) Beteiligungen; ~ interest in its own shares Anwartschaftsrecht auf die eigenen Aktien; ~ jurisdiction Billigkeitsgerichtsbarkeit; ~ levy vorläufige Beschlagnahme; ~ lien besitzloses Pfandrecht, Sicherungs-, Treuhandgut, sicherungsübereignete Gegenstände; ~ mortgage hypothekenähnliches Sicherungsrecht; ~ obligation obligatorische Verpflichtung; ~ owner wirtschaftlicher Eigentümer, Treuhandbegünstigter; ~ ownership wirtschaftliches Eigentum; ~ price angemessener Preis; ~ rate of interest (Br.) Zinsanspruch gegen den Treuhänder; ~ remedy Rechtsschutzmittel nach Billigkeitsrecht; ~ rescission durch Gerichtsurteil bedingte Vertragsauflösung; ~ right Anwartschaftsrecht, Billigkeitsanspruch; ~ rule [etwa] Recht und Billigkeit; ~ waste unzulässige Substanzschädigung; ~ title vorläufiges Eigentum, Eigentumsanwartschaft.

equitableness Billigkeit.

equities Dividendenpapiere, industrielle Wertpapiere, (Br.) Stammaktien, (law) Billigkeits-, Equityrechte;
free from the ~ unter Ausschluß aller persönlichen Einwendungen;
local ~ örtliches Aktienangebot; marketable ~ börsengängige Dividendenwerte; selected ~ ausgesuchte Anlagenwerte.

equity (business interest) Nettoanteil, (capital) Wert des Grundkapitals, Eigenkapital, (claim) billiger Anspruch, billige Forderung, Billigkeitsanspruch, (fairness in dealing) Rechtschaffenheit, Fairness, Treu und Glauben, Billigkeit, (law) Billigkeitsrecht, (in property, coll.) hypothekarische Belastung übersteigender Grundstückswert;
for reasons of ~ aus Gründen der Billigkeit;
common ~ Stammkapital; countervailing ~ ausgleichendes Billigkeitsrecht; latent ~ (internal relationship) geheimgehaltener (verdeckter) Anspruch; natural ~ [etwa] gesundes Rechtsempfinden; paramount ~ stärkerer Billigkeitsanspruch; perfect ~ (real-estate law) Eigentumstitel mit noch fehlender Grundbuchumschreibung, [etwa] Auflassungsanspruch; secret ~ verdeckter Anspruch; shareholders' ~ Nettoanteil der Aktionäre, Eigenkapital einer AG; total ~ (Br.) Eigenkapital; wife's ~ Ausgleichsanspruch der Ehefrau gegen das Vermögen des Ehemanns;
~ of opportunities Chancengleichheit; ~ of partners Teilhaberanspruch auf das Gesellschaftsvermögen zur Deckung eigener Schulden, Ausgleichsanspruch eines Gesellschafters; ~ of redemption Pfandauslösungs-, Hypothekenauslösungsrecht, Ablösungs-, Rückkaufsrecht; ~ to a settlement Ausgleichsanspruch der Ehefrau gegen das Vermögen des Ehemannes, Begünstigungsrecht der Ehefrau am Vermögen des Ehemannes; ~ of a statute entsprechende Gesetzesanwendung; ~ of stockholders (US) Nettoanteil der Aktionäre;
to build ~ (contract system) Eigenkapital ansparen; to have no ~ in the debtor keine Kapitalforderungen gegen den Schuldner durchsetzen können;
~ account Kapitalkonto; ~ accumulation Eigenkapitalbildung; ~ assets Anlagevermögen; ~ bank Aktienbank, Beteiligungsbank; to participate on an ~ basis sich kapitalmäßig beteiligen; ~ boom Aktienkonjunktur; ~ capital Eigenkapital; ~ court Billigkeitsgericht; ~ dilution Verwässerung des Eigenkapitals, Wertverschlechterung durch Grundstücksbelastung; ~ earnings Kapitalerträge, -einkünfte; ~ equipment Eigenkapitalausstattung; to raise ~ finance Kapital durch Aktienausgabe beschaffen; ~ financing Kapitalbeschaffung durch Aktienausgabe; ~ funding Hypothekenfonds; to plug the ~ gap for medium-sized companies Kapitalmarktlücke für Mittelbetriebe schließen; ~ holdings Aktien-, Wertpapierbeteiligungen; ~ interests Kapitalbeteiligung; ~ investment Kapitalbeteiligung an einer Gesellschaft, Beteiligung an Kapitalgesellschaften; ~ issue Aktienemission; ~ jurisdiction Zuständigkeit in Billigkeitssachen; ~ jurisprudence Rechtsprechung nach Billigkeitsrecht; ~ kicker bei der Darlehnsvergabe ausgehandelter Eigenkapitalerwerb; ~ law Billigkeitsrecht; ~ loan billiges Darlehen; ~ management Verwaltung von Aktienbeteiligungen; ~ market Aktienmarkt; ~ market investments Anlagemöglichkeiten im Aktienmarkt; ~ offerings Kapitalerhöhung; ~ owner Kapitaleigner; ~ ownership Eigenkapital; ~ participation Beteiligung am Stammkapital, Aktien-, Kapitalbeteiligung; ~ portefeuille (portfolio) Wertpapierportefeuille, Aktienportefeuille; ~ position Eigenkapitalverhältnisse; favo(u)rable ~ position günstiges Verhältnis des Nettoanteils; ~ prices (share value) Kurse der Dividendenwerte; ~ ratio Verhältnis der Aktiva zu den Passiva, Eigenkapitalkoeffizient, -quote; ~ receiver vom Gericht bestellter Vermögensverwalter; ~ receivership Vergleichsverwalterstellung, -position; ~ section Kapitalseite; ~ securities Dividendenpapiere; ~ share Stammanteil, Aktie mit normaler Dividendenberechtigung und Anteil am Liquidationswert der Gesellschaft; ~ shares Dividendenpapiere, Stammaktien; ~ share capital Stammkapital; government ~ shareholdings Staatsbeteiligungen an Aktiengesellschaften; to reduce one's ~ stake seinen Eigenkapitaleinsatz verringern; ~-starved company mit zu geringem Eigenkapital ausgestattete Gesellschaft; ~ stock Aktien-, Anteilskapital; ~ trading Geldaufnahme zu niedrigeren Zinssätzen als der Handelsgewinn, Fremdfinanzierung.

equivalence gleichwertiger Betrag, Gegenwert, Gleichwertigkeit;
~ of exchange Kurs-, Währungsparität.

equivalent (equal value) Gegenwert, Äquivalent;
to offer an ~ for damage done Gegenwert für den zugefügten Schaden anbieten;
~ (a.) (equal in value) gleichbedeutend, vom gleichen Wert, gleichwertig, äquivalent;
~ ransom entsprechendes Lösegeld; ~ units gleichartige Produktionseinheiten; ~ weight (paper) Gewicht per Quadratmeter.

equivocal zweideutig, doppelsinnig;
~ transactions fragwürdige Geschäfte.

equivocate (v.) doppelzüngig reden, Ausflüchte machen.

equivocation Zweideutigkeit, Wortverdrehung.

era Zeitalter, -rechnung, Ära, Epoche;
~ of scarcity Teuerungsperiode;
to mark an ~ Epoche einleiten.

eradicate (v.) ausrotten;
~ a disease Seuche ausrotten.

erase (v.) aus-, wegradieren, auslöschen;
~ from one's memory aus seinem Gedächtnis tilgen.

eraser Radiergummi.

erasement Ausradierung, (fig.) Vernichtung, Tilgung.

erasure Rasur, radierte Stelle.

erect (v.) bauen, aufstellen, (el.) [Oberleitungen] legen, (settle) stiften, gründen;
~ a building Gebäude errichten; ~ a new commonwealth neues Reich begründen; ~ a custom into law Gewohnheitsrecht zum Gesetz erheben; ~ a new government neue Regierung bilden; ~ a monument Denkmal aufstellen; ~ a printing press Druckpresse aufstellen; ~ a theory Theorie aufstellen.

erecting crane Montagekran.

erection Einrichtung, Montieren, Anbau, *(settlement)* Stiftung, Gründung;
 ~ **of a building** Gebäudeerrichtung;
 ~ **blue print** Montagezeichnung; ~ **cost** Errichtungs-, Montagekosten.

erector Montageleiter, Erbauer.

ergatocracy Arbeiterherrschaft.

ergonomics Arbeitsplatzanalyse.

erosion *(technical)* Verschleiß, Abnutzung;
 soil ~ Bodenerosion;
 ~ **from inflation** Inflationserosion; ~ **of profits** Gewinnerosion.

err *(v.)* sich irren, *(fig.)* auf Abwege geraten;
 ~ **on a point of law** Rechtsirrtum begehen; ~ **on the safe side** sichergehen; ~ **on the side of mercy** zu viel Gnade walten lassen.

errand Weg, Bestellgang, Botengang, Besorgung, Auftrag;
 to be on an ~ etw. zu besorgen (erledigen) haben; **to discharge an** ~ Auftrag ausführen, Bestellung machen; **to go (run) [on]** ~s Botengänge machen, besorgen; **to send s. o. on an** ~ j. eine Besorgung machen lassen; **to tell one's** ~ seinen Auftrag ausrichten;
 ~ **boy** Läufer, Laufbursche; ~ **goer** Botengänger.

errant tribes wandernde Stämme.

errata Berichtigungen, Druckfehlerverzeichnis.

erratic *(stock exchange)* uneinheitlich, sprunghaft.

erroneous irrtümlich, *(law)* rechtsirrtümlich;
 ~ **in point of law** rechtsirrig;
 ~ **assignment** ungültiger Rechtsübergang; ~ **entry** fehlerhafte Eintragung, Fehlbuchung; ~ **judgment** Fehlurteil.

error Irrtum, Fehler, Versehen, Schnitzer, *(law)* Formfehler, Verfahrensmangel, *(philately)* Fehldruck, *(print.)* Druckfehler;
 barring ~ Irrtum vorbehalten; **by** ~ irrtümlich;
 absolute ~ *(statistics)* absoluter Fehler; **approximation** ~ *(statistics)* Näherungsfehler; **ascertainment** ~ *(statistics)* Beobachtungsfehler; **clerical** ~ Schreibfehler; **common** ~ anerkannter Revisionsgrund; **compensating** ~ *(statistics)* ausgleichungsfähiger Fehler; **cross** ~s *(law)* Anschlußrevision; **discordant** ~ Irrtum infolge fehlender Willenseinigung; **fundamental** ~ grundlegender [Rechts]irrtum, Irrtum über die Vertragsgrundlage, *(appellate practice)* absoluter Revisionsgrund; **grammatical** ~ grammatikalischer Fehler; **harmful** ~ Revisionsfehler; **harmless** ~ unerheblicher Rechtsfehler; **heeling** ~ *(mar.)* Krängungsfehler; **interviewer** ~s bei Umfragen entstandene Fehler; **invited** ~ *(law)* absichtlicher Verfahrensfehler; **judicial** ~ Rechtsirrtum; **nonsampling** ~ *(statistics)* stichprobenfremder Fehler; **popular** ~ weitverbreiteter Irrtum; **printer's** ~ Druckfehler; **probable** ~ *(statistics)* wahrscheinlicher Fehler statistischer Mittelwerte; **processing** ~ *(statistics)* Aufbereitungsfehler; **radical** ~ fundamentaler Fehler; **reversible** ~ Revisionsgrund; **spelling** ~ Schreibfehler; **technical** ~ Formfehler; **total** ~ Gesamtmißweisung; **typographical** ~ Druck-, Satzfehler; **unbiassed** ~ *(statistics)* unverzerrter Fehler;
 ~ **in account** Rechenfehler; ~ **in addition** Additionsfehler; ~ **of calculation** Berechnungs-, Rechenfehler; ~ **in composition** *(print.)* Setzfehler; ~ **in computing** Berechnungsfehler; ~ **in equations** *(statistics)* Ansatzfehler; ~ **in estimating** Schätzungsfehler, irrtümliche Schätzung; ~ **of fact** Tatbestands-, Tatsachenirrtum; ~ **of first kind** *(statistics)* Fehler erster Ordnung; ~ **of judgment** falsches Urteil, falsche Beurteilung, Ermessensirrtum, Fehlurteil; ~ **in law** Rechtsirrtum; ~ **of observation** *(statistics)* Beobachtungsfehler; ~s **and omissions excepted** Irrtümer und Auslassungen vorbehalten; ~ **in persona** Irrtum über die Person; ~ **of the press** Druckfehler; ~ **of procedure** Verfahrensmangel; ~ **in reading off** Ablesefehler; ~ **apparent of record** offenbarer Irrtum; ~ **in the register** falsche Grundbucheintragung; ~ **as to the subject matter** Irrtum über den Vertragsgegenstand;
 to commit an ~ Fehler begehen (machen); **to convict s. o. of an** ~ jem. einen Irrtum nachweisen; **to correct an** ~ einem Fehler abhelfen, Fehler berichtigen; **to do s. th. in** ~ etw. versehentlich tun; **to lead s. o. into** ~ Irrtum bei j. erzeugen; **to rectify an** ~ Irrtum berichtigen; **to see the** ~ **of one's ways** seine Fehler einsehen; **to stand in** ~ sich im Irrtum befinden;
 ~ **band** *(statistics)* Fehlerbereich; ~ **indicator** *(computer)* Fehleranzeige; ~ **margin** Fehlerspielraum, -spanne, -wahrscheinlichkeit, Toleranz; ~ **probability** *(statistics)* Irrtums-, Fehlerwahrscheinlichkeit.

erudite Gelehrter;
 ~ *(a.)* gelehrt, belesen.

erupt *(v.)* *(volcano, war)* ausbrechen.

eruption | **of a volcano** Vulkanausbruch; ~ **of war** Kriegsausbruch.

escalate *(v.)* hochsteigern, -schaukeln, eskalieren, *(use escalator)* Rolltreppe benutzen;
 ~ **conventional war into nuclear warfare** konventionellen Krieg in einen Atomkrieg eskalieren.

escalating business regulation eskalierende Reglementierung der Wirtschaft.

escalation Steigerungsrate, *(mil.)* Steigerung, Hochschaukeln, Eskalation, *(prices, US)* Anpassung;
 ~ **of costs** Kosteneskalation; ~ **of defence costs** Eskalation der Verteidigungslasten;
 ~ **price** gleitender Preis; ~ **threat** Eskalationsdrohung.

escalator Rolltreppe, *(wage clause)* automatischer Ausgleich;
 ~ **adjustment** *(wages)* automatische Anpassung; ~ **clause** Wertsicherungs-, Gleit-, Indexklausel, *(prices)* gleitende Preisskala, Preisgleitklausel, *(wages)* Steigerungsklausel, Lohngleitklausel, gleitende Lohnklausel, -skala; **cost-of-living** ~ **contract** mit Preisgleitklausel ausgestatteter Vertrag; ~ **formula** Lohn-, Preisgleitklausel; ~ **panel** Rolltreppenschild; ~ **plan** Gleitklauselsystem; ~ **provision** Gleitklausel.

escapable cost vermeidbare Kosten.

escape Entkommen, Entrinnen, *(leakage)* Entweichen[lassen], *(relaxation)* Unterhaltung, Entspannung, Zerstreuung;
 actual ~ Gefängnisausbruch; **attempted** ~ Fluchtversuch; **fire** ~ Feuerleiter; **near** ~ knappes Entkommen; **negligent** ~ fahrlässiges Entweichen lassen; **voluntary** ~ Gefangenenbegünstigung bei der Flucht;
 ~ **of gas** Gasaustritt; ~ **from prison** Gefängnisausbruch; ~ **from shipwreck** Rettung als Schiffsbrüchiger;
 ~ *(v.)* flüchten, flüchtig werden;
 ~ **across the border** über die Grenze flüchten; **to narrowly** ~ **death** knapp dem Tode entgehen; ~ **from earth** *(spaceship)* Erdanziehungskraft überwinden; ~ **with one's life** mit dem Leben davonkommen; ~ **s. one for a moment** jem. im Augenblick entfallen; ~ **observation** der Beobachtung entgehen; ~ **prison** mit knapper Not einer Gefängnisstrafe entgehen; ~ **from prison** aus dem Gefängnis fliehen (entkommen); ~ **punishment** der Bestrafung (Strafe) entgehen; ~ **scot-free** unbestraft bleiben; ~ **from the shackles of state regulations** staatlichen Regulierungsfesseln entgehen; ~ **by the skin of one's teeth** mit einem blauen Auge davonkommen; ~ **from one's warders** seinen Bewachern entkommen;
 to foil s. one's ~ jds. Flucht vereiteln; **to have a hairbreadth** ~ um Haaresbreite entkommen; **to have a narrow (lucky)** ~ um Haaresbreite davonkommen; **to make one's** ~ sich aus dem Staube machen, erfolgreichen Fluchtversuch unternehmen;
 ~ **agent** Fluchthelfer; ~ **attempt** Fluchtversuch; ~ **clause** *(law of contract)* Rücktrittsklausel, *(US, tariff commission)* Konzessionsrücknahmeklausel, *(trade union)* Austrittsklausel; ~ **drain** Abflußkanal; ~ **hatch** Notausstieg, *(fig.)* Zufluchtsort zur Entspannung; ~ **literature** *(reading)* Entspannungslektüre, Unterhaltungsliteratur; ~ **period** Rücktrittsfrist; ~ **pipe** Abflußrohr; ~ **rocket** Rettungsrakete; ~ **route** Fluchtweg, -route; ~ **shaft** Rettungsschacht; ~ **slide** Notausstieg, -rutsche; ~ **suspect** Fluchtverdächtiger; ~ **trail** Fluchtweg; ~ **valve** Sicherheitsventil; ~ **velocity** *(spaceship)* Fluchtgeschwindigkeit; ~ **warrant** Haftbefehl für entsprungenen Häftling; ~ **way** *(mining)* Rettungsweg.

escapee Ausreißer, entsprungener Gefangener, Flüchtling.

escapism Vergnügungs-, Wirklichkeitsflucht.

escapist wirklichkeitsfremder Mensch;
 to become ~ sich den schönen Dingen des Lebens zuwenden.

escheat *(US)* Heimfall an den Fiskus, *(default of heirs)* Erbenlosigkeit, *(property escheated)* heimgefallenes Gut, dem Staat anheimgefallene Erbschaft;
 single ~ *(bailor)* Vermögenseinziehung;
 ~ **of land** Einziehung von Liegenschaften;
 ~ *(v.)* heimfallen, *(fall to the state)* dem Staat (Fiskus) verfallen, *(v./tr.)* konfiszieren;
 ~ **bonds** als Sicherheit gegebene Schuldverschreibungen zugunsten des Fiskus für verfallen erklären; ~ **an estate to s. o.** jem. etw. hinterlassen;
 to revert by ~ heimfallen, *(to state)* an den Fiskus fallen.

escheatage Heimfallrecht, *(reverting to the state)* Erbschaftsanfall an den Staat.

escheated succession Heimfallrechtsfolge.

escort Geleit, *(mar.)* Geleitfahrzeug, -schiff, *(mil.)* Ehren-, Schutzgeleit, Begleitmannschaft, Bewachung, Eskorte, Begleitung, Bedeckung, *(plant)* Arbeitseinweisung;

air ~ Begleitflugzeug; **convoy** ~ Geleitzug; **police** ~ Polizeibedeckung;
~ **of soldiers** Soldateneskorte;
~ (v.) Geleit geben, geleiten, eskortieren, *(plant)* einweisen;
~ **s. o. home** j. nach Hause begleiten; ~ **a prisoner** Gefangenen unter Bewachung abführen; ~ **a ship** einem Schiff Geleit geben; **to conduct a prisoner under** ~ Gefangenen unter Bewachung transportieren, Gefangeneneskorte durchführen;
~ **carrier** Geleitflugzeugträger; ~ **duty** Geleitschutzaufgaben; ~ **fighter** Begleitjäger; ~ **plan** Einweisungsschema; ~ **vessel** Begleitschiff, Geleitboot, Bewachungsfahrzeug; ~ **wagon** *(US)* Begleitwagen.
escorting party Geleitmannschaft.
escrow vorläufig hinterlegte Urkunde;
delivery in ~ Hinterlegung;
to hold in ~ treuhänderisch halten (verwahren); **to place in** ~ [bis zur Erfüllung der Vertragsbedingungen] hinterlegen; **to place a fund in** ~ Treuhänderfonds errichten; **to place an instrument in** ~ Urkunde hinterlegen (dem Treuhänder übergeben);
~ **account** Treuhandkonto; ~ **agreement** Treuhand-, Hinterlegungsvertrag; ~ **bonds** beim Treuhänder hinterlegte Obligationen; ~ **department** Hinterlegungsabteilung einer Bank; ~ **depository** Verwahrungsstelle für treuhänderisch hinterlegte Wertpapiere; ~ **holder** Hinterlegungsstelle, Treuhänder.
escutcheon Wappen, *(fig.)* Ehre, Ruf, *(name-plate)* Namensschild;
to blot one's ~ seinen Ruf schädigen.
espionage Spionage[geschäft];
suspected of ~ spionageverdächtig;
counter ~ Spionageabwehr; **industrial** ~ Werksspionage;
to combat ~ Spionage bekämpfen; **to commit** ~ Spionage[delikt] begehen;
_≗_ **Act** *(US)* Spionageabwehrgesetz; ~ **activity** Spionagetätigkeit; ~ **affair** Spionageaffäre; ~ **basis** Spionagezentrum; **by** ~ **means** auf dem Spionageweg; ~ **proceedings** Spionageverfahren; ~ **ring** Spionagering; ~ **work** Spionagetätigkeit.
espousal Parteinahme, Eintreten.
essay Aufsatz, Abhandlung, Studie, Ausarbeitung, *(new stamps)* Probeabdruck, *(school)* Arbeit, Aufsatz;
critical ~ kritischer Beitrag;
~ (v.) **a task** sich an einer Aufgabe versuchen;
~ **subject** Aufsatzthema.
essayist Literat.
essence Inbegriff, Kern, elementarer Bestandteil, *(perfume)* Wohlgeruch, Parfüm;
fifth ~ Quintessenz;
~ **of a book** Buchextrakt; ~ **of business** geschäftlicher Daseinsgrund; ~ **of a contract** wesentliches Vertragserfordernis, Vertragsinbegriff; ~ **of fraud** wesentliches Betrugsmerkmal; **very** ~ **of a matter** des Pudels Kern; ~ **of a will** wesentlicher Testamentsinhalt;
to be of ~ **for a contract** von wesentlicher Bedeutung für einen Vertrag sein.
essential Hauptsache;
~ (a.) wesentlich, *(vital)* unbedingt notwendig, lebensnotwendig, -wichtig, Hauptsache;
long experience ~ *(ad)* langjährige Erfahrung erforderlich;
~ **books** notwendige Bücher; ~ **elements** wesentliche Bestandteile (Erfordernisse); ~ **feature of s. one's policy** wesentlicher Zug einer Politik; ~ **foodstuffs** Grundnahrungsmittel; ~ **goods** lebenswichtige Güter; ~ **industry** kriegswichtiger Betrieb; ~ **influence of climate** entscheidender Klimaeinfluß; ~ **insanity** völlige Geisteskrankheit; ~ **part** Hauptbestandteil; ~ **provision** wesentliche Bestimmung; ~ **quality** wesentliche Eigenschaft; ~ **service** lebenswichtiger Betrieb; ~ **term** wesentlicher Vertragsinhalt; ~ **trade routes** *(US)* Liniendienst von besonderer volkswirtschaftlicher Bedeutung; ~ **work orders** *(Br.)* kriegsbedingte Einsetzung von Arbeitskräften.
essentials wesentliche Umstände, *(goods)* lebenswichtige Güter, *(US, politics)* Grundrechte;
production ~ wichtige Produktionsmittel;
~ **of a contract** wesentliche Vertragserfordernisse; ~ **of life** Lebensbedürfnisse; ~ **to registration** Eintragungsvoraussetzungen.
essentiality wesentliche Eigenschaft.
establish (v.) einrichten, einsetzen, gründen, errichten, stiften, anlegen, etablieren, ansiedeln, *(fix)* feststellen, -setzen, *(law court)* gerichtlich feststellen, *(prove)* einwandfrei nachweisen;
~ **o. s.** Geschäft errichten (gründen), sich etablieren (niederlassen), sich selbständig (ansässig) machen; ~ **s. o.** jem. zu einer Dauerstellung verhelfen;

~ **an agency** Vertretung einrichten; ~ **one's alibi** sein Alibi erbringen (nachweisen); ~ **o. s. as a bookseller** sich als Buchhändler niederlassen; ~ **a branch office** Filiale gründen; ~ **a business** Geschäft (Handelsfirma) errichten (gründen); ~ **o. s. as a businessman** sich selbständig machen, sich niederlassen; ~ **a new chair** Lehrstuhl errichten; ~ **o. s. in a citadel** sich in einer Festung festsetzen; ~ **one's claim** seinen Anspruch glaubhaft machen; ~ **a claim to a title** Eigentumsnachweis erbringen; ~ **a colony** Kolonie gründen; ~ **contact with s. o.** Verbindung (Kontakt) mit jem. aufnehmen; ~ **standard cost at a high level** Kosten hoch vorkalkulieren; ~ **o. s. in the country** sich auf dem Lande niederlassen; ~ **a credit** Kredit eröffnen; ~ **credibly** glaubhaft machen; ~ **a domicile** Wohnsitz begründen; ~ **beyond doubt** einwandfrei nachweisen; ~ **a fact** Tatsache beweisen; ~ **the facts** Sachverhalt ermitteln; ~ **a government** Regierung bilden; ~ **a new government** neue Regierung einsetzen; ~ **s. o. as governor** j. zum Gouverneur ernennen; ~ **o. s. in s. one's house** sich bei jem. einlogieren; ~ **one's identity** seine Identität nachweisen; ~ **o. s. in a job** sich beruflich durchsetzen; ~ **one's need of the property as the sole residence of o. s. or an adult member of one's family** als Hauseigentümer Eigenbedarf anmelden; ~ **s. o. in an office** j. in ein Amt einführen; ~ **order** Ordnung schaffen; ~ **peace** Frieden stiften; ~ **a prima facile case** schlüssig begründen und glaubhaft machen; ~ **priorities** Prioritäten setzen; ~ **high records** Höchstkurse aufstellen; ~ **close relations with s. o.** enge Beziehungen zu jem. aufnehmen; ~ **a legal relationship** Rechtsverhältnis begründen; ~ **one's reputation as a lawyer** sich als Anwalt einen Namen machen; ~ **one's residence** seinen Wohnsitz begründen; ~ **one's right** sein gutes Recht beweisen; ~ **a rule** Regel aufstellen; ~ **a scholarship** Stipendium einrichten; ~ **a new state** neuen Staat gründen; ~ **statement of accounts** Jahresabschluß feststellen; ~ **a tax on tobacco** Tabaksteuer einführen; ~ **a disputed will** Gültigkeit eines Testaments beweisen.
established gegründet, feststehend, *(employed)* fest angestellt;
long ~ alteingeführt, -eingesessen;
to be ~ *(claim)* feststehen, *(domiciled)* ansässig sein; **to be comfortably** ~ **in one's new house** sich im neuen Haus gut etabliert haben; **to become** ~ sich einbürgern; **to become firmly** ~ fester Bestandteil werden;
~ **bookseller** zugelassener Buchhändler; **well-**~ **business** gut eingeführtes Geschäft; ~ **church** *(Br.)* Staatskirche; ~ **civil servant** *(Br.)* festangestellter Beamter, Planstelleninhaber; ~ **credit** festbegründeter Kredit; ~ **custom** ständiger (eingeführter) Brauch; **well-**~**facts** feststehende Tatsachen; **well-**~**fortune** wohlfundiertes Vermögen; ~ **interpretation** anerkannte Auslegung; ~ **law** geltendes Recht; ~ **list** Angestelltenliste; ~ **merchant** selbständiger Kaufmann; ~ **officer** Beamter auf Lebenszeit; ~ **official** planmäßiger Beamter; ~ **place** *(Br.)* Geschäftssitz [einer Gesellschaft]; **well-**~ **position** angesehene Stellung; ~ **post** feste Anstellung, Planstelle; ~ **practice** bestehende Übung, *(law court)* ständige Rechtssprechung; ~ **prices** auf ein bestimmtes Niveau eingependelte Preise; ~ **principles of law** feststehende Rechtsgrundsätze; ~ **products** im Markt gut eingeführte Produkte; ~ **reputation** guter Ruf, Ansehen; ~ **truth** feststehende Wahrheit.
establishing| of contact Kontaktaufnahme;
~ **shot** charakteristischer Filmauftakt.
establishment *(abode)* Niederlassung, fester Wohnsitz, *(fixing)* Festsetzung, *(foundation)* Stiftung, *(government)* Stellenplan, *(group of plants)* Betriebszusammenfassung, *(house of business)* [Geschäfts]unternehmen, Firma, Geschäft, Betrieb, Anlage, Werk, Etablissement, *(instituting)* Einsetzung, Einrichtung, *(leadership)* Führungsschicht, tonangebende Gesellschaftsschicht, *(mar.)* Sollstärke, Mannschaftsbestand, *(mar. Br.)* Ausrüstungsnachweis, *(party)* Spitzenfunktionäre, *(personnel)* Personalbestand, Planstelle, *(place of business)* Geschäftsgrundstück, *(place in life)* Lebensstellung, Versorgung, Einkommen, Gehalt, *(plant)* Werk, Betrieb, *(setting up)* Gründung, Errichtung, Etablierung, Niederlassung [einer Firma];
on the ~ fest angestellt, in einer Planstelle;
banking ~ Bankinstitut, -geschäft; **branch** ~ Zweigbetrieb, -geschäft, Zweigniederlassung; **business** ~ Geschäftsbetrieb, geschäftliches Unternehmen; **charitable** ~ wohltätige Stiftung; **civil** ~ Beamtenschaft; **commercial** ~ gewerbliche Niederlassung; **consulting (fact-finding, guiding)** ~ Richtbetrieb; **dependent** ~s nichtselbständige Betriebseinheiten; **Eastern** ~ herrschende Gesellschaftsschicht in den Oststaaten; **educational** ~ Erziehungsanstalt; **vitally important** ~ lebenswichtiger Betrieb; **industrial** ~ Industrieunternehmen; **large** ~ Großbe-

trieb; **main** ~ Hauptniederlassung; **manufacturing** ~ gewerblicher Betrieb, Gewerbe-, Fabrikanlage, Fabrikationsbetrieb;
mercantile ~ Handelsunternehmen; **military** ~ Kriegsmacht,
Militär; **new** ~ Geschäftsneugründung; **one-man** ~ Einmannbetrieb; **naval** ~ Flotte; **peace** ~ *(mil.)* Friedensstärke; **permanent** ~ bleibende Einrichtung; **postal** ~ Postanstalt; **printing** ~
typographische Anstalt; **private** ~ Privatunternehmen, -be-
trieb; **research** ~ Forschungsinstitut; **retail** ~ Einzelhandelsbetrieb, -firma; **separate** ~ getrennter Haushalt, getrennte
Haushaltsführung; **war** ~ Kriegsstärke; **wholesale** ~ Groß-
handelsbetrieb;

~ **of an agency** *(US)* Errichtung einer Behörde; ~ **of branches**
Filialgründungen; ~ **in a budget** Stellenplan; ~ **of a cartel**
Kartellgründung; ~ **of a new chair** Lehrstuhlerrichtung, Einrichtung eines neuen Lehrstuhls; ~ **of a company** Gesellschaftsgründung; ~ **of a common customs tariff** Aufstellung eines
gemeinsamen Zolltarifs; ~ **of a connection** Herstellung einer
Verbindung; ~ **of contact with s. o.** Kontaktaufnahme mit jem.;
~ **of a corporation** Gesellschaftsgründung; ~ **of a credit** Krediteinräumung; ~ **of damage** Schadensnachweis; ~ **of diplomatic
relations** Aufnahme diplomatischer Beziehungen; ~ **of dower**
Einräumung eines Nießbrauchrechtes für die Witwe; ~ **of
enterprises abroad** Unternehmensgründungen im Ausland; ~
of a partnership Begründung eines Gesellschaftsverhältnisses;
~ **of paternity** Vaterschaftsnachweis; ~ **of a port** Hafenzeit; ~
of residence Wohnsitzbegründung; ~ **of servants** zahlreiche
Angestellte; ~ **of standards** Normenfestsetzung; ~ **of a new
state** Errichtung (Gründung) eines neuen Staates, Staatsgründung; ~ **of a tax** Steuererhebung; ~ **of a new tax** Einführung
einer neuen Steuer;

to be on the ~ auf der Gehaltsliste stehen, zu den Angestellten
gehören, Planstelle innehaben; **to belong to the** ~ etabliert sein;
to bring up a division on war ~ Division auf Kriegsstärke
auffüllen; **to enlarge an** ~ Unternehmen vergrößern; **to keep an
(a large)** ~ großes Haus führen; **to put s. o. on the** ~ jem. eine
Planstelle geben;

~ **charges** Generalunkosten; ~ **fund** Sozialversicherungsfonds;
~ **office** *(local government, Br.)* Personalamt; ~ **officer** *(Br.)*
Personalleiter; ~ **plan** Stellenplan.

estate *(assets)* Eigentum, [Gesamt]besitz, *(of bankrupt)*
Konkursmasse, *(interest in land)* Besitzrecht, *(landed property)*
Grundstück, Grund-, Landbesitz, Grundeigentum, Besitzung, Anwesen, Gut, *(left after death)* Erbschaftsmasse,
unverteilte Erbschaft, Nachlaß, *(property)* Vermögen[s-
masse], *(social standing)* Rang;
~**s** Liegenschaften;
absolute ~ unumschränktes Eigentum; **affected** ~ hypothekarisch belastetes Grundstück; **aggregate** ~ Gesamtnachlaß,
-vermögen; **agricultural** ~ landwirtschaftlicher Betrieb; **bankrupt's** ~ Konkursmasse; **base** ~ nachgeordneter Pachtbesitz;
big ~ große Besitzung; **brought in** eingebrachtes Gut;
building ~ baureifes Grundstück; **burdened** ~ hypothekarisch
belastetes Grundstück; **clear** ~ unbelastetes Grundstück;
conditional ~ bedingtes Eigentum; **contingent** ~ später anfallendes Eigentum; **council** ~ *(Br.)* soziale Wohnsiedlung; **country** ~ Landbesitz, -gut; **crown** ~ *(Br.)* Kronland, -gut;
decedent's ~ *(US)* Nachlaß; **derivative** ~ nachgeordnetes Recht
an einem Teilgrundstück; **determinable** ~ bedingtes Eigentumsrecht; **devolved upon s. o.** überkommene Erbschaft; **dominant** ~ herrschendes Grundstück; **encumbered** ~ hypothekarisch belastetes Grundstück; **entailed** ~ Familiengut, Fideikommiß, Majorat; **equitable** ~ sachenrechtsähnliches Recht,
Grundstücksnießbrauch; **executed** ~ ausgeübtes Immobiliar-
recht, in Besitz genommenes Grundstück; **executory** ~ aufschiebend bedingtes Grundstücksrecht; **expectant** ~ Anwartschaftsrecht, Nacherbschaft; **fast** ~ Grundvermögen, Immobilien; **the Fourth** ⊆ der Vierte Stand (Journalismus, Presse);
future ~ Anwartschaft, zukünftiges Besitzrecht; **housing** ~ aufgeschlossenes Gelände, Wohnsiedlung, -viertel, -block, Siedlungsgelände, Stadtrandsiedlung; **improved real** ~ im Wert
gestiegenes Grundstück; **industrial** ~ *(Br.)* Industrie-, Kom-
paktsiedlung; **insolvent** ~ überschuldeter Nachlaß, Nachlaßkonkurs; **intestate** ~ Nachlaß ohne letztwillige Verfügung;
joint ~ gemeinschaftlicher Grundbesitz; **landed** ~ Grundvermögen, Grundbesitz; **large** ~ ansehnlicher Besitz, Latifundie; **leasehold** ~
Erbpacht; **legal** ~ dingliches Eigentumsrecht; **life** ~ Liegen-
schaftsnießbrauch; **mixed** ~ *(US)* Erbpacht auf 99 Jahre; **mortgaged** ~ belastetes Grundstück; **movable** ~ bewegliches
Vermögen; **net** ~ reiner Nachlaß [nach Auszahlung der
Legate]; **original** ~ originäres Eigentumsrecht; **particular** ~
[etwa] Vorerbschaft; **personal** ~ bewegliche Habe, bewegliches

Vermögen, Mobilien, Mobiliarvermögen; **qualified** ~ auflösend bedingtes Nießbrauchrecht; **real** ~ unbewegliches Vermögen, Immobilien, Immobiliarvermögen, Grund[stücks]-
eigentum, Grund und Boden, Anwesen, Liegenschaften;
developed real ~ bebautes (erschlossenes) Grundstück; **residuary** ~ Restnachlaß, Nachlaß nach Zahlung aller Verbindlichkeiten; **Royal** ~ *(Br.)* Staatsdomäne; **separate** ~ eingebrachtes Gut, Vorbehaltsgut der Ehefrau, *(partner)* Sonder-,
Privatvermögen; **servient** ~ dienendes Grundstück; **settled** ~
treuhänderisch gebundenes Sondervermögen; **small** ~ *(Country Court Act, Br.)* Bagatellkonkurs; **solvent** ~ liquider Nachlaß; **suburban** ~ Stadtrandsiedlung; **tail** Fideikommiß; ~ **tail
female** nur an weibliche Deszendenz vererbbarer Besitz; ~ **tail
general** unbeschränkt vererblicher Besitz; ~ **tail male** Majorat;
taxable ~ steuerpflichtiger Nachlaß; **the Third** ⊆ *(history)* der
Dritte Stand; **total** ~ Gesamtnachlaß; **trading** ~ *(Br.)* Indu-
striepark; **trust** ~ Treuhandvermögen, -gut, treuhänderisch
verwaltetes Vermögen, *(deceased)* treuhänderisch verwalteter
Nachlaß, *(foundation)* Stiftungsvermögen; **undivided** ~ unverteilter Nachlaß; **unencumbered** ~ lastenfreies Grundstück;
vacant ~ herrenloser Nachlaß; **vested** ~ Herrschaftsrecht;

~ **in abeyance** noch nicht angetretene Erbschaft; ~ **without a
claimant** herrenloser Nachlaß; ~ **in common** Gesamthandseigentum, Miteigentum [bei verschiedenem Erwerbsgrund]; ~
upon (in) condition bedingter Besitz; ~ **in coparcenary** Besitzrecht mehrerer Erben; ~ **by the curtesy (in dower)** Witwennießbrauch; ~ **of a deceased person** Nachlaß; ~ **in dower**
lebenslängliches Besitzrecht der Witwe an einem Drittel des
beweglichen Nachlasses; ~ **and effects** Gesamtvermögen; ~ **by
elegit** zwangsverwaltetes Vermögen; ~ **free from encumbrances**
unbelastetes Grundstück; ~ **by the entirety** *(married couple)*
Gesamthandseigentum; ~ **in expectancy** Erbanwartschaft; ~ **in
fee simple** Voll-, Allodialeigentum, unbeschränktes Grundeigentum; ~ **in fee tail** erbrechtlich gebundenes Vermögen,
Fideikommiß; ~ **of inheritance** *(US)* ererbtes Vermögen, Nachlaß; ~ **with absolute inheritance** *(US)* Güter mit unbeschränkter Erbfolge; **legal** ~ **in land** Grundbesitz, Herrschaftsrecht an
einem Grundstück; ~ **per life** lebenslanger Grundstücksnießbrauch; **holy** ~ **of matrimony** heiliger Ehestand; ~ **in possession**
ausgeübtes Eigentumsrecht, unmittelbarer Grundbesitz; ~ **by
purchase** rechtsgeschäftlich erworbenes Eigentum; **the three** ~**s
of the realm** *(Br.)* die drei gesetzgebenden Faktoren; ~ **in
remainder** Anwartschaftseigentum; ~ **in reversion** Heimfallrecht; ~ **extending to the sea** bis zum Meer reichender Grundbesitz; ~ **in severalty** Einzelrechtsbesitz; ~ **by statute merchant**
zwangsverwaltetes Vermögen nach Londoner Stadtrecht; ~ **at
sufferance** *(US)* nach Pachtablauf stillschweigend weiterge-
währtes Besitzrecht; ~ **in tail** Grundbesitz mit gebundener
Erbfolge, Vorerbschaft, Fideikommiß; ~ **in joint tenancy**
Gesamthandsbesitz; ~ **for a term** zeitlich befristetes Besitzrecht; ~ **in usufruct** Grundstücksnießbrauch; **life** ~ **pour autre
vie** Besitzrecht auf Lebenszeit eines Dritten; ~ **at will** jederzeit
kündbares Pachtverhältnis; ~ **of wood and meadow land** aus
Wald und Wiesen bestehender Grundbesitz; ~ **for years** *(US)*
Grundstückspacht mit fester Pachtdauer; ~ **from year to year**
von Jahr zu Jahr verlängerte Pacht;

~ *(v.)* **out** verpachten;
to abandon a mortgaged ~ belastetes Grundstück aufgeben; **to
administer an** ~ Nachlaß verwalten, Konkursmasse zugunsten
des Gläubigers verwalten; **to alienate an** ~ Grundstück
umschreiben; **to be heir to an** ~ Grundbesitz erben; **to be in
charge of an** ~ Vermögen verwalten; **to bequeath s. o. the whole
of one's** ~ jem. sein ganzes Vermögen vermachen; **to break up
an** ~ Grundbesitz parzellieren; **to bring one's property into the
communal** ~ sein Vermögen in die Gütergemeinschaft einbringen; **to deed one's** ~ sein Vermögen übertragen; **to disencumber
an** ~ Grundbesitz entschulden; **to divide an** ~ Grundbesitz
parzellieren; **to divide a bankrupt's** ~ Konkursmasse ausschütten; **to enter an** ~ **at the Register of Deeds Office** *(US)* Grundstück im Grundbuch eintragen lassen; **to estimate an** ~
Grundstück abschätzen; **to free an** ~ **of encumbrances** Grundbesitz entschulden; **to have entire disposal of one's** ~ über sein
Vermögen frei verfügen können; **to lay claim to an** ~ Nachlaß
beanspruchen; **to lay out one's** ~ **for sale in lots** seinen Grundbesitz parzellieren; **to make over one's** ~ sein Vermögen vermachen; **to neighbo(u)r with an** ~ an ein Grundstück angrenzen; **to
own large** ~**s** umfangreichen Grundbesitz haben; **to parcel an** ~
Grundbesitz parzellieren; **to pay 40% out of the** ~ Konkursquote von 40% ausschütten; **to pay out of the trust** ~ aus der
Konkursmasse zahlen; **to plan an** ~ Nachlaßregelung vorsehen; **to settle the** ~ **of a deceased** Nachlaß eines Verstorbenen

regulieren; **to spend one's ~ in gaming** sein Vermögen verspielen (verwetten); **to value an ~** Grundbesitz steuerlich veranlagen; **to wind up an ~** Vermögensmasse ordnen;

~ **accounting** Nachlaßrechnungslegung; ~ **adviser** Vermögensberater; ~ **affairs** Nachlaßangelegenheiten; ~ **agency** *(Br.)* Immobilienbüro, -firma; ~ **agent** *(go-between, Br.)* Grundstücksmakler, Gütermakler, -agent, *(house steward)* Gutsverwalter; ~ **agent's fees** *(Br.)* Grundstücksmaklergebühr; ~ **assets** Nachlaßwerte; ~ **buildings** Wirtschaftsgebäude; ~ **car** *(Br.)* Kombiwagen; ~ **charges** Grundstückslasten; ~ **contract** Vertrag zur Begründung eines dinglichen Eigentumsrechtes; ~ **duties investment trust** *(Br.)* zur Vermeidung von Erbschaftssteuern errichteter Fonds.

estate duty *(Br.)* Erbschafts-, Nachlaßsteuer;
to avoid ~ *(Br.)* Erbschaftssteuer vermeiden; **to become liable to ~** *(Br.)* erbschaftssteuerpflichtig werden; **to charge ~** *(Br.)* Erbschaftssteuer veranschlagen;

~ **advantage** *(Br.)* Erbschaftssteuervorteil; ~ **allowance** *(Br.)* Erbschaftssteuerfreibetrag; ~ **charge** *(Br.)* Erbschaftssteuerbelastung; ~ **computation** *(Br.)* Erbschaftssteuerberechnung; ~ **credit** *(Br.)* Erbschaftssteuerfreibetrag; ~ **implication** *(Br.)* erbschaftsteuerliche Tragweite; ~ **interest** *(Br.)* Erbschaftssteuerzinsen; ~ **law** *(Br.)* Erbschaftssteuerrecht; ~ **legislation** *(Br.)* Erbschaftssteuergesetzgebung; ~ **liability** *(Br.)* Erbschaftssteuerfreigrenze; ~ **mitigation** *(Br.)* Erbschaftssteuerminderung, -milderung; ~ **office** *(Br.)* Nachlaßsteuerbehörde; ~ **position** *(Br.)* Erbschaftssteuersituation; **for ~ purposes** *(Br.)* für Erbschaftssteuerzwecke; ~ **rate** *(Br.)* Erbschaftssteuersatz; ~ **regulations** *(Br.)* Erbschaftssteuerrichtlinien; ~ **saving** *(Br.)* Erbschaftssteuerersparnis; ~ **valuation** *(Br.)* Erbschaftssteuerveranschlagung, -schätzung; ~ **value** *(Br.)* Erbschaftssteuerbetrag.

estate, surplus ~ funds zusätzlich für die Masseverteilung zur Verfügung stehende Mittel; ~ **house** Gutshaus; ~ **income** Einkünfte aus Grundbesitz, *(from deceased)* Nachlaßeinkünfte; ~ **inventory** Nachlaßverzeichnis, -inventar; ~ **management** Guts-, Grundstücksverwaltung; ~ **manager** Gutsverwalter, -inspektor, *(insurance company)* Immobilienverwalter; ~ **office** Maklerbüro; ~ **owner** Grundstückseigentümer; ~ **planning** Nachlaßregelung, -vorsorge; ~ **planning tax man** *(US)* Nachlaßsteuerexperte; ~ **property** Nachlaß-, Erbschaftsvermögen; ~ **rate** Erbschaftssteuersatz; ~ **security** Nachlaßwerte, -papiere; ~ **tax** *(US)* Erbschafts-, Nachlaßsteuer; **to speed up the collection of ~ taxes** *(US)* Einziehung von Erbschaftssteuern beschleunigen; ~ **tax outlay** *(US)* Erbschaftssteueraufwand; ~ **tax rate** *(US)* Nachlaßsteuersatz; ~ **tax savings** *(US)* Erbschaftssteuerersparnis, Nachlaßsteuerersparnis.

esteem Wertschätzung, Hochachtung;
~ *(v.)* respektieren, hohe Meinung haben;
~ **it a duty** es als Pflicht ansehen; ~ **highly** hochschätzen; ~ **it a privilege** es als Vorrecht betrachten;
to hold in high ~ wertschätzen.

estimable loss Verlustschätzung.

estimableness Schätzbarkeit.

estimate *(costs)* Vor-, Kosten[vor]anschlag, *(estimation)* Veranschlagung, Berechnung, Bewertung, [Ab]schätzung, Taxe, *(worth estimated)* Schätzwert;
in accordance with the ~s etatsmäßig; **at the lowest ~** nach niedrigster Schätzung; **on (at) a rough ~** grob überschlagen; **the ⌕ s** *(Br.)* Etat, Haushaltsplan, -voranschlag;
Annual ⌕ *(Br.)* Jahresvoranschlag; **approximate ~** annähernde Schätzung; **budgetary ~** Haushaltsvoranschlag; **building ~** Veranschlagung der Baukosten, Baukostenvoranschlag; **civil ~s** Voranschlag der Verwaltungsausgaben; **conservative ~** vorsichtige Schätzung; **cost ~** Kostenvoranschlag; **detailed ~s** ins Einzelne gehende Vorschläge; **fair ~** reiner Überschlag, angemessene Schätzung; **Naval ⌕** Marineetat, Flottenvorlage; **incorrect ~** falsche Schätzung; **labo(u)r [budget] ~** Voranschlag für Lohn- und Gehaltskosten; **official ~** amtliche Schätzung; **outside ~** möglichst genaue Schätzung; **plant ~s** Betriebsbudget; **preliminary ~** Kostenvoranschlag; **printing ~** Druckkostenvoranschlag; **rough ~** Überschlags[rechnung], rohe (grobe) Schätzung; **safe ~** vorsichtige Schätzung; **savings ~** Vorschau der Sparbewegungen; **supplementary ~s** Nachtragsetat, Haushaltsnachtrag; **uncritical ~** ungeprüfte Schätzung; ~ **of s. one's abilities** Beurteilung von jds. Fähigkeiten; ~**s free from bias** unverzerrte Schätzwerte; ~ **of a person's character** Charakterbeurteilung einer Person; ~ **of costs** Kostenvoranschlag; ~ **of the costs of construction** Schätzung der Herstellungskosten; ~ **of damage** Schadensberechnung; ~ **on demand** Voranschlag auf Wunsch; ~ **of expenditure** Ausgabenvoran-

schlag; ~ **of income** Einkommensschätzung; ~ **of a lease** Pachtanschlag; ~ **of productiveness** Rentabilitätsberechnung; ~ **of profits** Gewinn-, Ertragsschätzung; ~ **of the situation** *(mil.)* Lagebericht;
~ *(v.) (calculate)* berechnen, *(value)* [ab]schätzen, einschätzen, veranschlagen, beziffern, taxieren, bewerten;
~ **a character** Charakter beurteilen, Charakterbeurteilung vornehmen; ~ **the costs of a new house** Neubaukosten eines Hauses kalkulieren; ~ **the effect of a speech** Wirkung einer Rede berechnen; ~ **an estate** Grundstück abschätzen; ~ **the gains of an enterprise** Unternehmensertrag veranschlagen; ~ **a job of printing** Druckkostenauftrag veranschlagen; ~ **the productive capacity of land** Grundstück bonitieren; ~ **the repair of a building** Reparaturkosten eines Gebäudes veranschlagen; ~ **roughly** überschlagen; ~ **the value of land** Grundstückswert schätzen;
to ask a contractor to ~ for the repair of the buildings Bauunternehmer zu einer Reparaturkostenkalkulation auffordern; **to bring in the ⌕ s** *(Br.)* Budget (Haushalt, Etat) vorlegen (einbringen); **to come to double the ~** sich auf das Doppelte des Voranschlags belaufen; **to draw up the ⌕ s** *(Br.)* Haushaltsplan aufstellen; **to employ a more conservative ~** vorsichtige Schätzung (Kalkulation) zugrunde legen; **to exceed one's ~** seinen Voranschlag (Etat) überschreiten; **to form an ~** abschätzen, beurteilen; **to form an ~ of s. one's abilities** sich eine Ansicht über jds. Eignung bilden; **to form a correct ~ of s. th.** sich ein richtiges Bild über etw. verschaffen; **to form a true ~** richtig einschätzen; **to give an ~** Kostenanschlag machen; **to introduce the ⌕ s** *(Br.)* Haushalt einbringen; **to make an ~** Überschlag machen, veranschlagen; **to make an ~ of the costs** Kostenvoranschlag vornehmen; **to prepare the ~s** *(Br.)* Haushaltsplan aufstellen; **to put in an ~** Voranschlag einreichen; **to vote the ⌕ s** *(Br.)* Haushaltsplan genehmigen, Haushaltsvoranschlag bewilligen.

estimated geschätzt, veranschlagt;
it has been ~ schätzungsweise;
~ **account** veranschlagter Betrag, Schätzungsbetrag; ~ **amount** Schätzungsbetrag; ~ **charges** Kostenvoranschlag; ~ **costs** geschätzte (veranschlagte) Kosten, Sollkosten; ~ **earnings** geschätztes Einkommen; ~ **price** Schätzpreis, -wert; ~ **receipts** Solleinnahmen; ~ **time of arrival** *(airplane)* voraussichtliche Ankunftszeit; ~ **time of departure** *(airplane)* voraussichtliche Abflugzeit; ~ **value** veranschlagter Wert, Schätz-, Taxwert; ~ **weight** *(carrier)* geschätztes Gewicht.

estimating Kostenschätzung;
~ **clerk** Kalkulator; ~ **cost system** Kostenrechnungssystem mit vorausgeschätzten Kosten, Standardkostenrechnung; ~ **equation** *(statistics)* Schätzgleichung; ~ **office** Kalkulationsbüro.

estimation *(rough calculation)* Veranschlagung, Vor-, Überschlag, Abschätzung, Bewertung, *(estimate)* [Ein]schätzung, *(judgment)* Wertschätzung, Wertung, Würdigung, Beurteilung;
in the ~ of most people nach der Meinung der Mehrheit;
~ **of cost** Kosten-, Vorkalkulation;
to be in ~ in gutem Ruf stehen; **to be held in high ~** sich hoher Wertschätzung erfreuen; **to be rising in the ~ of the public** sich steigernder Wertschätzung in der Öffentlichkeit erfreuen; **to grow out of ~** seinen guten Ruf verlieren; **to lower s. o. in the ~ of right-thinking members of society generally** jds. Ansehen bei allen gerecht und billig Denkenden herabsetzen;
~ **price** Taxkurs.

estimator Schätzer, Taxator, Schätzgröße.

estop *(v.) (law)* klagehindernde Einrede vorbringen, rechtshemmenden Einwand erheben.

estoppage Ausschluß, Hemmung, Präklusion.

estopped durch eine Einrede (einen Einwand) gehindert.

estoppel rechtshemmender Einwand, prozeßhindernde Einrede, *(peremptory plea)* peremptorischer Einwand;
equitable ~ Unzulässigkeit der Ausübung eines Rechtes, Einrede der Unzulässigkeit des Rechtsweges;
~ **by conduct** Unzulässigkeit der Ausübung eines Rechts aufgrund eigenen Verhaltens; ~ **by deed** Unzulässigkeit einer Prozeßeinrede auf Grund einer urkundlich gegebenen Erklärung; ~ **by judgment** Einwand der Rechtskraftwirkung; ~ **by lashes** Verwirkungseinrede; ~ **by matter in pais** Einrede des eigenen schuldhaften Verhaltens; ~ **by negligence** Einrede des eigenen fahrlässigen Verhaltens; ~ **by record** Unzulässigkeit einer Einrede auf Grund einer protokollarisch aufgenommenen Erklärung; ~ **by representation** Rechtsscheinvollmacht; ~ **by verdict** Einrede der inneren Rechtskraft;
~ **certificate** Valutabescheinigung.

estovers Holzgerechtigkeit, *(alimony)* Unterhaltszahlung für die geschiedene Ehefrau, Alimente, *(allowance)* Unterhalt.

estrange *(v.)* seinem Zweck entfremden;
~ **o. s.** sich fernhalten; ~ **all s. one's friends** j. alle Freunde verlieren lassen; ~ **o. s. from politics** sich gänzlich von der Politik abwenden; ~ **o. s. from social life** sich von gesellschaftlichen Veranstaltungen fernhalten.

estrangement Entfremdung.

estray entlaufenes Haustier.

estreat *(Br.)* getreue Urteilsabschrift;
~ *(v.)* Protokollauszüge machen, Protokollauszüge dem Vollstreckungsbeamten übergeben, *(exact fine)* Geldstrafe eintreiben.

estrepe *(v.) (leasehold)* verwahrlosen lassen.

estrepement *(lease)* Verwahrlosung, Verwüstung.

estuary Mündungsgebiet.

etch *(v.)* ätzen.

etching Ätzung.

eternal beständig, unveränderlich;
~ **chatter** *(coll.)* ewiges Geschwätz.

ethic Ethos;
~ *(a.)* ethisch;
~ **advertising** lautere Werbung.

ethics Verhaltensregeln, ethische Grundsätze, Moral, Ethik, Sittenlehre;
legal ~ Berufsethik der Anwaltschaft; **professional** ~ Berufsethik, Standesehre, -pflicht;
~ **of a profession** Standespflichten, Berufsethos;
~ **code** Moralkodex; ~ **committee** *(US)* Parlamentsausschuß für Verhaltensweise von Abgeordneten, Ausschuß für Standesfragen.

ethical [berufs]ethisch, dem Berufsethos entsprechend, sittlich, moralisch, *(drug)* arzneimittelpflichtig;
not to be considered ~ dem Berufsethos widersprechen;
~ **advertising** ethische Werbung; ~ **behavio(u)r** standesgemäßes Verhalten; ~ **basis for education** sittliche Grundlagen für die Erziehung; ~ **duty** moralische Verpflichtung; ~ **principles** sittliche Grundsätze; ~ **products** anerkannte pharmazeutische Produkte; ~ **standards** Anstandsregeln; ~ **standards of a profession** Standespflichten eines Berufs.

ethnic volkstumsmäßig, völkisch.

ethnography Völkerbeschreibung, -kunde, Rassenkunde.

etiquette Etikette, gesellschaftliche Umgangsformen;
corporate ~ betriebliche Umgangsformen, Betriebsknigge; **legal** ~ Berufsethik der Anwälte; **medical** ~ ärztliche Berufsetiquette (Standespflichten);
~ **of the Bar** Standespflichten des Anwaltstandes; ~ **of the profession** Standesregeln.

euchre *(v.)* **s. o.** *(US sl.)* j. aufs Kreuz legen.

Eurobond|s auf dem Euro-Bondmarkt begebene internationale Anleihen;
~ **market** Eurokapitalmarkt, -anleihemarkt; ~ **market roundup** Zusammenfassung der wichtigsten Nachrichten über Entwicklungen auf dem Euromarkt.

Eurocard Euroscheckkarte.

Eurocheque *(Br.)* Euroscheck;
~ **clearing centre** Euroscheckverrechnungszentrale; ~ **scheme** Euroschecksystem.

Eurocontrol Internationale Flugsicherheitsbehörde.

Eurocrat Eurokrat.

Eurocredit Eurokredit;
~ **business** Eurokreditgeschäft; ~ **market** Eurokreditmarkt; **syndicated** ~ **sector** Eurokonsortialgeschäft.

Eurocurrencies Eurogeldmarkt.

Eurocurrency Dollarguthaben, Guthaben in konvertierbarer Währung;
~ **finance** Eurodollarfinanzierung; ~ **financing** Finanzierung auf dem Eurodollarmarkt; ~ **loan** Eurodollaranleihe; ~ **market** Eurodollarmarkt; ~ **money market rates** Geldmarktsätze des Eurodollarmarktes.

Eurodollar im Besitz von Nichtamerikanern befindlicher Dollar, Eurodollar;
~ **bond** Eurodollaranleihe; ~ **borrowings** Eurodollarverschuldung; ~ **market** Eurodollarmarkt.

Euromarket Europäische Wirtschaftsgemeinschaft.

Europe Europa;
Western ~ Westeuropa;
to envisage a ~ **of the future** europäisches Zukunftsbild entwerfen.

European Europäer;
to think as a ~ europäisch denken;

~ **Agreement on the Movement of Persons** Europäisches Übereinkommen über den Personenverkehr; ~ **Agricultural Equipment and Guarantee Fund** Europäischer Ausrichtungs- und Garantiefonds für die Landwirtschaft; ~ **Assembly** Europaparlament; ~ **Atomic Energy Community** *(EURATOM)* Europäische Atomgemeinschaft; ~**-based** in Europa stationiert; ~ **Broadcasting Agreement** Europäisches Rundfunkabkommen; ~ **Central Inland Transport Organization** Europäische Firmentranportorganisation; ~ **Combined Unit** *(EURCO)* künstliche europäische Währungseinheit; ~ **Commission** Europäische Kommission; ~ **Commission of Human Rights** Europäische Kommission für Menschenrechte; ~ **Committee for Coordination of Standards** Europäisches Komitee für Normung; ~ **Common Market** *(Br.)* Europäische Wirtschaftsgemeinschaft; ~ **Communities** Europäische Gemeinschaften; **to enter into the** ~ **Communities** den europäischen Gemeinschaftsorganisationen beitreten; ~ **Communities Act** Gesetz über die Europäischen Gemeinschaften; ~ **Communities Bill** Gesetz der Europäischen Gemeinschaften; ~ **Economic Community** *(EEC)* Europäische Wirtschaftsgemeinschaft; ~ **Coal and Steel Community** Europäische Gemeinschaft für Kohle und Stahl, Montanunion; ~ **Conference of Local Authorities** Europäische Kommunalkonferenz; ~ **Conference of Ministers of Transport** *(ECMT)* Europäische Transportministerkonferenz; ~ **Conference of Regional Planning Ministers** Europäische Raumordnungsministerkonferenz; ~ **Cultural Convention** Europäisches Kulturabkommen; ~ **Convention on Establishment** Europäisches Niederlassungsabkommen; ~ **convention on compulsory insurance against civil liability in respect of motor vehicles** Europäisches Übereinkommen über die obligatorische Haftpflichtversicherung für Kraftfahrzeuge; ~ **Convention on Social and Medical Assistance** Europäisches Fürsorgeabkommen; ~ **Court of Justice** Europäischer Gerichtshof; ~ **Court of Human Rights** Europäischer Gerichtshof für Menschenrechte; ~ **currency float** Europäischer Währungsverbund; ~ **Defence Community** Europäische Verteidigungsgemeinschaft; ~ **Development Fund** *(EDF)* Europäischer Entwicklungsfonds; ~ **Economic Community obligations** Freizügigkeitsbedingungen für Einwohner der EWG-Länder; ~ **Economic and Monetary Union** Europäische Wirtschafts- und Währungsunion; **whole** ~ **economy** gesamteuropäische Wirtschaft; ~ **elections bill** *(Br.)* Gesetz über die Direktwahlen zum Europaparlament; ~ **Executive Bodies** Europäische Exekutiven; ~ **family** europäische Völkerfamilie; ~ **Free Trade Association** *(EFTA)* kleine Freihandelszone; ~ **Fund** *(EF)* Europäischer Fonds; ~ **idea** Europagedanke; ~ **Investment Bank** Europäische Investitionsbank; ~ **joint float** europäischer Währungsverband; ~ **Market Regulations** Europäische Marktordnung; ~ **Monetary Agreement** *(EMA)* Europäisches Währungsabkommen; ~ **Nuclear Energy Agency** *(ENEA)* Europäische Kernenergieagentur; ~ **Nuclear Energy Community** *(ENEC)* Europäische Atomgemeinschaft (Euratom); ~ **Organization for Nuclear Research** Europäische Organisation für Kernforschung; ~ **Organization for the Safety of Air Navigation** Europäische Organisation zur Sicherung der Luftfahrt; ~ **Parliament** Europäisches Parlament; ~ **Payments Union** Europäische Zahlungsunion; ~ **plan** *(US)* Zimmervermietung ohne Frühstück; ~ **policy** Europapolitik; ~ **Productivity Agency** *(EPA)* Europäische Produktivitätszentrale; ~ **Recovery Program(me)** *(ERP)* Europäisches Wiederaufbauprogramm; ~ **Research Institute for Regional and Urban Planning** Europäisches Forschungsinstitut für Raumordnung und Stadtplanung; ~ **Society for Opinion and Marketing Research** *(ESOMAR)* Europäische Organisation von Marktforschungsinstituten; ~ **Social Fund** Europäischer Sozialfonds; ~ **Soil Charter** Europäische Bodenkarte; **[over]all-** **solution** gesamteuropäische Lösung; ~ **Space Research Organization** Europäische Organisation für Raumforschung; ~ **Union** Europaunion.

Europeanization Europäisierung.

Eurosterling Europfund.

Eurosyndicate index europäischer Börsenindex.

euthanasia Sterbehilfe.

evacuate *(v.)* evakuieren, aus-, umsiedeln, [Betrieb] aus-, verlagern, *(dwelling)* räumen, frei machen, *(troops)* verlegen;
~ **children to the country** Kinder aufs Land evakuieren; ~ **a contract** Vertrag aufheben; ~ **a fort** Festung räumen; ~ **a marriage** Ehe aufheben; ~ **a town** Stadt evakuieren.

evacuated evakuiert;
~ **zone** Evakuierungsgebiet.

evacuation Evakuierung, Abtransport, Abschub, *(corporation)* [Betriebs]verlagerung, Auslagerung, *(dwelling)* Räumung;

~ **of a contract** Vertragsaufhebung; ~ **of inhabitants** Aussiedlung der Einwohner;

~ **area** Umsiedlungs-, Evakuierungsgebiet; ~ **camp** Umsiedler, Evakuierungslager; ~ **hospital** *(US)* Ausweichlazarett; ~ **plan** Evakuierungsplan; ~ **test** Evakuierungsprobe.

evacuee Evakuierter, Aus-, Umsiedler, Bombenflüchtling.

evacuosis Flüchtlingspsychose.

evadable *(mil.)* umgehbar.

evade *(v.)* ausweichen, umgehen, *(tax)* hinterziehen;

~ **one's creditors** sich seinen Gläubigern entziehen; ~ **customs duty** Zollhinterziehung begehen; ~ **paying one's debts** sich um die Bezahlung seiner Schulden herumdrücken; ~ **definition** sich nicht definieren lassen; ~ **detection** der Entdeckung entgehen; ~ **a duty** sich einer Pflicht entziehen; ~ **one's enemies** sich seinen Feinden entziehen; ~ **the issue** Ausflüchte gebrauchen; ~ **justice** sich der gerichtlichen Verfolgung entziehen; ~ **the law** Gesetz umgehen; ~ **paying taxes** sich um die Steuerzahlung drücken, Steuern hinterziehen; ~ **punishment** sich der Strafe (Strafverfolgung) entziehen; ~ **[answering] a question** sich um die Beantwortung einer Frage herumdrücken; ~ **regulations** Bestimmungen umgehen; ~ **a rule** Vorschrift umgehen; ~ **military service** sich der Dienstpflicht entziehen, sich vom Wehrdienst drücken.

evaded income tax hinterzogene Einkommensteuer.

evader *(mil.)* Versprengter.

evading movement Ausweichbewegung, -manöver.

evaluate *(v.)* *(appraise)* bewerten, abschätzen, begutachten, *(ascertain amount)* zahlenmäßig bestimmen, berechnen, auswerten;

~ **on a hurry-up basis** Bewertung im Blitzverfahren vornehmen; ~ **claims** Forderungen bewerten; ~ **an employee** Leistungsfähigkeit eines Angestellten bewerten; ~ **evidence** Beweiswürdigung vornehmen; ~ **a work in material terms** Wert einer Arbeit in Zahlen berechnen.

evaluation Abschätzung, Taxierung, Bewertung, Wertbestimmung, -ermittlung, -berechnung;

executive ~ Bewertung von Führungskräften; **output** ~ Leistungsermittlung; **stock** ~ Bewertung von Lagerbeständen; ~ **of claims** Bewertung von Forderungen; ~ **of evidence** Beweiswürdigung; ~ **of furniture** Berechnung des Möbelwertes, Möbelbewertung; ~ **of a job** Arbeitsbewertung; ~ **of products** Warenbewertung; ~ **of reserves** Rückstellungen und Wertberichtigungen; ~ **system** Bewertungssystem; ~ **techniques** Bewertungsmaßstäbe; ~ **work** Auswertungstätigkeit.

evasion Ausflucht, Ausrede, *(avoiding)* Umgehen, Ausweichen, *(escape)* Entkommen, Flucht;

draft ~ *(US)* Umgehung des Militärdienstes, Drückebergerei vor dem Wehrdienst; **fiscal (tax)** ~ Steuerverkürzung, -hinterziehung; ~ **of currency laws** Umgehung von Devisenvorschriften; ~ **of customs duties** Zollhinterziehung; ~ **of one's duties** Pflichtverletzung, Außerachtlassung seiner Pflichten; ~ **of income tax** Hinterziehung der Einkommensteuer, Einkommensteuerhinterziehung; ~ **of a law** Gesetzesumgehung; ~ **of responsibility** Ausweichen vor der Verantwortung; ~ **of taxation** Steuerumgehung.

evasive ausweichend, voller Ausflüchte;

~ **action** Ausweichmanöver; **to take** ~ **action** Ausweichmanöver durchführen; ~ **answer** unverbindliche Antwort; ~ **reply** ausweichende Antwort.

eve Vorabend;

on the ~ **of great events** am Vorabend großer Ereignisse; **Christmas** ~ Weihnachtsabend; **to be upon the** ~ **of s. th.** unmittelbar bevor etw. stehen; ~ **of-poll issue** Auseinandersetzung in der Wahlzeit.

even gleich *(account)* schuldenfrei, ausgeglichen, *(number)* gerade, *(stock exchange, Br.)* glatt;

at ~ ohne Berechnung von Report- und Deportspesen; ~ *(v.)* gleichmachen, ebnen; ~ **out** *(prices)* sich einpendeln; ~ **out the market** Marktausgleich herbeiführen; ~ **out fluctuations in earning power** Ertragsschwankungen ausgleichen; ~ **up** *(account)* ausgleichen, *(stock exchange)* glattstellen; **to be** ~ **with s. o.** mit jem. quitt sein, jem. nichts mehr schuldig sein, *(rank equally)* mit jem. im gleichen Rang stehen; **to break** ~ *(business)* ohne Verlust (kostendeckend) arbeiten, sich noch finanziell rentieren, Gewinnschwelle erreichen; **to end** ~ *(print.)* mit voller Zeile abschließen; **to get** ~ **with s. o.** mit jem. abrechnen, mit jem. ins Reine kommen; **to make lines** ~ *(print.)* mit voller Zeile abschließen;

~-**aged** gleichaltrig; ~ **bet** Wette mit gleichem Einsatz; ~ **break** gleiche Chance, *(business)* gleicher Gewinn, Verlust; **of** ~ **date** gleichen Datums; **an** ~ **dozen** genau ein Dutzend; **to meet on** ~ **ground** unter gleichen Chancen kämpfen; ~-**handed justice** unparteiische Gerechtigkeit; ~ **lot** *(US)* Aktienpaket mit durch hundert teilbarem Nennwert; ~-**numbered page** Rückseite; ~ **odds** gleiche Chancen; ~ **page** Buchseite mit gerader Zahl; ~ **running** *(quality)* gleichmäßig; ~ **shares** gleiche Anteile; ~ **sum** runde Summe; ~-**tempered** gelassen, gleichmütig; **on** ~ **terms** im guten Einvernehmen; **to work on** ~ **terms** *(Australia)* umsonst arbeiten.

eveness Gleichheit, -förmigkeit;

~ **of disposition** seelisches Gleichgewicht; ~ **of opportunities** Chancengleichheit.

evening *(entertainment)* Abendunterhaltung;

musical ~**s** musikalische Abendveranstaltungen; **summer** ~ Sommerabend;

to spend a social ~ Abend in Gesellschaft verbringen;

~ **bulletin** Abendnachrichten; ~ **classes** Abend-, Fortbildungskursus; **to join** ~ **classes** Fortbildungsunterricht besuchen; ~ **dress** Abendanzug; **semi-**~ **dress** kleines Abendkleid; ~ **dress is optional** kein Zwang für einen Abendanzug; ~ **entertainment** Abendprogramm; ~ **gown** *(US)* kleines Abendkleid; ~ **mail** Abendpost; ~ **market** Abendbörse; ~ **meal** Abendessen; ~ **out** Ausgehabend; ~ **paper** Abendausgabe; ~ **party** Abendgesellschaft; ~ **performance** Abendvorstellung; ~ **school** *(Br.)* Fortbildungsschule; ~ **shift** Abendschicht; ~ **trade** Nachtbörse.

evening | **of the market** Herbeiführung eines Marktausgleichs; ~ **up** *(odd lots)* Spitzenausgleich, *(US, stock exchange)* Glattstellung; **forced** ~ **up** *(US)* Zwangsglattstellung; **usual weekend** ~-**up process** *(US)* übliche Glattstellungen am Wochenende; ~-**up transaction** *(US)* Glattstellungsgeschäft.

event Ereignis, Begebenheit, Vorfall, Vorkommnis, *(case)* Fall, *(sport)* sportliche Veranstaltung;

at all ~**s** in jedem Fall; **in the** ~ **of** im Falle; **in the** ~ **of death** im Todesfall; **in the** ~ **of success** im Erfolgsfall; **in the** ~ **of war** im Falle eines Krieges;

contingent ~ ungewisses Ereignis; **common** ~ alltägliches Ereignis; **fortuitous** ~ unvorhersehbares (zufälliges) Ereignis; **inevitable** ~ unvermeidbares Ereignis; **insured** ~ Versicherungsfall; **law-creating** ~ rechtsbegründendes Ereignis; **natural** ~ Naturereignis; **probable** ~ wahrscheinlich eintretendes Ereignis; **quite an** ~ besonderes Ereignis; **recent** ~**s** noch nicht lange zurückliegende Ereignisse; **sales** ~ verkaufsfördernder Umstand; **social** ~**s** gesellschaftliche Veranstaltungen; **unforeseen** ~ unvorhergesehenes Ereignis;

~ **of default** Verzugsfall; ~ **of international importance** Weltereignis; ~ **of loss** Schadensfall; ~ **of the war** Kriegsgeschehen; ~**s of the year** Veranstaltungen im Laufe des Jahres;

to act according to ~**s** nach den Umständen handeln; **to be outdated by the** ~**s** von den Ereignissen überholt sein; **to descend to more recent** ~**s** auf neuere Ereignisse zu sprechen kommen; **to influence** ~**s** Gang der Ereignisse beeinflussen.

eventual von unsicheren Ereignissen abhängig, eventuell.

eventuality Eventualität.

every | **man Jack**, ~ **mother's son** *(coll.)* Hinz und Kunz; **to enjoy** ~ **minute of one's holiday** die ganzen Ferien genießen; ~ **owner** jeder Kraftfahrzeughalter; ~ **person** *(law)* Jedermann.

everyday | **life** Alltagsleben; ~ **routine** Alltagsroutine.

everyone | **'s, in** ~ **mouth** in aller Munde; ~ **and his uncle** alle möglichen Leute.

everything | **I am possessed of** mein gesamtes Vermögen;

to be ~ **to s. o.** jds. ein und alles sein; **to think** ~ **of s. o.** große Stücke auf j. halten.

evict *(v.)* räumen, *(tenant)* exmittieren, heraussetzen, aus dem Besitz setzen, zur Räumung zwingen, Zwangsräumung betreiben;

~ **property from s. o.** von seinem Eigentum wieder Besitz ergreifen; ~ **a tenant for not paying his rent** Mieter wegen Mietschulden exmittieren.

evicted tenant hinausgesetzter Mieter.

eviction Besitzentsetzung, Exmittierung, [Zwangs]räumung;

actual ~ faktische Zwangsräumung (Exmittierung); **constructive** ~ Beeinträchtigung des Besitzes durch den Verpächter; **partial** ~ Exmittierung aus einzelnen Räumen; **total** ~ vollständiger Besitzentzug;

~ **for nonpayment of rent** Zwangsräumung wegen Mietschulden; ~ **of a tenant** Hinaussetzung eines Mieters; ~ **by title paramount** Besitzentziehung durch einen übergeordneten Dritten;

to sue for ~ auf Räumung klagen;

to enforce an administrative ~ decree von den Verwaltungsbehörden erlassenen Räumungsbefehl durchführen; ~ **notice** Räumungsbeschluß; ~ **order** Räumungsurteil, -beschluß; ~ **proceedings** Räumungsverfahren.

evidence Augenscheinlichkeit, Offenkundigkeit, Beweis[material], -mittel, -stück, -urkunde, *(indication)* Anzeichen, Spur, *(procedure)* Beweisverfahren, *(proof)* Beweis[material], -mittel, -urkunde, *(testimony)* Zeugnis, Zeugenaussage, *(witness)* Zeuge;

as ~ **of** zum Beweis für; **for lack (in the absence) of** ~ wegen mangels an Beweisen; **in** ~ deutlich sichtbar; **in default of** ~ aus Mangel an Beweisen; **no** ~ **on which you could hang a cat** nicht die Spur eines Beweises; **not one shred of** ~ nicht der Fetzen eines Beweises; **on very authentic** ~ aufgrund sehr authentischer Zeugnisse;

admissible ~ zugelassene Beweismittel; **best** ~ primäres Beweismittel; **character** ~ Leumundszeugnis; **circumstantial** ~ auf Indizien beruhender Beweis, Beweis aufgrund von Indizien, Indizienbeweis; **cogent** ~ zwingender Beweis; **collateral** ~ unterstützendes Beweismaterial; **collusive** ~ abgekartete Zeugenaussagen; **completed** ~ Abschluß der Beweisaufnahme, abgeschlossenes Beweisverfahren; **competent** ~ zulässiges Beweismaterial; **conclusive** ~ schlüssiger (zwingender) Beweis; **conflicting** ~ widersprechende Zeugenaussagen; **convincing** ~ überzeugendes Beweismaterial; **corroborating** ~ zusätzliches Beweismaterial; **cumulative** ~ zusätzliches Beweismaterial; **demonstrative** ~ Augenscheinsbeweis; **direct** ~ direkter Beweis; **newly discovered** ~ neuentdecktes Beweismaterial; **documentary** ~ Urkundenbeweis; **exonerating** ~ entlastende Zeugenaussage, Entlastungsbeweis; **expert** ~ Sachverständigengutachten; **external** ~ mittelbarer Urkundenbeweis; **extra-judicial** ~ außergerichtliche Beweisführung; **fabricated** ~ fabrizierte Beweismittel; **false** ~ falsche Zeugenaussagen; **flimsy** ~ nicht überzeugendes Beweismaterial; **fresh** ~ neues Beweismaterial; **hearsay** ~ Beweis von Hörensagen; **inadmissible** ~ unzulässiger Beweismaterial; **incompetent** ~ nicht zulässiges Beweismaterial; **incontestable** ~ einwandfreies Beweismaterial; **inculpatory** ~ Schuldbeweis; **indecisive** ~ unschlüssiges Beweismaterial; **indirect** ~ indirekter Beweis, Indizienbeweis; **internal** ~ in der Urkunde selbst liegende Beweiskraft; **intrinsic** ~ Urkundenbeweis; **King's** ~ *(Br.)* Kron-, Belastungszeuge; **legal** ~ rechtlich zugelassenes Beweismaterial; **mathematical** ~ zwingende Beweiskraft; **moral** ~ Wahrscheinlichkeitsbeweis; **opinion** ~ gutachtliche Beweisführung; **oral (parole)** ~ mündliche Zeugenaussage; **original** ~ mit Originalurkunden geführter Beweis; **partial** ~ Teilbeweis; **positive** ~ endgültiger (eindeutiger) Beweis; **presumptive** ~ Indizien-, Wahrscheinlichkeitsbeweis; **prima-facie** ~ glaubhafter Beweis, Beweis des ersten Anscheins; **primary** ~ primäre Beweismittel, Beweismittel erster Ordnung; **probable** ~ Wahrscheinlichkeitsbeweis; **probative** ~ bestätigendes Beweismaterial; **proper** ~ zulässiges Beweismittel; **Queen's** ~ *(Br.)* Kron-, Belastungszeuge; **real** ~ Beweis durch Augenscheinseinnahme, tatsächliche Beweisführung; **rebutting** ~ Gegenbeweis; **relevant** ~ Sachbeweis; **satisfactory** ~ aus-, hinreichendes Beweismaterial; **secondary** ~ mittelbarer Beweis, indirekte Beweismittel; **secondary documentary** ~ indirekter Urkundenbeweis; **second-hand** ~ Beweis aus zweiter Hand; **solid** ~ handfester Beweis; **state's** ~ *(US)* Kron-, Belastungszeuge, Beweismaterial der Staatsanwaltschaft; **striking** ~ eindeutiger Beweis; **substantive** ~ erhebliches Beweismaterial; **sufficient** ~ ausreichender Beweis; **supporting** ~ Beweisunterlage, -material; ~ **tendered** angebotener Beweis; **traditionary** ~ überlieferter Beweis; **unchallengeable** ~ unwiderlegbares Beweismaterial; **written** ~ Urkundenbeweis, schriftliche Beweisführung, schriftliches Beweismaterial;

~ **of age** Altersanzeichen; ~ **satisfactory to the company** für die Versicherungsgesellschaft ausreichender Beweis; ~ **of conformity as may be required** vertragsgemäße Belege; ~ **of a contract** Vertragsnachweis, -urkunde; ~ **of counsel** Rechtsgutachten; ~ **in court** gerichtliche Beweiserhebung; ~ **of debt** Schuldurkunde; ~ **for the defence** Entlastungsmaterial, -beweis; ~ **of guilt** Schuldbeweis; ~ **by inspection** Augenscheinsbeweis; ~ **having a bearing on the issue** erhebliches Beweismaterial; ~ **of indebtedness** Schuldurkunde, -titel; ~ **of insolvency** Nachweis der Zahlungsunfähigkeit; ~ **of insurability satisfactory to company** Nachweis der Versicherungsfähigkeit; ~ **of intention** Absichtsnachweis; ~ **sufficient in law** rechtserhebliches Beweismaterial, rechtserheblicher Beweis; ~ **of means** Mittel-, Vermögensnachweis; ~ **of memory** Nachweis der Merkfähigkeit; ~ **of payment** Zahlungsnachweis; ~ **for the prosecution** Belastungsmaterial; ~ **of prosperity** Wohlstandsmerkmale; ~ **of shipment** Versandnachweis; ~ **of success** Erfolgsnachweis; ~ **to support the verdict** urteiltragendes Beweismaterial; ~ **of title** Eigentumsnachweis; **conclusive** ~ **of title** Grundbuchvermutung; ~ **of ill will** Anzeichen böser Absichten; ~ **in writing** schriftliche Beweisführung;

~ *(v.)* dartun, beweisen, bestätigen, verkörpern, *(testify)* als Zeuge aussagen;

to acknowledge the ~ **of the facts** sich der Macht der Tatsachen beugen; **to adduce** ~ Beweis erbringen (antreten); **to admit in** ~ als Beweis zulassen; **to arrange the** ~ **against s. o.** Beweisergebnis zu jds. Ungunsten verfälschen; **to bar as** ~ nicht als Beweismittel zulassen; **to be** ~ als Beweis gelten; **to be in** ~ dem Gericht als Beweis vorliegen; **to be called on to give** ~ als Zeuge aufgerufen werden; **to be plain on the** ~ aufgrund der Beweiserhebung feststehen; **to be receivable in** ~ als Beweismittel zugelassen sein; **to bear** ~ Zeugnis ablegen; **to bring** ~ **forward** Beweis erbringen; **to call s. o. in** ~ als Zeugen benennen; **to collect** ~ Beweismaterial zusammenstellen; **to come up with** ~ mit Beweismaterial herausrücken; **to condemn s. o. on slight** ~ j. auf Grund geringer Indizien verurteilen; **to cook up** ~ Beweismaterial fälschen; **to cover up** ~ Beweismittel unterdrücken; **to decide whether a document is admissible as** ~ über die gesetzliche Beweiskraft einer Urkunde entscheiden; **to furnish** ~ **of s. th.** etw. beweisen, Beweis liefern, Belege beibringen (dartun); **to give** ~ Aussage machen, als Zeuge aussagen; **to give** ~ **in s. one's favo(u)r** zu jds. Gunsten aussagen, Zeugnis für j. ablegen; **to give** ~ **for (against) s. o.** für (gegen) j. aussagen; **to give false** ~ falsche Aussage machen; **to have** ~ **for a statement** Behauptung beweisen können; **to hear** ~ in die Beweisaufnahme eintreten, Beweisaufnahme vornehmen, Beweis erheben; **to hunt out (up)** ~ Beweismaterial aufstöbern; **to impound s. th. as** ~ etw. als Beweismittel beschlagnahmen; **to introduce** ~ Beweis antreten; **to lead** ~ Beweismaterial liefern; **to like to be very much in** ~ es darauf anlegen, in der Öffentlichkeit bemerkt zu werden; **to present for** ~ Beweismittel beibringen; **to produce** ~ Beweismaterial vorlegen, Zeugen stellen; **to put in as** ~ als (zum) Beweis anführen; **to put one's faith in s. one's** ~ sich auf jds. Zeugnis berufen; **to receive in** ~ als Beweismaterial zulassen; **to remove incriminatory** ~ **from the files** belastendes Beweismaterial aus den Akten verschwinden lassen; **to resist the** ~ Beweismaterial nicht zulassen; **to rule that the** ~ **is admissible** Beweisangebot für zulässig erklären; **to sift** ~ Beweismaterial sorgfältig prüfen; **to sum up the** ~ Beweisergebnis zusammenfassen; **to suppress** ~ Beweismittel unterdrücken; **to take** ~ Beweis erheben, Beweisaufnahme vornehmen; **to take s. one's** ~ j. als Zeugen vernehmen; **to take down the** ~ zu Protokoll nehmen, Protokoll aufnehmen; **to take exception to an** ~ Beweisergebnis nicht anerkennen; **to tender** ~ Beweis anbieten; **to turn King's (Queen's, *Br.*, state's, *US*)** ~ Kronzeuge werden, als Kronzeuge auftreten; **to weigh** ~ Beweis würdigen, Beweiswürdigung vornehmen; **to withhold** ~ Beweismaterial (Beweismittel) zurückhalten.

evidenced| by ausgewiesen durch; ~ **in writing** schriftlich nachgewiesen.

evident offenbar, augenscheinlich;
to make ~ klarstellen.

evidentiary, to be klar beweisen;
~ **facts** nachgewiesene Tatsachen.

evil Unheil, Übel, Schaden;
for good or ~ auf Gedeih und Verderb; **the lesser** ~ das kleinere Übel; **of two ~s choose the less** das kleinere Übel wählen;
to speak ~ **of s. o.** schlecht über j. sprechen;
~ **conduct** amoralisches Verhalten; ~ **day** Unglückstag; ~ **eye** *(fig.)* schlimmer Einfluß; **to look with an** ~ **eye on s. o.** j. scheel ansehen; **to have** ~ **forebodings** schlimme Vorahnungen haben; **to live an** ~ **life** unmoralisches Leben führen; ~ **news** katastrophale Nachrichten; ~ **reports afloat about s. o.** böse Gerüchte über j. im Umlauf; ~ **reputation** schlechter Ruf; ~ **tidings** schlechte Nachrichten.

evildoer Übeltäter.

evocation *(law)* Verweisung an ein höheres Gericht.

evoke *(v.)* **a case** Fall vor ein anderes Gericht ziehen.

evolution Fortschritt, *(mil.)* Stellungswechsel.

ex exklusive, ohne, ausschließlich, *(former)* früher, ehemalig, *(securities)* exklusive, abzüglich, *(shipping point)* ab;
~ **all** ausschließlich aller [Dividenden]rechte; ~ **ante** vorausberechnet; ~ **capitalization** ohne Anspruch auf Gratisaktien; ~ **car** ab Waggon; ~ **cathedra** von maßgeblicher Seite; ~ **contractus** vertraglich; ~ **coupon** ohne Kupon; ~ **dividend** ausschließlich Dividende; ~ **dock** *(US)* ab Kai; ~ **drawing** ohne Ziehung;

~ factory ab Fabrik (Werk); **~ gratia** ohne Anerkennung einer Rechtspflicht; **~ interest** ohne Zinsen; **~ London** ab London; **~ new** *(Br.)* ohne Bezugsrecht auf neue Aktien; **~ officio** von Amts wegen; **~ parte** auf Antrag; **~ quay [duty paid]** ab Kai [verzollt]; **~ post facto law** rückwirkendes Gesetz; **~ rights** ohne Bezugsrecht; **~ ship** frei ab Schiff; **~ stock dividend** *(US)* ohne Dividende mit Gratisschein; **~ warehouse** ab Lager; **~ works** ab Werk;

~-convict früherer Zuchthäusler; **~-employer** früherer Arbeitgeber; **~-farm price** Preis ab Hof; **~-mayor** alter Bürgermeister; **~-minister** ehemaliger Minister; **~-official** abgegangener Beamter.

ex officio von Amts wegen;

to act ~ von Amts wegen tätig werden; **to be present at a meeting ~** an einer Sitzung von Amts wegen (offiziell) teilnehmen;

~ member Mitglied kraft Amtes.

ex-service man Veteran.

exact genau, sorgfältig, exakt, präzise, *(rigoro(u)s)* streng, rigoros;

~ (v.) fordern, verlangen, erzwingen, *(fees)* erheben, *(payments)* eintreiben;

~ care and attention Sorgfalt und Aufmerksamkeit erfordern; **~ obedience** Gehorsam erzwingen; **~ payment of a debt from s. o.** Schulden bei jem. eintreiben;

to be ~ in business in Geschäften zuverlässig sein; **to be ~ in one's duties** seine Aufgaben sorgfältig erledigen; **to be ~ in one's payments** pünktlich zahlen, pünktlicher Zahler sein; **~ amount** genauer Betrag; **to tender the ~ amount** Nachschußsumme aufbringen; **~ copy of a document** wortgetreue Urkundenabschrift; **~ directions** genaue Anweisungen; **to give ~ details** genaue Details geben; **~ instrument** präzises Instrument; **~ interest** Zinsen auf Basis von 365 Tagen; **~ knowledge** umfassende Kenntnisse; **~ laws** strenge Gesetze; **~ memory** zuverlässiges Gedächtnis; **~ scholar** gewissenhafter Gelehrter; **~ translation** genaue (wortgetreue) Übersetzung; **~ value** genauer Wert; **his ~ words** seine tatsächlichen Worte.

exactable eintreibar.

exacting streng, genau;

to be too ~ with s. o. zu hohe Forderungen an j. stellen; **~ employer** anspruchsvoller Arbeitgeber; **~ task** anstrengende Arbeit.

exaction [Forderungs]beitreibung, *(exorbitant demand)* übertriebene Forderung;

~ of taxes Steuereintreibung.

exactness Genauigkeit, Exaktheit.

exactor Steuereintreiber.

exaggerate *(v.)* **one's claims** übertriebene Forderungen (Ansprüche) stellen.

exaggerated übertrieben, hochgeschraubt;

~ demand Übernachfrage; **~ price** übersetzter Preis; **to have an ~ sense of one's own importance** sich überbewerten; **~ value** zu hoch angesetzter Wert.

exaggeration Übertreibung, zu starke Betonung;

~ of value Überbewertung.

exalt *(v.)* im Rang erhöhen;

~ to the skies in den Himmel heben.

examination *(of accounts)* Revision, Prüfung, Kontrolle, Nachrechnung, Durchsicht, *(bankruptcy proceedings)* Vernehmung [des Gemeinschuldners], *(control)* Überrechnung, Kontrolle, *(criminal practice)* Befragung, Vernehmung, Verhör, *(investigation)* Untersuchung, [Über]prüfung, Einsichtnahme, *(patent office)* Patentuntersuchung, *(protocol)* Vernehmungsprotokoll, *(real-estate purchase)* Grundbucheinsicht, *(test)* Prüfung, Examen;

on ~ bei Prüfung; **on closer ~** bei näherer Besichtigung;

academic ~ akademische Prüfung, Universitätsexamen; **assembled ~s** gemeinsame Prüfung; **civil service ~** *(Br.)* Aufnahmeprüfung in den Staatsdienst; **close ~** genaue Prüfung; **[college] entrance ~** [Universitäts]aufnahmeprüfung; **competitive entrance ~** Bewerbungsprüfung; **cross-~** Kreuzverhör; **customs ~** Zollrevision; **direct ~** direkte Befragung, Zeugenvernehmung durch die benennende Partei; **end-of-year ~** Jahresschlußexamen, -prüfung; **entrance ~** Aufnahmeprüfung; **expert ~** fachmännische Überprüfung; **final ~** Abschlußprüfung; **hard ~** schwere Prüfung; **intermediate ~** Zwischenprüfung; **medical ~** ärztliche Untersuchung; **mental ~** Untersuchung auf den Geisteszustand; **oral ~** mündliches Examen, mündliche Prüfung; **overall ~** Generalüberholung; **pass ~** akademisches Schlußexamen; **post-mortem ~** Obduktion, Leichenschau; **preliminary ~** *(criminal law)* Vorprüfung; **previous**

~ Aufnahmeprüfung; private ~ Vernehmung durch den Einzelrichter; **promotional ~** Doktorexamen; **psychiatric ~** psychiatrische Untersuchung; **public ~** Vernehmung, Prüfungstermin; **qualifying ~** Fach-, Eignungsprüfung; **separate ~** getrennte Vernehmung; **stiffish ~** ziemlich schwere Prüfung; **term ~** Zwischenprüfung, -examen; **unassembled ~** Einzelexamen, -prüfung; **university ~** Aufnahmeverfahren, -prüfung; **viva voce ~** mündliche Prüfung; **written ~** schriftliche Prüfung, schriftliches Examen;

~ of business accounts Rechnungsprüfung; **~ of a long account** Belegprüfung; **~ of the baggage** *(US)* Gepäckrevision; **~ of a bankrupt** Vernehmung des Gemeinschuldners; **~ of the bill of health** Überprüfung des Gesundheitsattests; **~ of the books** Bücherrevision; **~-in-chief** erste Zeugenvernehmung, Zeugenbefragung durch den eigenen Anwalt; **~ of financial condition** Prüfung der wirtschaftlichen Verhältnisse; **~ of the goods** Besichtigung der Waren; **~ of luggage** *(Br.)* Gepäckrevision; **~ before a magistrate** Vernehmung durch den Einzelrichter; **~ on oath** eidliche Zeugenbefragung (Vernehmung); **~ of passports** Paßkontrolle; **~ of a prisoner** Gefangenenverhör, -vernehmung; **~ of proxies (power)** Vollmachtsüberprüfung; **~ of the soundness** Bonitätsprüfung; **~ of title** Grundbucheinsicht; **~ before trial** Zeugenvernehmung vor Verhandlungsbeginn; **~ of a witness** Zeugenvernehmung;

to apply for admission to an ~ sich zu einer Prüfung (einem Examen) melden; **to be in for an ~** vor einem Examen stehen; **to be permitted to sit for an ~** zu einer Prüfung zugelassen werden; **to be under ~** geprüft (untersucht) werden, *(criminal)* vernommen (verhört) werden; **to conduct a sophisticated ~ of the financial capacity** finanzielle Leistungsfähigkeit einer ausgeklügelten Überprüfung unterziehen; **to enter for an ~** sich zum Examen (zur Prüfung) melden; **to fail** *(Br.)* **(flunk,** *US)* **in an ~** Examen (Prüfung) nicht bestehen, durchfallen; **to go in (up) for an ~** sich einem Examen (einer Prüfung) unterziehen, in ein Examen gehen (steigen); **to have under constant ~** laufend prüfen; **to have a shy at an ~** Examensversuch riskieren; **to hold an ~** Examen (Prüfung) abhalten; **to hold a post-mortem ~** obduzieren; **to pass one's ~** sein Examen (seine Prüfung) bestehen (ablegen), sich erfolgreich einer Prüfung unterziehen; **to pass in the written ~** schriftliche Prüfung bestehen; **to pass one's school-leaving ~** sein Abitur machen; **to pass an ~ with hono(u)rs** Prüfung mit Auszeichnung bestehen; **to prepare o. s. for an ~** sich auf ein Examen (eine Prüfung) vorbereiten; **to present o. s. punctually for the ~** pünktlich zur Untersuchung kommen (erscheinen); **to put in for an ~** sich zu einer Prüfung anmelden; **to put s. o. through a searching ~** j. auf Herz und Nieren prüfen; **to qualify for an ~** Prüfungsvoraussetzungen erfüllen; **to reenter an ~** sich erneut zu einer Prüfung melden; **to shave through an ~** bei einer Prüfung gerade noch durchrutschen; **to sit for an ~** sich zum Examen melden, in ein Examen gehen (steigen), im Examen sitzen; **to subject s. o. to an ~** j. einer Prüfung unterziehen; **to take an ~** Prüfung (Examen) bestehen (machen); **to take s. one's ~** j. ins Verhör nehmen; **to take the ~ of a prisoner** Gefangenen einem Verhör unterziehen; **to undergo an ~** verhört (vernommen) werden; **to undergo a medical ~** sich ärztlich untersuchen lassen;

~ authorities Prüfungsgremium; **~ board** Prüfungsausschuß, -gremium; **~ department** *(patent office)* Prüfstelle; **~ fee** Prüfungsgebühr; **~ mark** Prüfungs-, Examensnote; **~ paper** schriftliche Prüfungsarbeit; **to give out the ~ papers** Prüfungsaufgaben bekanntgeben; **~ performance** Examensleistungen; **~ qualification** Examensnachweis; **~ question** Examens-, Prüfungsfrage; **~ report** Prüfungsbericht; **~ requirements** Prüfungsvorschriften; **~ result** Prüfungsergebnis; **~ room** Prüfungszimmer, *(doctor)* Untersuchungszimmer; **~ schools** *(Br.)* prüfungspflichtige Fächer; **~ score** Prüfungsergebnis; **~ system** Prüfungsverfahren; **~ technique** Prüfungsmethode.

examine *(v.)* prüfen, untersuchen, revidieren, *(account)* durchsehen, überprüfen, *(interrogate)* vernehmen, verhören, be-, ausfragen, *(records)* [Grundbuch] einsehen;

cross-~ ins Kreuzverhör nehmen;

~ accounts Rechnungen prüfen; **~ the bill of health** Gesundheitsattest überprüfen; **~ the books** Bücher prüfen (revidieren); **~ a building** Gebäude untersuchen; **~ a candidate** Kandidaten prüfen; **~ carefully** einer sorgfältigen Durchsuchung unterziehen; **~ as censor** zensieren; **~ closely** eingehend prüfen, beaugenscheinigen; **~ one's conscience** sein Gewissen befragen; **~ the goods** Ware prüfen; **~ item by item** Punkt für Punkt durchgehen; **~ into a matter** gründlich in eine Sache einsteigen; **~ on oath** eidlich vernehmen; **~ one by one** einzeln durchprüfen, durchmustern; **~ a pupil** Schüler prüfen; **~ old records** alte

Akten durchgehen; **to stop and ~ a ship** Schiff anhalten und durchsuchen; **~ a statement** Zusammenstellung prüfen; **~ thoroughly** gründlich erörtern; **~ a witness in a court of law** Zeugen gerichtlich vernehmen (einvernehmen).

examined copy mit dem Original verglichene Abschrift;
to be ~ on a subject in einem Fach geprüft werden.

examinee Prüfling, Examenskandidat.

examiner Untersucher, *(accountant)* Revisor, Prüfer, Kontroll-, Prüfungsbeamter, *(court)* Einzelrichter, *(customs)* Zollsachverständiger, *(interrogator)* Vernehmer, Verhörer, *(US, patent office)* Vorprüfer, Patentbeamter;
bank ~ Bankrevisor; **National ͦ** *(US)* Bundesprüfer für Bankinstitute; **medical ~** Vertrauensarzt; **special ~** mit der Vernehmung beauftragter Richter;
~ in chancery beauftragter Vernehmungsrichter.

examining, on bei Prüfung;
~ board Prüfungsgremium; **~ body** Prüfungsausschuß, -kommission; **~ judge (magistrate)** Untersuchungsrichter; **~ post** *(mil.)* Durchlaßposten.

example [Muster]beispiel, Exempel, *(sample)* Muster, Modell, *(warning)* warnendes Beispiel, Warnung;
beyond ~ beispiellos;
numerical ~ Zahlenbeispiel;
~ of advertising Werbebeispiel;
to follow s. one's ~ jds. Beispiel folgen; **to make an ~ of s. o.** j. zum Zweck der generellen Abschreckung bestrafen, Exempel an jem. statuieren; **to set a good ~** mit gutem Beispiel vorangehen.

excavate *(v.)* ausgraben, ausschachten;
~ a trench Graben ausheben; **~ a tunnel** Tunnel graben.

excavation Ausgrabung, *(cavity)* Höhle, Grube, *(railway)* Durchstich, Einschnitt;
~ site Baustelle.

exceed *(v.)* übersteigen, -schießen, -schreiten, *(predominate)* sich auszeichnen;
~ a prescribed amount Limit überschreiten; **~ one's authority** seine Vollmacht (Befugnisse) überschreiten; **~ the budget** Etat überschreiten; **~ s. one's expectations** jds. Erwartungen übertreffen; **~ one's instructions** seine Anweisungen (Instruktionen) überschreiten; **~ a limit** Limit überschreiten; **~ the speed limit** zulässige Geschwindigkeit (Geschwindigkeitsgrenze) überschreiten; **~ the prescribed period** Frist überschreiten; **~ one's powers** seine Befugnisse überschreiten; **~ one's rights** seine Rechte mißbrauchen; **~ in size and population** größen- und bevölkerungsmäßig übertreffen; **~ the sum of ...** Summe von ... übersteigen; **~ in value** wertmäßig übersteigen, an Wert übertreffen, im Wert übersteigen.

exceeding außerordentlich, äußerst;
~ of budget Haushaltsüberschreitung; **~ the speed limit** Überschreitung der Höchstgeschwindigkeit, Geschwindigkeitsüberschreitung;
~ *(a.)* übersteigend, mehr als;
not ~ in the aggregate one million dollars nicht mehr als insgesamt eine Million Dollar;
~ amount überschießender Betrag.

excel *(v.)* übertreffen, -ragen;
~ o. s. sich selbst übertreffen; **~ all one's rivals** gesamte Konkurrenz überflügeln.

excellence Vorzüglichkeit, Güte, ausgezeichnete Leistung.

excellency, Your Euer Exzellenz.

excellent erstklassig, vorzüglich, erlesen, von höchster Qualität;
~ piece of work hervorragende Arbeit.

excelsior *(print.)* Brillant;
~ *(a.)* von höchster Qualität, prima.

except *(v.)* *(exclude)* ausschließen, -nehmen, *(object)* Einwendungen erheben;
~ to a witness Zeugen ablehnen;
~ *(a.)* ausgenommen, außer;
~ as otherwise provided vorbehaltlich gegenteiliger Bestimmungen; **~ in time of war** Kriegszeiten ausgenommen.

excepted district *(education)* selbständiger Bezirk.

excepting ausgenommen, mit Ausnahme, *(deed)* vorbehaltlich.

exception Ausnahme, Ausschließung, *(document)* Vorbehalt, Vorbehaltsklausel, *(insurance contract)* Risikoausschluß, *(plea, US)* Einrede, Einwendung, [Verfahrens]einwand, *(specific clause in contract)* [in der Urkunde] ausgenommener Gegenstand, *(zoning)* Bauausnahmegenehmigung;
above ~ unanfechtbar; **by way of ~** ausnahmsweise;
declinatory ~ Einwand der Unzuständigkeit des Gerichts; **dilatory ~** aufschiebende Einrede; **general ~** Einrede des unschlüssigen Klagevorbringens; **marginal ~s** geringe Ausnahmen;

peremptory ~ peremptorische (rechtsvernichtende) Einrede; **solitary ~** einzige Ausnahme; **statutory ~** gesetzliche Ausnahme;
~ to classification Tarifänderung; **~ of no cause of action** Einrede der Unschlüssigkeit einer Klage; **~ to a rule** Ausnahmefall, -regel, Ausnahme von der Regel; **~ to a witness** Ablehnung eines Zeugen, Zeugenablehnung;
to admit of no ~ keine Ausnahme zulassen; **to make an ~ in s. one's case** bei jem. eine Ausnahme machen; **to take ~** Einwendungen erheben (machen), Anstoß nehmen, beanstanden; **to take ~ to an audit report** Revisionsbericht beanstanden; **to take ~ to evidence** Beweisergebnis nicht anerkennen; **to take ~ to a statement** einer Behauptung widersprechen; **to take ~ to a witness** Zeugen ablehnen;
~ sheet Tarifänderungsbescheid.

exceptionable tadelnswert, anstößig.

exceptional außergewöhnlich;
~ advantage Sondervorteil; **~ case** Sonder-, Ausnahmefall; **~ circumstances** außergewöhnliche Umstände, Ausnahme-, Sonderfall; **~ grant** Ausnahmebewilligung; **~ hardship** außergewöhnlicher Härtefall; **~ offer** Sonder-, Ausnahmeangebot; **~ opportunity** außergewöhnliche Gelegenheit; **~ position** Ausnahme-, Vorzugsstellung; **~ price** Sonder-, Ausnahmepreis; **~ provision** Sonder-, Ausnahmebestimmung; **~ rate** Ausnahme-, Sondertarif; **~ talent** einmalige Begabung; **~ tariff** Ausnahmetarif.

exceptionally cheap außergewöhnlich billig.

exceptive|clause Ausnahmebestimmung; **~ law** Ausnahmegesetz.

excerpt [Buch]auszug, Excerpt;
by the way of ~ auszugsweise;
out-of-context ~ aus dem Zusammenhang gerissene Stelle;
near-book ~ Buchauszug;
~ *(v.)* Auszug machen, ausziehen, exzerpieren.

excess *(outrage)* Exzeß, Ausschreitung, *(superabundance)* Übermaß, *(surplus amount)* Mehrbetrag, Überschuß;
in ~ im Übermaß, überflüssig; **in ~ of** mehr als;
~es Ausschreitungen;
~ of age Überalterung; **~ of authority** Vollmachtsüberschreitung; **~ of birth over death (in birth rates)** Geburtenüberschuß; **~ arising in consolidation** Konsolidierungsausgleichsposten; **~ of expenditure over revenues** Ausgaben-, Unkostenüberhang; **~ of exports** Ausfuhrüberschuß; **~ of imports over exports** Einfuhrüberschuß; **~ of income** Einnahmeüberschuß; **~ of population** Bevölkerungsüberschuß; **~ of granted powers** Überschreitung verliehener Befugnisse; **~ of provisions** überschüssige Vorräte; **~ of purchasing power** Kaufkraftüberhang; **~ of receipts over expenditure** Einnahmeüberschuß; **~ of tare** Übertara; **~es committed by the troops** von den Truppen verübte Ausschreitungen; **~ of weight** Mehrgewicht; **~ of work** Mehrarbeit, zusätzliche Arbeit, Arbeitsüberlastung;
~ *(v.)* *(Br., railway)* Zuschlagsfahrpreis erheben;
to act in ~ of one's rights seine Rechte mißbrauchen; **to be generous to ~** fast zu großzügig sein; **to be in ~ of the demand** Bedarf übersteigen; **to be in ~ of the sum required** benötigten Betrag überschreiten; **to be in ~ of the official wage rate** übertariflich bezahlt werden; **to commit ~es** Ausschreitungen begehen; **to drink to ~** übermäßig trinken; **to pay the ~ [on one's tickets]** Fahrpreiszuschlag zahlen;
~ amount überzahlter Betrag, Mehrbetrag; **~ application** Überzeichnung; **~ of loss background** Erfahrungen auf dem Gebiet der Exzedentenschadensversicherung; **~ baggage** *(US)* Gepäckübergewicht, Übergewicht, Mehrgepäck; **~ burden** *(Br.)* zusätzliche Verbrauchsteuerbelastung; **~ capacity** Überkapazität; **to work off its ~ capacity** seine Überkapazität loswerden; **~ charge** Kosten-, Gebührenzuschlag, *(life insurance)* Sicherheitszuschlag; **~ charges on income** Gewinn übersteigende Einkommensbelastungen; **~ check** Zusatzgepäckschein; **~ clause** *(insurance)* Sicherheitszuschlag; **~ condemnation** unberechtigte Enteignung; **~ consumption** Mehrverbrauch; **~ deductions** Sonderfreibetrag; **~ deductions account** Sonderfreibetragskonto; **~ demand** Nachfrageüberhang, Übernachfrage; **~ expenditure** Mehrausgaben; **~ fare** Fahrpreiszuschlag; **~ fee** Gebührenzuschlag, Zuschlagsgebühr; **~ freight** Frachtzuschlag, Überfracht; **~ hour** Überstunde; **~ insurance** Selbstbehalt; **~ liquidity** Liquiditätsüberhang, Überliquidität; **~ loan** *(US)* über den gesetzlichen Höchstbetrag hinausgehender Bankkredit; **~ loss insurance** Exzedentenrückversicherung; **~ luggage** *(Br.)* Mehr-, Übergewicht; **~-luggage charge** *(Br.)* Gewichtszuschlag; **~ money** Geldüberhang; **~ mortality** Sterblichkeitsüberhang; **~ offer** Überangebot; **~ payment of income**

tax Einkommensteuerüberzahlung; ~ **postage** Nachgebühr, Strafporto; **to trim** ~ **production** Produktionsüberschüsse beseitigen; ~ **profit** Wucher-, Über-, Sonder-, Kriegs-, Mehrgewinn; ~ **profits duty** *(Br.)* **(tax,** *US***)** Kriegs-, Übergewinn-, Sonder-, Mehrgewinnsteuer; ~ **profiteer** Wucherer, Kriegsgewinnler; ~ **reinsurance** Rückversicherung oberhalb des eigenen Risikos; ~ **loss reinsurance** Exzedentenrückversicherung; ~ **of loss ratio treaty** *(reinsurance)* Rückversicherungsvertrag zur verhältnismäßigen Begrenzung des Versicherungsrisikos; ~ **pressure** Überdruck; ~ **reserve** *(banking)* freie Rücklagen, *(US)* außerordentliche Reserve, Sonderrücklage; ~ **shares** zusätzlich angebotene Aktien; ~ **spending power** überschüssige Kaufkraft; **to mop** ~ **spending power** überschüssige Kaufkraft abschöpfen; ~ **supply** Überangebot; ~ **ticket** Zusatzfahrschein; ~ **of loss treaty** [Schadens]exzedentenvertrag; ~ **valuation** Mehrwertung; ~ **value** Mehrwert; ~ **vote** Nachbewilligung; ~ **weight** Mehr-, Übergewicht, Gewichtsüberschuß.

excessive übermäßig, übertrieben; ~ **in amount** zu hoch angesetzt; ~ **assessment** zu hohe Steuerveranlagung; ~ **bail** überhöhte Kaution; ~ **boom** überhitzte Konjunktur; ~ **charge** überhöhter Preis, wucherische Forderung; ~ **charges** übertriebene Gebühren; ~ **damages** übertrieben hohe Schadenersatzzuerkennung; ~ **demand** Überbedarf, -nachfrage, Nachfrageüberhang; **to make an** ~ **display of force** mißbräuchliche Machtdemonstration durchführen; ~ **drunkenness** gemeingefährliche Trunkenheit; ~ **encumbrance** Überschuldung; ~ **fine** Existenzgrundlage gefährdende Geldstrafe; ~ **indebtedness** Überschuldung; ~ **interest** Wucherzins[en]; ~ **labo(u)r** übermäßige Arbeit; ~ **price** Überpreis, überhöhter Preis; ~ **purchasing power** Kaufkraftüberhang; ~ **reserves** *(banking)* freie Reserven (Rücklagen); ~ **speed** überhöhte Geschwindigkeit; ~ **supply** Überangebot; ~ **supply of money** Geldüberhang; ~ **tax** überhöhte Steuer; ~ **or intemperate use of intoxicants** übermäßiger Alkoholgenuß.

excessively intoxicated unter übermäßigem Alkoholgenuß stehend, volltrunken.

exchange *(barter transaction)* Tauschgeschäft, -handel, *(capital assets)* Anlagenaustausch, *(circulation of bills)* Wechselverkehr, *(currency)* Währung, Valuta, Devisen, *(of goods)* [Aus]-tausch, Eintausch, Umtausch, *(interchange)* Auswechslung, *(market)* Börse, *(money ~)* Wechselstube, -stelle, *(of money)* Ein-, Umwechslung, *(object of exchange)* Tauschgegenstand, *(rate of exchange)* [Wechsel]kurs, *(reciprocal transfer)* Austausch von Landbesitz, *(tel.)* Fernsprechamt, -vermittlung, *(securities)* Umtausch [von Wertpapieren];
at the ~ **of** zum Kurs von; **at the current** ~ **of** zum Tageskurs von; **at the quoted** ~ zum angeführten Kurs; **in** ~ als Ersatz (Gegenleistung); **[quoted] on the** ~ an der Börse gehandelt, börsenfähig; **with** ~ *(US)* zuzüglich Einzugsspesen; **with a high rate of** ~ valutastark;
~s *(exchange market, Br.)* Devisenmarkt;
automatic ~ *(tel.)* Amt mit Selbstwähleinrichtung; **bank (banker's)** ~ Bankwechsel; **blocked** ~ blockierte Devisenbestände; **commercial** ~ Warenbörse; **commodity** ~ Warenbörse, Produktenbörse; **Consolidated** ℮ New Yorker Börse; **corn** ~ Getreidebörse; **cotton** ~ Baumwollbörse; **cross** ~ Wechselarbitrage; **cultural** ~ Kulturaustausch; **currency** ~ Devisenbörse; **current** ~ Tageskurs; **direct** ~ fester Umrechnungskurs; **dislocated** ~ zerrüttete Währung; **dollar** ~ Dollarwährung; **domestic** ~ Inlandwechsel; **dull** ~ flaue Börse; **employment** ~ *(Br.)* staatliche Arbeitsvermittlung; **evening** ~ Abendbörse; **favo(u)rable** ~ günstiger Kurs; **foreign** ~ ausländische Valuta, Devisen; **futures** ~ *(Br.)* Devisenterminhandel; **no goods** ~ kein Umtausch; **labour** ~ *(Br.)* Arbeitsamt; **local** ~ *(tel.)* Ortsamt; **long** ~ *(Br.)* langfristiger Devisenwechsel; **manual** ~ *(tel.)* Fernsprechvermittlung mit Handbetrieb; **nominal** ~ nomineller Kurs; **nontaxable** ~ steuerfreier Majoritätskauf; **part** ~ Teilzahlung; **pegged** ~ gestützter Wechselkurs; **private business** ~ eigene Telefonzentrale; **produce** ~ Produkten-, Warenbörse; **real** ~ bezahlter Kurs; **remaining foreign** ~ nicht ausgenutzte Devisenbeträge; ~ **the same** Wechselkurs unverändert; **share-for-share** ~ Umtauschverhältnis eins zu eins; **shipping** ~ Frachtenbörse; **short[-dated]** ~ kurzfristiger Wechsel; **stock** ~ Effekten-, Aktien-, Wertpapierbörse; **telephone** ~ [Telefon]zentrale, Fernsprechamt; **triangular** ~ dreiseitiges Verrechnungsabkommen; **true** ~ echtes Devisengeschäft; **trunk** ~ *(tel.)* Fernamt; **unfavo(u)rable** ~ ungünstiger Kurs; **variable** ~ variabler Kurs;
~ **of civilities** Austausch von Höflichkeiten; ~ **of commodities** Waren-, Güteraustausch; ~ **of currency** Geldumtausch; ~ **of**

the day Tageskurs; ~ **of dwellings** Wohnungstausch; ~ **of experiences** Erfahrungsaustausch; ~ **for forward (future,** *US***) delivery** Devisentermingeschäft; ~ **of goods** Waren-, Güteraustausch; ~ **of finished goods against raw materials** Austausch von Fertigwaren gegen Rohprodukte; ~ **of goods and services** Waren-, und Dienstleistungsverkehr; ~ **of ideas** Meinungs-, Gedankenaustausch; ~ **of information** Nachrichtenaustausch, Austausch von Informationen; ~ **of letters** Brief-, Schriftwechsel; ~ **of the market** Platzkurs; ~ **of notes** *(dipl.)* Notenwechsel, -austausch; ~ **of notes on the cancellation of passport requirements** Vereinbarung über Befreiung von Paßzwang; ~ **of patents** Patentaustausch; ~ **of populations** Bevölkerungsaustausch; ~ **of posts** Ämtertausch; ~ **of powers** Austausch der Vollmachten; ~ **of prisoners** Gefangenenaustausch; ~ **of ratifications** Austausch der Ratifizierungsurkunden; ~ **of services** Dienstleistungsverkehr; ~ **of shares (stock,** *US***)** Aktien[aus]-tausch; ~ **of shots** Kugelwechsel; ~ **for spot delivery** Devisenkassageschäft; ~ **of territory** Gebietsaustausch; ~ **without variation** keine Kursveränderungen; ~ **of views** Gedanken-, Meinungsaustausch;
~ **(v.)** [um]tauschen, ver-, austauschen, auswechseln, *(money)* [um]wechseln;
~ **blows** handgemein werden; ~ **civilities** Höflichkeiten austauschen; ~ **for** *(money)* wert sein; ~ **letters** korrespondieren; ~ **places** seine Plätze tauschen; ~ **into a new post** neuen Posten durch Tausch erhalten; ~ **presents** sich gegenseitig beschenken; ~ **prisoners** Gefangene austauschen; ~ **seats** Plätze tauschen; ~ **old shares for new** alte Aktien in neue eintauschen; **to be hammered on the** ~ *(Br.)* [an der Börse] für zahlungsunfähig erklärt werden; **to be long of** ~ *(US)* mit Devisen eingedeckt sein; **to gamble on the** ~ an der Börse spekulieren; **to give in** ~ einwechseln, in Tausch geben; **to list on the stock** ~ *(US)* zum Börsenhandel zulassen; **to make an** ~ Tausch vornehmen; **to peg the rate of sterling** ~ englische Währung stützen; **to suffer a loss in the** ~ **up to 10 per cent** Kurseinbuße bis zu 10% erleiden; **to surrender for** ~ zum Umtausch übergeben; **to take in** ~ als Tauschobjekt annehmen; **to take a car in part** ~ Auto in Zahlung nehmen;
~ **account** *(US)* Wechsel-, Valutakonto; ~ **accrual** Devisenzugänge; ~ **adjustment** Anpassung der Wechselkurse; ~ **advertising** Austauschinserat, Tauschanzeige; ~ **advice** Kursbericht, -notierung; ~ **agent** Börsenvertreter, Umtauschstelle [für Aktien]; ~ **agreement** Abkommen über den Zahlungsverkehr; ~ **allocation** Devisenquote; ~ **allotment** *(Br.)* Devisenzuteilung; ~ **allowance** Devisenzuteilung, -freibetrag; ~ **appreciation** Währungsaufwertung; ~ **arbitrage (arbitration)** Devisenarbitrage; **[foreign]** ~ **arrangements** Währungsbeziehungen, Zahlungsverkehr [mit dem Ausland]; ~ **assets** Devisenwerte; ~ **authorities** Devisenbehörde; ~ **authorization** Devisengenehmigung; ~ **balance** Devisenbilanz; ~ **balance in equilibrium** ausgeglichene Devisenbilanz; ~ **bank** Wechsel-, Devisenbank; ~ **bill of lading** Ersatzkonnossement; ~ **board** Kursanzeigetafel; ~ **broker** Wechsel-, Börsen-, Kurs-, Devisenmakler; ~ **brokerage** Wechselcourtage; ~ **business** Börsen-, Wechselgeschäft; **mere** ~ **business** Wechselreiterei; **to carry on** ~ **business** Wechselgeschäfte machen; ~ **calculation** Kursberechnung, Devisenrechnung; ~ **centre** Börsenplatz; ~ **charges** Wechselkosten; ~ **check** Austauschscheck; ~ **clause** Währungs-, Kursklausel; ~ **clearing** Devisenverrechnung; ~ **clearing agreement** Devisenabkommen; ~ **clearinghouse** Devisenverrechnungsstelle; ~ **commission** Wechselprovision; ~ **commission (committee)** Börsenkommission, -vorstand; ~ **commissionary** Börsenkommissar; ~ **commitments** Devisenengagements; ~ **compensation duty** Währungsausgleichszollzuschlag; ~ **control** offizielle Paritäts-, Devisenkontrolle, -bewirtschaftung; **to dismantle (lift)** ~ **controls** Devisenbewirtschaftung abbauen; ℮ **Control Act** *(Br.)* Devisenbewirtschaftungsgesetz; ~ **control authority** Devisenbehörde, -kontrollstelle; ~ **control regulations** Devisenbewirtschaftungsbestimmungen; ~ **control restrictions** Devisenbeschränkungen; ~~**controlling countries** Länder mit Devisenbewirtschaftung; ~ **copy** Austauschstück, Tauschexemplar; ~ **costs** Devisenaufwand, -kosten; ~ **credit** Devisen-, Fremdwährungskredit; ~ **deal** Tauschgeschäft; ~ **dealer** *(Br.)* Devisenhändler; ~ **dealings** *(Br.)* Devisenhandel, -geschäft; **forward** ~ **dealings** *(Br.)* Devisentermingeschäft; ~ **department** Devisenabteilung; ~ **depreciation** Währungsabwertung; ~ **difference** Kursdifferenz, -spanne; ~ **difficulties** schwierige Devisenlage; ~~**earning** devisenbringend; ~ **editor** Ausschnittsredakteur; ~ **embargo** Devisensperre; ℮ **Equalization Account** *(Br.)* Währungsausgleichsfonds; ℮ **Equalization Fund** *(US)* Währungsausgleichsfonds; ℮ **Equalization Grant** *(Br.)*

staatliche Ausgleichszuweisung; ~ **equation** Währungsausgleich; ~ **equilibrium** Zahlungsausgleich; ~ **expenditure** Devisenkosten; ~ **facilities** Devisenerleichterungen; ~ **fee** Devisengebühr; ~ **fluctuations** Kursschwankungen, Fluktuation der Devisenkurse; ~ **form** Umtauschformular; ~ **group** Austauschgruppe; ~ **guaranty** Kurssicherung; ~ **hall** Börsensaal; ~ **holdings** *(Br.)* Devisenbestände; ~ **intervention** Intervention der Währungsbehörden; ~ **lecturer** Austauschdozent; ~ **line** *(tel.)* Hauptanschluß, Amtsleitung; ~ **list** Kurszettel, -bericht, -notierung; ~ **loss** Währungs-, Devisenverlust; ~ **management** Devisenbewirtschaftung; ~ **market** Devisenmarkt; ~ **medium** Tauschmittel; ~ **member** Börsenmitglied; ~ **number** *(teletype writer)* Kennzahl; ~ **offer** Umtauschangebot; ~ **office** Wechselstube; ~ **operation** Umtausch-, Devisentransaktion, -geschäft; **forward** ~ **operations** Devisentermingeschäfte; ~ **order** *(airline)* Verrechnungsgutschrift, *(interline ticket)* Umtauschanweisung; ~ **outflow** Devisenabflüsse; ~ **outlet selling** Absatzbeschränkung auf ein Geschäft; ~ **parity** Währungs-, Kursparität; ~ **policies** Devisenpolitik; ~ **position** Devisenposition; ~ **premium** Agio; ~ **price** Umtauschpreis, *(stock exchange)* Börsenkurs; ~ **privilege** Umtauschrecht; ~ **proceeds** Devisenerlös, -ertrag; ~ **professor** Austauschprofessor; ~ **profit** Währungs-, Kursgewinn; ~ **program(me)** Austauschprogramm; ~ **quotation** Börsenkurs, -notierung; **telegraphic** ~ **quotation** Kursdepesche.

exchange rate Wechsel-, Umrechnungs-, Valuta-, Devisenkurs; **favo(u)rable** ~ günstiger Wechselkurs; **floating (flexible, free)** ~s bewegliche (freigegebene) Wechselkurse; **fluctuating** ~s schwankende Wechselkurse; **multiple** ~s multiple Wechselkurse; **official** ~ amtlicher Devisenkurs; **pegged** ~s feste Währungskurse;
to float the ~ Wechselkurs freigeben; **to keep down the Sterling** ~ Kurs des britischen Pfundes niedrig halten;
~ **arrangement** Wechselkursvereinbarung; ~ **change** Wechselkursänderung; ~ **depreciation** Verschlechterung des Wechselkurses; ~ **guarantee** Kursgarantie, -sicherung; ~ **guidelines** Wechselkursrichtlinien; ~ **policy** Wechselkurspolitik; ~ **regime** Wechselkurssystem; ~ **relationships** Wechselkursrelationen; ~ **structure** Wechselkursgefüge; ~ **surveillance** Wechselkursüberwachung; ~ **system** Wechselkurssystem.

exchange | rationing Devisenkontingentierung; ~ **regime** Wechselkurssystem; ~ **regulations** *(stock exchange)* Börsenordnung, *(control)* Devisenbestimmungen, -vorschriften; ~ **report** Börsenbericht; ~ **requirements** Devisenanforderungen; ~ **reserves** Devisenpolster, -reserve; ~ **restrictions** Devisen-, Zahlungsbeschränkungen, Devisenrestriktionen; ~ **restrictions on payments and transfers** Zahlungs- und Transferbeschränkungen, devisenrechtliche Beschränkungen; **foreign** ~ **risk** Kurs-, Währungsrisiko; ~ **risk guarantee** Währungsgarantie; ~ **rules** Devisenvorschriften; **to drop one's** ~ **seat** seine Mitgliedschaft bei der Börse (seinen Börsensitz) aufgeben; ~ **service** Wechseleinziehungsdienst; ~ **settlement** Devisenabrechnung; ~ **shortage** Devisenknappheit; ~ **slip** *(Br.)* Formular für gleichzeitige Ein- und Auszahlungen; ~ **stability** Kursstabilität; ~ **stabilization fund** *(US)* Währungsausgleichsfonds; ~ **standard** Wechselvaluta; ~ **statement** Devisenabrechnung; ~ **stringency** Devisenknappheit; ~ **student** Austauschstudent; **foreign** ~ **surplus** Devisenüberschuß; ~ **teacher** Austauschlehrer; ~-**teaching job** Austauschstelle; ~ **telegram** Kursdepesche; ~ **transaction** Tauschgeschäft, *(bill of exchange)* Devisengeschäft; **forward** ~ **transaction** Devisentermingeschäft; ~ **value** Tausch-, Börsen-, Marktwert.

exchangeability Vertauschbarkeit.
exchangeable aus-, vertauschbar, umtauschfähig;
~ **goods** Tauschprodukte; ~ **value** Tauschwert.
exchequer *(Bank of England, Br.)* Zentralkonto der Regierung bei der Staatsbank, *(Br.)* Staatskasse, Fiskus, *(Ministry of Finance)* Schatzamt, Finanzministerium, *(of a firm)* Finanzen, Kasse, Geldmittel;
common ~ Gemeinschaftskasse;
~ **aid** *(Br.)* staatliche Mittel; ♀ **and Audit Department** *(Br.)* Oberrechnungskammer, -hof; ~ **bill** *(former, Br.)* [kurzfristiger, verzinslicher] Schatzwechsel; ~ **bonds** *(Br.)* langfristige Schatzanweisungen; ~ **equalization grants** *(Br., till 1959)* Zuwendungen aus der Staatskasse an finanzschwache Gemeinden, Staatszuschüsse an die Gemeinden; ~ **money** Staatsmittel; ~ **return** *(Br.)* periodischer Bericht über das Zentralkonto der Regierung; ~ **stock** *(Br.)* Schatzanleihe; **6%** ~ **stocks** *(Br.)* sechsprozentige Staatsanleihe von 1970.
excisable [verbrauchs]steuerpflichtig, steuerbar;
~ **liquors** steuerpflichtige alkololische Getränke.

excise *(finance department, Br.)* Finanzverwaltung für indirekte Steuern, *(indirect tax)* indirekte Steuer, *(monopoly duty)* Monopolsteuer-, -gebühr, *(tax on consumption)* Waren-, Verbrauchssteuer, Akzise;
taxes, duties, imposts and ~s *(US)* Steuern, Zölle und Abgaben; ~ **on liquor** Getränkesteuer;
~ *(v.)* Verbrauchssteuer erheben, mit Verbrauchssteuer belegen, indirekt besteuern;
♀ **Account** *(Br.)* konsolidierter Staatsfonds; ~ **bond** Zollvermerk-, Zolldurchlaßschein; ~ **commission** *(US)* örtlicher Ausschuß für Schankkonzessionen; ~ **commissioner** Akziseneinnehmer; ~ **duty** *(Br.)* Warenabgabe [für Inlandswaren], Verbrauchssteuer; ~ **law** *(US)* Schanksteuergesetz; ~ **licence** *(US)* Schankkonzession, *(Br.)* Kraftfahrzeugbenutzungsgebühr; ~ **lieu property tax** *(US)* [etwa] Versicherungssteuer; ~ **office** *(Br.)* Akzisenamt, Regieverwaltung; ~ **officer** *(Br.)* Akziseneinnehmer; ~ **tax** *(US)* Verbrauchsabgabe, Sonderumsatz-, Gewerbe-, Konsumsteuer; ~ **warehouse** Steuerdepot, -lager.
exciseman *(Br.)* Akzisen-, [Verbrauchs]steuereinnehmer.
excite *(v.)* aufregen, *(photo)* [film]lichtempfindlich machen;
~ **customers' interest** Verbraucherinteresse hervorrufen; ~ **envy** Neid hervorrufen; ~ **interests to the highest pitch** allgemeine Anteilnahme zum Siedepunkt bringen; ~ **the mob** Pöbel anstacheln; ~ **the people to rebellion** Masse zum Aufruhr anstiften; ~ **a riot** Aufruhr auslösen.
excited crowd erregte Menge.
excitement Aufregung;
wild ~ wilde Erregung;
to be in a state of ~ ganz aus dem Häuschen sein; **to cause great** ~ große Aufregung hervorrufen; **to keep calm amid the** ~s im Gegensatz zu allen anderen einen kühlen Kopf behalten.
exciting spannend, nervenaufpeitschend;
~ **disaffection** Aufforderung zum Ungehorsam; ~ **novel** spannender Roman.
exclamation Ausruf, Geschrei;
~ **mark (point,** *US)* Ausrufungszeichen.
exclave Enklave.
exclude *(v.)* ausschließen, fernhalten;
~ **aliens from posts** Besetzung gewisser Stellen mit Ausländern nicht zulassen; ~ **unfounded claims** unbegründete Ansprüche nicht zulassen; ~ **immigrants form the country** Einwanderungsstopp vornehmen; ~ **all possibilities of doubt** alle Zweifelsfälle beseitigen; ~ **from a port** Hafenzugang verwehren; ~ **the general public** Öffentlichkeit ausschließen; ~ **both press and public** Presse und Öffentlichkeit ausschließen; ~ **s. o. from [membership in] a society** j. aus einem Verein ausschließen.
excluded ausgeschlossen;
~ **from a post** für eine Position nicht zugelassen.
excluding unter Ausschluß von, ausgenommen.
exclusion Ausschließung, Ausschluß, *(insurance)* Versicherungsbegrenzung, *(rejection)* Zurückweisung, Ablehnung;
to the ~ **of** unter Ausschluß von;
~ **of aliens** Einreiseverbot für Ausländer; ~ **of benefits** *(social insurance)* Leistungsausschluß; ~s **from gross income** steuerfreie Einkünfte; ~ **from inheritance** *(US)* Erbausschließung; ~ **of liability** Haftungsausschluß; ~ **of members** Mitgliederausschluß; ~ **of the [general] public** Ausschluß der Öffentlichkeit; ~ **of press and public from a meeting** Ausschluß der Presse und der Öffentlichkeit bei einer Versammlung; ~ **of a right** Rechtsausschluß; ~ **of warranty** Garantieausschluß;
~ **agreement** *(international arbitration)* Vertrag zur Ausschließung des ordentlichen Rechtsweges; ~ **law** *(US)* Einwanderungsgesetz; ~ **principle** *(price)* Ausschlußprinzip.
exclusive *(article)* Exklusivbericht;
~ *(a.)* nicht eingerechnet, ausschließlich, *(journalism)* exklusiv; ~ **of costs** ohne Kosten; ~ **of interest** mit Ausnahme der Zinsen; ~ **of any out building** *(covenant)* nur Wohngebäude gestattet; ~ **of packaging (wrapping)** Verpackung ausgenommen;
~ **agency** Alleinvertretung; ~ **agency contract** Alleinvertretungsvertrag; ~ **agent** Alleinvertreter; ~ **agreement** Exklusivvertrag; ~ **angle** *(advertising)* Ausschließlichkeitsaufhänger; ~ **bargaining agent** alleiniger Tarifpartner; **to move in** ~ **circles** in den obersten Gesellschaftskreisen verkehren; ~ **clause** Ausschließlichkeitsklausel, Ausschlußbestimmung; ~ **club** exklusiver Klub; ~ **contract** Exklusionsvertrag; ~ **control** alleinige Aufsichtsfunktion; ~ **dealer** *(US)* alleiniger Vertreter, Alleinvertreter; ~ **dealer arrangement** *(US)* Händlervereinbarung mit Ausschließlichkeitsklausel, Ausschließlichkeitsvertrag; ~ **dealing** *(US)* Markenbindung des Handels, Exklusivhandel; ~ **dealing contract** *(cartel law)* Ausschließlichkeitsvertrag; ~ **distribution** ausschließlicher Absatzweg, Alleinvertrieb,

Marktbindung des Handels; ~ **distribution franchise** *(US)* Alleinvertriebsrecht; ~ **distributor** Alleinvertriebsberechtigter; ~ **employment** einzige Beschäftigung; ~ **feature** Ausschließlichkeitsverhältnis; ~ **film** Exklusivfilm, alleiniges Vorführungsrecht; ~ **franchise** *(US)* Ausschließlichkeitsverpflichtung; ~ **hotel** Hotel der Spitzenklasse, Luxushotel; ~ **interview** Sonderinterview; ~ **jurisdiction** ausschließliche Zuständigkeit; **to have ~ jurisdiction in all cases** ausschließlich zuständig sein; ~ **licence** Alleinverkaufsrecht, Alleinlizenz, alleiniger Lizenznehmer; ~ **licensee** alleiniger Lizenzteilnehmer; ~ **listing** *(US, real-estate broker)* Alleinverkaufsrecht; ~ **model** Exklusivmodell; ~ **moving picture rights** Exklusivrechte für die Verfilmung; ~ **negotiating right** Alleinverhandlungsrecht; ~ **news** Exklusivnachricht; ~ **occupation** einzige Beschäftigung; ~ **owner** Alleininhaber; ~ **ownership** ausschließliches Eigentum; ~ **patterns** moderne Muster; ~ **possession** Alleinbesitz; ~ **power** ausschließliches Verfügungsrecht über den Nachlaß; ~ **privilege** Alleinverkaufsrecht; ~ **profession** exklusiver Berufszweig; ~ **reader** Exklusivleser; ~ **report** Exklusivbericht; ~ **representation** Alleinvertretung [eines Artikels]; ~ **right** Alleinberechtigung, Ausschluß-, Exklusivrecht; **to have the ~ rights in a production** alleiniges Herstellungsrecht haben; **to have the ~ rights for the sale of a car** alleiniges Verkaufsrecht (Generalvertretung) für ein Auto haben; ~ **sale** Alleinverkaufs[recht], Exklusivverkauf; ~ **sales agreement** Alleinverkaufsvereinbarung, Alleinvertretungs, -vertriebsvertrag; ~ **social circles** exklusive Gesellschaft; ~ **story** Exklusivbericht; ~ **use** alleiniges Nutzungsrecht; **to have an ~ voice in an election** begrenztes Wahlrecht haben.

exclusively | of all other causes allein auf den Unfall zurückzuführen; ~ **for public purposes** nur für öffentliche Zwecke vorgesehen.

exclusiveness, exclusivity Ausschließlichkeit, Exklusivität; ~ **stipulation** *(Br.)* Konkurrenzverbot, -ausschluß.

exculpate *(v.)* rechtfertigen, entlasten; ~ **s. o. from a charge** j. von einer Anklage (Schuld) freisprechen.

exculpation Entlastung, Rechtfertigung, Reinwaschung.

exculpatory rechtfertigend, entlastend; ~ **clause** *(trustee)* Entlastungs-, Freizeichnungsklausel; ~ **facts** entlastende Tatsachen; ~ **letter** Entschuldigungsbrief.

excursion kurze Reise, Abstecher, Ausflug, Vergnügungsreise, *(party of persons)* Reisegesellschaft, *(ride)* Ausfahrt; **cheap** ~ billige Einkaufstour; **school** ~ Schulausflug; **scientific** ~ wissenschaftliche Exkursion; ~ **into the country** Landpartie; **to go on an ~ to the mountains** Bergtour machen; **to make an ~** Ausflug machen; ~ **fares** Ausflugspreise; ~ **fare with minimum 14-day stay** Ferienbillet mit einem Mindestaufenthalt von zwei Wochen; ~ **rates** Touristen-, Ausflugstarif; ~ **steamer** Ausflugsdampfer; ~ **tariff** Touristen-, Ausflugstarif; ~ **ticket** Touristenkarte, Ferienbillet; ~ **traffic** Ausflugsverkehr; ~ **train** Ausflügler-, Sonder-, Vergnügungs-, Ferienzug.

excursionist Ausflügler, Vergnügungsreisender.

excusable entschuldbar; ~ **assault** zufällige unbeabsichtigte Körperverletzung; ~ **homicide** Tötung in Notwehr; ~ **neglect** unverschuldetes Versäumnis.

excuse Entschuldigung[sgrund]; **blind** ~ ungenügende Entschuldigung; **built-in valid** ~ absolut natürliche Entschuldigung; **lame (paltry)** ~ dürftige Entschuldigung; **poor (thin)** ~ billige Ausrede; **reasonable** ~ ausreichende Entschuldigung; **slim** ~ wenig überzeugende Ausrede; **trumped-up** ~ aus den Fingern gezogene Entschuldigung; **the first ~ to hand** erste greifbare Entschuldigung; ~ *(v.)* **s. one's absence** jds. Fernbleiben entschuldigen; ~ **s. o. from attendance** j. von der Teilnahme befreien; **to be absent without good ~** unentschuldigt fehlen; **to have one's ~ pat** Entschuldigung parat halten; **to offer as an ~** Entschuldigungsgrund angeben; **to send a written ~** schriftliche Entschuldigung vorlegen.

excused from attendance vom Erscheinen befreit.

excuss *(v.)* beschlagnahmen.

excussion Schuldeneintreibung.

exeat *(student, Br.)* Urlaub.

executable vollziehbar, aus-, durchführbar.

execute *(v.)* ausführen, vollenden, *(contract)* durchführen, Bedingungen erfüllen, *(function)* ausüben, verrichten, bewerkstelligen, *(instrument)* [rechtsgültig] ausfertigen, *(judgment)* vollstrecken, vollziehen, *(sales)* tätigen;

~ **an affidavit** eidesstattliche Erklärung abgeben; ~ **a change of front** *(mil.)* Frontwechsel durchführen; ~ **s. one's commands** jds. Befehle ausführen; ~ **a commission** sich eines Auftrags entledigen; ~ **a contract** Vertrag erfüllen; ~ **a criminal** Verbrecher hinrichten; ~ **a decree** Beschluß absetzen; ~ **a deed** Urkunde unterzeichnen; ~ **a legal document** Urkunde unterfertigen; ~ **a form** Formular ausfüllen; ~ **a judgment** Urteil vollstrecken; ~ **justice** Gesetz handhaben; ~ **a law** Gesetz durchführen; ~ **an office** Amt verwalten (ausüben); ~ **an order** Auftrag ausführen; ~ **an order at best** Auftrag bestens ausführen; ~ **orders in listed securities on a commission basis** Effektengeschäfte auf Provisionsbasis durchführen; ~ **a piece of work** Arbeit vollenden; ~ **a plan** Plan (Vorhaben) durchführen; ~ **a portrait** Gemälde erstellen; ~ **a power of attorney** Vollmacht ausstellen; ~ **under the rules** *(stock exchange)* zwangsweise abwickeln; ~ **a will** rechtsgültiges Testament errichten; ~ **a writ** gerichtliche Verfügung durchführen, Vollstreckungsbefehl erlassen.

executed aus-, durchgeführt; ~ **oral agreement** beiderseits erfüllter Vertrag; ~ **consideration** vorher empfangene (erbrachte) Gegenleistung; ~ **contract** erfüllter Vertrag; ~ **criminal** hingerichteter Verbrecher; ~ **estate** in Besitz genommenes Grundstück; ~ **remainder** feststehendes Anwartschaftsrecht; ~ **sale** erfüllter Kaufvertrag; ~ **trust** genau festgelegtes Treuhandverhältnis; ~ **use** gesetzlich zugestandener Gebrauch; ~ **writ** vollzogene gerichtliche Verfügung.

executing creditor Vollstreckungsgläubiger.

execution *(accomplishment)* Durch-, Ausführung, Vollziehung, Handhabung, *(of contract)* Durchführung, Erfüllung, *(criminal law)* Hinrichtung, Exekution, *(legal instrument)* Ausfertigung, Vollziehung, *(seizure)* Pfändung, [Zwangs]vollstreckung, *(writ)* Vollstreckungsauftrag; **by way of ~** im Wege der Zwangsvollstreckung; **exempt from ~** pfändungsfrei, unpfändbar; **ripe for ~** ausführungsreif; **subject to ~** der Zwangsvollstreckung unterliegend, pfändbar; **attachment ~** Vollstreckungsverfahren gegen einen Drittschuldner, Arrestvollziehung; **body ~** Inhaftierung; **defective ~** fehlerhafte Ausführung; **dormant ~** nur teilweise durchgeführte Vollstreckung, zurückgestellter Pfändungsauftrag; **due ~** *(will)* Errichtung in gehöriger Form; **equitable ~** Zwangsverwaltung mit Veräußerungsbefugnis; **forced ~** Zwangsabwicklung; **fresh ~** erneute Pfändung; **garnishee ~** Forderungspfändung; **general ~** Zwangsvollstreckung in das bewegliche Vermögen; **judgment ~** Vollstreckungsverfahren; **junior ~** nachrangige Vollstreckung; **partial ~** Teilausführung; **preliminary ~** vorläufige Pfändung; **public ~** öffentliche Hinrichtung; **special ~** vollstreckbare Ausfertigung, Vollstreckung in einen bestimmten Gegenstand; **uncompleted ~** noch nicht beendete Zwangsvollstreckung; **unsatisfied ~** fruchtlose Pfändung, erfolglose Zwangsvollstreckung; ~ **of an agreement** Durchführung eines Abkommens; ~ **of an authority** Vollmachtsausübung; ~ **of foreign awards** Vollstreckung ausländischer Schiedssprüche; ~ **of a bill** Rechnungsausstellung; ~ **of a building** Bauausführung; - **of a codicil** Erstellung eines Testamentsnachtrags; ~ **against a company (corporation, US)** Zwangsvollstreckung in das Gesellschaftsvermögen; ~ **of a contract** Vertragserfüllung; ~ **by creditors** Gläubigervollstreckung; ~ **of a deed (document)** Ausstellung einer Urkunde, Urkundenausfertigung; ~ **of one's duty** Pflichterfüllung; ~ **in force and operating** im Gange befindliche (gerade stattfindende) Zwangsvollstreckung; ~ **by hanging** Hinrichtung durch Erhängen; ~ **of hostages** Geiselerschießung; ~ **of instrument** Urkundenausfertigung; ~ **of judgment or decree** Vollstreckung aus einem Urteil; ~ **of the law** Gesetzesvollziehung; ~ **of an order** Auftragserledigung, Effektuierung eines Auftrags; ~ **of a policy** Ausstellung eines Versicherungsscheines, Policenausfertigung; ~ **of punishment** Strafvollzug; ~ **by sale of debtor's chattels** Zwangsversteigerung; ~ **levied by seizure** durch Pfändung vorgenommene Zwangsvollstreckung; ~ **of trust** Beendigung einer Treuhandverwaltung; ~ **of wages** Lohnpfändung; ~ **of a will** Testamentserrichtung; ~ **of work** Arbeitsausführung; **to ask for a stay in ~** Einstellung der Zwangsvollstreckung beantragen; **to be exempt from (liable to stay) ~** Vollstreckungsschutz genießen, nicht der Zwangsvollstreckung (dem Vollstreckungsaufschub) unterliegen, pfändungsfrei sein; **to be sold under ~** im Wege der Zwangsvollstreckung verkauft werden; **to be subject to ~** der Zwangsvollstreckung unterliegen; **to carry into ~** ausführen, vollstrecken; **to carry a judgment into ~** Vollstreckungsklausel erteilen; **to carry out an**

~ hinrichten, Hinrichtung durchführen; **to enforce a judgment by** ~ aus einem Urteil vollstrecken, Vollstreckung aus einem Urteil betreiben; **to grant a stay of** ~ Einstellung der Zwangsvollstreckung anordnen; **to have a writ of** ~ **for service** vollstreckbaren Schuldtitel haben; **to issue** ~ **against** Zwangsvollstreckung beantragen, Vollstreckungsauftrag erteilen; **to issue** ~ **for the amount of costs** Zwangsvollstreckung aus dem Kostenurteil betreiben; **to levy an** ~ Zwangsvollstreckung vornehmen; **to levy an** ~ **on s. one's goods** Zwangsvollstreckung gegen j. betreiben; **to levy** ~ **with respect to the costs** Zwangsvollstreckung aus dem Kostenurteil betreiben; **to levy** ~ **on the property** in das Vermögen vollstrecken; **to obstruct s. o. in the** ~ **of his duty** j. an der Ausübung seiner Pflichten hindern; **to put in an** ~ Pfändung vornehmen; **to put in an** ~ **and levy** Zwangsvollstreckung durchführen; **to put a plan into** ~ Plan (Vorhaben) durchführen; **to return an** ~ **unsatisfied (nulla bona, US)** Zwangsvollstreckung mangels Masse einstellen; **to satisfy an** ~ Zwangsvollstreckung durch Zahlung abwenden; **to stay** ~ Zwangsvollstreckung einstellen; **to stop the** ~ **of a decree** Beschluß aussetzen; **to suspend** ~ **temporarily** Zwangsvollstreckung vorübergehend einstellen; **to take in** ~ pfänden; ~ **creditor** Vollstreckungsgläubiger; ~ **deadline** Hinrichtungstermin; ~ **debtor** Vollstreckungsschuldner; ~ **lien** Vollstreckungspfandrecht, Arresthypothek; ~ **officer** Vollstreckungsbeamter; ~ **sale (US)** Zwangsversteigerung.

executionary order Hinrichtungsbefehl.

executioner Henker, Scharfrichter.

executive *(branch of government)* vollziehende Gewalt, Exekutive, *(employee, US)* leitender Angestellter, Führungskraft, Geschäftsführer, *(mil., US)* stellvertretender Kommandeur, *(state)* Präsident, Gouverneur, *(party)* Parteiführung, *(US)* erster geschäftsführender Beamter;

all-level ~s Führungskräfte aller Rangklassen; **big-company** ~ Konzernangestellter; **business** ~ kaufmännische Führungskraft; **chief** ~ *(US)* Vorstandsvorsitzer; **Chief** ⌀ *(US)* Oberste Führungsspitze; **collective** ~ Ausführungskollektiv; **construction** ~ leitender Angestellter in der Bauindustrie; **desk-bound** ~ Schreibtischstratege; **echelon-oriented** ~ Rangunterschiede beachtende Führungskraft; **field** ~ im Außendienst eingesetzte Führungskraft; **foreign-based** ~ im Ausland stationierte Führungskraft; **freshman** ~ junge Führungskraft; **fringe** ~ tantiemenberechtigte Führungskraft; **general** ~s Vorstand[smitglieder einer Aktiengesellschaft, ausführendes Organ; **highgrade (-ranking)** ~ *(US)* hochqualifizierter Beamter; **high-level** ~s Führungskräfte; **highly-paid** ~ *(US)* hochbezahlter Beamter; **junior** ~ Nachwuchskraft; **key international** ~s internationale Schlüsselkräfte; **leading** ~ führender (leitender) Angestellter; **level** ~ im Range gleichstehender Angestellter; **lower-echelon** ~s mittlere Führungskräfte; **middle management** ~ mittlere Führungskraft; **overtaxed** ~ zu hoch besteuerte Führungskraft; **party** ~ Parteivorstand; **resident** ~ ortsansässige Führungskraft; **sales** ~ Verkaufsleiter; **senior** ~ erfahrene Führungskraft; **articulate commercially aware senior** ~ streng kaufmännisch eingestellter leitender Angestellter; **supervisory** ~ Angestellter mit Überwachungsfunktionen; **take-charge** ~ initiativer Angestellter; **top** ~ Führungs-, Spitzenkraft; **up-and-coming** ~ erfolgreiche Nachwuchskraft; **woman** ~ Unternehmerin;

~ **of a corporation** *(US)* leitender Angestellter;

~ *(a.)* ausübend, vollziehend, exekutiv, *(managing)* verwaltend, leitend;

~ **ability** praktische Geschicklichkeit, Eignung als Leiter; **good** ~ **ability** Führungsqualitäten; ~ **act** Durchführungsgesetz; ~ **action** leitende Tätigkeit; ~ **administration** *(Br.)* Ministerialbürokratie; ~ **agency** durchführende Behörde; ~ **agent** vollziehendes Organ; ~ **agreement** Ministerialabkommen; **top** ~ **appointment** Spitzenposition; ~ **authority** vollziehende Gewalt; ~ **board** Generaldirektion, Vorstand; ~ **board committee** geschäftsführender Präsidialausschuß; ~ **body** Exekutivorgan; ~ **branch** ausführendes Organ, Verwaltungszweig; ~ **branch of government** vollziehende Behörde, Exekutive; ~ **capacity** führende (leitende) Tätigkeit; ~ **class** Schicht der leitenden Angestellten; ~ **-class car** Wagen für leitende Angestellte, Auto für gehobenere Ansprüche; ~ **command** *(mil.)* Ausführungskommando; ~ **- class prosperity** Wohlhabenheit der gehobeneren Bevölkerungsschichten; ~ **committee** Exekutiv-, Aktions-, Vollzugsausschuß, *(corporation, US)* geschäftsführender Vorstand; **National** ⌀ **Committee** *(Labour Party)* Parteivorstand; ~s' **company group protection** Gruppenversicherung für leitende Angestellte; ~ **compensation** Vergütung für leitende Angestellte; ~ **compensation package** massierte Sondervergün-

stigungen für leitende Angestellte; **to shed one's upright** ~ **control** seine beruflich anerzogene Zurückhaltung als leitender Angestellter aufgeben; ~ **council** *(EC)* Exekutiv-, Ministerrat, *(National Health Scheme, Br.)* [etwa] Landesgesundheitsamt; ~ **department** Vorstandsressort, *(ministry)* Ministerium; ~ **desk** Chefschreibtisch; ~ **dining room** Direktionskasino; ~ **duties** Führungsaufgaben; ~ **editor** Herausgeber; ~ **employee** leitender Angestellter, Führungskraft; ~ **evaluation** Beurteilung leitender Angestellter (von Führungskräften); ~ **expenses** Geschäftsführungskosten, Kosten der Geschäftsführung; ~ **fringes** zusätzliche Aufwendungen (Sondervergünstigungen) für leitende Angestellte; ~ **functions** Exekutivfunktionen, Führungsaufgaben, Vollzugsfunktionen; ~ **head** Leiter; ~ **head of the state** *(US)* Staatsoberhaupt; ~ **incentive plan** Leistungszulagensystem für leitende Angestellte; ~ **jet** Düsenflugzeug für Führungskräfte; **at** ~ **level** in führender (leitender) Stellung; ~ **management** verwaltungsmäßige Leitung, *(US)* Unternehmensleitung, Vorstand einer AG; ⌀ **Mansion** *(US)* Gouverneurswohnung; ~ **material** Nachwuchsreservoir; ~ **meeting** Vorstandssitzung; ~ **ministry** *(Br.)* Ministerialbürokratie; ~ **nature** Führungsfunktion; ~ **office** *(US)* Direktionsbüro; ~ **officer** *(US)* leitender Angestellter, Führungskraft, *(civil service, Br.)* Beamter [der öffentlichen Verwaltung], Vollzugsorgan, *(member of the board, US)* Vorstandsmitglied; **chief** ~ **officer** *(US)* Präsident eines Unternehmens, Vorstandsvorsitzender; ~ **order** *(US)* Durchführungsbestimmung, -verordnung; ~ **pardon** Gnadenerweis; ~ **pay package** Vergütungsangebot für Führungskräfte; ~ **performance** Leistung einer Führungskraft; ~ **perks** *(sl.)* Vergünstigungen für leitende Angestellte; ~ **personnel** leitende Angestellte, Führungskräfte; **to upgrade one's** ~ **personnel standards** Niveau seiner Führungskräfte heraufschrauben; ~ **portfolio (report)** Unternehmensbericht; ~ **position (post)** Führungsposten, leitende Stellung; **to move up to an** ~ **position** in eine führende Stellung gelangen; ~ **potential** unternehmerische Fähigkeiten; ~ **power** ausübende (vollziehende) Gewalt, Exekutive; ~ **promotion** Beförderung von Führungskräften; ~ **recruiter** Unternehmensberater; ~ **recruiting** Anwerben von Führungskräften, Unternehmensberatung; ~ **recruiting firm** Unternehmensberatungsfirma; ~ **requirements** Bedarf an Führungskräften, Führungskräftebedarf; ~ **responsibility** unternehmerische Verantwortlichkeit; ~ **retreat** Freizeitgelände für leitende Angestellte; ~ **rotation** turnusmäßige Versetzung leitender Angestellter; ~ **salaries** Vorstandsbezüge; ~ **search** Suche (Aufspürung) von Führungskräften; ~**-search consultant** Industrieberater; ~**-search unit** Team zur Aufspürung von Führungsnachwuchs; ~ **secretary** Vorstandssekretär[in]; ~ **selection** Auswahl von Führungskräften; ~ **session** Vorstandssitzung, *(US)* Geheimsitzung [des Senats]; ~ **shuffle** Umbesetzungen im Vorstand; ~ **skills** unternehmerische Eigenschaften; ~ **staff** Führungsstab; ~ **succession** Vorstandsnachfolge; ~ **suite** Vorstandsetage; **to make [it to] the** ~ **suite** Vorstandsposition erreichen, in den Vorstand gelangen, sich für die führende Schicht qualifizieren; ~ **talent** Führungsbegabung, -talent; ~ **top team** Führungsstab, -gruppe; ~ **trainee** Nachwuchskraft; ~ **training** betriebliche Fortbildung, Ausbildung von Führungskräften, Nachwuchsausbildung, -förderung; ~ **training program(me)** Ausbildungsprogramm für Führungskräfte; ~ **vice-president** *(US)* stellvertretender (geschäftsführender) Vorsitzender; ~ **warrant** *(asylum state)* Aufenthalts-, Asylgewährung; ~ **work** leitende Tätigkeit.

executor Vollzieher, Ausführender, *(law)* Testamentsvollstrecker;

~ **dative** gerichtlich bestellter Testamentsvollstrecker; **general** ~ mit allen Vollmachten vom Erblasser bestimmter Testamentsvollstrecker; **instituted** ~ testamentarisch eingesetzter Testamentsvollstrecker; **joint** ~ Mittestamentsvollstrecker; **limited** ~ Testamentsvollstrecker mit beschränkten Befugnissen; **literary** ~ Nachlaßverwalter eines Autors; ~ **nominate** testamentarisch bestellter Testamentsvollstrecker; **rightful** ~ ordnungsgemäß eingesetzter Testamentsvollstrecker; **special** ~ auftragsmäßig beschränkter Testamentsvollstrecker;

~ **to an estate** gerichtlich bestellter Testamentsvollstrecker; ~ **de son tort** nicht autorisierter Testamentsvollstrecker; ~ **by substitution** Ersatztestamentsvollstrecker; ~ **named in a will** testamentarisch bestimmter Testamentsvollstrecker;

to be appointed as ~ **under a will** als Testamentsvollstrecker [im Testament] vorgesehen sein; **to nominate an** ~ **of a will** Testamentsvollstrecker einsetzen (bestellen); **to renounce to act as** ~ **of an heir** auf die Ausübung seines Testamentsvollstreckeramtes verzichten;

~'s **account** Testamentsvollstreckerkonto; ~'s **bond** Kaution des Testamentsvollstreckers, Testamentsvollstreckerkaution; ~ **creditor** Nachlaßgläubiger mit Teilaufgaben eines Testamentsvollstreckers; ~'s **decree** Testamentsvollstreckerbestellung; ~-**trustee** Testamentsvollstrecker mit gleichzeitigem Auftrag der Vermögensverwaltung; ~'s **year** Todesjahr, in dem der Testamentsvollstrecker tätig wird.

executorial vollziehend;
~ **duties** Testamentsvollstreckertätigkeit.

executorship Testamentsvollstreckeramt;
~ **account** Anderkonto des Testamentsvollstreckers; ~ **law** Testamentsvollstreckerrecht.

executory vollziehend, vollstreckend, exekutiv, *(law)* wirksam werdend;
partially ~ teilweise erfüllbar;
~ **bequest** Anwartschaftsvermächtnis; ~ **consideration** zukünftige Gegenleistung; ~ **contract** noch nicht erfüllter Vertrag; ~ **decree** Vollstreckungstitel; ~ **device** aufschiebend bedingtes Vermächtnis, Nacherbeneinsetzung; ~ **estate** aufschiebend bedingtes Grundstücksrecht; ~ **gift** Schenkungsversprechen; ~ **interest** aufschiebend bedingtes dingliches Recht; ~ **limitation** aufschiebend bedingtes Vermächtnis; ~ **process** Vollstreckungsverfahren; ~ **purchase** Bedingungskauf; ~ **remainder** aufschiebend bedingtes Herrschaftsrecht; ~ **sale** noch zu erfüllender Kaufvertrag; ~ **trust** in das Belieben des Erben gestellte Stiftung; ~ **unilateral accord** Vertragsofferte, -angebot; ~ **use** Vorvermächtnis; ~ **warranties** vom Versicherungsnehmer abhängige Leistungen.

exemplar Muster, Vorbild, *(book)* Exemplar.

exemplary musterhaft, vorbildlich, *(monitory)* abschreckend, *(typical)* typisch;
~ **damages** über den verursachten Schaden hinausgehende Entschädigung, verschärfter Schadensersatz, Buße, Bußgeld.

exemplification *(law, US)* beglaubigte Abschrift, Erläuterung, Belegung durch Beispiele.

exemplified copy beglaubigte Abschrift.

exemplify *(v.)* erläutern, an Beispielen illustrieren, mit Beispielen belegen, *(by documents)* durch beglaubigte Abschrift beweisen, *(make attested copy)* gerichtlich beglaubigen;
~ **a deed** *(US)* beglaubigte Abschrift einer Urkunde anfertigen.

exempt Befreiter, Bevorrechtigter, Privilegierter, *(mil.)* UK-gestellter, vom Militärdienst Freigestellter;
tax-~s steuerfreie Wertpapiere;
~ *(a.)* befreit, frei (ausgenommen) von;
customs-~ zollfrei; **draft-~** *(US)* vom Militärdienst befreit, uk-, freigestellt; **tax-~** *(US)* steuerfrei;
~ **from charges** spesenfrei; ~ **from duty** zollfrei; ~ **from execution** pfändungsfrei, unpfändbar; ~ **from postage** portofrei; ~ **from seizure** pfändungs-, beschlagnahmefrei; ~ **from military service** freigestellt, vom Militärdienst befreit, unabkömmlich; ~ **from taxation** steuerfrei; ~ **from taxes** steuer-, zollfrei;
~ *(v.)* [von einer Steuer, Verpflichtung] befreien, *(mil.)* UK stellen, vom Militärdienst freistellen;
~ **completely from estate duty** völlig von der Erbschaftssteuer befreien; ~ **from income tax** einkommensteuerfrei machen, von der Einkommensteuer befreien; ~ **s. o. from jury duty** j. nicht auf die Schöffenliste setzen; ~ **s. o. from liability** jds. Haftung ausschließen; ~ **o. s. from liability** sich freizeichnen; ~ **s. o. from military service** j. vom Militärdienst befreien (freistellen); ~ **o. s. from a tax** sich von einer Steuer befreien; ~ **s. o. from a tax** jem. eine Steuer erlassen; ~ **a vehicle from the obligation to be registered** Fahrzeug von der Zulassungspflicht befreien;
to be ~ **from payment of contributions** von der Zahlung von Zwangsbeiträgen befreit sein; **to be** ~ **from taxes** keine Steuern zahlen, von Steuern befreit sein;
~ **amount** Freibetrag, *(mace-exempt)* pfändungsfreier Betrag, Pfändungsfreibetrag; **tax-~ amount** Steuerfreibetrag; ~ **commodities** nicht unter den Tarif fallende Waren; ~ **dealer** freier Börsenmakler [einer Kapitalsammelstelle]; **tax-~ note** steuerfreier Schuldschein; ~ **property** *(execution)* pfändungsfreies Vermögen; ~ **services** nicht unter den Spediteurtarif fallende Dienstleistungen.

exemptible befreibar.

exempting certificate Ausnahmebescheinigung.

exemption Befreiung, Enthebung, Entbindung, Ausnahme[stellung], Ausnahmeregelung, Sonderprivileg, *(execution)* unpfändbarer Besitz, pfändungsfreier Betrag, Pfändungsfreibetrag, *(income tax, US)* [Steuer]freibetrag, steuerfreier Betrag, *(mil.)* Freistellung, UK-Stellung, *(tariff)* Tarifausnahmen;
~**s** pfändungsfreie Gegenstände;

chartered ~ *(Br.)* Steuerfreiheit; **children's** ~ *(US)* Steuerfreibetrag für Kinder; **dependency** ~ *(US)* Steuerfreibetrag für Familienangehörige; **flat** ~ *(income tax, US)* pauschaler Freibetrag, steuerfreier Pauschalbetrag, Pauschfreibetrag; **lifetime** ~ *(US)* Erbschaftssteuerfreibetrag; **old-age** ~ *(US)* Altersfreibetrag; **outright** ~ *(US)* allgemein gewährter Steuerfreibetrag; **personal** ~ *(US)* persönlicher Steuerfreibetrag; **surviving spouse** ~ Erbschaftssteuerfreibetrag der überlebenden Ehefrau; **tax** ~ *(US)* Steuerfreibetrag; **withholding** ~ *(employee, US)* Lohnsteuerfreibetrag;
~ **from filing accounts** Befreiung von der Eintragungspflicht; ~ **from charges** Gebühren-, Abgabenfreiheit; ~ **for charities (charitable purposes)** Steuerfreibetrag für wohltätige Zwecke; ~ **from cost** Kostenbefreiung; ~ **from dividend restraint** *(Br.)* Befreiung von der Dividendenbegrenzungsverfügung; ~ **from [customs] duty** Abgaben-, Zollfreiheit; ~ **of estate duty** Erbschaftssteuerbefreiung; ~ **of examination** Erlaß eines Examens; ~ **from execution** Unpfändbarkeit, Vollstreckungsschutz; ~ **from income tax** *(US)* Einkommensteuerfreiheit; ~ **from inheritance tax** *(US)* Erbschaftssteuerfreibetrag; ~ **from liability** Haftungsausschluß; ~ **from postage** Portofreiheit; ~ **of property** *(US)* Vermögenssteuerfreibetrag; ~ **from social security payments** Freistellung von den Sozialversicherungsbeiträgen, Sozialversicherungsfreiheit; ~ **from seizure** Unpfändbarkeit, Pfändungsfreiheit, Vollstreckungsschutz; ~ **from military service** *(US)* Befreiung vom Militärdienst; ~ **from taxation** *(US)* Steuerbefreiung, -freiheit, Aufgabefreiheit;
to appeal to the court for ~ **from responsibility** negative Feststellungsklage erheben; **to be eligible for** ~ *(US)* Anspruch auf einen Steuerfreibetrag haben; **to claim** ~ **for particular stocks** *(US)* Erbschaftssteuerbefreiung für bestimmte Wertpapiere beantragen; **to grant** ~ *(US)* Steuerfreiheit gewähren; **to provide an** ~ **from registration** von der Registrierungspflicht ausnehmen; **to qualify for an** ~ *(US)* freibetragsberechtigt sein;
employee's withholding ~ **certificate** *(US)* Lohnsteuerfreibetragsformular; ~ **clause** *(Br.)* Ausnahme-, Freizeichnungs-, Freistellungsklausel; ~ **credit** *(US)* Steuerfreibetrag; ~ **increase** *(US)* Erhöhung des Steuerfreibetrages; **personal** ~ **increase** *(US)* Sonderausgabenerhöhung, Erhöhung der Freibetragsgrenze; ~ **laws** Unpfändbarkeitsbestimmungen, Vollstreckungsschutzgesetze; **[personal]** ~ **level** *(US)* Steuerfreibetragsgrenze, -höhe; ~ **limit** *(taxation, US)* Steuerfreigrenze; **estate-duty** ~ **limit** *(US)* Erbschaftssteuerfreigrenze; ~ **method** *(double taxation agreement)* Befreiungsmethode; ~ **minimum** *(taxation, US)* Mindestfreibetrag; ~ **order** Ausnahmeverfügung; ~ **privilege** Ausnahmerecht; ~ **provisions** Befreiungs-, Freistellungs-, Ausnahmebestimmungen.

exequatur Bestätigung eines Konsuls, Exequatur;
to grant the ~ das Exequatur erteilen; **to revoke the** ~ Exequatur zurückziehen.

exequies Totenfeier.

exercisable anwendbar.

exercise Gebrauch, Anwendung, Ausübung, Geltendmachung, *(school)* Übung, Übungsaufgabe, Arbeit, Übersetzung;
in ~ **of one's calling** in der Ausübung seines Berufs; **in** ~ **of one's duties** in Erfüllung seiner Dienstobliegenheiten;
graduation ~**s** Doktorexamen; **military** ~**s** militärische Übungen; **opening** ~**s** Eröffnungsfeierlichkeiten; **physical** ~**s** gymnastische Übungen; **religious** ~**s** Andachtsübungen; **rifle** ~ Gewehrexerzieren; **school** ~**s** Schulaufgaben, -arbeiten; **written** ~ schulische Arbeit;
~ **of discretion** Ermessensausübung; ~ **of judicial discretion** Ausübung des richterlichen Ermessens; ~ **of duties** Pflichtenwahrnehmung; ~ **of functions** Wahrnehmung von Aufgaben; ~ **of influence** Geltendmachung von Einfluß; ~ **of judgment** Ermessensgebrauch; ~ **of jurisdiction** Ausübung der Gerichtsbarkeit; ~ **of memory** Gedächtnisübung; ~**s in the North Sea** Flottenmanöver in der Nordsee; ~ **of an office** Verwaltung eines Amtes, Amtsausübung; ~ **of options** Ausübung des Prämienrechts, Optionsausübung; ~ **of an option to purchase** Ausübung einer Kaufoption; ~ **of power** Ausübung von Machtbefugnissen, Vollmachtsgebrauch; ~ **of a privilege** Geltendmachung eines Vorrechts; ~ **of a profession** Berufsausübung; ~ **of a right** Rechtsausübung; ~ **of subscription rights** Bezugsrechtsausübung; ~ **of a trade** Ausübung eines Gewerbes, Gewerbeausübung; ~ **of trusteeship functions** Ausübung treuhänderischer Funktionen; **free** ~ **of independent will** freie und ungehinderte Willensausübung;
~ *(v.)* *(rights, functions)* ausüben, geltend machen;
~ **a calling** Beruf ausüben; ~ **control** Aufsichtstätigkeit ausüben; ~ **the required degree of skill and diligence** die im Verkehr

erforderliche Sorgfalt anwenden; ~ **functions** Aufgaben wahrnehmen; ~ **one's influence** seinen Einfluß geltend machen; ~ **jurisdiction** Gerichtsbarkeit ausüben; ~ **one's mind** sich geistig beschäftigen; ~ **an office** Amt ausüben; ~ **an option** Prämienrecht (Optionsrecht) ausüben; ~ **s. one's patience** jds. Geduld strapazieren; ~ **power** Macht ausüben; ~ **a right** von einem Recht Gebrauch machen; ~ **the right to subscribe to new stock** Bezugsrecht ausüben; ~ **supervisory jurisdiction** als Aufsichtsinstanz tätig werden; ~ **a trade** Gewerbe ausüben; ~ **troops** Truppen ausbilden; ~ **one's voting rights** von seinem Stimmrecht Gebrauch machen; ~ **one's wits** seinen Verstand gebrauchen;
~ **book** [Schul]heft, Übungsbuch; ~ **ground** Exerzierplatz; ~ **lesson** Übung; ~ **price** Kurs im Zeitpunkt der Optionsausübung; ~ **station** Trainingsplatz.

exert (v.) anwenden, ausüben;
~ **o. s. to arrive early** Anstrengungen machen, rechtzeitig zu kommen; ~ **one's authority** seine Autorität geltend machen; ~ **all one's influence** seinen ganzen Einfluß aufbieten; ~ **pressure on s. o.** Druck auf j. ausüben; ~ **o. s. to the utmost** äußerste Anstrengungen unternehmen.

exertion Anstrengung, Bemühung, Arbeit, Mühe;
~ **of authority** Autoritätsanwendung; **skilfull ~ of a minimum of strength** vorsichtiger Einsatz eines Mindestmaßes von Kräften;
to be unequal to the ~s of travel(l)ing Reisestrapazen nicht gewöhnt sein; **to redouble one's ~s** seine Anstrengungen verdoppeln.

exhaust (car) Auspuff[rohr];
stainless steel-~ Auspuffanlage aus rostfreiem Stahl; **twin ~** Doppelauspuff;
~ (v.) erschöpfen, aufbrauchen, ausbeuten, (consume entirely) [vollständig] verbrauchen;
~ **o. s. in useless efforts** sich ohne jeden Erfolg abstrapazieren; ~ **the land** Raubbau treiben; ~ **the means (resources)** Mittel erschöpfen; ~ **s. one's patience** jds. Geduld erschöpfen; ~ **a quota** Kontingent erschöpfen; ~ **the remedies** Rechtsmittelweg erschöpfen; ~ **a subject** Thema erschöpfend behandeln; ~ **the water in a well** Brunnen leerpumpen (auspumpen); ~ **o. s. by hard work** sich durch harte Arbeit völlig kaputtmachen;
~ **box** Auspufftopf, Schalldämpfer; ~ **control** Auspuffkontrolle; ~ **cutout** Auspuffklappe; ~ **fan** Lüfter; ~ **pipe** Auspuffrohr; ~ **price** (US) Verkaufskurs ohne Deckungserhöhung; ~ **silencer** Auspufftopf; ~ **valve** Auspuffventil.

exhausted körperlich fertig, erledigt, (edition) vergriffen, (policy) abgelaufen, (reserves) erschöpft;
to have ~ one's mandate Grenzen seiner Vollmachtsbefugnisse erreicht haben;
~ **remedies** voll ausgeschöpfte Rechtsmittel.

exhaustion Erschöpfung, Abnutzung, (of land) Raubbau;
wasteful ~ Raubbau;
~ **of administrative remedies** Erschöpfung der verwaltungsmäßigen Rechtsmittel; ~ **of local remedies** (law of nations) Erschöpfung der innerstaatlichen Rechtsmittel; ~ **of reserves** Erschöpfung der Reserven.

exhaustation, to be in a state of in einem völligen Erschöpfungszustand sein.

exhausting ermüdend, anstrengend.

exhaustive erschöpfend, vollständig;
~ **cultivation** Raubbau; ~ **information** erschöpfende Auskunft.

exheredate (v.) (US) enterben.

exheredation (US) Enterbung.

exhibit (auditing) Status, Vermögensverhältnisse, (declaration) eidliche Erklärung, (document) Beweisstück, Beweismittel, als Beweis vorgelegte Urkunde, Beleg, Beweisschrift, Asservat, (enclosure) Anlage, Beilage, (exhibited article) Ausstellungsgegenstand, -stück, Schaustück, (exhibition) Ausstellung, (in pleading) schriftliche Eingabe;
~s Ausstellungsgüter, -artikel, (cinema) Reklamefotos;
permanent ~ Dauerausstellungsstück;
~ (v.) (goods) [Waren zum Verkauf] ausstellen, zeigen, zur Ansicht vorlegen, auslegen, (present formally) einreichen, vorlegen;
~ **to a bank** einer Bank vorlegen; ~ **a bill** Klage erheben; ~ **a charge** Anklage erheben; ~ **a greater degree of skill** besondere Geschicklichkeit anwenden; ~ **evidence** Beweis beibringen; ~ **a foundation (prize)** Stipendium ausschreiben; ~ **goods at a fair** Waren auf einer Messe ausstellen; ~ **goods in a shop window** Waren im Schaufenster auslegen; ~ **paintings in an art gallery** Gemälde in einer Galerie ausstellen; ~ **one's passport** seinen Paß vorzeigen; ~ **pictures** Filme vorführen; ~ **large profits**

große Gewinne ausweisen; ~ **s. th. to the public** etw. öffentlich ausstellen;
~ **hall** Ausstellungs-, Messehalle.

exhibited ausgestellt;
~ **articles** Ausstellungsgut, Messegüter, Exponate.

exhibiting (display) Ausstellen, Ausstellung, (production) Vorlage, Vorlegen;
~ **a charge of treason** Anklage wegen Hochverrats;
~ **firm** Aussteller, ausstellende Firma.

exhibition Ausstellung, Schau, Messe, (exhibit) Ausstellungsobjekt, ausgestellter Gegenstand, (of papers) Einreichung, (production) Vorlage, Vorzeigung, (scholarship, Br.) [Jahres]stipendium, (university) Veranstaltung;
on ~ ausgestellt;
art ~ Kunstausstellung; **continuous ~** Dauerausstellung; **export ~** Exportausstellung, -messe; **flying ~** Wanderausstellung; **industrial ~** Industrie-, Gewerbeausstellung; **international ~** Weltausstellung; **motor ~** Autoausstellung; **permanent ~** Dauerausstellung; **scholarships and ~s** (Br.) Stipendien und Preise; **school ~** Schulveranstaltung; **special ~** Fachmesse, Sonderausstellung; **travelling ~** Wanderausstellung; **universal (world) ~** Weltausstellung;
~ **of documents** Einreichung von Urkunden, Urkundenvorlage; ~ **of fashions** Modemesse; ~ **of a film** Filmvorführung; ~ **of household appliances** Haushaltsmesse; ~ **of one's knowledge** Anbringen seiner Kenntnisse; ~ **of bad manners** Vorführung schlechter Manieren; ~ **of pictures** Gemäldeausstellung; ~ **of works of art** Kunstausstellung;
to be on ~ öffentlich ausgestellt sein; **to make an ~ of o. s.** sich völlig vorbeibenehmen, sich zum allgemeinen Gespött (eine lächerliche Figur) machen; **to open an ~** Ausstellung eröffnen; **to stage an ~** Ausstellung veranstalten;
~ **board** Messe-, Ausstellungsleitung; ~ **buildings** Ausstellungsgebäude; ~ **corporation** Messe-, Ausstellungsgesellschaft; ~ **expenses** Ausstellungskosten; ~ **grounds** Messe-, Ausstellungsgelände; ~ **hall** Messe-, Ausstellungshalle; ~ **island** Ausstellungsinsel; ~ **premises** Ausstellungsräume; ~ **regulations** Messeordnung; ~ **room** Ausstellungsraum; ~ **site** Messe-, Ausstellungsfläche, -gelände; ~ **stand** Messe-, Ausstellungsstand; ~ **subject** Ausstellungsgegenstand; ~ **value** (moving-picture industry) erwartete Mindesteinnahmen.

exhibitioner (Br.) Stipendiat.

exhibitor Aussteller, Messeteilnehmer, -beschicker, Schausteller, (cinema) Kinobesitzer, (of documents) Einreicher;
foreign ~s ausländische Aussteller, Auslandsbeteiligung an einer Messe; **individual ~** Einzelaussteller.

exhilarant Anregungsmittel.

exhilarating news freudige Nachrichten.

exhort (v.) ermahnen, antreiben.

exhortation Ermahnung.

exhumation Leichenausgrabung, Exhumierung;
to grant an ~ order Einwilligung zur Exhumierung geben.

exhume (v.) exhumieren.

exigencies | of commercial and economic policy handels- und wirtschaftspolitische Erfordernisse;
to meet the ~ of this difficult period um den Anforderungen dieser schwierigen Zeit gerecht zu werden.

exigency, exigence Notlage, schwierige Lage, (pressing need) dringendes Bedürfnis, Erfordernis, (urgency) dringender Fall, Dringlichkeit;
~ **of a bond** Kautionszweck; ~ **of a writ** Tenor einer Gerichtsverfügung;
to be reduced to ~ in einer Notlage sein.

exigent dringend, dringlich;
to be ~ of s. th. etw. dringend benötigen.

exigible eintreibbar.

exile Exil, Landesverweisung, Ausweisung, Verbannung, (exiled person) Verbannter, Emigrant;
~**s from home** Heimatvertriebene;
~ (v.) ins Exil schicken, des Landes verweisen, ausweisen; ~ **o. s.** sich abkapseln; ~ **s. o. from his country** j. aus seinem Vaterland verbannen;
to go into ~ ins Exil gehen, emigrieren; **to live in ~** in der Emigration leben; **to send s. o. into ~** j. verbannen; **to set up a government in ~** Exilregierung bilden;
~ **government** Exilregierung.

exist (v.) bestehen, existieren, vorhanden sein, vorliegen;
~ **on very little** mit ganz wenig auskommen; ~ **in wretched circumstances** in schrecklichen Verhältnissen existieren; **able to ~** existenzfähig; **right to ~** Existenzberechtigung;
to cease to ~ (firm) eingehen, zu bestehen aufhören.

existence Vorhandensein, Existenz;
  continued ~ Fortbestand, Weiterbestehen; **hand-to-mouth** ~ unsichere Existenz;
  ~ **of a right** Bestehen eines Rechts; ~ **of a state of war** bestehender Kriegszustand;
  to be in ~ bestehen; **to build up an** ~ sich eine Existenz aufbauen; **to call into** ~ ins Leben rufen; **to lead a hand-to-mouth** ~ nahe am Existenzminimum leben; **to lead a happy** ~ vergnügtes Dasein führen; **to remain in** ~ weiterbestehen.
existing | claim bestehender Anspruch; ~ **creditor** dinglich gesicherter Gläubiger; ~ **debt** fällige Schuld; ~ **goods** im Eigentum des Verkäufers stehende Waren; ~ **indebtedness on a policy** Belastung durch die Abtretung der Police; ~ **law** bestehendes Gesetz; ~ **liabilities** bedingte und spätere Verpflichtungen; ~ **person** empfangenes, noch nicht geborenes Kind; ~ **practice** Gepflogenheit; ~ **public school** Internat und Internatsgelände; ~ **rights** allgemein gültige Rechtsansprüche; ~ **use** derzeitiger Verwendungszweck.
exit *(cinema)* Ausgang, *(fig.)* Abgang, Tod, *(journey out)* Ausreise, *(theater)* Abgang;
  emergency ~ Notausgang;
  to have free ~ **at all times** jederzeit herausgehen können; **to make one's** ~ *(theater)* abtreten;
  ~ **permit** Ausreiseerlaubnis, -genehmigung; ~ **point** [Autobahn]ausfahrt; ~ **staircase** Nottreppe; ~ **visa** Ausreisevisum.
exitus Tod, *(customs)* Ausfuhrzoll, *(lawsuit)* Ausgang.
exodus Aus-, Abwanderung, Auszug;
  general ~ allgemeiner Aufbruch; **rural** ~ Landflucht;
  ~ **of capital** Abwanderung von Kapital, Kapitalflucht; **industry-induced** ~ **from farm to factory** von der Industrialisierung ausgelöste Landflucht; ~ **of the people to sea and mountains for the summer holiday** sommerferienbedingte Massenabwanderung ans Meer und ins Gebirge.
exonerate *(v.)* entlasten, befreien, entbinden, freisprechen;
  ~ **s. o. from an obligation** j. von einer Verpflichtung (Pflicht) entbinden (entlasten); ~ **s. o. from responsibility** jem. die Verantwortung abnehmen.
exoneration Entlastung, Befreiung, Entbindung;
  ~ **clause** Freizeichnungsklausel.
exorbitance Maßlosigkeit, Habgier, Wucher.
exorbitant übertrieben, übermäßig, unerschwinglich, *(law)* ungesetzlich;
  ~ **bill** total überhöhte Rechnung; ~ **demand** unmäßige (übertriebene) Forderung; ~ **interests** überhöhte Zinsen, Wucherzinsen; ~ **price** exorbitanter Preis, Wucherpreis; **to cost an** ~ **price** unverschämt teuer sein; ~ **rates** übersetzter Tarif, *(interest)* wucherische Zinssätze.
exotic fremdländisch, exotisch.
expand *(v.)* erweitern, ausdehnen, ausweiten, *(v./i.)* sich entwickeln, aufblühen, expandieren;
  ~ **an argument** Argumentation vertiefen; ~ **one's business** sein Geschäft erweitern (ausdehnen); ~ **its engineering consultation service on an international basis** seinen technischen Beratungsdienst weltweit ausdehnen; ~ **the currency** Zahlungsmittelumlauf ausweiten; ~ **a pocket dictionary into a large volume** Taschenwörterbuch zu einem Großlexikon umarbeiten; ~ **at a lower rate** langsamer expandieren; ~ **government spending** Staatsausgaben ausweiten.
expanded *(print.)* breitlaufend;
  ~ **letters** breitlaufende Zeichen; ♃ **Program(me) for Technical Assistance** *(EPTA)* Technisches Hilfsprogramm der UNO; ~ **town** *(regional planning, Br.)* Entlastungsort, Trabantenstadt; ~ **type** *(print.)* breite Antiqua[schrift].
expanding universe expandierender Kosmos.
expansion Ausdehnung, Ausweitung, Ausbreitung, Erweiterung, *(accession)* Zuwachs, *(politics)* Expansion, Gebietsvergrößerung;
  consumer-led ~ konsumbedingte Expansion; **currency** ~ Ausweitung der Währung, Vermehrung des Zahlungsmittelumlaufs; **economic** ~ wirtschaftliche Expansion; **external turnover** ~ Ausweitung des Fremdumsatzes; **horizontal** ~ horizontale Ausdehnung; **industrial** ~ Industrieausweitung, industrielle Ausweitung (Ausdehnung); **territorial** ~ Gebietserweiterung; ~ **of assortment** Sortimentsausweitung; ~ **of a building** Anbau, Ausbau; ~ **of business** Ausbau eines Geschäfts, Geschäftserweiterung, -ausweitung; ~ **of capacity** Kapazitätsausweitung; ~ **of commerce** Handelsausweitung; ~ **of consumption** Konsumsteigerung; **[undue]** ~ **of credit** [übermäßige] Kreditausweitung; ~ **of currency** Ausweitung der Währung, Vermehrung des Zahlungsmittelumlaufs; ~ **of equipment** Vervollkommnung der Betriebsausstattung; ~ **of exports** Ausfuhrsteigerung; ~ **of a firm** Firmenvergrößerung; ~ **of liquidity** Liquiditätszunahme, -ausweitung; ~ **of machinery** Vervollkommnung des Maschinenparks; ~ **of membership** Mitgliederzuwachs; ~ **of the money supply** Geldausweitung, -schöpfung; ~ **of production** Produktionsausweitung; ~ **of sales** Umsatzausweitung; ~ **of territories** Gebietserweiterung; ~ **of the trade** Handels-, Wirtschaftsausdehnung, Geschäftsausweitung; ~ **of turnover** Umsatzausweitung, -steigerung;
  to check economic ~ expansionsdämpfende Politik betreiben; **to promote economic** ~ Expansion der Wirtschaft fördern;
  ~ **announcement** Mitteilung über die erfolgte Geschäftsausdehnung, Erweiterungsmitteilung; ~ **bottleneck** Expansionsengpaß; ~ **costs** Erweiterungskosten; ~ **curb** Expansionsbremse; ~ **forecast** Expansionsprognose; ~ **path** Expansionskurve; ~ **plan (program(me))** Erweiterungs-, Expansionsprogramm, Erweiterungsplan; ~ **scheme** Erweiterungsplan, -projekt; ~ **site** Expansionsgelände.
expansionary expansionsbedingt;
  ~ **force** Expansionskraft; **to switch policy to a strongly** ~ **line** Politik auf einen kräftigen Expansionskurs umstellen; ~ **phase** Expansionsphase; ~ **policy** Expansionspolitik.
expansionism Expansionsdrang, Expansionspolitik.
expansionist Expansionspolitiker;
  ~ *(a.)* expansiv;
  ~ **policy** Expansionspolitik; ~ **tendencies** Expansionsbestrebungen, -tendenzen; ~ **war finance** expansive Kriegsfinanzierung.
expansive expansiv, ausdehnend;
  ~ **monetary policy** expansive Geldpolitik; ~ **trend** konjunkturelle Ausweitung.
expatriate Ausgebürgerter, Verbannter, freiwillig im Ausland Lebender;
  German ~ Auslandsdeutscher;
  ~ *(v./i.)* auswandern, seine Nationalität aufgeben, in die Verbannung gehen, emigrieren, *(v./t.)* ausbürgern, expatriieren; ~ **o. s.** seine Nationalität aufgeben;
  ~ *(a.)* ausgebürgert.
expatriation Ausbürgerung, Expatriierung, Auswanderung, Aufgabe (Aberkennung) der Staatsangehörigkeit;
  ~ **allowance** Auslandszulage, -zuschuß.
expectable risk unkalkulierbares Risiko.
expectancy Erwartung, *(prospective possession)* Anwartschaft;
  legal ~ gesetzliche Anwartschaft; **pension** ~ Pensionsanwartschaft;
  ~ **of an inheritance** *(US)* Anwartschaft auf eine Erbschaft, Erbschaftserwartung; ~ **of life** *(insurance)* Lebenserwartung, mutmaßliche Lebensdauer.
expectant Anwärter;
  ~ *(a.)* erwartend, erwartungsvoll;
  ~ **estate** Erbanwartschaft, Nacherbschaft; ~ **heir** Erb[schafts]anwärter; ~ **mother** werdende Mutter; ~ **right** Anwartschaftsrecht; ~ **state** Erbanwartschaft.
expectation Aussicht, Erwartung, Hoffnung, *(future prospects)* Erbschaftserwartungen, Anwartschaft, *(statistics)* Erwartungswert;
  according to ~s erwartungsgemäß; **contrary to** ~s entgegen allen Erwartungen; **on tiptoe with** ~ brennend vor Erwartung; **mathematical** ~s mathematische Erwartungen; ~ **of demand** Nachfrageaussichten; ~ **of inflation** Inflationserwartung; ~ **of life** Lebenserwartung, mutmaßliche Lebensdauer; **average** ~ **of life** mittlere Lebensdauer; ~-**of-life tables** Sterblichkeitstabelle; ~ **of loss** Verlustkalkulation; **reasonable** ~ **of profit** berechtigte Gewinnerwartung; ~ **of victory** Siegeserwartung;
  to answer ~**(s)** nach Wunsch ausfallen; **to fall short of** ~s den Erwartungen nicht entsprechen; **to have** ~s **[from an aunt]** Erbaussichten [bei einer Tante] haben; **to have great** ~s größere Erbschaft zu erwarten haben;
  ~ **value** Vertragswert.
expectational cycle Erwartungsparameter.
expected erwartet, voraussichtlich;
  ~ **to rank** voraussichtliche Gläubiger; ~ **to sail** voraussichtliche Abfahrt; ~ **to win** als Wahlsieger eingestuft;
  ~ **deaths** *(insurance)* angenommene Todesfälle; ~ **life** *(asset)* gewöhnliche Nutzungsdauer; ~ **profit** imaginärer Gewinn; ~ **service** erwartete zusätzliche Dienstleistungen; ~ **time of arrival** voraussichtliche Ankunftszeit; ~ **value** durchschnittlicher Nutzungswert, Erwartungswert.
expedience Zweckmäßigkeit, Zweckdienlichkeit, Tunlichkeit.
expedient *(device)* Behelfs-, Hilfsmittel, Notbehelf;
  by way of ~ behelfsmäßig;

to hit upon an ~ Ausweg finden; **to resort to ~s** zu Notbehelfen greifen;

~ *(a.)* zweckmäßig, -entsprechend, tunlich;

~ **change of policy** angebrachte Änderung der Politik; ~ **solution of a difficulty** zweckmäßige Behebung einer Schwierigkeit.

expediment Mobiliarvermögen.

expedite *(v.)* befördern, absenden, expedieren, *(speed up)* beschleunigen, drängen auf;

~ **the business of the committee** Ausschußberatungen beschleunigen; ~ **matters** Dinge vorantreiben (beschleunigt bearbeiten).

expedited | freight Expreßgut; ~ **service** Eil-, Expreßdienst.

expediter Terminüberwacher.

expedition Expedition, Forschungs-, Entdeckungsreise, *(mil.)* Kriegs-, Feldzug, Unternehmen, *(speed)* Beschleunigung, Geschwindigkeit, Eile;

for the sake of ~ aus Gründen der Eilbedürftigkeit; **with the utmost** ~ mit äußerster Eile;

exploring ~ Forschungsreise; **hunting** ~ Jagdausflug; **military** ~ Feldzug, Kriegszug, militärische Expedition; **punitive** ~ Strafexpedition;

to furnish an ~ Expedition ausrüsten; **to go on an** ~ an einer Expedition teilnehmen; **to prepare an** ~ Expedition ausrüsten.

expeditionary force Expeditionskorps, -truppe.

expeditious geschäftig, emsig, prompt;

to be ~ **in business** prompt liefern;

~ **answer** prompte Antwort; ~ **messenger** flinker Bote.

expel *(v.)* ausstoßen, ausschließen, ausweisen, vertreiben, *(university)* relegieren;

~ **an alien** Ausländer abschieben (ausweisen); ~ **a child from school** Kind vom Schulbesuch ausschließen; ~ **from the hall** aus dem Saal weisen; ~ **from a party** aus einer Partei ausstoßen; ~ **s. o. from a society** j. aus einem Verein ausschließen; ~ **a student from college** Studenten von der Universität verweisen (relegieren).

expellee *(US)* Ausgewiesener, Flüchtling, Heimatvertriebener, *(student)* Relegierter.

expelling Ausweisung, *(student)* Relegation.

expend *(v.)* aufwenden, verwenden, *(money)* verwenden, auslegen, ausgeben, *(consume)* verbrauchen;

~ **all one's capital for equipment** sein gesamtes Kapital in die Ausstattung investieren; ~ **care** Sorgfalt anwenden; ~ **much time on s. th.** viel Zeit für etw. verwenden.

expendable verbrauchbar, kurzlebig;

~ **fund** Unkostenfonds; ~ **item** *(mil., US)* Verbrauchsartikel, *(Br.)* Verbrauchsmaterial; ~ **package** verlorene Packung, Einwegpackung; ~ **stores** *(Br.)* Verbrauchsmaterial; ~ **trust fund** Treuhandfonds mit freier Ertragsverwendung.

expender Verbraucher.

expenditure *(amount expended)* Ausgaben, [Kosten]aufwand, [Un]kosten, Spesen, *(consumption)* Aufwand, Verbrauch, *(laying out of money)* Ausgabe, Verausgabung, Aufwendungen, Auslagen;

at great ~ mit großem Geldaufwand;

actual ~ Istausgabe; **additional** ~ Mehraufwand, -ausgabe; **administrative** ~ Verwaltungsunkosten; **advertising** ~ Reklamekosten, Werbeausgaben; **aggregate** ~ Gesamtaufwand; **allowable** ~ steuerlich anerkannte Ausgabenposten (Aufwendungen); **anticipatory** ~ Ausgaben im Vorgriff; **average** ~ Havariegelder; **basic** ~ bleibende Unkosten; **budgetary** ~ Haushaltsausgaben; ~ **budgeted for** veranschlagte Ausgaben; ~ **not budgeted for** außerplanmäßige Ausgaben; **bureaucratic** ~ bürokratischer Aufwand; **capital** ~ aktivierungspflichtiger Aufwand, Kapitalaufwand, -verbrauch; **cash** ~ Barauflagen, -auslagen, -ausgaben; **consumer** ~ Verbraucherausgaben; **consumption** ~ Ausgaben für den Lebensunterhalt; **current** ~ laufende Ausgaben; **disallowable** ~ steuerlich nicht anerkannte Ausgaben; **estimated** ~ Sollausgaben; **extraordinary and outside** ~ außerordentliche und betriebsfremde Aufwendungen; **government (governmental)** ~ öffentliche Ausgaben, Staatsausgaben, Ausgaben der öffentlichen Hand; **growing** ~ wachsende Unkosten (Ausgaben); **heavy** ~ große Ausgaben; **increased** ~ Mehrausgaben; ~ **incurred** entstandene Kosten; **initial** ~ erstmalige Aufwendung, Anlage-, Installationskosten; **internal administrative** ~ Ausgaben für die innere Verwaltung; **lavish** ~ zügellose Ausgabenwirtschaft; **local** ~ *(US)* Kommunalausgaben, Aufwand der Gemeinden; **national** ~ Staatsausgaben; **net** ~ Nettoaufwand, Reinausgabe; **nonrecurring** ~ einmalige Ausgabe; ~ **occasioned** entstandene Aufwendungen; **office** ~ Büroaufwand, -unkosten; **operating** ~ Betriebsausgaben; **private** ~ private Ausgabe (Aufwendun-

gen); **professional** ~ Werbungskosten, -aufwand; **profuse** ~ übermäßige (verschwenderische) Ausgaben; **public** ~ Ausgabenwirtschaft der öffentlichen Hand, Staatsausgaben; **total public** ~ gesamte Ausgabenwirtschaft der öffentlichen Hände; **qualifying** ~ *(taxation)* für Abschreibungen zugelassener Kostenaufwand; **reduced** ~ Minderausgaben; **refundable** ~ erstattungsfähige Ausgaben; **returning** ~ wiederkehrende (laufende) Ausgaben; **routine** ~ tägliche Ausgaben; **ruinous** ~ ruinöser Aufwand; **social** ~ soziale Aufwendungen; **special** ~ Sonderausgaben; **tourist** ~ Ausgaben durch Ferienreisende; **unallowed** ~ nicht abgeschriebene Anschaffungskosten; **unforeseen** ~ unvorhergesehene Ausgaben; **wartime** ~ Kriegsausgaben; **welfare** ~ Fürsorge-, Sozialaufwendungen, Soziallasten, -ausgaben;

income and ~ Einnahmen und Ausgaben;

~ **not provided for in the budget** außerplanmäßige Ausgaben; ~ **on buildings** Bauinvestitionen; ~ **of a business** Geschäftsausgaben, -unkosten; ~ **on commissions** Provisionsaufwendungen; ~ **on education** Bildungsaufwand; ~ **to be charged to income** aus dem Erfolg zu deckende Aufwendungen; ~ **of money on armaments** Rüstungsetat, -ausgaben; ~ **on personnel** Personalaufwand; ~ **on additional plant** Kostenaufwand für Betriebserweiterungen; ~ **for relief** Aufwendungen für Unterstützungen; ~ **qualifying for relief** *(Br.)* bei der Steuer abzugsfähiger Ausgabenposten; ~ **on repairs** Reparaturkostenaufwand; ~ **on retirement pensions** Aufwendungen für die Altersversorgung; ~ **on staff** Personalaufwand; ~ **of the state** Staatsausgaben; ~ **for taxes on income, earnings and property** Aufwand für Steuern vom Einkommen, Ertrag und Vermögen; ~ **not allowable for tax purpose** steuerlich nicht anerkannte Ausgaben; ~ **for wages** Lohnaufwand;

to allocate one's ~ seine Ausgaben aufschlüsseln; **to axe** ~ Ausgaben beschneiden; **to be responsible for the** ~ Ausgabenwirtschaft zu verantworten haben; **to break down** ~ Spesen aufschlüsseln; **to control the** ~ Unkosten niedrig halten; **to cut** ~ **[down]** Ausgaben senken, Spesenetat kürzen; **to do away with wasteful** ~ unsinnige Ausgaben einschränken; **to entail large** ~ große Ausgaben verursachen; **to enter as** ~ als Ausgaben verbuchen; **to hold down** ~ Spesen niedrig halten; **to increase the** ~ Ausgaben erhöhen, Spesenetat vergrößern; **to incur** ~ **on agricultural building** Erhaltungsaufwand für landwirtschaftlich genutzte Gebäude haben; **to keep one's** ~ **within reasonable limits** Ausgaben auf ein vernünftiges Maß beschränken; **to plan one's** ~ sein Geld einteilen; **to put down one's** ~ seine Ausgabenwirtschaft beschränken; **to put a stop to** ~ Spesenaufwand begrenzen; **to refund the** ~ Spesen zurückerstatten; **to regulate one's** ~ seine Ausgabenwirtschaft in Ordnung bringen; **to suit one's** ~ sein Geld einteilen; **to suit one's** ~ **to one's income** mit seinem Einkommen auskommen, sich nach der Decke strecken; **to treat an** ~ **as properly attributable to capital** Ausgabe als aktivierungspflichtigen Aufwand behandeln;

~ **account** Aufwandskonto; **to go on** ~ **account** auf Spesenkonto gehen; **basic** ~ **accounts** bleibende Aufwandsposten; ~ **approach** Verwendungsrechnung des Volkseinkommens; ~ **authorization** Beschaffungsgenehmigung; ~ **ceiling** Ausgabenhöhe, Ausgabenplafond; ~ **committee** Ausgabenausschuß; ~ **controller** staatlicher Rechnungsprüfer; ~ **curve** Indifferenzkurve, Ausgabenkurve; ~ **cut** Ausgabeneinschränkung, -kürzung, -abstriche; ~ **exemption** Ausgabenfreibetrag; ~ **lag** Ausgabeverzögerung; **actual** ~ **outturn** tatsächlich vorgenommene Ausgaben; ~ **pattern** Ausgabenstruktur; ~ **rate** [höchstzulässiger] Unkostensatz; ~ **relief** Sonderausgabenfreibetrag; ~ **target** Ausgabenvorgabe; ~ **taxes** indirekte Steuern, Aufwandsteuern.

expense Ausgaben, Auslage, Aufwendungen, Spesen, Kosten;

after (deducting) ~s nach Abrechnung der Spesen; **all ~s included** mit Einschluß aller Kosten; **at one's own** ~ auf eigene Kosten; **at the** ~ **of** auf Kosten, zu Lasten; **at great** ~ sehr teuer; **at joint** ~ auf gemeinsame Kosten; **at my** ~ auf meine Kosten; **at public** ~ auf Kosten des Staates (Staatskosten); **at the** ~ **of quality** auf Kosten der Qualität; **at ship's ~s** auf Kosten der Reederei; **dividing [the] ~s** auf gemeinsame Kosten; **free of** ~ kostenfrei; **including the ~s** unter Einschluß (Einrechnung) der Spesen; **involving** ~ mit Kosten verknüpft (verbunden); **no ~s** *(bill of exchange)* ohne Kosten; **with all its attendant ~s** mit all den damit verbundenen Ausgaben; **with out-of-pocket** ~ gegen Erstattung der baren Unkosten;

accrued ~s entstandene Unkosten, Spesenforderungen, *(balance sheet)* antizipatorische Passiva; **actual ~s** Barauslagen; **additional ~s** zusätzliche Ausgaben, Neben[un]kosten; **administration ~s** *(trustee)* Kosten der Vermögensverwaltung;

administrative ~s Verwaltungskosten, -aufwand; **advanced ~** Spesen-, Kostenvorschuß; **advertising ~** Werbekosten; **annual ~s** Jahresausgaben; **building ~s** Baukosten; **business ~** Geschäftsunkosten; **capitalized ~s** kapitalisierte (aktivierte, auf Kapitalkonto übernommene) Ausgaben (Kosten); **cash ~s** Barauslagen; **casual ~s** gelegentliche Ausgaben; **claim ~s** Bearbeitungskosten, *(insurance)* Regulierungskosten; **collection ~** Einziehungs-, Inkassokosten; **connected ~s** notwendige Ausgaben; **constant ~s** fortlaufende Ausgaben; **contingent ~s** unerwartete Ausgaben; **~s covered** Kosten gedeckt, kostenfrei; **credit ~** Kreditkosten, -aufwand; **current ~s** laufende Ausgaben; **daily ~s** tägliche Ausgaben; **~s deducted** nach Abzug der Kosten; **deductible ~s** abzugsfähige Ausgaben; **deferred ~s** im voraus gezahlte Aufwendungen; **delivery ~s** Zustellungs-, Versandkosten; **departmental ~s** Abteilungskosten; **direct ~** unmittelbarer Kostenaufwand; **discharging ~** Entladungs-, Löschungskosten; **experimental ~** Versuchsaufwand; **extra ~** Sonderaufwendungen; **extraordinary and outside ~** außerordentliche und betriebsfremde Aufwendungen; **extravagant ~s** übermäßiger Aufwand; **factory overhead ~** Fertigungsgemeinkosten; **financial ~s** Finanzierungskosten, Finanzaufwand; **fixed ~s** Fix-, Generalunkosten, laufende Ausgaben; **~s charged forward** gegen Nachname der Kosten; **forwarding ~s** Versand[un]kosten, -spesen; **freight ~s** Versand-, Transportkosten; **future ~s** zukünftiger Aufwand; **general ~s** Generalunkosten, Gemein-, Handlungsunkosten; **head-office ~s** Unkosten der Zentrale; **heavy ~s** große (beträchtliche) Unkosten; **high ~s** bedeutende Ausgaben; **hospital ~s** Krankenhauskosten; **in-hospital medical ~s** im Krankenhaus anfallende Arztkosten; **household ~s** Kosten der Haushaltsführung, Wirtschaftsausgaben; **incidental ~s** Nebenausgaben, -kosten, -spesen; **all ~s included** mit Einschluß aller Kosten; **~s incurred** entstandene Kosten, gehabte Ausgaben; **indirect ~** mittelbarer Kostenaufwand, Gemeinkosten, allgemeine Unkosten; **insignificant ~s** unerhebliche Kosten; **~s involved** eingegangene Kosten; **irrecoverable ~s** nicht beitreibbare Kosten; **legal ~s** Gerichts-, Anwaltskosten; **living ~s** Lebenshaltungskosten; **local ~s** Platzspesen; **loading ~s** Verladekosten; **maintaining ~s** Unterhalt[ung]skosten, Erhaltungsaufwand; **maintenance ~** *(child)* Unterhaltskosten, -aufwand, Alimentationskosten; **management ~s** Verwaltungs-, Geschäftsführungskosten; **manufacturing ~s** Herstellungs-, Fertigungsgemeinkosten; **marketing ~s** Vertriebsunkosten; **medical ~s** Arztkosten; **minor ~s** kleinere Ausgaben; **~s necessarily incurred** notwendige Ausgaben; **noncash ~s** bargeldloser Kostenaufwand; **nonoperating ~s** *(balance sheet)* sonstige Ausgaben, betriebsfremde Aufwendungen; **nonproductive ~s** unproduktive Ausgaben; **nonrecurring ~s** einmalige (nicht wiederkehrende) Ausgaben; **office ~s** Geschäfts-, Bürounkosten; **operating ~s** Betriebsunkosten; **ordinary ~s** laufende (gemeine) Ausgaben; **organization ~** *(US)* Gründungskosten, -aufwand; **other ~** *(balance sheet)* andere Aufwendungen; **out-of-pocket ~s** effektive Ausgaben, *(Br.)* Barauslagen für Unkosten, verauslagte Spesen; **overhead ~s** Geschäfts-, Handlungsunkosten; **permissible ~** *(taxation)* abzugsfähige Unkosten; **personnel ~s** Personalaufwendungen; **petty ~s** geringfügige Ausgaben, kleine Spesen (Unkosten); **preliminary ~s** *(Br.)* vor der Gründung angefallene Ausgaben, Gründungskosten, -aufwand; **prepaid ~s** *(balance sheet)* vorausgezahlte Aufwendungen, transitorische Posten, aktive Rechnungsabgrenzungsposten; **preparation ~** Aufwand vor Produktionsaufnahme; **printing ~s** Druckkosten; **private ~s** persönliche Ausgaben; **productive ~s** werbende Ausgaben; **public ~s** Staatskosten; **real ~** Istausgabe; **official receiver's ~s** Massekosten; **recurrent ~s** regelmäßig wiederkehrende Ausgaben; **rehabilitation ~s** Wiederherstellungskosten; **reimbursed ~** erstattete Kosten; **rent ~s** Mietaufwand, -aufwendung; **running ~s** laufende Ausgaben, *(car)* Unterhaltungskosten; **security ~** Aufwendungen für Wertpapierbesitz; **selling ~s** Vertriebs[gemein]-, Verkaufsunkosten; **shipping ~s** Versandkosten, -spesen; **staff and material ~s** Personal- und Sachaufwand; **standing ~s** feste Unkosten; **sundry ~s** *(balance sheet)* sonstige Auslagen, verschiedene Ausgaben; **surgical ~s** Operationskosten; **testamentary ~s** Kosten der Testamentserrichtung, Testamentsvollstreckerkosten, Nachlaßkosten; **total ~** Gesamtausgaben, -kosten; **total ~s incurred** tatsächliche Gesamtausgaben; **transshipment ~s** Umladungskosten; **travelling ~[s]** Reisespesen, -[un]kosten; **uncontrollable ~s** von der Kostenstelle nicht beeinflußbare Kosten; **uncovered ~s** ungedeckte Ausgaben; **upkeep ~s** Unterhaltungskosten; **war ~** Kriegskosten; **working ~s** Betriebskosten;

~s of administration Kosten der Nachlaßverwaltung, Nachlaßverwaltungskosten; **~s provided for in the budget** im Etat vorgesehene Unkosten; **~s of building** Baukosten; **~ in carrying on business** laufende Geschäftsunkosten; **~ for composition** Satzkosten; **~s of construction** Erstellungskosten; **~s payable (defrayable) out of local contributions** zu Lasten der Gemeinde gehende Ausgaben; **~s necessarily incurred in performing one's duties** mit den Dienstobliegenheiten notwendigerweise im Zusammenhang stehende Aufwendungen; **~ against earnings** mit den Einkünften im Zusammenhang stehende Ausgaben; **~s of formation** Gründungskosten, -aufwand; **~ of a journey** Reisekosten; **~ of liquidation** Liquidierungsaufwand, -kosten; **~s of maintenance** Unterhaltungskosten, Erhaltungsaufwand; **~ of management and administration** Betriebs- und Verwaltungskosten; **~ of marketing** Vertriebs-, Absatzkosten; **~ on office requirements** Aufwendungen für Bürobedarf; **~ of operation** Betriebsausgaben; **~s for postage** Portokosten, -spesen; **~s of production** Herstellungskosten; **actual ~s of realization of the assets** bei der Versilberung tatsächlich angefallene Kosten; **~s not otherwise received** nicht anderweitig erstattete Kosten; **~s of receivership** Massekosten; **~s net of recoveries** *(insurance balance sheet)* Nettoaufwand zur Befriedigung von Regreßforderungen; **~s of registration** Eintragungsgebühren; **~ of [accruing from] representation** Repräsentationsaufwand; **~s of running** *(railway)* Betriebskosten; **~ for sale (of selling)** Verkaufsspesen, Vertriebsaufwand; **~ of the state** Staatsausgaben; **~s incurred by a trader in another capacity** in nichtgewerblicher Eigenschaft entstandene Ausgaben; **~s wholly and exclusively laid out for the purpose of the trade** in einem Gewerbebetrieb zwangsläufig anfallende Unkosten; **~s of travelling** Reiseunkosten, -spesen; **~ of trial** Verfahrenskosten; **~ of upkeep** Instandhaltungskosten; **~ of war** Kriegskosten;

~ is no object Kosten spielen keine Rolle;

~ (v.) für Spesen belasten, über Aufwand abrechnen;

~ in the year of occurence im Zeitpunkt der Entstehung als Unkosten verbuchen;

to absorb ~s Unkostenposten übernehmen; **to account for one's ~s** seine Spesen abrechnen; **to allocate general ~s** Gemeinkosten umlegen; **to allow s. o. his ~s** jem. seine Spesen ersetzen; **to apportion the ~s** Kosten aufteilen, Kostenaufteilung vornehmen; **to assess the members of the society with the ~s** Unkosten auf die Vereinsmitglieder umlegen; **to be an ~** Kosten machen (verursachen); **to be at the ~ of** ausgeben (bestreiten) müssen; **to be a great ~ to s. o.** jem. große Kosten verursachen; **to be lax in handling ~s** Spesenabrechnungen lasch behandeln; **to be liable for one's ~s** für seine Unkosten aufzukommen haben; **to be maintained at public ~** aus öffentlichen Mitteln unterhalten werden; **to be published at joint ~ of publisher and author** auf gemeinsame Kosten von Verleger und Autor veröffentlicht werden; **to bear the ~s** für die Kosten aufkommen, Kosten bestreiten; **to bear the ~ [on equal shares]** Kosten [zu gleichen Teilen] tragen; **to break down ~s** [Un]kosten (Spesen) aufschlüsseln; **to carry all ~s for s. o.** alle Kosten für j. tragen; **to charge an account with all the ~s** Konto mit sämtlichen Unkosten belasten, Unkosten über ein Konto buchen; **to charge to ~** Unkostenkonto belasten; **to charges ~s forward** Spesen nachnehmen; **to charge an ~ to the public debt** auf die Staatskasse übernehmen; **to clear ~s** Ausgaben abdecken; **not to clear one's ~s** seine Unkosten nicht hereinbekommen; **to contribute to the ~s** Unkostenbeitrag leisten; **to cover ~s** Ausgaben decken; **to curtail one's ~s** sich in seinen Ausgaben einschränken; **to cut down ~s** Unkostenetat (Spesenetat) kürzen, Ausgaben herunterschrauben; **to deduct ~s** Spesen absetzen, seine Unkosten abrechnen; **to defray the ~** Unkosten bestreiten, Kosten tragen; **to draw in one's ~s** sich in seinen Ausgaben einschränken; **to eagle-eye ~s** Spesen mit argwöhnischen Augen betrachten; **to enter as ~** als Ausgaben buchen; **to evaluate ~s** Kosten veranschlagen; **to figure out the ~s** Unkosten berechnen; **to get back one's ~s** seine Kosten decken; **to get rich at s. one's ~** sich auf jds. Kosten bereichern; **to go to ~** Kosten machen (verursachen) **to go to great ~s** sich in große Unkosten stürzen; **to go shares with s. o. in the ~** sich in die Unkosten mit jem. teilen; **to have all ~s paid** freigehalten werden; **to have gone to considerable ~s** beträchtliche Kosten aufgewandt haben; **to hold down ~s** Unkosten (Spesen) niedrig halten; **to include ~s** Kosten einrechnen; **to increase one's ~s** seinen Spesenetat vergrößern; **to incure heavy ~** beträchtliche Aufwendungen machen; **to indemnify s. o. for ~ incurred** jem. seine Spesen ersetzen; **to involve ~s** Kosten verursachen; **to involve much ~** mit großen Kosten verbunden sein; **to keep down the ~s** Spesenetat (Unkostenetat) niedrig halten; **to keep**

a **record of** one's ~s Spesenbelege sammeln;**to keep a strict account of** ~s Spesen genauestens überwachen; **to keep tabs on the** ~s Spesenwirtschaft im Auge haben; **to land s. o. with the** ~s jem. die Kosten aufbrummen; **to launch out into** ~s sich in Unkosten stürzen; **to limit** one's ~s sich einschränken; **to live at the** ~ **of others** auf anderer Leute Kosten leben, sich aushalten lassen; **to lump the** ~s Unkosten aufteilen; **to meet** ~s Kosten tragen, für die Kosten aufkommen; **to offer s. o.** $ 100 **and** ~s jem. 100 Dollar in der Woche und den Ersatz der Spesen anbieten; **to pay** ~s Kosten übernehmen; **to proportion** one's ~s **to** one's **income** seine Ausgaben den Einnahmen anpassen; **to put s. o. to great** ~ jem. große Kosten verursachen; **to put a stop to** ~s Unkosten abbremsen; **to recover** ~s sich für den Betrag seiner Spesen erholen; **to recover** one's ~s **properly incurred** gerechtfertigte Spesen erstattet bekommen; **to refund the** ~s Spesen begleichen, Ausgaben (Kosten) erstatten; **to reimburse the** ~ Spesen (Auslagen) vergüten; **to reimburse the witness for his** ~ dem Zeugen seine Kosten erstatten; **to restrict** one's ~s seine Ausgaben beschränken; **to retrench** Ausgaben einschränken; **to run on** ~s *(car)* auf Geschäftskosten laufen; **to save** ~s Kosten sparen; **to spare no** ~s keine Kosten scheuen.
expense account Spesen-, Aufwand-, Unkostenkonto, *(income tax, Br.)* absetzbare Geschäftsunkosten, *(statement of ~)* Unkostenaufstellung, Spesen-, Auslagenabrechnung;
to go on ~ auf Spesenkonto gehen; **to travel on** ~ zu Lasten des Spesenkontos verreisen;
~ **cutback (cutting)** Beschneidung des Spesenetats; ~ **deduction** Spesenabzüge; ~ **item** Spesenposten; ~ **restrictions** Einschränkung des Spesenaufwands, Speseneinschränkungen; ~ **rules** Spesenrichtlinien; ~ **spendings** Spesenaufwand, -ausgaben.
expense | allowance Aufwandsentschädigung; **to retain on a per-diem-plus-~ basis** auf Tages- und Unkostenbasis (Spesenbasis) beschäftigen; ~ **bill** Spesenrechnung; ~ **book** Unkostenbuch; ~ **budget** Spesen-, Unkostenetat, -anschlag; ~ **burden (charge)** Unkostenbelastung; ~ **category** *(Br.)* Kostenarten; ~ **classification** Spesen-, [Un]kostenaufgliederung; ~ **constants** gleichbleibende Ausgaben; ~ **control** Spesenkontrolle; ~ **distribution** Kostenverteilung; ~ **distribution sheet** Betriebsabrechnungsbogen; ~ **factor** Aufwands-, Spesen-, Kostenfaktor; ~ **figures** Aufwandszahlen, Kostenziffern; ~ **fund** Spesen-, Unkostenfonds; ~ **invoice** Unkostenaufstellung, -rechnung; ~ **item** Ausgabe-, Aufwands-, Spesenkosten; ~ **ledger** Unkostenhauptbuch; ~ **loading** *(insurance)* Spesen-, Unkostenbelastung, -verteilung; ~ **portion** Unkostenanteil; ~ **prepayment** Spesenvorschuß, Auslagenvorauszahlung; ~ **ratio** Unkostenanteil; ~ **report** Spesenabrechnung; **to submit** ~ **reports** Spesen-, Unkostenbelege einreichen; ~-**[report] reimbursement** Spesenrückerstattung; ~ **requirements** Kostenerfordernisse; ~ **rule** *(Br.)* Richtlinienerlaß für steuerabzugsfähige Ausgaben; ~ **sheet** Spesenabrechnung; ~ **voucher** Spesen-, Ausgabenbeleg; ~ **[is] no object** *(ad)* die Kostenfrage spielt keine Rolle.
expensive teuer, kostspielig, aufwendig;
to be ~ teuer sein; **to become more** ~ teurer werden, sich verteuern;
~ **advertising** kostspielige Werbung; ~ **car** Luxuswagen; ~ **hobby** kostspieliges Freizeitvergnügen; ~ **lawsuit** kostspieliger Prozeß.
expensively, to live auf großem Fuße leben.
experience Erfahrung, Praxis, Kenntnisse, Bewandertheit;
according to ~ erfahrungsgemäß; **based on** ~ auf Erfahrungen gegründet; **from my own** ~ aufgrund eigener Erfahrungen; **ample** ~ reiche Erfahrungen; **bad-debt** ~ Erfahrung mit faulen Schuldnern; **business** ~ Geschäftserfahrung, Routine; **driving** ~ Fahrpraxis; **field** ~ Erfahrungen im Außendienst, nachweisbare praktische Erfahrungen; **grey** ~ langjährige Erfahrung; **investment** ~ Erfahrungen im Anlagengeschäft; **ledger** ~ Erfahrung in der Führung des Hauptbuches; **long personal** ~ langjährige Praxis; **practical** ~ praktische (nachweisbare) Erfahrung, Lebenserfahrung; **previous** ~ Vorerfahrung; **professional** ~ Berufserfahrung; **punched-card** ~ Lochkartenerfahrung; **qualifying** ~ Qualifizierungsnachweis; **specialized** ~ Spezialerfahrung; **trial** ~ Erfahrung in Strafsachen; **wide** ~ große Erfahrungen;
~ **in business** geschäftliche Erfahrung, Geschäftserfahrung, -routine; ~ **as lecturer** Lektorenerfahrung; ~ **in trade** Geschäftserfahrung, -routine; ~ **of office work** Büroerfahrung;
~ *(v.)* **an advance** Kurssteigerung erfahren; ~ **a fresh decline** *(shares)* neuen Sturz erfahren; ~ **a decline in prices** Kursrückgang erleiden; ~ **a depression** *(prices)* fallen; ~ **difficulties** auf Schwierigkeiten stoßen; ~ **losses** Verluste erleiden; ~ **heavy trials** mit schweren Prüfungen fertig werden müssen;

to go through painful ~s schmerzliche Erfahrungen hinter sich bringen; **to have a nasty** ~ *(fam.)* widerliches Erlebnis haben; **to have previous** ~ Vorkenntnisse haben; **to have enough** ~ **for a position** über ausreichende Kenntnisse für eine Stellung verfügen; **to have had a wide** ~ **of men** seine Umwelt hinreichend kennengelernt haben; **to have** ~ **of teaching** über Unterrichtserfahrungen verfügen; **to know it by** ~ ein Lied davon singen können; **to lack** ~ über zu wenig Erfahrungen verfügen; **to profit by** ~ durch Erfahrung klug werden; **to relate** one's ~s über seine Erlebnisse berichten;
~ **rate** *(insurance)* auf Grund von Erfahrungen errechneter Entschädigungssatz, Erfahrungsrichtsatz; ~ **rating** Leistungsbeurteilung, -einstufung, *(pension scheme)* Gewinnverband; ~-**rating plan** Leistungsbeurteilungsschema, *(insurance)* auf Grund von Erfahrungen aufgestelltes Prämienschema; ~ **tables** Sterblichkeits-, Mortalitätstafeln.
experienced erfahren, versiert, bewandert, sachkundig, routiniert, gewandt;
~ **in business** geschäftskundig, -erfahren;
~ **nurse** erfahrene Krankenschwester.
experiment Versuch, Experiment, Probe;
as an ~ versuchsweise;
model ~ Modellverfahren;
~ *(v.)* versuchen, experimentieren;
~ **on s. th.** an einer Sache Versuche anstellen;
to make (try) ~ Versuche anstellen;
~ **farm** Versuchsgut, -farm; ~ **station** *(US)* Versuchsstation.
experimental experimentell;
~ **department** Forschungs-, Versuchsabteilung; ~ **design** Versuchsanordnung; ~ **engineer** Forschungsingenieur; ~ **error** Versuchsfehler; ~ **expense** Versuchsaufwand; ~ **farm** Versuchsgut; ~ **film** Experimentalfilm; ~ **gaming** Planspiele; ~ **group** Versuchsgruppe; ~ **institute** Versuchsanstalt; ~ **method** experimenteller Test; ~ **model** Versuchsmodell; ~ **road** Versuchsstraße; ~ **stage** Versuchsstadium; ~ **station** *(US)* Versuchsstation; ~ **testimony** Sachverständigenaussage; ~ **theater** Experimentiertheater; ~ **type** Versuchsmuster; ~ **year** Versuchsjahr.
experimentalize *(v.)* experimentieren, Versuche durchführen.
expert Fachmann, -gelehrter, Könner, Kenner, Spezialist, Autorität, Sachverständiger, Gutachter, Experte, *(factual knowledge)* Sachkenntnis, *(sworn appraiser)* beeidigter Sachverständiger;
according to the ~s nach Ansicht der Sachverständigen; **among** ~s in Fachkreisen, in der Fachwelt;
agricultural ~ landwirtschaftlicher Sachverständiger; **auditing** ~ Buchsachverständiger, Buchführungsexperte; **commerce-department** ~ Sachverständiger des Wirtschaftsministeriums; **functional** ~ Spezialist; **handwriting** ~ Schriftsachverständiger; **legal** ~ juristischer Sachverständiger; **marketing** ~ Marktsachverständiger, Fachmann für Fragen der Absatzförderung; **mining** ~ Bergbausachverständiger; **no-nonsense** ~ nüchtern denkender Sachverständiger; **qualified** ~ amtlich bestellter Sachverständiger; **quasi** ~ halber Sachverständiger; **sworn** ~ vereidigter Sachverständiger; **tax** ~ Steuerfachmann;
~ **on anti-trust law** Kartellspezialist; ~ **on business cycles** Konjunkturfachmann; ~ **in contracting** Vergabeexperte; ~ **appointed by the court** gerichtlich bestellter Sachverständiger, Gerichtssachverständiger; ~ **in economics** Wirtschaftsexperte; ~ **in handwriting** Schriftsachverständiger;
~ *(v.)* sachverständig überprüfen;
to appoint an ~ Gutachter ernennen; **to be an** ~ **in a matter** Sachverständiger in (Spezialist für) etw. (kompetent) sein; **to be an** ~ **on (in) economics** Wirtschaftsexperte sein; **to be informed by an** ~ von zuständiger Seite hören; **to call in (consult) an** ~ Sachverständigen zu Rate ziehen, Fachmann befragen; **to pose (set up) as an** ~ sich als Sachverständigen ausgeben; **to train** ~s **in arbitration** sachverständige Schiedsrichter ausbilden;
~ *(a.)* fachkundig, -männisch, erfahren, sachverständig, gutachtlich;
~ **advice** Sachverständigenurteil; **according to** ~ **advice** nach dem Urteil des Sachverständigen; **to give** ~ **advice** fachmännischen Rat erteilen; **to take** ~ **advice** Experten zur Konsultation hinzuziehen; ~ **assessor** sachverständiger Beisitzer; ~ **capacity** Sachverständigeneigenschaft; ~ **evidence** Sachverständigengutachten, gutachtliche Zeugenaussage; ~ **examination** fachmännische Überprüfung; ~'s **fee** Sachverständigengebühren; ~ **group** Sachverständigengruppe; ~ **guidance** sachkundige Beratung; ~ **inquiry** Sachverständigenuntersuchung; **to gain** ~ **knowledge** Fachkenntnisse erwerben; ~ **opinion** [Sachverstän-

digen]gutachten, gutachterliche Äußerung; ~'s report fachmännisches Gutachten, Bericht eines Sachverständigen, Sachverständigenurteil, -bericht; ~ **mail sorter** geschickter Briefsortierer; ~ **testimony** gutachtliche Aussage eines Sachverständigen; ~ **translation** kunstgerechte Übersetzung; ~ **tuition** Fachunterricht; ~ **witness** sachverständiger Zeuge; ~ **work** Facharbeit; ~ **workman** Facharbeiter; ~ **workmanship** Facharbeit; ~ **writer** Fachberichterstatter, -schriftsteller.

expertise Sachverständigengutachten, Expertise.

expertness Geschicklichkeit.

expilation Nachlaßunterschlagung.

expiration (becoming void) Erlöschen, Verfall, Fälligwerden, (termination) Zeitablauf, Ende;
after ~ of this period nach Ablauf dieser Frist; at the time of (on) ~ zur Verfallzeit, bei Verfall (Ablauf); payable at ~ bei Verfall zahlbar;
~ of a contract Vertragsablauf; ~ of credit Fälligwerden eines Kredits; ~ of a lease Pachtablauf, Beendigung eines Pachtvertrages; ~ of a patent Ablauf eines Patents; ~ of a period Fristablauf; ~ of the period of notice Ablauf der Kündigungsfrist; ~ of the period for redemption Ablauf einer Einlösungsfrist; ~ of policy Versicherungsablauf, Erlöschen einer Versicherung; ~ of the term fixed Ablauf der festgelegten Zeit; ~ of a term of office Beendigung einer Amtszeit; ~ of the term of partnership Ablauf des Gesellschaftsvertrages; ~ of time Zeitablauf; ~ of free time befristete Entladezeit; ~ of truce Ablauf (Beendigung) des Waffenstillstands;
to repay before the ~ of the period vor Verfallzeit bezahlen;
~ date Ablauf-, Verfalltermin; date of a patent Erlöschen eines Patentes; ~ list (insurance) Fälligkeitsliste; ~ notice Benachrichtigung über einen Fristablauf.

expire (v.) (become void) Gültigkeit verlieren, außer Kraft treten, verfallen, erlöschen, (come to an end) fällig werden, ablaufen, (contract) erlöschen;
~ by limitation verjähren.

expired (ticket) abgeknipst, ungültig;
to have ~ nicht mehr gültig sein, (letter of credit) ungültig [geworden] sein;
~ bill fälliger Wechsel; ~ cost unnützer Kostenaufwand; ~ licence erloschene Konzession; ~ patent erloschenes (abgelaufenes) Patent; ~ policy abgelaufene Police; ~ utility nicht mehr vorhandener (abgelaufener) Nutzungswert.

expiring ablaufend, verfallend;
~ date Verfalltag; ~ words of a dying man letzte Worte eines Sterbenden.

expiry Erlöschen, Verfall, Ablauf;
on ~ bei Erlöschen; on ~ of the lease bei Ablauf (Auslaufen) des Mietvertrages;
~ of a period (time limit) Fristablauf;
~ date Ablauftermin, Verfalldatum, -tag.

explain (v.) verständlich machen, auseinandersetzen, ausführlich explizieren, darlegen, erklären, erläutern;
~ o. s. sich rechtfertigen; ~ away als nicht existent darstellen, ausreden; ~ one's conduct sein Verhalten rechtfertigen; ~ in detail eingehend darlegen; ~ that one has been delayed by the weather seine Verspätung auf die Wetterverhältnisse zurückführen; ~ a passage Textstelle auslegen.

explanation Erläuterung, Darlegung, Erklärung;
~ with illustrative examples Erläuterung an Hand von Beispielen; ~ of signs Zeichenerklärung; ~ of terms Begriffserläuterung;
to come to an ~ with s. o. mit jem. eine Verständigung erzielen; to come in for an ~ einer Erläuterung bedürfen; to enter into long ~s langatmige Erläuterungen abgeben; to give an ~ of s. th. etw. erläutern; to give ~s for one's conduct Erklärungen für sein Verhalten abgeben; to need an ~ erklärungsbedürftig sein; to need no ~ keiner Erklärung bedürfen; to owe s. o. an ~ jem. Rechenschaft schuldig sein.

explanatory erklärend, erläuternd;
to be self-~ sich von selbst erklären;
~ annotations (notes) erläuternde Anmerkungen; ~ statement erklärende Feststellung, Erläuterung, Erläuterungsbericht.

expletive Füll-, Flickwort.

explicate (v.) erklären, auseinandersetzen.

explication Erläuterung, Erklärung.

explicit klar, bestimmt, deutlich, ausdrücklich;
to be quite ~ about a matter sich unmißverständlich über eine Sache äußern; to be more ~ in one's statements unmißverständliche Erklärung abgeben;
~ consent ausdrückliche Zustimmung; ~ declaration (statement) formelle Erklärung; ~ form entwickelte Schreibweise.

explode (v.) explodieren, zur Explosion bringen, (population) explosionsartig zunehmen;
~ a bomb Bombe hochgehen lassen; ~ with rage vor Wut platzen; ~ a superstition Aberglauben beseitigen; ~ a theory Theorie verwerfen.

exploded theory abgelehnte Theorie.

exploder Spreng-, Explosionsmittel.

exploit (v.) ausbeuten, ausnutzen, verwerten, auswerten;
~ one's friends seine Freunde ausnutzen; ~ a licence Lizenz verwerten; ~ a market situation Marktsituation ausnutzen; ~ a mine Bergwerk betreiben (in Betrieb nehmen); ~ a patent Patent verwerten; ~ public opinion sich die öffentliche Meinung dienstbar machen; ~ the national resources of a country Bodenschätze eines Landes ausbeuten; ~ slave labo(u)r Zwangsarbeiter einsetzen; ~ the working classes Arbeiterklasse ausbeuten.

exploitable verwertbar, ausbeutungsfähig, (mine) abbaufähig.

exploitation Ausbeutung, -nutzung, -wertung;
commercial ~ gewerbliche Verwertung, kommerzielle Ausbeutung; compulsory ~ Zwangsverwertung; illegal ~ gesetzwidrige Benutzung; industrial ~ industrielle Verwertung; monopolistic ~ monopolistische Ausbeutung; naked ~ schamlose Ausnutzung; ruthless ~ rücksichtslose Ausbeutung; wasteful ~ Raubbau;
~ of children Mißbrauch von Kindern; ~ of a country Erschließung eines Landes; ~ of a coal mine Betrieb eines Bergwerks; ~ of a licence Lizenzverwertung; ~ of a patent Patentverwertung; ~ of workers Ausbeutung von Arbeitern;
~ contract Ausbeutungsabkommen; ~ cost Ausbeutungs-, Verwertungskosten; ~ management Abbauwirtschaft; ~ rights Verwertungs-, Auswertungs-, Ausbeutungsrechte.

exploited foreign worker ausgebeuteter Gastarbeiter.

exploitee Ausgenutzter.

exploiter Benutzer, Verwerter.

exploiting a market situation Ausnutzung einer Marktsituation.

exploration Untersuchung, Erforschung, Erkundung, Sondierung, (mining) Probebohrung, (school) Orientierung;
space ~ Weltraumerkundung, Erforschung des Weltraums;
~ of the ground Bodenuntersuchung; ~ of the ocean depths Erforschung der Meerestiefen; ~ of planets Planetenerforschung;
~ activity Bohrtätigkeit; ~ concession Bohrlizenz; ~ course Orientierungskursus; ~ work Forschungstätigkeit.

exploratory | drilling Versuchs-, Probebohrung; ~ **expedition** Forschungs-, Entdeckungsreise; ~ **survey** (statistics) Vor-, Probeerhebung, Leitstudie; ~ **voyage** Entdeckungsreise.

explore (v.) untersuchen, sondieren, erforschen, erkunden;
~ a country Land erforschen; ~ the Arctic region Erkundung der Arktis vornehmen.

explorer Forschungsreisender, (US) Erdsatellit;
polar ~ Polarforscher.

exploring, to go auf Entdeckungsreise gehen.

explosion Sprengung, Detonation, Knall, Explosion;
bomb ~ Bombenexplosion; colliery ~ Grubenexplosion; firedamp ~ schlagende Wetter; population ~ Bevölkerungsexplosion; rental ~ explosionsartiges Ansteigen der Mietpreise; traffic ~ Explosion des Verkehrswesens; wage ~ Lohnexplosion;
~ of wrath Wutausbruch;
~ damage Explosionsschaden.

explosive Sprengstoff, explosiv, (fig.) aufbrausend;
to plant ~s heimlich Sprengstoff anbringen;
~ and dangerous articles Gefahrgüter im Straßenverkehr; ~ bomb Sprengbombe; ~ charge Sprengkörper, -ladung; ~ effect Sprengwirkung; ~ force Sprengkraft; ~ hazard Explosionsgefahr; ~ wave Explosionswelle.

exponent Typ, Exponent, Repräsentant;
~ of exchangeable value Exponent des Tauschwertes.

exponential smoothing (statistics) Prognoseverfahren für kurzfristige Bedarfsvorhersage.

export Export, [Waren]ausfuhr, (article) Exportgut, Ausfuhrartikel;
~s Ausfuhrartikel, -waren, -güter, Versand-, Exportartikel, (total export) Gesamtausfuhr;
additional ~ zusätzliche Ausfuhr; airbone ~ Ausfuhr auf dem Luftwege; capital ~ Kapitalausfuhr, -export; chief ~s Hauptausfuhrgüter; controlled ~s Exportlenkung; declining ~s rückläufige Exportentwicklung; gold ~ Goldausfuhr; increased ~s Export, Ausfuhrsteigerung; invisible ~s aktive Dienstleistungen, unsichtbare Ausfuhr; large-scale ~ Großexporte; manufactured ~s industrielle Aus-

fuhrartikel; **national** ~ Gesamtausfuhr; **pre-war** ~ Vorkriegsausfuhr; **rationed** ~ kontingentierte Exporte; **seaborne** ~s Ausfuhr auf dem Seewege; **temporary** ~ vorübergehende Ausfuhr; **total** ~s Gesamtausfuhr; **unrequired** ~s zur Begleichung von Auslandsschulden dienende Exporte, bilateraler Exportüberschuß; **visible** ~s sichtbare Ausfuhr, Warenausfuhr; ~s **in excess of imports** Ausfuhrüberschuß; ~ **of films** Filmexport; ~ **of recession** Ausfuhr in Rezessionszeiten;
~ **(v.)** ausführen, exportieren;
to be engaged in ~ im Außenhandel (Exportgeschäft) tätig sein; **to be geared to** ~ exportorientiert sein; **to be intended for** ~ für den Export bestimmt sein; **to curb** ~ Export drosseln; **to go for** ~ für den Export bestimmt sein; **to increase** ~ Ausfuhr erhöhen; **to produce for** ~ für das Exportgeschäft herstellen; **to raise (step up)** ~s Ausfuhr erhöhen; **to subsidize** ~ Ausfuhr fördern; ~ **achievements** Ausfuhrerfolge; ~ **advertising** Exportwerbung; ~ **agent** Exportvertreter, -agent; ~ **agreement** (cartel law) Ausfuhrabsprache; ~ **allocation** Export-, Ausfuhrzuteilung; ~ **article** Ausfuhr-, Exportartikel; ~ **association** (US) Exportverband; ~ **authorization** Ausfuhr-, Exportgenehmigung; ~ **ban** Ausfuhrverbot, -sperre; ~ **bank** Außenhandelsbank; ~ **bar** Goldausfuhrbarren; ~ **battle** Ausfuhr-, Exportschlacht; ~ **bill of lading** Ausfuhrkonnossement; ~ **bonanza** unerwartet hoher Ausfuhrerfolg; ~ **boom** Exportkonjunktur; ~ **bounty** Export-, Ausfuhrprämie, Exportbonus; ~ **bounty certificate** Exportbonusbescheinigung, Ausfuhrprämienschein; ~ **broker** Export-, Ausfuhragent; ~ **bullion point** Goldausfuhrpunkt; ~ **business** Export-, Ausfuhrgeschäft; ~ **business experience** Ausfuhrerfahrungen, Erfahrungen im Exportgeschäft; ~ **capacity** Exportkapazität; ~ **cartel** Ausfuhrkartell; ~ **catalog(ue)** Exportkatalog; ~ **center** Außenhandelsplatz; ~ **clearance** Ausfuhrabfertigung; ~ **clerk** Exportsachbearbeiter; ~ **commission merchant (house)** Ausfuhrkommissionär; ~ **commodities** Export-, Ausfuhrgüter, Ausfuhrwaren; ~ **company** Außenhandelsunternehmen, Exportgesellschaft; ~ **consignment** Exportsendung; ~ **content** Exportanteil, -quote; ~ **contract** Außenhandels-, Exportvertrag; ~ **control** Ausfuhrkontrolle, -lenkung, Außenhandelskontrolle; ~ **council** Ausfuhrförderungsgemeinschaft; ~ **country** Ausfuhrland; ~ **credit** Export-, Ausfuhrkredit; **fixed-rate** ~ **credit** festverzinslicher Exportkredit; ~ **credits guarantee** (Br.) [etwa] Hermesbürgschaft; ~ **credit guaranty department** (Br.) [etwa] Hermesgesellschaft, -versicherungsgesellschaft; ~ **credits insurance** Export-, Ausfuhrkreditversicherung; ~ **dealer** Exporthändler; ~ **declaration** (US) Exporterklärung, Ausfuhrdeklaration; ~ **deficit** Ausfuhrdefizit; Passivsaldo im Außenhandel; ~ **demands** Export-, Ausfuhrbedürfnisse; **[built-in]** ~ **department** [eingegliederte] Exportabteilung (Außenhandelsabteilung); ~-**dependent** exportabhängig; ~ **director** Leiter der Exportabteilung; ~ **documents** Ausfuhrpapiere; ~ **drive** Exportfeldzug, Ausfuhrförderung, forcierte Exportsteigerung; ~ **duty** Ausfuhrabgabe, -zoll, Ausgangs-, Exportzoll, -abgabe; **free of** ~ **duty** ausfuhrzollfrei; ~ **earner** Ausfuhrüberschußfaktor, Exportfaktor; ~ **earnings** Export-, Ausfuhrerlöse; **to stabilize** ~ **earnings** Exporterträge stabil halten; ~ **effort** Ausfuhranstrengungen; ~ **exchange** Exportdevisen; ~ **exhibition** Exportausstellung, -messe; ~ **expansion** Exportausweitung; ~ **facilities** Exporterleichterungen; ~ **factoring** Ausfuhrfaktoring; ~ **fall** Exportrückgang; ~ **figures** Ausfuhr-, Außenhandels-, Exportziffern; ~ **finance** Exportfinanzierung, Finanzierung von Exportgeschäften; ~ **finance concern** Exportfinanzierungsgesellschaft; ~ **financing** Export-, Ausfuhrfinanzierung; ~ **firm** Exporthaus, -firma; ~ **fluctuations** Schwankungen im Exporthandel; ~ **gold point** Goldausfuhrpunkt; ~ **goods** Ausfuhr-, Exportgüter; **mixed** ~ **group** Exportgemeinschaften; ~ **growth** Exportwachstum; ~ **guarantee** Ausfuhr-, Exportgarantie, -bürgschaft; ~ **house** Exportgeschäft, -firma; ℰ -**Import Bank of Washington** Einfuhr-Ausfuhr-Bank; ~ **incentive** Ausfuhranreiz, Exportvergünstigung; ~-**inclined** exportbewußt; ~ **increase** Export-, Ausfuhrsteigerung, -zunahme; ~ **industry** Exportindustrie; ~ **intelligence** (Br.) Export-, Ausfuhrnachrichten; ~ **invoice** Exportrechnung; ~ **item** Ausfuhr-, Exportartikel; ~-**led growth** exportindiziertes Wachstum; ~ **letter of credit** Exportakkreditiv; ~ **levy** Export-, Ausfuhrabgabe; ~ **licence** Ausfuhrgenehmigung, -bewilligung, Exportbewilligung; ~ **list** Ausfuhrliste; ~ **loan** Ausfuhr-, Exportkredit; ~ **manager** Leiter der Exportabteilung; **combination** ~ **manager** (US) selbständiger Exporthändler; ~ **market** Auslandsmarkt, Exportmarkt, -absatz; **to make inroads in the** ~ **market** Eroberungen auf dem Exportmarkt machen; ~ **merchant** Exportkaufmann, -firma; ~-**minded** ausfuhr-, exportbewußt, -interessiert; ~ **model**

Exportmodell; ~ **monopoly** Export-, Außenhandels-, Ausfuhrmonopol; ~ **obligations** Ausfuhrverpflichtungen; ~ **offer** Exportangebot; ~ **order** Ausfuhr-, Exportauftrag; ~ **order form** Exportauftragsformular; ~ **packer** auf Exportversand spezialisierter Verpackungsbetrieb; ~ **packing** Exportverpackung; ~ **pattern** Exportschema; ~ **payment lag** Rückstände bei der Begleichung von Exportforderungen; ~ **performance** Exportleistung; **weakening** ~ **performance** nachlassende Exportanstrengungen; ~ **permit** Ausfuhr-, Exportgenehmigung; ~ **point** oberer Goldpunkt; ~ **policy** Ausfuhr-, Exportpolitik; ~ **possibilities** Export-, Ausfuhrmöglichkeiten; ~ **potential** Exportmöglichkeiten; ~ **premium** Ausfuhrprämie; ~ **price** Ausfuhr-, Exportpreis; ~ **pricing** Festsetzung von Exportpreisen; ~ **profit margin** Ausfuhrgewinnspanne; ~ **program(me)** Ausfuhr-, Exportprogramm; **to set back the** ~ **program(me)** Exportprogramm zurückwerfen; ~ **prohibition** Ausfuhrverbot, -sperre; ~-**promoting** exportfördernd; ~ **promotion** Ausfuhr-, Exportförderung; ~-**promotion committee** Ausfuhrförderungsausschuß; ~ **prospects** Exportaussichten; ~ **publicity** Export-, Ausfuhrwerbung; ~ **quota** Export-, Ausfuhrkontingent; **initial** ~ **quota** Exportausgangsquote; **to fix** ~ **quotas** Export (Ausfuhr) kontingentieren; ~ **rates** Exporttarife; ~ **ratio** Ausfuhr-, Exportanteil; ~ **rebate** Ausfuhrrückvergütung; ~ **receipts** Exporteinnahmen; ~ **record** Ausfuhrrekord; ~ **regulations** Ausfuhrbestimmungen; ~ **requirements** Ausfuhrbedarf; ~ **restrictions** Export-, Ausfuhrbeschränkungen; ~ **revenue** Exporteinnahmen; ~ **sales** Auslandsabsatz, -umsatz; ~ **sales executive** Exportverkaufsleiter; ~ **sales note** Ausfuhrverkaufsrechnung; ~ **sample store** Ausfuhr-, Exportmusterlager; ~ **service division** [etwa] Exportberatungsstelle; ~ **share** Exportanteil; ~ **shipments** Exportlieferungen; ~ **specie point** Goldausfuhrpunkt; ~ **specification** (Br.) Ausfuhrerklärung; ~ **statistics** Export-, Außenhandels-, Ausfuhrstatistik; ~ **subsidiary** selbständige Exportfirma; ~ **subsidy** Export-, Ausfuhrförderung; -subvention; ~ **subsidy system** Ausfuhrförderungsverfahren; ~ **surplus** Export-, Ausfuhr-, Außenhandelsüberschuß; ~ **tariff** Ausfuhrzolltarif; ~ **tax** Ausfuhr-, Exportsteuer, Exportabgabe; ~ **tender** Ausfuhr-, Exportangebot; ~ **terms** Exportbedingungen; ~ **tonnage** Ausfuhrtonnage; ~ **trade** Export-, Außen-, Aktivhandel, Auslandsgeschäft, Ausfuhrwirtschaft; ℰ **Trade Act** (US) Außenhandelsgesetz; ~ **trade surplus** Außenhandelsüberschuß; ~ **transactions** Exportgeschäft; ~ **trend** Ausfuhr-, Exportentwicklung; ~ **value** Exportwert; ~ **volume** Außenhandels-, Ausfuhrvolumen.
exportable exportierbar;
~ **manpower** im Ausland einsatzfähige Arbeitskräfte.
exportation Ausfuhr, Export;
earmarked for ~ für die Ausfuhr bestimmt.
exported | **article** Exportartikel; ~ **goods** Ausfuhrgüter.
exporter Exporteur, Exportfirma, -händler;
direct ~ Exportfabrikant; **general** ~ Exporteur für mehrere Warengattungen; **prospective** ~ exportinteressierter Unternehmer;
~ **of capital** Kapitalexporteur;
~'**s credit** Ausfuhr-, Exportkredit.
exporting | **country** Ausfuhr-, Exportland; ~ **firm** Exportfirma.
expose (v.) aussetzen, preisgeben, (exhibit) ausstellen, -legen, (lay open) aufdecken, entlarven, (photo) belichten;
~ **o. s.** sich bloßstellen; ~ **a newborn child** neugeborenes Kind aussetzen; ~ **o. s. to criticism** sich Kritik zuziehen; ~ **o. s. to danger** sich Gefahren aussetzen; ~ **goods for sale** Waren feilhalten; ~ **goods in a shopwindow** Waren im Schaufenster zeigen; ~ **one's ignorance** seine Dummheit zur Schau stellen; ~ **for inspection** zur Ansicht auslegen; ~ **one's life** sein Leben riskieren; ~ **a plot** Verschwörung enthüllen; ~ **o. s. to ridicule** sich lächerlich machen; ~ **a substantial number of persons to serious risk of disease** größere Personenzahl einem ernsthaften Krankheitsrisiko aussetzen; ~ **to unnecessary risks** unnötigem Risiko aussetzen; ~ **a thief** Dieb entlarven.
exposed ungeschützt, preisgegeben, exponiert;
~ **to weather** den Wetterbilden ausgesetzt;
to be ~ zur Besichtigung aufliegen;
~ **child** ausgesetztes Kind; ~ **people** werblich erreichbarer Personenkreis; ~ **position** exponierte Lage.
exposé Denkschrift, Exposé.
exposition Darlegung, Erklärung, (US) [Verkaufs]ausstellung, Messe, (marketing) Darbietung, (photo) Belichtung[szeit];
industrial ~ Industrieausstellung;
~ **of a child** Kindesaussetzung; ~ **of a text** Textauslegung;
~ **corporation** Ausstellungsgesellschaft; ~ **officials** Ausstellungsleitung.

expositor Kommentator.

expository statute erläuterndes Gesetz, Erläuterungsgesetz.

expostulate *(v.)* ernste Vorhaltungen machen.

exposure Ausgesetztsein, *(building)* Lage, *(fig.)* Enthüllung, Entlarvung, Bloßstellung, *(of goods)* Darbietung, Ausstellung, *(photo)* Aufnahme, Belichtung[szeit];
~s *(fire insurance)* Nachbargefahr;
indecent ~ Erzeugung öffentlichen Ärgernisses; **southern ~** *(house)* Südlage;
~ **of a child** Kindesaussetzung; ~ **to light** *(photo)* Belichtung; ~ **of a plot** Aufdeckung einer Verschwörung; ~ **of goods for sale** Freihalten von Waren; ~ **against the sun** Gegenlichtaufnahme; **to die of** ~ erfrieren; **to threaten s. o. with** ~ jem. mit Enthüllungen drohen;
~ **hazard** *(fire insurance)* Nachbarschaftsrisiko; ~ **meter** Belichtungsmesser; ~ **table** Belichtungstafel; ~ **value** *(photo)* Lichtwert.

expound *(v.)* erläutern, erklären, auslegen;
~ **a law** Gesetz auslegen.

express *(delivery)* Eilbeförderung, -bestellung, *(letter)* Eilbrief, *(Br., messenger)* Eilbote, *(train)* Schnell-, Expreßzug, *(transported goods)* Expreßgut, *(US)* private Beförderung;
by ~ durch Eilboten, als Eilgut;
limited ~ *(US)* FD- (Fernschnell-) Zug; **long-distance** ~ FD-Zug; **local** ~ Nahverkehrsschnellzug;
~ *(v.)* ausdrücken, äußern, beschreiben, *(to send by express)* per Eilboten schicken, als Eilgut senden, *(US)* mit einem Privattransportunternehmen befördern;
~ **one's appreciation** seiner Wertschätzung Ausdruck verleihen; ~ **o. s. briefly** sich kurz fassen; ~ **o. s. with ease in French** geläufig Französisch sprechen können; ~ **expenditure in constant prices** Ausgaben in konstanten Preisen darstellen; ~ **a letter** Brief als Eilbrief (per Eilboten) schicken; ~ **the author's meaning** Ansicht des Autors wiedergeben; ~ **one's opinion** seine Meinung äußern; ~ **one's regrets** sein Bedauern zum Ausdruck bringen; ~ **o. s. strongly on a subject** sich unüberhörbar zu einem Thema äußern; ~ **in guarded terms** vorsichtig ausdrücken; ~ **one's thoughts on paper** seine Ansichten schriftlich niederlegen; ~ **one's willingness** sich bereit erklären; ~ **a wish** Anliegen vorbringen;
to send a parcel ~ Paket als Eilgut befördern lassen, Eilpaket aufgeben; **to travel** ~ D-Zug benutzen;
~ *(a.)* bestimmt, deutlich, ausdrücklich, *(Br.)* durch Eilboten, per Expreß, als Eilgut, *(US)* mit einem Privattransportunternehmen befördert;
~ **abrogation** ausdrückliche Außerkraftsetzung; **railway** ~ **agency** bahnamtlicher Rollfuhrdienst; ~ **agent** *(US)* Spediteur, Transporteur; ~ **agreement** ausdrückliche Abmachung; **per** ~ **airmail** per Luftpost Eilboten; ~ **assumpsit** Schuldanerkenntnis; **by** ~ **authority** mit ausdrücklicher Genehmigung; ~ **bill of lading** *(Br.)* Eilgutladeschein; ~ **boat** Schnellboot; ~ **bullet** Sondermunition; ~ **business** *(US)* Speditionsgewerbe, -geschäft; ~ **car** *(US)* Paketwagen; ~ **carriage** Eilgutbeförderung; ~ **classes** Beförderungsarten; ~ **classification** Tarifierung; ~ **cleaners** Schnellreinigung; ~ **colo(u)r** Bestreiten der Aktivlegitimation; ~ **company** *(US)* Eilgut-, Expreßgut-, Paketzustellungs-, Paketbeförderungsgesellschaft; ~ **condition** ausdrückliche Bedingung; ~ **consent** ausdrückliche Zustimmung; ~ **consideration** vertraglich erwähnte Gegenleistung; ~ **delivery** *(Br.)* Eil-, Expreßzustellung, -beförderung, *(US)* Beförderung durch ein privates Transportunternehmen; **to send by** ~ **delivery** *(Br.)* per Expreß zustellen; ~-**delivery fee** *(Br.)* Eilzustellgebühr; ~ **delivery limits** *(Br.)* Expresszustellungsbezirk; ~-**delivery service** *(Br.)* Eilzustelldienst; ~ **election** ausdrückliche Entscheidung für eine freiwillige Zuwendung; ~ **elevator** *(Br.)* Schnellaufzug; ~ **emancipation** Volljährigkeitserklärung; ~ **engine** Schnellzuglokomotive; ~ **forwarding** Eilbeförderung; ~ **freight** *(US)* Eilfracht, Eilgut; ~ **freight train** *(US)* Eilgüterzug; ~ **goods** *(Br.)* Eilfracht, Eilgut, *(US)* durch Paketpostgesellschaft beförderte Fracht; ~-**goods tariff** *(Br.)* Eilguttarif; **by** ~ **goods train** *(Br.)* als Eilgut; ~ **grant** ausdrückliche Gestattung; ~ **highway** *(US)* Schnellverkehrsstraße, Autobahn; ~ **image** absolutes Ebenbild; ~ **items** *(Br.)* Eilgutsendungen; ~ **journey** Blitzreise; ~ **lane** schneller Verkehrsweg; **reversible** ~ **lane** Einbahnschnellweg mit wechselnder Verkehrsrichtung; ~ **letter** *(Br.)* Eilbrief; ~ **line** Schnellverkehrslinie; ~ **liner** *(US)* Schnelldampfer; ~ **malice** Schädigungsabsicht; ~ **messenger** *(Br.)* Eilkurier, Eilbote; **by** ~ **messenger** *(Br.)* durch Eilboten, expreß; ~ **money order** *(US)* telegrafische Geldüberweisung; ~ **office** *(US)* Paketannahmestelle; ~ **package** *(US)* Eil-, Expreßpaket; ~ **paid** Eilgebühr (Eilbote)

bezahlt; ~ **parcel** *(Br.)* Schnell-, Eilpaket; **by** ~ **parcel post** *(Br.)* mit Eilpaket; ~ **permission** ausdrückliche Genehmigung, *(motorcar owner)* ausdrückliche Benutzungserlaubnis; ~ **postal delivery** *(Br.)* Schnellpostgut; **to come for this** ~ **purpose** eigens zu diesem Zweck kommen; ~ **request** ausdrückliche Aufforderung, ausdrückliches Verlangen; ~ **reservation** ausdrückliche Einschränkung; ~ **road (route)** *(US)* Schnellverkehrsstraße; ~ **service** Eilzustellungsdienst, Expreßgutverkehr; **same-day** ~ **post door-to-door service** Zustellungsdienst von Eilsendungen am gleichen Tag; ~ **speed** hohe Geschwindigkeit; **at** ~ **speed** im Eilzugtempo; ~ **statement** *(contract of employment)* ausdrückliche arbeitsvertragliche Bestimmung; ~ **term** *(law of contract)* ausdrückliche Vertragsvereinbarung; ~ **train** D- (Expreß-) Zug; **by** ~ **train** per Eilgut (Expreß); ~ **trust** gewillkürtes Treuhandverhältnis; ~ **van** Eilgutwagen; ~ **wagon** *(US)* Eilgutwagen; ~ **warranty** vertragliche Gewährleistung.

expressage *(US)* Sendung durch Paketbeförderungsgesellschaft, Eilgutfracht, *(charge, Br.)* Eilgutzustellungsgebühr.

expressed | in dollars auf Dollar lautend; ~ **in clear terms** klar ausgedrückt.

expressible ausdrückbar.

expression Äußerung, Ausdruck, *(mode of symbolism)* Ausdrucksweise, Diktion, *(phase of mood)* Tonfall, Betonung, Gefühl, *(phase)* Redensart;
beyond all ~ unaussprechlich;
colloquial ~ Ausdruck der Umgangssprache; **common** ~ allgemein üblicher Ausdruck; **faulty** ~ fehlerhafter Ausdruck; **literary** ~ gewählter Ausdruck; **local** ~ ortsgebundener Ausdruck; **low** ~ ordinärer Ausdruck; **obsolete** ~ veralteter Ausdruck; **slang** ~s Slangausdrücke; **technical** ~ Fachausdruck; **unguarded** ~ unglücklich gewählter Ausdruck; **wrong** ~ falsche Bezeichnung;
~ **of confidence** Vertrauensbeweis; ~ **of opinion** Meinungsäußerung; ~ **of sympathy** Beileids-, Sympathiebezeugung; ~ **of par values** Paritätenfestsetzung; ~ **of one's will** Willensäußerung;
to give eloquent ~ **to one's feelings** seinen Gefühlen beredten Ausdruck verleihen; **to give** ~ **to one's gratitude** seiner Dankbarkeit Ausdruck verleihen; **to give** ~ **to one's will** seinen Willen dokumentieren; **to withdraw an offending** ~ beleidigende Äußerungen zurücknehmen.

expressive force Ausdruckskraft.

expressly or impliedly ausdrücklich oder stillschweigend.

expressman *(US)* Angestellter einer Paketpostgesellschaft, Dienstmann.

expressway *(US)* Schnell[verkehrs]straße, Autobahn, *(urban motorway)* Stadtautobahn;
~ **building** *(US)* Autobahngebäude.

expromission Schuldübernahme.

expromissor Schuldübernehmer.

expropriate *(v.)* enteignen;
~ **privileges** Vorrechte beseitigen.

expropriated mine enteigneter Bergbaubetrieb.

expropriation Enteignung, Expropriierung;
~ **of alien property** Enteignung ausländischen Vermögens; ~ **for public purpose** Enteignung für öffentliche Zwecke;
~ **act** Enteignungsgesetz.

expulsion Verbannung, Vertreibung, Ausschluß, Ausweisung;
~ **of enemy nationals** Abschiebung feindlicher Ausländer; ~ **of a member of a club** Ausschluß eines Vereinsmitglieds; ~ **of a student** Relegation eines Studenten;
~ **order** Ausweisungsbefehl.

expunction Ausstreichung.

expunge *(v.)* löschen, streichen;
~ **a name from a list** Namen auf (von) einer Liste streichen.

expurgate *(v.) (pol.)* reinigen, säubern;
~ **a book** anstößige Stellen in einem Buch streichen.

expurgated edition of a book von anstößigen Stellen gereinigte Buchausgabe.

expurgator Zensor.

extemporaneous unvorbereitet, improvisiert, aus dem Stegreif.

extemporare, to speak aus dem Stegreif sprechen;
~ **address** Stegreifansprache.

extemporary unvorbereitet, improvisiert, aus dem Stegreif;
~ **speaker** Improvisator, Stegreifredner.

extemporize *(v.)* unvorbereitet sprechen.

extend *(v.)* ausdehnen, *(airplane)* Fahrgestell ausfahren, *(enlarge)* [Geschäft] ausbauen, erweitern, *(prolong)* prolongieren, verlängern, *(seize)* pfänden, *(shorthand)* [Kurzschrift] in Kurrentschrift übertragen, *(value)* [Land] bewerten, verschuldeten Besitz gerichtlich abschätzen;

~ o. s. sich ins Zeug legen;
~ **a balance** Saldo vortragen (übertragen); ~ **a bill of exchange** Wechsel prolongieren; ~ **one's business** sein Geschäft ausdehnen; ~ **carrier's lines** Ausweitung der Streckensätze genehmigen; ~ **a charter** Satzungsbefugnisse erweitern; ~ **the city boundaries** Stadtgrenzen erweitern; ~ **into another column** in eine andere Buchhaltungskolonne übertragen; ~ **a contract** Vertrag verlängern; ~ **a credit** Kreditverlängerung gewähren; ~ **a deed** Urkunde ausfertigen; ~ **a holiday** Urlaub verlängern; ~ **hospitality** Gastfreundschaft gewähren; ~ **an invoice** Rechnung spezifizieren; ~ **an invitation** Einladung aussprechen; ~ **one's jurisdiction** seinen Zuständigkeitsbereich erweitern; ~ **a lease** Pachtvertrag verlängern; ~ **s. one's leave** jds. Urlaub verlängern; ~ **the limits** Limit erhöhen; ~ **a passport** Paß verlängern; ~ **a patent** Patent verlängern; ~ **a period** Frist verlängern; ~ **help to the poor** Armen Hilfe anbieten; ~ **one's power** Machtbereich ausdehnen; ~ **one's premises** anbauen, ausbauen; ~ **protest** Protest erheben, (ship) Verklarung ablegen; ~ **a railway** Eisenbahnlinie ausbauen; ~ **as far as the river** sich bis zum Fluß hinziehen; ~ **the statute of limitations** Verjährungsfrist verlängern; ~ **a tax** jeden Steuerpflichtigen veranlagen; ~ **the term (time) of payment** Zahlungsaufschub gewähren; ~ **one's territory** sein Gebiet vergrößern; ~ **a ticket** Gültigkeitsdauer einer Fahrkarte verlängern; ~ **the time for filing an answer** Frist zur Abgabe einer Erklärung verlängern; ~ **the validity** Gültigkeit verlängern; ~ **a visit for a few days** Besuch um einige Tage verlängern; ~ **a welcome to s. o.** j. willkommen heißen; ~ **the works** Fabrikgelände erweitern.

extended prolongiert, verlängert, (print.) breit, (valued) bewertet, abgeschätzt, veranlagt;
to be ~ verlängert werden;
~ **benefit** (Br.) ins Ermessen gestellte Arbeitslosenunterstützung; ~ **bonds** (US) prolongierte Obligationen; ~ **cover** überstehender Buchdeckel; ~ **coverage** (fire insurance) zusätzlicher Versicherungsschutz, höhere Deckung; ~ **credit** (Br.) über ein halbes Jahr hinaus gewährter Exportkredit; ~ **family** Großfamilie; ~ **insurance** prämienfreie Versicherung; ~ **land** Grundstück, in das Zwangsvollstreckung betrieben wird; ~ **lease** zu gleichen Bedingungen verlängerter Pachtvertrag; ~ **leave** (mil.) Urlaubsverlängerung; ~ **letter** breite Schrift; ~ **list of repairs** umfangreiche Reparaturliste; ~**-play record** Langspielplatte; ~ **protest** (ship) Verklarung; ~**-term policy** prolongierte Kurzversicherungspolice; ~ **trip to Europe** längere Europareise; ~ **troops** (mil.) entfaltete Truppen; ~ **type** breite Drucktype; ~ **unemployment benefit** (Br.) Arbeitslosenhilfe für ausgesteuerte Arbeitslose, ins Ermessen gestellte Arbeitslosenunterstützung; **full** ~ **value** voller Schätzwert.

extending | a tax Steuerveranlagung verschiedener Steuerpflichtiger;
~ **table** (Br.) Ausziehtisch.

extensible ausbaufähig.

extension Erweiterung, Vergrößerung, Ausdehnung, (bankruptcy) Fristverlängerung, (to building) An-, Erweiterungsbau, (enlargement) Ausweitung, (interpretation) extensive Auslegung, (patent) Patentverlängerung, (photo) Kameraauszug, (prolongation) Verlängerung, Prolongation, (station) Nebenanschluß, -stelle, (tel.) Nebenanschluß, -stelle;
factory ~ Betriebserweiterung; **filing** ~ Verlängerung der Abgabefrist; **telephone** ~ Telefon-, Fernsprechanschluß; **university** ~ Erwachsenenbildung, Volksbildungswerk, Volkshochschule, Einrichtung von Abendkursen;
~ **of an accord** Verlängerung eines Abkommens; ~ **of a boundary** Grenzverlängerung; ~ **of business** Geschäftsausweitung; ~ **of capacity** Kapazitätsausweitung; ~ **of carrier's lines** Anhebung der Streckensätze; ~ **of a conflict** Ausweitung eines Konflikts; ~ **of credit** Kreditverlängerung; ~ **in demand** Nachfrageausweitung; ~ **of one's holiday** Urlaubsverlängerung; ~ **to a house** Vergrößerung eines Hauses, Hausanbau; ~ **of judgment** (Br.) Vollstreckbarkeitsanordnung für Urteile anderer Staaten; ~ **of jurisdiction** Zuständigkeitsausweitung; ~ **of leasehold** Pachtverlängerung; ~ **of leave** Urlaubsverlängerung; ~ **of the life of a patent** Patentverlängerung [um sieben Jahre]; ~ **of liquidity** Liquiditätsausweitung; ~ **of loan** Darlehns-, Kreditverlängerung; ~ **of note** Wechselprolongation; ~ **of operation** Ausweitung des Dienstleistungsfächers; ~ **of an order** Auftragserweiterung; ~ **of passport** Paßverlängerung; ~ **of the patent monopoly** Patentausdehnung; ~ **of payment** Zahlungsaufschub, Verlängerung der Zahlungsfrist; ~ **of the statutory period of limitation** Verlängerung der gesetzlichen Verjährungsfrist; ~ **of a railway** Ausbau einer Eisenbahnlinie; ~ **of Soviet influence** Ausdehnung des sowjetischen Einflußbe-

reiches; ~ **of time** Fristverlängerung, Nachfrist, zusätzliche Frist, Aufschub der Zahlungsfrist; ~ **of title** Landeinweisung; ~ **of validity** Verlängerung der Gültigkeitsdauer, Gültigkeitsverlängerung; ~ **of visa** Visaverlängerung; ~ **of war** Kriegsausweitung; ~ **of working hours** Verlängerung der Arbeitszeit;
to arrange with one's creditors sich mit seinen Gläubigern wegen eines Zahlungsaufschubs verständigen; **to build** ~**s** Ausbauten vornehmen; **to build an** ~ **to a hospital** Krankenhaus ausbauen, Erweiterungsbau zu einem Krankenhaus errichten; **to get an** ~ **for payment** Zahlungsaufschub erlangen; **to get an** ~ **of time** Fristverlängerung erreichen; **to request an** ~ um Zahlungsaufschub nachsuchen;
~ **agreement** Prolongationsabkommen, Stundungsvereinbarung; ~ **board** (tel.) Hauszentrale; ~ **cord** Verlängerungsschnur; ~ **course** Fortbildungs-, Volkshochschulkursus; ~ **key** Verlängerungsschlüssel; ~ **ladder** Auszieh-, Teleskopleiter; ~ **line** (tel.) Nebenanschluß; ~ **night** verlängerte Polizeistunde; ~ **piece** Verlängerungsstück; ~ **plan** Ausbauvorhaben; ~ **room** angebautes Zimmer; ~ **speaker** zusätzlicher Lautsprecher; ~ **student** [etwa] Volkshochschüler; ~ **table** (US) ausziehbarer Tisch, Ausziehtisch; ~ **work** [berufliches] Fortbildungswesen.

extensive ausgedehnt, umfassend;
to be ~ **in one's charity** äußerst freigebig sein;
~ **activities** intensive Tätigkeit; ~ **agriculture** extensive Wirtschaft; ~ **cultivation** extensive Wirtschaft; ~ **inquiries** ausgedehnte Untersuchungen; ~ **interpretation** extensive Auslegung; ~ **knowledge** umfassende Kenntnisse; ~ **margin** Wendepunkt der Gesamtertragskurve; ~ **rainfall** ergiebige Niederschlagsmenge; ~ **repairs** umfangreiche Reparaturen; ~ **researches** ausgedehnte Untersuchungen; ~ **trade** ausgedehnter Handel.

extent Umfang, Maß, Größe, Ausdehnung, (of a loan) Höhe, (seizure) Pfändung, (valuation, Br.) Abschätzung [von Land], Bewertung, (writ of execution) Beschlagnahme, Verfügung, Vollstreckungsbefehl;
to any ~ in beliebiger Höhe; **to the** ~ **of ...** bis zum Betrage von ...; **to the full** ~ in vollem Umfang; **to a large** ~ weitgehend; **to the** ~ **of such payment** bis zur Höhe der geleisteten Anzahlung; **immediate** ~ sofortige Beschlagnahme;
~ **in aid** Forderungspfändung; ~ **of a charge** Belastungshöhe; ~ **in chief** Pfändung eines Staatsschuldners; ~ **of credit** Kredithöhe; ~ **of damage** Schadenshöhe, -umfang, -ausmaß; ~ **of duty** Pflichtenumfang; **vast** ~ **of ground** riesiges Gelände; ~ **of liability** Umfang der Haftung, Haftungsumfang; ~ **.of loss** Schadenshöhe; ~ **of power of attorney** Vollmachtsumfang; ~ **of taxation relief** Umfang der Steuervergünstigung; ~ **of warranty** Garantieumfang;
to be liable to the ~ **of one's property** mit seinem ganzen Vermögen haften; **to work to the full** ~ **of one's powers** seine volle Arbeitskraft einsetzen.

extenuate (v.) mildern, verringern;
~ **s. one's guilt** jds. Schuld beschönigen.

extenuating circumstances mildernde Umstände.

extenuation Abschwächung, Beschönigung, (crime) Strafmilderung;
to plead poverty in ~ **of a theft** Armut als Strafmilderung für einen Diebstahl vorbringen.

exterior Außenansicht, (film) Außenaufnahme;
smooth ~ (person) verbindliches Wesen;
~ **(a.)** außen, äußerlich;
~ **advertising** Außenwerbung an Verkehrsmitteln; ~ **features of a building** Außenlinien eines Gebäudes; **to manufacture articles without** ~ **help** Waren ohne fremde Kräfte herstellen; ~ **possessions** auswärtige Besitzungen; ~ **shot** Außen-, Freilichtaufnahme; ~ **view** Außenansicht.

exterminate (v.) vernichten, ausrotten.

extermination Vernichtung, Ausrottung;
~ **camp** Vernichtungslager; ~ **campaign** Vernichtungsfeldzug.

exterminator Kammerjäger.

exterminatory war Vernichtungskrieg.

extern auswärtiger Schüler, Fahrschüler, Externer.

external | s Äußerlichkeiten, Nebensächlichkeiten;
to judge by ~**s** nach Äußerlichkeiten urteilen;
~ **(a.)** äußerlich, (foreign) auswärtig, ausländisch, außenwirtschaftlich, (perceptible) wahrnehmbar, sichtbar;
~ **account** Ausländerguthaben, (Br.) Devisen-, Auslandskonto; ~ **account area** Auslandskontenbereich; ~ **affairs** (Australia) Außenbeziehungen; ~ **affairs department** (Canada, Ireland) Außenministerium; ~ **aid** Auslandshilfe; ~ **assets** Auslandsvermögen, -anlagen, -werte; ~ **association** ausländische Vereinigung; ~ **audit** außerbetriebliche Revision; ~ **benefits**

volkswirtschaftliche Ersparnisse; ~ **bonds** Auslandsschuldverschreibungen; ~ **call** *(tel.)* Auslandsgespräch; ~ **combustion engine** Verbrennungsmotor; ~ **commerce** Außenhandel; ~ **commercial relations** Außenhandelsbeziehungen; ~ **communications** Auslandsmitteilungen; ~ **conditions** äußere Umstände; ~ **convertibility** freie Konvertierbarkeit; ~ **costs** volkswirtschaftliche Kosten; ~ **credit** Auslandskredit; ~ **credit transactions** Kreditverkehr mit dem Ausland; ~ **data** außerbetriebliche Unterlagen; ~ **debts** Auslandsschulden, äußere Staatsschuld; ~ **deficit** Zahlungsbilanzdefizit, Passivsaldo der Zahlungsbilanz; ~ **demand** Auslandsnachfrage; ~ **duties** Außenzölle; ~ **economic situation** außenwirtschaftliche Lage; ~ **economies** platzbedingte Kostenersparnisse eines gesamten Industriezweiges; ~ **economy** Außenwirtschaft; ~ **equilibrium** außenwirtschaftliches Gleichgewicht; ~ **evidence** äußerer Beweis, Beweis des äußeren Anscheins; ~ **examination** Abschlußprüfung außerhalb der Schule; ~ **examiner** auswärtiger Prüfer; ~ **force** Druck von außen; ~ **house organ** Kunden-, Aktionärszeitschrift; ~ **group** Auslandsgruppe; ~ **liabilities** Auslandsverbindlichkeiten; ~ **loan** Fremdwährungsanleihe, Auslandsanleihe, äußere Anleihe; ~ **mail service** *(US)* Auslandspostverkehr; ~ **make-up** Aufmachung eines Produkts; ~ **memory** *(data processing)* Externspeicher; ~ **national debt** Staatsverschuldung im Ausland; ~ **payments transactions** Zahlungsverkehr mit dem Ausland; ~ **position** außenwirtschaftliche Position; ~ **property** Auslandsvermögen; ~ **relationship** *(US)* Außenverhältnis; ~ **research** außerbetriebliche Forschung; ~ **sales** *(balance sheet)* Umsatz an die Kundschaft, Fremdumsatz; ~ **surplus** Zahlungsbilanzüberschuß, Aktivsaldo der Zahlungsbilanz; ~ **tariff** Außentarif; ~ **tax** Einfuhrzoll; ~ **trade** Außenhandel; ~ **traffic** Auslandsverkehr; ~ **turnover** Fremd-, Außenumsatz, Umsatz an die Kundschaft; ~ **value of money** Außenwert des Geldes; **increased** ~ **value of sterling** Außenwerterhöhung des Pfunds.

exterritorial exterritorial;
~ **privileges and rights** exterritoriale Vorrechte (Immunität), Exterritorialitätsrechte;
to possess ~ **status** Exterritorialitätsrechte genießen.

exterritoriality Exterritorialität.

extinct abgeschafft, aufgehoben, *(lapsed)* erloschen;
to become ~ *(firm)* erlöschen, eingehen;
~ **firm** im Handelsregister gelöschte Firma; ~ **law** aufgehobenes Gesetz; ~ **nation** ausgestorbenes Volk; ~ **title** erloschener Titel; ~ **volcano** erloschener Vulkan.

extinction *(of debt)* Tilgung, Löschen, *(destroying)* Vernichtung, Ausrottung, *(making extinct)* Löschung, *(right)* Untergang, Erlöschen;
close to ~ kurz vor dem Aussterben;
legal ~ Ungültigkeitserklärung; **partial** ~ teilweise Tilgung;
~ **of an action** Klageverjährung; ~ **of a claim** Erlöschen eines Anspruchs, Anspruchsverjährung; ~ **of debts** Schuldentilgung; ~ **of a firm** Erlöschen einer Firma, Löschung einer Firma im Handelsregister.

extinctive prescription Verjährung.

extinguish *(v.)* löschen, *(debt)* tilgen, *(fig.)* kaltstellen;
~ **s. o.** j. kaltstellen; ~ **an adversary** Gegner erledigen; ~ **an easement** Grunddienstbarkeit löschen; ~ **a fire** Feuer löschen (ersticken); ~ **a law** Gesetz abschaffen; ~ **a life** Leben auslöschen; ~ **a mortgage** Hypothek tilgen (amortisieren); ~ **opposition** Opposition zum Schweigen bringen.

extinguished *(easement)* erloschen.

extinguisher Zigarettentöter;
fire ~ Feuerlöscher.

extinguishment Löschung, Aufhebung, Tilgung, *(abolition)* Abschaffung;
~ **of a book account** Löschung einer Buchschuld; ~ **of common** Verlust des Allmenderechts; ~ **of a copyright** Erlöschen eines Urheberrechtes; ~ **of debts** Schuldentilgung; ~ **of an easement** Erlöschen einer Grunddienstbarkeit; ~ **of legacy** Vermächtnisfortfall; ~ **of lien** Pfanduntergang; ~ **of a mortgage** Hypothekentilgung, Hypothekenlöschung; ~ **of rent** Pachtfortfall durch Grundstückserwerb; ~ **of a right** Erlöschen eines Rechtes; ~ **of ways** Fortfall von Wegerechten.

extirpate *(v.)* vernichten, ausrotten.

extirpation Vernichtung, Ausrottung, *(waste)* Raubbau.

extol *(v.)* **s. o. to the skies** j. in den Himmel heben.

extorsive erpresserisch.

extort *(v.)* erpressen;
~ **a confession** Geständnis erpressen; ~ **contributions** Beiträge erzwingen; ~ **fees** unstatthafte Gebühren erheben; ~ **money from s. o.** Geld von jem. erpressen.

extortion Erpressung, *(extortionate charge)* Geldschneiderei, Wucher, *(by public officer)* passive Bestechung;
attempted ~ Erpressungsversuch;
~ **of fees** unstatthafte (überhöhte) Gebührenforderung; ~ **in office** Amtsunterschlagung.

extortionate|charge Geldschneiderei, Wucher; ~ **price** Wucherpreis.

extortioner Erpresser.

extra *(s. th. in addition)* Zugabe, Sonderleistung, *(charge added)* Zuschlag, *(film)* Komparse, *(labo(u)rer)* fallweise eingestellte Arbeitskraft, Aushilfe, *(newspaper, Br.)* Sonderausgabe, -nummer, Extrablatt, -ausgabe, *(special permit)* Sonderberechtigung, *(school)* Sonderfach, freiwilliges Nebenfach;
for a little ~ gegen geringen Aufpreis;
~**s** Nebengebühren, Neben-, Sonderausgaben, außerordentliche Ausgaben, Nebenkosten, *(US, extra equipment)* Sonderausrüstung, -ausstattung;
to absorb the ~**s** Sonderausgaben anderweitig ausgleichen; **to be charged for** ~ gesondert berechnet werden;
~ *(a.)* extra, besonders, *(extraordinary)* ungewöhnlich, außergewöhnlich, -ordentlich;
~ **allowance** Sonderentschädigung, -vergütung, *(technical)* Toleranz; ~**-big** übergroß; ~ **binding** Luxusausgabe; ~**-budgetary** außeretatmäßig; ~ **bus** Sonderomnibus; ~ **charge** [Sonder]zuschlag, [Preis]aufschlag; ~ **charges** Neben-, Extrakosten, Nebenspesen, außerordentliche Unkosten, Nebengebühren, Nachforderung, [Preis]aufschlag, Mehrpreis; **to make an** ~ **charge** Zuschlag berechnen; **to put on an** ~ **coach** Sonderwagen anhängen; ~ **colo(u)r** Spezialfarbe; ~**-continental** *(US)* außerhalb der westlichen Hemisphäre; ~ **costs** Extrakosten, *(law court)* Sonderaufwendungen, *(marginal cost)* Grenzkosten; ~ **discount** Sonder-, Extrarabatt; **dividend** Zusatzdividende, Bonus; ~ **draft** Extragewicht; ~ **duty** Nachsteuer, *(customs)* Zollaufschlag; ~ **edition** Sonderausgabe; ~ **engine** zusätzliche Lokomotive; ~ **equipment** *(US)* Sonderausrüstung; ~**-European** außereuropäisch; ~ **expenditure** Sonderausgaben; ~ **expenses** Sonderaufwendungen; ~ **expense insurance** Betriebsstillstandsversicherung; ~ **fare** Zuschlag[skarte]; ~**-fare train** Fernzug, D-Zug; ~ **fee** Extra-, Zusatzgebühr, Sonderhonorar; ~ **fine quality** allererste Qualität; ~ **flight** Sonderflug; ~ **freight** Mehrfracht, Frachtzuschlag; ~ **funds** Sondermittel; **to work an** ~ **half day** halben Tag zusätzlich arbeiten; ~**-hazardous employment** *(insurance)* besonders gefährliche Beschäftigung; ~ **high price** besonders hoher Preis; ~ **hour** Überstunde; ~ **income** Nebeneinkommen; ~ **interest** Zusatzzinsen; ~ **laydays** [Über]liegetage; ~ **luggage** *(Br.)* zuschlagspflichtiges Gepäck; ~**-marital relations** außereheliche Beziehungen; ~**-parliamentary opposition** außerparlamentarische Opposition; ~ **pay** Gehaltszulage; ~ **pay for entertainment** Repräsentationszulage; ~ **payment** außerordentliche Zahlung, Nachzahlung; ~ **performance** Sonderleistung; ~ **postage** Nachporto, Portozuschlag; ~ **premium** Zusatzprämie, Prämienzuschlag; ~ **profit** Nebenverdienst, außerordentliche Erträge, zusätzlicher Gewinn; ~ **profits** außerordentliche Erträge, zusätzlicher Gewinn; ~ **reprint** Sonderabdruck; ~ **services** *(official)* nicht vergütete Tätigkeit; ~ **sheet** *(print.)* Zuschußbogen; ~ **shift** *(mining)* Freischicht; ~ **special** *(Br.)* Sonderausgabe, Extrablatt, Nachtausgabe; ~ **strong binding** verstärkter Bucheinband; ~**-strong box** verstärkte Kiste; ~ **subject** Fakultativfach; ~ **sum for entertainment** Repräsentationszulage; ~ **task** *(school)* Strafarbeit; ~**-terrestrial** außerirdisch; ~ **ticket** Zuschlagskarte; ~ **time** Verlängerung[szeit]; ~ **towing charges** Schleppgebührzuschlag; ~ **train** Sonderzug; **to run** ~ **trains** Sonderzüge einsetzen; ~ **vires** *(lat.)* außerhalb der Zuständigkeit; ~ **weight** Übergewicht; ~ **work** Überstunden-, Mehrarbeit, *(school)* Strafarbeit.

extrabold *(print.)* fette Schrift, Fettdruck.

extract Auszug, Ausschnitt, Extrakt, Exzerpt, Abriß;
~ **of account** Konto-, Rechnungsauszug; ~ **from a book** Buchauszug; ~ **of the minutes** Auszug aus der Sitzungsniederschrift, Protokollauszug; ~ **of foreign newspapers** ausländische Pressestimmen; ~ **from records** Aktenauszug; ~ **from a registered statement** Handelsregisterauszug;
~ *(v.)* *(from book)* Auszüge machen, [aus einem Buch] ausziehen, exzerpieren, *(fig.)* herausholen, entlocken, *(mining)* zutage fördern;
~ **information from s. o.** Informationen aus jem. herausholen; ~ **money from s. o.** Geld bei jem. herausschinden;
to make (take) an ~ Auszug anfertigen, Auszüge machen; **to make** ~**s from a book** Buchauszüge anfertigen.

extracting plant Gewinnungsanlage.
extraction Abstammung, Abkunft, *(book)* Auszug, *(mining)* Gewinnung;
  to be of English ~ englischer Abstammung sein.
extractive industry Industrie der Bau, Steine und Erden.
extractor Trockenschleuder;
  ~ **fan** Fensterventilator.
extracurricular außerberuflich, *(subject)* außerplanmäßig.
extraditable auslieferbar;
  ~ **offence** auslieferungspflichtiges Verbrechen.
extradite *(v.)* *(law of nations)* ausliefern.
extradition Auslieferung;
  to refuse ~ Auslieferung ablehnen;
  ~ **law** Auslieferungsrecht; ~ **order** Auslieferungsersuchen; ~ **proceedings** Auslieferungsverfahren; ~ **rules** Auslieferungsbestimmungen; ~ **treaty** Auslieferungsvertrag; ~ **warrant** jederzeit widerrufliche Asylgewährung.
extradotal nicht zur Mitgift gehörig;
  ~ **property** *(US)* Vorbehaltsgut.
extrajudicial außerhalb der gerichtlichen Zuständigkeit, außergerichtlich;
  ~ **confession** außergerichtliches Geständnis.
extralegal außergesetzlich.
extramarital relations ehewidrige Beziehungen; ~ **relationship** ehewidriges Verhältnis.
extramatrimonial außerehelich.
extrametropolitan außerhalb der Großstadt.
extramural │ course *(Br.)* Hochschulkursus für Gasthörer; ~ **department** *(Br.)* für Gasthörer eingerichtetes Fachgebiet, Volkshochschulzweig; ~ **student** *(Br.)* Gasthörer, [etwa] Volkshochschüler; ~ **teaching** *(Br.)* Gastvorlesung; ~ **work** *(Br.)* Volkshochschulkursus.
extraneous fremd[artig], auswärtig, ausländisch;
  to be ~ **to s. th.** nicht zu etw. gehören;
  ~ **dividends** Substanz gefährdende Dividenden; ~ **evidence** außerhalb einer Urkunde liegende Beweismittel; ~ **expenses** Fremdaufwendungen; ~ **income** Sondereinnahmen, Fremderträge; ~ **influence** exogene Einflüsse; ~ **offense** nicht im vorliegenden Verfahren angeklagte Straftat; ~ **perils** *(insurance)* Sondergefahren.
extraofficial außeramtlich, nebenamtlich.
extraordinarily cheap außergewöhnlich billig.
extraordinary außerordentlich, besonders, außer-, ungewöhnlich;
  ~ **ambassador** Sonderbotschafter; ~ **average** Schadensausgleich; ~ **care** höchste Sorgfaltspflicht; ~ **case** *(criminal law)* außergewöhnlicher Fall; ~ **danger** *(master and servant)* ungewöhnliche Gefahr; ~ **depreciation** Sonderabschreibung; ~ **dividend** Superdividende; ~ **expenses** außerordentliche (außergewöhnliche) Aufwendungen, Fremdaufwendungen; ~ **flood** nicht vorhersehbare Überschwemmung; ~ **general meeting** *(Br.)* außerordentliche Hauptversammlung; ~ **hazard** durch andere Arbeitnehmer erhöhtes Risiko; ~ **help** fremde Hilfe; ~ **income** außerordentliche Erträge, Fremderträge; ~ **items** Fremd-, Sonderposten, Rechnungsabgrenzungsposten; ~ **meeting of shareholders** *(Br.)* außerordentliche Generalversammlung; ~ **motion of new trial** durch außergewöhnliche Umstände bedingter Wiederaufnahmeantrag; ~ **rainfall** ungewöhnliche Niederschlagsmenge; ~ **remedies** außerordentliche Rechtsbehelfe; ~ **repairs** außergewöhnliche Instandsetzungen; ~ **reserve** Sonderrückstellung; ~ **resolution** *(Company Act, Br.)* qualifizierter Mehrheitsbeschluß; ~ **risk** außergewöhnliche [durch den Arbeitgeber verursachte] Gefahr; ~ **services** außergewöhnliche Betreuung eines Invaliden; ~ **session of the court** Sondersitzung des Gerichts; ~ **value** *(freight)* ungewöhnlich hoher Frachtwert.
extraparliamentary außerparlamentarisch.
extrapolate *(v.)* *(statistics)* fortschreiben.
extrapolation *(statistics)* Fortschreibung.
extraprofessional außerberuflich.
extrasensory perception übersinnliche Wahrnehmung.
extraterrestrial außerirdisch.
extraterritorial nicht den Gesetzen des Gastlandes unterworfen, extraterritorial;
  ~ **air traffic** Auslandsluftverkehr; ~ **rights** Exterritorialrechte; ~ **risk** *(employee)* berufsfremdes Risiko; ~ **waters** Außengewässer.
extraterritoriality Extraterritorialität.
extravagance Übertriebenheit, Aufwand, Luxus, Verschwendung[ssucht];
  ~s törichte Streiche.

extravagant übertrieben, extravagant, verschwenderisch;
  ~ **expenses** übermäßiger Aufwand; ~ **taste** ausgefallener Geschmack.
extravaganza *(film, theater)* Ausstattungsstück.
extreme äußerste Maßnahme, höchster Grad, Extrem;
  to carry s. th. to ~s etw. zu weit treiben; **to fly to the opposite** ~ in das entgegengesetzte Extrem verfallen; **to go to** ~s vor nichts zurückschrecken; **to go from one** ~ **to the other** von einem Extrem ins andere verfallen; **to run to the** ~ bis zum Äußersten gehen;
  ~ **case** äußerster Notfall; ~ **cruelty** *(divorce case)* schwere Mißhandlung; ~ **danger** Gefahr für Leib und Leben; ~ **hazard** *(ship)* größte Seenot; ~ **left** äußerste Linke; ~ **mean** größter (kleinster) Mittelwert; ~ **necessity** dringende Notwendigkeit; ~ **old age** hohes Greisenalter; **to hold** ~ **opinions** extreme Ansichten vertreten; ~ **party** radikale Partei; ~ **patience** außergewöhnliche Geduld; ~ **penalty of the law** Todesstrafe; ~ **right** extreme Rechte; ~ **right-winger** Rechtsradikaler; ~ **value** Extremwert.
extremism, left-wing Linksextremismus.
extremist Fanatiker, *(pol.)* Radikaler, Ultra.
extremities, to be driven to zum Äußersten getrieben werden; **to be reduced to** ~ in größter Not sein; **to proceed to** ~ äußerste Maßnahmen ergreifen.
extremity äußerste Grenze, Spitze;
  ~ **of joy** Übermaß an Freude.
extricate │ *(v.)* **a carriage from the mud** Auto aus dem Schlamm herausholen; ~ **o. s. from danger** sich aus einer Gefahr befreien; ~ **o. s. from a difficulty** sich aus einer schwierigen Lage herausmanövrieren.
extrinsic nicht dazugehörend, unwesentlich, irrelevant;
  to be ~ **to s. th.** außerhalb einer Sache liegen;
  ~ **evidence** anderweitiger Beweis; ~ **value** äußerster Wert.
exuberance Überfluß, Fülle, üppiger Reichtum;
  ~ **of feeling** Gefühlsüberschwang.
exuberant üppig, überreichlich, *(fig.)* überschwenglich;
  ~ **spirits** sprudelnde Laune.
exalt *(v.)* **over s. o.** über j. triumphieren.
exurban shopping center *(US)* **(centre,** *Br.***)** außerhalb der Stadt gelegenes Einkaufszentrum.
exurbia Fabrikerrichtung auf der grünen Wiese.
eye *(fig.)* Gesichtskreis, Blickfeld;
  before (under) one's very ~ direkt vor jds. Nase; **in my** ~ nach meiner Meinung; **in the** ~s **of the law** vom Standpunkt des Gesetzes aus; **in the** ~s **of the world** nach dem allgemeinen Urteil; **up to the** ~s stark engagiert; **with an expert's** ~ mit den Augen eines Fachmanns; **with a fresh** ~ mit anderen Augen; **with other** ~s von einem anderen Standpunkt aus; **with an** ~ **to profit** in gewinnsüchtiger Absicht;
  artificial ~ Glasauge; **bird's-**~ Vogelperspektive; **black (bruised)** ~ blaues Auge; **cause-to-bid** ~s kauflüsterne Augen; **magic** ~ *(wireless)* magisches Auge; **private** ~ *(sl.)* Detektiv;
  ~ **to the main chance** Hauptaugenmerk auf das Wichtigste; **an** ~ **for an** ~ Auge um Auge; ~ **of the law** Auge des Gesetzes, Polizist;
  ~ *(v.)* **s. o. up and down** j. kritisch von oben bis unten mustern; ~ **with raised eyebrows** mit erheblicher Skepsis betrachten;
  to be in the public ~ im Brennpunkt des öffentlichen Interesses stehen; **to be all** ~s seine Augen überall haben; **to be up to the** ~s **in debt** bis über die Ohren verschuldet sein; **to be up to the** ~s **in work** bis über die Ohren in der Arbeit stecken; **to be a sheet in the wind's** ~ leichte Schlagseite haben; **to be mortgaged up to the** ~s bis übers Dach hinaus verschuldet sein; **to black s. one's** ~ jem. ein blaues Auge schlagen; **to build by** ~ nach Augenmaß bauen; **to catch the** ~ ins Auge fallen; **to catch s. one's** ~ jds. Aufmerksamkeit auf sich lenken, j. auf sich aufmerksam machen; **to catch the Speaker's** ~ *(parl.)* das Wort erhalten; **to clap** ~s **on s. th.** etw. zu Gesicht bekommen; **to close one's** ~s nicht sehen wollen; **to close one's** ~s **to the faults of s. o.** seine Augen vor den Fehlern eines anderen verschließen; **to do s. th. with one's** ~s **open** der Gefahr ins Auge sehen; **to find favo(u)r in s. one's** ~s vor jds. Augen Gnade finden; **to get into the public** ~ ins öffentliche Blickfeld geraten; **to give one's** ~ für sein Leben gern tun; **to give s. o. the glad** ~ jem. einen schäkernden Blick zuwerfen, mit jem. liebäugeln; **to have an** ~ **for s. th.** Blick (Auge) für etw. haben; **to have** ~s **at the back of one's head** einfach alles sehen; **to always have an** ~ **to business** stets nur ans Geschäft denken; **to have an** ~ **to one's own interests** seinen eigenen Vorteil im Auge haben; **to keep one's** ~s **peeled** *(sl.)* wie ein Schießhund aufpassen; **to keep s. o. under one's** ~ j. laufend überwachen (dauernd im Auge behalten); **to keep an** ~ **out for** Ausschau halten nach; **to keep a wary** ~ **on s. th.** wachsames

Auge auf etw. halten; **to lay** ~**s on** ein Auge werfen auf; **to lie in the** ~ **of the beholder** subjektive Empfindung eines Betrachters widerspiegeln; **to look s. o. straight in the** ~ jem. offen ins Auge schauen; **to look on a problem with a different** ~ Problem mit anderen Augen betrachten; **to make** ~**s at s. o.** jem. schöne Augen machen; **to marry s. o. with an** ~ **on her fortune** Frau wegen ihres Vermögens heiraten; **to mind one's** ~ *(coll.)* sich vorsehen; **to open s. one's** ~**s** jem. die Augen öffnen; **to pass through a needle's** ~ durch ein Nadelöhr gehen; **to pull the wool over s. one's** ~**s** *(US)* jem. Sand in die Augen streuen; **to see** ~ **to** ~ **with s. o.** mit jem. hundertprozentig übereinstimmen; **to see s. th. with half an** ~ etw. mit einem Blick (mühelos) sehen, etw. sofort herausfinden; **to see the whites in s. one's** ~ dem Gegner genau gegenüberstehen; **to shut one's** ~**s to the truth** seine Augen vor der Wahrheit verschließen; **to spring to the** ~ sofort ins Auge fallen; **to never take one's** ~**s off** in seiner Wachsamkeit niemals nachlassen; **to throw dust in s. one's** ~**s** jem. Sand in die Augen streuen; **to turn a blind** ~ seine Augen vor der Wirklichkeit verschließen, ein Auge zumachen; **to turn Nelson's** ~ **to breaches** über Verstöße hinwegsehen;

~ **appeal (catcher)** *(advertisement)* Blickfang; ~-**catching right-hand page** Aufschlagseite; ~ **contact** Augenverbindung; **at** ~ **level** in Augenhöhe; ~-**opener** überraschende Aufklärung, Überraschung, *(US sl.)* Frühschoppen; ~ **stopper** *(advertising)* Blickfang; ~ **witness** Augenzeuge; ~-**witness account** Augenzeugenbericht.

eyebrows, to cause some raised einiges Erstaunen hervorrufen; **to raise one's** ~ hochnäsig (entrüstet) aussehen.

eyehole Guckloch.

eyelid, not to bat an nicht mit der Wimper zucken; **to hang on by the** ~**s** an einem seidenen Faden hängen.

eyeservant Augendiener.

eyeservice Augendienerei.

eyeshot, within in Sichtweite.

eyesight Sicht.

eyesore unschöne Stelle, Dorn im Auge; **to be an** ~ **for s. o.** ein Dorn im Auge für j. sein.

eyeteeth, to cut one's seine Kinderschuhe austreten.

eyewash *(sl.)* Gewäsch, Geschwätz, fauler Zauber, Schmus.

eyre fliegendes Gericht.

F

F *(school, US)* Ungenügend, Sechs.
Fabian policy zauderndes Handeln, Verzögerungspolitik.
fable Fabel, erfundene Geschichte;
old wives' ~ Altweibergeschwätz;
to sort out fact from ~ Wahres vom Unwahren trennen;
~ **book** Fabel-, Märchenbuch; ~ **teller** Märchenerzähler; ~ **writer** Fabeldichter.
fableland Märchen-, Fabelland.
fablemonger Legendenerfinder.
fabler Fabelfans, Lügner.
fabric *(building)* Gebäude, Bau, *(reinforcement of concrete)* Stahldrahtgewebe, *(structure)* Struktur, Bau, Gefüge, *(texture)* Gewebe, Stoff, Fabrikat;
social ~ soziales (gesellschaftliches) Gefüge;
the whole ~ **of argument** das ganze Gerüst der vorgebrachten Argumente; ~ **of law** Rechtsgefüge; ~ **of society** soziales (gesellschaftliches) Gefüge, soziale (gesellschaftliche) Struktur;
to turn into ~ verarbeiten;
~ **fund** kirchliche Stiftung; ~ **gloves** Stoffhandschuhe; ~ **printing** Stoffdruck.
fabricant Hersteller, Fabrikant.
fabricate *(v.)* *(build)* bauen, errichten, *(forge)* fälschen, *(manufacture)* verfertigen, fabrizieren, erzeugen, herstellen, anfertigen;
~ **an accusation** falsche Anklage erheben; ~ **a book** Buch schreiben; ~ **a bridge** Brücke konstruieren; ~ **a document** Urkunde fälschen; ~ **ships** Schiffe bauen; ~ **a story** Geschichte erfinden; ~ **a will** Testament fälschen.
fabricated | **account** gefälschter Bericht; ~ **account of adventures** erfundene Abenteuergeschichte; ~ **document** gefälschte Urkunde; ~ **evidence** fabrizierte (konstruierte) Beweismittel; ~ **fact** vorgespiegelte (falsche) Tatsache; ~ **ship** zusammengebautes Schiff.
fabricating | **materials** Zulieferungsmaterial; ~ **parts** Zulieferungsteile.
fabrication *(building)* Bau, Errichtung, *(forging)* Fälschung, Erfindung, Lüge, *(manufacture)* Fabrikation, Anfertigung, Herstellung, Weiterverarbeitung;
pure ~ reine Phantasie;
~ **of automobiles** Autoherstellung; ~ **of a bridge** Brückenkonstruktion; ~ **of evidence** Herstellung falschen Beweismaterials; ~ **of government** Regierungsbildung; ~ **of a passport** Paßfälschung; ~**-in-transit** *(railroad)* Anwendung eines Durchgangstarifs für auf der Strecke formveränderte Frachtgüter;
~ **tax** Fabrikations-, Produktionssteuer.
fabricator Hersteller, Fabrikant, *(forger)* Fälscher.
fabulous fabelhaft, bombig;
~ **price** unerhörter Preis; ~ **wealth** unwahrscheinlicher (sagenhafter) Reichtum.
facade Fassade.
face Gesicht[sausdruck], Miene, *(coin)* Bild-, Vorderseite, *(document)* Wortlaut, *(exact amount)* genauer Betrag, *(mining)* Streb, Ort, *(nominal amount)* Nennwert, -betrag, Nominalwert, *(prestige)* Prestige, *(print.)* Typen-, Schriftbild, *(printing surface)* Druckoberfläche, bedruckte Vorderseite, *(reputation)* Ansehen, Ruf, Prestige;
for s. one's fair ~ um jds. schöner Augen willen; **in the** ~ **of danger** angesichts der Gefahr; **in the very** ~ **of day** bei hellichtem Tag; **in order to save one's** ~ aus Prestigegründen; **on the** ~ **of it** allem Anschein nach; **on the mere** ~ **of it** gleich beim ersten Blick;
poker ~ Pokergesicht;
~ **of affairs** Sachlage; ~ **of book** Titelseite; ~ **of a building** Vorderseite eines Gebäudes; ~ **of a clock** Zifferblatt; ~ **of a coin** Bildseite einer Münze; ~ **of debt** Nennbetrag einer Schuld; ~ **to** ~ unter vier Augen; ~ **of an instrument** genauer Wortlaut einer Urkunde; ~ **of invoice** Rechnungsbetrag; ~ **of judgment** Urteilsbetrag; ~ **of a mortgage** noch bestehende Hypothekenschuld; ~ **of a paper** Gesicht einer Zeitung; ~ **of policy** Versicherungswert; ~ **of record** Sitzungsprotokoll;
~ *(v.)* gegenüberstehen, entgegentreten, *(goods)* [durch Verpackung] ein besseres Äußeres geben;
~ **altered circumstances** geänderten Verhältnissen Rechnung tragen; ~ **down all objections** alle Einwände überkommen; ~ **down unpopularity** unpopuläre Maßnahmen in Kauf nehmen; ~ **the enemy** dem Feind die Stirn bieten; ~ **the facts** Tatsachen ins Gesicht schauen; ~ **the facts of life** sich mit den Gegeben-

heiten abfinden; ~ **the music** Suppe auslöffeln, die man sich eingebrockt hat; ~ **it (a matter) out** etw. mit größter Unverfrorenheit vertreten, Sache durchstehen; ~ **s. o. out of countenance** j. aus der Fassung bringen; ~ **the river** *(house)* mit der Front nach dem Fluß liegen; ~ **a street** *(window)* auf die Straße herausgehen; ~ **up to a danger** einer Gefahr ins Auge sehen;
to act in the ~ **of direct orders** gegen strikte Weisungen handeln; **to be regular on its** ~ *(check)* äußerlich in Ordnung sein; **to be void on its** ~ von Anfang an nichtig sein; **to bring persons** ~ **to** ~ Personen einander gegenüberstellen; **to exploit a** ~ *(mining)* Feld abbauen; **to fly in the** ~ **of s. o.** jem. widersprechen; **to fly in the** ~ **of facts** sich mit den Tatsachen nicht abfinden wollen; **to fly in the** ~ **of nature** gegen Naturgesetze angehen; **to fly in the** ~ **of providence** der Vorsehung in den Arm fallen; **to fly in the** ~ **of treaties** für Vertragsverletzungen agieren; **to have the** ~ so dreist sein, die Stirn haben; **to have to** ~ **s. th.** mit etw. konfrontiert werden; **to have a** ~ **as long as a fiddle** Leichenbittermiene aufsetzen; **to have the gallows in one's** ~ unheimlich aussehen; **to look s. o. in the** ~ j. durchbohrend ansehen; **to lose one's** ~ seinen guten Ruf verlieren, sein Ansehen einbüßen; **to make common cause in the** ~ **of common danger** sich angesichts einer gemeinsamen Gefahr zusammentun; **to pull a** ~ **as long as a fiddle** Gesicht wie drei Tage Regenwetter machen; **to put the best** ~ **on s. th.** einer Sache die beste Seite abgewinnen; **to put a bold** ~ **on s. th.** sich Unangenehmes nicht anmerken lassen; **to put a good** ~ **on one's actions** sein Tun bemänteln; **to put on a** ~ **of importance** sich wichtig machen; **to put a good** ~ **on a matter** gute Miene zum bösen Spiel machen; **to put a new** ~ **on things** neue Lage schaffen; **to put s. o. out of** ~ j. aus der Fassung bringen; **to put a new** ~ **on the business** einer Sache eine ganz andere Wendung geben; **to run one's** ~ *(US)* sein gutes Aussehen zur Krediterlangung ausnützen; **to save one's** ~ sein Ansehen (Gesicht, Prestige) wahren; **to set one's** ~ **against [doing]** opponieren, sich entschieden weigern; **to set one's** ~ **for home** seine Schritte heimwärts lenken; **to shut the door in s. one's** ~ jem. die Tür vor der Nase zuschlagen; **to succeed in the** ~ **of many difficulties** trotz zahlreicher Schwierigkeiten erfolgreich sein;
~ **amount** *(instrument)* Nominal-, Nennbetrag; ~ **amount insured by the policy** Versicherungssumme; ~**-to** ~ **discussion** Gespräch unter vier Augen; ~ **guard** [Draht]schutzmaske; ~**-to** ~ **interview** Befragung in Form eines persönlichen Gesprächs; ~**-lift** *(v.)* **the service stations** Tankstellen renovieren; ~**-lifting** Gesichtsstraffung, *(house)* Verschönerung, Renovierung; ~ **mask** Gesichtsmaske; ~ **mould** Schablone; **full-**~ **portrait** Porträt in Lebensgröße; ~ **rate** *(loan)* Nettosatz; ~ **saver** Vermeidung eines Prestigeverlustes; ~**-saving** Prestigeverlust vermeidend; ~ **value** Nominal-, Nennwert; **to take s. one's words at their** ~ **value** jds. Worte für bare Münze nehmen.
faced | **with bankruptcy** kurz vor dem Konkurs;
to be ~ **with a lawsuit** Prozeß zu gewärtigen haben; **to be** ~ **with s. th.** mit etw. konfrontiert werden; **to be** ~ **with ruin** dem Nichts gegenüberstehen.
facer plötzlich auftretende Schwierigkeit.
facet *(fig.)* Aspekt, Gesichtspunkt, *(precious stone)* Facette;
major ~**s of a business** wesentliche Aspekte eines Unternehmens.
facia Laden-, Firmenschild.
facial disfigurement *(insurance)* Verunstaltung des Gesichts.
facier äußere Erscheinung, Habitus.
facile geschickt, gewandt, *(easy to manage)* nachgiebig, fügsam, leicht zu überreden, *(Scot. law)* so beeinflußbar, daß Pflegschaft angeordnet werden muß;
to be ~ **in inventing lies** geschickter Lügner sein; **to have a** ~ **pen** gute Feder schreiben; ~ **victory** leicht errungener Sieg; ~ **worker** geschickter Arbeiter.
facilitate *(v.)* erleichtern, *(US)* fördern;
~ **payment** Zahlung erleichtern.
facilitation Förderung, Erleichterung;
~ **of payments** Zahlungserleichterungen; ~ **of trade** Förderung des Handelsverkehrs; ~ **of traffic** Verkehrserleichterung.
facilities *(advantages)* Erleichterungen, Möglichkeiten, Vorteile, Fazilitäten, *(appliances)* Anlagen, [Betriebs]einrichtungen, Vorrichtungen;
air-cargo terminal ~ Einrichtungen eines Luftfrachthafens; **bathing** ~ Bademöglichkeiten; **container** ~ Behälteranlagen; **credit** ~ Kreditfazilitäten; **defense- (defence-,** *Br.)* **financed** ~

vom Verteidigungsministerium finanzierte Anlagen; **educational** ~ Bildungsmöglichkeiten; **emergency** ~ Notstandsvorhaben; **engineering** ~ technische Einrichtungen; **full** ~ alle Möglichkeiten; **idle** ~ stilliegende Betriebsanlagen; **nondetachable** ~ im Handel unverwendbare Einbauten; **owned** ~ betriebseigene Fertigungsstätten; **payment** ~ Erleichterung der Zahlungsbedingungen; **port** ~ Hafenanlagen; **postal** ~ postalische Einrichtungen; **productive (production)** ~ Produktionseinrichtungen, -anlagen; **recreational** ~ Erholungsanlagen; **sanitary** ~ sanitäre Einrichtungen; **shipping** ~ [günstige] Versandmöglichkeiten; **sports** ~ Sportmöglichkeiten; **trade [promotive]** ~ Handelserleichterungen; **transport** ~ Transportmöglichkeiten;

~ **of payment** Zahlungserleichterungen; ~ **for the supply of information** Informationsmöglichkeiten; ~ **for old people** Altentagesstätten; ~ **for recreation** Erholungsanlagen; ~ **for sitting** Sitzgelegenheiten; ~ **for study** Studieneinrichtungen; ~ **for traffic** Verkehrserleichterungen; ~ **of transport** Transportmöglichkeiten; ~ **for travel** Reiseerleichterungen;

to grant certain ~ bestimmte Vorteile einräumen; **to offer** ~ **of payment** Zahlungserleichterungen anbieten.

facility [günstige] Gelegenheit, Möglichkeit, *(aptitude)* Gewandtheit, Geschicklichkeit, *(compliance)* Nachgiebigkeit, Gefälligkeit, *(plant, US)* Betrieb[sanlage], Werk;

air and naval ~ Luft- und Flottenstützpunkt;

~ **in speaking** Redegewandtheit;

to afford s. o. every ~ jem. jegliche Erleichterung gewähren; **to allow s. o. every** ~ **of improving his French** jem. laufend Gelegenheit zur Verbesserung seiner Französischkenntnisse gewähren; **to have great** ~ **in learning languages** Sprachbegabung haben;

~ **of payment clause** *(insurance)* Auszahlungsklausel; ~ **fee** Benutzungsgebühr.

facing Gegenüberstehen;

~ **of a brake** Bremsfutter;

to go through one's ~ seine Feuerprobe bestehen; **to put s. o. through his** ~s j. auf Herz und Nieren prüfen;

~ **brick** Blendstein; ~ **matter** *(advertising)* textanschließend; ~ **editorial matter** *(ad)* gegenüber redaktionellem Teil; ~ **slip** *(US)* Aufklebezettel, Paketadresse; ~ **text** gegenüber dem Text plazierte Anzeige.

facsimile Faksimile, genaue (getreue) Nachbildung, *(photography)* Fernfotografie, *(telegraphy)* Bildtelegrafie, -übertragung; ~ *(v.)* nachbilden, Faksimile herstellen;

to reproduce s. th. in (make a) ~ **of s. th.** etw. genau nachbilden (wiedergeben);

~ **apparatus** Bildfunkanlage, -gerät; ~ **document** Faksimileabschrift; ~ **edition** Faksimileausgabe; ~ **equipment** Bildübertragungsgerät; ~ **print** Faksimiledruck; ~ **probate** *(Br.)* beglaubigte Testamentsabschrift, wortgetreue Testamentsbestätigung; ~ **reprint** genauer (getreuer) Wiederdruck; ~ **signature** faksimilierte Unterschrift; ~ **stamp** Faksimilestempel; ~ **telegraph** Bildfunktelegraph; ~ **transmission** Bildübertragung; ~ **transmission service** Bildfunkdienst; ~ **transmitter** Bildsender.

fact Tatsache, Umstand, *(law)* Tatbestand, Tatumstände;

based on ~s tatsächlich; **in** ~ tatsächlich; **in** ~ **and law** in tatsächlicher und rechtlicher Hinsicht;

accomplished ~ vollendete Tatsache; **actual** ~s objektiver Tatbestand; **admitted** ~ anerkannte Tatsache; **basic** ~s grundlegende Tatsachen; **cold** ~ nackte Tatsache; **constituent** ~ Tatbestandsmerkmal; **dispositive** ~s rechtsbegründende Tatsachen; **divestitive** ~ den Verlust eines Rechtes nach sich ziehende Tatsache; **established** ~ feststehende Tatsache; **evidentiary** ~s beweiserhebliche Tatsachen; **hard** ~ nackte Tatsachen; **immaterial** ~s für die Entscheidung unerhebliche Tatsachen, unwesentlicher Sachverhalt; **investitive** ~ rechtsbegründete Tatsache; **jurisdictional** ~ für die Zuständigkeit bedeutsame Tatsache; **material** ~s wesentliche Tatsachen; **outstanding (positive)** ~ feststehende Tatsache; **real** ~s Sachverhalt; **striking** ~s nicht zu übersehende Tatsachen;

~s **of the case** Tatumstände, Sachverhalt; ~s **constituting the cause of action** klagebegründende Tatsachen; ~s **which are unnecessary to disclose** nicht offenlegungspflichtige Tatsachen; ~s **of experience** Erfahrungstatsachen; ~s **in issue** für die Entscheidung erhebliche Tatsachen; ~s **of life** Geheimnis des Lebens; ~ **with improve the risk** *(insurance)* risikoerhabsetzende Tatsachen; ~ **material to risk** für das Versicherungsrisiko wesentliche Tatsache; ~s **about turnover** Umsatzangaben; ~ **which the insurer's representative fails to notice on a survey** vom Versicherungsvertreter bei der Besichtigung nicht entdeckte Tatsachen;

to accept a statement as ~ Behauptung als gegeben hinnehmen; **to acknowledge the evidence of** ~s sich der Macht der Tatsachen beugen; **to adduce** ~s Tatsachen anführen; **to ascertain** ~s Tatsachen feststellen; **to be blind to the** ~s sich den Tatsachen verschließen; **to be founded on** ~(s) auf Tatsachen beruhen; **to be good in law and in** ~ rechtlich und sachlich begründet sein; **to come round to the** ~s sich mit den Tatsachen abfinden; **to conceal** ~s Tatsachen unterdrücken; **to lay** ~s **before a committee** Ausschuß mit den Tatsachen bekanntmachen (konfrontieren); **to pervert the** ~s Tatsachen verdrehen; **to prove with** ~s mit den Tatsachen untermauern; **to state the** ~s Tatsachen anführen, Tatsachenangaben machen; **to suppress important** ~s wichtige Tatsachen unterdrücken;

~ **finding** *(law court)* Tatsachenfeststellung; ~-**finding board** *(labo(u)r disputes)* Untersuchungsausschuß; ~-**finding committee** Untersuchungsausschuß; ~-**finding mission** Expertenkommission; **financial** ~-**finding mission** finanzielle Untersuchungskommisssion; ~-**finding survey** Lagebericht; ~-**finding tour** Inspektionsreise; ~ **sheet** Tatsachenzusammenstellung.

faction Faktion, Splitter-, Parteigruppe, Parteigruppierung, Interessentengruppe, Clique, *(party politics)* Vorherrschen von Parteigeist;

to split into petty ~s sich in Splittergruppen auflösen.

factional eigensüchtig.

factionalism Parteigeist.

factionary Parteigänger;

~ *(a.)* parteiisch.

factionist Parteigänger, -anhänger.

factious parteisüchtig;

~ **demand for goods** gewaltiger Warenbedarf; ~ **doings** Parteigetriebe; ~ **man** Parteigänger; ~ **spirit** Parteigeist.

factiousness Parteigeist.

factor Faktor, Moment, mitwirkender Umstand, *(agent)* [Verkaufs]kommissionär, [Abschluß]agent, Makler, Handelsvertreter, *(biol.)* Erbfaktor, *(factoring)* Warenbevorschusser, Absatzfinanzierungsinstitut, Factoringgesellschaft, -firma, *(US, garnishee)* Drittschuldner, *(manager)* Geschäftsführer, Disponent, *(Scotland)* Liegenschaftsverwalter;

contributory ~ fördernder Umstand; **cost** ~ Kostenfaktor; **cyclical** ~ konjunktureller Faktor; **decisive** ~ entscheidender Faktor; **deflationary** ~ deflationistischer Faktor; **determining** ~ maßgebender Umstand; **domestic** ~ Inlandsvertreter; **expense** ~s Kostenfaktoren; **foreign** ~ Auslandsvertreter; **home** ~ Inlandsvertreter; **income** ~ Einkommensfaktor, Leistungseinkommen; **judicial** ~ vom Gericht bestellter Pfleger; **market** ~s Marktfaktoren; **price-raising** ~ preiserhöhender Umstand; **rate-making** ~ preisbildender Faktor; **safety** ~ Sicherheitsfaktor;

~s **in the making of a nation** Umstände, die die Entstehung einer Nation fördern; ~ **of merit** Gütefaktor; ~s **that constitute an offence** strafbegründende Umstände; ~s **of production** Produktionsfaktoren; ~ **of safety** *(loan)* Sicherheitsfaktor; ~ **of value** Wertfaktor;

~ *(v.)* als Verwalter tätig sein, *(consignment)* auf Kommissionsbasis verkaufen;

~ **one's accounts** sich Betriebsmittelkredit durch Debitorenabtretung beschaffen; ~ **an estate** Gut verwalten;

to consider all ~s **involved** alle Faktoren berücksichtigen; **to make o. s. a great** ~ **in the economy** in der Wirtschaft eine große Rolle spielen; **to take a** ~ **into consideration** Umstand in Rechnung stellen;

~ **analysis** Faktorenanalyse; ~ **comparison** Merkmalsvergleich; ~ **cost** Kostenfaktor; ~ **credit** Punktbewertung; ~'s **fee** Faktorgebühr; ~'s **lien** *(US)* Kommissionärspfandrecht; ~ **loading** *(statistics)* Faktorbewertung; ~ **movement** Faktorwanderung.

factorage Kommissions-, Provisionsgebühr, *(agent's business)* Kommissionsgeschäft.

factored fabrikmäßig hergestellt, *(sold on commission)* auf Kommissionsbasis verkauft.

factoring *(US)* Warenbevorschussung, Ankauf offener Buchforderungen (von Warenforderungen), Debitorenverkauf;

maturity ~ Forderungsankauf mit bis zur Fälligkeit aufgeschobener Auszahlung; **nonnotification** ~ Forderungsankauf ohne Offenlegung der Abtretung; **notification (old-line)** ~ Forderungsankauf mit Anzeige an den Drittschuldner;

~ **agreement** Absatz-, Finanzierungsvertrag; ~ **chain** Faktoringkette; ~ **company** Faktoringgesellschaft; ~ **group** Faktoringgruppe; ~ **system** *(US)* Absatzfinanzierungssystem.

factorize *(v.)* faktorisieren, *(US)* Drittschuldner pfänden.

factorizing process *(US)* Pfändung eines Drittschuldners.

factory Fabrikationsstätte, Fabrik[anlage], Fabrikgebäude, Betrieb[sanlage], Werk-, Fertigungsanlage, *(body of factors)* Kaufmannschaft, *(police station, sl.)* Polizeistation, -wache, *(trading station)* Faktorei, Handelsniederlassung;
[direct] from ~ *(US)* ab Fabrik (Werk); **ex (loco)** ~ ab Werk; **in the** ~ in der Fabrik;
bonded ~ Fabrik zur Verarbeitung von Waren unter Zollaufsicht; **departmentalized** ~ *(US)* dezentralisierter Betrieb; **non-operating** ~ stillgelegter Betrieb; **ready-built** ~ Fabrik vom Fließband, Fließbandfabrik; **on-site** ~ an der Baustelle errichteter Betrieb; **strike-bound** ~ bestreikte Fabrik; **subassembly** ~ Montagewerk; **underground** ~ unterirdische Fabrik;
~ **together with plant complete** Fabrik mit Zubehör; ~ **at work** betriebsfertige Anlage;
to commission a new ~ neue Fabrik in Betrieb nehmen; **to erect a** ~ Fabrik bauen; **to manage a** ~ Fabrik leiten; **to open a** ~ Werk in Betrieb nehmen; **to run a** ~ Fabrik betreiben; **to run a** ~ **at a loss** Fabrik mit Verlust betreiben, in einer Fabrik mit Verlust arbeiten; **to set up a** ~ Fabrik anlegen; **to tie up a** ~ Fabrik stillegen; **to tool a** ~ Fabrik mit den notwendigen Maschinen ausstatten; **to work in a** ~ Fabrikarbeit leisten;
~ **account** Fabrikationskonto; ~ **overhead account** Fertigungs-, Fabrikationsgemeinkostenkonto; ~ **accounting** Fabrik-, Betriebsbuchhaltung; ⩜ **Acts** *(Br.)* Arbeitsschutzgesetzgebung, Gewerbeordnung; ~ **agreement** Betriebsvereinbarung; ~ **allowance of overtime** einem Betrieb zugestandene Überstundenzeit; ~ **area** Fabrikgelände; ~ **building** Fabrikationshalle, Fabrikgebäude; ~ **canteen** [Betriebs]kantine; ~ **chimney** Fabrikschornstein; ~ **committee** Betriebsrat; ~ **construction** Fabrikerrichtung; ~ **cost** Herstellungs-, Produktionskosten, Fabrikpreis; ~ **council** *(Br.)* Betriebsrat; ~ **deliveries** Fabrikauslieferungen; ~ **doctor** Werks-, Betriebsarzt; ~ **earnings** *(plant)* gesamte Lohnkosten; ~ **employment** industrielle Beschäftigung; ~ **equipment** Fabrikeinrichtung, Betriebseinrichtung; ~ **expenses** Herstellungs-, Produktions-, Fabrikationskosten; ~-**fabricated** fabrikmäßig hergestellt; ~ **farm** industriell betriebene Landwirtschaft; ~ **fleet** Betriebsfahrzeuge, Fahrabteilung; ~ **gate** Fabriktor; ~ **girl** Fabrikarbeiterin; ~ **guaranty policies** betriebliche Garantiezusagen; ~ **hand** Fabrikarbeiter; ~ **hooter** Fabriksirene; ~ **inspection** Gewerbeaufsicht, Gewerbepolizei; ~ **inspector** Gewerbeaufseher; ~ **inspectorate** Gewerbeaufsichtsamt; ~ **insurance** Betriebsversicherung; ~ **interference** Betriebseinmischung; ~ **inventory** Betriebsinventar; ~ **job** Fabrikarbeit; ~ **labo(u)rer** Fabrikarbeiter; ~ **law** Gewerberecht; ~ **ledger** Betriebshauptbuch; ~ **legislation** Arbeiterschutzgesetzgebung; ~-**made** fabrikmäßig hergestellt; ~-**made goods** Fabrikware; ~ **management** Betriebsführung, -leitung; ~ **manager** Betriebs-, Fabrikleiter; ~ **meeting** Betriebsversammlung; **to knuckle down to** ~ **muscle in the crunch** sich im Ernstfall den Betriebserfordernissen fügen; ~ **number** Fabriknummer; ~ **nursery** Betriebskindergarten; ~'**s occupier** Fabrikbesitzer; ~ **order** Betriebsanweisung; ~ **output** Fabrikationsausstoß; ~ **overheads** Fertigungsgemeinkosten; ~ **overhead account** Fertigungsgemeinkostenkonto; ~ **overhead rate** Fertigungsgemeinkostensatz; ~ **owner** Fabrikbesitzer, Betriebseigentümer; ~ **payroll** Betriebslohnliste; ~ **plot** Fabrikgrundstück; ~ **price** Erzeugerpreis, Fabrik[abgabe]preis, Preis ab Werk (Fabrik); ~ **product** gewerbliches Erzeugnis, Fabrikware; ~ **production** gewerbliche Produktion, Industrieerzeugung, -produktion; ~ **production of homes** Fließbandproduktion von Fertighäusern; ~ **profit** Fabrikationsgewinn; ~ **project** Fabrikprojekt; ~ **property** Betriebsgrundstück; ~ **railway** Werkbahn; *(motor trucks)* Ladefähigkeitsangaben; ~ **records** Betriebsunterlagen; ~ **regulations** gewerbepolizeiliche Anordnungen; ~ **rejects** Ausschußware; ~ **removal** Abbau von Betriebsanlagen; ~ **roadway** Werks-, Fabrikstraße; ~ **shipment** Versand ab Fabrik; ~ **sidings** Fabrikgleise; ~ **site** Industrie-, Werkgrundstück, Fabrikgelände; ~ **smokestack** Fabrikschornstein; ~ **snackshop** *(US)* Werks-, Betriebskantine; ~ **space** Produktionsfläche; ~ **spying** Werksspionage; ~ **stores** Fabriklager; ~ **supervision** Betriebsaufsicht; ~ **supplies** Betriebsstoffe, -materialien; ~ **system** Fabrikwesen, Faktoreisystem; ~ **town** Fabrikstadt; ~ **vessel** Fischverarbeitungsschiff; ~ **visit** Werks-, Betriebsbesuch; ~ **welfare worker** Sozialreferent eines Betriebes; ~ **woman** Fabrikarbeiterin; ~ **work** Fabrikarbeit; ~ **worker** Fabrikarbeiter; ~ **workload** Betriebsauslastung.
factual tatsächlich, wirklich, faktisch;
to be more ~ sich mehr an die Tatsachen halten;
~ **data (material)** Tatsachenmaterial; ~ **evidence** stichhaltige

Beweise; ~ **information** Sachinformation; ~ **knowledge** Sachkenntnisse; ~ **report** Tatsachenbericht; ~ **statement** Tatsachenbericht, objektive Sachdarstellung.
facultative freigestellt, fakultativ, wahlfrei, in das Ermessen gestellt;
~ **compensation** von freiem Ermessen abhängige Vergütung; ~ **enactment** Ermessensakt; ~ **money** fakultatives Geld; ~ **power** Ermessensbefugnis; ~ **reinsurance** *(reinsurer)* Rückversicherungsoption; ~ **studies** Wahlstudium; ~ **subject** Wahlfach.
faculties *(law of divorce)* finanzielle Lage des Ehemanns, Unterhaltsfähigkeit;
intellectual ~ geistige Fähigkeiten;
to be in possession of all one's ~ alle fünf Sinne beisammen haben.
faculty Können, Anlagen, Fähigkeit, Vermögen, Talent, *(authorization)* Erlaubnis, Ermächtigung, Befugnis, *(property)* Eigentum, Vermögen, *(university, US)* Lehrkörper, Fakultät, Kollegium;
mental ~ Geistesgaben; **perceptive** ~ Auffassungsgabe; **physical** ~ körperliche Leistungsfähigkeit;
⩜ **of Advocates** *(Scot.)* Anwaltschaft, -stand, -kammer; ~ **of discrimination** Unterscheidungsvermögen; ~ **of economics** volkswirtschaftliche Fakultät; ⩜ **of Law** Rechtsfakultät, juristische Fakultät; ⩜ **of Letters** philosophische Fakultät; ⩜ **of Medicine** medizinische Fakultät; ~ **of speech** Rednergabe, -begabung; ~ **of a university** Fakultät einer Universität;
to have a great ~ **of learning languages** große Sprachbegabung besitzen;
~ **adviser** *(US)* Studienberater; ~ **business** *(US)* Fakultätsangelegenheiten; ~ **committee** *(US)* Fakultätsausschuß; ~ **list** *(US)* Fakultätsverzeichnis; ~ **meeting** *(US)* Fakultätssitzung; ~ **member** *(US)* Fakultätsmitglied; ~ **principle of taxation** Steuerleistungsprinzip; **student-**~ **strike** *(US)* Fakultätsstreik.
fad Marotte, Schrulle, Laune, Steckenpferd, Liebhaberei, [zeitlich und örtlich] befristete Mode, Modetorheit;
the latest ~ neueste Marotte; **passing** ~ vorübergehendes Steckenpferd.
faddist Modefex.
fade *(v.)* *(film)* überblenden, verschwommen werden lassen, *(radio)* Schwund haben, *(sound)* leiser werden, *(stocks)* schwächer werden;
~ **away** abklingen; ~ **a curtain** Vorhang ausblenden; ~ **in** einblenden; ~ **out** *(film)* verklingen, *(photo)* abblenden; ~ **out a conversation** *(radio)* Stimmen verschwinden lassen; ~ **one scene into another** von einer Szene in die andere überblenden;
~-**in** *(photo)* Abblendung; ~-**out** *(investments)* Auslaufen, *(photo)* Ausblenden, -blendung, *(radio)* Fading; ~-**out formula** Auslaufformel; ~-**proof** *(suit)* farbecht.
fader Tonblende.
fading *(radio)* Fading, Schwund, Schwunderscheinung;
~ **in** Einblendung;
~ *(a.)* schwindend, *(colo(u)r)* unecht;
~ **control** Schwundausgleich; ~-**reducing antenna** schwundmindernde Antenne.
fag *(Br.)* Arbeitspferd, *(Br., sl.)* Glimmstengel, *(coll.)* Schinderei, Plackerei;
~ *(a.)* sich abplacken, sich abschinden, bis zur Erschöpfung schuften;
~ **end** Überbleibsel, *(cigarette)* Kippe; ~ **end of the term** letzte Semestertage; **to arrive at the** ~ **end** knapp vor Torschluß ankommen; **to be near its** ~ **end** fast beendet sein.
fagged out vollkommen ausgepumpt.
faggot Holz-, Reisigbündel, *(old shrivelled woman, Br.)* alte Schlampe;
~ **vote** erschlichene Wahlstimme.
fail *(in examination)* Durchgefallener;
without ~ unfehlbar;
~ *(v.)* *(go bankrupt)* Zahlungen einstellen, zahlungsunfähig werden, Bankrott (Konkurs) machen, bankrott werden, in Konkurs geraten (gehen), zusammenbrechen, *(engine)* aussetzen, absterben, *(examination)* durchfallen, -fliegen, nicht bestehen, *(harvest)* mißraten, *(machine)* ausfallen, *(neglect)* unterlassen, versäumen, *(not succeed)* mißlingen, versagen, scheitern, nicht zustande kommen, *(want)* mangeln, fehlen;
~ **to answer an invitation** auf eine Einladung nicht reagieren; ~ **to appear** *(at court)* nicht erscheinen, ausbleiben, Termin versäumen; ~ **in business** geschäftlich nicht reüssieren, zahlungsunfähig werden; ~ **half the candidates** Hälfte der Kandidaten durchfallen lassen; ~ **to comply with conditions** Bedingungen nicht erfüllen; ~ **with the critics** bei den Kritikern durchfallen; ~ **to get a connection** *(tel.)* keine Verbindung bekommen; ~

during a depression in einer Krisenzeit zusammenbrechen; ~ **in one's duty** seine Pflicht vernachlässigen; ~ **in an examination** [im Examen] durchfallen; ~ **with one's goal in sight** kurz vor dem Ziel aufgeben müssen; ~ **in one's hopes** sich in seinen Hoffnungen täuschen; ~ **for a million** Millionenkonkurs machen; ~ **to pay** zu zahlen versäumen; ~ **in perseverance** Durchhaltevermögen vermissen lassen; ~ **to obtain relief** mit einem Rechtsmittel nicht durchkommen; ~ **in respect for s. o.** es jem. gegenüber an Respekt fehlen lassen; ~ **to sell** sich nicht verkaufen lassen; ~ **in a suit** Prozeß verlieren; ~ **in one's undertakings** mit seinen Unternehmungen Schiffbruch erleiden; ~ **in three years running** dreijährige Mißernte hervorbringen;

~**-safe device** *(atomic bomber)* automatische Rückrufanlage; ~ **year** *(US)* Mißernte.

failed firm *(US)* zahlungsunfähige Firma.

failing Fehlen, Ausbleiben;

~ **to deliver up books** *(bankruptcy)* Nichtausfolgung von Rechnungsbüchern; ~ **to deliver up property** *(bankruptcy)* hintangehaltene Vermögensauslieferung; ~ **of record** Unvermögen der Beibringung einer Urkunde;

~ *(a.)* in Ermangelung, mangels;

~ **special agreement** in Ermangelung besonderer Absprachen; ~ **an answer** mangels Nachricht; ~ **circumstances** *(bank)* insolvent, zahlungsunfähig; ~ **him** im Falle seiner Abwesenheit; ~ **payment** mangels Zahlung; ~ **proof** mangels Beweises; ~ **a purchaser** in Ermangelung eines Käufers; ~ **a satisfactory reply** sofern nicht eine ausreichende Antwort eingeht; ~ **which** widrigenfalls; ~ **whom** im Fall seines Nichterscheinens; ~ **yield** mangels Ertrags;

~ **company** notleidendes Unternehmen.

failure Fehlen, Mangel, Ausbleiben, *(bankruptcy)* Konkurs, Bankrott, Fallieren, Zusammenbruch, *(default)* Ausbleiben, Versäumnis, *(el.)* Störung, *(ill success)* Mißerfolg, -lingen, Fehlschlag, -leistung, Erfolglosigkeit, *(insolvency)* Zahlungseinstellung, -unfähigkeit, *(machine)* Panne, Ausfall, Versagen, Aussetzen, *(negligence)* Unterlassung, Versäumnis, *(nonfulfilment)* Nichterfüllung, *(person)* Versagen;

bank ~ Bankzusammenbruch; **crop** ~ Mißernte; **current** ~ Stromausfall; **dead** ~ komplettes Fiasko; **engine** ~ Motorschaden; **financial** ~ finanzieller Zusammenbruch (Mißerfolg);

~ **to act** nicht ordnungsgemäß zustandegekommene (fehlerhafte) Verwaltungshandlung; ~ **to answer the roll call** Nichtanwesenheit bei der Namensverlesung; ~ **of appeal** versäumte Berufung; ~ **of a party to appear** Nichterscheinen vor Gericht, Ausbleiben beim Gerichtstermin, Terminversäumnis; ~ **to bargain collectively** Ablehnung einer Tarifvertragsverhandlung; ~ **of a battery** Versagen einer Batterie; ~ **to comply with** Nichteinhaltung; ~ **to comply with the time limit** Fristüberschreitung, -versäumnis; ~ **of consideration** Wegfall der (fehlende) Gegenleistung; ~ **properly to convene a meeting** unkorrekte Einberufung einer Versammlung; ~ **to cooperate** *(insurance law)* Ablehnung der Zusammenarbeit mit der Versicherungsgesellschaft im Prozeßfall; ~ **of crop** Mißernte; ~ **to meet the deadline** Fristüberschreitung; ~ **to deliver (meet delivery)** Nichterfüllung, -lieferung, Lieferungsversagen; ~ **to disclose** fehlende Offenlegung; ~ **to enforce rights** Nichtausnutzung von Rechten; ~ **to meet one's engagements** schuldhafte Nichterfüllung; ~ **of evidence** Beweisnot, fehlender Beweisantritt; ~ **in an examination** Versagen (Durchfall) in einer Prüfung; ~ **to file a return** Nichteinreichen der Einkommensteuererklärung; ~ **of good behavio(u)r** unqualifiziertes Verhalten; ~ **of issue** Erbenlosigkeit; ~ **of justice** Fehlurteil, Justizirrtum; ~ **of memory** Gedächtnisschwäche; ~ **to mention** Nichterwähnung; ~ **to muster a quorum** mangelnde Beschlußfähigkeit; ~ **to supply material information** mangelnde Information über wesentliche Tatsachen; ~ **to give notice** verabsäumte Benachrichtigung, Nichtanzeige; ~ **to meet one's obligations** Leistungsverzug; ~ **to observe a bye-law** Nichterfüllung von Statuten; ~ **to obey an order** Nichtbefolgung einer Anordnung; ~ **in any part** teilweise Nichterfüllung; ~ **to pay** Nichtzahlung; ~ **to pay a bill** Nichthonorierung eines Wechsels; ~ **to pay an instalment** Ratenverzug; ~ **of performance (to perform)** Erfüllungsmangel, mangelnde Vertragserfüllung, Nichterfüllung; ~ **of a plot** mißglücktes Attentat; ~ **of proof** Mißlingen eines Beweises, Beweisfälligkeit, -not; ~ **of a prophecy** Nichteintritt einer Prophezeiung; ~ **of record** mangelnde Vorlage [einer Urkunde]; ~ **to render a report** unterlassene Berichterstattung; ~ **in revenue** Einkommensteuerausfall; ~ **of title** Rechtsmangel; ~ **of trust** Nichtzustandekommen eines Treuhandvertrags;

to be a complete ~ totaler Versager sein; **to be a** ~ **as a lawyer** als Anwalt nicht reüssieren; **to be a social** ~ gesellschaftlich nicht erfolgreich sein; **to bring about the** ~ **of a plan** Plan scheitern lassen; **to end in a** ~ völlig danebengehen;

~ **rate** Ausfallrate, Ausfälle.

fair Messe, Ausstellung, Jahrmarkt;

at the ~ auf der Messe;

agricultural ~ landwirtschaftliche Ausstellung; **electric-goods** ~ Elektromesse; **engineering** ~ technische Messe; **fancy** ~ Wohltätigkeitsbasar; **food and drink** ~ Genuß- und Nahrungsmittelmesse; **industries** ~ Industrieausstellung, -messe; **international trade** ~ internationale Messe; **mechanic's** ~ Handwerkermesse; **outdoor** ~ Messe im Freigelände; **world** ~ Weltausstellung;

to attend a ~ Ausstellung (Messe) besuchen; **to exhibit goods at a** ~ Waren auf einer Messe ausstellen; **to frequent a** ~ Messe besuchen; **to hold a** ~ Messe abhalten; **to organize a** ~ Messe aufziehen; **to participate in a** ~ sich an einer Messe beteiligen; **to register to a** ~ sich zu einer Messe anmelden; **to send goods to a** ~ Messe beschicken;

~ **attendance** Messebesuch; ~**s' attraction** Messeattraktion; ~ **authorities** Messebehörde, Messeleitung, Ausstellungsleitung; ~ **bill** Messewechsel; ~ **building** Ausstellungs-, Messegebäude; ~ **catalog(ue)** Ausstellungs-, Messekatalog; ~ **day** Großmarkttag; ~ **dealer** Messebesucher; ~ **directory** Ausstellerverzeichnis; ~ **pass** Messeausweis; ~ **period** Messezeit; ~ **site** Ausstellungs-, Messegelände; ~ **test** Messetest; ~ **town** Messestadt; ~ **visitor** Messebesucher; ~ **week** Messewoche;

~ *(v.)* Reinschrift anfertigen;

to bid ~ sich gut anlassen; **to copy a letter out** ~ saubere Abschrift eines Briefes anfertigen; **to play** ~ ehrliches Spiel treiben; **to speak s. o.** ~ jem. schöne Worte machen; **to write out** ~ ins Reine schreiben, Reinschrift anfertigen;

~ *(a.) (air, water)* rein, klar, *(character)* unbescholten, makellos, fleckenlos, *(equitable)* reel, billig, gerecht, kulant, gefällig, angemessen, *(favo(u)rable)* günstig, aussichtsreich, vielversprechend, *(moderate)* mittelmäßig, *(note)* ausreichend, *(sky)* klar, wolkenlos;

pretty ~ ganz leidlich;

~ **enough** *(coll.)* vernünftig, sinnvoll; ~ **and equitable** der Billigkeit entsprechend; ~ **on its face** *(tax deed)* offenbar ohne Mängel; ~ **to middling** ziemlich gut bis mittelmäßig; ~ **and square** offen und ehrlich; ~ **and equitable** recht und billig; ~ **and reasonable** angemessen;

~ **abridgement** *(copyright law)* eigenständige Kürzungs- und Kompilationstätigkeit; ~ **accuracy** ausreichende Präzision; ~ **and proper legal assessment** ordnungsgemäße [Steuer]veranlagung; ~ **average quality** gute Durchschnittsqualität, Handelsgut mittlerer Art und Güte; ~ **business** leidlich gute Geschäfte; ~ **cash [market] value** Verkehrswert; ~ **chance of success** gute Erfolgschance; ~ **comment** zulässiges Werturteil; ~ **comment on a matter of public interest** Bemerkung in Wahrnehmung berechtigter Interessen; ~ **and reasonable compensation** angemessene Entschädigung (Vergütung); ~ **competition** freier Wettbewerb; **to arrive in** ~ **condition** *(goods)* in gutem Zustand eintreffen, unbeschädigt ankommen; ~ **and valuable consideration** vollwertige Gegenleistung; ~ **and reasonable contract** *(infant)* fairer Vertrag; ~ **copy** Reinschrift, druckfertiges Manuskript; ~ **damages** großzügige Entschädigung; ~ **Deal** *(US)* Sozialprogramm, -interventionismus; ~ **dealing** anständiges Geschäftsgebaren; ~ **demand** billige Forderung; ~ **employment practices** *(US)* Handhabung gleicher Arbeitsbedingungen für alle; ~ **equivalent** angemessener Gegenwert; ~ **and full equivalent for loss** voller und angemessener Verlustausgleich; ~ **estimate** angemessene Schätzung; ~ **field** echte Chance; ~ **game** jagbares Wild, *(fig.)* Freiwild; ~**-haired** *(fig.)* beliebt; ~**-haired boy of the manager** Liebling des Direktors; ~ **handwriting** passable Handschrift; ~ **hearing** einwandfreies rechtliches Gehör; ~ **heritage** annehmbare Erbschaft; ~ **income** angemessenes Einkommen; **to be a** ~ **judge of s. th.** ziemlich gutes Urteil über etw. abgeben können; ~ **knowledge or skill** ausreichende Sachkunde; ~ **labo(u)r standards** Mindestlohnnormen; ~ **market price** *(property)* marktgerechter Preis, Verkehrswert; ~ **market value** üblicher Marktpreis; **by means** auf ehrliche Weise; **to spoil s. one's** ~ **name** jds. guten Ruf beeinträchtigen; ~ **persuasion** Überredung ohne Zwang und Kniffe; ~ **play** redliches Verfahren; ~ **practices** anständiges Geschäftsgebahren; ~ **preponderance** *(law of evidence)* überwiegendes Beweisergebnis; ~ **price** angemessener (marktgerechter, üblicher) Preis; **to make** ~ **profits** anständige Gewinne erzielen; ~ **quality** durchschnittliche Qualität; **good** ~

qualities gute Qualitäten; ~ **rent** angemessene Miete; ~ **and accurate report** genauer und sachlicher Bericht; ~ **return** angemessener Gewinn; ~ **return on an investment** angemessene Rendite; ~ **sale** ordnungsgemäß durchgeführte Zwangsversteigerung; ~ **share** gerechter Anteil; ~ **speeches of politicians** gefällige (schönklingende) Politikerreden; ~ **terms** annehmbare Bedingungen; ~ **trade** (US) Lauterkeit des Wettbewerbs, Nichtdiskriminierung des Außenhandels, (price maintenance, US) Preisbindung; ~~**trade** preisbindungsmäßig; ≗ **Trade Act** (US) Gesetz über die Preisbindung von Markenartikeln; ~~**trade agreement** (US) Preisbindungsabkommen; ~~**trade policy** Außenhandelspolitik auf der Basis gegenseitiger Vorteile; ~~**trade practices** lautere Wettbewerbsmethoden, Preisbindungsmaßnahmen; ~~**trade pricing** (US) Preisbindung der zweiten Hand; ~~**trade rules** (US) Wettbewerbsregeln; ~ **trader** (US) Preisbinder; ~ **trading** vertikale Preisbildung; ≗ **Trading Act** (Br.) Gesetz über die Preisbindung von Markenartikeln; ~ **treat** (coll.) ne' Wucht; ~ **trial** gerechtes Verfahren, ~ **usage** (copyright) angemessener Gebrauch; ~ **valuation** Bewertung zum Verkehrswert; ~ **and reasonable value** angemessener Wert, Verkehrswert; ~ **cash market value** gemeiner Wert, üblicher Marktpreis; ~ **wages** angemessene Löhne; ~ **wage clause** (contract award) Zusicherung angemessener Löhne; ~ **warning** rechtzeitige Verwarnung; **to be in a** ~ **way to succeed** in einer Aufstiegsphase sein; ~ **wear and tear** allgemeine (übliche) Abnutzung; ~ **weather** gutes Wetter; ~~**weather friend** unzuverlässiger Freund, Wetterfahne; ~ **words** Schmeichelei; **to put s. o. off with** ~ **words** j. mit schönen Worten abspeisen; ~ **writing** saubere (gut leserliche) Handschrift.

fairgoer Messebesucher.
fairgoing Beziehen einer Messe.
fairground|s (US) Ausstellungs-, Messegelände;
   ~ **entertainers** Jahrmarktsleute.
fairing Jahrmarkts-, Messegeschenk.
fairly|situated günstig gelegen;
   to represent ~ **the financial position of a company** finanzielle Lage einer Gesellschaft richtig wiedergeben.
fairness Kulanz, (price) Angemessenheit;
   in ~ anständigerweise.
fairstead Messestand.
fairtime Messezeit.
fairway (mar.) Fahrwasser, -rinne.
fairy tale Märchen.
fairy-tale country Märchenland.
fairyland Wunderland, Zauberland.
fait accompli vollendete Tatsache.
faith Vertrauen, (fidelity) Redlichkeit, Pflichttreue, (rel.) Glaubensbekenntnis;
   in bad ~ bös-, schlechtgläubig, **in good** ~ in gutem Glauben, gutgläubig, auf Treu und Glauben;
   bad ~ Bösgläubigkeit; **full** ~ **and credit** (US) volle Anerkennung; **good** ~ guter Glaube, Treu und Glauben, Redlichkeit; **full** ~ **in business policy** Treu und Glauben im Geschäftsverkehr;
   to act in good ~ gutgläubig handeln; **to break s. one's** ~ jds. Vertrauen mißbrauchen; **to keep one's** ~ sein Wort halten; **to plead one's good** ~ sich auf seinen guten Glauben berufen; **to pledge one's** ~ sein Versprechen geben; **to put** ~ **in s. th.** einer Sache Glauben schenken;
   ~ **healing** Gesundbeten.
faithful pflichttreu, gewissenhaft, (story) wahrheitsgetreu;
   ~ **copy** zuverlässige Abschrift; ~**description** genaue Beschreibung; ~ **reproduction** genaue Wiedergabe; ~ **translation** wortgetreue Übersetzung.
faithfully yours hochachtungsvoll.
faithfulness Pflichttreue.
fake Nachahmung, Falsifikat, Fälschung, (product) Imitation;
   ~ (v.) nachahmen, imitieren, fälschen, (produce) aus schlechtem Material herstellen;
   ~ **a balance sheet** Bilanz fälschen (verschleiern, frisieren); ~ **a business report** Geschäftsbericht fälschen; ~ **a newspaper article** Zeitungsartikel zurechtschustern; ~ **up** frisieren, zurechtmachen;
   ~ (a.) nachgemacht, gefälscht;
   ~ **check customer** (US) Scheckfälscher; ~ **coin** falsche Münze; ~ **picture** Fälschung.
faked|balance sheet frisierte Bilanz; ~ **up** gefälscht; ~ **up for sale** für den Verkauf zurechtgemacht (frisiert).
faker (coll.) Fälscher, (peddler) Trödler.
fakery Tricks.
fakir (US) Straßenhändler mit Billigware.

fall (autumn, US) Herbst, (building) Einsturz, Zusammenbruch, -fallen, (criminal, sl.) Einbuchtung, (downward trend) Niedergang, Zusammenbruch, (of prices) Fallen, Sinken, Sturz, Rückgang, (rain) Niederschlagsmenge, (slope) Gefälle, Neigung, (stock exchange) Kurssturz, -einbruch, Baisse;
heavy ~ (prices) scharfer Rückgang; **sharp** ~ starkes Gefälle; **sheer** ~ (prices) plötzlicher tiefer Preissturz; **sudden** ~ (stock exchange) Kurseinbruch, Kurssturz;
rise and ~ Aufstieg und Untergang;
~ **in the bank rate** Heruntergehen des Diskontsatzes, Diskontsenkung; ~ **in the birth rate** Geburtenrückgang, -abnahme; ~ **of the currency** Geldentwertung; ~ **in demand** nachlassende Nachfrage, Nachfragerückgang, Auftragsrückgang; ~ **of the dollar** Dollarsturz; ~ **of an empire** Zusammenbruch eines Reiches; ~ **in employment** Beschäftigungsrückgang; ~ **in exports** Ausfuhr-, Exportrückgang; ~ **in fertility** Fruchtbarkeitsrückgang; ~ **of the government** Sturz der Regierung, ~ **of the hammer** Zuschlag; ~ **in interest rates** Zinsrückgang; ~ **in investment** Investitionsrückgang; ~ **of life** Herbst des Lebens; ~ **in population** Bevölkerungsabnahme, -rückgang; ~ **of potential** (el.) Spannungsabfall; ~ **in prices** Preis-, Kursrückgang, Kurssturz, Preisverfall, rückläufige Preistendenz; ~ **in production** Produktionsrückgang; ~ **in profits** Gewinnrückgang, -abnahme; **heavy** ~ **of rain** starke Regenfälle; ~ **of rents** Kursrückgang der Staatspapiere; ~ **in sales** Verkaufs-, Umsatzrückgang; ~ **in stocks** Weichen der Kurse, Kursrückgang; ~ **of temperature** Temperatursturz; ~ **in value** Wertrückgang; ~ **in the value of money** Geldwertverlust; ~ **in wages** Lohnabschwächung;
~ (v.) sich vermindern, abnehmen, fallen, sinken, (building) einstürzen, zusammenbrechen, einfallen, (criminal, sl.) eingebuchtet werden, (fortress) genommen werden, (government) gestürzt werden, (prices) fallen, stürzen, Rückgang (Kurseinbruch) erfahren, zurückgehen, (in war) im Kampf umkommen;
~ **aboard** (ships) zusammenstoßen; ~ **among thieves** unter die Räuber geraten; ~ **asunder** entzweigehen; ~ **back** (mil.) zurückweichen; ~ **back upon a forest** (mil.) sich in einen Wald zurückziehen; ~ **back on lies** zu Lügen seine Zuflucht nehmen; ~ **back upon s. th.** Rückhalt an etw. haben; **to have a sum put by to** ~ **back upon** auf Ersparnisse zurückgreifen können; ~ **behind** im Rückstand sein, ins Hintertreffen geraten; ~ **behind with one's correspondence** Briefschulden haben; ~ **behind with one's payments** mit seinen Zahlungen in Rückstand geraten; ~ **behind with one's rent** Miete schuldig bleiben; ~ **behind with one's work** Arbeitsrückstände haben; ~ **by the wayside** auf der Strecke bleiben; ~ **down** ein-, zusammenstürzen, einfallen, (fig.) Schiffbruch erleiden; ~ **down in the job** (coll.) beruflich versagen; ~ **due** fällig werden, verfallen; ~ **flat** nicht ankommen; ~ **for s. o.** für j. schwärmen; ~ **foul of** (ship) Kollision haben; ~ **foul of each other** sich in die Haare geraten; ~ **from one's position** seine Stellung verlieren; ~ **heir to s. th.** etw. erben; ~ **to the heirs on the father's side** der väterlichen Seite zufallen; ~ **ill** krank werden; ~ **in** einfallen, einstürzen, (bill of exchange) verfallen, (lease) ablaufen; ~ **in for s. th.** erbberechtigt werden, etw. erben; ~ **in with an arrangement** einem Vergleich zustimmen; ~ **in esteem** allgemeine Achtung (an Wertschätzung) verlieren; ~ **in with s. one's opinion** sich jds. Meinung anschließen; ~ **in price** Preis-, Kursrückgang erleiden; ~ **in with a request** Gesuch genehmigen; ~ **in a subject** in ein Gebiet fallen; ~ **in value** im Wert fallen, entwertet werden; ~ **in with s. one's view at once** mit jem. sofort übereinstimmen; ~ **into conversation** ins Gespräch kommen; ~ **into difficulties** in Schwierigkeiten geraten; ~ **into disuse** außer Gebrauch kommen; ~ **into a habit** Gewohnheit annehmen, sich angewöhnen; ~ **into the hands of s. o.** plötzlich unter jds. Kontrolle geraten; ~ **into line with** (fig.) konform gehen; ~ **into poverty** in Armut geraten, völlig verarmen; **not** ~ **into s. one's province** nicht zu jds. Zuständigkeit gehören; ~ **into a title** Erbschaft antreten; ~ **into a trap** in eine Falle geraten; ~ **off** sich nachteilig verändern, abnehmen, geringer werden, zurückgehen, nachlassen, (plane) abrutschen, (receipts) sich vermindern; ~ **off in quality** sich verschlechtern, in der Qualität nachlassen; ~ **on s. o.** (expenses) zu jds. Lasten gehen; ~ **directly on to the consumer** Verbraucher unmittelbar treffen; ~ **on evil days** laufend Pech haben; ~ **on one's face** (fig.) auf die Nase fallen; ~ **on one's feet** (fig.) immer auf die Füße fallen; ~ **on hard times** schwierige Zeiten durchstehen müssen; ~ **out of favo(u)r** in Ungnade fallen; ~ **over s. o.** vor jem. kriechen; ~ **over backwards** (fig.) sich beinahe umbringen; ~ **over each other for a new book** sich zu Dutzenden um einen Verlagsvertrag für ein neues Buch bemühen; ~ **over o. s. for the services of s. o.** sich ein Bein für j. ausreißen; ~ **short**

knapp werden; ~ **short in one's duty** seine Pflicht nicht hinlänglich erfüllen; ~ **short of expectations** Erwartungen nicht erfüllen; ~ **short of provisions** nicht genügend Lebensmittel haben; ~ **short of reality** weit hinter der Realität zurückbleiben; ~ **through** ins Wasser fallen (plan) mißlingen; **to s. one's share** jem. bei der Teilung zufallen; ~ **to work again** Arbeit wiederaufnehmen; ~ **under another category** unter eine andere Kategorie fallen; ~ **under the statute of limitations** der Verjährung unterliegen; ~ **under suspicion** in Verdacht geraten; ~ **upon s. o.** auf j. entfallen; ~ **vacant** vakant (frei) werden, unbesetzt sein; ~ **victim to a cost-reduction program(me)** Opfer eines Sparsamkeitsprogramms werden; ~ **within an agreement** unter einen Vertrag fallen; ~ **within article 5** in Paragraph 5 geregelt sein; ~ **within the budget** haushaltsrechtlich genehmigt sein; ~ **within a definition** unter eine Bestimmung fallen;

to be on the ~ (prices) fallen, sinken, weichen; **to be likely to** ~ (prices) zur Schwäche neigen; **to buy on a** ~ fixen, während der Baisse kaufen; **to cause a** ~ **in prices** auf die Kurse drücken; **to deal (go to, operate, speculate for) a** ~ auf Baisse spekulieren, konterminieren; **to get a** ~ **out of s. th.** (US) sich das Beste heraussuchen; **to have a sum put by to** ~ **back upon** sich einen Notgroschen als Reserve zurückgelegt haben; **to have s. o. to** ~ **back on** Rückhalt an jem. haben; **to purchase for a** ~ auf Baisse kaufen; **to ride for a** ~ (minister) auf den Rücktritt zusteuern; **to speculate for a** ~ konterminieren; **to take a** ~ **out of s. th.** (US coll.) sich das Beste aussuchen;

~**-back pay** (pieceworker) garantierter Mindestlohn, (dock worker, Br.) Anwesenheitsgeld; ~ **fashion** (US) Herbstmode; ~ **flat advertising** verpuffte Werbung; ~ **guy** (US sl.) Sündenbock; ~**-off in the economy** Konjunkturrückgang; ~**-off in imports** Einfuhrrückgang; ~**-off in new orders** Auftragsrückgang; ~ **merchandise** (US) Herbstartikel; ~ **registration at the school** (US) im Herbst erfolgende Schulanmeldungen.

fallacious trügerisch, irreführend.

fallacy Trugschluß;
popular ~ weitverbreiteter Irrtum.

fallen building clause Risikoausschluß bei Gebäudeeinsturz.

falling Fallen, Sinken, (party politics) Abfall;
~ **away** (party) Abfall; ~ **of the birth rate** Geburtenrückgang; ~ **of prices** Sinken der Preise; ~ **in sales** Absatz-, Umsatzrückgang;
~ (a.) sinkend, fallend, (market) rückgängig, -läufig;
to be ~ (prices) fallen;
~ **market** Baissemarkt; ~ **prices** weichende Kurse; ~ **short** Unzulänglichkeit.

falling-off (prices) Nieder-, Rückgang;
slight ~ leichter Rückgang;
~ **of business** Geschäftsrückgang; ~ **of orders** Auftragsrückgang; ~ **in sales** Abschwächung des Umsatzes, Absatz-, Umsatzrückgang.

fallout radioaktives Abfallmaterial, radioaktive Ausschüttung.

fallow brachliegendes Land;
to allow land to lie ~ Land brach liegen lassen;
~ **crop** Brachernte.

false falsch, unrichtig, (document) gefälscht, (faulty) fehlerhaft, (illegal) unrechtmäßig, rechtswidrig, (sham) nachgemacht, unecht;
to be ~ **to one's husband** Ehegatten hintergehen; **to be false to one's word** Versprechen nicht halten; **to play s. o.** ~ falsches Spiel mit jem. treiben;
~ **accounts** falsche Angaben; ~ **accusation** Falschanschuldigung; ~ **action** Scheinklage; ~ **alarm** blinder Alarm, falsche Meldung; ~ **answer** (pleading) bewußt falsches Klagevorbringen; ~ **arrest** unberechtigte Festnahme, Freiheitsberaubung; ~ **attack** Scheinangriff, Finte; ~ **balance sheet** gefälschte (frisierte) Bilanz; ~ **billing** (transportation business) falsche Gewichtsangabe; ~ **bottom** doppelter Boden; ~ **call** Fehlalarm; ~ **call rate** (alarm system) Fehlalarmprozentsatz; ~ **character** (Br.) Fälschung eines Arbeitszeugnisses; ~ **check** (US) (cheque, Br.) gefälschter Scheck; ~ **claim** unbegründete Forderung, unberechtigter Anspruch; ~ **coin** Falschgeld; ~ **coiner** Falschmünzer; ~ **coining** Falschmünzerei, Münzfälschung; ~ **colo(u)r** (fig.) betrügerische Aufmachung; **to sail under** ~ **colo(u)rs** (ship) unter falscher Flagge segeln, (fig.) seine wahren Motive verbergen; ~ **demonstration** falsche (unrichtige) Erklärung; ~ **door** blinde Tür; ~ **entry** Falschbuchung, Buchfälschung; ~ **evidence** Falschaussage; **to give** ~ **evidence** falsch aussagen; ~ **fact** (law of evidence) simulierte Tatsache; ~ **financial statement** falsche Bilanzerklärung; ~ **front** falsche Fassade, (sl.) Blendwerk; ~ **imprisonment** Freiheitsberaubung; ~ **instrument** gefälschte Urkunde; **to put a** ~ **interpretation on s.**

th. falsche (unrichtige) Auslegung von etw. vornehmen; ~ **issue** (counsel) irreführende Klagebegründung; ~ **judgment** Fehlurteil, unrichtiges Urteil; **to spread** ~ **news** Falschmeldungen verbreiten; ~ **lights and signals** irreführende Schiffssignale; ~ **making** (forgery) Fälschung; ~ **modesty** falsche Bescheidenheit; **to put** ~ **money in circulation** Falschgeld in Umlauf bringen; ~ **news** Falschmeldung; ~ **oath** Falscheid; ~ **papers** (banking) Kreditunterlagen mit gefälschten Angaben, (naut.) falsche Schiffspapiere; ~ **personnation** Annahme eines falschen Namens, Personenstandsfälschung; ~ **plea** verzögerndes Gegenvorbringen; **to be in a** ~ **position** auf der falschen Seite stehen; ~ **pretences** Vorspiegelung falscher Tatsachen; ~ **report** Falschmeldung; ~ **representation** vorsätzliche Täuschung; ~ **return** unrichtige Einkommensteuererklärung; ~ **start** Fehlstart; ~ **statement** falsche Angabe, (balancing) gefälschte Finanzaufstellung; ~ **and misleading statement** Vorspiegelung falscher Tatsachen; **to take a** ~ **step** Fehltritt tun; ~ **swearing** (Br.) Mein-, Falscheid, Eidesverletzung; ~ **take-off** (airplane) Fehlstart; ~ **tears** Krokodiltränen; ~ **token** (criminal law) gefälschte Urkunde; ~ **trade description** falsche Warenbezeichnung; ~ **verdict** Fehlurteil; ~ **weights** falsche Maße und Gewichte; ~ **witness** Falschaussage; **to bear** ~ **witness** falsches Zeugnis ablegen; ~ **words** (last will) Fehlbezeichnung.

falsehood vorsätzliche Unwahrheit;
injurious ~ Ruf-, Kreditschädigung;
~, **fraud and wilful imposition** (Scot.) Betrug;
to spread all sorts of ~ **about s. o.** jem. alles nur möglich Schlechte nachsagen.

falsely | impersonate (v.) Personenstandsfälschung begehen; ~ **represent o. s. to be a person holding office under Her Majesty** (Br.) Amtsanmaßung begehen.

falsework Lehrgerüst.

falsification Fälschung, (confutation) Widerlegung, (proving of errors) Nachweis eines falschen Rechnungspostens, (record) Urkundenfälschung, Falschbeurkundung;
~ **of accounts** (books) Fälschung von Rechnungsbüchern (Geschäftsunterlagen), Bücherfälschung, Kontenfälschung; ~ **of a balance sheet** Fälschung einer Bilanz, Bilanzfälschung; ~ **of competition** Wettbewerbsverzerrung; ~ **of documents** Urkundenfälschung; ~ **of a registry** Falschbeurkundung; ~ **of a statement** Widerlegung einer Erklärung.

falsificator Fälscher.

falsified | note gefälschte Banknote; ~ **signature** gefälschte Unterschrift.

falsifier Urkundenfälscher, (counterfeit) Falschmünzer.

falsify (v.) nachahmen, -machen, fälschen, verfälschen, Fälschung anfertigen, widerlegen, als falsch nachweisen, (disprove) Urteil als falsch hinstellen;
~ **the accounts** Bücher (Abrechnungen) fälschen; ~ **business records** Fälschungen in den Geschäftsbüchern vornehmen; ~ **an item in an account** Rechnungsposten fälschen; ~ **records** Urkunden [ver]fälschen; ~ **a story** Geschichte falsch wiedergeben.

falsifying a record Urkundenfälschung.

falter Schwanken, Zögern;
~ (v.) schwanken, zögern, (boom) nachlassen, abklingen;
~ **an excuse** Entschuldigung stammeln.

fame [guter] Ruf, Ruhm, Berühmtheit;
of ill ~ übelbeleumdet, berüchtigt;
literary ~ Schriftstellerruhm;
to seek ~ berühmt werden wollen.

famed berühmt, bekannt;
to become ~ **as a weather prophet** als erfolgreicher Wetterprophet gelten.

familiar Vertrauter, sehr guter Bekannter;
~ (a.) vertraut, wohlbekannt, familiär, vertraulich, (at ease) ungezwungen, intim, zwanglos;
ever ~ altbekannt; **too** ~ aufdringlich, zudringlich;
to be ~ **to** geläufig sein; **to be thoroughly** ~ **with s. th.** sich genau in etw. auskennen; **to be** ~ **with all office routine** mit allen Büroarbeiten vertraut sein; **to become** ~ **with s. th.** sich in etw. einarbeiten; **to make o. s.** ~ **with a language** sich mit einer Sprache vertraut machen;
~ **friend** enger Freund; **to be on** ~ **ground** sich in vertrauten Gefilden bewegen; ~ **quotation** geflügeltes Wort; **to have a** ~ **ring** sich bekannt anhören; ~ **spirit** Familiensinn, -geist; **to be on** ~ **terms with s. o.** sich mit jem. gut (auf vertrautem Fuß mit jem.) stehen, j. näher kennen.

familiarity Bekanntschaft, (easiness) Ungezwungenheit, familiärer Umgang, Vertrautheit, Zwanglosigkeit;
~ **with the law** Gesetzeskenntnis.

familiarization period Einarbeitungszeit.
familiarize *(v.)* sich einarbeiten;
~ **o. s. with s. th.** sich mit etw. vertraut machen; ~ **a new word** neues Wort einbürgern; ~ **o. s. with a foreign language** sich an eine Fremdsprache gewöhnen.
family Familie, Haushalt, *(lineage)* Herkommen, Abkunft, *(tribe)* Vorfahren, Stamm, Sippe, Geschlecht;
of good ~ aus gutem Hause; **of no special** ~ nicht zu einer bekannten Familie gehörend;
extended ~ *(sociology)* Großfamilie; **large** ~ kinderreiche Familie; **long-established** ~ alt-, erbeingesessene Familie; **my** ~ meine Angehörigen; **needy** ~ fürsorgebedürftige (unterstützungsbedürftige) Familie; **public-aid** ~ Sozialhilfe beziehende Familie; **rehoused** ~ umquartierte Familie; **respectable** ~ angesehene Familie; **two-person** ~ zweiköpfige Familie; **typical average** ~ Indexfamilie; **upper-income** ~ Familie mit höherem Einkommen; **whole** ~ ganze Familie;
~ **with dependent children** Familie mit in der Ausbildung befindlichen Kindern; ~ **dependent upon s. o. for support** unterhaltsberechtigte Familie; ~ **next door** benachbarte Familie; ~**-of-five** *(US)* fünfköpfige Familie; ~ **of languages** Sprachgruppe; ~ **of nations** Völkerfamilie; ~ **of great politicians** große Politikerfamilie; ~ **on relief** Sozialhilfe empfangende Familie; **to be in the possession of a** ~ im Familienbesitz sein; **to be one of the** ~ zur Familie gehören; **to belong to a** ~ **of good standing** zu einer guten Familie gehören; **to come of a good** ~ aus gutem Hause sein; **to force one's** ~ **on the town** *(US)* seine Familie auf die Fürsorge angewiesen sein lassen; **to have no life apart from one's** ~ ganz in seiner Familie aufgehen; **to maintain one's** ~ für seine Familie arbeiten, seine Familie unterhalten; **to utterly neglect one's** ~ seine Familie der Gefahr des Notstands aussetzen; **to provide for a large** ~ große Familie unterhalten; **to raise a** ~ Familie aufziehen; **to receive s. o. into his** ~ j. in seine Familie aufnehmen; **to return to the** ~ an die Familie zurückfallen; **to run in the** ~ in der Familie liegen, Familieneigenschaft sein; **to support a** ~ Lebensunterhalt einer Familie sicherstellen;
~ **accounting** Familienhaushaltsrechnung; ~ **affair** Familienangelegenheit; ~ **agency** *(US)* Eheberatungsstelle; ~ **allowance** *(Br.)* Familienzuschlag, -beihilfe, -zulage, -unterstützung, Kindergeld, *(US)* aus dem Nachlaß zu zahlender Unterhalt; ᵉ **Allowance Act** *(Br.)* Kindergeldgesetz; ~ **allowance deduction** *(Br.)* Kindergeldabzug; ~ **allowance scheme** *(Br.)* Kindergeldschema; ~ **appeal** *(advertising)* Ansprechen des Familiengefühls; ~ **archive** Familienarchiv; ~ **argument** Familienstreit; ~ **arrangement** Familienabkommen, Erbvertrag; ~ **assistance** Familienhilfe, -unterstützung; ~ **assistance program(me)** Familienbeihilfeprogramm; ~ **automobile** Familienauto, -fahrzeug; ~ **automobile doctrine** Kfz-Halterhaftung für Familienangehörige; ~ **background** Familienverhältnisse; ~ **benefit** *(New Zealand)* Familienbeihilfe, -unterstützung; ~ **bible** Hausbibel mit Familieneintragungen; ~ **bill** *(Br.)* Kindergeldgesetz; ~ **brand** Dachmarke; ~ **budget** Familienhaushaltsplan; ~ **business** Familienbetrieb, -unternehmen; ~**-buying power** Einkaufskraft einer Familie; ~ **car** Familienkutsche; ~ **car rule** Kfz-Halterhaftung für Familienangehörige; ~ **care** Familienfürsorge; ~ **casework** Familienfürsorge; ~ **casework agencies** Familienfürsorgeeinrichtungen; ~ **circle** Familienkreis, *(theater)* obere Galerie; ~ **commitments** Familienverpflichtungen; ~ **compact** Familienabkommen; ~ **company** Familiengesellschaft; ~ **composition** Zusammensetzung einer Familie; ~ **contract** Erbauseinandersetzungsvertrag; ~ **corporation** Familiengesellschaft; ~ **council** Familienrat; ~ **court** *(Br.)* Familiengericht; ~ **doctor** Hausarzt; ~ **dwelling** Familienwohnung; ~ **dynasty** Familiendynastie; **to be** ~**-employed** als mithelfendes Familienmitglied tätig sein; ~ **environment** durch die Familie bestimmte Umweltverhältnisse, häusliches Milieu; ~ **equalization fund** Familienausgleichskasse; ~ **estate** Familienbesitz, -gut, -vermögen; ~ **expenses** Haushaltungskosten; ~ **expenditure survey** *(Br.)* Indexvergleich der Familienlebensunterhaltskosten; ~ **firm** Familienbetrieb, -unternehmen; ~ **gathering** Familientreffen, -zusammenkunft; ~ **group** *(motorcar insurance)* Haushaltsangehörige; ~ **head** Familienoberhaupt; ~ **history** Familiengeschichte; ~ **holdings** Familienbesitz; ~ **hotel** Familienpension; ~ **house** Einfamilienhaus; ~ **household** Familienhaushalt; ~ **income** Familieneinkommen; ~ **income supplement** *(Br.)* Existenzminimumzuschuß; ~ **industry** Hauswirtschaft; ~ **insurance** Familienversicherung; ~ **jewels** Familienschmuck; ~ **law** Familienrecht; ᵉ **Law Reform Act** *(Br.)* Gesetz zur Reform des Familienrechts; ~ **lawyer** Familienanwalt; ~ **likeness** *(packaging)* Stilgleichheit bei der Verpackung; ~ **limitation** Begrenzung der Kinderzahl; ~ **lines** *(railway)* gemeinsam verwaltete Eisenbahngesellschaften; **to trace back one's** ~ **line** seinen Familienstammbaum zurückverfolgen; ~ **living** *(Br.)* Familienpfründe; ~ **living accommodation** Familienwohnung; ~ **magazine** Familienzeitschrift, Unterhaltungsmagazin; ~ **man** typischer Familienvater; **to be a** ~ **man** nur für seine Familie da sein; ~ **medical history** Familienkrankheiten; ~ **meeting** Familienrat; ~ **member** Angehöriger; ~ **minimum existence** Existenzminimum für eine Familie; ~ **name** Familienname; ~ **needs** Familienbedürfnisse; ~**-orientated** familienfreundlich; ~**-owned enterprise** Familienbetrieb; ~ **partnership** Familienunternehmen, -gesellschaft; ~ **passage** Familienüberführung; ~ **planning** Geburtenplanung, -regelung, Kinderzahlbegrenzung; **to provide** ~ **planning service and advice** bei der Familienplanung mit Rat und Tat zur Seite stehen; **free** ~ **passage** kostenlose Beförderung der Familienangehörigen; ~ **physician** Hausarzt; ~ **comprehensive high-ticket** ~ **policy** hochwertige Familienpauschalversicherung; ~ **pool** Familienstiftung; ~ **portrait** Ahnenbild; ~ **practitioner** Hausarzt; ~ **premium** Familienprämie; ~ **property** Familienvermögen; ~ **protection** Versorgung für Familienangehörige; ~ **provision** *(Br.)* gerichtlich festgesetzter Pflichtteil; ~ **purpose doctrine** Kfz-Halterhaftung für Familienangehörige; **to be unfit for** ~ **reading** sich zur Familienlektüre nicht eignen; ᵉ **Reform Act** *(Br.)* Volljährigkeitsänderungsgesetz; ~ **relation** Familienbeziehung; ~ **relocation** Umsiedlung einer Familie; ~ **research panel** Haushaltspanel; ~ **resemblance** Familienähnlichkeit; ~ **room** *(US)* Freizeitzimmer; ~ **row** Familienstreitigkeit; ~**-run concern** Familienunternehmen; ~ **saga** Familienroman; ~ **seat** Familiengut; ~ **sedan** Familienkutsche; ~ **service** Familienbetreuung; ~ **service rule** Kfz-Halterhaftung für Familienangehörige; ~ **settlement** *(Br.)* Erbauseinandersetzung, Abfindungs-, Erbeinsetzungsvertrag, Familienstiftung; ~ **situations** Familienereignisse; ~ **size** Familiengröße; ~ **size package** *(goods)* Groß-, Haushaltspackung; ~**-sized farm** *(US)* landwirtschaftlicher Familienbetrieb; ~ **skeleton** dunkler Punkt in der Familiengeschichte, Familienschande; ~ **status** Familienstand; ~ **ticket** Familienfahrschein; ~ **ties** Familienbande, -bindung; ~ **tree** Ahnentafel, Stammbaum; ~ **unit** *(unity)* Familieneinheit;; ~ **use** privater Verbrauch; ~ **vault** Erbbegräbnis; **to lay in the** ~ **vault** in der Familiengruft beisetzen; ~ **wage** Familienstandslohn; **in a** ~ **way** ungezwungen; **to be in the** ~ **way** in anderen Umständen sein; ~ **welfare** Familienfürsorge; **to do** ~ **work** Hausarbeit verrichten.
famine Hungersnot, Versorgungslücke;
coal ~ Kohlenmangel; **water** ~ Wassermangel;
~ **price** Wucherpreis; ~ **relief** Behebung der Versorgungsschwierigkeiten.
famish *(v.)* [fast] verhungern;
~ **a town** Stadt aushungern.
fan Fächer, *(enthusiastic devotee)* begeisterter Anhänger, Fan, *(technics)* Ventilator;
~ *(v.)* **deliberately** absichtlich schüren; ~ **the flame** *(fig.)* Leidenschaften entflammen; ~ **out** sich fächerförmig verbreiten, *(mil.)* ausschwärmen;
~ **aerial** Fächerantenne; ~ **club** Fanklub; ~ **delta** Schwemmdelta; ~ **driving** Ventilatorantrieb; ~ **jet engine** Stahltriebwerk; ~ **letters (mail)** Verehrerbriefe; ~ **marker** Markierungssender.
fanatic Fanatiker;
fresh-air ~ Frischluftanhänger.
fanciful trade name Phantasiebezeichnung.
fancy Phantasie, *(imagination)* Einbildung, Vorstellung, *(imaginary notion)* Eingebung, Einhalt, *(pet pursuit)* Vorliebe, Gefallen, Interesse, *(whim)* Schrulle, Laune;
a passing ~ kurzfristige Attraktion;
~ **for** lebhaftes Interesse für;
~ *(v.)* **o. s.** sich wichtig vorkommen, große Stücke von sich halten; ~ **o. s. as a speaker** sich für einen guten Redner halten; **to catch s. one's** ~ jds. Interesse erwecken; **to indulge one's** ~ einer Marotte nachgehen; **to take a** ~ **to s. th.** Gefallen an etw. finden; **to take the** ~ **of the public** beim Publikum Anklang finden, große Anziehungskraft auf das Publikum ausüben;
~ **article** Modeware, Mode-, Luxusartikel, modisches Produkt; ~ **ball** Kostümball; ~ **bread** Spezialbrot; ~ **business** Modegeschäft; ~ **dress [costume]** Maskenkostüm; ~**-dress ball** Kostüm-, Maskenball; ~ **fair** Modemesse; ~ **frame** *(US)* Zierrand; ~**-free** frei und ungebunden; ~ **goods** Galanterie-, Luxuswaren, Modeartikel; ~ **man** Zuhälter; ~ **name** Phantasiename; ~ **packaging** Luxuspackung; ~**-packed (in** ~ **packing)** in feiner Ausstattung; ~ **paper** Dekorations-, Luxuspapier; ~ **price** Phantasie-, Liebhaberpreis, Affektionswert; ~ **stocks** *(US)*

unsichere Spekulationspapiere; ~ **type** Zier-, Künstlerschrift; ~ **value** Liebhaberwert; ~ **woman** Mätresse; ~ **woods** Furnier-, Edelholz; ~ **word** *(trademark)* Phantasiewort.

fancymonger Modeschöpfer.

fancywork feine Handarbeit.

fanfare *(fig.)* Getue, Theater;
with ~ mit großem Trara.

fanfold form Leporellofalzung.

fanout Kontenausgleich.

fantasy Phantasie, Traumgebilde, Hirngespenst.

far fern, entfernt, weit gelegen;
to carry a joke too ~ mit einem Scherz zu weit gehen; **to carry modesty too** ~ seine Bescheidenheit übertreiben; **to go too** ~ zu weit gehen; **to go** ~ **towards overcoming s. one's financial troubles** jds. finanzielle Schwierigkeiten weitgehend beheben; **to go** ~ **towards making up for s. one's loss** jds. Verlust weitgehend decken; **not to go very** ~ **nowadays** heute nicht gerade viel ermöglichen; **to have gone too** ~ **to withdraw** sich zu weit vorgewagt haben; **to make one's money go** ~ mit seinem Geld lange auskommen; **to search** ~ **and wide for a missing child** überall nach einem verlorengegangenem Kind suchen;
~**-away times** vergangene Zeiten; **to be a** ~ **cry from** *(fig.)* weit entfernt sein von.

Far East Ferner Osten, Fernost.

Far Eastern | correspondent Fernostkorrespondent; ~ **policy** Fernostpolitik.

far | -fetched weit hergeholt, an den Haaren herbeigezogen; ~**flung activities** umfassender Wirkungskreis; ~**-off city** abgelegene Stadt; ~**-off cousin** weitläufig Verwandter; **to have a** ~**-reaching influence** über weitreichende Verbindungen verfügen; ~**-reaching proposals** folgenschwere Vorschläge; ~ **relations** entfernte Verwandte; ~**-sighted** weitblickend, umsichtig.

farce *(sl.)* Schwindel, Theater, *(theater)* Posse, Schwank;
knock-about ~ derbe Posse.

farcial | accusation absurde Beschuldigung; ~ **examination** geradezu lächerliches Examen; ~ **play** Possenspiel.

fare Fahrgeld, -preis, Passagier-, Überfahrtsgeld, *(food)* Kost, Nahrung, Speise, *(passenger carrier)* Fahrgast, Passagier, *(plane)* Flugpreis;
at a reduced ~ zu ermäßigtem Fahrpreis; **for no extra** ~ ohne zusätzliche Kosten, ohne Zuschlag;
~**s** Verkehrsausgaben, *(taxi driver)* Fuhren, Fahrten;
adult ~ Erwachsenenfahrkarte; **advanced purchase excursion** ~**s** *(Apex)* Ferientarif mit Vorausbuchung; **air[line]** ~ Flugpreis, -schein; **bargain-tour** ~ verbilligter Fahrpreis; **cheap** ~ verbilligter Fahrpreis; **excess** ~ Zusatzfahrschein, Fahrpreiszuschlag; **excursion** ~**s** Rundreise, Ausflugstarif; **full** ~ Fahrkarte zum vollen Fahrpreis, voller Fahrpreis; **half** ~ halber Fahrpreis, Fahrkarte zum halben Preis; **homely** ~ Hausmannskost; **low-cost** ~ billige Fahrkarte; **low seasonal** ~ ermäßigter Fahrpreis außerhalb der Saison; **meagre** ~ magere Kost; **minimum** ~ *(railway)* Mindestfahrpreis; **off-season** ~ Nachsaisonfahrschein; **ordinary** ~ Hausmannskost; **passenger** ~ Personentarif; **plain** ~ Hausmannskost; **plane** ~ Flugpreis; **railroad** ~ Eisenbahnfahrkarte; **reduced** ~**s** Fahrpreisermäßigung; **return** ~ *(Br.)* Rückfahrschein, -fahrkarte; **rock-bottom, no-amenities** ~ Billigflugpreisticket ohne Bordservice; **round-trip excursion** ~**s** Rundreise-, Ausflugstarif; **single** ~ Einzelfahrkarte, -preis, einfacher Fahrpreis; **standby** ~ kurz vor dem Abflug angebotener, verbilligter Flugschein; **supplemental** ~ Fahrpreiszuschlag;
budget ~ **on scheduled airlines** *(US)* Billigflugkarten für Linienflugzeuge;
all ~**s, please** Fahrkarten vorzeigen;
~ *(v.)* **badly** sich schlecht stehen; ~ **out** in die Welt hinausziehen; ~ **poorly** schlecht abschneiden;
to be fond of good ~ kein Kostverächter sein; **to have had only six** ~**s this day** *(taxi driver)* nur sechs Kunden am Tag gehabt haben; **to make money with** ~**s close to charter levels** mit an Charterpreisen angenäherten Flugtickets Geschäfte machen; **to pay one's** ~ seine Fahrkarte bezahlen; **to pay full** ~ vollen Fahrpreis bezahlen; **to tender the exact** ~ Fahrgeld abgezählt bereithalten;
~ **category** Fahrpreiskategorie; ~ **hike (increase)** Fahrpreiserhöhung; ~**s package** gebündeltes Flugkartenangebot; ~ **payments** Fahr- und Wegegelder; ~ **reduction** Fahrpreisermäßigung; ~ **schedule** Fahrpreisanzeiger; ~ **stage** *(Br.)* Fahrpreiszone, Tarifgrenze, Teilstrecke; ~ **structure** Fahrpreisgefüge; ~ **system** Fahrscheinwesen; **full-** ~ **ticket** Fahrkarte zum vollen Preis; **magnetically coded** ~ **ticket** durch Magnetcode verschlüsselte Fahrkarte.

farewell Abschied;
to bid s. o. ~ jem. Lebewohl sagen; **to bid an official** ~ **to s. o.** j. offiziell verabschieden;
~ **audience** Abschiedsaudienz; ~ **call** Abschiedsbesuch; ~ **celebration** Abschiedsfeier; ~ **dinner (party)** Abschiedsessen; ~ **letter** Abschiedsbrief; ~ **reception** Abschiedsempfang; ~ **speech** Abschiedsrede; ~ **visit** Abschiedsbesuch; ~ **words** Abschiedsworte.

farm landwirtschaftlicher Betrieb, Bauerngut, -hof, Pachthof, Farm, [Land]wirtschaft, Farm, *(building)* Guts-, Bauernhaus, *(taxation)* verpachteter Steuerbezirk;
dairy ~ Milchwirtschaft; **experimental** ~ Versuchsfarm; **factory** ~ industriell betriebene Landwirtschaft; **family-sized** ~ *(US)* von der Familie bewirtschafteter Bauernhof, landwirtschaftlicher Familienbetrieb; **home** ~ landwirtschaftlicher Eigenbetrieb; **leased** ~ Pachtgut; **highly mechanised and intensively cultivated** ~ vollmechanisierter und völlig durchorganisierter Landwirtschaftsbetrieb; **model** ~ Mustergut, -betrieb; **owner-operated** ~ *(US)* landwirtschaftlicher Eigenbetrieb; **oyster** ~ Austernzucht; **part-time** ~ landwirtschaftlicher Nebenbetrieb; **poultry** ~ Federvieh-, Geflügelzucht; **sprinkler-irrigated** ~ automatisch bewässerter Landwirtschaftsbetrieb; **submarginal** ~ landwirtschaftlicher Verlustbetrieb;
~ *(v.)* **(carry on farming)** Landwirtschaft betreiben, bebauen, wirtschaften, *(take on lease)* in Pacht nehmen, pachten;
~ **400 acres of land** 400 Morgen Land bewirtschaften; ~ **native labo(u)r** einheimische Arbeitskräfte dingen; ~ **land** Gut bewirtschaften; ~ **a lottery** Lotterieunternehmen pachten; ~ **out** verpachten, in Pacht geben, verdingen; ~ **out s. o.** jds. Unterhalt gegen Bezahlung einer Pauschale übernehmen; ~ **out children** Kinder gegen Bezahlung in Pflege geben; ~ **out composing** Satzarbeiten vergeben; ~ **out orders for many products** Aufträge in größerem Ausmaß produktionsmäßig verlagern; ~ **out to a consulting organization** an eine Beratungsfirma gegen Sonderhonorar vergeben; ~ **out a right to space in an exhibition** Ausstellungsraum vergeben; ~ **out taxes** Steuern verpachten; ~ **a tax** Steuer in Pacht nehmen;
to be brought up on a ~ auf dem Lande aufgewachsen sein; **to be settled on a** ~ auf einem Hof sitzen; **to let to** ~ in Pacht nehmen, pachten; **to manage (operate) a** ~ Bauernhof bewirtschaften; **to put s. o. into a** ~ jem. ein Pachtgut überlassen; **to work on a** ~ in der Landwirtschaft tätig sein;
~ **bailiff** *(Br.)* Gutsverwalter, Inspektor; ~ **bloc** Gruppe landwirtschaftlicher Interessenvertreter im Parlament, Grüne Front; ~ **boy** Landarbeiter; ~ **buildings** landwirtschaftliche Gebäude, Ökonomie-, Wirtschaftsgebäude; ~ **bureau** *(US)* Landwirtschaftsverband; ~ **concessions** landwirtschaftliche Tarifzugeständnisse; ~ **credit** Agrarkredit; ~ **Credit Administration** *(US)* Aufsichtsamt für Landwirtschaftskredite; ~ **credit agency** *(US)* landwirtschaftliches Kreditinstitut; ~ **credit system** *(US)* landwirtschaftliches Kreditwesen; ~ **crossing** niveaugleicher Bahnübergang; ~ **debtor** verschuldeter Landwirt; ~ **equipment** landwirtschaftliche Maschinen; ~ **family** Bauernfamilie; ~ **force** Landarbeiterschaft; ~ **implements** landwirtschaftliche Geräte (Maschinen); ~ **imports** Agrareinfuhren; ~ **importer** Importeur von Agrarerzeugnissen; ~ **income** Einkünfte aus der Landwirtschaft; ~ **labo(u)r** Landarbeit; ~ **labo(u)rer** Landarbeiter; ~ **labo(u)ring** Arbeit als landwirtschaftlicher Gehilfe; ~ **land** landwirtschaftliche Betriebsfläche, Flur-, Ackerland; ~ **lease** landwirtschaftlicher Pachtvertrag; ~**-lighting generator** Kleinaggregat; ~ **loan** Agrarkredit, Landwirtschaftskredit; ~ **loan bank** *(US)* landwirtschaftliche Genossenschaftsbank; ~ **loan bond** *(US)* Pfandbrief einer landwirtschaftlichen Genossenschaftsbank; ~ **losses** Verluste der Landwirtschaft; ~ **manager** *(US)* Gutsverwalter, -inspektor; ~ **management** *(US)* landwirtschaftliche Betriebsführung, Gutsbewirtschaftung; ~ **market** Markt für landwirtschaftliche Erzeugnisse; ~ **merger** Zusammenschluß von Landwirtschaftsbetrieben; ~ **minister** Landwirtschaftsminister; ~ **mortgage** Hypothek auf landwirtschaftlichen Grundbesitz; ~ **mortgage company** Realkreditinstitut; ~ **office** *(Br.)* Wirtschaftsgebäude; ~ **operation** Führung eines Landwirtschaftsbetriebes; ~ **output** landwirtschaftliche Produktion; ~ **place** Bauernhof; ~ **policy** Agrarpolitik; ~ **policy alignment** Anpassung der Agrarpolitik an die Europäische Gemeinschaft; ~ **prices** Preise landwirtschaftlicher Erzeugnisse, Agrarpreise; ~ **price level** Agrarpreisniveau; ~ **price support** *(US)* Stützung der Agrarpreise; ~ **produce (product)** landwirtschaftliches Erzeugnis, Agrarerzeugnis; ~ **production** Agrarproduktion; ~ **program(me)** [etwa] Grüner Plan; ~ **publication** landwirtschaftliches Fachblatt; ~ **real estate** Flur,

Ackerland, landwirtschaftliche Betriebsfläche, landwirtschaftlich genutztes Grundstück; ~ **road** Feldweg; ~ **servant** Hofknecht; ~ **stock** landwirtschaftliches Inventar, Viehbestand; ~ **subsidies** *(Br.)* Staatszuschüsse für den Ankauf landwirtschaftlicher Betriebe; ~ **surpluses** landwirtschaftliche Überschußprodukte; ~ **tenancy** Pacht eines Hofes; ~ **utensils** landwirtschaftliche Geräte; ~ **village** Bauerndorf; ~ **wages** Landarbeiterlöhne; ~ **wag(g)on** Ackerwagen; ~ **work** Feldarbeit; ~ **worker** Landarbeiter, landwirtschaftlicher Arbeiter.

farmer Bauer, Landwirt, Farmer, *(tenant)* Pächter;
baby ~ Kinderwärterin; **cattle** ~ Viehzüchter; **dairy** ~ Milchproduzent; **dirt** ~ Kleinbauer; **fruit** ~ Obstbauer; **house** ~ *(Br.)* Häusermakler; **oyster** ~ Austernzüchter; **produce-sharing** ~ Halbpächter; **sheep** ~ Schafzüchter; **stock** ~ Viehzüchter; **tenant** ~ Pächter; **tillage** ~ Landarbeiter;
~ **of revenues** Steuerpächter; ~ **working on shares** *(US)* Halbpächter;
to turn out a ~ Pächter abmeiern;
~**'s cooperative** landwirtschaftliche Genossenschaft, [etwa] Raiffeisenkasse; ~**'s institute** *(US)* landwirtschaftliches Institut; ~**s' movement** Bauernbewegung; **National** ⚷ **' Union** *(US)* Bauernverband.

farmery *(Br.)* Wirtschaftsgebäude.

farmhand *(US)* Knecht, Landarbeiter, landwirtschaftlicher Arbeiter.

farmhold Bauerngut.

farmholder *(US)* Gutsbesitzer.

farmhouse *(Br.)* Farm-, Bauern-, Gutshaus.

farming Acker-, Landwirtschaft, Ackerbau, *(leasing out)* [Ver]pachtung, Pachtbetrieb;
cottage ~ Kleinbauernbetrieb; **dairy** ~ Milchwirtschaft; **extensive (intensive)** ~ extensive (intensive) Bewirtschaftung; **fur** ~ Pelztierzucht; **large** ~ landwirtschaftlicher Großbetrieb; **mechanized** ~ mechanisierte Landwirtschaft; **poultry** ~ Geflügelzucht; **small** ~ landwirtschaftlicher Nebenbetrieb; **stock** ~ Viehzucht, -wirtschaft;
~ **on a large scale** landwirtschaftlicher Großbetrieb;
to be engaged in ~ Landwirtschaft betreiben;
~ *(a.)* landwirtschaftlich;
~ **association** landwirtschaftliche Genossenschaft; ~ **business** landwirtschaftliche Betriebsführung, Landwirtschaftsbetrieb; ~ **community** Dorfgemeinschaft; ~ **development loan** landwirtschaftlicher Erschließungskredit; ~ **implement** landwirtschaftliches Gerät; ~ **lease** Pachtvertrag; ~ **operations** landwirtschaftliche Tätigkeit; ~ **out** Verpachtung; ~ **products** landwirtschaftliche Erzeugnisse; ~ **purposes** landwirtschaftliche Zwecke; ~ **region** Landwirtschaftsgebiet; ~ **section of the population** selbstversorgender Bevölkerungsteil; ~ **stock** landwirtschaftliches Betriebsvermögen; ~ **utensils** landwirtschaftliche Geräte.

farmplace Bauernhof.

farmstead Bauernhof, -gut, Gehöft;
lonely ~ einsam gelegener Bauernhof;
~ **village** Bauerndorf.

farmtown *(Scot.)* Wirtschaftsgebäude.

farmwife Bauersfrau, Bäuerin.

farmyard Bauernhof, Guts-, Wirtschaftshof;
~ **buildings** Wirtschaftsgebäude.

farthing *(fig.)* Kleinigkeit.

fascicle Faszikel, *(part delivery)* Teillieferung.

fashion *(the elite)* die vornehme Welt, die oberen Zehntausend, *(form)* Form, Art, Gestalt, Sorte, *(good form)* [feine] Lebensart, -stil, Vornehmheit, *(style)* Mode, Zuschnitt;
according to the latest ~ nach der neuesten Mode; **after the** ~ nach Art (im Stil) von; **in** ~ modern; **in the latest** ~ nach dem neuesten Schnitt; **in its** ~ einigermaßen; **out of** ~ unmodern, veraltet; **in a roundabout** ~ auf Umwegen;
fall ~ *(US)* Herbstmode; **interseason** ~ Übergangsmode; **latest** ~ letzte Modeneuheit; **leading** ~ herrschende Mode; **present** ~ augenblickliche Mode; **prevailing** ~ überwiegende Mode; **rank and** ~ vornehme Welt; **rising** ~ kommende Mode; **summer** ~ Sommermode; **swift** ~ zügige Erledigung;
~**s in financing** modebedingte Finanzierungsmethoden; ~ **of the moment** augenblickliche Mode; ~ **of the period** gegenwärtige Mode;
~ *(v.)* zuschneiden, umarbeiten, modisch gestalten, nach der Mode verfertigen;
to be all the ~ neueste Mode (sehr beliebt) sein; **to be back in** ~ wieder in Mode sein; **to be the mirror of** ~ wie aus dem Modeheft geschnitten sein; **to behave in a strange** ~ sich seltsam aufführen; **to bring up a** ~ Mode aufbringen; **to change the** ~

der Mode eine andere Richtung geben; **to come into** ~ modern sein, günstige Aufnahme finden; **to come into** ~ **again** wieder aufkommen; **to come out of** ~ aus der Mode kommen; **to conform to the** ~ der Mode entsprechen; **to create a** ~ Mode aufbringen (kreieren); **to depend upon the** ~ der Mode unterworfen sein; **to do s. th. after a** ~ etw. nur oberflächlich tun; **to do s. th. army** ~ etw. mit militärischer Pünktlichkeit erledigen; **to do s. th. in a leisurely** ~ nach großmütterlicher Art erledigen; **to dress in the latest** ~ sich stets nach der neuesten Mode kleiden, modebewußt sein; **to follow the** ~ Mode mitmachen, sich nach der Mode richten, *(fig.)* der Zeitströmung folgen; **to get (go) out of** ~ unmodern werden; **to grow into** ~ modern werden; **to grow out of** ~ aus der Mode kommen; **to introduce a** ~ Mode aufbringen; **to lead (set) the** ~ [Mode] kreieren (bestimmen); **to speak in a rude** ~ sich eines groben Tons bedienen; **to strike out a new** ~ neue Mode aufbringen;
~ **adviser** Modeberater, -sachverständiger; ~ **articles** Modeware; ~ **artist** Modekünstler, -schöpfer; ~ **book** Modejournal; ~ **bureau** Modesalon; ~**-conscious** modebewußt; ~ **contrast** Modekontrast; ~ **design** Modezeichnung, -schöpfung; ~ **designer** Modeschöpfer; ~ **detail** modische Einzelheit; ~ **display** Modenschau; ~ **goods (items)** Modeartikel; ~ **house** Modesalon; ~ **house turnover** Umsätze der Modeindustrie; ~ **industry** Modeindustrie; ~ **journal** Modezeitschrift, -journal; ~ **knowledge** Modekenntnis; ~**-led** von der Mode beeinflußt; ~ **line** Modeartikel; ~ **look** geltende Mode; ~ **magazine** Modejournal, -zeitschrift; ~ **merchandise** Modeartikel; ~ **model** Modell; ~ **paper** Modezeitung, -journal; ~ **parade** Modenschau; ~ **pattern** Modezeichnung; ~ **photograph** Modefotograf; ~ **plate** Modebild, *(fig.)* Modepuppe; ~ **shift** Modeänderung; ~ **show** Modenschau; ~ **supplement** Modebeilage; ~ **syndicate letter** Modekolumne; **the** ~**s trade** Konfektionsindustrie; **wholesale** ~ **trade** Großkonfektion; ~ **trend** Modeentwicklung; **to set** ~ **trends** Mode beeinflussen; ~ **wear** Modeartikel; ~ **writer** Modeschriftsteller.

fashionable modisch, modern, vornehm, elegant;
to be currently ~ gerade Mode sein;
~ **complaint** Modekrankheit; ~ **hotel** schickes Hotel; ~ **quarters** gute Wohngegend; ~ **summer resort** eleganter Ferienort; ~ **world** obere Gesellschaftsschichten.

fashioner Gestalter.

fashioning Formgebung, Gestaltung.

fashionist Modeberater, -sachverständiger.

fashionmonger Modeschöpfer, -narr, -held, Stutzer, Geck.

fashionwear Modeartikel.

fast schnell, *(colo(u)r)* echt, *(dissipated)* flott, leichtlebig, emanzipiert, schnellebig, *(film)* stark lichtempfindlich, lichtstark, *(fixed)* fest, befestigt, sicher;
not ~ *(colo(u)r)* unecht; ~ **upon** dicht folgend;
~ **to light** lichtecht; ~ **in the mud** im Schlamm steckengeblieben;
to be ~ **aground** *(ship)* festsitzen; **to be five minutes** ~ *(clock)* fünf Minuten vorgehen; **to make a ship** ~ Schiff festlegen; **to play** ~ **and loose with s. o.** Katz und Maus mit jem. spielen, Schindluder mit jem. treiben; **to pull a** ~ **one on s. o.** *(sl.)* j. hereinlegen (aufs Kreuz legen), jem. einen Streich spielen;
~ **bill of exception** *(injunction suit, Georgia)* sofortige Beschwerde; ~ **breeder** schneller Brüter; ~ **buck** *(US sl.)* schnell verdientes Geld; ~**-colo(u)r** farbecht; ~ **estate** Grundvermögen; ~**-food franchise** Schnellrestaurantpacht, Konzession für eine Schnellgaststätte; ~**-food restaurant** Schnellgaststätte, -restaurant; ~ **freight** *(US)* Eilgut, -fracht; ~ **freight train** *(US)* Eilgüterzug; ~ **friends** unzertrennliche Freunde; ~ **goods traffic** *(Br.)* Eilgutverkehr; **by** ~ **goods train** *(Br.)* als Eilgut; ~ **lane** Schnellweg, Schnellfahrspur; **to lead a** ~ **life** flottes Leben führen; ~**-moving** schnell fahrend; ~**-moving goods** schnell umschlagende Ware; ~**-moving traffic** Schnellverkehr; ~ **route** Schnellzugverbindung; **hard and** ~ **rules** unbedingt einzuhaltende Regeln; ~**-selling item** schnellverkäuflicher Artikel, schnell umschlagende Ware, Selbstläufer; ~ **sleep** fester (tiefer) Schlaf; ~ **society** Luxusgesellschaft; ~**-spending** verschwenderisch; ~ **station** Schnellzugstation; ~**-talk** *(v.)* **s. o.** *(coll.)* jem. etw. einreden; ~ **train** D-, Eil-, Schnellzug; **to send goods by** ~ **train** Waren per Expreß schicken; ~ **watch** vorgehende Uhr; ~ **work** rasch erledigte Arbeit.

fasten *(v.)* befestigen, festmachen, *(ship)* verankern;
~ **an apprentice** Lehrlingsvertrag (Ausbildungsvertrag) abschließen; ~ **an article on s. o.** jem. einen Zeitungsartikel zuschieben; ~ **a door** Tür fest verriegeln; ~ **a crime upon s. o.** jem. die Schuld zuschieben; ~ **a nickname on s. o.** jem. einen Spitznamen beilegen; ~ **an obligation on s. o.** jem. eine Ver-

pflichtung auferlegen; ~ **on s. o. as an easy prey** j. als leichte Beute betrachten; ~ **the responsibility upon s. o.** jem. die Verantwortung zuschieben; ~ **up a box** Paket verschnüren.

fastidious anspruchsvoll, verwöhnt;
to be very ~ about one's dress was Kleidung angeht sehr pingelig sein; **to be ~ about one's food** am Essen herummäkeln.

fasting cure Fastenkur.

fastness Festigkeit, Haltbarkeit, *(colo(u)r)* Echtheit.

fat einträgliche Arbeit, *(theater)* Glanzstelle, Paradestück;
~'**s in the fire** der Teufel ist los;
to cut up ~ großes Vermögen hinterlassen; **to live on the ~ of the land** in Saus und Braus (wie Gott in Frankreich) leben;
~ *(a.)* einträglich, reichlich, lohnend, ergiebig;
~ **cat** *(sl.)* einflußreicher Hintermann; ~ **coal** bituminöse Kohle; ~ **job** bequeme Stellung; ~ **lands** fruchtbares Gebiet; ~ **lot of influence** herzlich wenig Einfluß; ~ **pocket book** dicke Brieftasche; ~ **profit** dicker Gewinn; ~ **purse** dicker Geldbeutel; ~ **salary** *(fam.)* dickes Gehalt; ~ **soil** fruchtbarer Boden.

fatal tödlich, mit tödlichem Ausgang, totbringend, *(fateful)* schicksalschwer, -haft, ominös, fatal;
to be ~ to s. one's plans das Ende von jds. Plänen bedeuten;
~ **accident** tödlicher Unfall; ~ **hour** Sterbestunde; **to have a ~ influence over s. o.** verhängnisvollen Einfluß auf j. ausüben; ~ **injury** tödliche Verletzung; ~ **thread** Lebensfaden.

fatalism Fatalismus.

fatalistic attitude fatalistische Einstellung.

fatalities Todesopfer, Unglücksfälle;
bathing ~ Badeunfälle.

fatality tödlicher Ausgang, Todesfall, Verkehrstod;
industrial ~ tödlicher Betriebsunfall;
~ **rate** Todesfallziffer.

fate Schicksal, Geschick, Los;
as sure as ~ todsicher;
the three ᵉ **s** Parzen, Normen;
to abandon s. o. to his ~ j. seinem Schicksal überlassen; **to meet one's ~ calmly** seinem Schicksal in Ruhe (gelassen) entgegensehen; **to seal s. one's ~** jds. Schicksal besiegeln; **to tempt one's ~** sein Schicksal herausfordern.

father Vater, Erzeuger, *(House of Commons)* Alterspräsident, *(society, Br.)* Vorsitzender;
adoptive ~ Adoptivvater; **city ~s** *(coll.)* Stadtväter; **foster ~** Pflegevater; **reputed ~** mutmaßlicher Vater;
~ **of the bar** Senior der Anwaltschaft; ᵉ **s of the Church** Kirchenväter; ~~-**in-law** Schwiegervater; ~ **to the poor** Beschützer der Armen;
~ *(v.)* Vaterschaft anerkennen;
~ **a book** sich als Autor eines Buches bekennen; ~ **a child upon s. o.** jds. Vaterschaft feststellen; ~ **a magazine article on s. o.** jem. einen Zeitschriftenaufsatz zuschreiben;
to act as ~ to s. o. Vaterstelle an jem. vertreten; **to be gathered to one's ~s** zu seinen Vätern versammelt werden; **to have been handed down from ~ to son for many generations** seit vielen Generationen von Vater auf Sohn übergegangen sein; **to play the heavy ~** sich als sehr nobel erweisen;
~'**s business** väterliches Geschäft; ᵉ **Christmas** *(Br.)* Weihnachtsmann; ~ **complex** Vaterkomplex; ᵉ '**s Day** *(US)* Vatertag; ~ **figure** geistiger Vater, Vaterfigur; **on the ~'s side** väterlicherseits; ~ **substitute** Vaterersatz; **heavy-~ tone** autoritäres Auftreten.

fatherhood Vaterschaft, *(House of Commons)* Alterspräsidium.

fatherland Vater-, Geburtsland.

fathom *(v.)* löten, sondieren;
~ **s. one's meaning** jds. Absichten ergründen.

fatigue [Arbeits]ermüdung, Erschöpfung, Überanstrengung, Strapaze, *(mil.)* Arbeitsdienst, *(techn.)* Ermüdung;
~**s incidental to a journey** mit einer Reise verbundene Anstrengungen;
~ **accident** auf Ermüdung zurückzuführender Unfall; ~ **allowance** Erholungszuschlag; ~ **clothes** *(mil.)* Drillich, Arbeitsanzug; ~ **curve** *(US)* Ermüdungskurve; ~ **detail** *(mil.)* Arbeitskommando; ~ **dress** Arbeitsanzug; ~ **duty** *(mil.)* Arbeitsdienst; ~ **party** *(mil.)* Arbeitskommando; ~ **test** Ermüdungsprobe; ~ **strength** *(metal)* Ermüdungsfestigkeit; ~ **uniform** Arbeitsanzug.

fatuous person Schwachsinniger.

fault *(commercial law)* Mangel, Fehler, Defekt, *(el.)* Leitungsfehler, Störung, *(culpable cause)* fehlerhaftes Verhalten, *(mining law)* Verwerfung;
scrupulous to a ~ von stärksten Skrupeln gepeinigt; **with all ~s** ohne Mängelgewähr; **with all ~s and imperfections** mit allen Mängeln und sonstigen Fehlern; **without ~** ohne Verschulden;

gross ~ grobe Fahrlässigkeit; **slight ~** leichte Fahrlässigkeit; ~ **attributable to** zuzurechnendes Verschulden;
~**s in a book** Mängel eines Buches; ~ **in the construction of a machine** Konstruktionsfehler einer Maschine; ~ **in the insulation of a cable** Isolationsfehler eines Kabels; ~ **of spelling** orthographischer Fehler;
to attribute the ~ to s. o. jem. die Schuld beimessen; **to be at ~ in an accident** an einem Unfall Schuld haben; **to be at ~ for an answer** um eine Antwort verlegen sein; **to be always finding ~** stets nur kritisieren; **to be free from ~** *(US)* frei von Verschulden sein; **to be generous to a ~** überaus großzügig sein; **to buy a car with all ~s** Auto ohne Garantie erwerben; **to commit a ~** Fehler machen, Fehltritt begehen; **to find ~ in s. o.** an jem. etw. auszusetzen haben; **to find ~ with s. th.** etw. beanstanden (bemängeln, tadeln); **to localize a ~** Fehler eingrenzen; **to smooth over a ~** Fehler bemänteln (beschönigen);
~ **localizer** *(tel.)* Störungssucher; ~ **plane** Bruchfläche.

faultfinder Beschwerdeführer, Nörgler, Besserwisser, *(tel.)* Störungssucher.

faultfinding Nörgelei, Besserwisserei, Beschwerdeführung, *(tel.)* Störungssuche;
~ **procedure** Verfahren zur Feststellung der Schuldigen.

faultiness Fehler-, Mangelhaftigkeit.

faulting *(geol.)* Verwerfung.

faultless einwand-, fehlerfrei;
~ **condition** fehlerloser Zustand; ~ **performance** tadellose Leistung.

faultsman *(tel.)* Störungssucher.

faulty mangelhaft, fehlerhaft, nicht einwandfrei, schadhaft, *(style)* nicht korrekt;
to be ~ in its manufacture Fabrikationsfehler haben;
~ **article** schlechte Ware; ~ **articulation** falsche Aussprache; ~ **contract** fehlerhafter Vertrag; ~ **control** Fehlschaltung; ~ **brakes** defekte Bremsen; ~ **design** Fehlkonstruktion; ~ **drafting of a document** Fehler bei der Abfassung einer Urkunde; ~ **expression** ungenauer Ausdruck; ~ **goods** nicht einwandfreie (fehlerhafte) Ware; ~ **mechanism** defekter Mechanismus; ~ **possession** widerrechtlicher Besitz; ~ **spacing** *(advertising)* falsche Raumaufteilung; ~ **statement** fehlerhafter Rechnungsauszug; ~ **workmanship** schlechte Ausführung.

favo(u)r *(aid)* Hilfe, Gefallen, Gefälligkeit, *(friendly regard)* Gunst, Wohlwollen, Gnadenbeweis, *(preference)* Vorzug, bevorzugte Behandlung, Privileg, Vergünstigung, *(television)* Bevorzugung bei Aufnahmen;
as a ~ aus Gefälligkeit; **awaiting the ~ of your reply** Ihrer gefälligen Antwort entgegensehend; **by ~ of** mit freundlicher Genehmigung von; **for ~ of publication in your columns** mit der Bitte um Veröffentlichung in Ihrem geschätzten Blatt; **in ~** beliebt, gefragt, begehrt; **in ~ of** zugunsten; **out of ~** *(goods)* nicht mehr gefragt; **for past ~s** für das erwiesene Wohlwollen; **under ~ of the night** unter dem Schutz der Nacht; **without fear or ~** unparteiisch;
high ~ Beliebtheit; **personal ~** persönlicher Gefallen; **your ~ of ...** Ihr geschätzter Brief vom ...;
~ *(v.)* begünstigen, bevorzugen, unterstützen, [mit Aufträgen] beehren;
~ **a creditor** Gläubiger begünstigen; ~ **one's father** *(coll.)* seinem Vater ähneln, auf seinen Vater kommen; ~ **s. th. without reservation** sich vorbehaltlos für etw. aussprechen; ~ **a scheme** Projekt befürworten;
to ask a ~ of s. o. Gefälligkeit von jem. erbitten; **not to ask for ~s** keine besonderen Ansprüche stellen; **to ask for the ~ of an answer** um Antwort bitten; **to balance in ~ of s. o.** jem. gutschreiben; **to be back in ~** wieder hoch im Kurse stehen; **to be in great ~** *(goods)* begehrt (beliebt, sehr gefragt) sein; **to be in s. one's ~** zu jds. Gunsten ausfallen; **to be in ~ with s. o.** bei jem. hoch im Kurse stehen; **to be all in ~ of s. th.** geschlossen dafür sein; **to be in ~ of a proposal** für einen Vorschlag sein; **to be out of ~** aus der Mode gekommen sein; **to be out of ~ with one's employer** es mit seinem Arbeitgeber verscherzt haben; **to be in ~ of votes for women** für das Frauenwahlrecht eintreten; **to confer a ~ on s. o.** jem. eine Gefälligkeit erweisen; **to curry ~** sich einschmeicheln; **to decide in s. one's ~** zu jds. Gunsten entscheiden; **to do a ~** Gefallen erweisen; **to draw a cheque in ~ of the treasurer** *(Br.)* Scheck auf den Schatzmeister ausstellen; **to find ~ in s. one's eyes** vor jds. Augen Gnade finden; **to grant s. o. a ~** jem. eine Gunst gewähren; **to grant special favo(u)rs to a customer** Kunden bevorzugt behandeln; **to heap ~s on s. o.** j. mit Gunstbeweisen überschütten; **to load s. o. with ~s** j. mit Gunstbeweisen überschütten; **to look on a plan with ~** einem Vorhaben positiv gegenüberstehen; **to obtain one's position**

more by ~ than by merit and abilities seine Position mehr der Protektion als Verdiensten und Fähigkeiten verdanken; **to react with ~** positiv reagieren; **to request the ~ of** s.'s **company to dinner** j. zum Abendessen einladen; **to show** s. o. **a ~** jem. eine Gunst erweisen; **to solicit a ~ of** s. o. j. um eine Gefälligkeit bitten; **to speak in** s. one's **~** für j. eintreten; **to stand high in** s. one's **~** bei jem. gut angeschrieben sein; **to win** s. one's **~** jds. Protektion erlangen; **to withdraw one's ~** seine Gunst entziehen; **to write out a check** (US) (cheque, Br.) **in** s. one's **~** zu jds. Gunsten einen Scheck ausstellen.

favo(u)rable günstig gesinnt, gewogen, geneigt, (promising) verheißungsvoll, vielversprechend;
to be ~ to a proposal einem Vorschlag zustimmen;
~ answer positive Antwort, günstiger Bescheid; **~ balance of trade** aktive Handelsbilanz; **~ conditions** günstige Bedingungen; **~ decision** obsiegendes Urteil; **~ exchange rate** günstiger Umrechnungskurs; **to look on** s. o. **with a ~ eye** j. wohlwollend behandeln; **~ price** günstiger Preis; **specially ~ rate** Sondertarif; **~ report** günstiger Bericht; **~ terms** günstige Preise; **on ~ terms** zu günstigen [Zahlungs]bedingungen.

favo(u)red begünstigt, bevorzugt;
to be ~ by circumstances von den Umständen profitieren; **to be ~ with an order** Auftrag erhalten;
most ~ nation clause Meistbegünstigungsklausel; **most ~ nation treatment** Meistbegünstigung.

favo(u)rite Günstling, Liebling, Favorit;
~s (market) Spitzenwerte;
least ~ am wenigsten gern gesehen;
to be the ~ of s. o. von jem. besonders bevorzugt werden; **to be** s. one's **~** jds. Liebling sein; **to play ~s** (US) parteiisch sein;
~ (a.) begünstigt, bevorzugt;
~ brand bevorzugte Marke; **~ dish** Leib-, Lieblingsgericht; **~ paper** Leib- und Magenblatt; **~ part-time** Lieblingszeitvertreib; **~ phrase** bevorzugte Redewendung; **~ remark** Lieblingsphrase; **~ son** (US pol.) bevorzugter Kandidat; **~ spot** Lieblingsplatz.

favo(u)ritism Günstlingswesen, -wirtschaft, Vetternwirtschaft;
~ in promotions Protektionswirtschaft bei Beförderungen;
to owe one's promotion to ~ seine Beförderung nur der Protektion verdanken.

fawn | (v.) on s. o. sich bei jem. einschmeicheln; **~ on a rich relative** vor einem reichen Verwandten katzbuckeln.

fear Furcht, Angst, Besorgnis;
in ~ of one's life in Todesängsten;
~ of death Todesangst; **~ of recession** Rezessionsbefürchtungen;
to have ~s Befürchtungen hegen, besorgt sein; **to have ~ for** s. one's **future** sich um jds. Zukunft große Sorgen machen; **to put** s. o. **in ~ of his life** jem. Todesängste einjagen; **to stand in great ~ of dismissal** ernsthaft seine Entlassung befürchten.

feasance (law) Erfüllung.
feasibility Ausführbar-, Gangbar-, Durchführbarkeit;
~ study Projekt-, Vorstudie.
feasible durchführbar, gangbar, tunlich;
not ~ untunlich;
to sound ~ glaubhaft (plausibel) klingen;
~ method of liquidation vernünftiger Vergleichsvorschlag.

feast Fest, Feier, Kirmes, (banquet) Festessen, Bankett, (rich entertainment) Augenweide, Labsal;
movable church ~s bewegliche Kirchenfeste;
~ of intelligent conversation Vergnügen an einem gescheiten Gespräch;
~ (v.) away the night Nacht durchfeiern; **~ one's friends** seine Freunde bewirten.

feat Glanzstück, Meisterstück;
brilliant ~ of engineering technische Meisterleistung.
feather Feder, Gefieder, (mood) Stimmung;
in high (full) ~ in gehobener Stimmung; **with a ~** mit dem kleinen Finger;
~ in one's cap Feder am Hut, (fig.) Pluspunkt, großes Verdienst, ehrenvolle Auszeichnung;
~ (v.) one's nest sein Schäfchen ins Trockne bringen;
to be in full ~ sich mächtig aufgetakelt haben; **to be in high ~** in glänzender Laune sein; **to crop** s. one's **~s** j. demütigen; **to show the white ~** seine Furcht deutlich zeigen; **to smooth one's crumpled ~s** seine Kaltblütigkeit wiedergewinnen; **to tar and ~** teeren und federn;
fine ~s make fine birds Kleider machen Leute.
featherbed Unterbett, (fig.) angenehmer Posten;
~ (v.) bevorzugen, (sl.) verweichlichen, (trade union, US) unnötige Arbeitskräfte einstellen;

~ the farmers Landwirtschaft subventionieren;
~ job (US) reine Sinekure; **~ landing** (parachuters) Federbettlandung; **~ treatment** bevorzugte Behandlung.
featherbedding Bevorzugung, Verwöhnung, (US) Bezahlung für eine nicht wirklich geleistete Arbeit, (US unionism) Anstellung nicht benötigter Arbeitskräfte;
~ of the farmers Subventionierung der Landwirtschaft;
~ practices (US) gewerkschaftliche Praktiken bei der Arbeitseinstellung.
featherbrain Schwachkopf.
featherweight (fig.) belanglose Sache.
feature Wesensmerkmal, Kennzeichen, Eigenheit, charakteristischer Zug, Charakteristikum, (advertising) Aufhänger, werbewirksames Element, Hauptmerkmal, (broadcasting) Hörfolge, Tatsachenbericht, (film) Hauptspielfilm, (newspaper) besonders aufgemachter (spezieller) Artikel, Sonderartikel, besondere Spalte, (featured person) Hauptperson, Star;
~s Gesichtszüge, Merkmale;
characteristic ~ charakteristisches Merkmal; **distinctive ~** Unterscheidungsmerkmal; **leading ~s** tonangebende Leute; **main ~s** Hauptmerkmal; **novel ~** Neuheitsmerkmal; **short ~** Beifilm; **special ~** besonderes Merkmal, Besonderheit, (newspaper) Sonderartikel; **star ~** Hauptfilm; **striking ~** verblüffende Ähnlichkeit;
~s of business Geschäftsmerkmale; **~s of a contract** Grundzüge eines Vertrages; **national ~s of a country** Topographie eines Landes; **geographical ~ of a district** geographische Merkmale eines Bezirkes; **~s of the ground** Terraineigenarten; **main ~s of foreign policy** Grundlinien der Außenpolitik; **unusual ~s in a political program(me)** ungewöhnliche Wesenszüge eines politischen Programms;
~ (v.) kennzeichnen, (film) in der Hauptrolle zeigen, (give prominence) Vorrang einräumen, besonders herausstellen, präsentieren;
~ a new actress neue Schauspielerin groß herausbringen; **~ an article** Zeitungsartikel groß aufmachen; **~ high-priced items** sich auf teure Qualitätserzeugnisse spezialisieren; **~ a landscape** Landschaft charakterisieren; **~ a piece of news** Nachricht groß aufmachen (in großer Aufmachung bringen);
to have no ~ in common überhaupt keine Ähnlichkeit haben; **to make a ~ of doing** s. th. sich angelegen sein lassen, etw. zu tun; **to make a special ~** Sonderangebot machen; **to make a special ~ of** s. th. sich auf etw. spezialisieren; **to make a ~ of sport** besondere Sportberichterstattung haben;
~ article großaufgemachter Artikel, Sonderartikel; **~ editor** verantwortlicher Redakteur für Titelgeschichten; **~ film** Hauptfilm; **~ page** Hauptseite; **~ picture** Hauptfilm; **two-~ program(me)** Doppelprogramm; **~ story** Titelgeschichte; **~ writer** Titelgeschichtenverfasser, Starjournalist.
featured, to be zur Schau (ausgestellt) werden, (news) aufgemacht werden;
~ articles Sonderangebot.
featureless uninteressant, (market) flau, matt, lustlos, (stocks) umsatzlos.
featuring of an article große Aufmachung eines Zeitungsartikels.
febrile | excitement fieberhafte Aufregung; **~ state** Fieberzustand.
fecund fruchtbar;
~ era in literature schöpferische Literaturperiode.
fed up, to be ~ with a th. (coll.) einer Sache überdrüssig sein, Nase voll haben, keine Lust mehr haben, sauer sein.
federacy Staatenbund, Föderation.
federal Föderalist;
~ (a.) bundesstaatlich, föderalistisch, föderativ, (unionistic, US) unionistisch, zentralistisch;
~ administration Bundesverwaltung; **ℓ Advisory Council** (US) [etwa] Zentralbankrat; **~ agency** (US) Bundesbehörde; **~ aid** Bundeshilfe, -zuwendung; **~ allowance** (US) Bundeszuschuß; **~ average** Bundesdurchschnitt; **ℓ Aviation Agency** (US) Flugsicherungsbehörde; **~ bank account** (US) [etwa] Girokonto bei der Landeszentralbank; **ℓ Budget** (US) Bundeshaushalt, -etat; **ℓ Bureau of Investigation (FBI)** (US) Bundeskriminalamt; **ℓ Chancellor** Bundeskanzler; **~ city** (US) Bundeshauptstadt; **ℓ Communications Act** (US) Fernmeldegesetz; **ℓ Communications Commission** (US) Bundesbehörde für Fernmeldewesen, Fernmeldebehörde; **~ constitution** Bundesverfassung; **~-controlled** vom Bund überwacht; **ℓ Corporation** (US) Bundesanstalt; **ℓ Court** (US) Bundesgericht; **ℓ Credit Union Act** (US) Gesetz über das Bundesaufsichtsamt für das Versicherungswesen; **~ currency** (US) Landeswährung; **~ debt** (US) Staatsschuld; **~ deposit insurance** (US) Einlagenversicherung; **ℓ**

Deposit Insurance Corporation *(US)* Bundesversicherungsanstalt für Krediteinlagensicherung; ⚥ **District** *(US)* Regierungssitz; ~ **employee** *(US)* Bundesbediensteter; ⚥ **Energy Administration** *(US)* Bundesenergiebehörde; ~ **expenditure** Bundesausgaben; ~ **export licence** Ausfuhrlizenz; ⚥ **Farm Loan bonds** *(US)* Pfandbriefe einer landwirtschaftlichen Genossenschaft; ⚥ **Farm Loan System** *(US)* landwirtschaftliches Genossenschaftswesen; ⚥ **Funds** *(US banking)* fundierte Staatspapiere, Staatsanleihen, Zentralbankgeld; ⚥ **Funds rate** *(US)* Tageskurs für Staatsanleihen; ⚥ **Government** *(US)* Bundesregierung; ~ **grant** *(US)* Bundeszuschuß; ⚥ **Housing Administration** *(US)* Bundesstelle für Wohnungsbau; ~ **income tax** *(US)* Einkommensteuer; ~ **instrumentality** *(US)* Bundesorgan; ⚥ **Insurance Contribution Act** *(US)* Sozialversicherungsgesetz; ⚥ **Insurance Loan Program** *(university, US)* Programm staatsverbürgter Studentendarlehn; ⚥ **Intermediate Credit Bank** *(US)* Bundeskreditinstitut für mittelfristige Agrarkredite; ~ **job appointment process** *(US)* Ernennungsverfahren für ein Bundesamt; ~ **judge** *(US)* Bundesrichter; ⚥ **Land Bank** *(US)* staatliche Landwirtschaftsbank; ~ **legislation** Gesetzgebung des Bundes, Bundesgesetzgebung; ⚥ **Maritime Commission** *(US)* Bundesschiffahrtsbehörde; ~ **matters** Bundesangelegenheiten; ⚥ **Mediation and Conciliation Service** *(US)* Oberste Schlichtungsbehörde; ~ **mediator** *(US)* Bundesschlichter; ⚥ **National Mortgage Association** *(US)* Bundesbehörde für Hypothekengewährung im sozialen Wohnungsbau; ~ **officer** *(US)* Bundesbeamter; ⚥ **Pension Guarantee Corporation** *(US)* Pensionsgarantiekasse; ~ **power** *(US)* Bundesgewalt; ⚥ **Power Commission** *(US)* Bundesenergiebehörde; ⚥ **Record Center** *(US)* Bundesarchiv; ~ **rediscount rate** *(US)* [etwa] Diskontsatz der Landeszentralbank; ⚥ **Reserve Act** *(US)* [etwa] Landeszentralbankgesetz; ⚥ **Reserve Agent** *(US)* [etwa] Landeszentralbankpräsident; ⚥ **Reserve Bank** *(US)* [etwa] Landeszentralbank; **to have a deposit account with the** ⚥ **Reserve Bank** *(US)* Konto bei der Landeszentralbank unterhalten; ⚥ **Reserve board** *(US)* [etwa] Landeszentralbankrat; ⚥ **Reserve chairman** [etwa] Bundesbankpräsident; ⚥ **Reserve City** *(US)* Sitz einer Landeszentralbank; ⚥ **Reserve credit** *(US)* [etwa] Landeszentralbankkredit; ⚥ **Reserve's discount rate** *(US)* Diskontsatz der Landeszentralbank; ⚥ **Reserve figures** *(US)* [etwa] Landeszentralbankzahlen; **to get most of the** ⚥ **Reserve services** *(US)* fast alle Einrichtungen der Landeszentralbank in Anspruch nehmen; ⚥ **Reserve System** *(US)* Zentralbankwesen; ⚥ **Savings and Loan Insurance Corporation** *(US)* Bundesaufsichtsamt für Bausparkassenwesen; ⚥ **Securities Act** *(US)* Bundeswertpapiergesetz; ⚥ **Security Agency** *(US)* Bundesversicherungsanstalt; ~ **state** Bundesstaat; ⚥ **Statement** *(US)* [etwa] Ausweis der Landeszentralbanken; ~ **subsidy** Bundeszuschuß; ~ **system** *(US)* Zentralbanksystem; ~ **tax** *(US)* Bundessteuer; ⚥ **Trade Commission** *(US)* Ausschuß zur Bekämpfung unlauteren Wettbewerbs; ~ **transfer tax** *(US)* Effektenumsatzsteuer; ~ **treasury** Staatskasse; ~ **unemployment tax** *(US)* Arbeitnehmerbeitrag zur Arbeitslosenversicherung; ⚥ **Works Agency** *(US)* Bundesamt für Arbeitsbeschaffung.

federalism Föderalismus, Partikularismus, Selbständigkeitsbestrebung, *(US)* Zentralismus.

federalist Föderalist;
~ *(a.)* föderalistisch.

federalization Zusammenschluß zu einem Staatenbund.

federate *(v.)* sich zu einem Bündnis vereinigen.

federated föderiert;
~ **state** Bundesstaat.

federation Zusammenschluß, *(association)* Verband, Vereinigung, *(federacy)* Staatenbund, [Kon]föderation;
economic ~ Wirtschaftsverband;
⚥ **of British Industries** [etwa] Arbeitgeberverband; ~ **of employers' organization** Arbeitgeberverband; **American** ⚥ **of Labor (AFL)** Amerikanischer Gewerkschaftsverband; ~ **of wholesale organizations** *(Br.)* Großhandelsverband; ~ **of workers' organization** Arbeitnehmerverband; ~ **of trade unions** Gewerkschaftsverband.

federative föderativ.

fee *(advertising)* Agenturvergütung, *(entrance money)* Eintrittsgeld, -gebühr, *(honorarium)* Honorar, Vergütung, Entgelt, *(remuneration)* Bezahlung, *(royalty)* Tantieme, *(school)* Schulgeld, *(sum payable to public officer)* [amtliche] Gebühr, Abgabe, Taxe, Sportel, *(university)* Studiengebühr, *(wages)* Lohn, Bezahlung;
at a modified ~ zu einer herabgesetzten Gebühr; **at a reduced** ~ für ein mäßiges Honorar; **for a small** ~ gegen geringe Gebühr; **liable to a** ~ gebührenpflichtig;

~**s as lately accumulated** letzthin angefallene Gebühren; **additional** ~ Zuschlagsgebühr; **admission** ~ Eintrittsgeld, -gebühr, Aufnahmegebühr; **annual** ~ Jahresgebühr; **application** ~ Anmelde-, Antragsgebühr; **apprentice** ~ Lehrgeld; **architect's** ~ Architektenhonorar; **attendance** ~s Präsenzgeld; **attorney's** ~ Anwaltshonorar; **auction (auctioneer's)** ~ Auktionskosten, -gebühren; **audit (auditing)** ~s Prüfungs-, Revisionsgebühren; **author's** ~ Tantieme, Autorenanteil; **base** ~ *(real estate)* befristetes Grundstücksnutzungsrecht, befristetes Immobiliarnutzungsrecht; **basic** ~ Grundgebühr; **boarding-school** ~ Internatskosten; **booking** ~ Vormerkgebühr; **brokerage** ~ Maklergebühr; **clerk's** ~s Schreibgebühr; **cloakroom** ~ Gepäckaufbewahrungsgebühr; **club** ~s Vereins-, Klubbeitrag; **collection** ~ Inkassogebühr; **comprehensive** ~ Pauschalgebühr; **conditional** ~ *(law)* fideikommissarischer Besitz; **consular** ~s Konsulatsgebühren; **consultation** ~ Beratungsgebühr; **copying** ~ Schreibgebühr; **counsel's** ~ *(Br.)* Anwaltsgebühren, -honorar; **court** ~s *(Br.)* Gerichtsgebühren, -kosten; **customhouse** ~s Zollgebühren; **determinable** ~ befristete Erbpacht; **development** ~ Erschließungsbeitrag; **director's** ~ Aufsichtsratstantieme; **discharging** ~s Entlade-, Löschungskosten; **docket** ~ Prozeßgebühr; **doctor's** ~ Arztrechnung, Liquidation; ~s **due** fällige Gebühren; **entrance** ~ Eintrittsgeld, Aufnahmegebühr; **examination** ~ Prüfungsgebühr; **excess** ~ Gebührenzuschlag; **expert's** ~ Sachverständigengebühren; **extra** ~ Sonderhonorar; **filing** ~s [Konkurs]anmeldegebühr; **fiscal** ~s fiskalische Gebühren; **fixed** ~ feste Gebühr; **flat** ~ fester Preis, Pauschalgebühr; **garage** ~[s] Standgeld; **handling** ~ Bearbeitungsgebühr; **initiation** ~ Aufnahme-, Eintrittsgebühr; **inspection** ~s Prüfungsgebühren; **insurance** ~ Versicherungskosten; **late** ~ Zuschlag[steuer], *(post, Br.)* Späteinlieferungsgebühr; **late-letter** ~ Nachtzustellungsgebühr; **lawyer's** ~ *(Br.)* Anwaltsgebühr; **legalization** ~ Beglaubigungsgebühr; **lending** ~ Leihgebühr; **licence** ~s Konzessions-, Lizenzgebühren; **limited (qualified)** ~ *(law)* an bestimmte Bedingungen geknüpftes Erbgrundstück, eingeschränktes Grundstücksrecht; **marriage** ~s standesamtliche Gebühren; **medical** ~ ärztliches Honorar; **minimum** ~ Mindestgebühr; **notarial** ~ Notariatsgebühr; **official** ~s amtliche Gebühren; **option** ~s Optionsgebühren; **parking** ~ Parkgroschen; **patent** ~ Patentgebühr; **porter's** ~ *(US)* Gepäckträgergebühr; **priority** ~ Gebühr für bevorrechtigte Abfertigung; **professional** ~ Honorar; **protest** ~s Protestspesen; **registration** ~ Anmelde-, Eintragungs-, Einschreibe-, Transfer-, Registergebühr; **remittance** ~ Überweisungskosten; **renewal** ~ *(patent law)* Verlängerungsgebühr; **retaining** ~ Anwaltsvorschuß, Prozeßberatungsgebühr; **returnable** ~ zurückzuerstattende Gebühr; **safe-custody** *(Br.)* ~ Depot-, Aufbewahrungsgebühr; **safe-deposit** ~ Depotgebühr; **school** ~s Schulgeld; **sheriff** ~s Gerichtsvollzieherkosten, -gebühren; **signing** ~ Zeichnungsgebühr; **skeleton** ~ Rahmengebühr; **solicitors'** ~ *(Br.)* Anwaltshonorar; **special** ~ Sondergebühr; **statistical** ~s statistische Gebühren; **stiff** ~ stramme Gebühr; **subscription** ~ Abonnements-, Subskriptionsgebühr; **transfer** ~ Übertragungs-, Transfergebühr; **tuition** ~s Schuldgeld; **underwriting** ~ Übernahmespesen; **user** ~ Benutzungsgebühr; **witness** ~ Zeugengebühr;

~**s as lately accumulated** letzthin angefallene Gebühren; ~**s paid in advance** Gebührenvorschuß; ~ **payable in addition to postage** zusätzliche Portogebühr; ~**s and subscriptions to professional bodies** Beiträge für Berufsverbände; ~ **for consultation** Beratungsgebühr; ~ **for custodianship** *(US)* Depotgebühr; ~**s incurred in obtaining a patent** Gebühren für die Erteilung eines Patents; ~ **and life rent** Eigentum und Nießbrauch; ~ **for presentation** Vorzeigegebühr; ~ **for safekeeping** Aufbewahrungsgebühr; ~ **contingent upon the success** Erfolgshonorar; ~ **incidental to a title** mit einem Eigentumsrecht verbundene Gebühr;

~ *(v.)* Gebühr bezahlen (entrichten), honorieren;
~ **a barrister (lawyer)** Honorar an einen Anwalt zahlen; ~ **a waiter** Trinkgeld geben;
to abate ~s Gebühren niederschlagen; **to be subject to a** ~ gebührenpflichtig sein; **to charge a** ~ Gebühr berechnen, erheben, Honorar liquidieren; **to collect a** ~ Gebühr einziehen; **to draw one's** ~s seine Tantiemen kassieren; **to exact** ~s Gebühren erheben; **to extort** ~s unstatthafte Gebühren fordern; **to hand out the papers on payment of a** ~ Unterlagen nach Zahlung einer Gebühr aushändigen; **to hold land in** ~ Land zu eigen haben; **to levy** ~s Gebühren erheben; **to pay the** ~s Gebühren entrichten; **to pay s. o. a** ~ j. honorieren; **to pocket large** ~s große Honorare einstreichen; **to raise a** ~ Gebühr erhöhen; **to reduce a** ~ Gebühr ermäßigen; **to refund** ~s Gebühren erstatten; **to remit** ~s Gebühren erlassen;

~ **arrangement** Gebührenabkommen; **to operate on a ~ basis** Honorarvereinbarung treffen; **~-charging** entgeltlich; ~ **cut** Gebührenherabsetzung; ~ **damages** Substanzschadensersatz; **~-farm** Erbpacht; ~ **farmer** Erbpächter; ~ **fund** Gebührenfonds; ~ **hike** Gebührenanstieg; ~ **income** Gebührenertrag; ~ **increase** Gebührenanhebung; ~ **note** Gebührenberechnung; ~ **payer** Gebührenzahler; ~ **scale** Gebührenstaffel; **compulsory ~ scale** verbindliche Gebührenstaffel; ~ **sheet** *(solicitor, Br.)* Gebührenrechnung; ~ **simple** Eigen-, Frei-, Erb-, Allodialgut, unbeschränkt vererbbares Grundeigentum; ~ **simple absolute** Grundeigentum; **conditional ~ simple** Fideikommißeigentum; ~ **splitting** Tantiemenaufteilung; ~ **system** *(agency business)* festes Gebührensystem; ~ **tail** Erbhof, Fideikommiß.

feeble schwächlich, hinfällig, *(not effective)* kraftlos, wirkungsarm, *(stock exchange)* schwach;
~ **argument** schwaches Argument; **~-minded** geistesschwach; **~-mindedness** Geistesschwäche; ~ **old man** hilfloser alter Mann; ~ **work** mäßige Arbeit.

feebling Schwächling.

feed Futter, Nahrung, *(machine)* Materialzuführung, *(theater)* Stichwort [für den Komiker];
on the ~ auf der Nahrungssuche; **out on ~** auf der Weide; ~ *(v.)* füttern;
~ at the high table tafeln; ~ **back waste material into the system** Abfallprodukte erneut industriell verwerten; ~ **down** abfressen; ~ **the fishes** *(sl.)* seekrank sein; ~ **in** *(computer)* eingeben; ~ **a machine with raw materials** einer Maschine Rohstoffe zuführen; ~ **out of s. one's hand** jem. aus der Hand fressen; ~ **paper into the typewriter** Papier in die Schreibmaschine einlegen (einspannen); ~ **straight through into the price** direkt auf die Preise durchschlagen; ~ **up** mästen;
to be off one's ~ keinen Appetit haben; **to have a good ~** erstklassig verpflegt werden;
~ **current** *(el.)* Gleichstrom; ~ **grain** Futtergetreide; ~ **store** *(US)* Futtermittelhandlung.

feedback Rückwirkung, *(el.)* Rückkopplung, *(cybernetics)* Informationsrückfluß, *(sociology)* Rückbeeinflußung;
~ **score** *(US, advertising)* Erfolgsmessung.

feeder Esser, *(airline)* Zubringerlinie, -flugzeug, *(print.)* Anleger, *(railway)* Zubringerzug, *(road)* Zubringer, *(theater)* Nebenfigur;
large ~ starker Esser;
~ **airport** Hilfsflugplatz; ~ **line** *(airplane)* Zubringerlinie, *(railway)* Zubringerlinie, Anschlußstrecke; ~ **liner** Zubringerflugzeug; ~ **machine (plane)** Zubringerflugzeug; ~ **plant** Zulieferungsbetrieb; ~ **road** Zubringer[straße]; ~ **service** Zubringerdienst.

feeding Füttern, Fütterung;
bottle ~ Flaschennahrung; **forcible ~** Zwangsernährung; ~ **of an account** Kontoanreicherung; ~ **in transit** Fütterung auf dem Transport;
~ **facilities** Verpflegungseinrichtungen.

feel Gefühl, Gefühlseindruck, Stimmung, Atmosphäre;
~ *(v.)* fühlen, empfinden, wahrnehmen, *(mil.)* Feinfühlung nehmen;
~ **in one's bones** Vorahnung haben; **not ~ bound to accept an offer** sich zur Annahme eines Angebots nicht verpflichtet fühlen; ~ **cheap** sich gedemütigt vorkommen; ~ **confident of success** sich seines Erfolges sicher sein; ~ **about in the dark for the electric light switch** im Dunkeln nach dem Lichtschalter tasten; ~ **the draught** *(Br.)* in arger Bedrängnis sein; ~ **the effects of an accident** Nachwirkungen eines Unfalls fühlen; ~ **the helm** *(ship)* dem Steuer gehorchen; ~ **at home** sich wohl fühlen; ~ **at home in a branch of knowledge** sich in einer Wissenschaft heimisch fühlen; ~ **a kindly interest towards s. o.** aufrichtige Anteilnahme an jds. Geschick haben; ~ **one's legs** Vertrauen fassen; ~ **for a penny in one's pocket** Kleingeld aus seiner Tasche holen; ~ **out the possibilities of a scheme** Erfolgschancen eines Vorhabens abtasten; ~ **not quite the thing** sich nicht besonders [wohl] fühlen; ~ **shaky** sich unwohl fühlen; ~ **with s. o. in his sorrow** an jds. Kummer Anteil nehmen; ~ **strongly about** entschiedene Ansichten haben; ~ **equal to a task** sich einer Aufgabe gewachsen fühlen; ~ **bad vibrations** negative Ausstrahlungen spüren; ~ **warm towards s. o.** jem. wohlgesonnen sein; ~ **one's way** sich tastend zurechtfinden; ~ **one's way towards an agreement** die Chancen eines Abkommens abtasten;
to get the ~ of work Arbeitserfahrung bekommen.

feeler *(fig.)* Fühler, Versuchsballon;
to throw out a ~ Fühler ausstrecken, Sache vorsichtig untersuchen.

feeling Gefühl;
class ~ Klassenbewußtsein; **good ~** Verträglichkeit; **hard ~** Ressentiment; **strong ~s** starke Überzeugung; **uncomfortable ~** ungutes Gefühl; **uneasy ~** unbehagliches Gefühl;
~s of guilt Schuldkomplex; ~ **of inferiority** Minderwertigkeitsgefühl; ~ **of the meeting** Stimmung der Versammlung;
to appeal to s. one's finer ~s an jds. Anstand appellieren; **to appeal to the ~s of an audience** Publikum gefühlsmäßig ansprechen; **to arouse favo(u)rable ~s for o. s. j.** günstig für sich einnehmen; **to be swayed by one's ~s** von seinen Gefühlen fortgerissen werden; **to contain one's ~s** seine Gefühle im Zaun halten, sich beherrschen; **to give utterance to one's ~s** seinen Gefühlen Ausdruck verleihen; **to give vent to one's ~s** seinen Gefühlen freien Lauf lassen; **to have a ~ of danger** Gefahr wittern; **to hurt s. one's ~s** jds. Gefühle verletzen; **to outrage s. one's ~s** jds. Gefühle mit Füßen treten; **to suffer a ~ of failure** sich für einen Versager halten;
~ **value** Gefühlswert.

feet | of clay verborgene Schwäche;
to be on one's ~ sich wieder erholt haben; **to be run off one's ~** sich die Beine ablaufen; **to carry s. o. off his ~** j. zu Begeisterungsstürmen hinreißen; **to fall on one's ~** immer auf die Füße fallen; **to feel its ~** *(country)* sein nationales Selbstvertrauen finden; **to find its ~ again** sich wieder fangen; **to get on its ~ again** *(business)* wieder flottwerden; **to have found its ~ again** *(market)* sich beruhigt (stabilisiert) haben; **to measure others' ~ by one's own last** andere nach sich beurteilen; **to put an enterprise on its ~ again** Unternehmen wieder in die Höhe bringen; **to set the budget on its ~ again** durcheinandergeratenen Etat sanieren.

feign *(v.)* heucheln, vortäuschen, simulieren, *(forge)* fälschen, *(invent)* erdichten, fingieren;
~ **death** sich totstellen; ~ **an excuse** Entschuldigung erfinden; ~ **illness** Krankheit simulieren.

feigned fingiert, falsch, simuliert;
~ **accomplice** Agent, Provokateur, Spitzel; ~ **action** Scheinprozeß; ~ **bid** Scheingebot; ~ **contract** Scheinvertrag; ~ **disease** simulierte Krankheit; **to write in a ~ hand** mit verstellter Handschrift schreiben; ~ **issue** Scheinverfahren; ~ **name** angenommener Name; ~ **payment** Scheinzahlung; ~ **purchase** Scheinkauf; ~ **trial** Scheinprozeß, -verfahren.

feint Scheinangriff, Ablenkungs-, Täuschungsmanöver;
~ *(v.)* durch eine Finte täuschen, Scheinangriff durchführen; ~ *(a.)* *(print., Br.)* schwach.

felicitate *(v.)* beglückwünschen, gratulieren.

felicitation Glückwünsche, Gratulation.

fellow Genosse, Gefährte, Kamerad, Kollege, *(associate)* Teilhaber, *(college)* Mitglied eines College, Dozent, *(contemporary)* Mitmensch, Zeitgenosse, *(of society)* Mitglied, *(university, Br.)* Stipendiat mit akademischem Titel;
jolly ~ fideles Haus; **school ~** Schulkamerad;
~s in crime Mittäter;
to be ~s zusammengehören; **to be hail-~-well-met with s. o.** dicke Tunke mit jem. (mit allen sofort vertraut) sein;
~ **board member** Vorstandskollege; ~ **boarder** Mitpensionär; ~ **Christian** Glaubensbruder; ~ **citizen** Mitbürger; ~ **conspirator** Mitverschwörer; ~ **convict** Knastbruder; ~ **counsellor** Ratsmitglied; ~ **countryman** Landsmann; ~ **creditor** Mitgläubiger; ~ **criminal** Mittäter; ~ **debtor** Mitschuldner; ~ **directors** Vorstandskollegen; ~ **disciple** Mitschüler; ~ **drawer** Mitaussteller eines Wechsels; ~ **employee (labo(u)rer)** Arbeitskollege, Mitarbeiter; ~ **feeling** Zusammengehörigkeits-, Solidaritätsgefühl; ~ **heir** Miterbe; ~ **human** Mitmensch; ~ **lodger** Zimmergenosse; ~ **man** Mitmensch; ~ **member** Kollege; ~ **member of the board** Vorstandskollege; ~ **partner** [Mit]gesellschafter, Teilhaber; ~ **passenger** Mitreisender, Reisegefährte; ~ **patriot** Landsmann; ~ **prisoner** Mitgefangener; ~ **pupil** Mitschüler; ~ **servant** *(US)* Mitangestellter, Arbeitskollege; **~-servant rule** Nichthaftung für durch Betriebsangehörige verursachte Schäden; ~ **soldier** Kriegskamerad; ~ **student** Studienkollege, Kommilitone; ~ **sufferer** Leidensgefährte; ~ **townsman** Mitbürger; **~-travel** *(v.)* mit dem Kommunismus sympathisieren, kommunistenfreundlich sein; ~ **traveller** Reisegefährte, *(pol.)* Sympathisant, Gesinnungsgenosse, kommunistischer Mitläufer, Kommunistenfreund, -sympathisant; ~ **unionist** *(US)* Mitglied derselben Gewerkschaft; ~ **worker** Mitarbeiter, Berufs-, Arbeitskamerad, Kollege.

fellowship Gemeinschaft, Kameradschaft, Kollegialität, Zusammengehörigkeit, *(of college)* Lehrkörper, *(company)* Gesellschaft, Genossenschaft, *(foundation, Br.)* Universitätsstipendium, *(fund)* Stipendienfonds, Forschungskredit, *(guild)*

Zunft, Gilde, *(membership)* Mitgliedschaft, *(religion)* Glaubensgemeinschaft;
good ~ gute Kameradschaft, Gemütlichkeit, Geselligkeit;
~ **of students** Studentengemeinschaft;
~ *(v.) (US)* in eine Gemeinschaft aufnehmen;
to admit to ~ als Vereinsmitglied aufnehmen; **to live in intellectual** ~ **with s. o.** sich gedanklich mit jem. völlig eins sein; **to sit for a** ~ im Doktorexamen stecken;
~ **scheme** Stipendiatssystem.

felo-de-se Selbstmörder.

felon Verbrecher.

felonious verbrecherisch, verräterisch;
~ **act** Verbrechen; ~ **assault** Mordversuch; ~ **homicide** Totschlag;
to be accused of loitering with ~ **intent** wegen Herumstreunens angezeigt werden.

feloniously in verbrecherischer Absicht.

felony Schwer-, Kapitalverbrechen, gemeingefährliches Verbrechen;
to compound a ~ Kapitalverbrechen begehen.

felt | pad Filzunterlage; **~-tip pen** Filzschreiber.

female Frau, Mädchen;
~ *(a.)* weiblich;
~ **acquaintance** Frauenbekanntschaft; ~ **heir** Erbin; ~ **labo(u)r** weibliche Arbeitskräfte; ~ **occupation** weibliche Beschäftigung, Frauenarbeit; ~ **operative** Arbeiterin; ~ **patient** Patientin; ~ **participation rate** Anteil weiblicher Arbeitskräfte; ~ **suffrage** Frauenstimmrecht; ~ **touch** *(advertising)* weibliche Note.

feme Frau;
~ **covert** Ehefrau; ~ **discovert** geschiedene Frau, Witwe; ~ **sole** ledige (alleinstehende, unverheiratete) Frau; ~ **sole trader** (merchant, *Br.*) selbständige Geschäftsfrau, Kauffrau.

feminism Frauenbewegung.

feminist Frauenrechtlerin.

fence Ein-, Umzäunung, Zaun, *(place of stolen goods, sl.)* Aufbewahrungsort für Diebesgut (Hehlerware), *(readiness in debate)* Debatierkunst, *(receiver of stolen goods)* Hehler;
on the ~ *(US)* unentschlossen, neutral;
wire ~ Metallgitter;
~ *(v.)* einzäunen, -hegen, -frieden, *(fig.)* Spiegelfechterei treiben, Ausflüchte machen, *(hunt, Br.)* zum Schongebiet erklären, *(receiver, sl.)* mit Diebesgut handeln, *(Scot.)* ungestörte Gerichtsverhandlung sicherstellen;
~ **in** einzäunen; ~ **off** abzäunen; ~ **out** abwehren; ~ **with a question** einer Frage ausweichen; ~ **securely** *(machinery)* gegen Unfälle sichern; ~ **a town with walls** Stadt mit Festungswällen umgeben;
to come down on the right side of the ~ Partei des Siegers ergreifen; **to come down on one or the other side of the** ~ sein Mäntelchen nach dem Winde hängen; **to come off the** ~ Neutralität aufgeben; **to mend one's ~s** *(US)* seine politischen Interessen wahren, nachbarliche Beziehungen verbessern; **to sit on (ride,** *US)* **the** ~ sich zu keiner Partei schlagen, unentschlossen sein, Zaungast sein, sich neutral verhalten;
~ **man** *(US)* unentschlossener Politiker; ~ **month** *(Br.)* Schonzeit; ~ **rider (sitter)** Unentschlossener; ~ **season (time)** *(Br.)* Schonzeit.

fencing *(enclosure)* Einzäunung, -friedigung, *(fig.)* Spiegelfechterei, Ausflüchte;
wire ~ Drahteinzäunung;
~ **provisions** *(machinery)* Absicherungsbestimmungen.

fend *(v.)* **| for o. s.** sich allein durchschlagen; ~ **off** abwehren; ~ **off a collision** *(ship)* Kollision vermeiden.

fender Schutzvorrichtung, *(fireplace)* Kaminvorsatz, *(locomotive)* Stoßfänger, *(mar.)* Fender, *(US)* Kotflügel;
~ **beam** *(railway)* Prellbock.

feoffee in (of) trust Fideikommißerbe.

feoffment Belehnung;
~ **in trust** Fideikommiß.

ferm Pachthof.

ferment *(fig.)* Gärung, innere Unruhe;
~ *(v.)* aufputschen;
to be in a state of ~ im Aufruhr sein.

ferret *(fig.)* Spion, Spitzel;
~ *(v.)* **out** aufspüren; ~ **out a secret** Geheimnis entdecken.

ferriage Überfahrts-, Fährgeld.

ferro-concrete Stahlbeton.

ferry Fähre, Fährschiff, *(airplane)* Überführungsdienst;
aerial ~ Fährbrücke; **trail** ~ fliegende Fähre; **train** ~ Fährschiff;

~ *(v.)* Fährdienst versehen, *(plane)* von der Fabrik zum Flugplatz fliegen, *(vehicles)* überführen, abliefern;
~ **a car across** Auto mit der Fähre übersetzen;
to take the ~ Fähre benutzen;
~ **bridge** Landungsbrücke, Trajekt; ~ **car** *(US coll.)* Privatwaggon für Stückgutladungen; ~ **command** *(airplane)* Überführungs-, Abhol-, Lieferkommando; ~ **craft** Fährboot; ~ **dues** Fährgeld; ~ **fare** Fährgeld; ~ **franchise** Fährkonzession; ~ **line** Überführungsroute; ~ **rocket** Landerakete, -fähre; ~ **service** Fährbetrieb; ~ **steamer** Fährdampfer; ~ **ticket** Fährschein.

ferryboat Fähre, Fährboot;
~ **advertising** Fährschiffwerbung.

ferryhouse Fährhaus.

ferryman Fährmann.

fertile fruchtbar, ergiebig, *(fig.)* schöpferisch, produktiv;
to be ~ **in excuses** jederzeit Ausreden bei der Hand haben;
~ **fields (soil)** fruchtbares Land; ~ **imagination** schöpferische Phantasie.

fertility rate Fruchtbarkeitsrate.

fertilizable bebauungsfähig.

fertilize *(v.)* **the soil** Boden düngen.

fertilizer künstlicher Dünger;
~ **industry** Düngemittelindustrie.

festal occasion festlicher Anlaß.

festival Festspiel, Festival;
~ **committee** Festausschuß.

festive festlich, feierlich;
~ **affair** gesellschaftliche Veranstaltung; ~ **board** Festtafel; ~ **season** Feiertage.

festivity Feier, Fest, Festlichkeit, festliche Stimmung.

festoon Girlande;
~ *(v.)* mit Girlanden schmücken.

fetch Herbeiholen, Bringen, *(trick)* Kniff, Trick;
~ *(v.)* [ab]holen, *(sell for)* einbringen, erzielen;
~ **and carry** niedrige Dienste verrichten, lediglich Handlanger sein; ~ **a doctor** Arzt holen; ~ **into port** in den Hafen einlaufen;
~ **a good price** sich gut verwerten (verkaufen) lassen, guten Preis erzielen.

fetter Fessel, *(fig.)* Zwang, Fessel, Hindernis;
~**s** Gefangenschaft;
~ *(v.)* [durch Schutzzölle] knebeln;
to burst one's ~s seine Fesseln sprengen; **to cast off the ~s of business** sich von geschäftlichen Sorgen frei machen.

fettle, in good in Form.

feud Fehde;
to be at ~ **with s. o.** mit jem. in Feindschaft leben.

feudal | system Lehnswesen; ~ **tenure** Lehnsbesitz.

feuilleton Feuilleton;
~ **supplement** Unterhaltungsbeilage.

feuilletonist Feuilletonschreiber.

feuilletonistic feuilletonistisch.

fever Fieber[zustand];
in a ~ in heller Aufregung.

fiasco Mißerfolg, Reinfall, Fiasko;
to be a ~ mit einem Fiasko enden.

fiat Machtanspruch, *(authorization)* Bestätigung, *(court order)* richterliche Verfügung, gerichtliche Anordnung;
joint ~ Konkurseröffnungsbeschluß;
~ **in bankruptcy** Konkursverwaltereinsetzung;
~ *(v.)* bevollmächtigen, zustimmen;
to give one's ~ **to s. th.** einer Sache zustimmen;
~ **money** *(US)* Papiergeld ohne Deckung, Buch-, Giralgeld; ~ **standard** Papierwährung.

fib Notlüge, kleine Schwindelei, Flunkerei;
to tell a ~ flunkern.

fibre Faserstoff, Textur, *(fig.)* Charakterstärke, Rückgrat;
man-made ~s Kunststoffe; **moral** ~ moralisches Rückgrat;
~ **direction** Laufrichtung.

fibreboard Holzfaserplatte.

fickle launisch, unbeständig;
to be ~ **with one's attentions** in seinen Neigungen schwanken;
~ **fortune** veränderliches Glück.

fiction Fiktion, *(literature)* Belletristik, Unterhaltungsliteratur, Roman;
general ~ gängiger Roman; **legal** ~ gesetzliche Fiktion; **light** ~ leichte Romanliteratur; **science** ~ Zukunftsroman;
~ **of law** gesetzliche Fiktion, Rechtsfiktion, -vermutung;
~ **character** Romanfigur; ~ **department** *(publishing house)* Romanabteilung; ~ **writer** Romanschriftsteller, Romancier.

fictional literature Unterhaltungsliteratur.

fictioner Romanschriftsteller.

fictitious fingiert, fiktiv, frei erfunden, *(assumed)* angenommen, *(counterfeit)* nachgemacht, unecht;
~ **account** Deckkonto; ~ **accounts** fingierte Rechnungen; ~ **action** Scheinprozeß; ~ **assets** fiktive Vermögenswerte; ~ **bargain** Scheingeschäft; ~ **bill** *(Br.)* Kellerwechsel; ~ **character of a novel** erfundene Romanfigur; ~ **claim** fingierter Anspruch; ~ **contract** Scheinvertrag; ~ **dividend** Scheindividende; ~ **liabilities** fingierte Kreditoren; ~ **marriage** Scheinehe; ~ **name** fingierter Name, Deckname, Pseudonym; ~ **payee** fingierter Remittent; ~ **payment** fingierte Zahlung; ~ **person** juristische Person; ~ **plaintiff** fingierte Prozeßpartei; ~ **price** fingierter Preis; ~ **profit** Scheingewinn; ~ **promise** unterstelltes Vertragsversprechen; ~ **purchase** Scheinkauf; ~ **sale** Schein-, Proformaverkauf; ~ **seizing** gesetzlich verfügte Besitzeinweihung; ~ **transaction** fingiertes Geschäft, Scheingeschäft; ~ **value** fiktiver Wert.

fiddle *(fam.)* Schwindel, Trick, *(nonsense)* dummes Zeug, *(stock exchange, London)* 1/16 Pfund, *(swindle, US. sl.)* kleine Schwindelei;
fit as a ~ kreuzfidel, putzmunter, kerngesund, quietschvergnügt;
~ *(v.) (sl.)* illegal erwerben;
~ **about** herumstümpern; ~ **away one's time** seine Zeit vertrödeln, seine Zeit verplempern; ~ **an income tax return** *(sl.)* bei der Einkommensteuererklärung betrügen; ~ **over a job** Sache austüfteln; ~ **while Rome burns** *(coll.)* sich mit Nichtigkeiten während einer Katastrophe beschäftigen; ~ **about one's room** in seinem Zimmer herumkramen;
to have a face as long as a ~ ganz bedeppert aussehen; **to play the first** ~ die erste Geige spielen; **to play second** ~ nur die zweite Geige spielen, wenig zu sagen haben, erst an zweiter Stelle rangieren.
fiddle-faddle Unsinn, Quatsch.
fiddlehead *(mar.)* Gallionsfigur.
fiddler *(loafer)* Müßiggänger.
fiddlestick *(fig.)* wertloses Zeug.
fiddling trivial, geringfügig;
a ~ **job** eine Geduldsprobe; ~ **little jobs** läppische Tätigkeit.
fide, bona gutgläubig, in gutem Glauben; **mala** ~ bösgläubig.
fidei | commission Fideikommiß, Nacherbschaft; ~ **commissary** Fideikommiß-, Nacherbe.
fidelity Aufrichtigkeit, Ehrlichkeit, *(accuracy)* Genauigkeit, Pflichttreue, *(television)* naturgetreue Wiedergabe;
contractual ~ Vertragstreue; **high** ~ naturgetreue Tonwiedergabe, Stereoklang;
~ **to one's principles** Festhalten an seinen Grundsätzen; ~ **of a translation** Genauigkeit einer Übersetzung;
to translate with the greatest ~ äußerst wortgetreu übersetzen;
~ **bond** Kaution gegen Veruntreuung, Kautionsverpflichtung; ~ **department** Garantieabteilung; **high** ~ **gram(m)ophone** Stereogrammophon; ~ **guarantee insurance** *(Br.)* Kautionsversicherung; ~ **insurance** *(US)* Kautions-, Garantieversicherung.
fiducial office Vertrauensposten.
fiduciaries, corporate Treuhandgesellschaft.
fiduciary Treuhänder, Vertrauensmann, -person;
~ *(a.)* treuhänderisch, anvertraut, *(notes)* fiduziär, ungedeckt; ~ **account** Treuhandkonto; ~ **accounting** treuhänderische Buchführung; ~ **activity** treuhänderische Tätigkeit; ~ **agent** Treuhänder; ~ **bond** Kautionsverpflichtung; ~ **capacity** Treuhändereigenschaft; **to act in** ~ **capacity** als Treuhänder handeln; **to be held in a** ~ **capacity** treuhänderisch verwaltet werden; ~ **coëmption** Kauf für einen Dritten; ~ **circulation** *(Br.)* ungedeckter Notenumlauf; ~ **contract** Treuhand-, Sicherungs-, Übereignungsvertrag; ~ **currency** ungedeckter Notenumlauf; ~ **debt** Schuld aufgrund eines Treuhandverhältnisses; ~ **debtor** Treunehmer; ~ **duty** treuhänderische Funktion; ~ **heir** Vorerbe; ~ **interest** treuhänderischer Anteil; ~ **[note] issue** *(Br., Bank of England)* ungedeckte Notenausgabe; **to limit the** ~ **issue** *(Br.)* Banknotenausgabe kontingentieren; ~ **limit** ungedeckte Notenausgabegrenze; ~ **loan** ungedeckter Personalkredit; ~ **money** Buch-, Giralgeld; ~ **nature** Vertrauensfunktion; ~ **note** *(Br.)* ungedeckte Banknote; ~ **note issue** *(Bank of England)* ungedeckte Banknotenausgabe; ~ **position** Vertrauensstellung; ~ **powers** treuhänderische Vollmachten; ~ **relations** Vertrauensbeziehung, -verhältnis; ~ **relationship** Treuhand-, Vertrauensverhältnis; ~ **standard** Papiergeldwährung.
fidget nervöse Unruhe.
field Feld, Acker[land] *(airport, mil.)* Feldflughafen, *(market)* Absatzgebiet, Markt, *(range)* Fach, Bereich, Amtsbereich, Fach-, Arbeits-, Sachgebiet, *(salesman)* Außendienst, *(scope)* Bereich, Bezirk, *(sport)* Sport-, Spielfeld, *(television)* Raster;

in the ~ im Außendienst; **in the economic** ~ auf wirtschaftlichem Gebiet; **in the** ~ **of agriculture** auf landwirtschaftlichem Gebiet; **in his** ~ auf seinem Gebiet, in seinem Fach; **in the** ~ **of public utilities** auf dem Gebiet der öffentlichen Versorgungsbetriebe; **in the social** ~ auf sozialem Gebiet; **out in the** ~ *(US)* nicht in Washington stationiert;
coal ~ Kohlenrevier, -lager; **badly cultivated** ~ schlecht bestelltes Feld; **diamond** ~ Diamantengebiet; **flying** ~ Flugplatz; **gold** ~ Goldgebiet; **hard-fought** ~ schwere Schlacht; **ice** ~ Eisscholle; **industrial** ~ industrieller Bereich; **landing** ~ Landeplatz; **mine** ~ Minengebiet; **oil** ~ Erdölgebiet, Ölvorkommen; **medium-priced** ~ mittlerer Preissektor; **pasture** ~ Wiese; **related** ~s verwandte Gebiete, benachbarte Fachgebiete; **tilled** ~ bestelltes Feld; **unlabo(u)red** ~ unbebautes Feld;
~ **of action (activity)** Tätigkeitsbereich, Arbeitsbereich, -feld; ~ **of application** Anwendungsbereich, -gebiet, Einsatzbereich, -gebiet; ~ **of art** Gebiet der schönen Künste; ~ **of attraction** attraktive Gegend; ~s **and branches** Außendienst und Filialen; ~ **of business activity** geschäftlicher Tätigkeitsbereich; **primary** ~s **of business** Hauptwirtschaftsgebiete; ~ **under cultivation** bestelltes Feld; **fair** ~ **and no favo(u)r** gleiche Bedingungen für alle; ~ **of finance** Finanzgebiet; ~ **of major professional interest** Hauptinteressengebiet; ~ **of knowledge** Wissensgebiet; ~ **of operation** Tätigkeitsgebiet, Arbeitsbereich; ~ **of politics** politisches Gebiet; ~ **of research** Forschungsgebiet; ~ **of study** Forschungs-, Arbeitsgebiet; ~ **of traffic** Verkehrswesen; ~ **of training** Ausbildungsbereich; **wide** ~ **of vision** weiter Gesichtskreis; ~ **of work** Aufgabenbereich;
~ *(v.) (mil.)* Soldaten ausrüsten;
to be outside s. one's ~ nicht in jds. Arbeitsgebiet fallen; **to open up a** ~ **of action for s. o.** Aufgabengebiet für j. schaffen; **to hold the** ~ Feld behaupten; **to leave s. o. in possession of the** ~ Feld für j. räumen; **to play the** ~ sich nicht festlegen; **to work in the** ~ im Außendienst tätig sein;
~ **agent** Vertreter im Außendienst; ~ **airport** Feldflughafen; ~ **allowance** *(mil.)* Front-, Mobilmachungszulage; ~ **auditor** Außenbeamter der Revision; ~ **bag** *(mil.)* Brotbeutel; ~ **base** *(mil.)* Etappengebiet, -ort; ~ **book** Flurbuch; ~ **boundary** Feldmark; ~ **control** Kontrolle des Außendienstes; ~ **costs** Plazierungskosten eines Produkts; ~ **corps engineers** Pioniertruppe; ~ **crops** Feldfrüchte; ~ **damage** Flurschaden; ~ **day** *(fig.)* ereignisreicher Tag, Galatag, *(mil.)* Truppenbesichtigung; **to have a** ~ **day** sich erfolgreich betätigen; ~ **dressing** *(mil.)* Verbandspäckchen; ~ **driver** *(US)* Feldhüter; ~ **engineers** *(Br.)* leichte Pioniertruppe; ~ **equipment** *(mil.)* feldmarschmäßige Ausrüstung; ~ **executive** Führungskraft im Außendienst; ~ **exercise** *(mil.)* Geländeübung; ~ **experience** Erfahrungen im Außendienst; ~ **force** im Außendienst eingesetzte Kräfte; **to back up the** ~ **forces** im Außeneinsatz tätige Kräfte verstärken; ~ **glass** Feldstecher; ~ **guide to** Kompendium über; ~ **hand** Landarbeiter; ~ **hospital** *(mil.)* fliegendes Lazarett, Hilfs-, Feldlazarett; ~ **hospital nurse** Rotkreuzschwester; ~ **interviewer** Befrager, Interviewer; ~ **interviewing** Befragung; ~ **inventory** Auslieferungs-, Außenlager; ~ **investigation** Umfrage, Marktforschung; ~ **investigator** Marktforscher, Interviewer; ~ **kitchen** Feldküche; ~ **manager** Außendienstbevollmächtigter, Gebietsverkaufsleiter; ~ **manoeuvre** *(Br.)* Felddienstübung; ~ **manual** *(mil.)* Felddienstordnung; ~ **map** Flurkarte; ~ **music** Marschmusik; ~ **name** Flurname; ~ **night** *(pol., Br.)* entscheidende Sitzung (Debatte); ~ **notes** Vermessungsnotizen; ~ **office** Außenstelle; ~ **officer** Außenbeamter; ~ **organization** Außenorganisation; ~ **pack** *(mil.)* Marschgepäck; ~ **postcard** Feldpostkarte; ~ **ration** *(mil.)* Feldverpflegung; ~ **records** Fachunterlagen; ~ **reeve** *(Br.)* Beauftragter für das Weideland; ~ **research** *(statistics)* Primärerhebung; ~ **sales force** Verkaufsorganisation; ~ **sales manager** Außenstellenleiter; ~ **service** Außendienst[tätigkeit]; ~ **study** Forschungsarbeit; ~ **staff** Mitarbeiter im Außendienst; ~ **survey** sorgfältige Untersuchung, *(marketing)* Absatz-, Marktforschung, Marktuntersuchung; **open-** ~ **system** Flurzwang; ~ **telephone** *(mil.)* Feldfernsprecher; ~ **test** [Produktions]probelauf; ~ **training** *(mil.)* Geländeübung, Gefechtsdienst; ~ **trip** Studienfahrt.
field warehouse *(US)* Lagerbetrieb, Außenlager;
~ **loan** Kredit gegen Sicherungsübereignung; ~ **receipt** Sicherungsübereignungs-, Lagerschein.
field warehousing *(US)* Lagerung sicherungsübereigneter Waren; ~ **organization** Lagerhausgesellschaft.
fieldwork Außenarbeit, -dienst, -einsatz, auswärtige Tätigkeit, *(interview)* individuelle Befragung, *(sociology)* Feldarbeit.
fieldworker Marktbefrager, *(sales force)* Außendienstmitarbeiter.

fifo (first-in, first-out) Fifoverfahren zur Vorratsbewertung, *(inventory valuation)* Zuerstentnahme der älteren Vorräte und Bilanzierung zum jeweiligen Buchwert, Realisationsprinzip.

Fifth Amendment, to plead the wegen möglicher Selbstbezichtigung die Aussage verweigern.

fifth│column *(pol.)* Fünfte Kolonne, Untergrundbewegung; ~‑**column activities** Untergrundtätigkeit; ~ **columnist** Untergrundkämpfer; ~ **essence** Quintessens; ~ **freedom rights** *(aviation, Br.)* besondere Luftverkehrsvergünstigungen; ⁎ **Teller** *(US)* [etwa] Reichsbankabrechnung; ~ **wheel at a coach** *(fig.)* fünftes Rad am Wagen, überflüssige Person.

fifty-fifty halbe-halbe.

fig Pfifferling, Kleinigkeit;
not to care a ~ for it keinen Deut darauf geben.

fight Gefecht, Kampf, Treffen, *(struggle)* Schlägerei, Streit;
in the thick of the ~ mitten im Kampfgetümmel;
hand-to-hand ~ Handgemenge; **prize ~** Wettkampf; **sham ~** Scheingefecht, Manöver; **sea ~** Seegefecht; **stand-up ~** regelrechter Kampf; **straight ~** Kampf zwischen zwei Kandidaten; **~ to a finish** Kampf bis zur Entscheidung; **~ against inflation** Inflationsbekämpfung; **~ for the market** Kampf um den Absatzmarkt; **~ against recession** Rezessionsbekämpfung;
~ *(v.)* kämpfen, *(law)* streiten;
~ an action at law sich in einem Prozeß verteidigen; **~ back a disease** einer Krankheit widerstehen; **~ for one's cause** für seine Sache kämpfen; **~ in defence of one's country** zur Verteidigung seines Landes kämpfen, sein Land verteidigen; **~ a duel** sich duellieren; **~ a fire** Feuer bekämpfen; **~ with their gloves off** sich einen erbarmungslosen Kampf liefern; **~ off a cold** Erkältung bekämpfen; **~ for one's own hand** seine Interessen wahren (vertreten); **~ it out** es ausfechten; **~ out the battle to the end** bis zum bitteren Ende kämpfen; **~ shy of s. o.** jem. aus dem Weg gehen; **~ shy of capital investment** vor Kapitalinvestitionen zurückschrecken; **~ for lower taxes** sich für niedrigere Steuern einsetzen; **~ through all the troubles** mit allen Schwierigkeiten fertig werden; **~ tooth and nail** sich mit Händen und Füßen wehren; **~ like vultures over the succession** wie Aasgeier um die Nachfolge kämpfen; **~ one's way** seinen Weg machen; **~ one's way at s. th.** sich mit etw. herumschlagen;
to have a hard ~ to make both ends meet sich schwer tun, mit seinen Mitteln auszukommen; **to have plenty of ~ left** noch über genügend Kampfgeist verfügen; **to put up little ~** wenig Kampfgeist zeigen; **to show ~** kampflüstern sein; **to start the ~** mit den Feindseligkeiten beginnen; **to take all the ~ of s. o.** j. seines ganzen Kampfgeistes berauben.

fighter Kämpfer, Schläger, Raufbold, *(mil.)* Jagdflugzeug;
~ airplane Jagdflugzeug; **~ bomber** Kampfbomber, -flugzeug, Jagdbomber, Jabo; **~ group** *(Br.)* Jagdgeschwader, *(US)* Jagdgruppe; **~ pilot** Jagdflieger; **~ plane** Jagdflugzeug; **~ umbrella** Jagdschutz; **~ wing** *(Br.)* Jagdgruppe, *(US)* Jagdgeschwader.

fighting Kämpfe, Gefecht;
street ~ Straßenkämpfe;
~ brand *(advertising)* Kampfmarke; **~ capacity** *(mil.)* Schlagkraft; **~ chance** Gewinnchance; **to live like a ~ cock** sich stets wie ein Kampfhahn aufführen; **~ efficiency** *(ship)* Kampfkraft; **~ force** Kampfkraft; **~ forces** Kampftruppe; **~ fund** *(union)* Streik-, Kampffonds; **~ line** Gefechtslinie; **~ strength** Kampfkraft; **to be on ~ terms** in Fehde miteinander liegen; **~ unit** Gefechtseinheit.

figurative sense übertragene Bedeutung.

figuratively in übertragenem (bildlichem) Sinne.

figure Gestalt, Form, *(amount)* Betrag, Wert, *(diagram)* Figur, Diagramm, *(illustration in a book)* Abbildung, Illustration, Tafel, *(metaphorical expression)* Redewendung, *(law of competition)* Bildzeichen, *(number)* Zahl, Ziffer, *(pattern)* Muster, *(personality)* Persönlichkeit, wichtige Person, *(price)* Preis;
at the best ~ bestens; **at a high ~** teuer; **at a low ~** billig; **by ~s** ziffernmäßig; **in round ~s** in einer runden Summe; **in ~s and words** in Ziffern und Worten;
average ~ Durchschnittszahl; **blind ~** undeutlich geschriebene Zahl; **bracketed ~** Klammerzahl; **central ~** *(drama)* zentrale Figur; **commerce department ~s** Ziffern des Wirtschaftsministeriums; **comparable (comparative) ~** Vergleichsziffer; **distinguished ~** bedeutende Erscheinung; **dominating ~** beherrschende Figur; **hard ~s** zuverlässiges Zahlenmaterial; **large ~** vierstellige Zahl; **magazine-reading ~s** Ziffern über den Leserkreis von Zeitschriften; **official ~s** amtliche Zahlen; **price ~s** Preisziffern; **provisional ~s** vorläufige Zahlen; **released Board of Trade ~s** vom Handelsministerium veröffentlichte Ziffern; **revised ~s** bereinigte Zahlen; **round ~** glatte (auf-, abgerundete) Zahl;

standard ~s of distribution Absatzkennzahlen; **greatest ~ of his era** bedeutendste Erscheinung seines Zeitalters; **leading ~s in finance, industry and trade** führende Persönlichkeiten des Finanz- und Wirtschaftslebens; **~s on sales volume** Umsatzangaben, -ziffern; **~ of speech** Redewendung; **mere ~ of speech** bloße Redensart;
~ *(v.)* (appear) darstellen, figurieren, *(calculate)* berechnen, in Zahlen angeben, ausrechnen, *(be conscious)* guten Klang haben;
~ o. s. sich im Geist vorstellen; **~ as s. o.** sich für j. anderen ausgeben;
~ on s. o. arriving early mit jds. früher Ankunft rechnen; **~ to s. one's credit** in jds. Guthaben stehen; **~ for an election** sich als Wahlkandidat bewerben; **~ in history** historische Rolle spielen; **~ large** große Rolle spielen; **~ on a list** auf einer Liste stehen; **~ for office** *(coll.)* sich um ein Amt bemühen; **~ out [at]** sich berechnen [auf], veranschlagt werden [auf], *(v. t.)* aus-, berechnen, *(US)* herausbekommen, austüfteln; **~ out the expense** Unkosten berechnen; **~ out at several millions** sich auf mehrere Millionen belaufen; **~ in the papers** in den Zeitungen erwähnt werden; **~ up** zusammenrechnen; **~ up the costs** Kosten veranschlagen (berechnen); **~ on a success** *(US)* mit einem Erfolg rechnen; **~ in the war** entscheidende Kriegsfunktionen ausüben;
not to allow credit beyond a certain ~ Kredit nur in einem bestimmten Rahmen gewähren; **to assess on ~s** auf Zahlen basieren; **to be smart at ~s** gut rechnen (mit Zahlen gut umgehen) können; **to buy at a low ~** billig erwerben; **to cast up ~s** zusammenrechnen, -zählen, addieren; **to cut a fine ~** gute Figur machen; **to cut a poor (sorry) ~** armselige Rolle spielen; **to do things on the big (go the whole) ~** *(US)* sich nicht mit Kleinigkeiten abgeben; **to drag down the overall profit ~s** Gesamtentwicklung der Gewinne negativ beeinflussen; **to draw funny ~s** Witzfiguren zeichnen; **to express in ~s** in Ziffern angeben; **to eyeball the ~s** Zahlen schätzen; **to fetch a high ~** hohen Preis erzielen; **to fill in the ~s** Zahlen einsetzen; **to gather ~s** Zahlenangaben gewinnen; **to juggle with ~s** Zahlenakrobatik betreiben; **to modify ~s for the sake of comparability** Ziffern zu Vergleichszwecken modifizieren; **to reach a respectable ~** erhebliche Umsätze machen; **to reckon one's ~s** seine Zahlen überprüfen; **to run into three ~s** *(costs)* in die Hunderte gehen; **to run into five ~s** *(income)* fünfstellig sein; **to sell at a high ~** gut (teuer) verkaufen; **to work out the ~s** Kalkulation vornehmen;
~ artist figürlicher Zeichner; **~ code** Zahlenkode, Telegraphenschlüssel.

figured iron Profileisen.

figurehead Gal(l)ions-, Repräsentationsfigur.

figuring Bezifferung;
~ [out] Berechnung.

filament Glühfaden.

filch *(v.)* klauen, stibitzen.

file Aktenstück, -bündel, -ordner, Kartei, Sammelmappe, Ordner, *(column)* Zug, *(data processing)* Datenmenge, *(mil.)* Reihe, Glied, *(of newspapers)* Jahrgang, Stoß Zeitungen, *(record)* Vorgang, *(register)* Liste, Verzeichnis, *(report)* Bericht;
for our ~s zu den Akten, für unser Archiv; **for your ~s** für die dortigen Akten; **in ~** *(mil.)* in Reih und Glied; **on ~** bei den Akten;
accordion (bellows) ~ Harmonikaakte; **alphabetic (box) ~s** alphabetisch geführte Akten; **basic-fact ~** Hauptakte; **bill ~** Wechselarchiv; **card-index ~** Karthothek, Kartei; **central ~** Zentralablage; **closed ~s** abgelegte (geschlossene) Akten; **credit ~** Kreditregistratur; **dead ~s** abgelegte Akten; **a deep ~** ganz geriebener Kunde; **departmental ~s** Aktenablage einer Abteilung; **in ~** Eingangskörbchen; **letter ~** Briefablage, -ordner, Schnellhefter; **map and plan ~** Kartenschrank; **master ~** Haupt-, Zentralkartei; **old ~** schlauer Fuchs; **ordinary ~s** übliche Akten; **personnel ~s** Personalakten; **ready-reference ~** griffbereite Akte; **single ~** Gänsemarsch; **tickler ~** Terminkalender; **wanted-person ~** Fahndungsbuch;
~ *(v.)* geltend machen, *(at court)* registrieren, gerichtlich eintragen lassen, *(clerk at court)* mit Eingangsvermerk versehen, *(documents)* [Akten, Briefe] ablegen, einordnen, zu den Akten nehmen, *(hand in)* vorlegen;
~ with *(petition)* einreichen bei, einbringen, vorlegen;
~ accounts with the Registrar of Companies *(Br.)* sich beim Gesellschaftsregister eintragen lassen, beim Gesellschaftsregister hinterlegen; **~ an action** Klage einreichen; **~ an application** Antrag stellen (einreichen); **~ an application for a patent** Patentanmeldung einreichen; **~ an application for seats with the**

secretary Plätze im Sekretariat bestellen; ~ **away** weglegen, zu den Akten legen, in einen Aktenordner einheften; ~ **a bankruptcy petition** Konkursantrag stellen; ~ **a bill** Gesetzesvorlage einreichen, *(commence a suit)* Prozeß austragen; ~ **past a catafalque** an einem Katafalk vorbeidefilieren; ~ **a claim** Anspruch anmelden; ~ **a claim in court** Forderung einklagen; ~ **a document** Urkunde zu den Akten nehmen; ~ **in** abheften; ~ **a dumping complaint** Dumpingklage erheben; ~ **an income-tax return** Einkommensteuererklärung abgeben; ~ **index cards** Karteikarten einreihen; ~ **information to one's newspaper** seiner Zeitung eine Nachricht zukommen lassen; ~ **a letter away** Brief abheften; ~ **letters in alphabetical order** Briefe alphabetisch ablegen; ~ **material departmentally** Akten abteilungsweise ablegen; ~ **a notice of appeal** Berufung einlegen; ~ **numerically** nummernmäßig ablegen; ~ **an objection to a bankrupt's discharge** Einspruch gegen die Entlastung eines Gemeinschuldners erheben; ~ **off** im Gänsemarsch abmarschieren; ~ **in order of date** chronologisch ablegen; ~ **out** aus den Akten heraussuchen; ~ **a paper** Antrag einreichen; ~ **a petition** Gesuch einreichen; ~ **a petition for an arrangement** Gläubigervergleich beantragen, Vergleichsantrag stellen; ~ **one's petition (a petition in bankruptcy)** Konkurs anmelden, Konkurseröffnungsantrag stellen; ~ **a petition for a divorce** Scheidungsklage einreichen; ~ **a plan** Vorschlag einreichen, *(bankruptcy)* Vergleichsvorschlag machen; ~ **a proof of claim** Ansprchsberechtigung nachweisen; ~ **a sentence carefully** *(coll.)* einen Satz sorgfältig ausfeilen; ~ **by subject matter** nach Sachgebieten ablegen; ~ **a suit** *(US)* Klage erheben; ~ **a will** Testament vorlegen;
to be on ~ bei den Akten sein; **to be retained in the** ~ bei den Akten bleiben; **to compile** ~s Akten anlegen; **to examine one's** ~s seine Akten durchgehen; **to have access to the** ~s Akteneinsicht haben; **to gnaw a** ~ *(fig.)* sich die Zähne ausbeißen; **to keep on** ~ [in den Akten] geordnet aufbewahren; **to locate** ~s Akten nachweisen; **to locate wanted** ~s with ease and speed benötigte Akten schnell und leicht beiziehen; **to misplace a** ~ Akte verlegen; **to open a** ~ Akte anlegen; **to place the correspondence on one's** ~s Korrespondenz ablegen; **to place a report on one's** ~s Bericht zu seinen Akten nehmen (in seinen Ordner einheften); **to put on** ~ in Vormerkung nehmen, vormerken; **to put on the** ~s zu den Akten nehmen; **to review one's** ~s seine Akten durchgehen; **to subjoin to the** ~s zu den Akten nehmen; **to take on** ~ zu den Akten nehmen;
~ **cabinet** Aktenschrank; ~ **card** Kartei-, Kartothekkarte; ~ **clerk** *(US)* Registrator, Registraturangestellter; ~ **copy** Aktendurchschlag, Ablage, Archivexemplar; ~ **cover** Aktendeckel; ~ **destroyer** Aktenwolf; ~ **folder** Aktenhefter, -ordner, Schnellhefter; ~ **heading** Aktenrubrik; ~ **index** Aktenverzeichnis; ~ **mark** Akten-, Eingangsvermerk; ~ **number** Akten-, Geschäftszeichen; **our** ~ **No. ...** unser Zeichen; ~ **reference** Akten-, Geschäftszeichen; ~ **signal** Kartenreiter; ~ **and use system** *(insurance commissioner, US)* Vorlage- und Einführungssystem; ~ **wrapper estoppel** *(patent law)* Einschränkung des Erteilungsverfahrens; ~ **wrapper history** *(patent)* Gesamtvorgang des Erteilungsverfahrens.

filed | for record abgelegt;
to be ~ zu den Akten (zdA); ~ **material** abgelegte Akten, Ablage; ~ **proceedings** gefertigte Schriftsätze.
filer *(US)* Registrator, Ordner;
delinquent ~ *(US)* Einreicher einer verspäteten Steuererklärung.
filial duty Kindespflicht.
filiate *(v.)* Vaterschaft eines unehelichen Kindes feststellen.
filiation *(US)* Abstammung, *(Scot., US)* Vaterschaftsfeststellung;
~**proceedings** *(US)* Vaterschaftsprozeß, -verfahren.
filibuster Freibeuter, *(US)* Obstruktion, Verschleppungstaktik; ~ *(v.)* *(US)* Obstruktion treiben, *(parl.)* Verabschiedung eines Gesetzentwurfs aufzuhalten (zu verschleppen) suchen.
filibusterer *(US)* Obstruktionspolitiker, Verschleppungstaktiker.
filing *(registration)* Anmeldung, Abgabe, Einreichen, Einreichung, Registrierung, Einordnung, [Akten]ablage;
upon ~ *(patent law)* bei der Anmeldung;
alphabetical ~ alphabetische Ablage; **central** ~ zentrale Ablage; **chronological** ~ chronologische Ablage; **classified** ~ Aktenablage nach Sachgebieten; **departmental** ~ Aktenablage einer Abteilung; **flat-top** ~ Flachablage; **geographical** ~ Ablage nach Orten; **horizontal** ~ Flachablage; **lateral** ~ bibliothekarische Ablage, Stehablage; **subject** ~ Ablage nach Sach-

gebieten; **suspended** ~ Hängeablage;
~ **of an action** Klageeinreichung, -erhebung; ~ **in alphabetical order** Aktenablage in alphabetischer Reihenfolge; ~ **of an application** Antragstellung; ~ **of an application for a patent** Patentanmeldung; ~ **of bankruptcy petition** Einreichung des Konkursantrages; ~ **of the formal charge** Anklageerhebung; ~ **of claim** Forderungsanmeldung; ~ **of a complaint** Abfassung einer Beschwerde; ~ **in order of date** Aktenablage in chronologischer Reihenfolge; ~ **of letters** Briefablage; ~ **of an Inland Revenue affidavit** Abgabe einer Erbschaftssteuererklärung; ~ **of the petition** Einreichung eines Ehescheidungsantrags; ~ **of records** Aktenablage; ~ **of a resolution** Einbringung eines Beschlußantrages, Resolutionseinbringung; ~ **of schedule** Erstellung einer Konkursbilanz; ~ **of a suit** *(US)* Klageeinreichung;
~ **box** Karteikasten; ~ **cabinet** Kartothek, Kartei, Aktenschrank; ~ **card** Ablagekartei; ~ **clerk** *(US)* Registrator, Registraturleiter, Archivar; ~ **costs** Eintragungsgebühren, *(bankruptcy)* Konkursanmeldegebühr; ~ **date** Abgabetermin, Anmelde-, Einreichungsdatum; ~ **drawer** Karteischublade; ~ **equipment** Ablagevorrichtung; ~ **extension** Verlängerung der Abgabefrist; ~ **fee** Eintragungsgebühr, *(bankruptcy)* Anmeldegebühr; ~ **jacket** Aktenhefter; ~ **office** Anmeldestelle; ~ **period** *(patent law)* Anmeldefrist; ~ **system** Ablagesystem; **central** ~ **system** zentrales Ablagewesen, Zentralregistratur; ~ **term** Abgabefrist.

fill *(newspaper)* Füller, *(US)* Geländeauffüllung, Erd-, Steindamm;
~ *(v.)* *(complete)* ausfüllen, ergänzen, *(appoint holder of post)* besetzen, *(discharge duties of post)* ausfüllen, *(post)* innehaben, versehen, bekleiden;
~ **the bill** *(Br., sl.)* hervorragende Stelle einnehmen, *(US)* alle Anforderungen erfüllen; ~ **a chair** Lehrstuhl besetzen; ~ **the [speaker's] chair** Vorsitz führen; ~ **a doctor's prescription** Rezept ausschreiben; ~ **s. one's mind** j. gedanklich beschäftigen; ~ **a need** einem Bedürfnis entsprechen; ~ **an office satisfactorily** Amt zur Zufriedenheit ausfüllen; ~ **an order** *(US)* Auftrag ausführen (erledigen); ~ **a part well** *(theater)* Rolle gut spielen; ~ **s. one's place** für j. eintreten, an jds. Stelle treten, jds. Stelle einnehmen; ~ **a post** Stelle besetzen; ~ **a post for some time** Stelle einige Zeit innehaben; ~ **all requirements (every requirements)** allen Anforderungen genügen; ~ **one's free time with reading** in seiner freien Zeit viel lesen; ~ **a truck** Waggon beladen; ~ **a vacancy** Stelle besetzen; ~ **the void** Lücke füllen.
fill in *(v.)* *(Br.)* [Formular] ausfüllen;
~ **an application form** Antragsformular ausfüllen; ~ **blank spaces** leere Stellen ausfüllen; ~ **a form carelessly** Formular flüchtig ausfüllen; ~ **the date** Datum einsetzen; ~ **the figures** Ziffern (Zahlen) einsetzen; ~ **a job** Stellung besetzen; ~ **one's name on an official form** seinen Namen in einem Formular einsetzen; ~ **an outline** Einzelheiten nachtragen; ~ **a program(me)** Ersatzprogramm senden; ~ **until s. o. returns** j. bis zu seiner Rückkehr vertreten.
fill out *(v.)* in die Breite ziehen;
~ **a bill** *(US)* Wechselformular ausfüllen; ~ **a blank** *(US)* Formular ausfüllen; ~ **a writ** Erlaß unterschreiben.
fill up *(v.)* *(complete)* vervollständigen, ergänzen;
~ **a form** *(Br.)* Vordruck ausfüllen; ~ **s. one's place** jds. Stelle einnehmen; ~ **with petrol (a tank)** volltanken, Tank vollmachen.
fill, to eat to one's sich sattessen.
fill-in Einfügsel;
~ **reorder** Bestellung zur Lagerauffüllung, Lagerbestellung.
filled, not in Blanko;
~ **to the brim** voll bis zum Rand; ~ **up** *(car)* aufgetankt;
to remain to be ~ noch besetzt werden müssen;
~ **orders** ausgeführte (erledigte) Aufträge.
filler *(newspaper)* Füllsel, Füller, Lückenbüßer, *(advertising)* Füllanzeige;
~ **freight** Zusatzladung; ~ **paper** Ersatzeinlagen für ein Ringbuch.
filling | of a contract (in of orders) Auftragserledigung, -abwicklung; ~ **in of a questionnaire** Ausfüllung eines Fragebogens; ~ **of vacancies** Neubesetzung erledigter Stellen; ~ **up** *(of form, Br.)* Ausfüllen;
~ **station** *(US)* Tankstelle.
fillip *(stimulus)* Ansporn, Anreiz, *(trivial thing)* Lappalie, Kleinigkeit;
not worth a ~ keinen Pfifferling wert;
to give a fresh ~ **to sales** Absatzansporn geben.
fill-up Füller, Lückenbüßer.

film Film, *(cinema)* Film, Kino, *(fibre)* Faser, Faden, *(pellicle)* Membrane;
~s Filmerzeugnisse, -industrie;
blood-and-thunder ~ Westernfilm; **colo(u)r** ~ Farbfilm; **documentary** ~ Kulturfilm; **fast** ~ besonders lichtempfindlicher Film; **feature** ~ abendfüllender Film; **free** ~ avantgardistischer Film; **full-length** ~ abendfüllender Film; **low-budget** ~ niedrig kalkulierter Film; **news** ~ Wochenschau; **quality** ~ gehaltvoller Film; **roll** ~ Rollfilm; **serial** ~ Film in Fortsetzungen; **silent** ~ Stummfilm; **synchronized sound** ~ synchronisierter Film; **talking** ~ Tonfilm; **three-dimensional** ~ dreidimensionaler Film; **topical** ~ aktueller Film, Aktualitätenschau; **unexposed** ~ unbelichteter Film;
~ **of dust** Staubschicht;
~ *(v.)* verfilmen, Film drehen;
~ **well** sich gut verfilmen lassen;
to cut a ~ Film schneiden; **to develop a** ~ Film entwickeln; **to distribute a** ~ Film verleihen; **to expose a** ~ Film belichten; **to go to the** ~s ins Kino gehen; **to have a** ~ **in the can** Film abgedreht haben; **to produce a** ~ Film herstellen; **to put a novel on the** ~ Roman verfilmen; **to release a** ~ Film zulassen (durch die Filmselbstkontrolle bringen, zum Verleih freigeben); **to shoot a** ~ Film drehen, Filmaufnahmen machen; **to show a** ~ Film vorführen; **to sink into a** ~ in einen Film investieren; **to unreel a** ~ Film ablaufen lassen;
~ **actor** Filmschauspieler; ~ **actress** Filmschauspielerin; ~ **addict** Filmnarr; ~ **advance** Filmvorschub; ~ **advertisement** *(Br.)* Filmwerbung, Kinoreklame, -werbung; ~ **aid** Filmunterstützung, -zuschuß; ~ **audience** Filmpublikum; ~ **author**: **to be in the** ~ **business** beim Film (in der Filmbranche) sein; ~-**distributing business** Filmverleih[geschäft]; ~ **camera** Filmkamera, Aufnahmeapparat; ~ **cartridge** Rollfilmspule; ~ **cement** *(photo)* Filmklebemittel; ~ **censorship** Filmzensur; ~ **censorship committee** Filmbewertungsausschuß; ~ **clip** Filmklammer; ~ **company** Filmgesellschaft; ~ **copy** Filmkopie, Musterabzug; ~ **critic** Filmkritik; ~ **director** [Film]regisseur; ~ **distribution** Filmverleih; ~ **distributor** Filmverleih, -unternehmen; ~ **exchange** Filmverleih, -börse; ~ **expert** Filmfachmann, -experte; **to have a** ~ **face** photogen sein; ~ **festival** Filmfestspiele; ~ **finance** Filmfinanzierung; ~ **financing** Filmfinanzierung; ~ **freak** Filmungeheuer; ~ **gauge** Filmbreite; ~ **hit** Kassenschlager; ~ **industry** Filmindustrie; ~ **journalist** Filmjournalist; ~ **library** Filmarchiv; ~ **magazine** Filmzeitschrift, *(photo)* Filmkassette; ~-**making** Filmherstellung; ~ **music** Filmmusik; ~ **pack** Filmpack; ~ **part** Filmrolle; ~ **people** Kinopublikum; ~ **performance** Filmvorführung; ~ **premiere** Filmuraufführung, -premiere; ~ **processing** Filmentwicklung; ~-**processing firm** Filmkopieranstalt; ~ **producer** Filmproduzent; ~-**producing center** *(US)* (**centre,** *Br.*) Film[produktions-]zentrum; ~ **production** Filmproduktion; ~ **projection booth** Filmvorführkabine; ~ **projection room** Filmvorführraum; ~ **projector** Filmprojektor; ~ **receipts** Filmeinnahmen; ~ **reel** Filmspule, -rolle; ~ **review board** freiwillige Filmkontrolle, Filmprüfstelle; ~ **rights** Film-, Verfilmungsrechte; **to ask for an option of the** ~ **rights of a book** an den Filmrechten eines Buches interessiert sein; ~ **rush** Filmrohfassung; ~ **scanning** Filmabtastung; ~ **script** Filmmanuskript; ~ **sets** Filmbauten; **to run a** ~ **show** Filmvorführung veranstalten; ~ **spectacular** Filmplakat; ~ **speed** *(camera)* Laufgeschwindigkeit, *(film)* Lichtempfindlichkeit; ~ **spool** Filmrolle; ~ **star** Filmstar; ~ **stock** noch nicht entwickelter Film; ~ **store** Filmarchiv; ~ **strip** Tonbildschau; ~ **studio** Filmstudio, -atelier; ~-**subsidy board** Filmförderungsanstalt; ~ **test** Eignungsprüfung für den Film; ~ **take-up spool** *(photo)* Filmführungsrolle; ~ **title** Filmtitel; ~ **trade** Filmverleih; ~ **transmission** Fernsehübertragung eines Films; ~ **workers' union** Gewerkschaft der Filmangestellten.
filmgoers Kino-, Filmpublikum, Kinobesucher.
filming site Drehort.
filmlet *(advertising)* Kurzfilm, Werbepost.
filmmaker Filmhersteller.
filmmaking Filmherstellung.
filmset *(v.)* im Photosatz herstellen.
filmsetting Photosatz.
filmslide Diapositiv.
filter Filter, Schmutzfänger;
band-pass ~ Bandfilter; **colo(u)r** ~ *(photo)* Farbfilter;
~ *(v.)* filtern, *(v./i.)* durchsickern, allmählich bekannt werden, *(mil.)* Nachrichten auswerten;
~ **in** *(Br.)* sich in den Verkehrsstrom einreihen; ~ **news** *(mil.)* Nachrichten auswerten; ~ **into the streaming traffic** sich in den flutenden Verkehr einreihen; ~ **through** *(news)* durchsickern;

~ **center** *(US)* (**centre,** *Br.*) Flugmeldezentrale; ~ **paper** Filterpapier; ~ **shot** Farbfilmaufnahme; ~ **tip** Filtermundstück; ~-**tipped cigarette** Filterzigarette.
filth Schmutz, Unrat, *(fig.)* obzöne Reden, unflätige Sprache.
filthy *(fig.)* moralisch verderblich, sittenverderbend.
final Schluß, Ende, *(newspaper)* Spätausgabe, letzte Ausgabe;
~s Schlußprüfung, -examen, Abgangsprüfung;
bar ~ juristisches Schlußexamen; **late night** ~ Spätausgabe;
~ *(a.)* definitiv, endgültig, abschließend, *(judgment)* rechtskräftig;
~ **and conclusive** rechtskräftig, endgültig;
to become ~ *(judgment)* rechtskräftig werden; **to take one's** ~s sein Schlußexamen machen;
~ **accord** Abschlußvereinbarung; ~ **account** Endabrechnung, Abschlußrechnung; ~ **act** *(dipl.)* Schlußakte; ~ **age** *(insurance)* Schlußalter; ~ **amount** Endwert; ~ **answer** definitive Antwort; ~ **architect's certificate** Bauabnahme; ~ **art work** Reinzeichnung; ~ **assembled product** Endmontageprodukt; ~ **assembly** Fertig-, Endmontage; ~ **balance** Endsaldo, Schlußbilanz; ~ **bill** Schlußabrechnung; ~ **cause** Endzweck; ~ **chapter** Schlußkapitel; ~ **clause** Schlußbestimmung; ~ **commission** Abschlußprovision; ~ **concord** *(Br.)* endgültige Regelung einer Streitigkeit; ~ **consumer** Endverbraucher; ~ **consumption pattern** Endnachfragestruktur; ~ **copy** Reinschrift; ~ **costs** *(law court)* gesamte Prozeßkosten; ~ **date** äußerster Termin, Endtermin; ~ **date for payment** äußerster Zahlungstermin; ~ **day of a school term** letzter Schultag; ~ **decision** Endurteil; ~ **declaration** *(turnover tax)* Abschlußmeldung; ~ **decree** *(divorce proceedings)* Endurteil; ~ **demand** Endnachfrage; ~ **destination** endgültiger Bestimmungsort; ~ **determination** endgültige Entscheidung; ~ **direction** endgültige Vorschrift; ~ **discharge** Abschlußbescheinigung, Rechnungsentlastung, Schlußbescheinigung; ~ **disposition** alles endgültig regelnder Schiedsspruch; ~ **distribution** Schlußverteilung; ~ **dividend** Schlußdividende, *(liquidation)* Schlußquote; **to make a** ~ **effort** letzte Anstrengung unternehmen; ~ **examination** Abgangs-, Abschlußprüfung; ~ **fee** Schlußgebühr; ~ **goods** Endprodukt; ~ **hearing** letzte mündliche Verhandlung, Schlußtermin; ~ **information given** Endbescheid; ~ **injunction** richterliche Schlußverfügung; ~ **instal(l)ment** Schlußzahlung, letzte Rate; ~ **inventory** Schlußinventar, Endbestand; ~ **judgment** letztinstanzliches Urteil, Definitiv-, Endurteil; ~ **leg** Schlußetappe; ~ **manufacturing estimates** endgültige Fertigungsplanung; ~ **meeting** Schlußverhandlung; ~ **negotiations** Schlußverhandlungen; ~ **observations** Schlußbemerkungen; ~ **order** Endentscheidung; ~ **passage** *(parl.)* letzte (dritte) Lesung; ~ **payment** Rest-, Abschlußzahlung; ~ **port** Bestimmungshafen; ~ **preparations** letzte Vorbereitungen; ~ **process** Vollstreckungsklausel; ~ **product** Endprodukt; ~ **proof** letzter Korrekturabzug, endgültiger Andruck; ~ **protocol** *(dipl.)* Schlußprotokoll; ~ **provisions** Schlußbestimmungen; ~ **pull** endgültiger Andruck; ~-**quarter figures** Vierteljahresendziffern; ~ **quotation** *(stock exchange)* Schlußkurs; ~ **receiver's receipt** *(purchase of public land)* Schlußquittung; ~ **record** Schlußprotokoll; ~ **recovery** *(US)* Prozeßgewinn in letzter Instanz, obsiegendes Endurteil; ~ **report** letzte Notierung, Schlußbericht; ~ **respite** letzte Frist; ~ **result** Schlußergebnis; **to give a** ~ **ruling** endgültig bescheiden; ~ **sailing** Verlassen des letzten englischen Hafens; ~ **salary** Endgehalt; ~ **scene** Schlußszene; ~ **sentence** Endurteil; ~ **session** abschließende Sitzung; ~ **settlement** *(estate)* Schlußabrechnung, -verteilung; ~ **solution** Endlösung; ~ **stage** Endstufe; ~ **stocktaking** Schlußinventur; ~ **stopping point** Endstation; ~ **submission** Schlußplädoyer; ~ **switch** Leitungswähler; ~ **term** Schlußsemester; ~ **throes** Schlußagonie; **to put the** ~ **touches on s. th.** einer Sache den letzten Schliff geben; ~ **trial** Hauptverhandlungstermin; ~ **utility** Grenznutzen; ~ **utility theory** Grenznutzenlehre; ~ **velocity** Endgeschwindigkeit; ~ **volume** Schlußband; ~ **vote** Schlußabstimmung.
finalist übrigbleibender Examenskandidat.
finality Endgültigkeit, Unwiderruflichkeit.
finalize *(v.)* *(production)* Produktionsentscheidung treffen;
~ **an agreement** Schlußprotokoll erstellen.
finally, to settle a matter ~ Sache endgültig regeln.
finance Finanzwirtschaft, Finanzen, Geldwesen, -wirtschaft, Finanzgebarung, *(science)* Finanzwissenschaft;
in charge of ~ finanziell verantwortlich;
~s Staatseinkünfte, -finanzen, Finanzlage;
additional ~ zusätzliche Geldbeträge; **big** ~ *(US)* Hochfinanz; **business** ~ betriebliche Finanzgebarung; **controlled** ~ Finanzkontrolle; **corporate** ~ Finanzwirtschaft von Körperschaften; **corporation** ~ *(US)* Finanzierung von Aktiengesellschaften; **a**

country's ~s Staatsfinanzen; **disordered** ~s zerrüttete Finanzverhältnisse; **governmental** ~ Staatsfinanzwirtschaft; **high** ~ *(US)* Großkapital, Hochfinanz; **hire-purchase** ~ *(Br.)* Finanzierung von Abzahlungsgeschäften; **home** ~ *(Br.)* öffentliche Finanzen; **local** ~ kommunales Finanzwesen, Gemeindefinanzen; **national** ~s Staatsfinanzen; **precarious** ~s mißliche Finanzlage; **public** ~s Finanzwissenschaft, öffentliches Finanzwesen, Staatsfinanzen; **shattered** ~s zerrüttete Finanzen; **sound** ~ gesunde Finanzgebarung; **strong** ~s günstige Finanzverhältnisse, gute Finanzlage (finanzielle Lage);
~s **of a state** Staatsfinanzen; ~ **of foreign trade** Außenhandels-, Exportfinanzierung;
~ *(v.) (devise ways)* finanziell ausarbeiten, *(engage in financial operations)* Geldgeschäfte machen, *(procure capital)* finanzieren, Kapital beschaffen, Geld bereitstellen, kapitalisieren;
~ **away** *(US)* [Geld] verschieben; ~ **a business** Geschäft finanzieren; ~ **the costs of an undertaking** Geldmittel für ein Unternehmen zur Verfügung stellen; ~ **an enterprise** Finanzierung eines Unternehmens übernehmen; ~ **government deficits by printing money** Staatsdefizite mittels der Notenbankpresse beseitigen; ~ **an institution** Geldmittel für ein Unternehmen auftreiben; ~ **one's money away** *(US)* sein Geld verspekulieren; ~ **out of cashflow** aus Bruttoerträgen finanzieren; ~ **permanently** durchfinanzieren; ~ **a railroad** Eisenbahnlinie finanzieren; ~ **a scheme** Finanzierung eines Unternehmens durchführen; ~ **up to 75%** bis zu 75% finanzieren; ~ **with short-term money** mit kurzfristigen Geldmitteln finanzieren;
to adjust one's ~s seine Finanzen regeln; **to be versed in questions of** ~ Finanzfachmann sein; **to furnish with** ~ finanzieren; **to have a genius for** ~ Finanzgenie sein; **to have one's** ~s **in such a shape that ...** finanziell so gestellt sein, daß ...; **to jeopardize one's** ~s seine Finanzlage gefährden; **to make** ~ **available on a revolving and reducing basis** Finanzierungsmittel revolvierend einsetzen; **to manage the** ~s Finanzangelegenheiten verwalten; **to offer favo(u)rable** ~ günstige Finanzierungsbedingungen anbieten; **to purge the** ~s **of a country** Finanzen eines Landes (Staatsfinanzen) in Ordnung bringen; **to put s. one's** ~s **on a healthy basis** j. finanziell sanieren; **to put the** ~s **of a country on a healthy footing** staatliches Sanierungsprogramm durchführen; **to shatter** ~s Finanzwirtschaft zerrütten;
~ **accounting** Finanzbuchhaltung; ~ **Act** *(Br.)* Haushaltsgesetz; ~ **activity** finanzielle Aktivitäten; ~ **administration** Finanzverwaltung; ~ **advertisement** Finanzanzeige; ~ **Bill** *(Br.)* Steuer-, Finanzvorlage; ~ **bill** *(US, banking)* Finanz[ierungs]-, Mobilisierungswechsel; **accepted** ~ **bill** *(US)* Finanzakzept, *(US, banking)* Finanzierungs-, Mobilisierungswechsel; ~ **budget** Finanzierungsetat; ~ **charges** Finanzierungskosten, -gebühr; ~ **commissioner** *(EC)* Finanzkommissar; ~ **committee** Finanzausschuß; ~ **company** [für einen Konzern tätige] Finanzierungsgesellschaft, Abzahlungsbank, Geldinstitut; **commercial** ~ **company** Finanzierungsgesellschaft, -träger; **personal** ~ **company** *(US)* Finanzierungsgesellschaft für Kleinkredite; **sales** ~ **company** Absatzfinanzierungsgesellschaft; ~ **Corporation for Industry** *(Br.)* [etwa] Industriekreditbank; ~ **demand** Finanzbedarf; ~ **department** Finanzabteilung, Kasse; ~ **division** Finanzabteilung, Kasse; ~ **equipment leasing** Finanzmiete beweglicher Wirtschaftsgüter; ~ **function** finanzieller Aufgabenbereich; ~ **group** Finanzgruppe; ~ **house** Finanzierungsinstitut, -gesellschaft, Teil-, Abzahlungsbank; ~ **house shares** Aktien einer Finanzierungsgesellschaft; ~ **leaders** führende Finanzleute; ~ **manager** Direktor der Finanzabteilung, Leiter des Finanz- und Rechnungswesens; ~ **markets** Finanzmärkte; ~ **minister** Finanzminister; ~ **Ministry** Finanzministerium; ~ **office** *(company)* Finanzressort; ~ **officer** Finanz-, Steuerbeamter, *(company)* Finanzvorstand; ~ **paper** Finanzierungstitel; ~ **section** Finanzabteilung; **public** ~ **situation** Lage der öffentlichen Haushalte; ~ **stamp** Effektenstempel; ~ **subsidiary** Finanzierungsgesellschaft; ~ **talks** Finanzierungsbesprechungen.

financed finanziert;
federally ~ vom Bund finanziert; **privately** ~ frei (auf privater Basis) finanziert; **state-**~ vom Staate finanziert.
financials Finanzverhältnisse.
financial finanziell, finanztechnisch, fiskalisch, geldlich, pekuniär, materiell, *(coll.)* flüssig, bei Kasse (Gelde);
~ **ability** finanzielle Leistungsfähigkeit; ~ **accountant** Finanzbuchhalter; ~ **accounting** Geschäfts-, Finanzbuchhaltung; ~ **advertisement** Finanzanzeige; ~ **advice** finanzielle Beratung; ~ **adviser** Finanzberater; ~ **affairs** Finanzangelegenheiten, Finanzierungs-, Geldgeschäfte; ~ **agency** auf Finanzierungsfragen spezialisierte Werbeagentur; ~ **agent** Finanz-, Darlehensmakler; ~ **agreement** Finanz[ierungs]abkommen; ~ **aid** finanzielle Hilfe, Finanz[bei]hilfe; ~ **aid by the state to political parties** staatliche Parteienfinanzierung; **to extend** ~ **aid** finanzielle Unterstützung gewähren; ~ **analysis** Finanzanalyse; ~ **analyst** Finanzfachmann, -experte, -berater, -analytiker; ~ **arrangement** finanzielle Abmachung, Finanzierungsplan; ~ **assets** Geldvermögen; ~ **assistance** finanzielle Hilfe (Unterstützung); ~ **authority** Währungsbehörde; ~ **autonomy** Finanzautonomie; ~ **backer** finanzieller Hintermann, Geldgeber; ~ **backing** finanzieller Rückhalt, finanzielle Rückendeckung (Unterstützung); ~ **basis** Kapitalbasis; ~ **beating** finanzielle Belastung; ~ **benefit** finanzielle Zuwendung, Vermögensvorteil; ~ **bleeding** finanzielle Ausblutung; ~ **bond** Kaution; ~ **budget** Finanzhaushalt; ~ **burden** finanzielle Belastung, Finanzlast; ~ **capacity** finanzielle Leistungsfähigkeit, Finanzkraft; ~ **centre** Finanz-, Bankenzentrum; ~ **circles** Finanzkreise, -welt; ~ **circumstances** Vermögensverhältnisse; **to be in good** ~ **circumstances** in guten finanziellen Verhältnissen leben; ~ **claims** vermögensrechtliche Ansprüche; ~ **collapse** finanzieller Zusammenbruch; ~ **column** *(newspaper)* Handels-, Wirtschaftsteil [einer Zeitung]; ~ **commentary** Börsenkommentar; ~ **commission (committee)** Finanzausschuß; ~ **community** Finanzwelt; ~ **company** Finanzierungsgesellschaft; ~ **compensation** finanzielle Entschädigung; ~ **condition** Finanz-, Vermögenslage, finanzielle Lage; **unsound** ~ **conditions** ungesunde Finanzlage; ~ **conduct** Finanzgebarung; ~ **conference** Finanzkonferenz; ~ **consultant** Finanzberater; ~ **contribution** finanzieller Zuschuß, *(EC)* Finanzbeitrag; ~ **control** Überwachung, Finanzkontrolle; ~ **controller** Leiter der Finanzabteilung; ~ **corporations** *(US)* Banken und Versicherungen; **to furnish** ~ **counsel** in Finanzierungsfragen beraten; ~ **counsel(l)ing** finanzielle Beratung, Beratung in Finanzierungsfragen; ~ **counsel(l)ing firm** Beratungsfirma für finanzielle Fragen; ~ **crisis** Geld-, Finanzkrise; ~ **cushion** Finanzierungspolster; ~ **data** finanzielle Angaben (Unterlagen); ~ **dealing** Finanztransaktion; ~ **dealings** Finanzgebaren; ~ **debts** Geldforderungen des Kapitalverkehrs; ~ **department** Finanzabteilung; ~ **details** Einzelheiten über finanzielle Abmachungen; ~ **difficulties** Finanzierungsschwierigkeiten; **to get (fall, run) into** ~ **difficulties** in Zahlungsschwierigkeiten geraten; **to get out of one's** ~ **difficulties** aus seinen Geldnöten herauskommen; ~ **director** Finanzdirektor; ~ **disaster** finanzielle Katastrophe; **to observe** ~ **discipline** sich finanziell diszipliniert verhalten; ~ **district** Banken-, Finanzzentrum; ~ **division** Finanzabteilung; ~ **drag** finanzielle Belastung; ~ **drain** finanzielle Belastung (Inanspruchnahme); ~ **duty** Finanzzoll; ~ **economist** Finanzmathematiker; ~ **editor** *(US)* Wirtschaftsredakteur; ~ **embarrassment** schlechte Finanzlage, Geldverlegenheit; ~ **enterprise** Finanzierungsinstitut; ~ **establishment** Kreditinstitut; ~ **executive** Finanzvorstand; ~ **expense** Finanzierungskosten, Kapitalaufwand; ~ **expert** Finanzsachverständiger; ~ **factor** Finanzfaktor; ~ **failure** finanzieller Zusammenbruch; **to distribute** ~ **favo(u)rs** finanzielle Vergünstigungen gewähren; ~ **field** finanzielles Gebiet, Finanzgebiet, -sektor; **to function in all** ~ **fields** erfolgreiche Finanzgeschäfte auf allen Gebieten abwickeln; **to put on a better (sounder)** ~ **footing** auf eine gesunde finanzielle Grundlage stellen; ~ **forecasting** Beurteilung der finanziellen Entwicklung, Finanzprognose; **to run the complete** ~ **function with emphasis on long-term** ~ **planning** für den gesamten Finanzsektor mit dem Schwerpunkt langfristiger Vorausplanungen verantwortlich sein; ~ **gap** Finanzierungslücke; ~ **gearing (leverage)** Fremdkapitalwirkung auf die Eigenkapitalrentabilität; ~ **handbook** Handbuch der Finanzen; ~ **handicaps** finanzbedingte Hemmnisse; ~ **hardship** finanzielle Misere; **to suffer** ~ **hardship** sich in bedrängten Finanzverhältnissen befinden; ~ **health** gesunde Finanzgebarung; **to put a bank's** ~ **health in question** Finanzkraft einer Bank in Frage stellen; ~ **help** finanzielle Unterstützung; ~ **house (institution)** Geld-, Kreditinstitut, Finanzierungsbank; **to put one's** ~ **house in order** seine Finanzwirtschaft in Ordnung bringen; ~ **incentives** finanzielle Anreize; **public** ~ **institution** öffentlich-rechtliches Kreditinstitut; ~ **interest** finanzielle Beteiligung, Finanzinteressen; ~ **interrelation** Kapitalverflechtung; ~ **instrument** Kreditinstrument; ~ **investment** Geldmarktanlage; ~ **investment manager** Anlageberater; ~ **journalist** Börsenjournalist; ~ **leader** führender Finanzmann; ~ **lease** Maschinenpachtvertrag [ohne Wartung]; ~ **legislation** Finanzgesetzgebung; **to be hard hit by one's** ~ **losses** schwer unter seinen finanziellen Verlusten leiden; ~ **machinery** Finanzapparat; ~ **management** Finanzplanung; ~ **manager** Finanzvorstand, Vorstandsmitglied für Finanzfragen; ~ **market** Markt für

Investitionspapiere, Finanz-, Geldmarkt, Finanzwirtschaft; ~ **market professionalist** Geldmarktexperte; ~ **matters** Finanzangelegenheiten; ~ **maze** Finanzwirrwarr; ~ **means** finanzielle (kapitalmarktreife) Mittel, Finanzierungsmittel; ~ **measures** Finanzgebarung, finanzielle Maßnahmen; ~ **men** Geschäftswelt; ~ **middleman** Finanz-, Kreditmakler; ~ **monopoly** Kreditmonopol; ~ **muscles** finanzielle Stärke; ~ **needs** finanzielle Bedürfnisse, Finanzbedarf; ~ **news** Börsenbericht, -nachrichten; **to highlight** ~ **news** Wirtschaftsnachrichten schwerpunktartig hervorheben; ~ **niceties** finanztechnische Feinheiten; ~ **obligation** finanzielle Verpflichtung; **to repudiate** ~ **obligations** sich finanziellen Verpflichtungen entziehen; **chief** ~ **officer** Kämmerer; ~ **operation** Finanztransaktion, -geschäft; **local** ~ **opinions** örtliche Finanzgrößen; ~ **organization** Finanzierungsinstitut; ~ **page** *(newspaper)* Wirtschaftsteil; ~ **paper** Handelsblatt, Börsenblatt, *(US)* Gefälligkeitswechsel; ~ **part** *(newspaper)* Handelsteil; **top local** ~ **people** führende Finanzleute am Platz; ~ **performance** Finanzgebarung, finanzielle Durchführung; ~ **plan** Finanzierungsverfahren; ~ **planning scheme** Finanzplanung, Finanzierungsübersicht; ~ **plight** finanzielle Misere; **from a** ~ **point of view** finanzpolitisch gesehen; ~ **policy** Geld-, Steuer-, Finanzpolitik, Finanzgebarung, -wirtschaft, Finanzen; **high-deficit** ~ **policy** extrem defizitäre Finanzpolitik; ~ **policy department** finanzpolitische Abteilung; ~ **position** Finanzverhältnisse, Finanz-, Vermögenslage, finanzielle Lage (Entwicklung); **sound** ~ **position** Kapitalkraft, -stärke; ~ **power** finanzielle Leistungskraft, Finanzkraft, -stärke, Geldmacht; ~ **press** Wirtschaftszeitungen; ~ **privilege** Finanzhoheit; ~ **probity** Korrektheit in finanziellen Dingen; ~ **program(me)** Finanzierungsprogramm; ~ **project** Finanzierungsprojekt; ~ **quarters** Finanzkreise; ~ **question** Geld-, Finanzfrage; ~ **rating** finanzieller Status, Finanzlage, -status; ~ **ratios** *(plant)* finanzwirtschaftliche Kennziffern; **for** ~ **reasons** aus finanziellen Gründen; ~ **records** finanzielle Unterlagen; ~ **reform** Finanzreform; ~ **relationship** kapitalmäßige Bindung; ~ **report** Jahresbericht, Bericht über die Vermögenslage; **for** ~ **reporting** für Handelsbilanzzwecke; **to develop** ~ **reporting** finanziell anstehende Fragen übersichtlich vortragen; ~ **requirements** Geld-, Finanz-, Kapitalbedarf; ~ **resources** Finanzierungsquelle, Geldmittel, Finanzkraft; ~ **responsibility** finanzieller Verantwortungssinn, *(US)* finanzielle Haftung; ~ **restrictions** finanzielle Beschränkungen; ~ **result** finanzielles Ergebnis; ~ **risk** finanzielles Risiko; ~ **sacrifice** finanzielles Opfer; ~ **savings** finanzielle Ersparnisse; ~ **scandal** Finanzskandal; ~ **sector** *(national income accounting)* Finanzierungssektor; ~ **Secretary to the Treasury** *(Br.)* Staatssekretär für Finanzen; ~ **section** Finanzabteilung; **to make** ~ **sense** sich finanziell auszahlen; ~ **service** finanzielle Hilfeleistung; ~ **service company** Finanzierungsgesellschaft; ~ **showing** finanzieller Eindruck; **to spend one's entire career on the** ~ **side** sich beruflich nur mit finanzwirtschaftlichen Fragen beschäftigen; ~ **situation** Finanz-, Vermögenslage; **to be in a poor (weak)** ~ **situation** finanziell schlecht gestellt sein; ~ **solvency** Zahlungsfähigkeit; ~ **soundness** Kreditfähigkeit, Solidität; **to tap** ~ **sources** Finanzquellen erschließen; ~ **sovereignty** Finanzhoheit; ~ **specialist** Finanzfachmann, -spezialist; ~ **squeeze** finanzieller Druck; ~ **stability** finanzielle Stabilität; ~ **standing** finanzielle Lage, Finanzlage, Kreditfähigkeit, Kapitalkraft, Bonität; **in good** ~ **standing** kapitalkräftig; ~ **state** Finanz-, Vermögenslage, -stand; ~ **statement** Status, Vermögensaufstellung, Bericht über die Vermögenslage, Finanzstatus, -ausweis, Jahres-, Bilanzabschluß; **descriptive** ~ **statement** erläuternde Finanzübersicht; **projected** ~ **statement** zukünftiger Finanzstatus; **special-purpose** ~ **statement** Finanzstatus für besondere Zwecke; ~ **statistics** Finanzstatistik; ~ **status** Finanzstatus, -ausweis, Vermögensaufstellung; ~ **staying power** finanzielle Durchhaltekraft; ~ **straits** Geldnot, -klemme, -sorgen; **to be in** ~ **straits** sich in finanziellen Schwierigkeiten befinden; **to continue in** ~ **straits** weiterhin in finanziellen Schwierigkeiten stecken; ~ **strength** Finanz-, Kapitalkraft, Kapitalstärke, -macht, finanzielle Stärke; ~ **structure** Finanz-, Kapitalstruktur; ~ **success** Kassenerfolg; **to receive** ~ **support** finanziell unterstützt werden; ~ **syndicate** Finanzkonsortium; ~ **system** Finanzwirtschaft, -system, -verfassung, Steuersystem; ~ **talks** Finanzbesprechungen, finanzielle Verhandlungen; ~ **term** Finanzausdruck; ~ **terminology** Finanzfachsprache; ~ **theory** Finanztheorie; ~ **Times All Share Index** auf 150 Aktien aufgebauter Index der Financial Times; ~ **transaction** Geldgeschäft, Finanztransaktion, Finanzierungsgeschäft; **to slide into deep** ~ **troubles** in ernsthafte finanzielle Schwierigkeiten geraten; ~ **undoing** finanzieller Ruin; ~ **vetting** Prüfung der Finanzver-

hältnisse auf Herz und Nieren; ~ **world** Finanzwelt, -leute; ~ **worth** Reinvermögen; ~ **wrongdoing** unkorrektes Finanzgebaren; ~ **year** *(Br., private)* Geschäfts-, Bilanz-, Betriebs-, Wirtschaftsjahr, *(state, Br.)* Finanz-, Rechnungs-, Haushalts-, Etatsjahr.

financially in finanzieller (geldlicher) Hinsicht;
~ **able** finanziell leistungsfähig; ~ **independent** finanziell selbständig; ~ **responsible** finanziell haftbar; ~ **situated** finanziell gestellt; ~ **sound (strong)** finanziell gesund, finanz-, kapitalkräftig, wohlfundiert; ~ **weak** finanz-, kapitalschwach;
to be better fixed ~ finanziell besser dastehen; **to be** ~ **interested** finanziell interessiert sein; **to do very nicely** ~ sehr gute Finanzergebnisse zeitigen; **to help s. o.** ~ j. finanziell unterstützen, jem. unter die Arme greifen; **to participate** ~ **in an enterprise** sich an einem Unternehmen finanziell beteiligen.

financier Finanzmann, Financier, Geldgeber, *(banker)* Bankier, *(capitalist)* Kapitalist, *(controller of finances)* Finanzbeamter, *(specialist)* Finanzexperte, -fachmann;
shady ~ zweifelhafter Geldverleiher, Finanzierungsschwindler;
~**s of dubious character** undurchsichtige Geldleute;
~ *(v.)* finanzieren, Finanzgeschäfte (Finanztransaktionen) durchführen.

financing Finanzierung, Kapitalbeschaffung;
accounts receivable ~ *(US)* Finanzierung durch Abtretung von Warenforderungen (Debitoren), Forderungsvorfinanzierung; **bill-of-lading** ~ Remboursgeschäft; ~ **campaign** ~ Finanzierung eines Wahlfeldzugs; **consumer** ~ Konsumfinanzierung; **convertible** ~ Finanzierung durch Ausgabe von Wandelschuldverschreibungen; **debt** ~ Finanzierung durch Abtretung von Debitoren (mittels Forderungsabtretung); **direct** ~ Direktfinanzierung; **direct placement** ~ Finanzierung durch unmittelbare Kapitalmarktunterbringung; **domestic** ~ Inlandsfinanzierung; **foreign-trade** ~ Außenhandelsfinanzierung; **government** ~ Staatsfinanzierung; **group** ~ Gemeinschaftsfinanzierung; **home** ~ Wohnungsbaufinanzierung; **interim** ~ Zwischenfinanzierung; **investment** ~ Finanzierung von Investitionen, Anlagenfinanzierung; **large-scale** ~ Finanzierung von Großprojekten; **leasehold** ~ Finanzierung durch Einräumung eines Erbbaurechtes; **loan-account** ~ Anleihefinanzierung; **longer-range** ~ längerfristige Finanzierungsmittel; **long-term** ~ langfristige Finanzierung; **marketing** ~ Absatzfinanzierung; **medium-range (medium-term)** ~ mittelfristige Finanzierung; **medium and long-term industrial** ~ mittel- und langfristiges Industriefinanzierungsgeschäft; **outside** ~ Finanzierung durch Fremdmittel, Fremdfinanzierung; **permanent** ~ Durch-, Endfinanzierung; **preliminary** ~ Vorfinanzierung; **production** ~ Produktionsfinanzierung; **purchase-money** ~ Kaufgeldfinanzierung; **self-**~ Eigen-, Selbstfinanzierung; **short-term** ~ kurzfristige Finanzierung; **standby** ~ Finanzierungsgarantie; **temporary** ~ Überbrückungsfinanzierung; **tight** ~ angespannter Finanzierungsmarkt; **war** ~ Kriegsfinanzierung;
~ **of the public deficits** Deckung der öffentlichen Defizite; ~ **of a campaign** Wahlkampffinanzierung; ~ **of hire-purchase transactions** *(Br.)* Finanzierung von Abzahlungsgeschäften; ~ **of new homes** Finanzierung von Eigenheimen; ~ **of housing** Wohnungsbaufinanzierung; ~ **of imports** Einfuhrfinanzierung; ~ **of industry** Industriefinanzierungen; ~ **of joint-stock companies** Finanzierung von Aktiengesellschaften; ~ **of a strike** Streikfinanzierung; ~ **of foreign trade** Außenhandelsfinanzierung;
to find favo(u)rable ~ günstige Finanzierungsmöglichkeiten beschaffen; **to handle one's own** ~ seine finanziellen Angelegenheiten selbst erledigen; **to incorporate flexibly in the overall** ~ flexibel in die Gesamtfinanzierung miteinbeziehen; **to switch** ~ sich anderweitig Finanzierungsrückhalt verschaffen; **to wrap up** ~ Finanzierung sicherstellen;
~ **agency** Finanzierungsgesellschaft; ~ **agreement** Finanzierungsvertrag, -vereinbarung; ~ **approval** Finanzierungsgenehmigung; ~ **assistance** Finanzierungshilfe; ~ **capabilities** Finanzierungsmöglichkeiten; ~ **charges (costs)** Finanzierungskosten; ~ **company** Finanzierungsgesellschaft; ~ **concept** Finanzierungskonzept; **in the** ~ **and distributing ends** bei Finanzierung und Verleih; ~ **expenses** Finanzierungskosten; ~ **facilities** Finanzierungserleichterungen; **long-term** ~ **funds** langfristige Finanzierungsmittel; ~ **institution** Finanzierungsinstitut; ~ **methods** Finanzierungsmethoden; ~ **operations** Finanzierungsgeschäfte; ~ **package** gebündeltes Finanzierungsangebot, komplettes Finanzierungsinstrument, Bündel finanzpolitischer Maßnahmen; ~ **plan** Finanzierungsplan; ~ **proposal** Finanzierungsvorschlag; ~ **requirements** Finanzie-

rungsbedarf; ~ **scheme** Finanzierungssystem, -schema; ~ **service** Finanzierungsleistung; ~ **statement** *(political party, US)* Finanzierungsnachweis; **to structure** ~ **vehicles** Finanzierungsmöglichkeiten schaffen.

find Fund, Entdeckung;
~ *(v.)* finden, feststellen, entdecken, herausbekommen, *(court of law)* für Recht erkennen, *(furnish)* ver-, beschaffen, auftreiben, *(procure)* versorgen, ausstatten, *(sl.)* klauen, organisieren; ~ **o. s.** seine Berufung erkennen; ~ **for o. s.** sich selbst versorgen; ~ **one's account in s. th.** Vorteil aus etw. ziehen; ~ **out an address** Adresse feststellen; ~ **bail** Bürgen stellen; ~ **one's bearings** seine Lage klar erkennen; ~ **a true bill** *(US)* Anklage für begründet erklären; ~ **o. s. in clothes** seine Bekleidung selbst finanzieren; ~ **correct** richtig befinden; ~ **against the defendant** Beklagten verurteilen; ~ **for the defendant** Klage abweisen, Angeklagten freisprechen; ~ **fault with s. th.** etw. bemängeln (beanstanden); ~ **favo(u)r** Eingang finden, abgenommen werden; ~ **favo(u)r with one's employer** von seinem Brötchengeber positiv beurteilt werden; ~ **in favo(u)r of s. o.** zu jds. Gunsten erkennen; ~ **one's feet** *(fig.)* selbständig werden; ~ **s. o. guilty of a charge** j. einer Anklage überführen; ~ **it in one's heart** es über sich bringen; ~ **s. o. at home** j. zu Hause antreffen; ~ **a language to present little difficulty** beim Erlernen einer Sprache keine großen Schwierigkeiten haben; ~ **one's level** Platz einnehmen, der einem zukommt; ~ **a job for s. o.** jem. eine Stellung verschaffen; ~ **a market** verlangt werden, Absatzmarkt haben; ~ **the money** Geld beschaffen; ~ **the money for a journey** Finanzierung einer Reise sicherstellen; ~ **the money for an undertaking** Geld für ein Unternehmen auftreiben; ~ **out** ermitteln, feststellen, *(patent)* feststellen; ~ **everybody out** niemanden antreffen; ~ **out the precise facts** genauen Sachverhalt feststellen; ~ **one's plan** seine Lesestelle wiederfinden; ~ **for the plaintiff** zugunsten des Klägers (antragsgemäß) entscheiden; ~ **a post for s. o.** Stellung für j. besorgen; ~ **a situation abroad** Stellung im Ausland finden; ~ **a warm supporter in s. o.** voll von jem. unterstützt werden; ~ **a transaction profitable** Nutzen aus einer Sache ziehen; ~ **a treasure** Schatzfund machen; ~ **a verdict of guilty** Schuldspruch verkünden; ~ **no way** keinen Ausweg finden; ~ **one's way** sich zurechtfinden;
to make s. o. ~ **his tongue** jem. die Zunge lösen;
~ **place (spot)** Fundort.

findable auffindbar.

finder Finder, *(customs)* Zolldurchsucher, *(photo)* Sucher, *(securities field)* Finanzmakler, *(wireless)* Peilfunkgerät;
to reward a ~ Finder belohnen;
~**'s fee** Maklerprovision; ~**'s reward** Finderlohn.

finding Finden, Entdeckung, *(court of arbitration)* Erkenntnisse (Feststellungen) des Gerichts, Befund, Ausspruch, Entscheidung, Urteil, *(investigation)* Untersuchungsergebnis, *(of lost property)* Fund, Fundgegenstand, -objekt;
according to the ~**s** nach den Feststellungen;
~**s** Prüfungsergebnisse, Schlußfolgerungen, *(artisan, US)* Handwerkszeug, *(court of appeal)* Revisionsergebnisse;
fault-~ Bemängelung, Beanstandung; **general** ~**s** Tatbestand; **positive** ~ ausdrückliche Feststellung;
~ **of capital** Kapitalbeschaffung; ~**s of a commission** Untersuchungsergebnis; ~**s of the court** Feststellungen des Gerichts; ~ **of fact** *(law court)* Tatsachenfeststellung, Tatbestand; ~ **of the jury** Geschworenenurteil, Urteil des Schwurgerichts; ~ **the means** Geldbeschaffung, -aufbringung, Kapitalbeschaffung; ~**s of an official report** amtliches Untersuchungsergebnis; ~**s of the police** Feststellungen der Polizei;
to accept a ~ **as binding** sich dem Schiedsrichterspruch unterwerfen; **to bring in a** ~ **against** auf Freispruch erkennen; **to make** ~**s** Feststellungen treffen; **to turn** ~**s to account** Untersuchungsergebnisse auswerten;
~ **list** *(library)* Kurzkatalog.

fine Geld-, Ordnungsstrafe, *(conveyancing)* Prozeßvergleich, *(law of tenure)* Pauschalzahlung, *(sum paid by way of composition)* Geldbuße, Reugeld, Strafsumme;
liable to a ~ mit einer Geldstrafe verbunden;
administrative ~ Buß-, Zwangsgeld; **default** ~ Versäumnisgebühr, Verspätungszuschlag; **heavy** ~ hohe Geldstrafe; **joint** ~ Gesamtgeldstrafe, kollektive Geldstrafe; **motoring** ~ Verkehrsstrafe, gebührenpflichtige Verwarnung; **nominal** ~ unbedeutende Geldstrafe;
~ **for default** Versäumnisgebühr, Verspätungszuschlag; ~ **left to the discretion of the judge** dem richterlichen Ermessen überlassene Geldstrafe; ~ **for disorderly conduct** Geldstrafe für ungebührliches Benehmen;

~ *(v.)* zu einer Geldstrafe verurteilen (verdonnern), mit einer Geldstrafe belegen, Buße auferlegen;
to assess a ~ Geldstrafe (Buße) festsetzen; **to get off with a** ~ mit einer Geldstrafe davonkommen; **to impose (levy) a** ~ Geldstrafe auferlegen; **to pass a** ~ **for illegal parking** Protokoll wegen falschen Parkens verpassen; **to pay a** ~ Geldstrafe zahlen; **to remit (revoke) a** ~ Geldstrafe erlassen; **to return a** ~ Geldstrafe bezahlen;
~ *(a.)* fein, verfeinert, *(gold, silver)* fein, rein, *(healthy)* gesund, *(superior)* ausgezeichnet, hervorragend, glänzend;
twelve carats ~ zwölfkarätig;
to be cut very ~ *(price)* scharf kalkuliert sein; **to cut (run) it** ~ ins Gedränge (Zeitnot) geraten; **to cut one's profit too** ~ zu niedrige Gewinnspanne haben; **not to put too** ~ **a point on it** *(coll.)* um das Kind beim Namen zu nennen; **to talk** ~ gebildet sprechen;
~ **adjustment** Feineinstellung; ~**-art gallery** Kunstgallerie; ~ **arts** schöne Künste; ~ **bank bill** erstklassiger Bankwechsel; **one** ~ **day** irgendwann einmal, *(story)* eines schönen Tages; ~ **dinner** schickes Essen; ~ **distinction** subtile Unterscheidung; ~ **excuse** jämmerliche Ausrede; **in** ~ **fettle** in guter Verfassung; ~ **force** unausweichliche Zwangslage; ~ **gold** Feingold; ~**-gold clause** Feingoldklausel; ~**-grain film** Feinkornfilm; ~**-hand copy** saubere Abschrift; **to act as a** ~ **hone** letzten Schliff geben; **to call things by** ~ **names** sich sehr gewählt ausdrücken; ~ **papers** *(Br.)* erstklassige Wechsel, prima Diskonten; ~ **pencil** harter Bleistift; ~ **piece of business** großartige Sache; ~ **print** *(warranty)* Kleingedrucktes, Garantieeinschränkungen; ~ **rate** *(US)* Leitzinssatz; ~ **scholar** großer Gelehrter; **with** ~ **screen** feingerastert; ~ **silk** empfindliche Seide; ~ **silver** Feinsilber; **to dress with** ~ **taste** sich geschmackvoll kleiden; **to have a** ~ **time** sich glänzend amüsieren; **to go over s. th.** **with a** ~ **tooth comb** etw. sehr sorgfältig prüfen; ~ **trade paper** erstklassiger Handelswechsel; ~**-tune** *(v.)* **an economy already at full capacity** Feinabstimmungen bei einer auf vollen Touren laufenden Wirtschaft abnehmen; ~ **tuning** *(radio)* Feinabstimmung; ~ **view** schöne Aussicht; ~ **work** Qualitätsarbeit; ~ **workman** guter Arbeiter.

fineness of gold Feinheitsgrad (Feingehalt) von Gold.

finest quality erstklassige Qualität.

finger *(clock)* Zeiger, *(informer, sl.)* Denunziant, Informant;
with a wet ~ mit dem kleinen Finger, mit Leichtigkeit;
professional ~ *(sl.)* berufsmäßiger Spitzel;
~ *(v.)* **s. one's money** jds. Geld einstecken;
to have a ~ **in the pie** seine Hand im Spiel haben; **to have a** ~ **in every pie** überall mitmischen; **to have one's** ~**s all thumbs** zwei linke Hände haben; **to keep one's** ~ **out of the pie** aus dem Spiel bleiben; **to keep one's** ~**s crossed for s. o.** jem. die Daumen drücken; **to lay (put) one's** ~ **on the evil** Finger auf eine offene Wunde legen; **not to lift a** ~ keinen Finger krumm machen, keine Hand rühren; **to put the** ~ **on s. o.** *(US sl.)* j. anschwärzen, j. verpfeifen; **not to stir a** ~ keinen Finger krumm machen; **to twist s. o. round one's little** ~ j. um den kleinen Finger wickeln; **to work one's** ~ **to the bone** sich die Hände wundarbeiten; **to have a little** ~ **ache** sich über seine Wehwehchen beklagen; ~ **alphabet** *(Br.)* Taubstummensprache; ~ **board** *(US)* Wegweiser; ~ **disk** *(tel.)* Wählscheibe; **to have s. th. at one's** ~ **ends** Sache wie am Schnürchen beherrschen; **to have the whole business at one's** ~**s' ends** sein Geschäft glänzend (aus dem FF) verstehen; ~ **language** Fingersprache; ~ **mark** Fingerabdruck; ~**-marked** voller Fingerabdrücke; ~ **plate** Schutzplatte, Türschoner; ~ **post** Wegweiser; ~ **stall** Fingerling; ~ **stop** *(typewriter)* Fingeranschlag; **to write (type) the ten-**~ **system** blindschreiben; ~ **tip** Fingerspitze; **at one's** ~ **tips** griffbereit; **always at your** ~ **tips** immer parat; **to be an Englishman to the** ~**-tips** typischer Engländer sein; **to have at one's** ~ **tips** im kleinen Finger haben, Sache wie am Schnürchen können, gründlich mit etw. vertraut sein, vollständig beherrschen.

fingerprint Fingerabdruck;
~ **s.o.** jem. Fingerabdrücke abnehmen;
to check ~**s** Fingerabdrücke untersuchen;
~ **indentification** Fingerabdruckverfahren.

finish Schluß, Ende, *(building)* Verputz, Ausbau, Fertigstellung, Nach-, Fertigbearbeitung, *(layout)* detailliertes Layout, *(paper)* Ausrüstung, *(refreshment house, Br., sl.)* bis nach Mitternacht offene Stampe, *(result of labo(u)r)* Vollendung, feine Qualität;
coated ~ Lackierung mit Schutzschicht; **poor** ~ schlechte Verarbeitung;
~ *(v.)* fertigstellen, fertig bearbeiten, beenden, *(el., gas, water)* installieren, *(meeting)* beschließen, *(perfect)* fertig bearbeiten, letzten Schliff geben, veredeln, *(stock exchange)* schließen;

~ **one's apprenticeship** auslernen, seine Ausbildung abschließen; ~ **s. o. off** j. völlig fertig machen; ~ **off a piece of work** Arbeitsvorgang abschließen; ~ **one's military service** seine Militärzeit beenden; ~ **up the evening at the theatre** nach dem Feierabend ins Theater gehen;
to be in at the ~ *(fig.)* in den Endkampf kommen, beim Schluß dabei sein; **to fight to the** ~ bis zum bitteren Ende kämpfen.

finished *(complete)* vollendet, vollkommen, erledigt, abgeschlossen, beendigt, beendet, fertig;
~ **art work** produktionsreife Zeichnung, Reinzeichnung; ~ **drawing** Endausführung einer Zeichnung, Reinzeichnung; ~ **gentleman** perfekter Gentleman; ~ **goods** Fertigwaren, -erzeugnisse; ~ **goods account** Fertigwarenkonto; ~ **goods inventory** Bestand an Fertigwaren; ~ **goods journal** Fertigwarenjournal; ~ **layout** Reinlayout; ~ **product** veredeltes Erzeugnis, Endprodukt, Veredelungs-, Fertigerzeugnis; **half-~ products** Halbfabrikate; **to convert into** ~ **products** zu Fertigwaren verarbeiten; **to translate a work with** ~ **skill** hervorragende Übersetzung eines Buches liefern; ~ **speaker** hervorragender Redner.

finishing Ausarbeitung, *(manufacture)* Veredelung, Über-, Neu-, Verarbeitung, Fertigstellung, *(el., gas, water)* Installation, Installierung;
~ **blow** Todesstoß; ~ **coat** Deckanstrich; ~ **industry** Veredelungsindustrie, -wirtschaft, verarbeitende Industrie; ~ **mill** Fertigstraße; ~ **off** Erledigung, Fertigmachen; ~ **operation** Fertigbearbeitung; ~ **plant** Veredelungsbetrieb; ~ **process** Veredelungsverfahren; ~ **school** Mädchenpensionat; **to give the** ~ **stroke** Gnadenstoß geben; ~ **time** *(plant)* Arbeitsschluß; **to add the** ~ **touches** letzten Schliff geben, letzte Hand anlegen.

fink Streikbrecher;
~ *(v.) (US sl.)* denunzieren.

fire Brand, [Groß]feuer, Feuersbrunst, *(fig.)* Begeisterung;
between two ~**s** *(fig.)* zwischen zwei Feuern; **liable to catch** ~ feuergefährlich; **on** ~ in Brand; **under** ~ unter Beschuß;
blue ~ bengalisches Feuer; **St. Elm's** ~ Elmsfeuer; **forest** ~ Waldbrand; **friendly** ~ *(insurance)* Nutzfeuer; **head** ~ *(US)* Lauffeuer; **hostile (unfriendly)** ~ *(insurance)* Schadenfeuer; **incendiary** ~ Feuer durch Brandstiftung; **intentional** ~ vorsätzlich gelegtes Feuer; **large** ~ Großfeuer;
~ **in one's belt** brennender Ehrgeiz; ~ **of a diamond** Funkeln eines Brillanten; ~ **in a coal mine** Grubenbrand; **running** ~ **of questions** Kreuzfeuer von Fragen; ~ **and sword** Feuer und Schwert; ~ **of youth** Begeisterungsfähigkeit der Jugend;
~ *(v.)* anzünden, in Brand stecken, *(catch ~)* Feuer fangen, sich entzünden, *(inflame)* anfeuern, inspirieren, *(mil.)* Feuer eröffnen, feuern, schießen, *(from service, coll.)* [feuern], herauswerfen, -schmeißen;
~ **away all one's ammunition** seine ganze Munition verschießen; ~ **the church bells** alle Kirchenglocken läuten lassen; ~ **upon a crowd** auf die Menge schießen; ~ **s. one's imagination** jds. Phantasie beflügeln; ~ **off a question** at s. o. j. mit einer Frage überfallen; ~ **a torpedo** Torpedo abschießen; ~ **up at the least thing** bei jeder Kleinigkeit aufbrausen;
to add fuel to the ~ *(coll.)* Öl ins Feuer gießen; **to be on** ~ in Brand stehen, brennen; **to be under** ~ stark angefochten werden; **to be destroyed by** ~ dem Feuer zum Opfer fallen; **to be insured against** ~ feuerversichert sein; **to be (fall) out of the frying pan into the** ~ vom Regen in die Traufe kommen; **to catch** ~ Feuer fangen, zu brennen beginnen; **to cease** ~ *(mil.)* Feuer einstellen; **to come under** ~ *(fig.)* heftig angegriffen werden; **to fight a** ~ Feuer bekämpfen; **to get on like a house on** ~ im Blitztempo vorankommen; **to go through** ~ **and water** den größten Gefahren trotzen; **to go through** ~ **and water for s.o.** für j. durchs Feuer gehen; **to have gone through the** ~ Feuerprobe bestanden haben; **to have suffered from** ~ Brandschaden haben; **to hire and** ~ *(coll.)* anstellen und entlassen; **to hold one's** ~ *(fig.)* sich Zurückhaltung auferlegen; **to light a wood** ~ Holzfeuer anzünden; **to open** ~ *(mil.)* Feuer eröffnen; **to play with** ~ *(fig.)* mit dem Feuer spielen; **to pull the chestnuts out of the** ~ Kastanien aus dem Feuer holen; **to put a country to** ~ **and sword** Land Brandschatzungen aussetzen; **to put a rapid** ~ **of questions on s. o.** j. mit Fragen bombardieren; **to raise** ~ brandstiften, Brandstiftung begehen; **to set on** ~ in Brand setzen; **to set the Thames on** ~ siebentes Weltwunder vollbringen; **to snatch out of the** ~ vor einer Katastrophe bewahren; **to strike** ~ Funken schlagen; **to take** ~ Feuer fangen, brennen; **not to be able to set the Thames on** ~ das Pulver nicht erfunden haben;
~ **adjuster** Brandschätzer; ~ **alarm** Feueralarm, *(apparatus)* Feuermelder; ~ **alarm point** Feuermeldestelle; ~ **alarm system**

Feuermeldeanlage, -system; ~ **apparatus** Feuerlöscher; ~ **area** Feuerausbruchsgebiet; ~ **or loss assessor** Brandschadenprüfer; ~ **authority** Feuerschutzbehörde; ~ **bar** Roststab; ~ **bell** Feuerglocke; ~ **belt** Feuergürtel; ~ **bill** *(mar.)* Brandrolle; ~ **blitz** Abwurf von Brandbomben; ~ **bomb** Brandbombe; ~ **brigade** *(Br.)* Feuerwehr, *(US)* örtliche freiwillige Feuerwehr; ~-**brigade measures** Sofortmaßnahmen, -programm; ~-**brigade team** *(Br.)* Feuerwehrmannschaft; ~ **call** Feueralarm; ~-**call system** Feuerwarnsystem; ~ **casualty insurer** Feuerversicherungsgesellschaft; ~ **certificate** feuerpolizeiliches Zeugnis; ~ **chief** Branddirektor; ~ **clay** Schamotte; ~ **company** *(Br.)* Feuerversicherungsgesellschaft, *(US)* Feuerlöschkommando, Feuerwehr; ~ **curtain** feuersicherer (eiserner) Vorhang; ~ **damage** Brand-, Feuerschaden; ~-**damaged** brandbeschädigt; ~ **department** *(insurance, Br.)* Feuerschadensabteilung; ~ **detector** automatischer (selbsttätiger) Feuermelder; ~ **direction** *(mil.)* Feuerleitung; ~ **director** *(anti aircraft defence)* Kommandogerät; ~ **district** Feuerbezirk; ~ **door** feuerfeste Tür; ~ **drill** Feuerwehrübung, Feuerlöschübung, Probefeueralarm; ~ **engine** Feuerwehrauto, -wagen, Motorspritze; ~ **escape** Feuerleiter, Nottreppe; ~ **exit** Notausgang; ~ **extinguisher** Feuerlöschgerät, -löscher; ~-**extinguishing apparatus** Feuerlöschanlage; ~ **fighter** Feuerwehrhauptmann; ~ **fighting** Brandbekämpfung; ~-**fighting damage** bei der Brandbekämpfung entstandener Schaden; ~-**fighting machine** Feuerlöschapparat, Feuerlöschwagen; ~ **fighting service** Feuerlöschdienst; ~-**fighting vehicle** *(craft)* Feuerlöschfahrzeug; ~ **gang** Bande von Brandstiftern; ~ **grate** Feuerrost; ~ **hazard** Feuergefahr, Brandrisiko; ~ **hook** Feuerhaken; ~ **hose** Feuerwehrschlauch; ~ **inspector** Brandmeister.

fire insurance Feuerversicherung, -assekuranz;
concurrent ~ gleichlaufende Feuerversicherung bei mehreren Gesellschaften;
~ **company** Feuer-, Brandversicherungsgesellschaft; ~ **fund** Brandkasse; ~ **loss adjustment** Brandversicherungsregulierung; ~ **policy** Feuerpolice; ~ **premium** Feuerversicherungsprämie; ~ **rates** Feuerversicherungstarif; ~ **risk** Feuerversicherungsrisiko.

fire|insurer Feuerversicherungsanstalt, -gesellschaft; ~ **lane** Feuerschneise; ~ **loss** Feuer-, Brandschaden; ~ **marshal** *(US)* Branddirektor; ~ **office** Feuerversicherungsanstalt, Brandkasse; ~ **party** Löschtrupp, -mannschaft; ~ **policy** *(Br.)* Feuerversicherungspolice; ~ **position** *(mil.)* Feuerstellung; ~-**power** *(mil.)* Feuerkraft; ~ **precautions** Feuerschutzvorkehrungen, Feuerverhütungsmaßnahmen; ~ **prevention** Feuerverhütung; ~ **protection** Feuerschutz, Brandverhütung; ~ **Protection Association** *(Br.)* Feuerschutzverband; ~ **protection organization** Brandverhütungsdienst; ~ **pump** Feuerlöschpumpe; ~ **raid** Abwurf von Brandbomben; ~ **raiser** *(Br.)* Brandstifter; ~ **raising** *(Br.)* Brandstiftung, -legung; ~-**resisting** feuerbeständig; ~-**resisting steel cabinet** feuerfester Stahlschrank; ~ **risk** Feuers-, Brandgefahr, -risiko; ~ **sale** *(US)* Verkauf feuerbeschädigter Waren; ~ **screen** Feuerschirm; ~ **station** *(ship, Br.)* Feuerlöschstation, -wache; ~ **storm** Feuersturm; ~ **support** *(mil.)* Feuerschutz, -unterstützung; ~ **testing station** *(Br.)* Versuchsanstalt zur Erforschung von Feuerursachen; ~ **tower** Leuchtturm, *(fireproof stairway)* feuersicherer Schacht; ~ **trench** *(mil.)* Schützengraben; ~ **truck** Löschfahrzeug; ~ **underwriter** Feuerversicherungsgesellschaft, -träger; ~ **wall** Brandmauer; ~ **waste** Feuerschaden; ~ **watch** Feuerwache; ~ **watcher** Brandwache, *(Br.)* Luftschutzwart; ~ **zone** *(mil.)* Feuerbereich.

firearm Schutzwaffe;
~**s certificate** *(Br.)* Waffenschein.
fireball Feuerball, Atompilz.
fireboard Kaminbrett.
fireboat *(mar.)* Feuerlöschboot.
firebox Brennkammer.
fireboy *(US)* Heizer.
firebrand *(fig.)* Unruhestifter, Aufwiegler;
~ **politics** revolutionäre Politik.
firebreak *(US)* Feuerschneise.
firebrick feuerfester Ziegel, Schamottestein.
firebug *(US sl.)* Brandstifter.
firecracker *(fireworks, US)* Frosch.
fired *(US sl.)* abgehalftert, gefeuert, entlassen;
to be ~ hinausfliegen.
firedamp *(mining)* schlagende Wetter, Grubengas.
fireeater *(fig.)* Streithahn, Eisenfresser.
fireflaught *(Scot.)* Wetterleuchten.
fireguard *(forestry)* Brandwache, *(fireplace)* Kamingitter.

firehouse *(US)* Spritzenhaus, Feuermeldestelle, -wache.
fireless cooker *(US)* Kochkiste.
firelight Feuerschein.
firelighter *(Br.)* Feueranzünder.
fireman Feuerwehrmann.
fireplace offener Kamin.
fireplug Hydrant, Wasseranschluß.
fireproof feuerbeständig, -fest;
~ **strong box** feuerfester Geldschrank; ~ **bulkhead** Brandschott; ~ **partition** Brandmauer; ~ **vault** feuerfestes Gewölbe.
fireproofing material feuerfestes Material.
fireroom Heizraum, Heizungskeller.
fireside Kamin, *(fig.)* häuslicher Herd, Daheim;
~ **chat** *(radio talk, US)* informelle Rundfunkansprache; **homely** ~ **scene** gemütliche Szene am häuslichen Kamin; ~ **tales** Kamingeschichten.
firetrap feuergefährdetes Gebäude.
firewarden *(US)* Brandwache.
firewood Brennholz.
firework Feuerwerk, *(fig.)* geistreicher Vortrag;
~**s** *(US, stock exchange)* plötzliche Hausse;
a spent ~ ausgebrannte Persönlichkeit;
to let off ~**s** Feuerwerk abbrennen;
~ **display** Feuerwerkvorführung.
fireworker Feuerwerker.
firing Anzünden *(coll.)* Entlassung, Herauswurf, *(fuel)* Brennmaterial, *(heating)* Heizung, Verbrennung *(mil.)* Schießen, Feuern;
oil ~ Ölfeuerung;
~**s in times of recession** rezessionsbedingte Entlassungen;
to be ~ **only on three cylinders** nur auf drei Töpfen laufen;
~ **line** *(mil.)* Kampffront; ~ **party (squad)** Hinrichtungs-, Exekutionskommando; ~ **position** *(mil.)* Feuerstellung; ~ **range** Schuß-, Reichweite.
firm [Handels]firma, Betrieb, Geschäft, Unternehmen, Gesellschaft, [Handels]haus, *(firm name)* Firmenname;
under the ~ **of** unter der Firma;
C-~ *(Br.) (Road and Rail Traffic Act)* Firma mit zugelassenem Werksverkehr; **affiliated** ~ Zweigniederlassung; **ailing** ~ notleidende Firma; **commercial** ~ Handelsfirma; **dissolved (defunct)** ~ erloschene Firma; **your esteemed** ~ Ihre geschätzte Firma; **executive recruiting** ~ Unternehmensberatung; **failed** ~ *(US)* zahlungsunfähige Firma; **fair-dealing** ~ reelles Geschäft, erstklassiges Unternehmen; **first-rate (first-class)** ~ erstklassige Firma, erstklassiges Unternehmen; **foreign** ~ Auslandsfirma; **import** ~ Importhaus; **independent** ~ unabhängige Firma; **law** ~ Anwaltsfirma, -büro; **leading** ~ führendes Haus; **long** ~ Schwindelfirma, -unternehmen; **efficiently managed** ~ rationell geführtes Unternehmen; **management consulting** ~ Unternehmensberatungsgesellschaft; **old-established** ~ alteingesessene Firma; **registered** ~ eingetragene Firma; **reliable** ~ vertrauenswürdige (reelle) Firma (Gesellschaft); **respectable** ~ achtbares (angesehenes) Haus; **shaky** ~ unzuverlässige Firma; **single** ~ Einzelfirma; **solid** ~ solides Geschäft, Unternehmen; **sound** ~ gut fundiertes Geschäft; **spot** ~ Barzahlungsgeschäft; **supplying** ~ Lieferfirma; **surveyed** ~ überprüfte Firma; **trading** ~ Handelshaus; **well-established** ~ gut eingeführte (alteingesessene) Firma; **well-reputed** ~ renommiertes Geschäft; **worldrenowned (universally known)** ~ Weltfirma, Firma mit Weltruf, weltbekannte Firma;
~ **of building contractors** Bauunternehmen; ~ **of investigators** Detektei, Detektivbüro; ~ **of lawyers** Anwaltsbüro, -firma; ~ **in liquidation** in Liquidation befindliche (abwickelnde) Firma; ~ **of good repute** renommierte Firma; ~ **of solicitors** Anwaltsfirma, -büro; ~ **of speculators** unsolides Geschäft; ~ **of stockbrokers** Maklerfirma, Börsenkommissionsgeschäft;
to bring a ~ **into existence** Firma gründen; **to effect the collection for a** ~ Inkassodienst für eine Firma besorgen; **to enter a** ~ in eine Firma eintreten; **to enter a** ~ **as partner** in eine Firma als Teilhaber eintreten; **to get in with a** ~ Geschäftsbeziehungen zu einer Firma aufnehmen; **to have a** ~ **entered in the register of companies** Firma handelsgerichtlich eintragen lassen; **to have a half interest in a** ~ an einer Firma hälftig beteiligt sein; **to let a** ~ **down** Firma herunterwirtschaften; **to manage a** ~ Firma (Gesellschaft) leiten; **to place an order for an article with a** ~ Artikel bei einer Firma in Auftrag geben; **to retire from a** ~ aus einer Firma ausscheiden; **to sign on behalf of a** ~ Unterschriftsvollmacht haben, unterschriftsberechtigt sein; **to transfer a** ~ **on paper** eine Gesellschaft nur auf dem Papier übertragen; **to travel for a** ~ Firma vertreten; **to turn a** ~ **into a joint stock company** *(Br.)* Firma in eine Aktiengesellschaft umwandeln;

~**'s assets** Geschäftsaktiva, Firmenvermögen; ~**'s bankruptcy** Firmenbankrott; ~**'s capital** Geschäfts-, Firmenkapital; ~**'s creditors** Geschäftsgläubiger; ~**'s debts** Gesellschaftsverbindlichkeiten; ~**'s name** Firmenname, -bezeichnung; ~ **optimum** Unternehmensoptimum; ~**'s participation** Firmenbeteiligung; ~ **property** Firmen-, Geschäftsvermögen; ~ **stamp** Firmenstempel; ~**'s traveller** Firmenvertreter;
~ *(v.)* sich festigen, fest werden;
~ **up** *(stock exchange)* festliegen, fester werden, anziehen [bis];
~ *(a.)* stationär, haltbar, sicher, *(fig.)* fest, beständig, standhaft, entschlossen, *(rate of exchange)* fest, unveränderlich;
~ **as a rock** felsenfest;
to be very ~ **in upholding one's authority** seine Autorität entschlossen bewahren; **to be** ~ **with children** Kindern gegenüber bestimmt auftreten; **to become** ~ *(prices)* fester werden; **to buy** ~ fest (auf feste Rechnung) kaufen; **to close** ~ *(stock exchange)* fest schließen; **to hold** ~ **to one's belief** an seinem Glauben festhalten; **to offer** ~ fest anbieten; **to remain** ~ *(prices)* sich halten; **to sell** ~ fest verkaufen; **to stand** ~ fest bleiben; **to turn** ~ fest werden;
to adapt a ~ **attitude** feste Haltung annehmen; **to maintain a** ~ **attitude** *(stock exchange)* fest bleiben; ~ **bargain** fester Abschluß; ~ **bid** festes (verbindliches) Angebot, *(dealer in securities)* festes Kaufgebot, Abnahmeverpflichtung; ~ **commitment** *(US)* feste (verbindliche) Hypothekenzusage; ~ **contract** verbindlicher Vertrag; **to put on a** ~ **countenance** entschlossenes Gesicht aufsetzen; ~ **deal** fester Abschluß; **to be on** ~ **ground** *(fig.)* festen Boden unter den Füßen haben; **to build on** ~ **ground** auf festem Untergrund errichten; **to rule with a** ~ **hand** mit fester Hand regieren; ~ **limit** feste Preisgrenze; ~ **market** feste Börse; **to take** ~ **measures** hart durchgreifen; ~ **offer** *(dealer in securities)* festes (bindendes, verbindliches) [Verkaufs]angebot, Abgabeverpflichtung; ~ **order** Fixauftrag; ~ **partisan** treuer Anhänger; ~ **policy** feststehende politische Linie; ~ **price** Festpreis, vertraglich vereinbarter Preis, Vertragspreis; ~ **prices** stabile Preise; ~ **purchase** Festkauf; ~ **quotation** verbindliches Preisangebot, *(stock exchange)* verbindliche Kursnotierung; ~ **rate** *(exchange)* Umtauschsatz; ~ **sale** fester Verkauf; ~ **stand** *(politics)* entschlossene Haltung; ~ **stock** *(US, stock exchange)* gehaltene Werte.
firming up of prices Festigung der Kurse.
firmly, to be ~ **against it** entschieden dagegen sein.
firmness Festigkeit, Entschlossenheit, *(stock exchange)* Festigkeit, feste Haltung;
with a certain cheerful ~ höflich, aber bestimmt;
~ **in calls** Festigkeit der Sätze für tägliches Geld; ~ **of the market** Festigkeit des Marktes; ~ **of prices** Preisstabilität.
first [Monats]erster, *(car)* erster Gang, *(edition)* Erstausgabe, *(railway)* Abteil erster Klasse, *(philat.)* Erstausgabe, *(university, Br.)* Eins, höchste Note;
from ~ **to last** vom Anfang bis zum Ende, immerfort;
~**s** erste (beste) Qualität, Erzeugnisse der besten Güteklasse;
~ **of exchange** Primawechsel;
~ *(a.)* zuerst, erstens, *(first-class)* erstklassig, -rangig, -stellig, vorzüglich;
ranking ~ erstrangig;
~ **of all** in erster Linie; ~ **and last** im großen Ganzen, durch und durch; ~ **or last** früher oder später;
to always come ~ stets oberstes Gebot sein; **to get a double** ~ Examen mit Auszeichnung bestehen; **to get a** ~ **in modern languages** im Fach für neuere Sprachen bei der Prüfung mit Eins abschließen;
~ **accrued** erstmals entstanden.
first aid erste Hilfe, Nothilfe;
to apply ~ **to s. o.** jem. erste Hilfe leisten.
first-aid | **association** Rettungsdienst; ~ **box (cupboard)** Verbandkasten; ~ **equipment** Unfallausrüstung, Einrichtungen für erste Hilfe; ~ **kit** Verbandspäckchen, -kasten; ~ **outfit** Notverbandskasten; ~ **post (station)** Unfallstation; ~ **service** *(Red Cross)* Hilfsdienst.
first | **aider** in erster Hilfe Ausgebildeter; ~ **allotment** ursprüngliche Emission; ~ **base** *(fig.)* Anfangsstufe; **not to get to** ~ **base** *(sl.)* nicht das Geringste erreichen; ~ **bid** Erstgebot; **at [the]** ~ **blush** nach dem ersten Anschein; ~ **board** *(stock exchange)* erste Kursnotierung, *(US)* erste Umsätze zwischen 10 und 12 Uhr [an der New Yorker Börse]; ~ **born** Erstgeborener; ~**-born** erstgeboren; ~ **call** erster Kapitalaufruf; ~ **charge** feste (dingliche) Belastung; ~**-chop** *(Br.)* prima, erstklassig; ~ **claim** Vorhand, erster Anspruch; ~ **class** höchste Stufe, *(railway)* erste Klasse, *(university, Br.)* höchste Note; **the** ~ **classes** die höheren Gesellschaftsschichten.

first-class erstklassig, ausgesucht, vorzüglich, prima, hervorragend, auserlesen, ausgezeichnet;
to go (travel) ~ erster Klasse reisen;
~ **cabin** Kabine in der ersten Klasse; ~ **carriage** Waggon erster Klasse; ~ **fare** Fahrkarte erster Klasse; ~ **hotel** erst[klassig]es Hotel; ~ **mail** *(matter) (US)* Briefpost; ~ **man** hervorragender Mann; ~ **misdemeanant** Verurteilter mit erleichtertem Strafvollzug; ~ **paper** erstklassiger Wechsel; ~ **passenger** Reisender in der ersten Klasse; ~ **quality** Produkt erster Wahl, erstklassige Qualität; ~ **railway carriage** erster Klasse Waggon; ~ **references** prima Referenzen; ~ **return to M** einmal Erster nach M und zurück; ~ **ticket** Fahrkarte erster Klasse; ~ **title** einwandfreier Eigentumstitel; ~ **work** vorzügliche Arbeit.

first | classer Erstkläßler; ~ **clerk** erster Prokurist, *(US)* Angestellter mit niedrigstem Gehalt; ~ **coat** Rohputz, Grundanstrich; ~ **come, ~-serve basis** Vorzugsbedienung des Erstkommenden; ~~**come, ~ served booking at the airport** Flugreservierungen billiger Flugscheine in der Reihenfolge des Eintreffens auf dem Flugplatz; ~ **cost** An-, Einkaufs-, Selbstkostenpreis, Gestehungskosten; ~ **cousin** Vetter ersten Grades; ~ **day cover** *(phil.)* Ersttagsbrief; ~ **degree burn** Verbrennung ersten Grades; ~ **devisee** Vorerbe; ~ **draft** Konzept; ~ **edition** Original-, Erstausgabe; ~ **engineer** Oberingenieur; ~ **family in the town** erste Familie in der Stadt; ~ **floor** *(Br.)* erstes Stockwerk, erster Stock, erste Etage, *(US)* Erdgeschoß, Hochparterre; **the ~ form** *(school, Br.)* erste Klasse [der Grundschule]; ~ **fruits** *(fig.)* erste Arbeitserfolge; ~ **gear** erster Gang; ~~**grade class** *(US)* erste Klasse [der Grundschule], Volksschulklasse; **at ~ hand** aus erster Hand; ~ **hand** bester Arbeiter; ~~**hand** direktbezogen; **to learn s. th. ~-hand** etw. aus erster Hand erfahren; ~~**hand information** Nachricht aus erster Hand; ~ **heir** nächster Erbanwärter; ~ **impression** *(law court)* erstmaliger Rechtsfall, *(run)* Schöndruck; ~~**in, ~-out** Zuerstentnahme der älteren Vorräte und Bilanzierung zum jeweiligen Buchwert; ~~**in, ~-out principle** *(inventory taking)* Realisationsprinzip; ~ **instalment** *(hire purchase)* Anzahlung, erste Rate; ~ **instance** erste Instanz; ~ **inventor** *(law of patents)* Ersterfinder; ~ **lady** *(US)* Frau des Präsidenten; ~ **let** erstmals vermietet; ~ **lien** erstrangiges Pfandrecht; ~ **lien collateral trust bonds** durch vorgehendes Pfandrecht an der hinterlegten Sicherheit gedeckte Pfandbriefe; ~ **line** *(mil.)* Elitetruppen; ⌂ **Lord of the Admiralty** *(Br.)* Marineminister; ⌂ **Lord of the Treasury** *(Br.)* Erster Lord des Schatzamtes; ~~**loss policy** Erstrisikoversicherung; ~ **mate** Obersteuermann; ~ **men in the country** hervorragende Persönlichkeiten eines Landes; ~ **mortgage** *(Br.)* erststellige (erstrangige) Hypothek; ~~**mortgage** erstrangig, -stellig; ~~**mortgage bonds** *(US)* durch erste Hypothek gesicherte Pfandbriefe; ~~ **mortgage trust bonds** *(US)* indirekt hypothekarisch gesicherte Pfandbriefe; ~ **name** Rufname, Vorname; **to be on a ~ name phone-calling basis** sich telefonisch mit Vornamen anreden; ~~**named** zuerst aufgeführt; ~ **night** Uraufführung, Premierenabend; ~ **nighter** Premierenbesucher; ~ **off** *(US sl.)* gleich jetzt; ~ **offender** noch nicht Vorbestrafter, Ersttäter; ~ **open water** Verschiffung erst bei eisfreiem Wasser; **at the ~ opportunity** bei der allerersten Gelegenheit; ~ **order goods** *(US)* Konsumgüter; ~~**page** *(US)* auf der ersten Seite [einer Zeitung]; ~ **papers** *(US)* vorläufige Einbürgerungspapiere; ~ **place** erster Platz; **to give s. o. the ~ place** jem. Vorrang einräumen; ~ **policy year** *(suicide clause)* erstes Versicherungsjahr; ~ **preference bonds** *(Br.)* erste Prioritätsobligationen; ~ **preferred stock** *(US)* erste Vorzugsaktien; ~ **premium** *(insurance)* Erstprämie; **to run off a ~ printing of 5.000 copies** Erstauflage von 5.000 Stück drucken; ~ **processing** erste Verarbeitung; ~ **product** Erstlingsarbeit; ~ **proof** erster Korrektur-, Rohabzug; ~ **purchaser** Ersterwerber; ~ **quality** prima Qualität.

first-rate ausgezeichnet, vorzüglich, erstklassig, ersten Ranges, prima;
to get on ~ sehr gut vorankommen;
~ **firm** erstklassiges Unternehmen; ~ **idea** famose Idee; **of ~ importance** von größter Wichtigkeit; **a ~ power** eine der Großmächte; ~ **quality** erstklassige Qualität; ~ **secretary** erstklassige, hervorragende Sekretärin; ~ **workmanship** hervorragende Arbeit.

first | reading *(bill)* erste Lesung; ~ **refusal** Vorkaufsrecht, Option, erstes Anrecht, Vorhand; ~ **refusal clause** Options-, Vorkaufsklausel; ~ **return** *(depletion)* erstmalige Aufführung [bei der Abschreibung]; ~ **right of purchase** Vorkaufsrecht; ~ **run** Schöndruck; ~ **secretary** Obersekretär; ~ **shift** Tagesschicht; **at ~ sight** anfangs, beim ersten Blick; ~ **son** ältester Sohn; ~ **speed** *(car, Br.)* erster Gang; ~ **steps in one's career** erste berufliche Schritte; ~ **storey** *(Br.)* erstes Stockwerk, *(US)*

Hochparterre; ~ **strike** *(atomic weapons)* Überraschungsangriff; ~ **teller** Kassierer für Auszahlungen; **not to know the ~ thing about** keine Ahnung von etw. haben; **to put things ~** Dringendem den Vorrang geben; **to see to it ~ thing in the morning** gleich morgen früh erledigen; **to succeed the very ~ time** gleich zu Anfang Erfolg haben; ~ **trial** Verhandlung erster Instanz; ~ **tier box** Loge im ersten Rang; **to buy in a shop for the ~ time** in einem Laden zum ersten Mal einkaufen; ~ **unpaid** *(bill of exchange)* Prima nicht; ~ **water** *(diamond)* erste Qualität, reinstes Wasser; ~ **year at school** erstes Schuljahr; **in one's ~ youth** in seiner Jugendzeit.

firstcomer Erster.

fisc *(Scot.)* Fiskus, Staatskasse.

fiscal Finanzbeamter, *(revenue stamp)* Steuermarke;
~ **1980** Steuersatz 1980;
~ *(a.)* steuerlich, fiskalisch, finanziell;
to take more positive ~ action next year im nächsten Jahr stärkere steuerliche Anreize schaffen; ~ **administration** Finanzverwaltung; ~ **agency** Finanzbehörde; ~ **agent** Vertreter des Fiskus, *(banking)* Zahlstelle; ~ **authorities** Finanz-, Steuerbehörden; **to close its ~ books** Steuerabschluß machen; ~ **boost** rasant angestiegenes Steueraufkommen; ~ **brake** Steuerbremse; ~ **budget** Staatsetat; ~ **burden** Lasten, Abgaben; ~ **charges** steuerliche Belastungen, Fiskallasten; ~ **committee** Steuerausschuß; ~ **concern** steuerliches Interesse; ~ **constituencies** fiskalische Dauerbelastungen; ~ **control** Steueraufsicht; ~ **cooperation** Beistand in Steuersachen; **to ride out a ~ crisis** mit einer Finanzkrise fertig werden; ~ **court** Finanzhof, -gericht; ~ **deficiencies** steuerpolitische Nachteile; ~ **deficit** Fehlbetrag im Staatshaushalt, Haushaltsfehlbetrag; ~ **device** Finanzplan; ~ **difficulties** fiskalische Schwierigkeiten, finanzielle Schwierigkeiten, *(city)* Steuernöte; ~ **division** Finanzabteilung; ~ **domicile** Steuerwohnsitz; ~ **drag** steuerliche Belastung, expansionsbedingte Steuerprogression, Steuerhemmschuh, -bremse; ~ **dues** Fiskusgebühren, fiskalische Gebühren; ~ **earnings** zu versteuernde Einnahmen; ~ **evasion** *(Br.)* Steuerverkürzung, -umgehung; ~ **expansion** Steuerausweitung; ~ **expert** Steuerexperte; ~ **fraud** Steuerbetrug, -hinterziehung; ~ **harmonization** Harmonisierung der Steuern; ~ **illusions** steuerliche Illusionen; ~ **immunity** Steuerfreiheit; ~ **instrument** Steuermittel; ~ **interest** Steuerinteresse; ~ **jurisdiction** Steuerhoheit; ~ **lands** Krongüter; ~ **management** Steuerverwaltung; ~ **manipulations** Steuermanipulationen; ~ **matters** Steuerfragen, -wesen; ~ **monetary policy** steuerpolitische Maßnahmen; ~ **monopoly** Steuermonopol; ~ **motive** Steuermotiv; ~ **offence** Steuer-, Zollvergehen; ~ **office** Finanzamt; ~ **officer** Finanzbeamter; ~ **opportunity** steuerliche Möglichkeit; ~ **orgy** Steuerorgie; ~ **penalty** Steuerstrafe; ~ **period** Geschäfts-, Rechnungsperiode, Steuerabschnitt, Buchungszeitraum; ~ **plan** Finanz-, Steuerplan; ~ **policy** steuerpolitische Maßnahmen, Finanz-, Fiskalpolitik; **overexpansive ~ and monetary policies** ausgeuferte steuer- und geldmarktpolitische Maßnahmen; ~ **policy initiatives** steuerpolitische Initiativen; ~ **privileges** steuerliche Privilegien; ~ **program(me)** Steuerprogramm; ~ **provisions** steuerrechtliche Vorschriften; ~ **prudence** vernünftige Anwendung der Steuergesetze; ~ **reform** Steuerreform; ~ **relationship** Steuerverhältnis; ~ **report** Finanz-, Geschäftsbericht; **to meet changing ~ requirements** Veränderungen der Steuerbedürfnisse Rechnung tragen; ~ **restraint** zurückhaltende Steuerpolitik; ~ **right** Finanzhoheit; ~ **situation** Finanzlage; ~ **stimulus** steuerlicher Anreiz; **to contradict extra ~ stimulus** besonderen Steueranreizen entgegenwirken; ~ **stimulus package** Steuerreizvorschläge; ~ **system** Finanz-, Steuersystem; ~ **taxes** Finanzzölle; ~ **techniques** steuertechnische Maßnahmen; ~ **treatment** steuerliche Behandlung; ~ **year** *(US)* Geschäfts-, Rechnungs-, Finanz-, Haushalts-, Etatsjahr, *(Br.)* Steuerjahr.

fiscalism Fiskalismus.

fiscality Steuerpolitik.

fiscalization Besteuerung.

fiscalize *(v.)* der Steuer unterwerfen, besteuern.

fish Fisch, *(chip)* Spielmarke, *(US sl.)* Dollar;
queer ~ komischer Kauz;
like a ~ out of water wie ein Fisch auf dem Trockenen;
neither ~, flesh nor good red herring weder Fisch noch Fleisch, nichts Halbes und nichts Ganzes; **a pretty kettle of ~** ziemliches Durcheinander, schöne Bescherung;
~ *(v.)* **for information** Informationen herauskitzeln; ~ **a pencil out of one's pocket** Bleistift aus seiner Tasche angeln; ~ **secrets out of s. o.** jem. Geheimnisse entlocken; ~ **in troubled waters** im Trüben fischen; ~ **up a mine** treibende Mine aus dem Wasser holen;

to be like a ~ out of water nicht in seinem Element sein; **to cry stinking ~** das eigene Nest beschmutzen; **to have other ~ to fry** Wichtigeres zu tun haben;

~ breeder Fischzüchter; **~ breeding** Fischzucht; **~ car** *(railway)* Fischwaggon; **~ carrier** Fischwagen; **~ commissioner** *(US)* Fischzuchtbeauftragter; **~ culture** Fischzucht; **~ net** Fischnetz; **~ sticks** Fischstäbchen.

Fisheries|department *(Br.)* Ministerialabteilung für Fischereifragen; **~ economics** Fischereiwirtschaft; **common ~ police** *(EC)* gemeinsame Fischfangpolizei.

fisherman Fischer, Angler, *(vessel)* Fischdampfer, Walfänger.

fishery Fischerei, Fischfang, *(right to take fish)* Fischereirechte; **coast ~** Küstenfischerei; **common ~** Fischereiabkommen, -gerechtsame; **deep-sea ~** Tiefseefischerei; **free ~** Fischereigerechtigkeit; **freshwater ~** Binnenfischerei; **in-shore ~** Küstenfischerei; **several ~** selbständiges Fischereirecht; **~ laws** Fischereigesetze; **~ protection** Fischereischutz.

fishhouse Fischhalle.

fishing Fischerei, Fischfang; **oyster ~** Austernfischfang; **to be ~ for compliments** auf Komplimente aus sein; **~ agreement** Fischereiabkommen; **~ area** Fanggebiet; **~ banks** flache Fischereigewässer; **~ boat** Fischerboot; **~ fleet** Fischereiflotte; **~ grounds** Fischgründe, -fanggebiet, -distrikt; **~ industry** Fischfangindustrie; **~ licence** Angelschein, Fischerlaubnis; **~ limits** Fischereigrenzen; **~ net** Fischnetz; **~ permit** *(US)* Angel-, Fischereischein; **~ port** Fischereihafen; **~ restrictions** Fischereibeschränkungen; **~ story** *(Br.)* Jägerlatein; **~ vessel** Fischfahrzeug; **~ zone** Fischereizone.

fishmonger Fischhändler.

fishpond, fishpool Fischteich.

fishwife Fischhändlerin.

fishyard Fischlagerstätte.

fishy *(sl.)* faul, verdächtig; **to sound ~** verdächtig klingen; **~ account** faule Geschichte; **~ business** dunkle Angelegenheit.

fission Atomspaltung; **~ bomb** Atombombe; **~ material** spaltbares Material.

fist *(print.)* Handzeichen; **~ law** Faustrecht; **~ note** Handzeichen.

fit Anfall *(mood)* Laune, Stimmung, Anwandlung, Einfall; **by ~s and starts** stoßweise; **apoplectic ~** Schlaganfall; **fainting ~** Ohnmachtsanfall; **~s of morality** moralische Anwandlungen; **to answer in a ~ of temper** mit einem Wutanfall antworten; **to beat s. o. into a ~** *(coll.)* j. spielend besiegen; **to fall into a ~** ohnmächtig werden; **to give s. o. a ~** *(coll.)* j. schrecklich aufregen; **to have a ~** Wutanfall bekommen, Zustände kriegen; **to have sudden ~s of energy** plötzlich äußerst tatendurstig werden; **to have a ~ of laziness** seine faulen Tage haben; **to almost have a ~ when seeing the bill** beim Anblick der Rechnung um ein Haar einen Schlaganfall bekommen; **to throw a ~** *(coll.)* ohnmächtig werden; **to work by ~s and starts** nur in Etappen arbeiten;

~ *(a.)* befähigt, tauglich, qualifiziert, geeignet, passend, *(healthy)* gesund, tauglich; **~ for acceptance** lieferfähig; **~ to carry arms** waffenfähig; **~ to drink** trinkbar; **~ to drive** fahrtüchtig; **~ to drop** zum Umfallen müde; **~ for duty** dienstfähig; **~ to eat** eßbar; **as ~ as a fiddle** in bester Verfassung, gesund wie ein Fisch im Wasser; **~ for habitation** bewohnbar; **dressed ~ to kill** geschmückt (geputzt) wie ein Pfingstochse; **~ for a king** eines Königs würdig, königlich; **~ to live** lebensfähig; **~ for printing** druckreif; **~ for service** diensttauglich; **~ for active service** kriegsverwendungs-, wehr-, felddienstfähig, kriegstauglich; **~ for service in the field** feldverwendungsfähig; **~ for transport** transportfähig; **~ to travel** reisefähig; **~ for work** erwerbs-, arbeitsfähig;

~ *(v.)* anpassen, ausrüsten, -statten, montieren; **~ a coal field** Kohlenfeld ausbeuten; **~ o. s. for one's new duties** sich auf seinen neuen Aufgabenbereich vorbereiten; **~ in one's holidays with s. one else** seine Urlaubspläne mit einem anderen abstimmen; **~ into a job** in Arbeit bringen; **~ a lock in ein Schloß passen; **~ s. o. to a nicety** jem. glänzend passen; **~ out** *(apartment)* einrichten, *(equip)* ausrüsten; **~ with new plumbing** neu installieren; **~ o. s. for a post** sich die für eine Stellung notwendigen Kenntnisse verschaffen; **~ a road for traffic** Straße instandsetzen; **~ [on] a suit** Anzug anprobieren; **~ o. s. into one's surroundings** sich seiner Umgebung anpassen; **~ on a tyre** Reifen aufziehen; **~ up** möblieren, ausstatten; **~ up a hotel with modern comforts and conveniences** Hotel auf das Modernste einrichten; **~ a workshop** Fabrik ausrüsten;

to be ~ for qualifiziert (tauglich) sein (für); **to be ~ for one's job** für seine Stellung geeignet sein; **to be passed ~** tauglich befunden werden; **to be as ~ as a fiddle** glänzend gelaunt (quietschvergnügt) sein; **to be hardly ~ to company** sich kaum vorzeigen können; **not to be ~ to hold a candle to s. o.** jem. nicht das Wasser reichen können; **to be reasonably ~ for habitation** für Wohnzwecke hinreichend geeignet sein; **to be ~ for nothing** zu nichts taugen; **not to be ~ for a position** für eine Stellung nicht geeignet sein; **to have nothing ~ to wear** nichts Geeignetes anzuziehen haben; **to make the punishment ~ the crime** angemessene Strafe verhängen; **to see ~ to adopt a suggestion** sich zur Annahme eines Vorschlags entschließen; **to decide on a ~ time** geeigneten Zeitpunkt festlegen.

fit-up *(theatre, Br.)* provisorische Bühne; **~ company** Wandertruppe.

fitment Einrichtungsgegenstand.

fitness *(for job)* Befähigung, Eignung, Qualifikation, *(ship)* Ladungstüchtigkeit; **physical ~** körperliche Tauglichkeit; **~ to drive** Fahrtüchtigkeit; **~ for employment** Arbeitsfähigkeit; **~ for habitation** Eignung für Wohnzwecke; **~ for a particular purpose** besondere Eignung (Zweckdienlichkeit) für etw.; **~ of property** Grundstückseignung; **~ for purpose** zugesicherte Eigenschaft, Zweckeignung; **~ for service** *(mil.)* Diensttauglichkeit; **~ for use** Einsatzfähigkeit; **national ~ campaign** Gesundheitsfeldzug.

fitout Ausrüstung.

fitted geeignet, qualifiziert; **to be ~ with modern comforts** mit allem Komfort ausgestattet sein; **~ accounts** unwidersprochener Kontokorrentsaldo.

fitter Schlosser, Installateur, Monteur, *(supplier, Br.)* Kohlenlieferant; **~ out** *(ship)* Reeder.

fitting Installation, Montage, Montieren, Installieren, *(apparatus)* Gerät, Apparat; **~s** *(apparatus)* Geräte, *(articles affixed)* Zubehör, *(furniture)* Einrichtung, Ausrüstungs-, Ausstattung[sgegenstände], Armaturen; **gas and electric-light ~s** Gas- und elektrische Anlagen; **office ~s** Büroeinrichtung; **shop ~s** Ladeneinrichtung; **~-on of a tyre** Aufziehen eines Reifens; **~-out** Ausstattung; **~-out of a vessel** Schiffsausrüstung; **~ together** Zusammenbau; **~-up of a machine** Montage einer Maschine; **to go to the tailor's for a ~** zum Schneider zur Anprobe gehen; **easy-~** bequem passend; **~ remark** zutreffende Bemerkung; **~ room** Kleiderkabine; **~ school** *(US)* Vorbereitungsschule; **~ shop** Montagewerkstatt.

five|r *(Br.)* Fünfpfundnote, *(US)* Fünfdollarnote; **~s** *(US)* fünfprozentige Papiere; **~-day week** Fünftagewoche; **~-and-dime store** *(US)* Einheitspreisgeschäft; **~-figure income** fünfstelliges Einkommen; **~ percenter** *(US)* Makler für Regierungsaufträge; **~-star hotel** Fünfsternehotel, Hotel erster Klasse; **~-year plan** Fünfjahresplan.

fix *(bribe, US)* Bestechung, *(dilema)*, Patsche, Klemme, *(drug)* Rauschgifteinheit, *(ship)* Besteckaufnahme, Standort, *(US sl.)* abgekartetes Spiel; **in good ~** *(US)* in gutem Zustand; **out of ~** kaputt, reparaturbedürftig; **~** *(v.)* befestigen, *(agree upon)* verabreden, vereinbaren, abmachen, *(appoint)* festsetzen, festlegen, bestimmen, fixieren, *(date of meeting)* anberaumen, *(mend)* reparieren, *(settle)* regeln, *(US sl.)* auf unehrliche Weise beeinflussen; **~ s. o.** *(US sl.)* j. bestechen; **~ the budget** Etat aufstellen; **~ damages** Entschädigung (Termin) festsetzen; **~ a date** Termin festsetzen (vereinbaren); **~ a date for a meeting** Sitzungstermin festsetzen, Sitzung ansetzen; **~ on a date** sich über einen Termin einigen; **~ dates in one's mind** sich Daten einprägen; **~ a day for a hearing in court** Gerichtstermin anberaumen; **~ one's departure** seine Abreise festsetzen; **~ a deposit for two months** Guthaben auf zwei Monate festlegen; **~ export quotas** Ausfuhr kontingentieren; **~ a hearing** [Gerichts]termin ansetzen; **~ the income tax** Einkommensteuerrichtlinien erlassen; **~ the income tax at 28%** Einkommensteuersätze in der Höhe von 28% festlegen; **~ a jury** *(US)* Geschworene bestechen; **~ a limit** Limit festsetzen, limitieren; **~ a meeting for twelve o'clock** Sitzung auf zwölf Uhr einberufen; **~ s. th. into one's memory** sich etw. einprägen; **~ a monument** Denkmal aufstellen; **~ a newspaper into the holder** Zeitung einspannen; **~ the position** *(ship)* Besteck nehmen, orten; **~ a price** Preis bestimmen (fixieren); ~ **the price of a new model** Preis für ein neues Modell festsetzen; ~ **quotas for import** Einfuhrkontingente verteilen; ~ **a rate** Kurs sichern; ~ **a rent** Mietpreis festsetzen; ~ **one's residence in a place** seinen Wohnsitz begründen; ~ **a royalty** Lizenzgebühr festlegen; ~ **suspicion on s. o.** Verdacht auf j. lenken; ~ **the tariff** Tarif festsetzen; ~ **up** (US) reparieren, in Ordnung bringen, (US sl.) versorgen, unterbringen; ~ **s. o. up for a job** Posten (Stellung) für j. finden; ~ **up a friend for the night** einem Freund ein Nachtquartier verschaffen; ~ **up a quarrel** Streit beilegen; ~ **up somewhere** sich eine Übernachtungsmöglichkeit suchen; ~ **things up with s. o.** sich mit jem. arrangieren; ~ **up a wireless station** Rundfunksender errichten (installieren); ~ **a time** Termin setzen; ~ **upon a little bungalow** sich zu einem kleinen Bungalowhaus entschließen; ~ **the value of an entry (item)** Buchungsposten valutieren; ~ **a watch** Uhr reparieren;

to be in a ~ in einer schlimmen Lage (in Verlegenheit) sein; **to get into a ~** in Verlegenheit (Schwierigkeiten) geraten; **to get o. s. into a bad ~** sich selbst hereinreiten; **to get out of a ~** sich aus der Klemme ziehen; **to get s. o. out of a ~** j. aus einer schwierigen Lage befreien; **to put on the ~** (US sl.) unter Druck setzen, Daumenschrauben ansetzen.

fixation of a photographic film Fixieren eines Films.

fixative Fixiermittel, (photo) Fixativ;
~ **bath** Fixierbad.

fixed bestimmt, ständig, unveränderlich, fest, festgelegt, (bill of exchange, Br.) ohne Respekttage, (sl.) bestochen;
to be ~ **on s. th.** auf etw. festgelegt sein; **to be well ~** (US) finanziell gut dran sein; **to become ~** (charge) sich konkretisieren; **to see one's daughters comfortably ~** seine Töchter gut versorgt wissen;
without ~ **abode** ohne festen Aufenthalt; ~ **allowance** Fixum; ~**-amount policy** Selbstbehalt ausschließende Versicherungspolice; ~ **ammunition** (mil.) Einheitsmunition; ~ **assets** (accounting) feste (fixe) Anlagen, Sache, Anlagevermögen, Sachanlagevermögen, immaterielle Anlagenwerte, Anlagegegenstände, Sachanlagen; ~**-assets account** Sachanlagenkonto; ~**-asset unit** feststehender Anlageposten; ~ **base** (double taxation agreement) feste Einrichtung; ~ **bill** (Br.) Präsiswechsel; ~ **budgets** für mehrere Jahre festgesetzte Etats; ~ **capital** festliegendes Kapital, Anlagekapital, feste (fixe) Kapitalsanlagen, ~**-capital asset** Gegenstand des Sachanlagevermögens; ~**-capital expenditure** Investitionsaufwand; ~**-capital goods** Investitionsgüter; ~ **charge** [etwa] Globalverpfändung, schwebende Schuld, besitzloses Pfandrecht mit wechselndem Besitz; ~ **charges** Generalkosten, feste Kosten (Spesen), Fix-, Festkosten; ~ **construction** (patent law) Bauwesen; ~ **contract price** vertraglich festgesetzter Preis; ~ **costs** Fixkosten, fixe (feste) Kosten; ~ **date** [fester] Termin, Terminvorschrift; ~**-date advertisement** Terminanzeige; ~ **date clause** Fixklausel; ~ **day** bestimmter Empfangstag, Termin, Frist; ~ **debentures** hypothekarisch gesicherte Schuldverschreibungen; ~ **debt** Obligations-, Dauerschuld; ~ **deductions** gleichbleibende (feststehende) Abzüge; ~**-[term] deposit** Festgeld, festes Geld, Einlage auf Depositenkonto, Termineinlage; ~ **depreciation** feststehende Abschreibungssätze; ~ **draft** Tratte ohne Respekttage; ~ **dues** feststehende Gebühren; ~ **exchange** Mengennotierung; ~ **exchange rates** feste Wechselkurse; ~ **expenses** Generalunkosten, laufende Ausgaben; ~ **fee** feste Gebühr; ~ **fund** (US) Investmentfonds mit feststehendem Portefeuille; ~ **furniture** fest eingebaute Möbel; ~ **idea** fixe Idee, Komplex; ~ **income** feststehende (ständige) Einkünfte, feststehendes Einkommen; ~ **indebtedness** langfristige Verschuldung; ~**-interest bearing** festverzinslich; ~**-interest securities** festverzinsliche Wertpapiere; ~ **investment** langfristige Kapitalanlage; ~ **investment trust** Kapitalanlagegesellschaft mit festgelegtem Effektenbestand; ~ **landing gear** (airplane) festes Fahrwerk; ~ **liabilities** feste (langfristige) Verbindlichkeiten; ~ **light** (mar.) Festfeuer; ~ **limits** (foreign exchange) feste Bandbreiten; ~ **loan** langfristiges Darlehen; ~ **margins of the exchange rates** feste Bandbreiten der Wechselkurse; ~ **mortgage** Festgeldhypothek; ~ **opinion** vorgefaßte Meinung; ~ **parity** feste Parität; ~ **period** fester Zeitraum; ~**-period order** Festauftrag auf bestimmte Zeit; **to have no ~ plans** keine festen Pläne haben; ~ **plant** festeingebaute Betriebsanlage; ~ **point** (data processing) Festkomma; ~ **price** gebundener Preis, Festpreis, (stock exchange) fester Kurs; **to sell goods only at ~ prices** nur zu Festpreisen verkaufen; ~**-price contract** Festpreisauftrag; ~**-price shop** Einheitspreisgeschäft; ~ **principles** feste Grundsätze; ~ **production coefficient** fester Produktionskoeffizient; ~ **property** Grundvermögen, Liegenschaften; ~ **rates** (Br.) in

Pence notierte Devisenkurse; ~ **ratio** festes Verteilungsverhältnis; ~ **resale price** in der zweiten Hand gebundener Preis; ~ **salary** festes Gehalt, Fixum; ~ **sample** festgelegte Stichprobe; ~ **selling prices** Preisbindung der zweiten Hand; ~ **shift** (enterprise) gleichbleibende Arbeitsschicht; ~ **station** feste Funkstelle; ~ **tail surface** (airplane) Leitwerkflosse; ~ **time** festgesetzte Zeit, Termin; ~ **time for delivery** Liefertermin; ~ **trust** (US) Kapitalanlagegesellschaft mit festem Effektenbestand; ~ **value loan** wertbeständige Anleihe.

fixing (determination) Festsetzung, -legung, Bestimmung, (fitting) Aufstellen, Montieren, Montage, (mar.) Berechnung;
~**s** (coll.) Ausrüstung[sgegenstände], (apparatus) Geräte;
~ **of a course** Kursbestimmung; ~ **of damages** Schadensfestsetzung; ~ **of a date** Terminbestimmung; ~ **of import quotas** Einfuhrkontingentierung; ~ **of a limit** Festsetzung von Höchstbeträgen; ~ **of a price** Ansatz eines Preises, Preisansatz, Preisfestsetzung, -legung; ~ **of quotas** Kontingentierung; ~ **of a trustee's remuneration** Festsetzung einer Treuhändervergütung; ~ **of wages** Lohnfestsetzung;
~ **agent** Fixier-, Bindemittel; ~ **bath** (photo) Fixierbad.

fixture feste Anlagen, Inventarstück, (event to occur) bevorstehendes Ereignis, (person in established place) Festangestellter, Planstelleninhaber, (sporting events) festliegende Veranstaltung, (time loan) kurzfristiger Kredit;
~**s** Zubehör;
agricultural ~**s** landwirtschaftliches Zubehör, Einbauten des Pächters; **domestic** ~**s** Wohnungseinbauten des Mieters; **immovable** ~ wesentlicher Grundstücksbestandteil; **movable** ~ entfernbarer Bestandteil; **ornamental** ~**s** der Verschönerung dienende Mietereinbauten; **small** ~ kleine Inventarstücke; **tenant's** ~ eingebaute Gegenstände des Pächters; **trade** ~**s** gewerbliche Mietereinbauten, (stock exchange) Wochengeld, wöchentliches Geld;
~**s and fittings** Einbauten und Zubehör des Mieters;
to become a ~ Zubehör (wesentlicher Bestandteil) werden, (fig.) feste Einrichtung werden; **to remove** ~**s** Zubehör entfernen.

fixup Kniff.

fizzle Steckenbleiben, Fiasko, Pleite;
~ **out** (v.) im Sande verlaufen.

flag Flagge, Fahne, (data processing) Leitcode, Fehleranzeige, (newspaper) Name, Titel, (stratified stone) Fliese, Steinplatte, (television) Lichtabdeckschirm;
black ~ Piratenflagge; **house** ~ Reedereiflagge; **merchant** ~ Handelsflagge; **national** ~ Staats-, Hoheitsflagge; **Red-Cross** ~ Rotkreuzflagge; **white** ~ weiße Fahne; **yellow** ~ Quarantäneflagge;
~ **of convenience** billige Handelsflagge, Billigkeitsflagge; ~ **of distress** Notflagge; ~ **of quarantine** Quarantäneflagge; ~ **of truce** weiße Fahne, Parlamentärsflagge;
~ (v.) beflaggen, (sag) abflauen, nachlassen, (signal) signalisieren, durch Flaggenzeichen warnen;
~ **a train** Zug anhalten;
to brandish (flourish) a ~ Fahne schwenken, to deck with ~**s** beflaggen; **to dip a** ~ Fahne senken; **to display one's** ~ Flagge zeigen; **to fly the** ~ **of** ... unter der Flagge ... von fahren; **to fly the** ~ **at half-mast** Flagge auf halbmast setzen; **to hoist one's** ~ Kommando übernehmen; **to lower one's** ~ Fahne einholen (niederholen); **to run up the** ~ Fahne aufziehen; **to show the** ~ (fig.) Farbe bekennen; **to show one's** ~ Flagge zeigen; **to strike one's** ~ Kommando abgeben; **to wave a red** ~ **to stop a train** mit der roten Flagge einem Zug entgegengehen;
~ **book** Flaggenbuch; ~ **carrier** nationale Fluggesellschaft; ~ **day** (Br.) Sammeltag für wohltätige Zwecke; ~ **discrimination** unterschiedliche Anwendung des Zolltarifs; ~ **salute** Flaggengruß; ~ **signal** Flaggensignal; ~ **station (stop, US)** Bedarfsanflughafen, (railway) Bedarfshaltestelle.

flagged beflaggt.

flagellate (v.) geißeln, peitschen.

flagging Fliesenlegen, (pavement) gepflasterter Gehweg, Trottoir; ~ (a.) nachlassend, abschwächend;
~ **interest** nachlassendes Interesse; ~ **tendency** Abschwächungstendenz.

flagman Fahnenträger, (sport) Starter, (railroad, US) Bahnwärter.

flagpole Fahnenmast.

flagrancy Schändlichkeit, Abscheulichkeit;
~ **of a crime** Ungeheuerlichkeit eines Verbrechens.

flagrant schamlos, schändlich;
~ **offence** flagrantes Verbrechen; ~ **injustice** schreiendes Unrecht; ~ **necessity** Notstand.

flagship Flaggschiff.
flagstaff Flaggenstock.
flagwagging Signalisieren.
flagwaver Agitator, *(coll.)* Chauvinist.
flagwaving Chauvinismus, Agitation.
flair feine Nase, Begabung;
  to have a ~ for bargains feine Nase für Gelegenheitskäufe haben; **to have a ~ for languages** sprachbegabt sein.
flamboyance Effekthascherei.
flame Flamme, Feuer;
  old ~ alte Flamme (Freundin);
  ~ of enthusiasm Begeisterungssturm;
  to be in ~s in Flammen stehen, brennen; **to commit one's manuscripts to the ~s** seine Aufzeichnungen verbrennen;
  ~ projector (thrower) Flammenwerfer.
flameproof feuerfest.
flank *(building)* Seite, *(mil.)* Flanke, Flügel;
  to take the enemy in ~ Flankenmanöver gegen den Feind durchführen;
  ~ attack Flankenangriff; **~ company** Anschlußkompanie; **~ defence** Flankenschutz; **~ fire** Flankenfeuer; **~ guard** Flanken-, Seitendeckung; **~ movement** Flankenbewegung.
flanking measures flankierende Maßnahmen.
flannel Flanell, *(fig.)* Liebedienerei.
flap *(airplane)* Landeklappe, *(sl.)* Durcheinander;
  ~ of an envelope Briefklappe.
flapper Fliegenklappe, *(sl.)* Denkzettel.
flare Leuchtkugel, -signal, *(fig.)* Ausbruch, Aufbrausen;
  ~ pistol Leuchtpistole.
flare-up Riesenspektakel.
flare up *(v.)* **at the least thing** bei der kleinsten Kleinigkeit aufbrausen.
flaring advertisement marktschreierische Werbung, sensationell aufgemachte Anzeige.
flash Aufleuchten, Blitz, Aufblitzen, *(brilliant burst)* Einfall, Idee, *(duration of a flash)* kurzer Augenblick, Blitzesschnelle, *(film, Br.)* Rückblende, -blick, *(mil., Br.)* Divisionszeichen, *(newspaper, radio)* Kurznachricht, *(thieves' language)* Gauner-, Vagabundensprache, *(torchlight, US)* Taschenlampe;
  in a ~ im Nu;
  news ~ kurze Nachrichtensendung;
  ~ of hope Hoffnungsstrahl; **~ of lightning** Blitz; **~ in the pan** kurzlebige Erscheinung; **~ of wit** Geistesblitz;
  ~ *(v.)* ausstrahlen, aufblitzen, *(move quickly)* sich blitzartig bewegen, flitzen, *(news)* durchsagen lassen;
  ~ a beam of light on s. th. Lichtstrahl auf etw. lenken; **~ a sudden light upon a mystery** Geheimnis schlagartig zum Vorschein bringen; **~ news across the world** Nachrichten über die ganze Welt verbreiten; **~ out a duty sign** Besetzzeichen ausstrahlen; **~ a portrait on the screen** Portrait auf die Leinwand werfen; **~ up on to a small display face** elektronisch auf eine kleine Bildfläche übertragen;
  to be ~ in the pan nach glänzendem Start versagen; **to do it in a ~** im Nu erledigen;
  ~ bomb *(mil.)* Leuchtbombe; **~ bulb** Blitzlichtlampe; **~ check** *(US)* **(cheque,** *Br.)* ungedeckter Scheck; **~ command** *(photocomposition)* Belichtungsbefehl; **~ flood** plötzliche Überschwemmung; **~ jewelry** Imitationsschmuck; **~ lamp** Blitzlichtlampe; **~ message** Blitztelegramm; **~ people** Gaunervolk; **~ report** vorläufiger Rechenschaftsbericht.
flashblack *(film)* Rückblende.
flashing | indicator *(car)* Blinker; **~ light** Blinkfeuer; **~ sign** Blinklichtwerbung; **~ signal** Leuchtsignal; **~ red warning (stop light)** Blinklicht[anlage].
flashlight Blitzlicht, *(torch, US)* Taschenlampe;
  ~ *(v.)* mit Blitzlicht fotografieren;
  ~ photography Blitzlichtaufnahme.
flashy glitzernd, glänzend.
flat Fläche, Ebene, *(apartment, Br.)* Etagen-, Mietwohnung, Appartement, *(blockhead, sl.)* Knallkopf, Einfaltspinsel, *(floor)* Stockwerk, Etage, *(house)* Mietshaus, *(lowland)* Flachland, Niederung, *(mar.)* Truppenlandungsboot, Leichter, *(Br., offset)* Film für Offset, *(railroad, US)* flacher offener Güterwagen, Plattformwagen, *(theater)* Kulisse, *(tyre, sl.)* Platter, Plattfuß, Reifenpanne;
  comfortable ~ bequeme Wohnung; **converted ~s** in Teilwohnungen umgebaute große Wohnung; **council ~** *(Br.)* Sozialwohnung; **five-roomed ~** Fünfzimmerwohnung; **freehold ~** *(Br.)* Eigentumswohnung; **furnished ~** möblierte Wohnung; **higher-bracket ~** Wohnung für gehobenere Ansprüche; **one-roomed ~** Einzimmerappartment; **owner-occupied ~** Eigen-

tumswohnung; **private-sector ~** freifinanzierte Wohnung; **rent-controlled ~** *(Br.)* dem Mieterschutz unterliegende Wohnung; **residential ~** Privatwohnung; **self-contained ~** abgeschlossene Mietwohnung, Wohnung mit eigenem Eingang, Etagenwohnung; **service ~** *(Br.)* Wohnung mit Bedienung, Wohnhotel; **small ~** kleine Wohnung; **working-class ~** Arbeiterwohnung;
  ~ in the attic Mansardenwohnung; **~ in a quiet neighbo(u)rhood** ruhig gelegene Wohnung;
  ~ *(a.)* *(level)* flach, platt, eben, *(photo)* ohne Schattierung, kontrastlos, *(selling badly)* schwer zu verkaufen, *(standard)* einheitlich, gleichmäßig, pauschal, *(stock exchange)* lustlos, flau, *(tyre)* platt, *(US, without interest)* ohne Berechnung aufgelaufener Zinsen, franko;
  ~ on one's back gänzlich herunter, abgewirtschaftet; **as ~ as a pancake** flach wie ein Pfannkuchen;
  to be ~ on its back völlig darniederliegen; **to be turned down ~** abgewimmelt werden; **to be working ~ out** *(coll.)* alle Reserven einsetzen; **to borrow money ~** zinslosen Kredit erhalten; **to fall ~** mißglücken, fehlschlagen, nicht ankommen, keinen Eindruck machen; **to furnish a ~** Wohnung möblieren; **to go ~ against s. one's orders** sich nicht an gegebene Anweisungen halten; **to go ~ with losing operations** Verlustgeschäft erleiden; **to lay a city ~** *(earthquake)* Stadt in einen Trümmerhaufen verwandeln; **to leave off ~** *(stock exchange)* flau (lustlos) schließen; **to leave s. o. ~** j. plötzlich verlassen; **to let a ~** *(Br.)* Wohnung vermieten; **to live in a ~** *(Br.)* eigene Wohnung haben; **to loan stocks ~** Wertpapiere zinslos lombardieren; **to open ~** *(stock exchange)* anfangs flau sein; **to rent a ~** *(Br.)* Wohnung vermieten; **to rent a ~ and take over the furniture** *(Br.)* Wohnung mieten und die Möbel übernehmen; **to sell stocks ~** Wertpapiere ohne Zinsvergütung veräußern; **to taste ~** schal schmecken;
  ~-bed press Flachdruckpresse; **~-bed printing** Flachdruck; **~ bonus** einheitliche Prämie, Pauschalprämie; **~ bonus system** Pauschalprämiensystem; **~ breaking** *(Br.)* Wohnungseinbruch; **~ broke** *(US sl.)* völlig pleite, gänzlich bankrott; **~ calculation** pauschale Berechnung; **~ car** *(US)* offener Güterwagen; **~ catcher** Zug-, Lockartikel; **~ charge** Pauschale; **~ coast** Flachküste; **~ conversation** langweilige Unterhaltung; **~ cost** Selbstkosten-, Gestehungspreis; **~ country** ebenes (flaches) Land, Flachland; **to give a ~ credit** zinslosen Kredit gewähren; **~ decision** klare Entscheidung; **~ denial** formelles Dementi; **to give a ~ denial** etw. rundweg ableugnen, glatt dementieren; **~ duplicator** Flachvervielfältiger; **~ dweller** *(Br.)* Appartmentbewohner, Miethausbewohner; **~ dwelling** App-artementwohnung; **~ exemption** *(US)* steuerlicher Pauschalfreibetrag, Pauschbetrag; **~ fare** *(short-distance transport)* Pauschalpreis, Einheitstarif; **~ fee** fester Preis, Pauschalgebühr, -honorar; **~ file** Schnellhefter; **~ house** *(Br.)* Mietshaus; **~ hunting** *(Br.)* Wohnungssuche; **~ increase** pauschale Erhöhung; **~-letting business** *(Br.)* Vermietungsgeschäft, Wohnungsgewerbe; **~ market** lustlose Börse; **~ no** glattes Nein; **~ nonsense** absoluter Unsinn; **~ price** Pauschalpreis; **~ printing** Flachdruck; **~ proof** Flachdruckabzug; **~ quotation** *(US)* Kursnotierung ohne aufgelaufene Zinsen.
flat rate einheitlicher Satz, Einheits-, Pauschalsatz, -gebühr, *(advertising)* Anzeigenfestpreis, *(el., US)* Kleinverbrauchertarif, *(taxation)* einheitlicher Steuersatz;
  ~ of contribution pauschaler Beitragssatz; **~ of pay** tarifliches Gehalt, Tarifgehalt.
flat-rate pauschal;
  ~ amount Pauschalbetrag; **on a ~ basis** pauschal; **~ bonus** Pauschalprämie; **~ car-licence fee** Kraftfahrzeugpauschalsteuer; **~ contribution** Grundbeitrag, *(social insurance)* Einheitsbeitrag; **~ freight** Pauschalfracht; **~ increase** Pauschalsatzerhöhung; **~ method** lineare Abschreibungsmethode; **~ reduction** genereller Lohnsteuerfreibetrag; **~ tariff** Kleinabnehmertarif.
flat | refusal glatte Ablehnung; **~ rent** Pauschalmiete; **~ salary** Pauschalgehalt; **~ shore** Flachküste; **~ speech** inhaltlose Rede; **~ stitching** Flachheftung; **~ sum** Pauschalbetrag; **~ tariff** Einheitstarif; **~ tile** Flachziegel; **~ tire (tyre,** *Br.)* Reifenpanne; **~ tuning** Grobabstimmung; **~ value** Pauschalwert; **~ warming** *(Br.)* Einweihungsfest; **~ yield** Pauschalsumme, Pauschalbetrag; **~ yield of an investment** *(Br.)* laufende [Anlagen]-verzinsung.
flatation Preisflaute.
flatcar *(US)* offener Güterwagen, Rungenwagen;
  piggyback ~ *(US)* Flachwagen für den Huckepackverkehr;
  ~ rate *(US)* Waggonfrachtsatz.

flatfoot *(sl.)* Polyp, Polizist.
flatfooted *(US)* offen, geradeheraus, *(Br.)* schwerfällig, phantasielos;
  to catch ~ *(US)* überrumpeln, auf frischer Tat erwischen.
flatiron Plätt-, Bügeleisen.
flatlet *(Br.)* kleine Wohnung, Kleinstwohnung.
flatlord *(Br.)* Vermieter einer Appartementwohnung.
flatness *(market)* Flaute, Flauheit, Lustlosigkeit;
  ~ in advertising business Anzeigenflaute.
flatsharer *(Br.)* Mitbewohner, -mieter;
  ~'s register *(Br.)* Mietnachweis für Gemeinschaftswohnungen.
flatsharing *(Br.)* Wohngemeinschaft.
flatted *(Br.)* in Appartements eingeteilt;
  ~ house Appartment-, Mietshaus.
flatten *(v.)* ebnen, *(cycle)* sich abflachen;
  ~ out *(airplane)* abfangen.
flattening | of economic growth Abflachung der Wachstumskurve; **~ out** *(airplane)* Abfangen.
flatter *(v.)* schmeicheln, Komplimente machen;
  ~ o. s. on one's cleverness sich in seiner Klugheit sonnen; **~ o. s. with hopes of success** sich Erfolgschancen vorgaukeln; **~ s. one's vanity** jds. Eitelkeit schmeicheln.
flatterer, mealy-mouthered glattzüngiger Schmeichler.
flattering schmeichelhaft, schmeichlerisch;
  to make ~ remarks schmeichelhafte Bemerkungen machen; **to speak in ~ terms of s. o.** in höchsten Tönen von jem. sprechen.
flattery Schmeichelei;
  mealy-mouthed ~ Süßholzraspelei.
flattop *(mar., US coll.)* Flugzeugträger.
flatware *(US)* Eßbesteck.
flatwork Mangelwäsche.
flaunt *(v.)* prunken;
  ~ advanced ideas sich mit fortschrittlichen Aussichten brüsten; **~ one's new riches** seinen neu erworbenen Reichtum zur Schau stellen.
flaunting of wealth, obscene Protzen mit seinem Reichtum.
flavo(u)r Aroma, Würze, *(fig.)* Atmosphäre, *(wine)* Bouquet;
  ~ of the Bohemian bohemienhafte Atmosphäre; **~ of romance** romantischer Beigeschmack;
  to get the full ~ of in den vollen Genuß kommen;
  ~ preference test Geschmackstest.
flaw *(sudden burst of wind)* Windstoß, Bö, *(defect)* Fehler, Defekt, schwacher Punkt, Manko, *(law)* Formfehler, *(manufacturing)* Fabrikationsfehler, *(reputation)* Makel, *(precious stone)* Wolke;
  ~ in s. one's character Charakterfehler; **~ in a pane of glass** Sprung in einer Fensterscheibe; **~ in reasoning** Fehler in der Beweisführung; **~ in a title** Rechtsmangel; **~ in a will** anfechtbares Testament;
  to offer a few ~s einige Fehler aufweisen.
flawless fehlerlos, makellos.
flea, to put a ~ in s. one's ear *(US sl.)* jem. einen Floh ins Ohr setzen; **to send s. o. away with a ~ in his ear** jem. gehörig den Kopf waschen;
  ~ bag *(sl.)* Schlafsack, Flohkiste; **~ bite** *(fig.)* Bagatelle; **~ market** Flohmarkt.
fledgeling *(Br.)* Grünschnabel.
flee *(v.)* Flucht ergreifen, fliehen;
  ~ away *(time)* wie im Fluge vergehen; **~ [from] a country** aus einem Lande flüchten; **~ in disorder** völlig aufgelöst fliehen; **~ from justice** sich der Strafverfolgung entziehen; **~ to the wall** sich in äußerster Notwehrlage befinden.
fleece Schäfchenwolke, *(stock exchange, sl.)* geprellter Börsianer;
  ~ *(v.)* prellen, rupfen;
  ~ s. o. of all his money j. um sein ganzes Geld betrügen; **~ s. o. of every halfpenny** jem. sein Geld bis zum letzten Heller abnehmen;
  to allow o. s. to be ~d sich betrügen lassen.
fleet [Kriegs]flotte, Luftflotte, *(bay)* Bai, Bucht, Gewässer;
  air (aerial) ~ Luftflotte; **battle ~** Schlachtflotte; **enemy ~** feindliche Flotte; **home ~** *(Br.)* Heimatflotte, Flotte in Heimatgewässern; **merchant ~** Handelsmarine; **ocean-going ~** Hochseeflotte; **truck ~** Lastkraftwagen-, Fuhrpark; **whaling ~** Walfangflotte;
  ~ of airplanes Flugzeuggeschwader; **~ of ambulances** Sanitätskolonne; **~ of cabs** Wagenpark; **~ of locomotives** Lokomotivpark; **~ of motorcars** Autokolonne; **~ of taxis** Taxiflotte; **~ of trucks** Fuhr-, [Last]kraftwagenpark; **~ of vehicles** Fuhr-, Wagenpark;
  ~ *(v.)* flitzen, *(mar.)* Position wechseln;

⚓ Air Arm *(Br.)* Marineluftwaffe; **~-book evidence** unzulässiges Beweismaterial; **~ buyer** Einkäufer von Firmenwagen; **~ buying** Fuhrparkankauf, Ankauf von Firmenwagen; **~ capacity** Handelsflottenkapazität; **~ car** Geschäfts-, Betriebs-, Firmenwagen; **~ discount** Prämiennachlaß bei Gruppenversicherung; **~ insurance** *(automobile)* Sammel-, Gruppenversicherung; **~ manager** Fuhrparkleiter; **own ~ operator** Besitzer eines eigenen Fuhrparks; **~ owner** Fuhrparkbesitzer; **~ plan** *(vehicle)* Gruppenversicherungssystem; **~ policy** *(insurance)* Flotten-, Gruppen-, Sammelpolice; **~ sale** *(vehicles)* Gruppenverkauf; **⚓ Street** *(London)* Zeitungs-, Presseviertel; **~ train** Geleitzug.
Flemish window Halbgeschoßfenster.
flesh Fleisch, *(fig.)* Menschengeschlecht;
  after the ~ nach Menschenart; **in the ~** in der Realität, leibhaftig, höchstpersönlich;
  ~ and blood Kinder, Verwandte; **one's own ~ and blood** sein eigen Fleisch und Blut;
  ~ *(v.)* **out a marketing organization** Absatzorganisation für zukünftige Aufgaben anreichern; **~ one's pen** zum ersten Mal die Feder führen;
  to demand one's pound of ~ auf seinem Schein bestehen; **to make s. one's ~ creep** j. erschaudern lassen, jem. kalt über den Rücken laufen.
fleshpots [of Egypt] üppiges Leben.
flex *(Br., el.)* Anschlußschnur, Litze.
flexibility Anpassungsfähigkeit, Flexibilität, Elastizität;
  built-in ~ *(cyclical policy)* eingebaute Flexibilität, *(tax system)* automatische Anpassungsfähigkeit;
  ~ of prices Elastizität der Preise, Preisflexibilität; **~ in production** Produktionsflexibilität.
flexible *(fig.)* anpassungsfähig, elastisch, *(price)* flexibel, *(techn.)* beweglich, nicht starr;
  ~ in thinking geistig beweglich;
  ~ binding flexibler Einband; **~ budget** elastischer Etat; **~ coupling** Gelenkkupplung; **~ currency** elastische Währung; **~ drive shaft** Kardanwelle; **~ exchange rate** flexibler Wechselkurs; **~ exchange-rate system** System flexibler Wechselkurse; **~ fund** *(US)* Investmentfonds mit auswechselbarem Portefeuille; **~ law** nachgiebiges Recht; **~ parities** flexible Wechselkurse; **~ provisions** elastische Bestimmungen; **~ rate** schwankender Wechselkurs; **~ response** *(atomic strategy)* wohlabgewogener Gegenschlag; **~ schedule** bewegliches Arbeitszeitprogramm; **~ tariff** dehnbarer Zolltarif, flexibler Tarif; **~ trust** *(US)* Kapitalanlagegesellschaft mit wechselndem Portefeuille; **~ use** elastische Handhabung [einer Vorschrift]; **~ working arrangement** gleitende Arbeitszeit; **~ working-hours scheme** System der gleitenden Arbeitszeit.
flexographic printing Druck mit Gummiklischee.
flextime *(Br.)* gleitende Arbeitszeit.
flick[s] *(Br., sl.)* Kintopp, Kino, Film;
  ~ *(v.)* **s. o. on the raw** j. an seiner wunden Stelle treffen; **~ knife** Schnappmesser.
flicker flackernde Flamme, *(fig.)* aufflackern, Funke, *(sl.)* Film;
  weak ~ of hope schwacher Hoffnungsschimmer;
  ~ *(v.)* *(speedometer needle)* hin und her pendeln;
  ~ out flackernd verlöschen;
  to raise barely a ~ of interest kaum Aufsehen erregen.
flies *(theater)* Soffitten;
  no ~ on s. o. nichts an jem. auszusetzen.
flier Flieger, Flugzeug, *(bus)* Schnellbus, *(leaflet, US)* Flugblatt, *(train)* Expresszug, *(US sl.)* Spekulationskauf eines Außenseiters, gewagte Spekulation.
flight *(distance covered)* Flugentfernung, -strecke, *(escape)* Flucht, *(flying)* Flug, Fliegen, [Flug]reise, Einflug, *(military formation)* Kette, *(staircase)* Treppenflucht, *(take-off)* Abflug, Flug;
  in the first ~ in vorderster Front; **in the highest ~** an führender Stelle;
  advanced booking ~ im voraus gebuchter Flug; **borderline ~** an der Grenze der Rentabilität liegender Flug; **commercial ~** Linienflug; **connecting ~** Flugverbindung; **contact ~** Flug mit Bodensicht; **cut down ~s** aufgehobener Flug; **domestic transfer ~s** Anschlußflüge im Inland; **gratuitous ~** Freiflug; **intelligence ~** Spionageflug; **long-distance ~** Langstreckenflug; **night ~** Nachtflug; **nonstop ~** Flug ohne Zwischenlandung; **normal ~** Normalflug; **off-peak ~s** gering belegte Flugzeiten; **one-line ~** Linienflug; **regular (scheduled, US)** ~ fahrplanmäßiger Flug; **round-the-world ~** Flug um die Welt; **thrift ~** verbilligter Flug; **trial ~** Probeflug; **visual ~** Flug mit Bodensicht; **walk-on daily ~** kurz vor Reiseantritt gebuchter Flug;

~ **in a balloon** Ballonflug; ~ **of capital** Kapitalflucht; ~ **from cash** Vermeidung von Bargeschäften; ~ **from the currency** Flucht aus der Währung; ~ **of the dollar** Dollarabwanderung; ~ **of fancy (imagination)** Schwung der Phantasie; ~ **of stairs** Treppenflucht; ~ **from taxation** Steuerflucht; ~ **over a territory** Überfliegen eines Gebiets;

to be scheduled for its first ~ zum Probeflug vorgesehen sein; **to call a** ~ Flug aufrufen; **to embark on one's** ~ seinen Flug antreten; **to follow the** ~ **of an aircraft by radar** Flugzeug auf dem Radarschirm verfolgen; **to handle a** ~ Flugzeug abfertigen; **to have a smooth** ~ ruhigen Flug haben; **to plan the first commercial** ~ erstmaligen Einsatz von Verkehrsflugzeugen vorsehen; **to put the enemy to** ~ Feind in die Flucht schlagen; **to seek safety in** ~ sein Heil in der Flucht suchen; **to take a** ~ fliegen; **to take to** ~ fliehen, weglaufen, flüchten;

~ **additions** zusätzliche Leistungen bei einem Flug; ~ **artefact** Flugkörper, -gerät; ~ **attendant** Flugbegleiter; ~ **bag** Flugtasche; ~ **cancellation** Flugstornierung; ~ **capital** Fluchtgelder, -kapital; ~ **captain** Flugkapitän; ~ **characteristics** Flugeigenschaften; ~ **control** Flugleitung; ~ **control personnel** Fluglotsen, -sicherungspersonal; ~ **coupon** Flugabschnitt, -schein, Bordkarte; ~ **crew** Flugzeugbesatzung; ~ **cutdown** aufgehobener Flug; ~ **date** Abflugtermin; ~ **deck** *(aircraft carrier)* Landedeck; ~**-deliver** *(v.)* mit dem Flugzeug transportieren; ~ **engineer** Bordmechaniker, -monteur; ~ **experience** Flugerfahrung; ~ **forecast** Flugwettervorhersage; ~ **formation** Flugformation; ~ **frequency** Flugfrequenz; ~ **home** Rückflug; **to process** ~ **information** Fluginformationen weiterleiten; ~ **instructions** Fluganweisung; ~ **instructor** Fluglehrer; ~ **line** Flugroute; ~ **manual** Bordhandbuch; ~ **mechanic** Flugzeugmechaniker; ~ **network** Flugverbindungsnetz; ~ **number** Flugnummer; ~ **path** Flugweg, -route, Einflugschneise; ~ **performance** Flugleistung; ~ **personnel** fliegendes Personal; ~ **plan** Fahrplan; ~ **recorder** Flugschreiber; ~ **refuelling** Auftanken in der Luft; ~ **reservation** Flug[platz]reservierung; ~ **route** Flugstrecke, -route; ~ **seat number** reservierte Flugplatznummer; ~ **segment** Flugbetriebsbereich; ~ **station** Abflugplatz; ~ **strip** behelfsmäßige Lande- und Startbahn; ~ **surveyance** Flugüberwachung; ~ **test** Flugerprobung, -test; ~**-test** *(v.)* flugtechnisch erproben; ~ **time** Flugzeit; ~ **track** Flugroute, -strecke; ~ **visibility** Flugsicht.

flighthouse Radarschiff.

flimflam Mumpitz.

flimsy durchsichtiges Papier, Seiden-, Durchschlagpapier, *(Br.)* Durchschlag, Kopie, *(train order)* Zuganordnung;
~ *(a.)* fadenscheinig;
~ **argument** schwaches Argument; ~ **evidence** nicht überzeugender Beweis.

flinch *(v.)* zurückweichen;
never to ~ **from one's duty** sich niemals seinen Pflichten entziehen.

fling *(scornful remark)* Stichelei, *(try, coll.)* Versuch;
~ **in the publishing business** kurzer Ausflug ins Verlagsgeschäft;
~ *(v.)* sich austoben;
~ **away one's hono(u)r** seine Ehre in den Staub treten; ~ **away one's money** mit dem Geld nur so um sich werfen; ~ **back the enemy** Feind zurückwerfen; ~ **caution to the wind** Vorsicht in den Wind schlagen; ~ **dirt at s. o.** jds. guten Ruf angreifen; ~ **all one's energy into s. th.** seine ganze Energie an etw. setzen; ~ **o. s. on a friend** sich einem Freund anvertrauen; ~ **off a restraining influence** sich von einem Einfluß freimachen; ~ **off without saying goodbye** ohne Aufwiedersehen zu sagen davonstürzen; ~ **o. s. about like a madman** sich wie ein Verrückter aufspielen; ~ **open a door** Tür aufstoßen; ~ **out at s. o.** j. mit Beleidigungen attackieren; ~ **out of the room** aus dem Zimmer stürzen; ~ **o. s. into a project** sich mit allen Kräften einem Projekt widmen; ~ **troops into the fray** Truppen in die Bresche werfen; ~ **up a task** eine Arbeit hinschmeißen; ~ **one's money out of the window** Geld aus dem Fenster schmeißen; ~ **up one's job** seine Stellung aufgeben;
to have one's ~ sich austoben; **to have had its initial** ~ **with the customers** erste Erfahrungen mit der Kundschaft hinter sich haben; **to take a** ~ **at a new job** sich in einem neuen Beruf versuchen.

flint Feuerstein, *(skinflint)* Geizhals;
to set one's face like a ~ **against a plan** sich mit Händen und Füßen gegen ein Projekt wehren; **to skin a** ~ geizig sein; **to wring water from a** ~ Wunder vollbringen;
~ **paper** Schmirgel-, Sandpapier.

flip | flop Umlegemappe; ~ **switch** *(el.)* Kippschalter.

flirt *(v.)* **with** *(fig.)* liebäugeln.

flit *(Br.)* Wohnungswechsel, Umzug.

flivver *(sl.)* alter Kasten, Karre, Schlitten, *(plane)* billige Kiste.

float *(airplane)* Schwimmer, Schwimmgestell, *(banking)* schwebende Überweisungen und Inkassi, *(currency)* freigegebener Wechselkurs, *(land law, US)* Landnahmeschein, *(life preserver)* Rettungsgürtel, *(mar.)* Floß, schwimmende Landebrücke, *(outstanding checks, coll.)* im Einzug befindliche Schecks, *(theater)* Rampenlicht, *(waggon)* Festwagen;
dirty ~ *(currency)* schmutziges Floaten; **downward** ~ ständiger Wertverlust; **independent** ~ unabhängige Pufferzeit;
~ *(v.)* schwimmen, *(circulate)* umlaufen, im Umlauf sein, *(drift along)* schweben, treiben, *(v./tr.)* *(flood)* unter Wasser setzen, überfluten, überschwemmen, *(give currency to)* in Umlauf bringen (setzen), *(mar.)* flottmachen, *(put on the market)* auf den Markt bringen, *(politics)* nicht gebunden sein, sich nicht festlegen;
not to ~ *(stock)* sich nicht verkaufen;
~ **about** *(rumo(u)r)* umgehen; ~ **around** *(US)* sich ohne festen Wohnsitz herumtreiben; ~ **a bond issue** Schuldverschreibungen ausgeben; ~ **a new business company** neue Gesellschaft gründen; ~ **the exchange rate** Wechselkurs freigeben; ~ **a loan** Anleihe lancieren (auflegen); ~ **s. o. into power** j. an die Macht bringen; ~ **a rumo(u)r** Gerücht lancieren; ~ **a wreck** Wrack flottmachen;
~ **bridge** Floßbrücke; ~ **chamber** Flutkammer; ~ **ledger** *(US)* Inkassowechselkonto; ~ **plane** Wasser-, Schwimmflugzeug.

floatable schwimmfähig, flößbar.

floatages *(Br.)* Strandgut.

floater *(casual, US)* Gelegenheitsarbeiter, *(of company)* Gründer, *(exhibition)* Ausstellungswagen, *(insurance)* Pauschalversicherung, *(mine adrift)* treibende Mine, *(politics)* parteiloser (schwankender) Wähler, *(stock exchange, Br.)* nicht notiertes (erstklassiges) Inhaberpapier, *(corrupt voter, US)* Wahlschwindler;
commercial ~ *(US)* Reisegepäckversicherung; **drummer** ~ *(US)* Versicherung für die Ausstattung eines Handlungsreisenden; **office** ~ *(US)* Versicherung der Büroeinrichtung; **personal** ~ *(Br.)* Reisegepäckversicherung für Privatreisende;
~ **policy** Pauschalversicherung.

floating Finanzierung, Finanzieren, *(exchange rate)* Wechselkursfreigabe, Freigabe der Wechselkurse, Floaten, Politik der schwankenden Wechselkurse;
bloc ~ Blockfloaten; **clean** ~ sauberes Floaten; **dirty** ~ schmutziges Floaten;
~ **of bonds** Emission (Ausgabe) von Obligationen; ~ **of a company** Gesellschaftsgründung; ~ **of a loan** Anleihebegebung;
~ *(v.)* schwimmend, treibend, *(circulating)* umlaufend, zirkulierend, im Umlauf befindlich, flottant, *(debt)* schwebend, unfundiert;
~ **accent** *(Br.)* schwankender Akzent; ~ **anchor** Treibanker; ~ **assets** Umlaufkapital, Betriebsmittel; ~ **battery** *(el.)* Pufferbatterie; ~ **block** gemeinsamer Wechselkursverbund, Währungsschlange; ~ **bridge** Tonnenbrücke, Schiffsbrücke; ~ **capital** Umlauf-, Betriebskapital, -vermögen, -mittel; ~ **cargo** unterwegs befindliche (schwimmende) Fracht; ~ **charge** *(Br.)* schwebende Schuld, Globalverpfändung, offene Gesamtbelastung, [etwa] besitzloses Pfandrecht mit wechselndem Objekt; ~ **crane** Ponton-, Schwimmkran; ~ **currencies** freigegebene Wechselkurse; ~ **debt** schwebende (unfundierte) Schuld, kurzfristige Staatsschuld; ~ **dock** Schwimmdock; ~ **equipment** Schiffspark; ~ **exchange rates** flexible (freigegebene) Wechselkurse, frei veränderliche Devisenkurse; ~ **hospital** Hospitalschiff; ~ **hotel** schwimmendes Hotel; ~ **ice** Treibeis; ~ **inspector** Kontrollbeamter; ~ **island** schwimmende Insel; ~ **liability** aufschiebend bedingte Verbindlichkeit; ~ **lien** Höchstbetragshypothek; ~ **light** Leuchtboje; ~ **mine** Treibmine; ~ **mortgage** Generalverpfändung; ~ **point** *(data processing)* Gleitkomma; ~ **policy** *(Br.)* Pauschal-, Generalpolice, *(fire insurance)* gleitende Neuwertversicherung; ~ **population** nicht seßhafter Bevölkerungsteil; ~ **pound** freigegebener Pfundkurs; ~ **rates of exchange** freie (frei gegebene) Wechselkurse, Wechselkursfreigabe, *(ocean freight)* Seefrachtsätze; ~ **rate issue in the local authority negotiable bond market** Ausgabe von mit variablen Zinssätzen ausgestatteten Kommunalanleihen; ~ **rumo(u)r** umlaufendes Gerücht; ~ **security** auswechselbare Kreditsicherheit; ~ **supply** tägliches (laufendes) Angebot; ~ **timbers of a wreck** treibende Wrackteile; ~ **trade** Seefrachthandel; ~ **value unit of account** wechselkursfreie Verrechnungseinheit; ~ **vote** Wechselwähler; ~ **voter** nicht parteigebundener Wähler; ~ **warehouse** schwimmendes Magazin; ~ **workshop** Reparaturschiff.

floatplane Wasser-, Schwimmflugzeug.

flock (aggregation) Schar, Haufen, Herde;
~s and herds Schafe und Rinder;
~ (v.) in Scharen herbeiströmen;
~ to the polls zur Wahl gehen; ~ together zusammenströmen, sich zusammenrotten;
to come in ~s in hellen Scharen kommen (herbeiströmen).
~ master Schafszüchter; ~ paper Samttapete.

flockman Schäfer.

flode-mark Flußlinie, Hochwasserstandszeichen.

flog (v.) peitschen;
~ o. s. (fig.) sich selbst zwingen; ~ along vorwärts treiben; ~ a competitor Konkurrenten ausstechen; ~ a dead horse sich um eine aussichtslose Sache kümmern, offene Türen einrennen, leeres Stroh dreschen; ~ on the market auf dem Markt verkloppen; ~ off verscherbeln.

flogging Prügelstrafe.

flong Matrizenkarton, Maternmappe.

flood strömende Wassermenge, Strömung, Hochwasser, Überschwemmung, (fig.) Flut, Fülle, Schwall;
the ~ Sintflut;
ebb and ~ Ebbe und Flut;
~ of abuse Flut von Beschimpfungen; ~ of callers Fülle von Besuchern; ~ of demands Konsumwelle; ~ of dollars Dollarstrom, -schwemme; ~ of donations Spendenstrom; ~ of law suits Prozeßlawine; ~ of letters Fülle von Briefen; ~ of light Flut von Licht; ~ of mail from the public zahlreiche Zuschriften aus der Öffentlichkeit; ~s of rain Regenfluten; ~ of words Wortschwall;
~ (v.) überschwemmen, -fluten;
~ the carburettor Vergaser ersaufen lassen; ~ with letters mit Briefen überschütten; ~ the market Markt überfluten (überschwemmen); ~ out property Grundvermögen durch Hochwasser vernichten; ~ a region Gebiet überfluten;
to be at the ~ steigen; to be swept away by the ~ vom Hochwasser fortgerissen werden; to cause ~s in the low-lying parts of the town Überschwemmungen in den niedriggelegenen Stadtteilen hervorrufen;
~ control Hochwasserkontrolle; ~ damage Überschwemmungsschaden; ~ disaster Hochwasserkatastrophe; ~ insurance Hochwasserversicherung; ~ plain Überschwemmungsgebiet; ~ prevention Hochwasserschutz, Vorkehrungen gegen Überschwemmungen; ~ risk Hochwasserrisiko; ~ tide Flut[zeit], Springflut; ~ waters Überschwemmung.

floodgate Schleusentor;
to open the ~s of one's passion Schleusen seiner Leidenschaft öffnen.

flooding Überschwemmung.

floodlight Flut-, Scheinwerferlicht;
~ (v.) mit Flutlicht anstrahlen;
~ projector Scheinwerfer, An-, Lichtstrahler.

floodlighting Flutlichtbeleuchtung, Flutlichtanlage.

floodlit von Scheinwerfern angestrahlt.

floodmark Hochwasserstandsmarke.

floodtide (fig.) Hochflut.

floor Fußboden, Diele, (minimum of prices, US) Mindestpreishöhe, Minimum, (parliament) Sitzungssaal, Plenum, (right to speak, US) Rederecht, Wort, (of a seam) Sohle, Liegendes, (sea) Grund, Boden, (stock exchange) Börsensaal, Parkett, (storey) Stockwerk, Geschoß, (television studio) Fernsehstudio;
on the ~ in der Fabrikhalle, am Arbeitsplatz;
asphalt ~ Asphaltboden; bare ~ nackter Fußboden; cement ~ Zementboden; dead ~ Blindboden; first ~ (Br.) erstes Stockwerk, (US) Hochparterre; ground ~ Erdgeschoß; house ~ Plenarsaal, Plenum; lower ~ Untergeschoß; main ~ Hauptverkaufsraum; price ~ Preisminimum; second ~ zweites Stockwerk; tile[d] ~ Plattenfußboden; top ~ oberstes Stockwerk; upper ~ Obergeschoß; wage ~ (US) Lohnminimum;
~ of a bridge Brückenbelag, -fahrbahn; ~ of the house Plenarsaal;
~ (v.) (car driving, sl.) mit Höchstgeschwindigkeit fahren;
~ an opponent Gegner erledigen; ~ a paper (fam., Br.) alle Examensfragen beantworten, Examen glänzend bestehen;
to ask for the ~ (US) ums Wort bitten; to be on the ~ (US) das Wort haben, (film) produziert werden; to carry the ~ (US) Parlament überzeugen; to cross the ~ of the House (Br.) zur Oppositionspartei übergehen; to demand the ~ (US) ums Wort bitten; to give the ~ to s. o. (US) das Wort an j. abgeben, jem. das Wort erteilen; to go on the ~ (US) das Wort ergreifen; to have the ~ (US) das Wort haben (erhalten); to hog the ~ (US sl.)

Redezeit mißbrauchen; to hold the ~ of the House (US) Versammlung durch seine Rede fesseln; to live on the first ~ im ersten Stock (auf der ersten Etage) wohnen; to make nominations from the ~ (US) Kandidaten im Plenum vorschlagen; to mop the ~ with s. o. (coll.) jem. eine gehörige Tracht Prügel verpassen; to occupy the whole of the first ~ (Br.) ganzes erstes Stockwerk bewohnen, (US) im Hochparterre wohnen; to take the ~ (US) das Wort ergreifen;
~ amendment (US) Änderungen durch das Plenum; ~ area Gebäudefläche; ~ broker (US) selbständiger Börsenmakler, Berufshandel; ~ check Anwesenheitskontrolle; ~ crossing (Br.) Übergang zur Oppositionspartei; ~ debate (US) Aussprache; ~ lamp Stehlampe; ~ leader (US) Einpeitscher, Parteiführer, Fraktionsführer; ~ manager (parl.) Berichterstatter, (warehouse, US) Abteilungsleiter; ~ member Börsenmitglied; ~ partner (US) Teilhaber einer Maklerfirma; ~ plan Stockwerks-, Raumverteilungsplan; ~ plan service Autoabzahlungsgeschäft; ~ planning Autofinanzierung für Händler; ~ price Mindestpreis; ~ show Kabarettvorstellung; ~ space Grund-, Bodenfläche, (exhibition) Ausstellungsfläche, (industry) Gewerbefläche; ~ space required Flächenbedarf; ~ space policy (Br.) Gewerbeflächensteuerung; ~ trader (US) auf eigene Rechnung spekulierendes Börsenmitglied, zugelassener Börsenhändler; ~ vote Plenarabstimmung, Abstimmung im Plenum; ~ weight capacity Tragfähigkeit eines Stockwerks.

floorcloth Fußbodenbelag.

floored, to be durchfallen.

floorer (fig.) unangenehme Nachricht.

flooring Fußbodenbelag.

floorwalker (US) Ladenaufsicht, Empfangschef.

flop (failure, sl.) wirtschaftlicher Mißerfolg, Fiasko, (person, sl.) Versager, Niete, (party politics, US) Überlaufen, Umschwenken, -fall, Parteiwechsel, (play) durchgefallenes Stück;
~ (v.) überlaufen, umschwenken, (play, sl.) durchfallen, (person) scheitern, Versager sein;
~ on the mat of the taxpayers den Steuerzahlern ins Haus flattern;
~ over (US) Partei wechseln; ~ down a heavy bag schweren Sack herunterplumpsen lassen;
to be a ~ mit einem Fiasko enden; to go ~ (play) Mißerfolg sein, durchfallen.

flophouse (US sl.) Asyl für Obdachlose, Penne.

flopped (play) durchgefallen.

flopper (US) Überläufer.

florid style überladener Stil.

florin (Br.) Zweishillingsstück, (Netherlands) Gulden.

flossy (US sl.) aufgedonnert, pompös.

flotage Strandgut.

flotation Schwimmen, Treiben, (of bills) Inumlaufsetzen, Inumlaufbringen, Begebung, (of capital) Kapitalbewegung, (of company) Gründung, (of a loan) Begebung, Lancieren;
new capital ~s Neuemissionen;
~ costs of a loan Anleihebegebungskosten;
~ of a company Gesellschaftsgründung.

flotilla Flottille;
~ leader Flottillenführer.

flotsam Treib-, treibendes Wrackgut, seetriftiges Gut;
~ and jetsam Strandgut.

flounce (v.) out of a party Partei überstürzt verlassen.

flounder (v.) nicht weiter wissen;
~ through a speech sich in einer Rede verhaspeln; ~ through a translation sich mit einer Übersetzung abquälen.

flourish Floskel, Schnörkel, schwülstige Redewendung;
~ of welcome Trompetenstoß zur Begrüßung;
~ (v.) florieren, blühen, gedeihen, (be flowery) Floskeln (Schnörkel) gebrauchen, schwülstig sprechen, (writer) auf der Höhe des Ruhmes sein;
~ goods Ware im Schaufenster auslegen; ~ a program(me) Programm ausschmücken;
to publish s. th. with a great ~ of trumpets etw. mit einem gewaltigen Trompetenstoß veröffentlichen.

flourishing trade schwunghafter Handel.

flow Strömung, (diction) Schwall, Erguß, Fluß, (flood) Überschwemmung, (output) Produktionsmenge, Leistung, (production) Arbeitsablauf, (travel of material) Produktionsmenge;
traffic ~ Verkehrsstrom;
~ of authority Durchsetzung der Autorität; ~ of capital Kapitalwanderung, -bewegung; ~ of capital interest Kapitalgüterstrom; ~ of cash Barmittelzufluß; ~ of commerce Handelsverkehr; ~ of commodities Warenverkehr; ~ of costs Kostenfluß;

~ **of credit** Kreditstrom; ~ **of dollars** Dollarfluß, -strom; ~ **of emigration** Flüchtlingsstrom; ~ **of funds** Mittelzufluß; ~ **of foreign funds** Devisenabfluß; ~ **of goods** Warenfluß; **free** ~ **of goods** freier Güterverkehr; ~ **of investment** Investitionsstrom; ~ **of merchandise** Warenfluß; ~ **of money** Geldumlauf; ~ **of incoming orders** Auftragszugang; ~ **of paper** Papierstrom; **even** ~ **of production** gleichmäßiger Produktionsablauf; ~ **of savings** Spargelderstrom; ~ **of settlers** Siedlerstrom; ~ **of the tide** Einsetzen der Flut; ~ **of tourists** Touristenstrom; ~ **of traffic** Verkehrsstrom; ~ **of words** Redefluß; ~ **of work** Arbeitsablauf; ~ **of world trade** Welthandelsströme;
~ **(v.)** [zu]fließen, strömen, *(abound)* überquellen, -schäumen, *(conversation)* dahinfließen, *(issue)* herrühren;
~ **back** *(money)* zurückströmen; ~ **over the banks** *(river)* aus dem Ufer treten; ~ **by heads** *(oil well)* stoßweise fließen; ~ **in** *(orders)* eingehen, hereinströmen; ~ **from industry and economy** *(wealth)* sich auf Fleiß und Sparsamkeit gründen; ~ **the land in summer** Land im Sommer überfluten; ~ **out** abfließen; ~ **into the sea** sich ins Meer ergießen;
to be on the ~ *(tide)* einsetzen; **to ensure a continuing** ~ **of tax** laufende Steuereingänge sicherstellen; **to have a ready** ~ **of language** wie ein Maschinengewehr reden;
~ **of funds accounts** Finanzstromrechnung; ~ **of funds approach** Verwendungsrechnung des Volkseinkommens; ~ **chart** Ablauf-, Flußdiagramm, Schaubild, *(data processing)* Datenflußplan; ~ **diagram** Arbeitsdurchlaufdiagramm; ~ **heater** Durchlauferhitzer; ~ **item** Flußgröße; ~ **mass** Fördermenge; ~ **process** Fließarbeit; ~ **process chart** Arbeitsablaufbogen; ~ **[-line] production** Fließbandproduktion; ~ **sheet** Verarbeitungsdiagramm; ~ **of funds statement** Ausweis über die Verwendung des Grundkapitals; ~ **system** Fließbandfertigung, Bandmontage; ~**-of-funds system** gesamtwirtschaftliche Finanzierungsrechnung; ~ **volume** Durchflußmenge.
flower Blume, *(fig.)* Blütezeit, *(choicest part)* das Beste, Auslese, *(ornament)* Ornament, Verzierung, *(print.)* Vignette;
in ~ in Blüte; **in the** ~ **of one's strength** im besten Mannesalter; **cut** ~ Schnittblume;
~ **of the army** Elite der Armee; ~ **of life** Blüte des Lebens; ~ **of the nation's manhood** Blüte der Nation; ~**s of speech** Redefloskeln;
~ **(v.)** blühen, *(fig.)* in höchster Blüte stehen;
to be in the ~ **of one's age** im besten Alter sein;
~ **arrangement** Blumenarrangement; ~ **bed** Blumenbeet; ~ **girl** *(Br.)* Blumenverkäuferin; ~ **market** Blumenmarkt; ♀ **People** Blumenkinder; ~ **shop** Blumenladen; ~ **show** Blumenausstellung;
no ~**s [by request]** Blumenspenden verboten.
flowery language blumenreiche Sprache;
to speak in a ~ Phrasendrescher sein.
flowing *(fig.)* flüssig, geläufig, schwungvoll, *(tide)* steigend.
flu | bug *(fam.)* Grippevirus; ~ **epidemic** Grippeepidemie.
fluctuate *(v.)* *(prices)* sich bewegen, schwanken, fluktuieren, steigen und fallen, *(stock exchange)* schwanken, in schwankender Haltung verkehren.
fluctuating unbeständig, schwankend, variabel;
~ **market** schwankender (unstabiler) Markt, Börsen-, Marktschwankungen; ~ **market value** veränderlicher Markt-, Kurswert; ~ **premium** veränderliches Agio; ~ **prices** schwankende Preise; ~ **quotations** schwankende Kursnotierungen; ~ **rates** schwankende Kurse.
fluctuation Schwanken, Schwankung, Fluktuieren, Fluktuation;
cyclical ~**s** Konjunkturschwankungen; **exchange** ~**s** Börsen-, Kursschwankungen; **market** ~**s** konjunkturelle Schwankungen; **price** ~**s** Preisschwankungen, -fluktuationen, Fluktuieren der Preise, Kursschwankungen; **seasonal** ~**s** jahreszeitlich bedingte Schwankungen, Saisonschwankungen;
~ **on bank accounts** Bewegung auf Bankkonten, Kontenumsätze; **cyclical** ~**s in business** Konjunkturschwankungen der Wirtschaft; ~**s of circulation** Auflageschwankungen; ~ **of costs** Kostenbewegung; ~**s of currency** Währungsschwankungen; ~ **of current** Stromschwankung; ~**s in demand** Nachfrageschwankungen; ~**s of the discount rate** Diskontbewegungen; ~ **in the exchange rate** Valuta-, Kursschwankungen; ~**s in the stock market [prices]** Börsen-, Aktienkursschwankungen, Schwankungen am Effektenmarkt; ~ **of the market** Kursschwankungen; ~**s in the money market** Geldmarktschwankungen; ~**s of prices** Kurs-, Preisbewegungen; ~**s of temperature** Temperaturschwankungen; ~**s in the value of money** Geldwertschwankungen;
to be subject to price ~**s** Kursschwankungen unterworfen sein; ~ **margin** Schwankungsbreite.

flue Rauchfang, Esse, Kamin.
fluency Geläufigkeit, Flüssigkeit.
fluent flüssig, geläufig, fließend;
to speak ~ **French** fließend Französisch sprechen;
~ **speaker** gewandter Redner.
fluff *(radio)* Versprecher, Sprechfehler;
~ **(v.)** *(theatre, Br., sl.)* Rolle mangelhaft beherrschen;
~ **one's lines** *(Br., sl.)* Rede abstottern.
fluid Flüssigkeit;
~ **(a.)** flüssig, leicht veränderlich, *(fig.)* geläufig;
~ **assets** *(US)* Umlaufvermögen; ~ **capital** *(US)* Umlaufkapital; ~ **coupling** hydraulische Kupplung; ~ **drive** Flüssigkeitskupplung, -getriebe; ~ **level** Flüssigkeitspegel; ~ **opinions** schwankende Aussichten; ~ **plans** leicht veränderliche Pläne; ~ **savings** noch nicht wieder angelegte Ersparnisse; ~ **state** *(industry)* Umwandlungsprozeß.
fluke *(fig.)* Glücksfall, Dusel.
fluky *(sl.)* unverdient.
flume Industriekanal.
flunk *(US sl.)* Drückeberger, Rückzieher, Versager;
~ **(v.) [out]** durchfallen, *(back out, US sl.)* Rückzieher machen.
flunkey *(US, servant)* Lakai, livrierter Diener, *(US, cringing person)* Speichellecker, *(stock exchange)* unerfahrener Börsenspekulant.
flunkeydom *(US)* Dienerschaft.
flunkeyism *(US)* Speichelleckerei, Kriecherei.
fluorescent schillernd;
~ **ink printing** Leuchtdruck; ~ **lamp** Leuchtstofflampe; ~ **light** Neonlicht; ~ **light strip** Neonröhre; ~ **screen** Leuchtschirm; ~ **tube** Leuchtstoffröhre.
flurry Windstoß, leichte Brise, *(flutter)* Aufregung, Unruhe, *(stock exchange)* plötzliche kurze Belebung, kurzer Börsenauftrieb;
in a ~ aufgeregt, nervös.
flush gewaltiger Wasserzufluß, *(feeling)* Aufwallung, Sturm, *(WC)* Spülung;
in the first ~ **of youth** in der Blüte der Jugend; **in the first** ~ **of victory** in der ersten Siegesbegeisterung;
~ **of orders** Auftragsstrom-, Flut von Aufträgen;
~ **(a.)** reichlich versehen, reich, *(plane)* eben, *(print.)* auf gleicher Höhe, ohne Einzug, bündig;
~ **left** linksbündig; ~ **right** rechtsbündig;
~ **of money** mit Geld wohl versehen;
~ **(v.) out the beneficial holders of voting shares** wahre Inhaber von Stimmrechtsaktien ausfindig machen; ~ **out a string of borrowers** größere Schar von Kreditnehmern aufscheuchen; **to be in the full** ~ **of health** von strotzender Gesundheit sein; **to be** ~ **of money** gut bei Kasse sein, Überfluß an Geld haben, äußerst flüssig sein; **to be pretty** ~ **with funds** recht gut bei Kasse sein; **to be very** ~ **with one's money** sorglos mit seinem Geld umgehen;
~ **blow** Volltreffer; ~ **deck** Glattdeck; ~ **paragraph** Absatz ohne Einzug; ~ **switch** *(el.)* Unterputzschalter; ~ **times** üppige Zeiten.
flushed | with sucess erfolgstrunken;
to be ~ **with** freudetrunken sein.
flusher Kanal-, Straßenreiniger.
flushing Wasserspülung.
fluster *(v.)* nervös machen.
flutter *(agitation)* Aufregung, Unruhe, *(motion picture)* Flattern, Unstetigkeit, *(sl.)* Spekulationsobjekt;
tape ~ unsteter Durchlauf eines Tonbands; **wing** ~ Vibrieren des Flugzeugs;
first ~ **of an upturn** erster Konjunkturanlauf;
~ **(v.) (tape)** unstet durchlaufen, *(wing)* vibrieren;
to be in a ~ **of excitement** völlig aus dem Häuschen sein; **to bring a** ~ **to s. one's heart** jds. Herz höher schlagen lassen; **to go to the races and have a** ~ auf dem Rennplatz einige Wetten legen; **to have a little** ~ ein paar Spielchen machen.
flux of money Geldumlauf.
fly Flieger, Flug, *(door)* Windfang, *(print.)* [Bogen]ausleger;
on the ~ *(fig.)* in ständiger Bewegung;
~**s** *(theat.)* Soffitten;
~ **in amber** seltenes Stück, Rarität; ~ **in the ointment** Haar in der Suppe;
~ **(v.) (plane)** fliegen, steuern, *(fugitive)* fliehen, *(time)* verfliegen, entrinnen, *(transport)* im Flugzeug befördern;
~ **about** *(rumo(u)r)* sich verbreiten; ~ **abroad** schnell bekannt werden; ~ **in an airplane** Flugzeug steuern, fliegen; ~ **to the arms** zu den Waffen eilen; ~ **around** *(US)* unruhig herumlaufen; ~ **the Atlantic** über den Atlantik fliegen; ~ **to bits** in

tausend Stücke zerspringen; ~ **blind** blindfliegen; ~ **before you buy** Produktionsaufträge erst nach positiv verlaufenen Modellversuchen erteilen; ~ **commercially** im Liniendienst fliegen; ~ **the country** aus dem Lande fliehen; ~ **a course** Kurs fliegen; ~ **a flag** unter einer Flagge fahren; ~ **free** umsonst fliegen; ~ **high** *(fig.)* hoch hinaus wollen; ~ **in** einfliegen; ~ **in troops** Truppen einfliegen; ~ **into a country** in ein Gebiet einfliegen; ~ **a kite** auf Gefälligkeitswechsel borgen, *(fig.)* Versuchsballon steigen lassen; ~ **nonstop** Direktflug durchführen; ~ **off the handle** *(US sl.)* aus dem Häuschen geraten; ~ **out** per Luftfracht transportieren; ~ **out at s. o.** ausfallend gegen j. werden; ~ **into a rage** in Wut geraten; ~ **by the seat of one's pants** *(sl.)* blindfliegen, *(fig.)* instinktiv handeln; ~ **over a territory** Gebiet überfliegen; ~ **at s. one's throat** j. plötzlich angreifen; ~ **the track** aus dem Gleis springen;
to make the feathers ~ hauen, daß die Fetzen fliegen; **to make the money ~** Geld mit vollen Händen ausgeben;
~-**by-night** Nachtvogel; ~-**by-night corporation** *(US)* Unternehmen von zweifelhaftem Wert; ~ **loft** *(theat.)* Soffitten; ~-**over** Stahlhochstraße, Straßenüberführung, *(aircraft)* Formationsflug; ~ **past** Formationsflug, Luftparade; ~ **posting** wilder Anschlag; ~ **power** *(stock certificate)* Blankoindossament; ~ **press** Schnellpresse; ~ **sheet** Flugblatt, *(directions for use)* Gebrauchsanweisung, Anleitung; ~ **under** [Straßen]unterführung.

flyable weather Flugwetter.
flyaway leichtfertiger Mensch.
flyboat schnelles Schiff.
flyer Flieger, *(US)* Spezialversandkatalog, *(fig.)* Senkrechtstarter.
flying Fliegen, Flug, *(aviation)* Fliegerei, Flugwesen;
blind ~ Blindflug; **contact** ~ Flug mit Bodensicht; **4 hours** ~ vier Flugstunden; **trick** ~ Kunstflug; **visual** ~ Flug mit Bodensicht;
~ **in** Einflug;
to keep the flag ~ Fahne hochhalten;
~ *(a.)* fliegend, flugtechnisch;
~ **accident** Flugunfall; ~ **activities** Fliegertätigkeit; ~ **allowance** Fliegerzulage; ~ **boat** Flugboot; ~ **bomb** Vergeltungswaffe; ~ **boom** Auftankvorrichtung in der Luft; ~ **bridge** Schiffsbrücke; ~ **center** Flugzentrum; ~ **circus** gemeinsam operierendes Geschwader; ~ **club** Fliegerklub; **to come off with** ~ **colo(u)rs** glänzenden Sieg erringen; ~ **column** *(mil.)* schnelle Kolonne; ~ **competition** Flugwettbewerb; ~ **condition** Flugzustand; ~ **conditions** Flugbedingungen; ~ **deck** Flugdeck; ~ **demonstration** Demonstrationsflug, Flugvorführung; ~ **equipment** Fliegerausrüstung; ~ **examination** Flugprüfung; ~ **exhibition** Wanderausstellung; ~ **experience** Flugerfahrung, -praxis; ~ **feat** fliegerische Leistung; ~ **field** kleiner Flugplatz, Flugfeld; ~ **ground** Fluggelände; ~ **height** Flughöhe; ~ **hour** Flugstunde; ~ **instruction** Flugunterricht; ~ **instructor** Fluglehrer; ~ **instruments** Flugüberwachungsinstrumente; ~ **laboratory** fliegendes Laboratorium; ~ **lane** Einflugschneise; ~ **machine** Flugapparat; ~ **man** Flieger; ~ **meeting** Flugwoche; ~ **model** Flugmodell; ~ **object** Flugkörper; ~ **officer** *(Br.)* Oberleutnant; ~-**off deck** Abflugdeck; ~ **personnel** fliegendes Personal, Flugpersonal; ~ **qualities** Flugeigenschaften; ~ **range** Aktionsradius, -bereich; ~ **risk** Flugrisiko; ~ **safe-deposit box** Flugzeugbehälter; ~ **safe-deposit box system** Flugzeugbehälterversand; ~ **safety** Flugsicherheit; ~ **saucer** fliegende Untertasse; ~ **schedule** *(US)* Flugplan; ~ **school** Fliegerschule; **contract** ~ **service** private Flugverkehrseinrichtungen; ~ **speed [under load]** Fluggeschwindigkeit [mit Belastung]; ~ **squad** Polizeistreife, Überfallkommando, *(Br.)* Sondereinsatzgruppe; ~ **squadron** fliegende Arbeitskolonne; ~ **start** fliegender Start; ~ **suit** Fliegeranzug; ~ **surveillance** Flugüberwachung; ~ **time** Flugzeit; ~ **training** Fliegerausbildung; ~ **trip** Flugreise; **to take a** ~ **trip** Flugreise machen; ~ **unit** fliegender Verband, Flugverband; **to pay a** ~ **visit** Stippvisite machen; ~ **weather** Flugwetter; ~ **weight** Fluggewicht; ~ **wing** Nurflügelflugzeug.
flyleaf *(bookbinding)* Vorsatz-, Deckblatt, Allonge.
f. o. b. frei an Bord.
foam|**extinguisher** Schaumfeuerlöscher; ~ **rubber** Schaumgummi.
fob *(v.)*|**s. o. off** j. hinhalten; ~ **s. o. off with a promise** j. mit einem Versprechen abspeisen; ~ **s. th. off on s. o.** jem. etw. andrehen.
focal|**distance** Brennweite; ~ **point** Brennpunkt; ~ **point of events** Brennpunkt der Ereignisse; ~ **plane shutter** *(photo)* Schlitzverschluß.
focus *(camera)* Einstellung, *(fig.)* Brenn-, Mittelpunkt;
in ~ scharf eingestellt; **out of** ~ unscharf;

~ **of attention** Brennpunkt des Interesses, Hauptanziehungspunkt; ~ **of conflict** Konfliktherd; ~ **of power** Machtzentrum; ~ **of unrest** Unruheherd;
~ *(v.)* **the camera** Entfernung einstellen; ~ **one's efforts on a problem** seine Bemühungen auf ein Problem konzentrieren; ~ **on** sich konzentrieren; ~ **on (for) infinity** *(photo)* auf unendlich einstellen; ~ **opera glasses to suit one's sight** Opernglas auf seine Sichtweite einstellen; ~ **a searchlight on an object** Suchscheinwerfer auf einen Gegenstand richten;
to come into ~ sich klar abzeichnen.
focusing|**camera** Mattscheibenkamera; ~ **interview** gezieltes Interview; ~ **magnifier** Einstellupe; ~ **mechanism** Scharfeinstellungsvorrichtung; ~ **scale** Entfernungsskala; ~ **screen** Mattscheibe.
fodder Futter;
cannon-~ Kanonenfutter;
to gather ~ sich Futter suchen.
foe Feind, Gegner;
~ **to progress** Fortschrittsgegner.
foetus Leibesfrucht.
fog Nebel, *(fig.)* Verwirrung, Unsicherheit, *(photo)* Schleier;
in a ~ *(fig.)* verwirrt;
drizzling ~ nieselnder Nebel; **go** ~ Nebelauflöser; **inland** ~ Landnebel; **thick** ~ dichter Nebel; **wet** ~ nässender Nebel;
~ *(v.)* in Nebel hüllen, einnebeln, *(v/i)* neblig werden, *(railway)* Nebelsignale auflegen;
~ **alarm** Nebelwarnung; ~ **bank** Nebelbank; ~ **bell** Nebelglocke; ~ **dispersal** Nebelauflösung; ~ **droplet (particle)** Nebeltröpfchen; ~ **lamp** Nebellampe; ~ **lights** Nebellampen, -scheinwerfer; ~ **signal (whistle)** Nebelsignal, -warnung.
foggy neblig, trüb, düster, *(fig.)* unklar, verworren, wirr, nebelhaft, *(photo)* verschleiert;
~ **idea** vage Idee; ~ **weather** nebliges Wetter, Nebelwetter.
foghorn Nebelhorn.
fogy Erzkonservativer, alter Knopp.
fogyish erzkonservativ.
foible *(fig.)* Schwäche, schwache Stelle.
foil Folie, Unterlage, *(hunting, Br.)* Fährte, Spur;
~ *(v.)* vereiteln, verhindern;
~ **s. one's plans** jds. Pläne vereiteln;
to serve as a ~ **for s. one's cleverness** als Beweis für jds. Klugheit dienen;
~ **paper** Folienpapier; ~ **printing** Foliendruck.
foist|*(v.)* anhängen, andrehen;
~ **o. s. upon s. o.** sich jem. aufdrängen; ~ **a book on an author** einem Autor ein Buch zuschreiben; ~ **a bad coin on s. o.** jem. ein falsches Geldstück andrehen; ~ **a spurious document on s. o.** jem. eine falsche Urkunde aufschwatzen; ~ **one's wares upon the public** seine schlechte Ware unter die Leute bringen.
fold Falz;
~ *(v.)* *(Br.)* zusammenbrechen, fallen, *(v/i)* sich zusammenfalten lassen, *(go bankrupt)* fallieren, bankrott werden, *(envelop)* einwickeln-, einschlagen, falzen, *(production)* einstellen;
~ **down a corner of a page** Eselohr in eine Seite machen; ~ **a letter** Brief zusammenfalten; ~ **s. th. in paper** etw. in Papier einschlagen (einwickeln); ~ **up** Geschäft aufgeben, aus einem Geschäft aussteigen; ~ **up a newspaper** Zeitung zusammenlegen;
to bring back the stray sheep into the social ~ verlorenes Schaf in den Schoß der Familie zurückführen; **to return to the** ~ *(party politics)* in den Schoß der Partei zurückkehren;
~-**in** *(advertising)* Anzeige mit eingefalteten Blättern.
folded printed sheet ausgedruckter Druckbogen.
folder *(cover for files)* Aktendeckel, Hefter, Mappe, *(folded circular)* Broschüre, Faltprospekt, -blatt;
file ~ Schnellhefter;
~ **of documents** Urkundenmappe.
folding|**bed** Klappbett; ~ **boat** Faltboot; ~ **box** Faltschachtel; ~ **camera** Klappkamera; ~ **chair** Klappstuhl; ~ **cot** Klappbett; ~ **doors** Flügeltür; ~ **machine** Falzmaschine; ~ **money** *(US coll.)* Papiergeld; ~ **postal card** Briefkarte; ~ **roof** *(car)* zusammenklappbares Verdeck; ~ **stool** Klappstuhl; ~ **table** Klapptisch.
foliate *(v.)* foliieren, paginieren, Seiten numerieren.
foliation Paginierung *(number of pages)* Blattzahl.
folio Folioblatt, -format, *(case for loose papers)* Umschlag, Mappe, *(ledger)* Kontobuchseite, *(number of words taken as unit)* Einheitswortzahl, *(page number)* Seitenzahl, -nummerierung, Paginierung, Kolumnenziffer, *(sheet of paper)* Folioformat;
large square ~ Atlasformat; **posting** ~ Angabe der Seitenzahl des Hauptbuches;

~ *(v.)* foliieren, paginieren, mit Seitenzahlen versehen;
~ **book** Buch in Folioformat, Foliant; ~ **reference** Bezugnahme auf Buchhaltungsbelege; ~ **size** Folioformat; ~ **volume** Folioband, Foliant.

folk Leute, *(Br.)* Verwandtschaft;
country ~ Landvolk; **simple** ~**s** einfache Leute;
~ **hero** Volksheld; ~ **memory** Volkstraditionen; ~ **music** Volksmusik; ~ **play** Volksstück; ~ **song** Volkslied; ~ **tale** Volkserzählung.

folksay volkstümliche Ausdrücke.

follow *(v.)* nachfolgen, *(go with)* begleiten, mitgehen, *(profession)* ausüben, Geschäft betreiben, *(pursue with hostility)* verfolgen;
~ **s.** one's advice sich nach jds. Rat richten; ~ **s.** one's argument sich jds. Beweisführung anschließen; ~ **a body to the grave** im Leichenzug mitgehen; ~ **other men's business** sich um anderer Leute Angelegenheiten kümmern; ~ **s. o. close[ly]** jem. auf dem Fuße folgen; ~ **the conservative party** mit der Führung der konservativen Partei einverstanden sein; ~ **copy** *(print.)* Manuskript wortwörtlich absetzen; ~ **a strict diet** streng nach Diät leben; ~ **the drum** *(coll.)* Soldat werden; ~ **out an enterprise** Unternehmen durchführen; ~ **s.** one's example jds. Beispiel befolgen; ~ **the fashion** sich nach der Mode richten, Mode mitmachen; ~ **s. o. to his grave (to the grave side)** jem. die letzte Ehre erweisen; ~ **only** one's own inclination sich nur nach seinen Neigungen richten; ~ **the law** Jurist werden; ~ **a line** *(pol.)* Linie verfolgen; ~ **another person in an disorderly manner** j. in aufrührerischer Weise verfolgen; ~ **a matter** einer Sache nachgehen; ~ **one's nose** seinem Instinkt folgen; ~ **on** gleich weitermachen; ~ **one's pleasure** seinem Vergnügen nachgehen; ~ **the plough (plow,** *US)* Bauer sein; ~ **the same profession** gleichen Beruf ausüben (haben); ~ **one's father's profession** in die Fußstapfen seines Vaters treten; ~ **s.** one's progress jds. berufliches Fortkommen im Auge behalten; ~ **the sea** Seemann werden; ~ **suit** gleichziehen, nachfolgen; ~ **s. th. through** Sache weiterverfolgen; ~ **in** s. one's tracks jds. Beispiel nacheifern; ~ **a trade** Gewerbe ausüben;
letter to ~ Brief folgt;
~**-on** Fortsetzungsanzeige; ~**-on contract** Anschlußauftrag; ~**-the-leader price policy** Preisführerschaftspolitik; ~ **shots** Folgeaufnahme; ~ **style** Satz nach vorliegendem Druckmuster.

follow-up weitere Verfolgung (Untersuchung) einer Sache, *(advertising)* nachfassende Befragung, *(salesman)* nachfassende Tätigkeit, Nachfolgeaktion;
~ **on correspondence** *(interview)* Nachfaßaktion; ~ **of orders** Terminüberwachung.

follow *(v.)* **up** nachfassen, energisch verfolgen, weiterverfolgen;
~ **an advantage** Vorteil wahrnehmen (ausnutzen); ~ **a clue** einem Hinweis nachgehen; ~ **a letter with a summons** seinem Brief einen Zahlungsbefehl folgen lassen; ~ **a matter** einer Sache nachgehen; ~ **a victory** Sieg ausnutzen.

follow-up | **advertising** Nachfaß-, Erinnerungswerbung; ~ **care** Nachbehandlung; ~ **file** Wiedervorlagenmappe; ~ **instruction** weitere Anweisung; ~ **letter** nachfassender Werbebrief, Folge-, Nachfaßbrief, Erinnerungsschreiben; ~ **mailings** Erinnerungspostwurfsendung; ~ **man** weiterer Vertreter; ~ **order** Anschlußauftrag; ~ **system** Wiedervorlageverfahren; ~ **training** anschließende Weiterausbildung; ~ **visit** nachfassender Besuch; ~ **work** nachfolgende (vervollständigende) Tätigkeit.

follower Nachfolger, *(partisan)* Anhänger, Mitläufer, Parteigänger, *(pursuer)* Verfolger;
~**s** Anhängerschaft;
camp ~ Marketender;
to be among s. one's ~**s** in jds. Gefolge sein.

following Anhängerschaft, Gefolge, Anhänger;
broad-based ~ Anhängerschar in allen Altersgruppen;
to build up a popular ~ Anhängerschaft in der großen Masse suchen; **to have a numerous** ~ zahlreiche Anhänger haben;
~ *(a.)* folgend, nachstehend;
~**-on advertisement** Anzeige im Rahmen einer Serie, Fortsetzungsanzeige; ~ **matter** *(advertisement)* textanschließend; ~ **resolution** nachstehende Entschließung.

foment *(v.)* pflegen, *(fig.)* fördern;
~ **strife** Streit schüren.

fomentation *(fig.)* Aufreizung, Schürung.

fond of vernarrt, versessen;
to be passionately ~ **reading** Leseratte sein; **to be** ~ **speaking ill of others** alle Leute gern schlecht machen; **to be** ~ **sweets** Naschkatze sein.

font *(print.)* Schriftgarnitur, kompletter Schriftsatz.

food Nahrung, Kost, Speise, Essen, *(victuals)* Nahrungs-, Lebensmittel, Verpflegung;
free ~ zollfreie Nahrungsmittel; **frozen** ~ tiefgekühlte Lebensmittel, Tiefkühlkost; **intellectual (mental)** ~ geistige Nahrung; **patent** ~**s** Markennahrungsmittel; **plain** ~ Hausmannskost; **processed** ~ verarbeitete Nahrungsmittel; **protective** ~ vitaminreiche Lebensmittel; **snatch** ~ Schnellgericht; **spare** ~ überflüssige Nahrungsmittel;
free ~ **and accommodation** freie Verpflegung und Wohnung;
~ **for controversy** Gegenstand für Auseinandersetzungen; ~ **for conversation** Stoff für die Unterhaltung, Gesprächsstoff; ~ **for thought** Stoff zum Nachdenken;
to adulterate ~ Nahrungsmittel verfälschen; **to be off one's** ~ keinen Appetit haben; **to dispense** ~ Nahrungsmittel verteilen; **to give s. o.** ~ **for thought** jem. Stoff zum Nachdenken geben; **to provide** ~ **for the mind** Geist anregen; **to quickfreeze** ~ Lebensmittel dem Tiefkühlverfahren unterziehen; **to ration** ~ Lebensmittel rationieren;
~ **ad** *(US)* Nahrungsmittelanzeige; ₰ **and Drug Act** *(Br.)* Lebensmittelgesetz; ₰ **and Drug Administration (FDA)** *(US)* Lebensmittelbehörde; ~ **allowance** Verpflegungszulage, Nahrungsmittelzuteilung; ~ **analyst** Nahrungsmittelchemiker; **National** ₰ **Bill** *(US)* Lebensmittelgesetz; ~ **card** Lebensmittelkarte; ~ **cart** *(airplane)* Servierwagen; ~ **chemist** Nahrungsmittelchemiker; ~ **conditions** Ernährungslage; ~ **conservation** Lebensmittelaufbewahrung, -einsparung; ~ **container** Lebensmittelbehälter; ~ **control** Lebensmittelkontrolle; ~ **controller** Lebensmittelkontrolleur; ~ **coupon** Lebensmittelkartenabschnitt; ~ **cut** Lebensmittelkürzung; ~ **deficit area** Nahrungsmittelzuschußgebiet; ~ **freezer** Tiefkühltruhe; ~ **gap** Nahrungsmittellücke; ~ **glut** Nahrungsmittelüberschüsse; ~ **hoarding** [Lebensmittel]hamstern; ~ **imports** Nahrungsmitteleinfuhr; ~ **industry** Nahrungsmittelindustrie; ~ **inspector** Lebensmittelkontrolleur, Fleischbeschauer; **in the** ~ **line** in der Lebensmittelbranche; ~ **manufacturer** Lebensmittelfabrikant; ~**-manufacturing industry** Lebensmittelindustrie; ~ **office** *(Br.)* Ernährungsamt; ₰ **and Agriculture Organization (FAO)** Ernährungs- und Landwirtschaftsorganisation; ~ **package (parcel)** Lebensmittelpaket; ~ **packer** Nahrungsmittelverpackungsbetrieb; ~ **poisoning** Lebensmittelvergiftung; ~ **position** Ernährungslage; ~ **prices** Lebens-, Nahrungsmittelpreise; ~ **price labelling** Lebensmittelauszeichnung; ~**-processing company** Lebensmittelverarbeitungsbetrieb; ~**-processing industry** Ernährungsindustrie; ~ **products** Nahrungsmittelprodukte; ~ **production** Ernährungswirtschaft; ₰ **for Peace Program** *(US)* Hilfsprogramm zur Kinderernährung in Entwicklungsländern; ~ **queue** Schlange vor einem Lebensmittelladen; ~ **ration** Lebensmittelration; ~ **rationing** Lebensmittelrationierung, Bewirtschaftung von Lebensmitteln; ~ **rent** Naturalrente; ~ **requirements** Lebens-, Nahrungsmittelbedarf; ~ **reserves** Nahrungsmittelreserven; ~ **retailer** Lebensmitteleinzelhändler; ~ **science** Ernährungswissenschaft; ~ **sector** Ernährungssektor; ~ **shares** (stocks, *US*) Lebensmittelaktien, -werte; ~ **shipment** Lebensmitteltransport, -versand; ~ **shop** Lebensmittelladen, -geschäft; ~ **shortage** Nahrungs-, Lebensmittelknappheit; ~ **situation** Ernährungslage; ~ **stamp benefit** kostenloser Lebensmittelabschnitt, Nahrungsmittelgutschein, Essensbon; ~ **stocks** Lebensmittelvorräte; ~ **subsidies** Nahrungsmittelzuschüsse; ~ **supplies** Lebensmittelvorräte; ~ **supply** Nahrungsmittelversorgung; ~ **surplus** Nahrungsmittelüberschuß; ~ **tax** Lebensmittelsteuer; ~ **ticket** Lebensmittelkartenabschnitt; ~ **value** Nährwert; ~ **waste** Lebensmittelverschwendung.

foodstuff Lebens-, Nahrungsmittel;
to preserve ~**s** Nahrungsmittel konservieren (haltbar machen).

fool Narr, Dummkopf, *(dupe)* Gimpel, Übervorteilter, *(idiot)* Schwachsinniger, Irrer, Idiot;
hopeless ~ hoffnungsloser Narr;
some ~ **of a politician** *(coll.)* irgend so ein Narr unter den Politikern;
~ *(v.)* **about (around)** sich herumtreiben, herumflanieren; ~ **about with one's wireless set** an seinem Radiogerät herumhantieren; ~ **away one's time** seine Zeit verplempern;
to be a ~ **for one's pains** weder Lohn noch gute Worte ernten; **to make a** ~ **of s. o.** j. zum Narren halten; **to make a** ~ **of o. s.** sich wie ein Narr aufspielen (lächerlich machen); **to play the** ~ Possen treiben;
fool's errand vergeblicher Gang, Metzgergang; **to go on a** ~**'s errand** etw. völlig umsonst tun; **to send s. o. on a** ~**' errand** j. in den April schicken; **to live in a** ~**'s paradise** im Schlaraffenland leben.

foolhardiness Draufgängertum.

foolproof ungefährlich, *(factory)* betriebssicher.

foolscap Propatria-, Kanzleipapier, Folioformat.

foot Fuß;
at ~ of the page unterstehend; at the ~ of the list am Ende der Liste;
~ of a page Seitenende, Ende einer Seite;
~ (v.) addieren;
~ a bill (US) Rechnung bezahlen, Unkosten tragen; ~ it sich auf die Socken machen; ~ up zusammenzählen, addieren; ~ up to DM 10.000 (debts) sich auf 10.000 DM belaufen; ~ up pretty high ziemlich hoch sein;
to be on ~ (project) im Gange sein; to get a bigger ~ in the market größeren Marktanteil erobern; to have one ~ in gaol (jail) mit einem Bein im Zuchthaus stehen; to have one ~ in the grave mit einem Fuß im Grabe stehen; to know the length of s. one's ~ jds. Schwächen genau kennen; to put one's ~ down Machtwort sprechen; to put one's ~ in it ins Fettnäpfchen treten; to put one's best ~ forward möglichst guten Eindruck machen; never to put a ~ wrong niemals einen Fehler machen; to set on ~ ins Werk setzen, auf die Beine stellen; to set a business on ~ Geschäft auf die Beine bringen; to set negotiations on ~ Verhandlungen in Gang bringen; to set an undertaking on ~ Sache lancieren (in Gang bringen); to start off on the wrong ~ Sache am falschen Ende anfassen;
~ brake Fußbremse; ~ line (print.) letzte Zeile, Unterschlag; ~ locker (mil.) Feldkiste; ~ log (US) Steg; ~ margin Fußsteg, unterer Rand; ~ passenger Fußgänger; ~ pavement Trottoir; ~ road Fußweg; ~ rule Zollstock; ~ starter (motorcycle) Tretanlasser; ~ switch Fußschalter; ~ tracks Fußspuren.
footage Filmstreifen.
football pools Fußballtoto.
footboard (vehicle) Trittbrett.
footboy Laufbursche, Page.
footbridge Fußgängerbrücke, -steg.
footgear Fußbekleidung, Schuhzeug.
foothold Stütze, Halt, (fig.) sichere Stellung;
to gain a ~ in another industry in einem anderen Industriebereich Fuß fassen.
footing (adding of columns) Addieren einzelner Posten, Kolonnenaddition, (entry money) Einstandsgeld, (status) Zustand, sichere Stellung, Lage, Status, (sum total) Gesamtsumme;
on an equal ~ paritätisch; on a statutory ~ auf gesetzlicher Grundlage;
friendly ~ freundschaftliches Verhältnis; peace ~ (mil.) Friedenstand, -stärke; war ~ (mil.) Kriegsstärke;
to be on an equal ~ with s. o. mit jem. im gleichen Range stehen; to be on a friendly ~ with s. o. freundschaftlich mit jem. verkehren; to be on a good ~ with s. o. gute Beziehungen zu jem. haben (unterhalten); to gain a ~ festen Fuß fassen; to get a ~ in society gesellschaftlich Fuß fassen; to lose one's ~ seinen Status verlieren; to pay one's ~ seinen Einstand geben; to put on a better financial ~ auf eine bessere finanzielle Grundlage stellen; to place two people on the same ~ zwei Menschen gleichberechtigt behandeln; to put on the same ~ gleichstellen.
footle Unsinn, Stuß;
~ (v.) töricht handeln;
~ away one's time seine Zeit mit Nichtigkeiten vertrödeln.
footlights (theater) Rampenbeleuchtung.
footmark Fußspur.
footloose industry standortungebundene Industrie.
footnote Fußnote, Anmerkung.
footpace (house) Treppenabsatz, Estrade, erhöhter Absatz.
footpath Fußpfad, (pavement) Trottoir, Bürgersteig.
footplate Wagentritt.
footprint Fußabdruck, Fußspur.
footrest Fußbank, Schemel, Fußraste.
footslogger (sl.) Infanterist.
footstep Tritt, Schritt, (print.) Antritt;
to follow in s. one's ~s in jds. Fußstapfen treten.
footwalk Laufgang.
footwall (mining) Liegendes.
footway Fußpfad, Bürgersteig.
footwear Schuhwerk, Fußbekleidung.
forage Viehfutter, (act of foraging) Beute-, Streif-, Raubzug;
green ~ Grünfutter;
~ (v.) among papers Papiere durchwühlen; ~ in one's pockets in seinen Taschen herumsuchen;
to find s. o. on a ~ in the kitchen (coll.) j. in der Küche beim Futtern antreffen.
forbear (v.) sich einer Sache enthalten;
~ to drink alcohol auf Alkohol verzichten; ~ to go into details sich Einzelheiten versagen; ~ a suit Klage unterlassen.

forbearance Stundung, Nachsicht, Zahlungsaufschub;
~ to sue Klageunterlassung;
to show ~ in dealing with people mit seinen Mitmenschen geduldig umgehen;
~ money Verzugszinsen.
forbid (v.) verbieten, untersagen.
forbidden verboten, untersagt;
~ by law gesetzlich verboten;
~ subjects of conversation verbotene Gesprächsthemen; fishing is ~ Angeln nicht erlaubt; the public are ~ to smoke in the garage Rauchen ist in der Garage nicht gestattet.
force Zwang, Gewalt[maßnahme], Druck, (employees) Belegschaft, (mil.) Militär, Streitkräfte, Heer, Truppen, (validity) Gültigkeit, Gesetzeskraft;
by ~ zwangsweise, gewaltsam, (politics) machtpolitisch; by sheer ~ mit nackter Gewalt; in ~ in Kraft, rechtsgültig; in full ~ vollzählig; owing to the ~ of circumstances unter dem Druck der Verhältnisse; still in ~ noch in Kraft, noch gültig;
~s Streitkräfte;
accelerative ~ Beschleunigungskraft; air ~ Luftwaffe, -streitkräfte; allied ~ alliierte Streitkräfte; armed ~s Streitkräfte; besieging ~s Belagerungstruppen; binding ~ bindende Kraft, Rechtskraft, -gültigkeit; brute ~ brutale Gewalt; centrifugal ~ Zentrifugalkraft; detective ~ Kriminalpolizei; foreign ~s ausländische Streitkräfte; irresistible ~ unwiderstehliche Gewalt; land ~s Landstreitkräfte; legal ~ Rechtskraft; ~ majeure höhere Gewalt; military ~s Streitkräfte; moral ~ moralische Stärke; multilateral ~ (mil.) multilaterale Streitmacht; naval ~s Seestreitkräfte; occupation ~s Besatzungstruppen, -macht; physical ~ physische Gewalt; police ~ Polizei[truppe]; probative ~ Beweiskraft; probatory ~ Beweiskraft; productive ~ Produktionskraft; rapid deployment ~ (mil.) strategische Eingreifreserve; relieving ~s Entsatztruppen; retroactive ~ rückwirkende Kraft; retrospective ~ rückwirkende Kraft; sea ~s Seestreitkräfte, -macht; spent ~ verlorene Autorität; stable ~ gleichbleibende Belegschaft; subsidiary ~ subsidiäre Geltung; task ~ (Br.) polizeiliche Sondereinheit, (plant) in Akkord arbeitende Belegschaft, (US) Arbeitsstab; superior ~ (law of negligence) höhere Gewalt; superior ~s (mil.) überlegene Streitkräfte; working ~ Belegschaft;
~s stationed abroad Truppen im Ausland; ~ of an agreement Gültigkeit eines Vertrages; ~ of appeal Rechtmäßigkeit einer Berufung; ~ of an argument Durchschlagkraft einer Beweisführung; ~ of arms Waffengewalt; ~ of character Charakterstärke; main ~ of demand Schwergewicht der Nachfrageentwicklung; ~ of men employed Gesamtbelegschaft; ~ of expression Aussagekraft; ~ and fear Gewalt oder Bedrohung; ~ of gravity Schwerkraft; ~ of habit Macht der Gewohnheit; ~ of law Gesetzeskraft; ~ of mortality Sterblichkeitserwartung; ~s of production Produktivkräfte; strong ~ of police starkes Polizeiaufgebot; third ~ in parliament dritte Kraft im Parlament; ~s of reaction reaktionäre Kräfte; powerful ~s in world affairs Machtfaktoren der Weltpolitik;
~ (v.) in die Notwendigkeit versetzen, zwingen, nötigen, forcieren, durchdrücken;
~ an action on the enemy Feind zur Schlacht zwingen; ~ a company into Chapter 10 proceedings (US) Gesellschaftskonkurs einleiten; ~ a confession from s. o. jem. ein Geständnis abpressen; ~ one's confidence upon s. o. jem. sein Vertrauen aufdrängen; ~ [open] a door Tür aufbrechen; ~ down (airplane) zur Notlandung zwingen; ~ down prices Preise drücken; ~ down the standard of work Leistungsniveau drücken; ~ one's entry sich gewaltsam Eintritt verschaffen; ~s. one's hand j. unter Druck setzen; ~ the hand of fortune dem Glück etwas nachhelfen; ~ issues Probleme ohne Rücksicht auf die Folgen lösen; ~ juice out of an orange Apfelsine auspressen; ~ the pace Tempo beschleunigen; ~ a pupil Ausbildung eines Schülers vorantreiben; ~ a ship on shore Schiff auf den Strand setzen; ~ s. o. to sign a paper j. zu einer Unterschrift zwingen; ~ a tip in s. one's hand jem. ein Trinkgeld aufnötigen; ~ up (prices) steigern, hinauftreiben, in die Höhe treiben; ~ one's way into government Regierungsgewalt erringen; ~ war upon a country einem Land den Krieg aufzwingen; ~ one's way through the crowd sich einen Weg durch die Menge bahnen; ~ one's way into a house sich gewaltsam Zugang zu einem Haus verschaffen; ~ out a few words of congratulation sich ein paar Glückwunschworte abringen; ~ o. s. to work hard sich zu harter Arbeit zwingen;
to attack with superior ~s mit überlegenen Kräften angreifen;
to back up the local field ~s die im Außendienst tätigen Kräfte

verstärken; **to be in** ~ gelten, in Kraft (gültig) sein, Geltung haben; **to be of no binding** ~ nicht bindend sein; **to be an international** ~ großen internationalen Einfluß ausüben, internationale Bedeutung haben; **to be no longer in** ~ nicht mehr gültig sein; **to be out in full** ~ in Scharen unterwegs sein; **to be overcome by** ~ **of one's emotions** von seinen Gefühlen überwältigt werden; **to bring up heavy ~s** größere Truppenmengen heranführen; **to bring a law into** ~ **again** Gesetz wieder zur Anwendung bringen; **to cease to have** ~ außer Kraft treten, kraftlos werden; **to come into** ~ in Kraft (Wirksamkeit) treten; **to come into** ~ **on the date of publication** mit dem Tag der Veröffentlichung in Kraft treten; **to have resort to** ~ zu Gewaltmaßnahmen greifen; **to have legal** ~ rechtskräftig sein; **to join ~s with** (mil.) Streitkräfte vereinigen; **to join the ~s** in die Armee eintreten; **to pool one's ~s** seine Kräfte gemeinsam einsetzen; **to put in** ~ zur Anwendung bringen; **to put into** ~ in Kraft treten lassen (setzen); **to put the law into** ~ Gesetz anwenden; **to raise ~s** Truppen aufstellen; **to remain in** ~ in Kraft bleiben; **to turn out in full** ~ geschlossen antreten; **to use** ~ Gewalt anwenden; **to use** ~ **in self-protection** (US) Gewalt in Notwehr anwenden; **to yield to** ~ der Gewalt weichen;

~ **account** städtisches Unternehmen auf eigene Rechnung; ~ **bill** (US) Gesetz über die Anwendung von Zwangsmaßnahmen; **~s capability** Truppenstärke; ♀ **Convention** Truppenvertrag; **~-fed** zwangsernährt; ~ **feed** (v.) gewaltsam (zwangsweise) ernähren; **~-land** (v.) Notlandung vornehmen; **~s newspaper** Soldatenzeitung; **~s reduction** Truppenreduzierung, -abbau; **~-water** (v.) notwassern.

forced (v.) erzwungen, gezwungen, dem Zwang unterworfen; ~ **agreement** Zwangsvergleich; ~ **call** Anlaufen eines Nothafens; ~ **course of exchange** Zwangsumrechnungskurs; ~ **currency** Zwangswährung; ~ **down** (airplane) zur Notlandung gezwungen; ~ **execution** Zwangsregulierung; ~ **feeding** Zwangsernährung; ~ **heir** (US) pflichtteilsberechtigter Erbe, Pflichtteilsberechtigter; ~ **heirship** (US) Pflichtteilsrecht; ~ **labo(u)r** Zwangsarbeit; ~ **landing** Notlandung; ~ **liquidation** Zwangsliquidation; ~ **loan** Krediterhöhung infolge Kontoüberziehung, Zwangsanleihe; ~ **march** Eilmarsch; ~ **quotations** fiktive Kurse; ~ **rate of exchange** Zwangs[umrechnungs]kurs; ~ **repatriation** Zwangsrepatriierung; ~ **sale** Zwangsverkauf, (auction) Zwangsversteigerung; ~ **sale by order of the court** gerichtlich angeordnete Zwangsversteigerung; **~-sale value** beim Zwangsverkauf erzielter Erlös; ~ **saving** Zwangssparen; ~ **selling** Zwangs-, Notverkäufe; ~ **statutory** ~ **share** (US) feste Nachlaßquote; ~ **sterilization** Zwangssterilisierung; ~ **style** gekünstelter Stil.

forcible gewaltsam, (fig.) eindrucksvoll, zwingend; ~ **detainer** unberechtigte Zurückhaltung, Herausgabeverweigerung; ~ **entry** verbotene Eigenmacht; ~ **entry into a building** Hausfriedensbruch; ~ **entry and detainer** Besitzstörungsklage; ~ **reason** stichhaltiger Grund; ~ **speaker** überzeugender Redner; ~ **trespass** Besitzstörung, verbotene Eigenmacht.

forcing Aufbrechen, (mil.) Erstürmen; ~ **up prices** Preistreiberei; ~ **house** (Br.) Treibhaus.

fore Vorderseite, Front; **to the** ~ (fig.) am Ruder; **well to the** ~ deutlich im Vordergrund; **~-and-after** in Kiellinie; **to be to the** ~ im Vordergrund stehen; **to be always to the** ~ **in a fight** immer an der vordersten Linie kämpfen; **to come to the** ~ ans Ruder kommen; **to find o. s. with nothing to the** ~ sich auf einmal völlig mittellos vorfinden; **to have come to the** ~ **recently** in letzter Zeit prominent geworden sein; **to have money to the** ~ Geld zur Verfügung haben; ~ **cabin** (Br.) vordere Kajüte; ~ **edge** (book) Außensteg; **in the** ~ **part of a train** am Zuganfang.

forebear Vorahn.
forebode (v.) prophezeien, weissagen; ~ **disaster** Vorahnungen eines Unglücks haben.
foreboding Prophezeiung, Weissagung.
forecast Vorausberechnung, -schau, Vorhersage, Voraussage, Prognose; **beyond all ~s** entgegen allen Prognosen; **district (local)** ~ (US) örtliche Wettervorhersagestelle; **economic** ~ Konjunkturvorschau; **financial** ~ Finanzvorschau; **mean-range** ~ Mittelfristvorhersage; **sales** ~ Umsatzprognose; **long-range weather** ~ langfristige Wettervorhersage; ~ **of national product** Schätzung der Sozialproduktentwicklung; ~ **of a slump** Baissevorhersage; ~ (v.) vorhersagen, voraussagen, im voraus schätzen, prognostizieren;

~ **the course of a business** Konjunkturprognose vornehmen; ~ **the future** Zukunft voraussagen; **to muffle one's** ~ **on prices** abgeschwächte Preisentwicklungsprognose abgeben; ~ **the weather** Wetter vorhersagen; ~ **amendment** Vorhersageänderung; ~ **budget** Konjunkturvorschau; ~ **chart** Vorhersagekarte; ~ **period** Vorhersagezeitraum.

forecaster (economics) Konjunkturberater, -politiker; **business** ~ Konjunkturprognostiker.
forecasting Voraussage, (business future) Konjunkturprognose; **business (economic)** ~ Konjunkturprognose, -vorschau, Wirtschaftsvorschau, Vorhersage wirtschaftspolitischer Entwicklungen; **long-range** ~ Langfristprognose; **sales** ~ Absatzvorschau; ~ **body** Prognosestelle; ~ **business** Prognosebranche; ~ **division** Abteilung für Konjunkturprognosen; ~ **error** Prognoseirrtum; ~ **method** Vorhersagemethode; **poor** ~ **records** miserable Prognoseerfolge; ~ **service** Prognosetätigkeit.
forecastle Vorderdeck, (merchant vessel) Logis.
foreclosable der Zwangsvollstreckung unterliegend, vollstreckungsfähig.
foreclose (v.) ausschließen, hindern, hemmen; ~ **on a mortgage** (US) aus einer Hypothek die Zwangsvollstreckung betreiben, (Br.) Hypothek (Pfand) für verfallen erklären; ~ **the mortgager's right of redemption** Recht des Hypothekenschuldners auf Grundstücksübertragung für immer ausschließen; ~ **an objection** Einwand übergehen.
foreclosed (mortgage) gekündigt; **not to be** ~ unkündbar sein.
foreclosure Ausschluß, (law) Rechtsausschließung, Präklusion, Verfallserklärung, (mortgage, US) Zwangsvollstreckung in das unbewegliche Vermögen; **strict** ~ rechtskräftige Verfallserklärung; **statutory** ~ Betreibung der Zwangsvollstreckung aus einer vollstreckbaren Urkunde, gesetzlich zugelassener Pfandverkauf; ~ **of a mortgage** Zwangsvollstreckung aus einer Hypothek; **to reopen** ~ Zwangsversteigerung aussetzen; ~ **action** (US) Vollstreckungsabwehrklage; **to bring a** ~ **action** (US) Vollstreckungsabwehrklage erheben; ~ **conveyance** (US) Grundstücksübertragung in der Zwangsversteigerung; ~ **decree** (US) Zwangsvollstreckungsbeschluß; ~ **order** (Br.) Pfandverfallsbeschluß, (US) Anordnung der Zwangsvollstreckung; ~ **order absolute** rechtskräftige Pfandverfallserklärung, endgültiger Pfandverfallsbeschluß; ~ **order insi** vorläufiger Pfandverfallsbeschluß; ~ **proceedings** Ausschlußverfahren, (US) Zwangsvollstreckungsverfahren; ~ **sale** (US) Pfandverkauf, Zwangsversteigerung; ~ **suit** (US) Vollstreckungsabwehrklage.
forecourt Vorhof.
foredate (v.) voraus-, vordatieren.
foredeck Vorderdeck.
foredoom Vorherbestimmung.
forefather Vorfahr, Ahn.
forefield Vorfeld, (mining) Ort.
forefront vorderste Reihe; **to be always in the** ~ **of the battle for voting rights** im Kampf für das Wahlrecht an vorderster Front stehen; **to loom in the** ~ hauptsächliches Nahziel sein; **to stand in the** ~ zu den Besten zählen.
foregift (Br.) Vorausbezahlung, (lease) Handgeld, Anzahlung.
foregoer Vorgänger, -läufer.
foregoing Vorstehendes; ~ **facts** vorstehender Sachverhalt.
foregone conclusion ausgemachte Sache, unvermeidlicher Schluß, Selbstverständlichkeit.
foreground Vordergrund, (mil.) Vorgelände; **to bring a question in the** ~ Problem auf den Tisch legen; **to keep o. s. in the** ~ sich in den Vordergrund spielen.
forehand rent (Br.) im voraus zahlbare Miete, Mietvorschuß.
foreign ausländisch, auswärtig, fremd, (not within the sphere of the court) von einem anderen Gericht abhängig; **to be** ~ **to s. one's nature** nicht zu jds. Charakter passen; ~ **acceptance** Außengeltung; **for** ~ **account** für fremde Rechnung; ~ **adjustment** im Ausland erfolgte Schadensregulierung; ~ **administrator** Auslandstestamentsvollstrecker; ~ **advertising** Auslandswerbung; ~ **affairs** auswärtige Angelegenheiten, Außenpolitik; **to be free to act in** ~ **affairs** in der auswärtigen Politik absolute Handlungsfreiheit besitzen; **~-affairs committee** Ausschuß für auswärtige Angelegenheiten; **~-affairs debate** Auslandsdebatte, Debatte über die Außenpolitik; ♀ **Affairs Minister** Außenminister; ~ **affiliate** ausländische Toch-

tergesellschaft, Auslandstochter; ~ **agency** (US) ausländische Bankagentur; ~ **agent** Auslandsvertreter; ~ **aid** (US) Entwicklungs-, Auslands-, Wirtschaftshilfe; **US-financed** ~ **aid** amerikanische Entwicklungshilfe; ⚖ **Aid Appropriation Act** (US) Entwicklungshilfegesetz; **~-aid fund** (US) Auslandshilfsfonds; **~-aid program** (US) Auslandshilfs-, Unterstützungsprogramm; **~-aid project** (US) Entwicklungshilfe-, Auslandsprojekt, -vorhaben; **~-aid spending** (US) Auslandshilfsgelder; ~ **amount** Devisenbetrag; ~ **application** Anmeldung im Ausland; ~ **apposer** (Br.) Revisor des Schatzamtes für Krongüter; ~ **assets** Devisen-, Fremdwerte; ~ **assets position** saldierte Auslandsguthaben; ~ **assignment** im Ausland vorgenommene Abtretung; ~ **attachment** Beschlagnahme ausländischen Eigentums; ~ **award** ausländischer Schiedsspruch; ~ **balance** Auslandsguthaben; ~ **bank** ausländisches Bankinstitut, Auslandsbank; ~ **banking corporation** (US) Auslandsbank; ~ **bank notes** ausländische Banknoten; ~ **bill [of exchange]** Fremdwährungswechsel; ~ **body** Fremdkörper; ~ **bonds** ausländische Obligationen; ~ **bonds issue** Auslandsemission; **~-born** im Ausland geboren; ~ **branch** Auslandsfiliale; ~ **broker** Makler in Auslandswechseln; **~-built** im Ausland hergestellt; ~ **business** Auslandsgeschäft; ~ **business trip** Geschäftsreise ins Ausland; ~ **call** (US) Auslandsgespräch; ~ **capital** Auslandskapital, ausländisches Kapital; **to bring ~ capital to a country** Auslandskapital anziehen; ~ **car** (railroad) Waggon einer anderen Gesellschaft; ~ **cartel** ausländisches Kartell; ~ **cash** [Geld]sorten, Bardevisen; ~ **charity** ausländische Stiftung; ~ **circulation** Auslandsverbreitung; ~ **clients** Auslandskundschaft; ~ **coins and notes** [ausländische] Sorten; ~ **collections** ausländische Inkassi; ~ **colony** Ausländerkolonie; ~ **commerce** (US) Außenhandel; ~ **commitments** außenpolitische Verpflichtungen; ~ **company** Auslandsgesellschaft; ~ **competition** Auslandskonkurrenz; ~ **control** Auslandskontrolle, Überfremdung; **~-controlled** überfremdet; ~ **corporate bonds** (US) Obligationen ausländischer Gesellschaften; ~ **corporation** (US) ausländische Gesellschaft; ~ **correspondence** Auslandskorrespondenz; ~ **correspondence clerk** (bank) Auslandskorrespondent; ~ **correspondence secretary** Fremdsprachensekretärin; ~ **correspondent** Auslandskorrespondent, -berichterstatter; ~ **countries (country)** Ausland; ~ **court** ausländisches Gericht, (US) Gericht eines anderen Bundesstaates;~ **coverage** Auslandsberichte; ~ **credit** Auslandskredit; ~ **credit balance** aktive Zahlungsbilanz; ⚖ **Credit Insurance Association** (US) [etwa] Hermesversicherungs AG; ~ **creditor** Auslandsgläubiger.

foreign currency ausländische Sorten (Währung), Devisen, Fremdwährung;
~ **account** Devisen-, Fremdwährungskonto; ~ **affair** Devisenaffäre; ~ **bonds** (US) ausländische Schuldverschreibungen, Fremdwährungsschuldverschreibungen; ~ **borrowings** Devisenausleihungen; ~ **claim** Devisenforderung; ~ **dealing** Devisenhandel; ~ **expenditure** Devisenaufwand; ~ **investment** Deviseninvestition; ~ **items** (balance sheet) Devisenbestände; ~ **loan** Währungskredit; ~ **notes** ausländische Banknoten; ~ **securities** ausländische Wertpapiere; ~ **trade** Devisenhandel; ~ **unit** ausländische Währungseinheit.

foreign | debit balance passive Zahlungsbilanz; ~ **debts** Auslandsverschuldung, -schuld, -forderung, äußere Schuld; ~ **debts proposal** Vorschlag zur Regelung der Auslandsschulden; ~ **debts service** Auslandsschuldendienst; ~ **demand** Auslandsnachfrage, -bedarf; ~ **department** Auslandsabteilung; ~ **deposits** Auslandseinlagen, Auslandsguthaben; ~ **divorce** in einem anderen Staat erfolgte Ehescheidung; ~ **dividends** ausländische Dividenden; ~ **document** ausländische Urkunde; ~ **dollar bonds** (US) Dollaranleihe fremder Staaten; ~ **domicile** Auslandswohnsitz; ~ **domination** Fremdherrschaft; ~ **dominion** (Br.) britisches Herrschaftsgebiet; ~ **earnings** Auslandsgewinne, -erträge; ⚖ **Economic Administration** (US) Verwaltungsstelle für Wirtschaftsfragen des Auslands; ~ **enlistment Act** (Br.) Verbotsgesetz gegen Wehrdienstableistung in fremden Staaten; ~ **equity** ausländisches Kapital, ausländische Beteiligung; ~ **equity capital** ausländisches Beteiligungskapital.

foreign exchange ausländischer Wechselkurs, Devisenkurs, (money) Devisen, Auslandsvaluten;
short of ~ devisenknapp;
blocked (frozen) ~ blockierte Devisen; **remaining ~** nicht ausgenutzte Devisenbeträge;
to apply for ~ Devisen beantragen; **to declare ~** Devisen anmelden;
~ **adjustments** Devisenwertberichtigungen; ~ **advice** Beratung

in Devisenangelegenheiten; ~ **adviser** Devisenberater; ~ **agreement** Devisenabkommen; ~ **allotments** (Br.) Devisenzuteilung; ~ **allowance** Devisenfreibetrag, -zuteilung; ~ **arbitrage (arbitration)** Devisenarbitrage; ~ **assets** Devisenguthaben, -bestände; ~ **authorities** Devisenbehörde; ~ **balance** Devisenbilanz; ~ **bank** Devisenbank; ~ **bill** Fremdwährungswechsel; ~ **broker** Devisenmakler; ~ **burden** Devisenbelastung; ~ **business** Devisenhandel; ~ **certificate** Devisenbescheinigung; ~ **clearing account** Devisenverrechnungskonto; ~ **clearing office** Devisenabrechnungsstelle; ~ **commission** Sortenprovision; ~ **commitments** Devisenengagements; ~ **contracts** Devisenabschlüsse; ~ **control** (US) Devisenbewirtschaftung, -überwachung; ~ **control board** (US) Devisenstelle; ~ **control legislation** (US) Devisengesetzgebung; ~ **control office** (US) Devisenstelle; ~ **costs** Devisenkosten, -aufwand; ~ **cost of imports** Deviseneinfuhrkosten; ~ **cover** Kurssicherung; ~ **credit** Devisen-, Fremdwährungskredit; ~ **crisis** Devisenkrise; ~ **cushion** Devisenpolster; ~ **dealer** Devisenhändler; ~ **dealings** Devisenverkehr, -handel; ~ **department** Devisenabteilung; ~ **deposits** Devisenguthaben, -bestände; ~ **earner** Devisenbringer; ~ **earnings** Devisenerträge, -einkünfte; ~ **equalization account** Devisenausgleichskonto; ~ **equalization fund** Devisenausgleichsfonds; ~ **exposure** Devisenlage; **to purchase ~ facilities** Devisenbestände erwerben; ~ **funds** Devisenbestände; ~ **futures** (US) Termindevisen; ~ **futures market** (US) Devisenterminmarkt; ~ **guaranty** Devisengarantie, Kurssicherung; ~ **holdings** Devisenguthaben, -bestände; ~ **inflow** Devisenzuflüsse; ~ **legislation** (US) Devisengesetzgebung; ~ **limit** Devisenplafond; ~ **list** Devisenkurszettel; ~ **losses** Devisenverluste; ~ **market** Devisen[termin]markt, -börse; ~ **offset** Devisenausgleich; ~ **offset agreement** Devisenausgleichsabkommen; ~ **outflow** Devisenabflüsse; ~ **permit** Devisengenehmigung, -bescheinigung; ~ **policy** Devisenpolitik; ~ **position** Devisenbestand, -position, -haushalt; ~ **position sheet** Devisenbilanz, -status; ~ **proceeds** Devisenerträge; ~ **profiteer** Devisenschieber; ~ **quota** Devisenkontingent; ~ **rates** Devisenkurse, -sätze; ~ **rationing** Devisenrationierung, -kontingentierung; ~ **regulations** Devisenkontrollbestimmungen, -bewirtschaftungsvorschriften, devisenrechtliche Bestimmungen; ~ **repatriation** devisenmäßige Vereinnahmung; ~ **requirements** Devisenerfordernisse; ~ **reserves** Devisenrücklage, -polster; **to be almost drained of ~ reserves** fast keine Devisenbestände mehr haben; ~ **restrictions** (US) Devisenverkehrsbeschränkungen, devisenrechtliche Beschränkungen, Devisenbewirtschaftung; ~ **return** Devisenrückfluß; ~ **risk** Kursrisiko; ~ **shortage** Devisenknappheit; ~ **spot dealings** Devisenkassahandel; ~ **squeeze** Devisendruck, -anspannung; **to deposit into the ~ stabilization fund** dem Währungsstabilisierungsfonds überweisen; **indirect ~ standard** Devisenwährung; ~ **statement** Devisenabrechnung; ~ **surplus** Devisenüberfluß; ~ **trader** Devisenhändler; ~ **transaction** Devisengeschäft; ~ **transfer** Devisentransfer.

foreign | excursion Auslandsreise; ~ **exhibitors** Auslandsbeteiligung an einer Messe; ~ **general average** große ausländische Havarie; **~-going ship (vessel)** Schiff auf großer Fahrt (Auslandsfahrt), im Übersehverkehr eingesetztes Schiff; ~ **government bonds** ausländische Staatsanleihen; **~-grown fruit** ausländisches Obst; **~-held** in Auslandsbesitz; ~ **holdings** Auslandsbesitz; ~ **holiday** Auslandsferienreise; ~ **income** Einkünfte im Ausland; ~ **indebtedness** Auslandsverschuldung; ~ **inquiry** Auslandsanfrage; ~ **interests** ausländische Beteiligungen, Auslandsbeteiligungen; **to be controlled by ~ interests** vom Ausland kontrolliert (überfremdet) sein; ~ **investments** Anlagen (Beteiligungen, Investitionen) im Ausland, Auslandsanlagen, Auslandsinvestitionen; **to plough (plow,** US) **in ~ investments** im Ausland anlegen; ⚖ **Investment Law** Auslandsinvestitionsgesetz; ⚖ **Investment Review Act** (Canada) Kontrollgesetz für ausländische Investitionen; ~ **issue** Auslandsemission; ~ **items** (US) Devisenpositionen; ~ **judgment** ausländisches Urteil, Urteil eines nicht zuständigen Gerichts; ~ **jurisdiction** ausländische Gerichtsbarkeit; ~ **labo(u)r** Gast-, Fremdarbeiter, ausländische Arbeitskräfte; ~ **language** fremde Sprache, Fremdsprache; **~-language advertising** fremdsprachliche Werbung; **~-language capability** Fremdsprachenbegabung; **~-language tuition** Fremdsprachenunterricht; ~ **law** ausländisches Recht; ~ **legion** (mil.) Fremdenlegion; ~ **lending** Krediteinräumung im Ausland; ~ **letter** Auslandsbrief; ~ **liabilities** Auslandsverbindlichkeiten; ~ **liquidations** (stock exchange) Auslandsverkäufe, ausländische Realisationen; ~ **living costs** Lebenshaltungskosten im Ausland; ~ **loan** Auslandsanleihe; **~-made product** ausländisches Erzeugnis; ~ **mail** Auslandspost; ~ **mail service** (Br.) Auslandsbriefverkehr; ~ **make** Auslandsfabrikat; ~ **market** ausländischer Absatzmarkt, Auslandsmarkt, *(stock exchange)* Markt der Auslandswerte; **to dump goods on ~ markets** Waren im Ausland billig auf den Markt bringen; **to shut out of the ~ market** vom Auslandsmarkt ausschließen; ~ **marriage** im Ausland geschlossene Ehe; ~ **matter** vor ein anderes Gericht gehörige Sache; ~ **member** auswärtiges Mitglied; ⚩ **Minister** Außenminister; **Deputy** ⚩ **Minister** Außenministerstellvertreter; **to call on the** ⚩ **Minister** im Außenministerium vorsprechen; ⚩ **Minister level** Außenministerebene; ~ **missions** Missionswesen im Ausland; ~ **money** ausländische Zahlungsmittel; ~ **money department** Sortenabteilung; ~ **money order** internationale Postanweisung; ~ **municipal bonds** *(US)* ausländische Kommunalanleihe; ~ **national** Ausländer; ~ **nationality** Ausländereigenschaft; ~ **news** Auslandsnachrichten; ~ **news editor** Auslandsredakteur; ~ **news report** ausländische Berichterstattung; ~ **notes** Sorten; ⚩ **Office** *(Br.)* Ministerium des Äußeren, Auswärtiges Amt; ~ **office spokesman** Sprecher des Auswärtigen Amtes; ⚩ **Operations Administration** *(US)* Auslandshilfsamt; ~-**owned** in ausländischem Besitz (Eigentum); ~-**owned balances** Auslandsguthaben; ~-**owned property** ausländisches Vermögen; ~ **ownership** ausländisches Vermögen, Auslandsbesitz; **to be under ~ ownership** Ausländern gehören; ~ **parcel post** Paketpost ins Ausland; **in ~ parts** *(Br.)* im Ausland; ~ **patent** Auslandspatent; ~ **payment** Auslandszahlung, Zahlung in Devisen; ~ **payments transactions** Zahlungsverkehr mit dem Ausland; ~ **pension** Auslandspension; ~ **plea** *(US)* Einrede (Einwand) der Unzuständigkeit; ~ **policy** auswärtige Politik, Außenpolitik; **to remain free to determine its own ~ policy** in außenpolitischen Entschlüssen frei bleiben; ~ **population** fremdländischer Bevölkerungsteil; ~ **port** Auslandshafen; ~ **possessions** Auslandsvermögen; ~ **postage** Auslandsporto, Auslandsposttarif; ~ **postage rates** Auslandspostgebühren; ~ **postal money order** Auslandspostanweisung; ~ **postcard** Auslandspostkarte; ~ **power** auswärtige Macht; ~ **press** Auslandspresse; ~ **price** Auslandspreis; ~ **product** ausländisches Fabrikat; ~ **property** ausländisches Eigentum (Vermögen), Auslandsvermögen; ~ **quota** Devisenkontingent; ~ **rails** *(US, stock exchange)* ausländische Eisenbahnwerte; ~ **relations** Auslandsbeziehungen; ~-**relations committee** Auswärtiger Ausschuß; ~ **relief** Auslandshilfe; ~ **representative** Auslandsvertreter; ~ **residence** Wohnsitz im Ausland; ~ **rule** Fremdherrschaft; ~ **rules** fremde Usancen; ~ **sales contract** Außenhandelsvertrag; ~ **sales figures** Außenhandelsziffern; ~ **school** Auslandsschule; ⚩ **Secretary** *(Br.)* Außenminister; ~ **sector** Außenwirtschaftsbereich; ~ **securities** ausländische Wertpapiere, Auslandswerte; ~ **service** *(US)* auswärtiger Dienst; ~ **service allowance** *(US)* Auslandszulage; ⚩ **Service Institute** *(US)* Diplomatenschule; ~ **service officer** *(US)* Beamter des Auswärtigen Dienstes; ~ **share** Auslandsaktie, ausländische Aktie; ~ **ship** ausländisches Schiff; ~ **shipment** Auslandssendung; ~ **shipper** Auslandsspediteur; ~ **situation** außenpolitische Lage; ~ **sojourn** Auslandsaufenthalt; ~ **stock** Valutapapier; ~ **stock exchange** Auslandsbörse; ~ **subject** Ausländer; ~ **subsidiary** selbständige Auslandstochter; ~ **tax relief** Steuervergünstigung für im Ausland erzielte Einkünfte.

foreign trade auswärtiger Handel, Außen-, Auslandshandel, Außenwirtschaft;
to be in the ~ *(ship)* auf Auslandsreise sein;
~ **activities** Außenhandelstätigkeit; ~ **agency** Außenhandelsstelle; ~ **agreement** Außenhandelsabkommen; ~ **balance** Außenhandelsbilanz; **active ~ balance** Aktivsaldo im Außenhandel; **adverse ~ balance** Passivsaldo im Außenhandel; ~ **center** *(US)* **(centre,** *Br.)* Außenhandelsplatz; ~ **certificate** Steuermannspatent für große Fahrt; ~ **contract** Außenhandelsvertrag; ~ **control** Außenhandelskontrolle; ~ **dealings** Außenhandelsabschlüsse; ~ **deficit** Passivsaldo im Außenhandel, Defizit im Außenhandel, Außenhandelsdefizit; ~ **department** Außenhandelsstelle; ~ **documents** Außenhandelspapiere; ~ **equilibrium** ausgeglichene Außenhandelsbilanz, außenwirtschaftliches Gleichgewicht; ~ **financing** Export-, Außenhandelsfinanzierung; ~ **monopoly** Außenhandelsmonopol; ~ **multiplier** Exportmultiplikator; ~ **official** Außenhandelsbeamter; ~ **policy** Außenhandelspolitik; ~ **surplus** Außenhandelsüberfluß; ~ **and service transactions** Waren- und Dienstleistungsverkehr mit dem Ausland; ~ **zone** Zollausschlußgebiet, Freihandelszone.

foreign | trading, to carry out Außenhandelsgeschäfte durchführen; ~ **trading station** Faktorei; ~ **transaction** Auslandsgeschäft; ~ **travel (trip)** Auslandsreise; ~ **vacation** Auslandsurlaub; ~ **valuation** *(customs)* Auslandswert; ~ **visitor** Auslands-

besucher; **to attract ~ visitors** Fremdenverkehr heben; ~ **voyage** Auslands-, Überseereise; ~ **will** Testament eines Ausländers; ~ **word** Fremdwort; ~ **worker** Fremd-, Gastarbeiter.

foreigner Ausländer, Fremder, *(product)* Auslandsprodukt, ausländisches Erzeugnis, *(security of a ~ government, Br.)* Auslandsobligation, *(vessel)* ausländisches Schiff; ~**s** *(stock exchange)* Auslandswerte, ausländische Werte.

foreignism fremdes Idiom, *(situation)* Ausländerei.

foreignize *(v.)* nach ausländischen Mustern gestalten.

forejudge *(v.)* aberkennen, *(banish)* verbannen.

forejudger *(Br.)* Ausschußurteil.

foreland Vorgebirge, Kap.

forelock, to take time by the Gelegenheit beim Schopf ergreifen; **to touch s. one's ~** j. ehrfurchtsvoll begrüßen.

foreman Vorarbeiter, Werkmeister, -führer, *(jury)* Wortführer, Obmann, Sprecher;
shop ~ Werkmeister.

foremanship Werksführerposten;
~ **training** Vorarbeiterausbildung.

forementioned vorerwähnt.

forename Vorname.

forensic gerichtlich, forensisch;
~ **medicine** Gerichtsmedizin; ~ **opinion** gerichtsmedizinisches Gutachten; ~ **term** juristischer Fachausdruck, Gerichtsausdruck.

forerunner Vorläufer, -gänger.

foresee *(v.)* **trouble** Schwierigkeiten voraussehen.

foreseeability Voraussehbarkeit.

foreseeable event voraussehbares Ereignis.

foreshadowing indicator Frühindikator.

foreship Vorderschiff.

foreshore Küstenvorland, Watt, Strand, Gestade.

foreside *(US)* Küstenland, Strand.

forest Forst, Wald, *(franchise)* Jagdrecht;
high (matured) ~ Hochwald; **mixed ~** Mischwald; **national ~** Staatsforst;
~ **of masts** Wald von Schiffsmasten; ~**s stretching for miles and miles** sich kilometerweit hinziehende Wälder;
~ *(v.)* aufforsten;
to cut down ~s Wälder abholzen;
~ **administration** Forstverwaltung; ~ **area** Waldfläche; ~ **court** Forstgericht; ~ **cover** Waldbestand; ~ **damage** Forstschaden; ~ **dweller** Waldbewohner; ~ **economics** Forstwirtschaft; ~ **fire** Waldbrand; ~ **guard** Forstschutzbeamter; ~ **helper** Forstwart; ~ **land** Waldgebiet, -land, -grundstück, Wälder; ~ **law** Forstrecht; ~ **management** Forstverwaltung; ~ **officer** Forstbeamter, Förster; ~ **product** Forstprodukt; ~ **protection** Forstschutz; ~ **range** Forstbezirk; ~ **ranger** *(US)* Förster, Forstwart; ~ **reserve** *(US)* Waldschutzgebiet; ~ **school** Forstschule; ~ **sheriff** Forstschutzbeamter; ⚩ **Service** *(US)* Bundesforstverwaltung; ~ **warden** Forstamtmann.

forestall *(v.)* vorwegnehmen, zuvorkommen, *(buy up)* vor-, aufkaufen;
~ **a competitor** der Konkurrenz zuvorkommen; ~ **the highway** Straßenverkehr behindern; ~ **the market** durch Aufkäufe den Markt beherrschen; ~ **a plot** Verschwörung unterlaufen; ~ **a raid on the treasury** *(coll.)* einer Attacke auf die Staatskasse zuvorkommen.

forestaller Aufkäufer.

forestalling produktionsorientierte Wirtschaftspolitik, Vorwegnahme, *(obstructing the highway)* Straßenbehinderung;
~ **the market** Aufkaufen.

forestation Aufforstung.

forestcraft Forstarbeiter.

forester Förster, Forstfachmann.

forestry *(forest law)* Waldland, -gebiet, Wälder, Forstwirtschaft, -fach;
~ **building** Forstgebäude; ~ **company** Forstwirtschaftsbetrieb; ~ **land** Waldgebiet; ~ **plantation** Waldanpflanzung.

foretell *(v.)* vorhersagen, voraussagen, wahrsagen.

forethought Vorsorge, -bedacht.

foretoken Anzeichen, Vorbedeutung.

forewarn *(v.)* vorwarnen.

forewoman Vorarbeiterin.

foreword Vorwort.

forfeit *(breach of contract)* Reugeld, Vertragsstrafe, *(for breach of rules)* Geldstrafe, Buße, *(forfeiture)* Verwirkung, *(freight)* Fehlfracht, Fautfracht, *(thing lost)* verfallener Gegenstand, verwirktes Pfand;
~ **of civil rights** Verlust der bürgerlichen Ehrenrechte; ~ **paid for overworking** Strafe für übermäßige Arbeit;

~ (v.) verlieren, als Pfand verlieren, *(confiscate)* einziehen, konfiszieren, beschlagnahmen, *(fail to keep an obligation)* vertragsbrüchig werden;

~ one's bail (bond) Kaution verwirken (verfallen lassen); **~ one's credit** seinen Kredit (guten Ruf) verlieren; **~ one's driving licence** *(Br.)* Führerschein entzogen bekommen (verlieren); **~ an estate by treason** sein Vermögen auf Grund eines Hochverratsprozesses verlieren; **~ s. one's esteem** jds. Achtung verlieren; **~ one's health** seine Gesundheit ruinieren; **~ one's hono(u)r** seiner Ehre verlustig gehen; **~ one's life** sein Leben verwirken; **~ the good opinion of one's friends** in den Augen seiner Freunde verlieren; **~ a patent** Patent verfallen lassen; **~ a penalty** Vertragsstrafe verwirken; **~ one's place** seine Stellung verlieren; **~ one's reputation** seinen guten Ruf verlieren; **~ a pledge** Pfand für verfallen erklären; **~ a right** eines Anspruchs verlustig gehen; **~ the right to a pension** Ruhegehaltsanspruch verlieren; **~ a security** Sicherheitsleistung für verfallen erklären, Kaution einbüßen; **~ shares** Aktienanteile für verwirkt erklären (kaduzieren); **~ one's tenancy** seinen Mietvertrag verletzen; **~ one's voting rights** sein Stimmrecht verwirken;

to pay a ~ Pfand geben; **to pay as a ~** Reugeld bezahlen; **to relinquish the ~** *(stock exchange)* Prämie verwirken; **to sell s. th. with a ~** etw. mit Verlust verkaufen;

~ clause Verwirkungsklausel; **~ money** Reugeld, Abstandssumme.

forfeitable einziehbar, verwirkbar, konfiszierbar.

forfeitableness Verwirkbarkeit, Konfiszierbarkeit.

forfeited verwirkt, verfallen, erloschen, eingezogen, konfisziert;

to be ~ to the state vom Staat konfisziert werden; **to become ~** verfallen; **to declare ~** *(shares)* kaduzieren;

~ pledge verfallenes Pfand; **~ right** verwirktes Recht; **~ shares** kaduzierte Aktien.

forfeiture *(confiscation)* Konfiskation, Vermögenseinziehung, Verwirkung, Verlust, Verfall, *(criminal act)* Einziehung, *(thing forfeited)* eingezogener Gegenstand, *(fine)* Buße, Einbüßung, Geldstrafe, *(loss of corporate franchise)* Konzessionsverlust, *(loss of office)* Amtsverlust;

~ of bond Pfandverwirkung, -verfall; **~ of citizenship** Entziehung (Aberkennung) der Staatsangehörigkeit; **~ of condition** Wegfall einer Bedingung; **~ of deposit** Depotverlust; **~ of a lease** Pachtverfallsklausel; **~ of one's driving licence** *(Br.)* Entzug des Führerscheins; **~ of a patent** Patentlöschung; **~ of a pension** Verwirkung eines Pensionsanspruchs; **~ of one's property** Vermögenseinziehung, -konfiskation; **~ of a right** Rechtsverwirkung; **~ of civil rights** Aberkennung der bürgerlichen Ehrenrechte; **~ of a seniority rank (right)** Rangverlust; **~ of shares** Kaduzierung von Aktien; **~ of tenancy** Verletzung eines Mietverhältnisses;

~ clause Verfallklausel.

forgather *(v.)* zusammenkommen;

~ s. o. j. zufällig treffen.

forge *(v.)* [ver]fälschen, nachmachen, *(commit forgery)* falschmünzen, Fälschung begehen;

~ ahead *(stock exchange)* Führung übernehmen; **~ ahead 13 points to 567** um 13 Punkte auf 567 steigen, **~ a bank note** Banknote fälschen; **~ a bill** Wechsel fälschen; **~ a check** *(US)* (cheque, *Br.*) Scheck fälschen; **~ coins** Falschmünzerei betreiben, falschmünzen; **~ a document** Urkunde verfälschen; **~ news** falsche Nachricht aufbringen; **~ a passport** Paßfälschung begehen; **~ a promissory note** Wechsel fälschen; **~ a signature** Unterschrift fälschen; **~ a will** Testament unterschieben;

~ shop Fälscherwerkstatt; **~ test** Echtheitsprobe.

forged gefälscht, falsch, *(document)* verfälscht, untergeschoben;

~ check *(US)* (cheque, *Br.*) gefälschter Scheck; **to pass ~ coins (put ~ notes) into circulation** Falschgeld in Umlauf setzen; **~ money** Falschgeld; **to utter a ~ document** Falschurkunde in Umlauf setzen; **~ instrument** verfälschte Urkunde, Falschurkunde; **~ note** gefälschte Banknote; **~ trademark** nachgemachtes Warenzeichen; **² Transfer Act** *(Br.)* Entschädigungsgesetz im Fall von Aktienmanipulation; **~ will** gefälschtes (untergeschobenes) Testament; **to produce a ~ will** gefälschtes Testament vorlegen.

forger Fälscher, Falschmünzer;

bill ~ Wechselfälscher;

~ of bank notes Banknotenfälscher; **~ of bills** Wechselfälscher; **~ of coins** Falschmünzer; **~ of documents** Urkundenfälscher; **~ of a signature** Unterschriftenfälscher;

~'s shop Fälscherwerkstatt.

forgery [Urkunden]fälschung, *(forged article)* Falsifikat;

attempted ~ Fälschungsversuch; **bill ~** Wechselfälschung, *(US)* Banknotenfälschung;

~ of bank notes Banknotenfälschung; **~ of bills** Wechselfälschung, *(US)* Banknotenfälschung; **~ of checks** Scheckfälschung; **~ of documents** Urkundenfälschung; **~ of an endorsement** Indossamentenfälschung; **~ of an instrument** Urkundenfälschung; **~ of passport** Paßfälschung; **~ of signature** Unterschriftenfälschung; **~ of stamps** Wertzeichenfälschung;

to be found guilty of ~ der Fälschung für schuldig befunden werden; **to commit ~** Fälschung begehen; **to prove to be a ~** sich als Fälschung herausstellen; **to put in a plea of ~** Fälschung einwenden, Fälschungseinwand erheben;

~ insurance Versicherung gegen Scheckfälschung.

forging press Falschgelddruckerei.

forgive *(v.)* *(penalty)* erlassen;

~ s. o. a debt jem. eine Schuld erlassen.

forgo *(v.)* *(remit)* erlassen, verzichten auf.

forisfamiliate *(v.)* bei Lebzeiten abfinden, *(renounce further shares)* auf weitere Erbansprüche verzichten.

forisfamiliated abgefunden.

forisfamiliation Abfindung bei Lebzeiten.

forjudge *(v.)* s. o. of s. th. jem. etw. aberkennen.

fork | of a road Weggabelung;

~ (v.) *(road)* sich trennen (gabeln);

~ out (up) *(sl.)* Geld herausrücken, tief in die Tasche greifen, blechen; **~ out a lot of money to the collector of taxes** größere Geldbeträge für die Steuer aufbringen müssen;

~ lift (truck) Gabel-, Hubstapler.

forlorn hope *(mil.)* Himmelfahrtskommando.

form Form, Gestalt, Figur, *(behavio(u)r)* gesellschaftliche Form, Höflichkeitsform, *(bidding)* Angebotsblankett, -formular, *(criminal conviction, sl.)* Vorstrafenregister, *(custom)* Sitte, [Ge]brauch, *(document with blanks)* Formular, Formblatt, Vordruck, *(efficiency)* Zustand, körperliche Verfassung, Leistungsfähigkeit, *(formality)* Förmlichkeit, Formalität, *(formula)* Formel, *(grade, Br.)* Schulklasse, *(print.)* Druckform, *(system)* Anordnung, Schema, Methode, System, *(technics)* Modell, Schablone;

as a matter of ~ aus formellen Gründen; **contrary to ~** formwidrig; **in bearer ~** auf den Inhaber lautend; **in bad ~** unschicklich; **in due ~** vorschriftsmäßig, ordnungsgemäß, in gültiger (gehöriger) Form, formgerecht; **in due ~ of law** in der vom Gesetz vorgeschriebenen Form; **in the ~ hereinafter set forth** in der im folgenden rechtlich festgelegten Form; **in tabloid ~** in konzentrierter Form; **a little off-~** nicht ganz in Form; **valid in ~ and fact** formell und materiell gültig; **without shape or ~** formlos;

application ~ Antrags-, Anmelde-, Bewerbungsformular; **bad ~** schlechte Manieren; **blank ~** Formvordruck; **check** *(US)* **(cheque, *Br.*) ~** Scheckformular, -vordruck; **common ~** anerkannte Formulierung; **dead ~s** leere Formalitäten; **entry ~** Antragsformular; **first ~** *(Br., school)* unterste Schulklasse; **higher ~s** *(Br.)* höhere Schulklassen; **income-tax ~** Einkommensteuerformular; **inquiry ~** Fragebogen; **legal ~** gesetzlich vorgeschriebene Form; **listing ~** *(banking)* Sammelaufgabeformular, *(stock exchange)* Zulassungsformular; **order ~** Auftragsformular, Bestellschein; **printed ~** Vordruck, Formblatt, gedrucktes Formular; **question ~** Fragebogen; **receipt ~** Quittungsvordruck, -formular; **registration ~** Anmeldeformular, polizeilicher Anmeldeschein; **reporting ~** *(insurance)* Risikoformular; **requisite ~** gehörige Form; **school ~** *(Br.)* Schulklasse; **set ~** Muster; **sixth ~** *(school)* Prima, oberste Klasse; **statutory ~** gesetzlich vorgeschriebene Form; **telegraph ~** Telegrammformular; **upper ~s** *(Br.)* höhere Schulklassen;

~ of acknowledgement [Schuld]anerkenntnisformular; **~ of action** Prozeßform; **~s of address** Anredeformen, Höflichkeitsfloskeln; **~ of application** Antragsformular; **~ of assignment** Abtretungsformular, -vordruck; **~ of authority** Antworttelegrammformular; **~s of business organization (undertakings)** Unternehmensformen, Gesellschaftsformen; **~ of claim** Anspruchformular; **~ of collateral** Besicherungsform; **~ of a contract** Vertragsform; **ancient ~s observed at the coronation** seit jeher übliche Krönungsbräuche; **~s of a court** gerichtliche Formalitäten; **two-tier ~ of education** zweigleisiger Ausbildungsgang; **~ of an enterprise** Unternehmensform; **~ of expropriation** Enteignungsmaßnahme; **~ of government** Staats-, Regierungsform, -system; **~ required by law** gesetzlich vorgeschriebene Form; **~ of motion** Antragsform; **~ of notice** Benachrichtigungsform; **set ~ of an oath** vorgeschriebene Eidesformel; **~ of payment** Zahlungsmodus, -weise; **standard ~ for presentation of loss and damages claim** Einheitsformular für die Anmeldung von Entschädigungsansprüchen; **~s of legal**

procedure Verfahrensformen, Rechtsverfahrensregeln; **common ~s of probate** einfache Feststellung der Gültigkeit eines Testaments; **~ of proxy** schriftliche Stimmrechtsermächtigung, Vollmachts-, Depot-, Stimmrechtsformular; **~s of purchase** Bezugsformen; **~ for claiming repayment of tax** Steuerrückerstattungsformular; **~ of renunciation** Verzichtsformular; **~ of resolution** Beschlußform; **~ of return** Einkommensteuerformular; **~ of statement** Bewertungsformular; **~ of the statute** gesetzliche Vorschrift; **~ of tender** Submissionsbogen; **combined ~ of transfer and power of attorney** kombiniertes Übertragungs- und Vollmachtsformular; **~ of wording** Formulierung;

~ (v.) (make up) formen, gestalten, gründen, konstituieren; **~ an acquaintance** Bekanntschaft machen; **~ a cabinet** Regierung bilden; **~ a child's character** Charakter eines Kindes bilden; **~ a class for beginners in English** Klasse für englischen Erstunterricht zusammenstellen; **~ themselves into a committee** sich zu einem Ausschuß konstituieren; **~ a company (Br.)** Gesellschaft gründen; **~ doubts** Zweifel hegen; **~ an estimate** [ab]schätzen; **~ a government (Ministry)** Regierung bilden; **~ into** umwandeln; **~ into line (mil.)** sich formieren; **~ a judgment** sich ein Urteil bilden; **~ an opinion** sich eine Meinung bilden; **~ a plan** Plan entwickeln; **~ into rank** sich formieren; **~ one's style on good models** seinen Schriftstil nach guten Beispielen entwickeln; **~ up** sich formieren;

to alter the ~ of government Staatsform ändern; **to appear in full ~** in großer Besetzung erscheinen; **to be in capital (cracking) ~ (US)** schwer in Form sein; **not to be in ~ (US)** nicht in Form sein; **to be off ~** nicht in Form sein; **to be in good and due ~** in guter Verfassung sein; **to be very observant of ~** sehr auf Formen halten; **to complete a ~** Formular (Vordruck) ausfüllen; **to cure a defect of ~** Formmängel heilen; **to execute a common ~ of transfer** üblichen Übertragungsvordruck rechtsgültig ausfertigen; **to fill in (up, out, US) ~** Formular ausfüllen; **to go through a ~ of marriage** morganatische Ehe schließen; **to have a well-proportioned ~** wohlproportioniert sein; **to invite s. o. to ~ a ministry** j. um die Übernahme eines Ministeriums bitten; **to pay too much attention to ~** zu sehr auf Formen Wert legen; **to prove a will in common ~** Testamentsvollstreckerzeugnis erteilen; **to reduce to a ~** auf eine Form bringen; **to take ~** Gestalt annehmen;

~ catalog(u)e (library) Fachkatalog; **~s close (Br., advertising)** Anzeigenschluß; **~s composition** Formularsatz; **~ entry** Facheintrag; **~ filling** Formularausfüllung; **~ letter** Muster-, Standard-, Formularbrief; **~ master (Br.)** Klassenleiter; **~ mate (Br.)** Klassenkamerad; **~ requirements** Formerfordernisse; **~ room (Br.)** Klassenzimmer; **to do s. th. for ~'s sake** um der Form zu genügen handeln; **~ setter** Setzer; **~ utility** verarbeitungsbedingter Nutzen.

forma pauperis, in im Armenrecht.

formal offizielle Angelegenheit;
~ (a.) formal, formell, in gehöriger Form, offiziell, konventionell, **(express)** ausdrücklich, **(methodical)** akademisch, schulmäßig, methodisch;
~ application formeller Antrag; **~ call** offizieller (formeller) Besuch, Höflichkeits-, Antrittsbesuch; **~ close** formeller Briefabschluß; **~ contract** formbedürftiger Vertrag; **~ defect** Formfehler; **~ denial** offizielles Dementi; **~ dinner** offizielles Essen; **~ dress** Gesellschaftsabendanzug; **~ ending** Schlußformel; **~ opening sitting** förmliche Eröffnungssitzung; **~ prize distribution** offizielle Preisverteilung; **~ receipt** formelle Quittung; **~ requirements** Formvorschriften, -erfordernisse; **to make a ~ speech** offizielle Ansprache halten; **to issue a ~ statement** offizielle Erklärung herausgeben; **~ transfer of property** rechtsgültige Vermögensübertragung; **to give s. o. a ~ warning** j. offiziell verwarnen; **~ way of procedure** Verfahrensform.

formalism Formalismus.

formalist Formenmensch, -wesen.

formalistic formalistisch.

formalities, customs Zollformalitäten; **legal ~** gesetzliche Erfordernisse (Formalitäten); **passport ~** Paßförmlichkeiten; **~ of contract** Vertragserfordernisse, -formalitäten; **~ at the frontier** Kontrolle an der Grenze; **~ of a lease** Formvorschriften eines Pachtvertrages; **~ of a will** Testamentserfordernisse; **to be no stickler for ~** nicht auf Formalitäten bestehen; **to comply with all necessary ~** vorgeschriebene Formalitäten erfüllen; **to dispense with ~** auf Förmlichkeiten verzichten.

formality Formvorschrift, Förmlichkeit, Formalität;
for the sake of ~ aus formellen Gründen;
empty ~ bedeutungslose Formalität; **legal ~** Rechtsformalität; **a mere ~** lediglich eine Formsache;

to receive s. o. with frozen ~ j. mit kühler Höflichkeit empfangen.

format Format;
in coffee-table ~ als großformatige Luxusausgabe.

formation Gestaltung, Gründung, Errichtung, **(arrangement of parts)** Anordnung, Zusammensetzung, Struktur, **(development)** Entwicklung, **(mil.)** Verband, Formation;
in open ~ in offener Schlachtformation;
battle ~ Schlachtordnung; **capital ~** Kapitalbildung; **new word ~** Neuwortschöpfung; **wealth ~** Vermögensbildung;
~ of blocs (pol.) Blockbildung; **~ of cartels** Kartellbildung; **~ of character** Charakterbildung; **~ of classes** Klassenentwicklung; **~ of a coalition** Koalitionsbildung; **~ of a combine** Konzernbildung, -entstehung; **~ of a company (corporation, US)** Gesellschaftsgründung; **~ of a concept** Begriffsbildung; **~ of a contract** Vertragsabschluß; **~ of fog** Nebelbildung; **~ of government** Regierungsbildung; **~ of partnership** Gesellschaftsgründung; **~ of prices** Preisbildung, -gestaltung; **~ of a state** Staatsgründung; **~ of a subsidiary firm** Filialgründung;
~ expenses Gründungskosten, -aufwand; **~ flight** Formationsflug; **~ flying** Fliegen im Verband.

formative | process Bildungsvorgang; **~ stage** Entwicklungsstadium; **~ years** entscheidende Jahre der Entwicklung; **~ years of a child** Entwicklungsjahre eines Kindes.

formed | action Klage mit vorgeschriebener Formulierung; **~ design** Überlegung, Vorsatz.

former früher, ehemalig, vormalig;
~ adjudication Rechtskrafteinrede; **~ acquittal** Berufung auf früherer Entscheidung; **~ customs** frühere Bräuche; **~ jeopardy** verwirkter Strafanspruch;
to be a mere shadow of one's ~ self nur noch ein Schatten seines früheren Ichs sein; **~ students** ehemalige Studenten.

formless formlos.

formula Formel, Schema, Vorschrift, **(common-law practice)** Klageformel;
constitutional ~ Verfassungsvorschrift; **hackneyed ~s** stereotype Formeln; **legal ~** Gesetzesformel, -vorschrift; **price ~** Preisformel; **specified ~** fester Verteilungsschlüssel;
~ for compound present value Zinsformel;
to find a ~ acceptable to all parties für alle annehmbare Formulierung finden;
~ deal (motion picture distributors, US) Abrechnung zu landesdurchschnittlichen Verleihsätzen; **~ flexibility** indikatorgebundene wirtschaftspolitische Maßnahmen.

formularization Formulierung.

formulary vorgeschriebene Form, **(collection of formulars)** Formal-, Vordruckssammlung, Formularbuch, **(medicine)** Rezeptbuch;
~ of an oath Eidesformel;
~ (a.) vorgeschrieben, vorschriftsmäßig, förmlich.

formulate (v.) abfassen, formulieren;
~ a program(me) Programm aufstellen; **~ proposals** Vorschläge ausarbeiten; **~ one's thoughts** seine Gedanken formulieren.

formulation Formulierung, Abfassung;
obscure ~ unklare Formulierung;
~ of an oath Eidesformel; **~ of a plan** Ausarbeitung eines Planes; **~ of a question** Fragestellung.

formulism Formalismus.

forsake (v.) im Stich lassen;
~ wife and children Frau und Kinder verlassen; **~ smoking** zu Rauchen aufhören.

forswear (v.) leidlich bestreiten, unter Eid vernehmen;
~ o. s. falsch (Meineid) schwören;
~ bad habits schlechte Angewohnheiten aufgeben; **~ a debt** Schuldverpflichtung unter Eid zurückweisen.

forsworn witness meineidiger Zeuge.

fort (mil.) Fort, Festung;
to hold the ~ Stellung halten.

fortaxed halb besteuert.

forte (fig.) starke Seite, Stärke.

forthcoming Erscheinen, **(Scot., law)** Hauptprozeß nach Pfändung;
~ (a.) entgegenkommend, hilfreich;
~ bond Sicherheitsleistung des Vollstreckungsschuldners; **~ books** Neuerscheinungen; **~ negotiations** bevorstehende Verhandlungen; **~ session** nächste Sitzung.

forthwith ohne Verzug, sofort.

fortification Befestigung, **(mil.)** Festungswerk, Befestigungsanlage, Grenzbefestigung.

fortified city befestigte Stadt.

fortify *(v.) (fig.)* moralisch stärken, *(mil.)* befestigen, mit Festungswerken schützen;
~ o. s. against s. th. sich gegen etw. wappnen; ~ o. s. against a cold sich gegen eine Erkältung schützen.

fortitude Seelenstärke.

fortnight's holiday Zweiwochenurlaub.

fortnightly *(Br.)* halbmonatlich, zweiwöchentlich, vierzehntägig; ~ **bill** Mediowechsel; ~ **commitments** Mediofälligkeiten; ~ **continuation** Medioprolongation; ~ **loan** Mediogeld; ~ **payment** Halbmonatszahlung; ~ **review** Halbmonatsschrift; ~ **settlement** Medioarrangement, -abrechnung, -liquidation.

fortress Festung, Fort, *(fig.)* sicherer Ort, Hort;
virtually impregnable ~ praktisch uneinnehmbare Festung; to deliver up a ~ to the enemy Festung dem Feind übergeben; ~ **town** Festungsstadt.

fortuitous zufällig, zufallsbedingt, unvermeidbar;
~ **collision** zufallsbedingte Schiffskollision; ~ **event** *(law)* Zufall, zufälliges Ereignis.

fortunate Glückskind;
the less ~ die weniger vom Glück Gesegneten.

fortune *(event)* Glück, Glücksfall, Zufall, *(property)* Vermögen, Mittel, Besitz, Hab und Gut, *(wealth)* Reichtum, Wohlstand;
entire ~ gesamtes Vermögen; **Goddess** ~ Glücksgöttin; **great** ~ großes Vermögen; **handsome** ~ beträchtliches Vermögen; **modest** ~ bescheidenes Vermögen; **sizable** ~ erhebliches Vermögen; **small** ~ kleines Vermögen; **vast** ~ unermeßliche Reichtümer;
~ **impossible to estimate** unübersehbares Vermögen; ~ **in reversion** zu erwartendes Vermögen, Anwartschaftsvermögen; ~s **of war** Kriegsglück;
to come into (inherit) a ~ reiche Erbschaft machen, Vermögen erben; to dissipate one's ~ sein Vermögen verprassen; to have ~ on one's side Glück haben; to make a ~ Vermögen erwerben; to make one's ~ sein Glück machen; to make one's ~ after the war sein Vermögen nach dem Krieg erwerben; to make a ~ out of a business Vermögen bei einem Geschäft verdienen; to marry a ~ reich heiraten, gute Partie machen; to read s. one's ~ jem. wahrsagen; to run through one's ~ sein ganzes Vermögen durchbringen; to seek one's ~ in a new country sein Glück in der Fremde suchen; to spend a ~ over one's business enorm viel Geld in sein Geschäft stecken; to spend a small ~ on s. th. kleines Vermögen für etw. ausgeben; to spend a small ~ on books sein ganzes Geld in Büchern anlegen; to try one's ~ sein Glück versuchen;
~ **hunter** Mitgiftjäger; ~ **hunting** Mitgiftjagd; ~ **seeker** Glücksritter; ~ **sheet** Aufstiegsmöglichkeitstabelle; ~ **teller** Wahrsager; ~**-telling** *(Br.)* Wahrsagen, Kartenlegen.

forty | **eight sheet poster** Mammutplakat; ~**-hour week** Vierzigstundenwoche; ~ **winks** *(coll.)* kleines Nickerchen.

forum Gerichtsort, örtliche Zuständigkeit, *(law)* Gerichtshof, Tribunal, *(public meeting, US)* Diskussionsveranstaltung;
~ **contractus** Gerichtsstand des Erfüllungsortes; ~ **domicili** Wohnsitzgerichtsstand; ~ **rei sitae** Belegenheitsgerichtsstand.

forward *(advanced)* fortgeschritten, *(stock exchange)* auf Ziel (Zeit);
balance carried ~ Saldovortrag; brought ~ Übertrag; charges ~ unter Nachnahme der Spesen; freight ~ Frachtbezahlung bei Warenankunft; please ~ bitte nachsenden; sum brought ~ Übertrag;
~ *(v.) (dispatch)* absenden, befördern, versenden, zusenden, expedieren, *(hasten)* beschleunigen, *(send on)* weiterbefördern, nachsenden;
~ **a new catalog(u)e** neuen Katalog versenden; ~ **by express train** als Eilgut befördern (versenden); ~ **goods by airfreight** Waren per Luftfracht versenden; ~ **goods to a customer** Kunden beliefern; ~ **goods to the market** Markt beschicken; ~ **goods by post** *(Br.)* **(mail,** *US)* Waren mit der Post befördern; ~ **letters to a new address** Briefe nachsenden; ~ **the mail** *(US)* Post expedieren; ~ **opinions** Ansichten äußern; ~ **s. one's plans** jds. Pläne fördern; ~ **by rail** mit der Bahn versenden;
to be ~ to help others hilfsbereit sein, anderen helfen; to be well ~ with one's work mit seiner Arbeit gut vorankommen; to bring ~ vorbringen; to bring ~ some new evidence neues Beweismaterial vorlegen; to buy ~ auf Lieferung (Zeit) kaufen; to carry ~ [Saldo] vortragen; to come ~ *(creditors)* sich melden; to date a check *(US)* (cheque, *Br.)* ~ Scheck vordatieren; to go ~ *(fig.)* Fortschritte machen; to sell ~ für zukünftige Lieferung (auf Zeit) verkaufen;
~ **account** Terminkonto; ~ **business** *(stock exchange)* Termingeschäft; ~ **buyer** Terminkäufer; ~ **buying** Terminkauf; ~ **cabin** Vorderkajüte; ~ **contract** Terminabschluß; ~ **cover** Kurssiche-

rung; ~ **crop** frühe Ernte; ~ **deal** *(Br.)* Zeit-, Termingeschäft; ~ **dealing** Devisentermingeschäft; ~ **delivery** Terminlieferung; ~ **dollar** Termindollar; ~ **exchange** Termindevisen, Devisenterminhandel; ~ **exchange deals** Devisentermingeschäfte; ~ **exchange market** Devisenterminmarkt; ~ **exchange operations** Devisenterminhandel, -geschäft; ~ **exchange rate** Devisenterminkurs; ~ **exchange transaction** Devisentermingeschäft; ~ **guaranty** Kurssicherung; ~ **integration** vertikales Betriebswachstum; ~ **linkage** absatzmäßige Verflechtung; ~ **line of defended localities** *(mil.)* Hauptkampflinie; ~ **market** Terminmarkt; ~ **money** Festgeld; ~ **movement** allgemeine Aufwärtsbewegung; ~ **operation** Termingeschäft; ~ **opinion** aufgeschlossene Ansichten; ~ **order** Terminauftrag; ~ **planning** Zukunftsplanung; ~ **price** Preis für künftige Lieferung; ~ **protest** voreiliger Protest; ~ **purchase** Kauf auf Zeit, Terminkauf; ~ **quotation** Terminnotierung; ~ **rate** Devisenterminkurs, Terminsatz; ~ **sale** Terminverkauf, Verkauf auf Lieferung; ~ **seat** Vordersitz; ~ **securities** Terminwerte, -papiere; ~ **seller** Terminverkäufer; ~ **statesman** aufgeschlossener Staatsmann; ~ **stock** Lagervorrat in der Verkaufsabteilung; ~ **strategy** *(mil.)* Verteidigung in der vordersten Linie, Vorwärtsstrategie; ~ **thinking** progressives Denken; ~ **transaction** Zeit-, [Devisen]termingeschäft; ~ **transactions in securities** Wertpapierterminhandel.

forwarded | **by** *(letter)* Absender;
to be ~ bitte nachsenden; not to be ~ nicht nachsenden;
~ **exchange deals** *(Br.)* Devisenterminhandel, -geschäft; ~ **goods** Versandwaren; ~ **telegram** nachgesandtes Telegramm.

forwarder [Ab]sender, *(merchant, US)* Beförderer, Spediteur;
freight ~ Güterexpedition;
~'s **note of charges** Speditionsrechnung; ~'s **receipt** Übernahmebescheinigung des Spediteurs.

forwarding *(book)* technische Vorbereitung, *(dispatch)* Versendung, Verschickung, Absendung, Übersendung, Versand, Expedition, Spedition, Beförderung, Abfertigung, *(sending on)* [Weiter]beförderung, Nachsendung;
international ~ internationale Spedition;
~ **of goods** Güterbeförderung, -transport; ~ **by rail** Bahnversand;
~ **address** Versandadresse; ~ **advice** Versandanzeige; ~ **agency** *(US)* Spediteur, Speditionsgesellschaft, -unternehmen, Versandbüro, -unternehmen; ~**agent** Spediteur; ~ **agent's certificate of receipt (FCR)** Übernahmebescheinigung des Spediteurs; ~ **book** Versandbuch; ~ **business** Transport-, Speditionsgeschäft, -gewerbe, Transportwesen; ~ **carrier** Absendespediteur, Absender; ~ **charges** Versandspesen, Speditionsgebühren; ~ **clerk** Expedient; ~ **commission** Speditionsgebühr; ~ **company** Transportgesellschaft; ~ **costs** Beförderungskosten; ~ **department** Versand-, Expeditionsabteilung; ~ **document** Frachtpapiere; ~ **expenses** Versandspesen, Speditionsgebühren; ~ **firm** Versand-, Speditionsgeschäft; ~ **house** Spediteur, Speditionsfirma, -betrieb; ~ **instructions** Versandvorschriften, -anweisungen, Transport-, Beförderungsanweisungen, -vorschriften, Leitwegangaben; ~ **merchant** *(US)* Spediteur; ~ **note** Versandmitteilung, Frachtbrief, Speditionsauftrag; ~ **office** Speditionsbüro, Abfertigungsstelle, Güterabfertigung, Expeditionsabteilung, *(railway)* Weiterleitungsstelle; ~ **point** Versandort, Abgangsbahnhof; ~ **route** Beförderungs-, Versandweg; ~ **schedule** Versandplan; ~ **station** Versandbahnhof, -station; ~ **terms** Versandbedingungen, -bestimmungen; ~ **trade** Speditionsgewerbe.

foster *(v.)* pflegen, fördern, begünstigen;
~ **the growth of heavy industries** Entstehung der Schwerindustrie begünstigen; ~ **a monopoly** Monopol fördern;
~ **brother** Pflegebruder; ~ **child** Pflegekind; ~ **daughter** Adoptiv-, Pflegetochter; ~ **father** Adoptivvater; ~ **home** Pflegeheim; ~ **mother** Adoptiv-, Pflegemutter; ~ **parents** Pflegeeltern; ~ **son** Pflege-, Adoptivsohn.

fosterage *(fig.)* Förderung, Pflege, Anregung.

fosterer Förderer.

foul Kollision, Zusammenstoß;
~ *(a.)* schmutzig, unrein, unsauber, stinkend, verpestet, übelriechend, *(berth)* ungünstig, *(coast)* gefährlich, *(print.)* unsauber, *(road)* verschmiert, *(rotten)* abscheulich, schlecht, verderbt, böse, *(ship)* in Kollision, *(unfair)* unehrlich, *(water)* verdorben, schlecht;
through ~ and fair durch dick und dünn; by fair means or ~ auf anständige oder unredliche Weise, auf jeden Fall;
~ *(v.) (run foul)* zusammenstoßen, beschmutzen, beflecken;
~ **a cable** Kabel verwickeln; ~ **s. one's name** jds. guten Ruf beschmutzen; ~ **a ship's course** Schiffskurs behindern;

to fall (run) ~ of the law mit dem Gesetz in Schwierigkeiten geraten; **to fight** ~ Spielregeln verletzen; **to make the air** ~ Luft verpesten; **to play s. o.** ~ j. hintergehen; **to run** ~ **of each other** *(ships)* zusammenstoßen; **to run** ~ **of a car** mit einem Auto zusammenstoßen;
~ **air** schlechte Luft, *(mining)* gebrauchte Wetter; ~ **bill of health** Gesundheitspaß mit Einschränkungen; ~ **bill of lading** einschränkendes (unreines) Konnossement; ~ **bottom** bewachsener Schiffsboden; ~ **case** *(print.)* verrutschter Buchstabe; ~ **chimney** verrußter Schornstein; ~ **copy** unsaubere Abschrift; ~ **deed** Infamie, Schandtat; ~ **means** unredliche Mittel; ~ **page** *(print.)* Schmutzseite; ~ **paper** Konzept, Strazze; ~ **play** Nichteinhalten der Spielregeln, verräterische Handlungsweise; ~ **player** Falschspieler; ~ **practices** Betrügereien; ~ **prison cell** schmutzige Gefängniszelle; ~ **proof** *(print.)* unkorrigierter Abzug; ~ **spoken** verleumderisch; ~ **weather** schlechtes (stürmisches) Wetter; ~ **wind** Gegenwind; ~ **words** obszöne Wörter.

found *(US)* inkl. Unterkunft und Verpflegung;
all ~ *(Br.)* freie Station; **not** ~ *(post office)* unauffindbar;
~ *(a.)* *(enterprise)* geschäftlich vertreten, *(person)* angetroffen, *(ship)* bevorratet;
~ **committing** auf frische Tat ertappt; ~ **within the district** im Gerichtsbezirk festgenommen; ~ **on premises** im Lokal angetroffen;
~ *(v.)* stiften, *(set up)* gründen, bauen, errichten;
~ **a chair** neuen Lehrstuhl errichten; ~ **a new city** Stadt gründen; ~ **an entail** Majorat errichten (stiften); ~ **a family** Familie gründen; ~ **a fortune** Grundlage für ein Vermögen legen; ~ **an opinion** Ansicht basieren; ~ **a scholarship** Stipendium stiften; ~ **a school** Stiftsschule errichten.

foundation Gründung, Gründungsakt, [Firmen]errichtung, Bildung, *(basement)* Unterlage, -bau, *(building)* Grundlegung, *(donation)* Schenkung, Fonds, Stipendium, *(endowed institution)* Anstalt, Stiftung, *(place of abode)* Niederlassung, erster Wohnsitz, *(supporting part)* Fundierung, *(theory)* Basis, Grundstock;
devoid of any ~ jeder Grundlage entbehrend; **on a steady** ~ auf sicherer Grundlage;
charitable ~ milde Stiftung, Stift; **richly endowed** ~ reich dotierte Stiftung; **private** ~ private Stiftung; **Rockefeller** ~ Rockefellerstiftung; **solid** ~ solide Grundlage;
~**s of a block of flats** Mietshauserrichtung; ~ **of a family** Familiengründung; ~ **of a house** Grundsteinlegung; ~**s of modern society** Grundlagen (Fundament) der modernen Gesellschaft; **to be on a** ~ von einer Stiftung leben, Stipendium haben, Stipendiat sein; **to be without any** ~ völlig unbegründet sein; **to exhibit a** ~ Stipendium ausschreiben; **to have no** ~ jeder Grundlage entbehren; **to lay the** ~ Grundstein legen; **to lay the** ~ **of a building** Fundament für ein Gebäude errichten; **to lay the** ~ **of a business** Geschäftsvoraussetzungen schaffen; **to lay the** ~**s of one's career** Grundstein für seine spätere Entwicklung legen; **to put s. o. on a** ~ jem. ein Stipendium gewähren; **to shake the** ~**s of society** Grundlagen der Gesellschaft erschüttern;
~ **block** Fundamentblock; ~ **board** Stiftungsamt; ~ **building** Stiftung, Stiftungsgebäude; ♀ **Day** Gründungstag; ~ **executives** Stiftungsvorstand; ~**'s income** Stiftungseinkünfte; ~ **school** Stiftsschule, Schulstiftung; ~ **stone** Grundstein; **to lay the** ~ **stone** Grundsteinlegung vornehmen.

foundationer *(Br.)* Stipendiat, Freiplatzinhaber, Freischüler.
founded | **on an affidavit** eidesstattlich glaubhaft gemacht; ~ **on a consideration** auf einer Gegenleistung beruhend; ~ **on contract** vertraglich begründet; ~ **on facts** auf Tatsachen beruhend, stichhaltig; ~ **in fraud** auf Betrug beruhend; ~ **in tort** aus unerlaubter Handlung;
to be ~ beruhen; **to be** ~ **on documents** urkundlich nachgewiesen sein.

founder Stifter, Gründer;
~ **of a business (firm)** Firmengründer;
~ *(v.)* *(fig.)* fehlschlagen, mißlingen, scheitern, *(ship)* sinken, verlorengehen;
to be the ~ **of a dynasty** Dynastie begründen;
~ **member** Gründungsmitglied; ~ **state** Gründerstaat.
founder's | **family** Gründerfamilie; ~ **meeting** konstituierende General-, Gründerversammlung; ~ **preference rights** Gründerrechte; ~ **profit** Gründergewinn; ~ **shares (stocks,** *US)* Gründeraktien, -anteile.
founding | **of subsidiaries** Filialgründung;
~ **body** Gründungsgremium; ~ **father** Begründer des Reichtums.
foundling Findling, Findelkind;
~ **hospital** Findlingsheim.

foundress Gründerin, Stifterin.
foundry [Schrift]gießerei;
~ **flimsy** Schriftgießereiabzug; ~ **proof** Revisionsabzug; ~ **type** Originalschrift für Handsatz.
fount Ölbehälter, *(fig.)* Born, *(print, Br.)* Schriftart;
~ **of all knowledge** *(coll.)* Universalgenie.
fountain Quelle, Brunnen, *(fig.)* Quelle, Ursprung;
~ **of wisdom** Weisheitsbrunnen; ~ **of youth** Jungbrunnen;
~ **pen** Füll[feder]halter.
fountainhead of all knowledge Quelle alles Wissens.
four, to be on all ~**s** *(law case)* mit einem früheren Rechtsstreit identisch (gleichgelagert) sein;
~~**colo(u)r block** Farbätzung; ~~**colo(u)r printing (process)** Vierfarbendruck; ~ **corners of an instrument** Urkundentext; ~ **corners of the world** entlegendste Gegenden der Welt; ~~**cycle engine** Viertaktmotor; ~~**cylinder motor** Vierzylindermotor; **to have an income of** ~ **figures** vierstelliges Einkommen haben; **the** ~ **hundred** *(US)* die oberen Zehntausend, Hautevolée; ~~**laned** vierspurig; ~~**letter word** obszönes Wort; **to get a** ~~**penny one** *(airplane, Br., sl.)* abgeschossen werden; ~~**power conference** Viermächtekonferenz; ~~**seater** *(car)* Viersitzer; ~~**wheel drive** Vierradantrieb.
fourth | **[bill] of exchange** Quartalswechsel; ~~**class matter** *(US)* Warensendungen, Paketpost; ~ **estate** *(Br.)* Presse, Zeitungswesen; ~ **grader** Viertkläßler;
fourteenth Amendment *(US, constitution)* Grundrechteanhang.
fowl Geflügel, Federvieh.
fox *(fig.)* Fuchs, Schlaukopf;
to set the ~ **to keep the geese** Bock zum Gärtner machen.
foxhole *(mil.)* Deckungsunterstand.
foyer Wandelhalle, -gang, Foyer.
fraction Bruch[teil], Fragment, *(communism)* Spaltergruppe;
by a ~ **of an inch** um Haaresbreite, mit knapper Not; **for the small** ~ **of a second** für einen Sekundenbruchteil;
improper ~ unechter Bruch; **proper** ~ echter Bruch; **vulgar** ~ gewöhnlicher Bruch;
~ **of the market** Marktanteil;
to escape death by a ~ **of an inch** um Bruchstücke dem Tod entgehen;
~ **stroke** Bruchstrich.
fractional geringfügig, unbedeutend, minimal;
~ **amount** Bruchteil; ~ **arithmetic** Bruchrechnung; ~ **bond** Teilschuldverschreibung; ~ **certificate** *(Br.)* Bruchteilsaktie; ~ **changes** *(stock exchange)* Veränderungen um Bruchteile eines Punktes, geringfügige Veränderungen; ~ **coin** Scheidemünze; ~ **coins** *(US)* Kleingeld; ~ **currency** *(US)* Scheidemünze; ~ **interest** Bruchteilswert, -anspruch; ~ **lot** *(US fam.)* nicht an der Börse gehandelte Abschnitte, *(New York stock exchange)* Paket mit weniger als 100 Aktien (Obligationen unter $ 1000 Nennwert); ~ **money** *(US)* Geldstücke unter Dollarwert; ~ **number** Bruchzahl; ~ **part** Bruchteil; ~ **reserves** *(banking)* vorgeschriebene Mindestreserven; ~ **share** Bruchteilsaktie, kleingestückelte Aktie; ~ **value** Bruchteilswert.
fractionalist Parteispalter, Abweichler.
fractionally, to lose abbröckeln.
fractionist *(communism)* Abweichler.
Fragile! Vorsicht! Zerbrechlich!
fragile *(ice)* brüchig;
~ **articles** Bruchwaren; ~ **health** schwache Gesundheit.
fragment Bruchstück, Überrest, Fragment;
~**s of a conversation** Brüchstücke einer Unterhaltung; ~ **of a fortune** Vermögensrest; ~**s of a meal** Überreste eines Mahles; ~ **appropriations** Geldbewilligung in Etappen.
fragmentary bruchstückartig, fragmentarisch;
~ **report** fragmentarischer Bericht.
frail zer-, gebrechlich;
~ **support** schwache Unterstützung.
frame Rahmen, Einrahmung, Umrandung, *(film)* Einzelbild, *(person)* Bezugrahmen, *(print.)* Schriftkasten, *(ship)* Gerippe, *(statistics)* Auswahlgrundlage, *(system)* Gefüge, System, Anordnung, Gebilde, *(statistics)* Auswahl-, Erhebungsgrundlage, *(television)* Rasterbild;
mortal ~ sterbliche Hülle;
~ **of mind** Gemüts-, Geistesverfassung; ~ **of reference** Bezugsrahmen, -system; ~ **of a writ** Form einer gerichtlichen Verfügung;
~ *(v.)* gestalten, bilden, *(devise falsely, sl.)* intrigieren, wühlen, *(print.)* [Satz] einfassen, *(words)* ausdrücken, formen;
~ **an accusation against s. o.** *(sl.)* Anschuldigungen gegen j. konstruieren; ~ **badly** sich ungünstig entwickeln; ~ **an estimate** Überschlag machen; ~ **a photograph** Photographie einrahmen;

~ **a plan** Plan entwerfen; ~ **a sentence** Satz formulieren; ~ **a ship** Schiffsgerippe bauen; ~ **a speech** Rede aufsetzen (entwerfen); ~ **a theory** Theorie aufstellen; ~ **up** (coll.) ausfeilen, einfädeln; ~ **well** (child) sich gut entwickeln;

to be in a cheerful ~ of mind bester Laune sein;

~ **aerial** Rahmenantenne; ~ **house** (US) Fachwerkhaus; ~ **story** Rahmengeschichte, -handlung; ~**-up** (US sl.) Machenschaften, Ränkespiel, abgekartetes Spiel, Komplott.

framed text umrandeter Text.

framer Verfasser.

framework Fachwerk, Rahmenwerk, Gerüst, (fig.) System, Gefüge, Rahmen, (waggon) Gestell;

conceptual ~ begrifflicher Bezugsrahmen; **legal ~** gesetzlicher Rahmen; **social ~** soziales Gefüge;

~ **of government** Regierungssystem; ~ **of society** Gesellschaftssystem;

to come within the ~ of a constitution unter eine Verfassung fallen;

~ **body** (airplane) Fachwerkrumpf.

framing Einfassung, -rahmung, (television) Bildeinstellung.

franchise (sole agency, US) Alleinverkaufsrecht, (asylum) Freistätte, Asyl, Zufluchtsort, (constitution) Verfassungs-, Grundrecht, (freedom of a city) Bürgerrecht, Freiheit, (Br., insurance) Mindestgrenze, Selbstbehalt, (licensing, US) Lizenz[vergabe], -betrieb, Konzessionserteilung, (privilege) Vorrecht, Sonderstellung, Privileg, Gerechtsame, (right of suffrage) aktives Wahl-, Stimmrecht, Wahlfähigkeit, -berechtigung, (taxation) Abgabefreiheit, (territory) Freibezirk;

elective ~ allgemeines Wahlrecht; **exclusive ~** (US) Alleinverkaufsrecht, -vertretung; **general ~** Rechtsfähigkeit; **household ~** (Br.) Stimmrecht des Haushaltungsvorstands; **local-government ~** (Br.) Wahlrecht für Kommunalwahlen; **personal ~** Verleihung der Rechtsfähigkeit; **preliminary ~** (US) Vorkonzession; **secondary (special) ~** (US) Konzessionsgewährung; ~ **for a bus service** Konzession für eine Omnibuslinie; ~ **of corporation** (US) Rechtspersönlichkeitsverleihung; ~ **de l'hôtel** Unverletzlichkeit des Gesandtschaftsgebäudes;

~ (v.) (US) Konzession verleihen, konzessionieren;

to have the ~ (Br.) Wahlrecht haben;

~ **agent** (US) Lizenzvertreter; ~ **agreement** (US) Lizenz-, Konzessionsvertrag; ~ **broker** (US) Lizenzmakler; ~ **business** (US) Konzessions-, Lizenzwesen; ~ **clause** (insurance, Br.) Frei-, Bagatell-, Selbstbehaltsklausel; ~ **company** (US) Lizenzabgabegesellschaft, Lizenzgeber; ~ **consultant** (US) Lizenzberater; ~ **dealer** (US) Lizenznehmer; ~ **field** (US) Konzessions-, Lizenzwesen; ~ **legislation** (US) Lizenzgesetzgebung; **to run a ~ operation** (US) Lizenzvertretung besitzen; ~ **operator** (US) Werbeflächenpächter an öffentlichen Verkehrsmitteln; ~ **owner** (US) Konzessionsinhaber; ~ **registration** (US) Lizenzregistrierung; ~ **registration statement** (US) Lizenzregistrierungserklärung; ~ **satellite** (US) lizensierte Tochtergesellschaft; ~ **seminar** (US) Generalvertreterseminar; **to supply ~ service** (US) Dienste einer Generalvertretung zur Verfügung stellen; ~ **show** (US) Lizenzmesse; ~ **sites** (US) Konzessionsgelände; ~ **tax** (US) Konzessionsabgabe.

franchised konzessioniert;

~ **distributor** (US) Generalvertreter.

franchisee (US) Konzessionsinhaber, -nehmer, Lizenznehmer, -inhaber.

franchiser (US) Lizenz-, Konzessionsvergeber, (privileged person) Privilegierter, (voting) stimmberechtigter Bürger.

franchising (US) Lizenz-, Konzessionserteilung, Konzessionierung, Lizenzvertretung, Alleinvertretung;

~ **industry** (US) Konzessionswesen.

frank Portofreiheit, (indication of ~) Franko-, Freivermerk, (letter sent free) portofreier Brief;

~ (a.) offen, freimütig, geradezu;

~ (v.) freimachen, portofrei machen, freistempeln, frankieren, (facilitate passage) freie Fahrt gewähren, (taxation) von der Steuer befreien;

~**-almoigne** Kirchenfreigut; ~ **bank** (Br.) Wittum; ~**-chase** Jagdduldung; ~ **concession of one's guilt** freimütiges Schuldeingeständnis; ~ **tenement** freies Grundeigentum.

franked | dividends nach Zahlung der Körperschaftssteuer gezahlte Dividenden; ~ **investment income** (Br.) nicht der Körperschaftssteuer unterliegende Kapitalerträge, körperschaftssteuerfreie Kapitalerträge, Kapitalerträge nach Steuerabzügen; ~ **payments** (Br.) körperschaftssteuerfreie Zahlungen, nach Steuerabzug geleistete Zahlungen.

franking Freimachung, Frankierung;

~ **of letters** (M.P.) Freimachungsprivileg;

~ **machine** (Br.) Freimachungs-, Frankiermaschine, Freistempler mit werblichem Aufdruck; ~ **privilege** (US) Portofreiheit, frei durch Ablösung; ~ **stamp** Briefmarkenstempel.

frankness to the point of insult schon bald an Beleidigung grenzende Offenheit.

frantic ungestüm, rasend;

to have a ~ amount to do schrecklich viel zu tun haben; ~ **applause** frenetischer Beifall; ~ **efforts** wilde Anstrengungen.

fraternal | association (US) Verein zur Förderung gegenseitiger Interessen; ~ **fighting** Brüderkrieg; ~ **group** Gemeinschaft; ~ **insurance** (US) Versicherungsverein auf Gegenseitigkeit, Sterbekasse; ~ **society** Verein zur Förderung gegenseitiger Interessen.

fraternity Bruderschaft, (American college) Studentenvereinigung, (union) Vereinigung, Interessengemeinschaft;

critical ~ Zunft der Kritiker;

~ **of the press** Journalistenvereinigung.

fraternization Verbrüderung, Fraternisierung.

fraternize (v.) sich verbrüdern, fraternisieren.

fraud Irreführung, betrügerisches Verhalten, Unterschlagung, Betrug;

actionable ~ arglistige Täuschung; **actual ~** vollendeter Betrug; **attempted ~** Betrugsversuch; **business ~** betrügerisches Geschäftsgebaren; **concealed ~** von vornherein beabsichtigter Betrug; **constructive (equitable) ~** Untreue, Unterschlagung, (law of contract) sittenwidriges Geschäft; **legal ~** Untreue; **moral ~** arglistige Täuschung; **pious ~** frommer Betrug; **tax ~** Steuerhinterziehung;

~ **on creditors** Gläubigerbetrug, -benachteiligung; ~ **in fact** vollendeter Betrug; ~ **on the minority** Benachteiligung einer Minderheit; ~ **in law** Untreue; ~ **on a power** betrügerischer Gebrauch einer Vollmacht; ~ **in treaty** betrügerische Ausstellung einer Urkunde;

to be guilty of ~ sich des Betrugs schuldig machen; **to commit a ~** Betrug begehen, betrügen; **to constitute a ~** Betrugstatbestand erfüllen; **to get money by ~** Geld auf betrügerische Weise erlangen; **to obtain by ~** erschleichen; **to perpetrate a ~ on the court** Gericht irreführen; **to prevent ~** (taxes) Steuerhinterziehung verhindern; **to show up a ~** Betrug entlarven;

~ **case** Betrugsfall; ~ **order** (post) Beförderungsverbot.

fraudulence of an action betrügerische Handlung.

fraudulency Betrügerei.

fraudulent betrügerisch, (dolose) arglistig, bösgläubig, -willig, dolos;

~ **act** Vertrauensmißbrauch; ~ **activity** betrügerische Handlung; ~ **alienation** Vollstreckungsvereitelung; ~ **alienee** bevorzugter Konkursgläubiger, (estate) bösgläubiger [Nachlaß]erwerber; ~ **assignment** Veräußerung mit dem Ziel der Gläubigerbenachteiligung; ~ **balance sheet** gefälschte Bilanz; ~ **bankrupt** betrügerischer Bankrotteur; ~ **bankruptcy** betrügerischer Bankrott, Konkursverbrechen; ~ **breach of trust** Untreue; ~ **clause** in arglistiger Absicht eingefügte Bestimmung; ~ **concealment** arglistiges Verschweigen; ~ **conversion** Veruntreuung, Unterschlagung; ~ **conveyance** Gläubigerbenachteiligung; **to make a ~ conveyance** [Konkurs]gläubiger benachteiligen; ~ **creditor** unredlicher Gläubiger; ~ **dealing** Betrugsmanöver; ~ **entry** Falschbuchung; ~ **gains** betrügerische Gewinne; ~ **impression** unerlaubter Nachdruck; **with ~ intent** in betrügerischer Absicht; ~ **misrepresentation** arglistige Täuschung, Vorspiegelung falscher Tatsachen; ~ **nature** Betrugscharakter; ~ **party** Betrüger; ~ **practices** betrügerische Machenschaften; ~ **preference** Gläubigerbegünstigung; **for ~ purposes** in Betrugsabsicht; ~ **removal** heimliches Entfernen [der Mietsachen]; ~ **representation** Vorspiegelung falscher Tatsachen; ~ **trading** betrügerische Geschäftsgebarung, Kundenbenachteiligung; ~ **transaction** Schwindelgeschäft; ~ **transfer** Übertragung des Schuldnervermögens mit dem Ziel der Gläubigerbenachteiligung.

fraudulently in betrügerischer Weise.

freak Laune, plötzliche Einfälle, (printing) Fehldruck;

~ **storm** ungewöhnlich heftiger Sturm.

free frei, befreit, (exempt) befreit, ausgenommen, verschont, (independent) frei, selbständig, unabhängig, ungebunden, (openhanded) freigebig, großzügig, (mar.) günstig, (unrestrained) uneingeschränkt, ungezwungen, zwanglos, (without cost) frei, gebührenfrei, spesenfrei, kostenlos, (not subject to a parent or guardian) volljährig;

accident-~ unfallfrei; **carriage-~** Fracht bezahlt; **cost-~** frei von allen Kosten; **duty-~** zollfrei; **fancy-~** frei und ungebunden; **post-~** portofrei; **postage ~** freigemacht; **rent-~** mietfrei; **tax-~** steuerfrei;

~ **on aircraft** frei an Bord des Flugzeugs; ~-**for-all** *(coll.)* allgemein zugänglicher Wettbewerb; ~ **alongside ship (vessel)** frei Längsseite Schiff; ~ **astray** keine besonderen Gebühren für fehlgeleitete Sendungen; ~ **of all average** nicht gegen große und besondere Havarie versichert; ~ **of average** frei von Havarie; ~ **from particular average** ~ frei von Teilhavarie; ~ **on bail** gegen Kaution (Bürgschaft) freigelassen; ~ **board amidships** frei Bord mittschiffs; ~ **on board (fob)** fob, franko Bord, frei Schiff, *(US)* frei Eisenbahn; ~ **on board and trimmed** frei an Bord und gestaut; ~ **from breakage** bruchfrei; ~ **from break and damage** frei von Bruch und Beschädigung; ~ **at building site** frei Baustelle; ~ **from business** unbeschäftigt; ~ **of debt** schuldenfrei; ~ **of capture and seizure** frei von Aufbringung und Beschlagnahme, Beschlagnahmerisiko ausgeschlossen; ~ **of [all] charge** kostenfrei, kostenlos, spesenfrei, gebührenfrei, unentgeltlich; ~ **of charge and postage paid** gratis und franko; ~ **and clear** *(estate)* frei und unbelastet, frei von Rechten Dritter; ~ **of commission** provisionsfrei, franko Provision; ~ **of the company of gentlemen** gesellschaftlich akzeptiert; ~ **of cost** kostenfrei; ~ **of customs duty** zollfrei; ~ **of damage** unbeschädigt, Schaden nicht zu unseren Lasten; ~ **of debt** schuldenfrei; ~ **from all deductions** ohne Abzüge jeder Art; ~ **from defects** mangel-, fehlerfrei; ~ **delivered** franko Bestimmungsort; ~ **docks** frei ab Kai; ~ **against documents** frei gegen Lieferschein; ~ **to the door** frei Haus; ~ **of duty** abgaben-, steuer-, zollfrei; ~ **and easy** frei und ungezwungen; ~ **from encumbrances** frei von Belastungen, lastenfrei; ~ **of expenses** kosten-, spesenfrei; ~ **from halo** *(film)* lichthoffrei; ~ **of ice** eisfrei; ~ **in and out and stowed** frei ein und aus und gestaut; ~ **of income tax** einkommensteuerfrei; ~ **of all income tax and capital-gains tax** einkommens- und kapitalgewinnsteuerfrei; ~ **of interest** zinsfrei, -los, unverzinslich; ~ **from legacy duty respectively** ohne Abzug anteiliger Erbschaftsteuern; ~ **overside** frei einschließlich Löschung im Ankunftshafen; ~ **of payment** franko; ~ **on plane** frei an Bord des Flugzeugs; ~ **on platform** frei Eisenbahngleis; ~ **of postage** *(US)* portofrei; ~ **on quay** frei Kai (Ufer); ~ **on rail** frei (franko) Bahnwagen (Waggon), frei Schiene; ~ **of riot and civil commotion** gegen Aufruhr und Bürgerkrieg nicht versichert; ~ **on sale** frei verkäuflich; ~ **of stamp** stempelsteuerfrei; ~ **station** bahnfrei, franko (frei) Bahnhof; ~ **station of departure** frei Abgangsbahnhof; ~ **station of destination** frei Bestimmungsbahnhof; ~ **on steamer** frei Schiff; ~ **of taxes** steuerfrei; ~ **on truck** *(Br.)* frei LKW ab Lager, frei Waggon; ~ **and unencumbered** unbelastet, hypothekenfrei; ~ **on the wag(g)on** frei auf den Wagen;
children [are] admitted ~ Kinder haben freien Eintritt;
~ *(v.)* befreien, in Freiheit setzen, Freiheit geben, *(commerce)* liberalisieren;
~ **s. o. of a burden** j. von einer Last befreien; **o. s. from one's commitments** alle Verpflichtungen loswerden; ~ **o. s. from debt** schuldenfrei werden; ~ **a debtor of his debts** Schuldner von seinen Schulden befreien; ~ **rationed goods** bewirtschaftete Ware freigeben; ~ **o. s. from s. one's grasp** sich von jds. Einfluß freimachen; ~ **a prisoner** Gefangenen freilassen; ~ **a property from a mortgage** Grundstück lastenfrei machen (entschulden); **to be** ~ *(member of parliament)* nicht dem Fraktionszwang unterliegen; **not to be** ~ **to act** nicht handlungsfähig sein; **to be** ~ **with one's advice** bereitwillig Ratschläge erteilen; **to be** ~ **from arrest** Immunität genießen; **to be** ~ **in business** Geschäfte großzügig abwickeln; **to be somewhat** ~ **in one's conversation** schlüpfrige Reden führen; **to be** ~ **and easy** sich völlig zwanglos benehmen; **to be** ~ **to fluctuate on the market** frei fluktuieren können; **to be** ~ **of the harbo(u)r** aus dem Hafen heraus sein; **to be** ~ **of s. one's house** bei jem. aus- und eingehen können; **to be** ~ **of illusions** keinerlei Illusionen haben; **to be** ~ **with one's money** nicht so genau rechnen, großzügig wirtschaften; **to be open** ~ **on Saturdays** sonnabends kostenlos zugänglich sein; **to be** ~ **from all preoccupations** überhaupt nicht voreingenommen sein; **to be delivered** ~ **railway station** frei Bahnsteig geliefert werden; **to be made** ~ **of s. th.** freien Zutritt zu etw. haben; **to break** ~ durchbrechen; **to break** ~ **from an influence** sich von einer Beeinflussung freimachen; **to be duty-**~ zollfrei sein; **to get off scot-**~ straffrei ausgehen; **to give s. th. away** ~ etw. kostenlos abgeben; **to have some time** ~ Zeit haben; **to import s. th.** ~ **of duty** etw. zollfrei einführen; **to make** ~ **with s. o.** sich jem. gegenüber zu viel herausnehmen; **to make s. o.** ~ **of a city** jem. das Bürgerrecht verleihen; **to run** ~ *(machine)* leer laufen; **to set s. o.** ~ j. auf freien Fuß setzen; **to set money** ~ Geld flüssig machen; **to shake o. s.** ~ **from all bias** jegliche Voreingenommenheit über Bord werfen;

~ **accommodation** freie Wohnung; **admission** ~ freier Eintritt; ~ **advertisement** Gratisanzeige; ~ **advertising** redaktionelle Werbung; ~ **allowance** Freigepäck; ~ **assets** frei verfügbare Guthaben; ~ **baggage allowance** *(US)* Freigepäck; ~ **balance** zinsloses (unverzinstes) Guthaben; ~ **balloon** Freiballon; ~-**banking system** *(US)* Bankenfreiheit; ~-**bench** Wittum, Witwennießbrauch; ~ **bonds** frei verfügbare (nicht als Sicherheit dienende) Obligationen; ~ **capital** zinsfreies Kapital; ~ **capital goods** Investitionsgüter für mehrere Zwecke; ~ **choice** freie Wahl; ♀ **Church** Freikirche; ~ **circulation of money** freier Geldumlauf; ~ **citizen** freier Bürger; ~ **city** freie Stadt; ~-**of-capture-and-seizure clause** Aufbringungs- und Beschlagnahmeklausel; ~-**on-board clause** Fob-Klausel; ~ **coinage** unbegrenztes Prägerecht; ~ **collective bargaining** Tarifvertragsfreiheit; ~ **competition** freier Wettbewerb, Wettbewerbsfreiheit; ~ **concert** Freikonzert; ~ **copy** Freiexemplar, -stück; ~ **currency** frei konvertierbare Währung; ~-**currency area** freier Währungsraum; ~-**currency country** nicht devisenbewirtschaftetes Land; ~ **day** freier Tag; ~ **deal** Gratisangebot; ~ **dealer** Kaufmannsfrau; ~ **delivery** kostenlose (portofreie) Zustellung, Lieferung frei Haus; ~-**delivery system** *(US)* kostenloses Zustellungswesen; ~ **demonstration in the home** kostenlose Hausvorführung; ~ **depreciation** Steuerfreiheit bis zur Anlagenabschreibung; ~ **determination** Entschlußfreiheit; ~ **discussion** offene Diskussion; ~ **dispatch** frei von Vergütung für gesparte Ladezeit; ~-**and-easiness** Ungezwungenheit; ~ **economy** freie Marktwirtschaft; ~ **elections** freie Wahlen; ~ **enterprise** freies Unternehmertum; ~-**enterprise principle (system)** Prinzip der freien Marktwirtschaft, marktwirtschaftliche Ordnung, freie Marktwirtschaft; ~ **enterpriser** Befürworter der freien Marktwirtschaft; ~ **entertainment** Gratisführung; ~ **entry** *(customs)* zollfreie Einfuhr, zollfreier Grenzübertritt, freier Zutritt; ~ **estate** erbschaftsteuerfreies Vermögen; ~ **exchange rate** beweglicher Wechselkurs; ~ **field of operations** selbständiges Tätigkeitsgebiet; ~ **film** avantgardistischer Film; ~ **fishery** *(rivers)* Fischereigerechtigkeit; **early** ~ **float** freie Pufferzeit; ~ **food** zollfreie Nahrungsmittel; ~ **food and accommodation** freie Kost und Station; ~-**for-all** offener Wettbewerb, *(free fight, US)* allgemeine Rauferei; ~-**form** zwanglos, ungezwungen; ~ **gangway** Landurlaub; ~ **gift** Werbegeschenk, Zugabe; **as a** ~ **gift** unentgeltlich, gratis; ~ **gift advertising** Werbung durch Musterverteilung, Zugabewerbung, Warenprobenverteilung; ~ **gift coupon** Gutschein; ~ **gold** reines Gold, *(US)* gesetzlich vorgeschriebene Reserven übersteigender Goldbestand, freies Gold; ~ **goods** zollfreie Waren, kontingentfreie Einfuhrware; **to allow (give) s. o. a** ~ **hand** jem. freie Hand lassen; ~-**handed** freigebig; ~-**hearted** freimutig, offenherzig; ~ **house** brauereiunabhängige Gastwirtschaft; ~ **import** [zoll]freie Einfuhr; ~ **income** frei verfügbares Einkommen; ~ **insertion** kostenlose Insertion, kostenloses Inserat; ~ **items** *(US)* spesenfreie Inkasso; ~ **journey** Freifahrt; ~ **labo(u)r** nicht gewerkschaftlich organisierte Arbeitskräfte; ~-**lance** Freischaffender; ~-**lance** *(a.)* freiberuflich, freischaffend; **to act as a** ~ **lance** freiberuflich arbeiten; ~-**lance artist** freier Graphiker; ~-**lance contributor** freiberuflicher Mitarbeiter; ~-**lance writer** freier Mitarbeiter, unabhängiger Journalist; ~-**lancer** *(newspaper)* freier Mitarbeiter; ~ **library** öffentliche Bibliothek; ~ **lighterage** Verladung von Stückgut ohne Aufschlag; ~ **line** *(tel.)* freie Leitung; ~ **list** Freiliste [zollfreier Gegenstände], Zollfrei-, Liberalisierungsliste; ~ **liver** Schlemmer, Genießer; ~ **loader** *(US sl.)* Schnorrer, Nassauer; ~ **loading** freie Beladung; ~ **loan** zinsloses Darlehen; ~ **luggage** *(Br.)* Freigepäck; ~ **luggage allowance** *(Br.)* Freigepäck; ~ **lunch** *(US)* kostenlose Mahlzeit; ~ **market** freier Markt, freie Marktwirtschaft, *(stock exchange)* offener Markt, Freiverkehrsmarkt; ~-**market economy** freie Marktwirtschaft; ~-**market fundamentalist** überzeugter Anhänger der freien Marktwirtschaft; ~-**market price** Freiverkehrskurs; ♀ **and Accepted Masons** Freimaurerorden; ~ **meals** Freitisch; ~ **membership** beitragsfreie Mitgliedschaft; ~ **moment** freie Minute; ~ **movement [of labo(u)r]** Freizügigkeit; ~ **movement of capital** freier Kapitalverkehr; ~ **movement of persons, services and capital** *(EC)* freier Personen-, Dienst- und Kapitalverkehr; ~ **offer** Gratisangebot; ~ **pass** Freifahrschein, Durchlaßschein; ~ **personalty** erbschaftssteuerfreies Mobiliarvermögen; ~ **place** *(school, Br.)* Freistelle; ~ **placer** *(Br.)* Freistelleninhalt; ~ **place systems** *(scholar, Br.)* Freistellenwesen; ~ **play** *(technics)* Spielraum; ~ **port** Freihafen; ~-**port area** Freihafengebiet; ~-**port shop** zollfreier Laden; ~-**port store** Freihafenlager; ~ **posting** Gratisplakat, Freiaushang; ~ **press** freie Presse; ~ **price** unabhängiger Preis; ~-**to-frontier price** *(EC)* Preis frei Grenze; ~ **publication** Gratiszeitung, -zeitschrift,

-blatt; ~ **puff** *(Br.)* kostenlose redaktionelle Werbung; ~ **quarters** freie Unterkunft; **to have ~ quarters** freigehalten werden; ~ **quota** Freigrenze, freies Kontingent; **~-ranging** auf allen Gebieten erfolgreich; **to allow s. o. ~ rein** jem. freie Hand lassen; ~ **reserves** *(US)* freie Rücklagen; ~ **response question** offene Frage; ~ **ride** Freifahrt, *(plane)* Freiflug, *(stock exchange)* kurze Haussespekulation; ~ **rider** gewerkschaftsfreier Arbeiter, Nichtgewerkschaftler, der an Tarifvergünstigungen teilnimmt; ~ **road** gebührenfreie Straße; **to give ~ run** freie Hand lassen; **~-sale system** *(airline)* ungebundener Flugkartenverkauf; ~ **sample** Freiexemplar, Gratismuster, -probe; ~ **school** unentgeltlicher Schulunterricht; ~ **scope** freie Hand, Handlungsfreiheit; ~ **share** Gratisaktie; ~ **shareholder** Bausparrer ohne Inanspruchnahme einer Bausparhypothek; ~ **ship** *(US)* nicht besteuertes ausländisches Schiff, Schiff eines neutralen Staates; ~ **space** *(marine)* Freiraum; ~ **speech** freie Meinungsäußerung; **~-spending** ausgabenfreudig; ~ **state** Freistaat; ~ **surplus** frei verfügbarer Überschuß; ~ **ticket** Freifahr-, Freikarte, *(lottery)* Freilos; ~ **time** Freizeit, *(loading)* gebührenfreie Ladezeit, *(railroad)* freie Liegezeit, *(unloading)* Abladefrist; ~ **and easy tone** ungezwungener Ton; ~ **trade** Freihandel, zollfreier Verkehr, Handelsfreiheit; **to stand for ~ trade** Freihandelsanhänger sein; **~-trade area** Freihandelszone, Zollausschlußgebiet; **~-trade area community** Freihandelsgemeinschaft; **~-trade association** Freihandelsgemeinschaft; **~-trade pledge** Freihandelsversprechen; **~-trade policy** Freihandelspolitik; **~-trade zone** Freihandelszone; ~ **trader** Freihändler, Anhänger des Freihandelssystems; ~ **translation** freie Übersetzung; ~ **transportation** *(US, carrier)* Freifahrscheinausgabe nur an Betriebsangehörige; ~ **trial** Gratisprobe, kostenlose Warenprobe; ~ **trip** Gratisreise; ~ **vote** freie Abstimmung [ohne Fraktionszwang]; ~ **white person** *(Naturalization Act, US)* Europäer; ~ **warren** Wildgehege, -reservat; ~ **will** Willensfreiheit; **of my own ~ will** aus freien Stücken; ~ **working** *(prices)* freies Spiel; ~ **world** freie Welt; ~ **zone** Freihafen[gebiet].

freeboot *(v.)* seeräubern.

freebooter Pirat, Freibeuter, Seeräuber.

freedom Freiheit, Unabhängigkeit, *(market)* Lebhaftigkeit, *(privilege)* Vorrecht, Privileg, *(unrestricted use)* Nutznießungsrecht;

academic ~ akademische Freiheiten; **political ~** politische Freiheit;

~ **of action** Aktions-, Handlungsfreiheit; ~ **of the air** Freiheit des Luftraums; ~ **from arrest** Immunität; ~ **of association** Vereinigungs-, Koalitionsfreiheit; ~ **of the borough** Bürgerrecht; ~ **of choice** Entscheidungsspielraum; ~ **of a city** Ehrenbürgerrecht; ~ **of a company** *(Br.)* Meisterrecht; ~ **of competition** Wettbewerbsfreiheit; ~ **of contract** Vertragsfreiheit; ~ **of entry into the market** jederzeit zugänglicher Markt, freier Marktzugang für jeden Anbieter; ~ **of establishment** *(EC)* Niederlassungsfreiheit; ~ **of exchange operations** freier Devisenverkehr; ~ **of expression and assembly** Rede- und Versammlungsfreiheit; ~ **of information** Informationsfreiheit; ~ **of movement** Bewegungsfreiheit, Freizügigkeit; ~ **of navigation on rivers** Schiffahrtsgerechtigkeit auf Flüssen; ~ **of opinion** Meinungsfreiheit; ~ **of the press** Pressefreiheit; ~ **of price formation** freie Preisbildung; ~ **of religion** Glaubensfreiheit; ~ **of the seas** Freiheit der Meere; ~ **to settle anywhere** Niederlassungsfreiheit; ~ **of speech** Recht der freien Meinungsäußerung, Redefreiheit; ~ **to strike** Streikrecht; ~ **from tax** Steuerfreiheit, Befreiung von Steuern; ~ **of trade** Freiheit der wirtschaftlichen Betätigung, Gewerbefreiheit; ~ **from wear and tear** Verschleißfestigkeit; ~ **of will** Willensfreiheit;

to bestow ~ on s. o. jem. die Freiheit schenken; **to give a friend the ~ of one's library** einem Freund die Benutzung seiner Bibliothek gestatten; **to have the ~ of s. th.** Benutzungsrecht von etw. haben; **to receive the ~ of a town** Ehrenbürger einer Stadt werden; **to rob s. o. of his ~** j. der Freiheit berauben; **to take out one's ~** Bürgerrechte erwerben; **to use ~s with s. o.** sich jem. gegenüber Vertraulichkeiten erlauben;

~ **fighter** Freiheitskämpfer; ~ **march** Freiheitsmarsch.

freehand [drawing] Faustskizze;

to draw ~ freihändig zeichnen.

freehold *(Br.)* freier Grundbesitz, freies Grundeigentum;

determinable ~ eigentumsähnliche Nutzung auf Lebenszeit; ~ **in law** gesetzlich vererbtes Grundeigentum; ~ **for life** Eigentum auf Lebenszeit;

to own the ~ über sein Grundeigentum frei verfügen können; ~ **estate** unbeschränktes Grundstückseigentum; ~ **factory** auf eigenem Grund und Boden errichtete Fabrik; ~ **farm** freier Bauernhof; ~ **flat** *(Br.)* Eigentumswohnung; ~ **house** Hausgrundstück; ~ **land** *(Br.)* parzellierter Grundbesitzanteil, unbebautes Grundstück, Siedlungsgrundstück; ~ **land and buildings** *(balance sheet, Br.)* bebaute und unbebaute Grundstücke; **~-land society** *(Br.)* Parzellierungsgesellschaft; ~ **owner** Grundstückseigentümer; ~ **property** Grundbesitz; ~ **reversion** Heimfall an den Grundstückseigentümer; ~ **securities** grundbuchliche Sicherheiten; ~ **tenure** freier Grundbesitz.

freeholder freier Grundeigentümer, unabhängiger Hausbesitzer.

freelance Freischaffender, freier Mitarbeiter;

~ *(a.)* freischaffend, freiberuflich;

to act as a ~ freiberuflich tätig sein;

~ **artist** freier Graphiker; ~ **contributor** freiberuflicher Mitarbeiter; ~ **importer** selbständige Importfirma; ~ **writer** freier Mitarbeiter, unabhängiger Journalist.

freeloader *(US sl.)* Schnorrer, Nassauer.

freeloading guest kostenlos beförderter Gast.

freely fluctuating exchange rates bewegliche Wechselkurse.

freeman Wahlberechtigter;

~ **of a city** Ehrenbürger;

to be admitted as ~ of a city zum Ehrenbürger ernannt werden.

freemason Freimaurer;

~s' lodge Freimaurerloge.

freemasonry Freimaurerei;

~ **of the press** instinktives Zusammengehörigkeitsgefühl der Presse.

freepost portofrei versandt;

~ **coupon** portofreier Gutschein.

freethinker Freidenker.

freeway *(US)* plankreuzungsfreie Fernverkehrsstraße, Autobahn;

six-lane ~ *(US)* Autobahn mit sechs Fahrbahnen;

~ **program** *(US)* Autobahnprogramm; ~ **ramp** *(US)* Autobahnauffahrt; ~ **system** *(US)* Autobahnnetz.

freewheel *(car)* Freilauf.

freewheeling seinen Neigungen folgend.

freeze Gefrieren, gefrorener Zustand, *(weather)* Frost;

deep ~ *(refrigerator)* Tiefkühlfach; **wage ~** Lohnstop;

~ **on new domestic bond issues** Emissionspause für Inlandsanleihen; **voluntary ~ on exports** freiwillige Exportbeschränkung; ~ **on pay and prices (incomes and wages)** Lohn- und Preisstopp; **to quick-~** tiefkühlen;

~ *(v.)* [ge]frieren, zu Eis werden, *(accounts)* einfrieren, blockieren, sperren, *(curtail civilian use)* rationieren, *(prices, US coll.)* auf bestimmter Höhe halten, *(wages, US coll.)* gesetzlich festlegen;

~ **action on a merger** Fusionsbeschluß inhibieren; ~ **s. one's blood** j. mit Schrecken füllen, jds. Blut frieren lassen; ~ **to death** erfrieren; ~ **out** *(sl.)* ausschließen, -schalten, *(stock exchange, sl.)* zusammenbrechen; ~ **s. o. out** j. kaltstellen; ~ **out the minority** Minderheit überstimmen; ~ **prices** *(US coll.)* Preisstopp durchführen, Preise amtlich auf einer bestimmten Höhe halten; ~ **up** *(airplane)* vereisen; ~ **wages** *(US coll.)* Lohnstopp durchführen;

to make one's blood ~ j. zu Tode erschrecken; **to put a ~ on hirings** Einstellungsstopp verfügen;

~ **conditions** Lohnstoppbestimmungen.

freezer Tiefkühltruhe;

ice-cream ~ Eismaschine.

freezing *(accounts)* Einfrieren;

price ~ Preisstopp; **quick ~** Tiefkühlverfahren; **wage ~** Lohnstopp;

~ **of credit** Kreditsperre; ~ **of debts** Einfrierung von Schulden; ~ **of funds** Mittelbindung, Bindung von Geldbeträgen; ~ **of payments** Stornierung von Zahlungen; ~ **of prices** *(US)* Preisstopp; ~ **of foreign property** Einfrierung ausländischer Guthaben; ~ **of wages** *(US)* Lohnstopp;

~ **box** Gefrierfach; ~ **chamber** *(Australia)* Kühlraum; ~ **level** Nullgradgrenze; **~-out** durch geschickte Manöver erreichter Ausschluß eines Teilhabers; ~ **point** Gefrierpunkt; ~ **process** Tiefkühlverfahren; ~ **temperature** Gefriertemperatur.

freight *(cargo)* Schiffsladung, *(hire of ship)* Schiffsmiete, *(~ line)* Frachtlinie, *(load)* Fracht, Frachtgut, Ladung, Ladegut, *(ocean freight, Br.)* Seefracht, *(tonnage)* Frachtraum, Laderaum, *(train)* Güterzug, *(transport charges)* Frachtkosten, -gebühr, -geld, Fuhrlohn, *(transportation of goods)* Frachttransport, -beförderung;

by ~ *(US)* per Frachtgut (Eisenbahn); **free of ~ and duty** frachtfrei verzollt; ~ **free (paid)** *(US)* frachtfrei, franko; **free of ~** franko, frachtfrei; **paying ~ as customary** in gewöhnlicher Fracht; **without ~** ohne Fracht;

additional ~ Mehrfracht, Frachtaufschlag; **advance[d]** ~ vorausbezahlte Fracht, Frachtvorschuß; **back** ~ Rückfracht, unvorhergesehene Fracht; ~ **back and forth** ausgehende und eingehende Fracht; **carload** *(US)* Waggonladung; **chartered** ~ Fracht laut Charterpartie; **clear** ~ Nettofracht; ~ **collect** *(US)* Fracht gegen Nachnahme, Frachtnachnahme; **dead** ~ tote Fracht, Ballastladung, -fracht; Fehl-, Rein-, Fautfracht; **discriminating** ~ Differentialfracht; **distance** ~ Distanzfracht; **extra** ~ Frachtzuschlag; **fast** ~ *(US)* Eilfacht, -gut, Schnellgut; ~ **forward** *(Br.)* Fracht gegen Nachnahme, Fracht bezahlt der Empfänger; **gross** ~ ganze Fracht, Bruttofracht; **home** ~ Rückfracht; ~~**in** Eingangsfracht; **interline** ~ von mehreren Spediteuren beförderte Fracht; **inward** ~ Eingangsfracht, *(US)* Frachtkosten für eingehende Waren; **joint** ~ gemeinsamer Frachttarif; **less-than-carload** ~ *(US)* Stückgut[sendungen]; **low-return** ~ langsame Rückfracht; **lump-sum** ~ Total-, Pauschalfracht; **minimum** ~ Mindestfracht; **net** ~ Nettofracht; **ocean** ~ See-, Transatlantikfracht; ~ **offered** Frachtangebot; **original** ~ Vorfracht; ~ **out** Hinfracht; **outgoing** ~ Ausgangsfracht; **outward** ~ abgehende Fracht (Ladung), Ausgangsfracht; ~ **outward and home** Hin- und Herfracht; **package** ~ *(US)* Stückgutsendung; ~ **payable** Fracht vorauszahlbar; ~ **payable abroad** im Ausland zahlbare Fracht; **paying** ~ *(US)* zahlende Fracht; **perishable** ~ leicht verderbliches Frachtgut; **phantom** ~ fiktive Transportkosten; ~ **prepaid** Fracht im voraus bezahlt, vorauszahlbare Fracht; **prorata** ~ anteilsmäßige Fracht, Distanzfracht; **railroad** ~ *(US)* Bahnfracht; **released** ~ Fracht zu ermäßigtem Tarif, Fracht zu herabgesetztem Wert; **respited** ~ gestundete Frachten; **return** ~ Rückfracht; **revenue** ~ *(US)* zahlende Fracht; **through** ~ durchgehende Fracht; **time** ~ in Raten gezahlte Fracht, Zeitfracht; **ton** ~ Tonnenfracht; **unremunerative** ~ nicht lohnende Fracht; **voyage** ~ Fracht für die ganze Reise, Reisefracht; **wrecked** ~ verlorene Fracht; **cost, insurance and** ~ **(cif)** Kosten, Versicherung und Fracht; ~ **by air** Luftfracht; ~ **and carriage** *(Br.)* See- und Landfracht; ~ **or carriage paid to A** See- oder Landfracht bis A bezahlt; ~ **and charges prepaid** fracht- und spesenfrei; ~ **as in charterparty** Fracht laut Charterpartie; ~ **and demurrage** Fracht- und Liegegeld; ~ **payable at destination** Fracht zahlbar am Bestimmungsort; ~ **and disbursement** Fracht und Auslagen; ~ **to be prepaid** Fracht im voraus zu bezahlen; ~ **pro rata** Distanzfracht; ~ **by the ton** Tonnenfracht;

~ *(v.) (hire a ship)* Schiff heuern, chartern, *(load)* befrachten, in Fracht nehmen, beladen, *(transport, US)* verfrachten, als Frachtgut befördern;

~ **upon delivery** Fracht nachnehmen; ~ **by parcels** Stückgüter laden; ~ **out a ship** Schiff verchartern; ~ **through** durchfrachten;

to absorb the excess ~ erhöhte Frachtkosten tragen; **to book** ~ Frachtraum belegen; **to charge** ~ Fracht[kosten] berechnen; **to engage the** ~ Fracht bedingen; **to haul** ~ Frachtgut befördern; **to sail on** ~ auf Fracht fahren; **to send s. th. by** ~ etw. als Frachtgut (per Fracht) schicken; **to stow** ~ Ladung verstauen; **to take in** ~ Ladung einnehmen, [Güter] verladen; **to take a ship to** ~ Schiff befrachten; **to trade on** ~ auf Fracht fahren;

~ **absorption** Frachtnachlaß; ~ **account** Frachtkonto, -rechnung; ~ **agency** *(US)* Güterabfertigungsstelle; ~ **agent** *(US)* Frachtspediteur, Leiter einer Güterabfertigungsstelle; ~ **airport** Frachtflughafen; ~ **area** Frachtzone; ~ **authorization** Frachtgenehmigung, -freigabe; ~ **bill** *(US)* Frachtbrief; ~ **bill number** *(US)* Frachtbriefnummer; ~ **boat** Frachtdampfer; ~ **booking** Belegung von Frachtraum, Frachtraumbelegung, -buchung; ~ **broker** Transport-, Schiffs-, Frachtmakler; ~ **brokerage** Frachtmaklergebühr; ~ **broking** Frachtmaklergeschäft; ~ **business** *(US)* Spedition[sgeschäft]; ~ **capacity** Frachtraum; ~ **car** *(US)* [geschlossener] Güterwagen, Waggon; **to spot a** ~ **car** *(US)* Güterwagen zur Entladestelle dirigieren; ~~**car shortage** *(US)* Waggonknappheit; ~ **carrier** Transportflugzeug, Frachtflugzeug; ~~**carrying aircraft** Frachtflugzeug; ~ **category** Verladeklasse; ~ **charges** Frachtkosten, -gebühren; **through-**~ **charges** Durchgangsfrachtgebühren; **to commute** ~ **charges** Frachtkosten bezahlen; ~ **claim** Frachtforderung [der Speditionsgesellschaft]; ~ **classification** Frachttarif; ~ **clerk** Speditionsangestellter; ~ **commodities** Frachtgüter; ~ **conductor** Warenaufseher; ~ **container** Transportbehälter; ~ **contract** Frachtvertrag; ~ **corporation** Frachtunternehmen; ~ **deficit** Frachtdefizit; ~ **delivery** Fracht-, Güterzustellung; ~ **density** Verkehrsdichte im Güterfernverkehr; ~ **depot** *(US)* Güterbahnhof, -niederlage; ~ **distributor** Güterumschlagstelle; ~ **elevator** *(US)* Waren-, Güteraufzug; ~ **engine** *(US)* Güterzuglokomotive; ~ **equalization** *(US)* Fracht-

ausgleich; ~ **expenses** *(US)* Frachtspesen, -kosten; ~ **facilities** günstige Frachtmöglichkeiten; ~ **forwarder** *(US)* Güterspediteur; ~ **handler** Frachtleiter; ~ **handling** Frachtumschlag; ~ **hauler** Frachtführer; ~ **house** *(US)* Warenlagerhaus, Güterschuppen; ~ **insurance** Fracht-, Gütertransportversicherung; ~ **integration committee** *(Br.)* Beratungsausschuß für Frachtintegrierungsfragen; ~ **line** Frachtstrecke; ~ **list** *(US)* Kontenzettel, Ladungsverzeichnis, Frachtbrief; ~ **locomotive** *(US)* Güterzuglokomotive; ~ **market** Frachtenmarkt, -börse; ~ **mile** Frachtkilometer; ~ **milage** nach Kilometern berechneter Frachttarif; ~ **note** *(Br.)* Frachtrechnung, -brief; ~ **office** *(US)* Frachtannahmestelle, Güterausgabe, -abfertigung; ~ **overcharge** zuviel erhobene Fracht[gebühr]; ~ **parity** Frachtparität; ~ **plane** Fracht-, Transportflugzeug; ~ **policy** Frachtpolice; ~ **quotation** Frachtnotierung; ~ **rate** Frachtrate, -satz; ~ **rates** Fracht-, Gütertarif; ~ **minimum rate** Mindestfrachtsatz; **ocean** ~ **rate** Transatlantikfrachtsatz; ~~**of-all-kinds rate** gleichmäßiger Frachtsatz; **returned** ~ **rate** verbilligter Frachtsatz für Leergut; ~ **and passenger rates** Beförderungspreis; ~~**rate increase** Frachttariferhöhung; ~ **receipt** Frachtquittung; ~ **reduction** Frachtermäßigung; ~ **release** Güterfreigabe, Frachterlaß; ~ **revenue** Frachterträgnisse, -einkünfte; ~ **revenue tariff** Frachttarif; ~ **room** Frachtraum; ~ **salesman** Frachtenmakler; ~ **service** Güterabfertigung, -beförderung, Frachtverkehr, -dienst; **lorry-size** ~ **service** *(Br.)* auf Mittelbetriebe zugeschnittener Frachtverkehr; ~ **shed** *(US)* Güterschuppen, -speicher, -halle; ~ **shipper** Frachtspediteur; ~ **space** Lade-, Fracht-, Schiffsraum; ~ **station** Güterschuppen; ~ **steamer** *(US)* Frachtschiff, -dampfer; ~ **storage** Güterlagerung; ~ **subsidy** Frachthilfe; ~ **system** Frachtwesen, Güterverkehr; **integrated** ~ **system** *(Br.)* integrierter Frachtverkehr; ~ **tariff** *(US)* Güter-, Frachttarif; ~ **terminal** Güterkopfstation; ~ **ton** Frachttonne, Gewichtstonne; ~ **tonnage** Nutzertrag-, Frachtraumfähigkeit, Gütertonnage; **[long-distance]** ~ **traffic** Güter[fern]verkehr, -frachtverkehr; **long-haul** ~ **traffic** Güterfernverkehr; **short-distance** ~ **traffic** Güternahverkehr; ~ **train** *(US)* Güterzug; **by** ~ **train** als Frachtgut; **by fast** ~ **train** *(US)* als Eilgut (Eilfracht); **expedited** ~ **train** *(US)* Schnellgüterzug; **local** ~ **train** *(US)* Nahgüterzug; ~~**train service** *(US)* Güterzugverkehr; ~ **transportation** *(US)* Gütertransport; ~ **truck** Fernverkehrslastwagen; ~ **vessel** Frachtschiff; ~ **waggon** *(US)* Güterwagen, Waggon; **heavy-duty** ~ **waggon** *(US)* schwerer Güterwaggon; ~ **warrant** *(US)* Frachtbrief; ~ **yard** *(US)* Güterbahnhof.

freightage Befrachtung, *(cargo)* Ladegut, Ladung, *(charges)* Frachtkosten, -gebühr, *(transportation)* Transport, Beförderung.

freighter Be-, Verlader, Ablader, Frachtführer, Be-, Verfrachter, *(aeroplane)* Frachtflugzeug, *(cargo steamer)* Frachtschiff, -dampfer, Frachter, *(ship ~)* Schiffsbefrachter, Reeder.

freighting *(chartering and loading of ships)* Chartern, Reederei, *(loading)* Befrachtung;
lump-sum ~ Befrachtung in Bausch und Bogen;
~ **by the case** Stückgutbefrachtung; ~ **by contract** Pauschalfracht; ~ **on measurement** Maßfracht; ~ **ad valorem** Befrachtung nach dem Wert; ~ **on weight** Befrachtung nach Gewicht; ~ **commission** Befrachtungsprovision; ~ **conditions** Befrachtungsbedingungen; ~ **voyage** direkte Beförderung von Seefracht.

freightless ohne Fracht (Ladung).

freightliner *(Br.)* mit Transportbehältern beladener Zug, Containerzug.

French | door Glastür; ~ **fold** Kreuzfaltung; **to take** ~ **leave** heimlich weggehen; ~ **roll** Weißbrötchen.

frequency Häufigkeit, *(el.)* Frequenz, Schwingungszahl, *(trains)* Verkehrshäufigkeit, Dichte;
high ~ Hochfrequenz; **proportional** ~ *(statistics)* proportionale Häufigkeit; **relative** ~ relative Häufigkeit;
~ **of accidents** Unfallhäufigkeit; ~ **of crimes** Häufigkeit von Verbrechen; ~ **of insertions** Anzeigenhäufigkeit; ~ **of loss** Schadenshäufigkeit; ~ **of publication** Erscheinungsweise, *(advertisement)* Häufigkeit des Erscheinens;
~ **band** Frequenzband; ~ **chart** Häufigkeitstabelle; **high-**~ **current** Hochfrequenzenstrom; ~ **curve** Häufigkeitskurve; ~ **discount** Mengenrabatt, Malrabatt, -staffel; ~ **and volume discount rates** Mal- und Mengenstaffel; ~ **distribution** Streuung; ~ **function** Häufigkeitsfunktion; ~ **movement** Häufigkeitsmoment; ~ **planning conference** Wellenkonferenz; ~ **range** Wobbelbereich; ~ **rate** Häufigkeitsverhältnis; ~ **study** Häufigkeitsstudie; ~ **table** Häufigkeitstabelle; ~ **theory of probability** Häufigkeitstheorie der Wahrscheinlichkeit.

frequent häufig [vorkommend], regelmäßig, beständig;
~ *(v.)* häufig aufsuchen, frequentieren;
~ **fairs** Messen besuchen, Märkte beziehen; ~ **a public house** Stammgast in einem Lokal sein;
to become ~ *(crime)* sich häufen;
~ **customer** Dauerkunde.
frequented stark besucht;
to be much ~ viel Zuspruch haben;
~ **way** befahrener Weg.
frequenter regelmäßiger Besucher (Gast).
fresh frisch, neu, *(blooming)* blühend, jugendlich, lebhaft, *(newly produced)* bisher unbekannt, *(unexperienced)* unerfahren, jung, *(tipsy, sl.)* beschwipst, angeheitert, *(unspoilt)* unverdorben, *(not used)* ungebraucht;
~ **from college** gerade von der Universität gekommen; ~ **in** gerade angekommen;
to be ~ **from the country** das erste Mal in der Stadt sein; **to be still** ~ **in one's memory** einem noch deutlich vor den Augen stehen; **to come** ~ **from college** Studium gerade beendet haben; **to get** ~ **with s. o.** unverschämt gegenüber jem. werden;
~ **air** kühle Luft; **in the** ~ **air** im Freien; **to admit** ~ **air into a room** Zimmer lüften; **to go out for some** ~ **air** frische Luft schöpfen gehen; ~-**air fiend** Frischluftfanatiker; ~-**air inlet** Frischluftzuführung; ~ **apprentice** unerfahrener Lehrling; ~ **breeze** frische Brise; ~ **chapter** neues Kapitel; ~-**comer** Neuling; ~ **contract** neuer Vertrag; ~ **copy** Neuausfertigung; **to put** ~ **courage into s. o.** jem. wieder Mut zusprechen; ~ **demand** erneute Kauflust; ~ **evidence** neu entdecktes Beweismaterial; **to meet** ~ **faces** neue Menschen kennen lernen; ~ **gale** stürmischer Wind; **to break** ~ **ground** etw. ganz Neues unternehmen; **to be a** ~ **hand in s. th.** Neuling (Novize) in einer Sache sein; **to throw** ~ **light on a subject** neue Informationen zu einem Thema beitragen; ~ **meat** Frischfleisch; ~ **news** gerade eingetroffene Nachrichten; ~ **novel** soeben erschienener Roman; ~ **outbreak of an epidemic** Rückkehr einer Epidemie; ~ **outbreak of fire** erneuter Feuerausbruch; **to set** ~ **papers** neue Prüfungsaufgaben stellen; ~ **paragraph** neuer Absatz; ~ **pursuit** sofortige Verfolgung; ~ **sheet of paper** neuer Bogen Papier; ~ **start** neuer Anfang; **to lay in a** ~ **stock** Neuanschaffungen machen; ~ **supplies** zusätzliche Lieferungen; ~ **troops** frische Truppen; ~ **vegetables** frisches Gemüse; ~ **water** Frischwasser; ~-**water college** *(US)* unbekanntes College, kleine Provinzschule; ~-**water damage** Süßwasserschaden; ~-**water fishing** Binnenfischerei; ~-**water sailor** unerfahrener Seemann.
fresher, freshman *(Br., sl.)* Student im ersten Semester.
freshness of mind Geistesfrische.
fret *(fig.)* Aufregung, Kummer;
~ **and fume of life** Widerwärtigkeiten des Lebens;
~ *(v.)* *(fig.)* sich Sorgen machen;
~ **and fume** vor Wut schäumen; ~ **one's life away** sich zu Tode ärgern; ~ **over trifles** sich über Kleinigkeiten aufregen;
to be on the ~ bekümmert sein.
friction Spannung, Mißhelligkeit, Reibung, Meinungsverschiedenheit;
economic ~ wirtschaftlicher Reibungskoeffizient;
political ~ **between two countries** politische Spannungen zwischen zwei Ländern.
frictional unemployment temporäre Arbeitslosigkeit, Fluktuationsarbeitslosigkeit.
fridge Kühl-, Eisschrank.
friend Freund, *(acquaintance)* Bekannter, *(countryman)* Landsmann, Kollege, *(favo(u)rer)* Gönner, Förderer, *(party member)* Parteigenossse;
approved ~ bewährter Freund; **bosom** ~ Busenfreund; **close** ~ intimer Freund; **fast** ~s unzertrennliche Freunde; **my hono(u)rable** ~ *(Br., parliament)* mein geschätzter Kollege (Herr Vorredner); **my learned** ~ mein geehrter Kollege; **next** ~ Prozeßpfleger eines Minderjährigen; **public** ~ öffentlicher Wohltäter; **tried** ~ zuverlässiger Freund;
~ **at court** einflußreicher Freund; **a good** ~ **of the poor** hilfreicher Gönner der Armen;
to be ~**s with s. o.** *(coll.)* mit jem. befreundet sein; **to have a large circle of** ~**s** über einen großen Freundeskreis verfügen; **to have influential** ~**s** über gute Beziehungen verfügen; **to have** ~**s at court** Protektion genießen; **to have** ~**s to stay** Logisbesuch haben; **to make** ~**s with everybody** sich mit allen Leuten gut stehen; **to make new** ~**s** seinen Freundeskreis erweitern.
friendly freundlich, befreundet, *(favo(u)rable)* hilfsbereit, wohlwollend;
to be ~ **to a cause** einer Sache wohlwollend (positiv) gegenüberstehen;

~ **arbitrator** Vermittler, Schlichter; ~ **arrangement** gütliche Einigung; ~ **fire** *(insurance)* Nutzfeuer; ~ **game (match)** Freundschaftsspiel; ~ **lead** *(Br.)* Wohltätigkeitsveranstaltung; ~ **nation** befreundeter Staat; ~ **neutrality** wohlwollende Neutralität; ~ **piece of advice** freundschaftlicher Ratschlag; **to give s. o. a** ~ **reception** j. freundlich aufnehmen; ~ **society** *(Br.)* Versicherungsverein auf Gegenseitigkeit, Unterstützungs-, Sterbe-, Hilfskasse, Wohltätigkeits-, Arbeiterhilfsverein; ~ **state** befreundeter Staat; ~ **suit** unter den Parteien abgestimmte Klage; **to be on** ~ **terms with s. o.** mit jem. auf freundschaftlichem Fuße stehen; **to do s. o. a** ~ **turn** jem. einen Freundesdienst leisten; ~ **understanding** gütliches Einvernehmen; ~ **winds** günstige Winde.
friendship Freundschaft;
promiscuous ~ leichtfertig geschlossene Freundschaft;
~ **treaty** Freundschaftsvertrag.
frigate Fregatte.
frills Extras, *(US, insurance)* neuartige Versicherungsleistungen;
no ~ keine Extraleistungen;
to put on ~ sich aufgeblasen benehmen; **to write without** ~ ungekünstelt (völlig natürlich) schreiben.
fringe *(fig.)* Randgebiet, -zone, *(outskirts)* äußerer Bezirk, Randbezirk;
on the ~**[s] of a forest** am Waldrand;
~**s** *(employees)* zusätzliche Sozialaufwendungen, Nebenleistungen;
executive ~ Sondervergünstigung [für leitende Angestellte]; **outer** ~**s of a city** Stadtrandgebiete; ~**s of civilization** Randzonen der Zivilisation; ~ **of a party** äußerster Parteiflügel;
~ *(v.)* **into the country** *(suburb)* ins Land übergehen;
to have touched only the ~ **of a question** in ein Problem überhaupt nicht eingedrungen sein; **to live on the** ~ **of society** zu den Asozialen gehören; **to touch the** ~**s of** nur am Rande berühren; ~ **activity** Randgebiete, -tätigkeit; ~ **area** Randgebiet; ~ **area parking** Parkrandgebiet; ~ **benefits** *(US, director)* Aufwandsentschädigung, Gewinnbeteiligung, *(pension provision)* Pensionsleistung, *(wage earner, US)* lohnunabhängige Einkommensteile, Lohnneben-, freiwillige Sozialleistungen, betriebliche Vergünstigungen; ~ **benefit program(me)** Gratifikations- und Vergünstigungswesen; ~ **cost** freiwilliger Sozialunkostenaufwand; ~ **executives** kostbare Arbeitskräfte; ~ **group** Sympathisantengruppe; ~ **increase** Erhöhung der Sondervergütungen; ~ **issues** *(labo(u)r agreement)* Bestimmungen über die Gewährung zusätzlicher Leistungen; ~ **militants** militante Randgruppen; ~ **outfit** unbedeutende Organisation; ~ **parking** Parken außerhalb der Ladenstadt; ~ **party** Splitterpartei; ~ **population** Randbevölkerung; ~ **supporter** Sympathisant.
frisk *(sl.)* Durchsuchung, Filzen;
~ *(v.)* *(sl.)* filzen.
frisket Retouchemaske.
fritter *(v.)* **away one's time** seine Zeit verplempern.
frivolous *(given to trifling)* leichtfertig, *(not worth notice)* belanglos, geringfügig, wertlos;
~ **or vexatious action** leichtfertige oder schikanöse Klage; ~ **answer** *(law)* ungenügende Antwort; ~ **argument** nicht stichhaltiges Argument; ~ **claim** leichtfertig erhobene Forderung; ~ **defence** leichtfertiges Gegenvorbringen; ~ **plea** schikanöser Einwand, Verschleppungsschriftsatz; ~ **remark** frivole Bemerkung.
frock *(clergy)* Priesterstand, *(politics)* Politiker, Abgeordneter.
frog *(US, railroad)* Gleiskreuzung.
frogman Froschmann.
frolic lustiger Streich, Scherz, Posse, Ausgelassenheit;
on a ~ **of one's own** zum eigenen Vergnügen.
front *(feigned appearance, coll.)* äußerer Anschein, Fassade, *(fig.)* Front, Organisation, *(of house)* Vorderseite, -front, Außenseite, Fassade, *(impudence)* Unverschämtheit, Frechheit, *(individual representing company)* Aushängeschild, Strohmann, nomineller Vertreter, *(mil.)* Front[gebiet], -richtung, -ausdehnung, Kampf-, Schlachtlinie, *(promenade, Br.)* Strandpromenade, *(subversive group)* Untergrundorganisation, *(theater)* Zuschauerraum;
at the ~ *(mil.)* im Felde; **in** ~ an der Spitze; **successful on all** ~**s** überall erfolgreich;
false ~ falsche Fassade; **hardened** ~ verhärtete Front; **home** ~ Heimatfront; **labo(u)r** ~ Arbeitsfront; **popular** ~ Volksfront; **put-up** ~ falsche Fassade; **sea** ~ Seeseite; **united** ~ gemeinsame Front, Einheitsfront; **warm** ~ *(weather)* Warmluftfront;
~ **of a building (house)** Vorderseite eines Gebäudes;
~ *(v.)* gegenüberstellen, konfrontieren;
~ **the sea** an der Küste liegen;

to be at the ~ an der Front (im Felde) stehen; **to come to the** ~ in den Vordergrund treten, bekannt werden, sich auszeichnen; **to come to the** ~ **again** *(topic)* wieder auftauchen (aktuell werden); **to fight on two** ~s an zwei Fronten kämpfen; **to form a united** ~ geschlossene Front bilden; **to go to the** ~ an die Front gehen; **to have the** ~ die Stirn haben; **to hurry soldiers to the** ~ Truppen an die Front werfen; **to present an unbroken** ~ intakte Frontlinie bilden; **to pull back the** ~ Front zurücknehmen; **to put a bold** ~ **on it** Mut zeigen; **to put up a** ~ *(US)* Schein wahren; **to roll up the** ~ *(mil.)* Front aufrollen; **to show a bold** ~ *(stock exchange)* feste Haltung zeigen;

~ **bench** *(Br.)* Minister-, Regierungsbank; ~ **bencher** *(Br.)* führender Parteipolitiker; ~ **building** Vordergebäude; ~ **carriage** erster Waggon; ~ **cover** erste Umschlagseite, Titelseite; ~ **desk** *(US, department store)* kaufmännischer Leiter; ~ **door** Haus-, Eingangs-, Vordertür, *(US sl.)* erstes Fahrzeug in einer Kolonne; ~-**door operation** *(Br.)* Liquiditätsbeschaffung durch Schatzwechselverkauf; ~-**end fee** hohe Provisionsgebühr; ~-**end load** hohe Anfangsbelastung, *(mutual fund)* hohe Provisionsbelastung beim Ersterwerb von Zertifikaten; ~-**end space** Türplakat; ~-**foot rule** Umlegung der Anliegerkosten aufgrund der Straßenfront; ~ **guard** Grenzschutz; ~ **line** *(mil.)* Kampffront, Frontlinie, -verlauf; ~-**line artillery piece** Frontgeschütz; ~-**line correspondent** Frontberichterstatter; ~-**line soldier** Frontsoldat; **to be in the** ~ **line of nationalization** von der Verstaatlichung am meisten bedroht sein; ~ **man** Untergrundkämpfer; ~ **matter** *(print., US)* Titelei, -kopf; ~ **name** *(US)* Vorname; ~ **office** Zentralbüro, Zentrale; ~-**office personnel** Stabspersonal; ~ **page** Kopf-, Vorder-, Hauptseite, Titelblatt, -seite; **to be spread across the** ~ **page** über die ganze erste Seite gehen; **to carry on the** ~ **page** auf der Titelseite bringen; **to hold the** ~ **page** erste Seite für Titelmeldungen freihalten; ~-**page headline** Schlagzeile auf der ersten Seite; ~-**page news** Schlagzeilennachrichten; ~ **pager** berühmte Persönlichkeit, Titelfigur; ~ **part of a train** Zuganfang; **to be in the** ~ **rank** zur Prominenz gehören; ~-**rank politician** Politiker der vordersten Linie, Spitzenpolitiker; ~-**road** *(US)* parallel zur Autobahn verlaufende Straße; ~ **room** Zimmer nach vorn, Vorderzimmer; ~ **runner** aussichtsreichster Kandidat, Spitzenkandidat, *(stock exchange)* Spitzenreiter; ~ **seat** Vordersitz; ~ **section** vorderer Teil einer Ausgabe; ~ **town** Grenzstadt, *(US)* Stadt an der Siedlungsgrenze; ~ **view** Vorderansicht, Aufriß; ~-**wheel drive** Frontantrieb; ~-**wheel drive car** Wagen mit Frontantrieb; ~ **yard** *(US)* Vorgarten, Vordergarten.

frontage Grundstück mit Straßenfront, *(of house)* Vorderfront, Frontlänge, -breite, *(mil.)* Frontabschnitt, Gefechtsbreite; **road** ~ Straßenfront, *(US)* parallel zur Autobahn verlaufende Straße.

frontager Straßen-, Uferanlieger, Vorderhausbewohner.

frontal | attack Frontalangriff; ~ **collision** Frontalzusammenstoß.

frontier [Landes]grenze, *(advance region, US)* Grenzgebiet, -bereich, Siedlungsgrenze, Zivilisationsgrenze, *(fig.)* Grenzbereich, Neuland;

delivered at ~ ab Grenzstation;

artificial ~ künstliche Grenze; **closed** ~ Grenzsperre; **controversial (disputed)** ~ strittige Grenze; **defined** ~ festgelegte Grenze;

~s **of knowledge** Grenzbereich des Wissens;

to adjust a ~ Grenze berichtigen; **to cross the** ~ Grenze überschreiten (passieren); **to live on the** ~ nahe der Grenze wohnen; **to open up new** ~s *(fig.)* Neuland eröffnen (erschließen);

~ **area** Grenzgebiet; ~ **certificate** Grenzbescheinigung; ~ **clash** Grenzzwischenfall; ~ **control** Grenzüberwachung, -kontrolle; ~ **control point** Zollgrenzstelle; ~ **crossing** *(EC)* Grenzüberschreitung, -gang; ~-**crossing** grenzüberschreitend; ~ **crossing costs** *(EC)* Grenzüberschreitungskosten; ~-**crossing goods** grenzüberschreitender Warenverkehr; ~-**crossing worker** Grenzgänger; ~ **customhouse** Grenzzollamt; ~ **dispute** Grenzstreitigkeit; ~ **district** grenznahe Gemeinde, Zollgrenzbezirk; ~ **fighting style** Partisanenkampfstil; ~ **formalities** Grenzformalitäten; ~ **fort** Grenzfestung; ~ **incident** Grenzzwischenfall, -konflikt; ~ **land** Grenzland, -gebiet; ~ **point** Grenzübergangspunkt; ~ **population** Grenzbevölkerung; ~ **post** Grenzpfahl, -stelle; **free at** ~ **price** *(EC)* Preis frei Grenze; ~ **province** Grenzprovinz; ~ **question** Grenzfrage; ~ **region** Grenzlandgebiet; ~ **revision** Grenzberichtigung, -bereinigung, -korrektur; ~ **river** Grenzfluß; ~ **service** *(Br.)* Grenzschutzdienst; ~ **stamp** Grenzstempel; ~ **station** Grenzstation, -posten, -übergangsbahnhof; ~ **town** Grenzstadt; [**local**] ~ **traffic** [kleiner] Grenzverkehr; ~ **worker** Grenzgänger; ~ **zone** Grenzstreifen, -gebiet, -zone.

frontiersman *(US)* Grenzbewohner.

fronting | and abutting unmittelbar angrenzend; ~ **the street** auf die Straße gehend.

frontispiece Titelbild, *(theater)* Proszenium.

frontrunner Spitzenkandidat, *(stock exchange)* Spitzenreiter.

frontsman *(Br.)* Straßenverkäufer.

frosh *(US)* Erstsemester, Student im ersten Semester.

frost Frost, Reif, *(fig., coll.)* Kühle, Frostigkeit, *(bad luck, sl.)* Mißerfolg, Reinfall;

when ~ **sets in** bei eintretendem Frost, bei Frosteinbruch; **dead** ~ totaler Reinfall; **ground** ~ Bodenfrost; **hard (sharp)** ~ beißende Kälte, klingender Frost; **slight** ~ leichter Frost;

~ **in s. one's manner** *(coll.)* frostiges Benehmen;

~ *(v.)* mit Eis (Reif) überziehen, *(fig.)* durch eisiges Benehmen abstoßen;

~ **over** sich bereifen, sich mit Eisblumen überziehen;

to turn out a ~ glatter Reinfall sein;

~-**free** frostfrei; ~ **injury** Frostschaden; ~ **insurance** Frostversicherung; ~ **period** Frostperiode; ~ **protection** Frostschutz; ~ **shake** Frostriß; ~ **signal** Frostwarnung.

frostbite Erfrierungserscheinung, Frostbeule.

frosted | glass Matt-, Milchglass; ~ **window-panes** bereifte Fensterscheiben.

frostiness Eiseskälte, *(fig.)* Frostigkeit.

frostproof frostbeständig.

frosty | answer frostige Antwort; ~ **reception** *(coll.)* eiskalter Empfang; ~ **weather** Frostwetter.

frostwork Eisblumen.

frown Stirnrunzeln, Ausdruck des Mißfallens;

~ *(v.)* **on s. th.** auf etw. mit Mißbilligung blicken; ~ **defiance on a crowd** Menge durch Blicke einschüchtern.

frowst verbrauchte Zimmerluft, Mief;

~ *(v.)* *(Br.)* Stubenhocker sein.

frowziness Schlampigkeit, Ungepflegtheit.

frozen zugefroren, mit Eis bedeckt, *(account)* eingefroren, blockiert, gesperrt, *(drug on the market)* schlecht verkäuflich, *(fig., US)* kalt, hart, *(not liquid)* nicht flüssig, *(price)* preisgebunden;

~ **out** *(US, stock exchange)* kaltgestellt; ~ **over** vereist, mit einer Eisschicht bedeckt;

~ **assets** eingefrorene Guthaben; ~ **capital** festliegendes Kapital; ~ **cargo** Gefrierladung; ~ **credit** eingefrorener Kredit; ~ **debts** Stillhalteschulden, eingefrorene Forderungen; ~ **fact** *(US)* unumstößliche Tatsache; ~ **food** tiefgekühlte Lebensmittel; ~-**food manufacturer** Tiefkühlnahrungsmittelbetrieb; ~ **goods** tiefgekühlte Waren; ~ **inventory** unabsetzbares Lager; ~ **meat** Gefrierfleisch; ~ **money** eingefrorene Gelder; ~ **price** eingefrorener Preis, Stoppreis; ~ **roads** vereiste Straßen; ~ **vegetables** Tiefkühlgemüse; ~ **zone** kalte Zone.

fruit Obst, *(profit)* Gewinn, Nutzen, *(result)* Ergebnis, Frucht, Resultat;

civil ~s Rechtsfrüchte; **dried** ~ Dörrobst; **natural** ~s natürliche Früchte; **old** ~ *(Br., sl.)* alter Knabe; **small** ~s Beerenobst;

~s **of crime** bei der Straftat erlangte Gegenstände; ~s **of industry** industrielle Erträge; ~ **of our labo(u)r** Ertrag unserer Arbeit; ~ **of much study** Resultat fleissiger Studiums;

to bear ~ *(fig.)* Früchte tragen, Ergebnisse zeigten; **to reap the** ~s Früchte ernten;

~ **car** Obstwaggon; ~ **fallen** Erträge nach der Trennung; ~ **jar** Einweckglas; ~ **juice** Fruchtsaft; ~ **machine** Glücks-, Spielautomat; ~ **ranch** *(US)* Obstfarm, -gut; ~ **salad** Obstsalat; ~ **stand** Obststand; ~ **tree** Obstbaum.

fruitful fruchtbar, ergiebig;

~ **career** erfolgreiche Laufbahn; ~ **rain** ergiebiger Regen.

fruition of one's labo(u)r Früchte seiner Arbeit.

fruitless efforts zwecklose Bemühungen.

frustrate *(v.)* vereiteln, durchkreuzen, zunichte machen;

~ **a contract** einem Vertrag die Geschäftsgrundlage entziehen, Vertrag nachträglich unmöglich machen; **the performance of a covenant** Vertragserfüllung nachträglich unmöglich machen; ~ **a deed** Urkunde ungültig machen; ~ **s. one's expectations** j. in seinen Erwartungen täuschen; ~ **a plan** Plan zunichte machen.

frustrated vereitelt, *(psych.)* gehemmt, verkrampft, frustriert;

~ **contract** unmöglich gewordener Vertrag; ~ **Contracts Act** *(Br.)* Gesetz über Leistungshindernisse bei der Vertragserfüllung; **Law Reform ~ Contracts Act** *(Br.)* Gesetz über den Wegfall der Geschäftsgrundlage.

frustrating | event Vertragserfüllung hinderndes Ereignis; ~ **factors** Verhinderungsgründe.

frustration Verhinderung, Vereitelung, *(law of contract)* objektive Unmöglichkeit, Leistungshindernis, *(psych.)* Frustration;

numero(u)s ~s zahlreiche Enttäuschungen; **original ~** ursprüngliche Unmöglichkeit; **supervening ~** nachträgliche Unmöglichkeit;
~ **of contract** nachträglich unmöglich gewordene Vertragserfüllung;
to cause the ~ of contract Geschäftsgrundlage wegfallen lassen.

fudge *(newspaper)* Raum für letzte Meldungen;
~ *(v.) (US sl.)* mogeln;
~ **up** zurechtstutzen.

fuel Brennstoff, Heizmaterial, *(for engines)* Betriebs-, Kraft-, Treibstoff, Benzin;
domestic ~ Hausbrand; **driving ~** Betriebsstoff; **high-octane ~** klopffestes Benzin; **liquid hydrogen ~** Treibstoff aus flüssigem Wasserstoff; **low-grade ~** minderwertiges Benzin; **solid ~** fester Treibstoff; **2-star ~** Normalbenzin;
~ *(v.)* tanken, *(ship)* bunkern, *(up)* Treibstoff einnehmen;
~ **the fires of the inflationary boom in business investments** Investitionskonjunktur inflationär anheizen; ~ **a ship** Schiff mit Treibstoff versehen;
to add ~ to the flames Leidenschaften entfachen; **to be low on ~** nicht mehr genug Benzin haben; **to heap ~ on the fire** Öl aufs Feuer gießen;
~ **allocation** Benzinzuteilung, -versorgung; ~ **bill** Brennstoffrechnung; ~ **consumption** Benzin-, Treibstoffverbrauch; ~ **consumption figure** Benzinverbrauchszahlen; ~ **consumption test (trial)** Benzinverbrauchstest; ~ **costs** Brennstoff-, Heizungskosten; ~ **cost increase** Benzinkostenerhöhung; ~ **crisis** Öl-, Brennstoffkrise; ~ **depot (dump)** Kraft-, Treibstofflager; ~ **economy** Treibstoffindustrie, sparsamer Treibstoffverbrauch; **to be good on ~ economy** wenig Treibstoff verbrauchen; **to be high on ~ economy** viel Treibstoff verbrauchen; ~ **economy improvements** treibstoffsparende Verbesserungen; ~ **engineering** Brennstofftechnik; ~ **feed** Brennstoffzu-, Benzinleitung; ~ **filter** Benzinfilter; ~ **gas** Heiz-, Betriebsgas; ~ **gauge** Benzinuhr; ~ **industry** Brennstoffindustrie; ~ **injection** Kraftstoffeinspritzung; ~ **injection engine (motor)** Einspritzmotor; ~ **mixture** Kraftstoffgemisch; ~ **monopoly** Treibstoffmonopol; ~ **oil** Brenn-, Heizöl; ~ **permit** Tankausweis; ~ **pipe** Benzin-, Kraftstoffleitung; ~ **price** Benzin-, Treibstoffpreis; ~ **price hike** Benzin-, Treibstoffpreiserhöhung; ~ **pricing** Benzinpreispolitik; ~ **pump** Benzinpumpe; ~ **requirements** Brennstoff-, Treibstoffbedarf; ~ **reserve** Benzin-, Brennstoffreserve, -vorräte; ~ **resources** Treibstoffquellen; ~ **-saving stove** sparsamer Ofen; ~ **savings** Treibstoffersparnisse; ~ **shortage** Treibstoff-, Energieverknappung; ~ **stop** Tankaufenthalt; ~ **storage** Treibstofflager, -lagerung; ~ **storage premises** Treibstoffdepot; ~ **supply** Treibstoff-, Benzin-, Brennstoffversorgung; ~ **system** Kraftstoffanlage; ~ **tank** Benzin-, Treibstofftank; **slip ~ tank** abwerfbarer Brennstoffbehälter; ~ **usage** Treibstoffverbrauch; ~ **yard** Betriebs-, Brennstofflager.

fuelling Treibstoffeinnahme, Tanken;
~ **station** Tankstation.

fug *(Br., coll.)* schlechte Luft, Mief.

fugitive Flüchtling, Ausreißer;
~ **from justice** flüchtiger Rechtsbrecher;
to be a ~ from justice fluchtverdächtig sein;
~ *(a.)* flüchtig, entflohen, geflohen, *(roaming)* vagabundierend, sich herumtreibend, *(short-lived)* kurzlebig, flüchtig;
~ **colo(u)rs** unechte Farben; ~ **criminal** flüchtiger Rechtsbrecher; ~ **debtor** flüchtiger Schuldner; ~ **felon** ausgebrochener Verbrecher; ~ **fund** Fluchtkapital; ~ **offender** flüchtiger Straftäter; ~ **oil** *(derrick)* ausströmendes Öl; ~ **soldier** Deserteur.

fulfil, fulfill *(US) (v.)* erfüllen, ausführen, zufriedenstellend vollziehen, vollbringen;
~ **a contract** Vertrag erfüllen; ~ **one's duty** seine Pflicht erfüllen; ~ **an obligation** Verpflichtung einhalten; ~ **a promise** Versprechen einlösen; ~ **the purpose** zweckentsprechend sein; ~ **the terms of reconstruction** den Umgründungsbedingungen gerecht werden.

fulfilment, fulfillment *(US)* Ausführung, Erfüllung, Vollziehung;
in ~ erfüllungshalber; **in ~ of a pledge** Erfüllung einer übernommenen Verpflichtung;
~ **of a contract** Vertragserfüllung; ~ **of a condition** Erfüllung einer Bedingung; ~ **of the notice period** Ablauf der Kündigungsfrist;
to defer ~ of supply contracts Erfüllung von Lieferverträgen aussetzen.

full *(utmost extent)* äußerster Grad, höchstes Maß;
~ *(a.)* voll, ganz, völlig, vollständig, *(in detail)* eingehend, ausführlich, genau, weitläufig, *(el.)* lautstark, *(hotel)* besetzt, *(without restraint)* unumschränkt;

at the ~ auf dem Höhepunkt; **in ~** voll, ungekürzt, per Saldo; **payment in ~** zum Ausgleich aller Forderungen; **to the ~** bis zum Letzten (Äußersten); **written in ~** ausgeschrieben;
~ **in the beams of a searchlight** in vollem Scheinwerferlicht; ~ **of beans** voller Lebenslust; ~ **to the brim** vollgestopft; ~ **in the face** direkt ins Gesicht; ~ **of himself** von sich eingenommen; ~ **of new ideas** voller neuer Ideen; ~ **of matter** inhaltsreich; ~ **out** mit höchster Geschwindigkeit; ~ **to overflowing** zum Platzen voll; ~ **up** *(Br.)* vollbesetzt;
to be ~ of o. s. (one's importance) von seiner Bedeutung überzeugt sein; **to be ~ of beans** lebenssprühend sein; **to be ~ of the news** von Nachrichten völlig beherrscht sein; **to be ~ up with business** total ausgelastet sein; **to be ~ up with coal (oil)** *(mar.)* vollgebunkert sein; **to enjoy o. s. to the ~** sich glänzend amüsieren; **to have one's hands ~** vollauf zu tun haben; **to have one's pockets ~ of money** Taschen voller Geld haben; **to pay in ~** voll bezahlen; **to pay in ~ or in instalments** im ganzen oder in Raten bezahlen; **to publish a letter in ~** Brief vollinhaltlich veröffentlichen; **to receipt in ~** per Saldo quittieren; **to work to the ~ at one's task** sein Äußerstes bei der Arbeit hergeben; **to write one's name in ~** seinen Namen ausschreiben;
~ **account** abschließende Rechnungslegung; ~ **address** volle (vollständige) Adresse; ~ **age** Mündigkeit, Volljährigkeit; **of ~ age** volljährig; **to attain ~ age** volljährig werden; ~ **allowance** *(ship)* volle Ration; ~ **amount** ganzer Betrag; ~ **answer** *(pleading)* vollständige Klagebeantwortung; ~ **annual value** voller Jahresertrag; ~ **-armed** in voller Rüstung; ~ **assembly** Plenum; ~ **authority** unumschränkte Vollmacht; ~ **benefit** voller Nutzen; ~ **binding** Ganzleineneinband; ~ **blood** von den gleichen Eltern abstammend; ~ **-blooded interpretation of a part** ausdrucksvolle Rollenwiedergabe; ~ **-blown** voll entwickelt, *(piece of news)* groß aufgemacht; ~ **-blown lawyer** versierter Anwalt; ~ **board** *(Br.)* Vollpension; ~ **-bottomed** mit großem Laderaum; ~ **bound** in Ganzleinen; ~ **cap** *(tyres)* Runderneuerung; ~ **cargo** volle Ladung; ~ **cloth** *(book)* Ganzleinen; ~ **or valuable consideration** geldwerte Gegenleistung; ~ **copy** vollständige Abschrift; ~ **costs** sämtliche Kosten, Vollkosten; ~ **-cost pricing** Vollkostenkalkulation; ~ **-cost principle** Vollkostenrechnung; ~ **court** ordnungsgemäß besetztes Gericht, Plenum; ~ **covenant deed** *(US)* Grundstücksübertragungsurkunde; ~ **coverage** *(insurance)* volle Risikoübernahme; ~ **crew** volle Besatzung; ~ **day** ausgebuchter Tag; ~ **defence** alle nur möglichen Einwendungen; ~ **details** genaue Angaben; ~ **discharge** endgültige Entlastung; ~ **dress** Gesellschafts-, Galaanzug; ~ **-dress** formell; ~ **-dress debate** *(parl.)* allgemeine Aussprache; ~ **-dress rehearsal** Generalprobe; ~ **economic price** nicht subventionierter (echter) Preis.

full employment Vollbeschäftigung;
to be in ~ vollbeschäftigt sein; **to move the economy toward ~** Vollbeschäftigungszustand in der Wirtschaft herbeiführen;
~ **budget** Staatshaushalt unter Vollbeschäftigungsbedingungen; ~ **economy** Vollbeschäftigungspolitik; ~ **gap** Vollbeschäftigungslücke; **to rush the economy back to ~ levels** Vollbeschäftigungszustand sofort wiederherstellen; **to drag the world economy up towards the ~ path** der Konjunktur weltweit wieder zur Vollbeschäftigung verhelfen; ~ **policy** Vollbeschäftigungspolitik; ~ **target** Vollbeschäftigungsziel; ~ **thesis** Vollbeschäftigungsthese.

full | face *(print.)* fette Schrift; ~ **-faced** *(print.)* fett; ~ **faith and credit** *(foreign judgment)* volle Gültigkeit; ~ **fare** voller Fahrpreis; **to pay ~ fare** vollen Preis zahlen; ~ **-fledged barrister** versierter Anwalt; ~ **-fledged professor** Vollprofessor; ~ **force of men** volle Besatzung; **in ~ gear** im höchsten Gang; ~ **-grown** ausgewachsen, erwachsen; ~ **hearing** ordnungsgemäßes rechtliches Gehör; **to wait a ~ hour** geschlagene Stunde warten; ~ **house** ausverkauftes Haus; ~ **indorsement** Vollgiro; ~ **information** ausführliche (genaue) Auskunft; ~ **interest admitted** Vollbeteiligung zugesagt; ~ **jurisdiction** sachliche Zuständigkeit; ~ **keyboard** *(typewriter)* Volltastatur; ~ **-leather binding** Ganzledereinband; ~ **-length** in voller Größe; ~ **-length film** abendfüllender Film; ~ **-length portrait** lebensgroßes Bild; **in ~ letters** voll ausgeschrieben; ~ **liability** Vollhaftung; ~ **liberty to act** volle Handlungsfreiheit; ~ **life** weder gestorben noch für tot erklärt; ~ **line** volle Zeile; ~ **-line department** reichlich sortimentiertes Warenhaus; ~ **-line forcing** Monopolzwang für den Ankauf von Komplementärerzeugnissen; ~ **load** volle Ladung, *(airplane)* Gesamtgewicht; ~ **lot** *(US)* [Börsen]abschlußeinheit; ~ **measure** *(print.)* voller Spaltensatz; ~ **member** ordentliches Mitglied, *(EC)* Vollmitglied; ~ **membership** Vollmitgliedschaft; **to get ~ membership** Vollmitglied werden; ~ **net** *(broadcasting)* Gemeinschaftssendung, *(price)* ohne jeden

Nachlaß; ~ **operating capacity** volle Betriebsleistung; ~ **out** Zeileneinrückung; ~ **ownership** Volleigentum; ~ **page** ganze Seite; ~-**page ad** (US) ganzseitiges Inserat, ganzseitige Anzeige; ~-**page newspaper advertisement** ganzseitige Anzeige, Ganzseiteninserat; ~-**page illustration** ganzseitige Abbildung; ~-**page rate** (advertising) Seitenpreis; ~ **paid** voll eingezahlt; ~-**paid stock** (US) voll eingezahlte Aktie; ~ **particulars** detaillierte Angaben, Näheres, alle (genaue) Einzelheiten; ~ **pay** voller Arbeitslohn, volles Gehalt; **to be retired on** ~ **pay** mit vollen Bezügen pensioniert werden; ~ **payment** Vollbezahlung; **in** ~ **and final payment** als endgültige Abfindung; ~ **position** (advertising) bevorzugte Plazierung, Vorzugsplatz, -plazierung; ~ **possession** unbeschränkter Besitz; ~ **powers** umfassende Vollmachten; ~ **price** voller (nicht herabgesetzter) Preis; ~-**price purchaser** Normalkäufer; ~ **professor** (US) ordentlicher Professor; ~ **proof** umfassender Beweis; ~ **quota** Vollkontingent; ~ **rates** volle Gebühren; ~ **rates of custom duties** allgemeiner Zolltarif; ~ **repayment** Rückzahlung in voller Höhe; ~ **right** Eigentum und Besitz; ~ **risk** volle Risikoübernahme; ~-**run edition ads** (US) Anzeigen in der Gesamtausgabe; ~ **scale** größten Ausmaßes; **to give** ~ **scope to s. o.** jem. völlig freie Hand lassen; ~ **screen** (film) Großaufnahme; ~ **service** (advertising) Beratung auf allen Gebieten; ~ **session** Plenarsitzung; ~ **set** (bill of lading) vollständiger Formularsatz, (documents) alle Ausfertigungen; ~ **set of samples** komplette Kollektion; ~ **settlement** vollständiger Ausgleich; ~ **showing** (advertising) Vollbelegung aller Anschlagstafeln in einem Bezirk; ~ **sister** leibliche Schwester; ~ **size** Normalgröße; ~ **speed** (mar.) Volldampf; ~ **statement** umfassende (vollständige) Erklärung; ~ **stop** Punkt; **to come to a** ~ **stop** (coll.) völlig zum Stillstand kommen; ~ **throttle** Vollgas; **at** ~ **tide** beim höchsten Wasserstand.

full-time hauptamtlich, -beruflich, ganztägig;
to run ~ im Schichtbetrieb laufen; **to work** ~ ganztägig arbeiten;
to employ on a ~ **basis** ganztägig beschäftigen; ~ **employment** ganztägige Beschäftigung, Ganztagsbeschäftigung; **to grow into a** ~ **employment** sich zu einer Ganztagsbeschäftigung entwickeln; ~ **job (profession)** ganztägige Beschäftigung (Arbeit), Ganztags-, Hauptbeschäftigung; ~ **role** Ganztagtätigkeit.

full | timer ganztägig Beschäftigter; ~ **title** Haupttitel; ~-**track vehicle** Raupenfahrzeug; ~ **up** (Br.) besetzt; ~ **value** Ersatz-, Versicherungswert; **at** ~ **value** vollgültig; ~ **weight** volles Gewicht; ~ **year** ganzes Jahr; ~ **year's course** ganzjähriger Lehrgang.

fuller information detaillierte Angaben.

fully | administered (estate) Einrede der Erschöpfung des Nachlasses; ~ **authorized** generalbevollmächtigt, mit allen Vollmachten ausgestattet; ~ **automatic** vollautomatisch; ~ **committed** zwecks Aburteilung dem Gericht übergeben; ~ **covered** (insurance) voll gedeckt (versichert); ~ **employed** vollbeschäftigt; ~ **entitled** vollberechtigt; ~ **fledged barrister** versierter Anwalt; ~ **licensed** mit unbeschränkter Schankkonzession; ~ **occupied** voll beschäftigt; ~ **paid [up]** voll eingezahlt; ~ **paid shares** voll eingezahlte Aktien; ~ **qualified** vollberechtigt; ~ **qualified workers** Vollarbeitskräfte; ~ **subscribed** voll gezeichnet;
until ~ **paid** bis zur endgültigen Bezahlung;
to be ~ **booked** (theater) ausverkauft sein; **to depress the pedal** ~ Gaspedal ganz durchtreten; **to take** ~ **two hours** zwei volle Stunden dauern; **to treat a subject** ~ Thema erschöpfend behandeln.

ful(l)ness (fig.) [Über]fülle, Reichtum;
in the ~ **of time** (bible) da die Zeit erfüllt war; **out of the** ~ **of his heart** im Überschwang seines Herzens;
to treat a subject with the ~ **due** Thema mit der gebotenen Ausführlichkeit behandeln.

fumble Herumtasten, stümperhafter Versuch;
~ (v.) ungeschickt jonglieren;
~ **around** herumfummeln; ~ **in the dark** im Dunkeln herumtasten; ~ **at a lock** an einem Schlüsselloch herumhantieren; ~ **in one's pockets for a key** nach einem Schlüssel in seinen Taschen tasten.

fume Dampf, Schwaden;
~ **of cigars** Zigarrenrauch;
~ (v.) s. o. j. beweihräuchern; ~ **because one is kept waiting** ungeduldig warten, bis man dran ist; ~ **over trifles** sich über Kleinigkeiten aufregen;
to be affected by the ~**s of jealousy** von Eifersucht verzehrt werden.

fumigate (v.) **a room** Zimmer desinfizieren.

fun Spaß, Zeitvertreib;
~ **and games** Possen;
to make ~ **of (poke** ~ **at) s. o.** j. zum Besten halten (lächerlich machen).

function (machine) Arbeitsweise, Funktion, (officeholder's duty) Amts[pflicht], -handlung, -tätigkeit, -verrichtung, Aufgabe, Funktion, [Dienst]obliegenheit, Geschäftsbereich, (social life) Empfang, gesellschaftliche Veranstaltung, (vocation) Beruf;
in his ~ **as magistrate** in seiner Eigenschaft als Magistratsbeamter; **outside one's** ~ außerdienstlich;
advisory ~ beratende Tätigkeit (Funktion); **banking** ~ Bankfunktion; **basic** ~**s** grundsätzliche Funktionen; **consular** ~**s** konsulare Funktionen; **double** ~ Doppelaufgabe; **executive** ~ Vollzugsfunktion; **governmental** ~**s** staatliche Funktionen; **honorary** ~ Ehrenamt; **interdependent** ~**s** voneinander abhängige Funktionen; **judicial** ~ richterliche Funktion; **legislative** ~ Gesetzgebungsfunktion; **managerial** ~ Aufgaben der Betriebsleitung; **ministerial** ~**s** vollziehende Funktionen; **official** ~ Amtshandlung; **society** ~ Empfang, gesellschaftliche Funktionen; **specific** ~ Sonderaufgabe, -funktion;
~ **of a committee** Ausschußfunktion; ~**s of a consul** konsularischer Aufgabenbereich; ~ **of coordinating** Koordinierungsaufgabe; ~ **of education** erzieherische Aufgaben; ~ **of a judge** richterliche Funktion; ~ **of money** Geldfunktion; ~**s of an officer of state** Funktionen eines Staatsbeamten; ~**s and powers** Aufgaben und Befugnisse; ~**s of society** Aufgaben der Gesellschaft;
~ (v.) arbeiten, tätig sein, amtieren, (mechanism) funktionieren;
~ **in all financial fields** erfolgreiche Finanzierungsgeschäfte auf allen Gebieten abwickeln; ~ **without friction** reibungslos funktionieren;
to carry out ~**s** Funktionen ausüben; **to carry out official** ~**s** dienstliche Aufgaben wahrnehmen; **to carry out** ~**s only under statutory authority** nur im Rahmen gesetzlicher Ermächtigung tätig werden; **to come within the scope of** ~ innerhalb des normalen Aufgabenkreises liegen; **to discharge one's** ~**s** seinen Pflichten nachkommen; **to exercise judicial** ~**s** richterliche Aufgaben wahrnehmen; **to fulfil[l] a** ~ Funktion ausüben; **to limit** ~**s** Aufgabenbereich beschränken; **to perform the** ~**s of servant and gardener combined** zugleich Hausangestellter und Gärtner sein;
~ **value** Gebrauchswert.

functional funktionell, fachlich, (official) amtlich, dienstlich, (statistics) repräsentativ;
~ **accounting** funktionale Kontenrechnung; ~ **architecture** zweckbestimmte Architektur; ~ **building** Zweckbau; ~ **capacity** Leistungsfähigkeit; ~ **claim** Funktionsanspruch; ~ **classification** Gliederung nach Sachgebieten, Berufsaufgliederung; ~ **commission** Fachausschuß; ~ **department** Fachabteilung, -referat; ~ **depreciation** Abschreibung auf Rationalisierungsinvestitionen; ~ **diagram** Arbeitsplan; ~ **disease (disorder)** Funktionsstörung; ~ **discount** Funktions-, Händlerrabatt; ~ **distribution** Funktionsgliederung; ~ **division of expenses** (US) funktionelle Kostenaufgliederung; ~ **expert** Spezialist; ~ **finance** antizyklische Konjunkturpolitik mittels steuerpolitischer Maßnahmen; ~ **grade** Funktionsstufe; ~ **manager** fachliche Führungskraft; ~ **middleman** Aufgabenverteiler, (advertising) Absatzmittler; ~ **object** Gebrauchsgegenstand; ~ **organization** (management) funktionale Organisation, Berufsverband; ~ **partition** funktionelle Trennung; ~ **protection** (law of nations) Schutz der internationalen Beziehungen; ~ **relationship** Funktionsverhältnis; ~ **representation** berufliche Vertretung in politischen Gremien; ~ **specialization** Aufgabenspezialisierung; ~ **statement** funktionale Kostenkalkulation; ~ **style** Stil der neuen Sachlichkeit; ~ **wholesaler** Engrosvertreter.

functionalism Zweckstil, Sachlichkeit.

functionary Funktionär, Amtsleiter, -walter, Angestellter; **nonpolicy-making** ~ untergeordneter Angestellter.

functioning Wirken, Arbeitsweise;
smooth ~ reibungsloser Ablauf;
~ **of the economy** Funktionieren der Volkswirtschaft;
~ (a.) im Betrieb.

fund (available assets) [flüssiges] Kapital, Geldsumme, (capital stock, Br.) Grund-, Stamm-, Betriebskapital einer Bank, (investment company) Anlagefonds, (money set apart) Fonds, zweckgebundene Vermögensmasse, [Sonder]vermögen, (stock) Vorrat;
accident ~ Betriebsunfallfonds; **aid** ~**s** Hilfsgelder; **available** ~ Bereitstellungsfonds, verfügbarer Fonds; **benevolent** ~ Wohltätigkeits-, Unterstützungsfonds; **bond** ~ Rentenfonds; **bonus**

~ Dividendenfonds; **bribery** ~ Bestechungsfonds; **cash-heavy** ~ liquider Fonds; **charity** ~ Wohltätigkeitsfonds; **closed-end** ~ Investmentfonds mit begrenzter Emissionshöhe, geschlossener Investmentfonds; **closed-end property** ~ geschlossener Immobilienfonds; **common** ~ Sondervermögen; **community** ~ gemeinsamer Fonds; **consolidated** ~ konsolidierte Staatsschuld; **contingency** ~ außerordentlicher Reservefonds, Not-, Sonderfonds; **contingent** ~ Not-, Sonderfonds; **cumulative** ~ thesaurierender Fonds; **depreciation** ~ Abschreibungsrücklage; **disability** ~ Invaliditätsfonds; **emergency** ~ Reservefonds; **employees' pension** ~ betriebliche Pensionskasse; **endowment** ~ Stiftungsvermögen; **exchange equalization** ~ Devisenausgleichsfonds; **expendable** ~ verfügbares Kapital, Unkostenfonds; **expendable trust** ~ Treuhandsfonds mit freier Ertragsverwendung; **fighting** ~ Kampffonds; **fixed** ~ Investmentfonds mit feststehendem Portefeuille; **semi-fixed** ~ Investmentsfonds mit begrenzt auswechselbarem Portefeuille; **flexible** ~ Investmentfonds mit auswechselbarem Portefeuille; **general** ~ allgemeine Rücklage, *(governmental accounting)* Staatskasse, allgemeine Etatsmittel, Steuermittel, Steuern und sonstige Einkünfte, öffentliches Vermögen; **general revenue** ~ Kommunalvermögen, Vermögen einer Kommune; **guarantee (guaranty)** ~ Garantie, Reservefonds; **imprest** ~ *(Br.)* Spesenvorschuß, *(petty cash)* Portokasse; **insurance** ~ Versicherungsfonds; **International Monetary** ~ Weltwährungsfonds; **investment** ~ Fonds einer Kapitalanlagegesellschaft, Anlagekapital, Investmentfonds; **joint union-industry** ~ gemeinsam von Industrie und Gewerkschaften errichteter Fonds; **leverage** ~ Investmentfonds mit Leihkapital; **loan** ~ Anleihekapital; **managed** ~ Investmentfonds mit veränderlichem Portefeuille; **mission** ~ Missionsfonds; **mixed** ~ gemischter Fonds; **mutual** ~ *(US)* Investment-, Kapitalanlagegesellschaft; **nonexpendable** ~ Thesaurierungsfonds; **old-age pension** ~ Pensionsfonds, -kasse; **open-end** ~ Investmentfonds mit beliebiger Investitionshöhe (unbeschränkte Anteilsausgabe), offener Investmentfonds; **operating** ~ Betriebsmittel; **original** ~ Grundstock; **outside** ~ Fremdkapital; **payroll** ~ Gehälterfonds; **pension** ~ Pensionskasse, -fonds; **permanent** ~ eiserner Bestand; **petty-cash** ~ Portokasse; **political** ~ politischer Fonds; **provident** ~ Unterstützungs-, Hilfskasse; **provident reserve** ~ außerordentliche Rücklage; **real-estate** ~ Immobilienfonds; **redemption** ~ Tilgungsfonds; **relief** ~ Hilfs-, Unterstützungsfonds; **renewal** ~ Erneuerungsfonds; **reserve** ~ Rücklagen, Rückstellung; **restricted** ~ Spezialfonds; **retiring** ~ Pensionsfonds, -kasse; **revolving** ~ *(governmental accounting, US)* rückzahlbare Staatssubvention, sich stets erneuernder Fonds; **safety** ~ Reserve-, Sicherheitsfonds, *(banking)* Mindestreserven; **secret** ~ Geheimfonds; **securities** ~ Wertpapierfonds; **security reserve** ~ Wertpapierrücklage; **separate** ~ Sonderfonds, getrennter Fonds; **separate political** ~ politischer Sonderfonds; **shareholding** ~ Aktienfonds; **sick-benefit** ~ Betriebskrankenkasse; **sickness** ~ Krankenkasse; **sinking** ~ Amortisations-, Tilgungsfonds; **slush** ~ Bestechungsfonds; **special** ~ Sonderfonds; **special assessment** ~ aus Sonderveranlagungen gebildeter Fonds, Sonderanlagenfonds; **special revenue** ~ Fonds zur Finanzierung von Sonderaufgaben, Sondervermögen; **specialized** ~ Spezialfonds; **share** ~ Aktienfonds; **stabilization** ~ Stabilisierungsfonds; **starter** ~ Startfonds; **state-operated** ~ vom Staat (Bund, staatlich verwaltetes) Sondervermögen; **strike** ~ Streikkasse, -fonds; **superannuation** ~ Pensionsfonds; **surplus** ~ nicht verbrauchte Etatsmittel; **sustentation** ~ Streikkasse; **testimonial** ~ privater Spesenfonds, Reptilienfonds; **trust** ~ Treuhandgelder, -vermögen, treuhänderisch verwaltetes Vermögen, *(foundation)* Stiftungsgelder, *(guardian)* Mündelgeld, -vermögen, *(investment* ~*)* Investmentfonds auf Basis eines Trusts, *(receivership)* Massekonto; **trust-and-agency** ~ von einer Treuhandgesellschaft verwaltetes Sondervermögen; **unemployment** ~ [etwa] Sondervermögen der Bundesanstalt für Arbeitslosenversicherung; **utility** ~ Sondervermögen öffentlicher Versorgungsbetriebe; **wage** ~ Lohnkasse; **welfare** ~ Unterstützungsfonds; **working-capital** ~ zweckgebundenes Sondervermögen, Fonds für Kommunalbetriebszwecke;

~ **of common sense** Portion gesunden Menschenverstands; ~ **of a company** Gesellschaftskapital; ~ **of** ~**s** Dachfonds; ~ **of information** Auskunftsquelle; ~ **open to the general public** Publikumsfonds; ~ **of amusing stories** unerschöpflicher Schatz amüsanter Geschichten;

~ *(v.) (convert floating debt, Br.)* [schwebende Schuld] fundieren, konsolidieren, kapitalisieren, *(finance)* finanzieren, *(invest, Br.)* Geld in Staatspapieren anlegen;

~ **the floating debt** Staatsschuld konsolidieren; ~ **government**

notes Schatzwechsel einlösen; ~ **interest arrears** Zinsrückstände kapitalisieren; ~ **a loan** Anleihe konsolidieren;

to be placed in a special ~ einem Sonderfonds zufließen; **to commit a** ~ **to the care of trustees** Vermögensfonds Treuhändern anvertrauen; **to convert a** ~ **to another purpose** Fondsvermögen anderweitig anlegen; **to create a** ~ Fonds bilden (errichten); **to endow a** ~ Fonds dotieren (alimentieren); **to have a perfect** ~ **of anecdotes** über einen unerschöpflichen Anekdotenschatz verfügen; **to have a rare** ~ **of perseverance** von unerschöpflicher Ausdauer sein; **to have a great** ~ **of wit** sehr geistreich sein; **to launch a** ~ Fonds gründen; **to liquidate a** ~ Fonds auflösen; **to make a** ~ **available** Fonds zur Disposition stellen; **to outperform a** ~ Fonds übertreffen; **to pay into a** ~ zu einem Fonds beisteuern; **to reestablish a** ~ Fonds auffüllen; **to run a hot** ~ Topf heißen Geldes verwalten; **to start a** ~ Subskriptionsliste auflegen, Sammlung veranstalten; **to take money out of a** ~ Geldbeträge aus einem Fonds entnehmen; **to vote a** ~ Fonds bewilligen;

~ **account** Fondskonto; ~ **administration** Kapitalverwaltung, *(investment fund)* Vermögensverwaltung; ~ **administrator** *(investment fund)* Vermögensverwalter; ~ **assets** Fondsvermögen; ~ **balance sheet** Vermögensbilanz; ~ **contribution** *(trade union)* Kampffondszuschuß; ~ **decision** *(investment trust)* Anlageentscheidung; ~ **financing** Fondsfinanzierung; ~ **group** Vermögenszusammenfassung; ~ **holdings** Fondsbestände; ~ **investment** Fondsanlage; ~ **liability** Fondsverpflichtung; ~ **management** Fondsverwaltung; ~ **manager** Vermögens-, Fondsverwalter; ~ **money** *(investment fund)* Anlagekapital; ~ **obligation** Fondsverpflichtung; ~ **pool** Sammelfonds; ~ **raiser** Mittelaufbringer, Geldeinsammler, -beschaffer; ~ **raising** Mittelaufbringung; ~**-raising activity (efforts)** Sammeltätigkeit; ~**-raising circuit** Reisetätigkeit für eine Sammelaktion; **to launch a** ~**-raising drive** große Sammelaktion starten; **sinking-** ~ **reserves** Amortisationsrücklagen; ~ **surplus** Fondsüberschuß; **sinking-**~ **tax** Anleihesteuer;

funds *(Br., government bonds)* Staatspapiere, -anleihen, *(pecuniary resources)* [Geld]mittel, Gelder, Finanzmittel, Kapital[ien], *(securities, US)* Effekten;

for lack of ~ mangels Barmittel; **in** ~ im Besitz verfügbarer Mittel, bei Kasse; **out of (without)** ~ mittellos, nicht bei Kasse; **returned for want of** ~ mangels Deckung zurück; **without** ~ **in hand** ohne Deckung (Guthaben);

the ~ *(Br.)* Staatsschulden, -papiere;

appropriated ~ bereitgestellte Mittel; **attached** ~ beschlagnahmte Geldbeträge; **available** ~ verfügbare (greifbare, flüssige, bereitstehende) Mittel; **bank** ~ Bankguthaben; **borrowed** ~ Fremdmittel; **British** ~ englische Staatsanleihe; **building society** ~ Bausparmittel; **consolidated** ~ *(Br.)* konsolidierte Anleihe, fundierte Staatsschuld, Konsols, Annuitäten; **corporate** ~ Gesellschaftsmittel; **current** ~ flüssige Mittel; **disposable** ~ verfügbares Geld, flüssige Gelder (Geldmittel); **dormant** ~ gerichtlich hinterlegtes Geld; **earmarked** ~ zweckbestimmte Mittel; **employed** ~ Betriebsvermögen, -mittel; **government[al]** ~ *(Br.)* Staatspapiere, -anleihen, fundierte Staatspapiere; **insufficient** ~ *(banking)* ungenügende Deckung, ungenügendes Guthaben; ~ **invested** angelegtes Geld; **liquid** ~ flüssige Mittel; **loan** ~ Kreditmittel; **necessary** ~ erforderliche Mittel, benötigte Gelder; **New York** ~ Barzahlung New York; **no** ~ *(banking)* keine Deckung, kein Guthaben; **operating** ~ Betriebsmittel; **original** ~ Stammkapital; **own** ~ eigene Mittel; **partnership** ~ Gesellschaftskapital; **permanent** ~ eiserner Bestand; **private** ~ privates Geld; **public** ~ *(Br., government annuities)* [fundierte] Staatspapiere, -anleihen, *(money on hand)* öffentliche Gelder (Mittel); **related** ~ verbundene Zweckvermögen; **sufficient** ~ genügende Deckung, ausreichendes Guthaben; **tied-up** ~ festliegende (festgelegte) Gelder; **transferable** ~ übertragbare Ausgabemittel; **trust** ~ Treuhandvermögen; **unapplied (unappropriated)** ~ nicht verwendete (verteilte) Mittel;

~ **in cash** Bar-, Kassenbestand; ~ **at disposal** verfügbare Mittel; ~ **on hand** flüssige Mittel, Geldmittel, eiserner Bestand; ~ **for housing** Mittel für den Wohnungsbau, Wohnungsbaumittel; ~ **for reconstruction** Wiederaufbaumittel; ~ **for reimbursement** Deckungsmittel; ~ **of a society** Vereinskasse; ~ **from outside sources** *(bank balance)* fremde Gelder;

to abstract ~ Vermögenswerte beiseiteschaffen; **to alienate** ~ **from their proper destination** Geldmittel anderen als den vorgesehenen Zwecken zuführen, Gelder zweckentfremden; **to be in** ~ flüssig (bei Kasse) sein, *(bank)* zahlungsfähig sein, *(firm)* kapitalkräftig sein; **to be out of** ~ nicht bei Geld (knapp bei Kasse) sein, *(bank)* zahlungsunfähig sein; **to buy** ~ Staatsanlei-

hen (Renten[werte]) kaufen; **to convert ~ to another purpose** Geldmittel anderweitig anlegen; **to deposit ~ with a trustee** Beträge für die Pensionskasse zurückstellen; **to earmark ~** Gelder zweckbestimmen; **to embezzle the ~ of a ward** Mündelvermögen unterschlagen; **to funnel ~ to one's own use** Vermögen für seine privaten Zwecke mißbrauchen; **to furnish with ~** mit Geldmitteln versehen, Deckung anschaffen; **to have ample ~** reichliche Mittel zur Verfügung haben; **to have ~ with a banker** Geld auf der Bank haben; **to have DM 10.000 in ~** 10.000 DM in Staatspapieren angelegt haben; **to have no ~ available** keine Geldmittel zur Verfügung haben; **to invest ~** Kapital anlegen; **to invest ~ in a scheme** sich mit Vermögenswerten an einem Unternehmen beteiligen; **to invest money in ~** *(Br.)* Geld in Staatsanleihen anlegen; **to ladle out ~** Geldmittel zur Verfügung stellen; **to make a call for ~** Kapitalerhöhung vornehmen; **to make the necessary ~ available** notwendige Mittel bereitstellen; **to misappropriate public ~** öffentliche Gelder unterschlagen; **to pool ~** Geld zusammenschießen; **to provide with ~** Geld beschaffen, für Deckung sorgen; **to put in ~** mit Geldmitteln versehen; **to put up ~** Geldmittel aufbringen; **to raise ~** Kapital beschaffen (aufnehmen), Mittel aufbringen (beschaffen); **to replenish its ~** *(party)* Kasse wieder auffüllen; **to supply s. o. with ~** j. mit Geldmitteln versehen; **to vote the ~** Haushaltsmittel (Etat) bewilligen;
sufficient~ **clause** *(banking)* Guthabenklausel; ~ **control** Mittelkontrolle; ~ **flow** Mittelzufluß; ~ **generation** Kapitalentstehung; ~ **statement** Verwendungs-, Vermögensnachweis, Bewegungsbilanz, Finanzflußrechnung.
fundable kapatalisierbar.
fundament Grundlage, Fundament;
~**s of bookkeeping** Grundbegriffe der Buchführung.
fundamental Grundlage, -prinzip, -zug, Fundament;
to reach a general agreement on ~s in den Grundsatzfragen zu einer Einigung gelangen;
~ *(a.)* grundlegend, grundsätzlich, elementar, fundamental;
~ **attitude** Grundhaltung, -einstellung; ~ **clause** Grundbedingung; ~ **colo(u)rs** Primärfarben; ~ **conception** Grundbegriff; ~ **contribution** grundlegender Beitrag; ~ **data** grundlegende Tatsachen; ~ **error** fundamentaler Irrtum; ~ **facts** grundlegende Tatsachen; ~ **freedoms** Grundfreiheiten; ~ **idea** Grundbegriff; ~ **issue** entscheidende Frage; ~ **law** Grundgesetz, Verfassung; ~ **paper** Grundsatzreferat; ~ **problem** Grundproblem; ~ **question** Grundsatzfrage; ~ **right** Grundrecht.
funded verzinslich angelegt, *(capitalized)* kapitalisiert, *(converted into permanent debt)* fundiert, *(invested in public funds)* in [fundierten] Staatspapieren angelegt;
~ **capital** angelegtes Kapital; **long-term ~ capital** langfristig angelegte Mittel; ~ **debt (indebtedness)** fundierte Schuld, *(Br.)* langfristige Anleiheschuld, Staatsanleihe; ~ **liability** konsolidierte Verbindlichkeit; ~ **loan** konsolidierte Anleihe, Staatsanleihe; ~ **property** Kapitalvermögen, *(Br.)* Besitz an Staatsanleihen; ~ **reserve** in verzinslichen Wertpapieren angelegter Reservefonds.
fundholder Fondsbesitzer, *(Br.)* Inhaber von Staatspapieren, Rentier, *(stockholder)* Aktionär.
fundholding *(Br.)* Besitz von Staatsanleihen.
funding *(conversion into permanent debt)* Schuldenkonsolidierung, Umwandlung [einer schwebenden in eine fundierte Schuld], Fundierung, Finanzierung, *(employee pension scheme)* Aussonderung von Betriebsmitteln für Versorgungszwecke der Angestellten, *(investing)* Anlage in Staatspapieren;
aggregate ~ Fundierung der Altersversorgungskosten; **multinational ~** multinationale Kapitalausstattung;
~ **of bank advances** Konsolidierung von Bankkrediten; ~ **of the floating debt** Konsolidierung der schwebenden Schuld; ~ **of a pension plan** Einrichtung (Ausstattung) einer Pensionskasse;
to delay its ~ Mittelbewilligung verzögern;
~ **bonds** Konsolidierungsschuldverschreibungen; ~ **debenture interests** *(Br.)* Zinsen in Form von festverzinslichen Schuldverschreibungen; ~ **loan** Konsolidierungsanleihe; ~ **operation** Fundierungstransaktion; ~ **program(me)** Konsolidierungsprogramm; ~ **provisions** Rückstellungen für Konsolidierungsaufgaben; ~ **stock** Konsolidierungsanleihe; ~ **system** Konsolidierungswesen.
fundless mittellos, ohne Kapitalien.
fundmonger Spekulant in Staatspapieren.
fundmongering Spekulation in Staatspapieren.
funeral Beerdigung, Begräbnis, Bestattung, Leichenbegräbnis, *(sl.)* Sache, Sorge;
state ~ Staatsbegräbnis;
to attend s. one's ~ an jds. Begräbnis teilnehmen; **to be none of**

my ~ mich nichts angehen; **to give s. o. a military ~** j. mit militärischen Ehren bestatten;
that's my ~ das ist meine Angelegenheit; **the ~ has been private** das Begräbnis hat in aller Stille stattgefunden;
~ **allowance** Sterbegeld; ~ **arrangements** Begräbnisvorkehrungen, Bestattungsvorkehrungen; ~ **bell** Totenglocke; ~ **benefit** Sterbebeihilfe, Begräbniszuschuß; ~ **car** Blumenwagen; ~ **ceremonies** Trauerfeier, Bestattungsfeierlichkeiten; ~ **chapel** Friedhofskapelle; ~ **cost (expenses)** Bestattungs-, Beerdigungs-, Begräbniskosten, Bestattungsgebühren; ~ **director** Beerdigungsunternehmen, Leichenbestatter; ~ **grant** Sterbezuschuß; ~ **home (house, parlor,** *US)* Leichenhalle; ~ **letter** Todesanzeige; ~ **march** Trauermarsch; ~ **oration** Leichen-, Grabrede; ~ **parlor** *(US)* Leichenhalle; ~ **procession** Leichen-, Trauerzug; ~ **sermon** Leichen-, Grabrede; ~ **service** Trauergottesdienst; ~ **society** Sterbekasse; ~ **undertaker** Leichenbestatter.
funerary urn Totenurne.
fungibility Vertretbarkeit, Fungibilität.
fungible fungibel, vertretbar, *(salable)* überall marktgängig;
~ **things** Gattungssachen.
funicular railway Drahtseilbahn.
funk *(Br., sl.)* riesige Angst, *(coward)* Angsthase, Hasenfuß;
blue ~ Mordsangst;
~ *(v.)* **out** *(US)* sich drücken;
to be in a blue ~ Dampf (Bammel) haben;
~**-hole** *(mil., sl.)* Heldenkeller.
funnel *(v.)* *(know-how)* kanalisieren.
funnies *(US sl.)* Witzseite einer Zeitung.
funny | business dunkle Geschichte, krumme Tour, zwielichtige Sache; ~ **man** *(theat.)* Hanswurst, Clown; ~ **paper** *(US)* Witzblatt, buntes Bilderheft.
fur Pelz;
~**s** Rauchwaren, Pelzwerk;
driving ~ Fahrpelz;
to make the ~ fly Streit heraufbeschwören, Unruhe stiften; ~ **coat** Pelzmantel; ~**-dresser** Pelzmacher.
furbish [up] *(v.)* auffrischen, herrichten;
~ **one's Latin** sein Latein aufpolieren; ~ **up an old tale** alte Geschichte wieder aufwärmen.
furlough *(official, soldier)* Urlaub;
on ~ beurlaubt;
six months' ~ Halbjahresurlaub;
~ *(v.)* beurlauben, Urlaub gewähren;
to go home on ~ Heimaturlaub antreten; **to grant ~ to an official** einem Beamten Urlaub gewähren; **to have a four-weeks' ~** vierwöchigen Urlaub haben; **to have a ~ every three years** alle drei Jahre urlaubsberechtigt sein;
~ **benefit** Urlaubsvergünstigung; ~ **certificate** *(US)* Urlaubsschein; ~ **rates** *(soldiers)* verbilligter Personentarif für Urlauber.
furnace Schmelz-, Hochofen;
oil-fired ~ mit Öl geheizter Kessel.
furnish *(v.)* *(fit up)* einrichten, versehen mit, *(provide)* versorgen, [be]liefern, ver-, beschaffen, *(supply with furniture)* einrichten, möblieren, ausstatten, ausrüsten;
~ **o. s.** sich einrichten; ~ **o. s. with s. th.** sich etw. anschaffen (besorgen); ~ **an army with supplies** Armee verproviantieren; ~ **capital** Kapital beschaffen; ~ **s. o. with cover (funds)** jem. Deckung zur Verfügung stellen; ~ **documents** Unterlagen beschaffen; ~ **satisfactory evidence** in der vorgeschriebenen Weise glaubhaft machen; ~ **an expedition** Expedition ausrüsten; ~ **a factory with current** elektrischen Strom in eine Fabrik legen; ~ **a house for s. o.** jem. ein Haus einrichten; ~ **s. o. with information** j. mit Nachrichten versorgen; ~ **a library with books** Bibliothek mit Büchern beliefern; ~ **s. o. with what he needs** j. mit allem Erforderlichen versorgen; ~ **an office** Büro möblieren; ~ **s. o. with full power** jem. uneingeschränkte Vollmacht erteilen; ~ **proof** Nachweis führen (liefern), Beweise erbringen; ~ **a return to the commissioners of Inland Revenue** *(Br.)* der Finanzverwaltung eine Einkommensteuererklärung vorlegen; ~ **a room** Zimmer möblieren; ~ **sound reasons** vernünftige Gründe vorbringen; ~ **security** Sicherheit leisten, Kaution stellen; ~ **services** Dienste leisten; ~ **a ship** Schiff ausrüsten; ~ **a bill with stamps** Wechsel verstempeln; ~ **a surety** Bürgen stellen.
furnished ausgestattet;
~ **apartment** möbliertes Zimmer; **to live in ~ apartments** möbliert wohnen; **to let a ~ apartment** möbliertes Zimmer vermieten; ~ **flat** möblierte Wohnung; ~ **house** möbliertes Haus; ~ **lettings** Vermietung möblierter Wohnungen; **well-~**

purse gut gespickte Börse; ~ **room** möbliertes Zimmer; **well-~ shop** gut eingerichteter Laden.

furnisher Lieferant, Lieferer;
~ **of capital** Kapitalgeber.

furnishing Lieferung, Versorgung, Ausstattung, Ausrüstung, *(equipment with furniture)* Möbelbeschaffung, Möblierung;
~**s** Mobiliar, Möbel, Einrichtungsgegenstände;
~**s and fixtures** Inventar, Mobiliar und Zubehör, Betriebs-, Geschäftseinrichtung;
house-~ firm Möbel- und Ausstattungsgeschäft; ~ **shop** Möbelgeschäft.

furniture Mobiliar, Möbel, Hausrat, Wohnungseinrichtung, *(print.)* Regletten, Stege;
household ~ Hausrat; **mental** ~ vorhandene Intelligenz, **office** ~ Büromöbel, -mobiliar; **secondhand** ~ gebrauchte Möbel; **unit** ~ Anbaumöbel;
~ **under distraint** einem Eigentumsvorbehalt unterliegende Möbel; ~ **of one's mind** vorhandene Intelligenz; ~ **of one's pocket** Geld; ~ **of a ship** Schiffsausrüstung;
to buy ~ on the hire-purchase *(Br.)* **(deferred payment, US) system** Möbel auf Abzahlung kaufen (abstottern); **to find one's ~** sich eigene Möbel anschaffen; **to have one's own ~** eigene Möbel haben; **to have one's ~ removed** seinen Umzug bewerkstelligen; **to invest in a new suite of ~** sich neue Möbel zulegen; **to lumber a room with ~** Zimmer mit Möbeln vollstopfen (überladen); **to store (warehouse, US) ~** Möbel auf den Speicher stellen; **to turn out s. one's ~** jds. Möbel ausräumen;
~ **broker** Händler mit alten Möbeln; ~ **builder** Möbelhersteller; ~ **car** Möbelwagen; ~ **dealer** Möbelhändler; ~ **and office equipment** Büroeinrichtung; ~ **exhibition** Möbelausstellung; ~ **industry** Möbelindustrie; ~ **manufacturer** Möbelfabrikant; ~ **mover** Möbelspediteur; ~ **packer** Möbelpacker; ~ **polish** Möbelpolitur; ~ **removal** Möbeltransport; ~ **remover** Möbelspediteur; ~ **shop (store, US)** Möbelgeschäft, -laden; ~ **van** Möbelwagen; ~ **warehouse** Möbelspeicher, -lager.

further zusätzlich, sonstig;
without troubling any ~ ohne sich weiter aufzuregen; **without ~ ado** ohne jedes Tamtam; **~ to our letter of yesterday** im Nachgang zu unserem gestrigen Schreiben;
~ *(v.)* fördern, unterstützen, behilflich sein;
~ **s. one's interests** jds. Interessen fördern; ~ **the cause of peace** Sache des Friedens fördern;
to go ~ into a matter Angelegenheit weiter (genauer) untersuchen; **to go no ~ into a matter** es dabei bewenden lassen;
~ **advance** erneute Darlehnsgewährung, Krediterhöhung; ~ **consideration** *(Br.)* Wiederaufnahmeantrag; **upon ~ consideration** nach weiterer Überlegung; ~ **cover** Nachschuß; **to ask for ~ credit** um zusätzlichen Kredit nachsuchen; **to go into ~ details** weitere Einzelheiten berichten; ~ **education** *(Br.)* Weiter-, Fortbildung; ~ **education college** weiterbildende (weiterführende) Schule; ~ **education course** *(Br.)* Volkshochschul-, Fortbildungskursus; ~ **education teacher** Volkshochschullehrer; **to remand a case for ~ enquiry** Fall zur weiteren Untersuchung zurückverweisen; ~ **hearing** Neuverhandlung; ~ **information** zusätzliche Angaben; ~ **instructions** *(jury)* weitere Belehrung, **without ~ loss of time** ohne jeden weiteren Zeitverlust; ~ **margin** Nachschuß; **until ~ notice** bis auf weiteres; ~ **proceedings** Neuverhandlung; ~ **orders** weitere Aufträge; ~ **particulars** nähere Einzelheiten, weitere Angaben; **with ~ reference to my letter of ...** unter weiterer Bezugnahme auf meinen Brief vom ...; ~ **signature required** *(bill, check)* zweite Unterschrift fehlt.

furtherance Unterstützung, Förderung;
in ~ of your aims zur Unterstützung Ihrer Ziele; **for the ~ of public welfare** für das Allgemeinwohl.

furtherer Förderer.

furtive verschlagen, hinterhältig.

fuse Zündschnur, Lunte, *(el.)* Sicherung;
time ~ Zeitzünder;
~ *(v.) (amalgamate companies)* fusionieren, verschmelzen, *(el., Br.)* durchbrennen;
to put in a new ~ neue Sicherung einsetzen;
~ **wire** *(el.)* Sicherungsdraht.

fusee Schwefelhölzchen, *(railroad, US)* Warnungssignal.

fuselage *(airplane)* Rumpf.

fusil(l)ade Massenerschießung;
~ *(v.)* erschießen, füsilieren.

fusion Fusion, Zusammenschluß, Verschmelzung, *(politics)* Koalition, Fusion;
~ **of political parties** Koalition politischer Parteien;
~ **bomb** Wasserstoffbombe.

fusionist Fusionsanhänger.

fuss unnötige Nervosität, übertriebene Geschäftigkeit, Getue, Wichtigtuer, Umstandskrämer;
~ *(v.)* **about s. o.** viel Wesens um j. machen;
to be in a fine ~ ziemlich durcheinander sein; **to get into a ~ about trifles** sich über Kleinigkeiten aufregen; **to kick up a ~** Umstände (Schwierigkeiten) machen.

fussy geschäftig, unnötig, nervös, *(bustling, US)* übertrieben heikel;
to be too ~ about one's clothes mit seiner Kleidung überpenibel sein.

fustian *(fig.)* Bombast, Schwulst.

fustigation Prügelstrafe.

fustiness Rückständigkeit.

fusty verstaubt, altmodisch, rückständig.

futile aussichtslos;
~ **attempt** vergeblicher Versuch.

future Zukunft, *(stock exchange)* Termingeschäft;
~**s** *(US)* Termingeschäfte, -handel, Lieferungskäufe;
business ~ Zukunft eines Unternehmens; **commodity ~s** *(US)* Warentermingeschäfte; **dark ~** freudlose Zukunft; **foreign exchange ~s** *(US)* Termindevisen; **healthy ~** vielversprechende Aussichten; **remote ~** ferne Zukunft;
~ *(a.)* zukünftig;
to be unconcerned about one's ~ sich über die Zukunft keine Gedanken machen; **to deal in ~s** Termingeschäfte betreiben; **to gear the ~** Weichen für die Zukunft stellen; **to have a great ~** große Zukunft vor sich haben; **to make out for a brilliant ~** glänzende Aussichten haben; **to make plans for the ~** Zukunftspläne machen; **to plan with relation to the ~** im Hinblick auf die Zukunft planen; **to provide (make provisions) for the ~** Zukunftssicherungen treffen, seine Zukunft sicherstellen, Alterssicherung treffen; **to ruin one's ~** seine Zukunftschancen vertun; **to save in anticipation of the ~** für die Zukunft vorsorgen; **to settle the ~ of one's children** seine Kinder sicherstellen;
to trade in ~s *(US)* Termingeschäfte abschließen;
to take on ~ account auf zukünftige Rechnung kaufen; ~**-acquired property** zukünftiger Vermögenserwerb; ~**s bargain** Termingeschäft, -abschluß; ~ **buyer** *(US)* Terminkäufer; ~**s cable rate** *(US)* Kabelsatz für Devisentermingeschäfte; ~ **candidate** *(US)* gemeinsamer Kandidat; ~**s commission man** *(US)* Terminkommissionär; ~ **contract** Lieferungsvertrag; ~**s contract** *(US)* Termingeschäft, -vertrag, Warentermingeschäft; ~**s deal (dealing)** *(US)* Fixkauf, -geschäft, festes Börsentermingeschäft; ~ **debt** noch nicht fällige Schuld; ~ **delivery** *(US)* Terminlieferung, spätere Lieferung; **to purchase for ~ delivery** *(US)* auf Termin kaufen; **to sell for ~ delivery** *(US)* auf Termin (Zeit) verkaufen; ~ **earnings** zukünftige Erträge, *(due to injury)* Verdienstausfall; ~ **estate** Anwartschaft, zukünftiges Vermögen; ~**s exchange** *(US)* Devisenterminhandel, Terminbörse, -geschäft; ~ **interests** zukünftige Ansprüche; ~**s market** *(US)* Terminmarkt, -börse; ~ **month** *(US)* Terminmonat; ~ **needs** zukünftiger Bedarf; ~**s operation** *(US)* Termingeschäft; ~ **orders** zukünftige Aufträge; ~ **outlook** Zukunftsschau; ~**s price** *(US)* Kurs für Termingeschäft, Terminkurs; ~ **project** Zukunftsprojekt; ~ **property** zukünftiges Vermögen; ~ **prospects** zukünftige Chancen; ~ **prospects of an undertaking** Zukunftsaussichten eines Unternehmens; ~**s purchase** *(US)* Terminkauf; ~**s rate** *(US)* Kurs für Devisentermingeschäfte, Terminsatz; ~ **research** Zukunftsforschung; ~ **right** Anwartschaft; ~**s sale** Verkauf auf Zeit, Terminverkauf; ~**s trading** *(US)* Terminhandel, -geschäft; ~**s trading operation** *(US)* Termingeschäft; ~ **trend** Entwicklungstendenz; ~ **use** zukünftige Verwertung.

futurology Zukunftsforschung, Futurologie.

fuzz *(US sl.)* Polyp.

fuzzy *(photo)* verschwommen.

G

gab Geschwätz, *(endless debate)* Quasselei, endlose Debatte.
gabble *(v.)* **over** unverständlich vorlesen.
gable Giebel;
~ **publicity** Giebelwerbung.
gabled house Giebelhaus.
gad Herumstreifen, Umherwandern;
on the ~ auf der Wanderschaft;
~ *(v.)* **on (abroad)** sich müßig herumtreiben.
gadabout Bummler, Müßiggänger, Herumtreiber, Pflastertreter.
gadfly *(fig.)* Störenfried.
gadget Gerät, Vorrichtung, Apparat, *(fig.)* Kniff, Schliche;
kitchen ~ Küchengerät;
~ **for opening tin cans** Büchsenöffner.
gadgetry technische Spielereien.
gaff Fischhaken;
penny ~ *(Br., sl.)* Bumslokal, Schmiere;
to give s. o. the ~ *(US sl.)* jem. das Leben sauer machen; **to stand the** ~ *(US sl.)* durchhalten, sich nicht kleinkriegen lassen.
gaffe Schnitzer, Fauxpas.
gaffer *(Br.)* *(foreman)* Vorarbeiter, Aufseher, Chef.
gag besonderer Einfall, *(fig.)* Knebelung, *(parl.)* Schluß (Abwürgen) der Debatte, *(theater)* witziger Einfall, Improvisation, Gag;
~ *(v.)* freie Meinungsäußerung unterdrücken (knebeln), *(theater)* improvisieren, extemporieren;
~ **a debate** Debatte abwürgen; ~ **the press** Presse mundtot machen.
gage *(US)* Maß, *(pledge)* [Unter]pfand, Bürgschaft, *(railway)* Spurweite;
~ *(v.)* verpfänden, *(appraise)* abschätzen, *(find capacity of)* eichen, *(measure)* [ab]messen;
~ **the height of a mountain** Höhe eines Berges berechnen;
to give s. th. as a ~ etw. als Pfand (Sicherheit) geben; **to lie to (be at)** ~ verpfändet sein.
gagging of debate Abwürgen einer Debatte.
gaieties Lustbarkeiten, Festlichkeiten.
gain *(amount of increase)* Zunahme, Zu-, Anwachs, *(profit)* Gewinn, Ertrag, Überschuß, Vorteil, Nutzen;
for purpose of ~ zu Gewinnzwecken; **with a** ~ **of seven points** mit einem Gewinn von 7 Punkten; **with the object of** ~ in gewinnsüchtiger Absicht;
~**s** *(emoluments, US)* Einkommen, Verdienst, Erwerb, Einkünfte, *(stock exchange)* [Kurs]gewinn;
capital ~ Kapitalgewinn, -einkommen; **ceasing** ~ entgangener Gewinn; **chargeable** ~ steuerpflichtiger Gewinn, veranlagungspflichtiger Gewinn; **clear** ~ Netto-, Reingewinn; **extra** ~ Nebengewinn; **ill-gotten** ~**s** unrechtmäßig erworbenes Gut; **material** ~**s** wesentliche Gewinne; **net** ~ Netto-, Reingewinn; **overseas** ~**s** in Übersee erzielte Gewinne; **net realized** ~ erzielter Nettogewinn; **striking** ~ auffallender Gewinn; **substantial** ~**s** *(stock exchange)* wesentliche Kursgewinne; **taxable** ~ besteuerungsfähiger Gewinn, Steuergewinn; **top** ~ *(stock exchange)* Spitzengewinn;
~ **in assets** Anlagenzugang; ~ **per cent** Prozentgewinn; ~ **derived from capital** Kapitalertrag; ~ **of exchange** Kursgewinn; ~ **to knowledge** Bereicherung des Wissens; ~ **in pages** Seitenzunahme; ~**s from sale of plant property** Erträge aus dem Abgang von Gegenständen des Anlagevermögens; ~**s from specialization** Spezialisierungsgewinne; ~ **in the stock market prices** Kursgewinnzuwachs; ~ **of time** Zeitgewinn; ~**s of trade** Handelsbilanzerträge, Wohlstandseffekte des Außenhandels; ~**s from valuation adjustments** Erträge aus Zuschreibungen zu Gegenständen des Anlagevermögens; ~ **in weight** Gewichtszunahme;
~ *(v.)* *(earn)* verdienen, erwerben, *(improve)* an Wert gewinnen, im Ansehen steigen, *(prices)* sich bessern, *(profit)* gewinnen, profitieren, *(yield)* einbringen;
~ **s. o. admittance** jem. Zutritt verschaffen; ~ **an advantage over one's competitors** seine Konkurrenten überflügeln; ~ **the battle** Schlacht gewinnen; ~ **by one's business** bei seinem Geschäft verdienen; ~ **one's cause** seinen Prozeß gewinnen; ~ **s. o. over for a cause** j. für eine Angelegenheit interessieren; ~ **the day** Sieg davontragen; ~ **one's destination** seinen Bestimmungsort erreichen; ~ **s. one's esteem** jds. Achtung erringen; ~ **experience** Erfahrungen sammeln; ~ **expert knowledge** Fachkenntnisse erwerben; ~ **a fortune** Vermögen erwerben; ~ **ground** Fortschritte machen, sich durchsetzen; ~ **the upper hand** Ober-

hand gewinnen; ~ **a hearing** Audienz erlangen; ~ **influence** Einfluß gewinnen; ~ **information** Informationen erhalten; ~ **land from the sea** dem Meer Land abgewinnen; ~ **one's living** seinen Lebensunterhalt verdienen; ~ **three minutes a day** *(clock)* am Tag drei Minuten vorgehen; ~ **s. o. over** j. für seine Interessen gewinnen; ~ **a point** Punkt gewinnen, *(fig.)* in einem bestimmten Punkt recht bekommen; ~ **three points** *(stock exchange)* sich um drei Punkte verbessern; ~ **in popularity** Popularität erlangen, volkstümlich werden; ~ **possession of s. th.** Besitzrecht an einer Sache erlangen; ~ **on one's pursuers** Vorsprung vor seinen Verfolgern erzielen; ~ **a reputation** in den Ruf kommen; ~ **nothing but ridicule** sich nur lächerlich machen; ~ **speed** schneller werden; ~ **strength slowly** langsam wieder zu Kräften kommen; ~ **a suit at law** *(US)* Prozeß gewinnen; ~ **time** Zeitgewinn erzielen; ~ **the top** an die Spitze kommen;
to have the ~ **in one's hands** sicherer Gewinner sein; **to make** ~**s** Gewinne verzeichnen; **to make** ~**s of s. th.** bei etw. gewinnen; **to make large** ~**s in the last election** bei der letzten Wahl große Gewinne erzielen; **to reap big** ~**s** Riesengewinne einstreichen; **to reap political** ~**s** sich politisch positiv auswirken; **to register small** ~**s** kleine Gewinne verzeichnen; **to share a** ~ Gewinn teilen;
~ **control** Lautstärkeregelung; ~ **sharing** *(bonus system)* Gewinnbeteiligung.
gainer Gewinner;
to be a large ~ **by a bargain** bei einem Geschäft groß verdienen.
gainful einträglich, gewinnbringend, vorteilhaft, lohnend *(occupation)* auf Erwerbseinkommen gerichtet;
to be ~**ly employed** erwerbstätig sein;
~ **employment (occupation)** Erwerbstätigkeit, einträgliche Beschäftigung; ~ **worker** Erwerbstätiger.
gainfully employed person Erwerbsperson, Erwerbstätiger.
gainings Verdienst, Ertrag, Gewinn, Einkommen, Einkünfte.
gainless unvorteilhaft, nicht einträglich.
gainsay *(v.)* **a statement** einer Behauptung widersprechen.
gala Festkleidung, *(feast)* Festlichkeit;
~ *(a.)* festlich, feierlich;
~ **dinner** Galadinner, Festessen; ~ **dress** Galauniform, -anzug; ~ **illumination** Festbeleuchtung; ~ **night** *(theater)* Festvorstellung; ~ **performance** Galaaufführung; ~ **week** Festwoche.
galaxy Milchstraße, Milchstraßensystem, *(fig.)* glänzende Schar;
~ **of talent** glänzende Versammlung begabter Persönlichkeiten.
gale Sturm, *(Br.)* periodische Pachtzahlung;
hanging ~ *(Br.)* Miet-, Pachtrückstände;
~ **day** *(Br.)* Pachttermin.
gall *(fig.)* bittere Erfahrung;
the ~ **of life** die Bitterkeiten des Lebens;
to dip one's pen in ~ Galle verspritzen.
gallant Kavalier, Galan.
gallery Galerie, Tribüne, *(arts)* Gemäldegalerie, *(mar.)* Laufgang, *(mining)* Strecke, Stollen, *(photo, US)* Fotoatelier, *(sports)* Zuschauer, Publikum, *(theater)* oberster Rang, Galerie;
portrait ~ Gemäldegalerie; **press** ~ Pressetribüne; **public** ~ Zuschauer-, Publikums-, Besuchertribüne; **rogues'** ~ Verbrecheralbum; **distinguished strangers'** ~ Prominenten-, Diplomatentribüne;
to play to the ~ nach Effekt haschen, an den Masseninstinkt appellieren;
~ **director** Galeriedirektor; ~ **play** Effekthascherei.
galleryite Galeriebesucher.
galley Galere, *(print.)* [Setz]schiff, *(ship)* Küche, Kombüse;
~ **proof** *(print.)* Fahnen-, Bürsten-, Korrekturabzug; ~ **slave** Galeerensträfling; ~**-west** *(US sl.)* verwirrt.
gallop, at a *(fig.)* im Eiltempo;
~ *(v.)* **through one's lecture** seine Vorlesung herunterrasseln; ~ **through one's work** seine Arbeit im Galopp erledigen.
galloping inflation galoppierende Inflation.
gallows Galgen;
to cheat the ~ der gerechten Strafe entrinnen; **to come to the** ~ gehängt werden; **to end on the** ~ am Galgen enden; **to have the** ~ **in one's face** Galgengesicht haben; **to send s. o. to the** ~ j. zum Tod durch Erhängen verurteilen;
~ **bird** Galgenvogel; ~ **mike** Hängemikrophon, Galgen.
Gallup|man Meinungsforscher; ~ **poll** Meinungsbefragung.

galore reichlich, genug, im Überfluß;
  to have cash ~ übermäßige Barreserven haben, äußerst liquide sein; **to have money** ~ Geld wie Heu haben.

galumptious *(sl.)* tipptopp.

galvanize galvanisieren;
  ~ *(v.)* **into life** zu neuem Leben erwecken.

gambit *(fig.)* erster Schritt, Eröffnung;
  calculated ~ *(US)* abgekartetes Spiel.

gamble Glücksspiel, *(speculation)* Spekulation;
  pure ~ reine Spekulation;
  ~ *(v.)* spielen, *(speculate)* [wild] spekulieren;
  ~ **on a fall** auf Baisse spekulieren; ~ **away one's fortune** sein Vermögen verspielen; ~ **with one's health** seine Gesundheit aufs Spiel setzen; ~ **in oil shares** in Ölaktien spekulieren; ~ **on the stock exchange** an der Börse spekulieren.

gambler [Glücks]spieler, *(stock exchange)* [Börsen]spekulant;
  common ~ gewerbliches Spielunternehmen.

gambling Glücksspiel, Hasardspiel, *(stock exchange)* waghalsiges Spekulieren;
  given to ~ vom Spielteufel besessen;
  commercialized ~ gewerbliches Glücksspiel;
  ~ **in futures** Differenzgeschäft; ~ **on the stock exchange** Börsenspekulation;
  ~ **contract** Spiel-, Wettvertrag; ~ **debts** Spielschulden; ~ **den (house)** Spielhölle; ~ **device** Glücksspielgerät; ~ **hell (hole,)** *(coll.)* Spielhölle; ~ **policy** *(life insurance)* Police für einen am Leben des Versicherten finanziell uninteressierten Begünstigten; ~ **resort** [Spiel]kasino, Spielbank; ~ **ring** Glücksspielring; ~ **table** Spieltisch; ~ **winning** Spielgewinn.

game Spiel, *(animal)* jagdbare Tiere, Wild, Wildbrett, *(apparatus)* Spielapparat, *(scheme)* Plan, Unternehmen, Trick, *(sl.)* Diebesbeute, *(pep, US)* Schneid, Kampfgeist;
  ~**s** *(athletic contest)* Wettkampf, *(fig.)* Schliche, Tricks;
  big ~ Großwild; **fair** ~ jagdbares Wild; **Olympic** ~**s** Olympische Spiele;
  ~ **of chance** Glücksspiel; ~ **of skill** Geschicklichkeitsspiel;
  ~ *(v.)* um Geld (hoch) spielen;
  ~ **away one's money (fortune)** sein Vermögen verspielen;
  to be ~ *(sl.)* zu allen Schandtaten bereit sein; **to be fair** ~ **for s. o.** Freiwild für j. sein; **to be in the advertising** ~ in Reklame machen, in der Werbebranche sein; **to be on the** ~ im gleichen Gewerbe tätig sein; **to be off one's** ~ nicht in Form sein; **to be playing a deep** ~ geheimnisvolle Dinge tun; **to beat s. o. at his own** ~ j. mit seinen eigenen Waffen schlagen; **to die** ~ als Held sterben; **to fly at too high** ~ sich zuviel vornehmen; **to have the** ~ **in one's hands** sicher gewinnen; **to know s. one's little** ~ wissen, was einer im Schilde führt; **to make** ~ **of s. o.** j. lächerlich machen; **to play s. one's** ~ jem. unabsichtlich helfen; **to play a double** ~ Doppelspiel betreiben; **to play the** ~ Spielregeln einhalten; **to play a dangerous** ~ gefährliches Spiel treiben; **to play a losing** ~ auf verlorenem Posten kämpfen (stehen); **not to play the** ~ **according to set rules** sich nicht nach den Spielregeln richten; **to see through s. one's** ~ jem. auf die Schliche kommen;
  ~ **act** Jagdgesetz; ~ **debt** Spielschuld; ~ **dog** Jagdhund; ~ **farmer** Jagdpächter; ~ **hog** *(US)* Jagdfrevler; ~ **hunter** Jäger; ~ **hunting** Jagd; ~ **laws** Jagdgesetze; ~ **license** *(US)* Jagdschein, -erlaubnis; ~**s master** Sportlehrer; ~ **plan** *(US)* Erfolgsstrategie; ~ **preserve** Wildpark; ~ **-park**, -gehege; ~ **season** Jagdzeit; **big-**~ **shooting** Großwildjagd; ~ **tenant** Jagdpächter; ~ **warden** Wildhüter.

gamebag Jagdtasche.

gamekeeper *(Br.)* Wildhüter, Forstaufseher.

gaming Spielen, Glücksspiel;
  to plead the ~ **act** Spieleinwand erheben; ~ **club** Spielklub; ~ **contract** Spiel-, Wettvertrag; ~ **house** [Spiel]kasino, -bank; ~ **loss** Spielverlust; ~ **room** Spielsaal; ~ **table** Spieltisch.

gammon *(Br.)* Humbug;
  ~ **and spinach** *(fig.)* Unsinn.

gammoner *(coll.)* Schwindler.

gamut *(fig.)* Skala, Reihe, Stufenleiter;
  the whole ~ **of feelings** gesamte Gefühlsskala;
  to run the whole ~ **of** ganze Skala durchlaufen.

gang Trupp, Gruppe, Schar, Rotte, *(company of workmen)* Arbeiterkolonne, *(gangsters)* Bande, *(print, US)* Sammelform, *(shift)* Schicht, Abteilung;
  breakdown ~ *(Br.)* Unfallhilfstrupp, -mannschaft;
  ~ **of burglars** Einbrecherbande; ~ **of convicts** Zuchthäuslerbande; ~ **of criminals** Verbrecherbande; **itinerant** ~ **of roadsmen** Straßenarbeiterkolonne;
  ~ *(v.)* **up** *(sl.)* sich zusammenrotten;
  ~ **boss** *(US)* Rotten-, Vorarbeiter; ~ **warfare** Bandenkrieg.

gangboard Laufplanke, Landungssteg.

ganger Rottenführer, Vorarbeiter.

gangplank Landungssteg, -brücke.

gangster *(US coll.)* bewaffneter Verbrecher, Bandit, Bandenmitglied, Gangster;
  ~**s** *(US)* Unterwelt.

gangsterism Verbrecher-, Bandenwesen.

gangway *(mining)* Sohlenstrecke, *(Br. parl.)* Quergang, *(passage)* Durchgang, Passage, *(ship)* Laufplanke, *(Br. theatre)* Gang [zwischen den Sitzen];
  free ~ Landurlaub; **main** ~ Sohlenstrecke.

gantlet *(US)* Spießrutenlaufen, *(railway)* Gleisverschlingung;
  to run the ~ *(US)* Spießruten laufen.

gantry *(railway)* Signalbrücke;
  ~ **crane** Gerüstkran.

Gantt progress chart *(statistics)* Arbeitsfortschrittsbild.

gaol *(Br.)* [Untersuchungs]gefängnis;
  ~ *(v.)* ins Gefängnis bringen (stecken);
  to be in ~ im Gefängnis sitzen, einsitzen; **to be sent to** ~ zu Gefängnis verurteilt werden; **to break** ~ ausbrechen; **to have one foot in** ~ mit einem Bein im Zuchthaus stehen;
  ~ **bird** Galgenvogel, Gewohnheitsverbrecher, Knastbruder, alter Sträfling; ~ **delivery** Aburteilung, *(popular speech)* Entweichenlassen von Gefangenen; ~ **limits** Gefängnisbereich.

gaoler *(Br.)* Gefangenenaufseher, Gefängniswärter.

gap Lücke, Loch, Öffnung, Spalt, *(airplane)* Tragflächenabstand, *(fig.)* Kluft, *(insurance)* Wartezeit;
  air ~ Luftloch; **deflationary** ~ Deflationslücke; **dollar** ~ Dollarlücke; **technological** ~ technologische Lücke; **white** ~ *(print.)* zu großer Zwischenraum;
  ~ **in an argument** Beweislücke; ~ **in a conversation** plötzliche Gesprächsstille; ~ **in the defence** Verteidigungslücke, Nahtstelle; ~ **in interest rates** Zinsgefälle; ~ **in one's knowledge** Bildungslücke; ~ **in the law** Gesetzeslücke; ~ **in the market** Marktlücke; **wide** ~ **between the views of two statesmen** großer Unterschied in den Auffassungen zweier Staatsmänner; ~ **in supplies** Angebots-, Versorgungslücke;
  to bridge the ~ überbrücken; **to bridge a** ~ **in the market** Marktlücke schließen; **to fill a** ~ Loch stopfen, Lücke ausfüllen; **to fill in the** ~ **in one's education** seine Bildungslücken schließen; **to find** ~**s in the market** Marktlücken ausfindig machen; **to stop (supply) a** ~ Lücke schließen;
  ~ **loan** Kredit für einen Spitzenbetrag.

garage Garage, Autohalle, *(aerodrome)* Hangar, *(repair shop)* Reparaturwerkstatt, *(stock exchange, US)* kleiner Börsensaal;
  floating ~ schwimmende Garage; **lockup** ~ Einzelgarage; **multi-storey** ~ Parkhochhaus; **open** ~ Sammelgarage, Garagenhalle; **parking** ~ Stockwerksgarage;
  ~ *(v.)* **a car** Auto einstellen (in die Garage fahren);
  ~ **attendant** Garagenwärter, Tankwart; ~ **company** Garagenfirma; ~ **remote-controlled** ~ **door** sich automatisch öffnende Garagentür; ~ **fee** Standgeld; ~ **keeper** Garagenbesitzer; ~ **keeper's liability insurance** Garagenhaftpflichtversicherung; ~ **proprietor** Garagenbesitzer; ~ **rent** Garagenmiete; ~ **sale** Gerümpelverkauf, *(US)* Werbeauftrag für eine ganze Verkehrslinie.

garaged in einer Garage abgestellt.

garageman Garagenarbeiter.

garb Amtskleid.

garbage *(books)* Schmutz, Schundliteratur, *(refuse, US)* Abfall, Müll;
  ~ **barrel** *(US)* Müll-, Abfalltonne; ~ **box** *(US)* Mülleimer, -kasten, -tonne; ~ **burner** *(US)* Müllverbrennungsanlage; ~ **can** *(US)* Müll-, Abfalleimer; ~ **cart** *(US)* Müllwagen; ~ **chute** *(US)* Müllschlucker; ~ **collection** *(US)* Müllabfuhr; ~ **collector** *(US)* Müllfahrer, -abfuhrunternehmer; ~ **conveyor** *(US)* Müllförderanlage; ~ **destructor** *(US)* Müllzerkleinerer; ~ **disposal** *(US)* Abfallbeseitigung; ~ **disposer** Abfallbeseitiger, Müllschlucker; ~ **dump** *(US)* Müllhalde, Schuttabladeplatz; ~ **gas heating** *(US)* durch Verwertung von Müllrückständen betriebene Gasheizung; ~ **incinerator** *(US)* Müllverbrennungsanlage; ~ **man** *(US)* Müllwerker; ~ **pickup** *(US)* Mülleimer; ~ **plant** *(US)* Müllverwertungsanlage; ~ **removal** *(US)* Abfallbeseitigung, Müllabfuhr; ~ **truck (wagon)** *(US)* Müllwagen.

garble entstellter Bericht;
  ~ *(v.)* **a report** Bericht verstümmeln (entstellen).

garden Garten[anlage];
  kitchen ~ Gemüsegarten; **market** ~ Handelsgärtnerei; **zoological** ~**s** Zoologischer Garten, Tiergarten;
  ~ *(v.)* im Garten arbeiten, Gartenbau treiben;
  to make a ~ Garten anlegen;

~ **chair** Gartenstuhl; ~ **city** Gartenstadt, Villenkolonie; ~ **designing** Gartenbau; ~ **frame** Mistbeetfenster; ~ **hose** Gartenschlauch; ~ **party** Gartenfest; **to lead s. o. up the ~ path** *(fam.)* j. an der Nase herumführen; ~ **plot** Gartenland, -grundstück; ~ **seat** Gartenbank, *(bus, Br,)* Holzsitz; ~ **stuff (truck,** *US)* Gartenerzeugnisse; ~ **suburb** *(Br.)* Gartenvorstadt; ~ **wall** Gartenmauer; ~ **weeding** *(fig.)* Durchforstung.

gardener Gärtner;
   landscape ~ Gartenarchitekt.

gardening Gartenbau, -arbeit;
   ~ **services** Gartenpflege; ~ **tools** Gartengeräte.

garland Girlande, Blumengewinde, *(fig.)* Siegespalme.

garner Getreidespeicher, *(fig.)* Kornkammer.

garnish Schmuck, Ornament, Verzierung;
   ~ *(v.) (decorate)* schmücken, verzieren, *(seize)* beim Drittschuldner pfänden, Pfändungsbescheid zukommen lassen, Zahlungsverbot erlassen, *(summon)* vorladen, *(trustee)* einem Treuhänder übergeben;
   ~ **a bank account** Bankkonto pfänden; ~ **the wages** Lohnpfändung vornehmen, Lohn pfänden.

garnishee Vorgeladener, *(third party debtor)* Drittschuldner;
   ~ *(v.)* vorladen;
   ~ **account** Sperrkonto [des Drittschuldners]; ~ **order** Pfändungs- und Überweisungsbeschluß; ~ **order absolute** endgültiges Zahlungsverbot; ~ **order nisi** vorläufiger Pfändungs- und Überweisungsbeschluß, vorläufiges Zahlungsverbot; ~ **proceedings** Forderungspfändungsverfahren; **to institute** ~ **proceedings** Forderung beim Drittschuldner pfänden lassen, Pfändungsforderung durchführen; ~ **summons** Zustellung eines Pfändungs- und Überweisungsbeschlußes an den Drittschuldner.

garnisher Forderungs-, Pfändungspfandgläubiger, Vollstreckungsgläubiger bei einer Forderungspfändung.

garnishment *(legal notice)* gerichtliche Vorladung, *(proceedings)* Zahlungs[leistungs]verbot an den Drittschuldner, Forderungspfändung, Forderungspfändungsverfahren, *(summons)* Vorladung;
   equitable ~ Verfahren zur Offenlegung der Vermögensverhältnisse, Offenbarungserklärung des Vollstreckungsschuldners; ~ **of wages** Lohnpfändung.

garment Kleidungsstück;
   ~ **rack** *(US)* Kleiderablage.

garret Dachstube, -kammer, Mansarde, Mansardenzimmer;
   to be wrong in the ~ nicht ganz richtig im Oberstübchen sein, nicht alle Tassen im Schrank haben;
   ~ **staircase** Bodentreppe; ~ **window** Dachluke.

garreteer *(impecunious author)* Zeilenschinder.

garreter Dachkammerbewohner.

garrison Garnison, Standort, *(fortress)* Besatzung;
   ~ *(v.)* **a town** Besatzung (Garnison) in eine Stadt legen;
   to keep ~ **in a town** in einer Stadt in Garnison liegen;
   ~ **commander** Standortkommandant; ~ **duty** Garnisonsdienst; ~ **state** Militärstaat; ~ **town** Garnisonsstadt.

garotte Erdrosselung.

gas Gas *(ballyhoo, coll.)* Aufschneiderei, *(gaslight)* Gaslicht, -flamme, *(mil.)* Giftgas, *(mining)* Grubengas, *(petrol, coll.)* Benzin;
   commercial ~ Ferngas; **laughing** ~ Lachgas; **lighting** ~ Leuchtgas; **natural** ~ Erdgas; **poison** ~ Kampf-, Giftgas; **town** ~ Fern-, Stadtgas;
   ~ *(v.)* mit Gas versorgen, *(mil.)* mit Gas töten;
   ~ **s. o.** *(sl.)* jem. blauen Dunst vormachen;
   to heat a room with ~ Zimmer mit Gas heizen; **to lay on the** ~ Gasleitung legen; **to pass** ~ *(sl.)* Prahlhans sein; **to run on** ~ *(US)* mit Benzin fahren; **to step on the** ~ Gas geben; **to turn off the** ~ Gas abstellen; **to turn on the** ~ Gas aufdrehen;
   ~ **air mixture** Brennstoffluftgemisch; ~ **attack** *(mil.)* Gasangriff; ~ **bill** Gasrechnung; ~ **board** Gaswerk; ~ **burner** Gasbrenner; ~ **burning** Gasfeuerung; ~ **chamber** Gaskammer; ~ **check** Gasdichtung; ~ **coke** Gaskoks; ~ **company** Gasgesellschaft; ~ **compound** Gasgemisch; ℒ **Consultative Council** *(Br.)* Beratung für Gasverbraucher; ~ **consumption** Gasverbrauch; ~ **coupon** *(US)* Benzingutschein; ~ **cylinder** Gasflasche; ~ **deal** Gaslieferungsvertrag; ~**-for-pipe deal** Röhrenverkaufsvertrag gegen Gasabnahmeverpflichtung; **natural** ~ **deposits** Erdgaslagerstätten; ~ **engine** Gasmotor; ~ **engineer** Gasfachmann; ~ **explosion** [Gruben]gasexplosion; ~ **field** Erdgasvorkommen; ~ **fire** Gasofen; ~ **fitter** Gasmann, Installateur; ~ **fittings** Gasinstallation; ~ **generation** Gaserzeugung; ~ **guzzler** Benzinschlucker, -fresser; ~**-guzzling car** Bezinschlucker; ~ **central heating** Gaszentralheizung; ~ **helmet** *(coal mine)* Gasmaske; ~

industry Gasindustrie, -wirtschaft; ~ **jet** Gasflamme; ~ **leakage** Gasaustritt; ~ **main** Gasleitung, -anschluß; ~ **mask** *(mil.)* Gasmaske; ~ **meter** Gaszähler; ~ **oven** Gasofen; ~ **pedal** Gaspedal; **to step on the** ~ **pedal** Gas geben; ~ **pipe** Gasrohr; ~ **pipeline** Gasleitung; **natural** ~ **pipeline** Erdgasleitung; ~ **pipelines network** Gaswerk; ~ **poisoning** Gasvergiftung; ~ **producer** Erdgaserzeuger; ~ **plant** Gaswerk; ~ **revenues** Erdgaseinkünfte; ~ **shortage** Erdgasknappheit; ~ **sign** Tankstellenhinweis; ~ **starter** *(airplane)* Gasanlasser; ~ **station** *(US)* Tankstelle; **commercial** ~ **supply** Ferngasversorgung; ~ **supply industry** Gaswirtschaft; ~ **tank** Gasbehälter, *(car)* Benzintank; ~ **turbine** Gasturbine; ~ **warfare** Gaskrieg.

gasateria *(US)* Selbstbedienungstankstelle.

gasfield Erdgasfeld.

gasholder Gasflasche.

gashouse *(US)* Gaswerk.

gasket Dichtung.

gaslight Gaslicht, -lampe.

gaslighter Gasanzünder.

gaslighting Gasbeleuchtung.

gasman Gasinstallateur, Gasmann, -kassierer.

gasoline *(US)* Benzin, Brenn-, Betriebsstoff;
   extra ~ *(US)* Benzin im Reservekanister;
   to run out of ~ *(US)* kein Benzin mehr haben;
   ~ **allowance** *(US)* Kraftstoffzuteilung, Benzinzuschuß; ~ **attendant** *(US)* Tankwart; ~ **can** *(US)* Benzinkanister; ~ **consumption** *(US)* Benzinverbrauch; ~ **container** *(US)* Benzinkanister; ~ **engine** *(US)* Benzinmotor; ~ **gauge** *(US)* Benzinstandsanzeiger, -uhr; ~ **price** *(US)* Benzinpreis; ~ **rail car** *(US)* Gliedertriebwagen; ~ **shortage** *(US)* Benzinknappheit; ~ **station** *(US)* Tankstelle; ~ **station attendant** *(US)* Tankwart; ~ **tax** *(US)* Benzinsteuer; ~ **truck** Lastwagen mit Gasgenerator.

gasp, at one's last in der Todesstunde;
   to be at its last ~ auf dem letzten Loche pfeifen.

gasper *(Br., sl.)* billige Zigarette, Glimmstengel.

gassy *(boastful)* aufgeblasen, eitel, *(mining)* schlagwetterreich.

gasworks Gasanstalt, -werk.

gate Eingang, Tor, *(aerodrome)* Flugsteig, *(entrance money)* Eintrittsgeld, *(expressway)* Autobahnabfahrt, *(firing, US)* Entlassung, Hinauswurf, *(passage)* [schmale] Durchfahrt, *(sport)* Besucherzahl, Zahl der verkauften Eintrittskarten, *(water)* Schleusentor;
   British ℒ **Paßkontrolle für Engländer; garden** ~ Gartentür;
   ~ *(v.) (Cambridge, Oxford)* Geldstrafe wegen überschrittener Ausgangszeit auferlegen;
   to get the ~ *(US)* hinausgeschmissen werden; **to give s. o. the** ~ *(US)* jem. einen Korb geben;
   ~ **bill** *(Oxford)* Geldstrafe wegen überschrittener Ausgangszeit; ~**-legged table** Klapptisch; ~ **meeting** Sportveranstaltung mit Eintrittsgeld; ~ **money** eingenommenes Eintritts-, Einlaßgeld; ~ **receipts** Kasseneinnahmen; ~**-type gear shift** *(car)* Kulissenschaltung.

gatecrash *(v.)* uneingeladen kommen;
   ~ **a meeting** sich in eine Versammlung einschmuggeln.

gatecrasher Eindringling, ungebetener Gast.

gatefold ausschlagbare Seite.

gatehouse Pförtnerhaus, *(railroad, US)* Bahnwärterhäuschen.

gatekeeper, gateman Pförtner, Torhüter, *(US, railroad)* Schranken-, Bahnwärter.

gatepost Türpfosten;
   between you and me and the ~ unter uns gesagt, streng vertraulich.

gateway Eingang, Einfahrt, Eingangstor, *(Restrictive Practices Court)* kartellunschädlicher Tatbestand;
   ~ **to fame** Eingangspforte zum Ruhm.

gather *(v.)* sammeln, anhäufen, *(congregate)* zusammenbringen, vereinigen, *(v./i.)* sich versammeln, *(bookbinding)* [in Lagen] zusammentragen, *(conclude)* schließen, folgen;
   ~ **in the crops** Ernte einbringen; ~ **in debts** Schulden einkassieren; ~ **from the evidence** aus dem Beweismaterial schließen; ~ **the facts** Tatsachen zusammentragen; ~ **one's friends together** seine Freunde um sich versammeln; ~ **information** Erkundigungen einziehen; ~ **in knots in the street** Gruppen in den Straßen bilden; ~ **the pages of a book** *(bookbinding)* Bogen eines Buches zusammentragen; ~ **from the papers** aus den Zeitungen erfahren; ~ **one's papers together** seine Papiere zusammenraffen; ~ **rents** Mieten einziehen; ~ **speed** schneller werden; ~ **from a statement** aus einer Erklärung schließen; ~ **strength** wieder zu Kräften kommen; ~ **taxes** Steuern kassieren; ~ **troops together** Truppen zusammenziehen; ~ **way** *(mar.)* Fahrt aufnehmen.

gatherer Sammler, *(bookbinding)* Zusammentragungsmaschine; **tax** ~ Steuereinnehmer.

gathering *(bookbinding)* Lage, *(collection)* Einsammeln, Erhebung [von Geldern], Geldsammlung, *(crowd)* Menschenansammlung, Menge, *(meeting)* Treffen, Tagung, Versammlung, Zusammenkunft;
at a public ~ auf einer öffentlichen Versammlung;
family ~ Familientreffen, -zusammenkunft; **industrial** ~ Wirtschaftstagung; **mammoth** ~ Massenversammlung;
~ **of the clan** Sippentag; **~-in of the crop** Ernteeinbringung; ~ **of speed** Geschwindigkeitszunahme; ~ **of strength** Wieder-zu-Kräften-Kommen;
to hold a ~ Versammlung abhalten.

gating *(university, Br.)* Ausgangsverbot.

gauge *(Br.)* Anzeiger, Meßgerät, *(bookbinding)* Klischeehöhenprüfer, *(draught of ship)* Tiefgang, *(measure)* [Eichmaß], Richtmaß, [Wasserstands]messer, Pegel, *(mil.)* Kaliber, *(print.)* Kolumnen-, Zeilenmaß, *(railway)* Spurweite;
broad ~ Breitspur; **narrow** ~ Schmalspur; **oil** ~ Ölstandsmesser; **petrol** ~ Benzinstandsmesser, -uhr; **standard** ~ Normalspur;
~ *(v.) (estimate)* [ab]schätzen, taxieren, beurteilen, *(find capacity of)* eichen, justieren, kalibrieren, *(measure)* abmessen;
~ **s. one's capacities** jds. Fähigkeiten beurteilen; ~ **s. one's character** jds. Charakter beurteilen; ~ **the content of a barrel** Faßinhalt berechnen; ~ **the market** Markt beurteilen; ~ **public opinion** öffentliche Meinung abschätzen; ~ **the progress made** Fortschritt abschätzen; ~ **the rainfall** Niederschlagsmenge messen; ~ **voting strength** Wahlmöglichkeiten kalkulieren;
to take the ~ aus-, abmessen;
~ **door** *(mining)* Wettertür.

gauger Eichmeister;
~**'s estimate** Eichschein.

gauging Eichung, Messung;
~ **office** Eichamt; ~ **rod** Eichstab.

gauntlet *(Br.)* Spießrutenlaufen;
to pick up the ~ Fehdehandschuh aufnehmen; **to run the** ~ Spießruten laufen; **to throw down the** ~ **to s. o.** jem. den Fehdehandschuh hinwerfen.

gavel *(US)* Auktionshammer;
~ **work** Frondienst.

gazette *(Br.)* Bundes-, Staatsanzeiger, Gesetz-, Amtsblatt, amtliches Organ, amtliche Zeitung;
diplomatic ~ diplomatisches Mitteilungsblatt; **official** ~ *(Br.)* amtliches Mitteilungsblatt; **police** ~ *(Br.)* Gerichtszeitung; **topical** ~ *(cinema)* Aktualitätenschau;
~ *(v.) (Br.)* amtlich (im Bundesanzeiger) bekanntgeben;
~ **an appointment** *(Br.)* Beförderung veröffentlichen; ~ **a case of bankruptcy** Konkursfall bekanntgeben; ~ **out** *(mil.)* verabschieden; ~ **to a regiment** zu einem Regiment versetzen;
to have one's name (appear) in the ~ auf der Liste der Konkurse (Konkursliste) stehen, bankrott sein;
~ **entries** *(Br.)* [etwa] amtliche Mitteilungen im Bundesanzeiger;
~ **writer** Journalist.

gazetted bankrupt für bankrott (zahlungsunfähig) erklärt.

gazetteer Journalist eines Amtsblattes, *(index)* Ortsnamenverzeichnis, -lexikon.

gazump *(v.) (Br.)* Grundstückspreis nachträglich erhöhen.

gear *(car)* Gang, Getriebe, *(ship)* seemännische Ausrüstung, *(tools)* Werkzeug, Gerät, Hausrat;
out of ~ im Leerlauf, [außer Betrieb], *(fig.)* in Unordnung; **in high** ~ in einem schnellen (hohen) Gang; **with full** ~ in höchster Übersetzung;
bottom ~ erster Gang; **camping** ~ Zeltausrüstung; **first** ~ *(car)* erster Gang; **fishing** ~ Angelgerät; **household** ~ Haushaltsartikel; **landing** ~ *(plane)* Landeknüppel; **loading** ~ Verladegerät; **low** ~ niedrigster (erster) Gang; **reverse** ~ Rückwärtsgang; **steering** ~ **of a ship** Steuerrad eines Schiffes;
~ *(v.) (adapt)* abstellen auf, *(set going)* in Gang setzen, *(car)* mit einem Getriebe versehen;
~ **to consumer needs** sich dem Verbraucherbedürfnis anpassen; ~ **the dollar value of contracts to gold** von Dollar auf Goldbasis umstellen; ~ **down** herunterschalten; ~ **a factory to s. th.** Fabrik auf etw. abstellen; ~ **for the future** Zukunftsweichen stellen; ~ **production to the capacity of a plant** betriebliche Produktionskapazität voll ausfahren; ~ **production to demand** Produktion der Nachfrage anpassen; ~ **the sum assured to the amount of the original loan** Versicherungssumme auf die ursprüngliche Kredithöhe abstellen; ~ **up** heraufschalten; ~ **up for election campaign** Wahlkampfvorbereitungen treffen;

to be out of ~ **(run in neutral)** ~ im Leerlauf sein; **to be thrown out of** ~ aus der Bahn geworfen sein; **to change into (engage) the second** ~ in zweiten Gang schalten; **to climb a hill on top** ~ Hügel ohne zu schalten herauffahren; **to run in neutral** ~ im Leerlauf sein;
~ **case** Getriebegehäuse; ~ **change** Gangschaltung; ~ **lever** Schalthebel; ~ **ratio** Übersetzungsverhältnis; ~ **shaft** Getriebewelle; ~ **wheel** Getrieberad.

gearbox Getriebe[gehäuse];
automatic ~ automatisches Getriebe.

geared | to export exportorientiert;
to be ~ **to** ausgerichtet sein auf; **to be** ~ **to the purchaser's age** auf das Alter des Erwerbers abgestellt sein.

gearing Getriebe, Triebwerk, *(capital)* festverzinslicher Anteil am Gesamtkapital;
high ~ Kapitalintensität; **low** ~ knappe Kapitaldecke, -ausstattung.

gearshift [Gang]schaltung;
~ **lever** Schalthebel.

gem Edelstein, *(fig.)* Perle, Juwel, Glanzstück, *(print.)* sehr kleiner Schriftgrad.

gene *(biol.)* Gen, Erbeinheit.

genealogical table (tree) genealogischer Stammbaum.

genealogize *(v.)* Ahnenforschung betreiben.

genealogy Abstammung, Geschlechterfolge.

general *(mil.)* General, Feldherr, Stratege;
advocate ~ *(EC)* Generalanwalt; **attorney** ~ *(Br.)* Generalstaatsanwalt; **Attorney** ~ *(US)* Justizminister; **consul** ~ Generalkonsul; **consulate** ~ Generalkonsulat; **director** ~ Generaldirektor; **inspector** ~ Generalinspekteur; **Postmaster** ~ Postminister; **secretary** ~ Generalsekretär; **Solicitor** ~ *(US)* stellvertretender Justizminister;
~ *(a.)* allgemein, generell, gemeinsam, gemeinschaftlich, *(customary)* allgemein verbreitet, üblich, landläufig, *(rough)* ungefähr, annähernd, unklar, unbestimmt;
~ **acceptance** unbedingte Wechselannahme, unbeschränktes Akzept; ~ **Account** *(International Monetary Fund)* Generalkonto; ~ **account** allgemeines Konto, *(bill)* Hauptrechnung; ~ **accountant** Finanzbuchhalter, Revisionsbeamter; ~ **accounting department** Finanzbuchhaltung; ~ **Accounting Office** *(US)* Bundesrechnungshof; ~ **advertising** überregionale Werbung; ~ **advertising rate** allgemeiner Anzeigentarif; ~ **agency** Generalvertretung; ~ **agency business** Generalvertretung; ~ **agent** Generalvertreter, -bevollmächtigter; ~ **agreement** Generalabkommen; ~ **Agreement on Tariffs and Trade (GATT)** Allgemeines Zoll- und Handelsabkommen; ~ **appearance** vorbehaltslose (uneingeschränkte) Klageeinlassung; ~ **arrangements to borrow (GAB)** allgemeine Kreditvereinbarungen; ~ **assembly** *(UNO)* Voll-, Generalversammlung, *(US)* gesetzgebende Körperschaft; ~ **assignment** *(banking)* Mantelzession; ~ **assignment for benefit of creditors** außerkonkursliche Abwicklung zugunsten der Gläubiger, Übertragung des Gesamtvermögens auf die Gläubiger; ~ **assumpsit** Schadenersatzklage wegen Nichterfüllung, allgemeine Schadenersatzverpflichtung; ~ **audit** Jahresabschlußprüfung; ~ **average** große Havarie; ~ **average contribution** gemeinsamer Havariebeitrag, Havarieumlage; ~ **average statement** große Havarie; ~ **balance sheet** Hauptbilanz; ~ **bequest** Geldsummenvermächtnis, aus dem Gesamtnachlaß zu leistendes Vermächtnis; ~ **bill of lading** Sammelkonnossement; ~ **bookkeeper** Hauptbuchhalter; ~ **bookkeeping department** Hauptbuchhaltung; ~ **bookseller** Sortimentsbuchhändler; ~ **building scheme** gesamtes Bebauungsprojekt, Generalbebauungsplan; ~ **burden** Handlungsunkosten; ~ **business** *(agenda)* Verschiedenes, *(insurance, Br.)* Sachversicherungsgeschäft; ~ **cargo** gemischte Ladung, Stückgut, Sammelladung; ~ **cargo liner** Linienfrachtschiff für Sammelladungen; ~ **cash** Betriebsmittel; **Advanced** ~ **Certificate of Education** *(Br.)* [etwa] Abiturientenzeugnis; **Ordinary** ~ **Certificate of Education** *(Br.)* [etwa] Zeugnis der mittleren Reife; ~ **challenge** grundsätzliche Geschworenenablehnung; ~ **charge** General-, Handlungsunkosten, *(Scot. law)* Frist zum Erbantritt; ~ **circulation** *(newspaper)* Gesamtauflage; ~ **clearing** *(London banks)* allgemeiner Verrechnungsverkehr; ~ **Commissioners of Income Tax** *(Br.)* Laienkollegium in Steuersachen; ~ **commodities** Sammelgüter; ~ **commodities trucking** Sammelguttransport; ~ **conception** Allgemeinbegriff; ~ **consumption** Massenkonsum; ~ **contingency reserve** allgemeine Delkredererückstellung; ~ **contractor** Generalunternehmer; ~ **cost** Gemeinkosten; ~ **Council** *(trade union, Br.)* ständiges Repräsentativorgan; ~ **counsel** Syndikus; ~ **court** *(Bank of England)* halbjährliche Generalversammlung; ~ **Court** *(US)*

gesetzgebende Körperschaft; ~ **credit** *(witness)* Glaubwürdigkeit; ~ **creditor** nicht bevorrechtiger Gläubiger; ~ **crossing** *(cheque, Br.)* allgemeiner Verrechnungsvermerk; ~ **custom** Landessitte, Gewohnheitsrecht; ~ **damage** unmittelbarer Schaden; ~ **damages** üblicher Schadenersatz; ~ **data** Allgemeines; ~ **dealer** *(Br.)* Gemischtwarenhändler, Krämer; ~ **delivery** *(US)* Ausgabestelle für postlagernde Sendungen; ~ **demurrer** Einwand der Unschlüssigkeit; ~ **denial** Bestreiten des gesamten Klagevorbringens; ~ **deposit** Sammeldepot; ~ **display** *(advertising)* Vollbelegung; ~ **distribution** allgemeiner Vertrieb; ~ **editor** Hauptschriftleiter; good ~ **education** gute Allgemeinbildung; ~ **election** Parlamentswahlen, allgemeine Wahlen; ~ **election day** Wahltermin, -tag; ~ **endorsement** Blankogiro; ~ **equilibrum** totales Gleichgewicht, Gleichgewicht bei allen Märkten; ~ **equilibrium theory** Gleichgewichtstheorie; ~ **estate** Gesamtvermögen; ~ **examination** Gesamtprüfung; ~ **execution** Zwangsvollstreckung in das bewegliche Vermögen; ~ **executives** Vorstandsmitglieder [einer AG]; ~ **exception** Unschlüssigkeitseinrede; ~ **executor** Nachlaßverwalter; ~ **expenses** General-, Handlungsunkosten; ~ **exporter** Exporteur mehrerer oder sämtlicher Warengattungen; ~ **failure of issue** Erbenlosigkeit; **to be a** ~ **favo(u)rite** überall beliebt sein; ~ **field** Allmende; ~ **findings** Tatbestand; ~ **foreman** Obermeister; ~ **franchise** staatlich verliehene Rechtsfähigkeit; ~ **freight** Stückgutfracht; ~ **freight carrier** Stückgutspediteur; ~ **fund** Rücklagenfonds, *(government accounting)* Steuern und sonstige Einkünfte, allgemeine Etatsmittel; ⌐ **Headquarters** Hauptquartier; ~ **hiring** von Jahr zu Jahr laufender Dienstvertrag; ~ **guardian** unbeschränkter Vormund; ~ **holiday** öffentlicher Feiertag; ~ **hospital** allgemeines Krankenhaus; ~ **idea** ungefähre Vorstellung; ~ **impression** Gesamteindruck; ~ **improvements** allgemein geplante Aufschließungsmaßnahmen; ~ **increase** *(tariff)* durchgehende Frachttariferhöhung; ⌐ **Index of Retail Prices** Einzelhandelspreisindex; ~ **indorsement** Blankoindossament; **to be a man of** ~ **information** vielseitig gebildet sein; ~ **instruction** Erläuterung juristischer Begriffe; ~ **insurance** normale Seeschadensversicherung; ~ **intent** allgemeine Willenseinrichtung; ~ **interest** *(hearsay evidence)* allgemeines Interesse; ~ **journal** Hauptbuch, Sammeljournal; ~ **jurisdiction** allgemeiner Gerichtsstand; ~ **knowledge** Allgemeinwissen, allgemeine Bildung; ~ **law** allgemeingültiges Gesetz; ~ **ledger** Hauptbuch; ~ **ledger account** Hauptbuchkonto; ~ **legacy** Geldsummenvermächtnis, aus dem Gesamtnachlaß zu leistendes Vermächtnis; ~ **letter of attorney in fact** Generalvollmacht; ~ **licensee** Generallizenznehmer; ~ **lien** allgemeines Zurückhaltungsrecht; ~ **line** Generallinie; ~ **line jobber** Großhändler mit mehreren Sortiment; ~ **listing** *(real-estate law)* gleichzeitige Vergabe an mehrere Makler; ~ **loan and collateral agreement** *(US)* laufender Vertrag zwischen Maklern und einer Bank zwecks Gewährung von Maklerdarlehn; ~ **maid** Alleinmädchen; ~ **management trust** Kapitalanlagegesellschaft mit veränderlichem Anlagefonds, Kapitalanlagegesellschaft mit eigenverantwortlicher Anlagenverwaltung; ~ **manager** Generaldirektor; ~ **medical council** *(Br.)* Bundesärztekammer; ~ **meeting** *(Br.)* Haupt-, Generalversammlung, *(society)* Mitgliederversammlung; **annual** ~ **meeting** *(Br.)* ordentliche Jahreshauptversammlung; **extraordinary** ~ **meeting** *(Br.)* außerordentliche Generalversammlung; ~ **merchandise** Stückgutfracht, *(US)* Gemischtwaren; ~ **mortgage** Gesamthypothek; ~ **mortgage bonds** *(US)* durch Gesamthypothek besicherte Schuldverschreibungen; ~ **obligation** allgemeine Verpflichtung; ~ **obligation bonds** *(municipal accounting)* Kommunalobligationen; ~ **office** Zentrale, Zentralbüro; ~ **officer** *(mil.)* Offizier im Generalsrang; ~ **operating expense** allgemeine Betriebsausgaben; ~ **opinion** allgemeine (landläufige) Meinung; ~ **orders** *(mil.)* Tagesbefehl; ~ **outlook** allgemeine Aussichten; ~ **outline of a scheme** Gesamtüberblick über ein Projekt; ~ **overhead** Handlungs-, Generalunkosten; ~ **overseer** Aufsichtsbehörde; ~ **owner** Eigentümer; ~ **pact** Rahmenvertrag; ~ **pardon** Amnestie; ~ **partner** unbeschränkt haftender Gesellschafter, Komplementär; ~ **partnership** Offene Handelsgesellschaft; ~ **plea** Rechtseinwand; ~ **policy** Generalpolice; ~ **post** ortsübliche Postzustellung; ~ **post office** Hauptpostamt; ~ **power of appointment** unbeschränkte Befugnis zur Einsetzung eines Begünstigten; ~ **power of attorney** Generalvollmacht; ~ **practice** übliches Verfahren; ⌐ **Practice Act** *(US)* Zivilprozeßordnung; ~ **practitioner** Hausarzt, praktischer Arzt; ~ **property** unbeschränktes Eigentum; ~ **property tax** *(US)* Vermögenssteuer; **the** ~ **public** die breite Öffentlichkeit; ~ **public-service station** im Interesse der Allgemeinheit errichteter Rundfunksender; ~ **publicity** Publikumswerbung; ~~

purpose aircraft Mehrzweckflugzeug; ~~**purpose contingency reserve** Garantierücklage, allgemeine Rücklage; ~~**purpose rates** allgemeingültiger Tarif; ~ **reader** Durchschnittsleser, Leserschaft; ~ **records** Buchungsunterlagen; ⌐ **Register** *(Br.)* Personenstandsregister; ⌐ **Register Office** *(Br.)* Hauptstandesamt; ~ **release** Verzicht auf alle gegenwärtige und zukünftige Ansprüche, völlige Entlastung, *(taxation)* allgemeine Steueramnestie; ~ **resemblance** vage Ähnlichkeit; ~ **restraint of trade** überall gültiges Konkurrenzverbot; ~ **retainer** ständige anwaltliche Tätigkeit bei Bedarf, *(fee)* Pauschalhonorar; ~ **rule** allgemeingültige Regel; **as a** ~ **rule** üblicherweise; ~ **sales manager** Absatz-, Verkaufs-, Vertriebsleiter; ~ **sales representative** Vertreter mehrerer Firmen; ~ **sales tax** allgemeine Umsatzsteuer; ~ **science** allgemeine Naturwissenschaft; ~ **servant** *(Br.)* Mädchen für Alles; ~ **service car** offener Güterwagen; ~ **service school** *(US)* [etwa] Generalstabsschule; ~ **sessions** [etwa] Schöffengericht; ~ **ship** Frachtschiff; ~ **shop** Gemischtwarenhandlung; ~ **staff** *(mil.)* Generalstab; ~ **staff officer** Generalstabsoffizier; ~ **stock** Stammaktie; ~ **storage** *(data processing)* Hauptspeicher; ~ **store** *(US)* Gemischtwarenhandlung; ~ **strike** Generalstreik; ~ **system theory** Systemtheorie; ~ **tail** auf Leiberserben beschränkte Rechtsnachfolge; ~ **tariff** *(customs)* Einheitstarif; ~ **taxes** allgemeine Steuern; ~ **tenancy** unbefristeter Pachtvertrag; ~ **term** *(US)* vollständige Kongreßsitzung; ~ **terms** allgemein gültige Bedingungen; **to explain s. th. in** ~ **terms** etw. in groben Zügen darlegen; ~ **ticket** *(US)* Abstimmung über mehrere Kandidaten auf einer Liste; ~ **traverse** allgemeines Bestreiten; ~ **usage** allgemeiner Brauch; **to be in** ~ **use** allgemein gebräuchlich sein; ~ **verdict** Geschworenenurteil; ~ **view** Totalansicht; ~ **warranty** Freistellung von Rechten Dritter für alle Zeit; ~ **welfare** allgemeines Wohl.

generalist Alleskönner.

generality allgemeine Redensart, *(general principle)* Allgemeingültigkeit;
   ~ **of a nation** Mehrheit einer Nation.

generalization Generalisierung, Verallgemeinerung.

generalize *(v.)* Verallgemeinerungen anstellen, verallgemeinern, generalisieren;
   ~ **the use of a new invention** neue Erfindung allgemein zur Anwendung bringen.

generally | accepted *(accounting principles)* überall anerkannt; ~ **binding** allgemein verbindlich.

generate *(v.)* hervorbringen, erzeugen;
   ~ **earnings** Einkünfte entstehen lassen; ~ **electricity** Elektrizität erzeugen.

generation Hervorbringung, Erzeugung, *(average lifetime of man)* Generation[sdauer];
   coming ~ Nachwuchs; **previous** ~**s** frühere Generationen; **rising** ~ heranwachsende Generation;
   ~ **of electricity** Stromerzeugnis;
   ~ **clash** Generationskonflikt; ~ **gap** Kluft zwischen den Generationen.

generator *(el.)* Generator.

generic term Sammelbegriff.

generosity Freigebigkeit, Großmütigkeit, Großmut.

generous freigebig, großzügig;
   to be ~ **with one's money** freigebig sein;
   ~ **gift** reichliches (großzügiges) Geschenk; ~ **harvest** gute Ernte; ~ **meal** üppige Mahlzeit; ~ **mood** Geberlaune; ~ **portion** volle Portion.

genetic engineering Veränderung der Erbanlagen.

Geneva | Conferences on the Law of the Sea Genfer Seerechtskonferenzen; ~ **convention** Genfer Konvention; ~ **Trade Conference** Genfer Handelskonferenz.

genial freundlich, jovial;
   ~ **climate** mildes Klima.

genius Genie, genialer Mensch;
   one's good ~ sein guter Geist;
   ~ **loci** Atmosphäre eines Platzes;
   to have a ~ **for finance** Finanzgenie sein; **to have a** ~ **for making friends** Freundschaften zu schließen wissen; **to have a** ~ **for languages** hervorragende Sprachbegabung besitzen; **to take a** ~ ein Genie erfordern.

genocide Völkermord.

genteel vornehm, elegant;
   ~ **class** Privilegiertenklasse; **to live in** ~ **poverty** selbst in der Armut Haltung zu wahren wissen; ~ **suburb** vornehmes Vorstadtviertel.

gentle freundlich, liebenswürdig;
   ~ **breeze** schwache Brise; ~ **calling** ehrenwerter Beruf; **the** ~ **and simple classes** vornehme und einfache Bevölkerungs-

schichten; ~ **craft** Angelsport; **of ~ extradition** von vornehmer Abkunft; ~ **family** gute Familie; ~ **reader** geneigter Leser; ~ **rebuke** sanfter Tadel; **the ~ sex** das schwache Geschlecht; ~ **slope** sanfter Abhang.

gentlefolk vornehme Leute.

gentleman Gentleman, Ehrenmann, Mann von Bildung, *(law)* Privatmann;
independent ~ Rentier;
~ **of colo(u)r** Farbiger; ~ **of fortune** Glücksritter; ~ **at large (of independent means)** Privatier; ~ **of the road** Wegelagerer, Straßenräuber; ~ **of the robe** Jurist; ~ **in waiting** Kammerherr, Kämmerer;
~ **farmer** Gutsbesitzer, Landwirt, Ökonom.

gentleman's agreement Vereinbarung auf Treu und Glauben, unverbindliche Gefälligkeitszusage.

gentlewoman vornehme Dame.

gentry *(Br.)* niederer Adel;
light-fingered ~ Zunft der Taschendiebe.

genuflection Hofknicks.

genuine echt, rein, lauter, unverfälscht, authentisch, *(business)* solid, reell;
~ **article** Markenartikel; ~ **coin** echte Münze; ~ **pearls** echte Perlen; ~ **purchaser** ernsthafter Reflektant; ~ **Rembrandt** echter Rembrandt; ~ **signature** ungefälschte Unterschrift.

genuineness of signature Echtheit der Unterschrift;
to have reason to doubt the ~ berechtigte Zweifel an der Echtheit einer Unterschrift haben.

geo-economic raumwirtschaftlich.

geographical | distribution gebietsmäßig aufgeteilter Verkauf; ~ **immobility** *(workers)* wohnungsbedingte Unbeweglichkeit; ~ **mobility** *(factor of promotion)* räumliche Mobilität; ~ **name** Ortsbezeichnung; ~ **sector** Gebiet.

geography, economic Wirtschaftsgeographie.

geometrical progression geometrische Progression.

geopolitical geopolitisch.

geopolitics Geopolitik.

geophysical year geophysikalisches Jahr.

geophysics Geophysik.

George *(aeronautics, sl.)* automatische Steuerung.

germ Mikrobe, Bakterie;
~ **of an idea** Keim (Ursprung) einer Idee;
~ **warfare** biologische Kriegsführung, Bakterienkrieg.

German type gotische Schrift, Frakturschrift.

germinal ideas unentwickelte Ideen.

gerontocracy Greisenherrschaft.

gerrymander *(US)* willkürliche Einteilung von Wahlbezirken, manipulierte Wahlkreisfestlegung;
~ *(v.)* **an election** (election districts) *(US)* Wahlschiebungen begehen; ~ **a piece of business** Angelegenheit manipulieren.

gerrymandering *(US)* Wahl[kreis]verschiebung.

gestation Schwangerschaft.

gestio Geschäftsführung.

gestor Geschäftsführer ohne Auftrag.

gesture Gebärde, Geste;
handsome ~ *(dipl.)* Geste, Sympathiebezeugung.

get *(Br., mining)* Ertrag, Fördermenge, Förderung, Ausbeute;
~**-off** *(airplane)* Abflug, Start, *(fig.)* Ausflucht, Drückebergerei; ~**together** *(US)* zwanglose Zusammenkunft;
~ *(v.)* *(earn)* verdienen, *(obtain)* bekommen, erhalten, erreichen; sich verschaffen, erlangen, *(purchase goods)* besorgen, auftreiben, [Waren] beziehen, *(succeed)* Erfolg haben, etw. ausrichten, *(win)* gewinnen;
~ **aboard** an Bord bringen, *(v./i.)* sich einschiffen; ~ **about** *(rumo(u)r)* umlaufen, umgehen; ~ **about a great deal** viel auf Reisen sein; ~ **above o. s.** sich überschätzen; ~ **across to an audience** beim Publikum ankommen; ~ **admission** Eintritt (Zutritt) erlangen; ~ **aground** kein Geld haben; ~ **ahead by leaps and bounds** ruckweise vorwärtskommen; ~ **ahead of s. o.** j. überrunden.

get *(v.)* **along** schaffen, vorankommen;
~ **on little money** mit wenig Geld auskommen; ~ **with people** mit den Leuten zurechtkommen; ~ **well** gute Fortschritte machen; ~ **well together** gut miteinander auskommen.

get *(v.)* **around a law** Gesetz umgehen.

get *(v.)* **at** Zugang erhalten;
~ **a th.** *(fam.)* auf etw. anspielen; ~ **s. o.** j. beeinflussen; ~ **the root of a trouble** einem Übel auf den Grund gehen; ~ **the truth** Wahrheit herausbekommen; ~ **a witness** Zeugen bestechen (bearbeiten).

get *(v.)* **away** fortschaffen, *(prisoner)* davonkommen, entkommen;

~ **early from a reception** Empfang frühzeitig verlassen; ~ **from one's environment** sich von Umwelteinflüssen freimachen; ~ **for the holidays** in den Ferien verreisen; ~ **from the office for a day** einen Tag nicht im Geschäft sein, sich einen Tag vom Büro freimachen; ~ **with it** ungestraft (mit einer Sache gerade noch) davonkommen.

get *(v.)* **back** zurückbekommen, -erhalten, [Geld] herausbekommen;
~ **into one's car** wieder in sein Auto einsteigen; ~ **one's own back on s. o.** sich bei jem. revanchieren.

get *(v.) | **the best of it** Sieg davontragen; ~ **s. th. on the brain** dauernd an etw. denken müssen; ~ **one's bread** seinen Lebensunterhalt verdienen, zur Sache kommen; ~ **behind** *(sl.)* unterstützen; ~ **by durchkommen**, ausreichen, *(car)* vorbeikommen; ~ **by on a low wage** mit einem niedrigen Lohn auskommen; ~ **clear** klarkommen; ~ **commodities from abroad** seine Ware außerhalb beziehen.

get *(v.)* **down | to business (brass tacks)** zur Sache kommen; ~ **to the facts** sich an die Tatsachen halten; ~ **on the emotional side of it** seinen Gefühlen freien Lauf lassen; ~ **s. one's speech** jds. Rede mitschreiben; ~ **a telephone conversation** Telefongespräch schriftlich festhalten; ~ **to one's work after the holidays** sich nach den Ferien an seine Arbeit machen.

get *(v.) | **an estate** Grundbesitzer werden, zu Grundbesitz gelangen; ~ **even with s. o.** *(US coll.)* es jem. heimzahlen; ~ **forward with one's work** mit seiner Arbeit vorankommen; ~ **forward in the world** zu Vermögen kommen; ~ **one's hand in** mit der Arbeit vertraut werden; ~ **it into one's head** es sich in den Kopf setzen; ~ **by heart** auswendig lernen; ~ **hold of** *(coll.)* erlernen; ~ **hold of s. o.** j. erwischen; ~ **home** *(remark)* voll verstanden werden; ~ **s. o. home** j. nach Hause schaffen; ~ **a hump (hustle)** sich beeilen.

get *(v.)* **in** *(bus, train)* einsteigen, *(parl.)* ins Parlament gewählt werden, *(party)* Regierungspartei werden, *(train)* einlaufen, ankommen;
~ **ahead of s. o.** jem. zuvorkommen; ~ **with s. o.** mit jem. gut zurechtkommen; ~ **for a constituency** sich um einen Wahlkreis bewerben; ~ **the crop** Ernte einbringen; ~ **debts** Schulden hereinbekommen; ~ **five minutes early** *(train)* fünf Minuten zu früh einlaufen; ~ **with a firm** Geschäftsbeziehungen zu einer Firma aufnehmen; ~ **one's hand** mit einer Arbeit vertraut werden; ~ **with influential people** mit einflußreichen Leuten anfreunden; ~ **s. o. to repair the television set** j. zur Reparatur des Fernsehers holen; ~ **taxes** Steuern hereinholen; ~ **up to time** *(train)* pünktlich einlaufen.

get *(v.)* **into | s. th.** in eine Sache einsteigen; ~ **an article into a paper** Zeitungsartikel unterbringen; ~ **a bus** in einen Bus einsteigen; ~ **a club** einem Verein beitreten, Vereinsmitglied werden; ~ **bad company** in schlechte Gesellschaft geraten; ~ **debt in** Schulden geraten; ~ **fooled in doing** sich verleiten lassen; ~ **bad habits** schlechte Gewohnheiten annehmen; ~ **a line of business** in eine Branche einsteigen; ~ **touch** Fühlung aufnehmen; ~ **s. o. into trouble** Geschichten über j. erzählen.

get *(v.) | **leave to go home** Heimaturlaub erhalten; ~ **a letter off** Brief expedieren; ~ **one's living** sein Auskommen haben, seinen Lebensunterhalt verdienen; ~ **low** *(price)* fallen; ~ **married** sich verheiraten; ~ **money out of s. o.** Geld aus jem. herausholen; ~ **one's money back** sein Geld zurückerhalten; ~ **six months** halbes Jahr Gefängnis bekommen; ~ **next to s. o.** *(US coll.)* jds. böse Absichten erkennen; ~ **nothing by it** leer ausgehen.

get *(v.)* **off** fortgehen, aufbrechen, abreisen;
~ **with s. o.** mit jem. anbandeln; ~ **cheaply** billig davonkommen; ~ **false coin** falsches Geld unterbringen (loswerden); ~ **one's daughter** Tochter verheiraten; ~ **the deep end** in Wut geraten; ~ **a duty** Verpflichtung loswerden; ~ **with a fine** mit einer Geldstrafe davonkommen; ~ **lightly** mit einem blauen Auge davonkommen; ~ **one's merchandise** seine Ware losschlagen; ~ **the rails** entgleisen; ~ **s. o.** *(barrister)* j. herauspauken; ~ **a letter off in good time** Brief noch rechtzeitig postieren; ~ **the train next station** bei der nächsten Station aussteigen.

get *(v.)* **on** zurecht-, vorwärtskommen, Fortschritte machen;
~ **with s. o.** mit jem. auskommen; ~ **without s. o.** sich ohne jem. behelfen; ~ **s. th. on s. o.** *(US)* etw. Kompromittierendes über j. erfahren; ~ **one's feet** sich zum Sprechen erheben; ~ **with the job** mit einer Arbeit zurechtkommen; ~ **in life** im Leben vorankommen; ~ **s. o.** mit jem. in Verbindung kommen, *(tel.)* sich mit jem. verbinden lassen; ~ **to s. o. at last** jem. zu guter Letzt hinter die Schliche kommen; ~ **with one's studies** mit seinem Studium vorankommen; ~ **in the world** seinen Weg machen.

get *(v.)* **out** herausholen, *(business)* Geschäft aufgeben, *(news)* bekanntwerden, herauskommen, *(publish)* herausbringen, veröffentlichen;

~ **of s. th.** aus einer Sache aussteigen; ~ **s. th. out of s. o.** etw. aus jem. herausbekommen; ~ **a balance sheet** Bilanz aufstellen; ~ **of bed on the wrong side** mit dem linken Fuß zuerst aufstehen; ~ **a book** Buch veröffentlichen; ~ **one's car** sein Auto herausfahren; ~ **a confession out of s. o.** j. zu einem Geständnis bringen; ~ **of a country** Land verlassen; ~ **of one's duties** sich um seine Verpflichtungen drücken; **s. o. out of a fix** jem. aus einer Klemme heraushelfen; ~ **of hand** außer Kontrolle geraten; ~ **without loss** seine Unkosten gerade decken; ~ **money out of s. o.** Geld aus jem. herauskitzeln; ~ **so much out of a property** so viel Rendite aus einem Vermögen erwirtschaften; **a secret** ~ **of s. o.** jem. ein Geheimnis entlocken; ~ **on time** *(newspaper)* rechtzeitig erscheinen; ~ **from under** *(US)* mit heiler Haut davonkommen; ~ **to the vote** zur Abstimmung bringen; **s. th.** ~ **of the way** etw. erledigen; ~ **a few words of thanks** ein paar Dankesworte stammeln.

get *(v.)* **over** ausführen, vollenden, *(fig.)* verwinden;
~ **one's financial losses** über seine finanziellen Verluste hinwegkommen; ~ **a serious illness** sich nach einer schweren Krankheit erholen; ~ **one's surprise** seine Überraschung überwinden.

get *(v.)* | **paid** bezahlt werden; ~ **possession** Besitz ergreifen; ~ **the price reduced** Preis herunterhandeln; ~ **only a small profit** nur geringen Nutzen erzielen; ~ **religion** *(fam.)* konvertieren; ~ **round** herumkommen, überreden, *(US)* [Gesetz] umgehen; ~ **round s. o.** *(fam.)* j. zu nehmen wissen; ~ **round a clause** um eine Bestimmung herumkommen; ~ **round every patient in a ward** jedem Kranken im Hospital einen Besuch abstatten; ~ **round the world** Weltreise machen, in der Welt herumkommen; ~ **the sack** *(sl.)* gefeuert werden; ~ **shut of s. o.** *(fam.)* j. loswerden; ~ **a station on one's radio set** Rundfunkstation auf seinem Apparat bekommen; ~ **a telegram** Telegramm erhalten.

get *(v.)* **through** durchkommen, Ziel erreichen, *(examination)* Examen (Prüfung) bestehen, *(tel.)* Verbindung bekommen;
~ **to s. o.** j. erreichen; ~ **a bill** einem Gesetz zur Annahme verhelfen; ~ **one's fortune** sein Vermögen aufzehren (durchbringen); ~ **a lot of correspondence** großen Teil seiner Korrespondenz erledigen; ~ **with one's work** mit seiner Arbeit fertig werden.

get *(v.)* | **thrown out** hinausgeschmissen werden; ~ **s. o. a ticket** jem. eine Fahrkarte besorgen; ~ **together** zusammenkommen; ~ **an army together** Heer aufstellen; ~ **one's thoughts together** sich geistig vorbereiten.

get *(v.)* **under** | **control** unter Kontrolle bekommen; ~ **a revolt** Aufstand niederschlagen; ~ **s. th. under way** etw. in Gang bringen.

get *(v.)* **up** aufstehen, sich erheben, *(arrange)* einrichten, veranstalten, organisieren, ins Werk setzen, *(document)* abfassen, *(organize)* einrichten, *(price)* [im Preis] steigen;
~ **the anchor** Anker lichten; ~ **an article for sale** Ware zum Verkauf ausstellen; ~ **a book** Buch aufmachen; ~ **a celebration** Fest veranstalten; ~ **to mischief** Böses im Sinn haben; ~ **a party for a birthday** Geburtstagsparty arrangieren; ~ **a performance for charity** Wohltätigkeitsveranstaltung zustande bringen; ~ **a petition** Eingabe aufsetzen; ~ **richly** *(book)* gut ausstatten; ~ **a role for a play** Rolle einstudieren; ~ **steam** *(fig.)* in Schwung kommen; ~ **a subject for an examination** Spezialfach für eine Prüfung vorbereiten; ~ **a sunken vessel** versunkenes Schiff heben.

get | **s. o. upon a subject** j. auf ein Thema bringen; ~ **what's coming to one** *(US)* seinen verdienten Lohn erhalten; ~ **wealth** zu Vermögen kommen; ~ **$ 8000 a year** 8000 Dollar im Jahr verdienen.

get-at-ability Zugänglichkeit.
get-at-able zugänglich.
getaway Flucht, Entkommen, *(airplane)* Abheben, *(bank robber)* Entkommen, *(car)* Anzugsvermögen;
~ **van** Fluchtwagen;
to make one's ~ sich aus dem Staub machen.
getter Empfänger.
getting Erhalten, Bekommen, *(mining, Br.)* Abbau, *(profit)* Gewinn, Erwerb;
~ **away** Abreise; ~ **back** Wiedererlangung, Zurückerlangen; ~ **into bad habits** Annahme schlechter Gewohnheiten; ~ **in of payment** Hereinbekommen einer Schuld; ~ **on** Vorankommen; ~ **on in one's career** berufliches Fortkommen; ~ **the right job** richtige Berufswahl; ~ **an order** Auftragseinholung, Akquisition (eines Auftrages); ~ **through** Bestehen eines Examens, Durchkommen.
getup Aufbau, Anordnung, *(book)* Aufmachung, *(dress)* Ausstaffierung, *(goods)* äußere Ausstattung, *(pep, US)* Energie, Unternehmungsgeist, Initiative, *(theater)* Inszenierung.

ghastly accident schrecklicher Unfall.
ghetto Judenviertel, Getto;
~ **area** Gettobezirk; ~ **resident** Gettobewohner.
ghost Gespenst, Geist, Spukgestalt, *(ghost writer)* Ghostwriter, literarischer Neger, *(optics)* unscharfes Bild, *(television)* Geister-, Doppelbild;
not the ~ **of a chance** nicht die geringste Aussicht (Chance);
~ *(v.)* für einen anderen anonym schreiben;
to see ~**s** Gespenster sehen;
~ **city** *(US)* verlassene Stadt; ~ **story** Gespenstergeschichte; ~ **town** Geisterstadt; ~ **view** *(advertising)* Innenbild eines Erzeugnisses, Werbebild; ~ **word** irrtümliche Wortbildung; ~ **writer** Redenverfasser, literarischer Neger, Ghostwriter.
ghostly | **atmosphere** gespenstige Atmosphäre; ~ **comfort** geistliche Tröstungen.
ghostwrite *(v.)* für die Veröffentlichung umschreiben.
giant *(fig.)* geistiger Riese;
~ **[size] package** Familien-, Haushaltspackung.
gift *(donation)* Zuwendung, Schenkung, Geschenk, *(right of granting)* Verleihungsrecht, *(in shop)* Zugabe, *(talent)* Fähigkeit, Gabe, Anlage;
as a (by free) ~ geschenk-, schenkungsweise;
absolute ~ Handschenkung, Schenkung unter Lebenden; ~**s accompanying s. o.** mitgeführte Geschenke; **birthday** ~ Geburtstagsgeschenk; **business** ~**s** Geschenke an Geschäftsfreunde; **Christmas** ~ Weihnachtsgeschenk; **free** ~ Zugabe, Werbegeschenk; **imperfect** ~ juristisch nicht abgeschlossene Schenkung; **lavish** ~ aufwendiges Geschenk; **liberal** ~ großmütige Schenkung; **onerous** ~ Schenkung unter Auflage; **residuary** ~ Rein-, Restvermächtnis; **spontaneous** ~ unerwartetes Geschenk; **substitutional** ~ Ersatzvermächtnis; **taxable** ~ steuerpflichtige Schenkung (Zuwendung); **tax-free** ~ steuerfreie Schenkung; **testamentary** ~ Schenkung von Todes wegen; **top-of-the-line** ~ kostbares Geschenk; **vested** ~ vollzogene Schenkung; **voluntary** ~ unentgeltliche Schenkung; **willing** ~ gern gegebenes Geschenk;
~**s for the benefit of a locality** Zuwendungen zur Landschaftsverbesserung; ~ **of cash** Bargeschenk; ~ **to charity** mildtätige Gabe, wohltätige Schenkung, Spende; ~ **of chattels** Schenkung beweglicher Gegenstände; ~**s held to be valid charitable trusts** als gemeinnützige Stiftungen anerkannte Zuwendungen; ~**s held to be not charitable** nicht als gemeinnützig anerkannte Zuwendungen; ~ **to a class of persons** Schenkung an einen bestimmten Personenkreis; ~**s to customers** Kundengeschenke; ~ **by deed** Schenkungsurkunde; ~**s of a habitual nature** Geschenke herkömmlicher Art; ~ **for language** Sprachbegabung; ~ **during life** Schenkung unter Lebenden; ~ **of money** Geldgeschenk; ~ **mortis causa** *(US)* Schenkung von Todes wegen; ~ **for organization** Organisationstalent; ~ **for presentation** Talent günstiger Selbstdarstellung; ~ **under seal** [etwa] notarielle Schenkung; ~ **inter vivos** Schenkung unter Lebenden; ~ **by will** Vermächtnis, Legat, Schenkung von Todes wegen;
~ *(v.)* schenken, verschenken;
to acquire s. th. (come to s. th.) by free ~ etw. im Schenkungswege erwerben; **to appreciate a** ~ Geschenk zu schätzen wissen; **to be in s. one's** ~ für die Stellenvergabe zuständig sein, von jem. vergeben werden; **to be in the** ~ **of a minister** im Rahmen der ministeriellen Zuständigkeit liegen; **to demand the return of a** ~ Schenkung widerrufen; **to have a** ~ **for mathematics** mathematisch begabt sein; **not to have the** ~ **of pleasing** keine Schmeicheleien sagen können; **to make a** ~ **of s. th. to s. o.** jem. etw. zum Geschenk machen, jem. etw. zuwenden; **to press a** ~ **on s. o.** jem. ein Geschenk aufdrängen; **to repudiate a** ~ Geschenk nicht annehmen;
free-~ **advertising** Zugabewerbung, Warenprobeverteilung; ~ **articles** Geschenkartikel; ~ **book** Geschenkausgabe, -buch, *(US)* Almanach, Taschenbuch; ~ **certificate** Gutschein zu Geschenkzwecken; **free** ~ **coupon** Gutschein, Wertgutschein; ~ **deed** Schenkungsversprechen, -urkunde; ~ **department** Geschenkartikelabteilung; ~ **enterprise** Prämienunternehmen; ~ **giving** Beschenken, *(shop)* Zugabewesen; ~ **horse** *(lit.)* Geschenk; **to look a** ~ **horse in the mouth** an einem Geschenk etwas auszusetzen haben; ~**-loan** *(v.)* als zinsloses Darlehen geben; ~ **package (parcel)** Geschenkpackung, Geschenkpaket, Liebesgabensendung; ~**-parcel program(me)** Spendenaktion; ~ **purchases** Geschenkeinkäufe; ~ **selection catalog(ue)** Geschenkartikelkatalog; ~ **selling** Geschenkartikelverkauf; ~ **shop** Geschenkartikelgeschäft, Andenkenladen; ~ **subscription** Geschenkabonnement; ~ **tax** *(US)* Schenkungssteuer; **to be subject to** ~ **tax** *(US)* schenkungssteuerpflichtig sein; ~ **tax**

benefits *(US)* Schenkungssteuervergünstigungen; ~ tax exclusion *(US)* Vermeidung der Schenkungssteuer; ~tax exemption *(US)* Schenkungssteuerfreibetrag; ~tax rate *(US)* Schenkungssteuersatz; ~ tokens *(postal savings association, Br.)* Guthabengutscheine; ~ valuation Steuerabschätzung eines Geschenks; ~ voucher Gutschein; ~ wrap *(v.)* geschenkmäßig verpacken; ~wrapped in Geschenkpapier eingepackt; ~wrapping Geschenkpackung.

gifted, highly hochbegabt.

giftwares Geschenkartikel.

gigantic publicity Riesenreklame.

gild *(v.)* vergolden, *(fig.)* gefälliges Aussehen geben; ~ a lie Lüge beschönigen; ~ the pill bittere Pille versüßen.

gilded vergoldet, *(fig.)* verschönert, beschönigt; ~ Chamber *(Br.)* Oberhaus; ~ youth Jeunesse dorée.

gilt *(sl.)* Draht, Moos, Kies; ~s *(Br.)* Kapitalmarktpapiere, mündelsichere Wertpapiere; long ~s *(Br.)* langfristige Rentenpapiere; ~s on tap zur Plazierung anstehende Anleihestücke; to take the ~ off the gingerbread der Sache den Reiz (Glanz) nehmen; ~ market Markt für mündelsichere Wertpapiere; ~ prices Kurse für mündelsichere Wertpapiere.

gilt-edged erstklassig, prima, *(Br.)* mündelsicher; to be ~ *(securities, Br.)* Mündelsicherheit genießen; ~ investment *(Br.)* mündelsichere Kapitalanlage; ~ list *(Br.)* mündelsichere Wertpapiere [in Börsenberichten]; ~ market *(Br.)* Markt für mündelsichere Wertpapiere (Staatsanleihen), Rentenmarkt; ~ sales *(Br.)* Umsätze in mündelsicheren Wertpapieren; ~ securities *(Br.)* mündelsichere Anlagepapiere; ~ stock *(Br.)* Staatsanleihepapiere, mündelsichere Wertpapiere.

gimbal joint Kardangelenk.

gimcrackery Kinkerlitzchen.

gimmick komplizierte Sache, *(tricks)* Dreh, Kniff, Mätzchen, *(US)* ausgefallene (sensationelle) Werbung, Reklametrick.

gimmickry technische Spielereien, Schaueffekte, Mätzchen.

ginger *(pep, coll.)* Mumm, Schneid; ~ *(v.)* up the production *(Br.)* Produktion hochtreiben; ~ group *(Br.)* radikale Politikergruppe.

gingerbread *(sl.)* Moneten, Kies.

gipsy Zigeuner[in].

girl, shop Ladenmädchen, Verkäuferin; ~ Friday *(Br.)* Schreibkraft; ~ typist Stenotypistin.

giro, national (postal) *(Br.)* Giro; bank ~ *(Br.)* Überweisung zu Lasten des Kreditkontos; national ~ *(Br.)* Postscheckwesen; postal ~ Postscheckwesen; ~ account Girokonto, *(Br.)* Postscheckkonto; to hold a ~ account Girokonto besitzen; to open a ~ account *(Br.)* Postscheckkonto einrichten; ~ account holder *(Br.)* Postscheckkontoinhaber; ~ administration *(Br.)* Postscheckamt; ~ banking service *(Br.)* Postscheckdienst; ~ card *(Br.)* Postscheckkarte; ~ centre *(Br.)* Postscheckamt; ~ cheque *(Br.)* Postscheck; ~ department *(Br.)* Postscheckabteilung, Giroabteilung; ~ service (system) *(Br.)* Postscheckdienst, -einrichtung, -verkehr; to use the post-office ~ system *(Br.)* per Postscheck überweisen; ~ transaction (transfer) *(Br.)* Postschecküberweisung; inter ~ transfer *(Br.)* Überweisungen von einem Postscheckkonto auf das andere; ~transfer slip *(Br.)* Überweisungsformular.

girobank | **services** *(Br.)* Postscheckeinrichtungen; National ~ services available at post offices Giroverkehr durch die Post.

gist Hauptpunkt, [des Pudels] Kern; ~ of an action Klagegrund; to catch the ~ das Wesentliche verstehen.

give Nachgeben, Elastizität; ~up Provisionsaufteilung; ~ and take gegenseitige Zugeständnisse; ~ *(v.)* geben, hin-, übergeben, überreichen, *(present)* schenken; ~ 8 per cent *(investment)* achtprozentige Verzinsung abwerfen; ~ account Bericht erstatten; ~ account of Rechenschaft ablegen, *(in books)* ausweisen, Abrechnung erteilen; ~ a good account of o. s. Erfolg haben; ~ advice avisieren; ~ it against s. o. gegen j. entscheiden; ~ aid and comfort begünstigen; ~ o. s. airs sich aufplustern (wichtig machen); ~ alms Almosen geben; ~ an average of ... Durchschnitt von ... gewähren.

give *(v.)* **away** weggeben, verschenken, *(betray)* verraten, *(wedding)* Braut übergeben; ~ a good chance gute Chance vertun; ~ the bride Braut zuführen; ~ all one's money sein ganzes Geld verschenken; ~ the prizes Preisverteilung vornehmen; ~ a secret Geheimnis ausplaudern; ~ the whole show sich die ganze Schau stehlen lassen.

give *(v.)* | **authority to** bevollmächtigen; ~ back zurückgeben, -erstatten; ~ s. o. back his liberty jem. seine Freiheit wiedergeben; ~ s. o. the bag *(coll.)* j. feuern; ~ bail Bürgschaft leisten, Kaution stellen; ~ s. o. the benefit of the doubt im Zweifelsfall zu jds. Gunsten entscheiden; ~ and bequeath vermachen, hinterlassen; ~ a clear (wide) berth sicheren Abstand halten; ~ s. o. best *(Br.)* j. als überlegen anerkennen; ~ a bill of exchange Wechsel ausstellen; ~ birth to gebären, *(fig.)* Unternehmen gründen; ~ s. o. one's blessing jem. seinen Segen geben; ~ bonds Sicherheiten bestellen; ~ bridle to freie Hand lassen; ~ a buying order Kaufauftrag erteilen; ~ 1 per cent call on a share for a month einer Aktie dont 1% auf einen Monat verkaufen; ~ into care in Verwahrung (Obhut) geben; ~ the case against s. o. Urteil zu jds. Ungunsten fällen; ~ colo(u)r gegnerischen Sachvortrag anerkennen; ~ one's compliments to s. o. sich jem. empfehlen lassen; ~ credit kreditieren; ~ s. o. into custody j. der Polizei übergeben; ~ damages Schadenersatz zuerkennen; ~ a day off Tag freigeben; ~ a decision Entscheidung fällen; ~ a description Beschreibung geben; ~ a discharge quittieren, Entlastung erteilen; ~ s. o. a disease Krankheit auf j. übertragen; ~ o. s. over to drinking der Trunksucht verfallen; ~ ear to zuhören; ~ one's ears for s. th. alles in der Welt für etw. geben; ~ effect to Rechtskraft verleihen; ~ employment beschäftigen; ~ evidence against s. o. gegen j. aussagen; ~ false evidence falsch aussagen; ~ the facts Tatsachenangaben machen.

give *(v.)* **for** verkaufen um; ~ the call *(stock exchange)* Vorprämie kaufen; ~ the put *(stock exchange)* Rückprämie verkaufen.

give | **forth** äußern, *(publish)* veröffentlichen, bekanntgeben; ~ full particulars ausführlich berichten; ~ generously freigebig sein; ~ as good as one gets mit gleicher Münze zurückzahlen; ~ grace Frist gewähren; ~ ground sich zurückziehen; ~ a handle Gelegenheit bieten; ~ a hearing Gehör schenken; ~ one's hono(u)r seine Ehre verpfänden.

give *(v.)* **in** nachgeben, ablassen, *(give in addition)* zugeben, *(hand in)* einreichen, übergeben, *(money)* Geld einschießen; ~ one's adhesion to a party seinen Parteieintritt bekanntgeben; ~ continuation in Report geben; ~ one's examination paper seine Prüfungsarbeit abgeben; ~ one's name sich auf einer Liste eintragen, sich eintragen lassen, *(parl.)* sich zur Wahl stellen; ~ to s. one's opinion sich jds. Meinung anschließen; ~ payment *(Louisiana)* in Zahlung geben.

give *(v.)* | **it to** heftig attackieren; ~ s. o. a job jem. Arbeit geben; ~ judgment Urteil [in einer Sache] erlassen; ~ lectures Vorlesungen halten; ~ one's life sein Leben einsetzen; ~ a lot to know viel dafür geben zu erfahren; ~ a matter every care Angelegenheit sorgfältig im Auge behalten; ~ s. o. his medicine jem. seine Arznei verabreichen; ~ one's money to the hotel manager to be looked after sein Geld dem Hoteltresor anvertrauen; ~ notice kündigen; ~ notice of loss Schadensanzeige erstatten; ~ s. o. the oath jem. den Eid zuschieben; ~ offence Anstoß (Ärgernis) erregen; ~ on *(London stock exchange)* in Prolongation geben, hineingeben; ~ an expert opinion Gutachten abgeben (erstatten).

give *(v.)* **out** *(announce)* ankündigen, bekanntmachen, -geben, *(distribute)* ausgeben, verteilen, *(supplies)* zu Ende gehen, erschöpft sein; ~ o. s. out as banker sich als Bankier ausgeben; ~ by contract [in Submission] vergeben; ~ the examination papers Prüfungsaufgabe bekanntgeben; ~ handbills Prospekte verteilen; ~ an interview *(US)* Interview gewähren; ~ a notice Bekanntmachung erlassen.

give *(v.)* | **over** aufgeben; ~ a piece of one's mind *(coll.)* etw. mißbilligen; ~ place Vorrang zuerkennen; ~ a good price guten Preis zahlen; ~ s. th. to the public etw. veröffentlichen; ~ a reading Vorlesung halten; ~ a receipt Quittung ausstellen; ~ a report Bericht erstatten; ~ one's respects to s. o. sich jem. empfehlen; ~ o. s. a rest sich eine Pause gönnen; ~ rise to verursachen, veranlassen, Anlaß geben; ~ rise to an action Klageanspruch begründen; ~ s. o. the sack *(sl.)* j. feuern; ~ security Sicherheit bestellen, Kaution stellen; ~ no signs of life kein Lebenszeichen geben; ~ and take Gewinn und Verlust durchschnittlich ausgleichen; ~ s. o. s. th. to think about jem. einen Denkzettel verpassen; ~ time stunden, Frist gewähren; ~ a toast Toast ausbringen; ~ s. o. to understand j. dahingehend informieren.

give *(v.)* **up** übergeben, -lassen, *(resign)* aufgeben, -stecken, *(reveal)* aufdecken, enthüllen, *(stock exchange)* Auftraggeber benennen; ~ s. o. *(doctor)* j. aufgeben; ~ o. s. up *(criminal)* sich freiwillig stellen; ~ o. s. up to s. th. sich einer Sache widmen;

~ **one's appointment** sein Amt abgeben; ~ **business** sich vom Geschäft zurückziehen, Geschäft aufgeben; ~ **one's (all) claims** auf seine (alle) Ansprüche verzichten; ~ **the crown** auf den Thron verzichten; ~ **effects to one's creditors** sich für zahlungsunfähig erklären; ~ **a fortress** Festung übergeben; ~ **a fortune for s. one's education** für jds. Erziehung ein Vermögen ausgeben; ~ **the keys of a city** Stadtschlüssel ausliefern; ~ **a newspaper** Zeitung abbestellen; ~ **to the police** der Polizei übergeben; ~ **all one possesses** sich von seinem ganzen Vermögen trennen; ~ **one's seat to s. o.** jem. seinen Platz überlassen; ~ **s. o. for lost** j. als vermißt melden.

give *(v.)* | **the value date** [Scheck] einbuchen; ~ **value for** Gegenleistung gewähren; ~ **voice to** äußern; ~ **way** *(member of parliament)* sich unterbrechen lassen, Zwischenfrage zulassen, *(mil.)* sich zurückziehen, *(prices)* nachgeben, abbröckeln, abflauen, *(scaffolding)* zusammenbrechen, *(ship)* ausweichen; ~ **way to one's emotions** sich seinen Gefühlsaufwallungen überlassen; ~ **way to traffic coming from the right** dem Rechtsverkehr Vorfahrt lassen; ~ **way to s. one's whims** jds. Launen nachgeben; ~ **s. o. a week** jem. eine Wochenfrist einräumen; ~ **s. o. what for** *(fam.)* sich j. gründlich vorknöpfen; ~ **s. o. s. th. in one's will** jem. etw. testamentarisch vermachen.

give-and-take Zusammenarbeit im Wege des Kompromisses; ~ **policy** Verständigungspolitik.

give-up *(stock exchange)* Offenlegung des Auftraggebers.

giveaway *(betrayal)* Verrat, Ausplaudern, *(leaflet)* Handzettel, *(seller, US)* [Verkäufer]prämie, Zugabe, Gutschein; ~ **price** Unterbietungs-, Schleuderpreis; ~ **show** Fernsehsendung mit Zuschauerbeteiligung.

given *(on document)* gegeben, ausgefertigt; ~ **in** als Zugabe; ~ **under my hand** von mir unterschrieben; **under the** ~ **conditions** unter den gegebenen Bedingungen; ~ **name** *(US)* Vor-, Taufname; **at the** ~ **price** zum festgesetzten Preis; ~ **sum** bestimmte Summe; **at a** ~ **time** zu einer bestimmten Zeit.

giver Geber, Schenker, Spender, *(of option money)* Prämienkäufer, Herein-, Reportnehmer, *(seller)* Verkäufer, Abgeber; ~ **of a bill** Wechselaussteller; ~ **for a call** Käufer einer Vorprämie; ~ **of a guarantee** Wechselbürge; ~ **of an option** *(Br.)* Prämienkäufer, Optionsgeber, Nachsteller; ~ **for a put** Verkäufer einer Rückprämie; ~ **of stock** Aktienverkäufer.

giver-out Materialausgeber.

giving | **of accounts** Rechnungslegung; ~ **away the prizes** Preisverteilung; ~ **back** Rückgabe; ~ **lessons** Stundengeben; ~ **out the awards** Preisverteilung; ~ **in payment** *(Louisiana)* In-Zahlung-geben; ~ **up [of a business]** Geschäftsaufgabe.

glad | **rags** *(sl.)* Sonntagskluft; ~ **tidings** frohe Nachricht.

gladhander *(US)* Popularitätshascher.

glamo(u)r Zauber, Blendwerk; ~**s** *(stock market, US)* Standard-, Spitzenwerte; ~ **of war** Kriegsverherrlichung; **to cast a** ~ **over s. o.** j. in seinen Bann schlagen; ~ **girl** Reklameschönheit; ~ **photographer** Modefotograf; ~ **stocks** *(US)* erstklassige Aktien, Standard-, Spitzenwerte; ~ **stock rating** *(US)* Einstufung als erstklassige Aktien.

glance flüchtiger Blick; **at a** ~ übersichtlich; ~ *(v.)* **briefly on** flüchtig streifen; ~ **over a letter** Brief überfliegen; ~ **at a subject** Thema flüchtig berühren; ~ **off a subject** von einem Thema abkommen; ~ **off s. o. like water off a duck's back** von jem. völlig unberührt abprallen; **to take a** ~ **at the newspaper headlines** Zeitungsüberschriften überfliegen; ~ **coal** Anthrazit.

glare grelles (blendendes) Licht; **in the full** ~ **of publicity** im Scheinwerferlicht der Öffentlichkeit.

glaring grell, blendend; ~ **abuses** skandalöse Mißbräuche; ~ **blunder** riesengroßer Fehler; ~ **colo(u)rs** schreiende Farben; ~ **headlights** aufgeblendetes Fernlicht; ~ **neon lights** grelles Neonlicht; ~ **poster** grellfarbiges Plakat.

Glass! Vorsicht! Glas!
amo(u)red ~ kugelsicheres Glas, Panzerglas; **eye** ~**es** Brille; **reinforced (wired)** ~ Drahtglas; **safety** ~ splitterfreies Glas, Sicherheitsglas; **weather** ~ Barometer; **to call for** ~**es all round** Runde spendieren; **to have had a** ~ **too much** ein Glas zuviel getrunken haben; **to wear** ~**es** Brillenträger sein; ~**-beaded screen** *(film)* Perlleinwand; ~ **case** Vitrine; ~ **claim** Glasschaden; ~ **eye** Glasauge; ~ **insurance** Fensterglasversi-

cherung; ~ **panel** Trennscheibe; ~**-roofed** mit einem Glasdach versehen; ~ **and china shop** Glas- und Porzellanladen; ~ **sign** Glasschild; ~ **wool** Glaswolle.

glasshouse Treibhaus, Gewächshaus, *(Br., mil., sl.)* Loch, Bau.

glassine Transparentpapier.

glassware Glassachen, -ware.

glassworks Glasfabrik, Glaserei.

glaze Glasur, Lasur, *(ice, US)* Glätte, Glatteis, *(polish)* Glasierfarbe; ~ *(v.)* verglasen, *(paper)* satinieren.

glazed | **cardboard** Preßpappe; ~ **frost** *(Br.)* Glatteis; ~ **paper** satiniertes (gestrichenes) Papier, Glanzpapier.

glazier Glaser.

glazing Glasscheibe, Fenster.

gleam schwacher Schein; ~ **of hope** Hoffnungsschimmer.

glean *(v.)* nachlesen, einsammeln; ~ **facts** Tatsachen zusammentragen; ~ **a field** Feld absammeln.

gleanings Lesefrüchte, Blütenlese.

glee Freude, Heiterkeit; **to be in high** ~ in Hochstimmung sein; ~ **club** Gesangverein.

glide Gleitflug; ~ *(v.)* gleiten, Gleitflug machen; ~ **into bad habits** schlechte Angewohnheiten annehmen; ~ **over the difficult passages** über schwierige Stellen hinweggleiten; ~ **past** *(years)* vergehen; ~ **landing** Gleitfluglandung; ~ **path** Funkleitweg.

glider Segelflieger, *(mar.)* Gleitboot, *(plane)* Gleit-, Segelflugzeug; ~ **bomb** *(mil.)* Gleitbombe; ~ **tug** Schleppflugzeug.

gliding Segelfliegen, -flug; **hang** ~ Drachensegeln; ~ **flight** Gleit-, Segelflug.

glimmer | **of hope** Hoffnungsschimmer; **not the least** ~ **of intelligence** kein Fünkchen von Intelligenz.

gloat *(v.)* **over the news** sich an den Neuigkeiten weiden.

global weltumspannend, -umfassend, global, pauschal; ~ **amount** Pauschalbetrag, -summe; ~ **capacity** Welt-, Gesamtkapazität; ~ **charges** Pauschalspesen; ~ **economics** Weltwirtschaft; ~ **insurance** Pauschalversicherung; ~ **offer** Globalangebot; ~ **quota** Globalkontingent; ~ **result** Gesamtergebnis; **to continue on a** ~ **scale** weltweit fortsetzen; ~ **settlement** pauschale Abgeltung (Regulierung); ~ **sum** Globalbetrag. Gesamtsumme; ~ **turnover** Gesamtumsatz; ~ **value adjustment** Sammelwertberichtigung.

globe Weltkugel, Globus; **to circle the** ~ Erdball umkreisen; **to cover the** ~ weltweit tätig sein; **to go round the** ~ Weltreise machen; ~ **trotter** Weltenbummler, Globetrotter.

globocrat Globetrotter.

gloom Düsternis, *(fig.)* Pessimismus, gedrückte Stimmung, *(US coll.)* Miesepeter, Schwarzseher; **to be cast into** ~ in Schwermut verfallen; **to cast a** ~ **over a village** gedrückte Stimmung in einem Dorf hervorrufen.

glory Ruhm, Ehre; ~ **in working for a good cause** Nimbus des Tätigseins für eine gute Sache; **to be the** ~ **of the age** einem Jahrhundert Glanz verleihen; **to send s. o. to** ~ *(coll.)* j. umbringen; ~ **hole** *(coll.)* Rumpelkammer.

gloss Glanz, Schimmer, *(note of explanation)* Glosse, Anmerkung, Randbemerkung; ~ **of respectibilty** Anstrich von Ehrbarkeit; ~ *(v.)* glossieren, Glossen schreiben, Randbemerkung machen; ~ **over** beschönigen, bemänteln; ~ **over s. one's faults** jds. Fehler bemänteln; **to cover one's actions with a** ~ **of legality** sein Handeln mit dem Mäntelchen der Legalität umgeben; **to put a** ~ **on the truth** Wahrheit beschönigen.

glossarist Kommentator.

glossary Spezialwörterbuch, Glossar; ~ **of terms** Begriffsdefinitionen.

glossy geschmeidig, *(picture page)* auf Glanzpapier gedruckt; ~ **deceit** raffinierter Betrug; ~ **magazine** reichbebildertes Magazin; ~ **photographic print** Hochglanzabzug.

glove Handschuh, *(fig.)* Fehdehandschuh; **without** ~**s** entschlossen, energisch; **to be hand in** ~ **with s. o.** sehr vertraut mit jem. sein, sich glänzend mit jem. verstehen; **to fit like a** ~ wie angegossen sitzen; **to handle s. o. with velvet ~s** j. mit Samthandschuhen behandeln; **to handle s. o. without ~s** j. schonungslos behandeln; **to take the ~s off** keine Umstände machen, unbarmherzig vorgehen; **to take up the ~** Fehdehandschuh aufnehmen; **to throw down the ~ to s. o.** jem. den Fehdehandschuh hinwerfen; **~ compartment** *(car)* verschließbares Handschuhfach.

glow Glühen, Glut;
in the first ~ of enthusiasm im ersten Ansturm der Begeisterung;
~ of youth Blüte der Jugend;
~ *(v.)* with zeal voller Eifer sein;
~ lamp (light) Glühlampe.

glowing glühend, leuchtend;
to be ~ with health vor Gesundheit strotzen;
~ account begeisterter Bericht;
to speak in ~ terms of s. o. voller Begeisterung (in glühenden Farben) von jem. sprechen.

glue Klebstoff, Leim;
~ *(v.)* kleben, leimen, kaschieren;
~ dispenser Gummierstift; **~ pot** Leimtopf.

glut *(market)* Überangebot, -fluß, -sättigung, -schwemmung, -häufung, Schwemme;
~ in the market Marktfülle, -schwemme, Überfüllung des Marktes; **~ of money** Geldüberfluß, -fülle, -überhang, -flüssigkeit, -anhäufung, -schwemme;
~ *(v.)* one's eyes on s. th sich nicht satt sehen können; **~ the market** Markt übersättigen (überschwemmen); **~ up the market** Markt versteifen.

glutted übersättigt, überhäuft.

glutting of the market Übersättigung des Marktes, Marktüberschwemmung.

glutton Vielfraß, Schlemmer;
~ for books Leseratte; **~ for work** arbeitswütiger Mensch.

gluttonous gierig, unersättlich.

go *(nasty business)* unangenehme Geschichte, dumme Sache, *(course)* Gang, Verlauf, *(fashion)* Mode, *(hit)* erfolgreiches Unternehmen, Treffer, *(illness, Br.)* Anfall, *(meal)* Portion, *(pep)* Energie, Schmiß, Schwung;
all the ~ der letzte Schrei; **at one (first) ~** beim ersten Anlauf; **full of ~** energisch, unternehmenslustig; **on the ~** immer unterwegs, *(fig.)* im Verfall begriffen;
capital ~ glänzender Erfolg; **a near ~** knappe Rettung;
~ *(v.)* gehen, *(be accepted)* angenommen (akzeptiert) werden, *(to be sold)* abgehen, verkaufen, (abgesetzt) werden, *(journey)* fahren, reisen, *(machine)* gehen, arbeiten, funktionieren, *(rumo(u)r)* kursieren, im Umlauf sein, sich verbreiten, *(time)* vergehen, verfließen, ablaufen, *(vehicles)* verkehren, fahren;
~ a begging Betteln gehen, *(goods)* nicht verlangt werden.

go *(v.)* **about** in Angriff nehmen, unternehmen, *(story)* verbreitet werden;
~ one's business sich um seine eigenen Angelegenheiten kümmern; **~ it carefully** sorgsam zu Werke gehen; **~ the country** Landpartie unternehmen; **~ a good deal** ziemlich viel ausgehen; **~ the streets** durch die Straßen bummeln; **~ one's usual work** seiner täglichen Beschäftigung nachgehen.

go *(v.)* **abroad** ins Ausland (außer Landes) gehen.

go *(v.)* **against | the plaintiff** *(judgment)* gegen den Kläger ergehen; **~ s. one's principles** gegen jds. Prinzipien verstoßen; **~ the tide** gegen den Strom schwimmen.

go *(v.)* **ahead** weitergehen, fortfahren, *(succeed)* erfolgreich vorwärtskommen;
~ fast rasch vorankommen; **~ at full speed** mit Hochdruck arbeiten; **~ sturdily** *(prices)* scharf anziehen.

go *(v.)* **all out** *(sl.)* sich bis zum Äußersten einsetzen.

go *(v.)* **along** weitermachen, fortfahren;
~ with seine Zustimmung dafür geben.

go *(v.)* **| among people** ausgehen; **~ any day** *(bank)* fallieren, bankrott gehen, jeden Tag pleite gehen können; **~ almost anywhere** *(currency)* fast überall [als Zahlungsmittel] angenommen werden; **~ armed** Waffen tragen; **~ astray** verlorengehen, abhanden kommen, sich verirren; **~ at it** etw. energisch in Angriff nehmen; **~ as follows** wie folgt lauten; **~ as high as** bis zu ... gehen; **~ as near as possible** möglichst billig verkaufen; **~ at fifty miles an hour** 80 Stundenkilometer fahren; **~ at twelve o'clock** *(mail)* um zwölf Uhr abgehen; **~ away** danebengehen; **~ away on business** geschäftlich verreisen.

go *(v.)* **back | on s. o.** zurückgehen, *(family)* abstammen;
~ on s. o. *(coll.)* j. in Stich lassen; **~ to the drawer** Regreß nehmen; **~ in one's native land** in seine Heimat zurückkehren; **~ to the last lesson** auf den Unterrichtsstoff der letzten Stunde eingehen; **~ on one's promise** sein Versprechen nicht einhalten.

~ on one's signature seine Unterschrift verleugnen; **~ to a subject** auf ein Thema zurückkommen; **~ to one's old ways** in seine alten Ansichten zurückfallen; **~ on one's word** sein Wort nicht halten.

go *(v.)* **| bail for s. o.** für j. bürgen; **~ bankrupt** bankrott machen, in Konkurs gehen; **~ a bear** auf Baisse spekulieren; **~ before** Vorrang haben; **~ behind** Hintergründe untersuchen; **~ behind a decision** Hintergründe einer Entscheidung ausleuchten; **~ behind the returns of an election** Wählerergebnis genauestens untersuchen; **~ behind s. one's words** doppelten Sinn aus jds. Worten herauszulesen versuchen; **~ better** Wetteinsatz erhöhen; **~ between** vermitteln.

go *(v.)* **beyond** überschreiten;
~ a contract nach dem Sinn eines Vertrages fragen; **~ one's instructions** über seine Weisungen hinausgehen; **~ the limit** Limit überschreiten.

go *(v.)* **| big** Riesenerfolg sein; **~ bull** auf Hausse spekulieren; **~ bust** Pleite machen.

go *(v.)* **by** vorbeigehen;
~ air from A to B von A nach B fliegen; **~ airplane** mit dem Flugzeug reisen, fliegen; **~ appearances** nur nach dem äußeren Anschein urteilen; **~ car** mit dem Auto fahren; **~ electricity** *(machine)* elektrisch betrieben werden; **~ entirely by what one's solicitor says** sich ganz nach den Weisungen seines Anwalts richten; **~ instructions** sich an Anweisungen halten; **~ the letter of the law** sich an den Buchstaben des Gesetzes halten; **~ the name of** unter dem Namen bekannt sein; **~ steamer** mit dem Dampfer fahren; **~ train** mit der Bahn fahren, Zug benutzen; **to let s. th. ~** einer Sache keine Beachtung schenken.

go | to Canossa nach Canossa gehen; **~ cheap** *(sl.)* billig weggehen; **~ Conservative** *(Br.)* konservative Partei wählen; **~ to court** vor Gericht gehen, prozessieren.

go *(v.)* **down** *(founder)* sinken, *(orders)* zurückgehen, *(price)* fallen, sinken, *(sales)* zurückgehen, *(have success)* Anklang finden, gut ankommen, *(from university, Br.)* Universität verlassen, seinen Abschluß machen;
~ in an examination in einem Examen durchfallen; **~ fighting** mit fliegenden Fahnen untergehen; **~ in history as a great statesman** in die Geschichte als großer Staatsmann eingehen; **~ like ninepins** wie die Kegel fallen; **~ to posterity** in die Nachwelt eingehen; **~ to the river** sich bis an den Fluß erstrecken; **~ a shaft** in eine Grube einfahren; **~ in value** Wertverlust erleiden; **~ with every soul on board** mit Mann und Maus untergehen; **~ very well with a provincial audience** beim Provinzpublikum besonders gut ankommen; **~ with s. o.** *(story)* von jem. geglaubt (geschluckt) werden; **~ well with s. o.** Anklang bei jem. finden; **not ~ well with the pupils** bei den Schülern schlecht ankommen; **~ without a fight** kampflos die Segel streichen.

go *(v.)* **| dry** Alkoholverbot einführen; **~ Dutch** getrennte Kasse machen; **~ equal shares** gleichen Anteil haben; **~ an errand** Botschaft ausrichten; **~ far** es weit bringen; **~ so far as ten years ago** soviel wert sein wie vor zehn Jahren; **~ fifty-fifty** halbehalbe machen; **~ flat** *(prices)* fallen.

go *(v.)* **for** gehen nach, holen;
~ o. s. auf eigene Rechnung arbeiten; **~ s. o.** *(US coll.)* für j. schwärmen, in j. verknallt sein; **~ a doctor** den Arzt holen; **~ nothing** als wertlos erachtet werden; **~ s. o. in the papers** j. in der Öffentlichkeit angreifen; **~ the plaintiff** zugunsten des Klägers ergehen; **~ a trip round the world** Weltreise unternehmen; **~ a walk** Spaziergang machen.

go *(v.)* **| from bad to worse** vom Regen in die Traufe kommen; **~ hard all day** ganzen Tag schwer arbeiten; **~ hence** *(suitor)* vom Gericht entlassen werden; **~ forward well** gut vorankommen; **~ further into a question** tiefer in eine Frage eindringen; **~ half and half with s. o.** sich mit jem. teilen, Halbpart machen; **~ heavily into the red** *(US)* schwere finanzielle Verluste erleiden; **~ as high as $ 400** *(auction)* bis zu 400 Dollar bieten.

go *(v.)* **in** hineingehen, *(begin)* anfangen, beginnen, *(money)* ausgegeben werden [für];
~ alphabetical order alphabetisch geordnet (aufgeführt) sein; **~ for** sich zuwenden (widmen), sich verlegen (spezialisieren) auf; **~ for an appointment** sich um eine Position bewerben; **~ for a candidate** Kandidaten unterstützen; **~ for a competition** sich an einem Wettbewerb beteiligen; **~ for a course of lectures** Vorlesung belegen; **~ for an examination** sich für eine Prüfung melden; **~ for law** Jura studieren; **~ for money** viel Geld zu verdienen suchen; **~ and out** freien Zugang haben; **~ for politics** Politiker werden; **~ in rags** ständig in Lumpen herumlaufen; **~ in rent and food** auf die Miete und Ernährung draufgehen; **~ for stamp-collecting** sich aufs Briefmarkensammeln werfen; **~ with s. o. in an undertaking** sich an einer Sache beteiligen.

go (v.) **into** (frequent) frequentieren, häufig besuchen, (investigate) untersuchen, (parl.) Parlamentssitz einnehmen, (participate) teilnehmen an, hineingehen in [ein Unternehmen], (profession) Beruf ergreifen;

~ **s. th.** sich intensiv mit etw. befassen; ~ **business** Kaufmann werden; ~ **debit** debitorisch werden; ~ **details (particulars)** sich mit Einzelheiten abgeben, auf Einzelheiten eingehen; ~ **the evidence** Beweismaterial durchsehen; ~ **exile** ins Exil gehen; ~ **a lengthy explanation of s. th** langatmige Erklärung über etw. abgeben; ~ **first (ground) gear** ersten Gang einschalten; ~ **mourning** Trauerkleidung tragen; ~ **opposition** in Opposition treten; ⸰ **Parliament** (Br.) Abgeordneter werden; ~ **partnership with s. o.** sich mit jem. assoziieren; ~ **politics** Politiker werden; ~ **deeply into a question** Problem eingehend untersuchen; ~ **society** gesellschaftlich ausgehen; ~ **s. one's statements** jds. Behauptungen sorgfältig prüfen.

go (v.) | **it** energisch auftreten, mit Schwung darauf losgehen; ~ **it alone** auf eigene Faust unternehmen; ~ **liberal at the by-election** bei der Nachwahl liberalen Kandidaten wählen; ~ **native** sich assimilieren, verwildern; ~ **nineteen to the dozen** das Blaue vom Himmel herunterschwätzen.

go (v.) **off** fort-, weggehen, (actor) abgehen, (lose consciousness) bewußtlos werden, (goods) weggehen, Absatz finden, (gun) losgehen, (marry, coll.) heiraten, (mine) explodieren, (train) abgehen;

~ **with a bang** Riesenerfolg sein; ~ **at the deep end** (US) sich unüberlegt auf etw. einlassen; ~ **in a fit** Anfall bekommen; ~ **with some treasured possessions** flüchten und einige Wertsachen mitnehmen; ~ **quickly** reißenden Absatz finden; ~ **the rails** entgleisen; ~ **rapidly** reißend weggehen; ~ **slowly** schwer verkäuflich sein, schlechten Absatz finden; ~ **smoothly** sich glatt abwickeln; ~ **to a good start** verheißungsvollen Anfang nehmen; ~ **the beaten track** vom rechten Wege abkommen; ~ **well** Erfolg haben; ~ **with the neighbo(u)r's wife** mit der Nachbarsfrau durchbrennen.

go (v.) **on** fortdauern, weitergehen, (actor) [auf der Bühne] auftreten, (keep talking) weiterreden, (time) verstreichen;

~ **at s. o.** über j. herziehen; ~ **books** auf den Erwerb von Büchern draufgehen; ~ **the dole** (Br.) Arbeitslosenunterstützung beziehen; ~ **an excursion (outing)** Ausflug machen; ~ **increasing** ständig zunehmen; ~ **to the next item on the agenda** sich dem nächsten Verhandlungspunkt zuwenden; ~ **a journey** auf eine Reise gehen, Reise machen (unternehmen); ~ **longer than expected** sich hinziehen; ~ **the parish** (Br.) der Gemeinde zur Last fallen; ~ **a relief fund** von einem Unterstützungsfonds leben; ~ **replacing with spares** immer neue Ersatzteile einsetzen; ~ **for seventy** sich den Siebzigern nähern; ~ **the stage** Schauspieler werden; ~ **trial** (person) vor Gericht kommen.

go (v.) **one better** übertreffen.

go (v.) **out** (appear in society) ausgehen, in Gesellschaft gehen, (bridge, US) einstürzen, zusammenbrechen, (depart from the country) außer Landes gehen, (extinct) ausgehen, erlöschen, (on strike) streiken, (minister) zurücktreten, ausscheiden, (news) bekannt (verbreitet) werden, (servant) Stellung außer Haus annehmen, (year) zu Ende gehen;

~ **all out for s. th.** sich intensiv (restlos) für etw. einsetzen; ~ **of business** Geschäft aufgeben; ~ **to business** ins Geschäftsleben eintreten; ~ **of fashion** aus der Mode kommen, unmodern werden; ~ **as governess** sich als Gouvernante Geld verdienen; ~ **a great deal** viele gesellschaftliche Veranstaltungen besuchen; ~ **on a limb** sich zu weit vorwagen; ~ **shopping** einkaufen gehen; ~ **of one's way** sich besondere Mühe geben, von der üblichen Tour seiner Politik abweichen; ~ **to work** auf Arbeit gehen.

go (v.) **over** (be adjourned) vertagt (zurückgestellt) werden, (inquire) untersuchen, überprüfen, besichtigen, (politician) Partei wechseln, übergehen, -wechseln;

~ **an account** Rechnung durchsehen (nachprüfen); ~ **big** Bombenerfolg sein; ~ **to the other camp** ins andere Lager überwechseln; ~ **a chapter again** Kapitel wiederholen; ~ **to the enemy** zum Feind überlaufen; ~ **the main facts again** Hauptdaten noch einmal durchnehmen; ~ **the ground thoroughly** Thema gründlich beleuchten; ~ **a house** Haus besichtigen; ~ **s. th. in one's mind** etw. geistig Revue passieren lassen; ~ **a piece of work** Arbeitsstück ausfeilen; ~ **to the other side** zur Konkurrenz gehen.

go (v.) | **overboard** (fig.) übertreiben; ~ **the pace** Geld mit vollen Händen ausgeben; ~ **to pieces** zusammenbrechen, zugrundegehen; ~ **in rags** in Lumpen herumlaufen; ~ **round to** kurz besuchen, formlosen Besuch machen, (supply all) für alle ausreichen, (rumo(u)r) umgehen, verbreitet werden; ~ **twenty miles round** Umweg von dreißig Kilometern fahren; ~ **security**

Bürgschaft leisten; ~ **and see s. o.** j. aufsuchen; ~ **shares** zu gleichen Teilen gehen; ~ **shopping** einkaufen gehen, Einkäufe machen; ~ **sick** (mil.) sich krank melden; ~ **slow** (workers) Bummelstreik durchführen; ~ **slow on orders** Aufträge nur zögernd erteilen; ~ **straight** (criminal) neuen Anfang machen, (train) durchfahren; ~ **swimmingly** glatt verlaufen.

go (v.) **through** sorgfältig durchgehen, (bill) angenommen werden, durchgehen, (luggage) durchsuchen;

~ **o. s.** (sl.) sich besaufen; ~ **an account again** Rechnung noch einmal durchgehen; ~ **gamely through an affair** Affäre mannhaft durchstehen; ~ **one's apprenticeship** seine Lehrzeit (Ausbildungszeit) absolvieren; ~ **the arguments again** Argumente noch einmal überprüfen; ~ **one's bills** seine Rechnungen durchgehen; ~ **a ceremony** Zeremonie absolvieren; ~ **clean through the door** (bullet) glatt die Tür durchschlagen; ~ **one's correspondence** eingegangene Post durchgehen (durchsehen); ~ **a dossier** sich mit einem Dossier vertraut machen; ~ **three editions** drei Auflagen erleben (haben); ~ **a fortune** Vermögen verjubeln (durchbringen); ~ **hardships** schwere Zeiten durchmachen; ~ **the hoops** Konkurs anmelden; ~ **a civil marriage** sich bürgerlich trauen lassen; ~ **all one's money** sein ganzes Geld ausgeben; ~ **a surgical operation** Operation überstehen; ~ **the whole program(me)** ganzes Programm ansehen; ~ **right (straight) through** (train) durchgehen; ~ **the town council** vom Gemeinderat gebilligt werden; ~ **with the undertaking** Unternehmen zu Ende führen.

go (v.) **to** | **s. o.** (inheritance) jem. zufallen; ~ **the bad** sich ungünstig entwickeln; ~ **the bar** Rechtsanwalt werden; ~ **charity** für wohltätige Zwecke bestimmt sein; ~ **the country** (pol.) Neuwahlen ausschreiben; ~ **court** vor Gericht gehen; ~ **great expense** sich in Unkosten stürzen; ~ **s. one's funeral** an jds. Leichenbegängnis teilnehmen; ~ **it** (US) sich an die Arbeit machen; ~ **law** prozessieren, vor Gericht gehen, Gerichtsweg beschreiten; ~ **pieces** (fig.) zusammenbrechen, zugrundegehen; ~ **press** in Druck gehen, gedruckt werden; ~ **protest** (bill) zu Protest gehen; ~ **sea** in See stechen; ~ **the eldest son** (title) auf den ältesten Sohn übergehen; ~ **war** Krieg eröffnen.

go (v.) **together** sich miteinander vertragen, (couple) miteinander gehen, (match) zusammenpassen.

go (v.) **under** (firm) bankrott werden, (founder) sinken, untergehen, (go to ruin) untergehen, zugrundegehen;

~ **the name of ...** im Namen von ... auftreten; ~ **unless business improves** ohne Konjunkturaufschwung pleite gehen; ~ **sail** (ship) auslaufen.

go (v.) **unpunished** unbestraft bleiben, straffrei ausgehen.

go (v.) **up** hinaufgehen, -fahren, (balloon) aufsteigen, (be candidate, Br.) sich bewerben, (building) errichtet (gebaut) werden, (curtain) hochgehen, (prices) steigen, anziehen, sich bessern, sich erhöhen, hinaufgehen, hochgehen, Aufschwung nehmen, (be ruined, US coll.) zugrundegehen, (university, Br.) Universität beziehen, zum Semesterbeginn wieder erscheinen;

~ **in s. one's estimation** in jds. Achtung steigen; ~ **everywhere** (buildings) überall gebaut werden; ~ **for one's examination** (Br.) ins Examen gehen, in eine Prüfung steigen; ~ **in flames** in Flammen aufgehen; ~ **a form** in die nächsthöhere Klasse versetzt werden; ~ **the line** (mil.) an die Front gehen; ~ **to London** nach London fahren; ~ **sharply** (prices) scharf anziehen.

go (v.) | **upon tick** (fam.) auf Pump kaufen; ~ **on one's way** sich auf den Weg machen; ~ **a long way** (money) lange reichen; ~ **a long way round** großen Umweg machen, (speech) durchschlagenden Erfolg zeitigen; ~ **the way of all things** den Weg allen Fleisches gehen; ~ **while the going is good** Gunst der Stunde ausnutzen; ~ **whistle** unbefriedigt weggehen.

go (v.) **with** harmonisieren, zusammenpassen;

~ **the crowd** sich der Mehrheit anschließen; ~ **the house** zum Haus gehören; ~ **an office** (salary) mit einem Amt verbunden sein; ~ **one's party** sich nach den Parteianordnungen richten; ~ **the tide** mit dem Strom schwimmen; ~ **the times** mit der Zeit mitgehen.

go (v.) **without** entbehren, ohne etw. auskommen;

~ **clay** Prozeß verlieren; ~ **a holiday** keine Ferienreise machen; ~ **saying** selbstverständlich sein, sich am Rande verstehen; ~ **supper** ohne Abendbrot bleiben.

go (v.) | **the whole hog** aufs Ganze gehen; ~ **wrong in early life** in der Jugend Dummheiten machen.

go, to be all the großen Zulauf haben, (fashion) höchst modern (der letzte Schrei, die große Mode) sein; **to be always on the** ~ laufend unterwegs sein; **to be full of** ~ voller Energie stecken, Mumm in den Knochen haben; **to be a near** ~ gerade noch gut gehen; **to be on the** ~ **all day** ganzen Tag auf den Beinen sein; **to have a** ~ dazwischentreten; **to have a** ~ **at s. th.** etw ausprobieren; **to have another** ~ weiteren Versuch unternehmen, erneut versuchen; **to have a bad** ~ **of flu** häßlichen Grippeanfall haben; **to have no** ~ keinen Schmiß haben; **to have nothing to** ~ **upon** keine Anhaltspunkte haben; **to have several** ~**es** mehrere Versuche anstellen; **to have several** ~**es at s. th.** mehrere Anläufe für etw. unternehmen; **to keep s. o. on the** ~ j. in Trapp halten; **to let it** ~ **at that** es dabei bewenden lassen; **to let s. th.** ~ **back** einer Sache keine Beachtung schenken; **to make a thing** ~ Schwung in etw. bringen, etw. zu einem Erfolg machen; **to make the bottle** ~ **round** Flasche kreisen lassen; **to want a hat to** ~ **with the dress** zum Kostüm einen passenden Hut benötigen.

go-ahead Unternehmungsgeist, Schwung, Schmiß, *(US, gogetter)* Draufgänger;
to get a quiet ~ stillschweigend genehmigt werden; **to receive the** ~ **on a project** freie Bahn (grünes Licht) für ein Vorhaben erhalten;
~ *(a.)* modern, fortschrittlich, unternehmend, unternehmungslustig, progressiv;
~ **business man** unternehmerisch eingestellter Geschäftsmann; ~ **times** avantgardistische Zeitepoche.

go-as-you-please ungeregelt, ungebunden, völlig ungezwungen.

go | -ashore clothes Ausgangsanzug; ~~**at-it young man** unternehmungslustiger junger Mann; ~~**between** Unterhändler, Zwischenträger, Vermittler, Mittelsmann; **to serve as a** ~~**between** als Vermittler tätig sein; **to give s. o. the** ~~**by** j. links liegen lassen; **to give s. o. the** ~~**by in the street** j. auf der Straße schneiden; ~~**cart** Kleinstrennwagen; ~~**devil** *(railway)* Materialwagen; **to have the** ~~**fever** Lampenfieber haben; ~ **fog** Nebelauflöser; ~~**getter** *(coll.)* energischer Mensch, Draufgänger, Raffke; ~~**getting** unternehmungslustig; ~~**home bonus** *(immigrant worker)* Repatriierungsprämie; ~~**home scheme** *(immigrant worker)* Repatriierungssystem; ~~**to meeting clothes** Ausgangsanzug; ~~**slow** *(Br.)* planmäßiges Langsamarbeiten, Arbeiten nach Vorschrift, Bummelstreik; ~~**slow policy** Politik des Bummelstreiks; ~~**slow strike** Arbeitsverlangsamung, Bummelstreik; ~~**slow tactics** Arbeitsverschleppung.

goal Ziel, Zweck, Ende, *(destination)* Bestimmungsort;
one's ~ **in life** jds. Lebensziel;
to specify the ~**s of discussion** Diskussionsziele abstecken;
~ **displacement** Zielverschiebung; ~ **judge** Zielrichter; ~ **line** Ziellinie; ~ **setting** Zielsetzung.

goat *(US sl.)* Sündenbock;
to get s. one's ~ j. auf die Palme bringen; **to play the giddy** ~ sich als Narr aufspielen; **to separate the sheep from the** ~**s** Schafe von den Böcken trennen.

gobbledygook *(US)* Kanzlei-, Behördensprache, schwulstiger Amtsstil.

gobo *(mike)* Schallschutz, *(television)* Blendschirm.

gocart Handwagen.

god-forsaken hole gottverlassenes Nest.

godchild Patenkind.

godfather Pate;
to act as ~ **to a child** bei einem Kind Pate stehen.

godmother Patentante.

godsend Gottesgeschenk, Glücksfall.

godspeed, to wish s. o. jem. glückliche Reise wünschen.

goggle box *(fam., television)* Glotzkasten, Glotze, Pantoffelkino.

goer Läufer.

goggles Schutzbrille.

going Abreise, Abfahrt, *(road condition)* Straßenzustand, -beschaffenheit;
good ~ gute Geschwindigkeit; **tough** ~ gehörige Schinderei;
close ~ **over** sorgfältige Prüfung; ~ **back on a friend** Verrat eines Freundes; ~ **back to school** Wiedereintritt in die Schule; ~ **back on one's word** Wortbrüchigkeit; ~ **to the country** Ausschreibung von Neuwahlen; ~ **down** *(person)* Abstieg; ~ **into effect** Wirksamwerden; ~ **in** Registrierung; ~ **off** Abreise; ~ **out** Ausgang; ~ **out of office** *(minister)* Rücktritt; ~ **to press** Drucklegung; ~ **into production** Produktionsaufnahme; ~ **through** *(documents)* Durchsicht; ~ **on strike** Streiken; ~ **up** Kurssteigerung;
~ *(a.)* arbeitend, gut gehend, im Betrieb (Gang);
~, ~ **gone!** *(auction)* zum ersten, zum zweiten, zum dritten; ~ **and coming** hin und zurück; ~ **at present** *(show)* im Augenblick aufgeführt;
to be still ~ **like the clappers** *(fam.)* immer noch tadellos funktionieren; **to be** ~ **on for sixty** sich den Sechzigern nähern; **to be** ~ **cheap** billig sein; **to be** ~ **strong** voller Energie stecken; **to give s. o. a** ~ **over** *(US)* j. ins Gebet nehmen; **to keep industry** ~ Produktion in Gang halten; **to set** ~ in Betrieb nehmen;

~ **concern** lebendes Geschäft, bestehendes Handelsgeschäft, im Betrieb befindliches Unternehmen, *(fig.)* gut funktionierende Sache; ~ **firm** gutgehendes Geschäft; ~ **market price** gängiger Marktpreis; ~ **over** *(US)* Rüge, Verweis; ~~**concern position** finanzielle Lage eines laufenden Betriebes; ~~**concern value (worth)** Betriebs-, Ertragswert; ~ **price** Tagespreis, Verkehrswert; ~~**to-press prices** letzte Kurse; ~ **rate** üblicher Lohntarif; ~ **rate of interest** derzeitiger Zinssatz; ~~**out-of-business sale** *(US)* Totalausverkauf; ~ **short** *(US)* Baissespekulation, Verkauf auf Baisse; ~ **value** Betriebswert; ~ **wage** üblicher Lohn; ~ **witness** abreisefertiger Zeuge.

goings Lauf der Welt;
~ **on** viel Betrieb;
strange ~~**on** seltsame Vorgänge.

golconda *(fig.)* Goldgrube.

gold Gold, *(coin)* Goldmünze, *(riches)* Reichtum, Geld;
as good as ~ goldrichtig; **on** ~ auf Goldbasis; **redeemable in** ~ in Gold rückzahlbar;
alloyed ~ Karat-, legiertes Gold; **bar** ~ Barrengold; **base** ~ schlechtes Gold; **twenty-four carat** ~ 24karätiges Gold; **clean** ~ reines Gold; **coined** ~ gemünztes Gold; **common** ~ 18karätiges Gold; **earmarked** ~ im Sonderdepot verwahrtes Gold, Goldreserve bei ausländischen Noteninstituten; **fine** ~ Feingold; ~ **18 carat fine** achtzehnkarätiges Gold; **free** ~ *(US)* die gesetzlich vorgeschriebenen Reserven übersteigender Goldbestand; **ingot** ~ Barrengold; **native** ~ gediegenes Gold; **parting** ~ Scheidegold; **pure** ~ reines (feines) Gold; **solid** ~ gediegenes Gold; **standard** ~ Münzgold, Gold von gesetzlichem Feinkorn; **sterling** ~ echtes Gold; **surplus** ~ Goldüberschuß; **true** ~ reines Gold; **virgin** ~ gediegenes Gold;
~ **in ingots** Stangengold; ~ **in nuggets** rohes Gold, Gold in Klumpen;
to be worth its weight in ~ unbezahlbar (nicht mit Gold zu bezahlen) sein; **to pay in** ~ in (mit) Gold bezahlen; **to demonetize** ~ Gold als Währungsunterlage aufgeben; **to hold** ~ **earmarked for foreign accounts** Gold für ausländische Rechnung im Depot halten; **to repatriate** ~ Goldabflüsse nach dem Inland zurückbringen; **to wash for** ~ Gold waschen;
~ **alloy** Goldlegierung; ~ **annuity** Goldrente; ~ **backing** Golddeckung; ~ **bar** Goldbarren; ~ **basis** Goldbasis; ~ **bloc** Goldwährungsblock; ~~**bloc countries** Goldblockländer; ~ **bonds** *(US)* Goldobligationen; ~ **brick** *(US sl.)* zweifelhafte Spekulation, Schwindel, Talmi; **to sell s. o. a** ~ **brick** j. anschmieren; **brooch** Goldbrosche; ~ **buck** *(US sl.)* Fanatiker; ~ **bugs** Goldklauseln; ~ **bullion** Gold in Barren, Goldbarren; ~~**bullion price** Goldbarrenpreis; ~~**bullion standard** Goldkern-, Goldbarrenwährung; ~ **buying** Goldankauf; ~~**buying price** Goldankaufspreis; ~ **certificate** *(US)* Goldzertifikat; ~ **circulation** Goldumlauf; ~ **clause** Goldklausel; ~ **clearance fund** *(US)* Goldausgleichsfonds; ~ **coast** *(US)* Goldküste, *(city, sl.)* vornehmes Viertel; ~ **coin** Goldmünze, -stück; **in** ~ **coin of the USA** in Goldwährung der USA; ~ **coins and bullions** Goldbestände; ~~**coin standard** Goldmünzwährung; ~ **coinage** Goldmünzprägung; ~ **consignment** Goldtransport, -sendung; ~ **consumption** Goldverbrauch; ~ **content** Goldgehalt; ~ **cover** Golddeckung; **to abolish (lift) the** ~ **cover** Golddeckung aufgeben; ~ **currency** Goldwährung; ~ **and silver currency** Doppelwährung; ~ **depositary certificate** Golddepotschein; ~ **digger** Goldgräber; ~ **diggings** Goldfundgebiet; ~ **dollar** Golddollar; ~ **drain** Goldabzug; ~ **embargo** Goldembargo, -einfuhrverbot; ~ **exchanges** Goldvaluten; ~~**exchange point** Goldausfuhrpunkt; ~~**exchange standard** Golddevisenwährung; ~ **export** Goldexport, -ausfuhr; ~ **export point** oberer Goldpunkt; ~ **field** Goldminenbezirk, -feld; ~ **fixing** *(London)* Festsetzung des Goldpreises; ~ **florin** Goldgulden; ~ **franc** Goldfranken; ~ **fund** Goldfonds; ~ **future contract** Goldtermingeschäft; ~ **hoard** Goldhortung; ~ **holdings** Goldbestände; ~ **import** Goldimport, -einfuhr; ~ **import point** unterer Goldpunkt; ~ **index** Goldindex; ~ **inflow** Goldzufluß; ~ **ingot** Goldbarren; ~ **loan** Goldanleihe; ~ **loss** Goldverluste; [two-tier] ~ **market** [gespaltener] Goldmarkt; **to split the** ~ **market into a free and an official market** Goldmarkt in einen freien und offiziellen Markt spalten; ~ **medal** Goldmedaille; ~ **mine** Goldmine, -grube, *(fig.)* Goldgrube; **a regular** ~ **mine** echte (wahre) Goldgrube; ~ **mining** Goldabbau; ~~**mining share** Goldminenaktie; ~ **movement** Goldbewegung; ~ **notes** *(US)* in Gold zahlbare Banknoten; ~ **outflow** Goldabfluß; ~ **parity** Goldparität; ~ **payment** Goldzahlung; ~ **piece** Goldstück; **to eat off** ~ **plate** auf goldenem Geschirr speisen; ~ **point** Goldpunkt; ~ **pool** Goldfonds; ~ **premium** Goldagio; ~ **price** Goldpreis; **two-tier price** gespaltener Goldpreis; ~ **printing** Goldprägung; ~

producing country Goldland; ~ **production** Goldgewinnung, -produktion; ~ **prospector** Goldsucher; ~ **purchaser** Goldankäufer; ~ **purchases** Goldankäufe; ~ **rate** Goldkurs; ~ **reserve** Bestand an Gold, Goldbestand, -reserve; ~ **rush** Goldfieber, -rausch; ~ **seeker** Goldsucher; ~ **settlement fund** *(Federal Reserve Banks, US)* Goldausgleichsfonds [der 12 Federal-Reserve-Banken]; ~ **shares** *(Br.)* Goldaktien; ~ **shipment** Goldsendung; ~ **shipment point** Goldpunkt; ~ **specie** Münzgold; ~ **specie standard** reine Gold[umlauf]währung; ~ **standard** Goldstandard, -währung; **to go off the** ~ **standard** Goldstandard, -währung aufgeben; **to support the** ~ **standard** für Aufrechterhaltung des Goldstandards eintreten; **to suspend the** ~ **standard** Goldstandard vorübergehend aufgeben; ~~-**standard country** Goldwährungsland; ~ **stock** Goldbestand, -vorrat, Goldaktie; ~ **strike** Goldfund; ~ **subscriptions** Goldeinzahlungen; ~ **supply** Goldangebot, -vorrat, -versorgung; ~ **trade** Goldhandel; ~ **tranche** *(International Monetary Fund)* Goldtranche; ~ **tranche rights** Goldtranchenziehungsrechte; ~ **transportation** Goldtransport; ~ **value** Goldwert; ~ **value basis** Goldwertbasis; ~ **value guarantee** *(International Monetary Fund)* Goldwertgarantie; **to carry a** ~~-**value guarantee** goldwertgesichert sein; ~ **washing** Goldwäscherei; ~ **withdrawal** Goldabzüge.

goldbrick *(mil., US)* Drückeberger, Soldat mit Druckposten; ~ *(v.) (US)* sich drücken.

goldbricking *(US)* Bummeln bei der Arbeit.

goldbug *(US sl.)* Verfechter des Goldstandards.

golden| **age** Glanzzeit; ~ **calf** Reichtum, Gold; **to worship the** ~ **calf** Reichtum anbeten; ~ **handshake** Abstandsgeld, phantastische Abfindungssumme [für vorzeitiges Ausscheiden; ~ **opinion** hohe Anerkennung; ~ **opportunity** glänzende Gelegenheit; ~~-**rod paper** Abdeckpapier; ~ **touch** *(advertising)* die goldene Note; ~ **wedding** goldene Hochzeit.

goldsmith Goldschmied.

goldsmithery Goldschmiedearbeit.

gone *(auction)* zugeschlagen, *(trade)* ruiniert; ~ **away, no address** unbekannt verzogen; **far** ~ weit fortgeschritten, in einer schwierigen Lage; ~ **case** hoffnungsloser Fall; ~ **concern position** finanzielle Verfassung im Falle einer Liquidation.

goner hoffnungsloser Fall.

gong Gong, elektrische Klingel; ~ *(v.) (police, Br.)* [Fahrzeug] durch Gongsignal stoppen.

good [öffentliches] Wohl, *(advantage)* Nutzen, Wert, Vorteil, *(balance sheet)* Habenseite, *(net profit)* Nettogewinn; **for** ~ ein für allemal; **for the** ~ **of one's health** zur Stärkung seiner Gesundheit; **for his own** ~ zu seinem eigenen Vorteil; **to the** ~ *(bank balance)* im Guthaben, auf der Kreditseite; **common** ~ Gemeinwohl; **public** ~ das öffentliche Wohl;
~ *(a.) (advantageous)* vorteilhaft, *(agreeable)* angenehm, *(authentic)* gültig, unverfälscht, authentisch, *(check)* in Ordnung, *(efficient)* fähig, befähigt, geeignet, *(financially sound)* zahlungs-, kreditfähig, gut, solid, solvent, sicher, *(morals)* rechtschaffen, redlich, *(skilful)* tüchtig, *(sound)* reell, *(valid)* rechtskräftig, -gültig;
as ~ **as new** fast neu; **as** ~ **as ready money** so gut wie Bargeld; **as** ~ **as settled** so gut wie erledigt;
~ **for** *(draft)* gut über den Betrag von; ~~-**for-nothing** wertlos; ~ **at languages** sprachbegabt; ~ **in law** rechtlich zulässig, rechtsgültig; ~ **for printing** druckreif, Imprimatur; ~ **for service** *(discharge of a civil servant)* im öffentlichen Interesse; ~ **for trade** handelsgünstig; ~ **until cancelled (recalled)** bis auf den Widerruf gültig; ~ **and valid** rechtsgültig;
to act for the common ~ im öffentlichen Interesse tätig sein; **to be £ 10 to the** ~ ein Guthaben von 10 Pfund haben; **to be** ~ **for its ordinary business engagements** seinen laufenden kaufmännischen Verpflichtungen stets nachkommen; **to be judged** ~ guten Ruf genießen; **to be** ~ **in law** zu Recht bestehen, rechtsgültig sein; **to be** ~ **for three months** noch drei Monate gültig sein; **to be too** ~ **for one's situation** bessere Stellung verdienen; **to be** ~ **for a sum** für einen Betrag gut sein; **to be** ~ **for a sum of £ 1000** für einen Betrag bis zu £ 1000 gut sein; **too** ~ **to be true** zu schön um wahr zu sein; **to be up to no** ~ nichts Gutes im Schilde führen; **to be as** ~ **as one's word** völlig zuverlässig sein; **to be** ~ **for several more years of service** auch in den nächsten Jahren noch leistungsfähig sein; **to become a power for** ~ guten Einfluß ausüben; **to come to the** ~ sich zum Guten wenden; **to do more harm than** ~ mehr schaden als nützen; **to give s. o. as** ~ **as one gets** jem. mit gleicher Münze heimzahlen; **to have gone for** ~ **and all** nie mehr zurückkommen; **to hold** ~ [noch] gelten; **not to keep** ~ **in hot weather** sich bei Hitze schlecht halten; **to labo(u)r for the common** ~ für die Allgemeinheit

arbeiten; **to leave the country for** ~ Land für immer verlassen; **to make** ~ gutmachen, erfolgreich sein, *(compensate)* ersetzen, vergüten, *(effect)* bewerkstelligen, *(expenses)* bezahlen, *(position)* sichern, *(promise)* erfüllen, *(statement)* beweisen, belegen; **to make** ~ **the casualties** Verluste auffüllen; **to make** ~ **one's claim** Gültigkeit seiner Forderung begründen; **to make** ~ **a defect** Mangel beseitigen; **to make** ~ **a loss** Verlust ausgleichen; **to make** ~ **on a note** Wechsel einlösen; **to return** ~ **for evil** Böses mit Gutem vergelten; **to settle down for** ~ sich für dauernd niederlassen; **to work for the** ~ **of the country** sich um das Wohl seines Landes verdient machen;
~ **bearing** gute Führung; ~ **merchantable abstract of title** [etwa] einwandfreier Grundbuchauszug; ~ **address** gute Wohngegend; ~ **articles** reelle Ware; **on** ~ **authority** aus zuverlässiger Quelle; ~ **bank note** echte Banknote; ~ **bargain** günstiger Kauf, Gelegenheitskauf; ~ **behavio(u)r** einwandfreie Führung; **to be in s. one's** ~ **books** bei jem. gut angeschrieben sein; ~ **and sufficient brakes** ausreichend funktionierende Bremsen; ~ **breeding** gute Manieren (Erziehung); ~ **business man** tüchtiger Geschäftsmann; ~ **cause** *(discharge)* Entlassungsgrund; ~ **cheap** wohlfeiler Kauf; ~~-**class** aus guter Familie; ~~-**class article** erstklassige Ware; ~~-**conditioned** in gutem Zustand; ~ **conduct** gutes Betragen; ~ **conduct certificate** Sitten-, Leumunds-, Führungszeugnis; ~~-**conduct prize** *(school)* Prämie für gute Führung; ≙ **Conduct Medal** *(mil.)* Auszeichnung für gute Führung; ~ **consideration** *(law)* Vertragsinteresse, Gegenleistung; ~ **country** *(Scot. law)* Geschworene; ~ **deal of money** ziemlicher Haufen Geld; ~ **debts** sichere Forderungen; ~ **defence** begründete Einrede; ~ **delivery** *(stock exchange)* einwandfreies Stück; **to constitute [a]** ~ **delivery** *(stock exchange)* lieferbar sein; ~ **and substantial depot** *(US)* für Personen- und Güterverkehr geeigneter Bahnhof; ~ **dollar** echter Dollar; **in** ~ **faith** in gutem Glauben, gutgläubig; ~~-**faith taker** gutgläubiger Erwerber; ~ **family** angesehene Familie; ~ **feeling** Sympathie, Wohlwollen; ~ **fellowship** gute Kameradschaft; ~~-**for-nothing (-naught)** Taugenichts, Tunichtgut; ~ **form** *(Br.)* guter Ton; ~ **fortune** Glückssträhne; **to prove a** ~ **friend** sich als wahrer Freund erweisen; ~ **general education** gute Allgemeinbildung; ~ **grace** Gunst; ~ **hand** fließende Handschrift; ~ **handwriting** schöne Handschrift; ~ **health** *(insurance)* gute Gesundheit; **to wait for a** ~ **hour** geschlagene Stunde warten; ~ **jury** unanfechtbare Geschworene; **to be a** ~ **life** *(insurance)* guten Lebensversicherungsaspiranten abgeben; **to live a** ~ **life** angenehmes Leben führen; ~~-**looker** gut aussehender Mensch; ~ **luck** viel Glück; ~ **man** sicherer Kunde; ~ **man for a position** geeigneter Mann für eine Stellung; ~ **and workmanlike manner** fachgerechte Behandlung; ~ **marriage** vorteilhafte Heirat; ~ **memory** gutes Gedächtnis; ~ **and lawful men** für eine Geschworenentätigkeit geeignete Männer; ~ **merchantable quality and condition** handelsübliche Güte und Beschaffenheit; ~ **midding** gut Mittel; ~ **middling quality** gute Mittelqualität; **to have a** ~ **mind to do s. th.** ziemlich fest zu etw. entschlossen sein; ~ **money** echtes Geld; **in** ~ **money** in klingender Münze; **to be earning** ~ **money** hoch bezahlt werden; ~~-**natured** gutmütig, gefällig; ~ **neighbo(u)r policy** Politik gutnachbarlicher Verbindungen; ~ **neighbo(u)rliness** gute Nachbarschaft, gutnachbarliches Verhältnis; ~ **news** angenehme (günstige, gute) Nachrichten; ~ **offices** *(international law)* Freundschafts-, Vermittlungsdienste, gute Dienste; ~ **opportunity** günstige Gelegenheit; **in** ~ **order and condition** in ordnungsgemäßem Zustand; ~ **people** Heinzelmännchen; ~ **place** gute Stellung; **of** ~ **position** in angesehener Stellung; ~ **receipt** gültige Quittung; ~ **record title** befriedigende Grundbucheinsicht; **of** ~ **reputation** unbescholten, angesehen; ~ **repute** guter (einwandfreier) Leumund; ~ **round sum** runde Summe; **to earn a** ~ **salary** schönes Gehalt haben; ~ **sense** gesundes Urteil; ~ **share** beträchtlicher Anteil; ~ **soil** fruchtbarer Boden; **to be in** ~ **spirits** sehr lebhaft sein; **no** ~ **talking about it** es hat keinen Zweck darüber zu sprechen; **to be on** ~ **terms with s. o.** auf gutem Fuß mit jem. stehen; **in** ~ **time** rechtzeitig; **to have a** ~ **time** sich glänzend amüsieren; ~ **title** einwandfreier Rechtstitel, unbestrittenes Eigentum; ~ **and clear record title, free from encumbrances** rechtsmängel- und lastenfreier Eigentumstitel; ~ **trade paper** diskontfähiger kurzfristiger Warenwechsel; **to be in** ~ **train** günstig stehen; ~ **turn** Gefälligkeit, Freundschaftsdienst; **to do s. o. a** ~ **turn** jem. einen guten Dienst erweisen, jem. gefällig sein; ~ **understanding** gutes Einvernehmen; ~ **use** korrekter Sprachgebrauch; ~ **value** reelle Waren; **to get** ~ **value for one's money** gute Ware für sein Geld bekommen; **to say a** ~ **word for s. o.** zu jds. Gunsten sprechen; ~ **works** karitative Tätigkeit.

goods *(merchandise)* Waren, Handelsware, -güter, -artikel, *(movable property)* Habe, bewegliches Vermögen, bewegliche Gegenstände, *(railway)* Güter[ladung], Fracht[gut], Ladung, *(US, stolen property)* Diebesbeute, *(textiles, US)* Textilien, Stoffe, *(train, Br.)* Güterzug;

by ~ *(Br.)* mit dem Güterzug, als Fracht;

advised ~ avisierte Ware; **~ afloat** schwimmende Güter, unterwegs befindliche Ware; **allocated ~** rationierte Waren; **ascertained ~** *(law)* Speziessachen; **available ~** verfügbare Ware; **bale ~** Ballengüter; **barrelled ~** Faßwaren; **bonded ~** Güter unter Zollverschluß, unverzollte Güter, Waren unter Zollverschluß, zollpflichtige Güter; **~ bought** Kaufsgut; **branded ~** Markenartikel, -ware, -erzeugnisse; **bulk[y] ~** sperriges Gut, Sperrgut, Massengüter; **business ~** Wirtschaftsgüter; **capital ~** Investitions-, Kapitalgüter; **~ carried** Güterverkehr; **carted ~** Rollgut; **choice ~** auserlesene (ausgesuchte) Ware; **cleared ~** verzollte Waren; **collective ~** öffentliche Einrichtungen; **commingled ~** vermischte (vermengte) Güter; **complementary ~** Komplementärgüter; **consignment ~** konsignierte Waren, Kommissionsware; **consumer (consumption) ~** Konsum-, Verbrauchsgüter, Verbrauchsgegenstände; **container-shipped ~** in Behältern versandte Waren; **contraband ~** Konterbande, Bann-, Schmuggelware; **convenience ~** der Bedürfnisbefriedigung dienende Güter, *(US)* persönliche Gebrauchsgegenstände; **coupon ~** markenpflichtige Waren; **damaged ~** beschädigte (zurückgesetzte) Ware; **debenture ~** Rückzollgüter; **defective ~** mangelhafte Güter, Waren; **derationed ~** freigegebene (nicht mehr bewirtschaftete) Waren; **destroyed ~** untergegangene Sachen; **dispatch ~** *(Br.)* Eilgut; **disposable ~** disponible (verfügbare) Waren; **domestic ~** einheimische Waren; **down-market ~** nicht marktkonforme Waren; **dry ~** *(US)* Textilwaren nach dem Meter, Schnittwaren; **durable ~** haltbare (langlebige) Wirtschaftsgüter, Gebrauchsgüter; **dutiable ~** zollpflichtige Waren (Güter); **duty-free ~** zollfreie Waren; **duty-paid ~** verzollte Güter; **economic ~** Wirtschaftsgüter; **essential ~** lebenswichtige Güter; **exchangeable ~** Tauschprodukte; **existing ~** im Eigentum des Verkäufers stehende Waren; **exported ~** ausgeführte (exportierte) Waren, Ausfuhrgüter; **express ~** *(Br.)* Eilfracht, -gut; **fancy ~** Luxusartikel, Neuheiten; **fashion ~** Modeartikel; **fast ~** *(Br.)* Eilfracht; **fast-moving (-selling) ~** leichtverkäufliche Ware, Ware mit hoher Umsatzgeschwindigkeit; **fast-~train** *(Br.)* Eilfracht; **faultless ~** fehlerfreie Ware; **faulty ~** mangelhafte Ware; **finished ~** Fertigerzeugnisse, -fabrikate; **first-rate ~** erstklassige Waren, Primawaren; **floating ~** schwimmende Ware; **forwarded ~** versandte Waren, Versandartikel; **fragile ~** zerbrechliche Ware; **free ~** zollfreie Waren; **frozen ~** tiefgekühlte Waren; **fully-manufactured ~** fertiggestellte Waren; **fungible ~** vertretbare Güter, Gattungssachen; **future ~** noch zu erzeugende Waren; **hard ~** *(US)* Gebrauchsgüter, -gegenstände; **hazardous ~** gefahrbringende Güter (Waren); **heavy ~** Schwergut; **high-grade ~** hochwertige Ware (Güter); **high-quality ~** hochqualifizierte Waren; **high-volume and highly acceptable branded consumer ~** hochwertige Massenkonsumgüter; **home-produced (home-made) ~** Inlandserzeugnisse, einheimische Fabrikate; **honest ~** unvermischte Waren; **hot ~** heiße (frisch gestohlene) Ware; **household ~** Haushaltsgeräte; **imported ~** Einfuhren, Einfuhrgüter, Importgüter; **impulse ~** spontan gekaufte Waren; **incoming ~** Wareneingang, -zugänge, eingehende Waren; **industrial ~** Industrieprodukte, Güter der gewerblichen Wirtschaft, gewerbliche Erzeugnisse, Produktionsgüter; **inferior ~** geringwertige (minderwertige) Waren; **inflation-prone ~** inflationsempfindliche Waren; **innocent ~** nicht geschmuggelte Waren; **insured ~** versicherte Erzeugnisse; **intermediate ~** Zwischenprodukte; **inventorial ~** lagerfähige Güter; **invoiced ~** fakturierte Ware; **job ~** Ramschware, Ausschußware; **lawful ~** *(international law)* unbeanstandete Ladung; **light ~** Leichtgut; **loose ~** Sturzgüter; **low-class (-quality) ~** minderwertige Ware; **low-duty ~** niedrig verzollte Waren; **lower-priced ~** Waren niedriger Preislage, billige Artikel; **luxury ~** Luxusartikel; **machine-made ~** maschinell hergestellte Waren, Fabrikware; **manufactured ~** Industrieprodukte, -erzeugnisse, industriell hergestellte Waren, gewerbliche Güter, Fertigerzeugnisse, -fabrikate; **fully manufactured ~** fertiggestellte Waren; **marked ~** gekennzeichnete Waren; **marketable ~** gängige (gut verkäufliche) Ware; **measured ~** sperrige (lose verladene) Güter, Sperrgut; **measurement ~** Maßgüter, nach Maß berechnete Ware; **medium-priced ~** Waren mittlerer Preislage; **medium-quality ~** Waren mittlerer Art und Güte; **memorandum ~** *(US)* unter Eigentumsvorbehalt überlassene Waren, in Kommission vergebene Waren; **miscel-**

laneous ~ Sammelgut; **missing ~** fehlende Waren; **mortgaged ~** verpfändete Waren; **movable ~** Mobilien, bewegliches Vermögen; **narrow ~** Kurz-, Bandwaren; **nondurable consumptive ~** kurzlebige Verbrauchsgüter; **nonessential ~** nicht lebensnotwendige Güter; **nonquota (nonrationed) ~** nicht bewirtschaftete (kontingentierte) Waren; **nonspecified ~** Gattungssachen; **nonstrategic ~** nicht kriegswichtige Waren; **onerous ~** unwirtschaftliche Artikel; **ordered ~** bestellte (in Auftrag gegebene) Waren; **outgoing ~** Warenausgang; **packaged ~** abgepackte Ware; **patent ~** Markenartikel; **highly perishable ~** [leicht] verderbliche Güter; **perished ~** verdorbene Waren; **picked ~** auserlesene Ware; **piece ~** nach dem Stück verkaufte Ware, Schnittware; **~ pledged** verpfändete (sicherungsübereignete) Sachen (Waren), Sicherungsgut; **poor-quality ~** Waren schlechter Qualität, minderwertige Waren; **prepackaged ~** Fertiggerichte; **prewar ~** Waren aus der Vorkriegszeit; **price-fixed ~** preisgebundene Waren; **price-maintained ~** preisgestützte (preisstabile) Waren; **prison-made ~** im Gefängnis hergestellte Waren; **prize ~** Prisengut; **producer (production) ~** Produktionsgüter; **prohibited ~** Schleich-, Schmuggelware; **quota (rationed) ~** bewirtschaftete (bezugsbeschränkte) Waren, kontingentierte Artikel; **~ received** Wareneingänge; **rejected ~** zurückgewiesene Waren; **required ~** Warenbedarf; **returnable ~** zurückgehende Waren; **returned ~** Rück-, Retourwaren, zurückgesandte Waren, Remittenden; **rough ~** Rohware, unfertige Ware; **rummage ~** Restwaren; **sacrificed ~** spottbillige Waren, *(average)* aufgeopferte Güter; **salable ~** gängige Ware; **scarce ~** Mangelware; **seasonal ~** Saisonartikel; **selected ~** auserlesene Ware; **semifinished ~** Halbzeug; **semi-luxury ~** Güter des gehobenen Bedarfs; **semimanufactured production ~** Halbfertigwaren der Produktionsgüterindustrie; **shipped ~** verschiffte (versandte) Waren, *(US)* Frachtgut; **shipwrecked ~** Schiffbruchsgüter; **shopping ~** erst nach Preisvergleich gekaufte Waren; **slow ~** Frachtgut; **slow-moving ~** Waren mit geringer Umschlagshäufigkeit (längerer Umschlagsdauer); **slow-selling ~** schlecht verkäufliche Ware; **smuggled ~** Schleich-, Schmuggelware; **soft ~** Textilwaren; **sold and delivered ~** gelieferte Waren; **specialty ~** Speziessachen, Markenartikel, Spezialartikel; **specified ~** beim Kaufabschluß bestimmte Waren, Speziessachen; **speed ~** *(Br.)* Eilgut; **spoilt ~** verdorbene Waren; **spot ~** sofort lieferbare Waren; **staple ~** Haupthandelsartikel, Stapelware, -güter; **sterling ~** gediegene Waren; **stocked ~** Warenbestand, -vorrat; **stolen ~** Diebesgut; **store ~** *(US)* gekaufte Ware; **stored ~** [ein]gelagerte Waren (Güter), Lagergut; **stranded ~** Strandgut; **strategic ~** Waren von kriegsgewichtiger Bedeutung; **substandard ~** unterdurchschnittliche Waren; **~ supplied** *(balance sheet)* Aufwendungen für bezogene Waren; **tainted ~** *(Br.)* von Nichtgewerkschaftlern hergestellte Waren; **tangible ~** materielle Güter; **tared ~** tarierte Waren; **trade ~** Handelsware, -güter; **trademarked ~** Markenartikel; **transit ~** Durchfuhrgut; **trashy ~** Schundware; **unascertained ~** *(law)* Gattungssachen; **unclaimed ~** herrenloses Gut; **uncleared ~** zollhängige Waren; **uncustomed ~** zollfreie Waren; **undeclared ~** nicht deklarierte (beim Zoll gemeldete) Waren, Schmuggelware; **undelivered ~** noch nicht gelieferte Waren; **unentered ~** noch nicht verzollte Waren; **unfinished ~** halbfertige Erzeugnisse, Halbfabrikate, -erzeugnisse; **union-label ~** *(US)* mit Gewerkschaftsetikett versehene Ware; **unpaid ~** unbezahlte Waren; **unsalable ~** schwer verkäufliche Waren; **utility ~** *(Br.)* Güter mit sozialem Preis, einfache Gebrauchsgüter; **valuable ~** Wertgegenstände; **war ~** Rüstungsgüter, kriegswichtige Erzeugnisse; **~, wares and merchandise** Erzeugnisse aller Art, Warenbestand; **warehouse ~** Güter unter Zollverschluß, Waren auf Lager, Lagererzeugnisse; **wet ~** flüssige Güter; **worldly ~** irdische Güter; **wrecked ~** Strandgut;

~ fit for acceptance lieferfähige Ware; **~ shipped on account** *(US)* auf Rechnung versandte Waren; **~ billed to customer** dem Kunden in Rechnung gestellte Ware; **~ in bond** unter Zollverschluß liegende Waren; **~ out of bond** verzollte Ware; **~ of small bulk** nicht sperrige Waren; **~ and chattels** Hab und Gut, bewegliche Sachen, bewegliches Eigentum (Vermögen); **~ in the process of clearing** zollhängige Waren; **~ in fair condition** annehmbare Ware; **~ on consignment (on commission)** in Kommission vergebene Waren, Kommissionsgut, -waren; **~ for consumption** Verbrauchs-, Konsumgüter; **~ of conspicuous consumption** aufwendige Verbrauchsgüter; **~ bought on credit** auf Kredit gekaufte Waren; **~ held up at the customs** vom Zoll beschlagnahmte Ware; **~ stopped at the customhouse** vom Zoll angehaltene (beschlagnahmte) Waren; **~ damaged in transit** auf dem Transport beschädigte Waren; **~ dangerous in them-**

selves von Natur aus gefährliche Sachen; ~ **to declare** anmelde-pflichtige Waren; **actual** ~ **ready for immediate delivery** effektive (abrufbereite) Waren; ~ **selling (going) like hot cakes (wildfire)** schnell vergriffene Waren; ~ **free of duty** Freigut; ~ **taken in execution** gepfändete Gegenstände; ~ **exhibited for sale** Ausstellungsartikel; ~ **intended for export** zur Ausfuhr bestimmte Ware, Exportartikel; ~ **free from fault** fehlerfreie Waren; ~ **to be forwarded** Speditionsgüter; ~ **on hand** Warenlager, Lagerbestand, lieferbare Waren; ~ **left on our hands** unbezahlte Ware; **heavy** ~ **laden in bulk** Sturzgüter; ~ **specified in the invoice attached** in beiliegender Rechnung verzeichnete Ware; ~ **not loaded due to lack of space** aus Raummangel nicht verladene Güter; ~ **of the first order** Konsum-, Verbrauchsgüter; ~ **of the second order** Investitions-, Produktionsgüter; ~ **of foreign origin** Waren ausländischer Herkunft, fremdländische Erzeugnisse; ~ **in parcels** Stückgut; ~ **which perish** verderbliche Ware; ~ **lying in pledge** verpfändete Waren; ~ **taken out of pledge** freigegebene Waren; ~ **in process** halbfertige Erzeugnisse, in der Herstellung befindliche Waren, Halbfabrikate, -erzeugnisse; ~ **in the process of clearing** zollhängige Waren; ~ **for further processing** Vorerzeugnisse; ~ **of British production** englische Erzeugnisse; ~ **of inferior quality** geringwertige Güter; ~ **at the railway depot** (Br.) bahnlagernde Güter; ~ **in request** Warenbedarf; ~ **en route** unterwegs befindliche Güter, Transitgüter; ~ **for sale** angebotene (käufliche, zum Verkauf stehende) Ware; ~ **on sale or return** Kommissionsware; ~ **to be shipped** (US) Frachtgüter; ~ **shipped on account** auf Rechnung versandte Waren; ~ **shipped in bulk** lose verladene (sperrige) Güter, Sperrgut; ~ **sold and delivered** gelieferte Waren; ~ **specified in the annexed invoice** in beiliegender Rechnung aufgeführte Waren; ~ **in stock** Warenbestand; ~ **in storage** eingelagerte Waren, Lagergut; ~ **in short supply** Mangelware; ~ **in transit** unterwegs befindliche Güter, Durchfuhrgut, Transitware, -güter; ~ **damaged in transit** auf dem Transport beschädigte Waren; ~ **for transshipment** Umladegut; ~ **sent on trial** Probesendung; ~ **in trust** Kommissionsware; ~ **in warehouse** eingelagerte Waren, Speichersachen; ~ **of inferior workmanship** minderwertige Waren;
to accept the ~ Warenlieferung abnehmen; **to accept delivery of** ~ Warenlieferung abnehmen; **to assure o. s. with** ~ sich Ware sichern; **to bail** ~ **to s. o.** jem. Waren vertragsmäßig übergeben; **to be left with** ~ auf seinen Waren sitzenbleiben; **to bill** ~ Waren in Rechnung stellen; **to bond** ~ Waren unter Zollverschluß legen; **to bring in** ~ Waren einführen; **to buy** ~ **at the sales** Waren auf einer Auktion kaufen; **to buy** ~ **wholesale** engros einkaufen; **to carry** ~ Fracht befördern; **to carry** ~ **at published fare on set schedules** Gütertransport zu öffentlich festgelegten Tarifsätzen durchführen; **to carry** ~ **in stock** Waren auf Lager halten; **to cart** ~ Waren per Achse befördern; **to catch s. o. with the** ~ (US) j. auf frischer Tat ertappen; **to clear** ~ **out of bond** Waren ausklarieren; **to collect** ~ Waren abnehmen; **to condition** ~ Waren konditionieren; **to convey** ~ **in transit** Waren im Durchgangsverkehr abwickeln; **to deliver the** ~ Ware liefern, (fig.) Erwartungen erfüllen; **to deliver** ~ **on board** Waren an Bord bringen; **to deliver** ~ **on sale or return** Waren in Kommission geben; **to demand** ~ **in replacement** Ersatzlieferung verlangen; **to detain** ~ Ware zurückbehalten; **to discharge** ~ Güter löschen; **to dispatch** ~ Güter befördern (verladen); **to dispatch** ~ **direct to s. o.** jem. Ware unmittelbar zuschicken; **to display** ~ **in the window** Ware im Fenster ausstellen; **to dispose of** ~ Waren absetzen; **to docket** ~ Waren etikettieren; **to dump** ~ Waren in großer Menge billig auf den Markt bringen, Warendumping betreiben; **to enter** ~ Waren beim Zoll deklarieren; **to enter** ~ **for consumption** Waren zum freien Verzehr einführen; **to expose** ~ **for sale** Waren feilhalten; **to flourish** ~ Ware auslegen; **to get** ~ **off** Waren absetzen; **to grade** ~ Waren nach Güteklassen einstufen, Waren sortieren; **to handle foreign** ~ ausländische Waren führen; **to have** ~ **bonded** Waren unter Zollverschluß lagern; **to have** ~ **delivered** Waren verabfolgen lassen; **to have** ~ **in stock** Waren führen; **to have the** ~ **on s. o.** (US) jem. gegenüber im Vorteil sein; **to hoard** ~ Waren horten; **to identify** ~ **by marks** Waren kennzeichnen; **to impose inferior** ~ **upon s. o.** jem. minderwertige Ware aufdrängen; **to install branded** ~ Markenartikel einbauen; **to intern** ~ (US) Waren ins Landesinnere versenden; **to introduce** ~ **into a country** Waren in ein Land einführen; **to keep** ~ Waren führen; **to keep tally of** ~ Waren auf einer Liste abhaken; **to lay in** ~ Waren auf Lager nehmen, Waren einlagern; **to lend money on** ~ Waren lombardieren; **to let** ~ **cheaply** Waren billig ablassen; **to levy a duty on** ~ Einfuhrzoll auf Waren erheben; **to load** ~ Güter verladen; **to lower the price of** ~ Warenpreis herunter-

setzen; **to make salvage of** ~ Güter aus einem verunglückten Schiff bergen; **to make a valuation of** ~ Waren abschätzen; **to manufacture** ~ **in various qualities** Waren verschiedenster Qualität herstellen; **to mark down** ~ Ware billiger auszeichnen (notieren); **to obtain** ~ Ware beziehen; **to offer** ~ **at 15 per cent off the regular price** Waren 15% unter Preis (mit einem 15prozentigen Abschlag vom Normalpreis) anbieten; **to order** ~ **[through a representative]** Waren [über einen Vertreter] bestellen; **to palm off** ~ **on s. o.** jem. Ware aufschwindeln; **to parcel out** ~ Ware in Partien aufteilen; **to pass off** ~ **as those of another make** (US) Waren unberechtigt als Markenartikel verkaufen (unter falschen Warenzeichen vertreiben); **to place** ~ Waren absetzen; **to place the** ~ **on the dock** Waren am Kai niederlegen; **to procure** ~ Ware beziehen; **to puff up** ~ Warenpreis in die Höhe treiben; **to push** ~ Waren aufdrängen; **to put** ~ **in stock** Waren auf Lager nehmen; **to rate** ~ (US) Waren zu einem bestimmten Frachttarif verwenden; **to realize** ~ Ware verwerten; **to receive** ~ Ware beziehen; **to reconsign** ~ Waren an neue Adresse weitersenden; **to recover shipwrecked** ~ Güter aus einem verunglückten Schiff bergen; **to refuse** ~ Warenabnahme verweigern; **to reject** ~ **delivered** Warenlieferung beanstanden; **to release** ~ **against payment** Waren freigeben; **to render** ~ **marketable** beschädigte Ware wieder zurechtmachen; **to repossess** ~ Waren wieder in Besitz nehmen; **to retake** ~ Sachen zurücknehmen; **to sell** ~ **easily** Waren flott absetzen; **to sell off** ~ Waren abstoßen; **to sell** ~ **under a secondary label** als zweitklassige Ware verkaufen; **to send** ~ **by rail** Waren mit der Bahn versenden; **to send** ~ **by fast train** Waren per Express schicken; **to serve a customer with** ~ Kunden mit Ware beliefern; **to set out** ~ **on a stall** Waren auf einem Stand zur Schau stellen; **to set too low a valuation on** ~ Waren unterbewerten; **to show a cheap line of** ~ billige Waren feilbieten; **to sign for the** ~ Wareneingang bestätigen; **to spread out** ~ **for sale** Waren zum Verkauf ausbreiten; **to stock varied** ~ verschiedene Warengattungen (alle Arten von Waren) führen; **to stop** ~ **in transit** kaufmännisches Zurückbehaltungsrecht ausüben; **to submit** ~ **to a careful examination** Waren einer genauen Untersuchung unterziehen; **to supply** ~ **on credit** Waren auf Kredit liefern; **to supply o. s. with** ~ sich mit Ware eindecken; **to take the** ~ **back** Waren zurücknehmen; **to take** ~ **on a consignment basis** Waren in Kommission nehmen; **to take delivery of** ~ Waren abnehmen; **to take up** ~ **to a large amount** Waren in großen Posten abnehmen; **to throw** ~ **on the market** Ware auf den Markt werfen; **to trace lost** ~ verlorengegangene Warenpartie wiederfinden; **to trade in** ~ Warengeschäfte machen; **to transport** ~ **by truck** Güter verfrachten; **to underbill** ~ (US) Waren zu niedrig deklarieren; **to unload** ~ Güter löschen; **to value** ~ Waren abschätzen (taxieren); **to venture** ~ Waren auf Spekulation übersenden; **to waggon** ~ Güter transportieren; **to warehouse** ~ Waren deponieren; **to wrap up** ~ Waren verpacken;
~ **account** Warenkonto, -rechnung; ~ **agent** (Br.) Bahnspediteur; ~**-bought ledger** Wareneingangsbuch; ~ **delivery** Warenlieferung; ~ **delivery and collection** (Br.) Rollfuhrdienst; ~ **department** (Br.) Güterabfertigung, -annahme, Warenabteilung; ~ **depository** Warendepot; ~ **depot** (Br.) Güterschuppen, Güterniederlage; ~ **engine** (Br.) Güterzuglokomotive; ~ **exchange** Produktenbörse; ~ **invoice** (Br.) Warenbegleitpapiere, Bahn[begleit]papiere; ~ **lift** (Br.) Lastenaufzug; ~ **line** (Br.) Güter[haupt]gleis; ~ **locomotive** (Br.) Güterzuglokomotive; ~ **loft** (Br.) Güterspeicher, -schuppen; ~ **and capital movement** Waren- und Kapitalverkehr; ~ **office** (Br.) Güterannahme, -abfertigung, -ausgabe, Frachtannahmestelle; ~ **platform** (Br.) Güterabladeplatz, -bahnsteig; ~ **purchase ledger** Wareneinkaufsbuch; ~ **quota** Warenkontingent; ~ **rates** (Br.) Gütertarif; ~ **service** (Br.) Güter-, Frachtverkehr; **by fast** ~ **service** (Br.) express; **to send by slow** ~ **service** (Br.) als Frachtgut schicken; ~ **shed** (Br.) Güterspeicher, -schuppen; ~ **station** (Br.) Güterbahnhof; ~ **tariff** (Br.) Gütertarif; ~ **trade** Warenhandel, -verkehr; ~ **traffic** Warenverkehr, (Br.) Güterverkehr, -transport, -bewegungen; **long-distance** ~ **traffic** (Br.) Güterfernverkehr, Frachtverkehr; **slow-**~ **traffic** (Br.) Waren-, Frachtgutverkehr; ~ **traffic across the border** grenzüberschreitender Verkehr; ~ **train** (Br.) Güterzug; **by** ~ **train** (Br.) als Fracht; **by fast** ~ **train** (Br.) express; ~ **and services transaction** Waren- und Dienstleistungsverkehr; ~ **transport** (Br.) Güterverkehr; ~ **truck** (Br.) offener Güterwagen; ~ **van** (Br.) gedeckter Güterwagen; ~ **value** Warenwert; ~ **vehicle** (US) Lastfahrzeug, Transportfahrzeug, Lastkraftwagen; ~ **waggon** (Br.) Güterwaggon, Frachtwaggon; ~ **warehouse** Lagerhaus, Warenspeicher; ~ **yard** (Br.) Güter[bahn]hof.

goodwill Firmenwert, Goodwill, geschäftliches Ansehen, guter Ruf, *(benevolence)* freundliche Einstellung, Bereitwilligkeit, Gefälligkeit, Wohlwollen, Gunst, *(customers)* [Stamm]kundschaft, Kundenkreis, Klientele, *(dipl.)* Verständigungsbereitschaft;
consolidated ~ Firmenwert eines Konzerns;
~ **of a business** immaterieller Firmenwert;
to acquire the ~ Kundschaft übernehmen; **to build up** ~ freundschaftliches Verhältnis schaffen; **to buy the** ~ **of a house** Firma mit der Kundschaft kaufen; **to gain s. one's** ~ jds. Wohlwollen erringen;
~ **account** Firmenwertkonto; ~ **advertising** institutionelle Werbung, Image-, Vertrauens-, Prestigewerbung; ~ **ambassador** Botschafter guten Willens; ~ **cruise** Freundschaftsreise, -fahrt; ~ **gift** Werbegeschenk; ~ **mission** Mission des guten Willens.
goody Bonbon, Prämie, *(US coll.)* Tugendbold.
gooseberry *(fig.)* Anstandswauwau.
gorilla *(US)* Leibwache.
goon *(US sl., labor troubles)* gewalttätiger Streikbrecher, Provokateur.
goose *(fig.)* Esel, Dummkopf;
to be unable to say bo to a ~ über die Maßen schüchtern sein; **to cook s. one's** ~ jem. arg mitspielen; **to kill the** ~ **that lays the golden eggs** Gans töten, die goldene Eier legt;
the ~ **hangs high** *(US coll.)* die Sache sieht vielversprechend aus.
gooseneck Hängemikrophon, Galgen.
Gordian Knot, to cut the gordischen Knoten durchhauen.
gospel *(fig.)* Evangelium, *(principle)* Grundsatz;
to take s. th. for ~ etw. für bare Münze nehmen;
~ **oath** Eid auf die Bibel; ~ **truth** Binsenwahrheit.
gossip Klatsch, Tratsch;
old ~ Klatschtante;
~ **column** *(newspaper)* Klatschspalte; ~ **columnist (writer)** Gesellschafts-, Klatschspaltenjournalist.
got up to the nines (to kill) aufgedonnert.
Gothic type *(print., Br.)* Fraktur.
gouache Gouachetechnik.
gourmet fare Feinschmeckerkost.
govern *(v.)* lenken, leiten, verwalten, *(rule)* herrschen, regieren, Zügel in der Hand haben, *(serve as a rule)* maßgebend sein;
~ **by injunctions** im Notverordnungswege regieren; ~ **s. one's policy** Richtschnur von jds. Politik sein; ~ **the choice of a representative** für die Auswahl eines Vertreters bestimmend (maßgebend) sein; ~ **on conservative lines** konservativ regieren; ~ **one's temper** seiner Erregung Herr werden, sein Temperament zügeln.
governable regierbar, lenkbar.
governance Regierungsgewalt, -herrschaft, *(form of government)* Regierungsform, Regime.
governed | by cost kostenbedingt; ~ **by what people say** von der Meinung Dritter beeinflußt;
to be ~ **by a law** unter ein Gesetz fallen; **to be** ~ **by the opinion of others** von den Meinungen Dritter abhängig sein;
~ **economy** gelenkte Wirtschaft.
governess Erzieherin, Hauslehrerin, Gouvernante.
governing regierend, herrschend, leitend, verwaltend;
self-~ selbstverwaltend;
~ **body** Verwaltungsgremium, Lenkungsausschuß, Kuratorium, Direktorium, Verwaltungsrat, Leitung, Vorstand; ~ **classes** herrschende Klassen (Schichten); ~ **commission** Kontroll-, Regierungsausschuß; ~ **committee** *(New York Stock Exchange)* Börsenvorstand; ~ **department** Ministerium; ~ **director** Einzel-, Alleinvorstand; ~ **idea** Leitgedanke; ~ **law** anwendbares Recht; ~ **market trends** marktbestimmende Entwicklungen; ~ **panel** Kuratorium; ~ **party** Regierungspartei; ~ **principle** Leitsatz; **self-**~ **territories** autonome Gebiete.
government [Staats]regierung, Verwaltung, Obrigkeit, Staat, Staatsverwaltung, *(agency)* Verwaltungsbehörde, *(cabinet, Br.)* Ministerium, Kabinett, *(direction)* Lenkung, Leitung, Führung, *(form of administration)* Regierungsform, -weise, *(territory)* Gouvernement, Statthalterschaft;
pro-~ regierungsfreundlich;
arbitrary ~ Willkürherrschaft; **big** ~ umfangreich konzipierter Regierungsapparat, *(US)* zentrale Regierungsgewalt; **broader-based** ~ Regierung auf breiter Grundlage; **caretaker** ~ *(Br.)* geschäftsführende Regierung, Übergangskabinett; **carpet** ~ Regierung politischer Abenteurer; **central (centralized)** ~ Zentralverwaltung, -regierung; **city** ~ Stadtverwaltung, städtische Verwaltung; **coalition** ~ Koalitionsregierung; **commission** ~ Ausschußverwaltung; **consolidated** ~ von einem Ministerium

ausgeübte Regierungsgewalt; **constitution-drafting** ~ mit der Ausarbeitung einer Verfassung beauftragte Regierung; **constitutional** ~ konstitutionelle Staatsform, *(Br.)* verfassungsmäßige Regierung; **the contracting** ~s die vertragsschließenden Regierungen; **coordinated** ~ auf mehrere Ministerien aufgeteilte Regierungsgewalt; **democratic** ~ demokratische Regierungsform; **depositary** ~ Verwahrerstaat; **established** ~ schon bestehende Regierung; **Federal** ~ *(US)* Bundesregierung; **foreign** ~ auswärtige Macht; ~ **general** Generalgouvernement; **hereditary** ~ Erbmonarchie; **host** ~ Gastland; **the incoming** ~ neue Regierung; **labo(u)r** ~ Arbeiterregierung, *(Br.)* von der Labour Party gebildete Regierung; **legal (legitimate)** ~ rechtmäßige Regierung, *(Br.)* örtliche Regierungsbehörde, Kommunal-, Gemeindeverwaltung; **majority** ~ Mehrheitsregierung; **member** ~ Regierung eines Mitgliedsstaates; **military** ~ Militärregierung, -verwaltung; **military-based right-wing civilian** ~ vom Militär gestützte rechts angesiedelte Zivilregierung; **minority** ~ Minderheitsregierung; **mixed** ~ gemischte Regierungsform; **monarchical** ~ Monarchie, monarchische Staatsform; **municipal** ~ Gemeindeverwaltung, städtische Verwaltung, Stadtverwaltung; **national** ~ Staatsregierung; **no-frills** ~ keine Sonderansprüche stellende Regierung; **opposite** ~ Gegenregierung; **parliamentary** ~ parlamentarische Regierungsform; **participating** ~ teilnehmende Regierung; **power-sharing** ~ Regierung mit geteilter Machtausübung; **provisional** ~ Interimsregierung, vorläufige Regierung; **puppet** ~ Marionettenregierung; **regional** ~ örtliche Regierungsbehörde, Bezirks-, Provinz-, Regionalregierung; **republican** ~ republikanische Staatsform, Republik; **responsible** ~ demokratische Regierung; **revolutionary** ~ Revolutionsregierung; **right-of-centre** ~ rechts von der Mitte angesiedelte Regierung; **self-**~ Selbstverwaltung, Autonomie; **shadow** ~ *(Br.)* Schattenkabinett; **signatory** ~ Unterzeichnerregierung; **stable** ~ stabile Regierungsverhältnisse; **state** ~ Staatsregierung; **territorial** ~ Territorialregierung; **Tory** ~ konservative Regierung; **totalitarian** ~ totalitäre Regierungsform; **unified (unitary)** ~ Einheitsregierung; **left-wing** ~ Linksregierung; **right-wing** ~ Rechtsregierung;
~ **of the day** jeweilige Regierung; ~ **in exile** Exilregierung; ~ **de facto** De-facto-Regierung; ~ **controlled by influence from outside** von äußeren Einflüssen beherrschte Regierung; ~ **by injunctions** Regierungsausübung durch Notverordnungen; ~ **de jure** anerkannte Regierung; ~ **of national safety** Regierung der nationalen Sicherheit; ~ **of mediocrities** aus Mittelmäßigkeiten bestehende Regierung; ~ **by the people** Volksregierung; ~ **in waiting** Schattenkabinett;
to accuse the ~ **of complacency** Regierung der Selbstzufriedenheit beschuldigen; **to administer the** ~ Regierungsgeschäfte wahrnehmen; **to advise the** ~ **on monetary policy** Regierung in Fragen der Währungspolitik beraten; **to approach a** ~ Schritte bei einer Regierung unternehmen; **to bring down the** ~ **on the budget issue** Regierung aus etatspolitischen Gründen stürzen; **to carry on the** ~ *(Br.)* Staatsgeschäfte führen; **to erect a new** ~ neue Regierung bilden; **to establish (form) a** ~ *(Br.)* Regierung bilden; **to institute a** ~ Regierung einsetzen; **to interfere with the established** ~ bestehende Regierung angreifen; **to lead to the fall of the** ~ zum Sturz der Regierung beitragen; **to make up a** ~ Regierung bilden; **to organize a** ~ Regierung zusammenstellen; **to overthrow the** ~ *(Br.)* Regierung stürzen; **to put a** ~ **out of office** Regierung stürzen; **to recognize a** ~ Regierung völkerrechtlich anerkennen; **to reshuffle the** ~ Regierung umbilden; **to resign from the** ~ *(Br.)* aus dem Kabinett ausscheiden; **to run the** ~ Regierungsgewalt innehaben; **to set up a** ~ **in exile** *(Br.)* Exilregierung bilden; **to support the** ~ *(Br.)* Regierungspolitik unterstützen; **to sustain the** ~ **in office** Regierung im Amt belassen; **to take over the** ~ *(Br.)* Regierung übernehmen; **to tender the** ~ **for a loan** sich um einen Staatskredit bemühen; **to turn out (upset) the** ~ Regierung stürzen;
~ **accounts** staatliches Rechnungswesen; ~ **accountant** staatlicher Rechnungsprüfer; ~ **action** staatliche Maßnahmen, Regierungstätigkeit; ~ **Actuary** amtlicher Versicherungsmathematiker; ~ **Advisory, Conciliation and Arbitration Service** *(Br.)* Schlichtungsstelle der Regierung für Arbeitskämpfe; ~ **affairs committee** staatlicher Untersuchungsausschuß; ~ **agency** *(US)* Verwaltungsbehörde, -stelle; ~ **agent** *(US)* Regierungsvertreter; ~ **aid** staatliche Finanzhilfe; ~ **aircraft** Regierungsflugzeug; ~ **allocations** Staatszuweisungen; ~ **annuities** *(Br.)* Staatsrenten, -anleihen, Rentenpapiere; ~ **apparatus** Regierungsmaschinerie; **to be responsive to the** ~'s **appeal** dem Wunsch der Regierung nachkommen; ~ **appointment** Staatsamt, -anstellung; ~ **appropriation** Staatsfonds; ~ **assistance**

Staatsbeihilfe; ~ **backing** staatliche Unterstützung; ~ **bank** Staatsbank; ~ **bidding process** staatliches Ausschreibungsverfahren; ~ **bill** Regierungsvorlage; **with ~ blessing** mit staatlicher Zustimmung; ~ **body** Regierungsstelle; ~ **bonds** *(US)* Staatspapiere, -anleihen, -obligationen, Renten; ~~**bond yield** Rentenrendite; ~ **borrowing** staatliche Kreditaufnahme, Staatsverschuldung; ~ **broker** *(Bank of England)* Börsenmakler [für öffentliche Anleihen]; ~ **business** Staatsaufträge, *(~ corporation)* Wirtschaftsunternehmung der öffentlichen Hand, Staatsunternehmen; ~ **capital** Staatskapital; ~ **circles** Regierungskreise; ~ **clearance** staatliche Genehmigung; ~ **clerk** Regierungsangestellter; ~ **clients** für den Staat beschäftigte Betriebe; ~ **coalition** Regierungskoalition; ~ **commission** Regierungsausschuß; ~ **communication** Regierungsmitteilung; ~ **communiqué** Regierungsverlautbarung, -erklärung; ~ **company** staatliche Gesellschaft; ~'s **conciliation service** staatliche Schlichtungsstelle; ~ **conciliator** staatlicher Schlichter; **without ~ consent** ohne Einwilligung der Regierung; ~ **consultations** Regierungsberatungen; ~ **consumption** staatlicher Verbrauch; ~ **contract** öffentlicher Auftrag, Staatsauftrag; **to be awarded a juicy ~ contract** fetten Staatsauftrag erhalten; **to hold ~ contracts** mit Staatsaufträgen beschäftigt sein; ~ **contracting** Vergabe von Staatsaufträgen; ~ **contractor** Betrieb mit Staatsaufträgen; ~ **control** staatliche Leitung (Lenkung), Bewirtschaftung, Staatskontrolle, -aufsicht, fiskalische Kontrolle; ~~**controlled** unter staatlicher Aufsicht; ~ **contractor** Betrieb mit Staatsaufträgen; ~ **corporation** *(US)* staatliches Unternehmen, Staatsbetrieb, staatliche Gesellschaft; ~ **credit** Staatskredit; ~ **crisis** Regierungs-, Staatskrise; ~ **data** behördliches Zahlenmaterial; **top-level ~ decision** auf höchster Ebene getroffene Staatsentscheidung; ~ **defeat** Regierungsniederlage; ~'s **deficit** Staatsdefizit, -fehlbetrag; ~ **delegate** Regierungsvertreter; ~ **department** *(Br.)* Ministerium, Behörde, Regierungsstelle; ~ **department concerned** fachlich zuständiges Ministerium; ~ **depository** *(US)* staatliche Kapitalsammelstelle; ~ **deposits** *(US)* Bankguthaben des Staates; ~ **director on the board** staatliches Aufsichtsratsmitglied; **to participate in a ~ drive** staatliche Initiative unterstützen; ~ **economic manipulation (management)** staatliche Wirtschaftslenkung; ~ **employee** Angestellter des öffentlichen Dienstes, Staatsbediensteter, -angestellter, *(US)* Beamter; ~ **employment** staatliche Anstellung; ~ **enterprise** Wirtschaftsbetrieb der öffentlichen Hand, staatliches Unternehmen, staatseigener Industrie-, Staats-, Regiebetrieb; ~ **expenditure** Ausgaben der öffenltichen Hand; **[direct] ~ expenditure** [unmittelbare] Staatsausgaben; ~ **ordinary expenditure and revenue** ordentlicher Staatshaushalt; ~ **experience** Regierungserfahrung; ~ **expert** Regierungssachverständiger; ~ **export credit insurance** staatliche Ausfuhrversicherung; ~ **financial credit** staatliche Kredithilfe; ~ **forces** Regierungstruppen; ~ **functionary** Staatsfunktionär; ~ **funds** fundierte Staatspapiere; **on ~ funds** auf Staatskosten; ~ **go-ahead** Genehmigung der Regierung; ~ **grant** Regierungszuschuß, staatliche Zuweisung; ~ **guidelines** staatliche Richtlinien; ~ **guarantee** Staatsgarantie, -bürgschaft; ~'s **handling** Behandlung durch die Regierung; ~ **handouts** Staatsgeschenke; ~ **help** Staatshilfe; ~ **house** Regierungs-, Gouverneursgebäude; ~ **information service** regierungsamtliches Informationswesen; ~ **instrumentalities** staatliche Stellen, Regierungseinrichtungen; ~ **intervention** staatliche Invention, Intervention seitens der Regierung; ~ **investigator** von der Regierung eingesetzter Untersuchungsbeamter; ~ **job** Staatsanstellung; ~ **land** staatliche Grundstücke (Ländereien); ~ **legislation** staatliche Gesetzgebung; ~ **level** Regierungsebene; ~ **liability** Amts-, Staatshaftung; ~ **life insurance** staatliche Lebensversicherung; ~ **loan** Staats-, Regierungsanleihe; ~ **majority** Regierungsmehrheit; ~ **man** Regierungsbeamter; **to focus on the ~ market** sich auf Staatsaufträge konzentrieren; ~ **mediator** staatlicher Schlichter; ~ **minister** Staatsminister; ~ **monopoly** Staatsmonopol; **to use ~ muscles** Staatsapparat einsetzen; **to set ~ nerves almost everywhere on edge** der Regierung den letzten Nerv töten; ~ **newspaper** Staatszeitung, offizielles Regierungsblatt; ~ **notes** *(Br.)* Schatzscheine; ⁀ **Notice** *(Br.)* Regierungserlaß; ~ **obligations** Staatsobligationen; ~ **office** öffentliches Amt, *(building)* Regierungsgebäude, -büro; ~ **officer** Regierungs-, Staatsbeamter; ~ **offices** Ministerien; ~ **official** *(Br.)* Staats-, Regierungsbeamter, staatlicher Beamter; **to displace a ~ official** *(Br.)* Staatsbeamten ablösen; ~~**operated plant** Staatsbetrieb; ~ **order** Regierungsanweisung, Staatsauftrag; ~ **organ** Staats-, Regierungsorgan; ~ **outlay** Staatsausgaben; ~~**owned** im Staatseigentum (Staatsbesitz), staatseigen; ~~**owned enterprise** staatliches Unternehmen, Regie-, Staatsbe-

trieb; ~ **ownership** Staatseigentum, Besitz der öffentlichen Hand; **to stay free of ~ ownership** der Verstaatlichung entgehen; ~ **paper** Staatsanleihe; ~ **papers** Staatspapiere, -dokumente; ~ **paralysis** Handlungsunfähigkeit der Regierung; ~ **participation** staatliche Beteiligung; ~ **partisan** Regierungsanhänger; ~ **party** *(Br.)* Regierungspartei; ~ **party to a convention** Vertragsregierung; ~ **pay increase** Beamtengehältererhebung; ~ **payrolls** staatlicher Personalaufwand; ~ **permission** staatliche Erlaubnis; ~ **plan** Regierungsplan, -programm; ~'s **policy** Regierungspolitik; **to approve at large of the ~'s policy** der Regierungspolitik im Großen und Ganzen zustimmen; ~ **portfolio** Ministerressort; **to obtain a ~ position through interest with a cabinet minister** Staatsstellung durch die Beeinflussung eines Kabinettsmitglieds erhalten; ⁀ **Printing Office** *(US)* Staatsdruckerei; ~ **proclamation** Regierungserklärung; ~ **procurement** staatliches Beschaffungswesen; ~ **program(me)** Regierungsprogramm; ~ **program(me) to stimulate economic activity** Konjunkturförderungsprogramm; ~ **project** Regierungsprojekt; ~ **promotion** staatliche Förderung, öffentliche Förderungsmaßnahmen; ~ **property** fiskalisches Eigentum, Staatsbesitz; ~ **protection** Polizeischutz; ~ **publications** *(US)* amtliche Veröffentlichungen; ~ **quarters** Regierungskreise; ~ **railway** *(Br.)* Staatsbahn; **in the ~ ranks** in den Reihen der Regierung; ~ **regulation** behördliche Anordnung, staatlicher Eingriff; ~ **representative** Regierungsvertreter; ~ **response** staatliche Reaktion; ~ **restrictions** staatliche Beschränkungen; ~ **revenue** *(Br.)* Staatseinnahmen, -einkünfte; ~ **salary** Beamtengehalt, staatliches Gehalt; ~ **sector** Regierungsbereich; ~ **securities** *(Br.)* Bundesanleihen, Staatsanleihe, -papiere; **to chip in ~ securities as a position of required reserves** zum Teil Bundesanleihen als Mindestreserve verwenden; ~ **service** Staatsdienst; **in ~ service** im Staatsdienst; **free ~ services** kostenlose staatliche Dienstleistungen; ~ **situation** Beamtenstellung, Staatsanstellung; ~ **speaker** Regierungssprecher; ~ **spending** *(Br.)* Staatsausgaben -finanzierung, Ausgaben der öffentlichen Hand; ~ **spending program(me)** *(Br.)* staatliches Ausgabenprogramm; ~ **spokesman** Regierungssprecher; ~~**sponsored** staatlich gefördert; ~ **stocks** *(Br.)* Staatsanleihen, -papiere; **to purchase ~ stocks through the Post Office savings department** *(Br.)* Staatsanleihe im Postsparkassenwege erwerben; ~ **study** Regierungsstudie; ~ **subsidy** staatliche Subvention, Staatszuschuß (Hilfeleistungen); ~ **supervision** Staatsaufsicht; ~ **support** staatliche Unterstützung; ~ **supporter** Regierungsanhänger; ~ **survey** Regierungsstudie; ~ **survival** Überleben der Regierung; ~ **system** Regierungssystem, -form; ~ **take-over** Übernahme durch den Staat; ~ **taxes** Staatsabgaben; ~ **tax take** staatliche Steuereinnahmen; ~ **telegram** Staatstelegramm; ~ **training center** *(US)* **(centre,** *Br.)* staatliches Umschulungslager; ~ **training contract** staatlicher Ausbildungsvertrag; ~ **unit** Regierungsstelle; **local ~ unit** Gemeinde.

governmental behördlich, staatlich;
anti-~ regierungsfeindlich;
~ **accounting** Staatsrechnungswesen; ~ **act** Staatsakt; ~ **action** Regierungs-, Verwaltungsmaßnahme, Regierungs-, Verwaltungstätigkeit; ~ **activity** Regierungstätigkeit; ~ **agency** *(US)* Regierungsbehörde, -stelle, Verwaltungsbehörde; ~ **assistance** staatliche Unterstützung; ~ **authorization** amtliche Bescheinigung; ~ **authority** *(US)* Regierungsbehörde; ~ **body** Regierungsorgan, -stelle, *(US)* Verwaltungsbehörde; **in its ~ capacity** in behördlicher (staatlicher) Eigenschaft; ~ **character** staatlicher Charakter; ~ **client** für den Staat arbeitender Betrieb; ~ **committee** Regierungsausschuß; **without ~ consent** ohne Einwilligung der Regierung; ~ **delegate** Regierungsvertreter; ~ **district** Regierungsbezirk; ~ **duties** Regierungs-, Staatsaufgaben; ~ **enterprise** Staats-, Regiebetrieb, Wirtschaftsunternehmen der öffentlichen Hand; ~ **expenditure** Staatsausgaben, Ausgaben der öffentlichen Hand; ~ **facility** staatliche Einrichtung, Regierungsgebäude; ~ **fee** Verwaltungsgebühr; ~ **finance** Staatsfinanzwirtschaft; ~ **forces** Regierungstruppen; ~ **function** Regierungsfunktion, staatliche Funktion; ~ **grant** Regierungs-, Staatsbeihilfe, -zuschuß; ~ **immunity** *(US)* Steuerfreiheit für staatliche Einrichtungen; ~ **income** Staatseinkommen; ~ **instrumentality** *(US)* vom Kongress bewilligte staatliche Stelle; ~ **level** Regierungsebene; ~ **life insurance** vom Staat abgeschlossene Lebensversicherung; ~ **machinery** Staatsapparat, -maschinerie; **to use ~ muscle** Staatsapparat einsetzen; ~ **obligations** *(US)* Staatsschuldverschreibungen; ~ **officer** *(US)* Staats-, Regierungsbeamter; ~ **planning** staatliche Bewirtschaftung; ~ **powers** Regierungs-, Staatsgewalt, staatliche Vollmachten; ~ **publication** amtliche Veröffentlichung; ~ **purpose** öffentlicher Zweck; ~ **relations**

Beziehungen zu Behörden- und Regierungsstellen; ~ **responsibilities** regierungsmäßige Verwaltungsaufgaben; ~ **subdivision**
nachgeordnete Verwaltungsbehörde; ~ **system** Regierungssystem; ~ **undertaking** Staatsbetrieb, -unternehmen; ~ **unit**
Gebietskörperschaft, Regierungsbehörde.

governmentalize (v.) reglementieren, von der Regierung abhängig machen.

governmentese Amtssprache.

governor oberster Verwaltungsbeamter, Gouverneur, Statthalter, (bank) Leiter, Vorstand, Präsident, Leiter, (fortress) Kommandant, (prison, Br.) Gefängnisdirektor, (ruler) Herrscher,
Regent, (tutor) Hauslehrer;
deputy ~ Vizepräsident, stellvertretender Gouverneur; ~ **general** Generalgouverneur; **Lieutenant** ~ (US) stellvertretender
Gouverneur; ~ **select** (US) designierter Gouverneur;
~ **of the central bank** Staatsbankpräsident; ~ **of the Bank of
England** Notenbankpräsident;
~ **generalship** Generalgouvernement.

governorship Statthalterschaft, (US) Gouverneursamt, -stelle.

gown Amtstracht, -gewand, (judge) Talar, (lawyer) Robe;
academic ~ akademische Tracht;
town and ~ Bürger- und Studentenschaft;
~ (v.) Talar anlegen.

grab unrechtmäßige Aneignung;
~ (v.) sich rücksichtslos aneignen;
~ **at an opportunity** Chance wahrnehmen;
to be up for ~s (fig.) für den Zugriff offenstehen; ~ **a job** (fam.)
Stellung ergattern; ~ **markets abroad** Auslandsmärkte mit
allen Mitteln erschließen;
~ **bag (barrel, box)** (US coll.) Glücksbeutel; ~ **raid** Raubüberfall; ~ **rope** (mar.) Sicherheitsleine.

grabman Ladendieb.

Grace (direct dialling, Br.) Direktwahlsystem.

grace Gnade, Gunst, Wohlwollen, [Zahlungs]frist, (delay) Nachfrist, (permission to take a degree, Br.) Zulassung zur
Promotion;
by ~ of the Senate durch Senatsbeschluß; **by way of** ~ auf dem
Gnadenwege; **in ~ of** zugunsten von; **with a bad** ~ widerwillig,
ungern; **with a good** ~ bereitwillig;
faithful ~ aus Loyalität gewährter Spielraum; **15 minutes** ~
akademisches Viertel; **a three days'** ~ (for payment of a bill)
dreitägiger Zahlungsaufschub;
airs and ~s überspanntes Benehmen, affektiertes Getue;
to be in s. one's bad ~s bei jem. in Ungnade sein; **to be in s. one's
good** ~s bei jem. gut angeschrieben sein; **to give a creditor a
week's** ~ seinem Gläubiger eine Frist von einer Woche gewähren; **to grant a [day's]** ~ [einen Tag] Frist gewähren; **to have the
~ to do s. th.** etw. anständigerweise tun;
~ **cup** Abschiedstrunk; ~ **note** Anstandsbrief; ~ **period** (credit)
tilgungsfreie Zeit.

graceless behavio(u)r taktloses Benehmen.

gradate (v.) stufenweise übergehen, (colo(u)rs) abstufen,
abtönen.

gradation Stufenleiter, Reihenfolge, Staffelung;
~s **of speed** Geschwindigkeitsstufen.

gradational abgestuft.

grade Rang[stufe], Grad, Klasse, (job evaluation, Br.) Lohnklasse, Besoldungsgruppe, (metal) Gehalt, (mil.) Dienstgrad,
(of quality) Güteklasse, -grad, Handelsklasse, Qualität, (US,
school) Klasse, (slope) Steigung, Gefälle, Neigung, (stage)
Stufe, Phase, (statistics) Rangordnungsgrad;
at ~ (railroad crossing, US) auf gleicher Höhe; **on the down** ~ im
Abstieg, fallend; **on the up** ~ im Aufstieg; **of finest** ~ erster
Qualität;
~s (elementary school, US) Grund, Volksschule, (elementary
school system, US) Volks-, Grundschulwesen;
~ **A** (US) erste Klasse; **elementary and secondary** ~s (US)
Grund- und Oberschulklassen; **higher** ~ gehobener Dienst;
salary ~ (Br.) Gehaltsstufe, -klasse, Besoldungsgruppe; **well
recognized** ~ gut eingeführte Sorte;
similar ~ **of bond** gleichartige Obligation; ~ **of fertility** Bonität;
like ~ **and quality** gleiche Beschaffenheit und Güte;
~ (v.) sortieren, ordnen, einstufen, einteilen, (quality) in Güteklassen einteilen, (US, school) zensieren;
~ **goods** Waren nach Güteklassen einstufen; ~ **the population
according to the income** Bevölkerung nach Einkommensklas-
sen einteilen; ~ **by sizes** der Größe nach sortieren;
to be on the down ~ (business) konjunkturellen Niedergang
erleben; **to be on the up** ~ (business) im Konjunkturauftrieb
sein; **to get a passing** ~ gute Examensnote erhalten; **to make the**

~ (coll.) guten Durchschnitt erreichen, Erfolg haben; **to receive
higher** ~s (US) bessere Zensuren erhalten; **to reduce to a lower**
~ (mil., US) degradieren; **to teach in the** ~s (US) Volksschulunterricht erteilen;
first-~ erstklassig; **high-**~ erstklassig, prima, hochwertig; **low-**
~ von minderer Qualität, minderwertig;
~ **crossing** (US) schienengleicher Bahnübergang (Kreuzung);
~ **description** (job evaluation) Tarifklassenbeschreibung; ~
label(l)ing Güteeinteilung durch Aufklebezettel, Güteklassen-
bezeichnung; **top-**~ **quality** erstklassige Qualität; ~ **school** (US)
Volks-, Elementar-, Grundschule; ~ **teacher** (US) Volks-,
Grundschullehrer.

graded | by size nach Größen sortiert;
~ **advertising rates** degressive Werbesätze; ~ **school** (US)
Grund-, Volks-, Elementarschule; ~ **tax** gestaffelte progressive (degressive) Steuer.

grader Planiermaschine;
fourth ~ (US) Viertkläßler.

gradient Gefälle, Steigung.

grading Klassifizierung, Einstufung, -gruppierung, Staffelung,
Güte[klassen]einteilung;
~ **of commodities** Wareneinteilung nach Güteklassen; ~ **of
premiums** Beitragsstaffelung;
~ **papers** Akademikernachweis; ~ **practice** Einstufungssystem;
~ **test** Einstufungstest.

gradual allmählich, stufenweise, graduell;
~ **increase in the cost of living** allmähliche Lebenskosten-
erhöhung.

gradualism stufenweise Anpassung, (pol.) Politik der kleinen
Schritte.

gradualist Anhänger der Politik der kleinen Schritte.

gradually stufenweise.

graduate (school, US) Absolvent, Abiturient, (university)
Akademiker, Graduierter, Doktor;
high school ~ (US) Mittelschüler;
~ **in law** Rechtsbeflissener;
~ (v.) promovieren, akademischen Grad erlangen, (US)
Abschlußprüfung (Abitur) machen, (classify) einstufen,
(taxes, wages) staffeln, (university) Diplom (akademischen
Grad) verleihen, graduieren;
~ **with a degree** mit einem akademischen Grad abgehen; ~
from Harvard seinen Doktor auf der Harvarduniversität
machen; ~ **in law** Doktor der Rechte erwerben; ~ **from a school**
Schule absolvieren; ~ **from high school** (US) Prüfung der mittleren Reife ablegen; ~ **a tax** Steuer festsetzen;
to be a high school ~ (US) abgeschlossene höhere Schulbildung
besitzen;
~ (a.) promoviert, graduiert, im Besitz eines akademischen
Grades;
~ **course** Graduiertenkursus; **to teach a** ~ **course** Doktoranden-
seminar abhalten; ~ **degree** Doktorgrad; ~ **education** Akade-
mikerausbildung; ~ **nurse** (US) ausgebildete Krankenschwester; ~ **securities** (US) amtlich notierte Werte; ~ **student**
Promovierter; ~ **study** Universitätsstudium.

graduated abgestuft, gestaffelt, (university) mit abgeschlossenem
Examen;
~ **contribution** (national security, Br.) nach Lohnstufen gestaffelte Sozialversicherungsbeiträge; ~ **income tax** gestaffelte
Einkommensteuer; ~ **interest** gestaffelte Zinsen, Staffelzinsen;
~ **pension scheme** (Br.) abgestuftes Sozialrentensystem; ~ **price**
gestaffelter Preis, Staffelpreis; ~ **tariff** gestaffelter Tarif, Staffeltarif; ~ **tax** gestaffelte Steuer, Klassensteuer; ~ **taxation**
gestaffelte (degressive) Besteuerung.

graduation Gradeinteilung, Staffelung, Abstufung, (commencement) Abschlußprüfung, (taking degree) Ablegung des
Abschlußexamens, Promotion, Erteilung (Zuerkennung)
eines akademischen Grades;
high-school ~ (US) Zeugnis der mittleren Reife;
~ **from a course** (US) Absolvierung eines Lehrgangs; ~ **from a
high school** (US) Abschlußprüfung der mittleren Reife; ~ **of
prices** Preiseinstufung; ~ **of wages** Lohnstaffelung;
~ **time** (student) Anmeldetermin.

graffiti Wandgekritzel.

graft (US) Korruption, durch Amtsmißbrauch erworbene Vorteile, Bestechungs-, Schmiergeld, aktive Bestechung, (mortgage) Formmangelheilung, (swindle) Schwindel, Schiebung,
(theft) Diebstahl, Veruntreuung;
~ (v.) schieben, ergaunern, sich bestechen lassen;
~ **scandal** Bestechungsskandal.

grafter (US, official) korrupter (bestochener) Beamter, (swindler) Schwindler, Schieber, Gauner.

grafting *(US)* Schmiergeldunwesen, Bestechung.

grain Getreide, Korn, *(paper)* Laufrichtung, *(pearl)* Gran, Grän;
  with a ~ of salt mit gewissen Einschränkungen, mit Vorbehalt;
  without a ~ of sense ohne Sinn und Verstand;
  bagged ~ Getreide in Säcken; **coarse ~s** Futtergetreide;
  not a ~ of hope nicht die geringste (kein Fünkchen) Hoffnung;
  not a ~ of common sense kein bißchen gesunder Menschenverstand;
  to go against s. one's ~ jem. gegen den Strich gehen; **to receive a few ~s of comfort** nur kümmerlichen Trost erhalten;
  ~ bills gegen Getreidelieferungen gezogene Wechsel; **~ broker** Getreidemakler; **~ cargo** Getreideladung; **~ crop** *(US)* Getreideernte; **~ crop estimate** *(US)* Ernteschätzung; **~ dealer** Getreidehändler; **~ deliveries** Getreidelieferungen; **~ direction** *(paper manufacturing)* Laufrichtung; **~ exchange** Getreidebörse; **~ exports** Getreideausfuhren; **~ futures** Getreidetermingeschäfte; **~ growing** Getreideanbau; **~ harvest** Getreideernte; **~ harvester** Mähmaschine, Bindemäher; **~ imports** Getreideeinfuhren; **~ market** Getreidemarkt; **~ merchant** Getreidehändler; **~ prices** Getreidepreise; **~ price adjustment** *(EC)* Angleichung der Getreidepreise; **~ production** Getreideproduktion; **~ purchases** Getreidekäufe; **~ rent** vergütetes Abernterecht; **~ storage** Getreidesilo; **~ trade** Getreidehandel; **~ weigher** Getreidewaage.

grained paper gekörntes Papier, Maserpapier.

grammalog(ue) *(stenography)* Kürzel.

grammar Grammatik, Sprachlehrenbuch;
  to know one's ~ seine Sprache beherrschen;
  ~ school *(Br.)* höhere Schule, humanistisches Gymnasium, *(US)* Mittelschule.

grammatical | blunder Sprachschnitzer; **~ error** Grammatikfehler.

gramophone Grammophon;
  ~ pickup Tonabnehmer; **~ recital** Grammophonvorführung; **~ record** Schallplatte.

grand *(US sl.)* tausend Dollar, *(music)* Piano, Flügel;
  concert ~ Konzertflügel;
  ~ (a.) großartig, grandios, imposant, *(of higher rank)* distinguiert, hochstehend, vornehm, prominent;
  to do the ~ auf vornehm machen;
  ~ air Vornehmheit; **~ entrance** Haupteingang; **~ gesture** großer Wurf; **~ jury** großes Geschworenengericht; **~ larceny** schwerer Diebstahl; **~ lodge** *(freemasonry)* Großloge; **º Old Party** *(US)* Republikanische Partei; **~ staircase** Haupttreppe; **to live in ~ style** aufwendiges Leben führen; **to have a ~ time** sich herrlich amüsieren; **~ total** End-, Gesamtsumme; **~ tour** große Besichtigungsreise.

grandfather clause *(carrier, US)* Befähigungsnachweisklausel.

grandmotherly *(pol.)* kleinlich.

grandstand Zuschauertribüne, Haupttribüne;
  ~ (v.) (US sl.) auf Effekt aus sein;
  ~ finish packender Endkampf; **~ play** Effekthascherei.

granger Landwirt, Farmer.

granite *(fig.)* Härte, Festigkeit;
  to bite on ~ auf eisernen Widerstand stoßen.

grant *(conveyance by written instrument)* urkundliche Übertragung, Übereignung, *(donation)* [schriftliche] Schenkung, *(of request)* Bewilligung, Gewährung, Erteilung, *(of right)* Verleihung, Konzession, *(sum granted)* Unterstützungssumme, [Kapital]zuschuß, finanzielle Hilfe, Subvention, *(university)* Stipendium, Ausbildungs-, Studienbeihilfe;
  in ~ nur urkundlich übertragbar;
  additional ~ nachträgliche Bewilligung, Nachbewilligung; **ancillary ~** *(Br.)* Bestätigung eines ausländischen Testaments; **annual ~** Jahreszuschuß; **block ~** zur freien Verfügung gewährter Zuschuß, Umstellungsbeihilfe; **capital ~** Zuschuß in Kapitalform, Kapitalzuschuß; **exceptional ~s** außerordentliche Zuwendung (Zuschüsse); **Exchequer Equalization º** *(Br.)* Ausgleichsleistungen an finanzschwache Gemeinden; **general ~** Mittelzuweisung an die Kommunen; **government[al] ~** öffentliche Subvention, Staatszuschuß; **maintenance ~** Unterhaltszuschuß, -beihilfe; **marriage ~** *(Br.)* Heiratsbeihilfe; **monetary ~** Geldbeihilfe, finanzieller Zuschuß; **office ~** Auflassung vom Amtswegen; **private land ~** Übertragung von öffentlichem Grundeigentum auf Privatpersonen; **public ~** Konzessions-, Lizenzerteilung; **rate deficiency ~s** *(Br.)* Ausgleichsleistungen an finanzschwache Gemeinden; **removal and lodging ~** *(Br.)* Umzugs- und Wohnungsbeihilfe; **specific ~** zweckgebundene Zuweisung, Zweckzuweisung; **state ~** staatlicher Zuschuß; **supplementary ~** Nachbewilligung; **training ~** Ausbildungszuschuß, -beihilfe;

~ of administration Anordnung der Nachlaßpflegschaft; **~ of administration de bonis non** Verwaltung bisher nicht erfaßter Nachlaßgegenstände; **~ of an advance** Vorschußbewilligung; **~s-in-aid** *(US)* Staats-, öffentliche Zuschüsse, Beihilfe, Subvention, *(Br.)* kommunale Finanzzuweisungen; **~ of a charter** Konzessionserteilung, -verleihung; **~ towards the cost of a university education** Zuschuß zum Universitätsstudium, Universitätszuschuß; **~ of credit** Kreditbewilligung; **~ by deed** urkundliche Übereignung; **~ of discharge** Entlastung des Gemeinschuldners, Befreiung von Konkursschulden; **~ of an easement** Einräumung einer Dienstbarkeit; **~ of land** Landbewilligung, -zuteilung; **~ of a lease** Pachtgewährung; **~ of letters of administration** Testamentvollstreckerbestellung; **~ of a licence** Lizenzgewährung; **~ of a loan** Darlehnsbewilligung; **~ of minerals** Bergwerksverleihung; **~ of money** Geldbewilligung; **~ of a patent** Patenterteilung; **~ of personal property** entgeltliche Vermögensübertragung; **~ of probate** Testamentsvollstreckerzeugnis; **~ of representation** Vertretungsnachweis; **~ of supply** *(parl.)* Steuerbewilligung; **~ to uses** Grundstücksauflassung;

~ (v.) (concede) gewähren, bewilligen, einräumen, zugeben, zugestehen, *(transfer)* übertragen, verleihen, formell überlassen;
  ~ additionally nachbewilligen; **~ administration** Nachlaßpflegschaft anordnen; **~ an advance** Vorschuß bewilligen; **~ aids** Beihilfen gewähren; **~ an allowance** Unterhaltszuschuß bewilligen; **~ an application without objection** Gesuch anstandslos bewilligen; **~ asylum** Asyl gewähren; **~ autonomy** Autonomie gewähren; **~ bargain and sell** Auflassungsgenehmigung erteilen; **~ a certificate** Attest ausstellen; **~ a charter (concession)** Konzession erteilen, Satzung verleihen, konzessionieren; **~ a credit** Kredit bewilligen; **~ and demise** Pachtbesitz einräumen; **~ a divorce** Scheidungsurteil verkünden, auf Scheidung erkennen; **~ an exemption** Steuerfreibetrag gewähren; **~ extension of time** Fristverlängerung zubilligen (gewähren); **~ s. o. facilities** jem. Erleichterungen gewähren; **~ a favo(u)r** Vergünstigung gewähren, Gunst erweisen; **~ and to freight let** Schiffscharter erteilen; **~ an injunction** einstweilige Verfügung erlassen; **~ interest** Zinsen gewähren (einräumen); **~ s. o. an interview** jem. ein Interview gewähren; **~ land** Land zuteilen; **~ a lease** als Pächter annehmen; **~ leave to appeal** Berufung zulassen; **~ a licence** Konzession (Lizenz) erteilen; **~ a loan** Darlehn geben; **~ a loan against securities** Wertpapiere lombardieren; **~ pardon** begnadigen; **~ a patent** Patent erteilen; **~ a pension** Pension bewilligen; **~ permission** Erlaubnis erteilen; **~ a petition** einem Antrag stattgeben, Gesuch genehmigen; **~ a privilege** Vorrecht einräumen; **~ a reduction** Nachlaß gewähren; **~ renewal of a draft** Wechsel prolongieren; **~ a request** einem Gesuch entsprechen (stattgeben); **~ a respite** stunden, Stundung gewähren, Frist einräumen, Zahlungsaufschub bewilligen; **~ in return** zum Ausgleich zur Verfügung stellen; **~ s. o. right** jem. ein Recht übertragen;
  to give s. o. a ~ of clemency jem. einen Gnadenerweis gewähren; **to lie in ~** nur urkundlich übertragbar sein; **to make a ~ to s. o.** jem. einen Zuschuß bewilligen; **to put in a claim for a ~** um die Bewilligung eines Zuschusses einkommen; **to receive a ~ of DM 200,-** Beihilfe von 200,- DM erhalten; **to receive a state ~** Staatszuschuß erhalten; **to withhold ~s** Finanzzuweisungen verweigern;
  ~-aided subventioniert, staatlich unterstützt, durch staatliche Zuschüsse unterstützt; **~-aided students** Stipendiaten; **~-back clause** *(licensing)* Rückübertragungsklausel; **~ formula** Unterstützungsformel; **~-making procedure** Zuschußverfahren; **~-paying authority** Ausbildungsförderungsstelle.

grantable *(to be conceded)* verleihbar, zu bewilligen, *(transferable)* übertragbar.

granted bewilligt, *(patent)* erteilt;
  to take s. th. for ~ für selbstverständlich halten; **to take a permission for ~** *(fam.)* mit einer Erlaubnis fest rechnen.

grantee Privilegierter, *(of charter)* Konzessionsinhaber, *(of sum granted)* Zuschußempfänger;
  ~ of an annuity Rentenempfänger, -berechtigter.

granting Zuteilung, Bewilligung, *(of charter)* Konzessions-, Lizenzerteilung;
  ~ of contracts Auftragsvergabe; **~ of a guarantee** Garantiegewährung; **~ of a lease** Pachteinräumung; **~ of a loan** Darlehnsgewährung, -bewilligung, Bereitstellung eines Kredits; **~ of a patent** Patenterteilung; **~ of a privilege** Einräumung eines Vorteils; **~ of renewals** Prolongationsgewährung; **~ of a right** Verleihung eines Rechtes, Rechtsverleihung; **~ of time** Fristbewilligung.

grantor Bewilligender, Verleiher [von Rechten], Zedent, *(US, of trust)* Stifter eines Treuhandverhältnisses;
~ **of a licence** Konzessionär; ~ **of power** Vollmachtgeber; ~ **of a trust** Treugeber;
~**s lien** Eigentümergrundschuld.

grapevine Weinstock, *(coll.)* Ente, Gerücht;
~ *(v.)* sich wie ein Lauffeuer verbreiten;
to have heard it on the ~ hinten herum gehört haben;
~ **telegraph** *(US, Australia)* lauffeuerartige Verbreitung, Flüsterpropaganda.

graph graphische Darstellung, Schaubild, Diagramm;
~ *(v.)* graphisch darstellen.

graphic graphisch, zeichnerisch, *(fig.)* anschaulich;
~ **art** graphische Darstellung, Grafik; ~ **design** Werbestil; ~ **formula** Konstruktionsformel; ~ **paper** Millimeterpapier; ~ **symbol** Schriftzeichen; ~ **writer** lebendiger Schriftsteller.

graphical representation graphische Darstellung.

graphologist, graphological expert Graphologe, Handschriftendeuter, Schriftsachverständiger.

graphology Graphologie.

grapple *(close hug in contest)* Handgemenge, *(mar.)* Enterhaken;
~ *(v.)* handgemein werden;
~ **with a difficulty** mit Schwierigkeiten kämpfen; ~ **with a problem** sich mit einem Problem auseinandersetzen.

grasp Reichweite, *(capability)* Verständnis, Fassungskraft, *(control)* Besitz, Herrschaft, Kontrolle, *(hold)* Griff;
~ *(v.)* verstehen, begreifen;
~ **an argument** Argument verstehen; ~ **a nettle** unangenehme Sache anfassen; ~ **an opportunity** Chance wahrnehmen; ~ **at a straw** nach einem Strohhalm greifen; **to be beyond s. one's** ~ jds. Fassungskraft übersteigen; **to have s. th. within one's** ~ etw. in Reichweite (Gewalt über etw.) haben; **to have a natural** ~ **for the theatrical side of an office** Auftrittsmöglichkeiten in einem Amt voll ausspielen; **to have a thorough** ~ **of a problem** Problem fest im Griff haben; **to have a good** ~ **of a subject** Fach gut beherrschen; **to have success within one's** ~ dem Erfolg zum Greifen nahe sein.

grass Gras, *(meadow)* Weideland, *(printer's, sl., Br.)* Aushilfsstellung;
~ *(v.)* *(inform the police, sl.)* denunzieren;
to be at ~ auf der Weide sein, *(fig.)* Ferien auf dem Lande machen; **to go to** ~ sich auf das Land zurückziehen; **to hear the** ~ **grow** das Gras wachsen hören; **not to let** ~ **grow under one's feet** keine langen Umstände machen, nicht lange zögern; **to send s. o. to** ~ j. abschieben; **to turn out animals to** ~ Vieh auf die Weide treiben.

grasshopper *(aeronautics)* Leicht-, Kleinflugzeug.

grassland Weideland, Wiese.

grassroots Wurzel, Quelle, *(US)* ländliche Gegend;
derived from the ~ aus dem Volke stammend;
~ *(a.)* volkstümlich, -verbunden;
~ **level** Parteibasis; ~ **political movement** volksverbundene politische Bewegung; ~ **rebellion** volkstümlicher Aufstand; ~ **support** Unterstützung durch die breite Masse; **to go down to** ~ **views** Meinung der breiten Masse des Volkes erforschen.

grateful letter Dankbrief.

gratification *(fee)* Honorar, *(remuneration)* Zuwendung, *(reward)* Lohn, Belohnung, *(satisfaction)* Befriedigung, Genugtuung, *(tip)* Trinkgeld.

gratify *(v.)* *(bribe)* bestechen, *(remunerate)* belohnen, vergüten;
~ **a child's thirst for knowledge** Wissensdrang eines Kindes befriedigen.

gratis gratis, ohne Entgelt, umsonst, unentgeltlich, frei;
to be admitted ~ freien Eintritt haben;
~ **copy** Freiexemplar.

gratitude Dankbarkeit, Erkenntlichkeit.

gratuitant Empfänger einer Zuwendung.

gratuities, no ~! Kein Trinkgeld!

gratuitous unentgeltlich, umsonst, gratis, frei, kostenlos, *(without consideration)* ohne Gegenleistung, *(without ground)* grundlos, unbegründet, willkürlich;
~ **advice** kostenloser Rat; ~ **allowance** Pension, Ruhegeld; ~ **article** Zugabe; ~ **assumption** willkürliche Annahme; ~ **bailee** unentgeltlicher Verwahrer; ~ **bailment** unentgeltliche Verwahrung; ~ **coinage** unentgeltliche Münzprägung; ~ **contract** unentgeltlicher Vertrag, einseitiger Vertrag; ~ **information** kostenlose Information; ~ **licensee** nicht gewerbsmäßiger Lizenznehmer; ~ **lie** grundlose Lüge; ~ **payment** Zahlung ohne Verpflichtung, unentgeltliche Zuwendung; ~ **service** kostenloser Kundendienst; ~ **suspicion** grundloser Verdacht; ~ **transfer** unentgeltliche Übertragung.

gratuitousness Unentgeltlichkeit.

gratuity *(bounty)* Abfindungssumme, *(money present)* Gratifikation, Zuwendung, [Sonder]vergütung, Geldgeschenk;
post-retirement ~ bei der Pensionierung gezahlte Abfindungssumme.

gratulation Beglückwünschung.

gravamen Beschwerde[grund].

grave Grab, letzte Ruhestätte, Begräbnisstätte;
common ~ Massengrab; **the pauper's** ~ Massen-, Armengrab; **to have one foot in the** ~ mit einem Fuß im Grab stehen;
~ *(a.)* ernst, schwerwiegend, erheblich;
~ **clothes** Toten-, Grabgewand; ~ **digger** Totengräber; ~ **news** schwerwiegende Nachrichten; ~ **situation** ernste Lage.

gravel path Kiesweg.

graven image Götzenbild.

graveside, to follow s. o. to the j. auf seinem letzten Gang begleiten.

gravestone Grabstein.

graveyard Gottesacker, Friedhof;
~ **insurance** unredlich erworbene Todesfallversicherung; ~ **shift** *(US sl.)* zweite Nachtschicht.

graving dock Trockendock.

gravitate *(v.)* **towards a city** von der Großstadt angelockt werden.

gravitational | **field** Schwerkraftfeld; ~ **force** Gravitationskraft.

gravity Feierlichkeit, Würde;
~ **of an appearance** gesetztes Auftreten; ~ **of an offence** Schwere eines Vergehens; ~ **of the international situation** Ernst der internationalen Lage; ~ **of a testimony** Gewicht einer Zeugenaussage.

gravure Gravur, Tiefdruck.

gravy *(bribe, sl.)* Bestechung, Schiebung;
~ **train** *(US sl.)* Futterkrippe, Druckposten; **to fall off the** ~ **train** *(US)* seinen Druckposten verlieren.

gray | **market** *(US)* grauer Markt; ~ **market operator** *(US)* Spekulant auf dem grauen Markt; ~ **matter** *(fig.)* Grütze, Verstand; ~ **prospects** trübe Aussichten.

graze Weiden, *(mil.)* Streifschuß;
~ *(v.)* weiden [lassen].

grazing | **land** Weideland; ~ **rights** Weiderechte.

grease Schmiermittel, *(bribe money, sl.)* Schmiergelder;
~ *(v.)* **s. one's palm** j. bestechen (schmieren), jem. Schmiergelder zahlen; ~ **the right palms** die richtigen Leute schmieren; ~ **the wheels** etw. durch Schmiergelder in Schwung bringen;
~ **monkey** *(US sl.)* Auto-, Flugzeugmechaniker; ~ **paint** Schminke; ~ **pencil** Fettstift; ~-**proof paper** fettdichtes Papier.

great *(Oxford)* Schlußexamen für den B. A.;
the ~ Prominente, Prominenz;
to be born ~ *(Br.)* in Großbritannien geboren sein; **to be a** ~ **one for spending money** groß im Geldausgeben sein; **to become** ~ *(Br.)* Britische Staatsangehörigkeit erlangen;
~ *(a.)* groß, wichtig, bedeutend, *(social life)* hochstehend;
~ **at** geschickt in;
~ **achievement** Großtat; **to live to a** ~ **age** hohes Alter erreichen; ~ **attraction** Hauptattraktion; ~ **cattle** Großvieh; ~ **depression** Weltwirtschaftskrise; ~ **fortune** großes Vermögen; ~ **go** *(Cambridge, sl.)* Schlußexamen für den B. A.; ~ **ignorance of grammar** große grammatische Lücken; ~ **issues** wichtige Probleme; ~ **landowner** Großgrundbesitzer; ~ **ledger** *(Br.)* Staatsschuldbuch; ~ **majority** erhebliche (überwiegende) Mehrheit; ~ **mogul** wichtige Persönlichkeit; ♔ **Powers** Großmächte; ~ **primer** *(print.)* anderthalb Cicero; ♔ **Seal** *(Br.)* Staatssiegel; **to have a** ~ **time** sich glänzend amüsieren; ♔ **Wall** Chinesische Mauer; ♔ **War** Erster Weltkrieg; ♔ **White Way** *(US)* New Yorker Theaterviertel; ~ **world** die oberen Zehntausend, gute Gesellschaft.

Greater London Council Verwaltungsbehörde von Großlondon.

greatness Prominenz, gesellschaftlich hoher Rang;
to inherit ~ *(Br.)* Britische Staatsangehörigkeit erben; **to register for** ~ *(Br.)* Britische Staatsangehörigkeit beantragen.

greed Habgier, Habsucht;
~ **of gain (for profits)** Gewinnstreben, -sucht.

greedy of gain gewinnsüchtig, profitgierig.

Greek, to be ~ **to s. o.** böhmische Dörfer für j. sein;
~ **gift** Danaergeschenk; ~ **Kalend** nie kommende Zeit.

green grün, *(concrete)* unabgebunden, *(inexperienced)* unerfahren, unreif;
village ~ Dorfanger;
~ **with envy** blaß vor Neid;
to be still ~ **at one's job** noch keine Berufserfahrung haben; **to keep s. one's memory** ~ jds. Gedächtnis auffrischen; **to make o.** ~ **with jealousy** j. vor Neid erblassen lassen;

~ belt Grüngürtel, -zone, -anlagen; **~ card** *(motorist)* grüne Karte, *(university, US)* Aufenthaltsgenehmigung; **~ Christmas** schneefreies Weihnachten; **~ cloth** Spieltisch; **~ currency** *(EC)* grüne Dollarwährung; **~-eyed monster** Eifersucht; **~ fingers** *(coll.)* glückliche Hand; **to have ~ fingers** *(coll.)* ein Händchen für Blumen haben; **~ food** *(cattle)* Grünfutter, *(man)* Gemüsekost; **~ label** *(Br.)* Zolletikett für Postpakete; **~-label service** *(Br.)* Postversand zollpflichtiger Artikel; **~ light** *(traffic regulations)* grünes Licht, *(fig.)* Zustimmung; **to give s. o. the ~ light** jem. grünes Licht geben; **~ money** *(EC)* Landwirtschaftsdollar; **~ old age** rüstiges Alter; **to live to a ~ old age** hohes Alter erreichen; **~ paper** *(Br.)* Informationsbericht, Arbeits- und Diskussionsunterlagen; **~ pound** *(EC)* grünes Pfund; **~ stamp** *(US)* Rabattmarke; **~ table** Spieltisch; **in the ~ tree** in guten Verhältnissen; **~ wedge** regionaler Grünbereich.

greenback *(US)* Banknote, Papiergeld [in den USA];
~ goods *(US sl.)* gefälschte Banknoten; **~ goods dealer** *(US sl.)* Banknotenfälscher.

greener *(sl.)* unerfahrener Ausländer.

greengrocer Obst- und Gemüsehändler.

greengrocery Obst- und Gemüsehandlung.

greenhorn *(fig.)* Grünschnabel.

greenhouse Treib-, Gewächshaus, *(airplane, sl.)* Vollsichtkanzel.

greenroom *(fig.)* Theaterklatsch.

Greenwich Mean Time Greenwicher Normalzeit.

greeting Anrede, Begrüßung;
~s Grüße, Empfehlungen;
~s card Glückwunschkarte; **~s telegram** Glückwunschtelegramm.

greffier Registrator, *(Channel Islands)* Notar.

grenade Handgranate.

grey|area Gebiet mit erhöhter Arbeitslosigkeit, unklares Gebiet, Grauzone; **~ book** *(pol.)* Graubuch; **~ market** grauer Markt; **~ matter** *(Br.)* Verstand, Grütze.

greyhound *(mar., sl.)* Ozeandampfer.

grid Gitter, Rost, *(electricity)* Verbund-, Überlandnetz, *(on maps)* Planquadrat, *(roads)* Straßennetz;
directional ~ Zielvorstellung, regionales Wachstum; **~ line** Rasterlinie; **~ reference** Planquadratangabe.

gridded map Gitternetzkarte.

gridiron Bratrost, *(railway)* Netzwerk, *(theater)* Schnürboden.

grief Sorge, Kummer, Gram;
to bring to ~ zugrunderichten; **to come to ~** zu Schaden kommen; **to redress a ~** Mißstand abstellen.

grievance Mißstand, Beschwerde[grund];
~ of the workers *(US)* Arbeitsstreitigkeiten;
to make a ~ of s. th. etw. zum Gegenstand einer Beschwerde machen; **to redress a ~** einer Beschwerde abhelfen; **to state one's ~** Beschwerde führen;
~ arbitration Schlichtungsverfahren in Beschwerdesachen; **~ committee** Schlichtungs-, Beschwerdeausschuß; **~ procedure** Schlichtungsverfahren.

grievous|bodily harm schwere Körperverletzung; **~ railway accident** schwerer Eisenbahnunfall; **~ taxes** harte Steuern.

grifter *(US sl.)* Schaubudenbesitzer.

grill Grill;
~ (v.) grillen, braten;
~ a criminal *(US sl.)* Verbrecher einem strengen Kreuzverhör unterwerfen.

grille Tür-, Fenstergitter, *(window)* Schalteröffnung, Sprechgitter.

grillroom Grillraum.

grim|determination unbeugsame Entschlossenheit; **~ humo(u)r** Galgenhumor; **to do s. th. out of ~ necessity** sich zu etw. in äußerster Not verstehen; **~ truth** grausame Wahrheit.

grime of a manufacturing town Schmutz einer Industriestadt.

grind *(steady hard work)* Paukerei, Büffelei, *(hardworking student, US sl.)* Streber, Büffler;
~ (v.) schinden, unterdrücken, *(coll.)* büffeln, pauken;
~ for an examination für ein Examen büffeln; **~ the faces of the poor** die Armen aussaugen; **~ to a halt** knirschend zum Stillstand kommen; **~ s. th. into s. one's head** jem. etw. eintrichtern; **~ it out** *(fam.)* etw. mühsam hochbringen; **~ down with taxes** übermäßig besteuern; **~ small** Kleinarbeit leisten; **~ away at one's studies** hart für die Universität arbeiten; **~ the wind** *(Br.)* in der Tretmühle sein;
to be back at the old ~ wieder in seiner Tretmühle sein;
~ house *(theater)* durchgehend geöffnetes Theater; **~ show** *(sl.)* Dauervorstellung.

grinder *(coach, Br., sl.)* Einpauker, Repetitor, *(sweater of workers)* Leuteschinder, Ausbeuter.

grinding poverty drückende Armut.

grindstone Schleifstein;
to hold s. one's nose to the ~ j. schwer arbeiten lassen, j. schinden.

grip Griff, Halt, *(comprehension)* Verständnis, Fassungskraft, *(domination)* Gewalt, Herrschaft, *(US, theater)* Kulissenschieber, *(valise)* Reisehandtasche;
in the ~ of vice in den Klauen des Lasters;
choking ~ Würgegriff;
~ on the economy Konjunkturbeherrschung; **~ on the market** Marktbeherrschung; **~ of a play on the audience** packende Wirkung eines Theaterstücks; **~ of the wheels** Greifen der Räder;
~ (v.) *(brakes)* greifen, fassen;
~ the attention of the audience seine Zuhörer packen;
to be at ~s with s. o. sich mit jem. auseinandersetzen; **to be at ~s with the enemy** mit dem Feind im Kampf stehen; **to establish a ~ on one's own party** seine Partei in den Griff bekommen; **to get to ~s with a problem** mit einem Problem fertig werden; **to have a good ~ on an audience** seine Zuhörer zu fesseln verstehen; **to have a ~ on the economy** Konjunktur fest in den Griff bekommen; **to have a good ~ of a problem** Problem schnell erfassen; **to have a good ~ of the situation** Situation voll beherrschen; **to take a ~ on (of) o. s.** sich fassen (beruhigen); **to take a ~ on s. o.** auf j. Einfluß ausüben;
~ brake Handbremse; **~ car** *(US)* Straßenbahnwagen.

gripe Gewalt, Macht, *(distress)* Elend, Not, Qual, *(techn.)* Kupplung, *(US sl.)* Meckerei, Murren;
in the ~ of a tyrant in der Gewalt eines Tyrannen;
~s *(coll.)* Kolik;
~ of poverty Zwang (Not) der Armut;
~ (v.) ergreifen, festhalten;
~ about *(US sl.)* meckern.

gripping story spannende (packende) Geschichte.

gripsack *(US coll.)* Handtasche, Reisetasche.

grist *(US coll.)* Menge;
to bring ~ to the mill Wasser auf jds. Mühle sein, *(yield)* einträglich sein, Profit bringen.

grit, true *(sl.)* Mumm;
~ in the machinery Sand im Getriebe.

groan *(v.)* **down** *(audience)* niederbrüllen.

groans of disapproval Mißfallensäußerungen.

grocer Lebensmittel-, Gemischt-, Kolonialwarenhändler;
~'s shop *(Br.)* **(store, US)** Lebensmittelgeschäft, Kolonialwarenhandlung; **~'s wares** Kolonialwaren.

groceries Gemischt-, Kolonialwaren, Lebensmittel.

grocery *(US)* Kolonialwarengeschäft, Gemischtwarengeschäft, -handlung;
~ business (trade) Kolonialwarenhandel; **~ outlet (store)** *(US)* Lebensmittelgeschäft, Gemischtwarenhandlung, Kolonialwarenhandlung, Kramladen; **~ shopping** Lebensmitteleinkauf; **to go ~ shopping** Lebensmittel einkaufen.

groceteria *(US)* Selbstbedienungsladen.

grog-shop verbotene Schnapsbrennerei.

groom Diener, Stallknecht;
~ (v.) a candidate for office *(US)* Kandidaten lancieren.

groove Furche, Graben, *(fig.)* Routine, Schablone, *(print.)* Signatur;
in the ~ *(fig.)* im richtigen Fahrwasser;
to fall into a ~ zur Routine werden; **to get into a ~** Schablonenmensch werden; **to travel in the same ~** im gewohnten Gleise bleiben.

grooving Falzung.

groovy *(fig.)* routinemäßig, schablonenhaft.

grope *(v.)* **in the dark** *(fig.)* im Dunkeln tappen.

gross Hauptteil, Gesamtheit, Ganzes, Gros, *(advertising)* Bruttotarifpreis, *(twelve dozen)* Gros;
by the ~ massenweise, in Bausch und Bogen, *(at wholesale)* im Großhandel; **in [the] ~** im ganzen, in Bausch und Bogen, brutto, *(law)* an der Person haftend;
box-office ~ Bruttokasseneinnahme;
~ (v.) brutto erbringen, Bruttoertrag abwerfen;
~ up Bruttogewinn erzielen, brutto erbringen, Bruttoertrag abwerfen;
to buy by [the] ~ in Bausch und Bogen kaufen; **to sell in the ~** engros verkaufen; **to weigh in the ~** brutto wiegen;
~ (a.) brutto, gesamt, total, *(coarse)* roh, unfein, ungebildet, vulgär, *(obscene)* unanständig, schmutzig;
~ abuse grober Mißbrauch; **~ adventure** Bodmereidarlehen; **~ amount** Roh-, Bruttobetrag; **~ annual value** Bruttomietwert; **~ assets** Roh-, Bruttovermögen; **~ average** Großhavarie; **~ aver-**

age hourly earnings Bruttodurchschnittsverdienst; ~ **average weekly earnings** durchschnittlicher Wochenverdienst; ~ **billings** Bruttofakturierungen; ~ **book value** Bruttobuchwert, Buchwert vor Abschreibungen; ~ **breach of duty** schwere Pflichtverletzung; ~ **carelessness** grobe Fahrlässigkeit; ~ **carrying capacity** Bruttotragfähigkeit; ~ **commission** Bruttoprovision; ~ **compensation** Bruttoentschädigung, Bruttoverdienst; ~ **debt** Gesamtschulden; ~ **delivery weight** Ladegewicht eines Fahrzeugs; ~ **deposits** gesamte Einlagen, Bruttoeinlagen, Einlagenbestand; ~ **dividend** Bruttodividende; ~ **domestic expenditures** Gesamtaufwand im Inland; ~ **domestic investment** gesamte Inlandsinvestitionen, Bruttoinlandsinvestitionen; ~ **domestic product** *(GDP)* Bruttosozialprodukt zu Marktpreisen; ~ **domestic product growth** Zunahme des Bruttoinlandsprodukts; ~ **earnings** Bruttoverdienst, -gewinn, -einnahmen, -einkommen; ~ **earnings figure** Bruttoertragsziffer; ~ **effect** *(machine)* Totalleistung; ~ **equivalent** Bruttogegenwert; ~ **error** schwerer Fehler; ~ **estate** Bruttovermögen, -nachlaß; ~ **estimated rental** *(house)* Bruttoertragswert; ~ **fault** grobe Fahrlässigkeit; ~ **fixed capital formation** Bruttoanlagenkapitalbildung; ~ **freight** Bruttofracht, ganze Fracht; ~ **hourly earnings (wages)** Bruttostundenverdienst; ~ **inadequacy** unzumutbar niedrige Entschädigung; ~ **income** Bruttoeinkommen, Roh-, Gesamteinkommen; **adjusted** ~ **income** *(US)* steuerpflichtiges Roheinkommen; ~ **income from wages and salaries** Bruttoeinkommen aus unselbständiger Arbeit; ~ **income tax** gesamt gezahlte Einkommensteuer; ~ **injury** grobes Unrecht; ~ **injustice** schreiende Ungerechtigkeit; ~ **insult** grobe Beleidigung; ~ **interest** Bruttozinsen; ~ **investment in fixed assets** Bruttoanlageninvestition; ~ **language** vulgäre Sprache; ~ **liability** *(US)* Bruttoverbindlichkeit; ~ **load** Bruttobelastung, Rohlast; ~ **loss** Rohverlust, Bruttoverlust, Bruttoverdienstausfall; ~ **margin** Betriebs-, Bruttohandelsspanne, Bruttomarge; ~ **merchandising margin** Bruttospanne ohne Skontoabzug; **variable** ~ **margin** Deckungsbeitrag; ~ **markup** Bruttogewinnspanne; ~ **misconduct** schwere Verfehlung; ~ **mistake** grober Fehler; ~ **money pool** Gewinnverteilungskartell.

gross national | **debt** National-, Staatsschuld; ~ **expenditure** Bruttosozialaufwand; ~ **expenditure at factor cost** Bruttosozialaufwand zu Faktorkosten; ~ **expenditure at market prices** Bruttosozialaufwand zu Marktpreisen; ~ **income** Brutto[volks]einkommen; ~ **product (GNP)** Bruttosozialprodukt; ~ **product at factor cost** Bruttosozialprodukt zu Faktorkosten; ~ **product gap** Vollbeschäftigungslücke; ~ **product key** Bruttosozialproduktschlüssel; ~ **product recovery** Bruttosozialproduktanstieg.

gross | **negligence** grobe Fahrlässigkeit; ~ **overcharge** flagrante Übervorteilung; ~ **pay** Bruttolohn; ~ **premium** Bruttoprämie; ~ **price** Brutto-, Rohpreis; ~ **principle** Bruttoprinzip; ~ **proceeds** Brutto-, Rohertrag; ~ **procedure** Rohertrag.

gross profit Roh-, Bruttogewinn;
~ **on sales** Brutto-, Warenrohgewinn;
~ **analysis** Rohgewinnanalyse; ~ **extra** Rohgewinnaufschlag; ~ **figures** Bruttogewinnziffern; ~ **margin** Bruttogewinnmarge; ~ **method** *(inventory)* Vorratbewertung mit Hilfe des Rohgewinns; ~ **rate** Rohgewinnsatz; ~ **ratio** Bruttogewinnverhältnis.

gross | **receipts** Bruttoertrag, Brutto-, Roheinnahmen; ~ **receivables** Bruttoforderungen, ~ **rent** Bruttopacht, -mietertrag; ~ **rental** Rohertrag, Bruttomiete, *(distributor)* Bruttoverleiheinnahmen; ~ **revenue** Roheinkünfte, Bruttoertrag; ~ **salary** Bruttogehalt; ~ **sales** Bruttowarenumsatz, -absatz; ~ **saving and investment accounts** Vermögensänderung der volkswirtschaftlichen Gesamtrechnung; ~ **savings** Bruttoersparnisse; ~ **sum** Gesamtsumme; ~ **surplus** Bruttoüberschuß, Rohüberschuß; ~ **terms** Laden und Löschen zu Lasten des Schiffes; ~ **ton** Bruttoregistertonne; ~ **ton mile** Bruttomeilentonne; ~ **tonnage** Bruttotonnage, -tonnengehalt; ~ **total** Bruttobestand; ~ **trading profit** Warenrohgewinn, Bruttogeschäftsgewinn; ~ **trading surplus** Bruttoreingewinn; ~ **turnover** Bruttoumsatz; ~ **value** Bruttowert; ~ **vegetation** üppige Vegetation; ~ **wage** Bruttolohn; ~ **weekly earnings** Bruttowochenverdienst; ~ **weight** Roh-, Bruttogewicht; ~ **working capital** Umlaufvermögen; ~ **yield** Bruttoertrag, *(stocks)* Bruttorendite.

grossing up Bruttoberechnung;
~ **up computation** Bruttoabrechnung.

grotesque *(print.)* Groteskschriften.

ground *(building site)* Bauplatz, -stelle, *(el.)* Erdanschluß, Erde, *(land)* Gelände, [Erd]boden, *(opinion)* Meinung, Ansicht, Haltung, Standpunkt, *(person's property in land)* Grund und Boden, Grundbesitz, -stück, *(reason)* [Beweg]grund, Ursache, *(region)* Gebiet, Gegend, *(theater)* Parterre;

above ~ oberirdisch, über Tage, *(fig.)* am Leben; **below** ~ unter Tage, begraben; **burnt to the** ~ bis zu den Grundmauern niedergebrannt; **down to the** ~ in jeder Weise vollständig; **from the** ~ **up** *(US)* ganz und gar, durch und durch; **on the** ~ mit der Begründung; **on the** ~ **that** aus dem Grunde daß; **on these** ~s aus diesen Gründen; **on German** ~ auf deutschem Gebiet; **on** ~s **of expediency** aus Zweckmäßigkeitsgründen; **on legal** ~s aus rechtlichen Gründen; **on personal** ~s aus persönlichen Gründen (Privatrücksichten); **on religious** ~s aus religiösen Gründen;

~s Ländereien, Felder, Acker, *(city)* städtische Anlagen, Garten-, Parkanlagen;

cogent ~ zwingender Grund; **common** ~ gemeinsame Basis, volle Übereinstimmung; **extensive** ~s umfangreiche Ländereien; **fishing** ~s Fischereigebiet, -distrikt; **football** ~ Fußballplatz; **forbidden** ~ nicht zugelassenes Thema; **hunting** ~ Jagdgebiet; **leased** ~ Pachtland; **reasonable** ~ stichhaltiger Grund; **recreation** ~ Kinderspielplatz, Erholungsgelände; **shooting** ~ Jagdrevier; **stamping** ~ Tummelplatz; **valid** ~s stichhaltige Gründe;

~ **of action** Klagegrund; ~s **for annulments** Anfechtungsgründe, *(judgment)* Aufhebungsgründe; ~s **of appeal** Berufungsgründe; ~s **for an application** Antragsbegründung; ~s **of attachment** Arrestgründe; ~ **of complaint** Beschwerdegrund; ~s **for a decision** Entscheidungsgründe; ~ **for dissolution** Auflösungsgründe; ~s **for divorce** Ehescheidungsgrund; ~s **for extradition** Auslieferungsgründe; ~s **for a judgment** Urteilsgründe; ~s **for litigation** Prozeßmaterial; ~s **of a mine** Grubenfeld; ~s **for giving notice** Kündigungsgrund; ~ **of nullity** Anfechtungsgrund; ~ **of opposition** *(patent law)* Einspruchsbegründung; **slippery** ~ **of politics** glattes Parkett der Politik; ~s **for removal** Entlassungsgrund; ~s **of rescission** Anfechtungsgründe; **sheer** ~s **of time** reiner Zeitmangel; ~ **for winding up** Liquidationsgrund;

~ *(v.)* gründen, bauen, errichten, *(airplane)* Startverbot erteilen, *(el.)* erden, *(opinion)* basieren, *(interest rates)* Tiefpunkt erreichen, *(ship)* auf Grund laufen, *(teacher)* in den Grundlagen unterrichten, Grundunterricht erteilen;

~ **the national airline** Linienfluggesellschaft lahmsetzen; ~ **an airplane** einem Flugzeug Startverbot erteilen; ~ **one's arguments on facts** seine Beweisführung auf Tatsachen stützen; ~ **a pupil in French** einem Schüler die Grundbegriffe im Französischen beibringen;

to act upon good ~s aus wohlüberlegten Gründen handeln; **to be on sure** ~ sich auf sicherem Boden bewegen; **to break the** ~ Absatzmarkt öffnen; **to break fresh** ~ Thema zum erstenmal behandeln, Neuland betreten; **to break new** ~ Neuland gewinnen; **to break into new high** ~ neue Höchstkurse erreichen; **to burn down to the** ~ durch Brand völlig zerstört werden; **to change one's** ~ seine Meinung ändern; **to cover a great deal (a lot) of** ~ gut vorankommen; **to cover much new** ~ große Mengen Neues zutage bringen; **to cut the** ~ **from under s. one's feet** jds. Argumente vorwegnehmen, jem. das Wasser abgraben; **to dash s. one's hopes to the** ~ *(fam.)* jds. Hoffnungen ein jähes Ende bereiten; **to dismiss for want of sufficient** ~s als unbegründet zurückweisen; **to establish** ~ Gründe vorbringen; **to establish a statutory** ~ **of opposition** *(tenant)* gesetzlich begründeten Widerspruch gegen eine Kündigung einlegen; **to excuse o. s. on the** ~s **of illness** sich mit Krankheit entschuldigen; **to fall to the** ~ *(plan)* mißlingen, scheitern; **to fall on fertile** ~ auf fruchtbaren Boden fallen; **to find common** ~ **for negotiations** gemeinsamen Boden für Verhandlungen (gemeinsame Verhandlungsgrundlage) finden; **to gain** ~ an Boden gewinnen, vorwärtskommen; **to get off the** ~ erfolgreichen Anfang machen; **to have extensive** ~s von großen Ländereien umgeben sein; **to have good** ~s gute Gründe haben; **to have [no]** ~s **for complaint** [keinen] Grund zur Beschwerde haben; **to hold one's** ~ *(prices)* sich behaupten (halten); **to lose** ~ an Boden verlieren; **to keep one's** ~ seinen Anspruch behaupten; **to maintain one's** ~ standhalten; **to make up for lost** ~ verlorenen Boden wiedergewinnen; **to move into new high** ~ neue Höchstkurse erreichen; **to push the market into new high** ~ Kurse zu neuem Höchststand bringen; **to shift one's** ~ seinen Standpunkt (seine Meinung) ändern, anders argumentieren; **to state the** ~ **of an appeal** *(taxation)* Steuerwiderspruch begründen; **to strike** ~ *(ship)* auflaufen auf den Grund; **to suit s. o. down to the** ~ j. hundertprozentig befriedigen, jem. voll in seinen Kram passen; **to till the** ~ Boden bewirtschaften; **to touch** ~ *(ship)* sinken, *(fig.)* zur Sache kommen; **to tread on forbidden** ~ verbotenes Thema berühren;

~ **alert** *(mil., airplane)* Startbereitschaft; ~ **annual** Jahrespacht; ~-**attack fighter** Erdkampfflugzeug; **to perform** ~-**breaking**

ceremonies Grundsteinlegung vornehmen; ~ **bridge** Knüppeldamm; ~ **clearance** *(airplane)* Bodenabstand; ~ **coat** Grundanstrich; ~ **colo(u)r** Grundfarbe; ~ **conditions** Geländeverhältnisse; ~ **connection** *(el.)* Erdung; ~ **control** Radarlandung; ~-**controlled approach** Radarblindlandung; ~ **crew** *(aerodrome)* Bodenpersonal; ~ **facilities** *(aerodrome)* Bodenanlagen.

ground floor Erd-, Untergeschoß, Parterre, *(US, price of shares)* Aktienvorzugspreise eines neugegründeten Unternehmens;
on the ~ *(house)* unten;
raised ~ Hochparterre;
to be in on the ~ von Anfang an dabei sein, Gründeranteil besitzen; **to get (be let) in on the ~** sich zu den Gründerbedingungen beteiligen, Gründeranteil erhalten, *(negotiations)* begünstigte Ausgangsposition haben; **to let in on the ~** Gründerbedingungen gewähren; **to live on the ~** zu ebener Erde (Parterre) wohnen;
~ **price** Ausverkaufspreis.

ground|fog Bodennebel; ~ **forces** Bodentruppen, Landstreitkräfte; ~ **game** *(Br.)* Niederwild; ~ **handling time** Abfertigungszeit; ~ **landlord** Grundeigentümer, Verpächter; ~ **law** Grundgesetz; ~ **lease** Grundstückspacht[vertrag], Erbbaurecht; ~ **level** *(house)* Bodenhöhe, Normal-, Erdgeschoßhöhe; **at ~ level** zu ebener Erde; ~ **lighting** Bodenbeleuchtung; ~-**to-air missile** Boden-Luftrakete; ~ **plan** Lage-, Gebäude-, Bau-, Grundplan, Grundriß; ~ **radar** Radarerdstation; ~ **rent** Grundabgabe, Reallast, Erbpachtzins; ~ **rent receipt** Pachtzinsquittung; **to break the ~ rules** gegen die elementarsten Bestimmungen verstoßen; ~ **rule** Grundregel; ~ **school** Spezialschule für Piloten; ~ **sheet** *(mil.)* Zeltbahn; ~ **speed** *(airplane)* Geschwindigkeit über Grund; ~ **staff** Bodenpersonal; ~ **station** Bodenstation; ~ **troops** *(mil.)* Bodentruppen, -verbände; ~ **warfare** Erdkrieg; ~ **water** Grundwasser; ~ **ways** *(mar.)* Ablaufbahn [beim Stapellauf].

groundage *(Br.)* Hafengebühr, Ankergeld.

grounded *(el.)* geerdet;
~ **down by taxation** übermäßig besteuert;
to be ~ in verankert sein in, *(airplane)* am Abflug verhindert sein; **to be well ~ in s. th.** wohlfundierte Kenntnisse von etw. haben; **to be ~ by fog** am Start durch Nebel verhindert sein; **to have been ~** *(pilot)* unter Flugverbot stehen;
well-~ rumo(u)r begründetes Gerücht; **well-~ theory** gut begründete Theorie.

grounding Fundament, Unterbau, *(teaching)* Anfangs-, Grundunterricht, Einführung;
good ~ *(fig.)* gute Unterlage;
~ **in economics** volkswirtschaftliche Grundkenntnisse; **basic ~ in marketing** Grundbegriffe der Absatzwirtschaft;
to have a good ~ in English über solide Kenntnisse in der englischen Sprache verfügen.

groundless|rumo(u)r grundloses Gerücht; ~ **suspicion** grundloser Verdacht.

groundman Erdarbeiter.

groundplot Bauplatz, -land, -grundstück.

groundwork Unter-, Grundlage.

group Gruppe, Klasse, *(US, airplane)* Geschwader, *(board of directors)* Ressort, *(business concern)* Konzern, *(ethnology)* Völkergruppe, *(mil.)* Verband, [Kampf]gruppe, *(parl.)* Fraktion, *(railway transport)* Sammelladung;
advisory ~ Beratergruppe; **age ~** Altersklasse, -gruppe; **blood ~** Blutgruppe; **breakaway ~** abgespaltene Gruppe; **buying ~** Einkaufsverband; **community ~** Gruppengemeinschaft; **consolidated ~** Konzerngruppe; **guerilla ~** Terroristen-, Partisanengruppe; **literary ~** literarischer Zirkel; **low price ~** niedrige Preisgruppe; **multiproduct ~** Konzern mit breitgestreutem Produktionsprogramm; **noncompeting ~** nicht konkurrierende Gruppe; **occupational ~** Berufsgruppe; **parliamentary ~** Fraktion; **political ~** politische Gruppe; **pressure ~** Interessen-, Machtgruppe; **salary ~** Gehaltsgruppe; **selling ~** Verkaufsverband; **sponsoring ~** Gruppe von Geldgebern; **standing ~ (UNO)** ständige Gruppe; **study ~** Studiengruppe, Arbeitsausschuß, -gemeinschaft; **tax ~** Steuerklasse; **twilight ~s** zwielichtige Gruppen; **wholesale-sponsored ~** vom Großhandel begünstigte Gruppe; **working ~** Arbeitsgruppe;
~ **of accounts** Kontengruppe; ~ **of actions** Gesamtheit der Maßnahmen; ~ **of banks** Bankenkonsortium, -gruppe; ~ **of brokers** Maklergruppe; ~ **of buildings** Gebäudekomplex; ~ **of buyers** Käuferkonsortium, -gruppe; ~ **for the common cause of ...** Förderkreis für ...; ~ **of companies** Konzern, Firmen-, Unternehmensgruppe; **well-balanced integrated ~ of complementary companies** wohlausgewogener Konzern mit einem breiten Sortiment integrierter Gesellschaften; **affiliate ~ of a**

corporation Konzerngruppe; ~ **of countries comprised** Länderkomplex; ~ **of dissidents** Dissidentengruppe; ~ **of figures** Zahlenkolonne; ~ **of functions** Funktionengruppe; ~ **of houses** Häuserkomplex; ~ **of individuals** Personengruppe; ~ **of industry** Industriezweig, Branche; ~ **of questions** Fragenkomplex; ~ **of sidings** Gleisanordnung; ~ **of solicitors** *(advertising)* Werbekontrolle; ~ **of ten** *(central banks)* Zehnerklub; ~ **of workmen** Arbeitergruppe;
~ **(v.)** [sich] gruppieren, anordnen, in Gruppen einteilen, klassifizieren;
to arrange articles in ~s paragraphenweise (in Paragraphen) zusammenstellen; **to bracket together in a ~** in einem Konzern zusammenfassen;
~ **accommodation** Gruppenanpassung; ~ **accounts** Konzernabschluß, -buchführung; ~ **accountant** Konzernbuchhalter; ~ **activities** Konzerngeschäfte, -tätigkeit; ~ **advertising** Gemeinschaftswerbung; ~ **annuity** *(US)* Gemeinschaftsrente; ~ **annuity insurance** kollektive Leibrentenversicherung; ~ **annuity pension plan** Gruppenrentenversicherungssystem; ~ **ascendancy** *(sociology)* Gruppenüberlegenheit; ~ **assets** Konzernvermögen; ~ **internal audit** konzerneigene Revision; ~ **balance sheet** Konzernbilanz; ~ **balance sheet total** Konzernbilanzsumme; ~ **banking** *(US)* Filialbankwesen, Bankgruppensystem; ~ **behavio(u)r** Massenverhalten; ~ **board** Konzernvorstand; ~ **bonus** Gruppenprämie; ~ **bonus plan** kollektives Gruppenprämiensystem; ~ **borrowing** Konzernkredite; ~ **break** *(el.)* Gruppenschalter; ~ **buyers** Gemeinschaftskäufer; ~ **buying** Sammeleinkauf; ~ **cash manager** Gelddisponent eines Konzerns; ~ **chairman** Konzernchef; ~ **charter rate** Reisegesellschaftstarif; ~ **cohesiveness** Gruppenkohäsion; ~ **commander** *(mil.)* Gruppenkommandeur; ~ **comparison** *(statistics)* Gruppenvergleich; ~ **compensation** Gruppenlohn; ~ **contribution** Gruppen-, Ressortbeitrag; ~ **creditor insurance** *(banking)* Kollektivlebensversicherung für Darlehensnehmer ungedeckter Kleinkredite; ~ **dealings** Konzerntransaktionen, -umsätze; ~ **decision** Gruppenentscheidung; ~ **demand** Konzernbedarf; ~ **depreciation** Gruppenabschreibung; ~ **discount** *(advertising)* Mengenrabatt bei Belegen mehrerer Zeitungen; ~ **discussion** Gruppendiskussion; ~ **dynamics** Gruppendynamik; ~ **executive** Gruppenleiter, leitender Konzernangestellter; ~ **factor** *(statistics)* Gruppenfaktor; ~ **financial director** Konzernfinanzchef; ~ **financial statement** Konzernbilanz; ~ **financing** Gemeinschaftsfinanzierung; ~**'s own funds** Konzerneigenmittel; ~ **incentive** Gruppenakkord; ~ **income** Konzernausschüttungen; ~ **index** Gruppenindex; ~ **instruction** Gemeinschaftsunterricht; ~ **insurance** Kollektiv-, Gruppen-, Betriebs-, Gemeinschaftsversicherung; ~ **contributory ~ insurance** Gruppenversicherung mit Beitragsleistung der Beteiligten; ~ **life insurance** Gruppenrisikoversicherung für vorzeitige Todesfälle, Kollektivlebensversicherung; ~-**term life insurance** Gruppenlebensversicherung; ~ **interaction** Gruppenwechselwirkung; ~ **interview** Gruppengespräch, -interview; ~ **leader** Kolonnenführer; ~**'s loss** Konzernverlust; ~ **manager** Gruppenleiter; ~ **management** Konzernleitung; ~ **marriage** Gruppenehe; ~ **member** *(going concern)* Konzerngesellschaft, -tochter, *(parl.)* Fraktionsmitglied; ~ **output** Gruppenleistung; ~ **payment** Akkordbezahlung; **with profits ~ pension scheme** gewinnbeteiligte Gruppenaltersversorgung; ~ **picture** Gruppenaufnahme; ~ **piece rate** Gruppenakkord[lohn]; ~ **piece work [plan]** Gruppenakkord[arbeit]; ~ **piecework system** Gruppenleistungslohnsystem; ~ **plan** *(transportation accounting)* Gruppenabschreibungsverfahren; ~ **policy** Sammel-, Gemeinschaftspolice; ~ **practice** Gruppenpraxis; ~ **production** Gruppenproduktion, -leistung; ~ **profit** Konzerngewinn; ~ **profit before taxation** Konzerngewinn vor Steuern; **executives' ~ company ~ protection** Gruppenversicherungsschutz für leitende Angestellte; ~ **rate** Pauschalsatz, *(railway)* Sammeltarif; ~-**rate travel** verbilligte Gruppen-, Sammelferienreise; **wholesale ~ rate** pauschalierter Gruppentarif; ~ **relationship** Konzernbeziehung, -verhältnis; ~ **result for the year** Konzernjahresergebnis; ~ **revenue before taxation** Konzernerträge vor Steuern; ~ **routing and charging equipment** *(tel.)* Direktwählsystem; ~ **scheme** *(insurance)* Gruppenversicherungssystem; ~ **share of profit** Konzerngewinnanteil; ~**'s sales** Konzernumsatz; ~ **solidarity** Gruppensolidarität; ~ **statement** Konzernausweis; ~ **tension** Gruppenspannung; ~-**term life insurance** Gruppenlebensversicherung; ~ **test** Gruppenprüfung; ~ **trading** Konzernhandel; ~ **training** Gruppenausbildung; ~ **treasurer** Finanzdirektor eines Konzerns; ~ **trip** Gruppenreise; ~ **tuition** Gruppenunterricht; ~ **turnover** Konzernumsatz; ~ **vehicle** Konzernfahrzeug; ~-**wide offer** Konzernangebot.

groupage Gruppierung;
~ **rate** Gruppentarif.
grouping Gruppierung, Gruppenbildung, Einteilung, Anordnung;
occupational (professional) ~ Berufskategorie;
~ **of balance-sheet items** systematische Ordnung der Bilanzposten; **age** ~ **of the population** Altersaufbau der Bevölkerung; ~ **of products** Zusammenführung zu einer Produktengruppe.
grow (v.) wachsen, zunehmen, (produce) ziehen, Getreide [an]bauen, (make progress) beruflich vorankommen, vorwärtskommen, (tension) sich erhöhen, zunehmen, (town) sich ausdehnen;
~ **considerably** beträchtlich zunehmen, sich beträchtlich erweitern; ~ **due** fällig werden; ~ **flat** (business) stocken; ~ **into fashion** Mode werden; ~ **into an awkward situation** sich unangenehm (bedenklich) entwickeln; ~ **on s. o.** steigenden Einfluß bei jem. gewinnen; ~ **out** (state) erwachsen, entstehen; ~ **out of bad habits** schlechte Angewohnheiten ablegen; ~ **out of one's clothes** aus seinen Kleidern herauswachsen; ~ **out of commercial considerations** aus handelspolitischen Erwägungen entstehen; ~ **out of fashion** aus der Mode kommen; ~ **out of a few towns** (state) aus einigen Städten zusammenwachsen; ~ **rapidly** überhandnehmen; ~ **more on the side of law and order** für Rechtsstaatlichkeit eintreten; ~ **stronger** sich verstärken; ~ **uneasy** in Unruhe geraten; ~ **up** auf-, heranwachsen, (custom) entstehen; ~ **upon s. o.** jem. zu gefallen anfangen; ~ **in volume** an Umfang zunehmen; ~ **in wisdom** weiser werden.
growable kultivierbar.
grower Pflanzer, Produzent, Züchter.
growing | of crops Feldfruchtanbau;
~ **child** heranwachsendes Kind; ~ **crop** Ernte (Früchte) auf dem Halm; ~ **debt** Schuldenanwachs, -zunahme; ~ **demand** wachsende Nachfrage; **potato-** ~ **district** Kartoffelanbaugebiet; ~ **insurance** Ernteversicherung; ~ **opinion** sich entwickelnde Meinung; ~ **season** Wachstumsperiode; ~ **timber** Holz auf dem Stamm; ~ **time** Wachstumszeit; ~ **wages** zunehmende Löhne.
grown-up Erwachsener;
~ (a.) erwachsen.
growth Wachsen, Wachstum, (development) Entwicklung, (extension) Ausdehnung, (increase) Anwachsen, Zunahme, -wachs, Vergrößerung, Ausdehnung, (stock) Wachstum;
of foreign ~ fremden Ursprungs, ausländisch;
company ~ Ausdehnung eines Unternehmens; **economic** ~ Wirtschaftswachstum, Entwicklung der Volkswirtschaft; **export-led** ~ exportbeeinflußtes Wachstum; **industrial** ~ industrielles Wachstum, Wachstum der Industrie; **investment-led** ~ durch Investitionen hervorgerufenes Wachstum; **long-term** ~ langfristige Wachstumsperiode; **market** ~ Wachstumsmarkt; **mushroom** ~ rapides Wachstum, rapide Zunahme; **native** ~**s** einheimische Bodenerzeugnisse; **noninflationary** ~ nicht inflationär bedingtes Wachstum; **rapid** ~ Überhandnahme; **slow economic** ~ geringe Wachstumsperiode;
~ **of balance sheet** Bilanzentwicklung; ~ **of business** Geschäftszunahme, -zuwachs; ~ **of capital** Kapitalzuwachs; ~ **in consumption** Konsumsteigerung; ~ **of demand** Nachfrageanstieg; ~ **in earnings** Ertragswachstum; ~ **in the economy** Konjunkturanstieg; ~ **of exports** Exportanstieg, Ausfuhrzunahme; ~ **in gross domestic product (gpd)** Wachstum des Bruttoinlandsprodukts; ~ **of income** Einkommenszunahme, -zuwachs, Ertragszunahme; ~ **of inventories** Lageranstieg, -zunahme; ~ **of population** Bevölkerungszunahme; ~ **of power** Machtzuwachs; ~ **in productivity** Produktivitätszunahme; ~ **of reserves** Anwachsen der Reserven, Rücklagenzunahme, -anstieg, Reservenzunahme; ~ **in sales** Umsatzsteigerung; ~ **in savings deposits** Spareinlagenzuwachs, -erhöhung; ~ **of trade** Ausdehnung (Zunahme) des Handels;
to limit the ~ **in its spending to 1% a year** Ausgabenzunahme auf 1% jährlich beschränken; **to reach full** ~ voll ausgewachsen sein; **to underwrite** ~ Wachstum finanzieren;
~ **area** Entwicklungsgebiet, Wachstumsgebiet; ~ **aspect** Wachstumsaspekt; ~ **assumption** Wachstumsannahme; **to raise** ~ **capital** neues Kapital zur Finanzierung von Entwicklungsaufträgen aufbringen; **accelerated** ~ **center** beschleunigtes Wachstumszentrum; ~ **curve** Wachstumskurve; ~ **era** Wachstumsperiode; ~ **factor** (securities) Wachstumsfaktor; ~ **favo(u)rites** Wachstumsfavoriten; ~ **fields** Wachstumsgebiete; ~ **financing** Wachstumsfinanzierung; ~ **forecast** Wachstumsprognose; ~ **halfpenny** (Br.) Mastviehabgabe; ~ **industry** Wachstumsindustrie; **to come to the end of the** ~ **line** Wachstumsgrenze erreicht haben; ~ **measurement** Wachstumsmessung; ~ **mentality** Wachstumsmentalität; ~ **model** Wachs-

tumsmodell; ~ **opportunities** Wachstumschancen; ~ **phase** Wachstumsphase; ~ **plan** Wachstumsvertrag; ~ **point** Entwicklungsschwerpunkt; ~ **poles** Wachstumspole; ~ **potential** Zuwachspotential; ~ **potentialities** (stocks) Wachstumsmöglichkeiten; ~ **process** Wachstumsprozeß; ~ **program(me)** Wachstumsprogramm; ~**-promoting** wachstumsfördernd; ~ **prospects** Wachstumsaussichten; ~ **ranking** Wachstumseinreihung; ~ **rate** Zuwachs-, Wachstumsrate, Wachstumstempo; **economic** ~ **rate** Wachstumsrate des Sozialprodukts; **zero** ~ **rate** zum Stillstand führende Wachstumsrate; ~ **rate of 17%** 17%ige Zuwachsrate; **to carry the whole economy to a decent** ~ **rate** der Gesamtwirtschaft zu angemessenen Wachstumsraten verhelfen; ~ **rate table** Wachstumstabelle; **year-to-year** ~ **ratio** jährliche Wachstumsrate; ~ **recession** Wachstumsrezession, -rückgang; ~ **record** Wachstumsnachweis; ~ **situation** Wachstumssituation; ~ **squeeze** Wachstumsbehinderung; ~ **stocks** Wachtumsaktien, -werte; **to switch into** ~ **stocks** in Wachstumswerte umsteigen; ~ **target** Wachstumsziel; ~ **term** Wachstumsgrad; ~ **trust** Wachstumsfonds; **no-**~ **year** kein Zuwachsjahr; **slow-**~ **year** langsames Wachstumsjahr; ~ **zone** Wachstumsgebiet.
grub (fig.) Arbeitstier, (penny-a-liner) Lohnschreiber, literarischer Tagelöhner, (ill-bred person) Prolet;
~ (v.) **along** sich schinden (abplagen).
grubber Arbeitstier.
grubstreet Schreiberlinge.
Grundy, Mrs. (Br.) die Leute.
Grundyism übertriebene Sittenstrenge.
Grundyite Sittenrichter.
guarantee (Br.) Bürgschaft, Bürgschaftsleistung, Garantie, Garantiehaftung, Gewähr[leistung], Zusicherung, (del credere) Delkredere, (guarantor) Garant, Gewährsmann, Bürge, (receiver of guarantee) Bürgschaftsnehmer, Bürgschaftsgläubiger, Kautions-, Sicherheitsnehmer, (security) Sicherheit, Kaution, (warranty) Garantieschein;
under our ~ auf unsere Verantwortung; **without** ~ ohne Gewähr, unter Ausschluß der Gewährleistung;
absolute ~ selbstschuldnerische Bürgschaft; **bank** ~ (Br.) Bankgarantie, -bürgschaft; **collateral** ~ Nebenbürgschaft; **collective** ~ (law of nations) kollektive Garantie; **commercial** ~ kaufmännische Bürgschaft, Garantieschein; **company** ~ Firmengarantie, Firmenbürgschaft; **conditional** ~ Ausfallbürgschaft; **continuing** ~ Dauergarantie, (US) Kreditbürgschaft; **credit** ~ Kreditbürgschaft; **deficit** ~ Ausfallbürgschaft; **expired** ~ abgelaufene (verfallene) Garantie; **fidelity** ~ (Br.) Kautionsversicherung; **government** ~ Staatsbürgschaft; **implied** ~ stillschweigend miteingeschlossene Garantie; **joint and several** ~ gesamtschuldnerische Bürgschaft; **local government** ~ Kommunalbürgschaft; **12-month** ~ Jahresgarantie; **mutual** ~ gegenseitiges Garantieversprechen; **new-product** ~ Garantie für gerade auf den Markt gebrachte Erzeugnisse; **reliable** ~ sichere Garantie; **several** ~ Einzelbürgschaft; **sole** ~ alleinige Bürgschaft; **specific** ~ auf einen Sonderfall beschränkte Bürgschaft; **special** ~ (US) Kreditbürgschaft; **specific** ~ Einzelbürgschaft; **standby** ~ (underwriters) Garantie des Direktabsatzes; **trustworthy** ~ einwandfreie Bürgschaft; **unlimited** ~ unbeschränkte Garantie; **a year's** ~ Garantie für ein Jahr, einjährige Garantie;
~ **of bill of exchange** Wechselbürgschaft, Aval, Wechselbürge; ~ **of delivery** Liefergarantie; ~ **payable on demand** bei Aufforderung fällig werdende Bürgschaft; ~ **under hand** einfaches (schriftliches) Bürgschaftsversprechen; ~ **of a loan** Anleihegarantie; ~ **under seal** notarielles Bürgschaftsversprechen; ~ **of tender** Bietungsgarantie; ~ **in writing** schriftliches Garantieversprechen;
~ (v.) (secure) sicherstellen, einstehen, gewährleisten, Gewähr übernehmen, sichern, (stand bail) bürgen, Bürgschaft leisten, sich verbürgen, (warrant) garantieren, Garantie leisten;
~ **for s. o.** Bürgschaft für j. übernehmen; ~ **due payment of a bill of exchange** Bezahlung eines Wechsels garantieren, Wechselbürgschaft übernehmen (leisten); ~ **a debt** sich für eine Schuld verbürgen; ~ **that the debts will be paid** Schuldenbezahlung garantieren; ~ **an endorsement** Indossament verbürgen; ~ **the genuineness of goods** für die Echtheit einer Ware bürgen (garantieren); ~ **s. o. from (against) a loss** jem. das Verlustrisiko abnehmen; ~ **a dividend to minority stockholders** Minderheitsaktionären eine Dividende garantieren; ~ **for the moiety** für die Hälfte Delkredere stehen; ~ **to pay (the payment of) a man's debt** für die Schulden eines Dritten Bürgschaft leisten; ~ **reciprocity** Gegenseitigkeit zusichern; ~ **the finest workmanship** für erstklassige Arbeit (Qualitätsarbeit) garantieren;

to ask for ~ Kaution verlangen; **to be ~ for** einstehen, bürgen, haften; **to call up a ~** Sicherheit in Anspruch nehmen; **to cancel a ~** Garantie annullieren; **to enter into a ~** Bürgschaft übernehmen; **to furnish a ~** Bürgschaft beibringen; **to go ~ for s. o.** für j. Bürgschaft übernehmen (leisten); **to hono(u)r a ~** Garantiezusage erfüllen; **to implement a ~** Garantie ausfüllen, einer Garantiepflicht nachkommen; **to leave s. th. as a ~** etw. als Sicherheit hinterlegen; **to limit a ~** Garantie einschränken; **to lose one's rights under a ~** seiner Garantieansprüche verlustig gehen; **to make a ~ stick** Garantieansprüche durchsetzen; **to offer ~** Delkredere anbieten; **to offer one's house as a ~** sein Haus als Sicherheit anbieten; **to pay up under one's ~** seinen Garantieverpflichtungen nachkommen; **to raise claims under a ~** Garantie in Anspruch nehmen, Garantieansprüche erheben; **to stand back of (behind, Br.) a ~** Garantieversprechen einlösen, Gewährleistungsansprüche erfüllen; **to stipulate for a ~** Garantie fordern; **to undertake a ~** Gewähr übernehmen;

~ agreement Garantieabkommen; **~ association (US)** Kautionsversicherungsgesellschaft; **~ bailer** Bürgschaftsnehmer; **~ bond** schriftliche Garantieerklärung, Garantieschein; **~ clauses** Bürgschaftsklauseln; **~ commission** Aval-, Bürgschafts-, Garantie-, Delkredereprovision; **~ company** Kautions-, Garantieversicherungsgesellschaft; **~ contract** Bürgschaftsversprechen, Garantievertrag; **~ deposit** Sicherheitshinterlegung, (insurance) Kautionsdepot; **~ form** Bürgschaftsformular; **~ fund (Br.)** Garantie-, Reservefonds, -mittel; **~ indebtedness** Bürgschaftsschuld; **~ insurance** Garantie-, Kredit-, Kautionsversicherung; **~ liability** Garantie-, Bürgschaftsverpflichtung; **~ offer** Garantieangebot; **~ pay** garantierte Mindestzahlung; **~ period** Garantiezeit, -frist; **~ registration card (seller)** Garantieschein; **~ securities** Kautionseffekten; **~ security account** Kautionseffektenkonto; **~ signature** Garantieunterschrift; **~ society (Br.)** Garantieversicherungs-, Kautionsversicherungsgesellschaft; **~ stock** nicht rückzahlbare Kapitaleinlage, Deckungsstock; **~ stocks (US)** Aktien mit Dividendengarantie; **~ undertaking** Garantieversprechen, -zusage.

guaranteed garantiert, mit Garantie, avaliert;

~ by per Aval; **~ by local authorities** kommunalverbürgt; **~ for cargo** garantiert ladebereit, Ladebereitschaft zugesichert; **to be ~ for one year** ein Jahr Garantie haben;

~ accounts verbürgte Außenstände; **amount ~** Garantiesumme, -betrag; **~ bill of exchange** avalierter Wechsel, Bürgschaftswechsel; **~ bond** schriftliche Garantieerklärung, Garantieschein; **~ bonds** Obligationen mit Kapital- und Dividendengarantie; **~ circulation** anerkannte Auflagenhöhe, Mindestauflage; **~ credit** Bürgschaftskredit; **~ day rate** garantierter Tageslohnsatz; **~ dividend** garantierte Dividende; **~ earnings** garantierter Verdienst; **~ employment** garantierte Mindestbeschäftigung; **~ hourly rate** garantierter Stundenlohntarif; **~ mail transfer (Br.)** garantierte briefliche Überweisung; **~ minimum circulation** garantierte Mindestauflage; **~ minimum wage for all trades** garantierter, absoluter Mindestlohn; **~ period** Garantiefrist, -zeit; **~ position (advertising)** zugesagte (garantierte) Plazierung; **~ price** Garantiepreis; **~ rate** garantiertes Grundgehalt; **~ stocks (Br.)** garantierte Schuldverschreibungen, (US) Aktien mit Dividendengarantie; **~ annual wage** garantierter Jahreslohn; **~ wage plan** Lohnabkommen mit garantierter Mindestbeschäftigungszeit; **~ week** garantierter Wochenlohn.

guarantor Bürge, Gewährsmann, Gewährsträger, Garant, Avalist;

absolute ~ selbstschuldnerischer Bürge; **conditional ~** Ausfallbürge; **joint ~** solidarischer Bürge; **joint ~s** Gesamtbürgen; **joint and several ~s** gesamtschuldnerische Bürgen, Gesamtbürgen; **several ~** Einzelbürge;

~ of a bill (note) Wechselbürge; **~ of a credit** Kreditbürge; **~ of payment** Zahlungsbürge;

to stand as ~ for s. o. für j. Bürgschaft leisten;

~ corporation Kautionsgesellschaft; **~ enquiry** Bürgenüberprüfung.

guaranty (law term) (US) Garantie, Garantieerklärung, Bürgschaftsleistung, Bürgschaft[sversprechen, -vertrag], Kaution, Gewähr[leistung], Zusicherung, (guarantee of bill of exchange) Wechselbürgschaft, (guarantor) Bürge, Gewährsmann, Garant, (security) Pfand, Sicherheit, Sicherheitssumme;

absolute ~ Bürgschaft ohne Einrede der Vorausklage, selbstschuldnerische Bürgschaft; **bank ~** Bankgarantie; **collateral ~** solidarische Haftung, Solidar-, Gesamtbürgschaft; **conditional ~** Ausfallbürgschaft; **continuing ~** Dauergarantie, Kredit-

bürgschaft; **fidelity ~** Schadloshaltungsbürgschaft, Amts-, Dienstbürgschaft; **general ~** Garantieangebot an unbestimmte Gläubiger; **joint and several ~ (US)** gesamtschuldnerische Bürgschaft; **special ~** Kreditbürgschaft, persönliche Bürgschaft; **specific ~ (US)** Garantievertrag;

~ of collection (US) Ausfallbürgschaft, Zahlungsgarantie; **~ of payment (US)** selbstschuldnerische Bürgschaft; **~ of title (US)** Rechtsmängelgewähr; **~ of title insurance (US)** Versicherung von Rechtsansprüchen auf Grundbesitz;

to act as a ~ for s. o. für j. bürgen (garantieren); **to ask for a ~** Garantie (Kaution) verlangen; **to give ~** Delkredere stehen (übernehmen); **to hono(u)r a ~** Garantiezusage erfüllen; **to pay a ~** Kaution leisten; **to pay under a ~** seinen Bürgschaftsverpflichtungen nachkommen; **to rescind a ~** Garantieversprechen für ungültig erklären; **to stand back of (behind, Br.) a ~** Garantieversprechen einlösen, Gewährleistungsansprüche erfüllen; **to stipulate for ~** Garantie fordern;

~ account Sicherstellungskonto; **~ agreement (contract) (US)** Bürgschafts-, Garantievertrag; **~ commission (US)** Garantieprovision; **~ company (US)** Kautionsversicherungs-, Garantiegesellschaft; **~ fund (banking)** Rücklagen-, Garantiefonds; **~ insurance (US)** Kautions-, Kreditversicherung; **~ of title insurance (US)** Versicherung von Rechtsansprüchen auf Grundbesitz, Rechtsmängelgewährleistungsversicherung; **factory ~ policies** betriebliche Garantiezusagen; **~ savings bank (New Hampshire)** Sparkasse mit zwei verschiedenen Einlageklassen.

guard Wache, Bewachung, (mil.) Wachmannschaft, (person) Wachmann, -posten, Sicherheitsbeamter, Wächter, (prison) Aufseher, Gefangenenwärter, -aufseher, (Br., railway train) Zugführer, Schaffner, Zugbegleiter (railroad, US) Bahnwärter;

off one's ~ unachtsam; **~s** Wachmannschaft;

advance ~ (mil.) Vorhut; **body ~** Leibwache; **coast ~** Küstenzollwache; **home ~ (Br.)** Bürgerwehr; **relieving ~** Ablösungsmannschaft; **standing ~** Dauerwachposten;

~ of hono(u)r Ehrenwache; **~ of a train (Br.)** Zugschaffner;

~ (v.) bewachen, bewahren, (take measures) Vorkehrungen treffen;

~ against accidents Unfälle verhüten; **~ a camp** Lager bewachen; **~ by clauses** durch vertragliche Bestimmungen absichern; **~ s. o. against danger** j. vor Gefahr schützen; **~ against disease** vor Krankheit schützen; **~ s. o. to his house** j. zu seinem Haus begleiten; **~ the interests** Interessen wahren; **~ one's life** sein Leben schützen; **~ prisoners** Gefangene bewachen; **~ one's reputation** auf seinen guten Ruf achten; **~ one's tongue** seine Zunge hüten; **~ a treasure** Schatz hüten;

to be on ~ Wache stehen (schieben); **to be on one's ~** auf der Hut sein; **to be off one's ~** unachtsam sein; **to inspect the ~ of hono(u)r** Ehrenformation (Ehrenwache, Ehrenkompanie) abschreiten; **to keep ~** Wache übernehmen; **to keep under close ~** unter strenger Aufsicht halten; **to keep a prisoner under ~** Gefangenen bewachen; **to march off under ~** unter Bewachung abführen; **to mount ~** Wache beziehen; **to put s. o. on his ~** Verdacht bei jem. erregen; **to relieve the ~** Wache ablösen; **to set a ~ on a house** Haus bewachen lassen; **to stand ~** Wache stehen;

~ boat Wachboot; **~ book (mil.)** Wachbuch; **~ chain** Sicherheitskette; **~ commander (mil.)** Wachhabender; **~ duty** Wachdienst; **to be on ~ duty** auf Wache stehen, Wache schieben; **~ lock** Sicherheitsschloß; **~ plate** Schutzblech; **~ ship** Wachboot.

guarded beaufsichtigt, bewacht, geschützt;

heavily ~ schwer bewacht;

to be ~ in one's behavio(u)r sich vorsichtig benehmen;

~ answer vorsichtige Antwort; **to express in ~ terms** vorsichtig ausdrücken.

guardian Vormund, Pfleger, Erziehungsberechtigter, (curator) Kurator, Verwahrer;

acting ~ Obervormund; **deputy ~** Gegenvormund; **domestic ~** vom Wohnsitzgericht bestellter Vormund; **general ~** Vormund; **joint ~** Gegen-, Nebenvormund; **legal ~** gesetzlicher Vormund, Erziehungsberechtigter; **natural ~** sorgeberechtigter Elternteil, natürlicher (gesetzlicher) Vormund; **official ~** Amtsvormund; **special ~** Pfleger, Mitvormund; **statutory ~** gesetzlicher Vormund; **testamentary ~** testamentarisch bestellter Vormund;

~ by appointment of [the high] Court [of Justice] gerichtlich bestellter Vormund, Amtsvormund; **~ by election** selbstgewählter (vom Mündel gewählter) Vormund; **~ ad hoc** Pfleger mit besonderem Auftrag; **~ ad litem** Prozeßpfleger; **~ by nature** Gewahrsamsinhaber eines Kindes, gesetzlicher Vormund;

for nurture sorgeberechtigter Elternteil; ~ **of the peace** Polizeibeamter; ~ **of the poor** *(Br.)* Armen-, Sozialpfleger, Fürsorgebeamter; ~ **of property** Vermögensverwalter; ~ **of the public interest** Hüter (Wahrer) des öffentlichen Interesses; ~ **by statute** testamentarisch bestellter Vormund; ~ **and ward** Vormund und Mündel;

to appoint a ~ Pfleger (Vormund) bestellen; **to be placed under a** ~ unter Vormundschaft stehen; **to place s. o. under the care of a** ~ j. unter Vormundschaft stellen;

~'**s allowance** Pflegegeld; ~ **angel** Schutzengel; ~ **neglect** Vernachlässigung der Vormundschaftpflichten.

guardianize *(v.)* als Vormund tätig sein.

guardianship Pflegeschaft, Vormundschaft[sverhältnis], Kuratel; **under** ~ unter Vormundschaft (Kuratel);

testamentary ~ Vormundschaft aufgrund letztwilliger Verfügung;

to admit under ~ unter Vormundschaft stellen; **to be under** ~ unter Vormundschaft stehen; **to be under the** ~ **of the laws** unter dem Schutz der Gesetze stehen; **to give an account of one's** ~ Vormundschaftsbericht erstellen; **to place a child under s. one's** ~ Kind unter jds. Vormundschaft stellen.

guarding of machinery Schutzvorrichtungen für Maschinenanlagen.

guardroom Wachlokal, -raum.

guardsman Wächter, Aufseher.

gubernatorial | election Gouverneurswahl; ~ **trip** Gouverneursreise.

guerilla Freischärler, Guerillakämpfer, Partisan, Bandenmitglied;

~ **action** Partisanentätigkeit; ~ **army** Partisanenstreitmacht; **to fight** ~ **campaigns** Partisanengruppen vernichten; ~ **chieftain** Partisanenführer; ~ **fighting** Partisanenbekämpfung; ~ **forces** Partisanen[streitmacht]; ~ **group** Freischärler, Partisanengruppe; ~ **leader** Partisanen-, Bandenführer; ~ **movement** Freischärler-, Partisanenbewegung; ~ **network** Terroristen-, Bandenorganisation; ~ **strike** ungesetzlicher (wilder) Streik; ~ **war[fare]** Guerilla-, Partisanen-, Bandenkrieg; **rival** ~ **war lords** rivalisierende Partisanenführer.

guess Vermutung, Schätzung, Mutmaßung;

anybody's ~ reine Vermutung; **educated** ~ begründete Vermutung.

guesstimate *(US sl.)* grobe Schätzung.

guesswork Vermutungen, Raterei.

guest *(hotel)* [Hotel]gast, Fremder, *(motorcar)* Mitfahrer;

free-loading ~**s** kostenlos beförderte Gäste; **house** ~ Gast des Hauses; **distinguished** ~ hoher Gast; **nonresident** ~ auswärtiger Gast; **paying** ~ zahlender Gast, Pensionär; **welcome** ~ willkommener Besuch;

landlord and his ~**s** Wirt und seine Gäste;

~ **of hono(u)r** Ehrengast; ~ **of the management** Gast des Hauses;

to appear as a ~ *(theater)* in einer Gastrolle auftreten; **to be a** ~ **of the management** umsonst wohnen, Gast des Hauses sein; **to put off one's** ~ seinen Gästen absagen; **to sign in** ~**s** Gäste aufnehmen; **to slight a** ~ Gast links liegenlassen;

~ **appearance** Gastvorstellung, -auftritt; ~ **card** Tischkarte; ~ **lecture** Gastvorlesung; ~ **night** *(club)* Gästeabend; ~ **part** *(theater)* Gastrolle; ~ **performance** Gastvorstellung; ~ **privileges** Gastvorrechte; **to extend** ~ **privileges** Gäste in seinen Klub einführen; ~ **professor** Gast-, Austauschprofessor; ~ **regulations** Hotelordnung; ~ **room** *(hotel)* Fremdenzimmer, *(private)* Besuchs-, Gastzimmer; ~ **speaker** Ehrenredner; ~ **worker** Gastarbeiter.

guestchamber Gäste-, Fremdenzimmer.

guesthouse Gasthaus, Fremdenheim, Gästehaus.

guidance Führung, Leitung, Anleitung, Richtlinie, Weisung, *(travellers)* [Touristen]betreuung;

for your ~ zu ihrer Orientierung; **under the** ~ **of** unter der Leitung von;

vocational ~ Berufsberatung;

~ **of production** Produktionslenkung; ~ **of agricultural production** *(EC)* Ausrichtung der landwirtschaftlichen Erzeugung; ~ **of trade** Wirtschaftslenkung;

to serve as ~ als Richtschnur dienen;

~ **clinic** Berufsberatungsinstitut; ~ **counsellor** *(US)* Jugendpsychologe; ~ **system** *(rocket)* Lenk-, Leitsystem.

guide *(adviser)* Ratgeber, Berater, *(directing principle)* Richtschnur, leitendes Prinzip, *(guidebook)* Reiseführer, -handbuch, *(manual)* Leitfaden, *(mil.)* Spähtrupp[mitglied], *(person)* Fremdenführer, *(punched card system)* Leitkarte, *(on roads)* Wegezeichen;

Alpine ~ Bergführer; **buyer's** ~ Führer für Einkäufer; **interviewer** ~ Leitfaden für den Interviewer; **museum** ~ Museumsführer; **official** ~ amtlicher Reiseführer; **pocket** ~ Führer im Taschenbuchformat; **railway** ~ Kursbuch, Fahrplan; **safe** ~ zuverlässiger Führer; **tourist** ~ Fremdenführer, Touristenführer;

~ **of cost** Kostenübersicht; ~ **to English literature** Einführung in die englische Literatur; ~ **to London** Führer durch London; ~ **to a museum** Museumsführer; ~ **to photography** Anleitung zum Fotografieren;

~ *(v.)* leiten, lenken, führen, *(act as guide)* als Reiseführer fungieren, *(instruct)* unterrichten, anleiten, belehren;

~ **a child's first steps** erste Schritte eines Kindes lenken; ~ **s. o. to his place** j. zu seinem Platz geleiten;

to take reason as one's ~ sich von Vernunftsgründen leiten lassen;

~ **beam** Funkleitstrahl; ~ **card** Leitkarte; ~ **price** *(EC)* Dienstleistungspreis; ~ **rail** Führungsschiene, *(print.)* Anlegeschiene; ~ **rope** *(balloon)* Schlepptau, -seil; ~ **sheet** *(advertising)* Sendeplan, *(interview)* Leitfaden.

guideboard Wegweisertafel.

guidebook Reisehandbuch, -führer, Fremdenführer; ~ **trade** Reisebuchhandel.

guided, to be ~ **by s. one's advice** sich nach jds. Ratschlägen richten; ~ **missile** Fernlenkgeschoß; ~ **weapon** Fernlenkwaffe.

guideline *(airplane)* Schlepp-, Leitseil, *(fig.)* Richtlinie, -schnur, *(print.)* Leitlinie;

pay ~**s** Lohnrichtlinien;

to act outside the ~**s laid down by the government** sich außerhalb der staatlich festgelegten Richtlinien bewegen; **to issue binding** ~**s** obligatorische Richtlinien festsetzen; **to keep within the** ~**s** sich innerhalb der Richtlinien halten;

~-**busting wage increase** staatliche Leitlinien desavouierende Lohnerhöhung; ~ **figures** Richtlinienziffern; ~ **indication** Orientierungshilfe; ~ **limit** Richtliniengrenze.

guidepost Wegweiser.

guideway Laufschiene.

guiding | control Lenkvorrichtung; ~ **line** Richtlinie; ~ **price** Richtpreis; ~ **principle** Leitprinzip, -gedanke, Richtschnur; ~ **principles** Leitsätze; ~ **thought** Leitgedanke.

guidon Wimpel, Standarte.

guild Zunft, Innung, Gilde, Fachschaft;

merchant ~ *(Br.)* Kaufmannsgilde; **trade** ~ Handwerkerzunft; ~ **socialism** Betriebssozialismus; ~ **system** Innungswesen.

Guildhall *(London)* Rathaus;

~ **sitting** Ratssitzung.

guillotine Guillotine, Fallbeil, *(parl.)* Obstruktionspolitik, Verzögerungstaktik;

~ *(v.)* Verzögerungstaktik anwenden;

~ **a debate** Debatte abwürgen;

~ **closure** *(parl., Br.)* Debattenabkürzung mittels beschränkter Redezeit; ~ **motion** Obstruktions-, Verzögerungsantrag; ~ **vote** *(Br.)* Abstimmung über den Schluß der Debatte.

guilt Schuld, *(culpability)* Strafbarkeit, -fälligkeit;

collective ~ Kollektivschuld; **war** ~ Kriegsschuld;

to admit one's ~ seine Schuld zugeben; **to admit one's** ~ **to the police** bei der Polizei ein Schuldgeständnis ablegen; **to incur** ~ straffällig werden; **to shake off the** ~ Schuldgefühl loswerden; **to shoulder the** ~ Schuld auf sich nehmen.

guiltiness Schuldbewußtsein.

guiltless unschuldig, schuldlos.

guilty schuldig, *(criminal)* strafbar, verbrecherisch;

to be ~ **of theft** sich des Diebstahls schuldig machen; **to be found** ~ **on a charge** einer Anklage für schuldig befunden werden; **to be found** ~ **on all counts** in allen Anlagepunkten für schuldig befunden werden; **to bring in** ~ für schuldig erklären; **to find s. o.** ~ j. schuldig sprechen, j. für schuldig erklären; **to find s. o. not** ~ j. freisprechen; **to plead** ~ sich schuldig bekennen; **to plead not** ~ Freispruch beantragen;

~ **behavio(u)r** schuldbewußtes Verhalten; ~ **conscience** schlechtes Gewissen.

guinea *(Br.)* Guinee *(21 Shilling)*;

~-**pig** *(Br.)* Versuchskaninchen, *(nominal director)* nominelles Aufsichtsratsmitglied.

guise Maske, Mantel, Verkleidung;

under the ~ **of** unter dem Vorwand; **under the** ~ **of friendship** aus angeblicher Freundschaft;

to put on the ~ **of benevolence** sich als Wohltäter aufspielen.

gulf Golf, Meerbusen, *(fig.)* Unterschied;

~ **between the rich and the poor** Kluft zwischen arm und reich;

to be put in the ~ *(Br., sl.)* niedrigstes Prädikat erhalten;
~ **stream** Golfstrom.
gum Klebstoff, *(philately)* Gummierung;
  with original ~ mit unbeschädigter Gummierung;
  ~ *(v.)* gummieren, mit einer Gummierung versehen;
  ~ **down** aufkleben; ~ **together** zusammenhalten; ~ **up the works**
  (fam.) Arbeit vermasseln.
gummed | envelope gummierter Umschlag; ~ **label** Klebezettel,
  -etikett, Aufkleber; ~ **paper** gummiertes Papier; ~ **tape** Klebestreifen; ~ **tape sealer** Klebeapparat.
gumption *(coll.)* gesunder Menschenverstand, Grütze, *(go)*
  Initiative, Unternehmungsgeist;
  to lack ~ keinen Mumm haben.
gumshoe *(US)* Gummiüberschuh, *(US sl.)* Polizist, Detektiv,
  Spitzel, Spion;
  ~ *(a.) (US sl.)* heimlich;
  ~ **campaign** Flüsterpropaganda; ~ **man** Detektiv.
gun Schuß-, Feuerwaffe, Gewehr, *(cannon)* Geschütz, Kanone,
  (US) Pistole, Revolver;
  under the ~ *(fig.)* unter Beschuß;
  air ~ Luftgewehr; **great** ~ *(sl.)* großes Tier; **machine** ~
  Maschinengewehr;
  ~ *(v.)* schießen, *(go hunting)* zur Jagd gehen;
  ~ **down** über den Haufen schießen; ~ **for support** *(US)* sich um
  Unterstützung bemühen;
  to blow great ~**s** *(storm)* heulen; **to stick to one's** ~**s** seine
  Stellung behaupten, *(fig.)* fest bleiben;
  ~ **licence** Waffenschein; ~ **registration** Waffenmeldepflicht; ~
  room *(mar., Br.)* Kadettenmesse; ~ **runner** Waffenhändler; ~
  running Waffenhandel.
gunboat Kanonenboot;
  ~ **diplomacy** Kanonenbootdiplomatie.
gunman *(US)* bewaffneter Verbrecher, *(US)* Revolverheld,
  (picket) bewaffneter Streikposten.
gunning | for stocks *(US)* Börsenmanöver der Baissepartei;
  to go ~ **for a burglar** Einbrecher verfolgen.
gunplay *(US sl.)* Schießerei.
gunpoint, to hold at mit dem Revolver in Schach halten.
gunrunner Waffenschmuggler.

gunrunning Waffenschmuggel.
gunshot Kanonen-, Gewehrschuß;
  in ~ in Schußweite;
  ~ **range** Kanonenschußweite.
gunsmith Büchsenmacher.
gush *(v.)* strömen, sich ergießen, *(fig.)* schwärmen;
  ~ **from a pipe** einem Rohr entströmen.
gusher *(US)* sprudelnde Ölquelle.
gushing compliments überschwengliche Komplimente.
gust [of wind] Windstoß, Windbö.
gusty böig.
guts *(sl.)* Schneid, Mumm;
  to have no ~ *(sl.)* Schlappschwanz sein; **to have no** ~ **in it**
  (speech) völlig farblos sein; **to have plenty of** ~ Mumm
  (Schneid) haben; **to have s. one's** ~ **for garters** sich zu revanchieren wissen.
gutter Gosse, Rinnstein, Straßengraben, *(advertising)* Innen-
  spalte, *(print.)* Bundsteg;
  to come from the ~ von der Straße aufgelesen sein; **to take s. o.**
  out of the ~ j. aus der Gosse auflesen;
  ~ **bleed** *(advertising)* Innenausschnitt; ~ **child** Gassenkind; ~
  journalism Skandaljournalismus; ~ **paper** Revolver-, Sensa-
  tions-, Skandalblatt; ~ **press** Schmutz-, Skandalpresse; ~ **stick**
  Bundsteg.
guttersnipe Straßenjunge, *(US)* Winkelmakler.
guy *(US sl.)* Bursche, Pfundskerl, *(running away, Br.)* Ausreißen,
  Verduften;
  swell ~ *(US fam.)* prima Kerl;
  ~ *(v.)* **the life out of s. o.** *(US)* mit jem. Schindluder treiben;
  to do a ~ *(Br., sl.)* verduften, abhauen.
guzzle, *(v.)* **away** versaufen, verprassen.
gymnasium *(sports)* Turn-, Sporthalle;
  high-school ~ Gymnasium.
gyratory *(traffic, Br.)* im Kreisverkehr.
gyrocompass Kreiselkompaß.
gyrograph Tourenzähler, -schreiber.
gyropilot *(airplane)* Selbststeuergerät, Kurssteuerung.
gyroplane Drehflügelflugzeug, Tragschrauber.
gyroscope | control Kreiselsteuerung; ~ **sextant** Kreiselkompaß.

H

h | -bomb *(mil.)* Wasserstoffbombe; **~-hour** Nullstunde.

habeas corpus Anordnung eines Haftprüfungstermins.

haberdasher Kurzwarenhändler, Herrenartikelgeschäft, -ausstatter.

haberdashery Herrenbekleidungsartikel, *(shop, US)* Herrenartikelgeschäft.

habilitate *(v.)* sich habilitieren, *(mining, US)* finanzieren, mit Betriebskapital ausstatten.

habilitation Habilitierung, *(mining)* Finanzierung.

habit Neigung, Gewohnheit, Gepflogenheit, *(professional dress)* Amts-, Berufskleidung;
from [force of] ~ aus [Macht der] Gewohnheit;
buying ~ Kaufgewohnheiten; **fast** ~ feste Gewohnheit; **nomadic** ~s Nomadengewohnheiten; **paying** ~s Zahlungsgebräuche, -gepflogenheiten; **regular** ~ feste Gewohnheit; **social** ~s gesellschaftliche Umgangsformen;
~ of consumption Konsumgewohnheit; **~ of mind** Geistesverfassung; **~ and repute** *(Scot. law)* nach Gewohnheit und Vermutung; **~s of savings** Spargewohnheiten;
to acquire a ~ of buying Kaufgewohnheit annehmen; **to fall (get, lapse) into bad** ~s schlechte Gewohnheiten annehmen; **to get (grow) out of a ~** Gewohnheit ablegen (aufgeben); **to make a ~ of it** es zur Gewohnheit werden lassen;
~-forming drugs Süchtigkeit hervorrufende Narkotika; **~ survey** Untersuchung über die Verbrauchergewohnheiten.

habitability Bewohnbarkeit.

habitable bewohnbar;
no longer ~ unbewohnbar;
to keep one's tenant house in ~ repair an einem Mietshaus die notwendigen Reparaturen vornehmen, sein Mietshaus in bewohnbarem Zustand halten.

habitancy dauernder Aufenthalt.

habitant Ein-, Bewohner.

habitat Wohngebiet, *(zool.)* Verbreitungsgebiet.

habitation Wohnung, *(place of abode)* Wohnsitz, Aufenthaltsort;
fit for ~ bewohnbar; **unfit for** ~ unbewohnbar, für Wohnzwecke ungeeignet;
human ~ menschliche Behausung;
~ tax Gebäudesteuer.

habitual gewöhnlich, gewohnheitsmäßig;
~ cinema-goer häufiger Kinobesucher; **~ criminal** Berufsverbrecher, Gewohnheitsverbrecher; **~ drunkard** Gewohnheitstrinker; **~[ly] persistent offender** *(Br.)* Gewohnheitsverbrecher.

habituate *(v.)* **o. s. to hard work** sich an schwere Arbeit gewöhnen.

habituation Gewöhnung.

habitué ständiger Besucher, Stammgast.

hack Tagelöhner, Gelegenheitsarbeiter, *(penny-a-liner)* Lohnschreiber, Schreiberling, Zeilenschinder, *(taxi, US)* Droschke, Taxi;
political ·· hack Gelegenheitspolitiker; **publisher's** ~ Lohnschreiber;
~ *(v.)* im Tagelohn arbeiten;
~ attorney Winkeladvokat; **~ licence** *(US coll.)* Taxikonzession; **~ stand** *(US)* Taxistand.

hackle, with one's ~s up gereizt, angriffslustig;
to get s. one's ~s up (make s. one's ~s rise) j. auf die Palme bringen.

hackney Droschke, Fiaker, *(hack)* Tagelöhner;
~ carriage öffentliches Beförderungsmittel; **~ coach (cab)** Mietkutsche, Droschke.

hackie *(US)* Taxichauffeur.

haggle Gefeilsche, Schacherei;
~ *(v.)* handeln, feilschen, schachern;
~ over (about) the price um den Preis feilschen.

haggler Schacherer, Feilscher.

haggling Preisfeilscherei.

Hague | Conventions Haager Abkommen; **~ Tribunal** ständiger Schiedsgerichtshof in Haag.

hail Hagel;
~ *(v.)* hageln;
~ from A in A beheimatet sein; **~ a taxi** Taxe heranwinken;
to be ~-fellow well met with s. o. mit jem. auf vertrautem Fuße stehen;
~ insurance Hagelversicherung.

haill, all and *(Scot. law)* das gesamte Anwesen.

hailstone Hagelkorn.

hailstorm Hagelwetter.

haimsucker *(Scot. law)* Hausfriedensbruch.

hair *(fig.)* Kleinigkeit;
against the ~ gegen den Strich; **by a** ~ um Haaresbreite; **to a** ~ haargenau; **without turning a** ~ ohne mit der Wimper zu zucken;
a ~ in one's neck *(Scot.)* Grund zur Beunruhigung;
to find a ~ in the soup Haar in der Suppe finden; **to get in s. one's ~s** j. nervös machen; **to get s. o. by the short** ~s *(sl.)* j. unter seiner Fuchtel haben; **to have s. o. in one's ~** *(US)* j. nicht ausstehen können; **to keep one's ~ on** *(sl.)* kaltes Blut bewahren; **to let down one's ~** *(fig.)* sich gehen lassen; **to lose one's ~** *(fig.)* seine Fassung verlieren; **to make s. one's ~ stand on end** einem die Haare zu Berge stehen lassen, jem. einen großen Schrecken einjagen; **to split ~s** Haarspalterei treiben; **not turn a ~** nicht mit der Wimper zu zucken;
~ compass Präzisionskompaß; **~ raiser** Schauergeschichte; **~-raising** haarsträubend; **~ space** *(print.)* halber Punkt.

hairbreadth Haaresbreite;
not to depart by a ~ from one's instructions sich haarscharf an seine Weisungen halten; **to escape by ~** um Haaresbreite entkommen;
~ escape äußerst knappes Entkommen.

haircutter [Damen]friseur.

haircutting saloon Damensalon.

hairdresser Friseur.

hairline Haarstrich, -linie;
to make a ~ distinction haarfeinen Unterschied machen.

hairpin bend Haarnadelkurve.

hairsplitter pedantischer Mensch.

hairsplitting Wortklauberei.

halcyon days ruhige Schönwettertage.

hale *(v.)* **off to prison** ins Gefängnis abführen.

half Hälfte, halber Anteil, *(school)* Halbjahr, Semester;
one's better ~ *(coll.)* jds. bessere Hälfte; **outward ~** *(railway)* Fahrkartenabschnitt für die Hinfahrt; **return ~** *(railway)* Rückfahrschein, -karte;
~ *(a.)* halb, *(fig.)* unvollkommen, oberflächlich;
to go ~ and ~ with s. o. Halbpart mit jem. machen; **to have ~ a mind to do s. th.** nicht übel Lust haben etw. zu tun;
not ~ bad *(coll.)* gar nicht so schlecht; **~-baked policies** nicht ausgegorene politische Ideen; **~ binding** Halblederband; **~ blood** Halbblut, Mischling; **~-bound** in Halbfranz gebunden; **~-bred** halbgebildet; **~-breed** Mischling, Halbblut; **~ brother** Halbbruder; **~-calf** Halbfranzband; **~ caste** Mischling, Halbblut; **~-cloth** Halbleinen; **~ commission** *(stock exchange)* halbe Provision; **~-commission man** *(Br.)* Vermittlungsagent eines Effektenmaklers; **~ compartment** *(railway)* Halbabteil; **~ crown** *(Br.)* halbe Krone; **~-day job** Teilzeit-, Halbtagsbeschäftigung; **~-day wage** Halbtagslohn; **~ dime** *(US)* Fünfcentstück; **~ dollar** *(US)* halber Dollar; **~ eagle** *(US)* Goldmünze zu 5 Dollar; **~-fare ticket** Fahrkarte zum halben Preis; **~-finished** halbfertig; **~-hearted attempt** halbherziger Versuch; **~ holiday** halber Arbeitstag, freier Nachmittag; **~-hourly bus service** halbstündlicher Omnibusverkehr; **to have a ~ interest in a firm** an einer Firma hälftig beteiligt sein; **~ knowledge** Halbwissen; **to be a ~ listener** nur mit halbem Ohr zuhören; **~-mast** halbmast; **~-mast** *(v.)* auf Halbmast setzen; **~-measure** *(print.)* zweispaltig; **~-page advertisement** halbseitige Anzeige; **~ pay** Warte-, Ruhegehalt, -geld, *(mil.)* Pension, Wartegeld; **on ~ pay** außer Dienst, verabschiedet; **to place on ~ pay** in den Wartestand versetzen, *(mil.)* pensionieren; **to sell out and go on ~ pay** sich pensionieren lassen; **~ pilotage** Bereitschaftsgeld [für einen Piloten]; **~-price** halber Preis; **to sell s. th. ~-price** etw. zum halben Preis verkaufen; **children ~-price** Kinder zahlen die Hälfte; **~ the profit** Quartalsmedio; **~ proof** Anscheinsbeweis; **~ rate** halber Fahrpreis; **~-seas over** *(coll.)* leicht angesäuselt; **~ share** halber Anteil, Hälfte, Halbpart; **~-shot** *(sl.)* fast betrunken; **~ sovereign** *(Br.)* Goldmünze zu 10 Shilling; **~ stock** *(US)* Aktie mit einem Pariwert von $ 50; **~ time** Halbzeit, *(worker)* halbe Arbeitszeit; **~-time** halbtägig; **to be on ~-time** nur halbtags arbeiten, in einem Teilbeschäftigungsverhältnis stehen; **~-time job** Teilzeit-, Halbtagsbeschäftigung; **~-time system** *(Br.)* Teilzeitbeschäftigungswesen; **~-time worker** Halbtagsarbeiter, Teilzeitbeschäftigter; **~-timer** Halbtagsarbeiter, Teilzeitbeschäftigter, *(student, Br.)* Werkschüler, -student; **~ title** *(print.)* Zwischen-, Schmutztitel; **~-tone** *(photo)* Halbton, gerastertes Bild, *(print.)* Autotypie; **~-tone block** Autotypieklischee; **~-tone shadings** Rastertönungen; **~-tongue**

Geschworenengericht für Ausländer; ~-**track** Räderraupen-fahrzeug; ~-**truth** Halbwahrheiten; ~-**weekly** halbwöchent-lich; ~-**willed** schwachsinnig; ~ **work** halbe Wochenarbeit; ~ **year** Halbjahr; ~ **yearly** halbjährlich; ~-**yearly dividend** Halb-jahresdividende; ~-**yearly instalment** Halbjahresrate; ~-**yearly payment** Halbjahreszahlung; ~-**yearly rest** Halbjahresab-schluß.

halfpenny, not to have a ~ **on o. s.** keinen Groschen Geld bei sich haben; **not to be a** ~ **the worth of it** keinen Pfifferling wert sein; **to turn up like a bad** ~ immer wieder auftauchen;
~ **post** (*Br.*) Drucksachen.

halfway, to meet auf halbem Wege entgegenkommen;
~ **house** auf halbem Weg gelegenes Gasthaus, (*fig.*) Kompro-miß, Entgegenkommen auf halbem Weg; ~ **measures** halbe (halbherzige) Maßnahmen, Kompromiß.

Halifax law Lynchjustiz.

hall Vestibül, Flur, Diele, (*college*) Speisesaal, (*corridor*) Gang, Korridor, Flur, (*guild*) Zunft-, Innungshaus, (*manor house, Br.*) Herrenhaus, (*Oxford*) Studentenwohnheim, Internat, (*US, university*) wissenschaftliche Vereinigung, Institut, Kollegium;
booking ~ Schalterhalle; **central** ~ (*post office*) Schalterhalle; **city** ~ (*US*) Rathaus; **conference** ~ Konferenz-, Sitzungssaal; **entrance** ~ Eingangshalle; **music** ~**s** (*US*) Konzerthalle; **parish** ~ Gemeindesaal; **Science** ⌖ (*US*) Naturwissenschaftliches Institut; **town** ~ (*Br.*) Rathaus; **waiting** ~ Wartesaal; ⌖ **of Justice** Justizpalast; ~ **of residence** (*Br.*) Studenten-wohnheim;
~ **bedroom** (*US*) kleines Schlafzimmer; ~ **boy** (*US*) Laufbur-sche; ~ **porter** Hausmeister; ~ **stand** Garderobe, Garderoben-ständer; ~ **tree** (*US*) Garderobenständer.

hallmark Feingehaltsstempel, (*fig.*) Merkmal, Charakteri-stikum;
~ (*v.*) stempeln, kennzeichnen, (*stamp with*) mit Feingehalts-stempel versehen, (*fig.*) kennzeichnen, Gepräge geben.

hallway (*US*) Vorplatz, Hausflur, Eingangshalle.

halt Halt, Stopp, Haltepunkt, (*railway, Br.*) Bedarfshaltestelle, (*mil.*) Rast;
to come to a ~ zum Stehen kommen; **to grind to a** ~ knirschend zum Stillstand kommen; **to speak with a** ~ zögernd sprechen; ~ **signal** Haltesignal, -zeichen.

halter (*fig.*) Henkerstod.

halting | argument hinkendes Argument; ~ **place** Rastplatz.

halve (*v.*) halbieren, auf die Hälfte reduzieren.

halves, to cry Halbpart verlangen; **to do s. th. by** ~ etw. nur halb tun; **to go** ~ **with s. o.** Hälfte der Kosten übernehmen, sich mit jem. in die Kosten teilen; **to go** ~ **in the expenses of a carriage** sich in die Fahrtkosten teilen.

ham (*sl.*) Funkamateur;
~ **actor** Amateurschauspieler.

hamesecken (*Scot. law*) Hausfriedensbruch.

hamlet Weiler, Flecken.

hammer Zwangsversteigerung;
~ **and sickle** Hammer und Sichel; ~ **and tongs** wild drauflos;
~ (*v.*) (*Br.*) für zahlungsunfähig erklären;
~ **away at a problem** hart an der Lösung eines Problems arbeiten; ~ **a defaulter** (*Br.*) jds. Zahlungsunfähigkeit bekannt-machen; ~ **down the lid of a box** Kistendeckel zunageln; ~ **an idea into s. one's head** jem. eine Idee eintrichtern; ~ **the market** (*US*) Preise durch Leerverkäufe drücken, Baisseangriff machen; ~ **out** ersinnen, erdenken, ausarbeiten; ~ **out policies** allgemeine Richtlinien ausarbeiten;
to bring to the ~ zwangsversteigern, versteigern, verauktionie-ren; **to come (go) under the** ~ versteigert werden; **to go at it** ~ **and tongs** mit Brachialgewalt angehen;
~ **price** Auktionspreis.

hammered, to be (*stockbroker, Br.*) für insolvent (bankrott, zahlungsunfähig) erklärt werden.

hammering (*broker*) Insolvenzfeststellung.

hamper Hemmnis, Hindernis, Fessel, (*container for fruits*) Ge-schenkkorb;
~ (*v.*) hindern.

hand Hand, (*a hand's breadth*) Handbreit, (*clock*) Zeiger, (*hand-writing*) Handschrift, (*help*) Hilfe, (*possession*) Besitz, Eigen-tum, (*performance*) Ausführung, Fertigkeit, (*ship*) Besat-zungsmitglied, Matrose, (*signature*) Unterschrift, (*skill*) Fingerspitzengefühl, Taktik, (*worker*) Gehilfe, [Hand]arbei-ter;
at ~ zur Hand, nahe [bevorstehend]; **at first** ~ aus erster Hand; **at my** ~**s** zu meinem Vorteil; **at second** ~ aus zweiter Hand, nicht unmittelbar; **by** ~ durch Boten; **for one's own** ~ im

eigenen Interesse, auf eigene Rechnung; **given under my** ~ **and seal** eigenhändig von mir unterschrieben und gesiegelt; **in** ~ (*in advance*) im voraus, pränumerando, (*cash*) bar, in klingender Münze, (*under control*) unter Kontrolle, (*stocked*) zur Verfü-gung, vorrätig, auf Lager; **in one's own** ~ eigenhändig; **in private** ~**s** in Privathand, in privater Hand; **in the turning of a** ~ im Handumdrehen; **off** ~ auf der Stelle, aus dem Stegreif; **on** ~ vorrätig, vorhanden, auf Lager, greifbar; **on every** ~ auf jeder Seite; **ready to one's** ~ in bequemer Nähe; **still on** ~ unbegeben; **to** ~ zur Hand, nahe; **under** ~ in einfacher Schriftform; **under the** ~ **of** unterzeichnet von; **under** ~ **and seal** unterschrieben und versiegelt; **with clean** ~**s** redlich; **with a heavy** ~ mit harter Hand, erbarmungslos; **with a high** ~ hochmütig, von oben herab, selbstherrlich; **with all** ~**s** mit Mann und Maus; **with one's own** ~ eigenhändig; **with strong** ~ gewaltsam;
~**s down** spielend, ohne Anstrengung, mühelos; ~ **and foot** (*fig.*) eifrig ergeben; ~ **and glove** auf vertrautem Fuß; ~ **to** ~ von Hand zu Hand; ~ **on heart** Hand aufs Herz; ~ **over** ~ (*fig.*) Zug um Zug, in rascher Folge;
~**s** Mannschaft, Belegschaft;
business ~ kaufmännische Handschrift; **clear** ~ deutliche Handschrift; **commercial** ~ kaufmännische Handschrift; **dead** ~ (*mortmain*) tote Hand; **factory** ~ Fabrikarbeiter; **farm** ~ Landarbeiter; **good** ~ gute Handschrift; **helping** ~ hilfreiche Hand; **an iron** ~ eiserne Zucht; **old** ~ alter Fachmann; **old parliamentarian** ~ erfahrener Abgeordneter (Parlamentsprak-tikus); **practised** ~ erfahrener Mann der Praxis (Praktiker); **running** ~ ausgeschriebene Handschrift, Kurrentschrift; **small** ~ gewöhnliche Korrespondenzschrift; ~**s wanted** Hilfskräfte gesucht;
~ (*v.*) aushändigen, übergeben, überreichen;
~ **down** (*court*) Urteil fällen; ~ **in** einreichen, eingeben, überge-ben, abliefern; ~ **in one's checks** seine Spielmarken einzahlen; ~ **in one's resignation** um seine Entlassung bitten, seinen Rück-tritt erklären; ~ **in a telegram** Telegramm aufgeben; ~ **s. o. a letter** jem. einen Brief aushändigen; ~ **on news** Nachrichten weiterleiten; ~ **s. o. out of a car** jem. aus dem Auto helfen; ~ **out the wages** Löhne auszahlen; ~ **over** aushändigen, herausgeben, verabfolgen, abliefern; ~ **over one's authority** seine Vollmachten delegieren; ~ **over the command** Kommando übergeben; ~ **over a draft to a bank for collection** Tratte der Bank zum Einzug überlassen; ~ **over the money direct** Geld unmittelbar übergeben; ~ **over papers on payment of fees** Papiere nach Zahlung der Gebühren aushän-digen; ~ **over to the police authorities** den Polizeibehörden übergeben; ~ **over one's property to s. o.** sein Vermögen auf j. übertragen; ~ **a boy a punishment** (*US fam.*) einem Schüler eine Strafe verpassen; ~ **s. th. round** etw. herumreichen; ~ **s. o. a long tale of woe** jem. seine Leidensgeschichte erzählen; ~ **it to s. o.** (*US sl.*) jds. Überlegenheit anerkennen;
to act with a high ~ sich tyrannisch (despotisch) aufführen; **to allow s. o. a free** ~ jem. freie Hand lassen; **to be able to turn one's** ~ **to anything** praktisch mit allem fertig werden; **to be at** ~ kurz bevorstehen; **to be in** ~ in Arbeit sein, bearbeitet werden; **to be a capital** ~ **at s. th.** etw. meisterhaft (aus dem Effeff) verstehen; **to be delivered by** ~ von einem Boten überbracht werden; **to be a good** ~ **at** sehr geschickt (geübt) in etw. sein; **to be on** ~ **at all times** ständig anwesend sein; **to be in the** ~**s of moneylenders** von Wucherern ausgebeutet werden, Geldverlei-hern ausgeliefert sein; **to be a good** ~ **at s. th.** etw. glänzend verstehen; **to be** ~ **in glove with s. o.** sehr vertraut mit jem. sein, sich glänzend mit jem. verstehen; **to be unlikely to change** ~**s** in festen Händen sein; **to be on s. one's** ~**s** jem. zur Last fallen; **to be lost with all** ~**s** mit Mann und Maus untergehen; **to be a new** ~ **to s. th.** Neuling in einer Sache sein; **to be quite out of** ~ nicht zu bändigen sein; **to be short of** ~**s** Leute brauchen; **to bind s. o.** ~ **and foot** (*fig.*) j. vollkommen aktionsunfähig machen; **to bring a gentle but firm** ~ **into the management** Zügel behutsam aber fest in die Hände nehmen; **to change** ~**s** Besitzer wechseln, in andere Hände übergehen; **to come to** ~ eintreffen, in jds. Hände gelangen; **to dismiss all one's** ~**s** seine gesamte Beleg-schaft entlassen; **to end up in the** ~**s of liquidators** nur noch liquidiert werden können; **to fall into the** ~**s of a blackmailer** einem Erpresser in die Hände fallen; **to feed out of s. one's** ~ jem. völlig hörig sein, jem. aus der Hand fressen; **to fight** ~ **to** ~ handgemein werden; **to fight for one's own** ~ seine eigenen Interessen vertreten; **to get one's** ~ **in** in Schwung kommen; **to get a big** ~ reichen Beifall ernten; **to get s. th. off one's** ~**s** eine Sache loswerden; **to get one's** ~ **on s. th.** etw. in die Finger bekommen; **to get out of** ~ außer Kontrolle geraten, nicht mehr zu bändigen sein, (*troops*) Mannszucht verlieren; **to get the**

upper ~ Oberhand gewinnen; **to give one's ~ on a bargain** durch Handschlag besiegeln; **to give a bill from ~** Wechsel aus der Hand geben; **to give s. o. free ~** jem. freie Hand lassen; **to give a helping ~ to s. o.** jem. hilfreich zur Seite stehen; **to give a performer a big ~** *(coll.)* einem Darsteller großen Applaus zollen; **to give her ~ to a suitor** Bewerbung annehmen; **to go ~ in ~ with s. o.** *(fig.)* mit jem. Schritt halten; **to go on one's ~s and knees** auf allen vieren kriechen; **to hang heavy on one's ~s** *(time)* langsam vergehen; **to have a ~ for s. th.** mit etw. umgehen können; **to have a ~ in** beteiligt sein an (bei), seine Finger im Spiel haben; **to have s. th. in ~** sich mit etw. beschäftigen; **to have on one's ~s** zur Verfügung haben; **to have s. th. on one's ~s** mit etw. belastet sein; **to have no ~ in an affair** mit einer Sache nichts zu tun haben, an einer Sache nicht beteiligt (unschuldig) sein; **to have one's ~s full** alle Hände voll zu tun haben; **to have one's ~ in** gut in Schuß sein; **to have an empty house on one's ~s** leerstehendes Haus zu verkaufen (vermieten) haben; **to have so much money in ~** so viel Geld zur Verfügung haben; **to have still some money on ~** Reserven haben; **to have one's ~ in the till** über die Kasse verfügen; **to have an open ~** offene Hand haben; **to have s. o. on (in) the palm of one's ~** j. völlig in der Hand haben; **to have a piece of news first ~** Nachricht aus erster Hand haben; **to have one's ~ tied** nicht Herr seiner Entschlüsse sein; **to have s. th. (an affair) well in ~** Situation völlig unter Kontrolle haben; **to join ~s** sich verbünden; **to keep one's ~ in** nicht aus der Übung geraten; **to keep one's ~ in at s. th.** an etw. beteiligt sein; **to keep a firm ~ on** Kontrolle über etw. ausüben; **to lay ~s on s. th.** Besitz von etw. ergreifen; **to lay violent ~s on o. s.** Selbstmord begehen; **to lay violent ~s on s. o.** jem. Gewalt antun; **to learn s. th. at first ~** etw. unmittelbar (aus erster Hand) erfahren; **to lend a ~** hilfreich sein, Hand anlegen; **to let one's temper get out of ~** Selbstbeherrschung verlieren; **not lift a ~** keinen Finger rühren; **to live by one's ~s** von seiner Hände Arbeit leben; **to live close at ~** um die Ecke herum wohnen; **to live from ~ to mouth** von der Hand in den Mund leben, jeden Pfennig brauchen; **to make one's ~** Profit erzielen; **not to move ~ or foot** keinen Finger rühren; **to pass into the ~s of** in die Hände von jem. übergehen; **to pass into other ~s** in fremde Hände übergehen; **to pass through many ~s** durch viele Hände gehen, häufig den Besitzer wechseln; **to play into the ~s of s. o.** jem. in die Hände arbeiten; **to purchase first ~** aus erster Hand kaufen; **to put o. s. in the ~s of** sich jem. anvertrauen; **to put last ~ to** letzte Hand anlegen; **to put the matter in ~** Auftrag bearbeiten; **to put a matter into the ~s of a lawyer** Sache einem Rechtsanwalt übergeben; **to put one's ~ to the plough** Hand ans Werk legen; **to put one's ~ to a task** an eine Sache herangehen, Sache in Angriff nehmen; **to resign into s. one's ~s** in jds. Hände legen; **to rub one's ~s** *(fig.)* sich die Hände reiben; **to rule with a heavy ~** strenges Regime führen; **to rule s. o. with a high ~** j. despotisch behandeln; **to send a letter by ~** Brief durch Boten überbringen lassen; **to set one's ~ to a document** Urkunde mit seiner Unterschrift versehen; **to show one's ~** *(fig.)* seine Karten aufdecken; **to sign in one's own ~** eigenhändig unterschreiben; **to spend money with both ~s** Geld mit vollen Händen ausgeben; **to strengthen one's ~** seine Position verstärken; **to strike ~s upon a bargain** über einen Handel einig werden; **to take in ~** unternehmen, übernehmen; **to take s. o. by the ~** *(fig.)* j. in seine Obhut nehmen; **to take gifts with both ~s** von beiden Parteien Geschenke nehmen; **to take one's life in one's ~s** sein Leben mutwillig aufs Spiel setzen; **to take the law into one's own ~s** sich selbst Recht schaffen, zur Selbsthilfe schreiten; **to take a ~ in the business** sich an einer Sache beteiligen; **to take too much on ~** sich zuviel vornehmen; **to take on 200 extra ~s** zusätzlich zweihundert Arbeiter einstellen; **to take a ~ in the work** o. s. sich selbst an die Arbeit machen; **to throw in one's ~** sich verloren geben; **to try one's ~ at editing a magazine** sich an die Herausgabe einer Zeitschrift wagen; **to wait on s. o. ~ and foot** j. von hinten und vorne bedienen, jem. jeden Wunsch von den Augen ablesen; **to win ~s down** leichten Sieg davontragen; **to write in a rude ~** ungelenke Handschrift haben; **to write in a small ~** zierliche Handschrift haben; **to write a letter in one's own ~** Brief eigenhändig schreiben; **to write a good ~** schöne Handschrift haben;

all ~s on deck! alle Mann an Deck!;

~ **atlas** Handatlas; ~ **baggage** *(US)* Handgepäck; ~ **bell** Tischglocke; ~ **brake** Handbremse; ~ **composition** Handsatz; ~ **compositor** Handsetzer; ~ **dynamo** handbetriebener Dynamo; ~ **edge** Schattierung; **to lead a ~-to-mouth existence** von der Hand in den Mund leben; ~-**to-~ fight** Kampf Mann gegen Mann; ~ **grenade** Handgranate; ~ **labo(u)r** Handarbeit; ~ **labo(u)rer** Handarbeiter; ~ **lettering** gezeichnete Schrift; ~ **list**

kurze Liste; ~ **luggage** *(Br.)* Handgepäck; ~-**me-down** *(fam., US)* Konfektions-, Fertiganzug, Anzug von der Stange, *(a.)* von der Stange (fertig) gekauft; ~ **money** Handgeld; ~**s-off policy** Nichteinmischungspolitik; ~ **paper** Büttenpapier; ~-**picked candidate** sorgfältig ausgesuchter Kandidat; ~ **print** Handabzug; **within ~-reach** mit der Hand zu greifen; ~ **sale** Kaufabschluß durch Handschlag; ~ **setting** Handsatz; ~-**sign** *(v.)* handschriftlich unterzeichnen; ~ **signal** Wink (Zeichen) mit der Hand; ~-**signed** handsigniert; ~ **stamp** Briefstempel; **not do a ~'s turn** keinen Finger rühren.

hand-to-mouth | buying unmittelbare Bedarfsdeckung, reiner Bedarfskauf, Einkäufe zur sofortigen Verwendung; ~ **existence** unsichere Existenz; **to lead a ~ existence** nahe am Existenzminimum leben; **to switch to a ~ ordering pace** Auftragserteilung nur im Bedarfsfall vornehmen.

hand | print Handabzug; ~ **tool** Handwerkzeug; ~ **tooling** Handbearbeitung; ~-**written** mit der Hand geschrieben, handschriftlich.

handbag Handköfferchen, -tasche;
~ **snatching** Handtaschenraub.

handbill Flugblatt, -zettel, Reklame-, Werbeprospekt, Hand-, Reklamezettel, Werbeblatt;
to give out ~s Flugblätter verteilen;
~ **distribution** Flugblattverteilung.

handbook Hilfs-, Handbuch, Nachschlagewerk, *(bookmaker)* Wettbuch, *(guidebook)* Reiseführer.

handcar *(US)* Draisine mit Handbetrieb.

handcart Handkarren, -wagen.

handclap Händeklatschen.

handcuff | s Handschellen;
~ *(v.)* Handschellen anlegen;
to clap ~ on s. o. jem. Handschellen anlegen.

handful Handvoll, *(person difficult to control)* lästige Person, Nervensäge;
~ **of coins** Handvoll Münzen;
to be a ~ for s. o. jem. sehr zu schaffen machen; **to throw away ~s of money** mit dem Geld nur so um sich werfen.

handgrip Handgriff, Händedruck;
to come to ~s handgemein werden.

handgun Handfeuerwaffe.

handicap *(fig.)* Hindernis, Erschwerung, Benachteiligung;
economic ~ wirtschaftliche Belastung; **time ~** zeitlicher Nachteil;
to be under a great ~ financially finanziell stark benachteiligt sein; **to be under a heavy ~** schwer benachteiligt sein.

handicapped benachteiligt, [körper]behindert;
~ **children** Sorgenkinder; ~ **person** Körperbehinderter; ~ **worker** körperbehinderter Arbeiter.

handicapping Benachteiligung.

handicraft handwerklicher Beruf, Handwerk, *(firm)* Handwerks-, Gewerbe[betrieb], *(manual skill)* Handfertigkeit;
local ~ ortsansässiges Gewerbe; **one-man ~** [handwerklicher] Einmannbetrieb;
to exercise a ~ Handwerk ausüben, Handwerker sein;
~ *(a.)* gewerbetreibend;
~ **business** Handwerksbetrieb; ~ **pursuits (trade)** Handwerksberuf.

handicraftsman Handwerker.

handicraftsmanship Handwerkertum.

handie-talkie *(mil., US)* Feldfunksprechgerät.

handiness Handlichkeit, Geschicklichkeit.

handiwork Handarbeit.

handkerchief Taschentuch;
to throw the ~ to s. o. jem. sein Wohlwollen zu erkennen geben.

handle Handgriff, *(fig.)* Handhabe, *(car)* Kurbel, *(pretext)* Handhabe, Angriffspunkt, Vorwand, *(pump)* Schwengel;
up to the ~ *(US)* bis zum Äußersten;
front-door ~ Vordertürgriff; **starting ~** *(car)* Anwerfer;
~ *(v.)* *(item)* manipulieren, *(manage)* behandeln, handhaben, sich befassen, bearbeiten, bewältigen, erledigen, *(trade)* handeln [in, mit], Handel treiben, *(transport)* befördern, weiterleiten;
~ **s. o. carefully** vorsichtig mit jem. umgehen (verfahren); ~ **with care in carriage** Transport vorsichtig behandeln; ~ **a case** Angelegenheit bearbeiten; ~ **a large degree of independence with great accuracy** selbständige Stellung gewissenhaft ausfüllen; ~ **easily** sich leicht handhaben lassen; ~ **s. o. without gloves (mittens)** j. nicht gerade mit Glacéhandschuhen anfassen; ~ **s. o. with kid gloves** j. mit Glacéhandschuhen behandeln; ~ **foreign goods** ausländische Waren führen; ~ **imported goods** Importwaren einführen; ~ **an item** Posten

manipulieren; **~ a lot of business** viele Sachen gleichzeitig erledigen; **~ a lot of money** größere Geldsumme verwalten; **~ a matter** Angelegenheit besorgen; **~ large orders** große Aufträge bearbeiten; **~ a ship** Schiff manövrieren; **~ a situation in a masterly manner** Situation meisterhaft beherrschen; **any sort of business** Geschäfte aller Art erledigen; **~ stocks and bonds** Wertpapiere handeln; **~ a subject delicately** Thema delikat behandeln; **~ large sums of money** große Geldbeträge verwalten; **~ traffic** Verkehr bewältigen;
to be hard to ~ schwer zu behandeln sein; **to give s. o. a** ~ **against o. s.** jem. eine Handhabe gegen sich geben; **to give a** ~ **for calumny** der Verleumdung Tür und Tor öffnen; **to have a** ~ **to one's name** *(coll.)* Titel führen; **to rough-**~ brutal behandeln; **~ bar** *(bicycle)* Lenkstange.
handler *(police)* Hundeführer.
handling Abwicklung, Handhabung, Manipulation, Bearbeitung, Aus-, Durchführung, *(operating methods)* Betriebsabwicklung, *(transportation)* Beförderung, Weiterleitung;
proper ~ sachgemäße Behandlung; **rough** ~ unsachgemäße Behandlung;
~ of an affair Bearbeitung einer Angelegenheit; **~ an agency** Agenturleitung; **~ on board** Umstauen an Bord; **~ of calls** Gesprächsabwicklung; **~ of cargo** Umstauen der Ladung; **~ of customers' orders** Bearbeitung von Kundenbestellungen; **~ of the economy** Konjunktursteuerung; **~ of flights** Flugabfertigung; **~ of public funds** Verwaltung öffentlicher Mittel; **~ of an order** Auftragsbearbeitung; **~ of return of unsold copies** Remittendenbearbeitung; **~ stolen goods** *(Br.)* Hehlerei; **~ of traffic** Verkehrsbewältigung;
~ capacity Umschlagkapazität; **~ characteristic** Bedienungseigenschaft; **~ charge** *(stock exchange)* Manipulationsgebühr; **~ charges** Umschlagspesen, Bearbeitungsgebühren; **~ costs** Bearbeitungs-, Abwicklungs-, Verwaltungskosten; **~ equipment** Verladeanlage, -einrichtung; **~ fee** Bearbeitungsgebühr; **~ place** Abfertigungsstelle; **~ platform** Verladegerüst, Ausladebrücke; **~ qualities** *(car)* Fahreigenschaften; **special ~ parcel** *(US)* Schnellpaket; **~ time** Bearbeitungszeit, *(factory)* Materialtransportzeit.
handmade handgearbeitet, -gemacht, *(paper)* handgeschöpft;
~ paper Büttenpapier.
handout *(beggar, US sl.)* Almosen, Gabe, *(leaflet)* [Werbe]prospekt, Broschüre, Waschzettel, *(press release)* Pressenotiz, freigegebenes Pressematerial;
to cadge ~s um milde Gaben betteln; **~ material** Informationsmaterial.
handover of power Machtübergabe.
handrail [Treppen]geländer.
handsale Handkauf.
handsel *(gift)* Begrüßungs-, Einstandsgeschenk, *(earnest money)* An-, Handgeld, *(wedding)* Hochzeitsgeschenk [des Bräutigams], *(new year)* Neujahrsgeschenk;
~ *(v.)* zum ersten Mal gebrauchen, einweihen; **~ a dealer** Händler erstmalig einschalten; **~ a shop** zum erstenmal in einem Laden kaufen.
handseller Straßenhändler.
handset Handapparat, Hörer.
handshake, golden Sonderbonus, Entlassungsabfindung;
to give s. o. the golden ~ j. wegloben.
handsome hübsch, staatlich, *(generous)* nobel, großzügig, freigebig;
~ fortune ansehnliches Vermögen; **~ price** erheblicher Preis; **~ profit** stattlicher Gewinn; **~ residence** stattliches Herrenhaus; **~ treatment** großzügige Behandlung.
handsorting Aussortierung mit der Hand;
~ method Ablegeverfahren.
handwork Handarbeit.
handworkman Handarbeiter.
handwriting Handschrift, *(manuscript)* Manuskript, *(print.)* Schreibschrift;
in ~ eigenhändig geschrieben;
current ~ flüssige Handschrift; **developed** ~ ausgeschriebene Handschrift; **legible** ~ saubere Handschrift; **readable** ~ gut lesbare Handschrift; **sprawling** ~ gespreizte Handschrift; **shocking** ~ miserable Handschrift;
the ~ **on the wall** böses Omen;
to disguise one's ~ seine Handschrift verstellen; **to make out a** ~ Handschrift entziffern;
~ analysis Handschriftendeutung, -untersuchung; **~ expert** Schriftsachverständiger.
handwritten holographisch, mit der Hand geschrieben;
~ application handschriftliche Bewerbung.

handy handlich, greifbar, leicht erreichbar;
to come in ~ zustatten kommen; **to always keep a first-aid kit** ~ Verbandskasten immer parat haben;
~ man Gelegenheitsarbeiter, Aushilfsarbeiter, -kraft, Faktotum; **~ size** handliches Format; **~ way** eingängige Methode.
hang Abhang, Abschüssigkeit, Senkung, *(fig.)* Hang, Neigung, *(US coll.)* Bedeutungsweise;
~ *(v.)* hängen, aufhängen, *(fig.)* hängen, schweben, *(jury, US)* keine Einigung erzielen, *(put to death)* aufhängen, henken.
hang *(v.)* **about** sich herumtreiben;
~ at street corners for the pubs to open herumlungernd auf das Öffnen der Kneipen warten.
hang *(v.)* | **around on the street corners** *(sl.)* an den Straßenecken herumstehen; **~ back** zaudern, unentschlossen sein; **~ in the balance** noch unentschieden (in der Schwebe) sein, auf der Kippe stehen.
hang *(v.)* **by** | **the eyelids** an einem seidenem Faden hängen; **~ a hair** an einem seidenen Faden hängen; **~ a single thread** an einem seidenen Faden hängen; **~ the wall** ungenützt bleiben.
hang *(v.)* | **s. o. in effigy** j. symbolisch aufhängen; **~ fire** *(fig.)* auf sich warten lassen; **~ heavy** *(time)* langsam vergehen, dahinschleichen; **~ a lamp from the ceiling** Lampe an der Decke aufhängen; **~ on s. one's lips** an jds. Lippen hängen.
hang *(v.)* **on** sich festhalten (festklammern), *(show perseverance)* nicht aufgeben, ausdauernd sein;
~ to s. o. j. weiterhin in Sicht behalten; **~ like grim death** bis zum Umfallen aushalten.
hang *(v.)* **out** *(loiter, sl.)* heraushängen, herumlungern, *(sl.)* kampieren;
~ flags flaggen, Fahnen aufhängen.
hang *(v.)* **round** *(US)* herumlungern.
hang *(v.)* **together** zusammenhalten.
hang *(v.)* **up** verzögern, *(tel.)* Telefonhörer auflegen;
~ a plan definitely Plan endgültig aufgeben; **~ wallpaper** tapezieren, Tapete anbringen.
hang, not to care a ~ sich überhaupt nicht darum kümmern; **to get the** ~ **of s. th.** sich in etw. einarbeiten, Bogen herausbekommen; **to let things go** ~ sich den Teufel um etw. kümmern (scheren);
~ gliding Drachenfliegen.
hangar *(aircraft)* Hangar, Flugzeughalle, *(coaches)* Schuppen.
hanger Aufhängevorrichtung;
~-on Schmarotzer, *(pol.)* Mitläufer; **paper-**~ Tapezierer; **~ card** Hängeplakat.
hanging Erhängen, Hinrichtung durch den Strang;
~s Wandbehang, Tapete;
paper ~ Tapezieren;
~ indent *(print.)* eingerückter (eingezogener) Satz; **~ matter** todeswürdiges Verbrechen; **~ sign** Hängeschild.
hangman Henker.
hangout *(US sl.)* Bude, Treffpunkt, Stammkneipe.
hangover *(remains)* Überbleibsel, *(sl.)* Katzenjammer, Kater.
Hank *(BBC, Br.)* frühere Nachmittagssendungen.
hanker *(v.)* **after wealth** dem Reichtum nachjagen.
hankering after fame Ruhmsucht.
hanky-panky Hokuspokus.
Hansard *(Br.)* amtliches Parlamentsprotokoll.
hansardize *(v.)* *(Br.)* einem Abgeordneten frühere Ausführungen entgegenhalten.
haphazard zufällig, vom Zufall bestimmt;
at ~ aufs Geratewohl;
~ sampling unkontrollierte Stichproben, stichprobenartige Marktuntersuchung.
happen *(v.)* vorgehen, sich ereignen, eintreten, passieren, zustandekommen, *(US coll.)* zufällig hereingeschneit kommen.
happening Ereignis, Vorkommnis.
happenstance notes *(US fam.)* Randkommentar.
happy glücklich, beglückt, *(coll.)* angeheitert, leicht beschwipst;
~-go-lucky fashion unbekümmerte Lebensweise; **~ New Year** glückliches Neujahr; **~ touch** *(advertising)* freundliche Note.
harakiri Harakiri.
harangue Tirade, *(speech)* leidenschaftliche Rede;
~ *(v.)* **the mob** zur Menge reden.
haranguer leidenschaftlicher Redner.
harbo(u)r [See]hafen, *(refuge)* Herberge, Zufluchtsort, Unterschlupf;
artificial ~ künstlicher Hafen; **cold** ~ Nachtasyl; **commercial** ~ Handelshafen; **icebound** ~ vereister Hafen; **ice-free** ~ eisfreier Hafen; **inner** ~ Binnenhafen; **land-locked** ~ Binnenhafen; **man-of-war** ~ Kriegshafen; **natural** ~ natürlicher Hafen; **open** ~ offener Hafen; **outer** ~ Außenhafen; **tidal** ~ Gezeitenhafen;

short-term ~ for one's cash kurzfristige Barmittelanlage; **~ of refuge** Nothafen, Zufluchtsort; **~ of transshipment** Umschlaghafen;

~ (v.) anlegen, im Hafen ankern, (fig.) Zuflucht gewähren, beherbergen;

~ s. o. jem. Obdach gewähren; **~ a dog** Hund halten; **~ a grudge against s. o.** Groll gegen j. hegen; **~ an escaped prisoner** einem entsprungenem Verbrecher Unterschlupf gewähren; **~ suspicion** Verdacht hegen; **~ thoughts of revenge** Rachegedanken hegen;

to be free of the ~ aus dem Hafen heraus sein; **to call at a ~** Hafen anlaufen; **to clear the ~** aus dem Hafen auslaufen; **to clean out a ~** Hafen ausbaggern; **to enter ~** [in den Hafen] einlaufen; **to fetch the ~** Hafen erreichen; **to give ~ to a criminal** einem Verbrecher Unterschlupf gewähren; **to leave ~** [aus dem Hafen] auslaufen; **to offer ~ to s. o.** jem. ein Obdach anbieten; **to remain off the ~** auf der Reede ankern; **to steam out of the ~** Hafen verlassen;

~ authority Hafenamt, -behörde; **~ barrage** Hafensperre; **~ board** Hafenbehörde, Hafenmeisteramt, -verwaltung; **~ charges** Hafengebühren; **~ craft** Hafenfahrzeug; **~ docks** Hafenanlagen; **~ dues** Hafengebühren, Hafenzoll, Hafenabgaben; **~ duties** Hafendienst; **~ entrance** Hafeneinfahrt; **~ facilities** Hafenanlagen, -einrichtungen; **~ guard** Hafenpolizei, -wache; **~ installations** Hafenanlagen, -einrichtungen; **~ line** Hafenabgrenzung; **~ master** Hafenmeister, -aufseher, -kommissar, -inspektor; **~ mouth** Hafeneinfahrt; **~ police** Hafenpolizei; **~ railway** Hafenbahn; **~ rates** Hafengebühren; **~ regulations** Hafenordnung; **~ risk** Hafengefahr; **~ station** Hafenbahnhof; **~ service** Hafenleistungen; **~ tug** Hafenschlepper; **~ watch** Hafenwache.

harbo(u)rage Schutz, Zuflucht.

harbo(u)rer Beherberger.

harbo(u)ring Gewährung von Unterschlupf;
~ of criminals Verstecken von Verbrechern.

harbourless ohne Hafen, (fig.) obdachlos.

hard hart, (US, alcohol) hochprozentig (difficult to bear) schwierig, anstrengend, mühsam, (prices) hoch, starr, (severe) streng, hart;

as ~ as adamant stahlhart; **as ~ as nails** von eiserner Gesundheit, (fig.) ohne falsche Sentimentalitäten; **~ to come by** schwer zu erwischen; **~ to deal with** unzugänglich, schwer zu nehmen; **~ and fast** (agreement) unbedingt bindend, ausnahmslos; **~ to please** schwer zu befriedigen; **~ to understand** schwerverständlich; **~ up** in schlechten Verhältnissen, ohne Geld, schlecht bei Kasse, auf dem Trockenen;

to be ~ at it tüchtig an der Arbeit sein; **to be ~ on s. o.** streng zu jem. sein, Strenge gegenüber jem. zeigen; **to be as ~ as a flint** (fam.) Herz von Stein haben; **to be ~ of hearing** schwerhörig sein; **to be ~ hit** große Verluste erlitten haben; **to be as ~ as nails** (fam.) in erstklassiger Verfassung sein; **to be ~ put to it to do** Schwierigkeiten bei etw. haben, etw. auf dem Halse haben; **to be ~ up for** schwer im Druck sein, finanziell knapp sein; **to be ~ up for an excuse** kaum eine Entschuldigung finden können; **to be ~ put to it in großer Verlegenheit sein; to be ~ set to find money** schwer Geld auftreiben können; **to be ~ up for money** sich in Geldverlegenheit befinden, kaum Geld haben; **to be ~ to please** schwer zufriedenzustellen sein; **to be ~ to sell** sich schwer verkaufen lassen; **to follow ~ upon s. o.** jem. dicht auf den Fersen sein; **to run s. o. ~** j. an einem strengen Zügel führen; **to work ~** schwer arbeiten; **to work ~ for one's living** sich sein Brot schwer verdienen;

~-acquired knowledge hart erarbeitetes Wissen; **~ ankle** (dial.) Bergarbeiter; **to be a ~ blow for s. o.** j. schwer treffen; **~-boiled** hartgesotten, kaltschnäuzig; **~-boiled egg** (fig., sl.) hartgesottener Bursche; **~ board** Hartfaserplatte; **~ book** schweres Buch; **~-bought experience** teuer bezahlte Erfahrungen; **~ case** (US) unverbesserlicher Verbrecher; **~ cases** unbillige Entscheidungen; **~ cash** (cash on hand) Barbestand, (coin) Hartgeld; **~ coal** Anthrazit; **~ coal mining** Steinkohlenbergbau; **~ colo(u)rs** grelle Farben; **~-contrast picture** Kontrastfoto; **~ copy** geschriebener Text, Klartext; **~ core** (engineering, Br.) fester Untergrund, Schotterlage, (unemployment) dauernder Arbeitslosenbestandteil; **~ core in borrowing** unabgebauter laufender Kreditbedarf; **~-core** (fam.) knallhart; **~ core hiring program(me)** Einstellungsprogramm für Dauerarbeitslose; **~-core thinking** Grundsatzdenken; **~-core unemployed** Bodensatz der Arbeitslosen, (a.) zum Bodensatz [der Arbeitslosen] gehörend; **~-core worker** Dauerarbeitsloser; **~ cover** Leineneinband; **~-cover** (a.) mit festem Einband; **~ currency** harte Währung; **~-currency account** Hartwährungskonto; **~-**

~ currency country Hartwährungsland, währungsstarkes Land; **~-currency shop** Geschäft, in dem nur mit Devisen eingekauft werden kann; **~ dollar** harter Dollar; **~ drinks** starke Getränke; **~-earned money** schwer (sauer) verdientes Geld; **~ earnings** sauer verdientes Geld; **~ facts** unumstößliche (nackte) Tatsachen; **~ fate** grausames Schicksal; **~ finish** Feinputz; **~-finished** fest verarbeitet; **~ frost** strenger Frost; **~-got fortune** mühsam erworbenes Vermögen; **~-handed** (fig.) tyrannisch; **~ hat** Arbeitgeberhut; **~-headed** realistisch, geschäftsmäßig, praktisch, nüchtern; **~-hearted** hartherzig; **~ hole** (sl.) Kriminalbeamter; **~ job** schwerer Beruf; **~ knot** fester Knoten; **~ labo(u)r** (US) Zwangsarbeit, Zuchthaus; **~ language** schwer zu erlernende Sprache; **~ liner** Befürworter einer harten Politik; **~ lines** Pech; **~ liquors** scharfe Getränke; **~-living money** (Br., mil.) konvertierbares Geld; **~-lying money** (Br., mil.) Raumbeschränkungszulage; **~ luck** nicht verdientes Schicksal; **~ master** gestrenger Meister; **~ metal** Hartmetall; **~ money** Hartgeld, (currency) frei konvertierbares Geld; **to call s. o. ~ names** jem. nichts ersparen; **~-nosed** kaltrechnend; **~ nut to crack** harte Nuß, schwieriges Problem; **~ paper** (photo) hartes Papier; **~ pressed (-pushed) debtor** schwer bedrängter Schuldner; **~ print** (photo print) harter Abzug; **~ problem** schwieriges Problem; **~ reading** schwere Lektüre; **~ rubber** Hartgummi; **~-and-fast rules** absolut bindende Vorschriften, strenge Regeln; **~ sell** Holzhammermethode, aggressive Verkaufspolitik; **~-sell** (a.) (US) reaktionär, orthodox; **~ selling** Anwendung aggressiver Verkaufsmethoden, Verkaufen um jeden Preis; **to be ~-set to find money** in großer Geldverlegenheit sein; **~-shell** (US coll.) unnachgiebig, kompromißlos; **to be a ~ spot** (stock exchange, US) festliegen; **~ student** ausdauernder Gelehrter; **~ stuff** (sl.) Alkohol; **~ style** uneleganter Stil; **to say ~ things to s. o.** ganz unverblümt mit jem. sprechen; **~ thinking** angestrengtes Nachdenken; **~ times** schlechte Zeiten; **to have a ~ time of it** mit Schwierigkeiten zu kämpfen haben, schwere Zeiten durchmachen; **to learn it the ~ way** Lehrgeld zahlen; **~ winter** strenger Winter; **~ wood** (sl.) Stehplatzkarte; **~ work** schwere Arbeit, Schwerarbeit; **~ worker** fleißiger Arbeiter; **~-working** fleißig.

hardboard Hartfaserplatte.

harden (v.) (fig.) sich verhärten, (prices) anziehen, steigen, fester werden, sich festigen;
~ the body sich abhärten; **~ o. s. to the cold** (fam.) sich gegen Kälte abhärten; **~ s. one's heart** jds. Herz verhärten; **~ the roads** Straßen austrocknen lassen.

hardened criminal verstockter Verbrecher.

hardening (prices) Anziehen, Festigung;
~ of the market (tendency) Versteifung am [Geld]markt.

hardgoods devisenstarke Waren.

hard[i]ness Härte, Widerstandsfähigkeit, Ausdauer.

hardliner Verfechter eines harten Kurses.

hardpan niedrigster Stand;
~ price (US coll.) niedrigst stehende Kurse.

hardship Härte, Not, Bedrängnis, (hard to bear) Mühsal, Beschwerde, Ungemach;
to do ~ to s. o. jem. hart zusetzen; **to lead to undue ~** zu unbilliger Härte führen;
~ allowance Härtezulage, -ausgleich; **special ~ allowance** (Br.) besondere Härtezulage bei Berufsunfähigkeit; **~ case** Härtefall; **~ clause** Härteklausel; **~ post** Stellung mit Härtezulage.

hardstand Flugzeugabstellplatz.

hardtack Schiffszwieback, (sl.) Moos, Moneten, Kies.

hardtop Limousine ohne feste Mittelstreben.

hardware Metall-, Eisenwaren, (data processing) Maschinenausrüstung;
builder's ~ Baumaterialien;
~ department Haushaltungsabteilung; **builder's ~ merchant** Baumaterialienhändler.

hardwareman Metall-, Eisenwarenhändler.

hare Hase;
mad as a March ~ total verrückt;
~ and hounds Schnitzeljagd;
to run with the ~ and hunt with the hounds es mit beiden Seiten halten; **to start a ~** dem Gespräch eine neue Richtung geben.

hark (v.) **back** (fig.) zurückgreifen auf.

harlequin Hanswurst, Kasperl.

harm Nachteil, Schaden, Verletzung;
grievous bodily ~ schwere Körperverletzung;
to do a great ~ großen Schaden anrichten; **to mean no ~** nichts Böses im Sinn haben; **to see no ~ in s. th.** nichts Böses darin sehen;
out of ~'s way in Sicherheit.

harmful nachteilig, schädlich;
  to be ~ to s. one's interests jds. Interessen schädigen;
  ~ publications jugendgefährdende Schriften.

harmless unschädlich;
  to save s. o. ~ j. schadlos halten;
  ~ error unerheblicher Rechtsfehler; **~ talk** harmloses Gespräch.

harmonic *(fig.)* harmonisch;
  ~ balance *(car)* Stabilisator; **~ plane** *(tide, US)* Nullebene.

harmonization *(tariff)* Abstimmung, Harmonisierung, *(text)* Angleichung;
  ~ of customs duties *(EG)* Zollharmonisierung; **~ of taxation** Steuerangleichung.

harmonize *(v.)* harmonisieren, abstimmen, *(taxes)* harmonisieren, angleichen, *(texts)* in Übereinstimmung bringen;
  ~ with s. o. mit jem. harmonisieren.

harmony Einigkeit, Einklang, Eintracht;
  ~ of interests Interessenübereinstimmung; **~ in international affairs** internationale Übereinstimmung;
  to be in ~ with public opinion mit der öffentlichen Meinung übereinstimmen; **to live in perfect ~** harmonisches Dasein führen.

harness Ausrüstung;
  in ~ in der täglichen Arbeit;
  ~ *(v.)* (natural forces) nutzbar machen;
  to be in ~ mitten in der Arbeit stehen; **to die in ~** in den Sielen (in der Ausübung seines Berufs) sterben; **to get back into ~ again** *(fam.)* wieder in die Tretmühle zurückkehren; **to run (work) in double ~** eng zusammenarbeiten;
  ~ cop *(US sl.)* uniformierter Polizist; **~ maker** Sattler; **~ making** Sattlerei.

harp Harfe;
  ~ *(v.)* upon the same string dauernd auf einem Thema herumreiten.

harpoon Harpune;
  ~ *(v.)* harpunieren.

harrow Egge;
  ~ *(v.)* s. one's feelings jds. Gefühle verletzen;
  to be under the ~ in großer Not sein.

harry *(v.)* verheeren, verwüsten;
  ~ one's debtors seine Schuldner laufend bedrängen.

harsh|judge strenger Richter; **~ judgment** hartes Urteil; **to exchange ~ words with s. o.** sich gegenseitig beschimpfen.

harshly, to deal ~ with s. o. hart mit jem. umspringen.

harum-scarum flatterhafter Mensch;
  to do s. th. in a ~ way etw. in Teufelseile erledigen.

harvest [Getreide]ernte, *(fig.)* Ertrag, Gewinn, Erfolg;
  bad ~ Mißernte; **bountiful ~** überreiche Ernte; **generous ~** gute Ernte; **heavy ~** reiche Ernte; **liberal (overflowing) ~** überreiche Ernte; **rich ~** reiche Ernte; **small ~** magere Ernte; **standing ~** Ernte auf dem Halm; **wheat ~** Weizenernte;
  ~ *(v.)* Ernte einbringen, [ab]ernten;
  to get in (win) the ~ Ernte einbringen; **to reap the ~ of one's hard work** Früchte harter Arbeit ernten; **to yield a rich ~ of information** umfangreiches Informationsmaterial zutage fördern;
  ~ collection Ernteeinbringung; **~ festival** Dankgottesdienst, Erntedankfest; **~ fluctuations** Ernteertragsschwankungen; **~ home** Erntefest; **~ prospects** Ernteaussichten; **~ report** Erntebericht; **~ time** Erntezeit; **at ~ time** während der Ernte; **~ work** Erntearbeit; **~ worker** Erntearbeiter.

harvester Erntearbeiter, Schnitter, *(machine)* Mähdrescher;
  volunteer ~ *(US)* Erntehelfer.

harvesting Ernteeinbringung;
  ~ expenses Kosten der Ernteeinbringung; **~ period** Erntezeit; **~ waggon** Erntewagen.

hash Durcheinander, Mischmasch, *(coll.)* alter Kohl, *(stupid fellow)* Dummkopf;
  to make a ~ of it etw. verpatzen, *(fam.)* Durcheinander anrichten; **to settle s. one's ~** jem. einen Strich durch die Rechnung machen; **to settle s. one's ~ in a couple of articles** j. mit ein paar Zeitungsartikeln völlig erledigen;
  ~ house *(US sl.)* billiges Speisehaus, Bumslokal.

hasp and staple *(Scot. law)* Schlüsselübergabe.

haste Eile, Geschwindigkeit;
  to make ~ sich beeilen.

hasten *(v.)* zur Eile antreiben;
  ~ s. one's death jds. Tod beschleunigen.

hastiness Eilfertigkeit, Voreiligkeit.

hasty eilfertig, eilig, hastig;
  ~ bridge *(mar.)* Behelfsbrücke; **to jump to a ~ conclusion** voreilige Schlußfolgerung ziehen; **~ obstacle** Schnellsperre.

hat Hut, *(fig.)* Kardinalswürde;
  under one's ~ geheim, für sich; **~ in hand** unterwürfig;
  bad ~ *(Br., sl.)* übler Kunde;
  to go round with the ~ Beiträge (Spenden) sammeln; **to hang up one's ~** sich häuslich niederlassen; **to keep the news under one's ~** Nachrichten für sich behalten; **to pass the ~ round for s. o.** Sammelaktion für j. starten; **to take one's ~ off to s. o.** jem. den Vorrang zuerkennen; **to talk one's ~ off to s. o.** jem. in Grund und Boden reden; **to talk through one's ~** *(sl.)* faseln, Kohl reden; **to throw one's ~ into the ring** sich um einen Posten bewerben;
  ~ money Primgeld; **~ shop** Hutladen; **~ tree** *(US)* Hutständer.

hatch *(mar.)* Luke;
  under ~es unter Deck, *(fig.)* in der Klemme, *(sl.)* erledigt;
  ~ *(v.)* a plot Verschwörung aushecken;
  to cover and secure the ~es Luken schließen.

hatchback Fließheck.

hatched rule Strichlinie.

hatchel *(v.)* **s. o.** j. durchhecheln.

hatchet Kriegsbeil;
  to bury the ~ Streit (Kriegsbeil) begraben; **to throw the ~** aufschneiden; **to take up the ~** Kriegsbeil ausgraben.

hatching *(fig.)* aushecken.

hatchway Luke.

hatmaker Hutmacher.

hatrack Hutablage.

hatstand Hutständer.

hatter Hutmacher;
  as mad as a ~ völlig übergeschnappt.

haul Schleppen, Ziehen, *(distance covered)* Transportweg, -strecke, *(fig.)* Fischzug, Beute, Fund, *(transport)* Schleppertransport;
  line ~ Linienverkehr; **long ~s** Fernverkehr; **short ~s** Nahverkehr;
  ~ of coal Ladung Kohlen; **good ~ of fish** reicher Fischzug; **long ~s on the railway** *(US)* Güterfernverkehr;
  ~ *(v.)* ziehen, schleppen, befördern, transportieren, *(fig.)* seinen Kurs ändern, *(mining)* fördern, *(wind)* umspringen;
  ~ s. o. over the coals j. tüchtig herunterputzen; **~ down a flag** Flagge niederholen; **~ down one's flag** kapitulieren; **~ freight** Frachtgut befördern; **~ off** *(mar.)* abdrehen; **~ up** zur Verantwortung ziehen;
  to get a fine (make a good) ~ schönen Gewinn (fette Beute) machen;
  long-and-short ~ clause *(US)* günstigere Frachtklausel; **long ~ [freight] traffic** *(US)* Güterfernverkehr; **long-~ truck** *(US)* Fernlaster.

haulage Ziehen, Schleppen, Transport, Beförderung, *(cartage)* Rollfuhr, *(charges)* Beförderungs-, Abroll-, Transportkosten, *(mining)* Förderung;
  road ~ Güterkraftverkehr; **long-distance road ~** *(Br.)* Fernlastverkehr;
  ~-contracting business Fuhr-, Rollfuhrunternehmen; **~ contractor** Transport-, Rollfuhrunternehmen, Fernspediteur; **~ firm** Transport-, Speditionsfirma; **road ~ industry** Speditionsgewerbe.

hauler, haulier *(Br.)* Schlepper, Fuhrunternehmer, -mann, Spediteur, Frachtführer;
  general ~ allgemeines Güterfernverkehrsunternehmen.

hauling Ziehen, Schleppen, Abschleppen, Beförderung, Transport;
  local ~ örtlicher Zubringerdienst (Zustelldienst); **long-distance ~** *(US)* Güterfernverkehr;
  ~ cable Zugseil; **~ costs** Zubringer-, Zustellungskosten; **~ gallery** *(mining)* Abbauförderstrecke; **~ line** *(mar.)* Wurfleine; **~ plant** *(mine)* Förderanlage; **~ rates** Streckentarif; **~ rope** Schleppseil.

haunt Schlupfwinkel, Lieblingsplatz;
  busy ~s of men Treffpunkt vielbeschäftigter Männer;
  ~ *(v.)* spuken, umgehen, *(frequent)* sich ständig aufhalten;
  to go back to one's old ~s alte Erinnerungen auffrischen.

have Besitzender, Reicher, *(Br., sl.)* Betrug, Schwindel;
  ~-not Habenichts; **~s and ~-nots** Reiche und Arme;
  ~ *(v.)* haben, besitzen;
  ~ s. o. *(Br., sl.)* j. hereinlegen (beschummeln); **~ advice** ärztlichen Rat einholen; **~ authority over s. o.** Befehlsgewalt über j. haben; **~ the care of s. o.** für j. Sorge tragen, Sorgerecht für j. haben; **~ enough coal in** ausreichenden Kohlenvorrat eingelagert haben; **~ a conference** Besprechung abhalten; **~ the decorators in** Maler im Haus haben; **~ s. o. down** j. als Logiergast haben; **~ s. o. down for an explanation** Erklärung von jem.

verlangen; ~ **a hand in** beteiligt sein; ~ **at hand** zur Verfügung haben; **to** ~ **and to hold** *(conveyancing)* über den Eigentumsübergang einig sein; ~ **s. th. by heart** etw. auswendig können; ~ **s. o. in hono(u)r** j. in Ehren halten; ~ **s. o. in for dinner** abends einen Gast eingeladen haben; ~ **original jurisdiction** in erster Instanz zuständig sein; ~ **the key of the riddle** Lösung eines Rätsels wissen; ~ **s. o. on** j. zum Besten haben; ~ **s. th. on** etw. vorhaben; ~ **s. th. on s. o.** *(US sl.)* belastendes Material gegen j. haben; ~ **nothing on** nichts vorhaben, keine Verabredung haben; ~ **nothing on s. o.** *(coll.)* kein Druckmittel gegen j. haben, jem. in keiner Weise überlegen sein; ~ **nothing on tomorrow evening** morgen abend frei sein; ~ **it out** Meinungsverschiedenheit austragen; ~ **it out with s. o.** etw. endgültig mit jem. bereinigen, sich mit jem. auseinandersetzen, jem. den Zahn ziehen; ~ **one's pocket picked** bestohlen werden; ~ **a police record** vorbestraft sein; ~ **power to dispose** verfügungsberechtigt sein; ~ **a quorum** beschlußfähig sein; ~ **recourse against s. o.** Regreß gegen j. nehmen; ~ **one's sleep out** sich richtig ausschlafen; ~ **it from a reliable source** aus verläßlicher Quelle erfahren; ~ **s. o. up** Logierbesuch haben; ~ **s. o. up for exceeding the speed limit** j. wegen Überschreitung der Geschwindigkeitsbegrenzung anzeigen; ~ **a vote** stimmberechtigt sein; ~ **done writing** mit dem Schreiben fertig sein; ~ **5000 pounds a year** jährlich 5000 £ verdienen;
hard-to-~ girl am meisten gefragtes Modell.

haven Hafen, *(asylum)* Asyl, Freistätte;
tax ~ Steuerparadies;
~ **of rest** Zufluchtsort.

haversack *(mil.)* Brotbeutel, Proviantasche;
~ **ration** *(Br.)* Marschverpflegung.

having Habe, Eigentum, Besitz[ung].

havoc Verwüstung, Verheerung;
to cause ~ schwere Verwüstungen verursachen; **to play** ~ **in the streets** Verheerungen in den Straßen anrichten; **to play** ~ **on s. th.** sich verheerend auf etw. auswirken.

hawk Halsabschneider, Wucherer;
~ *(v.)* hausieren [gehen];
to know a ~ **from a handsaw** zwischen zwei verschiedenen Dingen wohl unterscheiden können.

hawker Hausierer, fliegender Händler, Wandergewerbetreibender, Straßenhändler;
~**'s licence** Wandergewerbeschein.

hawking Hausieren, Wander-, Hausierergewerbe, Handel im Umherziehen, nichtpermanente Verkaufstätigkeit.

hay | in stack frei gestapeltes Heu;
to make ~ **of s. th.** etw. durcheinanderwerfen; **to make** ~ **of an argument** Argument ad absurdum führen; **to make** ~ **while the sun shines** das Eisen schmieden, solange es heiß ist;
~**-bote** Holzentnahmerecht zum Ausbessern von Hecken und Zäunen.

haycock Heuschober.

hayloft Heuboden.

haywire *(US sl.)* hoffnungsloses Durcheinander;
to go ~ *(sl.)* schiefgehen, total verrückt werden.

hazard Gefahr, Gefahrenquelle, Wagnis, Risiko, *(chance)* Zufall, *(game)* Glücksspiel, *(insurance law)* versicherbares Risiko, Versicherungsrisiko;
at all ~**s** unter allen Umständen; **at the** ~**s of one's life** unter Lebensgefahr;
accident ~ Unfallrisiko; **bonus** ~ Risikoprämie; ~**s not covered** ausgeschlossene Risiken; **fire** ~**s** Feuergefahr; **industrial** ~ Betriebsrisiko; **moral** ~ Risiko falscher Angaben des Versicherten, subjektives [Versicherungs]risiko; **occupational** ~ Berufsgefahr; **physical** ~ tatsächliches (natürliches) Risiko; ~**s of the sea** Seegefahr; ~ **of war** Kriegsrisiko, -gefahren;
~ *(v.)* *(risk)* aufs Spiel setzen, riskieren, *(venture)* wagen;
~ **one's life** sein Leben riskieren; ~ **a remark** Bemerkung riskieren;
to pose ~**s** Gefahren heraufbeschwören; **to run a** ~ etw. riskieren, Risiko eingehen;
~ **bonus** Gefahrenzulage, Risikoprämie; ~ **classification** *(insurance)* Risikoklassifizierung.

hazardous *(business)* riskant, gefährlich;
~ **contract** von einem unbestimmten Ereignis abhängiger Vertrag, Risikovertrag; ~ **goods** gefährliche Güter; ~ **insurance** Risikoversicherung; ~ **negligence** Leichtfertigkeit; ~ **occupation** gefährlicher Beruf; ~ **situation** gefährliche Lage, *(job)* gefährlicher Arbeitsplatz; ~ **speculation** gewagte Spekulation; ~ **work bonus** Risikoprämie.

haze Dunstschleier, feiner Nebel;
~ *(v.)* *(US)* schikanieren.

haziness Diesigkeit.

hazing *(US)* Schikanieren.

hazy dunstig, diesig, leicht nebelig, *(coll.)* beschwipst, benebelt, *(fig.)* unklar, nebelhaft, verschwommen.

head Kopf, Haupt, *(aggregation, Br.)* Anzahl, Menge, Ansammlung, *(cape)* Landspitze, Vorgebirge, Kap, *(category)* Kategorie, Abschnitt, Rubrik, Kapitel, *(chief)* [An]führer, Oberhaupt, Chef, Leiter, Vorsteher, Prinzipal, Vorstand, *(coin)* Kopf, *(crisis)* Höhepunkt, Entscheidung, Krise, *(headache, coll.)* Brummschädel, Kater, *(item)* [Rechnungs]posten, *(leading position)* Spitze, höchste Stelle, Kommandostelle, führende Stellung, *(ling.)* Oberbegriff, *(newspaper)* Kopfleiste, Schlagzeile, Überschrift, Titelkopf, *(of page)* Kopf, *(reason)* Verstand, *(school)* Direktor, *(sea)* Schaumkrone, *(ship)* Bug, *(source of a stream)* Quelle, *(top)* Spitze, Kopf;
at the ~ **of affairs** an der Spitze; **at the** ~ **of the column** an der Kolonnenspitze; **at the** ~ **of the poll** mit den meisten Stimmen; **by a short** ~ um eine Nasenlänge; **by the** ~ **and heels** gewaltsam; **down by the** ~ *(fig.)* angeheitert, *(mar.)* vorlastig; **from** ~ **to foot** vom Scheitel bis zur Sohle; **off one's** ~ übergeschnappt; **off one's own** ~ auf dem eigenen Mist gewachsen; **on this** ~ über dieses Kapitel; **on your** ~ **be it** auf deine Verantwortung; **out of one's** ~ *(US)* nicht zurechnungsfähig, ohne klaren Verstand; **over my** ~ über mein Begriffsvermögen; **over s. one's** ~ über jds. Kopf hinweg; **over** ~ **and heels** bis zum Hals; **over the** ~ **of others** bevorrechtigt; **per** ~ pro Kopf;
~ **over heels** Hals über Kopf; **ten dollars a** ~ 10 Dollar pro Stück (Person);
clear ~ kluger Kopf; **crowned** ~**s** gekrönte Häupter; **department** ~ Abteilungsleiter; **responsible** ~ verantwortlicher Leiter; **spread** ~ ganzseitige Überschrift; **two-line** ~ zweizeilige Überschrift;
~ **of an agency** *(US)* Behördenleiter; ~**s of an agreement** Hauptpunkte einer Vereinbarung; ~ **of a bridge** Brückenkopf; **real** ~ **of the business** eigentlicher Kopf des Unternehmens; ~ **of a cask** Faßboden; ~ **of cattle** Stück Rindvieh; ~**s of a charge** Klagepunkte; ~ **of the class** Klassenerster, Primus; ~ **of a delegation** Chefdelegierter, Delegationschef; ~ **of a department** Abteilungsvorstand, -leiter, *(US)* Minister; ~ **of a family** Haushaltungsvorstand, -haupt; ~ **for figures** Zahlensinn; ~ **of the firm** Firmen-, Geschäftsinhaber; ~ **of the government** *(Br.)* Regierungschef; ~**s of government** Spitzen der Behörden; ~ **of the household** Haushaltungsvorstand; ~ **of a jetty** Molenkopf; ~ **of a letter** Briefkopf; ~ **of a list** Spitze einer Liste; ~ **of a mission (post)** Missionschef; ~**s of negotiations** Hauptverhandlungspunkte; ~ **of page** Kopf einer Seite; ~ **and shoulders above the others** einsame Spitze; ~**s of a speech** Hauptpunkte einer Rede; ~ **and front of a speech** wesentlicher Inhalt einer Ansprache; ~ **of state** Staatsoberhaupt; ~**s or tails** *(of coin)* Kopf oder Adler (Wappen); ~ **and front of an undertaking** Seele eines Unternehmens; ~ **of water** Wassersäule;
~ *(v.)* rubrizieren, *(direct)* richten, steuern, lenken, *(furnish with heading)* mit dem Kopf (Titel) versehen, betiteln, *(lead)* anführen, an der Spitze stehen, leiten, *(take the lead)* Spitze bilden;
~ **for bankruptcy** auf den Konkurs zusteuern; ~ **one's class** Klassenerster sein; ~ **an expedition** Expeditionsführer sein; ~ **a letter with certain words** üblichen Briefanfang wählen; ~ **a list** Liste eröffnen (anführen), an der Spitze einer Liste stehen; ~ **off a quarrel** Streit verhindern; ~ **off an awkward question** unangenehme Frage abwimmeln; ~ **the poll** bestes Abstimmungsergebnis erzielen; ~ **a rebellion** Aufstand leiten, Rebellenführer sein; ~ **a riot** Kopf eines Aufstandes sein; ~ **a ship for the harbo(u)r** Schiff zum Hafen steuern; ~ **south** *(house)* Südlage haben; ~ **up** ansteigen;
to be at the ~ **of** vorstehen; **to be on s. one's** ~ jds. Schuld sein; **to be at the** ~ **of affairs** regieren; **to be at the** ~ **of the business** Geschäft leiten; **to be** ~ **over heels in debt** total verschuldet sein; **to be at the** ~ **of a list** Liste anführen; **to be at the** ~ **of a party** Parteiführer sein; **to be at the** ~ **of the poll** größte Stimmenzahl erzielt haben; **to be** ~ **and shoulders above the rest** den anderen haushoch überlegen sein; **to be over the** ~**s of an audience** sein Publikum überfordern; **to be promoted over s. one's** ~ außer der Reihe befördert werden; **to be put over s. one's** ~ anderen bei Beförderungen überspringen; **to be unable to make** ~ **or tail of it** etw. überhaupt nicht verstehen; **to be weak in the** ~ nicht sehr intelligent sein; **to bring a matter to a** ~ etw. zum Klappen bringen, Entscheidung mit Gewalt herbeiführen; **to bury one's** ~ **in the sand** Kopf in den Sand stecken; **to collide** ~ **on** frontal zusammenstoßen; **to collide with a ship** ~ **on a pier** frontal mit dem Landungssteg zusammenstoßen (kollidieren); **to come to**

a ~ Krisenpunkt erreichen, sich zuspitzen; **to drag in a subject by the ~ and ears** Gesprächsthema an den Haaren herbeiziehen; **to gather ~** überhandnehmen; **to give s. o. his ~** j. an der langen Leine laufen lassen; **to give orders over s. one's ~** sich mit seinen Anordnungen über j. hinwegsetzen; **to give s. o. a swelled ~** j. eingebildet machen; **to go to the ~** (success) jem. in den Kopf steigen; **to have a bad ~** (sl.) Brummschädel haben; **to have a good ~ for business** guter Geschäftsmann (kaufmännisch gewandt) sein; **to have a ~ for figures** gut mit Zahlen umgehen können; **not to have a ~ for heights** leicht schwindlig werden; **to have a good ~ for languages** sprachbegabt sein; **to have a ~ for politics** politische Begabung haben; **to have one's ~ screwed on the right way** kluges Köpfchen haben; **to have a good ~ on one's shoulders** gesunden Menschenverstand besitzen; **to hit the nail on the ~** Nagel auf den Kopf treffen; **to keep its ~** (stocks) sich behaupten; **to keep one's ~** kaltes Blut bewahren; **to keep a cool ~** kühlen Kopf bewahren; **to keep one's ~ shut** (sl.) das Maul halten; **to keep one's ~ tucked in** (fam.) kein Risiko eingehen; **to keep one's ~ above water** sich über Wasser halten; **to lay our ~s together** die Köpfe zusammenstecken; **to let s. o. have his ~** j. am langen Zügel laufen lassen; **to lose one's ~** seinen Kopf verlieren; **to make ~ against s. o.** jem. die Stirn bieten; **to make a story up out of one's ~** sich eine Geschichte aus den Fingern saugen; **to pay s. o. so much a ~** soundso viel pro Kopf zahlen; **to put an old ~ on young shoulders** der Jugend Weisheit lehren wollen; **to put ~s together** Köpfe zusammenstecken, dunkle Pläne schmieden; **to put ideas into s. one's ~** jem. Flausen in den Kopf setzen; **to put s. th. out of one's ~** Plan aufgeben; **to ram one's ~ against the wall** mit dem Kopf durch die Wand wollen; **to reckon in one's ~** im Kopf ausrechnen; **to run in s. one's ~** jem. im Kopf herumgehen; **to sell a house over s. one's ~** Haus gegen jds. Willen verkaufen; **to suffer from a swelled ~** an Größenwahn leiden; **to take the ~** Führung übernehmen; **to take it into one's ~** sich etw. in den Kopf setzen; **to talk over the ~s of one's audience** sein Publikum überfordern; **to talk s. one's ~ off** j. besoffen (jem. ein Loch in den Bauch) reden; **to treat a question under several ~s** Frage unter verschiedenen Aspekten behandeln; **to turn s. one's ~** jem. den Kopf verdrehen; **to walk with one's ~ in the air** seine Nase hoch tragen; **to win by a ~** um Kopfeslänge gewinnen; **to work out in one's ~** im Kopf ausrechnen; **to work out at five pounds a ~** auf 5 Pfund pro Kopf zu stehen kommen;
~ **agency** Generalagentur, -vertretung; ~ **agent** Generalvertreter; ~ **bookkeeper** Ober-, Hauptbuchhalter; ~ **cashier** Hauptkassierer; ~ **clerk** leitende Fachkraft, Geschäftsführer, Bürovorsteher; ~ **cook** Chefkoch; **cook and bottle washer** (fam.) wichtigste Person des Betriebes; ~ **count** Kopfzählung; ~ **counter** (sl.) Nasenzähler, (marketing, sl.) Marktforscher; ~ **doctor** Chefarzt; ~ **fire** (US) Lauffeuer; ~ **firm** Stammhaus; ~ **foreman** Vorarbeiter; ~ **foremost** kopfüber; ~ **gate** Schleusentor; ~ **house** Warteraum vor Kopfbahnsteigen; ~-**hunt** Kopfjagd, (fig.) Jagd auf Nachwuchskräfte; ~-**hunter** Kopfjäger, (US) Nachwuchsjäger; ~ **lamp** Scheinwerfer; ~ **lessee** Hauptvermieter; ~ **manager** Generaldirektor, Betriebsleiter; ~ **margin** oberer weißer Rand, Kopfsteg; ~ **money** (bounty offered, US) Kopfgeld, -steuer; ~ **note** Hauptsätze (Zusammenfassung) eines Urteils; ~ **office** Hauptbüro, -geschäftsstelle, -sitz, Direktion, Zentrale; ~-**office account** Konto beim Stammhaus; ~-**office accounting** Rechnungslegung der Hauptgeschäftsstelle; ~-**office expense** Unkosten der Zentrale; ~-**office management** Hauptverwaltung; ~-**on** rechtwinklig zum Verkehrsfluß; **to meet (strike) ~-on** frontal zusammenstoßen; ~-**on advertising** Werbung an einem Verkehrsknotenpunkt; ~-**on attack** Frontalangriff; ~-**on clash** (fig.) frontaler Zusammenstoß, Frontalzusammenstoß; ~-**on collision** frontaler Zusammenstoß; ~-**on location** bevorzugte Plazierung von Außenwerbung; ~-**on position** (advertising) Werbung an einem Verkehrsknotenpunkt; ~ **organization** Spitzenverband, -organisation, Gesamtverband; ~ **packer** Packmeister; ~ **physician** Chefarzt; ~ **rest** (car) verstellbare Kopfstütze; ~ **rules** (print.) Kopfleiste; ~ **saleswoman** Direktrice; ~ **shrinker** (sl.) Psychologe; ~-**start program(me)** kopflastiges Programm; ~ **tax** (US) Einwanderungssteuer; ~ **wind** Gegenwind; ~ **word** (dictionary) Stichwort.
headband (print.) Kopfleiste.
headed angeführt, geleitet, (titled) überschrieben, betitelt;
~ **by the Foreign Minister** unter Führung des Außenministers.
heading Kopfstück, -teil, -ende, (airplane) Flugrichtung, (conversation) Thema, Gesprächspunkt, (letter) Briefkopf, (mar.) Kompaßkurs, (mining) Stollen, (printing) [Kapitel]überschrift, Kopf, Titel, Rubrik;

general ~ Sammelüberschrift; **main ~** Haupttitel; **tariff ~** Zollposition;
~ **of a balance sheet** Bilanzposten; ~ **on the customs tariff** Position des Zolltarifs, Zollposition;
to fall under the ~ unter die Rubrik fallen; **to give a ~** betiteln; ~ **industry** Spitzenindustrie.
headless kopflos, führerlos.
headland Landzunge, -spitze, Kap.
headlight Scheinwerfer;
dipped (nondazzle) ~s abgeblendete Scheinwerfer; **to dim (dip) the ~s** Scheinwerfer abblenden.
headline Überschrift, Blickfang-, Schlagzeile, (book) Kopfzeile, (broadcasting) schlagzeilenartige Meldung;
blind ~ ungeschickte Schlagzeile; **news ~s** (broadcast) Nachrichten in Kurzfassung; **scare ~** sensationelle Überschrift;
~ (v.) mit einer Überschrift (Schlagzeile) versehen;
to get the ~s Schlagzeilen für sich in Anspruch nehmen; **to make ~s** Schlagzeilen liefern; **to take the ~s** Schlagzeilen machen.
headlined, to be Schlagzeilen machen.
headliner Schlagzeilenverfasser, (theater) Hauptdarsteller, (US) Hauptperson;
civic ~s (US) Prominenz, prominente Bürger.
headlong Hals über Kopf;
to drive ~ into a slump kopfsprungartigen Konjunkturrückgang erfahren; **to plunge ~ into a description** sich kopfüber in eine eingehende Beschreibung stürzen; **to rush ~ to one's ruin** sich seinem Untergang mit Riesenschritten nähern;
~ **decision** unüberlegte Entscheidung; ~ **flight** panikartige Flucht.
headman Führer, Vorsteher, (Br.) Vorarbeiter.
headmaster (school) Direktor, Schulvorstand, -leiter, (elementary school) Rektor.
headphone (tel.) Kopfhörer.
headpiece (brains, coll.) kluger Kopf, (print.) Kopf-, Zierleiste.
headquarter (v.) (coll.) seinen Hauptsitz haben, Hauptbüro eröffnen.
headquarters (fire brigade) Feuerwehrkommando, (mil.) Standort, Hauptquartier, Kommandantur, Kommandobehörde, Gefechtsstand, Stabsquartier, (office) Hauptgeschäftsstelle, -sitz, -führung, Zentrale, (place of residence) [Haupt]aufenthaltsort, (police) Polizeidirektion;
general ~ oberste Heeresleitung;
~ **of an agency** Hauptsitz (Hauptzentrale) einer Behörde;
to have its ~ at ... Hauptniederlassung in ... haben.
headrest Kopfstütze, -lehne.
headright (US) Siedlungsanspruch.
headroom lichte Höhe;
to have the ~ for a substantial budget stimulus genügend Plafond für erhebliche Haushaltsbelebungen haben.
headset Kopfhörer.
headship oberste Leitung, leitende Stellung, Vorsitz, Vorstand, (school) Direktorstelle.
headsman Scharfrichter.
headstick (print.) Kopfsteg.
headstone Eck-, Grundstein, (grave) Grabstein.
headstream (river) Oberlauf.
headstrong halsstarrig, dickköpfig.
headwaiter Ober-, Zahlkellner.
headwater (river) Quellgebiet.
headway (mar.) Geschwindigkeit, Fahrt voraus, (mining, Br.) Hauptstollen, Vortriebsstrecke, (progress) Vorankommen, Fortschritt;
to make ~ Fortschritte machen, vorankommen.
headwork geistige Arbeit, Kopfarbeit.
headworker geistiger Arbeiter, Kopfarbeiter.
heal (v.) heilen, kurieren, (fig.) ausgleichen, versöhnen;
~ **the breach between two persons** Versöhnung zwischen zwei Menschen herbeiführen; ~ **s. o. from a disease** j. von einer Krankheit heilen.
healall Allheilmittel.
healer Gesundbeter, Heilpraktiker, (fig.) Aussöhner.
healing Genesung, Gesundung.
health Befinden, Gesundheitszustand, -wesen;
for reasons of ~ gesundheitshalber; **in the best (pink) of ~** bei bester Gesundheit; **in glowing ~** bei blühender Gesundheit; **bad ~** schlechte Gesundheit; **impaired ~** geschwächte Gesundheit; **improved ~** gestärkte Gesundheit; **mental ~** Geistesverfassung; **physical ~** Gesundheit; **public ~** öffentliches Gesundheitswesen; **sound ~** einwandfreier Gesundheitszustand;

~ **of earnings** gesunde Ertragslage; ~ **and sanitation** Gesundheitswesen;

to be in bad ~ gesundheitlich schlecht dran sein; **to be in the best of** ~ bei bester Gesundheit sein; **to be broken in** ~ zerrüttete Gesundheit haben; **to be in poor** ~ kränkeln; **to be in rude** ~ vor Gesundheit strotzen; **to drink to the** ~ **of s. o.** Toast auf jds. Gesundheit ausbringen, auf jds. Wohl trinken; **to have poor** ~ schwache Konstitution haben; **to inquire after s. one's** ~ sich nach jds. Gesundheit erkundigen; **to look the picture of** ~ vor Gesundheit strotzen; **to recruit one's** ~ seine Gesundheit wiederherstellen; **to risk one's** ~ seine Gesundheit aufs Spiel setzen; **to travel for one's** ~ Erholungsreise machen;

~ **activities** Gesundheitsmaßnahmen; ~ **administration** Gesundheitswesen; ~ **board** Gesundheitsamt; ~ **care** Gesundheitsfürsorge, -vorsorge; ~ **care system** Gesundheitsvorsorgewesen; ~ **center** *(US)* **(centre,** *Br.***)** Ambulatorium, Gesundheitszentrum; ~ **certificate** ärztliches Attest, Gesundheitsattest, -nachweis; ~ **check on the firm** *(US)* Gesundheitsbonus der Firma; ~ **conference** Hygienekonferenz; ~ **contribution** Krankenversicherungsbeitrag; ~ **Department** *(US)* Gesundheitsministerium; ~ **and Welfare Department** *(US)* Sozialamt; ~**-endangering** gesundheitsgefährdend; **public** ~ **facilities** Gesundheitseinrichtungen; ~ **fields** Gesundheitswesen; ~ **food store** Reformhaus; ~ **hazards** *(employment)* gesundheitliche Risiken, Gesundheitsrisiko; ~ **insurance** Krankenversicherung; **compulsory** ~ **insurance** *(Br.)* Kassenzwang; **National** ~ **Insurance** *(Br.)* Staatliche Krankenversicherung; **to subscribe to a** ~ **insurance** *(Br.)* [Kranken]kassenmitglied sein; ~ **insurance fund** Krankenkasse; **national** ~ **insurance plan** *(Br.)* Kassensystem; ~ **law** Gesundheitsgesetzgebung; ~ **measures** Gesundheitsmaßnahmen; ~ **officer** Beamter des Gesundheitsamtes, *(quarantine officer, US)* Quarantänearzt, Amtsarzt; **cooperation** ~ **plan** gemeinsames Gesundheitsprogramm verschiedener Unternehmen; ~ **protection** Gesundheitsvorsorge; ~ **provisions** Gesundheitsauflagen, -bestimmungen; **to free s. o. for** ~ **reasons** j. aus gesundheitlichen Gründen entlassen; ~ **resort** Bad, [Luft]kurort; ~ **resort supplement** Bäderbeilage; ~ **risk** Gesundheitsrisiko; **public (national,** *Br.***)** ~ **service** öffentlicher (staatlicher) Gesundheitsdienst, öffentliches Gesundheitswesen; ~ **services** *(Br.)* Einrichtungen der Gesundheitspflege; ~ **service benefit** Krankenkassenleistung; ~ **service charges** *(Br.)* Krankenkassengebühren; ~ **service fees** *(Br.)* vom staatlichen Gesundheitsamt gezahlte Arzthonorare; ~ **service patient** *(Br.)* Kassenpatient; ~ **service provisions** Krankenkassenbestimmungen; ~ **service system** Krankenkassensystem; **public** ~ **specialist** Hygieniker; ~ **and decency standard of living** angemessener Unterhalt, Lebensstandard; ~ **statistics** Gesundheitsstatistik; ~ **surgeon** Quarantänearzt; ~ **visitor** Gesundheitsfürsorger; **employee** ~ **welfare** betriebliche Gesundheitspflege; ~ **welfare benefit** Krankenzulage.

healthful gesundheitsfördernd.

healthguard *(Br.)* Quarantänearzt.

healthy nicht anfällig, gesund;

~ **criticism** nützliche Kritik; **to put the finances of a country on a** ~ **footing** Staatsfinanzen sanieren; **to have a** ~ **look** gesund aussehen; ~ **sign** ermutigendes Anzeichen; ~ **way of living** gesunde Lebensweise.

heap Haufen;

~ **of books** Fülle von (Haufen) Bücher; **a** ~ **of people** Unmasse Menschen; ~**s of time** eine Masse Zeit;

~ *(v.) (fig.)* überhäufen, überschütten;

~ **injuries (insults) upon s. o.** j. mit Schmähungen überschütten; ~ **favo(u)rs upon s. o.** j. mit Gunstbezeigungen überschütten; ~ **up riches** Reichtümer ansammeln; ~ **together** zusammentragen, -häufen;

to be struck all of a ~ *(coll.)* völlig durcheinander (platt) sein; **to feel** ~**s better** sich unendlich besser fühlen; **to have** ~**s of things to do** alle Hände voll zu tun haben; **to knock s. o. all of a** ~ j. völlig sprachlos machen; **to lie about in** ~**s** massenhaft herumliegen.

heaped measure gehäuftes (gerütteltes) Maß.

hear *(v.)* hören, *(interrogate)* vernehmen, verhören, *(learn)* erfahren, anhören, vernehmen;

~ **s. th. about s. o.** etw. über j. erfahren; ~ **an argument by counsel** anwaltliche Darstellung entgegennehmen, mündlich verhandeln; ~ **a case** Fall verhandeln; ~ **a case in chambers** *(Br.)* Verhandlung unter Ausschluß der Öffentlichkeit führen; ~ **a child his lesson** einem Kind seine Aufgabe abfragen; ~ **a deputation** Abordnung anhören; ~ **and determine** richterlich entscheiden; ~ **the evidence** Beweis erheben, Beweiserhebung

vornehmen; ~ **a lecture** Vorlesung [regelmäßig] hören; ~ **a petition** Gesuch entgegennehmen; ~ **the parties** den Parteien rechtliches Gehör gewähren; ~ **a piece of news** Neuigkeit erfahren; ~ **regularly from one another** in ständigem Kontakt miteinander bleiben; ~ **witness** Zeugen vernehmen, in die Zeugenvernehmung eintreten;

to like to ~ **o. s. talk** sich gern reden hören.

heard, to be ~ **next month** *(case)* nächsten Monat anstehen; **to ask that a case may be** ~ **in camera** Antrag auf Ausschluß der Öffentlichkeit stellen.

hearer Zuhörer.

hearing Gehör, Anhörung, *(audience)* Audienz, *(interrogation)* Vernehmung, Verhör, Voruntersuchung, *(law court)* Gerichtsverhandlung, Termin, [mündliche] Verhandlung, *(listening to arguments)* rechtliches Gehör, *(parl.)* öffentliche Anhörung, Anhörungsverfahren;

at the ~ **on** im Termin von; **in s. one's** ~ in jds. Gegenwart; **in the** ~ **of strangers** in Gegenwart fremder Personen; **out of** ~ außer Hörweite;

closed-door ~ Anhörung hinter verschlossenen Türen; **congressional** ~ *(US, senate)* öffentliche Ausschußsitzung; **court** ~ Anhörung durch das Gericht, Gerichtsverhandlung; **deferred** ~ vertagte Verhandlung; **fair** ~ rechtliches Gehör; **final** ~ Schlußverhandlung, -termin; ~**-impaired** hörgeschädigt; **interlocutory** ~ Vor-, Zwischenverfahren; **preliminary** ~ Voruntersuchung; **public** ~ öffentliche Verhandlung; **unfair** ~ ungerechtes Verfahren;

~ **in court** Gerichtsverhandlung; ~ **in public** öffentliche Anhörung;

~ **of an appeal** Berufungsverhandlung; ~ **of an application** Verhandlung über einen Antrag; ~ **in camera (chambers,** *Br.***)** Verhandlung unter Ausschuß der Öffentlichkeit; ~ **of a case** [Gerichts]verhandlung einer Sache; ~ **of evidence** Beweisaufnahme, -termin, -erhebung, Zeugenvernehmung; ~ **before the immigration office** *(US)* Verhandlung vor den Einwanderungsbehörden; ~ **de novo** erneute Verhandlung; **trial** ~ **of a singer** Probeauftritt einer Sängerin (eines Sängers); ~ **of witnesses** Zeugenvernehmung;

to adjourn a ~ Verhandlung vertagen, Termin absetzen; **to assign a day for a** ~ **in court** Termin zur mündlichen Verhandlung anberaumen; **to be down for** ~ zur Verhandlung anstehen; **to be given a full** ~ Fall komplett vortragen können; **to be refused a** ~ keine Anhörung finden; **to begin with the** ~ **of evidence** in die Beweisaufnahme eintreten, zur Beweisaufnahme schreiten; **to bring to** ~ Verhandlung ansetzen; **to come up for** ~ **next week** nächste Woche verhandelt werden; **to condemn s. o. without a** ~ j. ohne Anhörung verurteilen; **to defer the** ~ Verhandlung vertagen; **to fix a** ~ Verhandlung (Termin) anberaumen; **to gain a** ~ *(at court)* angehört werden, sich eine Audienz verschaffen; **to get a** ~ angehört werden, zu Wort kommen; **to give s. o. a fair** ~ j. unparteiisch anhören; **to give petitioners a** ~ Gesuche mündlich entgegennehmen; **to grant s. o. a** ~ j. anhören; **to have a keen sense of** ~ ausgezeichnetes Gehör haben; **to hold a** ~ *(US, senate)* Vernehmung durchführen; **to put (set) a case down for** ~ Termin für eine Sache ansetzen, mündliche Verhandlung anordnen, anberaumen;

~ **aid** Hörapparat; ~ **date** *(liquidation)* Verhandlungs-, Anhörungstermin; ~ **officer** *(US)* Verwaltungsrichter; ~ **room** Verhandlungszimmer, Vernehmungszimmer.

hearsay Hörensagen;

to have it only from ~ nur vom Hörensagen wissen;

~ **evidence** Beweis vom Hörensagen (aus zweiter Hand).

hearse Leichenwagen.

heart Herz, *(center)* Mittelpunkt, Kern, innerer Teil, *(character)* Mut, Festigkeit, mannhafter Charakter;

after one's own ~ wunschgemäß; **at** ~ im innersten Wesen; **at the** ~ **of** im Mittelpunkt; **by** ~ auswendig; **from one's** ~ frisch von der Leber weg; **from the bottom of one's** ~ aus ganzem Herzen; **in** ~ guten Mutes; **in good** ~ *(land)* in ausgezeichnetem Zustand; **in one's** ~ insgeheim; **in his** ~ **of** ~**s** im tiefsten Grunde seines Herzens; **in the** ~ **of the forest** im Waldesinneren; **out of** ~ mutlos; **to one's** ~**'s content** nach Herzenslust; **with my whole** ~ mit Leib und Seele; **with** ~ **and soul** von ganzem Herzen, mit Leib und Seele;

~ **of a city** Kern einer Stadt, Stadtkern; **the very** ~ **of a matter** des Pudels Kern;

to be at the ~ **of s. th.** Kern einer Sache bilden, innerstes Wesen ausmachen; **to be etched on s. one's** ~ **in acid** unauslöschlich in jds. Herz eingegraben sein; **to be in good** ~ zuversichtlich sein; **to be in strong** ~ bester Laune sein; **to break s. one's** ~ jem. das

Herz brechen; **to come to the ~ of the matter** auf den Kern einer Sache vorstoßen; **to cry one's ~ out** sich die Augen ausweinen; **to cut s. o. to the ~** j. bis ins Innerste seines Herzens treffen; **to desire s. th. with all one's ~** etw. von ganzem Herzen wünschen; **to do s. th. with a light (heavy) ~** etw. leichten (schweren) Herzens tun; **to eat one's ~ out** sich vor Kummer verzehren; **to feel a great gladness at ~** im Innersten seines Herzens glücklich sein; **to find the ~ to do** es übers Herz bringen; **not to find it in one's ~** es nicht über sich bringen; **to have the ~** gefühllos genug sein; **to have s. th. at ~** etw. von Herzen wünschen; **to have one's ~ in one's boots** Herz in der Hosentasche haben; **to have one's ~ in one's mouth** hündische Angst (Herzklopfen) haben; **to have one's ~ in the right place** das Herz auf dem richtigen Fleck haben; **to have set one's ~ on doing s. th.** sein Herzblut an etw. gesetzt haben; **to have a ~ of stone** Herz aus Stein haben; **to have s. one's welfare at ~** um jds. Wohlsein besorgt sein; **to have one's ~ in one's work** ganz in seiner Arbeit aufgehen, mit dem Herzen bei der Arbeit sein; **to indulge o. s. to one's ~'s content** sich nach Herzenslust wohl sein lassen; **to lay to ~** beherzigen; **to learn s. th. by ~** etw. auswendig lernen; **to open one's ~ to s. o.** jem. sein Herz ausschütten; **to pluck up ~** sich ein Herz fassen; **to put new ~ into s. o.** jem. wieder Mut machen; **to put one's ~ and soul into one's work** mit Leib und Seele bei der Sache sein; **to put fresh ~ into the troops** den Truppen neuen Auftrieb geben; **to ruin others with a light ~** andere leichtherzig zugrunderichten; **to set one's ~ on s. th.** sein Herz an etw. hängen; **to set s. one's ~ at rest** j. beruhigen; **to take s. th. to ~** sich etw. zu Herzen nehmen; **to take the ~ out of s. o.** j. gänzlich entmutigen; **to throw o. s. ~ and soul into a business** sich einer Sache mit allen Fasern seines Herzens verschreiben; **to wear one's ~ upon one's sleeve** sein Herz auf der Zunge tragen;
~ **attack** Herzanfall; ~ **complaint** Herzfehler, -leiden; ~ **failure** Herzfehler, Herzinfarkt; **to make a ~-felt appeal** jem. ernsthaft ins Gewissen reden; **to express one's ~-felt thanks** seinen tiefempfundenen Dank aussprechen; ~ **pacemaker** Herzschrittmacher; ~ **strain** Herzbeanspruchung; ~ **trouble** Herzleiden.

heartache Kummer, Sorge.
heartbreaker Herzensbrecher.
hearten (v.) ermutigen.
heartening news herzerfrischende Neuigkeiten.
hearth Herd, Feuerstelle, (fig.) Heim, Haus;
without ~ **or home** heimatlos.
hearth, open-~ furnace Siemens-Martin Ofen.
heartstrings innerste Gefühle;
to play upon s. one's ~ jem. das Herz zerreißen.
heartthrob (fig.) Schwarm, Ideal.
hearty herzlich, tiefempfunden;
~ **appetite** herzhafter Appetit; **to give one's ~ approval to a plan** einem Plan von ganzem Herzen zustimmen; ~ **timber** gesundes Holz.
heat (agitation of mind) Leidenschaftlichkeit, Erregtheit, (extortion, US sl.) Folterung [zwecks Aussage], (med.) Fieberhitze, (meteorology) Hitzeperiode, (phys.) Wärme, (rage) Wut, Zorn, (single effort, US) größte Anstrengung;
at one ~ in einer einmaligen Kraftanstrengung; in the ~ of the debate auf dem Höhepunkt der Debatte; in the ~ of the moment im Eifer (in der Hitze) des Gefechts; out of a white ~ of emotion aus größter Erregung;
~ **of summer** Sommerhitze;
~ (v.) [be]heizen, (fig.) heftig erregen, erhitzen;
~ **the passions** Leidenschaften entflammen; ~ **a room with gas** Zimmer mit Gas heizen;
to reply with some ~ ziemlich erregt antworten; **to turn on the ~** alles aufbieten, ganze Kraft einsetzen; **to work o. s. up into a white ~** sich zur größten Erregung steigern;
~ **barrier** (airplane) Hitzemauer, -grenze; ~ **energy** Wärmeenergie; ~ **flash** (atomic bomb) Hitzeblitz; ~ **lightning** Wetterleuchten; ~-**proof (-resisting)** hitzebeständig, feuerfest; ~-**treatment** (metal) thermische Behandlung, Wärmevergütung; ~ **unit** (phys.) Wärmeeinheit; ~ **wave** Hitzewelle.
heated geheizt, (fig.) erhitzt, erregt;
~ **car service** Waggonheizungsdienst; ~ **debate (discussion)** hitzige Diskussion; **to make a ~ reply** erregt antworten.
heater Heizer, (apparatus) Heizgerät, -körper;
dish ~ Warmhalteplatte; electric ~ elektrischer Heizofen; gas ~ Gasofen; oil ~ Ölheizofen;
~ **car** heizbarer Waggon.
heath (Br.) Heide[land].
heather, to take to the (Scot.) Bandit werden.
heating [Be]heizung;
electric ~ elektrische Heizung; hot-air ~ Warmluftheizung;

~ **of buildings** Gebäudeheizung; ~ **by steam** Dampfheizung; **to have oil ~** mit Öl heizen, Ölheizung haben; **to turn off the ~** Heizung abstellen; **to turn on the ~** Heizung anstellen;
~ **apparatus** Heizgerät; ~ **cushion** Heizkissen; ~ **expenses** Heizkosten; ~ **installation** Heizungsanlage; ~ **oil** Heizöl; ~ **pad** Heizkissen; ~ **plant** Heizungsanlage; ~ **power** Heizwert; ~ **season** Heizperiode; **to install a ~ system** Heizung installieren.
heatstroke Hitzschlag.
heave Heben, Hochziehen;
~ **of the sea** Seegang;
~ (v.) **the anchor** Anker lichten; ~ **coal** Kohlen trimmen; ~ **the lead** loten; ~ **and set** (ship) stampfen; ~ **in sight** in Sicht kommen.
heaven Himmel, (climate) [Klima]zone;
~ **on earth** Himmel auf Erden;
to move ~ and earth Himmel und Hölle in Bewegung setzen.
heaver, coal Kohlentrimmer.
heavies (stock exchange, Br.) Eisenbahnaktien.
heavier-than-air schwerer als Luft.
heavily | loaded schwer beladen; ~ **wooded** dichtbewaldet;
~ **in debt** stark verschuldet;
to be ~ fined mit einer hohen Geldstrafe belegt werden; **to be ~ taxed** hoch besteuert werden; **to go off ~** sich schwer verkaufen, nur langsam weggehen; **to land too ~** (airplane) harte Landung machen; **to lose ~** große (schwere) Verluste haben; ~ **travelled line** stark befahrene Linie (Strecke).
heaviness Gewicht, Druck;
~ **of the market** Gedrücktheit des Marktes.
heaviside layer Heavisideschicht.
heavy (beer, Br., sl.) Starkbier, (bodyguard) Leibwächter, (theater) Schurke;
~ (a.) schwer, (book) langweilig, fad, (harvest) ergiebig, reich, (order) umfangreich, groß, bedeutend, (stock exchange) gedrückt, flau, schlecht;
~ **in debt** stark verschuldet; ~ **as lead** schwer wie Blei; ~ **of sale** schwer zu verkaufen; ~ **with sleep** schlaftrunken;
to be very ~ on coal (machine) viel Kohle verbrauchen; **to hang ~ on one's hands** (time) dahinschleichen; **to lie ~ on one's conscience** Gewissen erheblich belasten;
~ **armament** schwere Artillerie; ~-**armed** schwer bewaffnet; ~ **baggage** großes Gepäck; ~ **beer** Starkbier; ~ **buyer** Großeinkäufer, -abnehmer; ~ **buying** Großabnahme; ~ **charge on the budget** beträchtliche Etatsbelastung; of ~ **consequences** mit weitreichenden Folgen; ~ **consumer** Großverbraucher; ~ **crop** hervorragende Ernte; ~ **current** (el.) Starkstrom; ~ **dealer** Händler mit großen Umsätzen; ~ **drinker** starker Trinker; ~-**duty** hochbesteuert; ~-**duty engine** Hochleistungsmotor; ~-**duty truck** Schwerlastwagen; ~ **expenditure** große (beträchtliche) Ausgaben; ~-**face type** Plakatbuchstabengröße; ~ **fall in stocks** heftiger (starker) Kursrückgang; ~ **fine** hohe Geldstrafe; ~ **firm (house)** bedeutende Firma; ~ **frame** fette Umrandung, Trauerrand; ~ **goods** Schwergut; **to rule with a ~ hand** mit eiserner Hand regieren; ~ **indebtedness** starke Verschuldung; ~ **industries** Schwerindustrie; ~ **industry shares** Aktien der Schwerindustrie; ~-**laden** schwer beladen; ~ **lift** Schwergut; ~-**lift charge** Schwergutaufschlag; ~-**lift crane** Schwerlastkran; ~ **lines** (railway shares) [hochstehende] Eisenbahnaktien [englischer Hauptlinien]; ~ **losses** schwere (hohe) Verluste; ~ **market** infolge nachlassender Nachfrage gedrückter Markt; ~ **meal** schwer verdauliche Mahlzeit; ~ **metal** Schwermetall; ~ **money** ungemünztes Geld; ~ **oil** Schweröl; ~ **orders** umfangreiche Aufträge; ~ **parts** (theater) tragische Rollen; ~ **rails** (Br.) Eisenbahnpapiere; **to be ~ reading** schwer verdauliche Lektüre darstellen; ~ **responsibility** hohe Verantwortung; ~ **road** schwer zu befahrende Straße; ~ **sea** schwere See; ~ **sky** düsterer Himmel; ~ **soil** lehmiger Boden; ~ **swell** (Br.) Gernegroß, Stutzer; ~ **taxes** hohe (drückende) Steuern; ~ **tidings** schlechte Nachrichten; ~ **traffic** starker Verkehr; ~ **traffic line** Hauptverkehrslinie; ~ **truck market** Lastwagenmarkt; ~ **type** Fettdruck; ~ **undertaking** schwieriges Unternehmen; ~ **water** Schwerwasser; ~ **work** Schwerarbeit.
heavyweight (US coll.) Prominenter, gewichtige Persönlichkeit.
hebdomadal wöchentlich.
hecatomb großes öffentliches Opfer, Massenmord.
heck of a row Heidenspektakel.
heckle (v.) quälen, piesacken, (in meeting) durch Zwischenrufe aus dem Konzept bringen, ins Kreuzverhör nehmen.
heckler Zwischenrufer.
hectic hektisch, unruhig;
~ **fever** Schwindsucht; **to lead a ~ life** hektisches Leben führen;
to have a ~ time keinen Augenblick Ruhe haben.

hectograph Hektograph, Vervielfältigungsgerät;
~ *(v.)* hektographieren, vervielfältigen.
hedge Hecke, Umzäunung, *(fig.)* Mauer, Barriere, *(stock exchange)* Deckungs-, Sicherungsgeschäft;
~ **against inflation** Inflationssicherung, -damm; ~ **of police** Polizeisperre;
~ *(v.)* ausweichen, sich drücken, kneifen, *(stock exchange)* Sicherungsgeschäft abschließen, sich gegen Verluste sichern, *(witness)* unklare Antworten geben, sich nicht festlegen wollen;
~ **against a bet** sich gegen den Verlust einer Wette sichern; ~ **all bets** sich nach allen Seiten absichern; ~ **in (off)** mit einer Hecke umgeben; ~ **in a piece of ground** Grundstück einzäunen; ~ **a rate** Kurs sichern; ~ **s. o. in with rules and regulations** jem. jegliche Bewegungsfreiheit nehmen;
to come down on the wrong side of the ~ auf dem falschen Bein Hurrah schreien; **not to grow on every** ~ nicht jeden Tag anzufinden sein; **to place a** ~ Deckungsgeschäft unterbringen; **to put** ~**s in a contract** Vertrag verklausulieren; **to sit on the** ~ *(fam.)* sich reserviert verhalten;
~ *(a.)* minderwertig, schlecht, *(nearly illegal)* zweifelhaft, nicht ganz koscher;
~ **bird** Landstreicher, Vagabund; ~ **bote** *(tenant)* Holzgerechtigkeit; ~ **buying** Vorratseinkäufe; ~ **clause** *(US)* Schutzklausel, Vorbehalt[sklausel]; ~ **lawyer** Winkeladvokat; ~ **marriage** heimliche Ehe; ~ **press** Revolverblatt; ~ **school** schlechte Schule; ~ **selling** Deckungs-, Sicherungsverkauf; ~ **writer** Schreiberling.
hedged | in by clauses verklausuliert;
to be ~ **about with qualifications** mit Einschränkungen abgesichert sein.
hedgehog *(mil.)* Igelstellung.
hedgehop *(v.) (airplane, sl.)* tief fliegen, heckenspringen.
hedgehopper *(sl.)* Heckenspringer, Tiefflieger.
hedger Drückeberger.
hedgerow Baumhecke.
hedging *(stock exchange)* Abschluß von Deckungsgeschäften, Gegendeckung;
~ **sale** Deckungsverkauf; ~ **transaction** Deckungsgeschäft.
heebie-jeebies *(US sl.)* Katzenjammer.
heed Sorgfalt, Behutsamkeit;
to give ~ **to an order** Anordnung befolgen; **to pay** ~ **to s. th.** etw. sorgfältig beachten; **to take little** ~ **of s. one's criticism** jds. Kritik in den Wind schlagen.
heedless unbesonnen, rücksichtslos;
~ **of public opinion** ohne Rücksicht auf die öffentliche Meinung.
heel Ferse, Absatz, *(scoundrel, US sl.)* Schurke, *(ship)* Krängung, *(shoe)* Hacken;
back on one's ~**s** zurückgedrängt, in der Defensive; **down (out) at** ~ *(Br.)* mit abgetretenen Absätzen, heruntergekommen, verwahrlost, zerlumpt; **in the** ~**s of the hunt** *(Irish)* in letzter Minute; **under the** ~ **of a cruel dictator** in der Gewalt eines grausamen Diktators; **upon one's** ~**s** dicht auf den Fersen;
~ **of Achilles** Achillesferse, wunder Punkt; **head over** ~**s** Hals über Kopf;
~ *(a.)* verwahrlost, verkommen, vernachlässigt, schäbig;
~ *(v.)* sich an jds. Fersen heften, *(court favo(u)r)* katzbuckeln, radfahren, *(ship)* sich auf die Seite legen, krängen, *(supply with, US sl.)* ausstaffieren, versorgen;
to be carried away with the ~**s foremost** tot weggetragen werden; **to be dragged in the** ~**s of s. o.** in jds. Kielwasser schwimmen; **to be under the** ~ **of the invader** unter einer Invasionsarmee schmachten; **to clap by the** ~**s** einsperren; **to cool one's** ~**s** sich die Beine in den Bauch stehen; **to dig one's** ~**s in** sich auf die Hinterbeine setzen; **to follow at (upon) s. one's** ~**s** jem. auf dem Fuße folgen; **to follow on the** ~**s of war** zu den Kriegsfolgen gehören; **to give a** ~ *(ship)* krängen; **to have the** ~**s of s. o.** j. überholen; **to have the police on one's** ~**s** von der Polizei gejagt werden; **to kick one's** ~**s** sich die Beine in den Bauch stehen; **to kick up one's** ~**s** *(US sl.)* sich köstlich amüsieren; **to lay by the** ~**s** ins Gefängnis stecken; **to show a clean pair of** ~**s** sich aus dem Staube machen; **to take to one's** ~**s** sein Heil in der Flucht suchen; **to tread upon s. one's** ~**s** jem. auf dem Fuße folgen; **to tread on each other's** ~**s** *(events)* dicht aufeinander folgen; **to turn on one's** ~ auf dem Absatz kehrt machen.
heeled *(sl.)* mit Geld ausgerüstet;
well ~ *(sl.)* stinkreich.
heeler *(US coll.)* blind ergebener Anhänger, Wahlmacher.
heft *(US)* Einfluß.
hegemony Vormachtstellung, Hegemonie.

height Höhe, *(fig.)* Höhepunkt, Gipfel;
at the ~ **of one's career** auf dem Gipfel seiner Laufbahn;
barometric ~ Barometerhöhe;
~ **of ambition** Gipfel des Ehrgeizes; ~ **of clouds** Wolkenhöhe; ~ **of fashion** neueste Mode; ~**-to-paper** Schrifthöhe; ~ **above sea level** absolute Höhe;
to be at the ~ **of one's glory** Gipfel des Ruhms erreicht haben; **to lose** ~ *(airplane)* absacken;
~ **sickness** Höhenkrankheit.
heighten *(v.)* erhöhen, vergrößern, steigern.
heir [gesetzlicher] Erbe;
alternative ~ Ersatzerbe; ~ **apparent** *(Br.)* gesetzlicher (zukünftiger) Erbe; **appointed** ~ eingesetzter Erbe; **beneficiary** ~ Erbe mit Beschränkung auf das Nachlaßverzeichnis, nach Inventarerrichtung beschränkt haftender Erbe; **bodily** ~ leiblicher Erbe, ~ **collateral** Erbe in der Seitenlinie (dritter Ordnung); **conventional** ~ Vertragserbe, Erbe auf Grund eines Erbvertrages; ~ **expectant** Erb[schafts]anwärter; **fiduciary** ~ Vorerbe; **forced** ~ *(US)* Pflichtteilsberechtigter; ~ **general** *(US)* Universalerbe, gesetzlicher Erbe; **immediate** ~ nächster Erbe; **instituted** ~ *(Scot.)* Testamentserbe, eingesetzter Erbe; **irregular** ~ Erbscheinserbe; **joint** ~**s** Miterben; **last** ~ *(Br.)* letzter Erbe; **lawful** ~ rechtmäßiger Erbe, Noterbe; **legal** ~ gesetzlicher Erbe; **legitimate** ~**s** legitime Erben; **lineal** ~ Linearerbe; **living** ~**s** lebende Erbberechtigte; **male** ~ nächster männlicher Erbberechtigter; ~ **natural** ~ mit dem Erblasser in direkter Linie verwandter Erbe, Erbe durch Geburtsrecht; ~ **presumptive** *(Br.)* mutmaßlicher Erbe, nächster gesetzlicher Erbanwärter, Präsumtiverbe; **representative** ~ Ersatzerbe; **reversionary** ~ Nacherbe; **rightful** ~ gesetzlicher (rechtmäßiger) Erbe; **sole** ~ Universal-, Alleinerbe; **special** ~ Fideikommißerbe; **statutory** ~ *(US)* gesetzlicher Erbe; **substituted** ~ Ersatzerbe; **supposititious** ~ falscher Erbe; **testamentary** ~ *(US)* testamentarisch bestimmter Erbe; ~ **unconditional** Erbe ohne Verpflichtung der Inventarerrichtung; **universal** ~ Gesamt-, Universalerbe; ~ **whatsoever** gesetzlicher Erbe;
~ **by adoption** Adoptiverbe; ~**s and assigns** Rechtsnachfolger; ~ **of the blood** Erbe aufgrund der Verwandtschaft; ~ **of one's body** leiblicher Erbe; ~ **by customs** *(Br.)* Erbe entsprechend dem Ortsgebrauch; ~ **by device** *(US)* testamentarischer Erbe, Testamentserbe; ~ **to personal estate** Mobiliarerbe, Erbe des beweglichen Vermögens; ~ **in inspectancy** Erbschaftsanwärter; ~**-at-law** *(US)* gesetzlicher Erbe, Intestaterbe; ~ **of line** Erbe in gerader Linie (erster Ordnung); ~ **of provision** Testamentserbe, testamentarisch bestimmter Erbe; ~ **in tail** Vorerbe; ~ **to the throne** Thronanwärter, -folger;
to appoint an ~ Erben einsetzen; **to be** ~ **to an estate** Nachlaßgrundstück erben; **to be** ~ **to a splendid fortune** glänzendes Vermögen erben; **to be left** ~ **to s. one's estate** jds. Besitz erben; **to become s. one's** ~ j. beerben; **to declare o. s. as** ~ sich als Erben benennen; **to design an** ~ Erben bestimmen; **to fall** ~ **to a property** Vermögen erben; **to fall to the** ~**s on the father's side** auf die Erben der väterlichen Seite entfallen; **to institute s. o. as one's** ~ j. zu seinem Erben einsetzen; **to make s. o. one's** ~ j. zu seinem Erben bestimmen; **to own as** ~ als Erben anerkennen; **to pass to the** ~**s** auf die Erben übergehen; **to recognize s. o. as a lawful** ~ j. als rechtmäßigen Erben anerkennen; **to vest in the** ~ **at law** auf den gesetzlichen Erben übergehen;
~ **apparency** unzweifelhaftes Erbrecht; ~**'s certificate** *(US)* Erbschein.
heirdom Erbe, Erbschaft;
to come into an ~ Erbschaft antreten.
heirloom Erbstück.
heirship Erbeneigenschaft, *(US)* Erbschaftsrecht;
forced ~ *(US)* Pflichtteilsrecht;
~ **movables** *(Scot.)* Dreißigster.
held *(law court)* entschieden, erkannt;
~ **covered** *(insurance)* gedeckt; ~ **for damages** schadensersatzpflichtig; ~ **up by fog** durch Nebel aufgehalten; ~ **for postage matter** *(US)* wegen ungenügender Frankierung zurückbehalten; ~ **in suspension** suspendiert;
to be ~ **over** *(Br.)* im Portefeuille behalten werden; **to be** ~ **up** festsitzen, *(train)* liegenbleiben; **to be** ~ **up by bandits** von Wegelagerern überfallen werden; **to be** ~ **up for lack of money** wegen fehlender Mittel nicht gestartet werden.
helibus Hubschrauberbus.
helicopter Hubschrauber;
attack ~ Kampfhubschrauber; **military** ~ Militärhubschrauber;
~ **bus** Hubschrauberbus; ~ **hire** Hubschraubermiete; ~ **terminal** Hubschrauberlandeplatz.

helidrome Hubschrauberlandeplatz.
heliograph Lichtsprechgerät.
heliographic printing Lichtpausverfahren.
heliotrope Lichtsprechgerät.
heliotype Lichtdruck.
helipilot Hubschrauberpilot.
heliport Start- und Landebahn für Hubschrauber, Hubschrauberlandeplatz.
hell *(fig.)* Hölle, *(print.)* Defektkasten, *(prison)* Verlies, Gefängnis, Kerker;
  for the ~ of it ohne besonderen Grund; **ride ~ for leather** so
  schnell wie möglich; **to ~ and gone** *(sl.)* total ruiniert;
  gambling ~ Spielhölle;
  ~ upon earth Hölle auf Erden; **~ of a note** *(sl.)* etw. völlig
  Ungewöhnliches; **~ to pay** schwere Strafe; **~ of a time** schreckliche Zeit;
  to be in a ~ of a temper Mordswut haben; **to give s. o. ~** jem. die
  Hölle heiß machen, jem. einheizen; **to give the enemy ~** dem
  Feind tüchtig einheizen; **to have a ~ of a time** schwere Zeiten
  durchmachen müssen; **to like s. o. a ~ of a lot** j. schrecklich gern
  haben; **to make a ~ of a noise** *(sl.)* Höllenlärm veranstalten; **to
  make a ~ of a conman** *(US)* erstklassigen Schwindler abgeben;
  to make s. one's life a ~ [upon earth] jem. das Leben zur Hölle machen; **to kick up (raise) ~** Mordskrach schlagen; **to suffer
  ~ on earth** die Hölle auf Erden haben; **to work like ~** wie
  der Teufel arbeiten;
  ~-bender gewaltige (wilde) Sauftour; **to be ~-bent on s. th.** wie
  der Teufel hinter etw. her sein; **~ bomb** *(sl.)* Wasserstoffbombe; **~ cat** Furie; **~-fire** Höllenlärm; **~'s kitchen** *(US sl.)*
  Verbrecherviertel; **~ night** *(brotherhood, US)* Einführungs-
  abend; **~ raiser** Unruhestifter.
hellhole *(sl.)* Höllenplatz.
hellkite Unmensch.
hello girl *(US coll.)* Telefonfräulein.
helm *(fig.)* Führung, Herrschaft, *(ship)* Steuer, Ruder;
  ~ of the state Staatsruder;
  to be at the ~ *(fig.)* am Ruder sein, herrschen; **to be at the ~ of
  the state** Staatsschiff leiten.
helmet Helm;
  crash ~ Sturzhelm; **steel ~** Stahlhelm; **tropical ~** Tropenhelm.
help Hilfsdienst, Hilfe[leistung], Unterstützung, Beihilfe, *(help-
ers)* Aushilfspersonal, Hilfspersonal;
  by the ~ of the darkness im Schutz der Dunkelheit;
  home ~ Haushaltshilfe; **lady ~** *(US)* Hausangestellte; **little or
  no ~** wenig oder gar keine Hilfe; **mother's ~** Kindermädchen;
  past ~ verloren; **positive ~** praktische Hilfe; **unstinting ~** großzügige Hilfe;
  ~ to the memory Gedächtnisstütze;
  ~ o. s. sich bedienen, zugreifen; **~ s. o. with one's advice** jem.
  mit einem Rat dienlich sein; **~ down** *(fig.)* zum Untergang
  beitragen; **~ s. one's downfall** zu jds. Sturz beitragen; **~ out**
  aushelfen, als Aushilfe arbeiten;
  ~ (v.) helfen, Hilfe leisten, unterstützen, fördern;
  to appeal to s. o. for ~ j. um Hilfe bitten; **to come to s. one's ~**
  jem. zu Hilfe kommen; **to lend effective ~ to s. o.** wirkliche
  Hilfe für j. sein; **to promise one's ~** Hilfsversprechen abgeben;
  to refuse ~ to s. o. jem. Hilfe verweigern;
  ~ scheme Hilfs-, Notdienst; **~ wanted** *(newspaper)* Stellenangebot; **~-wanted ads** *(US)* Stellenanzeigen.
helper Helfer, Gehilfe, Hilfsperson, -arbeiter, -kraft;
  ~s Hilfspersonal.
helping Helfen, Hilfe;
  second ~ *(restaurant)* zweite Portion;
  ~ (a.) hilfreich, helfend;
  to lend a ~ hand behilflich sein, unter die Arme greifen.
helpless hilflos, unpraktisch;
  ~ invalid hilfloser Krüppel.
helplessness, utter gänzliche Hilflosigkeit.
helpmate Gehilfe, Gefährte.
helterskelter Durcheinander;
  ~ (a.) Hals über Kopf.
helve Griff, Stiel;
  to throw the ~ after the hatchet Flinte ins Korn werfen.
hem Saum, Einfassung;
  ~ (v.) about (around) umgeben, einschließen; **~ and haw** nicht
  mit der Sprache herauswollen.
hemmed in by enemies von Feinden umringt.
hemisphere Hemisphäre, Erdkugel.
hen party *(coll.)* Kaffee-, Damenkränzchen.
henchman Gefolgsmann, Anhänger, *(politics)* Opportunist,
Konjunkturritter.

henpecked unter dem Pantoffel;
  ~ husband Pantoffelheld.
hep *(US sl.)* im Bilde;
  to be ~ to anything sich auf alles verstehen.
herald Ausrufer;
  ~ (v.) in feierlich einführen.
heralded, widely groß herausgestellt.
herbage *(Br.)* Weiderecht.
herd Herde, Rudel, Masse, großer Haufen;
  common ~ Pöbel;
  ~ of cattle Viehherde;
  ~ (v.) people Menschen zusammenpferchen;
  ~ instinct Herdentrieb, -instinkt.
herdbook Herd-, Stammbuch.
herding Viehhüten;
  ~ of people Zusammenpferchung von Menschen.
hereditability Erblichkeit.
hereditable erblich, erbfähig, vererbbar;
  ~ bond *(Scot.)* Hypothek.
hereditaments *(Br.)* Grundbesitz, *(US)* vererblicher [Vermö-
gens]gegenstand, Erbschaft, -gut, Erbbesitz, Erbe, *(succession)* Erbfolge;
  corporeal ~ *(Br.)* Grundbesitz, *(US)* bewegliche Erbschaftsge-
  genstände; **incorporeal ~** vererbte Rechte, nicht körperliche
  Vermögensgegenstände, Immaterialgüterrechte.
hereditary erblich, vererbbar;
  ~ beliefs Überlieferungen; **~ disease** erbliche Belastung, angeborene Krankheit, Erbkrankheit; **~ enemy** Erbfeind; **~ monarchy** Erbmonarchie; **~ portion** Pflichtteil; **~ proprietor**
  Erbschaftsbesitzer; **~ security** *(Scot.)* Hypothek; **~ share** *(US)*
  gesetzlicher Erbteil; **~ state** Erbstaat; **~ succession** *(US)* gesetzliche Erbfolge; **~ taint** erbliche Belastung.
hereinafter nachstehend.
hereunder aufgrund dieser Vorschrift.
herewith hiermit.
heritability Erblichkeit, Erbfähigkeit.
heritable *(Scot., US)* vererblich, -bar;
  ~ bond dinglich gesicherte Schuldurkunde; **~ estate** Nachlaßgegenstand; **~ property** *(Scot. law)* Grundbesitz; **~ rights** *(Scot.
  law)* Grundstücksrechte; **~ security** dingliche Sicherheit,
  Hypothek.
heritage Erbschaft, -gut, Erbe, *(Scot.)* Grundbesitz;
  archaeological ~ archäologisches Kulturgut;
  ~ in danger gefährdete Kulturgüter;
  to preserve the ~ kulturelles Vermächtnis erhalten.
heritor Erbschaftsbesitzer.
hermit Einsiedler.
heroic action Heldentat.
herring, to draw a red ~ across the trail Täuschungsmanöver
durchführen.
herringbone Fischgrätenmuster.
hesitant *(market)* zurückhaltend.
hesitate *(v.)* Bedenken haben, zögern, zaudern, unschlüssig sein;
  ~ at nothing vor nichts zurückschrecken;
  to make s. o. ~ j. stutzig machen.
hesitation Unschlüssigkeit, Zögern, Schwanken, *(of buyers)*
Zurückhaltung;
  without ~ ohne Bedenken.
heterodyne *(broadcasting)* Überlagerung;
  ~ (v.) überlagern;
  ~ receiver Überlagerungsempfänger, Superhet.
hew *(v.)* | **close to the line** *(US)* vorsichtig vorgehen; **~ out a career
for o. s.** sich mühsam hocharbeiten; **~ one's way through dense
jungle** sich einen Weg durch den Urwald bahnen.
heyday Blüte-, Glanzzeit;
  to be in the ~ of one's glory auf dem Gipfel seines Ruhmes
  stehen; **to be in the ~ of youth** in der Blüte der Jugend stehen; **to
  have a ~** sein ganzes Können ausspielen.
hiatus Öffnung, Lücke, *(advertising)* Sommerpause;
  ~ in demand Nachfragelücke.
hick *(US sl.)* Hinterwäldler;
  ~ town *(US sl.)* Provinzstadt, Kleinkleckersdorf.
hidden verborgen, geheim;
  ~ assets freie Rücklagen, stille Reserven; **~ defect** versteckter
  (verborgener) Mangel; **~ hand** *(fam.)* okulte Einflüsse; **~ meaning** versteckte Bedeutung; **~ offer** *(advertisement)* versteckte
  Offerte, verstecktes Angebot; **~ persuader** geheimer Verfüh-
  rer; **~ price increase** versteckte Preiserhöhung [durch Quali-
  tätsminderung]; **~ reserves** stille Reserven, freie Rücklagen; **~
  tax** versteckte (verschleierte) Steuer; **~ threat** versteckte Drohung; **~ unemployment** nicht sichtbare Arbeitslosigkeit.

hide Versteck, *(fig.)* Fell, Haut;
~ *(v.)* verstecken, verbergen, beiseite schaffen;
~ **away a secret in one's heart** Geheimnis in seinem Herzen verschließen; ~ **away a treasure** Schatz verbergen; ~ **one's candle (light) under a bushel** sein Licht unter den Scheffel stellen; ~ **s. o. from justice** j. der Gerechtigkeit entziehen; ~ **out** *(US)* sich [vor der Polizei] verbergen; ~ **up a scandal** Skandal vertuschen; ~ **the views** Aussicht versperren;
to save one's ~ seine eigene Haut retten, seinen Kopf aus der Schlinge ziehen; **to tan s. one's** ~ jem. eine Tracht Prügel verabreichen;
~ **hunter** *(US)* Pelzjäger; ~**out** *(coll.)* Versteck; **guerilla** ~**out** Partisanenunterschlupf.

hidebound *(fig.)* kleinlich, engherzig;
~ **etiquette** starres Zeremoniell.

hideous crime scheußliches Verbrechen.

hiding Verstecken, Verbergen, *(flogging, coll.)* Tracht Prügel;
to be in ~ sich verbergen; **to come out of** ~ sein Versteck verlassen; **to give s. o. a** ~ jem. eine Tracht Prügel verabreichen; **to go into** ~ in den Untergrund gehen; **to take a** ~ *(fig.)* Schlappe einstecken müssen;
~ **place** Versteck.

hierarchic hierarchisch.

hierarchy Hierarchie;
~ **of diplomatic agents** diplomatische Rangordnung; ~ **of needs** Bedürfnispyramide.

hi-fi *(US, fam.)* mit getreuer Tonwiedergabe, Stereo.

higgle *(v.)* hausieren [gehen].

higgledy-piggledy kunterbunt durcheinander, wie Kraut und Rüben.

higgler Trödler, Hausierer.

higgling Feilschen.

high Höchststand, *(business)* Aufschwungsjahr, *(gear)* höchster Gang, Schnell-, Geländegang, *(weather, coll.)* Hochdruckgebiet;
all-time ~ *(stock exchange)* einmaliger Höchststand; **closing** ~ Kulminationshöchststand; **a new** ~ neues Hoch; **record** ~ Rekordhöhe;
to be at an all-time ~ *(prices, US)* höher denn je stehen; **to move to another (reach a) new** ~ erneuten (neuen) Höchsstand erreichen;
~ *(a.)* hoch, *(under the influence of drugs, sl.)* auf der Reise, auf dem Trip, *(price)* hochstehend, teuer;
definitively too ~ effektiv zu hoch;
as ~ **as** bis zum Preis von; ~ **and dry** *(person)* kaltgestellt, auf dem toten Gleis, *(ship)* gestrandet; ~ **and low** überall; ~ **up in the skies** wie im siebenten Himmel;
to be ~ hoch im Kurse stehen; **to be** ~ **and mighty** sich als feinen Herrn aufspielen; **to be** ~ **in office** hohe Stellung bekleiden; **to be** ~ **up in the civil service** hohe Staatsstellung innehaben; **to continue** ~ Höchstkurs beibehalten; **to fly** ~ hoch fliegen, *(fig.)* hoch hinaus wollen, ehrgeizige Pläne haben; **to get** ~ *(narcotics)* Rausch bekommen; **to go as** ~ **as DM 10.000,-** bis zu 10.000,- DM gehen; **to hold one's head** ~ seinen Kopf hoch tragen, stolz sein; **to pay** ~ teuer bezahlen; **to play** ~ mit hohem Einsatz spielen; **to put the** ~**-and-mighty** sich aufspielen; **to ride** ~ **in public esteem** hochangesehen sein; **to rule** ~ hoch im Kurs stehen; **to run** ~ *(emotions)* toben, *(prices)* gestiegen sein, *(sea)* hoch gehen; **to search** ~ **and low for s. th.** an allen Ecken und Enden nach etw. suchen; **to shift into** ~ höchsten Gang einschalten; **to walk with one's head** ~ Nase hoch tragen;
~ **affairs** wichtige Angelegenheiten; ~**-altitude aircraft** Höhenflugzeug; ~**-altitude flying** Höhenflug; ~ **area** Hochdruckgebiet; ~ **Authority** Hohe Behörde; ~ **bailiff** Obergerichtsvollzieher; ~**-born** von vornehmer Abstammung; ~**-bracket people** Einkommensteuerzahler in den oberen Steuerstufen; ~**-brow** Intellektueller, Schöngeist, *(a.)* intellektuell, schöngeistig; ~**browism** intellektueller Hochmut; ~**-caliber (calibre,** *Br.)* hochqualifiziert; ~ **change** Hauptbörse; ~ **Church** *(Br.)* Hochkirche; ~**-class** erstklassig, hochwertig; ~**-class goods** hochqualifizierte Erzeugnisse, Produkte erstklassiger Qualität; ~**-class hotel** erstklassiges (Ia) Hotel; ~**-class investment** erstklassige Kapitalanlage; ~**-class residential area** vornehme Wohngegend; ~**-class robbery** Hochstapelei; ~**-colo(u)red description** übertriebene Darstellung; ~ **command** *(mil.)* Oberkommando; ~ **Commission** Hochkommission; ~ **Commissioner** Hochkommissar; ~ **condition** vorzüglicher Zustand; **the** ~ **Contracting Parties** die hohen Vertragsschließenden, hohe Vertragsparteien; ~**-cost** hochwertig; **at a** ~ **cost** zu teuren Preisen; ~**-cost enterprise** kapitalintensives Unternehmen; ~**coupon** hochrentierlich; ~ **Court of Admiralty** *(Br.)* Prisenge-

richt; ~ **Court of Justice** *(Br.)* Oberster Gerichtshof; ~ **day** Festtag; ~ **degree of care and diligence** äußerste Sorgfaltspflicht; ~**-density area** verkehrsdichte Gegend; ~**-duty goods** hochbesteuerte Artikel; ~ **earner** Großverdiener; ~ **expenses** bedeutende Ausgaben; ~ **explosive** hochexplosiver Sprengstoff; ~**-falutin language** schwülstige Sprache, hochtrabendes Geschwätz; ~ **farming** intensive Bodenbewirtschaftung, Intensivkultur; **in** ~ **favo(u)r** in besonderer Gunst; ~ **fever** starkes Fieber; ~**-fidelity** getreue Tonwiedergabe, Stereo; **to buy at a** ~ **figure** teuer einkaufen; ~ **finance** *(US)* Hochfinanz, Hochstapelei; **to write in a** ~**-flown style** hochgestochen schreiben; ~ **frequency** Hochfrequenz; ~**-frequency amplifier** Hochfrequenzverstärker; ~ **flying** auf vollen Touren laufend; ~ **gear** höchster Gang; **to be in** ~ **gear** auf Hochtouren laufen; **to shift into** ~ **gear** höheren Gang einschalten; ~**-geared** *(capital)* überkapitalisiert; ~**-geared capital** hohes Fremdkapital; ~ **gearing** Erhöhung der Fremdkapitalintensität; ~ **German** Hochdeutsch; ~ **gloss print** Hochglanzabzug; ~**-grade** erstklassig, hochwertig, -gradig, prima; ~**-grade fuel** Qualitätsbenzin; ~**-grade goods** Qualitätserzeugnis; ~**-grade investments** erstklassige Kapitalanlagen; ~**-grade issues** hochwertige Papiere (Erzeugnisse); ~**-grade official** höherer Beamter; ~ **ground** Anhöhe; **to shoot into new** ~ **ground** *(US)* in rascher Steigerung neue Höchstkurse erreichen; ~ **hand** Willkür-, Gewaltherrschaft; **with a** ~ **hand** arrogant, aufgeblasen; ~ **hat** Zylinder; ~**-hat** *(US sl.)* Snob, Geck; **to be on one's** ~ **horse** aufgeblasen sein; **to ride the (get on one's)** ~ **horse** auf einem hohen Roß sitzen; ~ **ideals** hohe Ideale; ~**-income people** Leute mit hohem Einkommen; ~ **interest** hohe Zinsen; ~ **jinks** *(coll.)* Bombenstimmung; **to be for the** ~ **jump** auf den Henker warten; ~ **key** heller Bildschirm; ~**-keyed** leicht nervös; ~**-level** hochgelegen, *(fig.)* von hohem Niveau, *(qualified)* hochqualifiziert; ~ **level of prices** Hochstand der Preise; ~**-level business** Hochkonjunktur; ~ **life** Luxusleben; ~ **living** Wohlleben; ~ **mind** noble Gesinnung; ~ **money** *(US)* teures Geld; ~ **mortality** hohe Sterblichkeitsrate; ~**-mortality parts** Teile mit hoher Verschleißquote; ~ **multiple company** Unternehmen mit einem hohen Kursertragsmultiplikator; ~**-octane** mit hoher Oktanzahl; ~**-octane gasoline** klopffestes Benzin; ~ **official** hoher Beamter; **to have a** ~ **opinion of s. o.** gute Meinung von jem. haben; **of a** ~ **percentage** hochprozentig; ~ **percentage of moisture** hoher Feuchtigkeitsgrad; ~ **performer** überdurchschnittliche Erfolgsaktie; ~**-pitched emotions** erhabene Gefühle; ~**-pitched roof** steiles Dach; ~ **places** führende politische Kreise; ~ **position** hohe Stellung; ~**-potential** hochqualifiziert; ~**-powered** hochleistungsfähig; ~**-powered money** Zentralbankgeld; ~**-powered salesman** hervorragender (rasanter) Verkäufer, Verkaufskanone; ~ **premium** hohe Prämie; ~ **pressure** Hochdruck; ~**-pressure** *(a.)* nachdrücklich, energisch; ~**-pressure** *(v.)* **customers** Kunden bearbeiten; ~**-pressure advertising** in rascher Folge wiederholte Werbung; ~**-pressure area** Hochdruckgebiet; ~**-pressure engine** Hochleistungsmotor; ~**-pressure salesmanship** rasante Verkaufstechnik, Anwendung besonders intensiver Verkaufsmethoden; **to fetch a** ~ **price** hohen Preis erzielen; ~**-price period** Preiskonjunktur; ~**-price rate system** System der progressiven Leistungslohns, überproportionales Akkordlohnsystem; ~**-price work** überproportionale Akkordarbeit; ~**-priced** hochstehend, *(goods)* kostspielig, teuer, *(securities)* höher bewertet, hochstehend; ~**-priced commodities** teure Produkte; **of** ~ **quality** hochwertig; ~**-quality products** Qualitätserzeugnisse, Produkte des gehobeneren Bedarfs; ~**-ranking official** höherer Beamter; ~ **rate** hoher Kurs[stand]; **to be at a** ~ **rate** teuer sein; ~ **rate of interest** hoher Zinssatz; **to establish new** ~ **records** neue Höchstkurse erreichen; **of** ~ **repute** hochangesehen; **of** ~ **rank** hochgestellt; **to take a** ~ **rank** hoch gewertet werden; ~**-ranking** hochstehend; ~ **respect** tiefer Respekt; ~**-rise building** Hochhaus; ~**-rise hotel** Hochhaushotel; ~ **roller** *(US)* Modegeck; ~ **salary** hohes Gehalt; ~ **school** *(US)* Mittel-, Ober-, Realschule, höhere Lehranstalt; **senior** ~ **school** höhere Lehranstalt; **senior** ~**-school student** *(US)* Real-, Oberschüler; ~**-school graduate** *(US)* [etwa] Abiturient; ~ **seas** hohe (offene) See, offenes Meer; **to be on the** ~ **side** *(prices)* ziemlich hoch sein; ~ **size** *(advertisement)* Hochformat; ~ **society** obere Zehntausend; ~**-sounding phrases** hochtönende Phrasen; ~**-sounding title** hochtrabender Titel; ~ **speed** hohe Geschwindigkeit, *(mar.)* äußerste Kraft; ~**-speed lens** *(photo)* lichtstarkes Objektiv; ~**-speed memory** *(data processing)* Schnellspeicher; ~**-speed printer** Schnelldrucker; ~**-speed train** Schnellverkehrszug; **in** ~ **spirits** in gehobener Stimmung; ~ **spot** *(US)* wichtiger Punkt, Hauptsache; **to hit the** ~ **spot** kurz das Wichtigste erwähnen, *(actor)* herausragende Rolle spielen; ~ **spot of the evening** Höhepunkt des Abends; **to play for ~ stakes** um einen hohen Einsatz spielen; ~ **standing** guter Ruf; **of ~ standing** hochangesehen; ~ **stepper** *(fig.)* affektierte Person; ~ **street** Hauptgeschäftsstraße, Hauptstraße; **~-strung nerves** überempfindliche Nerven; ~ **summer** Hochsommer; **~-tasted** pikant; ~ **tea** *(Br.)* Tee mit Sondergerichten; ~ **temperature** hohe Temperatur; **political ~ tension** politische Hochspannung; **~-tension transmission cable** Hochspannungsleitung; **~-tension wire** Hochspannungsleitung; **to speak of s. o. in ~ terms** in hohen Tönen von jem. sprechen; **~-ticket instalment sales** hochwertige Abzahlungsverkäufe; ~ **tide** Hochwasser, Flut, *(fig.)* Gipfel-, Höhepunkt; ~ **time** höchste Zeit, *(sl.)* Heidenspaß, *(carousel, sl.)* Gelage, Zecherei; **to have a ~ time** luxuriöses Leben führen; **~-toned** *(fig.)* hochgesinnt; **~-toned finishing school for girls** hochfeines Mädchenpensionat; ~ **Tory** *(Br.)* engstirniger Konservativer; ~ **tory** *(Br.)* Rechtsradikaler; ~ **treason** Landes-, Hochverrat; **~-up** *(coll.)* hochgestellte Persönlichkeit, hohes Tier; **to live ~ up** hoch wohnen; **to set a ~ value on s. th.** etw. hoch einschätzen; **~-value goods** hochwertige Erzeugnisse; **~-volume branded goods** Massengüter der Markenindustrie; ~ **wages** hohe Löhne; ~ **water** Hochwasser; ~ **watermark** Flutmarke; ~ **wind** heftiger Wind; **~-wing aircraft** Hochdreher.

highball *(cocktail, US)* Highball, *(railroad, US)* Freifahrtssignal.

highbinder Erpresser.

highbrow *(coll.)* intellektuell.

higher, to bid mehr bieten, überbieten; **to go (run) ~** [im Preis] aufschlagen; **to rate ~** höher bewerten;
~ **classes** Oberschicht; ~ **echelon** höhere Instanz; ~ **education** Hochschulbildung; ~ **forms** höhere Schulklassen; ~ **goods** Güter höherer Ordnung; ~ **grades of the civil service** höherer Staatsdienst; **~-grade officials** höhere Beamtenschaft; ~ **industrial classes** gehobenere Wirtschaftsschichten; ~ **National Certificate in Business Studies** Diplomvolkswirtzeugnis; **to appoint s. o. to a ~ post** j. befördern; ~ **ranking** höherstehend; **of ~ value** höher bewertet.

highest | amount Höchstbetrag; ~ **bid** Höchstgebot; ~ **bidder** Meistbietender; **to sell to the ~ bidder** meistbietend verkaufen; ~ **in, first out** am teuersten eingekauft, zuerst verkauft; ~ **level** Höchststand; ~ **price** Höchstpreis, -kurs.

highflier überspannte Person.

highflyer Hochstapler.

highflying überspannt, übertrieben, extravagant.

highhanded von oben herab, anmaßend;
to be ~ with s. o. j. arrogant behandeln; ~ **government** Willkürherrschaft.

highhandedness Anmaßung, Willkür.

highjacker Luftpirat, Flugzeugentführer.

highjacking Flugzeugentführung, Luftpiraterie.

highlands Hochland.

highlight *(photo)* Glanzlicht;
~s Glanzpunkte;
~ **of a story** Höhepunkt einer Geschichte; **~s of a town** führende Persönlichkeiten einer Stadt;
~ *(v.)* unterstreichen, hervorheben, richtig zur Wirkung bringen;
~ **half-tone** Hochlichtautotypie.

highlighted schlaglichtartig beleuchtet.

highly in hohem Grade, *(fig.)* anmaßend;
to think too ~ of s. o. j. überschätzen, hohe Meinung von jem. haben;
~ **gifted** hoch begabt; ~ **paid** hochbezahlt; ~ **placed official** hochgestellter Beamter.

highness Höhe;
His Royal ~ Seine königliche Hoheit;
~ **of character** Charakterstärke.

highroad Land-, Hauptstraße;
~ **to success** sicherer Erfolgsweg.

highway öffentlicher Verkehrsweg, Haupt-, Fernverkehrs-, Kraftfahrstraße, Landstraße erster Ordnung, Chaussee, *(fig.)* sicherster und bequemster Weg;
adjoining ~ angrenzende Landstraße; **arterial ~** Durchgangs-, Fernverkehrsstraße; **common ~** Landstraße; **community ~** *(US)* Land-, Feldweg; **divided ~** *(US)* zweigeteilte (doppelte) Fahrbahn; **express ~** *(US)* Schnellverkehrsstraße, Autobahn; **interstate ~** *(US)* durch mehrere Bundesstaaten führende Fernverkehrsstraße; **main ~** Straße erster Ordnung; **major ~** Hauptverkehrsstraße, vorfahrtsberechtigte Straße; **multistrip ~** *(US)* Fernverkehrsstraße (Autobahn) mit Parallelbahnen; **private ~** Anliegerstraße; **public ~** öffentlicher Verkehrsweg; **six-lane ~** *(US)* sechsbahnige Fernverkehrsstraße;

~ **of commerce** Handelsstraße; **~s of speculation** Spekulationsmöglichkeiten;
to be on the ~ to success auf einem sicheren Erfolgsweg sein, Schlüssel zum Erfolg in der Tasche haben; **to dedicate (open) a ~** Verkehrsweg für die Benutzung freigeben; **to keep a ~ in repair** Landstraße instandhalten; **to obstruct a ~** Straße blockieren, Verkehrsbehinderung darstellen; **to peg the ~** Landstraße entlangtrotten;
~ Act *(US)* Straßenbau- und Unterhaltungsgesetz; ~ **authority** Straßenbaubehörde; ~ **builder** Straßenbauer; ~ **carrier** *(US)* Beförderungs-, Transportgesellschaft; **~ Code** *(Br.)* Straßenverkehrsordnung; ~ **construction** Straßenbau; ~ **crossing** Bahnkreuzung; ~ **department** Straßenbauamt; ~ **depot** Straßenmeisterei; ~ **driver** Fernlastfahrer; ~ **engineer** Straßenbauingenieur; ~ **engineering** Straßenbauwesen; ~ **ganger** Straßenräuber; ~ **laws** *(US)* Straßenunterhalts- und Benutzungsgesetze; ~ **marker** Fernstraßenverkehrsschild; ~ **network** Fernstraßenverkehrsnetz; ~ **parish** Straßenbaubezirk; ~ **patrol** Verkehrsstreife; ~ **patrolman** motorisierte Verkehrsstreife; ~ **program** *(US)* Verkehrs-, Fernstraßenprogramm; ~ **project** *(US)* Fernstraßenprojekt; ~ **rate** *(Br.)* Straßenunterhaltsabgabe; ~ **robber** Straßenräuber; ~ **robbery** Straßenraub; ~ **route** Fernverkehrsstraße; ~ **sign** Verkehrsschild; ~ **speed** *(US)* Autobahngeschwindigkeit; ~ **surveyor** Beamter des Straßenbauamts; ~ **system** Straßenverkehrswesen; ~ **tax** *(US)* Straßenbenutzungsgebühr; ~ **toll** Verkehrsunfallziffer; ~ **traffic** Straßenverkehr; ~ **transportation** *(US)* Güterfernverkehr; ~ **user fee (tax,** *US)* Straßenbenutzungsgebühr.

highwayman Wegelagerer, Straßenräuber *(Br.)* Straßenbahnarbeiter.

hijack *(v.)* Raubüberfälle auf Schmuggelfahrzeuge durchführen;
~ **an airplane** Flugzeug kapern (entführen); ~ **a truck** Lastwagen ausrauben.

hijacker Straßenräuber, *(of airplane)* Luftpirat, Flugzeugentführer;
~'s airfield Piratenflugplatz.

hijacking Flugzeugentführung, Luftpiraterie, Kapern eines Flugzeuges;
~ **insurance** Versicherung gegen Flugzeugentführungen.

hike *(US, prices)* Anstieg, Steigen;
~ **in energy imports** gestiegene Energieeinfuhren; ~ **in interest rates** Anstieg der Zinssätze;
~ *(v.)* wandern, marschieren, *(prices, US coll.)* steigen.

hiker Wanderer, Tramp.

hill Hügel, Anhöhe;
over the ~s *(fig.)* auf dem absteigendem Ast, *(US sl.)* fahnenflüchtig; **up ~ and down dale** bergauf und bergab;
~ *(v.)* sich hügelartig erheben;
to take the ~ in top gear bergige Straßen im Schnellgang fahren;
~ **climbing** Bergfahrt; **~-climbing efficiency** *(car)* Steigleistung; ~ **farming subsidies** *(Br.)* Agrarzuschüsse für von der Natur benachteiligte Gebiete; ~ **folk** Bergbewohner.

hillbilly *(US)* Hinterwäldler.

hillside Abhang, Berghang.

hillsite erhöhte Lage.

hilltop Bergspitze.

hilly hügelig;
~ **road** steile Straße.

hillybilly hinterwäldlerisch.

hind *(Br.)* Bauer, Landbewohner;
to get on one's ~ legs *(fig.)* sich auf die Hinterbeine stellen.

hinder *(v.)* abhalten, aufhalten, hemmen, hindern;
~ **and delay** Vollstreckung zu vereiteln suchen; ~ **s. o. in answering a letter** j. von der Beantwortung eines Briefes abhalten.

hindmost letzter;
the devil takes the ~ den Letzten beißen die Hunde.

hindrance Hemmnis, Hindernis.

hindsight zu späte Einsicht.

hinge Scharnier, Gelenk, *(fig.)* kritischer Punkt, Angelpunkt, *(philately)* Klebefalz;
off the ~s aus den Fugen (Angeln);
ball-joint ~ Kugelgelenk;
~ *(v.)* mit einem Scharnier versehen;
~ **on an alliance** von einem Bündnis abhängig sein.

hint Hinweis, Andeutung, Wink, Fingerzeig, *(stock exchange)* Börsentip;
by ~s auf Umwegen;
broad ~ Wink mit dem Zaunpfahl; **driving ~s** Fahrzeuganleitungen;

~s **for housewives** Ratschläge für Hausfrauen;
~ *(v.)* Hinweis geben, Andeutung machen;
to give a ~ Hinweis geben; **to jot down a few** ~s **for s. o.** jem. einige Hilfsanweisungen hinterlassen; **to know how to take a** ~ blitzschnell reagieren; **to take a (the)** ~ es sich gesagt sein lassen.

hinterland Landesinnere, *(shop, city)* Einzugsgebiet.

hip *(roof)* Gratanfall;
to catch s. o. on the ~ jds. schwache Stelle angreifen; **to have s. o. in the** ~ j. in seiner Gewalt haben; **to smite s. o.** ~ **and thigh** j. erbarmungslos zugrunde richten;
~ **bath** Sitzbadewanne; ~ **boot** Waffenstiefel; ~ **flask** Taschenflakon; ~ **pocket** Hüftentasche; ~ **roof** Walmdach.

hippodrome Pferdezirkus.

hirable vermietbar.

hire Miete, *(payment for* ~*)* Mietpreis, -zins, Miete, *(act of hiring, US)* An-, Einstellung, *(sailor)* Heuer, *(wage)* [Arbeits]lohn;
for ~ zu vermieten, *(taxi)* frei; **on** ~ mietweise, vermietet, *(ready to be hired)* zu vermieten;
~ **of money** Leihkapital; ~ **for a safe** Safemiete; ~ **for use** Sachmiete; ~ **for work and labo(u)r** Werklieferungsvertrag;
~ *(v.)* mieten, pachten, *(engage, US)* einstellen, anstellen, *(hire out)* vermieten, *(mar.)* heuern;
~ **s. o.** *(US)* j. in Sold nehmen; ~ **an attorney** *(US)* sich einen Anwalt nehmen; ~ **a car** Auto mieten; ~ **a concert hall** Konzerthalle anmieten; ~ **a crew** Mannschaft anmustern; ~ **by the day** in Tagelohn nehmen; ~ **labo(u)r** *(US)* Arbeitskräfte einstellen; ~ **a murderer** Mörder dingen; ~ **out** *(US)* ausleihen, vermieten; ~ **o. s. out** sich verdingen; ~ **a sailor** Matrosen anheuern; ~ **a servant** Hausangestellte engagieren;
to let on ~ vermieten; **to let s. th. out on** ~ etw. vermieten; **to pay for the** ~ **of a hall** Saalmiete bezahlen; **to take on** ~ leihen, mieten; **to take a car on** ~ Auto mieten; **to work for** ~ gegen Entgelt arbeiten;
~ **car** Mietwagen; ~ **car driver** Mietwagenfahrer; ~ **charges** Mietgebühren; ~ **payment** Mietpreis.

hire-purchase *(Br.)* Raten-, Abzahlungskauf, -geschäft, Kauf auf Abzahlung, Abstottern;
on ~ *(Br.)* auf Abzahlung[sbasis], auf Raten;
~ *(v.)* **s. th. to a customer** *(Br.)* einem Kunden etw. auf Abzahlung verkaufen;
to borrow through ~ *(Br.)* Abzahlungskredit aufnehmen; **to buy on** ~ *(Br.)* auf Abschlagszahlung (Ratenzahlung) kaufen; **to hold on** ~ *(Br.)* als Ratenzahler besitzen; **to sell on** ~ *(Br.)* auf Abzahlung verkaufen;
⸰ Act *(Br.)* Raten-, Abzahlungsgesetz; ~ **activities** *(Br.)* Abzahlungsgeschäfte; ~ **advertisement** *(Br.)* Anzeigenserie auf Abzahlungsbasis; ~ **agreement** *(Br.)* Teil-, Ab-, Ratenzahlungsvertrag; ~ **and conditional sale agreement** *(Br.)* Abzahlungsvertrag mit Eigentumsvorbehalt; **to be subject to a** ~ **agreement** *(Br.)* noch bezahlt werden müssen; ~ **borrowings** *(Br.)* Abzahlungskredite; ~ **card** *(Br.)* Karteikarte eines Abzahlungskunden; ~ **charges** *(Br.)* Abzahlungskosten, -gebühr; ~ **commitments** *(Br.)* Teil-, Abzahlungsverpflichtungen; ~ **company** *(Br.)* Abzahlungsfinanzierungsgesellschaft; ~ **contract** *(Br.)* Teil-, Raten-, Abzahlungsvertrag; ~ **creditor** *(Br.)* Abzahlungsgläubiger; ~ **debts** *(Br.)* Abzahlungsverschuldung; ~ **finance** *(Br.)* Finanzierung von Abzahlungsgeschäften; ~ **finance company (house)** *(Br.)* Kundenkreditbank, Abzahlungsfinanzierungsgesellschaft, -firma; ~ **finance shares** Aktien einer Abzahlungsfinanzierungsgesellschaft; ~ **form** *(Br.)* Abzahlungsformular; ~ **hazard** *(Br.)* Abzahlungsrisiko; ~ **instalment** *(Br.)* Abzahlungsrate; ~ **interest** *(Br.)* Abzahlungsbetrag; ~ **paper** *(Br.)* Ratenzahlungs-, Abzahlungswechsel; ~ **period** *(Br.)* Abzahlungszeitraum; ~ **price** *(Br.)* Preis bei Ratenzahlung, Abzahlungspreis; ~ **regulations** *(Br.)* Abzahlungsbestimmungen; ~ **repayment** *(Br.)* Rückführung eines Abzahlungsvertrages; ~ **restrictions** *(Br.)* Einschränkung der Abzahlungsgeschäfte; ~ **sale** *(Br.)* Ratenzahlungsgeschäft, -verkauf; ~ **sales** *(Br.)* Abzahlungsumsätze; ~ **restrictions** Einschränkung des Abzahlungsgeschäfts; ~ **system** *(Br.)* Ratenzahlungssystem, Abzahlungswesen; **to buy furniture on the** ~ **system** *(Br.)* Möbel auf Abzahlung (Raten, Stottern) kaufen; **to sell on the** ~ **system** *(Br.)* auf Abzahlung verkaufen; ~ **terms** *(Br.)* Abzahlungsbedingungen; ~ **transaction** *(Br.)* Abzahlungs-, Teilzahlungsgeschäft.

hired ver-, gemietet, *(taxi)* besetzt;
~ **aircraft** Charterflugzeug; ~ **car** Mietwagen; ~ **carriage** Mietfuhre; ~ **girl** Hausangestellte; ~ **gun** Söldner; ~ **hand** Landarbeiter; ~ **help** Aushilfsarbeiter, -kraft; ~ **man** Lohnarbeiter, Tagelöhner; ~ **troops** Söldnertruppen.

hireling Mietling, Söldner, *(a.)* käuflich, feil, gedungen.

hirer Mieter, Vermieter, *(of labo(u)r)* Arbeitgeber, Dienstherr, *(hire purchase, Br.)* Abzahlungsverpflichteter;
~ **of a safe** Safemieter.

hiring Mieten, Vermieten, *(worker)* An-, Einstellung;
centralized ~ zentralisiertes Einstellungssystem; **preferential** ~ bevorzugte Einstellung;
~ **and hiring** *(US)* Anstellung und Entlassung; ~ **of furniture** Möbelmiete; ~ **during a strike** Arbeitseinstellungen in einer Streikperiode; ~ **of tarpaulins** Gestellung von Planen; ~ **of a thing for use** Mobiliarmiete; ~ **at will** Arbeitseinstellung auf unbestimmte Zeit;
maximum ~ **age** höchstzulässiges Einstellungsalter; ~ **agreement** Mietvertrag, *(servant)* Dienstvertrag; ~ **charge** Mietgebühr, Miete; ~ **conditions** *(US)* Einstellungsbedingungen; ~ **limit** Einstellungsgrenze; ~ **out** Vermietung, *(person)* Verdingung; ~ **quota** Einstellungsquote; ~ **rate** Einstellungsrate; ~ **regulations** Anstellungsbestimmungen; ~ **scheme** Anwerbungsplan; ~ **subsidy** Einstellungszuschuß.

hiss *(v.)* *(theater)* auspfeifen.

histogram *(statistics)* Säulendiagramm, Staffelbild.

historiate *(v.)* historisches Hintergrundmaterial zur Verfügung stellen.

historic geschichtlich, historisch;
~ **cost** Herstellungs-, ursprüngliche Anschaffungskosten, *(public-utility accounting)* angefallene Ist-, nachträglich errechnete Selbstkosten; ~ **depreciation** Abschreibung nach Anschaffungswerten; ~ **event** historisches Ereignis; ~ **profit target** Ertragsziel aufgrund nachträglich errechneter Selbstkosten; ~ **record** Kriegstagebuch; ~ **spot** geschichtlich bedeutsamer Ort.

historical geschichtlich;
~ **criticism** Quellenkritik; ~ **film** historischer Film; ~ **geography** Geschichtsgeographie; ~ **novel** historischer Roman; ~ **painting** historisches Gemälde; ~ **record** Quellenbeleg; ~ **school** *(economics)* historische Schule; ~ **waters** auf Gewohnheitsrecht beruhende Hoheitsgewässer.

history *(career)* [Lebens]geschichte, -lauf, Werdegang;
family and personal ~ *(life insurance)* Familien- und eigene Krankheiten; **contemporary** ~ Gegenwartsgeschichte; **literary** ~ Literaturgeschichte; **natural** ~ Naturgeschichte; **personal** ~ Angaben zur Person;
~ **of art** Kunstgeschichte; ~ **of civilization** Kulturgeschichte; ~ **of literature** Literaturgeschichte; ~ **of mind** Geistesgeschichte; ~ **of misconduct** *(employee)* fortgesetztes ungehöriges Verhalten;
to go down in ~ in die Geschichte eingehen; **to have a** ~ Vergangenheit haben; **to know the inner** ~ **of an affair** Hintergründe eines Falles kennen;
to expunge from the ~ **books** historisch ungeschehen machen; ~ **lesson** Geschichtsstunde; **to write for a personal** ~ **form** Personalfragebogen erbitten; **permanent** ~ **record** laufend fortgeführte Personalunterlagen; ~ **sheet** Personalbogen.

histrionic Schauspieler;
~ **ability** schauspielerische Begabung; ~ **art** Schauspielkunst.

histrionics Effektenfahrerei.

hit *(collision)* Zusammenstoß, -prall, *(sarcastic remark)* Spitze, *(song)* Schlager, *(success)* Treffer, Erfolg, glücklicher Zufall;
lucky ~ Glücksfall; **smash** ~ durchschlagender Erfolgsfilm; **song** ~ Schlagererfolg, Hit;
~ **or miss** aufs Geratewohl; ~ **at politicians** auf die Politiker gezielte Bemerkung;
~ *(v.)* treffen, *(erect, US)* errichten, *(combustion engine)* laufen; ~ **the right answer** richtige Antwort finden; ~ **a blot** Achillesferse ausfindig machen; ~ **on all four cylinders** *(car)* auf allen Töpfen gut laufen; ~ **s. one's fancy** jds. Geschmack treffen; ~ **it** *(coll.)* Nagel auf den Kopf treffen; ~ **it big** großen Treffer erzielen; ~ **a man when he is down (below the belt)** *(fig.)* jds. ungünstige Lage ausnutzen; ~ **the nail on the head** Nagel auf dem Kopf treffen; ~ **an all-time low** absoluten Tiefstand erreichen; ~ **off** improvisieren; ~ **it off with s. o.** *(coll.)* sich mit jem. gut vertragen, gut (glänzend) miteinander auskommen; ~ **off a political personage** politische Persönlichkeit improvisieren; ~ **s. o. off to a T** j. täuschend ähnlich nachahmen; ~ **out blindly** sich wie der Teufel im Weihwasser benehmen; ~ **the taste of the public** Publikumsgeschmack treffen; ~ **upon a plan for making money** gute Verdienstmöglichkeit ausfindig machen; ~ **the right road** auf die richtige Straße kommen; ~ **upon a solution** Lösung finden; ~ **one's stride** richtig auf Touren kommen; ~ **town** *(US coll.)* in der Stadt gut ankommen; ~ **on the right word** auf das richtige Wort kommen;

to attempt s. th. ~ or miss etw. auf jeden Fall versuchen; **to be ~ in one's pride** *(fam.)* in seinem Stolz getroffen sein; **to draw a ~** Glückstreffer machen; **to have a sly ~ at s. o.** satirische Bemerkung über j. machen; **to have never ~ it off** nie miteinander ausgekommen sein; **to make a ~** *(US)* Bombenerfolg sein; **~-off** *(sl.)* geschickte Darstellung; **~ parade** Schlagerparade.

hit-and-run flüchtig;
  ~ accident Fahrer-, Unfallflucht; **~ charge** Anklage wegen Fahrerflucht; **to be prosecuted on a ~ charge** wegen Fahrerflucht angeklagt sein; **~ driver** flüchtiger Fahrer, Unfallflüchtiger; **~ driving** Fahrerflucht; **~ offence** Fahrerfluchtvergehen; **~ raid** *(mil.)* Stippangriff; **~ strike** wilder Streik; **~ victim** Opfer eines Fahrerfluchtvergehens.

hitch Hindernis, Störung, Haken;
  serious ~ in the negotiations ernsthafte Stockung in den Verhandlungen;
  ~ *(v.)* festmachen, *(agree, coll.)* sich vertragen, übereinstimmen, *(mil.. sl., US)* seinen Wehrdienst absolvieren;
  ~ a carriage onto the train Waggon anhängen; **~ up to a job** *(US)* sich an die Arbeit machen; **~ a ride** sich im Auto mitnehmen lassen; **~ one's waggon to a star** sich ein hohes Ziel stecken, hoch hinauswollen;
  to go off without a ~ reibungslos ablaufen; **to serve a ~ with a law firm** sich in einem Anwaltsbüro die Sporen verdienen.

Hitchcock appeal *(advertising)* kriminalistischer Stimmungseffekt.

hitchhike *(coll.)* Autofahren per Anhalter, *(advertising)* in eine Sendung eingeblendete Werbung für Nebenprodukte;
  ~ *(v.)* *(coll.)* Auto zum Mitfahren anhalten, per Anhalter fahren, trampen.

hitchhiker Anhalter, Tramper.

hitchhiking Autostopp, Trampen.

hive Menschenmenge;
  ~ of industry Industriezusammenballung; **~ of money** Geldschatz;
  ~ *(v.)* sammeln, aufbewahren, *(live together)* gemeinsam hausen, zusammenwohnen.

hive *(v.)* **off** verselbständigen, sich abspalten, *(colony)* selbständig werden;
  ~ profitable activities to the private sector ertragreiche Teilgebiete wieder reprivatisieren; **~ parts** teilreprivatisieren; **~ a service** Tätigkeit (Dienst) einstellen; **~ state industries** Staatsbetriebe reprivatisieren, Reprivatisierung verstaatlichter Industriebetriebe durchführen.

hive off of parts Teilreprivatisierung.

hived-off fragments teilreprivatisierte Fragmente.

hiving off Verselbständigung, *(industry)* Reprivatisierung;
  ~ operations Reprivatisierungsmaßnahmen; **~ process** Verselbständigungsprozeß.

hoard Ansammlung, [heimlicher] Vorrat;
  a miser's ~ Hamsterlager eines Geizkragens;
  ~ of anecdotes Anekdotenschatz; **~ of money** Geldschatz;
  ~ *(v.)* horten, anhäufen, ansammeln, hamstern;
  ~ supplies Vorräte horten; **~ up** ansammeln, aufspeichern; **~ up treasure** Vermögen ansammeln.

hoarder Hamsterer;
  food ~ Lebensmittelhamsterer;
  ~ of money Geldhamsterer.

hoarding Hortung, Ansammlung, Aufstapelung, Hamstern, Hamsterei, *(billboard, Br.)* Reklamefläche, Anschlagbrett, Litfaßsäule, *(fence)* Bretter-, Bauzaun;
  advertisement ~ Reklamewand; **inventory ~** Lagerhortung; **labo(u)r ~** Hortung von Arbeitskräften;
  ~ of money Geldhortung; **~ of supplies (provisions)** [Lebensmittel]hamsterei;
  ~ place Versteck; **~ purchases** Hamsterkäufe.

hoarfrost Raureif.

hoary altersgrau, ehrwürdig.

hoax Flunkerei, *(newspaper)* Falschmeldung, Zeitungsente, *(mockery)* Schabernach, Fopperei;
  to play a ~ on s. o. jem. einen Schabernack spielen.

hobble *(coll.)* Klemme, Patsche.

hobbledehoy Schlacks, Tolpatsch.

hobby Liebhaberei, Steckenpferd;
  to make a ~ of photography Amateurfotograf sein; **to paint as a ~** in seiner Freizeit malen; **to ride one's pet ~** sein Steckenpferd reiten.

hobby horse Steckenpferd;
  to start on one's ~ auf sein Lieblingsthema zu sprechen kommen.

hobnail *(fig.)* Bauerntölpel.

hobnob auf gut Glück;
  ~ *(v.)* eng befreundet sein.

hobo *(US)* Landstreicher, Tippelbruder.

hoboism *(US)* Landstreichertum.

Hobson's choice Zwangslage.

hock *(US sl.)* Pfand;
  in ~ verschuldet, *(pawned)* verpfändet, *(in prison)* im Kittchen;
  ~ *(v.)* verpfänden.

hocus-pocus Hokuspokus, Gaunertrick.

hodge-podge Sammelsurium;
  ~ act Sammelgesetz.

hodmen of literature literarische Tagelöhner.

hoe Hacke;
  ~ *(v.)* **up weeds** Unkraut jäten;
  to have a hard row ~ es schwer im Leben haben.

hog marktfähiges Schlachtschwein, *(coll.)* Schmutzfink;
  ~ *(v.)* *(coll.)* rücksichtslos fahren;
  ~ the road niemanden vorbeilassen, rücksichtslos fahren, Chausseeschreck sein;
  to go the whole ~ ganze Arbeit leisten, nicht auf halbem Wege stehen bleiben;
  ~ caller *(US sl.)* tragbarer Lautsprecher; **~-tied to business** ans Geschäft gefesselt.

hogshead großes Faß.

hogwash Plunder.

hoist Lastenaufzug;
  ammunition ~ *(warship)* Munitionsaufzug;
  ~ *(v.)* **[out] a boat** Boot aussetzen; **~ casks and crates aboard** Fässer und Kisten an Bord hieven; **~ coal** Kohle befördern; **~ s. th. upon s. o.** jem. etw. aufschwätzen; **~ a flag** Flagge hissen; **~ in a seaplane** Seeflugzeug an Bord nehmen;
  to be ~ with one's own petard den eigenen Ränken zum Opfer fallen.

hoistaway *(US coll.)* Aufzug.

hoisting *(mine)* Schachtförderung;
  ~ in of the boats Anbordnahme der Boote; **~ of a flag** Hissen einer Flagge;
  ~ cable Flaschenzug, Förderseil; **~ engine** Hebewerk, Ladekran; **~ engineer** Aufzugsarbeiter; **~ shaft** Förderschacht.

hoistway Aufzugsschacht.

hold Halt, Griff, *(controlling influence)* Einfluß, Macht, *(detention)* Haft, *(possession)* Gewahrsam, *(print.)* Stehsatzanweisung, *(prison)* Gefängnis, *(ship)* Schiffs-, Stau-, Laderaum;
  ~ on the resources Rückgriff auf die Hilfsquellen;
  ~ *(v.)* [fest]halten, *(anchor)* halten, *(court)* entscheiden, *(meeting)* abhalten, *(objection)* bestehenbleiben, *(possess)* im Besitz (in Verwahrung) haben, innehaben, besitzen, *(prices)* sich halten, *(retain)* rückbehalten, *(be tenant)* gepachtet haben;
  to have and ~ besitzen;
  ~ s. th. against s. o. jem. etw. vorwerfen; **~ aloof** sich abseits halten; **~ back** zurück-, einbe-, vorenthalten, *(buyers)* sich zurückhalten; **~ back on bringing in planned new capacity** Zurückhaltung bei der Verwirklichung bereits geplanter Kapazitätsausweitungen üben; **~ back information** Informationsmaterial zurückhalten; **~ down** unterdrücken, niederhalten; **~ s. o. down** j. im Griff haben; **~ down a claim** *(Br.)* seinem Grundstücksanspruch aussetzen; **~ down the exchange rate** Wechselkurs niedrighalten; **~ a job down** *(coll.)* Beruf weiter ausüben; **~ the pedal down** *(US)* Gaspedal durchtreten; **~ forth** dozieren, Rede schwingen; **~ forth to the crowd** Volksrede halten; **~ forth at length on s. th.** sich an einem Thema festbeißen; **~ forth a profit** mit einem Gewinn winken; **~ in** in Schach halten; **~ in with s. o.** jds. Freundschaft bewahren; **~ in one's temper** sein Temperament zügeln; **~ the line** *(tel.)* am Apparat bleiben; **~ off** ab-, fernhalten, *(storm)* nicht ausbrechen; **~ off the enemy** Feind abwehren; **~ off people** Mitmenschen zurückstoßen; **~ on** *(tel.)* am Apparat bleiben; **~ onto the market** Marktanteil halten; **~ onto one's oil shares** seine Ölaktien durchhalten; **~ out** *(fortress)* sich halten, *(make offer)* Angebot machen, *(supplies)* reichen; **~ out s. o.** *(Br.)* *(company)* jem. scheinbar Vertretungsmacht zuordnen; **~ out at s. o.** *(US coll.)* jem. etw. verheimlichen; **~ out against an attack** einem Angriff standhalten; **~ out the carrot to get more investments** mit immer weiteren Investitionen winken; **~ out to the end** bis zum Schluß durchhalten; **~ out a hand to s. o.** jem. bei der Überbrückung von Schwierigkeiten helfen; **~ out little hope for recovery** nur geringe Besserungschancen versprechen können, nur geringe Hoffnung auf eine Besserung machen können; **~ o. s. out as a partner** *(US)* sich als Gesellschafter ausgeben; **~ out for higher price** besseres Angebot abwarten; **~ out bright prospects to s. o.** jds. Zukunft in leuchtenden Farben malen; **~ over** verschie-

ben, *(Br., cheque)* im Portefeuille behalten, *(official)* über die festgelegte Zeit in Amt bleiben, *(payment)* stunden, *(tenant)* Räumung verzögern, sich auszuziehen weigern; ~ **s. th. over s. o.** jem. mit etw. drohen; ~ **over a bill** Wechsel prolongieren; ~ **over a matter to the next meeting** Angelegenheit bis zur nächsten Sitzung zurückstellen; ~ **over the rest of the goods** restliche Ware zurückbehalten; ~ **together** zusammenhalten; ~ **the nation together** Volk bei der Stange halten; ~ **one's staff together** seine Belegschaft zusammenschweißen; ~ **under a lease** gepachtet haben; ~ **s. th. up** etw. verzögern; ~ **up foodstuffs** Lebensmittel zurückhalten; ~ **up one's hands** sich ergeben; ~ **up the hands of s. o.** j. unterstützen; ~ **up payment pending enquiries** Zahlungen während der Untersuchung zurückstellen; ~ **up its price** sich im Preis halten; ~ **s. o. up to ridicule** j. lächerlich machen (der Lächerlichkeit preisgeben); ~ **up traffic** Verkehr anhalten (hindern); ~ **up a train** *(US)* Zug ausrauben; ~ **up well** *(securities)* sich gut behaupten; ~ **with s. o. (s. one's opinion)** mit jem. übereinstimmen;

~ **an action** Prozeß fortsetzen; ~ **an appointment** Amt innehaben; ~ **an argument** Beweis aufrechterhalten; ~ **one's audience** sein Publikum fesseln; ~ **the bag** *(coll.)* leer ausgehen, *(stock exchange)* auf seinen Wertpapieren sitzen bleiben; ~ **to bail** Stellung einer Kaution anordnen; ~ **s. o. at bay** j. auf respektvollem Abstand halten; ~ **the boards** *(play)* auf dem Spielplan bleiben; ~ **a brief** *(Br.)* vor Gericht (anwaltlich) vertreten, *(coll.)* j. verteidigen; ~ **no brief for** *(coll.)* Verteidigung ablehnen; ~ **a candle to ...** *(coll.)* Vergleich zu ... aushalten; ~ **in all cases** *(rule)* überall gelten; ~ **s. o. on charge of theft** *(US)* j. unter der Bezichtigung des Diebstahls festhalten; ~ **in check** in Schach halten; ~ **one's choice** bei seiner Wahl bleiben; ~ **a conference** Besprechung abhalten; ~ **a conversation** Gespräch führen; ~ **copy** Korrekturen lesen; ~ **one's course** Kurs halten; ~ **court** Gerichtsverhandlung leiten, verhandeln, Gerichtssitzung abhalten; ~ **for the court** für das Gericht verwahren; ~ **a debate** Diskussion leiten; ~ **s. o. for the whole debt** j. für die ganze Schuld haftbar machen, vom Schuldner die gesamte Summe verlangen; ~ **by one's decision** bei seiner Entscheidung bleiben; ~ **deliberations** Beratungen abhalten (pflegen); ~ **in demesne** Grundeigentum besitzen; ~ **an election** Wahl durchführen; ~ **s. o. in great esteem** hohe Meinung von j. haben; ~ **an examination** Prüfung abhalten; ~ **a feast** *(Br.)* Fest veranstalten; ~ **the fort** Festung halten, *(fig.)* Stellung halten; ~ **good** zutreffen, *(law)* in Kraft bleiben, gelten, gültig sein; ~ **one's ground** sich behaupten, seine Stellung halten; ~ **one's hand** nichts unternehmen; ~ **one's head high** Nase hoch im Wind tragen; ~ **as hostage** als Geisel nehmen; ~ **intercourse with s. o.** Beziehungen mit jem. unterhalten; ~ **the key to the puzzle** Schlüssel des Rätsels kennen; ~ **land** Grundstückseigentümer sein; ~ **on lease** als Pächter besitzen; ~ **level** Kursstand halten; ~ **s. o. liable** j. haftpflichtig (haftbar) machen; ~ **the line** *(tel.)* am Apparat bleiben; ~ **the accused man to be innocent** *(jury)* Angeklagten wegen erwiesener Unschuld freisprechen; ~ **the market** Stützungsaktion unternehmen, Markt beherrschen; ~ **a mass of details in one's head** Fülle von Einzelheiten behalten; ~ **a meeting** Versammlung (Sitzung) abhalten; ~ **s. o. for murder** j. unter Mordverdacht festhalten; ~ **an office (a position)** Amt bekleiden (innehaben), amtieren, *(political party)* an der Macht sein, regieren; ~ **strange opinions** seltsame Ansichten vertreten; ~ **one's own** sich halten, seine Stellung behalten (behaupten), *(business)* seine Marktstellung behaupten; ~ **one's own with the best** mit den Besten konkurrieren können; ~ **one's own against all comers** sich gegen alle Widersacher behaupten; ~ **a parley** Waffenstillstandsverhandlungen führen; ~ **Parliament** Parlament einberufen; ~ **one's peace** sich ruhig verhalten, den Mund halten; ~ **that a plan is impracticable** Plan für undurchführbar halten; ~ **pleas** vor Gericht verhandeln; ~ **six people** *(car)* sechs Sitzplätze haben; ~ **in pledge** als Pfand besitzen; ~ **no prejudice** kein Vorurteil haben; ~ **its price** seinen Preis beibehalten; ~ **s. o. prisoner** j. in Haft halten; ~ **a professorship** Professur (Lehrstuhl) innehaben; ~ **s. o. to his promise** j. auf sein Versprechen festnageln; ~ **property as a trustee** Vermögen treuhänderisch verwalten; ~ **a public inquiry** öffentliche Untersuchung durchführen; ~ **the purse** Kasse führen, Kassenwart sein; ~ **a railway train** Zug anhalten; ~ **o. s. in readiness** sich bereithalten; ~ **one's reputation cheap** sich überhaupt nicht um seinen Ruf kümmern; ~ **one's reputation dear** sehr um seinen guten Ruf besorgt sein; ~ **o. s. responsible** sich verantwortlich fühlen; ~ **s. o. responsible** sich an j. halten; ~ **s. o. responsible for the damage** j. für den Schaden haftbar machen; ~ **the road well** *(car)* gute Straßenlage haben; ~ **in safe custody** verwahren; ~ **seven shares** sieben Aktien besitzen; ~

shares in a business Geschäftsanteile besitzen; ~ **the stage** *(play)* sich auf der Bühne behaupten, auf dem Spielplan bleiben; ~ **stocks** Aktien besitzen; ~ **sound stocks** auf guten Werten sitzen bleiben; ~ **stocks for a rise** Aktien in Erwartung von Kurssteigerungen (für eine Haussebewegung) zurückhalten; ~ **stocks as security** Aktien als Sicherheit halten; ~ **sway over the world** Welt beherrschen; ~ **one tenth of the paid-up capital** ein Zehntel des eingezahlten Kapitals vertreten; ~ **one's tongue** seine Zunge hüten; ~ **true** gültig bleiben, gelten; ~ **on trust** als Treuhänder verwalten; ~ **a trustee to an account** Treuhänder für ein Konto verantwortlich machen; ~ **a view** Ansicht vertreten; ~ **a wager** Wette halten; ~ **water** wasserdicht sein, *(argument)* stichhaltig sein; **[not]** ~ **water** *(fig.)* [nicht] stichhaltig sein; ~ **s. o. to his word** j. auf sein Versprechen festnageln;

to break out of the ~ mit dem Löschen der Ladung beginnen; **to get** ~ **of s. o.** j. erwischen; **to get a** ~ **on s. o.** j. unter seinen Einfluß bekommen; **to get** ~ **of s. th.** Wind von etw. bekommen; **to get** ~ **of a secret** Geheimnis aufdecken; **to have a firm** ~ sicher beherrschen; **to have a great** ~ **over s. o.** großen Einfluß bei jem. besitzen; **to keep a tight** ~ **of s.** th. etw. fest im Griff haben; **to lay (put) in** ~ in Haft nehmen; **to lose one's** ~ **on realities** sich vom Boden der Wirklichkeit entfernen; **to maintain one's** ~ **over a district** Bezirk im Griff behalten; **to take** ~ **of** Besitz ergreifen; **to take** ~ **of the housework** Haushalt leiten; **~-back pay** bis zur Erstellung der Lohnliste einbehaltene Löhne; **~-harmless agreement** Haftungsübernahmevertrag, Vereinbarung über die Freistellung von Schadenersatzverpflichtungen; **~-out** verteidigungsfähiger Schlupwinkel.

holdall Reisetasche, *(coll.)* Konversationslexikon.

holdback Hindernis, *(door)* Türstopper;

~ **pay** *(US)* einbehaltene Lohngelder.

holder *(land)* Pächter, *(mar.)* Schauermann, *(property, stocks)* Inhaber, Besitzer;

account ~ Konteninhaber, -besitzer; **actual** ~ augenblicklicher (gegenwärtiger) Inhaber; **bicycle** ~ Fahrradständer; **bona-fide** ~ gutgläubiger Besitzer (Inhaber); **cigar** ~ Zigarrenspitze; **coupon** ~ Kuponinhaber, -besitzer; **debenture** ~ Pfandbrief-, Obligationen-, Schuldverschreibungsinhaber; **former** ~ ursprünglicher Inhaber; **joint** ~ Miteigentümer, -besitzer; **joint-account** ~ Inhaber eines Gemeinschaftskontos; **legal (lawful)** ~ rechtmäßiger Inhaber; **licence** ~ Lizenznehmer, Konzessionär; **loan** ~ Anleihebesitzer; **majority** ~ Mehrheitsaktionär; **mala-fide** ~ schlechtgläubiger Inhaber, unredlicher Besitzer; **minority** ~ Minderheitsaktionär; **patent** ~ Patentinhaber; **previous** ~ Vorbesitzer, Vordermann, Vorgänger; **prior** ~ Vorbesitzer, früherer Inhaber; **registered** ~ *(Br.)* eingetragener Aktionär; **season-ticket** ~ Dauerkarteninhaber; **small-fund** ~ Kleinrentner; **small** ~ *(Br.)* Kleinbauer, -landbesitzer, Siedler; **stake** ~ Parzellenbesitzer; **stall** ~ Standinhaber; **subsequent** ~ Nachbesitzer, -mann; **third** ~ *(mortgage)* Drittbesitzer; **ticket** ~ Fahrkarteninhaber; **true** ~ rechtmäßiger Inhaber;

~ **of an annuity** Rentenempfänger, -berechtigter; ~ **of bank stock** Bankaktionär; ~ **of a banking account** Bankkontoinhaber; ~ **of a bill of exchange** Wechselinhaber, -gläubiger; ~ **of a cheque** *(Br.)* **(check,** *US)* Scheckinhaber; ~ **of a cheque card** *(Br.)* Scheckkarteninhaber; ~ **of debt claims** Forderungsinhaber; ~ **in due course** Indossant, rechtmäßiger (legitimierter) Wechsel-, Scheckinhaber, *(innocent* ~ *for value)* gutgläubiger Inhaber; ~ **of a large estate** Großgrundbesitzer; ~ **in bad faith** bösgläubiger Besitzer; ~ **in good faith** gutgläubiger Besitzer (Inhaber); ~ **of a letter of credit** Kreditbriefinhaber; ~ **of a licence** Konzessionsinhaber, Lizenznehmer; ~ **of a lien** Pfandgläubiger, -halter; ~ **of a mortgage** Hypothekengläubiger; ~ **of a note** Wechselinhaber; ~ **of a patent** Patentinhaber; ~ **of a pension** Rentenempfänger, Pensionsberechtigter; ~ **of a pledge** Pfandgläubiger; ~ **of power** Gewaltinhaber; ~ **of a power of attorney** Vollmachtsinhaber; ~ **of record** *(US)* eingetragener Aktionär; ~ **of a right** Rechtsinhaber; ~ **of s. one's securities** Gläubiger von Sicherheiten, Pfandgläubiger, Effekteninhaber; ~ **of shares** Aktionär; ~ **of staff shares** Belegschaftsaktionär; ~ **of stocks** Wareneigentümer, *(securities, US)* Aktionär; ~ **for the time being** jeweiliger Inhaber; ~ **on trust** Treuhänder; **bona-fide** ~ **for value without notice** rechtmäßiger Wechselinhaber (Scheckinhaber); **innocent** ~ **for value** gutgläubiger Inhaber; ~ **for value of a bill** Inhaber einer Wechselgutschrift;

to be made out in the name of the ~ auf den Inhaber lauten; **~'s right** Rechte des Wechselinhabers.

holding *(interest)* Beteiligung, Anteil, *(land held, Br.)* Pachtung, Pacht-, Zinsgut, *(possession)* [Grund]besitz, Bestand, *(stocks held)* Aktienbesitz, *(store)* Vorrat, Lager;

agricultural ~ (Br.) landwirtschaftlich genutzter Grundbesitz, Pachtgut; **bill** ~s Wechselstand; **collateral** ~s Lombardbestand; **discount** ~s Bestand an Diskonten; **diversified** ~s weitgestreute Anlagebeteiligungen; **financial** ~ finanzielle Beteiligung; **foreign** ~s Auslandsbesitz; **gold** ~s Goldbestand; **gold and foreign-exchange** ~s Gold- und Devisenbestände; **long-term** ~s langfristige Anlagen; **majority** ~ Mehrheitsbeteiligung; **maximum personal** ~ höchstzulässiger Bestand pro Person; **minority** ~ Minderheitsbeteiligung; **net** ~s Nettobestände; **paper** ~s Effektenbesitz; **pre-war** ~s Vorkriegsbeteiligungen; **real-estate** ~s Immobilienbesitz; **small** ~ (Br.) landwirtschaftlicher Kleinbetrieb, Kleinlandbesitz, (shares) Kleinbesitz an Aktien;

~s of acceptances Akzeptbestand; ~s in banks Bankbeteiligungen; ~s in a business enterprise Geschäftsanteile; gold and silver ~s of a country Münzbestände eines Landes; ~ of the courts ständige Rechtsprechung der Gerichte; ~ down prices Preisbegrenzung; average ~ of the goods in store Durchschnittsbestand des Warenlagers; ~ of land Land-, Grundbesitz; ~s of a library Bibliotheksbestände; ~ the line preisstabilisierende Maßnahmen; ~ the market (US) Marktstützung; ~ of a meeting Abhaltung einer Versammlung; ~ of money Kassenhaltung; ~ out (Br.) Sichausgeben als Gesellschafter, Duldung des Rechtsscheins; ~ over (tenant) verzögerte Räumung, Besitz nach Pachtablauf, Auszugsverweigerung; ~ of a captured position (mil.) erfolgreiche Verteidigung einer eroberten Stellung; ~s of securities Wertpapierportefeuille; ~s of shares Aktienbesitz; ~ of outdoor advertising sites Stellennetz; ~ the statutory meeting Abhaltung der Hauptversammlung; ~s of stocks Vorratshaltung, (securities, US) Aktienbesitz; ~ of units Zertifikatsbesitz;

to add to one's ~s monthly monatlich zu seinen Beständen zukaufen; to be ~ (fair) abgehalten werden; to divide (parcel out) land into small ~s Land parzellieren; to have ~s in several companies mehrere Beteiligungen besitzen, an verschiedene Gesellschaften beteiligt sein; to increase one's ~s of cash Erhöhung der Barbestände vornehmen, Liquidität anreichern; to reveal one's ~s to the tax authorities seine Beteiligungen den Steuerbehörden offenlegen;

Agricultural ᴼ Act (Br.) Pachtgesetz; ~ altitude (airplane) Warteflughöhe; ~ area (airplane) Warteraum; ~ attack (mil.) Bindung von Feindkräften, Scheinangriff; ~ capacity (vehicle) Fassungsvermögen; ~ company Holding-, Dachgesellschaft; intermediate (interposed) ~ company Zwischenholding; operating ~ company tätige Holdinggesellschaft; top ~ company übergeordnete Holding-, Dachgesellschaft; ~-company system Holdingsystem; ~ cost Lagerhaltungskosten; ~ ground (mar.) Ankergrund; ~ operation Dauerbeschäftigung; ~-out partner (Br.) Scheingesellschafter; ~ period (income tax) Besitzdauer; ~ power (mil.) Durchsteh-, haltevermögen; ~ room Kühlraum; small ~ system Parzellierungswesen; ~ times (shop) Bedienungszeit.

holdover (advertising) nicht gebrachte Anzeige, (carry-over) Übertrag, (concession) übertragene Konzession, (sl., hangover) Kater, (official) über die Pensionszeit hinaus bleibender Beamter, (repeater) Repetent, sitzengebliebener Schuldner, (rest) Überbleibsel, Rest;
~s (US) am nächsten Tag eingelöste Schecks und Wechsel; ~ credit Überbrückungskredit.

holdup (railway) Betriebsstockung, -störung, Panne, (robbery, US) Straßenraub, bewaffneter Überfall, (traffic) Verkehrsstockung, -stauung;
~ on the underground railway Verzögerung des U-Bahnverkehrs;
personal ~ insurance (US) Überfallversicherung; ~ man (US) Straßenräuber.

hole (awkward situation) Klemme, mißliche Lage, (prison) Gefängniszelle, (underground habitation) Elendsquartier, Loch;
in the ~ pleite, bankrott;
godforsaken ~ gottverlassenes Nest, Kleinkleckersdorf; inspection ~ Schau-, Guckloch; wretched little ~ kümmerliche Bude;
~ in the air Luftloch; ~ in s. one's coat Fleck auf jds. weißer Weste; rotten ~ of a place kümmerliches Loch, (fam.) Rattennest; ~ in the wall (sl.) Kleinstbetrieb;
~-and-corner heimlich und anrüchig;
to be full of ~s (road) voller Straßenlöcher sein; to be in a ~ in der Patsche sitzen; to find o. s. in a ~ in einer vertrackten Lage sein; to get s. o. out of a ~ jem. aus der Klemme (Patsche) helfen; to make ~s in one's capital sein Kapital anbrechen; to

make a large ~ in one's savings großes Loch in jds. Ersparnisse reißen; to pick ~s in an argument Beweisführung zerpflücken; to put s. o. in a ~ j. in die Enge treiben;
~-and-corner business anrüchiges Geschäft; ~-and-corner dealings undurchsichtige Geschäfte; ~-and-corner methods undurchsichtige Methoden; ~-puncher Locher.

holiday (US) [arbeits]freier Tag, Ruhetag, (Br.) gewöhnlicher Feiertag, (festival day) Festtag, (school) schulfreier Tag, (vacation, Br.) Ferien, Ferientag, Urlaub, Erholungsaufenthalt;
on ~ auf Urlaub, in den Ferien;
bank ~ (Br.) Bankfeiertag; Christmas ~s Weihnachtsferien; Easter ~s Osterferien; a fortnight's ~ 14tägiger Urlaub; legal ~ gesetzlicher Feiertag; a month's ~ ein Monat Urlaub; official ~ gesetzlicher Feiertag; paid ~ (Br.) bezahlter Urlaub, Feiertag; public ~ gesetzlicher Feiertag; school ~s (Br.) Schulferien; short ~ kleine Ferienreise (Urlaubsreise); summer ~ (Br.) große Ferien, Sommerferien; three weeks' ~ dreiwöchiger Urlaub; ~s with pay (Br.) bezahlter Urlaub;
to allow two weeks ~ zwei Wochen Urlaub genehmigen; to ask for a fortnight's ~ um zwei Wochen Urlaub einkommen; to be on [one's] ~ Urlaub machen, in den Ferien sein, Ferien haben; to be away on ~ auf Urlaub sein; to curtail one's ~ Urlaub vorzeitig beenden; to get away for the ~s in den Ferien (im Urlaub) verreisen; to give s. o. a ~ jem. einen Tag frei geben; to go for one's (on) ~ in die Ferien reisen, Erholungsurlaub machen; to go on ~ through a travel agency Ferienreise über ein Reisebüro buchen; to have a ~ freien Tag (Ferien) haben, freihaben; to make ~ Fest feiern, Feiertag bezahlen; to put in for three days ~ um einen dreitägigen Urlaub bitten; to run a ~ sich eine Urlaubsreise leisten; to stagger the ~ Urlaub aufteilen; to take a ~ sich einen Tag frei nehmen; to take a month's ~ in summer einmonatlichen Sommerurlaub machen; to take one's ~s seinen Urlaub nehmen; to take separate ~s getrennten Urlaub machen; to want a ~ urlaubsreif sein;
~ accommodation Ferienunterkunft, -unterbringung, -quartier; ᴼs with Pay Act (Br.) Urlaubsvergütungsgesetz; ~ address Ferienanschrift, Urlaubsanschrift; basic ~ allowance Grundbetrag des Urlaubsgeldes; annual ~ allowance of £ 1300 in foreign currencies jährliche Devisenzuteilung von 1300 Pfund für Urlaubsreisen; to break their long-standing ~ arrangements vom alterprobten Ferienrhythmus abweichen; ~ booking Ferien-, Urlaubsreservierung; ~ budget Urlaubsetat, Ferienbudget; ~ camp Ferienlager, -siedlung, Erholungsheim; ~ chalet Ferienhaus, -bungalow; ~ clothes Sonntagskleider, Freizeitkleidung; ~ course Ferienkursus; ~ crowds Scharen von Urlaubern (Feriengästen), Urlaubsströme, -massen; ~ cruise Kreuzfahrt; ~ entitlement Urlaubsanspruch; ~ exchange Ferienaustausch; ~ excursion Ausflug; ~ expense in den Ferien ausgegebenes Geld; ~ facilities Urlaubs-, Ferieneinrichtungen; ~ gift Mitbringsel; ~ ground Feriengegend, Vergnügungspark; ~ guide Ferienführer, -handbuch; ~ home Ferienhaus; ~ insurance Ferienversicherung; ~ layoffs Entlassungen während der Urlaubszeit; in ~ mood in Ferienstimmung; money-saving ~ package billige Sonderangebote für die Urlaubszeit; ~ paradise Ferien-, Urlaubsparadies; ~ pay Urlaubsgeld, Feiertagszuschlag, doppelte Entlohnung für Arbeit an gesetzlichen Feiertagen; accrued ~ pay Urlaubsgeldrückstände; ~ politician Biertischpolitiker; ~ post Ferienbeschäftigung; ~ poster Ferienplakat; ~ reading Ferienlektüre; ~ region Urlaubs-, Feriengebiet; ~ remuneration Urlaubsgeld, Ferienvergütung, -geld; accrued ~ remuneration zustehendes Urlaubsgeld; ~ replacement (Br.) Urlaubsvertretung; ~ residence Ferienwohnung; crowded ~ resort stark besuchter (überlaufener) Ferienort; ~ rush Ferienandrang; ~ schedule Ferien-, Urlaubsordnung; ~ season Urlaubs-, Ferienzeit; ~ shutdown Stillegung in der Ferienzeit, ferienbedingte Schließung; ~ snapshot Urlaubsphoto; ~ specials Ferientarif; ~ spot Ferien-, Urlaubsort; ~ stay Ferienaufenthalt; ~ task (school) Ferienarbeit, -aufgabe; ~ time Ferienzeit; ~ tour Ferienreise; ~ trade Touristenbranche; ~ traffic Urlaubsverkehr; ~ travel Urlaubs-, Ferienreise; ~ village Feriendorf; ~ visit passage bezahlte Urlaubsreise, Ferientransportvergütung, Ferienreisekosten.

holidayer, holidaymaker Urlauber, Ferienreisender, Erholungssuchender, Sommerfrischler.

hollow Höhle, Hohlraum, (drain) Abzugskanal;
~ (a.) hohl;
to beat s. o. ~ (coll.) j. mit Leichtigkeit schlagen;
~ friendship falsche Freundschaft; ~ peace Scheinfriede; ~ victory (fam.) trügerischer Sieg.

holograph eigenhändig geschriebenes Testament;
~ (a.) eigenhändig geschrieben.

holographic will eigenhändig geschriebenes Testament.

Holy | Father Papst; **to have a ⁰ fear** *(fam.)* Heidenangst haben; **⁰ orders** Priesterweihe; **~ See** päpstlicher Stuhl.

homage Huldigung, Ehrerbietung, *(oath of allegiance)* Treueeid; **in ~ to s. o.** aus Verehrung für j.;

to render ~ to s. o. for a discovery jem. seine Hochachtung für eine Entdeckung bezeugen.

home Wohnung, Haus, Heim, *(abode)* Aufenthalt, Zufluchtsort, *(asylum)* Asyl, Heim, Institut, Anstalt, *(native land)* Heimat-[land], Mutterland, *(residence)* ständiger Wohnort;

at ~ zu Hause, *(country)* im Lande, in der Heimat, *(fig.)* in seinem Element, *(jour)* Empfangstag; **not at ~** kein Gästeempfang; **at ~ and abroad** im In- und Ausland; **away from ~** abwesend, verreist; **on my returning ~** bei meiner Rückkehr; **in the privacy of the ~** in der Intimsphäre; **on his way ~** auf seiner Rückreise; **without permanent ~** ohne festen Wohnsitz; **additional ~** Zweitwohnung; **broken ~** kaputte Ehe; **council ~** *(Br.)* Sozialwohnung; **flat ~** Bungalowhaus; **harvest ~** Erntefest; **maternity ~** Entbindungsheim; **mental ~** Nervenheilanstalt; **mobile ~** transportables Haus; **national ~** Heimstätte; **new ~s authorized** Neubaubewilligungen; **nursing ~** Privatklinik; **orphans' ~** Waisenhaus; **own ~** Eigenheim; **permanent ~** ständige Wohnstätte; **remand ~** Jugendgefängnis; **sailors' ~** Seemannsheim; **single-family ~** Einfamilienhaus; **stately ~** großes Herrenhaus, Landsitz; **poor suburban ~** ärmliche Vorstadtwohnung;

~ for the aged Altersheim; **~ of the fine arts** Wiege der schönen Künste; **~ for the blind** Blindenanstalt; **boarding ~ for dogs** Hundepension; **~ for the elderly** Altenwohnheim; **~ for incurables** Trinkerheilanstalt; **new ~s purchased with conventional mortgages** auf dem Hypothekenmarkt finanzierte Hauskäufe; **~ of rest** Ruheplatz; **~ close to work** betriebsnahe Wohnung; **~** *(v.)* nach Hause zurückkehren, *(aircraft)* zum Heimatflughafen zurückkehren, Heimathafen mittels Leitstrahls anfliegen, *(live in)* sein Heim haben, wohnen, *(rocket)* automatisch auf ein Ziel zusteuern;

~ in Zielansteuerung vornehmen; **~ s. o.** j. in einem Heim unterbringen;

to be away from ~ auf Reisen (verreist) sein; **to be at ~** Gäste empfangen; **to be at ~ with s. th.** mit einer Sache vertraut sein, von einer Sache etw. verstehen; **not to be at ~ to anyone** niemanden empfangen; **to be back ~** wieder zu Hause sein; **to be perfectly at ~ with a subject** in einem Teilgebiet wohlbewandert sein; **not to be at ~ for s. o.** für j. nicht zu sprechen sein; **to be very pleasant in one's own ~** in seinen eigenen vier Wänden völlig gelöst sein; **to be at ~ in society** gesellschaftlich völlig sicher sein; **to bring ~ to s. o.** für j. lebendig werden lassen; **to bring s. th. ~ to s. o.** jem. über etw. die Augen öffnen; **to bring a charge (crime) ~ to s. o.** Anklagepunkte gegen j. beweisen, j. überführen, jem. ein Verbrechen nachweisen; **to bring war ~ to the people** Zivilbevölkerung in Kriegsaktionen einbeziehen; **to buy a ~ of one's own** Eigenheim erwerben; **to come ~ on s. o. some day** mit jem. eines Tages abrechnen; **to drive s. th. ~ to s. o.** jem. etw. klarmachen; **to feel at ~ in a branch of knowledge** sich in einer Wissenschaft heimisch fühlen; **to feel perfectly at ~ on a subject** auf einem Gebiet völlig zu Hause sein; **to feel at ~ in a foreign language** Fremdsprache wie seine Muttersprache sprechen; **to furnish one's ~** sich einrichten; **to get prisoners back to their ~s** Gefangene repatriieren; **to give s. o. a ~** j. bei sich aufnehmen; **to go ~** *(remark)* genau (auf der richtigen Stelle) sitzen; **to have a ~ of one's own** eigene Wohnung (eigenes Heim) haben; **to leave ~** von zu Hause fortgehen; **to long for ~** sich nach der Heimat sehnen; **to look on a place as one's ~** sich an einem Ort wie zu Hause fühlen; **to make for ~** sich nach Hause begeben; **to make o. s. at ~** es sich bequem machen; **to make one's ~ in the country** sich auf dem Lande niederlassen; **to own one's ~** Eigenheimbesitzer sein; **to press a pedal ~** Gaspedal blockieren; **to return to one's old ~** in seine alten Jagdgründe zurückkehren; **to see s. o. ~** j. nach Hause begleiten; **to see one's old ~ again** seine Heimat wiedersehen; **to serve ~s with cable television services** Häuser an das Kabelfernsehnetz anschließen; **to set up a ~** seinen eigenen Hausstand begründen; **to stay at ~** zu Hause bleiben; **to strike ~** seine Wirkung nicht verfehlen;

~ *(a.)* heimisch, *(mar.)* landwärts, *(native)* inländisch, einheimisch;

~ address Privatanschrift, Wohnsitzadresse; **~ affairs** *(Br.)* Innenpolitik, innenpolitische Fragen (Angelegenheiten); **~ agency** Inlandsvertretung; **~ appliances** Haushaltsgeräte; **~ army** im Inland stationierte Streitkräfte; **~ bank** Hausbank; **~ base** Heimatbasis; **~ battalion** *(Br.)* Ersatztruppenteil; **~ build-**

~er *(US)* Eigenheimbesitzer; **~ building** *(US)* Eigenheimerrichtung; **~ building and loan association** *(US)* Bausparkasse; **~ building industry** *(US)* Wohnungsbauwirtschaft; **~ business** Inlandgeschäft; **~ buyer** Eigenheimerwerber, Hauskäufer; **~ buying** Eigenheimerwerb; **~ car** *(railway)* eigener Waggon; **~ care** häusliche Betreuung; **~ cinema** Heimkino; **~ circle** Familienkreis; **~ club cooperative apartment houses** *(US)* gemeinsam erbaute Mehrfamilienhäuser; **~ comforts** häusliche Bequemlichkeiten; **~-coming weekend** *(US)* internatsfreies Wochenende; **~ commodities** Landesprodukte, einheimische Waren; **~ low-cost construction** billiger Wohnungsbau; **~ consumption** Inlandsverbrauch, -bedarf; **~ consumption value** Inlandswert; **~ cooking** Hausmannskost; **~ correspondent** Inlandskorrespondent; **The ⁰ Counties** *(Br.)* Grafschaften rings um London; **~ country** *(Br.)* Mutterland, Heimatland; **~ currency** Landeswährung, Binnenwährung; **~ currency issues** nur im Inland gültige Banknoten; **~ debit** *(US)* eigener Scheck; **~ defence** Landesverteidigung; **~ delivery** Hauszustellung, Lieferung frei Haus; **~ demand** einheimischer, inländischer Bedarf, Binnen-, Inlandsnachfrage; **⁰ Department** *(US)* Innenministerium, Ministerium des Inneren; **~ descriptions** *(Br.)* heimische Wertpapiere; **~ dweller** Eigenheimbesitzer; **~ economic class** *(US)* Hauswirtschaftsunterricht; **~economics** *(US)* Hauswirtschaftslehre; **~ economy** Binnenwirtschaft; **~-entertaining** Hauseinladung; **~ entertainment** Zeitvertreib zu Hause; **~ environment** häusliche Verhältnisse (Umgebung); **~ exhibition** Eigenheimausstellung; **~ farm** landwirtschaftlicher Eigenbetrieb; **~ financing** Wohnungsbau-, Eigenheimfinanzierung; **to keep the ~ fires burning** Sicherheit des Vaterlandes gewährleisten; **~ fleet** *(Br.)* Flotte in Heimatgewässern; **~-folks** Familienmitglieder; **~ forces** *(mil.)* im Inland stationierte Streitkräfte; **~ freezer** Tiefkühltruhe; **~ freight** Her-, Rückfracht; **~ front** Heimatfront; **on the ~ front** auf innenpolitischem Gebiet; **~-front problem** innerpolitisches Problem; **~ furnishings** Wohnungseinrichtung; **~ garage** Eigenheimgarage; **~ garden** eigener Garten; **~ ground** *(sport)* Vereinsgelände; **to visit customers on their ~ ground** Kunden in ihren eigenen vier Wänden besuchen; **~-grown** einheimisch, im Lande erzeugt; **⁰-Grown Cereals Authority** *(Br.)* Dienststelle zum verstärkten Inlandgetreideanbau; **⁰ Guards** *(Br.)* Bürgerwehr, Miliz; **~ help** Mütterhilfe; **~ helper system** vom Betrieb gestellte stundenweise Haushaltshilfen; **~ improvements** Schönheitsreparaturen; **~-improvement loan** zur Instandsetzung der Wohnung gewährtes Darlehen; **~ industry** einheimische Industrie, *(carried on at home)* Haus-, Heimindustrie, *(EC)* einzelstaatlicher Wirtschaftszweig; **to foster ~ industries** einheimische Industrie fördern; **~-foreign insurance** *(Br.)* Korrespondenzversicherung; **~ insurer** Eigenheimversicherungsgesellschaft; **~ journey** Heim-, Rückreise; **~ joys** Freuden des Familienlebens; **⁰ Judiciary Committee** Rechtsausschuß des Repräsentantenhauses; **~ paid ~ leave** bezahlter Heimaturlaub; **~ leave earned at the rate of four days per calendar month** viertägiger Urlaubsanspruch pro einmonatliche Tätigkeit; **~ lessons** Schulaufgaben; **~ life** Familienleben; **~ loan** Inlandsanleihe; **~ lot** *(US)* Wohngrundstück; **~ mail** *(Br.)* Inlandpost; **~ manufacture[s]** Inlandsproduktion, inländische Erzeugnisse; **~ market** Inlands-, Binnenmarkt; **~-market orders** Inlandsaufträge; **~-market price** Inlandspreis; **~ minister** *(India)* Innenminister; **~ mission** Innere Mission; **~ mortgage** Eigenheimhypothek; **~ mortgage loan** auf dem Eigenheim abgesichertes Hypothekardarlehen; **~ news** Inlandsnachrichten; **~ office** *(in a private house)* Arbeitsplatz zu Hause, *(US)* Zentrale, Hauptbüro, *(Br.)* Innenministerium; **~ office inquiry** *(Br.)* Untersuchungsbericht des Innenministeriums; **~ office minister** *(Br.)* Innenminister; **~-office tour of duty** Pflichtaufenthaltszeit in der Zentrale; **~ order** Inlandsauftrag; **~ organization** Inlandsorganisation; **~ ownership** Eigenheimbesitz, Haus- und Grundstücksbesitz; **~-owning member** Eigenheimbesitzer; **~ policy (politics)** Innenpolitik; **~ port** Heimathafen; **~ posting** Verwendung im Innendienst; **to push ~ prices out of reach of ordinary people** Erwerb eines Eigenheims für Normalverbraucher unerschwinglich machen; **~ produced** im Inland erzeugt; **~-produced goods** heimische Fabrikate, Inlandserzeugnisse; **~ producer** Inlandserzeuger; **~ products** einheimische Erzeugnisse; **~ purchase** Eigenheimerwerb; **~ rails (railways, Br.)** einheimische Eisenbahnwerte; **~ rate** Inlandstarif; **~ rental** Wohnungsmiete; **~ requirements** Inlands-, Eigenbedarf [eines Landes], einheimischer Bedarf; **~ reserves** *(mil.)* Landsturm; **~ rule** Selbstverwaltung, -regierung; **~ ruler** Autonomievorkämpfer; **~ safe** *(Br.)* Privatsafe; **~ sales** Inlandsabsatz, -geschäft, -umsatz; **~ sales manager** Inlandverkaufsleiter; **⁰**

Secretary *(Br.)* Innenminister; ~ **securities** *(Br.)* inländische Wertpapiere; ~ **seeker** Eigenheiminteressent; ~ **service** Inlandsdienst; ~ **service assurance** *(Br.)* Volks-, Kleinlebensversicherung; ~ **service salesman** Hausierer, [Haustür]vertreter; ~ **shares** *(Br.)* inländische Aktien; ~ **signal** *(railway)* Einfahrtssignal; ~ **site** Wohngrundstück; ~ **state** Heimatstaat; ~ **station** *(railway)* End-, Heimatbahnhof; ~ **stocks** *(Br.)* inländische Wertpapiere; ~ **television** Heimkino; ~-**television cartridge** Fernsehkassette für das Heimkino; ~ **territory** *(US)* Heimatgebiet; ~ **town** Heimatstadt; ~-**town customer** Kunde im Stadtgebiet; ~ **towner** *(US)* Ortsansässiger; ~ **trade** *(Br.)* Binnen-, Inlandshandel, -wirtschaft; ~-**trade navigation** Küstenverkehr; ~ **trade ship** Küstenschiff; ~ **trading** *(Br.)* Inlandsgeschäft; ~ **traffic** Binnenverkehr; ~ **truth** ungeschminkte Wahrheit, Binsenwahrheit; **to tell s. o. a few ~ truths** jem. gehörig die Meinung sagen; ~ **use** *(Br.)* Verbrauch im Inland, Inlandsverbrauch; ~-**use entry** *(Br.)* Einfuhrdeklaration für Inlandsverbrauch; ~ **value** Inlandswert; ~-**value declaration** Zolleingangserklärung; ~ **visitation** [ärztlicher] Hausbesuch; ~ **waters** Hoheitsgewässer.

homebody *(US coll.)* häuslicher Mensch, Stubenhocker.
homebound auf dem Rückflug (der Heimreise) befindlich.
homebred einheimisch, *(fig.)* steif, ungehobelt;
  with ~ courtesy mit angeborener Höflichkeit.
homecome Heimkehr.
homecomer Heimkehrer.
homecoming Heimkehr;
  ~ **prisoner** Heimkehrer; ~ **weekend** *(US)* Wochenendurlaub zu Hause.
homecroft *(Br.)* Heimstätte, Eigenheim in Stadtnähe, *(labo(u)rer)* Arbeitersiedlung, landwirtschaftliche Nebenerwerbssiedlung;
  ⁓ **Scheme** *(Br.)* Heimstättenwerk.
homecrofter *(Br.)* Heimstättenbesitzer.
homekeeping häuslich.
homeland Heimat-, Vaterland.
homeless heimat-, wohnung-, obdachlos.
homelessness Obdachlosigkeit.
homelike wie zu Hause.
homely einfach, häuslich, hausbacken;
  ~ **atmosphere** vertraute Atmosphäre.
homemade selbstgemacht, inländisch, einheimisch;
  ~ **commodities (goods)** einheimische Waren.
homemaker Hauswirtschaftsleiterin.
homemaking Hauswirtschaftslehre, Haushaltsführung.
homeowner *(US)* Haus-, Eigenheimbesitzer;
  ~**s' loan corporation** *(US)* Bausparkasse.
homer Brieftaube.
homesick heimwehkrank;
  to be ~ Heimweh haben.
homesickness Heimweh.
homespun *(fig.)* schlicht, einfach.
homestall Herrenhaus.
homestead *(US)* Heimstätte, landwirtschaftliche Nebenerwerbssiedlung, Eigenheim;
  business ~ *(US)* gewerblich genutztes Eigenheim; **rural ~** *(US)* unter Vollstreckungsschutz stehende landwirtschaftliche Betriebsstätte; **stock-raising ~** *(US)* gewerblich genutztes Eigenheim mit Viehzucht; **urban ~** *(US)* landwirtschaftliche Nebenerwerbssiedlung;
  ~ *(v.) (US)* Eigenheim erwerben;
  ⁓ **Act** *(US)* Heimstättengesetz; ~-**aid benefit association** *(US)* Bausparkasse; ~ **corporation** *(US)* Terrainparzellierungsgesellschaft, gemeinnützige Siedlungsgesellschaft; ~ **estate** *(US)* Heimstättengrundstück; ~ **exemption** *(US)* Zwangsvollstreckungsfreibetrag für Heimstätten; ~ **exemption laws** *(US)* [etwa] Vollstreckungsschutzgesetze für landwirtschaftliche Nebenbetriebe; ~ **law** *(US)* Heimstättenrecht; ~ **lease (selection)** *(Australia)* Landpachtung; ~ **lot** *(US)* Heimstättengrundstück; ~ **right** *(US)* Heimstättenvollstreckungsschutz, Heimstättenrecht.
homesteader *(US)* Heimstätten-, Eigenheimbesitzer, Siedler.
homeward | bound auf der Heimreise begriffen, nach der Heimat bestimmt; **to be ~ bound** *(ship)* auf der Rückreise sein; ~-**bound ship** nach dem Heimathafen fahrendes Schiff; ~ **cargo** Rückladung; ~ **journey** Heimreise; ~ **voyage** Heimfahrt; ~ **way** Heimweg.
homework Hausindustrie, Heimarbeit, *(school)* Hausarbeit, -aufgaben;
  written ~ schriftliche Hausaufgabe;
  to do one's ~ Schulaufgaben machen.

homeworker Heimarbeiter.
homicidal | attempt versuchte Tötung, Tötungsversuch; ~ **lunatic** mordlustiger Irrer.
homicide Tötung;
  culpable ~ Totschlag; **excusable ~** Tötung bei Vorliegen von Schuldausschließungsgründen, Notwehr; **felonious ~** Mord, Totschlag; **justifiable ~** gerechtfertigte Tötung; **negligent ~** fahrlässige Tötung; **wilful ~** vorsätzliche Tötung;
  ~ **by misadventure** Unfall mit tödlichem Ausgang; ~ **by necessity** rechtlich notwendige Tötung; ~ **in self-defence** Tötung in Notwehr;
  to commit ~ in self-defence in Notwehr töten;
  ~ **squad** Mordkommission; ~ **trial** Verfahren wegen Mordes, Mordprozeß.
homily *(fig.)* Moralpredigt.
homing *(airplane)* Ziel-, Senderanflug;
  ~ **device** Zielanfluggerät; ~ **pigeon** Brieftaube; ~ **station** Funkleitstelle, -station; ~ **vehicle** Zielflugkörper.
homogeneous product homogenes Produkt.
homogenizing Gleichschaltung.
homologate *(v.)* bestätigen, beglaubigen.
homologation *(Scot.)* Vertragsbestätigung.
honest rechtschaffen, redlich, ehrlich, *(fair)* reell;
  to be quite ~ about it es ganz ehrlich meinen;
  ~ **folk** redliche Leute; ~ **goods** unvermischte Ware; ~-**to-goodness Republican** *(US)* aufrichtiger Republikaner; ~ **opinion** ehrliche Meinung; **to earn an ~ penny** ehrlich sein Brot verdienen; ~ **piece of work** sauberes Stück Arbeit; ~ **profits** ehrliche Gewinne; ~ **weight** volles Gewicht.
honesty Ehrlichkeit, Redlichkeit;
  ~ **pays** Ehrlichkeit zahlt sich aus; ~ **is the best policy** ehrlich währt am längsten.
honey Honig, *(US)* Liebling, Schatz;
  ~ **to my soul** Balsam für meine Seele.
honeymoon Flitterwochen, Hochzeitsreise;
  ~ *(v.)* Flitterwochen verbringen.
honorarium Honorar.
honorary ehrenamtlich;
  to serve in an ~ capacity ehrenamtlich tätig sein; ~ **chairman** Ehrenpräsident, -vorsitzender; ~ **debt** Ehrenschuld; ~ **degree** Ehrendoktor; ~ **duties** ehrenamtliche Funktionen (Aufgaben); ~ **freeman** Ehrenbürger; ~ **function** Ehrenamt; ~ **member** Ehrenmitglied; ~ **membership** Ehrenmitgliedschaft; ~ **office (position)** Ehrenamt; ~ **pay** Ehrensold; ~ **president** ehrenamtlicher Präsident, Ehrenvorsitzender; ~ **rank** ehrenhalber verliehener Rang; ~ **secretary** ehrenamtlicher Sekretär; ~ **title** ehrenhalber verliehener Titel; ~ **trustee** ehrenamtlich tätiger Treuhänder.
hono(u)r Ehre, *(respect)* Hochachtung, Respekt, Ehrerbietung, *(school)* besondere Auszeichnung;
  to s. one's ~ zu jds. Ehren; **upon my ~** auf Ehrenwort;
  ~**s** Ehrenverleihungen;
  academic ~s akademische Ehrungen (Auszeichnungen); **the last ~s** Grabgeleit; **military ~s** militärische Ehren beim Begräbnis; **New Year's ~s** Beförderungen zum Neujahrstag; **professional ~** Standesehre;
  ~ *(v.)* [be]ehren, *(accept bill)* akzeptieren, annehmen, *(pay bill)* einlösen, bezahlen, honorieren;
  ~ **a bill at maturity** Wechsel bei Verfall einlösen; ~ **a ceremony with one's presence** Festakt durch seine Anwesenheit auszeichnen; ~ **a check** Scheck einlösen; ~ **s. o. with one's confidence** j. mit seinem Vertrauen auszeichnen; ~ **an invitation** einer Einladung Folge leisten; ~ **on presentation** bei Vorlage honorieren; ~ **one's signature** seine Unterschrift einlösen;
  to attain the highest ~s zu den höchsten Würden aufsteigen; **to be an ~ to one's country** seinem Vaterland zur Zierde gereichen; **to be an ~ to one's school** seiner Schule Ehre machen; **to be on one's ~ to do s. th.** moralisch zu etw. verpflichtet sein; **to be bound in ~ to do** anstandshalber tun müssen; **to carry off the ~s** Siegespalme davontragen; **to come out of an affair with ~** sich mit Eleganz aus einer Affäre ziehen; **to consider it an ~ to do s. th.** etw. als Ehre betrachten; **to do the ~s** als Gastgeber[in] fungieren; **to fling away one's ~** auf seine Ehre pfeifen; **to forfeit one's ~** seiner Ehre verlustig gehen; **to grant s. o. military ~s** jem. militärische Ehren erweisen; **to hold s. o. in great ~** große Hochachtung vor jem. haben; **to hold a banquet in ~ of s. one's arrival** anläßlich jds. Anwesenheit ein Essen geben; **to leave a fortress with all the ~s of war** ehrenvollen Abzug aus einer Festung erhalten; **to make it a point of ~ to do s. th.** etw. als Ehrensache ansehen; **to meet with due ~** gehörig honoriert werden; **to obtain first-class ~s** sein Examen mit Eins abschlie-

ßen, Prädikatsexamen machen; **to pass with ~s** mit Auszeichnung bestehen; **to pay ~s to s. o.** jem. Respekt bezeigen; **to pay the last ~s to s. o.** jem. das letzte Geleit geben (die letzten Ehren erweisen); **to pledge one's ~** seine Ehre verpfänden; **to prepare due ~** Annahme vorbereiten; **to put s. o. on his ~** jem. auf sein Ehrenwort hin trauen; **to put up a statue in ~ of s. o.** jem. ein Denkmal errichten; **to receive s. o. with all due ~s** j. mit allen ihm gebührenden Ehren empfangen; **to render the last ~s** letzte Ehren erweisen; **to state on one's ~** auf Ehre und Gewissen versichern; **to take ~s in mathematics** seinen Abschluß in höherer Mathematik machen;

~'s degree *(Br.)* Prädikatsexamen, mit Auszeichnung erworbener Doktorgrad; **~s list** *(Br.)* Vorschlagsliste für Ordensverleihungen; **~s man** *(Br.)* **(student, US)** Prädikatsabsolvent; **for ~'s sake** um der Ehre zu genügen; **~s system** Auszeichnungssystem.

hono(u)rable ehrenhaft, achtbar;
  ~ burial ehrenhaftes Begräbnis; **~ calling** ehrenvoller Beruf; **~ discharge** *(mil.)* ehrenhafte Entlassung; **my ~ friend** der Herr Vorredner; **~ intentions** Heiratsabsichten; **the ~ member for A** *(Br.)* der Abgeordnete für A; **~ mention** ehrenvolle Erwähnung; **to conclude an ~ peace** ehrenvollen Frieden abschließen; **~ salary** anständiges Gehalt; **~ understanding** *(restraint of trade)* formlose Wettbewerbsabrede.

hono(u)red bill eingelöster Wechsel.

hood *(car)* Dach, Verdeck, *(engine, US)* Motorhaube, *(US sl.)* Gangster;
  pointed ~ Spitzgiebel;
  to lower the ~ Verdeck öffnen.

hoodlum *(US sl.)* Raufbold, Strolch, Rowdy.

hoodoo *(US)* Unglücksbringer.

hoof *(v.)* | **out** *(sl.)* hinauswerfen;
  to be under the ~ unterdrückt werden; **to beat (pad) the ~** auf Schusters Rappen reisen; **to buy cattle on the ~** Schlachtvieh lebend erwerben; **to show the cloven ~** Pferdefuß sehen lassen.

hoofer *(US sl.)* Revuegirl.

hook Haken, Öse, *(advertising)* Blickfang, Aufhänger, *(river)* scharfe Krümmung;
  by ~ or by crook auf Biegen und Brechen; **off the ~** von der Stange, *(sl.)* abgehauen; **off the ~s** in Unordnung; **on one's own ~** *(sl.)* auf eigene Faust (Gefahr);
  clothes ~ Kleiderhaken;
  ~ and eye Haken und Öse; **~, line and sinker** *(fig.)* mit allem Drum und Dran;
  ~ (v.) a husband *(coll.)* Ehemann ergattern; **~ in** einhaken; **~ it** *(sl.)* abhauen, türmen; **~ up** mit einem Haken befestigen, *(broadcasting stations)* zusammenschalten;
  to sling one's ~ türmen, sich aus dem Staub machen;
  ~-and-ladder truck *(US)* Rettungswagen [der Feuerwehr].

hooked, to become ~ on s. th. *(sl.)* süchtig auf etw. werden, von etw. besessen sein.

hookup *(broadcasting)* Gemeinschaftsschaltung, Zusammenschaltung, *(plan of assemblage)* Schaltschema, -bild, *(politics)* Zusammenschluß, Bündnis;
  to be on one's own ~ sich selbständig gemacht haben; **to speak over a countrywide ~** über alle Sender sprechen.

hooligan *(coll.)* Rowdy, Straßenlümmel.

hooliganism Rowdytum.

hoop Band, Faßreifen;
  to go through the ~s Konkurs anmelden, sich bankrott erklären; **to put s. o. through the ~** jem. das Leben zur Hölle machen;
  ~ iron Bandeisen.

hooper rating Hörerstatistik.

hoopla *(US sl.)* Rummel.

hoot *(car, Br.)* Hupe, *(factory)* Fabriksirene;
  ~ (v.) a speaker down Redner auspfeifen; **~ a play off the stage** Theaterstück auszischen;
  not to be worth a ~ keinen Pfifferling wert sein; **not to care a ~ (two ~s)** *(sl.)* sich einen Dreck um etw. kümmern, einem völlig schnuppe sein.

hooter Sirene, *(car)* Hupe, *(factory, ship)* Sirene.

hop *(airplane)* kurzer Überlandflug, Kurzflug, *(dance, sl.)* Schwoof;
  ~ (v.) across schnell herüberfahren; **~ the freight** als blinder Passagier mitfahren; **~ it** *(sl.)* türmen, abhauen; **~ off** *(airplane, sl.)* starten; **~ the ocean** Ozean überqueren; **~ a train** *(US)* auf einen Zug aufspringen; **~ the twig** *(sl.)* verduften, abhauen; **~ upwards** sprunghaft ansteigen, nach oben klettern;
  to be always on the ~ herumwirtschaften;
  ~ sacking grobe Sackleinwand.

---

hope Hoffnung, Vertrauen, Zuversicht;
  to be past all ~ hoffnungsloser Fall sein; **to have high ~s for s. th.** auf etw. große Hoffnungen setzen;
  ~ chest *(US)* Aussteuertruhe.

horizon Horizont, *(fig.)* [geistiger] Horizont, Gesichtskreis.

horizontal Querformat;
  ~ (a.) horizontal, waagerecht;
  ~ amalgamation horizontaler Zusammenschluß; **~ combine** horizontales Kartell, Horizontalkonzern; **~ contract** horizontaler Vertrag; **~ expansion** horizontale Ausdehnung; **~ files** Flachregistratur, -ablage, Horizontalablage; **~ increase in salaries of ten per cent** *(US)* einheitlicher zehnprozentiger Gehaltsanstieg; **~ integration** horizontale Eingliederung, Verschmelzung von Konkurrenzfirmen; **~ mobility** Faktormobilität; **~ spacing** Zeichendichte; **~ tail surfaces** Höhenleitwerk; **~ union** Fachgewerkschaft.

horn *(airplane)* Leitflächenhebel, *(car)* Hupe;
  on the ~s of a dilemma zwischen Skylla und Charybdis, in einer Zwickmühle;
  fog ~ Nebelsirene, -horn; **hunting ~** Jagdhorn; **motor ~** Autohupe;
  ~ of plenty Füllhorn;
  to come out of the little end of the ~ den Kürzeren ziehen; **to draw (pull) in one's ~s** Rückzieher machen; **to honk the ~** Hupe betätigen; **to put s. o. on the ~s of a dilemma** jem. die Wahl zwischen zwei Möglichkeiten geben;
  ~-book Fibel, Elementarbuch; **~-book law** rudimentäre Rechtskenntnisse; **~ push** Hupen.

horoscope Horoskop.

horror Schreck, Grausen, Entsetzen;
  ~s of war Kriegsgreuel;
  to have a ~ of publicity Abscheu vor der Öffentlichkeit haben; **~ film** Gruselfilm; **~ novel** Schauerroman; **~ weapon** Abschreckungswaffe.

horse Pferd, *(mil.)* Kavallerie, *(print.)* Anlegetisch, *(school, US sl.)* Eselsbrücke;
  cart ~ Wagenpferd; **coach ~** Kutschpferd; **dark ~** völliger Außenseiter; **draught ~** Zugpferd; **light ~** *(mil.)* leichte Kavallerie; **race ~** Rennpferd; **stalking ~** Deckmantel, Vorwand, *(politics)* Strohmann, Marionettenfigur;
  ~ of another colo(u)r völlig andere Angelegenheit; **~ and foot** *(mil.)* Kavallerie und Infanterie;
  ~ (v.) around *(fam.)* herumalbern;
  to be on one's high ~ auf einem hohen Roß sitzen, von oben herab sein; **to back the wrong ~** aufs falsche Pferd setzen; **to come off the high ~** klein und häßlich werden; **to eat like a ~** wie ein Scheunendrescher fressen; **to flog a dead ~** leeres Stroh dreschen, offene Türen einrennen, seine Energien verschwenden; **not to look a gift ~ in the mouth** einem geschenkten Gaul nicht ins Maul schauen; **to mount (ride) the high ~** sich aufs hohe Roß setzen; **to put the cart before the ~** Pferd beim Schwanz aufzäumen; **to swap ~s midstream** *(fig.)* Pferde mitten im Strom wechseln; **to work like a ~** wie ein Pferd arbeiten;
  ~ box Pferdetransportwagen; **~-and-buggy** hoffnungslos veraltet, vorsintflutlich; **to be beyond the ~-and-buggy stage** über das Anfangsstadium hinaus sein; **~ car** Pferdewaggon; **to grin through a ~ collar** primitive Witze machen; **~ coper (dealer)** Pferdehändler; **to be a judge of ~ flesh** etw. von den Pferden verstehen; **~ Guards** *(fig., Br.)* Oberkommando, Generalstab; **~ holder** Pferdehalter; **~-marine** *(fig.)* Person am falschen Platz; **to be in the ~ marines** *(hum.)* zur reitenden Gebirgsmarine gehören; **[straight] from the ~'s mouth** *(sl.)* aus erster Quelle; **~ opera** *(sl.)* Wildwestfilm; **~ race** Pferderennen; **~ sense** gesunder Menschenverstand; **~ trading** Pferdehandel.

horseback Pferderücken;
  on ~ zu Pferd;
  ~ opinion *(US)* allererste Meinung.

horseleech Wucherer.

horseplay grober Unfug.

horsepower Pferdestärke, PS.

horseshoe table Hufeisentafel.

horticultural gärtnerisch, gartenbaulich;
  ~ products Gartenbauerzeugnisse; **~ show** Gartenbauausstellung.

horticulture Gartenbau.

hose Schlauch;
  garden ~ Gartenschlauch; **rubber ~** Gummischlauch.

hosiers Herrenausstattungsgeschäft.

hosiery Wirkwaren, Trikotagen, *(factory)* Strumpf[waren]fabrik;
  ~ manufacture Strumpfindustrie.

hospitable gastfreundlich, aufnahmebereit, aufgeschlossen;
to be ~ to new ideas neuen Ideen aufgeschlossen gegenüberstehen.
hospital Krankenhaus, -anstalt, Klinik, Hospital, *(mil.)* Lazarett;
base ~ Kriegslazarett; **clearing ~** *(Br.)* Feldlazarett; **cottage ~** Kleinkrankenhaus; **fever ~** Krankenhaus für ansteckende Krankheiten, Quarantänelazarett; **field ~** Feldlazarett; **foundling ~** Findlingsheim; **general ~** allgemeines Krankenhaus; **health-service ~** Krankenhaus des staatlichen Gesundheitsdienstes; **isolation ~** Quarantänelazarett; **maternity ~** Entbindungsanstalt; **mental ~** *(Br.)* Irrenanstalt, Heil- und Pflegeanstalt; **military ~** Lazarett; **public ~** gemeinnütziges, öffentliches Krankenhaus; **Red Cross ~** Rotkreuzkrankenhaus; **teaching (training) ~** Lehrkrankenhaus; **voluntary ~** *(Br.)* durch Subventionen unterhaltenes Krankenhaus, subventioniertes Krankenhaus;
~ for mental diseases *(US)* Heil- und Pflegeanstalt; **~ financed by voluntary efforts** durch freiwillige Spenden (privat) getragenes Krankenhaus, durch Subventionen unterhaltenes Krankenhaus, Privatklinik;
to admit s. o. into ~ j. in ein Krankenhaus aufnehmen; **to be under treatment in ~** im Krankenhaus behandelt werden; **to build an extension to a ~** Krankenhaus ausbauen; **to enter a ~** Krankenhaus aufsuchen; **to lie in ~** im Krankenhaus liegen, Krankenhauspatient sein; **to rush s. o. to the ~** j. auf schnellstem Wege zum Krankenhaus bringen; **to send s. o. to ~** j. ins Krankenhaus einweisen; **to take s. o. to ~** j. ins Krankenhaus einliefern; **to walk the ~s** klinische Semester absolvieren;
~ accommodation Krankenhausversorgung; **~ administration** Krankenhausverwaltung; **~ aid** Krankenhaushelfer; **~ apprentice** *(ship, US)* Stationsschwester; **~ attendant** Krankenwärter; **~ battalion** *(mil.)* Sanitätsabteilung; **~ bed** Krankenhausbett; **[in-]benefit** Krankenhauszuschuß; **~ benefit insurance** Krankenhauszusatzversicherung; **~ bill** Krankenhausrechnung; **~ blanket** Krankenhausdecke; **~ board** Krankenhausverwaltung; **~ building** Krankenhausbau; **~ care** Krankenhausbehandlung, -pflege; **~ carriage** Krankenwagen; **~ charge** Krankenhauskosten; **~ consultant** Krankenhausfacharzt; **~ contract** Auftrag zum Bau eines Krankenhauses; **~ costs** Krankenhauskosten; **cost containment** Eindämmung der stetig steigenden Krankenhauskosten; **~ doctor** Krankenhausarzt; **~ entrance** Krankenhauseinfahrt; **~ expenses** Krankenhauskosten; **~ fee** Krankenhaustagegeld; **~ finance** Krankenhausfinanzen; **~ kitchen** Krankenhausküche; **~ management** Krankenhausverwaltung; **~ management committee** Krankenhausverwaltungsausschuß; **~ nurse** Krankenschwester; **~ orderly** *(mil.)* Sanitätssoldat; **~ patient** Krankenhauspatient, -insasse; **~ planning** Planungen für den Krankenhausbau; **~ premises** Krankenhausgebäude; **~ prescription** Krankenhausrezept; **~ provision** Krankenhausversorgung; **~ review** Krankenhausinspektion; **~ room and board** Krankenhausunterbringung; **~ services** Krankenhausleistungen; **~ ship** Lazarettschiff; **~ specialist** Krankenhausfacharzt; **~ stay** Krankenhausaufenthalt; **~ train** Lazarettzug; **~ treatment** Krankenhausbehandlung; **~ unit** Lazaretteinheit; **~ visit** Krankenhausbesuch; **~ ward costs** Krankenhauspflegekosten; **~ worker** Krankenhaushelfer.
hospitaler Krankenhauspatient, -insasse.
hospitalism Krankenhaussystem, -zustände.
hospitality Gastlichkeit, Gastfreundschaft;
to be big on ~ für Gastfreundschaft berühmt sein; **to enjoy Her Majesty's ~** *(fam.)* im Gefängnis sitzen; **to show s. o. ~** jem. Gastfreundschaft gewähren.
hospitalization *(US)* Einlieferung (Einweisung) in ein Krankenhaus, stationäre Krankenhausbehandlung, Krankenhausaufenthalt, -aufnahme;
~ insurance *(US)* Zusatzversicherung für Krankenhausaufenthalt; **~ records** *(US)* Krankenhausunterlagen.
hospitalize *(v.) (US)* in ein Krankenhaus einweisen, j. ins Krankenhaus aufnehmen (einliefern).
host [Quartier]wirt, Gastgeber, Veranstalter, Hausherr, *(innkeeper)* Herbergsvater, Gastwirt, *(quantity)* Masse, [Un]menge;
~ (v.) beherbergen;
a whole ~ of children ganzer Haufen von Kindern; **~ of gnats** Mückenschwarm; **the ~s of heaven** die himmlischen Heerscharen; **~ of ideas** Fülle von Ideen; **~ of questions** Fülle von Fragen; **to act as the ~** als Gastgeber[in] fungieren; **to be a ~ in o. s.** ein ganzes Regiment ersetzen; **to be faced with a ~ of difficulties** unendlichen Schwierigkeiten gegenüberstehen; **to reckon without one's ~** seine Rechnung ohne den Wirt machen;

~ community Gastgebergemeinschaft; **~ country** Aufnahmestaat, Gastland; **~ government** Gastregierung; **~ member** gastgebendes Vereinsmitglied; **~ state** Gastland; **~ town** gastgebende Stadt.
hostage Geisel;
held as ~ als Geisel festgehalten;
to give ~s to fortune sich Gefahren aussetzen; **to keep a ~** als Geisel behalten; **to leave a further ~ for the future** weiteren Konfliktstoff schaffen; **to take ~s** Geiseln nehmen;
~ taking Geiselnahme; **~-taking operation** Geiselnahmeaktion.
hostel Herberge, *(Br.)* Studenten-, Wohnheim;
youth ~ Jugendherberge;
~ for drifters Obdachlosenasyl;
~ accommodation Wohnheimunterbringung; **youth ~ association** Jugendherbergsverband.
hosteler Jugendherbergsbenutzer.
hostess Gastgeberin, Hausfrau *(attendant)* Empfangsdame, Hostesse;
air ~ Stewardeß, Reisebegleiterin;
~ (v.) Gastgeber[in] sein.
hostile feindlich, feindselig;
~ to reform reformfeindlich;
to be ~ to s. o. jem. feindlich gesinnt sein;
~ act feindselige Handlung, Feindhandlung; **~ army** feindliche Armee; **~ assistance** neutralitätswidrige Beistandsleistung; **~ crowd** feindselige Menge; **to make a ~ demonstration against s. o.** j. öffentlich verhöhnen; **~ embargo** völkerrechtswidriges Embargo; **~ feelings** feindselige Einstellung (Stimmung); **~ fire** *(insurance)* Schadensfeuer; **~ possession** widerrechtlicher Besitz; **~ power** Feindmacht; **~ territory** Feindgebiet, -land; **~ witness** parteiischer Zeuge.
hostilities Feindseligkeiten;
at the outbreak of ~ beim Ausbruch von Feindseligkeiten;
active ~ Kampfhandlungen;
to begin ~ Feindseligkeiten eröffnen; **to cease ~** Feindseligkeiten einstellen; **to continue ~** Feindseligkeiten fortsetzen; **to open ~** Feindseligkeiten eröffnen; **to resume ~** Feindseligkeiten wiederaufnehmen; **to start ~** Feindseligkeiten eröffnen; **to suspend ~** Feindseligkeiten einstellen.
hostility Feindseligkeit, Gegnerschaft;
to feel no ~ towards s. o. keine Feindschaft gegen j. hegen; **to show persistent ~ towards s. o.** jem. fortgesetzt feindlich begegnen.
hostler Stall-, Pferdeknecht, *(US)* Lokomotivwärter.
hot heiß, *(el.)* unter Strom stehend, *(note)* neu ausgegeben, *(oil)* illegal gepumpt und verschifft, *(radioactive, sl.)* radioaktiv, *(sensational)* aufregend, höchst interessant, sensationell, *(stolen goods)* heiß, leicht identifizierbar, illegal, geschmuggelt;
boiling ~ kochend heiß;
~ and bothered aufgeregt, verwirrt; **~ under the collar** aufgebracht, verärgert; **~ and strong** tüchtig, gründlich; **~ to suffocation** erstickend heiß;
~ (v.) (engine) beschleunigen;
~ up sich erhitzen;
to be ~ on s. one's heels jem. direkt auf den Fersen sein; **to be ~ for reform** auf Reformen brennen; **to be ~ on the trail** heiße Spur verfolgen; **to blow ~ and cold** sein Mäntelchen nach dem Wind hängen, abwechselnd positiv und negativ reagieren; **to catch it ~** Rüffel einstecken müssen; **to get all ~ and bothered** stinkewütend werden; **to get ~ over an argument** sich bei einer Debatte erhitzen; **to get ~ under the collar** auf die Palme gebracht werden; **to give it ~ to s. o.** jem. gründlich einheizen; **to go ~ and cold all over** einem kalt und heiß den Rücken herunterlaufen; **to keep a dish ~** Mahlzeit warmhalten; **to make it ~ for s. o.** jem. die Hölle heiß machen, jem. einheizen; **to make a place too ~ for s. o.** j. zum Verschwinden (Abzug) zwingen; **to run ~ (engine)** sich heiß laufen;
~ air Heißluft, *(fig.)* blauer Dunst; **to let off ~ air** Wichtigkeiten von sich geben; **~-air balloon** Heißluftballon; **~-air dryer** Wäschetrockner; **~-air heating** Heißluftheizung; **~-air pipe** Warmluftrohr; **~ bill** noch nicht plazierter Schatzwechsel; **~ blast** Fön; **~ blood of youth** Heißblütigkeit der Jugend; **~-blooded** leidenschaftlich; **~ box** *(railroad, US)* heißgelaufenes Kugellager; **to sell like ~ cakes (dogs)** wie warme Würstchen (Semmeln) weggehen; **~ cargo** Erzeugnisse eines bestreikten Betriebs; **~ dog** heißes Würstchen; **~ goods** frisch gestohlene Ware; **~ money** heißes Geld; **~-money outflow** Abfluß heißer Gelder; **red-~ news** *(coll.)* sensationelle Nachrichten; **~ plate** Koch-, Heizplatte; **~ potato** *(fig.)* heißes Eisen; **~ press** Heißmangel; **~ pursuit** *(law of nations)* Verfolgungsrecht, Nacheile; **~ rod** *(US sl.)* frisiertes Auto; **~ seat** heikle Situation, *(airforce,*

sl.) Schleudersitz, *(US)* elektrischer Stuhl; ~ **seller** hervorragender Verkaufsschlager; ~ **spring** Thermalquelle; ~ **stuff** *(sl.)* Könner, tolle Sache, erstklassige Qualität, *(US)* Sensationsnachricht; **to be going to have a ~ time** vor ernsthaften Auseinandersetzungen stehen; ~ **trail** frische Fährte; ~ **type** Bleisatz; ~ **war** heißer Krieg; **to get into ~ water** sich in die Nesseln setzen; **to get into ~ water with s. o.** es mit jem. zu tun bekommen; ~**-water bottle** Wärmflasche; ~**-water connections** Heißwasseranlage; ~**-water heating** Warmwasserheizung; **during the ~ weather** in der Hitzeperiode; ~ **wire** *(pol.)* heißer Draht.

hotbed Mist-, Frühbeet, *(fig.)* Brutstätte;
~ **of corruption** Korruptionssumpf; ~ **of intrigue** Intrigennest; ~ **of vice** Brutstätte des Lasters.

hotchpot Einbeziehung von Vorausempfängen bei der Nachlaßverteilung, Ausgleichsverfahren;
capital ~ Kapitalausgleich;
~ **of ideas** Ideenmischmasch;
to bring into ~ auf das Erbteil anrechnen; **to put into** ~ Ausgleichung vornehmen;
to bring into ~ **advances** als Vorausempfang anrechnen; ~ **calculation (computation)** Ausgleichsberechnung, Berechnung der Ausgleichspflicht; ~ **clauses** Ausgleichsklauseln; ~ **provisions** Ausgleichsbestimmungen; **statutory** ~ **requirements** gesetzliche Bestimmungen über den Ausgleich von Vorausempfängen, Ausgleichspflicht.

hotchpotch Sammelsurium, *(meal)* Eintopfgericht, *(law)* Ausgleichspflicht.

hotel Hotel, Gasthof, -haus;
commercial ~ Hotel für Geschäftsreisende, Durchgangshotel; **downtown** ~ *(US)* im Stadtzentrum gelegenes Hotel; **exclusive** ~ Hotel der Spitzenklasse; **floating** ~ schwimmendes Hotel; **high-class** ~ erstklassiges Hotel; **high-rise** ~ Hochhaushotel; **local** ~**s** Hotels am Platze; **de-luxe** ~ Luxushotel; **luxury** ~ Luxushotel, Hotel der Spitzenklasse; **medium-priced** ~ Hotel der mittleren Preisklasse, Hotel der Mittelklasse; **old-line** ~ altrenommiertes Hotel; **private** ~ *(Br.)* Pension; **residential** ~ Familienpension; **second-class** ~ zweitklassiges Hotel; **station** ~ Bahnhofshotel; **swell** ~ feudales Hotel; **upper-bracket** ~ Hotel der gehobenen Mittelklasse;
to book a ~ *(Br.)* Hotelzimmer bestellen; **to cancel a room at a** ~ Hotelzimmer abbestellen; **to check in with a** ~ sich bei einem Hotel anmelden; **to check out of a** ~ Hotel nach Rechnungsbegleichung verlassen; **to lodge at a** ~ in einem Hotel wohnen; **to put up at a** ~ sich in einem Hotel einlogieren; **to register with a** ~ Anmeldezettel im Hotel ausfüllen; **to run up a bill in a** ~ große Hotelrechnung haben; **to secure a room in a** ~ Hotelzimmer bestellen; **to stay at a** ~ in einem Hotel wohnen; **to telegraph to a** ~ **for a reservation** Hotelzimmer telegrafisch bestellen;
~ **accommodation** Hotelmöglichkeiten, -unterbringung, -quartier; **to book** ~ **accommodation in advance** Hotelreservierung vornehmen; ~ **bar** Hotelbar; ~ **bed** Hotelbett; ~ **bedroom** Hotelzimmer; ~ **bedroom surplus** überschüssige Hotelbetten; ~ **bill** Hotelrechnung; ~ **booking** Hotelreservierung; ~ **broker** Hotelnachweis; ~ **building** Hotelgebäude; ~ **bus** Hotelbus; ~ **business** Hotelgewerbe, -industrie; ~ **and restaurant business** Gaststättengewerbe; ~ **capacity** Hotelkapazität; ~ **car** *(US)* Schlafwagen mit Speisewageneinrichtung; ~ **chain** Hotelkette; ~ **clerk** Empfangschef; ~ **company** Hotelbetrieb; ~ **concierge** Hotelportier; ~ **dining room** Hotelrestaurant; ~ **directory** Hotelanzeiger; ~ **employee** Hotelangestellter; ~ **and catering employees** Angestellte des Hotel- und Gaststättengewerbes; ~ **expenses** Hotelkosten, -spesen; ~ **field** Hotelwesen; ~ **guide** Hotelverzeichnis; ~ **industry** Beherbergungsgewerbe, Hotelgewerbe; ~ **lobby** Hotelhalle; ~ **management** Hoteldirektion, -führung; ~ **manager** Hoteldirektor; ~ **operation** Hotelbetrieb; ~ **porter** Hotelportier; ~ **proprietor** Hotelbesitzer, Gastwirt; ~ **Proprietors Act** *(Br.)* Gesetz zur Beschränkung der Gastwirtshaftung; ~ **register** Fremdenbuch; ~ **regulations** Haus-, Gäste-, Hotelordnung; ~ **reservation** Zimmerreservierung; ~ **room** Hotelzimmer; **to book a** ~ **room** Hotelzimmer bestellen; **to update a** ~ **room** Hotelzimmer modernisieren; **to work from a** ~ **room** vom Hotelzimmer aus seiner Arbeit nachgehen; ~ **safe deposit** Hotelaufbewahrung; ~ **servants** Hotelpersonal; ~ **site** Hotelgelände, -grundstück; ~ **size** Hotelgröße; ~ **staff** Hotelangestellte, -personal; ~ **subsidiary** Hotelfiliale; ~ **suite** Zimmerflucht, Suite; **company** ~ **suite** betriebseigene Hotelsuite; ~ **trade** Hotelgewerbe, -industrie, -wesen; ~ **unit** Hoteleinheit; ~ **voucher** Hotelgutschein; ~ **worker** Hotelangestellter.

hotelhood Hoteleigenschaft.

hotelize *(v.)* in ein Hotel verwandeln.

hotelkeeper Gastwirt, Wirt, Hotelbesitzer, Hotelier.

hotfoot, to follow ~ **on the heels of the retreating enemy** dem fliehenden Feind auf dem Fuße folgen.

hothouse Treib-, Gewächshaus.

hotpot Fleisch- und Gemüseeintopf.

hottest part of the election Siedepunkt des Wahlkampfes.

hound Jagdhund, *(despicable person)* Schurke, Hund;
movie ~ Kinonarr;
~ *(v.)* **a dog at s. o.** Hund auf j. hetzen; ~ **on pursuers** Verfolger antreiben;
to follow the ~**s** an einer Parforcejagd teilnehmen; **to run with the hare and hunt with the** ~**s** es mit beiden Seiten halten.

hounded by one's creditors von seinen Gläubigern bedrängt.

hour Stunde, *(school)* Unterrichtsstunde, *(television)* feststehende Sendung, *(university)* anrechenbare Stunde;
after ~**s** nach der Geschäftszeit, nach Dienstschluß (Feierabend, Ladenschluß), *(stock exchange)* nachbörslich; **before** ~**s** *(stock exchange)* vorbörslich; **at an unearthly** ~ in aller Herrgottsfrühe; **at the eleventh** ~ *(fig.)* kurz vor zwölf, fast zu spät; **at the** ~ **indicated** zur bezeichneten Stunde; **at an** ~**'s notice** ohne jede Vorankündigung, mit einstündiger Kündigung; **before** ~**s** *(stock exchange)* vorbörslich; **by the** ~ stundenweise; **for** ~**s [on end]** stundenlang; **in an evil** ~ zu einer ungünstigen Zeit; **in the** ~ **of death** in der Todesstunde; **out of** ~**s** außerhalb der Dienstzeit; **until all** ~**s** bis spät in die Nacht; ~**s absent** Fehlstunden; **actual** ~**s** *(employment)* tatsächlich geleisteter Stundendurchschnitt, effektive Arbeitszeit; **business** ~**s** Geschäftsstunden, -zeit, Dienststunden; **the children's** ~ *(wireless)* Kinderfunk; **closing** ~**s** Ladenschluß[zeiten]; **crowded** ~**s** Hauptverkehrszeit; **loose (off)** ~ Freistunde; **office** ~**s** Dienst-, Büro-, Geschäftszeit; **official** ~**s** *(stock exchange)* Börsenzeit; **rush** ~**s** Hauptgeschäftszeit, Stoßzeit; **school** ~**s** Schulstunden; **slack** ~**s** schwache Verkehrszeit; **the small** ~**s** frühe Morgenstunden; **shop** ~**s** Verkaufszeiten, Geschäftszeit; **solid** ~ geschlagene Stunde; **visiting** ~**s** *(hospital)* Besuchszeit; ~**s actually worked** tatsächlich geleistete Arbeitsstunden; **working** ~ Arbeitszeit, Dienststunden;
~**s of attendance** Dienst-, Bürozeit, *(doctor)* Sprechstunden; **by** ~ Stunde um Stunde; ~ **of cause** *(Scot. law)* Terminzeit; ~ **of death** Todesstunde; ~**s of employment** Arbeits-, Beschäftigungszeit; **two** ~**s on end** zwei geschlagene Stunden; **maximum** ~**s of employment** Höchstarbeitszeit; **an** ~ **from here** eine Wegestunde von hier; ~**s of opening** Eröffnungszeit; **final** ~ **of trading** Börsenschluß; ~**s for trading on the stock exchange** Börsenzeit; **actual** ~**s of work** effektive Arbeitszeit; **contractual** ~**s of work** vertraglich vereinbarte Arbeitszeit; **scheduled** ~**s of work** festgesetzte Arbeitszeit;
to be dealt with after ~**s** *(stock market)* im Telefonverkehr gehandelt werden; **to do s. th. out of** ~**s** etw. außerhalb der Dienstzeit erledigen; **to give s. o. a bad quarter of an** ~ jem. eine unangenehme Viertelstunde bereiten; **to keep late** ~**s** lange aufbleiben; **to keep regular** ~**s** regelmäßige Dienststunden einhalten; **to move an** ~ **ahead** eine Stunde vorgehen; **to pay s. o. by the** ~ j. stundenweise bezahlen; **to reckon** ~**s of overtime** Überstundenzeit anrechnen; **to reduce** ~**s** Arbeitszeit verkürzen; **to run every** ~ *(bus)* stundenweise verkehren; **to take** ~**s over s. th.** stundenlang für etw. benötigen; **to work long** ~**s** lange arbeiten; **to work staggered** ~**s** Schicht arbeiten;
~**s convention** Arbeitszeitabkommen; **eight-**~**s day** Achtstundentag; ~ **hand** *(clock)* Stundenzeiger; **three** ~**s journey** dreistündige Reise; ~**s limit** Stundenbegrenzung; ~ **plate** *(clock)* Ziffernblatt.

hourglass Sanduhr.

hourly stundenweise, stündlich;
~ **bus service** stündlicher Busverkehr; ~ **compensation** Stundenlohnvergütung; **average** ~ **earnings** Durchschnittsstundenlohn; ~ **efficiency** [menschliche] Stundenleistung; ~ **employee** auf Stundenlohnbasis Beschäftigter; ~ **output** [maschinelle] Stundenleistung; ~ **payroll** Lohnabrechnung; ~ **rate** Stundenlohnsatz, -tarif; **guaranteed** ~ **rate** garantierter Stundenlohntarif; ~ **service of trains** stündlicher Zugverkehr; **to live in an** ~ **threat of discovery** jede Minute entdeckt zu werden befürchten; ~ **wage** Stundenlohn.

house Haus, Heim, Wohnung, *(dynasty)* Familie, Geschlecht, Dynastie, *(firm)* Handelsfirma, -haus, *(household)* Haushaltung, *(parl.)* Abgeordnetenhaus, Parlament, Kammer, *(school)* Internat, *(Br., stock exchange)* Börse, *(theater)* Zuschauerraum, Theatervorstellung, *(townhall)* Ratsversammlung;
at my [private] ~ bei mir zu Hause; **at the rear of the** ~ hinter dem Haus; **like a** ~ **on fire** blitzschnell, mit Windeseile; **on the** ~ auf Kosten des Gastwirts (des Hauses);

The ⚲ *(Br.)* *(coll.)* Londoner Börse;
ample ~ geräumiges Haus; **ancient ~** sehr altes Haus; **apartment ~** Mietshaus; **bachelor ~** Junggesellenbude; **banking ~** Bankhaus, -geschäft, Bank; **beer ~** Bierwirtschaft; **boarding ~** Fremdenpension; **business ~** Handels-, Geschäftshaus; **capacity ~** *(theater)* ausverkauftes Haus; **carriage ~** Remise; **charity ~** Pflegeheim; **chief ~** Stammhaus; **coffee ~** Café; **commercial ~** Handelsfirma, Geschäfts-, Handelshaus; **commission ~** Maklerfirma; **company ~** Werkswohnung; **contiguous ~** angrenzendes Haus; **controlled ~** *(Br.)* der Mieterschutzgesetzgebung unterliegendes Haus; **cooperation apartment ~** Wohnhaus einer Siedlungsgesellschaft, in genossenschaftlichem Besitz stehendes Mietshaus; **country ~** Landhaus; **crowded ~** *(theater)* gut besetztes (besuchtes) Haus; **detached ~** einzelstehendes (freistehendes) Haus; **discount ~** Diskontbank; **disorderly ~** Bordell; **duplex ~** Doppelhaus; **dwelling ~** Wohnhaus; **eating ~** Gasthaus, Speiselokal; **engine ~** Maschinenhaus; **executive-level ~** Haus für gehobene Ansprüche; **first ~** *(cinema)* Frühvorstellung; **flatted ~** Mietshaus; **frame ~** Fachwerkhaus; **free ~** brauereiunabhängige Gastwirtschaft; **full ~** *(theater)* volles Haus; **furnished ~** möbliertes Haus; **good ~** *(theater)* volles Haus; **guest ~** Gästehaus; **issuing ~** Emissionshaus, -bank; **low-rent ~** billiges Mietshaus; **Lower ⚲** erste Kammer, Volkskammer, Unterhaus; **manor ~** Gutshaus, Schloß, Herrensitz; **mansion ~** Herrenhaus, -sitz; **no ~** beschlußunfähiges Parlament; **occupied ~** bewohntes Haus; **one-family ~** Einfamilienhaus; **opera ~** Operngebäude, Oper; **~ opposite** gegenüberliegendes Haus; **originating ~** *(issue of securities)* Konsortialführerin; **owner-occupied ~** Eigenheim; **overcrowded ~** überbelegtes Haus; **packed ~** *(theater)* volles Haus; **packing ~** Warenlager, *(factory, US)* Konservenfabrik; **precut ~** Fertighaus; **prefabricated ~** im Montagebau hergestelltes Fertighaus; **private ~** Privathaus; **public ~** Gastwirtschaft, Kneipe, Lokal; **publishing ~** Verlagshaus, Verlag; **quakeproof ~** erdbebensicheres Haus; **remand ~** *(Br.)* Jugendstrafanstalt; **rent-free ~** mietfreies Haus; **rooming ~** Mietshaus für Einzelmieter; **scattered ~s** verstreut liegende Häuser; **second ~** *(theater)* zweite Vorstellung; **single-family ~** Einfamilienhaus; **small ~** *(theater)* schlecht besetztes Haus; **solvent ~** zahlungsfähige Firma; **split-level ~** Haus mit zweierlei Niveau; **sponging ~** *(Br.)* Schuldgefängnis; **sporting ~** übelbeleumdetes Haus; **straggling ~s** verstreut liegende Häuser; **substantial ~** solides Geschäft; **tenement ~** Mietshaus; **terrace[d] ~** Reihenhaus; **three-stor(e)y ~** dreistöckiges Haus; **tied ~** brauereiabhängige Gastwirtschaft, Vertragsrestaurant; **tippling ~** Trinkstube; **tool ~** Geräteschuppen; **town ~** Stadthaus; **old trading ~** alte Firma; **two-family ~** Doppelhaus; **Upper ⚲** Oberhaus, zweite Kammer; **vacant ~** leerstehendes Haus;
~ of accommodation Herberge, Absteigequartier; **~ advertised for sale** zum Verkauf angebotenes Haus; **⚲ of Assembly** gesetzgebende Körperschaft; **~ on the border** Grenzhaus; **~ of call** Herberge, Absteigequartier; **~ of cards** *(fig.)* Kartenhaus; **⚲ of Commons** *(Br.)* Unterhaus; **~ under construction** im Bau befindliches Haus; **~ of correction** *(US)* Besserungsanstalt; **⚲ of Delegates** *(Virginia)* Unterhaus; **~ of detention** Untersuchungsgefängnis, Haftlokal; **~ of ill fame** Freudenhaus, Bordell; **~ with a garage attached** Haus mit angebauter Garage; **~ of God** Gotteshaus; **~ and home** Haus und Hof; **⚲ of Keys** *(Isle of Man)* Unterhaus; **~ inexpensive to run** billig zu bewirtschaftendes Haus; **~ of issue** Emissionshaus; **⚲ of Lords** *(Br.)* Oberhaus; **~ of mourning** Trauerhaus; **⚲s of Parliament** *(Br.)* Parlamentsgebäude; **~ of refuge** Heim sittlich Gefährdeter; **⚲ of Representatives** *(US)* Unter-, Abgeordnetenhaus, Repräsentantenhaus; **~s offered for sale** *(newspaper)* Häusermarkt; **~ for sale with immediate possession** sofort bezugsfertiges Haus; **~ of good (high) standing** angesehene Firma; **end ~ of a street** letztes Haus einer Straße; **~ of worship** Gotteshaus;
~ *(v.)* *(provide with)* Wohnraum zur Verfügung stellen, beherbergen, unterbringen;
~ s. o. immediately jem. sofort eine Wohnung besorgen; **~ one's old books in an attic** alte Bücher in einer Dachkammer abstellen; **~ one's family** seiner Familie eine Wohnung besorgen;
to address the ~ das Wort ergreifen; **to admit into a ~** in ein Haus einlassen; **to be confined to the ~** Haus hüten müssen; **to bid for a ~** auf ein Haus bieten; **to break into a ~** in ein Haus einbrechen; **to bring the ~ down** stürmischen Beifall auslösen (erzielen); **to build a ~** Haus bauen; **to burn like a ~ on fire** lichterloh brennen; **to buy a ~ free from all debt** Haus lastenfrei erwerben; **to buy a ~ for its materials** Haus auf Abbruch kaufen; **to dismantle a ~** Haus abreißen; **to draw a full ~**

(lecture) großen Zulauf haben; **to eat s. o. out of ~ and home** jem. die Haare vom Kopf fressen; **to empty a ~** Haus räumen; **to enter the ⚲** *(Br.)* Parlamentsmitglied werden; **to establish o. s. in a ~** sich in einem Haus einrichten; **to have a ~ of one's own** eigenes Haus haben, Hauseigentümer sein; **to have neither ~ nor home** nirgendwo zu Hause sein; **to have a drink on the ~** an einer Lokalrunde teilnehmen; **to insure one's ~ against fire** sein Haus feuerversichern; **to keep ~** seinen eigenen Haushalt haben, *(debtor, Br.)* sich vor seinen Gläubigern verstecken; **to keep the ~** nicht ausgehen; **to keep ~ for s. o.** jem. die Wirtschaft führen; **to keep to the ~** nicht ausgehen; **to keep a good ~** behagliches Leben führen; **to keep open ~** gastfreies Haus führen; **to keep ~ together** zusammenleben; **to live in one's very ~** ganz für sich (allein) leben; **to look over a ~** Haus besichtigen; **to make a ⚲** *(parl., Br.)* für eine Abstimmung die erforderliche Mehrheit haben, zur Beschlußfähigkeit erforderliche Anzahl von Parlamentsmitgliedern zusammenbringen; **to make a ~ over in several apartments** Haus in Eigentumswohnungen umbauen; **to make o. s. heard in every part of the ~** im ganzen Theater gut verstanden werden; **to manage s. one's ~** jem. den Haushalt führen; **to move into a ~** in ein Haus einziehen; **to move out of a ~** aus einem Haus ausziehen; **to occupy a ~** Haus bewohnen; **to offer s. o. a ~ for $ 45.000** jem. ein Haus für 45.000 Dollar anbieten; **to offer one's ~ as a guarantee** sein Haus als Sicherheit anbieten; **to order s. o. out of the ~** j. aus seinem Haus weisen; **to play at keeping ~** wie Mann und Frau leben; **to play to an empty ~** *(theater)* vor leeren Bänken spielen; **to put before the ⚲ for consideration** dem Parlament zur Beratung vorlegen; **to put (set) one's ~ in order** seine Angelegenheiten in Ordnung bringen; **to put one's own ~ in order first** zuerst vor der eigenen Tür kehren; **to ravage a ~** Haus plündern; **to rebuild a ~** Haus wiederaufbauen; **to remain in a ~ during lifetime** lebenslängliches Wohnrecht besitzen; **to render a ~ free from the provisions of the Rent Restriction Act** *(Br.)* Mieterschutzbestimmungen für ein Haus aufheben; **to rent a ~ with immediate possession** sofort bezugsfähiges Haus mieten; **to search a ~** Haussuchung vornehmen; **to sell a ~ over s. one's head** Haus gegen jds. Willen verkaufen; **to set up ~** eigenen Hausstand errichten (gründen); **to shut up ~** Haus zuschließen; **to take a ~ for a year** Haus für ein Jahr mieten; **to turn a ~ into flats** Haus in Wohnungen umbauen; **to turn the whole ~ upside down** das ganze Haus auf den Kopf stellen; **to vacate a ~** Haus räumen, aus einem Haus ausziehen; **to value a ~ at $ 40.000** Hauswert mit 40.000 Dollar festsetzen;
~ ad *(publisher, US)* Eigenanzeige; **~ advertising** *(agency)* Eigenwerbung; **~-to-~ advertising** an der Haustür verteiltes Werbematerial, Haushaltswerbung; **~ agency** Häusermakler, Wohnungsvermittlung, *(advertising)* [haus]eigene (vorgeschobene) Werbeagentur, Hausagentur; **~ agent** *(Br.)* Häuser-, Grundstücks-, Wohnungs-, Immobilienmakler; **~ approval** Zustimmung der Plenums; **under ~ arrest** unter Hausarrest; **~ barge** *(Br.)* Hausboot; **~ bill** trassierter eigener Wechsel, Filialwechsel; **⚲ Bill** *(parl.)* Parlamentsgesetz; **~ brand** Haus-, Eigenmarke; **~ burning** Brandstiftung; **~ buyer** Hauskäufer; **~ call** *(doctor)* Hausbesuch; **~-to-~ canvassing** Akquirieren; **~ car** *(railway)* gedeckter Güterwagen; **~ career** parlamentarische Laufbahn; **~ chambermaid** *(Br.)* Hausmädchen; **~ charge** *(restaurant)* Couvert, Gedeck; **~ check** *(US)* Haussuchung; **~ cleaning** Hausreinigung, *(business, US sl.)* mit Entlassungen verbundene Reorganisation; **political ~ cleaning** *(US sl.)* politisch bedingte Entlassungen; **spring ~ cleaning** Frühjahrsputz; **~ coal** Hausbrand; **~-to-~ collection** Haussammlung; **⚲ committee** *(parl.)* Parlamentsausschuß; **~ committee** *(clubs)* Präsidium; **~-connection box** *(el.)* Hausanschlußkasten; **~ construction** Hauserrichtung, -bau; **~ conversion** Hausumbau; **~ deal** Hauskauf; **~ delivery** Lieferung frei Haus; **~ detective** Hausdetektiv; **~-to-~ distribution** Postwurfsendung; **~ dog** Haushund; **~ dress** Hausanzug; **~ duty** Gebäude-, Haussteuer; **inhabited ~ duty** Hauszinssteuer; **~ farmer** *(Br.)* Häusermakler; **~ flag** Reedereiflagge; **⚲ floor** *(US)* Plenum; **~ furnisher** Möbelgeschäft; **~ furnishing** Möblierung eines Hauses; **~ guest** Logiergast, *(inn)* Gast des Hauses; **~-hunt** *(v.)* auf Wohnungssuche gehen; **~ hunter** Wohnungssuchender; **~ hunting** Wohnungssuche; **~ improvements** Schönheitsreparaturen; **~ item** *(Br.)* eigener Scheck; **~ jobber** *(Br.)* Häusermakler; **~ journal** Werkszeitung, Hauszeitschrift; **⚲ Judiciary Committee** *(US)* Rechtsausschuß des Repräsentantenhauses; **~ knacker** *(Br.)* Aufkäufer von Häusern zwecks Untervermietung; **~-letting** Hausvermietung; **~ modernization** Wohnhausmodernisierung; **~ mover** Möbelspediteur; **~ moving** Umzug; **~ number** Hausnummer; **~ organ** *(US)* Betriebszeitung, Betriebs-,

Werkszeitschrift; **external ~ organ** Aktionärszeitschrift; **~ painter** Maler, Dekorateur; **~ party** geselliges Beisammensein über mehrere Tage; **~ phone** Haustelefon; **~ physician** diensthabender Arzt, *(hotel)* Hausarzt; **~ plate** Hausplakette; **~ porter** Hausmeister; **⌀ price** *(Br.)* Börsenpreis; **~ property** Hausgrundstück, Haus-, Grundbesitz; **to invest one's money in ~ property** sein Geld in Wohngrundstücken anlegen; **~ purchase** Hausankauf, -erwerb; **~ property purchase** Hauserwerb; **~-purchase insurance** *(life insurance)* Hypothekentilgungsversicherung; **~ purchaser** Hauskäufer; **first-time ~ purchaser** Ersterwerber eines Hauses; **~ raising** *(US)* Hausbau mit Nachbarschaftshilfe; **~ refuse** Küchenabfall; **~ rent** Hausmiete; **⌀ Rules Committee** *(US)* Geschäftsordnungsausschuß; **~ search** Hausdurchsuchung; **~-to-~ selling** Direktverkauf durch Vertreter (an der Haustür); **~ staff** Anstaltsärzte; **~ steward** Hausverwalter; **~ surgeon** Anstaltschirurg; **~ tax** Wohngebäudesteuer; **~ track** Betriebsgleis, -anschluß; **~ trailer** Wohnwagen; **~ wag(g)on** Wohnwagen; **⌀ Ways and Means Committee** *(US)* Haushaltsausschuß.

house-to-house | advertising Haushaltswerbung; **~ canvassing** Akquirieren; **~ collection** Haussammlung; **~ selling** Direktverkauf an der Haustür (an Verbraucher).

houseboat Haus-, Wohnboot;
~ *(v.)* auf einem Hauboot wohnen.

housebote Holzentnahmerecht für Hausreparaturen.

housebound ans Haus gefesselt.

houseboy Hausdiener.

housebreak *(v.)* Einbruchsdiebstahl begehen.

housebreaker Einbrecher, *(pulling down houses)* Abbruchunternehmen.

housebreaking Einbruch, Einbruchsdiebstahl, *(pulling down)* Abbruch, Abreißen;
~ contractor Abbruchunternehmen; **~ tools** Einbruchswerkzeuge.

housebroken *(dog)* stubenrein.

housebuilding Wohnungs-, Hausbau, Gebäudeherstellung;
subsidized ~ Erstellung von Sozialwohnungen.

housefather Haushaltungsvorstand.

housefurnishing Haushaltsutensilien, Hausrat.

household Haushalt, -stand, Familiengemeinschaft, Wirtschaft;
the ⌀ *(Br.)* königliche Hofhaltung;
common ~ gemeinsamer Haushalt; **composite ~** gemischter Haushalt; **joint ~** häusliche Gemeinschaft, gemeinsame Haushaltsführung; **private ~s** private Haushalte; **the Royal ~** *(Br.)* Hofhaltung;
to be one of the ~ zur Familie gehören; **to have a large ~** über zahlreiche Bedienstete verfügen; **to scrimp one's ~** mit dem Haushaltsgeld geizen;
~ *(a.)* alltäglich, vertraut;
~ appliances Haushaltsgeräte; **~ arts** Haushaltskunst, -lehrgang; **~ assets** Haushaltsgegenstände; **~ bill** Haushaltsrechnung; **~ bread** selbstgebackenes Brot; **~ budget survey participant** Berichtsfamilie einer Haushaltsausgabenbefragung; **~ coat** Familienwappen; **~ consumer** Haushalt als Verbrauchereinheit; **~ consumption** Haushaltsverbrauch; **~ delivery** Direktlieferung an die Haushalten; **~ duties** Haushaltsarbeiten; **~ economics** Hauswirtschaftslehre; **~ economy** Hauswirtschaft; **~ edition** Familienausgabe; **~ effects** Haushaltsgegenstände, Hausrat; **~ employee** Hausangestelle[r]; **~ equipment** Haushaltsgeräte; **~ essentials** lebenswichtige Haushaltsgüter; **~ expenses** Haushaltungskosten, Wirtschaftsgeld; **~ furnishings** Wohnungseinrichtung; **~ furniture** Hausrat, Wohnmöbel; **electric-powered ~ gadget** elektrisches Haushaltsgerät; **~ goods** Hausrat, Haushaltsgegenstände, Mobiliar; **~ head** Haushaltungsvorstand; **~ help** Haushaltshilfe; **~ income** Haushaltsgeld; **~ insurance** Hausratsversicherung; **~-moving industry** Umzugsgewerbe; **~ name** geflügeltes Wort; **~ operating costs** Kosten der Haushaltsführung, Haushaltungskosten; **~-purchasing behavio(u)r** Einkaufsverhalten bei Anschaffungen für den Haushalt; **~ refuse** Küchenabfall; **~ requirements** Haushaltsbedarf; **~ servant** Hausangestellte[r]; **~ stuff** Hausrat, Haushaltsgegenstände; **~ troops** Gardetruppen, Leibgarde; **~ utensils** Haushaltungsgegenstände; **~ wares** Haushaltswaren, Haushaltungsgegenstände; **~ wear** Hauskleidung; **~ word** Alltagswort.

householder *(head of household)* Haushaltungsvorstand, *(inhabitant)* Hausbewohner, *(owner)* Hauseigentümer, -besitzer;
~ and lodgers Mieter und Vermieter;
~'s insurance Haushaltsversicherung; **~ policy** kombinierte Hausratsversicherung.

householding Hausverwaltung.

housekeep *(v.)* Haushalt führen;
~ for o. s. für sich selbst sorgen müssen.

housekeeper Haushälterin, Wirtschafterin, *(occupier)* ständiger Hausbewohner;
resident ~ im Haushalt lebende Haushaltshilfe;
to be a good ~ gut wirtschaften können;
~ allowance (relief, *Br.)* Steuerfreibetrag für Hausangestellte.

housekeeping Haushalt[sführung], *(US)* Hausverwaltung;
light ~ leichte Hausarbeit;
to be good at ~ sich gut auf die Haushaltsführung verstehen; **to facilitate ~** Bewirtschaftung erleichtern; **to give up ~** seinen Haushalt auflösen; **to set up ~** seinen Hausstand gründen;
~ allowance Haushaltungsgeld; **~ book** Wirtschafts-, Haushaltungsbuch; **~ chores** Hausarbeiten; **~ crew** Instandsetzungsmannschaft; **~ money** Wirtschafts-, Haushaltsgeld; **to make the ~ money stretch** mit dem Haushaltsgeld auskommen.

houseless obdachlos;
~ desert unbewohnte Wüste.

housemaid Zimmer-, Stubenmädchen.

houseman Hausdiener.

housemaster Haushaltungsvorstand, *(Br.)* Schulgruppen-, Heimleiter, *(boarding school, Br.)* Hausaufseher.

housemate Haus-, Stubengenosse.

housemating Hausgemeinschaft.

housemistress *(boarding school, Br.)* Hausaufseherin.

housemother Hausmutter, Heimleiterin.

houseowner Hausbesitzer, -eigentümer.

houseownership Hausbesitz.

houseroom Wohnraum;
to give s. o. ~ j. ins Haus nehmen; **not to give it ~** es nicht einmal geschenkt nehmen.

housetop Dach;
to proclaim from the ~s öffentlich verkünden.

housetrained *(dog)* stubenrein.

housewares Haushaltungsgegenstände.

housewarming [party] Einstands-, Einzugsfest, Einweihungsfeier;
to give a ~ Haus einweihen.

housewear Haushaltskleidung.

housewife Hausfrau;
~ *(v.)* geschickt wirtschaften.

housewifely haushälterisch.

housework Hausarbeit;
to do ~ im Haushalt arbeiten.

housing *(carrying charges)* Transportkosten zum Packhof, *(casing)* Gehäuse, *(charges)* Lagergeld, *(house building)* Wohnungsbau, *(lodging)* Wohnung, Herberge, Obdach, *(providing shelter)* Unterbringung, Beherbergung, Wohnungsbeschaffung, -wesen, *(storage)* Lagerung;
additional ~ zusätzlicher Wohnraum; **controlled ~** bewirtschafteter Wohnungsmarkt; **differential gear ~** Differentialgehäuse; **factory-built ~** industriell hergestellte Wohnung, vorfabrizierte Wohnungseinheit; **free ~** kostenlose Wohnungsgestellung; **low-cost ~** billige Wohnung; **federally financed low-cost ~** *(US)* sozialer Wohnungsbau; **low- (moderate-) income ~** sozialer Wohnungsbau; **mass-produced ~** Massenproduktion von Wohnungseinheiten; **modular ~** vorfabrizierte Wohnungseinheiten, Modellwohnung; **multiple unit ~** Mehrzweckwohnung; **permanent ~** Dauerwohnung; **poor ~** Notstandsquartier; **prefab ~** *(coll.)* vorfabrizierte Wohnung; **public ~** öffentlicher (gemeinnütziger) Wohnungsbau; **publicly-provided ~** staatlich bereitgestellte Wohnungen; **rural ~** ländliches Wohnungswesen; **subsidized ~** Unterstützung bei der Wohnungsbeschaffung, Wohnungs[bau]hilfe; **substandard ~** unzulängliche Unterkunft; **temporary ~** Behelfsunterkünfte, -unterbringung; **upgraded ~** verbesserte Unterbringung; **upper-level ~** Wohnung für gehobene Ansprüche;
~ of refugees Unterbringung von Flüchtlingen; **~ of the poor** Unterbringung der Armen;
to procure a ~ Wohnung beschaffen; **to provide ~** Wohnung beschaffen;
National ⌀ Act *(Br.)* Wohnungsbaugesetz; **⌀ Administration** *(US)* Wohnungsbauministerium; **Central ⌀ Advisory Committee** *(Br.)* Wohnungsberatungsstelle; **National ⌀ Agency** *(US)* Wohnungsamt, -behörde; **~ aid** Wohnungsfinanzierung, -beihilfe; **~ aid bill** Wohnungsbauförderungsgesetz; **~ allowance** Wohnungsentschädigung, -zuschuß, -geld; **~ analyst** Wohnungsbauexperte; **~ area** Wohngebiet; **to make one's own ~ arrangements** sich selbst eine Wohnung besorgen; **~ assistance** Wohnungsbeihilfe, -entschädigung; **~-assistance sheme** Wohnungsbeihilfewesen; **~ association** *(Br.)* Woh-

nungsbaugesellschaft, -genossenschaft, gemeinnütziger Wohnungsbauverband; **~ and finance association** Wohnungsbaufinanzierungsgesellschaft; **~ authority** Wohnungsbehörde, -amt; **~ bank** Bank für Wohnungsfinanzierungen; **~ bill** Wohnungsbaugesetz; **~ boom** Wohnungsbaukonjunktur; **~ campaign** Wohnungsbaufeldzug; **~ code** baupolizeiliche Verordnung; **~ commission** Wohnungsausschuß; **~ complex** Wohnhauskomplex; **~ conditions** Wohn[ungs]verhältnisse; **~ construction** Wohnungsbau; **~ control** Wohnungzwangswirtschaft, Bewirtschaftung des Wohnungsmarktes, Wohnraumbewirtschaftung; **~ cooperative** Wohnungsbaugenossenschaft; **~ costs** Wohnungskosten; **~ counselling** Wohnungsberatung; **~ credit** Wohnungsbeschaffungskredit; **~ crisis** Krise auf dem Wohnungsmarkt, Wohnungsbaukrise; **~ deal** Hausverkauf; **~ demand** Wohnungsbedarf; **~ density** Wohnungsdichte; **~ department** (Br.) Wohnungsbaubehörde; **~ department allocation** Wohnungsbaukontingent; **~ development** Wohnsiedlung; **~-development plan** (Br.) Wohnungsbauprojekt; **~ and urban development** Wohnwesen und Stadtentwicklung; **~ difficulties** Wohnungsschwierigkeiten; **~ discrimination** Wohnungsdiskriminierung; **~ estate** aufgeschlossenes Gelände, Wohnviertel, -block, -siedlung, Siedlung[sgelände], Stadtrandsiedlung; **new ~ estate** neue Wohnsiedlung, neues Wohnviertel; **suburban ~ estate** Stadtrandsiedlung; **~ executive** Leiter des Wohnungswesens; **~ expenditure** Aufwendungen für den Wohnungsbau; **~ expert** Wohnungsbauexperte; **~ facilities** Wohnmöglichkeiten; **~ famine** Wohnungsnot; **~ finance** Wohnungsfinanzierung; ⏣ **Finance Act** (Br.) Gesetz zur Finanzierung des sozialen Wohnungsbaus; **~ and home financing** Wohnungsfinanzierung; ⏣ **and Home Financing Agency** Wohnungsfinanzierungsgesellschaft; **~ gap** fehlender Wohnungsraum; **~ industry** Wohnungswirtschaft; **~ innovations** neue Wohnungsbaumethoden; **~ inquiry** Wohnungsbestandsaufnahme; **~ land** Wohngrundstücke; **~ law** Wohnungsbaugesetz; **local ~ law** Ortsstatut; **~ legislation** Gesetzgebung für den Wohnungsbau; **~ loan** Wohnungs-, -baudarlehen; **~ loan scheme** Baukreditvorhaben; **~ management** Wohnungsverwaltung; **~ manager** Wohnungsverwalter; **~ market** Wohnungsmarkt; **~ mortgage** Eigenheimhypothek; **~ needs** Wohnungsbedarf; **~ office** Wohnungsamt; **~ ordinance** Wohnungsbaustatut; **~ permit** Baugenehmigung; **~ policy** Wohnungsbaupolitik; **~ position** Wohnungssituation, Lage am Wohnungsmarkt; **~ price** Mietpreis, -kosten, Kosten einer Wohnung; **~ problem** Wohnungsproblem, -not; **~ program(me)** Wohnungsbauprogramm; **assisted ~ program** (US) [etwa] Wohngeldprogramm; **low-cost ~ program(me)** Programm für die Beschaffung billiger Mietwohnungen; **federally financed low-cost ~ project** (US) vom Bund finanziertes soziales Wohnungsbauprojekt; **public ~ project** staatliches Wohnungsbauprojekt; **~ prototype** Muster-, Modellwohnung; **~ purchase by instalment** Hauserwerb im Abzahlungswege; **~ quality** Wohnungsqualität; **~ question** Wohnungsfrage; **~ rehabilitation** Wohnungsinstandsetzung; **high ~ rent** hohe Wohnungsmiete; ⏣ **Rents and Subsidies Act** (Br.) Mieterschutz- und Wohngeldgesetz; **~ requirements** Wohn[ungs]bedarf; **~ scene** Wohnungsmarktlage; **~ scheme** Wohnungsbauvorhaben; **~ segregation** im Wohnungswesen ausgeübte Rassentrennung; **~ shortage** Unterdeckung von Wohnungen, Wohnungsdefizit, -not, -knappheit, -mangel; **~ society** (Br.) gemeinnützige Wohnungsbaugesellschaft; **~ solution** Lösung der Wohnungsfrage; **~ space** Wohnraum; **~ standard** Wohnstandard; **~ starts** neu angefangene Wohnungseinheiten, Neubauten; **~ statistics** Wohnungsstatistik; **~ stock** Wohnungsangebot, Häuserhalde; **~ stocks** Aktien von Wohnungsbaugesellschaften; ⏣ **Subsidies Act** (Br.) Wohnungsbauförderungsgesetz; **~ subsidy** Wohnungsgeld; **single-tested ~ subsidy** von einer individuellen Bedürftigkeit abhängig gemachtes Wohngeld; **~ supply** Wohnungsangebot; **~ survey** Haushaltserhebung; **council-rated ~ tenure** mit Mitteln des sozialen Wohnungsbaus finanzierter Wohnungsanteil; **~ unit** Wohnungseinheit; **privately financed ~ unit** frei finanzierte Wohnung; **~ upturn** Wohnungsbaukonjunktur.

hovel Schuppen, (cottage) Elendsquartier, Loch.

hoveler Bergungsboot, Küstenfahrzeug.

hovercraft Schwebeschiff, Luftkissenfahrzeug, -boot.

howdy (v.) s. o. j. begrüßen.

howf (Scot.) Lieblingsaufenthalt.

howl Geheul, Gebrüll, (wireless) Pfeifen;
   ~ of protest Protestgeschrei;
   ~ (v.) with the pack (fam.) mit den Wölfen heulen; **~ down a speaker** Redner niederschreien.

howler (el.) Summer, (radio) Pfeifen, Heulen, (sl.) grober Schnitzer;
   to come a ~ in eine Patsche geraten, Pech haben.

howling | **of the storm** Heulen des Sturms;
   ~ injustice schreiende Ungerechtigkeit; **~ mistake** grober Schnitzer; **~ success** kolossaler Erfolg; **~ wilderness** trostlose Wüste.

hoy Leichter.

Hoyle, according to genau nach Vorschrift.

hoyman Leichterkapitän.

hub Knotenpunkt, (fig.) Angelpunkt, (wheel) Radnabe;
   from ~ to tire (US) vollständig, total; **up to the ~** (US) bis zum Hals, ganz und gar;
   ~ of commerce Handelszentrum; **~ of industry** industrielles Zentrum; **~ of the universe** Mittelpunkt (Nabel) der Welt; **~ of the financial world** Finanzzentrum;
   to be honest up to the ~ grundehrliche Haut sein.

hubble-bubble Stimmengewirr.

hubbub Rummel.

huckster (advertising, US) Werbeagent, Reklamefachmann, (street trader) Hausierer, Straßenverkäufer;
   ~ (v.) verhökern, Schacher treiben, (peddle) hausieren.

huckstering, political politischer Kuhhandel.

huckstery Hökerladen.

huddle Wirrwarr, Unordnung;
   ~ (v.) over hinpfuschen; **~ through a piece of work** bei einer Arbeit pfuschen; **~ up** durcheinanderwerfen; **~ up an agreement** Vertrag zusammenpfuschen;
   to go into a ~ with s. o. Geheimbesprechung mit jem. führen.

hue Farbe, Farbton, Kolorit;
   ~ and cry Verbrecherjagd, (London police) Fahndungsausschreibung; **~s of the rainbow** Regenbogenfarben;
   to raise a ~ Steckbrief gegen j. erlassen; **to raise a ~ and cry after s. o.** Fahndung für j. ausschreiben, Verfolgungsjagd durchführen; **to raise a ~ and cry against new tax proposals** gegen neue Steuervorschläge Sturm laufen; **to take on the ~ of death** Totenblässe annehmen.

huff Aufbrausen;
   ~ (v.) aufbringen, beleidigen, (hector) herumkommandieren, ärgern;
   ~ s. o. into s. th. jem. etw. aufzwingen;
   to go off in a ~ wütend davonlaufen; **to take ~ at s. th.** etw. übelnehmen.

huff-duff Funkpeilgerät.

huffish übelnehmerisch.

hug Umarmung;
   ~ (v.) o. s. sich beglückwünschen; **~ to the coast** sich nahe an der Küste halten; **~ an opinion** zäh an einer Ansicht festhalten; **~ a prejudice** Vorurteil haben.

huge | **collection of samples** gewaltiges Musterlager; **~ price** enormer Preis.

huggermugger Unordnung, Durcheinander;
   to live in a ~ fashion völlig ungeordnetes Leben führen.

huggery (Br.) Postenjägerei.

hulks Schiffsgefängnis.

hull (airplane, ship) Rumpf, (insurance) Schiffskasko;
   ~ and machinery (insurance) Kasko und Maschinen;
   ~ insurance [Schiffs]kaskoversicherung; **~ interest** Kaskointeresse; **~ policy** Kaskopolice; **~ insurance underwriter** Kaskoversicherer.

hullabaloo Spektakel, Tumult.

hullo girl (fam.) Telefonfräulein.

hum Summen, Brummen;
   busy ~ of a large city Großstadtgeräusche;
   ~s and haws verlegenes Geräusper; **~ of voices** Stimmengemurmel;
   ~ (v.) with activity in vollem Betrieb sein;
   to make things ~ Sache in Schwung (Leben in die Bude) bringen.

human menschlich;
   ~ appeal (advertising) Ansprechen menschlicher Gefühle; **~ being** menschliches Wesen, Mensch; **~ capital** menschliches Kapital; **~ ecology** Sozialökologie; **~ engineering** Arbeitsplatzgestaltung, Ergonomie; **~ factor** menschliche Seite; **~ factor in business** Mensch im Betrieb; **~ foibles** menschliche Schwächen; **to be unfit for ~ habitation** unbewohnbar sein; **to bear no regard for ~ life** rücksichtslos über Menschenleben hinweggehen; **~ nature** menschliche Natur; **~ necessity** menschlicher Bedarf; **~ race** Menschengeschlecht; **~ relations** zwischenmenschliche Beziehungen, Kontaktpflege; **~ relations in industry** Mitarbeiterbeziehungen im Betrieb; **~ resource accounting** Humanver-

mögensrechnung; ~ **rights** Menschenrechte; ~ **rights clauses** Menschenrechtsbestimmungen; ~ **rights commission** Menschenrechtskommission; ~ **rights drive** Engagement für die Menschenrechte; ~ **rights movement** Menschenrechtsbewegung; ~ **rights violation** Verletzung der Menschenrechte; ~ **side** das Menschliche - Allzumenschliche; ~ **touch** menschliche Note, Förderung zwischenmenschlicher Beziehungen; ~ **trade** Menschenhandel.

humane menschenfreundlich, human, *(tending to refinement)* humanistisch;
~ **learning** humanistische Bildung; **Royal ⚬ Society** Gesellschaft zur Errettung Ertrinkender.

humanitarian|concerns humanitäre Belange; ~ **endeavo(u)rs** humanitäre Bestrebungen.

humanities Geisteswissenschaften;
~ **department** geisteswissenschaftliche Abteilung.

humanity Menschlichkeit, Humanität;
to treat s. o. with ~ j. menschlich behandeln.

humanization Humanisierung.

humanize *(v.)* humanisieren, zivilisieren.

humankind Menschengeschlecht.

humanly possible menschenmöglich.

humble bescheiden, demütig, anspruchslos;
~ *(v.)* **o. s. in the dust** sich selbst erniedrigen; ~ **s. one's pride** jds. Stolz demütigen;
to be very ~ **to one's superiors** behördenfromm sein;
of ~ **birth** von niedriger Abstammung; ~ **classes** einfache Bevölkerungsschichten; ~ **occupation** unansehnlicher Beruf; **in my** ~ **opinion** nach meiner unmaßgeblichen Meinung; **to eat** ~ **pie** zu Kreuze kriechen, sich demütigen; **under my** ~ **roof** unter meinem bescheidenen Dach; **to do things on a** ~ **scale** auf einem bescheidenen Niveau leben; **my** ~ **self** meine Wenigkeit; **your** ~ **servant** Ihr ergebenster Diener.

humbled, to be sich ganz klein fühlen.

humbug Schwindel, Mache, Humbug, Mumpitz;
~ *(v.)* **a lot of money from s. o.** von jem. viel Geld erschwindeln.

humbugger Schwindler.

humdinger tolle Sache, *(US sl., engine)* reibungslos laufender Motor.

humdrum eintönig, langweilig, fade;
~ **existence** langweiliges Dasein; **to live a** ~ **life** eintöniges Leben führen; **to be engaged in** ~ **tasks** mit langweiligen Arbeiten beschäftigt sein; ~ **work** monotone Arbeit.

humid air feuchte Luft.

humidity Luftfeuchtigkeit, Feuchtigkeitsgehalt.

humiliating peace terms erniedrigende Friedensbedingungen.

humiliation Demütigung, Erniedrigung.

hummer Summer, *(humdinger, sl.)* tolle Sache, *(person, sl.)* Betriebsnudel.

humming schwungvoll, stark.

humo(u)r Komik, Humor, *(mood)* Stimmung, Laune;
not in the ~ **for work** arbeitsunlustig;
~ **of the situation** Situationskomik;
~ *(v.)* **s. o.** j. aufheitern; ~ **s. one's fancy** jds. Phantasie anregen;
to be in a giving ~ in Schenkerlaune sein; **to be in a good** ~ guter Laune sein.

humorist Spaßvogel.

humorous paper Witzblatt.

hump Buckel, Höcker, *(critical period)* kritische Zeit, Krise;
~ **in the road** Straßenunebenheit;
~ *(v.)* trampen, auf Arbeitsuche sien;
~ **it** sich dranhalten;
to be over the ~ über den Berg sein; **to get the** ~ *(fam.)* Stinkwut bekommen; **to give s. o. the** ~ jem. auf die Nerven gehen; **to live on one's** ~ *(fam.)* von seinem Fett zehren.

humpty dumpty kleiner dicker Kerl, Stöpsel.

hunch *(coll.)* Vorahnung;
to have a ~ Verdacht hegen.

hundred *(Br.)* hundert Pfund;
not a ~ **miles from here** *(hum.)* ganz in der Nähe; **to go a** ~ **miles an hour** 140 Stundenkilometer fahren; **a** ~ **per cent American** hundertprozentiger Amerikaner.

hundred|-percenter Hurrapatriot, Ultranationaler; ~**-percentism** Hurrapatriotismus.

hundredweight Zentner.

hung up *(US, speculator)* festgefahren, festgelegt.

hunger Hunger;
~ **for excitement** Sensationsgier; ~ **for knowledge** Wissensdurst;
~ *(v.)* **after praise** *(fam.)* nach Anerkennung dürsten;
to die of ~ an Hunger sterben;

~ **blockade** Hungerblockade; ~ **cure** Abmagerungsdiät; ~ **march** Hungermarsch; ~ **marcher** Hungermarschierer; ~~ **stricken** ausgehungert; ~ **strike** Hungerstreik; ~~**strike** *(v.)* in einen Hungerstreik eintreten; **to go on a** ~ **strike** in einen Hungerstreik eintreten; ~ **striker** Hungerstreik Durchführender.

hungry, as ~ **as a hunter** hungrig wie ein Wolf;
to be ~ **for knowledge** wissensdurstig sein.

hunker *(US sl.)* Reaktionär, Stockkonservativer.

hunkerous *(US sl.)* reaktionär, rückschrittlich, stockkonservativ.

hunky *(US sl.)* eingewanderter Hilfsarbeiter;
~ *(a.)* *(US sl.)* prima, in Butter.

hunt Jagdgebiet, Revier, *(fig.)* Verfolgung, Jagd;
~ **for a criminal** Verbrecherjagd;
~ *(v.)* jagen, *(search)* verfolgen, fahnden;
~ **for a lost book** nach einem verlorengegangenen Buch suchen;
~ **down a criminal** Verbrecher aufspüren; ~ **after fortune** dem Glück nachjagen; ~ **after glory** ruhmsüchtig sein; ~ **out an old diary** altes Tagebuch auffinden; ~ **out of society** gesellschaftlich in den Bann tun; ~ **a trail** Spur verfolgen; ~ **up old friends** alte Freunde aufsuchen; ~ **up old records** alte Unterlagen wiederfinden; ~ **from the village** aus dem Dorf jagen; ~ **high and low for a missing will** überall (an allen Ecken und Enden) nach einem verschwundenen Testament forschen;
to find s. th. after a long ~ etw. nach langem Suchen finden.

hunter Jäger, *(dog)* Jagdhund;
curio ~ Antiquitätensammler; **dowry** ~ Mitgiftjäger; **fortune** ~ Mitgift-, Glücksjäger; **house** ~ Wohnungssuchender; **legacy** ~ Erbschleicher; **lion** ~ Prominentenjäger; **place** ~ Stellenjäger.

hunting Jagd, Jagen, *(search)* Suche, *(radar)* Abtastvorrichtung; **bargain-**~ Jagd nach Gelegenheitskäufen, *(stock market)* Effektenspekulation; **house** ~ Wohnungssuche;
to go a-~ auf die Jagd gehen;
~ **box** Jagdhütte; ~ **dog** Jagdhund; ~ **ground** Jagdrevier, -gebiet, Jagdgelände; **happy** ~ **ground for collectors** Sammlereldorado; ~ **horn** Jagdhorn; ~ **licence** Jagdschein; ~ **lodge** Jagdhütte; ~ **permit** *(US)* Jagdschein; ~ **seat** Jagdschlößchen.

hurdle Hürde, Schwierigkeit;
to clear all the ~s alle Hürden nehmen.

hurdy gurdy Drehorgel, Leierkasten.

hurl *(v.)* schleudern;
~ **an accusation into s. one's face** jem. eine Anklage ins Gesicht schleudern; ~ **o. s. into the fray** sich ins Getümmel stürzen; ~ **invectives** Beschimpfungen ausstoßen; ~ **reproaches on s. o.** jem. heftige Vorwürfe machen.

hurly burly Aufruhr, Tumult.

hurricane Orkan, Wirbelsturm;
~ **of applause** Beifallssturm;
to let loose a ~ **of abuse** *(fam.)* Flut von Verwünschungen ausstoßen;
~ **deck** Sturm-, Promenadendeck; ~ **lamp** Windlaterne.

hurried übereilt, gehetzt;
to be ~ **on by the police** von der Polizei zum Weitergehen aufgefordert werden;
to write a few ~ **lines** schnell ein paar Zeilen schreiben; ~ **meal** hastige Mahlzeit.

hurry Eile, Hast;
in a ~ in großer Eile; **in the** ~ **of business** im Drang der Geschäfte;
~ **of modern life** Geschäftigkeit unserer Tage;
~ *(v.)* hasten, sich beeilen, *(expedite)* schnell befördern;
~ **into one's clothes** in seine Kleider fahren; ~ **a coal wag(g)on** *(Br.)* Kohlenwagen fahren; ~ **on** antreiben; ~ **soldiers to the front** Truppen an die Front werfen; ~ **over a task** Arbeit flüchtig erledigen; ~ **up** vorwärtstreiben, *(v./i.)* sich beeilen;
to be in too great a ~ **to make money** einfach nicht zum Geldverdienen kommen;
~ **call** Notruf; ~~**skurry** Überstürzung.

hurst Hain, Wäldchen.

hurt Verletzung, Verwundung, *(damage)* Schaden, Beschädigung;
~ **to s. one's pride** Kränkung von jds. Stolz; ~ **of s. one's reputation** Beeinträchtigung von jds. gutem Ruf;
~ *(v.)* verwunden, verletzten, *(damage)* Schaden zufügen, schädigen;
~ **s. one's feelings** jds. Gefühle verletzen; ~ **s. one's interests** jds. Interessen beeinträchtigen.

hurtful nachteilig, schädlich;
to be ~ **to s. one's interests** jds. Interessen beeinträchtigen;
~ **rumo(u)rs** rufschädigende Gerüchte.

hurtle *(v.)* zusammenprallen, -stoßen.

husband Ehemann, Gatte;
 ship's ~ Schiffsagent, Korrespondentreeder;
 ~ **wife** Eheleute;
 ~ *(v.)* bewirtschaften, *(economize)* sparsam (haushälterisch) umgehen;
 ~ **one's resources** mit seinen Vorräten pfleglich umgehen; ~ **one's strength** mit seinen Kräften haushalten;
 to live as ~ **and wife** wie Mann und Frau leben.
husband's | authorization ehemännliche Genehmigung; ~ **responsibility for wife's expenditure** Haftung des Ehegatten für im Rahmen der Schlüsselgewalt getätigte Ausgaben; ~ **tea** schwacher Tee.
husbandage Schiffsagentengebühr.
husbanding Bewirtschaftung, Bebauung;
 ~ **of capital** vorsichtiger Kapitaleinsatz.
husbandman Landwirt, Bauer.
husbandry *(economy)* sparsame Wirtschaft, *(farming)* Acker-, Landwirtschaft;
 animal ~ *(US)* Viehzucht; **good** ~ einwandfreie Wirtschaftsführung.
hush Schweigen, Stille;
 the ~ **before the storm** die Stille vor dem Sturm;
 ~ *(v.)* **up** vertuschen, totschweigen;
 ~ **affair** vertuschte Angelegenheit; ~**-hush** erhöhte Geheimhaltungsstufe; ~ **money** Schweigegeld; **big-**~ **object** supergeheimer Gegenstand, Geheimprojekt; ~ **police** Geheimpolizei; ~ **ship** U-Bootfalle; ~ **shop** *(Br.)* Kneipe.
husk *(fig.)* wertlose Hülle.
hustings Tribüne, Rednerbühne.
hustle Gedränge, Getriebe, *(coll.)* Schwung, Tempo;
 ~ **and bustle** Gedränge und Gehetze;
 ~ *(v.)* mit Hochdruck arbeiten;
 ~ **through the crowd** sich einen Weg durch die Menge bahnen, sich durchdrängen; ~ **s. o. into a decision** j. zu einer Entscheidung drängen; ~ **a thief into the van** Dieb in die grüne Minna verfrachten;
 to get a ~ **on** *(US, fam.)* sich sputen.
hustler *(coll.)* Arbeitstier, rühriger Mensch, *(US sl.)* Geschäftemacher, Ganove.
hut Bude, Hütte, *(mil.)* Baracke;
 ~ *(v.)* in Baracken unterbringen;
 Alpine ~ Berghütte;
 ~ **builder** Barackenaufsteller; ~ **camp** Barackenlager.
hutch Verschlag.
hutment Barackenlager.
hybrid Bastard;
 ~ **bill** *(Br.)* gemischte Gesetzesvorlage, Interessenvorlage.

hydraulic | brake Öldruckbremse; ~ **dock** Schwimmdock; ~ **engineer** Wasserbauingenieur; ~ **engineering** Wasserbaukunst; ~ **power** hydraulische Kraft; ~ **shock absorber** Flüssigkeitsstoßdämpfer.
hydro-electric power station Wasserkraftwerk.
hydrofoil [boat] Tragflächenboot.
hydrogen bomb Wasserstoffbombe.
hydrographic | map Seekarte; ~ **Office** Seewarte.
hydroplane Wasserflugzeug.
hygiene Gesundheitspflege, Hygiene.
hygienic | conditions sanitäre Verhältnisse; ~ **facilities** sanitäre Anlagen.
hyperemployment Über-, Vollbeschäftigung.
hyperinflation übermäßige Inflation, anormale Inflationsrate.
hypermarket Einkaufszentrum.
hypersincerity übertriebene Ehrlichkeit.
hypersonic velocity Überschallgeschwindigkeit.
hyphen Bindestrich, Trennungszeichen.
hyphenate *(v.)* mit einem Bindestrich versehen.
hyphenated American naturalisierter Amerikaner.
hyphenation Silbentrennung;
 ~ **program(me)** *(terminal)* Silbentrennungsprogramm.
hypnotic | sleep Hypnoseschlaf; ~ **state** Hypnosezustand.
hypocrite Heuchler, Scheinheiliger.
hypothec Hypothek, *(Scot. law)* Verpächterpfandrecht an Vieh und Ernte.
hypothecary hypothekarisch, pfandrechtlich;
 ~ **action** Zwangsvollstreckungsklage; ~ **claim** Hypothekenforderung; ~ **debts** Hypothekenschulden; ~ **right** Hypotheken-, Grundstückspfandrecht; ~ **security** Pfandsicherheit, hypothekarische Sicherheit; ~ **value** *(US)* Beleihungs-, Lombardwert.
hypothecate *(v.)* verpfänden, *(mortgage)* hypothekisieren, *(ship)* verbodmen;
 ~ **securities** Wertpapiere lombardieren, Effekten beleihen (lombardieren).
hypothecated asset sicherungsübereigneter Vermögensgegenstand.
hypothecation Verpfändung, Beleihung, Hypothekisierung, *(securities)* Beleihung, Lombardierung, *(ship)* Verbodmung;
 ~ **of goods** Warenlombard; ~ **of securities** Lombardierung von Wertpapieren;
 ~ **bond** Bodmereischein; ~ **certificate** *(US)* Lombardschein; ~ **value** Beleihungs-, Lombardwert.
hypothecator Hypothekenschuldner.
hypothesis Hypothese, Vermutung.
hypothetical | question hypothetische Frage; ~ **yearly tenancy** hypothetische Jahrespacht.

I

ice Eisschicht, *(fig.)* Zurückhaltung, Reserviertheit;
   nipped by ~ vom Eis eingeschlossen; **on thin** ~ *(fig.)* in einer gefährlichen Situation;
   anchor ~ Grundeis; **drifting (floating, loose, moving)** ~ Treibeis; **ground** ~ Grundeis; **open** ~ fahrbares Eis;
   to break the ~ *(fig.)* Situation auflockern; **to cut no** ~ keinerlei Wirkung zeigen, keinen Eindruck machen, nicht ziehen; **to cut no** ~ **with s. o.** *(fam.)* jem. nicht imponieren, j. unbeeindruckt lassen; **to keep on** ~ *(US)* auf Lager haben, in Reserve (petto) halten; **to keep food on** ~ Lebensmittel konservieren; **to put on** ~ *(US)* sich sichern, sicherstellen; **to skate on thin** ~ sich auf dünnes Eis wagen (auf eine gefährliche Sache einlassen);
   ~ **age** Eiszeit; ~ **apron** *(bridge)* Eisbrecher; ~ **breaker** *(ship)* Eisbrecher; ~ **cap** Eisdecke, *(Northpole)* Eiskappe; ~ **car** *(railway)* Eiswaggon; **mixed** ~ **cream** gemischtes Eis; ~**-cream cone** Hörnchen [für Eis]; ~ **cube** Eiswürfel; ~ **field** Eisfeld; ~**-free harbo(u)r** eisfreier Hafen; ~ **jam** Eisstoß; ~ **layer** Eisschicht; ~ **machine** Eismaschine, Gefrierapparat; ~ **making** Eisherstellung; ~ **mist** Frostnebel; ~ **pack** *(med.)* Eisbeutel; ~ **pantomime** Eisrevue; ~ **parlo(u)r** Eisdiele; ~ **Patrol** *(mar.)* Eismeldedienst; ~ **pilot** Eislotse; ~ **safe** Eiskasten; ~ **sheet** Eisdecke, Inlandseis; ~ **show** Eisrevue; ~ **storm** Eisregen; ~ **stream** Gletscher.
iceberg Eisberg.
icebound zu-, eingefroren;
   to become ~ einfrieren.
icebox *(US)* Eis-, Kühlschrank.
icebreaker Eisbrecher.
icehouse Eiskeller.
iceman *(US)* Eisverkäufer.
icing Vereisung, *(refigerator car)* Eisversorgung;
   ~ **on the cake** Zuckerguß, *(fig.)* Zugabe, Bonus;
   ~ **charge** Eisversorgungsgebühr; ~ **station** Bahnhof zur Ergänzung des Eisvorrats.
icy road vereiste Straße.
idea Idee, Begriff, Vorstellung, Gedanke, Einfall;
   basic ~ Grundbegriff; **exploded** ~ überwundener Standpunkt; **half-baked** ~s unausgegorene Ideen; **inventive** ~ *(patent law)* Erfindungsgedanke; **leading** ~ Grundgedanke; **long-range** ~ Vorstellung auf lange Sicht; **stereotyped** ~ Klischeebegriff; **untried** ~ unerprobte Idee;
   ~ **of cartels** Kartellidee;
   to be dominated by one ~ von einer fixen Idee besessen sein; **to be a man full of new** ~s ideenreiche Persönlichkeit sein; **to enter into s. one's** ~s in jds. Sinn handeln; **to feed on** ~s sich auf Ideenreichtum verlassen; **to force one's** ~s **on other people** anderen Leuten seine Ansichten aufdrängen; **to get an** ~ **into one's head** sich etw. in den Kopf setzen; **to give a general** ~ **of a book** Überblick über ein Buch geben; **to have no** ~ **of s. th.** keine Ahnung von etw. haben; **to have a poor** ~ **of s. one's abilities** j. schlecht beurteilen können; **to have some** ~ **of the export business** ein bißchen vom Exportgeschäft verstehen; **to present one's** ~s seine Ansichten vortragen; **to start an** ~ **on its way** für eine Idee werben;
   ~s **man** *(advertising, Br.)* Ideenspezialist, -gestalter, -anreger; ~**-monger** Ideenverbreiter.
ideal Wunschbild, Ideal[vorstellung];
   ~ *(a.)* ideal, vollkommen, mustergültig;
   ~ **candidate** Bewerberideal; ~ **capacity** Betriebsoptimum; ~ **car** Traumauto; ~ **home** Traumhaus; ~ **standard** optimale Standardkosten; ~ **weather for a holiday** ideales Ferienwetter.
ideality Vorstellungskraft.
identical gleichlautend, -bedeutend, übereinstimmend, identisch;
   ~ **copy** gleichlautende Abschrift; ~ **statements** gleichlautende Erklärungen; ~ **twins** eineiige Zwillinge.
identifiable kenntlich, feststellbar, identifizierbar;
   ~ **property** feststellbare Vermögenswerte.
identification Feststellung der Persönlichkeit (Nämlichkeit), Kennzeichnung, Identifikation, *(establishing identity)* Legitimation, Erkennung;
   ~ **of a criminal** Identifizierung eines Verbrechers; ~ **of persons killed in a road accident** Identifizierung von Verkehrsopfern; ~ **of source** Offenlegung der Informationsquelle;
   ~ **card** Personalausweis, Kennkarte; ~ **card case** Ausweishülle; ~ **disk** *(mil. US)* Erkennungs-, Identitätsmarke; ~ **mark** Erkennungs-, Nämlichkeitszeichen; ~ **papers** Ausweis-, Personal-, Legitimationspapiere, Personalausweis; ~ **parade**

Gegenüberstellung, Konfrontation; ~ **plate** *(motor car)* polizeiliches Kennzeichen; ~ **tag** *(mil.)* Erkennungsmarke; ~ **words** *(tel.)* Buchstabierwörter.
identify *(v.)* identifizieren, kennzeichnen, Identität bestätigen (feststellen);
   ~ **o. s.** sich ausweisen; ~ **o. s. with s. o.** sich in j. hineinversetzen, sich mit jem. identifizieren (solidarisch erklären); ~ **goods by marks** Waren kennzeichnen; ~ **o. s. with the majority** sich der Mehrheit anschließen; ~ **o. s. with the new political party** neugegründete politische Partei unterstützen; ~ **a strange ship** Nationalität eines Schiffs ausmachen.
identifying badge Kennmarke.
identity Identität, Nämlichkeit, [Personen]gleichheit, *(patent law)* Wesens-, Patentgleichheit, *(personality)* Persönlichkeit, Individualität;
   of known ~ von Person bekannt; **payable upon submission of proof of** ~ bei Nachweis der Legitimation auszahlbar; **mistaken** ~ Personenverwechslung, Identitätsirrtum;
   ~ **of invention** gleiche Erfindung; ~ **of the subject matter** *(insurance)* Nämlichkeit des Versicherungsgegenstands; ~ **of political opinions** Gleichheit der politischen Ansichten;
   to be arrested because of mistaken ~ auf Grund einer Identitätsverwechslung festgenommen werden; **to establish the** ~ **of s. o.** jds. Identität feststellen; **to prove one's** ~ sich legitimieren (ausweisen);
   ~ **card** *(papers)* [Personal]ausweis, Kennkarte; ~ **certificate** Identitätsnachweis, Nämlichkeitszeugnis; ~ **disk** Erkennungsmarke; ~ **papers** Personalausweis.
ideological rift, to bridge the ideologische Risse überbrücken.
ideology Ideologie;
   totalitarian ~ totalitäre Ideologie.
idiograph Handelsmarke.
idiographic signature eigenhändige Unterschrift.
idiom Spracheigentümlichkeit, idiomatische Redewendung, Redensart;
   to be at home with ~s volksnah zu reden verstehen.
idiomatic idiomatisch.
idiomatically, to express o. s. idiomatische Redewendung gebrauchen.
idiot Idiot, Geistesschwacher, Schwachsinniger.
idiotic geistesschwach, idiotisch.
idle müßig, untätig, *(capital)* unproduktiv, unausgenutzt, tot, brachliegend, zinslos, *(groundless)* grundlos, unbegründet, *(lazy)* faul, träge, müßig, arbeitsscheu, *(not operating)* außer (nicht im) Betrieb, stillstehend, leerlaufend, *(unoccupied)* unbeschäftigt, erwerbslos, untätig, *(without worth)* wertlos, nichtig;
   ~ *(v.)* *(engine)* leerlaufen;
   ~ **about** herumtrödeln; ~ **about the streets** auf den Straßen herumflanieren; ~ **away one's time** seine Zeit vergeuden (verplempern);
   to be ~ feiern, *(machine)* brachliegen, stillstehen, unausgenutzt sein; **to let one's money lie** ~ sein Geld nicht arbeiten lassen; **to lie** ~ *(capital)* nicht arbeiten; **to run** ~ *(factory)* stilliegen, *(machine)* außer Betrieb sein; **to stand** ~ ungenutzt bleiben; **not to stand** ~ **by** nicht tatenlos zusehen;
   ~ **apprentice** fauler Lehrling; ~ **capacity** *(US)* ungenutzte Kapazität, Leerlaufkapazität; ~ **capital** totes Kapital; **out of** ~ **curiosity** aus blanker Neugier; ~ **facilities** stilliegende Betriebsanlagen; ~ **fellow** Faulenzer; ~ **gossip** leeres Geschwätz; ~ **hours** Mußestunden; ~ **money** brachliegendes (nicht angelegtes) Kapital; ~ **motion** Leerlauf; ~ **period** Liegezeit; ~ **and disorderly person** *(Br.)* Arbeitsscheuer, liederliche Person; ~ **plant** stilliegende Fabrikanlage; ~**-plant expenses** Stillstandskosten; ~ **pretext** unberechtigter Vorwand; ~ **rumo(u)r** grundloses Gerücht; ~ **talk** Gewäsch; ~ **tenement** leerstehende Wohnung; ~ **threat** leere Drohung; ~ **time** Warte-, Verlustzeit, Warteverlust, *(production process)* verlorene Zeit, Brache, Leerlaufzeit; ~**-time report** Stillstandsbericht; ~ **workman** unbeschäftigter Arbeiter.
idleness Untätigkeit, Müßigkeit, *(worker)* Arbeitsscheu;
   to eat the bread of ~ Müßiggang treiben; **to live in** ~ seine Zeit vertun.
idler Müßiggänger, Faulenzer, *(railway)* leerer Waggon;
   ~ **car** Rungenwagen für überhängende Ladung.
ignition *(motor car)* Zündung;
   battery ~ Batteriezündung;

~ **battery** Zündbatterie; ~ **circuit** Zündstromkreis; ~ **key** Zündschlüssel; ~ **lever** Zündverstellhebel; ~ **timing** Einstellung der Zündung, Zündpunkteinstellung.

ignominous schimpflich, ehrenrührig;
~ **peace** Schandfrieden.

ignominy Schmach, Schimpf, Schande.

ignorance Unwissenheit, Unkenntnis, Nichtwissen;
accidental ~ Unkenntnis nebensächlicher Umstände; **culpable** ~ schuldhafte Unkenntnis; **essential** ~ Unkenntnis wesentlicher Umstände; **involuntary** ~ zwangsläufige Unkenntnis; **utter** ~ gänzliche Unwissenheit; **voluntary** ~ schuldhaftes Nichtwissen, schuldhafte Unkenntnis;
~ **of fact** Nichtkenntnis tatsächlicher Umstände; ~ **of the law** Unkenntnis des Gesetzes;
to be in complete ~ **of s. one's plans** keine Ahnung von jds. Plänen haben; **to display one's** ~ sich ein Armutszeugnis ausstellen; **to keep s. o. in** ~ j. in Unkenntnis lassen; **to plead** ~ Einwand der Unkenntnis vorbringen, sich auf Unkenntnis berufen; **to plead** ~ **in excuse of one's conduct** Unkenntnis des Gesetzes vorschützen; **to trade upon other people's** ~ mit der Dummheit der Leute Geschäfte machen.

ignorant of in Unkenntnis von, unkundig;
to be ~ nicht wissen;
~ **conduct** dämliches Benehmen.

ignore *(v.)* nicht beachten (kennen), außer Acht lassen, ignorieren;
~ **a bill of indictment** Klage als unbegründet abweisen, Anklage verwerfen; ~**a complaint** Beschwerde zurückweisen; ~ **s. one's existence** j. völlig ignorieren; ~ **an insult** Beleidigung übersehen; ~ **an invitation** auf eine Einladung nicht reagieren; ~ **an objection** Einwand nicht anerkennen; ~ **an order** Anordnung nicht beachten (mißachten); ~ **a prohibition** Verbot überschreiten; ~ **rude remarks** Unverschämtheiten überhören; ~ **a signal** *(railway)* Signal überfahren.

Iliad *(fig.)* langer Bericht;
an ~ **of woes** Kette von Unglücksfällen.

ill Übel, Unglück, Mißgeschick;
~ *(a.)* krank, *(bad)* schlimm, schlecht, böse, übel, *(dangerous)* gefährlich;
to be dangerously ~ lebensgefährlich erkrankt sein; **to can** ~ **afford the time and money** sich weder zeitlich noch geldlich leisten können; **to be** ~ **at ease** in großer Unruhe sein, sich unbehaglich fühlen; **to be taken (fall)** ~ krank werden; **to be** ~**off** schlimm dran sein; **to pretend to be** ~ Krankheit vorschützen; **to speak** ~ **of one's neighbo(u)rs** seine Nachbarn anschwärzen;
~**-advised** schlecht beraten; ~**-assorted** zusammengewürfelt; ~ **at ease** befangen, ungeeignet; ~ **blood** böses Blut, Feindschaft; ~**-bred** ungebildet, unerzogen; ~ **breeding** schlechte Erziehung; ~**-conditioned** schlecht beschaffen, *(goods)* in schlechtem Zustand; ~ **conduct** schlechte Führung; ~**-disposed** übelgesinnt; **to be** ~**-disposed towards s. o.** j. nicht leiden können; ~**-educated** mit schlechter Schulbildung; ~ **fame** schlechter Ruf; ~**-feeling** Ressentiment; ~ **fortune** Mißgeschick; ~**-founded** schlecht begründet, unbegründet, abwegig; ~**-gotten** unrechtmäßig erworben; ~**-health** schlechter Gesundheitszustand; **to allege** ~ **health as a reason** Krankheit als Grund angeben; ~**-humo(u)r** schlechte Laune; ~**-judged attempt** Versuch am untauglichen Objekt; ~ **luck** Pech; ~**-managed** schlecht bewirtschaftet; ~**-mannered** unmanierlich; ~ **manners** schlechte Manieren; ~**-matched** schlecht zusammenpassend; ~ **nature** Bösartigkeit; ~ **omen** böses Vorzeichen; ~**-prepared** schlecht vorbereitet; ~**-qualified** ohne die erforderlichen Eigenschaften; ~**-reputed** übel beleumdet; **to be** ~**-serving** Bärendienst erweisen; ~**-set** *(book)* schlecht gedruckt; ~ **success** Erfolglosigkeit, Mißerfolg; ~**-tempered** schlecht gelaunt; ~**-timed** ungelegen, zeitlich schlecht abgestimmt; ~**-treat** *(v.)* mißhandeln; ~**-treatment** schlechte Behandlung, Mißhandlung; **to do s. o. an** ~ **turn** jem. einen bösen Streich spielen; ~**-usage** *(crew)* schlechte Behandlung; ~**-used** mißbraucht; **to think o. s.** ~**-used** sich ausgenutzt fühlen; ~ **will** böser Wille.

illegal unrechtmäßig, ungesetzlich, rechtswidrig, widerrechtlich, verboten;
~ **act** rechtswidrige (widerrechtliche) Handlung; ~ **activities** illegale Tätigkeit; ~ **conditions** ungesetzliche (rechtlich unzulässige) Bestimmungen; ~ **conduct** rechtswidriges Verhalten; ~ **consideration** gesetzwidrige (rechtlich unzulässige) Gegenleistung (Vertragsleistung); ~ **contract** sittenwidriger Vertrag; ~ **dealing** verbotener Handel; ~ **interest** Wucherzinsen; ~**lottery** nicht genehmigte Lotterie; ~**love** verbotene Liebe; ~ **operation** verbotener Eingriff; ~ **practices** *(Br.)* rechtswidrige Wahlpraktiken; ~ **proceedings** ungesetzliches Verfahren; ~ **profit** unrechtmäßiger Gewinn; ~ **strike** wilder Streik; ~ **trade** Schmuggel, Schleichhandel, völkerrechtlich verbotener Handel; ~ **transaction** illegale Geschäfte.

illegality Rechts-, Gesetzwidrigkeit, Ungesetzlichkeit, Unrechtmäßigkeit, Illegalität.

illegibility Unleserlichkeit.

illegible unleserlich.

illegitimacy Ungültigkeit, Unrechtmäßigkeit, *(bastardy)* uneheliche Geburt, Unehelichkeit.

illegitimate ungesetzlich, *(born out of wedlock)* nicht-, außerehelich;
~ *(v.)* verbieten, für ungesetzlich erklären;
~ **child** uneheliches (lediges) Kind, Bastard; **of** ~ **descent** unehelicher Abkunft; ~ **statement** unberechtigte Erklärung.

illegitimation Ungültigkeitserklärung.

illiberal knauserig.

illicit unerlaubt, verboten, rechts-, gesetzwidrig, ungesetzlich;
~ **betting** unerlaubte Wettgeschäfte; ~ **cohabitation** Konkubinat; ~ **dealer** Schwarzhändler; ~ **diamond buying** *(South Africa)* unerlaubter Diamantenankauf; ~ **distiller** Schwarzbrenner; ~ **distillery** Schwarzbrennerei; ~ **profits** unerlaubte Gewinne; ~ **sales** Schwarzverkauf; ~ **trade** Schleich-, Schwarzhandel; ~ **work** Schwarzarbeit.

illimitable unbegrenzbar.

illiquid nicht flüssig, *(bank)* illiquide, zahlungsunfähig, *(claim)* unbewiesen;
~ **position** angeschlagene Liquiditätsposition.

illiquidity fehlende Liquidität, Illiquidität, Zahlungsunfähigkeit.

illiteracy Analphabetentum, Bildungsmangel.

illiterate Analphabet;
~ *(v.)* ungebildet, analphabetisch;
~ **letter** Brief voller Fehler.

illness Krankheit, Leiden;
on account of ~ krankheitshalber;
occupational ~ Berufskrankheit; **severe** ~ *(insurance)* schwere Krankheit;
~**es of children** Kinderkrankheiten;
to be absent through ~ wegen Krankheit fehlen; **to be compelled by** ~ **to resign** aus Krankheitsgründen aufgeben müssen; **to have a slight** ~ indisponiert sein; **to insure against** ~ Krankenversicherung abschließen; **to introduce an** ~ Krankheit einschleppen;
~ **costs** Krankheitskosten; ~ **frequency rate** Erkrankungsziffer, Krankenausfallquote.

illocable nicht vermietbar, unvermietbar.

illuminate *(v.)* beleuchten, *(Br.)* festlich illuminieren, *(fig.)* aufklären;
~ **a difficult passage in a book** schwierige Buchstelle erläutern.

illuminated│advertising Leuchtreklame; ~ **indicator** Leuchtschirm; ~ **letter** Leuchtbuchstabe; **poorly** ~ **room** dunkles Zimmer.

illuminating lichtspendend, *(fig.)* aufschlußreich;
~ **effect** Leuchteffekt; ~ **engineer** Beleuchtungsingenieur, -techniker; ~ **engineering** Beleuchtungstechnik; ~ **gas** Leuchtgas; ~ **oil** Leuchtöl; ~ **talk** klärendes Gespräch.

illumination *(Br.)* [Fest]beleuchtung, *(fig.)* Erleuchtung, Aufklärung;
artificial ~ künstliche Beleuchtung; **dimmed** ~ *(car)* abgeblendetes Licht; **full** ~ *(car)* Fernlicht.

illusion Sinnestäuschung, Illusion, falsche Vorstellung, Einbildung;
optical ~ optische Täuschung;
to cherish an ~ sich einer Illusion hingeben; **to lend o. s. to** ~**s** sich in Illusionen wiegen; **to work off an** ~ **on s. o.** j. zu einer Illusion verleiten.

illusory illusorisch, täuschend, trügerisch.

illustrate illustriert;
~ *(v.)* erläutern, illustrieren;
~ **with examples** mit Beispielen belegen.

illustrated, richly reich bebildert;
~ **by lantern slides** durch Lichtbilder veranschaulicht; ~ **paper** Illustrierte; **well** ~ **textbook** reich bebildertes Lehrbuch.

illustration Abbildung, Illustration, Bild, *(making clear)* Erläuterung, Illustration, *(patent law)* bildliche Darstellung;
text ~**s** Abbildungen im Text;
~ **of the letterpress** Textabbildung;
to tie in ~**s in a text** Text illustrieren;

illustration 474

~ **board** Malkarton; ~ **printing** Illustrationsdruck; **calendered or glazed ~-printing paper** satiniertes oder kalandriertes Illustrationsdruckpapier.

illustrative erläuternd, erklärend;
~ **data** Anschauungsmaterial; ~ **phrase** Anwendungsbeispiel.

image bildliche Darstellung, Bild[nis], Ebenbild, *(advertising)* Meinungs-, Leitbild, *(imagination)* Vorstellungsbild, Idee, *(symbol)* symbolische Darstellung;
brand ~ Werbe-, Markenstil; **career** ~ berufliches Image; **corporate** ~ Leitbild eines Unternehmens; **faulty** ~ fehlerhaftes Fernsehbild; **public** ~ Erscheinungsbild in der Öffentlichkeit;
~ *(v.)* abbilden, bildlich darstellen;
to be the very (living) ~ **of s. o.** jem. wie aus dem Gesicht geschnitten sein; **to cultivate an** ~ Image pflegen; **to speak in ~s** in Metaphern sprechen; **to stand like a wooden** ~ *(coll.)* wie ein Ölgötze darstehen;
~ **building** Leitbilderstellung; ~-**building program(me)** Leitbildprogramm; ~ **dissector** *(television)* Bildzerleger[röhre]; ~ **merchant** Meinungsmanipulator; ~ **polishing** Imagepflege; ~-**rating system** System zur Erforschung der Kundenmeinung; ~ **worship** Götzendienst.

imaginary nur in der Einbildung vorhanden, imaginär, fingiert;
to create ~ **difficulties** künstliche Schwierigkeiten machen; ~ **grievances** eingebildete Beschwerden; ~ **profit** Scheingewinn; ~ **value** Schein-, Affektionswert.

imagination Einbildungs-, Vorstellungskraft, Phantasie, *(idea)* Gedanke, Einfall;
in the ~ im Geist;
to have a lively ~ lebhafte Phantasie haben.

imaginative|power Vorstellungskraft; ~ **writer** phantasievoller Schriftsteller.

imagine *(v.)* sich vorstellen, konstruieren, sich einbilden, *(treason, Br.)* planen.

imbalance Unausgewogenheit, Ungleichgewicht;
~ **in world payments** unausgeglichene Weltzahlungsbilanz.

imbasing|of coinage Münzverschlechterung; ~ **of money** Münzverschlechterung.

imbecile Geistesschwacher, Schwachsinniger;
~ *(a.)* geistesschwach, schwachsinnig;
~ **remarks** törichte Bemerkungen.

imbecility Geistesschwäche, Schwachsinn.

imbroglios [politische] Komplikationen.

imbue *(v.)* **s. o. with prejudices** j. mit Vorurteilen erfüllen.

imbued|with one's own importance von seiner eigenen Bedeutung erfüllt; ~ **with patriotism** patriotisch angehaucht;
to be ~ **with a sense of one's own importance** ganz von der Bedeutung der eigenen Persönlichkeit erfüllt sein.

imitate *(v.)* nachmachen, -ahmen, kopieren;
~ **s. one's style** jds. Stil kopieren; ~ **s. o. to the life** j. täuschend nachahmen.

imitated nachgeahmt, unecht, künstlich.

imitation Nachahmung, Imitation, *(counterfeit)* Fälschung, Falsifikat, *(free translation)* freie Übersetzung;
beware of ~s vor Nachahmungen wird gewarnt;
colo(u)rable ~ täuschend ähnliche Nachahmung; **inferior** ~ geringwertige Nachahmung;
~ **of trademarks** Nachahmung (Fälschung) von Warenzeichen;
~ **art paper** satiniertes Papier; ~ **diamond** Straß; ~ **firearm** Scheinpistole; ~ **goods** Nachahmungen; ~ **jewellery** Imitationsschmuck; ~ **leather** Kunstleder; ~ **pearl** unechte Perle; ~ **stamp** nachgemachte Briefmarke.

imitative|arts bildende Künste; ~ **product** nachgeahmtes Erzeugnis.

imitator Fälscher, Imitator.

immaculate makellos;
~ **book** fehlerfreies Buch.

immanent contradiction Grundwiderspruch.

immaterial unwesentlich, unerheblich, unwichtig, *(incorporal)* unkörperlich, immateriell;
~ **to the subject** nicht zum Thema gehörig;
to be ~ **to s. o.** jem. gleichgültig sein;
~ **averment** *(pleading)* unerhebliche [Prozeß]behauptung, unerhebliches Vorbringen; ~ **facts** unwesentliche Tatsachen; ~ **issue** für die Entscheidung unwesentlicher Punkt; ~ **objection** unerheblicher Einwand; ~ **statement** rechtsunerhebliche Erklärung; ~ **variance** *(proof of character)* geringfügige Abweichung.

immature unreif;
~ **creditor nation** Staat mit aktiver Handelsbilanz; ~ **debtor nation** Staat mit passiver Handelsbilanz;
~**[d]** unausgereift, unentwickelt, *(not yet due)* noch nicht fällig.

immediate unverzüglich, augenblicklich, sofort, *(first hand)* unmittelbar, aus erster Hand, direkt, *(urgent)* dringend;
~ **action** Sofortmaßnahmen; **to take** ~ **action** sofort reagieren; ~ **annuity** sofort fällige Rente; ~ **approach** unmittelbarer Zufahrtsweg; ~ **benefit** sofortiger Versicherungsschutz; ~ **cause** unmittelbare Ursache; ~ **control** *(motor vehicle)* vollständige Beherrschung; ~ **credit account** *(US)* Einlagenkonto mit sofortiger Scheck- und Wechselgutschrift; ~ **delivery** umgehende (sofortige) Lieferung; **for** ~ **delivery** sofort lieferfähig; ~ **demand** Nachfragestoß; ~ **descent** unmittelbare Abstammung; ~ **family** engste Familie; ~ **future** nächste Zukunft; ~ **heir** nächster Erbe; ~ **heir to the throne** unmittelbarer Thronerbe; ~ **information** Information aus erster Hand; ~ **matter** *(law court)* Sofortsache; **to receive an** ~ **month's warning** einmonatliche Kündigung erhalten; ~ **neighbo(u)r** unmittelbarer Nachbar; ~ **notice** *(insurance)* sofortige Benachrichtigung [vom Eintritt des Versicherungsfalls]; ~ **object** Nahziel; ~ **occupation** sofort bezugsfähig; ~ **parties to a bill** unmittelbare Wechselbeteiligte; ~ **payment** sofortige Zahlung; **my** ~ **plans** meine augenblicklichen Pläne; **with** ~ **possession** *(house)* sofort bezugsfähig; ~ **reply** sofortige (umgehende) Antwort, postwendend; ~ **reversion** unmittelbares Heimfallrecht; ~ **steps** Sofortmaßnahmen; ~ **urgency** höchste Dringlichkeit; **in the** ~ **vicinity** in unmittelbarer Nachbarschaft (Nähe).

immediately gleich, sofort, unverzüglich;
~ **effective** sofort wirksam, mit sofortiger Wirkung.

immemorial unvordenklich;
~ **possession** *(Lousiana)* Besitz seit unvordenklichen Zeiten; ~ **usage** uralter Brauch, uralte Gepflogenheit, Ersitzung.

immerse *(v.)* **o. s. in a conversation** sich in ein Gespräch vertiefen.

immersed|in debt völlig verschuldet;
to be ~ **in a book** in ein Buch versunken sein; **to be** ~ **in one's work** in seiner Arbeit aufgehen.

immersion *(fig.)* Vertieftsein, Vertiefung;
~ **heater** Tauchsieder.

immigrant Einwanderer;
to admit ~s Einwanderung zulassen; **to exclude ~s from the country** Einwanderungsstop erlassen;
~ **labo(u)r** Gastarbeiter; ~ **remittances** Überweisungen von Einwanderern; ~ **vote** Wahlstimmen der Einwanderer; ~ **wage** Gastarbeiterlohn; ~ **worker** Gastarbeiter.

immigrate *(v.)* zu-, einwandern;
~ **foreign labo(u)r** ausländische Arbeitskräfte einsetzen.

immigration Zu-, Einwanderung, *(immigrants arrived)* Einwandererzahl;
⁓ **Act** *(Br.)* Einwanderungsgesetz; ⁓ **and Nationality Act** *(US)* Einwanderungs- und Staatsangehörigkeitsgesetz; ~ **authorities** Einwanderungsbehörden; **to be held up by the** ~ **authorities** von den Einwanderungsbehörden festgehalten werden; ~ **bar** Einwanderungsstop; ~ **control** Einwanderungskontrolle; ~ **country** Einwanderungsland; ~ **department** Einwanderungsabteilung; ~ **issue** Einwanderungsfrage; ~ **law** Einwanderungsrecht; ~ **office** Einwanderungsbehörde; ~ **officer** Einwanderungsbeamter; ~ **papers** Einwanderungspapiere; ~ **permit** Einwanderungsbewilligung; ~ **policy** Einwanderungspolitik; ~ **proceedings** Einwanderungsverfahren; ~ **quota** Einwanderungskontingent, -quote; ~ **regulations** Einwanderungsbestimmungen; ~ **restrictions** Einwanderungsbeschränkungen; ~ **scheme** Einwanderungsprojekt; **US** ⁓ **and Naturalization Service (INS)** Einwanderungs- und Einbürgerungsbehörde der USA; ~ **visa** Einwanderungsvisum.

imminence nahes Bevorstehen, drohende Gefahr, Gefahr im Verzug.

imminent, to be unmittelbar bevorstehen;
~ **danger** unmittelbare (unmittelbar bevorstehende) Gefahr.

imminently dangerous article lebensgefährlicher Gegenstand.

immobility Immobilität.

immobilization Festlegung, Einfrieren, *(coins)* Einziehung;
~ **of capital** Kapitalfestlegung; ~ **of funds** Bindung von Geldbeträgen, Mittelbindung; ~ **of liquid funds** Liquiditätsbindung; ~ **of troops** Bindung von Truppenverbänden.

immobilize *(v.)* festlegen, einfrieren, (coins) aus dem Verkehr ziehen;
~ **a body of troops** feindliche Truppenverbände binden; ~ **capital** Kapital festlegen.

immobilized handlungsunfähig;
~ **money** festgelegte Mittel.

immoral gegen die guten Sitten verstoßend, sittenwidrig, unsittlich, unmoralisch;
~ **conduct** sittenwidriges (unsittliches) Verhalten; ~ **consideration** sittenwidrige Gegenleistung; ~ **contract** sittenwidriger

Vertrag, Vertrag gegen die guten Sitten; **to lead an ~ life** unsittlichen Lebenswandel führen; **~ offence** Sittlichkeitsverbrechen.

immorality Sittenlosigkeit, unsittlicher Lebenswandel, *(contract)* Sittenwidrigkeit.

immovable unbeweglich, *(fig.)* entschlossen, unerschütterlich;
~s Liegenschaften, Immobilien, unbewegliches Vermögen, unbewegliche Sachen;
~ estate Liegenschaften; **~ fixture** wesentlicher Bestandteil; **~ property** unbewegliches Vermögen, *(US)* unbeweglicher Nachlaß.

immune immun, geschützt, frei;
to have become ~ to the drawbacks of one's job gegen beruflichen Ärger abgestumpft sein.

immunity Freiheit, Immunität, Privileg, Unverletzlichkeit, Sonderrecht;
diplomatic ~ diplomatische Immunität; **legal ~** strafrechtliche Immunität; **parliamentary ~** parlamentarische Immunität, Abgeordnetenimmunität;
~ of corporation tax *(US)* Steuerfreiheit einer Aktiengesellschaft; **~ from a disease** Immunität gegen eine Krankheit; **~ from prosecution** Strafverfolgungsfreiheit; **~ from punishment** Strafausschließungsgrund; **~ from taxes** Abgaben-, Steuerfreiheit; **~ of witness** Zeugnisverweigerungsrecht;
to claim ~ from taxes Abgabenfreiheit verlangen; **to enjoy diplomatic ~** diplomatische Immunität genießen; **to grant ~** Immunität gewähren; **to have ~ against any legal proceedings** aufgrund seiner Immunität sich jedem Gerichtsverfahren entziehen; **to waive (withdraw) ~** Immunität aufheben.

immunize *(v.)* immunisieren.

impact Belastung, Druck, *(advertisement)* Einwirkung, Stoßkraft, Intensität, Wirkungswert, -möglichkeit, *(projectile)* Aufschlag;
~ of inflation Inflationsdruck, -auswirkungen; **~ on liquidity** Liquiditätsauswirkung, -druck; **~ of a tax** *(Br.)* Steuerbelastung;
~ area *(missile)* Aufschlaggebiet; **~ damage** Kollisionsschaden; **~ effect** *(demand)* Stoßwirkung, Anstoßeffekt; **~ price elasticity** Initialpreiselastizität; **~ study** Untersuchung der Werbewirksamkeit; **~ test** Anzeigentest.

impair *(v.)* vermindern, beeinträchtigen, beschädigen, verschlechtern, schmälern;
~ s. one's credit jds. Kreditfähigkeit schädigen; **~ one's health by overwork** sich durch Überarbeitung gesundheitlich schädigen; **~ s. one's interests** Interessen beeinträchtigen (verletzen); **~ investment** Investitionskürzungen vornehmen; **~ the obligations of a contract** Vertragsverpflichtungen abschwächen; **~ s. one's reputation** Rufmord an jem. begehen.

impaired| capital [durch Verlust] vermindertes Kapital; **~ credit** geschwächter Kredit; **~ fortune** gefährdetes Vermögen; **seriously ~ health** ernsthaft gefährdete Gesundheit.

impairing the obligation of contracts Beeinträchtigung vertraglicher Verpflichtungen.

impairment *(capital)* Kapitalschmälerung, *(of rights)* Schmälerung, Beeinträchtigung;
~ of capital Kapitalverminderung, -schmälerung; **~ of one's mental faculties (a mental nature)** Beeinträchtigung seiner geistigen Fähigkeiten (Verstandeskräfte); **~ of health** Beeinträchtigung der Gesundheit; **~ of a physical nature** Beeinträchtigung des körperlichen Wohlbefindens; **~ of value** Beeinträchtigung des Wertes, Wertminderung.

impanel *(v.)* in eine Liste eintragen, *(jurors, US)* in die Geschworenenliste eintragen, Geschworenenliste aufstellen.

impanelment Eintragung in die Geschworenenliste.

imparl *(v.)* Schlichtungsbefugnisse haben.

imparlance Einräumung einer Erwiderungsfrist;
general ~ Vertagung zur Vorbereitung der mündlichen Verhandlung.

impartial unbefangen, unparteiisch, unvoreingenommen, vorurteilslos;
~ chairman *(labo(u)r relations)* unparteiischer Vorsitzender; **~ jury** unvoreingenommene Geschworene.

impartiality Unbefangenheit, Unparteilichkeit, Objektivität, Sachlichkeit, Unvoreingenommenheit.

impassable unwegsam, unbefahrbar, unpassierbar;
~ road unpassierbare Straße.

impeach *(v.)* in Frage stellen, in Zweifel ziehen, *(bring accusation)* beschuldigen, Anklage erheben, wegen Amtsmißbrauchs anklagen;
~ s. o. with a crime j. eines Verbrechens anklagen (beschuldigen); **~ s. one's hono(u)r** jds. Ehre herabsetzen; **~ a judge for**

taking bribes Richter der Bestechlichkeit beschuldigen; **~ s. one's motives** jds. Motive in Zweifel ziehen; **~ a public officer** Amtsanklage erheben; **~ a witness** *(US)* Glaubwürdigkeit eines Zeugen erschüttern.

impeachable anklagbar;
~ for waste *(tenant)* haftbar für Substanzschäden;
~ contract anfechtbarer Vertrag; **~ motive** zweifelhafte Motive.

impeachment Infragestellung, Bezweifelung, *(impeaching)* Beschuldigung, Anklage, Anklageerhebung, *(ministers)* Parlaments-, Ministeranklage;
~ of annuity *(Br.)* Beeinträchtigung der Ertragsfähigkeit; **~ of waste** *(tenant)* Haftung des Pächters für (Schadensersatzklage wegen) Substanzverschlechterung; **~ of a witness** *(US)* Erschütterung der Glaubwürdigkeit eines Zeugen.

impeccable makellos, einwandfrei.

impecuniosity Geldmangel, Mittellosigkeit.

impecunious unbegütert, mittellos.

impede *(v.)* verhindern, behindern, aufhalten, hemmen;
~ the course of justice in den Gang der Rechtpflege eingreifen; **~ the enemy's movements** Feindbewegungen stören; **~ progress** dem Fortschritt im Wege stehen; **~ the liberty to work** Betätigungsfreiheit behindern; **~ the service of process** Zustellung vereiteln; **~ traffic** Verkehr behindern.

impediment gesetzlicher Hinderungsgrund, Behinderung;
absolute ~ absolutes Ehehindernis; **dirimant ~** Ehenichtigkeitsgrund; **prohibitive ~** Eheverbot; **relative ~** relatives Ehehindernis;
~ to marriage Ehehindernis; **~ on the road** Verkehrshindernis; **~s to trade** Handelsschranken; **~ to traffic** Verkehrsbehinderung;
to be an ~ to foreign trade Außenhandel erschweren; **to be an ~ to s. one's promotion** Hinderungsgrund für jds. Beförderung abgeben; **to have an ~ in one's speech** Sprachfehler (Sprachstörungen) haben.

impedimenta *(law)* Ehehindernisse, *(mil.)* Troß, Gepäck.

impeding the liberty to work Behinderung der Betätigungsfreiheit; **~ the service of process** Zustellungsvereitelung.

impel *(v.)* antreiben, vorwärtsstreiben;
~ a nation to greater efforts Nation zu größeren Anstrengungen bewegen.

impelled by secret motives von geheimen Motiven angetrieben.

impend *(v.)* unmittelbar bevorstehen, drohend schweben.

impending, to be nahe bevorstehen;
~ arrival kurz bevorstehende Ankunft.

impenetrable undurchdringlich;
~ secret unergründliches Geheimnis.

imperative gebieterisch, unumgänglich, *(law)* zwingend;
~ duty unumgängliche Verpflichtung; **~ need** dringende (unumstößliche) Notwendigkeit; **~ order** Mußvorschrift.

imperfect unvollkommen, fehlerhaft, mangelhaft, *(law)* nicht durchsetzbar;
~ competition *(US)* unvollkommener Wettbewerb, ungleiche Wettbewerbsbedingungen; **~ market** unvollkommener Markt, Markt mit monopolistischem Verhalten; **~ obligation** nicht einklagbare Verpflichtung, Naturalobligation; **~ ownership** zeitlich begrenztes Eigentumsrecht; **~ title** aufschiebend bedingtes Eigentum; **~ trust** ungenau festgelegtes Treuhandverhältnis.

imperfection Fehlerhaftigkeit, Schwäche, Unvollkommenheit, *(print.)* Defektbuchstabe.

imperforate *(stamps)* nicht perforiert.

imperial *(Br.)* das Britische Weltreich betreffend, *(magnificent)* großartig, herrlich, *(sovereign)* souverain, gebietend, *(of superior size)* außerordentlich groß;
⌀ Defence College *(Br.)* Kriegsakademie; **~ generosity** grandiose Großzügigkeit; **~ interests** Interessen des britischen Reiches; **~ preference** *(Br.)* Vorzugszoll im Commonwealth, Vorzugstarif, Zollbegünstigung; **~ standards** *(Br.)* gesetzliche Maße und Gewichte; **~ taxes** *(Br.)* Staatssteuern.

imperialism Imperialismus, Weltmachtpolitik.

imperialist Imperialist.

imperil *(v.)* gefährden;
~ one's good name seinen guten Namen riskieren; **~ national security** Staatssicherheit gefährden.

impermeable to water wasserdicht.

impermissible unstatthaft.

impersonal unpersönlich;
~ account totes Konto, Sachkonto; **~ discussion** sachliche Diskussion; **~ entity** Sachgesamtheit; **~ interest** sachliches Interesse; **~ ledger** Sachkontobuch; **~ taxes** Sachsteuern.

impersonate *(v.)* verkörpern, darstellen, personifizieren;
  to falsely ~ sich fälschlich für einen anderen ausgeben.
impersonation Verkörperung, Darstellung, Personifikation;
  false ~ falsche Namensführung.
impertinence Ungehörigkeit, Unverschämtheit, *(irrelevancy)* Irrelevanz, Unschlüssigkeit, Unerheblichkeit.
impertinent | averment nicht zur Sache gehörige Prozeßbehauptung, unerhebliches Vorbringen; ~ **remarks** unverschämte Bemerkungen.
impetuous remarks unüberlegte Bemerkungen.
impetus Aufschwung, Auftrieb;
  ~ **to combination** steuerliche und wirtschaftliche Impulse zum Konzernzusammenschluß; ~ **towards expansion** Wachstumsimpuls; ~ **to trade** Anreiz für die Ausdehnung des Handels; **to furnish additional** ~ zusätzliche Auftriebskräfte verleihen; **to give fresh** ~ **to s. th.** einer Sache neuen Schwung verleihen.
impignoration Verpfändung.
impinge *(v.)* widerrechtlich eingreifen;
  ~ **upon each other** *(interests)* aufeinanderstoßen.
impingement Zusammenstoß, *(encroachment)* Übergriff.
implant *(fig.)* einprägen.
implead *(v.)* anklagen, verklagen, (US) [etwa] Streit verkünden.
impleaded [mit]verklagt.
impleader [etwa] Streitverkündung.
implement Zubehör, Werkzeug, Arbeitsgerät, Bedarfsgegenstand, *(fulfil(l)ment of contract)* Vertragserfüllung;
  ~s Utensilien, Zubehör, Handwerkszeug;
  agricultural (farm) ~s landwirtschaftliches Gerät; **gardening** ~s Gartengeräte; **writing** ~s Schreibutensilien;
  ~s **of husbandry** landwirtschaftliche Geräte; ~s **and machinery** *(factory)* Inventar; ~s **of trade** Handwerks-, Arbeitsgeräte, Betriebsinventar; ~s **of war** Kriegsrüstung;
  ~ *(v.)* erfüllen, aus-, durchführen;
  ~ **an agreement** Abkommen durchführen; ~ **a guarantee** einer Garantiezusage nachkommen; ~ **a law** Gesetz durchführen; ~ **an obligation** einer Verpflichtung nachkommen; ~ **the provisions of a convention** Bestimmungen eines Abkommens in Kraft setzen; ~ **step by step** schrittweise durchführen.
implementation Erfüllung, Durch-, Ausführung;
  ~ **of a contract** Vertragserfüllung, -ausfüllung;
  ~ **clauses** Durchführungsbestimmungen, Anwendungsmodalitäten; ~ **program(me)** Durchführungsplan; ~ **stages** Durchführungsetappen.
implementing | agency ausführende Dienststelle; ~ **regulations** Durchführungsbestimmungen.
implicate *(v.)* mit einbegreifen, implizieren, *(involve deeply)* mitbelasten, mit hineinbeziehen, verwickeln;
  ~ **s. o. in a crime** j. in ein Verbrechen mit hineinbeziehen; ~ **an official in a bribery scandal** Beamten in einen Bestechungsskandal verwickeln.
implicated in a crime in ein Verbrechen verwickelt.
implication Begleiterscheinung, stillschweigende (selbstverständliche) Folgerung, Vermutung;
  by ~ ohne weiteres, stillschweigend;
  necessary ~ *(construing)* allein in Betracht kommende (zwingende) Bedeutung;
  ~ **into contract** stillschweigend vereinbarter Vertragsinhalt; ~ **of law** Rechtsfolgerung; ~s **of a war** Begleiterscheinungen eines Krieges; **full** ~ **of words** volle Tragweite von Worten;
  to carry an ~ Tragweite haben; **to renew by** ~ stillschweigend verlängern.
implicit mit inbegriffen, stillschweigend einbegriffen, mitverstanden, gesetzlich vermutet, gefolgert, impliziert;
  ~ **in the contract** im Vertrag mit einbegriffen; ~ **agreement** stillschweigendes Übereinkommen; ~ **assent** stillschweigende Zustimmung; ~ **faith** blindes Vertrauen; ~ **interest** kalkulatorischer Zins; ~ **obedience** unbedingter (absoluter) Gehorsam; ~ **recognition** stillschweigende Anerkennung; ~ **trust** blindes Vertrauen.
implied vermittelt, gefolgert, sich aus den Umständen ergebend, stillschweigend, mutmaßlich;
  ~ **residually** stillschweigend inbegriffen;
  ~ **agreement** stillschweigende Vereinbarung; ~ **assumption** stillschweigende Annahme; ~ **authority** vermutete Vollmacht; ~ **condition** stillschweigende [Vertrags]bedingung; ~ **consent** stillschweigende Zustimmung; ~ **contract** konkludent abgeschlossener Vertrag; ~ **covenant** stillschweigend enthaltene Verpflichtung; ~ **duties** *(labo(u)r law)* stillschweigend eingeschlossene Pflichten des Arbeitnehmers; ~ **guarantee** gesetzliche Gewährleistung; ~ **intention** mutmaßlicher Parteiwille; ~ **licence** *(patent law, Br.)* zu vermutende Lizenzvergabe; ~

malice vermuteter Vorsatz; ~ **obligation** mitübernommene Verpflichtung; ~ **offer** mitvermutetes Angebot; ~ **powers** *(US pol.)* vermutete (implizierte, unterstellte) Befugnisse; ~ **terms** im Dienstvertrag mit eingeschlossene Rechte und Pflichten; ~ **trust** Kraft Gesetzes entstandenes Treuhandverhältnis; ~ **waiver** stillschweigender Verzicht; ~ **warranty** *(US)* gesetzliche Gewährleistung.
implore *(v.)* flehen, bitten;
  ~ **a judge for mercy** Richter um Gnade anflehen.
imply *(v.)* in sich einschließen, besagen, implizieren;
  ~ **consent** Zustimmung beinhalten.
impolicy unkluges Vorgehen.
impolitical unpolitisch, unüberlegt.
imponderables Imponderabilien.
import Einfuhr, Import, Auslandszufuhr, *(meaning)* Inhalt, Sinn;
  ~s Einfuhr[waren], Importartikel;
  capital ~ Kapitalimport, -einfuhr; **credit-based** ~s kreditabhängige Importe; **cut-price** ~s billige Importe; **direct** ~s unmittelbare Einfuhren; **food** ~ Nahrungs-, Lebensmitteleinfuhr; **free** ~ zollfreie Einfuhr; **higher-quality** ~s hochwertigere Einfuhren; **increased** ~s Einfuhrsteigerung; **indirect** ~s mittelbare Einfuhren; **invisible** ~s unsichtbare Einfuhr, passive Dienstleistungen; **low-priced** ~s billige Importe; **nonquota** ~s nicht kontingentierte Einfuhrartikel; **principal** ~s Haupteinfuhrwaren; **quota** ~s kontingentierte Einfuhren; **reduced-tariff** ~s zollermäßigte Importe; **token** ~s symbolische Importe (Einfuhren); **total** ~s Gesamteinfuhr; **visible** ~s sichtbare Einfuhren, Wareneinfuhr;
  ~s **from abroad** ausländische Einfuhren; ~ **on joint account** Einfuhr auf Partizipationsrechnung; ~ **of foreign capital** ausländische Kapitaleinfuhr; ~s **in excess of exports** Einfuhrüberschuß; **free** ~ **of goods** freie Wareneinfuhr; **clandestine** ~ **of goods** unerlaubte Wareneinfuhr; ~s **free of payment** unentgeltliche Einfuhren; ~ **of a statement** Bedeutung einer Erklärung;
  ~ *(v.)* importieren, [Waren] einführen;
  ~ **duty-free** zollfrei einführen; ~ **freely** ungehindert einführen; ~ **goods into a country** Waren in ein Land einführen; ~ **labo(u)r from another district** Arbeitskräfte aus anderen Bezirken herbeiholen;
  to book ~s sich Importe sichern; **to choke back** ~s Einfuhr drosseln; **to curb** ~s Einfuhr drosseln; **to decontrol** ~s Einfuhr liberalisieren; **to grasp the full** ~ **of words** volle Tragweite von Worten begreifen; **to impose** ~s *(US)* Importware zwecks Zollfestsetzung klassifizieren; **to increase** ~s Einfuhr erhöhen; **to restrict (slow down)** ~s Importe drosseln, Einfuhrtempo verlangsamen;
  ~ **agent** Import-, Einfuhragent; ~ **allocation** Einfuhrzuteilung; **auto** ~ **man** Autoimporteur; ~ **application** Einfuhrantrag; ~ **arrangement** Einfuhrregelung; ~ **authorization** Einfuhrbewilligung; ~ **ban** Einfuhrverbot; ~ **bar** Einfuhrhindernis; ~ **business** Importgeschäft; ~ **certificate** Einfuhrschein, Einfuhrunbedenklichkeitsbescheinigung; ~ **charges** *(EC)* Einfuhrabgaben; ~ **clearance** Einfuhrbescheinigung; ~ **commerce** Passivhandel; ~ **commission agent** Einfuhrkommissionär; ~ **control** Einfuhrkontrolle; ~ **credit** Import-, Einfuhrkredit; ~ **cuts** Einfuhrkürzungen; ~ **cutbacks** Import-, Einfuhrkürzungen; ~ **damage** Einfuhrnachteile; ~ **dealer** Einfuhrhändler, Importeur; ~ **department** Importabteilung; ~ **deposit** *(Br.)* Importdepot; ~ **duty** Einfuhrzoll, -abgabe; **to liquidate** ~ **duty** *(US)* Importabgabe endgültig aufheben; ~ **entitlement account** Einfuhrberechtigungskonto; ~ **entry** Einfuhrdeklaration; ~ **equalization fee (tax,** *US)* Einfuhrausgleichsabgabe; ~ **excise tax** *(US)* Einfuhrsteuer, -verbrauchsabgabe; ~ **factoring** Importfaktoring; ~ **figure** Einfuhrziffer; ~ **firm** Importhaus; ~ **free list** Freiliste zollfreier Gegenstände; ~ **gain** Importgewinn; ~ **gold point** Goldeinfuhrpunkt; ~ **goods** Einfuhrwaren; ~ **handicap** Einfuhrhemmnis; ~ **house** Importfirma; ~ **industry** Importindustrie; **to simplify** ~ **inspection requirements** Kontrollbestimmungen bei der Einfuhr vereinfachen; ~ **letter of credit** Importkreditbrief, -akkreditiv; ~ **levy** Einfuhrabgabe, *(EC)* Abschöpfungsbetrag; ~ **licence** Einfuhrbewilligung, Importgenehmigung, -lizenz; ~ **licensing** Importgenehmigungsverfahren; ~ **limitation** Einfuhrbegrenzung; ~-**limitation agreement** Einfuhrbegrenzungsabkommen; ~ **list** Einfuhrliste; ~ **markup** Einfuhraufschlag; ~ **merchandise** Einfuhrwaren; ~ **merchant** Importkaufmann, Einfuhrhändler; ~ **monopoly** Einfuhrmonopol; ~ **payment leads** vorrangig geleistete Zahlungen für Importe; ~ **permit** Einfuhrbewilligung, -genehmigung, -erlaubnis; ~ **price** Einfuhrpreis; ~ **procedure** Einfuhrverfahren; ~ **prohibition** Einfuhr-, Importverbot; ~ **quota** Einfuhr-

kontingent, Importquote; **to fix ~ quotas** Einfuhr kontingentieren; **~ rate** Einfuhrzoll; **~ reduction** Einfuhrrückgang; **~ regulations** Import-, Einfuhrbestimmungen; **to tighten ~ regulations** verschärfte Einfuhrbestimmungen erlassen; **~ requirements** Einfuhrbedarf, -bedürfnisse; **~ restraints** Einfuhrbeschränkungen; **~ restrictions** Beschränkung der Einfuhren, Import-, Einfuhrbeschränkungen; **to put on ~ restrictions** Einfuhrbeschränkungen einführen; **~ specie point** unterer Goldpunkt; **~ statistics** Einfuhrstatistik; **~ subsidy** Importsubvention; **~ surcharge** Einfuhrzusatzabgabe, Importabgabe; **~ surplus** Einfuhrüberschuß; **to switch off the ~ tap** Einfuhrhahn zudrehen; **~ tariff** Einfuhrzoll; **~ tide** Einfuhrwelle; **~ trade** Einfuhr-, Passiv-, Importhandel; **~ -geschäft; ~ trade bookseller** Importbuchhändler; **~ transaction** Einfuhr-, Importgeschäft; **~ trust receipt** Sicherungsübereignungsschein für Importware; **~ value** Einfuhrwert.

importability Einführbarkeit.

importable einführbar, importierbar.

importance Wichtigkeit, Bedeutung;
of ~ von Belang; **of secondary ~** von untergeordneter Bedeutung;
overriding ~ übermäßige Bedeutung;
to attach no ~ to keine Bedeutung (Gewicht) beimessen; **to be of basic ~** von grundlegender Bedeutung sein; **to be of secondary ~** nebensächliche Rolle spielen.

important wichtig, bedeutend;
very ~ person *(vip)* hochgestellte Persönlichkeit.

importation Import, Einfuhr, Zufuhr;
~s Einfuhrwaren, -artikel;
passed for temporary ~ vorübergehend zur Einfuhr zugelassen; **~ in bond** Einfuhr unter Zollverschluß; **~ of gold** Goldeinfuhr; **~ of goods** Wareneinfuhr; **~ of goods in minimum commercial quantities** Wareneinfuhr in handelsüblichen Mindestmengen.
to grant duty-free ~ zur Einfuhr zollfrei zulassen;
temporary ~ papers Zollpapiere für vorübergehende Einfuhr.

imported | from England aus England eingeführt;
~ articles (commodities, goods) Import-, Einfuhrwaren.

importer Importeur, Importkaufmann, Einfuhrhändler, Warenbezieher.

importing | country Import-, Einfuhrland; **~ firm (house)** Importfirma; **~ industry** Importindustrie.

importunate aufdringlich, lästig;
~ claims hartnäckige Forderungen.

importune *(v.)* behelligen, belästigen;
~ a husband for more money Ehemann dringend um mehr Geld bitten.

importunity Belästigung, Behelligung, Zudringlichkeit.

impose *(v.)* *(obligation)* auferlegen, aufbürden, verhängen, *(print.)* ausschießen, *(taxes)* auferlegen, ausschreiben;
~ upon s. o. jem. etw. aufdrängen (aufschwindeln);
~ charges Abgaben erheben; **~ one's company on s. o.** sich jem. aufdrängen; **~ conditions upon s. o.** jem. Bedingungen auferlegen; **~ new duties** neue Zollbestimmungen erlassen; **~ an embargo** Embargo verhängen; **~ a fine** auf eine Geldstrafe erkennen; **~ inferior goods upon s. o.** jem. minderwertige Ware aufdrängen; **~ upon s. one's kindness** jds. Güte mißbrauchen; **~ martial law** Kriegsrecht verhängen; **~ upon s. one's good nature** jds. Gutmütigkeit ausnutzen; **~ an obligation** Verpflichtung auferlegen; **~ a penalty on s. o.** gegen j. eine Strafe erkennen; **~ respect** Hochachtung abnötigen; **~ restrictions** Beschränkungen festsetzen; **~ sanctions** Sanktionen auferlegen; **~ silence on s. o.** jem. Stillschweigen auferlegen; **~ a tax on the people** neue Steuer einführen (erheben).

imposed from on high von oben aufgezwungen.

imposing repräsentativ;
~ display of knowledge imponierende Wissensdarbietung; **~ table** *(print.)* Metteurtisch.

imposition Auferlegung, Aufbürdung, Verhängung, *(imposture)* Betrug, Betrügerei, *(levy)* [öffentliche] Abgabe, Auflage, Steuer, *(overreaching)* Übervorteilung, *(print.)* Umbruch, *(school, Br.)* Strafbarkeit;
~ of martial law Verhängung des Kriegsrechtes, Kriegsrechtverhängung; **~ on s. one's kindness** Mißbrauch von jds. Güte; **~ of a penalty** Verhängung einer Strafe; **~ of taxes** Besteuerung, Steuerausschreibung.

impossibility, absolute absolute Unmöglichkeit; **manifest ~** offenbare Unmöglichkeit; **partial ~** teilweise Unmöglichkeit; **permanent ~** dauernde Unmöglichkeit; **practical ~** praktische Unmöglichkeit; **prior ~** ursprüngliche (anfängliche) Unmöglichkeit; **relative ~** Unvermögen; **supervening ~** nachträgliche Unmöglichkeit;

~ of performance of contract Unmöglichkeit der Vertragserfüllung.

impossible unmöglich, *(impracticable)* undurchführbar;
absolutely ~ absolut unmöglich; **legally ~** rechtlich unmöglich; **physically ~** materiell (physisch) unmöglich; **relatively ~** relativ unmöglich;
~ consideration unmögliche Vertragsleistung; **~ contract** unmöglicher Vertrag; **~ situation** unmögliche Situation;

impost Abgabe, Steuer, *(import duty)* Einfuhrzoll;
~s Gefälle;
~ (v.) (imports, US) Importware zwecks Zollfestsetzung klassifizieren.

imposter Hochstapler, Schwindler, Betrüger.

imposture Betrug, Betrügerei, Hochstapelei, Schwindel;
to make a living by lying and ~ sich durch Lug und Trug durchs Leben schlängeln.

impound *(v.)* in gerichtliche Verwahrung geben, mit Beschlag belegen, beschlagnahmen, sicherstellen;
~ a document Urkunde in gerichtliche Verwahrung nehmen; **~ stray cattle** verlassenes Vieh einsperren.

impoundage, impounding gerichtliche Verwahrung;
~ of contraband goods Beschlagnahme von Kontrabande.

impoverish *(v.)* verarmen, an den Bettelstab bringen;
~ a people Land verarmen lassen; **~ the soil** Boden erschöpfen.

impoverished | by doctors' bills durch Arztrechnungen fast am Bettelstab; **~ in men** menschenarm;
~ land ausgelaugter Boden; **the ~ state of my exchequer** meine kümmerlichen Finanzen.

impoverishment Verarmung, Aussaugung;
~ of the mind geistige Erschöpfung; **~ of the soil** Bodenerschöpfung, -auslaugung; **~ of the working class** Verelendung der Arbeiterklasse.

impracticability Unausführbarkeit, objektive Unmöglichkeit.

impracticable unaus-, undurchführbar, *(impassable)* unbefahrbar, unpassierbar;
~ idea nicht realisierbare Idee; **~ scheme** undurchführbarer Plan.

impregnable | arguments unwiderlegbare Argumente; **~ fortress** uneinnehmbare Festung.

impregnate *(v.)* imprägnieren.

impregnation Schwängerung, *(fig.)* Durchdringung, Befruchtung.

impresario Impresario.

imprescriptibility Unersitzbarkeit, Unverjährbarkeit.

imprescriptible unersitzbar, unverjährbar, nicht der Verjährung unterliegend.

impress Ausdruck, Stempel, Impressum, *(characteristic)* charakteristisches Merkmal;
~ (v.) Stempel aufdrücken, *(levy for public service)* beschlagnahmen, requirieren;
~ [o. s. on] s. o. j. beeindrucken, Eindruck auf jem. machen; **~ the railwaymen into military service** Eisenbahner dienstverpflichten; **~ s. o. unfavo(u)rably** ungünstigen Eindruck bei jem. hinterlassen; **~ sailors** Matrosen gewaltsam anwerben; **~ a seal upon s. th.** Siegel auf etw. aufdrücken;
to leave an ~ upon one's age seinem Zeitalter seinen Stempel aufdrücken;
~ copy Korrekturabzug.

impressed | seal Prägestempel; **~ stamp** eingedrucktes Postwertzeichen.

impression Eindruck, Wirkung, *(imprinting)* Aufdruck, *(print.)* Abdruck, Neudruck;
colo(u)red ~ Farbdruck; **foul ~** schlechter Abdruck; **fraudulent ~** unerlaubter Nachdruck, Raubdruck; **good ~** guter Abzug; **mat ~** Mattdruck; **new ~** neue, unveränderte Auflage; **proof ~** Probeabzug;
first ~ of 5000 copies Erstauflage von 5000 Stück; **~ of a seal** Siegelabdruck, -aufdruck;
to leave an ~ on s. o. Eindruck bei jem. zurücklassen; **to make a strong ~ on the House** im Parlament einen großen Eindruck hinterlassen.

impressive | scene packende Szene; **~ silence** eindrucksvolle Stille.

impressment gewaltsame Dienstverpflichtung, Zwangsrekrutierung, -verpflichtung.

imprest *(Br.)* Vorschuß [aus öffentlichen Mitteln];
~ (v.) (Br.) Vorschuß gewähren;
~ account *(Br.)* Spesen-, Vorschußkonto; **~ accountant** *(Br.)* Vorschußempfänger; **~ fund** *(Br.)* [Spesen]vorschuß, *(petty cash)* Bargeld-, Portokasse; **~ money** *(Br.)* Handgeld; **~ system** *(Br.)* bargeldloser Zahlungsverkehr.

imprimatur *(fig.)* Zustimmung, Billigung, *(print.)* Druck-erlaubnis.

imprint Aufdruck, Abdruck, *(fig.)* Gepräge, Stempel, *(print.)* Erscheinungs-, Druckvermerk, Pflichtandruck, Impressum; **no** ~ ohne Verlagsangabe; **printer's** ~ Angabe des Druckers; **publisher's** ~ Druckvermerk, Impressum;
~ *(v.) (stamp)* abdrucken, drucken, auf-, ein-, bedrucken;
~ **on one's memory** seinem Gedächtnis einprägen; ~ **a letter with a postmark** Briefstempel aufdrücken.

imprinting Herstellervermerk, Eindruck.

imprison *(v.)* verhaften, gefangensetzen, ins Gefängnis werfen, einsperren, inhaftieren, einbuchten.

imprisoned, to be im Gefängnis sitzen, inhaftiert (in Untersuchungshaft) sein;
person ~ Inhaftierter.

imprisonment Freiheitsentziehung, Festsetzung, Verhaftung, Inhaftierung, Haft, Gefangenhaltung;
under pain of ~ *(US)* bei einer Gefängnisstrafe von; **false** ~ unberechtigte Festnahme, Freiheitsberaubung; **life** ~ lebenslängliche Freiheitsstrafe; **ordinary** ~ Polizeihaft; ~ **for debt** Schuldhaft; ~ **in the second degree** Strafhaft; ~ **in the first division** Polizeihaft; ~ **with hard labo(u)r** *(US)* Zuchthausstrafe; ~ **for life** lebenslängliche Freiheitsstrafe; ~ **without the option of a fine** Gefängnisstrafe ohne Geldersatzstrafe; ~ **before trial** Untersuchungshaft;
to be liable for ~ sich einer Gefängnisstrafe aussetzen, mit Gefängnis bestraft werden; **to be sentenced to three years** ~ zu drei Jahren Gefängnis verurteilt werden; **to inflict** ~ auf eine Gefängnisstrafe erkennen; **to serve a sentence of** ~ Gefängnisstrafe absitzen.

improbation Feststellungsklage auf Unechtheit einer Urkunde.

improbity Unehrlichkeit.

impromptu Improvisation, *(speech)* Stegreifrede;
~ *(a.)* aus dem Stegreif, unvorbereitet, improvisiert;
to speak ~ aus dem Stegreif (unvorbereitet) sprechen;
~ **event** Improvisation; ~ **performance** Stegreifvorstellung; ~ **speech** unvorbereitete Rede, Stegreifansprache.

improper unrichtig, *(traffic)* verkehrswidrig, unvorschriftsmäßig, *(indecent)* anstandswidrig, ungebührlich, unsittlich, unanständig;
~ **conduct** ungehöriges Benehmen; ~ **cumulation of actions** unzulässige Klagenhäufung; ~ **dress** unpassende Bekleidung; ~ **fraction** unechter Bruch; ~ **influence** sittenwidrige Beeinflussung; ~ **language** unanständige Redeweise; ~ **navigation** fehlerhaftes Handeln an Bord; ~ **packing** unsachgemäße Verpackung; ~ **person** Mensch mit schlechtem Ruf; ~ **legal proceedings** unzuständiges Gerichtsverfahren; ~ **signalling** verkehrswidrige Blinkeranzeige; ~ **storage** fehlerhafte (unsachgemäße) Verstauung; ~ **use** mißbräuchliche Verwendung, unzulässiger Gebrauch; ~ **use of confidential information** Mißbrauch vertraulicher Kenntnisse; **to make** ~ **use** mißbrauchen.

improprieties, to commit sich unschicklich benehmen.

impropriety ungehöriges Benehmen, Ungehörigkeit.

improvability Verbesserungsfähigkeit, *(land)* Kultivierbarkeit.

improvable verbesserungsfähig, *(land)* kultivierbar, anbaufähig.

improve *(v.) (become better)* sich bessern, Fortschritte machen, *(make better)* verbessern, aufbessern, vervollkommnen, *(land)* kultivieren, melioren, *(market)* erholen, sich kräftigen, Aufschwung nehmen, *(refine)* veredeln, verfeinern, *(relations)* ausbauen, verbessern, *(rise)* steigen;
~ **an acquaintance** Bekanntschaft pflegen (kultivieren); ~ **away** durch Verbesserungsversuche verderben; ~ **away one's profits** seine Gewinne aufzehren; ~ **the conditions of the poor** bessere Lebensbedingungen für die Armen herbeiführen; ~ **considerably** bedeutenden Aufschwung nehmen; ~ **one's natural gifts by study** eine natürliche Begabung durch Lernen fördern; ~ **in health** seine Gesundheit festigen; ~ **on s. one's ideas** durch jds. Ideen gefördert werden; ~ **a lot by building on it** *(US)* Wertsteigerung eines Geländes durch Bebauung erzielen; ~ **in manners** sich durch bessere Manieren auszeichnen; ~ **on the mode of tillage** Kultivierungsmethode verbessern; ~ **the occasion** Gelegenheit ausnutzen; ~ **o. s. of an offer** sich ein Angebot zunutze machen; ~ **a property** Werterhöhungen an einem Grundstück vornehmen; ~ **industrial premises** Werterhöhungen auf Industriegrundstücken vornehmen; ~ **whole sections of a town** ganze Stadtteile sanieren; ~ **the shining hour** *(fam.)* von einer Gelegenheit profitieren; ~ **one's stocks of learning** seine Kenntnisse erweitern; ~ **in one's studies** sich vervollkommnen; ~ **one's time** seine Zeit gut nutzen; ~ **with use** bei der Benutzung an Wert gewinnen; ~ **the value** Wert erhöhen; ~ **in value** im Wert steigen; ~ **virgin land** Neuland kultivieren.

improved verbessert, vervollkommnet;
~ **goods** veredelte Erzeugnisse; ~ **health** gestärkte Gesundheit; ~ **land** melioriertes Land; ~ **site** erschlossenes Gelände.

improvement *(advance)* Steigen, Anziehen, Steigerung, Erholung, *(agriculture)* Bodenverbesserung, Melioration, *(betterment of building)* Verbesserung, Werterhöhung, *(economics)* Aufwärtsbewegung, -tendenz, *(increase)* Erhöhung, Vermehrung, *(law of patents)* Zusatzpatent, Patentverbesserung, *(progress)* Fortschritt, *(refining)* Veredelung, *(stock market)* Kursanstieg;
open to ~ kultivierungsfähig;
~s werterhöhende Aufwendungen, *(land)* Meliorationen; **allround** ~s Verbesserungen auf der ganzen Linie; **beneficial** ~s wertsteigernde Meliorationen; **far-reaching** ~s durchgreifende Verbesserungen; **the very latest** ~s allerletzte Verbesserungen; **local** ~s örtlich begrenzte Aufschließungsmaßnahmen, Ausbau von Gemeindeanlagen; **marked** ~ merkliche Besserung, entschiedener Fortschritt; **moral** ~ moralische Erklärung; **necessary** ~s werthaltende Gebäudeverbesserungen; **patentable** ~s patentfähige Verbesserungsvorschläge; **pension** ~s Verbesserung der Pensionsleistungen; **permanent** ~ dauernde Wertverbesserung; **price** ~s Preissteigerungen, *(stock exchange)* Kursaufbesserungen; **the so-called** ~s die sogenannten Errungenschaften; **social** ~ soziale Aufbauarbeit; **soil** ~ Meliorationen; **widely spread** ~ *(stock exchange)* Kursanstieg auf breiter Front; **street** ~ Straßenerschließung; **technological** ~s Verbesserungen nach dem Stand der Technik, entwicklungsbedingte Verbesserungen; **transportation and housing** ~ Verbesserung der Verkehrs- und Wohnungsbedingungen; **valuable** ~s werterhöhende Aufwendungen; **voluntary** ~ Verschönerungsarbeiten;
~ **in the balance of payments** Verbesserung der Zahlungsbilanz; ~s **of buildings** *(US)* bauliche Verbesserungen, Gebäudewerterhöhungen; ~s **of business premises** *(US)* Werterhöhungen von Geschäftsgebäuden; ~ **in climate** Klimaverbesserungen; ~ **in one's social conditions** gesellschaftlich verbesserte Stellung; ~s **in dwellings** Wohngebäudeverbesserungen; ~ **in earnings** Ertragsverbesserung; ~ **in health** Festigung der Gesundheit; ~ **of a house** Werterhöhung eines Hauses; ~s **in house buildings** Fortschritte im Wohnungsbau; ~ **of land** Meliorationen, Bodenverbesserung; ~ **in liquidity** Liquiditätsverbesserung; ~ **of an occasion** Wahrnehmung einer Gelegenheit; ~ **in pay** Gehaltsaufbesserung; ~ **in prices** Preiserhöhung, *(stock exchange)* Kursanstieg, -aufbesserung; ~ **in profits** verbesserte Gewinnsituation; ~ **in quality** Qualitätsverbesserung; ~ **in rates** Tarifverbesserung; ~ **of real estate** Werterhöhung eines Grundstücks; ~ **in roads** Straßenerneuerung, -verbesserung; **general** ~ **of whole sections** allgemeine Sanierung ganzer Stadtteile; ~ **in the situation** *(policy)* Lageverbesserung; ~ **in sterling exchange** Verbesserung im Pfundkurs; ~ **in stocks** Erholung der Aktienkurse; ~ **in trade** zunehmendes Geschäft; ~ **of the trade balance** Verbesserung der Handelsbilanz; ~ **in value** Erhöhung des Wertes, Werterhöhung; ~ **in the weather** Wetterverbesserung;
to be an ~ Fortschritt darstellen; **to be an** ~ **on** s. o. j. übertreffen; **to constitute a technical** ~ technischen Fortschritt darstellen; **to show signs of** ~ leichte Besserung aufweisen;
~ **area** *(Br.)* Erschließungs-, Sanierungsgebiet; **general** ~ **area** *(Br.)* für Hausmodernisierungen bestimmtes Sanierungsgebiet; **to set up industrial** ~ **areas** industrielle Sanierungsgebiete schaffen; ~ **bonds** *(US)* der Verbesserung öffentlicher Anlagen dienende Kommunalanleihe; ~ **company** Meliorationsunternehmen; ~ **course** Fortbildungskursus; ~ **factor** auf den Produktivitätszuwachs abgestellter jährlicher Lohnsteigerungsbetrag; **local** ~ **fund** Meliorationsfonds; ~ **grants** Instandsetzungszuschüsse, Wohngebäude-, Meliorationszuschüsse; ~ **industry** Veredelungswirtschaft; ~ **lease** *(New South Wales)* mit Meliorationsauflagen vergebene Pacht; ~ **loan** Meliorationskredit; ~ **mortgage bonds** *(US)* an zweiter und dritter Stelle gesicherte Schuldverschreibungen zur Erstellung öffentlicher Anlagen; ~ **notice** *(health service, Br.)* Verbesserungsauflage; ~ **patent** Vervollkommnungs-, Verbesserungs-, Zusatzpatent; ~ **purpose** Meliorationszweck; ~ **scheme** Abänderungsplan; ~ **trade** Veredelungsverkehr.

improver Anlernling, Praktikant, Volontär.

improvidence *(administrator)* Ungeeignetheit, Unzuverlässigkeit.

improvident unbedacht, leichtsinnig.

improving, to be aufwärts gehen; **to be** ~ **at the close** *(stock exchange)* sich bei den Schlußkursen erholen.

improvisation unvorbereiteter Veranstaltung, Improvisation.

improvisator Stegreifdichter.

improvise *(v.)* aus dem Boden stampfen, improvisieren.

improvised | bed Notbett; ~ **law** hastig zusammengestoppeltes Gesetz; ~ **meal** improvisierte Mahlzeit; ~ **speech** Stegreifrede.

imprudence Unvorsichtigkeit.

impugn *(v.)* anfechten, bestreiten;
~ **the character of a witness** Glaubwürdigkeit eines Zeugen in Zweifel ziehen; ~ **a claim** Forderung bestreiten; ~ **a piece of evidence** Beweisstück ablehnen.

impugnable bestreitbar, anfechtbar.

impugnment | of a claim Bestreiten einer Forderung; ~ **of a testimony** Bestreiten einer Zeugenaussage; ~ **of a witness** Zeugenablehnung.

impulse Antrieb, Auftrieb, Aufschwung, Drang, Anstoß, Impuls, Elan;
on the first ~ beim ersten Anblick;
charitable ~ wohltätige Anwandlung; **current** ~ Stromimpuls, -stoß; **irresistible (uncontrollable)** ~ *(insanity)* unwiderstehlicher Drang; **rash (sudden)** ~ unüberlegte Handlung; **vital** ~ Lebenselan;
~ **to trade** Aufschwung des Handels;
to act on ~ impulsiv handeln; **to act on the** ~ **of the moment** einer augenblicklichen Eingebung folgend handeln; **to do s. th. on a sudden** ~ einer plötzlichen Laune nachgehen; **to feel an irresistible** ~ unwiderstehlichen Drang verspüren; **to give an** ~ **to s. th.** Anstoß zu etw. geben; **to yield to** ~ sich verleiten lassen; ~ **buyer** Spontankäufer; ~ **buying** auf Grund plötzlicher Überlegung zustande gekommene Einkäufe, Impuls-, Spontan-, Stimmungskäufe; ~ **goods (items)** *(US)* spontan gekaufte Waren, Impulskaufgegenstände.

impulsion *(fig.)* Impuls, Anreiz, Anstoß;
to act at the ~ **of s. o.** auf jds. Anregung handeln.

impulsive impulsiv, leicht erregbar, gefühlsbeherrscht;
to be ~ **in one's actions** impulsiv handeln;
~ **nature** impulsives Temperament.

impunity Straflosigkeit, Straffreiheit;
with ~ straflos.

impure schmutzig, unsauber;
~ **air** unsaubere Luft; ~ **motive** unanständiges Motiv.

imputability Zurechenbarkeit.

imputable zurechenbar, zuschreibbar.

imputation Beschuldigung, Bezichtigung, Unterstellungen, Verdacht, Zurechnung;
defamatory ~ verleumderische Beschuldigung;
~ **of s. one's character** Angriff auf jds. Leumund; ~ **of payment** *(debtor)* Zweckbestimmung einer Zahlung;
to be under an ~ bezichtigt werden;
~ **system** *(corporation tax, Br.)* Anrechnungs-, Zurechnungssystem, Körperschaftssteueranrechnung.

impute *(v.)* zurechnen, beschuldigen, bezichtigen;
~ **an accident to the driver's carelessness** Unfall auf die Unvorsichtigkeit des Fahrers zurückführen; ~ **to an author** einem Autor zuschreiben; ~ **a crime to s. o.** jem. ein Verbrechen anlasten; ~ **a fault to s. o.** jem. einen Fehler anlasten; ~ **a tax** Steuer anrechnen.

imputed zugeschrieben;
~ **cost** kalkulatorische (nicht erfaßte) Kosten; ~ **interest** zugerechnete Zinsen; ~ **item** kalkulatorischer Posten; ~ **knowledge** unterstellte (fingierte) Kenntnis, Kennenmüssen; ~ **negligence** *(US)* zurechenbare (zu vertretende) Fahrlässigkeit Dritter; ~ **notice** zurechenbare Kenntnis; ~ **price** Schattenpreis; ~ **rent** kalkulatorische Miete; ~ **value** veranschlagter (abgeleiteter) Wert.

in innen, drinnen, *(additional)* als Zugabe, obendrein, *(Br.)* nach London, *(fashion)* in Mode, modern, *(mar.)* im Hafen, festgemacht, *(pol.)* an der Macht, am Ruder, *(possession)* im Besitz, *(train)* angekommen, da;
~**s** *(pol.)* Regierungspartei;
~**s and outs** *(fig.)* Feinheiten, Winkelzüge; **the** ~**s and outs of a house** alle Ecken und Winkel eines Hauses;
to be ~ *(candidate)* gewählt sein, *(pol.)* an der Macht sein, regieren, *(train)* gerade angekommen sein; **to be** ~ **for it** *(sl.)* dran sein; **to be** ~ **for s. th.** etw. zu gewärtigen haben; **to be** ~ **with s. o.** mit jem. auf vertrautem Fuß stehen; **to be always** ~ **and out of hospital** alle Nasen lang im Krankenhaus sein; **to be** ~ **with all the best people** glänzende Verbindungen haben; **to be** ~ **for a competition** sich an einem Wettbewerb beteiligen; **to be** ~ **and out of the market** *(US)* kurzfristige Börsenspekulationen durchführen; **to be** ~ **for a period of prosperity** glänzenden Zeiten entgegensehen; **to be well** ~ **on a deal** *(fam.)* die besten Chancen haben; **to be well** ~ **at headquarters** von höchster Stelle protegiert werden; **to know s. o.** ~ **and out** j. genauestens

kennen; **to be well** ~ **with s. o.** sich glänzend mit jem. verstehen; **to fall** ~ **with s. th.** mit etw. übereinstimmen; **to go** ~ **for s. th.** sich einer Sache unterziehen; **to know the** ~**s and outs of a matter** Affäre in allen Verästelungen kennen; **to throw** ~ als Zugabe gewähren;
~**-between** Zwischenhändler; ~**-and-**~ **breeding** Inzucht; ~**-clearer** *(Br.)* Bankbevollmächtigter im Verrechnungsverkehr; ~**-depth analysis** Tiefenanalyse; ~**-fighting** *(fig.)* Nahkampf; ~**-flight convenience** Flugkomfort; ~**-flight movie** während des Fluges gezeigter Film; ~**-flight service** Betreuung während des Fluges; ~**-going crowd** hereinströmende Menschenmenge; ~**-going tenant** übernehmender Pächter; ~**-grade salary decrease** tarifliche Niedereinstufung; ~**-hospital benefits** Krankenhausbeihilfen; ~**-house** *(US)* betriebseigen; ~**-house control** innerbetriebliche Überwachung; ~**-house consultant unit** betriebliche Beratergruppe; ~**-house fund** versicherungseigener Investmentsfonds; ~**-house rule** innerbetriebliche Richtlinien; ~**-law** *(coll.)* angeheirateter Verwandter; ~**-line engine** Reihenmotor; ~**-maintenance** Unterhaltung armer Krankenhauspatienten; ~ **party** Regierungspartei; ~**-plant** *(US)* innerbetrieblich; ~**-plant printing** *(US)* Hausdruckerei; ~**-plant shop** *(Br.)* Betriebs-, Werksladen; ~**-plant training** *(US)* Werkstattausbildung; ~**-service seminar** Betriebsseminar; ~**-service training** *(US)* innerbetriebliche Berufsförderung (Fortbildung); ~**-store promotion** *(US)* im Laden betriebene Verkaufsförderung; ~ **train** angekommener Zug.

inability Unvermögen, Unfähigkeit, *(law)* subjektive Unmöglichkeit;
in case of ~ im Unvermögensfall; **in case of** ~ **to pay** bei Zahlungsunfähigkeit;
legal ~ Rechtsunfähigkeit; **prospective** ~ voraussichtliches Unvermögen;
~ **of deciding in one's own case** Unvermögen in eigener Sache zu entscheiden; ~ **to pay** Zahlungsunfähigkeit; ~ **to perform** Unmöglichkeit der Leistung; ~ **to supply goods** Lieferunfähigkeit; ~ **to support o. s.** Erwerbsunfähigkeit.

inaccessibilty Unzugänglichkeit.

inacessible nicht betretbar, unzugänglich, *(person)* unnahbar;
~ **document** unerreichbare Urkunde.

inaccuracy Ungenauigkeit;
~ **of a translation** Ungenauigkeit einer Übersetzung.

inaccurate ungenau, falsch, unrichtig;
~ **account** unrichtiges Konto; ~ **copy** fehlerhafter Abdruck; ~ **information** ungenaue Angaben; ~ **statement** falsche Erklärung; ~ **translation** ungenaue Übersetzung.

inaccurately, to translate ungenau übersetzen.

inacquaintance mangelnde Bekanntschaft.

inaction Untätigkeit;
to be reduced to ~ zur Untätigkeit verurteilt sein.

inactive untätig, träge, *(business)* still, *(mil.)* nicht aktiv, außer Dienst, *(stock exchange)* flau, unbelebt, reserviert, lust-, umsatz-, geschäftslos;
~ **account** umsatzloses (totes) Konto; ~ **capital** brachliegendes Kapital; ~ **habits** müßige Gewohnheiten; ~ **market** lustlose Börse; ~ **money** gehortetes Geld; ~ **official** untätiger Beamter; ~ **securities** Effekten mit geringen Umsätzen; ~ **status** Wartestand.

inactivity Untätigkeit, *(business)* Stille, Flaute, *(stock exchange)* Flaute, Lustlosigkeit;
~ **market** ~ Lustlosigkeit der Börse; **masterly** ~ Politik des Gewährenlassens.

inadaptable nicht anpassungsfähig.

inadequacy Unangemessenheit, Mißverständnis, *(insufficiency)* Unzulänglichkeit;
~ **of a quorum** Beschlußunfähigkeit.

inadequate unangemessen, unzulänglich, nicht ausreichend, inadequat;
~ **of a quorum** beschlußunfähig;
to be ~ **to a purpose** dem Zweck nicht entsprechen;
~ **arrangement** unzureichende (jämmerliche) Organisation; ~ **consideration** unangemessene Gegenleistung; ~ **damages** durch Schadenersatz nicht gutzumachender Schaden; **to decide on** ~ **grounds** aufgrund magerer Beweise entscheiden; ~ **information** ungenügende Informationen; ~ **notice** unzureichende Benachrichtigung; ~ **organization** jämmerliche Organisation; ~ **price** völlig unzulänglicher Preis; ~ **remedy** *(common law)* ungeeigneter Rechtsbehelf; ~ **resources** nicht ausreichende (unzulängliche) Kapitalmittel; ~ **style** kümmerlicher Stil.

inadequately provided ungenügend ausgerüstet.

inadmissibilty Unzulässigkeit.

inadmissible unzulässig, unstatthaft;
~ **assets** *(excess profit tax, US)* steuerfreie Wertpapiere; ~ **evidence** nicht zugelassenes Beweismaterial; ~ **proposal** unannehmbarer Vorschlag.

inadmitted assets *(insurance accounting)* im Liquidationsfall geringwertige Anlagegüter.

inadvertence Sorglosigkeit, Unachtsamkeit.

inadvertent unbeabsichtigt, unabsichtlich, versehentlich;
~ **action** Zufallshandlung.

inadvertently versehentlich, aus Versehen.

inadvisable nicht empfehlenswert (ratsam).

inalienability Unübertragbarkeit, Unveräußerlichkeit.

inalienable unveräußerlich, unübertragbar.

inane fade, albern, geistlos;
~ **remark** geistlose Bemerkung.

inanimate schwunglos, fade, *(market)* flau, unbelebt, matt, lustlos;
~ **conversation** langweilige Unterhaltung.

inanimateness Schwunglosigkeit, *(market)* Flaute, Lustlosigkeit.

inappellable keine Berufung zulassend, unanfechtbar.

inapplicability Unanwendbarkeit.

inapplicable unanwendbar;
to be ~ entfallen.

inappreciable ganz geringfügig.

inapproachability Konkurrenzlosigkeit.

inapproachable konkurrenzlos.

inappropriate ungeeignet, unangemessen, unzweckmäßig;
~ **speech** deplazierte Rede.

inapt ungeeignet, untauglich.

inaptitude Ungeeignetheit, Untauglichkeit.

inarticulate undeutlich;
~ **with drink** sinnlos besoffen; ~ **with rage** vor Wut sprachlos.

inattention | to one's business Vernachlässigung seines Geschäfts;
to have fits of ~ zeitweise völlig weggetreten sein.

inaugural *(president, US)* Antrittsrede;
~ **address** *(US)* Übernahme-, Antrittsrede; ~ **ceremonies** Eröffnungs-, Einweihungsfeierlichkeiten; ~ **convention** Gründerparteitag; ~ **flight** Jungfernflug; ~ **issue** Erstausgabe; ~ **lecture** Antrittsvorlesung; ~ **speech** Antrittsrede.

inaugurate *(v.)* einweihen, -setzen, inaugurieren, eröffnen;
~ **an air service** Fluglinienverkehr aufnehmen; ~ **a building** Gebäude seiner Bestimmung übergeben; ~ **a new era in travel** neue Reisemöglichkeiten erschließen; ~ **a fête** Fest aus der Taufe heben; ~ **a life insurance** Lebensversicherung abschließen; ~ **a monument** Denkmal enthüllen; ~ **a new policy** neue Politik einleiten; ~ **the President of the United States** Präsidenten der USA in sein Amt einführen; ~ **reforms** Reformen einführen; ~ **a ship canal** Schiffahrtskanal einweihen; ~ **a new system** neues Verfahren einführen.

inauguration *(building)* Einweihung, Eröffnung, *(monument)* Enthüllung, *(office)* Amtseinsetzung;
~ **of a new policy** Einleitung einer neuen Politik; ~ **of the President of the USA** Amtseinführung des amerikanischen Präsidenten;
~ **address** Antrittsrede; ~ **Day** *(US)* Amtseinführung.

inauspicious moment ungünstiger Moment.

inboard im Schiffsraum befindlich;
to take the anchor ~ Anker an Bord nehmen;
~ **cargo** Innenladung.

inborn angeboren.

inbound auf der Heimfahrt befindlich;
~ **common** nicht eingefriedete Almende; ~ **ship** für den Heimathafen bestimmtes Schiff.

inbred angeboren.

incalculability Unberechenbarkeit.

incalculable unberechenbar, *(of persons)* unzuverlässig;
~ **loss** unermeßlicher Verlust.

incandescent lamp Glühlampe.

incapability Unfähigkeit, Untauglichkeit, *(law)* Geschäftsunfähigkeit;
~ **to commit a crime** Strafunmündigkeit; ~ **of being elected** Wahlunfähigkeit; ~ **of giving evidence** Zeugnisunfähigkeit; ~ **of holding public office** Unfähigkeit zur Bekleidung öffentlicher Ämter; ~ **of making a will** Testierunfähigkeit; ~ **of succeeding to an estate** Erbunfähigkeit; ~ **to work** Arbeitsunfähigkeit.

incapable ungeeignet, untauglich, unfähig;
permanently ~ *(law)* dauernd geschäftsunfähig;
~ **of acting** handlungsunfähig; ~ **of acting in law** geschäftsunfähig; ~ **of crime** strafunmündig; ~ **of deception** des Betrugs nicht fähig; ~ **of being elected** passiv wahlunfähig; ~ **of giving evidence** zeugnisunfähig; ~ **of entering into contract** vertragsunfä-

hig; ~ **of holding public office** unfähig zur Bekleidung eines öffentlichen Amtes; ~ **of improvement** nicht [mehr] verbesserungsfähig; ~ **of making a will** testierunfähig; **declared ~ of managing one's own affairs** geschäftsunfähig, entmündigt; ~ **of managing one's own affairs in some jurisdictions** beschränkt geschäftsfähig; ~ **of proof** nicht beweisbar; ~ **of reparation** nicht wiedergutzumachen; ~ **of succeeding to an estate** erbunfähig; ~ **of (to) work** arbeitsunfähig, erwerbsunfähig;
to be ~ of managing one's own affairs seine eigenen Angelegenheiten nicht mehr besorgen können; **to be ~ of repair** nicht mehr repariert werden können; **to have s. o. declared ~ of managing his own affairs** j. entmündigen (für geschäftsunfähig) erklären lassen;
~ **child** unmündiges Kind.

incapacitate unfähig machen, *(deprive of legal requisites)* für unfähig erklären, disqualifizieren;
~ **s. o.** *(law)* j. entmündigen.

incapacitated arbeitsunfähig, *(legally incapable)* entmündigt, geschäftsunfähig;
temporarily ~ vorübergehend nicht arbeitsfähig;
to become permanently ~ dauernd erwerbsunfähig werden;
partly ~ person Person mit verminderter Erwerbsfähigkeit; ~ **person** Geschäftsunfähiger, Entmündigter; ~ **worker** arbeitsunfähig gewordener Arbeiter, Invalide, Erwerbsunfähiger.

incapacitation *(law)* Aberkennung der Rechtsfähigkeit, Entmündigung;
~ **for work** Arbeitsunfähigkeit.

incapacity Untüchtigkeit, Unfähigkeit;
legal ~ mangelnde (beschränkte) Geschäftsfähigkeit, Rechtsunfähigkeit; **mental ~** Geschäftsunfähigkeit wegen Geisteskrankheit; **partial ~** Teilinvalidität; **permanent ~** dauernde Erwerbsunfähigkeit; **total ~** Vollinvalidität, Erwerbsunfähigkeit;
~ **to act in law** Geschäftsunfähigkeit; ~ **to contract** Geschäftsunfähigkeit; ~ **through drunkenness** Geschäftsunfähigkeit wegen Volltrunkenheit; ~ **for employment** Arbeits-, Erwerbsunfähigkeit; ~ **to inherit** Erbunfähigkeit; ~ **of a staff** Untauglichkeit des Personals; ~ **to sue** mangelnde Aktivlegitimation, fehlende Prozeßfähigkeit, Prozeßunfähigkeit; ~ **for making a will** Testierunfähigkeit; ~ **to work** Arbeits-, Erwerbs-, Berufs-, Dienstunfähigkeit;
to be under some personal ~ to sue nicht prozeßfähig sein, keine Prozeßfähigkeit besitzen.

incarcerate *(v.)* einsperren, inhaftieren.

incarceration Inhaftierung, Freiheitsentzug.

incendiarism Brandstiftung, *(fig.)* Aufwiegelung.

incendiary Brandstifter, *(mil.)* Brandbombe;
~ *(a.)* brandstifterisch, *(fig.)* aufwieglerisch, aufrührerisch;
~ **bomb** Brandbombe; ~ **fire** Feuer durch Brandstiftung; ~ **loss** auf Brandstiftung beruhender Schaden; ~ **letter** *(Scot.)* Drohbrief; ~ **material** Brandmaterial; ~ **newspaper article** Hetzartikel; ~ **speech** Hetzrede.

incentive [Leistungs]anreiz, Antrieb, Ansporn, *(finance)* Anreizeffekt, *(salesman)* Leistungsprämie;
buying ~ Kaufanreiz; **output-oriented ~** produktionsbezogene Prämie; **profit-sharing ~** Gewinnbonus;
~ **to crime** Antrieb zum Verbrechen; ~ **to invest** Investitionsanreiz; ~ **for saving** Sparanreiz; ~ **to work** Arbeitsanreiz;
to lack ~ *(market)* lustlos sein;
~ *(a.)* anspornend, antreibend;
to carry ~ arrangements besondere Leistungsprämien einschließen; ~ **bonus** Leistungszulage, Prämie; **to extend ~ coverage** Leistungsentlohnung ausdehnen; ~ **operation** Akkordarbeit; ~ **pay** Leistungslohn, Mehrverdienst; ~ **pay agreement** Leistungslohnabkommen; ~ **pay figuration** Leistungslohnerrechnungen; ~ **plan** spezielles Leistungsprämiensystem, Prämienwesen; ~ **premium** Gratiskupon, Anreizprämie; ~ **program(me)** Prämienprogramm; ~ **rate** Leistungslohnsatz; ~ **rebate** Anspornrabatt; ~ **taxation** zyklisches Steuersystem; ~ **wage** Leistungs-, Erfolgslohn; ~ **wage plan (system)** Leistungslohnsystem, -entlohnung, leistungsbezogenes Entlohnungssystem.

incept *(v.)* *(habilitate)* sich habilitieren;
~ **in arts** sich zum M. A. qualifizieren.

inception Beginn, Anfang, *(Cambridge)* Qualifikation zum M. A., *(habilitation)* Habilitation, Habilitierung, *(suit in court)* Prozeßbeginn;
~ **of an enterprise** Gründung eines Unternehmens; ~ **of a product** Herstellungsbeginn eines Erzeugnisses;
~ **date of a policy** Beginn der Versicherungslaufzeit.

incessant | rain Dauerregen; ~ **worries** unaufhörlicher Verdruß.

inch *(advertisement)* Anzeigengrundmaß, *(fig.)* Kleinigkeit, Bißchen;
by ~es Schritt für Schritt; **within an ~** um ein Haar;
every ~ a soldier jeder Zoll ein Soldat;
~ (a.) zollbreit, -dick;
~ (v.) open a door Tür Spalt breit öffnen; **~ one's way forward** zentimeterweise vorankommen;
to be within an ~ of fight knapp vor einer Prügelei stehen; **not to depart an ~ from s. one's orders** jds. Anweisungen bis zum I-Tüpfelchen ausführen; **to dispute the ground ~ by ~** sich detailliert auseinander setzen, Punkt für Punkt ausdiskutieren; **not to give way an ~** keinen Fußbreit weichen; **to know every ~ of the neighbo(u)rhood** Nachbarschaft wie seine Hosentasche kennen.
inched staff Zollstock.
inchmeal zollweise, Schritt für Schritt;
to take a town ~ Stadt stückchenweise (in Etappen) erobern.
inchoate angefangen, unvollständig, rudimentär;
~ agreement einseitig unterzeichneter Vertrag; **~ bill of exchange** noch nicht vollständig ausgefülltes Wechselformular; **~ cheque** *(Br.)* nicht fertig ausgefüllter Scheck; **~ crime** nicht vollendetes Verbrechen, unvollendete Straftat; **~ instrument** unvollständige Urkunde, *(Br.)* Blankoakzept; **~ interest** Anwartschaftsrecht; **~ right** Anwartschaftsrecht, *(patent law)* angemeldetes Patentrecht; **~ right of dowry** Anwartschaft auf das Witwenpflichtteilsrecht; **~ stage** Anfangsstadium; **~ state** in Entstehung begriffener Staat.
inchoateness Anfangsstadium.
incidence *(distribution)* Ausdehnung, Verbreitung, Verteilung, *(ore, oil)* Vorkommen, Häufigkeit, *(range of influence)* Wirkungs-, Einflußbereich, -gebiet;
tax ~ Steuerwirkung;
~ of a duty Steueranfall; **~ of gold** Goldvorkommen; **~ of loss** Schadenshäufigkeit, -anfall; **~ of a tax** Auswirkung einer Steuer, Steuerbelastung, -anfall, -wirkung; **~ of taxation** Steueranfall, -wirkung, -inzidenz.
incident zufälliges Ereignis, Zufall, Begebenheit, Vorfall, Vorkommnis, Nebenumstand, Begleiterscheinung, *(law)* Nebensache, *(pol.)* Zwischenfall;
air ~ Luftzwischenfall; **frontier ~** Grenzzwischenfall; **~s of a journey** Reisezwischenfälle;
to hear of an ~ von einem Vorfall Kenntnis bekommen;
~ (a.) vorkommend, *(law)* abhängig, gehörig;
~ in the diplomatic service mit den Verpflichtungen im diplomatischen Dienst zusammenhängend;
to be ~ to a piece of land mit einem Grundstück verbunden sein.
incidental gelegentlich, beiläufig, zufällig, nebensächlich, nebenher entstanden;
~ upon folgend auf; **~ to employment** *(risk)* berufsgebunden; **~ to a journey** reiseüblich;
to be ~ verbunden sein, dazugehören; **to be ~ to the normal activity of a business** im Rahmen des üblichen Geschäftsverkehrs liegen;
~ acquaintance Gelegenheitsbekanntschaft; **~ earnings** Nebenverdienst; **~ expenses** Nebenausgaben, -kosten; **~ expenses of production** unproduktive Kosten; **~ income** Nebeneinkommen; **~ meeting** Zufallstreffen; **~ music to play** Bühnen-, Filmmusik; **~ plea of defence** *(Br.)* *(defense, US)* Verteidigungseinwand; **~ powers** dazugehörige Befugnisse, der Satzung nach zustehende Vollmachten; **~ profit** Nebengewinn; **~ provisions** Nebenbestimmungen; **~ receipts** Nebeneinkünfte; **~ remark** gelegentliche Bemerkung, Zwischenbemerkung.
incidentals unvorhergesehene Ausgaben, Nebenkosten, -ausgaben.
incinerate *(v.)* einäschern, verbrennen.
incineration Einäscherung, Feuerbestattung.
incinerator Verbrennungsofen, Verbrennungsanlage.
municipal ~ kommunale Müllverbrennungsanlage.
incisive criticism beißende Kritik.
incite *(v.)* anstiften, verleiten, aufhetzen;
~ s. o. to a crime j. zu einem Verbrechen anstiften; **~ a riot** zur Aufruhr anstiften; **~ s. o. to work** j. zur Arbeit antreiben; **~ workmen against their masters** *(Br.)* Arbeiter gegen ihre Arbeitgeber aufhetzen.
incitement Anregung, Triebfeder, *(instigation)* Anstiftung, Aufhetzung.
inciter Antreiber.
incivility Unhöflichkeit.
incivism mangelnder Bürgersinn, Unbotmäßigkeit.
inclearing *(cheque, Br.)* gesamter Abrechnungsbetrag.

inclination Zug, Neigung, Hang, Vorliebe;
~ to buy Kaufneigung, -lust, -interesse; **~ to duty** angeborenes Pflichtgefühl; **~ to invest** Investitions-, Anlagebereitschaft; **~ to merge** Fusionsneigung; **~ to sell** Verkaufs-, Abgabeneigung;
to follow only one's own ~s nur seinen Neigungen leben; **to have an ~ towards s. o.** Zuneigung für j. empfinden.
incline Gefälle, *(railway)* Ablaufberg;
~ (v.) Neigung haben, geneigt sein;
~ one's ear to s. o. *(fig.)* jem. sein Ohr leihen; **~ lower** im Preis niedriger werden; **~ to pity** mitleidig gestimmt sein; **~ to rise** *(market)* zur Festigkeit neigen; **~ one's steps towards a place** seine Schritte zu einer Stelle lenken.
inclined **to buy** aufnahmefähig, kaufwillig;
to be ~ to fall *(prices)* zur Schwäche neigen; **to be favo(u)rably ~ towards s. th.** einer Sache wohlwollend gegenüberstehen; **to be well ~ towards s..o.** jem. äußerst wohlgesonnen sein; **to feel ~** disponiert (geneigt) sein;
~ plane schiefe Ebene; **~ railway** *(US)* Standseilbahn.
inclose *(v.)* [als Anlage] beifügen, beilegen, *(encompass)* einengen, umgeben;
~ a jury Geschworene einschließen.
inclosed herewith an-, beiliegend.
inclosed land umfriedetes Grundstück.
inclosure Anlage, Beilage, *(right of common, Br.)* Befreiung von der Allmendepflicht;
~s *(US)* Landeinfriedungen.
~ Act *(Br.)* Gesetz über die Privatisierung von Gemeindeland.
include *(v.)* einbeziehen, einschließen, umfassen, enthalten, [mit]einrechnen;
~ in the agenda auf die Tagesordnung setzen; **~ s. o. among one's friends** j. zu seinen Freunden zählen; **~ in a report** in einem Bericht mit aufnehmen; **~ in one's will** in seinem Testament bedenken.
included mitinbegriffen, einschließlich;
not ~ nicht mitinbegriffen; **not ~ in the price** im Preis nicht eingeschlossen; **breakfast is not ~** Frühstück ist nicht eingerechnet;
postage ~ einschließlich Porto.
including einschließlich, inbegriffen, inklusive;
~, up to and einschließlich und bis zu;
~ all charges alle Kosten eingeschlossen, einschließlich aller Spesen.
inclusion Einbeziehung, -schließung, *(min.)* Einschluß;
~ in the agenda Aufnahme in die Tagesordnung; **~ of conditions** Aufnahme von Bedingungen; **~ of a word in a dictionary** Aufnahme eines Wortes in ein Wörterbuch.
inclusive einschließlich, eingerechnet, inklusiv;
~ of interest Zinsen einschließlich;
~ charge Gesamtgebühr; **~ price** Pauschalpreis; **~ sum** Globalbetrag; **~ survey** allgemeine Vermessung; **~ terms** *(at a hotel)* alles inbegriffen.
incognito Inkognito, unerkannt, unter fremdem Namen;
to preserve one's ~ sein Inkognito nicht lüften; **to travel ~** unter fremdem Namen reisen.
incognizance Unkenntnis.
incoherence Unvereinbarkeit, Widersprüche.
incoherent unzusammenhängend.
income Einkommen, Einnahmen, Einkünfte, *(investment fund)* Erträge, Erträgnisse;
accrued ~ *(balance sheet)* antizipative Erträge; **accumulated ~** *(trust)* thesaurierte Einkünfte; **actual ~** tatsächlich erzieltes Einkommen, tatsächliche Einkünfte; **additional ~** zusätzliches Einkommen, Nebeneinkünfte, -einnahmen, -einkommen; **adjusted gross ~** *(US)* steuerpflichtiges Bruttoeinkommen; **aggregate ~** Gesamteinkommen; **annual ~** Jahreseinkommen, -ertrag; **guaranteed annual ~** garantiertes Jahreseinkommen; **assessable ~** *(US)* steuerpflichtiges (veranlagungspflichtiges) Einkommen; **assured ~** sicheres (festes) Einkommen; **average ~** Durchschnittseinkommen; **big ~** hohes Einkommen; **bunched ~** längerfristig in einem Steuerjahr anfallendes Einkommen; **business ~** Einkünfte aus Gewerbebetrieb, Geschäftseinnahmen; **per capita ~** pro-Kopf Einkommen; **cash ~** Bareinnahmen; **casual ~** Nebeneinkünfte; **charitable ~** Einkünfte aus wohltätigen Spenden; **clear ~** Nettoeinkommen; **consumer ~** Verbrauchereinkommen; **corporate ~** *(US)* Gesellschaftseinkommen; **current ~** im Rechnungsjahr anfallendes Einkommen; **deferred ~** *(accounting, US)* im voraus eingegangene Erträge, antizipatorische Passiva, Rechnungsabgrenzungsposten; **accrued expense and deferred ~** *(balance sheet, US)* Rechnungsabgrenzungsposten; **dependable ~** verläßliches (sicheres) Einkommen; **derived ~** abgeleitetes Ein-

kommen; **discretionary** ~ frei verfügbares Einkommen; **disposable personal** ~ *(social accounting, US)* frei verfügbarer Einkommensanteil nach Steuern, Nettoeinkommen nach Steuerabzug; **distributable** ~ zur Ausschüttung kommende Erträge; **dividend** ~ Dividendenerträgnisse; **domestic** ~ Inlandseinkünfte; **earned** ~ Erwerbseinkommen, Einkünfte aus gewerblicher Tätigkeit; **entire** ~ Gesamteinkommen; **estate** ~ *(Br.)* Einkünfte aus Land- und Forstwirtschaft; **exempt** ~ steuerfreies Einkommen; **excess preference** ~ überprozentuale Sondereinkünfte; **extra** ~ Nebeneinkünfte; **extraneous** ~ Fremderträge; **extraordinary** ~ außerordentliche Einnahmen; **extraordinary and outside** ~ *(balance sheet)* außerordentliche und betriebsfremde Erträge; **family** ~ Familieneinkommen; **farm** ~ Einkünfte aus Land- und Forstwirtschaft; **fast-mounting** ~ rasch steigendes Einkommen; **financial** ~ Finanzerträge; **fixed** ~ festes (ständiges) Einkommen; **foreign** ~ ausländische Einkünfte; **government[al]** ~ Staatseinkünfte; **gross** ~ Roh-, Reineinnahme, Bruttoeinkommen; **guaranteed** ~ garantiertes Einkommen; **hard-currency** ~ harte Deviseneinnahmen; **high** ~ hohes Einkommen; **individual** ~ Privateinnahmen, -einkünfte; **industrial** ~ Einkünfte aus Gewerbebetrieb; **interest** ~ Zinserträgnisse; **investment** ~ Einkommen aus Kapitalvermögen, Kapitaleinkünfte, *(insurer's dividend)* Gewinnbeteiligung; **franked investment** ~ *(Br.)* körperschaftssteuerfreie Kapitalerträge; **fairly large** ~ höheres Einkommen; **larger** ~ höheres Einkommen; **life** ~ lebenslängliches Einkommen; **low** ~ niedriges Einkommen; **maximum relevant** ~ für die Körperschaftssteuerberechnung infragekommendes Höchsteinkommen; **middle-bracket** ~ mittleres Einkommen; **miscellaneous** ~ vermischte Einkünfte, Einkommen verschiedenster Art, sonstige Einkünfte; **mixed** ~ Einkünfte aus selbständiger und nichtselbständiger Arbeit; **money** ~ Geldeinnahmen; **national** ~ Sozialprodukt, Volkseinkommen; **net** ~ reiner Nettoüberschuß, Reineinkommen, Nettoeinkommen, -einnahme; **per capita net** ~ Nettoeinkommen pro Kopf der Bevölkerung; **net operating** ~ Betriebsreineinnahme; **net-of-tax-**~ einkommensteuerfreie Einkünfte; **nominal** ~ Nominaleinkommen; **nonfranked** ~ *(Br.)* Kapitalerträge vor Steuerabzug; **nonoperating** ~ *(balance sheet)* betriebsfremde Erträgnisse; **nonrecurring** ~ unregelmäßiges Einkommen, einmalige Erträgnisse; **nontaxable** ~ steuerfreies Einkommen; **nontrading** ~ nicht gewerbsmäßige Einkünfte; **occupational** ~ Einkünfte aus selbständiger Arbeit (freiberuflicher Tätigkeit); **omitted** ~ bei der Steuererklärung nicht aufgeführte Einkünfte; **operating** ~ Betriebseinnahmen, betriebliche Einkünfte; **original** ~ Anfangseinkommen; **other** ~ *(balance sheet)* sonstige Einkünfte; **outside** ~ Nebeneinkünfte; **overseas** ~ überseeische Einkünfte; **periodic** ~ *(balance sheet)* periodenfremde Erträge; **permanent** ~ ständige Einkünfte, festes Einkommen; **personal** ~ Privateinkünfte, Einkünfte natürlicher Personen; **preference** ~ steuerlich begünstigte Einkünfte; **premium** ~ Prämieneinnahmen; **prepaid** ~ *(balance sheet)* antizipatorische Passiva, im voraus eingegangene Erträgnisse; **pretax** ~ Einkommen vor [Abzug der] Steuern, Brutto-, Vorsteuereinkommen, unversteuertes Einkommen; **principal** ~ Haupteinkommen; **professional** ~ Einkünfte aus freiberuflicher Tätigkeit; **property** ~ Einkünfte aus Land- und Forstwirtschaft; **real** ~ Real-, Effektiveinkommen; **realized** ~ tatsächlich verbrauchtes Einkommen; **regular** ~ festes (regelmäßiges) Einkommen, regelmäßige Einkünfte; **relevant** ~ zu Steuerzwecken festgesetzte Einkünfte; **rent[al]** ~ Mieteinnahmen; **retained** ~ *(US)* unverteilter Reingewinn, stehengelassener (thesaurierter) Gewinn, Gewinnrücklage; **retirement** ~ Versorgungs-, Pensionsbezüge, Ruhegehalt, -geldbezüge; **scanty** ~ knappes Einkommen; **self-employment** ~ Einkünfte aus selbständiger Tätigkeit; **settled** ~ festes Einkommen; **similar** ~ ähnliche Erträge; **sinking-fund** ~ Erträge des Amortisationsfonds; **small** ~ geringes Einkommen; **spendable** ~ für Ausgaben [frei] zur Verfügung stehendes Einkommen, Nettoeinkommen; **stable** ~ wertbeständiges Einkommen; **statutory** ~ [dreijähriges] Durchschnittseinkommen; **steady** ~ regelmäßige Einkünfte; **subsidiary** ~ Nebeneinkünfte; **sufficient** ~ ausreichendes Einkommen; **surplus** ~ überschüssiger Gewinn; **tax-exempt** ~ steuerfreie Einkünfte; **taxable** ~ steuerpflichtiges Einkommen; **taxed** ~ versteuertes Einkommen; **total** ~ Gesamteinkommen; **total joint** ~ gemeinsames Gesamteinkommen; **total net** ~ Jahreseinkommen; **trading** ~ Einkünfte aus Gewerbebetrieb, Gewerbeertrag; **unearned** ~ *(accounting)* antizipatorische Passiva, im voraus eingegangene Erträge, *(investment)* Kapital-, arbeitsloses (fundiertes) Einkommen, Kapitalertrag, Vermögenseinkünfte; **unbudgeted** ~ außerplan-

mäßige Einnahmen; **unfranked [investment]** ~ *(Br.)* der Körperschaftssteuer unterliegende Kapitalerträge; **unrelated business** ~ *(settlement)* steuerpflichtiger Einkommensteil; **untaxable** ~ steuerfreies Einkommen; **wage** ~ Erwerbseinkommen, Einkünfte aus nicht selbständiger Tätigkeit; **wife's** ~ Einkünfte aus selbständiger Tätigkeit; **wife's earned** ~ Erwerbseinkommen der Ehefrau; **yearly** ~ Jahreseinkommen;

net ~ **from abroad** auswärtige Nettoeinkünfte; ~ **from affiliates** Erträge von Tochtergesellschaften, Erträge aus Beteiligungen; ~ **arising in the United Kingdom** in England anfallendes Einkommen; ~ **in arrears** rückständige Einkünfte; ~ **due to a bankrupt** dem Gemeinschuldner zustehende Einkünfte; ~ **in the $ 15.000 - 20.000 bracket** Einkommen zwischen 15.000 und 20.000 Dollar; ~ **from buildings and landed property (real estate)** Einkünfte aus unbeweglichem Vermögen; ~ **from a business** Gewerbeertrag; **gross** ~ **from business** gewerbliches Bruttoeinkommen; ~ **from business and property** gewerbliche Einkünfte und solche aus Vermögensnutzung; ~ **from a camping site** Zeltplatzeinkünfte; ~ **per capita** pro Kopf-Einkommen; ~ **from capital [investment]** Einkünfte aus Kapitalvermögen, Gewinn aus Kapitalanlagen; ~ **from a carpark** Parkplatzeinnahmen; ~ **not charged under any other heading** *(income-tax form, Br.)* sonstige Einkünfte; ~ **from a ghostwritten column** Einkünfte aus einer von Dritten verfaßten Zeitungskolumne; ~ **received under deduction of tax at sources** der Quellenbesteuerung unterliegende Einkünfte (Erträge); ~ **from dividends** Dividendenerträgnisse, -einkünfte; ~ **from employment** Einkünfte aus nichtselbständiger Tätigkeit; ~ **subject to exchange control** den Devisenbeschränkungen unterliegende Einkünfte; ~ **of a fund** Fondserträge; ~ **from a garage** Einkünfte aus der Vermietung von Garagenplätzen; ~ **from instalment sales** Einkünfte aus Abzahlungsgeschäften; ~ **from interest** Zinserträge, Kapitaleinkünfte; ~ **from investments** Erträge aus Beteiligungen, Einkünfte aus Anlagevermögen (Kapitalvermögen); ~ **from other investments** Erträge aus anderen Finanzanlagen; ~ **received in kind** Naturaleinkommen; ~ **issuing out of land** Einkünfte aus Grund und Boden; ~ **from occupation of lands** *(Br.)* Einkünfte aus Land- und Forstwirtschaft; ~ **for life** Einkommen auf Lebenszeit; ~ **commensurate with one's needs** die Lebensbedürfnisse deckendes Einkommen; ~ **of nonrecurring nature** außergewöhnliche Erträge; ~ **arising from any office or employment of profit** Einkünfte aus nichtselbständiger Arbeit; ~ **from ownership of land** *(US)* Einkünfte aus Eigentum an Grund und Boden, grundsteuerpflichtige Einkünfte; ~ **arising from participation in the capital and profits of a company** Einkünfte aus Kapital- und Gewinnanteilen einer Gesellschaft; ~ **received from pensions** Versorgungs-, Pensionsbezüge, Ruhegehalt; ~ **from profession or vocation** *(Br.)* Einkünfte aus selbständiger Arbeit (freiberuflicher Tätigkeit); ~ **from profit transfer agreements** Erträge aus Gewinnabführungsverträgen; ~ **of property** Vermögenseinkünfte; ~ **derived from landed property** Einkünfte aus Land- und Forstwirtschaft; ~ **from real property** *(double taxation)* Einkommen aus unbeweglichem Vermögen (aus Eigentum in Land- und Forstwirtschaft); ~ **from rents and profits of land** Einkünfte aus Vermietung und Verpachtung; ~ **from sales** Umsatzerlöse, Veräußerungswinne; ~ **from scholarship** Einkünfte aus einem Stipendium; ~ **from securities** *(income-tax form, Br.)* Einkünfte aus Kapitalvermögen (Wertpapierbeständen); ~ **from foreign securities** Erträge von auswärtigen Wertpapieren; ~ **from self-employment** *(Br.)* Einkünfte aus selbständiger Tätigkeit; ~ **received from social insurance** Bezüge aus der Sozialversicherung; ~ **from service transactions** Erträge aus Dienstleistungen; ~ **from subsidiaries** Erträgnisse aus Beteiligungen; ~ **from surrender-of-profits agreements** Erträge aus Gewinnabführungsverträgen; ~ **before** ~ **taxes** Erträge vor Steuern; ~ **wholly liable to** ~ **tax** voll steuerpflichtiges Einkommen; ~ **exempt from taxation (taxes)** steuerfreies (unversteuertes) Einkommen; ~ **liable to tax** steuerpflichtiges Einkommen; ~ **chargeable (liable) to corporation tax** körperschaftssteuerpflichtiges Einkommen; **net** ~ **after taxes** Nettoerträge nach Steuern; ~ **derived from trading abroad** im Ausland erzielte gewerbliche Einkünfte; ~ **reinvested in units** in neuen Kapitalanteilscheinen angelegte Kapitalerträge; ~ **from wages** Einkünfte aus nichtselbständiger (unselbständiger) Tätigkeit; ~ **above the living wage** freies Einkommen [über dem Existenzminimum]; ~ **of the wife** Einkünfte der Ehefrau; ~ **from work** Einkünfte aus nichtselbständiger Tätigkeit; ~ **for the year** Jahresgewinn; **net** ~ **for the year** Jahresüberschuß;

to anticipate one's ~ sein Einkommen im voraus verbrauchen; **to augment one's** ~ sein Einkommen vermehren; **to average**

one's ~ seine Einkünfte über mehrere Jahre verteilen; **to base taxation on the ~** Einkommen zur Besteuerungsgrundlage nehmen; **to be eligible for ~** einkommensberechtigt sein; **to be out of proportion to one's ~** zum Einkommen in keinem Verhältnis stehen; **to be paid out of ~** aus dem laufenden Einkommen bezahlt werden; **to be taxable as ordinary ~** normal zu versteuern sein; **to bring in a good ~** gute Rendite erwirtschaften; **to charge ~ at the basic rate** Einkünfte mit den Sätzen des unteren Proportionalbereichs versteuern; **to charge unfranked ~ to corporation tax only** *(Br.)* Kapitalerträge lediglich der Körperschaftssteuer unterwerfen; **to combine a high ~ with capital security in the long term** langfristige Kapitalsicherheit mit hohen Erträgen kombinieren; **to come from current ~** aus dem laufenden Einkommen gespeist werden; **to constitute taxable ~** steuerpflichtiges Einkommen darstellen; **to derive (draw) ~** Einkünfte beziehen; **to determine an ~** Einkommen ermitteln; **to double one's ~** sein Einkommen verdoppeln; **to equalize ~** Einkommen angleichen; **to exceed one's ~** über seine Verhältnisse leben; **to give rise to immediate ~** sich sofort in Erträgnissen niederschlagen; **to have as ~** einnehmen;**to have a fat ~** dicke Gelder verdienen; **to have an independent ~** (~ **of one's own**) Privatvermögen (Privateinkünfte) haben; **to have a large ~** viel Geld verdienen; **to have no ~ in one's own right** über kein eigenes Einkommen verfügen; **to have a steady ~** sein gesichertes Brot haben; **to include the gross dividend as part of one's statutory total ~** Bruttodividende als Teil des steuerpflichtigen Gesamteinkommens deklarieren; **to live on one's ~** von seinen Einkünften (seiner Rente) leben; **to live up to one's ~** mit seinem Einkommen auskommen; **to make a good ~** schönes Einkommen haben; **to make up one's ~** sein Einkommen erhöhen; **to outrun one's ~** über seine Verhältnisse leben; **to receive ~ from securities without deduction of ~ tax** Wertpapiererträge kapitalertragssteuerfrei erhalten; **to report as taxable ~** [als Einkommen] versteuern; **to report one's pro-rata share of a limited partnership as one's own ~** Erträge aus seiner Kommanditbeteiligung als persönliches Einkommen versteuern; **to report as ~ for the year** als in diesem Jahr erzieltes Einkommen behandeln; **to return the details of one's ~** detaillierte Einkommenssteuererklärung abgeben; **to set aside part of one's ~** Einkommensteile zurücklegen; **to spread out ~** Einkommen aus Steuergründen über die Jahre verteilen; **to suit one's expenditure to one's ~** mit seinem Einkommen auskommen; **to supplement one's ~ by journalism** seine Einkünfte durch journalistische Betätigung aufbessern; **to take heavy tolls of one's ~** großen Einkommensteil verschlingen; **to tax ~** Einkommen besteuern; **to tax ~ at the source** Einkommen (Einkünfte) steuerlich an der Quelle erfassen; **to understate one's ~** sein Einkommen zu niedrig angeben; **to value an ~** Einkommensteuer festsetzen;

~ account Ertragsrechnung, *(balance sheet)* Einnahmeseite der Gewinn- und Verlustrechnung; **national ~ accounting** Volksvermögensrechnung, volkswirtschaftliche Gesamtrechnung; **~ and expenditure account** *(corporation)* Bericht über die Einnahmen- und Ausgabenentwicklung, Ertrags-, und Aufwandsrechnung; **earned ~ allowance** *(Br.)* Freibetrag für Berufstätige; **wife's earned ~ allowance** *(Br.)* zusätzlicher Steuerfreibetrag für das Erwerbseinkommen der Ehefrau; **~ analysis** Ertragswertanalyse; **~ averaging** Einkommensverteilung auf mehrere Jahre, Durchschnittsbesteuerung; **~ basis** Rendite [eines Wertpapiers]; **~ beneficiary** Einkommensbegünstigter; **~ benefit** Einkommensgewinn; **~ bonds** Gewinnschuldverschreibungen; **~ and adjustment bond** Besserungsschein; **~ bondholder** Inhaber eines Besserungsscheines; **~ bracket** Einkommenssteuergruppe, -klasse, Tarifgruppe; **[high] ~ brackets** [hohe] Steuerklassen; **to be in low ~ brackets** einer niedrigen Steuerstufe angehören; **to be eligible for the earned ~ ceiling rate of 50%** nur mit dem halben Steuersatz versteuert werden; **~ changes** Einkommensveränderungen; **~ class** Einkommenssteuerklasse, -gruppe; **lower ~ class** niedrigere Einkommensgruppe; **middle-income classes** mittlere Einkommensschichten; **~ control** Einkommenskontrolle; **~ cost** Einkaufspreis; **~ debentures** *(Br.)* gewinnabhängige verzinsliche Schuldverschreibungen; **~ deductions** Erlössschmälerungen, Abzüge vom steuerpflichtigen Einkommen, betriebsfremder Aufwand; **~ determination** Erfolgs-, Einkommensermittlung; **~ differences** Einkommensunterschiede; **~ differential** Einkommensgefälle; **~ distribution** Einkommensverteilung; **~ division** Einkommensschichtung; **~ earner** *(US)* Einkommensbezieher; **~ effect** Einkommenseffekt; **~ elasticity** Einkommenselastizität der Nachfrage; **~ elements** Einkommensteile; **~ engineering** *(US)* Budget-, Haushaltsauf-

stellung; **~ expenditure** Investitionen zur Erzielung kurzfristiger Kapitalerträge; **~ expenditure model** *(Keynes)* Einkommensmodelle; **upper ~ family** gut verdienende Familie; **~ figures** Einkommensziffern; **~ floor** Einkommenshöhe; **~ gain** Einkommenszuwachs, -anstieg; **~ gap** Einkommensabstand; **to operate on an ~ gap** mit Defizit arbeiten; **~ gearing** Fremdkapitalwirkung auf die Eigenkapitalrentabilität; **~ group** Einkommenssteuerklasse, -gruppe, -schicht; **~ growth** Einkommenzuwachs; **~ growth rate** Einkommenszuwachsrate; **~ guarantee** Einkommensgarantie; **~ hotchpot** Einkommensausgleich; **~ increment** Einkommenssteigerung; **~ item** Einnahmeposten; **~ level** Einkommensstufe, -höhe; **~ limit** [Einkommensteuer]freigrenze; **low ~ neighbo(u)rhood** niedrige Einkommensgegend, Armeleuteviertel; **~ maintenance** Einkommenssicherung; **~-maintenance payments** [Einkommens]-unterstützungszahlungen; **high-~ people** hohe Einkommensbezieher; **~ policy** Rentenversicherung zugunsten eines überlebenden Dritten; **~ policies** *(Br.)* Lohn- und Einkommenspolitik; **[safe] ~ producer** [sicherer] Einkommensfaktor; **~ producing factor** Einkommensfaktor; **~-yielding property** Einkünfte aus Kapitalvermögen; **~ property appraisal** Ertragswertabschätzung; **~ protection insurance** Garantieversicherung für gleichbleibendes Einkommen; **~ qualification** *(Br.)* Mindesteinkommen; **~ realization** Gewinnrealisierung; **~ receipts** Vereinnahmung von Erträgen; **~ receiver** Einkommensempfänger; **~ redistribution** Einkommensumverteilung; **~ relief** *(Br.)* Einkommenssteuerfreibetrag; **earned ~ relief** *(Br.)* Freibetrag für Berufstätige (Arbeitseinkünfte); **~ return** *(US)* Rendite, Kapitalerträgnis, -ertrag; **nonoutput-linked ~ rise** nicht produktionsgekoppelte Ertragssteigerung; **to be higher up in the ~ scale** zu den Besserverdienenden zählen; **~ schedule** *(Br.)* Einkommenssteuertabelle; **~ security** gesichertes Einkommen; **~ sheet** Einkommenssteuererklärung, -aufstellung, -formular; **~ splitting** Einkommensaufteilung, Splitting; **~ statement** *(US)* Gewinn- und Verlustrechnung, Einkommensaufstellung, (~ *sheet*) Einkommenserklärung; **comparative ~ statement** *(US)* vergleichende Gewinn- und Verlustrechnung; **cursory ~ statement** *(US)* kurzfristige Erfolgsrechnung; **~ statement charges to reserve** *(US)* Rücklagenvortrag in einer Gewinn- und Verlustrechnung; **minimum ~ statement content** *(US)* Mindestumfang einer Einkommenssteuererklärung; **~ supplement** *(US)* Staatszuschuß zum Einkommen; **~ support** Verbesserung der Einkommensverhältnisse; **~ surplus** Einkommensüberschuß; **~ surtax** Mehreinkommensteuer, Einkommenssteuerzuschlag.

income tax Einkommensteuer;
free of ~ [einkommen]steuerfrei; **in levying ~** bei Veranlagung (Festsetzung) der Einkommensteuer;
additional ~ *(Br.)* Einkommenssteuerzuschlag; **assessed ~** veranlagte Einkommensteuer; **basic rate ~** zum Grundtarif anfallende Einkommensteuer, einheitlicher Grundsteuersatz; **corporate (corporation) ~** Körperschaftssteuer; **deferred federal ~** *(US)* Einkommenssteuerrückstellung; **evaded ~** hinterzogene Einkommensteuer; **graduated ~** gestaffelte Einkommensteuer; **federal ~** *(US)* übliche Einkommensteuer; **higher-rate ~** mit einem höheren Tarif anfallende Einkommensteuer; **individual ~** *(US)* veranlagte Einkommensteuer; **normal ~** *(US)* übliche Einkommensteuer; **personal ~** *(US)* Einkommensteuer; **withholding ~** *(US)* Lohnsteuerabzug;
~ on corporations *(US)* Körperschaftssteuer; **~ on individuals** *(US)* Einkommensteuer für natürliche Personen; **~ on profits distributed** Einkommensteuer auf ausgeschüttete Gewinne; **~ upon return of investments** *(US)* Kapitalertragssteuer;
to attract ~ on only 50% nur den halben Einkommenssteuersatz auslösen; **to be liable to ~** einkommensteuerpflichtig sein; **to cheat one's ~** Einkommensteuer hinterziehen; **to exempt from ~** von der Einkommensteuer befreien; **to fix the ~** Einkommenssteuerrichtlinien erlassen; **to increase ~ by 10 per cent** zehnprozentige Erhöhung des Einkommenssteuersatzes vornehmen; **to scale up ~** Einkommensteuersätze erhöhen; **to suffer ~ at the basic rate at source** *(dividend)* einem einheitlichen Körperschaftssteuersatz vor der Ausschüttung unterworfen sein; **to withhold ~** *(US)* Lohnsteuer einbehalten;
~ account Einkommenssteuerkonto; **~ accounting** Einkommenssteuerbuchführung; **~ accrual** fällige Einkommensteuer; **~ Act** *(Br.)* Einkommenssteuergesetz; **~ and Corporation Taxes Act** *(Br.)* Einkommens- und Körperschaftssteuergesetz; **~ age exemption** altersbedingte Einkommenssteuerfreigrenze; **~ allowance** Einkommenssteuerfreibetrag; **~ allowance increase** Erhöhung des Einkommenssteuerfreibetrages; **~ amendment**

Einkommensteuernovelle; ~ **angle** Einkommenssteuerge-
sichtspunkt; ~ **appeal** Einspruch gegen eine Einkommenssteuerveranlagung; ⚖ **Appeal Tribunal** [etwa] Bundesfinanzhof; ~
assessment Einkommenssteuerveranlagung, Einkommens-
steuerbescheid; **to make an ~ assessment upon s. o. j.** zur
Einkommensteuer veranlagen; ~ **authority** Finanzamt; ~ **base**
Einkommenssteuerbemessungsgrundlage; ~ **bill** (US) Ein-
kommensteuerbescheid, -veranlagung; ~ **blank** (US) Einkommenssteuerformular; ~ **bracket** Einkommenssteuerstufe; ~
calculation Einkommenssteuerberechnung; ~ **case** Einkom-
menssteuersache; ~ **certificate** (US) Steuerzuschlag bei Steuer-
zwangsvollstreckung; ~ **tax changes** Einkommenssteuer-
änderungen; ~ **collector** Einkommenssteuerbearbeiter; ~
computation Einkommensteuerberechnung; ~ **credit** (US)
Einkommenssteuererleichterung, -freibetrag, -vergünstigung;
~ **cut** Einkommenssteuersenkung, -herabsetzung; ~ **declaration** (Br.) Einkommenssteuererklärung; **to notarize an ~ declaration** (Br.) Einkommenssteuererklärung in notarieller Form
vornehmen; ~ **deductions** Abzüge vom steuerpflichtigen Einkommen, Einkommenssteuerabzüge; ~ **deficiency** Einkom-
menssteuerausfall; ~ **depreciation allowance** im Rahmen der
Einkommensteuer gewährte Abschreibungsvergünstigungen;
~ **directives** Einkommenssteuerrichtlinien; ~ **division** Einkom-
menssteuerabteilung; ~ **dodger** Einkommenssteuerhinterzie-
her; ~ **evasion** Einkommenssteuerhinterziehung; **personal ~
exemption** (US) persönlicher Steuerfreibetrag; ~ **form** Einkommenssteuerformular; ~ **implementation ordinance** Ein-
kommenssteuerdurchführungsverordnung; ~ **increase** Ein-
kommenssteuererhöhung; ~ **indexation** Einkommenssteuer-
indexierung; ~ **investigator** Steuerprüfer, -fahnder; **personal ~
job** einkommenssteuerliche Tätigkeit; ⚖ **Law** (US) Einkommenssteuergesetz; ~ **law** Einkommenssteuerrecht; ~ **legislation** Einkommenssteuergesetzgebung; ~ **liability** Einkom-
menssteuerschuld; ~ **list** Hebeliste; ~ **litigation** Einkommens-
steuerverfahren; ~ **load** Einkommenssteuerbelastung; **to
escape the ~ net** der Einkommensbesteuerung gänzlich entgehen; ~ **obligation** Einkommenssteuerverpflichtung; ~ **office**
Finanzamt; ~ **payer** Einkommenssteuerzahler; ~ **payment**
Einkommenssteuerzahlung; ~ **practice** Handhabung der Ein-
kommenssteuerbestimmungen; ~ **preparation** Bearbeitung der
Einkommenssteuererklärung; ~ **principles** Einkommenssteu-
ergrundsätze; ~ **progression** Einkommenssteuerprogression;
for ~ purposes aus Einkommenssteuergründen, für Einkom-
menssteuerzwecke; **for basic rate ~ purposes** zwecks Sicherstellung des Einkommenssteuergrundtarifs; **[personal] ~ rate**
Einkommenssteuersatz, -tarif; **top marginal ~ rates** höchste
Einkommenssteuersätze; **to abolish the top three earned ~ rates**
die drei höchsten Steuerklassen gewerblich versteuerten Einkommens beseitigen; ~ **rebate** Einkommenssteuerrückerstat-
tung; ~ **receipts** Aufkommen an Einkommensteuer; ~
reduction Einkommenssteuerermäßigung; ~ **reference number**
Einkommenssteuernummer; ~ **reform** Einkommenssteuerre-
form; ~ **regulations** Einkommenssteuervorschriften, -be-
stimmungen; ~ **relief** (Br.) Einkommenssteuervergünstigung,
-erleichterung, -freibetrag; **to qualify (rank) for ~ relief** (Br.) zu
Einkommenssteuervergünstigungen berechtigen, (Br.) ein-
kommenssteuerbegünstigt sein; ~ **return** Einkommenssteuererklärung; **consolidated ~ return** Einkommenssteuererklärung im Konzernverband; **to fail to file an ~ return** keine
Einkommenssteuererklärung abgeben; **to file one's ~ return**
Einkommenssteuererklärung abgeben; ~ **return blank (form)**
Einkommenssteuerformular; **to be removed from the ~ rolls
entirely** völlig von der Einkommensteuer freigestellt werden; ~
rules Einkommenssteuerrichtlinien; **to be subject to special ~
rules** mit Ausnahmesätzen besteuert werden; ~ **safeguards**
einkommenssteuerliche Vorsichtsmaßnahmen; ~ **scale** Ein-
kommenssteuergrundtabelle; ~ **service** Beratung in Einkom-
menssteuerfragen; ~ **standard rate** Mindesteinkommens-
steuersatz; ~ **statement** (US) Einkommenssteuererklärung; **to
make an ~ statement** (US) sein Einkommen angeben, Einkommenssteuererklärung fertigen; ~ **statute** (US) Einkommensteuergesetz; ~ **surcharge (surtax)** (Br.) Einkommenssteuerzuschlag; ~ **system** Einkommenssteuersystem; ~ **treatment**
steuerliche Behandlung bei der Einkommenssteuerveranlagung; ~ **year 1980** Steuerjahr 1980; ~ **yield** Einkommenssteu-
eraufkommen.
income | unit Bezeichnung des Einkommenssteuerzahlers; ~
value Ertragswert; ~ **yield** Einkommensertrag.
incomeless ohne Einkommen.
incomer Ankömmling, neu Zugezogener, (successor) Nachfolger
[im Miet-, Pachtverhältnis].

incoming Eintreffen, Ankommen;
~s [Zahlungs]eingänge, Einkünfte, Einnahmen;
~s **and outgoings** Eingänge und Ausgänge;
~ **of a train** Einlaufen eines Zuges;
~ (a.) ankommend, eingehend, -laufend, (accruing) erwach-
send, entstehend, anfallend, (order) einlaufend;
~ **exchanges** (US) von der Verrechnungsstelle eingehende
Schecks; ~ **goods** Wareneingang; ~ **long-distance call** (tel.)
ankommendes Ferngespräch; ~ **mail** Posteingang; ~ **mayor**
neuer Bürgermeister; ~ **officer** neu eintretender Beamter; ~
orders Auftragseingänge; ~ **partner** neu eintretender Gesellschafter; ~ **profit** anfallende Erträge; ~ **stocks** Lager-, Waren-
zugänge; ~ **tenant** neuer Mieter; ~ **tide** Flut; ~ **year**
beginnendes Jahr.
incommensurable number Primzahl.
incommensurate (inadequate) unangemessen, ungenügend, (incommensurable) nicht vergleichbar.
incommode (v.) Unannehmlichkeiten verursachen.
incommodious lästig, unbequem, beschwerlich.
incom(m)unicado vom Verkehr mit anderen abgeschnitten.
incommunication Haft ohne Sprecherlaubnis.
incommutable nicht umwandelbar (austauschbar).
incomparable nicht vergleichbar.
incompatibility Unvereinbarkeit.
incompatible unverträglicher Mensch;
~ (a.) unvereinbar, widersprüchlich;
~ **interests** widerstreitende Interessen; ~ **offices** nicht gleichzeitig bekleidbare Ämter.
incompact lose, unverpackt.
incompetence, incompetency (inability) Unfähigkeit, Untauglichkeit, (judge) Inkompetenz, Unzuständigkeit, Nichtzuständig-
keit, Nichtbefugnis, (US) mangelnde Geschäftsfähigkeit;
~ **of evidence** (US) Unzulässigkeit von Beweismitteln; ~ **to
succeed** Erbunfähigkeit; ~ **to act as a witness** Unfähigkeit,
Zeuge zu sein.
incompetent Geschäftsunfähiger;
mental ~ Geistesschwacher, Geschäftsunfähiger;
~ (a.) (not able) unfähig, (incapacitated by law, US) nicht
geschäftsfähig, unzurechnungsfähig, geschäftsunfähig, (evidence) unzulässig, nicht zur Sache gehörig, unfähig, (not
legally qualified) nicht befugt, unzuständig;
mentally ~ (US) geistesschwach, -krank;
~ **to act** handlungsunfähig; ~ **to make a contract** geschäfts-,
vertragsunfähig; ~ **to do one's job** beruflich ungeeignet; ~ **to
make a will** testierunfähig;
to adjudge ~ (US) für geschäftsunfähig erklären; **to be thoroughly ~ to do s. th.** für etw. schlechthin ungeeignet sein; **to be
~ to advise in a matter** in einer Angelegenheit keinen Rat
erteilen können; **to weed out the ~s** Unfähige herausschmeißen;
~ **evidence** unzulässiges Beweismaterial; ~ **witness** (US) rechtlich unzulässiger Zeuge.
incomplete unvollzählig, unvollständig;
~ **contract** unvollständiger Vertrag.
incompletely signed Unterschrift unvollständig.
incompleteness (contract) Unvollständigkeit.
incompliance Nichterfüllung.
incomprehensible unverständlich.
incomputable unberechenbar.
inconclusive (evidence) nicht schlüssig (überzeugend), unschlüssig, widerlegbar.
inconclusiveness mangelnde Schlüssigkeit, Widerlegbarkeit.
incongruity Mißverhältnis, mangelnde Übereinstimmung, Unvereinbarkeit, Widersinnigkeit.
incongruous unvereinbar, widerspruchsvoll.
inconsequence Folgewidrigkeit.
inconsiderable unbeträchtlich.
inconsiderate rücksichtslos, taktlos.
inconsistency Unvereinbarkeit, [innerer] Widerspruch, Nichtübereinstimmung.
inconsistent (contradictory) unvereinbar, widerspruchsvoll,
widersprüchlich, inkonsequent, (incompatible) unvereinbar;
to be ~ im Widerspruch stehen;
~ **statements** einander widersprechende Aussagen.
incontestability Unanfechtbarkeit;
~ **clause** Unanfechtbarkeitsklausel.
incontestable unanfechtbar, unstreitig;
~ **evidence** unwiderlegbares Beweismaterial.
inconvenience Unannehmlichkeit[en], Ungelegenheiten;
~ **of living far from town** Unbequemlichkeiten des Lebens auf
dem Lande;

~ (v.) in Verlegenheit bringen;
to be an ~ to s. o. jem. zur Last fallen; **to manage s. th. at great personal ~** auf Kosten größter persönlicher Unannehmlichkeiten mit etw. fertig werden; **to put s. o. to great ~(s)** jem. große Unannehmlichkeiten bereiten.

inconvenienced, not to be unduly keine unbilligen Unbequemlichkeiten erleiden.

inconvenient unbequem, lästig;
at a most ~ time zu sehr ungelegener Zeit.

inconvertibility (banknotes) Nichteinlösbarkeit, (debentures) Nichtumwandel-, Nichtkonvertierbarkeit, (goods) Nichtumsetzbarkeit.

inconvertible (banknotes) nicht einlösbar, (debentures) nicht konvertierbar, unkonvertierbar, (goods) nicht umsetzbar;
~ paper currency Papierwährung ohne Einlösungszwang.

incoordinate nicht koordiniert.

incoordination mangelnde Koordinierung.

incorporate (v.) vereinigen, verbinden, zusammenschließen, (admit to university) Externen an einer Universität zulassen, (constitute as corporation) juristische Person gründen, [amtlich] als Aktiengesellschaft eintragen, registrieren, inkorporieren, (unite with) einverleiben, verbinden;
~ one bank with another Banken fusionieren; **~ into a book** in ein Buch einarbeiten; **~ one's business** seine Firma in eine Kapitalgesellschaft umwandeln; **~ a club** Verein ins Vereinsregister eintragen lassen; **~ a railway company** einer Eisenbahngesellschaft Korporationsrecht verleihen; **~ all the latest discoveries** alle neuesten Entdeckungen berücksichtigen; **~ fields in an estate** Grundstücksparzellen zusammenschreiben; **~ with others** mit anderen fusionieren; **~ into a parish (town)** eingemeinden; **~ suggestions in a plan** Anregungen in einem Entwurf verarbeiten; **~ a state into another** Staat einem anderen einverleiben;
~ (a.) (incorporeal) unkörperlich, immateriell, (registered) einverleibt, inkorporiert, amtlich eingetragen;
~ bank nicht eingetragene Bank.

incorporated inkorporiert, registriert, als juristische Person eingetragen, (US) [amtlich als AG] eingetragen;
not ~ keine Körperschaft, (US) keine Kapitalgesellschaft;
~ in the United Kingdom mit Sitz in England;
to be ~ Rechtspersönlichkeit erlangen; **to be ~ in A** seinen Sitz in A haben; **to be ~ a member of a college** in ein College aufgenommen werden; **to be ~ in another firm** in einer anderen Firma aufgehen;
~ accountant (Br.) staatlich geprüfter Bücherrevisor, öffentlich bestellter Buchprüfer; **~ bank** (US) Aktienbank; **~ body** Körperschaft; **~ business** Gesellschaftsunternehmen; **~ city** kreisfreie Stadt; **~ company** (Br.) handelsgerichtlich eingetragene Gesellschaft, rechtsfähige Handelsgesellschaft, (US) Aktiengesellschaft; **~ law society** Anwaltskammer; **~ society** eingetragener (rechtsfähiger) Verein; **~ town** Stadtgemeinde.

incorporation (incorporated body) Korporation, Körperschaft, (forming of corporation, US) Inkorporierung, Körperschaftsbildung, Gesellschaftsgründung, (registration) [amtliche] Eintragung, Registrierung, (town) Eingemeindung, (uniting with) Einverleibung, Einbeziehung, Eingliederung, Aufnahme;
compulsory ~ Zwangsregistrierung, -eintragung;
~ of a field into an estate Zusammenschreibung von Grundstücksparzellen; **~ of provinces** Einverleibung von Provinzen; **~ of a territory** Einverleibung fremden Staatsgebiets; **~ of a town** Erhebung zur kreisfreien Stadt;
~ fee Eintragungsgebühr; **~ tax** Körperschaftsgründungssteuer.

incorporator Gründer, Gründungsmitglied.

incorporeal unkörperlich, immateriell;
~ chattels Immaterialgüterrechte; **~ hereditament** nichtkörperliche Vermögensgegenstände, vererbliche Rechte; **~ property** immaterielle Vermögensrechte; **~ right** immaterielles Güterrecht; **~ things** nicht körperliche Gegenstände.

incorrect unrichtig, ungenau, fehlerhaft, falsch;
~ act Inkorrektheit; **~ conduct** ungehöriges Benehmen; **~ expression** Ungenauigkeit im Ausdruck; **~ indorsement** (US) unvollständiges Indossament; **~ text** fehlerhafter Text, Sprachungenauigkeit.

incorrectly | addressed unrichtig adressiert; **~ printed** verdruckt.

incorrectness Unrichtigkeit, Ungenauigkeit.

incorrupt unbestechlich, (goods) gut erhalten, frisch, (text) fehlerlos.

incorruptible unbestechlich.

incoterms Regeln für die Auslegung handelsüblicher Vertragsformeln, internationale Lieferklauseln.

increasable vergrößerungsfähig.

increase (accumulation) Auflaufen, (advance) Ansteigen, Erhöhung, Steigerung [der Preise], (agriculture) Bodenertrag (augmentation) Vermehrung, Vergrößerung, Wachstum, Erweiterung, Zunahme, Zulage, (increment) Zuwachs, (pay) Zulage, Gehaltserhöhung, (profit) Nutzen, Ertrag, Gewinn, (wages) Lohnzulage;
on the ~ im Zunehmen;
17% ~ 17%ige Zuwachsrate; **plus £ 3500 ~** Erhöhung um 3500 Pfund; **appreciable ~** spürbare Erhöhung; **capital ~** Kapitalerhöhung; **exemption ~** Erhöhung des Steuerfreibetrags; **fringe ~** Erhöhung der Sondervergünstigungen; **general ~** allgemeiner Lohnanstieg; **hoped-for ~** erhoffte Gehaltserhöhung; **interest ~** Zinserhöhung; **net ~** Nettoerhöhung; **population ~** Bevölkerungszunahme; **postal ~** Erhöhung der Postgebühren; **price ~** Preis-, Kursanstieg; **proportional ~** entsprechende Zunahme; **revenue ~** Erhöhung des Steueraufkommens; **salary ~** Gehaltserhöhung; **slight ~** leichte Zunahme; **steady ~** ständige Zunahme;
~ in allowance (income tax) Freibetragserhöhung; **~ in the amount of bank credit** Erhöhung des Kreditvolumens; **~ in fixed assets** Zunahme des Anlagevermögens; **~ in the bank rate** (Br.) Diskonterhöhung; **~ of business** Geschäftszunahme; **~ in business activity** Konjunkturbelebung; **~ in (of) capital** Kapitalerhöhung; **~ in capital investments** Erweiterungsinvestitionen; **~ of capital stock** (US) Kapitalaufstockung, -erhöhung; **~ in charges** Gebührenanhebung; **~ in child benefit** (Br.) Kindergelderhöhung; **~ in child population** Zunahme des Kinderprozentsatzes; **~ in claims** Anhäufung von Rechtsansprüchen; **~ in consumption** Verbrauchssteigerung; **~ in cost** Kostensteigerung, -anstieg; **~ of credit** Krediterhöhung; **~ in crime** Verbrechenszunahme; **~ of currency** Geldvermehrung; **~ in demand** wachsende Nachfrage; **~ for dependants** Kinderzuschlag, Zuschlag für abhängige Familienangehörige; **~ of deposits** Einlagenzuwachs; **~ of [their] special deposits with the Bank of England** [etwa] Mindestreservenerhöhung bei der Bundesnotenbank; **~ in depreciation allowances for industries** Erhöhung der industriellen Abschreibungsbeträge; **~ in the discount (rediscount, US) rate** Diskonterhöhung, Erhöhung des Diskontsatzes; **~ of duties** Zollerhöhung; **~ in efficiency** Leistungssteigerung; **~ in equity** Eigenkapitalerhöhung; **~ of exports** Exportsteigerung; **~ in finished goods** Fertigwarenanstieg; **~ in freight rates** Frachterhöhung; **~ in the gold backing for the gold currency** Erhöhung der Golddeckung der Währung; **~ of hazard** Risiko-, Gefahrerhöhung; **~ of imports** Einfuhranstieg; **~ of investment** Investitionszuwachs; **~ of knowledge** Erweiterung der Kenntnisse, Verbreiterung des Wissens; **~ in landing fees** Erhöhung der Landegebühren; **~ in liquidity** Liquiditätsverbesserung, -anreicherung; **~ of notes in circulation** Erhöhung des Banknotenumlaufs; **~ in output** Produktionssteigerung; **~ in pay** Gehaltserhöhung; **~ of penalty** Strafverschärfung; **~ in population** Bevölkerungszunahme; **~ in power** Machtzuwachs; **~ in the power of backbenchers** Machtzunahme der Hinterbänkler; **~ of premium** Prämienerhöhung; **~ in prices** Verteuerung, Preisanstieg; **allround ~ in prices** allgemeine Preissteigerung; **~ in oil prices** Ölpreiserhöhung; **simultaneous ~ in prices** gleichzeitiges Anziehen der Preise; **~ in production** Produktionserhöhung; **~ in productivity** Produktivitätssteigerung; **~ in profit** Ertragssteigerung; **~ in purchasing power** Kaufkraftsteigerung; **~ in quotas** Quotenerhöhung; **~ in range of goods** Sortimentserweiterung; **~ in rank** Rangerhöhung; **~ in rates** Tariferhöhung; **~ in real income** Realeinkommenssteigerung; **~ in receipts** Mehreinkommen, -einnahmen, Zunahme der Einkünfte; **~ in the rediscount rate** (US) Diskontsatzerhöhung; **~ of rent** Mieterhöhung; **~ in required reserves** (US) Mindestreservenerhöhung; **~ in revenue** Einnahmenanstieg; **~ in the risk** Erhöhung des Risikos, Gefahrenerhöhung; **~ in sales** Belebung des Absatzes, Kaufbelebung; **~ of salary** Gehaltszulage; **~ in savings** Zunahme der Spartätigkeit; **~ of share capital** (Br.) Kapitalerhöhung, -aufstockung; **~ in share prices** Kursanstieg; **~ in shipments** Lieferzunahme; **~ in taxation [of 10%]** [zehnprozentige] Steuererhöhung; **~ in taxes** (taxation) Steuererhöhung, -vermehrung; **~ in trade** Aufschwung des Handels; **~ in turnover** Umsatzsteigerung; **~ in unemployment** Zunahme der Arbeitslosigkeit, Arbeitslosenanstieg; **~ in value** Erhöhung des Wertes, Wertsteigerung; **percentage ~ in value** prozentualer Preisanstieg; **~ in wages** Lohnanstieg, -erhöhung; **~ in weight** Gewichtszunahme;
~ (v.) (advance) erhöhen, steigern, vermehren, (v. i.) sich erhöhen (vermehren), anwachsen, [an]steigen, zunehmen;

~ **the borrowings at the bank** Bankkredit in erhöhtem Maße in Anspruch nehmen; ~ **the capital stock** *(US)* Kapital verstärken (erhöhen); ~ **the original capital by ...** Grundkapital um ... erhöhen; ~ **the cost of goods** Warenpreise heraufsetzen; ~ **a credit** Kredit erhöhen; ~ **their special deposits with the Bank of England** [etwa] Mindestreserven bei der Bundesnotenbank erhöhen; ~ **the expenditure** Ausgaben erhöhen; ~ **exports** Export steigern; ~ **further** *(prices)* weiter anziehen; ~ **in numbers** zahlenmäßig zunehmen; ~ **in numbers again** sich erneut vermehren; ~ **paper circulation** Notenumlauf steigern; ~ **in price** im Preis steigen, teurer werden, *(v. tr.)* Preiserhöhung vornehmen, Preis heraufsetzen; ~ **productivity** Produktivität steigern; ~ **s. one's salary** jem. eine Gehaltserhöhung gewähren; ~ **speed** Geschwindigkeit erhöhen; ~ **the taxes** Steuern erhöhen; ~ **in value** im Wert steigen, wertmäßig zunehmen; ~ **one's vigilance** seine Wachsamkeit verdoppeln; ~ **in volume** volumenmäßig zunehmen; ~ **wages** Löhne erhöhen;
to approve an ~ **in capital** Kapitalerhöhung genehmigen; **to be on the** ~ im Zunehmen begriffen sein, Steigerung aufweisen; **to find its way into an** ~ **of current assets** sich in einem Anstieg des Umlaufvermögens niederschlagen; **to show an** ~ Steigerung aufweisen;
percentage ~ **basis** prozentuale Erhöhungsbasis; ~ **forecast** Zuwachsvorhersage, -prognose.
increased, to be sich erhöhen;
~ **care** erhöhte Sorgfalt; ~ **consumption** Konsumerhöhung; ~ **cost of living** gestiegene Lebenshaltungskosten; ~ **demand** Bedarfszunahme, Mehrbedarf; ~ **exports** Exportsteigerung; ~ **interest** erhöhte Zinsen; ~ **output** Mehrprodukt; ~ **pay** Lohnzulage; ~ **wealth** Vermögenszunahme.
increasing zunehmend, steigend;
to go on ~ immer noch steigen;
~ **costs** Kostenzunahme; ~ **return** zunehmende Erträge.
incredible unglaubhaft, unglaublich;
to spend ~ **sums of money** unwahrscheinliche Geldbeträge ausgeben.
increment Zunahme, [Wert]zuwachs, Erhöhung, *(profit)* Gewinn, Mehrertrag;
annual ~ *(salary)* jährliche Gehaltssteigerung; **current annual** ~ *(forestry)* regelmäßiger Jahreszuwachs; **fixed-percentage value** ~ prozentual festgelegte Wertsteigerung; **marginal** ~ Mindestwerterhöhung; **pension** ~ Pensionsaufstockung, -erhöhung; **plottage** ~ Wertsteigerung bei Zusammenlegung; **price** ~ Wertzuwachs durch erhöhte Preise; **quality** ~ Qualitätssteigerung, -verbesserung; **salary** ~ Gehaltserhöhung, -aufbesserung; **unearned** ~ *(land)* unverdienter Wertzuwachs; **wage** ~ *(Br.)* Lohnerhöhung; **yearly** ~ *(salary)* jährliche Gehaltssteigerung;
~ **per cent** prozentualer Anstieg;
~ **income tax** Gewinnzuwachs-, Mehreinkommensteuer; **property** ~ **tax** Wertzuwachssteuer; ~ **value** Wertzuwachs; ~ **value duty** Wertzuwachssteuer.
incremental | **capital output ratio** marginaler Kapitalkoeffizient; ~ **cost** nahe der Rentabilität liegende Kosten, Grenzkosten; ~ **scale** Gehaltssteigerungstabelle.
incriminate *(v.)* beschuldigen, anklagen;
~ **o. s.** sich selbst belasten (bezichtigen).
incriminated [politisch] belastet;
less ~ minderbelastet.
incriminating | **admission** belastendes Zugeständnis von Tatsachen; ~ **circumstance** belastender Umstand; ~ **documents** belastende Beweisstücke; ~ **evidence** *(law suit)* Belastungsmaterial.
incrimination Inkriminierung, Belastung;
political ~ politische Belastung.
incriminatory belastend;
~ **statement** *(accused)* belastende Aussage.
incroachment Beeinträchtigung.
incubation period Inkubationszeit.
incubus *(fig.)* bedrückende Last.
inculpate *(v.)* beschuldigen, anklagen.
inculpatory belastend.
incumbency Pfründenbesitz, *(sphere of action)* Amtsbereich.
incumbent *(benefice)* Pfründeninhaber, *(office)* Stelleninhaber;
to be ~ **upon s. o.** jem. obliegen.
incumber *(v.)* belasten, hypothekisieren.
incumbered verschuldet, belastet.
incumbrance [Grundstücks]last, Hypothekenbelastung;
earlier ~ Vorlast;
to be subject to prior ~**s** grundbuchlich vorbelastet sein.
incumbrancer Hypotheken-, Pfandgläubiger.
incur *(v.)* eingehen, übernehmen, auf sich nehmen, sich zuziehen;
~ **a danger** sich einer Gefahr aussetzen; ~ **debts** Schulden

machen; ~ **a duty** steuerpflichtig sein; ~ **no expense** *(bill of exchange)* ohne Kosten; ~ **heavy expenses** sich in große Unkosten stürzen; ~ **a fine** Geldstrafe verwirken; ~ **liabilities** sich Verpflichtungen aufladen; ~ **large losses** hohe Verluste erleiden; ~ **an obligation** Verpflichtung übernehmen; ~ **a penalty** Strafe verwirken, sich strafbar machen; ~ **punishment** sich strafbar machen; ~ **a risk** Risiko übernehmen (eingehen); ~ **s. one's suspicions** jds. Verdacht auf sich lenken.
incurable unheilbar Kranker;
~ **defect** unheilbarer Mangel; ~ **disease** unheilbare Krankheit; ~ **drunkard** Quartalssäufer; ~ **insanity** unheilbare Geisteskrankheit;
incuriosity Interesselosigkeit.
incurious uninteressiert, interesselos.
incurred expenses gehabte Ausgaben.
incurrence of debts Schuldenaufnahme.
incurring a liability Eingehen einer Verbindlichkeit.
incursion Einbruch, Einfall, Raub-, Streifzug;
~**s into the capital** Angreifen des Kapitals; ~**s on my leisure time** Attacken auf meine Freizeit;
to make ~**s into the capital** Kapital angreifen; **to make** ~**s into an enemy's country** Raubzüge ins Feindgebiet unternehmen.
incursionist Eindringling.
indebt *(v.)* verschulden.
indebted verschuldet, schuldenbelastet, *(obliged)* [zu Dank] verpflichtet;
not ~ schuldenfrei;
to be ~ **to a large amount to s. o.** jem. einen großen Betrag schulden; **to be contingently** ~ aus Giroverbindlichkeiten schulden; **to be deeply** ~ **to s. o.** tief in jds. Schuld stehen; **to be** ~ **by a thousand dollars** 1000 Dollar Schulden haben; **to be** ~ **to s. o. for information** Informationen verdanken.
indebtedness Verschuldung, Verschuldetsein, Schulden[last], Verbindlichkeiten, Verpflichtungen, *(sum owed)* Schuldensumme, -betrag;
bank ~ Bankverschuldung; **bond** ~ Anleiheschulden; **excessive** ~ Überschuldung; **involuntary** ~ *(county)* unaufschiebbare Zahlungsverpflichtung; **long-term** ~ langfristige Verschuldung; **net** ~ Nettoverschuldung; **rural** ~ Verschuldung der Landwirtschaft; **short-term** ~ kurzfristige Verbindlichkeiten; **state** ~ Staatsverschuldung; **voluntary** ~ *(county)* Kommunalverpflichtungen bei ausgeglichenem Haushalt;
~ **to affiliates** *(balance sheet, US)* Verbindlichkeiten gegenüber Konzerngesellschaften; ~ **of local authorities** Kommunalverschuldung;
to clear up one's ~ seine Schulden zurückführen.
indecency Unsittlichkeit, Unanständigkeit;
public ~ Erregung öffentlichen Ärgernisses.
indecent unsittlich, unzüchtig;
~ **advertising** anstößige Werbung; ~ **assault** Nötigung zur Unzucht; ~ **exhibition** sittenwidriges Zurschaustellen; ~ **liberties** unzüchtige Handlung; ~ **publication** unzüchtige Veröffentlichung.
indecipherable unleserlich, nicht zu entziffern.
indecisive evidence unschlüssiges Beweismaterial.
undecorous behavio(u)r ungehöriges (unziemliches) Verhalten.
indefeasible unanfechtbar, unverletzlich;
~ **interest** unantastbarer Anspruch; ~ **right** unzichtbarer Rechtsanspruch; ~ **title** unanfechtbarer Anspruch.
indefensible nicht vertretbar, unhaltbar;
to be wholly ~ völlig unentschuldbar sein.
indefinable undefinierbar.
indefinite unbestimmt, unbegrenzt;
~ **leave** unbegrenzter Urlaub; ~ **legacy** Gattungsvermächtnis; ~ **payment** *(Scot., law)* allgemeine Schuldenrückzahlung.
indefinitely auf unbestimmte Zeit.
indeliberate unabsichtlich, unüberlegt.
indelible | **ink** Kopiertinte; ~ **pencil** Tintenstift.
indelibly engraved on the mind unvergeßlich dem Gedächtnis eingeprägt.
indelicacy Taktlosigkeit.
indelicate taktlos, ohne Zartgefühl;
~ **act** Unanständigkeit; ~ **word** unanständiges Wort.
indeliverable nicht lieferbar.
indemnification Entschädigung, Vergütung, Schadloshaltung, Ersatzleistung, Schadenersatz, Abfindung, Abstandsgeld, *(reimbursement of penalty)* Sicherstellung;
capital ~ Kapitalabfindung; **governmental** ~ staatliche Entschädigung; **special** ~ Sondervergütung;
to pay s. o. a sum by way of ~ jem. etw. im Entschädigungswege zahlen.

indemnified schadlos.

indemnify *(v.)* *(compensate)* entschädigen, Entschädigung gewähren, Schadloshaltung zusagen, schadlos halten, vergüten, Schadenersatz leisten, *(secure)* sichern, *(give immunity from punishment)* der Verantwortlichkeit entbinden, *(secure)* sicherstellen, sichern;
~ **o. s.** sich schadlos halten; ~ **s. o. for expenses incurred** jem. seine Spesen ersetzen; ~ **s. o. for a hardship** jem. einen Härteausgleich gewähren; ~ **s. o. for a loss** j. für einen Verlust entschädigen; ~ **a minister** Minister von der Anschuldigung der Überschreitung seiner Befugnisse freisprechen; ~ **the owner of property taken for public use** enteigneten Eigentümer entschädigen.

indemnitee *(US)* Entschädigungsberechtigter.

indemnitor *(US)* Haftungsschuldner.

indemnity *(amount of damages)* Entschädigungsbetrag, -summe, Schadenersatz, *(compensation)* Entschädigung, Abfindung, Schadloshaltung, -erklärung, *(documentary credit)* Versprechen der Schadloshaltung, *(exemption)* Straflosigkeit, Amnestie, *(politics)* nachträgliche Billigung, Indemnität, *(security)* Sicherstellung, -heit, *(stock exchange, US)* Prämiengeschäft;
bound to allow ~ zum Schadenersatz verpflichtet;
accident ~ Unfallentschädigung; **cash** ~ Mankogeld; **commercial** ~ Schadensersatz des Verkehrswertes; **fair** ~ großzügige Entschädigung; **implied** ~ stillschweigend übernommene Entschädigungsverpflichtung; **land** ~ Entschädigungsgrundstück; **lump-sum** ~ Pauschalabfindung; **monetary** ~ Geld-, Barabfindung; **third-party** ~ Haftpflicht gegenüber Dritten; **war** ~ Kriegsentschädigung;
~ **for costs** Kostensicherheit; ~ **for expropriation** Enteignungsentschädigung; ~ **against liability** Haftungsfreistellung, -ausschuß;
to pay full ~ **to s. o.** jem. den Schaden in voller Höhe ersetzen; **to waive (renounce) a claim to** ~ auf Schadensersatzansprüche verzichten;
~ **account** Abfindungskonto; ~ **bond** Schadlos-, Ausfallbürgschaft, Garantieverpflichtung; ~ **clause** Haftungsfreistellungsklausel, Ausfallklausel; ~ **company** Konkursversicherungsgesellschaft; ~ **contract** Garantie-, Schuldübernahmevertrag; ~ **form** Garantievertragsformular; ~ **fund** Entschädigungskasse; ~ **insurance** Schadensversicherung; ~ **land** *(for railroads)* Ersatzgrundstück; ~ **letter** *(Br.)* Garantieverpflichtung, Ausfallbürgschaft; ~ **limit** höchste Entschädigungssumme; ~ **loan** Tilgungsschuld; ~ **period** *(insurance)* Leistungsdauer; ~ **policy** Haftpflichtversicherungspolice; **to file an** ~ **policy from an insurance company with the department** der Aufsichtsbehörde gegenüber den Nachweis einer Schadensversicherung erbringen.

indenization Einbürgerung.

indent Vertragsurkunde, *(indenture)* [gesiegelter] Vertrag, *(export order)* Warenbestellung aus dem Ausland, Auslandsbestellung, Auslandsauftrag, *(mil., Br.)* Requisition, *(print.)* Einrückung, Einzug;
closed (specific) ~ Auslandsbestellung eines bestimmten Markenerzeugnisses; **open** ~ Auslandsbestellung einer Gattungsware; **ration** ~ *(Br.)* Bezugsschein;
~ *(v.)* *(document)* Vertragsurkunde im Duplikat aufsetzen, *(mil.)* requirieren, beitreiben, *(order)* Waren im Ausland bestellen, [Auslands]auftrag erteilen, *(print.)* einrücken, Zeile einziehen;
~ **s. o.** j. in die Lehre (Ausbildung) geben, j. als Lehrling verpflichten; ~ **upon s. o. for s. th.** bei jem. etw. bestellen; ~ **the first line of each paragraph** bei jedem Absatz die erste Zeile einrücken;
~ **merchant** Indentkaufmann.

indentation *(line of printing)* Einzug, Einrückung.

indented im Ausbildungs-, Lehrlingsverhältnis, *(bound by contract)* vertraglich verpflichtet, *(print.)* eingerückt, eingezogen;
~ **coast** eingeschnittene Küste; ~ **deed** synallagmatischer Vertrag; ~ **line** eingerückte Zeile.

indention *(print.)* Einrücken [einer Zeile].

indentor überseeischer Käufer.

indenture *(apprentice)* Lehr-, Berufsausbildungsvertrag, *(instrument of contract under seal)* [gesiegelte] Vertragsurkunde, *(instrument in duplicate)* in mehreren Ausfertigungen vorliegende Vertragsurkunde, *(list)* [amtliche] Liste;
under an ~ auf Grund eines Vertrages;
trust ~ *(US)* Treuhandvertrag;
~ **of apprenticeship** Lehrlings-, Ausbildungsvertrag; ~ **of assumption** Übernahmevertrag; ~ **of lease** Pachtvertrag; ~ **of mortgage** Hypothekenbewilligungsurkunde, -brief;

~ *(v.)* in die Lehre (zur Ausbildung) geben, durch Lehrvertrag verpflichten, als Gesellen einstellen;
to be bound by ~ vertraglich gebunden (in der Berufsausbildung) sein; **to be out of one's** ~**s** ausgelernt (Lehre beendet, Ausbildung abgeschlossen) haben; **to bind by** ~ in die Lehre (zur Ausbildung) geben; **to take up one's** ~**s** in ein Ausbildungsverhältnis eintreten;
~ **trust** Wertpapiersondervermögen; ~ **trustee** für ein Wertpapiervermögen bestellter Treuhänder.

indentured vertraglich verpflichtet, *(apprentice)* im Ausbildungs-, Lehrlingsverhältnis;
~ **labo(u)r** zwangsverpflichtete Arbeitskräfte.

independence Unabhängigkeit, Selbständigkeit, *(competency)* hinreichendes Auskommen;
comfortable ~ finanzielle Unabhängigkeit; **economic** ~ wirtschaftliche Unabhängigkeit; **judicial** ~ richterliche Unabhängigkeit; **political** ~ politische Unabhängigkeit;
to gain (reach) ~ seine Unabhängigkeit gewinnen; **to have acquired a modest** ~ gewisse Unabhängigkeit erreicht haben; **to live a life of** ~ unabhängiges Leben führen; **to secure** ~ Unabhängigkeit erhalten;
~ **Day** *(US)* Unabhängigkeitstag; ~ **movement** Unabhängigkeitsbewegung.

independency *(politics)* unabhängiger Staat.

independent *(broadcasting)* freier Sender, *(in politics)* unabhängiger Politiker, Parteiloser, *(voter)* unabhängiger Wähler;
~**s** *(union, US)* unabhängige Gewerkschaften;
to vote for the ~**s next election** bei der nächsten Wahl die freie Wählergemeinschaft wählen;
~ *(a.)* selbständig, [finanziell] unabhängig, ungebunden, selbständig, frei, im Besitz hinreichender Mittel, *(pol.)* unabhängig, fraktionslos, parteilos;
to be ~ auf eigenen Füßen stehen; **to be** ~ **of one's parents** nicht auf seine Eltern angewiesen sein; **to be** ~ **of trains, trams and buses** von den öffentlichen Verkehrsmitteln unabhängig sein;
~ **accountant** *(US)* Wirtschaftsprüfer; ~ **activities** selbständige Tätigkeit; ~ **adjuster** selbständiger Schadensabschätzer; ~ **advice** *(trust deed, will)* unparteiische Beratung; ~ **agency** *(US)* unabhängige Bundesverwaltungsbehörde; **to put on an** ~ **air** *(fam.)* sich aufspielen (brüsten); ~ **banking system** unabhängiges Bankwesen; ~ **Broadcasting Authority** Verwaltungsrat der unabhängigen Rundfunk- und Fernsehgesellschaften; ~ **businessman** selbständiger Gewerbetreibender; **in an** ~ **capacity** in freiberuflicher Tätigkeit, selbständig; ~ **contract** selbständiger Vertrag, Vertrag über selbständige Leistungen; ~ **contractor** selbständiger Unternehmer; ~ **covenant** abstrakte Verpflichtung; ~ **financing** Eigenfinanzierung; ~ **firm** selbständige Firma; ~ **fortune** Vermögen, das unabhängig macht; ~ **gentleman** Rentner, Privatier; ~ **income** freiberufliche Einkünfte; **to have an** ~ **income** Privatvermögen besitzen, privatisieren; ~ **means** eigenes Vermögen; **to be of** ~ **means** finanziell unabhängig sein; ~ **outlet** unabhängiges Einzelhandelsgeschäft; ~ **patent** selbständiges Patent; ~ **proof** selbständiger Beweis; ~ **retail trade** ungebundener Einzelhandel; ~ **retailer** selbständiger Einzelhändler; ~ **store** *(US)* selbständiges Einzelhandelsgeschäft; ~ **television** kommerzielles Fernsehen; ~ **thinker** selbständiger Denker; ~ **union** unabhängige Fachgewerkschaft; ~ **witness** freiwilliger Zeuge.

indeterminable unbestimmbar.

indeterminate unbestimmt, unsicher;
~ **bonds** *(US)* Obligationen mit erst nach einer gewissen Laufzeit festgesetztem Rückzahlungstermin; ~ **damages** unbezifferter Schadenersatz; ~ **debate** ergebnislose Diskussion; ~ **ideas** unklare Ideen; ~ **obligation** Gattungsschuld; ~ **sentence** *(US)* Strafe von unbestimmter Dauer, Rahmenstrafe.

index Inhalts-, Namenverzeichnis, Index, [Sach]register, Tabelle, Kennziffer, *(fig.)* Wegweiser, Fingerzeig, *(index file)* Kartei, Karthotek, *(pointer)* Anzeiger, Nachweiser, *(print.)* Hand[zeichen];
tied to the ~ indexgebunden, -gekoppelt;
all-share ~ allgemeiner Aktienindex; **alphabetical** ~ alphabetisches Verzeichnis; **business** ~ Handelsregister; **card** ~ Kartei, Kartothek; **chain** ~ verketteter Index; **cost-of-living** ~ Lebenskosten-, Lebenshaltungsindex; **crossed weight** ~ gekreuzter Index; **Dow Jones** ~ *(US)* Aktienkursindex; **expurgatory** ~ Index der katholischen Kirche; **industrial ordinary** ~ Index der als typisch erachteten Stammaktien; **industrial production** ~ Produktionsindex; **overall** ~ Gesamtindex; **price** ~ Preisindex; **adjusted production** ~ bereinigter Produktionsindex; **national-production** ~ Index der industriellen Nettoproduktion; **quantum** ~ Mengenindex; **share-price** ~ *(Br.)*

Aktenindex; **stock-exchange** ~ Börsenindex; **subject** ~ Sachkatalog, -verzeichnis; **thumb** ~ *(book)* Daumenindex; **trade** ~ Handelsindex; **unweighted** ~ unbewerteter Index; **weighted** ~ gewogener Index; **wholesale-price** ~ Großhandelsindex; ~ **of general business activity** Konjunkturindex; ~ **of abnormality** Abnormalitätsindex; ~ **of association** Assoziationsindex; ~ **based on 1914 averages as 100** auf den Durchschnitt von 1914 mit 100 bezogener Index; ~ **of building (construction) costs** Baukostenindex; ~ **of consumer prices** Verbraucherpreisindex; ~ **of employment** Beschäftigungsindex; ~ **of total gain from trade** Index des gesamten Handelsgewinns; ~ **of industrial production** Index der industriellen Nettoproduktion, Produktionsindex; ~ **of inflation** Inflationsindex; ~ **of members** *(Br.)* Aktionärsverzeichnis; ~ **of names** Namensverzeichnis; ~ **of orders booked** Auftragsliste; ~ **of retail prices** Einzelhandelspreisindex; ~ **of securities** Effektenindex; ~ **of industrial shares** Industrieaktienindex; ~ **of share prices** Aktienindex, Index der Aktienkurse; ~ **of stocks** *(US)* Index der Aktienkurse, Aktienindex; ~ **of wholesale prices** Großhandelsindex; ~ *(v.)* mit einem Inhaltsverzeichnis versehen, registrieren; ~ **oil prices to industrial goods** Ölpreis an Industrieproduktpreise koppeln; **to be an** ~ **of a country's prosperity** Gradmesser für den Wohlstand eines Landes sein (darstellen); **to compile an** ~ Register zusammenstellen; **to enter an item on an** ~ Posten in ein Verzeichnis aufnehmen; **to put a book on the** ~ Buch verbieten; ~ **board** *(US, cardboard)* Karteikartenpapier; ~ **card** Karteikarte; ~ **clause** Indexklausel; ~ **clip** Karteireiter; ~ **curve** Indexkurve; ~ **figures** Indexzahlen; ~ **file** Kartei, Kartothek; ~ **finger** Zeigefinger; ~ **fund** an den Aktienindex gekoppelter Investmentfonds, Indexfonds; ~ **heading** Sachregisterrubrik; ~ **linked** mit einem Index gekoppelt; ~ **linking** Indexverbindung, -kopplung; ~ **letter** Anfangsbuchstabe.

index number *(statistics)* Index[zahl], Indexziffer, Meßziffer, Katalognummer;
composite ~ Generalindex; **cross-weighted** ~ gekreuzter Index; **weighted** ~ gewogener Index; ~ **of cost of living** Lebenskosten-, Lebenshaltungsindex; ~ **of securities** Effektenindex; ~ **of wholesale prices** Großhandelsindex; ~ **valuation** Bewertung anhand des Wirtschaftsindex; ~ **wage** an den Lebenshaltungsindex gebundener Lohn, Indexlohn; ~ **wage provisions** auf den Lebenshaltungsindex abgestimmte Lohnregelung; ~ **wage rise** Indexlohnerhöhung.

indexation Indexierung, Indexbindung; **tax** ~ Steuerindexierung; ~ **of personal tax allowances** Indexierung von Steuerfreibeträgen; ~ **of taxes** Steuerindexierung; ~ **of tax threshold** Indexierung der Steueranfangsbeträge (des unteren Proportionalbereichs); ~ **package** gesamte Steuerindexierung; ~ **system** Indexsystem.

indexed and annotated mit Sachregister und Anmerkungen versehen.

Indian | **Ink** Ausziehtusche; · **summer** Altweiber-, Spätsommer.

indicate *(v.)* zeigen, darauf hinweisen, bezeichnen, anzeigen; ~ **one's plans** seine Pläne kurz andeuten.

indicated, as wie angegeben; ~ **amount** angegebener Betrag.

indication Anzeichen, Hinweis, Anhaltspunkt, Fingerzeig; **according to all** ~s nach allen Anzeichen; **with no** ~ **of the year** ohne Jahreszahl; ~ **of origin** Ursprungsbezeichnung, -vermerk; ~ **of place** Ortsangabe; ~ **of price** Preisangabe; ~ **of publisher** Verlagsangabe; ~ **of references** Angabe von Referenzen; ~ **of route** *(letters)* Leitvermerk; ~ **of storm** Sturmanzeichen; **to give early** ~s **of one's talent** seine Begabung frühzeitig erkennen lassen.

indicative hinweisend, andeutend; ~ **evidence** angetretener Beweis; ~ **price** *(EC)* Hinweispreis.

indicator Indikator, Meßgröße, Gradmesser, *(car)* Winker, *(monetary policy)* Indikator;
sensitive leading business ~ bedeutsamer konjunkturempfindlicher Indikator; **direction** ~ Fahrtrichtungsanzeiger; **distance** ~ *(car)* Kilometerzähler; **economic** ~ Konjunkturindikator, -barometer; **key** ~ Schlüsselbarometer; **lagging** ~ nachhinkender Konjunkturindikator; **speed** ~ Geschwindigkeitsmesser; **train** ~ Ankunfts- und Abfahrtstafel; **true** ~ überzeugender Beweis; ~ **of business** Konjunkturbarometer; ~s **to inflation** Inflationsindikatoren; ~ **of production** Produktionsbarometer; ~ **arm** Winkerarm; ~ **board** Anzeigetafel, Tableau; ~ **card (diagram)** Leistungsdiagramm.

indict *(v.)* anklagen, öffentliche Anklage erheben, verklagen.

indictable an-, verklagbar, strafrechtlich verfolgbar, strafwürdig, strafbar; ~ **offence** Verbrechen, schweres Vergehen, Schwurgerichtssache; ~ **offender** [Kriminal]verbrecher, Straftäter.

indicted for (on charge of) complicity als Mittäter angeklagt.

indictee Angeklagter.

indicter *(criminal law)* Ankläger; **to assume the role of** ~ Anklagerolle übernehmen.

indictment Beschuldigung, formelle Anklage[schrift], Anklageerhebung, -verfügung, Eröffnungsbeschluß; **fresh** ~ neuer Anklagepunkt; **to bring in (lay) an** ~ **against s. o.** Anklage gegen j. erheben; **to exclude from** ~ Anklage fallenlassen; **to find an** ~ dringenden Tatverdacht bestätigen; **to prefer an** ~ Anklageschrift vorlegen; **to quash an** ~ Verfahren einstellen; **to traverse an** ~ Gegenbeweis führen.

indictor Ankläger.

indifference Gleichgültigkeit, Interesselosigkeit; **to show** ~ **to s. one's fate** von jds. Schicksal nicht beeindruckt sein.

indifferent unbeteiligt, unparteiisch, uninteressiert, gleichgültig; **to remain** ~ neutral bleiben.

indigence Vermögenslosigkeit, Armut, Bedürftigkeit.

indigene Einheimischer, Eingeborener.

indigent [unterstützungs]bedürftig, arm; ~ **insane person** mitteloser Geisteskranker.

indigestible diet unverdauliche Kost.

indigestion Magenverstimmung; ~ **in the market** Marktverstimmung.

indignation Entrüstung, Empörung; ~ **meeting** Protestversammlung.

indignity Beschimpfung, Kränkung, Beleidigung, Schmähung, *(divorce suit, US)* seelische Grausamkeit.

indirect mittelbar, nicht unmittelbar, indirekt, *(law)* nicht in direkter Linie ererbt;
~ **action** *(advertising)* Prestigewerbung; ~ **arbitration** indirekte Arbitrage; ~ **bill** Domizilwechsel; ~ **claim** Schadenersatzforderung für mittelbar zugefügten Schaden; ~ **cost** Fertigungsgemeinkosten; ~ **damage** mittelbarer Schaden; ~ **department** Hilfskostenstelle; ~ **dialling system** *(tel.)* Durchwahlsystem; ~ **elections** indirekte Wahlen; ~ **evidence** mittelbarer Beweis, Indizienbeweis; ~ **exchange** indirekte Devisenarbitrage; ~ **expenses** allgemeine Geschäftsunkosten, Fertigungsgemeinkosten; ~ **exporting** unsichtbare Ausfuhr; ~ **initiative** *(US)* von den Wählern ausgehender Gesetzantrag; ~ **labo(u)r cost** Gemeinkostenlöhne; ~ **liability** Eventualverbindlichkeit; ~ **lighting** indirekte Beleuchtung; ~ **material** Hilfs-, Gemeinkostenmaterial; ~ **means** Umwege, Umschweife; ~ **opinion method** indirekte Befragungsmethode; ~ **possession** mittelbarer Besitz; ~ **production** mittelbare Produktion; ~ **rates** *(Br.)* per Pfund notierte Devisenkurse; ~ **relief** *(double taxation)* Anrechnungsverfahren; ~ **road** Umweg; ~ **route** Umwegstrecke; ~ **selling** Verkauf durch Mittelsleute; ~ **speech** *(gr.)* indirekte Rede; ~ **tax** indirekte Steuer; ~ **tax increase** Erhöhung der indirekten Steuern; ~ **way** Umweg.

indirection indirektes Vorgehen; **by** ~ auf Umwegen.

indirectly auf Umwegen.

indiscipline Disziplinlosigkeit.

indiscrete step unkluger Schritt.

indiscretion Vertrauensbruch, Indiskretion.

indiscriminate unterschiedslos, wahllos; ~ **charity** kritiklose Wohltätigkeit.

indiscriminating unterschiedslos, wahl-, kritiklos.

indiscrimination Unterschiedslosigkeit, Kritiklosigkeit.

indispensable unerläßlich, unentbehrlich, unabkömmlich; ~ **parties** notwendige Streitgenossen.

indisposed nicht aufgelegt, abgeneigt, indisponiert.

indisposition Unpäßlichkeit, Verstimmung.

indisputability Unbestreitbarkeit.

indisputable unbestreitbar, unstreitig.

indistanter unverzüglich.

individual Einzelperson, natürliche Person, Individuum;
private ~ Privatmann, -person; **shady** ~s zweifelhafte Existenzen; **to act merely as an** ~ lediglich als Privatperson handeln; ~ *(a.)* einzeln, eigentümlich, persönlich, besonders, individuell, charakteristisch; ~ **account** Einzelkonto; ~ **achievement** Einzelleistung; ~ **air outlet** Einzelbelüftung; ~ **amount** Einzelbetrag; ~ **apartment**

eigene Wohnung; ~ **area** Einzelbereich; ~ **assets** Privatvermögen [eines Gesellschafters]; ~ **bank return** *(US)* Ausweis der New Yorker Girozentrale; ~ **banker** *(US)* Privatbankier; ~ **bargaining** Einzeltarifverhandlung; ~ **bond** persönlicher Schuldschein; ~ **case** vorliegender Fall, Einzelfall; ~ **consumer** Einzelverbraucher; ~ **cost** Einzelkosten; ~ **credit** Personalkredit; ~ **creditor** Privatgläubiger; ~ **debts** Privatschulden [eines Gesellschafters]; ~ **deposits** Guthaben privater Kundschaft; ~ **earnings** pro Kopf-Einkommen; ~ **entrepreneur** Einzelunternehmer; ~ **estate** persönliches Vermögen [eines Gesellschafters]; ~ **firm** *(US)* Einzelfirma; ~ **income** Privateinkünfte; ~ **income tax** *(US)* Einkommensteuer; ~ **initiative** Privatinitiative; ~ **insurance** Individual-, Einzelversicherung; ~ **insurer** Einzelversicherer; ~ **ledger** Kundenbuch; ~ **licence** Einzelgenehmigung; ~ **location** *(advertising)* Sonderplacierung; ~ **member** Einzelmitglied; ~ **order** Einzelauftrag; ~ **output** Einzelproduktion, Einzelanfertigung; ~ **person** Individuum, Einzelperson; ~ **piece rate** Einzelakkordsatz; ~ **piecework** Einzelakkord; ~ **producer** Einzelerzeuger; ~ **production** Einzelanfertigung; ~ **property** Privatvermögen; ~ **proprietor** *(US)* alleiniger Geschäftsinhaber; ~ **proprietorship** *(US)* Einzelfirma; ~ **purchaser** Einzelkäufer; ~ **rate** Einzelakkordsatz; ~ **resident of the United States** natürliche Person mit Wohnsitz in den USA; ~ **statement** *(US)* Einzelbilanz; ~ **style** charakteristischer Stil; ~ **tax burden** steuerliche Individualbelastung; ~ **valuation** Einzelbewertung; ~ **vendor** Einzelverkäufer; ~ **wage** Einzellohn; ~ **wealth** Privatvermögen; ~ **weight** Stückgewicht.

individually namentlich, persönlich, jeder für sich, einzeln;
to be ~ liable persönlich haften.

individualism persönliche Note, Persönlichkeit, Individualität, Individualismus;
rugged ~ krasser Individualismus.

individualist Einzelgänger, Individualist.

indivisible performance unteilbare Leistung.

indoctrinate *(v.)* unterweisen, schulen;
~ **s. o. with an idea** jem. eine Idee eintrichtern.

indoctrination Unterweisung, Schulung.

indolence Trägheit.

indoor im Hause;
to have to stay ~s Hausarrest haben; **to keep ~s** das Haus hüten;
~ **aerial** Zimmer-, Innenantenne; ~ **dress** Hauskleidung; ~ **installation** Hausinstallation; ~ **meeting** geschlossene Versammlung; ~ **photo** Innenaufnahme; ~ **plant** Zimmerpflanze; ~ **relief** anstaltsinterne Unterstützung; ~ **shot** *(film)* Innenaufnahme; ~ **staff** Hauspersonal; ~ **swimming pool** Hallenbad; ~ **work** Haus-, Heimarbeit.

indorsable girierbar, indossabel, indossierbar.

indorse *(v.)* indossieren, girieren, begeben, durch Indossament übertragen;
~ **back** durch Giro zurückbegeben; ~ **in full** voll girieren.

indorsed mit Giro (Indossament) versehen;
~ **in blank** mit Blankoindossament versehen, in blanko giriert; **amount** ~ eingelöster Betrag; **duly** ~ ordnungsgemäß giriert.

indorsee Girat, Indossat, Indossatar;
~ **in due course** gutgläubiger Indossatar.

indorsement Giro, Indossament, Indossierung, *(insurance)* Versicherungsnachtrag, *(sanction)* Bestätigung, *(writing on back of document)* Rückseitenvermerk;
transferable by ~ durch Indossament übertragbar, indossabel; **without** ~ ungiriert;
absolute ~ *(US)* unbeschränktes Giro; **accommodation** ~ Gefälligkeitsindossament; **blank** ~ Blankoindossament, -giro; **conditional** ~ bedingtes (beschränktes) Giro; ~ **confirmed** Giro bestätigt; **direct** ~ *(US)* Vollgiro; **fiduciary** ~ fiduziarisches Indossament; **forged** ~ gefälschtes Indossament, Girofälschung; **full** ~ Vollgiro; **general** ~ Blankoindossament; **irregular** ~ ungenaues Giro, Indossament nicht in Ordnung; **official** ~ amtliche Bestätigung; **partial** ~ Teilindossament; **per pro.** ~ Prokuraindossament; **pledge** ~ Pfandindossament; **post** ~ Nachindossament; **proper** ~ ordnungsgemäßes Giro; **qualified** ~ Giro ohne Verbindlichkeit (Obligo), beschränktes Indossament; **regular** ~ gewöhnliches Giro; **required** Giro fehlt; **restrictive** ~ beschränktes Giro (Indossament), Ermächtigungs-, Inkassoindossament, Rektaindossament; **special** ~ Vollgiro, -indossament; **unauthorized** ~ unbefugtes Indossament;
~ **in blank** Blankoindossament, Blankogiro; ~ **of a cheque** Girierung eines Schecks; ~ **on a document** Vermerk auf einer Urkunde; ~ **of a firm** Firmenindossament; ~ **in full** Vollgiro; ~ **after maturity** Nachindossament; ~ **on a policy** Policenver-

merk; ~ **per procuration** Prokuraindossament; ~ **supra protest** Indossament nach Protest; ~ **in representative capacity** Prokuraindossament; ~ **without recourse** Giro ohne Verbindlichkeit (Obligo); ~ **of trustee** Treuhandgiro; **special** ~ **of writ** *(Br.)* abgekürzte Klagebegründung, Zustellungsvermerk mit Rechnungslegung;
to place a ~ indossieren; **to transfer by** ~ durch Giro übertragen;
~ **stamp** Girostempel.

indorser Girant, Indossant, Begebender;
accommodation ~ Gefälligkeitsgirant; **intermediate** ~ Zwischengirant; **preceding (previous, prior)** ~ Vordermann; **qualified** ~ Girant ohne Verbindlichkeit; **subsequent** ~ Hinter-, Nachmann; **unqualified** ~ Blankogirant;
~'**s liability** Wechselhaftung, Giroverbindlichkeit.

indorsing a cheque *(Br.)* **(check,** *US)* Girierung eines Schecks.

induce *(v.)* veranlassen, bewegen, verleiten, anstiften;
~ **s. o. to change his mind** j. zu einer Meinungsänderung veranlassen; ~ **men to strike** Arbeiter zum Streik verleiten.

induced veranlaßt, *(el.)* sekundär, induziert;
~ **consumption** Verbrauchssteigerung; ~ **current** *(el.)* Induktionsstrom; ~ **investment** Investitionssteigerung.

inducement Anreiz, Anteil, Antrieb, Beweggrund, Veranlassung, Verleitung, *(contracting)* Interesse, *(criminal evidence)* Tatmotiv, *(introduction)* einleitende Tatsachenfeststellung, *(pleading)* zusammenfassende Klagebegründung;
direct ~ *(union official)* unmittelbare Anstiftung zum Vertragsbruch;
~**s of a business career** Berufsaussichten; ~ **to buy** Kaufanreiz; ~ **to enter a contract** Verleitung zum Vertragsabschluß; ~ **to fund** Fundierungsanreiz; ~ **of infringement** Anstiftung zur Patentverletzung; ~**s of a large town** Großstadtverlockungen; **to hold out an** ~ **to s. o.** jem. etw. als Anreiz bieten.

inducing breach of contract Verleitung zum Vertragsbruch, Anstiftung zum Vertragsbruch.

induct *(v.)* *(mil., US)* [zum Militärdienst] einziehen, einberufen, *(in office)* einsetzen, einführen.

inductee *(mil., US)* Einberufener, Eingezogener, Eingerückter, Rekrut.

induction *(el.)* Induktion, *(mil., US)* Einberufung, Einziehung, Einrücken, *(in office)* Einsetzung, Einführung;
~ **order** *(US)* Gestellungs-, Einberufungsbefehl; ~ **pipe** *(engine)* Ansaugrohr; ~ **station** *(US)* Einberufungsort.

indulge *(v.)* nachsichtig sein, gewähren lassen;
~ **in s. th.** sich mit etw. abgeben; ~ **a debtor** einem Schuldner Zahlungsaufschub gewähren; ~ **in extravagances** sich Extravaganzen leisten; ~ **one's taste** seiner Neigung frönen, sich leisten; ~ **s. one's whims** jds. Launen nachgeben.

indulgence *(favo(u)r)* Entgegenkommen, Vergünstigung, *(priority)* Vorrecht, Privileg, *(respite)* Zahlungs-, [Wechsel]stundung, *(self-gratification)* Freizeitbeschäftigung;
~ **in gambling** Spielleidenschaft; ~ **of a guest** einem Gast bezeigtes Entgegenkommen;
to ask s. one's ~ j. um Nachsicht bitten; **to grant s. o. every** ~ äußerst nachsichtig gegenüber jem. sein.

indulgent judge milder Richter.

industrial Gewerbetreibender, Industrieller, *(worker)* Industriearbeiter;
~**s** *(stock exchange)* Industriepapiere, -werte, *(stock exchange report)* Industriemarkt;
~ *(a.)* industriell, gewerblich, *(industrialized)* mit starker Industrie, industrialisiert, *(belonging to industrial life insurance)* Arbeiterlebensversicherung betreffend, *(person)* in der Industrie beschäftigt;
highly ~ hochindustrialisiert;
~ **accession** Bearbeitungszuschlag; ~ **accident** Dienst-, Arbeits-, Fabrik-, Betriebsunfall; ~ **accident insurance** Betriebsunfallversicherung; ~ **accident prevention** Betriebsunfallverhütung; ~ **accident reserve** Rückstellungen für Betriebsunfälle; ~ **accomplishment** Wirtschaftserfolg; ~ **accounting** Betriebsbuchhaltung, industrielles Rechnungswesen; ~ **accounting system** Industriekontenrahmen; ~ **accounts** *(agency)* Industriekundschaft; ~ **achievements** industrielle Leistungen; ~ **action** Arbeitskonflikt, betriebliche Kampfhandlung, Arbeitskampf; **irregular** ~ **action short of a strike** *(Br.)* streikähnliche rechtswidrige Kampfmaßnahmen; ~ **activity** gewerbliche Tätigkeit; ~ **administration** Betriebswirtschaft; ~ **advance** öffentlicher Kredit an einen Gewerbebetrieb; ~ **advertiser** Anzeigenblatt der Wirtschaft; ~ **advertising** Werbung für Industrieerzeugnisse, Produktions-, Investititionsgüterwerbung; ~ **adviser** *(US)* Betriebsberater; ~ **affiliations** Industrie-

verbindungen; ~ **agency** Agentur für Industriewerbung; ~ **agreement** Tarif-, Lohnabkommen; ~ **arbitration** gewerbliche Schiedsgerichtsbarkeit; ≗ **Arbitration Board** *(Br.)* Gewerbeschiedsgericht; ~ **area** Industriegebiet; ~ **art** Gewerbegraphik; ~ **artist** Werbegraphiker; ~ **association** *(US)* Fach-, Wirtschafts-, Industrieverband; ~ **assurance** *(Br.)* Kleinlebensversicherung; ≗ **Assurance and Friendly Societies Act** *(Br.)* Lebensversicherungen und Sterbekassengesetz; ≗ **Assurance Commissioner** *(Br.)* Aufsichtsbehörde für Kleinlebensversicherer; ~ **average** Industriedurchschnitt; ~ **award** tarifrechtlicher Schiedsspruch; ~ **bank** Industrie-, Kredit-, Gewerbebank; **skeletal ~ base** zum Skelett abgemagertes Industriereservoir; ~ **bill** Industrieakzept; ~ **bonds** Industrieanleihen, -obligationen; ~ **borrower** Kreditnehmer aus der Industrie; ~ **broker** Grundstücksmakler für gewerbliche Grundstücke; ~ **building** gewerblich genutztes Gebäude; ~ **business** *(life insurance)* Kleinlebensversicherungsgeschäft; ~ **buyer** Einkäufer für die Industrie; ~ **canteen** Betriebskantine; ~ **capacity** industrielle Kapazität; ~ **capital** Gewerbe-, Industriekapital; ~ **capitalism** Industriekapitalismus; ~ **census** Betriebszählung; ~ **center** *(US)* **(centre,** *Br.)* Industriezentrum; ~ **charges** gewerbliche Abgaben; ~ **circles** Industriekreise; ~ **city** Industrie-, Fabrikstadt; ~ **class** Fabrikarbeiterschaft; ~ **code** Gewerbeordnung; ~ **collateral** *(US)* Sicherheit durch Hinterlegung von Industrieaktien; ~ **colony** Industrieansiedlung, mit öffentlichen Mitteln unterhaltene Arbeitersiedlung; ~ **combination** industrieller Zusammenschluß, Industriekonzern; ~ **commission** Sozialversicherungsbehörde; ~ **commodities** Güter der gewerblichen Wirtschaft; ~ **community** Industriegebiet; ~ **company** Industriebetrieb; ~ **complex** Industriekomplex; ~ **concentration** wirtschaftliche Konzentration, Betriebskonzentration; ~ **concern** Industrieunternehmen, -betrieb, -konzern; ~ **conference** Wirtschaftsbesprechung; ~ **conflict** Arbeitskonflikt; ~ **conscription** *(US)* Arbeitsdienstpflicht; ~ **conglomerate** Industriekonzern; ~ **construction** Industriebauten; ~ **consumer** gewerblicher Verbraucher, Großabnehmer; ~ **consumption** gewerblicher Verbrauch, Großabnahme; ~ **control** Wirtschaftskontrolle, Gewerbeaufsicht; ~ **cooperation [society]** gewerbliche Genossenschaft; ~ **corporation** Industrieunternehmen; ~ **cost accounting** betriebliches Rechnungswesen; ~ **counsellor** Wirtschafts-, Industrieberater; ~ **country** Industriestaat; ≗ **Arbitration Court** *(Br.)* Gewerbegericht, Schlichtungsausschuß, Berufungsgericht in Arbeitsstreitigkeiten; ~ **credit** Industriekredit; ~ **cross-section** wirtschaftlicher Querschnitt; ~ **customer** Industrieabnehmer; ~ **death benefit** Sterbegeld für Betriebsunfälle; ~ **death benefit for widows and other dependants** *(Br.)* Invalidenrente für Familienangehörige; ~ **democracy** mitbestimmte Wirtschaft, Wirtschaftsdemokratie; ~ **design** industrielle Formgebung, Gebrauchsmuster; ~ **designer** Formgestalter, technischer Zeichner, Gebrauchsgraphiker; ~ **development** Industrieansiedlung, *(planning)* industrielle Erschließung; ~ **development certificate** *(Board of Trade, Br.)* Standortbescheinigung; ~ **development company** Erschließungsgesellschaft; ~ **diamond** Industriediamant; ~ **disablement benefit** *(Br.)* Versehrten-, Erwerbsunfähigkeitsrente; ~ **discipline** Betriebsdisziplin; **prescribed ~ disease** *(Br.)* Berufskrankheit; ~ **dismantling** [Industrie]demontage; ~ **display** Schau industrieller Erzeugnisse; ~ **dispute** Arbeitsstreitigkeit, -kampf; ≗ **Disputes Tribunal** *(Br.)* Berufungsgericht für Arbeitsstreitigkeiten; ~ **distributor** Großhändler für Industriebetriebe; ~ **district** Industriebezirk, -gegend; ~ **division** Industriezweig, Sparte, Fachgruppe; ~ **domain** Wirtschaftsbereich; ~ **economy** gewerbliche Wirtschaft; ~ **education** Betriebsausbildung; ~ **efficiency** Leistungsfähigkeit der Wirtschaft; ~ **empire** Wirtschaftsimperium; ~ **employee** Fabrikangestellter; ~ **employment** industrielle Tätigkeit, Gewerbetätigkeit; ~ **emporium** wirtschaftliche Schlüsselstellung; ~ **engineer** Wirtschaftsingenieur; ~ **engineering** *(US)* Fertigungssteuerung, Betriebstechnik; ~ **enterprise** gewerblicher Betrieb, Industrieunternehmen, -betrieb; ~ **equipment** Betriebsausrüstung; ~ **equities** Industrieaktien, -werte; ~ **espionage** Industrie-, Wirtschaftsspionage; ~ **estate** *(Br.)* Industriegelände, -erwartungsland, -siedlung; ~ **executive** *(US)* Gewerbeaufseher; ~ **exhibition** Industrie-, Gewerbeausstellung; ~ **expansion** wirtschaftliche Expansion, Betriebsausweitung; ~ **expansion program(me)** Wirtschaftsprogramm; **to slow down ~ expansion** Wachstum der Industrie verlangsamen; ~ **expansion program(me)** Wirtschaftsprogramm; ~ **experience** Industrieerfahrungen; ~ **fair** Industriemesse; ~ **fatality** tödlicher Betriebsunfall; ~ **features** *(stock exchange)* Industriewerte; ~ **finance** Wirtschaftsfinanzierung; ~ **finance company** Wirtschaftsfinanzierungsgesellschaft, Konsum-, gewerbliche Kreditgenossenschaft; ~ **and Commercial Finance Corporation Ltd** *(Br.)* [etwa] Industriekreditbank; ~ **floor space** industrielle Nutzfläche; ~ **fluctuation** konjunkturbedingte Schwankungen der Wirtschaft; ~ **gathering** Wirtschaftstagung; ~ **geography** Wirtschaftsgeographie; ~ **giant** Industriegigant; ~ **goods** Industrieprodukte, Investitions-, Produktionsgüter; ~ **group** Industriegruppe; ~ **growth** Wachstum der Industrie; ~ **hazard** Betriebsrisiko; ~ **health** Arbeitshygiene, betriebliches Gesundheitswesen; ~ **hereditaments** Fabrik oder Werkstatt; ~ **hub** Industriezentrum; ~ **hygiene** Betriebshygiene; ~ **illness** Berufskrankheit; ~ **income** Einkünfte aus Gewerbebetrieb; ~ **index** Industrieindex; ~ **information** gewerbliche Öffentlichkeitsarbeit; ≗ **Injuries Act** *(Br.)* Sozialversicherungsgesetz; ~ **injuries benefit** *(Br.)* Sozialversicherungsleistungen bei Arbeitsunfällen (in Berufsschadensfällen), Betriebsunfallrente; ~ **injuries scheme** Sozialversicherungssystem; ~ **injuries system** Berufsunfallversorgung; ~ **injury** Betriebs-, Berufsunfall, Arbeitsunfall, Dienstbeschädigung, Berufsschaden; ~ **injury benefit** Arbeitsunfähigkeitsrente; ~ **installations** industrielle Anlagen, Industrieanlagen; ~ **[life] insurance** Kleinlebens-, Volksversicherung; ~ **insurance agent** festangestellter Versicherungsvertreter; ~ **insurance fund** Betriebskrankenkasse; ~ **intervention** wirtschaftspolitische Intervention; ~ **inventory** Fabriklager; ~ **investment** Vermögensanlage in Industriewerten; ~ **issues** Industriewerte, -emissionen; ~ **jurisdiction** Gerichtshoheit in Arbeitsrechtsfragen; ~ **labo(u)rer** Fabrikarbeiter; ~ **land** Betriebs-, Industriegrundstück, -gelände; ~ **law** *(Br.)* Gewerbe-, Arbeitsrecht; ~ **leader** Wirtschaftsführer; ~ **library** Werksbibliothek; ~ **licence** Produktionskonzession; ~ **life** Wirtschaftsleben; ~ **life insurance** Kleinlebensversicherung; ≗ **Life Office Association** *(Br.)* Verband der Kleinlebensversicherungen; ~ **line** Betriebseisenbahn; ~ **list** *(stock exchange)* Kurszettel der Industriewerte; ~ **loan** Industrieanleihe; ~ **loan company** gewerbliche Kreditgenossenschaft; ~ **loan society** gewerblicher Kreditverein; ~ **location policy** Ansiedlungspolitik, ~ **machine** *(US)* Industrieorganisation; ~ **magazine** industrielle Fachzeitschrift; ~ **magnate** Großindustrieller; ~ **management** Betriebsführung, *(business administration)* Betriebswirtschaft; ~ **manager** Betriebsführer; ~ **manufactures** gewerbliche Fertigwaren; ~ **market** Absatzmarkt für industrielle Erzeugnisse, Investitionsgütermarkt, *(stock exchange)* Industriemarkt; ~ **market research** Produktionsgütermarktforschung; ~ **marketing** Absatzwirtschaft; **basic ~ materials** Industriegrundstoffe; ~ **medicine** Betriebsmedizin; ~ **ministry** Industrieministerium; ~ **mobility** regionale Mobilität der Betriebe; ~ **mobilization** Mobilisierung (Mobilmachung) der Wirtschaft; ~ **monopoly** Wirtschafts-, Industriemonopol, Kartell; ~ **museum** Gewerbemuseum; ~ **nation** Industrieland; ~ **news** Wirtschaftsnachrichten; ~ **news service** Nachrichtendienst für die Wirtschaft; ~ **occupation** gewerblicher Beruf; ~ **ordinary index** Index als typisch erachteter Stammaktien (industrieller Stammaktien); ~ **organization** Industrieverband, *(Br.)* Industriebetriebslehre; ~ **output** Industrieerzeugung, -ausstoß, -produktion; ~ **participation** industrielle Beteiligung; ~ **partnership** *(US)* Arbeitergewinnbeteiligung; ~ **patronage** Wirtschaftsbevormundung; ~ **paymaster** industrielle Finanzierungsquelle; ~ **payroll** Betriebslohnliste; ~ **peace** Arbeitsfrieden; ~ **pension** Sozialversicherungsrente bei Vollinvalidität; ~ **pension plan** betriebliche Altersversorgung; ~ **plan** Industrieprogramm; ~ **plant** Wirtschaftsbetrieb, Industrie-, Fabrikanlage, Werk; ~ **plant reserve** industrielle Reservekapazität; ~ **policy** sektorale Strukturpolitik; ~ **potential** Industriepotential; ~ **power** Industrienation; **unfair ~ practices** unlautere Arbeitskampfmethoden; **to constitute an unfair ~ practice** Tarifvertragsbruch darstellen; ~ **price** Fabrik[abgabe]preis; ~ **prison** Arbeitshaus; ~ **proceeds** Betriebsertrag; ~ **process** Produktions-, Herstellungsprozeß; ~ **procurement** Beschaffung von Industrieerzeugnissen; ~ **producer** Industrieller, Fabrikant; ~ **producer price** industrieller Erzeugerpreis; ~ **products** gewerbliche Erzeugnisse, Produktionsmittel, Zwischenprodukt; ~ **production** Industrieproduktion; ~ **production index** Produktionsindex; **to step up ~ production** Industrieproduktion erhöhen; ~ **property protection** gewerblicher Rechtsschutz; ~ **profit** Betriebsgewinn; ~ **project** Fabrikprojekt; ~ **property** gewerbliches Eigentum, *(land)* Industriegrundstück, gewerblich genutztes Grundstück; ~ **property rights** gewerbliche Schutzrechte; ~ **and provident society** *(Br.)* Erwerbsgenossenschaft, Konsumgenossenschaft, -verein; ~ **psychologist** Betriebspsychologe; ~ **psychology** Betriebspsychologie; ~ **purposes** gewerbliche Zwecke; ~ **railroad** *(US)* (railway, Br.) Betriebseisenbahn; ~ **recovery** Wirtschaftsbelebung; ~ **reformatory** (US) Besserungsanstalt; **to establish a new ~ regime** neues Industriezeitalter heraufführen; ~ **region** Fabrikgegend; ~ **regulations** gewerbepolizeiliche Bestimmungen; ~ **relations** Beziehungen zwischen dem Betrieb und überbetrieblichen Institutionen; ⌂ **Relations Act** (Br.) Gesetz zur Regelung der Beziehungen zwischen Arbeitnehmern und Arbeitgebern (Sozialpartnern), Sozialpartnergesetz; ~ **relations counsellor** Berater des Personalchefs; ~ **relations court** Schiedsgericht für Arbeitssachen, Schiedsgericht für Streitigkeiten zwischen Betrieben und Gewerkschaften; **to reject the ~ relations package** Bündel von Vorschlägen zur Regelung der Beziehungen zwischen den Sozialpartnern ablehnen; ~ **relations policy** Personalpolitik; ~ **report** Industriebericht; ~ **research** betriebswissenschaftliche Untersuchung; ~ **resources** industrielle Hilfsquellen; ~ **responsibility** Fürsorgefunktionen der gewerblichen Wirtschaft; ~ **restructuring** Umstrukturierung der Industrie; ~ **resurgence** Wiederaufbau der Wirtschaft; ~ **retail store** werkseigener Verkaufsladen, [Werks]kantine; **[diminishing] ~ return** [abnehmender] Wirtschafts-, Gewerbeertrag; ~ **revolution** industrielle Umwälzung (Revolution); ~ **sabotage** Wirtschaftssabotage; ~ **safety** Betriebssicherheit; ~ **sales** Industrieumsätze, industrieller Absatzmarkt; ~ **sanitation** betriebliche Gesundheitspflege; ~ **savings** Betriebs-, Werksparen; ~ **school** (Br.) Gewerbeschule, (US) Erziehungsanstalt für straffällige Jugendliche; ~ **science** Industriebetriebslehre; ~ **secret** Betriebsgeheimnis; ~ **section** Industriegegend; ~ **sector** industrieller Bereich; ~ **securities** Industriewerte, -papiere; ~ **self-government** Selbstverwaltung der Wirtschaft; ~ **selling** Direktverkauf, Beziehungskauf; ~ **service** Industrieberatungsdienst; ~ **shares** Industriewerte; ~ **sickness insurance fund** Betriebskrankenkasse; ~ **site** Fabrikgrundstück, Industrieareal; ~ **social work** Betriebsfürsorge; ~ **society** Erwerbsgenossenschaft; ~ **and provident society** (Br.) Produktions- und Konsumverein, Erwerbs- und Wirtschaftsgenossenschaft; ⌂ **and Provident Societies Act** (Br.) Erwerbs- und Wirtschaftsgenossenschaftsgesetz, Konsumvereinsgesetz; ~ **sociologist** Betriebssoziologe; ~ **sociology** Betriebssoziologie; ~ **state** Industriestaat; ~ **statistics** Gewerbestatistik; ~ **stocks** (US) Industrieaktien, -werte; ~ **store** betriebseigener Laden; ~ **strife** Arbeitskampf; ~ **subsidies** Industriesubventionen; ~ **supplies** Industrielieferungen; ~ **system** Wirtschaftssystem; ~ **tax** Gewerbesteuer; ~ **town** Industrie-, Fabrikstadt; ~ **track** Fabrik-, Betriebsgleis; ~ **training** Fach-, Gewerbe-, Berufsausbildung; ⌂ **Training Act** (Br.) Berufs-, Gewerbeausbildungsgesetz; ~ **training board** (Br.) Berufsausbildungsstelle, Fortbildungsstelle; ~ **transference** Industrieumsetzung; ~ **tribunal** (Br.) Arbeits-, Gewerbegericht; ~ **trust** (US) Finanzierungsgesellschaft für Industriebedarf; ~ **undertaking** Industrieunternehmen; ~ **union** Industrie-, Betriebs-, Fachgewerkschaft; ~ **union council** Betriebsratsvereinigung; ~ **unionism** fachliches Gewerkschaftswesen; ~ **unit** Industrieanlage, Fabrikbetrieb; **large-scale ~ units** industrielle Großanlagen; ~ **use** industrielle Nutzung, gewerblicher Zweck, Gewerbezweck; ~ **user** gewerblicher Verbraucher; ~ **value** wirtschaftlicher Wert; ~ **wages** Industriearbeiterlöhne; ~ **warfare** Wirtschaftskrieg; ~ **wealth** Industrievermögen; ~ **welfare** Betriebsfürsorge; ~ **welfare work** Arbeiter-, Betriebsfürsorge; ~ **widow's pension** (Br.) Hinterbliebenenrente; ~ **work** industrielle Tätigkeit, Gewerbetätigkeit; ~ **worker** Industrie-, Fabrikarbeiter.

industrialism Gewerbetätigkeit, Industrialismus.

industrialist Industrieller, Gewerbetreibender;
big ~ Großindustrieller; **top ~** führender Industrieller.

industrialization Industrialisierung;
forced-draft ~ Zwangsindustrialisierung;
~ **program[me]** Industrialisierungsprogramm.

industrialize (v.) industrialisieren.

industrialized | **highly** hochindustrialisiert; **less ~** industrieschwach;
to become ~ zur Industrie werden;
~ **country** Industrieland, -staat; ~ **nation** Industriestaat.

industries, hard-goods devisenstarke Industriezweige; **high-type ~** hochwertige Industrieanlagen; **higher-taxed ~** höher besteuerte Industriezweige; **protected ~** (US) durch Schutzzölle geförderte Industriezweige; **recession-hit ~** von der Rezession besonders betroffene Industriesparten; **regulated ~** (US) gebundene Industriezweige; **resource-based ~** von Bodenschätzen abhängige Wirtschaftszweige; **secondary ~** weiterverarbeitende Industrie; **service ~** Dienstleistungsgewerbe; **service-oriented ~** dienstleistungsorientierte Industriezweige;

soft-goods ~ devisenschwache Industriezweige; **sweated ~** unterbezahlte Industriezweige; **seasonally unstable ~** saisonabhängige Industriezweige;
~ **with low employment output ratio** Industriezweige mit geringen Arbeitsintensitätsquoten im Verhältnis zur Gesamtproduktion;
to regulate the ~ of a country Wirtschaft eines Landes lenken;
to shut down whole ~ ganze Industriebranchen (Industriesparten) stillegen;
~ **fair** [Industrie]messe, -ausstellung.

industrious arbeitsam, fleißig, (industrial) gewerblich, industriell.

industry Industrie, (assiduity) Fleiß, Betriebsamkeit, (branch of ~) Branche, Gewerbe-, Wirtschafts-, Industriezweig, gewerbliche Wirtschaft, (entrepreneurs) Unternehmerschaft;
aero ~ Luftfahrtindustrie; **agricultural ~** Industrie für landwirtschaftliche Betriebsmittel; **armament ~** Rüstungsindustrie; **automobile (automotive, US) ~** Auto-, Kraftfahrzeugindustrie; **auxiliary ~** Hilfsindustrie; **banker-controlled ~** von den Banken beherrschte Industrie; **basic ~** Grund[stoff]industrie; **boot and shoe ~** Schuhindustrie; **bounty-fed ~** (Br.) subventionierte Industrie; **brewing ~** Brauereigewerbe; **building ~** Bauindustrie, -gewerbe, -wirtschaft; **capital-goods ~** Investitionsgüter-, Kapitalgüterindustrie; **car ~** Autoindustrie; **cement ~** Zementindustrie; **chemical ~** chemische Industrie; **close-knit ~** engverzahnter Industriezweig; **clothing ~** Bekleidungsindustrie; **coal, iron and steel ~** Montanindustrie; **coal-mining ~** Kohlenbergbau; **competing ~** Konkurrenzbetriebe; **construction ~** Bauindustrie; **consumer (consumption [goods]) ~** Konsum-, Verbrauchgüterindustrie; **continuous ~** sämtliche Phasen durchführender Industriebetrieb; **cotton ~** Baumwollindustrie; **covered ~** in die Arbeitslosenfürsorge miteinbezogene Industrie; **dangerous ~** gefährliches Gewerbe; **depressed ~** von der Krise betroffene Industriezweige; **domestic ~** einheimische Industrie; **electrical engineering ~** elektrotechnische Industrie; **electricity ~** Elektroindustrie; **embryo ~** noch in der Entwicklung begriffene Gewerbe; **engineered ~** metallverarbeitende Industrie; **essential ~** produktionswichtige Industrie; **export-oriented ~** exportintensive Industrie; **extractive ~** Industrie der Steine und Erden; ~ **that is falling off** an Bedeutung verlierender Industriezweig; **farming ~** Industrie für landwirtschaftliche Betriebsmittel; **[non]ferrous ~** [Nicht]eisenmetallindustrie; **finishing ~** verarbeitende Industrie, Veredlungswirtschaft; **food-processing (-manufacturing) ~** Lebensmittelindustrie; **foot-loose ~** standortunabhängige Industrie; **forest ~** forstwirtschaftlicher Betrieb; **fuel ~** Brennstoffindustrie; **glass ~** Glasindustrie; **heavy ~** Schwerindustrie; **heavy engineering ~** Schwermaschinenindustrie; **highly geared ~** kapitalintensive Industrie; **home ~** einheimische Industrie; ~ **still in its infancy** noch in den Kinderschuhen steckende Industrie; **infant ~** schutzzollbedürftige Industrie; **intra-state ~** (US) auf einen Staat beschränkte Industrie; **iron ~** Eisenindustrie; **iron and steel ~** Hüttenindustrie; **ironworking ~** eisenverarbeitende Industrie; **large-scale ~** Großindustrie; **leading ~** führende Industrie; **leather ~** Lederindustrie; **light ~** Leichtindustrie; **liquid fuel ~** Kraftstoffindustrie; **local ~** ortsansässige Industrie; **local-service ~** Nahverkehrsgewerbe; **machine-tool ~** Werkzeugmaschinenindustrie; **manufacturing ~** verarbeitende Industrie; **mechanical ~** Maschinenbauindustrie; **medium-sized ~** Mittelbetrieb; **metallurgical ~** Metallindustrie; **metal-working ~** metallverarbeitende Industrie; **mining ~** Montanindustrie; **monopolistic (monopolized) ~** Monopolindustrie; **motor-car ~** (Br.) Kraftfahrzeugindustrie; **nation-wide ~** (US) überregionale Industrie; **new ~** neuer Wirtschaftszweig; **nuisance ~** Emissionsbetrieb; **octopied ~** dezentralisierter Großbetrieb; **overcrowded ~** übersetzter Industriezweig; **oil ~** Ölindustrie; **paper ~** Papierindustrie; **power ~** Energiewirtschaft; **plastics ~** Kunststoffindustrie; **plastics-processing ~** kunststoffverarbeitende Industrie; **precision engineering ~** feinmechanische Industrie; **primary ~** Grundstoffindustrie; **private ~** Privatbetrieb; **processing ~** Verarbeitungs-, Vered(e)lungsindustrie; **producer-goods ~** Produktionsgüterindustrie; **production ~** Produktionsmittelindustrie; **protected ~** zollpolitisch geschützte Industrie; **railroad ~** Eisenbahnindustrie; **regimed ~** unter staatliche Aufsicht gestellter Industriezweig; **retail ~** Einzelhandelsgewerbe; **seasonal ~** saisonbedingte Industrie; **seasonnally unstable ~** durch Saisonschwankungen beeinflußte Industrie; **self-contained ~** autarker Industriezweig; **service ~** Dienstleistungsgewerbe; **sheltered ~** (Br.) zollpolitisch-geschützte Industrie; **shipping ~** Schiffahrtsindustrie; **short-staffed ~** unterbesetzter Gewerbezweig; **small**

[-scale] ~ Kleinbetriebe; **sophisticated** ~ Industrie für Güter des gehobenen Bedarfs; **stable** ~ bodenständige Industrie; **stable-volume** ~ volumenmäßig gleichbleibende Wirtschaft; **state-owned** ~ Staatsbetrieb; **steel** ~ Stahlindustrie; **steel-using** ~ stahlverarbeitende Industrie; **subsidized** ~ staatlich subventionierte Industrie; **sugar [-cane]** ~ Zuckerindustrie; **surrounding** ~ Nachbarindustrie; **sweated (sweatshop)** ~ unterentlohntes Gewerbe; **textile** ~ Textilindustrie; **tourist** ~ Fremdenverkehrsgewerbe; **toy** ~ Spielwarenindustrie; **traditional** ~ traditionelle Industrie; **tyre and rubber** ~ Gummiwaren- und Reifenindustrie; **undermanned** ~ Industrie mit Arbeitermangel; **unorganized** ~ gewerkschaftsfreie Wirtschaft; **[un]sheltered** ~ *(Br.)* [nicht] durch Staatsaufträge oder hohe Zollmauern unterstützte Industriezweige; **vital** ~ lebenswichtiger Industriezweig; **war** ~ Rüstungsindustrie; **wartime** ~ Kriegsindustrie; **wood-manufacturing** ~ holzverarbeitende Industrie; **wood-pulp** ~ Zelluloseindustrie; **woodworking** ~ holzverarbeitende Industrie; **wool(l)en** ~ Wollindustrie;
~ **overtaken (bypassed) by industrialization** durch Industrialisierung überholtes Gewerbe; ~ **that is falling off** an Bedeutung verlierende Industrie; ~ **still in its infancy** noch in den Kinderschuhen steckende Industrie; ~ **producing at its maximum output** mit voller Ausnutzung der Kapazität arbeitende (voll ausgelastete) Industrie;
to benefit local ~ einheimische Industrie steuerlich begünstigen; **to bring an** ~ **under state control** Industriezweig unter Staatsaufsicht stellen; **to buy o. s. into an** ~ sein Kapital in einem Gewerbe anlegen; **to control an** ~ Industriezweig beherrschen; **to create an** ~ Industrie ins Leben rufen; **to create** ~ **from the ground up** Industriebetrieb auf der grünen Wiese beginnen; **to cross over into a new** ~ in eine andere Branche überwechseln; **to gain a foothold in another** ~ in einem anderen Industriebereich Fuß fassen; **to nurse an infant** ~ neugegründeten Industriezweig fördern; **to originate an** ~ neuen Industriezweig begründen; **to nationalize** ~ Industrie verstaatlichen; **to put** ~ **on short weeks** Kurzarbeitswochen in der Industrie auslösen; **to retool** ~ Industrie neu ausrüsten;
~ **association** Industrieverband; **all-** ~ **average** gesamter Industriedurchschnitt; ~ **competition** industrieller Wettbewerb; ~ **complex** Industriekomplex; ~ **contractor** Industrielieferant; ~ **development** industrielle Entwicklung; ~ **executives** industrielle Führungskräfte; ~ **experiences** Industrieerfahrungen; ~ **figures** industrielle Daten; ~ **giant** Industriegigant; ~ **group** Industriegruppe; ~ **growth** Wachstum der Industrie; ~ **label** gewerbliche Schutzmarke; ~ **leader** industrieller Vorreiter; ~ **management** führende Wirtschaftskreise; ~ **negotiator** Verhandlungspartner auf Seiten der Industrie; ~ **observer** Beobachter aus Kreisen der Industrie; ~ **obsolescence** Industrieüberalterung; ~ **outlet** Geschäft mit Industriekundschaft; ~ **panel** Industrieausschuß; ~ **pension** Industriepension; ~ **ratio** Industriekoeffizient; ~ **recruiter** Anwerber von Arbeitskräften; ~ **sales** Industrieabsatz; ~ **slump** industrielle Rezession; **according to** ~ **sources** wie aus Industriekreisen verlautet; ~ **spending** Kapitalaufwand der Wirtschaft; ~ **standard** Industrienormung; ~ **statistics** Gewerbestatistik; ~ **trend** industrielle Entwicklung; ~**-wide** in der ganzen Industrie geltend; ~**-wide bargaining** Tarifverhandlungen für einen gesamten Industriebereich.
inebriate Betrunkener, Trunksüchtiger;
~ **asylum** Trinkerheil-, Entziehungsanstalt.
inebriation Trunkenheit, Trunksucht.
inedited nicht redigiert.
ineffective unwirksam, wirkungslos, *(workman)* arbeitsunfähig;
to become ~ außer Kraft treten, unwirksam werden;
~ **speaker** wirkungsloser Redner.
ineffectual wirkungslos;
~ **attempt** fruchtloser Versuch; ~ **treatment** erfolglose Behandlung.
inefficiency of labo(u)r Arbeitsunfähigkeit.
inefficient untauglich, wirkungslos, unwirksam, kraftlos, unwirtschaftlich, unrationell, *(person)* leistungsunfähig, untüchtig.
inelastic | **demand** unelastische Nachfrage; ~ **supply** unelastisches Angebot.
ineligibility Ungeeignetheit, Unfähigkeit, Nichtwählbarkeit, Ausschluß vom passiven Wahlrecht, Unfähigkeit zur Bekleidung eines Amtes, Untauglichkeit;
~ **for naturalization** Einbürgerungsunfähigkeit.
ineligible ungeeignet, nicht qualifiziert *(law)* unfähig, *(mil.)* untauglich, *(to hold an office)* nicht qualifiziert für, ausgeschlossen von, nicht wählbar, unwählbar;

to be ~ **for a position** für eine Position nicht geeignet sein; **to declare a member** ~ **to use the resources of the fund** Mitglied von der Inanspruchnahme der Fondsmittel ausschließen;
~ **location** ungünstige Belegenheit; ~ **paper** *(US)* nicht diskontfähiger Wechsel.
inept ungehörig, unpassend, nichtig, ungültig.
inequality Ungleichheit, Verschiedenheit;
~ **of income** Einkommensungleichheit; ~ **of pay** Lohnungleichheit; ~ **in wealth** Vermögensungleichheit;
to lessen the ~ **of income** Ungleichgewichtigkeiten der Einkommensverteilung mindern; **to suffer** ~ **of status** nicht gleichberechtigt sein.
inequitable unbillig, ungerecht;
~ **rates** ungerechte Versicherungssätze.
inequity Unbilligkeit, Ungerechtigkeit.
inert träge, faul, untätig.
inertia Untätigkeit, Trägheit;
~ **factor** Trägheitsfaktor.
inessential unwesentlich;
to omit ~s Unwichtiges auslassen.
inestimable unschätzbar.
inevitable | **accident** unvermeidliches Ereignis; ~ **fate** unentrinnbares Schicksal;
to resign o. s. to the ~ sich in Unvermeidbares fügen.
inexact fehlerhaft, ungenau.
inexecutable nicht durchführbar, unausführbar.
inexecution of a contract Nichterfüllung eines Vertrages.
inexhaustible unerschöpflich.
inexpediency Unzweckmäßigkeit;
~ **of raising taxes** Untunlichkeit von Steuererhebungen.
inexpedient unzweckmäßig, zweckwidrig.
inexpensive billig, wohlfeil.
inexperienced | **in business** geschäftlich unerfahren;
~ **driver** Fahrer ohne Verkehrserfahrung; ~ **sailor** unbefahrener Seemann; ~ **worker** ungelernter Arbeiter.
infamous unehrenhaft, der bürgerlichen Ehrenrechte verlustig;
~ **behavio(u)r** standeswidriges Verhalten; ~ **crime** unehrendes (ehrloses) Verbrechen; ~ **person** *(US)* der bürgerlichen Ehrenrechte Entkleideter; ~ **punishment** Zuchthausstrafe; ~ **traitor** schändlicher Verräter.
infamy Ehrlosigkeit, *(law)* Verlust der bürgerlichen Ehrenrechte.
infancy Kinder-, Säuglingsalter, *(law)* Unmündigkeit, Minderjährigkeit, *(early period)* Anfangsstadium;
in its ~ in den Kinderschuhen;
natural ~ Kindesalter [bis sieben Jahre];
~ **of an industry** erste Anfänge einer Industrie; ~ **of a nation** Anfangsstadium einer Nation;
to be still in its ~ noch im Aufbaustadium sein; **to plead** ~ Einwand der Minderjährigkeit erheben;
~ **status** Minderjährigkeitsstellung.
infant Minderjähriger [unter 18 Jahren];
to be binding upon an ~ Minderjährigen vertraglich binden;
~ *(a.) (law)* minderjährig, minorenn, unmündig;
~ **beneficiary** minderjähriger Leistungsberechtigter; ~ **children** minderjährige Kinder, Minderjährige; ~ **colony** junge Kolonie; ~**'s contract** Vertrag eines Minderjährigen; ~**-death rate** Kindersterblichkeitsrate; ~ **food** Säuglingsnahrung; ~ **industry** schutzzollbedürftige (junge) Industrie; ~ **member of a partnership (partner)** minderjähriger Teilhaber; ~ **mortality** Säuglingssterblichkeit; ~s **Relief Act** *(Br.)* Schutzgesetz für Minderjährige; ~ **school** *(Br.)* Vor-, Kleinstkinderschule; ~ **state** junger Staat; ~ **teacher** Kinderlehrer; ~ **welfare** Säuglingsfürsorge.
infanthood Säuglingsalter.
infantile *(fig.)* im Anfangsstadium;
~ **diseases** Kinderkrankheiten.
infantry Fußvolk, Infanterie.
infatuate *(v.)* verblenden, betören;
~ **s. o. with an idea** jem. eine Idee in den Kopf setzen.
infeasible undurchführbar, unausführbar.
infect *(v.)* anstecken, infizieren, *(law)* mit dem Makel der Ungesetzlichkeit behaften;
~ **the air** Luft verpesten; ~ **s. o. with an opinion** jem. eine ungünstige Meinung beibringen.
infected district verseuchtes Gebiet.
infection Infektion, Ansteckung, *(fig.)* schlechter Einfluß, *(law)* Makel der Ungesetzlichkeit;
auto-~ Selbstinfektion;
to catch ~ sich infizieren (anstecken); ~ **period** Infektionszeit.
infectuous disease ansteckende Krankheit, Infektionskrankheit.

infer *(v.)* folgern, schließen;
~ **a term** Schlußfolgerungen aus einer Vertragsbestimmung ziehen.
inference Schlußfolgerung, Rückschluß;
to make ~**s** Schlüsse ziehen; **to negative an** ~ Vermutung widerlegen.
inferential proof Indizienbeweis.
inferior Untergeordneter, -gebener, Tieferstehender;
~ *(a.)* minderwertig, mittelmäßig, ziemlich schlecht, zweitklassig, [im Wert] geringer, *(freight train)* nicht vorfahrtsberechtigt, *(print.)* unter der Schriftlinie, tiefstehend, *(of rank)* untergeordnet, niedriger, geringer, tieferstehend;
to be ~ **to s. o.** jem. nachgeordnet sein, hinter jem. zurückstehen; **to be in no way** ~ **to s. o.** jem. in keiner Hinsicht nachstehen; **to be** ~ **to s. o. in merit** geringere Verdienste als ein anderer aufweisen;
~ **court of law** unteres (niedrigeres) Gericht, Gericht mit sachlich beschränkter Zuständigkeit; ~ **goods** minderwertige Ware; ~ **officer** untergeordneter Beamter; ~ **piece of work** zweitklassiges Werk; ~ **position** unbedeutende (untergeordnete) Stellung; **to be in an** ~ **position** in untergeordneter Stellung sein; ~ **product** minderwertiges Erzeugnis; ~ **quality** schlechte (geringere) Qualität; ~ **services** untergeordnete Tätigkeit; ~ **workmanship** minderwertige Arbeit.
inferiority geringere Qualität, Minderwertigkeit;
~ **in numbers** zahlenmäßige Unterlegenheit;
~ **complex** Minderwertigkeitsgefühl.
infernal machine Höllenmaschine.
infertile soil unfruchtbares Land.
infest *(v.)* verheeren, heimsuchen, *(flood)* überschwemmen;
~ **the streets** Straßen unsicher machen.
infidel ungläubig. nicht rechtgläubig.
infidelity Untreue, Treubruch;
conjugal ~ eheliche Untreue, Ehebruch.
infiltrate *(v.)* infiltrieren, einsickern, einschleusen;
~ **the enemy lines** durch die feindlichen Linien durchsickern; ~ **into an organization** Organisation unterwandern, in eine Organisation einschleusen.
infiltration Eindringen, Infiltration, Unterwanderung, Durchdringung, *(mil.)* Einsickerung;
~ **of an organization** Unterwanderung einer Organisation; ~ **of spies** Einschleusung von Spionen;
to advance by ~ langsam einsickern.
infinite series unendliche Reihe.
infinitesimal industry *(US)* Zwergbetrieb, -unternehmen.
infirm schwach, schwächlich, gebrechlich, *(feeble of mind)* geistesschwach, *(fig.)* unfundiert, *(voidable)* anfechtbar;
to be ~ **of purpose** unentschlossen sein;
~ **argument** unfundiertes Argument; ~ **support** schwache Unterstützung.
infirmarian Spitalvorsteher.
infirmary *(mil.)* Krankenrevier, *(old people)* Spital;
poor-law ~ Armenspital.
infirmative *(law)* entlastend;
~ **consideration** Entlastungspunkt; ~ **fact** entlastende Tatsache.
infirmity *(feebleness)* Gebrechlichkeit, Schwäche, *(stock exchange)* Schwäche, *(voidableness)* Anfechtbarkeit, *(weakmindedness)* Geistesschwäche;
~ **of purpose** Unentschlossenheit.
inflame *(v/i.)* sich entflammen;
~ **the popular feeling** Volksleidenschaft erregen.
inflammable brennbar;
~ **cargo** feuergefährliche Ladung.
inflammatory | **article** Hetzartikel; ~ **speech** aufreizende Rede, Hetzrede.
inflatable boat Schlauchboot.
inflate *(v.)* aufblähen, in die Höhe treiben, übermäßig steigern, *(tyre)* aufpumpen;
~ **the currency** Geldumlauf künstlich steigern, Inflation herbeiführen.
inflated aufgeblasen, hochmütig, *(economy)* inflationär;
~ **with pride** vor Stolz geschwellt; ~ **currency** Inflationswährung; ~ **language** schwülstige Sprache; ~ **prices** künstlich überhöhte Preise; ~ **stocks** zu hoher Lagerbestand, überhöhte Lagerhaltung; ~ **style** bombastischer Stil; ~ **value** [künstlich] erhöhter Wert, Inflationswert.
inflater Preistreiber, *(stock exchange)* Haussier, Haussespekulant.
inflation Geldaufblähung, Inflation, [Geld]entwertung, *(council)* Aufgeblasenheit, *(pomposity)* Schwülstigkeit;

cost ~ Kosteninflation; **cost-push** ~ durch Produktionskostensteigerung ausgelöste (kostentreibende) Inflation, Kostendruckinflation; **credit** ~ Kreditausweitung; **creeping** ~ schleichende Inflation; **demand** ~ Nachfrageinflation; **demand-pull** ~ nachfrageüberhangbedingte Inflation, durch Nachfrageüberhang ausgelöste Inflation; **demand-shift** ~ durch Nachfrageverschiebungen ausgelöste Inflation; **double-digit** ~ zweistellige Inflationsrate; **food-price** ~ Inflation der Nahrungsmittelpreise; **government-spending-boosted** ~ durch Staatsausgaben angeheizte Inflation; **hidden** ~ versteckte Inflation; **home-grown** ~ hausgemachte Inflation; **pent-up** ~ gesteuerte Inflation; **price-frozen** ~ preisgestoppte Inflation; **runaround** ~ unaufhaltsame Inflation; **runaway** ~ galoppierende (zügellose) Inflation; **wage-fuelled** ~ durch Lohnsteigerungen angeheizte Inflation; **wage-led** ~ durch Lohnerhöhungen ausgelöste Inflation; **wage-push** ~ durch Lohnsteigerung bedingte Inflation; **war-caused** ~ kriegsbedingte Inflation; **wildfire** ~ verheerende Inflation;
~ **in cost** Kosteninflation; ~ **of the currency** Geldinflation; **runaway** ~ **of prices** sich überstürzende Preisinflation;
to battle ~ Inflation bekämpfen; **to bring** ~ **under control** Inflation in den Griff bekommen; **to curb** ~ Inflation bremsen (dämpfen); **to cure** ~ Inflation in den Griff bekommen; **to encourage** ~ Inflation fördern; **to fuel** ~ Inflation anheizen; **to halt** ~ der Inflation Einhalt gebieten; **to hedge against** ~ **by gearing the dollar value of contracts to gold** Abschlüsse durch Umstellung von Dollar auf Goldbasis inflationssicher machen; **to hold** ~ **down to the level of international competitors** Inflationssteigerung auf dem gleichen Niveau wie die internationale Konkurrenz halten; **to hold the line on** ~ Inflation zurückdrängen; **to keep up with** ~ sich den Inflationssätzen anpassen; **to kindle** ~ Inflation anheizen; **to level-peg** ~ Inflation stabilisieren; **to make** ~ **worse** inflationelle Entwicklung vorantreiben; **to prime** ~ Inflation anheizen; **to put a brake on** ~ Inflation abbremsen; **to rekindle the** ~ Inflation neu beleben; **to resort to** ~ Inflation als letztes Hilfsmittel anwenden; **to rise with** ~ inflationsbedingt steigen; **to slow down** ~ Inflationsrate verlangsamen; **to squeeze** ~ **out of their system** der Inflation den Nährboden entziehen; **to take a strong stand against** ~ Inflation stärker bekämpfen; **to tend to** ~ inflationsorientiert sein; **to undergo** ~ Inflationszeit durchmachen;
~ **accounting** Erfassung der Inflationsentwicklung; ~**-adjusted** inflationsbereinigt; ~ **alert** Inflationswarnung; ~ **antidote** Gegenmittel gegen die Inflation; ~ **bias** inflationäre Verzerrung; ~ **boom** inflationistische Konjunktur; ~ **danger** Inflationsgefahr; ~ **explosion** explosive Inflationssteigerung; ~ **factor** Inflationsmoment; ~ **fighting** Inflationsbekämpfung; ~ **forecast** Inflationsprognose; ~ **gain** Inflationsgewinn; ~**-hedged** inflationsgeschützt; ~**-induced** inflationsbedingt; ~ **pace** Inflationstempo; ~ **phobia** Inflationsangst, -hysterie; ~ **plateau** zeitweilige Inflationsstabilität; ~ **potential** Inflationszunahme; ~**-prone goods** inflationsempfindliche Waren; ~ **proof** inflationssicher; ~**-proof investment** inflationssichere Kapitalanlage; **built-in** ~ **proofing** automatische Inflationssicherung; ~ **proofing of wages** Inflationssicherung der Löhne; ~ **rate** Geldentwertungsrate, Inflationsrate; **single-figure** ~ **rate** einstellige Inflationsrate; **after** ~ **retention** nach Abrechnung der inflationsbedingten Erhöhung; ~ **revival** Wiederaufleben der Inflation; ~ **shelter** Schutz vor inflationären Entwicklungen, Inflationsschutz.
inflationary inflationistisch, inflationsbedingt, inflationär;
~ **adjustment** Inflationsausgleich; ~ **chaos** Inflationschaos; ~ **danger** Inflationsgefahr; ~ **climate** Inflationsklima; ~ **expectations** Inflationserwartungen; ~ **experiences** Inflationserfahrungen; ~ **factor** Inflationsfaktor; ~ **fever** Inflationsfieber; ~ **forces** Inflationskräfte; **to grapple with** ~ **forces** inflationäre Kräfte in den Griff bekommen; ~ **gain** Inflationsgewinn; ~ **gap** *(government expenditure)* inflatorische Lücke, Inflationslücke; ~ **hike** inflationärer Preisanstieg; ~ **impact** Inflationsdruck; ~ **period** Inflationszeit; ~ **policy** Inflationspolitik; ~ **pressure** Inflationsdruck; ~ **profit** Inflationsgewinn; ~ **psychology** Inflationspsychologie; ~ **revival** Wiederbelebung der Inflation; ~ **signposts** Inflationshinweise; ~ **spiral** Inflationsschraube, Inflations-, Lohn-Preisspirale; ~ **squeeze** Inflationsdruck; ~ **tendencies** inflationistische Tendenzen; **to curb the** ~ **tendencies** inflatorische Tendenzen eindämmen; ~ **threat** Inflationsdrohung; ~ **times** Inflationszeit; ~ **trend** inflationistische Tendenz; ~ **upsurge** rasante Inflationszunahme.
inflationist Inflationist, Inflationsanhänger;
~ *(a.)* inflationistisch, inflationär;
~ **period** Inflationszeit.

inflatory effect inflationistische Wirkung.

inflexible unbeugsam, unerschütterlich;
~ **code of morals** starrer Sittenkodex.

inflict *(v.)* auferlegen, aufzwingen, zufügen;
~ **s. th. upon s. o.** jem. etw. aufbürden; ~ **one's company on s. o.** *(fam.)* sich jem. aufbürden; ~ **damage** Schaden zufügen; ~ **the death penalty upon a murderer** Mörder zum Tode verurteilen; ~ **disciplinary punishment on s. o.** j. disziplinarisch belangen; ~ **a fine on s. o.** Geldstrafe gegen j. verhängen; ~ **punishment on s. o.** jem. eine Strafe auferlegen, Strafe gegen j. verhängen.

infliction Auferlegung;
~ **of damage** Schadenszufügung; ~ **of a fine** Auferlegung einer Geldstrafe; ~**s put upon the people** dem Volk auferlegte Leiden.

inflow Zustrom, Zufluß, *(air)* Einfließen, *(investment trust)* Mittelaufkommen;
~ **of capital** Kapitalzufluß; ~ **of cash** Kassenzugänge; ~ **of foreign currency** Devisenzufluß; ~ **of funds** Mittelzufluß; ~ **of liquidity** Liquiditätszufluß; ~ **swelling the money supply** durch Devisenzuflüsse bewirkte Geldausweitung; ~ **into savings accounts** Zugang bei den Spareinlagen.

influence Einfluß, Einwirkung, Macht, *(person)* einflußreiche Persönlichkeit;
under the ~ **of intoxicating liquor (alcohol)** unter Alkoholeinfluß;
cyclical ~ Konjunktureinfluß; **favo(u)rable** ~ günstiger Einfluß; **undue** ~ *(law)* unzulässige Beeinflussung, Sittenwidrigkeit, psychischer Zwang;
~ **for good** positiver Einfluß; ~ **of rationalization** Rationalisierungseffekt;
~ *(v.)* beeinflussen, Einfluß ausüben, bewirken;
~ **the course of events** in den Gang der Ereignisse eingreifen; ~ **s. o. for the good** j. positiv beeinflussen;
to be an ~ **in politics** einflußreiche politische Persönlichkeit sein; **to be under the** ~ **of alcohol** in angetrunkenem Zustand sein; **to be under the** ~ **of s. o.** unter jds. Einfluß stehen, von jem. beeinflußt werden; **to break free from an** ~ sich von jds. Einfluß frei machen; **to bring** ~ **to bear on s. o.** seinen Einfluß bei jem. geltend machen; **to come under the** ~ **of s. o.** unter jds. Einfluß geraten; **to exercise** ~ Einfluß ausüben; **to exercise one's** ~ **on s. o.** auf j. einwirken; **to exercise one's** ~ **on behalf of s. o.** seinen Einfluß zu jds. Gunsten geltend machen; **to exert one's** ~ seinen Einfluß ausüben; **to exert undue** ~ **on s. o.** j. unter Druck setzen, j. einschüchtern; **to have far-reaching** ~ über weitreichende Beziehungen verfügen; **to have** ~ **with s. o.** Einfluß bei jem. haben; **to owe one's position to** ~ seine Stellung Beziehungen verdanken; **to use one's** ~ **on behalf (in favo(u)r) of s. o.** seine Beziehungen für j. einsetzen; **to use undue** ~ **with the maker of a will** j. bei der Abfassung eines Testaments in unzulässiger Weise beeinflussen;
~ **peddler** Regierungskontakter.

influenced by an anticyclone im Bereich einer Hochdruckzone.

influential einflußreich, einflußvermögend;
~ **circles** maßgebende Kreise; **to have** ~ **friends** gute Beziehungen haben; ~ **politician** einflußreicher Politiker.

influenza epidemic Grippeepidemie.

influx Zufluß, [Waren]zufuhr, *(air)* Einfließen;
~ **of aliens** Fremdenzustrom; ~ **of capital** Kapitalzufluß, -strom; ~ **of cash** Barmittelzufluß; ~ **of foreign exchange** *(US)* Devisenzuflüsse; ~ **of funds (money)** Mittelflüsse; ~ **of liquidity** Liquiditätszufluß; ~ **of refugees** Flüchtlingstrom; ~ **of visitors** Besucherstrom; ~ **of wealth** Wohlstandszunahme.

inform *(v.)* unterrichten, Nachricht geben, mitteilen, informieren, bescheiden, benachrichtigen, orientieren, *(denounce)* anzeigen, Strafanzeige erstatten, denunzieren;
~ **s. o.** jem. Bescheid geben, j. unterrichten; ~ **o. s. about s. th.** sich über etw. Kenntnis verschaffen; ~ **the administration of a decision** Entscheidung auf dem Verwaltungswege bekanntgeben; ~ **against s. o.** j. anzeigen, Strafanzeige gegen j. erstatten, Denunziationen gegen j. vorbringen, j. denunzieren; ~ **s. o. of one's intended departure** j. über seine beabsichtigte Abreise in Kenntnis setzen; ~ **the police** Polizei verständigen.

informal formlos, formfrei, zwangslos, informell, unzeremoniell, *(irregular)* regel-, formwidrig;
~ **balance** asymmetrische Anordnung; ~ **commission** informeller Ausschuß; ~ **contract** formfreier Vertrag; ~ **conversation** informelles Gespräch, zwangloses Gespräch; ~ **dress** zwangloser Anzug; ~ **expression** familiärer Ausdruck; ~ **gathering** zwangloses Treffen (Zusammensein); ~ **interview** Stegreifinterview; ~ **investigation** inoffizielle Untersuchung; ~ **meeting** zwanglose Zusammenkunft; ~ **record** *(bookkeeping)* inoffizielle Buchungsunterlage; ~ **visit** informeller Besuch.

informality Formlosigkeit, Zwanglosigkeit, *(irregularity)* Formfehler, Mangel der gesetzlichen Form.

informally. to meet nicht offiziell (zwanglos) zusammentreten.

informant Gewährsmann, Berichterstatter, Informant, Auskunftsperson, -geber, *(by way of accusation)* Erstatter einer Anzeige, Denunziant, *(interview)* Befragter;
to refuse to disclose the name of one's ~ seinen Gewährsmann nicht preisgeben.

information Benachrichtigung, Verständigung, Unterrichtung, Information, Kenntnis, Aufschluß, Orientierung, *(accusation)* [Straf]anzeige, formelle Anzeige, Denunziation, *(attorney)* Anklage, *(data processing)* Programmieren, Programmiergabe, *(news)* Auskunft, Bescheid, Nachricht, Meldung, Mitteilung, Informationsmaterial, Informationen, Unterlagen, Berichte, Aufschlüsse;
according to the latest ~ nach den neuesten Informationen; **for** ~ zur Kenntnisnahme, informationshalber; **for** ~ **and further action** zur Kenntnis und weiteren Veranlassung; **upon** ~ **and belief** *(US)* nach bestem Wissen und Gewissen;
confidential ~ vertrauliche Mitteilung (Information, Kenntnisse); **correct** ~ richtige Information; **criminal** ~ Strafanzeige; **false** ~ falsche Auskunft; **first-hand** ~ Nachrichten aus erster Hand; **further** ~ weitere Angaben; **general** ~ allgemeine Bildung; **inadequate** ~ unzureichende Information; **inside** ~ vertrauliche Mitteilung (Unterrichtung); **mechanical** ~ technische Information; ~ **obtained** eingezogene Erkundigungen; **postal** ~ Auskunft in Postangelegenheiten; **precise** ~ genaue Auskunft; **privileged** ~ durch Aussageverweigerungsrecht geschützte Mitteilung; **relevant** ~ zweckdienliche Auskünfte; **reliable** ~ zuverlässige Angaben (Auskunft); **restricted** ~ vertrauliche Mitteilung; **satisfactory** ~ befriedigende Auskunft; **secret** ~ Geheiminformation; **tariff** ~ Zollauskunft; **trade** ~ wirtschaftlicher Informationsdienst; **vague** ~ zweifelhafte Auskunft; **wrong** ~ falsche Auskunft;
~ **of intrusion** Verfahren wegen Besitzstörung öffentlicher Ländereien; ~ **in the nature of a quo warranto** Verfahren wegen Konsessionserschleichung; ~ **in my possession** mir zur Verfügung stehende Informationen; ~ **straight from the horse's mouth** Informationen aus erster Quelle;
to apply to s. o. for ~ sich an j. um Auskunft wenden; **to ask for detailed** ~ Einzelheiten erfragen; **to be required to give** ~ auskunftspflichtig sein; **to check up on** ~ Auskunft überprüfen; **to collect** ~ Erkundigungen einziehen, Auskünfte einholen, Nachrichten beschaffen; **to contact the** ~ sich bei der Information melden; **to convey** ~ Informationen zukommen lassen; **to decline** ~ Auskunft verweigern; **to disclose confidential** ~ Informationsmaterial preisgeben; **to dismiss an** ~ Verfahren einstellen; **to extract (get)** ~ Informationen herausholen; **to ferret out** ~ Informationsmaterial ausgraben; **to file an** ~ *(Br.)* Anklage erheben; **to furnish** ~ Auskunft erteilen; **to gather** ~ **about s. o.** Erkundigungen über j. einziehen, sich über j. informieren (Informationen verschaffen); **to gather** ~ **upon s. th.** wegen einer Sache Erkundigungen einziehen; **to give** ~ *(US)* Anzeige erstatten; **to give s. o. false** ~ j. falsch informieren; **to go in quest of** ~ **about s. o.** Erkundigungen über j. einholen; **to handle** ~ informatorische Aufgaben erfüllen; **to have no** ~ **as to s. th.** über etw. nicht unterrichtet sein; **to lay** ~ **against s. o. with the police** *(Br.)* Anzeige gegen j. bei der Polizei erstatten, j. bei der Polizei anzeigen; **to lodge** ~ amtlich berichten; **to lodge** ~ **against s. o.** Klage gegen j. erheben; **to obtain (receive)** ~ Auskunft erhalten; **to obtain** ~ **from outside sources** Auskünfte von dritter Seite erhalten; **to prefer an** ~ Strafanzeige erstatten; **to procure** ~ Auskunft einholen; **to put** ~ **at s. one's fingertips** j. mit stets griffbereiten Auskünften versorgen; **to rely for** ~ **on s. o.** übliche Informationen über j. einholen; **to request** ~ um Auskunft bitten; **to secure** ~ sich informieren (Informationen beschaffen); **to swap** ~ **on tax loaders** Informationen über Steuersünder austauschen; **to volunteer some** ~ von sich aus Informationsmaterial zur Verfügung stellen;
~ **activity** Informationstätigkeit; ~ **agency** Informationsbüro, -stelle; ~ **agreement** *(tender)* Vereinbarung über den Austausch von Submissionsinformationen; ~ **bank** Informationsbank; ~ **booth** *(US)* Auskunftsstelle; ~ **bureau** *(US)* Auskunftei, Informations-, Auskunftsbüro; ~ **center** *(US)* **(centre, Br.)** Nachrichtenstelle, Auskunftsbüro; ~ **department** Auskunftsabteilung; ~ **desk** Informationsstand, Auskunftstelle, -schalter; ~ **disclosure** Veröffentlichung von Informationsmaterial; ~ **input** Programmeingabe; ~ **kit** Informationsprospekt; ~ **manager** Leiter der Marktforschung; ~ **media** Nachrichtenorgane, Medien; ~ **minister** Informationsminister; ~ **needs** Informationsbedürfnis; ~ **office** Informations-

stelle, -amt; **central ~ office** zentrale Auskunftsstelle; **government ~ office** staatliches Auskunftsbüro; **~ officer** Pressereferent; **~ output** Programmausgabe; **~ program(me)** Informationsprogramm; **~ retrieval** *(data processing)* Informationswiedergewinnung; **~ service** Informationsdienst, -quelle; **~ sharing** Informationsaustausch; **~ sharing agreement** Abkommen zur gegenseitigen Unterrichtung; **~ stand** *(fair)* Informations-, Auskunftsstand; **~ system** Informationssystem; **~ window** Auskunftsschalter.

informational│activity Informationstätigkeit; **~ record** Informationsbericht.

informative informatorisch, informativ, aufschlußreich;
~ advertising Informationswerbung; **~ book** informierendes Buch; **~ labeling** *(US)* **(labelling,** *Br.)* Ursprungsauszeichnung, Herkunftsbezeichnung; **~ talk** informatives Gespräch.

informed unterrichtet, informiert, im Bilde;
well ~ gut unterrichtet; **to be ~** Bescheid erhalten; **to keep s. o. ~** j. auf dem laufenden halten;
in ~ quarters in unterrichteten Kreisen.

informer Anzeigenerstatter, Denunziant;
common ~ Spitzel, berufsmäßiger Denunziant; **police ~** Polizeispitzel;
to turn ~ seine Komplizen preisgeben;
~ system Spitzelwesen.

infract *(v.) (US)* übertreten, brechen, verstoßen, verletzen;
~ neutrality Neutralität verletzen.

infraction Verstoß, Verletzung, Übertretung;
shop ~ Verstoß gegen die Betriebsordnung;
~ of faith Treubruch; **~ of the law** Gesetzesverletzung; **~ of regulations** Übertretung von Anordnungen; **~ of a treaty** Vertragsbruch, -verletzung.

infractor Übertreter.

infrastructural project Infrastrukturvorhaben.

infrastructure Infrastruktur;
~ development Entwicklung der Infrastruktur; **~ investments** infrastrukturelle Investitionen.

infrequent visitor seltener Gast.

infringe *(v.)* verstoßen, verletzen, *(contract, patent)* verletzen, brechen;
~ a copyright Urheberrecht verletzen; **~ a law** gegen ein Gesetz verstoßen; **~ an obligation** einer Verpflichtung nicht nachkommen; **~ a patent** Patentrecht verletzen; **~ the provisions** den Bestimmungen zuwiderhandeln; **~ s. one's rights** in jds. Rechte eingreifen; **~ a rule** gegen eine Regel verstoßen; **~ a trademark** Warenzeichenrecht verletzen; **~ a trust** Treuhandpflicht verletzen.

infringement Eingriff, Übergriff, *(contract)* Verstoß, Verletzung, *(law)* Übertretung, Verletzung, *(patent law)* Patentverletzung;
contributory ~ Beihilfe bei einer (mittelbare) Patentverletzung; **public ~** offenkundige Verletzung;
~ of the articles Satzungsverstoß; **~ of the constitution** Verfassungsbruch; **~ of a contract** Vertragsbruch, -verletzung; **~ of a copyright** Urheberrechtsverletzung; **~ of registered design** *(Br.)* Verletzung eines Gebrauchsmusters; **~ of a law** Gesetzesverletzung; **~ of letters patent** Patentverletzung, -bruch; **~ of s. one's rights** Übergriff (Eingriff) in jds. Rechte; **~ of a trademark** Warenzeichenverletzung, Markenfälschung; **~ of a treaty** Vertragsverletzung;
to bring an action for ~ of patent against s. o. Patentverletzungsklage gegen j. anstrengen; **to constitute an ~ of a patent claim** Tatbestand der Patentverletzung erfüllen; **to sue for ~ of a patent** auf Patentverletzung klagen;
~ action Patentwiderspruchsklage; **~ case** Patentverletzungsfall; **~ proceedings** Patentverletzungsverfahren; **~ suit** *(patents)* Patentverletzungsklage.

infringer Rechtsverletzer, *(patent law)* Verletzer eines Patents.

infringing party *(patent law)* Patentverletzer.

infuse *(v.)* einträufeln, einflößen;
~ new life into s. o. jem. neuen Lebensmut schenken.

infusion│of funds Geldspritze; **~ of money** Geldzufluß.

ingather *(v.) (Scot.)* einziehen, beitreiben.

ingenious erfinderisch, genial, *(of things)* sinnreich.

ingenuity Erfindungsgabe, Einfallsreichtum.

ingoing Amtseintritt, *(fig.)* gründlich, sorgfältig;
~ *(a.) (lease)* antretend; **~ tenant** neuer Mieter (Pächter).

ingot│of gold Goldbarren; **~ of steel** Stahlblock;
~ *(v.)* zu Barren verarbeiten;
~ iron Flußstahl.

ingrain *(v.)* tief verwurzeln.

ingrained prejudice tief verwurzeltes Vorurteil.

ingratiate *(v.)* **o. s. with s. o.** sich bei jem. beliebt machen.

ingratiation Liebedienerei.

ingratitude Undankbarkeit.

ingredient Bestandteil;
chief ~s Hauptbestandteile; **primary ~s** Grundbestandteile.

ingress Eintritt, freier Zutritt;
free ~ and egress freier Ein- und Auslauf.

ingrossing Kopieherstellung.

inhabit *(v.)* bewohnen, seinen Wohnsitz haben.

inhabitable bewohnbar.

inhabitancy ständiger Aufenthalt, Wohnort, -sitz.

inhabitant Be-, Einwohner, Ansässiger;
~s Einwohnerschaft, Ortsbewohner, Bevölkerung;
capital ~ *(Br.)* Gemeinderatsmitglied; **local ~** Ortseinwohner; **~ of a house** Hausbewohner; **~ of a town** Stadtbewohner, Bürger;
~ tax Einwohnersteuer.

inhabitation Wohnort, Wohnsitz.

inhabited bewohnt;
~-house duty *(Br.)* Hauszinssteuer.

inhere *(v.)* anhaften, innewohnen.

inherent anhaltend, innewohnend, zugehörig;
to be ~ in the blood im Blute liegen;
~ defect (vice) *(law of contract)* innewohnender Mangel; **~ delay** unvermeidbare Arbeitsunterbrechung; **~ deterioration** innerer Verderb, leichte Verderblichkeit; **~ powers** *(US)* originäre (aus der Rechtsnatur sich ergebende) Befugnisse; **~ right** angeborenes (durch Geburt erworbenes) unveräußerliches Recht; **~ vice or nature of the subject matter insured** innerer Verderb oder natürliche Beschaffenheit des versicherten Gegenstandes.

inherently dangerous in sich selbst gefährlich.

inherit *(v.)* erbberechtigt sein, j. beerben, erben;
~ s. th. from s. o. etw. von jem. erben; **~ a characteristic from one's father** charakteristische Eigenschaft von seinem Vater erben; **~ equally** zu gleichen Teilen erben; **~ an estate** Erbschaft machen; **~ a fortune** im Erbgang zu einem Vermögen gelangen; **~ a house** Haus erben; **~ jointly** miterben, gemeinsam erben; **~ a title** Titel erben.

inheritability Vererbbarkeit.

inheritable erblich, erbfähig, *(transmissible by descent)* im Erbweg übertragbar, vererblich, vererbbar;
~ blood legitime Erbfolge.

inheritance *(US)* Nachlaß, Hinterlassenschaft, Erbschaft, Erbe, Erbgut, Erbbesitz;
by ~ im Erbwege (Erbgange), erblich;
family ~ Familienerbstück; **general ~** ererbtes Vermögen, Nachlaß; **linear ~** lineare Erbfolge;
~ in abeyance ruhende Erbschaft; **~ consisting of a house** aus einem Haus bestehende Erbschaft;
to acquire by ~ im Wege der gesetzlichen Erbfolge erwerben; **to come into an ~** Erbschaft machen, in den Genuß einer Erbschaft gelangen; **to disclaim an ~** Erbschaft ausschlagen; **to enter upon an ~** Erbschaft antreten; **to exclude from an ~** von der Erbfolge ausschließen; **to receive s. th. by ~** etw. im Erbschaftswege erhalten; **to reckon on an ~** auf eine Erbschaft spekulieren; **to take by ~** erben;
~ Act *(Br.)* Erbschaftsgesetz; **~ claim** Nachlaßforderung; **~ exemption** *(US)* Erbschaftssteuerfreibetrag; **~ tax** *(US)* Nachlaß-, Erbschaftssteuer; **~ tax payment** *(US)* Erbschaftssteuerzahlung; **~ taxation** *(US)* Erbschaftssteuerwesen.

inherited audience Zuhörer der vorausgegangenen Sendung.

inheritor *(US)* Erbe.

inhibit *(v.)* untersagen, verbieten.

inhibition Verbot, Untersagung, *(land register, Br.)* Eintragungsverbot, Vormerkung, *(process to distrain debtor)* gerichtliches Veräußerungsverbot;
government ~ staatliches Verbot;
~ against a wife *(Scot.)* Beschränkung (Entzug) der Schlüsselgewalt;
to feel (have) no ~s keine Hemmungen haben.

inhibitory *(judgment)* inhibierend, verbietend.

inhospitable unwirtlich, ungastlich, unbewohnbar;
~ coast unwirtliche Küste.

inhuman treatment unmenschliche Behandlung.

inhumanity Unmenschlichkeit.

inimical feindselig, nachteilig;
~ to health gesundheitsschädlich.

iniquitous bösartig, schlecht;
~ oppression widerrechtliche Unterdrückung.

iniquity Frevelhaftigkeit, *(Scot., law)* widerrechtliche richtliche Entscheidung.

initial Anfangsbuchstabe, Initiale, Paraphe, Handzeichen;
~ *(v.) (sign with initials)* abzeichnen, paraphieren;
~ **the accounts** Rechnungen abzeichnen; ~ **a document** Urkunde mit seinem Handzeichen versehen;
to append one's ~s to s. th. etw. abzeichnen (paraphieren);
~ *(a.)* anfänglich;
~ **adjustment** Nulleinstellung; ~ **allocation** Erstausstattung; ~ **allowance** *(Br.)* erhöhte Sonderabschreibung für Neuanschaffungen, Sofort-, Anfangsabschreibung; ~ **application** Erstanmeldung; ~ **assignment** Anfangsstellung; ~ **balance sheet** Eröffnungsbilanz; ~ **campaign** *(advertising)* Einführungsfeldzug; ~ **capital** Anfangs-, Ausgangs-, Gründungs-, Einlegekapital; ~ **capital allowance** Sofort-, Erst-, Anfangsausstattung; ~ **capital expenditure** Einrichtungs-, Anlagekosten; ~ **capitalization** Erstausstattung; ~ **carrier** Aufgabespediteur; ~ **charge** *(investment fund)* einmalige Gebühr, Ausgabespesen; ~ **contact** erste Kontaktaufnahme; ~ **cost** Anschaffungspreis; ~ **credit balance** *(ECU)* Anfangsguthaben; ~ **debit balance** *(ECU)* Anfangsschuld; ~ **deposit** *(bank)* Anfangseinlage; ~ **development expenses** Anfangs-, Anlaufkosten; ~ **difficulties** Anfangsschwierigkeiten; ~ **dividend** *(Br.)* Abschlagsdividende; ~ **equipment** Erstausrüstung, -ausstattung; ~ **expenses** Anfangskosten *(insurance)* Abschlußkosten; ~ **export quota** Export-, Ausfuhrkontingent; ~ **form** Grundausstattung, -modell; ~ **guaranty deposit** *(insurance)* Anfangskaution; ~ **inventory** Anfangsinventar; ~ **investments** Erstinvestitionen; ~ **issue** Erstausstattung; ~ **letter** Anfangsbuchstabe; ~ **meeting** Eröffnungssitzung; ~ **operation** Inbetriebsetzung; ~ **order** Erstauftrag; ~ **outlay** Anschaffungskosten; ~ **payment** Anzahlung; ~ **performance** *(theater)* Premiere; ~ **period** Anlaufzeit; ~ **placing** Erst-, Anfangseinstufung; ~ **placing of securities** Erstabsatz von Wertpapieren; ~ **point** *(shipment)* Abgangsort; ~ **position** *(mil.)* Ausgangsstellung; ~ **premium** Anfangsprämie; ~ **production** Anfangsproduktion; ~ **purchase** Ersterwerb, -kauf; ~ **reserve** *(life insurance)* Anfangsreserve [für das nächste Jahr]; ~ **salary** Anfangsgehalt; ~ **sales** Erstverkäufe; ~ **share** Einlage, ~ **stages of an undertaking** Anfangsstadium eines Unternehmens; ~ **stock** *(inventory)* Anfangsbestand, Eröffnungsbestand; ~ **subscription** Erstzeichnung; ~ **surplus** *(corporation, US)* Reingewinn vor Eintragung ins Handelsregister, Überschußvortrag; ~ **symptoms** Anfangssymptome; ~ **terminus** Abgangsstation; ~ **training** Grundausbildung; ~ **value** Anfangs-, Anschaffungswert; ~ **waiting period** *(insurance)* [Anfangs]wartezeit; ~ **years** Anfangsjahre; ~ **yield** Anfangsrendite.

initialize *(v.)* abzeichnen, paraphieren.

initial(l)ed│check *(US)* (**cheque**, *Br.*) Scheck mit geprüfter Unterschrift; ~ **paper** Monogrammpapier.

initiate Anfänger, Neuling, Adept;
~ *(v.)* Anstoß geben, beginnen, Anfang machen, Initiative ergreifen, einleiten, *(instruct)* anlernen, einarbeiten, einführen, *(pol.)* als Erster beantragen;
~ **s. o.** j. in den Anfangsgründen unterrichten; ~ **into a club** in einen Verein (Klub) einführen; ~ **a deal** Geschäft einleiten; ~ **legislation** Gesetzesvorlage einbringen, Gesetzgebung initiieren; ~ **negotiations** Verhandlungen einleiten; ~ **a plan** Plan zur Ausführung bringen; ~ **a new policy** als erster ein neues politisches Programm beantragen; ~ **[legal] proceedings against s. o.** Prozeß gegen j. anstrengen; ~ **proceedings for rescission of a contract** auf Vertragsaufhebung klagen; ~ **a reform** Reform in Gang setzen; ~ **business relations** Geschäftsbeziehungen anbahnen; ~ **s. o. in a science** j. in die Anfangsgründe einer Wissenschaft einführen; ~ **s. o. into a secret** j. in ein Geheimnis einweihen; ~ **s. o. into a secret society** j. in eine Geheimgesellschaft aufnehmen;
~ **member of a secret society** Mitglied eines Geheimbundes.

initiated eingeführt, eingeweiht.

initiating│and structuring of multinational financing Einleitung und Abwicklung multinationaler Finanzierungsgeschäfte;
~ *(a.)* federführend.

initiation Einleitung, -führung, Beginn, *(ceremonies)* Aufnahmefeierlichkeiten, Einführungszeremonie;
~ **into an office** Amtseinführung;
to bar the ~ of a prosecution Strafverfolgung unterbrechen;
~ **ceremony** Aufnahmezeremonie; ~ **fee** Aufnahme-, Eintrittsgebühr.

initiative erster Schritt, Initiative, *(pep)* Unternehmungsgeist, Schwung, *(pol., US)* Gesetzesinitiative, *(Switzerland)* Volksbegehren;

on the ~ of auf Anstoß (Anregung) von; **on one's own ~** aus eigenem Entschluß;
legislative ~ gesetzgeberische Initiative; **private ~** persönliche Initiative; **trade-policy ~s** handelspolitische Anregungen;
to be lacking ~ keine Initiative besitzen; **to do s. th. on one's own ~** etw. aus eigenem Antrieb tun, selbst initiativ werden; **to take the ~** die Initiative ergreifen, den ersten Schritt tun.

initiatory *(a.)* einleitend, einführend;
~ **ceremonies** Einweihungszeremonien; ~ **steps** einleitende Schritte.

inject *(v.)* einspritzen;
~ **fear into s. o.** jem. Furcht einflößen (einjagen).

injection Einspritzung, Injektion;
~ **of new capital** Kapitalspritze;
~ **syringe** Injektionsspritze.

injunction Vorschrift, [dringender] Hinweis, Auflage, *(judicial order)* einstweilige Verfügung, gerichtliche Anordnung (Unterlassungsverfügung);
blanket ~ *(labo(u)r dispute)* globale einstweilige Verfügung; **final ~** endgültiges Unterlassungsurteil; **interim (interlocutory) ~** einstweilige Verfügung; **labor ~** *(US)* einstweilige Verfügung in arbeitsrechtlichen Streitigkeiten; **mandatory ~** gerichtliche Verfügung zur Vornahme einer Handlung [wegen einer gegenständlichen Leistung]; **ex parte ~** Verfügung im einseitigen Verfahren (ohne Anhörung der Gegenseite); **parting ~** Abschiedsermahnung; **permanent ~** bis zum Gerichtsurteil gültige Verfügung; **perpetual ~** zeitlich unbeschränkte gerichtliche Verfügung (Unterlassungsverfügung); **preliminary ~** einstweilige Unterlassungsverfügung; **preventive ~** vorbeugendes Unterlassungsurteil; **prohibitory ~** auf Unterlassung gerichtetes Verbot; **provisional ~** vorläufige (einstweilige) Verfügung; **restrictive ~** einstweilige Verfügung zur Durchsetzung einer Konkurrenzklausel; **temporary ~** *(US)* befristete richterliche Verfügung; **to restrain ~** Unterlassungsverbot; ~ **restraining transfer** Unterlassungsverfügung gegen eine Aktienübertragung;
to appeal an ~ Beschwerde gegen eine einstweilige Verfügung einlegen; **to ask for (claim) an ~** einstweilige Verfügung beantragen; **to award an ~** gerichtliche Verfügung erlassen; **to cancel (discharge, dissolve) an ~** einstweilige Verfügung aufheben; **to file an application for an ~** Antrag auf Erlaß einer einstweiligen Verfügung stellen; **to give strict ~s to s. o.** jem. ganz genaue Anweisungen geben, jem. dringend einschärfen; **to grant an ~** einstweilige Verfügung erlassen; **to grant an ~ ex parte** einstweilige Verfügung ohne mündliche Verhandlung erlassen; **to impose a judicial ~ upon s. o.** jem. ein gerichtliches Verfügungsverbot auferlegen; **to seek an ~** einstweilige Verfügung beantragen; **to sue for an ~** auf Unterlassung klagen;
~ **suit** Unterlassungsklage.

injunctive│power Möglichkeit zur Erlangung einer einstweiligen Verfügung; ~ **proceedings** Verfahren zwecks Erlaß (Antrag auf) einer einstweiligen Verfügung; ~ **process** einstweiliges Verfügungsverfahren; ~ **relief** Möglichkeit des Erlasses einer einstweiligen Verfügung; **to use an ~ route** Weg der einstweiligen Verfügung beschreiten; ~ **suit** Verfahren zur Erlangung einer einstweiligen Verfügung, Unterlassungsklage.

injure *(v.) (damage)* beschädigen, Schaden (Körperverletzung) zufügen, *(impair)* schädigen, beeinträchtigen;
~ **an article of merchandise** Verkaufsgegenstand beschädigen; ~ **one's health** seine Gesundheit schädigen; ~ **s. one's interests** jds. Interessen (Rechte) beeinträchtigen; ~ **s. one's pride** jds. Stolz treffen; ~ **s. one's reputation** jds. gutem Ruf Abbruch tun.

injured verletzt, *(damaged)* beschädigt;
badly ~ schwerbeschädigt; **fatally ~** tödlich verletzt; **party ~** Benachteiligter, *(accident)* Beschädigter, Verletzter;
the dead and the ~ Unfalltote und Unfallverletzte;
to be ~ on duty sich eine Dienstverletzung zuziehen;
with an ~ air mit gekränkter Miene; ~ **party** Geschädigter, Verletzter; **in an ~ voice** mit beleidigter Stimme.

injuries Schäden, Verletzungen;
internal ~ innere Verletzungen; **personal ~** Personenschäden; ~ **to a building due to the wet** auf Nässe zurückzuführende Gebäudeschäden;
to receive severe ~ schwer verletzt werden.

injurious schädlich, verderblich, nachteilig;
~ **to health** gesundheitsschädlich;
to be gravely ~ to the national economy Volkswirtschaft ernstlich gefährden; **to be ~ to social order** soziale Ordnung stören; **to prove ~ to s. one's interests** sich für jds. Interessen nachteilig auswirken; **to prove ~ to s. one's reputation** jds. gutem Ruf Abbruch tun, jds. Ruf beeinträchtigen;

~ **affection** *(real estate)* Wertminderung; ~ **falsehood** *(Br.)* geschäftsschädigende Behauptungen, Kreditschädigung; ~ **language** Schimpfreden; ~ **words** *(Louisiana)* beleidigende Worte, Verleumdung.

injuriously affected nachteilig betroffen, geschädigt.

injury Unrecht, Unbill, Ungerechtigkeit, *(damage)* [Be]schädigung, Schaden, Nachteil, *(impairment)* Beeinträchtigung, *(hurt)* [Körper]verletzung, *(infringement)* [Rechts]verletzung; **to the ~ of s. o.** zu jds. Nachteil; **with the purpose of ~** in benachteiligender Absicht;

absolute ~ Verletzung von Mitgliedschaftsrechten; **accidental ~** unfallbedingte Verletzung, Unfallverletzung; **bodily ~** Körperverletzung; **civil ~** einklagbarer Schaden; **compensable ~** ersetzbarer Schaden; **constructive ~** fingierter Schaden; **continuing ~** Dauerschaden; **disabling ~** Dienstbeschädigung; **fatal ~** tödliche Verletzung; **industrial ~** Betriebs-, Berufsschaden, (wiedergutzumachender) Arbeitsunfall; **irreparable ~** nicht ersetzbarer Betriebsschaden; **mental ~** Nerven-, Hirnschaden; **minor ~** geringfügige Verletzung; **nonaccidental ~** schuldhafte Verletzung; **occupational ~** Betriebs-, Berufs-, Arbeitsunfall; **permanent ~** lebenslängliche Körperbeschädigung, Dauerschaden; **personal ~** Personenschaden, Körperverletzung; **physical ~** Körperverletzung; **positive ~** unmittelbarer Schaden; **private ~** einklagbare Verletzung; **real ~** Ehrverletzung; **relative ~** mittelbare Rechtsverletzung; **reparable ~** finanziell gutzumachende Beschädigung; **serious ~** schwere Körperverletzung; **slight ~** geringer Schaden; **verbal ~** [Formal]beleidigung;

~ **caused by accident** Unfallverletzung, -schaden, unfallbedingte Körperverletzung; ~ **to a building** Gebäudeschaden; ~ **done by frost** Frostschaden; ~ **suffered by goods** Warenbeschädigung; ~ **to health** Gesundheitsschaden, gesundheitlicher Schaden; ~ **sustained in the line of duty** Dienstverletzung; ~ **to the neighbo(u)rhood** Belästigung der Nachbarschaft; ~ **to person** Personenschaden; ~ **to property** Sachbeschädigung, -schaden; ~ **past redress** nicht wiedergutzumachender Schaden; ~ **to one's reputation** Kreditgefährdung, -schädigung; ~ **to the tyre** Reifenschaden, -panne; ~ **at work** Betriebs-, Arbeitsunfall, Berufsschaden;

to be an ~ Schaden darstellen; **to do an ~** Schaden tun (zufügen), beschädigen; **to do an ~ to s. one's feelings** jds. Gefühle verletzen; **to inflict an ~** Schaden zufügen; **to suffer ~** benachteiligt werden;

~ **accidents** Unfälle mit Verletzten; ~ **benefit** *(Br.)* Versehrtengeld, Unfallrente.

injustice Unrecht, Ungerechtigkeit; **to do s. o. an ~** jem. ein Unrecht zufügen.

ink Tinte, *(stamp pad)* Stempelfarbe; **Chinese ~** Ausziehtusche; **copying ~** Kopiertinte; **indelible ~** Urkundentinte; **Indian ~** Ausziehtusche; **marking ~** Zeichentinte; **printer's ~** Druckerschwärze; **stamping ~** Stempelfarbe; **to sling ~** *(sl.)* sich schriftstellerisch betätigen; ~ **blot** Tintenklecks; ~ **eraser** Tintenradiergummi; ~ **glass** Tintenfaß; ~ **pad** Stempelkissen; ~ **pencil** Kopierstift.

inker *(telegraphy)* Morseschreiber.

inking Farbgebung; ~ **ribbon** Farbband; ~ **roller** Farbwalze.

inkling Andeutung, Wink; **to get an ~ of s. th.** Wind von etw. bekommen; **to have an ~ of s. th.** dunkle Ahnung von etw. haben.

inkpot Tintenfaß.

inkslinger *(sl.)* Tintenkleckser, Schreiberling.

inkslinging *(sl.)* Tintenklecksereien.

inkstand Schreibgarnitur.

inlaid floor Parkettfußboden.

inland In-, Binnenland, Landesinnere; **to explore the ~** Landesinnere erforschen; **to go ~** landeinwärts gehen;

~ *(a.)* inländisch, binnenländisch, *(native)* einheimisch, im eigenen Land erzeugt, *(towards the interior)* landeinwärts, ins Landesinnere;

~ **account** im Inland geführtes Konto; ~ **air traffic** Inlandluftfahrt; ~ **bill of exchange** *(Br.)* Inlandswechsel; ~ **carrier** Binnenfrachtführer; ~ **city** Landstadt; ~ **coin** Landesmünze; ~ **commodities** Landesprodukte; ~ **communication** Binnenverkehr; ~ **customs office** Binnenzollamt; ~ **duty** Inlandsabgabe, Binnenzoll; ~ **ice** Gletschereis; ~ **letter** Inlandbrief; ~ **mail** *(Br.)* Inlandpost; ~ **marine insurance** *(US)* Binnentransportversicherung; ~ **market** Binnenmarkt; ~ **money order** Inlandspostanweisung; ~ **navigation** Binnenschiffahrt; ~ **parcel** Inlandspaket; ~ **payments** Inlandszahlungen; ~ **[rate of]**

postage Inlandsporto; ~ **port** Binnenhafen; ~ **producer** inländischer Erzeuger; ~ **product (produce)** einheimisches Erzeugnis (Fabrikat), Landesprodukt; ~ **rate** Binnentarif; ~ **postage rates** Inlandsposttarif; ~ **revenue** *(Br.)* Aufkommen an indirekten Steuern, Staatseinkünfte, Steuereinnahmen, *(authority, Br.)* Finanzverwaltung; ⌁ **Revenue affidavit** *(Br.)* beeidigte Steuererklärung, Erbschaftssteuerformular; ⌁ **Revenue Authorities** *(Br.)* Einkommensteuer-, Finanzbehörden; ⌁ **Revenue Department** *(Br.)* Finanzverwaltung; ⌁ **Revenue Office** *(Br.)* Finanzverwaltung, Finanz-, Steueramt; ⌁ **Revenue officer** *(Br.)* Steuerbeamter; ⌁ **Revenue Official** *(Br.)* Finanz-, Steuerbeamter; ⌁ **Revenue receipts** *(Br.)* Steuereinnahmen, Staatseinkünfte; ⌁ **Revenue section** *(Br.)* Einkommensteuerabteilung; ⌁ **Revenue stamp** *(Br.)* Stempel-, Steuermarke; ⌁ **Rules of the Road** *(US)* Binnenschiffahrtsordnung; ~ **sea** Binnenmeer; ~ **selling price** Inlandspreis; ~ **state** Binnenstaat; ~ **tariff** Binnenzoll; ~ **telegram** *(Br.)* Inlandstelegramm; ~ **town** Landstadt; ~ **trade** Binnenhandel; ~ **traffic** Binnenverkehr; ~ **transport[ation]** Binnentransport; ~ **transportation insurance** Binnentransportversicherung; ~ **transportation system** *(US)* Binnentransportsystem; ~ **waters** Binnengewässer; ~ **waters navigation** *(US)* Binnenschiffahrt; ~ **waters transportation** Binnenschiffahrtsverkehr; ~ **waterway** Binnenschiffahrtsweg; ~ **waterways bill of leading** Ladeschein, Binnenkonnossement; ~ **waterway craft** Binnenschiffe; ~ **waterways insurance** Binnenschiffahrtsversicherung; ~ **waterways transport** Binnenschiffahrtsverkehr.

inlander Binnen-, Inländer.

inlay Einlegearbeit, Intarsie, *(wood)* Furnierholz; ~ *(v.)* furnieren.

inlaying of floors Parkettierung.

inlet Einlaß, Einfahrt, Bucht, *(port)* Hafeneinfahrt; ~ **pipe** Einlaufrohr, Zulaufleitung; ~ **valve** Ansaugventil.

inmate Bewohner, Insasse, Hausgenosse; **camp ~** Lagerinsasse.

inmost feelings innerste Gefühle.

inn Gasthof, -stätte, Herberge; **common ~** Gasthof, -wirtschaft; ⌁**s of Chancery** *(Br.)* Anwaltsvereinigung; **to keep an ~** Gastwirtschaft betreiben; **to put up at an ~** in einem Gasthof absteigen.

innate courtesy angeborene Höflichkeit.

innavigable nicht schiffbar, *(vessel)* nicht seetüchtig.

inner innen befindlich, *(fig.)* geistig, seelisch; ~ **area** Sanierungsgebiet; ~ **barrister** *(Br.)* [etwa] Justizrat; **to belong to the ~ circle** zum Kreis der Vertrauten gehören; ~**-city market** Immobilienmarkt für Stadtkerngrundstücke; ~ **court** Hinterhof; ~ **door** Innentür; ~ **form** *(print.)* Widerdruckform; ~ **harbo(u)r** Binnenhafen; ~ **life** Innenleben; **to satisfy the ~ man** *(coll.)* den Bedürfnissen seines Magens genügen; ~ **margin** weißer Innenrand; ~ **meaning** verborgener Sinn; ~ **page** Innenseite; ~ **relationship** *(US)* Innenverhältnis; ~ **reserves** *(finance)* stille Reserven; ~ **tube** Schlauch; ~ **tube valve** Schlauchventil.

inning *(marsh)* Marschland, *(time of power)* Herrschaftszeit; ~**s** *(Br.)* günstige Gelegenheit; **to have their ~s** *(party)* an der Macht (am Ruder) sein; **to have had a long ~s** schon lange am Ruder sein.

innkeeper Gastwirt, Gasthausbesitzer; ~**'s liability** Gastwirtshaftung.

innocence Unschuld, Schuldlosigkeit, *(goods)* Unverdächtigkeit; **to pretend ~** Unschuld vorschützen; **to protest one's ~** seine Unschuld beteuern; **to prove s. one's ~** jds. Schuldlosigkeit ergeben.

innocent unschuldig, schuldlos, *(goods)* unverdächtig, *(legal)* gesetzlich erlaubt; ~ **of a charge** unschuldig im Sinne der Anklage; **as ~ as a new-born child** so unschuldig wie ein neugeborenes Kind; ~ **of ideas** ohne jede Ideen, völlig ideenlos; **village ~** Dorftrottel; **to be ~ of a crime** Verbrechen nicht begangen haben;

~ **agent** *(criminal law)* willenloses Werkzeug; **to put on an ~ air** unschuldige Miene aufsetzen; ~ **amusement** harmloses Vergnügen; ~ **conveyances** *(Br.)* zulässige Pächterverfügungen; ~ **goods** nicht geschmuggelte Waren; ~ **holder for value** gutgläubiger Besitzer; ~**-looking person** naiv wirkender Mensch; ~ **material** unschädlicher Stoff; ~ **misrepresentation** unbeabsichtigte Falschdarstellung; ~ **passage** *(law of nations)* friedliche Durchfahrt; ~ **purchase** gutgläubiger Erwerb; ~ **purchaser** gutgläubiger Erwerber; ~ **trade** erlaubter Handel neutraler Staaten; ~ **trespass** versehentliches Betreten eines Grundstücks; ~ **woman** unberührte Jungfrau, unbescholtene Frau.

innominate nicht klassifiziert;
~ **contract** atypischer Vertrag.
innovate *(v.)* Neuerungen einführen.
innovation Einführung von Neuerungen, Innovation, Neuerung;
to make technical ~s in industry neue technologische Verfahren in der Industrie einführen.
innovator Pionier.
innuendo versteckte Andeutung, Wink, *(law)* erläuternde Bemerkung;
to throw out ~s against a minister diskriminierende Bemerkungen über einen Minister fallen lassen.
inobservance Nichtbeachtung, -befolgung.
inoccupation Beschäftigungs-, Erwerbslosigkeit.
inoccupied beschäftigungs-, erwerbslos.
inoculate *(v.)* impfen;
~ **s. o. with new ideas** jem. neue Ideen einimpfen.
inoculation Impfung;
preventive ~ Schutzimpfung.
inoffensive unschädlich.
inofficial inoffiziell, nicht amtlich, offiziös;
~ **dealings** *(stock exchange)* Freiverkehr; ~ **market** Freiverkehrsmarkt.
inofficious pflichtwidrig;
~ **testament** Testament, das den Pflichtteilsberechtigten ausschließt, unwirksames Testament.
inoperative *(ineffectual)* unwirksam, ungültig, *(not in operation)* nicht im Betrieb befindlich, untätig;
to be ~ keine Geltung mehr haben; **to become** ~ außer Kraft treten, ungültig werden;
~ **account** *(Br.)* umsatzloses Konto.
inopportune unangebracht, unangemessen, unzeitgemäß;
~ **remarks** unangebrachte Bemerkungen.
inordinate *(excessive)* übermäßig, *(not regulated)* unregelmäßig, regellos;
to keep ~ **hours** unregelmäßig schlafen.
inpatient stationärer Patient, Anstaltspatient.
inpayment Einzahlung.
inpensioner *(Br.)* Insasse eines Invalidenhauses.
inpouring passengers hereinströmende Fahrgäste.
input *(data processing)* Eingabe, Eingangswert, Einsatzinformation, Einsatzmenge, *(statistics)* kalkulierbare Vorleistungen im Produktionsprozeß;
~**-output analysis** Input-Output-Analyse; ~ **coefficient** Produktionskoeffizient; ~ **data** Eingabedaten; ~ **file** Eingabekartei; ~**-output structure** industrielle Verflechtungsstruktur; ~ **price** Kostengüterpreis; ~ **tax** Vorsteuer.
inquest gerichtliche Untersuchung;
coroner's ~ Obduktion, amtliche Totenschau, amtliches Leichenschauverfahren;
~ **to fix damages** Untersuchung zur Schadensfeststellung; ~ **of lunacy** gerichtliche Untersuchung im Entmündigungsverfahren; ~ **of office** *(Br.)* amtliche Untersuchung zur Feststellung etwa angefallenen Kronguts;
to hold an ~ **on a body** Leiche obduzieren.
inquire *(v.)* nachfragen, Rückfrage halten, sich erkundigen, Erkundigungen einziehen, untersuchen, sich umhören;
~ **after s. o.** sich nach jem. erkundigen; ~ **into s. th.** etw. untersuchen, eingehende Erkundigungen nach etw. anstellen; ~ **into the assets of a debtor** Schuldner auspfänden; ~ **into a crime** Verbrechen untersuchen; ~ **for a book at a shop** sich im Laden nach einem Buch erkundigen; ~ **for the manager** um den Geschäftsführer bitten; ~ **into a matter** Angelegenheit untersuchen; ~ **s. one's name** j. nach seinem Namen fragen; ~ **into s. one's position** sich eingehend nach jds. Verhältnissen erkundigen; ~ **the price** nach dem Preis fragen, Preis erfragen; ~ **about trains** sich nach den Zügen erkundigen; ~ **one's way** sich nach dem Weg erkundigen; ~ **in writing** schriftlich anfragen.
inquired for gefragt, begehrt.
inquirendo *(interests of the crown)* Untersuchungsvollmacht.
inquirers, serious ernsthaft interessierte Reflektanten.
inquiries extending over several years sich über Jahre erstreckende Untersuchungen;
to make ~ Erkundigungen einziehen, Umfrage halten; **to make unofficial** ~ sich unter der Hand erkundigen.
inquiring mind wißbegieriger Mensch.
inquiry Nachforschung, -frage, Anfrage, Erkundigung, *(census)* Erhebung, *(investigation)* Untersuchung, Auskunftsersuchen, Ermittlung;
on ~ auf Nachfrage; **for the purpose of** ~ zwecks Nachforschung; **regarding your** ~ bezüglich ihrer Anfrage; **without** ~ *(stock exchange)* nicht gesucht;

extensive ~ umfassende Untersuchung; **further** ~ weitere Erkundigungen; **judicial** ~ gerichtliche Untersuchung, Ermittlungsverfahren; **official** ~ amtliche Untersuchung (Erhebungen), Enquete; **parliamentary** ~ parlamentarische Untersuchung; **preliminary** ~ gerichtliche Voruntersuchung; **statistical** ~ statistische Erhebung; **steady** ~ beständige Nachfrage; **telephoned** ~ telefonisch übermittelte Anfrage; **thorough** ~ eingehende Untersuchung;
~ **as to prices** Preisanfrage;
to conduct an ~ Untersuchung durchführen; **to hold an** ~ Untersuchung durchführen; **to hold an** ~ **behind closed doors** Untersuchung hinter verschlossenen Türen (unter Ausschluß der Öffentlichkeit) durchführen; **to hold a judicial** ~ Ermittlungsverfahren einleiten; **to hold an official** ~ offizielle Untersuchung durchführen; **to institute an** ~ Untersuchung einleiten; **to make an** ~ Anfrage richten; **to make an** ~ **into a case** Fall untersuchen; **to open a judicial** ~ gerichtliche Untersuchung eröffnen; **to order an** ~ Untersuchung veranlassen; **to remand a case for further** ~ Fall zur weiteren Untersuchung zurückverweisen; **to set up an** ~ Untersuchung einleiten;
~ **agency** Auskunftei; ~ **agent** *(Br.)* Privatdetektiv; ~ **board** Untersuchungsausschuß; ~ **fee** Gebühr für Nachfrageschreiben; ~ **form** Fragebogen, Anfrageformular; ~ **office** *(Br.)* Auskunftsbüro, -stelle, Auskunftei, *(railway)* Auskunftsschalter.
inquisition *(coroner)* Leichenschau, *(inquiry)* gerichtliche (amtliche) Untersuchung, *(proceedings)* Untersuchungsprotokoll;
~ **in lunacy** *(Br.)* Untersuchung auf den Geisteszustand.
inquisitive neugierig, wißbegierig;
to be ~ **of s. th.** etw. genau wissen wollen.
inquisitor Untersuchungsbeamter, -richter.
inroad Überfall, Eindringen, *(fig.)* Ein-, Übergriff, Inanspruchnahme;
to make ~s Wirkungen erzielen; **to make ~s upon one's capital** sein Kapital angreifen; **to make ~s upon the enemy** Feind überfallen; **to make vast ~s in the market** entscheidenden Markteinbruch erzielen; **to make ~s upon s. one's savings** Loch in jds. Ersparnisse reißen; **to make ~s upon s. one's time** jem. die Zeit stehlen.
inrush | of tourists Touristenstrom; ~ **of water** Wasserflut.
ins and outs | of a matter alle Einzelheiten (Seiten) einer Sache;
to know the ~ **of a question** Frage in allen Einzelheiten kennen.
insane geisteskrank, wahnsinnig, verrückt, unzurechnungsfähig;
certifiably ~ nachgewiesenermaßen geisteskrank; **incurably** ~ unheilbar geisteskrank;
to become ~ geisteskrank werden; **to be certified** ~ für unzurechnungsfähig erklärt werden; **to declare s. o.** ~ j. für geisteskrank erklären;
~ **asylum** *(US)* Irren-, Heil- und Pflege-, Nervenheilanstalt; ~ **delusion** Zwangsvorstellung; ~ **idea** tolle Idee; ~ **person** Geisteskranker, Wahnsinniger, Unzurechnungsfähiger.
insanitariness Gesundheitsschädlichkeit.
insanitary gesundheitsschädlich.
insanitation unhygienischer Zustand.
insanity Geisteskrankheit, -gestörtheit, Wahnsinn;
adolescent ~ Jugendwahnsinn; **circular (maniacal-depressive)** ~ manisch-depressives Irresein; **compulsive** ~ Zwangspsychose; **emotional** ~ Affektpsychose; **habitual** ~ chronische Geisteskrankheit; **idiophatic** ~ angeborene Geisteskrankheit; **involutional** ~ senile Geistesschwäche; **legal** ~ Unzurechnungsfähigkeit; **moral** ~ krankhafte Hemmungslosigkeit; **settled** ~ Geisteskrankheit infolge chronischen Alkoholismus;
~ **induced by intoxication** Unzurechnungsfähigkeit wegen Volltrunkenheit;
to certify s. one's ~ j. für geisteskrank erklären.
insatiable | of glory ruhmsüchtig; ~ **of power** machthungrig;
~ **appetite** ungezügelter Appetit.
inscribe *(v.)* [in eine Liste] eintragen, einschreiben, einzeichnen, registrieren, *(dedicate)* widmen, zueignen, *(finance)* Namensaktionäre registrieren, *(monument)* mit einer Inschrift versehen;
~ **in a book** in ein Buch einschreiben; ~ **across the face of a bill** auf der Vorderseite eines Wechsels girieren; ~ **a tomb with a name** Namen in ein Grabmal einmeißeln.
inscribed eingetragen, registriert;
~ **stock** *(Br.)* börsenmäßig gehandelte Buchwerte, Schuldbuch-, Giroforderungen, -titel.
inscription Einschreibung, -tragung, -zeichnung, *(of book)* Zueignung, Widmung, *(securities)* Registrierung von Namenspapieren, *(words inscribed)* In-, Aufschrift;
~**s** *(Br.)* Namensaktien;
~ **book** Anmeldebuch; ~ **form** Anmeldeformular.

inscrutable ways of providence unergründliche Wege der Vorsehung.

insect *(fig.)* lästiger Mensch, Ungeziefer.

insecure unsicher, gefährlich, riskant;
~ **building** baufälliges Gebäude; ~ **credit** ungedeckter Kredit; ~ **investment** unsichere Kapitalanlage; ~ **life of a conspirator** gefährliches Leben eines Verschwörers; ~ **load** unbefestigte Ladung; **to be in an ~ position** sich in einer kritischen Lage befinden.

insecurity Unsicherheit, Gefährlichkeit;
job ~ berufliche Unsicherheit; ~ **in share prices** Aktienkursunsicherheit; ~ **of tenure** Mietunsicherheit.

inseminate *(v.)* **in s. one's mind** in jds. Gedächtnis einprägen.

insensible sinnlos, unverständlich;
not to be ~ of s. one's kindness sich jds. Freundlichkeit bewußt sein; **to be ~ to pain** schmerzunempfindlich sein.

insensitive | to light lichtunempfindlich;
to be ~ to political realities den politischen Realitäten nicht entsprechen.

inseparable untrennbar.

insert Einfügung, Einschaltung, *(advertising)* Inserat, Anzeige, *(extra leaf, US)* Beilage, Beilagenprospekt, Beihefter, Beileger, *(postal service)* Drucksache;
~**s** *(advertising, US)* Inneneinlage, Zeitungsbeilage, Beilagenprospekt;
furnished ~**s** angelieferte Beilagen;
~ *(v.) (in newspaper)* [Anzeige] einrücken lassen, inserieren, *(place)* einfügen, einsetzen;
~ **an advertisement in a newspaper** Anzeige in eine Zeitung einrücken; ~ **blotting paper between the sheets** Löschpapier zwischen Papierbögen legen; ~ **in brackets** in Klammern setzen; ~ **in a catalog(ue)** in einen Katalog aufnehmen; ~ **a clause** Paragraph (Klausel) einfügen (aufnehmen); ~ **a coin in a slot machine** Münze in einen Automaten einwerfen; ~ **a leaf into a file** Blatt in ein Ringbuch einlegen; ~ **a line** Zeile einfügen; ~ **a new paragraph in an essay** neuen Absatz in einen Artikel einarbeiten.

insertion Einschaltung, Zusatz, *(advertisement)* Anzeige, Annonce, Inserat, *(el.)* Zwischenschaltung, *(terminal)* Texteinschub;
~ **of an advertisement** Anzeigenaufgabe; ~ **of an announcement in a newspaper** Bekanntmachung in der Zeitung; ~ **of a clause** Aufnahme einer Klausel; ~ **and size** Auftragsumfang; ~ **mark** Verweisungszeichen; ~ **order** schriftlicher Anzeigenauftrag mit genauer Plazierungsangabe; ~ **schedule** Erscheinungsplan.

inset Einlage, Beilage, *(advertising)* Einschaltseite, Zeitungsbeilage, *(map, diagram inserted)* Nebenkarte, Einsatz;
~ **handle** *(car)* versenkbarer Türgriff; ~ **portrait** eingeblendetes Bild.

inshore an der Küste, küsteneinwärts;
to keep ~ sich in Küstennähe halten;
~ **fisheries** Küstenfischerei.

inside Innenteil, -seite, *(car)* Innenplatz, *(print.)* Innenseite, *(period of time, Br., coll.)* mittlerer Teil, Mitte;
~**s** innerste Gedanken;
~ *(a.)* im Innern befindlich, innen, inwendig;
~ **and contents unknown** innere Beschaffenheit und Inhalt unbekannt;
to be ~ on a matter *(US fam.)* Hintergründe kennen; **to come to Paris for the ~ of a week** für eine knappe Woche nach Paris kommen; **to do s. th. ~ of two days** *(US)* etw. in weniger als zwei Tagen erledigen; **to finish a work ~ of a week** *(US)* Arbeit innerhalb einer Woche erledigen; **to get right ~ a part** *(fam.)* völlig in einer Theaterrolle aufgehen; **to know the ~ of an affair** Interna einer Sache kennen; **to know a subject ~ out** Sache gründlich beherrschen; **to know a town ~ out** Stadt wie seine Hosentasche kennen; **to look into the ~ of s. th.** etw. gründlich untersuchen; **to turn everything ~ out** alles total umkrempeln; **to walk on the ~ of the pavement** an der Häuserseite des Bürgersteiges gehen;
~ **address** Privatanschrift; ~ **board** *(US)* Führungsgremium aus leitenden Angestellten; ~ **back cover** dritte Umschlagseite; ~ **broker** *(Br.)* amtlich zugelassener Makler; ~ **data** interne Ergebnisse; ~ **director** *(US)* Vorstandsmitglied; ~ **dope** *(US sl.)* vertrauliche Presseinformation; ~-**drive car** Innenlenker; ~ **front cover** vierte Umschlagseite; ~ **information** *(coll.)* Information aus erster Hand, vertrauliche Unterrichtung; ~ **job** *(sl.)* mit Hilfe von Hausbewohnern durchgeführter Diebstahl; **to speak with ~ knowledge** Hintergründe kennen; ~ **money** Innen-

geld; ~ **pages of a newspaper** Innenseiten einer Zeitung; ~ **seat in a bus** Innenplatz in einem Autobus; ~ **story** Hintergrundbericht, Blick hinter die Kulissen; **to have the ~ track** im Vorteil sein.

insider Eingeweihter, Mitglied;
~**s** eingeweihte Kreise, *(Br.)* Börsenmakler, Berufshandel;
~ **information** vertrauliche Unterrichtung, Information über betriebsinterne Vorgänge; ~ **trading** Berufshandel.

insidious disease heimtückische Krankheit.

insight Einsicht, Einblick;
~ **into human character** psychologisches Einfühlungsvermögen;
to gain an ~ into s. th. Einsichten in etw. gewinnen; **to shed valuable ~ into** wertvolle Erkenntnisse ergeben.

insignia of rank Dienst-, Rangabzeichen, Emblem.

insignificance Bedeutungslosigkeit, Lappalie.

insignificant unbedeutend, unerheblich, belanglos, bedeutungslos, minimal;
~ **person** Mensch ohne Einfluß; **to occupy an ~ place in society** keine Rolle in der Gesellschaft spielen; ~ **sum** geringfügige Summe.

insinuate *(v.)* andeuten, anspielen auf;
~ **o. s. into s. one's favo(u)r** sich bei jem. einschmeicheln; ~ **s. th. nasty** bösartige Einflüsterungen vornehmen; ~ **o. s. into society** in das Gesellschaftsleben Eingang finden.

insinuating manner einschmeichelndes Wesen.

insinuation Anspielung, versteckte Andeutung, *(ingratiation)* Einschmeichelung;
~ **of infidelity** Einflüsterungen von Untreue; ~ **of a will** Einreichung (Vorlage) eines Testaments.

insipid abgestanden, schal;
~ **compliments** fade Komplimente; ~ **tale** abgeschmackte Geschichte.

insist *(v.)* bestehen, dringen;
~ **upon one's innocence** seine Unschuld beteuern, nicht schuldig plädieren; ~ **on obedience** Gehorsam fordern; ~ **on payment** auf Bezahlung bestehen; ~ **upon a point** Punkt besonders hervorheben; ~ **on one's rights** auf seinen Rechten bestehen.

insistence Beharrlichkeit, Nachdruck;
with great ~ mit eindringlichen Worten (großem Nachdruck).

insistent beharrlich, hartnäckig, nachdrücklich;
to be ~ on s. th. auf einer Sache bestehen; **to become more ~ in one's demands** in seinen Forderungen radikaler werden.

insociable ungesellig.

insolation Sonneneinstrahlung.

insolvable | bank notes nicht einlösbare Banknoten; ~ **debts** unbezahlbare Schulden.

insolvency Insolvenz, Unvermögen, Überschuldung, Zahlungsunfähigkeit, -einstellung, Fallissement, Bankrott;
in case of ~ im Unvermögensfall, bei Zahlungsunfähigkeit;
commercial ~ kaufmännische Zahlungsunfähigkeit, Geschäftsinsolvenz; **involuntary ~** von den Gläubigern beantragtes Vergleichsverfahren; **national ~** Staatsbankrott; **open ~** allgemein bekannte Zahlungsunfähigkeit; **voluntary ~** vom Gemeinschuldner beantragtes Vergleichsverfahren;
~ **of an estate** Nachlaßüberschuldung;
to be in a state of ~ zahlungsunfähig sein; **to be verging on ~** kurz vor der Zahlungsunfähigkeit stehen; **to declare one's ~** sich für zahlungsunfähig erklären, seine Zahlungen einstellen;
~ **guarantee fund** *(Br.)* Insolvenzenfonds; ~ **laws** *(Br.)* Vergleichsordnung; ~ **proceedings** Vergleichsverfahren; ~ **statistics** Insolvenzenstatistik; ~ **statute** *(US)* Vergleichsordnung.

insolvent Zahlungsunfähiger, zahlungsunfähiger Schuldner;
~ *(a.)* überschuldet, zahlungsunfähig, illiquide, insolvent, bankrott;
~ **at the time of preference** zum Zeitpunkt der Gläubigerbegünstigung zahlungsunfähig;
to be adjudged ~ für bankrott erklärt werden; **to become ~** zahlungsunfähig werden; **to declare o. s. ~** sich für zahlungsunfähig erklären, seine Zahlungen einstellen;
~ **company** Gemeinschuldner; ~ **debtor** Zahlungsunfähiger, Gemein-, Konkursschuldner; ~ **estate** Konkursmasse, *(inheritance)* überschuldeter (illiquider, konkursreifer) Nachlaß; ~ **law** *(statute, US)* Vergleichsordnung.

inspect *(v.)* beaugenscheinigen, besichtigen, Einsicht nehmen, inspizieren, untersuchen, prüfen;
~ **the books** Bücher revidieren (einsehen); ~ **a car** [Auto]inspektion durchführen; ~ **checks** *(cheques, Br.)* Wechsel überprüfen; ~ **documents** Urkunden einsehen; ~ **the documents of title** Grundbuchunterlagen prüfen; ~ **the extent of a damage** Schaden besichtigen; ~ **the gas meter** Gaszähler ablesen; ~ **the**

goods Ware prüfen; ~ **the land register** Grundbuch einsehen; ~ **troops** Truppen inspizieren; ~ **a witness** Zeugen vernehmen.

inspecting|officer Prüfungsbeamter; ~ **order** Prüfungsauftrag, *(goods lying at dock)* Besichtigungsschein.

inspection Prüfung, Besichtigung, Kontrolle, Einsichtnahme, Revision, *(car)* Inspektion, *(food)* Qualitätskontrolle;
by ~ nach Augenmaß; **for [your kind]** ~ zur [gefälligen] Ansicht; **on second** ~ bei nochmaliger Durchsicht; **subject to** ~ Besichtigung vorbehalten, prüfungspflichtig; **under sanitary** ~ unter gesundheitspolizeilicher Aufsicht;
check ~ Kontrolluntersuchung; **close** ~ gründliche Prüfung; **curtailed** ~ abgebrochene Prüfung; **customs** ~ Zollrevision, -untersuchung; **factory** ~ gewerbepolizeiliche Überprüfung, Gewerbeaufsicht; **free** ~ **invited** kein Kaufzwang; **hurried** ~ eilige Besichtigung; **judicial** ~ richterlicher Augenschein; **local** ~ Ortsbesichtigung, Augenscheinnahme; **medical** ~ amtsärztliche Untersuchung; **obligatory** ~ Prüfungspflicht; **passport** ~ Paßkontrolle; **public** ~ jedermann mögliche Einsichtnahme; **sanitary** ~ gesundheitspolitische Aufsicht, Überwachung durch die Gesundheitsbehörden; **shipping-point** ~ Prüfung am Versandort; **tax** ~ Steuerprüfung; **trade** ~ Gewerbeaufsicht;
~ **of boilers** Dampfkesselüberwachung; ~ **of books** Einsichtnahme in die (Revision der) Geschäftsbücher; ~ **of documents** Einsichtnahme in Urkunden, Urkundeneinsicht; ~ **of goods** Besichtigung der Ware; ~ **of mines** Grubenaufsicht, Prüfung der Grubensicherheit; ~ **of property** *(Br.)* Augenschein, *(land)* Grundstücksbesichtigung; ~ **of the records** Akteneinsicht; ~ **of the register** Registereinsicht, *(Br.)* Grundbucheinsicht; ~ **of troops** Truppenbesichtigung;
to be available for ~ zur Einsicht zur Verfügung stehen; **to be open to public** ~ öffentlich zur Einsicht ausliegen; **to buy after** ~ nach Besicht kaufen; **to carry out an** ~ **on the spot** Besichtigung an Ort und Stelle durchführen; **to grant** ~ Einsicht gestatten; **to hold an** ~ Besichtigung abhalten (durchführen); **to open for** ~ zur Besichtigung freigeben; **to subject s. th. to close** ~ etw. einer sorgfältigen Untersuchung (Überprüfung) unterziehen; **to submit for s. one's kind** ~ jem. zur gefälligen Einsichtnahme übersenden;
~ **bureau** *(carrier business)* Prüfungsstelle; ~ **car** *(railway)* Draisine; ~ **certificate** Prüfungsbescheinigung; ~ **committee** Prüfungs-, Abnahmekommission; ~ **cost** Prüfungs-, Abnahmekosten; ~ **department** *(insurance)* Prüfungsabteilung; ~ **diagram** Prüfungsdiagramm; ~ **fee** *(acceptance test)* Prüfungsgebühr; ~ **hole** Schauloch; ~ **laws** gesetzliche Vorschriften über Qualitätsprüfungen; ~ **lot** Prüfungsposten, *(statistics)* Los; ~ **personnel** Prüfungspersonal, Abnahmebeamte; ~ **procedure** Abnahmeverfahren; ~ **process** Inspektions-, Prüfungsverfahren; ~ **service** Inspektionsdienst durch Versicherungsexperten; ~ **stamp** Prüfungssiegel, Kontrollmarke; ~ **ticket** Kontrollzettel; ~ **tour** Besichtigungsreise, -fahrt.

inspector Aufseher, Aufsichtsbeamter, Prüfer, Inspektor, *(customs)* Zollaufseher, -beamter, *(police)* Polizeiinspektor;
chief ~ *(Br.)* höherer Polizeibeamter; **customs** ~ Zollinspektor, -aufscher, beamter; **factory** ~ Gewerbeaufseher; **food** ~ Lebensmittelkontrolleur; ~ **general** Oberinspektor; ⍦ **General** *(mil., US)* Generalinspekteur; **new business** ~ Versicherungsinspektor; **police** ~ *(Br.)* Polizeikommissar; **road** ~ Straßenaufseher; **ticket** ~ Fahrkartenkontrolleur;
~ **of agents** Versicherungsinspektor; ⍦ **of Foreign and Colonial Dividends** *(Br.)* Aufsichtsstelle für koloniale und auswärtige Dividendenwerte; ~ **of mines** Grubenaufseher, -aufsichtsamt; ~ **of schools** [etwa] Schulrat; ⍦ **of Taxes** *(Br.)* Finanzamtsleiter; ~ **of weights and measures** Eichmeister; ~ **of works** Bauaufsichtsbehörde;
~**'s district** Aufsichtsbezirk; ~**'s report** Prüfungs-, Revisionsbericht.

inspectoral staff Aufsichtspersonal, Inspektionsstab.

inspectorate Aufseheramt, *(district)* Aufsichtsbezirk;
factory ~ Gewerbeaufsichtsamt;
~ **of schools** *(Br.)* Schulaufsichtsamt.

inspectorship Oberaufsicht;
state ~ Staatsaufsicht.

inspiration plötzlicher Einfall, Inspiration;
under the ~ **of** auf Veranlassung von;
to have a sudden ~ plötzliche Eingebung haben.

inspire *(v.)* anspornen, anfeuern, ermutigen, beeinflussen;
~ **s. o. with confidence** jem. Vertrauen einflößen; ~ **s. o. with respect** jem. Respekt einflößen.

inspired *(rumo(u)r)* inspiriert;
~ **with hope** von Hoffnung beflügelt;
~ **article** lanzierter Artikel.

instability Veränderlichkeit, Unbeständigkeit, *(currency)* Unsicherheit;
~ **of demand** Nachfrageinstabilität.

instable unsicher, unbeständig, nicht stabil.

install *(v.)* installieren, *(in office)* einführen, -weisen, -setzen, *(el.)* Leitung legen, *(machine)* aufstellen, installieren, *(in office)* einführen, -weisen, -setzen;
~ **a college president** Präsidenten eines College einführen; ~ **an engine** Motor einsetzen (einbauen); ~ **a heating system** Heizung installieren; ~ **a lighting system** Lichtleitungen legen; ~ **a machine** Maschine installieren; ~ **a minister into a new charge** Minister in sein Amt einführen; ~ **s. o. in an office** j. in sein Amt einweisen (einsetzen); ~ **o. s. in a place** sich auf einem Platz niederlassen.

installation *(factory)* Betriebseinrichtung, Werk, installierte Anlage, Fabrikanlage, *(into office)* Einführung, Einsetzung, *(setting up)* Installierung, Einbau, Montage;
heating ~ Heizungsanlage; **lighting** ~ Lichtanlage; **military** ~s militärische Anlagen;
~ **subject to approval** genehmigungsbedürftige Anlagen; ~ **of a central heating** Einbau einer Zentralheizung; ~s **under construction** *(balance sheet)* Anlagen im Bau;
to make the ~ **of expensive plant pay** Rentierlichkeit einer kostspieligen Fabrikeinrichtung sicherstellen;
~ **charges** *(tel.)* Kosten der Anschlußeinrichtung; ~ **cost** Aufstellungs-, Einbaukosten; **on site** ~ **cost** bauseitig anfallende Installationskosten.

installed, duly wohlbestallt;
to be comfortably ~ **in a new home** bequem in einer neuen Wohnung eingerichtet sein.

instal[l]ment *(of book)* Lieferung, *(installation)* Aufstellung, Installierung, Einbau, Montage, *(into office, Br.)* Amtseinsetzung, Bestallung, Einführung, *(part delivery)* Teillieferung, *(part payment)* Raten-, Ab-, Teilzahlung, Rate, *(publication)* Fortsetzung;
as an ~ **against balance due** als Teilzahlung auf den geschuldeten Betrag; **by** - s in Teillieferungen, ratenweise, in Raten, auf Teilzahlung; **by stated** ~s in festgelegten Raten; **in monthly** ~s in monatlichen Raten (Teilbeträgen); **in seven** ~s *(newspaper)* in sieben Fortsetzungen; **payable in 4** ~s in 4 Raten zahlbar;
aid ~s in Raten gewährte Hilfszahlungen; **amortization** ~ Amortisationsquote, -rate; **annual** ~ jährliche Ratenzahlung; **final** ~ letzte Rate, Schlußrate, Abschlußzahlung; **first** ~ Anzahlung, erste Rate; **monthly** ~ Monatsrate; **past-due** ~ überfällige Rate; **petty** ~s geringfügige Teilzahlungen; **semiannual** ~ Halbjahresrate; **sinking-fund** ~ Tilgungs-, Ablösungsrate; **tax** ~ *(US)* Einkommensteuervorauszahlung; **yearly** ~ Jahresrate;
~ **of amortization** Tilgungsrate; ~ **of a publication** Lieferungswerk; ~ **of purchase price** Kaufpreisrate; ~ **of rent** monatliche Miete;
to appear in ~s in Fortsetzungen erscheinen; **to be an** ~ **behindhand** mit einer Rate im Rückstand sein; **to be published in** ~s in Fortsetzungen veröffentlicht werden; **to buy by** ~s auf Abzahlung kaufen; **to buy a motorcar and pay for it by monthly** ~s Auto im Teilzahlungswege erwerben; **to fall behind with an** ~ mit einer [Teilzahlungs]rate in Rückstand sein; **to issue a loan in** ~s Anleihe in Stücken ausgeben; **to pay an** ~ Rate bezahlen, Teilzahlung leisten; **to pay by (in)** ~s in Raten zahlen; **to pay in small** ~s in kleinen Raten abzahlen; **to pay a subscription in** ~s Subskription in Raten bezahlen; **to spread** ~s **over several months** Teilzahlungsraten auf mehrere Monate verteilen; **to vote credits in** ~s Kredit nur ratenweise bewilligen;
~ **account** Teilzahlungskonto; ~ **allotment** *(Br.)* Anleihezuteilung im Teilzahlungswege; ~ **basis** Teilzahlungsgrundlage; ~ **bonds** *(US)* serienweise rückzahlbare Obligationen; ~ **business** Raten-, Teilzahlungsgeschäft; **retail** ~ **business** Teilzahlungskredite für Einzelhändler; ~ **buying** Abzahlungskauf, Teilzahlungsgeschäft; **to lift restrictions on** ~ **buying** Beschränkungen auf dem Teilzahlungsgebiet aufheben; ~ **buying system** Teilzahlungswesen; ~ **charges** Teilzahlungskosten; ~ **collections** Inkasso von Ratenzahlungen; ~ **contract** Abzahlungs-, Teilzahlungsvertrag; ~ **credit** Teil-, Abzahlungskredit; **productive** ~ **credit** Teilzahlungskredit für Produktivgüter; **retail** ~ **credit** Teilzahlungskredit für Einzelhändler; ~ **credit business** Teil-, Abzahlungsgeschäft; ~ **credit extension** Ausweitung des Teilzahlungsgeschäfts; ~ **credit outstanding** Gesamtsumme der Teilzahlungskredite, Teilzahlungsvolumen; ~ **debt** Abzahlungsverpflichtungen; ~ **finance** Finanzierung von Teilzahlungsgeschäften; ~ **finance company** Teilzahlungskreditbank; ~ **finance subsidiaries** abhängige Teilzahlungsgesellschaften; ~

financing Teilzahlungsfinanzierung; ~ **house** *(US)* Teilzahlungsunternehmen, Kundenkreditbank; ~ **interest** Teil-, Abzahlungsgebühr; ~ **land sales** Grundstücksverkäufe auf Teilzahlungsbasis; ~ **loan** Teilzahlungskredit; ~ **equipment loan** *(US)* Teilzahlungskredit mit Eigentumsvorbehalt; ~ **method of accounting** Buchungsmethode mit Realisierung der Rohgewinne bei Rateneingang; ~ **mortgage** Amortisationshypothek; ~ **note** *(US)* Schuldschein mit Unterwerfungsklausel; ~ **obligations** Teilzahlungsverpflichtungen; ~ **option** ratenweise Bezahlung der Erbschaftssteuer; **to select an ~ option** Ratenzahlung wählen; ~ **option assets** in Raten nachlaßversteuerte Gegenstände; ~ **order** Anordnung von Ratenzahlungen; ~ **payment** Teil-, Abschlags-, Ratenzahlung; ~ **plan** Ab-, Raten-, Teilzahlungssystem; **on the ~ plan** auf Teilzahlung[s-basis]; **sinking-fund ~ plan** Tilgungsplan; **to buy on the ~ plan** im Teilzahlungswege erwerben, auf Teilzahlung (Raten) kaufen; ~**-plan financing** Teilzahlungsfinanzierung; ~ **price** Raten, Teilzahlungspreis; ~ **purchase** Kredit-, Ratenkauf; ~ **receivables** *(balance sheet, US)* Teilzahlungsverträge, -verpflichtungen; ~ **restrictions** Einschränkungen der Abzahlungsgeschäfte; ~ **sale (selling)** Abzahlungsverkauf, Teilzahlungsverkauf; **high-ticket ~ sales** hochwertige Teilzahlungsgeschäfte; ~ **sales contract** Ratenzahlungsvertrag; ~ **shares** in Raten zahlbare Aktien; ~ **system** Abzahlungs-, Raten-, Teilzahlungssystem; **to buy (pay) on the ~ system** in Raten zahlen, auf Teil-, Abzahlung kaufen; ~ **transaction** [einzelnes] Teilzahlungsgeschäft.

instance Fall, Beispiel, *(entreaty)* Er-, Ansuchen, dringende Bitte, *(law court)* Instanz;

at the ~ of auf Vorschlag (Antrag, Veranlassung) von; **for ~** zum Beispiel; **in the first ~** an erster Stelle, in erster Linie, *(judicial proceedings)* in der ersten Instanz; **in a given ~** in einem Einzelfalle; **in the last ~** in letzter Instanz;

higher ~ höhere Instanz; **lower ~** untere Instanz, Vorinstanz; **second ~** Beschwerde, Berufungsinstanz;

~ **of espionage** Spionagefall;

~ *(v.)* als Beispiel anführen;

to quote an ~ Beispiel anführen.

instant kurzer Augenblick, Moment, *(inst.)* laufenden (lfd.) Monats, unverzüglich;

on the ~ sofort, im Nu, augenblicklich; **on the 8th ~** am 8. des lfd. Monats;

the last ~ Ende des laufenden Monats; **particular ~** bestimmter Zeitpunkt;

~ **coffee** Pulverkaffee; ~ **dismissal** fristlose Entlassung; **to be in ~ need of help** sofortiger Hilfe bedürfen; ~ **print shop** Sofortdruckerei; ~ **relief** sofortige Erleichterung.

instantaneous unverzüglich, blitzschnell;

~ **action** Sofortaktion; ~ **crime** Einzelstraftat; ~ **exposure** sofortige Entwicklung; ~ **photograph** Momentaufnahme.

instanter, instantly sofort, unverzüglich.

instate *(v.)* **in office** in ein Amt einsetzen.

instigate *(v.)* aufhetzen, anstiften;

~ **a malefactor** Verbrecher anstiften; ~ **a strike** zu einem Streik aufhetzen.

instigation Aufhetzung, Anstiftung;

at the ~ of auf Veranlassung von.

instigator of a crime Anstifter eines Verbrechens.

instil(l) *(v.)* einflößen;

~ **a new doctrine into the people** dem Volk eine neue politische Doktrin einträufeln (eingeben, oktroieren).

instinct Instinkt, *(talent)* Begabung;

by ~ instinktiv;

~ **of self-preservation** Selbsterhaltungstrieb;

to bring out sexist ~ Gleichberechtigungsinteresse erwecken; **to have an ~ for crime** verbrecherische Anlagen haben.

institorial power *(clerk)* Geschäftsführungsbefugnis.

institute Einrichtung, Institut, Akademie, Anstalt, Gesellschaft, *(appointed heir, Scot.)* Erstberechtigter, *(building)* Anstaltsgebäude, *(order)* Vorschrift, Verordnung, *(statute)* Statut, Grundgesetz, *(university)* Universitätsinstitut;

~**s** Gesetzessammlung;

Farmers' ~ *(US)* Landwirtschaftsinstitut; **mechanics' ~** Handwerksordnung; **research ~** Forschungsinstitut; **teachers' ~** Lehrerseminar; **town-planning ~** Institut für Städteplanung; **~ of Bankers** *(Br.)* Bankiervereinigung; ~ **for business-cycle research** Konjunkturinstitut; **~ for Economic Research** Wirtschaftsforschungsinstitut; ~ **of export** Ausfuhrinstitut; **~ of Management** Managementinstitut; **~ for Population Research** Demoskopisches Institut; **~ of Transport** *(Br.)* Institut zum Studium von Verkehrsfragen;

~ *(v.)* *(establish)* einführen, einrichten, einsetzen, gründen, *(enact)* anordnen, verordnen, *(set in operation)* einleiten;

~ **an action at law** Sache vor Gericht bringen; ~ **[bankruptcy] proceedings against** [Konkurs]verfahren einleiten; ~ **s. o. into a benefice** jem. eine Pfründe aussetzen; ~ **a code of laws** Gesetzessammlung in Kraft setzen; ~ **criminal proceedings** Strafverfahren einleiten; ~ **a government** Regierung einsetzen; ~ **s. o. as heir** *(US)* j. als Erben einsetzen; ~ **inquiries** Nachforschungen anstellen; ~ **an inquiry** Untersuchung einleiten; ~ **investigations** Ermittlungen einleiten; ~ **a law** Gesetz einführen; ~ **into an office** in ein Amt einsetzen; ~ **a society** Gesellschaft ins Leben rufen; ~ **a suit** *(US)* Klage einreichen (anstrengen);

~**-cargo clause** *(Br.)* zusätzliche Frachtdeckungsklausel, Klausel für Seewarenversicherung; ~**-war clauses** Kriegsklauseln; ~ **leader** Institutsleiter.

institution *(building)* Anstalts-, Institutsgebäude, *(corporate establishment)* Anstalt, Institut, *(established order)* Einrichtung, *(establishing)* Errichtung, Gründung, Stiftung, Eröffnung, *(habit, coll.)* eingefleischte Gewohnheit, *(law of inheritance)* Erbeinsetzung, *(law practice)* Prozeßbeginn, *(person)* bekannte Person, *(society)* Stiftung, Gesellschaft, *(sociology)* Institution, Einrichtung, *(statute)* Verordnung, Satzung, Statut;

banking ~ Bankinstitut; **charitable ~** wohltätige (milde) Stiftung, Versorgungsanstalt, karikative Einrichtung; **educational ~** Bildungsanstalt; **financial ~** Geld-, Finanz-, Kreditinstitut; **governmental ~** staatliche Einrichtung; **investing ~** Kapitalsammelstelle; **legal ~** Rechtseinrichtung; **literary ~** literarische Gesellschaft; **mental ~** Heil- und Pflegeanstalt; **mercantile ~** Wirtschaftsinstitut; **nonprofit-making ~** gemeinnützige Einrichtung; **penal ~** Straf[vollzugs]anstalt; **permanent ~** feststehende (ständige) Einrichtung; **philanthropic ~** gemeinnützige Einrichtung; **public ~** öffentliche Einrichtung, öffentlich-rechtliche Anstalt, gemeinnütziges Unternehmen; **publicly-owned credit ~** öffentlich-rechtliches Kreditinstitut; **union ~** gewerkschaftliche Einrichtungen;

~ **of bankruptcy proceedings** Einleitung eines Konkursverfahrens; ~ **to a benefice** Pfründeneinsetzung; ~ **for the blind** Blindenanstalt; ~ **of customs** Begründung von Gebräuchen; **~ of the European Community** Organe der Europäischen Gemeinschaft; ~ **of an heir** *(US)* Erbeinsetzung; ~ **for inebriates** Trinkerheilanstalt; ~ **of an inquiry** Einleitung einer Untersuchung; ~ **of legal proceedings** Einleitung eines gerichtlichen Verfahrens; ~ **of restrictions** Einführung von Beschränkungen; ~ **of rules** Einführung von Regeln; ~ **of winding-up proceedings** Einleitung des Liquidationsverfahrens;

to place s. o. in an ~ for defectives for examination j. zur Überprüfung seines Geisteszustands in eine Anstalt einweisen.

institutional angeordnet, verordnet, eingesetzt, institutionell, *(economy)* auf weite Sicht abgestimmt;

~ **accounts** Konten von Kapitalsammelstellen; ~ **advertising** *(US)* Eigen-, Vertrauens-, Goodwill-, Repräsentations-, Firmenwerbung, firmeneigene Werbung; **to prosper on ~ business** im Kapitalanlagegeschäft erfolgreich sein; ~ **buyer** Kapitalsammelstelle; ~ **campaign** Goodwillwerbung; ~ **care** geschlossene Fürsorge, Anstaltspflege; ~ **clients** Kapitalanleger, Anlagepublikum; ~ **fund manager** Verwalter des Vermögens einer Kapitalsammelstelle; ~ **life** Anstaltsaufenthalt; ~ **investor (lender)** institutionelle Anleger, Kapitalsammelstelle; ~ **investor services** Beratungsdienst für Kapitalanlagestellen; **to come under ~ liquidation** von einer Kapitalanlagestelle abgestoßen werden; ~ **money manager** Geldhändler von Kapitalsammelstellen; ~ **monopoly** Meinungsmonopol; ~ **problem** Institutionsproblem; ~ **saver** institutioneller Sparer; ~ **selling** Effektenverkauf an Kapitalsammelstellen; ~ **trading** außerbörslicher Effektenverkehr mit Kapitalsammelstellen; ~ **treatment** Anstaltsbehandlung; ~ **unit of government** staatliche Kapitalanlagestelle; ~ **user** Behördenkundschaft.

institutionalization Institutionalisierung.

institutionalize *(v.)* verfassungsmäßig fixieren, institutionalisieren.

institutor Gründer, Stifter, *(lawsuit)* Kläger;

~ **of a law** Gesetzgeber.

instruct *(v.)* *(direct)* anweisen, Anweisung geben, Weisungen erteilen, beauftragen, *(impart knowledge)* unterweisen, instruieren, *(inform)* unterrichten, informieren, *(school)* anleiten, ausbilden, Unterricht erteilen;

~ **o. s.** sich unterrichten; ~ **s. o.** jem. einen Auftrag erteilen; ~ **an agent** Vertreter orientieren; ~ **an attorney** *(US)* Anwalt beauftragen; ~ **a class** Schulklasse unterrichten; ~ **a clerk in bookkeeping** Angestellten in die Buchführung einweisen; ~ **a** committee Ausschuß mit Weisungen versehen; ~ **s. o. of a fact** j. über einen Sachverhalt instruieren; ~ **jurors** *(US)* Geschworene über die wesentlichen Rechtsgrundsätze belehren; ~ **a solicitor** *(Br.)* Anwalt beauftragen (mit Weisungen versehen); ~ **a representative** *(US)* seinen Abgeordneten mit Weisungen versehen; ~ **s. o. how to do his work** jem. Arbeitsanweisungen erteilen.

instructed, as weisungs-, auftragsgemäß; ~ **in** bekannt mit.

instruction *(direction)* Anordnung, [An]weisung, Instruktion, Auftrag, Vorschrift, Verhaltungsmaßregel, *(practice)* Informationsbeschaffung, *(teaching)* Unterweisung, Ausbildung, Belehrung, Unterricht;

according to (in accordance with, as per) ~s vorschrifts-, weisungs-, instruktions-, auftragsmäßig; **contrary to** ~ gegen ausdrückliche Anweisungen; **pursuant to your** ~s gemäß Ihren Instruktionen; **under** ~s of auf Anweisung von; ~s Verhaltungsmaßregeln, Instruktionen;

audo-visual ~ Unterricht mit Lehrfilmen; **driving** ~ Fahrunterricht; **forwarding** ~s Versandanweisung; **full-time** ~ ganztägige Ausbildung; **mandatory** ~s *(US)* verbindliche Anweisungen; **official** ~s Dienstanweisungen, gesetzliche Vorschriften, Dienstvorschriften; **operating** ~s Betriebsanordnungen, -anweisungen; **packing** ~s Verpackungsvorschriften, Versandanweisungen; **peremptory** ~ *(to jurors)* bindende Rechtsbelehrung; **private** ~ Privatunterricht; **self-**~ Selbstunterricht; **service** ~ *(post)* Beförderungsbestimmungen; **shipping** ~s *(US)* Versandanweisung; **strict** ~ ausdrückliche Anweisung; **trade-policy** ~s handelspolitische Instruktionen; **written** ~s schriftliche Anweisungen (Instruktionen);

~ **to counsel (solicitor)** *(Br.)* Anweisungen an den Anwalt; ~ **for dispatch of goods** Versandanweisung; ~ **on the job** Ausbildung am Arbeitsplatz; ~s **to jurors** *(US)* Rechtsbelehrung der Geschworenen; **individual** ~ **by post** individuelles Fernstudium; ~s **for use** Gebrauchsanweisung;

to act contrary to ~s Anordnungen zuwiderhandeln; **to act upon** ~ weisungsgemäß verfahren, Anweisungen Folge leisten; **to ask for** ~s Weisungen einholen; **to await** ~s Anweisungen abwarten, auf Anordnungen warten; **to carry out (comply with, follow) an** ~ Weisung ausführen (befolgen); **to comply with** ~s **received** sich nach den empfangenen Weisungen richten; **to disregard (contravene) an** ~ einer Weisung zuwiderhandeln; **to give** ~s Anweisungen erteilen, Anordnungen erlassen (geben); **to give s. o.** ~s jem einen Auftrag (Instruktionen) erteilen; **to give** ~s **to a solicitor** *(Br.)* Anwalt mit Weisungen versehen; **to go beyond one's** ~s seine Anweisungen überschreiten; **to lay strict** ~s **on s. o.** jem. genaue Anweisungen geben; **to receive** ~s Direktiven erhalten; **to receive full and particular** ~s detaillierte Anweisungen erhalten; **to receive full-time** ~ **at an university** ganztägiges Universitätsstudium absolvieren;

~ **book** Lehrbuch; ~ **booklet** Gebrauchsanweisung, Anleitungsheft; ~ **card** Arbeitsanweisung; ~ **manual** Betriebs-, Dienstanweisung, Handbuch für Ausbildungsfragen; ~ **sheet** Bedienungsanleitung, *(interviewer)* Befragungsvorschrift.

instructional lehrreich, belehrend; ~ **film** Kultur-, Lehrfilm; ~ **method** Ausbildungsmethode; ~ **trip** Informationsreise.

instructive book Lehrbuch.

instructor Kursleiter, Ausbilder, *(university, US)* Dozent; **chief** ~ Ausbildungsleiter.

instrument *(measuring device)* Apparat, Meßgerät, *(document)* Dokument, Urkunde, Beweisstück, *(fig.)* Handhabe, *(implement)* Gerät, Werkzeug, Instrument, *(commercial paper, US)* Handelspapier, *(person used)* Handlanger;

assignable ~ übertragbares Papier; **authentic** ~ echte (beglaubigte) Urkunde; **bearer** ~ Inhaberpapier; **complete** ~ ausgefüllte Urkunde; **dial** ~ *(tel.)* Wähleinrichtung; **effective** ~ gültige Urkunde; **endorsable** ~ indossables Papier; **international** ~ internationales Vertragswerk; **legal** ~ Rechtsdokument; **lost** ~ abhanden gekommene Urkunde; **musical** ~ Musikinstrument; **negotiable** ~ begebbares Wertpapier; **nonnegotiable** ~ Rektapapier; **order** ~ Orderpapier; **original** ~ Originalurkunde; **perfect** ~ eingetragene Urkunde; **supplemental** ~ Zusatzdokument; **testamentary** ~ Testament; **transferable** ~ übertragbares Papier; **trust** ~ Treuhandvertrag;

~ **of abdiction** Abdankungsurkunde; ~ **of acceptance** *(law of nations)* Annahmeurkunde; ~ **of accession** Beitrittsurkunde; ~ **of appeal** Berufungsschriftsatz; ~ **appointing a proxy** Stimmrechtsermächtigung, Bevollmächtigungsurkunde; ~ **of appointment** Bestallungsurkunde; ~ **of approval** Genehmigungsurkunde; ~ **of assignment** Abtretungs-, Zessionsurkunde; ~ **to bearer** Inhaberpapier; ~ **of charge** Hypothekenbewilligungs-,

Belastungsurkunde; ~ **of credit** verkehrsfähiges (begebbares) Papier; ~ **of no effect** wertloses Papier; ~ **of evidence** Beweisurkunde, -mittel; ~ **of notification** Notifikationsurkunde; ~ **to order** Orderpapier; ~ **not to order** Rektapapier; ~ **payable to bearer** Inhaberpapier; ~ **payable to order** Orderpapier; ~ **payable to joint payers** an verschiedene Zahlungsempfänger zahlbares Papier; ~ **of payment** Zahlungsmittel; ~ **of economic policy** wirtschaftspolitisches Instrument; ~s **of monetary policy** Geldmarktinstrumentarium; ~ **of ratification** Ratifikations-, Ratifizierungsurkunde; ~ **of saisine** *(Scot., law)* Auflassungsurkunde; ~ **of signature** Unterzeichnungsurkunde; ~ **of title** Eigentums-, Besitztitel; ~ **of transfer** Übertragungsurkunde; ~s **of war** Kriegswerkzeuge;

to alter an ~ Urkunde abändern; **to be the** ~ **of another's crime** willenloses Werkzeug eines Verbrechers sein; **to be a mere** ~ **in the hands of another** bloßes Werkzeug in der Hand eines anderen sein; **to deliver an** ~ Urkunde aushändigen; **to execute an** ~ Urkunde ausfertigen; **to fly by** ~s nur nach den Instrumenten (blind) fliegen; **to give out an** ~ Papier begeben; **to provide** ~s Mittel und Wege bieten; **to reform an** ~ *(US)* Urkunde berichtigen; **to turn out** ~s **of war** Kriegsmaterial herstellen;

~ **board** Instrumenten-, Armaturenbrett; ~ **flight plan** Blindflugplan; ~ **flight rules** Blindflug-, Instrumentenflugregeln; ~ **flying** Blindfliegen, -flug; ~ **landing** Nebel-, Blindfluglandung; ~ **making** Instrumentenbau; ~ **name plate** Geräteschild; ~ **panel** *(car)* Instrumentenskala.

instrumental dienlich, förderlich;

to be ~ **in doing s. th.** bei etw. behilflich sein; **to be** ~ **in finding well paid work for a friend** sich hilfreich bei der Beschaffung einer gut bezahlten Stellung für einen Freund erweisen; **to be largely** ~ **in a matter** weitgehend in einer Angelegenheit tätig werden; **to be** ~ **to a purpose** Beitrag zu einem Zweck leisten;

~ **capital** Produktivkapital; ~ **cause** mitwirkende Ursache; ~ **disturbance** Gerätestörung; ~ **error** Instrumentenfehler; ~ **goods** Produktionsgüter; ~ **music** Instrumentalmusik; ~ **scale** Instrumentenskala.

instrumentality Mitwirkung, Zweckdienlichkeit;

by s. one's ~ durch jds. Vermittlung.

instrumentation Instrumentenausrüstung.

insubordinate widersetzlich;

~ **conduct** Widersetzlichkeit, Gehorsamsverweigerung.

insubordination Widersetzlichkeit, Gehorsamsverweigerung, Ungehorsam, Auflehnung, Meuterei.

insufficiency Unzulänglichkeit, Ungültigkeit, *(affidavit)* Unvollständigkeit [einer eidesstattlichen Erklärung], *(equity pleading)* mangelnde Substantiierung;

~ **of assets** mangelnde Deckung; ~ **in an office** mangelnde Eignung für ein Amt.

insufficient unzulänglich, ungenügend, nicht ausreichend, *(law)* rechtsungültig, nichtig, *(person)* untauglich;

~ **assets** unzureichende Aktiva; ~ **food supplies** unzureichende Nahrungsmittelvorräte; ~ **funds** *(bill of exchange)* ungenügende Deckung; ~ **means** nicht ausreichende Mittel; ~ **packing** mangelhafte Verpackung, Verpackungsfehler.

insufficiently | paid ungenügend frankiert; ~ **stamped** ungenügend verstempelt.

insular isoliert, alleinstehend, *(narrow-minded)* engstirnig, stur; ~ **climate** Inselklima; ~ **mind** *(fam.)* sturer Gesell; ~ **prejudices** kleinliche Vorurteile.

insularity Insellage, *(position)* isolierte Lage; ~ **of outlook** *(Br.)* Engstirnigkeit.

insulate *(v.)* *(el.)* isolieren, *(isolate)* absondern, isolieren.

insulating | switch *(el.)* Trennschalter; ~ **tape** Isolierband.

insulation Isolierung.

insulator *(el.)* Isolator, Nichtleiter.

insult Ehrenkränkung, Beschimpfung, Beleidigung;

studied ~ vorsätzliche Beleidigung;

~ **to s. one's hono(u)r** Ehrenkränkung;

~ *(v.)* beleidigen, beschimpfen;

~ **s. o. with odious suspicions** j. durch abscheuliche Verdächtigungen kränken;

to add ~ **to injury** Sache noch schlimmer machen; **to offer an** ~ **to s. o.** j. beleidigen; **to pocket an** ~ Beleidigung schlucken.

insulting | behavio(u)r beleidigendes Verhalten; ~ **language** beleidigende Ausdrücke.

insurability Versicherungsfähigkeit, Versicherbarkeit.

insurable versicherbar, versicherungsfähig;

~ **interest** versicherbares Interesse, Versicherungsinteresse; **to have an** ~ **interest** finanziell interessiert sein; ~ **property** versicherbare Vermögensgegenstände; ~ **risk** versicherbares Risiko, Versicherungsrisiko; ~ **value** Versicherungswert.

insurance Versicherung, *(premium paid)* Versicherungsprämie, *(sum insured)* Versicherungssumme;
covered by ~ durch Versicherung gedeckt; **exempt from ~** versicherungsfrei; **in the field of ~** auf dem Versicherungsgebiet;
accident ~ Unfallversicherung; **personal accident ~** private Unfallversicherung; **travel(l)ers' accident ~** Reiseunfallversicherung; **accident benefit ~** Unfallversicherung; **accounts receivable ~** *(US)* Debitorenversicherung; **additional ~** Extra-, Zusatzversicherung; **air passengers' ~** Fluggastversicherung; **aircraft ~** Luftfahrtversicherung; **airport liability ~** Flugplatzversicherung; **all-in (-loss) ~** Gesamt-, General-, Universalversicherung; **all-risks ~** Einheitsversicherung; **annuity ~** Leibrentenversicherung; **art property and jewel(le)ry ~** Wertgegenständeversicherung; **assessment ~** Lebensversicherung auf Gegenseitigkeit; **auto-travel ~** Kraftfahrreiseversicherung; **[compulsory] automobile ~** *(US)* Kraftfahrzeug[haftpflicht]-versicherung; **automobile collision ~** Kaskoversicherung; **automobile personal liability and property damage ~** *(US)* Haftpflicht- und Kaskoversicherung; **aviation ~** Flugzeug-, Luftfahrtversicherung; **bad-debts ~** Kreditversicherung; **baggage ~** *(US)* Reisegepäckversicherung; **bank-burglary and robbery ~** Versicherung gegen Bankeinbruch und Bankraub; **blanket ~** Kollektivversicherung; **bodily injury ~** öffentlich-rechtliche Haftpflichtversicherung; **boiler ~** Dampfkesselversicherung; **bonds ~** Kautionsversicherung; **bottomry ~** Bodmereiversicherung; **builder's risk ~** Bauunternehmerhaftpflichtversicherung; **burglary ~** Einbruchsdiebstahlversicherung; **burial ~** Sterbeversicherung; **business ~** Betriebsverlustversicherung, Versicherung leitender Angestellter; **business interruption ~** Betriebsstillstandsversicherung, Versicherung gegen Betriebsunterbrechung; **business partnership ~** Teilhaberversicherung; **capital redemption ~** Sparversicherung; **cargo ~** Güter-, Frachtversicherung; **~ carried** unterhaltene (aufrechterhaltene) Versicherung; **casualty ~** *(US)* Schadens-, Unfallhaftversicherung; **cattle ~** Viehversicherung; **check (cheque,** *Br.***) alteration and forgery ~** Versicherung gegen Scheckfälschungen; **child endowment ~** Aussteuer-, Ausbildungsversicherung; **collateral ~** zusätzliche Versicherung, Nebenversicherung; **collective ~** Gruppen-, Kollektivversicherung; **collision ~** Kollisions-, Kaskoversicherung; **commercial ~** Delkredere- und Vertrauensschadens-, Handelsrisiko-, Garantieversicherung; **commercial accident ~** Betriebsunfallversicherung; **commission ~** Versicherung gegen entgangene Provisionsgebühr; **common carrier's ~** Güterverlustversicherung; **common carrier's legal liability ~** Spediteurhaftpflichtversicherung; **compensation ~** *(US)* Arbeiterunfallversicherung; **complementary ~** Ergänzungs-, Zusatzversicherung; **comprehensive ~** Universalversicherung; **comprehensive motorcar ~** *(Br.)* Teilkaskoversicherung; **comprehensive automobile and property damage ~** *(US)* Teilkaskoversicherung; **compulsory ~** obligatorische Versicherung, Pflicht-, Zwangsversicherung; **concurrent ~** Parallelversicherung; **consequential damage (loss) ~** Versicherung gegen mittelbaren Schaden, Folgeschädenversicherung; **contingency ~** Versicherung gegen besondere Risiken; **voluntarily continued ~** freiwillige Weiterversicherung; **contract ~** Submissionsversicherung; **contractors' public liability and property damage liability ~** Unternehmerhaftpflicht- und Sachschadenversicherung; **contributory ~** Versicherung mit Selbstbehalt; **contributory group ~** Gruppenversicherung mit Beitragsleistung der Beteiligten; **convertible term ~** Risikoumtauschversicherung; **conveyance ~** Haftpflichtversicherung im Grundstücksverkehr; **cooperative ~** genossenschaftliches Versicherungswesen; **corporative ~** Gemeinschaftsversicherung; **credit ~** Kreditversicherung; **crop ~** Ernteversicherung; **deferred ~** zurückgestellte Versicherungsbeiträge; **deferred annuity ~** abgekürzte Lebensversicherung; **direct ~** Erst-, Direktversicherung; **disability (disablement) ~** Unfall-, Invaliditätsversicherung; **double ~** Mehrfach-, Doppelversicherung; **earthquake ~** Erdbebenversicherung; **educational endowment ~** Ausbildungsversicherung; **elevator ~** Fahrstuhlversicherung; **employers' liability ~** Unternehmer-, Betriebshaftpflichtversicherung; **endowment ~** Versicherung auf den Erlebensfall, Versorgungs-, Aussteuerversicherung; **engineering ~** Maschinenbetriebs-, Maschinenbruchversicherung; **excess ~** Exedenten-, Überversicherung; **expired ~** abgelaufene Versicherung; **explosion ~** Explosionsversicherung; **extended ~** aufgestockte (prolongierte) Versicherung; **extra ~** Zusatzversicherung; **factory ~** Betriebsversicherung; **fidelity ~** *(US)* Kautions-, Garantieversicherung; **fidelity guarantee ~** *(Br.)* Garantie-, Kautionsversicherung;

fire ~ Feuer-, Brandversicherung; **first-loss ~** Erstrisikoversicherung; **fleet ~** Kraftfahrzeugsammelversicherung; **flood ~** Überschwemmungsversicherung; **fraternal ~** Bruderschaftsversicherung; **free ~** kostenloser Versicherungsschutz; **freight ~** Frachtversicherung; **frost ~** Frostversicherung; **full-coverage collision ~** hundertprozentige Kaskoversicherung; **full-coverage theft ~** vollgedeckte Diebstahlversicherung; **funeral-cost ~** Sterbefallversicherung; **furniture-in-transit ~** Umzugsversicherung; **garage keeper's liability ~** Garagenbesitzerhaftpflichtversicherung; **garage liability ~** Garagenhaftpflichtversicherung; **general ~** normale Seeschadenversicherung; **glass ~** Fensterglasversicherung; **governmental life ~** Lebensversicherung für Staatsangestellte; **ground-rent ~** Versicherung zur Einhaltung von Reallastverpflichtungen; **group ~** Kollektiv-, Gruppen-, Gemeinschaftsversicherung; **group disability ~** Sammelunfallversicherung; **group life ~** Gruppenrisikoversicherung für vorzeitige Todesfälle; **group term life ~** Gruppenlebensversicherung; **guaranty ~** Kautionsversicherung; **guaranty-of-title ~** *(US)* Versicherung von Rechtsansprüchen auf Grundbesitz, Rechtsmängelgewährleistungsversicherung; **hail ~** Hagelversicherung; **hazardous ~** Elementarschadensversicherung; **health ~** *(Br.)* Krankenversicherung; **hi[gh]-jacking ~** Versicherung gegen Flugzeugentführung; **home ~** Hausversicherung; **hospital benefit ~** Krankenhaus-Zuschußversicherung; **house and contents ~** Hausratsversicherung; **householder's comprehensive ~** kombinierte Haus- und Hausratsversicherung, verbundene Wohngebäudeversicherung; **hull ~** *(airplane, ship)* Kaskoversicherung; **indemnity ~** Schadenverlustversicherung; **individual ~** Einzelversicherung; **industrial injuries ~** *(Br.)* Berufsunfallversicherung; **industrial [life] ~** *(US)* Volks-, Kleinlebensversicherung; **inland transportation ~** Binnentransportversicherung; **inland waterways ~** Binnenschiffahrtsversicherung; **international motor ~** internationale Autoversicherung; **jewel(le)ry ~** Juwelenversicherung; **leasehold ~** *(US)* Pachtausfallversicherung, Versicherung für [entgangenen Gewinn] für im Werte gestiegene Grundstücke; **public liability ~** öffentlich-rechtliche Haftpflichtversicherung; **life ~** Lebensversicherung; **joint life ~** Überlebensversicherung; **ordinary life ~** *(US)* Großlebensversicherung; **straight (whole) life ~** Lebensversicherung auf den Todesfall; **lightning ~** Blitzschlagversicherung; **limited pay[ment] ~** Lebensversicherung mit abgekürzter Prämienlaufzeit, abgekürzte Lebensversicherung; **livestock ~** Viehversicherung; **loss-of-profit ~** Geschäftsausfall-, Folgeschaden-, Gewinnverlustversicherung; **low-premium ~** Versicherung mit ermäßigten Prämiensätzen; **low-rate ~** Kleinlebensversicherung; **luggage ~** *(Br.)* Reisegepäckversicherung; **machinery ~** Maschinenhaftpflichtversicherung; **malpractice ~** Versicherung gegen Kunstfehler; **manufacturers' public liability and property damage liability ~** Unternehmerhaftpflicht- und Schadenversicherung; **marine (maritime) ~** Seetransportversicherung; **marine hull ~** Schiffskaskoversicherung; **marriage-portion ~** Aussteuerversicherung; **maternity ~** Mutterschaftsversicherung; **matured ~** fällige Versicherung; **medical ~** Krankenversicherung; **mercantile open-stock ~** Diebstahlversicherung offener Warenlager; **mobile ~** Kraftfahrzeugversicherung; **more specific ~** spezielle Schadensversicherung; **mortgage guaranty ~** Hypothekengarantieversicherung; **motor ~** Kraftfahrzeugversicherung; **motor car ~** *(Br.)* Auto-, Kraftfahrzeugversicherung; **motor-car liability ~** Kraftfahrzeughaftpflichtversicherung; **motor renewal ~** Erneuerung einer Kraftfahrzeugversicherung; **motor-vehicle ~** Kraftfahrzeugversicherung; **mutual ~** Versicherung auf Gegenseitigkeit, Gegenseitigkeitsversicherung; **National ~** *(Br.)* Sozialversicherung; **national health ~** *(Br.)* Krankenversicherung; **nonmandatory ~** freiwillige Versicherung; **occupancy ~** Besitzversicherung; **old-age ~** Renten-, Altersversicherung; **old-line life ~** normale Todesfallversicherung; **optional ~** fakultative Versicherung; **ordinary long-term ~** Versicherung auf den Lebensfall; **overseas ~** Überseeversicherung; **own ~** Selbstversicherung; **owner's liability ~** Eigentümerhaftpflichtversicherung; **paid-up ~** beitragsfreie (prämienfreie) Versicherung; **parcel-post ~** *(US)* Paketpostversicherung; **participating ~** Versicherung mit Gewinnbeteiligung; **partnership ~** Teilhaberversicherung; **paymaster robbery ~** Kassenraubversicherung; **pecuniary ~** Vermögensversicherung; **pedal-cycle ~** Fahrradversicherung; **permanent [partial] disability ~** Versicherung im Fall von Dauer-, Teilinvalidität; **permanent health ~** unbegrenzte Versicherung im Krankheitsfall; **personal ~** Individualversicherung; **personal holdup ~** Versicherung gegen Raubüberfall; **personal liability ~** Privathaftpflichtversicherung; **plate-glass** ~ Spiegel-, Fensterglasversicherung; **pluvious** ~ Regenversicherung; **prepaid** ~ vorausbezahlte Versicherung; **previous** ~ Vorversicherung; **private** ~ Privatversicherung; **producer's liability** ~ Gewährleistungsversicherung des Warenherstellers; **professional** ~ Berufshaftpflichtversicherung; **profit** ~ Gewinnversicherung; **property** ~ Sachversicherung; **property damage liability** ~ Sachschadenversicherung; **property owner's liability** ~ Hauseigentümerhaftpflichtversicherung; **protection and indemnity** ~ *(Br.)* seerechtliche Reederhaftpflichtversicherung; **pure endowment** ~ Kapitalversicherung auf den Erlebensfall; **rail transportation** ~ *(US)* Bahntransportversicherung; **rain** ~ Regenversicherung; **rainfall** ~ Regenversicherung; **reciprocal** ~ Gegenseitigkeits-, Reziprozitätsversicherung; **registered-mail** ~ Versicherung für eingeschriebene Postsendungen, Valorenversicherung; **reinstatement** ~ gleitende Neuwertversicherung; **renewable** ~ Versicherung mit ermäßigter Anfangsprämie; **rent** ~ Mietausfall-, -verlustversicherung; **rental value** ~ Mietausfallversicherung; **reporting** ~ Inventarversicherung mit der Auflage von Veränderungsmeldungen; **residence** ~ Gebäudeversicherung; **residence burglary** ~ Einbruch-, Diebstahlversicherung; **riot and civil commotion** ~ Aufruhrversicherung; **robbery** ~ Raubüberfallversicherung; **safe-deposit box** ~ Depotversicherung; **securities** ~ Wertpapierverwahrungsversicherung; **shipping** ~ *(US)* Transportversicherung; **short-period** ~ unter einem Jahr abgeschlossene Versicherung; **sick[ness]** ~ *(US)* Krankenversicherung; **single-premium** ~ Lebensversicherung gegen Zahlung einer einmaligen Prämie; **smoke** ~ Rauchversicherung; **social** ~ *(US)* Sozialversicherung; **special** ~ Versicherung für zusätzliches Transportrisiko; **sprinkler leakage** ~ Versicherung gegen Wasserschaden bei Feuerlöschanlagen; **state** ~ staatliche Versicherung, Staatsversicherung; **storm and tempest** ~ Sturmschädenversicherung; **strike** ~ Streikversicherung; **subscribed (subscribers')** ~ Abonnentenversicherung; **subsequent** ~ Nachversicherung; **supplementary** ~ Zusatzversicherung; **surety** ~ Untreue-, Kautionsversicherung; **surety bonds** ~ Bürgschaftsversicherung; **surgical fees** ~ Operationskostenversicherung; **survivor's (survivorship)** ~ Hinterbliebenen-, Überlebensversicherung; **tenant's liability** ~ Mieterhaftpflichtversicherung; **term** ~ abgekürzte Versicherung, Versicherung auf Zeit, Risiko-, Kurzversicherung; **theft** ~ Diebstahlversicherung; **third-party [indemnity]** ~ Haftpflichtversicherung; **third-party accident** ~ *(Br.)* Unfallhaftpflichtversicherung; **title** ~ *(US)* Versicherung gegen Rechtsmängel bei Grundstückserwerb; **tornado** ~ *(US)* Sturmversicherung; **tourists' baggage floater** ~ *(Br.)* globale Reisegepäckversicherung; **tourist weather** ~ Reisewetterversicherung; **transport** ~ Transportversicherung; **transportation** ~ *(US)* Transportversicherung; **travel** ~ Reiseversicherung; **travel(l)ers' accident** ~ Reiseunfallversicherung; **unemployment** ~ Arbeitslosenversicherung; **unoccupied buildings** ~ Versicherung gegen Schäden an unbewohnten Gebäuden; **use and occupancy** ~ Betriebsunterbrechungsversicherung; **voluntary** ~ freiwillige Versicherung; **war risk** ~ Versicherung gegen Kriegsgefahr; **warehouseman's liability** ~ Speicher-, Lagerversicherung; **water-damage** ~ Wasserschadenversicherung; **weather** ~ Reisewetterversicherung; **whole-life** ~ Lebensversicherung auf den Todesfall, reine Todesfallversicherung; **windstorm** ~ Sturmschäden-, Windbruchversicherung; **workmens' compensation** ~ *(US)* Unternehmerhaftpflicht-, Arbeiter-, Berufsunfallversicherung; **worldwide** ~ *(US)* Wertsachenversicherung [unabhängig vom Aufbewahrungsort der Gegenstände];

~ **on the body** Kaskoversicherung; ~ **against breakage** Bruchschädenversicherung; ~ **on cargo** Frachtversicherung; ~ **of crop** Ernteversicherung; ~ **against damage by hail** Hagelversicherung; ~ **against damage to property** Sachschadenversicherung; ~ **of delivery in time** Versicherung des Interesses an rechtzeitiger Lieferung; ~ **in force** laufende Versicherung; ~ **on freight** Frachtversicherung; ~ **of goods in transit** Gütertransportversicherung; ~ **on hull and appurtenances** *(ship)* Kaskoversicherung; ~ **of liability** Haftpflichtversicherung; ~ **against loss by redemption (redemption at par)** Kursverlustversicherung; ~ **of merchandise** Warenversicherung; ~ **of a person** Personenversicherung; ~ **with limited premium** Versicherung mit abgekürzter Prämienzahlung; ~ **on a premium basis** Versicherung gegen Prämie; ~ **for private medical treatment** *(Br.)* private Krankenversicherung; ~ **of property** Sachversicherung; ~ **of rights or financial interest** Vermögensversicherung; ~ **against all risks** Versicherung gegen alle Gefahren; ~ **by single payment** Versicherung gegen einmalige Prämienzahlung; ~ **of structure** Gebäudeversicherung; ~ **of structure and**

contents Gebäude- und Mobiliarversicherung; ~ **in transit** Transitversicherung; ~ **of value** Valoren-, Wertversicherung; **to arrange an** ~ Versicherung (Versicherungsvertrag) abschließen; **to buy** ~ sich versichern lassen; **to cancel an** ~ Versicherung aufheben; **to carry** ~ *(US)* versichert sein; **to carry** ~ **against legal liability** *(US)* gesetzliche Haftpflichtversicherung unterhalten; **to continue** ~ **of a class written previously** *(Br.)* bisher betriebene Versicherungssparte weiter betreiben; **to cut back on** ~s weniger Geld für Versicherungen vorsehen; **to effect an** ~ Versicherung abschließen; **to introduce an** ~ Versicherung vermitteln; **to maintain an** ~ **in force** Versicherungsschutz aufrechterhalten; **to place an** ~ Versicherung abschließen; **to pledge an** ~ Versicherungsanspruch verpfänden; **to provide an** ~ Versicherung decken; **to receive £ 10.000** ~ Versicherungssumme in Höhe von 10.000 £ ausgezahlt bekommen; **to reinstate an** ~ Versicherung wiederaufnehmen; **to sell** ~ als Versicherer tätig sein; **to take out an** ~ sich versichern lassen, Versicherungspolice erwerben; **to write** ~ als Versicherer tätig sein, Versicherung übernehmen;

prepaid ~ **account** Versicherungsvorauszahlungskonto; **National ⌾ Act** *(Br.)* Sozialversicherungsgesetz; ~ **adjuster** Versicherungs-, Schadensregulierer, Schadenssachverständiger; ~ **advice** Versicherungsberatung; ~ **agency** Versicherungsagentur, -vertretung, -büro; ~ **agent** Versicherungsagent, -vertreter, Akquisiteur; ~ **application** Versicherungsantrag; ~ **appraisal** Abschätzung zu Versicherungszwecken; ~ **aspects** Versicherungslage; ~ **auditor** Versicherungsrevisor, -prüfer; ~ **bank** Versicherungsanstalt; ~ **basis** Versicherungsgrundlage; ~ **beneficiary** Versicherungsbegünstigter; ~ **benefit** Versicherungsleistung; **social** ~ **benefits** Sozialversicherungsleistungen; **to maintain** ~ **benefits in the face of inflation** inflationsunabhängige Versicherungsleistungen gewährleisten; ~ **branch** Versicherungszweig; ~ **broker** Versicherungsmakler; ~ **business** Versicherungsbetrieb, -wesen; **general** ~ **business** *(Br.)* Sachversicherungsgeschäft; **to be engaged in the** ~ **business** im Versicherungsgewerbe tätig sein; ~**-buying public** Versicherungspublikum, -kundschaft; ~ **canvasser** [Versicherungs]akquisiteur; ~ **carrier** Versicherungsträger, -unternehmer; ~ **case** Versicherungsfall; ~ **certificate** Versicherungszertifikat, -bescheinigung; ~ **charges** Versicherungslasten, -kosten, -gebühren; ~ **charges on a packet** Paketversicherungsgebühr; ~ **claim** Versicherungsanspruch; **to settle** ~ **claims** Versicherungsansprüche regulieren; ~ **claim adjuster** Schadensregulierer, -festsetzer, Versicherungssachverständiger, -inspektor; ~ **classification** Einteilung in Gefahrenklassen; ~ **clause** Versicherungsklausel, -bestimmung; ~ **clerk** Versicherungsangestellter, -bearbeiter; ~ **collector** Versicherungseinnehmer; ⌾ **Commissioner** *(US)* Versicherungsaufsichtsbeamter; ~ **committee** *(health insurance)* Sozialversicherungsausschuß; ⌾ **Companies Act** *(Br.)* Gesetz über Versicherungsgesellschaften; ~ **company** Versicherungsgesellschaft, -anstalt; **joint-stock** ~ **company** Versicherungsgesellschaft auf Aktien; **mutual life** ~ **company** Lebensversicherungsverein auf Gegenseitigkeit; **to make a claim on one's** ~ **company** seine Versicherungsgesellschaft in Anspruch nehmen; ~ **conditions** Versicherungsbedingungen; ~ **and financial service conglomerate** Versicherungs- und Finanzierungskonzern; ~ **consumer** Versicherungsnehmer; ~ **contract** Versicherungsvertrag; **to conclude (enter into) an** ~ **contract** Versicherungsvertrag abschließen; **to discharge an** ~ **contract** Versicherungsvertrag erfüllen; **national** ~ **contributions** *(Br.)* Sozialversicherungsbeiträge; **social** ~ **contributions** *(US)* Sozialversicherungsbeiträge; ~ **contributor** Versicherungspflichtiger; ~ **corporation** *(US)* Versicherungsgesellschaft; **mutual** ~ **corporation** *(US)* Versicherungsgesellschaft auf Gegenseitigkeit; **stock** ~ **corporation** *(US)* Versicherungsgesellschaft auf Aktien; ~ **costs** Versicherungskosten; ~ **counsellor** Versicherungsberater; ~ **cover** Versicherungsschutz, Schadensversicherungssumme, Deckungshöhe; ~ **coverage** Versicherungsschutz; **business** ~ **coverage** Deckungsumfang der für den Betrieb abgeschlossenen Versicherungen; ~ **demand** Versicherungsbedarf; ~ **department** Versicherungsaufsichtsamt; ~ **disputes** Versicherungskontroversen; ~ **dividend** *(US)* Gewinnanteil; ~ **document** Versicherungsurkunde; ~ **dodger** pflichtwidrig nicht versicherter Fahrer; ~ **draft** *(US)* Versicherungswechsel; ~ **engineer** Spezialist für Feuerversicherungen; ~ **enterprise** Versicherungsunternehmen; ~ **examiner** Versicherungsprüfer; ~ **expense** Versicherungskosten; ~ **fee** *(post)* Versicherungsgebühr; ~ **fraud** Versicherungsbetrug; ~ **fund** Deckungsstock, Versicherungsstock; **National ⌾ Fund** *(Br.)* Sozialversicherungsstock; ~ **green card** grüne Versicherungskarte; ~ **holder** Versicherungsnehmer; **to build an ~ holding company** Versicherungsholding gründen; **~ industry** Versicherungsindustrie, -gewerbe, -wirtschaft; **~ instal(l)ment** Versicherungsrate; **~ investment salesman** Vertreter der Versicherungsbranche; **~ law** Versicherungsrecht; **& Law** (US) Versicherungsaufsichtsgesetz; **~ lawyer** (US) Versicherungsanwalt; **~ legislation** gesetzliche Vorschriften über das Versicherungswesen; **~ liability** Versicherungspflicht; **~ line** Versicherungsfach, -zweig; **~ market** Versicherungsmarkt; **~ matters** Versicherungswesen; **~ merger** Zusammenschluß von Versicherungsgesellschaften; **~ messenger** Versicherungsbote; **~ money** Versicherungssumme; **~ need** Versicherungsbedürfnis; **~ note** vorläufiger Deckungs-, Versicherungsschein; **~ office** Versicherungsanstalt, -büro, -agentur, -gesellschaft; **mutual ~ office** (Br.) Versicherungsverein auf Gegenseitigkeit; **~ officer (official)** Versicherungsbeamter; **~ operations** Versicherungstätigkeit; **~ option** wahlfreie Kapital- oder Rentenzahlung; **extended-term ~ option** Wahlrecht der beitragsfreien Lebensversicherung; **~ papers** Versicherungsunterlagen; **~ parlance** Versicherungssprache; **~ payment** Versicherungsleistung; **~ period** Versicherungszeit, -dauer; **~ plan** Versicherungssystem; **no-fault ~ plan** verschuldensfreies Versicherungssystem.

insurance policy Versicherungspolice, -schein;
all-risks ~ Globalpolice; **life ~** Lebensversicherungspolice; **open ~** Generalversicherungspolice; **paid-up ~** beitragsfreie Versicherungspolice; **standard fire ~** Einheitsfeuerversicherungspolice;
to surrender an ~ Versicherung zurückkaufen; **to take out an ~** Versicherung abschließen, sich versichern lassen;
~ acquisition costs Abschlußkosten für Versicherungspolicen.

insurance | portfolio Versicherungsbestand; **~ premium** Versicherungsprämie, -beitrag; **to be liable to pay ~ premiums** versicherungspflichtig sein; **~ principal** Kapitalsumme einer Versicherung; **~ proceeds** Entschädigungszahlungen einer Versicherungsgesellschaft; **~ profession** Versicherungsgewerbe; **~ profit** Gewinn im Geschäftsjahr einer Versicherungsgesellschaft; **~ rate** Versicherungssatz, -prämie, -tarif, Prämiensatz; **~ recovery** Versicherungsentschädigung, -zahlung; **~ reform** Versicherungsreform; **~ register** Versicherungsunterlagenverzeichnis; **state ~ regulations** Bestimmungen des Versicherungsaufsichtsamtes; **statutory ~ requirements** gesetzliche Versicherungserfordernisse; **~ reserve** Prämienreserve, Selbstversicherungsrücklage, Rückstellung für Eigenversicherung; **~ results** Geschäftsergebnisse von Versicherungsgesellschaften; **~ risk** Versicherungsrisiko; **~ salesman** Versicherungsvertreter; **contributory ~ scheme** beitragspflichtiges Versicherungssystem; **national ~ scheme** (Br.) Sozialversicherungswesen; **~ section** (Department of Trade, Br.) Ministerialabteilung für das Versicherungswesen; **~ share** Versicherungsaktie; **~ slip** Versicherungsformular, (marine insurance) Beteiligungsnote; **~ solicitor** (Br.) Versicherungsanwalt; **~ stock** (US) Versicherungsaktie; **contributory ~ system** beitragspflichtiges Versicherungssystem; **~ surveyor** Versicherungssachverständiger; **~ tariff** Prämien-, Versicherungstarif; **unemployment ~ tax** Arbeitslosenversicherungsbeitrag [des Arbeitgebers]; **~ taxation** Versicherungsbesteuerung; **~ technician** Versicherungsmathematiker; **~ tester** Versicherungsprüfer, -sachverständiger; **~ trade** Versicherungsgewerbe; **~ transaction** Versicherungsgeschäft; **~ travel(l)er** Versicherungsreisender, -vertreter; **automatic ~ treaty** Generalrückversicherungsvertrag; **~ trust** (US) Treuhandvereinbarung zur Direktauszahlung im Versicherungsfall; **~ umbrella** Versicherungsschutz; **underwriter** Versicherungsträger, Assekuranzversicherung; **~ valuation** (life insurance) Festsetzung des Rückkaufwertes; **~ value** festgesetzter Rückkaufwert einer Versicherung; **~ warranties** Zusicherungen des Versicherungsunternehmens; **~ wrinkles** Versicherungskniffe; **~ writer** Versicherungsagent, -vertreter.

insurant (US) Versicherter, Versicherungsnehmer.

insure (v.) versichern, sich versichern lassen, Versicherung abschließen, (guarantee) garantieren, verbürgen, sicherstellen; **~ o. s. for £ 20.000** sich für 20.000 £ lebensversichern; **~ against possible accidents** Unfallversicherung abschließen; **~ for a larger amount** nachversichern; **~ a debt** Bürgschaft leisten, Delkredere stehen; **~ one's house against fire** sein Haus feuerversichern; **~ against illness** sich für den Krankheitsfall versichern, Krankenversicherung abschließen; **~ one's life** sein Leben versichern; **~ against one's legal liability for injury or damage to others** sich gegen die Folgen der gesetzlichen Haftpflicht versichern; **~ one's own life for the benefit of the other** sich gegenseitig lebensversichern; **~ against loss** gegen Scha-

den versichern; **~ against loss of business profit following a fire** sich gegen Brandfolgeschäden versichern; **~ a number in a lottery** auf eine besondere Lotterienummer setzen; **~ in an insurance office** bei einer Versicherungsgesellschaft versichern; **~ at a low premium** zu einer niedrigen Prämie versichern; **~ against a risk** Risikoversicherung abschließen; **~ s. th. against all risks** für etw. eine Generalpolice nehmen; **~ against third-party risks** gegen Haftpflicht versichern; **~ a ship out and home** Schiff für die Hin- und Rückreise versichern; **~ below value** zu niedrig versichern.

insured Versicherter, Versicherungsnehmer;
~ (a.) versichert;
currently ~ (US) laufend versichert; **elsewhere ~** anderweitig versichert; **fully ~** (US) vollversichert;
amount ~ Versicherungssumme, Deckungsbetrag; **object ~** versicherter Gegenstand; **original ~** (reinsurance) Hauptversicherter; **period ~** Versicherungszeit; **subjectmatter ~** versicherter Gegenstand; **sum ~** Versicherungssumme; **value ~** Versicherungswert;
~ account (US) versichertes Konto; **~ bank** der staatlichen Depositenversicherung angeschlossene Bank; **~ event** Versicherungsfall; **~ letter** (Br.) Wertbrief; **~ mail** versicherte Postsendung; **~ parcel** (Br.) Wertpaket; **~ party** Versicherungsnehmer; **~ pension plan** bei Versicherungen abgedecktes Betriebspensionssystem; **~ person** Versicherter, Versicherungsnehmer; **~ value** Versicherungswert, -summe.

insuree Versicherter.

insurer Versicherer, Versicherungsgeber, -träger;
~s Versicherungsgesellschaft;
composite ~ Pauschalversicherungsnehmer; **individual ~** Einzelversicherer; **maritime ~** Seeassekurant, -versicherer; **non-tariff ~** (motor insurance, Br.) tariffreie Kraftfahrzeugversicherungsgesellschaft; **original ~** Erstversicherer; **recognized ~** staatlich genehmigter Versicherungsträger;
to act as ~ als Versicherer tätig sein.

insurgence Aufruhr, -lehnung, Rebellion, Revolte, (international law) Revolte.

insurgent Aufständischer, Aufrührer, Rebell, (party politics, US) Abweichler;
~ (a.) aufständisch, -rührerisch;
~ army Rebellenheer; **~ forces** Rebellentruppen; **~ government** Revolutionsregierung; **~ sea** aufrührerisches Meer; **~ troops** aufständische Truppen.

insuring clause Festlegung des Versicherungsumfangs.

insurrection Aufstand, Aufruhr, Revolte, Erhebung;
to rise in ~ sich erheben (empören).

insurrectional aufrührerisch.

insurrectionism aufrührerische Gesinnung.

insurrectionist Rebell, Aufständischer, Aufrührer.

intact unverletzt, unversehrt, intakt;
~ seal intaktes Siegel;
to keep one's reputation ~ seinen guten Ruf bewahren; **to live on the interest and keep one's capital ~** von den Zinsen leben und sein Kapital nicht angreifen.

intaglio Gravur, Schnitt;
~ printing Tiefdruck.

intake Einnehmen, (mining) Wetter, (reclaimed land) Moor-, Marschland;
caloric ~ Kalorienmenge;
~ of food Nahrungsaufnahme; **annual ~ of 100.000 National Service men** Hunderttausend Wehrpflichtige pro Jahr;
~ valve Einlaßventil.

intangible | s of value immaterielle Werte von Bedeutung;
~ (a.) unkörperlich, immateriell, (fig.) unbestimmt, vage;
~ arguments vage Beweisgründe; **~ assets** immaterielle Vermögenswerte; **~ property** immaterielles Vermögen; **~ value** immaterieller Wert, (firm) Firmenwert, (mortgage) Geldwert.

integer programming ganzzahlige Programmierung.

integral wesentlich, integriert, vollständig;
~ part of a contract wesentlicher Vertragsbestandteil.

integrate (v.) integrieren, eingliedern, konzentrieren, zusammenfassen, (racial policy) Rassenschranken aufheben.

integrated umfassend, integriert;
fully ~ voll integriert;
to be economically ~ in Verbundwirtschaft arbeiten;
~ bar gesamte Anwaltschaft; **~ commercial** eingeblendete Werbesendung; **~ data** zusammengefaßte Daten; **~ economy** Verbundwirtschaft; **~ public utility system** integrierte Versorgungsbetriebe; **~ school** (US) Schule ohne Rassentrennung; **~ store** (US) Filialbetrieb, Kettenladen; **~ trust** vertikaler Konzern.

integration Zusammenschluß, Integration, Eingliederung, Konzentration, *(racial policy, US)* Aufhebung der Rassenschranken;
backward ~ vertikales Betriebswachstum mit Angliederung einer vorgelagerten Produktionsstufe; **economic** ~ wirtschaftliche Integration; **forward** ~ vertikales Betriebswachstum mit Angliederung einer nachgelagerten Produktionsstufe; **horizontal** ~ horizontaler Zusammenschluß; **political** ~ politische Integration; **progressive** ~ schrittweise Eingliederung; **school** ~ *(US)* rassisch gemischtes Schulsystem; **vertical** ~ vertikaler Zusammenschluß;
~ **of markets** Marktverflechtung;
~ **movement** Konzentrationsbewegung; ~ **period** Integrationszeitraum; ~ **process** Integrationsprozeß.
integrity persönliche Lauterkeit, Integrität;
business ~ geschäftliche Lauterkeit.
intellect Verstand, Intellekt;
~**s of an age** große Geister eines Zeitalters; ~ **of the country** *(coll.)* Intelligenzschicht des Landes.
intellectual Verstandesmensch, Intellektueller;
~**s** Intelligenz;
~ *(a.)* geistig, verstandesgemäß, intellektuell;
~ **activity of a country** geistiges Leben eines Landes; ~ **being** vernunftbegabtes Wesen; ~ **exercise** Gedankenspiel; ~ **faculties** geistige Fähigkeiten; ~ **heavy-weight** Intelligenzbestie; ~ **life** Geistesleben; ~ **occupation** geistiger Beruf; ~ **person** intelligenter Mensch; ~ **powers** Verstandeskräfte; ~ **property** geistiges Eigentum; ~ **pursuits** geistiger Beruf.
intellectualist Intellektueller, Verstandesmensch.
intelligence Intelligenz[quote], Klugheit, Verstand, *(information)* Nachricht[en], Auskunft, Mitteilung, *(mil.)* Nachrichten-, Geheimdienst, Abwehr, Spionage;
clandestine ~ geheimes Nachrichtenmaterial; **general** ~ Allgemeinbildung; **latest** ~ neueste Nachrichten; **military** ~ Geheim-, Spionage-, Nachrichtendienst; **secret** ~ Geheiminformationen; **shipping** ~ Schiffahrtsnachrichten; **university** ~ Nachrichten aus dem Universitätsleben;
~ **with the enemy** Verbindung mit dem Feind;
to gather ~ *(mil.)* Nachrichten einziehen; **to have secret** ~ **of the enemy's plans** geheime Informationen über die feindlichen Absichten vorliegen haben; **to receive** ~ **of s. th.** Nachricht über etw. erhalten; **to score high in an** ~ **quotient test** gutes Ergebnis bei der Prüfung des Intelligenzquotienten erzielen;
~ **activity** Spionagetätigkeit; ~ **agency** Geheimdienst, Abwehr-, Spionagestelle; **Central** ⚏ **Agency** *(US)* Geheimdienst; ~ **agent** Geheimagent, Spion; ~ **bureau (department)** Auskunftsabteilung, *(mil.)* Nachrichtenabteilung; ~ **correlation** Wechselbeziehungen zweier Intelligenzen; ~ **courier** Geheimkurier; ~ **department** *(mil.)* Nachrichtendienst, -abteilung; ~ **director** Abwehrchef; **Naval** ⚏ **division** Abwehrdienst der Marine; ~ **evaluation** Nachrichtenauswertung; ~ **expert** Nachrichten-, Geheimdienstexperte; ~ **flight** Spionageflug; ~ **material** Informationsmaterial der Abwehr; ~ **network** Spionagenetz; ~ **office** Informations-, Nachrichtenstelle, -büro, *(US)* Stellenvermittlung für Hausangestellte, *(espionage)* Abwehrstelle; ~ **officer** Abwehr-, Nachrichtenoffizier, Beamter des Geheimdienstes; ~ **operation** Tätigkeit (Aktion) des Geheimdienstes; ~ **operative** Geheimdienstler; ~ **oversight board** *(US)* Überwachungsbehörde des Nachrichtendienstes; ~ **quotient** Intelligenzquotient; ~ **satellite** Nachrichtensatellit; ~ **service** *(mil.)* Nachrichtendienst; ~ **setup** Geheimdienstorganisation; ~ **source** Nachrichtenquelle; ~ **test** Begabtenprüfung, Intelligenzprüfung, -test.
intelligencer Nachrichtenüberbringer, Zwischenträger, *(secret agent)* Kundschafter, Geheimagent, Spion.
intelligent klug, gescheit, intelligent;
to be ~ **of a subject** sich in einem Gebiet bestens auskennen;
~ **answers to questions** intelligente (kluge) Fragenbeantwortung.
intelligibility Allgemeinverständlichkeit.
intelligible verständlich, begreiflich.
intemperance Ausschweifung, Trunksucht.
intend *(v.)* beabsichtigen, vorhaben, planen, *(law)* Vorsitz haben;
~ **an action** Klage anstrengen; ~ **one's own advantage** sich selbst um sein Fortkommen kümmern; ~ **one's business** sich um seine Sachen kümmern; ~ **no harm** nichts Böses vorhaben; ~ **marriage** ernsthafte Absichten haben; ~ **a novel for the screen** Roman für die Verfilmung vorsehen; ~ **for the medical profession** sich zur ärztlichen Laufbahn entschließen; ~ **to purchase** reflektieren, kaufinteressiert sein.
intendance Verwaltung, Oberaufsicht, *(mil.)* Intendantur.

intendancy Aufsichtsamt, Intendantenamt, *(district)* Verwaltungsbezirk.
intendant Verwalter, Oberaufseher, Intendant.
intended berechnet, beabsichtigt;
~ **for export** für den Export bestimmt;
to be ~ **for the medical profession** für die ärztliche Laufbahn bestimmt sein; ~ **to be recorded** *(conveyancing)* zur Eintragung ins Grundbuch vorgesehen sein;
my ~ **[husband]** mein Zukünftiger; ~ **wife** Verlobte.
intending | buyer (purchaser) Kaufinteressent, -reflektant; ~ **subscriber** interessierter Abonnent.
intendment, common *(law)* wahre Bedeutung;
~ **of the law** Sinn des Gesetzes; ~ **of a testator** wirklicher Wille des Erblassers.
intense stark, angespannt, *(photo)* hell, stark, intensiv;
~ **study** intensives Studium; ~ **young lady** sehr gefühlsbetontes Mädchen.
intenseness of study angestrengtes Studium.
intensification Intensivierung, *(photo)* Verstärkung.
intensifier Verstärker.
intensify *(v.)* intensivieren;
~ **restrictions** Beschränkungen verschärfen.
intensity Intensität, Heftigkeit, *(el.)* Stromstärke, *(photo)* Dichtigkeit;
caloric ~ Heizwert;
~ **of competition** Wettbewerbsintensität.
intensive intensiv, Ertrag (Produktivität) steigernd, ertragssteigernd;
capital-~ kapitalintensiv; **labo(u)r-**~ arbeitsintensiv;
~ **advertising** Intensivwerbung; ~ **agriculture** intensive Wirtschaft; ~ **bombardment** Flächenbombardierung; ~ **care unit** Intensivstation; ~ **cultivation of land** intensive Bodenbewirtschaftung; ~ **margin** Nullpunkt des Grenzertrages; ~ **methods of agriculture** intensive Bewirtschaftungsmethoden; ~ **propaganda** verstärkte Propaganda; **to make an** ~ **study of a subject** Thema sehr intensiv studieren (untersuchen).
intent Absicht, Ziel, Plan, Vorsatz, *(law)* Sinn, wahre Bedeutung;
to all ~**s and purposes** im Endeffekt, praktisch; **with** ~ absichtlich, vorsätzlich; **with** ~ **to defraud** in betrügerischer Absicht; **without evil** ~ in keiner bösen Absicht;
common ~ *(of word)* allgemeine Bedeutung; **criminal** ~ verbrecherische Absicht, strafrechtlicher Vorsatz; **dishonest** ~ unredliche Absicht; **general** ~ allgemeine Willensrichtung; **legislative** ~ Wille des Gesetzgebers; **specific** ~ *(criminal law)* fester (konkreter) Vorsatz;
~ **of agreement** Vertragswille; ~ **to defame** Verleumdungsabsicht; ~ **to defraud** Betrugsabsicht, betrügerische Absicht; ~ **to delay or defeat creditors** vorsätzliche Gläubigerbenachteiligung; ~ **to enter** Beitrittsabsicht; ~ **of the parties** Parteiwille;
~ *(a.)* versessen, erpicht;
~ **on business** geschäftlich interessiert; ~ **on pleasure** vergnügungssüchtig;
to ask the jury whether the act was committed with ~ den Geschworenen die Frage nach dem Vorsatz des Täters vorlegen; **to be** ~ **on one's business** sich nur für sein Geschäft interessieren; **to be** ~ **on getting to the office in time** auf jeden Fall pünktlich im Büro sein wollen;
~ **application** ernstliche Bewerbung.
intention Absicht, Willensrichtung, -erklärung, Wille, Vorhaben, *(criminal law)* Vorsatz;
with good ~**s** in guter Absicht;
declared ~ erklärter Wille; **defective** ~ Willensmangel; **incidental** ~ Nebenabsicht; **serious** ~**s** Heiratsabsichten;
~ **to appropriate** Zweckbestimmungsabsicht; ~ **to damage** Schädigungsabsicht; ~ **to release a debt** beabsichtigter Schulderlaß; ~ **to deceive** Täuschungsabsicht; ~ **of fraud** Betrugsabsicht; ~ **of a law** Gesetzesabsicht; ~ **to create legal obligation** auf das Eingehen gesetzlicher Verpflichtungen gerichteter Wille; ~ **to make a gift** Schenkungsabsicht; ~ **of the parties** Parteiwille; ~ **to resign** Rücktrittsabsicht;
to act with the most hono(u)rable ~**s** aus ehrenhaften Motiven handeln; **to be paved with good** ~**s** mit besten Absichten (guten Vorsätzen) gepflastert sein; **to court a woman with hono(u)rable** ~**s** ernsthafte Absichten haben; **to do s. th. with the best** ~**s** mit besten Absichten an etw. herangehen; **to grasp s. one's** ~**s** jds. Gedanken begreifen; **to look for an evil** ~ **in everything** in allem nur Nachteiliges sehen; **to make known one's** ~**s** Heiratsantrag machen.
intentional absichtlich, vorsätzlich.
intentious to buy kaufinteressiert.
inter *(v.)* begraben, bestatten, beisetzen.

Inter-American Development Bank Entwicklungsbank für die lateinamerikanischen Länder.

interact *(v.)* sich gegenseitig beeinflussen.

interaction Wechselwirkung.

interagency Vermittlung;
~ **agreement** zwischen Sonderorganisationen der UNO abgeschlossenes Verwaltungsabkommen; ~ **committee** interministerieller Ausschuß; ~ **group** interministerielle Arbeitsgruppe.

interagent Vermittler, Mittelsmann.

interallied interalliiert;
~ **debt** interalliierte Schulden.

interbank | **balances** gegenseitige Bankverpflichtungen; ~ **clearings** Lokalumschreibungen, Ortsclearing im internen Bankverkehr; **in** ~ **dealings** im Verkehr der Banken untereinander, im Bankverkehr; ~ **payments** Zahlungen im Bankverkehr, Überweisungsverkehr; ~ **rate** Eurogeldmarktzinssatz.

interborough in mehreren Stadtteilen gelegen.

interbourse von Börse zu Börse gehandelt;
~ **securities** internationale (international gehandelte) Wertpapiere.

interbreed *(v.)* kreuzen, vermischen.

intercalary | **day** Schalttag; ~ **year** Schaltjahr.

intercalate *(v.)* einschalten, einschieben.

intercalation Einschaltung.

intercede *(v.)* **for s. o.** für j. eintreten, sich für j. verwenden (einsetzen), für j. als Fürsprecher auftreten;
~ **with the father for the son** für den Sohn beim Vater ein gutes Wort einlegen.

interceder Fürsprecher, Vermittler.

intercept abgefangener (aufgefangener) Funkspruch (Brief);
~ *(v.)* Weg abschneiden, *(catch)* ab-, auffangen, *(connection)* unterbrechen;
~ **the enemy's bombers** feindlichen Bombenverband abfangen;
~ **a letter** Brief abfangen; ~ **a messenger** Boten abfangen; ~ **telephone calls** Telefongespräche abhören; ~ **the trade** Handel behindern; ~ **the traffic** Verkehr stoppen; ~ **the view** Aussicht versperren.

interceptable parts auswechselbare Teile.

interception Unterbrechung, *(letters)* Auf-, Abfangen, *(tel.)* Abhören;
~ **by the censor** Anhalten von Post durch die Zensur; ~ **of documents** Urkundenunterdrückung;
~ **station** Abhörstelle.

interceptor *(airplane)* Abfangjäger, *(civil engineering)* Auffangkanal, Sammler, *(wireless)* Abhörstation;
~ **fighter (plane)** Abfangjäger.

intercession Vermittlung, Intervention, Eintreten, Fürsprache, *(law)* Schuldübernahme, *(pol.)* Vorstellungen;
to make ~ **for s. o.** zu jds. Gunsten intervenieren.

intercessional vermittelnd.

intercessor Vermittler, Fürsprecher.

intercessory vermittelnd.

interchange Austausch;
holiday ~ Ferienaustausch;
~ **of civilities** Austausch von Höflichkeiten;
~ *(v.)* austauschen, -wechseln, *(barter)* Tauschhandel treiben, *(cause to alternate)* abwechseln;
~ **letters** Briefe austauschen; ~ **service** Umsteigemöglichkeit.

interchangeability principle Austauschprinzip.

interchangeable auswechselbar, austauschbar;
~ **bonds** auswechselbare Namenschuldverschreibungen; ~ **manufacturing** Herstellung auswechselbarer Maschinenteile; ~ **parts** auswechselbare Teile.

interchapter eingeschobenes Kapitel.

intercitizenship *(US)* doppelte Staatsangehörigkeit bei einzelnen Bundesstaaten, Mehrstaatenangehörigkeit.

intercity | **check** (cheque, *Br.*)**-clearing service** Scheckaustausch innerhalb einer Stadt; ~ **differential** Ortsklassen[lohn]ausgleich; ~ **railway** Bahnlinie zwischen zwei Städten, Nahverkehrsverbindung; ~ **train** Nahverkehrszug.

intercoastal trade Küstenhandel.

intercom *(coll.)* Haus-, Wechselsprechanlage, *(airplane)* Bordsprechanlage, Bordtelefon.

intercommonage gemeinsames Weiderecht.

intercommunicate *(v.)* miteinander in Verbindung stehen (in Verbindung treten).

intercommunication Zwischenverkehr, gegenseitiger Verkehr;
~**s** Nachrichtenverbindungen;
~ **system** Bordsprech-, Gegensprechanlage.

intercommunion vertrauter Verkehr.

intercommunity harmonisches Zusammenleben.

intercompany inner-, zwischenbetrieblich;
~ **charge on income** konzerninterne Ertragsbelastungen; ~ **claims** Konzernforderungen; ~ **debts** Konzernschulden (Verbindlichkeiten); ~ **elimination** *(consolidated balance sheet)* Konzernausgleich; ~ **liabilities** Konzernverbindlichkeiten; ~ **loan** Konzernkredit, -darlehn; ~ **loss** Konzernbuchverlust; ~ **operations** Geschäftsverkehr zwischen Konzerngesellschaften; ~ **price** Verrechnungspreis; ~ **profit** Konzernbuchgewinn; ~ **rate** Verrechnungskurs; ~ **relations** Konzernbeziehungen; ~ **sales** Verkäufe innerhalb des Konzerns (zwischen Konzerngesellschaften), Konzernumsatz, Innenumsätze; ~ **squaring** Konzernausgleich; ~ **transactions** konzerninterne Umsätze.

interconnected miteinander verbunden, *(el.)* vermascht.

interconnecting flight Anschlußflug.

intercontinental | **ballistic missile** Interkontinentalrakete; ~ **bomber** Interkontinentalbomber.

interconvertible gegenseitig austauschbar, auswechselbar.

intercorporate konzernintern;
~ **privilege** *(US)* Schachtelprivileg; ~ **relations** Konzernbeziehungen, -verhältnisse; ~ **stockholding** *(US)* wechselseitige Aktienbeteiligungen, Schachtel[besitz], -beteiligung; ~ **tax on dividends** Körperschaftssteuer auf Dividenden aus Schachtelbeteiligungen.

intercourse Umgang, [Geschäfts]verkehr, Handelsverbindung;
business ~ geschäftliche Beziehungen; **diplomatic** ~ diplomatischer Verkehr; **social** ~ gesellschaftlicher Verkehr; **to hold** ~ **with s. o.** zu jem. Beziehungen unterhalten; **to live in daily** ~ **with great writers** täglichen Umgang mit berühmten Schriftstellern pflegen.

interdepartmental ressortmäßig;
~ **agreement** Ressortabkommen; ~ **business** gemeinsam (mehrere Abteilungen) interessierende Fragen; ~ **committee** interministerieller Ausschuß; ~ **conference** Ressort-, Abteilungsleiterbesprechung; ~ **transfer** Versetzung von einer Abteilung in die andere.

interdepend *(v.)* [gegenseitig] voneinander abhängen.

interdependence gegenseitige Abhängigkeit, Interdependenz;
economic ~ wirtschaftliche Verflechtung;
~ **of two processes of manufacture** Abhängigkeit zweier Herstellungsverfahren voneinander.

interdependent untereinander zusammenhängend, gegenseitig abhängig, ineinandergreifend.

interdict Untersagung, Verbot, *(injunction)* Verfügungsverbot;
~ *(v.)* verbieten, untersagen;
~ **s. o.** j. eines Rechtes verlustig erklären; ~ **trade with foreign nations** Handelsverkehr mit dem Ausland untersagen.

interdiction Untersagung, Verbot, *(law)* Entmündigung;
~ **of commerce (commercial intercourse)** Handelsverbot, totales Embargo; ~ **of lunacy** Entmündigung wegen Geisteskrankheit;
to impose judicial ~ **upon s. o.** jem. ein gerichtliches Verfügungsverbot auferlegen.

interest *(advantage)* Vorteil, Interesse, Belange, Nutzen, Nutznießung, *(importance)* Bedeutung, Interesse, Wichtigkeit, *(on loan)* Zinsen, Zinsfuß, -satz, Verzinsung, *(right)* [An]recht, Anspruch, *(risk)* Versicherungsinteresse, *(share)* [finanzielle] Beteiligung, Anteil, Anteilsrecht;
and ~ zuzüglich Stückzinsen; **as** ~ zinsweise; **at** ~ auf Zinsen; **at legal** ~ zum gesetzlichen Zinsfuß; **bearing** ~ verzinslich, zinstragend; **bearing no** ~ unverzinslich; **no** ~ **charged** franko Zinsen; **cum** ~ einschließlich Stückzinsen; **detrimental to our** ~**s** unseren Interessen abträglich; **ex** ~ ohne Zinsen; **free of** ~ zinslos, unverzinslich; **in the public** ~ im öffentlichen Interesse; **of considerable** ~ von ziemlicher Bedeutung; **of general** ~ von allgemeinem Interesse; **in the** ~ **of the truth** um der Wahrheit zu dienen; **of present** ~ von aktuellem Interesse; **paying [no]** ~ [un]verzinslich; **plus** ~ mit Zinsen; **with** ~ mit [Berechtigung auf] Zinsen; **without** ~ unverzinslich, franko Zinsen; **yielding** ~ verzinslich;
~**s** Interessengruppe, Interessenten, Interessengemeinschaft, *(business)* Geschäfte, Belange, *(possessions)* Besitz;
absolute ~ absolutes Recht; **accrued** ~ aufgelaufene [aber noch nicht fällige] Zinsen, Zinsenzuwachs, *(bonds)* Stückzinsen; **accrued** ~ **payable** *(balance sheet, US)* entstandene (noch nicht fällige) Zinsverbindlichkeiten; **accruing** ~ auflaufende Zinsen; **accumulated** ~ aufgelaufene [und fällige] Zinsen; **annual** ~ Jahreszinsen, jährliche Zinsen; **anticipatory** ~ Zinsvorauszahlungen; **average** ~ Durchschnittszinsen; **back** ~ rückständige Zinsen, Zinsrückstände; **bank** ~ Bankzinsen; **the banking** ~ Bankkreise; **beneficial** ~ Nießbrauch[recht], Nutznießung *(insurance)* Versicherungsanspruch des Begünstigten; **the brew-**

ing ~ Brauereigewerbe; **British** ~s englische Interessentengruppe; **building society** ~ Bauspar[vertrags]zinsen; **business** ~ Geschäftsanteil; **business** ~s Geschäftswelt, -interessen; **chief** ~ Hauptinteresse; **clashing** ~s widerstreitende Interessen; **commercial** ~s kaufmännische Interessen, Handelsinteresse; **common** ~ Anknüpfungspunkt; **the common** ~ das allgemeine Beste; **compensatory** ~ Unkosten gerade deckende Zinsen; **compound** ~ Zinseszinsen; **conditional** ~ bedingtes Anrecht; **conflicting** ~s widerstreitende Interessen, Interessenskollision, -konflikt; **contingent** ~ bedingtes Recht; **contract** ~ vereinbarter Zinsfuß, -satz; **controlling** ~ Mehrheitsbeteiligung, ausschlaggebender Kapitalanteil; **conventional** ~ üblicher Zinsfuß, -satz; **credit** ~ Habenzinsen; **credited** ~ gutgeschriebene Zinsen; **current** ~ laufende Zinsen; **customary** ~ landesüblicher Zins; **daily** ~ Tageszinsen; **debit** ~ Sollzinsen; **deferred** ~ transitorische Zinsen; **determinable** ~ auflösend bedingtes Nutzungsrecht; **divergent** ~s divergierende Interessen, Interessenkollision; **due** zu zahlende Zinsen, Haben-, Aktivzinsen, Zinsforderungen; ~ **earned** Zinsertrag, Habenzinsen; **earned not collected** (balance sheet) noch nicht eingegangene Zinserträge; **economic** ~s Wirtschaftsinteressen; **equated** ~ gestaffelte Zinsen, Staffelzinsen; **equitable** ~ Anwartschaftsrecht, Rückübereignungsanspruch des Sicherungsgebers; **exact** ~ (US) auf der Basis von 365 Tagen berechnete Zinsen; **excessive** ~ Wucherzinsen; **financial** ~ Kapitalbeteiligung, -interesse; **funding debenture** ~ Zinsen in Form von festverzinslichen Schuldverschreibungen; **foreign** ~s Auslandsbeteiligungen; **future** ~ Anwartschaft; **general** ~s allgemeines Interesse; **government** ~s staatliche Beteiligungen; **graduated** ~ Staffelzinsen; **gross** ~ Bruttozinsen; **guaranteed** ~ Zinsgarantie; **illegal** ~ Wucherzinsen; **imputed** ~ kalkulatorische Zinsen; **incompatible** ~s widerstreitende Interessen; **increased** ~ erhöhte Zinsen; **industrial** ~s Industriebeteiligungen; **instalment** ~ Zinsrate; **insurable** ~ versicherbares Interesse, Versicherungsinteresse; **interim** ~ Zwischenzinsen; **interlocking** ~s Interessenverflechtung; **intermediate** ~ Zwischenzinsen; **the iron** ~ die Eisenindustrie; **joint** ~ Gesamthandseigentum; **landed** ~s Großgrundbesitz[er]; **leasehold** ~ Pacht-, Mietanspruch; **legal** ~ rechtlich anerkanntes Interesse, (legal interest rate) gesetzliche Kontokorrentzinsen; **legitimate** ~ berechtigtes Interesse; **life** ~ Nutzungsrecht auf Lebenszeit, lebenslänglicher Nießbrauch, lebenslängliche Nutznießung; **loan** ~ Darlehns-, Anleihezinsen; **local** ~ Lokalinteresse; **the long** ~ Hausseengagement; **lucrative** ~ zu erwartender Gewinn; **majority** ~ Mehrheitsbeteiligung; **majority controlling** ~ ausschlaggebende Mehrheitsbeteiligung; **marine (maritime)** ~ Bodmereizins; **maximum** ~ höchstzulässiger Zinssatz; **mercantile** ~s kaufmännische Interessen; **mesne** ~ Zwischenzins; **mining** ~ Bergwerksinteressen; **minority** ~ Minderheitsanteil, Minoritätsbeteiligung; **moneyed** ~ Kapitalinteressen, Finanzwelt; **mortgage** ~ Hypothekenzinsen; **multiple** ~s vielseitige Interessen; **mutual** ~ gegenseitiges (gemeinsames) Interesse; **national** ~ nationale Belange, nationales Interesse, Staatsinteresse; **net** ~ Nettozinsen; **net** ~ **paid** Zinsmehraufwand; **nominal** ~ Nominalverzinsung; **one-third** ~ Drittelbeteiligung; **one's own** ~ sein eigenes Ich; **ordinary** ~ (US) auf Basis von 360 Tagen berechnete Zinsen; **outside** ~ außerhalb des eigentlichen Studiums liegendes Interesse; **outstanding** ~ fällige Zinsen, Zinsaußenstände; ~ **paid** Zinsaufwand, -einnahmen; **partnership** ~ Gesellschaftsanteil; **past due** ~ überfällige Zinsen; ~ **payable** fällige Zinsen, Passivzinsen; **pecuniary** ~ finanzielles Interesse; **penal** ~ Verzugszinsen; **principal and** ~ Kapital und Zinsen; **private** ~s Privatangelegenheiten; **producing** ~s Produktionsinteresse; **prohibited** ~ nicht versicherungsfähiges Interesse; **protected** ~ steuerlich abzugsfähige Zinsen; **property** ~ Vermögensanteil; **public** ~ öffentliche Belange, öffentliches Wohl (Interesse); **pure** ~ Nettozinsen; ~ **receivable** (US) ausstehende Zinsen, Aktivzinsen; **accrued** ~ **receivable** (US) entstandene (noch nicht fällige) Zinsforderungen; **received** ~ Zinseingang; **reciprocal** ~ gegenseitig in Rechnung gestellte Zinsen; **red** ~ Sollzinsen; **redeemable** ~ ablösliche Zinsen; ~ **returned** Rückzinsen; **reversionary** ~ Anwartschafts-, Rückfallsrecht, Heimfallsanspruch, Nacherbschaftsrecht; **running** ~ laufende Zinsen; **sectional** ~ s lokale Interessen; **self-** ~ Eigennutz; **semi-annual** ~ halbjährliche Zinsen; **shipping** ~ Reedereibetrieb, -geschäft; **the shipping** ~ Schiffahrtsinteressen, die Handelsschiffahrt; **short** ~ (marine insurance) Überversicherung, (stock exchange) Baisseengagement; **simple** ~ einfache (gewöhnliche) Zinsen; **statutory** ~ gesetzlicher Zinssatz; **storage** ~ Lagergebühren; **subordinate** ~ untergeordnete Interessen; **sundry investments and** ~s (balance sheet) verschiedene Beteiligungen; **transient** ~ vorübergehen-

des Interesse; **true** ~ Nettozinsen; **undivided** ~ Nutznießung zur gesamten Hand; **unearned** ~ (balance sheet) transitorische Zinserträge; **unpaid** ~ rückständige Zinsen, Zinsrückstand; **untaxed** ~ unversteuerte Zinsen; **usurious** ~ Wucherzinsen; **vested** ~s wohlerworbene Rechte; **vital** ~s lebenswichtige Interessen; **warm** ~ reges Interesse; **yearly** ~ **paid** jährlich gezahlte Zinsen; ~ **debited to an account** einem Konto angelastete Zinsen; ~s **with the administration** Beziehungen zu Behörden; ~ **collected in advance** Zinsvorauszahlungen; ~ **on advances credited (payable on advances)** (balance sheet) Zinsen auf gewährte Vorschüsse; ~ **per annum** jährliche Zinsen; ~ **on arrears** Verzugszinsen; ~ **on bank loans** Bankzinsen; ~ **upon bonds** Obligationenzinsen; ~ **paid to a building society** Bausparzinsen und Tilgung; ~ **from building societies** vereinnahmte Bausparzinsen; ~ **in business** Geschäftsinteresse, -beteiligung, -anteil; ~ **on capital** Kapitalzinsen, -verzinsung; ~ **on capital accounts (outlay)** Verzinsung der Anschaffungskosten, Kapitalverzinsung; ~ **on loan capital** Darlehnszinsen; ~ **on credit balances** Habenzinsen; ~ **on current account** Kontokorrentzinsen; ~ **on current debts** Verzinsung der laufenden Schulden; ~ **on debit balances** Einlage-, Debit-, Sollzinsen; ~ **for default (delay, detention)** Verzugszinsen; ~ **on deposits** Depositen-, Bank-, Habenzinsen; ~ **on ordinary deposits** übliche Sparzinsen; ~ **on deposits with a trustee savings bank** Zinsen von einem Spartguthaben; ~ **on deposit account** (Br.) Sparbuchzinsen; ~ **on estate duty** (Br.) Erbschaftssteuerzinsen; ~ **in excess of a reasonable commercial rate** über handelsübliche Sätze hinausgehende Verzinsung; ~ **in expectancy** Anwartschaftsrecht; ~ **and similar expenses** Zinsen und zinsähnliche Aufwendungen; ~ **in a firm** Kapital-, Geschäftsanteil; **American** ~s **in Germany** amerikanische Kapitalbeteiligungen in Deutschland; ~ **on indebtedness** Schuldzinsen; ~s **as an individual** Privatinteressen; ~ **upon** ~ Zinseszinsen; ~ **on investments** Anlagenverzinsung, Zinsen aus Kapitalanlagen; **the** ~ **at issue** beteiligte Interessen; ~ **in the job** berufliches Interesse; ~ **in land** Grundbesitz-, -stücksanteil; **beneficial** ~ **in land** Nießbrauch an einem Grundstück; ~ **of legatee** Vermächtnisanspruch; ~ **on a loan** Kredit-, Darlehnszinsen; ~ **of money** Geldzins; ~ **on borrowed money** Kreditzinsen; ~ **on mortgage** Hypothekenverzinsung; ~ **in the nature of investments** (balance sheet) beteiligungsähnliche Ansprüche; ~ **or no** (insurance) Verzicht auf Nachweis eines versicherbaren Interesses; ~ **on overdraft** Überziehungskreditzinsen; ~ **on fluctuating overdrafts** Zinsen aus Kontokorrentkrediten; ~ **of each partner in the profits** Gewinnanteil jedes Teilhabers; ~ **in the patent exploitation** Beteiligung an der Patentverwertung; ~ **on principal** Kapitalverzinsung; ~ **pro and contra** Soll- und Habenzinsen, Kredit- und Debetzins; ~ **in the profit** Gewinnbeteiligung; ~ **in property** vermögensrechtlicher Anspruch, Eigentumsanspruch; ~ **at the rate of 4%** Zinsen zum Satz von 4%; ~ **in real estate** Grundbesitz, Grundstücksanteil; ~ **not taxed before receipt** noch nicht versteuerte Zinserträge; ~ **on securities** Wertpapier-, Effektenzinsen; ~ **in shares** Aktienbeteiligung; ~ **on shares** Stückzinsen; ~ **of the state** Staatsinteresse; ~ **in succession** Erbanwartschaft; ~ **in tail** erbfolgemäßig festgelegtes Besitzrecht; ~ **as usual** übliche Zinsen, ~ **in a vessel** Schiffsanteil, -beteiligung; ~s **pour autre vie** Ansprüche während der Lebenszeit eines Dritten; **true** ~ **in s. one's welfare** aufrichtiges Interesse an jds. Wohlergehen;

~ (v.) Teilnahme (Interesse) erwecken, interessieren, (make partner) beteiligen, zum Teilhaber machen, als Partner aufnehmen;

~ **o. s. in s. th.** sich für etw. interessieren; ~ **s. o. in s. th.** j. zur Beteiligung an etw. veranlassen; ~ **s. o. in a cause (plan)** jds. Interesse an einer Angelegenheit (für ein Vorhaben) wecken; **to act in s. one's** ~ jds. Interessen wahrnehmen, für fremde Rechnung tätig werden; **to act adversely to s. one's** ~ gegen jds. Interessen handeln; **to act in one's own** ~ im eigenen Interesse handeln; **to add the** ~ **to the capital** Zinsen zum Kapital schlagen; **to add** ~ **to the debt half-yearly** Debetzinsen halbjährlich in Rechnung stellen; **to affect the** ~s Interessen berühren; **to allow** ~ Zinsen vergüten; **to allow the back** ~ **to accumulate** Zinsrückstände entstehen lassen; **to ascertain** ~ Zinsen berechnen, Zinsberechnung durchführen; **to attend to s. one's** ~ jds. Interessen vertreten (wahrnehmen); **to be in s. one's** ~ in jds. Interesse liegen; **to be of little** ~ von geringer Bedeutung sein; **to be loyal to s. one's** ~ jds. Interessen wahren (ordnungsgemäß wahrnehmen); **to be out at** ~ auf Zinsen ausgeliehen sein; **to be prejudicial to s. one's** ~ sich nachteilig auf jds. Interessen auswirken; **to be void of** ~ kein Interesse finden; **to bear** ~ Zinsen tragen, sich verzinsen, verzinslich sein; **to bear** ~ **at [at the rate of] 6%** sich mit 6% verzinsen, 6% Zinsen bringen; **to** borrow at ~ Geld zu Zinsen ausleihen; **to bring in** ~ Zinsen einbringen; **to bring s. o. into one's** ~ j. für sich gewinnen; **to bring ~s into conflict** Interessenkollision hervorrufen; **to build defences for one's** ~s seine Interessen verteidigen; **to buy an** ~ **in a firm** Geschäftsanteil (Firmenanteil) übernehmen; **to capitalize** ~ Zinsen zum Kapital schlagen; **to carry** ~ Zinsen abwerfen (einbringen); **to carry a low rate of** ~ niedrig verzinslich sein; **to cast** ~ Zinsen ausrechnen; **to channel one's** ~ seine Interessen in eine bestimmte Richtung lenken; **to charge** ~ Zinsen berechnen (belasten, erheben); **to charge** ~ **[on both sides]** Zinsen [gegenseitig] in Rechnung stellen (berechnen); **to claim relief for** ~ **paid on a debt** Steuervergünstigungen für gezahlte Zinsen beantragen; **to collide (come into collision) with s. one's** ~s mit jds. Interessen kollidieren; **to compound** ~ **quarterly** Zinsen vierteljährlich berechnen; **to compute** ~ Zinsen ausrechnen; **to compute 5 per cent** ~ 5% Zinsen berechnen; **to consult one's own** ~ seine eigenen Interessen (seinen Vorteil) im Auge haben (bedenken), an sich selbst denken; **to create** ~ großes Interesse hervorrufen; **to dispose of one's** ~ **in a firm** seinen Geschäftsanteil veräußern; **to earn good** ~ sich gut verzinsen; **to excite world-wide** ~ weltweites Echo finden; **to feel an** ~ **in s. th.** an etw. interessiert sein; **to feel no great** ~ **in politics** sich für Politik wenig interessieren; **to focus one's** ~ sein Interesse auf einen Punkt vereinigen; **to found on mutual** ~ auf Gegenseitigkeit gründen; **to give s. o. financial** ~ **in a business** j. an einem Geschäft beteiligen; **to give s. o. a joint** ~ **in an affair** j. an einer Sache partizipieren lassen; **to grant an** ~ **of 6 per cent** auf etw. 6% Zinsen geben, etw. mit 6% verzinsen; **to guard** ~s *(broker)* Interessen wahren; **to have an** ~ beteiligt sein, Vermögensinteresse haben; **to have** ~ **with s. o.** bei jem. Kredit haben; **to have an** ~ **in a business** an einem Geschäft beteiligt sein, Geschäftsanteil besitzen; **to have** ~s **in common** gemeinsame Interessen haben; **to have an** ~ **in a company of $ 100.000** mit 100.000 Dollar an einer Gesellschaft beteiligt sein; **to have** ~ **at court** über einflußreiche Beziehungen verfügen; **to have an** ~ **in an enterprise** an einem Unternehmen finanziell beteiligt sein; **to have an** ~ **in an estate** erbberechtigt sein; **to have an eye to one's own** ~s seinen eigenen Vorteil im Auge haben; **to have outside** ~s besondere Interessensgebiete haben; **to have an** ~ **in the profit** am Gewinn beteiligt sein; **to have a direct** ~ **in s. th.** an etw. unmittelbar interessiert sein; **to have no money** ~ **in a concern** an einem Unternehmen finanziell nicht beteiligt sein; **to hold a 10%** ~ mit 10 Prozent beteiligt sein, zehnprozentige Beteiligung besitzen; **to hold controlling** ~ Aktienmehrheit besitzen; **to impair (injure) s. one's** ~s jds. Interessen beeinträchtigen; **to interfere with one's own private** ~s eigenen Interessen entgegenstehen; **to invest money at** ~ Geld verzinslich anlegen; **to invest a sum at 6 per cent** ~ Betrag zu 6% anlegen; **to keep down** ~ Zinsniveau niedrighalten; **to lend free of** ~ zinsfrei ausleihen; **to lend at short** ~ kurzfristiges Darlehen gewähren; **to lend out money at** ~ Geld auf Zinsen ausleihen; **to live on the** ~ **received from one's capital** von den Zinsen seines Vermögens leben; **to loan on** ~ auf Zinsen ausleihen; **to look after s. one's** ~s jds. Interessen vertreten (wahrnehmen); **to look after one's own** ~s seinen Vorteil zu wahren wissen; **to lose** ~ das Interesse verlieren; **to make** ~ **with s. o.** Kredit bei jem. in Anspruch nehmen; **to make default in the payment of** ~ mit den Zinszahlungen in Verzug sein; **to obtain s. one's** ~ j. für sich gewinnen; **to obtain a government position through** ~ **with a cabinet minister** Staatsstellung durch die Beeinflussung eines Kabinettmitgliedes erhalten; **to offer s. o. an** ~ **in one's business** jem. eine Beteiligung an seinem Geschäft anbieten; **to operate against the public** ~ sich gegen das öffentliche Interesse richten; **to pay** ~ verzinsen, Zinsen zahlen; **to pay** ~ **in advance** Zinsvorauszahlungen leisten; **to pay** ~ **when due** Zinsen laufend bezahlen; **to pay 8 per cent** ~ **on a loan** Kredit mit 8% verzinsen, 8% Zinsen für einen Kredit bezahlen; **to prejudice seriously s. one's** ~s jds. Interessen ernstlich schädigen; **to promote s. one's** ~s jds. Angelegenheiten fördern; **to protect** ~s *(broker)* Interessen wahren; **to purchase an** ~ Kapitalanteil kaufen; **to purchase an** ~ **in a trading partnership** Geschäftsanteil an einer offenen Handelsgesellschaft erwerben; **to put out at** ~ verzinslich (zinstragend) anlegen; **to put one's money out at** ~ Geld auf Zinsen ausleihen, sein Geld arbeiten lassen (nutzbringend anlegen); **to raise the** ~ Zinsfuß (Zinssatz) erhöhen; **to reduce the** ~ Zinssatz (Zinsen) senken; **to repay an injury with** ~ *(fam.)* sich überlegen zu rächen wissen; **to represent s. one's** ~s jds. Belange vertreten; **to run counter to s. one's** ~s jds. Interessen verletzen (zuwiderlaufen); **to safeguard one's** ~s seine Interessen wahren; **to secure** ~s Beteiligungen erwerben; **to sell one's** ~ seinen Geschäftsanteil (seine Beteiligung) verkaufen; **to serve the**

public ~ dem öffentlichen Interesse dienen; **to show** ~ **in one's work** seiner Arbeit Interesse entgegenbringen; **to sit at a high** ~ hohe Zinsen zahlen müssen; **to study the** ~s **of s. o.** jds. Vorteil im Auge haben; **to suit s. one's** ~s jds. Interessen dienen; **to take an** ~ **in s. th.** sich etw. angelegen sein lassen, sich für etw. interessieren, Interesse an etw. nehmen; **to take a fresh** ~ **in life** neuen Lebensmut gewonnen haben; **to take no further** ~ desinteressiert sein; **to take an** ~ **in a firm** sich an einer Firma beteiligen; **to take no great** ~ **in politics** sich für Politik kaum interessieren, politisch nicht interessiert sein; **to travel abroad in the** ~s **of a business firm** Geschäftsinteressen einer Firma im Ausland wahrnehmen; **to uphold** ~s Interessen wahrnehmen; **to use one's** ~ **on s. one's behalf** seine Beziehungen für j. einsetzen; **to work in the** ~s **of humanity** aus humanitären Gründen für eine Sache tätig werden; **to work out** ~ Zinsen ausrechnen; **to yield** ~ sich verzinsen, Zinsen tragen (abwerfen); **to yield high** ~ hohe Rendite erzielen.

interest account Zinsenkonto, Zinsberechnung; **collectible** ~ Zinsensammelkonto; **equated** ~ Staffelrechnung.

interest | allocation Zinsdotierung; ~ **arbitrage** Zinsarbitrage; **to fund** ~ **arrears** Zinsrückstände kapitalisieren; ~ **balance** *(US)* täglicher Zinsberechnung zugrunde liegender Kontosaldo, Zinssaldo; **compound** ~ **basis** Zinseszinsbasis; ~-**bearing** verzinslich, zinstragend; **fixed** ~-**bearing** festverzinslich; ~-**bearing capital** Zinskapital; ~-**bearing investment** verzinsliche Kapitalanlage; ~-**bearing securities** verzinsliche Wertpapiere; ~ **bonds** an Stelle von Zinsen ausgegebene Obligationen, Gratisobligationen anstelle von Barverzinsung; ~ **burden** Zinsbelastung; ~ **ceilings** Höchstzinsen; ~ **certificate** Zinsvergütungsschein; ~ **charges** Zinsbelastung, -satz, Zinsenlast, *(balance sheet)* Zinsen[dienst]; **excessive** ~ **charge** wucherische Zinsforderung; ~ **clause** Zinsklausel, *(bill of exchange)* Zinsversprechen; ~ **component** Zinsbestandteil; ~ **computation** Zinsberechnung; ~ **cost** Habenzinsen, Zinsenaufwand; ~ **coupon** Zinsschein, -abschnitt, -kupon; ~ **coupons payable to bearer** Inhaberzinsschein; ~ **crediting** Zinsgutschrift; ~ **due date** Zinstermin; **to redeem at an** ~ **date** zu einem Zinstermin ablösen; ~ **deduction** steuerliche Absetzung der Zinsen; ~ **differential** Zinsgefälle; ~ **differential subsidy** Zinsausgleichsleistung; ~ **earned figures** Zinsertragszahlen; ~ **earnings** Zinsertrag, -einnahmen, -überschuß; ~ **equalization tax** *(US)* Zinsausgleichssteuer; ~ **expenditure** Zinsaufwendungen, -aufwand, Zinsendienst; ~ **expense** Zinslast, -aufwand, -aufwendungen; ~ **factor** zugkräftiges Werbeelement, Aufmerksamkeitsfaktor; ~-**free** zinsfrei, zinslos, unverzinslich; ~-**free loan** unverzinsliches Darlehen; ~ **group** Interessentengruppe, -verband; ~ **income** Zinserträgnisse, -erträge; ~ **instal(l)ment** Zinsrate; ~ **level** Zinsniveau; ~ **loss** Zinsverlust, -ausfall; ~ **lottery** Prämienlotterie; ~ **margin** Zinsmarge; **compound** ~ **method of depreciation** Zinseszinsabschreibungsmethode; ~ **numbers** Zinszahlen, -nummern; ~-**paying period** Zinsperiode; ~ **payments** Zinszahlungen; ~ **payment date** Zinstermin; ~ **premium** Zinsbonus; ~ **profit** Zinsgewinn.

interest rate Zinssatz, -fuß, -ausstattung; **debtor** ~ Sollzinssatz; **long-term** ~ Zinssatz für langfristige Kredite, Sätze für langfristige Gelder; **market-related** ~ marktgängiger Zinssatz; **minimum** ~ Mindestzinssatz; **short-term** ~ Zinssätze für kurzfristige Gelder, Geldmarktzinsen; **to adjust** ~ Zinsen anpassen; **to edge** ~s **down** Zinssätze allmählich senken; **to pay high** ~s hohe Zinsen zahlen; **to raise the** ~s Zinsen erhöhen; **to reduce the** ~ Zinsen senken; ~ **adjustment** Zinsanpassung; ~ **ceiling** Zinshöchstsätze; ~ **changes** Zinssatzänderungen; ~ **cut** Herabsetzung der Zinssätze; ~ **development** Zinssatzentwicklung; ~ **expectation** Zinserwartungen; ~ **level** Zinsniveau; ~ **relief** Zinsvergünstigung; ~ **risk** Zinsrisiko; ~ **situation** Zinssituation; ~ **structure** Zinsgefüge, -struktur; ~ **subsidy** Zinszuschuß.

interest | rebate (reduction) Zinsnachlaß, -verbilligung; ~ **receipts** Zinseingänge; ~ **receivable** *(US)* Zinsforderungen; ~ **relief** Zinsnachlaß; ~ **relief grant** Zinszuschußdarlehen, Zinserleichterungszusage, Zinszuschüsse; ~ **savings** Zinsersparnisse; **determinable** ~ **securities** variabel verzinsliche Papiere (Aktienwerte); **fixed-** ~ **securities** festverzinsliche Papiere; ~ **sensitivity** Zinsempfindlichkeit; ~ **share** Beteiligungsquote; ~ **sheet** Zinsbogen; ~ **stabilization** Zinsstabilisierung; ~ **statement** Zinsenaufstellung, -berechnung, -note; ~ **suit** *(probate court)* Klage auf Ausstellung eines Testamentsvollstreckungszeugnisses; ~ **surplus** Zinsüberschuß; ~ **table** Zinstabelle; ~ **ticket** Zinsschein; ~ **voucher (warrant)** Zinsabschnitt, -kupon, -schein, -beleg; ~ **yield** Zinsertrag, Rendite; ~-**yielding** rentierlich, verzinslich.

interested [mit]beteiligt, *(bias(s)ed)* parteiisch;
  to be ~ reflektieren; **to be ~ in s. th.** sich für etw. interessieren;
  to be ~ in British funds sein Geld in englischer Staatsanleihe angelegt haben; **to be financially ~ in a business** an einem Unternehmen finanziell (kapitalmäßig) beteiligt sein; **to be legitimately ~** berechtigte Interessen haben; **to be ~ in shipping** sein Geld in der Schiffsindustrie angelegt haben; **to become financially ~** sich finanziell beteiligen wollen;
  ~ audience aufmerksam zuhörendes Publikum; **~ listener** aufmerksamer Zuhörer; **~ motives** eigennützige Beweggründe; **~ parties** Interessenten, Beteiligte; **~ partner** Teilhaber; **~ party** Beteiligter; **~ witness** parteiischer (voreingenommener) Zeuge.
interestedness Beteiligtsein, Voreingenommenheit.
interfactory comparative studies Betriebsvergleiche.
interfere *(v.)* sich einmischen, sich ins Mittel legen, intervenieren, *(impair)* störend beeinflussen, stören, beeinträchtigen, *(patent law, US)* sein Prioritätsrecht geltend machen;
  ~ in s. one's affairs sich in jds. Angelegenheiten einmischen; **~ with an application** *(patent)* mit einer Patentanmeldung kollidieren; **~ with private business** in die Privatwirtschaft eingreifen; **~ in a dispute** sich in eine Auseinandersetzung einschalten; **~ with the course of justice** Lauf der Gerechtigkeit aufhalten; **~ with the established government** bestehende Regierung angreifen; **~ in family quarrels** sich in Familienstreitigkeiten einmischen; **~ with s. one's interests** jds. Interessen beeinträchtigen (verletzen); **~ with one's private interests** seinen eigenen Interessen entgegenstehen; **~ with the operation of a rule** Anwendung einer Regel verhindern; **~ with s. one's plans** jds. Pläne durchkreuzen; **~ with s. one's possessions** j. im Besitz stören; **~ in what does not concern one** sich in Dinge einmischen, die einen nichts angehen;
  to allow pleasure to ~ with duty seine Vergnügungen mit dem Pflichtenkreis kollidieren lassen.
interfered beeinträchtigt.
interference Aufeinandertreffen, Zusammenstoßen, Eingreifen, Einschreiten, Intervention, Dazwischentreten, Störung, Beeinträchtigung, Einmischung, Eingriff, *(clashing of interests)* Interessenkonflikt, *(patent)* Kollision, Patenteinspruch, Geltendmachung der Prioritätsrechte, Anfechtungsklage im Patentverfahren, Anfechtungsverfahren, *(radio)* Störung, Überlagerung;
  illegitimate ~ verbotene Eigenmacht; **judicial ~** gerichtlicher Eingriff in die Verwaltung; **state ~** staatliche Einmischung; **unwarrantable ~** verbotene Eigenmacht;
  ~ from foreign broadcasting stations Störung durch ausländische Rundfunkstationen; **~ with private business** Eingriffe in die Privatwirtschaft; **~ in the business of others** Einmischung in anderer Leute Sachen, Geschäftsstörung; **~ with competitors** Konkurrenzkampf; **~ of interests** Interessengegensatz; **~ with a possession** Besitzstörung;
  to brook no ~ keine Einmischung dulden; **to go into ~** *(patent law)* bis zur Austragung des Streits zurückgestellt werden; **to keep ~ at a minimum** Einmischungen auf ein Mindestmaß beschränken;
  ~ proceedings *(patent law)* Verfahren zur Feststellung eines Prioritätsrechtes, Prioritätsverfahren.
interfering störend, *(el.)* sich überlagernd;
  ~ claims *(patent law)* widerstreitende (kollidierende) Ansprüche; **~ inventions** *(patent law)* kollidierende Erfindungen; **~ patent** Kollisionspatent; **~ signal** Störsignal.
interfirm comparative studies Betriebsvergleiche.
interfund|borrowing haushaltsrechtliche Kreditgewährung; **~ settlement** Haushaltspostenausgleich.
intergovernmental zwischenstaatlich;
  ~ agency zwischenstaatliche Einrichtung; **~ agreement (arrangement)** formloses Regierungsabkommen; **~ bodies** zwischenstaatliche Organisationen; **⌀ Committee for European Migration (ICEM)** zwischenstaatliches Komitee für europäische Auswanderung; **~ conference** zwischenstaatliche Regierungskonferenz; **~ consultations** zwischenstaatliche Beratungen; **⌀ Maritime Consultative Organization** zwischenstaatliche beratende Schiffahrtsorganisation.
intergroup eliminations konzerninterne Verrechnungen.
interim einstweilige Regelung, Interim;
  at ~ provisorisch; **in the ~** in der Zwischenzeit, vorläufig, einstweilig;
  short-term ~ kurzfristige Zwischenhilfe;
  to take over the duties of a post in the ~ Ferienvertretung übernehmen;
  ~ *(a.)* einstweilig, in der Zwischenzeit, zwischenzeitlich, vorläufig, interimistisch;

~ account Zwischen-, Interims-, Durchlaufkonto, Zwischenabschluß; **~ administration** Übergangsregierung; **~ agreement** vorläufige Vereinbarung; **~ aid** Überbrückungshilfe; **~ alimony** vorläufige Unterhaltsregelung; **~ audit** in der Berichtszeit vorgenommene Revision; **~ balance [sheet]** Zwischenbilanz, -abschluß; **~ bill** Zwischenrechnung, Interimswechsel; **~ bond** vorläufiger (kurzfristiger) Schuldschein; **~ cabinet** Zwischenregierung; **~ calculation** Zwischenkalkulation; **~ certificate** Interimsschein; **~ closing** *(bookkeeping)* Bücherabschluß vor dem Jahresende, Zwischenabschluß; **~ commission** Interimskommission; **~ committee** Interimsausschuß; **~ committitur** Anordnung der Untersuchungshaft; **~ copyright** vorläufiges Urheberschutzrecht; **~ credit** Zwischenkredit; **~ curator** *(of prisoner)* vorläufiger Vermögensverwalter; **~ deal** Zwischenabkommen; **~ decision** Zwischenentscheidung, -bescheid; **~ decree** Zwischenurteil; **~ development** vorläufiger Erschließungsplan; **~ dividend** Zwischen-, Abschlags-, Interimsdividende; **~ earnings statement** *(US)* Zwischenbilanz; **~ factor** vorläufiger Konkursverwalter; **~ financial reporting** Zwischenbilanzierung; **~ financial statement** Zwischenbilanz; **~ financing** Zwischenfinanzierung; **~ increase** vorläufige Tariferhöhung; **~ injunction** einstweilige Verfügung; **~ interest** Zwischenzinsen; **~ licence** vorläufige Konzession; **~ loan** Zwischenkredit; **as an ~ measure** als Zwischenlösung; **~ officer** für eine Übergangsperiode eingesetzte Amtsperson; **~ order** vorläufige Anordnung; **~ period** Zwischenzeit; **~ rate** Übergangstarif; **~ receipt** vorläufige Quittung, Interims-, Zwischenquittung; **~ receiver** vorläufiger Verwalter, einstweiliger Treuhänder; **~ relief** vorläufige Unterstützung; **~ reply** Zwischenbescheid; **~ report** Zwischenbericht; **~ result** Zwischenergebnis; **~ rule** Zwischenregierung; **~ share** Interimsaktie; **~ solution** einstweilige Regelung, Zwischenlösung; **~ state** vorübergehendes Staatsgebilde; **~ statement** Zwischenbilanz, -abschluß; **~ stock certificate** *(US)* Interimsaktie; **~ treaty** Zwischenabkommen.
interindustry cooperation *(US)* unternehmerische Zusammenarbeit.
interinsurance exchange *(US)* Schadensteilungsverband.
interior Inneres, Innenraum, *(inland)* Landesinnere, Binnenland, *(photo)* Innenaufnahme, *(pol.)* innere Angelegenheiten;
  continental ~ Inneres eines Kontinents; **forest ~** Waldgemälde; **~ of a building** Gebäudeinneres;
  ~ *(a.) (domestic)* in-, binnenländisch;
  ~ bank *(US)* Regionalbank; **~ courtesy lights** *(car)* Innenbeleuchtung; **~ customs post** *(US)* Binnenzollstelle; **~ debt** Inlandsverschuldung; **~ decoration** Innenausstattung, -dekoration; **~ decorator** Innendekorateur; **~ designer** Innenarchitekt; **~ dimensions** Innenabmessungen; **~ display** Innenauslage, [Waren]auslage innerhalb des Ladens; **~ drainage** Binnenentwässerung; **~ economy** *(administration)* Materialverwaltung; **~ equipment** Inneneinrichtung, -ausstattung; **~ market** Binnenmarkt; **~ minister** Innenminister; **~ ministry officials** Beamte des Innenministeriums; **~ town** Binnenstadt; **~ trade** Binnenhandel; **~ view** Innenansicht.
interjacent dazwischenliegend.
interject *(v.)* **a remark** Bemerkung einwerfen.
interjection Zwischenruf.
interlaced scanning *(television)* Zeilensprungverfahren.
interlacing of capital Kapitalverflechtung.
interlard *(v.)* **with quotations** mit Zitaten spicken.
interleaf Zwischenblatt, Durchschuß.
interleave *(books)* durchschießen.
interlibrary loan auswärtiger Leihverkehr.
interline Zwischenzeile, -linie, *(print.)* Durchschuß[linie];
  ~ *(v.)* dazwischenschreiben, Zeilen einfügen, *(print.)* durchschießen;
  ~ a translation in a text Übersetzung zwischen den Text schreiben;
  ~ fare Teilstreckenfahrpreis; **~ freight** von mehreren Spediteuren beförderte Fracht, Streckenfracht; **~ passenger service** Teilstreckenpersonenverkehr; **~ revenues** Teilstreckeneinnahmen; **~ ticket** Teilstreckenfahrkarte.
interlinear zwischen den Zeilen, zwischenzeilig, *(print.)* blank; **~ space** Zeilenabstand.
interlineation of a text Textinterpolation.
interlined|with corrections mit Korrekturen zwischen den Zeilen;
  ~ manuscript Interlinearmanuskript.
interlinked directorship *(Br.)* Schachtelaufsichtsrat.
interlock *(v.)* ineinandergreifen, -schachteln, verflechten, *(railway)* [Signale] verriegeln.

interlocked verschachtelt, miteinander verflochten;
~ **enterprises** verflochtene Unternehmen.
interlocking [Überkreuz]verflechtung, Verschachtelung, *(railway)* Verblockung, Verriegelung;
~ *(a.)* ineinandergreifend, integrierend;
~ **of several undertakings** Verschachtelung verschiedener Unternehmungen;
~ **arrangements of production** produktionsmäßige Verflechtung; ~ **combine** Konzernverflechtung; ~ **directorate** *(US)* Personalunion bei Verwaltungen verschiedener Gesellschaften, Schachtelaufsichtsrat; ~ **holdings of firms** Konzernzusammenhänge; ~ **interest** *(US)* Schachtel[beteiligung]; ~ **liquidity in world markets** weltbedingte Liquiditätsverhältnisse; ~ **question** korrespondierende Frage; ~ **relationship** Unternehmensverbindungen, Organschaft; ~ **rights** Schachtelprivileg; ~ **stock ownership** Verschachtelung des Aktienkapitals.
interlocution Unterredung, Gespräch, *(law)* vorläufiges Urteil, Zwischenurteil.
interlocutor Gesprächspartner, -teilnehmer, *(Scot., US)* Zwischenurteil, Gerichtsbeschluß.
interlocutory *(during a conversation)* gesprächsweise, ins Gespräch eingeflochten, *(Scot.)* einstweilig, vorläufig;
~ **application** Verfahrensantrag; ~ **costs** im Laufe des Verfahrens anfallende Gerichtskosten; ~ **decision** Zwischenentscheidung; ~ **decree** Zwischenurteil; ~ **form** Gesprächsform; ~ **hearing** Zwischenverhör; ~ **injunction** einstweilige Verfügung mit gewisser Dauerregelung; ~ **judgment** Zwischenurteil; ~ **order** Zwischenverfügung; ~ **proceedings** Vor-, Inzidentfeststellungsverfahren; ~ **relief** vorläufiger Rechtsschutz; ~ **sentence** Entscheidung einer Nebenfrage.
interlope *(v.) (intrude into business)* sich [in die Geschäfte anderer] eindrängen, sich unbefugt einmischen, *(traffic without licence)* wilden Handel (unkonzessioniertes Gewerbe) betreiben.
interloper *(intruder)* Eindringling, *(trader without licence)* wilder (unkonzessionierter) Händler, Schleich-, Schwarzhändler.
interlude Zwischenspiel, Posse;
~s **of bright weather** dazwischenliegende Schönwetterperiode.
intermarriage Mischheirat.
intermarry *(v.)* gemischte Ehe schließen, untereinander heiraten.
intermeddle *(v.)* | **in s. one's business** sich in jds Angelegenheiten einmischen; ~ **with what does not concern one** sich in Dinge einmischen, die einen nichts angehen.
intermeddling Einmischung.
intermediary Mittelsmann, -person, *(mediator)* Vermittler, *(product)* Zwischenprodukt, *(trader)* Zwischenhändler;
to act as ~ als Vermittler auftreten, vermitteln;
~ *(a.)* dazwischenliegend, vermittelnd;
~ **bank** *(US)* eingeschaltete Bank; ~ **bearer** Zwischenträger; ~ **trade** Zwischenhandel.
intermediate Vermittler, Verbindungsmann, *(attorney)* Zwischenprüfung;
~ *(a.)* dazwischenliegend, zwischenzeitlich, *(direct)* mittelbar, indirekt;
~ *(v.)* dazwischentreten, als Vermittler auftreten, vermitteln, intervenieren;
~ **account** Zwischenabrechnung; ~ **agent** Zwischenvertreter, Vermittler; ~ **area** *(unemployment politics)* Grauzone; ~ **authority** mittelbarer Zeuge; ~ **broker** Zwischenmakler; ~ **buyer** Zwischenkäufer; ~ **carrier** Zwischenspediteur; ~ **colo(u)r** Mittelfarbe; ~ **credit** mittelfristiger Kredit, Zwischenkredit; ⚷ **Credit Bank** *(US)* Staatliche Landwirtschaftsbank; ~ **day** *(Br., stock exchange)* Unterbrechungstag; ~ **depot** *(US)* Zwischenstation; ~ **examination** Zwischenexamen; ~ **financing** Zwischenfinanzierung; ~ **frequency** *(radio)* Zwischenfrequenz; ~ **goods** Zwischenprodukt, Halbfabrikat; ~ **grades** *(US)* vierte bis siebte Schulklassen; ~ **holding company** Zwischenholding; ~ **indorser** Zwischengirant; ~ **input** Vorleistung; ~ **lag** Anlaufverzögerung; ~ **order** richterliche Zwischenverfügung; ~ **port** Zwischenhafen; ~ **position** Zwischenstellung, vorübergehende Stellung; ~ **product** Halbfabrikat; ~-**range ballistic missile** Mittelstreckenrakete; ~ **reply** Zwischenbescheid; ~ **school** *(US)* Mittelschule; ~ **seller** Zwischenverkäufer; ~ **stage** Zwischenstadium; ~ **station** Zwischenstation; ~-**term** mittelfristig; ~-**term credit** mittelfristiger Kredit; ~ **ticket** *(US)* Übergangsfahrschein; ~ **toll** Teilstreckengebühr; ~ **trade** Zwischenhandel; ~ **transactions** Vorumsätze; ~ **trial** *(attorney)* Zwischenprüfung; ~ **value** Zwischenwert; ~ **voucher** Eigenbeleg; ~ **witness** mittelbarer Zeuge.
intermediation Dazwischentreten, Vermittlung.
intermediator Vermittler.

interment Begräbnis, Bestattung.
intermezzo Zwischenspiel, Intermezzo.
interminable debate nicht endenwollende Diskussion.
intermingle *(v.)* vermischen.
interministerial interministeriell.
intermission Unterbrechung, Aussetzen, Pause;
without ~ fortwährend, ohne Unterlaß;
to work without ~ ununterbrochen arbeiten.
intermit *(v.)* unterbrechen, zeitweilig aussetzen.
intermittent nicht ständig unterbrochen;
~ **ad campaign** *(US)* periodisch unterbrochene Werbemaßnahmen; ~ **easement** zeitweilig ausgeübte Dienstbarkeit; ~ **fever** Wechselfieber; ~ **light** Blinklicht; ~ **manufacturing** Produktion nur auf Bestellung; ~ **unemployment** vorübergehende Arbeitslosigkeit.
intermix *(v.) (goods)* sich vermischen.
intermixture of goods *(law)* [Waren]vermischung.
intern *(US)* Hilfsarzt, Pflichtassistent, *(hospital patient)* Krankenhausinsasse, *(person interned)* Internierter;
~ *(v.)* internieren, *(med., US)* als Assistenzarzt tätig sein;
~ **goods** *(US)* Waren ins Landesinnere versenden; ~ **an insane person** Geisteskranken in eine Anstalt verbringen.
internal innerstaatlich, binnen-, inländisch, heimisch, *(plant)* innerbetrieblich, *(pol.)* innenpolitisch, *(university)* im College wohnend;
~ **account** Inlandskonto; ~ **administrative expenditure** Ausgaben für die innere Verwaltung; ~ **affairs** innere (innerpolitische) Angelegenheiten; ~ **air route** Inlandfluglinie; ~ **air traffic** Inlandsflugverkehr; ~ **arrangements** interne Abmachungen (Regelungen); ~ **audit** innerbetriebliche (betriebseigene) Revision; ~ **audit office** *(local government, Br.)* Gemeindeprüfungsamt; ~ **auditor** betriebseigener Revisor, Innenrevisor, *(local government, Br.)* Gemeinderechnungsprüfer; ~ **bonds** Inlandsschuldverschreibungen, -anleihe; ~ **boom** Inlandskonjunktur; ~ **charges** inländische Abgaben; ~ **check** Betriebsprüfung, -kontrolle; ~ **combustion engine** Explosions-, Verbrennungsmotor; ~ **commerce** *(US)* Binnenhandel; ~ **consumption** Inlandsverbrauch; ~ **control** innerbetriebliche Erfolgskontrolle; ~ **currency** Binnengewährung; ~ **debt** interne Schuld, Inlandsschuld, -verschuldung; ~ **duty** Binnenzoll; ~ **economic equilibrium** binnenwirtschaftliches Gleichgewicht; ~ **economic trend** Binnenkonjunktur; ~ **economies of scale** interne Kostendegression; ~ **economy** *(administration)* Materialverwaltung; ~ **effects** private Erträge (Kosten); ~ **evidence** innerer Beweis; ~ **frontiers** *(EC)* Binnengrenzen; ~ **improvements** *(US)* werterhöhende Investitionen, Kanal-, Landstraßen- und Eisenbahnbauten; **to suffer** ~ **injuries in an accident** sich bei einem Unfall innere Verletzungen zuziehen; ~ **issue** Inlandsemission; ~ **lag** Anlaufverzögerung; ~ **law** innerstaatliches Recht; ~ **legislation** inländische Gesetzgebung; ~ **liabilities** Inlandsverbindlichkeiten; ~ **loan** Inlandsanleihe; **to be absorbed by the** ~ **market** im Inland aufgenommen werden; ~ **memory** *(programming)* Internspeicher; ~ **migration** Binnenwanderung; ~ **monopoly** Binnenmonopol; ~ **national debt** innere Staatsschuld; ~ **navigation** Binnenschiffahrt; ~ **organ** Betriebszeitung; ~ **partition** Zwischenwand; **to maintain** ~ **peace** für Aufrechterhaltung von Ruhe und Ordnung sorgen; ~ **police** *(US)* innerstaatlich ausgeübte Polizeibefugnisse; ~ **politics** Innenpolitik; ~ **price** Verrechnungspreis; ~ **revenue** Staatseinkünfte aus inländischen Steuern und Abgaben, Steueraufkommen, -einnahmen; ⚷ **Revenue Authorities** *(US)* Finanz-, Steuerbehörde; ⚷ **Revenue Code** *(US)* Abgabenordnung; ⚷ **Revenue Office** *(US)* Einkommensteuerbehörde; ⚷ **Revenue Service** *(US)* Einkommensteuerverwaltung; ⚷ **Revenue taxes** *(US)* inländische Steuern und Abgaben; ~ **service** *(airline)* Inlandsflugverkehr; ~ **specialist** *(med.)* Internist; ~ **strain** innenpolitische Spannungen; ~ **student** Internatsangehöriger; ~ **tariff** Binnenzoll; ~ **taxes** innerstaatliche Steuern; ~ **trade** Binnenhandel; ~ **transaction** Buchhaltungsvorgang; ~ **transportation** *(US)* Binnentransport; ~ **transportation system** *(US)* Binnentransportsystem, -wesen; ~ **transportation technician** *(US)* Binnentransportsachverständiger; ~ **voucher** Eigenbeleg; ~ **war** Bürgerkrieg; ~ **waters** innerstaatliche Gewässer, Binnengewässer.
internation *(US)* Internierung.
international *(politics)* Mitglied einer Internationale;
~s international gehandelte Wertpapiere;
~ *(a.)* international, weltpolitisch, zwischenstaatlich;
⚷ **Advertising Association** *(IAA)* Internationaler Werbeverband; ~ **agreement** internationaler Vertrag; ⚷ **Agreement on Railway Freight Traffic** Internationale Übereinkunft über den

Eisenbahnfrachtverkehr; ~ **air law** internationales Luftrecht; ⁰̴ **Air Transport Association** *(IATA)* Internationaler Luftverkehrsverband; ~ **arbitration** internationale Schiedsgerichtsbarkeit; ⁰̴ **Association for the Protection of Industrial Property** Internationaler Verband zum Schutz gewerblichen Eigentums; ⁰̴ **Association of Universities** Internationaler Hochschulverband; ⁰̴ **Atomic Energy Agency** *(IAEA)* Internationale Atomenergiekommission; ⁰̴ **Bank for Reconstruction and Development** Internationale Wiederaufbaubank, Weltbank; ~ **banking** internationales Bankwesen; ⁰̴ **Bar Association** Internationale Anwaltsvereinigung; ~ **business** Weltwirtschaft; ⁰̴ **Chamber of Commerce** Internationale Handelskammer; ~ **check** *(US)* Reisescheck; ⁰̴ **Civil Aviation Organization** *(ICAO)* Internationale Verkehrsluftfahrtorganisation; ~ **claim** völkerrechtlicher Anspruch; ~ **classification of goods** Warenklasseneinteilung; ⁰̴ **Code [of Signals]** internationales Signalbuch; ~ **commerce** Welthandel; ~ **commodity agreement** internationales Rohstoffabkommen; ~ **community** gesamte Welt, Völkergemeinschaft; ~ **confederation** internationale Vereinigung; ⁰̴ **Confederation of Free Trade Unions** Internationaler Bund freier Gewerkschaften; ~ **conference** internationale Konferenz; ~ **consignment note** internationaler Frachtbrief; ~ **convention** internationales Übereinkommen (Abkommen); ⁰̴ **Convention for Prevention of Pollution of the Sea by Oil** Ölverschmutzungsabkommen; ~ **Cooperation Administration** *(ICA)* *(US)* Auslandshilfsamt, Amt für internationale Zusammenarbeit; ⁰̴ **Cooperative Alliance** Internationaler Genossenschaftsverband; ~ **copyright** internationales Verlagsrecht; ⁰̴ **Court of Justice** Internationaler Gerichtshof; ⁰̴ **Development Agency** Internationale Entwicklungsstelle; ⁰̴ **Development Association** *(IDA)* Internationale Entwicklungsorganisation; ~ **double taxation** internationale Doppelbesteuerung; ~ **economics** Außenwirtschaftstheorie, -lehre, -politik, Wirtschaftslehre der außenwirtschaftlichen Beziehungen; ~ **exchange** Devisen; ~ **exchange market** internationaler Devisenmarkt; ~ **exhibition** Weltausstellung; ⁰̴ **Federation of Airline Pilots' Associations** *(IATA)* Internationale Pilotenvereinigung; ⁰̴ **Federation for Housing and Planning** Internationaler Verband für Wohnungswesen, Städtebau und Raumplanung; ⁰̴ **Federation of Trade Unions** Internationale Gewerkschaftsvereinigung; ⁰̴ **Finance Cooperation** *(IFC)* internationale Finanzierungsgesellschaft; ~ **issuing business** Auslandsemissionsgeschäft; ⁰̴ **Criminal Police Organization** Interpol; ~ **justice** völkerrechtliche Rechtspflege; ~ **labo(u)r code** Weltarbeitsrecht; ⁰̴ **Labo(u)r Conference** Weltarbeitskonferenz; ⁰̴ **Labo(u)r Office** Internationales Arbeitsamt, Weltarbeitsamt; ⁰̴ **Labo(u)r Organization** Internationale Arbeiterorganisation; ~ **law** internationales Recht, Völkerrecht; ~ **private law** internationales Privatrecht; **public ~ law** Völkerrecht; **contrary to ~ law** völkerrechtswidrig; **under ~ law** völkerrechtlich; ~ **law of the sea** Seevölkerrecht; ⁰̴ **Law Commission** *(UNO)* Völkerrechtskommission; ~ **lending** internationaler Kreditverkehr; ~ **liquidity** Weltwährungsreserven; ~ **mail** Weltpost; ~ **map** Weltkarte; ~ **maritime traffic** internationaler Seeverkehr; ~ **market** *(stock exchange)* Markt für international gehandelte Wertpapiere; ~ **monetary conference** Weltwährungskonferenz; ⁰̴ **Monetary Fund** Weltwährungsfonds; ~ **monetary system** internationales Währungssystem; ~ **money** *(coll.)* Gold; ~ **money order** Auslandspostanweisung; ~ **multiplier** Volkswirtschaftsmultiplikator; ~ **nautical mile** internationale Seemeile; ~ **obligations** internationale Verpflichtungen; ⁰̴ **Organization of Employers** Internationale Arbeitgeberorganisation; ~ **payments** zwischenstaatlicher Zahlungsverkehr; ~ **personality** Völkerrechtssubjekt; ~ **Postal Union** Weltpostverein; ~ **price** Weltmarktpreis; ⁰̴ **Refugee Organization** *(IRO)* Weltflüchtlingsorganisation; ~ **relations** zwischenstaatliche Beziehungen; ~ **reply coupon** internationaler [Rück]antwortschein; ~ **responsibility** völkerrechtliche Haftung; ⁰̴ **River Community** Internationale Flußanliegergemeinschaft; ~ **road signals** internationale Verkehrszeichen; ~ **road traffic** internationaler Straßenverkehr; ⁰̴ **Sanitary Regulations** internationale Gesundheitsvorschriften; ~ **securities** international gehandelte Effekten (Wertpapiere); ~ **settlement** internationale Niederlassung; ⁰̴ **Shipping Federation** Internationaler Reederverein; ~ **situation** Weltlage; ⁰̴ **Standard Industrial Classification of all Economic Activities** *(SSIC)* internationale Wirtschaftszweigsystematik; ~ **standards** völkerrechtliche Verhaltensnormen; ⁰̴ **Standard Classification of Occupation** internationale Berufssystematik; ⁰̴ **Standardization Organization** Internationaler Normenausschuß; ~ **stocks** *(US)* international gehandelte Wertpapiere; ⁰̴ **Telecommunications Union** *(S.T.U.)* internationaler Fernmeldeverein; ~ **territory** Völkergemeinschaftsgebiet; ~ **trade** Welthandel; **Standard** ⁰̴ **Trade Classification** Internationales Warenverzeichnis für den Außenhandel; ⁰̴ **Trade Conference** Internationale Wirtschaftskonferenz; ⁰̴ **Trade Organization** Internationale Handelsorganisation; ~ **trade unionism** internationales Gewerkschaftswesen; ~ **trademark** international geschütztes Warenzeichen; ~ **transit** internationaler Durchfuhr-, Transitverkehr; ~ **union** Weltverband; ⁰̴ **Union of Local Authorities** Internationaler Gemeindeverband; ~ **unit** *(statistics)* international gebräuchliche Maßeinheit; ~ **usage** internationale Gepflogenheiten; ~ **waters** internationale Gewässer; ⁰̴ **Working Men's Association** Internationale [Arbeitervereinigung]; ⁰̴ **Youth Hostel Federation** Internationale Jugendherbergsverband.

internationalist Völkerrechtsspezialist.

internationalization Internationalisierung.

internationalize *(v.)* internationalisieren.

internationally | minded international eingestellt; ~ **orient[at]ed** international ausgerichtet.

internee Internierter.

internist *(med.)* Internist.

internment Internierung; ~ **camp** Internierungslager.

interoffice | communication direkt geschaltetes Telefonnetz; ~ **memo** innerbetrieblicher Aktenvermerk; ~ **slip** Laufzettel.

interparliamentary | committee interparlamentarischer Ausschuß; ⁰̴ **Union** Interparlamentarische Union.

interpellant Interpellant.

interpellate *(v.)* Zwischenfrage stellen, parlamentarische Anfrage richten, interpellieren.

interpellation Zwischenfrage, parlamentarische (kleine) Anfrage, Interpellation, *(caveat)* Einspruch, Einrede, *(citation, Br.)* Vorladung.

interpenetration gegenseitige Durchdringung, Verflechtung.

interphone *(US)* *(mil.)* Bordsprechanlage, *(tel.)* Haussprechanlage, -telefon.

interplanetary aviation interplanetarische Raumfahrt.

interplant transfer innerbetriebliche Versetzung.

interplay Zusammenspiel, Wechselwirkung; ~ **of colo(u)rs** kombinierte Farbwirkung; ~ **of forces** wechselseitiges Kräftespiel.

interplea Einwand der mangelnden Passivlegitimation.

interplead *(v.)* Streit verkünden, Interventionsklage erheben.

interpleader Streitverkündigung, Drittwiderspruchs-, [Haupt]- interventionsklage, Einwand der mangelnden Passivlegitimation; ~ **issue** Gläubigerstreit; ~ **proceedings** Nebeninterventionsverfahren; ~ **summons** Ladung bei der Zwangsvollstreckungsintervention.

interpolate *(v.)* einschalten, einflicken, einsetzen, einschieben, *(mathematics)* interpolieren; ~ **a bank** Bank einschalten.

interpolated clause eingeschobener Satz.

interpolation Einschiebung, Einschaltung, Interpolation.

interpose *(v.)* sich ins Mittel legen, intervenieren, vermitteln; ~ **one's authority** seinen Einfluß geltend machen; ~ **a counterclaim** Gegenforderung stellen; ~ **in a dispute** in einem Streit vermitteln; ~ **an objection** Einspruch einlegen, Widerspruch erheben; ~ **a remark** Bemerkung einflechten; ~ **one's veto** von seinem Vetorecht Gebrauch machen.

interposition Vermittlung, Fürspruch, Dazwischentreten.

interpret *(v.)* auslegen, interpretieren, erklären, *(translate)* dolmetschen, als Dolmetscher fungieren; ~ **a contract** Vertrag auslegen; ~ **a difficult passage in a book** Buchpassage interpretieren; ~ **extensively** weit auslegen; ~ **restrictively** einschränkend auslegen; ~ **s. one's silence as refusal** jds. Schweigen als Ablehnung werten; ~ **a role** Rolle darstellen; ~ **strictly** eng auslegen.

interpretable übersetzbar, auslegbar.

interpretation Auslegung, Auswertung, Interpretation, Deutung, *(translation)* mündliche Übersetzung, Verdolmetschung; **authentic ~** maßgebliche Auslegung; **close ~** enge Auslegung; **court ~** gerichtliche Auslegung; **extensive ~** ausdehnende Auslegung; **extravagant ~** unberechtigte (unzulässig weite) Auslegung; **judicial ~** richterliche Auslegung; **liberal (unrestricted) ~** freie (weite) Auslegung; **limited (restricted, rigid) ~** enge (strenge) Auslegung; **narrow ~** enge Auslegung; **predestined ~** Auslegung aufgrund vorgefaßter Meinung; **proper ~** richtige Auslegung; **several ~s** mehrere Auslegungsmöglichkeiten; **simultaneous ~** Simultanübertragung; **statutory ~** Gesetzesauslegung; **strained ~** erzwungene (forcierte) Auslegung;

~ **of balance sheet** Bilanzanalyse; ~ **of a contract** Vertragsauslegung; ~ **of data** Datenauswertung; ~ **of a law** Gesetzauslegung; ~ **of statistics** Auswertung von Statistiken;
to admit of two ~s zwei Auslegungsmöglichkeiten zulassen; **to give a new** ~ umdeuten; **to put a restrictive ~ on** einschränkend auslegen; **to put a wide ~ on** weit auslegen (interpretieren); **to put a wrong ~ on s. one's actions** jds. Handlungsweise falsch auslegen;
~ **clause** Auslegungsbestimmung, -vorschrift.

interpreter Übersetzer, Dolmetscher;
conference ~ Konferenzdolmetscher; **court** ~ Gerichtsdolmetscher; **sworn** ~ vereidigter Dolmetscher;
to act as an ~ **to a meeting** als Dolmetscher in einer Sitzung fungieren; **to call in an** ~ Dolmetscher zuziehen; **to supply an** ~ Dolmetscher stellen;
~ **examination** Dolmetscherprüfung; ~ **school** Dolmetscherschule.

interpretership Dolmetscheramt, -funktion, -tätigkeit.

interracial strife Rassenkonflikt.

interregional zwischengebietlich.

interregnum Übergangsregierung.

interrelated untereinander zusammenhängend;
~ **company** Schachtelgesellschaft, -unternehmen.

interrelation wechselseitige (gegenseitige) Beziehung;
capital ~ Kapitalverflechtung.

interrelationship gegenseitige Beziehung;
close ~ Verzahnung.

interrogate (v.) verhören, be-, ausfragen, vernehmen;
~ **a witness** Zeugen einvernehmen.

interrogatee Verhörter, Befragter.

interrogation Vernehmung, Verhör, Befragung;
~ **by police officers** polizeiliche Vernehmung; ~ **of a prisoner** Gefangenenvernehmung; ~ **of a witness** Zeugeneinvernahme; ~ **mark (note)** Fragezeichen; ~ **officer** Vernehmungsoffizier.

interrogative headline (Br.) (newspaper) Überschrift in Frageform.

interrogator Vernehmungsbeamter, Befrager, (politics) Interpellant.

interrogatories schriftlicher Beweisfragebogen, Beweisfragen;
to deliver ~ schriftliche Fragen an die gegnerische Prozeßpartei stellen.

interrogatory gerichtliche Frage.

interrupt (v.) unterbrechen, aufhalten, stören, (prescription) hemmen, unterbrechen;
~ **the debate with a question** während der Debatte eine Frage stellen; ~ **the flow of commerce between two countries** Handlungsbeziehungen zwischen zwei Ländern zum Stillstand bringen; ~ **prescription (period of limitation,** Scot., law) Verjährung unterbrechen; ~ **a speaker** Redner stören (unterbrechen); ~ **the view** Aussicht versperren.

interrupted unterbrochen;
to have been ~ (negotiations) ruhen.

interruption Unterbrechung, Störung, Stockung, (machine) Betriebsstörung, (remark) Zwischenbemerkung, (temporary cessation) vorübergehende Unterbrechung;
without ~ ununterbrochen;
~ **of business** Unterbrechung des Geschäftsbetriebs; ~ **of the period of limitation (prescription,** Scot.) Unterbrechung (Hemmung) der Verjährung; ~ **of a sentence** Strafaussetzung; ~ **of a speech** Unterbrechung eines Redners; ~ **of the statute of limitations** Unterbrechung der Verjährungsfrist; ~ **of traffic** Verkehrsstörung; ~ **of unemployment** unterbrochene Beschäftigungszeit; ~ **in the voyage** Reiseunterbrechung; ~ **in working hours** Arbeitsunterbrechung;
to work six hours without ~ sechs Stunden hintereinander arbeiten.

intersect (v.) schneiden, sich kreuzen.

intersection Kreuzungspunkt, (US) Straßenkreuzung;
~~**-free** (US) kreuzungsfrei.

interspace Zwischenraum, -zeit.

intersperse (v.) **a speech with quotations** Rede mit Zitaten spicken.

interstate zwischenstaatlich, (US) zwischen den einzelnen Bundesstaaten;
~ **commerce** (US) Handel zwischen den Einzelstaaten, zwischenstaatlicher Handel; ~ **commerce commission** (US) Bundesverkehrsbehörde; ~ **law** internationales Privatrecht; ~ **relations** zwischenstaatliche Beziehungen; ~ **shipment** zwischenstaatlicher Versand; ~ **trade barriers** zwischenstaatliche Handelsschranken.

interstellar interstellar.

interterritorial zwischenstaatlich.

interurban zwischen den Städten verkehrend;
~ **bus** Überlandomnibus; ~ **traffic** Überlandverkehr.

interval Zwischenraum, Interval, (broadcasting) Pausenzeichen, (theater) Pause;
at ~s dann und wann;
bright ~s (weather) Aufheiterungen; **lucid** ~ (insane) lichter Augenblick; **meal** ~ Mittagspause;
~ **of half an hour** halbstündiger Abstand; ~ **of publication** Erscheinungsintervall; ~**s between starting times of trains** Zugabstände; ~ **of fair weather** Schönwetterperiode;
to hold meetings at short ~s rasch aufeinanderfolgende Sitzungen abhalten; **to leave at short ~s** (buses) in kurzen Abständen verkehren; **to meet at regular ~s** in regelmäßigen Zeitabständen zusammenkommen; **to start at ~s of an hour** stündlich starten;
~ **signal** (radio) Pausenzeichen.

intervenant Nebenintervenient.

intervene (v.) dazwischentreten, sich einmischen, sich einschalten, intervenieren, (law) Prozeß beitreten;
~ **in an action** einem Rechtsstreit beitreten; ~ **in the affairs of a neighbo(u)ring country** in einem Nachbarland intervenieren; ~ **in the internal affairs of a country** sich in die inneren Angelegenheiten eines Landes einmischen; ~ **in an agreement** einem bestehenden Vertrag beitreten; ~ **in s. one's defence** sich für j. ins Mittel legen; ~ **in a dispute** bei einem Streit vermitteln; ~ **in case of need** als Notadressat intervenieren; ~ **to little purpose** mit seiner Intervention fast nichts erreichen; ~ **on a reasonable scale to buy dollars** im mäßigen Umfang Dollarinterventionskäufe durchführen.

intervener Vermittler, (law) Nebenintervenient;
to appear as ~ als Nebenintervenient auftreten.

intervenient Intervenient;
~ (v.) dazwischenliegend.

intervening‖act Interventionshandlung; ~ **agency (cause)** Unterbrechung des Kausalzusammenhangs; ~ **damages** während des Rechtsstreits erhöhter Schadensersatz; ~ **pages** dazwischenliegende Seiten; ~ **party** Nebenintervenient; ~ **period** Zwischen-, Übergangszeit, -periode; ~ **use** Zwischennutzung.

intervention Einmischung, Einschaltung, Dazwischentreten, Vermittlung, Einschreiten, (policy) Intervention, Einspruchserhebung, (third party) Nebenintervention, Beitritt zum Rechtsstreit, Prozeßbeitritt;
armed ~ bewaffnete Intervention, bewaffnetes Eingreifen; **economic** ~ wirtschaftspolitische Intervention; **government** ~ staatliche Intervention; **police** ~ polizeiliches Einschreiten; **state** ~ Interventionismus, staatliche Intervention;
direct ~ **in the economy** staatliche Intervention in die Wirtschaft; ~ **supra protest** Ehrenintervention, -eintritt;
to use all its D-mark in ~s sämtliche DM für Interventionskäufe verwenden;
~ **agency** (EC) Interventionsstelle; ~ **board for agricultural produce** Einfuhr- und Vorratsstelle für landwirtschaftliche Erzeugnisse; ~ **buying** (International Monetary Fund) Interventionskäufe; ~ **expenditure** Interventionskosten; ~ **measures** (EC) Interventionsmaßnahmen; ~ **point** (Federal Reserve Bank) Interventionspunkt; ~ **policy** Interventionspolitik; ~ **price** (EC) Interventionspreis, (stock exchange) Interventionskurs; ~ **scheme** Interventionsplan.

interventionism Interventionismus.

interview Unterredung, Besprechung, [Befragungs]gespräch, Zusammenkunft, Interview;
checklist ~ im einzelnen festgelegtes Interview; **depth** ~ Tiefeninterview; **employment** ~ persönliche Vorstellung, Einstellungsgespräch; **exclusive** ~ Exklusivgespräch; **face-to-face** ~ Befragung in Form eines mündlichen Gesprächs; **focused** ~ zentriertes Interview; **informal** ~ Stegreifinterview; **initial** ~ Eingangsgespräch; **open-ended (qualitative)** ~ informelles Interview; **oral** ~ mündliche Befragung; **personal** ~ mündliches Interview; **private** ~ persönliche Zusammenkunft; **quantitative** ~ im einzelnen festgelegtes Interview; **stolen** ~ erlistetes Interview; **telephone** ~ telefonisches Interview; **televised** ~ Fernsehinterview;
~ (v.) Interview geben, interviewen;
to arrange an ~ Interview zustande bringen; **to come for an** ~ sich persönlich vorstellen; **to cover leisurely in an** ~ in einem Gespräch ganz nebenbei anschneiden; **to favo(u)r s. o. with an** ~ jem. ein Interview gewähren; **to fudge an** ~ bei einem Interview Blech reden; **to grant an** ~ Interview geben, Unterredung bewilligen; **to refuse to give any ~s to journalists** der Presse jedes Interview verweigern;

~ bias einseitig verfälschte Befragung; **~ guide** Interview-anweisung.

interviewee Befragter, Interviewter.

interviewer Gesprächspartner, [Markt]befrager;
~ bias Umfragefehler; **~ outline** Leitfaden für die Befragung.

interviewing units Befragungseinheiten.

interweave *(v.)* **truth with fiction** Dichtung und Wahrheit miteinander vermischen.

interzonal interzonal;
~ agreement Interzonenabkommen; **~ traffic** Interzonenverkehr.

intestable nicht testierfähig.

intestacy Fehlen eines Testaments;
partial ~ nur teilweise verfügter Nachlaß;
to claim under an ~ gesetzliches Erbrecht geltend machen; **to go by ~** an die gesetzlichen Erben fallen.

intestate Intestaterblasser;
~ *(a.)* ohne letztwillige Verfügung (Testament) [verstorben], nicht testamentarisch vermacht;
to die ~ ohne Erbregelung sterben, ohne letztwillige Verfügung [zu hinterlassen] sterben;
~ decedent *(US)* Erblasser ohne Testament; **~ estate** gesetzlicher Erbe; **to succeed to an ~ estate** als Intestaterbe (gesetzlicher Erbe) erben; **~ succession** gesetzliche Erbfolge, Intestaterbfolge; **~ successor** gesetzlicher Erbe.

intestinal disorders politische (innere) Unruhen.

intestine war Bürgerkrieg.

intimacy Vertraulichkeit, Intimität, *(illicit sexual intercourse)* ehewidrige Beziehungen;
to be on terms of ~ auf vertrautem Fuße stehen.

intimate *(v.)* ankündigen, bekanntmachen, *(give notice)* mitteilen, *(hint)* andeuten, zu verstehen geben;
~ one's approval of a plan einem Plan seine Zustimmung geben, sein Einverständnis mit einem Plan zu verstehen geben; **~ one's intention** von seiner Absicht Kenntnis geben;
~ *(a.)* vertraut, persönlich, privat, befreundet;
to be ~ with the great mit berühmten Persönlichkeiten vertraulichen Umgang pflegen; **to become ~ with s. o.** mit jem. intime Beziehungen aufnehmen;
to tell a friend ~ details of one's life einem Freund vertrauliche Dinge aus seinem Leben anvertrauen; **~ diary** persönliches Tagebuch; **~ friend** Vertrauter; **~ knowledge** genaue Sachkenntnis; **~ nature of a conversation** vertrauliche Gesprächsführung; **to be on ~ terms with s. o.** mit jem. auf vertrautem Fuße stehen.

intimation Ankündigung, Bekanntmachung, *(hint)* Andeutung, Wink, *(notification)* Mitteilung;
~ of gratitude Dankesbezeugung.

intimidate *(v.)* einschüchtern, abschrecken;
~ a witness Zeugen einschüchtern.

intimidation Einschüchterung, Nötigung, Drohung;
~ of voters *(US)* Nötigung von Wählern; **~ of witnesses** Zeugeneinschüchterung, -nötigung;
to surrender to ~ Einschüchterungen nachgeben.

intolerable cruelty *(law of divorce)* unerträgliche Grausamkeit.

intolerance Intoleranz, Unduldsamkeit.

intolerant unduldsam, intolerant;
to be ~ of a drug Medizin nicht vertragen; **to be ~ of opposition** Widerspruch nicht ertragen können.

intoxicant Rauschmittel.

intoxicate *(v.)* betrunken machen, *(fig.)* berauschen.

intoxicated betrunken;
~ with pride aufgeblasen;
to drive a car while ~ *(US)* Kraftfahrzeug im Zustand der Trunkenheit fahren;
~ person unter Alkoholeinfluß stehende Person, Betrunkener.

intoxicating liquors alkoholische Getränke.

intoxication Trunkenheit, Alkoholvergiftung;
to get exhilarated to the point of ~ about s. th. Sache ungeheuer interessant finden.

intoximater Alkoholpegelmeßgerät.

intra-|Community Trade *(EC)* Handel innerhalb der EG-Länder; **~ enterprise conspiracy** Absprache zwischen Konzernunternehmen; **~ European trade** innereuropäischer Handel; **~ muros** nicht öffentlich; **~ vires** ermächtigt, befugt, im Rahmen der Satzung, satzungsgemäß.

intrabrand competition innerbetrieblicher Markenwettbewerb.

intracollegiate innerhalb einer Universität.

intractable child schwer erziehbares Kind.

intradepartmental innerbetrieblich, *(plant)* innerbetrieblich.

intragovernmental agreement Regierungsabkommen.

intramural nicht öffentlich, innerhalb des Universitätsbezirkes, auf die Studenten (Universität) beschränkt.

intransigence Kompromißlosigkeit, Radikalismus.

intransigent politischer Starrkopf, Radikaler;
~ *(a.)* *(pol.)* kompromißlos, radikal.

intraorganizational conference *(tel.)* Konferenzschaltung.

intraregional innergebietlich.

intrastate *(US)* innerstaatlich;
~ commerce *(US)* Wirtschaftsverkehr in einem Bundesstaat; **~ rate** *(US)* in einem Bundesstaat geltender Tarif; **~ shipment** *(US)* binnenstaatlicher Versand.

intrenched camp *(mil.)* Feldschanze.

intrenchment *(mil.)* Verschanzung, Feldbefestigung.

intricate verwickelt, verworren, knifflig;
~ plot *(novel)* komplizierte Handlung.

intrigue Intrigen, Umtriebe, Quertreibereien, Machenschaften, Ränkespiel;
~ *(v.)* intrigieren, Ränke schmieden, *(fascinate)* fesseln, interessieren, faszinieren;
~ to get s. o. an appointment jem. durch Intrigen zu einer Anstellung verhelfen.

intriguer Ränkeschmied, Intrigant.

intrinsic wirklich, innerlich, eigentlich, *(private)* privat, geheim, vertraut;
~ defect innerer Mangel; **~ evidence** unmittelbarer Urkundenbeweis; **~ value** wirklicher (wahrer) Wert, *(commercial establishment)* Basiswert; **~ worth** *(person)* innerer Wert.

introduce *(v.)* *(bring forward)* zur Sprache bringen, *(bring into use)* einführen, in den Verkehr bringen;
~ o. s. [by name] sich [selbst] vorstellen; **~ a bill before parliament** Gesetzesantrag (Gesetzentwurf) einbringen; **~ a business** Geschäft anbahnen; **~ at court** bei Hofe vorstellen; **~ customs duties** Zölle einführen; **~ s. o. in his duties** j. in sein Amt einweisen; **~ evidence** Beweis antreten; **~ on the exchange** *(Br.)* an der Börse einführen; **~ a new fashion** neue Mode aufbringen; **~ goods into a country** Waren in ein Land einführen; **~ new ideas into a business** neue Ideen in einer Firma zum Tragen bringen, Neuerungen in einem Geschäft einführen; **an illness** Krankheit einschleppen; **~ an insurance** Versicherung vermitteln; **~ a lecturer to the audience** Vortragenden dem Publikum vorstellen; **~ into the market** auf den Markt bringen; **~ s. o. in s. one's presence** jem. einem Dritten vorstellen; **~ s. o. to a process** j. mit einem Verfahren bekannt machen; **~ s. o. into a room** j. in ein Zimmer hereinführen; **~ a subject into a conversation** Gesprächsthema anschneiden.

introduced by empfohlen durch;
to be ~ to society gesellschaftlich eingeführt werden.

introduction Einführung, Empfehlung, *(illness)* Einschleppen, *(listing, Br.)* Einführung [von Effekten an der Börse], *(preface)* Vorwort, *(preliminary statement)* Einleitung, Einführung, *(presentation)* [persönliche] Vorstellung, Bekanntmachung;
new-product ~ Einführung eines neuen Artikels;
~ all around allgemeine Vorstellung; **~ of a bill** Einbringung eines Gesetzentwurfes; **~ of business** Anbahnung eines Geschäfts, Geschäftsanbahnung; **~ of convertibility** Übergang zur Konvertierbarkeit; **progressive ~ of a common customs tariff** schrittweise Einführung eines gemeinsamen Zolltarifs; **on the exchange** *(Br.)* Börseneinführung; **~ of goods into a country** Wareneinfuhr in ein Land; **~ to English literature** Einführung (Leitfaden) in die englische Literatur; **~ of a motion** Antragstellung; **~ of a motion of censure** Einbringung eines Mißtrauensvotums;
to give s. o. an ~ to s. o. jem. eine Einführung für j. mitgeben; **to write an ~ to a book** Einleitung schreiben, Buch einleiten; **~ price** Einführungspreis.

introductory einleitend;
~ campaign *(advertising)* Einführungswerbung; **~ chapter** einführendes Kapitel; **~ course** Anfängerkursus; **~ discourse** Einleitungsrede; **~ exercises** Vorübungen; **~ gift** Werbe-, Einführungsgeschenk; **~ law** Einführungsgesetz; **~ letter** Einführungsschreiben; **~ material** *(advertising)* bei der Einführung verwendetes Werbematerial; **~ matter** *(print.)* Vorbogen; **~ number** *(periodical)* Einführungsheft; **~ offer** Sonderangebot; **~ rate** Einführungstarif, *(magazine)* Einführungspreis; **~ remarks** einleitende Bemerkungen; **~ report** Einführungsbericht; **~ steps** einleitende Schritte; **~ words** einführende Worte.

intromission *(assumption of authority)* unberechtigte Einmischung, *(dealings of agent, Br.)* Selbsthilfeverkauf, *(Scot., law)* Geschäftsführung ohne Auftrag, *(property of deceased person)* Nachlaßaneignung;
necessary ~ *(married couple)* berechtigte Nachlaßpflege.

intromit (v.) (Scot., law) sich unberechtigt einmischen.

introspection Selbstprüfung.

introversion Introvertiertheit.

introvert introvertierter Mensch;
~ (v.) one's mind sich auf sein Innenleben einstellen.

intrude (v.) sich eindrängen, lästig werden, (law) Besitz stören;
~ o. s. upon s. o. sich jem. aufdrängen; ~ o. s. into a business sich in eine Sache einmischen; ~ o. s. into a meeting sich selbst einladen; ~ upon s. one's privacy jds. Intimsphäre verletzen, sich in jds. Privatsachen einmischen; ~ one's views upon others anderen Leuten seine Ansichten aufdrängen; ~ upon s. one's time jem. die Zeit stehlen.

intruder ungebetener Gast, Eindringling, (air force) feindliches Einzelflugzeug, (law) Besitzstörer.

intrusion Einmischung, Aufdrängen, Aufdringlichkeit, (law) Besitzstörung, gesetzwidrige Besitznahme;
~ upon a company Inanspruchnahme ungewünschter Gastlichkeit; ~ of s. one's privacy Verletzung der Intimsphäre Dritter, Einmischung in anderer Leute Privatsachen; ~ upon s. one's time Inanspruchnahme von jds. Zeit;
to make an ~ upon s. o. j. belästigen, sich jem. aufdrängen.

intrust (v.) Treuhandvertrag abschließen, zu treuen Händen übergeben.

intuition Intuition, Fingerspitzengefühl;
to have an ~ plötzliche Eingebung haben.

intuitive intuitiv;
~ knowledge unmittelbare Kenntnis.

inundate (v.) überschwemmen, -fluten.

inundated überschwemmt;
~ with applications for a post mit Bewerbungsschreiben überschüttet.

inundation of tourists Touristenstrom.

inurbane unhöflich, ungehobelt.

inure (v.) abhärten, (take effect) wirksam werden, in Kraft treten;
~ to the benefit zugutekommen; ~ to the heir den Erben zufallen.

inurement Gewöhnung, Gebrauch.

invade (v.) einfallen, eindringen, Einfall machen, (fig.) überlaufen, überschwemmen;
~ a building in ein Gebäude eindringen; ~ a city (tourists) Stadt überschwemmen; ~ a country in ein Land einfallen; ~ s. one's house (fam.) j. plötzlich besuchen, Invasion bei jem. veranstalten; ~ the principal (US) Kapital angreifen; ~ s. one's privacy jds. Intimsphäre verletzen; ~ another person's rights in jds. Rechte übergreifen.

invader Eindringling.

invading army (force) Invasionsarmee.

invalid Kranker, Gebrechlicher, (mil.) Invalide, (worker) Dienst-, Arbeitsunfähiger;
permanent ~ dauernd Erwerbsunfähiger, Vollinvalide;
~ (v.) zum Invaliden machen, (mil.) aus der Armee als untauglich entlassen;
to be ~ außer Kraft sein; to be ~ed home (mil.) als Invalide entlassen werden; to become ~ außer Kraft treten; to declare a marriage ~ Ehe für nichtig erklären; to make (render) ~ außer Kraft setzen;
~ (a.) (disabled) invalide, dauernd dienst-, arbeitsunfähig, dienstuntauglich, (not valid) ungültig, unwirksam, kraftlos, nichtig;
~ argument nicht überzeugendes Argument; ~ assignment nichtige Abtretung; ~ carriage Selbstfahrer; ~ chair Rollstuhl; ~ check (US) (cheque, Br.) unvollständiger Scheck; ~ claim unwirksamer Rechtsanspruch; ~ contract ungültiger Vertrag; ~ diet Krankenkost; ~ letter of credit ungültiger Kreditbrief; ~ soldier Invalide; ~ will ungültiges Testament.

invalidate (v.) für ungültig (kraftlos) erklären, unwirksam machen, Gültigkeit aufheben, (law) außer Kraft setzen;
~ an act Gesetz außer Kraft setzen; ~ an agreement (a contract) Vertrag annullieren; ~ an argument Argument entkräften; ~ a judgment Urteil kassieren; ~ securities Wertpapiere für kraftlos erklären; ~ a will Testament für ungültig erklären.

invalidated bonds außer Kurs gesetzte Schuldverschreibungen.

invalidation Aufhebung, Ungültigkeitserklärung, Annullierung, (law) Kraftloserklärung;
~ of evidence Entkräftung von Beweismaterial; ~ of a judgment Urteilsaufhebung; ~ of securities Kraftloserklärung von Wertpapieren;
~ suit Nichtigkeitsverfahren.

invalidism Invalidität.

invalidity Rechtsungültigkeit, Ungültigkeit, Nichtigkeit, (US, invalidness) Arbeits-, Dienstunfähigkeit, Invalidität;

legal ~ Unwirksamkeit; partial ~ Teilunwirksamkeit;
to set up ~ Ungültigkeit geltend machen;
~ allowance (benefit) (US) Erwerbs-, Arbeitsunfähigkeitsrente; noncontributory ~ pension beitragsfreie Invalidenrente.

invaluable unschätzbar, unbezahlbar.

invariable (market) gleichbleibend, unveränderlich;
~ practice of the courts ständige Rechtssprechung.

invasion Einfall, Invasion, Überfall, (encroachment) Übergriff, Verletzung;
~ of cold air Kälteeinbruch; ~ of a city by tourists Überschwemmung einer Stadt durch Touristen, Touristen-, Fremdeninvasion einer Stadt; ~ of privacy Verletzung der Intimsphäre; ~ of s. one's rights Eingriff in jds. Rechte;
~ attempt Invasionsversuch; ~ period Invasionszeit.

invasive|tourists aufdringliche Touristenströme; ~ war Angriffskrieg.

invective Schmährede, Schmähung, Beschimpfung;
to bombard s. o. with ~s j. mit Schmähungen überhäufen.

inveigh (v.) against the weather über das Wetter schimpfen.

inveigle (v.) verlocken, -leiten, -führen;
~ s. o. into investing his money unwisely j. zu Fehlinvestitionen verleiten.

inveigled, to be ~ in[to] a plot in eine Verschwörung verwickelt sein (werden); to become ~ in politics in politische Dinge (Machenschaften) verstrickt werden.

inveiglement Verlockung, Verleitung;
to be proof against all ~s gegen alle Verlockungen gefeit sein.

invent (v.) erfinden, Erfindung machen.

invented word Kunstwort.

invention Erfindung;
cognate ~s verwandte Erfindungen; employee ~ Angestelltenerfindung; epoch-making ~ bahnbrechende Erfindung; joint ~ gemeinsame Erfindung; labo(u)r-saving ~ arbeitssparende Erfindung; latest ~ neueste Erfindung, Modeneuheit; patentable ~ patentfähige Erfindung; patented ~ patentierte Erfindung; ~ sought to be patented zum Patent angemeldete Erfindung; prior ~ ältere Erfindung; pure ~ Ammenmärchen; most useful ~ äußerst nützliche Einrichtung; works ~ Betriebserfindung;
~ made by employees Angestelltenerfindung;
to abandon an ~ Erfindung fallen lassen; to amount to ~ Erfindungshöhe haben (erreichen); to base an ~ Patent auf eine Basis stützen; to be full of ~s (newspaper) voller erfundener Geschichten sein; to exploit an ~ Erfindung verwerten; to impose secrecy on an ~ Erfindung unter Geheimschutz stellen; to patent an ~ Erfindung zum Patent anmelden; to perfect an ~ Erfindung auf den neuesten Stand bringen; to produce an ~ Gegenstand der Erfindung herstellen; to put an ~ to commercial use Erfindung gewerblich verwerten; to reduce an ~ to practice Erfindung praktisch verwerten; to refine upon another's ~ Erfindung eines anderen vervollständigen; to take out a patent for ~ Erfindung patentieren lassen; to tell s. o. a story of one's own jem. seine Darstellung eines Falles geben;
~s exhibition Erfinderausstellung.

inventive erfinderisch;
~ faculty (skill) Erfindungsgabe, Erfindereigenschaft; ~ merit Erfindungshöhe; to deny the ~ step Erfindungshöhe verneinen.

inventiveness (patent law) Erfindungshöhe.

inventor Erfinder;
employee ~ Angestellter als Erfinder, Arbeitnehmererfinder; fellow ~ Miterfinder; joint ~ Miterfinder; original ~ eigentlicher Erfinder; prior ~ Ersterfinder;
~'s right Erfinderrecht; ~'s royalty Patent-, Lizenzgebühr.

inventories Lager-, Warenbestände, (balance sheet, US) Vorräte, Bestände;
~ at the lower of cost or market Warenbestände zum Anschaffungs- oder niedrigerem Marktpreis angesetzt;
to build up ~ Lagervorräte ansammeln.

inventorship, joint Erfindergemeinschaft.

inventory (list of goods) Inventar[verzeichnis], -liste, Bestandsnachweis, -liste, -verzeichnis, Lagerbestandsverzeichnis, (inventory taking, US) Bestandsaufnahme, Inventur, (list of securities) Stückeverzeichnis, (schedule made by executor) Nachlaßinventar, -verzeichnis, (stock on hand, US) Vorräte, Inventar, Lager-, Warenbestand;
basic ~ Normalbestand [an Waren]; beginning ~ Anfangsinventar, -bestand; book ~ (US) Buchinventar, Lagerbefundbuch, Buchwert der Lagerbestände; business ~ Geschäftsinventar; closing ~ Endbestand, Schlußinventur, Bestand zum Jahresende; continuous ~ buchmäßiges (laufend geführtes) Inventar, fortlaufende Lagerbestandsfeststellung; employee

skills ~ Fähigkeitenverzeichnis; **ending** ~ Schlußinventar; **estate** ~ Nachlaßverzeichnis, -inventar; **estimated** ~ geschätzter Lagerbestand; **finished-goods** ~ Fertigwarenlager, -bestand; **going** ~ laufendes Inventar; **goods-in-process opening** ~ Halbfabrikate-Anfangsbestand; **initial** ~ Bestand zum Jahresbeginn; **low** ~ geringer Lagerbestand, geringe Lagervorräte; **maximum** ~ Maximalbestand an Vorräten; **merchandise** ~ Warenbestand, -lager; **opening (original)** ~ Anfangs-, Eröffnungsinventar; **parts** ~ Bestand an Fabrikaten; **perpetual** ~ *(US)* buchmäßig (laufend) geführtes Inventar, permanente Inventur, Buchinventur; **physical** ~ körperliche Bestandsaufnahme, tatsächlich aufgenommenes Inventar; **plant** ~ Betriebsinventar; **previous** ~ Vorinventur; **raw-material[s]** ~ Rohstoffbestände, -lager; **record** ~ Buchinventur; **running** ~ laufendes Inventar; **target** ~ Plan-, Sollbestand; **test** ~ Teilinventur; **top-heavy** ~ übervolles Lager; **unsold** ~ Lagerbestand; **work-in-process** ~ *(US)* Halbfabrikate-Anfangsbestand;

~ **at cost** Inventar zum Anschaffungspreis; ~ **of fixtures** Zubehörliste; ~ **of goods** Wareninventar; ~ **of household furniture** Mobiliarverzeichnis; ~ **of property** Vermögensverzeichnis, -aufstellung, *(bankruptcy proceedings)* Masseverzeichnis; ~ **of technical terms** Fachwörterbestand;

~ *(v.)* Verzeichnis anlegen, Inventar aufnehmen, inventarisieren, Inventur machen;

~ **at $ 5000** Inventarwert von 5000 Dollar haben;

to be part of the ~ zum Inventar gehören; **to draw up an** ~ Inventar aufnehmen, Bestandsverzeichnis anlegen; **to keep down an** ~ Lager knapp halten, Lagervorräte knapp bemessen, vorsichtige Lagerpolitik betreiben; **to liquidate an** ~ *(US)* Lager (Vorräte) abbauen; **to observe an** ~ Inventur überwachen; **to put into the** ~ in Lagervorräten anlegen; **to reduce** ~ Lager abbauen; **to take an** ~ Bestandsaufnahme machen, inventarisieren; **to take** ~ **in January** im Januar Inventur machen;

~ **account** Inventar-, Warenbestands-, Sachkonto; ~ **accumulation** Bestandsauffüllung, Lagerauffüllung, -anreicherung; ~ **adjustment** Lagerangleichung; ~ **audit** Inventar-, Bestandsprüfung; ~ **book** Inventarbuch; ~ **building** Lagerproduktion, -bestandsauffüllung; ~ **build-up** Vorratsanstieg, Lagerauffüllung; ~ **buying** Lagereinkäufe; ~ **card** Inventarkarte; **perpetual** ~ **card** Lagerkarte; ~ **certificate** *(US)* Bestandprüfungsbescheinigung, Inventurprüfungsbescheinigung; ~ **changes** Änderungen in der Lagerhaltung, Lagerbestandsveränderungen; ~ **checking** Inventar-, Lagerkontrolle, -prüfung; ~ **classification** Bestandseingruppierung; ~-**conscious** lagerbewußt; ~ **control** Lager-, Vorratsbewirtschaftung, Bestands-, Lagerbestandskontrolle; ~ **control system** Lagerkontrollsystem; ~ **controller** Lagerhaltungspezialist; ~ **cut-off date** Inventurtag, -termin; ~ **cutting** Vorratsabbau, Lagerabbau; **average** ~ **cycle** Umschlagsdauer; ~ **decrease** Lagerabgang; ~ **decumulation** Lager-, Vorratsabbau; ~ **figures** Bestandszahlen; ~ **perpetual** ~ **file** laufende Bestandskartei; ~ **fluctuations** Lagerhaltungs-, Inventarwertschwankungen; ~ **group** Waren-, Lagergruppe; ~ **growth** Lagerzunahme; ~ **holdings** Lagerbestände; ~ **increase** Lagerauffüllung, Auffüllung der Lagerbestände; ~ **investments** Lagerinvestitionen, Vorratsinvestitionen; ~ **investment cycle** Lagerzyklus; ~ **item** Inventarposten, Posten des Bestandsverzeichnisses; ~ **liquidation** *(US)* Lagerabbau; ~ **list** Bestandsverzeichnis; ~ **loan** Lagerfinanzierung durch mittel- oder langfristige Kredite; ~ **loss** Bestandsverlust; ~ **markup** Rohgewinnaufschlag auf den Inventarwert; ~ **number** Inventarnummer, *(library)* Inventarisierungsnummer; ~ **observation** Inventurüberwachung; ~ **period** Inventarfrist; ~ **picture** Lagerbild; **to knock the** ~ **picture out of focus** Lagerpolitik völlig durcheinanderbringen; ~ **price** Inventurpreis; ~ **price decline** *(balance sheet, US)* Wertminderung der Vorräte; ~ **pricing** Vorrätebewertung, Bestands-, Inventarbewertung; ~ **proceedings** Warenbestandsaufnahme, Inventurarbeiten; ~ **profit** Lager-, Buchgewinn; ~ **protection** Preisgarantie für Lagerbestände; ~ **quantity** Inventurmenge; ~ **recession** Lagerrezession; ~ **record** Inventurverzeichnis; ~ **reduction** Bestandsverminderung, Lagerabbau; ~ **register** Bestandsbuch, -verzeichnis, Inventurbuch, Lagerverzeichnis; ~ **reserve** Rückstellung für Lagerabwertungen; ~ **sale** Inventurausverkauf; ~-**sales ratio** Lagerumsatzverhältnis; ~ **schedule** Inventarverzeichnis, -aufstellung, Bestandsverzeichnis; ~ **sheet** Inventarverzeichnis, -blatt, -aufstellung; ~ **shortage** Lagermanko, -defizit, Bestandsfehlbetrag; ~ **shrinkage** Bestandsverlust, Schwund; ~ **size** Lagerumfang, -größe, -ausdehnung; **perpetual-**~ **system** laufende Lagerkontrolle; ~ **taking** Aufnahme der Bestände, Inventar[aufnahme], Be-

standsaufnahme; ~ **target** lagerpolitisches Ziel; ~ **turnover** Umschlagshäufigkeit des Lagerbestands, Lagerumschlag; ~ **turnover ratio** Lagerumschlagsverhältnis; ~ **valuation** Vorräte-, [Lager]bestandsbewertung; ~ **valuation adjustment** *(national income accounting)* Lagerbewertungsausgleich, Wertberichtigung der Lagerbestände; ~ **valuation changes** Änderungen in der Bestandsbewertung; ~ **valuation method** Lagerbewertungsmethode; ~ **value** Lagerbestands-, Inventarwert; ~ **verification** Inventur-, Bestandsprüfung; ~ **woes** Lagerschwierigkeiten; ~ **writedown** *(US)* Lager-, Bestands-, Inventarabschreibung.

inverse umgekehrt, entgegengesetzt;

~ **order** *(alienation of land)* umgekehrte Reihenfolge; ~ **probability** *(statistics)* Rückschlußwahrscheinlichkeit; **to be in** ~ **proportion** im umgekehrten Verhältnis stehen; ~ **value** Umkehrwert.

inversion Umkehrung.

invert *(v.)* umkehren, umdrehen;

~ **a sentence** Satz umstellen.

inverted | commas Anführungszeichen, -striche; ~ **flight** Rückenflug.

inverter *(tel.)* Sprachverzerrer, Invertergerät.

invest *(v.)* investieren, [Geld] anlegen, unterbringen, [Kapital] einschießen, plazieren, *(law)* einsetzen [in], *(mil.)* belagern, einschließen, zernieren;

~ **in s. th. of one's own** sich selbst etw. anschaffen;

~ **advantageously** zinstragend anlegen, günstig investieren; ~ **one's fortune in life annuities** sich in eine lebenslängliche Rente einkaufen; ~ **5% of their assets in chattel paper** 5% des Anlagevermögens in Beleihungen beweglichen Vermögens investieren; ~ **s. o. with authority** j. mit Vollmacht versehen, j. bevollmächtigen; ~ **capital** Kapital anlegen, investieren; ~ **o. s. in one's coat** sich mit seinem Mantel umhüllen; ~ **funds in a scheme** sich mit Vermögenswerten an einem Unternehmen beteiligen; ~ **in public funds** in Staatspapieren anlegen; ~ **in house property** Hausbesitzer werden, Wohngrundstücke erwerben; ~ **the management of a bank in s. o.** jem. die Leitung einer Bank übertragen; ~ **one's money to good account (advantage)** sein Geld gut (vorteilhaft, gewinnbringend) anlegen; ~ **money in a business** Geld in ein Geschäft stecken; ~ **one's money in a business enterprise** sich an einem geschäftlichen Unternehmen beteiligen; ~ **one's money in real estate** sein Geld in Grundstücken anlegen; ~ **one's money in stock** sein Geld in Wertpapieren anlegen; ~ **one's money in stocks and shares** sein [ganzes] Geld in Aktien anlegen; ~ **at short notice** kurzfristig (befristet) anlegen; ~ **s. o. with an office** j. mit einem Amt bekleiden; ~ **with full powers (authority)** mit allen Vollmachten versehen (ausstatten); ~ **in initial publicity** für die Einführungskampagne investieren; ~ **safely** sicher anlegen; ~ **one's savings in a business enterprise** seine Ersparnisse in ein Geschäftsunternehmen stecken; ~ **primarily in securities** seine Anlagen hauptsächlich in Wertpapieren tätigen; ~ **only in short-term gain** nur für sofort rentierliche Investitionen vornehmen; ~ **the situation with additional horrors** Situation noch schrecklicher machen; ~ **£ 1000 in government stock** 1000 Pfund in Staatspapieren anlegen (investieren); ~ **a subject with interest** Thema interessant gestalten; ~ **in a new suit(e) of furniture** *(Br.)* sich neue Möbel zulegen; ~ **a town closely** *(mil.)* Stadt fest einschließen;

to be ready to ~ Anlagebereitschaft zeigen.

invested finanziell angelegt, investiert;

~ **with discretionary powers** mit Vollmacht den Umständen entsprechend zu handeln;

to be ~ **with full authority** alle nur möglichen Vollmachten erhalten haben; **to be** ~ **in a business** im Geschäft stecken;

~ **capital** eingesetztes (angelegtes) Kapital, Anlagekapital, -vermögen; ~ **money** angelegtes Geld.

investee Investitionsempfänger.

investigate *(v.)* untersuchen, erforschen, überprüfen, revidieren, Revision vornehmen, *(inquire)* einer Sache nachgehen, ermitteln;

~ **the causes of a railway accident** Ursachen eines Eisenbahnunglücks untersuchen; ~ **affairs of a company** Geschäfte einer Gesellschaft der Revision unterziehen; ~ **a crime** wegen eines Verbrechens ermitteln; ~ **the facts more thoroughly** Tatsachen noch gründlicher prüfen; ~ **ownership of a company** Eigentumsverhältnisse einer Gesellschaft untersuchen; ~ **s. th. statistically** statistische Erhebungen über etw. anstellen.

investigating | activity Ermittlungtätigkeit; ~ **authority** Ermittlungsbehörde; ~ **committee** Ermittlungs-, Untersuchungsausschuß; ~ **magistrate** Untersuchungsrichter; ~ **officer** Ermittlungsbeamter; ~ **panel** Untersuchungsausschuß.

investigation Untersuchung, [Über]prüfung, Revision, *(inquiry)* Nachforschung, Ermittlung, Erhebung, Erforschung;
upon ~ bei näherer Untersuchung;
analytical ~ analytische Untersuchung; **close** ~ eingehende (gründliche) Untersuchung; **consumer** ~ Untersuchung des Verbrauchermarktes; **criminal** ~ Voruntersuchung, staatsanwaltliche Ermittlungen, Ermittlungen der Kriminalpolizei; **curious** ~ genaue Untersuchung; **extensive** ~s umfangreiche Ermittlungen; **informal** ~s informelle Ermittlungen; **judicial** ~ gerichtliche Untersuchung; **preliminary** ~ Voruntersuchung; **scientific** ~ wissenschaftliche Untersuchung; **statistical** ~s statistische Erhebungen; **systematic** ~ systematische Untersuchung;
~ **of accidents** Unfalluntersuchung; ~ **of behavio(u)r** Verhaltensforschung; ~ **of a case** Prüfung eines Rechtsfalles; ~ **of a company's affairs** Revision der Geschäfte einer Gesellschaft; ~s **of ownership** Prüfung der Eigentumsverhältnisse; ~s **by the police** polizeiliche Ermittlungen; ~ **of title** Prüfung der Eigentums- und Grundpfandrechte (Belastungsverhältnisse); **to be under** ~ Ermittlungsverfahren vor sich haben; **to cause** ~s **to be made** Nachforschungen anstellen lassen; **to conduct an** ~ Untersuchung anstellen; **to drop** ~s Ermittlungen einstellen; **to fail to make a reasonable** ~ keine gründliche Untersuchung vornehmen; **to have an** ~ **in charge** Untersuchung leiten; **to make** ~s **on the spot** Untersuchungen (Erhebungen) an Ort und Stelle durchführen; **to weather an** ~ Untersuchung überstehen; ~ **cost** Untersuchungs-, Ermittlungskosten; ⊵ **Department** *(Br.)* [etwa] Bundeskriminalamt; ~ **service** Zollfahndungsdienst.
investigative|**agency** Fahndungsbehörde; ~ **costs** Untersuchungskosten; ~ **process** Untersuchungsverfahren; ~ **reporting** auf Recherchen beruhende Reportage; ~ **unit** Zollfahndungsstelle; ~ **work** Untersuchungstätigkeit.
investigator mit einer Untersuchung Beauftragter, Untersuchungs-, Ermittlungsbeamter, Rechercheur, *(marketing)* Marktbefrager.
investigatory|**committee** Untersuchungsausschuß; ~ **force** Untersuchungsstab; ~ **matter** Untersuchungsfall, Ermittlungssache.
investing, formula Wertpapieranlage nach dem System der Durchschnittskostenminderung;
~ **institution** Kapitalsammelstelle; ~ **member** *(loan society, Br.)* noch nicht zugeteilter Bausparer; ~ **public** anlageinteressiertes (anlagesuchendes) Publikum, Anlage-, Kapitalmarktpublikum.
investiture Amtseinsetzung, Bestallung.
investive fact rechtsbegründende Tatsache.
investment *(building society)* Bausparsumme, *(capital invested)* [Kapital]anlage, Vermögensanlage, *(investing)* Investierung, Investition, Anlegung, Plazierung, *(investiture)* Bestallung, *(mil.)* Belagerung, Blockade, Zernierung, *(money put in)* [Kapital]einlage, Einschuß, Beteiligung, Anlage[kapital];
~s *(balance sheet)* finanzielle Beteiligungen, Wertpapiere, Effektenportefeuille;
~s **abroad** Auslandsanlagen, -investitionen, Investitionen im Ausland, auswärtige Investitionsvorhaben; **aggressive** ~s spekulative (risikoreichere) [Kapital]anlagen; **attractive** ~ attraktive Kapitalanlagen; **autonomous** ~ von wirtschaftlichen Überlegungen unabhängige Investitionen; **beginning** ~ Gründungseinlage; **branch** ~ Investitionen in Filialbetrieben; **capital** ~ langfristige Kapitalanlage, Kapitalverwertung, Investitionsaufwand, Investitionskapital, Anlageinvestition, langfristig angelegtes Kapital; **capital-seeking** ~ anlagesuchendes Kapital; **choice** ~ erstklassige (ausgesuchte) Kapitalanlage; **current** ~s vorübergehende Anlagen; **direct** ~s mit eigener Betätigung gekoppelte Investitionen, Direktinvestitionen; **domestic** ~s Inlandsinvestitionen; **earning** ~ gewinnbringende Kapitalanlagen; ~s **effected** Investitionsleistungen; **equipment** ~s Investitionen für den Maschinenpark, Ausstattungsinvestitionen; **estate** ~ Grundstücksanlage; **excessive** ~ übermäßige Investitionen, Überinvestition; **false** ~s Fehlinvestitionen; **financial** ~ Geldmarktanlage; **first-mortgage** ~s Kapitalanlagen in Ersthypotheken; **fixed** ~ feste Kapitalanlage; **fixed-capital** ~ Anlagevermögen; **fixed-deposit** ~ Anlagen auf Depositenkonto; **fixed-income** ~ festverzinsliche Werte; **fixed-property** ~ Anlagevermögen; **foreign** ~ Auslandsanlagen, -investitionen; **gilt-edged** ~ *(Br.)* mündelsichere (erstklassige) Kapitalanlage; **good** ~ vorteilhafte Anlage; **centrally planned government** ~ dirigistisch gelenkte staatliche Investitionen; **gross corporate** ~ Bruttoinvestitionen der Wirtschaft; **gross private domestic** ~s Bruttoinlandsinvestitionen; **high-grade** ~

erstklassige Anlage; **higher-yielding** ~s höherverzinsliche Anlagewerte; **impaired** ~s Anlagenveränderung; **improper** ~ *(trust fund)* gesetzwidrige (bestimmungswidrige) Kapitalanlage; **induced** ~ Investitionssteigerung; **industrial** ~ Vermögensanlage in Industriewerten; **initial** ~s Anfangsinvestitionen; **intangible** ~[s] immaterielle Anlagewerte, Kapitalanlage in immateriellen Werten; **interest-bearing** ~ zinsbringende Kapitalanlage, *(securities)* festverzinsliche Anlagepapiere; **legal** ~s *(US)* mündelsichere [Kapital]anlage; **liquid** ~ leicht realisierbare Kapitalanlagen; **long-lived (-term, -time)** ~ auf lange Sicht vorgenommene Investitionen, langfristige Kapitalanlage (Investitionen), *(balance sheet, US)* Wertpapiere des Anlagevermögens; **manufacturing** ~s Investitionen auf dem Fertigungssektor; **minimum** ~ Mindesteinlage; **mistaken** ~s Fehlinvestitionen; **narrower-range** ~s *(trustee, Br.)* mündelsichere Papiere der ersten Auswahlstufe; **negative** ~ Lagerabbau; **net** ~ Nettoinvestitionen; **new** ~ Neuinvestition, -anlage; **noncommutable** ~ nicht ablösbare Kapitalanlage; **nonoperating fixed** ~ außerbetriebliche Anlagen; **nonquoted** ~s *(Br.)* nicht an der Börse notierte Wertpapiere; **nonspeculative** ~ Kapitalanlage zu Rendizwecken; **obligatory** ~ Pflichteinlage; **original** ~ Gründungseinlage, Anfangskapital; **other** ~s *(balance sheet)* diverse Anlagewerte; **outside** ~ außerbetriebliche Kapitalanlage; **paying** ~ vorteilhafte (gewinnbringende) [Kapital]anlage; **permanent** ~ langfristige Kapitalanlage, Daueranlage; **planned** ~ Investitionsplanung; **poor** ~ schlechte Kapitalanlage, schlechte Anlagewerte; **portfolio** ~ indirekte Investitionen, Kapitalanlage in Wertpapieren, Wertpapieranlage, Portfolioinvestment; **prime** ~ mündelsichere (erstklassige) Kapitalanlage; **private** ~ private Kapitalanlage; **productive** ~ produktive Kapitalanlage; **productivity-improving** ~ produktivitätsfördernde Kapitalinvestitionen; **profitable (remunerative)** ~ lohnende (ertragreiche) Kapitalanlage, vorteilhafte Investitionen; **prudent** ~ ordnungsgemäß vorgenommene Kapitalinvestition; **public** ~[s] [Kapital]investitionen der öffentlichen Hand; **quoted** ~s *(Br.)* börsengängige Wertpapiere; **real** ~ echte Investition; **real-estate** ~s Anlagen in Grundstücken (Grundbesitz), Investitionen im Immobiliensektor; **safe** ~ sichere [Kapital]anlage; **selected** ~s *(Br.)* ausgesuchte Anlagewerte; **short-term** ~s kurzfristige [Kapital]anlagen; **sleeping** ~ stille Beteiligung; **social** ~s soziale Investitionen; **special situation** ~ risikoreichere (spekulative) [Kapital]anlagen; **speculative** ~ Kapitalanlagen zu Spekulationszwecken; **stock** ~ Aktienbesitz; **tax** ~ steuerbegünstigte Kapitalinvestition; **temporary** ~ kurzfristige Anlage, Zwischenanlage, *(balance sheet, US)* Wertpapiere des Umlaufvermögens; **total** ~ Gesamtinvestitionen, *(balance sheet of investment fund)* Wertpapiervermögen insgesamt; **trade** ~ *(Br.)* Vermögensanlage im Interesse des Geschäftsbetriebes; **trust** *(US)* *(trustee, Br.)* ~s mündelsichere Kapitalanlage; **unproductive** ~ unproduktive Kapitalanlage; **unprofitable** ~ unvorteilhafte Kapitalanlage; **unquoted** ~ *(Br.)* an der Börse nicht notierte Wertpapiere, nicht börsenfähige Wertpapiere; **widerrange** ~s *(trustee, Br.)* mündelsichere Papiere bestimmter in England an den Börsen notierter Gesellschaften;
~ **from abroad** auswärtige Kapitalinvestitionen; ~ **in fixed assets** Anlageinvestitionen; ~ **in the business** Geschäftseinlage; ~ **of capital** Geldanlage, Kapitalinvestierung, Anlage von Kapitalien; ~ **of one's capital** Vermögensanlage; ~ **in human capital** Bildungsinvestition; **employee** ~s **in the capital of a business** Belegschaftsaktien; ~ **in capital goods** Kapitalanlagegüterinvestition; ~s **in companies** Beteiligungen an Gesellschaften, *(balance sheet)* Beteiligungsbestand; ~s **at cost** Wertpapiere zu Anschaffungskosten; ~s **in default** notleidende Kapitalanlagen; ~ **of funds** Anlage von Geldbeträgen, Kapitalinvestition; **short-term** ~ **of funds** kurzfristige Mittelanlage; **sundry** ~s **and interests** *(balance sheet)* verschiedene Beteiligungen; ~ **in quick-return labo(u)r-cost displacing equipment** Maschinenparkinvestitionen mit dem Ziel rascher Ertragssteigerung durch Verringerung der Lohnquote; ~ **with a useful life of ten years** Anlagegüter mit einer zehnjährigen Nutzungsdauer; ~ **in men** Ausbildungskosten, für Arbeitskräfte aufgewandte Personalinvestitionen; ~ **in mortgages** Hypothekenanlage; ~ **in plant and equipment** Betriebsausstattung; ~ **in plant and machinery** Betriebs- und Maschinenparkinvestitionen; ~ **of net profit** Verwendung des Reingewinns; **commercial** ~ **in property** gewerbsmäßige Anlagen im Immobiliensektor; ~s **undertaken for rationalization purposes** Rationalisierungsinvestitionen; ~ **in research** Aufwendungen für Forschungsarbeiten; ~ **in securities** Anlage in Wertpapieren, Wertpapieranlage, Finanzierungs-, Portefeuilleinvestitionen, *(balance*

sheet) Wertpapierbestand; ~ **in foreign securities** Auslandsinvestitionen; ~ **in show pieces** Paradeinvestitionen; ~ **in stocks** Lagerinvestitionen; ~**s in subsidiaries and associated companies** Beteiligungen an Tochter- und Konzerngesellschaften; ~ **in training** Ausbildungsinvestitionen; ~ **at valuation** Effektendepot zum Taxwert; ~**s in war loans** Anlage in Kriegsanleihe; **to attract** ~ **to poorer regions** attraktive Anlagebedingungen für industriell weniger erschlossene Gebiete schaffen; **to bring forward more** ~ Investitionszunahme zustandebringen; **to check** ~ Investitionen (Investitionstätigkeit) bremsen; **to convert** ~ **into a nontaxable form** in eine steuerfreie [Kapital]anlage umwandeln; **to court** ~s Investitionstätigkeit hofieren; **to cut back on** ~ Investitionstätigkeit verringern; **to derive income from an** ~ Einkommen aus einer Vermögensanlage beziehen; **to dole out in overseas** ~ für Investitionen im Ausland auswerfen; **to earmark for** ~ für Investitionszwecke bestimmen; **to effect** ~s Investitionen vornehmen; **to hold down** ~ **in new facilities** Neuanlagegeschäft drosseln; **to make an** ~ Geld anlegen; **to make long-term** ~s langfristig anlegen; **to make** ~**s in real estate** Geld in Grundstücken anlegen, Investitionen auf dem Immobiliensektor vornehmen; **to make a good** ~ vorteilhaft anlegen; **to make greater** ~ mehr investieren; **to place in** ~**s** in Anlagewerten investieren; **to plow** *(US)* **(plough,** *Br.***) in foreign** ~**s** im Ausland anlegen, Auslandsinvestitionen vornehmen; **to realize an** ~ Beteiligung realisieren (abgeben); **to receive £ 500 from** ~**s** 500 Pfund an Kapitaleinkünften haben; **to repatriate earnings from foreign** ~**s** ausländische Anlagenerlöse devisenmäßig vereinnahmen; **to rush into new** ~ überstürzte Investitionen vornehmen; **to single out for** ~ zur Anlage empfehlen; **to slow down** ~ Investitionstempo drosseln; **to switch** ~**s** Anlageveränderungen vornehmen;
~ **account** Anlagekonto, Depot-, Einlage-, Beteiligungskonto, Vermögensänderungskonto, Konto Beteiligungen, *(building society)* Bausparkonto, *(National Savings Bank, Br.)* Postsparkonto; ~ **accounting** Anlagebuchführung; ~ **activities** Investitionstätigkeit; **brisk** ~ **activity** flottes Investitionstempo; **to stImulate** ~ **activity** Investitionstätigkeit beleben; ~ **advice** *(Br.)* Kapitalanlageberatung; ~ **adviser** Anlage-, Effektenberater; **professional** ~ **adviser** hauptberuflicher Anlageberater; ~ **Adviser Act** Anlageberatergesetz; ~ **advisory agreement (contract)** Anlageberatungsvertrag; ~ **advisory service** Anlageberatung; ~ **affiliate** abhängige Kapitalanlagegesellschaft; ~ **aid** Investitionsbeihilfe; **to remove the no-**~ **alibi** Alibi für mangelnde Investitionsbereitschaft beseitigen; ~ **allowance** *(Br.)* Abschreibungen für Investitionen, Steuervergünstigung für Kapitalanlagen, Investitionsfreibetrag, 130%ige Abschreibung für Anlagegüter; ~ **analysis** Anlagenanalyse, -beratung, *(securities)* Portefeuilleberatung; ~ **analyst** Anlagenberater, *(securities)* Portefeuilleberater; ~ **angles** Anlagegesichtspunkte; ~ **anticipation** erwartete Investitionshöhe; ~ **application form** Wertpapieranlageformular; ~ **appraisal** Anlagenbewertung, Rentabilitätsschätzung einer Investition, Investitionsrentabilitätsschätzung; **flexible** ~ **approach** bewegliche (flexible) Anlagepolitik; ~ **area** Anlagebereich; ~ **assistance** Investitionshilfe; **speculative** ~ **attraction** Anreiz zu spekulativer Anlage; ~ **backlogs** Investitionsüberhang; ~ **ban** Investitionsverbot; ~ **bank[er] (banking house)** *(US)* Anlage-, Effekten-, Gründungsbank, Emissionshaus, -bank; **European** ~ **Bank** Europäische Investitionsbank; ~ **banking** Anlage-, Investitions-, Effektenbank-, Emissionsgeschäft, Bankgeschäft in Anlagewerten; ~ **banking firm** Emissionsfirma; ~ **banking functions** Funktionen des Anlagegeschäfts; ~ **banking house** *(US)* Emissionshaus, -bank; ~ **banking job** Anlagen-, Investitionsberatung; ~ **barometer** *(US)* Kursbarometer für Anlagewerte; ~ **bills** Anlagepapiere; ~ **bonds** festverzinsliche Anlagepapiere, -werte; ~ **bonus** Investitionszulage; ~ **boom** Investitionskonjunktur; ~ **broker** Makler für hochwertige Anlagepapiere; ~ **business** Anlagegeschäft; ~ **buying** Anlagekäufe; ~ **capital** Anlage-, Investitionskapital; ~ **certificate** Investmentanteil, -zertifikat; ~ **charges** Anlagekosten; ~ **clauses** Anlagebestimmungen; ~ **climate** Investitionsklima; ~ **club** Verein für Kapitalanlageinteressenten; ~ **commitments** Anlageverpflichtungen; ~ **commitment process** Entstehung der Anlagebereitschaft; ~ **committee** Investitionsausschuß, *(investment fund)* Anlagenausschuß; ~ **community** Anlagepublikum.
investment company Kapitalanlage-, Investmentgesellschaft, Effektenemissionsgeschäfte betreibende Bank;
closed-end ~ Kapitalanlagegesellschaft mit geschlossenem Anlagefonds; **diversified** ~ Kapitalanlagegesellschaft mit gesetzlich vorgeschriebener Risikostreuung; **management** ~ Kapital-

anlagegesellschaft mit freizügiger Anlagepolitik; **open-end** ~ Investmentgesellschaft mit beliebiger Emissionshöhe; **registered** ~ zugelassene Kapitalanlagegesellschaft; **regulated** ~ *(US)* steuerlich privilegierte Kapitalanlagegesellschaft;
~ **Act** Kapitalanlagegesetz; ~ **portfolio** Wertpapierfonds einer Investmentgesellschaft.
investment | consultant Anlageberater; ~ **contract** Kapitalanlagevertrag; **public** ~ **control** staatliche Investitionskontrolle; **to scrap** ~ **controls** Investitionskontrollen weniger scharf handhaben; ~ **costs** Investitionsaufwand; ~ **counsel[or]** *(US)* Effekten-, Anlageberater; ~ **counselling** *(US)* Anlageberatung; ~ **counselling firm** *(US)* Anlageberatungsfirma; ~ **counselling position** *(US)* Beratungsposition für Investitionsfragen; ~ **credit** Investitions-, langfristiger Anlagekredit; ~ **criterion** Investitionskriterium; ~ **currency** *(Br.)* Fremdwährungsmittel für Auslandsinvestitionen; ~ **currency market** *(Br.)* Kapitalmarkt für Fremdwährungsinvestitionen; **to go through an** ~ **currency pool** *(Br.)* Devisen für Auslandsinvestitionen über einen Dollarsonderfonds erwerben; ~ **cycle** Investitionszyklus; ~ **dealer** *(US)* Effektenhändler; ~ **decision** *(investment trust)* Investitionsentschluß, -entscheidung; **capital** ~ **decision-making** Investitionsentscheidung; ~ **demand** Anlagebedürfnis, Investitionsnachfrage; ~ **demand curve** Nachfragekurve für Investitionskapital; ~ **department** Effektenabteilung; ~ **disposition** Anlageverfügung; ~ **dollars** *(Br.)* für Auslandsinvestitionen verfügbare Dollarguthaben; ~ **earnings** Anlage-, Beteiligungserträge, -erlöse, -erträgnisse; ~ **elimination** Anlagenausgliederung; ~ **enthusiasm** Anlagebegeisterung; ~ **environment** Umwelteinflüsse des Anlagegeschäfts; ~ **estate** *(investment trust)* Anlage-, Kapitalvermögen; ~ **expenditures** Investitionsaufwand; ~ **expense** Anlagenaufwand, Investitionskosten; ~ **experience** Anlagenerfahrung, Erfahrungen im Investitionsgeschäft; ~ **failure** Fehlinvestition; ~ **famine** bitter fehlende Investitionen (Investitionsvorhaben); ~ **financing** Finanzierung von Investitionen, Anlagenfinanzierung; ~ **firm** Beteiligungsfirma; ~ **function** Investitionsfunktion; ~ **fund** Anlagekapital, *(investment trust)* Investmentfonds, Fonds einer Kapitalanlagegesellschaft; **open-end** ~ **fund** Investmentfonds mit unbeschränkter Anteilezahl; **open-end real-property** ~ **fund** offener Immobilienfonds; ~ **fund certificate** Investmentanteil, -zertifikat; ~ **fund unit** *(Br.)* Investmentanteil, -zertifikat; ~ **gain** Anlagegewinn, Investitionsvorteil; ~ **goal** Anlageziel; ~ **goods** Investitionsgüter; **high-quality** ~ **goods** hochwertige Investitionsgüter; ~ **grant** Investitionszuschuß; ~ **guaranty treaty** Investitionsschutzabkommen; ~ **habits** Anlagegewohnheiten; ~ **holdings** Anlagenbesitz; ~ **house** Anlageberatungsfirma; ~ **incentive** Investitionsanreiz; ~ **income** Einkünfte aus Kapitalvermögen, Kapitaleinkünfte, -einkommen, -erträge, *(insurer's dividend, US)* Gewinnbeteiligung; **net** ~ **income** Nettoanlageeinkommen; ~ **income surcharge** Steuerzuschlag für Kapitalerträge, Steuerzuschlag für Einkünfte aus Kapitalvermögen; ~ **industry** Investitionsgüterindustrie; ~ **inflow** *(building society)* Zugänge an Bausparverträgen; ~ **institution** [Kapital]anlageinstitut; ~ **intentions** Investitionsabsichten, Kapitalanlagevorhaben; ~ **interest** Anlageinteresse; ~ **ledger** Konto Investierungen (Anlagen), Anlagekonto; ~ **letter** *(US)* Garantiezusage für den Nichtverkauf von Aktien; ~**-like feature** anlageähnlicher Charakter; ~ **loan** Investitionsanleihe, -kredit; ~ **loss** Anlageverlust; ~ **management** Verwaltung von Kapitalanlagen, Anlagen-, Effektenverwaltung *(investment trust)* Anlagenberatung; ~ **management service** Beratungsdienst in Vermögensfragen; ~ **manager** *(investment fund)* Anlageberater; ~ **market** Markt für Anlagewerte, Anlagemarkt; ~ **matters** Anlagefragen; ~ **media** *(US)* Anlagemöglichkeiten; ~ **merit** Anlagevorteil; ~ **middlemen** Anlagenvermittler; ~ **multiplier** Investitionsmultiplikator; ~ **newsletter** Anlageinformationsbrief; ~ **object** Anlageobjekt; ~ **objective** Anlageziel; ~ **opportunities** Anlagemöglichkeiten; ~ **outlays** Investitionsaufwand; ~ **outlet** Anlage-, Investitionsmöglichkeit; ~ **owner** Anlagenbesitzer; ~ **paper** Anlagepapier, -titel; **to skew the** ~ **pattern towards shorter-lived projects** Investitionstätigkeit einseitig auf kurzfristige Projekte verschieben; ~ **payment sales** Abzahlungsgeschäft; ~ **performance** Anlagetätigkeit, Investitionsleistung; **[capital]** ~ **plan** Investitionsprogramm, -vorhaben; **monthly** ~ **plan** Sparvertrag mit monatlichen Raten; ~ **policy** Investitions-, Anlagepolitik, *(investment fund)* Anlagebestimmungen; ~**s portfolio** Effektenportefeuille; ~ **premium** Investitionszulage; ~ **problem** Anlageproblem; ~ **process** Investitionsprozeß; ~ **productivity** Kapitalproduktivität; ~ **profit** Kapitalgewinn, Gewinn aus Beteiligungen; ~ **program(me)** Anlage-, Investitionsprogramm; ~ **project** Investitionspro-

jekt, -vorhaben; ~ **promotion** Förderung von Investitionsvorhaben, Investitionsförderung; ~ **property** Investitionsgrundstück; ~ **proposal** Investitionsantrag; ~ **purpose** Anlagezweck; **for ~ purposes** als Kapitalanlage; ~ **quota** Investitionsquote; ~ **rating** (US) Anlagenbewertung, -schätzung; ~ **ratio** Investitionsquote; **good ~ records** gute Investitionsergebnisse; ~ **recovery** Anlagendeckung; **to trigger an ~ recovery** Wiederbelebung der Investitionstätigkeit auslösen; ~ **requirements** Anlagenbedarf; ~ **reserve** Kapitalreserve; ~ **reserve fund** für Zeiten wirtschaftlichen Niedergangs zur Verfügung stehender Investitionsfonds, Kapitalverlustrücklage; ~ **restrictions** Anlage-, Investitionsbeschränkungen; ~ **return** (revenue, Br.) Erträge aus vorgenommenen Investitionen, Kapitalverzinsung, -ertrag, (shares) Kapital-, Anlagerendite; ~ **risk** Investitions-, Anlagerisiko; ~ **route** Investitionsweg; ~ **rules** Anlagerichtlinien; ~ **sales drive** Werbefeldzug für Kapitalanlagen; ~ **saving** Investmentsparen; **~-saving curve** Investitionssparkurve; ~ **schedule** Investitionstabelle; ~ **securities** (US) Inhaberschuldverschreibungen, erstklassige Anlagepapiere, -werte; ~ **services** Effektenberatungstätigkeit; **mutual ~ share** Investmentzertifikat; ~ **slump** Tiefstand bei Anlageinvestitionen; ~ **spending** Ausgaben für Investitionszwecke, Investitionsausgaben, Kapitalinvestition; ~ **spurt** Investitionsanstrengung; ~ **standards** Anlagegrundsätze; ~ **stock** Anlagepapiere; ~ **sum** Investitionsbetrag; ~ **supervision** Anlagenüberwachung; ~ **surcharge** Steuerzuschlag auf Kapitaleinkünfte; ~ **surge** Investitionsflut; ~ **target** Investitionsziel; ~ **tax credit** steuerliche Erleichterungen (Steuervergünstigungen) für Investitionen, steuerliche Investitionsprämie; ~ **tax incentive** steuerlicher Anreiz für Investitionen, Investitionszulage; ~ **total** Investitionsbestand; ~ **trend** Investitionstendenz.

investment trust Investmenttrust, -gesellschaft, Effektenfinanzierung, Kapitalanlagegesellschaft;
closed-end ~ Investmentgesellschaft, Kapitalgesellschaft mit konstantem Anlagenkapital; **fixed ~** Effektengesellschaft mit festgelegtem Effektenbestand; **management ~** nach eigenem Ermessen anlegende Kapitalgesellschaft;
~ **buying** Anlagenkäufe einer Investmentgesellschaft; ~ **certificate** an der Börse gehandeltes Investmentzertifikat, Anteilschein; ~ **company** Kapitalanlagegesellschaft; ~ **manager** Geschäftsführer einer Kapitalanlagegesellschaft; ~ **securities** Fondswerte eines Investmenttrustes.

investment|turnover Kapitalumschlag; ~ **underwriter** (US) Emissionshaus; ~ **upturn** Investitionsaufschwung; ~ **value** Investitions-, Anlagewert; ~ **vehicle** Anlagemedium; ~ **yield** Anlageverzinsung.

investor Kapitalanleger, -geber, (building society) Bausparer;
~s Anlagepublikum;
big ~ Großanleger; **foreign ~** ausländischer Kapitalanleger; **high-bracket ~** Kapitalgeber mit hoher Einkommensteuerprogression; **individual ~** einzelner Kapitalanleger; **institutional ~** Kapitalsammelstelle, institutioneller Anleger; **long-term ~** Daueranleger; **private ~** privater Anleger; **professional ~** Kapitalanlagestelle; **seasoned ~** erfahrener Kapitalanleger; **small ~** Kleinanleger; **trusting ~** vertrauensvoller Kapitalanleger; **would-be ~** Anlageinteressent;
~**'s balance** (building society) Bausparguthaben; ~ **confidence** Vertrauen des Anlagepublikums; ~ **demand** Anlegerbedürfnisse; ~**'s interest** (building society) Bausparzinsen; ~**'s pessimism** Anlagepessimismus; ~ **protection society** Schutzvereinigung von Wertpapierbesitzern; ~ **relations** Anlegerpflege, Pflege des Anlagepublikums.

inviability (diplomats) Unverletzbarkeit, Immunität.
inviable unverletzlich.
invigilate (v.) (Br.) Aufsicht führen;
~ **at an examination** Examenskandidaten beaufsichtigen.
invigilation (Br.) Aufsichtsführung, Beaufsichtigung.
invigilator (Br.) Aufsicht[sführender], Aufseher.
invigorate (v.) **business** Wirtschaft ankurbeln.
invigoration of business Ankurbelung der Wirtschaft.
invisible|s unsichtbarer Handel, unsichtbare Dienstleistungen, (balance of payment) Dienstleistungsverkehr mit dem Ausland;
~ **(a.)** unsichtbar;
~ **balance** unsichtbare Ein- und Ausfuhr, Dienstleistungsbilanz; ~ **earnings** Einkünfte aus unsichtbaren Geschäftstransaktionen; ~ **exports** unsichtbare Ausfuhr, aktive Dienstleistungen; ~ **imports** unsichtbare Einfuhren, passive Dienstleistungen; ~ **ink** unsichtbare Tinte; ~ **items of trade** unsichtbare Posten der Leistungsbilanz; ~ **supply** unsichtbare Bestände; ~ **trade** Dienstleistungsverkehr.

invitation Einladung, Aufforderung, (solicitation) Ausschreibung;
written ~ schriftliche Einladung;
~ **to bid** (US) Ausschreibung, Aufforderung zur Abgabe von Angeboten (Submissionen); ~ **to contract** Aufforderung zur Abgabe eines Angebots; ~ **to lunch** Einladung zum Mittagessen; ~ **to the public to subscribe to a loan** Subskriptionsaufforderung, -einladung für eine Anleihe; ~ **to tender (for tenders)** Konkurrenzausschreibung; **public ~ to tender** öffentliche Ausschreibung, Aufforderung zur Abgabe von Angeboten, Angebotsausschreibung; **closed (restricted) ~ for tenders** beschränkte Ausschreibung; ~**s for tenders with discretionary award of contracts** freihändige Ausschreibung; ~ **to treat** (contract law, Br.) Aufforderung, ein Angebot abzugeben, Geschäftsanbahnung;
to accept an ~ einer Einladung Folge leisten; **to be an ~ to buy** zum Kauf einladen; **to cancel (decline, refuse) an ~** Einladung absagen; **to come at s. one's ~** jds. Einladung Folge leisten; **to mail (send) out ~** Einladungen verschicken; **to send out an ~ to tender** Ausschreibung veranstalten, ausschreiben;
~ **card** Einladungskarte; ~ **list** Einladungsliste; ~ **performance** Privatvorstellung.

invite (v.) einladen, auffordern, ausschreiben;
~ **(v.) s. o. in** j. hereinbitten; ~ **applications for a position** Stelle ausschreiben; ~ **applications for shares** (Br.) zur Aktienzeichnung auffordern; ~ **bids** (US) Auftrag ausschreiben; ~ **public competition** öffentlichen Wettbewerb ausschreiben; ~ **criticism** Kritik herausfordern; ~ **discussion** um Diskussionsbeiträge bitten; ~ **offers** zu Angeboten auffordern; ~ **shareholders to subscribe the capital** Aktionäre zur Zeichnung auffordern; ~ **subscriptions for a loan** Anleihe [zur Zeichnung] auflegen; ~ **tenders for a building** Gebäude im Submissionswege ausschreiben; ~ **tenders for a piece of work** Ausschreibung veranstalten.
invited error bewußt herbeigeführter Verfahrensfehler.
invitee geschäftlicher Besucher.
inviting country einladendes Land.
invocation Anrufung, Beschwörung;
~ **of aid** Hilfsersuchen; ~ **of an article** Berufung auf einen Artikel; **colo(u)rable cause or ~ of jurisdiction** Zuständigkeitsbegründung im Fall wissentlich falscher Anschuldigung; ~ **of papers** (law court) Anforderung von Akten, Aktenanforderung.
invoice [Waren]rechnung, -verzeichnis, Begleitrechnung, Lieferschein, Faktura, Nota, (delivery) Sendung, Lieferung;
as indicated in enclosed ~ laut beiliegender Rechnung; **as per ~** laut Faktura (Rechnung); **as per ~ on the other side** laut umstehender Rechnung; **on examining (checking) your ~** beim Durchgehen Ihrer Faktura; **on transmitting the ~** bei Übersendung der Faktura;
commercial ~ Handelsfaktura; **consular ~** Konsulatsfaktura; ~ **continued** Rechnungsübertrag; **corrected ~** berichtigte Rechnung; **customs ~** Zollfaktura; **itemized ~** spezifizierte Rechnung; **legalized ~** beglaubigte Faktura; **original ~** Originalfaktura; **postdated ~** nachdatierte Rechnung; **priced ~** mit Preisen versehene Faktura; **proforma ~** Proforma-, fingierte Rechnung, Konsignationsfaktura; **provisional ~** vorläufige Rechnung; **purchase ~** Einkaufsrechnung; **sales ~** Ausgangs-, Verkaufsrechnung; **shipping ~** (US) Versandrechnung; **standardized ~** Normalrechnung; **sterling ~** in Pfund zahlbare Rechnung; **supplementary ~** Zusatzrechnung; **supplier's ~** Lieferantenrechnung; ~ **total** Rechnungsbetrag;
~ **(v.)** Faktura erteilen, fakturieren, (enter in invoice) in Rechnung stellen;
~ **from a country** einklarieren;
to cancel an ~ Rechnung ungültig machen; **to check an ~** Probe auf eine Rechnung machen, Rechnung überprüfen; **to enter in the ~** auf die Rechnung setzen; **to follow up ~s** [den Eingang von] Rechnungen überwachen; **to get the consular ~s legalized** Konsulatsfakturen beglaubigen lassen; **to handle ~s** Rechnungen bearbeiten; **to make out an ~** Rechnung ausstellen (schreiben); **to order against ~** auf Rechnung bestellen; **to pass an ~** Rechnung bewilligen; **to prepare an ~** Rechnung ausstellen; **to question an ~** Rechnung beanstanden; **to receipt an ~** Rechnung quittieren; **to sell at a loss on the ~** unter dem fakturierten Wert verkaufen; **to verify by ~s** mit Rechnungen belegen;
~ **amount** Rechnungsbetrag; ~ **auditing** Rechnungsprüfung; ~ **book** Einkaufs-, [Eingangs]fakturen-, Rechnungsbuch; ~ **bureau** Fakturenbüro; ~ **clerk** Fakturist; ~ **cost** Bruttoeinkaufspreis; ~ **department** Fakturenabteilung; **combination sales-order-shipper ~ form** kombiniertes Auftrags- und Versandrechnungsformular; ~ **number** Rechnungsnummer; ~

price Rechnungs-, Fakturapreis; ~ **register** Faktura-, Einkaufsbuch; ~ **stamp** Fakturastempel; ~ **supervision** Überwachung eingehender Rechnungen; ~ **value** Faktura-, Rechnungswert; ~ **weight** Rechnungsgewicht; ~ **work** Fakturierungsarbeiten.

invoiced, as laut Faktura (Rechnung);
~ **amount** Rechnungsbetrag, -preis; ~ **charge** fakturierter Betrag; ~ **goods** fakturierte Waren; ~ **price** fakturierter Preis, Fakturapreis, Rechnungsbetrag; ~ **sale** fakturierter Umsatz.

invoicing Rechnungserteilung, -ausstellung;
~ **of accounts** Rechnungserstellung; ~ **of goods** Fakturieren, Fakturierung;
~ **machine** Fakturiermaschine.

invoke (v.) anführen, zitieren;
~ **the aid of the court** Gericht anrufen; ~ **an article** sich auf einen Artikel berufen; ~ **papers into court** Urkunden als Beweismaterial zulassen; ~ **the provisions of a statute** sich auf Gesetzesbestimmungen berufen;
~ **a precedent** Präzedenzfall anführen.

involuntary unfreiwillig, unabsichtlich, unter Zwang;
~ **action** willenlose Handlung; ~ **assignment for the benefit of creditors** zur Befriedigung der Gläubiger zwangsweise vorgenommene Vermögensübertragung auf einen Treuhänder; ~ **bankrupt** Zwangsgemeinschuldner; ~ **bankruptcy** durch Gläubigerantrag herbeigeführter Konkurs; ~ **conversion** Zwangskurs; ~ **deposit** zufälliges Verwahrungsverhältnis; ~ **discontinuance** Verfahrensaussetzung von Amts wegen; ~ **indebtedness** unaufschiebbare Zahlungsverpflichtung; ~ **liquidation** Zwangsliquidation; ~ **manslaughter** fahrlässige Tötung; ~ **payment** Zahlung aufgrund arglistiger Täuschung; ~ **servitude** Zwangsarbeit; ~ **transfer** Forderungsübergang kraft Gesetzes.

involve (v.) (draw into) hineinziehen, verwickeln, (have as result) mit sich bringen, zur Folge haben, einschließen, -begreifen;
~ **s. o. in a sorry business** j. in eine unangenehme Sache mit hineinziehen; ~ **additional charges** mit weiteren Kosten verbunden sein; ~ **s. o. in a crime** j. zum Komplizen eines Verbrechens machen; ~ **o. s. in debt** sich verschulden, sich in Schulden stürzen; ~ **much expense** große Unkosten verursachen, hohe Kosten nach sich ziehen; ~ **a great increase in the national debt** erhebliche Erhöhung der Staatsverschuldung auslösen (zur Folge haben); ~ **the forfeiture of property** Einziehung des Vermögens zur Folge haben; ~ **s. one's living in London** jds. Wohnsitz in London notwendig machen (bedingen); ~ **s. o. in a quarrel** j. in einen Streit hineinziehen; ~ **s. o. in trouble** sich Schwierigkeiten einbrocken.

involved verwickelt, kompliziert, (included) einbegriffen;
amount ~ betroffener Betrag, (law court) Streitwert; **personally** ~ persönlich engagiert (betroffen);
to be ~ auf dem Spiele stehen; **to be deeply** ~ **in debt** stark (hoch) verschuldet sein; **to be** ~ **in s. one's ruin** in jds. Zusammenbruch mit hineingerissen werden; **to become** ~ **in one's speech** sich verheddern; **to get** ~ **in a conspiracy** in eine Verschwörung verwickelt werden.

involvement verwickelte Angelegenheit, Schwierigkeit, [Geld]verlegenheit, (engagement) Beteiligtsein, Engagiertsein;
financial ~ finanzielle Folgewirkung;
~ **in business** wirtschaftliche Verquickung;
to run down one's ~ sein Engagement abbauen.

invulnerable unverwundbar;
~ **arguments** unanfechtbare Argumente.

inward binnen-, inländisch, ins Inland;
~ **bill of lading** Importkonnossement; ~**-bound** auf der Heimreise (Heimfahrt) begriffen, nach der Heimat bestimmt; ~ **duty** (Br.) Eingangs-, Binnenzoll; ~ **manifest** Zolleinfuhrerklärung; ~ **meaning** eigentliche Bedeutung; ~ **passage** Rückfahrt; ~ **trade** (Br.) Einfuhrhandel; ~ **traffic of a port** Schiffsverkehr im Hafen.

ionosphere Ionosphäre.

iota (fig.) Kleinigkeit, Tüttelchen;
not an ~ kein Jota;
not to yield an ~ **of one's privileges** kein Jota nachgeben.

IOU Schuldschein, -anerkenntnis.

ipso jure unmittelbar kraft Gesetzes, von Rechts wegen.

iron Eisen;
as hard as ~ so hart wie Stahl, stahlhart;
shooting ~ (sl.) Schießeisen; **soft** ~ Weicheisen;
~ (v.) bügeln;
~ **out initial difficulties** Anfangsschwierigkeiten bereinigen; ~ **out a road with a steam roller** Straße mit der Dampfwalze glattwalzen;
to have a few more ~**s in the fire** mehrere Eisen im Feuer haben;

to put a man in ~s j. Fesseln anlegen; **to rule with a rod of** ~ mit eiserner Hand regieren; **to strike while the** ~ **is hot** das Eisen schmieden, solange es heiß ist;
~ (a.) eisern, (fig.) unerbittlich, grausam, kalt;
to have an ~ **constitution** eiserne Konstitution haben; ~ **concrete** Stahlbeton; ~ **curtain** (pol.) eiserner Vorhang; ~ **dross** Hochofenschlacke; ~ **and Steel Federation** (Br.) Eisen- und 0Stahlvereinigung; ~ **foundry** Eisengießerei; **to rule with an** ~ **hand** mit eiserner Hand regieren; ~ **horse** (coll.) Dampfroß, Lokomotive; ~ **law of wages** eisernes Lohngesetz; ~ **lung** (med.) eiserne Lunge; ~ **man** (sl., US) Dollar; ~ **note** (fam.) erstklassig abgesicherter Schuldschein; ~ **ore** Eisenerz; ~ **ore mining** Eisenerzbergbau; ~ **and nonferous metals production** Eisen- und Nichteisenmetallerzeugung; ~ **ration** eiserne Ration, eiserner Bestand; ~**-safe clause** Geldschrankklausel; ~ **scrap** Schrotteisen; ~ **and steel shares** Montanaktien; ~ **will** (fam.) eiserner Wille.

ironbound | coast zerklüftete Küste; ~ **traditions** erstarrte Überlieferungen.

ironclad (fig.) geharnischt, starr;
~ **clause** unumgehbare Klausel; ~ **motor** Panzermotor; ~ **oath** unverbrüchlicher Eid; ~ **rule** unumstößliche Regel.

ironmaster (Br.) Eisenhüttenbesitzer.

ironmonger (Br.) Metallwarenhändler.

ironsmith Grobschmied.

ironwork Eisenkonstruktion;
~s Eisenhütte.

ironworker Hüttenarbeiter, Stahlbaumonteur.

ironworking industry eisenverarbeitende Industrie.

irony of fate Ironie des Schicksals.

irradiate (v.) **a patient** Patienten [ultraviolett] bestrahlen.

irradiation Strahlungsintensivität;
~ **injury** Strahlenschädigung.

irrebuttable unwiderlegbar;
~ **presumption** unwiderlegbare Vermutung.

irreclaimable (soil) nicht anbaufähig (kulturfähig).

irreconcilable unversöhnlich;
~ **enemies** unversöhnliche Gegner; **two** ~ **statements** zwei widersprüchliche Angaben.

irrecoverable debts uneinbringliche (nicht eintreibbare) Schulden.

irredeemable (annuities, bonds) unkündbar, untilgbar, unablösbar, (paper currency) nicht einlösbar;
~ **annuity** unablösbare Rente; ~ **bonds** nicht tilgbare (unkündbare) Schuldverschreibungen; ~ **currency** nicht in Gold einlösbare Währung; ~ **debenture** (Br.) unkündbare Obligation; ~ **foreign exchange standard** Golddevisenwährung; ~ **loss** unersetzlicher Verlust; ~ **paper money** nicht einlösbares Papiergeld; ~ **security** Obligation ohne Tilgungsrate.

irredentist Irredentist.

irreducible minimum for repairs Mindestbetrag für Reparaturen.

irrefutable nicht widerlegbar, unwiderlegbar;
~ **fact** unbestreitbare Tatsache.

irregular (mil.) Zeitfreiwilliger, (partisan) Freischärler, Partisan, (worker) gelegentlich Beschäftigter;
~s zweite Wahl, minderwertige Produkte;
~ (a.) (law) regel-, vorschriftswidrig, (stock exchange) uneinheitlich, schwankend, nicht einheitlich, (mil.) irregulär;
~ **action of a machine** ungleichmäßiger Lauf einer Maschine; ~ **conduct** ungehöriges Benehmen; ~ **customer** Laufkunde; ~ **deposit** Sammel-, Summenverwahrung; ~ **document** unvollständige Urkunde; ~ **employment** Gelegenheitsbeschäftigung; ~ **indorsement** ungenaues Giro; **at** ~ **intervals** in unregelmäßigen Abständen; ~ **judgment** von der ständigen Rechtssprechung abweichendes Urteil; ~ **marriage** nicht voll anerkannte Ehe; ~ **payments** unregelmäßige Zahlungen; ~ **physician** Kurpfuscher; ~ **proceedings** ungesetzliches (unter Formfehlern leidendes) Verfahren; ~ **process** mangelhafte Zustellungsurkunde; ~ **troops** irreguläre Truppen.

irregularity Unregelmäßigkeit, Vorschrifts-, Regelwidrigkeit, abnormer Zustand, (law) Formfehler, Verfahrensverstoß, (stock exchange) Uneinheitlichkeit;
on account of an ~ **in the indorsement** wegen eines Formfehlers im Giro;
legal ~ formaler Verfahrensverstoß, Verfahrensmangel;
~ **of appointment** verfahrenswidrige Bestallung; ~ **of ground** Unebenheit des Bodens; ~ **in the proceedings** Verfahrensmangel; ~ **in service** Zustellungsmangel;
to commit an ~ sich Unregelmäßigkeiten zuschulden kommen lassen.

irregularly drawn Formfehler in der Ausstellung.

irrelevancy Nebensächlichkeit.

irrelevant belanglos, irrelevant, *(foreign to the subject)* nicht zur Sache gehörig, *(law)* unerheblich;
~ **allegation** prozeßunerhebliches Vorbringen; ~ **answer** unschlüssige Klageerwiderung;
to make ~ **remarks** nicht beim Thema bleiben.

irremediable unheilbar.

irremovability Unabsetzbarkeit, Unkündbarkeit.

irremovable nicht absetzbar, unabsetzbar, unkündbar, *(pauper)* nicht abschiebbar.

irreparable unersetzlich;
~ **damages** Schadensersatz nicht wiedergutzumachenden Schadens; ~ **injury** nicht wiedergutzumachender Schaden; ~ **loss** unersetzlicher Verlust.

irrepealable unwiderruflich, unersetzbar.

irrepleviable *(pledge)* uneinlösbar.

irreproachable conduct untadeliges Verhalten.

irresistable, irresistible|force unwiderstehliche Gewalt; ~ **impulse** *(criminal)* unwiderstehlicher Trieb.

irrespective of ohne Rücksicht auf, unabhängig von, ganz gleich ob;
~ **franchise** ohne Freiteil.

irresponsibility Nichthaftbarkeit, Nichtverantwortlichkeit, *(incapability)* Unzurechnungsfähigkeit.

irresponsible *(law)* Unzurechnungsfähiger;
~ *(a.)* unverantwortlich, verantwortungslos, *(insolvent)* zahlungsunfähig, *(not answerable)* nicht verantwortlich, unzurechnungsfähig;
to be quite ~ unzurechnungsfähig sein; **to entrust serious business to** ~**s** wichtige Geschäftsangelegenheiten ungeeigneten Leuten übertragen;
~ **behavio(u)r** verantwortungsloses Benehmen; ~ **debtor** unzuverlässiger Schuldner; ~ **servant** nicht haftender Erfüllungsgehilfe.

irretrievable unersetzlich, unwiederbringlich;
~ **loss** unersetzlicher Verlust.

irretrievably broken *(marriage)* unheilbar zerrüttet.

irreverential respektlos.

irreversible nicht umkehrbar, unwiderruflich;
~ **lease** unkündbarer Pachtvertrag.

irrevocability Unwiderruflichkeit.

irrevocable unwiderruflich, unumstößlich;
~ **[letter of] credit** *(US)* unwiderruflich bestätigtes Akkreditiv, unwiderruflicher Kreditbrief; ~ **decision** unwiderrufliche Entscheidung; ~ **judgment** unumstößliches Urteil; ~ **statement** unwiderrufliche Erklärung; ~ **trust** unwiderrufliche Stiftung.

irrigable bewässerbar.

irrigate *(v.)* bewässern, berieseln;
~ **desert areas** Wüstengebiete bewässern; ~ **by means of water channels** mit Hilfe kleiner Kanäle bewässern.

irrigation Bewässerung, Berieselung;
artificial ~ künstliche Bewässerung;
~ **bond** *(US)* Schuldverschreibungen zur Finanzierung von Bewässerungsprojekten; ~ **canal (channel)** Bewässerungsgraben, -kanal; ~ **district** Bewässerungsbezirk; ~ **plant (works)** Bewässerungsanlagen; ~ **scheme** Bewässerungsprojekt; ~ **system** Bewässerungssystem; ~ **water** aus Bewässerungsprojekten gewonnenes Wasser.

irritant clause *(Scot. law)* Pachtverfalls-, Nichtigkeitsklausel.

island Insel, *(advertising)* alleinstehend, *(traffic)* Verkehrsinsel;
floating ~ Eisberg; **street** ~ Verkehrsinsel;
~ *(v.)* auf einer Insel aussetzen;
~ **position** *(advertising)* Inselplazierung; ~ **site** Inselgelände; ~ **universe** Milchstraßensystem.

islander Inselbewohner.

isobaric chart Druckwetterkarte.

isolate *(v.)* isolieren.

isolated isoliert, abgesondert;
~ **case** Einzel-, Sonderfall; ~ **farm** Einzelfarm; ~ **house** einzelstehendes Haus; ~ **instance** Einzelfall; ~ **selling** homogenes Monopol; ~ **transaction** *(US)* zulässiges Einzelgeschäft, vereinzeltes Rechtsgeschäft.

isolation Absonderung, *(pol.)* Isolierung;
~ **hospital** Quarantänekrankenhaus, Seuchenlazarett.

isolationism Isolationismus;
to retreat into ~ isolationistische Politik wieder aufnehmen.

isolationist Isolationist;
to turn ~ sich dem Isolationismus zuwenden.

isolationistic isolationistisch;
~ **policy** isolationistische Politik, Politik des Isolationismus.

isometric standard Preisindexwährung.

isonomy Rechts-, Gesetzesgleichheit.

issuable emittierbar, emissionsfähig, *(law)* anstehend, schlüssig;
~ **defence** sachliche Einwendung; ~ **matter** zur Entscheidung anstehende Sache; ~ **term** anstehender Gerichtstermin.

issuance *(US)* Ausgabe, Aus-, Verteilung;
~ **of checks** *(US)* Scheckausstellung; ~ **of a deed** *(US)* Ausstellung einer Urkunde; ~ **of a law** Erlaß eines Gesetzes; ~ **of licence** *(US)* Lizenzerteilung; ~ **of material** *(US)* Materialausgabe; ~ **of notes** Wechselausstellung; ~ **of an order** Erlaß einer Verfügung (Verordnung); ~ **of orders** *(mil.)* Befehlsausgabe; ~ **of paper money** Papiergeldausgabe; ~ **of passports** Paßausstellung; ~ **of policy** Ausfertigung einer Police; ~ **of rations** Rationenausgabe; ~ **of shares (stocks,** *US)* Aktienausgabe, -emission; ~ **of a visa** *(US)* Visumausstellung.

issue *(bill of exchange)* Ausstellung, *(common law)* klägerische Zusammenstellung des Prozeßmaterials, *(distribution)* Verabfolgung, Ausgabe, Lieferung, *(income from land)* Einkünfte aus Land- und Forstwirtschaft, *(law court)* Streitfrage, -punkt, Fall, *(loan)* Begebung, Auflegung, *(mil.)* Ausgabe, Verteilung, *(newspaper)* Nummer, Ausgabe, *(of order)* Erlaß, Ausgabe, *(pol.)* Streit-, Kern-, Angelpunkt, *(presentation)* Vorzeigung, *(proceeds)* Erlös, Ertrag, *(progeny)* Kind[er], Abkommen-, Nachkommen[schaft], Leibeserben, *(publishing)* Herausgabe, Ausgabe, Veröffentlichung, *(result)* Ergebnis, Ausgang, Resultat, *(securities)* Emission, Reihe, Ausgabe, Serie;
at ~ strittig, streitig, im Streit befangen; **capable of** ~ emissionsfähig; **irrelevant to the** ~ rechtlich unerheblich; **per** ~ je Ausgabe; **without** ~ kinderlos, ohne Nachkommenschaft;
bond ~ Anleiheemission; **cabinet** ~ Kabinettfrage; **capital** ~**s** Emissionstätigkeit; **collateral** ~ Nebenfrage; **debenture** ~ Emission von Schuldverschreibungen, Obligationenausgabe; **domestic** ~ Inlandsemission; **feigned** ~ hypothetische Streitfrage; **first** ~ erste Serie; **formal** ~ verfahrensmäßig zulässige Einlassung; **free** ~ **and entry** freies Kommen und Gehen; **fresh** ~ neue Serie; **general** ~ *(law)* allgemeines Bestreiten; **high-risk** ~**s** risikoreiche Werte; **home-currency** ~**s** im Inland ausgegebene Banknoten; **immaterial** ~ unwesentlicher Einwand, nicht entscheidungserhebliche Frage; **industrial** ~**s** Industrieemissionen, -werte, -papiere, -anleihen; **inferior** ~ Unterpariausgabe; **internal** ~ Inlandsemission; **junior** ~**s** durch nachstehende Hypothek gesicherte Obligationsserie, *(shares)* junge Aktien; **legal** ~ Rechtsfrage; **legitimate** ~ eheliche Nachkommen; ~ **living** lebende Nachkommen; **main** ~ Kernpunkt; **male** ~ männliche Nachkommenschaft; **master** ~ Hauptproblem, -streitpunkt; **material** ~ wesentlicher Einwand, für die Entscheidung bedeutsame Frage; **note** ~ Banknotenausgabe; **original** ~ Originalausgabe; **privileged** ~**s** bereinigte Emissionen; **public** ~ öffentliche Emission; **real** ~ eigentliches Problem; **recent** ~ Neuemission; **reduced** ~ Minderausgabe; **second** ~ zweite Serie; **security** ~ Wertpapieremission; **senior** ~ mit Vorrechten ausgestattete Anleiheausgabe; **share** ~ Aktienausgabe; **side** ~ Nebenfrage; **small** ~ Kleinverkauf; **special** ~ Sondereinwendungen, Bestreiten einzelner Punkte; **stock** ~ *(US)* Aktienausgabe; **superior** ~ Überpariausgabe; ~**s traded** gehandelte Aktien; **unfavo(u)rable** ~ ungünstiger Ausgang;
~ **of assessment** Fertigstellung einer Steuerveranlagung; **[new]** ~ **of bank-notes** Banknotenausgabe; ~ **of a bill of exchange** Wechselausstellung; ~ **of bonds** Ausgabe von Obligationen; **serial** ~ **of bonds** Serienemission, Emission in Serien; **further** ~ **of capital** Kapitalerhöhung; ~ **of a check** *(US)* (cheque, *Br.*) Scheckausstellung; ~ **of new coinage** Ausgabe neuer Münzen; ~**s of the day** Tagesfragen; ~ **of debentures** Obligationenausgabe, *(Br.)* Pfandbriefausgabe; ~ **of a dispute** juristische Streitfrage; **free** ~ **and entry** freies Kommen und Gehen; ~ **of an estate** Einkünfte aus Grundbesitz; ~ **of fact** Sachverhalt, Tatfrage, -sache; **special** ~ **on Germany** *(newspaper)* Deutschlandausgabe; ~ **of law** Rechtsfrage; ~ **of a letter of credit** Ausstellung eines Kreditbriefes (Akkreditivs); ~ **of a loan** Begebung (Emission) einer Anleihe, Anleihebegebung; ~ **of loan capital** Begebung von Obligationen; ~ **of monopoly** Monopolfrage; ~ **of a newspaper** Herausgabe einer Zeitung; **most recent** ~ **of a newspaper** neueste Nummer einer Zeitung; ~**s on offer** Emissionsangebot; ~ **of an order** Erlaß einer Verfügung; ~ **of paper currency** Papiergeldausgabe; ~ **above par** Überpariemission; ~ **at par** Pariemission; ~ **below par** Unterpariemission; ~ **of a passport** Ausstellung eines Reisepasses, Paßausstellung; ~ **of a patent** Patenterteilung; ~ **of a periodical** Zeitschriftenexemplar; ~**s and profits** Grundstückserträge; ~ **of a prospectus** *(Br.)* Auflegung zur Zeichnung durch Prospekte, Prospektherausgabe; ~ **to the public** öffentliche Zeichnung; ~ **for sale** Feilhalten; ~ **of securities** Effekten-,

Wertpapieremission; ~ **of shares** *(Br.)* Aktienausgabe, -emission; ~ **of shares at a discount** *(Br.)* Unterpariausgabe von Aktien; ~ **of shares at a premium** *(Br.)* Überpariemission von Aktien; ~ **of stamps** Briefmarkenausgabe; ~ **of stocks** *(US)* Aktienausgabe, -emission; **main ~ of a suit** Prozeßinhalt; ~ **in tail** erbberechtigte Nachkommenschaft; ~ **by tender** Aktienemission im Submissionswege; ~ **of tickets** Fahrkartenausgabe; ~**s from the underground** U-Bahnausgänge; **good ~ of an undertaking** guter Ausgang eines Unternehmens;

~ *(v.)* *(bill of exchange)* ausstellen, *(book)* herausgeben, veröffentlichen, *(certificate)* [Zeugnis] ausstellen, *(come from)* ent-, herstammen, herkommen, abstammen, *(distribute)* verabfolgen, ausgeben, *(income)* zufließen, *(notes)* in Umlauf setzen, ausgeben, emittieren, *(order)* [ergehen] erlassen, *(in pleading)* sich widersprechende Standpunkte vertreten, *(policy)* ausfertigen, *(result)* endigen, resultieren, *(shares)* ausgeben;

~ **bank-notes** Banknoten in Umlauf setzen; ~ **to the bearer** auf den Inhaber ausstellen; ~ **a bill of exchange** Wechsel ausstellen (ziehen); ~ **bonds** Obligationen ausgeben; ~ **a certificate** Bescheinigung ausstellen; ~ **a check against an account** Guthabenscheck ausschreiben; ~ **bad checks** *(US)* ungedeckte Schecks ausstellen, Scheckbetrug begehen; ~ **a [formal] decree** Beschluß (Verordnung) ergehen lassen; ~ **a draft on** s. o. Wechsel auf j. ziehen; ~ **execution against** Zwangsvollstreckung betreiben, Vollstreckungsauftrag erteilen; ~ **from a good family** aus einer guten Familie stammen; ~ **out of land** *(income)* aus der Land- und Forstwirtschaft stammen; ~ **a letter of credit** Akkreditiv eröffnen, Kreditbrief ausstellen; ~ **a loan** Anleihe begeben; ~ **a newspaper** Zeitung herausgeben; ~ **in numbers** in Heften liefern; ~ **an order** Verfügung (Verordnung, Bestimmung) erlassen, *(mil.)* Befehl erlassen; ~ **a patent** Patent erteilen; ~ **a prospectus** Prospekt lancieren; ~ **provisions** Lebensmittel ausgeben; ~ **additional rations** Zusatzverpflegung ausgeben; ~ **securities at a discount** Wertpapiere unter Pari emittieren; ~ **securities at a premium** Wertpapiere über Pari emittieren; ~ **shares at a discount** *(Br.)* Aktien unter Pari ausgeben; ~ **shares at a premium** *(Br.)* Aktien über Pari ausgeben; ~ **stamps** Briefmarken ausgeben; ~ **a statute in bankruptcy** Konkurs anmelden; ~ **a summons** Ladung verfügen, gerichtlich laden, vorladen; ~ **a warrant for the arrest of** s. o. Haftbefehl gegen j. erlassen; ~ **a writ** Klageschriftsatz mit Ladung zustellen;

to argue political ~**s** über politische Fragen diskutieren; **to be at ~ with** s. o. sich mit jem. über etw. streiten; **to be in ~** Gegenstand von Verhandlungen sein, *(controversial)* bestritten werden, streitig sein; **to be at ~ on a question** Frage diskutieren; **to be continued in our next ~** Fortsetzung in unserem nächsten Heft; **to bring a matter to an ~** Sache zur Entscheidung bringen; **to bring to a successful ~** zum erfolgreichen Abschluß bringen; **to bring a campaign to a successful ~** Werbefeldzug erfolgreich abschließen; **to buy new stamps on the day of ~** Briefmarken am Tag der Ausgabe kaufen; **to define the ~** Streitgegenstand festsetzen; **to die without ~** ohne Nachkommenschaft sterben; **to dispose of an ~** Emission begeben; **to evade the ~** Ausflüchte gebrauchen; **to face an ~** einem Problem gegenüberstehen; **to force an ~** Entscheidung erzwingen; **to join ~ upon the defence** sich zur Hauptsache einlassen; **to join ~ with** s. o. gegenteilige Behauptung vorbringen; **to leave ~** Nachkommenschaft hinterlassen; **to leave an ~ up in the air** Frage völlig offen lassen; **to lie at ~** in der Schwebe sein; **to make ~s to the army** Lieferungen für die Armee durchführen; **to make a new ~ of capital** Kapitalerhöhung vornehmen; **to obscure the ~** Gründe verschleiern; **to place an ~** Emission plazieren; **to place a question on a new ~** Frage einer neuen Entscheidung zuführen; **to plead the general ~** gesamtes Klagevorbringen bestreiten; **to point to a happy ~ of the negotiations** auf einen glücklichen Ausgang der Verhandlungen hindeuten; **to pool ~s** *(US)* sich zu gegenseitigem Vorteil vereinigen; **to put a claim in ~** Forderung bestreiten; **to raise an ~** Rechtsfrage aufwerfen; **to raise the whole ~** ganzen Sachverhalt anschneiden; **to retire outstanding ~s** fällige Emissionen zurückkaufen; **to set out the ~** Streitfall darlegen; **to settle an ~** sich mit der Gegenpartei einigen; **to stand on an ~** zu einer Frage stehen; **to state an ~** Frage aufwerfen; **to take ~** strittige Punkte ausdrücklich behaupten; **to take ~ with** s. o. anderer Meinung mit jem. sein; **to wait for the ~ of events** Gang der Ereignisse abwarten;

~ **audience** von einer Sendung erfaßte Zuhörerzahl; ~ **bank** Noten-, Emissionsbank; ~ **date** Erscheinungstermin; ~ **department** *(Bank of England)* Emissionsabteilung, Notenausgabestelle; **property ~ form** Materialausgabeschein; ~ **house** Emissionshaus; ~ **par** *(Br.)* Parikurs; ~ **premium** Emissions-

agio; ~ **price** Ausgabe-, Emissionskurs, Erstausgabe-, Abgabepreis; ~ **production** Herstellung einer Heftnummer; ~ **project** Emissionsvorhaben; **capital ~ restrictions** Emissionssperre; ~ **roll** Prozeßakten; ~ **room** *(ship)* Proviantkammer; ~ **stamp** Stempelsteuer; ~ **value** Ausgabewert; ~ **volume** Emissionsvolumen; ~ **waiting list** *(advertising)* Warteliste.

issued, to lautend auf;
  to be ~ ergehen, *(stock exchange)* erscheinen;
  ~ **capital** *(Br.)* **(capital stock,** *US***)** effektiv ausgegebenes Kapital, gezeichnetes (zur Zeichnung aufgelegtes) Grundkapital.

issueless *(US)* ohne Nachkommen.

issuer Emittent, Aussteller, Ausgeber;
  ~ **of a loan** Anleihegeber; ~ **of a passport** Paßaussteller.

issuing Ausstellung, Ausgabe;
  security ~ Emissionsgeschäft;
  ~ **of books** *(library)* Bücherausgabe; ~ **bad checks** *(US)* Scheckbetrug; ~ **of patents** Patenterteilung; ~ **a prospectus** Veröffentlichung eines Prospekts; ~ **of a warehouse warrant** Lagerscheinausstellung;
  ~ **activity** Emissionstätigkeit; ~ **agency** Emissionsstelle; ~ **authority** ausstellende Behörde; ~ **bank[er]** Emissionsbank, *(letter of credit)* Akkreditivbank; ~ **business** Emissionsgeschäft; ~ **company** emittierende Gesellschaft, Emissionshaus, -gesellschaft; ~ **date** Ausgabedatum, -tag, Ausstellungsdatum; ~ **expenses** Emissionskosten; ~ **group** Emittentengruppe; ~ **house** *(Br.)* Emissionshaus, Finanzierungsbank; ~ **office** Ausgabe-, Emissionsstelle; ~ **place** Ausstellungs-, Ausgabeort; ~ **price** Anfangskurs, Ausgabekurs; ~ **result** Emissionsergebnisse; ~ **syndicate** Emissions-, Begebungskonsortium; ~ **transaction** Emissionsgeschäft.

it *(US coll.)* der Gipfel, die Höhe.

italic *(print.)* kursiv;
  ~ **type** Kursivschrift.

italicize *(v.)* kursiv drucken, durch Kursivdruck hervorheben.

itch brennendes Verlangen, Sucht, Gelüst;
  ~ **for money** Geldgier; ~ **for praise** Ruhmsucht;
  (v.) **after hono(u)r** ruhmsüchtig sein.

itching *(fig.)* lüstern, begierig;
  to have an ~ palm offene Hand haben.

itchless *(fig.)* unbestechlich.

item Punkt, Gegenstand, Einzelheit, -posten, *(article of sale)* Verkaufsgegenstand, *(bill)* Geld-, Rechnungsposten, Abschnitt, *(bookkeeping)* Position, [Buchungs]posten, Buchung, Abschnitt, *(data processing)* Datenwort, *(GATT)* Tarifnummer, *(newspaper)* Nachricht, Zeitungsnotiz, Abschnitt, Artikel, *(paragraph)* Ziffer [in einem Abkommen], *(post)* Postsendung;
  by ~s postenweise;
  accruing ~s entsprechende (noch nicht fällige) Posten; **availability ~s** *(US)* langfristige Einlagen; **balance-sheet ~s** Bilanzposten; **big-ticket ~s** Luxusartikel; **booked ~s** eingetragene Posten; **bookkeeping ~s** Buchungsposten; **budget ~** Haushaltstitel; **cash ~** Kassenposten, Bareingang; **collection ~** Inkassowechsel; **combined ~s** Sammelsendungen; **company-manufactured capitalized ~s** aktivierte Eigenleistungen; **credit ~** Haben-, Gutschrift-, Kreditposten; **current assets ~** Posten des Umlaufvermögens; **debatable ~s** bestreitbare Posten; **debit ~** Debet-, Lastschriftposten; **deferred ~** Rechnungsabgrenzungsposten; **do-it-yourself ~s** Bastelware, -artikel; **expense ~** Ausgabeposten; **express ~s** Eil[gut]sendungen; **fast-selling ~** schnell verkäuflicher Artikel; **hard-to-sell ~s** schwer verkäufliche Waren; **higher-margin ~** ertragsintensivere Verkaufsartikel; **house ~** *(Br.)* eigener Scheck; **important ~** wesentlicher Punkt; **intercompany ~** innerbetriebliche Posten, Rechnungsposten inner Organgesellschaft; **interesting ~** interessanter Artikel; **large ~** großer Posten; **ledger ~** Hauptbuchposten; **local ~** Lokalartikel; **missing ~s** fehlende Postsendungen; **monitory ~** *(balance sheet)* Merkposten; **news ~** Presse-, Zeitungsnotiz, -artikel; **nonrecurring ~** einmaliger Rechnungsposten; **open ~** offene Position; **out ~s** *(US)* Abschnitte auf auswärtigen Plätzen; **out-of-stock ~** nicht auf Lager befindlicher Warenposten; **out-of-town ~** Abschnitt auf auswärtige Plätze; **overlapping ~s** sich überschneidende Posten; **patented ~s** einzelne Patentgegenstände; **pay ~** kostenvergütete Position; **preference ~** steuerlich begünstigter Posten; **press ~** Zeitungsnotiz; **pro-memoria ~** *(balance sheet)* Merkposten; **rationed ~** bewirtschafteter (rationierter) Artikel; **receivable ~s** *(US)* debitorische Posten; **recorded ~** eingetragener Posten; **registered ~s** eingeschriebene Sendungen; **separate ~** Sonderposten; **single ~** Einzelbetrag, -posten; **small-ticket ~s** geringwertige Wirtschaftsgüter; **not squared ~** unbeglichener Posten;

surplus ~ Überschußposten; **suspense (transitory)** ~ durchlaufender (transitorischer) Posten, Durchgangsposten; **in-transit** ~ durchlaufender Posten; **uncollectable** ~ nicht betreibbarer Posten; **unpaid** ~ offener Posten; **urgent** ~s dringende Postsendungen; **valuation** ~ Wertberichtigungsposten; **wire fate** ~ Abschnitte mit telegrafischer Eingangsanzeige;

~ **of account** Rechnungsposten; ~**s on the agenda (of business)** Punkte auf der Tagesordnung, Tagesordnungspunkte; ~**s in a balance sheet** Bilanzposten; ~ **of a bill** Rechnungsposten; ~ **included in the budget** Etatsposten, Titel des Haushaltsplans, Haushaltsartikel; ~**s of business** Punkte der Tagesordnung; ~**s [received] for collection** Inkassoposten, Einzugswerte; **fourth** ~ **of the contract** vierter Vertragsparagraph; ~ **in dispute** strittiger Punkt; ~**s of expense (expenditure)** Ausgabeposten; **incidental** ~ **of expense** Nebenausgabe; ~**s hard to get rid off** schwerverkäufliche Artikel; ~**s below the line in the balance sheet** Positionen unter dem Strich; ~ **of news** Nachrichtenmeldung, Zeitungsnotiz; ~**s assigned in pension** *(bank balance)* Pensionsgegenstände; **first** ~ **on a program(me)** erste Nummer auf dem Programm; ~ **of property** Vermögensgegenstand; ~ **in the revenue** Einnahmeposten; ~ **not squared** unbeglichener Posten; ~ **not in stock** nicht auf Lager befindliche Ware; ~**s liable to surcharge** *(Br.)* zuschlagspflichtige (nachgebührenpflichtige) Sendungen; ~ **in transit** durchlaufender Posten, Durchgangsposten; ~ **of value** Wertgegenstand;

~ *(v.)* eintragen, notieren, vermerken, verzeichnen; **to allow an** ~ **in an account** Rechnungsposten anerkennen; **to cancel an** ~ Posten stornieren (austragen); **to carry an** ~ **forward** Posten übertragen; **to credit an** ~ Posten kreditieren (gutschreiben); **to debit an** ~ Posten belasten; **to deduct an** ~ **from an account** Rechnungsposten abziehen; **to enter an** ~ **in the ledger** Posten im Hauptbuch eintragen; **to examine** ~ **by** ~ Punkt für Punkt durchgehen; **to fix the value of an** ~ Buchungsposten valutieren; **to give the** ~**s** Details mitteilen; **to list** ~**s** Posten aufführen; **to lump** ~ **together** Posten zusammenwerfen; **to number the** ~**s in a catalog(ue)** Katalogposten numerieren; **to pass an** ~ **to the current account** Posten auf dem Kontokorrent verbuchen; **to post an** ~ Posten eintragen

(buchen); **to scratch an** ~ **of an account** Rechnungsposten streichen; **to specify** ~**s** Posten einzeln aufführen; **to strike off an** ~ Posten streichen; **to take out an** ~ Posten ausziehen; **to tick off** ~**s in an account** Rechnungsposten abhaken; **to verify the** ~**s of a bill** Rechnungsposten kontrollieren;

~ **man** *(US)* Berichterstatter.

itemization *(US)* einzelne Aufführung, Einzelaufzählung, Spezifikation, Aufgliederung;

~ **of an account** Aufführung einzelner Buchungsposten; ~ **of costs** Kostenaufgliederung.

itemize *(v.)* *(US)* einzeln aufführen, näher angeben, spezifizieren, detaillieren, nach Posten aufgliedern, listenmäßig aufführen;

~ **accounts** einzelne Rechnungsposten angeben (spezifizieren); ~ **a bill** Rechnung spezifizieren; ~ **costs** Kosten aufgliedern.

itemized | **account** spezifizierte Rechnung; ~ **appropriation** detaillierte Mittelzuweisung; **to demand an** ~ **bill** spezifizierte Rechnung verlangen; ~ **costs** *(US)* Einzelkosten; ~ **schedule** *(US)* Einzelaufstellung.

itinera[n]cy Teilnehmer einer Dienstreise, Reisegesellschaft.

itinerant umherziehend, im Umherziehen, reisend, ambulant;

~ **dealer** Hausierer, Wander-, Reisegewerbetreibender; ~ **exhibition** Wanderausstellung; ~ **judge** innerhalb eines Bezirks reisender Richter; ~ **library** Wanderbibliothek; ~ **life** Wanderleben; ~ **merchant** Wandergewerbetreibender; ~ **peddling** Hausierhandel, Hausieren, Reise-, Wander-, Hausierergewerbe; ~ **salesman** Wandergewerbetreibender, Hausierer; ~ **showman** Schaubudenbesitzer; ~ **trade** Hausierhandel, Reise-, Wandergewerbe; ~ **trader** Hausierer, Reisehändler, ambulanter Händler, Wandergewerbetreibender; ~ **trading** Wander-, Reisegewerbe; ~ **tribunal** fliegender Gerichtsstand; ~ **trophy** *(sport)* Wanderpreis; ~ **vendor** *(US)* herumziehender Händler, Hausierer, Wandergewerbetreibender; ~ **[agricultural] worker** [landwirtschaftlicher] Wander-, Saisonarbeiter.

itinerary *(account of travels)* Reisebeschreibung, Reiseführer, *(register of places)* Reiseroute, -plan.

itinerate *(v.)* umherziehen.

itineration Geschäftsreise.

ivory towered wirklichkeitsfremd.

J

jabber Geplapper, Gewäsch;
~ (v.) schnattern, plappern, tratschen.
jack (car) Wagenheber, (day labor) Gelegenheitsarbeiter, Tagelöhner, Handlanger, (el.) Buchse, Steckdose, (sl.) Moos, Kasse;
before one can say ♂ **Robinson** im Handumdrehen (Nu);
every man ~ jedermann; **lifting** ~ Hebevorrichtung; **pilot's** ~ Lotsenflagge;
♂ **Ketch** (Br.) Henker; **~-o'-lantern** Elmsfeuer; **~-in-office** aufgeblasener Bürokrat, Paragraphenreiter; **~-of-all-trades** Allerweltskerl, Alleskönner, Faktotum, Universalgenie, Hans Dampf in allen Gassen;
~ (v.) **-all** Handlangerdienste leisten; ~ **up s. o.** j. auf Touren bringen; ~ **up a car** Auto aufbocken; ~ **up prices** (coll.) Preise erhöhen (anheben); ~ **up s. o.** j. auf Touren bringen;
~ **easy** (coll.) gleichgültig; ~ **flag** Gösch; ~ **pot** (US sl.) illegaler Fonds; **to hit the** ~ **pot** Hauptgewinn bekommen, großes Glück haben; **~-pot winner** Kassenschlager; ~ **tar** (coll.) Teerjacke.
jackanapes Stutzer, Geck.
jackaroo (Australia) Grünhorn, Neuling.
jackdaw Meckerer, Nörgler.
jacket Jacke, Jackett, (machine) Zylindermantel, (paper wrapper) Schutzumschlag;
dust ~ [Buch]schutzumschlag; **life** ~ Schwimmweste;
to dust s. one's ~ j. durch prügeln.
jacketing Verkleidungsmaterial, (coll.) Tracht Prügel.
jackhead pit (mining) blinder Schacht.
jackstraw Strohpuppe.
jactation Prahlerei.
jactitation falsche Behauptung, Berühmung;
~ **of marriage** (Br.) Vorspielung der Eheschließung.
jactivous durch Versäumnisurteil verloren.
jag (US sl.) Schwips;
to be on the ~ Bummel machen; **to have a** ~ **on** einen sitzen haben.
jail (US) Haftanstalt, [Untersuchungs]gefängnis;
county ~ Bezirksgefängnis;
~ (v.) ins Gefängnis werfen;
~ **on corruption charge** wegen Bestechung zu einer Gefängnisstrafe verurteilen;
to be in ~ **on convictions for other crimes** Gefängnisstrafe für andere Verbrechen absitzen; **to hold in** ~ **without formal charge** ohne Anklageerhebung im Gefängnis festsetzen; **to put in** ~ inhaftieren, einsperren;
~ **delivery** (US) gewaltsame Gefangenenbefreiung; ~ **sentence** (US) Gefängnisstrafe; **to draw** ~ **terms** zu einer Gefängnisstrafe verurteilt werden.
jailbird (sl.) Knastbruder.
jailbreaker (US) Ausbrecher.
jailbreaking (US) Gefängnisausbruch.
jailer Gefängnisaufseher, -wärter.
jailhouse (US) Gefängnis.
jaloppy (coll. US, airplane) alte Mühle, (car) alte Klapperkiste.
jam Gedränge, Volksgewühl, (of fruit) Marmelade, (photo offset) Papierstau, (predicament, coll.) mißliche Lage, Klemme, (radio, television) Störung, (traffic) Verkehrsdurcheinander, -stau, Verstopfung, Stockung, Stauung;
real ~ (Br., sl.) Mordsspaß; **street (traffic)** ~ Verkehrsstockung, -stauung, Stau;
~ **in the money market** (US) Geldmarktenge, -klemme;
~ (v.) blockieren, versperren, verstopfen, (crowd) sich hineinquetschen (drängen), (radio, television) stören;
~ **a bill through Congress** (US) Gesetz durchpeitschen; ~ **one's brakes on** mit voller Kraft bremsen; ~ **one's clothes into a small suitcase** seine Kleider in einen kleinen Koffer stopfen; ~ **the enemy's stations during the war** Empfang feindlicher Rundfunkstationen in Kriegszeiten stören; ~ **the passage with people** Leute in einem Korridor zusammendrängen;
to be in a ~ in der Klemme sitzen, in Geldverlegenheit sein; **to get into a** ~ in Schwierigkeiten geraten; **to want** ~ **on it** (fam.) Extrawurst haben wollen;
~ **jar** Marmeladenglas; **~-packed** vollgestopft, brechend voll; ~ **resistance** Störwiderstand; ~ **session** (swing music) Improvisationsspielen; **~-up** Zeitdruck.
jamboree Pfadfindertagung, (sl.) Saufgelage.
jammed brechend voll;
to be ~ (traffic) sich stauen; **to be** ~ **in the ice** im Eis festsitzen.

jammer (radio) Störsender.
jamming Betriebsstörung, (radio television) Störung durch andere Sender, Störsendung;
spot ~ Störung eines Kanals (einer Frequenz);
~ **on a brake** plötzliche Bremsbetätigung;
~ **transmitter** Störsender; ~ **wave** Störwelle.
jangle (v.) plappern, tratschen.
janitor (US) Pförtner, Hausmeister, -verwalter, Gebäudeverwalter;
~ (v.) (US) als Hausmeister tätig sein.
janitress (US) Hausmeisterin.
January sales (Br.) Winterschlußverkauf.
jar Gefäß, Kanne, Krug, (discordance) Uneinigkeit, Streit, Zank, (discordant sound) Knirschen, Knarren, Kreischen;
family ~ Familienkrach; **~s of a motor cycle** Erschütterungen eines Motorrads; **unpleasant** ~ **to the nerves** Nervensäge;
~ (v.) nicht übereinstimmen, sich widersprechen, (colo(u)rs) sich beißen;
~ **on s. one's feelings** jds. Gefühle verletzen; ~ **[on] the nerves** auf die Nerven gehen; ~ **open** (carriage door) aufspringen; ~ **the whole house** (machine) ganze Haus erfüllen;
♂ **Tar** Matrose, Teerjacke.
jargon Fach-, Standes-, Berufssprache, (nonsense) Kauderwelsch;
lawyer's ~ Juristendeutsch;
~ **of radio** Kauderwelsch der Rundfunkamateure;
to know the ~ **of the stage** Theaterjargon beherrschen.
jarring| **of the nerves** Nervenanspannung, -reizung;
~ (a.) schrill, mißtönend;
~ **colo(u)rs** sich beißende Farben; ~ **interests** gegeneinanderstehende Interessen, Interessengegensätze;
to sound a ~ **note in the concert of praise** in den Lobesgesang einen Mißton hereintragen; ~ **opinions** widerstreitende Meinungen.
Jason clause (ship) Versicherungsklausel gegen verborgene Mängel.
jato unit Düsenstarthilfe.
jaundice (fig.) Voreingenommenheit.
jaunt kleine Vergnügungsreise, Ausflug, Spritztour;
on a ~ auf einer Spritztour (einem Bummel);
round-the-world ~ Weltflugreise;
~ (v.) bummeln, Spritztour (Vergnügungsreise) machen.
javelin formation Kolonnenflug.
jaw (sl.) Standpauke, Gardinen-, Strafpredigt;
to leave s. o. with his ~ **dropped** j. mit offenem Mund stehen lassen;
~ **boning** Wirtschaftssteuerung durch Überredung.
jawbreaker schwer auszusprechendes Wort.
jay (sl.) Dummkopf;
~ **hawker** (sl.) Partisan.
jaywalk (v.) Verkehrszeichen nicht beachten, verkehrswidrig über die Straße gehen.
jaywalker unachtsamer Fußgänger, Verkehrssünder.
jaywalking verkehrswidrige Straßenüberquerung.
jazzed up (sl.) aufgedonnert.
jealous eifersüchtig, neidisch;
~ **of one's rights** sehr auf die Wahrung seines Rechtes bedacht;
to be ~ **of s. one's good name** jem. seinen guten Namen neiden.
jealousy of rank Standesneid.
jeans Arbeitsanzug.
Jedbury justice Lynchjustiz.
jeep Kübel-, Geländewagen, (airforce, US) kleiner Amphibienwagen, Verbindungsflugzeug.
jeer (v.) **s. o. off the stage** j. durch Zwischenrufe von der Bühne vertreiben.
jell (public opinion) sich herauskristallisieren.
jeopardize| (v.) in Gefahr bringen, gefährden, riskieren, aufs Spiel setzen;
~ **one's business** geschäftliche Verluste riskieren; ~ **one's finances** sich in finanzielle Ungelegenheiten bringen; ~ **s. one's interests** jds. Interessen gefährden; ~ **one's life** sein Leben einsetzen (riskieren).
jeopardizing a creditor's interests Gläubigergefährdung.
jeopardy Gefahr, Gefährdung, Risiko;
double ~ abermalige Strafverfolgung;
~ **of life and limb** Gefahr der Verurteilung zu einer schweren Strafe;

to be in ~ of one's life in Lebensgefahr schweben, *(accused)* der Gefahr einer Verurteilung ausgesetzt sein; **not to be in ~ of life for the same offence** nicht zum zweiten Mal angeklagt werden können;
~ assessment *(income tax)* sofortige Steuerveranlagung wegen befürchteten Steuerausfalls.

Jericho *(coll.)* weit entfernter Ort;
go to ~ geh dahin, wo der Pfeffer wächst.

jerk plötzlicher Stoß, Schlag;
at one ~ auf einmal; **by ~s** ruckweise;
the ~s *(US)* Verzückungen;
~ *(v.)* into action ruckweise in Gang kommen;
to put a ~ in it *(sl.)* mit Schwung drangehen; **to stop with a ~** *(train)* ruckartig (mit einem Ruck) anhalten.

jerkwater *(railroad, coll., US)* Zubringerzug;
~ town Provinznest.

jerky|ride in a bus Schüttelfahrt in einem Omnibus; **~ style** sprunghafter Stil.

jerque *(v.) (Br.)* zollamtlich untersuchen;
~ note *(Br.)* Eingangszollschein, Klarierungsbrief.

jerquer *(Br.)* zollamtlicher Prüfer, Zollbeamter.

jerry *(Br., sl.)* Spelunke, Kneipe, deutscher Soldat;
~ *(v.)* -build *(Br.)* mit schlechtem Material bauen; **~-builder** Bauspekulant; **~-built** unsolide gebaut, als Behelf, provisorisch; **~ shop** *(Br., sl.)* Spelunke.

jerrycan *(Br.)* Spritkanister.

jest Spaß, Witz;
full of ~ voll witziger Einfälle;
standing ~ Zielscheibe ständigen Gelächters;
to turn everything into a ~ alles verspotten.

jester Spaßmacher.

jesting lächerlich, unbedeutend;
no ~ matter keine Sache zum Spaßen.

jet Düse, Stahlrohr, *(gush of liquid)* Strom, Fluß, Strahl;
regular ~ konventionelles Düsenflugzeug; **roundtrip ~** Rundreise im Düsenflugzeug;
~ of fire Feuerstrahl;
~ age Düsenzeitalter; **~-age aircraft** Flugzeug des Düsenzeitalters; **~-age hotel** Düsenzeitalterhotel; **~ aircraft** Düsenflugzeug; **commercial ~ aircraft** Düsenverkehrsflugzeug; **~ aircraft engine** Düsenflugzeugmotor; **~ airliner** Düsenverkehrsflugzeug; **~ bomber** Düsenbomber; **~ carburettor** Düsen-, Einspritzvergaser; **all-cargo ~ clipper** Universalfrachtdüsenflugzeug; **~ cargo plane** Düsenfrachtflugzeug; **~-commute** *(v.)* täglich im Düsenflugzeug ins Büro fliegen; **~ commuter** Düsenflugzeugpendler; **~ drive** Düsenstrahlantrieb; **~ engine** Düsentriebwerk, -motor; **~ fare** Düsenflugschein; **~ fighter** Turbojäger; **~ fleet** Düsenflugzeugflotte; **~ flight** Düsenflug; **~ freight** Düsenfrachtgut; **~ freightage** Düsenfracht; **~ freighter** Düsenfrachter, Düsenfrachtflugzeug; **~ fuel** Düsentreibstoff; **~ helicopter** Düsenhubschrauber; **~ jockey** *(sl.)* Düsenpilot; **~ plane** Düsenverkehrsflugzeug; **~ pilot** Düsenpilot; **~ plane** Düsenflugzeug; **~ port** Düsenflugzeughafen; **~-propelled** mit Strahlantrieb versehen; **~ propeller** Turbopropeller; **~ propulsion** Düsenantrieb; **~-propulsion plane** Düsenflugzeug; **~ service** Düsenflugzeugverkehr; **~-style** düsenartig; **~ transport** Düsentransportflugzeug, -maschine.

jetliner Düsenflugzeug.

jetsam Seewurf[gut], Strandgut;
flotsam and ~ treibendes Wrack- und Strandgut, Schiffbruchsgüter.

jettison See-, Notwurf;
~ of cargo Ladungswurf;
~ *(v.)* a bill *(fam.)* Gesetzentwurf fallenlassen; **~ the cargo** [Waren] über Bord werfen;
to make ~ Güter über Bord werfen.

jettisonable abwerfbar.

jetty Mole, Landungsplatz, Anlegestelle.

jewel Edelstein, *(fig.)* Juwel, Schatz, Kleinod;
~s of the crown Kronjuwelen; **~ of a servant** Perle;
~ house Schatzkammer.

jewel(l)er Juwelier[geschäft].

jewel(le)ry|box Schmuckkassette; **~ insurance** Juwelen-, Schmuckversicherung; **~ shop** Juwelierladen.

jib *(v.) (Br.)* abgeneigt sein;
~ at a job Arbeit nicht machen wollen; **~ at working overtime** *(Br.)* Überstunden ablehnen;
~ door Geheim-, Tapetentür.

jibe *(v.) (US coll.)* übereinstimmen, in Einklang stehen.

jiffy, in a im Nu.

jig *(sl.)* Streich.

jigger *(bicycle, sl.)* alte Kiste.

jiggery-pokery *(Br., coll.)* Hokuspokus.

jigsaw puzzle Zusammensetzspiel.

jilt *(v.)* **at s. o.** jem. einen Korb (den Laufpaß) geben.

Jim|Crow *(US)* Neger; **~ Crowism** *(US)* Rassendiskriminierung.

jingle Geklingel, Gebimmel, *(slogan)* Slogan, Werbespruch;
~ *(v.)* sich reimen;
~ in a pocket (money) in der Tasche klimpern.

jingo Chauvinist, Hurrapatriot;
~ party chauvinistische Partei.

jingoism Chauvinismus, Hurrapatriotismus.

jingoist Chauvinist.

jingoistic chauvinistisch.

jingjams Säuferwahnsinn, *(fig.)* Kribbeln.

jinks Ausgelassenheit, *(US sl.)* Pechvogel, Unglücksrabe;
to hold high ~ sehr ausgelassen sein.

jinx Unglücksrabe, Pechvogel.

jitney *(US sl.)* billiger Autobus, billiges Verkehrsmittel.

jitters *(US sl.)* Zappeligkeit;
to have the ~ Heidenangst haben.

jitterbug *(sl.)* Nervenbündel.

Job's comforter schlechter Tröster.

Job's-tears Krokodilstränen.

job *(criminal act)* krumme Sache, Schiebung, Profitgeschäft, *(duty)* Aufgabe, Pflicht, *(employment, coll.)* Arbeit, [An]stellung, Stelle, Position, Posten, Arbeitsplatz, -stelle, -verhältnis, Beruf, Berufsarbeit, -tätigkeit, Beschäftigung, *(piece of business)* Geschäft, Auftrag, *(piece of work)* [Stück] Arbeit, Leistung, *(print.)* Satz-, Akzidenzarbeit;
by the ~ in (auf) Akkord, im Stücklohn, stückweise, *(for a lump sum)* zu einem Pauschalpreis; **having a ~** berufstätig; **on the ~** bei der Arbeit; **out of a ~** arbeitslos;
alternate ~ Ausweichberuf; **~s available** offene Arbeitsplätze; **bad ~** Fehlschlag, Pfuscherei, *(sl.)* krumme Sache; **basic ~** Hauptaufgabe; **beginning ~** Anfangsberuf; **blind-alley ~** Beruf ohne Fortkommensmöglichkeit, Stellung ohne Aufstiegsmöglichkeit; **boring ~** langweilige Arbeit; **a boy's ~** kinderleichte Sache; **clear-cut ~** übersehbare Berufsposition; **cushy ~** Druckposten; **easy ~** Kinderspiel; **entry-level ~** neu angefangener Beruf; **fat ~** bequeme Stellung, ruhiger Posten; **fiddling little ~s** unbedeutende Tätigkeiten; **full-time ~** ganztägige Beschäftigung; **government ~** Beschäftigung im Staatsdienst, Staatsstellung; **higher-grade ~s** höher qualifizierte Arbeitsplätze; **higher-level ~** *(US)* gehobene Stellung; **key ~** Schlüsselstellung; **labo(u)ring ~** Stellung als ungelernter Arbeiter; **odd ~** Gelegenheitsarbeit; **~s offered** offene Stellen; **highly paid ~** hochdotierte Stellung; **permanent ~** feste Stellung, Dauerstellung; **plant ~** Arbeitsplatz in einer Fabrik; **prestige ~** angesehener Arbeitsplatz; **priority ~** vordringliche Arbeit, *(key position)* Schlüsselstellung; **private-sector ~s** Arbeitsplätze in der Privatwirtschaft; **professional ~** Berufsposition; **public works ~** Arbeitstätigkeit im Rahmen öffentlich erteilter Aufträge; **put-up ~** *(sl.)* abgekartetes Spiel, Mache, Machwerk, Schiebung; **restricted ~** gebundene Arbeit; **routine ~** mechanische Arbeit; **rush ~** Eilauftrag; **scarce ~** Mangelberuf; **shopfloor ~** Fabrikarbeit; **similar ~** gleichartiger Beruf; **skilled factory ~** Facharbeiterberuf; **soft ~** ruhiger Posten, Druckposten; **terminal ~** Beruf ohne Aufstiegsmöglichkeit (Zukunftsaussichten); **~s threatened** gefährdete Arbeitsplätze; **top-pay-ing ~** hochbezahlter Beruf; **top-priority ~** vordringlichste Aufgabe; **tough ~** schweres Stück Arbeit; **well-paid ~** gut bezahlte Stellung; **white-collar ~** [gehobene] Büroarbeit, Stehkragenberuf;
~ outside agriculture außerlandwirtschaftlicher Arbeitsplatz; **~s awaiting attention** noch zu erledigende Arbeiten; **~s for the boys** Ämter für siegreiche Parteianhänger; **~ in hand** in Angriff genommene Arbeit; **~ with good prospects** zukunftsträchtige Stellung, chancenreiche Position;
~ *(v.)* (deal corruptly) öffentliches Amt mißbrauchen, Schiebungen begehen, in die eigene Tasche wirtschaften, veruntreuen, *(deal in stocks, Br.)* mit Aktien handeln, Maklergeschäfte betreiben, Wertpapierhändler (Makler) sein, *(do odd jobs)* Gelegenheitsarbeiten verrichten, *(purchase and resell, US)* Zwischenhandel treiben, im Zwischenhandel verkaufen, *(sublet)* Arbeit auf feste Rechnung geben, im Akkord vergeben, *(undertake work at agreed price)* Arbeit auf feste Rechnung übernehmen, *(wholesale business, US)* Großhandel betreiben, *(work for own advantage)* öffentliches Amt in gewinnsüchtiger Weise mißbrauchen, Amtsmißbrauch begehen, Korruption begehen, schieben, *(work by the job)* in Akkord (gegen Stücklohn) arbeiten;

~ s. o. off sich j. vom Halse schaffen; ~ in bills Wechselmakler sein; ~ a contract Auftrag an seine Lieferanten weitervergeben; ~ out (Br.) weitervergeben; ~ out a building contract Bauauftrag im Submissionswege vergeben; ~ out many functions viele Aufgabengebiete außerbetrieblich erledigen lassen; ~ s. o. into a well-paid post jem. durch unsaubere Machenschaften eine gute Stellung verschaffen; ~ shares Kursmakler sein; to apply for a ~ sich um eine Stelle bewerben, um eine Beschäftigung nachsuchen; to be at a dead end in one's ~ beruflich in einer Sackgasse sein; to be back on the ~ Arbeit wieder aufgenommen haben; to be fit for one's ~ sich für einen Beruf eignen; to be looking for a ~ auf Stellungssuche sein; to be on the ~ fleißig arbeiten, (sl.) auf dem Posten (rührig) sein; to be cut out for a ~ für eine Aufgabe wie geschaffen sein; to be out of a ~ arbeitslos (beschäftigungslos, ohne Beschäftigung) sein; to be paid by the ~ im Akkord bezahlt werden; to be unfit for a ~ sich für einen Beruf nicht eignen; to be up to one's ~ seiner Aufgabe gewachsen sein; to blame one's ~ for one's psychological ills psychologische Schwierigkeiten auf seine Arbeitstätigkeit zurückführen; to butcher a ~ Arbeit verpfuschen; to create a ~ for s. o. Arbeitsplatz für j. schaffen; to do a ~ Arbeit verrichten, Beschäftigung ausüben; to do one's ~ well in seinem Beruf erfolgreich sein; to do s. one's ~ j. zugrunderichten; to do a first-class ~ ausgezeichnete Arbeit leisten; to do one's ~ well in seinem Beruf erfolgreich sein; to do odd ~s Gelegenheitsarbeiten verrichten; to fill a ~ through selection consultants Position durch Einschaltung einer Beratungsfirma besetzen; to find a ~ Arbeit finden; to find s. o. a ~ jem. eine Beschäftigung verschaffen; to fix s. o. up with a ~ jem. eine Stellung besorgen; to free ~s Arbeitsplätze freimachen; to gag at a ~ sich vor einer Arbeit ekeln; to get the right ~ richtige Berufswahl treffen; to get a ~ by push seine Stellung Protektion verdanken; to get on the ~ am Arbeitsplatz erscheinen; to give s. o. a ~ j. in sein Geschäft einstellen; to give up one's ~ seine Stellung aufgeben; to give s. th. up as a bad ~ Sache als erfolglos abtun; to go with the ~ mit dem Arbeitsverhältnis im Zusammenhang stehen; to groom s. o. for a ~ j. für einen Beruf trimmen; to have a ~ Arbeit haben, im Berufsleben stehen; to have a fine ~ glänzende Stellung haben; to have a little ~ for s. o. etw. für j. zu erledigen haben; to have a part-time ~ Halbtagsbeschäftigung haben; to have a ~ in prospect Stellung in Aussicht haben; to have a regular ~ einer regelmäßigen Beschäftigung nachgehen; to hold a ~ Stelle innehaben; to hold down a ~ (US) seine Stellung behalten; to kick s. o. out of his ~ j. abschießen; to know one's ~ [inside out] sein Fach (Handwerk) gründlich verstehen; to land a ~ Arbeitsplatz ergattern; to learn on the ~ seine Berufsausbildung am Arbeitsplatz bekommen, durch seine Arbeit hinzulernen; to lie down on the ~ auf der faulen Haut liegen; to look for a ~ auf Arbeitsuche sein, Arbeit suchen; to lose one's ~ seine Stellung verlieren; to lure labo(u)r into other ~ Arbeitskräfte zum Berufswechsel verleiten; to make a bad ~ Arbeit sabotieren; to make the best of a bad ~ retten, was zu retten ist; to make a good ~ of s. th. etw. gut erledigen; to make a professional ~ of s. th. etw. fachgemäß ausführen; to make a thorough ~ of it ganze Arbeit leisten; to offer another ~ in substitution Ersatzarbeitsplatz anbieten; to pack up one's ~ seine Stellung aufgeben; to put s. o. on to a ~ jem. eine Stellung verschaffen; to put in for a ~ sich um eine Stellung bewerben; to put one's ~ right Beanstandungen bei einer geleisteten Arbeit beseitigen; to put out a ~ on commission Arbeit in Regie vergeben; to quit one's ~ (US) seine Stellung aufgeben; to reeducate on the ~ am Arbeitsplatz umschulen; to scent a ~ Arbeitsplatz ausfindig machen; to set s. o. a ~ jem. eine bestimmte Aufgabe geben; to shake down in a ~ sich an einen Beruf gewöhnen; to slack at one's ~ bei der Arbeit trödeln; to start on a ~ Stelle (Stellung) anbieten; to stay off one's ~ Arbeit niederlegen; to stay on the ~ Stellung beibehalten; to stick to a ~ seinem Beruf weiterhin nachgehen; to strip s. o. off a ~ j. von einer Aufgabe entbinden; to switch a ~ Berufswechsel vornehmen; to tackle a ~ Aufgabe erledigen; to tag for a ~ für einen Beruf gewinnen; to take a ~ Stellung annehmen; to throw up one's ~ seine Stellung aufgeben; to toss out of ~s arbeitslos (brotlos) machen; to trade ~s Arbeitsplätze tauschen; to try to find a ~ Arbeit suchen; to turn down a ~ Stellung ablehnen; to turn down ~s on offer angebotene Arbeitsmöglichkeiten ablehnen; to work by the ~ im Akkord arbeiten;

~ (a.) im Akkord;

on-the-~ accident Arbeitsunfall; ~ analysis (US) Berufsanalyse, Arbeitsstudie, Arbeitsplatzuntersuchung; ~-analysis formula (US) für Berufsanalysen verwendete Formel; ~ analyst Berufsstatistiker; ~ applicant Stellenbewerber; ~ application Stellenbewerbung; ~ assignment berufliche Aufgabe, Arbeitsaufgabe; ~ attendance Einhaltung der Arbeitsstunden; ~ availability Bereitstellen von Arbeitsplätzen; computerized ~ bank Berufsspeicherungsanlage; ~ boredom Arbeitsunlust; ~ breakdown Arbeitsplatz-, Tätigkeitsbeschreibung; ~ candidate Stellungsuchender, Bewerber; ~ card Auftragsabrechnungskarte; executive ~ category Klasse der gehobenen Angestellten; ~ centre (Br.) Arbeitsvermittlung, Stellenbörse; ~ changes Arbeitsplatzwechsel; ~ characteristics Berufskennzeichen, -merkmale, Arbeitscharakteristika; ~ classes Berufsklassen, -gruppen; ~ classification (US) Berufszugehörigkeit; ~ classification index (US) Berufsgruppenindex; ~ comparison scale Arbeitsvergleichsskala; ~ competition Berufswettbewerb; ~ competitor (US) Mitbewerber; ~ compositor Akzidenzsetzer; ~ conditions Arbeits-, Berufsbedingungen, Umwelteinflüsse; ~ content (US) Arbeitsinhalt; ~ cost ledger Auftragskostenbuch; ~ cost sheet Auftragskostensammelblatt; ~ cost system Kostenrechnung für Einzelfertigung; ~ costing Auftragskostenrechnung, Kostenrechnungssystem; ~ counselling (US) Arbeitnehmerberatung, Berufsberatung; ~ counsellor (US) Berufsberater; ~-creating agency Arbeitsbeschaffungsstelle; ~-creating measures Arbeitsbeschaffungsmaßnahmen; ~-creating power Arbeitsbeschaffungsmöglichkeit; ~ creation Arbeitsbeschaffung; ~-creation palliative steuerliche Erleichterungen bei der Schaffung von Arbeitsplätzen; ~ creation program(me) Arbeitsbeschaffungsprogramm; ~ cutback Arbeitskräfteabbau; ~ description (US) Arbeitsplatz-, Stellen-, Tätigkeitsbeschreibung; ~ dictionary (US) Berufsverzeichnis; ~ difficulty allowance Zuschlag für schwierige Arbeiten; ~ dilution Arbeitseinteilung nach Befähigungen; ~ disaster berufliche Katastrophe; ~ discrimination (US) berufliche Diskriminierung, Benachteiligung im Arbeitsleben; ~ duties Berufsaufgaben; ~ economics training Berufsförderung leitender Angestellter; ~ efficiency berufliche Leistungsfähigkeit; ~ enlargement Arbeitsplatzausweitung; ~ enthusiasm Berufsbegeisterung; ~ environment berufliche Umgebung (Umwelt); ~ etiquette berufliche Umgangsformen; ~ evaluation (US) Arbeitswertung; ~ evaluation scale (US) Vergleichstabelle für das Arbeitsbewertungsverfahren; ~ evaluation system (US) Arbeitsbewertungsmethode; ~ factor Arbeits-, Bewertungsmerkmal; ~ families berufsgleiche Gruppen; ~ family Berufseinheit; ~ getting Stellenvermittlung; ~ goods Ramsch-, Partie-, Schleuderware; ~ goods shop (trade) Partiewarengeschäft, Ramschladen; ~ grading berufliche Einstufung; ~ hazard Berufsgefahr, -risiko; ~-hop (v.) Arbeitsplatz (Beruf) häufig wechseln; ~-hopping häufiger Berufswechsel (Arbeitsplatzwechsel); ~ hunter Stellenjäger, Stellungssuchender; ~ hunting Arbeitssuche, Stellenjagd; ~ identification Arbeits-, Berufsbezeichnung; ~ insecurity Unsicherheit im Berufsleben, berufliche Unsicherheit; ~ instability berufliche Unbeständigkeit; ~ instruction Arbeitsunterweisung, -einwirkung; ~ instruction training Anleitungsverfahren für die Berufsausbildung; ~ interview Berufsgespräch; ~ jockey Postenjäger; ~ joy Arbeitslust, -befriedigung; ~ knowledge Berufskenntnis; to help s. o. up the ~ ladder jem. größere Berufschancen gewähren; ~ layout Arbeitsplatzgestaltung; ~ leasing Zeitarbeit; ~ line Ramsch-, Partie-, Schleuderware, Kleinserie; ~ loss Stellungs-, Arbeitsplatzverlust; ~ lot Warenposten zweiter Wahl (mit kleinen Fehlern), Restposten, Ramschwaren, -partie, Partieware; to buy as a ~ lot partieweise kaufen; to buy books as a ~ lot Bücher in Bausch und Bogen kaufen; to sell a ~ lot im Ramsch verkaufen; ~-lot buying Ramsch[waren]kauf; ~-lot production Kleinserienfertigung; odd-~ man Gelegenheitsarbeiter; ~ market Stellen-, Arbeitsmarkt; ~ mobility berufliche Beweglichkeit; executive ~ mobility freie Berufsmöglichkeit für leitende Angestellte; ℓ's news Hiobsbotschaft; ~ number Kostennummer für einzelne Arbeiter, Arbeitsauftragsnummer; ~ offer Stellenangebot; ~ office Akzidenzdruckerei; ~ opening offene Stelle, Arbeitsplatz; ~ openings offene Stellen; ~ operation Fertigungsvorgang; ~ opportunity Erwerbs-, Arbeitsmöglichkeit; ~ order (US) Verarbeitungsanweisung, Fabrikationsauftrag; ~-order cost accounting (US) Arbeitsauftragskosten-, Stückerfolgsrechnung, Zuschlags-, Serienkalkulation; ~ order cost card (US) Kostenrechnungskarte; ~ order cost sheet (US) Kostenrechnungsblatt; ~-order costing (US) Kostenrechnungssystem für auftragsweise Fertigung; ~-order number (US) Fabrikationsauftragsnummer; ~ pattern Stellenbesetzungsplan; ~ peace Arbeitsfriede; ~ performance Arbeits-, Berufsleistung; ~ pinch Beschäftigungsnotlage; ~ placement (US) Stellenvermittlung; ~ placement program (US) Programm zur Schaffung von Arbeitsplätzen; ~

pricing Lohnkostenkalkulation; ~ **printer** Akzidenzdrucker; ~ **printing** kleinere Druckarbeiten, Akzidenzdruck; ~ **processing** Lohnveredelung; ~ **production** (US) Einzelfertigung, -fabrikation, Auffertigung; ~ **program(me)** Arbeitsbeschaffungsprogramm; ~ **prospects** Berufsaussichten; ~ **provider** Arbeitgeber; ~ **quandaries** berufliche Schwierigkeiten; ~ **questionnaire** beruflicher Fragebogen; ~ **queue** Arbeitslosenschlange; ~ **ranking** berufliche Rangordnung; ~ **rate** Stücklohn-, Akkordrichtsatz, Akkordlohnsatz; ~ **rating** (US) berufliche Bewertung nach dem Punktverfahren, Arbeitsbewertung; ~**-rating system** (US) Arbeitsbewertungsverfahren nach dem Punktsystem; **industrial ~ ratio** Industriebesatz; ~ **record** berufliche Vergangenheit, beruflicher Werdegang; ~ **reduction** Verringerung von Arbeitsplätzen; ~ **relations training** Ausbildungsprogramm zur Verbesserung des Betriebsklimas; ~ **relationship** Berufsverhältnis; ~ **release scheme** (Br.) Bonussystem für Frühpensionierung; ~ **report** Arbeitsbericht; ~ **requirements** Berufserfordernisse; ~ **responsibility** berufliche Verantwortung; ~ **reservation** Berufsbeschränkung; ~ **retention** Beibehaltung des angestammten Berufs; ~ **rotation** (US) Arbeitsplatzwechsel [innerhalb eines Betriebes], Stellenrotation, Ringtausch; ~ **satisfaction** (US) berufliche Befriedigung, Arbeitsfreude, -befriedigung, berufliche Zufriedenheit; ~**-satisfactory items** zur beruflichen Befriedigung beitragende Merkmale; **short-term ~-saving exercise** kurzfristig unternommene Anstrengungen zur Sicherung von Arbeitsplätzen; ~**-saving rescue** Rettungsmaßnahmen zur Erhaltung von Arbeitsplätzen; ~ **scene** Berufssituation; ~ **security** Sicherheit des Arbeitsplatzes, berufliche Sicherheit; ~ **seeker** (US) Stellungssuchender; **first-~ seeker** Anwärter auf den ersten Arbeitsplatz; **to run free ads for ~ seekers** (US) Stellengesuche kostenlos veröffentlichen; **to be ~-sensitive** sich empfindlich auf Arbeitsplätze auswirken; ~ **seniority** (US) Dienstalter; ~ **shop** (US) Einzelanfertigungsbetrieb, Spezialteilebetrieb; ~ **shop operation** (US) Einzelanfertigung; ~ **shop sequencing** (Br.) Maschinenbelegungsplan; ~ **shortage** Knappheit an Arbeitsplätzen, Arbeitsplatzverknappung; ~ **simplification** Arbeitsvereinfachung; ~ **situation** Arbeitsmarktlage; ~ **slash** Stellenkürzung; ~ **slot** (US sl.) Berufsposition; ~ **specialization** (US) berufliche Spezialisierung; ~ **specification** (US) Arbeitsplatzbeschreibung; **to match ~ specifications** beruflichen Anforderungen entsprechen; ~ **standardization** Berufsnormung; ~ **start** Berufsstart, -beginn; ~ **status** Berufsstatus, berufliche Position; ~ **success** Berufserfolg; ~ **switch** Verschiebungen im Gesamtbereich aller Arbeitsplätze; ~ **tape** (terminal) Arbeitsband; ~ **ticket** (US) Akkord-, Arbeitslaufzettel; ~ **time** Arbeits-, Stückzeit; ~ **title** Berufsbezeichnung; **[on-the-] ~ training** (US) Ausbildung am Arbeitsplatz, Berufsausbildung; ~**-training process** (US) berufliches Ausbildungsverfahren; ~ **vacancy** unbesetzter Arbeitsplatz; ~ **wage** Akkordlohn, Stücklohn; ~ **work** Arbeit im Akkord, Stück-, Akkordarbeit, (job printing) Akzidenzdruck; **to do ~ work** im Akkord arbeiten; ~ **worker** Stück-, Akkordarbeiter.

jobber (casual labo(u)rer) Gelegenheitsarbeiter, (day labo(u)rer) Tagelöhner, Dienstmann, Handlanger, (middleman, US) Zwischen-, Großunternehmer, -händler, Grossist für Partiewaren, (piece worker, US) Akkordarbeiter, Stücklohnarbeiter, (speculator) Schieber, Börsenspekulant, (stock exchange, Br.) Effekten-, Fondshändler, [Börsen]makler, Wertpapierhändler;
desk ~ Grossist ohne eigenes Lager (mit Streckengeschäft); **exchange ~** Sortenhändler; **general-line ~** Großhändler für alle Warengattungen; **land ~** Güter-, Immobilien-, Grundstücksmakler, Grundstücksspekulant; **local ~** Platzmakler; **odd ~** Gelegenheitsarbeiter; **rack ~** (US) Absatzmittler, Realgroßhändler, Großlieferant; **speciality ~** (US) Spezialitätengroßhändler; **wagon ~** (US) Grossist mit eigenem Lager;
~ **in bills** (Br.) Wechselreiter; ~ **in securities** (Br.) Fonds-, Wertpapierhändler;
~ **system** (Br.) Börsenhändlersystem; ~'s **trade** Großhandelsgewerbe; ~'s **turn** (Br.) Kursgewinn eines Maklers.

jobbery Amts-, Vertrauensmißbrauch, Geschäftemacherei, Schiebung, Korruption, Durchstecherei, Unterschlagung, Veruntreuung, (stock market) Börsenspekulation;
municipal ~ kommunale Durchstechereien.

jobbing (buying and reselling, US) Zwischen-, Großhandel, (job work) Akkord-, Stücklohnarbeit, (print.) Akzidenzdruck, (speculation) Spekulation[sgeschäft], (stock exchange dealings, Br.) Börsen-, Effektenhandel, Maklergeschäft, (wholesale business, US) Großhandel, (casual work) Gelegenheitsarbeit;
land ~ Grundstücksspekulation;

~ **in bills** Wechselarbitrage, -spekulation; ~ **in contangos** (Br.) Reportgeschäft;
~ (a.) auf Stück (im Akkord) arbeitend;
~ **backwards** Effektenhandel mit Hinweis auf die Erfolgsgeschichte des Unternehmens; ~ **business** Maklergeschäft; ~ **gardener** Lohngärtner; ~ **hand** Akkordarbeiter; ~ **house** (US) Großhandelshaus, (brokerage) Maklerfirma; ~ **man** Gelegenheitsarbeiter; ~ **production** Auftrags-, Kleinserienfertigung; ~ **tailor** Flickschneider; ~ **work** (print.) Akzidenzarbeit; ~ **workman** Stücklohnarbeiter.

jobholder (US) Arbeitnehmer, Festangestellter, Stelleninhaber; **public ~** (US) Staatsangestellter, Beamter.

jobbing|face Akzidenzschrift; ~ **work** Akzidenzsatz.

jobholding Festhalten an einem Beruf.

jobless (US) erwerbs-, arbeitslos;
~ **army** Arbeitslosenarmee; ~ **claims** Arbeitslosenforderungen; ~ **percentage** Arbeitslosenprozentsatz; ~ **picture** Bild des Arbeitslosenmarktes; ~ **rate** Arbeitslosenziffer, -prozentsatz, -quote; ~ **roll** Arbeitslosenverzeichnis; ~ **total** Arbeitslosengesamtzahl.

joblessness (US) Arbeitslosigkeit.

jobman Akkordarbeiter.

jobmaster (Br.) Wagenverleiher.

jobshop sequencing (Br.) Maschinenbelegungsplan, Reihenfolgeplanung.

jockey (Br.) Handlanger;
~ (v.) deichseln, zuwegebringen;
~ **s. o. away** j. hinweglotsen; ~ **s. o. out of his job** j. um seinen Arbeitsplatz bringen; ~ **s. o. out of his money** j. um sein Geld betrügen; ~ **s. o. into an office** jem. aufgrund seiner Beziehungen zu einem Amt verhelfen; ~ **for position** sich mit allen nur erdenkbaren Mitteln um eine Position bemühen; ~ **a transaction** sich an einem Kuhhandel beteiligen; ~ **s. o. in a transaction** j. bei einem Geschäft übervorteilen.

jockeying Springen von einer Warteschlange zur anderen.

Joe Miller Kalauer.

jog Stoß, Schütteln;
~ (v.) **along** seinen Lauf nehmen; ~ **along comfortably** gut vorankommen; ~ **up and down** (bus) hin- und herschütteln; ~ **s. one's memory** jds. Gedächtnis auffrischen; ~ **on somehow** sich irgendwie durchwursteln; ~ **s. o. up and down** (bus) j. durchschütteln;
to give s. one's memory a ~ jds. Gedächtnis auffrischen; **to go along at an esay ~** dahintrotten.

jogtrot Trott, Schlendrian, Tretmühle;
monotonous ~ of life monotones Alltagsleben;
~ (v.) **along** sich durchwursteln; ~ **s. one's memory** jds. Gedächtnis auffrischen; ~ **on somehow** irgendwie weiterkommen;
to go back to the ~ of the office wieder in die berufliche Tretmühle zurückkehren.

John| Bull typischer Engländer; ~ **Doe** fingierter Kläger, fiktive Prozeßpartei; ~ **Hancock** (signature) Friedrich Wilhelm.

Johnny (Br., sl.) Stutzer, Bummler;
~ **Raw** Neuling, Grünschnabel; ~**-on-the-spot** (US) Hans Dampf in allen Gassen.

join Verbindungsstelle, Fuge, Naht, Bindeglied;
~ (v.) sich zusammentun (vereinigen, verbinden), (associate) beitreten;
~ **an action** einem Prozeß beitreten; ~ **the army** zum Militär einrücken, ins Heer eintreten; ~ **an association** Vereinsmitglied werden; ~ **a band of robbers** sich einer Räuberbande anschließen; ~ **battle** Kampf aufnehmen; ~ **s. o. in a bottle of wine** mit jem. eine Flasche Wein trinken; ~ **a cartel** sich zu einem Kartell zusammenschließen; ~ **two causes of action** zwei Ansprüche in einer Klage geltend machen; ~ **a class** an einem Kursus teilnehmen; ~ **more closely** sich enger anschließen; ~ **a club** einem Verein beitreten; ~ **the colo(u)rs** Soldat werden; ~ **a company** Gesellschafter werden; ~ **company with s. o.** sich zu jem. gesellen, jem. Gesellschaft leisten; ~ **in the conversation** sich an der Unterhaltung beteiligen; ~ **documents to a report** einem Bericht Unterlagen beifügen; ~ **evening classes** Abendschule besuchen; ~ **one's father's firm** in das väterliche Geschäft eintreten; ~ **a firm as an associate (a partner)** in eine Firma als Teilhaber eintreten; ~ **forces** (mil.) Streitkräfte vereinigen; ~ **hands with s. o.** zusammenarbeiten, gemeinsame Sache machen, einander unterstützen; ~ **interests with s. o.** mit jem. gemeinsame Sache machen; ~ **issue** sich auf eine Klage (zur Hauptsache) einlassen; ~ **a lawsuit** (US) einem Prozeß beitreten; ~ **together in liability** sich solidarisch erklären; ~ **the majority** sich der Mehrheit anschließen, (die) sich zu seinen

Vätern versammeln; ~ **an island with the mainland** Insel mit dem Festland verbinden; ~ **a party** Parteimitglied werden, einer Partei beitreten; ~ **as party to an action** als Streitgenosse mitverklagen; ~ **as plaintiff** als Streitgenosse klagen; ~ **in a protest** sich einem Protestschritt anschließen; ~ **two persons in marriage** zwei Menschen verheiraten; ~ **one's ship** sich einschiffen; ~ **a society** einem Verein beitreten; ~ **stock with s. o.** sein Kapital mit jem. zusammenschießen; ~ **a treaty** (law of nations) einem Vertrag beitreten; ~ **the ranks** ins Heer eintreten; ~ **a river** in einen Fluß einmünden; ~ **up** (mil.) sich stellen, Soldat werden, einrücken; ~ **one's unit** sich bei seinem Truppenteil einfinden.

joinder Verbindung, Zusammenfügung;
~ **of actions** Klageverbindung, -häufung, Prozeßverbindung; ~ **of causes of action** objektive Klagenhäufung, Klagenverbindung; ~ **in demurrer** Eingehen auf die Zulässigkeit eines Rechtseinwands; ~ **of error** (criminal law) Revisionserwiderung; ~ **of issue** Klageeinlassung, Einlassung zur Hauptsache; ~ **of offences** Zusammenfassung mehrerer Straftaten in einer Anklage; ~ **of parties** Streitgenossenschaft, Nebenintervention; ~ **in pleading** Festlegung des strittigen Sachverhalts; ~ **of offences** Einbeziehung von Einzelstraftatbeständen.

joined beigefügt, anliegend, beigeheftet.
joiner Bauschreiner, -tischler.
joinery Schreinerei.
joining Verbindung, Zusammenfügung, (juncture) Treffpunkt, (film) Klebestelle;
~ **Europe** Anschluß an Europa; ~ **of a firm** Geschäftseintritt.

joint Verbindung, Gelenk, (bookbinding) Falz, (railway) Schienenstoß, (sl.) Spelunke, Bumslokal;
out of ~ (fig.) aus den Fugen;
ball-and-socket ~ Kugelgelenk;
to put s. one's nose out of ~ (fig.) Favorit an Stelle eines anderen werden;
~ (a.) gemeinsam, gemeinschaftlich, solidarisch, verbunden, (obligated in common) gemeinschuldnerisch, zur gesamten Hand;
to come out top ~ gemeinsam an der Spitze liegen;
~ **account** gemeinsame Rechnung, gemeinsames Konto, Konsortial-, Metakonto; **for** ~ **account** auf gemeinsame Rechnung; ~**account money** Konsortialgeldbeträge; ~**account party** Metakontoinhaber; ~ **action** gemeinsames Vorgehen, (lawsuit) Prozeß als Streitgenossen; **to take** ~ **action** gemeinsam vorgehen; ~ **adventure** gemeinsames Unternehmen, Gemeinschaftsunternehmen, (US) Beteiligungs-, Gelegenheitsgesellschaft, Beteiligungsgeschäft; ~ **advertising** Gemeinschaftswerbung; ~ **agent** (carrier) Vertreter mehrerer Spediteure; ~ **agreement** (labo(u)r relations) Lohnabkommen mehrerer Firmen mit einer Gewerkschaft, Tarifabkommen; ~ **ambassador** gemeinsamer Botschafter; ~ **[and survivor] annuity** Überlebensrente; ~ **annuity survivor pension plan** Pensionssystem mit Zahlung von Überlebensrenten; ~ **applicants** gemeinsame Anmelder; ~ **appointment** gemeinsame Einsetzung; ~ **apprenticeship committee** Betriebsausbildungsausschuß; ~ **arbiter** gemeinsamer Schlichter; ~ **attorney** Mitbevollmächtigter; ~ **author** Mitverfasser, -autor; ~ **authority** (local government, Br.) Zweckverband; ~ **authorship** Mitverfasser-, Mitautorenschaft; ~ **bargain** gemeinsames Geschäft; ~ **beneficiaries** gemeinschaftlich Bedachte; ~ **board (body)** (Br.) Zweckverband; ~ **bonds** von mehreren Gesellschaften ausgegebene Obligationen; ~ **business [venture]** Metageschäft; ~ **capital** Gesellschaftskapital; ~ **cargo** Sammelladung; ~ **cause** gemeinsame Sache; ~ **collateral** gemeinsame Sicherheit; ~ **commissary** Mitbevollmächtigter; ~ **commission** gemischte Kommission; ~ **committee** (Br., parl.) gemischter Ausschuß, (local government, Br.) kommunale Arbeitsgemeinschaft; ~ **compact** Gemeinschaftsvertrag; ~ **complaint** gemeinsame Beschwerde; ~ **composition** Gesamtvergleich; ~ **concurrence** gemeinschaftliche Zustimmung; **to settle a trade dispute by** ~ **consultation** Arbeitskampf im Wege gemeinsamer Besprechungen beilegen; ~ **contract** gemeinschaftlicher Vertrag; ~ **contractor** Mitkontrahent, -unternehmer; ~ **convention** (US) gemeinsame Sitzung von Kongreß und Einzelstaatparlamenten; ~ **costs** Schlüssel-, Umlagekosten; ~ **council** Gewerkschaftsausschuß; ~ **credit** Konsortialkredit; ~ **creditor** Gesamthandsgläubiger; ~ **debt** gemeinschaftliche Schuld; ~ **debtors** Gesamt-, Mit-, Solidarschuldner; ~ **defendant** Mitbeklagter; ~ **demand** verbundene Nachfrage, Komplementärbedarf; ~ **demand goods** (US) Komplementärgüter; ~ **deposit** Gemeinschaftsdepot; ~ **director** Mitdirektor; ~ **directorship** Mitleitung; ~ **editor** Mitherausgeber; ~ **editorial board** Redak-

tionsgemeinschaft; ~ **efforts** vereinigte Anstrengungen; ~ **employer** gemeinsamer Arbeitgeber; ~ **enterprise** Gemeinschaftsunternehmen, Gelegenheitsgesellschaft; ~ **establishment** Gemeinschaftsgründung; ~ **estate** gemeinsames Vermögen, Miteigentum zur gesamten Hand; ~ **executor** Mittestamentsvollstrecker; **to be published at the** ~ **expense of publisher and author** auf Kosten von Autor und Verleger veröffentlicht werden; ~ **family** Gesamtfamilie; ~ **fiat** Konkurseröffnungsbeschluß gegen Gesamtschuldner; ~ **financing** Mitfinanzierung; ~ **floating** Blockfloaten; ~ **founder** Mitgründer; ~ **guarantors** Mit-, Gesamtbürgen; ~ **guaranty** solidarische Haftung; ~ **guardian** Gegen-, Neben-, Mitvormundschaft; ~ **heir** (US) Miterbe; ~ **heritage** (US) Miterbschaft, gemeinsame Erbschaft; ~ **hiring hall** gemeinsames Stellenvermittlungsbüro von Arbeitgeber- und Arbeitnehmerseite; ~ **holder** Mitinhaber, -besitzer; ~ **household** gemeinsame Haushaltsführung; ~ **industrial council** paritätisch besetzter Betriebsausschuß, ständig tagendes Arbeitsschiedsgericht; ~ **industry of husband and wife** Erwerbstätigkeit beider Ehegatten; ~ **interest** Gesamtbeteiligung; ~ **invention** Gemeinschaftserfindung; ~ **inventor** Miterfinder; ~ **labo(u)rer** Mitarbeiter; ~ **legatee** Mitvermächtnisnehmer; ~ **lessee** Mitpächter; ~ **liability** gesamtschuldnerische Haftung; ~ **life insurance** Gegenseitigkeitsversicherung; ~ **lives** (life insurance) verbundene Leben; **during their** ~ **lives** solange sie beide leben; ~ **management** gemeinsame Leitung, (employees) Mitbestimmung; ~ **manager** Mitdirektor, [Direktions]kollege; ~ **mandatory** Mitbeauftragter; ~ **meeting** gemeinsame Sitzung; ~ **mortgage** Gesamthypothek; ~ **negligence** zum Unfall führende Fahrlässigkeit mehrerer Personen; ~ **negotiating panel** gemeinsamer Verhandlungsausschuß; ~ **nominee** Gemeinschaftskandidat; ~ **obligation** Gesamtverpflichtung; ~ **obligee** gemeinsamer Gläubiger; ~ **obligor** Mitschuldner; ~ **occupancy** Mitbesitz; ~ **occupant** Mitbesitzer; ~ **offence** gemeinsam begangene Straftat; ~ **offender** Mittäter; ~ **operation** gemeinsames Vorgehen, Gemeinschaftsbetrieb; ~ **option** gemeinsam ausgeübte Option; ~ **owner** Miteigentümer, (ship) Mit-, Partenreeder; ~ **owners** gemeinsame (gemeinschaftliche) Eigentümer; **to be** ~ **owners** gemeinsam besitzen; ~ **ownership** Eigentum zur gesamten Hand, Miteigentum, (shipping) Parten-, Mitreederei; **to have** ~ **ownership over (of) s. th.** etw. im Gesamthandseigentum besitzen; ~ **partner** Teilhaber, Mitinhaber; ~ **partnership** Teilhaberschaft; ~ **patent** Gemeinschaftspatent; ~ **pension** Überlebensrente; ~ **plaintiff** Nebenkläger; ~ **police authority** (Br.) kommunaler Zweckverband für Polizeifunktionen; ~ **policy** verbundene Lebensversicherungspolice; ~ **possession** Mitbesitz; ~ **power of attorney** Gesamtvollmacht, Kollektivvollprokura; ~ **principal** Gesamtkapital; ~ **producer** Gesamthersteller; ~ **product** Verbundprodukt, Kuppelprodukt; ~ **production** verbundene Produktion; ~ **production council** (Br.) Arbeitgeber-Arbeitnehmerproduktionsausschuß; **on** ~ **profit and loss** auf gemeinschaftlichen Gewinn und Verlust; ~ **promise** gemeinsames Versprechen; ~ **promissory note** solidarischer trockener Wechsel; ~ **property** Gesamthandseigentum, Gütergemeinschaft; **to hold** ~ **property** Gesamthandseigentum besitzen; ~ **property interest** Gesamthandseigentumsrecht; ~ **proprietor** Teilhaber, Miteigentümer, -inhaber; ~ **proprietorship** Miteigentum; ~ **purchase** Gemeinschaftseinkauf; ~ **purchaser** Miterwerber; ~ **purse** gemeinsame Kasse; ~ **purse arrangement** auf gemeinschaftliche Rechnung betriebenes Geschäft; ~ **rate** (railway) Sammeltarif; ~ **rate selling** Tariflohnbestimmung durch Vorstand und Betriebsrat; ~ **report** gemeinsamer Bericht; ~ **research** gemeinsames Forschungsunternehmen; ~ **resolution** (pol.) gemeinsame Entschließung, Gemeinschaftsbeschluß; ~ **respondent** Mitverklagter; ~ **responsibility** gemeinsame Haftung; ~ **return** (income tax, US) gemeinsame Veranlagung von Ehegatten; ~ **right** gemeinschaftlicher Anspruch; ~ **sales agency** Verkaufsgemeinschaft; ~ **security** Solidarbürgschaft; ~ **seller** Mitverkäufer; ~ **services** (ENEA) Gemeinschaftsvorhaben; ~ **session** (parl.) gemeinsame Sitzung; ~ **shareholders** (Br.) Mitaktionäre; ~ **shares** gemeinschaftliche Anteile; ~ **signatory** Mitunterzeichner; ~ **signature** Kollektivzeichnung; ~ **statement** gemeinsame Erklärung.

joint stock Gemeinschaftsfonds, Gesellschaftskapital, (Br.) Aktienkapital;
~ **bank** Aktienbank; ~ **brewery** Aktienbrauerei; ~ **company** (Br.) Aktiengesellschaft, AG, (US) Kommanditgesellschaft auf Aktien; ~ **company with limited liability** (Br.) Aktiengesellschaft ohne Nachschußpflicht; ~ **insurance company** Versicherungsgesellschaft; ~ **corporation** (US) Aktiengesellschaft; ~ **land bank** (US) Landwirtschaftsbank auf Aktien.

joint | suitor Nebenpartei; ~ **supply** gemeinsames Angebot, Kupplungsangebot; ~ **surety** Mitbürgschaft, Mit-, Solidarbürge; ~ **tariff** Sammeltarif; ~ **tenancy** Mitbesitz, -pacht, *(tenure by two persons)* Gesamthandseigentum; ~ **tenant** Gesamthandseigentümer; ~ **title** Eigentum zur gesamten Hand; ~ **tort** gemeinsam begangene unerlaubte Handlung; ~ **tortfeasors** Mit-, Gemeinschaftstäter, Mittäterschaft; ~ **translator** Mitübersetzer; ~ **trespass** gemeinsam begangene Besitzstörung; ~ **trial** gemeinsames Strafverfahren; ~ **trustee** Gegentreuhänder; ~ **undersigner** Mitunterzeichner; ~ **undertaking** Gemeinschaftsunternehmen, Partizipationsgeschäft; ~ **use** gemeinschaftliche Nutznießung, Mitbenutzung, Mitgebrauch; ~ **user** Mitbenutzer; ~ **venture** Beteiligungsgeschäft, Gemeinschaftsunternehmen, gemeinschaftliche Beteiligung, *(contracting)* Arbeitsgemeinschaft, *(banking)* Metageschäft, *(ownership)* Beteiligungsverhältnis; ~ **venture agreement** Gemeinschaftsabkommen, Arbeitsgemeinschaft; ~ **venture company** Beteiligungsgesellschaft; ~ **warrant** Gesamtbürgschaft; ~ **warrantor** Solidar-, Gesamtbürge; ~ **warranty** Solidarhaftung, -bürgschaft; ~ **will** *(US)* gemeinsames Testament; ~ **working** Gemeinschaftsbetrieb.

joint and several gesamtschuldnerisch, gemeinsam, solidarisch; ~ **bond** gesamtschuldnerisches Zahlungsversprechen; ~ **bonds** von mehreren Gesellschaften ausgegebene Obligationen; ~ **contract** Gesamtschuldverhältnis; ~ **credit** Gemeinschaftskredit; ~ **creditor** Gesamtgläubiger; ~ **debt** Gesamt-, Solidarschuld; ~ **debtor** Gesamtschuldner; ~ **liability** gesamtschuldnerische (gemeinsame, solidarische) Haftung; ~ **note** *(US)* gesamtschuldnerisches Zahlungsversprechen; ~ **obligation** gesamtschuldnerische Verpflichtung, Gesamtverbindlichkeit; ~ **responsibility** gesamtschuldnerische Haftung.

jointist Inhaber eines verbotenen Alkoholausschanks.

jointly zusammen; **to be sued** ~ gemeinschaftlich verklagt werden; **to inherit** ~ zusammen erben, miterben; **to own a house** ~ Haus gemeinsam besitzen; **to possess s. th.** ~ etw. gemeinsam besitzen; **to render** ~ **liable** als Streitgenossen (solidarisch) haftbar machen; **to start a company** ~ **with s. o.** gemeinsam eine Gesellschaft gründen; ~ **acquired property** gemeinsame Anschaffungen, *(US)* Errungenschaftsgemeinschaft; ~ **owned** im gemeinsamen Eigentum; ~ **entitled person** Mitberechtigter.

jointly and severally liable insgesamt und einzeln (gesamtschuldnerisch) haftbar; **to be** ~ als Gesamtschuldner (gesamtschuldnerisch) haften; **to own a house** ~ Haus gemeinsam besitzen; **to use** ~ mitbenutzen; ~ **owned** im gemeinsamen Eigentum; ~ **owned assets** Gesamthandsvermögen.

jointress, jointuress nießbrauchberechtigte Witwe.
jointure Wittum, Leibgedinge, Nießbrauchrecht der Witwe am Mannesvermögen; ~ *(v.)* Leibgedinge aussetzen; **to settle a** ~ **on one's wife** seiner Frau ein Wittum aussetzen.

joke Witz; **no** ~ keine Kleinigkeit, ernsthafte Sache; **practical** ~ Schabernack, Streich; ~ **of the village** Dorftrottel, Gespött der Stadt; **to play a practical** ~ **on s. o.** jem. einen Streich spielen; **to see a** ~ Witz verstehen.

joker *(pol., US sl.)* Hintertür, absichtliche Unwirksamkeitsklausel.

jolly (boat) Jolle.
jolt Ruck, Stoß; ~ **of electric current** Stromstoß; ~**s of the road** holprige Straßenstellen; ~ *(v.) (bus)* rattern; ~ **along** dahinholpern; **to throw a severe** ~ **into s. th.** einer Sache einen schweren Stoß versetzen.

josh *(US sl.)* Verulkung, Veräppelung; ~ *(v.)* hänseln, veräppeln, hochnehmen.

jostle Zusammenstoß; ~ *(v.)* anrempeln, -puffen; ~ **with s. o. for s. th.** sich mit jem. um etw. drängeln; ~ **each other** einander ins Gehege kommen; ~ **s. o. out of the way** j. zur Seite stoßen; ~ **one's way to the front** sich nach oben durchboxen.

jostlement Gedrängel.
jot Jota, Deut; **not one** ~ **or tittle** kein bißchen; ~ *(v.)* **down** aufschreiben, notieren.

jotter Notizbuch.
jottings kurzer Vermerk, Notizen.
journal Tagebuch, *(bookkeeping)* Journal, Memorial, Primanote, *(periodical)* Zeitschrift, *(press)* [Tages]zeitung, *(railway)* Fahrtbericht, *(ship)* Logbuch, *(technical)* Achsschenkel, Zapfen; **the ~s** *(parliament, Br.)* Protokollbuch, Parlamentsberichte; **bills-payable** ~ *(US)* Wechselverfallbuch; **bills-receivable** ~ *(US)* Wechseldebitorenbuch; **cash** ~ Kassenjournal; **cash disbursements** ~ Kassenausgangsjournal; **cash receipts** ~ Kasseneingangsjournal; **economic** ~ Wirtschaftszeitung; **evening** ~ Abendblatt; **fashion** ~ Modezeitschrift; **finished-goods** ~ Fertigwarenjournal; **general** ~ Hauptbuch; **ledger** ~ Hauptbuch und Journal; **ledgertype** ~ in Tabellenform geführtes Hauptbuch, amerikanisches Journal; **monthly** ~ Monatszeitschrift; **multi-column** ~ Mehrspaltenjournal; **petty-cash** ~ Portokassenbuch; **private** ~ Geheimbuch; **professional** ~ Fachzeitschrift; **purchase** ~ Wareneingangsbuch; **purchase returns** ~ Einkaufsretourenjournal; **requisition** ~ Warenbeschaffungsjournal; **sales** ~ Warenausgangsbuch, Verkaufsjournal; **sales return** ~ Rückwarenbuch; **scientific** ~ wissenschaftliche Zeitschrift; **simple** ~ Journal für einfache Buchführung; **technical** ~ Fachzeitschrift; **trade** ~ Handelsblatt; **two-column** ~ Zweispaltenjournal; ~ **of a society** Vereinsblatt; ~ *(v.)* in ein Tagebuch eintragen, *(journalize)* Journal führen; **to bring the cash through the** ~ Kasse journalisieren; **to maintain a** ~ Journal führen; **to post into the** ~ ins Journal übertragen; **to run through the** ~ Journal durchlaufen; **to suppress a** ~ Zeitung verbieten; ~ **bearing** Zapfenlager; ~ **book** Journal, Tagebuch; ~ **entry** Journaleintragung, -buchung; **compound** ~ **entry** zusammengefaßte Journalbuchung; ~ **form** Journalblatt; ~ **item** Journalposten; ~ **number** Geschäftszeichen; ~ **voucher** Buchungsbeleg.

journalese Zeitungsstil, -sprache, -jargon.
journalism Journalismus, Berichterstattung, Zeitungs-, Pressewesen, Publizistik.
journalist Journalist, Publizist, Schriftsteller, *(editor)* Schriftleiter, *(keeper of diary)* Tagebuchführer; **broadcast** ~ Rundfunkreporter; **financial** ~ Börsenberichterstatter, -journalist; **independent** ~ freier Journalist; **lady** ~ Journalistin; **investigative political** ~ auf politischem Gebiet recherchierender Journalist; **sensational** ~ reißerisch schreibender Journalist; **to be a** ~ Beruf eines Journalisten ausüben.

journalistic publizistisch, journalistisch; ~ **experience** journalistische Erfahrungen; ~ **literature** Tagesliteratur; ~ **skills** journalistische Fähigkeiten.

journalization Eintragung ins Journal.
journalize *(v.)* ins Journal eintragen, Journal führen, *(write a diary)* Tagebuch führen, *(write for newspapers)* für [Tages]zeitungen schreiben.

journey [Tages]reise, Weg, Route; ~ **abroad** Auslandsreise; ~ **back** Rück-, Herfahrt; **day's** ~ Tagesreise; **a four hours' train** ~ vierstündige Eisenbahnfahrt; **leisure** ~ Reise in Etappen; **long** ~ weite Reise; **nonstop** ~ Reise ohne Unterbrechungen; **official** ~ Dienstreise; **omnibus** ~ Autobusfahrt; **outward** ~ *(Br.)* Aus-, Hinreise; **return** ~ Rückreise; **sea** ~ Schiffsreise; ~ **there and back** Hin- und Rückfahrt; ~ **by air** Flug[reise]; ~ **on business** Geschäftsreise; ~ **full of incidents** Reise mit zahlreichen Zwischenfällen; ~ **for pleasure** Vergnügungsreise; ~ **on Shanks' mare** Reise auf Schusters Rappen; **to arrange for a** ~ Reisevorbereitungen treffen; **to break one's** ~ **at X.** seine Reise in X unterbrechen; **to continue one's** ~ seine Reise fortsetzen; **to go on a** ~ verreisen, Reise unternehmen; **to interrupt one's** ~ seine Reise unterbrechen; **to make a** ~ **halfway round the world** halbe Weltreise unternehmen; **to make ([under]take) a** ~ Reise unternehmen; **to proceed on (resume) one's** ~ seine Reise fortsetzen; **to prosecute a** ~ **with utmost speed** Reise mit größter Beschleunigung fortsetzen; **to set out (start) on a** ~ Reise antreten; **to start on the return** ~ Rückreise antreten; **to write an account of a** ~ Reisebericht verfassen; **to reach one's** ~**'s end** sein Reiseziel erreichen.

journeyer Reisender.
journeyman Wanderbursche, *(worker)* Lohnarbeiter, Geselle, Gehilfe, Handlanger; **full-fledged** ~ voll ausgebildeter Geselle; ~ **clock** Kontrolluhr; ~**'s examination** Gesellenprüfung; **approved** ~**'s rate** Gesellenlohn; ~ **wages** Gehilfen-, Gesellenlöhne.

journeywork Routinearbeit, *(badly paid work)* schlecht bezahlte (niedrige) Arbeit.

joy ride Spazierenfahren, Spazier-, Schwarz-, Vergnügungsfahrt, Spritztour.

joy-ride *(v.)* Vergnügungsfahrt (Spritztour) machen, Schwarzfahrt unternehmen.

joy | riding Vergnügungs-, Schwarzfahrt; ~ **stick** *(airplane, coll.)* Steuerknüppel.

jubilee [Dienst]jubiläum;
  diamond ~ sechzigjähriges Jubiläum; **silver** ~ fünfundzwanzigjähriges Jubiläum, silberne Hochzeit; ~ **stamp** Jubiläumsmarke.

judge, Richter, Beisitzer, *(connoisseur)* Fachmann;
  the ~s Richterkollegium;
  alternate ~ stellvertretender Richter; **appellate** ~ Berufungs-, Revisionsrichter; **assistant** ~ Hilfsrichter; **associate** ~ beisitzender (beigeordneter) Richter, Beisitzer; **challenged** ~ abgelehnter Richter; **chief** ~ Gerichtspräsident; **circuit** ~ herumreisender Richter; **city ~** *(US)* Friedensrichter; **corrupt** ~ käuflicher Richter; **court of appeal** ~ Berufungsrichter; **district** ~ Bezirks-, Amtsrichter; **lay** ~ Laienrichter; **learned** ~ gelehrter Richter; **~ ordinary** *(US)* ordentlicher Richter; **partial** ~ voreingenommener Richter; **presiding** ~ vorsitzender Richter; **probate** ~ *(US)* Nachlaßrichter; **professional** ~ Berufsrichter; **puisne** ~ untergeordneter Richter, Beisitzer; **regular** ~ ordentlicher Richter; **senior** ~ dienstältester Richter; **side** ~ Beisitzer; **~ sitting** vorsitzender (den Vorsitz führender) Richter; **supervising** ~ aufsichtsführender Richter; **trial** ~ *(US)* erstinstanzlicher Richter, Vorderrichter; **vacation** ~ *(Br.)* Ferienrichter, Richter während der Ferienzeit; **venal** ~ bestechlicher Richter;
  ~ of appeal Berufungsrichter; **~ in bankruptcy** Konkursrichter; **~ in chambers** Einzelrichter; **~ of character** Menschenkenner; **~ sitting in court** vorsitzender (amtierender) Richter; **~ of election** *(US)* Wahlprüfer; **~ of fact** Vorderrichter; **~ de facto** als Richter fungierende Person; **~s at a flower show** Preisrichterkollegium auf einer Blumenausstellung; **~ in lunacy** Vormundschaftsrichter; **~ of police** *(Scot.)* Polizeirichter; **~ pro tempore** Hilfsrichter;
  ~ *(v.)* beurteilen, entscheiden, *(law court)* Recht sprechen, richterlich entscheiden, Urteil fällen;
  ~ by appearance nach dem äußeren Aussehen entscheiden; **~ in favo(u)r of s. th.** sich für etw. entscheiden; **~ it necessary to do s. th.** etw. für notwendig halten; **~ others by o. s.** Dritte nach seinen eigenen Fähigkeiten messen; **~ in the last resort** letztinstanzlich entscheiden;
  to be a ~ of s. th. sich auf etw. verstehen; **to be a fair ~ of s. th.** ziemlich gutes Urteil über etw. abgeben können; **to be appointed ~** zum Richter ernannt werden; **to be no ~** kein Fachmann sein; **to challenge a ~** Richter ablehnen; **to come before the ~** vors Gericht kommen; **to constitute s. o. a ~** j. als Richter einsetzen; **to disqualify a ~** Richter von der Ausübung des Richteramtes ausschließen; **to leave it to the country to ~** Urteil der öffentlichen Meinung überlassen;
  ~ advocate *(Br.)* Kriegsgerichtsrat, *(US)* Militäranwalt; **~ Advocate-General** Präsident des Kassationshofes; **~'s certificate** Kostenbescheinigung, -feststellungsbeschluß; **~ delegate** beauftragter Richter; **~-made** auf richterliche Entscheidung beruhend; **~-made law** Richterrecht; **~'s minutes (notes)** handschriftliche richterliche Protokollnotizen; **~'s orders** richterliche Verfügung; **~'s rules** *(Br.)* Verhörrichtlinien.

judgment *(ability to judge)* Entscheidungsfähigkeit, *(court of law)* richterliche Entscheidung, Gerichtsurteil, -entscheidung, Urteilsspruch, *(discretion)* Ermessen, *(opinion)* Meinung, Gutdünken, *(process of judging)* Urteilsfällung, Beurteilung;
  in my ~ nach meinem Befinden; **in the ~ of the management** nach Ansicht der Geschäftsführung;
  as appears from the ~ of the court wie aus dem Urteil hervorgeht;
  alternative ~ nach den Wünschen der unterlegenen Partei auszufüllendes Leistungsurteil; **business** ~ kaufmännisches Urteilsvermögen; **clear** ~ gesundes Urteilsvermögen; **conditional** ~ bedingtes Endurteil; **consent** ~ Prozeßvergleich; **contra-dictory** ~ kontradiktorisches Urteil; **declaratory** ~ Feststellungsurteil; **default** ~ Versäumnisurteil; **deficiency** ~ Ausfallurteil; **domestic** ~ inländisches Urteil; **dormant** ~ nicht mehr vollstreckbares Urteil, verjährtes Urteil; **enforceable** ~ vollstreckbares Urteil; **provisionally enforceable** vorläufig vollstreckbares Urteil; **enforced** ~ vollstreckte Entscheidung; **favo(u)rable** ~ obsiegendes Urteil; **final** ~ rechtskräftiges (letztinstanzliches) Urteil; **foreign** ~ im Ausland ergangenes Urteil;

interlocutory ~ Zwischenurteil, -entscheidung; **irregular** ~ von der ständigen Rechtssprechung abweichendes Urteil, verfahrenswidrig ergangenes Urteil; **junior** ~ Vorurteil; **money** ~ Zahlungsurteil; **nice** ~ kritisches Urteil; **~ over** *(US)* Regreßurteil; **personal** ~ Leistungsurteil; **previous** ~ früheres Urteil; **provisional** ~ vorläufiges Urteil, Vorbehaltsurteil; **reserved** ~ vorsichtige Stellungnahme; **reversible** ~ der Aufhebung unterliegendes Urteil; **simulated** ~ erschlichenes Urteil; **situational** ~ Situationserkenntnis; **snap** ~ vorschnelles Urteil; **sound** ~ gesundes Urteilsvermögen; **subjective** ~ subjektives Urteil; **summary** ~ Urteil im Urkundenprozeß, abgekürztes Urteil; **unsatisfied** ~ nicht vollstrecktes Urteil; **value** ~ Werturteil; **void** ~ nichtiges Urteil;
  ~ of board of directors Vorstandsbeschluß; **~ of character** Menschenkenntnis, -beurteilung; **~ by confession** *(US)* Anerkenntnisurteil; **~ by consent** Anerkenntnisurteil; **~ for costs** Kostenurteil, -entscheidung; **~ by default** Versäumnisurteil; **~ of dismissal** ablehnende Entscheidung, abweisendes Urteil; **~ in error** Revisionsurteil; **~ of execution** Vollstreckungsbefehl; **~ liable to stay off execution** dem Vollstreckungsaufschub unterliegendes Urteil; **~ at interim** Zwischenurteil; **~ at law** rechtskräftiges Urteil; **~ on the merits** Entscheidung in der Hauptsache, Sachurteil; **~ in personam** Leistungsurteil; **~ given for the plaintiff** Urteil zugunsten des Klägers; **~ quashed on a point of law** aus Rechtsgründen aufgehobenes Urteil; **~ of recovery** *(US)* rechtskräftiges Urteil; **~ in rem** Gestaltungsurteil, Urteil mit Wirkung für und gegen alle; **~ in restraint** nach Klageverzicht ergehendes Urteil; **~ on verdict** Sachurteil; **~ on a special verdict** bei unstreitigem Sachverhalt ergehendes Urteil;
  to acquiesce in a ~ Urteil annehmen; **to act with ~** verständnisvoll handeln; **to affirm a ~** Urteil bestätigen; **to appeal against a ~** Rechtsmittel (Berufung) einlegen; **to arrest ~** Urteil (Verfahren) aussetzen; **to carry a ~ into execution** Vollstreckungsklausel erteilen; **to carry out a ~** Urteil vollstrecken; **to come up for ~** verhandelt werden; **to confess ~** Urteil anerkennen; **to confirm a ~** Urteil bestätigen; **to deliver a ~** Urteil fällen; **to deliver ~ by default** Versäumnisurteil ergehen lassen; **to deliver a ~ in the first instance** in erster Instanz entscheiden; **to enforce (execute) a ~** Urteil vollstrecken; **to enter into ~ with s. o.** in Beratungen mit jem. eintreten; **to execute a ~** Urteil vollstrecken; **to fight a case to find ~** Prozeß bis zur letzten Instanz durchfechten; **to file a ~** Vollstreckbarkeit eines Urteils beantragen; **to form one's ~** sich ein Urteil bilden; **to found a ~ on an award** Urteil auf einen Schiedsspruch gründen; **to give ~** Urteil sprechen; **to give one's ~** seine Meinung äußern; **to give ~ in favo(u)r of s. o.** Prozeß zu jds. Gunsten entscheiden, zu jds. Gunsten anerkennen; **to hand down ~** Urteil verkünden; **to have a sound ~** Urteilsvermögen besitzen; **to move an arrest of ~** Aussetzung eines Urteils (Urteilsaussetzung) beantragen; **to obtain a ~** Urteil erwirken; **to obtain ~ against a debtor** Urteil gegen einen Schuldner erwirken; **to pass ~** Urteil fällen; **to pass an adverse (unfavo(u)rable) ~ on s. th.** etw. abfällig beurteilen; **to pass a ~ for the plaintiff in a suit** Urteil zugunsten des Klägers erlassen; **to pass ~ on a prisoner** Angeklagten aburteilen; **to pass ~ on a work** *(fam.)* Werturteil über eine Arbeit fällen; **to perfect ~** *(US)* Urteil vervollständigen; **to pronounce a ~** Urteil fällen; **to pronounce a ~ in open court** Urteil öffentlich verkünden; **to quash a ~ on a point of law** Urteil aus Rechtsgründen aufheben; **to render ~** Urteil sprechen; **to reopen a ~** Verfahren wieder aufnehmen; **to reserve a ~** Urteilsverkündung aussetzen; **to reverse one's ~** seine Meinung ändern; **to reverse a ~ on appeal** Urteil in der Berufungsinstanz aufheben; **to review a ~** Urteil der Vorinstanz überprüfen; **to satisfy a ~** sich aus einem Urteil befriedigen; **to secure a ~** Urteil erwirken; **to set aside a ~** Urteil aufheben; **to set forth the reasons for a ~** Urteil begründen; **to sit in ~ upon s. o.** über j. zu Gericht sitzen; **to sit in ~ on a case** Fall verhandeln; **to squash a ~** Urteil aufheben; **to stay a ~** Vollstreckung eines Urteils aussetzen; **to submit to s. one's ~** jds. Belieben stellen, jem. anheimstellen; **to suspend a ~** Urteilsverkündung aussetzen, Vollstreckung eines Urteils aussetzen; **to sustain a ~** Urteil bestätigen; **to uphold a ~** Urteil bestätigen; **to use one's best ~** nach bestem Ermessen handeln; **to vacate a ~** Urteil aufheben (umstoßen); **to vacate a ~ on appeal** Urteil in der Berufungsinstanz aufheben;
  ~ book Urteilsregister; **~ cap** Richterkappe; **~s column** Gerichtsspalte; **~ creditor** Vollstreckungsgläubiger; **~ day** Tag des letzten Gerichts; **~ debt** gerichtlich anerkannte (vollstreckbare) Forderung, Vollstreckungsforderung; **debtor** Vollstreckungsschuldner; **~ [debtor] summons** *(Br.)* Konkursandrohung mit Zahlungsbefehl, Vorladung wegen Nichtbezah-

lung der Urteilsschuld, Antrag auf Beugehaft; ~ **docket** Prozeßregister; ~ **execution** vollstreckbare Urteilsausfertigung; ~ **hall** Gerichtssaal; ~ **lien** *(US)* gerichtlich festgestelltes Zurückbehaltungsrecht, *(real estate)* Arrest-, Zwangshypothek; ~ **limit** gerichtliche festgesetzte Schadensersatzgrenze; ~ **note** Schuldschein mit Unterwerfungsklausel, Schuldanerkenntnisschein; ~ **paper** beglaubigter Urteilsentwurf; ~-**proof** *(US)* nicht pfändbar, nicht der Zwangsvollstreckung unterliegend, nicht betreibbar, pfändungsfrei; ~ **rate** *(fire insurance)* Selbsteinschätzung; ~ **record** Sitzungsprotokoll; ~ **roll** Urteilsurkunde mit Ladungsnachweis; ~ **sample** *(statistics)* subjektiv ausgewählte Stichprobe; ~ **sampling** bewußte Auswahl, *(marketing)* stichprobenartig durchgeführte Meinungsforschung; ~ **seat** Richterplatz, -sitz, -stuhl; ~ **summons** Antrag auf Beugehaft.

judgeship Richteramt.
judicable gerichtsfähig, *(case)* verhandlungsreif.
judicative zum Urteil befähigt;
~ **power** Urteilskraft.
judicator Rechtssprecher.
judicatory richterlich, gerichtlich;
~ **power** richterliche Gewalt; ~ **tribunal** Gerichtshof.
judicature Rechtssprechung, -pflege, *(law court)* Gerichtshof, *(tenure of office)* Amtsperiode;
᷄ **Act** *(Br.)* Gerichtsverfassungsgesetz.
judice, sub rechtshängig.
judicial gerichtlich, richterlich, *(criminal)* kritisch, scharf im Urteil;
quasi ~ gerichtsähnlich;
~ **and extrajudicial** gerichtlich und außergerichtlich;
~ **act** gerichtliche (richterliche) Entscheidung; ~ **action** gerichtliches Verfahren; ~ **admission** Geständnis vor Gericht; ~ **authorities** Justiz-, Gerichtsbehörden; ~ **authority** richterliche Gewalt, Ermächtigung, Gerichtsbarkeit; ~ **bench** Richterbank; ~ **bond** Kaution; ~ **branch** Justizwesen; ~ **bribery** Richterbestechung; ~ **business** gerichtliche Tätigkeit; **to speed** ~ **business** gerichtliches Verfahren beschleunigen; **in his** ~ **capacity** in seiner Eigenschaft als Richter; ~ **circuit** *(US)* Gerichtsbezirk; ~ **cognizance** Kenntnis des Gerichts; ~ **conception** Rechtsauffassung; ~ **confession** gerichtliches Geständnis; ~ **construction** richterliche Auslegung; ~ **control** richterliche Nachprüfung; ~ **convention** aufgrund einer Gerichtsanordnung getroffene Vereinbarung; ~ **corruption** Richterbestechung; ~ **court** Gerichtshof; ~ **custom** Rechtsgewohnheit; ~ **day** Gerichtstag; ~ **decision** richterliche Tätigkeit, richterliche (gerichtliche) Entscheidung, Gerichtsurteil; ~ **declaration** Erklärung vor Gericht, eidesstattliche Erklärung; ~ **declaration of law** ständige Rechtssprechung; ~ **department** Justizverwaltung; ~ **dictum** richterliche Meinungsäußerung; ~ **discretion** richterliches Ermessen; ~ **district** Gerichtsbezirk; ~ **divorce** Ehescheidung; ~ **document** Gerichtsurkunde, Prozeßakte; ~ **enquiry** gerichtliche Untersuchung; ~ **entitlement** Rechtstitel; ~ **error** Justizirrtum; ~ **evidence** Beweiserhebung, -mittel; ~ **factor** gerichtlich bestellter Pfleger (Vermögensverwalter), *(Scot.)* vom Gericht eingesetzter Verwalter (Pfleger), Nachlaßverwalter; ~ **faculty** Unterscheidungsvermögen; ~ **function** richterliche Funktion, Richteramt; **to discharge** ~ **functions** richterliche Funktionen ausüben (wahrnehmen); ~ **hearing** mündliche Verhandlung, Gerichtsverhandlung; ~ **inquiry** gerichtliche Untersuchung; ~ **inspection** richterlicher Augenschein; ~ **knowledge** Kenntnis des Gerichts, gerichtsnotorisch; ~ **legislation** Rechtsschöpfung durch die Gerichte; ~ **mind** kritischer Verstand; ~ **mortgage** *(Louisiana)* gerichtlich entstandenes Pfandrecht; ~ **murder** Justizmord; ~ **notice** Gerichtskenntnis; ~ **oath** vom Richter abgenommener Eid; ~ **office** Richteramt; ~ **officer** Justizbeamter, Richter; ~ **opinion** Urteilsbegründung; ~ **order** Gerichtsbeschluß, gerichtliche (richterliche) Verfügung; ~ **panel** Rechtsausschuß; ~ **power** richterliche Gewalt, Justizhoheit; **to be invested with** ~ **powers** mit richterlicher Gewalt ausgestattet sein; ~ **proceedings** Gerichtsverhandlung, gerichtliches Verfahren; **to take** ~ **proceedings** Rechtsweg beschreiten; ~ **process** Vorladung vor Gericht; ~ **protection** Rechtsschutz; ~ **question** vom Gericht zu entscheidende Frage; ~ **records** Gerichtsakten; **to obtain** ~ **redress** gerichtliche Abhilfe erzielen; ~ **reform** Justizreform; ~ **remedy** Rechtsbehelf; ~ **rent** gerichtlich festgesetzte Miete; ~ **review of administrative action** *(US)* richterliche Nachprüfung von Verwaltungsmaßnahmen, Normenkontrolle; ~ **ruling** Gerichtsentscheidung; ~ **sale** *(Scot.)* gerichtlich angeordneter Verkauf, Zwangsversteigerung; ~ **separation** Trennung von Tisch und Bett, gerichtliche Trennung; ~ **sequestration** gericht-

liche Beschlagnahme; ~ **statistics** Gerichtsstatistik; ~ **survey** Lokaltermin; ~ **system** Rechtssystem, -pflege; ~ **township** *(US)* Gerichtsbezirk; ~ **trustee** gerichtlich bestellter Treuhänder; ᷄ **Trustees Act** *(Br.)* Pflegschaftsgesetz; ~ **writ** richterliche Anordnung (Verfügung).
judiciary Gerichtswesen, -verfassung, -system, Richterstand, *(US)* richterliche Gewalt;
~ *(a.)* gerichtlich, richterlich;
᷄ **Act** *(US)* Gerichtsverfassungsgesetz; ~ **committee** Rechtsausschuß; ~ **proceedings** Prozeßverfahren.
judicious verständig, einsichtsvoll, abgewogen.
judiciousness Wohlabgewogenheit.
jug Krug, Kanne, *(clink, sl.)* Kittchen, Kasten, Knast;
~ *(v.)* ins Kittchen stecken;
to be in ~ eingelocht sein, im Kittchen sitzen; **to put in** ~ *(fam.)* einlochen.
juggernaut Moloch, *(truck)* Riesentransporter, -laster, Lastzug;
~ **of war** Kriegsmoloch.
juggle Taschenspielerei, -trick, Hokuspokus;
financial ~ Finanzschwindel;
~ *(v.)* jonglieren, *(practice imposture)* schwindeln, manipulieren, frisieren;
~ **with s. o.** falsches Spiel mit jem. treiben; ~ **the accounts** Konten frisieren; ~ **with the facts** Tatsachen verfälschen; ~ **with s. one's feelings** mit jds. Gefühlen Schindluder treiben; ~ **with figures** mit Zahlen jonglieren; ~ **s. o. out of his money** jem. das Geld aus der Tasche ziehen.
juggler Taschenspieler, Zauberkünstler, Jongleur, *(impostor)* Betrüger.
jugglery Jonglieren.
jugular vein *(fig.)* Lebensader.
juice Saft, *(sl.)* Sprit, Schnaps;
fruit ~ Fruchtsaft; **orange** ~ Orangensaft;
to let s. o. stew in his own ~ j. im eigenen Saft schmoren lassen;
to step on the ~ **Gas** geben.
juicy saftig, interessant, spannend.
juke | box Musikautomat; ~ **joint** *(US sl.)* Spelunke, Tanzlokal, Restaurant mit Plattenautomat.
jumble Ramsch, Trödel, *(confused mixture)* Wirrwarr, Durcheinander;
~ **of words** Mischmasch von Worten;
~ *(v.)* **up** durcheinanderbringen, -werfen;
~ **sale** *(Br.)* Ramschverkauf; ~ **shop** *(Br.)* Trödel-, Ramschladen.
jumbled story verwirrte Geschichte.
jumbo Trampel, Elefantenküken, *(person, Br., sl.)* Leuchte, Kanone;
~ *(a.)* *(US)* riesengroß;
~ **jet** Riesendüsenflugzeug; ~ **size** kolossale Größe.
jump Sprung, Satz, *(advantage, US coll.)* Vorsprung, -gabe, Vorteil, *(burglary, Br., sl.)* Ding, Einbruch, *(film)* Umsprung [von Nah- und Fernaufnahme], *(journey)* Reisestrecke, *(parachutist)* Fallschirmabsprung, *(prices)* sprunghaftes Emporschnellen, rasanter (sprunghafter) Anstieg, *(promoting)* Übergehen;
on the ~ zerfahren, nervös, ruhelos;
the ~**s** *(sl.)* Säuferwahnsinn;
price ~**s** Preis-, Kurssprünge;
~ **in costs** plötzlicher Kostenanstieg; ~ **in crime** Anstieg der Kriminalität, Zunahme der Verbrechen; ~ **in a curve** Bruch in einer Kurve; ~ **in earnings** sprunghafter Ertragsanstieg; ~ **in exports** plötzlicher Ausfuhranstieg; ~ **in imports** plötzlicher Einfuhranstieg; ~ **in incomes** sprunghafter Einkommensanstieg; ~ **in orders** kräftiger Auftragsanstieg; ~ **in prices** Preis-, Kurssprünge, plötzliche Preissteigerung; ~ **in production** rasanter Produktionsanstieg; **40%** ~ **in salary** 40%iger Gehaltsanstieg; ~ **in sales** plötzlicher Umsatzanstieg;
~ *(v.)* *(prices)* emporschnellen, plötzlich steigen, sprunghaft ansteigen, *(in promotion)* überspringen, *(railroad, US)* auf-, abspringen, *(typewriter)* springen;
~ **back into the fray** sich wieder ins Getümmel stürzen; ~ **one's bail** *(US)* Bürgschaft schießen (Kaution verfallen) lassen; ~ **on the bandwaggon** zur erfolgreichen Partei umschwenken, Mitläufer sein; ~ **at a bargain** Gelegenheit beim Schopf ergreifen; ~ **one's camera** sich seinen Photoapparat schnappen; ~ **channels** *(US)* Instanzenweg nicht einhalten; ~ **a claim** *(US)* sich einen Mutungsanspruch anmaßen; ~ **to a conclusion** voreiligen Schluß ziehen; ~ **down s. one's throat** jem. über den Mund fahren (aufs Dach steigen); ~ **into new high ground** *(prices)* sprunghaft steigen und einen neuen Höchstkurs erzielen; ~ **the gun** sich einen unfairen Vorteil verschaffen; ~ **a locality** *(US)* Gegend verlassen; ~ **s. one's nerves** jem. auf die Nerven gehen; ~ **off**

their office blocks aus dem Geschäft der Errichtung von Bürogebäuden aussteigen; ~ **at an offer** *(fam.)* sich über ein Angebot freuen; ~ **at an opportunity** mit beiden Händen zugreifen; ~ **out of the frying pan into the fire** vom Regen in die Traufe kommen; ~ **out of a moving train** aus einem fahrenden Zug abspringen; ~ **prices** Preise sprunghaft erhöhen; ~ **into new purchase** sich auf Neuerwerbungen stürzen; ~ **a question on s. o.** jem. mit einer Fragestellung überraschen; ~ **the queue** sich vordrängeln; ~ **the rails** entgleisen; ~ **out of one's skin** aus der Haut fahren; ~ **a stronghold** befestigte Stellung im Sturm nehmen; ~ **from one subject to another** Gesprächsthemen ununterbrochen wechseln; ~ **on the stock exchange** an der Börse kräftig steigen; ~ **to it** *(sl.)* etw. mit Schwung in Angriff nehmen; ~ **into a taxi** sich in ein Taxi stürzen; ~ **the track** entgleisen; ~ **a train** *(US)* Zug ohne Fahrkarte benutzen, schwarzfahren; ~ **up** emporschnellen, plötzlich steigen; **to be all of a** ~ schlechtes Nervenkostüm haben; **to be one** ~ **ahead of one's competitors** der Konkurrenz immer um eine Nasenlänge voraus sein; **to be for the high** ~ sich auf das Schlimmste gefaßt machen müssen; **to be ~ed at** sehr gefragt sein; **to get the** ~ **on s. o.** *(US)* jem. den Rang ablaufen; **to get the** ~ **on one's competitors** *(US)* seine Konkurrenz überflügeln; **to go up with a** ~ *(stock exchange)* plötzlich in die Höhe gehen; **to have the ~s** an Säuferwahnsinn leiden; **to keep s. o. on the ~** *(coll.)* j. in Trapp halten; **to stay one** ~ **ahead of s. o.** jem. stets einen Schritt voraus sein;

~ **area** *(parachutist)* Absprungsgebiet; ~ **master** *(parachutist)* Absetzer; ~ **seat** *(car, US)* Klappsitz.

jumped-up improvisiert, *(arrogant, coll.)* hochgestochen.

jumping-off | place Endstation; ~ **point** *(parachutist)* Absprungspunkt.

jumping seat *(car)* Klappsitz.

jumping | of the metals Entgleisen; ~ **over of details** stillschweigende Auslassung von Einzelheiten;
political ~-jack politischer Hampelmann.

jumpy, to make s. o. j. nervös machen.

junction Treffpunkt, *(mil.)* Vereinigung, *(railway)* [Eisenbahn]knotenpunkt, Zweigstation, Anschlußbahnhof, Eisenbahnanschluß, *(road)* [Straßen]kreuzung, *(siding)* Gleisanschluß, Anschlußgleis;
main ~ Hauptknotenpunkt; **police-controlled** ~ Kreuzung mit polizeilicher Verkehrsregelung; **traffic** ~ Verkehrsknotenpunkt;
~ **box** *(el.)* Anschlußdose; ~ **canal** Verbindungskanal; ~ **line** Anschlußgleis; ~ **point** Frachtknotenpunkt; ~ **rail** Verbindungsgleis; ~ **railway** Anschlußbahn.

juncture *(crisis)* [kritischer] Zeitpunkt, Krisis, Krisenzeit, *(connection)* Verbindungsstelle;
at this ~ an dieser Stelle, in diesem Augenblick.

jungle Dschungel, *(hobo camp, US sl.)* Landstreicherlager;
tangled ~ **of facts** undurchdringliches Dickicht von Tatsachen; **to cut a passage through the** ~ sich einen Weg durch den Urwald bahnen;
~ **market** *(stock exchange, Br.)* Markt für westafrikanische Bergwerksaktien; ~ **warfare** Dschungelkrieg.

junior Junior, *(in office)* Untergeordneter;
~ *(a.)* junior, jünger [als], *(lower in rank)* untergeordnet, nachrangig, niedriger;
~ **accountant** Hilfsprüfer; ~ **barrister** jüngerer Teilhaber einer Sozietät, Juniorpartner; ~ **bonds** durch nachstehende Hypothek gesicherte Schuldverschreibungen; ~ **bondholder** Neubesitzer; ~ **branch** Jugendorganisation; ~ **championship** Jugendmeisterschaft; ~ **clerk** Bürohilfe; ~ **counsel** [etwa] Anwaltsassessor; ~ **creditor** nachrangiger Gläubiger; ~ **detention Centre** *(Br.)* Jugendstrafanstalt; ~ **employee** Jungarbeiter [14 - 18 Jahre]; ~ **execution** Anschlußpfändung; ~ **forms** *(Br.)* die ersten vier Volksschulklassen, Grundschulklassen; ~ **group** Juniorengruppe; ~ **high school** *(US)* [etwa] Real-, Mittelschule; ~ **hospital doctor** Assistenzarzt; ~ **issue** durch nachstehendes Pfandrecht gesicherte Serie von Obligationen, *(US)* Sammelaktien; ~ **lawyer** [etwa] Anwaltsassessor; ~ **lien** jüngeres (nachstehendes) Pfandrecht; ~ **lien bond** durch nachrangige Hypothek gesicherte Obligation; ~ **management** unterste Unternehmensführung; ~ **minister** Staatsminister; ~ **mortgage** *(US)* nachstellige Hypothek; ~ **office staff** untergeordnetes Büropersonal; ~ **officer** subalterner Beamter; ~ **partner** Juniorpartner; ~ **right** *(Br.)* Erbübergang auf den jüngeren Sohn; ~ **salesman** Nachwuchskraft im Verkauf; ~ **school** *(Br.)* Grundschule; ~ **security** zweitrangige Sicherheit; ~ **staff** dienstjüngere Belegschaft; ~ **stocks** junge Aktien; ~ **writ** später zugestellte Klage.

juniority *(lower position)* untergeordnete Stellung.

junk Trödel, Kram, Altmaterial, Plunder, wertloses Zeug, *(garbage)* Abfall, Gerümpel, *(rejects)* Ausschuß[ware], *(scrap)* Schrott, *(ship)* Dschunke;
~s alte Sachen;
~ *(v.) (sl.)* zum alten Eisen werfen, ausrangieren;
~ **auto** *(car)* ausrangiertes Auto, Schrottwagen; ~ **car tax** Autoverschrottungsgebühr; ~ **collector** Müllfahrer; ~ **dealer** Schrott-, Altwaren-, Abfallhändler, Trödler; ~ **goods** Ramsch[waren]; ~ **heap** *(US)* Müllkippe, *(car, sl.)* schrottreifes Auto, Schrottauto; ~ **market** Schrottmarkt; ~ **peddler** Trödelhändler; ~ **pile** Ausschußlager; ~ **shop** Trödel-, Ramschladen, Schrotthandlung; ~ **value** Schrottwert; ~ **yard** Kippe, Abfallhalde, Schrottplatz, Autofriedhof.

junked | auto Schrottauto, -wagen; ~**-up** *(car)* frisiert.

junket Vergnügungsfahrt, Landpartie, Picknick, *(banquet)* Schmaus, Festessen, *(pleasure excursion, US)* Vergnügungsreise auf öffentliche Kosten;
~ *(v.)* Landpartie machen, picknicken, *(US)* sogenannte Dienstreise auf öffentliche Kosten unternehmen.

junketing party *(US)* Picknick, Landpartie.

junkie Rauschgiftsüchtiger.

junking Verschrottung.

junkman Altwarenhändler, Trödler.

junky kitschig.

junta Junta;
~ **member** Juntamitglied.

junto Clique, Klüngel, Interessensgruppe.

jural juristisch;
~ **relations** juristische Beziehungen.

jurat *(Br.)* unterschriebene eidliche Zeugenaussage, *(juror)* Schöffe.

juration Eidesabnahme.

juramentado, to go *(US)* Amok laufen.

jurator Geschworener.

juratory eidlich.

jurisconsult Rechtsgelehrter.

juridical gerichtlich, rechtlich, juristisch;
~ **act** Rechtshandlung; ~ **comparison** Rechtsvergleich; ~ **day** Verhandlungstag [des Gerichts]; ~ **person** *(US)* juristische Person.

jurisdiction Entscheidungsgewalt, -befugnis, Rechtsprechung, *(authority)* Zuständigkeit, Gerichtsbarkeit, *(state)* Hoheitsbereich, *(territory)* Gerichtsbezirk;
administrative ~ Verwaltungsgerichtsbarkeit; **appellate** ~ Berufungsgerichtsbarkeit, Zuständigkeit als Berufungsinstanz; **auxiliary** ~ hilfsweise gegebene Zuständigkeit; **civil** ~ Zuständigkeit in bürgerlichen Rechtsstreitigkeiten; **common-law** ~ Rechtssprechung nach gemeinem Recht; **concurrent** ~ mehrfache Zuständigkeit, nichtausschließliche Gerichtsbarkeit, Wahlgerichtsstand; **contentious** ~ streitige Gerichtsbarkeit; **coordinate** ~ konkurrierende Gerichtsbarkeit; **criminal** ~ Zuständigkeit in Strafsachen; **cumulative** ~ zusätzliche Gerichtsbarkeit; **disciplinary** ~ Disziplinargerichtsbarkeit; **discretionary** ~ Befugnis zu Ermessensentscheidungen, Ermessensbefugnis; **domestic** ~ innerstaatliche Zuständigkeit; **equitable** ~ Rechtsprechung nach Billigkeitsrecht; **equity** ~ Zuständigkeit im Equityverfahren; **exclusive** ~ ausschließliche Zuständigkeit (Gerichtsbarkeit); **federal** ~ *(US)* Bundesgerichtsbarkeit; **fiscal** ~ Steuerhoheit; **foreign** ~ fremde Zuständigkeit; **general** ~ allgemeine Zuständigkeit; **industrial** ~ Zuständigkeit in arbeitsrechtlichen Streitigkeiten; **international** ~ internationale Schiedsgerichtsbarkeit; **limited** ~ Sonderzuständigkeit; **maritime** ~ Seegerichtsbarkeit; **matrimonial** ~ Zuständigkeit in Ehesachen; **national** ~ *(Br.)* inländische Gerichtsbarkeit; **noncontentious** ~ freiwillige Gerichtsbarkeit; **original** ~ erstinstanzliche Zuständigkeit; **probate** ~ Zuständigkeit in Vormunds und Nachlaßsachen; **removal** ~ *(US)* bundesgerichtliche Zuständigkeit; **special** ~ Sondergerichtsbarkeit; **summary** ~ einzelrichterliche (niedere) Zuständigkeit; **supervisory** ~ Aufsichtsbefugnis; **tax** ~ Zuständigkeit in Steuersachen; **territorial** ~ örtliche Zuständigkeit; **union** ~ ausschließliches Vertretungsrecht einer Gewerkschaft; **venue** ~ Zuständigkeit für einen Gerichtsstand; **voluntary** ~ freiwillige Gerichtsbarkeit;
general ~ **of a court** allgemeine Zuständigkeit eines Gerichts; ~ **of an exceptional court** Sondergerichtsbarkeit; ~ **in personam** Hoheitsrechte über eine natürliche Person; ~ **in probate matters** Gerichtsbarkeit in Nachlaßsachen; ~ **in rem** sachliche Zuständigkeit; ~ **over the subject matter** sachliche Zuständigkeit;

to be subject to ~ der Gerichtsbarkeit unterstehen; **to come within the ~ of a court** zur Zuständigkeit eines Gerichts gehören; **to come within the ~ of the administrative courts** in die Kompetenz der Vewaltungsgerichte fallen; **to confer ~ on a court** Zuständigkeit eines Gerichts begründen; **to decline ~** sich für unzuständig erklären; **to establish ~** Zuständigkeit begründen; **to exercise ~** Hoheitsrechte ausüben, *(law court)* Recht sprechen; **to extend ~** Zuständigkeitsbereich erweitern; **to have [no] ~ over** [nicht] zuständig sein für; **to have appellate ~** Rechtsmittelinstanz sein; **to lie within the ~** zum Gerichtsbezirk gehören; **to refuse to acknowledge a ~** Zuständigkeit ablehnen;
~ **clause** Zuständigkeitsvereinbarung, obligatorische Schiedsgerichtsklausel; ~ **notice** Kenntnis des Gerichts, gerichtsnotorische Tatsachen.

jurisdictional gerichtlich;
~ **amount** *(US)* Streitsumme, -wert; ~ **basis** Rechtsgrundlage; ~ **clause** *(law of nations)* Gerichtsklausel; ~ **dispute** Zuständigkeitsstreit, *(labo(u)r union, US)* gewerkschaftliche Auseinandersetzung; ~ **facts** prozessuale Voraussetzungen; ~ **plea** Einwand der Unzuständigkeit; ~ **question** Zuständigkeitsfrage; ~ **waters** Hoheitsgewässer.

jurisprudence Rechtswissenschaft, -lehre;
comparative ~ vergleichende Rechtswissenschaft; **medical ~** Gerichtsmedizin.

jurisprudential rechtswissenschaftlich.

jurist Rechtsgelehrter, *(student, Br.)* Rechtsstudent.

juristic | act Rechtshandlung, -geschäft; ~ **person** *(US)* juristische Person.

juror Geschworener, *(awarder of prizes)* vereidigter Preisrichter;
to challenge ~s Geschworene ablehnen; **to serve as a ~** als Geschworener tätig sein;
~**'s book** Geschworenenverzeichnis.

jury Sachverständigen-, Prüfungsausschuß, *(court)* Geschworene, Schwurgericht, Geschworenenausschuß;
common ~ Geschworenenbank; **coroner's ~** Totenschau; **fair ~** unparteiisches Geschworenengericht; **grand ~** *(US)* Anklagejury, großes Geschworenengericht; **hung ~** blockiertes Geschworenengericht; **mixed ~** maßgebendes Geschworenengericht; **petty ~** *(US)* Urteilsjury; **special ~** beruflich qualifiziertes Geschworenengericht; **struck ~** besonders ausgewähltes Geschworenengericht; **trial ~** Schwurgericht;
to apply for one's case to be heard by a ~ Schwurgerichtsverhandlung beantragen; **to be (serve) on a ~** auf der Geschworenenbank sitzen; **to draw the ~** Geschworene auslosen; **to impanel a ~** Geschworene einsetzen; **to instruct the ~** die Geschworenen belehren; **to strike a ~** Geschworene auswählen;
~ **award** Geschworenenspruch; ~ **box** Geschworenenbank; ~ **fixing** *(US)* Bestechung von Geschworenen, Geschworenenbestechung; ~ **list (panel)** Geschworenenliste; ~ **service** Geschworenentätigkeit; **to be called to ~ service** als Geschworener einberufen werden; **to be exempt from ~ service** nicht als Geschworener verpflichtet werden können; ~ **tampering** Geschworenenbestechung; ~ **trial** Geschworenengericht, -verhandlung.

juryman Geschworener.

just gerecht, angemessen, billig, *(agreeing with pattern)* richtig, genau, passend, gehörig;
~ **and equitable** gerecht und billig; ~ **to a minute** absolut zutreffend; ~ **out** *(book)* gerade erschienen; ~ **prior** unmittelbar vorhergehend; ~ **and reasonable** gerecht und zumutbar; ~ **at that spot** genau an dieser Stelle; ~ **the thing** genau das Richtige; **to be ~ an ordinary man** einfacher Durchschnittsmensch sein; **to sleep the sleep of the ~** Schlaf des Gerechten schlafen;
~ **allowance** berechtigte Aufwendungen; **without ~ cause** ohne ausreichenden (gerechtfertigten) Grund; **to speak for a ~ cause** sich für eine gerechte Sache einsetzen; ~ **compensation** angemessene Entschädigung; ~ **conduct** richtiges (korrektes) Verhalten; ~ **debt** rechtsgültige Schuld; **a ~ and lawful decision** gerechte und billige Entscheidung; **to receive one's ~ deserts** seine gerechte Strafe erhalten; ~ **indignation** berechtigte Empörung; ~ **opinion** vernünftige Ansicht; **to give a ~ picture** richtiges Bild der Lage zeichnen; ~ **proceeding** gerechtes Verfahren; **to cut s. th. to the ~ proportions** etw. auf das richtige Maß zurückbringen; ~ **reward for s. one's actions** wohlverdienter Lohn für jds. Handlungen; ~ **statement** wahre Feststellung; ~ **title** rechtmäßiger Anspruch; ~ **will** absoluter Rechtstitel; ~ **value** *(taxation)* Verkehrswert.

justice Gerechtigkeit, Rechtmäßigkeit, *(adherence to fact)* Richtigkeit, *(fairness)* Billigkeit, *(judge)* Richter, *(jurisdiction)* Gerichtsbarkeit, Justiz;
in ~ von Rechts wegen;
chief ~ Gerichtspräsident; **commutative (distributive) ~** ausgleichende Gerechtigkeit; **lay ~** Laienrichter; **law ~** Bagatellgerichtsbarkeit; **poetical ~** ausgleichende Gerechtigkeit; **retributive ~** ausgleichende Gerechtigkeit; **social ~** soziale Gerechtigkeit; **summary ~** Schnellgerichtsbarkeit; **swift ~** Lynchjustiz; **venal ~** käufliche Justiz;
~ **of appeal** *(Br.)* Berufungsrichter; ~ **of a claim** Rechtmäßigkeit eines Anspruchs; ~ **of the forest** *(Br.)* Forstgericht; ~ **of the peace** *(US)* Friedens-, Amtsrichter; **Chief ⚖ of the United States** Bundesgerichtspräsident; **⚖ of the Peace** Friedensrichter;
to administer ~ Recht sprechen; **to be brought to a speedy ~** rasch abgeurteilt werden; **to bring s. o. to ~** j. gerichtlich belangen; **to bring a criminal to ~** Verbrecher aburteilen; **to dispense ~** Rechtspflege ausüben; **to dispute the ~ of a claim** Berechtigung eines Anspruchs bestreiten; **to do ~ to o. s.** sein wahres Können zeigen; **to do ~ to s. o.** jem. Gerechtigkeit widerfahren lassen; **to do ~ to a meal** *(fam.)* bei einer Mahlzeit tüchtig zulangen; **to evade ~** sich der richterlichen Verfolgung entziehen; **to interfere with the course of ~** Lauf der Gerechtigkeit anhalten; **to pervert the course of ~** Recht beugen; **to revive ~** Gerechtigkeit wiederherstellen; **to stand with ~** für die Gerechtigkeit eintreten; **to stand in the way of ~** der Gerechtigkeit in den Arm fallen; **to warp ~** Recht beugen;
~ **announcement** Mitteilung des Justizministeriums; **⚖ Ayres** *(Scot. law)* Gerichtsbezirk; ~ **box** Richterstand;; ~ **broker** bestechlicher Richter; ~**'s clerk** Geschäftsstellenleiter; **⚖ Department** *(US)* Justizministerium; ~ **seat** *(Br.)* Forstgericht.

justiceship Richteramt.

justiciable einer Gerichtsbarkeit unterworfen.

justiciary Justiziar;
~ *(a.)* gerichtlich, gesetzlich;
~ **court** *(Scot. law)* Oberstes Gericht für Strafsachen.

justifiability Rechtmäßigkeit.

justifiable berechtigt, gerechtfertigt, vertretbar;
to be ~ zu Recht bestehen;
~ **cause for suspicion** Grund für hinreichenden Verdacht; ~ **complaint** berechtigte Beschwerde; ~ **controvery** Rechtsstreitigkeit; ~ **criticism** berechtigte Kritik; ~ **homicide** Tötung bei Vorliegen von Rechtfertigungsgründen.

justification Rechtfertigung, Rechtfertigungsgrund, *(governmental accounting)* Begründung für angeforderte Etatsmittel, *(print.)* Justierung, Ausschluß, *(slander)* Wahrheitsbeweis;
written ~ schriftliche Entschuldigung;
~ **and privilege** Wahrnehmung berechtigter Interessen;
to plead ~ *(libel suit)* sich auf Wahrnehmung berechtigter Interessen berufen.

justified berechtigt, gerechtfertigt, begründet;
fully ~ decision rechtmäßige Entscheidung; ~ **space** *(setting)* variabler Zwischenraum.

justify *(v.)* *(administer justice)* Recht sprechen, rechtfertigen, verteidigen, *(bondsman)* sich als Bürge qualifizieren, *(print.)* justieren, ausschließen, *(pronounce free from guilt)* von Schuld freisprechen;
~ **the action of the government** Regierungsmaßnahme rechtfertigen; ~ **bail** Nachweis ausreichender Sicherheit führen, seine Zahlungsfähigkeit nachweisen; ~ **a lunch as business expense** Mittagessen über Spesen abrechnen; ~ **a statement** Erklärung gutheißen; ~ **a trip with good business reasons** Geschäftsreise mit zwingenden Gründen belegen.

justifying bail Nachweis der Zahlungsfähigkeit.

justness Gerechtigkeit, *(exactness)* Richtigkeit, Genauigkeit, *(fairness)* Billigkeit.

juvenile Jugendlicher, *(bookshop)* Kinderbuch;
~ *(a.)* jugendlich, jung;
~ **adult** *(Br.)* Jugendlicher, Heranwachsender; ~ **book** Jugendbuch; ~ **cases** *(criminal court)* Jugendsachen; ~ **delinquency** Jugendkriminalität, -täterschaft; ~ **delinquent** jugendlicher Täter; **to be labelled as ~ delinquent** als jugendlicher Straftäter eingestuft werden; ~ **employment** Beschäftigung von Jugendlichen; ~ **fiction** Jugendroman; ~ **literature** Jugendliteratur; ~ **offender** jugendlicher Täter; ~ **prisoner** jugendlicher Strafgefangener; ~ **stage** Entwicklungsstadium; ~ **wrongdoing** unerlaubte Handlungen Jugendlicher.

juxta position *(patent law, Br.)* patentfähige Zusammensetzung.

K

K ration *(mil.)* hochkonzentrierte Sonderration.
Kaiser's Geburtstag *(US sl.)* Lohntag.
Kale *(US sl.)* Pinke-Pinke.
kangaroo|s *(Br.)* westaustralische Bergwerksaktien;
  ~ *(v.)* *(US sl.)* aufgrund gefälschten Beweismaterials verurteilen;
  ~ **closure** *(pol., Br.)* Abkürzung der Debatte auf bestimmte Punkte; ~ **court** *(US sl.)* Scheingerichtshof.
Kayducer *(US sl.)* Zugschaffner.
keek *(US sl.)* Wirtschaftsspion.
keel Kiel;
  ~s Kohlenschiffe;
  on an even ~ *(fig.)* ausgeglichen;
  to lay down a ~ auf Kiel legen, Schiffsbau beginnen; **to put back on an even ~** in ein ruhigeres Fahrwasser zurückbringen; **to remain on an even ~** ausgeglichene Konjunkturpolitik betreiben.
keelage Kielgeld, Hafengebühren.
keen *(competition)* scharf, *(good looking, US sl.)* geschniegelt, schick;
  ~ **to enjoy life** lebenslustig; **as ~ as mustard** *(coll.)* Feuer und Flamme, ganz versessen, sehr erpicht;
  to be ~ on s. th. auf etw. erpicht sein; **not to be very ~ on it** nicht sehr daran interessiert sein; **to be ~ on money-making** aufs Geldverdienen aus sein;
  ~ **appetite** Heißhunger; **to be a ~ businessman** hinter seinen Geschäften her sein; ~ **competition** scharfer Wettbewerb; ~ **demand** hektische Nachfrage; **to have a ~ eye for a bargain** Nase für gute Geschäfte haben; ~ **intelligence** scharfer Intellekt; ~ **interest** lebhaftes Interesse; **to be a ~ judge of men** Scharfblick bei der Menschenbeurteilung zeigen; ~ **lawyer** scharfsinniger Anwalt; **to have a ~ mind** scharfsinnig sein, über Scharfsinn verfügen; **to be ~-nosed** guten Riecher haben; ~ **observer of contemporary affairs** neugieriger Beobachter des Zeitgeschehens; ~ **prices** überhöhte Preise; ~ **sarcasm** beißender Sarkasmus; ~ **sense of guilt** echtes Schuldgefühl; **to be ~-witted** scharfsinnig sein.
keep *(food)* Verpflegung, *(livelihood)* Unterhalt, Kost;
  for ~s kannst' du behalten, *(coll., US)* endgültig;
  ~ *(v.)* behalten, *(contract)* einhalten, *(employ)* halten, *(have charge of)* verwahren, aufbewahren, *(have on sale)* [Ware] führen, auf Lager halten, *(meeting)* abhalten, *(newspaper, US)* halten, abonnieren, *(provide for)* unterhalten, *(remain in good condition)* sich halten, *(shop)* betreiben, führen;
  ~ **o. s.** sich selbst unterhalten, seinen Lebensunterhalt selbst verdienen; ~ **o. s. to o. s.** Eigenbrötler sein; ~ **s. th. to o. s.** etw. für sich behalten;
  ~ **an account** Konto unterhalten; ~ **an account of expenses** über Ausgaben Buch führen; ~ **accounts** Rechnungsbücher führen, ordentliche Buchführung unterhalten; ~ **s. o. advised** j. auf dem laufenden halten; ~ **an animal** Tier halten; ~ **apart** getrennt aufbewahren; ~ **an appointment** Verabredung einhalten; ~ **an article** Artikel führen; ~ **an assembly** Versammlung abhalten; ~ **nothing back from one's friends** seinen Freunden alles erzählen; ~ **on one's balance** *(fig.)* sich im Zaun halten; ~ **the ball rolling** Sache in Gang halten; ~ **one's bed** das Bett hüten; ~ **one's birthday** seinen Geburtstag feiern; ~ **boarders** Pensionäre haben, Pension betreiben; ~ **body and soul together** gesund bleiben; ~ **books** Bücher führen; ~ **the car straight** Auto im Schuß haben; ~ **the cash** Kassierer sein, Kassenwart abgeben; ~ **cave** *(Br., sl.)* Schmiere stehen; ~ **Christmas** Weihnachtsfest feiern; ~ **Christmas in the old style** alte Weihnachtsbräuche bewahren; ~ **o. s. in clothes** seine Kleidung selbst bezahlen; ~ **s. o. company** jem. Gesellschaft leisten; ~ **company with s. o.** *(sl.)* miteinandergehen; ~ **one's composure** Haltung bewahren; ~ **the composition standing** Satz stehen lassen; ~ **confined** gefangenhalten; ~ **a copy of a letter** Briefdurchschlag behalten; ~ **one's own counsel** seine Meinung für sich behalten, sich um seine eigenen Sachen kümmern; ~ **currently** fortlaufend führen; ~ **s. o. in custody** j. in Gewahrsam halten; ~ **dark** *(coll.)* alles im Dunkeln lassen; ~ **for a later date** für einen späteren Zeitpunkt aufheben; ~ **a diary** Tagebuch führen; ~ **s. o. for dinner** j. zum Essen dabehalten; ~ **one's engagements** seinen Verpflichtungen nachkommen; ~ **a family** seine Familie ernähren; ~ **a feast** Fest feiern; ~ **the field** *(mil.)* Feldzug fortsetzen; ~ **on's foot** den Anstand wahren; ~ **the gates of a town** Stadttore bewachen; ~ **going** in Gang halten; ~

firm *(prices)* fest bleiben; ~ **one's hair on** seine Ruhe bewahren; ~ **one's hand in** nicht aus der Übung kommen; ~ **in harness** zur Arbeit anhalten; ~ **one's head above water** sich durchs Leben schlagen; ~ **s. o. at home** j. zu Hause behalten; ~ **one hop ahead of s. o.** jem. stets um einen Schritt voraus sein; ~ **early hours** früh aufstehen; ~ **late hours** lange aufbleiben; ~ **s. o. going** j. über Wasser halten; ~ **house** seinen eigenen Haushalt haben, *(Br.)* sich vor seinen Gläubigern verstecken, Konkursvergehen begehen; ~ **a disorderly house** Bordell betreiben; ~ **open house** sehr gastfrei sein; ~ **house for s. o.** jem. den Haushalt führen; ~ **indoors** zu Hause bleiben; ~ **s. o. indoors** j. im Haus festhalten; ~ **s. o. informed** j. laufend unterrichten; ~ **an inn** Gastwirtschaft betreiben, Hotelier sein, Hotel führen; ~ **[to] the land aboard** sich nach der Küste halten; ~ **[to] the law** Gesetz einhalten (beobachten); ~ **old letters** alte Briefe aufbewahren; ~ **one's letters under lock and key** seine Korrespondenz verschlossen aufbewahren; ~ **a stiff upper lip** sich nicht erweichen lassen; ~ **a list** Verzeichnis (Liste) führen; ~ **s. th. locked up** etw. unter Verschluß halten; ~ **the middle of the road** Mittelweg einschlagen; ~ **the minutes** Protokoll führen; ~ **money at a bank** Geld bei einer Bank stehen haben; ~ **the news to o. s.** Neuigkeiten für sich behalten; ~ **note of s. th.** Notiz über etw. anfertigen; ~ **an office** Amt innehaben; ~ **s.o. in the office** j. im Büro aufhalten; ~ **open** offenhalten; ~ **[back] one's payments** seine Zahlungen einhalten; ~ **the peace** öffentliche Ruhe und Ordnung bewahren; ~ **a policy alive** Versicherungspolice aufrechterhalten; ~ **posted** auf dem Laufenden halten; ~ **the pot boiling** sein Leben fristen; ~ **s. o. in prison** j. im Gefängnis festhalten; ~ **a promise** Versprechen halten; ~ **ready** bereithalten; ~ **record of s. th.** Aufzeichnungen über etw. machen; ~ **records** amtliche Unterlagen aufbewahren, Akten führen; ~ **in repair** anfallende Reparaturen erledigen, in ordnungsgemäßem Zustand halten; ~ **in safe custody** sicher aufbewahren, verwahren; ~ **for sale** feilhalten; ~ **the sea** Seeherrschaft behalten; ~ **separate** getrennt halten; ~ **a servant** sich eine Hausangestellte leisten; ~ **a shop** Laden führen (besitzen); ~ **a grocer's shop** Lebensmittelladen besitzen; ~ **s. o. short of money** j. knapp [bei Kasse] halten; ~ **the stage** sich auf der Bühne behaupten; ~ **steady** *(prices)* sich behaupten; ~ **in stock (store)** auf Lager halten, Artikel führen; ~ **to the subject** beim Thema bleiben, sich auf das Thema beschränken; ~ **Sunday** Sonntag heiligen; ~ **a good table** auf das Essen Wert legen; ~ **in suspense** in der Schwebe halten, *(creditors)* [Gläubiger] hinhalten; ~ **a bill in suspense** Wechsel Not leiden lassen; ~ **tabs on s. o.** j. im Auge behalten; ~ **term** *(Term of Court, Br.)* Jurastudium beenden, *(Br.)* [auf der Universität] studieren; ~ **terms** Verbindung aufrechterhalten; ~ **the New York Times** die New York Times halten (lesen); ~ **things ticking over** Dinge in Gang halten; ~ **track** informiert (auf dem laufenden) bleiben; ~ **track of costs** Kosten im Griff behalten; ~ **a treaty** Vertrag einhalten; ~ **in touch** in Verbindung bleiben; ~ **s. o. waiting** j. warten lassen; ~ **one's way** seinen Kurs fortsetzen; ~ **working** Arbeit fortsetzen; ~ **turning up** immer wieder auftauchen; ~ **a wife and seven children** Ehefrau und sieben Kinder unterhalten; ~ **abreast of the times** mit der Zeit Schritt halten; ~ **aloof** sich abseits halten; ~ **asunder** getrennt halten.
keep *(v.)* **at|s. th.** an einer Sache festhalten (dranbleiben);
  ~ **s. o. with appeals for money** j. fortlaufend um Geld angehen; ~ **s. o. 4 dollars a day** j. für vier Dollar täglich verpflegen.
keep *(v.)* **away** fernhalten;
  ~ **s. o.** j. abhalten; ~ **for a few days** ein paar Tage fernbleiben.
keep *(v.)* **back** zurück[be]halten;
  ~ **the crowd** Menge zurückhalten; ~ **s. th. from s. one's wages** etw. von jds. Lohn einbehalten (zurückbehalten).
keep *(v.)* **down** (Preise) niedrig halten;
  ~ **costs** Kosten niedrig halten; ~ **expenses** Unkosten (Spesen) niedrig halten; ~ **interest** Zinsen bei Fälligkeit bezahlen; ~ **a people by force** Volk unterdrücken; ~ **prices down** Preissteigerungen verhindern.
keep *(v.)* **in** zu Hause bleiben, *(print.)* kompreß setzen, Satz stehenlassen;
  ~ **with a customer** Kunden pflegen; ~ **one's hand** Hände im Spiel behalten; ~ **money** mit Geld versehen; ~ **a pupil in** Schüler nachsitzen lassen.
keep *(v.)* **off** nicht näher kommen lassen;
  ~ **a subject** sich von einem Thema fernhalten.

keep *(v.)* **on** | **at s. o.** *(fam.)* j. immer weiter schikanieren; ~ **the light** Licht brennen lassen; ~ **searching** unaufhörlich suchen; ~ **an old servant** altem Dienstboten das Gnadenbrot geben.

keep *(v.)* **out** sich heraushalten, *(print.)* mit Abständen setzen; ~ **of debt** sich schuldenfrei halten; ~ **s. o. of his money** jem. sein Geld vorenthalten; ~ **strictly of s. th.** sich prinzipiell aus einer Sache heraushalten.

keep *(v.)* **to** | **an agreement** sich an eine Vereinbarung halten; ~ **a student to his career of teacher** Studenten zum Festhalten an seinem Lehrerberuf bewegen; ~ **a strict diet** sich einer strengen Diät befleißigen; ~ **s. o. to his promise** j. auf sein Versprechen festnageln.

keep *(v.)* **up** aufrechterhalten, *(prices)* weiter hoch bleiben; ~ **appearances** den Schein wahren; ~ **a business** Geschäft fortführen; ~ **a correspondence** Schriftwechsel unterhalten; ~ **one's credit** seinen guten Ruf bewahren; ~ **old customs** alten Bräuchen anhängen; ~ **to date** sich auf dem Laufenden halten; ~ **s. o. to date** j. auf dem laufenden halten; ~ **a large house** großes Haus unterhalten; ~ **with the Joneses** *(Br.)* mit den Nachbarn Schritt halten; ~ **one's payments** seinen Zahlungsverpflichtungen nachkommen; ~ **the price of goods** Preise aufrechterhalten; ~ **one's spirits** Mut nicht sinken lassen; ~ **with the times** mit der Zeit Schritt halten.

keep | *(v.)* **the fire under** des Feuers Herr werden; ~ **within a limit** Limit einhalten.

keep, **not to be able to** ~ **money** mit Geld nicht umgehen können; **to be here for** ~**s** *(sl.)* für dauernd bleiben; **not to be worth one's** ~ das Pulver nicht wert sein; **to earn one's** ~ sich selbst ernähren; **not to earn one's** ~ seinen Unterhalt nicht verdienen; **to give s. th. to s. o. to** ~ jem. etw. in Verwahrung geben; **to have s. th. for** ~**s** etw. umsonst bekommen; **to have one's parents to** ~ seine Eltern unterhalten müssen; **to work for one's** ~ gegen freie Station arbeiten.

keeper *(attendant)* Wächter, *(bookkeeper)* Buchhalter, *(gamekeeper)* Förster, *(holder)* Verwahrer, *(lender)* Vermieter, Verleiher, *(museum)* Konservator, Kustos, *(owner)* Inhaber, Besitzer, *(prison)* Gefängniswärter, Gefangenenaufseher; **boardinghouse** ~ Pensionsinhaber; **lighthouse** ~ Leuchtturmwärter; **park-**~ Parkwächter; ~ **of an animal** Tierhalter; ~ **of the archives** Archivar; ~ **of a bawdy house** Bordellbesitzer; ~ **of a dog** Hundebesitzer; ~ **of the forest** Forstverwalter; ~ **of a gambling den** Spielhöllenbesitzer; ~ **of the privy purse** *(Br.)* Intendant der Zivilliste; ~ **of a railway bookstall** *(Br.)* Bahnhofsbuchhändler; ~ **of the records** *(US)* Urkundsbeamter; ~ **of the Great Seal** *(Br.)* Staatssiegelbewahrer; ~ **of the touch** *(Br.)* Münzstättenleiter.

keeping *(care)* Pflege, Obhut, *(charge)* Gewahrsam, Verwahrung, Aufsicht, Haft, *(harmony)* Einklang, Übereinstimmung, *(livelihood)* Unterhalt, Unterhaltung, Kost; **for safe** ~ zur sicheren Aufbewahrung; ~ **back** Zurückhaltung; ~ **books** Rechnungsführung; ~ **a gambling house (place)** Unterhaltung einer Spielbank; ~ **house (bankruptcy law)** verstecken vor den Gläubigern; ~ **in** *(pupil)* Arrest, Nachsitzenlassen; ~ **of minutes** Protokollaufbewahrung; ~ **out** Heraushaltung; ~ **the peace** Aufrechterhaltung von Ruhe und Ordnung; ~ **lost property** Fundunterschlagung; ~ **of records** Urkunden-, Unterlagenführung; ~ **for sale** Feilhaltung; **to be in** ~ **with s. th.** im Einklang mit etw. stehen, mit etw. übereinstimmen; **to be in safe** ~ in guter Obhut sein; **to have s. th. in one's** ~ etw. in Verwahrung haben; ~ **room** *(US)* Wohnzimmer.

keeperless *(gate)* unbewacht.

keepsake, for a zum Andenken.

kemp *(US sl.)* Schnauferl.

ken *(fig.)* Horizont, Wissensbereich.

Kennedy round *(GATT)* Zolltarifsenkung.

kennel Hundehütte, *(gutter)* Gosse, Rinnstein, *(US sl.)* armselige Behausung, Loch; **stone** Rinnstein;

kentish fire Mißfallenskundgebung.

kentlage *(mar.)* Ballasteisen.

kept, to be ~ **in** *(pupil)* nachsitzen müssen; **to be** ~ **here by business** hier geschäftlich aufgehalten werden; ~ **woman** ausgehaltenes Frauenzimmer.

kerb Bordschwelle, *(stock exchange, Br.)* Freiverkehrsmarkt, Freiverkehr, Nachbörse; ~ **[-stone] broker** *(Br.)* Freiverkehrsmakler; ~ **exchange** *(Br.)* Freiverkehrsbörse; ~ **market** *(Br.)* Freiverkehrsmarkt; ~ **prices** *(Br.)* Freiverkehrskurse; ~ **stone** Bordstein.

kerbside Bürgersteigseite.

kernel of power Machtzentrum.

kettle *(US sl.)* Taschenuhr; **pretty** ~ **of fish** *(US sl.)* schöne Bescherung; **to be a different** ~ **of fish** etw. ganz anderes sein; ~ **stitch** *(bookbinding)* Kettenstich.

ketchup, in the *(US sl.)* in den roten Zahlen.

key Schlüssel, *(advertising)* Kennziffer, -wort, Chiffre, Schlüsselzahl, Kontrollziffer, *(architecture)* Schlußstein, *(computer)* Drucktaste, *(el.)* Druckkontakt, -taste, *(fig.)* Schlüssel, Lösung, *(leading position)* Schlüsselposition, *(map)* Zeichenerklärung, -schlüssel, *(mil.)* beherrschende Stellung, Macht, *(motion picture)* Filmstreifenmarkierung, *(pitch of tone)* Tonart, *(print.)* Setzteil, Schließteil, *(railway)* Schienenkeil, *(typewriter)* Taste; **all in the same** ~ monoton; **in** ~ in Ordnung; **in a minor** ~ in trauriger Stimmung; **clear entry** ~ *(computer)* Lösch- und Korrekturtaste, Konstanttaste; **distribution** ~ Verteilerschlüssel; **golden (silver)** ~ Bestechungsgeld; **listening** ~ *(tel.)* Mithörtaste; **master** ~ Hauptschlüssel; **morse** ~ Morseschlüssel; **skeleton** ~ Nachschlüssel; ~ **to a cipher** Codeschlüssel; ~ **of distribution** Verteilungsschlüssel; ~ **to a riddle** Auflösung eines Rätsels; ~ **to signs** Zeichenerklärung; ~ **to the political situation** Schlüssel zur politischen Lage; ~ **to hit success** Schlüssel zum Erfolg; ~ **for the use of teachers only** Lösungsheft, -buch, Übersetzungsschlüssel;

~ *(v.)* *(newspaper advertisement)* mit Kennziffer (Schlüsselwort) versehen, *(print.)* füttern, unterlegen, *(terminal)* tasten, eingeben; ~ **in** eingeben, -tasten; ~ **into a machine a personal code number** in einen Apparat seine Kodenummer eingeben; ~ **one's publicity** sich die Aufmerksamkeit seiner Kundschaft sichern; ~ **up** erhöhen; ~ **up a crowd** Menge in Aufregung versetzen;

to be in ~ **with** übereinstimmen; **to be the** ~ **to sales** Absatzmarkt öffnen; **to have got the** ~ **of the street** nicht ins Haus hineinkommen können, ausgesperrt sein; **to hold the** ~ **of one's own fate** sein Schicksal in den eigenen Händen halten; **to hold the** ~ **to a country's political future** Schlüsselstellung für die politische Zukunft eines Landes besitzen; **to keep under lock and** ~ hinter Schloß und Riegel halten; **to leave the** ~ **in the lock** Schlüssel stecken lassen; **to speak in a high** ~ hohe Stimmlage haben; **to speak in a sharp** ~ in scharfem Ton sprechen; **to touch the right** ~ richtigen Ton anschlagen; **to turn the** ~ abschließen; **to turn it over ready to turn a** ~ schlüsselfertig übergeben;

~ **aid** Schlüsselkraft; ~ **appointments** [Besetzung von] Schlüsselpositionen; ~ **area** ausschlaggebendes Gebiet; ~ **avenue** Erfolgsweg; ~ **bit** Schlüsselbart; ~ **body** Schlüsselorgan; ~ **businessmen** führende Geschäftsleute; ~ **cabinet posts** Schlüsselpositionen im Kabinett; ~ **center** *(US)* **(centre,** *Br.)* Schlüsselstelle; ~**-cold** *(dial.)* interesselos; ~ **community leader** führende Persönlichkeit; ~ **company people** führende Leute im Betrieb; ~ **costs** Hauptunkosten; ~ **concern** Hauptbedenken; ~ **currency** Leitwährung; ~ **customer** wichtiger Kunde; ~ **data** Schlüsselziffern; ~ **date** Stichtag; ~ **demand** Hauptforderung; ~ **details** wichtige Einzelheiten; ~ **drawing** Originalzeichnung; ~ **economies** Schlüsselbetriebe; ~ **employees (executives)** Schlüsselkräfte; ~ **facts** Schlüsselmaterial; ~ **factor** Schlüsselzahl, -faktor; ~ **feature** Hauptmerkmal; ~ **figure** Schlüsselfigur, -zahl; ~ **financial nation** finanzstarkes Land; ~ **holdings** Schlüsselbeteiligungen; ~ **indicator** Schlüsselbarometer; ~ **industrial emporium** wirtschaftliche Schlüsselstellung; ~ **industry** lebenswichtiger Betrieb, Schlüsselindustrie; ~ **issue** Schlüsselfrage; **[turn]-**~ **job** Schlüsselstellung; ~ **link** Hauptverbindung; ~ **man** Schlüsselkraft, Hauptperson, *(organization)* Verbindungsmann, *(indispensable worker)* unentbehrliche Arbeitskraft; **to tempt a** ~ **man away from his employers** Schlüsselkraft wegengagieren; ~ **map** Übersichtskarte; ~ **market** Verbrauchergruppe in einer Schlüsselposition; ~ **members** wichtigste Mitglieder; ~ **money** Handgeld, Anzahlung, *(tenant)* Mietvorauszahlung, Abstandsgeld, verlorener Baukostenzuschuß; ~**-money rates** Geldleitsätze; ~ **number** Kennziffer, Chiffre; ~ **objective** Hauptanliegen, -ziel; ~ **office** Schlüsselstellung; ~ **official** Beamter in Schlüsselposition; ~ **paper** führende Zeitung; **to play a** ~ **part in Parliament** Schlüsselfigur im Parlament abgeben; ~ **people** Schlüsselkräfte; ~ **performance** Haupttätigkeit; ~ **performance area** Haupttätigkeitsgebiet; ~ **personnel** Schlüsselkräfte; ~ **plant** Schlüsselbetrieb; ~ **plate** *(print.)* Randplatte, -form; ~ **position (post)** Schlüssel-, leitende Stellung; **to earmark for a** ~ **position** für eine Schlüsselstellung ausersehen; ~ **price** marktentscheidender Preis; ~ **product lines** Fertigungsprogramme von entscheidender Bedeutung; ~ **provision** Schlüsselbedingung; ~ **punch** Locher; ~ **quality** wichtigste Eigenschaft; ~ **question** Schlüsselfrage; ~ **rate** *(banking)* Leitzinssatz, *(insurance)* nach Gefahrenklassen eingeteilte Grundprämie; ~ **ratio** Schlüsselzahl; ~ **resource** Hauptquelle; ~ **ring** Schlüsselring, -bund; ~ **road** Hauptverkehrsweg; **to play a ~ role** Schlüsselfigur abgeben; ~ **service** Schlüsseldienst; ~ **state official** erster Staatsdiener; ~ **station** *(broadcasting, US)* programmgestaltender Sender, Hauptsender; ~ **step** Schritt von entscheidender Bedeutung; ~ **strategic position** strategische Schlüsselposition; ~ **supply** Hauptversorgungsbasis; ~ **symbols** grafische Zeichen; ~ **task** Hauptaufgabe; ~ **years** entscheidende Jahre; ~ **union leaders** gewerkschaftliche Spitzenfunktionäre; ~ **vote** entscheidende Abstimmung; **to swing a ~ vote** Entscheidung bei einer Abstimmung herbeiführen; ~ **witness** wichtigster (entscheidender) Zeuge; ~ **word** Stich-, Schlüsselwort; ~ **worker** hochqualifizierter Facharbeiter, Schlüsselkraft, Spezialist.

keyboard *(typewriter)* Tastatur, Tastenfeld, -reihe;
~ *(v.)* mit Linotype (Monotype) setzen, tasten.

keyboarding Dateneingabe.

keyed mit Tasten versehen, *(ciphered)* chiffriert, verschlüsselt;
to be ~ up erregt (gespannt, aufgeregt) sein;
~ **address** Kennziffer-anschrift; ~ **advertising** Kennziffer-, Chiffrewerbung, Kennzifferanzeige; ~ **coupon** Kennzifferkupon; ~ **layout** Tastaturbelegung.

keyhole, to peep through the durchs Schlüsselloch gucken.

keying Kennziffernausstattung;
~ **of advertisements** Chiffrewerbung, Zeitungswerbung unter Kennziffer, Anzeigenkennzeichnung;
~ **error** Tastfehler.

keyless watch sich automatisch aufziehende Uhr.

keynote Grundton, *(fig.)* Grund-, Hauptgedanke, *(party politics, US)* Parteilinie;
~ **of an exhibition** Grundgedanke einer Ausstellung; ~ **of a policy** politisches Leitmotiv; ~ **of a speech** Hauptthema einer Rede;
~ *(v.)* als Grundgedanke enthalten, *(party politics, US)* Parteilinie festlegen (verkünden);
to strike the ~ das Wesentliche einer Sache berühren;
~ **address (speech)** *(US)* richtungsweisende Rede; ~ **idea** *(advertising)* Hauptgedanke, Grundidee; ~ **speaker** tonangebender Sprecher.

keynoter *(US)* Programmredner, Verkünder des Parteiprogramms, [Partei]programmatiker.

keypoint *(fig.)* Schwerpunkt, *(mil.)* Schlüsselpunkt, -stellung;
~ **operator** Sammelspediteur.

keypunch Streifenlocher.

keystone Schlußstein, *(fig.)* Stütze, Grundpfeiler;
~ **of a policy** Hauptträger einer Politik;
to be a ~ in the defence program(me) Schlüsselposition im Verteidigungsprogramm einnehmen.

keystroke Tastenanschlag.

khaki, to get into Soldat werden.

kibe [aufgesprungene] Frostbeule;
to tread on s. one's ~ jem. auf die Zehen treten, jds. Gefühle verletzen.

kibitz *(US sl.)* Kiebitz, unerbetener Ratgeber;
~ *(v.)* *(US sl.)* Kiebitz abgeben, kiebitzen.

kibosh *(US sl.)* Mumpitz;
to put the ~ on s. th. einer Sache den Garaus machen.

kick *(fashion)* neuester Modefimmel, letzter Schrei, *(fig.)* Nervenkitzel, *(pep)* Energie, Mumm, *(grounds of complaint, US)* Beschwerdegrund, *(stimulation of liquor, US sl.)* Schwips, Affe;
all the ~ modisch, der letzte Schrei; **just for ~s** nur zum Spaß;
~ *(v.)* *(grumble, coll.)* nörgeln;
~ **o. s.** *(sl.)* sich selbst widerlich finden; ~ **in** *(US sl.)* Geld reinbuttern;
~ **about** planlos in der Gegend herumlaufen; ~ **back** *(US sl.)* Hehlerware zurückgeben; ~ **the beam** gewogen und zu leicht befunden werden; ~ **s. one's bottom** *(fam.)* j. in den Hintern treten; ~ **the bucket** *(sl.)* abkratzen; ~ **the crutches from under a scheme** Plan praktisch zunichtemachen; ~ **the door in** Tür eintreten; ~ **a man when he's down** *(fam.)* Gestürzten attackieren; ~ **a man downstairs** j. herausschmeißen; ~ **one's heels** sich die Beine in den Bauch stehen, seine Zeit vertrödeln; ~ **it** *(US)* Lasten loswerden; ~ **off** *(sl.)* dran glauben müssen; ~ **s. o. out** j. auf die Straße setzen (rausschmeißen); ~ **over** *(US sl.)* ausrauben; ~ **against partiality** sich gegen parteiische Behandlung wehren; ~ **against the pricks** wider den Stachel löcken; ~ **over the traces** über die Stränge schlagen; ~ **against the treatment one is receiving** sich schlechte Behandlung nicht gefallen lassen; ~ **up** *(parl., Br.)* ins Oberhaus versetzen; ~ **up a dust** viel Staub aufwirbeln; ~ **up earnings** Gewinne hochschrauben; ~ **up a fuss** Krach schlagen, randalieren; ~ **up a row (shindy)** randalieren; ~ **upstairs** durch Beförderung kaltstellen, *(Br.)* ins Oberhaus befördern; ~ **a public man upstairs** öffentlich bekannte Persönlichkeit die Treppe heraufbefördern; ~ **one's way into the headlines** seinen Weg in die Schlagzeilen machen;
to be getting its ~s *(sl.)* zum Knüller werden; **to be on a new ~** sich für eine neue Sache begeistern; **to get the ~** *(Br., coll.)* Laufpaß bekommen, rausfliegen, gefeuert werden; **to get a ~ out of s. th.** etw. höchst interessant finden; **to get more ~s than halfpence** wenig Dank (mehr Prügel als Lob) ernten; **to have a ~** *(US sl.)* einen sitzen haben; **to have a ~ against s. th.** etw. dagegen haben; **to have no ~ left** alle Lebensgeister verloren haben; **to lack a certain ~** nicht gerade spannend sein;
~ **starter** Tretanlasser, Kickstarter; ~-**up** *(US sl.)* Krach, Aufruhr, Spektakel.

kick-out *(US sl.)* Rausschmiß.

kickback *(coll.)* Blitzreaktion, *(US)* Schmiergeld [eines Arbeiters an den Vorarbeiter], *(commission)* erzwungene Provisionszahlung, *(thief)* Rückgabe von Diebesgut.

kicker *(motor, sl.)* Hilfsmotor, *(chronic protester, US)* Nörgler, Quertreiber, Meckerer.

kicking *(child)* Bocken;
to lie ~ about the house im ganzen Haus herumliegen.

kickoff *(coll.)* Aufbruch, Eröffnung, Start, *(US sl.)* fristlose Entlassung.

kickup *(sl.)* Krach, Spektakel.

kid *(US)* Kind, Jugendlicher, *(sl.)* Grünschnabel;
~**s** *(US)* Heranwachsende;
~ *(v.)* foppen, aufgießen, verkohlen;
~ **s. o. j.** anpflaumen; ~ **o. s.** sich selbst veräppeln;
~ **appeal** Werbeansprache auf dem Wege über das Kind; ~ **glove** Glacéhandschuh; **to fight one's way through life with ~ gloves** die Bandagen beim Kampf durchs Leben nie ablegen; **to handle s. o. with ~ gloves** j. mit Glacéhandschuhen anfassen.

kid-glove sanft, zart, wählerisch;
~ **methods** Samthandschuhmethoden;
to give s. o. ~ treatment j. mit Glacéhandschuhen anfassen.

kidding, all ~ aside *(US)* Scherz beiseite.

kidnap Menschenraub, [Kindes]entführung;
~ *(v.)* entführen, Menschenraub begehen;
~ **attempt** mißglückte Entführung, Entführungsversuch;
to be ~-free ohne Entführungen sein.

kidnapper [Kindes]entführer, Menschenräuber.

kidnapping Entführung, Menschenraub.

kidney, to be of the right vom richtigen Schlage sein.

kidvid *(television)* Kindersendung, *(fam.)* Kinderfernsehen.

kill Tötung, *(hunting)* Strecke, erlegtes Wild, Jagdbeute, *(mar.)* Zerstörung, Versenkung;
~ *(v.)* töten, umbringen, erschlagen, *(annul)* für ungültig erklären, stornieren, *(broadcasting)* ausfallen lassen, *(el.)* abschalten, *(mil.)* zerstören, abschießen, *(print.)* zu Streichsatz erklären, *(theater)* durch Kritik vernichten;
~ **o. s.** sich umbringen; ~ **an airplane** Flugzeug abschießen; ~ **a bill in parliament** Gesetzantrag zu Fall bringen; ~ **two birds with one stone** zwei Fliegen mit einer Klappe schlagen; ~ **the fatted calf** Wiedersehensfest feiern, Willkommensschmaus veranstalten; ~ **an engine** Motor abwürgen; ~ **all feelings of humanity** alle humanitären Anwandlungen abwürgen; ~ **s. one's hopes** jds. Hoffnungen zunichtemachen; ~ **by inches** zu Tode quälen; ~ **with kindness** mit Freundlichkeiten überhäufen; ~ **the nerve of a tooth** Nerv eines Zahnes abtöten; ~ **off** abmurksen, umbringen, abschlachten, ausrotten; ~ **off the hero in the last chapter** Helden im letzten Kapitel sterben lassen; ~ **a passage** Teil einer Nachricht unterdrücken; ~ **a proposal** Vorschlag scheitern lassen; ~ **the sound of footsteps** *(carpet)* Fußtritte verschlucken; ~ **a story** Zeitungsartikel streichen; ~ **time** Zeit totschlagen; ~ **a wire** Telegramm widerrufen; ~ **a word** Wort löschen; ~ **o. s. with work** sich überarbeiten (zu Tode arbeiten);
to be dressed to ~ todschick sein, sich mächtig herausstaffiert haben; **to be out to ~** *(fam.)* auf Eroberungen aus sein.

killable schlachtreif.

killed | in action [im Krieg] gefallen; ~ **instantly** *(accident)* sofort tot;
to be ~ in an accident tödlich verunglücken;
~ **matter** gestrichener Text.

killer Mörder, *(fig.)* Metzger, Schlächter;
  humane ~ Schreibtischmörder; **vermin ~** Ungeziefervertilgungsmittel.
killing Töten, Tötung, Mord, *(hunting)* Strecke, Jagdbeute, *(stock exchange, coll.)* hoher Spekulationsgewinn;
  germ ~ Abtötung von Bakterien; **mercy ~** Gnadentod, Euthanasie;
  ~ by misadventure unverschuldete Tötung; **~ a policeman** Mord eines Polizeibeamten, Polizistenmord;
  to be out for quick ~ *(fam.)* schnell Gewinn machen wollen; **to make a ~ in bonds** hohe Spekulationsgewinne in festverzinslichen Papieren erzielen;
  ~ (a.) mörderisch, anstrengend;
  ~ glance mörderischer Blick; **~ pace** mörderisches Tempo; **~ time** Schlachtzeit, *(fig.)* köstliche Zeit.
killjoy Störenfried, Spielverderber.
kilo charge *(book trade)* Kilogebühr.
kin *(relation)* Sippe, Geschlecht, Familie, Verwandter, Angehöriger, Verwandtschaft;
  next of ~ nächste Verwandte;
  collateral ~ Verwandte[r] in der Seitenlinie; **lineal ~** Verwandte[r] in der direkten Linie;
  ~ (a.) blutsverwandt;
  to be of ~ to s. o. mit jem. verwandt sein; **to come of good ~** aus einer guten Familie stammen.
kind *(matter)* Gegenstand, Sache, *(quality)* Qualität, *(sort)* Art, Klasse, Gattung, Sorte;
  in ~ in natura; **in cash or in ~** in bar oder in Sachleistungen;
  nothing of the ~ nichts dergleichen; **of average ~ or quality** von mittlerer Art und Güte; **of the same ~** gleichartig;
  the literary ~ literarisch Interessierte;
  ~s of income Einkommensarten; **~ of securities** Effektengattung; **~ of soil** Bodenbeschaffenheit; **~ of type** Schriftart;
  to be the ~ of man who hits back zu den Leuten gehören die sich nichts gefallen lassen; **to be ~ of queer** etw. wunderlich sein; **to go by some ~s of fiction** den Klischeevorstellungen in einigen Romanen Glauben schenken; **to have a ~ of suspicion** vagen Verdacht haben; **to pay in ~** in Naturalien zahlen; **to repay s. o. in ~** j. mit gleicher Münze zurückzahlen;
  ~ (a.) gütig, freundlich;
  ~ to animals tierlieb;
  ~ act gute Tat; **~ answer** gefällige Antwort; **to give s. o. a ~ reception** j. freundlich aufnehmen; **to give a proposal a ~ reception** Vorschlag in freundlicher Erwägung ziehen; **with ~ regards** mit freundlichen Grüßen; **~ words** freundliche Worte.
kindle *(v.)* anzünden, *(fig.)* anfeuern, entflammen, *(v./t.)* Feuer fangen, entzünden;
  ~ for eagerness vor Eifer sprühen; **~ a fire** Feuer anmachen; **~ the interest of an audience** seine Zuhörer begeistern, Publikum zur Begeisterung hinreißen; **~ the passions** Leidenschaften entfachen.
kindling Anmachholz.
kindred Verwandtschaft;
  of ~ blood blutsverwandt;
  ~ languages verwandte Sprachen.
kinescope Bildwiedergaberöhre;
  ~ recording Fernsehaufzeichnung.
king König, Monarch, *(railroad, sl.)* Zugschaffner;
  oil ~ Ölkönig, -scheich; **railroad ~** *(US)* Eisenbahnkönig;
  to crown s. o. ~ j. zum König krönen.
king-craft Regierungskunst.
king size Übergröße, *(advertising)* Königsformat;
  ~ (a.) überdurchschnittlich groß.
king's | advocate *(Br.)* Kronanwalt; **~ Bench [Division]** *(Br.)* Gericht[shof] erster Instanz; **~ bounty** Ausfuhrprämie; **~ counsel** *(Br.)* Justizrat; **~ evidence** belastendes Beweismaterial; **to turn ~ evidence** Kronzeugen abgeben; **~ highway** öffentliche Landstraße; **~ keys** *(Scot. law)* Brecheisen [bei Vollstreckung]; **~ peace** Landfrieden.
kingdom Königreich;
  gone to ~ come im Jenseits sein;
  to expediate s. o. to ~ come j. ins Jenseits befördern.
kingpin *(coll.)* Hauptperson, beherrschende Persönlichkeit.
kingship Königtum.
kink *(fig.)* Schrulle;
  to have got a ~ in the brain im Oberstübchen nicht ganz richtig sein.
kinky überspannt, schattenhaft.
kinsfolk Familienangehörige, Verwandtschaft.
kinship Anverwandtschaft, Verwandtschaftsverhältnis.
kinsman Familien-, Sippenangehöriger.

kiosk, newspaper ~ Zeitungskiosk.
kiss | -off *(US sl.)* fristlose Kündigung;
  ~ (v.) the book auf die Bibel schwören; **~ the dust** *(coll.)* ins Gras beißen; **~ s. th. goodbye** etw. wegwerfen; **~ out** *(US sl.)* um seinen Anteil bringen; **~ the post** ausgeschlossen sein; **~ the rod** sich einer Strafe beugen.
kit Ausrüstung, -stattung, Handwerkszeug, *(entire set of anything, coll.)* Kram, Sammelsurium, *(journalism)* Pressemappe, *(publicity)* im einzelnen vorbereitetes Programm;
  do-it-yourself ~ Handwerkskasten; **military ~** Soldatengepäck; **repair ~** Reparaturwerkzeuge; **skiing ~** Skiausrüstung; **tool ~** *(car)* Werkzeugausstattung; **the whole ~ and boiling** die ganze Sippschaft;
  ~ and [ca]boodle *(US sl.)* die ganze Baggage (Sippschaft); **~ of tools** Satz Werkzeuge;
  ~ (v.) up ausstaffieren;
  to pack up one's ~ sein Bündel schnüren;
  ~ bag Handwerkstasche, *(mar.)* Kleider-, Seesack; **~ inspection** Spindrevision.
kitchen Küche[nabteilung], *(caboose, US sl.)* Dienstabteil;
  ~ cabinet Küchenschrank, *(US)* Ratgebergruppe [des Präsidenten]; **~ drain** Küchenablauf, Ausguß; **~ facilities** Kochmöglichkeit; **~ gadget** Küchengerät; **~ garden** Gemüsegarten; **~ maid** Küchenmädchen; **~ police** *(mil.)* Küchendienst; **~ sink** Ausguß; **~-sink arguments** Argumente aus der Gosse; **~-sink drama** Wohnküchendrama; **~ staff** Küchenpersonal; **~ stuff** Küchenabfälle; **~ unit** Einbauküche; **~ utensils** Küchengeräte.
kitchener *(Br.)* Küchenherd.
kitchenette Küchennische.
kitchenware Küchengeschirr.
kite Papierdrache, *(bill, sl.)* Keller-, Reit-, Gefälligkeitswechsel, *(British Standards Institute)* Qualitätsbescheinigung, *(plane, sl.)* Mühle, Kiste, *(rascal)* Halunke, Gauner, *(underworld use, US sl.)* Kassiber;
  advertising ~ Reklamedrachen;
  ~ (v.) (anchor) fassen, *(bill, Br.)* Reitwechsel ausstellen, sich durch Wechselreiterei Kredit beschaffen, sich gegenseitig Schecks ausstellen, *(check, US)* Scheckbetrag fälschen;
  to fly a ~ *(coll.)* Gefälligkeitswechsel ziehen, Reitwechsel ausstellen;
  ~ balloon Fesselballon; **~ mark** *(Br.)* Qualitätszeichen, Standardnormstempel.
kiteflyer *(Br., coll.)* Aussteller ungedeckter Wechsel.
kiteflying Loslassen eines Versuchsballons, *(Br., coll.)* Wechselreiterei.
kith and kin *(Br.)* eigenes Fleisch und Blut.
kiting | checks *(US)* Ziehung von Schecks auf durch noch nicht eingegangene Inkassi, vorgetäuschte Guthaben; **~ stocks** *(US)* Hinauftreiben von Aktienkursen.
kittens, to have ~ *(US sl.)* seinen Gefühlen freien Lauf lassen, Dampf ablassen.
kittle | cattle schwer zu behandelnde Leute; **~ question** heikle Frage.
kitty gemeinsame Kasse, Sammeltasse, *(money pooled, sl.)* Sparbüchse.
klupper *(US sl.)* träger Arbeiter.
knack Kunstgriff, Trick, Kniff, *(aptness)* Gewandtheit, Fertigkeit, *(clever contrivance)* praktische Vorrichtung;
  ~ of pleasing Kunst des Gefallens;
  to get into the ~ of s. th. sich in etw. hineinfinden, mit etw. zurechtkommen; **to have the ~ of it** etw. glänzend verstehen, den Bogen heraushaben; **to have a ~ with children** sich gut auf Kinder verstehen; **to have the happy ~ of saying the right thing** glückliche Gabe besitzen, stets das Richtige zu sagen; **to have lost the ~ of s. th.** aus der Übung gekommen sein.
knacker Abbruchunternehmer, *(Br.)* Abdecker, Notschlachter, Tierkörperverwerter, *(of ship)* Schiffsausschlachter.
knapsack Tornister, Rucksack.
knee *(technics)* Kniestück, -rohr;
  on the ~s of gods im Schoße der Götter;
  to ask s. o. on one's bended ~ j. kniefällig bitten; **to bring s. o. to his ~s** j. auf die Knie zwingen; **to force a company to its financial ~s** Unternehmen aus finanziellen Gründen auf die Knie zwingen;
  ~-high to a grasshopper *(US coll.)* Dreikäsehoch; **~-hole writing desk** Diplomatenschreibtisch.
knell Grabgeläut, *(fig.)* Todeswarnung.
knife Dolch, Messer;
  pocket ~ Taschenmesser; **poor ~** schlechter Esser;
  ~ (v.) s. o. *(US sl.)* jem. einen Dolchstoß versetzen, j. abschießen;

to get one's ~ into s. o. j. gefressen haben; **to have a horror of the ~** sich vor Operationen fürchten; **to lay a ~ and fork for s. o.** für j. mitdecken; **to play a good ~ and fork** gut und reichlich essen.

knight *(fig.)* Kavalier, Ritter, Beschützer;
~s **of the post** käufliche Zeugen; ~ **of the road** Handlungsreisender, *(driver)* höflicher Fahrer, *(robber)* Straßenräuber;
⚥**-Marshal** *(Br.)* Hofmarschall; ~ **service** *(fig.)* ritterliche Tat.

knit Stinkarbeit;
~ **together by common interests** eng durch gemeinsame Interessen verbunden;
~ *(v.)* **up a plot** *(fam.)* Komplott aushecken.

knitted goods Strickwaren, Trikotagen.

knock Schlag, Stoß, *(motor)* Klopfen, *(US sl.)* beißende Kritik;
~ *(v.)* schlagen, stoßen, *(US sl.)* schlechte Presse haben;
~ **about** sich herumtreiben, unstetes Leben führen, *(goods)* im Umlauf (erhältlich) sein; ~ **against s. o.** j. zufällig treffen; ~ **them in the aisles** *(US sl.)* sein Publikum von den Sitzen reißen; ~ **down** *(misappropriate railroad fares, US coll.)* Fahrgeld veruntreuen, *(auction)* Zuschlag erteilen, zuschlagen, *(car)* anfahren, *(lower in price, coll.)* stark drücken, *(machinery)* [für Transportzwecke] in Bestandteile zerlegen, *(US sl.)* gesellschaftlich einführen; ~ **down books** Bücher verramschen; ~ **down a customer** *(sl.)* Kunden abspenstig machen; ~ **down a house** Haus abreißen; ~ **s. o. down for a song** *(fam.)* j. um eine Gesangseinlage bitten; ~ **down the till** *(sl.)* sich an der Ladenkasse vergreifen; ~ **into a cocked hat** *(sl.)* in Stücke schlagen, total fertigmachen; ~ **one's head against** in Konflikt geraten; ~ **in** *(university, sl., Br.)* Einlaß begehren; ~ **in the head** *(fig.)* [Plan] zunichtemachen; ~ **s. o. into the middle of next week** j. in hohem Bogen hinauswerfen; ~ **it** *(sl.)* Fahrzeug anhalten; ~ **off** schnell erledigen, *(kill, sl.)* umbringen, *(police raid, US sl.)* ausheben, *(from price)* vom Preis abziehen (herunterhandeln), Preisabstrich vornehmen, *(work, sl.)* Arbeit einstellen, Feierabend (Schicht) machen; ~ **s. th. off** etw. erledigen; ~ **off an article for a magazine** Zeitungsartikel herunterschreiben; ~ **off a bank** *(sl.)* Bank berauben; ~ **off ten dollars from a bill** zehn Dollar von einer Rechnung abziehen; ~ **s. one's head off** *(coll.)* j. spielend übertreffen; ~ **off a line or two to s. o.** *(sl.)* jem. ein paar Zeilen schreiben; ~ **off a lot of work** Riesenberg von Arbeit bewältigen; ~ **the top off its inflation mountains** Spitze des Inflationsberges beseitigen; ~ **out** *(auction, Br.)* Käuferring bilden, unter sich verkaufen; ~ **o. s. out** *(sl.)* fasziniert (völlig weg) sein; ~ **the bottom out of a financial speculation** finanziellen Spekulationen den Boden entziehen; ~ **stupid ideas out of s. o.** jem. törichte Ideen austreiben; ~ **out a letter** Brief herunterschreiben; ~ **over an ill-reputed bookmaking parlo(u)r** *(sl.)* berüchtigte Wettbude hochgehen lassen; ~ **over a store** *(sl.)* Laden ausplündern; ~ **s. o. for a row** *(sl.)* j. ungemein beeindrucken; ~ **sideways** aus der Bahn werfen; ~ **together** etw. schnell zusammenhauen, improvisieren; ~ **up** wecken, *(arrange)* improvisieren; ~ **o. s. up** *(fam.)* sich völlig aufreiben; ~ **up against s. o.** j. zufällig treffen; ~ **up a garage out of an old hen house** Garage aus einem alten Hühnerhaus zusammenbauen; ~ **up a meal** Essen in die Pfanne hauen;
to be a big ~ to one's family *(sl.)* für seine Familie kaum zu ertragen sein; **to have the ~~in on s. o.** *(sl.)* j. auf dem Kicker haben; **to know s. o. by his ~** j. an einer frappanten Bewegung erkennen; **to take the ~** *(sl.)* schweren finanziellen Schlag abbekommen;
~~**-for-~** **agreement** *(motor car insurance)* gegenseitige Regreßverzichterklärung; ~~**-over** *(US sl.)* Raubüberfall.

knockabout kleine Segeljacht, *(handyman, Australia)* Gelegenheitsarbeiter, *(US sl.)* wilde Rauferei;
~ *(a.)* unstet, unruhig, zigeunerhaft, strapazierfähig;
~ **comedian** Taschenspieler, Gauner; ~ **life** Zigeunerleben; ~ **performance** Clownvorstellung.

knockdown zerlegbarer Gegenstand, *(auction)* Zuschlag, *(bad news)* niederschmetternde Nachricht, *(fist fight)* Rauferei, *(store money stolen, US sl.)* Plündern der Portokasse, *(US sl.)* gesellschaftliche Einführung;
~ *(a.)* zerlegbar, zusammenlegbar, *(economics)* mindest, äußerst, niedrigst;
~ **furniture** zerlegbare Möbel; ~ **kit** auf dem Autofriedhof abgestelltes Auto, Schrottwagen; ~ **price** Werbe-, Spottpreis, *(auction)* äußerster Preis, Mindestpreis.

knocked about in transit beim Transport beschädigt.

knocked down zu Transportzwecken auseinandergenommen, zerlegt;
~ **for a song** für einen Spottpreis zugeschlagen;
at a ~ price *(Br.)* spottbillig;
to be ~ by a motor car von einem Auto angefahren werden.

knocked out abgeschlafft, betrunken;
~ **by the news** von den Nachrichten überwältigt;
to be ~ in an examination im Examen durchfallen; **to be ~ in a tournament** in einem Turnier ausscheiden.

knocking down [Versteigerungs]zuschlag, Zuschlagserteilung;
~ **copy** *(Br.)* herabsetzende (aggressive) Werbung, herabsetzender Werbetext.

knocking-off time Feierabend.

knockout vernichtende Niederlage, *(Br.)* Ringbildung, Scheinauktion, *(merchandise, sl.)* Verkaufsschlager, *(striking thing, US)* tolle Sache;
~ **for a fiction story** *(sl.)* erstklassiger Romanentwurf;
~ **agreement** Bietungsabsprache; ~ **auction** Scheinauktion; **to sell s. th. at a ~ price** etw. im Ringkauf verkaufen; ~ **system** Ausscheidungssystem.

knockup Trainingsspiel.

knot Knoten, Seemeile, *(fig.)* Schwierigkeit, Verwicklung, Problem, *(mil.)* Epaulette, *(naut.)* Knoten;
Gordian ~ Gordischer Knoten; **marriage ~** Band der Ehe; **porter's ~** *(porter)* Schulterkissen;
~ **of friends** enger Freundeskreis; ~ **of vehicles** Fahrzeuganhäufung;
~ *(v.)* mit einem Knoten befestigen;
~ **a parcel firmly** Paket fest verschnüren; ~ **together** zusammenknoten;
to get into ~s völlig durcheinandergeraten; **to stand about in ~s** in Gruppen (Menschentrauben) zusammenstehen; **to tie a ~ in one's handkerchief** *(fam.)* Knoten ins Taschentuch machen.

knotty | **problem** kompliziertes Problem; ~ **question** schwierige Frage.

know *(v.)* kennen, wissen, im Bilde sein, erfahren;
in the ~ *(coll.)* im Bilde; **before you ~ where you are** im Handumdrehen;
~ **better than** so viel Verstand haben; **not to ~ s. o. from Adam** keine Ahnung haben, wer j. ist; ~ **s. o. like a book** j. in- und auswendig kennen; ~ **one's business** sein Geschäft verstehen; ~ **one's distance** wissen, wie weit man gehen kann; ~ **English** Englisch verstehen; ~ **s. one's little game** wissen, was j. im Schilde führt; ~ **s. th. by heart** etw. auswendig kennen; ~ **how to behave** sich zu benehmen wissen; ~ **how to drive a car** Autofahren können; ~ **how the land lies** wissen, wie der Hase läuft; ~ **how to treat children** mit Kindern umzugehen wissen; ~ **by name** den Namen nach kennen; ~ **one's onions (oil, oats)** sein Handwerk verstehen, wissen, wo der Barthel seinen Most holt; ~ **s. th. perfectly** umfassende Kenntnisse auf einem Gebiet haben; ~ **all one's neighbo(u)r's proceedings** alles wissen, was beim Nachbarn vorgeht; ~ **one from the other** zwei Menschen auseinanderhalten; ~ **the rights of a case** Sache in- und auswendig kennen; ~ **the ropes** *(mar.)* Seemannshandwerk verstehen, seine Sache verstehen, eingeweiht sein; ~ **s. o. by sight** von Sehen her kennen; ~ **a thing or two** in der Welt Bescheid wissen, kein Dummkopf sein; ~ **the time of day** wissen, was es geschlagen hat; ~ **a town like the back of one's hand** Stadt wie seine eigene Westentasche kennen; ~ **one's way about** sich auskennen (zurechtfinden); ~ **what's what** sich auf etw. bestens verstehen; ~ **where the shoe pinches** wissen, wo der Schuh drückt; ~ **on which side one's bread is buttered** auf seinen Vorteil bedacht sein;
to be in the ~ eingeweiht (im Bilde) sein; **to come to ~** erfahren; **to get to ~ s. o.** j. kennen lernen; **to get to ~ the details of a business** sich in ein Geschäft einarbeiten; **to let ~** Nachricht geben, benachrichtigen; **not ~ what s. o. is driving at** nicht wissen, worauf j. hinaus will;
~~**-all** Schlaumeier, Besserwisser; ~~**-all manner** allwissende Miene; ~ **nothing** Dummkopf.

know all men *(conveyancing)* hiermit sei allen kundgetan.

know-how praktisches Wissen, praktische Erfahrungen, Fachkenntnisse;
industrial ~ industrielle Produktionserfahrungen, praktische Betriebserfahrung; **manufacturing ~** spezielle Produktionskenntnisse.

knowing klug, intelligent, scharfsinnig, *(US sl.)* elegant, fesch, schick;
to assume a ~ air Eingeweihten spielen; ~ **dog** durchtriebener Kerl; ~ **faculties** Erkenntniskräfte; ~ **glance** bedeutsamer Blick; **a ~ one** ein Schlauberger.

knowingly wissentlich, bewußt;
~ **and wilfully** vorsätzlich.

knowledge Kennen, Wissen, *(law)* Kenntnis;
contrary to one's ~ wider besseres Wissen; **to my certain ~** wie ich genau weiß;

to the best of one's ~ and belief nach bestem Wissen und Gewissen;

actual ~ tatsächliche (unmittelbare) Kenntnis; **allround** ~ umfassende Kenntnisse, globales Wissen; **commercial** ~ kaufmännische Kenntnisse; **common** ~ Allgemeinwissen; **well-digested** ~ gut verarbeitete Erkenntnisse; **expert** ~ Fachkenntnisse; **extensive** ~ umfassendes Wissen, vielseitige Kenntnisse; **full** ~ genaue Kenntnisse (Sachkenntnis); **general** ~ allgemein bekannte Tatsachen; **imputed** ~ unterstellte (zurechenbare) Kenntnis; **in-depth** ~ gründliche Kenntnisse; **intimate** ~ genaue Sachkenntnis; **medical** ~ ärztliche Kenntnisse; **personal** ~ Kenntnis aus eigener Wahrnehmung; **practical** ~ auf Erfahrung beruhende Kenntnisse, praktische Erfahrung; **profound** ~ profundes Wissen; **scanty** ~ dürftige Kenntnisse; **special (specialized, technical)** ~ Fachkenntnisse; **slight** ~ oberflächliche Kenntnisse; **thorough** ~ gründliche Kenntnisse; **up-to-the-minute** ~ allerneueste Erkenntnisse; **working** ~ verwertbare Kenntnisse;

~ **of banking** Erfahrungen im Bankgeschäft; ~ **of business** Geschäftskenntnisse, -erfahrung; ~ **of a line of business** Branchenkenntnisse; **fluent** ~ **of English** fließende englische Sprachkenntnisse; ~ **of the law** Rechtskenntnisse, juristische Kenntnisse; ~ **of life** Lebenserfahrung; ~ **of markets in Europe** Kenntnisse der europäischen Marktsituation;

to apply one's ~ seine Kenntnisse verwerten; **to be a matter of common** ~ allgemein bekannt sein; **to come to the** ~ **of s. o.** Kenntnis erhalten, jem. zu Ohren kommen; **to have a thorough** ~ **of s. th.** in etw. gut beschlagen sein; **to have recourse to the superior** ~ **of specialists** Dienste hervorragender Fachleute in Anspruch nehmen können; **to have a working** ~ **of a foreign language** sich in einer Fremdsprache ausreichend verständigen können; **to have** ~ **of another's peril** Kenntnis von der Gefährdung eines anderen besitzen; **to have a** ~ **of several languages** mehrere Sprachen beherrschen; **to have no** ~ **of the ways of the world** sich in der großen Welt nicht auskennen; **to increase one's** ~ seinen Wissensstand erweitern; **to keep s. th. from s. one's** ~ etw. von jem. fernhalten; **to know or to be chargeable with** ~ *(criminal law)* kennen oder kennen müssen; **to marry**

without the ~ **of one's parents** ohne das Einverständnis seiner Eltern heiraten; **to put all** ~ **in the window** mit seinem Wissen prahlen; **to speak from one's own** ~ aufgrund eigener Erfahrungen sprechen; **to speak with full** ~ **of the facts** in Kenntnis aller Tatsachen sprechen;

special ~ **not required** *(advertisement)* besondere Kenntnisse nicht erforderlich.

knowledgeable klug, intelligent;

to be ~ **of the structure, taxation and pricing in their particular financial markets** sich in den Struktur-, Steuer- und Preisproblemen ihrer spezialisierten Märkte für Investitionspapiere auskennen.

known bekannt, notorisch;

not ~ *(letter)* unzustellbar;

to be ~ **to the police** Vorstrafenregister haben; **to become** ~ *(author)* Durchbruch erzielen; **to come to be** ~ bekannt werden; **to have** ~ **better days** früher in guten Verhältnissen gelebt haben, bessere Tage gesehen haben; **to have never** ~ **trouble** nie Schwierigkeiten gehabt haben; **to make o. s.** ~ sich bekanntmachen (vorstellen); **to make s. one's misdeeds** ~ **to the police** jds. Missetaten der Polizei melden; **to make one's plans** ~ seine Pläne enthüllen;

~ **facts** feststehende Tatsachen; ~ **heirs** feststehende Erben; **of** ~ **identity** von Person bekannt; ~ **loss** *(freight)* erkannter Verlust.

knuck *(US sl.)* Taschendieb.

knuckle *(joint)* Gelenk;

a bit near the ~ *(fam.)* etw. unanständig; **near the** ~ *(coll.)* bis an die Grenze des Anständigen;

~ *(v.)* **down** *(US sl.)* ernsthaft arbeiten; ~ **under** nachgeben, sich unterwerfen, klein beigeben;

to be pretty near the ~ äußerst heikel sein; **to rap s. o. over the** ~**s** jem. einen Verweis erteilen;

~ **duster** *(sl.)* Schlagring.

kotow, kowtow *(fam.)* Katzbuckeln, Kriechen.

kraft paper *(US)* braunes Packpapier.

kudos *(coll.)* Ruhm, Ehre;

for the sake of ~ von Ehrgeiz angetrieben.

L

L Seitenflügel, *(US coll.)* Hochbahn;
  ⁻ **plate** Fahrschülerzeichen; ~ **train** Hochbahnzug.
la-di-da *(fam.)* affektiert.
lab *(US)* Labor;
  ~ **block** Laborgebäude.
label *(branded goods)* Schutzmarke, *(codicil)* Testamentsnachtrag, Kodizill, *(short name)* Bezeichnung, Benennung, *(parcel)* Paketzettel, -adresse, Aufkleber, *(parchment)* Pergamentstreifen, Bändchen, *(adhesive stamp)* Aufklebemarke, *(ticket)* Etikett, Anhänge-, Bezeichnungsschild, Anhänge-, Aufklebe-, Warenadreßzettel;
  under a new ~ *(party)* mit einem neuem Programm;
  adhesive ~ Klebezettel; **airmail ~** Luftpostkleber; **baggage ~** *(US)* Gepäckanhänger, -adresse, -zettel; **gummed ~** Aufklebeadresse; **industrial ~** gewerbliche Schutzmarke; **luggage ~** *(Br.)* Gepäckadresse, -anhänger, -zettel; **part-of-speech ~** Wortartbezeichnung; **paste-on ~** Aufklebeadresse; **price ~** Preiszettel; **quality ~** Gütezeichen; **stick-on ~** Beklebezettel; **tie-on ~** Anhänger, Anhängezettel;
  ~ *(v.)* mit Etikett versehen, etikettieren, [Waren] [aus]zeichnen, beschildern, beschriften, kennzeichnen, bezetteln, *(assign to category)* kategorisieren, einstufen, klassifizieren, eingruppieren, *(number)* numerieren, *(write address on)* mit Aufschrift versehen;
  ~ **an article for sale** Gegenstand mit Preiszettel versehen, Artikel auszeichnen; ~ **a criminal** zum Verbrecher abstempeln; ~ **s. o. as a demagogue** j. als Demagogen bezeichnen;
  to place a ~ on s. o. jem. als ... abstempeln; **to put ~s on one's luggage** *(Br.)* sein Gepäck mit Adressenanhängern versehen; **to sell under a secondary ~** als zweitklassige Ware verkaufen;
  ~ **holder** Kofferanhänger.
labelling Etikettierung, Be-, Kenn-, Auszeichnung, Markierung, Kategorisierung, Unterteilung, *(prices)* Preisauszeichnung;
  descriptive ~ übliche Etikettierung; **informative ~** Ursprungs-, Herkunftsbezeichnung;
  ~ **machine** Etikettiermaschine; ~ **provisions** Kennzeichnungs-, Auszeichnungsbestimmungen; ~ **requirements** Kennzeichnungsvoraussetzungen.
laboratory Labor[atorium] *(fig.)* Werkstatt, -stätte;
  flying ~ fliegendes Laboratorium; **manned orbiting ~** bemanntes Weltraumlaboratorium;
  ~ **animal** Versuchstier; ~ **apparatus** Laborgerät; ~ **assistant** Laborant; ~ **equipment** Laboratoriumsausstattung; ~ **experiment** Laborexperiment; ~ **test** Laboruntersuchung; ~ **work** Labortätigkeit; ~ **worker** Laborant.
laborious mühsam, mühselig;
  ~ **task** schwierige Arbeit; ~ **style of writing** schwerfälliger Briefstil; ~ **undertaking** schwieriges Unternehmen.
Labo(u)r Arbeiterklasse, -schaft, *(Br.)* Arbeiterpartei.
labo(u)r Arbeit[skraft], Tätigkeit, *(operatives)* Arbeiterklasse, -schaft, Arbeitskräfte, *(ship)* Schlingern, Stampfen;
  casual ~ Gelegenheitsarbeit; **child ~** Kinderarbeit; **colo(u)red ~** schwarze Arbeitskräfte; **compulsory ~** Zwangsarbeit; **common ~** ungelernte Arbeit, Handarbeit; **conscript ~** zwangsverpflichtete Arbeitskräfte; **convict ~** Zuchthausarbeit; **drafted ~** dienstverpflichtete Arbeitskräfte, Fremdarbeiter; **farm ~** Landarbeit; **female ~** weibliche Arbeitskräfte; **foreign ~** ausländische Arbeitskräfte, Fremdarbeiter; **free ~** unorganisierte Arbeiterschaft; **hard ~** Zwangsarbeit, Zuchthaus; **juvenile ~** Jugendarbeit; **lost ~** vergebliche Mühe; **manual ~** körperliche Arbeit, Handarbeit; **manufacturing ~** [gesamte] Fabrikationslöhne; **marginal ~** unrentable Arbeitskräfte; **native ~** eingeborene Arbeitskräfte; **nonunion ~** nicht organisierte Arbeiter[schaft]; **ordinary ~** gewöhnliche Arbeit; **organized ~** *(US)* gewerkschaftlich organisierte Arbeiter; **paid ~** bezahlte Arbeitskräfte, Lohnarbeit; **peasant ~** landwirtschaftliche Arbeitskräfte; **prison ~** Gefangenenarbeit; **qualified ~** geschulte Arbeitskräfte; **road ~** Straßenbauarbeit; **semi-skilled ~** angelernte Arbeitskräfte; **skilled ~** Facharbeiter; **specialized ~** Spezialkräfte; **strike-free ~** am Streik nicht beteiligte Arbeitskräfte; **surplus ~** überschüssige Arbeitskräfte; **union ~** gewerkschaftlich organisierte Arbeitskräfte; **unorganized ~** gewerkschaftlich nicht organisierte Arbeitskräfte; **unpaid farm ~** unbezahlte landwirtschaftliche Arbeitskräfte; **unskilled ~** ungelernte Arbeitskräfte; **untrained ~** ungelernte Arbeitskräfte, Hilfsarbeiter; **white ~** weiße Arbeitskräfte; **work-in-process ~** Halbfabrikatelöhne;

material and ~ Material und Arbeitslöhne; ~ **and capital** Arbeitnehmer und Arbeitgeber; ~ **of Hercules** Herkulesarbeit; ~ **of love** freiwillige (gern getane) Arbeit;
  ~ *(v.)* sich abmühen, anstrengen, [schwer] arbeiten, sich abarbeiten, *(ship)* schlingern, stampfen;
  ~ **for s. th.** sich um etw. abmühen; ~ **an argument** bei einer Beweisführung bis ins Einzelne gehen; ~ **under a constant anxiety** von ständiger Furcht geplagt sein; ~ **under a burden** mit einer schweren Last leben; ~ **at a (for the) cause of peace** sich für die Sache des Friedens einsetzen; ~ **under difficulties** unter schwierigen Verhältnissen arbeiten, mit Schwierigkeiten zu kämpfen haben; ~ **under a dillusion** sich Illusionen hingeben; ~ **up a hill** sich einen Berg heraufackern; ~ **a jury** Geschworene zu beeinflussen suchen; ~ **under a misapprehension** sich in einem Mißverständnis befinden; ~ **a point** auf einen strittigen Punkt ausführlich eingehen; ~ **through the heavy sea** *(ship)* durch das aufgewühlte Meer stampfen; ~ **under a sense of wrong** Gefühl des Unrechts haben;
  to direct ~ Arbeitskräfte einsetzen; **to displace human ~ by machinery** menschliche Arbeitskräfte ersetzen; **to earn one's living by manual ~** seinen Lebensunterhalt mit seiner Hände Arbeit verdienen; **to go ~** *(constituency, Br.)* Labourpartei wählen; **to hire ~** *(US)* Arbeitskräfte einstellen; **to immigrate (import) ~** ausländische Arbeitskräfte heranziehen; **to lure ~ into other jobs** Arbeitskräfte zum Berufswechsel verführen; **to procure ~** Arbeit verschaffen; **to recruit ~** Arbeiter einstellen; **to save ~** Arbeitskräfte sparen; **to sweat ~** Arbeitskräfte ausbeuten;
  ~ **agreement** *(trade union, US)* Tarif-, Kollektivvertrag; ~ **allocation** Arbeitszuweisung, -einsatz; ~ **arbitration** Schlichtung von Arbeitsstreitigkeiten; ~ **arrangements** Arbeitsvereinbarungen; ~ **association** Arbeitnehmervereinigung; ~ **attaché** Sozialattaché; ~ **bank** *(US)* Gemeinwirtschafts-, Gewerkschaftsbank; ~ **banking** *(US)* Gewerkschaftsbankwesen; ~ **battalion** Arbeitskommando; ~ **boycott** *(US)* Arbeitsboykott; ~ **budget** Lohn- und Gehaltsetat; **Incorporated** ⁻ **Bureau** *(US)* Beratungsstelle für Gewerkschaftsfragen; ~ **camp** Arbeitslager, Strafkolonie; ~ **candidate** *(Br.)* Kandidat der Labour Party; ~ **case** Arbeitsprozeß; ~ **charges** Arbeitskostenbelastung, Lohnkostenanteil; ~ **circles** Gewerkschaftskreise; ~ **college** Arbeiterhochschule; ~ **colony** Arbeitersiedlung; ~ **committee** Gewerkschaftsausschuß; ~ **conditions** [betriebliche] Arbeitsverhältnisse; ~ **conflict** *(US)* Lohn-, Arbeitsstreitigkeit; ~ **conscription** Arbeitsdienstpflicht; **to be liable to ~ conscription** arbeitsverpflichtet werden; **to have a low ~ content** arbeitsextensiv sein; ~ **copartnership** Gewinnbeteiligung der Arbeitnehmer; ~ **cost** Lohnkosten, *(balance sheet)* Arbeitslöhne; ~ **cost** Fertigungslöhne; **indirect ~ cost** Gemeinkostenlöhne; ~ **cost index** Lohnkostenindex; **work-in-process ~ costs** Halbfabrikatelöhne; ~ **cost trend** Arbeitskostenentwicklung; ~ **council** Betriebsrat; ~ **court** *(US)* Arbeitsgericht; ~ **court order** Arbeitsgerichtsbeschluß; ⁻ **Day** *(US)* Arbeitsfeiertag; ~ **demand** Nachfrage nach Arbeitskräften, Arbeitsbedarf; ⁻ **Department** *(US)* Arbeitsministerium; ~ **displacement** Ersetzung der menschlichen Arbeitskraft; ~**-displacing machines** Arbeitskräfte ersetzende Maschinenanlagen; ~ **disputes** arbeitsrechtliche Streitfragen, Tarifstreitigkeiten; ~ **disturbances** Arbeiterunruhen; ~ **division** Arbeitsteilung; ~ **division process** Arbeitsaufteilungsverfahren; ~ **economics** Arbeitswissenschaft, -ökonomie; ~ **efficiency** Arbeitsleistung; ~ **efficiency variance** Leistungsgradabweichung; ~ **employment costs** Arbeitskosten; ~ **estimate** Gehalts- und Lohnkostenvoranschlag; ~ **exchange** *(Br.)* Arbeitsnachweis[stelle]; **to report to the ~ exchange** *(Br.)* sich beim Arbeitsamt melden; ~ **exchange officer** *(Br.)* Arbeitsamtsleiter; ~ **exertion** körperliche Anstrengung; ~ **flux** Arbeitsplatzwechsel; **potential ~ force** Arbeitskräftepotential, -reserve; ~ **force** Arbeitskräfte, Beschäftigtenzahl, Belegschaft; **total possible ~ force** Arbeitskräftereserven; **to reduce the ~ force** Arbeitskräfte abbauen; **to redeploy the ~ force** Arbeitskräfte umdisponieren; ~**-force dropouts** Belegschaftsabgänge; ~ **glut** Überangebot an Arbeitskräften; ~ **government** Arbeiterregierung; ~ **grade** Arbeitsbefähigung für eine bestimmte Arbeit; ~ **hoarding** Horden von Arbeitskräften; ~**-importing country** Gastarbeiterland; ~ **inspection** Gewerbeaufsicht; ~**-intensive** arbeitsintensiv; ~ **item** Gehalts-, Lohnposten; ~ **jurisdiction** Arbeitsgerichtsbarkeit; ~ **law** Arbeitsrecht; ~ **law violator** Übertreter arbeits-

rechtlicher Bestimmungen; ~ **leader** *(US)* Gewerkschaftsführer; [**protective**] ~ **legislation** Arbeiterschutzgesetzgebung; ≗ **majority** *(Br.)* Mehrheit der Labour Party; ~ **management** betriebliche Personalpolitik; ~ **management committee** Arbeitnehmer-Arbeiter-Ausschuß; **~-management contract** betriebliche Lohnvereinbarung; **~-management relations** Arbeitgeber-Arbeitnehmerverhältnis; ≗ **Management Relations Act** *(US)* [etwa] Betriebsverfassungsgesetz; ~ **market area** Einzugsgebiet; **free (tight) ~-market** gut (knapp) besetzter Arbeitsmarkt; **to enter the ~ market** erstmals im Beschäftigungsverhältnis stehen (auf den Arbeitsmarkt kommen); ~ **market clearing** Arbeitsmarktausgleich; ~ **market policy** Arbeitsmarktpolitik; ~ **market policy measures** arbeitsmarktpolitische Maßnahmen; ~ **market situation** Arbeitsmarktlage; ~ **material** Arbeitsmaterial; ~ **mayor** *(Br.)* [etwa] SPD-Bürgermeister; ~ **member** *(Br.)* Abgeordneter der Arbeiterpartei; ~ **movement** Arbeiterbewegung; **~'s national support** Arbeiterstimmenunterstützung im ganzen Land; ~ **needs** Arbeitskräftebedarf; **International ≗ Office** Internationales Arbeitsamt; ~ **organization** *(US)* Gewerkschafts-, Arbeiterorganisation; ~ **outlook** Arbeitskräftevorschau; ≗ **Party** *(Br.)* Labour-, Arbeiterpartei; ~ **party credentials** *(Br.)* Empfehlungen seitens der Labour Party; **local ~ party's general management committee** Ortsverbandsausschuß; ~ **pass** Arbeitserlaubnisschein, -genehmigung; ~ **peace** Arbeitsfrieden; ~ **performance** Arbeitsleistung; ~ **permit** *(Br.)* Beschäftigungs-, Arbeitsgenehmigung, -erlaubnis; ~ **picture** Beschäftigungsbild; ~ **piracy** *(US)* Abwerbung von Arbeitskräften; ~ **policy** Arbeitsmarktpolitik; **company ~ policy** betriebliche Gewerkschaftspolitik; ~ **pool** Arbeitsreserve; **unfair ~ practices** *(US)* unlautere Arbeitskampfmethoden; ~ **press** *(US)* Gewerkschaftspresse; ~ **problems** Arbeiterfragen; ~ **productivity** Arbeitsproduktivität, -leistung; ~ **question** Arbeiterfrage; ~ **rate** Lohnstundensatz; **common ~ rate** Durchschnittslohn; ~ **rates** Lohnkosten; ~ **recruitment** Anwerbung von Arbeitskräften; ~ **reform** *(US)* Gewerkschaftsreform; ~ **reform bill** *(US)* Gewerkschaftsreformgesetz; ~ **relations** Arbeitgeber-, Arbeitnehmerverhältnis; ~ **relations director** Arbeitsdirektor; ~ **report** Arbeitsbericht; ~ **representation** Arbeitnehmervertretung; ~ **representative** Arbeitnehmervertreter; ~ **representative on the board** Vertreter der Arbeitnehmerseite im Aufsichtsrat; ~ **requirements** Bedarf an Arbeitskräften, Arbeitskräftebedarf; ~ **research association** *(US)* Gewerkschaftsinstitut; ≗ **rule** Labourregierung; ~ **saving** Einsparung von Arbeitskräften; **~-saving devices (appliances)** arbeitsparende Einrichtungen; **~-saving machines** Maschinen zur Einsparung von Arbeitskräften; ~ **scarcity** Mangel an Arbeitskräften, Arbeitermangel; ~ **scheme** Arbeitsordnung; ~ **separation** Entlassung von Arbeitskräften, Arbeitsabgänge; ~ **settlement** Arbeitersiedlung; ~ **shortage** Verknappung an Arbeitskräften; ~ **situation** Arbeitsmarktlage; ~ **spy** *(US)* von der Arbeitgeberseite bezahlter Spion; ~ **standards** Arbeitsbedingungen; **fair ~ standards** gerechte Arbeitsnormen; ~ **statistics** Arbeitsstatistik; ~ **stoppage** Arbeitseinstellung; ~ **strike** Arbeiterausstand; **~-only subcontracting** Arbeitskräfteeinsatz lediglich im Unterlieferantenverhältnis; ~ **supply** verfügbare Arbeitskräfte, Arbeitskräfteangebot; **better quality ~ supply** höher qualifizierte Arbeitskräfte; **excess ~ supply** Arbeitskräfteüberschuß; **~'s national supply** Unterstützung durch Arbeiterstimmen im ganzen Land; **potential ~ supply** Arbeitskräftepotential; ~ **support** Unterstützung durch Arbeiterkreise; ~ **surplus** Überschuß an Arbeitskräften; **~-tax matter** *(Br.)* steuerbedingte Lohnkosten; **~-tight economy** angespannte Arbeitsmarktlage; ~ **time ticket** Zeitlohnzettel; ~ **trouble** Arbeiterunruhen; ~ **turnover** Arbeitsplatzwechsel, betriebliche Fluktuationsrate; ~ **union** *(US)* Gewerkschaft; ~ **union affiliation** *(US)* Gewerkschaftszugehörigkeit; ~ **union due** *(US)* Gewerkschaftsbeitrag; ~ **union official** *(US)* Gewerkschaftsfunktionär; ~ **unrest** Arbeiterunruhen; ~ **upheaval** Arbeiteraufstand; ~ **vote** Arbeiterstimmen; ~ **welfare** Arbeiterfürsorge.

labo(u)red style of writing umständliche Schreibweise.

labo(u)rer [ungelernter] Arbeiter, Hand-, Lohnarbeiter;
agricultural ~ Landarbeiter; **casual** ~ Gelegenheitsarbeiter; **day** ~ Tagelöhner; **factory** ~ Fabrikarbeiter; **farm** ~ Landarbeiter, landwirtschaftlicher Arbeiter; **fellow** ~ Arbeitskollege; **forced** ~ Zwangsarbeiter; **foreign** ~ Gast-, Fremdarbeiter; **hired** ~ Lohnarbeiter; **industrial** ~ gewerblicher Arbeiter, Fabrikarbeiter; **manual** ~ Handarbeiter; **permanent** ~ Stammarbeiter; **skilled** ~ Facharbeiter; **slave** ~ Zwangsarbeiter; **unskilled** ~ ungelernter Arbeiter.

labo(u)ring arbeitend, werktätig;
to be ~ under an accusation mit einer Beschuldigung leben müssen; ~ **classes** Arbeiterbevölkerung; ~ **man** Werktätiger, Arbeiter; **to pull the ~ oar** *(fam.)* gewaltige Arbeitsanstrengung unternehmen.

lace Spitze, *(uniform)* Litze;
shoe ~s Schnürsenkel;
~-curtain *(Irish, sl.)* wohlhabend, betucht.

lacerate *(v.)* quälen, mißhandeln;
~ **s. one's feelings** jds. Gefühle verletzen.

laches Trägheit, *(law)* fahrlässige Versäumnis [der rechtzeitigen Geltendmachung einer Forderung], Verwirkung;
~ **of entry** Nichteintritt einer Erbschaft; ~ **in bringing suit** Klageverwirkung;
to plead ~ as a defense (defence, *Br.)* **to a suit** Prozeßverschleppungseinwand vorbringen.

lack Mangel, Fehlen, Knappheit;
for ~ of evidence mangels Beweises; **for ~ of time** aus Zeitmangel;
~ **of ability** mangelnde Eignung; ~ **of adjustment** Anpassungsmängel; ~ **of articulation** Mangel an selbstbewußtem Auftreten; ~ **of authority** fehlende Vertretungsmacht; ~ **of capital** Kapitalmangel, -knappheit; ~ **of care** mangelnde Sorgfalt; ~ **of commitment** fehlendes Engagement; ~ **of communication** Kommunikationsschwierigkeiten; ~ **of confidence** mangelndes Vertrauen; ~ **of conformity** *(goods delivered)* Vertragswidrigkeit; ~ **of consent** fehlende Einwilligung; ~ **of consideration** fehlende Gegenleistung; ~ **of delivery** Mangel des Erfüllungsgeschäftes; ~ **of demand** mangelnde Nachfrage; ~ **of due diligence** mangelnde Sorgfalt; ~ **of discernment** mangelnde Einsicht; ~ **of endorsement** fehlendes Giro; ~ **of faith** mangelndes Vertrauen; ~ **of feed** Futtermangel; ~ **of food** Lebensmittelmangel, -knappheit; ~ **of form** Formmangel, -fehler; ~ **of funds** fehlende Geldmittel; ~ **of private investment** fehlende Kapitalinvestitionen der privaten Wirtschaft, Stagnation der privaten Investitionstätigkeit; ~ **of judgment** mangelnde Urteilskraft; ~ **of jurisdiction** mangelnde Zuständigkeit, Unzuständigkeit; ~ **of knowledge** Unkenntnis; ~ **of liquidity** Liquiditätsbeengung, -klemme; ~ **of management mobility** Unbeweglichkeit des Vorstands; ~ **of means** Mittellosigkeit, Bedürftigkeit; ~ **of money** Geldknappheit; ~ **of payment** Ausbleiben der Zahlung; ~ **of production** Produktionsausfall; ~ **of quorum** Beschlußunfähigkeit; ~ **of sales** ungenügender Umsatz; ~ **of support** mangelnde Unterstützung; ~ **of title** fehlender (mangelnder) Rechtsanspruch, Rechtsmangel; ~ **of transport** fehlende Transportmöglichkeiten; ~ **of utility** Nutzungsmangel; ~ **of political vision** mangelnde politische Weitsicht;
~ *(v.) (money)* fehlen, knapp sein;
~ **capital** zu knappe Kapitaldecke haben; ~ **no clients** über mangelnde Kundschaft nicht zu klagen haben; ~ **experience** über zu wenig Erfahrungen verfügen; ~ **for nothing** nichts entbehren müssen, es an nichts fehlen haben;
~-all Habenichts, armer Schlucker.

lackey Lakai, livrierter Diener, *(fig.)* Speichellecker, Kriecher.

lacking fehlend, mangelnd.

lackluster, lacklustre *(Br.)* lustlos, matt.

ladder Leiter, *(stockings, Br.)* Laufmasche;
accommodation ~ Schiffsleiter; **extension** ~ ausziehbare Leiter; **gangway** ~ Fallreep; **peg** ~ Stangenleiter; **social** ~ *(fam.)* gesellschaftliche Schicht;
~ **of success** Erfolgsleiter;
to bring s. o. back down the ~ j. die Erfolgsleiter wieder herunterfallen lassen; **to climb a rung of the social** ~ gesellschaftlich wieder ein Stück vorankommen; **to kick down the** ~ sich undankbar nach dem Aufstieg erweisen; **to reach the top of the** ~ an die Spitze gelangen; **to see through a** ~ das Offensichtliche erkennen; **not see a hole in the** ~ total betrunken sein;
~-proof laufmaschenfest.

lade *(v.)* [be]laden, ein-, verladen;
~ **goods to a vessel** Schiff befrachten.

laden [be]laden, befrachtet;
heavily ~ hoch beladen;
~ **in bulk** mit Massengut beladen; ~ **with parcels** mit Stückgut befrachtet; ~ **with responsibilty** mit Verantwortung belastet; **fully ~ ship** voll beladenes Schiff.

ladies' | paper Modejournal; ~ **president** Präsidentin; ~ **supplement** Frauenbeilage.

lading Verladen, Beladen, *(freight)* Ladung, Fracht;
to take in ~ Fracht einnehmen;
~ **charges** Ladegebühren, Ladekosten; ~ **port** Verlade-, Versandhafen.

lady Dame;

~ of the house Hausherrin; **~-in-waiting** diensttuende Hofdame;

to play the fine ~ die große Dame spielen;

~ almoner *(Br.)* Sozialbetreuerin; **~ bookkeeper** Buchhalterin; **~ cashier** Kassiererin; **~ clerk** kaufmännische Angestellte; **~ help** *(Br.)* Haustochter, Stütze der Hausfrau, **~ housekeeper** Haushälterin; **~'s maid** Kammerzofe; **~ mayoress** Bürgermeisterfrau; **a ~'s man** Schürzenjäger; **~ President** Präsidentin; **~ reader** Lektorin; **~ secretary** Sekretärin; **~ typist** Stenotypistin.

ladykiller Schürzenjäger, Herzensbrecher.

lag Verzögerung, Rückstand, Zurückbleiben, *(aerodynamics)* Rücktrift, *(criminal)* Galgenvögel, Sträfling, *(el.)* Phasenverschiebung;

cultural ~ zurückgebliebene kulturelle Entwicklung; **earnings ~** Einkommensnachholbedarf; **old ~** ausgekochter Verbrecher; **time ~** zeitliche Verzögerung;

~ in collection Inkassorückstand; **~ in investments** stagnierende Investitionstätigkeit; **~ in orders** Auftragslücke;

~ (v.) verzögern, zurückbleiben, *(criminal, sl.)* in die Zwangsjacke stecken;

~ behind nachhinken; **~ behind s. o.** hinter jem. zurückbleiben.

lagan Seewurf.

laggard Bummler, Trödler, *(a.)* träge, lässig, saumselig.

lagger auf Bewährung entlassener Zuchthäusler.

laid|low by sickness durch Krankheit gehindert; **~ off** *(US)* personalmäßig abgebaut; **~ out** *(sl.)* betrunken; **~ up** ans Bett gefesselt, bettlägerig;

to be ~ up with flu wegen einer Grippe das Bett hüten müssen; **~ paper** gestreiftes Papier.

lair *(agriculture)* Bodenbeschaffenheit.

laird *(Scotland)* Großgrundbesitzer.

laity Nichtfachleute.

lake, by auf dem Binnenwege;

~ district Seengebiet.

lam *(US sl.)* Abhauen, Verduften;

on the ~ *(sl.)* auf Achse, *(fugitive)* auf der Flucht;

~ (v.) verduften, abhauen, *(sl.)* Zeche prellen;

to take it on the ~ *(US sl.)* sich aus dem Staube machen.

lamb *(stock exchange, sl.)* unerfahrener Spekulant;

like ~ and salad alles in Butter;

to be anything but the snow-white ~ kein Unschuldslämmchen mehr sein.

lame lahm, hinkend.

lame duck Niete, Versager, lahme Ente, *(stock market, US)* ruinierter Spekulant, *(pol., sl.)* aus dem Amt scheidender (durchgefallener) Politiker;

~ bill *(sl.)* aussichtsloser Gesetzentwurf; **~ government** handlungsunfähige Regierung; **~ session** *(US)* Sitzungsperiode nach den Wahlen; **~ terms** behinderte Regierungszeit.

lame|excuse unzureichende Entschuldigung; **~ story** unglaubwürdige Geschichte.

lament *(v.)* beklagen, jammern;

~ *(v.)* over one's misfortune über seine Mißhelligkeiten lamentieren.

lamentable occurrence bedauerliches Ereignis.

lamp Lampe, Laterne;

ceiling ~ Deckenlampe, -leuchte; **festoon ~** Soffittenlampe; **head ~** *(car)* Scheinwerfer; **oil ~** Öllampe; **pocket ~** Taschenlampe; **reading ~** Leselicht; **safety ~** Grubenlaterne; **spirit ~** Spirituslampe; **side ~s** Begrenzungslichter; **standard ~** Stehlampe; **street ~** Straßenlaterne; **table ~** Tischlampe; **tubular ~** Soffittenlampe; **wall ~** Wandleuchte;

~ *(v.)* leuchten, mit Lampen versehen;

to pass on the ~ *(fig.)* Fackel weitergeben; **to smell of the ~** nach Arbeit aussehen, *(style)* sorgfältig ausgefeilt sein;

~ bracket Lampenhalter; **~ holder** Fassung; **~ hour** Kilowattstunde; **~ oil** *(fig.)* nächtliches Studium, Nachtarbeit; **~ shade** Lampenschirm; **~ standard** Straßenlaterne.

lampoon Pamphlet, Schmähschrift;

~ *(v.)* Pamphlet verfassen.

lamppost Laternenpfahl;

between you and me and the ~ vertraulich, ganz unter uns.

lamplight Lampenlicht.

lamplighter Laternenanzünder.

lamster *(sl.)* entsprungener Zuchthäusler.

land *(balance sheet)* Grundstücke, Immobilienbesitz, *(country)* Land, Volk, Einwohner, *(district)* Gegend, Bezirk, Landschaft, *(landed property)* Grundbesitz, Grundstück, Grund und Boden, Gelände, *(national resources)* natürliche Reichtümer, *(as opposed to sea)* Land, *(soil)* Boden, Grund;

by ~ auf dem Landwege, per Achse; **by ~ and sea** über Land und Meer; **incident to a piece of ~** mit einem Grundstück verbunden;

~s Ländereien, Liegenschaften;

abandoned ~ aufgegebenes Grundstück; **accommodation ~s** zu Spekulationszwecken aufgekaufte Grundstücke; **~ compulsorily acquired** zwangsenteignetes Grundstück; **adjacent (adjoining) ~** Nachbargrundstück; **agricultural ~** landwirtschaftlich genutztes Grundstück; **arable ~** Ackerland; **barren ~** nicht anbaufähiges Land; **bounty ~s** Schenkungsland; **cleared (cultivated) ~** urbar gemachtes (bestelltes) Land, Neubruch; **crown ~s** Staatsdomänen; **cut-over ~** abgeholztes Grundstück; **debatable ~** umstrittenes Gebiet; **demesne ~** selbstbewirtschaftetes Land; **developed ~** Bauland, baureifes Land, erschlossenes Gelände; **privately-developed ~** privat erschlossenes Land; **dominant ~** herrschendes Grundstück; **donation ~s** Landschenkungen; **dry ~** festes Land; **~ enclosed** eingefriedetes Grundstück; **~ enclosed within other ~s** Enklave; **extended ~** Grundstück, in das Zwangsvollstreckung betrieben wird; **foreign ~** Ausland; **forest ~** Waldland, -grundstück[e]; **forested ~** forstwirtschaftlich genutzte Fläche; **heavy ~** schwerer Boden; **idle ~** unerschlossenes Gelände; **impoverished ~** ausgesaugter Boden; **marginal ~** marginaler Boden; **meadow ~** Weideland; **mineral ~** bergbaufähiges Land; **money ~** testamentarisch zum Verkauf vorgesehenes Grundvermögen; **native ~** Vater-, Heimatland; **new ~** *(US)* unbebautes Grundstück (Land); **no-man's ~** Niemandsland; **overflowed ~** überfluteter Landstrich; **Promised ~** Land der Verheißung; **public ~** Almende, Gemeindeland, Grundstücke der öffentlichen Hand; **rank ~** fruchtbarer Boden; **recorded ~** grundbuchlich eingetragenes Grundstück; **registered ~** *(Br.)* ins Grundbuch eingetragenes Grundstück, eingetragener Grundbesitz; **relinquished ~** aufgegebenes Grundstück; **school ~s** öffentliche Grundstücke zur Finanzierung von Schulbauten; **seated ~** erschlossenes Gelände; **servient ~** dienendes Grundstück; **settled ~** der Verfügungsfreiheit entzogener Grundbesitz, Fideikommiß; **shop ~** *(fam.)* Domäne der Warenhäuser; **~ taken** enteignetes Grundstück; **theater ~** Theaterdomäne; **third-party ~** *(balance sheet)* fremde Liegenschaften; **undulating ~** wellenförmiges Gelände; **unregistered ~** *(Br.)* grundbuchlich nicht eingetragenes Grundstück, vom Grundbuch nicht erfaßtes Grundstück; **unseated (undeveloped) ~** unerschlossenes Gelände; **central urban ~** zentral gelegenes Bauland; **used ~** genutztes Grundstück; **waste ~** Brachland;

~ subject to compulsory acquisition für Zwangsenteignung in Frage kommendes Bauland; **~ and buildings, real estate** *(balance sheet, US)* Grundstücke und Gebäude, unbebaute und bebaute Grundstücke; **~, buildings, plant and machinery** *(balance sheet, Br.)* Sachanlagen; **~ and chattels** Grundeigentum und bewegliche Sachen; **~ ripe for development** Bauerwartungsland; **~s, tenements and hereditaments** *(US)* Liegenschaftsrechte (Liegenschaften) aller Art; **~ on lease** Pachtland; **~ of make-believe** Utopia; **~ flowing with milk and honey** Land, wo Milch und Honig fließt, Schlaraffenland; **~ that may be mortgaged** belastungsfähiges Grundstück; **~ conveyed by way of mortgages** hypothekarisch belastetes Grundstück; **~ of plenty** Schlaraffenland; **~ farmed on scientific principles** nach wissenschaftlichen Erkenntnissesn bewirtschaftetes Land; **~ out at rent** verpachtetes Grundstück; **~ as security** Grundstückssicherheit; **~ conveyed on trust** treuhänderisch übereignetes Grundstück; **~ held on trust for sale** von einer Vermögensverwaltung zum Verkauf angebotenes Grundstück;

~ *(v.)* (discharge) [Waren] ausladen, löschen, *(go ashore)* landen, anlegen, an Land gehen, *(set ashore)* ans Land bringen, *(of ship)* anlegen;

~ s. o. j. für etw. gewinnen; **~ s. o. with s. th.** jem. etw. einbrocken; **~ an airliner safely** sichere Flugzeuglandung durchführen; **~ an assignment** Rolle ergattern; **~ s. o. in an awkward position** j. in eine schiefe Lage bringen; **~ like a cat** Schwierigkeiten entgehen; **~ in a strange city without money** in einer fremden Stadt ohne Geld festsitzen; **~ a criminal** Verbrecher schnappen; **~ o. s. in great difficulties** sich erhebliche Schwierigkeiten zuziehen; **~ in a ditch** in einem Graben landen; **~ on one's feet** wieder auf die Füße fallen; **~ s. o. in a nice fix** j. ganz schön in die Klemme bringen; **~ on s. o. for a fortnight** *(fam.)* bei jem. zwei Wochen bettknüllen; **~ a fortune** Vermögen machen; **~ goods** Güter löschen; **~ a job** Stellung finden; **~ s. o. a job** jem. eine Stellung besorgen; **~ passengers quickly** Passagiere schnell ausschiffen; **~ s. o. in prison** *(fam.)* j. im Gefängnis enden lassen; **~ a prize** sich einen Preis holen; **~**

safely *(airliner)* glatt landen; ~ **on the sea** auf dem Wasser landen; ~ **second** als Zweiter durch Ziel gehen; ~ **s. o. at the station** j. beim Bahnhof absetzen;

to acquire ~ **in advance of development** Vorratsgelände erwerben; **to assemble parcels of** ~ Grundstücke zusammenschreiben; **to assure** ~ Grundstück auflassen; **to be attached with the** ~ mit einem Grundstück verbunden sein; **to bear with the** ~ *(ship)* aufs Land zuhalten; **to bring** ~ **under cultivation** Land in Kultur nehmen; **to buy some** ~ Grundbesitz erwerben; **to buy** ~ **on a large scale** Grundstücksareal aufkaufen; **to charge one's** ~ sein Grundstück belasten; **to charge** ~ **as security** Grundstück zu Sicherungszwecken belasten; **to come in to** ~ zur Landung ansetzen; **to come in sight of** ~ Land sichten; **to convey** ~ Grundstück auflassen; **to devise** ~ **held in socage** Erbpachtgrundstück vermachen; **to enter** ~ *(US)* sich als Grundstückserwerber eintragen lassen; **to farm 400 acres of** ~ 400 Morgen bewirtschaften; **to have** ~ **by entireties** gemeinsamen Grundbesitz haben; **to hold** ~ Land (Grundeigentum) besitzen, Grundeigentümer sein; **to know how the** ~ **lies** wissen, wie der Hase läuft; **to lay** ~ **out in a community** Grundstücke erschließen; **to make** ~ *(ship)* Land anlaufen (sichten); **to obtain** ~ **for development** Bauerwartungsland erwerben; **to own acres of** ~ Grundbesitzer sein; **to parcel** ~ **into small holdings** Grundstücksparzellierung vornehmen; **to reclaim** ~ Neuland gewinnen; **to reduce** ~ **to public purpose** Land für öffentliche Zwecke verwenden; **to run with the** ~ auf einem Grundstück lasten; **to see how the** ~ **lies** sehen, wie der Hase läuft; **to send by** ~ mit Fahrgelegenheit versenden; **to settle** ~ *(ship)* vom Land abhalten; **to surrender** ~ Grundstück auflassen; **to take** ~ **by descent** Grundbesitz erben; **to take** ~ **on lease** Grundstück pachten; **to touch** ~ landen; **to transfer** ~ Grundstück auflassen; **to travel by** ~ zu Lande reisen; **to turn one's** ~ **into money** sein Grundvermögen flüssig machen; **to use** ~ **for agricultural purposes** Grund und Boden landwirtschaftlich nutzen; **to work on the** ~ Landarbeiter sein;

~ **acquisition** Land-, Grundstückszuweisung, -erwerb; ⁰ **Act** Agrargesetz; ~ **action** Grundstücksprozeß; ~ **agency** *(US)* Immobilien-, Maklerbüro, Grundstücksmakler; ~ **agent** *(US)* Grundstücks-, Gütermakler, *(steward, Br.)* Gutsverwalter; ~ **appreciation** Bodenschätzung, Grundstücksbewertung, Bonitierung; ~ **area** Grundstücksfläche; ~ **army** *(mil.)* Landheer, -streitkräfte; ~ **assembly** Parzellenvereinigung; ~ **bank** Hypotheken-, Grundkreditbank; ~-**based aircraft** auf Flugplätzen stationierte Flugzeuge; ~ **bonds** *(US)* landwirtschaftliche Pfandbriefe; ~ **boom** Baulandkonjunktur; ~ **border** Landesgrenze; ~-**borne trade** Binnenhandel; ~ **breeze** Landwind; ~ **broker** *(Br.)* Grundstücks-, Immobilienmakler; ~ **carriage** Beförderung auf dem Landwege, Landtransport; ~ **carrier** Transportunternehmer, Fernspediteur; ~ **ceilings** Grundstückshöchstpreise; ~ **certificate** *(Br.)* [etwa] Grundbuchauszug; ~ **charge** Belastung von Grundbesitz, Grundstücksbelastung, Reallast; **local** ~ **charges** kommunale Grundstückslasten; **registered** ~ **charge** *(Br.)* [etwa] Buchgrundschuld; **unregistered** ~ **charge** *(Br.)* [etwa] Briefgrundschuld; ⁰ **Charges Act** *(Br.)* Grundlastengesetz; ⁰ **Charges Register** *(Br.)* Belastungsverzeichnis nicht eingetragener Grundstücke; ~ **claim** *(US)* Rechtsanspruch auf Landzuteilung; ⁰**s Clauses Act** *(Br.)* Gesetz über die Bodeninanspruchnahme durch die öffentliche Hand, Enteignungsgesetz; ~ **college** landwirtschaftliche Hochschule; ~ **company** Terrain-, Grundstücksgesellschaft; ~ **consolidation** Flurbereinigung; ~ **contract** [obligatorischer] Grundstücksverkauf; ~ **corridor** Landkorridor, -zugang; ~ **cost** Grundstückspreis; ~ **court** *(St. Louis, US)* Gericht für Grundstückssachen; ~ **credit** Grundstückskredit; ~ **credit company** Bodenkreditanstalt; ~ **cruiser** *(fam.)* Panzerwagen, Tank; ~ **damages** Enteignungsentschädigung; ~ **deal** Grundstücksgeschäft; ~ **deed** Besitzurkunde; ⁰ **Department** *(US)* Bundesamt für den Grundbesitz der öffentlichen Hand; ~ **developer** Grundstückserschließungsgesellschaft; ~ **development** Erschließung von Baugelände; ~ **development project** Baulanderschließungsprojekt; ~ **district** *(US)* Grundbuchbezirk; **undeveloped** ~ **duty** *(Br.)* Bauland-, Bauplatzsteuer; ~ **economy** Immobilienwirtschaft; ~ **estate** Grundeigentum; ~ **forces** *(mil.)* Landstreitkräfte, -heer, -macht; ~ **gabel** Bodenzins; ~-**grabber** spekulativer Landaufkäufer, Grundstücksspekulant; ~ **grabbing** spekulativer Landerwerb, -aufkauf; ~ **grant** *(US)* Landzuweisung; ~-**grant bonds** *(US)* durch Verpfändung von Eisenbahnstrecken gesicherte Eisenbahnobligationen; ~-**grant procedure** *(US)* Landzuweisungsverfahren; ~-**grant road** *(US)* mit öffentlichen Mitteln gebaute Straße; ~-**grant university** *(US)* staatlich geförderte Universität; ~ **hun-**

ger Landhunger; ~-**hungry** landhungrig; ~ **improvements** [Grundstücks]meliorationen, Landverbesserungen; ⁰**Improvement Acts** *(Br.)* Meliorationsgesetze; ~ **improvement company** Finanzierungsgesellschaft für Grundstücksmeliorationen; ~ **indemnity** Entschädigungsgrundstück; ~ **jobber** Güter-, Immobilien-, Grundstücksmakler, -spekulant; ~-**jobbing** Güter-, Grundstücksspekulation; ~ **law** Boden-, Grundstücksrecht; ~ **laws** Agrargesetze; **to get on one's** ~ **legs** sich wieder auf dem Lande zurechtfinden; ~ **link** Landverbindung, -brücke; ~ **loan** Bodenanleihe; ~ **measuring** Land-, Feldvermessung; ~ **mine** *(mil.)* Landmine; ~ **mortgage bank** Bodenkreditanstalt; ~ **nationalization** Verstaatlichung von Grund und Boden; ~ **office** *(US)* Bundesamt für Grundstücke der öffentlichen Hand; ~-**office business** *(fam., US)* flottgehendes Geschäft, Bombengeschäft; ~ **patent** *(US)* Landzuweisungsurkunde; ~ **plane** Landflugzeug; ~ **power** Landmacht; ~ **price** Boden-, Grundstückspreis; ~ **purchase** Land-, Grundstückskauf; **compulsory** ~ **purchase** Zwangsenteignung; ~ **question** Agrarfrage, -problem; ~ **reclamation** Landgewinnung, Urbarmachung; ~ **records** *(US)* Grundstücksregister; ~ **reform** Bodenreform; ~ **reeve** Hilfskraft eines Gutsverwalters; ~ **reformer** Bodenreformer; ~ **register** *(Br.)* Grundbuch; ~ **registration** *(Br.)* Eintragung von Grundbesitz, Grundbucheintragung; ⁰ **Registration Act** *(Br.)* [etwa] Grundbuchordnung; **compulsory** ~ **registration area** *(Br.)* grundbuchpflichtiges Gebiet; ~ **registration rules** *(Br.)* Grundbuchbestimmungen; ⁰ **Registry** *(Br.)* Kataster-, Grundbuchamt; ~ **registry fees** *(Br.)* Grundbuchgebühren; ~ **registry general map** *(Br.)* [etwa] Grundbuchblatt; ~ **and tenant relationship** Miet-, Pachtverhältnis; ~ **requirements** Flächenbedarf; ~ **revenues** Grundstückseinkünfte; ~ **risk** *(insurance)* Landtransportrisiko; ~ **route** Landweg; ~ **sales** Grundstücksverkäufe; ~ **scrip** *(US)* staatlicher Landzuweisungsschein; ~ **service** *(mar.)* Landdienst; ~ **settlement** *(India)* Landzuweisungsvereinbarung; ~ **settlement board** Ansiedlungskommission; ~ **settlement society** Siedlungsgenossenschaft, -gesellschaft; ~ **shares** *(Br.)* Aktien von Terraingesellschaften; ~ **shark** Matrosenausbeuter; ~ **speculation** Boden-, Grundstücksspekulation; ~ **speculation company** Terraingesellschaft; ~ **speculator** Grundstücksspekulant; ~ **station** *(radio)* Bodenstation; ~ **steward** *(Br.)* Gutsverwalter; ~ **subdivision** Landaufteilung; ~ **surveying** Gelände-, Grundstücks-, Landvermessung, Geländeaufnahme; ~ **surveyor** Vermessungsbeamter, Landmesser; ~ **surveyor and valuer** Katasterbeamter; ~ **tax** *(US)* Grundabgabe, Grundsteuer; ~ **tax parish** *(US)* Grundsteuerveranlagungsstelle; ~-**taxer** Grundsteuerbefürworter; ~ **tenant** Grundpächter; ⁰ **Tenure Act** *(Rhodesia)* Landpachtgesetz; ~ **tie** Mauerstütze; ~ **tenure** Grundstückspacht; ~ **transfer** Grundstücksübertragung; ⁰ **Transfer Act** *(Br.)* [etwa] Grundbuchordnung; ~ **transport** Landtransport, Beförderung auf dem Landwege; ~ **tribunal** *(Br.)* Enteignungsausschuß, Schiedsstelle in Enteignungsfragen; ~ **trust** Grundstückgenossenschaft; ~ **use** Flächen-, Grundstücksnutzung; ~-**using** raumbeanspruchend; ~ **valuation** Grundstücksbewertung; ~ **value** Grundstücks-, Bodenwert; ~ **value tax** Wertzuwachssteuer für Grundstücke; ~ **waiter** *(Br.)* Zollinspektor [im Küstenverkehr]; ~ **warfare** Landkrieg; ~ **warrant** *(US)* Landzuweisungsschein; ~ **wind** Landwind; ~ **worker** Landarbeiter.

landbridge Landbrücke.

landed begütert, *(discharged)* gelöscht;
~ **aristocracy** Großgrundbesitzer, Junker; **on** ~ **basis** incl. Löschen und Leichtern; ~ **estate** Grundeigentum, -besitz, Landbesitz, Ländereien; ~ **gentry** *(Br.)* Gutsbesitzer, Landadel; ~ **interest** Großgrundbesitz[er]; ~ **men** Grundstücksbesitzer; ~ **price** Preis frei Bestimmungshafen; ~ **property** Grundbesitz, Landeigentum, Liegenschaften, Landbesitz; **to have** ~ **property** Liegenschaften besitzen; ~ **proprietor** Grundstückseigentümer; ~ **security** Grundpfandrecht; ~ **servitude** Grunddienstbarkeit; ~ **terms** Verkaufspreis einschließlich Fracht- und Entladungskosten, franko Löschung; ~ **weight** Anlandgewicht.

landfall Erdrutsch, *(inheritance)* unerwartete Erbschaft, *(plane)* Landung, Landen.

landfill Geländeauffüllung.

landholder Grundeigentümer, -besitzer, *(tenant)* Pächter.

landholding Land-, Grundbesitz, Pacht.

landing Landung, Landen, *(discharge)* Ausladen, Löschung [einer Ladung], Ausschiffung, *(hallway)* Vorplatz, *(place of ~)* Auslade-, Lande-, Anlegeplatz, *(platform)* Perron, Bahnsteig, *(staircase)* Treppenabsatz, Podest;

on ~ beim Landen;

balked ~ *(US)* Fehllandung; **belly ~** Bauchlandung; **blind ~** Blindlandung; **dead-stick ~** Landung mit abgestelltem Motor; **emergency (forced) ~** Notlandung; **faulty ~** mißglückte Landung; **instrument ~** Blindlandung; **safe ~** glatte Landung; **~ and delivery** Landung und Ablieferung;

to clear up for full-stop ~ Landeerlaubnis erteilen; **to dispute a ~ by the enemy** einer feindlichen Landung Widerstand leisten; **to effect a ~** landen; **to make a bad ~** schlecht landen; **to make an emergency ~** Notlandung vornehmen; **to make a good ~** glatt landen;

~ account Landeschein; **~ angle** *(plane)* Ausrollwinkel; **~ area** *(mil.)* Landegebiet, -platz, Landungsgebiet; **~ beam** Gleit-, Landungsstrahl; **~ bill** *(ship)* Landungsrolle; **~ book** Löschungsbuch; **~ certificate** Löschungsbescheinigung, Löschschein; **~ charges** Landungs-, Löschkosten; **~ and service charge** Lande- und Wartegebühren; **~ chassis** Landegestell; **~ clearance** *(aircraft)* Landegenehmigung; **~ conditions** Landebedingungen; **~ craft** *(mil.)* Landungsboot; **~ deck** Flugdeck; **~ detachment** *(mil.)* Landungskorps; **~ facilities** Landeeinrichtungen; **~ fee** Landegebühr; **~ field** Landeplatz, Rollfeld; **~ flare** Bordlandefackel; **~ floodlight** Landebahnleuchte; **~ force** *(mil.)* Landungstruppe, amphibische Truppe; **~ forecast** Landevorhersage; **~ gear** Fahrwerk, Landegestell; **~ ground** Landeplatz, Rollfeld; **advanced ~ ground** Gefechtslandeplatz; **~ light** Landefeuer; **~ mark** Landezeichen; **~ notice** Frachtankunftsbenachrichtigung; **~ operation** *(mil.)* Landungsunternehmen; **~ order** Löscherlaubnis, *(Br.)* Zollpassierschein; **~ party** *(mil.) (Br.)* Kommandounternehmen, Landungstrupp, amphibische Truppe; **~ permit** Löscherlaubnis; **~ place (platform)** Anlegestelle, Landeplatz; **~ ramp** Landesteg; **~ rates** Löschungskosten; **~ restrictions** Landeverbot; **~ rights** Landerecht; **~ ship** Landungsboot; **~ site** Landeplatz; **~ speed** Landegeschwindigkeit; **~ stage** Güterlandeplatz, schwimmende Landungsbrücke, *(ship)* Flugdeck; **~ strip** Landebahn, Rollfeld; **~ surveyor** *(Br.)* Oberzollaufseher; **~ ticket** Landungskarte; **~ waiter** *(Br.)* Hafenzollbeamter, Zollinspektor im Küstengebiet; **~ weight** Gewicht am Eingangsort, Landungsgewicht.

landlady Hauswirtin, Vermieterin.

landless ohne Grundbesitz.

landlocked landeingeschlossen;
~ harbo(u)r vom Land eingeschlossener Hafen.

landlord *(innkeeper)* Gastwirt, *(landowner)* Gutsherr, *(lessor)* Mietherr, Vermieter, Verpächter, Hauswirt, *(owner of a house)* Hausbesitzer, -eigentümer;
ground ~ *(Br.)* Verpächter; **large- (many-) acred ~** Großgrundbesitzer;
~ and tenant *(law)* Miet- und Pachtrecht;
to be heavily balanced in the ~'s favo(u)r *(law court)* sehr vermieterfreundlich sein; **to lure private ~s back into the market** freifinanzierten Wohnungsbau ankurbeln;
~ and Tenant Act *(Br.)* Mieterschutzgesetz; **~'s fixtures** fest installierte Einrichtungsgegenstände; **~'s liability** Vermieterhaftpflicht; **~'s property tax** *(Br.)* Besteuerung des Nutzungswertes des eigengenutzten Einfamilienhauses; **~'s warrant** Vollstreckungsauftrag aus Vermieterpfandrecht.

landloper Vagabund.

landlubber Landratte.

landman Landbewohner, -ratte.

landmark Grenzstein, Markstein, Grenzmal, Geländemarke, Feldmarkung, *(fig.)* Wendepunkt, *(mar.)* Seezeichen, Landmarke;
~s in history Meilensteine der Geschichte;
to plant a ~ Markstein setzen; **to shift a ~** Markstein versetzen (verrücken); **to stand out as ~** wahre Meilensteine in der Entwicklung bedeuten;
~ case grundlegender Fall; **~ decision** herausstehende Entscheidung.

landmine *(mil.)* Landmine.

landowner Grund-, Land-, Gutsbesitzer, Grundeigentümer;
adjoining ~ Grundstücksnachbar.

landownership Grundbesitzertum.

landowning grundbesitzend.

landplane Landflugzeug.

landrover geländegängiger Kraftwagen.

landscape Landschaft;
natural ~ Naturlandschaft;
~ (v.) landschaftlich verschönern;
to be a blot on the ~ Landschaft verschandeln;
~ architect (gardener) *(US)* Gartenarchitekt; **~ gardening** *(US)* Landschaftsgestaltung; **~ painter** Landschaftsmaler.

landscaper Gartenarchitekt.

landscapist Landschaftsmaler.

landsick *(ship)* schwer manövrierfähig.

landslide Erdrutsch, *(pol.)* [völliger] Umschwung, Umwälzung;
democratic ~ großer Stimmenzuwachs für die Demokraten;
~ sweep *(election victory)* überwältigender Wahlsieg.

landslip Erdrutsch, *(Br.)* Umschwung, überwältigender Wahlsieg;
Conservative ~ überwältigender Wahlsieg der konservativen Partei.

landsman unerfahrener Matrose.

landward landeinwärts gelegen;
~ area *(Scotland)* ländliches Gebiet.

landwash Brecherlinie.

lane Pfad, [Feld]weg, Spur, *(airplane)* Flugschneise, *(passage)* Durchgang, Gasse, *(ship)* Fahrtroute, festgelegter Kurs, *(little street)* Gasse, *(strip of roadway)* Fahrbahn, Spur;
air ~ Flugschneise; **central ~** Mittelfahrbahn; **deceleration ~** Fahrbahn für Langsamfahrzeuge; **filter ~** Spur für Linksabbieger; **four-traffic ~** vierbahnige Straße, Straße mit vier Fahrbahnen; **inside ~** weißer Trennungsstrich, innerer Randstreifen; **left-hand traffic ~** linke [Auto]fahrbahn; **nearside ~** innerer Randstreifen; **offside (outside) ~** äußere Fahrbahn; **safety ~** Fußgängerzone; **three-~** mit drei Fahrbahnen; **~ of traffic** Fahrspur, -bahn;
to change from one ~ to another Fahrbahn wechseln; **to form a ~** Gasse (Spalier) bilden; **to pass through a ~ of people** durch eine Menschengasse (Spalier von Menschen) gehen;
~ discipline Fahrbahndisziplin; **~ marking** Fahrbahnmarkierung; **carriageway ~ markings** Autobahnmarkierungen; **~ route** Schiffahrtsroute; **~ straddling** vorschriftswidriger Fahrbahnwechsel; **four-~ traffic** vierspuriger Verkehr; **improper ~ usage** falsche Fahrbahnbenutzung.

language Rede, Redeweise, Sprache, *(terminology)* Fachsprache, Phraseologie, Terminologie;
in plain ~ *(telegram)* nicht verschlüsselt;
abusive ~ Schmähungen, Beschimpfungen, Schimpfreden; **bad ~** ordinäre Ausdrucksweise; **business ~** Handelssprache; **coded ~** verschlüsselter Text; **commercial ~** Handelssprache; **dead ~** tote Sprache; **defamatory ~** beleidigende Ausdrücke; **derivative ~** Tochtersprache **direct ~** direkte Rede; **electronic ~** Computersprache; **flash ~** Gaunersprache; **foreign ~** Fremdsprache; **hard ~** schwer zu erlernende Sprache; **inflated ~** schwülstige Ausdrucksweise; **kindred ~s** verwandte Sprachen; **law ~** *(legal)* Rechtssprache, Sprache der Juristen; **living ~** lebende Sprache; **medical ~** medizinische Fachsprache; **modern ~** lebende Sprache; **national ~** Landessprache; **native ~** Muttersprache; **offensive ~** ärgerniserregende Worte; **official ~** Amtssprache; **original ~** Muttersprache; **parliamentary ~** parlamentarische Ausdrucksweise; **primary ~** gesprochene Sprache; **strong ~** Kraftausdrücke; **technical ~** Fachsprache; **vile ~** vulgäre Ausdrucksweise;
~ of diplomacy Sprache der Diplomaten, Diplomatensprache; **~ of economics** Wirtschaftssprache; **~ of the gutter** Ausdrucksweise der Gosse; **~ of instruction** Unterrichtssprache;
to acquire a ~ Sprache erlernen; **to have great facility in learning a ~** Sprachtalent besitzen; **to have a great command of a ~** Sprache völlig beherrschen; **to have a working knowledge of a ~** einige Kenntnisse in einer Sprache haben; **to master a ~** Sprache beherrschen; **to polish a ~** Sprachkenntnisse auffrischen; **to read modern ~s** moderne Sprachen studieren; **to read o. s. into a ~** sich in eine Sprache einlesen; **to speak the same ~** *(fig.)* die gleiche Sprache sprechen; **to study ~s** Fremdsprachen studieren; **to take up modern ~** neuere Sprachen studieren; **to use bad ~** Schimpfworte gebrauchen;
~ ability Sprachbegabung; **~ allowance** Sprachenzulage; **~ barrier** Sprachschranke, -hindernis; **~ bill** Sprachenverordnung; **additional ~ capability** zusätzliche Sprachkenntnisse; **~ class** Sprachenklasse; **~ course** Sprachkursus; **~ department** *(foreign office)* Sprachendienst; **~ equality** Sprachengleichberechtigung; **~ gap** Sprachlücke; **~ laboratory** Sprachlabor; **~ law** Sprachenregelungsgesetz; **~ master** *(Br.)* Sprachlehrer; **~ module** *(terminal)* Silbentrennungsprogramm; **~ needs** Spracherfordernisse; **~ relationship** Sprachverwandtschaften; **~ school** Sprachschule; **~ service** Sprachendienst; **~ teacher** Sprachlehrer; **foreign ~ training** Fremdsprachenausbildung; **foreign ~ tuition** fremdsprachlicher Unterricht.

languaged sprachkundig.

languid matt, erschöpft, schwach, *(market)* interesselos, flau, matt, schleppend, lustlos.

languidness Interesselosigkeit.

languish *(v.)* erschlaffen, ermatten, *(business)* darniederliegen;
~ **in prison** im Gefängnis schmachten.
languishing interesselos;
~ **illness** schleichende Krankheit; ~ **interest** erlahmendes Interesse; ~ **trade** darniederliegender Handel.
lantern Laterne;
Chinese ~ Lampignon; **dark** ~ Blendlaterne; **projection** ~ Bildwerferlampe; **signalling** ~ Signallampe; **street** ~ Straßenlaterne;
~ **of science** Leuchte der Wissenschaft;
~ **jack** Irrlicht; ~ **lecture** Lichtbildvortrag; ~ **light** *(raised skylight)* Oberlichtfenster; ~ **slide** Diapositiv; ~ **slide lecture** Lichtbildvortrag.
lap *(bookbinding)* Falz, *(sport)* Runde;
in fortune's ~ im Schoße des Glücks; **in the** ~ **of the Gods** in den Sternen geschrieben; **in the** ~ **of luxury** von Luxus umgeben.
lappage *(adverse possession)* Interessenskonflikt.
lapped in luxury von Luxus umgeben.
lapse *(decay)* Verfall, *(law)* Heim-, Verfall, Erlöschen, *(mistake)* Fehlleistung, Fehler, Versehen, Lapsus, Entgleisung;
after a ~ **of three months** nach Ablauf von drei Monaten;
~ **from true belief** Abfall vom wahren Glauben; ~ **of a testamentary bequest** Vermächtniswegfall; ~ **of a contract** Erlöschen eines Vertrages; ~ **of a copyright** Erlöschen des Urheberrechts; ~ **from one's duty** Pflichtversäumnis; ~ **of justice** Justizirrtum; ~ **of a legacy** Hinfälligkeit eines Vermächtnisses; ~ **of memory** Gedächtnisversagen; ~ **of offer** Gegenstandsloswerden eines Angebots; ~ **of a patent** Erlöschen (Auslaufen) eines Patents; ~ **of the pen** Schreibfehler; ~ **of a policy** Policenverfall; ~ **of style** Stilbruch; ~ **of time** Frist-, Zeitablauf; **long** ~ **of time** lange Zeitspanne; ~ **of the tongue** Versprecher; ~ **from virtue** moralische Entgleisung; ~ **of five years** Zeitspanne von fünf Jahren;
~ *(v.) (become void)* verfallen, erlöschen, außer Kraft treten, unwirksam werden, *(criminal law)* [Strafverfahren] einstellen, *(legacy)* ausfallen, *(offer)* gegenstandslos werden, *(revert to)* heimfallen, *(time)* verstreichen, vergehen, ablaufen;
~ **to s. o.** *(estate)* auf j. übergehen; ~ **away** *(time)* verstreichen; ~ **into barbarism** in die Barbarei zurückfallen; ~ **into bad habits** schlechte Gewohnheiten annehmen; ~ **back into idleness** in den Müßiggang zurückfallen; ~ **into obscurity** in Vergessenheit geraten; ~ **criminal proceedings** *(Br.)* Strafverfahren einstellen; ~ **into silence** dem Schweigen anheimfallen; ~ **from virtue into vice** moralisch entgleisen;
to allow a right to ~ Recht erlöschen (verfallen) lassen; **to be in** ~ verfallen, verjähren; **to plead** ~ **of time** Einrede der Verjährung vorbringen.
lapsed verfallen;
to have ~ verfallen (verjährt) sein;
~ **copyright** erloschenes Urheberrecht; ~ **devise** ungültige testamentarische Verfügung; ~ **legacy** hinfällig gewordenes Vermächtnis; ~ **patent** verfallenes Patent; ~ **policy** ungültige (verfallene) Versicherungspolice; ~**-policy book** Versicherungsablaufregister.
lapsing | of legacy Legatsverfall;
~ **schedule** Kostenverteilungsschema.
larcener *(US)* Dieb.
larcenous | action Diebstahlhandlung; ~ **intent** Diebstahlvorsatz.
larceny *(US)* Diebstahl;
compound (grand, mixed) ~ schwerer Diebstahl; **petty** ~ Mundraub, leichter Diebstahl; **simple** ~ einfacher Diebstahl;
~ **by bailee (finder)** Fundunterschlagung; ~ **from the person** Taschendiebstahl; ~ **in a store** Ladendiebstahl;
to commit ~ Diebstahl begehen.
large beträchtlich, groß, umfangreich, *(coll.)* großspurig, protzig, pompös, *(extensive)* umfassend, ausgedehnt, weitgehend;
at ~ auf freiem Fuß; **by and** ~ in großen und ganzen; **in the** ~ in großem Umfang, großangelegt;
as ~ **as life** in Lebensgröße;
the public at ~ das Publikum in seiner Gesamtheit;
to approve at ~ **of the government's policy** der Regierungspolitik im großen und ganzen zustimmen; **to be still at** ~ noch auf freiem Fuß sein; **to grow** ~**er and** ~**er** immer größer werden; **to leave a subject at** ~ Frage unentschieden lassen; **to scatter accusations at** ~ alle und jeden beschuldigen; **to set a prisoner at** ~ einem Gefangenen die Freiheit schenken; **to speak at** ~ **on a subject** sich umfassend zu einem Thema äußern; **to talk** ~ *(sl.)* in den Tag hineinreden, angeben, aufschneiden; **to turn up again as** ~ **as life** so als ob nichts gewesen wäre wieder auftauchen; **to write at** ~ in allen Einzelheiten schildern;

~**-area economy** Großraumwirtschaft; ~ **attitude** vorurteilsfreie Stellungnahme; **to draw a** ~ **audience** großes Publikum anlocken; ~ **bond** *(Br.)* Schuldverschreibung mit Nennwert über 1000 $; ~ **building site** Großbaustelle; ~ **charge** *(sl.)* Bonze, hohes Tier; ~ **charity** hochherzige Mildtätigkeit; ~ **chemical concern** Großbetrieb der chemischen Industrie; ~ **contract** Großabschluß; ~ **corporations** *(US)* Großindustrie; ~ **customer** Großabnehmer; ~ **discretion** erheblicher Ermessensspielraum; ~ **establishment** Großbetrieb; ~ **estate** ansehnlicher Besitz; ~ **expenditure** großer Aufwand; ~ **exporter** Großexporteur; ~ **family** kinderreiche Familie; ~ **farmer** Großbauer; **middle and** ~ **farmers** Mittel- und Großlandwirte; ~ **fortune** großes Vermögen; ~**-handed** freigiebig; ~ **hospitality** großzügige Gastfreundschaft; ~ **hotel** großes Hotel; ~ **income** hohes Einkommen; ~ **industrial concerns** *(Br.)* Großindustrie; **to incur** ~ **losses** große (hohe) Verluste erleiden; ~**-lot production** Massenerzeugung; ~**-lot trader** *(stock exchange)* Pakethändler; ~ **meal** reichliche Mahlzeit; ~ **merchant** Großhändler; ~**-minded** vorurteilsfrei, -los, frei von Vorurteilen; ~ **octavo** Großoktav; ~ **order** Großauftrag; ~ **panel** Großfläche; ~ **powers** umfangreiche (umfassende) Vollmachten; ~ **producer** Serienfabrikant; **to buy and sell on a** ~ **scale** Großunternehmen haben; **to open a business on a** ~ **scale** Geschäft großzügig aufziehen.
large-scale großangelegt, umfangreich, ausgedehnt;
~ **advertiser** Unternehmen mit umfangreichem Werbeprogramm; ~ **attack** Großangriff; ~ **business** Großbetrieb, -unternehmen; ~ **consumer** Großverbraucher; ~ **consumer advertising** breitgestreute Verbraucherwerbung; ~ **enterprise (establishment)** Großbetrieb, -unternehmen; ~ **exports** Großexporte; ~ **industrial concern** *(Br.)* großindustrielles Unternehmen, Großkonzern; ~ **industrial units** industrielle Großanlagen; ~ **industry** Großindustrie, -betrieb; ~ **investor** Großanleger; ~ **manufacture** Serien-, Massenherstellung; ~ **map** Karte in großem Maßstab; ~ **operations** Großeinsatz; ~ **producer** Massenwarenhersteller; ~ **production** Massen-, Serienproduktion; ~ **retailing** Massenfilialbetrieb.
large | share in the management entscheidender Anteil an der Geschäftsführung; ~ **size** Großformat; ~**-sized** im Großformat, großformatig; ~ **space ads** *(US)* großflächige Anzeigen; ~ **sum** großer Betrag; ~ **test** Großversuch; ~ **treatment of a subject** umfassende Themenbehandlung; ~ **user** Großverbraucher, -abnehmer; ~ **views** weitherzige (liberale) Ansichten; ~ **volume** großformatiges Buch; **to be in a** ~ **way of business** bedeutendes Geschäft haben; **to see things in a** ~**way** die Dinge im großen Maßstab sehen; **to trade in a** ~ **way** Großbetrieb haben, umfangreiche Geschäfte abwickeln.
largesse Freigiebigkeit.
lark Jux, Ulk;
to rise with the ~ mit den Hühnern aufstehen.
larry *(sl.)* Schaufensterbummler.
lash *(punishment)* Prügelstrafe;
~ *(v.)* **one's listeners into a fury** seine Zuhörer in Wutausbrüche hineinsteigern; ~ **out into expenditure** phantastische Kosten verursachen; ~ **out against the government** Regierung scharf angehen; ~ **s. o. with one's tongue** beleidigende Vorwürfe gegen j. erheben;
to be under the ~ **of criticism** *(fam.)* beißender Kritik ausgesetzt sein.
lashings | to drink Unmenge von Getränken; ~ **of whisky** Ströme von Whisky.
last *(v.)* fortdauern, bestehen, ausreichen;
~ **s. o. out** j. überleben; ~ **till three o' clock** sich bis drei Uhr ausdehnen (hinziehen);
~ *(a.)* äußerst, zuletzt, letzter, *(latest)* neuester;
to be ~ **in** als letzter eingestellt sein; **to be near one's** ~ seinem Ende nahe sein; **to stick to one's** ~ bei seinem Leisten bleiben; **while the money** ~**s** solange das Geld reicht;
~ **assize** *(fig.)* das letzte Gericht; ~ **attention** äußerste Aufmerksamkeit; ~ **bid** letztes Gebot; ~ **clear chance** *(car)* letzte Ausweichmöglichkeit; ~ **column** Schlußspalte; ~ **consumer** Endverbraucher; ~ **day** Schlußtag; ~**-day business** Ultimogeschäft; ~**-day money** Ultimogeld; ~**-ditch weapons** Endsiegwaffe; ~**-ditcher** Linksradikaler; ~ **heir** *(Br.)* Staat als Erbe; ~ **illness** Todeskrankheit; ~**-in, first-out** *(inventory taking, US)* Zuerstentnahme der neueren Vorräte und Bilanzierung zum jeweiligen Buchwert; ~**-in, first out basis** Entlassungsverfahren nach der Anzienität; ~**-mentioned** letzterwähnt; ~**-minute appeal** Appel in letzter Minute; ~ **name** Familien-, Zuname; ~ **news** letzte Meldungen; ~ **page** letzte Seite; **to share one's** ~ **penny with s. o.** sein letztes Geld mit jem. teilen; ~ **quotation**

Schlußnotierung; **~ resort** letzte Instanz; **to pay one's ~ respects to s. o.** jem. die letzten Ehren erweisen; **~ sickness** Todeskrankheit; **~ speaker** Vorredner; **~ survivor** Letztlebender; **in the ~ term** im letzten Semester; **the ~ thing** *(fashion)* das Allerneueste; **~ will [and testament]** letzter Wille, Testament; **the ~ word** *(fashion)* der letzte Schrei; **~ year** Vorjahr.

lastage Ballast, Schiffszoll.

lasting *(durable)* haltbar, dauerhaft, *(enduring)* anhaltend, beständig, dauernd;
  ~ for a period of six months sechs Monate gültig;
  ~ peace dauerhafter Friede; **~ value** bleibender Wert.

latch Klinke, Druck-, Schnappschloß;
  on the ~ nur eingeklinkt;
  ~ *(v.)* **on to s. th.** *(sl.)* etw. endlich ergattern.

latchkey Hausschlüssel, Drücker;
  ~ kid (child) Schlüsselkind.

late verspätet, spät, *(former)* früher, ehemalig, *(lately deceased)* [kürzlich] verstorben;
  ~ of ehemals wohnhaft in;
  a bit ~ in the day *(fam.)* ein bißchen spät; **~ in life** in vorgerücktem Alter; **~ at night** in vorgerückter Stunde;
  to be ~ Verspätung haben; **~** lange aufbleiben;
  ~ arrival Verspätung; **~ bag** *(Br.)* Briefkasten mit Spätleerung; **~ burgomaster** Altbürgermeister; **~ capitalism** Spätkapitalismus; **~-closing Saturday** verkaufsoffener Sonnabend; **~-comer** Nachzügler; **~ cutoff of the admission** späte Kassenschließung; **~ delivery** Spätzustellung; **~ fee** *(Br.)* Extraporto für spät ausgelieferte Briefe, Späteinlieferungsgebühr, *(US)* Strafgebühr; **at a ~ hour in the day** zu später Stunde; **to keep ~ hours** lange aufbleiben, Nachtvogel sein; **~ letter** zu spät aufgegebener Brief; **~ minister** früherer Minister; **~-night final** Nachtausgabe; **~ opening** Abendverkauf; **~ pass** *(mil.)* Nachturlaubsschein; **~ period** *(med.)* Inkubationszeit; **~ residence** ehemalige Wohnung; **~ shopper** Späteinkäufer; **~ starter** Spätzünder; **~ summer** Spät-, Nachsommer.

latent versteckt, verborgen, geheim, latent;
  ~ abilities latente Fähigkeiten; **~ ambiguity** versteckte Mehrdeutigkeit; **~ defects** verborgene Mängel; **~ disagreement** versteckter Dissens; **~ equity** verdeckter Anspruch; **~ image** latentes Bild; **~ injury** äußerlich nicht erkennbare Verletzung; **~ partner** stiller Teilhaber; **~ period** *(med.)* Inkubationszeit; **~ reserve** stille Reserve.

later will jüngeres Testament.

lateral Seitenteil, *(mining)* Nebenstollen;
  ~ *(v.)* seitlich;
  ~ branch *(family tree)* Seitenlinie; **~ combination** vertikaler Konzern; **~ deviation** seitliche Abweichung; **~ line** *(railway)* Nebenlinie; **~ view** Seitenansicht.

latest | creation jüngste Modeschöpfung; **~ date** Schlußtermin; **~ fashion** neueste Mode; **the very ~ improvements** allerletzte Verbesserungen; **~ intelligence** neueste Nachrichten; **very ~ news** allerletzte Nachrichten; **~ novelties** letzte Neuheiten.

lath Latte, Leiste;
  ~ and plaster Putzträger und Putz.

Latin Latein;
  thieves' ~ Gaunersprache;
  ~-American Free-Trade Association (LAFTA) Lateinamerikanische Freihandelszone.

latitude *(fig.)* Bewegungsfreiheit, Spielraum, *(geography)* Breite, *(photo)* Belichtungsspielraum;
  south ~ südlicher Breitengrad;
  ~ in selection Auswahlumfang; **~ of thought** Gedankenfreiheit; **to allow s. o. great ~** jem. große Freiheiten gewähren; **to allow much ~ in political belief** absolute politische Meinungsfreiheit gestatten; **to relate facts with considerable ~** es mit der Wiedergabe von Tatsachen nicht besonders nehmen; **to translate with some ~** frei (nicht allzu wörtlich) übersetzen.

latitudinarian freizügig.

latrine Latrine.

latrocinium *(lat.)* Straßenraub.

latter grass zweite Heuernte.

lattice Gitterfenster, -tür;
  ~ sampling Stichprobenverfahren im Gittermuster.

laudatory speech Lobrede.

laugh Lachen, Gelächter;
  ~ *(v.)* **at difficulties** Schwierigkeiten nicht ernst nehmen; **~ from the wrong side of the mouth** himmelhochjauchzend-zu-Tode-betrübt sein; **~ up one's sleeve** sich ins Fäustchen lachen; **to have the ~ on one's side** Lacher auf seiner Seite haben.

laughing stock Zielscheibe des Gespötts.

laughter, to roll up with sich einen Ast lachen.

launch *(airplane)* Abschuß, Katapultstart, *(boat)* Barkasse, *(launching)* Stapellauf;
  motor ~ Motorbarkasse;
  ~ into life Eintritt ins Leben;
  ~ *(v.)* *(airplane)* katapultieren, mit Katapult starten, *(rocket)* abschießen, *(ship)* vom Stapel laufen (lassen);
  ~ s. o. j. lancieren;
  ~ into abuse of s. o. in Verwünschungen über j. ausbrechen; **~ an advertising campaign** Werbefeldzug starten; **~ an aircraft into the air** Flugzeug starten; **~ an appeal** Aufruf erlassen, Sammelaktion starten; **~ an attack upon the enemy** Feind angreifen; **~ a boat from a ship** Boot zu Wasser lassen; **~ censures against s. o.** j. einer Kritik unterziehen; **~ a corporation on an acquisition drive** mit einem Unternehmen in großzügiger Weise Beteiligungen erwerben; **~ s. o. into eternity** *(fam.)* j. ins Jenseits befördern; **~ an idea** mit einem Plan an die Öffentlichkeit treten; **~ an inquiry on a question** Untersuchungsausschuß zur Lösung einer Frage einsetzen; **~ a young man into business** jungen Mann [geschäftlich] unterbringen; **~ into a discussion** sich in eine Unterhaltung (Diskussion) stürzen; **~ a loan** Anleihe auflegen; **~ s. th. on the market** etw. auf den Markt bringen (auf dem Markt einführen), *(advertising)* großangelegte Einführungsreklame aufziehen; **~ a mine** Mine auslegen; **~ a new business enterprise** neues Geschäft (Unternehmen) gründen; **~ an offensive** Offensive beginnen; **~ into a massive sales drive** sich in eine gewaltige Absatzkampagne stürzen; **~ out** großzügig Geld ausgeben; **~ out an argument** mit neuen Argumenten kommen; **~ out into expenses** sich in Unkosten stürzen; **~ out into explanations** sich in Erklärungen flüchten; **~ out into extravagance** sich in extravagante Ausgaben (Extravaganzen) stürzen; **~ out into the sea** in See stechen; **~ out in the sea of life** sich ins volle Leben stürzen; **~ a new passenger line** neue Passagierlinie in Betrieb nehmen; **~ out on a voyage of discovery** auf eine Entdeckungsreise gehen; **~ into politics** in die Politik einsteigen; **~ a proclamation** Proklamation erlassen; **~ a new product** neues Erzeugnis herausbringen; **~ a rocket** Rakete abfeuern; **~ a son into the world** Sohn seine ersten Schritte unternehmen lassen; **~ threats against an opponent** Drohungen gegen einen Widersacher ausstoßen; **~ a torpedo** Torpedo abschießen;
  ~ ad[vertising] *(US)* Einführungsanzeige, -werbung.

launched, to be vom Stapel laufen.

launcher Abschußvorrichtung, *(airplane)* Katapult, Flugzeugschleuder.

launching Starten, In-Gang-Setzen, *(airplane)* Abschießen, Start, *(ship)* Stapellauf, *(rocket)* Abschuß;
  ~ on the market Einführung auf dem Markt;
  ~ area Startgebiet; **~ ceremony** Schiffstaufe; **~ cost** Start-, Anlaufkosten; **~ device** Abschußvorrichtung; **~ facilities** Abschußanlagen; **~ failure** Abschußpanne; **~ pad** *(rocket)* Abschußstelle, -rampe, Startrampe; **~ platform** Abschußbühne; **~ platform for peace** Ausgangsbasis für Friedensverhandlungen; **~ point** *(rocket)* Abschußrampe, -stelle; **~ ramp** Ablaufbahn; **~ range for rockets** Raketenabschußplatz; **~ site** Abschußgelände, Startbahn, -platz; **~ test** Testkampagne; **~ way** Ablaufbahn.

launderette Schnellwäscherei.

laundress Waschfrau.

laundry Waschanstalt, Wäscherei;
  to hang out the ~ Wäsche aufhängen, *(sl.)* Fallschirmtruppen absetzen.

laundryman Wäschereiangestellter.

laureate Preisträger;
  ~ wreath Lorbeerkranz.

laurels *(fig.)* Lorbeeren, Ruhm;
  to look to one's ~ auf seinen Ruhm bedacht sein; **to rest on one's ~** sich auf seinen Lorbeeren ausruhen; **to win ~** Lorbeeren ernten.

lava [stream] Lava[strom].

lavatory Waschgelegenheit, -raum, Toilette, Klosett;
  public ~ Bedürfnisanstalt;
  ~ attendant Toilettenwärter, -frau.

lavender Lavendel;
  to lay s. o. out in ~ *(sl.)* j. in Samt und Seide kleiden; **to lay up in ~** für die Zukunft beiseitelegen.

lavish *(v.)* verschwenden, reichlich spenden, spendieren;
  ~ *(a.)* freigiebig, verschwenderisch;
  ~ with one's money sehr freigebig mit seinem Geld;
  to be ~ with verschwenderisch umgehen;
  ~ expenditure zügellose Ausgabenwirtschaft; **to live in a ~ style** auf großem Fuße leben.

lavishly, to spend verschwenderisch Geld ausgeben.

law Recht, *(enactment)* Gesetz, Statut, Edikt, *(jurisprudence)* Rechtswissenschaft, -gelehrsamkeit, *(legal procedure)* [gerichtliches] Verfahren, Prozeß;

according to ~ von Rechts wegen; **at** ~ gerichtlich; **by** ~ gesetzlich, von Rechts wegen; **by operation of** ~ kraft Gesetzes; **bound by** ~ rechtlich (gesetzlich) verpflichtet; **when the** ~ **comes into effect** bei Inkrafttreten des Gesetzes; **by operation of** ~ kraft Gesetzes; **contrary to** ~ rechtswidrig; **designated (fixed) by** ~ gesetzlich bestimmt (festgelegt); **in** ~ gesetzmäßig; **in conformity with the** ~ gesetzmäßig; **in fact and in** ~ rechtlich und tatsächlich; **learned in** ~ juristisch ausgebildet; **outside the** ~ außergesetzlich; **pending at** ~ rechtshängig; **prescribed by** ~ gesetzlich vorgeschrieben; **relevant in** ~ rechtserheblich; **required by** ~ gesetzlich vorgeschrieben; **under the** ~ aufgrund des Gesetzes, nach dem Gesetz; **under English** ~ nach englischem Recht; **under public** ~ öffentlichrechtlich; **under the** ~ **in force** nach geltendem Recht; **valid in** ~ rechtsgültig, -kräftig; **when the** ~ **comes into effect** bei Inkrafttreten des Gesetzes; **within the meaning of the** ~ im Sinne des Gesetzes;

in ~ **and in fact** rechtlich und tatsächlich;

absolute ~ Naturrecht; **accepted international** ~ geltendes Völkerrecht; **adjective** ~ Prozeßrecht, formelles Recht, Verfahrensrecht; **loosely administered** ~ ungenau angewandtes Gesetz; **administrative** ~ Verwaltungsrecht; **admiralty** ~ Seerecht; **agrarian** ~s Bodenreformgesetze; **international air** ~ internationales Luftrecht; **antitrust** ~s Kartellgesetzgebung; ~ **applicable** anwendbares Gesetz; **banking** ~ Bankgesetz; **bankrupt (bankruptcy)** ~ Konkursrecht; **binding** ~ zwingendes Recht; **budget** ~ *(US)* Haushaltsrecht; **business** ~ Gewerberecht; **cardinal** ~ oberstes Gesetz; **case** ~ auf früheren Entscheidungen beruhendes Recht, Präzedenz-, Richter-, Fallrecht; **civil** ~ bürgerliches Recht, Zivilrecht; **club** ~ Recht des Stärkeren, Faustrecht; **codified** ~ kodifiziertes Recht; **cogent** ~ zwingendes Recht; **commercial** ~ Handelsrecht; **common** ~ gemeines Recht, Landrecht; **company** ~ *(Br.)* Recht der Kapitalgesellschaften, Aktien-, Gesellschaftsrecht; **comparative** ~ vergleichendes Recht; **comprehensive** ~ umfassendes Gesetz; **conflicting** ~s sich widersprechende Gesetze; **constitutional** ~ Verfassungsrecht; **contract** ~ Schuldrecht; **cooperative** ~ *(US)* Genossenschaftsgesetz; **corporation** ~ *(US)* Aktienrecht; **criminal** ~ Strafrecht; **crown** ~ *(Br.)* Strafrecht; **customary** ~ Gewohnheitsrecht; **dead** ~ ungültiges Gesetz; **decree** ~ Not-, Rechtsverordnung; **domestic** ~ innerstaatliches Recht, Heimat-, Landesrecht; **dormant** ~ unanwendbar gewordenes Gesetz; **draft** ~ Gesetzentwurf; **economic** ~ ökonomisches Gesetz; **economic** ~s Wirtschaftsgesetzgebung; **enacted** ~ Gesetzesrecht; **established** ~ geltendes (bestehendes) Recht; **existing** ~ geltendes Recht; **ex-post-facto** ~ rückwirkendes Gesetz; **exclusion** ~ *(US)* Einwanderungsgesetz; **factory** ~ Gewerberecht; **family** ~ Familienrecht; **federal** ~ *(US)* Bundesrecht, -gesetz; **flexible** ~ nachgiebiges Recht; **forest** ~ Forstrecht; **foreign** ~ ausländisches Recht; **game** ~s Jagdrecht; **general** ~ allgemein geltendes Recht; **governing** ~ anwendbares Recht; **Halifax** ~ summarisches Rechtsverfahren; **immigration** ~ Einwanderungsgesetz; **industrial** ~ *(Br.)* Gewerbe-, Arbeitsrecht; **insolvency** ~ Vergleichsordnung; **inspection** ~ Warenprüfungsvorschriften; **insurance** ~ Versicherungsrecht; **internal** ~ nationales Recht; **international** ~ internationales Recht, Völkerrecht; **introductory** ~ Einführungsgesetz; **judge-made** ~ Richterrecht; **labo(u)r** ~ Arbeitsrecht; **local** ~ Ortsrecht, *(US)* Kommunalrecht; **lynch** ~ Lynchjustiz; **maritime** ~ See[handels]recht; **matrimonial** ~ Eherecht; **martial** ~ Kriegs-, Standrecht; **mercantile** ~, ~ **merchant** Handelsrecht; **military** ~ Militärstrafrecht, Kriegs-, Standrecht; **mixed** ~s Schuld- und Sachenrecht; **moral** ~ Sittengesetz; **municipal** ~ innerstaatliches Recht, Gemeinde-, Kommunalrecht; **national** ~ Landesrecht, innerstaatliches (inländisches) Recht; **natural** ~ Naturrecht; **naval** ~ Seerecht; **nonretroactive** ~ nicht rückwirkendes Gesetz; **obsolete** ~ nicht mehr angewendetes, formell noch nicht aufgehobenes Gesetz; **operative** ~ gültiges Gesetz; **organic** ~ Grundgesetz, Verfassung; **patent** ~ *(US)* Patentrecht; **paramount** ~ Verfassungsrecht; **parliamentary** ~ parlamentarische Geschäftsordnung; **penal** ~ Strafrecht; **peremptory** ~ unabdingbares (zwingendes) Recht; **personal** ~ Immunitätsrecht; **political** ~ Staatsrecht; **poor** ~ Armen-, Fürsorgerecht; **positive** ~ positives (geltendes) Recht, Satzungsrecht; **private** ~ Privat-, Zivilrecht; **international private** ~ internationales Privatrecht; **prize** ~ Prisenrecht; **probate** ~ Testaments-, Nachlaßrecht; **procedural** ~ Verfahrensrecht; **provisional** ~ Übergangsgesetz; **public** ~ öffentliches Recht,

Staatsrecht; **public international** ~ Völkerrecht; **quarantine** ~ Quarantänevorschriften; **real** ~ Sachenrecht; **real-estate** ~ Grundstücksrecht; **reinforced** ~ verschärftes Gesetz; **relevant** ~ anwendbares Recht; **retroactive (retrospective)** ~ rückwirkendes Gesetz, Gesetz mit rückwirkender Kraft; **revenue** ~ Steuerrecht; **settled** ~ allgemein anerkannter Rechtssatz; **shipping** ~ Schiffahrtsrecht; **special** ~ Sonderrecht; **state** ~ *(US)* einzelstaatliches Recht; **statute** ~ Gesetzesrecht, kodifiziertes (geschriebenes) Recht; **statutory** ~ geschriebenes Recht; **strict** ~ strenges Gesetz; **subsidiary** ~ subsidiär geltendes Recht; **substantive** ~ materielles Recht; **sumptuary** ~s Luxusgesetzgebung; **tacit** ~ Gewohnheitsrecht; **territorial** ~ innerstaatliches Recht; **trademark** ~ Warenzeichenrecht; **tribal** ~ Stammesrecht; **unconstitutional** ~ verfassungswidriges Gesetz; **uniform** ~ Vereinheitlichungsgesetz; **unwritten** ~ Gewohnheitsrecht; **workmen's compensation** ~ *(Br.)* Gewerbeunfallversicherungsgesetz; **written** ~ geschriebenes Recht;

~ **of agency** Recht der Stellvertretung; ~ **as amended on** Gesetz in der Fassung von; ~ **of arms** Kriegsrecht; ~ **of bankruptcy** Konkursrecht; ~ **on bills of exchange** Wechselrecht; ~ **on the books** verabschiedetes Gesetz; ~ **of the case** materielle Rechtskraft; ~ **of causation (causality)** Verursachungsgesetz; ~ **of collective bargaining** Tarifvertragsrecht; ~ **of commorientes** Vermutung des erstversterbenden Älteren bei gemeinsamem Tod; ~ **of comparative costs** *(Ricardo)* Gesetz der komparativen Kosten; ~ **of conflicts** *(US)* internationales Privatrecht; ~ **of contract** Schuldrecht, Recht der Schuldverhältnisse; ~ **of copyright** Urheberrechtsgesetz; ~ **of customs** Zollgesetz; **general** ~ **of demand** Gesetz von Angebot und Nachfrage; ~ **of decedent's estate** *(US)* Erbfolgerecht, -gesetz; ~ **of diminishing return** Gesetz vom abnehmenden Bodenertrag; ~ **fallen into disuse** nicht mehr angewandtes Recht; ~ **of divorce** Ehescheidungsrecht; ~ **of establishment** Niederlassungsrecht; ~ **of evidence** Beweisrecht; ~ **of exchange** Wechselrecht; ~ **of the flag** Recht des Heimathafens; ~ **in force** gültiges Recht, geltendes Gesetz; ~ **of indifference** Prinzip der Preisunterschiedslosigkeit; ~ **of inheritance** Erbrecht; ~ **of insurance** Versicherungsrecht; ~ **of the jungle** Faustrecht; ~ **of the land** geltende Rechtsnormen; ~ **of marque** Völker-, Retorsionsrecht; ~ **of marriage** Eherecht; ~ **of master and servant** *(Br.)* Arbeitsrecht; ~ **of mortgages** Hypothekenrecht; ~ **of nations** Völkerrecht, internationales (zwischenstaatliches) Recht; ~ **of nature** Naturrecht; ~ **of large numbers** Gesetz der großen Zahlen; ~ **made for the occasion** aus besonderem Anlaß erlassenes Gesetz; ~ **and order** öffentliche Ruhe und Ordnung; ~ **of partnership** Gesellschaftsrecht; ~ **of procedure** Verfahrens-, Prozeßrecht; ~ **of diminishing marginal productivity** Gesetz der abnehmenden Grenzproduktivität; ~ **of property** *(Br.)* Liegenschafts-, Sachenrecht; ~ **of real property** Liegenschaftsrecht; ~ **of reciprocity** Recht der Gegenseitigkeit; ~s **and regulations** Gesetze und sonstige Rechtsvorschriften; ~ **of domestic relations** *(US)* Familienrecht; ~ **of returns to scale** Gesetz vom abnehmenden Ertragszuwachs; ~ **of the road** Straßenverkehrsrecht; ~ **of sales** Recht des Kaufvertrages; ~ **of self-preservation** Selbsterhaltungstrieb; ~ **of the staple** Marktrecht; ~ **of succession** Erb[folge]recht; ~ **of supply and demand** Gesetz von Angebot und Nachfrage; ~ **of torts** Recht der unerlaubten Handlungen; ~ **as to trade unions** Koalitionsrecht; ~ **of war** Kriegsrecht;

~ *(v.) (coll.)* vor Gericht gehen;

to abide by a ~ Gesetz befolgen; **to abrogate a** ~ Gesetz abschaffen (aufheben); **to abolish a** ~ Gesetz aufheben; **to act contrary to a** ~ gegen ein Gesetz verstoßen; **to administer a** ~ Gesetz anwenden; **to apply a** ~ Gesetz anwenden; **to back a** ~ **with action** Gesetz mit Inhalt anfüllen; **to be above the** ~ über dem Gesetz stehen; **to be amenable to** ~ dem Gesetz unterliegen; **to be at** ~ prozessieren, Prozeß führen; **to be bound by** ~ dem Zwang des Gesetzes unterworfen sein; **to be caught in the meshes of a** ~ in die Schlingen eines Gesetzes verstrickt sein; **to be equal before the** ~ vor dem Gesetz gleich sein; **to be good in** ~ rechtlich zulässig sein; **to be good in** ~ **and in fact** rechtlich und sachlich begründet sein; **to be governed by** ~ unter ein Gesetz fallen; **to be governed by the** ~ **of domicile** nach dem Recht des Wohnsitzes beurteilt werden; **to be in the** ~ als Rechtsanwalt tätig (Jurist) sein; **to be a** ~ **unto o. s.** sich zum Gesetzgeber aufspielen; **to be locked firmly into** ~ fest durch Gesetze gebunden sein; **to be under the guardianship of the** ~ unter dem Schutz des Gesetzes stehen; **to be regulated by** ~ durch Gesetz geregelt sein; **to be up against the** ~ mit dem Gesetz in Konflikt geraten sein; **to be bred up for the** ~ für die juristische Laufbahn bestimmt werden; **to be treated in** ~ **in one's own right** rechtlich als Träger von Rechten und Pflichten gelten; **to become ~ in Kraft treten; to break a ~** Gesetz verletzten (übertreten, brechen); **to bring a ~ into action** Gesetz zur Anwendung bringen; **to cancel a ~** Gesetz aufheben; **to carry out** Gesetz anwenden; **to circumvent a ~** Gesetz umgehen; **to claim the benefit of a ~** Schutz eines Gesetzes in Anspruch nehmen; **to come to an arrangement is better than going to ~** ein magerer Vergleich ist besser als ein fetter Prozeß; **to come under the (within the provisions of a) ~** in den Anwendungsbereich eines Gesetzes (unter ein Gesetz) fallen; **to comply with a ~** Gesetz befolgen; **to conform o. s. to the ~** sich dem Gesetz unterwerfen; **to construe a ~** Gesetz auslegen; **to consult the ~** im Gesetz[buch] nachschlagen; **to contravene the ~** dem Gesetz zuwiderhandeln; **to disobey a ~** Gesetz nicht befolgen; **to dispense a ~** Gesetz anwenden; **to dodge a ~** Gesetz umgehen; **to enact a ~** Gesetz erlassen; **to enforce the ~** den Gesetz Geltung verschaffen, dem Gesetz Nachdruck verleihen; **to evade a ~** Gesetz umgehen; **to execute a ~** Gesetz durchführen; **to expound a ~** Gesetz auslegen; **to extinguish a ~** Gesetz abschaffen; **to give effect to a ~** Gesetz in Kraft setzen; **to give a measure the force of ~** Maßnahme gesetzlich verankern; **to go in for ~** sich für die juristische Laufbahn entscheiden; **to go to ~** Rechtsweg beschreiten, klagen; **to go to ~ with s. o.** j. verklagen (gerichtlich belangen), gegen j. prozessieren; **to go to the ~ (barrister)** Anwaltspraxis ausüben; **to have become ~** zum Gesetz geworden sein; **to have the ~ on s. o.** j. gerichtlich belangen, gegen j. gerichtlich vorgehen; **to have recourse to the ~** Prozeß anstrengen, prozessieren, Gerichte anrufen; **to have the ~ on one's side** im Recht sein; **to infringe a ~** Gesetz verletzen; **to invalidate a ~** Gesetz außer Kraft setzen; **to keep within the ~** sich an das Gesetz halten; **to lay down the ~** Gesetz auslegen; **to lay down the ~ about (fig.)** selbstherrlich auftreten, arrogant proklamieren, sich überheblich äußern; **to maintain the ~** für ein Gesetz eintreten; **to maintain ~ and order** öffentliche Ruhe und Ordnung aufrechterhalten; **to make ~s** Gesetze machen; **to make a ~ of no effect** Gesetz wirkungslos machen; **to obey a ~** Gesetz befolgen; **to observe a ~** Gesetz befolgen; **to offend against a ~** gegen ein Gesetz verstoßen; **to pass into ~** Gesetzeskraft erhalten, Rechtkraft erlangen; **to practise ~** als Rechtsanwalt tätig sein, Anwaltspraxis betreiben, Anwaltsberuf ausüben; **to proclaim martial ~** Kriegsrecht verhängen; **to promulgate a ~** Gesetz verkünden; **to put the ~ into force (operation)** Gesetz anwenden; **to put the ~ into motion** Gesetzesmaschinerie in Bewegung setzen; **to put the ~ into operation in all its rigo(u)r** Gesetz mit aller Strenge anwenden; **to read ~** Rechtswissenschaft (Jura) studieren; **to read up on a ~** im Gesetz nachlesen; **to repeal a ~** Gesetz aufheben; **to rescind a ~** Gesetz außer Kraft setzen; **to respect the ~** dem Gesetz Achtung zollen; **to revise a ~** Gesetz abändern; **to revoke a ~** Gesetz aufheben; **to run counter to a ~** dem Gesetz zuwiderhandeln; **to run foul of a ~** mit dem Gesetz in Konflikt geraten; **to set a ~ at naught** Gesetz mißachten; **to settle a matter without going to ~** Angelegenheit außergerichtlich erledigen; **to stand good in ~** rechtsgültig sein; **to strain a ~** einem Gesetz Gewalt antun; **to stretch ~** (in unberechtigter Weise auslegen); **to study ~ (US)** sich des Studiums der Rechte befleißigen, Jura (Rechtswissenschaft) studieren; **to submit o. s. to the ~** sich dem Gesetz unterwerfen; **to sue under a ~** aufgrund eines Gesetzes klagen; **to suspend the operation of a ~** Gesetz vorübergehend außer Kraft setzen; **to take the ~ into one's own hands** eigenmächtig vorgehen, sich selbst Recht verschaffen; **to transgress (trespass) a ~** Gesetz übertreten; **to vary from a ~** vom Gesetz abgehen; **to violate a ~** Gesetz verletzen (brechen); **~-abiding** die Gesetze beachtend, gesetzestreu; **~-abidingness** Gesetzestreue; **~ of Property Act (Br.)** Bodenrechtsreformgesetz; **~ adviser** Rechtsberater, -beistand; **~ agent** Rechtsvertreter, (Scot.) Rechtsanwalt; **~ blank** Urkundenformular; **~ book** Gesetzbuch, juristisches Buch; **~ business** Rechtsangelegenheit, -sache; **~ conduct** Prozeß führen; **~ case** Rechtsfall, Prozeß[sache]; **~ charges** Prozeß-, Gerichtskosten; **~ commission (Br.)** Rechtskommission; **~ committee (New York stock exchange)** Rechtsbeirat; **~ of the Sea Conference** Seerechtskonferenz; **~ costs** Gerichts-, Prozeß-, Verfahrenskosten, Kosten der Rechtsverfolgung; **~ court** Gericht[shof]; **~-creating event** rechtsbegründendes Ereignis; **~ day (bond, mortgage)** Verfallstag; **~ department** Rechtsabteilung; **~ enforcement** Gesetzanwendung, -durchsetzung, Exekutive; **~ enforcement authorities** Vollstreckungsbehörde; **~-enforcement leader** Polizeichef; **~ enforcement officer** Vollzugsbeamter, Exekutivorgan; **~ expenses** Gerichtskosten; **~ faculty** juristische Fakultät; **~ firm** Anwaltsfirma, -kanzlei, -büro; **common-**

~ jurisdiction Rechtssprechung nach gemeinem Recht; **~ language** Rechtssprache; **~ library** Rechtsbibliothek; **~ list (Br.)** Anwaltsverzeichnis, -gutachten; **~ memorandum (US)** Rechtsausführungen, -gutachten; **~ office (US)** Rechtsanwaltsbüro; **~ officer** Gerichtsperson, Justizbeamter; **~ officer of the Crown (Br.)** Rechtsberater der Krone; **~ partner** Sozius; **~ practice** Anwaltspraxis, -tätigkeit; **~ proceedings** gerichtliches Verfahren; **~ reform** Rechtsreform; **~ reports** Entscheidungssammlung; **~ reporting** Berichterstattung über Rechtsfälle; **~ review** juristische Zeitschrift; **~ school (Br.)** Rechtsakademie, (US) juristische Fakultät; **~ society (Br.)** Anwaltsverein; **~-society examination (Br.)** Anwaltsprüfung; **~ student** Rechts-, Jurastudent, Student der Rechte, Rechtsbeflissener; **~ studies** juristisches Studium, Jura-, Rechtsstudium; **~ teacher** Rechtslehrer; **~ term** Sitzungsperiode, (legal expression) juristischer Ausdruck; **~ training** juristische Ausbildung; **~ treaty** normativer Vertrag; **~ writer** juristischer Schriftsteller, Kommentator.

lawbreaker Gesetzesbrecher, -übertreter.

lawbreaking Gesetzesübertretung, -verstoß.

lawful rechtmäßig, rechtsgültig, gesetzlich, gesetzmäßig, zulässig, (document) gültig;
~ act Rechtshandlung; **~ age** Volljährigkeit, Mündigkeit; **to reach ~ age** volljährig (mündig) werden; **~ authority** zuständige Behörde; **~ cause** gesetzlicher Grund; **~ claim** berechtigter Anspruch; **~ currency** gesetzliches Zahlungsmittel; **~ damages** gesetzlich begründeter Schadensanspruch; **~ day** Werktag; **~ discharge** Entlastung des Gemeinschuldners; **to disturb s. o. in the ~ enjoyment of a right** j. im Genuß eines Rechtes stören; **~ entry (real estate)** berechtigte Wiederinbesitznahme; **~ goods (US)** zum Export freigegebene Waren, keine Konterbande; **~ heir** rechtmäßiger Erbe; **~ issue (last will)** gesetzliche Erben, Nachkommenschaft; **~ man** freier Mann; **~ marriage** gültige Heirat; **~ money (US)** gesetzliches Zahlungsmittel; **~ owner** rechtmäßiger Eigentümer; **~ possession** rechtmäßiger Besitz; **~ prize** völkerrechtlich anerkannte Prise; **~ rate (railway)** gültiger Tarif; **~ representative** rechtmäßiger Vertreter, (executor) Nachlaßverwalter, (real property) gesetzlicher Erbe; **~ reserve (banking, US)** gesetzlich vorgeschriebene Reserve, Mindestreserve; **~ ruler** rechtmäßiger Herrscher; **~ share** rechtmäßiger Anteil, (inheritance) Pflichtteil; **~ things in action** gesetzliche Forderungsrechte; **no ~ trade** verbotenes Gewerbe.

lawfulness Gesetz-, Rechtmäßigkeit.

lawgiver Gesetzgeber.

lawgiving Gesetzgebung;
~ (a.) gesetzgebend.

lawless ungesetzlich, unrechtmäßig, gesetzwidrig;
~ man Geächteter; **~ times** Zeiten der Gesetzlosigkeit.

lawlessness Ungesetzlichkeit, Unrechtmäßigkeit, Gesetzwidrigkeit.

lawmaker Gesetzgeber.

lawmaking Rechtsschöpfung, Gesetzgebung;
~ power Gesetzgebungsbefugnis.

lawsuit (US) [Zivil]prozeß, Klage, Rechtsstreit;
adversary ~ streitiges Verfahren; **expensive ~** kostspieliger Prozeß; **pending ~** anhängiger Prozeß;
to be cast in a ~ Prozeß verlieren; **to be faced with a ~** Prozeß zu gewärtigen haben; **to be involved in a ~** in einen Rechtsstreit verwickelt sein; **to bring a ~ against s. o.** Prozeß gegen j. anstrengen; **to carry on a ~** prozessieren, Prozeß führen; **to commence a ~** Prozeß anfangen; **to conduct a ~ for a client** Prozeß für einen Mandanten führen; **to duck a ~** Prozeß verhindern; **to engage in a ~** Prozeß anfangen; **to engage in a dishonest ~** sich in einen üblen Rechtsstreit einlassen; **to have a ~ with s. o.** mit jem. einen Prozeß führen; **to join a ~** einem Prozeß beitreten; **to lose one's ~** seinen Prozeß verlieren; **to protract a ~** Prozeß verschleppen; **to recover in one's ~** seinen Prozeß gewinnen; **to settle a ~ amicably** Prozeß durch Vergleich erledigen; **to venture a ~** es auf einen Prozeß ankommen lassen; **to win a ~** Prozeß gewinnen.

lawyer (person versed in law) Jurist, Rechtsgelehrter, (solicitor) [Rechts]anwalt;
businessman's ~ Wirtschaftsanwalt, -jurist; **common ~** Zivilrechtler; **conveyancing ~** Fachanwalt für Grundstückssachen; **corporation ~ (US)** Verbandsanwalt; **full-fledged ~** versierter Anwalt; **guardhouse ~ (sl.)** unaufgeforderter törichter Ratgeber; **industrial ~** Wirtschaftsrechtler; **insurance ~** Versicherungsanwalt; **intending ~** zukünftiger Anwalt; **international ~** auf internationales Recht spezialisierter Anwalt; **office ~ (US)** beratender Anwalt; **patent ~** Patentanwalt; **pettifogging ~** Winkeladvokat; **Philadelphia ~ (US fam.)** gerissener Anwalt;

practising ~ praktizierender Anwalt; **quirky** ~ gerissener Anwalt; **rising** ~ aufstrebender Anwalt; **slick** ~ raffinierter Anwalt; **standing** ~ mit der ständigen Vertretung beauftragter Rechtsanwalt; **property (real-estate)** ~ auf Immobilien spezialisierter Anwalt; **tax** ~ *(US)* Anwalt in Steuersachen, Steueranwalt;

~ **of wide experience** sehr erfahrener Anwalt;

~ *(v.)* Prozeß führen, *(practise as a lawyer)* als Rechtsanwalt tätig sein;

to be a failure as a ~ als Anwalt nicht reüssieren; **to consult a** ~ Anwalt zu Rate ziehen; **to engage the services of a** ~ sich einen Anwalt nehmen; **to pass o. s. off as a** ~ sich als Anwalt ausgeben; **to put a matter into the hands of a** ~ Angelegenheit einem Anwalt übergeben (übertragen); **to retain a** ~ Anwalt zur dauernden Beratung engagieren;

~**'s fee** Rechtsanwaltsgebühren; ~**'s opinion** *(US)* Anwaltsgutachten.

lax nachlässig, lasch;

~ **in morals** moralisch angeknackst;

to be ~ **in one's conduct** sich gehen lassen; **to be** ~ **in carrying out one's duties** seine Pflichten nicht sehr ernst nehmen; **to be** ~ **in handling expenses** Spesenabrechnungen lasch behandeln; ~ **conscience** elastisches Gewissen; ~ **discipline** schlechte Disziplin; ~ **ideas** vage Ideen; ~ **morals** lockere Sitten; ~ **use of a word** ungenaue Benutzung eines Wortes.

laxity Laschheit, Laxheit;

~ **in one's duties** schlampige Pflichtenerledigung.

lay *(expedition of thieves)* Räuber-, Diebesbande, *(sl., job)* Betätigungsfeld, Beschäftigung, Branche, Job, *(terms of sale, US)* Verkaufsbedingungen, *(whaling voyage)* Anstellung mit Gewinnbeteiligung, Beteiligungslohn;

at a good ~ *(US)* zu günstigen Bedingungen;

~ **of the land** Hügeligkeit;

~ *(a.)* laienhaft, nicht fachmännisch;

~ *(v.)* legen, *(ascertain damages)* Schadenersatz feststellen;

~ **an ambush** Hinterhalt legen; ~ **attachment** mit Beschlag belegen; ~ **bare** offenlegen; ~ **a bomb (an egg)** *(entertainer, sl.)* totalen Reinfall erleben; ~ **a building in ashes** Gebäude zu Schutt und Asche verbrennen; ~ **a cable** Kabel verlegen; ~ **one's case before the commission** seinen Fall dem Ausschuß vorlegen; ~ **s. th. at s. one's charge** jem. etw. zur Last legen; ~ **chickie** *(sl.)* Schmiere stehen; ~ **claim to** Anspruch erheben; ~ **claim to an estate** Anspruch auf einen Nachlaß erheben, Nachlaß beanspruchen; ~ **a complaint** Beschwerde einlegen; ~ **a country under contribution** einem Land Kontributionen auferlegen; ~ **the course** *(mar.)* Kurs festlegen; ~ **one's damages** seine Schadensersatzansprüche begründen; ~ **s. th. at s. one's door** jem. etw. in die Schuhe schieben; ~ **embargo** Schiffsarrest anordnen; ~ **fast** festsetzen, -nehmen; ~ **the foundation** Fundament legen; ~ **the foundation for one's future success** Grundlagen für seine späteren Erfolge schaffen; ~ **hands on** in Besitz nehmen; ~ **violent hands upon o. s.** Selbstmordversuch begehen; ~ **s. o. fast by the heels** j. einholen und gefangensetzen; ~ **one's heart bare** aus seinem Herzen keine Mördergrube machen; ~ **one's homage to s. one's feet** jem. seine Ehrerbietung bezeigen; ~ **so much on a horse** soundsoviel auf ein Pferd wetten; ~ **an indictment against s. o.** schriftliche Klage gegen j. einreichen; ~ **strict injunctions on s. o.** jem. genaue Anweisungen geben; ~ **an information** Anzeige erstatten; ~ **complete information before the House** Parlament vollständig unterrichten; ~ **land fallow** Land brachlegen; ~ **the land** Land ansteuern; ~ **low an empire** Reich zerstören; ~ **mines** Minen verlegen; ~ **a mistake to s. one's charge** einen Fehler anlasten; ~ **a novel in England** Roman in England spielen lassen, Schauplatz eines Romans nach England verlegen; ~ **o. s. open to criticism** sich der Kritik aussetzen; ~ **open a plot** Komplott enthüllen; ~ **paper** *(sl.)* ungedeckte Schecks benutzen; ~ **to rest** zur ewigen Ruhe betten; ~ **siege to a town** Stadt belagern; ~ **a ship alongside the quay** Schiff am Kai festmachen; ~ **little store by** geringachten, wenig von halten; ~ **a story** Geschichte ansiedeln; ~ **stress (weight) on** Gewicht (Wert) auf etw. legen; ~ **the table for breakfast** Frühstückstisch decken; ~ **heavy taxes on tobacco** Tabak hoch besteuern; ~ **a trap** Falle stellen; ~ **the venue** Klage einbringen; ~ **a wager** Wetteinsatz vornehmen; ~ **the land waste** alles herunterbrennen, verbrannte Erde hinterlassen.

lay aboard *(v.)* sich längsseits legen.

lay aside *(v.)* zurücklegen, beiseite legen, *(cease to consider)* aufgeben, verwerfen, ad acta legen;

~ **all ambition** jeden Ehrgeiz fahren lassen; ~ **one's dignity** seine Würde vergessen; ~ **money for one's old age** für sein Alter sparen.

lay away *(v.)* *(US)* Ware zurücklegen.

lay before *(a.)* vorlegen;

~ **s. th. before s. o.** jem. etw. zur Ansicht vorlegen; ~ **s. o. the dangers he is running** jem. die ihm bevorstehenden Gefahren deutlich klarmachen; ~ **s. o. all the facts of a case** jem. den Sachverhalt im einzelnen vortragen (einen Fall in allen Einzelheiten darstellen); ~ **facts before a committee** Ausschuß mit den Tatsachen bekannt (vertraut) machen; ~ **a case (matters) before the court** Fall dem Gericht vortragen, Gericht mit einer Sache befassen; ~ **the House** Gesetzesantrag einbringen; ~ **complete information before the House** Parlament voll unterrichten; ~ **a report before a meeting** einer Versammlung Bericht erstatten.

lay by *(v.)* *(save)* beiseite-, zurücklegen, sparen.

lay down *(v.)* *(machine, US)* Panne haben, *(office)* niederlegen, *(plan)* aufzeichnen, *(rules)* aufstellen, *(save up)* zurücklegen, *(ship)* auf Stapel legen;

~ **o. s.** sich zum Schlafen legen; ~ **one's arms** seine Waffen strecken; ~ **conditions for s. o.** Bedingungen für j. festsetzen; ~ **a floor with linoleum** Zimmer mit Linoleum auslegen; ~ **an indictment** Anklage erheben; ~ **the law** gebieterisch auftreten; ~ **one's life** sein Leben opfern; ~ **a map of the district** Bezirkskarte aufnehmen; ~ **an office** Amt niederlegen; ~ **plans for a holiday** Ferienpläne machen; ~ **prices** Preise festsetzen; ~ **a principle** Grundsatz aufstellen; ~ **a railway** Eisenbahnlinie bauen; ~ **reasons** Gründe anführen; ~ **general rules** allgemeingültige Regeln aufstellen; ~ **a ship** Schiff auf Kiel legen; ~ **a time limit** Frist (Termin) setzen; ~ **tools** streiken, in den Streik treten.

lay in *(v.)* sich eindecken mit, anschaffen, Vorräte anlegen, *(coal mine)* auflassen, schließen;

~ **goods** Waren einlagern (auf Lager nehmen); ~ **provisions** Vorräte anlegen; ~ **a good stock of books** sich gut mit Büchern eindecken; ~ **stocks pretty heavily** sich kräftig eindecken, erhebliche Lagerankäufe tätigen; ~ **stores for the winter** Wintervorräte anlegen.

lay off *(v.)* beiseite legen, *(survey)* abstecken, ausmessen, *(US sl.)* nicht länger belästigen, *(workers)* entlassen, abbauen;

~ **a bet** *(bookmaker)* Wette teilweise woanders plazieren; ~ **at short notice** kurzfristig entlassen; ~ **part of heavy bets with colleagues** *(bookmaker)* größere Wetten teilweise bei anderen Buchmachern plazieren; ~ **a risk** *(insurance company)* Rückversicherung abschließen, sich rückversichern; ~ **o. s. for a week** sich für eine Woche ins Bett legen; ~ **workmen during a business depression** in der Depression Arbeiter vorübergehend entlassen.

lay on *(v.)* *(fam.)* organisieren, *(tax)* auferlegen;

~ **on colo(u)rs** Farben auftragen; ~ **duties on imports** Einfuhrzoll erheben; ~ **gas to a house** Haus an die Gasversorgung anschließen; ~ **hands on** Besitz ergreifen; ~ **violent hands on o. s.** Selbstmord begehen; ~ **one's hopes on s. o.** seine Hoffnungen auf j. setzen; ~ **gas and water** Gas und Wasseranschlüsse verlegen; ~ **strict injunctions on s. o.** jem. genaue Anweisungen geben; ~ **the shelf** *(Br.)* zu den Akten legen; ~ **special trains** Sonderzüge einsetzen; ~ **the table** *(pol., US)* auf unbestimmte Zeit zurücklegen; ~ **it on thick (with a trowel)** dick auftragen.

lay out *(v.)* *(display)* auslegen, zur Schau stellen, *(plan)* entwerfen, *(print.)* aufmachen, gestalten, *(spend)* ausgeben, -legen, vorschießen;

~ **o. s. out** es sich bequem machen; ~ **a cable** Kabel verlegen; ~ **a corpse** Leichnam aufbahren; ~ **a garden** Garten anlegen; ~ **goods** Waren auslegen; ~ **mines** Minen verlegen; ~ **money** Geld ausgeben; ~ **one's money carefully** sein Geld sorgfältig anlegen; ~ **a printed page** Layout für eine Seite fertigstellen.

lay over *(v.)* *(break journey, US)* Reise unterbrechen;

~ **for a week** um eine Woche verschieben.

lay | *(v.)* **s. o. under a necessity (an obligation)** j. zu etw. zwingen; ~ **s. o. under an obligation** jem. eine Verpflichtung auferlegen; ~ **a country under contribution** einem Land Kontributionen auferlegen; ~ **s. o. under restrictions** je. Beschränkungen auferlegen.

lay up *(v.)* *(ship)* aus der Fahrt ziehen, außer Dienst stellen, *(store)* [Vorräte] zurücklegen, ansammeln, sparen;

~ **a car** Auto unterstellen; ~ **for** *(ship)* Kurs nehmen auf; ~ **money** Geld zurücklegen; ~ **provisions** Vorräte anlegen; ~ **s. th. for a rainy day** Notpfennig zurücklegen; ~ **a ship for repairs** Schiff in Reparatur nehmen.

lay *(v.)* **a tax upon land** Grundsteuern erheben.

lay, not to be on one's old nicht mehr in der alten Stellung sein; **to sell one's farm at a good** ~ *(US)* seinen Hof äußerst günstig verkaufen; **to steer by the** ~ **of the land** sich nach der Küstenlinie orientieren.

lay | **-away** *(US)* zurückgelegte Ware; ~ **brother** Laienbruder; **~-by** *(road)* Ausweichstelle, Park-, Rastplatz; ~ **clerk** Küster; ~ **corporation** weltliche Gesellschaft; ~ **days** Liegezeit, Liegetage, Löschzeit; **extra ~-days** Extraliegetage; ~ **figure** Schaufensterpuppe, *(fig.)* Marionette, Strohpuppe; ~ **judge** *(US)* Laienrichter; ~ **mind** *(fam.)* Laienansicht; ~ **people** Geschworene; ~ **person** Laie, Nichtfachmann; ~ **system** *(fishing)* an Kapitän und Mannschaft verteilter Versteigerungserlös; ~ **worker** *(parish)* Gemeindehelfer.

layabout Streuner, Tagedieb, Herumlungerer.

layer Schicht, Lage;
in ~s lagenweise.

laying | **down of an office** Verzicht auf ein Amt; ~ **down of a ship** Kiellegung eines Schiffes; **~-in of provisions** Vorratsanlage, -sammlung; **~-off of personnel** [vorübergehender] Personalabbau; ~ **on of taxes** Auferlegung von Steuern; ~ **out** Aufmachung, Gestaltung, Auslage; ~ **out of money** Geldausgabe, Ausleihen von Geld; ~ **up** Überliegezeit; ~ **up of a ship** Außerdienststellung eines Schiffes;
~ **days** Lösch-, Ladezeit, Liegezeit.

layman Laie, Nichtfachmann, -jurist;
in ~'s **terms** laienhaft ausgedrückt.

layoff [vorübergehender] Personalabbau, vorübergehende Entlassung, *(strike)* Arbeitseinstellung;
massive ~s *(strike)* Massenentlassungen; **recession ~s** rezessionsbedingte Entlassungen; **steel ~s** Entlassungen bei der Stahlindustrie;
~ **benefit (pay)** Entlassungsentschädigung; **reduced ~ pay** gekürzte Entlassungsabfindung.

layout Plan, Anordnung, Anlage, *(advertisement)* Aufriß, Konzeption, Layout, Ideen-, Rohskizze, *(book, newspaper)* Satzspiegel, *(display of goods)* Ausgestaltung des Verkaufsraums, Aufmachung, *(division of sales areas)* Aufschlüsselung von Verkaufsgebieten, *(working regulations)* Arbeitsschema, -anweisungen;
departmental ~ Anordnung der Betriebsanlagen; **page ~** Aufmachung einer Seite; **workplace ~** Arbeitsplatzgestaltung; ~ **of the equipment** Lageplan; ~ **of a letter** Briefanordnung; ~ **of rooms** Raumverteilung, -anordnung; **practical ~ of a workshop** zweckmäßige Einrichtung einer Werkstatt;
to make a ~ Layout anfertigen;
~ **department** Planungsabteilung; ~ **man** Entwurfsgraphiker, Metteur; ~ **plan** Werksplanung.

layouter Entwurfsgraphiker.

layover Fahrtunterbrechung, *(airplane crew)* Ruhezeit.

laystall *(Br.)* Müllablagerungsstelle.

lazaret(te) Aussätzigenspital, *(quarantine)* Quarantäneschiff, -station.

laze *(v.)* **away** mit Nichtstun verbringen;
~ **one's time** seine Zeit verbummeln.

lazy faul, träge;
to have a ~ fit Anwandlung von Faulheit haben; ~ **river** träge dahinfließender Fluß.

lazybones Faulpelz.

leach *(v.)* durchsickern.

lead führende Rolle, Führung, Leitung, Vorsprung, *(el.)* Leitungsdraht, Kabel, *(hint)* Anhaltspunkt, Hinweis, Fingerzeig, *(insurance company)* Einführung, *(mar.)* Senkblei, Blei, *(metallic element)* Blei, *(mining)* Ader, Gang, *(newspaper article)* kurz zusammenfassende Einleitung, *(for pencil)* Mine, *(print.)* Durchschuß, *(seal)* Plombe, *(theater)* führende Rolle, Hauptrolle, *(window)* Fensterblei, Bleieinfassung;
~s *(print.)* Zeilenzwischenräume, Durchschußmaterial;
~s **and lags** Phasenverschiebung; ~s **for investors** Hinweise für das Anlagegeschäft; ~s **and lags in trade** Schwankungen im Handelsverkehr;
~ *(v.)* leiten, leitende (führende) Stellung einnehmen, führen, an der Spitze stehen, *(adduce evidence)* Beweismaterial liefern, *(law)* Verhandlung führen, *(mar.)* loten, *(pane)* in Blei fassen, *(print.)* durchschießen, *(seal)* versiegeln, plombieren;
~ **the army** Heer führen; ~ **s. o. astray** j. auf Abwege führen, j. verführen; ~ **back to a subject** auf ein Thema zurückkommen; ~ **a blind man** Blinden führen; ~ **s. o. captive** j. gefangen abführen; ~ **all competitors** gesamte Konkurrenz übertreffen; ~ **the Conservatives** Konservative Partei führen; ~ **to a discovery** zu einer Entdeckung führen; ~ **s. o. a dog's life** jem. die Hölle auf Erden bereiten, jem. das Leben zur Hölle machen; ~ **up to the final event of a drama** zum dramatischen Höhepunkt führen; ~ **a miserable existence** kümmerliches Dasein fristen; ~ **an expedition** Expedition leiten; ~ **to the fall of the government** Sturz der Regierung herbeiführen; ~ **the fashion** modebe-

stimmt sein, Mode machen; ~ **s. o. up the garden path** j. an der Nase herumführen; ~ **the House** Unterhaus anführen; ~ **a good life** angenehmes Leben führen; ~ **into a mistake** zu einem Fehler verleiten; ~ **a movement** an der Spitze einer Bewegung stehen; ~ **a mutiny** Meuterei anführen; ~ **s. o. by the nose** j. an der Nase herumführen; ~ **an orchestra** Orchester dirigieren; ~ **out a matter** *(print.)* Satz spationieren ~ **a party** Partei führen; ~ **to a rebellion** Aufstand auslösen; ~ **to a good result** gutes Resultat zeitigen; ~ **s. o. into temptation** j. in Versuchung führen; ~ **the troops on to victory** mit den Truppen einen Sieg erringen; ~ **the van** Spitze anführen; ~ **visitors in** Besucher hereinführen; ~ **up to a war** zum Krieg führen, Kriegsursache sein, Kriegsausbruch hervorrufen; ~ **the way** richtigen Weg zeigen, vorangehen; ~ **s. o. out of his way** j. von seinem Weg abbringen; ~ **a witness** einem Zeugen Suggestivfragen stellen; ~ **the world** führende Position in der Welt ausüben;
to cast the ~ Lot auswerfen, loten; **to follow s. one's ~** jds. Beispiel folgen; **to get the ~ out of one's pants** *(sl.)* voll in Aktion treten, *(fam.)* Ton angeben; **to give s. o. a ~** jem. mit gutem Beispiel vorangehen; **to have the ~** Führung innehaben; **to have ~ in one's pants** *(sl.)* Blei an den Füßen haben; **to have ~ in one's pencil** *(sl.)* sehr vital sein; **to have considerable ~ over s. o.** j. fest im Griff haben; **to keep one's dog on the ~** Hund an der Leine führen; **to keep one's ~ over s. o.** Vorsprung vor jem. behalten; **to play juvenile ~s** *(theater)* jugendliche Heldenrollen spielen; **to retain the ~** Vorrangstellung beibehalten; **to seal with ~** plombieren, versiegeln; **to swing the ~** *(Br., sl.)* krankfeiern, sich drücken; **to take the ~** an die Spitze treten, Führung (Vorsitz) übernehmen; **to take the conversational ~** Gesprächsführung an sich reißen;
~ **balloon** *(sl.)* Reinfall; ~ **coffin** Bleisarg; **permissible ~ content** zulässiger Bleigehalt; **~-in** *(advertising)* Anfang (suggestiver Beginn) einer Anzeige, *(broadcasting)* Ansage; ~ **line** Lotleine; **~-pipe cinch** *(sl.)* Kinderspiel; ~ **off** betonter Texteinsatz; ~ **story** *(news broadcasting)* Hauptnachricht, wichtigste Nachricht, *(advertisement)* Spitze; ~ **time** Einführungszeit.

leaden | **seal** Zollplombe, -siegel; ~ **sky** bleierner Himmel.

leader Leiter, Führer, *(advertisement)* Blickführungslinie, *(article of trade)* Zug-, Anreiz-, Lockartikel, *(counsel, Br.)* erster Anwalt, Kronanwalt, *(film)* Vorspann, Startband, *(music)* Dirigent, *(press, Br.)* Leitartikel;
~s führende Persönlichkeiten, *(print.)* Leit-, Tabellenpunkte, *(question)* Suggestivfrage, *(stock market)* führende Marktwerte, Favoriten;
dominant ~ Führerpersönlichkeit; **floor ~** Fraktionsführer; **future ~s** Führungsnachwuchs; **industrial ~** Wirtschaftsführer; **labo(u)r ~** Gewerkschaftsführer; **loss ~** *(US)* Lockartikel, Lockvogelangebot; **party ~** *(Br.)* Parteiführer; **team ~** Mannschaftsführer; **troop ~** Truppenführer;
~ **of a cartel** Kartellvorreiter; ~s **in the community** führende Persönlichkeiten; ~ **for the defence** Hauptverteidiger; ~ **of a delegation** Delegationsleiter; ~ **of an expedition** Expeditionsleiter; ~ **of a gang** Rädels-, Bandenführer; ~ **of the House of Commons** *(Br.)* Sprecher des Unterhauses; ~ **of industry** Wirtschaftsführer; ~ **of the opposition** *(Br.)* Oppositionsführer; ~ **of a parliamentary party** Fraktionsführer; ~ **of a party** Parteiführer; **traditional ~s on prices** seit je führende Werte; ~s **of society** Spitzen der Gesellschaft;
to be a ~ in a field auf seinem Gebiet führend sein; **to be the ~ of a party** Parteiführer sein; **to be cut out for a ~** Führernatur sein; **to become the ~ in establishing pricing policies** Preisführerschaft übernehmen;
loss-~ item *(US)* Lockartikelposten; ~ **principle** Führerprinzip; ~ **writer** *(Br.)* Leitartikler.

leaderette kurzer Leitartikel, *(Br.)* Glosse.

leadership führende Rolle, Führerschaft, Führung, Leitung;
under the ~ unter der Führung;
to be appointed to the ~ of the House of Commons zum Führer des Unterhauses ernannt werden; **to claim ~** Führungsrolle beanspruchen; **to lack ~** keine Führungsqualitäten besitzen; **to pass on the administration ~** Leitung der Verwaltung abgeben; **to provide ~** Führungsqualitäten an den Tag legen;
~ **community** Führungsschicht; ~ **contender** an den Führungseigenschaften Zweifelnder; **to flex one's ~ muscles** seine Führereigenschaften ausprobieren; ~ **forum** Führungsgremium; ~ **personnel** Führungskräfte; ~ **potential** Führungspotential; ~ **position** Führungsstellung, führende Position; ~ **qualities** Führereigenschaften; **in the ~ ranks** in führenden Kreisen.

leading Führung, Leitung, Lenkung;
~ *(a.)* führend, federführend, leitend, maßgebend, entscheidend, tonangebend;

to be ~ in its line of business führend auf dem Markt (in seiner Branche) sein;

~ agent of a firm Hauptrepräsentant einer Firma; **~ article** Leitartikel; **~ bank** Konsortialführerin; **~ business** Hauptbeschäftigung; **~ case** Präzedenzfall; **~ class** führende Schicht; **~ counsel** *(Br.)* leitender (erster) Anwalt; **~ currency** Leitwährung; **~ decision** grundsätzliche Entscheidung; **~ executive** leitender Angestellter; **~ fact** Hauptsache; **~ fashion** herrschende Mode; **~ fashion house** führender (erster) Modesalon; **~ figures in finance, industry and trade** führende Persönlichkeiten des Finanz- und Wirtschaftslebens; **~ firm** führendes Haus; **~ group** Führungsgruppe; **~ hand** Geschäftsführer; **~ idea** Leitgedanke; **~ indicator** Vorindikator; **~ lady** *(theater)* Hauptdarstellerin; **~ light** *(mar.)* Kurs-, Richtfeuer; **~ in and out line** Zufuhrgleis; **~ man** führende Persönlichkeit, *(theater)* Hauptdarsteller; **~ men of the day** führende Tagespolitiker; **~ motive** Hauptmotiv; **~ paper** führende Zeitung; **~ part** führende Rolle; **~ partner** Hauptteilhaber; **~ people** führende Persönlichkeiten, Spitzen der Gesellschaft; **~ people in the world of art** meinungsgebende Persönlichkeiten in der Kunstwelt; **~ price** Richtpreis; **~ principle** oberster Grundsatz; **~ question** Suggestivfrage; **~ role** Führungsrolle; **~ shares** *(stock exchange)* Spitzenwerte, führende Werte; **~ shareholder** Hauptaktionär; **~ ship** Kolonnenschiff; **~ spirit of an enterprise** Seele eines Unternehmens; **~ statesman** führender Staatsmann; **in ~ strings** in den Kinderschuhen; **to conduct in ~ strings** am Gängelband führen; **~ story** *(advertisement)* Spitze, *(broadcasting)* wichtigste Nachricht, Hauptnachricht; **~ underwriter** Erstversicherer; **~ topics of the hour** Hauptgesprächsstoff; **~ wire** *(el.)* Leitungsdraht.

leadtime Vorlaufzeit.

leaf Blatt, *(table)* Einlagebrett;

counterfoil and ~ Kontrollabschnitt und Abreißblatt; **gold ~** Blattgold;

~ of a table Einlegebrett eines Tisches;

~ *(v.)* through *(US)* durchblättern;

to have a quick ~-through etw. rasch durchblättern; **to take a ~ out of s. one's book** sich j. zum Muster (als Beispiel) nehmen, jds. Beispiel folgen; **to turn over a ~** umblättern; **to turn over a new ~** *(fam.)* neuen Anfang machen, neues Leben anfangen.

leaflet Zettel, Flug-, Werbeblatt, Flugschrift, -zettel, kleiner Prospekt, [Werbe]broschüre.

league Bündnis, Bund, Verband, Liga, *(covenant)* Vereinbarung, Abkommen;

♀ of Nations Völkerbund; **~ of states** Staatenliga;

~ *(v.)* sich verbünden.

leak wasserundichte Stelle, *(mar.)* Leck, *(fig.)* undichte Stelle, *(el.)* Verluststrom;

inspired ~ gezielte Indiskretion;

~ of information Informationslücke;

~ *(v.)* out durchsickern; **~ water** wasserdurchlässig sein.

leakage Leckage, Leckwerden, Verlust, Schwund, Abnahme, Abgang, *(allowance for ~)* Schwundvergütung, *(of capital)* Kapitalverlust, *(news)* Durchsickern, Indiskretion;

free from ~ frei von Leckage;

~ and breakage Leckage und Bruch; **~ of state secrets** Bekanntwerden von Staatsgeheimnissen;

~ clause Leckageklausel.

leaked, to be *(news)* durchsickern.

leaky *(ship)* undicht;

~ memory unzuverlässiges Gedächtnis.

lean *(soil)* unfruchtbar, *(unprofitable)* unvorteilhaft;

~ *(v.)* (tend to) neigen, tendieren, sympathisieren;

~ against *(sl.)* Razzia durchführen; **~ on a friend's advise** vom Rat eines Freundes abhängig sein; **~ on s. o. for aid** auf jds. Hilfe angewiesen sein; **~ upon others for guidance** sich gern fremder Führung anvertrauen; **~ a hand on s. o. to do s. th.** j. kräftig unter Druck setzen; **~ towards mercy** für einen Gnadenbeweis plädieren; **~ towards an opinion** einer Meinung zuneigen; **~ over backward** *(coll.)* sich die Beine für etw. ausreißen; **~ to romance** romantisch eingestellt sein; **~ towards socialism** sozialistische Neigungen haben; **~ on others for support** auf fremde Hilfe bauen; **~ upon** *(mil.)* sich anlehnen;

~ coal Magerkohle; **~ concrete** Magerbeton; **~ harvest** schlechte Ernte; **~ mixture** Spargemisch; **~-to** Anbau; **~-to roof** Pultdach; **~-to shed** angebauter Schuppen; **~ type** *(print.)* magere Schrift; **~ wages** kümmerliche Löhne; **~ work** *(print.)* schlechter Satz; **~ year** Verlust-, Defizitjahr.

leaning Neigung, Vorliebe, Tendenz;

criminal ~s kriminelle Veranlagung; **ideological ~s** ideologische Neigungen;

~ towards pacifism pazifistische Neigungen;

to have conservative ~s konservativ eingestellt sein.

leaps, by sprungweise, sprunghaft; **by ~s and bounds** außerordentlich rasch;

~ in the dark Sprung ins Ungewisse; **~ in employment** Beschäftigungsanstieg;

~ *(v.)* auflodern, hochschießen;

~ ahead in die Höhe schnellen; **~ to a conclusion** voreiligen Schluß ziehen; **~ to the eye** ins Auge springen; **~ into fame** mit einem Schlag berühmt werden; **~ at an offer** sich auf ein Angebot stürzen; **~ at an opportunity** Gelegenheit beim Schopfe fassen; **~ right into romance** kopfüber ein romantisches Abenteuer führen; **~ from one topic to another** laufend das Thema wechseln; **~ up** sprunghaft steigen;

to progress by ~s and bounds glänzend (mit Riesenschritten) vorankommen; **to rise by ~s and bounds** *(prices)* sprunghaft ansteigen.

leapfrog *(v.)* *(mil.)* in überschlagendem Einsatz vorgehen lassen.

leapfrogging Sprungrevision;

~ bargaining Tarifverhandlungsmethode mit überschlagendem Einsatz; **~ investment** rollender Investitionseinsatz.

leaping flames auflodernde Flammen.

learn *(v.)* lernen, *(hear)* erfahren, *(from a letter)* entnehmen, ersehen;

~ s. th. about s. o. etw. über j. in Erfahrung bringen; **~ by heart** auswendig lernen; **~ a foreign language** Fremdsprache erlernen; **~ one's lessons** seine Schulaufgaben machen; **~ from a master** bei einem Meister in die Lehre gehen; **~ from one's mistakes** aus seinen Fehlern lernen; **~ the truth** Wahrheit erfahren.

learned | in the law juristisch ausgebildet;

my ~ friend *(parl., Br.)* mein geehrter Kollege; **~ judge** gelehrter Richter; **~ man** Gelehrter; **~ periodical** wissenschaftliche Zeitschrift; **~ professions** akademische Berufe; **~ society** wissenschaftliche Gesellschaft; **~ treatise** gelehrte Abhandlung;

to have ~ wissen, im Bilde sein;

it is ~ *(newspaper)* man erfährt, es verlautet.

learner Anlernling, Lehrling, *(automobile)* Anfänger;

to be a quick ~ rasche Auffassungsgabe haben;

~-driver Fahrschüler.

learning Wissen, Können;

the new ~ Zeit des Humanismus; **observational ~** Lernen durch Beobachtung; **polite ~** Literatur;

~ of languages Sprachenlernen; **~ of lessons** Erledigung der Schulaufgaben;

to be a man of great ~ großes Wissen besitzen;

~ capacity Aufnahmefähigkeit; **~ process** Lernprozeß; **to be in the ~ process** noch in den Lehrjahren sein, noch in der Ausbildung stecken.

leasable [ver]pachtbar;

~ area Pachtfläche, -land.

lease Verpachtung, -mietung, Pacht, Miete, *(contract)* langfristiger Pacht-, Mietvertrag, Pacht-, Mietverhältnis, *(instrument)* Pachturkunde, *(period)* Pacht-, Mietzeit, Pachtdauer;

on ~ mietweise, zur Miete, pachtweise; **on expiration of the, when the ~ expires** nach Ablauf der Pacht (des Mietvertrages); **building ~** *(Br.)* Erbbauvertrag; **commercial ~** Mietvertrag für gewerblich genutzte Räume; **concurrent ~** Obermietverhältnis; **conditional ~** im Grundstückseigentum umwandelbares Pachtverhältnis; **determinable ~** befristetes Pacht-, Mietverhältnis; **equipment ~** Maschinenpachtmiete; **extended ~** zu gleichen Bedingungen verlängerter Pachtvertrag; **farm ~** landwirtschaftliche Pachtung; **financial ~** Maschinenpachtvertrag ohne Wartung; **ground ~** Grundstückspacht[vertrag]; **head ~** Hauptpachtverhältnis; **homestead ~** *(US)* auf 28 Jahre vergebene Pacht, Erbpacht; **improvement ~** mit Meliorationsauflage vergebene Pachtung; **irrevertible ~** unkündbarer Pachtvertrag; **landlord-repairing ~** Pacht ohne Erhaltungsverpflichtung; **long-term ~** langjähriger Mietvertrag (Pachtvertrag); **low ~** billige Pacht (Miete); **master ~** Hauptmietvertrag; **mining ~** Bergwerksberechtigung; **moderate ~** mäßige Pacht (Miete); **ninety-nine years' building ~** 99-jähriges Erbbaurecht; **parole ~** mündlicher Mietvertrag (Pachtvertrag); **perpetually renewable ~** ständig verlängerbarer Pachtvertrag; **proprietary ~** Hauptmiet-, Hauptpachtvertrag; **repairing ~** Miet-, Pachtvertrag mit Instandhaltungsklausel; **reversionary ~** Anschlußpacht, Nachlaßpacht; **service ~** *(US)* Maschinenpacht- und -wartungsvertrag; **short ~** kurzfristiger Miet-, Pachtvertrag; **special ~** Sonderpachtverhältnis; **tenant-repairing ~** Pacht mit Instandhaltungs- und Reparaturpflicht, Erhaltungspacht; **written ~** schriftlicher Pachtvertrag;

~ **of assets** Anlagenpachtung; ~ **of business premises** Miete eines Geschäftslokals, Mietvertrag über gewerblich genutzte Räume; ~ **determinable at the end of seven years** Siebenjahresvertrag; ~ **determinable on the death of the lessor** Pachtvertrag, der am Todestag des Verpächters endet; ~ **of a dwelling** Hausmiete; ~ **of a farm** landwirtschaftliche Pachtung; ~ **of a house** Hausvermietung; ~ **of land** Grundstückspacht; ~ **for life** Pacht auf Lebenszeit, Erbpacht auf Lebenszeit eines Dritten; **a new ~ of (on) life** neue Lebenszuversicht; ~ **with the option to buy** Mietkauf; **renewable ~ at the option of the tenant** auf Wunsch des Pächters verlängerter Pachtvertrag; ~ **for a fixed period** Pachtvertrag für einen bestimmten Zeitraum; ~ **in perpetuity** Erbpacht; **bargain basement ~ of property** billige Grundstückspacht; ~ **for a term of years** Pacht auf Zeit; ~ **on time** Zeitpacht; ~ **of trade** Pacht eines Gewerbebetriebes;

~ *(v.)* **[out]** [ver]pachten, [ver]mieten;

~ **the advertisement business** Anzeigenteil pachten; ~ **for agricultural use** zur landwirtschaftlichen Nutzung verpachten; ~ **business property** Geschäftsgrundstück vermieten; ~ **on the landlord's terms** zu den Vertragsbestimmungen des Eigentümers mieten;

to be rented on ~ verpachtet sein; **to cancel a ~** Pacht aufheben; **to draw up a ~** Pachtvertrag aufsetzen; **to enter into a ~** Pachtvertrag (Mietvertrag) abschließen; **to extend a ~** Mietvertrag verlängern; **to grant a ~** vermieten, verpachten; **to hold land under a ~** Grundstück gepachtet haben; **to let on (put out to) ~** verpachten, vermieten, in Pacht geben; **to purchase a 99-year ~ of office premises** 99jähriges Erbbaurecht an einem Bürogrundstück erwerben; **to record a ~** Mietvertrag (Pachtvertrag) registrieren lassen; **to renew a ~ on a hand-to-mouth basis** Pachtvertrag jeweils im letzten Augenblick provisorisch verlängern; **to renew the ~ of a house** Mietvertrag eines Hauses erneuern; **to sign a ~** Mietvertrag abschließen; **to take a (on) ~** pachten, in Pacht nehmen, mieten; **to take a house on ~ for several years** mehrjährigen Mietvertrag über ein Haus abschließen; **to take a ~ of a piece of land** Grundstück pachten; **to take a new ~** neuen Mietvertrag abschließen; **to take a new ~ of life** neues Leben beginnen; **to take on 99 years' ~** Erbbauvertrag über 99 Jahre abschließen; **to terminate a ~** Mietvertrag (Pachtvertrag) kündigen (aufheben);

~ **arrangement** Pachtvereinbarung; ~ **back** Rückkaufgarantie; ~ **broker** Agent für Grundstückspachten, Pachtmakler; ~ **brokerage** Grundstückspachtvermittler; ~ **expiration** Pachtablauf; **printed ~ form** Pachtvertragsformular; ~**-lend** *(US)* Pacht- und Leihvertrag; ~**-lend deliveries** *(US)* Lieferungen auf Pacht- und Leihbasis; ~ **payment** Pachtzahlung; ~ **period** Miet-, Pachtzeit, -dauer; ~ **renewal** Miet-, Pachtverlängerung; ~ **store** Mietspeicher; ~ **system** Gefangenenarbeitssystem; ~ **value** Pachtwert.

leased vermietet, verpachtet;

to be ~ for long terms in Erbpacht vergeben sein;

~ **car** *(US)* Mietauto, -wagen, Leihwagen; ~ **company** *(US)* Pachtgesellschaft; ~ **facilities** im Leasingverfahren gepachtete Anlagen; **farm** verpachteter (gepachteter) Hof; ~ **land** Pachtgrundstück, -land; ~ **property** Pachtgrundstück, Mietgegenstand; ~ **territory** *(law of nations)* Pachtgebiet.

leasehold Pacht[besitz], Pachtgrundstück, gepachteter Grundbesitz, Pachtung, Zeitpacht, Mietbesitz, -grundstück; **life ~** Pachtung auf Lebenszeit; **long-term ~** Erbpacht; **parole ~** mündlicher Pachtvertrag;

~ **area** Pachtgebiet; ~ **building** Miet-, Pachtgebäude, Mietshaus, Zinshaus; ~ **deed** Miet-, Pachtvertrag; ~ **enfranchisement** Pachtablösung; ~ **estate** Pachtgrundstück, -gut; **to surrender a ~ estate** Pachtrecht übertragen; ~ **financing** Finanzierung von Miethäusern; ~ **house** Pachtgebäude; ~ **improvements** Werterhöhungen während der Pachtzeit; ~ **insurance** Pachtgutversicherung; ~ **interest** Pachtrecht, -anspruch; ~ **land** Pachtgrundstück, -land; ~ **land and buildings** *(balance sheet, Br.)* Pachtbesitz; ~ **mortgage** Verpfändung eines Pachtanspruchs; ~ **premises (property)** gepachteter Grundbesitz, gepachtetes Pachtgrundstück, Mietgegenstand; ~ **Reform Act** *(Br.)* Pachtreformgesetz; ~ **reversion** Heimfallrecht von Unterpachtgrundstücken; ~ **tenure** Pachtbesitz; ~ **territory** *(law of nations)* Pachtgebiet.

leaseholder Pächter, Mieter.

leaseless ohne Pachtverhältnis.

leasemonger Pachtmakler, Vermietungsbüro.

leaser Verpächter.

leash, to put a ~ on s. th. scharfe Kontrolle auf etw. anwenden.

leasing [Ver]pachten, Pacht[ung], Mieten, *(financing)* Leasing, *(letting out)* Vermieten, Vermietung;

consumer goods ~ Konsumgütervermietung; **equipment ~** Vermietung der Ausrüstung; **financial equipment ~** Miete für bewegliche Wirtschaftsgüter; **fleet ~** Vermietung ganzer Fuhrparks; **maintenance ~** Wartungsmiete; **plant ~** Vermietung ganzer Betriebsanlagen; **sales-back ~** *(US)* Anlagenerwerb durch eine Leasinggesellschaft mit gleichzeitiger Vermietung an den Verkäufer; **service ~** Vermietung unter Übernahme von Nebenleistungen; **short ~** kurzfristiges Mietgeschäft; **truck ~** Fahrzeugvermietung;

~ **of a house** Hausmiete; ~**, renting and hiring** An- und Vermieten;

~ **agreement** Leasingvertrag; ~ **arrangement** Leasingvertrag; **cross-frontier ~ business** grenzüberschreitendes Leasinggeschäft; ~ **company** Leasinggesellschaft; ~ **department** Miet-, Pachtabteilung.

least kleinster, geringster;

~ **of all** am allerwenigsten;

to cost at ~ mindestens kosten; **not to mention in the ~** völlig bedeutungslos sein; **to say the ~ of it** gelinde ausgedrückt; ~**-cost combination** Minimalkostenkombination.

leather Leder, *(underworld use, sl.)* Börse, Brieftasche;

imitation ~ Kunstleder;

nothing like ~ eigner Herd ist Goldes Wert;

~ **and prunella** nur ein rein äußerlicher Unterschied; ~ **articles** Lederwaren; ~ **binding** *(US)* Lederband; ~ **industry** Lederindustrie; ~ **suitcase** Lederkoffer; ~ **upholstery** *(car)* Lederpolster.

leatherneck *(US sl.)* Ledernacken.

leave Erlaubnis, Genehmigung, Zulassung, *(of absence, US)* Urlaub, Ferien, *(mil.)* Abschied;

by ~ of court mit gerichtlicher Erlaubnis; **on ~** beurlaubt; **on temporary ~** zeitweilig beurlaubt; **with your ~** mit Ihrer Genehmigung;

additional ~ zusätzlich bewilligter Urlaub, Nachurlaub; **annual ~** Jahresurlaub; **compassionate ~** Urlaub aus familiären Gründen; **full-pay ~** vollbezahlter Urlaub; **generously paid ~** großzügig bezahlte Urlaubsregelung; **home ~** Heimaturlaub; **shore ~** Landgang; **short ~** Kurzurlaub; **special short ~** Sonderurlaub; **sick ~** Krankheits-, Genesungsurlaub; **a six months' ~** halbjähriger Urlaub; **study ~** Bildungsurlaub; **terminal ~** noch zustehender Urlaub;

~ **of absence** genehmigter Urlaub, Sonderurlaub, Beurlaubung; ~ **to appeal** Zulassung der Berufung; ~ **of court** gerichtliche Erlaubnis; ~ **to go out** Ausgangsurlaub; ~ **to land** Landeerlaubnis; ~ **and licence** Einwand der Genehmigung des Grundstückseigentümers; ~ **with[out] pay** [un]bezahlter Urlaub;

~ *(v.)* lassen, *(bequeath)* hinterlassen, vermachen, vererben, *(job)* Stellung aufgeben, gehen, *(person)* weggehen, abreisen, *(ship)* auslaufen, *(submit for consideration)* anheimstellen, *(train)* gehen, abfahren;

~ **in abeyance** in der Schwebe (offen) lassen; ~ **one's address** seine Adresse hinterlassen; ~ **s. th. alone** sich in etw. nicht einmischen; ~ **the army for the law** vom Heer zum Anwaltsberuf überwechseln; ~ **a balance of $ 1000 to your debit** Saldo von $ 1000 zu Ihren Lasten aufweisen; ~ **one's bag in the cloakroom** seinen Koffer zur Gepäckaufbewahrung geben; ~ **blank** unausgefüllt lassen; ~ **in bond** unter Zollverschluß lassen; ~ **the Cabinet** aus der Regierung ausscheiden; ~ **the chair** Sitzung aufheben; ~ **s. th. to chance** dem Zufall überlassen; ~ **s. o. in charge of s. th.** jem. etw. zu getreuen Händen übergeben; ~ **the Church** aus der Kirche austreten; ~ **in the cold** *(coll.)* vernachlässigen; ~ **a competitor behind** *(fam.)* der Konkurrenz das Nachsehen geben; ~ **the country** außer Landes gehen; ~ **much to be desired** viel zu wünschen übrig lassen; ~ **s. o. to his devices** j. sich selbst überlassen; ~ **to s. one's discretion** in jds. Ermessen stellen; ~ **s. o. flat** j. sitzen lassen; ~ **s. o. free to do what he wants** jem. vollkommene Freiheit lassen; ~ **off bad habits** schlechte Angewohnheiten ablegen; ~ **s. th. hanging in the air** etw. in der Schwebe lassen; ~ **harbo(u)r** auslaufen; ~ **the house** ausgehen; ~ **s. o. a house** jem. ein Haus vermachen; ~ **s. th. at s. one's house** etw. bei jem. einstellen; ~ **the impression** Eindruck hinterlassen; ~ **no issue** keine Nachkommen hinterlassen; ~ **one's job** seine Stelle aufgeben; ~ **the jury to find their verdict** Geschworene zwecks Urteilsfindung entlassen; ~ **a legacy to s. o.** Vermächtnis für j. aussetzen; ~ **a matter over** Entscheidung einer Angelegenheit dem Zufall überlassen; ~ **medicine for the law** jetzt anstatt von Medizin jetzt Jura studieren; ~ **a message for s. o.** jem. etw. ausrichten lassen; ~ **one's money to s. o.** jem. sein Geld vermachen; ~ **all one's money to charity** sein Vermögen für wohltätige Zwecke bestimmen; ~ **for New York** nach New

York auswandern; ~ **nothing to accident** nichts dem Zufall überlassen; ~ **nothing but debts** nichts als Schulden hinterlassen; ~ **off work** Feierabend machen; ~ **a page blank** Seite frei lassen; ~ **a political party** aus einer Partei austreten; ~ **a port** auslaufen; ~ **out a possibility** Möglichkeit nicht berücksichtigen; ~ **s. o. with a problem** j. mit einem Problem konfrontieren; ~ **a profit** Gewinn abwerfen; ~ **one's property to one's wife** sein Vermögen seiner Frau hinterlassen; ~ **the rails** entgleisen; ~ **the reader to judge** dem Leser das Urteil überlassen; ~ **on record** protokollieren lassen; ~ **s. o. without a roof over his head** jem. das Dach über dem Kopf wegnehmen; ~ **school** mit der Schule fertig sein, von der Schule abgehen; ~ **a servant in charge of the house** Hausangestellten zur Kontrolle im Hause lassen; ~ **the service** aus dem Dienst ausscheiden; ~ **one's situation** seine Stellung aufgeben; ~ **no stone unturned** alle Hebel in Bewegung setzen, nichts unversucht lassen; ~ **a strip** *(sl.)* Bremsspuren hinterlassen; ~ **the track** entgleisen; ~ **unpaid** unbezahlt lassen; ~ **at one's own volition** von sich aus kündigen; ~ **one's wife** seine Ehefrau verlassen; ~ **by will** testamentarisch vermachen; ~ **word for s. o.** Nachricht für j. hinterlassen; ~ **work** streiken; ~ **half one's work till the next day** Hälfte der Arbeit bis zum nächsten Tag lassen.

leave about herumliegen lassen.

leave behind zurücklassen;
~ **s. o. behind** jem. den Rang ablaufen; ~ **one's luggage behind** sein Gepäck vergessen.

leave off *(cease)* aufhören mit, einstellen, *(train)* abfahren;
~ **flat** *(stock exchange)* flau schließen; ~ **studying law** sein Rechtsstudium abbrechen; ~ **smoking** mit dem Rauchen (zu rauchen) aufhören; ~ **s. o. well off** j. in guten Verhältnissen zurücklassen; ~ **work** Feierabend machen.

leave *(v.)* **out** | **of an agreement** aus einem Vertragsverhältnis entlassen; ~ **the details** Einzelheiten weglassen; ~ **a letter** Buchstaben vergessen (auslassen).

leave over übriglassen;
~ **a matter over** Sache auf sich beruhen lassen.

leave, to apply (ask) for ~ Urlaub beantragen, Urlaubsgesuch einreichen; **to be on long** ~ große Ferien haben; **to be on** ~ **of absence** genehmigten Urlaub verbringen; **to be done out of one's** ~ **every time** jedesmal um seinen Urlaub gebracht werden; **to be eligible for** ~ urlaubsberechtigt sein, Urlaubsanspruch haben; **to break** ~ nicht genehmigten Urlaub nehmen; **to come in for a** ~ Antrag auf Beurlaubung (Urlaubsantrag) stellen; **to extend a** ~ Urlaub verlängern; **to give** ~ Erlaubnis erteilen, Urlaub bewilligen, beurlauben; **to give s. o. four weeks'** ~ j. für vier Wochen freistellen; **to go back to England on** ~ seinen Urlaub in England nehmen; **to go on** ~ auf Urlaub gehen, seinen Urlaub antreten; **to go home on** ~ Heimaturlaub nehmen; **to grant** ~ Erlaubnis erteilen, Urlaub bewilligen, beurlauben; **to grant** ~ **to appeal** Berufung zulassen; **to have two weeks'** ~ 14 Tage Urlaub haben; **to have** ~ **to stay away from the office tomorrow** für den morgigen Tag freigenommen haben; **to obtain a month's** ~ Monatsurlaub bekommen; **to overstay one's** ~ seine Urlaubszeit überschreiten; **to put in for three days'** ~ dreitägigen Urlaub beantragen; **to refuse** ~ **to appeal** Berufung versagen; **to take one's** ~ seinen Urlaub nehmen; **to take one's** ~ **of s. o.** sich von jem. beurlauben; **to take French** ~ sich unauffällig empfehlen (heimlich entfernen); **to take** ~ **of one's friends** sich von seinen Freunden verabschieden; **to take** ~ **of pleasure** den Vergnügungen entsagen; **to take** ~ **of one's senses** verrückt spielen; **to turn over the** ~**s of a book** Buchseiten umblättern;
take it or ~ **it** nach deinem Belieben; **all** ~ **is stopped** totale Ausgangssperre;
~ **book** *(mil.)* Urlaubsliste, -buch; ~~**breaking** Urlaubsüberschreitung; **generous** ~ **conditions** großzügige Urlaubsregelung; ~ **day** freier Tag; ~ **entitlement** Urlaubsanspruch; ~ **schedule** *(US)* Urlaubsplan; ~~**taking** Abschied; ~ **train** Urlauberzug.

leaving Abgang, Ausgang, *(bequest)* Hinterlassenschaft, *(ship)* Ausreise;
~**s** Reste, Restanten, Abfall;
school-~ Schulabgang, -entlassung;
~ **of a steamer** Dampferabfahrt; ~ **without notice** Nichteinhaltung der Kündigungsfrist; ~ **out** Weglassung;
~ **certificate** *(Br.)* Arbeitszeugnis, *(school)* Abgangszeugnis; ~ **dinner** Abschiedsessen; ~ **examination** Abgangsprüfung; **assistants'** ~ **examination** *(book trade)* Abschlußprüfung zum Assistenten im Buchhandel; ~~**off time** Arbeitsschluß; ~ **shop** *(sl.)* Trödler.

leblang *(v.) (sl.)* verbilligte Theaterkarten verkloppen.

lection Lektion, Lesart, Variante.
lector *(US)* Lektor.
lectorship *(US)* Dozenten-, Lektorenstelle, Dozentur.
lecture Vorlesung, Vortrag, Referat, *(course of lectures)* Vorlesungszyklus, *(lectureship)* Lektorat, *(variation in text)* Lesart, Variante;
first (inaugural) ~ Antrittsvorlesung; **lantern** ~ Lichtbildvortrag; **open** ~ öffentliche Vorlesung; **overlapping** ~**s** sich zeitlich überschneidende Vorlesungen; **paid** ~ honorierter Vortrag; **public** ~ öffentlicher Vortrag; **three-hour** ~ dreistündige Vorlesung; **university extension** ~**s** Vorlesungen auf der Volkshochschule; **video-type** ~ auf einem Fernsehband aufgenommene Vorlesung;
~ **with discussion** Seminar; ~ **with slides** Lichtbildervortrag;
~ *(v.)* Vorlesungen halten, vortragen, lesen, dozieren;
~ **s. o.** j. schulmeistern; ~ **on s. th.** Vortrag über etw. halten; ~ **on ancient history** alte Geschichte lesen; ~ **to students** Vorlesungen halten;
to attend a ~ sich einen Vortrag anhören, *(student)* Vorlesung besuchen; **to be a constant attendant at a course of** ~**s** Vorlesungen regelmäßig besuchen; **to curtail a** ~ Vorlesung vorzeitig abbrechen; **to cut** ~**s** in Vorlesungen fehlen, Vorlesungen schwänzen; **to deliver (give) a** ~ Vorlesung (Vortrag) halten, lesen; **to get a** ~ abgekanzelt werden; **to hear** ~**s** Vorlesungen besuchen (belegen); **to prevent a** ~ **taking place** Vorlesung verhindern; **to print one** ~**s** seine Vorlesungen in Buchform erscheinen lassen; **to ramp up some** ~**s out of old notes** aus alten Aufzeichnungen eine Vorlesungsreihe zusammenschustern; **to read a** ~ Vorlesung halten; **to sit a** ~ **out** bis zum Schluß eines Vortrags (einer Vorlesung) bleiben; **to take [good] notes at a** ~ Vorlesungen [ausführlich] mitschreiben; **to turn out to a** ~ sich zur Abwechslung einen Vortrag anhören; **to write up one's notes on a** ~ Vorlesungsaufzeichnungen überarbeiten;
~ **circuit** Vortragsreise; ~ **fee** Vortragshonorar, *(university)* Vorlesungsgebühr; ~ **hall** Vorlesungssaal; ~ **list** Vorlesungsliste, -verzeichnis; **to take** ~ **notes** Vorlesung mitschreiben; ~ **room** Vorlesungssaal, Hörsaal; ~ **system** Vorlesungssystem; ~ **theater (theatre,** *Br.***)** Aula; **to go on a** ~ **tour** auf eine Vortragsreise gehen.
lecturer Vortragender, *(publisher)* Lektor, Referent, *(university)* [Privat]dozent, Lehrbeauftragter;
principal ~ Studienleiter; **senior** ~ festangestellter Privatdozent, Assistenzprofessor;
~ **scale** Gehaltsstaffel für Dozenten.
lectureship Lehrauftrag, Dozentur, Lektorat, *(course of lectures)* Vorlesungsreihe.
lecturess Dozentin, Vortragende.
lecturette kleine Vorlesung, Kurzreferat.
lecturing Abhalten von Vorlesungen;
~ **duties** Dozenten-, Lektoraufgaben, -tätigkeit.
ledger Hauptbuch, *(register)* Register;
accounts-payable ~ *(US)* Kontokorrentbuch für Kreditoren; **accounts-receivable** ~ *(US)* Kontokorrentbuch für Debitoren; **branch** ~ Hauptbuch einer Filiale, Filialbuchführung; **building** ~ Gebäudekonto; **creditors'** ~ Gläubigerbuch, Kreditorenbuch; **customers'** ~ Kundenkonto, Debitorenbuch; **daily mail** ~ Brieftagebuch; **expense** ~ Unkostenhauptbuch; **factory** ~ Betriebshauptbuch; **general** ~ Hauptbuch [mit sämtlichen Hauptbuchkonten]; **goods-bought** ~ Wareneinkaufsbuch; **goods-sold** ~ Warenverkaufsbuch; **great** ~ Staatsschuldbuch; **loose-leaf** ~ [Hauptbuch in] Loseblattbuchführung; **payroll** ~ Lohn-, Gehaltsliste; **plant** ~ Betriebs- und Ausstattungshauptbuch; **plant and equipment** ~ Betriebs- und Ausstattungshauptbuch; **private** ~ Privatkontenbuch; **property** ~ Anlagenbuch; **purchase** ~ Kreditorenbuch; **securities** ~ Effektenbuch; **shareholders'** ~ Aktienbuch; **stockholders'** ~ *(US)* Aktienbuch; **stores** ~ Lagerhauptbuch; **subscribers'** ~ Zeichnungsliste; **subsidiary** ~ Hilfskontobuch, Nebenbuch;
to balance the ~ Hauptbuch abschließen (saldieren); **to enter into the** ~ in das Hauptbuch eintragen; **to keep the** ~ das Hauptbuch führen; **to post an item in the** ~ Posten ins Hauptbuch eintragen; **to post up the** ~ Hauptbuch vollständig nachtragen;
~ **abstract** Hauptbuchauszug; ~ **account** Hauptbuchkonto; ~ **asset** *(insurance accounting)* im Hauptbuch eingetragener Anlageposten; ~ **book** Hauptbuch; ~ **clerk** Buchhalter; ~ **control** Hauptbuchkontrolle; ~ **experience** Erfahrung in der Führung des Hauptbuchs; ~ **folio** Hauptbuchfolio; ~ **item** Hauptbuchposten; ~ **journal** in Tabellenform geführtes Hauptbuch, amerikanisches Journal; ~ **keeper** Hauptbuchführer; ~~**keeping staff** Personal der Hauptbuchhaltung; ~

paper gutes Schreibpapier; ~ **postings** Hauptbucheintragungen; ~ **report** Hauptbuchauszug; ~ **sheet** Kontoblatt; ~ **transfer** Umbuchung im Hauptbuch; ~**-type journal** amerikanisches Journal; ~ **work** Hauptbuchführung.

lee *(mar.)* Lee[seite], *(sheltered place)* windgeschützte Stelle;
under the ~ unter dem Schutz;
~**s of society** Abschaum der Gesellschaft;
to drain the cup to the ~ Becher bis zur bitteren Neige leeren;
~ **shore** Leeküste; **on a** ~ **shore** in Schwierigkeiten; ~ **side** Leeseite.

leech *(fig.)* Blutsauger, Parasit;
~ *(v.)* **s. o.** *(borrow, sl.)* j. bluten lassen;
to stick like a ~ wie eine Klette festhängen.

leet, short Bewerber, Kandidatenliste, Liste der zur engeren Wahl Anstehenden;
to eat the ~ Bedingung einstecken müssen.

leeway *(mar.)* Abtrift, *(room for action, coll.)* Spielraum, Bewegungsmöglichkeit;
to have considerable ~ **to make up** genügend Spielraum haben.

left linke Seite;
the ~ *(pol.)* die Linke, der linke Flügel;
anti-Market ~ EG-feindliche Linke; **bottom** ~ *(page)* links unten; **extreme** ~ äußerste Linke; **moderate** ~gemäßigte Linke;
to be very far to the ~ sehr weit links stehen; **to keep to the** ~ sich links halten, links fahren; **to overtake on the** ~ links überholen; **to place one's viewpoint** ~ **of centre** sich politisch links von der Mitte eingruppieren; **to swing violently to the** ~ sich heftig nach links orientieren;
~ *(a.)* übrig[geblieben];
~ **on hand** übrig, auf Lager geblieben; ~ **till called for** postlagernd; ~ **at station to be called for** bahnlagernd;
to ask to be ~ **out of an agreement** an einer Vereinbarung nicht teilnehmen wollen; **to be** ~ **in abeyance** in der Schwebe bleiben; **to be better** ~ **unsaid** besser ungesagt bleiben; **to be** ~ **with goods** auf seinen Waren sitzenbleiben; **to be** ~ **over** übrigbleiben, restieren; **to be** ~ **over from a sale** vom Verkauf übrigbleiben; **to get nicely** ~ *(coll.)* ganz schön hereingelegt werden; **to be** ~ **to one's purchase** von seiner Hände Arbeit leben; **to gather together what was** ~ **of the fortune** Vermögensüberreste zusammensuchen;
~**-hand corner** *(book)* linke Ecke; ~**-handed marriage** morganatische Ehe; ~**-hand side** *(balance sheet)* Debet-, Passivseite; ~**-hand side of a street** linke Straßenseite; ~**-hand traffic** Linksverkehr; ~**-hand twist** *(pol.)* Linksdrall; ~**-handed compliment** zweifelhaftes Kompliment; ~**-handed person** Linkshänder; ~ **luggage** *(Br.)* zur Aufbewahrung gegebenes Gepäck; ~**-luggage office** *(Br.)* Handgepäckaufbewahrung, Gepäckaufbewahrungsstelle; ~**-luggage ticket** *(Br.)* Gepäckaufbewahrungsschein; ~**-off clothing** abgelegte Kleider; **top** ~ **position** *(page)* links oben; ~ **turn** Linksschwenkung; **no** ~ **turn** Linksabbiegen verboten; ~ **turn signal** Linksabbiegersignal; **the** ~ **wing** Linksgruppe; **extreme** ~**-wing** linksradikal; ~**- or right-wing** links- oder rechtsextrem.

left-wing | **cartel** Linkskartell; ~ **coalition** Linkskoalition; ~ **extremism** Linksextremismus; ~ **gain** Zuwachs der Linken; ~ **government** Linksregierung; **to break the** ~ **grip** Einfluß des linken Flügels zurückdrängen; ~ **militants** linkslastige militante Kräfte; ~ **opposition** Linksopposition; ~ **party** Linkspartei; **under** ~ **pressure** unter dem Druck des linken Flügels; ~ **organization** linksstehende Organisation; ~ **program(me)** Programm der Vereinigten Linken; ~ **radical** Linksradikaler; ~ **revolt** revolvierender linker Flügel; ~ **socialist** Linkssozialist; ~ **victory** Wahlsieg der Linksparteien; ~ **votes** Linksstimmen.

left | **winger** Zugehöriger des linken Flügels, Linkspolitiker, Anhänger einer Linkskoalition, Linker; ~ **wingism** Koalitionspolitik mit der Linken.

leftism *(pol.)* Linksorientierung.

leftist *(pol.)* Anhänger der Linken, Linkspolitiker;
to be a ~ links stehen;
~ *(a.)* linksgerichtet, sozialistisch;
~ **press** Linkspresse.

leftovers, leftover stocks Reste, Restanten.

lefty *(sl.)* Linksradikaler.

leg Bein, *(airplane)* Teilstrecke, *(journey)* Abschnitt, Teil, Etappe, *(railway)* Linie;
on one's ~**s** gut situiert; **on its last** ~**s** klapprig, kurz vor dem Zusammenbruch;
~ *(v.)* **it** seine Beine gebrauchen;
to be on one's ~**s** *(speaker)* Rede stehend halten; **to be on one's hind** ~**s** sich wieder erholt haben, wieder auf die Beine kommen; **to be on one's last** ~**s** am Ende sein, auf dem letzten Loch

pfeifen; **to be carried off one's** ~**s** hinweggeschwemmt werden; **to feel (find) one's** ~**s** *(fig.)* Vertrauen fassen, Selbstvertrauen gewinnen; **to get on one's** ~**s** sich erheben; **to get on one's** ~**s again** wieder Fuß fassen; **to get s. o. on his** ~**s again** j. wieder flottmachen; **to give s. o. a** ~ **up** jem. Unterstützung angedeihen lassen, *(fam.)* j. in den Sattel helfen; **to have** ~**s** *(mar.)* sehr schnell sein; **to have been on one's** ~**s all day** ganzen Tag auf den Beinen (unterwegs) gewesen sein; **to have not a** ~ **to stand on** überhaupt keine Rechtfertigung haben; **to make a** ~ seinen Kratzfuß machen; **to pull s. one's** ~ sich einen Spaß mit jem. erlauben; **to put one's best** ~ **foremost** sich beeilen; **to run s. o. off his** ~**s** jem.; **to set a business on its** ~**s** Sache auf die Beine bringen; **to shake a** ~ Tanzbein schwingen, *(sl.)* seinen höchsten Gang einschalten; **to show a** ~ *(coll.)* aus dem Bett steigen; **to stand on one's own** ~**s** *(fig.)* auf eigenen Füßen stehen; **to stretch one's** ~**s** sich die Beine vertreten, Spaziergang machen; **to take to one's** ~**s** *(fam.)* seine Beine in die Hand nehmen; **to walk s. o. off his** ~**s** j. müde laufen; **to write off a bad** ~ sich ans Bein binden;
to give ~ **bail** sich aus dem Staube machen, Fersengeld geben; ~ **man** *(sl.)* Lokalreporter; ~ **pulling** Fopperei.

legacy Vermächtnis, Legat, testamentarische (letztwillige) Zuwendung, *(pol.)* politisches Vermächtnis;
absolute ~ unbedingtes Vermächtnis; **accumulative (additional)** ~ Zusatzvermächtnis; **alternative** ~ Hauptwahlvermächtnis; **cash** ~ Barvermächtnis; **conditional (contingent)** ~ bedingtes Vermächtnis; **cumulative** ~ Zusatzvermächtnis; **demonstrative** ~ beschränktes Gattungsvermächtnis, Geldvermächtnis; **general** ~ Quoten-, Geldsummen-, Gattungsvermächtnis; **indefinite** ~ Erbeinsetzung auf den beweglichen Nachlaß; **lapsed** ~ durch Tod des Bedachten erledigtes Vermächtnis; **modal** ~ mit Auflagen versehenes Vermächtnis; **pecuniary** ~ Geldvermächtnis, -legat; **preferential** ~ Vorausvermächtnis; **residuary** ~ Vermächtnis des gesamten beweglichen Restnachlasses (nach Abzug von Legaten und Kosten); **special (specific)** ~ Einzelvermächtnis; **statutory** ~ *(Br.)* Pflichtteil; **trust** ~ vom Treuhänder verwaltetes Vermächtnis; **universal** ~ Universalsukzession; **vested** ~ unabdingbares Vermächtnis;
~ **in hotchpot** ausgleichspflichtige letztwillige Zuwendung; ~ **of residue** letztwillige Zuwendung; ~ **of shame** *(fam.)* Anstandsvermächtnis; ~ **of shares** Aktienlegat;
to abate the amount of a ~ Vermächtnis kürzen; **to admeasure a** ~ Legat aussetzen; **to be enriched by a** ~ von einem Vermächtnis profitieren; **to bequeath a** ~ Vermächtnis aussetzen; **to come into a** ~ Vermächtnisnehmer sein; **to leave a** ~ **to s. o.** Vermächtnis für j. aussetzen; **to subtract a** ~ Legat einbehalten;
~ **duty** *(Br.)* Erbschaftsteuer [auf den beweglichen Nachlaß]; ~ **hunter** Erbschleicher; ~ **hunting** Erbschleicherei; ~ **monger** Erbschleicher; ~ **tax** Vermächtnissteuer.

legal *(based on law)* gesetzlich, gesetzmäßig, juristisch, *(lawful)* rechtmäßig, legal, *(valid)* [rechts]gültig, rechtskräftig;
~ **act** Rechtshandlung, Willenserklärung; ~ **action** Prozeß; **to allow** ~ **action** Rechtsweg zulassen; ~ **acumen** juristischer Scharfsinn; ~ **adoption** Annahme an Kindes Statt; ~ **advice** Rechtsberatung; **to take** ~ **advice** sich juristisch beraten lassen; ~ **adviser** juristischer Berater; ~ **affairs** Rechtsangelegenheiten; ~ **age** gesetzliches Mindestalter, Volljährigkeit; ~ **age of consent to marriage** heiratsfähiges Alter; ~ **agent** Rechtsvertreter, gesetzlicher Vertreter; **free** ~ **aid** *(US)* Rechtshilfe, unentgeltlicher Rechtsbeistand, *(Br.)* Armenrecht; ~ **aid certificate** *(Br.)* Armenrechtszeugnis; ~ **aid office** *(Br.)* Rechtsberatungsstelle; ~ **aid society** Rechtsschutzverein; ~ **arguments** rechtliche Begründung, Rechtsausführungen; ~ **assets** frei verfügbare Nachlaßgegenstände; ~ **assistant** juristischer Mitarbeiter; ~ **authority** Justiz-, Gerichtsbehörde; ~ **basis** gesetzliche Grundlage, Rechtsgrundlage; ~ **battle** Rechtsstreit; ~ **benefit** Rechtsvorteil; ~ **bonds** *(US)* mündelsichere Schuldverschreibungen; ~ **cap** Kanzleibogen; ~ **capacity** Rechts-, Geschäftsfähigkeit; ~ **capacity to sue** Prozeßfähigkeit; ~ **capital** festgesetztes Eigenkapital; ~ **career** juristische Laufbahn; ~ **cause** unmittelbare Ursache; ~ **charges** gesetzliche Gebühren, *(Br.)* Anwaltsgebühren; ~ **claim** gesetzlicher Anspruch, Rechtsanspruch, Forderungsrecht; ~ **coin** gesetzliches Zahlungsmittel; ~ **committee** Rechtsausschuß; ~ **community** gesetzlicher Güterstand; ~ **concept[ion]** Rechtsbegriff, -auffassung, -vorstellung; ~ **conclusion** Rechtsfolgerung; ~ **condition** gesetzliche Bedingung; ~ **contract** rechtsgültiger Vertrag; ~ **correspondence** juristischer Schriftwechsel; ~ **costs** *(Br.)* Rechts-, Gerichtskosten; ~ **counsel** *(US)* Rechtsberater; **to hire** ~ **counsel** *(US)* sich juristisch beraten lassen; ~ **cruelty** *(divorce proceedings)* seelische Grausamkeit, Mißhandlungen;

~ **custodian** amtliche Hinterlegungsstelle; ~ **custom** *(US)* Gewohnheitsrecht; ~ **day** Gerichtstag; ~ **debts** einklagbare Forderungen; ~ **debt margin** *(municipal accounting)* zugelassene Überschuldung; ~ **decision** rechtskräftiges Urteil, Gerichtsentscheidung; ~ **department** Rechtsabteilung, juristische Abteilung; ~ **dependent** Unterhaltsberechtigter; ~ **detriment** Rechtsnachteil; ~ **dictionary** Rechtswörterbuch; ~ **disadvantage** Rechtsnachteil; ~ **disability** Geschäfts-, Rechtsunfähigkeit; ~ **discretion** richterliches Ermessen; ~ **dispute** Rechtsfrage; ~ **distributee** Pflichtteilsberechtigter; ~ **document** öffentliche Urkunde; ~ **domicile** gesetzlicher Wohnsitz, Gerichtsstand; ~ **duty** Rechtspflicht; ~ **duty to use care** gesetzliche Sorgfaltspflicht; ~ **eagle** *(sl.)* höchst gerissene Staranwalt; ~ **editor** für Rechtsfragen zuständiger Redakteur; ~ **education** juristische Ausbildung; ~ **effect** Rechtswirkung; ~ **entity** juristische Person, Rechtsfigur, -persönlichkeit; ~ **estate** dingliches Eigentumsrecht; ~ **ethics** juristische Standespflichten; ~ **evidence** zugelassenes Beweismaterial; ~ **excuse** gesetzlicher Schuldausschließungsgrund; ~ **expert** juristischer Sachverständiger, Jurist; ~ **expression** Rechtsbegriff; ~ **extinction** Ungültigkeitserklärung; ~ **fare** gesetzlich festgelegter Fahrpreis; ~ **fees** Anwaltsgebühren; ~ **fiction** juristische (gesetzliche) Fiktion; ~ **force** Rechtskraft, -gültigkeit, -wirksamkeit, Gesetzeskraft; **of** ~ **force** rechtskräftig, -wirksam; **of no** ~ **force** rechtsunwirksam; **to have** ~ **force** Rechts-, Gesetzeskraft haben; ~ **form** Rechtsform; ~ **formalism** Rechtsformalismus; ~ **formality** Rechtsformalität, juristische Formalität; ~ **framework** gesetzlicher Rahmen; ~ **fraud** Untreue, Unterschlagung; ~ **functions** juristische Aufgaben; ~ **government** rechtmäßige Regierung; ~ **ground** Rechtsgrund; **to have firmer** ~ **ground** bessere Rechtsposition haben; ~ **guardian** gesetzlicher Vormund; ~ **hazard** juristisches Risiko; ~ **heir** rechtmäßiger Erbe; ~ **holiday** *(US)* gesetzlicher (öffentlicher) Feiertag; ~ **hypothec** gesetzlich entstandene Hypothek; ~ **incapacity** Rechts-, Geschäftsunfähigkeit; ~ **injury** Rechtsverletzung; ~ **insanity** Geschäftsunfähigkeit wegen Geisteskrankheit, Unzurechnungsfähigkeit; ~ **instrument** Rechtsdokument; ~ **interest** rechtlich anerkanntes Interesse, *(real estate law)* Grundstücksrecht; ~ **interest in land** Recht an einem Grundstück; ~ **interest rate** gesetzlicher Zinssatz, -fuß; ~ **investment** *(US)* mündelsichere Kapitalanlage (Anlagepapiere); ~ **issue** *(last will)* Nachkommen; **to be in** ~ **jeopardy** einem Strafverfahren ausgesetzt sein; ~ **knowledge** Rechtskenntnis; ~ **language** Juristen-, Rechtssprache, Sprache der Juristen; ~ **lexicon** Rechtswörterbuch; ~ **liability** gesetzliche Haftpflicht, *(public accountant)* gesetzliche Haftung des Betriebsprüfers; ~ **liability insurance** Haftpflichtversicherung bis zur Höhe der gesetzlichen Haftpflicht; ~ **literature** Rechtsliteratur, juristische Literatur; ~ **malice** vermuteter Vorsatz; ~ **man** rechtsfähige Person, Rechtspersönlichkeit; ~ **marriage** rechtsgültige Ehe; **in** ~ **and nonlegal matters** gerichtlich und außergerichtlich; ~ **maxim** Rechtsmaxime, -grundsatz; ~ **mind** juristischer Verstand; ~ **mortgage** *(Br.)* Ersthypothek; ~ **name** Vor- und Nachname; ~ **negligence** Außerachtlassen der im Verkehr erforderlichen Sorgfalt; ~ **notice to quit** gesetzlich zugelassene Kündigung; ~ **obligation** rechtliche Verpflichtung, Rechtspflicht; ~ **obligation to support** Unterhaltspflicht; ~ **offence** Rechtsverletzung; ~ **officer** Justizbeamter; ~ **opinion** Rechtsgutachten; ~ **order** gesetzliche Anweisung; ~ **owner** formeller Eigentümer; ~ **person** juristische Person, Rechtspersönlichkeit; ~ **personality** Rechtspersönlichkeit; ~ **phrase** Rechtsausdruck, juristischer Fachdruck; ~ **phraseology** Rechtssprache; ~ **position** Rechtslage, -stellung, -position; ~ **possessor** rechtmäßiger Besitzer (Eigentümer); ~ **practitioner** Rechtskundiger, Jurist; ~ **prejudice** Rechtsnachteil; ~ **presumption** Rechtsvermutung; ~ **principle** Rechtsprinzip, -grundsatz; ~ **proceeding** Gerichtsverfahren; **to carry on (institute)** ~ **proceedings** prozessieren, gerichtliche Schritte einleiten; **to take** ~ **proceedings for the recovery of debts** Schulden einklagen; **by** ~ **process** auf dem Rechtswege, gerichtlich; ~ **procedure** Prozeßwesen; ~ **profession** Anwaltsberuf, Anwaltschaft; **to go into the** ~ **profession** Jurist werden, Juristenlaufbahn einschlagen; ~ **protection** Rechtsschutz; ~ **provision** gesetzliche Bestimmung; ~ **publication** rechtswirksame Veröffentlichung; ~ **quay** *(Br.)* Zollkai; ~ **qualification** juristische Ausbildung; ~ **question** Rechtsfrage; ~ **rate** *(railway)* anerkannter Tarif; ~ **rate of interest** gesetzlicher Zinssatz; **for** ~ **reasons** aus Rechtsgründen; ~ **redress** gerichtliche Abhilfe, Rechtsmittel; **to create** ~ **relations** Rechtsverhältnis begründen; ~ **relationship** Rechtsverhältnis; ~ **remedy** gesetzliche Abhilfe, Rechtsmittel; ~ **representative** gesetzlicher (rechtmäßiger) Vertreter; ~ **requirement** *(banking)* gesetzlich

vorgeschriebenes Deckungsverhältnis; ~ **rescission** von den Parteien vereinbarte Vertragsaufhebung; ~ **personal representative** Testamentsvollstrecker; ~ **reserve** *(banking, life insurance)* gesetzliche Rücklage; ~ **residence** gesetzlicher Wohnsitz; **not to accept** ~ **responsibilities** Rechtsfolgen ausschließen; ~ **reversion** [siebenjähriges] Umwandlungsrecht; ~ **right** Rechtsanspruch [nach Landrecht]; ~ **rule** Rechtsnorm, -satz; ~ **security** *(US)* mündelsichere Anlage; ~ **separation** Trennung von Tisch und Bett, Ehetrennung; ~ **sequence** Rechtsfolge; ~ **session** Sitzungsperiode; **to apply a new** ~ **standard** neue Rechtsnormen zur Anwendung bringen; ~ **standing** Rechtsstellung; ~ **standing in court** prozessuale Stellung; ~ **status** Rechtsstellung; **to acquire** ~ **status** Rechtsposition (Rechtsstellung) erlangen; **to have** ~ **status** rechtsfähig sein; **to take** ~ **steps against s. o.** Rechtsweg gegen j. beschreiten; ~ **strike** ordnungsgemäß durchgeführter Streik; ~ **subrogation** Rechtsübergang; ~ **successor** Rechtsnachfolger; ~ **succession** Rechtsnachfolge; ~ **system** Rechtssystem; ~ **tender** gesetzliches Zahlungsmittel; ~ **tender bonds** *(US)* in gesetzlichen Zahlungsmitteln zahlbare Obligationen; ~ **tender notes** *(US)* als gesetzliches Zahlungsmittel geltende Banknoten; ~ **term** juristischer Fachausdruck, Rechtsausdruck; ~ **thing in action** gesetzliches Forderungsrecht; ~ **title** Volleigentum; ~ **training** juristische Ausbildung; **to have had** ~ **training** juristisch aus-, vorgebildet sein; ~ **transaction** Rechtsgeschäft; **to be brought to a** ~ **trial** ordnungsgemäß abgeurteilt werden; ~ **usufruct** Nießbrauch an Rechten, Rechtsnießbrauch; ~ **validity** Rechtsgültigkeit; ~ **view** Rechtsauffassung; ~ **viewpoint** Rechtsstandpunkt; ~ **voter** Wahlberechtigter; ~ **wilfulness** bewußte Nichtbeachtung gesetzlicher Haftpflicht; ~ **writer** juristischer Schriftsteller; ~ **year** Abschluß-, Kalenderjahr.

legalese *(US sl.)* juristischer Fachjargon.

legalism Rechtsformalismus, Juristensprache, Paragraphenreiterei.

legality Gesetz-, Rechtsmäßigkeit, Rechtsgültigkeit; **to challenge the** ~ **of official actions** Rechtmäßigkeit amtlicher Maßnahmen nachprüfen lassen.

legalization amtliche Beglaubigung, Legalisierung.

legalize *(v.) (make lawful)* Rechtsgültigkeit verleihen, amtlich beglaubigen (bestätigen), legalisieren; ~ **an invoice** Faktura beglaubigen.

legally gesetzlich, rechtmäßig; ~ **adopted** ordnungsgemäß adoptiert; ~ **binding** rechtsverbindlich; ~ **contributing cause of injury** entscheidende Ursache einer Verletzung; ~ **committed** aufgrund eines Haftbefehls inhaftiert; ~ **competent** geschäftsfähig; ~ **constituted court** ordnungsgemäß besetztes Gericht; ~ **determined** gesetzlich festgelegt; ~ **effective** rechtswirksam; ~ **justifiable** juristisch vertretbar (haltbar); ~ **liable** haftpflichtig, haftbar; ~ **operating automobile** zugelassenes Auto; ~ **protected** gesetzlich geschützt; ~ **qualified** zugelassen; ~ **qualified voter** in der Wahlliste eingetragener Wähler; ~ **resident** mit Wohnsitz; ~ **responsible** voll verantwortlich, geschäftsfähig; ~ **sufficient evidence** für die Urteilsfindung ausreichendes Beweismaterial.

legate Legat, päpstlicher Gesandter.

legatee Testamentserbe, Vermächtnisnehmer; **general** ~ Generalvermächtnisnehmer; **residuary** ~ Nachvermächtnisnehmer; **sole** ~ *(US)* Universalerbe, Gesamterbe; **specific** ~ Einzelvermächtnisnehmer; **universal** ~ Universal-, Haupterbe.

legation Gesandschaft, *(building)* Gesandschaftsgebäude, *(personnel)* Gesandschaftspersonal.

legator Erblasser, Vermächtnisgeber, Testator.

legatorial erblasserisch.

legend Sage, Legende, *(print.)* Bildunterschrift, Legende, *(on coin)* Umschrift, *(explanatory statement)* Erklärung.

legerdemainist Gaukler, Taschenspieler.

legible leserlich, lesbar.

legion Legion; **British** ⌖ Frontkämpferverband; **Foreign** ⌖ Fremdenlegion; ⌖ **of Hono(u)r** Ehrenlegion.

legionary Legionär, *(Br.)* Angehöriger des Frontkämpferverbands.

legislate *(v.)* Gesetze erlassen; ~ **against gambling** Gesetz gegen Glückspiele erlassen; ~ **a corporation into existence** Körperschaft durch Gesetzgebung ins Leben rufen; ~ **s. o. out of office** j. durch Amtsaufhebung um seine Stellung bringen.

legislation Gesetzgebung; **antilabo(u)r** ~ gewerkschaftsfeindliche Gesetzgebung; **commercial** ~ Handelsgesetzgebung; **consumer protection** ~

Gesetzgebung zum Schutz des Verbrauchers; **cost-increasing** ~ Kostenlawine auslösende Gesetzgebung; **concurrent** ~ konkurrierende Gesetzgebung; **emergency** ~ Notstandsgesetzgebung; **foreign-exchange** ~ Devisengesetzgebung; **industrial** ~ Gewerbegesetzgebung; **internal** ~ Landesgesetzgebung; **labo(u)r** ~ Arbeiter[schutz]gesetzgebung; **municipal (national)** ~ inländische Gesetzgebung; **permissive** ~ Kannbestimmungen; **prolabo(u)r** ~ gewerkschaftsfreundliche Gesetzgebung; **prospective** ~ zukünftige Gesetzgebung; **retroactive (ex-post-facto)** ~ Gesetzgebung mit rückwirkender Kraft; **social** ~ Sozialgesetzgebung; **subordinate** ~ delegierte Gesetzgebung; **watered-down** ~ verwässerte Gesetzgebung;
~ **in force** geltende Gesetzgebung; ~ **by reference** Änderungsgesetzgebung;
to alter the ~ **in force** gültige Gesetze abändern; **to enact** ~ Gesetze erlassen; **to initiate** ~ Gesetze einbringen, Gesetzgebung initiieren; **to update** ~ Gesetzgebung auf den neuesten Stand bringen.

legislative Legislative, gesetzgebende Gewalt;
quasi-~ gesetzgebungsähnlich;
~ **act** Gesetzgebungsakt; **by** ~ **action** auf dem Gesetzgebungsweg; ~ **assembly** gesetzgebende Versammlung; ~ **body** gesetzgebende Körperschaft; ~ **branch** gesetzgebendes Organ; ~ **budget** (US) Haushaltsgesetz; ~ **business** Angelegenheit des Gesetzgebers; ~ **committee** Gesetzgebungsausschuß; ~ **council** gesetzgeberischer Rat; ~ **court** Verwaltungs-, Sondergericht; ~ **department** (US) Legislative; ~ **expenses** Kosten der Rechtsprechung; ~ **function** Gesetzgebungsfunktion; ~ **initiative** gesetzgeberische Initiative; ~ **intent** Absicht des Gesetzgebers; ~ **investigation** (parl., US) Ausschußuntersuchung; ~ **motive** Motiv des Gesetzgebers; ~ **package** Gesetzespaket; ~ **period** Legislaturperiode; ~ **policy** Gesetzgebungspolitik; ~ **power** gesetzgebende Gewalt, Legislative; ~ **prerogative** Gesetzgebungskompetenz; ~ **probe of banking practices** (US) Bankenenquete; ~ **procedure** Gesetzgebungsverfahren; ~ **process** Gesetzgebungsverfahren; ~ **program(me)** Gesetzgebungsprogramm; ~ **proposal** Gesetzesvorschlag; ~ **provisions** Rechtsvorschriften; ~ **reforms** Reformen des Gesetzgebers; ~ **session** Legislaturperiode; ~ **style** Gesetzgeberstil; ~ **treaty** normativer Vertrag;
~ (a.) gesetzgebend, gesetzlich, legislativ.
legislator Gesetzgeber.
legislatorial gesetzgeberisch.
legislature (lawmaking body) Legislative, gesetzgebende Körperschaft, (period) Legislaturperiode, (US) Parlament [eines Einzelstaates].
legist Rechtskundiger, -gelehrter, Jurist.
legitim (Scot.) Pflichtteil.
legitimacy Gesetz-, Rechtmäßigkeit, (lawful birth) eheliche Geburt, Ehelichkeit, Legitimität;
to contest the ~ Ehelichkeit anfechten.
legitimate rechtlich, rechtmäßig, gesetzlich, gesetzmäßig, begründet, (of birth) ehelich, legitim;
~ (v) legalisieren, (bastard) für ehelich erklären;
~ **birth** eheliche Geburt; ~ **business expenses** steuerlich anerkannte Geschäftsunkosten; ~ **child** eheliches Kind; ~ **claim** berechtigter Anspruch; ~ **conclusion** berechtigte Schlußfolgerung; ~ **consignee** Empfangsberechtigter; ~ **costs** rechtlich zulässige Kosten; ~ **descent** eheliche Abstammung; ~ **doubt** berechtigter Zweifel; ~ **government** rechtmäßige Regierung; ~ **hope** berechtigte Hoffnung; ~ **interest** berechtigtes Interesse; ~ **king** rechtmäßiger König; ~ **offspring** eheliche Abkömmlinge; ~ **portion** Pflichtteil; ~ **proceedings** rechtmäßiges Verfahren; **to use public money for** ~ **purposes only** öffentliche Gelder bestimmungsgemäß ausgeben; ~ **reasons** berechtigte Gründe.
legitimation Legitimation, Legitimierung, Legalisierung, (bastard) Ehelichkeitserklärung;
~ **of a child** Anerkenntnis eines Kindes; ~ **by subsequent matrimony** Legitimation durch nachfolgende Heirat.
legitimization Legitimation, Legitimierung.
legitimatize (v.) legitimieren.
leisure Muße, frei verfügbare (freie) Zeit, Freizeit;
at ~ unbeschäftigt, [dienst]frei; **at one's** ~ in seiner Freizeit;
to be seldom at ~ selten Zeit zur Muße haben; **to do s. th. at** ~ etw. in aller Ruhe tun; **to enjoy some** ~ seine Freizeit genießen; **to have** ~ **for reading** Zeit zum Lesen haben; **to scant s. o. in** ~ jem. nur geringe Freizeit lassen;
~ **activities** Freizeitgestaltung, -bereich; ~ **area** Freizeitgebiet; ~ **business** Freizeitindustrie; ~ **complex** Freizeitkomplex; ~ **education** Fortbildungsmöglichkeiten in der Freizeit; ~ **facility**

Freizeitanlage; ~ **hours** dienstfreie Zeit, Mußezeit, Muße-, Ruhestunden; ~ **industry** Freizeitindustrie; ~ **interests** Freizeitinteressen; ~ **items** Freizeitartikel; ~ **package** Freizeitangebot; ~ **products** Freizeiterzeugnisse, -artikel; ~ **pursuit** Freizeitbeschäftigung; ~ **time** freie Zeit, Freizeit; **to organize one's** ~ **time** seine Freizeit gestalten; **to spend one's** ~ **time** seine Freizeit verbringen; **to throw away one's** ~ **time** seine Freizeit vergeuden; ~**-time activities** Freizeitgestaltung; ~**-time market** Freizeitmarkt; ~**-time needs** Freizeitbedürfnisse; ~**-time service** Freizeitdienstleistungen; ~ **wear** Freizeitkleidung.
leisured frei, müßig, nicht arbeitsmäßig verplant;
~ **classes** begüterte Klassen, wohlhabender Bevölkerungsteil.
leisurely gemächlich, ohne Hast;
to do s. th. in a ~ **fashion** sich Muße für etw. nehmen; ~ **journey** Reise in Etappen; ~ **pace** gemächliches Tempo; ~ **walk along the boulevards** gemächlicher Bummel über die Prachtstraßen.
lemon (sl.) Niete, Versager.
lend (fam.) Anleihe;
~ (v.) [ver]leihen, ausleihen, Darlehen geben;
~ **o. s. to s. th.** sich zu etw. hergeben;
~ **one's aid to s. th.** einer Sache Unterstützung gewähren; ~ **[out] books** Bücher ausleihen; ~ **on bottomry** auf Bodmerei geben; ~ **on collateral** Lombardkredit gewähren, lombardieren; ~ **for consumption purposes** Konsumkredit gewähren; ~ **day-to-day money** Tagesgeld ausleihen; ~ **dignity to s. th.** einer Sache Würde verleihen; ~ $ 2500 **on the documents** Dokumente mit 2500 Dollar beleihen; ~ **one's ear to s. o.** jem. zuhören (Gehör gewähren); ~ **an employee to s. o.** Angestellten zu jem. abstellen; ~ **long-term bond finance direct to major companies** größeren Unternehmen mit langfristigen Obligationen eine direkte Finanzierung gewähren; ~ **s. o. a helping hand** jem. behilflich sein; ~ **o. s. to illusions** sich Illusionen hingeben; ~ **itself to meditation** zur Meditation anregen; ~ **money on collateral** Effekten lombardieren; ~ **money on contango** Reportgeschäfte machen; ~ **money on goods** Waren lombardieren; ~ **money on an insurance policy** Versicherungspolice beleihen; ~ **money at interest** Geld auf Zinsen ausleihen; ~ **money free of interest** Kapital zinsfrei ausleihen; ~ **money on mortgage** Darlehen gegen Hypothekenbestellung geben, Hypothekardarlehen gewähren; ~ **one's name to s. th.** seinen Namen zu etw. hergeben; ~ **an officer** (mil.) Offizier abstellen; ~ **out** ausleihen; ~ **on seccurity** besicherten Kredit gewähren; ~ **at short interest** kurzfristiges Darlehen gewähren; ~ **one's soul to one's work** mit ganzer Seele bei der Arbeit sein; ~ **stock** Aktien ausleihen; ~ **money on stock** Aktien (Wertpapiere) lombardieren; ~ **o. s. to a transaction** sich zu einer Sache hergeben; ~ **up to 100 per cent of the valuation of a house** Haus zu 100% seines Wertes beleihen.
lend-lease (v.) (US) in Leihpacht überlassen.
Lend-Lease Act (US) Pacht- und Leihgesetz; ~ **Administration** (US) Pacht- und Leihverwaltung; ~ **aid** (US) Pacht- und Leihhilfe; ~ **bills** (US) Pacht- und Leihvertrags-Schulden; ~ **system** (US) Pacht- und Leihsystem.
lendable beleihbar.
lender Ausleiher, Verleiher, Anleihe-, Kredit-, Darlehnsgeber;
capital ~ Kapitalgeber; **marginal** ~ letztbereiter Kreditgeber; ~ **on bottomry** Bodmereigeber; ~ **of capital** Geld-, Kapitalgeber; ~ **of last resort** (Bank of England) letzte Refinanzierungsmöglichkeit, [etwa] Bundesnotenbank; ~ **of money** Geldverleiher;
to act as a ~ **of last resort** Rediskontkontingente zur Verfügung stellen.
lending Ver-, Ausleihen, Kredit-, Darlehnsgewährung, -bewilligung;
international ~ internationaler Kreditverkehr; **personal** ~ Personalkredite;
~ **on collateral (security)** Gewährung eines Lombardkredits; ~ **on current account** Kontokorrentausleihungen; ~ **on loan account** Kreditgewährung; ~ **to foreigners** Auslandskredite; ~ **to a group** Konzerndarlehen; ~ **or loaning money or credit** Darlehns-, Kreditgewährung; ~ **of money** Geldausleihung; ~ **to nonbank customers** Ausleihungen an Nichtbanken; ~ **to nonresidents** Darlehnsgewährung an Devisenausländer, Auslandskredite; ~ **out** Ausleihung;
government ~ **agency** staatliche Darlehnskasse; ~ **business** (banking) Darlehns-, Aktivgeschäfte, Debitorengeschäft; ~ **country** Gläubigerland; ~ **fee** Leihgebühr; ~ **institute** (institution) Darlehnsinstitut, Geldinstitut; ~ **library** Leihbibliothek; ~ **limit** Beleihungsgrenze; ~ **obligations** Ausleihungsverpflichtungen; **qualified** ~ **officer** erfahrener Kreditsachbearbeiter; ~ **operation** Darlehnsgeschäft; ~ **policy** Darlehns-, Kreditpolitik; ~ **power** Kreditpotential; ~ **practices** Darlehnsusancen;

program(me) Darlehns-, Kreditprogramm; ~ **rate** *(US)* Lombard-, Leih-, Kreditsatz; **public ~ right** Ausleihungsbefugnis; ~ **society** Vorschußverein; ~ **stop** Kreditsperre; ~ **terms** Ausleihungsbedingungen.

length Länge, Dauer, *(book)* Umfang;
at ~ ungekürzt; **at great ~** sehr ausführlich; **wave ~** Wellenlänge;
~ **of conversation** Gesprächsdauer; ~ **of copy** Manuskriptlänge; ~ **of credit** Kreditdauer; ~ **of employment** Beschäftigungsdauer, -zeit; **average ~ of holiday** durchschnittliche Urlaubsdauer; ~ **of life** Lebensdauer; ~ **of line** Zeilenlänge; ~ **of notice** Kündigungsfrist; ~ **of a road** Straßenlänge; ~ **of service** Dienstzeit, -alter; ~ **of stay** Aufenthaltsdauer; ~ **of time** Zeitdauer; **reasonable ~ of time** angemessene Frist; ~ **of time needed for a job** benötigte Arbeitszeit;
to carry scepticism to some ~ Skeptizismus ziemlich weit treiben; **to dwell at too great ~ on details** sich in Einzelheiten verlieren; **to go to all ~s** aufs Ganze gehen; **to go to any ~ for s. o.** alles für j. tun; **to go to great ~s** sich sehr bemühen; **to go the whole ~** bis zum Äußersten gehen; **to go to the ~ of crime** bis an den Rand eines Verbrechens gehen; **to keep s. o. at arm's ~** j. auf Distanz halten; **to know the ~ of s. one's foot** jds. Schwächen (Grenzen) kennen; **to lecture s. o. at great ~** jem. eine ausführliche Gardinenpredigt halten; **to make a stay of some ~** sich eine gewisse Zeit aufhalten; **to speak at some ~ on a subject** sich eingehend über ein Thema verbreiten; ~ **margin** Längentoleranz.

lengthen *(v.)* | **life** Leben verlängern; ~ **out** sich in die Länge ziehen.

lengthening of working hours Arbeitszeitverlängerung.

lengthy weitschweifig, langatmig.

leniency Nachsicht, Milde.

lens *(photo)* Linse;
supplementary ~ Vorsatzlinse;
~ **screen** Gegenlichtblende.

leonine | **contract** leoninischer Vertrag; ~ **partnership** leoninische Gesellschaft.

leper policy Aussätzigenpolitik.

lese majesty Majestätsbeleidigung.

lesion Schädigung, Funktionsstörung.

less ab[züglich], minus;
~ **charges** abzüglich Unkosten; ~ **interest accrued** unter Abzug der Zinsen; ~ **tax** nach Steuern.

less-than-carload *(railroad, US)* Stückgut[sendung];
~ *(a.)* als Stückgut;
~ **delivery** Stückgutzustellung; ~ **freight** *(US)* Stückgutsendung; ~ **freight charges** Stückguttarif; ~ **lot** *(US)* Stückgut; ~ **shipment** Stückgutsendung; ~ **traffic** Stückgutverkehr.

less-than-truckload *(US)* Lastwagenteilsendung, Stückgut;
~ **rate** Stückguttarif.

lessee Pächter, Mieter;
master ~ Hauptmieter.

lessen *(v.)* vermindern, herabsetzen;
~ **s. one's services** jds. Verdienste schmälern; ~ **one's speed** seine Geschwindigkeit vermindern.

lessening of tensions Verminderung von Spannungen.

lesser of two evils das kleinere Übel.

lesson Lektion, Lehr-, Unterrichtsstunde, *(school work)* Schularbeit, Aufgabe, *(warning)* Denkzettel, Lektion;
private ~s Nachhilfestunden, -unterricht;
~**s in deportment** Anstandsunterricht; ~**s of experience** auf Erfahrung gegründete Lehren; ~**s in French** Französischunterricht;
~ *(v.)* Unterricht erteilen;
to be a ~ for s. o. Lehre für j. sein; **to cancel a ~** Unterricht ausfallen lassen; **to draw a ~ from s. o.** Unterricht von jem. erhalten; **to give ~s** Stunden geben, Unterricht erteilen; **to give private ~s** Privat-, Nachhilfeunterricht geben; **to learn one's ~** durch Fehler weise werden; **to prepare one's ~s** seine Schularbeiten machen, sich für die Schule vorbereiten; **to read s. o. a ~** jem. einen Verweis erteilen; **to take ~s from s. o.** Unterricht bei jem. nehmen.

lessor Verpächter, Vermieter;
master ~ Hauptvermieter;
~ **of a flat** Vermieter eines Appartements;
to allow the ~ to view the state of repair of the premises dem Verpächter ein Inspektionsrecht über den Reparaturzustand auszuüben gestatten; **to revert to the ~** dem Erbpächter zufallen;
~ **company** verpachtende Gesellschaft; ~**'s lien** Vermieterpfandrecht.

let *(Br.)* Vermieten, Vermietung, Verpachtung;
without ~ or hindrance ohne jede Behinderung;
not to get a ~ for one's house keinen Mieter für sein Haus finden;
~ *(v.)* lassen, erlauben, *(lease)* vermieten, verpachten;
~ **alone** in Ruhe lassen; ~ **a bail** Haftverschonung gegen Kautionsstellung gewähren; ~ **bygones be bygones** Vergangenes ruhen lassen; ~ **the cat out of the bag** *(coll.)* Katze aus dem Sack lassen; ~ **a boat for hire for the purpose of pleasure only** Boot zu reinen Vergnügungszwecken vermieten; ~ **at commercial rents** gewerbsmäßig verpachten; ~ **for $ 4000 a year** 4000 Dollar im Jahr an Miete bringen; ~ **a farm to a tenant** Hof verpachten; ~ **a flat** *(Br.)* Wohnung vermieten; ~ **o. s. go** sich gehen lassen; ~ **o. s. go on a subject** sich zu einem Thema uneingeschränkt äußern; ~ **fall a hint of one's intentions** Andeutung über seine Absichten fallen lassen; ~ **have** überlassen; ~ **on hire** vermieten, verpachten; ~ **a house furnished** Haus möbliert vermieten; ~ **it go at that** es dabei bewenden lassen; ~ **a matter drop** Sache fallenlassen; ~ **an opportunity slip** sich eine Gelegenheit entgehen lassen; ~ **it pass** durchgehen lassen, darüber hinwegschauen; ~ **at a full rent** zu normalen Sätzen verpachten; ~ **at a full commercial rent** zu Geschäftszwecken vermieten; ~ **on an annual agricultural tenancy** jahrweise zur landwirtschaftlichen Nutzung verpachten; ~ **well** sich gut vermieten lassen.

let *(v.)* **down** herunterlassen, *(fig.)* im Stich (aufsitzen) lassen;
~ **s. o. by £ 100** j. um hundert Pfund bringen; ~ **the fire** Feuer ausgehen lassen; ~ **a firm** Firma herunterwirtschaften; ~ **s. o. gently** j. auf eine Zurücksetzung schonend vorbereiten;
to have been badly ~ ganz schön hereingelegt worden sein.

let in *(v.)* einlassen, *(deceive)* betrügen, hereinlegen;
~ **o. s.** sich selbst Zugang verschaffen; ~ **o. s. for** sich auf etw. einlassen, sich auf den Hals laden; ~ **s. o. for s. th.** jem. etw. einbrocken (aufhalsen); ~ **s. o. in for the expenses** j. gegen Erstattung der Spesen beteiligen; ~ **s. o. on a good thing** *(stock exchange)* j. an einem guten Geschäft beteiligen; ~ **o. s. with a latch-key** Tür mit einem Drücker öffnen; ~ **s. o. on a secret** j. in ein Geheimnis einweihen;
to have been ~ for a speech zu einer Rede verdonnert worden sein.

let *(v.)* **s. o. into** | **a building** j. in ein Gebäude hereinlassen; ~ **a secret** j. in ein Geheimnis einweihen.

let off *(v.)* laufen *(davonkommen)* lassen, *(fire)* abfeuern;
~ **s. o.** jem. die Strafe erlassen; ~ **s. o. from his engagement** j. freigeben; ~ **fireworks** Feuerwerk veranstalten; ~ **flat** möblierte Wohnung vermieten; ~ **a house into flats** Haus in Einzelwohnungen (an Einzelmieter) vermieten; ~ **with a fine** mit einer Geldstrafe davonkommen lassen; ~ **s. o. a penalty** jem. eine Strafe erlassen; ~ **a property as a whole** Grundstück pauschal vermieten.

let *(v.)* **out** ausplaudern, *(discharge, sl.)* feuern, *(give out on contract)* Auftrag vergeben, *(let on lease)* verpachten;
~ **the air of the tyres** Luft aus den Reifen herauslassen; ~ **on hire** bewegliche Sachen vermieten; ~ **on lease** verpachten; ~ **works and supplies** Arbeiten und Lieferungen vergeben;
to be ~ on bail gegen Kaution freigelassen werden.

let *(v.)* | **s. o. over the factory** jem. eine Fabrikbesichtigung gestatten; ~ **s. o. through an exam** *(fam.)* j. durch ein Examen durchlassen.

let *(v.)* **up** aufhören, ablassen;
~ **on a pursuit** Verfolgung aufgeben.

let *(a.)* vermietet, verpachtet;
to be ~ with immediate possession bezugsfertig zu vermieten; ~**-alone principle** Grundsatz des freien Wettbewerbs (der freien Wirtschaft); ~**-out** *(fig.)* Schlupfloch.

letch for power *(sl.)* Machtgier.

letdown plötzliche Flaute, Rückgang, Abnahme, Nachlassen;
~ **in sales** Abschwächung des Umsatzes, Absatzflaute, Absatz-, Umsatzrückgang.

lethal weapon *(Scot.)* tödliche Waffe.

letoff *(punishment)* Erlassen einer Strafe.

letout *(sl.)* Rausschmiß, Gefeuertwerden.

letter *(character)* Buchstabe, *(epistle)* Brief, Schreiben, *(one who lets)* Vermieter, Verpächter, *(print.)* Type, Schrift[art];
by ~ in Briefform, brieflich, schriftlich; **in accordance with the ~ of the law** formalrechtlich; **in ~ and in spirit** dem Buchstaben und dem Inhalt nach; **in receipt of your ~** im Besitz Ihres Briefes; **in reply to your ~** in Beantwortung Ihres Briefes; **to the ~** buchstäblich; **when looking through my ~s** bei Durchsicht meiner Korrespondenz; **with reference (referring) to your ~** mit Bezugnahme auf Ihr Schreiben;
~**s** Briefschaften;

accompanying ~ Begleit, Anschreiben; **adjustment** ~ ausgleichender Brief; **allotment** ~ *(Br.)* Bezugsrechtsmitteilung, Zuteilungsschein, -anzeige; **anonymous** ~ anonymer Brief; **attached** ~ anliegendes Schreiben, Anlage; **battered** ~ beschädigter (lädierter) Buchstabe; **begging** ~ Bettelbrief; **black** ~ *(print.)* Faktur; **blackmailing** ~ Erpresserbrief; **blind** ~ unbestellbarer Brief; **block** ~s Druckbuchstaben, -schrift, Blockschrift; **bread-and-butter** ~ Kutscherbrief; **broken** ~ beschädigter Buchstabe; **business** ~ Geschäftsbrief; **cable** ~ Brieftelegramm; **caller's** ~ postlagernder Brief; **capital** ~ großer Buchstabe; **chain** ~ Kettenbrief; **circular** ~ Rundschreiben; ~s **citatory** schriftliche Vorladung; **collection** ~ Inkassoschreiben; **commercial** ~ Geschäftsbrief; **compound** ~ *(print.)* Doppelbuchstabe; **confidential** ~ vertraulicher Brief; **congratulatory** ~ Gratulations-, Glückwunschschreiben; **covering** ~ Begleitschreiben; ~s **credential** *(dipl.)* Beglaubigungsschreiben; **cut-out** ~ aus ausgeschnittenen Buchstaben zusammengesetzter Brief; **day** ~ [Tages]brieftelegramm; **dead** ~ unbestellbarer Brief; ~s **dismissory** Entlassungsschreiben; **double** ~ Doppelbrief; **draft** ~ Briefentwurf; **dropped** ~ ausgefallener Buchstabe; **enclosed** ~ anliegendes Schreiben; ~s **exchanged** frühere Korrespondenz; **express** ~ *(Br.)* Eilbrief; **follow-up** ~ *(advertising)* nachfassender Werbebrief; **form** ~ Briefmuster; **handwritten** ~ Handschreiben; **illuminated** ~ handkolorierter Buchstabe; **incoming** ~ Briefeingang; **insured** ~ *(Br.)* Wertbrief; **late** ~ zu spät aufgegebener Brief; **libellous** ~ beleidigendes Schreiben; **local** ~ Ortsbrief; **misplaced** ~ Irrläufer; **model** ~ Briefmuster; **monitory** ~ Erinnerungs-, Mahnschreiben, Mahnbrief; **night** ~ *(US)* Brieftelegramm; **official** ~ amtliches Schreiben, Amtschreiben, *(school)* blauer Brief; **open** ~ offener Brief; **outgoing** ~ auslaufender Brief; ~s **overt** Patenturkunde; **[post]-paid** ~ frankierter Brief; **patent** ~ Bestallungs-, Ernennungs-, Patenturkunde; **personal** ~ persönlicher Brief; **post-office-box** ~ postlagernder Brief; **posted** ~ mit der Post beförderter Brief; **pre-collection** ~ letzte Mahnung vor der Zwangsbeitreibung; **prepaid** ~ frankierter Brief; **previous** ~s vorhergehende Briefe; **private** ~ Privatbrief; **process** ~s vervielfältigte Briefe; **raised** ~ erhabener Buchstabe; **recommendatory** ~ Empfehlungs-, Befürwortungs-, Einführungsschreiben; **registered** ~ eingeschriebener Brief, Einschreiben; **resignation** ~ Austrittserklärung; **returned** ~ zurückgesandter Brief; ~s **rogatory** *(US)* Rechtshilfeersuchen; **Roman** ~[s] *(print.)* Antiqua[schrift], -buchstaben; **rubricated** ~s Buchstaben in roter Schrift; **sales** ~ Verkaufsbrief; **sea** ~ Schiffspaß; **second-class** ~ Briefdrucksache; **separate** ~ Sonderschreiben; **short-paid** ~ ungenügend frankierter Brief; **small** ~ Kleinbuchstabe; **special delivery** ~ *(US)* Eilbrief; **specimen sales** ~ Musterverkaufsbrief; **split** ~ Bezugsrechtsschreiben; **stamped** ~ frankierter Brief; ~s **testamentary** *(US)* Testamentsvollstreckerzeugnis; **thank-you** ~ Dankesbrief; **threatening** ~ Drohbrief; **unclaimed** ~ nicht abgeholter (unbehobener) Brief; **undated** ~ undatierter Brief; **unpaid** ~ unfrankierter Brief; **unregistered** ~ gewöhnlicher Brief; **warrant** ~ *(US)* Garantieschein; **strongly worded** ~ geharnischter Brief; **your esteemed** ~ Ihr geschätztes Schreiben;

~s **of abolition** *(prosecution)* Einstellungsanweisung; ~ **of acceptance** Annahmeerklärung; ~ **confirming an acceptance** Bestätigungsbrief; ~ **before action** einer Klage vorausgehender Anwaltsbrief; ~ **of acknowledgment** Bestätigungsbrief; ~s **of administration** Testamentsvollstreckerzeugnis; ~ **of administration with the will annexed** Testamentsvollstreckerbestellung durch das Gericht; ~ **of advice** Avis[brief], Anzeige, Benachrichtigungsschreiben; ~ **of advocation** Ansichziehen einer Sache durch ein höheres Gericht; ~ **of allotment** *(Br.)* Bezugsrechtsmitteilung, Zuteilungsanzeige; ~ **of apology** Absage-, Entschuldigungsbrief; ~ **of application** Antragsformular, Bewerbungsschreiben, *(for shares, Br.)* Zuteilungsantrag; ~ **of appointment** Ernennungs-, Bestallungsurkunde; ~ **of approbation** Genehmigungsschreiben; ~ **of attorney** Bevollmächtigungsschreiben, *(lawsuit, US)* Prozeßvollmacht; ~ **of authority** Bevollmächtigungsschreiben, *(letter of credit)* Akkreditivermächtigung; ~ **of authorization** Ermächtigungsschreiben; ~s **of business** *(Br.)* Gewerbelizenz; ~ **to be called for** postlagernder Brief; ~ **of charge** *(banking, Br.)* Zweckbestätigung; ~ **in clear** Klarschriftbrief; ~ **of commendation** Belobigungsschreiben; ~ **of complaint** Beschwerdebrief; ~ **of condolence** Kondolenzbrief, -schreiben; ~ **of congratulation** Gratulations-, Glückwunschschreiben; ~ **of consignment** Frachtbrief; ~ **of conveyance** Frachtbrief; ~ **of convocation** Einberufungsschreiben; ~[s] **of credence** *(dipl.)* Beglaubigungsschreiben.

letter of credit Akkreditiv, [Reise]kreditbrief; **circular** ~ Reisekredit-, Zirkularkreditbrief; **commercial** ~ *(US)* unwiderruflicher Warenkreditbrief, Rembourskredit; **confirmed** ~ bestätigtes Akkreditiv, bestätigter Kreditbrief; **direct** ~ an eine bestimmte Bank gerichteter Kreditbrief; **documentary** ~ Dokumentarakkreditiv; **export** ~ Exportkreditbrief; **import** ~ Importkreditbrief; **irrevocable** ~ unwiderrufliches Akkreditiv; **mutual** ~ Gegenakkreditiv; **open** ~ Inhaberkreditbrief; **revocable** ~ widerruflicher Kreditbrief, widerrufliches Akkreditiv; **revolving** ~ sich automatisch erneuerndes Akkreditiv; **sight** ~ Kreditbrief, bei dem die dagegen gezogenen Wechsel bei Sicht fällig sind; **straight** ~ Kreditbrief, dessen Gültigkeit sofort nach Finanzierung der darin spezifizierten Waren erlischt; **traveller's** ~ Reisekreditbrief; **unconfirmed** ~ unbestätigtes Akkreditiv; ~ **not yet utilized** noch nicht ausgenutzter Kreditbrief.

letter | **of no date** undatierter Brief; ~ **of delegation** Ermächtigungsschreiben, Inkassovollmacht; ~ **of dismissal** Entlassungsschreiben; ~ **to the editor** Eingesandt; ~ **of engagement** Anstellungsschreiben; ~ **of exchange** Wechsel, Tratte; ~ **to follow** Brief folgt; ~ **of grace** Moratorium; ~ **of grant** Bewilligungsschreiben; ~s **of guardianship** *(US)* Anordnung der Vormundschaft, Pflegschaftseinsetzungsbeschluß; ~ **in hand** vorliegender Brief; ~ **of hypothecation** *(Br.)* Verpfändungsurkunde beim Warenrembours; ~ **of indemnity** Ausfallbürgschaft, *(US)* Konnossementsgarantie; ~ **of indication** *(Br.)* **(identification)** beigefügte Unterschriftsprobe, Korrespondentenliste; ~ **of inquiry** schriftliches Auskunftsersuchen; ~ **of instruction** Verhaltensanweisung, schriftliche Anweisung; ~ **of intent** Bereitschafts-, Absichtserklärung; ~ **of introduction** Einführungs-, Empfehlungsbrief; ~ **of invitation** Einladungsschreiben; ~ **of the law** Buchstabe des Gesetzes; ~ **of licence** Fristverlängerung, Stundungsvereinbarung, *(bankruptcy proceedings)* Stillhalteerklärung der Gläubiger, Schuldenmoratorium; ~ **of lien** *(Br.)* Verpfändungsurkunde; ~ **offering a loan** schriftliches Darlehnsangebot; ~s **of intimation** *(Scot.)* Vorführungsbefehl; ~ **of naturalization** Einbürgerungsurkunde; ~ **of marque** Kaperbrief; ~ **requesting payment** Mahnbrief; ~ **of pledge** Verpfändungsurkunde; ~ **of postponement** Rangrücktrittserklärung; ~ **exempt from postage** portofreier Brief; ~ **of protection** Moratorium; ~ **of recall** *(dipl.)* Ab-, Zurückberufungsschreiben; ~ **of recommendation** Empfehlungsschreiben, Befürwortungsbrief; ~ **of recredentials** *(dipl.)* Bestätigungsschreiben; ~ **of regret** Absagebrief, *(stock exchange, Br.)* Mitteilung über die Ablehnung einer Aktienzuteilung; ~ **of reminder** Mahnbrief; ~ **of remittance** Rimessebrief; ~ **of renunciation** *(Br.)* Verzichtschreiben [auf Aktienzuteilung]; ~ **of reply** Antwortbrief; ~ **of representation** *(balance sheet)* Vollständigkeitserklärung; ~s **of request** *(Br.)* Rechtshilfeersuchen; ~ **of resignation** *(trade union)* Austrittserklärung; ~ **of respite** Stundung, Moratorium; ~ **of safe conduct** Geleitbrief; ~ **of setoff** *(bank)* Aufrechnungsvereinbarung; ~ **of sympathy** Beileidsbrief; ~ **of thanks** Danksagungsbrief, Dankbrief; ~ **terminating employment** Kündigungsbrief; ~ **of transmittal** Anschreiben, Begleitbrief; ~ **of trust** Sicherungsschein, Treuhandvereinbarung; ~s **that have passed between us** die zwischen uns gewechselten Briefe, unsere Korrespondenz; **solicitor's** ~ **of undertaking** schriftliche Verpflichtungserklärung eines Anwalts; ~ **of withdrawal** Kündigungsschreiben; ~ *(v.)* beschriften, mit Buchstaben bezeichnen;

to acknowledge the receipt of a ~ Briefempfang bestätigen; **to answer a** ~ Brief beantworten; **to be flooded with** ~s mit Briefen überflutet werden; **to break the seal of a** ~ Brief unberechtigt öffnen; **to bring a** ~ **to a close** Brief abschließen; **to build a** ~ Brief aufsetzen; **to call for a** ~ Brief abholen; **to carry out an order to the** ~ Auftrag buchstabengetreu ausführen; **to cash a** ~ **of credit** Kreditbrief einlösen; **to collect (fetch) one's** ~s **from the post office** seine Briefe von der Post abholen; **to confirm a** ~ Brief (brieflich) bestätigen; **to date a** ~ **ahead** Brief vordatieren; **to dead a** ~ Brief für unbestellbar erklären; **to deliver a** ~ Brief zustellen; **to dispatch a** ~ Brief absenden (aufgeben); **to draw up a** ~ Brief aufsetzen; **to drop a** ~ **into a mail box** Brief einwerfen; **to express a** ~ Brief als Eilbrief schicken; **to file a** ~ **away** Brief abheften; **to follow up a** ~ **with a summons** seinem Brief einen Zahlungsbefehl folgen lassen; **to get a** ~ **off** Brief expedieren; **to give a** ~ **an attractive look** Brief in ansprechender Form schreiben; **to go by the** ~ **of the law** sich an den Buchstaben des Gesetzes halten; **to grant** ~s **of administration** Testamentsvollstrecker einsetzen; **to hand s. o. a** ~ jem. einen Brief aushändigen; **to head a** ~ Brief beginnen; **to inform s. o. by** ~ j. brieflich unterrichten; **to intercept a** ~ Brief abfangen; **to**

issue a ~ **of credit** Kreditbrief ausstellen, Akkreditiv eröffnen; **to keep** ~**s** Brief aufheben; **to keep a copy of a** ~ Briefkopie behalten; **to keep the** ~ **of an agreement** Vereinbarung hundertprozentig erfüllen; **to let a** ~ **circulate** Brief umgehen (zirkulieren) lassen; **to lose a** ~ **in detail** Brief nicht in allen Einzelheiten mitbekommen; **to mail a** ~ *(US)* Brief zur Post geben; **to make a** ~ **private** Brief als persönlich kennzeichnen; **to misdirect a** ~ Brief fehlleiten; **to obey to the** ~ unbedingten Gehorsam leisten; **to open the** ~**s** Wahlbestimmen auszählen; **to open one's** ~**s** Post öffnen (aufmachen); **to open a** ~ **of credit** Akkreditiv eröffnen; **to pen a** ~ Brief verfassen; **to post a** ~ *(Br.)* Brief zur Post geben; **to read into a** ~ aus einem Brief herauslesen; **to receive** ~**s** Post bekommen; **to reply (respond) to a** ~ Brief beantworten; **to round off a** ~ Brief wirkungsvoll abschließen; **to run off a** ~ **on the typewriter** Brief auf der Schreibmaschine herunterrasseln; **to scribble a** ~ Brief hinhauen; **to send a** ~ **by hand** Brief durch Boten zustellen; **to send a** ~ **by registered post** *(Br.)* **(special handling, US)** Brief per Einschreiben schicken; **to sort out** ~**s** Briefe [ein]ordnen, Briefe aussortieren; **to stick to the** ~ **of an agreement** Vertrag wörtlich auslegen; **to suppress a** ~ Brief unterschlagen; **to take a** ~ **to the post office** Brief zur Post bringen; **to take out** ~**s of administration** sich zum Testamentsvollstrecker bestellen lassen; **to trace (track) down a** ~ Brief ausfindig machen; **to take one's stand on a** ~ sich auf einen Brief stützen; **to understand from a** ~ einem Brief entnehmen; **to write a** ~ **to s. o.** jem. einen Brief schreiben; **to write a** ~ **in a disguised hand** Brief mit verstellter Handschrift schreiben; ~ **bag** Briefbeutel, Postsack; ~ **balance** *(Br.)* Briefwaage; ~ **bomb** Briefbombe; ~ **book** Brieftage-, Kopierbuch, Briefordner; ~**s-despatched book** *(Br.)* Briefausgangsbuch; ~**s received book** Briefeingangsbuch; ~~**bound** am Buchstaben des Gesetzes klebend; ~ **box** Briefabholfach, Briefeinwurf; **to clear the** ~ **box** Briefkasten leeren; **to drop into the** ~ **box** Brief einwerfen; ~ **box system** *(espionage)* Briefkastensystem; ~ **calendar** Terminkalender; ~ **card** *(Br.)* Briefkarte; ~ **carrier** *(Br.)* Briefsortierer, *(US)* Briefträger; ~ **case** Brieftasche, -mappe, *(print.)* Setzkasten; **automatic** ~ **coding** *(sorting)* automatisches Briefverteilungssystem; ~**s column** Leserbriefspalte; ~ **cover** Briefumschlag; ~ **cutter** Brieföffnungsmaschine; ~ **delivery** Briefzustellung; ~~**directing scheme** Briefleitverfahren; ~ **drop** Briefeinwurf; ~ **file** Briefordner, Schnellhefter; ~~**folding machine** Brieffaltemaschine; ~ **founder** *(print.)* Schriftgießer; ~ **founding** Schriftguß; ~ **foundry** Schriftgießerei; ~ **learning** Buchgelehrsamkeit; ~ **lock** Buchstabenschloß; ~ **messenger** Briefbote; ~ **office** Postamt; ~ **opener** Brieföffner; ~~**opening machine** Brieföffnungsmaschine; ~ **pad** Briefblock; ~ **page** Leserbriefseite; ~ **paper** Briefpapier; ~**s patent** Patenturkunde; **to be** ~~**perfect** *(fig.)* äußerst korrekt sein, *(theater)* rollenfest sein; **to be** ~~**perfect in one's part** seine Rolle perfekt beherrschen; ~~**collecting place** Briefsammelstelle; ~~**directing place** Briefleitstelle; ~ **post** *(Br.)* Briefpost; **first-class** ~ **post** *(Br.)* vorrangig zugestellte Briefe; ~ **posting** Briefaufgabe, -einlieferung; **localized first-class** ~ **posting timetables** ortsgebundene Zeittafeln über die Abfertigung von Briefpost; **to maintain one's** ~ **prices among the cheapest in Europe** die niedrigsten Briefportotarife in Europa besitzen; ~ **punch** Locher; ~ **rate** *(Br.)* Briefporto; ~ **remittance** briefliche Überweisung; ~ **scales** *(US)* Briefwaage; ~~**sealing machine** Briefverschlußmaschine; ~ **sorter** Briefsortierer; **mechanized** ~ **sorting** automatische Briefsortiereinrichtung; ~ **spacing** Spationieren, Sperren; ~ **stamper** Briefstempel; ~ **stocks** *(US)* Aktien mit beschränkter Verwendungsfähigkeit; ~ **style** Briefstil; ~ **telegram** Brieftelegramm; ~ **traffic** Zahl der beförderten Briefe; ~ **worship** Buchstabengläubigkeit; ~ **writer** Briefschreiber; ~ **writing** Briefschreiben.

lettered studiert, gebildet.

lettergram Brieftelegramm.

letterhead Briefkopf, Schreibpapier mit eingedrucktem Briefkopf, *(business use)* Geschäftsbogen.

lettering Schriftschreiben, -zeichen, Buchstabenbezeichnung, Beschriften, Aufdruck;
~ **of a book cover** Buchaufdruck.

letterless ohne Post.

letterpress *(text)* Text, Druck, *(print.)* Briefkopier-, Druckerpresse;
~ **printing** Buchdruck.

letterweight Briefbeschwerer.

letting Verpachtung, Vermietung;
furnished ~**s** Vermietung möblierter Zimmer;
~ **of contract** *(US)* Auftragsvergabe; ~ **in** Einlassen, Einlaß; ~ **of lease** Verpachtung, Vermietung; ~ **out** *(prisoner)* Entlas-

sung; ~ **of rooms** Zimmervermietung; ~ **furnished or unfurnished rooms** Vermietung möblierter oder nicht möblierter Zimmer; ~ **of works and supplies** Auftragsvergabe; ~ **conditions** Pacht-, Mietbedingungen; ~ **expenses** Vermietungsaufwand; ~ **value** Miet-, Pachtwert.

lettuce *(sl.)* Papiergeld.

letup Unterbrechung, Nachlassen, Pause;
no ~ **in s. one's endeavo(u)rs** nie nachlassende Bemühungen; ~ **in inflation** nachlassende Inflation;
to work twelve hours without a ~ zwölf Stunden hindurch ununterbrochen arbeiten.

level [gleiche] Höhe, Niveau, Maßstab, *(land)* Fläche, ebenes Land, Ebene, *(mining)* Sohle, *(rank)* Rang, Stand, Stellung, Ansehen, *(technics)* Wasserwaage;
at all ~**s** auf allen Ebenen; **at cabinet** ~ auf Regierungsebene; **at executive** ~ in führender Stellung; **on a** ~ *(fig.)* auf gleicher Stufe (Ebene); **on the** ~ *(coll.)* ehrlich, offen; **on the highest** ~ auf höchster Ebene; **on the same** ~ auf gleicher Höhe (Stufe); **on middle-management** ~ auf dem Gebiet der mittleren Führungskräfte;
air ~ Lufthöhe; **astronomical** ~ astronomische Höhe; **bargain** ~ niedrigster Preis (Kurs); **Foreign Minister** ~ Außenministerebene; **government** ~ Regierungsebene; **high** ~ hoher Stand; **higher social** ~ höhere gesellschaftliche Ebene; **highest** ~ Höchstniveau; **inventive** ~ Erfindungshöhe; **low** ~ Tiefstand; **lowest** ~ *(prices)* Tiefststand; **peak** ~ Höhepunkt; **prescribed** ~ vorgeschriebene Höhe; **pre-oil-crisis** ~ Niveau vor der Ölkrise; **pre-war** ~ Vorkriegsstand; **price** ~ Kurs-, Preisniveau; **purchasing** ~**s** Stufen des Beschaffungsprozesses; **same** ~ gleiche Stufe; **sea** ~ Meeresspiegel; **subsistence** ~ Existenzminimum; **two-page** ~ doppeltes Priesniveau; **wage** ~ Lohnniveau; **water** ~ Grundwasserspiegel; **year-ago** ~ Vorjahrsniveau;
~ **of economic activity** Konjunkturniveau; ~ **of alcohol** Alkoholspiegel; ~ **of armaments** Rüstungsstand; ~ **of aspiration** Anspruchsniveau; **high** ~ **of public borrowing** hohe Kreditaufnahme der öffentlichen Hand; **general** ~ **of business** allgemeine Wirtschaftslage; **low** ~ **of industrial capacity utilization** geringer Auslastungsgrad der industriellen Kapazitäten; ~ **of earnings** Ertragsniveau; ~ **of education** Bildungsstand, -niveau; ~ **of efficiency** Leistungsgrad; ~ **of employment** Beschäftigungsstand; **the lowest** ~ **ever** absoluter Tiefstand; ~ **of exchange** Kursstand; ~ **of existence** Existenzstufe; **intermediate** ~ **of government** zweite staatliche Ebene; ~ **of income** Einkommensniveau; ~ **of inflation** Inflationsniveau; ~ **of invention** *(patent law)* Erfindungshöhe; ~ **of languages** Sprachenniveau; ~ **of liquidity** Liquiditätsgrad; **general** ~ **of liquidity and gearing** allgemeines Liquiditäts- und Kapitalintensitätsniveau; ~ **of living** *(US)* Lebensstandard; ~ **of management** Führungsniveau, -schwelle; ~ **of market demand** Marktsituation; ~ **of organization** Organisationsstufe; ~ **of output** Produktionsstand; ~ **of performance** Leistungsniveau, -stand; ~ **of population** Bevölkerungsstand; ~ **of premium** gleichbleibende Prämie; ~ **of prices** Preisstand, -niveau, *(stock exchange)* Kursstand; **high** ~ **of prices** Hochstand der Preise; **low** ~ **of prices** gedrücktes Kursniveau; ~ **of commodity prices at wholesale** Großhandelsindex; ~ **of production** Produktionsstand, -höhe, -niveau; ~ **of productivity** Produktivitätsniveau, -stand; ~ **of reassurance** Sicherheitsgrad; ~ **of relief** Unterstützungshöhe; ~ **of significance** *(statistics)* Signifikanzgrad; ~ **of spending** Ausgabenhöhe; ~ **of supply** Versorgungsstand; ~ **of technology** Stand der Technik; ~ **of unemployed** Grad der Arbeitslosigkeit; ~ **of wages** Lohnniveau; ~ **in the previous year** Vorjahresstand;
~ *(v.)* auf gleiche Höhe bringen, [ein]planieren, einebnen, nivellieren, ausgleichen, gleichmachen, *(US sl.)* ehrlich sein, Wahrheit sprechen;
~ **with s. o.** *(sl.)* j. anständig behandeln; ~ **an accusation against s. o.** Beschuldigungen gegen j. vorbringen; ~ **a building with the ground** Gebäude abreißen; ~ **down** *(wages)* Löhne herabsetzen; ~ **a road down** Straße planieren; ~ **with the ground** dem Erdboden gleichmachen; ~ **off** planieren, *(airplane)* abfangen, *(recession)* sich abschwächen; ~ **up** nach oben ausgleichen, *(wages)* erhöhen; ~ **up prices** Preise hinaufschrauben;
to be on a ~ **with s. o.** mit jem. auf gleicher Stufe stehen; **to be up to the** ~ an das Niveau heranreichen; **to carry to higher price** ~**s** zu Kurssteigerungen führen; **to come down to s. one's** ~ auf jds. Niveau herabsteigen; **to do one's** ~ **best** alles in seinen Kräften stehende tun; **to draw** ~ **with s. o.** mit jem. gleichziehen, j. einholen; **to find one's own** ~ Platz einnehmen, der einem zukommt; **to fix the** ~ **of pay** Gehaltsrahmen festlegen; **to have found one's own** ~ seinen Platz in der Gesellschaft eingenom-

men haben; **to hit a new ~** neuen Höhepunkt erreichen; **to hold talks at the ~ of ambassadors** Gespräche auf Botschaftsebene durchführen; **to maintain the same ~ of prices** Preise auf dem gleichen Niveau halten; **to make ~ with the ground** dem Erdboden gleichmachen; **to push to a ~** hinaufschrauben; **to raise the ~ of prices** Preisniveau anheben; **to reduce to a ~** auf ein Niveau zurücknehmen; **to remain below year-before ~s** hinter dem Vorjahresergebnis zurückbleiben; **to rise to the ~ of s. o.** jds. gesellschaftliches Niveau erreichen; **to upgrade the ~** Niveau anheben;

~ (a.) flach, eben, waagerecht, horizontal;

~ annuity gleichbleibende Rente; **~ crossing** *(Br.)* schienengleicher Übergang; **~ ground** ebenes Gelände; **~ life** geregeltes Leben; **to have a ~ head** in sich ruhen, ausgeglichen sein; **~-pegging** stabilisierter Kursstand; **to hold a high-~ position** führende Stellung einnehmen; **~ premium** gleichbleibende Prämie; **~-premium system** Kapitaldeckungsverfahren; **~ printing** Flachdruck; **~ road** ebene Straße; **~ stress** *(phonetics)* schwebende Betonung; **top-~ talks** Gespräche auf höchster Ebene.

level(l)er *(pol.)* Gleichmacher.
levelheaded vernünftig, nüchtern, ausgeglichen.
levelheadedness, to show political politische Besonnenheit zeigen.
levelling Ausgleichen, Planierung, Nivellierung;

~ out of business fluctuations Konjunkturausgleich; **~ of classes** Abschaffung der Klassenunterschiede; **~ down** *(wages)* Herabsetzung; **~ of premiums** *(insurance)* Bildung von Durchschnittsprämien; **~ up** Erhöhung;

~ price *(EC)* Ausgleichspreis; **~ process** Nivellierungsprozeß.
levelment Nivellierung.
levelness Ausgeglichenheit.
lever Hebel, Brechstange, *(fig.)* moralisches Druckmittel;
~ watch Ankeruhr.
leverage *(capital)* festverzinslicher Anteil am Gesamtkapital, *(fig.)* Einfluß, Macht, Druckmittel, Hebelwirkung, *(profit)* zum Umsatz disproportionale Tendenz, Disproportionalität, *(stocks)* Verhältnis von Obligationen und Vorzugsaktien zu Stammaktien;

financial ~ disproportionaler Finanzstatus;
to have no ~ to be able to bring to bear on s. o. keine Druckmöglichkeiten gegen j. besitzen;
~ company *(US)* auf mehreren Wegen finanzierter Investmentfonds; **~ effect** Hebelwirkung; **~ factor** Verhältnis des Fremdkapitals zum Eigenkapital; **high ~ factor** hoher Verschuldungsgrad; **~ fund** *(US)* Investmentfonds mit Leihkapital; **~ point** disproportionaler Gewinnpunkt; **~ stock** Stammaktien mit großem Anteil an Vorzugsaktien.
leveraged, to be highly hohen Verschuldungsgrad aufweisen;
~ position disproportionale Gewinnsituation.
leviable eintreibbar, steuer-, zollpflichtig.
levy Eintreibung, *(collecting of tax)* [Steuer]erhebung, -veranlagung, abgabe, *(contribution)* Beitrag, Umlage, *(distraint)* Pfändung, Beschlagnahme, *(EC)* Abschöpfung[sbetrag], *(mil.)* Truppen-, Zwangsaushebung, Aufgebot, *(tax)* Umlage, Abgabe, Steuer[satz];

ammunition ~ *(Br.)* Munitionssteuer; **betterment ~** Wertzuwachsabgabe; **capital ~** Kapital-, Vermögensabgabe; **capital gains ~** Kapitalzuwachssteuer; **compulsory ~** Zwangsabgabe; **equitable ~** vorläufige Beschlagnahme; **general ~** Massenaufgebot; **intracommunity ~** *(EC)* innergemeinschaftlicher Abschöpfungsbetrag; **yearly pension ~** Jahresbeitrag zum Pensionsfonds; **political ~** Parteiumlage; **excess-profits ~** *(Br.)* Übergewinnsteuer; **property ~** Vermögensabgabe; **special ~** Sonderabgabe; **tax ~** Steuererhebung;

~ of costs Kostenerhebung; **~ of distress** Pfändung, Beschlagnahme; **subsequent ~ of duties** Nacherhebung von Zöllen, Nachverzollung; **~ of execution** Betreiben der Zwangsvollstreckung; **~ on exports** Ausfuhr, Exportabgabe; **~ on imports** Einfuhrabgabe; **~ on premium income** Abgabe auf die Prämieneinkünfte; **~ in kind** Naturalabgabe; **~ in mass** Einberufung aller Wehrfähigen; **~ on real estate** Abgabe auf das Grundvermögen;

~ (v.) beschlagnahmen, pfänden, zwangsvollstrecken, *(EC)* abschöpfen, *(mil.)* [Truppen] ausheben, *(tax, contribution)* erheben, eintreiben;

~ by direct assessment zur Einkommensteuer veranlagen; **~ an army** Truppen ausheben, Heer aufstellen; **~ an attachment order** Pfändungsbeschluß erlassen, Beschlagnahme anordnen (verfügen); **~ blackmail on s. o.** j. erpressen, Erpressung an jem. begehen; **~ a charge** Gebühr erheben; **~ contributions** Kontributionen erheben; **~ by deduction at source** Quellenbesteuerung vornehmen; **~ a distress on** Pfändung vornehmen

(ausbringen), mit Beschlag belegen, beschlagnahmen; **~ duties** mit Abgaben belegen; **~ customs duties** Zölle erheben; **~ a duty on goods** Einfuhrzoll auf Waren erheben; **~ on s. one's estate** (goods, property, an execution) Zwangsvollstreckung gegen j. betreiben; **~ execution into the company's property** in das Gesellschaftsvermögen vollstrecken; **~ execution with respect to the costs** Zwangsvollstreckung aus dem Kostenurteil betreiben; **~ a fee** Gebühr erheben; **~ a fine on s. o.** jem. eine Geldstrafe auferlegen; **~ $ 100 a year for the pension fund** Jahresbeitrag von 100 Dollar für den Pensionsfonds erheben; **~ on land** Grundbesitz besteuern; **~ on the entire property** gesamtes Vermögen beschlagnahmen; **~ a ransom** Lösegeld fordern; **~ a rate** Tarif erheben; **~ taxes** Abgaben (Steuern) erheben, besteuern; **~ a tax on capital** Vermögenssteuer erheben; **~ a tax on dividend distribution** Kapitalertragssteuer erheben; **~ taxes on capital** Vermögenssteuer erheben; **~ taxes on land** Grundbesitz besteuern; **~ troops** Truppen ausheben; **~ war upon s. o.** Krieg gegen jem. führen;

to authorize the ~ of a tax Steuererhebung genehmigen; **to charge a ~** *(EC)* Abschöpfung erheben; **to collect a political ~ from its members** Beitrag zu einer politischen Aktion einsammeln; **to impose a ~** *(EC)* Abschöpfungsbetrag erheben; **to make a ~ on capital** Vermögenssteuer erheben;

~ court *(Delaware)* Steueraufsichtsbehörde.
levying | of charges Gebührenerhebung; **~ a distress** Betreibung der Zwangsvollstreckung, Pfändung.
lexer *(sl.)* Jurastudent.
lexical lexikographisch.
lexicographer Wörterbuchverfasser.
lexicon Wörterbuch, Lexikon;
practical ~ Reallexikon;
~ of business Wirtschaftswörterbuch.
ley Brachland.
liabilities *(balance sheet)* Passiva, Passivmasse, -bestand, -seite, *(in bankruptcy)* Schulden, Konkursmasse, *(obligations)* Verbindlichkeiten, Verpflichtungen, Schulden;

assets and ~ Aktiva und Passiva;
accrued ~ *(balance sheet, US)* aufgelaufene [aber noch nicht fällige] Verpflichtungen, antizipative Schulden; **bank notes ~** Verpflichtungen aufgrund der Ausgabe von Banknoten; **business ~** Geschäftsschulden; **capital ~** Kapitalverschuldung; **contingent ~** *(balance sheet, Br.)* Rückstellung für zweifelhafte Schulden (Dubiosen), Eventualverpflichtungen, -verbindlichkeiten; **current ~** *(balance sheet)* kurzfristige Verbindlichkeiten; **customers' ~** Verpflichtungen der Kundschaft; **deferred ~** im voraus eingegangene [zunächst passivierte] Einnahmen; **deposit ~** Verbindlichkeiten aus Depositenkonten, Kontokorrentverbindlichkeiten; **direct ~** *(US)* unbedingte und unbestrittene Verbindlichkeiten; **existing ~** bestehende Verbindlichkeiten; **external ~** Auslandsverbindlichkeiten; **fictitious ~** fiktive Kreditoren; **fixed ~** gleichbleibende Verbindlichkeiten, *(long-term)* langfristige (fundierte) Verbindlichkeiten; **foreign ~** Auslandsverbindlichkeiten, -verpflichtungen; **~ incurred** eingegangene Verpflichtungen; **indirect ~** *(balance sheet)* Eventualverbindlichkeiten; **intercompany ~** Konzernverbindlichkeiten; **internal ~** Inlandsverbindlichkeiten; **long-term ~** *(balance sheet)* langfristige Verbindlichkeiten; **maturing ~** fällig werdende Verbindlichkeiten; **minimum ~** Mindestreserve, -verpflichtungen; **net ~** Nettoverbindlichkeiten nach Abzug der liquiden Aktiva; **other ~** *(balance sheet)* sonstige Verbindlichkeiten; **outstanding ~** *(balance sheet)* ausstehende Verbindlichkeiten; **quick ~** kurzfristige Verbindlichkeiten; **reserve-carrying foreign ~** mindestreservepflichtige Auslandsverbindlichkeiten; **secondary ~** *(balance sheet, US)* Eventualverbindlichkeiten; **secured ~** gesicherte (sichergestellte) Verbindlichkeiten; **shareholders' ~** *(Br.)* Einzahlungspflicht der Aktionäre, Aktionärsverpflichtungen; **short-term ~** kurzfristige Verbindlichkeiten; **sight ~** sofort fällige Verbindlichkeiten; **sundry ~** *(balance sheet)* sonstige Verbindlichkeiten; **suspense ~** transitorische Passiva; **third-party ~** fremde Verbindlichkeiten; **time ~** befristete Verbindlichkeiten; **total ~** *(balance sheet)* Gesamtverbindlichkeiten; **unrecorded ~** nicht belegte Verbindlichkeiten; **unsecured ~** ungesicherte Verbindlichkeiten, *(bankruptcy)* gewöhnliche Konkursforderungen;

~ on account of acceptances (from the acceptance of bills) *(balance sheet)* Verbindlichkeiten aus der Annahme gezogener Wechsel, Akzeptverbindlichkeiten; **customers' ~ on acceptances** *(balance sheet)* Akzeptverbindlichkeiten der Kundschaft; **contingent ~ in respect of acceptances** Verpflichtungen aus geleisteten Akzepten; **~ of a bank** *(balance sheet)* Kundeneinlagen; **~ to banks** *(balance sheet)* Verbindlichkeiten gegenüber

Kreditinstituten; **~ on account of endorsements on bills discount-ed** Giroverbindlichkeiten; **~ of the banking department** *(Br.)* Verpflichtungen der Bank von England; **~ upon bills** Verpflichtungen aus noch nicht eingelösten Wechseln, Wechselverpflichtungen; **~ for foreign bills negotiated** *(balance sheet)* Verbindlichkeiten für weiterbegebene Auslandswechsel; **~ for possible calls on shares** Einzahlungsverpflichtungen auf nicht voll eingezahlte Aktien; **~ on outstanding claims** *(insurance)* Schadensreserve; **~ of contract** vertragliche Verpflichtungen, Vertragsverpflichtungen; **~ to credit institutions** *(bank balance)* Verbindlichkeiten gegenüber Kreditinstituten; **~ payable on demand** Sichtverbindlichkeiten; **~ and shareholder's equity** Verbindlichkeiten und Eigenkapital; **~ of the estate** Nachlaßverbindlichkeiten; **~ in foreign exchange** Devisenverpflichtungen; **~ arising from guarantees and warranty contracts** Verbindlichkeiten aus Bürgschaften und Gewährleistungsverträgen; **~ from the issue and endorsement of bills** *(balance sheet)* Verbindlichkeiten aus der Begebung und Übertragung von Wechseln; **~ other than above** *(balance sheet)* sonstige Verbindlichkeiten; **~ to outsiders** *(consolidated balance sheet)* Verpflichtungen gegenüber Dritten; **~ due on presentation** Sichtverbindlichkeiten; **~ of equal priority** gleichrangige Verbindlichkeiten; **~ subject to reserve requirements** rücklagepflichtige Verbindlichkeiten; **~ for a term of at least four years** Verbindlichkeiten mit einer Laufzeit von mindetens vier Jahren;

to acknowledge ~ Schulden anerkennen; **to carry as ~** *(balance sheet)* als Passiva behandeln, passivieren, auf der Passivseite aufführen; **to contract ~** Verpflichtungen (Verbindlichkeiten) eingehen; **to discharge one's ~** seinen Verbindlichkeiten nachkommen; **to escape one's ~** sich seinen Schulden entziehen; **to incur ~** Verpflichtungen eingehen; **to involve ~** Verpflichtungen nach sich ziehen; **to meet one's ~** seinen Verbindlichkeiten nachkommen; **to wind up ~** Verbindlichkeiten ordnen; **~ adjustment** Schuldenregelung, *(Br.)* Schuldnervergleich; **~ adjustment order** *(Br.)* gerichtliche Vergleichsregelung; **~ side** *(balance sheet)* Passivseite.

liability *(bankrupt)* Schuldenmasse, *(debt)* Schuld, Obligo, *(obligation)* Verpflichtung, Verbindlichkeit, *(responsibility)* Haftung, Haftpflicht, -barkeit, Verantwortlichkeit, *(title of credit side)* Passivseite, -schuldposten, Posten auf der Passivseite;
free from (without) ~ ohne Obligo (Verbindlichkeit), unverbindlich; **with denial of ~** ohne Anerkennung einer Rechtspflicht;
absolute ~ unbeschränkte Haftung, Gefährdungshaftung; **acceptance ~** Akzeptverpflichtung; **bank ~** Bankverbindlichkeit; **capital ~** Kapitalverpflichtung; **civil ~** zivilrechtliche Schadenersatzverpflichtung (Haftung), Passivlegitimation; **collective ~** Kollektivhaftung; **contingent ~** bedingte Verpflichtung, Eventualverpflichtung, Ausfallhaftung; **contractual ~** vertragliche Haftung (Verpflichtung), Vertragshaftung; **corporate ~** Firmenhaftung; **criminal ~** Zurechnungsfähigkeit; **cross ~** *(ships)* gegenseitige Haftung; **direct ~** unbestrittene und unbedingte Verbindlichkeit; **double ~** *(stockholder of a bank, US)* doppelte Haftung; **employers' ~** Unfallhaftpflicht der Arbeitgeber; **endorser's ~** Giroverbindlichkeit, Wechselhaftung, Regreßpflicht; **extended ~** Haftungserweiterung; **existing ~** bestehende Verbindlichkeit; **floating ~** aufschiebend bedingte Verbindlichkeit; **full ~** Vollhaftung; **funded ~** langfristige Verbindlichkeit; **government ~** Staatshaftung; **gross ~** *(US)* Gesamtverbindlichkeit, -verpflichtung; **income-tax ~** Einkommensteuerschuld; **individual ~** persönliche Haftung; **joint ~** gemeinsame (solidarische) Verbindlichkeit (Haftung), Gesamt-, Solidarhaftung; **joint and several ~** gesamtschuldnerische Haftung (Verpflichtung); **landlord's ~** Haftung des Vermieters; **legal ~** gesetzliche Haftung (Haftpflicht), Rechtsverpflichtung; **limited ~** beschränkte Haftung, Haftungsbeschränkung; **liquidated ~** festgestellte Verbindlichkeit; **matured ~** fällige Verbindlichkeit (Schuld); **maximum ~** Haftpflichthöchstgrenze; **minimum ~** Haftpflichtmindestgrenze; **noncontractual ~** außervertragliche Haftung; **occupier's ~** Haftung des Grundstückseigentümers; **original ~** ursprüngliches Schuldverhältnis; **over ~** *(US)* Regreßpflicht; **owner's ~** Eigentümerhaftung; **personal ~** persönliche Haftung; **preexisting ~** bereits bestehende Verpflichtung; **primary ~ [to pay]** unmittelbare Verpflichtung, selbstschuldnerische Haftung; **prorata ~** anteilmäßige Haftung; **public ~** allgemeine Haftpflicht; **reserve ~** *(stock issue)* Nachschußpflicht; **secondary ~** *(US)* sekundäre Haftung, Eventualverbindlichkeit, Ausfallhaftung; **several ~** Individualhaftung, individuelle Haftung;

single ~ Einzelhaftpflicht; **state ~** Staatshaftung; **statutory ~** gesetzliche Haftpflicht; **strict ~** unbeschränkte Haftung, Gefährdungshaftung; **tax ~** Steuerschuld, -pflicht; **third-party personal injury ~** gesetzliche Haftpflicht; **tortious ~** Haftung aus unerlaubter Handlung; **unlimited ~** unbeschränkte Haftung (Haftpflicht); **unliquidated (unascertained) ~** der Höhe nach unbestimmte Verbindlichkeit; **unsecured ~** ungesicherte Verbindlichkeit, nicht bevorrechtigte Forderung; **vicarious ~** Haftung für den Erfüllungsgehilfen (fremdes Verschulden);
~ to render account Rechnungslegungspflicht; **~ for animals** Tierhalterhaftung; **~ for baggage** *(US)* Haftpflicht für das Reisegepäck; **~ to bankruptcy jurisdiction** Haftung nach konkursrechtlichen Bestimmungen; **~ to further call** Nachschußpflicht; **~ of common carrier** Spediteurhaftung; **~ for compensation** Schadensersatzpflicht; **~ of principal contract** Hauptverbindlichkeit; **~ to contribute** Beitragspflicht; **~ of a contributory** *(Br.)* Haftung eines nachschußpflichtigen Gesellschafters, Nachschußpflicht; **~ for damages** Schadensersatzpflicht; **~ for death or bodily injury to third parties** Haftung im Todesfall oder für Körperverletzungen; **~ for contracted debts** Schuldenhaftung, Haftung für eigene Schulden; **~ to declare** Deklarationspflicht; **~ for defects** Mängelhaftung; **~ to diseases** Anfälligkeit für Krankheiten; **~ to discover** Vorlage-, Auskunftspflicht; **~ of drawer** Ausstellerhaftung; **~ of employer** Haftung des Arbeitgebers; **~ for endorsement** Wechselhaftung; **~ to explode** *(product)* Explosionsgefahr; **~ towards guests** Gastwirtshaftung; **~ of an heir** Erbenhaftung; **~ of indorser** Indossantenhaftung; **~ attaching to the inheritance** Nachlaßverbindlichkeit; **legal ~ for injury** gesetzliche Schadensersatzpflicht; **~ of innkeeper** Gastwirtshaftung; **~ of liquidator** Haftung eines Liquidators; **~ for losses** Haftung für Schaden, Schadenshaftung; **~ for (to provide) maintenance** Unterhaltspflicht; **~ of members** Mitgliederhaftung; **~ for fraudulent misrepresentation** Haftung infolge Vorspiegelung falscher Tatsachen; **~ for negligence of servants** Haftung für Fahrlässigkeit von Erfüllungsgehilfen; **~ for negligence in tort** Haftung aus unerlaubter Handlung; **~ for noncompliance** Haftung wegen Untätigkeit; **~ of an official** Beamtenhaftung; **~ for omissions** *(prospectus)* Haftung für Weglassung wichtiger Angaben; **~ of the owner** Eigentümerhaftung; **~ of partner** Gesellschafterhaftung; **~ of retiring partners** Haftung ausscheidender Gesellschafter; **~ for partnership debts** Haftung für Gesellschaftsschulden; **~ to pay** Zahlungsverpflichtung, -pflicht; **~ to pay taxes** Steuerpflicht, -schuld; **~ to penalty** Strafbarkeit; **~ to recourse** Regreßpflicht, -haftung; **~ to give additional security** Zuschußpflicht; **~ for military service** Wehrdienstpflicht; **~ of shipowner** Reederhaftung; **~ created by statute** gesetzliche Haftung, satzungsmäßige Verpflichtung; **~ of stockholder** *(US)* Aktionärsverpflichtung; **~ to be sued** Passivlegitimation, Prozeßfähigkeit; **~ to support a wife** *(US)* Unterhaltspflicht gegenüber der Ehefrau; **~ in tort** Haftung aus unerlaubter Handlung; **~ of a trustee** Treuhänderhaftung;
to absolve from ~ von der Haftung befreien; **to accept (assume) ~ for** Verantwortung übernehmen für; **to attract ~ in tort** aus unerlaubter Handlung haften; **to be exonerated from ~** von der Haftung befreit werden; **to be under ~** verpflichtet sein; **to carry an insurance against legal ~** gesetzliche Haftpflichtversicherung unterhalten; **to carry limited ~ in a partnership** kommanditistisch beteiligt sein; **to contract a ~** Haftung eingehen; **to decline a ~** Verpflichtung ablehnen; **to deny ~ under a policy** Haftpflicht aufgrund der Versicherungsbedingungen ablehnen; **to discharge a ~** Verpflichtung erfüllen, einer Verbindlichkeit nachkommen; **to discharge from all ~** von jeglicher Haftung befreien; **to exempt (free) s. o. from a ~** j. von einer Verbindlichkeit (Haftung, Haftpflicht) befreien; **to meet one's ~** seiner Verpflichtung (Verbindlichkeit) nachkommen; **to negative ~** Haftpflicht (Haftung) ausschließen; **to reduce one's ~** seinen Haftungsumfang beschränken; **to release s. o. from a ~** j. von einer Verbindlichkeit (Haftpflicht) befreien; **to restrict unlimited ~ towards guests** Gastwirtshaftung beschränken;
~ account Passivkonto; **~ accrual** antizipative Schuld; **Employers' ^{&} Act** Betriebshaftpflichtgesetz; **~ bond** absolut gültiger Unfallverpflichtungsschein; **~ certificate** *(US)* Erklärung des Vorstands über dem Prüfer zur Verfügung gestellte Unterlagen, Vollständigkeitserklärung; **~ claim** Schadensersatzforderung, -klage; **~ clause** Haftungsklausel; **limited ~ company** Gesellschaft mit beschränkter Haftung (GmbH); **~ coverage** Haftungsumfang; **~ dividend** durch Ausgabe von Schuldverschreibungen gezahlte Dividende; **~ entry** *(issue of an indemnity)* Haftungsbuchung; **~ explosion** explosionsartige Haftungszunahme; **~ insurance** Haftpflichtversicherung; **employ-**

ers' ~ **insurance** Betriebs-, Unternehmerhaftpflichtversicherung; **legal** ~ **insurance** Haftpflichtversicherung bis zur Höhe der gesetzlichen Haftung; **[employers']** ~ **insurance law** Haftpflichtgesetz; ~ **item** *(balance sheet)* Passiv-, Schuldposten; ~ **ledger** Wechselobligo, -konto; **to concentrate on** ~ **lines** sich auf das Unfallhaftpflichtgeschäft konzentrieren; ~ **loss** Haftungsschaden; **general** ~ **policy** Haftpflichtversicherungspolice, -vertrag; ~ **provisions** Haftungsvorschriften; ~ **reserve** aufgelaufene [aber noch nicht fällige] Verbindlichkeiten; ~ **suit** Haftpflichtprozeß; ~ **verification** Bewertung von Verbindlichkeiten.

liable *(answerable)* haftbar, haftpflichtig, *(obliged)* verpflichtet, verbunden, verantwortlich, unterworfen;

individually (personally) ~ persönlich haftbar; **primarily** ~ unmittelbar (selbstschuldnerisch) haftbar; **secondarily** ~ subsidiär haftbar (haftpflichtig); ~ **jointly and severally** gesamtschuldnerisch haftbar; **vicariously** ~ als Erfüllungsgehilfe haftbar;

~ **to render account** rechenschafts-, rechnungspflichtig; ~ **to breakage** zerbrechlich; ~ **to charges** gebührenpflichtig; ~ **to a commission** provisionspflichtig; ~ **for compensation** schadensersatzpflichtig; ~ **under a contract** vertraglich verpflichtet; ~ **to contribute (contribution)** beitragspflichtig; ~ **for (to pay) damages** entschädigungs-, schadenersatzpflichtig; ~ **to discount** rabattfähig; ~ **to discover** auskunftspflichtig; ~ **to duty** abgabe-, zollpflichtig; ~ **to execution** der Zwangsvollstreckung unterliegend; ~ **to render information** auskunftspflichtig; ~ **by law** gesetzlich verpflichtet; ~ **to maintain** unterhaltspflichtig; ~ **to make good a loss** schadenersatzpflichtig; ~ **for military service** wehrpflichtig; ~ **at once** unmittelbar haftpflichtig; ~ **to pay** zahlungsverpflichtet; ~ **to pay customs duty** zollpflichtig; ~ **to pay taxes** steuer-, abgabenpflichtig; ~ **to penalty** strafrechtlich verantwortlich; ~ **to recourse** regreßpflichtig; ~ **to make restitution** rückerstattungspflichtig; ~ **to respond in damages** zum Schadenersatz verpflichtet; ~ **to give security** kautionspflichtig; ~ **to stamp duty** stempelsteuerpflichtig; ~ **to subscription** beitragspflichtig; ~ **to be sued** passiv legitimiert, prozeßfähig; ~ **to be sued for damages** schadenersatzpflichtig; ~ **to support** unterhaltspflichtig; ~ **for such tax** steuerpflichtig; **to be** ~ haftbar sein, haften; **to be** ~ **to do** dazu neigen, zu tun; **to be** ~ **to contribute to the assets of a company** *(Br.)* nachschußpflichtig sein; **to be** ~ **on an executory contract** aus einem schwebend wirksamen Vertrag haften; **to be** ~ **up to one's contribution** bis zur Höhe seiner Einlage haften; **to be** ~ **to a customer to the extent of a loss** einem Kunden in Höhe des entstandenen Schadens haftbar sein; **to be** ~ **jointly and severally** als Gesamtschuldner (gesamtschuldnerisch) haften; **to be** ~ **personally (individually)** ~ persönlich haftbar sein; **to be** ~ **for damages** schadenersatzpflichtig sein; **to be** ~ **for one's wife's debts** für die Schulden der Ehefrau aufkommen müssen; **to be** ~ **for the debt of the principal** für den Hauptschuldner haften; **to be** ~ **for a defect** für einen Mangel haften, der Mangelhaftung unterliegen; **to be** ~ **to execution** der Zwangsvollstreckung unterliegen; **to be** ~ **for expenses** für Unkosten aufzukommen haben; **to be** ~ **to the extent of one's property** mit seinem ganzen Vermögen haften; **to be** ~ **to imprisonment** einer Gefängnisstrafe unterliegen; **to be** ~ **to income tax** der Einkommensteuer unterliegen, einkommensteuerpflichtig sein; **to be** ~ **in law for the results of one's own negligence** für die Folgen seiner Fahrlässigkeit rechtlich haftbar sein; **to be** ~ **without limitation** unbeschränkt haften; **to be** ~ **for partnership debts** als Gesellschafter haften; **to be** ~ **to be prosecuted by one's debtors** von seinen Gläubigern belangt (verklagt) werden können; **to be** ~ **to replace the damaged goods** zur Nachlieferung verpflichtet sein; **not to be** ~ **for more than one's rat(e)able share of a loss** nur bis zur Höhe seines verhältnismäßigen Verlustanteils haften; **to be** ~ **to prosecution** sich strafbar machen, strafrechtlicher Verantwortung unterliegen; **to be** ~ **to seasickness** leicht seekrank werden; **to be strictly and absolutely** ~ aus Gefährdung haften; **to be** ~ **for the torts of one's agent** für unerlaubte Handlungen seines Vertreters haften; **to be vicariously** ~ für den Erfüllungsgehilfen haftbar sein (haften); **to be vicariously** ~ **for acts of negligence by employees** für fahrlässige Handlungen seiner Angestellten als Erfüllungsgehilfen haften; **to be** ~ **for voluntary waste** für vorsätzliche Beschädigung haften; **to become** ~ **on a bill** wechselrechtlich haften; **to hold s. o.** ~ j. verantwortlich (haftbar) machen; **to make o. s.** ~ **to a fine** sich dem Risiko der Verhängung einer Geldstrafe aussetzen.

liaise *(v.)* Verbindung aufnehmen, *(mil.)* als Verbindungsoffizier fungieren;

~ **with the press** ständig mit der Presse Verbindung halten.

liaison Zusammenarbeit, Kontakt, Verbindung;

close ~ **between departments** enge Zusammenarbeit zwischen einzelnen Abteilungen;

~ **committee** Verbindungsausschuß; ~ **consultant (man)** *(US)* Kontakt-, Verbindungsmann; ~ **duties** Verbindungsaufgaben; ~ **mission** Verbindungsbüro; ~ **office** Verbindungsstelle; ~ **officer** Verbindungsoffizier.

libel Ehrverletzung, Verleumdung, Beleidigung, *(Admiralty case, US)* Klage;

criminal ~ strafbare Verleumdung; **seditious** ~ hochverräterische (staatsgefährdende) Veröffentlichung; **trade** ~ Anschwärzung der Konkurrenz;

~ *(v.)* verleumden, Verleumdung veröffentlichen, beleidigen, *(file a suit, Scot.)* Klageschrift einreichen, anklagen;

to bring an action of ~ **against s. o.** Beleidigungsprozeß gegen j. anstrengen; **to serve s. o. with a writ for** ~ j. wegen Beleidigung verklagen; **to sue a newspaper for** ~ Beleidigungsklage gegen eine Zeitung anstrengen; **to utter a** ~ **against s. o.** j. beleidigen (verleumden), Verleumdung gegen j. begehen;

to lay o. s. open to a ~ **action** sich eine Beleidigungsklage zuziehen; ~**'s repetition** Wiederholung einer Beleidigung; ~ **suit (writ)** Beleidigungsprozeß, Verleumdungsklage.

libellant *(admiralty case)* Kläger.

libellee *(Br.)* Beklagter.

libeller *(Br.)* Verleumder.

libellous ehrenrührig, beleidigend, verleumderisch;

~ **per se** offensichtlich beleidigend;

~ **statement** verleumderische Erklärungen, ehrenrührige Behauptung.

liberal fortschrittlich eingestellter Mensch, *(pol.)* Liberaler, Mitglied der Liberalen Partei;

~ *(a.)* liberal, *(generous)* freigebig, *(gift)* großzügig, *(translation)* frei;

to be ~ **in business** in Geschäften großzügig sein; **to be** ~ **of money** in Geldangelegenheiten großzügig sein; **to be** ~ **of promises** großzügige Versprechungen machen; **to go** ~ liberale Partei wählen;

~ **arts** *(US)* Geisteswissenschaften; ~ **bastion** liberale Bastion; ~ **cloak** liberales Mäntelchen; ~ **construction or interpretation** weite Auslegung; ~ **donor** großzügiger Spender; ~ **education** allgemeinbildende Erziehung; ~ **gift** großmütiges Geschenk; ~ **giver to charity** großzügiger Spender; ~ **harvest** überreiche Ernte; ~ **manner** unbefangenes (ungezwungenes) Auftreten; ~**-mindedness** freiheitlich gesinnt, liberal; ~ **offer** großzügiges Angebot; ~ **Party** Liberale Partei; ~ **professions** freie Berufe; ~ **provisions** reiche Vorräte; ~ **settlement** kulante Bedingungen; ~ **supply of food and drink** großzügige Bereitstellung von Genußmitteln und Getränken; ~ **system of public schools** freier Schulzugang; ~ **thinker** freiheitlicher Denker; ~ **trade** liberalisierte Wirtschaft; ~ **trade policy** liberale Handelspolitik; **to take a** ~ **turn** sich liberal verhalten.

liberalism Liberalismus;

to smack of ~ liberalistisch angehaucht sein; **to stem back** ~ Liberalismus eindämmen.

liberality Unvoreingenommenheit, Liberalität, *(generosity)* Großzügigkeit, Freigebigkeit.

liberalization Liberalisierung;

trade ~ wirtschaftliche Liberalisierung, Liberalisierung des Handels;

~ **of depreciation allowances** liberalisierte Abschreibungspolitik;

~ **agreement** Liberalisierungsabkommen; ~ **codex** Liberalisierungskodex; ~ **measures** Liberalisierungsmaßnahmen.

liberalize *(v.)* *(pol.)* zum Liberalismus bekehren;

~ **a list of items** Warenliste liberalisieren.

liberalized capital account liberalisiertes Kapitalkonto.

liberally, to reward s. o. j. großzügig belohnen.

liberate *(v.)* befreien, [Gefangene] freilassen, *(loot)* plündern;

~ **capital** Kapital flüssig machen; ~ **the mind from prejudices** sich von Vorurteilen freimachen.

liberation Befreiung, Freilassung;

~ **of capital** Flüssigmachen von Kapital; ~ **of a nation** Befreiung eines Volkes;

~ **movement** Befreiungsbewegung; ~ **organization** Befreiungsarmee, -front.

liberee befreiter Kriegsgefangener.

liberties| of the City of London Londoner Bürgerrechte;

to take ~ sich Freiheiten herausnehmen; **to take** ~ **with s. one's property** sich an fremdem Vermögen vergreifen; **to take** ~ **with a text** Text frei auslegen;

~ **clause** *(contract of affreightment)* Sonderrechtsklausel.

libertinism Zügellosigkeit, Sittenlosigkeit.

liberty Freiheit, *(privilege)* Sonderrecht, *(school, sl.)* schulfreier Tag;

civil ~ bürgerliche Freiheit, *(US)* verfassungsmäßig garantiertes Bürgerrecht; **constitutional** ~ von der Verfassung gewährleistete Freiheit; **natural** ~ Freiheit der Person; **personal** ~ persönliche Freiheit, Freizügigkeit, Niederlassungsfreiheit; **political** ~ staatsbürgerliche Freiheit, Bürgerrecht; **religious** ~ Religionsfreiheit;

free ~ **of action** uneingeschränkte Bewegungsfreiheit; ~ **to appeal** Berufungsmöglichkeit; ~ **to come and go** Freizügigkeit, Niederlassungsfreiheit; ~ **of conscience** Gewissensfreiheit; ~ **of contract** Vertragsfreiheit; ~ **of the globe** *(marine insurance)* regional unbeschränkter Versicherungsschutz; ~ **of movement** Freizügigkeit; ~ **of a port** Hafenanlauferlaubnis; ~ **of the press** Pressefreiheit; ~ **of the rules** *(prisoner)* offene Haftunterbringung; ~ **of trade** Gewerbefreiheit;

to be at ~ **to do s. th.** Erlaubnis haben, etw. zu tun; **to be at** ~ **to appeal** Berufungsmöglichkeit haben; **not to be always at** ~ nicht immer verfügbar sein; **to have** ~ **of choice** freie Wahl haben; **to have full** ~ **of action** volle Handlungsfähigkeit haben; **to leave at** ~ auf freiem Fuße lassen; **to remit s. o. at** ~ j. wieder in Freiheit setzen; **to restore s. o. to** ~ jem. die Freiheit wiedergeben;

~ **boat** Urlauberschiff; ~ **bonds (loan)** *(US)* Kriegsanleihe; ~ **man** Matrose auf Landurlaub; ~ **ship** *(US)* Truppentransportschiff; ~ **ticket** *(mar.)* Landurlaub.

librarian Bibliothekar.

librarianship Bibliothekarberuf.

library Bücherei, Bibliothek, *(film record)* Archiv;

businessman's ~ kaufmännische Bibliothek; **circulating** ~ Leihbibliothek; **comprehensive** ~ umfassende Bibliothek; **film** ~ Filmarchiv; **free** ~ öffentliche Bibliothek, Stadtbibliothek, Volksbibliothek, -bücherei; **lending** ~ Leihbibliothek, öffentliche Bibliothek; **private** ~ Privatbibliothek; **public** ~ öffentliche Bibliothek, Stadtbücherei; **reference** ~ Präsenzbibliothek; **special[ized]** ~ Spezial-, Fachbibliothek; **travelling** ~ Reisebibliothek; **well-stocked** ~ gut ausgestattete Bibliothek; ⌂ **of Congress** *(US)* Kongreßbibliothek; ~ **of program(me)s** Programmbibliothek; ~ **for public reference** öffentliche Nachschlage-, Präsenzbibliothek;

to be a walking ~ *(fam.)* wandelndes Konservationslexikon sein;

~ **binding** Bibliothekseinband; **particularly strong** ~ **binding** stabiler Bibliothekseinband; ~ **book** Bibliotheksbuch; ~ **budget** Bibliotheksetat; ~ **card** *(US)* Benutzerkarte; ~ **case** Bücherschrank; ~ **edition** Ausgabe im Großformat; ~ **rebate** Bibliotheksnachlaß; ~ **science** Bibliothekswissenschaft; ~ **tax** Pflichtexemplarbestimmung; ~ **ticket** Benutzerkarte.

licence, license *(US)* *(book)* Druckbewilligung, *(burial)* Bestattungskonzession, *(land)* Benutzungsrecht, *(patent law)* Patentausnutzung, *(marriage)* Heiratserlaubnis, *(motorcar)* Führerschein, *(permit)* Erlaubnis[schein], [amtliche] Genehmigung, Berechtigungsnachweis, *(real property)* Grundstücksbenutzungsrecht, *(sale)* Verkaufsrecht, *(servant)* vorübergehendes Wohnrecht, *(trade, business or calling)* Lizenz, Konzession, Gewerbeschein, -berechtigung, Zulassung, *(university)* Befähigungsnachweis, -zeugnis;

subject to a ~ lizenzpflichtig; **under a** ~ aufgrund einer Zulassung; **under** ~ **from the author** mit Genehmigung des Autors;

A ~ *(Road and Rail Traffic Act, Br.)* allgemeine Güterfernverkehrgenehmigung; **building** ~ Baugenehmigung; **business** ~ Geschäftserlaubnis, Gewerbekonzession; **bloc** ~ *(patent law)* Pauschallizenz; **broadcast-transmitting** ~ Sendeerlaubnis; **C** ~ *(Road and Railway Traffic Act, Br.)* Güterfernverkehrgenehmigung für Werksverkehr; **car** ~ Zulassungspapiere; **common** ~ *(Br.)* Heiratserlaubnis; **compulsory** ~ Zwangslizenz; **corporation** ~ Gesellschaftskonzession; **cross** ~s Lizenzaustausch; **dog** ~ Hundesteuermarke; **driving** *(Br.)* **(driver's,** *US)* ~ Führerschein, Fahrerlaubnis; **international driving** ~ internationaler Führerschein; **excise** ~ *(Br.)* Schankkonzession; **exclusive** ~ Einzelkonzession, Alleinlizenz; **executory** ~ Konzession für später; **expired** ~ erloschene Konzession; **export** ~ Ausfuhrgenehmigung; **express** ~ ausdrücklich gewährte Konzession; **defined field** ~s Lizenzen auf technischem Anwendungsgebiet; **game** ~ Jagdschein, -erlaubnis; **general** ~ Generallizenz; **grantback** ~ *(US)* Rücklizenz; **gun** ~ *(Br.)* Waffenschein; **hack** *(US)* Taxikonzession; **hawker's** ~ Wandergewerbeschein; **high** ~ *(intoxicating liquors)* Sonderkonzession; **hunting** ~ Jagdschein; **implied** ~ stillschweigend gewährte Lizenz; **import** ~ Einfuhrgenehmigung, -bewilligung; **individual** ~ Einzelgeneh-

migung; **interim** ~ vorläufige Konzession; **justice's** ~ *(Br.)* Schankkonzession; **liquor** ~ Wirtshausgenehmigung, [Schank]konzession; **local taxation** ~ gebührenpflichtige Genehmigung; **manufacturing** ~ Herstellungslizenz; **marriage** ~ Heiratserlaubnis; **mining** ~ Mutung, Bergbaukonzession; **motor-vehicle** ~ Kraftfahrzeugzulassung, -papiere; **nonexclusive** ~ einfache Lizenz; **occasional** ~ Sondererlaubnis; **off-~** *(Br.)* Schankrecht über die Straße; **on-** *(Br.)* Schankrecht im eigenen Betrieb; ~ **outwards** Warenausfuhrgenehmigung; **pedlar's** ~ Hausiererlaubnis, Wandergewerbeschein; **poetic** ~ dichterische Freiheit; **printer's** ~ Erlaubnis zum Betrieb einer Druckerei; **professional** ~ Genehmigung zur Ausübung eines Berufes; **publican's** ~ Wirtshausgenehmigung, [Schank]konzession; **real-estate** ~ Makler-, Immobilienkonzession; **registrars'** ~ standesamtliche Heiratserlaubnis; **rod** ~ Angelschein; **royalty-free** ~ gebührenfreie Lizenz; **shooting** ~ Jagdschein; **simple** ~ jederzeit widerrufliche Erlaubnis; **special** ~ Sondergenehmigung, *(Br.)* besondere Heiratserlaubnis; **theater** ~ Theaterkonzession; **trade (trading)** ~ Handelserlaubnis, Gewerbekonzession; **trademark** ~ Warenzeichenlizenz; **unrestricted** ~ unbeschränkte Lizenz; **wireless** ~ Rundfunkgenehmigung;

~ **to drive a car** Fahrerlaubnis, Führerschein; ~ **to export** Ausfuhrgenehmigung; ~ **to carry firearms** Waffenschein; ~ **to import** Einfuhrgenehmigung; ~ **to manufacture** Herstellungslizenz; ~ **to operate** Zulassung zum Geschäftsbetrieb; ~ **to operate a motor vehicle** Fahrerlaubnis; ~ **revocable at pleasure** jederzeit widerrufliche Konzession; ~ **to practise as doctor** ärztliche Zulassung, Approbation; ~ **to print** Druckerlaubnis; ~ **of right** *(Br.)* Zwangslizenz; ~ **for the sale of alcoholic drinks** Schankkonzession; ~ **to sell** Verkaufserlaubnis, -genehmigung, Konzession; ~ **to carry on a trade** Gewerbeschein; ~ **to use** Benutzungsschein; ~ **for value** gebührenpflichtige Lizenz.

license *(v.)* *(US)*, **license** *(Br. and US)* *(book)* freigeben, zulassen, *(business)* konzessionieren, Konzession (Lizenz) erteilen, lizensieren, [amtlich] genehmigen, erlauben, behördliche Genehmigung erteilen, zulassen, *(theater)* zur Aufführung freigeben;

~ **a candidate for the ministry** j. ministrabel machen; ~ **a doctor to practise medicine** einem Arzt die Zulassung (Approbation) erteilen; ~ **a firm** Lizenz an eine Firma vergeben; ~ **s. o. to keep an inn** Gastwirtskonzession erteilen; ~ **a lawyer** Anwalt zulassen; ~ **liquor selling** Alkoholausschank konzessionieren; ~ **a pilot** Pilotenprüfung abnehmen, Pilotenschein ausstellen; ~ **a play** Theaterstück genehmigen; ~ **s. o. to sell drinks** jem. die Schankkonzesion erteilen;

to apply for a ~ Konzession (Lizenz) beantragen; **to be built under** ~ **from the ministry of defence** nach vom Verteidigungsministerium vergebenen Lizenzen gebaut werden; **to build under** ~ lizenzmäßig herstellen; **to disqualify a** ~ Führerschein einziehen; **to do s. th. under** ~ etw. nach eingeholter Genehmigung tun; **to endorse a** ~ Eintragung auf dem Führerschein vornehmen; **to exploit a** ~ Lizenz verwerten; **to forfeit one's** ~ seine Lizenz verlieren; **to grant a** ~ Lizenz erteilen, konzessionieren; **to grant a** ~ **in respect of a copyright** urheberrechtliche Lizenz erteilen; **to hold a** ~ Konzession innehaben, Lizenz besitzen; **to issue a** ~ Genehmigung (Konzession) erteilen; **to marry on a** ~ mit Sondergenehmigung heiraten; **to obtain a** ~ **under false pretences** sich eine Lizenz erschleichen; **to revoke a** ~ Konzession (Lizenz) entziehen; **to show a** ~ Berechtigungsnachweis erbringen; **to suspend a** ~ *(US)* Lizenz (Konzession) zeitweilig außer Kraft setzen; **to take out a** ~ sich einen Erlaubnisschein beschaffen, sich eine Konzession verschaffen; **to take out a** ~ **for a car** Kraftfahrzeugzulassung einholen; **to take out a dog** ~ Hund anmelden; **to take out a** ~ **for a year** *(Br.)* Führerschein für ein Jahr erwerben; **to withdraw a** ~ Lizenz entziehen;

~ **agreement** Lizenzvertrag; **cross** ~ **agreement** Lizenzaustauschvertrag; ~ **application** Genehmigungsantrag; ~ **arrangement** Lizenzabkommen; ~ **business** Konzessionswesen; ~ **buying** Konzessionserwerb; ~ **duty** Lizenzgebühr; ~ **fee[s]** Genehmigungs-, Lizenzgebühr[en], *(Br.)* Schankerlaubnissteuer; ~ **form** Bezugsschein; ~ **holder** Konzessions-, Lizenzinhaber, Konzessionär; ~ **income** Lizenzeinkünfte, -erträge; ~ **insurance** Versicherung gegen Nichterneuerung der Konzession; ~ **number** *(US)* polizeiliches Kennzeichen, Autonummer; **dealer's** ~ **number** rote Nummer [des Autoverkäufers]; ~ **plate** *(US)* polizeiliches Kennzeichen, Zulassungs-, Nummernschild; ~ **proceedings** Konzessions-, Lizenzverfahren; **renewal** Konzessions-, Lizenzerneuerung; ~ **revocation** Konzessionsentziehung, Lizenzrückruf; ~ **requirements** Lizenzvoraussetzungen; ~ **system** Konzessionssystem; ~ **tag** Steuermarke; ~ **tax** Lizenzgebühr, *(US)* Gewerbesteuer.

licenced, licensed amtlich zugelassen, befugt, konzessioniert, privilegiert;

to be ~ berechtigt, (lizenziert, zugelassen, befugt) sein, Konzession besitzen; **to be duly ~** patentamtlich berechtigt sein; **to be ~ to sell s. th.** Vertriebs-, Verkaufskonzession für etw. haben; **to be ~ to sell drinks** Schankkonzession besitzen;

~ **company** konzessionierte Gesellschaft; ~ **construction** Lizenzbau; ~ **dealer** Vertragshändler; ~ **firm** Lizenznehmer; ~ **house** (Br.) Lokal mit Schankkonzession, konzessioniertes Wirtshaus; ~ **person** Konzessionsinhaber; ~ **physician** (US) approbierter Arzt; ~ **pilot** zugelassener Pilot; ~ **premises** (Br.) konzessionierter Ausschank, Lokal mit Schankkonzession; ~ **quarter** Bordellviertel; ~ **saloon** Lokal mit Schankkonzession; ~ **trade** konzessionierter Alkoholhandel; ~ **traffic** konzessioniertes Gewerbe; ~ **undertaking** konzessioniertes Unternehmen; ~ **victualler** (Br.) Gastwirt mit Schankkonzession.

licencee, licensee (Br.) Lizenz-, Konzessionsinhaber, Konzessionär, Lizenznehmer, -träger, (motor vehicle, US) Führerscheininhaber, (patent law) Patentberechtigter, (publican) Schankkonzessionär, (servant) vorübergehend Wohnberechtigter;

bare ~ geduldeter Benutzer; **exclusive ~** alleiniger Lizenzinhaber, Inhaber einer Ausschließlichkeitslizenz; **general ~** Generallizenznehmer;

~ **by invitation** zutrittsberechtigte Person, Zutrittsberechtigter.

licencing, licensing (Br.) [amtliche] Zulassung, Genehmigung, Lizenz-, Konzessionserteilung, Modellverpachtung;

cross ~ (patent law) Lizenzaustausch, gegenseitige Lizenzerteilung, Paketlizenzen; **exclusive ~** alleinige Patentausnutzung; **multiple ~** (patent law) Erteilung von Parallellizenzen an mehrere Lizenznehmer; **compulsory package ~** Zusammenfassung von Lizenzen; **mandatory package ~** Vergabe von Paketlizenzen;

~ **of motor vehicles** Kraftfahrzeugzulassung; ~ **of patents** Patentvergabe; ~ **of process** Lizenzierung eines Herstellungsverfahrens;

~ **Act** Gaststättengesetz; ~ **activity** Lizenzausübung; ~ **agency** Konzessionsbehörde; ~ **agreement** Lizenzabkommen; **cross ~ arrangement** (US) Lizenzaustauschvereinbarung; **multiple ~ agreement** Mehrfachlizenzabkommen; ~ **authority** (Br.) für Schankkonzessionen zuständige Behörde; ~ **committee** Konzessionsausschuß; ~ **contract** Lizenzvertrag; ~ **hours** Ausschankzeiten; ~ **income** Lizenzeinkünfte; ~ **law** Schankgesetz; ~ **magistrate** Beamter für Konzessionserteilungen; ~ **ordinance** Lizenzgewährung; ~ **procedure** Zulassungsverfahren; ~ **provisions** Genehmigungsvorschriften; ~ **regulations** Konzessionsbestimmungen; ~ **requirements** gewerbepolizeiliche Voraussetzungen; ~ **restrictions** Lizenz-, Konzessionsauflagen; ~ **system** Konzessionswesen; ~ **ties** Lizenzverpflichtungen.

licenser, licensor (Br.) Lizenzgeber, Konzessionserteiler.

lick Schuß, Spritzer, (US) Kraftaufwand;

a ~ and a promise schlampige Arbeit;

at full ~ (sl.) mit größter Geschwindigkeit;

~ (v.) s. o. (sl.) j. verdreschen; ~ **the beach** (waves) Ufer bespülen; ~ **inflation** mit der Inflation fertig werden; ~ **the roof** (flames) am Dach emporzüngeln; ~ **into shape** in die richtige Form bringen, zurechtbiegen; ~ **an article into shape** Verkaufsartikel zurechtmachen; ~ **a recruit into shape** Rekruten bimsen; ~ **s. one's shoes** vor jem. kriechen;

not to do a ~ of work (US) keinen Finger rühren.

licking Niederlage;

to take one's ~ like a man Niederlage ohne mit der Wimper zu zucken einstecken.

lid (mil.) Funker, (restraint, US coll.) Zügelung, Einschränkung;

with the ~ off unter Aufdeckung aller Scheußlichkeiten;

to keep a ~ on costs Kosten niedrig halten; **to keep a ~ on prices** gegen Preiserhöhungen scharf vorgehen; **to put the ~ on** (Br.) einer Sache die Krone aufsetzen; **to raise the ~** nicht mehr scharf durchgreifen; **to slap an iron ~ on a city** Stadt mit starker Hand regieren.

lie, white **lie** Notlüge;

~ **of the ground** Belegenheit;

~ (v.) (appeal, claim) zulässig sein, (order) vorliegen;

~ **on (with) s. o.** jem. obliegen; ~ **against s. o.** (action) gegen j. anhängig sein; ~ **along** (mar.) krängen; ~ **along the river** sich entlang des Flusses erstrecken; ~ **along the shore** in Küstensichtweite entlangsegeln; ~ **in ambush** im Hinterhalt liegen; ~ **at anchor** vor Anker liegen; ~ **at the bank** (money) in der Bank sein, auf der Bank liegen; ~ **like a book** wie gedruckt lügen; ~ **heavy on s. one's conscience** schwer auf jds. Gewissen lasten; ~ **dormant** sich nicht verzinsen; ~ **down** keinen Widerstand leisten; ~ **down under an insult** Beleidigung einstecken; ~ **fallow** brach liegen; ~ **in franchise** (property) herrenlos sein; ~ **through a forest** (road) durch einen Wald führen; ~ **like a gas-meter** (fam.) lügen, daß sich die Balken biegen; ~ **in grant** urkundlich übertragbar sein; ~ **on s. one's hands** unverkauft bei jem. liegenbleiben; ~ **at s. one's heart** jem. am Herzen liegen; ~ **idle** brachliegen, stillstehen; ~ **idle at the bank** ungenutzt auf dem Konto stehen; ~ **in livery** der Auflassung bedürfen; ~ **low** sich verbergen, abwarten, (coll.) ganz unauffällig leben, (sl.) auf eine günstige Gelegenheit warten; ~ **at s. one's mercy** von jds. Gnade abhängen; ~ **under an obligation** verpflichtet sein; ~ **off the land** vom Land abhalten; ~ **open to attacks** Angriffen ausgesetzt sein; ~ **over** (remain unpaid) nicht zur Verfallszeit bezahlt werden, aufgeschoben werden, (be paid too late) nicht rechtzeitig bezahlt werden; ~ **in prison** Insasse eines Gefängnisses sein; ~ **away s. one's reputation** jds. Ruf durch Lügen untergraben; ~ **in ruins** in Trümmern liegen; ~ **under [a] sentence of death** zum Tode verurteilt werden; ~ **in state** feierlich aufgebahrt sein; ~ **under [the] suspicion of murder** unter Mordverdacht stehen; ~ **on the table** (letter) nicht offiziell zur Kenntnis genommen sein; ~ **in one's throat** das Blaue vom Himmel herunterlügen; ~ **under a charge of theft** des Diebstahls beschuldigt werden; ~ **up** von der Arbeit ausruhen, (ship) außer Dienst (Fahrt) sein, aufliegen; ~ **in wait** im Hinterhalt liegen; ~ **with s. o.** in jds. Macht liegen; ~ **with the author** in die Verantwortung des Autors fallen;

to act a ~ durch Handlungen bewußt irreführen; **to allow a motion ~ over** mit der Zurückstellung eines Antrags einverstanden sein; **to find out how the ground ~s** herausfinden wie der Hase läuft; **to get an idea of the ~ of the land** sich im Gelände orientieren; **to give s. o. the ~** j. Lügen strafen; **to give s. o. the ~ direct** formelles Dementi abgeben; **to know where one's interests ~s** seine Interessenslage herausfinden; **to let a matter ~ over** Angelegenheit zurückstellen; **let sleeping dogs ~** schlafende Hunde nicht wecken;

~**-abed** Langschläfer; ~ **detector** Lügendetektor.

lien Zurückbehaltungs-, Pfandrecht;

agricultural ~ Erntepfandrecht; **artisan's ~** (US) gewerbliches Zurückbehaltungsrecht; **attorney's ~** Zurückbehaltungsrecht des Rechtsanwalts [an Dokumenten usw.], Aktenzurückbehaltungsrecht; **bank[er]'s ~** (Br.) Verwertungsrecht einer Bank; **carrier's ~** Spediteur-, Frachtführerpfandrecht; **charging ~** Sicherungsübereignung, (solicitor) [Akten]zurückbehaltungsrecht; **common-law ~** gesetzliches Zurückbehaltungsrecht; **concurrent ~** gleichrangiges Pfandrecht; **consummate ~** Pfandrecht aufgrund eines rechtskräftigen Urteils; **conventional ~** vertraglich vereinbartes Pfandrecht, Vertragspfandrecht; **equitable ~** Sicherungsgut; **execution ~** Pfändungs-, Vollstreckungspfandrecht, Zwangs-, Arresthypothek; **factor's ~** Kommissionärs-, Treuhandpfandrecht; **first ~** vorgehendes Pfandrecht; **floating ~** (US) Sicherungsrecht in wechselnder Höhe; **general ~** allgemeines Pfandrecht (Zurückbehaltungsrecht); **implied ~** gesetzlich vermutetes Zurückbehaltungs-, Pfandrecht; **inchoate ~** Pfandrecht aufgrund eines noch nicht rechtskräftigen Urteils; **judgment ~** (US) gerichtlich festgestelltes Grundstückspfandrecht; **junior ~** nachstehendes (jüngeres) Pfandrecht; **lessor's ~** Vermieterpfandrecht; **maritime ~** Schiffspfandrecht; **materialman's ~** Zurückbehaltungsrecht aus Werklieferungsvertrag; **mechanic's ~** (US) gewerbliches Zurückbehaltungsrecht; **mortgage ~** Grundpfandrecht; **municipal ~** kommunales Pfandrecht auf ein Anliegergrundstück; **paramount ~** vorrangiges Pfandrecht; **particular ~** Zurückbehaltungsrecht an einem bestimmten Gegenstand; **possessory ~** Zurückbehaltungsrecht, Besitzpfand; **prior ~** (US) ranghöheres (bevorrechtigtes) Pfandrecht; **retaining ~** (lawyer) Zurückbehaltungsrecht; **second ~** zweitrangiges Pfandrecht; **secret ~** (vendor) Eigentumsvorbehalt; **seller's ~** Zurückbehaltungsrecht des Verkäufers; **senior ~** älteres Pfandrecht; **special (specific) ~** Pfandrecht an einer bestimmten Sache; **statutory ~** gesetzliches Pfandrecht; **tax ~** Steuerpfandrecht; **vendor's [for unpaid purchase money] ~** Eigentumsvorbehalt des Verkäufers, (real estate) Restkaufgeldhypothek; **warehouseman's ~** Lagerhalterpfandrecht;

~ **by agreement** Vertragspfandrecht; ~ **on a cheque** (Br.) (check, US) Zurückbehaltungsrecht an einem Scheck; ~ **upon cargo** Zurückbehaltungsrecht des Frachtführers; ~ **of a covenant** Eingangsformel einer Urkunde, einleitender Teil eines Vertrages; ~ **of factor at common law** Zurückbehaltungsrecht des Kommissionärs, Kommissionärspfandrecht; ~ **on goods** Zurückbehaltungsrecht; ~ **by operation of law** gesetzliches Zurückbehaltungsrecht (Pfandrecht); ~ **obtained through legal**

proceedings im Prozeßweg begründetes Pfandrecht; ~ **on real estate** Grundpfandrecht; ~ **of record** eingetragenes Pfandrecht;

to be secured by a ~ pfandrechtlich gesichert sein; **to be subject to the** ~ **of a judgment** der Zwangsvollstreckung unterliegen; **to constitute (create) a** ~ Pfandrecht bestellen; **to enforce a** ~ Pfandrecht verwerten; **to exercise a** ~ Pfandrecht ausüben; **to have a** ~ **[up] on a cargo** Zurückbehaltungsrecht an einer Ladung haben; **to have a** ~ **on the personal property of the debtor** Pfandrecht an den Gegenständen des persönlichen Gebrauchs seines Schuldners haben; **to lay a** ~ **on s. th.** Zurückbehaltungsrecht (Pfandrecht) an einer Sache geltend machen; **to lose the** ~ Pfandrecht verlieren; **to spread a** ~ Pfandrecht erweitern; **to vacate a** ~ Pfandrecht aufheben; **to waive a** ~ auf die Ausübung eines Pfandrechts verzichten;

~ **account** Begründung für ein Pfandrecht; ~ **claimant** Pfändungsberechtigter; ~ **creditor** *(US)* Pfandgläubiger, *(bankruptcy)* dinglich abgesicherter Gläubiger; ~ **date** Entstehungstermin einer Steuerschuld; ~ **letter** *(Br.)* Verpfändungs-, Pfandurkunde.

lienee Pfandschuldner, Verpfänder, Sicherungsgeber.

lienor *(US)* Zurückhaltungsberechtigter, Sicherungsnehmer.

lieu Ort, Stelle;

in ~ an Stelle von; **in** ~ **of payment** an Zahlungs Statt; **in** ~ **of performance** an Erfüllungs Statt;

~ **land** *(condemnation)* Ersatzgrundstück; ~ **tax** Ersatzsteuer.

life Leben, *(agreement)* Gültigkeits-, Geltungsdauer, Laufzeit, *(biography)* Biographie, Lebensdarstellung, *(~ insurance)* Lebensversicherungspolice, *(period of duration)* Nutzungsdauer, *(social activity)* gesellschaftliche Veranstaltungen;

as large as ~ in Lebensgröße; **dangerous to** ~ lebensgefährlich; **during his natural** ~ auf Lebenszeit; **during the** ~ **of the contract** während der Vertragsdauer; **for** ~ für den Rest des Lebens, lebenslänglich, auf Lebenszeit (Lebensdauer); **not for the** ~ **of me** um keinen Preis der Welt; **from the** ~ nach der Natur (dem lebenden Modell); **to the** ~ lebenstreu; **with all the pleasure in** ~ mit dem allergrößten Vergnügen;

agreed ~ *(debt)* vereinbarte Laufzeit; **animal** ~ Tierwelt; ~ **assured** Lebensversicherter; **bad** ~ *(insurance)* unterdurchschnittliche Lebenserwartung; **busy** ~ arbeitsreiches Leben; **conjugal** ~ Eheleben; **country** ~ Leben auf dem Lande; **cultural** ~ kulturelles Leben; **dog's** ~ Hundeleben; **economic** ~ Nutzungsdauer; **eternal** ~ ewiges Leben; **my early** ~ meine Jugend; **expected** ~ *(of equipment)* geschätzte Nutzungsdauer; **family** ~ Familienleben; **fashionable** ~ Modewelt; **good** ~ *(life insurance business)* gesunder Versicherungsnehmer, Versicherter mit überdurchschnittlicher Lebenserwartung; **high** ~ Luxusleben; **intellectual** ~ Geistesleben; **limited** ~ begrenzte Lebensdauer; **low** ~ die kleinen Leute; **married** ~ Ehestand, -leben; **natural** ~ natürliche Lebenszeit eines Menschen; **private** ~ Intimsphäre; **probable** ~ mutmaßliche Lebensdauer; **professional** ~ Berufsleben; **proper** ~ wirkliche Lebensdauer; **remaining** ~ Restnutzungsdauer; **service** ~ *(machine)* Nutzungs-, Lebensdauer; **social** ~ geselliges Leben, Gemeinschaftsleben; **still** ~ ruhiges Leben; **[sub]standard** ~ [unter]durchschnittliche Lebensdauer; **total** ~ Gesamtlebensdauer; **town** ~ Leben in der Stadt; **useful** ~ Nutzungsdauer; **vacuous** ~ müßiges Leben; **working** ~ Arbeitsjahre;

~ **of an agreement** Laufzeit eines Vertrages, Vertragsdauer; ~ **in being** verbleibende Lebenszeit; ~ **of a bond** Laufzeit einer [Kommunal]obligation; ~ **of building** Gebäudenutzungsdauer; ~ **of a government** Regierungszeit; ~ **of a lease** Laufzeit eines Mietvertrages (Pachtvertrages); ~ **of a letter of credit** Laufzeit eines Akkreditivs; ~ **and limb** Leib und Leben; ~ **of a loan** Darlehnsdauer; ~ **of a patent** Gültigkeitsdauer (Laufzeit) eines Patents, Patentdauer; ~ **of a partnership** Beteiligungsdauer; ~ **of a policy** Policendauer; ~ **in the diplomatic service** Diplomatenleben; ~ **of a ship** Lebensdauer eines Schiffes; ~ **and soul of a company** Seele eines Unternehmens; ~ **of a steamship** Lebensdauer eines Dampfers;

to assure one's ~ **with a company** *(Br.)* sich lebensversichern; **to be apprehensive for one's** ~ um sein Leben besorgt sein; **to be full of** ~ lebhaft (interessiert) sein; **to be in danger of one's** ~ sich in Lebensgefahr befinden; **to be the** ~ **of the conversation** zur Gesprächsbelustigung beitragen; **to be a matter of** ~ **and death** um Tod und Leben gehen; **to beat s. o. within an inch of his** ~ j. fast zu Tode prügeln; **to carry one's** ~ **in one's hands** sein Leben riskieren; **to come to** ~ Bewußtsein wieder erlangen; **to endanger the** ~ **of a substantial number of persons** das Leben einer größeren Anzahl von Menschen gefährden; **to escape with** ~ **and limb** das nackte Leben retten; **to give new** ~ **to s. o.** jem.

seinen Lebensmut wiedergeben; **to give** ~ **to s. th.** etw. ins Leben rufen; **to have an easy** ~ bequemes Dasein führen; **to have led an adventurous** ~ bewegtes Leben hinter sich haben; **to have no regard for human** ~ rücksichtslos über Menschenleben hinweggehen; **to have the time of one's** ~ sich köstlich amüsieren; **to enter public** ~ ins öffentliche Leben eintreten; **to have a** ~ **for tax purposes of twenty five years** steuerliche Nutzungsdauer von 25 Jahren haben; **to hold an office (a post) for** ~ auf Lebenszeit (lebenslänglich) angestellt sein; **to insure one's** ~ Lebensversicherung abschließen; **to lay down one's** ~ **for s. o.** sein Leben für j. hingeben; **to lead a fast** ~ flottes Leben führen; **to lead a steady** ~ solides Leben führen; **to lead a** ~ **of pleasure** vergnügtes Dasein führen; **to lead the** ~ **of Riley** *(US coll.)* sorgenfreies Leben führen; **to live all one's** ~ **in A** sein ganzes Leben in A zubringen; **to live half of one's** ~ **on one's job** Hälfte seines Lebens beruflich verbringen; **to live a secluded** ~ abgeschlossen (zurückgezogen) leben; **to live a** ~ **of independence** unabhängiges Leben führen; **to lose one's** ~ **by accident** Unfalltod erleiden, bei einem Unfall sterben; **to put** ~ **into an enterprise** *(fam.)* Leben in die Bude bringen; **to recall s. o. to** ~ j. wiederbeleben; **to result in great loss of** ~ viele Todesopfer fordern; **to retire from active** ~ in den Ruhestand treten; **to risk one's** ~ sein Leben einsetzen (aufs Spiel setzen); **to run for one's** ~ sein Leben retten; **to sacrifice one's** ~ sein Leben hingeben; **to save s. one's** ~ j. aus Todesgefahr retten; **to see** ~ in der Welt herumkommen, seine Erfahrungen machen; **to sell one's** ~ **dearly** sein Leben teuer verkaufen; **to set one's** ~ **on a chance** sein Leben aufs Spiel setzen; **to squander** ~ **routinely** sein Leben bedenkenlos wegwerfen; **to take one's own** ~ freiwillig aus dem Leben scheiden, Selbstmord begehen; **to take s. one's** ~ j. umbringen; **to take one's** ~ **in one's hands** sein Leben bewußt aufs Spiel setzen; **to talk away one's** ~ sich um Kopf und Kragen reden; **to write s. one's** ~ jds. Biographie schreiben;

~ **annuitant** Leibrentenempfänger; **[whole]** ~ **annuity** lebenslängliche Rente, Leibrente; ~ **annuity company** Rentenanstalt.

life assurance *(Br.)* Lebensversicherung;

deferred ~ aufgeschobene Lebensversicherung; **free** ~ prämienfreie Lebensversicherung; **industrial** ~ Volks-, Kleinlebensversicherung; **more than one** ~ Lebensversicherung über verbundene Leben; **ordinary** ~ Großlebensversicherung; **straight** ~ Versicherung auf den Todesfall, Todesfallversicherung; **whole** ~ Lebensversicherung auf den Todesfall, reine Todesfallversicherung;

~ **arrangements** *(Br.)* steuerliche Behandlung von Lebensversicherungsprämien; ~ **company** Lebensversicherungsgesellschaft; ~ **contract** Lebensversicherungsvertrag; ~ **policy** Lebensversicherungspolice; ~ **premium** Lebensversicherungsprämie; ~ **protection** Lebensversicherungsschutz.

life | belt *(Br.)* Rettungsgürtel; ~ **beneficiary** lebenslänglich Begünstigter, lebenslänglicher Nutznießer; ~ **blood** *(fig.)* Lebensenergie; ~ **branch** Lebensversicherungsabteilung; ~ **buoy** Rettungsboje; ~ **car** *(mar.)* Rettungswagen; ~ **companion** Lebensgefährte; ~ **company** Lebensversicherungsgesellschaft; ~ **contingency** *(insurance)* von der Lebensdauer abhängiges Risiko, Lebensrisiko; ~ **contract** Vertrag auf Lebenszeit; ~ **coverage** Lebensversicherungsschutz; ~ **cycle** Lebensablauf; ~**-and-death struggle** Kampf auf Leben und Tod; ~ **director** lebenslänglich bestelltes Vorstandsmitglied; ~ **estate** [lebenslänglicher] Grundstücksnießbrauch; **to create a** ~ **estate** Nießbrauch bestellen; ~ **expectancy** Lebenserwartung; ~ **fund** *(life insurance)* Prämienreserve; ~ **history** Lebensgeschichte; ~ **imprisonment** lebenslängliches Gefängnis, lebenslängliche Zuchthausstrafe (Haft); ~ **income** lebenslängliches Einkommen.

life insurance Lebensversicherung;

assessment ~ Lebensversicherung auf Gegenseitigkeit; **business** ~ Partner-, Teilhaberversicherung; **combined endowment and whole-**~ gemischte Versicherung auf den Erlebens- und Todesfall; **governmental** ~ Lebensversicherung für Staatsangestellte; **group** ~ Sammel-, Kollektivlebensversicherung; **high-value** ~ hochwertige Lebensversicherung; **industrial** ~ *(US)* Volks-, Kleinlebensversicherung; **joint** ~ wechselseitige Überlebensversicherung; **limited-pay** ~ *(US)* Lebensversicherung mit abgekürzter Prämienzahlung; **mutual** ~ Lebensversicherung auf Gegenseitigkeit; **noncancellable** ~ unkündbare Lebensversicherung; **ordinary** ~ *(US)* Lebensversicherung auf den Todesfall, Großlebensversicherung; **paid-up** ~ voll eingezahlte Lebensversicherung; **renewable term** ~ befristete Lebensversicherung mit Verlängerungsrecht, verlängerungsfähige Risikolebensversicherung; **salary reduction (savings)** ~ Lebensversicherung, bei der die Prämien vom Gehalt abge-

bucht werden; **straight ~** Versicherung auf den Todesfall, Todesfallversicherung; **term ~** Risikolebensversicherung; **whole ~** Lebensversicherung auf den Todesfall, Todesfallversicherung; **wholesale ~** globale Lebensversicherung;
~ in force Lebensversicherung mit laufender Beitragszahlung; **~ with (without) profits** *(Br.)* Lebensversicherung mit (ohne) Gewinnbeteiligung; **~ war risk included** Lebensversicherung mit Einschluß der Kriegsgefahr;
to buy a ~ Lebensversicherung abschließen;
~ agent Lebensversicherungsvertreter; **~ company** Lebensversicherungsgesellschaft; **mutual ~ company** Lebensversicherungsgesellschaft auf Gegenseitigkeit; **~ contract** Lebensversicherungsvertrag; **~ cover (coverage)** Lebensversicherungsschutz; **~ elements** Lebensversicherungscharakter; **~ fund** Prämienreserve einer Lebensversicherungsgesellschaft; **~ holdings** Vermögensfonds einer Lebensversicherungsgesellschaft; **~ office** Lebensversicherungsbüro; **~ policy** Lebensversicherungspolice; **20-payment ~ policy** Lebensversicherungspolice mit auf 20 Jahre abgekürzter Laufzeit; **~ premium** Lebensversicherungsprämie; **~ protection** Lebensversicherungsschutz; **~ relief** *(Br.)* Freibetrag für Lebensversicherung; **business ~ trust** Treuhandgesellschaft zur Verwaltung einer Teilhaberversicherung.

life│-insured savings account *(US)* mit einer Lebensversicherung gekoppeltes Sparkonto; **~ interest** lebenslängliche Nießbrauch, lebenslänglicher Nießbrauch; **determinable ~ interest** auflösend bedingtes lebenslängliches Nutzungsrecht; **to invest one's money at ~ interest** sein Vermögen in einem Leibrentenvertrag anlegen; **~ jacket** Schwimmweste; **~ land** Pachtung auf Lebenszeit; **~ line** Lebensader, *(fig.)* Rettungsanker, *(mar.)* Rettungsleine, *(mil.)* lebenswichtige Verbindungs-, Kommunikationslinie, *(traffic)* Verkehrsader; **to swim between the ~ lines** im abgetrennten Gebiet schwimmen; **~ manager** Leiter einer Lebensversicherungsabteilung; **~ member** Mitglied auf Lebenszeit; **~ membership** lebenslängliche Mitgliedschaft; **~ net** Sprungtuch; **~ office** Lebensversicherungsbüro; **~ pattern** Lebensgewohnheiten; **to set the ~ pattern of the community** Rahmen des Gemeinschaftslebens bestimmen; **~ pension** lebenslängliche Pension; **~ pensioner** Leibrentner; **to take out policies on one's key men** seine Schlüsselkräfte lebensversichern; **~ policy** Lebensversicherungspolice; **limited-payment ~ policy** abgekürzte Lebensversicherungspolice; **permanent ~ policy** jährlich kündbare Lebensversicherungspolice; **~ policy with profits** gewinnbeteiligte Lebensversicherungspolice; **~ policy qualifying for relief** *(Br.)* steuerbegünstigte Lebensversicherungspolice; **to take out a ~ policy** Lebensversicherung abschließen, sein Leben versichern; **~ preserver** *(mar., US)* Schwimmweste, Rettungsgürtel; **~ raft** Rettungsfloß; **~ rate** Prämiensatz einer Lebensversicherung; **~ rocket** Rettungsrakete; **~ sentence** lebenslängliche Freiheitsstrafe; **~ shot** Aufnahme aus dem täglichen Leben; **~ signal** Rettungsbojensignal; **~ size** Lebensgröße; **above ~ size** überlebensgroß; **average ~ span** normale Lebensdauer; **~ story** Szene aus dem täglichen Leben; **~ strings** Lebensfaden; **~ style** Lebensstil; **~ subscription** einmaliger Beitrag auf Lebenszeit; **~ tables** Sterblichkeitstabelle, Sterbetafel; **~ tenancy** lebenslänglicher Nießbrauch [an einem Grundstück]; **to hold a ~ tenancy of a house** lebenslänglichen Nießbrauch an einem Haus (lebenslängliches Wohnrecht) haben; **~ tenant** lebenslänglicher Nießbraucher; **~ tenure** Amt auf Lebenszeit, lebenslängliche Anstellung; **~ underwriter** Lebensversicherer.

lifeboat Rettungsboot, *(sl.)* Umwandlung einer Todes- in eine lebenslange Haftstrafe;
~ Association Lebensrettungsgesellschaft; **~ station** Rettungsstation.

lifeguard Leibwache, *(US)* Rettungswache, -schwimmer.

lifehold Nießbrauch, lebenslängliche Grundpacht;
~ *(a.)* auf Lebenszeit.

lifeholder lebenslänglicher Nießbraucher.

lifeless leblos, *(fig.)* schwunglos, temperamentlos, *(stock exchange)* lustlos, matt, flau.

lifelessness Flaute, Lustlosigkeit.

lifelong lebenslang, -länglich.

lifemanship erfolgreiches Auftreten.

lifer *(prison)* lebenslängliche Freiheitsstrafe, *(prisoner)* Lebenslänglicher.

liferent *(Scot.)* Nießbrauch auf Lebenszeit, lebenslängliche Rente, Leibrente;
~ *(v.)* lebenslängliche Rente aussetzen.

liferenter *(Scot.)* lebenslänglicher Nießbraucher, Leibrentner.

lifesaver Lebensretter.

lifesaving Lebensrettung;
~ apparatus Lebensrettungsgerät; **~ medal** Lebensrettungsmedaille; **~ service** Rettungsdienst.

lifetime Lebenszeit;
all one's ~ Zeit seines Lebens; **in one's ~** bei Lebzeiten; **once in a ~** sehr selten;
~ career Gesamtlaufbahn; **~ gift** Schenkung unter Lebenden.

lifework Lebensarbeit, -werk.

lifo *(inventory taking)* Zuerstentnahme der neueren Vorräte und Bilanzierung zum jeweiligen Buchwert.

lift Aufheben, *(Br.)* Aufzug, *(advancement)* Beförderung, *(in car)* Mitfahrgelegenheit, *(contribution)* Beistand, Hilfe, Unterstützung, *(plane)* Auftrieb, *(prices)* Steigen, Aufschwung;
air ~ Luftbrücke; **dead ~** *(fig.)* vergebliche Anstrengungen; **goods ~** *(Br.)* Warenaufzug; **heavy ~** schwere Last; **high-speed ~** *(Br.)* Schnellaufzug;
~ *(v.)* hochheben, aufheben, beseitigen, *(fig.)* auf eine höhere Ebene heben, *(mist)* weggehen, sich verziehen, steigen, *(plagiarism)* plagiieren, *(collect rents)* Mieten kassieren, *(pilfer)* stehlen, klauen;
~ one's hand against s. o. handgreiflich gegen j. werden; **~ a ban** Verbot aufheben; **~ the bar** Verjährung unterbrechen; **~ cattle** *(Br.)* Vieh stehlen; **~ the censorship** Zensur aufheben; **~ a control** *(trade)* Bewirtschaftungsmaßnahmen aufheben; **~ up one's head** sein Haupt erheben; **~ up the heel against** unfreundlich behandeln, mit Undankbarkeit vergelten; **~ a passage from an author** jem. plagiieren; **~ s. o. of poverty** jem. aus der Armut heraushelfen; **~ a promissory note** Schuldschein bezahlen; **~ prices** Preise hochschrauben; **~ restrictions on instal(l)ment buying** Beschränkungen auf dem Abzahlungsgebiet aufheben; **~ the top** *(stock exchange, US)* Höchstkurs heraufsetzen;
to get a ~ mitgenommen werden; **to get a ~ up in the world** gesellschaftlich erfolgreich sein; **to give s. o. a ~** jem. im Auto mitnehmen; **to have a ~** *(fam.)* Gehaltsaufbesserung erfahren; **to have a ~ home** Gelegenheit zur Rückfahrt finden; **to ride down in a ~** *(Br.)* mit dem Fahrstuhl herunterfahren; **to take the ~ to the tenth floor** *(Br.)* Aufzug zum zehnten Stock nehmen;
~ attendant (boy, Br.) Fahrstuhlführer; **~ boy** *(Br.)* Fahrstuhlführer; **~ company** *(Br.)* Fahrstuhlgesellschaft; **~ shaft** *(Br.)* Aufzugsschacht; **~ ticket** *(Br.)* Skiliftfahrschein; **~ truck** Hubstapler; **~ van** Möbeltransportbehälter.

lifter *(sl.)* Langfinger.

lifting Aufhebung;
~ of the banking secrecy Aufhebung des Bankgeheimnisses; **~ of fixed retail prices** *(book trade)* Aufhebung der Ladenpreise; **~ of quota controls** Aufhebung von Kontingentskontrollen; **~ crane** Hebekran.

ligan Seewurf.

light [Tages]licht, *(lighter, sl.)* Zigarettenanzünder, *(law)* Recht auf ungehinderten Lichtzutritt, *(mar.)* Leuchtfeuer, -turm;
according to his ~s nach dem Maß seiner Einsicht; **by the ~ of a candle** bei Kerzenlicht; **in the ~ of** angesichts von, im Zeichen von; **in favo(u)rable ~** in günstigem Licht;
advertising ~s Reklamebeleuchtung; **ancient ~s** *(Br.)* Licht- und Fensterrecht; **artificial ~** künstliche Beleuchtung; **coast ~** Leuchtfeuer; **clearance ~** *(airplane)* Begrenzungslicht; **dashboard ~** Armaturenbeleuchtung; **defective ~** defekte Lichtanlage; **flashing ~** Blinkfeuer; **floating ~** Leuchtboje; **fluorescent ~** Neonlicht; **green ~** freie Fahrt, *(fig.)* offizielle Erlaubnis, grünes Licht; **harbo(u)r ~** Hafenfeuer; **intermittent ~** Blinkfeuer; **landing ~** Landefeuer, *(airport)* Landelicht; **leading ~s** führende Leute; **navigation ~s** Navigationslichter; **neon ~** Neonlicht; **parking ~** Parklicht; **position (running, US) ~** *(airplane)* Positionslichter, *(car)* Begrenzungslicht; **rear ~** Heck-, Rücklicht; **red ~** *(traffic beacon)* Rot; **revolving ~** Dreh-, Blinkfeuer; **signal ~** Bake, Signalbake; **traffic ~s** Verkehrsampel; **traffic indicator ~s** Blinklichtanlagen;
shining ~s of an age Glanzgestalten eines Zeitalters; **~ of one's countenance** seine Zustimmung; **~ of day** Tageslicht; **shining ~ of the day** Leuchte einer Epoche; **leading ~s of a party** Gesellschaftsspitzen; **~ and shade** Licht und Schatten;
~ *(v.)* upon a rare book in a secondhand bookshop beim Antiquar auf ein seltenes Buch stoßen; **~ a lamp** Lampe anzünden; **~ out** *(sl.)* sich dünne machen; **~ up** hell beleuchten, aufleuchten;
to act according to one's ~s seinen Verstandeskräften entsprechend handeln; **to appear in one's true ~** sich im wahren Licht zeigen; **to appear in the ~ of a scoundrel** sich als Schurke entpuppen; **to be charged with driving without ~** wegen Fahrens ohne Licht angeklagt sein; **to bring to ~** ans Tageslicht befördern, aufdecken; **to cast a doubtful ~ on s. th.** zweifelhaftes Licht auf eine Sache werfen; **to come to ~** ans Tageslicht

kommen, sich herausstellen; **to do one's best according to one's** ~ das Beste aus sich machen (herausholen); **to have new** ~ **upon s. th.** neue Erkenntnisse über etw. gewonnen haben; **to hide one's** ~ **under a bushel** sein Licht unter den Scheffel stellen; **to make** ~ **of an accusation** Anklage nicht ernst nehmen; **to make** ~ **of a piece of advice** Ratschlag nicht beachten; **to make** ~ **of dangers** Gefahren auf die leichte Schulter nehmen; **to place s. one's conduct in a false** ~ jds. Verhalten falsch deuten; **to put o. s. in a good** ~ sich ins rechte Licht setzen; **to put s. th. in a favo(u)rable** ~ etw. günstig darstellen; **to put s. th. in its true** ~ etw. ins rechte Licht rücken; **to receive green** ~ **for a project** grünes Licht für ein Vorhaben erhalten; **to return** ~ *(ship)* ohne Ladung zurückfahren; **to see the** ~ *(fam.)* die Wahrheit erkennen, kapieren; **to see the red** ~ *(fam.)* Floh ins Ohr gesetzt bekommen; **to see the** ~ **of day** das Licht der Welt erblicken, *(book)* veröffentlicht werden; **to set the facts in true** ~ Tatsachen ins rechte Licht rücken; **to see the** ~ **of a joke** Pointe eines Witzes begreifen; **to see a matter in a new** ~ Angelegenheit jetzt ganz anders beurteilen; **to shed** ~ **on s. th.** Licht auf etw. werfen; **to show s. o. a** ~ j. aufklären; **to show o. s. in good** ~ sich ins rechte Licht setzen; **to stand in s. one's** ~ jds. Vorankommen behindern; **to stand in one's own** ~ sich selbst um die Früchte seiner Arbeit bringen; **to stop a neighbo(u)r's** ~ einem Nachbarn die Sicht verbauen; **to throw a new** ~ **on a matter** Angelegenheit in neuem Licht erscheinen lassen; **to travel** ~ mit nur wenig Gepäck reisen; **to view s. one's conduct in a favo(u)rable** ~ jds. Verhalten positiv beurteilen;
~ *(a.)* leicht, von geringem [spezifischen] Gewicht, *(bright)* hell, licht, *(drink)* von geringem Alkoholgehalt, *(ship)* unbeladen, leer;
~ **aircraft** Leichtflugzeug; ~ **attack of illness** leichte Krankheit; ~ **beacon** Leuchtbake, -feuer; ~ **beer** leichtes Bier; ~ **breeze** leichte (schwache) Brise; ~ **buoy** Leuchtboje; ~ **cargo** Leichtgut; **to have a** ~ **character** liederlichen Lebenswandel führen; ~ **coin** *(US)* untergewichtige Münze; ~ **comedy** leichte Komödie; ~ **cruiser** leichter Kreuzer; ~ **displacement** Leertonnage; **red-~ district** Hurenviertel; ~ **draught** *(ship)* Tiefgang des leeren Schiffes; ~ **dues** *(mar.)* Leuchtfeuergebühren; ~ **-duty vehicle** Hilfsfahrzeug; ~ **-earned** leicht verdient; ~ **effect** Lichteffekt, -wirkung; ~ **engine** alleinfahrende Maschine; ~ **expense** geringe Ausgaben; ~ **field artillery** leichte Feldartillerie; ~ **filter** *(photo)* Lichtfilter; ~ **-fingered** *(sl.)* diebisch; **to be** ~ **-fingered** Mein und Dein verwechseln; ~ **-fingered gentry** Zunft der Taschendiebe; ~ **freight** Leichtgüter; ~ **goods** Leichtgüter; ~ **hand** *(fig.)* verständisvolles Vorgehen; *(fast)* ohne Gepäck, *(ship)* nicht voll bemannt; ~ **housekeeping** leichte Hausarbeit; ~ **industries** Leichtindustrie; ~ **literature** Unterhaltungsliteratur; ~ **marching order** *(mil.)* leichtes Marschgepäck; **no** ~ **matter** keine Kleinigkeit; ~ **metal** Leichtmetall; ~ **obstruction** Lichtverbauen; ~ **oil** Leichtöl; ~ **plane** Leichtflugzeug; ~ **plant** Leichtanlage; ~ **profits** mäßiger Gewinn; ~ **punishment** milde Strafe; ~ **railway** *(Br.)* Klein-, Seiten-, Schmalspurbahn; ~ **reading** leichte Lektüre; ~ **signal** Signalanlage; ~ **soil** leichter Boden; ~ **taxation** geringe Besteuerung; ~ **trading** schwacher [Börsen]umsatz; ~ **van** leichter Lastwagen; ~ **vessel** Leuchtschiff; ~ **wave** Leichtwelle; ~ **weights** zu leichte Gewichte; ~ **work** leichte Arbeit; ~ **year** *(astronomy)* Lichtjahr.
lighted, dim abgeblendet;
~ **by electricity** elektrisch beleuchtet;
~ **road** beleuchtete Straße.
lighten *(v.)* erleichtern, *(illuminate)* be-, erleuchten, *(ship)* ableichtern, löschen, Ladung verringern, teilweise entladen;
~ **one's conscience** sein Gewissen erleichtern; ~ **a ship's cargo** ableichtern, Ladung verringern, teilweise entladen; ~ **a sentence** Strafe mildern, Strafmaß herabsetzen; ~ **s. one's task** jds. Aufgabe erleichtern; ~ **taxes** Steuern senken, Steuererleichterungen gewähren.
lightening Erleuchtung, *(ship)* Leichterung, Ableichtern; ~ **of the burden of the state** Erleichterung der Staatslast; ~ **of taxation** Steuererleichterungen.
lighter Leichter, Kahn;
cigarette ~ Feuerzeug;
~ **-than-aircraft** Luftballon;
~ *(v.)* in einem Leichter befördern.
lighterage *(price for unloading by lighters)* Löschungsgebühren, *(price for use of lighters)* Leichtergebühren, *(removal of cargo)* Löschung durch Leichterung, Schutentransport;
~ **charges** Leichterungskosten, Leichtergebühren.
lighterhire Leichtermieter.
lightface *(print.)* magere Schrift.
lighterman Leichterschiffer.

lightfast lichtecht.
lighthead leichtfertiger Mensch.
lighthouse Leuchtturm;
revolving ~ Drehfeuer;
~ **charges** Leuchtfeuergebühren; ~ **keeper** Leuchtturmwärter.
lighthouseman Leuchtturmwächter.
lighting Beleuchtung[sanlage];
electric ~ elektrische Beleuchtung; **indirect** ~ indirekte Beleuchtung; **interior** ~ Innenbeleuchtung; **street** ~ Straßenbeleuchtung;
~ **of a vehicle** Fahrzeugbeleuchtung;
~ **arrangement** Lichtverhältnisse; ~ **effects** *(theater)* Beleuchtungseffekte; ~ **engineer** Beleuchtungstechniker; ~ **equipment** Beleuchtungsanlage; ~ **expenses** Beleuchtungskosten; ~ **expert** Beleuchtungsfachmann; ~ **fixture** Beleuchtungskörper; ~ **regulations** *(car)* Beleuchtungsvorschriften; ~ **-up time** Einschaltzeit für Straßenbeleuchtung (Autoscheinwerfer).
lightly leicht, wenig, *(frivolous)* leichtfertig, *(with levity)* liederlich, locker;
~ **equipped** schlecht ausgerüstet;
to bear s. th. ~ etw. mit Gelassenheit tragen; **to eat** ~ schwacher Esser sein; **to get off** ~ noch gut davonkommen sein; **to sit** ~ **upon s. o.** j. kaum belasten; **to speak** ~ **of s. th.** leichtfertig über etw. reden; **to think** ~ **of s. th.** etw. geringschätzen; **to touch** ~ **on a delicate matter** heikles Thema äußerst vorsichtig angehen; **to travel** ~ mit wenig Gepäck reisen;
~ **come,** ~ **go** wie gewonnen so zerronnen.
lightness *(weight)* Leichtigkeit.
lightning [Blitz]schlag;
as quick as ~ blitzschnell; **like greased** ~ *(fam.)* wie ein geölter Blitz;
ball ~ Kugelblitz; **chain[ed]** ~ Kettenblitz; **sheet** ~ Flächenblitz; **summer** ~ Wetterleuchten;
to be struck by ~ vom Blitzschlag getroffen werden;
~ **call** *(tel.)* Blitzgespräch; ~ **clause** Blitzschlagklausel; ~ **conductor** *(Br.)* *(rod)* Blitzableiter; ~ **damage** Blitzschäden; ~ **insurance** Versicherung gegen Blitzschlag; ~ **progress** *(fam.)* rasanter Fortschritt; **to make a** ~ **retort** schlagfertig antworten; ~ **rod** *(airforce, sl.)* Düsenkampfflugzeug; **with** ~ **speed** mit Blitzgeschwindigkeit; ~ **storm** Gewitter; ~ **strike** spontaner Streik; ~ **war** Blitzkrieg.
lightship Feuerschiff.
lightweight stationery dünnes Briefpapier.
likelihood Wahrscheinlichkeit, *(statistics)* Mutmaßlichkeit.
likely-looking vielversprechend, aussichtsreich.
likeness Gleichheit, Ähnlichkeit;
family ~ Familienähnlichkeit;
~ **of his father** Abbild seines Vaters;
to have one's ~ **taken** sich photographieren lassen.
liking Zuneigung, Gefallen;
~ **for business** geschäftliches Interesse;
to take an immediate ~ **for (to) each other** sich sofort sympathish sein.
limb Glied, Körperteil;
out on a ~ *(coll.)* in einer gefährlichen Lage, sehr im Nachteil;
~ **of the law** Arm des Gesetzes;
to escape with life and ~ mit einem blauen Auge davonkommen.
limbless *(US)* Amputierter.
limbo Rumpelkammer, *(condition of neglect)* Verwahrlosung;
~ **of fools** Narrenparadies;
to be dumped into ~ *(Br.)* als nutzlos weggeworfen werden; **to go in** ~ in den Papierkorb wandern.
limelight Rampenlicht [der Öffentlichkeit];
in the ~ im Licht der Öffentlichkeit; **fond of the** ~ publicitysüchtig;
to be in the ~ im Blickpunkt der Öffentlichkeit stehen.
limit *(boundary)* Grenze, Linie, *(commodity exchange)* zugestandene Preisschwankung pro Tag, *(duration of validity)* Gültigkeitsdauer, *(maximum amount)* Höchst-, Maximalbetrag, *(price)* Preisgrenze, Limit, *(rate)* festgesetzte Menge, Satz, *(restriction)* Begrenzung, Schranke;
in ~**s** Zutritt gestattet; **to the** ~ bis zur Höhe von; **within** ~ in Grenzen, maßvoll, im Rahmen; **within the** ~**s of the city** innerhalb der Stadtgrenzen; **within local** ~**s** im lokalen Maßstab; **without** ~**s** schrankenlos;
age ~ Altersgrenze, Mindestalter; **cartage** ~ Zustell-, Lieferbezirk; **credit** ~ *(Br.)* Kreditlinie; **debt** ~ *(municipal accounting)* Verschuldungsgrenze; **well defined** ~**s** genau bestimmte Grenzen; **extreme** ~ äußerster Termin; **feasible** ~ ausführbares Limit; **fiduciary** ~ Höchstgrenze für ungedeckte Notenaus-

gabe; **firm ~** Festorder; **increased ~** *(liability insurance)* erhöhte Versicherungssumme; **inferior ~** frühestmöglicher Zeitpunkt; **large ~** ausgedehntes Limit; **legal ~** *(note issue)* Deckungsgrenze; **lower ~** untere Grenze, Mindestgrenze; **lowest ~** letzter Preis; **manageable ~s** angemessene Grenzen; **maximum ~** Höchstgrenze; **minimum ~** Mindestgrenze; **narrow ~** enge Grenzen, knappes Limit; **off ~s** *(US)* Zutritt verboten; **office ~** *(insurance)* Deckungsgrenze, Höchstbetrag; **practicable ~** ausführbares Limit; **rate ~** *(postal service)* Höchstgewicht; **size ~** *(postal service)* Höchstgröße; **speed ~** zugelassene Höchstgeschwindigkeit; **standard ~** *(liability insurance)* normale Versicherungssumme; **superior ~** spätmöglicher Zeitpunkt; **three-mile ~** Dreimeilengrenze, -zone; **time ~** Zeitraum, -spanne, Frist, *(speaker)* Redezeit; **upper ~** Höchstgrenze; **utmost ~** äußerste Grenze;

~ of authority Vollmachtsbeschränkung; **agreed ~ for check** vereinbartes Scheckausstellungslimit; **~ of compensation** Entschädigungsgrenze, Höchstentschädigung; **~ of cover** *(insurance)* Deckungsgrenze; **~ of credit** *(Br.)* Beleihungsgrenze, Kreditlinie; **~ impracticable of execution** unausführbares Limit; **~s to growth** Grenzen des Wachstums, Wachstumsgrenzen; **~ of human performance** Grenzen menschlicher Leistungsfähigkeit; **~ of indemnity** *(insurance)* Haftungsgrenze; **~s of port** Hafenbereich; **basic ~ for property damage** versicherter Sachschadensgrundbetrag; **~ of speed** Geschwindigkeitsgrenze; **~ on television spending in campaigns** Begrenzung der Fernsehwahlkosten; **~ of territorial waters** Höchstgrenze [auf dem Meer]; **~ of time** zeitliche Begrenzung; **~ of tolerance** Toleranz; **~ on votes** Stimmrechtsbeschränkung; **formal ~ on wage increase (rises)** *(Br.)* gesetzlich festgelegte Lohnsteigerungsbegrenzung, Höchstgrenze für Lohn- und Gehaltssteigerungen;

~ *(v.)* begrenzen, *(price)* limitieren, Limit vorschreiben, *(restrict)* ein-, beschränken, kontingentieren, *(set bounds)* begrenzen, Grenzen setzen;

~ o. s. to three aspects of a subject sich auf drei Aspekte eines Themas beschränken; **~ an estate** befristetes Eigentumsrecht gewähren; **~ expenditure** Aufwandsetat (Ausgaben) beschranken; **~ o. s. to strict necessities** sich auf das unbedingt Notwendige beschränken; **~ a price** Preis-, Kurslimit festsetzen; **~ the time allotted to each speaker** Redezeit beschränken; **to be bound to a ~** an ein Limit gebunden sein; **to be straining the ~s of s. one's patience** jds. Geduld überfordern; **to be within the ~ of an overdraft** sich im Rahmen eines Überziehungskredits halten; **to cancel a ~** Kreditlimit aufheben; **to confine s. one's authority within certain ~s** jds. Machtbefugnisse auf ein gewisses Ausmaß einschränken; **to exceed the ~** *(broker)* Limit ([Preis]grenze) überschreiten; **to go beyond the ~** über das Limit hinausgehen; **to go for the ~** *(US)* bis zum Äußersten gehen; **to fix the ~s of the debate beforehand** Redezeit von vornherein festlegen (begrenzen); **to fix an extreme ~ for a budget** Etathöchstgrenze festsetzen; **to impose ~s on one's expenditure** sich Einschränkungen auferlegen; **to keep within the ~** sein Limit einhalten; **to keep one's expenditure within reasonable ~s** Ausgaben auf ein vernünftiges Maß einschränken; **to lend money without ~s** schrankenlos Geld verleihen; **to observe a time ~** Frist einhalten; **to raise the ~** Limit erhöhen; **to raise the ~ on personal loans** Ausleihungshöchstgrenze für Personalkredite anheben; **to reach the age ~** Altersgrenze erreichen; **to reach the ~s of one's resources** an der Grenze seiner Mittel ankommen; **to reduce one's ~** sein Limit einschränken; **to set a ~** Limit festsetzen; **to set a ~ to the expenses** Ausgaben der Höhe nach beschränken;

~ order *(broker, US)* limitierter [Börsen]auftrag, limitierte Order, Limitauftrag; **~ pricing** monopolistische Niedrigpreispolitik.

limitation Be-, Einschränkung, Begrenzung, Kontingentierung, *(prescription)* Verjährung[sfrist], *(restrictive condition)* Begrenzung eines Besitzrechts, *(time assigned)* vorgeschriebene Frist;

collateral ~ *(interest in estate)* bedingtes Nutzungsrecht; **constitutional ~** Verfassungsbeschränkung; **contingent ~** zeitlich beschränktes Fideikommiß; **family ~** Begrenzung der Kinderzahl; **membership ~** Begrenzung der Mitgliederzahl; **population ~** Begrenzung der Bevölkerung; **statutory ~** gesetzliche Verjährungsfrist, Verjährungsbestimmungen; **time ~** Klageerhebungsfrist, Verjährung;

~ of action Klageverjährung, -ausschlußfrist; **~ of an administration** Verwaltungsgrenzen; **~ of armaments** Rüstungsbeschränkung, -begrenzung; **~ of authority** Zuständigkeitsbeschränkung, Vollmachtsbeschränkung; **~ of a claim** Anspruchsverjährung; **~ of credit** Kreditrestriktion; **~ of (on) dividends** Dividendenbeschränkung; **~ of an estate** Grundstücksabgrenzung; **~ of a lesser estate** Einräumung eines beschränkten Eigentumsrechtes; **~ of exports** Ausfuhrbeschränkung; **~ of fees** Gebührenkürzung; **~ of hours** Arbeitszeitbeschränkung; **~ of imports** Einfuhrbeschränkung; **10% a year ~ on dividend increases** jährliche Begrenzung des Dividendenanstiegs auf 10%; **~ of the fiduciary issue** Kontingentierung der Banknotenausgabe; **~ of jurisdiction** Einschränkung der Zuständigkeit, Zuständigkeitsbegrenzung; **~ in law** *(estate)* zeitlich begrenztes Nutzungsrecht; **~ of liability** Beschränkung (Einschränkung) der Haftung, Haftungsbeschränkung; **~ of liability by contract** vertragliche Haftungsbeschränkung; **~ of membership** Begrenzung der Mitgliederzahl; **~ of output** Produktionsbeschränkung; **~ of criminal proceedings** Strafverfolgungsverjährung; **~s upon production** Produktionsbeschränkungen, -begrenzungen; **~ of profits** Gewinnbeschränkung; **~ of the right to alienation** Veräußerungsbeschränkung; **~ of right to vote (voting power)** Stimmrechtsbeschränkung; **~ of time** *(criminal proceedings)* [Straf]verjährung; **~s written into warranties** Verjährungsbestimmungen von Garantiezusagen; **to accept a £ 6 a week ~ on pay increases** sich mit maximal 30,- DM Wochenlohnanstieg zufrieden geben; **to be barred by ~** verjährt sein; **to enter the city ~s** in die Stadt hineinfahren; **to extend the term of ~ prescribed** Verjährung unterbrechen; **to impose ~s upon s. one's liberty of action** jds. Bewegungsfreiheit einengen; **to know one's ~s** seine Grenzen kennen; **to scrap ~s on industry** industrielle Beschränkungen aufheben;

⌐ Act *(Br.)* Verjährungsgesetz; **to apply the ⌐ Act** *(Br.)* Verjährungsbestimmungen anwenden; **~ over** Nacherbschaft; **~ period** Verjährungsfrist; **to recommence the ~ period** Verjährungsfrist wieder zum Laufen bringen; **~ provisions** Verjährungsbestimmungen; **~ table** Verjährungstabelle; **~ title** voller Rechtstitel.

limited *(US)* Bus (Zug) mit beschränkter Platzzahl;

~ *(a.)* beschränkt, begrenzt, limitiert, *(company)* mit beschränkter Haftung, *(politics)* konstitutionell, *(railway)* mit beschränkter Platzzahl;

~ by guaranty mit beschränkter Nachschußpflicht; **~ by shares** auf die Einlage beschränkt; **~ in time** zeitlich begrenzt, befristet;

~ administration zeitlich begrenzte Nachlaßverwaltung; **~ appeal** eingeschränkte Berufsmöglichkeit; **~ audit** abgekürzte Prüfung; **~ authority** begrenzte Vollmacht, abgegrenzter Auftrag; **~ authority to sign** eingeschränkte Unterschriftsvollmacht; **~ capacity** beschränktes Fassungsvermögen, *(legal capacity)* beschränkte Geschäftsfähigkeit; **of ~ capacity** beschränkt geschäftsfähig; **~ cheque** *(Br.)* limitierter Scheck; **private ~ company** *(Br.)* Gesellschaft mit beschränkter Haftung; **public ~ company** *(Br.)* [etwa] Aktiengesellschaft; **~ [liability] company** *(Br.)* **(corporation,** *US)* [etwa] Gesellschaft mit beschränkter Haftung (GmbH); **~ condition** Marktenge; **~ court** Gericht mit beschränkter Zuständigkeit; **~ credit** Kredit in begrenzter Höhe; **~ depositary** *(Federal Reserve System, US)* Depotbank mit Beschränkungen in der Annahme von Depots; **~ dividend** limitierte Dividende; **~-dividend corporation** Gesellschaft mit gesetzlich vorgeschriebener Dividendenbeschränkung; **~ divorce** *(US coll.)* Trennung von Tisch und Bett; **~ edition** begrenzte Auflage; **~ executor** regional (zeitlich) beschränkter Nachlaßverwalter; **~ express** D-Zug mit Platzkartenzwang; **~ function wholesaler** *(US)* beschränkt zugelassener Großhändler; **~ government** konstitutionelle Regierung; **~ guarantee (guaranty)** befristete Garantie; **~ horizon** *(fig.)* Beschränktheit; **~ intelligence** beschränkte Intelligenz; **~ or special jurisdiction** besondere Zuständigkeit; **~ legal tender** beschränkt gültiges Zahlungsmittel; **~ liability** beschränkte Haftung; **~ life assets** Kapitalanlagegüter mit beschränkter Lebensdauer; **~ mail** Bahnpost; **~ market** nur beschränkt aufnahmefähiger Markt, beschränkte Absatzmöglichkeiten, begrenzter Absatzmarkt; **~ means** begrenzte Mittel; **~ monarchy** konstitutionelle Monarchie; **~ order** Limit, limitierte [Börsen]order; **~ owner** Nießbrauchberechtigter; **~ partner** beschränkt haftender Teilhaber (Gesellschafter), Kommanditist; **~ partner's liability** Kommanditistenhaftung; **~ partnership** Kommanditgesellschaft; **⌐ Partnership Act** *(Br.)* Gesetz über Kommanditgesellschaften; **~ payment insurance** Lebensversicherung mit abgekürzter Prämienzahlung; **~ payment life policy** *(US)* abgekürzte Lebensversicherung, Lebensversicherung mit abgekürzter Prämienzahlung; **~ period** *(action for divorce)* Lebenszeit; **~ policy** Police mit beschränktem Risiko; **~ power**

of appointment beschränktes Bevollmächtigungsrecht; ~ **premium** abgekürzte Prämienzahlung; ~ **price** Limitpreis, *(stock exchange)* Kurslimit; **~-price store** *(US)* Kleinpreisgeschäft, Billigwarenhaus; ~ **publication** Sonderdruck; **to have only ~ resources** nur über beschränkte Mittel verfügen; ~ **sphere of activity** beschränkter Wirkungskreis; ~ **taxability (tax liability)** beschränkte Steuerpflicht; ~ **ticket** verbilligte Fahrkarte; ~ **train** Platzkartenzug; ~ **veto** eingeschränktes Vetorecht; ~ **view** begrenzter Gesichtskreis.

limitedness of the market Marktenge.

limitless | ambition grenzenloser Ehrgeiz; ~ **ocean** unendlicher Ozean.

limousine Limousine;
to provide door-to-airport ~ service Kraftfahrzeuge für den Transport zum Flugplatz stellen.

limping standard hinkende Währung.

linage *(advertising)* Anzeigenraum, Zeilenzahl, *(payment for literary work)* Zeilenhonorar.

linear increase of taxation lineare Steuererhöhung.

line Zeile, Linie, *(agent's order)* Vertreterbestellung, *(boundary)* Grenze, Linie, *(branch of business)* Branche, Geschäfts-, Gewerbezweig, Kategorie, *(broadcasting)* Relaisverbindung, *(cable)* Kabel, *(class of goods)* Warengattung, -sortiment, Artikel, Sorte, Posten, Partie, *(cord)* Seil, Tau, Schnur, *(cord used in measuring)* Maßband, *(of descent)* Verwandtschafts-, Abstammungslinie, *(direction)* Richtschnur, -linie, *(gas, water)* Leitung, *(insurance)* Zeichnungs-, Versicherungshöchstgrenze, Höchstbetrag, *(mark)* Strich, *(matter)* Sache, Angelegenheit, *(method)* Art und Weise, Verfahren, Methode, *(mil.)* Linie, Schützengraben, *(mil., Br.)* Zelt-, Barackenreihe, *(newspaper)* Zeile, *(order for goods)* [Waren]auftrag, Bestellung, *(outline)* Kontur, Zug, *(production)* Fertigungsserie, *(railway truck)* Fahr-, Eisenbahngleis, Schienenstrang, Geleise, *(sphere of business)* Fach, Arbeits-, Fachgebiet, Tätigkeitsfeld, Wirkungskreis, [Aufgaben]gebiet, *(staff members)* Linienkräfte, *(organized system of transport)* Verkehrsunternehmen, *(telecommunication)* Fernverbindung, *(tel.)* [Amts]leitung, Anschluß, *(television)* Abtast-, Bildzeile, *(traffic)* Verkehrs-, Omnibus-, Eisenbahnlinie, *(transportation company)* Eisenbahn-, Autobus-, Luftverkehrsgesellschaft, *(troops)* Kampf-, Fronttruppe;

~s Los, Geschick, Lage, *(marriage licence)* Trauschein, *(school)* Strafarbeit, *(sequence of ideas)* Richtlinien, Grundsätze, Prinzipien;

above the ~ *(Br.)* zum ordentlichen Etat (Haushalt) gehörig; **all along the ~** auf der ganzen Linie; **along commercial ~s** nach kommerziellen Gesichtspunkten; **along these ~s** nach diesen Richtlinien (Grundsätzen), auf diese Weise; **behind the ~s** hinter der Front, in der Etappe; **below the ~** *(balance sheet)* unter dem Strich, *(Exchequer, Br.)* nicht zum ordentlichen Haushalt gehörig; **by the ~** zeilenweise; **by rule and ~** sehr sorgfältig, ganz genau; **down the ~** auf der ganzen Linie; **in direct ~** in unmittelbarer Abstammung, in direkter Linie; **in the firing ~** im vordersten Schützengraben; **in the food ~** in der Lebensmittelbranche; **in the male ~** in der männlichen Linie; **in my ~** in meinem Fach; **in ~ of his duty** *(US)* in Ausübung seines Dienstes; **in ~ with** in Übereinstimmung mit; **on the ~s** nach dem Muster; **on the ~s laid down** nach den festgelegten Grundsätzen; **out of ~** unmodern, nicht schick, *(price)* außer Ordnung geraten; **true to the party ~** linientreu;

the ~ Äquator;

actor's ~s Theaterrolle; **agate ~** *(advertising)* Anzeigenmaß, -zeile; ~ **ahead** Kiellinie; **ascending ~** *(kinsfolk)* aufsteigende Linie; **assembly ~** Montage-, Fließband; **banking ~** Bankfach; **base ~** *(advertising)* Schlußaussage; **belt ~** *(US)* Gürtelbahn; **best-selling ~** am besten verkäufliche Artikel; **blank ~** vorgedruckte Linie; **branch ~** Gleisabzweigung, Zweigbahn, Nebenlinie; **broken ~** *(tel.)* unterbrochene Verbindung, *(traffic regulation)* unterbrochene Trennlinie, Leitlinie; **building ~** Baugewerbe, -fach, *(building law)* Fluchtlinie; **bus ~** Omnibuslinie; **busy ~** *(US)* besetzte [Telefon]leitung, besetzter Anschluß; **catch ~** Stichwortzeile; **cheap ~** preiswerte Ware, billige (zweitklassige) Warenpartie; **center ~** Mittellinie; **collateral ~** *(descent)* Seitenlinie; **colo(u)r ~** Rassenschranke; **commercial ~** kaufmännisches Fach; **communication ~s** Verkehrsverbindungen, -weg; **competitive ~** Konkurrenzerzeugnisse; **connecting ~** Verbindungsbahn; **continuous white ~** *(traffic)* durchgezogene Trennungslinie; **credit ~** *(US)* eingeräumter Kredit, Kreditrahmen, -linie; **crossed ~** *(tel.)* falsche Verbindung; **differential ~** Linie mit Vorzugstarif; **direct ~** *(descent)* direkte Linie (Abstammung); **direct exchange ~** *(tel.)* Haupt-

anschluß; **displayed ~** hervorgehobene Titelzeile; **disused ~** tote Bahnlinie; **dotted ~** punktierte (gestrichelte) Linie; **double-tracked ~** zweispurige Bahn; **double white ~** *(traffic)* doppelter Trennungsstrich; **down ~** *(Br.)* von London; **enemy's ~s** feindliche Linien; **engaged ~** *(Br.)* besetzte Leitung, besetzter Anschluß; **your esteemed ~s** Ihr geschätztes Schreiben; **exchange ~** *(tel.)* Amtsleitung, Hauptanschluß; **extension ~** *(tel.)* Nebenanschluß; **fault ~** Verwerfungslinie; **feeder ~** Anschlußstrecke, Zubringer; **feint ~s** schwache Linierung; **female ~** *(descent)* weibliche Linie; **fighting ~** Kampflinie; **front ~** *(mil.)* Front[linie]; **full ~** gesamtes Sortiment; **genealogical ~** Abstammungslinie; **gross ~** *(insurance)* Höchstgrenze; **guiding ~** Richtlinie; **[hang-]clothes ~** Wäscheleine; **hard ~** *(pol.)* harte Linie, Pech, Unglück; **high-priced ~** teures Erzeugnis; **high-risk ~** Versicherungszweig mit hohem Risiko; **hot ~** *(international politics)* heißer Draht; **industrial ~** Betriebs-, Fabrikgleis; **junction ~** Verbindungsbahn; **~s laid down** gegebene Richtlinie; **leading ~** Spezialität, Reklameartikel; **leased ~** *(tel.)* gemietete Fernleitung; **life ~** Rettungsleine, *(fig.)* Rettungsanker; **local ~** Vorortzug; **local service ~** Zubringer; **loop ~** *(railway)* Nebenstrecke; **low-priced ~s** billige Artikel; **main ~** *(railway)* Hauptlinie, -strecke; **male ~** männliche Linie, Mannesstamm; **marriage ~s** *(Br.)* Heiratsurkunde; **maternal ~** mütterliche Linie, Abstammung; **net ~** *(insurance)* Höchstgrenze des Selbstbehalts; **new ~** Absatz, neue Zeile; **oil ~** Ölleitung; **open (overhead) ~** *(tel.)* oberirdische Leitung, Freileitung; **party ~** *(tel., US)* gemeinsamer [Telefon]anschluß; **the party ~** politisches Programm, Parteiprogramm; **paternal ~** väterliche Abstammung; **popular ~** begehrter Artikel; **private ~** *(tel.)* Privatanschluß; **broadly diversified product ~** breit gestreutes Warensortiment; **quality ~** Qualitätserzeugnis; **railway** *(Br.)* **(railroad,** *US)* ~ Eisenbahnlinie, -gleis; **run-of-the-mill ~** einfaches Durchschnittserzeugnis; **secondary ~** Nebenlinie; **self-effacing ~** zurückhaltender Verlauf; **service ~** Dienstleitung; **shared ~** *(tel.)* gemeinsamer Telefonanschluß; **shipping ~** Schiffahrtslinie; **side ~** Nebenprodukt, *(occupation)* Nebenbeschäftigung; **Southern ~** Südbahn; **special ~** Spezialität; **splitting-up ~** Abstellgleis; **stage ~** *(bus)* Städteverkehr; **steamship ~** Dampferlinie, -route; **straight ~** Bauflucht, *(border)* geradliniger Verlauf; **subscriber's ~** *(tel.)* Teilnehmeranschluß; **tapped ~** angezapfte Telefonleitung; **telephone ~** Telefonleitung; **through ~** durchgehende Linie; **tramway ~** Straßenbahnlinie; **transversal ~** Seitenlinie; **trunk ~** *(railway)* Hauptlinie, -verkehrstraße, -strecke, *(tel.)* Stamm-, Fernleitung, Fernverbindung; **two ~s** *(tel.)* zwei Anschlüsse; **unused ~** totes Gleis; **up ~** *(Br.)* Strecke nach London; **white ~** leerer Raum, Durchschuß; **zero ~** Nullinie;

~ **of action** Handlungsweise, Vorgehen; ~ **of argument** Beweisführung; ~ **of ascent** Verwandtschaftsgrad; ~ **of battle** Kampflinie, vorderste Linie; ~ **of buildings** Häuserreihe; ~ **of business** Geschäftszweig, Branche; **all ~s of business** alle Geschäftszweige; **deep ~s of care** tiefe Sorgenfalten; ~ **of commerce** *(US)* Handels-, Wirtschaftszweig, -sparte, Branche; **~s of communication** Verbindungslinie, Verkehrsstrecke, *(fig.)* Informationsweg, Nachrichtenweg, -verbindungen; ~ **of conduct** Lebenswandel; ~ **of consanguinity** Blutsverwandtschaft; ~ **of credit** *(US)* Kreditgrenze, -linie, Höchstkredit; **second ~ of defence** *(clearing banks, Br.)* zweite Verteidigungslinie; ~ **of demarcation** Demarkations-, Grenzlinie; ~ **of departure** Abfahrtsgleis; ~ **of deposit** *(US)* durchschnittlicher Kreditsaldo eines Depositenkontos; ~ **of discount** durchschnittliche Höhe eines Bankkredits; ~ **of duty** *(mil.)* Dienstart; **boundary ~s of an estate** Grundstücksgrenze; ~ **of fire** Schußlinie; ~ **of goods** Warensortiment; ~ **of industry** Industriezweig, -sparte; ~ **of insurance** Versicherungszweig, -sparte; ~ **by itself** Extrazeile, freistehende Zeile; ~ **of manufacture** Fabrikationszweig; ~ **of moving traffic** Fahrzeugkolonne; **first ~ of a paragraph** Absatz; **main ~s of a party's policy** parteipolitische Programmpunkte; ~ **of people waiting to go to a cinema** Schlange wartender Kinobesucher; **~s of policy** politische Richtschnur, Richtlinien der Politik; ~ **of post** Postroute; ~ **of proceeding** Vorgehensweise; ~ **of product** [Waren]sortiment; ~ **of production** Produktionszweig; **~s of promotion** Beförderungsrichtlinien; ~ **of last resistance** letzte Widerstandslinie; ~ **between right and wrong** Grenze zwischen Recht und Unrecht; ~ **of samples** Musterkollektion; ~ **of sight** Blickrichtung; ~ **and staff** Betriebsführung und Mitarbeiter; ~ **of stockings** Partie Strümpfe; ~ **of succession** Erblinie; ~ **of support** Reservetruppen; ~ **of thinking** Denkweise; ~ **of thought** Gedankenkette; ~ **of trade** Erwerbszweig; ~ **of travel** Reiseroute; **~s on which an understanding can be reached** Einigungsmodalitäten;

~ *(v.)* liniieren, *(bring into agreement)* zu einheitlichem Handeln zusammenschließen;

~ **in a conto(u)r** Konturen aufzeichnen; ~ **in** einzeichnen; ~ **the kerb** am Bürgersteig Spalier stehen; ~ **off** abgrenzen; ~ **paper** Papier linieren; ~ **one's pocket** in die eigene Tasche wirtschaften; ~ **one's purse well** sich mit genügend Geld ausrüsten; ~ **the route** Spalier bilden; ~ **the streets** Spalier bilden; ~ **through** aus-, durchstreichen; ~ **up** sich zusammenschließen, *(queue up, US)* in einer Schlange anstehen, *(mil.)* in Reihen antreten; ~ **up public opinion** Übereinstimmung der öffentlichen Meinung herbeiführen; ~ **up the troops** Truppen aufstellen; ~ **up against wage restraint** sich gegen eine Politik der Zurückhaltung bei Tarifverhandlungen aussprechen;

to adhere to a ~ **of conduct** an einer bestimmten Verhaltensweise festhalten; **to adjust a** ~ Zeile ausschließen; **to adopt an anti-communist** ~ antikommunistische Politik betreiben; **to adopt a new** ~ neuen Kurs einschlagen; **to be in the banking** ~ im Bankfach tätig sein; **to be behind the** ~**s** sich hinter der Front aufhalten, in der Etappe leben; **to be employed in a** ~ in einer Branche beschäftigt sein; **to be in** ~ **with** übereinstimmen mit; **to be in the** ~ vom Fach sein; **to be in** ~ **with one's best interests** mit seinen eigenen Interessen bestens übereinstimmen; **to be in the book** ~ im Buchhandel tätig sein; **to be in the brokerage** ~ als Makler tätig sein; **to be again moving broadly in** ~ **with the gross national product** mit dem Bruttosozialprodukt praktisch wieder gleichgezogen haben; **not to be in** ~ **with one's character** nicht zu jds. Charakter passen; **to be of a good** ~ aus gutem Hause stammen; **to be hard** ~**s on s. o.** *(fam.)* Unglück für j. darstellen; **to be the last of one's** ~ der Letzte seines Stammes sein; **to be sure of one's** ~**s** *(actor)* seine Rolle beherrschen, rollenfest sein; **to be on the** ~ **to the private secretary** mit der Privatsekretärin telefonieren; **to be s. one's** ~ in jds. Fach schlagen; **to be out of s. one's** ~ nicht in jds. Fach schlagen; **to be successful all along the** ~ auf der ganzen Linie erfolgreich sein; **to begin a new** ~ Absatz machen; **to bring into** ~ in Einklang bringen, anpassen, gleichstellen; **to bring s. o. into** ~ j. auf Vordermann bringen; **to buy the** ~ Meinung übernehmen; **to buy a** ~ **completely** sich einem Verfahrensmodus vollinhaltlich anschließen; **to buy s. one's** ~ **of thinking** sich von jem. überzeugen lassen; **to change one's** ~ **of business** Geschäftszweig ändern; **to check up on a** ~ Telefonleitung überprüfen; **to choose the** ~ **of least resistance** Weg des geringsten Widerstandes gehen; **to close a** ~ Bahnlinie stillegen; **to come into** ~ gleichschalten; **to come off the** ~**s** Fließband verlassen; **to come from a good** ~ aus einer guten Familie stammen; **to come into** ~ **with the majority** *(fam.)* sich der Mehrheit anschließen; **to come on the** ~ ans Telefon kommen; **to cross the** ~ *(ship)* Äquator überqueren; **to cut across all the** ~**s** sich über alles hinwegsetzen; **to deal in a** ~ Artikel führen; **to deal in larger** ~**s of shares** über größere Aktienpakete verfügen; **to diversify one's product** ~**s** sein Warensortiment auffächern; **to divide a** ~ *(print.)* Zeile abbrechen; **to draw the** ~ Grenze ziehen; **to draw a** ~ **somewhere** irgendwo eine Grenze ziehen; **to draw hard and fast** ~**s** scharfe Grenze ziehen; **to drop s. o. a** ~ **(few** ~**s)** jem. ein paar Zeilen schreiben; **to engage the** ~ **for twenty minutes** Telefonleitung für zwanzig Minuten blockieren; **to engage in a** ~ **of business** in einem Geschäftszweig arbeiten; **to establish a** ~ **of credit** *(US)* Kreditlinie festsetzen; **to establish a regular** ~ [Dampfer]verbindung einrichten; **to fall into** ~ *(mil.)* sich in die Marschkolonne einordnen (einreihen); **to fall into** ~ **with s. o.** sich jds. Ansichten anschließen; **to follow the party** ~ den von der Partei festgesetzten Grundsätzen folgen, Parteidisziplin bewahren; **to follow the** ~ **of least resistance** Richtung des geringsten Widerstands einschlagen; **to get a** ~ **on s. th.** Informationen über etw. erhalten; **to get into the** ~ **of traffic** sich in den Verkehrsstrom einordnen (einreihen); **to get off the** ~ Telefongespräch beenden; **to give s. o.** ~ **enough** jem. genügend Freiheiten gewähren (gewähren lassen); **to go down the** ~ *(US)* gefeuert (hinausgeworfen) werden; **to go down the** ~ **for s. o.** *(US)* für j. durchs Feuer gehen; **to go up the** ~ *(mil.)* an die Front gehen; **to go into the front** ~**s** zur Front gehen; **to govern on conservative** ~**s** nach konservativen Grundsätzen regieren; **to hand s. o. a** ~ jem. etw. verkaufen; **to hold the** ~ *(tel.)* am Apparat bleiben; **to hold the** ~ **on costs** Kostenniveau halten; **to hold the** ~ **on prices** Preise stabil halten; **to indent a** ~ Zeile einrücken; **to inspect the** ~**s** Zeltlager besichtigen; **to keep to the** ~**s** Zeilen halten; **to keep to one's own** ~ sich von anderen unabhängig machen; **to keep s. o. to a** ~ **of policy** j. politisch festlegen; **to lay down** ~**s** Richtlinien geben; **to lay down the broad** ~**s of a work** große Linien eines Werkes aufzeigen; **to lay out the** ~ Strecke abstecken; **to leave the** ~ *(tel.)* Gespräch unterbrechen; **to leave a** ~ **blank** Zeile leer

lassen (aussparen); **to lie in s. one's** ~ in jds. Fach schlagen; **to mark by a dotted** ~ durch eine punktierte Linie kennzeichnen; **to obtain a** ~ **of credit to run for a year** *(US)* Kreditlinie für ein Jahr erhalten; **to overstep the** ~**s of good taste** gegen den guten Geschmack verstoßen; **to peg out a** ~ Linie festlegen; **to proceed on certain** ~**s** sich nach bestimmten Weisungen richten; **to project beyond the building** ~ Baufluchtlinie nicht einhalten; **to pursue a** ~ **of business** einem Geschäftszweig nachgehen; **to put it on the** ~ *(sl.)* blechen, berappen; **to read between the** ~**s** zwischen den Zeilen lesen; **to redraw the** ~**s** Versicherungsbedingungen neu fassen; **to retire within one's** ~**s** *(mil.)* sich geordnet zurückziehen; **to roll off the** ~ Fließband verlassen; **to run a cheap** ~ billige Artikel verkaufen; **to save a** ~ Zeile einsparen; **to sell its losing** ~ mit Verlust arbeitenden Fertigungsbetrieb verkaufen; **to set up a committee on the following** ~**s** Ausschuß nach folgenden Grundsätzen zusammensetzen; **to shoot a** ~ *(sl.)* angeben; **to space out the** ~**s** Zeilen auslaufen lassen; **to specialize in a** ~ sich auf einen Artikel spezialisieren; **to stand in the** ~ sich [in einer Reihe] anstellen; **to step out of** ~ aus der Reihe tanzen; **to study one's** ~**s** seine Rolle einstudieren; **to study a subject on sound** ~**s** Thema sehr methodisch angehen; **to take an apparently neutral** ~ **towards the money market** dem Geldmarkt gegenüber strikt neutral verhalten; **to take a hard** ~ feste Position beziehen; **to take a rigid** ~ strenge Haltung einnehmen, energisch vorgehen; **to take the** ~ *(coll.)* Ansicht (Meinung) vertreten; **to take one's own** ~ nach seiner eigenen Methode vorgehen; **to take a strong** ~ energisch vorgehen; **to toe the** ~ sich auf das Parteiprogramm festlegen; **to trace back one's family** ~ Familienstammbaum zurückverfolgen; **to trace a flat** ~ *(stocks)* kein Kursanstieg aufweisen; **to translate life into** ~ **and colo(u)r** Leben mit Stift und Farbe einfangen; **to wait in a** ~ in einer Schlange warten; **to work on the** ~**s of s. o.** nach jds. Erfahrungen arbeiten; **to write a** ~ *(underwriter)* Teilrisiko übernehmen;

~ **activity** Tätigkeit in einer Branche; ~ **advertising** Produktionswerbung; **twenty-**~ **article** zwanzigzeiliger Artikel; ~ **block** Strichätzung; ~**-blocking device** Gleissperre; ~ **border** Linienumrandung; ~ **break** *(railway)* Streckenausfall; **one-business** Spezial-, Fachgeschäft; ~ **charge** *(tel.)* Grundgebühr; ~ **chart** Linienschaubild, -diagramm; ~ **control** *(television)* Zeilensteuerung; ~ **cord** Leitungsschnur; ~ **cost** Fernschreibmietgebühr; ~ **cut** *(US)* Strichklischee; ~ **drawing** Feder-, Strichzeichnung; ~ **drop** *(el.)* Spannungsabfall; ~ **etching** Strichätzung; ~ **executive** Produktionsleiter; ~ **fault** *(tel.)* [Leitungs]störung; ~ **filling** Zeilenauffüllung; ~ **flyback** *(television)* Zeilenrücklauf; **full** ~ **forcing** *(US)* Abnahmezwang für alle Produkte; ~ **frequency** *(television)* Zeilenfrequenz; ~**-haul movement** Linienverkehr; ~**-haul rate** Streckensatz; ~ **length** Zeilenbreite; ~ **manager** Fachgebietsleiter; ~ **measure** Zeilenmaß; ~ **navigation** Linienschiffahrt; ~ **officer** leitender Angestellter; ~ **organization** Geschäftsgliederung in Abteilungen; ~**-organizing ability** organisatorische Branchenbegabung; ~ **plate** Strichätzung; ~ **position** verantwortliche Führungsposition; ~ **production** Produktion am laufenden Band; ~ **relationship** Anweisungsbeziehung; **limited-**~ **retailer** *(US)* Fachhändler; ~ **sale** *(advertising)* Werbeabschluß für eine bestimmte öffentliche Verkehrslinie; ~ **service** *(railway)* Außendienst; ~**-of-battle ship** Linienschiff; ~ **shooter** *(sl.)* Angeber, Aufschneider; ~ **shooting** *(sl.)* Angabe; **one-**~ **shop** Fach-, Spezialgeschäft; ~ **shutup** Fertigungsaufgabe; ~**-and-staff principle** Stablinienprinzip; ~**-up** Aufstellung, Anordnung, Team, *(mil.)* Aufmarsch, *(queuing)* Warteschlange; ~**-up of Afro-Asian powers** Machtblock afrikanischer und asiatischer Staaten.

lineage Abkunft, Abstammung, Sippe;
~ **crest** Familienwappen.

lineal in gerader Linie, gradlinig, linear, direkt;
~ **ancestor** Vorfahre in gerade Linie; ~ **consanguinity** Blutsverwandtschaft; ~ **descendant** unmittelbarer Abkömmling, direkter Nachkomme; ~ **descent** gradlinige Abstammung, direkte Nachfolge; ~ **heir** leiblicher Erbe, Leibeserbe; ~ **promotion** Beförderung der Reihe nach; ~ **relative** unmittelbarer Verwandter; ~ **succession** Nachfolge (Erbfolge) in gerader Linie.

lineally, to be ~ **descended from s. o.** unmittelbar von jem. abstammen.

linen Leinen, Leinwand;
to wash one's dirty ~ **in public** *(fig.)* öffentlich seine schmutzige Wäsche waschen;
~ **towel** Leinenhandtuch; ~ **trade** Leinwarenhandel; ~ **warehouse** Weißwarengeschäft.

linear|increase of taxation lineare Steuererhöhung; ~ **measure** Längenmaß; ~ **programming** lineare Planungsrechnung.

lineman *(railway)* Streckenarbeiter, *(tel.)* Störungssucher.
linen | draper *(Br.)* Weißwarenhändler; ~ **paper** Leinenpapier.
liner Linienschiff, -flugzeug, Übersee-, Passagierdampfer;
cargo ~ Linienfrachtschiff; **general cargo** ~ Stückgutdampfer; **ocean (transatlantic)** ~ Übersee-, Ozeandampfer; ~ **conference** Linienverkehrskartell; ~ **freight** Stückgutfracht; ~ **freighting** Stückgutbefrachtung; ~**s' rates** Frachtraten nach den Bedingungen des Linienverkehrs; ~ **service** Linienverkehr; ~ **terms** Linienschiffahrtbestimmungen; ~ **transport** Warenbeförderung auf Schiffen regulärer Linien; ~ **tonnage** Linienschiffstonnage.
linewalker Leitungsüberwacher, Streckengeher.
linger *(v.)* verweilen, sich aufhalten, noch bleiben, *(dawdle)* bummeln, trödeln, zögern, *(remain existent)* sich halten, fortleben, lebendig bleiben, *(v./tr.)* sich in die Länge ziehen;
~ **about (around)** herumlungern; ~ **around the house** sich in der Nähe des Hauses aufhalten; ~ **over one's cups** bei seiner Flasche Wein sitzen bleiben; ~ **on** *(custom)* noch geübt werden; ~ **behind others** hinter den anderen hertrödeln; ~ **out one's days on a sickbed** auf dem Krankenbett dahinsiechen; ~ **over a subject** sich weit und breit über ein Thema auslassen; ~ **away one's time** seine Zeit verplempern.
lingering | disease schleichende Krankheit; ~ **look** sehnsüchtiger Blick.
lingo Kauderwelsch, Fachjargon.
linguist Sprachforscher;
to be a good ~ Sprachtalent haben, sprachgewandt sein.
linguistic | area Sprachgebiet; ~ **atlas** Sprachenatlas; ~ **minorities** sprachliche Minderheiten; ~ **enclave** Sprachinsel; ~ **map** Sprachatlas; ~ **problem** Sprachenproblem; ~ **stock** Sprachfamilie.
lining Futter[stoff], *(bookbinding)* Kapitalband, *(civil engineering)* Auskleidung, *(el.)* Isolierung, *(fixing of boundaries, Scot.)* Grenzlinienfestlegung.
link Bindeglied, Verbindung, Band, Anknüpfungspunkt, *(chain)* Kettenglied, *(machine)* Zwischen-, Gelenkstück;
~**s** Beziehungen;
capital ~ Kapitalverflechtung; **golf** ~**s** Golfplatz; **missing** ~ fehlendes Glied;
~**s with corresponding banks** Korrespondenzbankverbindungen; ~ **in a chain of evidence** fehlendes Beweisglied; ~ **between the past and the future** Verbindung zwischen Gestern und Morgen; ~ **to gold** Bindung an den Goldpreis;
~ *(v.)* in Verbindung bringen, verbinden, [aneinander] anschließen;
~ **records** Akten zusammenheften; ~ **up** *(spaceship)* zusammenkoppeln; ~ **up one's land** Grundstücksparzellen vereinigen; ~ **up transmitters** Sender zusammenschließen;
~ **s. o. with an affair** j. mit einer Angelegenheit in Verbindung bringen;
to be ~**ed with a canal** durch einen Kanal verbunden sein; **to be** ~**ed with the West** mit dem Westen liiert sein; ~ **course** Einführungskurs.
linkage Verknüpfung, individuelle Verflechtungsbeziehungen;
~ **of risks** *(insurance)* Risikoverbindung.
linkup Konzerngruppe, *(spaceships)* Koppelmanöver.
linotype *(print.)* [Zeilenguß]setzmaschine, Linotype.
lion Löwe, *(person of interest)* Berühmtheit, Größe, Prominenter; **literary** ~ Größe in der Literatur; **social** ~ Gesellschaftslöwe; ~ **of the day** Held des Tages; **a** ~ **at home, a mouse abroad** zu Hause ein Tyrann und draußen ein Feigling; ~**s of a place** Sehenswürdigkeiten eines Ortes; ~ **in the way** eingebildete Gefahr;
to beard the ~ **in his den** sich in die Höhle des Löwen wagen; **to make a** ~ **of s. o.** jem. Prominentenrechte zuerkennen; **to show s. o. the** ~**s** jem. die Sehenswürdigkeiten zeigen;
~ **hunter** Prominentenjäger; ~**'s share** Löwenanteil; **to rouse the sleeping** ~ schlafenden Löwen wecken; **to twist the** ~**'s tail** über die Briten herziehen.
lionize *(v.)* Gesellschaftslöwe sein;
~ **s. o.** j. [als Berühmtheit] herumreichen; ~ **Paris** Sehenswürdigkeiten von Paris besuchen.
lip Lippe, *(impudent speech, sl.)* Unverschämtheit;
to button up one's ~**s** *(sl.)* Geheimnis bewahren; **to give s. o. a** ~ *(sl.)* Lippe gegenüber jem. riskieren; **to hang on s. one's** ~**s** jem. gespannt zuhören; **to keep a stiff upper** ~ die Ohren steif halten; ~ **devotion** geheuchelte Ergebenheit; ~ **language** Lautsprache; ~ **reading** Ablesen der Worte von den Lippen; ~ **service** geheuchelte Ergebenheit.
liquid flüssig, liquid, sofort realisierbar;
highly ~ hochliquide;

to be ~ ausreichend liquide Mittel haben;
~ **assets** flüssige (verfügbare, liquide) Mittel (Gelder), Aktiva hoher Liquiditätsstufe, flüssiges Vermögen, *(balance sheet, US)* Umlaufvermögen; **to be short of** ~ **assets** liquiditätsbeengt sein; ~ **capital** liquide Mittel, Umlaufkapital; ~ **current assets** kurzfristiges Umlaufsvermögen; ~ **debt** sofort fällige Forderung; ~ **deficit** Liquiditätsdefizit; ~ **duplicator** Umdruckvervielfältiger; ~ **food** flüssige Nahrung; ~ **form** liquide Form; **to hold savings in** ~ **form** Ersparnisse liquide angelegt haben; ~ **funds** liquide Mittel; ~ **holdings** liquide Bestände; ~ **hydrogen** Flüssigwasserstoff; ~ **investments** leicht realisierbare Kapitalanlagen, liquide Reserven der Wirtschaft; ~ **loan** Liquiditätskredit; ~ **market** Börse mit ausreichenden Umsätzen; ~ **measure** Flüssigkeitsmaß; ~ **position** Flüssigkeits-, Liquiditätsposition, -bilanz, Flüssigkeit [der Bilanz], *(banking)* Liquiditätsstatus; **to maintain a** ~ **position** ausreichende Liquidität unterhalten; ~ **proof of a demand** schriftlicher Forderungsnachweis; ~ **ratio** Liquiditätskennziffer, *(bank)* Liquidität ersten Grades; ~ **reserves** *(banking business)* sofort realisierbare (liquide) Reserven, Mindest-, Liquiditätsreserven; ~ **resources** flüssige (liquide) Mittel; ~ **securities** leicht absetzbare (sofort realisierbare) Papiere; ~ **strength** kurzfristig realisierbare Vermögenswerte, hoher Liquiditätsgrad; ~ **surplus** Liquiditätsüberschuß.
liquidatable realisierbar.
liquidate *(v.) (account)* abrechnen, abwickeln, glattstellen, saldieren, *(customs, US)* Importabgaben endgültig festsetzen, *(debt)* bezahlen, begleichen, abtragen, tilgen, Schuldenregelung vornehmen, *(even up)* glattstellen, *(firm)* liquidieren, abwickeln, auflösen, *(v./i.)* in Liquidation gehen, liquidieren, *(get rid of)* liquidieren, töten;
~ **the assets of a bankrupt** Konkursmasse liquidieren; ~ **a business** Geschäft auflösen; ~ **a company** Gesellschaft auflösen (liquidieren); ~ **a bankrupt's affairs** Konkurssache abwickeln; ~ **damages** Schadenersatz feststellen; ~ **debts** Schulden begleichen; ~ **an inventory** *(US)* Lager abbauen; ~ **a loan** Kredit abwickeln; ~ **one's portfolio at the bottom of the market** sein Effektenportefeuille am Börsentiefstpunkt abstoßen; ~ **one's securities** seine Papiere realisieren; ~ **shares** Aktien flüssig machen; ~ **one's stock of goods** sein Lager abstoßen.
liquidated festgestellt, festgesetzt, beziffert, *(debt)* getilgt, geregelt;
~ **account** der Höhe nach feststehender Saldo; ~ **claim** festgestellter (ziffernmäßig bestimmter) Anspruch; ~ **damages** festgesetzte (vorausgeschätzte) Schadenssumme, Konventionalstrafe; ~ **damages clause** Konventionalstrafklausel; ~ **debt** bezahlte Schuld; ~ **demand** festgestellte Forderung, einvernehmlich geregelter Bedarf; ~ **sum** berechenbare Summe, feststehender Betrag.
liquidating | agent Liquidator; ~ **balance sheet** Liquidationsbilanz; ~ **bank** Abwicklungsbank; ~ **distribution** Masseverteilung; ~ **dividend** Liquidationsquote, -anteil, Konkursquote; ~ **market** *(US)* auf umfangreiche Glattstellungen hin schwacher Markt; ~ **office** Abwicklungsamt; ~ **partner** abwickelnder Geschäftsteilhaber; ~ **trust** Liquidationsmasse; ~ **value** Abschreibungswert, Liquidationswert.
liquidation *(account)* Abrechnung, Abwicklung, *(company)* Liquidation, Liquidierung, Abwicklung, Auflösung, *(debt)* Abtragung, Bezahlung, Tilgung, *(evening up)* Glattstellung, *(realization)* Flüssigmachung, Realisation, Verkauf gegen bar; **in** ~ in Liquidation;
adjudicated ~ Zwangsauflösung, -liquidation; **formal** ~ offizielle Liquidation; **inventory** ~ *(US)* Lagerabbau; **involuntary** ~ Zwangsliquidation; **taxable** ~ Verteilung auf die Aktionäre; **voluntary** ~ freiwillige Liquidation, Selbstauflösung; **members' voluntary** ~ Eigenliquidation;
~ **of an annuity** Rentenablösung; ~ **by arrangement** Liquidationsvergleich; ~ **of assets** Anlagenverkauf, -verwertung; ~ **of a business** Geschäftsauflösung; ~ **of a company** Firmenliquidation; ~ **of debts** Begleichung von Schulden, Schuldentilgung; ~ **of a fund** Auflösung eines Fondsvermögens, Fondsauflösung; ~ **of holdings** Flüssigmachen von Kapitalanlagen; ~ **of inventories** *(US)* Lagerabstoßung; ~ **of long positions** *(stock exchange)* Glattstellung von Hausse-Engagements; ~ **of property** Vermögensliquidation; ~ **of speculations** Glattstellungen; ~ **subject to the supervision of the court** gerichtliche Liquidation, Liquidation unter Aufsicht des Gerichts;
to carry out a ~ Abwicklung durchführen; **to come in for heavy** ~**s** *(stock market)* umfangreichen Gewinnrealisationen (Glattstellungen) unterworfen sein; **to enter (go) into** ~ in Liquidation treten; **to sign in** ~ in Liquidation zeichnen;

~ **account** Abwicklungs-, Liquidationskonto; ~ **certificate** Liquidationsanteilschein; ~ **damages** Liquidationsverlust; ~ **dividend** Schlußdividende, *(bankruptcy)* Liquidations-, Konkursquote; ~ **expense** Liquidationskosten; ~ **fee** Abwicklungsgebühr; ~ **fund** Tilgungsfonds; ~ **office** Liquidationskasse; ~ **plan** Liquidationsvorschlag, -plan; **to ease** ~ **problems** Liquidation erleichtern; ~ **proceedings** Abwicklungs-, Konkurs-, Liquidationsverfahren; ~ **sale** Liquidationsverkauf; ~ **value** Abwicklungs-, Liquidationswert.

liquidator Liquidator, Abwickler, Masseverwalter, *(customs, US)* Taxator, Schätzer;

official ~ *(Br.)* gerichtlich bestellter Liquidator; **provisional** ~ vorläufig bestellter Liquidator (Abwickler);

~ **appointed by the court** gerichtlich bestellter Liquidator; ~ **of an estate** Konkursverwalter; ~ **for the purpose of winding up** freiwillig bestellter Liquidator; ~ **in winding up by the court** Zwangsliquidator, Konkursverwalter;

~'s **accounts** Abrechnung des Liquidators (Abwicklers); ~'s **duties** Aufgaben eines Liquidators; ~'s **expenses** Kosten des Liquidators; ~'s **power** Vollmachten eines Liquidators.

liquidatorship Abwickleramt, Amt eines Liquidators.

liquidity [Geld]flüssigkeit, Liquidität;

ample ~ Liquiditätsfülle; **bank** ~ Bankenliquidität, Liquidität des Bankensystems; **corporate** ~ Firmenliquidität, Liquidität einer Aktiengesellschaft; **newly created** ~ Liquiditätsausweitung; **domestic** ~ Inlandsliquidität; **excess** ~ Liquiditätsüberhang, Überliquidität; **financial** ~ Barliquidität; **increasing** ~ Liquiditätszunahme, -anreicherung; **primary (secondary, tertiary)** ~ liquide Mittel erster (zweiter, dritter) Ordnung; **reduced** ~ eingeengte Liquidität, Liquiditätsschwierigkeiten; **surplus** ~ Liquiditätsüberhang, Überliquidität; **total** ~ Gesamtliquidität; **unconditional** ~ *(special drawing rights)* uneingeschränkte Liquidität; **world** ~ internationale Liquidität, Weltwährungsreserve;

~ **in assets** Vermögens-, Primärliquidität; ~ **of a balance sheet** Bilanzliquidität; **of a bank** Bankenliquidität; ~ **of the Federal Reserve System** *(US)* Notenbankliquidität; **interlocking** ~ **in world markets** weltbedingte Liquiditätsverhältnisse; **to absorb** ~ Liquiditätsabschöpfung vornehmen; **to be based on** ~ liquiditätsmäßig sichtbar werden; **to be a source of** ~ liquiditätspolitische Möglichkeiten darstellen; **to be a strain on** ~ Liquiditätsanspannung darstellen; **to build** ~ für Liquidität Sorge tragen, liquiditätspolitische Maßnahme treffen; **to clamp down on** ~ Liquiditätsbestimmungen verschärfen; **to cut domestic banking** ~ Liquidität des inländischen Bankapparates verknappen; **to establish enough** ~ für eine ausreichende Liquiditätsdecke sorgen; **to have no effect on** ~ liquiditätspolitisch neutral sein; **to imply true** ~ wahres Bild der Liquiditätsverhältnisse aufzeigen; **to increase** ~ Liquidität anreichern; **to lack** ~ liquiditätsbeengt sein; **to maintain** ~ für ausreichende Liquidität Sorge tragen; **to rebuild** ~ Liquiditätsverbesserung erzielen, Liquidität verbessern; **to reduce** ~ Liquiditätsüberhang abbauen; **to require greater** ~ verstärkte Liquiditätsbedürfnisse haben; **to strain** ~ angespannte Liquiditätspolitik betreiben; **to withdraw** ~ Liquidität entziehen;

~ **afflux** Liquiditätszustrom; ~ **arrangements** Liquiditätsabsprache, -dispositionen; ~ **aspect** Liquiditätsaspekt; ~ **assistance** Liquiditätshilfe; ~ **balance** Liquiditätsbilanz; ~ **basis** Liquiditätsgrundlage; ~ **battle** Liquiditätsschlacht; ~ **bind** Liquiditätsbeengung; ~ **control** Liquiditätskontrolle; ~-**creating effect** Liquiditätsauswirkung, -effekt; ~ **crisis** Liquiditätskrise; ~ **deficit** Liquiditätsdefizit; ~ **differential** Liquiditätsgefälle; ~ **difficulties** Liquiditätsschwierigkeiten; ~ **improvement** Liquiditätsverbesserung; ~ **level** Liquiditätsniveau; **to establish itself firmly on the international** ~ **map** sich auf internationalen Märkten eines ausgezeichneten Liquiditätsrufes erfreuen; ~ **management** Liquiditätssteuerung, Gelddisposition; ~ **manager** Gelddisponent; ~ **margin** Liquiditätsspielraum; ~ **measures** Liquiditätsmaßnahmen; ~ **pinch** Liquiditätsbeengung, -klemme; **to squelch talk of** ~ **pinch** um das Liquidationsgerede zu beenden; ~ **position** Liquiditätsstatus; ~ **preference** Liquiditätsvorliebe, -neigung, -streben; ~ **preference theory** *(Keynes)* Liquiditätstheorie; ~ **pressure** Liquiditätsdruck; ~ **problem** Liquiditätsproblem; **to contain one's** ~ **problems** Liquiditätsauswirkungen abschwächen; ~ **ratio** Liquiditätsverhältnis, -grad, -koeffizient, *(banking)* Liquidität zweiten Grades; **cash** ~ **ratio** Barliquidität; **total** ~ **ratio** Gesamtliquidität; **to build up a higher** ~ **ratio than the minimum** höheren Liquiditätsgrad als notwendig erzielen; ~-**reducing** liquiditätsvermindernd; ~-**reducing factors** liquiditätsbelastende Faktoren; ~ **requirements** Liquiditätserfordernisse,

-vorschriften; ~ **reserve** Liquiditätsreserve; ~ **rules** Liquiditätsrichtlinien, -grundsätze; ~ **shortage** eingeengte Liquidität, Liquiditätsknappheit, -verknappung; ~ **squeeze** Liquiditätsdruck; ~ **test** Liquiditätsprüfung; ~ **trap** Liquiditätsfalle; ~ **trough** Liquiditätsmulde; ~ **worries** Liquiditätssorgen.

liquor Alkohol, alkoholisches Getränk;

under the influence of ~ alkoholisiert, unter Alkoholeinfluß; **the worse for** ~ betrunken;

~s Spirituosen;

~ *(v.)* **s. o. up** j. mit alkoholischen Getränken traktieren; **to sleep off one's** ~ seinen Rausch ausschlafen;

~ **dealer** Spirituosenhändler; ~ **excise** *(US)* Steuer auf alkoholische Getränke, Alkoholsteuer; ~ **licence** Schankkonzession; ~ **selling** Spirituosenverkauf; ~ **shop** Spirituosengeschäft; ~ **store** *(US)* Spirituosengeschäft, -handlung; ~ **tax** *(US)* Steuer auf alkoholische Getränke; ~ **tax certificate** *(US)* Schankkonzession; ~ **trade** Spirituosenhandel.

list Liste, Register, [Adressen]verzeichnis, Aufstellung, *(docket, Br.)* Terminkalender, *(legal voters)* Verzeichnis der Wahlberechtigten, *(stock exchange, US)* an der Börse eingeführte Effekten, *(stock exchange, Br.)* Kursblatt;

as per enclosed ~ gemäß der anliegenden Liste; **on the** ~ auf der Liste;

absentees' ~ Abwesenheitsliste; **alphabetical** ~ alphabetisches Verzeichnis; **annual** ~ Jahresverzeichnis; **Army** ~ *(mil.)* Rangliste; **black** ~ Boykottliste, schwarze Liste, *(bankruptcy)* Insolventenliste; **cargo** ~ Ladeverzeichnis; **cause** ~ *(law court)* Terminkalender; **check** ~ Strich-, Kontrolliste, *(voters, US)* Wählerliste; **civil** ~ *(Br.)* Zivilliste; **commercial** ~ Liste der Handelssachen; **credit** ~ Liste der kreditfähigen Kunden, *(theater)* Verzeichnis der beteiligten Schauspieler; **crew** ~ Mannschaftsliste, Musterrolle; **danger** ~ *(hospital)* Liste der Schwerkranken; **decline** ~ *(insurance company)* Verzeichnis abzulehnender Risiken; **desiderata** ~ Fehlliste; **duty** ~ *(mil.)* Dienstplan; **electoral** ~ Wählerliste; **exchange** ~ *(Br.)* Kurszettel; **free** ~ Freiliste [zollfreier Gegenstände]; **freight** ~ Ladungsverzeichnis, Versandliste; **general** ~ Einheitstarif; **local** ~ Gemeindeliste; **membership** ~ Mitgliedsliste, -verzeichnis; **nominal** ~ Namensverzeichnis, **official** ~ *(stock exchange, Br.)* amtliche Börsennotierung, amtlicher Kurszettel, amtliches Kursblatt, *(US)* Verzeichnis börsengängiger Wertpapiere; **passenger** ~ Passagierliste; **passing out** ~ *(theater)* Kontermarke; **price** ~ Katalog mit Preisangaben, Preisverzeichnis, -liste; **priority** ~ Dringlichkeitsliste; **prohibited** ~ Verbotsliste; **publisher's monthly** ~ Monatsverzeichnis der Neuveröffentlichungen; **recommended** ~ Empfehlungsliste; **registration** ~ Wählerliste; **reliable** ~ Liste auf die man sich verlassen kann; **retired** ~ Liste der Beamten im Ruhestand; **sailing** ~ Liste der Abgangsdaten; **salary** ~ Gehaltsliste; **seniority** ~ Anziennistätsliste; **share** ~ Aktionärsverzeichnis; **shipping** ~ Liste der Abgangsdaten; **shopping** ~ Einkaufszettel; **sick** ~ Krankenliste; **signatory** ~ Liste der Zeichnungsberechtigten; **single** ~ *(parl.)* Einheitsliste; **specie** ~ Geldsortenzettel; **stock-exchange** ~ *(Br.)* Kursblatt; **stop** ~ schwarze Liste, Boykottliste; **subscription** ~ Subskriptionsliste; **tax** ~ Steuerrolle, *(real estate)* Verzeichnis der säumigen Steuerzahler; **the** ~ *(stock exchange, Br.)* Liste der börsenfähigen Wertpapiere; **trade** ~ Preisliste, Geschäftskatalog; **unfair** ~ *(US)* schwarze Liste, Boykottliste; **uniform** ~ Einheitstarif; **voting** ~ Wählerliste; **waiting** ~ Warteliste; **wine** ~ Weinkarte;

~ **of abbreviations** Abkürzungsverzeichnis; ~ **of accidents** Unfalliste; ~ **of applicants** Bewerberliste; ~ **of applications** *(Br.)* Zeichnungsliste; ~ **of arrivals** Fremdenliste; ~ **of articles** Warenliste; ~ **of assets** Vermögensverzeichnis, *(bankruptcy)* Masseverzeichnis, *(estate)* Nachlaßverzeichnis; ~ **of assets and liabilities** Vermögens-, Masseverzeichnis, Finanzstatus; ~ **of awards** Gewinnliste [bei der Preisverteilung]; ~ **of bills for collection** Wechselinkassoliste; ~ **of books** Bücherverzeichnis, -liste; ~ **of books available** Verzeichnis lieferbarer Bücher; ~ **of cabinet members** Kabinettsliste; ~ **of candidates** Anwärter-, Partei-, Kandidatenliste; ~ **of charges** Gebührenordnung; ~ **of code names** Decknamenverzeichnis; ~ **of commitments** Obligoliste; ~ **of commodities** Warenverzeichnis; **a** ~ **of contributories** Tabelle der unbedingt Nachschußpflichtigen; ~ **of correspondents** Korrespondentenliste; ~ **of creditors of a bankrupt** Konkurstabelle; ~ **of the crew** Mannschaftsliste, Musterrolle; ~ **of customers** Kundenliste; ~ **of dilapidations** *(Br.)* Reparaturliste; ~ **of directors** Vorstandsverzeichnis; ~ **of drawings** Auslosungsliste; ~ **of electors** Wahlliste; ~ **of employees** Angestelltenverzeichnis; ~ **of exchange** Liste der Wechselkurse; ~ **of foreign exchange** *(Br.)* Devisenkurszettel; ~ **of exhibitors** Ausstellerverzeichnis; ~ **of fares** Eisenbahntarif; ~ **of goods liable to pay customs** Negativliste ~ **of localities** Ortsverzeichnis; ~ **of members** Mitgliederverzeichnis, *(Br.)* Aktionärsliste; ~ **of names** Namensverzeichnis, -liste; ~ **of nominees** Kandidatenliste; ~ **of offers** Angebotsverzeichnis; ~ **of orders** Auftrags-, Bestellliste; ~ **of parities** Paritätenliste; ~ **of participants** Teilnehmerliste; ~ **of passengers** Passagierliste; ~ **of proscribed persons** Proskriptionsliste; ~ **of taxable persons** Steuerliste; ~ **of precedence** Rangliste; ~ **of prices** Preisliste, *(Br.)* Kursblatt, -zettel; ~ **of prices of securities** Effektenkurszettel; ~ **of priorities** Dringlichkeitsliste; ~ **of prizes** Gewinnliste; ~ **of products** Warenverzeichnis; ~ **of taxable property** Vermögensteuerliste; ~ **of new publications** Verzeichnis neu erschienener Werke; ~ **of [market] quotations** Börsen-, Kurszettel, -blatt; ~ **of real estates** Grundstücksverzeichnis; **stockbroker's ~ of recommendations** Liste empfohlener Börsenwerte; ~ **of requirements** Bedarfsliste; ~ **of sailings** Aufstellung der Abgangsdaten; ~ **of salaries** Gehaltsliste; ~ **of securities** Effektenverzeichnis; ~ **of shareholders** *(Br.)* Aktionärsverzeichnis; **voting ~ of shareholders** *(Br.)* Liste der stimmberechtigten Aktionäre; ~ **of authorized signatures** Unterschriftenverzeichnis; ~ **of speakers** Rednerliste; ~ **of spellers** Fernsprechalphabet; ~ **to starboard** *(ship)* Schlagseite nach Steuerbord; ~ **of stock exchange quotations** *(Br.)* Kursblatt, -zettel; ~ **of stockholders** *(US)* Aktionärsverzeichnis; ~ **of subscribers** Subskriptions-, Abonnentenliste; ~ **of suppliers** Lieferantenliste; ~ **of those present** Anwesenheitsliste; ~ **of titles** *(book trade)* Titelaufnahme; ~ **of trains** Fahrplan; ~ **of voters** Wählerliste; ~ **of shares** Wunschzettel;

~ *(v.)* in einer Liste eintragen, in eine Liste aufnehmen, [listenmäßig] erfassen, registrieren, aufzeichnen, verzeichnen, *(catalog(ue))* katalogisieren, *(inventory)* inventarisieren, in ein Inventar aufnehmen, *(stock exchange, US)* [Effekten] an der Börse einführen (notieren), zum Börsenhandel zulassen;

~ **all one's books** Bücherverzeichnis anlegen; ~ **assets** *(US)* Liste des zu versteuernden Vermögens aufstellen; ~ **in a catalog(ue)** in einen Katalog aufnehmen; ~ **documents** Dokumente aufnehmen; ~ **one's engagements** seine Verabredungen notieren; ~ **items** Posten aufführen; ~ **officially** amtlich notieren; ~ **property with a broker** *(US)* einem Makler Grundstückseigentum an die Hand geben; ~ **property for taxation** zu versteuerndes Vermögen aufstellen, Vermögen steuerlich erfassen; ~ **to starboard** *(ship)* Schlagseite nach Steuerbord haben;

to add to a ~ in eine Liste aufnehmen; **to be on a ~** auf einer Liste stehen; **to be at the bottom of the ~** letzter Kandidat sein; **to be on the active ~** *(mil.)* im aktiven Dienst stehen; **to be on the cause ~** zur Verhandlung anstehen; **to be at the head of a list** Liste anführen; **to be on the reserve ~** *(mil.)* der Reserve angehören; **to be on the short ~** in die engere Wahl kommen; **to be on the danger ~** *(hospital)* zu den schweren Fällen zählen; **to be put on the short ~** in die engere Wahl kommen (gezogen werden); **to be struck from the ~** *(insolvency)* für zahlungsunfähig erklärt werden; **to build up a ~** Liste zusammenstellen; **to check off a name on a ~** jds. Namen auf der Liste abhaken; **to come bottom of (low on) a ~** ganz am Ende (weit unten auf) einer Liste stehen; **to compile (draw up) a ~** Liste aufstellen; **to draw up a ~ of items of business** Tagesordnungspunkte zusammenstellen; **to enrol(l) (enter) in a ~** in eine Liste eintragen; **to enter in an official ~** amtlich registrieren; **to enter the ~s** an einem Wettbewerb teilnehmen; **to figure on a ~** auf einer Liste stehen; **to go into a broader ~ of equities** breitgestreute Wertpapierkäufe tätigen; **to head a ~** an der Spitze einer Liste stehen, Liste anführen (eröffnen); **to look down a ~** Liste durchsehen; **to maintain a ~** Adressenverzeichnis auf dem neuesten Stand halten; **to make out (up) a ~** Liste aufstellen; **to prepare a ~** Liste anfertigen; **to put into a ~** in ein Verzeichnis aufnehmen; **to put one's name on a ~** sich in eine Liste eintragen; **to put s. one's name on the ~ of speakers** jds. Namen in die Rednerliste eintragen; **to put on the retired ~** in den Ruhestand versetzen, pensionieren; **to put forward a ~ of candidates** Kandidatenliste aufstellen; **to reel off one's ~ of woes** übliche Platte seiner Krankheiten abspielen; **to register on a ~** *(US)* sich (seinen Namen) auf einer Liste eintragen; **to rent ~s** *(list broker, US)* Adressenverzeichnisse leihweise zur Verfügung stellen; **to sell ~s** *(list broker)* Adressenverzeichnisse verkaufen; **to stand first on a ~** Liste anführen; **to strike (take) a name off the ~** Namen von einer Liste streichen; **to top a ~** Liste anführen (eröffnen); **to withdraw from a ~** von einer Liste streichen;

~ **broker** Adressenbüro, -verlag; **commercial ~ house** gewerbliches Adressenbüro; ~ **owner** Inhaber eines Adressenverlags,

-büros; ~ **price** Listen-, Katalogpreis; **suggested ~ price** empfohlener Listenpreis; **to sell closer to ~ prices** sich beim Verkauf strenger an Listenpreise halten; **to sell under ~ prices** Listenpreise unterbieten; **sample ~** Listenauswahl; ~ **system** *(voting)* Listen[wahl]system, Listenwahl.

listed in eine Liste (ein Verzeichnis) aufgenommen, registriert, *(of stocks, US)* börsenfähig, an der Börse zugelassen (eingeführt), amtlich notiert, *(taxation)* [steuerlich] erfaßt;

~ **above the market price** oberhalb des Kurswertes notiert; ~ **securities** *(US)* an der Börse eingeführte (zugelassene) Werte; ~ **stock** *(US)* amtlich notierte Werte.

listen | *(v.)* **to s. o.** jem. Gehör schenken, jds. Rat folgen; ~ **to advice** Ratschläge beachten; ~ **in to other people's conversation** Gespräche Dritter belauschen; ~ **with both ears** sehr genau (gespannt) zuhören; ~ **to s. o. with one's third ear** jem. im Unterbewußtsein zuhören; ~ **to a few home truths** ein paar Binsenweisheiten einstecken müssen; ~ **in** *(broadcasting)* sich eine Rundfunksendung anhören, *(tel.)* Telefongespräch abhören, *(university)* Vorlesungen hören, ohne immatrikuliert zu sein; ~ **to the Prime Minister** Ansprache des Premierministers [im Rundfunk] anhören; ~ **in tonight** sich das abendliche Rundfunkprogramm anhören; ~ **to reason** auf einen Rat hören, ein Wort mit sich reden lassen, Vernunft annehmen; ~ **for the telephone bell** auf das Telefon aufpassen.

listener Rundfunkhörer, *(tel.)*;
~~**-in** Rundfunkhörer, *(tel.)* Mithörer;
to be primarily a ~ hauptsächliche Aufgabe im Zuhören sehen; ~ **research** Hörerumfrage, -analyse.

listenership *(US)* Hörerschaft;
~ **research** *(US)* Hörerumfrage [zu einer bestimmten Sendung].

listening | **in** Rundfunkhören;
~ **area** Sendebereich; ~ **audience** Hörerpublikum; ~ **device** Mit-, Abhörvorrichtung; ~ **key** Mithörtaste; ~ **post** *(mil.)* Horchposten; ~ **service** *(mil.)* Abhördienst.

lister *(US)* Steuerbeamter.

listing Katalogisierung, Inventarisierung, Registrierung, *(real estate, US)* Maklerbeauftragung, -auftrag, *(of stocks, US)* amtliche Notierung, Börseneinführung, -zulassung;
exclusive ~ ausschließlicher Maklerauftrag; **multiple ~** Maklerkartell; **open ~** Verkaufsauftrag an mehrere Grundstücksmakler;
~ **of property** *(US)* Inventar-, Vermögensaufstellung; ~ **of property for taxation** *(US)* Vermögensteuererklärung; ~ **of real estate** Registrierung von zum Verkauf stehenden Grundbesitzes; ~ **of securities** *(US)* Börsenzulassung von Wertpapieren, Wertpapierzulassung;
official ~ notice *(stock exchange, US)* Zulassungsbescheid, Börsenzulassungsbescheid; ~ **requirements** *(stock exchange, US)* Voraussetzung für die Börseneinführung.

listless schwunglos, interesselos, teilnahmslos;
~ **trading** *(US)* Freiverkehr.

literacy Gebildetsein, geistige Bildung.

literal Druckfehler;
~ *(a.)* wörtlich, wortgetreu, buchstäblich, *(true to the fact)* nicht übertrieben, wahrheitsgetreu;
~ **acceptation of the law** buchstabengetreue Gesetzesauslegung; ~ **annihilation** buchstäbliche Vernichtung; ~ **contract** schriftlicher Vertrag, Vertrag in Schriftform; ~ **description** genaue Beschreibung; ~ **error** Druckfehler; ~ **meaning of a word** eigentliche Wortbedeutung, wörtliche Bedeutung; **to be ~-minded** alles wortwörtlich nehmen; ~ **notation** Buchstabenbezeichnung; ~ **proof** schriftliche Beweismittel; **to take s. th. in a ~ sense** etw. wortwörtlich nehmen; ~ **transcript** wortgetreue Übertragung; ~ **translation** wortgetreue Übersetzung.

literalism buchstäbliche Auslegung, Buchstabenglaube.

literalization wörtliche Auslegung.

literalize *(v.)* buchstäblich auslegen.

literally | **famished** buchstäblich verhungert;
to carry out an order too ~ Anweisungen übergenau befolgen; **to translate ~** wortgetreu übersetzen.

literary literarisch, schriftstellerisch;
~ **activity** schriftstellerische Tätigkeit; ~ **agent** Verlagsvermittler; ~ **artist** Erzählertalent; ~ **capacity** schriftstellerische Begabung; ~ **composition** *(copyright law)* eigenschöpferische Leistung, individuelle Gestaltung, Schriftwerk; ~ **critic** Literaturkritiker; ~ **earnings** Büchereinnahmen; ~ **editor** Feuilletonredakteur; ~ **expression** gewählter Ausdruck; ~ **gems** literarische Kostbarkeiten; ~ **history** Literaturgeschichte; ~ **item** Büchersendung; ~ **language** Schriftsprache; ~ **man** gebildeter Mann, Literat; ~ **piracy** Plagiat, Diebstahl geistigen

Eigentums; ~ **profession** Schriftstellerberuf, Schriftstellerei; ~ **property** geistiges Eigentum, Urheber-, Autorenrechte; ~ **review** Literaturblatt, -beilage; ~ **society** literarische Gesellschaft; ~ **star** literarische Größe; ~ **style** Schriftstil; ~ **supplement** Literaturbeilage; ~ **tools** literarische Hilfsmittel; ~ **work** schriftstellerische Tätigkeit, Schriftwerk.

literator Kritiker.

literature Schrifttum, Literatur, *(printed matter)* Drucksachen, Prospekte;
elegant ~ Belletristik; **free** ~ kostenloses Informationsmaterial; **pertinent** ~ einschlägige Literatur; **specialized** ~ Fachliteratur; **travel** ~ Reiselektüre;
~ **for the blind** Blindensendungen; ~ **on request** auf Wunsch Übersendung von Informationsmaterial; ~ **sent gratis on request** kostenlos angeforderte Prospekte; ~ **of a subject** Fachliteratur;
to be engaged in ~ schreiben, Schriftsteller sein, schriftstellern; **to take to** ~ sich literarisch betätigen.

lithographic establishment lithographische Anstalt.

lithography Steindruck, Lithographie.

lithoprint *(v.)* lithographieren.

litigable strittig.

litigant [at law] Prozeßpartei, -führer.

litigate *(v.)* Rechtsstreit führen, prozessieren;
~ **a cause** Prozeß anhängig machen; ~ **a claim** Forderung einklagen; ~ **a commercial dispute** wirtschaftliche Auseinandersetzung gerichtlich austragen.

litigation Rechtsstreit, Prozeß, Prozessieren;
in ~ rechtshängig, streitbefangen; **in case of** ~ im Streitfall; **international** ~ Prozeß vor dem internationalen Gerichtshof; **patent** ~ Patentstreit;
to bring into ~ rechtshängig werden lassen; **to drop one's** ~ seine Klage zurücknehmen;
to withdraw from one's ~ **claim** seine Prozeßforderung zurückziehen; ~ **costs** Prozeßkosten; ~ **expenses** *(US)* Gerichtskosten; ~ **list** Prozeßverzeichnis; ~ **work** Prozeßtätigkeit.

litigator *(US)* Prozeßpartei.

litigiosity *(Scot.)* Rechtshängigkeit.

litigious *(quarrelsome)* prozeßsüchtig, *(subject to litigation)* prozeßhängig, strittig, streitig;
~ **forms** Prozeßformen; ~ **person** Querulant; ~ **right** nur gerichtlich durchsetzbares Recht.

litigiousness Prozeßsucht.

litiscontestation Beginn eines Rechtsstreits.

litter Durcheinander, herumliegender Abfall, Papierreste;
~ *(v.)* **papers about the floor** Papier über den ganzen Fußboden verstreuen; ~ **up one's room** sein Zimmer völlig durcheinanderbringen;
to make a ~ **of a room** Chaos in seinem Zimmer anrichten; **to pick up one's** ~ **after a picnic** Picknickabfälle einsammeln; ~ **bin (basket)** Abfallbehälter.

little Kleinigkeit;
in ~ in kleinem Maßstab;
~ *(a.)* klein, geringfügig, unbedeutend, *(miserable)* gemein, erbärmlich, armselig;
~ **by** ~ nach und nach; ~ **or nothing** fast nichts;
to be ~ **known** kaum bekannt sein; **to get** ~ **out of it** nur geringen Nutzen (Gewinn) von etw. haben; **to think** ~ **of s. o.** nicht sehr viel von jem. halten;
~ **business** geringer Umsatz; ~ **discomforts** geringfügige Unbequemlichkeiten; **poor** ~ **efforts** rührende Bemühungen; ~ **farmer** Kleinbauer; ~ **go** *(Cambridge)* Zulassungsprüfung, *(sl.)* unermüdlicher Versuch; ~ **grey cells** *(sl.)* menschliches Gehirn; ~ **or no help** wenig oder gar keine Hilfe; ~ **minds** kleine Geister; **a** ~ **money** ein bißchen Geld; **no** ~ **pains** viel Mühe; ~ **theatre** *(Br.)* Kammerspiele, Kleinbühne; ~ **things** Nebensächlichkeiten; ~ **schemes** kleine Intrigen; ~ **school** *(sl.)* Jugendgefängnis; ~ **way** kurze Strecke Weges; **to know s. one's** ~ **ways** jds. Schliche kennen; **a** ~ **while** ein Weilchen.

littleness Geringfügigkeit, Kleinigkeit.

lit up like a Christmas tree (Times Square, a church) *(sl.)* betrunken wie eine Strandhaubitze.

live *(broadcasting)* Live-, Direktsendung, -übertragung;
during their joint ~**s** *(life insurance)* solange sie beide leben;
~ *(v.)* leben, existieren, sich ernähren, *(reside)* wohnen;
~ **for o. s.** nur für sich leben; ~ **abroad** seinen Wohnsitz im Ausland haben; ~ **to a great age** hohes Alter erreichen; ~ **on air** von fast nichts leben; ~ **a full all-round life** erfülltes Leben haben; ~ **apart** getrennt leben; ~ **in furnished apartments** möbliert wohnen; ~ **five blocks from here** fünf Straßen weiter wohnen; ~ **on bread and water** von Wasser und Brot leben; ~ **on**

one's capital von seinem Kapital leben, sein Vermögen aufzehren; ~ **on cash earnings** seinen Lebensunterhalt mit bar entlohnten Gelegenheitsarbeiten fristen; ~ **on charity** von der Wohltätigkeit leben; ~ **in easy circumstances** in guten Verhältnissen leben; ~ **in straitened circumstances** in äußerster Armut leben; ~ **close at hand** um die Ecke herum wohnen; ~ **in clover** reinste Fettlebe sein; ~ **in comfort** behagliches Leben führen; ~ **in cramped conditions** in bedrängten Verhältnissen leben; ~ **in the country** auf dem Lande leben; ~ **through a crisis** Krise durchstehen; ~ **at daggers drawn** auf gespanntem Fuße leben; ~ **next door** nebenan wohnen; ~ **on s. one's doorstep** jem. das Haus einlaufen; ~ **down an incident in one's career** mit Rückschlägen in seiner beruflichen Entwicklung fertig werden; ~ **down prejudice** mit Vorurteilen fertig werden; ~ **economically** sparsam wirtschaften; ~ **at s. one's expense** jem. auf der Tasche liegen; ~ **on the fat of the land** in Saus und Braus leben; ~ **off government checks** *(US)* (cheques, *Br.*) von staatlicher Unterstützung leben; ~ **in s. one's family** zur Familie gehören; ~ **from hand to mouth** von der Hand in den Mund leben; ~ **happily with s. o.** glückliches Leben mit jem. führen; ~ **high** Luxusleben führen; ~ **high on the hog** *(sl.)* aufwendig (auf großem Fuße) leben, großen Aufwand treiben; ~ **high up** hoch wohnen; ~ **honestly** ehrliches Leben führen; ~ **through sheer horror** absolute Schreckenszeit durchmachen; ~ **in a house rent-free** mietfrei in einem Hause wohnen; ~ **with the husband** mit dem Ehemann zusammenleben; ~ **in huts** in Baracken leben; ~ **in** am Arbeitsplatz leben; ~ **off the income** vom Kapital leben; ~ **on s. one's income** jem. auf der Tasche liegen; ~ **on one's wife's income** sich von seiner Frau ernähren lassen; ~ **up to one's income** immer gleich alles ausgeben; ~ **and let** ~ leben und leben lassen; ~ **a double life** Doppelleben führen; ~ **half of one's life on one's job** Hälfte seines Lebens beruflich verbringen; ~ **a good life** angenehmes Leben führen; ~ **an obscure (a retired) life** zurückgezogen leben; ~ **a riotous life** in Saus und Braus leben; ~ **a life of independence** unabhängiges Leben führen; ~ **as a lodger (in lodgings)** zur Miete wohnen; ~ **like a lord** Herrenleben führen, wie Gott in Frankreich (wie ein Fürst) leben; ~ **at rack and manger** *(Br.)* auf großem Fuße (in Saus und Braus) leben, sich auf Kosten anderer Leute amüsieren; ~ **above one's means** über seine Verhältnisse leben; ~ **within one's means** mit seinem Geld auskommen; ~ **on prior means** von seinem Vermögen leben; ~ **on one's name** von seinem guten Namen zehren; ~ **in dire need** in äußerster Armut leben; ~ **through the night** diese Nacht überleben; ~ **out** nicht im Haus (außerhalb) wohnen, *(US)* auswärts in Stellung sein; ~ **by one's pen** sich als Schriftsteller sein Brot verdienen; ~ **perforce** notgedrungen leben; ~ **up to one's principles** seinen Grundsätzen gemäß leben; ~ **in wretched poverty** in jämmerlichen Verhältnissen leben; ~ **in privacy** zurückgezogen leben; ~ **up to one's promise** sein Versprechen verwirklichen lassen; ~ **on one's relations** seinen Verwandten auf der Tasche liegen; ~ **on one's reputation** von früheren Erfolgen zehren; ~ **up to one's reputation** seinem guten Ruf Genüge leisten; ~ **within a few seconds run of the station** ein paar Schritte vom Bahnhof entfernt wohnen; ~ **on one's salary** von seinem Gehalt leben; ~ **like a saint** wie ein Heiliger leben; ~ **on a large scale** auf großem Fuße leben; ~ **down a scandal** Skandal überleben; ~ **in the shadow** Schattendasein führen; ~ **one's full span** sein Leben bis zur Neige auskosten; ~ **through a storm** Sturm überstehen; ~ **in grand style** in Saus und Braus leben, aufwendiges Leben führen; ~ **by the sweat of one's brow** von seiner Hände Arbeit leben; ~ **on borrowed time** nicht mehr lange zu leben haben; ~ **together** zusammen wohnen (leben); ~ **out of town** auswärts wohnen; ~ **up to the letter of a contract** Vertrag bis zum letzten I-Tüpfelchen erfüllen; ~ **upon the parish** von der öffentlichen Hand (Wohlfahrt) unterstützt werden; ~ **through two wars** zwei Kriege miterlebt haben; ~ **and cohabit together as husband and wife** wie Eheleute zusammenleben; ~ **in a small way** sehr bescheiden (in dürftigen Verhältnissen) leben; ~ **well** üppig leben; ~ **on one's wife** von den Einkünften seiner Frau leben; ~ **within o. s.** sich nur mit sich selbst beschäftigen; ~ **on one's wits** sich mehr oder weniger ehrlich durchs Leben schlagen; ~ **by the work of one's hand (by working)** von seiner Hände Arbeit leben; ~ **on £ 5000 a year** mit 5000 Pfund im Jahr auskommen; ~ *(a.)* lebend, lebendig, *(broadcasting)* unmittelbar übertragen, direkt, *(el.)* unter Spannung, stromführend, eingeschaltet, *(print.)* druck-, gebrauchsfertig;
to broadcast (transmit) ~ direkt senden (übertragen), Livesendung ausstrahlen, live senden;
~ **announcement** *(advertising)* Direktwerbedurchsage; ~ **assets** wohlfundierte Anlagewerte; ~ **axle** Differentialachse; ~ **birth**

Lebendgeburt; ~ **broadcast** Direktübertragung; **real ~ burglar** richtiger Einbrecher; ~ **campaign** *(advertising)* direkte Werbedurchspruchserie; ~ **cartridge** scharfe Patrone; ~ **coals** glühende Kohlen; ~ **[television] coverage** Direktübertragung; ~ **headline** lebender Kolumnentitel; ~ **letter book** Tageskopiebuch; ~ **load** Nutz-, Verkehrslast; **to be a ~ man** auf Draht sein; ~ **matter** druckfertiger Satz; ~ **park** Wildpark; ~ **program(me)** Direktsendung; ~ **question** aktuelle Frage; ~ **rail** Stromschiene; ~ **steam** Kesseldampf; ~ **storage** Garagendienst bei Tag und Nacht; ~ **transmission** Direktübertragung; ~ **weight** Lebendgewicht; ~ **wire** unter Strom stehende Leitung, stromführende Leitung, *(fig.)* energiegeladener Mensch; **to be a real ~ wire** *(fam.)* Energiebündel sein; **to be the ~ wire in a concern** Antriebskraft eines Unternehmens sein.

lived in bewohnt.

livelihood Nahrung, [Lebens]unterhalt, Auskommen, Existenz[grundlage];
to deprive s. o. of his ~ j. um seine Existenzgrundlage (Lohn und Brot) bringen; **to earn one's** ~ seinen Lebensunterhalt verdienen; **to earn an honest** ~ bürgerlichen Beruf ausüben; **to earn one's ~ by teaching** sich durch Stundengeben ernähren; **to fear for one's** ~ sich um seine Existenz Sorgen machen; **to pick up a scanty ~** *(Br.)* sein knappes Auskommen haben; **to scrabble for one's** ~ sich für seinen Lebensunterhalt abplacken (abrackern) müssen; **to seek a ~** sein Auskommen suchen.

liveliness *(market)* Lebhaftigkeit.

lively kräftig, vital, *(stock exchange)* flott, lebhaft;
to make things ~ for s. o. jem. kräftig einheizen;
~ **debate** lebhafte Debatte; ~ **description** lebendige Beschreibung; ~ **idea** lebhafte Vorstellung; ~ **imagination** lebhafte Phantasie; **to take a ~ interest in s. th.** lebhaftes Interesse an etw. nehmen; ~ **recollection** deutliche Erinnerung; **to have a ~ time of it** aufregende Zeiten erleben.

livery *(allowance of food)* Deputat, *(dress)* Livree, *(peculiar dress)* [Amts]tracht, *(stables, US)* Mietstallung, *(servants collectively)* Dienerschaft, *(transition)* Übergabe, Übertragung[s]urkunde];
at ~ *(horse)* in Verpflegung; **in ~** livriert; **out of ~** in gewöhnlicher Kleidung;
~ **of seizin** Besitzübertragung, -einweisung, -verschaffung;
to receive in ~ in Besitz übernehmen; **to sue out one's ~** *(Br.)* auf Grundbuchumschreibung klagen, um Übertragung seines Erbgutes nachsuchen;
~ **company** *(London)* Handwerksgilde; ~ **conveyance** für die öffentliche Personenbeförderung zugelassenes Fahrzeug; ~ **horse** Mietpferd; ~ **servant** livrierter Dienst; ~ **stable** Mietstallung.

liveryman Pferdeverleiher.

liverymen *(Br.)* Zunftmitglieder.

livestock Vieh[bestand], lebendes Inventar;
~ **car** Viehwagen; ~ **clause** *(insurance, Br.)* Klausel für Verschiffung lebender Tiere; ~ **dealer** Viehhändler; ~ **insurance** Viehversicherung; ~ **production** Tierzucht; ~ **ranger** Viehzüchter; ~ **waggon** Viehwagen.

living Leben, Wohnen, Aufenthalt, *(livelihood)* Nahrung, [Lebens]unterhalt, Auskommen, Existenz;
capable of making a ~ erwerbsfähig; **unable to earn one's ~** erwerbsunfähig; **while ~** bei Lebzeiten;
cheap ~ billige Lebensweise; **extravagant ~** aufwendige Lebensführung; **fat ~** fette Pfründe; **gracious ~** eleganter Lebensstil; **plain ~** schlichte Lebensweise; **high-style ~** aufwendige Lebensführung; **poor ~** magere Pfründe; **substandard ~** asoziale Wohnweise;
~-**in** Wohnung beim Arbeitgeber; ~ **in adultery** ehebrecherisches Verhältnis; ~ **in the country** Leben auf dem Lande; **to be fond of good ~** gern gut tafeln; **to dispense s. o. from the necessity of earning his** ~ jede Notwendigkeit entheben seinen Lebensunterhalt selbst zu verdienen; **to earn one's ~** seinen Lebensunterhalt verdienen; **to earn a bare ~** nur das Allernotwendigste verdienen; **to earn a ~ by manual labour** seinen Lebensunterhalt durch seiner Hände Arbeit verdienen; **to get a sufficient ~** genug zum Leben verdienen; **to make a ~** Fortkommen finden; **to make a good ~** reichliches Auskommen haben; **to make a precarious ~** unsichere Existenz haben; **to make a ~ out of it** seinen Lebensunterhalt damit verdienen; **to make one's own ~** sich selbst unterhalten (ernähren); **to scrape for one's ~** sein Leben fristen, sich für seinen Lebensunterhalt abplacken (abrackern) müssen; **to work for one's ~** für seinen Lebensunterhalt arbeiten; **to work hard for one's ~** hart arbeiten müssen; **to wrest a ~ from the soil** dem kargen Boden seinen Lebensunterhalt abringen;

~ *(a.)* lebend, wohnhaft, *(active)* tätig;
~ **alone** alleinstehend; ~ **with husband** zusammenwohnend; ~ **separate and apart** *(income tax statement)* getrennt lebend; ~ **together** zusammenlebend;
~ **accommodation** Wohnung, Wohnmöglichkeit; ~ **accommodations** Wohnverhältnisse; ~ **allowance** Unterhaltszuschuß; ~ **conditions** Existenzbedingungen, Lebensbedingungen, -verhältnisse; ~ **cost (expenses)** Lebenshaltungskosten; **family ~ expenses** Lebensunterhaltskosten einer Familie; ~ **habits** Lebensgewohnheiten; ~ **image** getreues Abbild; ~ **language** lebende Sprache; ~ **memory** Rückerinnerung der heute noch Lebenden; **within ~ memory** seit Menschengedenken; ~ **pledge** Grundstücksübertragung gegen Kaufpreisstundung; ~-**out allowance** Wohnungsgeld; ~ **quarter** Wohnviertel; ~ **room** Wohnzimmer; ~ **room gig** *(sl.)* Fernsehauftritt; ~ **space** *(pol.)* Lebensraum; ~ **standard** Lebensstandard; ~ **tent** Wohnzelt; ~ **trust** *(US)* lebenslängliche Treuhandverwaltung; ~ **wage** Mindestlohn, Existenzminimum; **still ~ witness** noch lebender Zeuge.

lizard *(sl.)* Briefkasten.

lizzie *(car, sl.)* alter Klapperkasten.

Lloyd's Londoner Versicherungsbörse.

load Fuhre, Last, Ladung, Fracht, *(fig.)* Last, Bürde, *(insurance)* Verwaltungskostenzuschlag, *(liquor, sl.)* Schluck Alkohol, *(loading capacity)* Tragfähigkeit, *(machine)* Belastung, Arbeitsleistung, *(work)* Arbeitspensum;
~**s** *(quantities, coll.)* Masse, Scharen, Unmengen;
additional ~ Beiladung; **breaking** ~ Bruchlast; **coach** ~ Wagenladung; **dead** ~ tote Last; ~ **evenly distributed** gleichmäßig verteilte Last; **deck** ~ Deckladung; **electric** ~ Strombelastung; **financial** ~ finanzielle Belastung; **full** ~ volle Belastung (Ladung); **gross** ~ Bruttobelastung; **maximum** ~ Höchstbelastung; **maximum useful** ~ Höchstzuladung; **net** ~ Nutzlast; **no** ~ Nullast; **paying** ~ *(railway)* Nutzlast; **peak** ~ Spitzenbelastung; **permissible** ~ Höchstbelastung; **rated** ~ berechnete Leistung; **safe[ty]** ~ zulässige Belastung (Beanspruchung); **tax** ~ steuerliche Belastung; **total** ~ Bruttobelastung; **unit** ~ Verladeeinheit; **useful** ~ Nutzlast; **welfare** ~ Belastung des Fürsorgeetats;
~ **of care** Sorgenlast; ~ **of coal** Kohlenladung; ~ **on one's conscience** Gewissensbelastung; ~**s of debts** Berge von Schulden, Schuldenberg; ~ **of furniture** Möbelladung; ~ **of hay** *(sl.)* Schnorrer; ~**s of money** große Menge Geld; ~ **on a motor** Belastung eines Motors; ~ **on a section** *(railway)* Streckenbelastung; ~ **of a ship** Schiffsladung; **heavy ~ on one's shoulders** schwere Verantwortung; ~**s of tourists** Touristenstrom; ~ **of a waggon** Waggonladung; ~ **of work** Haufen Arbeit;
~ *(v.)* ein-, beladen, etw. [auf]laden, *(add to the selling price)* Aufschlag vornehmen, *(adulterate)* verfälschen, *(encumber)* belasten, *(insurance)* Prämienzuschlag für Verwaltungskosten erheben, *(narcotics, sl.)* Narkotika einnehmen, *(put aboard)* befrachten, verladen, *(stock exchange)* stark kaufen, *(supply abundantly)* überlasten -laden, *(take aboard)* Ladung übernehmen (einnehmen);
~ **for A** Ladung nach A übernehmen; ~ **s. o. with abuse** j. mit Beschimpfungen überhäufen; ~ **in bulk** *(ship)* Sturzgüter laden; ~ **a cargo** Ladung einnehmen; ~ **a cart** Fuhre beladen; ~ **a dice** Würfel fälschen; ~ **the dice against s. o.** j. in unfairer Weise benachteiligen; ~ **s. o. down with s. th.** j. bis zum Hals vollstopfen; ~ **s. o. with favo(u)rs** jem. übermäßige Beweise seiner Gunst zukommen lassen; ~ **a film** Film einlegen; ~ **with gifts** mit Geschenken überschütten, überreich beschenken; ~ **s. o. with hono(u)rs** j. mit Ehrungen überhäufen; ~ **in** einladen; ~ **one's memory** sein Gedächtnis belasten; ~ **out** ausladen; ~ **down s. o. with parcels and packages** j. mit Päckchen und Paketen beladen; ~ **in parcels** Stückgut laden; ~ **passengers** Fahrgäste aufnehmen; ~ **s. o. with praise** j. mit Lob überschütten; ~ **a slide** Platte in eine Kassette einlegen; ~ **up** *(v./i.)* ein-, aufladen, Ladung einnehmen, *(buy)* große Mengen einkaufen; ~ **on a waggon** auf einen Waggon laden, Waggon beladen; ~ **s. o. with work** jem. viel Arbeit aufhalsen;
to carry a heavy ~ on one's shoulders große Verantwortung tragen; **to give way under the ~ of misfortunes** unter der Last der Unglücksfälle zusammenbrechen; **to have a ~ on one's mind** Problem mit sich herumschleppen; **to have ~s s. of money** im Geld schwimmen; **to take a ~ off s. one's mind** jem. einen Stein vom Herzen nehmen;
~ **capacity** Trag-, Ladefähigkeit; ~ **cargo** Ladepforte; ~ **displacement** Wasserverdrängung, Ladetonnage, -gewicht; ~ **draft** *(Br.)* **(draught)** *(mar.)* Ladetiefgang; ~ **factor** Kapazitätsausnutzungsgrad, Kapazitätsauslastungsquotient, *(airplane)*

Auslastung; ~ **limit** Beladungsgrenze; ~ **line** Ladelinie, -marke; **subdivision** ~ **line** Schottenladelinie; ~ **platform** *(car)* Ladefläche; **~-rate tariff** Tarif nach normalem Verbrauch; ~ **test** Belastungsprobe; ~ **waterline** Ladelinie.

loaded befrachtet, verladen, vollbeladen, *(drunk, sl.)* ganz schön geladen;
  heavily ~ schwer beladen;
  ~ **in bulk** als Schüttgut verladen; ~ **with cares** von Sorgen überlastet; ~ **with securities** mit Effekten stark eingedeckt; ~ **up with** mit einem reichlichen Vorrat versehen;
  ~ **arm** geladene Waffe; ~ **cane** Totschläger; ~ **dice** falscher Würfel; ~ **premium** *(insurance)* Zuschlagsprämie.

loader Verlader;
  chief ~ Verladeaufseher.

loadability Verladefähigkeit.

loading [Be]laden, Auf-, Ver-, Einladen, *(airplane)* Belastung, *(freight)* Ladung, Fracht, *(instalment system, Br.)* Aufschlag, *(insurance)* Prämienaufschlag für die Verwaltungskosten, Verwaltungskostenzuschlag, -anteil, Prämienzuschlag, *(investment trust)* Ausgabenzuschlag zuzüglich Erwerbskosten der Wertpapiere, *(production)* zu den Gestehungskosten hinzutretende Generalunkosten, *(putting aboard)* Verladung, Befrachten, *(ship)* Schiffsladung, *(statistics)* Zuschlag zur Erzielung eines gewogenen Indexes;
  commercial ~ raumsparende Verladung; **daily** ~s Tagesversand; **maximum permissible** ~ zulässige Höchstbeladung; **multiple** ~ Verladung mehrerer Stückgutladungen; **off** ~ Entladung, Löschung; **ship** ~ Schiffbeladung;
  ~ **on the berth** Stückgutbeladung, -befrachtung; ~ **in bulk** Sturzgüterbefrachtung; ~ **of goods** Verladung der Ware; ~ **for London** Verladung nach London; ~ **of the slides** Einlegung von Platten in eine Kassette; ~ **and unloading** Ein- und Ausladen, Laden und Löschen;
  to be ~ Ladung nehmen; **to finish** ~ **up** Ladungsvorgang beenden;
  ~ **area** Ladefläche; ~ **bay** Ladeplatz; ~ **berth** Verladekai, Ladestelle, -platz; ~ **bridge** Verladebrücke; ~ **capacity** *(vehicle)* Fassungsvermögen, Nutzlast; ~ **carrier** Verladespediteur; ~ **charges** Verlade-, Aufladegebühr, -spesen; ~ **costs** Beladungskosten; ~ **crane** Ladekran; ~ **crew** Verlademannschaft; ~ **days** Verladefrist; **unit** ~ **device** Verladevorrichtung für Stückgut; ~ **dock** Ladedock; ~ **equipment** Ladevorrichtung; ~ **facilities** Verladeanlagen; ~ **gauge** Begrenzung der Ladung; ~ **gear** Verladeeinrichtung, -vorrichtung; ~ **hands** Lademannschaft; ~ **hatch** Ladeluke; ~ **jack** Ladebühne; ~ **ledge** Ladebühne; ~ **limit** Belastungsgrenze; **daily** ~ **list** Tagesversandmeldung; ~ **officer** Verladeaufseher; ~ **pamphlet** Verladevorschrift; ~ **permit** Ladeerlaubnis; ~ **place** Verladeort; ~ **plant** Verladeanlage, -einrichtung; ~ **platform** Ladebühne, -rampe; ~ **point** Verladeort, Ladestelle; ~ **port** Versand-, Verladehafen; ~ **profit** *(insurance)* Aufschlagsgewinn; ~ **quay** Verladekai; ~ **ramp** Verladerampe; ~ **regulations** Verladebestimmungen; ~ **and unloading report** Verzeichnis der einsatzbereiten Waggons; ~ **risk** Verladerisiko; ~ **space** Laderaum, -fläche; ~ **station** Verladestation, -bahnhof; ~ **system** Verladesystem; ~ **tackle** Ladevorrichtung; ~ **test** Belastungsprobe; ~ **time** Beladefrist; ~ **track** Ladegleis; ~ **wharf** Verladekai.

loadmanage Hafenschleppergebühr.

loadshedding *(el.)* Abschaltung ganzer Stromnetze.

loadsman Hafenpilot.

loaf Leib Brot, *(loafing, coll.)* Bummeln, Faulenzen, *(US, dish)* Frikadelle;
  ~ *(v.)* bummeln, herumlungern;
  ~ **on s. o.** auf jds. Kosten faulenzen; ~ **about the streets** in den Straßen herumlungern; ~ **away one's time** seine Zeit vertrödeln;
  to be on the ~ bummeln, faulenzen; **to use one's** ~ *(fam.)* seinen Verstand gebrauchen.

loafer Müßiggänger, Bummler.

loan Anleihe, Darlehn, Kredit, *(advance)* Vorschuß, *(lending)* [Aus]leihen, Leihgabe;
  as a ~ leihweise, als Leihgabe; **on** ~ geliehen, leihweise; **by way of** ~ *(US)* leih-, vorschußweise; **thrown out of** ~s *(stocks)* nicht lombardfähig;
  ~s Leihgeld, Ausleihungen, Kredite, Anleihemittel;
  accommodation ~ Überbrückungskredit; **accommodation endorsement** ~ Kredit gegen Wechselbürgschaft; **additional** ~ Zusatzdarlehen; **agricultural** ~ *(US)* Agrar-, Erntefinanzierungskredit; **allotted** ~s **not yet collected** noch nicht abgehobene ausgeloste Anleihestücke; **amortized (amortizing)** ~ Amortisationsdarlehn, -anleihe, Tilgungsdarlehn; **authorized**

~ **genehmigtes** Darlehn; **bank** ~ Bankkredit, -darlehn; **bottomry** ~ Bodmereigeld; **bridging** ~ Überbrückungskredit; **broker's** ~ *(US)* Maklerdarlehen; **budgeted** ~s etatisierte Kreditmittel; **business** ~ Betriebsmittelkredit; **call** tägliches Geld, Tagesgeld; **cash** ~ Bardarlehn; **civic** ~ *(US)* öffentliche Anlage; **clearance** ~ Tagesgeld; **collateral** ~ Darlehn aufgrund börsengängiger Wertpapiere, Lombardkredit, -darlehn; **commercial** ~ Geschäftskredit, Warenkredit; **commercial bank** ~ Bankkredit mit 30 - 90 Tagen Laufzeit; **commodate** ~ Leihe; **commodity** ~ Warenkredit; **consolidated** ~ konsolidierte Anleihe; **construction** ~ Baudarlehn; **consumption** ~ Klein-, Konsumentenkredit; **conversion** ~ Konversionsanleihe; **corporate** ~ *(Br.)* kommunale Anleihe; **corporation** ~ *(Br.)* Kommunalanleihe; **crop** ~ Ernte[finanzierungs]kredit; **customer's** ~ Kundenkredit; **day** ~ Tagesgeld; **day-to-day** ~ Tagesgeld, *(Br.)* täglich fälliges Darlehn an Börsenmakler; **dead** ~ dubioses Darlehn, wegen Nichtrückzahlung verlängertes kurzfristiges (eingefrorenes) Darlehn; **debenture** ~ Obligationsanleihe; **defense** *(US)* **(defence, Br.)** Verteidigungsanleihe; **demand** ~ *(US)* tägliches (täglich fälliges) Geld, Tagesgeld, sofort fälliger Kredit; **deposit** ~ Bankkredit für bargeldlose Überweisungen; **domestic** ~ Inlandsanleihe; **Eurocurrency** ~ Eurodollaranleihe; **export financing** ~ Ausfuhrfinanzierungsanleihe; **external** ~ Auslandsanleihe, -kredit; **farm** ~ Landwirtschaftskredit; **fiduciary** ~ ungesicherter Personalkredit; **first-mortgage** ~ durch erststellige Hypothek gesicherter Kredit; **fixed** ~ Festgeld; **fixed interest-bearing** ~ festverzinsliche Anleihe; **fixed-value** ~ wertbeständige Anleihe; **floating-rate** ~ Anleihe mit freigegebenem Wechselkurs; **forced** ~ Krediterhöhung infolge Kontoüberziehung, Zwangsanleihe; **foreign** ~ Auslandsanleihe, -kredit, äußere Anleihe; **foreign-currency** ~ Währungskredit; **free** ~ zinsfreies Darlehn; **frozen** ~ eingefrorener Kredit; **funding** ~ konsolidierte Anleihe, Kapitalisierungsanleihe; **gap** ~ Überbrückungskredit, Kredit für einen Spitzenbetrag; **gilt-edged** ~ *(Br.)* mündelsichere Anleihe; **government[al]** ~ Staatsanleihe, öffentliche Anleihe; **gratuitous** ~ unentgeltliche Leihe; **home-improvement** ~ Instandsetzungskredit; **indexed** ~ indexgebundene Anleihe; **industrial** ~ Industrieanleihe; **inland** ~ innere Anleihe; **intercompany** ~ konzerninternes Darlehn; **interest-bearing** ~ verzinsliches Darlehn; **interim** ~ Zwischen-, Überbrückungskredit; **internal** ~ Inlandsanleihe; **international** ~ internationale Anleihe; **low-interest** ~ zinsverbilligtes Darlehn; **irredeemable** ~ unkündbare (untilgbare) Anleihe; **land** ~ Bodenkredit; **line-of-credit** ~ *(US)* Kredit in festgesetzter Höhe; **liquid** ~ Liquiditätskredit; **livestock** ~ *(US)* Darlehn zur Finanzierung der Viehwirtschaft; **local-authority** ~ *(Br.)* Kommunalanleihe; **long-sighted** ~ langfristiges Darlehn; **long-term (-time)** ~ langfristiger Kredit; **lottery** ~ Auslosungsanleihe; **maritime (marine)** ~ Bodmereidarlehn; **medium-term** ~ mittelfristiger Kredit; **mixed** ~ durch verschiedenartige Sicherheiten gedeckter Kredit; **money** ~ Kassendarlehn; **monthly** ~ Ultimo-, Monatsgelder; **morning** ~ *(broker, US)* Tagesgeld; **mortgage** ~ hypothekarisch gesichertes Darlehn, Hypothekendarlehn; **municipal** ~ Stadt-, Kommunalanleihe; **national** ~ Staatsanleihe; **ninety days** ~ Dreimonatsgeld; **no-purpose** ~ nicht zweckgebundener Kredit; **noninterest** ~ zinsloses Darlehn; **noninterest-bearing** ~ unverzinsliche Anleihe; **nonliquid** ~ eingefrorener Kredit; **outside** ~ amtlich nicht notierte Anleihe; **overnight** ~ innerhalb 24 Stunden rückzahlbarer Kredit; **oversubscribed** ~ überzeichnete Anleihe; **perpetual** ~ unkündbare Rentenanleihe; **personal** ~ Personalkredit; **policy** ~ Policenbeleihung; **precarious** ~ jederzeit kündbares Darlehn; **preference (preferential)** ~ Vorzugs-, Prioritätsanleihe; **pre-war** ~ Vorkriegsanleihe; **primary** ~ Hauptkredit; **prior-lien** ~ erststelliges Darlehn; **private** ~ privater Kredit; **productive** ~ Produktionskredit; **prohibited** ~ verbotene Kreditgewährung; **public** ~ öffentliche Anleihe, öffentlicher Kredit, Staatsanleihe; **purchase-money** ~ Warenbeschaffungskredit; **qualifying** ~ *(Br.)* steuerbegünstigter Anschaffungskredit; **quoted** ~ notierte Anleihe; **real-estate** ~ hypothekarisch besicherter Kredit, Grundstückskredit; **reconstruction** ~ Wiederaufbauanleihe, -darlehn, -kredit; **redeemable** ~ ablösbare Anleihe, Tilgungsdarlehn; **redemption** ~ Tilgungs-, Amortisationsanleihe; **relief** ~ Notstandskredit; **repaid** ~ zurückfließende Darlehnssumme; **respondentia** ~ Bodmerei auf die Schiffsladung; **revalorized** ~ aufgewertete Anleihe; **revolving-fund** ~ sich automatisch erneuernder Kredit; **seasonal** ~ Saisonkredit; **secured** ~ besicherter (gedeckter) Kredit, garantierte Anleihe; **security** ~ Kredit gegen Wertpapierlombard, Lombardkredit; **self-liquidating** ~ *(US)* kurzfristiger Warenkredit; **short [-sighted (-time)]** ~ kurzfristiger Kredit; **sight** ~

gegen Sichtwechsel gewährtes Darlehn; **sinking-fund ~** Tilgungsanleihe; **small ~** Kleinkredit; **small business administration ~** *(US)* Mittelstandskredit; **small personal ~** persönlicher Kleinkredit; **state ~** Staatsanleihe, staatliche Kreditmittel; **stock-exchange ~** kurzfristiges Darlehn an Börsenmakler; **stopgap ~** Überbrückungskredit; **straight ~** auf einmal in voller Höhe fälliges Darlehn; **street ~** *(US)* kurzfristiges Darlehn an Börsenmakler; **subordinated ~** nachrangig gesichertes Darlehn; **subscribed ~** voll gezeichnete Anleihe; **tax-exempt ~** steuerfreie Anleihe; **term ~** mittelfristiges Darlehn; **three-per-cent ~** dreiprozentige Anleihe; **tied ~** zweckgebundene Anleihe, zweckgebundenes Darlehn; **time ~** *(US)* Darlehn mit bestimmter Laufzeit, festes Geld, Festgeld; **trade ~** *(US)* Warenkredit; **trustee ~** *(US)* mündelsichere Anlage; **uncovered (unsecured) ~** unbesichertes Darlehn, Personalkredit, offener Kredit, Blankokredit; **undated ~** unbefristeter Kredit; **unfrozen ~** freigegebene Anleihe; **unsafe ~** unsicherer Kredit; **unsecured ~** unbesichertes Darlehn; **untied ~** nicht zweckgebundenes Darlehn; **victory ~** *(Br.)* Kriegsanleihe; **war ~** Kriegsanleihe;
~ for account of others Darlehnsgewährung für fremde Rechnung; **~s en bloc** Globaldarlehn; **~ against borrower's note** Schuldscheindarlehn, Solawechselkredit; **~ on bottomry** Bodmereigeld; **~ at call** täglich kündbares Darlehn; **~s in circulation** in Umlauf befindliche Anleihen; **~ on collateral** besichertes Darlehn, Lombardkredit; **~ for consumption** Klein-, Konsumentenkredit; **~ in current account** Kontokorrentkredit; **~ to customer** Kundendarlehn; **~ on debentures** Obligationenanleihe; **~ repayable on demand** täglich kündbares Darlehn; **~s and discounts** Lombard- und Diskontgeschäfte; **~ made to an employee** betriebliches Darlehn; **~ to employee written off** abgeschriebenes Angestelltendarlehn; **~ for exchange** kostenloses Warendarlehen; **~ on a gold basis** Goldanleihe; **~ on goods** Warenlombard; **~ made to the government** der Regierung eingeräumter Kredit; **~ for the improvement of property** Kredit für Gebäudewerterhöhungen; **~ to an infant** einem Minderjährigen gewährter Kredit; **~ at (on) interest bearing interest at 8%** achtprozentige Anleihe; **~ without interest** zinsloses Darlehn; **~ on merchandise** Warenlombard; **~ on mortgage** hypothekarisch gesichertes Darlehn, Hypothekardarlehn; **~ on notice** kündbares (zeitlich befristetes) Darlehn; **~ on overdraft** Überziehungs-, Kontokorrentkredit; **~ with payment of weekly interest** Darlehn mit wöchentlicher Zinszahlung; **~ for the purpose of improvement** Meliorationsdarlehn; **~ for the purpose of investment** Investitionskredit; **~ redeemable by lot** auslosbare Anleihe; **~ on securities (upon collateral securities)** besicherter Kredit, abgesichertes Darlehn, Lombarddarlehn, -kredit, Effektenlombard; **~ without security** unbesicherter Kredit; **~ on stock** Effektenlombard; **~ on trust** Personalkredit; **~ for use** Gebrauchsüberlassung, Leihe; **~ advanced for use in the business** Betriebs[mittel]kredit; **~ by the week (with payment of weekly interest)** Darlehn mit wöchentlicher Zinszahlung; **~s from social and welfare funds** *(balance sheet)* Verbindlichkeiten gegenüber Sozialeinrichtungen; **~s for a term of at least four years** Ausleihungen mit einer Laufzeit von mindestens 4 Jahren;
~ *(v.)* [out] [aus]leihen, gegen Zinsen ausleihen, Darlehn gewähren, Kredit geben;
to gift-~ als geschenktes Darlehn geben;
~ on collateral gegen Sicherheit Kredit gewähren; **~ on interest** auf Zinsen ausleihen; **~ on short periods** auf kurze Frist ausleihen;
to amortize a ~ Darlehn tilgen; **to apply for a ~** Darlehn beantragen; **to award a ~** Anleihe gewähren; **to be thrown out of ~s** *(securities)* als Lombardunterlage nicht gewertet werden; **to call in a ~** Anleihe kündigen; **to contract a ~** Anleihe abschließen (kontrahieren), Darlehn aufnehmen; **to convert a ~** Anleihe konvertieren; **to cover over a ~** Anleihe überzeichnen; **to draw a ~ in tranches** Anleihe in Abschnitten in Anspruch nehmen; **to float a ~** Anleihe lancieren (auflegen, begeben); **to fund a ~** Anleihe konsolidieren; **to grant a ~** Kredit (Anleihe) gewähren, Darlehn geben; **to grant a ~ on s. th.** etw. beleihen; **to grant ~s on security** besicherte Darlehen gewähren; **to have s. th. on ~** etw. zur Leihe haben; **to have more bad ~s to write off than usual** mehr als üblich faule Kredite abschreiben müssen; **to invite subscriptions for a ~** Anleihe zur Zeichnung auflegen; **to issue a ~** Anleihe begeben; **to issue a ~ in instalments** Anleihe in Tranchen auflegen (in Stücken ausgeben); **to launch a ~** Anleihe auflegen; **to make payments on a ~** Rückzahlungen auf einen Kredit leisten; **to meet a ~ when due** fälligen Kredit zurückzahlen; **to negotiate a ~** Anleihe vermitteln; **to oblige s.**

o. **with a ~** jem. mit einem Darlehn aushelfen; **to obtain a ~ of money by application** beantragtes Darlehn erhalten; **to offer s. o. a ~ of s. th.** jem. etw. auf Kreditbasis anbieten, jem. eine Kreditofferte machen; **to offer a ~ for subscription** Anleihe zur Zeichnung auflegen; **to oversubscribe a ~** Anleihe überzeichnen; **to pay off a ~** Darlehn zurückzahlen; **to place a ~** Anleihe unterbringen (auf den Markt bringen); **to pull out of a ~** sich aus einem Anleihekonsortium zurückziehen; **to put money out to ~** Gelder ausleihen; **to put out on ~** verleihen; **to put a ~ into the hands of a syndicate** Anleihe an ein Konsortium übertragen; **to raise a ~** Anleihe (Kredit, Darlehn) aufnehmen; **to raise a ~ on an estate** Hypothekarkredit aufnehmen; **to recall a ~** Darlehn kündigen; **to redeem a ~** Darlehn tilgen, Anleihe zurückzahlen (tilgen); **to refinance a ~** Kredit refinanzieren; **to repay a ~** Kredit abdecken, Darlehn zurückzahlen; **to replenish a ~** zusätzliche Sicherheiten stellen; **to return a ~ ahead of schedule** Anleihe vorzeitig zurückzahlen; **to revalidate a ~** Anleihe aufwerten; **to service a ~** Zinsendienst einer Anleihe durchführen; **to subscribe for (to, Br.) a ~** Anleihe zeichnen; **to supplement a ~** Ergänzungskredit gewähren; **to sweeten a ~** *(sl.)* erstklassige Sicherheiten stellen; **to take up a ~** Darlehn aufnehmen; **to take a portion of a ~** Anleihe teilweise (Anleihentranche) übernehmen; **to turn thumbs down on a ~** Kreditanfrage ablehnen; **to underwrite a ~** Anleihe fest übernehmen;
~ account Darlehns-, Kreditkonto; **to stop a ~ account** Entnahmen von einem Kreditkonto begrenzen; **~ administration** Anleihebetreuung; **~ agent** Darlehnsvermittler; **~ agreement** Darlehns-, Kreditvertrag, Anleiheabkommen; **~ application** Darlehnsantrag, Kreditantrag, -ersuchen; **~ appraisal** Kreditprüfung; **~ assistance** Darlehnshilfe; **~ association** Darlehnskasse; **building and ~ association** Bausparkasse; **~ backing** Darlehnssicherheit; **~ balance** Kreditsaldo; **~ bank** *(Br.)* Kreditbank, -anstalt, Darlehnsbank, -kasse, Lombardbank; **agricultural ~ bank** Landwirtschaftsbank; **~ broker** Darlehnsvermittler; **~ business** Darlehns-, Anleihegeschäft, *(securities)* Lombardgeschäft; **personal ~ business** Personalkreditgeschäft; **~ capital** *(Br.)* Fremd-, Leih-, Anleihekapital; **~-capital duty** *(Br.)* Anleihesteuer; **~ ceiling** Kreditplafond; **~ certificate** Hinterlegungschein einer Girozentrale; **~ charges** Kredit-, Darlehnsgebühren; **~ clause** Anleiheklausel; **~ collection** ausgeliehene Sammlung, Leihgabe; **~ commissioners** Finanzierungsstelle für öffentliche Arbeiten; **~ commitments** Darlehnsverpflichtungen, Anleiheverpflichtungen; **unused ~ commitment** nicht in Anspruch genommene Kreditfazilität; **to lock in one's ~ commitments** seine Kreditfazilitäten äußerst behutsam in Anspruch nehmen; **~ committee** Anleihe-, Kreditausschuß; **small ~ company** *(US)* Darlehnskassenverein; **~ contract** Darlehns-, Anleihevertrag; **~ conversion** Anleihekonversion; **~ council** Anleihegremium; **~ creditor** Darlehnsgläubiger, Kreditgeber; **~ crowd** *(US)* Maklergruppe, die Aktien borgen oder ausleihen will; **~ debtor** Anleiheschuldner; **~ default** unmöglich gewordene Kreditrückführung; **~ demand** Kreditbedürfnisse, -bedarf, -nachfrage, Anleihebedarf; **~ department** Anleiheabteilung, Kreditabteilung; **personal ~ department** Personalkreditabteilung; **~ embargo** Anleihesperre; **~ envelope** Sicherheitenmappe; **~ fee** Kreditbearbeitungsgebühr; **~ financing** Anleihefinanzierung; **~ function** *(banking)* Anleihegeschäft; **~ fund** Darlehnskasse, Anleihefonds, Anleihekapital; **soft ~ fund** Anleihefonds für währungsschwache Länder; **~ funds** Kredit-, Darlehnsmittel; **~ guarantee (guaranty)** Anleihegarantie; **~ holder** Anleihebesitzer, -gläubiger, Obligationär; **~ insurance** Kreditversicherung; **~ interest** Darlehns-, Anleihezinsen; **~ interest claim** Darlehnszinsforderung; **~ interest received** vereinnahmte Darlehnszinsen; **~ issues and interest-bearing treasury bonds** Anleihen und verzinsliche Schatzanweisungen; **~ ledger** *(US)* alphabetisches Darlehnskonto; **small ~ lending** Kleinkreditgeschäft; **~ loss** Kreditverlust; **~ market** *(US)* Anleihemarkt; **~ money** Darlehnsbetrag; **~ negotiations** Anleiheverhandlungen; **~ offer** Anleiheangebot; **~ office** Darlehnskasse, Vorschußkasse, *(pawnbroker)* Pfandleihanstalt, Leihhaus; **~ officer** Kreditsachbearbeiter; **~ package** gebündelte Kredite, Anleihebündel; **~ pact** Kreditabkommen; **~ participation** Anleihebeteiligung; **~ policy** Kreditpolitik; **~ portfolio** Kreditplafond; **~ premium** Anleiheagio; **~ project** Anleiheprojekt; **~ rate** Darlehns[zins]satz; **average business ~ rate** Durchschnittssatz für Geschäftskredite; **~-to-price ratio** Kreditpreisverhältnis; **~ receipt** Darlehnsquittung, Schuldschein; **~ redemption** Anleiheablösung, -rückzahlung, -tilgung; **~ register** *(Br.)* Journal zur chronologischen Verbuchung gewährter Darlehen; **~ regulations** Anleihebestimmungen; **~ repayment** Darlehnsrückzahlung; **~ report** Anleihebe-

richt; ~ **request** Darlehnsgesuch; ~ **restrictions** Kreditrestriktionen; ~ **sanction** Darlehns-, Anleihegenehmigung, Kreditzustimmung; ~ **scandal** Anleiheskandal; ~ **section** Darlehnsabteilung; ~ **service** Anleiheverzinsung, Anleihedienst; ~ **shark** *(US)* Halsabschneider, wucherischer Geldverleiher, Wucherer, Kredithai; ~ **sharking** *(US)* wucherischer Geldverleih; ~ **society** *(Br.)* Kredit-, Darlehnsverein, -gesellschaft, Kreditgenossenschaft; **mutual ~ society** *(Br.)* Vorschuß-, Darlehnskassenverein auf Gegenseitigkeit; **remedial ~ society** *(Br.)* gemeinnützige Pfandleihgesellschaft; **to issue ~ stock** *(Br.)* Anleihe ausgeben; ~ **stock interest** Anleihezinsen; ~ **stockholder** Anleihegläubiger, -zeichner; ~ **subscriber** Anleihezeichner; ~ **subscription** Anleihezeichnung; ~ **subscription price** Anleihezeichnungskurs; ~ **system** Darlehnssystem; ~ **talks** Kreditverhandlungen, Anleihegespräche; ~ **terms** Anleihebedingungen, Anleiheausstattung; ~ **ticket** Kreditauskunftsbogen; ~ **value** Beleihungs-, Lombardwert; **to be waiting at the ~ window** am Darlehnsschalter Schlange stehen.
loanable verleihbar;
~ **capital** Leihkapital; ~ **funds** ausgeliehene Mittel, Leihgelder; ~ **market** Kreditmarkt.
loaned|display geliehenes Ausstellungsmaterial; ~ **employee** abgestellter Angestellter.
loanee Darlehnsnehmer.
loaner Darlehnsgeber.
loaning rate *(US)* Zinssatz im Fixgeschäft.
loanmonger Darlehns-, Finanzmakler, Anleihevermittler.
lobby *(hall)* [Vor]halle, Vestibül, breiter Korridor, Vorraum, *(parliament)* Wandelgang, -halle, *(pressure group)* Interessen-, Machtgruppe, Lobby, *(theater)* Vor-, Wandelhalle, Foyer;
division ~ *(parl., Br.)* Abstimmungshalle;
~ **of a hotel** Hotelhalle; ~ **of a theater** Foyer;
~ *(v.)* Lobbytätigkeit ausüben, Interessen vertreten, Abgeordnete beeinflussen (bearbeiten);
~ **a bill** Gesetz [als Interessent] beeinflussen; ~ **correspondent** Vertrauensjournalist; ~ **through** *(US)* Gesetz durch Beeinflussung durchbringen; ~ **for higher subsidies** Abgeordnete wegen der Erhöhung von Zuschüssen beeinflussen.
lobbying Beeinflussung von Abgeordneten;
~ **for higher subsidies** Einflußnahme auf die Gewährung höherer Zuschüsse; ~ **of members of parliament** Beeinflussung von Abgeordneten;
~ **activities** Lobbytätigkeit, Interessenvertretung; ~ **fee** Lobbyhonorar; ~ **group** Interessengruppe, Lobby; ~ **office** Kontaktbüro.
lobbyism *(US)* Lobbyismus, -tätigkeit, Interessenvertretung, Einflußnahme, Beeinflussung von Abgeordneten.
lobbyist Interessenvertreter, Lobbyist;
vendable ~ bezahlter Interessentenvertreter.
lobster *(sl.)* Pfuscher, Stümper;
~ **shift** Mitternachtsschicht.
local *(inhabitant)* Ortsbewohner, *(newspaper)* Lokales, *(post office, Br.)* Ortsdienst, *(pub, Br.)* Kneipe, *(trade union, US)* Ortsverein, *(train)* Nah-, Vorortszug;
~ *(a.)* örtlich, ortsansässig, ortsgebunden, heimisch, kommunal, local, *(address)* hier;
to be ~ nicht weit verbreitet sein; **to pop into the ~ for a pint** zum Abendschoppen gehen;
~ **acceptance** Platzakzept; ⌒ **Act** Ortsstatut; ~ **action** Klage am Gerichtsstand der belegenen Sache; ~ **administration** Gemeindeverwaltung; ~ **advertising** Anzeigenwerbung ortsansässiger Firmen, Lokalwerbung, Ortsanzeigen; ~ **affairs** Kommunalangelegenheiten; ~ **agent** Platz-, Bezirksvertreter; ~ **agreement** Ortstarif; ~ **aid post** *(US)* Truppenverbandsplatz; ~ **anaesthetic** Lokalanästesie; ~ **appeal tribunal** *(industrial benefit, Br.)* Sozialgericht; ~ **area** Ortsbezirk, Region; ~ **assessment** Veranlagung durch die Gemeinde, Gemeindeumlagen; ~ **attachment** örtliche Bindung; ~ **attorney** *(US)* am Gerichtsort praktizierender Anwalt; ~ **attraction** *(mar.)* Ortsabweichung; ~ **authorities** *(US)* Kommunal-, Ortsbehörden, Gemeindeverwaltungen, -verbände, kommunale Gebietskörperschaften (Verwaltungseinheiten); ~ **authorities' investment** Investitionen im kommunalen Bereich; ~ **authorities stock** *(US)* Kommunalpapiere; ~ **authority** Kommunalbehörde; ~ **authority bond** *(US)* Kommunalschuldschein; ~ **authority negotiable bond market** kommunaler Anleihemarkt; ~ **authority loan** *(Br.)* Kommunaldarlehn, -anleihe; ~ **authority market** Markt für Kommunalanleihen; ~ **bank** Bank am Platze; ~ **bill** Platzwechsel; ~ **board** Gemeindeausschuß; ~ **bond** *(Br.)* Kommunalschuldverschreibung, -obligation; ~ **bonus** Ortszuschlag, -zulage; ~ **branch** Ortsgruppe, *(bank)* Zweigstelle, Filiale;

budget Kommunal-, Gemeindehaushalt; ~ **budgeting** Gemeindehaushaltswesen; ~ **business** Platz-, Lokogeschäft; ~ **by-law** *(Br.)* Ortsstatut; ~ **call** *(tel.)* Ortsgespräch; ~ **campaign** örtlich begrenzte Werbeaktion; ~ **charge** *(tel.)* Ortsgebühr; ~ **charges** *(banking)* Platzspesen; ~ **chattel** mit dem Grundstück verbundene bewegliche Sache; ~ **cheque** *(Br.)* Platzscheck; ~ **colo(u)r** Ortskolorit; ~ **concerns** Ortsangelegenheiten, Lokalverhältnisse; **of ~ concern** zum Aufgabenbereich einer Gemeinde gehörig; ~ **conditions** örtliche Verhältnisse; ~ **constitution** Kommunalverfassung; ~ **consumption** örtlicher Verbrauch, Platzverbrauch; ~ **corporation** *(US)* Gebietskörperschaft; ~ **council** Ortsbehörde, Stadt-, Gemeinderat; ~ **court** *(Br.)* örtliches Gericht, *(US)* einzelstaatliches Gericht; ~ **currency** Landeswährung; ~ **customs** Ortsgebrauch, Platzusance; ~ **customer** täglicher Kunde, Stammkunde; ~ **debts** Gemeindeschulden; ~ **delivery** Ortszustellung; ~ **district council** Gemeinderat; ~ **division** Kommunaleinheit; ~ **doctor** ortsansässiger Arzt; ~ **draft** Platzwechsel; ~ **education authority** Kreisschulamt; ~ **elections** *(Br.)* Kreistags-, Gemeinderats-, Kommunal-, Bezirkswahlen; ~ **election results** Kommunalwahlergebnis; ⌒ **Employment Act** *(Br.)* Gesetz zur regionalen Strukturverbesserung; ~ **examination** *(Br.)* Universitätsprüfung der Abiturienten an einer Schule; ~ **exchange** *(tel.)* Ortsvermittlung; ~ **express** Vorortszug; ~ **expression** ortsgebundener Ausdruck; ~ **fee** Ortsgebühr; ~ **finance** Kommunal-, Gemeindefinanzen; ~ **[finance] officer** Kommunal[finanz]beamter; ~ **food officer** *(Br.)* Ernährungsamt, Kartenausgabestelle; ~ **freight** *(US)* Rollgutverkehr, Fracht im Nahverkehr; ~ **freight train** *(US)* Nahgüterzug.
local government *(Br.)* [kommunale] Selbstverwaltung, kommunale Behörde, Gemeindeverwaltung, Kommunalverwaltung; ⌒ **Act** *(Br.)* Kommunalverwaltungsgesetz, Gemeindeordnung; ~ **council** kommunale Vertretungskörperschaft; ~ **elections** *(Br.)* Kommunalwahlen; ~ **functions** kommunale Selbstverwaltungsfunktionen; ~ **finance** kommunale Finanzen, Kommunalfinanzierung; ~ **jobs** kommunalpolitische Aufgaben; ~ **law** Gemeinde-, Kommunalrecht; ~ **officer** *(Br.)* Kommunalbeamter, städtischer Beamter.
local|habit Ortsgebrauch; ~ **habitation** Aufenthaltsort; ~ **health authority** Kreisgesundheitsamt; ~ **horizon** sichtbarer Horizont.
local improvement Ausbau der Gemeindeanlagen; ~ **assessment** Erschließungsbeitrag; ~ **bonds** Kommunalobligationen für den Ausbau der Gemeindeanlagen, Meliorationsobligationen; ~ **fund** Meliorationsfonds.
local|industrial union örtliche Fachgewerkschaft; ~ **influence** kommunale Einflüsse, einflußreiche Stellung als Ortsansässiger; ~ **information** an Ort und Stelle eingeholte Informationen; ~ **inspection** Augenscheinnahme, Lokaltermin; ~ **interests** Lokalinteressen; ~ **influence** kommunale Einflüsse; ~ **item** Lokalartikel; ~ **jurisdiction** örtliche Zuständigkeit; ~ **knowledge** Platz-, Ortskenntnis; ~ **land charge** kommunale Grundstückslast; ~ **law** örtliches Recht, Ortsrecht, *(US)* Kommunalrecht; ~ **legislation** kommunale Gesetzgebung; ~ **letter** Ortsbrief; ~ **line service** Zubringerdienst; ~ **man** Ortsansässiger; ~ **manager** *(Br.)* Bezirksdirektor; ~ **map** Spezialkarte; ~ **market** Lokalmarkt; ~ **name** Ortsbezeichnung; ~ **needs** örtliche Bedürfnisse; ~ **news** Lokalnachrichten; ~ **newspaper** Lokalzeitung, -blatt; ~ **notable** Lokalgröße; ~ **office** örtliche Niederlassung; ~ **officer** *(Br.)* Kommunalbeamter; ~ **option** *(US)* örtliche Volksabstimmung über Gewährung von Schankkonzessionen; ~ **paper** Heimat-, Lokalzeitung; ~ **people** Ortsbewohner; ~ **picture** Lokalkolorit; ~ **plan** *(Br.)* Flächennutzungsplan; ~ **planning authority** Orts-, Kreisplanungsbehörde; ~ **police** Ortspolizei; ~ **politician** Kommunalpolitiker; ~ **politics** Lokal-, Kommunalpolitik; **to be active in ~ politics** sich kommunalpolitisch betätigen; ~ **prejudice** *(state court, US)* örtlich begründete Vorurteile; ~ **prepays** *(railway)* Vorausfrachten im Ortsverkehr; ~ **press** Lokalpresse; ~ **price** Lokalpreis; ~ **pub** *(Br.)* Dorfkneipe; ~ **purchases** Platzkäufe; ~ **quarrels** lokale Streitigkeiten; ~ **radio** Ortsender; ~ **railway** Vorort-, Lokalbahn; ~ **report** Platzbericht; ~ **rate** Ortstarif, *(advertising)* Anzeigentarif für ortsansässige Firmen; ~ **rates** ortsübliche Sätze, *(Br.)* Kommunalabgaben, -steuern, Gemeinde-, Grundsteuern; ~ **reception** *(radio)* Ortsempfang; ~ **record** Ortsregister; ~ **report** Platzbericht; ~ **requirements** lokaler Bedarf, Kommunalbedarf; ~ **resident** Ortsansässiger, -einwohner, -kundiger; ~ **revenue** Gemeindeeinnahmen; ~ **road** Kreisstraße; ~ **rules** regional bedingte Verordnungen; ~ **scale** kommunale Ebene; ~ **self-government** kommunale Selbstverwaltung, Gemeindehoheit; ~ **services** Kommunallei-

stungen; ~ **service line** Zubringerlinie; ~ **shipper** Spediteur am Platze; ~ **sign** Ortskennzeichen; ~ **situation** örtliche Belegenheit; ~ **staff** ortsansässiges Personal; ~ **statute** Ortsstatut; ~ **stocks** Lokalwerte; ~ **stringer** Lokalkorrespondent; ~ **subscriber** (tel.) Ortsteilnehmer; ~ **talents** Lokalgrößen; ~ **tariff** Binnenschiffahrtstarif; ~ **tax** (US) Kommunal-, Gemeindesteuer, -abgaben, Kommunalsteuer für aus Verbesserung öffentlicher Einrichtungen entstandene Werterhöhung; ~ **tax system** (US) Kommunalsteuerwesen; ~ **taxation Act** (Br.) Kommunalsteuerergesetz; ~ **taxation licence** gebührenpflichtige Konzession; ~ **telegram** Ortstelegramm; ~ **term** Lokalausdruck, ortsüblicher Ausdruck; ~ **terms** Platzbedingungen; ~ **time** Ortszeit; ~ **topography** örtliche Beschaffenheit; ~ **trade** Platzgeschäft; ~ **trade council** (Br.) Ortsverband; ~ **traffic** Vorort-, innerstädtischer Verkehr, Orts-, Nahverkehr, (tel.) Ortsgespräch; **to accommodate** ~ **traffic** dem Ortsverkehr dienen; ~ **train** Nah-, Vorortszug; ~ **express train** für den Nahschnellverkehr eingesetzter Zug; ~ **transaction** Platzgeschäft; ~ **union** (US) Ortsverein; ~ **unit of government** Kommunalverwaltungsstelle, -einheit; ~ **usage** Ortsgebrauch, Platzusance; ~ **venue** örtlich zuständiges Gericht; ~ **veto** örtlicher Einspruch; ~ **wage** ortsüblicher Lohn; ~ **wants** örtlicher Bedarf; ~ **weekly** örtlich erscheinendes Wochenblatt; ~ **wine** Landeswein.

localism Ortsausdruck, (sectionalism) Provinzialismus, Lokalpatriotismus.

localist Lokalpatriot.

locality Ort, Lokalität, (minerals) Fundort, (bump of ~) Ortssinn, (site) Örtlichkeit, Lage;
  in this ~ in dieser Gegend;
  ~ **of the deed** Ort des Verbrechens, Tatort; ~ **of a lawsuit** örtliche Zuständigkeit für einen Prozeß;
  to have a good bump of ~ guten Ortssinn haben.

localizable lokalisierbar.

localization örtliche Beschränkung (Festlegung), Lokalisierung;
  ~ **of a conflict** Lokalisierung eines Konflikts; ~ **of a fault** Fehlereingrenzung; ~ **of an industry** Ansiedlung einer Industrie, Industriekonzentration; ~ **of labo(u)r** Zusammenballung von Arbeitskräften.

localize (v.) örtlich festlegen (beschränken), lokalisieren.

localized crisis Teilkrise.

localizer (aviation) Landekurssender, Leitstrahlbake.

locally am Ort;
  ~ **situate** belegen;
  to be well known ~ ortsbekannt sein.

locality Ort, Lokalität, (minerals) Fundort, (site) Örtlichkeit, Lage;
  obscure ~ gänzlich unbekannter Ort.

locate (v.) örtlich festlegen, lokalisieren, (assign place) Platz anweisen, (discover) ausfindig machen, feststellen, (establish o. s., US) sich niederlassen, (ansiedeln), (let on hire) in Pacht geben, (mining claim, US) Grenzen einer Bergwerkskonzession festlegen;
  ~ **the enemy** Feind ausfindig machen; ~ **a factory** Fabrikgelände (Standort für eine Fabrik) auswählen; ~ **a fault** Fehler eingrenzen; ~ **a gang** Verbrecherbande aufspüren; ~ **industry** Gewerbe ansiedeln; ~ **a land warrant** Landzuteilung vornehmen; ~ **the lines of a property** (US) Grundstücksgrenzen festlegen; ~ **one's office** sein Büro unterbringen; ~ **a new office** neues Büro einrichten; ~ **a quotation** Zitat (Stelle) auffinden; ~ **a railroad** Streckenführung einer Eisenbahnlinie festlegen; ~ **the scene in A** Schauplatz nach A verlegen; ~ **a school in the suburbs** Schule im Stadtrandgebiet ansiedeln; ~ **the seat of a disease** Entstehungsherd einer Krankheit ausfindig machen, Krankheit lokalisieren; ~ **a town on the map** Stadt auf einer Karte finden.

located gelegen, (bank) zugelassen;
  ~ **in A** mit dem Sitz in A;
  to be ~ Sitz haben, (US) belegen sein, liegen, Sitz haben, (person) domizilieren, ansässig (stationiert) sein; **to be physically** ~ **in** ... geographisch in ... gelegen sein; **to be** ~ **in the area in which a law is valid** sich im Geltungsbereich eines Gesetzes befinden.

locating device (airplane) Ortungsgerät.

location (advertising) Plazierung, Raum für Außenwerbung, (airplane) Abstellplatz, (corporation) juristischer Sitz, (defining of boundaries, US) Absteckung, Abmessung, Grenzbestimmung, (film) Ort für Aufnahmen, Filmgelände, (leasing) Verpachtung, Vermietung, (library use, US) Platz, (mining) [Festlegung einer] Bergwerkskonzession, zugewiesenes Schürfrecht, Mutung, zugewiesenes Schürffeld, (place of settlement) Niederlassung, (placing) Anlegung, (plot) [abgestecktes] Stück

Land, (position) Lage, Standort, Belegenheit, Stellung, Platz, Stelle, (process of locating, US) Lokalisierung, Grenzbestimmung, örtliche Festlegung, Ansiedlung, (railway) Abstecken einer Strecke, (service of person) Dienstort, vorübergehende Abstellung, (settlement) Niederlassung, Siedlung, (trust) Zulassungsort, (wireless operator) Standort;
  in a desirable ~ verkehrsgünstig gelegen, in schöner Lage; **on** ~ (film) außerhalb des Studios, im Außengelände; **business** ~ geschäftliche Niederlassung; **head-on** ~ (advertisement) bevorzugte Plazierung; **high-rent** ~ Geschäftsgegend mit hohen Mieten; **individual** ~ (advertising) Sonderstelle, -plazierung, (outdoor advertising) mit einem einzigen Plakat belegte Werbefläche; **ineligible** ~ ungünstige Belegenheit; **present** ~ derzeitiger Aufbewahrungsort; **present** ~ **unknown** jetziger Aufenthaltsort unbekannt;
  ~ **of business assets** Belegenheit von Betriebsvermögen; ~ **of debts** Erfüllungsort für Geschäftsschulden; **suitable** ~ **for new factories** gute Standortlage für neue Fabriken; ~ **of industry** Ansiedlung von Industriebetrieben; **planned** ~ **of industry** gesteuerte Industrieansiedlung; ~ **of land** Grundstücksbelegenheit; ~ **of office** Geschäfts-, Amtssitz; ~ **of principal office** Hauptgeschäftssitz; ~ **of the registered office** Gesellschaftssitz; ~ **of officials** Stationierung von Beamten; ~ **of page** (advertising) Seitenlayout; ~ **of property** Grundstücksbelegenheit;
  to be in a pleasant ~ schön gelegen sein; **to pinpoint the** ~ **of a radio operator** Standort eines Funkers anpeilen;
  ~ **analysis** Standortanalyse; ~ **of Office Bureau** (Br.) Amt für Standortplanung von Bürobetrieben; ~ **caterer** Vertragslieferant von Filmgesellschaften bei Außenaufnahmen; ~ **factor** Standortfaktor, (US) Immobilienmakler; ~ **filming** Außenaufnahmen; ~ **model** Standortmodell; **industrial** ~ **policy** Standort-, Ansiedlungspolitik; ~ **preference** Standortpräferenz; **part-**~ **production** teilweise im Aufnahmegelände hergestellte Filmproduktion; ~ **sheet** (railroad) Einsatzliste.

locational | **advantage** Standortvorteil; ~ **choice** Standortwahl.

locative calls (deed) Geländepunkte.

locator (US) Landmesser, (civil law, US) Vermieter, Verpächter.

lock Schloß, Verschluß, (receiver of stolen goods, sl.) Hehler, (sluice) Schleuse, (vehicles) Stockung, Verstopfung, (of wheel) Bremsvorrichtung;
  under ~ **and key** hinter Schloß und Riegel;
  canal ~ Kanalschleuse; **dead** ~ Verriegelungsschloß; **letter-keyed** ~ Kombinationsschloß; **mortise** ~ Einsteckschloß; **safety** ~ Sicherheitsschloß; **Yale** ~ Sicherheitsschloß;
  ~, **stock and barrel** mit allem Drum und Dran, mit Sack und Pack;
  ~ (v.) ver-, zuschließen, (be blocked) blockiert werden, (canal) mit Schleusen ausstatten, (ship) schleusen, (truck) zugehen;
  ~ **away** weg-, verschließen, ver-, absperren; ~ **the door against s. o.** jem. die Tür verschließen; ~ **down** (ship) hinabschleusen; ~ **s. o. in** j. einsperren, -einschließen; ~ **o. s. in** sich einschließen; ~ **off** durch Schleusen absperren; ~ **out** (labo(u)rers) aussperren; ~ **a ship** Schiff durchschleusen; ~ **up** (print.) im Formkasten festmachen, Form schließen; ~ **up capital** Kapital blockieren (festlegen); ~ **up all one's capital in land** sein ganzes Vermögen in Grundstücken anlegen; ~ **a prisoner** Gefangenen einsperren; ~ **up a stock** Werte festlegen; ~ **the wheels of a car** Räder eines Autos blockieren;
  to keep under ~ **and key** unter Verschluß halten; **to pick a** ~ Schloß mit einem Dietrich aufbrechen; **to put under** ~ **and key** auf Nummer Sicher bringen;
  ~ **charges (dues)** Schleusengeld; ~ **gate** Schleusentor; ~ **keeper** Schleusenwärter.

lockage Schleusengeld.

lockbox verschließbare Kassette, Schließfach.

locked | **out** ausgesperrt;
  ~ **by mountains** von Bergen umschlossen;
  to be ~ **in ice** im Eis festsitzen; **to be** ~ **up** (capital) festliegen; **to be** ~ **up in land** in Grundstücken angelegt sein; **to get** ~ **up by the police** ins Polizeigefängnis kommen; **to have a secret safely** ~ **away in one's breast** Geheimnis tief in seinem Busen verschließen;
  ~ **warehouse** Zollager.

locker (customs officer, Br.) Zollaufseher, -inspektor, (drawer) Schließfach, (mil.) Spind;
  not a shot in the ~ kein Pfennig Geld;
  to go to Davy Jones' ~ (sl.) im Meer ertrinken;
  ~ **plant** Tiefkühlaufbewahrung; ~ **room** Umkleideraum, -kabine.

locking | **up of capital** Kapitalfestlegung;
  central ~ **system** zentrales Verschlußsystem.

lockman Schleusenwärter.

lockout Ausschluß, Aussperrung;
  general ~ Massenaussperrung;
  ~ actions Aussperrungsmaßnahmen.

locksman Schleusenwärter.

locksmith Schlosser.

locksmithery Schlosserei.

lockup Verschließen, *(asylum)* Irrenanstalt, *(car)* Autobox, Einzelgarage, *(confinement)* Haft, Gewahrsam, *(invested capital)* feste Kapitalanlage, festgelegtes Kapital, *(frozen capital)* eingefrorenes Kapital, *(print.)* Metteur, *(prison, US)* Polizei-, Untersuchungsgefängnis, Haftanstalt, *(renewed note)* prolongiertes Papier, *(school, Br.)* Schulschluß;
  military ~ Haftlokal;
  ~ of capital *(Br.)* Festlegung von Kapitalien;
  ~ garage verschließbare Garage; **~ house** provisorisches Gefängnis; **~ shop** *(Br.)* nur von der Straße zugänglicher Laden.

locomotive [engine] Lokomotive;
  in these ~ days in dieser reiselustigen Zeit; **~ repairs** Lokomotivreparatur; **~ works** Lokomotivfabrik.

locum|tenancy *(lat.)* Stellvertretung; **~ tenens** *(lat.)* Stellvertreter; **to act as ~ tenens for a doctor** als Arztvertreter fungieren.

locution Redewendung.

lode *(drain, Br.)* Entwässerungsgraben, *(mining)* Gang, Flöz, Ader.

lodeman Hafenpilot.

lodemanage Lotsengeld.

lodestar Leitstern.

lodge *(hut)* Hütte, *(freemasonry)* Loge, *(porter)* Pförtnerloge, -haus, *(residence of college head, Br.)* Amtswohnung, *(summer house)* Sommer-, Wochenendhaus, *(temporary dwelling place)* Bleibe, vorübergehende Wohnung;
  hunting ~ Jagdhütte; **porter's ~** Pförtnerloge;
  ~ (v.) (deposit) hinterlegen, in Verwahrung geben, deponieren, *(establish as resident)* unterbringen, *(file)* einreichen, *(quarter)* aufnehmen, unterbringen, einquartieren, *(reside as a lodger)* zur Miete (als Mieter) wohnen, logieren;
  to board and ~ s. o. j. unterbringen und versorgen;
  ~ an appeal Berufung (Rechtsmittel, Einspruch) einlegen; **~ a caution** Vormerkung eintragen; **~ a completed certificate** ausgefülltes Zertifikat abgeben; **~ a check** Scheck einreichen; **~ a claim** Forderung anmelden; **~ with s. o. a claim for $ 5000** jem. eine Forderung über 5000 Dollar einreichen; **~ a complaint** Beschwerde vorbringen (einlegen); **~ a credit in favo(u)r of s. o.** Kredit zu jds. Gunsten eröffnen; **~ documents** Urkunden vorlegen; **~ elsewhere** ausquartieren; **~ s. o. in goal** j. ins Gefängnis einsperren; **~ at a hotel** im Hotel wohnen; **~ information against s. o.** j. anzeigen, Anzeige gegen j. erstatten; **~ a life policy as security** Lebensversicherungspolice zur Besicherung hinterlegen; **~ money with s. o.** Geld bei jem. hinterlegen (deponieren); **~ s. o. over night** j. eine Nacht unterbringen; **~ an objection** Einspruch erheben; **~ for payment** zur Zahlung hereingeben; **~ power in s. one's hands** jem. Vollmacht geben (erteilen); **~ administrative powers** Verwaltungsbefugnisse übertragen; **~ a proof of debt with the official receiver** Forderung beim Konkursverwalter anmelden; **~ a protest** Protest einlegen; **~ in the registry** jds. polizeiliche Anmeldung entgegennehmen; **~ as security** als Sicherheit hinterlegen; **~ shipwrecked persons in the school** Schiffbrüchige vorübergehend in der Schule unterbringen; **~ a tender** Angebot einreichen; **~ one's valuables in the bank** seine Wertsachen ins Bankdepot geben; **~ in the warehouse** aufs Lager bringen; **~ porter** Hotelportier.

lodgeman *(Br.)* Hotelportier.

lodger [Unter]mieter, *(boarder)* zahlender Gast, Pensionär, Kostgänger;
  fellow ~ Mitbewohner; **householders and ~s** Mieter und Vermieter;
  to live as a ~ zur Miete wohnen; **to make a living by taking in ~s** vom Vermieten leben; **to take in ~s** Zimmer vermieten;
  ~ franchise Mieterwahlrecht.

lodging Logis, [Miet]wohnung, Unterkunft, Behausung, möbliertes Zimmer, *(boarding)* Unterbringung, Beherbergung, *(residence, Br.)* Aufenthalt, Wohnsitz, *(residence for college head)* Amtswohnung, *(warehousing)* Lagern;
  ~s möbliertes Zimmer;
  board and ~ Unterkunft und Verpflegung, Kost und Logis; **free board and ~** freie Station; **furnished ~s** möblierte[s] Zimmer; **a night's ~** Unterbringung für eine Nacht, Nachtquartier; **unfurnished ~s** Leerzimmer;

~ of appeal Einlegung eines Rechtsmittels, Berufungseinlegung; **~ of a caution** Eintragung einer Vormerkung; **~ of money** Deponierung (Hinterlegung) von Geld; **~ of security** Sicherheitsleistung;
  to find ~ for a night Unterkunft für eine Nacht finden; **to have ~ with** einquartiert sein; **to let ~s** *(Br.)* Zimmer vermieten; **to let furnished ~** möbliert vermieten; **to live in ~s** zur Miete wohnen; **to live in furnished ~s** möbliert wohnen; **to stay in private ~** zur Miete wohnen; **to take ~** sich einmieten, [möblierte] Wohnung mieten; **to take ~s with s. o.** bei jem. einziehen;
  ~ allowance *(mil.)* Wohnungsgeldzuschuß; **~ bill** Wohnungszuweisungsschein; **~ bureau** Wohnungsnachweis, Quartieramt; **~ conditions** Wohnungsverhältnisse; **~ letter** Zimmervermieter; **~ money** Miete für ein Zimmer, *(allowance)* Wohngeldzuschuß; **~ place** Nachtquartier; **~ room** gemietetes Zimmer.

lodginghouse [billige] Pension, Fremdenheim, Hotel garni;
  common ~ *(Br.)* Obdachlosenasyl;
  ~ keeper Pensionsinhaber.

lodgment *(deposit of customer)* Bankdepot, *(depositing)* Hinterlegung, Deponierung, *(lodging of documents)* Urkundenhinterlegung, gerichtliche Hinterlegung, *(lodging)* Mietwohnung, *(mil.)* befestigte Stellung, Verschanzung, *(settlement)* Niederlassung;
  ~ of a check Scheckeinreichung; **~ of a complaint** Beschwerdeeinlegung; **~ of a protest** Protesterhebung;
  to effect ~ sich verschanzen; **to find a ~** vorteilhafte Stellung finden;
  ~ office Hinterlegungsstelle.

loft *(attic room)* Dachgeschoß, -boden, Speicher, *(warehouse)* Lagerhaus aus unabgeteilten Stockwerken;
  ~ (v.) auf dem Speicher aufbewahren;
  ~ building *(US)* Speichergebäude; **~ rental** Speichermiete; **~ space** *(US)* Speicherraum.

lofty moral authority überlegene moralische Autorität.

log [Holz]klotz, Block, *(airplane)* Betriebstagebuch, *(broadcasting)* Sendeprogramm, *(logbook)* Tagebuch, Schiffsjournal, *(mining, oil)* Bohrbericht;
  as easy as rolling off a ~ *(US)* kinderleicht; **in the ~** unbehauen; **~s** Rundholz;
  ~ (v.) abholzen, *(enter in logbook)* in ein Logbuch eintragen; **to roll a ~ for s. o.** *(US)* jem. helfen;
  ~ board *(Br.)* Wachtafel; **~ cabin (hut)** Blockhaus, -hütte; **~ college** *(US)* Blockhausschule; **~ hut** Blockhütte; **~ slate** Logtafel.

logarithmic chart logarithmische Darstellung.

logboard *(mar., Br.)* Wachtafel.

logbook *(car, US)* Fahrtnachweis, Kontrollbuch, *(ship)* Schiffsjournal, Bord-, Logbuch;
  official ~ Schiffstagebuch.

loggerheads, to be at sich in den Haaren liegen.

logging Holzfällen.

logistic *(mil.)* logistisch, Nachschubwesen betreffend;
  ~s Logistik, Nach- und Rückschub, Nachschubwesen.

logistical|apparatus logistischer Apparat; **~ problem** Nachschub-, Versorgungsproblem; **~ support** logistische Versorgung.

logotype Namens-, Firmenschriftzug, Markenname.

logroll *(v.)* Kuhhandel betreiben;
  ~ a law *(pol., US)* Gesetze durch gegenseitige Unterstützung durchbringen.

logrolling *(pol., US)* politischer Kuhhandel.

logroller *(US)* am Kuhhandel Beteiligter.

loiter *(v.)* herumlungern, sich herumtreiben, [bei der Arbeit] bummeln;
  ~ the hours away Stunden abbummeln.

loiterer Bummler.

loitering Herumtreiben, -stehen, Bummelei;
  ~ with intent to commit an offence Herumtreiben in gesetzwidriger Absicht.

loll *(v.)* sich räkeln.

lolly *(Br., sl.)* Moneten, Kies, Moos.

lollygag *(v.) (sl.)* faulenzen.

lombard Pfandleiher, Geldwechsler;
  ~ loan Lombardkredit, -darlehn; **~ rate** Lombardsatz; **~ Street** Londoner Geldmarkt.

London|Debt Agreement Londoner Schuldenabkommen; **~ equivalent** Londoner Parität; **~ exchange** Devise London; **~ parity** Londoner Parität; **~ rates** Londoner Wechselkurs; **~ weighting allowance** Londoner Ortszuschlag.

lone allein, einzeln;
  ~ wolf Einzelgänger.

lonely abgelegen, verlassen;
~ **pay** Entschädigungsprämie für automatisationsbedingte Arbeitskürzung; ~ **spot** einsame Gegend.
long *(stock exchange, US)* Haussier, *(vacation, US)* große Ferien;
~**s** *(brokers who are long)* Haussiers, *(securities)* unkündbare Wertpapiere;
~**s and shorts** Hausse- und Baissegeschäft; **the ~ and the short of it** um es kurz zu machen;
~ *(a.)* lang, weit, *(betting)* durch höheren Wetteinsatz gekennzeichnet, langfristig, *(above the norm)* übergroß, *(stock exchange)* auf Kurssteigerungen wartend, [gut] eingedeckt;
~ **in oil** mit hohem Ölgehalt;
~ *(v.)* verlangen, sich sehnen;
~ **for s. one's return** sehnsüchtig auf jds. Rückkehr warten;
to be ~ of cash flüssig sein; **to be ~ of exchange** *(US)* mit Devisen eingedeckt sein; **to be ~ of the market** *(US)* mit Effekten hinreichend versehen sein, Wertpapiere in Erwartung einer Preissteigerung zurückhalten; **to be ~ of stock** *(US)* mit Aktien eingedeckt sein; **to be away for ~** lange weg (abwesend) sein; **not to be ~ in making up one's mind** sich schnell entschließen, von schneller Entschlußkraft sein; **to borrow ~** langfristig ausleihen; **to buy ~** Haussekauf tätigen, auf Hausse spekulieren; **to known the ~ and the short of a matter** Geschichte in allen Einzelheiten kennen;
~ **account** *(US)* Engagements der Haussepartei, *(Br.)* Hausseposition; ~**-ago** Vergangenheit; ~ **arm** *(sl.)* Bulle, Polyp; ~**-arm** *(v.) (sl.)* per Anhalter reisen; **to have a ~ arm** weitreichenden Einfluß haben; ~, **heavy or bulky articles** Sperrgut; ~ **bill** langfristiger Wechsel, *(account)* große (hohe) Rechnung; ~ **bond** über zwanzigjährige Anleihe; ~ **cable** Fernkabel; ~ **credit** langfristiger Kredit; ~ **custom** alter Brauch; ~ **date** Wechsel auf lange Sicht; ~**-dated** langfristig; ~**-dated gilt** *(Br.)* börsengängiges Staatspapier mit über zehnjähriger Laufzeit; ~**-dated investment** langfristige Kapitalanlage; ~**-dated paper** *(Br.)* langfristiges Papier, langfristiger Wechsel; ~ **day** Arbeitszeit mit Überstunden.
long-distance weite Strecke, *(tel.)* Fernamt, -vermittlung;
~ *(v.)* Ferngespräch führen;
~ **air operation** Langstreckenflugbetrieb; ~ **blockade** Seesperre; ~ **cable** Fernkabel; ~ **cable system** Fernkabelnetz; ~ **call** Ferngespräch, -verbindung, -anruf, *(Europe)* Auslandsgespräch; ~ **charges** *(tel.)* Ferngesprächsgebühren; ~ **connection** Fernverbindung; ~ **connector** *(tel.)* Fernleitungswähler; ~ **dialling** Fernleitungswahl; ~ **flight** Langstreckenflug; ~ **freight traffic** Güterfernverkehr; **to pinch profitable ~ freight traffic from the roads** gewinnträchtigen Güterfernverkehr von den Straßen verdrängen; ~ **freight train** *(US)* Ferngüterzug; ~ **goods traffic** *(Br.)* Güterfernverkehr; ~ **haulage (hauling)** *(US)* Güterfernverkehr; ~ **lorry driver** Fernfahrer; ~ **line** Fernleitung, -linie; ~ **mover** Fernspediteur; ~ **operator** Fernamt; ~ **phone call** Ferngespräch; ~ **reception** Fernempfang; ~ **road haulage** Fernlastverkehr; ~ **road train** *(US)* Fernlastzug; ~ **road traffic** Fernlastverkehr; ~ **route** Fernverkehrslinie, -verbindung, -strecke; ~ **supply** Fernversorgung; ~ **telephone connection** Fernverbindung; ~ **traffic** Fernverkehr; ~ **train** Fernschnellzug; ~ **transport** Ferntransport, -beförderung, *(US)* Güterfernverkehr.
long | dozen großes Dutzend; ~ **draft** langfristiger Wechsel; **to be ~ drawn out** langwierig sein; ~ **drawn explanation** langatmige Erklärung; ~ **drawn-out visit** übermäßig langer Besuch; ~**-established** alteingesessen; ~ **exchange** *(US)* langfristiger Devisenwechsel; **to pull a ~ face** langes Gesicht machen; ~ **family** große (kinderreiche) Familie; ~**-felt want** langjähriger Wunsch; ~ **figure** vierstellige Zahl; ~ **firm** *(Br.)* Schwindelfirma; ~**-form report** *(auditing)* detaillierter Revisionsbericht; ~ **green** *(US sl.)* Papiergeld; ~ **guess** unsichere Schätzung; ~ **hand** gewöhnliche Schreibschrift, Kurrentschrift; ~ **haul** lange Strecke; ~ **hauls [on the railway]** Güterfernverkehr; ~**-haul driver** Fernlastfahrer; ~**-haul freight traffic** Güterfernverkehr; ~**-haul jet** Fernverkehrsdüsenflugzeug; ~**-haul transport** Güterferntransport; ~ **and short haul** Nah- und Fernverkehrstransport; ~**-haul route** Langstreckenroute; ~**-haul truck** Fernlastwagen; ~**-haul trucker** Fernlastfahrer; ~ **haulage** Fernlastverkehr; ~ **hours** lange Arbeitszeit; ~ **interest** *(US)* Engagements der Haussepartei, *(Br.)* Hausseposition; ~ **job** langwierige (zeitraubende) Arbeit; ~ **journey** weite Reise; ~ **lease** langjähriger Mietvertrag (Pachtvertrag); ~ **list** umfangreiche Liste; ~**-lived assets** langlebige Wirtschaftsgüter, Anlagevermögen; ~**-lived consumer goods** langlebige Konsumgüter; ~ **market** *(US)* nicht mehr aufnahmefähiger Markt; ~ **measure** Längenmaß; ~ **memory** weitreichendes Gedächtnis; ~ **moun-**

tain village abgelegenes Gebirgsdorf; ~ **notice** frühzeitig erfolgte Kündigung; ~ **order** Verkaufsauftrag über eigene Aktien; ~ **paper** langfristiges Papier; ~**-period loan** langfristiges Darlehn; ~**-playing record** Langspielplatte; ~ **position** Hausseposition; ~ **premium** hohe Prämie; ~ **price** *(gross price)* hoher Preis, *(retail price)* Bruttokleinhandelspreis; **to give a ~ price for s. th.** viel für etw. bezahlen; ~ **priced** teuer; ~ **primer** *(print.)* Korpus; ~ **pull** *(US)* Effektenspekulation auf lange Sicht; **on the ~ pull** auf längere Sicht gesehen; **to be a purchase for the ~ pull** *(US)* als spekulative Anlage auf lange Sicht gelten; ~ **purse** wohl gespickte Börse.
long-range weittragend, -reichend, langfristig;
~ **armament** Fernkampfwaffen; ~ **bomber** Langstrecken-, Fernbomber; ~ **civil aircraft** Fernverkehrsflugzeug; ~ **communication** Weitverkehr; ~ **forecasting** Langfristprognose; ~ **direction finding** Funkfernpeilung; ~ **navigation** Fernschifffahrt; ~ **planning** langfristige Planung, Planung auf weite Sicht; ~ **rocket** Fernrakete; ~ **weapon** Fernkampfwaffe.
long | rate *(bill of exchange)* Devisenkurs für langfristige Wechsel, *(insurance)* Prämiensatz für über ein Jahr ausgestellte Versicherungsprämie; ~**-rate policy** für mehr als ein Jahr ausgestellte Versicherungspolice; ~ **robe** Anwaltsrobe; **to be a gentleman of the ~ robe** Jurist sein, dem Juristenstand angehören; ~ **room** *(London)* Zollabfertigungshalle; **in the ~ run** im Endergebnis, auf lange Sicht; ~**-run average costs** langfristige Durchschnittskosten; ~ **sale** Effektenverkauf aus eigenen Beständen, Hausseverkauf; ~ **service** langjährige Dienstzeit, *(mil.)* längere Dienstverpflichtung; ~**-service employee** langjähriger Angestellter; ~**-service man** *(mil.)* Langdienender; ~ **shot** *(sl.)* Fernaufnahme; ~ **side** Längsseite, *(stock exchange, US)* Haussepartei; **to be on the ~ side of the market** *(US)* Wertpapiere in Erwartung einer Kurssteigerung zurückhalten; **to buy ~ side** *(US)* auf Hausse spekulieren; ~ **sight** *(fig.)* Weitblick; ~**-sighted** *(fig.)* umsichtig, weitblickend; ~**-sighted draft** langfristiges Papier; ~**-sighted weather forecast** langfristige Wettervorhersage; ~ **of standing** seit längerer Zeit bestehend, althergebracht; ~**-standing account** lange bestehendes Konto; ~**-standing invitation** schon lange ausgesprochene Einladung; ~ **Sterling** langfristiger Pfundwechsel auf London; ~ **stock** *(US)* effektiv im Besitz befindliche Aktien; **to be s. one's ~ suit** *(fig.)* jds. Stärke sein.
long-term langfristig;
~ **appointment** Dauerstellung; ~ **benefit** sich erst zukünftig auswirkender Vorteil; ~ **bond (note)** langfristige Schuldverschreibung; ~ **business** *(Br.)* Personenversicherung; ~ **compensation** *(income tax)* Einkünfte für in mehreren Jahren geleistete Arbeit; ~ **contract** langfristiger Vertrag; ~ **credit** langfristiger Kredit; ~ **engagements** langfristige Verpflichtungen; ~ **holding of shares** langfristiges Durchhalten von Aktien; ~ **indebtedness** langfristige Verschuldung; ~ **investment** langfristige Kapitalanlage; ~ **lease** langfristiger Mietvertrag; ~ **liability (obligation)** langfristige Verbindlichkeit; ~ **program(me)** langfristiges Investitionsprogramm; ~ **prospects** Aussichten auf lange Sicht; ~ **supply arrangement** langfristiges Lieferabkommen.
long | ton *(Br.)* Bruttotonne; ~ **vacations** *(US)* große Ferien, *(Br.)* Gerichtsferien; **to take ~ views** vorausschauend denken; ~ **wave** Langwelle; ~ **way round** großer Umweg; ~**-winded** langatmig.
longboat Barkasse, Beiboot.
longbow, to draw (pull, use) the große Geschichten erzählen.
longevity pay *(US)* Prämie für langjährige Betriebszugehörigkeit.
longhair *(sl.)* Intellektueller.
longhand gewöhnliche Handschrift.
longshoreman *(US)* Schauermann, Kai-, Dock-, Hafenarbeiter.
look Blick, *(appearance)* Aussehen, *(face)* Miene, Geschichtsausdruck;
new ~ geändertes Aussehen, *(fashion)* neue Mode; ~**-in** kurzer Besuch; **no ~-in with a strong competition** geringe Chance bei starker Konkurrenz; ~ **over** Überprüfung; ~ **see** *(Br., sl.)* Sichumsehen; ~ **through** Durchsicht, Prüfung; ~ *(v.) (search)* fahnden.
look *(v.)* **about for a job** sich nach einer Stellung umsehen.
look *(v.)* **after | a child** sich um ein Kind kümmern; ~ **the household** Haushalt besorgen; ~ **s. one's interests** jds. Interessen wahrnehmen.
look *(v.)* **at** einsehen;
~ **the battery of a car** Autobatterie überprüfen; ~ **s. one's proposal** jds. Vorschlag prüfen.
look *(v.),* **never ~ back** *(fig.)* gut vorankommen; ~ **bad** schlechtstehen; ~ **down a list** Liste durchsehen; ~ **downwards** *(prices)*

sinken; **~ for a job** sich nach einer Stellung umsehen; **~ forward to the pleasure of a first order** einem Erstauftrag gern entgegensehen; **~ forward to s. one's reply** auf jds. Antwort warten; **~ in on s. o.** j. kurz besuchen; **~ in at the office** kurz im Büro hereinschauen; **~ into a matter** sich eine Sache ansehen, Angelegenheit prüfen; **~ on** Zuschauer sein; **~ on with s. o.** mit jem. mitlesen; **~ on (upon) s. o. as an authority on a subject** j. auf einem Gebiet als Kapazität betrachten; **~ out for s. o.** nach jem. Ausschau halten; **~ out for s. th.** sich nach etw. umsehen; **~ out on the seafront (room)** aufs Meer hinausgehen; **~ over an account** Rechnung durchsehen (prüfen); **~ over a correspondence** Briefwechsel sichten; **~ over a house** Haus besichtigen; **~ round** besichtigen, (fig.) alle Möglichkeiten prüfen; **~ round a town** Stadt besichtigen; **~ through s. o.** j. wie Luft behandeln; **~ through a bill** Rechnung überprüfen; **~ through one's notes** seine Notizen durchsehen; **~ to s. o. for help** von jem. Hilfe erwarten; **~ into a matter** Angelegenheit besorgen; **~ to a better distribution of wealth** bessere Vermögensverteilung herbeiführen wollen; **~ to profit** mit Gewinn rechnen.

look (v.) **up (in a book)** nachschlagen, (business) sich erholen, (prices) aufschlagen, in die Höhe gehen;
~ **s. o. up** j. besuchen; **~ s. o. up and down** j. sorgfältig mustern; **~ to s. o. as a leader** zu seinem Führer aufschauen; **~ a passage** Stelle nachlesen; **~ a train** sich einen Zug heraussuchen; **~ a word in a dictionary** Wort im Wörterbuch nachschlagen.

look (v.) **upon s. o. as a likely candidate** j. als geeigneten Bewerber ins Auge fassen.

look, to get a ~ in (fam.) Chance erhalten; **to have a good ~ at it** sich eine Sache genau ansehen; **to have a ~ round the town** Stadtrundgang unternehmen; **to have a ~-see (Br.)** sich die Sache mal ansehen; **to take a cool ~** einer Sache kühl ins Auge schauen.

looker | -in Fernsehteilnehmer; **~-on** Zuschauer.

looking | over the books bei Durchsicht der Bücher;
to be ~ for a job auf Stellungssuche sein; **to be ~ up (shares)** steigen, im Kurs anziehen.

lookout sorgfältige Beobachtung, (gambling house) Schmieresteher, (guard) Beobachtungsposten, (prospects) Aussichten, (ship) Schiffswache, Ausguck, Krähennest;
bad ~ schlechte Aussichten; **primary ~ (forestry)** Feuerwache; **to be on the ~ for bargains** auf Gelegenheitskäufe aus sein; **~ man (post)** Beobachtungsposten; **~ point** Aussichtspunkt.

loop (aviator) Schleife, (el.) geschlossener Stromkreis, Schleife, (railway) Nebenlinie;
~ antenna Rahmenantenne; **~ line** Nebenlinie, Zweigbahn; **~ station** Kopfbahnhof.

loophole Hintertürchen, Ausweg;
~ in the law Gesetzeslücke.

loose frei, (novel) schlüpfrig, (unpacked) unverpackt, lose;
~ or in packages lose oder verpackt;
~ (v.) (mar.) Anker lichten;
~ an arrestment Beschlagnahme aufheben;
to go on the ~ Bummel unternehmen; **to have a screw ~** nicht ganz richtig im Kopf sein; **to play fast and ~ with father's money** leichtsinnig mit Vaters Geld umgehen;
~ argument schlechtes Argument; **~ capital** brachliegendes Kapital; **~ cash (change)** Münz-, Kleingeld; **~ colo(u)rs** nicht waschechte Farben; **~ combinations (cartel, US)** lockere Vereinbarungen, kartellähnliche Zusammenschlüsse; **~ connection (el.)** Wackelkontakt; **in ~ cover** broschiert; **~ criminal** auf freiem Fuß befindlicher Verbrecher; **at a ~ end** ohne regelmäßige Beschäftigung; **~ ends** unerledigte Kleinigkeiten; **~ funds** frei verfügbare Mittel; **~ hour** freie Stunde, Freistunde; **~ insert** Beilage; **~-knit combinations** vertragliche Wettbewerbsbeschränkungen; **~-leaded (print.)** mit breitem Durchschuß.

loose-leaf Einlageblatt;
~ account Loseblattkonto; **~ binder** Loseblatt-, Ringbuch, Sammelmappe, Schnellhefter; **~ book** Loseblatt-, Ringbuch; **~ catalog(ue)** Katalog mit losen Seiten; **~ edition** Loseblattwerk; **~ form** Loseblattmethode; **~ ledger** Loseblattbuchführung; **~ notebook** Loseblattbuch; **~ system** Loseblattsystem.

loose | leaves lose Blätter; **~ line** Ausgangszeile; **~ money** Kleingeld; **in ~ order (mil.)** entwickelt; **~ papers** zerstreute Papiere; **~ paragraphs** einzelne Paragraphen; **~ pieces of information** zusammenhanglose Nachrichten; **~ rate** überdurchschnittlich hoher Lohntarif; **to ride s. o. with a ~ rein** j. am langen Zügel führen; **~ sale** Verkauf in Bausch und Bogen, Engrosverkauf; **~ sheet** loses Blatt; **to have a ~ tongue** Geheimnisse ausplaudern; **~ translation** ungenaue Übersetzung; **~ warehouse** Engrosgeschäft.

loosen | (v.) discipline Disziplin lockern; **~ the lid on tight money** Geldmarktverknappung beseitigen; **~ one's purse-strings** seinen Geldbeutel öffnen; **~ up (money)** billiger werden.

loot Haufen Geld, (plunder) Kriegsbeute, (thieve) Diebesgut;
~ of a bank Bankraub;
~ (v.) berauben, plündern;
~ a city Stadt plündern.

looter Plünderer.

lop (v.) the staff (US) Belegschaft reduzieren.

lord Gebieter, Machthaber, (proprietor) Grundherr;
~ (v.) it over s. o. sich jem. gegenüber als Herr aufspielen;
to live like a ~ wie ein Fürst (Gott in Frankreich) leben;
♀ Advocate (Scot.) Kron-, Generalstaatsanwalt; **♀ Chancellor (Br.)** Lordkanzler; **♀ Commissioners of the Treasury (US)** Finanzministerium; **♀'sDay Act (Br.)** Gesetz über die Einhaltung der Sonntagsruhe; **♀ Mayor (Br.)** Oberbürgermeister; **♀ President of the Council (Br.)** ehrenamtlicher Präsident des Geheimen Staatsrates; **♀ Privy Seal (Br.)** Lordsiegelbewahrer; **♀ Provost (Scot.)** Oberbürgermeister.

loro account Vostrokonto.

lorry (Br.) Lastkraftwagen, -auto, LKW, (mining) Förderwagen, Hund, (railway, Br.) Lore, offener Güterwagen, Rungenwagen;
by ~ (Br.) mit Lastkraftwagen;
heavy ~ (Br.) schwerer Lastwagen;
~ (v.) (Br.) mit Lastwagen befördern;
~-borne (Br.) mit Lastwagen befördert;
~ driver (Br.) LKW-, Fernlastfahrer; **~ freezer (Br.)** Tiefkühllastwagen; **~ load (Br.)** Lastwagenladung; **~ production (Br.)** Lastwagenproduktion.

lose (v.) verlieren, einbüßen, zusetzen, (forfeit) [einer Sache] verlustig gehen, (prices) zurückgehen;
~ an action Prozeß verlieren; **~ the battle for public opinion** Schlacht um die Gunst der öffentlichen Meinung verlieren; **~ a bill** Gesetzesantrag nicht durchbringen; **~ o. s. in a book** beim Lesen eines Buches alles um sich herum vergessen; **~ business** Kundschaft verlieren; **~ a case** in einem Prozeß unterliegen; **~ a clear thousand dollars** glatte tausend Dollar verlieren; **~ ten minutes a day (watch)** pro Tag zehn Minuten nachgehen; **~ one's debts** unbezahlt bleiben; **~ ground (prices)** zurückgehen; **~ a little ground** geringe Verluste hinnehmen müssen; **~ heavily** schwere Verluste erleiden; **~ interest** Interesse an etw. verlieren; **~ one's job** seine Stellung verlieren; **~ one's labo(u)r** sich umsonst bemühen; **~ a lawsuit** Prozeß verlieren; **~ one's life** sterben; **~ money by a bad investment** sich verspekulieren, Fehlinvestition vornehmen; **~ a motion** Antrag nicht durchbringen (durchbekommen); **~ one's position** seine Stellung verlieren; **~ the post** zu spät zur Post gehen; **~ at the rate of ten pounds a week** wöchentlich zehn Pfund zusetzen; **~ a right** eines Rechtes verlustig werden; **~ one's senses** verrückt werden; **~ on a speculation** sich verspekulieren; **~ track of s. th.** etw. aus den Augen verlieren; **~ one's train** seinen Zug verpassen; **~ on a transaction** bei einem Geschäft Verluste erleiden; **~ in value** an Wert verlieren, Wertminderung erleiden; **~ votes** Stimmenverlust erleiden; **~ the war** Krieg verlieren.

loser, money ~ Verlustträger, Verlierer;
to be a ~ zusetzen; **to be a bad ~** schlechter Verlierer sein; **to be a ~ to a considerable amount** bedeutenden Betrag verloren haben.

losing verlorenes Geld, Verlust;
~s and winnings Gewinn und Verlust;
~ (a.) verlustbringend, unrentabel;
~ bargain schlechtes Geschäft, Verlustgeschäft, -abschluß; **~ battle** verlorene Schlacht; **~ business** Verlustgeschäft; **to play a ~ game** aussichtslose Sache betreiben; **to sell its ~ line (concern)** Verlustbetrieb verkaufen; **~ operation** Verlustgeschäft; **to go flat with ~ operations** Verlustgeschäfte erleiden; **~ party** unterliegende Partei; **~ price** Verlustpreis, nicht die Selbstkosten deckender Preis; **~ sale** Verlustverkauf.

loss Verlust, (balance sheet) Verlustanteil, (damage) Schaden, Einbuße, Einbüßung, (disadvantage) Nachteil, Ausfall, (fidelity bond) Unterschlagung, (insurance) Versicherungsschaden, Schadensfall, Wertminderung, (shrinkage) Schwund, Abgang;
after ~ nach Eintritt des Schadensfalles; **after charging off all ~es** nach Abschreibung aller Verluste; **at a ~** mit Verlust; **at the time of ~** während einer Verlustperiode; **causing a ~** verlustbringend; **in case (the event) of ~** im Schadensfall, im Verlustfall, (insurance) bei Eintritt des Versicherungsfalles; **involving heavy ~es** verlustreich; **upon the occurrence of a ~** beim Eintritt des Schadensfalles, beim Schadenseintritt; **showing a ~** verlustaufweisend; **without any ~ of time** ohne Zeitverlust;

~es *(balance sheet)* Abgänge, *(mil.)* Verluste, Ausfälle; **accidental** ~ zufälliger Schaden; **accounting** ~ buchmäßiger Verlust, Buchverlust; **actual** ~ eingetretener (tatsächlicher) Verlust, *(insurance)* Verlust in Höhe des Zeitwerts [des versicherten Gegenstandes], Sachschaden; ~ **[not] allowable** steuerlich [nicht] anerkannter Verlust; **annual** ~ Jahresverlust; **anticipated** ~ vorweggenommener Verlust; **average** ~ Verlust durch allgemeine Havarie, Havarieschaden; **bad-debt** ~**es** *(US)* Verluste aus zweifelhaften Forderungen; **book** ~ buchmäßiger Verlust, Buchverlust; **business** ~ Betriebs-, Geschäftsverlust; **capital** ~ Kapitalverlust; ~ **carried forward** *(balance sheet, Br.)* Verlustvortrag; **clear** ~ Nettoverlust; **concealed** ~ *(carrier)* nicht erkannter Verlust; **consequential** ~ mittelbarer Verlust, Folgeschaden; **considerable** ~ empfindlicher Verlust; **constant** ~ Dauerverlust, -schaden; **constructive** ~ in Geld abzulösender Schaden; **constructive total** ~ *(insurance)* durch Aufgabe des Schiffes entstandener (konstruktiver) Totalverlust, fingierter Totalschaden; **corporate** ~**es** *(US)* Firmenverluste; **dead** ~ *(sl.)* reiner (unwiederbringlicher, endgültiger, totaler) Verlust, Totalverlust; ~ **deductible** *(income tax)* steuerlich abzugsfähiger Verlust, Verlustabzug; **direct** ~ unmittelbarer Verlust, versicherter Schaden, *(fire insurance)* unmittelbarer Dauerschaden; **emergency** ~ Elementarschaden; **estimable** ~ abschätzbarer Verlust, Verlustkalkulation; **exchange** ~ durch Kursschwankungen entstandener Verlust; **farm** ~**es** landwirtschaftliche Verluste; **fire** ~ Brandschaden; **foreign exchange** ~ Devisenverlust; **gross** ~ Bruttoschaden, -verlust, Rohverlust; **heavy** ~ großer (schwerer) Verlust, Großschaden; **incalculable** ~ unermeßlicher Verlust; **incendiary** ~ durch Brandstiftung verursachter Schaden; ~ **incurred** eingetretener Verlust; **insignificant** ~ geringfügiger Verlust; **irrecoverable (irretrievable)** ~ unersetzlicher Verlust; **irredeemable** ~ uneinbringlicher Verlust; **known** ~ *(carrier)* erkannter Verlust; **marginal** ~ Verlustspitze; **marine** ~ Verlust auf See; **markdown** ~ durch Preisherabsetzung entstandener Verlust; **mining** ~**es** Abbauverluste; **natural** ~ natürlicher Schwund; **net** ~ Rein-, per-Saldo-, Nettoverlust; **nonbusiness** ~ nicht geschäftsbedingter Verlust; **nontrading** ~ nicht betriebsbedingter Verlust; **normal** ~ natürlicher Schwund; **occurred** ~ entstandener Schaden; **operating** ~ laufender Betriebsverlust, Geschäftsverlust; **overall** ~ Gesamtverlust; **partial** ~ Teilverlust, -schaden, Partialschaden; **pecuniary** ~ Geldverlust, Vermögensschaden; **property** ~ Vermögensschaden; **protracted** ~ lang anhaltender Schaden; **rental** ~ Mietverlust; **salvage** ~ *(marine insurance)* Versicherungsschaden nach Abzug der geretteten Waren, Bergungsschaden; **serious** ~ empfindlicher Schaden; **severe** ~ schwerer Verlust, Großschaden; **shock** ~ *(insurance)* Katastrophenschaden; **sustained** ~ erlittener Schaden; **surety** ~**es** *(balance sheet)* Verluste aus Bürgschaften; **taxable** ~ Steuerverlust; **terminal** ~ Verlust im Jahr der Beendigung des Geschäftsbetriebs; **total** ~ Totalverlust, -schaden; **total** ~ **only** nur gegen Totalverlust; **trading** ~ Betriebs-, Geschäftsverlust; **trivial** ~ unerheblicher Schaden; **uninsured excess** ~ nicht durch Exzedentenrückversicherung gedeckter Verlust; **underwriting** ~ *(insurance company)* Verlust im Geschäftsjahr; **unrelieved** ~ steuerlich nicht verwerteter Verlust; **use and occupancy** ~ Betriebsunterbrechungsschaden; **vacancy** ~ Mietausfall; **wage** ~ Lohnausfall;

~ **of the adventure** Ausfall des Unternehmens; ~ **arising from first-year allowance** auf Abschreibung im Anschaffungsjahr zurückzuführender steuerlicher Verlust; ~ **in assets** Anlagenabgang; ~ **of baggage** *(US)* Gepäckverlust; ~ **as shown in the balance sheet** ausgewiesener Bilanzverlust; ~**es of circulating capital** Umlaufskapitalverluste; ~**es chargeable against the year** aus dem Jahresertrag zu tilgende Verluste; ~ **of consortium** *(married couple, Br.)* Beeinträchtigung der Lebensgemeinschaft; ~ **of contract** nicht zustande gekommener Vertragsabschluß; ~ **of custom** Kundenverlust, Einbuße an Kundschaft; ~ **or damages** Schaden jeder Art; ~ **from bad debts** *(US)* Verlust aus zweifelhaften Forderungen, Kundenausfälle; ~**es caused by operational deficiencies** Verlustquellenrechnung; ~ **of earnings** Verdienstausfall, Ertragsverlust, -ausfall; ~ **of earning capacity** Verlust der Arbeitsfähigkeit; ~ **of efficiency** Leistungsverlust; ~ **of employment** Verlust des Arbeitsplatzes; ~ **of equipment** Geräteverlust; ~ **on exchange** Kursverlust; ~ **on export income** Exporterlösverlust; ~ **of face** Prestigeverlust; ~ **by fire** Brand-, Feuerschaden; ~**es on foreign exchanges** Devisenverluste; ~ **of franchise** *(US)* Konzessionsverlust; ~ **of ground** Gebietsverlust, *(mil.)* Geländeverlust; ~ **available for group relief** *(Br.)* für den Konzernausgleich zur Verfügung stehender Verlust; ~**es on the growth side** Wachs-

tumsverluste; ~ **of heat** Wärmeverlust; ~ **of income** Einkommensverlust, -ausfall; ~ **incurred by breach of contract** Vertrauensschaden; ~ **claimable on insurance** Schadensanspruch gegen die Versicherung; ~ **fully covered by insurance** durch die Versicherung voll gedeckter Schaden; ~ **not compensated by insurance** von der Versicherung nicht gedeckter Schaden; ~ **of interest** Zinsverlust, -ausfall; ~ **on investments** Verlust aus Kapitalanlagen, Anlagenverlust; ~ **of job** Arbeitsplatzverlust; ~ **by leakage** Verlust durch Auslaufen; ~ **in letting** Miet-, Pachtausfall; ~ **of life** Verlust an Menschenleben; ~ **on loss** ein Verlust nach dem anderen; ~ **of overseas markets** Verlust überseeischer Absatzgebiete; ~ **of money** Geldverlust; ~ **of nationality** Verlust der Staatsbürgerschaft, Ausbürgerung; ~ **occasioned by breach of contract** durch Vertragsbruch entstandener Schaden, Vertrauensschaden; ~ **of office** Stellungsverlust; ~ **of output** Produktionsverlust; ~ **of pay** Lohnausfall; ~ **from insured peril only** nur auf die versicherte Gefahr zurückzuführender Schaden; **national** ~ **in potential output** nicht genutzte volkswirtschaftliche Wachstumsmöglichkeit; ~ **in price** Kursverlust; ~ **of priority** Rangverlust; ~ **of production** Produktionsausfall, -verlust; ~ **of profits** Geschäftsverlust, Gewinnrückgang; Ertragseinbuße; ~ **of prospective profits** entgangener Gewinn; ~ **of property** Vermögensverlust, -schaden; ~ **of property values** Verlust von Vermögenswerten; ~ **of publicity** Prestigeverlust, Öffentlichkeitsschaden; ~**es recoverable under a contract of insurance** versicherungsmäßig gedeckte Verluste; ~ **available for relief** steuerlich absetzbarer Verlust; ~ **of rent** Mietverlust, -ausfall; ~**es on retirement of fixed assets** Verluste aus dem Abgang von Gegenständen des Anlagevermögens; **recession-induced** ~ **of revenue** rezessionsbedingter Steuerausfall; ~ **of a right** Rechtsverlust, Verlust eines Rechtes; ~ **of civil rights** Verlust der bürgerlichen Ehrenrechte; ~ **of service** Kündigung eines Angestelltenverhältnisses; ~ **of services of the spouse** *(Br.)* Verlust der Arbeitskraft des Ehepartners; ~ **of a ship with all hands** Schiffsuntergang mit der gesamten Besatzung; ~ **of a ship at sea** Schiffsverlust, -untergang; ~ **on the spot** Platzverlust; ~ **of status** Statusverlust; ~ **of substance** Substanzverlust; ~ **of tax** Steuerverlust; ~ **of time** Zeitverlust; ~ **of tonnage** Tonnageverlust; ~ **of trade** Betriebsverlust, Handelsrückgang; ~ **in transit** Gewichtsverlust auf dem Transport, Transportschaden, -verlust; ~ **of use** Gebrauchsentzug, Nutzungsausfall, *(rent-a-car)* Mietausfall; ~ **in value** Wertverlust, -minderung; ~ **of useful value** *(depreciation, Br.)* unvorhergesehene Entwertung; ~ **in value owing to damage** *(waste)* Wertminderung; ~ **in the value of money** Geldwertverlust; ~ **of votes** Stimmenverlust; ~ **of wages** Lohnausfall; ~**es in war** Kriegsverluste, Ausfälle; ~ **of wealth** Vermögensverlust; ~ **in weight** Gewichtsschwund, -abgang, -verlust; ~ **chargeable against the year** aus dem Jahresertrag zu tilgender Verlust; ~**es brought forward from previous years** aus den Vorjahren vorgetragene Verluste;

to absorb ~**es** Verluste auffangen; **to allow** ~**es in venture capital companies to be set off against personal income tax liabilities** Verrechnung von Spekulationsverlusten mit Einkommensteuerschulden gestatten; **to apportion** ~**es evenly over several years** Verluste gleichmäßig über mehrere Jahre verteilen; **to assess a** ~ Schaden abschätzen; **to be at a** ~ **for money** in Geldverlegenheit sein; **to be at a** ~ **for words** keine Worte finden, in Wortverlegenheit sein; **to be crippled by a** ~ **of supplies** durch Vorratsengpässe aktionsunfähig sein; **to be a dead** ~ **to s. o.** für j. völlig unbrauchbar sein; **to be exposed to a** ~ einem Verlust ausgesetzt sein; **to be liable for a** ~ für einen Schaden aufkommen müssen (haftbar sein); **to be responsible for a** ~ für einen Schaden haften; **to bear a** ~ Verlust tragen; **to buy at a** ~ mit Verlust einkaufen; **to carry back a** ~ Verlust zurücktragen, Verlustrücktrag vornehmen; **to carry forward a** ~ **for one year** Verlust ein Jahr steuerlich vortragen; **to carry forward long-term** ~**es** Verluste längerfristig vortragen; **to carry on at a** ~ weiter mit Verlust arbeiten; **to claim damages for** ~ **of expectation of life** Schadensersatz für geringer gewordene Lebenserwartung verlangen; **to charge off (deduct)** ~**es** Verluste abschreiben; **to close with a** ~ mit Verlust abschließen; **to cover all** ~**es** alle Schäden decken; **to cut a** ~ Verlust verhüten; **to cut one's** ~**es** rechtzeitig zu spekulieren aufhören, seine Verluste abschreiben (abbuchen); **to discover the** ~ **of a document** Verschwinden einer Urkunde entdecken; **to estimate the** ~ Schaden feststellen (ermitteln); **to get off without a** ~ sich salvieren, ohne Verlust davonkommen; **to guarantee s. o. against a** ~ jem. das Verlustrisiko abnehmen; **to have a heavy** ~ schwere Verluste haben; **to hold s. o. harmless from a** ~ j. von einer Schadenersatzverpflichtung freistellen; **to incur heavy** ~**es** große

Verluste erleiden; **to inflict a serious ~** schweren Verlust zufügen; **to make allowances for ~es** Verluste berücksichtigen; **to make good (up for) a ~** Schaden ersetzen (vergüten), Verlust decken; **to make a ~ in lettings** Mietverlust erleiden; **to make a ~ in a trade or business** steuerlich anerkannte geschäftliche Verluste erleiden; **to make up for one's ~es** seine Verluste ausgleichen; **to meet with a ~** Verlust (Schaden) erleiden (erfahren); **to notch up a ~** Verlust erzielen; **to notify the police of a ~** Verlustanzeige bei der Polizei abgeben; **to offset earlier ~es** Verlustausgleich herbeiführen (vornehmen); **to operate at a ~** mit Verlust arbeiten; **to participate in a ~** an einem Verlust beteiligt sein; **to put down to ~** als Verlust buchen; **to put the ~ at DM 1000** Verlust auf 1000 DM beziffern; **to reckon up one's ~es** seinen Verlust berechnen, Verlustbilanz aufstellen; **to recoup one's ~es in gaining on the stock exchange** seine Verluste durch Börsenspekulationen wieder hereinbekommen; **to recover a ~ (insurance)** Schaden decken; **to recover one's ~es (stock exchange)** seine Verluste ersetzt bekommen, sich von einem Schaden erholen; **to reimburse s. o. for his ~es** jds. Verluste übernehmen; **to result in a ~** mit Verlust abschließen; **to retrieve a ~** Verlust wieder einbringen; **to run at a ~** mit Verlust arbeiten; **to safeguard against ~es** sich vor Verlusten schützen; **to save from a ~** vor Verlust bewahren; **to secure against a ~** sich gegen einen Verlust schützen; **to sell at a ~** mit Verlust verkaufen; **to set the ~ against earned income** Verluste mit dem erzielten Einkommen verrechnen; **to settle a ~** Schadensfall regeln; **to share in a ~** sich an einem Verlust beteiligen; **to share a ~ rat(e)ably** Verlust anteilig tragen; **to show a ~** Verlust aufweisen, mit Verlust abschließen; **to stand a ~ (Ausfall) tragen; **to suffer ~ of prestige** Prestigeverlust erleiden; **to suffer a severe ~** empfindliche Einbuße erleiden; **to sustain a ~** Verlust erleiden; **to turn paper ~es into actual ~es** Buchverluste durch Verkäufe in echte Verluste umwandeln; **to undergo a ~** Verluste erfahren; **to work at a ~** mit Unterbilanz arbeiten;

~ account Verlustkonto; **profit and ~ account** Gewinn- und Verlustkonto, Ergebnisrechnung; **~ and gain account (US)** Gewinn- und Verlustkonto; **~ adjuster** Regulierungsbeamter; **~ adjustment** Schadensregulierung; **~ advice** Schadensanzeige; **~ assessment** Schadensfeststellung, -abschätzung; **~ assessor (Br.)** Schadensabschätzer, Regulierungsbeamter; **~ balance** Verlustsaldo; **~ carryback (US)** Verlustrücktrag; **~ claim** Schadenersatzklage; **~ and damage claim (transportation)** Transportschadensforderung; **~-payable clause** Schadenersatzklausel; **to plunge into the ~ column** in die Verlustzone (rote Ziffern) geraten; **~ compensation** Verlustausgleich; **~ deduction** Verlustabzug; **~ experience** Schadenserfahrung, -verlauf; **~ expert (insurance)** Schadensabschätzer; **~ figures** Verlustzahlen, -ziffern; **~ frequency** Schadenshäufigkeit; **all-~ insurance (US)** Gesamtversicherung; **~ of profits insurance** Gewinnverlustversicherung; **~ leader, ~-leader item** Verlustträger, **(shop)** Reklamepreis, Lockartikel, Lockvogelangebot, Köder; **to be ~-leading** Verlustpreise hinnehmen; **~ limitation** Verlustbegrenzung; **~ maker** Verlustträger; **~ payee** Schadenersatzberechtigter; **~ payment** Auszahlung der Schadenssumme; **~ prevention** Schadensverhütung; **~ preventive work** Unfallverhütungstätigkeit; **~-producing factor** Verlustfaktor; **~ ratio** Verlustquote, **(insurance)** Schadensquote; **with a no-~ record** ohne einen einzigen Verlust; **~ relief (Br.)** Verlustabzug, **(income-tax statement, Br.)** Verlustanrechnung; **~ repartition** Verlustaufteilung; **~ reserve (insurance)** Schadensreserve, Rücklage für laufende Risiken, Rückstellung für Verluste; **~ selling** Verlustverkauf von Anreizwaren; **~ settlement** Schadensregulierung; **~ side** Verlustseite; **~ statistics** Verluststatistik.

lost verloren, abhanden gekommen, in Verlust geraten, **(broken down)** ruiniert;

~ or not ~ (marine insurance) ohne Rücksicht auf Verlust der Ladung; **~ at sea** untergegangen;

to be ~ verlorengehen, **(motion)** durchfallen, nicht angenommen werden, **(ship)** verunglücken, untergehen; **to be ~ in applause** im Beifall untergehen; **to be ~ with all hands** mit der ganzen Besatzung untergehen; **to be ~ at sea** Seemannstod erleiden; **to be ~ upon s. o.** keinen Eindruck auf jem. machen; **to get ~** abhanden kommen, verloren gehen; **to give up for ~** als verloren betrachten;

~ bill of exchange abhandengekommener Wechsel; **~ cause** aussichtslose Sache; **~ check (US) (cheque, Br.)** abhandengekommener Scheck; **~ discount** Diskontverlust; **~ freight** Frachtverlust, -ausfall; **~ instrument** abhandengekommene Urkunde; **~ opportunity** verlorene Gelegenheit; **~ papers** verlegte Unterlagen (Urkunden); **~ pay** Lohnausfall; **~ profit**

entgangener Gewinn; **~ property** verlorene Gegenstände, Fundsachen; **~-property office** Fundbüro; **~ time** Verlustzeit; **~-time accident** Unfall mit Arbeitsausfall; **~ usefulness** Entwertung, Abschreibung; **to pay s. o. the ~ value of s. th.** jem. den Verlust von etw. ersetzen.

lot Teil, Anteil, **(book trade)** Partie, **(duty, Br.)** Abgabe, Steuer, **(film)** Aufnahme-, Freigelände, Drehort, **(goods)** Waren-, Lieferposten, Partie, Sendung, **(item)** Posten, Artikel, **(lottery)** Los, **(plot of land, US)** Bauplatz, Stück Land, [Grundstücks]parzelle, Flurstück, Gelände, **(production)** Herstellungsposten, Erzeugnis, **(set)** Satz, **(taxation)** Steueranteil;

by casting ~s durch das Los; **in ~s** in Partien, posten-, partienweise; **in small ~s** in kleinen Quantitäten; **in ~s of 5 to 10 units** in Partien von 5 - 10 Stück;

attractive ~ (book trade) Reizpartie; **auction ~** Auktionsposten; **bad ~ (coll.)** übler Kerl, Miststück; **broken ~** Partieware, Restposten, **(stock exchange)** Bruchschluß; **building ~ (US)** Bauparzelle, -platz; **city ~ (US)** städtischer Bauplatz; **diverse ~** gemischte Gesellschaft; **empty ~ (US)** nicht bebautes Grundstück; **even (full) ~** voller Börsenschluß; **inspection ~** Prüfungsposten; **job ~** Partie-, Ramschwaren; **landscaped ~ (US)** vom Gartenarchitekten angelegtes Grundstück; **less-than-carload ~ (US)** Stückgutsendung; **neighbo(u)ring ~ (US)** Nachbargrundstück; **odd ~** Restpartie, **(stock exchange)** Bruchschluß; **parking ~ (US)** Parkplatz; **small ~s** kleine Partien; **the whole ~** die ganze Gesellschaft;

new ~ of hats Kollektion neuer Hüte; **a ~ of money** eine Menge (Masse) Geld, Geld wie Heu; **a ~ of poppycock** völliger Quatsch; **~s of room** viel Platz; **~s of good things** jede Menge schöne Sachen; **~(s) of time** viel (eine Masse) Zeit;

~ (v.) verlosen, durch Los zuteilen;

~ out in Partien aufteilen, **(land)** parzellieren;

to be redeemed by ~ zur Rückzahlung ausgelost werden; **to buy in one ~** in Bausch und Bogen (im Ramsch) kaufen; **to buy as a job ~** Partie von etw. (partieweise) kaufen; **to call out the ~s** Lose ausrufen; **to cast ~s** Lose ziehen, losen; **to cast in one's ~ with s. o.** jds. Schicksal teilen; **to choose by ~** durch das Los wählen; **to dispose of a ~ at reduced prices** Partie zu zurückgesetzten Preisen abgeben; **to divide into ~s (US)** parzellieren; **to draw ~s** Lose ziehen, losen; **to draw securities by ~** Papiere auslosen; **to fall to s. one's lot** auf jds. Anteil entfallen; **to have a ~ on one's mind** seinen Kopf ziemlich voll haben; **to have ~s of money** Geld wie Heu haben; **to have no part or ~ in s. th.** keinerlei Anteil an einer Sache haben; **to pay scot and ~ (Br.)** Steuern nach Vermögen bezahlen; **to receive a new ~ of hats** neue Warensendung von Hüten erhalten; **to redeem by ~** zur Rückzahlung auslosen; **to see quite a ~ of s. o.** j. ziemlich häufig sehen; **to sell in ~s** partieweise verkaufen; **to settle s. th. by ~** etw. durch das Los entscheiden lassen; **to spend ~s of money** eine Menge Geld ausgeben; **to subdivide into ~s** in Parzellen aufteilen; **to take the whole ~** ganzen Restposten abnehmen; **to throw in one's ~ with s. o.** sich mit jem. solidarisch erklären; **to waste a ~ of time** viel Zeit vergeuden;

~ acceptance sampling Abnahmemuster; **~ book (US)** Kataster, Flurbuch; **~ completion (book trade)** Partieergänzung; **~ completion period** Partieergänzungszeitraum; **~ item** Partiestück; **~ money (auction sale)** Auktionsgebühr; **~ number** Losnummer; **economic ~ size** wirtschaftliche Losgröße; **job ~ trade** Partiewarengeschäft.

lottery Verlosung, Ausspielung, Lotterie, **(affair of chance)** Glückssache, Lotteriespiel;

charity ~ Tombola; **class (Dutch) ~** Klassenlotterie; **Genoese ~** Zahlenlotterie; **interest ~** Prämienanleihe; **number ~** [Zahlen]lotterie; **serial ~** Serienlotterie;

to draw a ~ Ausspielung vornehmen; **to draw a prize in the ~** in der Lotterie gewinnen, Lotteriegewinn machen; **to draw securities by ~** Wertpapiere auslosen; **to ensure a number in a ~** auf eine besondere Lotterienummer setzen; **to put in the ~** in der Lotterie setzen; **to take part in a ~** in einer Lotterie spielen;

~ agent Lotterieeinnehmer; **~ bond** Lotterie-, Los-, Prämien-, Auslosungsanleihe; **~ drawing** Losziehung, Verlosung; **~ gambling** Lotteriespiel; **~ list** Ziehungsliste; **~ loan** Prämienanleihe; **~ number** Losnummer; **~ office** Lotterieeinnahme, -annahme; **~ prize** Lotteriegewinn; **~ sampling (statistics)** Auslosungs-, Stichprobenverfahren, Zufallsauswahl; **~ tax** Lotteriesteuer; **~ ticket** [Lotterie]los; **to take ~ tickets** in der Lotterie spielen; **~ wheel** Lotterietrommel, Glücksrad.

lotto Zahlenlotto.

loud laut, **(colo(u)r)** schreiend;

to be ~ in one's admiration seine Bewunderung laut äußern; **to be ~ in one's complaints** sich gewaltig (lautstark) beschweren;

~ **applause** starker Beifall; ~ **criticism** heftige Kritik; ~ **dress** auffallende Kleidung; ~ **lie** offensichtliche Lüge; ~ **offence** schreiende Missetat; ~ **pattern** aufdringliches Muster; ~ **streets** lärmende Straßen.

loudspeaker Lautsprecher;
high-power ~ Großlautsprecher;
~ **advertising** Lautsprecherwerbung; ~ **paging** Ausrufen; ~ **paging device** [Lautsprecher]ausrufanlage; ~ **van** Lautsprecherwagen; ~ **waggon** Lautsprecherwagen.

lounge Aufenthaltsraum, Hotelhalle, *(lounging)* Bummeln, Faulenzen, *(stroll)* Bummel, gemütlicher Spaziergang, *(theater)* Foyer;
hotel ~ Hotelhalle, -diele, Gesellschaftsraum, Aufenthaltsraum für Hotelgäste;
~ *(v.)* herumlungern;
~ **away the time** Zeit vertrödeln;
~ **chair** Klubsessel; ~ **lizard** Salonlöwe, Eintänzer, Gigolo; ~ **suit** *(Br.)* Sakko-, Straßenanzug.

lounger Müßiggänger, Faulenzer.

lousy | **with cash** *(sl.)* Taschen voller Geld;
~ **dinner** *(coll.)* miserables Essen.

love, for neither ~ nor money nicht für Geld und gute Worte;
~ **in a cottage** Liebesheirat ohne finanzielle Grundlage; ~ **of country** Vaterlandsliebe;
~ *(v.)* **to hate** Haßliebe empfinden;
not to be had for ~ nor money weder für Geld noch für gute Worte käuflich sein; **to play for** ~ um die Ehre spielen; **to work for** ~ umsonst arbeiten;
~ **affair** Liebesaffäre; ~**begotten** unehelich; ~ **child** *(Br.)* uneheliches Kind; ~ **match** Liebesheirat; ~ **story** Liebesroman, -geschichte.

low *(car)* erster Gang, *(stock market, US)* Tiefstand;
~ **of the cycle** tiefster Punkt der Konjunkturkurve;
~ *(a.)* niedrig, gering, tief, *(prices)* billig, gedrückt;
artificially ~ künstlich niedrig gehalten;
~ **in cash** knapp bei Kasse; **of ~ birth** von einfacher Herkunft; **to be ~** *(prices)* niedrig stehen; **to be still bumping along near its ~ for the year** immer noch auf dem Jahrestiefstpunkt verharren; **to be running** ~ knapp werden; **to buy** ~ billig einkaufen; **to feel** ~ deprimiert sein; **to lie** ~ sich vorsichtig verhalten; **to live** ~ kümmerliches Dasein fristen; **to play** ~ nur niedrige Einsätze riskieren; **to play it ~ down** *(fam.)* Sache herunterspielen; **to reach a new** ~ *(US)* neuen Tiefststand erreichen; **to run** ~ knapp werden, ausgehen; **to sell** ~ wohlfeil verkaufen;
~ **area** Tiefdruckgebiet; ~ **birth rate** niedrige Geburtenziffer; ~**brow** kulturloser (primitiver, geistig anspruchsloser) Mensch; ~**budget film** niedrig kalkulierter Film; ~**class** von geringer Qualität, minderwertig; ~ **comedy** Posse; ~ **company** üble Gesellschaft; ~ **consumption** sparsamer (geringer) Verbrauch; ~**consumption lamp** im Verbrauch billige Lampe; ~**cost** preiswert; ~**-cost deal** Niedrigpreisangebot; ~**-cost housing** sozialer Wohnungsbau; ~**-cost production** mit niedrigen Selbstkosten (geringen Unkosten) hergestellte Produktion, mit geringen Unkosten (niedrigen Selbstkosten) arbeitende Industrie; ~**-cost productive facilities** günstige Produktionsverhältnisse; ~**-cost transportation** niedrige Versandkosten; **the ⌾ Countries** Niederlande; ~ **diet** substanzlose Kost; ~**-down** *(sl.)* Sonderinformation, Hintergrundmaterial; ~**-down behavio(u)r** unanständiges Verhalten; ~**-down business** schmutzige Angelegenheit; ~**-down methods** unsaubere (üble) Methoden; ~**-down trick** schmutziger Trick; ~**-duty goods** niedrig verzollte Waren; ~ **estimate** niedrige Schätzung; ~ **expression** ordinärer Ausdruck; ~ **forms of life** niedere Lebensformen; **to be in ~ funds** nicht gut bei Kasse sein; ~ **gear** niedriger Gang; ~**-geared** *(capital)* unterkapitalisiert; ~**-geared capital** zu niedrig bemessenes Kapital; ~ **gearing** Herabsetzung des Fremdkapitalanteils; ~**-grade** von minderer Qualität, minderwertig; ~**-grade fuel** minderwertiges Benzin; **to get in ~ habits** in schlechte Gesellschaft geraten; ~ **income** geringes (niedriges) Einkommen; ~**-key treatment** miserable Behandlung; ~ **Latin** Küchenlatein; ~ **lease** billige Miete (Pacht); ~ **level** Niedrigzone; ~ **level of prices** Tiefstand der Kurse; **to break far below the previous ~ levels** weit unter den letzten Tiefpunkt fallen; **to carry the prices to a new ~ level** Kurse auf einen neuen Tiefstand bringen; ~**-level attack** *(plane)* Tiefangriff; ~**-level flight** Tiefflug; ~ **life** Leben der unteren Schichten; ~ **manners** schlechte Manieren; ~ **oil consumption** niedriger Ölverbrauch; ~ **orders** untere Klassen; ~ **paid** gering bezahlt; ~ **part of a town** übel beleumdeter Stadtteil; ~**-pass filter** *(el.)* Hochfrequenzdrossel; ~ **point** Tiefstand [der Kurse]; ~ **price** niedriger Preis; **at a ~ price** billig; ~**-price competition** Konkurrenz mit niedri-

gen Preisen; ~**-price countries** Billigpreisländer; ~**-price group** niedrige Preisgruppe; ~**-priced** billig, niedrig im Preis (bewertet), *(stock exchange)* niedrignotierend; **steadily** ~**-priced** anhaltend billig; ~**-profile** mit flachem Profil; ~ **rate** niedriger Satz (Kurs); **at a ~ rate of interest** zu niedrigen Zinsen, zinsgünstig; **to buy at a ~ rate** wohlfeil kaufen; ~**-rate articles** niedrig verzollte Waren; ~ **reserve** knappe Reserven; **to be in ~ spirits** deprimiert sein; ~ **standard of living** niedriger Lebensstandard; **in a ~ state of health** in schlechtem Gesundheitszustand; ~ **station in life** bescheidene Berufsposition; ~ ⌾ **Sunday** Weißer Sonntag; ~ **taste** schlechter Geschmack; ~ **tension** *(el.)* Niederspannung; ~ **tide** Ebbe; ~ **traffic short hops** Kurzstreckenverbindung; ~ **value lands** *(US)* billiger Grund und Boden; ~ **voltage** niedrige Spannung; ~ **wages** niedrige Löhne; ~ **water** *(fig.)* Ebbe, *(scarcity of money)* Geldmangel; **to be in ~ water** schlecht bei Kasse sein; ~**-watermark** Niedrigwassermarke, *(fig.)* Tiefstpunkt, -stand; ~**-wing aircraft** Tiefdecker.

lower *(a.)* niedriger;
~ *(v.)* herab-, heruntersetzen, herunterdrücken, ermäßigen, senken, herabmindern, *(v./intr.)* fallen, sinken;
~ **o. s.** sich selbst erniedrigen; ~ **the bank rate** *(Br.)* Diskontsenkung vornehmen; ~ **a boot** Boot herunterlassen; ~ **o. s. by taking bribes** sich durch Annahme von Bestechungsgeldern korrumpieren lassen; ~ **the currency** Währung verschlechtern; ~ **the discount rate** Diskontsatz herabsetzen (ermäßigen); ~ **a flag** Flagge senken; ~ **the price of goods** Warenpreise heruntersetzen (ermäßigen); ~ **the rate of interest** Zinssatz herabsetzen; ~ **the rediscount rate** *(US)* Diskontsatz herabsetzen (ermäßigen); ~ **the rents** Mieten herabsetzen; ~ **one's sights** seine Ziele zurückschrauben; ~ **s. one's spirits** *(fam.)* j. enttäuschen; ~ **in value** an Wert verlieren;
to be appreciably ~ beträchtlich niedriger sein; **to rule** ~ sich billiger stellen;
~ **berth** untere Koje; ~ **bid** niedrigeres Gebot; ~ **boy** *(Br.)* Schüler der Unterstufe; ~**-bracket** zur unteren Steuergruppe gehörend; ~ **case** *(print.)* Kasten für Kleinbuchstaben; ~ **case letter** Kleinbuchstabe, Minuskel; ~ **class** untere Klassen, *(income tax)* Gruppe mit niedrigem Einkommen; ~ **classman** jüngeres Semester; ~ **of cost or market principle** *(balancing)* Niederstwertprinzip; **valued at the** ~**-of-cost-or-market price** *(balance sheet)* bewertet zum Einstands- oder Marktwert; ~ **court** nachgeordnetes (unteres) Gericht; ~ **deck** Zwischendeck; **the ~ deck** *(Br.)* Mannschaftsgrade; ~ **estimate** niedrigere Schätzung; ~ **form** *(school)* Unterstufe; ~**-grade civil servant** *(Br.)* Beamter des einfachen Dienstes; ~ ⌾ **House** Unterhaus; ~**-income brackets** unterer Einkommensbereich; ~ **instance** Vorinstanz; ~**-level official** unterer Beamter; ~ **life** Leben der unteren Schichten; ~ **management** untere Führungsebene; ~ **middle classes** Kleinbürgertum; ~**-price limit** Niedrigstpreisgrenze; ~**-price policy** Preisherabsetzungspolitik; ~**-priced** verbilligt; ~ **school** Unter- und Mittelstufe [an höheren Schulen].

lowering Herab-, Heruntersetzung;
~ **of the bank (discount) rate** *(Br.)* Diskontsenkung, -ermäßigung; ~ **of fares** Fahrpreisermäßigung; ~ **of prices** Preisherabsetzung, -senkung, *(stock exchange)* Kursabschwächung; ~ **of the rate of rediscount** *(US)* Diskontherabsetzung; ~ **of taxation** Steuerherabsetzung, -ermäßigung; ~ **of the time loan rate** Abschwächung der Sätze für festes Geld.

lowest | **bid** geringstes Gebot, Mindestgebot; ~ **bidder** Mindestbietender; ~ **contractor** Mindestfordernder; ~ **freight** Mindestfracht; ~ **level** Tiefststand; ~ **level of prices** niedrigstes Preisniveau, *(stock exchange)* niedrigster Kursstand; ~ **percentage** Mindestgehalt; ~ **price** niedrigster (äußerster) Preis, *(stock exchange)* niedrigster Kurs; ~ **quotation** niedrigster Kurs; ~ **taker** Wenigstfordernder; ~ **yield** Mindestrendite, -ertrag.

lowly einfach;
~ **cottage** bescheidenes Häuschen.

lowness, in the ~ of my circumstances in Anbetracht meiner bitteren Notlage;
~ **of spirits** Deprimiertheit.

loyal treu ergeben, loyal, staatstreu;
to be ~ to the interests of s. o. jds. Interessen sorgfältig wahrnehmen; **to be ~ to one's party** Parteidisziplin üben;
~ **buyer** zuverlässiger Kunde; ~ **subject** treuer Untertan; ~ **supporter** treuer (loyaler) Anhänger.

loyalist Regierungstreuer, treuer Parteianhänger;
~ **strike** Solidaritätsstreik; ~ **troops** regierungstreue Truppen.

loyalty Loyalität;
~ **board** *(US)* Überprüfungsstelle für Sicherheitsrisiken; ~ **oath** *(US)* Treueeid; ~ **program** *(US)* Loyalitätsprogramm.

lubricant Schmiermittel.
lubricate einfetten, schmieren, ölen.
lubrication Schmieren, Schmierung, Ölen.
lubricator Schmiermittel.
lucid | explanation deutliche Erklärung; ~ **literary style** klarer Stil.
luck Schicksalsfügung, Glück, Zufall;
as ~ **would have it** wie der Zufall es wollte;
bad ~ Pechsträhne; **hard** ~ nicht verdientes Schicksal;
~ **of the draw** Glück bei der Auslosung, Auslosungszufall;
~ **(v.) out** (US) Glück haben;
to be in ~ Glücksträhne haben; **to be down on one's** ~ vom Pech verfolgt, in einer üblen Lage sein, Pechsträhne haben; **to be out of** ~ Unglück haben; **to have the devil's own** ~ vom Teufel begünstigt sein, unverschämtes Glück haben; **to have a run of bad** ~ Pechsträhne haben, vom Pech verfolgt werden; **to keep s. th. for** ~ etw. als Glücksbringer behalten; **to push one's** ~ sein Glück aufs Spiel setzen; **to try one's** ~ sein Glück versuchen; **to try one's** ~ **at the gaming tables** sein Glück im Spielsaal ausprobieren;
~ **money** Glücksgeld, (stock trading) Preisnachlaß; ~ **penny** Glückspfennig; **to be in** ~'**s way** Glücksträhne haben.
lucky | at cards Glück im Spiel;
to be bloody ~ unverschämtes Glück haben; **to strike it** ~ (US fam.) Glückstreffer landen, das große Los ziehen;
~ **bag (dip)** (Br.) Glücksbeutel, Krabbelsack; ~ **bargee** Glückskind; ~ **beggar** Glückspilz; ~ **day** Glückstag; ~ **dog** Glückspilz; **to make a** ~ **guess** hundertprozentig richtig liegen; ~ **hit (shot)** Glückstreffer; ~ **incident** Glücksfall; ~ **star** Glücksstern; **to be born under a** ~ **star** Sonntagskind sein; **to thank one's** ~ **stars** von Glück sagen; **to run into a** ~ **streak** auf eine Glücksträhne stoßen; ~ **strike** (US) Glückstreffer.
lucrative rentabel, gewinnbringend, lukrativ, ertragreich, einträglich;
~ **bailment** entgeltliche Verwahrung; ~ **business** einbringliches Geschäft; **to be a** ~ **business** gute Rendite abwerfen; ~ **office** besoldetes Amt; ~ **position** einträgliche Position (Stellung); ~ **succession** (Scot. law) vorteilhafter Erwerb; ~ **transaction** lukratives Geschäft.
lucrativeness Einträglichkeit, Ergiebigkeit, Rendite.
lucre Gewinn, sittenwidrige Bereicherung, Profit;
for ~ aus Gewinnsucht;
filthy ~ gemeine Profitgier.
lucrum cessans (Latin) entgangener Gewinn.
luculent | explanation einleuchtende Erklärung; ~ **proof** überzeugender Beweis.
lug (coll.) Last, Ladung, (US coll.) Affektiertheit;
~ **(v.)** zerren, schleppen;
~ **in a story** Geschichte mit allen Mitteln ins Gespräch bringen.
luggage (Br.) [Reise]gepäck, Passagiergut;
carry-on ~ (airplane) mit ins Flugzeug genommenes Handgepäck; **extra** ~ zuschlagspflichtiges Gepäck; **free** ~ Freigepäck; **heavy** ~ großes Gepäck; **left** ~ Aufbewahrungsgepäck; **overweight** ~ Gepäck mit Übergewicht, Gepäckübergewicht; **personal** ~ Handgepäck; **registered** ~ aufgegebenes Gepäck; ~ **in advance** Passagiergut; ~ **in excess** Übergewicht; ~ **travelling with the passenger** Handgepäck;
to carry ~ **with one** Gepäck mit sich führen; **to check the** ~ sein Gepäck aufgeben; **to check out the** ~ Gepäck ausgeben; **to collect one's** ~ sein Gepäck (bei der Gepäckaufbewahrung) abholen; **to deliver** ~ Gepäck zustellen; **to examine the** ~ Gepäck zollamtlich revidieren; **to get the** ~ **through the customs** sein Gepäck zollamtlich revidieren lassen; **to have one's** ~ **registered** sein Gepäck aufgeben; **to run the** ~ **to the station** Gepäck zum Bahnhof befördern; **to see to the** ~ für das Gepäck sorgen, Gepäck besorgen; **to send one's** ~ **in advance** sein Gepäck aufgeben; **to take charge of the** ~ sich um das Gepäck kümmern;
~ **area** (car) Gepäckraum; ~ **boot (compartment)** Kofferraum; ~ **carrier** (bicycle) Gepäckträger; ~ **check** Gepäckschein; ~ **chit** Gepäckschein; ~ **clerk** Gepäckabfertiger; ~ **compartment** (car) Gepäckraum; ~ **counter** Gepäckschalter; ~ **examination** zollamtliche Gepäckrevision; ~ **grid** (car) Kofferbrücke, Gepäckhalter; ~ **guard** Fahrladeschaffner; ~ **insurance** Reisegepäckversicherung; ~ **label** Gepäckanhänger, -adresse; ~**-label holder** Anhänger; ~ **lift** Gepäckaufzug; ~ **locker** Gepäck-, Schließfach; **left-~ office** Gepäckannahme, -aufgabe, -abgabestelle, -schalter, -aufbewahrungsstelle; **to claim one's things from the left-~ office** sein Gepäck bei der Gepäckaufbewahrung abholen; **to leave one's things at the** ~ **office** sein Gepäck abgegeben haben; ~**-office clerk** Abfertigungsbeam-

ter; ~ **platform** Gepäck-, Güterbahnsteig; ~ **porter** Gepäckträger; ~ **rack** Gepäcknetz; ~ **receipt** Gepäckaufbewahrungsschein; ~ **registration window** Gepäckschalter; ~ **room** Aufbewahrungs-, Gepäckraum; ~ **stand** Gepäckständer; ~ **tag** Gepäckanhänger; **[left]** ~ **ticket** Gepäck[hinterlegungs]schein; ~ **traffic** Gepäckverkehr; ~ **trolley** Gepäckkarren; ~ **van** Gepäckwagen, Packwagen.
lukewarm support laue Unterstützung.
lull Ruhepause, vorübergehendes Abklingen, (stock exchange) Geschäftsstille, Flaute, (wind) Abflauen;
~ **in business** geschäftliche Flautezeit, Geschäftsstockung; ~ **in the conversation** Gesprächspause; ~ **in fighting** Kampfpause; ~ **in the storm** Nachlassen des Sturms; ~ **in the wind** Flaute;
~ **(v.) (wind)** abnehmen, -flauen, nachlassen;
~ **s. o. with false hopes** j. mit falschen Hoffnungen einlullen; ~ **s. one's suspicions** jds. Argwohn zerstreuen.
lumber (Canada, US) Bau-, Nutzholz, (refuse household goods) überflüssiger Ballast, Trödel, (rumble) Gerümpel, Plunder;
~ **(v.)** unordentlich aufstapeln, (move clumsily) rumpeln, poltern, (saw timber) Holz sägen;
~ **one's mind with useless bits of information** sein Gedächtnis mit unnötigen Informationseinzelheiten belasten; ~ **a room with furniture** Zimmer mit Möbeln vollstopfen; ~ **a story with details** Erzählung mit Einzelheiten überladen; ~ **up** sinnlos vollstopfen;
~ **industry** Holzwirtschaft; ~ **room** Rumpelkammer.
lumberjack (US) Holzfäller.
lumberman (Canada, US) Holzfäller.
lumberyard Holzplatz.
luminescent lamp Leuchtstoffröhre.
luminous | -figure representation Leuchtzifferanzeige; ~ **signs** Leuchtschrift; ~ **speaker** glänzender Redner.
lump Masse, große Menge;
all of a ~ alles auf einmal; **in the** ~ im ganzen (Durchschnitt), in Bausch und Bogen, pauschal[iert];
~ **of money** Unmenge Geld; ~ **of selfishness** pure Selbstsucht;
~ **(v.)** zusammenwerfen;
~ **one's all on a horse** alles auf ein Pferd setzen; ~ **into a category** in einen Topf werfen; ~ **the expenses** Unkosten aufteilen; ~ **it** (sl.) es dabei bleiben lassen; ~ **items together** (balance sheet) Posten zusammenwerfen; ~ **many items under a heading** viele Punkte unter einer Überschrift zusammenfassen; ~ **with** in einen Topf werfen, über einen Kamm scheren;
to be a ~ **of selfishness** stets nur an sich denken; **to buy in the** ~ im Ramsch (in Bausch und Bogen) kaufen; **to fix in the** ~ pauschalieren; **to have a** ~ **in one's throat** vor Aufregung nicht sprechen können, wie zugeschnürte Kehle haben; **to pay in the** ~ im ganzen bezahlen; **to sell in the** ~ in Bausch und Bogen verkaufen;
~ **allowance** Pauschalabschreibung; ~ **bargain** (mining) Stückgedinge; ~ **coal** Stückkohle; ~ **fee** Pauschalgebühr; ~ **freight** Pauschalfracht; ~ **indemnity** Pauschalentschädigung; ~ **price** Pauschalpreis.
lump sum einmalige Summe, Pauschalbetrag, -summe, Pauschale;
~ **of capital** pauschaler Kapitalbetrag;
~ **agreement** Pauschalvertrag, -vereinbarung; ~ **allotment** Pauschalzuteilung; ~ **allowance** Pauschalvergütung; ~ **appropriation** Pauschalzuweisung; **on a** ~ **basis** pauschal; ~ **charges** Pauschalgebühr; ~ **charter** Pauschalcharter; ~ **contract** Pauschalvertrag, Werkvertrag zu einem Pauschalpreis; ~ **deductions** Pauschalabsetzungen; ~ **expenditure** Pauschalausgaben; ~ **fee** Pauschalhonorar; ~ **freight** Pauschalfracht; ~ **investment** Pauschalanlage; ~ **payment** Pauschalzahlung, -entschädigung, pauschale Vergütung (Abfindung); ~ **payout** Abfindungszahlung; ~ **pension** pauschalierte Pensionszahlung; ~ **price** Pauschalpreis; ~ **purchase** Großeinkauf; ~ **rate** Pausch[al]satz; ~ **settlement** pauschale Regulierung, Pauschalregulierung, -abfindung, Kapitalabfindung; ~ **subsidy** Pauschalsubvention; ~ **tax** Pauschalsteuer; ~ **work** pauschal übernommene Arbeit, Pauschalakkord.
lumped-order terms of sale monatliche Abrechnungsbedingungen.
lumper Hafenarbeiter, Schauermann.
lumping | sale Pauschalverkauf, (real estate) Zwangsversteigerung eines Grundstückskomplexes.
lunacy Geisteskrankheit, -störung, geistige Unzurechnungsfähigkeit;
~ **proceedings** Entmündigungsverfahren.
lunar | landing Mondlandung; ~ **probe** Mondrakete, -sonde; ~ **surface** Mondoberfläche.

lunatic Geisteskranker, -gestörter, -schwacher;
~ *(a.)* geisteskrank, geistesgestört, -schwach;
to be found ~ by inquisition *(Br.)* nach amtlicher Untersuchung für geisteskrank befunden werden;
~ **asylum** Irren-, Nervenheilanstalt; ~ **fringe** *(coll.)* Hundertfünfzigprozentiger.
lunch zweites Frühstück, Gabelfrühstück, Imbiß, Mittagessen;
business ~ geschäftliche Mittagsverabredung; **quick** ~ Schnellgericht; **simple** ~ einfaches Mittagessen;
~ *(v.)* Mittagessen einnehmen;
to ask s. o. for ~ j. zum Frühstück einladen; **to justify a** ~ **as business expense** Mittagessen über Spesen abrechnen; **to order s. th. for** ~ etw. zum Mittagessen bestellen;
~ **allowance** Mittagessenzuschuß; ~ **break** Mittagspause; ~ **counter** Imbißstube; ~**-counter car** Eisenbahnzug mit Kücheneinrichtung; ~ **hour** Mittagszeit; ~ **time** Mittagszeit; ~**-time stroll** Mittagsspaziergang.
luncheon [Mittag]essen, Imbiß;
anniversary ~ Jubiläums-, Gedächtnisessen;
to ask s. o. to stay for ~ j. zum Mittagessen auffordern;
~ **commitment (engagement)** Mittagsverabredung, Verabredung zum Mittagessen; **free** ~ **facilities** freier Mittagstisch; ~ **meeting** Mittagsverabredung, ~ **meeting session** Arbeitsessen; ~ **quarter** Mittagstisch; ~ **voucher** Essenmarke; **to buy** ~ **vouchers** im Abonnement essen.
luncheonette Imbißstube, Schnellgaststätte.
lung of a city Großstadtlunge.
lurch Hang, Neigung, *(ship)* Schlingern;
~ *(v.)* schlingern, rollen, *(pilfer)* mausern, stibitzen, klauen;
~ **across the street** über die Straße taumeln;
to leave in the ~ im Stich lassen.
lure Lockartikel, -vogel, -mittel, Köder;
~ *(v.)* anlocken, ködern;
~ **s. o. away from his duty** jem. seinem Pflichtenkreis entfremden; ~ **away with an offer of better pay** mit dem Angebot höherer Bezahlung abwerben; ~ **labo(u)r into other jobs** Arbeitskräfte zum Berufswechsel verführen (abwerben); ~ **s. o. with bright prospects** jem. eine glänzende Zukunft in Aussicht stellen; ~ **back into one's sphere of influence** j. in seinen Einflußbereich zurückführen.
lurk Schlupfwinkel, Versteck, *(Br., sl.)* Kniff, Schlich, Trick;
on the ~ auf der Lauer;
~ *(v.)* **away** sich wegstehlen (fortschleichen); ~ **in s. one's mind** *(suspicion)* weiterhin schlummern.
lurking | **passion** schlummernde Leidenschaft; ~ **place** Schlupfwinkel, Versteck.

lush *(drunken person, sl.)* Säufer, *(intoxicating liquor)* Stoff.
lust | **of power** Machtgier;
~ *(v.)* **for revenge** nach Rache dürsten.
luster, lustre *(Br.)* Schein, *(chandelier)* Kronleuchter, Kristallanhänger, *(fig.)* Glanz;
~ **of pearls** Perlenglanz, -schimmer;
to add fresh ~ **to a name** einem Namen neuen Glanz verleihen.
luxuriance Üppigkeit, Fülle, Reichtum.
luxuriant üppig, wuchernd;
~ **imagination** üppige Phantasie.
luxuriate *(v.)* üppig leben;
~ **in details** in Einzelheiten schwelgen; ~ **in one's new life** Luxus seines neuen Lebens in allen Einzelheiten genießen; ~ **in opulence** im Luxus schwelgen.
luxuries Luxusartikel, -waren, -güter;
not to be able to enjoy ~ sich nichts leisten können; **to get few** ~ sich wenig leisten können;
~ **tax** Luxussteuer.
luxurious schwelgerisch, luxuriös;
~ **hotel** Luxushotel, Hotel der Spitzenklasse; ~ **life** Luxusleben.
luxury Luxus, Aufwand, *(item)* Luxusgegenstand;
in the lap of ~ vom Luxus umgeben;
to afford ~ sich Luxus leisten können; **to live (be rolling) in** ~ Luxusleben führen; **to wallow in** ~ im größten Luxus leben;
~ **apartment** Luxuswohnung; ~ **article** Luxusartikel; ~ **car** Luxusauto; ~ **flat** Komfortwohnung; ~ **goods** Luxusgüter, -artikel, -waren; ~ **and semi-~ goods** Güter des gehobenen Bedarfs; ~ **hotel** Luxushotel, Hotel der Spitzenklasse; ~ **housing** Luxuswohnung; ~ **imports** Luxuswareneinfuhr; ~ **industry** Luxuswarenindustrie; ~ **life** Luxusleben; ~ **liner** Luxusflugzeug, -schiff, -dampfer; ~ **ocean** ~ Luxusdampfer; ~ **ocean liner** Luxusdampfer; ~ **package** Luxusausführung; ~ **resort** mondäner Kurort, Luxuskurort; ~ **saloon** Luxuslimousine; ~ **tax** Luxussteuer; ~ **trade** Handel mit Luxusgütern, Luxuswarenhandel.
lyceum Schulgebäude, *(lecture room)* Vortrags-, Vorlesungssaal, *(US)* [etwa] Volkshochschule, -bildungsverein.
lying | **down** Unterwerfung;
~ **in state** öffentliche Aufbahrung;
to be ~ **ill in bed** krank zu Bette liegen; **to leave one's papers** ~ **about** seine Unterlagen herumliegen lassen; **to take it** ~ **down** klein beigeben;
~ **idle** *(money)* brachliegend, ungenutzt; ~**-in hospital** Entbindungsheim.
lynch *(v.)* lynchen;
~ **law** Lynchrecht, -justiz.

M

M-day Mobilmachungstag.
macadam Schotterdecke, -straße.
macadamize *(v.)* beschottern.
macadamized road Schotterstraße.
mace *(parl.)* Amtsstab, *(police)* Knüppel, *(sl.)* Schwindel;
~-**bearer** *(Scot.)* Gerichtsdiener; ~-**proof** *(US)* pfändungsfrei, nicht der Zwangsvollstreckung unterliegend.
macer *(Scot.)* Gerichtsdiener.
Mach|number Machzahl; ~ **two** doppelte Schallgeschwindigkeit.
machinable bearbeitbar, maschinell herstellbar.
machinal maschinell, maschinenmäßig.
machinations Intrigen, Umtriebe;
political ~s politische Intrigen;
to upset ~s Machenschaften vereiteln.
machine Maschine, Apparat, Vorrichtung, Mechanismus, *(gearing)* Triebwerk, Getriebe, *(literature)* Kunstgriff, *(politics, US)* Organisation, Apparat, *(vehicle)* Fahrzeug;
~s *(pol.)* Funktionäre, Führungsgremium;
adding ~ Addiermaschine; **addressing** ~ Adressiermaschine; **automatic** ~ Automat; **calculating** ~ Rechenmaschine; **copying** ~ Kopierpresse; **democratic** ~ *(US)* Apparat der Demokratischen Partei; **duplicating** ~ Vervielfältigungsmaschine; **franking** ~ Frankiermaschine; **invoicing** ~ Fakturiermaschine; **key-operated** ~ Maschine mit Tastenbedienung; **labo(u)r-saving** ~s arbeitssparende Maschinen; **party** ~ *(fam.)* Parteiapparat, -organisation; **perfect** ~ vollendete Erfindung; **political** ~ Parteiapparat; **printing** ~ Druckpresse; **slot** ~ Münzautomat; **three-bank** ~ dreireihige Schreibmaschine; **type-setting** ~ Satzgerät, -maschine;
~s and equipment *(balance sheet)* Maschinen und Ausstattung; ~ **in operating condition** betriebsbereite (einsatzbereite) Maschine; ~ **of government** Regierungsapparat;
~ *(v.)* mit der Maschine (maschinell) herstellen;
to be a mere ~ reinster Automat sein; **to be working the** ~ **at the other end** Gegenstelle bedienen; **to mark by** ~ maschinell auszeichnen; **to operate a** ~ Maschine arbeiten lassen; **to put a** ~ **to further trials** weitere Versuche mit einer Maschine anstellen; **to reduce s. o. to a mere** ~ j. zur reinsten Maschine herabwürdigen; **to replace a** ~ Maschine ersetzen; **to rest a** ~ Maschine anhalten; **to send a** ~ **on free trial** Maschine kostenlos zum Ausprobieren zusenden; **to start a** ~ Maschine in Betrieb setzen; **to stop a** ~ Maschine abstellen;
~ **accountant** Maschinenbuchhalter; ~ **accounting** Maschinenbuchführung; ~ **age** Maschinenzeitalter; ~ **burden unit** Maschinen-, Platzkostensatz; ~ **composition** *(print.)* Maschinensatz; ~ **downtime** *(US)* Maschinenbrachezeit; ~-**finished paper** maschinenglattes Papier; ~ **fitter** Maschinenschlosser, Mechaniker; ~ **gun** Maschinengewehr; ~ **hour** Maschinenstunde; ~ **hour rate** Maschinenstundensatz; ~-**idle time** Maschinenausfallzeit; ~ **language** Maschinensprache; ~-**made** maschinell hergestellt; ~ **operator** Bedienungskraft einer Maschine; ~-**posted** maschinell gebucht; **bookkeeping** ~ **operator** Maschinenbuchhalter; ~ **posting** maschinelle Buchung; ~ **products** Maschinenerzeugnisse; ~ **production** Serien-, Massenherstellung; ~ **rental** Maschinenmiete; ~ **setting** *(print.)* Maschinensatz; ~ **shop** Maschinenbaufirma, -werkstatt, -halle, Reparaturwerkstätte; ~ **tabulation** maschinelle Tabellierung; ~ **time** Nutzungszeit einer Maschine; ~ **tool** Werkzeugmaschine; ~ **tools industry** Werkzeugmaschinenindustrie; ~ **wear** maschinelle Abnutzung; ~ **work** Maschinenarbeit; ~ **works** Maschinenfabrik.
machinery Maschinen[anlage], Maschinenpark, maschinelle Anlagen, technische Ausstattung, *(fig.)* Apparat, Räderwerk;
administrative ~ Verwaltungsapparat; **agricultural** ~ landwirtschaftliche Maschinen; **party** ~ Parteiapparat; **printing** ~ Maschinenpark einer Druckerei; **regular** ~ offizielle Kanäle;
~ **for consultation** Konsultationsapparat, -mechanismus; ~ **of credit** Kreditapparat; ~ **and equipment** *(balance sheet)* Maschinen und Geräte, Betriebsausrüstung; ~ **of government** Staatsmaschinerie, Regierungsapparat; ~ **in operation (use)** in Betrieb (in Benutzung, im Gebrauch) befindliche Maschinen; ~ **and plant** *(balance sheet)* Maschinen und maschinelle Anlagen; ~, **plant and equipment** *(balance sheet)* Maschinen und maschinelle Anlagen;
to install (lay down) new ~s neue Maschinen aufstellen;
~ **account** Maschinenanlagenkonto; ~ **builder** Maschinenbauer,

-hersteller; ~ **fair** technische Messe; ~ **insurance** Maschinenversicherung; ~ **production** maschinelle Herstellung, Maschinenproduktion; ~ **replacement** Erneuerung des Maschinenparks.
machining maschinelle Bearbeitung;
~ **allowance** Zuschlag für maschinelle Bearbeitung; ~ **method** Bearbeitungsmethode; ~ **operation** Bearbeitungsvorgang; ~ **time** Arbeitszeit [einer Maschine].
machinist Machinist, Maschinenschlosser, -bauer, Konstrukteur, *(mar.)* Deckoffizier.
mackle *(print.)* Doppeldruck, verwischter Druck.
macro economics Makroökonomie.
macroeconomic model of income determination gesamtwirtschaftliches Kreislaufmodell.
mad wahnsinnig, verrückt;
as ~ **as a March hare (hatter)** total verrückt;
to get ~ **at s. o.** *(US. fam.)* über j. verärgert sein; **to go** ~ durchdrehen;
~ **dog** tollwütiger Hund; ~ **point** fixe Idee.
made gemacht, hergestellt, angefertigt;
American-~ in Amerika hergestellt; **foreign-**~ im Ausland hergestellt; **home-**~ selbstgemacht; **ready-**~ konfektionell hergestellt, fertig, von der Stange;
~ **in Germany** in Deutschland hergestellt;
~ **known** zur Kenntnis gebracht, *(writ of scire facias)* zugestellt; ~ **to last** auf Dauer gearbeitet, dauerhaft gemacht; ~ **to measure** maßgefertigt, -gearbeitet; ~ **of money** *(fam.)* steinreich; ~ **to order** auf Bestellung gemacht (angefertigt); ~ **out to** lautend auf; ~ **out to order** an Order ausgestellt; ~ **up** fertiggestellt; ~ **up for sale** verpackt;
German-~ **article** deutsches Fabrikat; ~ **bill** *(Br.)* indossierter Wechsel; ~ **ground** aufgeschütteter Boden; ~-**up clothes** Konfektionsware, -kleidung; ~-**up story** erfundene Geschichte.
madhouse Irrenanstalt.
madman Geisteskranker, Wahnsinniger.
madness Wahnsinn.
maelstrom of war Kriegsstrudel.
magazinable für Zeitschriftenveröffentlichungen geeignet.
magazine Warenlager, [Waren]niederlage, Magazin, Speicher, Vorratsraum, *(film)* Filmmagazin, *(mil.)* Munitions-, Nachschub-, Proviantlager, *(newspaper)* Magazin, Unterhaltungszeitschrift, [illustrierte] Zeitschrift, Illustrierte;
educational ~ bildende Zeitschrift; **glossy** ~ reich bebilderte Zeitschrift; **highly selective** ~ hochqualifizierte Zeitschrift; **illustrated** ~ Illustrierte; **principal** ~ Hauptniederlage;
~ *(v.)* *(edit)* Zeitschrift herausgeben, *(store)* aufspeichern, lagern;
to leaf through a ~ *(US)* Zeitschrift durchblättern; **to subscribe for (take in, Br.) a magazine** Zeitschrift abonnieren;
~ **advertisement (advertising)** Zeitschriftenreklame, -werbung; ~ **article** Zeitschriftenartikel; ~ **business** Zeitschriftenhandel; ~ **field** Zeitschriftenmarkt; ~ **printing** Zeitschriftendruck; ~ **readership** Zeitschriftenleserkreis; ~ **reading figure** Ziffern über den Leserkreis von Zeitschriften; ~ **rights** Veröffentlichungsrechte für Zeitschriften; ~ **salesman** Zeitschriftenhändler; ~ **solicitor** *(US)* Zeitschriftenwerber; ~ **subscription** Zeitschriftenabonnement.
magazinist Mitarbeiter einer Zeitschrift.
magic Magie, Zauber[kraft];
the ~ **of a great name** magische Kraft eines großen Namens;
~ **eye** magisches Auge; ~ **formula** Zauberformel.
magister Graduierter, Wissenschaftler.
magisterial obrigkeitlich, amtlich, behördlich, *(law court)* richterlich;
~ **character** Magistratscharakter; ~ **decree** Verwaltungserlaß; ~ **district** *(US)* Verwaltungsbezirk; ~ **precinct** *(US)* örtlicher Zuständigkeitsbereich, Amtsgerichtsbezirk; ~ **pronouncement** amtliche Verlautbarung; ~ **rank** obrigkeitliche Stellung.
magistracy Magistrat, Obrigkeit, Amt, *(law court)* Richterschaft, *(precinct)* Amtsbezirk.
magistrate *(US)* [öffentlicher] Beamter, staatlicher Funktionär, Verwaltungsbeamter, Amtmann, *(officer with judicial powers)* [Friedens]richter, richterlicher Beamter, *(officer with criminal jurisdiction)* Haftrichter, *(Scot.)* Bürgermeister, Ratsherr;
chief ~ *(Scot.)* Regierungschef, erster Staatsdiener, Präsident, *(town)* Bürgermeister, oberster Verwaltungsbeamter; **committing** ~ Untersuchungsrichter; **district** ~ Bezirksrichter; **exam-**

ining (investigating) ~ Untersuchungsrichter; police ~ (US) Verkehrsrichter; stipendiary ~ (Br.) Berufs-, Friedensrichter; resident ~ (Ireland) Verkehrsrichter;
~s entitled to adjudicate zuständige Behörden; ~ in bankruptcy Konkursrichter;
to be brought before the ~ dem Richter vorgeführt werden;
~'s certificate behördliche Bescheinigung; ~s (Br.) (~'s, US) court Schnellrichter, (South Carolina) Amtsgericht.
magistrateship Magistratsamt, Amtsperiode.
magnate Magnat;
armaments ~ Rüstungsindustrieller; industrial ~ Großindustrieller; territorial ~ Großgrundbesitzer;
~ of finance Finanzmagnat; ~ of industry Großindustrieller.
magnetic magnetisch, (fig.) fesselnd, faszinierend;
~ attraction magnetische Anziehungskraft; ~ field Magnetfeld; ~ mine magnetische Mine; ~ needle Kompaßnadel; ~ papertype Lochstreifen; ~ personality faszinierende Persönlichkeit; ~ sound recorder Magnettongerät; ~ tape Magnet-, Tonband.
magnifier Lupe, Vergrößerungsglas.
magnify (v.) vergrößern;
~ a difficulty Schwierigkeit übertreiben.
magnifying|glass Vergrößerungsglas, Lupe; ~ lens Vergrößerungslinse.
maid [Haus]mädchen, (unmarried woman) Junggesellin;
~ of hono(u)r (Br.) Ehren-, Hofdame, (US) Brautjungfer;
to do without a ~ sein Dienstmädchen abschaffen, ohne Dienstmädchen auskommen;
~ servant Dienstmädchen, Hausangestellte.
maiden junge unverheiratete Frau;
~ assize (Br.) Gerichtssitzung ohne Kriminalfall; ~ modesty mädchenhafte Bescheidenheit; ~ name Geburts-, Mädchenname; ~ soil jungfräulicher Boden; ~ speech (parl.) erste Rede, Erstlings-, Jungfernrede; ~ trip (voyage) Probe-, Jungfernfahrt, (airplane) Erstflug.
maidenhead Jungfräulichkeit.
mail Post[sendung], Postsachen, Brief-, Paketpost, (bag) Postbeutel, -sack, (delivery of postal matters) Postversand, (Scot. law) Miete, (vehicle) Postauto, -zug, -flugzeug;
by ~ per Post; by the first ~ mit der ersten Post; by the next ~ mit der nächsten Post; by return of ~ postwendend, umgehend; by surface ~ (US) mit gewöhnlicher Post; by today's ~ mit der heutigen Post; with the same ~ mit gleicher Post;
~s Brief-, Paketpost, Postsachen;
arriving ~ eingehende Post; bulk ~ Postwurfsendung; closed ~ versiegelte Postsäcke im zwischenstaatlichen Durchgangsverkehr; daily ~ Tagespost; damaged ~ beschädigte Post; delivered ~ zugestellte Post; departing ~ ausgehende (abgehende) Post; domestic ~ Inlandspost; early ~ Morgenpost; filed ~ Ablage; first-class ~ (US) Paketpost; foreign ~ Auslandspost; fourth-class ~ (US) Paketpost; incoming ~ eingehende Post, Posteingang; interoffice ~ betriebsinterner Briefverkehr; inward ~ Inlandspost; letter ~ Briefpost; limited ~ (railway) Bahnpost; local ~ Ortspost; metered ~ durch Freistempler freigemachte Post; morning ~ Morgenpost; outgoing ~ Briefausgang, ausgehende (abgehende) Post; outward ~ Auslandspost; registered ~ Einschreibsendung; second-class ~ (US) Zeitungspost; special ~ Extrapost; special-delivery ~ Eilbotensendung; third-class ~ (US) Drucksachen; undeliverable ~ unzustellbare Postsendungen; undelivered ~ noch nicht zugestellte Post;
~s and duties (Scot.) Grundzins;
~ (v.) (US) mit der Post senden, zum Versand bringen, zur Post geben, auf der Post aufliefern;
~ a letter at the post office Brief bei der Post aufgeben; ~ in one's order postalisch Auftrag erteilen; ~ out versenden; ~ parcels Pakete aufgeben;
to carry ~ Post befördern; to collect the ~ Briefkasten leeren; to dispatch (dispose of) the ~ Post abfertigen (erledigen); to do (go through) one's ~ seine Post (seine schriftlichen Verpflichtungen) erledigen, seine Post durchsehen; to forward the ~ Post expedieren; to get lost in the ~ auf dem Postweg verlorengehen; to open the ~ Post[sachen] öffnen; to receive ~ Post bekommen; to sell by ~ im Postversandwege verkaufen; to send a letter by air ~ Brief per Luftpost schicken;
direct ~ advertising Drucksachen-, Einzelwerbung durch die Post, Postwerbung; ~ advertising reply Werbeantwort; ~ advice briefliche Benachrichtigung; ~-back form mit der Post zurückgeschickter Fragebogen; ~ ballot Wahlschein; ~ boat Postschiff, -dampfer, Paketboot; ~ boycott Briefboykott; ~ car[riage] (railway) Postwagen; ~ carrier Postbote; ~ cart (Br.)

Handwagen des Postboten; ~ classification Postversandarten; ~ clerk (US) Angestellter einer Speditionsabteilung; ~ coach (Br.) Postomnibus; ~ collection Postabholung; ~ credit Postlaufkredit; ~ day Posttag; ~ delivery Postzustellung, -auslieferung; ~ department Expedition[sabteilung]; ~ dispatch Postabfertigung; ~ distribution centre Briefsammelstelle; ~ drop Briefannahmestelle; ~ fraud Postbetrug, Irreführen der Post; ~-in premium Zugabe gegen eingesandten Kupon; registered ~ insurance Postwertversicherung; direct ~ literature Postwurfprospekt; ~ matter Postsendungen, -sachen, -gut.
mail order Auftrag durch die Post, Postauftrag, -versand;
to do ~s Aufträge postalisch erledigen.
mail-order durch Versandgeschäft;
~ advertising Versandhauswerbung; ~ business Versandgeschäft, -handel; ~ business boom Hausse im Versandhausgeschäft; ~ catalog(ue) Versandhauskatalog; ~ company Postversandfirma; ~ contract Versandgeschäftsauftrag; ~ department Postversandabteilung, Expedition; to practise ~ distribution durch das Versandhaussystem absetzen; ~ establishment [Post]versandunternehmen; ~ field Versandhauswesen; ~ film-processing firm Filmkopierwerk und Versand; ~ firm (house) Versandhaus, -geschäft, -unternehmen; ~ publicity Postversandwerbung; ~ retailer über ein Versandhaus anlieferndes Einzelhandelsgeschäft; ~ sales Versandhausumsätze; ~ selling Versandverkauf; ~ store Auslieferungsstelle einer Versandfirma; ~ wholesaler Versandgroßhändler.
mail|payer (Scotch law) Mieter; ~ payment (remittance) briefliche Überweisung; in-the-~ price Preis frei Haus; ~ privilege (US) Portovergünstigung für bestimmte Postsendungen; ~ questionnaire (questionary) brieflich versandter Fragebogen; ~ research (survey) postalische Befragung; ~ robbery Postdiebstahl, -raub.
mail service (US) Postdienst, -verkehr, -zustellung;
external ~ Auslandspostverkehr; internal ~ Inlandspostverkehr; transit ~ Durchgangspostverkehr;
~, passenger and parcel service Post-, Passagier- und Paketschiffahrt;
to suspend ~ Postverkehr einstellen.
mail|station (US) Postamt; ~ steamer Postdampfer, Paketboot; ~ strike Postarbeiterstreik; ~ theft Postdiebstahl; ~ survey brieflich angestellte Marktuntersuchung; two-tiered ~ system zweistufiges Posttarifsystem; ~ teller Kassierer für postalisch eingehende Überweisungen; ~ train Postzug; by ~ train als Frachtgut; ~ transfer Überweisung durch die Post, Postüberweisung, briefliche Auszahlung; ~ van Paketpostwagen.
mailable postalisch zu befördern, zum Postversand zugelassen, postversandfähig.
mailbag Postbeutel, -sack.
mailbox (US) Briefeinwurf, -kasten [im Hause].
mailed postalisch aufgegeben, von der Post befördert;
~ application schriftlicher Antrag; ~ fist (fig.) Gewaltandrohung, -anwendung.
mailer Postabfertiger, (cotter) Pachthäusler, (mailing machine, US) Adressiermaschine, Frankierautomat.
mailguard (Br.) Begleitperson.
mailing (US) Auflieferung (Aufgabe) bei der Post, Postversand, (Scot.) Pachtgut, -zins.
~s Postversandmaterial;
unaddressed ~ Postwurfsendung;
~ address (US) Postanschrift; ~ bag Musterbeutel; ~ carton Versandkarton; ~ charges Porto-, Postgebühren; ~ clasp Musterklammer; ~ clerk Postabfertiger; ~ costs Versandkosten; ~ date Versandtermin, Postabgangsdatum; ~ department Expedition[sabteilung]; ~ equipment Postabfertigungsgerät; ~ expenses Post-, Versandgebühren; ~ fees Postgebühren; ~ list (US) Postversandliste, Adressenkartei, -verzeichnis; to add s. one's name to the ~ list (US) j. in die Adressen-, Postversandliste aufnehmen; ~-list control Adressenkontrolle; ~-list revision Adressenüberprüfung; ~-list source Adressenquelle; ~ machine Adressiermaschine, Frankierautomat; ~ office Versandbüro, -stelle; ~ piece Postwurfsendung; ~ room Postabfertigungsraum; ~ schedule Adressenplan; ~ scheme (Br.) Plan für Postversandwerbung; ~ shot Postwerbeexemplar; ~ table Briefsortiertisch; ~ tube Papp-, Versandrolle.
mailman (US) Briefträger, Postbote.
mailplane Postflugzeug.
mailroom Postabfertigungsraum.
maim (v.) verstümmeln, zum Krüppel machen.
main Festland, Kontinent, (cable) Hauptkabel, (principal part) Hauptsache, -punkt, (principal pipe) Hauptleitung, -rohr, (principal railroad, US) Hauptlinie;

in the ~ hauptsächlich; **with might and** ~ mit aller Kraft, mit aller Gewalt;
street ~ Hauptrohr;
~ *(a.)* vorwiegend, hauptsächlich;
~ **accomplishment** Hauptleistung; ~ **act** höhere Gewalt; ~ **artery** Hauptverkehrsweg; ~ **body of an army** Gros eines Heeres; ~ **branch** Hauptfiliale, -stelle; ~ **building** Hauptgebäude; ~ **business** Hauptgeschäft; ~ **cable** Hauptstromkabel; ~ **catalog(ue)** Hauptkatalog; ~ **clearing station** *(US)* Hauptverbandsplatz; **to have an eye to the ~ chance** sich um seine eigenen Interessen kümmern, seinen eigenen Vorteil im Auge haben; ~ **claim** *(patent)* Hauptanspruch; ~ **column** Hauptspalte; ~ **comfort** bester Komfort; ~ **committee** Hauptausschuß; ~ **constituent** Hauptbestandteil; ~ **contract** Grundvertrag; ~ **contractor** Hauptlieferant, Generalunternehmer; ~ **crop** erste Ernte; ~ **current of traffic** Hauptverkehrsstrom; ~ **customer** wichtigster Kunde, Hauptkunde; ~ **deck** Oberdeck; ~ **difficulties** Hauptschwierigkeiten; ~ **dish** Hauptgericht; ~ **drag** *(sl.)* Hauptverkehrsstraße; ~ **drain** Hauptkanal; ~ **edition** Hauptausgabe; ~ **effect** *(statistics)* Haupteffekt; ~ **establishment** Hauptniederlassung; ~ **feature** Hauptmerkmal; ~ **features of a speech** Hauptaussage einer Rede; ~ **force** nackte Gewalt; ~ **fuse** *(electricity)* Hauptsicherung; ~ **hatch** Großluke; ~ **highway** Landstraße erster Ordnung; ~ **interview** *(employment)* Einstellungsbefragung; ~ **issue** Hauptfrage, -problem, *(law)* Hauptsache; ~ **junction** Hauptknotenpunkt; ~ **line** Haupttelegraphenlinie, *(airplane)* Hauptfluglinie, *(railway)* Hauptlinie, *(sl.)* Hauptsache im Leben; ~ **line of resistance** *(mil.)* Hauptkampflinie; ~ **market** Hauptabsatzgebiet; ~ **object in life** wesentliches Lebensziel; ~ **office** *(US)* Zentrale, Hauptverwaltung, -stelle, -büro, -niederlassung; ~ **opinion** herrschende Meinung; ~ **place of business** Hauptgeschäftssitz; ~ **point** Hauptsache; ~ **post office** Hauptpostamt; ~ **reason** Hauptgrund; ~ **road** Landstraße erster Ordnung; ~ **route** Hauptstrecke; ~ **sea** offene See; ~ **seat of activity** Hauptniederlassung; ~ **sewer** Hauptkanal; ~ **source** Hauptbezugsquelle; ~ **squeeze** *(sl.)* Boß, Chef; ~ **staircase** *(tenement house)* Haupttreppe; ~ **station** Hauptbahnhof; ~ **stem** *(US)* Hauptverkehrslinie; ~ **street** *(US)* Hauptstraße, Ausfallstraße; ~ **subject** Hauptfach; ~ **supplier** Hauptlieferant; ~ **support** Hauptstütze; ~ **thing** Hauptsache; ~ **topic** Hauptthema; ~ **track** Hauptlinie; ~ **travel(l)ed-road** stark befahrene Straße; ~ **type** Grundschrift; ~ **worry** Hauptsorge.
mainland Festland, Kontinent.
mainpernable kautionsfähig.
mains Hauptleitung, *(el.)* Stromnetz, *(sewerage)* Kanalisation;
operating on the ~ *(wireless)* mit Netzanschluß;
town ~ städtische Kanalisation;
to connect to the ~ an die Kanalisation (das Stromnetz) anschließen; **to take one's power from the** ~ ans E-Werk angeschlossen sein;
~ **breakdown** Strom-, Netzausfall; ~ **input** Netzanschluß; ~ **receiving set** Netzempfänger; ~ **voltage** *(el.)* Netzspannung.
mainstay of the city's finances Rückgrat der städtischen Finanzen.
mainstream Haupttendenz, Hauptrichtung, *(adherents)* Großteil der Anhänger;
~ **of traffic** Hauptverkehrsstrom;
~ **corporation tax** Hauptkörperschaftsteuer; ~ **policy** Schwerpunktpolitik.
maintain *(v.) (affirm)* behaupten, *(carry on)* aufrechterhalten, weiterführen, beibehalten, *(keep in repair)* warten, instandhalten, instandsetzen, *(prices)* stützen, halten, *(support)* unterhalten, betreuen, versorgen;
~ **themselves** *(prices)* sich halten (behaupten);
~ **an action** Prozeß führen; ~ **an action in one's own name** im eigenen Namen klagen; ~ **an airport** für die Instandhaltung eines Flugplatzes Sorge tragen; ~ **an attitude** Haltung beibehalten; ~ **blocks** klischieren; ~ **books** Bücher führen; ~ **one's candidature** *(Br.)* seine Kandidatur aufrechterhalten; ~ **the contrary** Gegenteil behaupten; ~ **a correspondence** Briefwechsel führen; ~ **the deliveries** Lieferungen fortsetzen, weiter liefern; **jointly** ~ **a dependant** Angehörigen gemeinsam unterhalten; ~ **at public expense** aus öffentlichen Mitteln unterhalten; ~ **a family** Familie ernähren; **to neglect to** ~ **one's family** Unterhalt seiner Familie vernachlässigen; ~ **a friendship** Freundschaft bewahren; ~ **one's ground** standhalten; ~ **that one is innocent of a charge** seine Schuldlosigkeit in einer Strafsache behaupten; ~ **the law** für das Gesetz eintreten; ~ **an open mind on a question** einer Frage aufgeschlossen gegenüberstehen; ~ **an office** Geschäftsstelle unterhalten; ~ **order** Ordnung aufrechterhalten; ~ **a patent** Patent aufrechterhalten; ~ **s. o. in**

a position j. in einer Stellung belassen; ~ **prices** Preisgefüge aufrechterhalten; ~ **fixed resale prices** Preisbindung der zweiten Hand beibehalten; ~ **a railway (railroad,** *US)* Eisenbahnlinie für den öffentlichen Verkehr unterhalten; ~ **diplomatic relations with a country** diplomatische Beziehungen zu einem Land unterhalten; ~ **one's reputation** seinen guten Ruf behaupten; ~ **reserves** Reserven unterhalten; ~ **one's rights** seine Rechte wahren; ~ **a road** Straße unterhalten (instandhalten); ~ **a son at the university** Sohn auf der Universität studieren lassen; ~ **the speed** Geschwindigkeit beibehalten; ~ **a speed of 80 miles an hour** 120 km Stundendurchschnitt fahren; ~ **a suit** *(US)* Prozeß fortsetzen; ~ **a good understanding** in gutem Einvernehmen leben; ~ **its value** seinen Wert behalten; ~ **a war** Krieg führen; ~ **one's wife in the style she is accustomed to** seiner Ehefrau den gewohnten Lebensstandard bieten.
maintainability Haltbarkeit, *(airplane)* Wartbarkeit.
maintainable erhaltungspflichtig, *(airplane)* zu warten.
maintained *(stock exchange)* behauptet;
to be ~ Unterhalt beziehen, *(prices)* sich halten;
~ **price** gebundener Preis.
maintainer Betreuer.
maintaining│capital intact Abschreibung im Rahmen der volkswirtschaftlichen Gesamtrechnung; ~ **resale prices** Preisbindung der zweiten Hand, Einhaltung von Wiederverkaufspreisen.
maintenance *(keeping in repair)* [laufende] Unter-, Instandhaltung, Wartung[sdienst], *(keeping up)* [Aufrecht]erhaltung, Wahrung, *(criminal law)* illegale Unterstützung einer prozeßführenden Partei, *(obligation to pay)* Unterhaltspflicht, *(subsistence)* [Lebens]unterhalt, Unterhaltzahlung, Unterstützung, Unterhaltsmittel;
entitled to ~ unterhaltsberechtigt;
building ~ Gebäudeunterhaltung; **current** ~ Unterhaltungsaufwand, laufende Instandhaltung, Wartungskosten; **deferred** ~ aufgeschobene Reparaturen; **matrimonial** ~ ehelicher Unterhalt; **minimum** ~ notwendiger Lebensunterhalt; **preventive** ~ vorbeugende Instandhaltung; **reasonable** ~ angemessener Unterhalt; **resale price** ~ Preisbindung der zweiten Hand; **secured** ~ *(Br.)* gesicherte Unterhaltszahlung; **separate** ~ *(US)* Unterhalt bei Getrenntleben;
~ **of an account** Kontounterhaltung; ~ **of an automobile** Fahrzeugunterhaltung; ~ **of a building** Gebäudeinstandhaltung; ~ **of the crew** Mannschaftsverpflegung; ~ **of dues** Einziehung von Gewerkschaftsbeiträgen durch den Betrieb; ~ **of a family** Unterhalt einer Familie; ~ **of law and order** Aufrechterhaltung der öffentlichen Sicherheit und Ordnung; ~ **of liquidity** *(banking)* Liquiditätsvorsorge; ~ **of membership** Aufrechterhaltung der Mitgliedschaft, *(trade union)* aufrechterhaltene Gewerkschaftsmitgliedschaft als Beschäftigungsvoraussetzung; ~ **of order and security** Aufrechterhaltung der öffentlichen Ruhe und Ordnung; ~ **of the poor** Fürsorge [für die Armen]; ~ **of prices** Preisstützung, -bindung, Aufrechterhaltung des Preisgefüges; ~ **of a quorum** Beibehaltung der Beschlußfähigkeit; ~ **and repair** Unterhalt und Instandsetzung; ~ **of resale prices by local dealers** Preisbindung der zweiten Hand durch die örtlichen Händler; ~ **of one's rights** Wahrung seiner Interessen; ~ **of public roads and highways** Unterhaltung (Instandhaltung) von Straßen und öffentlichen Wegen; ~ **suitable to s. one's station in life** standesgemäßer Unterhalt; ~ **of structure** Gebäudeerhaltung; ~ **of tombs** Grabstättenpflege; ~ **of way** *(railway)* Streckenunterhaltung;
to award ~ Unterhalt zuerkennen; **to be responsible for** ~ unterhaltspflichtig sein; **to claim** ~ Unterhaltsansprüche stellen (geltend machen); **to make contributions towards the costs of** ~ Beitrag zu den Unterhaltskosten leisten; **to provide** ~ **for s. o.** jem. Unterhalt gewähren; **to share the** ~ gemeinsam für den Unterhalt aufkommen; **to sue for** ~ Unterhaltsklage erheben (anstrengen);
~ **advertising** Erhaltungswerbung; ~ **agreement** *(trade union)* vereinbarte Zwangsmitgliedschaft; ~ **allowance** Unterhaltszahlung, -zuschuß, -beihilfe; ~ **arrears** rückständige Unterhaltszahlungen, Unterhaltsrückstände; ~ **assessment** Instandhaltungsumlage; ~ **backlog** Nachholbedarf bei Instandsetzungsarbeiten; ~ **bond** *(coll.)* Garantie der Herstellungsfirma; ~ **budget** Wartungsetat; ~ **charges** Instand-, Unterhaltskosten, Wartungs-, Erhaltungsaufwand; ~ **claim** Unterhaltsanspruch; ~ **clause** *(last will)* Versorgungsbestimmung; ~ **contract** Wartungsabkommen; ~ **cost** Instandhaltungs-, Betriebs-, Wartungs-, Unterhaltungskosten, Erhaltungsaufwand; ~ **cost estimate** Schätzung der Unterhaltungskosten; ~ **cycle** Wartungs-, Unterhaltungszyklus; ~ **department** Instandset-

zungsabteilung; ~ **employees** Instandhaltungs-, Wartungspersonal; ~**-of-way employee** Streckenarbeiter; ~ **engineer** Wartungsingenieur; ~ **engineering** Instandhaltungs- und Pflegemaßnahmen; ~ **estimate** Schätzung des Unterhaltungsaufwands; ~ **expense** Instandhaltungs-, Instandsetzungs-, Unterhaltungskosten; ~ **expense account** Unterhaltungsaufwands-, Instandhaltungskonto; ~ **facilities** Wartungsanlagen; ~ **fee** *(US)* Vertragsstrafe; ~ **grant** Unterhaltszuschuß, -beihilfe; ~ **hall** Reparaturhalle; ~ **instruction** Instandhaltungsvorschrift; ~ **man** Wartungsmonteur; ~ **manager** Leiter der Instandhaltungsabteilung; ~ **obligation** Unterhaltspflicht; **to evade one's** ~ **obligations** sich seiner Unterhaltspflicht entziehen; ~ **order** *(Br.)* Unterhaltsurteil; ~ **payments** Unterhaltszahlungen, Unterstützungszahlungen; ~ **people** Wartungspersonal; ~ **personnel** Wartungspersonal; ~ **proceedings** Unterhaltsverfahren; ~ **reserve** Rückstellung für Instandhaltungskosten; ~ **section** Instandhaltungsabteilung; ~ **service** [Maschinen]wartung; ~ **staff** *(railway)* Betriebspersonal; **universal** ~ **standards** allgemein übliche Instandhaltungsrichtwerte; ~ **wages** das Existenzminimum deckender Lohn; **general** ~ **work** laufende Instandsetzungsarbeiten; **postponed** ~ **work** unterlassene Instandhaltung; ~ **workers** Wartungskräfte.

maintenor *(Br.)* außenstehender Prozeßtreiber.

maisonette *(French)* kleine Etagenwohnung, Kleinwohnung.

maitre Oberkellner;
~ **d'hôtel** Hotelbesitzer.

Majesty Majestät;
during Her ~**'s pleasure** bis auf Widerruf; **on Her** ~**'s service** *(Br.)* frei durch Ablösung, portofreie Dienstsache.

major Großjähriger, Mündiger, Volljähriger, *(mil.)* Major, *(~ subject, US)* Hauptfach, *(supervising workman, Br.)* Vorarbeiter;
~ *(v.) (US)* als Hauptfach studieren;
~ **on** *(fig.)* sich konzentrieren auf; ~ **in business administration** *(US)* sich auf Betriebswirtschaft spezialisieren; ~ **in a subject** *(US)* in einem Fach mit Auszeichnung bestehen;
~ *(a.)* größer, *(of full age)* volljährig, mündig;
~ **concern** Hauptanliegen; ~ **consumer goods** hochwertige Gebrauchsgüter; ~ **and minor fault rule** *(collision of vessels)* Beweispflicht für das Mitverschulden; ~ **objective** Hauptziel; ~ **overhaul** *(machinery)* umfassende Überholung; ~ **part of the assembly** Versammlungsmehrheit; ~ **part of the revenue** Haupteinnahmequelle; ~ **portion** Hauptanteil; ~ **repair** größere Reparatur; ~ **road** Vorfahrtstraße; ~ **selling day** Hauptverkaufstag; ~ **subordinate** Hauptuntergebener; ~ **supplier** Hauptlieferant; ~ **swing** *(US)* Marktentwicklung über einen größeren Zeitraum; ~ **vote** von der Mehrheit abgegebene Stimmen.

majoritarian rule Mehrheitsherrschaft.

majority Überzahl, Mehrheit, Majorität, *(full age)* Mündigkeit, Volljährigkeit, *(mil.)* Majorsrang, *(of votes)* Stimmenmehrheit;
after ~ nach Erreichung der Volljährigkeit; **by a** ~ **of votes** durch Mehrheitsbeschluß; **in the** ~ **of cases** in der Mehrzahl der Fälle; **overruled by the** ~ von der Mehrheit überstimmt;
absolute ~ absolute Majorität; **adverse** ~ Mehrheit gegen den Antrag; **antigovernment** ~ regierungsfeindliche Mehrheit; **bare** ~ einfache [Stimmen]mehrheit; **clear** ~ einfache Mehrheit; **comfortable** ~ sichere Mehrheit; **coupon** ~ Mehrheit parteitreuer Abgeordneter; **crushing** ~ erdrückende Mehrheit; **government's** ~ Regierungsmehrheit; **hair's-breadth** ~ hauchdünne Mehrheit; **large** ~ große Mehrheit; **left-wing** ~ Linksmajorität, -mehrheit; **narrow** ~ knappe Mehrheit; **overall** ~ absolute Mehrheit; **overwhelming** ~ überwältigende Mehrheit; **paper-thin** ~ hauchdünne Mehrheit; **parliamentary** ~ Parlamentsmehrheit; **particular (qualified)** ~ qualifizierte Mehrheit; **proportionate** ~ anteilsmäßige Mehrheit; **prospective** ~ erwartete Mehrheit; **relative** ~ relative Mehrheit; **requisite** ~ erforderliche Mehrheit; **silent** ~ schweigende Mehrheit; **simple** ~ einfache Mehrheit; **small** ~ geringe Mehrheit; **special** ~ qualifizierte Mehrheit; **three-fourths** ~ Dreiviertelmehrheit; **two-thirds** ~ Zweidrittelmehrheit; **vast** ~ überwiegende Mehrheit; **waver-thin** ~ hauchdünne Mehrheit; **whooping** ~ überwältigende Mehrheit; **working** ~ arbeitsfähige Mehrheit;
~ **in amount** *(company)* kapitalmäßige Mehrheit; ~ **in amount of claim** *(bankruptcy proceedings)* Mehrheit nach der Höhe der angemeldeten Forderungen; ~ **of the Cabinet** Kabinettsmehrheit; ~ **of the committee** Ausschußmehrheit; ~ **of a company** Gesellschaftsmehrheit; ~ **of creditors** Gläubigermehrheit; ~ **of creditors in number and value** zahlen- und forderungsmäßige Gläubigermehrheit; ~ **of qualified electors (voters)** Mehrheit

der abgegebenen Stimmen; ~ **in interest** anteilsmäßige Mehrheit; ~ **of members** Mehrheit nach Köpfen; ~ **in number** zahlenmäßige Mehrheit; ~ **in number and three-fourths in value** Mehrheit der erschienenen Gläubiger und 3/4 Mehrheit der angemeldeten Forderungen; ~ **in number and value of creditors** zahlen- und wertmäßige Gläubigermehrheit; ~ **in value of the creditors** Gläubigermehrheit nach der Höhe der angemeldeten Forderungen; ~ **of shares (stock, US)** Aktienmehrheit; ~ **of stock-holders** *(US)* kapitalmäßige Aktionärsmehrheit; ~ **of votes** Mehrzahl der abgegebenen Stimmen, Stimmenmehrheit; ~ **of those present and voting** Mehrheit der stimmberechtigten Anwesenden; ~ **of the workers** Gros der Arbeiter;
to attain one's ~ volljährig werden, Volljährigkeit erreichen; **to be in control of a** ~ über eine Mehrheit verfügen; **to be a few votes short of a** ~ um wenige Stimmen von der Majorität entfernt (in der Minderheit) sein, um wenige Stimmen unterliegen; **to be in a** ~ Mehrheit haben; **to be elected by a large** ~ mit großer Mehrheit gewählt werden; **to beat by a** ~ überstimmen; **to carry a vote by an overwhelming** ~ bei der Abstimmung eine überwältigende Mehrheit erhalten; **to combine with a** ~ in der Mehrheit aufgehen; **to command a** ~ **in the Senate** über eine Mehrheit im Senat verfügen; **to control a** ~ **of votes** über die Stimmenmehrheit (Majorität) verfügen; **to elect by an absolute** ~ mit absoluter Mehrheit wählen; **to form the** ~ Mehrheit bilden; **to gain a** ~ Mehrheit erhalten; **to have a** ~ **on the board** über eine Vorstandsmehrheit verfügen; **to have the** ~ **on one's side** über die Mehrheit verfügen, Stimmenmehrheit haben; **to identify o. s. with the** ~ sich der Mehrheit anschließen; **to install a left-wing** ~ Linksmajorität herbeiführen; **to lack an outright** ~ keine ausreichende Mehrheit haben; **to muster a robust** ~ sichere Mehrheit zusammenbringen; **to obtain the necessary** ~ erforderliche Mehrheit erzielen; **to pass by a simple** ~ mit einfacher Mehrheit verabschieden; **to poll a** ~ **of votes** Mehrheit der abgegebenen Stimmen erhalten; **to reach one's** ~ volljährig werden; **to receive the** ~ **cast** Mehrheit der abgegebenen Stimmen erhalten; **to secure a** ~ Mehrheit aufbringen (erzielen); **to secure a** ~ **of votes cast** Mehrheit der abgegebenen Stimmen erhalten; **to side with the** ~ sich der Mehrheit anschließen; **to swing a** ~ *(US)* über eine Mehrheit verfügen; **to take a decision by a simple** ~ Beschluß mit einfacher Mehrheit fassen;
~ **approval** Zustimmung der Mehrheit; ~ **control** Majoritätsstellung; ~ **decision** Mehrheitsbeschluß; ~ **demand** Forderungen der Mehrheit; ~ **election** Mehrheitswahl; ~ **government** Mehrheitsregierung; ~ **holding** Mehrheitsbeteiligung; ~ **interest** Mehrheitsbeteiligung; ~ **leader** *(parl.)* Mehrheitsführer; ~ **opinion** *(US)* Mehrheitsvotum; ~**-owned** im Mehrheitsbesitz, majorisiert; ~**-owned subsidiary** Tochtergesellschaft mit Mehrheitsbeteiligung der Mutter; ~ **ownership** Mehrheitsbeteiligung; ~ **party** Mehrheitspartei; **to hold** ~ **power** Vormachtstellung einnehmen; ~ **report** Mehrheitsbericht; ~ **representation** *(trade union)* Mehrheitsvertretung; ~ **resolution** Mehrheitsbeschluß; ~ **rights** Mehrheitsrechte; ~ **rule** *(election)* Mehrheitssystem, -prinzip; ~ **shareholder** *(Br.)* Besitzer der Aktienmehrheit, Mehrheitsaktionär; ~ **stake** Majoritätsbeteiligung; ~ **stock** *(US)* Aktienmehrheit; ~ **stock participation** *(US)* Mehrheitsbeteiligung; ~ **stockholder** *(US)* Mehrheitsaktionär, Besitzer der Aktienmehrheit; **to command** ~ **support** sichere Mehrheit haben; **to gain** ~ **support** Mehrheit für sich gewinnen; ~ **verdict** Mehrheitsurteil; ~ **view** Auffassung der Mehrheit; ~ **vote** Mehrheitsbeschluß, -abstimmung, -wahl; Stimmenmehrheit; **to step up** ~ **voting** Abstimmung nach Mehrheitsgrundsätzen forcieren; ~ **whip** Fraktionsführer der Parlamentsmehrheit.

majuscule Großbuchstabe, großer Anfangsbuchstabe.

make Erzeugnis, Fabrikat, Marke, Warenzeichen, *(brand)* [Marken]produkt, *(electric circuit)* Schließen, *(condition)* Beschaffenheit, Verfassung, Zustand, *(form)* Ausführung, Ausfertigung, Machart, *(literature)* Fassung, Stil, *(manufacture)* Herstellung, Produktion, Fabrikation, *(machine)* Bauart, Typ, *(maker's wage)* Macherlohn, *(output)* Ausstoß, Produktion[smenge];
of best English ~ beste englische Qualität; **of first-class** ~ in hervorragender Verarbeitung; **of first-rate** ~ erstklassig; **of French** ~ Erzeugnis französischer Herkunft; **on the** ~ *(sl.)* profitgierig, hinter dem Gelde her;
best ~ bestes Fabrikat; **first-rate** ~ erstklassiges Fabrikat; **foreign** ~ ausländisches Fabrikat; **inferior** ~ minderwertiges Fabrikat; **our own** ~ unser eigenes Fabrikat (Eigenfabrikat); **popular** ~ gut eingeführte Marke (Ware); **standard** ~ Normalausführung;
~ **of car** Automarke;

~ *(v.)* machen, *(execute in legal form)* ordnungsgemäß ausstellen, *(gain)* verdienen, *(manufacture)* fabrizieren, [ver]fertigen, erzeugen, herstellen, anfertigen, produzieren, *(port)* [Hafen, Land] anlaufen, *(print.)* druckfertig machen;

~ **s. o.** jds. Glück machen; ~ **absolute** rechtskräftig werden lassen; ~ **one's accounts with s. o.** mit jem. abrechnen; ~ **the acquaintance** Bekanntschaft machen, kennenlernen; ~ **an acquisition** erwerben; ~ **an address** Ansprache halten; ~ **allowance for** berücksichtigen; ~ **an allowance** [Preis] nachlassen, Rabatt geben; ~ **s. o. an allowance of $ 500 a year** jem. einen jährlichen Unterhaltsbetrag von 500 Dollar gewähren; ~ **amends** Schadenersatz leisten; ~ **an application** Antrag stellen; ~ **an appointment** Verabredung treffen; ~ **a long arm** sich gewaltig anstrengen; ~ **an arrangement with s. o.** Vereinbarung mit jem. schließen; ~ **an assignment** übertragen, zedieren; ~ **an audience** Zuhörerzahl schätzen; ~ **an award** Schiedsspruch fällen; ~ **a bargain** Geschäft abschließen; **to intend to ~ one's son a barrister** seinen Sohn für die Anwaltslaufbahn bestimmen; ~ **the best of it** das Beste herausholen; ~ **the best of a bad job** *(bargain)* retten, was zu retten ist; ~ **the best of one's way home** so schnell als möglich nach Hause zurückkehren; ~ **the best-seller list** *(US)* Bestseller sein; ~ **a bill of exchange** ausstellen; ~ **binding** verbindlich machen; ~ **blocks** klischieren; ~ **bones about** sich zieren (anstellen); ~ **no bones about it** nicht viel Federlesens machen; ~ **a book** Wetten annehmen; ~ **bricks without straw** aus nichts etw. machen, etw. aus dem Nichts aufbauen; ~ **a building** Gebäude errichten; ~ **it one's business** sich eine Sache angelegen sein lassen; ~ **a business of politics** im Hauptberuf Politiker sein; ~ **a successful businessman** erfolgreichen Geschäftsmann abgeben; ~ **a change in the program(me)** Programmänderung vornehmen; ~ **one's choice** seine Wahl treffen; ~ **the circuit** *(el.)* Kontakt schließen; ~ **a clean breast of it** sich etw. von der Seele reden; ~ **common cause** gemeinsame Sache machen; ~ **a complaint** Beschwerde einlegen, sich beschweren; ~ **a contract** Vertrag machen (abschließen); ~ **a conveyance** Übereignung vornehmen; ~ **a copy** Abschrift anfertigen; ~ **a good deal by** gutes Geschäft tätigen; ~ **a dead set** festen Entschluß fassen; ~ **a decision** Entscheidung fällen; ~ **a declaration** Erklärung abgeben; ~ **default** nicht bezahlen, seinen Verpflichtungen nicht nachkommen, *(fail to appear)* Gerichtstermin versäumen; ~ **a degree** akademischen Grad erlangen; ~ **demands on s. one's time** jds. Zeit beanspruchen; ~ **no difference** keinen Unterschied ausmachen; ~ **in the same direction** in die gleiche Richtung weisen; ~ **a discovery** Entdeckung machen; ~ **the whole distance in a week** gesamte Strecke in acht Tagen zurücklegen; ~ **distribution in stock** Gratisaktien verteilen; ~ **do with** mit etw. zurechtkommen; **do and mend** selbst wieder instandsetzen und sich behelfen; ~ **an effort** Anstrengung unternehmen; ~ **an emergency landing** Notlandung vornehmen, notlanden; ~ **an end of s. th.** einer Sache ein Ende machen; ~ **both ends meet** mit seinem Einkommen auskommen; ~ **an entry** Eintragung (Buchung) vornehmen; ~ **one's escape** erfolgreichen Fluchtversuch unternehmen; ~ **evident** beweisen, klarstellen; ~ **an exhibition** Ausstellung veranstalten; ~ **an expedition** Expedition unternehmen; ~ **in s. one's favo(u)r** zu jds. Gunsten sprechen; ~ **a fool of o. s.** sich blamieren; ~ **a fortune** Vermögen machen; ~ **free with s. o.** sich jem. gegenüber Vertraulichkeiten herausnehmen; ~ **a friend of s. o.** sich mit jem. befreunden; ~ **a garden** Garten anlegen; ~ **a friendly gesture to s. o.** freundliche Geste jem. gegenüber machen; ~ **good** ersetzen, vergüten; ~ **good arrears** Rückstände begleichen; ~ **good a damage** Schaden ersetzen; ~ **good a deficiency (loss)** Schaden decken, für einen Schaden aufkommen, Verlust abdecken; ~ **good gossip** Stoff für die Klatschtanten abgeben; ~ **one's hand** Profit machen (erzielen); ~ **a hash of s. th.** etw. verpatzen; ~ **hay while the sun shines** das Eisen schmieden, solange es heiß ist; ~ **headway** Fortschritte machen; ~ **s. o. one's heir** j. zu seinem Erben bestimmen; ~ **for home** sich auf den Heimweg machen; ~ **first honors** *(US)* erste Auszeichnungen erhalten; ~ **an excellent husband** ausgezeichneten Ehemann abgeben; ~ **one's influence fee** seinen Einfluß zur Geltung bringen; ~ **inquiries** Erkundigungen einziehen; ~ **intrigues** Ränke schmieden; ~ **it** *(US)* es schaffen; ~ **it tough** schwieriges Problem aus einer Sache machen; ~ **a bad job of s. th.** etw. verpatzen; ~ **a journey** Reise unternehmen; ~ **s. o. a judge** j. zum Richter ernennen; ~ **a judgment** sich ein Urteil bilden; ~ **known** bekanntgeben; ~ **land** Land ausmachen; ~ **s. th. last** sich etw. einteilen; ~ **a law** Gesetz machen; ~ **a law of no effect** Gesetz wirkungslos machen; ~ **s. o. liable for s. th.** j. haftbar machen; ~ **light of** als nicht schwierig behandeln; ~ **a lip** seine Verachtung zeigen; ~ **a**

living seinen Lebensunterhalt verdienen; ~ **a loan** Kredit gewähren; ~ **margin** *(print.)* Randbreite festsetzen; ~ **one's mark** sein Handzeichen setzen, unterschreiben, *(fig.)* einflußreichen Posten bekommen; ~ **good marks at school** gute Zensuren in der Schule erhalten; ~ **one's market** sein Warenlager absetzen; ~ **a matter of conscience** seinem Gewissen folgen; ~ **to measure** nach Maß anfertigen; ~ **a mess of s. th.** etw. verpatzen (vermurksen); ~ **money** Geld verdienen; ~ **money by economies** einsparen; ~ **money of s. th.** etw. veräußern; ~ **money of an execution** Zwangsvollstreckung realisieren; ~ **the most of s. th.** intensiven Gebrauch von etw. machen; ~ **a mountain out of a molehill** aus der Mücke einen Elefanten machen; ~ **a poor mouth** Armut vorschützen; ~ **s. one's mouth water** jem. das Wasser im Munde zusammenlaufen lassen; ~ **a move** Zug machen, *(coll.)* Initiative ergreifen; ~ **much of** als bedeutsam hinstellen; ~ **a name for o. s.** sich einen Namen machen; ~ **s. o. a newcomer** j. für einen Neuling halten; ~ **a note** Wechsel ausstellen; ~ **nothing of it** für unwichtig halten; ~ **oath and depose** als Zeuge unter Eid aussagen; ~ **objections** Einwände erheben; ~ **an offer** Angebot (Offerte) abgeben; ~ **to order** auf Bestellung anfertigen; ~ **a new organization** neue Organisation ins Leben rufen; ~ **an out** *(print.)* etw. zu setzen vergessen; ~ **one of the party** mitmachen; ~ **payable** zahlbar stellen; ~ **payment** Zahlung leisten; ~ **an additional (supplementary) payment** Nachzahlung leisten; ~ **one's peace with** Frieden schließen, Streit beilegen; ~ **plans** Pläne schmieden; ~ **into the political scene** *(sl.)* sich politisch engagieren; ~ **into port** in den Hafen einlaufen; ~ **twenty pounds a day** zwanzig Pfund am Tag verdienen; ~ **a practice of it** Gewohnheit daraus machen; ~ **s. o. a president** j. zum Präsidenten wählen; ~ **a price** Preis festsetzen (bestimmen); ~ **prize of** als Prise nehmen; ~ **a profit** Gewinn erzielen; ~ **a profit of $ 100.000** 100.000 Dollar verdienen; ~ **progress** vorankommen, Erfolg haben; ~ **a promissory note** Schuldschein ausstellen; ~ **propaganda** Werbetrommel rühren; ~ **provision for** Vorkehrungen treffen, *(balance sheet)* Rücklage bilden; ~ **public** veröffentlichen; ~ **a public notice** öffentlich bekanntgeben; ~ **a purchase** Einkauf tätigen; ~ **purparty** Ländereien aufteilen; ~ **a query** Rückfrage halten; ~ **a quorum** beschlußfähig sein; ~ **random tests** Stichproben machen; ~ **s. th. read differently** in andere Worte fassen; ~ **excellent reading** hervorragende Lektüre abgeben; ~ **ready** zurichten; ~ **a reduction** Rabatt gewähren, Abzug vornehmen; ~ **remittance** in bar überweisen, remittieren; ~ **a report** Bericht erstatten; ~ **a request** Gesuch einreichen; ~ **a return** Einkommensteuererklärung abgeben; ~ **a road** Straße anlegen; ~ **a rule** Regel aufstellen; ~ **a sacrifice** Opfer bringen; ~ **sail** Reise antreten; ~ **samples** Warenproben zusammenstellen; ~ **for the open sea** in See stechen; ~ **a search for contraband** nach Konterbande fahnden; ~ **s. o. smart** j. Schmerzensgeld zahlen lassen; ~ **a special provision about** besondere Bestimmung vorsehen; ~ **a speech** Rede halten; ~ **a statement** Erklärung abgeben; ~ **for stock** lagermäßig herstellen; ~ **sure** auf Nummer Sicher gehen; ~ **a table of statistics** statistische Tabelle aufstellen; ~ **terms** Bedingungen stellen; ~ **a testament** Testament errichten; ~ **good time** gut vorankommen; ~ **things hum** *(sl.)* Leben in die Bude bringen; ~ **a town** *(US)* Stadt besichtigen; ~ **a train** Zug erreichen (erwischen); ~ **trouble** Schwierigkeiten bereiten; ~ **o. s. understood** sich verständlich machen; ~ **use** gebrauchen, verwerten, Gebrauch machen; ~ **full use** voll auswerten (ausnutzen); ~ **valid** validieren, gültig machen; ~ **void** annullieren, anfechten; ~ **wages** durch Mehrarbeit eine Lohnerhöhung erzielen; ~ **s. o. wait** j. hinhalten, j. warten lassen; ~ **war upon a country** Krieg gegen ein Land führen; ~ **way** Platz machen; ~ **one's way in the world** Erfolgsmensch sein; ~ **fair weather** schmeicheln; ~ **heavy weather** *(fig.)* nur unter Schwierigkeiten vorankommen; ~ **a will** Testament errichten; ~ **work** unnötig komplizieren; ~ **short work of** kurzen Prozeß machen; ~ **the worst of s. th.** etw. gänzlich heruntermachen;

all I ~ by (on) it mein ganzer Verdienst.

make away sich davonmachen (aus dem Staube machen), beiseite schaffen;

~ **with o. s.** Selbstmord begehen; ~ **with a document** Urkunde beseitigen; ~ **with one's fortune** sein Vermögen durchbringen.

make for ansteuern, Kurs haben auf;

~ **s. th.** etw. garantieren; ~ **one's advantage** sich zu jds. Vorteil (günstig auf j.) auswirken; ~ **better reception** *(aerial)* Empfang verbessern; ~ **the open sea** in See stechen.

make off losschlagen, veräußern;

~ **with s. th.** sich mit etw. aus dem Staube machen; ~ **with the cash** mit der Kasse durchbrennen; ~ **with an umbrella** Schirm versehentlich mitnehmen.

make out *(draw up)* ausstellen, ausfertigen, *(fill out)* ausfüllen, *(find out)* ausfindig machen, feststellen, herausbekommen, *(list)* aufstellen, *(have success, US)* gut abschneiden;
~ **o. s. out cleverer than one really is** sich für klüger halten, als man in Wirklichkeit ist; ~ **an account** Rechnung ausstellen; ~ **to bearer** auf den Inhaber ausstellen; ~ **a bill of exchange** Wechsel ausstellen; ~ **in blank** blanko ausstellen; ~ **a case** Klage begründen; ~ **a check** *(US)* **(cheque,** *Br.***) to s. o.** Scheck auf j. ausstellen; ~ **a document in duplicate** Urkunde in doppelter Ausfertigung ausstellen; ~ **a handwriting** Handschrift entziffern; ~ **of the harbo(u)r** aus dem Hafen auslaufen; ~ **an inscription** Inschrift entziffern; ~ **an invoice** Rechnung ausstellen; ~ **a list** Aufstellung anfertigen, Liste erstellen; ~ **out the meaning of a letter** Briefinhalt verstehen; ~ **the money** Geld herbeischaffen; ~ **a passport** Paß ausstellen; ~ **a road** Weg markieren; ~ **together badly** schlecht miteinander auskommen.
make over *(alternate, US)* umarbeiten, umändern, *(transfer)* abtreten, übertragen, übereignen;
~ **the business to one's son** Geschäft auf seinen Sohn übertragen; ~ **a debt** Forderung abtreten; ~ **one's estate** sein Vermögen hinterlassen (vermachen); ~ **one's estate in fee** Fideikommiß errichten; ~ **the whole of one's property to a trust** sein gesamtes Vermögen einer Stiftung vermachen.
make up *(accounts)* ausgleichen, *(compensate)* wiedergutmachen, ersetzen, *(dispute)* beilegen, *(document)* verfassen, abfassen, *(go to a coach)* Nachhilfeunterricht nehmen, *(list)* aufstellen, *(print.)* umbrechen, *(put together)* zusammenstellen, *(supply deficiency)* vervollständigen, vollmachen;
~ **an account** Konto abschließen; ~ **one's accounts** seine Bücher abschließen, Jahresabschluß machen; ~ **one's accounts with s. o.** mit jem. abrechnen; ~ **an amount** Defizit ersetzen; ~ **a considerable amount** beträchtliche Summe darstellen; ~ **the average** Dispache aufmachen; ~ **a balance sheet** Bilanz aufstellen; ~ **a bed for the unexpected guests** für unerwartete Gäste ein Bett aufstellen; ~ **the cash** Kassensturz machen; ~ **on a competitor** Konkurrenten schlagen; ~ **for a deficiency** Verlust wiedereinbringen (ausgleichen, decken); ~ **the deficiency** Fehlendes ergänzen; ~ **the deficit** Fehlbetrag decken; ~ **the difference** Unterschied ausgleichen; ~ **the even money** Saldo ausgleichen; ~ **one's income** sein Einkommen erhöhen; ~ **an inventory** Lagerbestand (Inventur) aufnehmen, Inventur machen; ~ **it up** wiedergutmachen; ~ **it up with s. o.** sich mit jem. versöhnen; ~ **leaway** *(fig.)* Versäumtes nachholen; ~ **a list** Liste aufstellen; ~ **for one's losses** sich erholen; ~ **for lost ground** verlorenes Gelände wiedergewinnen; ~ **one's mind** sich entschließen, Entschluß fassen; ~ **the missing number of a publication** seine Sammlung vervollständigen; ~ **a page of type** Druckseite fertigmachen; ~ **a parcel** Paket packen; ~ **to influential people** sich Vorteile bei einflußreichen Leuten verschaffen; ~ **a prescription** Arznei verordnen; ~ **a new railway guide** neuen Fahrplan zusammenstellen; ~ **the requisite sum** fehlende Summe ergänzen (aufbringen); ~ **a shortage** Fehlbetrag ausgleichen; ~ **sleep** Schlaf nachholen; ~ **a speech** Rede ausarbeiten; ~ **statistics** Statistik aufstellen; ~ **a story** Geschichte erfinden; ~ **for lost time** verlorene Zeit aufholen (einbringen); ~ **a train of cars** Zugfolge zusammenstellen;
to be on the ~ *(fam.)* aufs Geld aus sein.
make | believe Spiegelfechterei, Vorstellung, Heuchelei, Heuchler; ~ **and break** *(techn.)* Unterbrecher; ~**-good** *(advertising)* kostenlose Ersatzanzeige, *(broadcasting)* Ersatzwerbedurchspruch; ~**-job policy** Arbeitsbeschaffungspolitik; ~ **and mend** *(mil., Br.)* Putz- und Flickstunde; ~**-out artist** *(sl.)* erfolgreicher Verführer; ~ **ready** *(printing)* Zurichtung; ~**-ready time** *(production)* Vorbereitungszeit.
make-up Verfassung, Struktur, Zusammensetzung, -stellung, *(cosmetics)* kosmetische Mittel, *(examination, US)* Wiederholungsprüfung, nachgeholter Kurs, *(film)* Ausstattung, -staffierung, *(laying out)* Aufmachung, Ausstattung, Verpackung, *(print.)* Umbruch, Klebespiegel;
~ **of a book** Buchausstattung; ~ **of the cabinet** Zusammensetzung des Kabinetts; ~**of packets** Verpackung von Paketen; ~ **of a society** Zusammensetzung eines Vereines;
~ **galley** Setzschiff; ~ **man** Umbruchredakteur; ~ **pay** *(US)* Akkordzuschlag; ~ **proof** Umbruchkorrektur; ~ **regulations** *(post)* Aufmachungsbestimmungen; ~ **section** Mettageabteilung; ~ **wages** *(piece work)* Ausgleichslohn; ~ **work** Aufholarbeit, nachgeholte Arbeitszeit.
make work *(trade union)* Arbeitsbeschaffungspraktiken;
~ **increase in government spending** zur Arbeitsbeschaffung vorgenommene Erhöhung der Staatsausgaben.

makebate Störenfried, Unruhestifter.
makefast Festmacheboje.
maker *(of bill)* Wechselgeber, -aussteller, *(drawer)* Aussteller *(manufacturer)* Hersteller, Produzent, Erzeuger, Fabrikant; **accommodation** ~ Gefälligkeitsaussteller; **balance** ~ Bilanzersteller; **joint** ~ *(bill of exchange)* Mitaussteller;
~ **of a note** Ausstellung eines Solawechsels; ~ **up** *(print.)* Metteur;
~**'s number** Fabriknummer; ~**'s trademark** Herstellungszeichen.
makeshift Notbehelf, Aushilfe, Lückenbüßer, Surrogat, Provisorium;
~ *(a.)* behelfsmäßig, provisorisch;
~ **construction** Behelfskonstruktion.
makeweight Gewichtszugabe, *(makeshift)* Lückenbüßer, Notbehelf;
to be the ~ Zünglein an der Waage sein.
making [An]fertigung, Herstellung, Fabrikation, Erzeugung, *(quantity manufacture)* Produkt, *(structure)* Bauart, Zusammensetzung;
material and ~ Material und Löhne;
~**s** *(earnings)* Verdienst, Einnahmen, Profit;
~ **away** Vernichtung; ~**s of a great man** Qualitäten einer Persönlichkeit; ~ **a false entry** Vornahme einer Falschbuchung; ~ **an offer** Abgabe einer Offerte; ~ **a profit** Gewinnerzielung; ~ **of a will** Testamentsabfassung, -errichtung;
to be in the ~ noch nicht fertiggestellt sein; **to have the ~s of it** Zeug dazu haben.
making out *(document)* Ausfertigung, Ausstellung;
~ **of an account** Rechnungsausstellung; ~ **a check** *(US)* **(cheque,** *Br.***)** Scheckausstellung; ~ **of a list** Listenaufstellung.
making | over Übertragung, -eignung; ~ **payments for customers** Durchführung von Zahlungsaufträgen von Kunden; ~ **of program(me)s** Programmgestaltung.
making up Entschädigung;
~ **the account** *(books)* Abschluß der Bücher, Kontenabschluß; ~ **a balance sheet** Bilanzaufstellung; ~ **the budget** Haushalts-, Etataufstellung; ~ **the cash** Kassenabschluß; ~ **an inventory** Inventuraufstellung; ~ **and imposing** *(print.)* Umbruch; ~ **a list** Listenaufstellung; ~ **for losses** Verlustausgleich; ~ **of one's mind** Meinungsbildung; ~ **of monthly reports** Zusammenstellung von Monatsberichten; ~ **of trains** Zugzusammenstellung.
making-up | day *(Br.)* Prämienerklärungs-, Reporttag, zweiter Liquidationstag; ~ **price** *(Br.)* Lieferungs-, Abrechnungskurs, Liquidationspreis, -kurs.
mala fide in bösem Glauben, bös-, schlechtgläubig, arglistig, unredlich;
~ **purchaser** bösgläubiger Erwerber.
mala fides Bösgläubigkeit, Arglist.
maladjusted *(person)* milieugestört.
maladjustment schlechte Anpassung, Mißverhältnis, *(sociology)* Fehlanpassung, Milieustörung;
~ **in the balance of payments** Störungen der Zahlungsbilanz; ~ **of prices** Preisschere.
maladminister *(v.)* schlecht verwalten.
maladministration Mißwirtschaft, Korruption;
~ **of justice** Rechtsbeugung, Ämterkauf.
maladministrator Betrüger.
malady chronische Krankheit;
social ~ soziale Zerrüttung.
malcontent Mißvergnügter, politischer Agitator;
~ *(a.)* mit der Regierung unzufrieden.
maldistribution schlechte (mangelhafte) Verwaltung;
~ **of wealth** ungleiche Vermögensverteilung.
male | heir männlicher Erbe; ~ **line [of descent]** Mannesstamm; ~ **person** Person männlichen Geschlechts.
malediction üble Nachrede, Verleumdung.
malefaction Missetat, Verbrechen.
malefactor Misse-, Übeltäter.
malevolence Böswilligkeit, Arglist.
malevolente mißgünstig, feindselig.
malfeasance gesetzwidrige Handlung, rechtswidriges Handeln, fehlerhafte Amtsführung, Gesetzesübertretung;
~ **in office** Vergehen im Amt, Amtsvergehen.
malfeasant gesetzwidrig, kriminell.
malfunction Panne, Defekt;
~ *(v.)* schlecht funktionieren, Defekt, Mißbildung haben, [technische] Panne haben;
to warn of any ~ **in the lighting, braking and fuel systems** Versagen der Lichtanlage, der Bremsvorrichtungen und des Treibstoffsystems anzeigen.

malice Arglist, Böswilligkeit, Vorsatz, Dolus;
with ~ **aforethought (prepense)** in böswilliger Absicht, vorsätzlich;
actual ~ Schädigungsabsicht; ~ **aforethought** vorbedachte böse Absicht, Vorsatz; **constructive** ~ unterstellter Verbrechensvorsatz; **express** ~ Schädigungsabsicht; **general** ~ kriminelle Veranlagung; **implied** ~ vermutete böse Absicht; **legal** ~ vermuteter Vorsatz; **particular** ~ Rachedurst; **premeditated** ~ Tötungsvorsatz; **universal** ~ Hang zum Verbrecher; ~ **in fact** Schädigungsabsicht; ~ **in law** Vorsatz.

malicious arglistig, boswillig, vorsätzlich, heimtückisch; ~ **abandonment** *(spouse)* böswilliges Verlassen; ~ **abuse of legal process** Vollstreckungsmißbrauch; ~ **accusation** leichtfertige (falsche) Anschuldigung; ~ **act** vorsätzliche Handlung; ~ **arrest** Freiheitsberaubung im Amt, rechtswidrige Festnahme, ungerechtfertigte Verhaftung; ~ **falsehood** *(Br.)* Anschwärzung; ~ **gossip** üble Nachrede; ~ **injury** vorsätzliche Körperverletzung; ~ **intent** böswillige Absicht; ~ **killing** vorsätzliche Tötung, Mord; ~ **mischief** *(Scot., US)* vorsätzliche Sachbeschädigung; ~ **prosecution** mutwilliges Prozessieren; ~ **remarks** hämische Bemerkungen; ~ **trespass** vorsätzliche (mutwillige) Sachbeschädigung; ~ **use in process** Vollstreckungsmißbrauch.

malign *(v.)* **an innocent person** Unschuldigen verleumden.

malinger *(v.)* sich krank stellen, Krankheit vorschützen, simulieren.

malingerer Scheinkranker, Simulant, Drückeberger.

malingering Simulieren.

malnutrition Unterernährung, schlechte Ernährung.

malpractice gesetzwidriges Verhalten, gesetzwidrige Handlungsweise, ungehöriges Verhalten, strafbare Handlung, *(official)* Amtsmißbrauch, *(physician)* Kunstfehler, Pfuscherei, *(professional misconduct)* Vernachlässigung der beruflichen Sorgfaltspflicht, standeswidriges Verhalten;
professional ~ Kunstfehler;
~ **insurance** Versicherung gegen Kunstfehler.

malproduction Überproduktion.

malt tax *(Br.)* Malzsteuer.

maltreat *(v.)* mißhandeln.

maltreatment schlechte Behandlung, Mißhandlung, *(surgeon)* Kunstfehler.

malversation korruptes Verhalten, Veruntreuung, Unterschleif, *(malpractice)* Amtsmißbrauch;
~ **of public money** Amtsunterschlagung.

mama's boy Muttersöhnchen.

mammon Mammon, irdische Güter, Reichtum;
to worship ~ dem Mammon dienen.

mammoth | business enterprise Mammutkonzern, -unternehmen;
~ **losses** Riesenverluste.

man Mensch, Mann, Person, *(servant)* Diener, Angestellter, *(mar.)* Matrose, *(mil.)* Soldat;
per ~ pro Person;
allround ~ Alleskönner; **best** ~ Trauzeuge; **colo(u)red** ~ Farbiger, **confidence** ~ Hochstapler; **contact** ~ Kontakter, Verbindungsmann, Behördenvermittler; **credit** ~ Kreditfachmann; **educated** ~ gebildeter Mensch; **family** ~ verheirateter Mann; **ideas** ~ *(advertising, Br.)* Ideenspezialist, -gestalter; **key** ~ Schlüsselkraft, Hauptperson, unentbehrliche Arbeitskraft, *(liaison)* Verbindungsmann; **moral** ~ Mensch mit moralischen Grundsätzen; **odd-job** ~ Gelegenheitsarbeiter; **old** ~ Chef; ~ **overboard** Mann über Bord; **public** ~ Mann der Öffentlichkeit; **reliable** ~ zuverlässiger Mann; **self-made** ~ Autodidakt; **set-up** ~ guter Mann; **underground** ~ Grubenarbeiter; **university** ~ Akademiker; **waiting** ~ Diener;
~ **of action** Tatmensch; ~ **to bank on** ein Mann auf den man sich verlassen kann; ~ **of business** Geschäfts-, Kaufmann; **one's** ~ **of business** jds. geschäftlicher Vertreter; ~ **of great discretion** sehr besonnener Mann; ~ **of education** gebildeter Mann; ~ **of established position** angesehener Mann; ~ **of estate** Mann von hohem Rang; ~ **of figures** Zahlenmensch; ~ **Friday** treu ergebener Diener; **the** ~ **of the hour** der Mann des Tages; ~ **of ideas** ideenreicher Mensch; ~ **of impulse** impulsiver Mensch; ~ **of influence** einflußreiche Persönlichkeit; ~ **of iron** erbarmungsloser Mann; ~ **of law** Vertreter des Gesetzes; ~ **of letters** Gelehrter, Wissenschaftler; ~ **of mark** markante Persönlichkeit; ~ **of means (property)** begüterter Mann; ~ **on parole** bedingt Entlassener; ~ **of many parts** vielseitiger Mann; ~ **of another paste** Mensch von ganz anderem Schlag; ~ **of pleasure** Genußmensch; ~ **of poise** ausgeglichener Mensch; ~ **of prestige** angesehene Persönlichkeit; ~ **on the spot** örtlicher Vertreter; ~ **of straw** vorgeschobene Person, Strohmann; ~ **in the street**

Durchschnittsmensch; ~ **about town** Gesellschaftsmensch, Salonlöwe; ~**-of-war** Kriegsschiff; ~ **of all work** Hans Dampf in allen Gassen, Faktotum; ~ **of the world** Weltmann; ~ **and men** Arbeitgeber und Arbeitnehmer;
~ *(v.) (ship)* bemannen;
~ **a fortress** Besatzung in eine Festung legen; ~ **and supply a ship** Schiff ausrüsten;
to be a ~ **of caliber** Format haben; **to be a** ~ **of the widest culture** umfassende Bildung haben; **to be an Oxford** ~ in Oxford studiert haben; **to be one's own** ~ selbständig sein; **to be the strong** ~ **in the organization** der starke Mann in einem Verband sein; **to feel a new** ~ sich wie neugeboren fühlen; **to know s. o. and boy** j. schon als Jungen gekannt haben; **to launch a young** ~ **in business** jungen Mann unterbringen; **to live as** ~ **and wife** wie Mann und Frau zusammenleben; **to play the** ~ sich mutig zeigen; **to satisfy the inner** ~ Mahlzeit zu sich nehmen;
~**-days lost** verlorene Arbeitstage; ~**-hour** Arbeitsstunde; **nominal** ~**-hour** Sollarbeitsstunde; ~**-hours lost** verlorene Arbeitsstunden, Ausfallstunden, Arbeitsverlust, -zeitausfall; ~**-hours worked** geleistete Arbeitsstunden (Arbeitszeit); **no** ~**'s land** Niemandsland; ~**-made** von Menschenhand geschaffen, künstlich; ~**-made customs** menschliche Gebräuche; ~ **midwife** Geburtshelfer; ~**-made fibres** Kunststoffe; ~ **output** Ausstoß pro Arbeitsstunde; ~ **rating** Leistungseinstufung.

manacles Handfesseln.

manage *(v.) (administer)* verwalten, führen, *(conduct)* [Betrieb] leiten, Geschäft führen, *(contrive)* fertigbringen, bewerkstelligen, zurechtkommen, zustande bringen, einrichten, *(control)* beaufsichtigen, dirigieren, *(get on)* sich durchbringen, lavieren, *(get up)* veranstalten, organisieren, *(handle)* behandeln, handhaben, bedienen, umgehen mit, *(household)* vorstehen, leiten, *(jockey)* einfädeln, deichseln, *(landed property)* bewirtschaften, *(makeshift)* sich behelfen, möglich machen, es schaffen, auskommen;
~ **s. o.** j. zu nehmen wissen; ~ **with $ 100** mit 100 Dollar auskommen können; ~ **one's own affairs** seine eigenen Angelegenheiten erledigen; ~ **s. one's affairs** jds. Angelegenheiten besorgen; ~ **the affairs of State** Staatsangelegenheiten führen; ~ **a sailing boat** mit einem Segelboot zurechtkommen; ~ **a business** Geschäft führen; ~ **increased diversity** der Führung einer immer breitgefächerten Unternehmensgruppe gerecht werden; ~ **to do** es hinkriegen; ~ **an estate** Gut bewirtschaften; ~ **without help** ohne Hilfe auskommen; ~ **in spite of lack of funds** auch ohne Geldmittel zurechtkommen; ~ **without help** ohne Hilfe auskommen; ~ **a household** Haushalt leiten; ~ **it** etw. schaffen; ~ **on less** mit weniger auskommen; ~ **with little money** mit wenig Geld durchkommen; ~ **a matter** Sache deichseln; ~ **on one's pay** mit seinem Gehalt auskommen; ~ **a piece of work** Arbeit bewältigen; ~ **real estate** Immobilienbesitz verwalten; ~ **on a modest salary** mit einem bescheidenen Gehalt auskommen; ~ **somehow** sich irgendwie behelfen; ~ **the stage effects with great skill** hervorragender Bühnenbildner sein; ~ **a town** Stadtverwaltung leiten;
to have a fortune to ~ Vermögensverwaltung haben; **to know how to** ~ **s. o.** j. zu nehmen wissen.

manageable handlich, leicht zu regulieren, gefügig, willfährig, folgsam;
~ **proportion** überschaubares Ausmaß.

managed | bonds Schuldobligationen über eine breitgestreute Anlagesumme; ~ **currency** manipulierte Währung; ~ **economy** Planwirtschaft; ~ **fund** *(US)* Investmentfonds mit auswechselbarem Wertpapierbestand; ~ **money** Papiergeld ohne Deckung; ~ **trust** *(US)* Kapitalanlagegesellschaft mit wechselndem Portefeuille.

management *(administration)* Verwaltung, Betrieb, *(company)* Geschäftsleitung, Verwaltungsspitze, Direktion, [Geschäfts-]vorstand, *(conducting of business)* Leitung, Geschäfts-, Betriebsführung, -leitung, *(entrepreneurship)* Unternehmertum, *(executives)* leitende Angestellte, Führungskräfte, *(handling)* Handhabung, Behandlung, *(of house, US)* Hausverwaltung, *(of landed property)* Bewirtschaftung, *(organizational talent)* Organisationstalent, *(railway)* Betriebsplan;
in the judgment of the ~ nach Ansicht der Geschäftsleitung; **under new** ~ nach Geschäftsübernahme, unter neuer Leitung; **advanced** ~ mittlere Führungsschicht; **aggressive** ~ unternehmerischer Vorstand; **bad** ~ schlechte Betriebsführung; **brand** ~ Markenbetreuung; **business** ~ Geschäfts-, Wirtschaftsführung, Betriebswirtschaft; **central** ~ Zentralverwaltung; **co-** ~ Mitbestimmung; **corporate** ~ Geschäftsleitung; **debt** ~ *(US)* Bundesschuldenverwaltung; **demand** ~ Nachfragesteuerung; **editorial** ~ redaktionelle Leitung; **effective** ~ *(double taxation)*

tatsächliche Geschäftsleitung; **executive** ~ Geschäftsleitung; **factory** ~ Betriebs-, Fabrikleitung, Betriebsverwaltung; **farm** ~ Gutsverwaltung, landwirtschaftliche Betriebsführung; **general** ~ Gesamtgeschäftsführung; **ill** ~ schlechte Verwaltung, Mißwirtschaft; **industrial** ~ Betriebsführung; **internal** ~ Betriebsleitung; **investment** ~ Verwaltung von Kapitalanlagen; **middle** ~ *(US)* mittlere Führungsschicht (Führungskräfte); **multiple** ~ Unterstützung der obersten Führungskräfte durch Arbeitnehmervertreter; **personnel** ~ Personalverwaltung; **plant** ~ Betriebsleitung; **poor** ~ schlechte (mangelhafte) Geschäftsführung; **production** ~ Führung eines Produktionsbetriebes; **proper** ~ ordnungsgemäße Bewirtschaftung; **prudent** ~ umsichtige Leitung; **scientific** ~ wissenschaftliche Betriebsführung; **shop** ~ Betriebsleitung; **sole** ~ alleinige Geschäftsführung; **strong** ~ energische Geschäftsführung; **superannuated** ~ pensionsreifer Vorstand; **top** ~ oberste Führungskräfte, Unternehmensspitze, Zentralverwaltung;

~ **by alternatives** Betriebsführung durch das Angebot von Variationsmöglichkeiten; ~ **of a case** Prozeßführung; ~ **of cash funds** Verwaltung von Zwischenanlagebeträgen; **central** ~ **of a combine** Konzernleitung; ~ **by communication and participation** Betriebsführung nach Informierung und Anhörung; ~ **of a corporation** Verwaltungsspitze einer Gesellschaft; ~ **of the national debt** Bundesschuldenverwaltung; ~ **by decision rules** Betriebsführung anhand eines Verhaltenskatalogs; ~ **by delegation** Betriebsführung im partizipativen Führungsstil; ~ **of direction and control** Betriebsführung im autoritären Stil; ~ **of the economy** staatliche Stabilitätspolitik; ~ **of an estate** Gutsverwaltung; ~ **by exception** *(US)* Betriebsführung nur in Ausnahmefällen (nach Ausnahmeprinzipien); **poor** ~ **of expenditure** schlechte Ausgabenwirtschaft; ~ **of a fair** Messeleitung; ~ **of a firm** Unternehmens-, Firmenleitung; ~ **of a hospital** Krankenhausverwaltung; ~ **of a house** Haushaltsführung; ~ **by innovation** Betriebsführung durch ständiges Streben nach Systemerneuerung; ~ **and labo(u)r** Tarifpartner; ~ **of land** Bodenbewirtschaftung; ~ **of men** Menschenführung; ~ **by motivation** Betriebsführung durch Darlegung überzeugender Beweggründe; ~ **by objectives** Betriebsführung durch Zielvorgabe; ~ **of a program(me)** Durchführung eines Programms; ~ **of property** Grundstücks-, Vermögensverwaltung; ~ **by results** zielgesteuerte Unternehmensführung; ~ **of securities** Effektenverwaltung; ~ **of a ship** technische Bedienung eines Schiffes; ~ **by system** Betriebsführung durch Systematisierung aller Leitungs- und Kontrolltätigkeiten; ~ **by teaching** Betriebsführung mittels weitgehender Weiterbildung;

to assume the ~ **of affairs** Erledigung von Sachen in die Hand nehmen; **to be due to bad** ~ auf schlechte Verwaltung zurückzuführen sein; **to be under new** ~ neue Geschäftsführung haben; **to change the** ~ Vorstand auswechseln; **to copy the** ~ **of the money supply on the fiscal side** Geldversorgung der Wirtschaft mit steuerlichen Maßnahmen unterstützen; **to dismantle central** ~ zentralgesteuerte Verwaltungsspitze auflösen; **to draft in a new** ~ neue Geschäftsführung einsetzen; **to have a voice in the** ~ in der Verwaltung (Leitung) mitzureden haben; **to have a technical 50 - 50 voice in the** ~ ziffernmäßig zu 50% an der Geschäftsführung beteiligt sein; **to invest the** ~ **of a bank in s. o.** jem. die Leitung einer Bank übertragen; **to represent** ~ **in labo(u)r disputes** Unternehmertum in arbeitsrechtlichen Auseinandersetzungen vertreten; **to resign from** ~ von der Geschäftsführung zurücktreten; **to share (take part) in the** ~ an der Geschäftsführung teilnehmen; **to structure one's** ~ **from scratch** Führungsgremium von Grund auf umstrukturieren; **to supply the** ~ **with advice** dem Vorstand beratend zur Verfügung stehen; **to take a large share in the** ~ an der Geschäftsführung entscheidend beteiligt sein;

~ **ability** Führungsqualitäten; ~ **accountancy** betriebliche Rechnungsprüfung; ~ **accountant** betrieblicher Rechnungsprüfer; ~ **accounting** Rechnungswesen für bestimmte Betriebsführungsbedürfnisse; **to supply** ~ **advice** dem Vorstand beratend zur Verfügung stehen; ~ **adviser** Unternehmens-, Vorstandsberater, Berater der Geschäftsführung; ~ **advisory committee** Beratungsgremium des Vorstands; ~ **agreement** Geschäftsführungsvereinbarung; ~ **appointments** Positionen für Führungskräfte; ~ **appraisal** Unternehmensbewertung; ~ **audience** Managerlesekreis; ~ **audit** Vorstandsbewertung; ~ **board** Vorstandsgremium; ~ **cabinet** *(US)* aus Nachwuchskräften zusammengesetzte Betriebsführung; ~ **cadre** Verwaltungskader; ~ **career** Unternehmerlaufbahn, Verwaltungskarriere; ~ **cash-incentive scheme** Tantiemenregelung für leitende Angestellte; ~ **center** Ausbildungszentrum für Führungskräfte; ~ **changes** Vorstandswechsel, Wechsel (Veränderung) im Vor-

stand; ~ **committee** Verwaltungsausschuß, geschäftsführender Ausschuß, Geschäftsführungsausschuß, *(local government, Br.)* Hauptausschuß; ~ᵉ **Committee** *(EG)* Direktorium; ~ **company** *(US)* Betriebsführungsgesellschaft, *(investment fund, US)* Verwaltungsgesellschaft; ~ **concept** Vorstandskonzeption; ~ **consultancy** Unternehmens-, Vorstandsberatung; ~ **consultant** Unternehmens-, Betriebs-, Vorstands-, Industrieberater; ~ **consulting** Betriebs-, Unternehmensberatung; ~ **consulting firm** Unternehmensberatung[sgesellschaft], Beratungsfirma; ~ **consulting organization** Unternehmensberatungsgesellschaft; ~ **contract** Verwaltungs-, Vorstandsvertrag; ~ **control** Vorstandsbereich, -ressort; ~ **council** Direktorium; ~ **counsellor** Unternehmens-, Betriebs-, Industrie-, Vorstandsberater; **top-level** ~ **decision** Entscheidung auf höchster Ebene; ~ **decline** stetig nachlassende Führungsqualifikationen; ~ **department** Verwaltungsabteilung; ~ **development scheme** Nachwuchsförderungswesen; ~ **education** Nachwuchsausbildung; ~ **efficiency** Leistungsfähigkeit des Vorstandes; ~ **engineer** hervorragender Betriebsführer; ~ **engineering** *(US)* Betriebstechnik; ~ **expense** Geschäftsführungs-, Verwaltungskosten; [**general**] ~ **experience** unternehmerische Erfahrung, Unternehmererfahrung; **to be heavy on organizational** ~ **experience** erhebliche Erfahrungen in der Leitung eines Unternehmens haben; ~ **expertise** Führungskunst; ~ **fee** Vorstandsvergütung, Geschäftsführungshonorar, *(investment trust)* Verwaltungskosten, -gebühr; ~ **fee bonus** *(investment trust)* Prämie für erfolgreiche Verwaltungstätigkeit, Verwaltungsprämie; **general** ~ **field in industry** Aufgabengebiet im Vorstandsbereich; ~ **flexibility** bewegliche Führungsmethoden; ~ **functions** Führungstätigkeit, -aufgaben, Betriebsführungsfunktionen; ~ **fund** Investmentfonds mit veränderlichem Portefeuille; ~ **game** Betriebsplanspiel; ~ **goal** bestmögliche Belegschaftsverwendung; ~ **group** Führungsgruppe; ~ **guide** Handbuch für die Geschäftsführung; ~ **hierarchy** Betriebshierarchie; ~ **incentive** Verwaltungsprämie; ~ **information** Information der Führungskräfte; ~ **input** Einsatz von Führungspersonal; ~ **inventory** Stellenbesetzungsplan für Führungskräfte; ~ **investment company** Kapitalanlagegesellschaft mit Freizügigkeit in der Anlagepolitik; **to retool their** ~ **knowledge** ihr Führungsinstrumentarium umrüsten; ~ **level** Führungsniveau, -höhe, -schwelle; **on middle** ~ **level** auf dem Gebiet der mittleren Führungskräfte; ~ **office** Verwaltungsbüro, -gebäude; ~ **organization** Verwaltungsorganisation, Betriebsorganisation; ~ **participation** betriebliche Mitbestimmung; ~ **perfection** Führungswirksamkeit; ~ **permission** Genehmigung durch die Geschäftsleitung; ~ **personnel** Führungskräfte; ~ **planning** Betriebs-, Unternehmensplanung; ~ **policy** Betriebs-[führungs]-, Unternehmenspolitik; ~ **position** leitende Position, Führungsposition; **top-level** ~ **position** Spitzenposition; ~ **practice** Betriebsführungspraxis; ~ **principles** Grundsätze der Betriebsführung; ~ **problems** Probleme der Geschäftsführung; ~ **profession** führende Berufsschicht; ~ **rating** Vorstandsbeurteilung; ~ **ratio** Verhältnis der leitenden Angestellten zur Belegschaft, betriebswirtschaftliche Proportion; ~ **report** Vorstandsbericht; ~ **representative** Unternehmensvertreter; ~ **reserve group** *(US)* Führungsnachwuchsgruppe; ~ **of exchange risk** Eingrenzung der Wechselkursrisiken; ~ **science** Wissenschaft von der Betriebsführung, Betriebsführungswissenschaft; ~ **science research** Forschungstätigkeit im Bereich der Betriebsführung; **to come into the** ~ **scene** in den Vorstand gelangen, seinen Vorstandsaufstieg bewerkstelligen; ~ **secretary** Direktionssekretär[in]; ~ **seminar** Nachwuchsseminar; ~ **shares** *(US)* Vorstandsaktien, Genußscheine für den Vorstand; ~ **sharing** *(US)* Beteiligung an der Geschäftsführung; ~ **skills** Führungsqualitäten; ~ **stock** *(US)* Vorstandsaktien; ~ **strategy** langfristige Unternehmenspolitik, Betriebsführungspolitik; ~ **strike** Streik der Führungskräfte; ~ **structure** Führungsstruktur; ~ **study** Studium der Betriebsführung; ~ **style** Führungsstil; ~ **subject** Betriebsführungsfach; ~ **survey** Untersuchung über die Führungskräfte; ~ **switch** Austausch von Vorstandsmitgliedern; ~ **talent** Führungsqualitäten, -begabung; ~ **team** Führungsgruppe, Verwaltungskörper, -rat; **top** ~ **team** Spitzengremium; **to hold one's** ~ **team** seine leitenden Angestellten an sich binden; ~ **technique** Betriebsführungsverfahren, Führungsmethoden; **sophisticated** ~ **techniques** raffinierte Betriebsführungsmethoden; **to update its** ~ **techniques** Führungsapparat modernisieren; ~ **trainee** Nachwuchskraft, Führungsnachwuchs; ~ **trainee (training) course** Ausbildungskurs für Nachwuchskräfte; ~ **training** Ausbildung von Führungskräften, Nachwuchsausbildung; ~ **training adviser** Berater in der Nachwuchsschulung; ~ **trust** Kapitalanlagegesellschaft mit freizügiger Anlagepolitik, nach eigenem Ermessen anlegende Kapitalgesellschaft; **general ~ trust** Investmentgesellschaft mit breitgestreutem Aktienportefeuille (umfassendem Anlagefonds); ~ **ultimatum** Ultimatum der Geschäftsführung.

managemental unternehmerisch.

manager (administration) Verwalter, Leiter, Vorsteher, (broadcasting, film, theater) Regisseur, Intendant, Impresario, (conductor of business) Betriebsleiter, -führer, Geschäftsführer, Unternehmensleiter, Direktor, (estate) Bewirtschafter, Verwalter, Gutsinspektor, (film actress) Manager, persönlicher Berater, (law, Br.) vom Gericht eingesetzter Treuhänder, (managing clerk) Disponent, Faktor, (organizer) Veranstalter, Organisator;

~s Direktion, Vorstand;

acting ~ Betriebsleiter, geschäftsführender Direktor; **advertising ~** Leiter der Werbeabteilung, Werbechef, Propagandaleiter; **assistant ~** stellvertretender Direktor; **bank ~** Bankdirektor; **branch ~** Filialleiter, -vorsteher; **business ~** kaufmännischer Leiter, Geschäftsführer; **chief ~** Betriebsleiter, Hauptgeschäftsführer; **city ~** (US) Amtsbürgermeister, Oberstadtdirektor; **commercial ~** kaufmännischer Leiter; **credit ~** Leiter der Kreditabteilung; **data-processing ~** Leiter der Datenverarbeitung; **departmental ~** Abteilungsleiter (Direktor); **deputy ~** stellvertretender Geschäftsführer (Direktor); **district ~** Gebietsleiter; **estate ~** Guts-, Grundstücksverwalter, Gutsinspektor; **export ~** Exportleiter; **factory ~** Betriebs-, Werksleiter, Fabrikdirektor; **farm ~** Gutsverwalter, -inspektor; **financial (finance) ~** Leiter des Finanz- und Rechnungswesens; **functional ~** fachliche Führungskraft; **general ~** geschäftsführendes Vorstandsmitglied, Betriebsführer, (US) Generaldirektor; **head ~** Betriebsleiter, Generaldirektor; **hotel ~** [Hotel]geschäftsführer, -direktor; **immediate ~** unmittelbarer Vorgesetzter; **information ~** Leiter der Marktforschung; **marketing ~** Leiter der Abteilung Absatzförderung, Vertriebsleiter; **merchandise ~** Leiter der Ein- und Verkaufsabteilung; **office ~** Büroleiter; **operations (plant) ~** (US) Betriebsleiter, -direktor; **owner-~** Alleinunternehmer, selbständiger Betriebsleiter; **personnel ~** Leiter der Personalabteilung, Personaldirektor, -chef; **production ~** Produktionsleiter; **prospective ~s** Führungsnachwuchs; **publicity ~** Leiter der Public-Relations-Abteilung; **sales ~** Verkaufsleiter, Leiter der Verkaufsabteilung; **sales promotion ~** Leiter der Verkaufsförderung; **saving ~** sparsamer Verwalter; **special ~** gerichtlich bestellter Geschäftsführer, Einzelliquidator; **staff ~** Personalchef; **stage ~** Intendant; **store ~** Geschäftsführer; **technical ~** technischer Direktor (Leiter); **top-level ~** oberste Führungskraft; **top-performing ~** äußerst erfolgreicher Geschäftsführer; **traffic ~** Betriebsaufseher; **woman ~** Geschäftsführerin; **works ~** (Br.) Betriebs-, Werks-, Fabrikleiter;

receiver and ~ (Br.) Vermögensverwalter mit Geschäftsführungsbefugnis;

~ of a bank Bankdirektor; **~ of a branch office** Filialleiter; **~s of a conference** (parliament) Mitglieder eines Vermittlungsausschusses; **~ of credit** Kreditfachmann; **~ of a hotel** Hoteldirektor; **~ of men** Menschenführer;

to appoint a ~ Geschäftsführer bestellen; **to ask for the ~** Geschäftsführer verlangen; **to be a bad ~** nicht einteilen können; **to be an excellent ~** sehr gut wirtschaften können; **to remove a ~** Geschäftsführer abberufen;

~'s authority Geschäftsführungsbefugnis; **~ education** Managerausbildung; **~ thinking** Managerdenkweise; **~ underwriter** Konsortialführer.

manageress Geschäftsführerin, Betriebsleiterin.

managerial führend, geschäftsleitend, unternehmerisch, direktorial;

high ~ agent (US) Abteilungsleiter; **~ appointments** Berufung in leitende Stellungen; **~ assistance** Führungshilfe; **~ behavio(u)r** (US) Verhalten einer Führungskraft; **in a ~ capacity** in leitender Stellung; **~ class** Unternehmerschicht; **~ decisions** Maßnahmen der Betriebsleitung; **~ disease** Managerkrankheit; **~ duties** Direktionsaufgaben; **~ economics** (US) allgemeine Betriebswirtschaftslehre; **~ employee** leitender Angestellter; **~ task force** Sondereinsatzgruppe der Geschäftsführung; **~ function** Unternehmerfunktion; **~ group** Betriebsgruppe; **~ hierarchy** Hierarchie der leitenden Angestellten; **at ~ level** auf Führungs-, Vorstandsebene; **~ market** Managerleserkreis; **~ occupation** leitende Berufsfunktion, führende Stellung; **high-income ~ people** hochverdienendes Management, Führungskräfte mit hohem Einkommensniveau; **~ policy** Unternehmenspolitik; **~ position (post)** führender Posten,

Führungsposten, leitende Stellung; **~ prerogative** Unternehmervorrecht; **~ problems** Probleme der Betriebsführung, Führungsprobleme; **~ qualities** Unternehmereigenschaften; **~ ranks** betriebliche Rangordnung; **~ representation** Unternehmervertretung; **~ revolution** Managerrevolution; **~ secretary** Vorstandssekretär[in]; **~ staff** Verwaltungskörper, Geschäfts-, Betriebsleitung, Führungskräfte; **~ state** Betriebsimperium; **~ system** Unternehmertum; **~ success** Erfolg als Unternehmer; **~ talent** unternehmerische Fähigkeiten, Unternehmerbegabung; **~ techniques** Führungsmethoden; **new ~ techniques** neue Methoden in der Unternehmensführung; **~ work** Arbeit von Führungskräften.

managership Geschäftsführertätigkeit, Managertum.

managing Geschäftsführung, Betriebsleitung, Verwaltung;

~ (a.) (conducting) leitend, geschäftsführend, verwaltend, (economizing) wirtschaftlich, sparsam;

~ agent Geschäftsführer; **~ board** Verwaltung, Verwaltungsrat, Vorstand, Direktorium; **~ body** geschäftsführendes Organ; **~ clerk** Geschäftsleiter, -führer, Bevollmächtigter, Prokurist, Bürovorsteher, leitender Angestellter; **~ committee** Vorstand, geschäftsführender Ausschuß, Direktionsausschuß, Verwaltungsausschuß; **~ company** (Br.) Verwaltungsgesellschaft; **~ director** (Br.) geschäftsführendes Vorstandsmitglied, Generaldirektor, Betriebs-, Geschäftsführer; **~ directors** geschäftsführender Verwaltungsrat einer AG; **~ directorship** Vorstandsvorsitz; **~ editor** Chef vom Dienst; **~ man** Vertreter der Geschäftsführung, (estate) Gutsverwalter, -inspektor; **~ owner of a ship** Korrespondenzreeder; **~ partner** geschäftsführender Gesellschafter (Teilhaber); **~ position** leitende Position, Führungsposten, -position; **~ president** geschäftsführender Präsident; **to fulfil(l) a ~ role** Verwaltungsaufgabe wahrnehmen.

manche-present Bestechungsgeschenk.

Manchester | goods Baumwolltextilien; **~ policy** Manchestertum; **~ school** Manchesterschule.

mandamus gerichtliche Verfügung an eine untergeordnete Instanz;

alternative ~ Gegeneinwände gestattende Gerichtsverfügung; **interlocutory ~** (Br.) einstweilige Verfügung; **peremptory ~** zwingende Gerichtsverfügung.

mandarin (coll.) hoher Beamter, (Br., sl.) rückständiger Parteiführer;

~ mountain Moloch der Beamtenhierarchie.

mandat Befehl, Erlaß, Vorschrift, (proxy) Auftrag, Vollmacht, Mandat.

mandatary Beauftragter, Bevollmächtigter, [Prozeß]bevollmächtigter, Auftragsnehmer, Sachverwalter, (treaty of Versailles) Mandatsträger, -regierung.

mandate (banking) Kontovollmacht, (contract of bailment) Mandat, [Mandats]auftrag, Vollmacht, Geschäftsbesorgungsvertrag (court order) Vollstreckungsbefehl, Verordnung, Erlaß, Verfügung, Weisung, (international law) Mandat[sauftrag], (mandated territory) Mandatsgebiet, (order) Verordnung, Erlaß, Weisung, Verfügung, (parl.) Mandat, (power of attorney) Prozeßvollmacht;

dividend ~ Inkassoauftrag für Dividendenerträgnisse; **electoral ~** Abgeordnetenmandat; **international ~** unter internationaler Aufsicht ausgeübtes Mandat; **written ~** schriftliche [Bank]vollmacht;

~ (v.) einem Mandat unterstehen;

~ a country to one of the Powers einem Staat (einer Großmacht) ein Mandat über ein Land übertragen;

to confer a ~ on a power einem Staat ein Mandat übertragen; **~ form** Vollmachtsformular, (banking) Verzeichnis der Unterschriftsberechtigten; **~ government** Mandatsregierung; **~s system** (League of Nations) Mandatssystem.

mandated | area Mandatsgebiet; **~ colony** Kolonialmandat, Mandatskolonie; **~ territory** Mandatsgebiet.

mandatee Beauftragter, Bevollmächtigter.

mandator Auftrag-, Vollmachtgeber, Mandant.

mandatory Bevollmächtigter, Mandatsträger, (international law) Mandatsmacht, -regierung;

~ (a.) obligatorisch, zwingend, zwangsläufig, unabdingbar, pflichtgemäß, verbindlich, verpflichtet;

~ by law vom Gesetz vorgeschrieben;

to make s. th. ~ upon s. o. jem. etw. vorschreiben;

~ clause (US) Mußvorschrift; **~ injunction** einstweilige Verfügung wegen einer gegenständlichen Leistung; **~ instructions** (US) verbindliche Anweisungen; **~ power** Mandatsmacht, -regierung; **~ provision** (US) unabdingbare (zwingende) Bestimmung, Mußvorschrift; **~ statutory provisions** zwingende gesetzliche Bestimmung; **~ removal** zwangsweise Entlassung; **~ requirements** unabdingbare Voraussetzungen; **~ retirement** Zwangspensionierung; **~ retiring age** festgelegtes (vorgeschriebenes, obligatorisches) Pensionsalter (Ruhestandsalter); **~ settlement** Zwangsregelung; **~ state** Mandatsträger, -staat; **~ statute** zwingendes Gesetz; **~ writ** gerichtliche Verfügung.

manhandle *(v.)* **a drunkard** mit einem Betrunkenen unsanft umgehen.

manhole Einsteigloch, Luke;
~ cover *(road)* Schachtdeckel.

manhood Mannesalter, Volljährigkeit;
to reach ~ mannbar werden;
~ suffrage männliches Wahlrecht.

manhunt *(trainees)* Nachwuchsjagd.

manhunter Nachwuchsjäger.

manifest öffentliche Erklärung, Manifest, *(customs)* Zolldeklaration, *(invoice)* Lade-, Warenverzeichnis, Ladungsmanifest, Frachtliste, -brief, *(party politics)* Wahlaufruf, *(public manifestation)* Kundgebung;
bonded ~ Freigut; **cargo ~** Ladeverzeichnis; **inward ~** Zolleinfuhrerklärung; **outward ~** Zollausfuhrerklärung;
~ *(v.)* offenbaren, darlegen, manifestieren, kundtun, verkünden, *(demonstrate)* Kundgebung veranstalten;
~ great activity Geschäftigkeit entfalten; **~ a cargo** Ladung[sverzeichnis] anmelden; **~ itself** *(disease)* zum Ausbruch kommen; **~ the truth of a statement** Richtigkeit einer öffentlichen Erklärung bestätigen;
to split ~s on transatlantic flights wechselweise Benutzung von Charter- und Linienflugzeugen im Transatlantikverkehr ermöglichen;
~ *(a.)* offenkundig, augenscheinlich, deutlich, klar, offenbar, handgreiflich, manifest;
~ freight beim Zoll vorzulegende Exportsendung; **~ injustice** offenkundige Ungerechtigkeit; **~ ton** *(water carrier)* Ladungseinheit, -tonne.

manifestant Abgeber eines Ladungsverzeichnisses, *(partaker of manifestation)* Kundgebungsteilnehmer.

manifestation Offenbarung, Manifestation, *(party)* Wahlprogramm, *(politics)* politische Kundgebung, Demonstration;
~ of life Lebensäußerung; **~ of time** Zeit-, Fristnachweis.

manifesto *(US)* Grundsatzerklärung, Proklamation;
election ~ Wahlproklamation.

manifold hektografierter Abzug, Durchschlag, Kopie;
~ *(v.)* vervielfältigen, hektografieren;
~ *(a.)* mannigfaltig, vielfach, vielseitig, vielseitig verwendbar;
~ book Durchschreibebuch; **~ classification** *(statistics)* Mehrfacheinteilung; **~ duties** vielseitige Aufgaben; **~ form of entry** Mehrfachformular für Eintragungen; **~ paper** Vervielfältigungspapier, Saugpost; **~ plug** Vielfachstecker; **~ system** Vervielfältigungssystem, -methode; **~ traitor** Verräter in mehrfacher Hinsicht; **~ writer** Vervielfältigungsapparat.

manifolder Vervielfältigungsapparat.

manifolding Vervielfältigungsarbeiten;
~ machine Vervielfältigungsapparat.

manipulable *(market)* beeinflußbar.

manipulate *(v.)* *(cook)* frisieren, zurechtstutzen, *(handle)* handhaben, behandeln, *(influence)* manipulieren, künstlich beeinflussen, deichseln, schieben;
~ accounts Bücher frisieren; **~ the currency** Währung manipulieren; **~ election returns** Wahlergebnisse verfälschen; **~ exchange rates** Wechselkurse manipulieren; **~ the market** *(stock exchange)* Markt beeinflussen, Börsenkurse manipulieren; **~ s. th. towards objectives** durch geschickte Kniffe etw. seinem Ziel näherbringen; **~ stocks** Aktien manipulieren; **~ one's supporters** seine Anhänger bei der Stange halten; **~ the trading profit by means of general provisions** Betriebsgewinn durch allgemeine Rückstellungen manipulieren; **~ voters** Wähler beeinflussen.

manipulation Handhabung, Behandlung, Manipulation, Manöver, *(stock exchange)* Kursbeeinflussung, -manipulierung;
~s unsaubere Machenschaften (Praktiken);
business (fraudulent) ~ betrügerisches Geschäftsgebaren; **~ of accounts** Kontenfälschung; **~ of the currency** Manipulation der Währung, Währungsmanipulation; **~ of an election** Wahlschwindel, -manipulation, Manipulation einer Wahl; **~ of the market** Kursmanipulation; **~ on the stock exchange** Börsenmanöver;
to make a lot of money by clever ~s of the stock market viel Geld durch geschickte Börsenmanöver verdienen; **to upset ~s** Machenschaften vereiteln.

manipulator Manipulierer, *(stock exchange)* Kursbeeinflusser.

manipulatory manipulierend.

mankind Menschheit, Menschengeschlecht.

mannequin Mannequin, Vorführdame;
~ parade Modenschau.

manner *(conduct)* Auftreten, Benehmen, Umgangsformen, *(method of procedure)* Verfahren, Modus, Methode, Art und Weise, *(style)* Manier, Stilart;
by no ~ of means unter keinen Umständen; **in a grand ~** auf großem Fuße;
as to the ~ born wie hineingeboren;
~s Benehmen, Umgangsformen, Manieren, Sitten, Gebräuche;
bad ~s schlechte Manieren; **business ~** Geschäftsgebaren; **the grand ~** altmodisches Benehmen; **liberal ~** unbefangenes Auftreten; **pothouse ~s** Benehmen wie in der Kneipe; **rustic ~** bäuerisches (ungehobeltes) Benehmen; **shocking bad ~s** *(fam.)* absolut unmögliche Manieren; **soft ~s** höfliches Auftreten; **unrefined ~s** unfeines Benehmen;
~ of calculation Berechnungsart; **~ of conveyance** Beförderungsart; **~ of delivery** Versandform; **sparse ~ of fighting** aufgelockerter Kampfstil; **all ~ of political goals** alle möglichen politischen Ziele; **~ of interpretation** Auslegungsweise; **~ of packing** Verpackungsart; **~ of payment** Zahlungsweise, -modus; **all ~ of things** alles Mögliche; **~ of voting** Wahlverfahren, -methode; **~ of working** Arbeitsweise, -verfahren;
to answer in an easy ~ ungezwungen antworten; **to have an awkward ~** sich linkisch benehmen; **to have bad ~s** schlechte Manieren haben; **to have quite a ~** distinguiert auftreten; **to make one's ~s** sich verbeugen; **to teach s. o. ~s** j. Mores lehren.

mannerism gekünstelter Stil.

mannerliness gutes Benehmen, gute Kinderstube.

manning *(ship)* Bemannung;
~ level Ebene für Personalentscheidungen; **to cut ~ levels** Personalbestand abbauen; **to reduce ~ levels in other departments** Belegschaftsstärke in anderen Abteilungen abbauen; **~ table** *(US)* fachlich aufgegliederte Personalkartei, Stellenbesetzungsplan.

manor Rittergut, Land-, Herrensitz, *(history)* Grundherrschaft, *(US)* Pachtland;
reputed ~ früheres Rittergut;
~ house Gutshaus, Schloß, Herrensitz.

manorial herrschaftlich;
~ rights Grundeigentümerrechte.

manoeuvre *(Br.)* **manoeuver** *(US)* Manöver, Schachzug, Kunstgriff, Manipulieren, Manipulation, Finte, schlaues Vorgehen, *(mar.)* Flottenmanöver, *(mil.)* Truppenbewegung, -übung, [Luft]manöver;
army ~s Heeresmanöver; **fleet ~s** Flottenmanöver; **underhand ~** geheime Machenschaften, Intrigen;
~ of diversion Ablenkungsmanöver; **~s of a politician** Machenschaften eines Politikers;
~ *(v.)* geschickt zu Werke gehen, manövrieren, manipulieren;
~ off the East coast an der Ostküste Manöver durchführen; **~ s. o. into a corner** *(fam.)* j. in eine ausweglose Lage manövrieren; **~ the enemy out of a position** Feind aus einer Stellung vertreiben; **~ a friend into a good job** einem Freund eine gute Stellung besorgen; **~ s. o. out of s. th.** j. aus etw. herausmanövrieren; **~ one's car into a difficult parking space** sein Auto in eine schwierige Parklücke hereinmanövrieren; **~ for position** *(fam.)* sich in eine gute Stellung hineinmogeln.

manoeuvrability Manövrierfähigkeit, *(fig.)* Beweglichkeit;
~ of a car Beweglichkeit eines Autos.

manoeuvrable manövrierfähig, beweglich.

manoeuvrer Taktiker, Schlaumeier, Intrigant.

manpower menschliche Arbeitskraft, Leistungsfähigkeit eines Mannes, *(labo(u)r force)* verfügbare Arbeitskräfte, Personalbestand, *(mil.)* Menschenmaterial, *(total strength)* Iststärke;
exportable ~ im Ausland einsetzbare Arbeitskräfte; **rural ~** landwirtschaftliche Arbeitskräfte; **skilled ~** ausgebildete Fachkräfte; **surplus ~** Überschuß an Arbeitskräften; **technical ~** Fachkräfte;
to [make] call on ~ Arbeitskräfte in Anspruch nehmen; **to cut down military ~** Iststärke herabsetzen; **to recruit ~** *(US)* Arbeitskräfte einstellen;
~ [forecasting] approach Arbeitskräftebedarfsansatz; **~ budget** Personaletat; **~ control** Arbeitslenkung; **~ development program(me)** betriebliches Fortbildungsprogramm; **~ establishment** Personalbestand; **~ front** Arbeitskräftefront; **~ inventory** Personalkartei; **~ management** Arbeitseinsatz; **~ market** Arbeitsmarkt; **~ need** Arbeitskräftebedarf; **~ planning** Arbeits-

kräfteeinsatz, Personalplanung; ~ **policy** personalpolitische Grundsätze eines Unternehmens; ~ **program(me)** Arbeitsbeschaffungsprogramm; ~ **requirements** Arbeitskräftebedarf; ~ **reserve** Arbeitskräftereservoir; ~ **resources** Bestand an Arbeitskräften; **to buy** ~ **resources** Nachwuchskräftebedarf decken; ~ **savings** Einsparung von Arbeitskräften; ~ **shortage** Mangel an Arbeitskräften, Arbeitskräftemangel; ~ **situation** Arbeitsmarktlage; ~ **strength** Belegschaftsstärke; ~ **surplus** Überschuß an Arbeitskräften; ~ **training** Ausbildung von Arbeitskräften; ~ **training program(me)** *(US)* Programm für Schulung ungelernter Arbeiter; ~ **withdrawal** Truppenabzug.

mansard Mansarde;
~ **roof** Mansardendach.

manservant Diener.

mansion herrschaftliches Wohnhaus, Gutshaus;
~s *(Br.)* Mietskaserne, -haus, Wohngebäude;
~ **and lands pertaining to** Gutshaus und dazugehörende Ländereien;
~ **house** Herrenhaus, -sitz.

manslaughter vorsätzliche Körperverletzung mit tödlichem Ausgang, fahrlässige Tötung, Totschlag;
involuntary ~ fahrlässige Tötung; **misdemeanor** ~ *(US)* Vergehen mit Todesfolge; **voluntary** ~ vorsätzliche Tötung [im Affekt].

manslayer Totschläger.

manslaying Totschlag.

manticulate *(v.)* Taschendiebstahl begehen.

mantle *(fig.)* Schutz-, Deckmantel, *(company)* Mantel;
to adopt a ~ sich einen Standpunkt zu eigen machen; **to inherit s. one's** ~ in jds. Rolle schlüpfen;
~ **children** später legitimierte Kinder.

mantrap Fußangel, *(fig.)* Falle.

manual *(handbook)* Vorschriften-, Instruktions-, Handbuch, Leitfaden, Manual, Führer, *(interviewer)* Gebrauchsanweisung, Leitfaden, *(mil.)* Dienstvorschrift;
accounting ~ Leitfaden für das Rechnungswesen; **field writer's** ~ Handbuch für Interviewer; **shorthand** ~ Handbuch für Stenographie; **sign** ~ eigenhändige Unterschrift;
~ *(a.)* mit der Hand, manuell;
~ **alphabet** Fingeralphabet; ~ **aptitude** manuelle Begabung; ~ **mechanical bookkeeping** Durchschreibebuchhaltung; ~ **control** Handbedienung; ~ **delivery** tatsächliche Übergabe, *(donation)* Erfüllung eines Schenkungsversprechens; ~ **exchange** Fernsprechvermittlung mit Handbetrieb; ~ **gift** Handschenkung; ~ **labo(u)r** körperliche Arbeit; ~ **labo(u)rer** Handarbeiter; ~ **operation** Handbedienung; ~ **possession** tatsächlicher Besitz; ~ **press** Handpresse; ~ **rate** *(insurance)* Ausgangstarif; ~ **rates** *(Oklahoma Inspection Bureau)* sozialer Unfallversicherungstarif; ~ **seal** Handsiegel; ~ **shifting** *(car, US)* Handschaltung; ~ **sign** ~ eigenhändige Unterschrift; ~ **skill** Handfertigkeit; ~ **training** Werkunterricht; ~ **typesetting** Handsatz; ~ **work** körperliche Arbeit, Handarbeit; ~ **worker** ungelernter Arbeiter, Handarbeiter.

manually signed handschriftlich unterzeichnet, eigenhändig unterschrieben.

manufactory Fabrikations-, Herstellungsbetrieb, Fabrik[gebäude], Werk;
to set up a ~ Fabrikationsbetrieb einrichten.

manufacture Herstellung, Verarbeitung, Fabrikation, fabrikmäßige Herstellung, Verfertigung, Anfertigung, Produktion, Ausstoß, *(line of industry)* Industrie-, Fabrikationszweig, *(manufactured article)* Industrieprodukt, hergestellter Artikel, Erzeugnis, Fertigware, Fabrikat, Fabrikwaren;
apparel ~ Konfektionsindustrie; **direct-marketing** ~ Fabrikhandel; **domestic** ~ einheimisches Fabrikat; **durable** **~s** Dauergüter; **nondurable** **~s** Verbrauchsgüter; **home (inland)** ~ einheimisches Fabrikat; **industrial** **~s** gewerbliche Fertigwaren; **large-scale** ~ Massenherstellung, Großserienfertigung; **semi-** **~s** Halbfabrikate; **serial** ~ Reihen-, fabrikmäßige Herstellung, Serienfabrikation; **wholesale** ~ Massenfabrikation;
~ **to customer's specification** Einzelanfertigung;
~ *(v.)* fabrikmäßig (maschinell) herstellen, fabrizieren, Produktionsstätten unterhalten, produzieren, erzeugen, anfertigen, ausstoßen *(work up)* verarbeiten;
~ **goods in various qualities** Waren verschiedenster Qualität herstellen; ~ **under licence** Herstellungslizenz ausnutzen; ~ **news** *(fam.)* Neuigkeiten fabrizieren; ~ **public opinion** öffentliche Meinung künstlich beeinflussen (manipulieren);
to be faulty in its ~ Fabrikationsfehler haben; **to discontinue the** ~ Herstellung einstellen; **to supply a defect in** ~ Fabrikationsfehler beseitigen.

manufactured fabrikmäßig hergestellt;
properly ~ ordnungsgemäß hergestellt;
~ **article** Fabrikware, -erzeugnis, Fertigfabrikat; ~ **goods (items)** Fabrikware, Industriewaren, -artikel; ~ **products** industriell hergestellte Produkte, Industrieprodukte, -erzeugnisse; ~ **stage** Fabrikationsstadium.

manufacturer Fabrikant, Hersteller[firma], Industrieller, Erzeuger, Produzent, *(owner)* Fabrikbesitzer;
direct-marketing (-selling) ~ direkt absetzender Hersteller, Fabrikhändler; **diversified** ~ Herstellungsbetrieb mit einem breiten Produktionsprogramm; **lower-cost** ~ billigerer Herstellungsbetrieb;
~ **of cars** Auto[mobil]fabrikant; ~ **and retailer** Selbstverkäufer.

manufacturer's│agent *(US)* Industrie-, Werks-, Fabrikvertreter, Vertreter von Herstellungsfirmen; ~ **brand** Fabrikmarke; ~ **catalog(ue)** Preisliste, -verzeichnis; ~ **cost** Herstellungskosten, Selbstkostenpreis des Herstellers; ~ **cost price** Fabrikationspreis, Industrievertriebskosten; ~ **excise** *(US)* Herstellerumsatz-, Fabrikatsteuer; ~ **export agent** *(US)* Exportvermittler; ~ **goods** Produktionsgüter; ~ **liability** Haftung des Herstellers, Produzentenhaftung; ~ **liability doctrine** Grundsatz der Produzentenhaftung; **not to sell below the** ~ **list prices** Listenpreise des Herstellers einhalten; ~ **mark** Warenzeichen, Fabrikmarke; ~ **number** Herstellungs-, Fabrikationsnummer; ~ **price** Herstellungspreis; ~ **product** Firmenerzeugnis; ~ **public liability insurance** Betriebshaftpflichtversicherung; ~ **representative** Werksvertreter; ~ **sales price** Verkaufspreis ab Fabrik; ~ **own shop** betriebseigene Verkaufsfiliale; ~ **sign** Fabrikzeichen; ~ **tax** Herstellerumsatz-, Fabrikationssteuer; ~ **warranty** Haftung des Herstellers, Produzentenhaftung.

manufacturing [fabrikmäßige] Herstellung, Verarbeitung, Fabrikation, Produktion;
mobile-home ~ Herstellung transportabler Häuser; **quantity** ~ Massenherstellung, -erzeugung, Serienproduktion;
~ *(a.)* gewerbetreibend, fabrikatorisch, herstellend, fabrizierend;
to expand into ~ sich zusätzlich auf die Herstellung verlegen;
~ **account** Fabrikationskonto; ~ **summary account** Fabrikationssammelkonto; ~ **acquisition** betriebliche Neuerwerbung; ~ **activity** Produktions-, Fabrikationstätigkeit; ~ **agreement** Herstellungsvertrag; ~ **analysis** Arbeitsplanung im Rahmen der Fertigungsplanung; ~ **basis** Produktionsbasis; ~ **branch** Fabrikations-, Industriezweig; ~ **business** Gewerbebetrieb; ~ **capacity** Fabrikationskapazität; ~ **center** *(US)* Industrie-, Produktionszentrum; ~ **clause** *(books, US)* Urheberschutzklausel; ~ **company** *(Br.)* Produktionsgesellschaft, Fabrikationsbetrieb, Herstellungsbetrieb, -firma; ~ **complex** Fabrikkomplex; ~ **concern** Produktions-, Fabrikationsbetrieb; ~ **consumer** gewerblicher Verbraucher; ~ **corporation** *(US)* Produktionsgesellschaft, Fabrikations-, Herstellungsbetrieb; ~ **cost** Anfertigungs-, Fabrikations-, Herstellungs-, Produktionskosten; ~ **cost control** Produktionskostenkontrolle; ~ **cost sheet** Fabrikationskostenaufstellung; ~ **country** Herstellungsland; ~ **defect** Fabrikationsfehler; ~ **department** Produktionsabteilung, Fertigungsabteilung; ~ **district** Fabrikbezirk, -gegend, Industriegebiet; ~ **division** Herstellungs-, Fabrikations-, Produktionsabteilung; ~ **economics** Produktionskostensenkung; ~ **efficiency** Produktionsleistung; ~ **engineer** Betriebsingenieur; ~ **enterprise (establishment)** gewerblicher Betrieb, Fertigungs-, Produktions-, Fabrikations-, Herstellungsbetrieb, Fabrikanlage; ~ **expenses** Fertigungskosten; ~ **facilities** Produktions-, Herstellungsanlagen; ~ **firm** Herstellerfirma; ~ **group** Herstellergruppe; ~ **income** Einkommen aus Gewerbebetrieb, Betriebseinkommen; ~ **industry** verarbeitende Industrie, Erzeuger-, Fertigungsindustrie; ~ **investment** Investitionsaufwand im Fertigungssektor; ~ **knowhow** industrielle Produktionserfahrung; ~ **knowledge** Fabrikationskenntnisse; ~ **labo(u)r** Fabrikationslöhne; ~ **licence** Fabrikations-, Herstellungslizenz; ~ **loss** Betriebsverlust; ~ **man** Hersteller; ~ **method** Bearbeitungs-, Fabrikations-, Herstellungs-, Produktionsverfahren; ~ **monopoly** Herstellungs-, Produktions-, Fabrikationsmonopol; ~ **nation** Industriestaat; ~ **operations** Produktionsvorgang, Fabrikations-, Herstellungsbetrieb; ~ **order** Produktions-, Fabrikationsauftrag; ~ **output** Produktions-, Fabrikausstoß; ~ **place** Produktionsstätte, Herstellungswerk, Industrie-, Fabrikationsbetrieb, Fabrikanlage; ~ **population** Arbeiterbevölkerung; ~ **price** Fabrik[ations]-, Herstellungspreis, Macherlohn; ~ **process** Herstellungs-, Fabrikationsmethode, Produktionsvorgang, -prozeß, Fertigungsverfahren, Fabrikations-, Herstellungsprozeß, -verfahren, Fa-

brikationsablauf; **efficient ~ process** rationelles Fertigungsverfahren; **~ profit** Produktions-, Fabrikationsgewinn; **~ program(me)** Fertigungs-, Fabrikationsprogramm, Produktionsplan; **~ project** Fabrikations-, Herstellungsprojekt; **for ~ purposes** für Fabrikationszwecke; **~ quarter** Fabrikviertel; **~ requirements** betriebstechnische Anforderungen; **~ rights** Fabrikations-, Herstellungsrechte; **~ schedule** Fertigungs-, Fabrikations-, Produktionsplan; **~ secret** Fabrikationsgeheimnis; **~ sector** Produktionssektor; **~ service** Herstellungs-, Produktionsverfahren; **~ society** Produktivgenossenschaft; **~ statement** Aufgliederung der Produktionskosten, Produktionsbilanz; **~ study** Fabrikationsstudie; **~ subsidiary** Zulieferungsbetrieb; **~ tag** Laufzettel; **~ technique** Herstellungsverfahren; **~ time** Fertigungszeit; **~ town** Industrie-, Fabrikstadt; **~ trade** Fabrikationsgewerbe, gewerbliche Wirtschaft; **~ volume** Fabrikationsvolumen; **~ wages** Produktions-, Fertigungslöhne; **~ zone** Fabrikationszentrum.

manure Düngemittel.

manuscript Manuskript, *(print.)* Satz-, Druckvorlage;
in ~ handschriftlich; **printed as ~** als Manuskript gedruckt; **to cast off a ~** Manuskript absetzen; **to correct a ~** Manuskript verbessern; **to go through a ~ for typing errors** Manuskript auf Schreibfehler durchsehen; **to review a ~** Manuskript kritisch überprüfen; **to send a ~ to the printers** Manuskript in die Setzerei geben; **to set up a ~** Manuskript absetzen;
~ (a.) handgeschrieben, *(typewriter)* maschinengeschrieben; **~ department** *(library)* Handschriftenabteilung.

map Landkarte, *(plan projection)* Meßtischblatt, Geländekarte;
off the ~ abgelegen, unzugänglich, *(fig.)* veraltet; **on the ~** *(fig.)* in Rechnung zu stellen, beachtenswert;
general (outline, skeleton) ~ Übersichtskarte; **free beat-the-jam ~** kostenlose Landkarte zur Umgehung von Verkehrsstauungen;
~ of a city Stadtplan; **~ on a scale 1/100.000** Karte im Maßstab 1:100.000; **~ of a town** Stadtplan; **~ of the world** Weltkarte;
~ (v.) kartographisch aufnehmen, darstellen;
~ the basin of a river Flußbettkarte zeichnen; **~ out** genau aufzeichnen; **~ out a new career** neuen Beruf planen; **~ out a course of action** Aktionsplan ausarbeiten; **~ out a future** Zukunft vorausplanen; **~ out a route** Reiseroute auf der Karte festlegen; **~ out one's time** sich seine Zeit einteilen;
to be off the ~ nicht mehr zur Diskussion stehen; **to be very much on the ~ now** im Augenblick weitgehend im Vordergrund stehen; **to have slid off the ~** von der Landstraße verschwunden sein; **to put s. th. on the ~** dafür sorgen, daß die Wichtigkeit einer Sache bekannt wird; **to put s. th. on the ~ for s. o.** etw. für j. erreichbar machen; **to wipe a whole city off the ~** ganze Stadt ausradieren;
~ board Kartenbrett; **~ case** Kartenbehälter; **~ cover** Kartenfutteral; **~ exercise** *(mil.)* Planspiel; **~ grid** Koordinatennetz; **~ holder** Kartenhalter; **~ maker** Kartograph; **~ making** Kartenzeichnen, Kartographie; **~ making from aerial photos** Luftbildvermessung; **~ projection** Kartenprojektion; **~ reading** Kartenlesen; **~ scale** Kartenmaßstab.

mapper Kartograph, Kartenzeichner.

mapping Kartenaufnahme, Kartographie.

mar *(v.)* zugrunderichten, ruinieren;
~ s. one's work jds. Werk zunichtemachen; **to make or ~ s. o.** *(fam.)* jds. Glück oder Unglück bedeuten.

marathon *(fig.)* Dauerwettkampf;
~ negotiations Marathonverhandlungen.

maraud *(v.)* plündern, marodieren.

marauder Plünderer, Räuber, Marodeur.

marble Marmor;
not to have all one's ~s *(sl.)* nicht alle beisammen haben.

march [Fuß]marsch, *(frontier)* Grenzgebiet;
dead ~ Totenmarsch; **forced ~** Eil-, Gewaltmarsch; **military ~es** Marschmusik; **parade ~** Parademarsch; **past ~** Vorbeimarsch, Parade;
~ of events Gang der Ereignisse; **~ of prices** Preisanstieg; **~ of progress** fortschrittliche Entwicklung; **inflationary ~ of wages** inflationeller Lohnanstieg, Lohninflation;
~ (v.) marschieren, vorrücken, *(frontier)* gemeinsame Grenze haben;
~ in einrücken, einmarschieren; **~ off** *(prisoner)* abführen; **~ past** vorbeimarschieren; **~ through** durchmarschieren; **~ up and down the station platform** auf dem Bahnsteig auf- und abmarschieren;
to steal a ~ upon s. o. jem. zuvorkommen (die Schau stehlen, den Rang ablaufen);
~ orders Marschbefehl.

marching | in Einmarsch; **~ through** Durchmarsch;
~ column Marschkolonne; **~ money** Reisegeld, *(mil.)* Verpflegungsgeld; **~ order** Marschausrüstung; **~ orders** *(Br.)* Marschbefehl, *(fam.)* Ausführungsbestimmungen; **in full (heavy) ~ orders** feldmarschmäßig; **to be under ~ orders** Marschbefehl haben; **to give s. o. his ~ orders** *(fam.)* j. entlassen; **~ rations** Marschverpflegung.

mare's-nest Zeitungsente.

margin *(annotation)* Randbemerkung, *(cover)* Deckung, Deckungsspanne, Anschaffung, *(difference)* Marge, Differenz, Spielraum, [Verdienst-, Gewinn-, Handels]spanne, Unterschied zwischen Einkaufs- und Verkaufspreis, Bruttogewinn, *(exchange rate)* Bandbreite, *(insurance)* Verwaltungskostenzuschlag, *(limit)* Grenze [der Leistungsfähigkeit], Rentabilitätsgrenze, *(net earnings)* Überschuß, Reingewinn, *(print.)* [unbedruckter] Rand, Abstand, *(stock exchange)* Deckungsbetrag, Hinterlegungs-, Sicherheitssumme, Einschuß, *(typewriter)* [Seiten]rand;
as per ~ wie nebenstehend; **named in the ~** nebenstehend vermerkt; **on the ~** am Rande;
additional ~ *(broker)* zusätzliche Deckung, Nachschußzahlung [beim Lombardgeschäft]; **bled ~** bis in die Schrift hinein beschnittener Rand; **bottom ~** unterer weißer Rand; **credit ~** Kreditgrenze, -spielraum; **cropped ~** zu stark beschnittener Rand; **dealer's ~** Großhandels-, Gewinnspanne; **extensive ~** Extensitätsgrenze; **fixed ~** *(exchange rate)* feste Bandbreiten; **foot ~** unterer Rand; **gross ~** Brutto-, Rohgewinnspanne; **gross merchandising ~** Bruttospanne ohne Skontoabzug; **head ~** oberer weißer Rand; **inner ~** Innenrand; **intensive ~** Intensitätsgrenze; **liquidity ~** Liquiditätsspielraum; **maximum ~** Höchstspanne; **narrow ~** geringe Verdienstspanne; **net ~** Reingewinn; **opened ~** aufgeschnittener Rand; **post-tax ~** Gewinnspanne nach Begleichung (Abzug) der Steuern; **product line ~** Branchenhandelsspanne; **profit ~** Verdienst-, Gewinn-, Handelsspanne; **retail ~** Einzelhandelsgewinnspanne; **safety ~** Sicherheitsmarge; **shoestring ~** *(US, broker)* völlig ungenügende Deckung; **smallest of ~** geringste Gewinnspanne; **tail ~** unterer weißer Rand; **top ~** oberer weißer Rand; **trade ~** Handelsspanne; **variable gross ~** Bruttogewinn, Deckungsbeitrag; **wholesale ~** Großhandelsspanne; **wide ~** großer Spielraum, *(typewriter)* breiter Rand; **working ~** Reservebetrag für unvorhergesehene Fälle;
~ of consciousness Bewußtseinsschwelle; **~ of consumption** Sättigungsgrad; **~ of credit** Kreditspielraum; **~ of cultivation** Bebauungsgrenze, Kultivierungsgrenze; **~ of dumping** Dumpingspanne; **~ of error** Fehlerspielraum; **~ of the exchange rate** Bandbreite der Wechselkurse, Wechselkursbandbreite; **~ for unforeseen expenses** Reserve für unvorhergesehene Ausgaben; **~ of fluctuation** Schwankungsbreite; **wider ~ of fluctuation** größere Bandbreiten; **~ of income** Einkommensgrenze; **commercial ~ per item** Waren-, Einzelhandelsspanne; **~ [between the rates] of interest** Zinsgefälle, Spanne verschiedener Zinssätze, Zinsspanne; **prescribed ~s of free liquidity** vorgeschriebene freie Liquiditätsreserven; **~ of preference** Präferenzspanne; **~ of production (productiveness)** Rentabilitätsgrenze, Grenznutzen; **~ of profit** Verdienst-, Gewinn-, Handelsspanne, [Gewinn]marge, *(banking)* Zinsspanne, *(limit)* Ertragsgrenze; **pretax ~ of profit** Gewinnspanne vor Steuerabzug; **~ of profitableness** Rentabilitätsgrenze, Grenznutzen; **~ of safety** Sicherheitskoeffizient, -faktor; **on the sales ~** Verkaufsspanne; **~ of solvency** *(insurance companies)* Liquiditätsmarge; **~ of subsistence** Existenzgrenzbereich;
~ (v.) mit einem Rand versehen, *(specify with a note)* mit Randbemerkungen versehen, *(stock exchange)* Einschuß leisten, Deckung anschaffen, Einschußzahlung machen, durch Hinterlegung einer Sicherheitssumme decken;
~ up zusätzliche Sicherheit leisten, *(broker)* Deckung für Kursverluste stellen;
to allow s. o. some ~ jem. einen gewissen Spielraum zugestehen; **to allow a ~ for mistakes** mögliche Fehler einkalkulieren; **to buy on ~** *(US)* gegen Sicherheitsleistung kaufen; **to cut ~s** Verdienstspannen herabsetzen; **to deposit a ~ in cash** *(US)* Bareinschuß leisten, Bardeckung anschaffen; **to escape death by a narrow ~** mit knapper Not dem Tode entgehen; **to go near the ~** gefährliches Spiel treiben; **to leave a ~** Spielraum gewähren, sich rentieren, Gewinn abwerfen; **to leave a good ~** guten Überschuß abwerfen; **to make ~** *(print.)* Randbreite festsetzen; **to provide a substantial ~ for saving** erhebliche Sparmöglichkeiten gewähren; **to purchase on ~** gegen Sicherheitsleistung ankaufen; **to put up a ~** Einschußzahlung leisten; **to put up more ~** Nachschußzahlung leisten; **to reserve a ~** Spielraum lassen;

to sell on ~ *(US)* gegen Sicherheitsleistung verkaufen; **to set ~s** *(US)* Einschußbetrag festlegen; **to write on the ~** Randbemerkungen machen;

~ **account** *(stock broker, US)* Hinterlegungs-, Einschußkonto; **contribution ~ accounting** Deckungsbeitragsrechnung; ~ **borrowing** *(US)* Einschußpflicht; ~ **business (buying)** *(US)* Effektendifferenzgeschäft; ~ **call** *(US)* Aufforderung zur Leistung einer Einschußzahlung im Effektendifferenzgeschäft; **narrow ~ line** enge Gewinnspanne; ~ **rate** *(securities, US)* Lombardsatz, -gebühr; ~ **release** *(typewriter)* Randauslösung; ~ **requirements** *(stock exchange, US)* Einschußbedarf im Effektendifferenzgeschäft, Mindesteinzahlungsbetrag; ~ **rules** *(stock exchange, US)* Kreditbeschränkungsbestimmungen; ~ **stop** *(typewriter)* Randauslösung; ~ **system** *(US)* Effektenkauf mit Sicherheitsleistung; ~ **trading** *(US)* Effektendifferenzgeschäft; ~ **transaction** *(US)* Effektendifferenzgeschäft.

marginal knapp (gerade noch) rentabel, kostendeckend, zum Selbstkostenpreis, *(printed on the margin)* auf den Rand gedruckt, *(sociology)* als Außenseiter geltend, gesellschaftlich nicht voll akzeptierbar;

~ **account** *(US)* [Gewinnspanne lassendes] Einschußkonto; ~ **adjustment** Tarifanpassung in Grenzfällen; ~ **analysis** Grenzplankostenrechnung; ~ **approach** Lösung durch Differentation; **to operate on a ~ basis** gerade die Selbstkosten decken; ~ **belt** Randmeer; ~ **benefits** freiwillige Sozialleistungen; ~ **borrower** Grenzkreditnehmer; ~ **buyer** letztinteressierter Käufer; ~ **capital-output ratio** Grenzkapitalkoeffizient; ~ **case** Grenzfall; ~ **category** *(statistics)* Randklasse; ~ **classification** Randeinteilung; ~ **company** Gesellschaft an der Grenze der Rentabilität, Grenzbetrieb; ~ **constituency** *(Br.)* Wahlbezirk mit knapper Stimmenmehrheit, umstrittener Wahlbezirk; ~ **consumer** Endverbraucher; ~ **costing** *(Br.)* Teil-, Grenzplankostenrechnung; ~ **costs** Mindest-, Grenzkosten, nahe der Rentabilitätsgrenze stehende Kosten; ~ **cost pricing** Marginalkostenpreis; ~ **credit** *(Br.)* Wechselkreditbrief; ~ **deposit account** *(Br.)* Teilgutschriftskonto für ausländische Wechsel; ~ **desirability** Grenznutzen; ~ **district** Grenzbezirk; ~ **disutility of labo(u)r** *(US)* Grenze der Arbeitswilligkeit, Grenzopfer, Arbeitsunlustigkeit; ~ **earnings** Grenzertrag; ~ **efficiency of capital** Grenzleistungsfähigkeit des Kapitals; ~ **exceptions** geringfügige Ausnahmen; ~ **firm** Betrieb an der Grenze der Rentabilität, Grenzbetrieb; ~ **gloss** Randglosse; ~ **growth contribution** marginaler Wachstumsbeitrag; ~ **income** Grenzertrag, Deckungsbeitrag, Bruttogewinn; ~ **income statement** Ergebnisrechnung auf der Basis variabler Kosten; ~ **increment** Aufnahmegrenze des Marktes; ~ **inscriptions** *(coin)* Umschrift; ~ **labo(u)r** unrentable Arbeitskräfte; ~ **land** an der Grenze der Rentabilität liegendes Land; ~ **lender** letztbereiter Kreditgeber; ~ **man** *(sociology)* Randpersönlichkeit; ~ **mine** unrentable Zeche; ~ **net product** Nettogrenzprodukt; ~ **note** Randbemerkung, Marginalie, *(banking business, Br.)* Teilquittung, *(contract, Scot.)* Vertragszusatz; **to make ~ notes in a book** Buch mit Randbemerkungen versehen; ~ **payment** Differenzzahlung; ~ **principle** Grenzprinzip; ~ **producer** Betrieb an der Grenze der Rentabilität, Grenzbetrieb, -produzent; ~ **product** Grenzprodukt; ~ **product curve** Grenzvertragskurve; ~ **production** Produktion an der Kostengrenze (innerhalb der Rentabilität liegende) Produktion; ~ **productivity** an der Grenze der Rentabilität liegende Ertragsfähigkeit, Grenzproduktivität; ~ **productivity of labo(u)r** Grenzproduktivität der Arbeit; ~ **productivity theory of wages** Grenzproduktivitätstheorie; ~ **profit** Grenzertrag, -nutzen, Gewinnminimum, Rentabilitätsschwelle; ~ **propensity to consume** an der Grenze liegende Konsumbereitschaft, marginale Konsumfreudigkeit; ~ **propensity to export** marginale Exportquote; ~ **propensity to save** an der Grenze liegende Sparfreudigkeit; ~ **propensity to spend** marginale Ausgabenneigung; ~ **purchaser** unschlüssiger Käufer; ~ **rate** Steuerhöchstsatz; ~ **rate of substitution** Grenzrate der Substitution; ~ **receipt** *(banking, Br.)* Teilquittung; ~ **relief** *(Br.)* ermäßigter Steuersatz für die untersten Einkommensgruppen, Steuerermäßigung in Grenzfällen; ~ **return** Grenzertrag; ~ **revenue** Grenzertrag, -einnahmen; ~ **rules** *(stock exchange, US)* einschränkende Bestimmungen für Lombardkredite; ~ **sales** gerade noch rentabler (an der Rentabilitätsschwelle liegender) Absatz, Verkäufe zum Selbstkostenpreis; ~ **sea** *(law of nations)* Randmeer; ~ **seat** *(parl.)* unsicherer (knapp gehaltener) Parlamentssitz; ~ **seller** letztinteressierter Verkäufer, Grenzanbieter; ~ **space** *(print.)* Randbreite; ~ **supply** Spitzenangebot; ~ **tax rate** *(income tax)* Eingangssteuersatz; ~ **tax rate of 98%** Steuerhöchstsatz von 98%; ~ **theory of distribution** Theorie der Grenzproduktivität; ~ **theory of value** Grenznutzentheorie; ~ **trading** Effektendifferenzgeschäft; ~ **translation** mäßige Übersetzung; ~ **tribe** Grenzstamm; ~ **undertaking** Grenzbetrieb; ~ **unit** letzte Produkteinheit; ~ **unit cost** Grenzkosten für die letzte Produkteinheit; ~ **utility** Grenznutzen; ~ **utility of labo(u)r** Grenznutzen der Arbeit; ~ **utility school** Grenznutzenschule; ~ **utility theory** Grenznutzentheorie, -lehre; ~ **value** Grenzwert; ~ **weather conditions** Randwetterbedingungen; ~ **yield** Grenzertrag.

marginalia Randbemerkungen.

marginalist theory Grenznutzentheorie.

marginalize *(v.)* mit Randbemerkungen versehen.

marginally, to be only ~ dependent on purchases abroad nur für die Spitzenbedarfsdeckung auf ausländische Einfuhren angewiesen sein.

marina Seepromenade.

marine Marine, Seewesen;

~s Marinetruppen;

tell that to the horse ~ das kannst du deiner Großmutter erzählen;

merchant (mercantile) ~ Handelsmarine;

~ **adventure** Seegefahr, -risiko; ~ **band receiver** Seefunkempfänger; ~ **barometer** Schiffsbarometer; ~ **belt** Küstenhoheitsgewässer, *(law of nations)* Hoheitsgewässer, Randmeer; ~ **cable** Seekabel; ~ **carrier** Seefrachtführer; ~ **chart** Seekarte; ~ **communications** Nachrichtennetz der Seestreitkräfte; ~ **contract** Seebeförderungsvertrag; ~ **corps** *(US)* Marinekorps; ~ **court** *(US)* Seegericht; ~ **engine** Schiffsmotor; ~ **engineer** Schiffsingenieur; ~ **engineering** Schiffsmaschinenbau; ~ **forces** Seestreitkräfte; ~ **hospital** *(US)* Krankenhaus für Matrosen; ~ **infantry** Marineinfanterie; ~ **inspector** *(insurance company)* Schiffsinspektor.

marine insurance See[schadenstransport]versicherung;

inland ~ Binnentransportversicherung;

~ **Act** *(Br.)* Seetransportversicherungsgesetz; ~ **broker** Seeversicherungsmakler; ~ **certificate** *(US)* Seeversicherungspolice; ~ **company** Transport-, Seeversicherungsgesellschaft; ~ **contract** Seetransportversicherungsvertrag; ~ **merchant** Seeversicherungsmakler; ~ **premium** Seeversicherungsprämie; ~ **underwriter** Seetransportversicherer.

marine interest Bodmereizinsen; ~ **law** Seerecht; ~ **league** Seemeile; ~ **loan** Bodmereidarlehn; ~ **loss** Verlust auf See; ~ **manager** Leiter des Seeversicherungsgeschäfts; ~ **map** Seekarte; ~ **meteorology** Meereswetterkunde; ~ **perils** See[transport]gefahr, Seerisiko; ~ **policy** Seetransportversicherungspolice; ~ **products** Meeresprodukte; ~ **rate** Prämiensatz der Seeversicherung; ~ **registry** *(Br.)* Eintragung ins Schiffsregister; ~ **registry office** *(Br.)* Schiffsregisteramt; ~ **researcher** Meeresforscher; ~ **risk** See[transport]gefahr, Seerisiko; ~ **society** *(Br.)* Kadettenanstalt; ~ **station** Hafenbahnhof; ~ **store** *(Br.)* Trödelgeschäft, Trödelladen; ~ **stores** Schiffsbedarf; ~ **surveying** Vermessung der Küstengewässer; ~ **surveyor** amtlich bestellter Schiffssachverständiger, nautischer Experte; ~ **trade** Seehandel; ~ **transport** Beförderung auf dem Seeweg, Seetransport; ~ **transportation company** Seetransportgesellschaft; ~ **underwriter** See[schadens]versicherer; ~ **warfare** Seekrieg.

mariner Schiffer, Seemann, Matrose;

master ~ Handels-, Schiffskapitän.

marital ehelich, ehemännisch;

~ **affection** eheliche Zuneigung; ~ **bond** Eheband; ~ **capacity** Ehefähigkeit; ~ **coercion** Nötigung der Ehefrau; ~ **control** *(Br.)* Verwaltungs- und Nutznießungsrecht des Ehemannes am eingebrachten Gut der Ehefrau; ~ **deduction** *(estate tax, US)* Freibetrag der Ehefrau; ~ **domicile** ehelicher Wohnsitz; ~ **duties (obligations)** eheliche Pflichten; ~ **partner** Ehegatte; ~ **portion** *(Louisiana)* Pflichtteilsanspruch der Ehefrau; ~ **relations** eheliche Beziehungen; ~ **relations clinic** Eheberatungsstelle; ~ **rights and duties** ehe[männ]liche Rechte und Pflichten; ~ **status** Familienstatus.

maritime seefahrend;

~ **Administration** *(US)* Schiffahrtministerium; ~ **adventure** Seeunternehmen; ~ **affairs** Schiffahrtsangelegenheiten; ~ **assistance** Bergung und Hilfeleistung; ~ **belt** Küstenhoheitsgewässer; ~ **blockade** Seeblockade; ~ **cause** Seerechtsfall; ~ **city** Hafenstadt; ~ **claim** Seeschadenssumme, seerechtlicher Anspruch; ~ **climate** Seeklima; ~ **commerce** [Über]seehandel, Kauffahrtei; **Federal ~ Commission** *(US)* Bundesamt für die Handelsschiffahrt, Seeamt; **Intergovernmental ~ Consultative Organization** Zwischenstaatliche Beratende Schiffahrtsorganisation; ~ **contract** Schiffahrtsvertrag; ~ **contract of affreightment** Befrachtungsvertrag, Seefrachtvertrag; ~ **country** Küstenland; ~ **court** Seeamt; ~ **declaration** Verklarung; ~ **disaster** Schiffahrtskatastrophe; ~ **fishing** Seefischerei; ~ **freight** Seefracht; ~ **harbo(u)r** Seehafen; ~ **hypothecation** *(US)* Schiffspfandrecht; ~ **industry** Schiffsindustrie; ~ **insurance** Seeversicherung; ~ **insurer** Seeassekurant, -versicherer; ~ **intercourse** Seeverkehr; ~ **interest** Bodmereizinsen; ~ **jurisdiction** Seegerichtsbarkeit; ~ **law** Seerecht; ~ **lien** Seerückbehaltungs-, Schiffspfandrecht; ~ **life** Seemannsleben; ~ **loan** Bodmereidarlehn; ~ **matters** Schifffahrtsangelegenheiten; ~ **nation** Seefahrervolk; ~ **navigation** Seeschiffahrt; ~ **perils** Seetransportgefahr; ~ **policy** Seeversicherungspolice; ~ **port** Seehafen; ~ **power** Seemacht, -staat; ~ **profit** Bodmereiprämie; ~ **province** Küstenprovinz; ~ **reign** Seeherrschaft; ~ **risk** Seetransportgefahr; ~ **safety** Sicherheit auf See; ~ **service** seemännische Dienstleistung; ~ **shipping** Seeschiffahrt; ⚓ **State** *(Br.)* Offiziere und Mannschaften der Kriegsmarine; ~ **territory** Seehoheitsgebiet; ~ **tort** auf hoher See begangene unerlaubte Handlung; ~ **town** Küstenstadt; ~ **trade** Seehandel; ~ **traffic** Seeverkehr; ~ **transport** Seetransport.

mark *(analphabetic)* Merk-, Handzeichen, Kreuz, *(badge)* Abzeichen, *(beacon)* Bake, Leitzeichen, *(cattle)* Brandmal, *(German currency)* Mark, *(distinction)* Rang, Bedeutung, *(mar.)* Landmarke, *(quality)* Marke, Nummer, Qualität, Sorte, *(school)* Note, Zensur, *(sign)* Charakteristikum, [Kenn]zeichen, Eigentumszeichen, Marke, Markenzeichen, Markierung, Bezeichnung, [Merk]mal, *(stain)* Fleck, *(stamp)* Stempel, *(standard)* gewünschte Norm, *(stock exchange, Br.)* Kursfestsetzung, Notierung, *(ticketing label)* Preiszettel, -zeichen, -angabe, Warenzettel, [Waren]auszeichnung, *(trademark)* Handels-, Fabrik-, Schutzmarke, Warenzeichen;

as a ~ of my esteem als Beweis meiner Wertschätzung; **below the ~** unterdurchschnittlich; **beside the ~** nicht zur Sache gehörig; **not up to the ~** nicht auf der Höhe; **of ~** beachtenswert; **to the occasion** zur Feier des Tages; **up to the ~** den Erwartungen entsprechend, tadellos; **wide of the ~** fehl am Platz, unangebracht; **within the ~** innerhalb der erlaubten Grenzen;

~s Zensur, Noten, Zeugnis;

adjusting ~ Einstellzeichen; **assembly ~** Montagezeichen; **bad ~s** *(school)* schlechte Note (Zensur); **blocked ~** *(Germany)* Sperrmark; **boundary ~** Grenzzeichen, -mal; **check ~** Kontrollzeichen; **certification ~** *(US)* Güte-, Verbandszeichen; **collective ~** *(US)* Verbandszeichen, -marke; **common ~** Gemeindeweide; **deceptive ~s** irreführende Warenzeichen; **distinctive ~** Unterscheidungsmerkmal, Kennzeichen; **easy ~** *(sl.)* leichte Beute, Gimpel; **examination ~s** Examens-, Prüfungsnoten; **file ~** Eingangsvermerk; **finger ~** Fingerabdruck; **good ~** gute Note; **guiding ~** Verweisungszeichen; **hall-~** Feingehaltsstempel; **high ~s** gute Noten; **identification ~** Nämlichkeits-, Erkennungszeichen; **late ~** Tadel für Zuspätkommen; **load-line ~** Lademarke; **low ~** Tiefpunkt; **manufacturer's ~** Fabrik-, Herstellermarke; **misleading ~s** irreführende Kennzeichen; **not my ~** nicht mein Geschmack; **jointly owned ~s** Handelszeichen im gemeinschaftlichen Eigentum; **paper ~** Wasserzeichen; **price ~** Preiszettel, -auszeichnung; **proof-correction ~s** Korrekturzeichen; **punctuation ~s** Interpunktations-, Satzzeichen; **question ~** Fragezeichen; **reference ~** Verweisungszeichen; **registered ~** Registermarke; **service ~** Dienstmarke, -abzeichen; **water ~** Wasserstandsmarke;

~s of old age Alterserscheinungen, -anzeichen; **~ of confidence** Vertrauensbeweis; **~ of correction** Korrekturzeichen; **~ of favo(u)r** Gunstbezeigung; **~ of origin** Ursprungsbezeichnung; **~ for pilots** Orientierungszeichen für Piloten; **~ of quality** Güte-, Qualitätszeichen; **~ of good will** Beweis guten Willens;

~ *(v.)* markieren, bezeichnen, *(articles of gold)* stempeln, *(be characteristic)* kennzeichnen, charakteristisch sein, *(designate by ~)* be-, kennzeichnen, *(price tag)* auszeichnen, *(school)* zensieren, Noten erteilen, *(select)* bestimmen, ausersehen, *(stock exchange)* notieren;

~ one's approval seine Zustimmung bezeigen; **~ a bale of merchandise** Warenballen kennzeichnen; **~ the bounds of an estate** Grundstücksgrenze darstellen; **~ a case** Kiste beschriften; **~ a cheque** *(Br.)* Scheck bestätigen; **~ clearly consigned goods** Konsignationsware genau kennzeichnen; **~ one's clothes with one's name** seine Kleidung namentlich kennzeichnen; **~ off a distance on the map** Entfernung auf der Karte abstecken; **~ equal distances along a line** gleiche Abstände auf einer Linie eintragen; **~ by a dotted line** durch eine punktierte Linie kennzeichnen; **~ down** *(goods)* billiger (niedriger) auszeichnen, [im] Preis herabsetzen, *(note)* aufzeichnen, vormerken, niederschreiben, *(stock exchange)* niedriger notieren; **~ s. o.**

~ down j. für etw. vormerken; **~ a book down half the price** Buchpreis auf die Hälfte reduzieren; **~ down the discount rate** Diskontsenkung vornehmen; **~ down the price of an article** Warenpreis herabsetzen; **~ down for sale** Verkaufspreis herabsetzen; **~ s. o. down as one's successor** j. zu seinem Nachfolger bestimmen; **~ an era** charakteristisch für ein Zeitalter sein; **~ with a hot iron** brandmarken; **~ a leader** *(qualities)* Führer auszeichnen; **~ by machine** maschinell auszeichnen; **~ to the market** *(stock exchange, US)* besicherten Kredit dem Wert der gestellten Sicherheit anpassen; **~ off** abtrennen, abgrenzen, mit Pfählen abstecken; **~ out** ausersehen (vorsehen) für, *(cancel)* ausstreichen, *(plan)* entwerfen, *(price tag)* mit Preisangaben versehen, auszeichnen, *(trace out)* abgrenzen; **~ out boundaries** Grenzen festlegen; **~ out a claim** Grundstück abstecken; **~ out a course** Reiseroute festlegen; **~ out for a brilliant future** glänzende Zukunftsaussichten haben; **~ out a path** Weg bezeichnen (kennzeichnen); **~ a place on the map** Ort auf einer Karte markieren; **~ s. o. as an easy prey** j. als leichte Beute betrachten; **~ out a plot of a ground** Parzelle abstecken; **~ s. o. out for promotion** j. zur Beförderung vorsehen; **~ an examination paper** Prüfungsarbeit durchsehen; **~ prices** mit Preiszetteln versehen; **~ a pupil absent** abwesenden Schüler aufschreiben; **~ retail merchandise** Einzelhandelsartikel auszeichnen; **~ with the selling price** mit dem Verkaufspreis auszeichnen; **~ stock** *(stock exchange, Br.)* Kurswerte notieren; **~ with a white stone** als Glückstag bezeichnen; **~ timber [for sawing]** Bäume [zum Fällen] markieren; **~ time** *(fig.)* nicht von der Stelle kommen, *(stock exchange)* fast unverändert bleiben; **~ the trend of public opinion** Entwicklung der öffentlichen Meinung erkennen lassen; **~ up** *(give credit)* anschreiben, *(prices)* mit einem höheren Preis auszeichnen, *(stock exchange)* höher notieren; **~ up the discount rate** Diskontsatz heraufsetzen; **~ the wrecks in a channel** Schiffswracks in einem Kanal mit Baken versehen;

to adjust an instrument by guide ~s Instrument nach Richtwerten einstellen; **to be an easy ~** *(sl.)* leicht beschwindelt werden können (hereinzulegen sein); **to be too easy a ~** viel zu naiv (nicht raffiniert genug) sein; **to be below the ~** unter dem Durchschnitt sein; **to be near the ~** der Wahrheit nahekommen; **to be not up to the ~** nicht in Ordnung sein; **to be quite off the ~** arg danebenhauen; **to be quick on the ~** *(motor)* gutes Startvermögen haben; **to be up to the ~** den Anforderungen entsprechen; **to bear the ~ of a strong conviction** Ausdruck einer starken Überzeugung sein; **to bear every ~ of poverty** überall Armutszeichen aufweisen; **to bring home bad ~s** schlechtes Zeugnis mitbringen; **to come up to the ~** allen Anforderungen entsprechen; **not to feel quite up to the ~** sich nicht ganz wohl (auf der Höhe) fühlen; **to give s. o. full ~s** jem. höchste Anerkennung zollen; **to give s. o. a good ~** jem. eine gute Note geben; **to hit the ~** ins Schwarze treffen, Erfolg haben; **to leave one's ~ upon s. th.** einer Sache sein Gepräge geben; **to leave one's ~ upon one's time** seiner Zeit seinen Stempel aufdrücken; **to lodge an objection to the ~** *(stock exchange, Br.)* gegen eine Kursfestsetzung protestieren; **to make one's ~** sein Handzeichen setzen, sein Kreuz machen, *(fig.)* einflußreiche Position erlangen, sich einen Namen machen; **to make a ~ in the calendar** sich einen Tag rot im Kalender anstreichen; **to make one's ~ on the life of the country** dem Leben eines Volkes seinen Stempel aufdrücken; **to miss the ~** vorbeischießen, danebenhauen; **to obtain full ~s** in allen Fragen voll bestehen; **to overshoot the ~** über die Stränge schlagen; **to put a ~ on** mit Kennzeichen versehen;

~ book Klassenbuch; **moot ~** Gemeindeversammlung; **~ signature** Unterschrift eines Analphabeten.

markdown *(US)* niedrigere Auszeichnung, Preisherabsetzung, -nachlaß, Rabatt, *(reduced article, US)* im Preis herabgesetzte Ware, *(writedown)* Abschreibung;

~ of securities Neubewertung von Effekten;

~ cancellation Aufhebung der Preisherabsetzung; **~ of the rights issue** Bezugsrechtsabschlag; **~ loss** durch Preisherabsetzung entstandener Verlust; **~ price** herabgesetzter Kleinhandelspreis, Handelsabschlag; **~ revision** Überprüfung der Preisherabsetzungen.

marked gekennzeichnet, bezeichnet, markiert, *(fig.)* ausgeprägt, deutlich, spürbar, *(price)* mit Preisen versehen, ausgezeichnet;

~ and numbered gezeichnet und numeriert;

to be ~ *(stock exchange, Br.)* notiert werden; **to be strongly ~** *(tendency)* deutlich zu spüren sein; **to be ~ by a decline of prices** im Zeichen der Baisse stehen; **to be ~ down** *(stock exchange)* niedriger notiert werden; **to be ~ down for s. th.** für etw. bestimmt (vorgesehen) sein; **to be ~ up** höher notieren;

to be a man of ~ **ability** bedeutende Qualitäten besitzen; ~ **absence of supporters** kaum vorhandene Anhänger; **very ~ accent** deutlich spürbarer Akzent; **with ~ attention** mit gespannter Aufmerksamkeit; ~ **check** *(US)* gekennzeichneter Scheck; ~ **cheque** *(Br.)* bestätigter Scheck; **with ~ composure** mit zur Schau getragener Ruhe; ~ **decline** ausgeprägter Rückgang; ~ **difference** sichtbarer Unterschied; ~**-down price** herabgesetzter Preis; ~ **goods** ausgezeichnete Waren; ~ **improvement** *(stock exchange)* deutliche Besserung; **to treat s. o. with ~ incivility** j. betont unhöflich behandeln; ~ **inflation** erhebliche Inflation; ~ **list** Belegungsliste; ~ **shares** *(Br.)* abgestempelte Aktien; **strongly ~ tendency** deutlich spürbare Tendenz; ~ **transfer** *(Br.)* Übertragungsurkunde [über Effektenverkäufe]; ~**-up price** heraufgesetzter Preis.

markedly | **polite** erstaunlich höflich; ~ **wrong** ausgesprochen falsch.

marker Aufschreiber, Anmerker, *(bookmark)* Lesezeichen, *(I.O.U., sl.)* Schuldversprechen, *(mil., airplane)* Leuchtbombe, *(for marking ground)* Markierstein, *(sport)* Markiergerät, *(signpost, US)* Straßen-, Verkehrsschild;
~ **of goods** Warenauszeichner.

market Markt, *(business situation)* Handelsverkehr, Wirtschaftslage, *(market day)* Markttag, *(demand)* Nachfrage, *(fair)* Messe, Jahrmarkt, *(franchise)* Marktgerechtigkeit, -recht, *(marketing)* Absatz, Abnehmer, *(money market)* Geldmarkt, *(market price)* Marktpreis, Kurs, *(profit)* Umsatz, Gewinn, Vorteil, *(seat of trade)* Markt, Handelsplatz, *(source of supply)* Bezugsquelle, *(state of the market)* Marktlage, *(stock exchange)* Börse, Verkehr, *(store)* Laden, Geschäft, *(trade)* Handel, *(trading area)* Absatzmarkt, -gebiet, -bereich, -möglichkeit, *(traffic)* Marktbesuch, -verkehr, *(value)* Marktwert;
at the ~ *(US)* zum Börsenkurs, bestens; **at today's ~** auf der heutigen Börse; **close to the ~** marktnah; **in conformity with the ~** marktgerecht; **in keeping with the ~** marktkonform; **in the ~** auf dem Markt, am Platze; **in the free ~** außerbörslich; **in a rising ~** bei steigenden Kursen; **obtainable on the ~** an der Börse gehandelt; ~ **off** *(US)* Kurse abgeschwächt; **on the ~** zum Verkauf; **when the ~ opens** bei Börsenbeginn; **with a brisk ~** bei guten Umsätzen;
active ~ lebhafter Markt; **advancing ~** steigende Marktpreise; **greatly agitated ~** stürmisch bewegte Börse; **agricultural ~** Markt für landwirtschaftliche Erzeugnisse, Agrarmarkt; **assured ~** sicherer Absatzmarkt; **bear ~** Baisse; **bearish ~** Baissestimmung; **black ~** Schwarzmarkt, schwarzer Markt; **bond ~** Markt für festverzinsliche [Wert]papiere, Renten-, Pfandbriefmarkt; **boom ~** Hausse; **brisk ~** lebhafte Börse; **broad ~** aufnahmefähiger Markt; **bull ~** Hausse; **bullish ~** Haussestimmung; **buoyant ~** steigende Tendenz aufweisender (fester) Markt; **buyers' ~** Käufermarkt; **call-money ~** Markt für Tagesgeld; **capital ~** Emissionsmarkt, Kapitalmarkt; **cash ~** *(stock exchange)* Kassamarkt; **cattle ~** Viehmarkt; **central ~** Haupt-, Erzeugergroß-, Zentralmarkt; **cheerful ~** lebhafte Börse; **chief ~** Hauptmarkt; **colonial ~** Markt für Kolonialwerte; **commodity ~** Waren-, Rohstoffmarkt, Produkten-, Warenbörse; **Common ~** Gemeinsamer Markt; **competitive ~** freier Markt; **very competitive ~** Markt mit starkem Wettbewerb; **consols ~** Markt für Staatsanleihen; **consumer ~** Verbrauchsgütermarkt; **copper ~** Markt für Kupferwerte; **corporate bond ~** Markt für industrielle Schuldverschreibungen; **over-the-counter ~** *(US)* Markt für nicht notierte Werte, Freiverkehrsmarkt, Freiverkehr, Telefonhandel; **covered ~** Markthalle; **curb ~** *(US)* Freiverkehr[sbörse], Freiverkehrsmarkt; **dead ~** flauer Markt, lustlose Börse; **declining ~** fallende Kurse; **demoralized ~** äußerst gedrückt liegender Markt; **depressed ~** Baissemarkt, gedrückt liegender Markt; **discount ~** *(Br.)* Diskontmarkt; **disturbed ~** bewegte Börse; **domestic ~** Binnen-, Inlandsmarkt, inländischer Absatzmarkt; **down ~** rückläufige Kurse, abgeschwächte Börse; **dull ~** lustloser Markt, Flaute; **easy ~** Markt mit großem Warenangebot, *(stock exchange)* freundliche Börse; **employment ~** Arbeits-, Stellenmarkt; **equity ~** Aktienmarkt; **exchange ~** *(Br.)* Devisenmarkt; **Eurocurrency ~** Eurodollarmarkt; **export ~** Auslands-, Ausfuhr-, Exportmarkt; **farm ~** Markt für landwirtschaftliche Erzeugnisse, Agrarmarkt; **featureless ~** lustlose Börse; **financial ~** Markt für Investitionspapiere; **firm ~** feste Börse (Kurse); **fish ~** Fischmarkt; **flat ~** lustlose Börse; **fledging ~** gerade flügge gewordener Absatzmarkt; **fluctuating ~** schwankende Nachfrage; **foreign ~** ausländischer Markt, Auslandsmarkt, -absatz; **foreign-exchange ~** Devisenmarkt; **forward ~** Terminmarkt; **free ~** offener Markt, freie Marktwirtschaft, *(stock*

exchange) Freiverkehrsmarkt; **freight ~** Frachtenbörse; **fresh ~** Markt für Frischprodukte; **futures ~** Terminmarkt; **gilt-edged ~** *(Br.)* Markt für mündelsichere Wertpapiere (Staatsanleihen); **glutted ~** mit Waren überschwemmter (übersättigter) Markt; **gray ~** *(US)* grauer Markt; **greatly agitated ~** stürmisch bewegte Börse; **guaranteed ~** garantiertes Absatzgebiet; **heavy ~** gedrückter Markt, schleppender Absatz; **high-priced ~** teurer Markt; **home ~** Inlands-, heimischer Markt; **imperfect ~** heterogener Markt; **inactive ~** lustloser Markt, Flaute; **industrial ~** Markt für Industriewerte; **inland ~** Binnen-, Inlandsmarkt; **inofficial ~** Freiverkehrsmarkt; **international ~** Markt für international gehandelte Wertpapiere, Weltmarkt; **investment ~** Markt für Anlagewerte, Anlagemarkt; **jungle ~** *(Br.)* Markt für westafrikanische Bergwerksaktien; **kerb ~** *(Br.)* Freiverkehrsmarkt; **labo(u)r ~** Arbeitsmarkt; **leading ~** tonangebende Börse; **lifeless ~** matte Börse; **limited ~** beschränkt aufnahmefähiger Markt; **liquidating ~** auf umfangreiche Glattstellungen hin schwache Börse; **lively ~** lebhafter Börsenverkehr; **long ~** *(US)* nicht mehr aufnahmefähiger Markt; **major ~** Hauptabsatzgebiet; **mining ~** Montanmarkt; **miscellaneous ~** Markt für verschiedene Wertpapiere; **mixed ~** uneinheitliche Kurse; **money ~** Geldmarkt; **municipal ~** Markt für Kommunalpapiere; **narrow ~** Marktenge, *(stock exchange)* lustloser Markt, geringe Umsätze; **national ~** Absatz im ganzen Bundesgebiet; **new issue ~** Emissionsmarkt; **next ~** nächster Markttag; **nominal ~** fast umsatzlose Börse; **nonadmitted ~** *(insurance business, US)* Markt der in einem Einzelstaat nicht zugelassenen Versicherungsgesellschaften; **off-board ~** *(US)* Markt für nicht notierte Wertpapiere; **oligopolistic ~** von wenigen Anbietern bestimmter Markt; **open ~** *(market free to all)* offener Markt[verkehr], Offenmarkt, *(outside market)* Freiverkehr; **open-air ~** im Freien abgehaltener Markt; **outside ~** Freiverkehrsmarkt, -kurs, außerbörslicher Kurs; **out-of-town ~** *(US)* Regionalbörse; **overbought ~** *(US)* wegen spekulativer Ankäufe nicht mehr aufnahmefähiger Markt; **overseas ~** Überseemarkt, Markt für Überseewerte, überseeischer Markt, überseeisches Absatzgebiet; **oversold ~** *(US)* bei fallenden Kursen nicht mehr aufnahmefähiger Markt; **overstocked ~** übersättigter (mit Waren überschwemmter) Markt; ~ **overt** *(Br.)* offener Markt, Verkauf am offenen Markt; **pegged ~** *(US)* unveränderlicher Markt; **perfect ~** vollkommener Markt, homogener Markt; **poor ~** schlechter Absatz, schlecht bestückter Markt; **present ~** effektiver Markt; **primary ~** *(US)* Vormarkt, Aufkaufmarkt; **primary commodities ~** Grundstoffmarkt; **principal ~** Hauptabsatzgebiet; **produce ~** Waren-, Produktenmarkt; **promising ~** günstiger Absatzmarkt; **property ~** *(Br.)* Immobilien-, Grundstücksmarkt; **public transport commuter ~** Absatzmarkt auf öffentlichen Nahverkehrsmitteln; **quality ~** Qualitätsmarkt; **quiet ~** geringe Umsätze; **railway (railroad, US) ~** *(stock exchange)* Markt für Eisenbahnwerte; **ready ~** aufnahmefähiger Markt; **real-estate ~** *(US)* Grundstücks-, Immobilienmarkt; **receptive ~** aufnahmebereiter Markt; **regional ~** Regionalmarkt; **relevant ~** *(US)* maßgeblicher Markt; **resistant ~** widerstandsfähiger Markt; **restricted ~** eng abgegrenzter Absatzmarkt; **rigged ~** *(US)* Markt mit spekulativ beeinflußten Kursen; **rights ~** *(US)* Markt für Bezugsrechte; **rising ~** steigende Kurse, Hausse[markt], Marktsteigerung; **sagging ~** abgeschwächter Markt, schwache Börse; **scanty ~** schlecht befahrener Markt; **seaboard ~** Küstenhandelsplatz; **secondary ~** Markt zweiter Ordnung; **security ~** Wertpapier-, Effektenbörse; **seller's ~** Verkäufermarkt; **sensitive ~** empfindlich reagierende Börse; **settled ~** Stapelplatz; **share ~** *(Br.)* Aktienmarkt; **shrivel(l)ing ~** schrumpfender Marktanteil; **sick ~** *(US)* uneinheitliche und lustlose Börse; **slack ~** Flaute, Geschäftsstille; **sluggish ~** Geschäftsunlust; **small ~** enger Markt; **soft ~** nicht sehr aufnahmefähiger Markt; **spot ~** Kassamarkt, Barverkehr; **stagnant ~** stagnierender Markt, Absatzstockung; **standard ~** tonangebende Börse; **steady ~** feste Börse; **stiff ~** stabile Marktlage; **stock ~** Wertpapierbörse, Wertpapier-, Aktienmarkt; **street ~** *(Br.)* Nachbörse, Freiverkehr; **strong ~** feste Börse; **terminal ~** Schlußbörse; **the ~** *(stock exchange)* Standort des Marktes; **thin ~** geringe Umsätze; **trading ~** stagnierender Markt; **under-supplied ~** *(stocks)* nicht genügend belieferter Markt; **unofficial ~** *(Br.)* Freiverkehrsmarkt; **unprecedented ~** absolut einmalige Nachfrage; **untapped ~** unerschlossene Absatzgebiete; **virgin ~** jungfräulicher Markt; **wage ~** Lohnbörse; **weak ~** schwache Börse; **weekly ~** Wochenmarkt; **wholesale ~** Großhandelsmarkt; **wholesale produce ~** Produktengroßhandelsbörse; **world ~** Weltmarkt;

~ **for bonds** Pfandbriefmarkt; ~ **for cattle** Viehmarkt; ~ **for chemicals (chemical shares,** *Br.*) Chemiemarkt; ~ **for construction** Baumarkt; ~ **of consumption** Verbrauchermarkt; ~ **for futures [delivery]** Terminmarkt, -börse, Markt für Termingeschäfte; ~ **for long-term funds** Markt für langfristige Gelder; ~ **of issue** Emissionsmarkt; ~ **for mortgages** Hypothekenmarkt; ~ **for fixed-interest bearing securities** Markt für festverzinsliche Wertpapiere; ~ **in floating-rate local authority securities** Markt für wechselkursungebundene Kommunalwerte; ~ **for stocks** *(Br.)* Effektenmarkt; ~ **well stocked with goods** gut beschickter Markt;

~ *(v.) (deal)* handeln, Handel treiben, Märkte besuchen, einkaufen, markten, *(put on the ~, US)* auf den Markt bringen, *(sell)* auf dem Markt verkaufen, absetzen;

~ **one's block of shares** sein Aktienpaket auf dem Markt unterbringen; ~ **equity securities** Dividendenwerte auf dem Markt unterbringen; ~ **rail freight more aggressively** Möglichkeiten im Eisenbahnfrachtverkehr der Kundschaft marktgerechter darstellen; ~ **securities to the public** Papiere auf dem Kapitalmarkt unterbringen;

to apportion the ~ Markt aufspalten; **to be at the** ~ auf dem Markt sein; **to be in the** ~ Abnehmer sein, Interesse haben, sich interessieren für, als Käufer auftreten, Bedarf haben, *(house)* zum Verkauf [auf dem Grundstücksmarkt] angeboten sein; **to be on the** ~ *(stock exchange)* angeboten werden, zu haben sein; **to be absorbed by the internal** ~ im Inland aufgenommen werden; **to be found on the** ~ auf dem Markt vertreten sein; **to be in and out of the** ~ *(US)* kurzfristige Börsenspekulation durchführen; **to bear the** ~ Kurse drücken; **to blanket the entire** ~ ganzen Markt erfassen; **to boom the** ~ Kurse in die Höhe treiben; **to bridge a gap in the** ~ Marktlücke schließen; **to bring on the** ~ auf den Markt bringen; **to bring one's eggs (hogs) to the wrong (bad)** ~ schlechtes Geschäft machen, seine Pläne ins Wasser fallen sehen; **to bring one's pigs to a pretty (the wrong)** ~ aufs falsche Pferd setzen; **to bull the** ~ auf Hausse kaufen; **to calm the** ~ Markt beruhigen; **to carry pigs to the** ~ Geschäfte machen wollen; **to carve out wider** ~**s** weitere Märkte (Absatzgebiete) erschließen; **to close in quiet** ~**s** bei ruhigen Schlußkursen liegen; **to come into the** ~ [zum Verkauf] angeboten werden, auf den Markt kommen, *(stock exchange)* angeboten werden, zu haben sein; **to come to a good (bad)** ~ gut (schlecht) verkaufen; **to come out of the** ~ *(stock exchange)* aus dem Markt herauskommen, angeboten werden; **to command the** ~ Markt beherrschen; **to congest the** ~ Markt überschwemmen; **to conquer a** ~ Markt erobern; **to control the** ~ Markt beherrschen; **to corner the** ~ Markt aufkaufen; **to create a** ~ Absatzmarkt schaffen; **to cultivate the** ~ Marktpflege betreiben; **to depress the** ~ Kurse drücken; **to divide the** ~ Markt aufteilen; **to dominate the** ~ Markt beherrschen; **to dump goods on a foreign** ~ Waren im Ausland billig auf den Markt bringen; **to even out the** ~ Marktausgleich herbeiführen; **to find a** ~ verlangt werden, Absatzfeld haben; **to find a ready** ~ guten Absatz haben (finden), sich rasch verkaufen; **to find new** ~**s for one's manufactures** neue Märkte (Absatzgebiete) für seine Erzeugnisse erschließen; **to find gaps in a** ~ Marktlücken finden; **to flog on the** ~ auf dem Markt verkloppen; **to flood (flow) the** ~ Markt überschwemmen; **to force the** ~ Markt forcieren; **to force out of the** ~ vom Markt vertreiben; **to frequent** ~**s** Märkte beziehen; **to gauge the** ~ Marktbeurteilung vornehmen; **to get a bigger foot in the** ~ größeren Marktanteil erhalten; **to give a fillip to the** ~ der Börse Auftrieb geben; **to glut the** ~ Markt überschwemmen; **to go long of the** ~ Papiere halten, um die Kurse hochzutreiben; **to have an effect on the** ~ Markt beeinflussen; **to have a ready** ~ **for sale** jederzeit verkäuflich sein; **to have recourse to the** ~ Markt in Anspruch nehmen; **to hold a** ~ Markt abhalten; **to hold on the** ~ Marktanteil halten; **to hold the** ~ Stützungsaktion unternehmen; **to jump into the** ~ plötzlich Kaufaufträge erteilen; **to launch on the** ~ auf den Markt werfen; **to lose a** ~ günstige Verkaufsgelegenheit vorübergehen lassen; **to make a** ~ *(stock exchange)* künstliche Nachfrage nach Aktien hervorrufen, Gegenmine legen, Kurse hochtreiben; **to make a** ~ **of s. th.** etw. losschlagen; **to make up a** ~ Absatzgebiet erschließen; **to manipulate the** ~ Markt beeinflussen; **to meet with a ready (speedy)** ~ aufnahmefähigen Markt (guten Absatz) finden; **to mesmerize the** ~ Börse faszinieren; **to milk the** ~ Markt durch Spekulationsmanöver ausplündern; **to move down** ~ billigen Sektor des Marktes gewinnen; **to open up new** ~**s** neue Märkte erobern (Absatzgebiete erschließen); **to overstock the** ~ Markt überschwemmen; **to place on the** ~ Markt beschicken; **to play the** ~ *(coll.)* an der Börse (in Aktien) spekulieren; **to purchase in the open** ~ am offenen Markt kau-

fen; **to play the stock** ~ an der Börse (in Aktien) spekulieren; **to put on the** ~ auf den Markt bringen; **to put the** ~ **into a free fall** Börsenkurse ungehindert fallen lassen; **to put an article on the** ~ Artikel einführen; **to recover a** ~ Absatzgebiet zurückerobern; **to regain the** ~ Markt wiedergewinnen; **to regulate the** ~ Markt kontrollieren; **to rescue the** ~ Stützungsaktion unternehmen; **to rig the** ~ *(Br.)* Kurse unzulässsig beeinflussen (in die Höhe treiben); **to romp into a** ~ Markt spielend erobern; **to sell at the** ~ *(US)* zum Börsenkurs verkaufen; **to sell in the open** ~ am offenen Markt verkaufen; **to send goods on the** ~ Markt beschicken; **to share in the expanding** ~ sich an der Marktausweitung beteiligen; **to stag the** ~ Markt durch Konzertzeichnungen beeinflussen; **to stimulate the** ~ Markt beleben; **to supply a** ~ Markt beliefern; **to swamp the** ~ Markt überschwemmen; **to take off (out of) the** ~ aus dem Markt nehmen; **to tap a** ~ Markt erschließen, auf dem Markt in Erscheinung treten; **to throw on the** ~ auf den Markt werfen; **to unload stocks on the market** Markt mit Aktien überschwemmen; **to understand the** ~ Absatzverhältnisse (Markt) kennen; **to wait out the** ~ *(sl.)* Märkte durch Zurückhaltung beeinflussen; **to win back** ~**s** Märkte (Absatzgebiete) zurückgewinnen; **to win a new** ~ neuen Markt erobern;

~ **acceptance** Aufnahme durch den Markt; **agency** Marktstelle, Börsenvertretung; ~ **analysis** Marktuntersuchung, -forschung, -analyse, -kenntnis, Konjunkturdiagnose; ~ **analyst** Marktbeobachter, Konjunkturdiagnostiker; ~ **appraisal** Verkehrswertschätzung; ~ **appreciation** *(investment fund)* Bewertungsmethode; ~ **area** Absatzgebiet, -markt; ~ **assessment** Marktbewertung; **assumption** Markteroberung; ~ **audit** Marktuntersuchung; ~ **average** durchschnittliche Kursentwicklung, Durchschnittskurs, -preis; ~ **barometer** Börsenbarometer; ~ **basket** Markttasche, *(statistics)* Warenkorb; ~ **behavio(u)r** Marktverhalten; ~ **boom** [Börsen]hausse; ~ **break** Börsensturz; ~ **capacity** Aufnahmefähigkeit des Marktes; ~ **capitalization value** Kapitalisierungsmarktwert; ~ **changes** Marktveränderungen; ~ **changes in interest rates** Änderung der Zinskonditionen; ~ **comment** Börsenbericht; **Open ~ Committee** *(US)* Offenmarktausschuß; ~ **competition** *(carrier)* Tarifwettbewerb; ~ **concentration** Absatzkonzentration; ~ **condition(s)** Marktlage, Konjunkturlage, Absatzverhältnisse, -bedingungen, Marktbedingungen; ~ **conduct** Verhalten auf dem Markt; ~ **contact** Marktberührung; ~ **control** Marktbeherrschung; ~ **coverage** Absatzanteil, -erfassung; ~ **crier** Marktschreier, -ausrufer; ~ **dabbler** Börsendilettant; ~ **data** Absatzzahlen, -ziffern; ~ **day** Markttag, Wochenmarkt, *(stock exchange)* Börsentag; ~ **dealer** Händler; ~ **debut** erster Börsenauftritt; ~ **decline** Kursrückgang; ~ **demand** Marktbedürfnis, -bedarf; ~ **development** Marktentwicklung; ~ **discount** *(Br.)* Privatdiskont; ~**-distorting** marktverzerrend; ~ **distortion** Marktverzerrung; ~ **dominance** Marktbeherrschung; ~**-dominating** marktbeherrschend; ~**-dominating enterprise** marktbeherrschendes Unternehmen; ~ **domination** Marktbeherrschung; ~ **dues** Marktgebühren, -abgaben, Standgebühren; ~ **economy** freie Marktwirtschaft; **outside the sphere of the** ~ **economy** außerhalb des marktwirtschaftlichen Bereichs; ~ **exploration** Markterkundung, Erkundung von Absatzmärkten; ~ **factor** Marktfaktor; ~ **facts** Marktdaten; **to run against the** ~**'s favo(u)r** sich nicht marktkonform entwickeln; ~ **financing** Absatzfinanzierung; ~ **flexibility** Nachfrageflexibilität; ~ **fluctuations** konjunkturelle Schwankungen, Konjunkturschwankungen, *(stock exchange)* Kursschwankungen; ~ **forces** Marktkräfte, -macht; ~ **and non** ~ **forces** Kräfte innerhalb und außerhalb des Marktes; ~ **forecast** Konjunktur-, Marktprognose; ~ **gap** Marktlücke; ~ **garden** Handelsgärtnerei; ~ **gardening** Handelsgärtnerei; ~ **groupings** Käufergruppen; ~ **growth** Wachstumsmarkt; ~ **guide** Marktführer; ~ **hole** Marktlücke; ~ **house** *(Br.)* Markthalle; ~ **inactivity** Lustlosigkeit des Effektenmarktes; ~**-induced** marktbedingt; ~ **information** Marktuntersuchung; ~ **inquiry** Marktanalyse; ~ **intelligence** umfassende Marktinformationen; ~ **investigation** Marktbeobachtung, -forschung; ~ **knowledge** Marktkenntnis; ~ **leader** Marktführer; ~ **leaders** führende Börsenwerte, Spitzenreiter; ~ **letter** *(US)* Börsenbrief, täglicher Marktbericht; ~ **level** Preisniveau; ~ **loss** Kursverlust; ~ **maker** Gegenspekulant, Kursfestsetzer; ~ **making** Kurstreiberei, -spekulation, Gegenspekulation; ~ **manipulator (operator)** Kursspekulant; ~ **mechanism** Marktmechanismus; ~ **model** Modellfall; ~ **monopoly** Absatzmonopol; ~ **news** Börsenbericht; ~ **nexus** Marktkomplex; ~ **observation** kontinuierliche Marktbeobachtung, -forschung; ~ **operation** Marktbeherrschung, Börsentransaktion; **open** ~ **operation** Offenmarktgeschäft; ~ **opportunity** Absatzmöglichkeit; ~ **order** *(US)* Marktanweisung, *(stock exchange, US)* unlimitierter Börsenauftrag, Billigst-, Bestauftrag, Bestensorder; **Common ⁰ Organization** Marktordnung der EG; **national ~ organizations** einzelstaatliche Marktordnungen; **~-oriented** marktorientiert; ~ **orientation** Marktorientierung; ~ **outlook** Konjunkturaussichten; ~ **participation** Marktbeteiligung; ~ **partner** Marktpartner; ~ **partnership** *(Br.)* Vereinigung zweier Börsenmitglieder der Londoner Börse; ~ **pattern** Probemuster; ~ **penetration** Marktdurchdringung; ~ **performance** Absatzleistung; ~ **performers** führende Börsenwerte; ~ **place** Marktplatz; **to come into the ~ place** zum Verkauf kommen; **to turn the world into a global ~ place** seine Erzeugnisse auf dem ganzen Erdball verkaufen; ~ **planning** Absatzplanung; **open ~ policy** Offenmarktpolitik; ~ **position** Marktlage, -position, Absatzposition; **to adapt o. s. flexibly to ~ possibilities** sich den Marktmöglichkeiten flexibel anpassen; ~ **potential** Absatzmöglichkeit, Marktpotential; **[dominant] ~ power** wirtschaftliche Machtstellung, marktbeherrschende Stellung; ~ **price** Marktpreis, *(US)* Wiederbeschaffungswert, *(cost of market, whichever is lower)* Wert nach dem Niederstwertprinzip, *(stock exchange)* Effekten-, [Börsen]kurs, Kurswert; **at current ~ price** zum Marktpreis; **fair ~ price** marktgerechter Preis; **usual ~ prices** marktgängige (gültige) Preise; ~ **price list** Marktbericht; ~ **process** Marktbildungsprozeß; ~ **profit** Kursgewinn; ~ **prospects** Absatzerwartungen, Konjunkturaussichten; ~ **purchasing** günstiger Materialeinkauf; ~ **quota** Absatzkontingent, Marktanteil; ~ **quotation** [Börsen]notierung, -kurs, Kursnotierung; ~ **rally** Markterholung; ~ **rate** Marktpreis, *(discount rate, Br.)* Diskontsatz [der Londoner Banken und Wechselmakler], Geldmarktsatz, *(stock exchange, US)* Tages-, [Börsen]kurs, Kurswert; **fluctuating ~ rate** *(US)* veränderlicher Kurs; **short-term ~ rate** kurzfristiger Geldsatz; ~ **rate of discount** *(Br.)* Privatdiskontsatz; ~ **rates of interest** Geldmarktsätze; ~ **ratio** *(US)* Marktverhältnis; ~ **reaction** Börsenreaktion; ~ **recession** Konjunkturrückgang; ~ **regulation** Marktordnung; ~ **report** Markt-, Handels-, Preisbericht, *(stock exchange)* Kurs-, Börsenbericht; **money-~ report** Geldmarktbericht; ~ **representative** Einkaufs-, Verkaufsagent, Einkäufer; ~ **research** Marktuntersuchung, Absatz-, Marktforschung, Konjunkturtest; **~-research agency (organization)** Marktforschungsinstitut; ~ **research group** Marktforschungsgruppe; ~ **research specialist (worker)** Konjunkturforscher; ~ **researcher** Konjunkturforscher; ~ **resistance** Marktwiderstand, Widerstandsfähigkeit des Marktes; ~ **rigger** Kurstreiber; ~ **rigging** Kurstreiberei, Börsenmanöver, -manipulation; ~ **rumo(u)r** Börsengerücht; ~ **saturation** Marktsättigung; ~ **schedule** listenmäßiger Nachweis einer Nachfrageentwicklung; ~ **segment** Teilmarkt; ~ **segmentation** Marktaufteilung, Aufteilung des Absatzmarktes; ~ **selling value** gewöhnlicher Verkaufswert; ~ **sentiment** Stimmung an der Börse, Börsenstimmung; ~ **share** Marktanteil; ~ **share trend** Marktanteilsentwicklung; ~ **sharing** Marktaufteilung; **~-sharing agreement** Marktabrede, Vertriebsabsprache; ~ **situation** Marktlage, Absatzverhältnisse, -lage; **poor ~ situation** schlechte Absatzlage; ~ **size** Marktgröße; ~ **softening** Kursabschwächung; ~ **spots** *(US)* Effekten mit Sonderbewegungen; ~ **square** Markt[platz]; ~ **stand** Marktbude; ~ **standard** Marktrichtwert; ~ **statistics** Absatzstatistik; ~ **structure** Marktgefüge, -struktur; ~ **study** Marktuntersuchung, Markt-, Absatzstudie; ~ **supervision** Marktkontrolle; ~ **supply** Marktangebot, -belieferung; ~ **survey** Marktuntersuchung, -analyse; ~ **survey method** *(advertising budget)* Geschäftsentwicklung und Absatzmethode; ~ **swing** *(US)* Konjunkturwende; ~ **syndicate** Börsenkonsortium; ~ **system** Marktwirtschaft; ~ **terms** Börsenusancen; ~ **territory** Absatz-, Marktgebiet; ~ **testing** Marterkundung; ~ **tip** Börsentip; ~ **top** Höchstkurs; ~ **town** *(Br.)* Stadt mit Marktrecht, Marktflecken; ~ **train** Marktzug; ~ **transaction** Börsentransaktion, -geschäft; ~ **trend** Konjunktur-, Marktentwicklung, -tendenz, Trend; ~ **trend analysis** Konjunkturdiagnose; ~ **truth** Börsenwahrheit; ~ **upsurge** Emporschnellen der Kurse; ~ **valuation** Marktbewertung; ~ **value** Gemein-, Kauf-, Marktwert, *(stock exchange)* Kurswert, Tageskurs, notierter Kurs, Notierung, *(trading value)* Verkehrswert; **fair ~ value** üblicher Marktwert; **fair and reasonable ~ value** angemessener Wert, Verkehrswert; **fair-cash ~ value** gemeiner Wert, üblicher Marktpreis; **fluctuating ~ value** veränderlicher Kurs; **lower ~ value** niedriger Zeitwert; **open ~ value** *(inheritance tax, Br.)* Verkehrswert; **total ~ value** Gesamtkurswert; ~ **volume** Marktgröße, -volumen, -umfang; ~ **ware(s)** Marktware; ~ **watchman** Hallenaufseher; ~ **weakness** Marktschwäche.

marketability Marktfähigkeit, -gängigkeit, Börsenfähigkeit.

marketable *(salable)* marktfähig, marktbar, von marktfähiger Güte, marktgängig, absatzfähig, gang-, umsetz-, lieferbar, verkäuflich, *(stock exchange)* börsenfähig, -gängig, notiert, umlauffähig;

easily ~ leicht realisierbar;

to render goods ~ beschädigte Waren wieder zurechtmachen; ~ **equities** börsengängige Dividendenwerte; ~ **parcels** börsenübliche Stückzahl; ~ **prices** herrschende Marktpreise; ~ **products** verkaufsfähige (gängige) Ware; ~ **securities (stocks)** börsengängige (börsen-, marktfähige) Wertpapiere (Effekten); ~ **securities at cost** *(balance sheet, US)* Wertpapiere zu Ankaufskursen; **readily ~ staples** leicht realisierbare Waren; ~ **title** vollgültiger Rechtstitel; ~ **title [to land]** gerichtlich festgestellter Eigentumsanspruch; ~ **value** Markt-, Verkaufswert.

marketeer *(US)* Verkäufer, Händler, *(stock exchange)* Abgeber, Verkäufer.

developmental ~ aufgeschlossener Absatzfachmann; **pro ~** *(Br.)* Anhänger der britischen Zugehörigkeit zur Europäischen Gemeinschaft.

marketer *(US)* Marktbezieher, -besucher, *(marketing specialist)* Absatzfachmann.

marketing Lehre vom Warenabsatz, Gesamtheit aller absatzfördernder Maßnahmen, Absatzwirtschaft, -planung, Absatz[wesen], -bemühungen, -politik, Marktschaffung, -versorgung, Vertrieb[slehre], *(goods)* Marktvorräte, -waren; **~s** *(purchase)* Markteinkäufe, *(sales)* Marktverkäufe;

agricultural ~ Absatz landwirtschaftlicher Erzeugnisse; **associative (cooperative) ~** genossenschaftliches Absatzwesen; **commodity ~** Warenabsatz, -vertrieb; **direct ~** Direktabsatz, -vertrieb, individuelle Absatzpolitik; **industrial ~** Absatz von Industrieerzeugnissen; **innovatory ~** schöpferische Absatzpolitik; **orderly ~** *(US)* Vertriebs-, Absatzkontrolle, Selbstbeschränkungsabkommen; **organized ~** organisiertes Absatzwesen; **total ~** Gesamtabsatz;

~ **of an article** Gesamtheit der absatzfördernden Maßnahmen für einen Artikel; ~ **of securities** Effektenabsatz, -einführung; **to do one's ~** seine Einkäufe machen; **to go ~** auf den Markt gehen, *(commission agent)* Provisionsgeschäfte machen;

~ **activity** Vertriebs-, Absatztätigkeit; ~ **adviser** Vertriebs-, Absatzberater; ~ **agency** Vertriebsagentur, Verkaufsbüro, Absatzvertretung; ~ **agreement** Vertriebs-, Absatzvereinbarung; ~ **analysis** Markt- und Absatzanalyse; ~ **analyst** Absatzfachmann; ~ **area** Absatzbereich, -gebiet, Verkaufsgebiet; ~ **arrangement** Marktabrede, -absprache, -vereinbarung; ~ **association** Absatzvereinigung, absatzwirtschaftlicher Verband; ~ **audit** vertriebs- und marktpolitische Unternehmensanalyse; ~ **background** Marktlage; ~ **backing** Absatzunterstützung; ~ **behavio(u)r** marktorientiertes Verhalten; ~ **board** Absatzausschuß, Verteiler-, Absatzkontrollstelle; ~ **campaign** Absatzfeldzug, Werbekampagne, projektorientierte Aktion; ~ **cartel** Vertriebs-, Absatzkartell; ~ **center** Handelsplatz; ~ **channels** Absatzwege; ~ **company** Vertriebsgesellschaft; ~ **concept** Absatzdenken; ~ **conception** Absatzkonzeption; ~ **conditions** Vertriebs-, Absatzverhältnisse, -bedingungen; ~ **consultant** Fachmann (Berater) in den Fragen der Absatzförderung, freiberuflicher Vertriebsberater, freiberuflicher Berater in Absatzfragen; ~ **consulting** freiberufliche Vertriebsberatung; ~ **contract** Vertriebs-, Absatzvereinbarung; ~ **control** Absatzkontrolle; ~ **cooperative** Vertriebs-, Verwertungs-, Absatzgenossenschaft; ~ **corporation** *(US)* Vertriebsgesellschaft; ~ **costs** Absatz-, Vertriebskosten; ~ **data** Absatzzahlen, Vertriebsunterlagen; ~ **department** Vertriebs-, Marketingabteilung; ~ **difficulties** Absatzschwierigkeiten; ~ **director** Leiter der Vertriebsabteilung, Vertriebsdirektor; ~ **division** *(department of commerce, US)* Absatzforschungsabteilung; ~ **drive** Absatzfeldzug; ~ **economies** Einsparungen durch Verbesserungen des Absatzsystems; ~ **economist** Vertriebsfachmann; ~ **efficiency** Leistungsfähigkeit des Vertriebs-, Absatzapparates; ~ **efforts** Absatz-, Vertriebsanstrengungen; ~ **entry** Markterschließung; ~ **executive** Vorstandsmitglied für Absatz und Vertrieb, Vertriebs-, Marketingfachmann; ~ **expense(s)** Vertriebsunkosten; ~ **experience** Absatzerfahrung; ~ **expert** Marktsachverständiger, Fachmann für Fragen der Absatzförderung; ~ **facilities** Vertriebs-, Absatzwesen; ~ **field** Vertriebs-, Absatzwesen; ~ **financing** Absatzfinanzierung; ~ **functions** absatzwirtschaftliche Funktionen, Vertriebsfunktionen; ~ **gimmick** Absatzgag; ~ **goal** Absatz-, Vertriebsziel; **to run into ~ headaches** Schwierigkeiten bei der Absatzplanung bekommen; ~ **information** Vertriebs-, Absatzkunde; ~ **inquiry** Marktuntersuchung-, analyse; ~ **institution** Vertriebs-, Absatzeinrichtung; ~ **investigation** Absatzstudie; ~ **knowhow** Absatz-, Vertriebserfahrungen; ~ **knowledge** Absatzkunde; ~ **leadership** hervorragende absatztechnische Fähigkeiten; ~ **legislation** Vertriebsgesetzgebung; ~ **machinery** Vertriebsapparat, Absatzwirtschaftler, Verkaufsförderer; ~ **man** Vertriebsfachmann, Absatzwirtschaftler, -fachmann, Verkaufsförderer; ~ **manager** Vertriebsleiter, Leiter der Abteilung Absatzförderung (Vertriebsabteilung); ~ **mentality** absatzbewußte Mentalität; ~ **methods** Vertriebs-, Absatzmethoden; ~-**minded** absatz-, vertriebsbewußt; ~ **mindedness** Absatzbewußtsein; **to grow in ~ mindedness** sich immer mehr dem Absatzdenken zuwenden; ~ **mix** *(US)* Absatzplanung; ~ **net** Einkaufsnetz; ~ **operations** marktwirtschaftliche Maßnahmen; ~ **opportunity** Absatzchance, -möglichkeit; ~ **order** *(agricultural goods, US)* Absatzverordnung; ~-**oriented** absatzbewußt; ~ **orientedness** Absatzbewußtsein; ~ **organization** *(EG)* Marktorganisation; ~ **outlet** Einzelhandelsgeschäft; ~ **outlook** Absatzaussichten, -konjunktur; ~ **people** Absatzfachleute; ~ **personnel** Vertriebspersonal; ~ **picture** Absatzbild; ~ **plan** Absatzplanung; ~ **planning** Absatzplanung; ~ **policy** Vertriebs-, Absatzpolitik; ~ **practices** Verkaufspraktiken; ~ **problem** Absatzfrage; ~ **procedure** **(process)** Vertriebs-, Absatzverfahren; ~ **product** Vertriebs-, Absatzprodukt; ~ **program(m)e** Absatz-, Vertriebsprogramm; ~ **proposal** Vertriebs-, Absatzvorschlag; ~ **quota** Absatzquote, -kontingent, Sollvorhaben für den Absatz; ~ **regulation** *(EG)* Marktordnung; ~ **regulatory** Marktordnung; ~ **research** Markt-, Absatzforschung, Marktanalyse; ~ **research study** Vertriebs-, Absatzstudie; ~ **researcher** Absatz-, Marktforscher; ~ **resource** Absatzbereitschaft; ~ **season** Verkaufssaison; ~ **specialist**, Vertriebs-, Absatzfachmann, Absatzspezialist; ~ **statistics** Absatzstatistik; ~ **structure** Absatzstruktur; ~ **study** Absatz-, Vertriebsstudie; ~ **subsidiary** Vertriebsgesellschaft; ~ **surplus** Absatzüberschuß; ~ **survey** Marktanalyse; **field ~ survey** Marktforschung an Ort und Stelle; ~ **system** Absatzwesen, Vertriebssystem; ~ **technique** Absatz-, Vertriebstechnik; ~ **terminology** Verkaufsterminologie; ~ **terms** Begriffe des Absatzwesens (Vertriebswesens); ~ **territory** Absatzbezirk; ~ **transaction** absatzwirtschaftliche Maßnahmen; ~ **venture** Auftreten auf dem Markt, Marktuntersuchung; ~ **year** *(EG)* Getreidewirtschaftsjahr.

marketman Marktbesucher, -bezieher.

marking Be-, Kennzeichnung, Markierung, *(check, US)* Bestätigungsvermerk, *(prices)* Preisauszeichnung, *(stock exchange, Br.)* Kursnotierung;
~**s** *(stock exchange)* Tagesumsätze;
deceptive ~ falsche Bezeichnung; **national** ~ *(airplane)* Hoheitsabzeichen;
~ **of articles patented** Kennzeichnung von Markenerzeugnissen; ~ **of a check** *(US)* Bestätigung eines Schecks, Scheckbestätigung; ~ **out of a claim** Grenzziehung, Vermarkung, Grundstücksabsteckung;
~ **clerk** *(stock exchange, Br.)* Kursmakler; ~ **department** Preisermittlungsabteilung; ~ **ink** Wäsche-, Zeichentinte; ~ **instructions** Kennzeichnungsbestimmungen; ~ **machine** Kennzeichnungsmaschine; **to be in good** ~ **name** *(Br.)* zum Zahlstellengeschäft zugelassen sein; ~ **pencil** Signier-, Markierungsstift; ~ **requirements** Kennzeichnungsvorschriften.

markon *(US)* Kalkulationsaufschlag.

marksman Schreibunkundiger, Analphabet, *(mil.)* Scharfschütze.

markup Artikel-, Stück-, Einzel-, Wareneinzelspanne, Handelsspanne, Kalkulationsaufschlag, *(customs)* Aufschlag, *(difference between cost and retail price of merchandise)* Rohgewinnaufschlag [auf den Einkaufspreis], *(pricing)* höhere Auszeichnung, Preiserhöhung;
import ~ Aufschlag auf den Einfuhrpreis; **inventory** ~ Rohgewinnaufschlag auf das Warenlager; **product line** ~ Branchenhandelsspanne;
~ **on cost** Kalkulationsaufschlag auf den Einstandspreis; ~ **on prices** Preiserhöhung, höhere Preisauszeichnung; ~ **on retail prices** Kalkulationsaufschlag auf den Verkaufspreis; ~ **on selling prices** Handelsspanne;
to put a flat ~ **on all items** bei allen Artikeln einheitlich dieselbe Handelsspanne berechnen;
~ **cancellation** Aufhebung der Preiserhöhungen; ~ **percentage** Bruttogewinnsatz; ~ **pricing** an der Nachfrageelastizität orientierte Preiskalkulation.

marline rate *(advertising, US)* Anzeigenzeilenkosten pro Umsatz von 1 Milliarde Dollar.

marmor *(v.)* **book edges** Bücherschnitte marmorieren.

maroon *(v.)* auf einer einsamen Insel aussetzen, *(sl., Br.)* herumlungern.

marooner Seeräuber, Pirat.

marque Kaperschiff.

marquee großes Zelt, *(hotel)* Schirmdach, *(circus use, sl.)* Haupteingang.

marriage Ehe[stand], Eheschließung, Heirat, *(advertising)* Verschmelzung zweier Entwürfe;
at the time of ~ zum Zeitpunkt der Eheschließung; **by** ~ angeheiratet; **related by** ~ verschwägert;
bigamous ~ Bigamie; **church** ~ kirchliche Trauung; **common-law** ~ Ziviltrauung, -ehe, standesamtlich geschlossene Ehe, standesamtliche Trauung; **communal** ~ Gruppenehe; **compassionate** ~ wilde Ehe; **consensual** ~ mündlich geschlossene Ehe; **fictitious** ~ Scheinehe; **lawful** ~ gültige Ehe; **lefthand** ~ Eheschließung zur linken Hand, morganatische Ehe; **mixed** ~ gemischte Ehe, Mischehe; **morganatic** ~ morganatische Ehe; **plural** ~ Polygamie; **Scotch** ~ formlose Eheschließung; **secret** ~ heimliche Ehe; **valid** ~ rechtsgültige Ehe; **void** ~ ungültige Ehe, Nichtehe; **voidable** ~ anfechtbare Ehe;
~ **of convenience** Konventionalheirat; ~ **of interest** Geldheirat; ~ **in name only** Scheinehe; ~ **by proxy** Ferntrauung; ~ **in a registry office (in the office of a superintendent registrar,** *Br.)* standesamtliche Trauung;
to announce a ~ Eheschließung anzeigen; **to annul a** ~ Ehe für nichtig erklären; **to be an impediment to** ~ Ehehindernis darstellen; **to bring about a** ~ Ehe stiften; **to celebrate (contract) a** ~ Ehe eingehen (schließen), eheliche Verbindung eingehen, Trauung vollziehen; **to give s. o. in** ~ j. verheiraten; **to have a** ~ **nullified by decree of court** Ehe für nichtig erklären lassen; **to make a brilliant** ~ glänzende Partie machen; **to refuse an offer of** ~ Heiratsantrag ablehnen; **to take s. one's hand in** ~ mit jem. die Ehe eingehen, sich mit jem. verheiraten;
~ **Act** *(Br.)* Ehegesetz; **Foreign ~ Act** *(Br.)* Gesetz über Eheschließungen im Ausland; ~ **antenuptial ~ agreement** vorehelicher Güterrechtsvertrag; ~ **allowance** Ehegattenfreibetrag; ~ **articles** vorläufiger Ehevertrag; ~ **barrier** Eheverbot; ~ **bond** Ehebund; ~ **broker** Heiratsvermittler[in]; ~ **brokerage** Heiratsvermittlung; ~ **brokerage contract** Ehevermittlungsvertrag; ~ **ceremony** Trauung, Eheschließung[sfeierlichkeit, -akt], Trauungszeremonie; **to undergo a ~ ceremony** sich trauen lassen; ~ **certificate** Trauschein, Heiratsurkunde; ~ **consideration** Schadenersatz wegen Bruches des Eheversprechens; ~ **contract** *(US)* Güterrechtsvertrag; ~ **dispensation** Ehedispens; ~ **document** Heiratsurkunde; ~ **failure** gescheiterte Ehe; ~ **grant** Ehestandsbeihilfe; ~ **guidance** Eheberatung; ~ **guidance council** Eheberatungsstelle; ~ **guidance counsellor** Eheberater; ~ **law** Eherecht; ~ **licence** *(US)* Ehegenehmigung, -konsens, Heiratserlaubnis; ~ **lines** *(Br.)* Trauschein; ~ **loan** Ehestandsdarlehen; ~ **needs of a woman** Heiratszulage; ~ **notice book** *(Br.)* Aufgebots-, Heiratsregister; ~ **officer** *(diplomatic service, Br.)* Konsulatsbeamter mit der Berechtigung, Eheschließungen vorzunehmen; ~ **outfit** Aussteuer; ~ **portion** Mitgift, Aussteuer, Heiratsgut; ~ **portion insurance** Aussteuerversicherung; ~ **promise** Eheversprechen; ~ **rate** Zahl der Eheschließungen pro Kopf der Bevölkerung; ~ **ring** Trauring, Ehering; ~ **rites** Hochzeitszeremoniell; ~ **service** Trauung; ~ **settlement** Ehevertrag; ~ **statistics** Heiratsstatistik; ~ **tie** eheliches Band, Eheband.

marriageable ehetauglich, -mündig, heiratsfähig, mannbar;
~ **age** heiratsfähiges Alter, Heiratsalter.

marriageableness Ehemündigkeit, -tauglichkeit, Heiratsfähigkeit.

married verheiratet;
~ **at a registry** standesamtlich getraut;
of an age to be ~ heiratsfähig sein; **to be happily** ~ in glücklicher Ehe leben; **to get** ~ Ehe schließen, sich verehelichen;
~ **allowance** *(married couple, Br.)* Ehegattenfreibetrag für Verheiratete; ~ **couple** Eheleute; ~ **life** eheliche Gemeinschaft, Eheleben; ~ **man** Verheirateter, Ehemann; ~ **people** Eheleute; ~ **state** Ehestand; ~ **woman** Ehefrau; ~ **women's property act** *(Br.)* Gesetz über die güterrechtliche Stellung der Ehefrau.

marrow Kern, Wesentliches;
to the ~ bis aufs Mark;
pith and ~ **of a statement** Quintessenz einer Erklärung.

marry *(v.)* heiraten, Ehe schließen, sich verehelichen;
~ **again** sich wiederverheiraten, zweite Ehe eingehen; ~ **over the broomstick** zur linken Hand heiraten; ~ **into a business** in ein Geschäft einheiraten; ~ **into a family** einheiraten; ~ **a fortune** reich heiraten; ~ **without the knowledge of one's parents** ohne Einverständnis seiner Eltern heiraten; ~ **money** Geldheirat eingehen, nach Geld heiraten; ~ **off** verheiraten, unter die Haube bringen.

marrying Verheiratung, *(stock exchange)* Antrag;
~ **man** Ehekandidat.
marsh Sumpfland.
marshal *(court of law, Br.)* Urkundsbeamter, Gerichtsschreiber, *(executioner, US)* Vollzugs-, Vollstreckungsbeamter, *(festival)* Festordner, Zeremonienmeister, *(fire department, US)* Feuerwehrhauptmann, *(mil.)* Marschall, *(police)* Bezirkspolizeichef; **Air** ~ Luftmarschall; **city** ~ *(US)* Polizeidirektor; **fire** ~ *(US)* Branddirektor, Feuerwehrhauptmann; **knight** ~ *(Br.)* Hofmarschall;
~ **of the diplomatic corps** Protokollchef;
~ *(v.)* ordnen, ordnungsgemäß aufstellen, arrangieren, *(mil.)* in Schlachtordnung aufstellen, *(railway)* rangieren, zusammenstellen, verschieben;
~ **one's arguments** seine Gründe zusammenstellen; ~ **assets** Aktiva [im Konkurs] (Verteilungsplan) feststellen; ~ **a company at table** Tischordnung machen; ~ **creditors** Rangordnung der Gläubiger festlegen, Gläubigerrangordnung feststellen; ~ **facts** Tatsachenmaterial zusammentragen; ~ **military forces** Streitkräfte aufmarschieren lassen; ~ **liens** Pfandobjekte erfassen; ~ **securities** Sicherheiten aufteilen, Konkurstabelle aufstellen.
marshal(l)ing An-, Einordnung, *(railway)* Rangieren;
~ **assets** *(bankruptcy)* Feststellung der Aktiva, Rangordnung der Sicherheiten, Aufstellung eines Verteilungsplans; ~ **liens** Feststellung der Rangordnung von Pfandobjekten; ~ **remedies** Gläubigerbeschränkung; ~ **securities** Aufteilung der Sicherheiten, Aufstellung der Konkurstabelle;
~ **yard** *(Br.)* Rangier-, Verschiebebahnhof.
marshland Sumpfland, Moor.
mart Handelszentrum, Jahrmarkt, *(auction room)* Auktionsraum.
martial kriegerisch, militärisch, soldatisch;
~ **array** Schlachtaufstellung.
martial law Stand-, Kriegsrecht;
according to ~ standrechtlich;
to be under ~ unter Standrecht stehen; **to declare (proclaim)** ~ Standrecht verhängen; **to lift** ~ Kriegsrechtverhängung wieder aufheben; **to try by** ~ vor ein Standgericht stellen.
martial| music Militärmusik; ~ **spirit** Kampfesmut.
martyr Märtyrer;
to die a ~ **in the cause of science** sein Leben im Dienst der Wissenschaft opfern; **to make a** ~ **of o. s.** sich als Märtyrer aufspielen.
martyrdom Märtyrertum.
mascot Glücksbringer, Maskottchen, Talisman;
radiator ~ Kühlerfigur.
mash *(fig.)* Mischmasch, Gemisch.
mask *(masquerade)* Maske, Maskierung, Verkleidung, Maskerade, *(mil.)* Tarnung, Blende, *(photo)* Vorsatzscheibe, *(pretext)* Vorwand, Schein, *(print.)* Abdeckrahmen, Decker;
under the ~ **of** unter dem Schein; **under the** ~ **of night** im Schutze der Nacht;
carnival ~ Karnevalsmaske; **death** ~ Totenmaske; **gas** ~ Gasmaske; **oxygen** ~ Sauerstoffmaske; **protective** ~ Schutzmaske;
~ *(v.)* *(mil.)* tarnen;
~ **one's enmity under an appearance of friendliness** seine Feindschaft mit angeblicher Freundschaft tarnen; ~ **out** *(reproduction)* abdecken, ausdecken, retouchieren; ~ **a ship under a neutral flag** Schiff unter einer falschen neutralen Flagge laufen lassen;
to put on a ~ Maske aufsetzen, sich maskieren; **to throw off one's** ~ Maske fallen lassen.
masked maskiert, *(mil.)* getarnt, *(ship)* mit falschen Papieren versehen;
~ **advertising** Schleichwerbung; ~ **ball** Maskenball; ~ **gun** getarntes (verstecktes) Geschütz; ~ **headlight** Tarnscheinwerfer; ~ **troops** getarnte Truppen.
masking Maskierung, *(fig.)* Verstellung, Schauspielerei, Theater;
~ **out** *(reproduction)* Ab-, Ausdecken;
~ **paper** Abdeckpapier; ~ **tape** Klebestreifen.
masquerade Maskenfest, -kostüm;
~ *(v.)* maskiert umhergehen;
~ **under a false name** sich hinter einem falschen Namen verstecken.
masquerader Maskenzugteilnehmer, Schwindler.
mass Masse, Anhäufung, -sammlung, *(aggregation)* Gesamtheit, Aggregat, Komplex, *(bankruptcy)* Konkursmasse, *(church)* Messe;
the ~**es** die Allgemeinheit, die breiten Massen;
in the ~ im großen und ganzen;

~ **of assets** Anlagenkomplex, Vermögens-, Aktivmasse; ~ **of the audience** Mehrzahl der Zuhörer; ~ **of errors** Unmenge von Fehlern; ~ **of evidence** Fülle von Beweisen; ~ **of imports** überwiegender Teil der Einfuhr; ~ **of letters** Fülle von Briefen; ~ **of manoeuvre** *(Br.)* strategische Reserve; ~ **of mistakes** Fehleranhäufung; **great** ~ **of people** breite Bevölkerungsschichten; ~ **of the population** Masse des Volkes; ~ **of snow** Schneemassen; ~ **of traffic** Ansammlung von Fahrzeugen; ~ **of troops** Truppenansammlung;
~ *(v.)* sich ansammeln, massieren;
~ **troops on the frontier** Truppen an der Grenze zusammenziehen;
to be a ~ **of bruises** *(coll.)* überall blaue Flecken haben; **to gather in** ~**es** massiert in Erscheinung treten;
~ **action** massierte Aktionen; ~ **advertising** Massenwerbung; ~**-announcement exchange** Fernsprechansagedienst; ~ **appeal** Massenanreiz; ~ **approach** Massenansprache; ~ **arrests** Massenverhaftungen; ~ **attack** *(mil.)* massierter Angriff; ~ **circulation** Massenauflage; ~ **circulation media** Massenmedia; ~**-circulation paper** Massenblatt; ~ **communications** Massenmedia; ~ **consumption** Massenverbrauch; ~ **demonstrations** Massendemonstrationen; ~ **deportation** Massendeportation; ~ **discount** Mengenrabatt; ~ **dismissal** Massenentlassungen; ~ **display** Massenauslage; ~ **effect** Massenwirkung; ~ **entertainment** Massenbelustigung, -veranstaltung; ~ **execution** Massenerschießung, -hinrichtung; ~ **grave** Massengrab; ~ **housing** Massenunterbringung, -wohnsiedlung; ~ **hysteria** Massenhysterie; ~ **income** Masseneinkommen; ~ **jump** *(mil.)* Massenabsprung; ~ **magazine** Massenblatt; ~ **markets** Massenmärkte; ~**-market** *(v.)* in großen Mengen auf den Markt bringen; ~ **marketing** Massenabsatz; ~ **media** Massenmedien; ~ **meeting** Massenversammlung; ~ **movement** Massenbewegung; ~ **murder** Massenmord; ~ **murderer** Massenmörder; ~ **observation** *(Br.)* Meinungsforschung bei der gesamten Bevölkerung; ~ **picketing** massiertes Streikpostenaufgebot; ~**-produce** *(v.)* fabrikmäßig herstellen, in Massen produzieren; ~**-produce** *(v.)* **its service** aufgrund von Massenproduktion einen einheitlichen Service leisten; ~**-produced** in Serien[produktion] (fabrikmäßig) hergestellt; ~**-produced article** Serien-, Massenartikel; ~ **producer** Massenhersteller.
mass production Massenerzeugung, -herstellung, -produktion, -fabrikation, fabrikmäßige Herstellung, Serienproduktion, -herstellung;
standardized ~ Fließbandarbeit, Herstellung am laufenden Band;
~ **car** Serienwagen; ~ **enterprise (firm)** Groß-, Massenhersteller; ~ **industry** Massengüterindustrie; ~ **society** Massenproduktionsgesellschaft.
mass| purchasing power Massenkaufkraft; ~ **rally** Massenversammlung; ~ **response** Massenzuspruch; ~ **selling** Massenverkauf, -absatz, -vertrieb; ~ **strike** Generalstreik; ~ **suggestion** Massensuggestion; ~ **transit** Massentransport; ~ **transit problems** Probleme des Massentransports; ~ **transport[ation]** Massentransport; ~ **transport system** Massentransportsystem; ~ **unemployment** Massenarbeitslosigkeit; ~ **unit** Masseneinheit; ~ **vaccination** Massenimpfung.
Massachusetts Trust *(US)* treuhänderisch geleitetes Unternehmen.
massage parlo(u)r Massagesalon.
massacre Massaker, Massentötung, -mord, Blutbad;
~ *(v.)* Blutbad anrichten, massakrieren, Massenmord begehen.
massive massig, massiv;
~ **layoffs** Massenentlassungen.
mast [Antennen]mast, Schiffsmast, *(airship)* Ankermast;
electric ~ Laternenpfahl, Kandelaber;
to sail before the ~ im Mannschaftsgrad zur See fahren.
master *(captain)* Kapitän, Schiffer, *(corporation)* Leiter, Vorsteher, *(craft)* Handwerksmeister, Chef, *(law court)* protokollführender Gerichtsbeamter, *(employer)* Principal, Arbeitgeber, Geschäfts-, Dienstherr, Vorgesetzter, *(law officer, Br.)* Rechtspfleger, *(law officer, US)* Hilfsrichter, *(owner)* Besitzer, Eigentümer, *(person skilled in trade)* [Werk]meister, *(record)* Matrize, *(school, Br.)* Lehrer, Studienrat, *(title)* Magister, *(university college, US)* Rektor;
billet ~ *(mil.)* Quartiermeister; **form** ~ Klassenlehrer; **little** ~ *(journeyman, Br.)* Geselle, *(undercontractor)* Unterlieferant; **mathematics** ~ *(Br.)* Mathematiklehrer; **old** ~ *(art)* alter Meister; **special** ~ Gerichtsbeauftragter, -vertreter; **taxing** ~ Kostenfestsetzungsbeamter;
~**[s] and men (servant)** Arbeitgeber und Arbeitnehmer;

~-at-arms Schiffsprofos; **~ of Arts** Magister der freien Künste; **~ of business administration** graduierter Betriebswirt; **~ of ceremonies** Zeremonienmeister, Protokollchef, *(US)* Conferencier; **~ in chancery** Rechtspfleger; **~ of city planning** *(US)* Planungsingenieur; **~ of coasting vessel** Küstenschiffer; **~ of common law** *(Br.)* Urkundsbeamter der Geschäftsstelle, Rechtspfleger; **≗ of the Crown office** *(Br.)* [etwa] Staatsanwalt; **~ of economics** graduierter Volkswirt; **~ in English** *(Br.)* Englischlehrer; **~ of the house** Hausherr; **~ of law** Magister der Rechte; **~ in lunacy** *(Br.)* Gerichtsbeauftragter im Entmündigungsverfahren, Aufsichtsbeamter in Nervenheilanstalten; **~ of the mint** Münzwardein; **≗ of the Rolls** *(Court of Appeal, Br.)* Oberster Richter; **≗ of Science** Magister der Naturwissenschaften; **~ of a trading vessel** Kapitän eines Handelsschiffes, Handelskapitän;

~ *(v.)* meistern, beherrschen, bewältigen, *(lead)* leiten, führen; **~ a difficulty** Schwierigkeit bewältigen; **~ one's feelings** sich beherrschen; **~ a foreign language** Fremdsprache beherrschen; **~ the intricacies of municipal finances** kompliziertes Gebiet der Kommunalfinanzen beherrschen; **~ a situation** Situation meistern; **~ a subject** Fach beherrschen;

to be one's own ~ unabhängig sein; **to be ~ of a large fortune** über ein großes Vermögen verfügen können; **to be ~ in one's own house** völlig frei entscheiden können, Herr im Hause sein; **to be ~ of the situation** Herr der Lage sein; **to be ~ of a subject** Fachgebiet beherrschen; **to be ~ of one's time** über seine Zeit frei verfügen können; **to make o. s. ~ of s. th.** etw. in seinen Besitz bringen; **to make o. s. ~ of a language** Sprache im Selbststudium erlernen;

like ~ like man wie der Herr so's Geschirr;

~ *(a.)* hauptsächlich, wichtigst;

~ agreement Manteltarifabkommen; **~ attendant** Hafenmeister; **~ bedroom** *(US)* Elternschlafzimmer; **~ budget** Gesamtetat, -haushaltsplan; **~ builder** Baumeister, -unternehmer; **~ card** Leit-, Stamm-, Grundkarte; **to obtain one's ~'s certificate** sein Kapitänspatent bekommen; **~ charge** *(US)* Kreditkarte; **~ clock** Kontrolluhr; **~ control account** Hauptkontrollkonto; **~ copy** *(cinema)* Originalkopie, *(law of contract)* maßgebliches Exemplar; **~ craftsman** Handwerksmeister; **~ of science in business administration degree** Doktor der Betriebswissenschaft; **to take one's ~ degree** sein Doktorexamen machen; **~ file** Zentralkartei; **~ freight agreement** Rahmenfrachtabkommen; **~ group contract** Sammelversicherungsvertrag; **~ hand** Fachmann, Spezialist, Meister; **~ key** Haupt-, Nachschlüssel; **~ mariner** Handelskapitän, Kapitän auf großer Fahrt; **~ mechanic** Vorarbeiter, Werksmeister; **~ mould** Originalform; **~ paper** Umdruckoriginalpapier; **~ pay record** Lohnkonto; **~ plan** umfassender Plan, Gesamtkonzeption; **~ plate** Originalklischee; **~ policy** *(life insurance)* Gruppen-, Rahmenpolice; **~ print** vollendeter Photoabzug; **~ register** Klassenbuch; **~ and servant relation** Dienst[vertrags]verhältnis; **~ sample** *(statistics)* Ausgangsstichprobe; **~ schedule** Gesamtplan; **~ scheduling** Gesamtplanung; **~ scheme with profits endowment assurance** *(Br.)* gewinnbeteiligte Gruppenversicherung auf den Erlebensfall; **~ sergeant** *(US mil.)* Haupt-, Stabsfeldwebel; **~ stroke** Glanzstück, Meisterleistung, -zug; **~ stroke of diplomacy** meisterhaft diplomatischer Schachzug; **~ summary sheet** Betriebsabrechnungsbogen; **~ switch** Hauptschalter; **~ tenant** Hauptmieter; **~ touch** Feineinstellung; **~'s wages** Kapitänsheuer; **~ workman** Werkmeister, Vorarbeiter.

masterly performance Meisterleistung.
mastermind *(US)* Kapazität, Köpfchen, Kanone;
~ *(v.)* hinter den Kulissen wirken.
masterpiece Meisterstück.
mastership Lehramt, *(organization of employers)* Arbeitgebervereinigung;
to attain a ~ in es zur Meisterschaft bringen; **to enter upon a ~** Lehramt antreten.
masterwork Meisterstück.
mastery Herrschaft, Gewalt;
to gain the ~ Oberhand gewinnen.
masthead *(newspaper)* Impressum.
mat Matte, Abtreter, Vorleger, *(photo)* Wechselrahmen, Passepartout, *(print.)* Matrize;
~s Matern;
beer ~ Bierfilz, -deckel;
~ *(v.)* mit Matten auslegen;
to be on the ~ *(sl.)* zur Rechenschaft gezogen werden, es ausbaden müssen; **to have s. o. on the ~** j. zurechtweisen;
~ *(a.)* glanzlos, matt;
~ service Materndienst.

match Gegenstück, *(contest)* Wettspiel, -kampf, Match, *(item)* Ware, Artikel gleicher Qualität, *(splinter of wood)* Streichholz; **football ~** Fußballspiel; **a good ~** gute Partie; **safety ~** Sicherheitszündholz; **shouting ~** lautstarkes Rededuell; **spent ~** abgebranntes Streichholz;
perfect ~ of colo(u)rs vollkommene Farbenübereinstimmung;
~ *(v.)* (to be able to contend with) es aufnehmen können, *(find material that matches)* etw. Passendes finden, *(harmonize)* zusammenpassen, dazu passen, *(make equal)* anpassen, passend zusammenstellen, *(v./i.)* sich verheiraten, *(tax statement)* anpassen;
~ against aufwiegen; **~ new cars on the market** neue Autotypen auf dem Markt einführen; **~ costs and revenues** Kosten den Erträgen anpassen; **~ s. one's grade** dieselbe Qualität liefern wie; **~ the sample** mit dem Muster übereinstimmen; **~ one's strength against s. o.** seine Kräfte gegen j. messen; **~ well** gut zusammenpassen; **~ with** vergleichen mit;
to be a ~ for s. o. sich mit jem. messen können; **to be a ~ for s. th.** einer Sache gewachsen sein; **to be more than a ~ for s. o.** j. in die Tasche stecken; **to be up to the ~** auf der Höhe sein; **to make a ~ of it** Heirat zustandebringen; **to make a good ~** gute Partie machen; **to meet one's ~** seinen Mann (seinesgleichen) finden; **to meet more than one's ~** seinen Meister finden;
~ monopoly Zündwarenmonopol.
matchable zusammenpassend.
matchboarding Täfelung.
matchbook, matchbox Streichhölzchenheft, Streichholzschachtel;
~ advertising Zündholzwerbung.
matched| colo(u)r Mischfarbe; **~ groups** Parallelgruppen; **~ orders** *(US)* Börsenaufträge zum gleichzeitigen Kauf und Verkauf des gleichen Wertpapiers; **~ samples** abgestimmte Vergleichsstichproben.
matching *(balance sheet)* Anpassung, periodische Abgrenzung von Aufwand und Ertrag;
~ clause Anpassungsklausel.
matchless *(economics)* konkurrenzlos.
matchmaker Streichholzfabrikant, *(marriage)* Ehestifter, Heiratsvermittler.
matchmaking Streichholzfabrikation, *(marriage)* Ehevermittlung.
matchmark Montagezeichen.
matchwood Streichhölzerholz;
to make ~ of s. th. etw. kurz und klein schlagen, Brennholz aus etw. machen.
mate Arbeitskamerad, Gefährte, *(helper)* Handlanger, Gehilfe, *(husband)* Ehegatte, *(merchant marine)* Steuermann, Maat, *(ship)* Steuermann, Maat;
chief ~ erster Offizier;
~ *(v.)* words with deeds den Worten Taten folgen lassen;
~'s receipt Steuermannsquittung, Steuermanns-, Bordempfangsschein, Auslieferungs-, Verladeschein, Verladebescheinigung.
material Werkstoff, Substanz, Material, Baustoff-, *(accessories)* Zubehör, Bestandteil, *(woven fabric)* Stoff, *(scientific work)* Hilfsquelle, Unterlagen;
auxiliary ~s Hilfsstoffe; **building ~** Baumaterial, Baustoff; **chief ~** Hauptmaterial; **~s consumed** *(balance sheet)* Materialverbrauch; **crude ~** Rohmaterial; **defective ~** fehlerhaftes Material, Materialfehler; **direct ~** Produktions-, Fertigungsmaterial, unmittelbar benötigtes Material; **faulty ~** Materialfehler; **fission ~** spaltbares Material; **indirect ~** Gemeinkostenmaterial; **insulating ~** Isolationsmaterial; **low-value ~** minderwertiges Material; **office ~s** Büroeinrichtung[sgegenstände]; **photographic ~s** Photozubehör; **raw ~** Roh-, Werkstoff; **reliable ~** bewährtes Material; **~s requisitioned** Materialanforderungen; **war ~** Kriegsmaterial; **worked ~** aufgearbeitetes Material; **working ~** Betriebsmaterial; **writing ~s** Schreibutensilien, -materialien;
labo(u)r and ~s Arbeitslohn und Materialkosten;
~s on hand Materialbestand; **~s fit for the job** verarbeitungsfähiges Material; **~s unfit for the job** ungeeignetes (unbrauchbares) Material; **~ on order** bestelltes Material; **~ in process of production** in Verarbeitung befindliches Material; **~ required for production** für die Produktion erforderliche Materialien; **indirect ~s and supplies** Materialgemeinkosten; **~ for thought** Stoff zum Nachdenken;
not to be ~ to the point in question für den infragekommenden Punkt unerheblich sein; **to buy a house for its ~** Haus auf Abbruch kaufen; **to collect ~ for a scientific work** Material für eine wissenschaftliche Arbeit zusammenstellen; **to disseminate**

propaganda ~ Propagandamaterial verteilen; **to provide** ~ **for discussion** Diskussionsstoff abgeben; **to tool** ~ Material einsetzen;

~ *(a.)* materiell, körperlich, leiblich, substantiell, *(essential)* ausschlaggebend, unumgänglich, wesentlich, *(relevant)* rechtserheblich, relevant, einschlägig;

~ **accounting** Materialabrechnung; ~ **allegation** wesentliche Prozeßbehauptung; ~ **alteration** *(instrument)* rechtserhebliche Veränderung; ~ **analysis** Rohstoffeindeckungsplan; ~ **assets** Sachwerte; ~ **budget** Materialkostenplan, **direct** ~ **budget** Materialkostenplan, Materialbedarfsplanung; ~ **car** Materialienwaggon; ~ **change** *(bill of exchange)* nachträgliche Wechseländerung; ~ **change of user** *(building, Br.)* wesentliche Gebrauchsänderung; ~ **circumstance** in der Sache begründeter (wesentlicher) Umstand; ~ **comforts and pleasures** materielle Vorzüge und Annehmlichkeiten; **to have enough for one's** ~ **comforts** sich ein angenehmes Leben leisten können; ~ **concealment** *(insurance law)* Verschweigen wesentlicher Umstände (Tatsachen); ~ **consequence** sachliche Folgerung; ~ **consumption** Materialverbrauch; ~ **control** Materialkontrolle, -prüfung; ~ **costs** sachliche Ausgaben, Materialkosten; **direct** ~ **cost** direkter Materialaufwand; **indirect** ~ **costs** Materialgemeinkosten; ~ **cost burden rate** Materialgemeinkostenzuschlag, -satz; ~ **costing** Materialkostenermittlung; ~ **damage** Schaden wirtschaftlicher Art, Sachschaden; ~ **data** wesentliche Angaben; ~ **defect** Materialfehler; ~ **detriment** wesentlicher (erheblicher) Nachteil; ~ **discomfort** erhebliche Belästigung; ~ **evidence** beweiserhebliche Zeugenaussage; ~ **expenditure** Sachaufwand; ~ **expenses** Sachaufwendungen, Sachkosten; ~ **fact** *(insurance contract)* wesentliche Tatsache; **to suppress** ~ **facts** wesentliche Tatsachen verschweigen; ~ **flow** Werkstoffdurchlauf; ~ **goods** Materialien, Sachgüter; ~**s handling** *(US)* Material-, Werkstoffbehandlung, -bearbeitung; ~ **interests** Beteiligungen von erheblichem Umfang; ~ **issue** für die Entscheidung wesentlicher Punkt; ~ **item** *(balance sheet)* wesentlicher Bilanzposten;~**s management** Materialverwaltung; ~ **misrepresentation** absichtliches Verschweigen von für die Versicherungsgesellschaft wesentlichen Umständen; ~ **needs** materielle Bedürfnisse; ~ **period** rechtserheblicher Zeitraum; ~ **point of view** weltliche Betrachtung der Dinge; ~**s prices** Materialpreise; ~ **property** Sacheigentum; ~ **provision** wesentliche Bestimmung; ~ **purchases** Rohstoffkäufe; ~**-received report** *(US)* Materialempfangsbescheinigung; ~ **requirements** Materialbedarf; ~ **requisition** Materialanforderung; ~ **requisition slip** Materialentnahmeschein; ~ **resources** Rohstoffquellen; **to have been of a** ~ **service to s. o.** jem. wesentliche Dienste geleistet haben; ~ **shortage** Materialknappheit, Materialverknappung; **raw** ~ **substitution** Werkstoffumstellung, -ersatz; ~ **supplies** Materialvorrat; ~ **terms** wesentliche Bestimmungen; ~ **testing** Materialprobe, -prüfung; ~**s testing office** Materialprüfungsamt; **at the** ~ **time** zu der betreffenden Zeit; ~ **train** Materialzug; ~ **value** Barverkaufswert; ~ **wellbeing** körperliches Wohlbefinden; ~ **witness** Hauptzeuge.

materialism, dialectic dialektischer Materialismus; **historical** ~ historischer Materialismus.

materialist Materialist.

materialize *(v./i.)* sich erfüllen, sich verwirklichen, Gestalt annehmen, *(v./tr.)* in die Wirklichkeit umsetzen, realisieren.

materialman Baustoffhändler.

maternal von mütterlicher Seite;

~ **care** mütterliche Pflege; ~ **hospital** Entbindungsheim; ~ **line** Abstammung mütterlicherseits; ~ **mortality** Müttersterblichkeit; ~ **property** mütterliches Vermögen; ~ **welfare** Mütterfürsorge.

maternity Mutterschaft;

~ **allowance (benefit, fee, relief)** Wochenhilfe, -geld; ~ **care** Entbindungsfürsorge; ~ **center** *(US)* **(centre,** *Br.***)** Mütterberatungsstelle; ~ **child welfare centre** *(Br.)* Betreuungsstelle für Mutter und Kind; ~ **grant** *(Br.)* Mütterbeihilfe; ~ **home** Entbindungs-, Wöchnerinnenheim; ~ **hospital** Entbindungsanstalt; ~ **insurance** Mutterschaftsversicherung; ~ **leave** Entbindungsurlaub; ~ **pay** Mutterschaftsgeld; ~ **period** Mutterschutzfrist; ~ **ward** *(hospital)* Entbindungsabteilung; ~ **welfare** Mutterschaftsfürsorge; ⚖ **and Child Welfare Act** *(Br.)* Fürsorgegesetz für Mutter und Kind.

mathematical|expectation mathematische Erwartung; ~ **reserve** Deckungsrücklage, -kapital.

mathematics|of distribution Vertriebsmathematik; ~ **of finance** Finanzmathematik; ~ **of marketing** Absatzmathematik.

matinée Nachmittagsvorstellung, Matinee.

matriarchy Matriarchat.

matriculate Immatrikulierter;

~ *(v.)* sich immatrikulieren (einschreiben), *(admit to membership)* als Vereinsmitglied aufnehmen;

~ **a student** Studenten immatrikulieren; ~ **for university entrance** sich an einer Universität matrikulieren.

matriculation Immatrikulation;

~ **examination** *(Br.)* Zulassungsprüfung [zur Universität].

matrimonial ehelich;

extra-~ außerehelich;

~ **action** Klage in Ehesachen; ~ **adviser** Eheberater; ~ **agency** Heiratsvermittlung[sbüro]; ~ **agent** Heiratsvermittler; ~ **assets** eheliches Vermögen; ~ **causes** Ehesachen; ~ **cohabitation** eheliches Zusammenleben; ~ **differences** eheliche Differenzen, Ehezwistigkeiten; ~ **domicile (home,** *Br.***)** eheliche Wohnung, Ehewohnung, ehelicher Wohnsitz, Wohnsitz zur Zeit der Eheschließung; ⚖ **Home Act** *(Br.)* Gesetz zum Schutz der ehelichen Wohnung, ~ **home and contents** *(Br.)* Familienheim und Mobiliar; ~ **jurisdiction** Zuständigkeit in Ehesachen; ~ **law** Eherecht; ~ **maintenance** *(Br.)* ehelicher Unterhalt; ~ **obligations** eheliche Pflichten; ~ **offence** ehewidriges Verhalten, Eheverfehlung, -widrigkeit; ~ **offence of desertion** böswilliges Verlassen; ~ **order** *(Br.)* Anordnung des Getrenntlebens; ~ **problem** Eheproblem; ~ **proceedings** Verfahren in Ehesachen; ~ **property rights** ehelicher Güterstand; ~ **regime** *(US)* eheliches Güterrecht; ~ **suit** Klage in Ehesachen; ~ **troubles** eheliche Schwierigkeiten.

matrimony eheliche Verbindung, Ehestand;

to be joined in holy ~ in den Stand der heiligen Ehe treten.

matrix Matrize, Mater;

~ **of pacifism** pazifistischer Nährboden;

~ **board** Maternpappe; ~ **service** Matern-, Korrespondenzdienst.

matron Hausdame, Wirtschafterin, *(prison)* Aufseherin, *(school)* Heimleiterin.

matter Stoff, Material, *(affair)* Angelegenheit, Sache, *(business)* Geschäft, *(case)* vorliegende Sache, schwebender Fall, Streit-, Verhandlungsgegenstand, *(evidence)* Beweisthema, *(manuscript)* abzusetzendes Material, zu setzender Text, Drucksatz, Manuskript, *(substance of book)* Gegenstand, Inhalt;

as ~**s stand** wie die Dinge liegen; **for that** ~ insoweit, was das betrifft; **in the** ~ **of** bezüglich, in Sachen von; **in** ~**s educational** in Erziehungsfragen;

~**s** Umstände, Dinge;

business ~**s** geschäftliche Angelegenheiten; **commercial** ~**s** Handelssachen; **first-class** ~ *(US)* Brief- und Paketsendungen; **second-class** ~ *(US)* Zeitungen und Zeitschriften; **third-class** ~ *(US)* Paketdrucksachen; **fourth-class** ~ *(US)* Paketpost, Mustersendungen; **dead** ~**s** *(print.)* abgelegter Satz, Ablegesatz; **editorial** ~ redaktioneller Teil; **hanging** ~ todeswürdiges Verbrechen; **immediate** ~ Sofortsache; **inquired** ~ *(stock exchange)* Geld gesucht; ~ **insured** versicherter Gegenstand; **no laughing** ~ ernste Angelegenheit; **leaded** ~ durchgeschossener Satz; **life-and-death** ~ Fragen, bei denen es um Leben und Tod geht; **no light** ~ keine Kleinigkeit; **live** ~ *(print.)* druckfertiger Satz; **mail** ~ *(US)* Postsache; **mixed** ~ *(print.)* gemischter Satz; **money** ~ Geldfrage, -angelegenheiten; **nude** ~ nur auf Zeugenaussage beruhender Beweis; **personal** ~**s** persönliche Angelegenheiten; **postal** ~ *(Br.)* Postsache; **plain** ~ *(print.)* glatter Satz; **pressing** ~ dringende Angelegenheit; **printed** ~ Drucksache; ~ **read** gelesener Stoff, beendete Lektüre; **reading** ~ Lesestoff; **restricted** ~ geheime Dienstsache; **routine** ~ Routinesache; **security** ~ Geheimsache; ~**s spiritual and temporal** geistliche und weltliche Angelegenheiten; **standing** ~ *(print.)* Stehsatz; **stated** ~ Sachvortrag; **straight** ~ glatter Satz; **subject** ~ vorliegende Sache, behandelter Gegenstand; **subordinate** ~ Nebensache; **summary** ~**s** Fälle zur Erledigung im Schnellverfahren;

~ **and manner** Gehalt und Gestalt; **mind and** ~ Geist und Materie;

~ **of abatement** Rechtsmangel; ~ **of arrangement** Verhandlungssache; ~ **calling for attention** vordringliche Angelegenheit; ~ **of bankruptcy** Konkurssache; ~ **of business** geschäftliche Angelegenheit, Geschäftssache; ~ **of competence** Kompetenzfrage; ~ **of public concern[ment]** gemeinsame Belange, öffentliche Angelegenheit; ~ **of official concern** amtliche Angelegenheit, Dienstsache; ~ **of conscience** Gewissenssache, -frage; ~ **of consequence** wichtige Angelegenheit; ~ **of construction** Auslegungsfrage; ~ **in controversy** Anlaß für scharfe Kontroversen, Streitgegenstand; ~ **of course** Selbstverständlichkeit, Alltägliches; ~**s to be dealt with** anstehende Fragen; ~ **in deed** urkundlich nachweisbare Tatsache; ~ **of**

delicacy heikle Angelegenheit; ~ **of discretion** Ermessensfrage; ~ **for discussion** Diskussionsgegenstand; ~ **in dispute** fragliche Angelegenheit, *(law court)* Streitgegenstand; ~ **for distribution** *(print.)* Ablegesatz; ~ **of fact** *(US)* Tatsache, wirklicher Vorfall, *(law)* Tatfrage; ~-**of-fact** sachlich, nüchtern, prosaisch; ~-**of-factness** Phantasielosigkeit, Positivismus; ~ **of form** Form-, Verfahrensfrage; ~ **of habit** Gewohnheitssache; ~ **in hand** vorliegende Sache; ~ **of secondary importance** zweitrangige Angelegenheit; **subject** — **of invention** Gegenstand der Erfindung; ~ **in issue** strittige Angelegenheit, Streitgegenstand; ~ **of knack** Gewohnheitssache; ~ **of law** Rechtsfrage; ~ **of life and death** Lebens-, Existenzfrage; ~ **of luck** Glückssache; ~ **of opinion** Ansichtssache; ~ **in pais** tatsächliches Vorbringen; ~ **of prestige** Geltungs-, Prestigefrage; ~ **in question** fragliche Angelegenheit; ~ **of record** aktenmäßig verbürgte Tatsache; ~ **for reflection** Stoff zum Nachdenken; ~ **of remedy** prozeßrechtliche Frage; ~ **of routine** Routineangelegenheit; ~s **of state** Staatsangelegenheiten; ~ **of subsistence for man** Existenzfrage; ~ **of substance** wesentliche (materiellrechtliche) Frage; ~ **of taste** Geschmacksfrage; ~ **of time** Zeitfrage; ~ *(v.)* von Bedeutung sein, ausmachen;
~ **to s. o.** für j. von Bedeutung sein; ~ **a good deal** Erhebliches ausmachen; ~ **little to s. o.** jem. ziemlich gleichgültig sein; **to be a** ~ **of arrangement** besprochen werden müssen; **to be a** ~ **of common knowledge** allgemein bekannt sein; **to be a** ~ **of record** aktenmäßig feststehen, aktenkundig sein; **to be no trifling** ~ keine Bagatelle sein; **to be conversant with a** ~ mit einer Sache vertraut sein; **to be strict in the** ~ **of discipline** strenge Auffassungen in Disziplinarangelegenheiten vertreten; **to carry** ~s **too far** es zu weit treiben; **to check up on a** ~ *(US)* Angelegenheit überprüfen; **to clear up a** ~ Angelegenheit klären; **to cost a** ~ **of $ 100** etwa 100 Dollar kosten; **to crowd a** ~ *(US)* Sache vorantreiben; **to discuss a** ~ über eine Angelegenheit beraten; **to handle a** ~ Angelegenheit erledigen (besorgen); **to help** ~s **Situation** verbessern; **to keep track of a** ~ Sache im Auge behalten; **to leave all money** ~s **to s. o.** jem. alle finanziellen Angelegenheiten überlassen; **to look into a** ~ **again** Sache erneut prüfen; **to place a** ~ **in s. one's hands** jem. die Erledigung einer Angelegenheit übertragen; **to provide** ~ **for discussion** Diskussionsbeitrag leisten, Diskussionsgegenstand abgeben; **to put a** ~ **in s. one's hands** jem. eine Aufgabe übertragen; **to rule on a** ~ in einer Sache entscheiden; **to see clear in a** ~ in einer Sache klar sehen; **to settle a** ~ **without going to law** Angelegenheit außergerichtlich erledigen; **to speak to the** ~ zur Sache (zum Thema) sprechen; **to take** ~s **easy** Sache leicht nehmen; **to take a** ~ **in hand** Sache in die Hand nehmen; **to touch [upon] a delicate** ~ kitzligen Punkt (heißes Eisen) berühren; **to wangle a** ~ Sache deichseln.
matter-of-fact person Tatsachenmensch.
mature *(v.)* fällig (zahlbar) werden;
~ **on the 15th** am 15. fällig werden; ~ **during the years** Reifeprozeß durchmachen;
~ *(a.)* *(due)* fällig, abgelaufen, zahlbar, *(perfected)* durchdacht, reiflich erwogen, ausgereift, *(person)* geistig entwickelt, reif;
as severally ~ wie jeweils fällig;
to be of ~ **age** reiferen Alters sein; **after** ~ **consideration** nach sorgfältigen Erwägungen; ~ **creditor nation** starker Industriestaat mit passiver Handelsbilanz; **to give a question** ~ **deliberation** sich eine Sache reiflich überlegen; ~ **individual** ausgereifte Persönlichkeit; ~ **plan** ausgereifter Plan.
matured verfallen, fällig, *(wine)* abgelagert;
to have not ~ **properly** *(wine)* noch nicht ausgereift (genügend abgelagert) sein;
~ **capital** fälliges Kapital; ~ **claim** fällige Forderung; ~ **coupon** noch nicht zur Zahlung eingereichter Kupon; ~ **liability** fällige Verbindlichkeit.
maturing | on fällig werdend, fällig;
~ **liability** in Kürze fällige Verbindlichkeit; ~ **portion** fällige Tranche.
maturity Fälligkeit, Verfall[zeit], *(insurance)* Versicherungsfall;
at (on) ~ bei Fälligkeit (Verfall), zur Verfallszeit; **before (prior to)** ~ vor Verfall (Eintritt der Fälligkeit); **by** ~ *(insurance)* durch Ablauf; **on** ~ bei Fälligkeit; **payable at** ~ bei Fälligkeit zahlbar; **till** ~ bis zum Verfall; **with a** ~ **of** fällig am;
average [term of] ~ Durchschnittsverfallzeit; **current** ~ innerhalb eines Jahres fällige Verbindlichkeit; **short** ~ kurze Verfallszeit;
~ **of age** Reife des Alters; ~ **of a bill** Ablauf eines Wechsels; ~ **on demand** Fälligkeit bei Sicht; ~ **three months after date of issue** Fälligkeit drei Monate nach Ausgabedatum; ~ **of judgment** Urteilsreife; ~ **of one year** einjährige Laufzeit;

to bring to ~ zur Reife bringen; **to defer (delay)** ~ Verfall (Fälligkeit) aufschieben; **to have a** ~ **of twenty years** zwanzigjährige Laufzeit haben; **to pay at** ~ Zahlungsfrist einhalten; **to pay before** ~ vorausbezahlen, vor Fälligkeit bezahlen; **to pay a bill of exchange at** ~ Wechsel bei Fälligkeit einlösen;
~ **age** *(insurance)* Endalter; ~ **basis** Rendite einer Obligation unter Zugrundelegung der Gesamtzeit; ~ **claim** Fälligkeitsanspruch; ~ **date** Fälligkeitstag, -termin, -datum, Verfalldatum; ~ **index (tickler,** *US)* Terminkalender, Verfallbuch; ~ **value** Fälligkeitswert.
maverick *(pol.)* Einzelgänger, Außenseiter, unabhängiger Politiker;
~ *(v.)* sich absondern.
maxim *(established principle in law)* Rechtsgrundsatz;
~s **of equity** billigkeitsrechtliche Grundsätze.
maximalist Ultraradikaler.
maximization of profit Gewinnmaximierung.
maximum Höchstbetrag, *(bid)* Höchstgebot, *(price)* Höchstsatz, -preis, *(upper limit)* Höchstgrenze, Optimum;
~ **that may be advanced** höchster Beleihungswert;
~ *(a.)* höchstzulässig, maximal;
~ **advance** Beleihungshöchstsatz; ~ **age** Höchstalter; ~ **amount** Höchstbetrag; ~ **bank advance** Höchstbetrag eines Banksaldos; ~ **benefit** größtmöglicher Nutzen, Höchstvergünstigung; ~ **borrowing requirement** Kreditbedarfsspitze; ~ **capacity** *(production)* Höchstkapazität, Spitzenleistung, Produktionsoptimum, *(carrying power)* Tragfähigkeit; ~ **deficiency** *(coins)* Fehlergrenze; ~ **demand** Spitzennachfrage; ~ **depreciation** höchster zugelassener Abschreibungssatz; ~ **dividend** Höchstdividende; ~ **efficiency** Höchstleistung; ~ **employment** Höchstbeschäftigung, Beschäftigungsoptimum; ~ **figure** Höchstziffer; ~ **fine** Höchstgeldstrafe; ~ **hiring age limit** *(US)* Höchsteinstellungsalter; ~ **holding** Höchstbesitz; ~ **hours of labo(u)r (work)** Höchstbeschäftigungszeit; ~ **import duty** höchster Einfuhrzoll; ~ **liability** Haftpflichthöchstgrenze; ~ **likelihood estimation** *(statistics)* Schätzung nach dem höchsten Wahrscheinlichkeitswert; ~ **limit** Höchstgrenze; ~ **linage** *(ad)* Höchstgrenze; ~ **load** äußerste Belastung, Höchstbelastung, Grenzlast; ~ **loan value** Beleihungsgrenze, höchster Beleihungswert; ~ **long-time returns** anhaltende Höchsteinnahmen; ~ **margin** Höchstspanne; ~ **membership** Mitgliederhöchststand; ~ **mortgage interest rate** Hypothekenhöchstsatz; **to establish** ~ **noise levels for airliners of between 102 and 108 decibels** Höchstwerte von 102 - 108 Phon für Flugzeuge zulassen; ~ **number** Höchstzahl; ~ **odd linage unit** größte unreguläre Zeileneinheit; ~ **output** Produktionsoptimum, Maximalleistung, Höchstleistung, -produktion; ~ **penalty** Höchststrafe; ~ **performance** Höchstleistung; ~ **power** Höchstleistung; ~ **price** Höchstpreis, *(stock exchange)* Höchstkurs; ~ **productive efficiency** produktive Höchstleistung [eines Menschen]; ~ **punishment** Höchststrafe; ~ **quota** Höchstkontingent; ~ **rate** Höchstsatz, -preis, *(carrier)* Höchsttarif, *(foreign exchange)* Höchstkurs, *(insurance)* Höchstprämie; ~ **rate of interest** Höchstzinssatz; ~ **rebate** Höchstrabatt; ~ **salary** Höchstgehalt; ~ **selling price** höchster Verkaufspreis; ~ **sentence** Höchststrafe; ~ **social advantage** *(taxation)* höchstmöglicher Einkommensausgleichseffekt; ~ **speed** Höchstgeschwindigkeit; ~ **strength** *(mil.)* Höchststärke; ~ **tariff** Maximaltarif, -zoll, *(insurance)* Höchsttarif; ~ **and minimum tariff** Doppeltarif; ~ **tax rate** Steuerhöchstsatz; ~ **temperature recorded** höchster bisher aufgezeichneter Temperaturwert; ~ **time apportionment** *(tax)* höchstzulässige Verteilung auf mehrere Jahre; ~ **time limit** Höchstdauer; ~ **useful load** Höchstzuladung; ~ **value** oberste Wertgrenze, Maximal-, Höchstwert; ~ **wage(s)** Höchst-, Spitzen-, Maximallohn; ~ **weight** Höchstgewicht; ~ **wholesale price** Großhandelshöchstpreis.
maxirecession Maxirezession.
maxirecovery höchstmögliche Konjunkturerholung.
Mayflower Van Lines *(US)* Lastentaxidienst.
mayfly Eintagsfliege.
mayhem Verstümmelung.
mayor [Ober]bürgermeister;
deputy ~ stellvertretender Bürgermeister; **Lord** ♀ *(Br.)* Oberbürgermeister;
to stand as a ~ für das Amt des Oberbürgermeisters kandidieren;
~'s **court** Stadtgericht.
mayoral election Oberbürgermeisterwahl.
mayoralty Bürgermeisteramt.
maze Labyrinth, Irrgarten;
to be in a ~ verwirrt sein.

meadow Wiese, Matte, Anger, Aue;
~ *(v.)* als Heuwiese benutzen.
meadowland Grünland.
meagre dürftig, kärglich;
~ **attendance at the council meeting** schwach besuchte Ratssitzung; ~ **fare** magere Kost; **to be at work on a ~ subject** sich mit einem Thema beschäftigen, das nichts hergibt.
meal Mahlzeit, *(bore, sl.)* langweilige Angelegenheit;
free ~s freie Kost; **gourmet ~** Schlemmermahl; **in-flight ~s** während des Fluges verabreichte Mahlzeiten; **light ~** leichte Mahlzeit; **meagre ~** karges Mahl, kümmerliche Mahlzeit; **spare ~** bescheidene Mahlzeit; **welfare ~s** kostenlos ausgegebene Mahlzeiten;
to furnish ~s without charge kostenlos Essen ausgeben; **to get one's own ~s** sich seine Mahlzeiten selbst bereiten; **to prepare a ~** Mahlzeit zubereiten; **to provide ~s free** Wohlfahrtsspeisungen vornehmen; **to take one's ~s in the hotel** im Hotel speisen, seine Mahlzeiten im Hotel einnehmen;
~s allowance Verpflegungszuschuß; **~ break** Mittagspause; **four-~ course** Mahlzeit mit vier Gängen; **~ ticket** Beköstigungs-, Essensbon; **to buy ~ tickets** im Abonnement essen; **~ voucher** Essens-, Verpflegungsmarke, Essensbon.
mealtime Essenszeit.
mealy-mouthed, to be geziert (affektiert) sprechen.
mean Mittel[weg (-strecke)], *(value)* Durchschnitts-, Mittelwert;
arithmetical ~ Durchschnitt, Mittelwert; **corrected ~** korrigierter Mittelwert; **extreme ~** größter Mittelwert; **golden (happy) ~** goldener Mittelweg; **working ~** provisorischer Durchschnitt;
~ *(a.) (average)* mittel, durchschnittlich, *(base)* kleinlich, schäbig, filzig;
to be ~ beyond expression fürchterlicher Geizkragen sein; **to be rather ~ over money matters** in finanziellen Dingen etw. kleinlich sein; **to feel rather ~ for not helping more** schlechtes Gewissen wegen seiner geringen Hilfeleistung haben;
to take a ~ advantage of s. o. j. in der widerlichsten Weise ausnutzen; **no ~ artist** bedeutender Künstler; **~ average** gewogener Mittelwert; **of ~ birth** von niedriger Abkunft; **~ capacity** Durchschnittskapazität; **no ~ city** Stadt von einiger Bedeutung; **~ competition** unlauterer Wettbewerb; **~ course** mittlerer Kurs; **~ deviation** lineare Stellung; **~ draught** mittlerer Tiefgang; **~ due date** mittlerer Verfalltag; **~ high water** mittleres Hochwasser; **~ house** schäbiges Haus; **~ individual** schäbiges Individium; **~ job** *(US)* langweilige Tätigkeit; **~ life** mittlere Lebensdauer; **~ low tide** mittleres Niedrigwasser; **~ number** Durchschnittszahl, Mittelwert; **to have no ~ opinion of o. s.** große Meinung von sich haben, sich für bedeutend halten; **~ output** Durchschnittsleistung; **~ range forecast** Mittelfristvorhersage; **~ rank** niederer Rang; **~ rascal** niederträchtiger Schuft; **~ rate of exchange** Mittel-, Durchschnittskurs; **~ reserve** *(policy year)* Mittelrückkaufswert; **to be no ~ scholar** bedeutender Gelehrter sein; **~ spot rate** Kassamittelkurs; **~ streets** armselige Straßen; **~ surroundings** kümmerliche Umgebung; **~ tare** Durchschnittstara; **~ temperature** Durchschnittstemperatur; **~ time** mittlere Ortszeit; **~ trick** gemeiner (übler) Trick; **~ value** Durchschnittswert;
~ *(v.)* beabsichtigen, meinen, *(earmark)* bestimmen, ausersehen, *(word)* bedeuten;
~ business ernsthaft reflektieren, ernstlich interessiert sein; **~ a great deal for s. o.** jem. viel bedeuten; **~ no harm** nichts Böses wollen; **~ a house for one's daughter** Haus testamentarisch für seine Tochter bestimmen; **~ a lot for s. o.** viel für j. bedeuten; **~ no offence** keine beleidigende Absicht hegen; **~ one's son to succeed** seinen Sohn als Nachfolger vorgesehen haben; **~ war** Krieg bedeuten; **~ well by s. o.** freundliche Absichten gegenüber jem. hegen.
meaning Meinung, *(word)* Bedeutung, Sinn;
pregnant with ~ bedeutungsvoll; **within the ~ of this law** im Sinne dieses Gesetzes;
figurative ~ übertragene Bedeutung; **inner ~** verborgener Sinn; **primary ~** Hauptbedeutung; **secondary ~** *(trademark, US)* Nebenbedeutung;
~ of a word Wortbedeutung;
to distort the ~ of the text Sinn eines Textes entstellen; **to give s. o. a ~ look** jem. einen bedeutungsvollen Blick zuwerfen; **to take a new ~** neue Bedeutung gewinnen.
means [Geld]mittel, Einkommen, Geld, Kapital, *(method)* Weg, Methode, *(property)* Vermögen;
according to one's ~ seinen Möglichkeiten entsprechend; **by ~ of** vermittels, durch; **by fair ~ or foul** im Bösen oder im Guten; **by some ~ or other** auf irgendeine Weise; **by unlawful ~** unter

Anwendung unerlaubter Mittel; **of small ~** minderbemittelt; **with inadequate ~** behelfsmäßig; **without ~** unbemittelt, unversorgt, mittellos;
adequate ~ entsprechende Mittel; **ample ~** reichliche Mittel, hinlängliches Kapital; **available ~** flüssige (verfügbare) Mittel; **compulsory ~** Zwangsmittel; **constitutional ~** verfassungsmäßige Mittel; **current ~** Umlaufvermögen; **independent ~** eigenes Vermögen; **insufficient ~** unzureichende Mittel; **limited ~** bescheidene (begrenzte, geringfügige) Mittel; **narrow ~** knappe Mittel; **private ~** private Mittel, Privatvermögen; **slender ~** unzureichende Mittel;
ways and ~ *(pol.)* Geldbeschaffung, -bereitstellung;
~ of access *(Factory Act)* sicherer Zugang; **~ of carriage** Transportmittel; **~ of coercion** Zwangsmittel; **~ of communication** Kommunikations-, Verkehrsmittel, Nachrichtenmittel; **~ of conveyance** Beförderungsmittel, Transportmöglichkeiten; **~ to an end** Mittel zum Zweck; **no ~ of escape** kein Fluchtweg; **~ of evidence** Beweismittel; **~ of existence** Existenzmittel; **~ for fighting fire** Feuerbekämpfungsmittel; **major ~ of income** Haupteinnahmequelle; **~ of livelihood (living)** Erwerbsquelle; **~ of mass communication** Massenmedien; **~ of payment** Zahlungsmittel; **~ of production** Produktionsmittel; **~ of saving** Sparmöglichkeiten; **~ of stimulus** wirtschaftliche Belebungsmittel; **~ of subsistence (support)** Existenzmittel, Unterhalt; **~ of extending the trade** zur Handelsausweitung zur Verfügung stehende Mittel; **~ of transportation** *(US)* Beförderungs-, Transport-, Verkehrsmittel;
to adjust the ~ to an end Mittel dem Zweck anpassen; **to be beyond s. one's ~** für j. nicht erschwinglich sein; **to be deficient in ~** nicht genügend Mittel haben; **to be a man of ~** Vermögen besitzen; **to be without ~** mittellos sein; **to be of independent ~** finanziell unabhängig sein; **to contribute according to one's ~** seinen Verhältnissen entsprechend beitragen; **to contrive ways and ~** Mittel und Wege finden; **to have ample ~ at one's disposal** reichliche Mittel zur Verfügung haben; **to have considerable ~** bedeutendes Vermögen haben; **to have inadequate ~** nur unbedeutende finanzielle Mittel besitzen; **to have recourse to foul ~** zu unredlichen Mitteln greifen; **to justify the ~** Mittel rechtfertigen; **not to lie within s. one's ~** nicht im Rahmen von jds. Möglichkeiten liegen; **to live on one's private ~** von seinem Privatvermögen leben; **to live beyond (above) one's private ~** über seine Verhältnisse leben; **to prove one's lack of ~** seine Bedürftigkeit nachweisen; **to use every possible ~ to do s. th.** alle nur möglichen Mittel einsetzen;
~ test *(Br.)* Bedürftigkeitsnachweis, Überprüfung des finanziellen Status, *(credit rating)* Kreditprüfung; **~ and purpose test** Kreditwürdigkeit- und -verwendungsprüfung; **~ test limit** Bedürftigkeitsgrenze.
measurable meßbar;
to come within a ~ distance of success dem Erfolg greifbar nahe sein.
measure Maß, Meßinstrument, Ausmaß, Umfang, Grad, Höhe, *(action)* Maßnahme, -regel, *(enactment, Br.)* gesetzliche (gesetzgeberische) Maßnahme (Verfügung), *(print.)* Zeilen-, Satz-, Kolumnenbreite, *(unit of measurement)* Maßstab, Verhältnis;
as a temporary ~ als vorübergehende Maßnahme; **beyond the ~ of** außerhalb des Rahmens von; **by any ~** welchen Standpunkt man auch einnimmt; **in a large ~** im großen Umfang; **in some ~** bis zu einem gewissen Grad; **made to ~** nach Maß angefertigt, maßgearbeitet; **out of all ~** außerordentlich, über alle Maßen; **weights and ~s** Maße und Gewichte;
agrarian ~s Agrarmaßnahmen; **coercive ~s** Zwangsmaßnahmen; **corrective ~** Abhilfemaßnahmen; **cubic ~** Hohlmaß; **demographic ~s** bevölkerungspolitische Maßnahmen; **disciplinary ~** Disziplinarmaßnahmen; **drastic ~** durchgreifende Maßnahmen; **economizing ~s** Sparmaßnahmen; **emergency ~** Notstandsmaßnahmen; **extreme ~s** letztes Mittel; **financial ~s** finanzielle Maßnahmen; **half ~** halbe Maßnahme; **heaped ~** gehäuftes Maß; **incisive ~** einschneidende Maßnahme; **interim ~** Zwischenlösung; **land ~s** Maßnahmen für die Landwirtschaft; **legal ~s** juristische Schritte; **liquid ~** Flüssigkeitsmaß; **precautionary (preventive) ~** vorbeugende Maßnahmen; **preliminary ~s** vorbereitende Maßnahmen; **protective ~s** Schutzmaßnahmen; **radical (strong) ~s** drastische Maßnahmen; **square ~** Flächenmaß; **tape ~** Maßband; **trade ~s** handelspolitische Maßnahmen; **well-timed ~** Schachzug;
~s of adjustment Anpassungsmaßnahmen; **~ of assistance** Hilfsmaßnahmen; **~ of capacity** Hohlmaß; **~ of care** Sorgfaltsgrad; **~ of coercion** Zwangsmaßnahme; **~s of conciliation** Versöhnungsschritte; **~s of control** Kontroll-, Aufsichtsmaß-

nahmen; ~ **of damage** Schadensumfang, -bemessung; ~ **of damages** Umfang der Schadensersatzberechnung, Schadensersatzhöhe; ~**s of economy** Sparmaßnahmen; ~ **of length** Längenmaß; ~ **of precaution** Vorsichtsmaßnahme; ~**s of public security** Sicherheitsmaßnahmen; ~ **of value** Wertmesser, -maßstab; ~**s short of war** kriegsähnliche Handlungen;

~ *(v.)* be-, er-, abmessen, Messungen vornehmen, *(fig.)* vergleichen, abschätzen, *(tailor)* Maß nehmen;

~ **off** abmessen; ~ **out** aus-, zuteilen; ~ **out a mine** Bergwerk markscheiden; ~ **up to s. o.** *(US)* jem. gewachsen sein; ~ **up favo(u)rably with others** im Vergleich mit anderen günstig abschneiden; ~ **up to one's task** *(US)* seiner Aufgabe gewachsen sein;

~ **changes of temperature** Temperaturschwankungen messen; ~ **s. o. with one eye** sich ein Urteil über j. bilden; ~ **income net of tax** Reineinkommen zugrundelegen; ~ **the length of a room** Zimmer der Länge nach ausmessen; ~ **out a mine** Bergwerk markscheiden; ~ **a piece of ground** Grundstück ausmessen; ~ **one's skill with a rival** seine Fähigkeiten gegenüber der Konkurrenz ausprobieren; ~ **the speed of a car** Geschwindigkeit eines Autos feststellen; ~ **one's spending by one's means** seine Ausgabenwünsche nach seinen Einnahmemöglichkeiten ausrichten; ~ **one's strength with s. o.** seine Kräfte mit jem. messen; ~ **swords with s. o.** *(fig.)* sich mit jem. messen; ~ **the tonnage of a ship** Schiffstonnage feststellen; ~ **up one's position** *(US)* notwendige Qualifikation für eine Position mitbringen;

to adopt ~**s** Maßnahmen ergreifen; **to buy** ~ nach Maß kaufen; **to cancel** ~**s** Maßnahmen rückgängig machen; **to close upon** ~**s** sich über Maßregeln einigen; **to do away with s. th. as a** ~ **of economy** etw. aus Sparsamkeitsgründen aufgeben; **to do everything with due** ~ bei allem und jedem Maß halten; **to drive s. o. to extreme** ~**s** jem. zum Äußersten treiben; **to employ hard** ~**s** strenge Maßnahmen ergreifen, durchgreifen; **to give s. o. full** ~ jem. gut gewogen verkaufen; **to give the** ~ **of one's feelings** seinen Gefühlen beredten Ausdruck geben; **to give a** ~ **the force of law** einer Maßnahme Gesetzeskraft verleihen; **to have a suit made to** ~ Maßanzug bestellen; **to know no** ~ maßlos sein; **to pass** ~ Maßnahmen beschließen; **to retain a sense of** ~ sich Sinn für Maßhaltung bewahren; **to seal weights and** ~**s** Maße und Gewichte stempeln; **to sell by** ~ nach Maß verkaufen; **to set** ~ Maßstäbe setzen; **to set** ~**s to one's ambition** seinen Ehrgeiz zügeln; **to take [all due]** ~**s** [alle erforderlichen] Maßnahmen ergreifen; **to take s. one's** ~ jds. Charakter beurteilen, sich ein Urteil über j. bilden; **to take appropriate** ~**s** das Erforderliche veranlassen; **to take drastic** ~**s** energisch gegen etw. einschreiten; **to take extreme** ~**s** zum Äußersten schreiten; **to take faulty** ~**s** falsche Maßnahmen ergreifen; **to take legal** ~**s** rechtliche Schritte ergreifen, Rechtsweg einschlagen; **to take strong** ~**s against reckless drivers** harte Maßnahmen gegen rücksichtslose Autofahrer ergreifen; **to take the** ~ **of the housing market** Entwicklung des Wohnungsmarktes vorherbestimmen; **to take the** ~ **of a room** Raumverhältnisse abschätzen (abmessen); **to take s. one's** ~**s for a suit** jem. Maße für einen Maßanzug nehmen;

~ *(a.)* nach Maß angefertigt, maßgearbeitet;

~ **cargo (goods)** Sperrgut.

measured abgemessen, *(calculated)* wohlüberlegt, abgewogen;

~ **by** gemessen an; ~ **in the clear** im Lichten gemessen;

to get ~ **for a suit of clothes** sich zu einem Anzug Maß nehmen lassen;

~ **distance** Stoppstrecke; ~ **language** gemäßigter Ton; ~ **mile** geometrische Meile; **with** ~ **steps** mit gemessenen Schritten; **to speak in** ~ **terms** sich maßvoll ausdrücken; ~ **ton** Raumtonne; **to speak in a** ~ **tone** gemäßigte Sprache gebrauchen, sich Mäßigung auferlegen; ~ **words** abgewogene Worte.

measurement Messung, Vermessen, Maßbestimmung, *(mining)* Markscheidung, *(tonnage)* Tonnengehalt;

~**s of a room** Ausmaße eines Zimmers; ~ **of a ship** Schiffsvermessung;

to take s. one's ~ **for a suit** jem. zu einem Anzug Maß nehmen;

~ **account** Maßrechnung; ~ **cargo (goods)** Sperrgut, sperrige Ladung; ~ **ton** Raumtonne.

measurer Feld-, Landmesser.

measuring Vermessung;

~ **apparatus** Meßvorrichtung; ~ **cable** *(el.)* Prüfkabel; ~ **instrument** Meßinstrument; ~ **rod** Maßstab; ~ **tape** Bandmaß; ~ **tool** Maßvorrichtung.

meat Fleisch, *(restaurant)* Fleischspeise, -gericht;

butcher's ~ Schlachtfleisch; **carcase** ~ Frischfleisch; **chilled** ~ Kühlfleisch; **frozen** ~ Gefrierfleisch;

~ **of a book** wesentlicher Buchinhalt;

to make cold ~ **of s. o.** *(sl.)* Hackfleisch aus jem. machen; **to put** ~ **around the bones** Sache mit Substanz versehen;

~ **broth** Fleischbrühe; **preserved-**~ **factory** Fleischkonservenfabrik; ~ **house** *(fam.)* Schlachthof; ~ **inspection** Fleischbeschau; ~ **packer** Fleischverarbeitungsbetrieb; ~ **packing** Fleischverarbeitung; ~ **packing industry** Fleischkonservenindustrie; ~ **run** *(railroad use, sl.)* Schnellzug; ~ **safe** Fliegenschrank; ~ **tea** Vesper.

meatman *(US)* Metzger.

meatwaggon *(sl.)* Rettungswagen.

mechanic Mechaniker, Monteur, Maschinist, *(artisan)* Handwerker, *(car)* Autoschlosser;

dental ~ Dentist; **master** ~ Handwerksmeister; **motor** ~ Autoschlosser;

average ~ **skilled in the art** *(patent law)* Durchschnittsfachmann;

~ *(a.)* handwerklich;

~**'s lien** Zurückbehaltungsrecht des Handwerkers, bevorrechtigte Handwerkerforderung.

mechanical mechanisch, handwerksmäßig, maschinell, *(automated)* automatisch, selbsttätig, *(fig.)* gewohnheitsgemäß, schablonenartig, mechanisch, unwillkürlich;

to do one's work ~**ly** wie eine Maschine arbeiten;

~ **arm** Armprothese; ~ **bookkeeping** Maschinenbuchführung, Durchschreibebuchhaltung; ~ **devices** mechanische Vorrichtungen; ~ **dodge** *(coll.)* Handwerkskniff; ~ **drawing** Konstruktionszeichnung; ~ **effect** *(machine)* Nutzeffekt; ~ **engineer** Maschinenbauingenieur; ~ **engineering** Maschinenbau; ~ **engineering company** Maschinenbaufirma; ~ **engineering industry** Maschinenbauindustrie; ~ **engineering product** Maschinenbauerzeugnis; ~ **equipment** Maschinenanlage; ~ **equivalent** *(patent law)* mechanisch gleichwerter Gegenstand; ~ **information** technische Information; ~ **operation** Bearbeitungsvorgang; ~ **pencil** *(US)* Füllbleistift; ~ **press** Schnellpresse; ~ **process** mechanisches Verfahren; ~ **skill** handwerkliche Fähigkeiten (Geschicklichkeiten); ~ **transport** *(mil.)* Lastwagentransport; ~ **treatment** Weiterverarbeitung; ~ **typesetting** Maschinensatz.

mechanics Mechanik, Mechanismus, Konstruktion von Maschinen;

practical ~ Maschinenlehre; **precision** ~ Feinmechanik;

~ **of advertisement** Werbetechnik; ~ **of play-writing** Aufbau eines Theaterstücks.

mechanism Vorrichtung, Mechanismus;

~ **of government** Verwaltungsmaschinerie, -apparat.

mechanization Mechanisierung, *(mil.)* Motorisierung.

mechanize *(v.)* auf Maschinenbetrieb umstellen, mechanisieren, *(mil.)* motorisieren.

mechanized|division Panzergrenadierdivision; ~ **farming** mechanisierte Landwirtschaft; ~ **forces** *(mil.)* mechanisierte Verbände, Panzereinheiten.

medal Medaille, Schaumünze, *(reward)* Ehrenmedaille, Auszeichnung, Orden;

commemorative ~ Denkmünze; **service** ~ Dienstmedaille;

~ *(v.)* mit einer Ehrenmedaille auszeichnen, dekorieren;

to sport all one's ~**s** *(fam.)* alle Orden und Auszeichnungen tragen.

meddle *(v.)* sich einmischen;

~ **in other people's affairs** sich in fremde Angelegenheiten einmischen; ~ **with one's papers** in seinen Unterlagen herumhantieren.

media Media, Medien, Werbeträger, Reklamemittel;

advertising ~ Werbemittel, -träger; **commissionable** ~ provisionspflichtige Medien; **communication** ~ Werbemedien; **the instant** ~ Rundfunk und Fernsehen; **mass** ~ Massenmedien, *(Br.)* Rundfunk und Fernsehen; **national** ~ überregionale Werbeträger;

to place advertisements in various ~ Anzeigen bei verschiedenen Werbeträgern plazieren;

~ **allocation** Aufteilung auf die verschiedenen Werbeträger, Streuung; ~ **analysis** Werbeträgeranalyse; ~ **audience combination** Zielgruppenkombination von Werbeträgern; ~ **campaign** Werbe-, Mediafeldzug; **broadcast** ~ **campaign** über Rundfunksender ausgestrahlte Werbekampagne; **to run a** ~ **campaign** Werbeaktion in den Massenmedien durchführen; ~ **clerk** Mediasachbearbeiter; ~ **concept** Werbekonzeption; ~ **cost** Werbekosten; ~ **coverage** Berichterstattung in den Nachrichtenmitteln; ~ **department** Werbeabteilung; ~ **details** alle Einzelheiten eines Werbemittels; ~ **director** Leiter der Abteilung Streuung; ~ **evaluation** Bewertung als Werbeträger; ~ **man** Streuplaner; ~ **manager** Medialeiter; ~**-oriented** auf Meinungsmedien ausgerichtet; ~ **planner** Mediaplaner; ~ **planning** Mediaplanung; ~ **person** Vertreter der Massenmedien; ~ **research** Überprüfung von Werbeträgern, Media-, Werbeträgerforschung; ~ **schedule** Streuplan; ~ **selection** Mediaauswahl; ~**strategy** Festlegung der Media; ~ **survey** Werbeträgerforschung; ~ **vehicle** Werbeträger.

medial line Mittellinie.

median Zentralwert, *(statistics)* Halbwert;
~ *(a.)* in der Mitte liegend;
~ **income** *(US)* mittleres Einkommen; ~ **point** *(math.)* Mittelpunkt; ~ **wage** Durchschnittslohn; ~ **waves** *(radio)* Mittelwellen.

mediate *(v.)* vermitteln, Vermittler spielen, schlichten;
~ **a peace** Frieden vermitteln; ~ **a settlement** Abkommen zustandebringen;
~ **descent** mittelbare Erbfolge; ~ **powers** *(agent)* Nebenbefugnisse; ~ **testimony** Zeugnis vom Hörensagen.

mediation Vermittlung, Schlichtung, Fürsprache;
through his ~ durch seine Fürbitte;
~ **agency of the government** staatliche Schlichtungsstelle; ~ **board** Schiedsgericht[shof]; ~ **commission (committee)** Schlichtungs-, Vermittlungsausschuß; ~ **function** Schlichtungsaufgabe; ~ **period** Vermittlungszeit; **to bring a complaint before an outside** ~ **service** neutrale Schlichtungseinrichtungen in Anspruch nehmen.

mediator Unterhändler, Vermittler, Schlichter.

mediatorship Vermittleramt.

Medicaid *(Br.)* Gesundheitsdienst für Bedürftige.

medical *(coll.)* Mediziner, *(mil., sl.)* ärztliche Untersuchung;
~ *(a.)* ärztlich, medizinisch;
to take ~ **advice** ärztlichen Rat einholen; ~ **adviser** ärztlicher Berater; ~ **aid scheme** ärztliches Versorgungswerk; ~ **aircraft** *(law of nations)* Sanitätsflugzeug; ~ **appeal tribunal** ärztliches Beschwerdegericht; ~ **assistance** ärztliche Fürsorge, Krankenfürsorge; ~ **attendance (attention)** ärztliche Behandlung (Betreuung, Versorgung, Dienstleistungen, Bemühungen); **to have** ~ **attention** ärztlich behandelt werden; ~ **attendant** Krankenwärter; ~ **benefits** ärztliche Leistungen; ~ **board** Gesundheitsamt; ~ **care** ärztliche Versorgung; ~ **care for the aged** Krankenversorgung älterer Menschen; ~ **certificate** ärztliche Bescheinigung, [ärztliches] Attest; ~ **commission** Ärztekommission; ~ **consultant** Facharzt; ~ **costs** Arztkosten; ~ **course** Medizinstudium; ~ **department** Gesundheitsdienst; ~ **establishment** Ärzteschaft; ~ **evidence** medizinischer Sachverständigenbeweis; ~ **examination** ärztliche Untersuchung; **compulsory** ~ **examination** Pflichtuntersuchung; ~ **examiner** *(insurance business, Br.)* Vertrauensmann, -arzt, Amtsarzt, *(postmortem examination)* Leichenbeschauer; ~ **expenses** Arztkosten; ~ **expert** Facharzt; **free** ~ **facilities** kostenlose ärztliche Betreuung; ~ **faculty** ärztliche Fakultät; ~ **fee** ärztliches Honorar; ~ **history** Krankengeschichte; ~ **inspection** ärztliche Kontrolle, *(Br.)* amtsärztliche Untersuchung; ~ **insurance** Krankenversicherung; ~ **jurisprudence** Gerichtsmedizin; ~ **knowledge** ärztliche Kenntnisse; ~ **man** Arzt, Doktor; ~ **officer [of health]** *(Br.)* Amts-, Schul-, Bezirks-, Fürsorgearzt; **to come before the** ~ **officer** Visite hinter sich bringen; ~ **opinion** ärztliches Gutachten; ~ **orderly** Sanitäter; ~ **payment coverage** *(US)* Insassenunfallversicherung; ~ **plan** Krankenversicherungsschutz; ~ **practices committee** Zulassungsausschuß für Kassenärzte; **qualified** ~ **practitioner** praktischer Arzt; ~ **profession** Arztberuf, Ärzteschaft; ~ **record** Krankenblatt; ~ **referee** *(US)* Vertrauens-, Amtsarzt; ~ **report** Krankheitsbericht; **subsidized** ~ **scheme** Zuschüsse im Krankheitsfall; ~ **science** medizinische Wissenschaft; ~ **services** Gesundheitsdienst, ärztliche Verrichtung (Tätigkeit); ~ **specialist** Facharzt; ~ **stores** Sanitätsmaterial; ~ **student** Medizinstudent; ~ **superintendent** Chefarzt; ~ **treatment** ärztliche Behandlung; **to be under** ~ **treatment** Patient sein; **to give s. o.** ~ **treatment** j. ärztlich behandeln; **to give s. o. private** ~ **treatment** j. privat behandeln; ~ **ward** internistische Abteilung.

medicament Arzneimittel, Medikament;
~ *(v.)* Medikamente verabfolgen.

medicamentation Heilmittelverabfolgung.

Medicare *(Br.)* Gesundheitsfürsorge für über 65jährige.

medicate *(v.)* medizinisch behandeln.

medicated bath Heilbad.

medication medizinische Behandlung.

medicinal medizinisch, heilkräftig;
~ **herbs** Heilkräuter; ~ **spring** Heilquelle.

medicine Medizin, Heilkunde, Arznei;
forensic (legal) ~ Gerichtsmedizin;

---

to give s. o. a dose of his own ~ *(fam.)* Gleiches mit Gleichem vergelten; **to practise** ~ ärztlichen Beruf ausüben; **to study** ~ Medizin studieren; **to swallow one's** ~ *(fig., US)* die Pille schlucken, sich abfinden; **to take one's** ~ seine Medizin nehmen, *(fig.)* sich dreinfügen (abfinden);
~ **chest** Bord-, Reise-, Hausapotheke; ~ **man** Medizinmann, Zauberer.

mediocre mittelmäßig, zweitklassig;
to rise above the ~ sich aus der Masse hervorheben.

mediocrity Mittelmäßigkeit, *(man)* Dutzendmensch.

medicolegal gerichtsmedizinisch.

meditate *(v.)* meditieren, nachsinnen, grübeln;
~ **mischief** Unheil ausbrüten.

meditation Meditation.

medium Mittler, Mittel, Medium, Organ, *(advertisement)* Reklame-, Werbeträger, -mittel, *(middling quality)* Mittelware, *(print.)* Medianpapier, *(surroundings)* Umgebung, Milieu, *(terminal)* Datenträger, *(tool)* Arbeitsgerät;
through the ~ **of** durch Vermittlung von; **through the** ~ **of a goods agent** *(Br.)* mit Hilfe (unter Inanspruchnahme) eines Bahnspediteurs; **through the** ~ **of the press** durch die [Mitwirkung der] Presse;
~**s** *(Br., government securities)* Papiere mit mittlerer und längerer Laufzeit;
advertising ~ Werbeträger, -mittel; **circulating** ~ Umlaufs-, Tauschmittel; **commissionable** ~ provisionspflichtiges Medium; **consumer advertising** ~ Werbeträger für die Verbraucherwerbung; **currency** ~ Zahlungsmedium; **good** ~ *(quality)* mittelfein; **just** ~ goldener Mittelweg; **news** ~ Nachrichtenmittel; **social** ~ soziales Milieu;
~ **for advertising** Werbe-, Reklamemittel, Werbeträger; ~ **of currency** *(circulation, exchange)* Valuta, *(exchangeable article)* Tauschmittel, *(rate)* Mittelkurs; ~ **of payment** Zahlungsmittel; **to stick to a happy** ~ goldenen Mittelweg einschlagen;
~ *(a.)* mittelmäßig, gewöhnlich, *(print.)* halbfett;
good ~ *(quality)* mittelfein;
~ **capacity** mittelmäßige Begabung; ~**-dated** mittelfristig; ~ **enterprise** Mittelbetrieb, mittelgroßes Unternehmen; ~ **and small-scale enterprises** Mittel- und Kleinbetriebe; ~**-faced** *(print.)* halbfett; ~ **goods** Mittelware, mittlere Qualität; ~ **owner** Eigentümer eines Werbemittels; ~**-powered car** mittelstarker Wagen; ~ **price** Durchschnitts-, Mittelpreis; ~ **price range** mittlere Preislage; ~**-priced goods** Waren mittlerer Preislage; ~ **quality** mittlere Qualität, Mittelsorte, zweite Wahl; ~**-quality goods** Waren mittlerer Qualität und Güte, Produkte mittlerer Qualität; ~**-range bomber** Mittelstreckenbomber; ~**-range nuclear weapon** für mittlere Entfernungen vorgesehene Nuklearwaffen; ~**-ranking state** Staat mittlerer Größe; ~ **rule** halbfette Linie; ~ **shot** *(film)* Halbtotale; ~ **size** Durchschnitts-, Mittelgröße; ~**-sized** in mittlerer Größe, mittelgroß; ~**-sized business (establishment)** mittlerer Betrieb, mittleres Unternehmen, Mittelstandsunternehmen, gewerblicher Mittelbetrieb; ~ **sorts** mittlere Qualitäten; ~ **and long term** mittel- und langfristig; ~**-term credit** *(Eurodollar market)* mittelfristiger Kredit; ~ **unit** *(terminal)* Speicher; ~ **waves** Mittelwellen.

medley Durcheinander, Mischmasch, *(gathering)* gemischte Gesellschaft, *(music)* Potpourri.

meek sanft[mütig], mild;
as ~ **as a lamb** lammfromm.

meet *(US sl.)* Treffpunkt, *(railroad use, sl.)* Eisenbahnknotenpunkt;
~ *(v.)* treffen, sich versammeln (begegnen), *(company, parl.)* tagen, zusammentreten, *(comply with)* nach-, entgegenkommen, erfüllen, *(pay)* begleichen, tragen, *(satisfy)* befriedigen;
~ **s. o.** j. kennenlernen, *(fam.)* jem. halbwegs entgegenkommen; ~ **with an accident** Opfer eines Unfalls werden, verunglücken; ~ **with approval** auf Zustimmung stoßen, gebilligt werden; ~ **a bill** Rechnung begleichen, *(bill of exchange)* Wechsel einlösen (honorieren); ~ **s. one's case** jds. Problem lösen; ~ **quite by chance** sich ganz zufällig treffen; ~ **one's commitments (engagements)** seinen Verpflichtungen nachkommen; ~ **the claims of one's creditors** seine Gläubiger befriedigen; ~ **competition** konkurrenzfähig sein; ~ **the deadline** Frist einhalten; ~ **the demand** Nachfrage befriedigen, Bedarf decken; ~ **the demands for payment** Zahlungsansprüche befriedigen; ~ **a doctor in consultation** Arzt konsultieren; ~ **one's draft** sein Akzept einlösen; ~ **no end of interesting people** eine Fülle interessanter Menschen treffen; ~ **all expenses** alle Kosten bestreiten; ~ **the eye** sichtbar sein; ~ **one's fate calmly** seinem Schicksal in Ruhe entgegensehen; ~ **s. o. half way** jem. auf halbem Wege entgegenkommen; ~ **at regular intervals** in regelmäßigen Zeitab-

schnitten zusammentreten; ~ **one's liabilities** seine Verpflichtungen (Verbindlichkeiten) erfüllen; ~ **short-term liabilities** kurzfristige Verbindlichkeiten abdecken; ~ **with a loss** Verlust erleiden; ~ **with losses on the stock exchange** Kursverluste hinnehmen müssen; ~ **with objections** Einwänden begegnen; ~ **one's obligations** seinen Verpflichtungen nachkommen; ~ **with obstacles** Hindernisse begegnen; ~ **the parliament** *(government)* sich dem Parlament stellen; ~ **payments** Teil-, Ratenzahlungen einhalten; ~ **s. o. at the appointed place** j. an der bezeichneten Stelle finden; ~ **with due protection** *(bill)* honoriert werden; ~ **with a kind reception** freundlich aufgenommen werden; ~ **with a refusal** sich eine Absage holen; ~ **[practical] requirements** den Anforderungen [der Praxis] entsprechen; ~ **one's reward** seinen Lohn erhalten; ~ **as of right** automatisch zusammentreten; ~ **s. o. at the station** j. vom Bahnhof abholen; ~ **all trains** *(buses)* überall Anschluß haben; ~ **troubles halfway** Vorkehrungen gegen Unannehmlichkeiten treffen; ~ **a long-felt want** langjähriges Bedürfnis befriedigen; ~ **wishes half-way** den Wünschen auf halbem Wege entgegenkommen; ~ **up with s. o.** *(US)* mit jem. zusammentreffen; ~ **the workers** über Löhne diskutieren;
to arrange to ~ s. o. Verabredung mit jem. treffen; **to make both ends ~** mit seinem Einkommen auskommen; **to send s. o. to ~ s. o.** j. zum Abholen schicken;
pleased to ~ you erfreut, Sie kennen zu lernen.

meeting Besprechung, Beratung, Sitzung, Versammlung, Konferenz, Tagung, Zusammenkunft, -sein, -treffen, Begegnung; **annual general ~** *(Br.)* ordentliche Jahreshaupt-, Generalversammlung; **board [of directors] ~** Vorstandssitzung; **adjourned ~** nach der Vertagung fortgesetzte Sitzung; **all-day ~** ganztägige Sitzung; **called ~** besonders einberufene [Aktionärs]versammlung; **cabinet ~** Kabinettssitzung; **class ~** Aktionärsversammlung der gleichen Aktiengattung, gruppenweise stattfindende Aktionärsversammlung; **closed-door ~** geschlossene Sitzung; **committee ~** Ausschußsitzung; **company ~** *(Br.)* Haupt-, Gesellschafterversammlung; **company-wide ~** Konzerntagung; **corporate (corporation) ~** *(US)* Haupt-, Gesellschafterversammlung; **creditors' ~** Gläubigerversammlung; **directors' ~** Vorstands-, Direktionssitzung; **extraordinary general ~** *(Br.)* außerordentliche Hauptversammlung; **family ~** Familienratsbesprechung; **final ~** Schlußversammlung; **general ~** ordentliche Hauptversammlung; **informal ~** zwanglose Zusammenkunft; **initial ~** Eröffnungssitzung; **joint ~** gemeinsame Sitzung; **mass ~** Massenversammlung, -kundgebung; **ministerial ~** Ministertreffen, -konferenz; **on-the-spot ~** sofort einberufene Tagung; **open ~** Versammlung unter freiem Himmel; **ordinary ~** *(Br.)* ordentliche Hauptversammlung; **overflow ~** Parallelversammlung; **packed ~** überfüllte Versammlung; **panel ~** *(US)* Zusammenkunft ausgesuchter Diskussionsmitglieder, Diskussionsveranstaltung; **periodical ~s** regelmäßige Zusammenkünfte; **plenary ~** Vollversammlung; **policy ~** geschäftspolitische Tagung; **political ~** politische Versammlung; **preliminary ~** Vorversammlung; **private ~** nicht öffentliche Sitzung; **public ~** öffentliche Versammlung (Sitzung); **regular ~** *(US)* ordentliche Hauptversammlung; **requisitioned ~** auf Antrag der Aktionäre einberufene Hauptversammlung; **sales ~** Vertretertagung; **secret ~** geheime Zusammenkunft; **seditious ~** staatsgefährdende Versammlung; **small-group ~** Treffen im kleinen Kreis; **special ~** Sondersitzung, **(company)** außerordentliche Hauptversammlung; **stated ~** ordentliche Hauptversammlung; **statutory ~** gesetzlich vorgeschriebene Generalversammlung; **summit ~** Gipfeltreffen; **town ~** *(US)* Gemeindeversammlung, Stadtratssitzung; **unlawful ~** ungesetzliche Versammlung;
~ **of the [executive] board** Vorstandsitzung [einer Gesellschaft]; ~ **of the board of directors** Aufsichtsratssitzung; ~ **of the Cabinet** Kabinettssitzung; ~ **in camera** Sitzung unter Ausschluß der Öffentlichkeit; ~ **of cars** Autozusammenstoß; ~ **of Congress** Kongreßsitzung; ~ **of contributories** Versammlung nachschußpflichtiger Gesellschafter; ~ **of creditors** Gläubigerversammlung; ~ **debt repayment** Schuldentilgungsmaßnahmen; ~ **of directors** Vorstands-, Direktionssitzung; ~ **of experts** Sachverständigenkonferenz; ~ **of incorporators (to organize)** Gründungsversammlung; ~ **of members** Mitgliederversammlung; ~ **of minds** *(law of contract)* Willeneinigung, Übereinstimmung der Willenserklärungen; ~ **called at short notice** kurzfristig einberufene Versammlung; **annual ~ of the parish** jährliche Bürgerversammlung; ~ **in a private place** privat abgehaltene Versammlung; ~ **in a public place** öffentlich abgehaltene Versammlung; ~ **[not] open to the public** [nicht]öffentliche Sitzung; ~ **of shareholders** *(Br.)* **(stockholders,** *US)* Aktionärs-,

Haupt-, Generalversammlung; **special ~ of stockholders** *(US)* außerordentliche Generalversammlung; **the ~ to be held tomorrow** morgen stattfindende Versammlung (Sitzung);
to absent o. s. from a ~ sich von einer Versammlung fernhalten; **to address a ~** in einer Versammlung das Wort ergreifen; **to address a ~ on an off-the-record basis** vertrauliches Thema in einem Kreis behandeln; **to adjourn a ~** Versammlung (Sitzung) vertagen; **to appoint a day for a ~** Sitzung anberaumen; **to assist at a ~** an einer Versammlung teilnehmen; **to attack the regularity of a ~** Ordnungsmäßigkeit einer Versammlung bestreiten; **to attend (be present at) a ~** bei einer Tagung (Versammlung) anwesend sein, einer Versammlung beiwohnen; **to break up a ~** Versammlung gewaltsam auflösen; **to bring up a conclusion in a ~** Resolution in einer Versammlung einbringen; **to call a ~** Sitzung (Versammlung) einberufen; **to call a ~ at short notice** Sitzung mit Fristverkürzung einberufen; **to call a general ~ to order** *(US)* Hauptversammlung eröffnen; **to call a ~ of shareholders** *(Br.)* **(stockholders,** *US)* Hauptversammlung einberufen; **to close a ~** Sitzung schließen; **to constitute a valid ~** Satzungserfordernisse für eine Hauptversammlung erfüllen; **to convene (convoke) a ~** Versammlung einberufen; **to cover a ~ of shareholders** *(Br.)* **(stockholders,** *US)* über eine Hauptversammlung berichten; **to declare a ~ closed** Sitzung schließen; **to dissolve a ~** Versammlung auflösen; **to fix a ~** Sitzung einberufen (anberaumen); **to hold a ~** Versammlung (Tagung) abhalten; **to hold a ~ in accordance with the regulations** Versammlung entsprechend den vorgeschriebenen Regularien abhalten; **to hold a ~ on a formal basis** alle Formalitäten bei einer Hauptversammlung beachten; **to hold ~s on the factory floor** Versammlungen im Betriebsgelände abhalten; **to hold a public ~** öffentliche Versammlung abhalten; **to leave a ~ under protest** Sitzung unter Protest verlassen; **to monopolize a ~** Verhandlungsleitung in einer Sitzung an sich reißen; **to open the ~** Sitzung (Tagung, Versammlung) eröffnen (für eröffnet erklären); **to overstaff a ~** zu einer Sitzung zuviel Teilnehmer einladen; **to park a ~** große Anzahl von Anhängern in eine Versammlung dirigieren; **to postpone a ~** Versammlung vertagen; **to preside over a ~** in einer Sitzung den Vorsitz führen; **to prohibit a ~** Versammlung verbieten; **to put a resolution to the ~** der Versammlung einen Resolutionsentwurf vorlegen; **to run a ~** Sitzung leiten; **to schedule a ~ for ten o'clock** *(US)* Sitzung für zehn Uhr festsetzen; **to set up a ~** Versammlung einberufen; **to settle a day for a ~** Sitzungstermin festlegen; **to shift a ~ to a hotel** Sitzung in ein Hotel verlegen; **to summon a general ~** *(Br.)* Hauptversammlung einberufen; **to turn out for a ~** Versammlung besuchen; **to walk out of a ~** Versammlung verlassen; **to wind up a ~ with a short speech** Versammlung mit einem kurzen Schlußwort beenden;
~ **clothes** Sonntagsanzug; **company ~s column** *(newspaper)* Hauptversammlungsspalte; ~ **day** Sitzungstag; **annual ~ day** Hauptversammlungstermin; ~ **hall** Versammlungs-, Tagungshalle, Gemeindehaus; ~ **message** Tagungsbotschaft; ~ **monopolizer** Gesprächsbeherrscher; ~ **participant** Tagungs-, Sitzungsteilnehmer; ~ **place** Tagungs-, Versammlungsort, Treffpunkt; **to arrange [for] a ~ place** Treffpunkt ausmachen; **to fix a ~ place** Treffpunkt festlegen; ~ **practice** Hauptversammlungserfahrungen; ~ **procedure** Versammlungsablauf, -procedere; ~ **room** Tagungs-, Sitzungssaal; ~ **time** Bürozeit.
meetinghouse Andachtshaus.
megaphone Sprachrohr, Megaphon.
megaton Million Tonnen;
~ **bomb** Bombe von 1000 Kilotonnen.
meliorate *(v.)* verbessern, veredeln, *(soil)* meliorieren.
melioration Verbesserung, Veredelung;
~s Grundstücksmeliorationen.
mellow reif, saftig, *(wine)* süß, *(tipsy, sl.)* beschwipst, angeheiratet;
of ~ age gereiften Alters.
melon *(US)* außerordentliche Dividende, Gratisaktie, grösserer Bonus;
to cut a ~ außerordentliche Dividende [in Form von Gratisaktien] ausschütten;
~ **cutting** Ausschüttung einer außerordentlichen Dividende.
melt *(v.)* schmelzen, flüssig werden;
~ **away** dahinschmelzen, -schwinden; ~ **down** einschmelzen; ~ **into a drizzle** *(fog)* in einen Nieselregen übergehen; **in s. one's hands** *(money)* in jds. Händen wie Schnee in der Sonne schmelzen; ~ **into tears** zu Tränen gerührt werden.
melted | out *(sl.)* abgebrannt, total pleite; ~ **snow** Schmelzwasser.
melting Verschmelzung;
to be gradually ~ away immer weniger werden;

~ **furnace** Schmelzofen; ~ **heat** schwüle Hitze; ~ **point** Schmelzpunkt; ~ **pot** *(fig.)* Schmelztiegel; **to go into the** ~ **pot** sich einer völligen Umwandlung unterziehen; **to put into the** ~ **pot** gänzlich ummodeln; **to put everything back into the** ~ **pot** alles wieder in Frage stellen.

member Mitglied, Angehöriger, *(building)* Bauteil, *(building society, Br.)* Bausparer, *(of company, Br.)* Gesellschafter, Aktionär;

advanced ~ *(building society, Br.)* zugeteilter Bausparer; **alternative** ~ *(Br.)* Ersatzmitglied; **duly appointed** ~ ordnungsgemäß gewähltes Mitglied; **associate** ~ assoziiertes Mitglied; **board** ~ Vorstands-, Aufsichtsratmitglied; **borrowing** ~ *(Br.)* zugeteilter Bausparer; **cabinet** ~ Regierungs-, Kabinettsmitglied; **card-carrying** ~ eingetragenes Mitglied; **committee** ~ Ausschußmitglied; **conference** ~ Tagungs-, Konferenzteilnehmer; **congress** ~ Kongreßteilnehmer; **consultant** ~ beratendes Mitglied; **consumer** ~ Mitglied einer Verbrauchergenossenschaft; **coopted** ~ hinzugewähltes (kooptiertes) Mitglied; **deputy** ~ stellvertretendes Mitglied; **dissenting** ~ nicht zustimmender Aktionär; **enrolled** ~ eingetragenes Mitglied; **ex-** ~ früheres Mitglied; **ex-officio** ~ Mitglied kraft Amtes; **foreign** ~ auswärtiges (ortsfremdes) Mitglied; **founder** ~ Gründungsmitglied; **freshman** ~ neues Vereinsmitglied; **full** ~ Vollmitglied, ordentliches Mitglied; **habitual** ~ ständiges Vereinsmitglied; **honorary** ~ Ehrenmitglied; **inactive (nonactive)** ~ inaktives Mitglied; **investing** ~ *(building society, Br.)* ansparender (noch nicht zugeteilter) Bausparer; **key** ~**s** wichtigste Mitglieder; **life** ~ Mitglied auf Lebenszeit; **needy** ~ in Not geratenes Mitglied; **new** ~ neues Mitglied; **nominal** ~ Mitläufer; **nonpermanent** ~ nicht ständiges Mitglied; **ordinary** ~ vollberechtigtes Mitglied; **original** ~ Gründungsmitglied; **paid-up** ~ voll bezahlter Angehöriger; **panel** ~ Diskussionsteilnehmer; **part-time** ~ nicht ständiges Mitglied; **party** ~ Parteimitglied; **paying** ~ förderndes Mitglied; **permanent** ~ ständiges Mitglied; **private** ~ einfaches Parlamentsmitglied; **regular** ~ ordentliches Mitglied; **subscribing** ~ beitragzahlendes Mitglied; **trade** ~ Mitglied eines Berufsverbandes; **unadvanced** ~ *(building society, Br.)* noch nicht zugeteilter Bausparer; **union** ~ Gewerkschaftsmitglied; **voting** ~ stimmberechtigtes Mitglied; **withdrawing** ~ ausscheidendes Mitglied;

~ **of an academy** Akademiemitglied; ~ **of the army** [etwa] Bundeswehrangehöriger; ~ **of an association** Verbands-, Vereinsmitglied; ~ **of the audience** Zuhörer; ~ **of the executive board** *(US)* Vorstandsmitglied; ~ **of the board of directors** Aufsichtsratmitglied; ~ **of the cabinet** Regierungs-, Kabinettsmitglied; ~ **of a cartel** Kartellmitglied; ~ **of a chamber** Kammermitglied; ~ **of a club** Vereinsmitglied; **assistant** ~ **of a committee** Ersatzmitglied eines Aussschusses; ~ **of a company** *(Br.)* Gesellschafter; ~ **of Congress** *(US)* Parlaments-, Kongreßmitglied; ~ **of a corporation** *(US)* Gesellschafter; ~ **of local council** Gemeinderatsmitglied; ~ **of the crew** Besatzungsmitglied; ~ **of the directorate** Direktoriumsmitglied; ~ **of the family** Familienmitglied; ~ **of a firm** Teil-, Mitinhaber einer Firma, Firmeninhaber; ~**s above the gangway** einflußreiche Abgeordnete; ~**s below the gangway** *(Br.)* mit der offiziellen Parteipolitik nicht einverstandene Mitglieder; ~ **of the government** *(Br.)* Regierungs-, Kabinettsmitglied; ~ **of the House of Commons** Unterhausmitglied; ~ **of the House of Representatives** *(US)* Kongreßabgeordneter; ~ **of the managing committee (management)** Vorstandsmitglied; ~ **of Parliament** *(Br.)* Unterhausmitglied, Abgeordneter; ~**s present and voting** anwesende und abstimmende Mitglieder; ~ **of the press** Pressevertreter; ~ **as of right** Mitglied kraft Amtes; **corresponding** ~ **of a society** korrespondierendes Mitglied einer Gesellschaft; ~ **of the staff** Mitarbeiter; ~ **of the stock exchange** Börsenmitglied; ~ **of a trip** Reiseteilnehmer; ~ **of the university** Universitätsangehöriger;

to admit as ~ **to one's ranks** Mitgliederzahl vergrößern; **to admit as** ~ als Mitglied aufnehmen; **to be a** ~ **of Parliament** Abgeordneter sein; **to become a** ~ **of an association** Vereinsmitglied werden; **to cease to be a** ~ als Mitglied (Aktionär) ausscheiden; **to drop a** ~ **from the rolls** j. von der Mitgliederliste streichen; **to elect s. o. as a** ~ j. zum Mitglied wählen; **to expel a** ~ Mitglied ausschließen; **to mail out to** ~**s** *(US)* an die Mitglieder verschicken; **to select s. o. as** ~ j. zum Mitglied wählen; **to strike a** ~ **off the list** Mitglied ausschließen;

~ **banks** *(US)* Mitgliederbanken [des Federal-Reserve-Systems]; ~ **bank balance held as reserve** *(US)* [etwa] bei der Landeszentralbank unterhaltene Mindesteinlagen; ~ **bank borrowings** *(US)* Inanspruchnahme von Krediten bei der Landeszentralbank; ~**'s capital** Gesellschafterkapital; ~ **check** Mitgliedsscheck; ~ **corporation** Mitgliedsfirma; ~ **country** Mit-

gliedsstaat; ~ **currency** *(OECD)* Mitgliederwährung; ~ **dues** Mitgliederbeiträge; ~ **firm** Mitgliedsfirma; ~ **form provided** beigefügte Mitgliederklärung; ~ **governments** Mitgliedsregierungen; ~**'s mortgage** *(Br.)* Bausparhypothek; ~**s' roll** Mitgliederverzeichnis, -liste; ~ **state** Mitgliedsstaat.

membership Mitgliederschaft, Zugehörigkeit, *(collective body of members)* Mitgliederzahl;

association ~ korporative Mitgliedschaft, Verbandszugehörigkeit; **club** ~ Vereinszugehörigkeit; **compulsory** ~ Zwangsmitgliedschaft, Beitrittszwang; **continued** ~ aufrechterhaltene Mitgliedschaft; **dual** ~ Doppelmitgliedschaft; **ex-officio** ~ Mitgliedschaft von Amts wegen; **fluctuating** ~ wechselnder Mitgliederbestand; **free** ~ beitragsfreie Mitgliedschaft; **full** ~ Vollmitgliedschaft; **honorary** ~ Ehrenmitgliedschaft; **individual** ~ Einzelmitgliedschaft; **large** ~ große Mitgliederzahl; **maximum** ~ Mitgliederhöchststand; **paid-up** ~ beitragszahlende Mitglieder; **union** ~ Gewerkschaftszugehörigkeit, -mitgliedschaft;

~ **of the cabinet** Regierungszugehörigkeit;

to acquire ~ Mitgliedschaft erwerben; **to admit to** ~ als Mitglied aufnehmen; **to apply for** ~ **of a club** sich bei einem Verein anmelden; **to be ineligible for** ~ als Mitglied nicht in Betracht kommen; **to cancel one's** ~ aus einem Verein austreten; **to declare one's** ~ **of a club** seinen Beitritt zu einem Verein erklären; **to discontinue** ~ Mitgliedschaft aufheben; **to exclude s. o. from** ~ j. von der Mitgliedschaft ausschließen; **to expand** ~ Mitgliedschaftskreis erweitern; **to get full** ~ Vollmitglied werden; **to propose for** ~ zur Aufnahme als Mitglied vorschlagen; **to put a name down for** ~ Mitgliedschaft für j. beantragen; **to renew one's** ~ seine Mitgliedschaft erneuern; **to withdraw from** ~ seine Mitgliedschaft aufgeben;

~ **application** Mitgliedschaftsantrag; ~ **association** *(US)* nicht eingetragener Verein; **[annual]** ~ **card** Mitgliedskarte; ~ **charge** Mitgliedsgebühr; ~ **committee** Mitgliedschaftsausschuß; ~ **contribution** Mitgliedsbeitrag; ~ **corporation** *(US)* eingetragener Verein, gemeinnützige Gesellschaft; ~ **drive** Mitgliederwerbung; ~ **dues** *(US)* Mitgliedsbeitrag; ~ **fee** Mitgliedsbeitrag; ~ **form provided** beigefügte Mitgliederklärung; ~ **interest** Mitgliedsanteil, -schaftsrecht; ~ **limitation** Mitgliederbegrenzung; ~ **list (roll)** Mitgliederliste, -verzeichnis; ~ **number** Mtgliedsnummer; ~ **privileges** Mitgliedschaftsvorrechte; ~ **register** Mitgliederverzeichnis; ~ **requirements** Mitgliedschaftsvoraussetzungen; ~ **rights** Mitgliederrechte; ~ **selection** Mitgliederauswahl; ~ **supervision** Mitgliederüberwachung; ~ **terms** Mitgliedschaftsbedingungen; ~ **ticket** Mitgliedsausweis.

memo Memorandum, Promemoria, Notiz; ~ **book** Notizbuch; ~ **pad** Notizblock.

memoir Lebensgeschichte, *(essay)* Denkschrift, Exposé; ~**s** Memoiren, Denkwürdigkeiten; **war** ~**s** Kriegserinnerungen.

memoirist Memoirenschreiber.

memorabilia Denkwürdigkeiten.

memorandum *(articles of agreement)* Vereinbarung, Vertragsurkunde, *(bill)* Kommissionsschein, -note, *(diplomatic note)* diplomatische Note, *(lease)* Beschreibung eines Pachtgrundstücks, *(marine insurance)* Haftungsausschuß (Haftungsbeschränkung) für leicht verderbliche Ware, *(pol.)* Denkschrift, *(record of events)* kurze Aufzeichnung der vereinbarten Punkte, Aktenvermerk, Exposé, Memorandum, *(short notice)* Notiz, Vermerk, Gedächtnisstütze, *(summary of terms of agreement)* Auszug aus den Vertragsbestimmungen, *(statement of goods sent)* Bordereau, Lieferschein [im Kommissionsverkauf];

common ~ *(Lloyd's, Br.)* Deckungsausschluß für Bruchschäden; **annexed** ~ beigefügtes Exposé; **law** ~ *(US)* Rechtsgutachten; **urgent** ~ Dringlichkeitsvermerk; **written** ~ schriftliche Vereinbarung;

~ **of agreement** *(international law)* schriftlich abgefaßte Vereinbarung; ~ **of alteration** *(patent law)* abgeänderter Patentantrag, Änderungsanmeldung; ~ **of appearance** *(Br.)* Einlassungserklärung; ~ **and articles** *(Br.)* Gesellschaftsstatuten, Gründungsurkunde und Satzung; ~ **of association** *(Br.)* Gründungsurkunde, Gesellschaftsvertrag, -statuten; ~ **and articles of association** *(Br.)* Gesellschaftsstatuten, Satzung, ~ **of charge** Grundstücksbelastungsurkunde; ~ **of deposit** Hinterlegungsurkunde, *(securities)* Effektenverzeichnis; ~ **in error** schriftliche Irrtumserklärung; ~ **for file** Aktenvermerk; ~ **of insurance** *(Br.)* vorläufiger Deckungsschein; ~ **of law** *(US)* Rechtsgutachten; ~ **of equitable mortgage under hand** schriftliche Sicherungsvereinbarung; ~ **of partnership** Gesellschaftsvertrag; ~ **of pledge** Verpfändungsurkunde; ~ **of registration** Eintragungs-

vermerk; **~ of satisfaction** *(mortgage, Br.)* Löschungsbewilligung, löschungsfähige Quittung; **~ in writing** schriftliche Vereinbarung;
to be shipped on ~ kommissionsweise versandt werden; **to make a** ~ Exposé anfertigen; **to send on a** ~ *(jewels)* in Kommission senden;
~ articles *(insurance, mortgage)* vom Versicherungsschutz ausgeschlossene Gegenstände; **~ bill** Kommissions-, Lieferschein; **~ book** *(bookkeeping)* Memorial, Manual, Kladde, *(notebook)* Notizbuch; **~ buying** Kauf mit Rückgaberecht; **~ card index** *(bookseller)* Vormerkkartei; **~ check** *(US)* befristeter Scheck; **~ clause** *(marine insurance)* Haftungsbeschränkung, -ausschluß, Freizeichnungsklausel; **~ collection** *(railway)* Frachtnachnahme; **~ column** Vermerkspalte; **~ copy of bill of lading** ungezeichnete Konossementskopie; **~ dating** *(US)* besonders vereinbarte Zahlungsbedingungen; **~ goods** *(package)* *(US)* Kommissionsware; **~ outlines** Grundzüge einer Vereinbarung; **~ pad** Notizblock; **~ sale** Verkauf auf Kommissionsbasis, Kommissionsverkauf, Kauf auf Probe; **~ sheet** Tagesordnung.
memorial *(to authorities)* Eingabe, Bitt-, Denkschrift, *(dipl.)* informelle Note, *(law, Br.)* zu den Akten einzureichender Urkundenauszug, *(monument)* Ehrenmal, Gedenkstätte, *(UNO, statement of facts)* Schriftsatz;
war ~ Kriegerdenkmal;
to present (submit) a ~ Eingabe machen, Denkschrift einreichen; **to proclaim a national** ~ zum Nationaldenkmal erklären;
~ address Gedächtnis-, Gedenkrede; **~ ceremony** Gedenkfeier; **⌂ Day** *(US)* Heldengedenktag; **~ park** *(US)* Friedhof; **~ publication** Festschrift; **~ service** Gedenkstunde, Gedächtnisgottesdienst; **~ stone** Gedenk-, Grundstein; **~ tablet** Gedenkplatte, -tafel; **~ wreath** Gedenkkranz.
memorialist Memoirenschreiber.
memorialize *(v.)* Bittschrift einreichen, *(commemorate)* Gedenkfeier abhalten.
memorization Auswendiglernen.
memorize *(v.)* im Gedächtnis behalten, auswendig lernen;
~ one's lines seine Ansprache auswendig lernen.
memory Merkfähigkeit, Gedächtnis, Andenken, Erinnerung, *(data processing)* Dauerspeicher, *(power of recognition)* Erinnerungsfähigkeit;
beyond ~ vor Menschendenken; **from** ~ aus dem Gedächtnis, auswendig; **to the best of my** ~ soweit ich mich erinnern kann; **within living** ~ noch in Erinnerung vieler Lebender; **within the ~ of man** seit Menschengedenken;
defective ~ schlechtes Gedächtnis; **legal** ~ Menschengedenken; **long** ~ weitreichendes Gedächtnis; **photographic** ~ visuelles Gedächtnis; **treacherous** ~ unzuverlässiges Gedächtnis; **vague** ~ verschwommene Erinnerung; **well-stocked** ~ geschultes Gedächtnis;
bad ~ for dates schlechtes Zahlengedächtnis; **~ for places** Ortsgedächtnis;
to aid ~ Gedächtnis stützen; **to be a blurred** ~ dunkel in Erinnerung; **to burden one's ~ with unnecessary dates** sein Gedächtnis mit unnützen Zahlen belasten; **to call to** ~ sich ins Gedächtnis zurückrufen; **to escape s. one's** ~ jds. Gedächtnis entfallen; **to dwell in s. one's** ~ in jds. Gedächtnis haften bleiben; **to have a bad ~ for dates** schlechtes Zahlengedächtnis haben, sich Daten nicht merken können; **to have a bad ~ for names** kein Namensgedächtnis haben; **to have a pleasant ~ of s. o.** sich gern an j. erinnern; **to have a ~ like a sieve** Gedächtnis wie ein Sieb haben; **to have a weak** ~ schwaches Gedächtnis haben; **to imprint on one's** ~ seinem Gedächtnis unauslöschlich einprägen; **to jog s. one's** ~ jds. Gedächtnis auffrischen; **to lose one's** ~ sein Gedächtnis verlieren; **to refresh one's** ~ sein Gedächtnis auffrischen; **to retain a clear** ~ **of s. th.** klare Erinnerung an etw. behalten haben; **to slip one's** ~ seinem Gedächtnis entgleiten; **to speak from** ~ frei sprechen; **to task one's** ~ sein Gedächtnis belasten; **to treasure s. one's** ~ jds. Andenken in Ehren halten; **to trust one's ~ too much** sein Gedächtnis überfordern;
~ access *(data processing)* Speicherzugriff; **~ aid** Gedächtnisstütze, -hilfe; **~ book** *(US)* Notizbuch; **~ error** Erinnerungsfehler; **~ image** Erinnerungsvorstellung; **~ performance** Merkfähigkeit; **~ measurement** Messung der Erinnerungsfähigkeit; **~ retention** Gedächtnisvermögen, -speicherung; **~ sketch** Gedächtnisskizze; **~ souvenir** bleibende Erinnerung; **auditory ~ span** Erinnerungsvermögen; **~ test** Gedächtnistest; **~ unit** Datenspeicher; **~ value** Erinnerungswert.
men | of light and leading führende Fachleute; **~ of station** Leute von Rang;
~'s room Herrentoilette.

menace drohende Gefahr, Bedrohung;
potential ~ mögliche Gefahr;
~ to s. one's safety Bedrohung der Sicherheit; **~ to world peace** Bedrohung des Weltfriedens;
~ *(v.)* **with war** Kriegsdrohungen ausstoßen.
ménage Haushalt.
mend Besserung, *(mended place)* Stopf-, Flickstelle, ausgebesserte Stelle;
~ *(v.)* reparieren, ver-, ausbessern, flicken, *(correct)* berichtigen, verbessern;
~ one's efforts seine Anstrengungen verdoppeln; **~ one's fences** *(US)* seine politischen Interessen wahren (nachbarlichen Beziehungen verbessern); **~ the fire** Feuer schüren, nachlegen; **~ invisibly** kunststopfen; **~ one's manners** sich bessere Manieren zulegen; **~ one's market** seine Handelsbedingungen verbessern; **~ matters** Situation verbessern; **~ one's pace** seinen Schritt beschleunigen; **~ one's ways** seine Fehler einsehen; **~ a broken window** zerbrochene Fensterscheibe reparieren;
to be on the ~ auf dem Wege der Besserung sein.
mendable ausbesserungs-, reparaturfähig.
mendicancy Bettelei, Betteln.
mending Ausbessern, Flicken;
invisible ~ Kunststopfen;
to be ~ nicely *(patient)* sich gut erholen.
menial Knecht, Diener, Lakai;
pampered ~ Lakaiennatur;
~ *(a.)* zur Dienerschaft gehörig, *(mean)* gemein, niedrig;
~ offices niedrige Dienste; **to obtain a ~ task** untergeordnete Beschäftigung finden.
mental geistig, intellektuell;
~ aberration krankhafte Störung der Geistestätigkeit; **~ ability** geistige Fähigkeit; **~ activity** Geistestätigkeit; **~ age** altersbezogener Intelligenzgrad; **~ alienation** geistige Störung, Geistesstörung; **~ anguish** seelisches Leid, seelischer Schmerz; **~ arithmetic** Kopfrechnen; **~ asylum** Nervenheilanstalt; **~ breakdown** Nervenzusammenbruch; **~ capacity or competence** Handlungsfähigkeit, *(law)* Zurechnungsfähigkeit; **~ case** Fall von Geisteskrankheit, Geisteskranker; **~ condition** Geistesverfassung; **~ cruelty** *(divorce, US)* seelische Grausamkeit; **~ defect** Geistesstörung, -schwäche; **~ defective** *(Br.)* Geistesschwacher, -gestörter; **~ defectiveness** Geistesschwäche; **~ deficiency** Störung der Geistestätigkeit; **~ delusion** Sinnestäuschung; **~ derangement** krankhafte Störung der Geistestätigkeit; **~ disablement** geistige Behinderung; **~ disease** Geisteskrankheit, -störung; **~ disorder** Geistesstörung, -krankheit, -schwäche; **to suffer from ~ disorder** geistesgestört sein; **~ disposition** geistige Veranlagung; **temporary disturbance of ~ faculties** vorübergehende Störung der Geistestätigkeit; **~ element** *(offence)* subjektiver Tatbestand; **~ faculties** Geistesgaben; **~ healing** psychologische Heilmethode; **~ health** Geistesverfassung; **⌂ Health Act** *(Br.)* Entmündigungsgesetz, Irrenfürsorgegesetz; **~ health service** Betreuung geistig Behinderter und Geisteskranker; **~ home** *(hospital, US)* Heil- und Pflegeanstalt, Nervenheilanstalt; **~ illness** Geisteskrankheit; **~ image** geistige Vorstellung; **~ incapacity (incompetency)** Geschäfts-, Unzurechnungsfähigkeit; **~ infirmity** Geistesschwäche; **~ injury** psychischer Schaden, geistiger Defekt, Dachschaden; **~ injury claims** auf psychische Berufsschäden gegründete Ersatzansprüche; **~ institution** *(US)* Heil- und Pflegeanstalt, Irrenanstalt; **~ patient** Geisteskranker; **~ picture** Vorstellungsbild; **~ powers** geistige Fähigkeiten, Geisteskraft; **~ process** Denkvorgang; **~ reservation** geheimer Vorbehalt, Mentalreservation; **~ set** geistige Einstellung; **~ shock** [Nerven]schock; **~ specialist** Nerven-, Irrenarzt; **~ state** Geisteszustand; **~ test** psychologischer Test, Intelligenzprüfung; **~ welfare officer** Sozialfürsorge für Geisteskranke; **~ work** geistige Arbeit.
mentally | defective geistesschwach, unzurechnungsfähig; **~ deranged** geistesgestört, -krank; **~ disordered** geisteskrank, -gestört, -schwach; **~ disordered person** Geisteskranker; **~ ill** geisteskrank; **~ retarded** geistig zurückgeblieben.
mentality Geisteskraft, Mentalität;
average ~ Durchschnittsmentalität.
menticide *(brain washing)* Gehirnwäsche.
mention *(v.)* Erwähnung, Hinweis, Vermerk;
hono(u)rable ~ ehrenvolle Erwähnung;
~ in dispatches ehrenhafte Erwähnung im Heeresbericht;
~ *(v.)* erwähnen, anführen;
~ individually namentlich anführen; **~ s. one's name** sich auf j. berufen; **~ s. o. in one's will** j. in seinem Testament bedenken; **to give individual ~ to s. o.** j. einzeln erwähnen.

mentioned | above oben erwähnt; **afore** ~ vorgenannt;

to be hono(u)rably ~ *(school)* Belobigung erhalten; **to be ~ in dispatches** *(mil., Br.)* im Kriegsbericht lobend erwähnt werden.

mentition Falschaussage.

mentor Mentor, Berater, Ratgeber, Helfer.

menu Karte, Menü, Speisenfolge;

to be off the ~ nicht auf der Speisekarte stehen;

~ card Speisekarte.

mercantile handeltreibend, kaufmännisch, geschäftlich;

~ academy Handelshochschule; **~ advice** Handelsbericht; **~ affairs** Geschäftsleben, Handelssachen; **~agency** Handelsvertretung, -agentur, *(US)* Kreditauskunftei; **~agent** *(Br.)* Kommissionär, Handelsvertreter, Makler; **~ bank** Handelsbank; **~ bill** Warenwechsel; **~ broker** Handelsmakler; **~ business** Warenhandel; **~ career** kaufmännische Laufbahn; **~ class** Kaufmanns-, Handelsstand; **~ community** Kaufmannschaft; **~ concern** Handelsfirma, Wirtschaftskonzern; **~ connections** Handelsbeziehungen; **~ credit** Warenkredit; **~ creditor** Warengläubiger; **~ directory** Branchenverzeichnis; **~ doctrine** Merkantilismus; **~ enterprise (establishment)** Handelsniederlassung, -firma; **~ house** Handelshaus, -firma, Geschäftshaus; **~ open stock insurance** Einbruchversicherung für Warenlager; **~ safe insurance** Einbruchversicherung von Waren und Wertpapieren in Safes von Geschäftsunternehmen; **~ interests** kaufmännische Interessen; **~ law** See-, Verkehrs- und Handelsrecht; **~ line** Kaufmannsfach; **~ marine** Handelsmarine, Kauffahrtei; **~ men** Kaufleute; **~ nation** Handelsvolk, handeltreibende Nation; **~ operations** Handelsverkehr, geschäftlicher Verkehr; **~ paper** Warenpapier, -wechsel, -akzept; **~ partnership** *(US)* Offene Handelsgesellschaft; **~ practice** Handelsbrauch; **~ pursuits** kaufmännische Tätigkeit, Handelsbetrieb; **~ report** Bericht einer Kreditauskunftei; **~ risk** Geschäftsrisiko; **~ school** Anhänger des Merkantilsystems; **~ spirit** Handelsgeist; **~ store** *(US)* Ladengeschäft; **~ system** Merkantilsystem; **~ term** Handelsausdruck; **~ theory** Merkantilismus; **~ town** Handelsstadt; **~ transaction** Handelsgeschäft, geschäftliche Transaktion; **~ vessel** Handelsschiff.

mercantilism Merkantilismus, Freihandelspolitik, *(commercialism)* Krämergeist.

mercantilist Merkantilist, Freihändler.

mercantilistic merkantilistisch.

mercenarily aus Gewinnsucht, für Geld.

mercenary Mietling, *(mil.)* Söldner;

~ (a.) geldsüchtig, feil, käuflich, *(hired)* gedungen;

~ marriage Geldheirat; **~ troops** Söldnertruppe.

merchandise Waren, [Handels]güter, -ware, Artikel, Erzeugnis, *(inventory)* Warenlager, *(technique)* Vertriebs- und Verkaufssteuerung;

as-in ~ zurückgesetzte (reduzierte) Ware; **branded ~** Markenartikel; **convict-made ~** von Strafgefangenen hergestellte Waren; **~ displayed** zur Schau gestellte (ausgestellte) Waren; **fashion ~** Modeartikel; **high-cost ~** Waren in hoher Preislage; **higher-margin ~** Waren mit hoher Gewinnspanne; **falsely marked ~** falsch bezeichnete Waren; **marked-down ~** im Preis herabgesetzte Ware; **nonperishable ~** unverderbliche Waren; **price-fixed ~** preisgebundene Waren; **price-bound ~** preisgebundene Erzeugnisse; **purchased ~** bezogene Waren; **quality ~** Qualitätsware; **shopworn ~** vom langen Liegen im Laden wertgeminderte Waren, Ladenhüter; **slow-moving ~** langsam verkäufliche Ware; **spring ~** Frühjahrsartikel; **staple ~** Haupterzeugnisse; **trademarked ~** Markenartikel; **up-to-date ~** neueste Artikel;

goods, wares and ~ Hab und Gut;

~ on account Waren auf Kredit; **~ shipped by air** auf dem Luftwege beförderte Güter; **~ at the beginning of the month** Bestand am Monatsanfang; **~ on consignment** Kommissionsware; **~ intended for export** Ausfuhr-, Exportgüter; **~ on hand** Warenbestand; **~ on memorandum** *(US)* Kommissionsware; **~ on order** in Auftrag gegebene (bestellte) Waren; **~ in storage** eingelagerte Waren; **~ in transit** unterwegs befindliche Ware, Transitware; **~ lying in a warehouse** Konsignationsware;

~ (v.) *(US)* Handel treiben, handeln, Geschäfte machen, kaufen und verkaufen, *(sales promotion)* dem Publikum empfehlen, Absatzplanung betreiben;

~ account Warenkonto; **~ accounting** Warenbuchhaltung; **~ allowance** Warenrabatt; **~ appeal** Kaufanreiz; **~ arrangement** Warenanordnung; **~ assortment** Warensortiment; **~ balance** *(US)* Handelsbilanz; **~ broker** Waren-, Produktenmakler; **~ budget** Mittel für die Warenbeschaffung; **~ car** Güterwagen; **~-category [profit] margin** Warengruppenspanne; **~-category statistics** Warengruppenstatistik; **~ checker** Warenprüfer; **~**

classification Wareneinstufung; **~ committee** Einkaufsausschuß; **~ control** Warenkontrolle; **~ cost** Einkaufskosten abzüglich Warenskonto; **~ creditor** Warengläubiger; **~ debtor** Warenschuldner; **~ department** Warenabteilung; **~ inventory** Warenverzeichnis, -inventar, *(balance sheet)* Warenbestand, *(stock)* Warenlager; **~ investment** Warenvorrat; **~ item** Warenposten; **~ knowledge** Warenkunde; **~ lines** Warensortiment; **~ manager** *(department)* kaufmännischer Leiter eines Warenhauses, Leiter der Ein- und Verkaufsabteilung; **~ manual** Warenhandbuch; **gross ~ margin** Bruttoverdienstspanne; **~ mark** *(Br.)* Warenzeichen; **~ Marks Act** *(Br.)* Warenzeichengesetz; **~ mix** Zusammensetzung des Sortiments; **~ movement** Warenbewegung; **~ offerings** Warenangebot; **~ plan[ning]** Wareneinkaufssystem; **~ procurement** Warenbeschaffung; **~ procurement cost** Warenbeschaffungskosten; **~ purchases** Wareneinkäufe; **~ receivables** *(balance sheet, US)* Warenforderungen; **~ return** Warenrückgabe; **~ scheme** Verkaufsplan; **~ selection** Warenauswahl; **~ shipment** Warenversand; **~ shortage** Warenknappheit; **~ storage space** Warenlagerraum; **~ stock** Warenlager; **~ testing bureau** Warenprüfstelle; **~ trade** Warenhandel; **~ trade balance** Warenhandelsbilanz **~ trade surplus** Warenhandelsüberschuß; **~ traffic** Waren-, Güterverkehr; **~ transaction** Warentransaktion; **~ transfer** Wareneigentumsübereignung; **~ turnover** Lagerumschlag, Warenumsatz; **~ valuation** Lagerbewertung; **~ warehouse** Warenspeicher.

merchandiser beratender Verkäufer.

merchandising Steuerung von Vertrieb und Verkauf, Absatzvorbereitung durch Vertriebsplanung, Absatzförderung, Verkaufspolitik, -förderung, *(retail business)* Präsentation der Waren im Einzelhandelsgeschäft;

retail ~ Einzelhandelsvertrieb;

~ concern Handelsfirma, -unternehmen; **~ department** Vertriebsabteilung; **~ director** Leiter der Verkaufsförderungsabteilung; **~ earnings** Erträge aus dem Warengeschäft; **~ efficiency** erfolgreiche Vertriebspolitik; **~ establishment** Handelsfirma; **~ experience** Verkaufserfahrung; **~ function** Warenlagerfunktion; **~ manager** Vertriebsdirektor; **gross ~ margin** Bruttogewinnsatz; **~ operation** Warentransaktion; **~ organization** Vertriebsorganisation; **~ plan** Verkaufsförderungsplan; **~ policy** Verkaufspolitik; **to formulate ~ policy** Verkaufspolitik festlegen; **~ risk** Absatzrisiko; **~ scheme** Absatz-, Verkaufsplan; **~ show** Warenmesse; **~ statistics** Warenstatistik; **~ support** Verkaufsunterstützung bei Einzelhändlern; **~ technique** Warenkunde.

merchandisable verkaufs-, absatzfähig.

merchant [Groß]kaufmann, *(agent)* Vertreter, Handlungsreisender, *(exports)* Exportkaufmann, *(purchaser)* Einkäufer, *(shopkeeper, US)* Ladenbesitzer, Einzelhändler, Krämer, *(trader)* Händler, *(wholesaler)* Großhändler;

~s Kaufmannschaft, [Groß]kaufleute, Handelskreise;

city ~ Kaufherr; **coal ~** Kohlenhändler; **commission ~** Kommissionär; **established ~** selbständiger Kaufmann; **export ~** Exportkaufmann; **forwarding ~** *(US)* Spediteur; **feme-sole ~** *(Br.)* selbständige Geschäftsfrau; **import ~** Importkaufmann, Importeur; **~ law** Handelsrecht; **speed ~** Schnellfahrer, rücksichtsloser Autofahrer; **wine ~** Weinhändler; **wholesale ~** Großhändler;

~ (v.) Warenhandel betreiben;

to turn ~ kaufmännischen Beruf ergreifen;

~s' accounts kaufmännische Buchführung; **~ adventurer** Überseespekulant; **~ appraiser** *(revenue office)* Schätzer im Zollbescheidverfahren; **~ apprentice** Handelslehrling, kaufmännisch Auszubildender; **~ bank** *(Br.)* Handelsbank, kaufmännisches Akzepthaus, Akzept-, Remboursbank; **~ banking** *(Br.)* Remboursgeschäft; **to expand its ~ banking arm** *(Br.)* seine Handelsbankfunktionen ausdehnen; **~'s basket** *(statistics)* Warenkorb; **~ captain** Kapitän bei der Handelsmarine; **~'s clerk** kaufmännischer Angestellter, Handlungsgehilfe; **armed ~ cruiser** bewaffneter Handelskreuzer; **~ flag** Handels-, Reedereiflagge; **~ fleet** Kauffahrtei-, Handelsflotte, -marine; **warriddled ~ fleet** durch den Krieg stark mitgenommene Handelsflotte; **~'s goods** Handelsware; **~ guild** Kaufmannsinnung; **~'s house** Kaufhaus; **~ marine** Handelsmarine; **~ marine industry** Schiffahrtsindustrie; **~ middleman** Kommissionär; **~ navy officer** Angestellter der Handelsmarine; **~'s office** Kontor; **~s' prices** Engrospreise; **~ prince** Magnat, Kaufherr, Wirtschaftsführer; **~'s rules** Handelsusancen; **~ seaman** Angehöriger der Handelsmarine; **~ service** Handelsschiffahrt, -marine, Seehandel; **[warbuilt] ~ ship** [im Krieg gebautes] Handelsschiff; **~ ship order** Handelsschiffsauftrag; **~ shipper** *(Br.)* Exporthändler; **~ shipping** *(Br.)* Handelsschiffahrt, Seehandel;

ᵒ **Shipping Act** *(Br.)* Handelsschiffahrtsgesetz; ᵒ **Shipping Regulations** *(Br.)* Handelsschiffahrtsverordnung; ~ **shop** Kaufladen; ~ **trading** Großhandel; ~ **venturer** Spekulant; ~ **vessel** Kauffahrtei-, Handelsschiff; ~**'s wife** Kaufmannsfrau.

merchantability handelsübliche Qualität.

merchantable lieferbar, *(salable)* verkäuflich, gangbar, marktgängig;
   not ~ unverkäuflich;
   in a ~ **condition** in handelsfähigem Zustand; ~ **quality** Ware mittlerer Art und Güte, marktübliche Qualität, marktgängige Ware; ~ **title** rechtsmängelfreies Eigentum.

merchantableness Lieferbarkeit, Verkäuflichkeit, Gangbarkeit, Gängigkeit, handelsübliche Qualität.

merchanthood kaufmännisches Gewerbe.

merchanting *(Br.)* überseeisches Warenbörsengeschäft;
   ~ **trade** *(Br.)* Transithandel; ~ **transactions** *(Br.)* Transitgeschäfte.

merchantlike kaufmännisch, geschäftsmäßig.

merchantman Handelsschiff, Kauffahrer, -fahrteischiff.

merchantry kaufmännisches Gewerbe.

mercy Gnade, Gnadenrecht;
   with a recommendation to ~ mit einer Empfehlung für den Gnadenweg;
   to be at the ~ **of the waves** den Wellen preisgegeben sein; **to be put (left) to s. one's** ~ jds. Willkür ausgeliefert sein; **to petition for** ~ Gnadengesuch einreichen; **to show no** ~ keine Gnade walten lassen; **to throw o. s. on s. one's** ~ sich jem. auf Gnade und Ungnade ausliefern;
   ~ **killing** Euthanasie, Gnadentod.

mere | form reine Formsache; ~ **imagination** reine Einbildung; ~ **motion** unbeeinflußte Willenshandlung; ~ **right** besitzloses Eigentum; **to sell for a** ~ **song** spottbillig verkaufen; ~ **trifle** bloße Kleinigkeit.

merge *(v.)* zusammenschließen, -legen, *(business enterprise)* verschmelzen, sich vereinigen, fusionieren, *(v./i.)* aufgehen in;
   ~ **into curiosity** in Neugier umschlagen; ~ **in an Empire** in einem Imperium aufgehen; ~ **into one large organization** sich in einem großen Unternehmen zusammenschließen; ~ **in one person** *(rights)* sich in eine Person vereinigen.

merged, half teilweise fusioniert.

merger *(absorption by larger estate)* Aufgehen [eines Besitzes in einem größeren], *(amalgamation)* Verschmelzung, Fusion[ierung], [Firmen]zusammenschluß, *(criminal law, US)* Konsumtion, *(rights)* Vereinigung von Rechten in einer Person, Konfusion, *(shares)* Zusammenlegung;
   bank ~ Bankenfusion; **conglomerate** ~ Fusion branchenfremder Unternehmen; **corporate** ~ Zusammenschluß von Gesellschaften, Gesellschaftsfusion; **downstairs** ~ Fusion der Mutter- mit der Tochtergesellschaft; **full-fledged** ~ komplette Fusion; **government-aided** ~ staatlich geförderte Fusion; **horizontal** ~ Fusion von Konkurrenzunternehmen; **industrial** ~ industrieller Zusammenschluß, Konzentrationsvorgang; **proposed** ~ Fusionsvorschlag; **vertical** ~ vertikale Fusion, vertikaler Zusammenschluß;
   ~ **of banks** Bankenfusion; ~ **of charges on property** Konfusion von Grundstückslasten und -rechten; ~ **of contract** Novation; ~ **of funds** Kapitalzusammenlegung; ~ **by operation of law** gesetzliche Konfusion; ~ **of rights of action** Aufgehen der Klageansprüche;
   to block a ~ einer Fusion im Wege stehen; **to freeze action on** ~ Fusionsbeschluß inhibieren; **to rule on** ~**s** für Fusionsgenehmigungen zuständig sein; **to undo a** ~ Fusion rückgängig machen;
   ~ **accord** Fusionsvereinbarung; ~ **activity** Fusionsgeschäftigkeit; ~ **agreement** Fusionsvereinbarung, -vertrag; ~ **application** Fusionsantrag; ~ **arrangement** Fusionsabkommen; ~ **bid** Fusionsangebot; ~ **candidate** Fusionskandidat; ~ **clearance** *(US)* Fusions-, Konzentrationsgenehmigung; ~ **company** fusionierende Gesellschaft; ~ **control** Fusionskontrolle; ~ **decision** Fusionsbeschluß; ~ **fever** Fusionsfieber; ~ **front** Fusionsfront; **to play the** ~ **game** sich an dem Fusionsspiel beteiligen; ~ **movement** Fusionsbewegung; ~ **offer** Fusionsangebot; ~ **partner** Fusionspartner; ~ **plan** Fusionsplan; ~ **possibilities** Fusionsmöglichkeiten; ~ **pressure** Fusionsdruck; **to dominate in the** ~ **scene** im Fusionsgeschäft den Ton angeben; ~ **statement** Fusionserklärung; ~ **talks** Fusionsgespräche, -verhandlungen; ~ **trend** Fusionstendenz.

merit Verdienst, Vorzug, Wert;
   on its ~**s** gesondert, für sich allein; **on its own** ~**s** an und für sich betrachtet; **on the** ~**s or in terms of amount** dem Grunde oder der Höhe nach; **upon the** ~**s** nach materiellem Recht; **without** ~**s** unbegründet;

~**s of a case** für die Beurteilung wesentliche Umstände eines Falls, Tatbestandsmerkmale; ~**s of the defence** wesentliches Vorbringen der Verteidigung;
   ~ *(v.)* **reward** Belohnung verdienen;
   to admit a claim on the ~**s** Anspruch dem Grunde nach anerkennen; **to be destitute of** ~**s** jeder Grundlage entbehren; **to deal with a case upon its** ~**s** in der Hauptsache (materiellrechtlich) entscheiden; **to decide (judge) a case on its** ~**s** Fall allein aufgrund der ihm innewohnenden Umstände entscheiden; **to decide on the** ~**s of each particular case** von Fall zu Fall entscheiden; **to discuss s. th. on its** ~**s** Sache ihrem wesentlichen Inhalt nach besprechen; **to dismiss a claim on the** ~**s** Klage als unbegründet abweisen; **to examine the** ~**s of a claim** Schlüssigkeit eines Anspruchs prüfen; **to give judgment on its** ~**s** in der Hauptsache entscheiden; **to go into the** ~**s of a case** Für und Wider einer Sache erörtern; **to have no** ~ nicht begründet sein; **to make a** ~ **of being punctual** sich viel auf seine Pünktlichkeit zugutehalten; **to make a** ~ **of s. th.** sich auf eine Sache etw. einbilden; **to regard an appeal as being without** ~**s** Einspruch für unbegründet halten; **to rest (stand) on its own** ~**s** für sich allein beurteilen; **to take great** ~ **to o. s. for s. th.** sich große Verdienste um etw. erwerben; **to treat s. o. according to his** ~**s** j. nach seinen Verdiensten behandeln;
   ~ **bonus** Leistungsprämie, -zulage; ~ **increase** *(US)* Lohnerhöhung aufgrund besonderer Leistung, Leistungszulage; ~ **pricing system** *(motorcar insurance, US)* Kraftfahrzeugversicherungssystem mit Prämien für unfallfreies Fahren; ~ **rating** *(US)* Leistungseinstufung, -beurteilung, Personalbeurteilung; ~**-rating sheet** *(US)* Leistungsbeurteilungsblatt; ~ **rating system** *(US)* Leistungsbeurteilungssystem, -prinzip; ~ **salary increase** *(US)* Leistungszulage; ~ **system** *(US)* allein auf Fähigkeiten beruhendes Beförderungswesen, Leistungsprinzip; ~ **wants** meritorische Bedürfnisse, Kollektivbedürfnisse.

meritocracy Leistungsgesellschaft.

meritorious | conduct verdienstvolles Verhalten; ~ **consideration** auf einer Anstandspflicht begründete Leistung; ~ **defence** materiell-rechtliche Einwendung.

merry heiter, *(tipsy)* angeheitert, beschwipst;
   ~ **as the day is long** quietschvergnügt; ~ **as a lark (cricket)** kreuzfidel;
   to be ~ **in one's cups** vergnügten Umtrunk halten, einen kleinen sitzen haben; **to make** ~ feiern; **to make** ~ **over s. th.** sich über etw. belustigen, sich über etw. lustig machen.

merry-go-round Karussel, *(fig.)* circulus vitiosus, *(traffic)* Rund-, Kreisverkehr, *(pol.)* Wahlkarussel;
   to be on a ~ pausenlos unterwegs sein.

merrymaker Schmauser, Zecher.

merrymaking Belustigung, Gelage.

mesh Masche;
   ~ *(v.)* *(fig.)* umstricken, umgarnen.

meshes Netzwerk, Geflecht, *(fig.)* Netze, Schlingen;
   ~ **of political intrigue** politisches Intrigengespinst; ~ **of railways** Eisenbahnnetz; ~ **of a spider's web** Spinnengewebe;
   to be caught in the ~ **of the law** in den Schlingen des Gesetzes verstrickt sein; **to draw into one's** ~ in sein Netz ziehen; **to entangle s. o. in the** ~ **of intrigue** j. in ein Netz von Intrigen verwickeln.

mesne dazwischenliegend, *(legal term)* zwischenzeitlich;
   ~ **assignment** dazwischenliegende Abtretung; ~ **incumbrance** kurzfristige Zwischenbelastung; ~ **interest** Zwischenzins; ~ **process** *(US)* gerichtliche Zwischenverfügung; ~ **profits** *(Br.)* unrechtmäßig erworbene Grundstücksfrüchte.

mess [Offiziers]messe, Kasino, *(mar.)* Regimentstisch, *(meal)* Portion, *(state of confusion)* Durcheinander, Unordnung, Schlamassel;
   officers' ~ Offizierskasino;
   ~ **of pottage** Linsengericht;
   ~ *(v.)* *(mil., mar.)* im Kasino essen;
   ~ **around** *(sl.)* Zeit verplempern; ~ **in** *(US)* sich unberechtigt einmischen; ~ **up** in Unordnung bringen, verpfuschen; ~ **up all one's plans** alle Vorbereitungen durcheinanderbringen;
   to be in a ~ in der Patsche sitzen; **to be in a pretty** ~ *(house)* in desolatem Zustand sein; **to clear up the** ~ die Schweinerei in Ordnung bringen; **to get into a** ~ in eine Klemme geraten; **to make a nice** ~ **of it** etw. Schönes anrichten; **to make a** ~ **of a job** Arbeit miserabel erledigen; **to turn into a** ~ sich in ein Tohuwabohu verwandeln;
   ~ **attendant** Kassinoordinanz; ~ **council** Kasinovorstand; ~ **hall** Kasino[raum], Kantine, Messe; ~ **kit** *(mil., US)* Kochgeschirr; ~ **quarters forward** Mannschaftsraum; ~ **sergeant** *(mil.)* Küchenbulle; ~**-up** *(coll.)* Durcheinander, Mißverständnis.

message Nachricht, Bestellung, Mitteilung, Benachrichtigung, Bericht, Bescheid, Botschaft, *(advertising)* Werbeaussage, -argumentation, *(broadcasting)* Durchsage, *(sovereign)* Adresse, *(US)* Ansprache, Sendschreiben [des Präsidenten];
New Year's ~ Neujahrsansprache; **President's** ⚲ Botschaft des Präsidenten an den Kongress; **repeated** ~ *(telegraph form)* Kontrolltelegramm; **state of the union** ~ *(US)* Regierungserklärung; **telephone[d]** ~ telefonische Mitteilung (Benachrichtigung), fernmündliche Nachricht; **telegraphed** ~ Drahtnachricht; **urgent** ~ eilige Nachricht; **verbal** ~ mündliche Mitteilung; **wireless** ~ Funkspruch, -meldung; **written** ~ schriftliche Mitteilung;
~ **in code** verschlüsselte Nachricht; ~ **of greetings** *(US)* Glückwunschtelegram; ~ **by telegraph** Drahtnachricht;
~ *(v.)* Nachricht übermitteln;
to bear (carry) a ~ Botschaft überbringen; **to deliver** ~s **for s. o.** Botengänge für j. erledigen; **to get the** ~ etw. richtig aufnehmen; **to go on a** ~ etw. für jem. erledigen; **to leave a** ~ Mitteilung hinterlassen; **to put across the** ~ zu verstehen geben; **to run** ~s Botendienste tun, Botengänge erledigen; **to send a** ~ **by telephone** Nachricht telefonisch übermitteln; **to take a** ~ Mitteilung entgegennehmen; **to write a** ~ **in cipher** Botschaft chiffrieren;
~ **authenticator** Mitteilungsbestätigungswort; ~ **bearer** Nachrichtenträger, -übermittler; ~ **card** *(mil.)* Meldekarte; ~ **center** *(US)* **(centre,** *Br.)* Meldekopf, Nachrichtensammelstelle; ~ **form** Depeschen-, Telegrammformular; ~ **number** *(publishing business)* Meldenummer.

messenger [Eil]bote, Läufer, *(bank)* Kassenbote, *(court)* Gerichtsdiener, *(court of bankruptcy)* Masseverwalter, *(dipl.)* Kurier, *(forerunner)* Verkünder, Vorbote, *(mil.)* Meldeläufer;
by ~ durch Boten;
bank ~ Bank-, Kassenbote; **express** ~ *(Br.)* Kurier, Eilbote; **hotel** ~ [Hotel]page; **Queen's** ~ königlicher Kurier; **special** ~ *(US)* Eilbote; **telegraph** ~ Telegrammbote;
~ **at arms** *(Scot.)* Zustellungsbeamter;
to dispatch a ~ Boten entsenden, Kurier abfertigen; **to intercept a** ~ Boten abfangen;
~ **boy** Laufbursche, Botenjunge; ~ **dog** Meldehund; ~'s **fee** Botenlohn, Bestellgebühr, -geld; ~ **pigeon** Brieftaube; ~ **service** Botendienst; **Foreign** ⚲ **Service** Kurierabteilung.
messing allowance *(mil.)* Verpflegungsgeld.
messuage Wohnhaus mit dazugehörigem Landbesitz.
messy job Drecksarbeit.
metachronism Fristberechnungshelfer.
metage Meßgebühr, Meß- und Wagengeld.
metal Metall, *(road)* Schotter;
~s *(Br.)* Eisenbahnschienen;
base ~ unedles Metall; **nonferrous** ~s Nichteisenmetalle; **precious** ~ Edelmetall;
~ *(v.)* beschottern;
to run off the ~s entgleisen;
all-~ **airplane** Metallflugzeug; ~ **blind** Blechrolladen; ~ **block** Metallklischee; ~ **cut** Metallklischee; ~ **exchange** Metallbörse; ~ **fabricating** Metallverarbeitung; ~ **industry** Metallindustrie; ~ **manufactures** Metallwaren; ~ **mining** Erzbergbau; ~ **processing industry** metallverarbeitende Industrie; ~ **sign** Metallschild; ~ **strapping** Bandeisensicherung; ~ **trades** Metallbranche; ~ **worker** Metallarbeiter; ~ **workers union** Metallarbeitergewerkschaft.
metal(l)ed | road Schotterstraße; ~ **surface** Schotterdecke.
metallic | cover Metalldeckung; ~ **currency (money)**Metall-, Hartgeld; ~ **standard** Metallwährung.
metal(l)ing *(railway)* Schienenverlegung, *(roads)* Beschotterung.
metalware Metallwaren.
metamorphosis, social soziale Umwandlung.
metaphrase wörtliche Übersetzung.
metayer *(Br.)* Halbpächter;
~ **system** Natural-, Halbpachtsystem.
mete *(v.)* | [out] **punishment** Strafe zumessen; ~ **rewards** Belohnungen austeilen;
~s **and bounds** *(piece of land)* Grenzlinien;
to know one's ~s **and bounds** seine Grenzen kennen.
meteor Meteor, *(fig.)* flüchtige Erscheinung.
meteoric career kometenhafte Laufbahn.
meteorological | message Wettermeldung, -nachricht, *(mil.)* Barbarameldung; ~ **briefing** mündliche Wetterberatung; ~ **divide** Wetterscheide; **medium-term** ~ **forecast** mittelfristige Wettervorhersage; ~ **observation** Wetterbeobachtung; ~ **office** Wetteramt, -warte, -station; ~ **satellite** Wettersatellit; ~ **watch office (station)** Flugwetterüberwachungsstelle.

meteorologist Wetterbeobachter, Meteorologe.
meter Meßinstrument, Messer, Zahlwert;
gas ~ Gasuhr; **electric (current)** ~ Stromzähler; **exposure** ~ Belichtungsmesser; **parking** ~ Parkuhr; **water** ~ Wasseruhr;
~ *(v.)* messen;
to read the gas ~ Gasverbrauch ablesen;
~ **board** Zählertafel; ~ **reader** Elektrizitäts-, Strom-, Gaszähler, -ableser, *(airforce, sl.)* Kopilot; ~ **reading** Zählerstand.
metered mail *(US)* **(post,** *Br.)* vom Freistempler freigemachte Post.
method Weg, Verfahren, Verfahrensweise, Art und Weise, Methode, System;
approved ~ bewährte Methode; **comparative** ~ Kostenvergleichsmethode; **cost or market whichever is the lower** ~ *(balance sheet)* Niederstwertprinzip; **industrial** ~ industrielles Verfahren; **low-down** ~s unsaubere Methoden; **new managerial** ~s neue Methoden in der Unternehmensführung; **observational** ~s Beobachtungsmethoden; **out-of-date** ~s veraltete Methoden; **short-cut** ~ Abkürzungsverfahren; **working** ~ Fabrikationsverfahren;
~ **of application** Anwendungsverfahren; ~ **of approach** Annäherungsmethode; ~ **of assessment** Veranlagungsmethode; ~ **of calculation** Berechnungsart, Kalkulationsmethode; ~ **of compensation** Ausgleichsrechnung; **unfair** ~s **of competition** unlauterer Wettbewerb; ~ **of computation** Berechnungsmethode; ~ **of construction** Bauart, -methode, -weise; ~ **of depreciation** Abschreibungsart, -methode; **declining balance** ~ **of depreciation** degressive Abschreibungsmethode; **straight-line** ~ **of depreciation** lineare Abschreibungsmethode; ~ **of dispatch** Versandweise; ~ **of financing** Finanzierungsmethode, -weise, -art; **new** ~ **of illumination** neues Beleuchtungssystem; **inhuman** ~s **of interrogation** unmenschliche Verhörmethoden; ~ **of investigation** Untersuchungsmethode; ~ **of levying** Erhebungsverfahren; ~ **of management** Verwaltungsmethoden; ~ **of operation** Arbeitsweise, -methode; ~ **of overlapping maps** *(statistics)* koordinierte Doppelauswahl; ~ **of packing** Verpackungssystem; ~ **of payment** Zahlungsmodus, -weise; ~ **of production** Produktionsverfahren; ~[s] **of quoting** Notierungsart, -usance; ~ **of granting relief** für die Berechnung von Steuerermäßigungen angewandte Methode; ~ **of repaying** Rückzahlungsweise; ~ **of shipment** Versandsystem; ~ **of taxation** Besteuerungsart, -verfahren; ~ **of teaching** Unterrichtsmethode; ~[s] **of trading** Handelsusance; ~ **of transport** Fortbewegungsmethode, Transportsystem; ~ **of valuation** Bewertungsmethode; ~ **of voting** Abstimmungsmodus, -methode; ~ **of working** Arbeitsmethode;
to adopt a ~ Methode anwenden; **to work with** ~ methodisch arbeiten;
~**s-time measurement** Elementarzeitbestimmungssystem.
methodical methodisch, planmäßig;
~ **work** systematische Arbeit.
métier Gewerbe, Handwerk, *(fig.)* Fach-, Spezialgebiet.
metric system metrisches System, Dezimalsystem.
metrication *(Br.)* Umstellung auf das metrische System.
Metro *(coll., Br.)* U-Bahn;
⚲ **concept** Großstadtkonzept; ⚲ **government** Großstadtverwaltung.
Metroland *(Br.)* mit der U-Bahn erreichbare Stadtbezirke.
metroliner *(US)* Nahverkehrsschnellzug.
metropolis Hauptstadt;
commercial ~ Handelsmetropole.
metropolitan haupt-, großstädtisch;
~ **area** Großstadtgebiet; ~ **authority** Großstadtverwaltung; ~ **cheque** *(Br.)* Scheck auf Groß-London; ~ **clearing** *(Br.)* Stadtclearing in Groß-London; ~ **consumer** Großstadtverbraucher; ~ **country** Mutterland; ~ **development** Großstadtentwicklung; ~ **district** Großstadtgebiet; ~ **government** Großstadtverwaltung; ~ **stipendiary magistrate** *(London)* Berufsrichter; ~ **office** *(US)* Stadtbüro; ~ **paper** Großstadtausgabe; ~ **plan** *(advertising)* Ortsverbreitungsplan; ~ **police** *(London)* Stadtpolizei; ⚲ **Police Commissioner** *(Br.)* Chef der Polizeikräfte Groß Londons; ~ **railway** *(Br.)* Stadtbahn, [Londoner] U-Bahn; ~ **region** Großstadtgebiet; ~ **suburb** Großstadtvorort; ~ **territories** Mutterland; ~ **territory** Großstadtgebiet.
mettle Enthusiasmus, Eifer;
full of ~ von echtem Schrot und Korn; **on one's** ~ auf Trapp gebracht;
to put s. o. on his ~ jds. Ehrgeiz anstacheln; **to show one's** ~ alle seine Künste zeigen; **to try s. one's** ~ j. auf die Probe stellen.
mew | s *(Br.)* zu Apartmentwohnungen umgebaute Ställe;
~ *(v.)* **o. s. up from the world** sich von der Welt zurückziehen.

Mexican promotion *(raise)* Rangerhöhung ohne Gehaltserhöhung.
mezzanine Zwischenstock.
mezzotint technique Schabemanier.
miche *(v.) (dial.)* Schule schwänzen.
Michey Bordradargerät.
microcircuit Mikroschaltkreis.
mircoeconomics Mikroökonomie.
microfilm Mikrofilm;
~ *(v.)* Mikrofilmaufnahmen machen;
~ **processor** Entwicklungsgerät für Mikrofilme.
micrograph mikrografische Darstellung.
microphone Mikrophon;
directional ~ Richtmikrophon; **remote-control** ~ Mikrophon mit Fernbedienung;
to plant a ~ verstecktes Mikrofon anbringen;
~ **key** Sprechtaste.
microphotographic mikrofotografisch.
microprint Mikrodruck.
microscope Mikroskop.
microprocessor kleiner Datenverarbeiter.
microwave Ultrakurzwelle;
~ **wave link** Richtfunkverbindung.
mid mitten in, in der Mitte befindlich;
in ~ **air** mitten in der Luft; ~**-air collision** Zusammenstoß in der Luft; **to be in** ~**-career** seine Laufbahn noch nicht abgeschlossen haben; ~**-European Time** mitteleuropäische Zeit; ~**channel** Schiffahrtsrinne; **in-~ construction** mitten in der Bauzeit; ~**-leg deep in water** knietief im Wasser; ~**-month** Medio; ~**-month account** Medioabrechnung; **in** ~**-ocean** auf offener See; **to quit in** ~**-terms** mitten in der Ausbildung aufhören; ~**-year demands** Anforderungen zum Halbjahresultimo; ~**-year settlement** Halbjahresabrechnung.
midday snack Mittagsmahlzeit.
middle Zentrum, Mitte, *(journalism)* Feuilleton;
~ **of the river** Flußmitte; ~ **of the street** Straßenmitte;
~ *(a.)* mittel..., *(quality)* mittelmäßig;
to be in the ~ **of reading** intensiv mit einer Lektüre beschäftigt sein; **to keep to the** ~ **of the road** Mittelkurs halten;
~**-aged** von mittlerem Alter; ~ **article** *(Br.)* Feuilleton; ~**-bracket income** mittleres Einkommen, Einkommen in der mittleren Steuerklasse; ~ **break** *(wireless)* Sendezeichen während des Programms; ~ **class** Mittelstand; ~**-class** zum Mittelstand gehörig, mittelständisch, bürgerlich; **lower** ~ **class** untere Mittelschicht; ~ **income classes** mittlere Einkommensschichten; **upper** ~ **classes** gehobener Mittelstand; ~**-class family** bürgerlicher Haushalt; ~**-class prejudices** bürgerliche Vorurteile; ~**-class professional people** gebildete Mittelschicht; ~**-class residential area** bürgerliche Wohngegend; ~**-class society** mittelständische (bürgerliche) Gesellschaft; ~ **course** Mittelweg; **to take a** ~ **course** Mittelweg einschlagen; ~ **deck** Mitteldeck; ~ **East** Mittelost; ~**-grade diplomat** Diplomat der mittleren Beamtenlaufbahn; ~**-income classes** mittlere Einkommensschichten; ~ **latitude** mittlere Breite; ~ **life** mittleres Lebensalter; ~ **line of main channel** Mitte des Hauptschiffahrtsweges; ~ **management** *(US)* mittlere Führungsschicht (-ebene, -kräfte); ~ **[market,** *Br.***) price** Mittelkurs, -preis; **to maintain a** ~ **position** Mittelkurs halten; ~ **quality** Mittelqualität; ~**-ranking states** Staaten mittlerer Größe; ~**-rate** mittelmäßig; ~ **roader** Durchschnittswähler; ~ **school** *(Br.)* Mittelschule; ~ **school course** *(Br.)* Mittelschulbildung; ~ **size** Mittelgröße; ~**-sized** von mittlerer Größe, mittelgroß; ~ **thread** *(stream)* Mittellinie; ~ **watch** *(ship)* Mitternachtswache; ~ **way** *(economics)* gemischte Wirtschaftsform; ~ **West** mittlerer Westen.
middle-of-the-road neutral, unabhängig;
~ **conduct** Steuerung eines gesunden Durchschnittskurses; ~ **voter** Durchschnittswähler.
middle-of-the-roaders Politiker des gemäßigten Parteiflügels.
middleman *(broker)* Zwischenhändler, Makler, *(go-between)* Mittelsmann, -person, Vermittler, *(retailer)* Wiederverkäufer;
functional ~ Zwischenmakler; **merchant** ~ Kommissionär; **produce** ~ Produktmakler;
~**'s business** Zwischenhandel; ~**'s profit** Zwischengewinn.
middling mittelfein, -mäßig, von mittlerer Art und Güte;
good ~ mittelgut; ~ **large** mittelgroß;
to be feeling only ~ sich nicht besonders wohl fühlen;
good ~ **quality** gute Mittelsorte; ~ **size** mittlere Größe.
middlings Mittelsorte, Ware mittlerer Art und Güte.
midget submarine Kleinst-U-Boot.
midnight│appointment *(politics, US)* Beamteneinstellung kurz vor Beendigung der Regierungszeit; ~ **deadline** *(US)* Schluß-

termin Mitternacht; ~ **hours** Mitternachtsstunden; **to burn the** ~ **oil** sich in den Abendstunden fortbilden, Nachtarbeiter sein; ~ **shift** Mitternachtsschicht.
midshipman Seekadett.
midsummer Hochsommer.
midtown area im Stadtzentrum gelegenes Gebiet;
to operate in or near ~**s** *(airplane)* im Nahverkehr eingesetzt sein.
midway *(exhibition, US)* Haupt-, Mittelstraße.
midwife Hebamme.
midwifery service Hebammendienst.
midyear Jahresmitte, *(coll., US)* Prüfungszeit um die Jahresmitte;
~ **demands** Anforderungen zum Halbjahresultimo; ~ **dividend** Halbjahresdividende; ~ **movements of funds** Kapitalbewegung zum Halbjahresultimo; ~ **settlement** Halbjahresabschluß, -rechnung.
mien Gebaren, Haltung.
miff Unlust, Mißmut.
might Stärke, Macht;
with ~ **and main** mit Leibeskräften;
to work with all one's ~ wie der Teufel arbeiten.
migrant Auswanderer;
~ **worker** Wanderarbeiter.
migrate *(v.)* fortziehen, auswandern;
~ **into a country** einwandern.
migration, internal Binnenwanderung; **seasonal** ~ saisonbedingte Wanderung, Saisonwanderung;
~ **from an area** Abwanderung aus einem Gebiet; ~ **of capital** Kapitalabwanderung, -flucht; ~ **from the countryside** Landflucht; ~ **of the people** Völkerwanderung; ~ **of rural workers** Abwanderung landwirtschaftlicher Arbeitskräfte;
net ~ **change** Wanderungssaldo, -bilanz; **net** ~ **gain** Wanderungsgewinn; **net** ~ **loss** Wanderungsverlust.
migratory│grounds Verbreitungsgebiet; ~ **life** Wanderleben; ~ **worker** Wanderarbeiter.
mild milde, sanft;
as ~ **as a lamb** lammfromm;
to put it ~**[ly]** um es gelinde auszudrücken;
~ **air** milde Luft; ~ **attempt** schüchterner Versuch; ~ **punishment** leichte Strafe.
mildewed sheet *(book trade)* Schimmelbogen.
mike *(US sl.)* Mikrofon.
mile, Admiralty *(Br.)* englische Seemeile; **air** ~ Luftmeile; **nautical (sea)** ~ Seemeile; **statute** ~ englische Landmeile;
to eat up ~**s** Kilometer verschlingen; **to feel** ~**s better** *(coll.)* sich unendlich besser fühlen;
~**-eater** Kilometerfresser; **three-**~ **limit** Dreimeilengrenze; ~ **post** Meilenstein.
mil(e)age gefahrener Kilometer, *(allowance for travel(l)ing expense)* Fahrtentschädigung, Kilometergeld, *(car)* Kilometerstand, *(compensation per mile)* Zeugengeld, *(length in miles)* Meilenzahl, Länge in Meilen, *(rate per mile)* Fahrpreis pro Meile, Kilometerpreis;
road ~ *(of railroad)* Streckenlänge;
~ **per gallon** Kraftstoffverbrauch auf 100 km;
~ **allowance** Kilometergeld; ~ **basis** *(railway)* Kilometerberechnungsgrundlage; **to pay on a** ~ **basis** nach einem Kilometerschlüssel bezahlen; ~ **book** *(US)* Fahrscheinheft; ~ **car** *(railroad)* auf Kilometerbasis vermieteter Waggon; **low-**~ **car** wenig gefahrenes Auto; ~ **charge** Kilometergeld; **to get better** ~ **and saving money every mile one drives** billiger im Verbrauch sein je mehr man fährt; ~ **rate** *(car)* Kilometertarif, -satz, *(railway)* Differenzfrachtsatz; ~ **recorder** Kilometerzähler; ~ **tax** *(US)* Güterverkehrs-, Transportsteuer; ~ **ticket** *(US)* Fahrkarte eines Fahrscheinheftes.
mil(e)ometer Kilometerzähler.
milestone Kilometerstein, *(fig.)* Meilenstein, Markstein.
milieu Milieu, Umwelt.
militancy Kriegszustand;
~ **of consumers** Konsumentenaggressivität.
militant streitbar, aggressiv.
militarism Militärherrschaft, Militarismus.
militarist Militarist, Fachmann in militärischen Angelegenheiten.
military Militär, Soldaten, Truppen;
~ *(a.)* militärisch;
~ **academy** *(Br.)* Kriegsakademie; **to be of** ~ **age** im militärpflichtigen Alter sein; ~ **aid** Militärhilfe; ~ **airplane (aircraft)** Militärflugzeug; ~ **alliance** Militärbündnis; ~ **area** Kriegs-, Sperrgebiet; ~ **assistance** militärische Hilfeleistung, Militär-

hilfe; ~ **attaché** Militärattaché; ~ **authorities** Militärbehörden; ~ **band** Militärkapelle; ~ **base** Militärbasis, *(US)* Militärstützpunkt; ~ **budget** Verteidigungshaushalt, -etat; ~ **buildup** Aufbau einer Rüstungsindustrie; ~ **business** Rüstungsgeschäft; ~ **causes** *(Br.)* militärgerichtliche Fälle; ~ **censorship** Militärzensur; ~ **chest** Kriegskasse; ~ **commission** Kriegs-, Militärgericht; ⚬ **Committee** *(ATLANTIC TREATY)* Militärausschuß; ~ **contract** Rüstungsauftrag; ~ **coup** Militärumsturz; ~ **court** Militärgericht; ~ **custody** Militärgewahrsam; ~ **dictatorship** Militärdiktatur; ~ **duty** Wehrdienst; ~ **establishment** stehendes Heer; ~ **facilities** militärische Anlagen; ~ **forces** Armee, Streitkräfte; ~ **government** Militärregierung; ~ **hospital** Lazarett; ~ **household** Verteidigungshaushalt; ~ **installations** militärische Einrichtungen (Anlagen); ~ **intelligence** ausgewertete Feindnachrichten, *(Br.)* Nachrichtendienst, Gegenspionage; ~ **junta** militärische Junta, Militärjunta; ~ **jurisdiction** Militärgerichtsbarkeit, Kriegs-, Standrecht; ~ **law** Militärstrafrecht, Wehrrecht; ~ **man** Krieger, Soldat, Militär; ~ **mission** Militärmission; ~ **necessity** übergesetzlicher Notstand im Kriegsfall; ~ **offense** *(US)* Militärstraftat; ~ **officer** Berufsoffizier; ~ **order** Strafrecht, Soldatenstand; ~ **outlays** Militärausgaben; ~ **painter** Schlachtenmaler; ~ **pay** Wehrsold; ~ **pay book** Soldbuch; ~ **personnel** Militärangehörige; ~ **plane** Militärflugzeug; ~ **police** Militärpolizei, Feldjägertruppe; ~ **potential** militärisches Potential, Kriegspotential; ~ **profession** Soldatenberuf; ~ **purchases** Rüstungskäufe; ~ **regime** Militärregime; ~ **reprisals** militärische Repressalien; ~ **resources** Kriegspotential; ~ **rule** Militärherrschaft; ~ **school** *(US)* Kadettenanstalt; ~ **service** Wehrdienst, Militärdienstzeit; **fit for ~ service** militärdiensttauglich; **liable to ~ service** militär-, dienstpflichtig; **compulsory ~ national service** allgemeine Wehrpflicht; ~ **security service** militärischer Sicherheitsdienst; **to do one's ~ service** seiner Dienstpflicht genügen; **to impress workmen into ~ service** Arbeiter dienstverpflichten; ~ **service book** Wehrpaß; ~ **spending** Militärausgaben; ~ **state** Soldatenstand; ~ **stores** Kriegsmaterial; ~ **testament (will)** formloses Militärtestament; ~ **training** militärische Ausbildung; ~ **tribunal** Militärgericht, ~ **truck** Militärfahrzeug; ~ **zone** Militärgebiet.

militia Bürger-, Landwehr, Miliz.

milk, skimmed Magermilch;
~ **for babes** leicht verständliche Literatur; ~ **and honey** Überfülle schöner Dinge; ~ **of human kindness** Milch der frommen Denkungsart; ~ **and water** *(fig.)* sentimentales Gewäsch;
~ *(v.) (US)* ausbeuten, *(fig.)* schröpfen, melken, *(tel.)* anzapfen;
~ **s. o.** j. ausnehmen; ~ **the market** *(stock exchange, US)* Markt durch Spekulationsmanöver ausplündern; ~ **the pigeon** den Mohren weiß waschen; ~ **the till** Portokasse plündern;
~ **bar** Milchbar; ⚬ **Board** *(Br.)* Milchhandelsbehörde; **to be on a ~ diet** Milchdiät durchführen; ~ **marketing board** Molkereigenossenschaft; ~ **float** *(Br.)* Milchwagen; ~ **round** tägliche Route; ~ **run** *(airforce, US sl.)* Routineflug, -einsatz; ~ **shake** Milchmischgetränk; ~ **support price** Milchstützungspreis; ~ **waggon** *(sl.)* grüne Minna.

milking *(tel.)* Anzapfen, *(US)* Ausbeutung eines Unternehmens.

milksop Muttersöhnchen, Schlappschwanz.

milky way Milchstraße.

mill Mühle, *(factory)* Fabrik, Werk, *(iron works)* [Roh]eisenwerk, *(print.)* Druckwalze, *(prison, sl.)* Gefängnis, Kittchen;
ex ~ ab Fabrik (Werk);
coffee ~ Kaffeemühle; **cotton ~** Spinnerei; **paper ~** Papierfabrik; **rolling ~** Walzwerk; **saw ~** Sägewerk;
~ **out of work** stillgelegter Betrieb;
~ *(v.)* fräsen;
to have been through the ~ viel durchgemacht haben; **to have gone through the ~** harte Ausbildung hinter sich haben; **to put s. o. through the ~** j. in eine harte Schule schicken; **to work in a ~** in einer Fabrik arbeiten, Fabrikarbeiter sein;
~ **hand** Fabrikarbeiter; ~ **owner** Fabrikbesitzer; ~ **privilege** *(riparian proprietor)* Mühlengerechtigkeit; ~ **shutdown** Fabrikschließung; ~ **site** Mühlengrundstück; ~ **supply house (firm)** Zuliefer[ungs]firma; ~ **town** *(Br.)* Fabrikstadt.

millboard starke Pappe, Buchbinderpappe.

millenium Jahrtausend.

milliard *(Br.)* Milliarde.

millimetre line Millimeterzeile.

milline *(US)* Tausenderpreis;
~ **rate** *(US) (advertising)* Preiskoeffizient per 1.000.000 Leser.

millinery *(Br.)* Modewaren.

milling in transit *(cereals)* Zwischenmahlrecht;
~ **industry** Weizenindustrie.

million Million;
a thousand ~s *(Br.)* Milliarde;
~s of people Unmasse Menschen;
to have ~s and ~s millionenschwer sein.

millionnaire Millionär.

millowner Fabrikbesitzer, Industrieller.

millsite Werksgrundstück.

millstone Mühlstein;
to be between the upper and the nether ~ von zwei Seiten her unter Druck stehen; **to see into a ~** das Gras wachsen hören.

mimeograph Vervielfältigungsapparat;
~ *(v.)* vervielfältigen;
~ **paper** Saug-, Abzugspost.

mimeographing Vervielfältigung;
~ **department** Vervielfältigungsbüro.

mimic warfare Scheinkrieg.

minable coal abbauwürdige Kohle.

mince, not to ~ matters kein Blatt vor den Mund nehmen.

mincemeat Hackfleisch, Gehacktes;
to make ~ of s. o. Hackfleisch aus jem. machen.

mind Sinn, Gemüt, *(brains)* Verstand, *(intention)* Absicht, Vorhaben, Zweck, *(memory)* Erinnerung, Gedächtnis, *(opinion)* Meinung, Ansicht;
bearing in ~ in dem Bewußtsein; **in the back of their ~s** in ihren Hintergedanken; **of sound ~** geistig gesund; **of unsound ~** geisteskrank, -gestört, geistig umnachtet; **of a worldly ~** materiell eingestellt; **out of sight, out of ~** aus den Augen aus dem Sinn; **average ~** Duchschnittsmensch; **the human ~** der menschliche Geist; **probing ~** sondierender Geist; **public ~** öffentliche Meinung;
~ **prone to doubt** skeptischer Geist; ~ **and memory** *(testator)* Testierfähigkeit; **two ~s with but a single thought** zwei Seelen und ein Gedanke;
~ *(v.) (care)* sich kümmern, sorgen;
~ **one's P's and Q's** *(coll.)* wie auf Eiern gehen; ~ **the shop** Kunden bedienen;
to alter one's ~ sich anders besinnen; **to be all of one ~** allseitig übereinstimmen; **to be in one's right ~** bei vollem Verstand sein; **to be of s. one's ~** jds. Ansichten teilen; **to be of the greatest ~s of his time** einer der größten Geister seiner Zeit sein; **to be in two ~s** geteilter Meinung (unschlüssig) sein, schwanken; **to be fresh in one's ~** noch gut in Erinnerung haben; **to be out of one's ~** seinen Verstand verloren haben, von Sinnen sein, durchgedreht haben; **to be in one's right ~** bei klarem Verstand sein; **to be of sound ~** bei vollem Verstand sein; **to be uneasy in one's ~** sich unbehaglich fühlen; **to bear in ~** im Gedächtnis behalten, Rechnung tragen; **to blow one's ~** explodieren; **to boggle the ~** stutzig machen; **to broaden the ~** Horizont erweitern; **to call s. th. back to ~** sich etw. ins Gedächtnis rufen; **to cast one's ~ back** sich im Geist zurückversetzen; **to change one's ~** sich anders besinnen; **to close one's ~ to s. th.** sich gegen etw. verschließen; **to cross s. one's ~** jem. plötzlich in den Sinn kommen; **to disturb s. one's peace of ~** jds. Seelenfrieden stören; **to exercise one's ~** sein Gehirn strapazieren; **to exercise one's ~ fully and freely** von seinen Verstandeskräften ungestört und vollen Gebrauch machen; **to find s. th. to one's ~** etw. nach seinem Geschmack finden; **to get an idea fixed in one's ~** sich etw. in den Kopf setzen; **to give one's ~ to s. th.** sich einer Sache befleißigen; **to give s. o. a good piece of one's ~** jem. gehörig die Meinung sagen; **to have in ~** beabsichtigen; **to have a good ~** ziemlich entschlossen sein; **to have half a ~ to do** weitgehend dazu neigen; **to have little ~ to do s. th.** wenig Lust haben etw. zu tun; **to have s. th. on one's ~** etw. auf dem Herzen haben, von etw. beunruhigt sein; **to keep an open ~** für alles aufgeschlossen sein; **to know one's ~** eigene Meinung haben; **to leave an impression on s. one's ~** Eindruck bei jem. hinterlassen; **to let one's ~ run upon s. th.** vor etw. träumen; **to lose one's ~** den Verstand verlieren; **to make up one's ~** sich schlüssig werden, sich entschließen; **to pass out of one's ~** in Vergessenheit geraten; **to put s. o. in ~ of s. th.** j. an etw. erinnern; **to put s. th. out of one's ~** sich etw. aus dem Kopf schlagen; **to read s. one's ~** jds. Gedanken lesen; **to relieve one's ~** sein Gewissen erleichtern; **to rouse the public ~** öffentliche Meinung erregen; **to set one's ~ on a holiday in Spain** sich einen Spanienurlaub in den Kopf gesetzt haben; **to speak one's ~** seine Meinung ungeniert äußern, reden, wie einem der Schnabel gewachsen ist; **to take s. one's ~ away** j. ablenken; **to take one's ~ off s. th.** seine Aufmerksamkeit von etw. abwenden; **to take s. one's ~ of his sorrows** jem. eine Sorgenlast abnehmen;
~ **campaign** Propagandakrieg; ~ **cure (healing)** Psychotherapie; ~ **reader** Gedankenleser; ~ **reading** Gedankenlesen.

minded eingestellt, bewußt;
politically ~ politisch interessiert;
to become air-~ flugbegeistert sein; **to be food-~** Gourmet sein; **commercially** ~ **men** kommerziell eingestellte Leute; **theater-~ people** Theateramateure.
mindful | of one's duties pflichtbewußt;
to be ~ berücksichtigen; **to be** ~ **of one's good name** auf seinen guten Ruf bedacht sein; **to be** ~ **of the nation's welfare** sich um das Wohlergehen der Nation Sorgen machen.
mine Zeche, Bergwerk, Grube, *(explosive)* Mine;
~s *(shares)* Montanwerte, -papiere, Bergwerksaktien, Kuxe;
abandoned ~ verlassener Bau; **aerial** ~ Luftmine, -torpedo; **captive** ~ eigengenutztes Bergwerk; **coal** ~ Kohlenbergwerk, Grube; **contact** ~ Tretmine; **exhausted** ~ totes Gebirge; **expropriated** ~ enteigneter Bergbaubetrieb; **floating** ~ Treibmine; **gold** ~ Goldader, *(fig.)* Goldgrube; **shutdown** ~ aufgelassene Grube;
~ **of anecdotes** Anekdotenschatz; ~ **of information** Fundgrube an Informationen; **~s and plants** Bergwerks- und Hüttenanlagen;
~ *(v.) (coal)* abbauen, fördern, *(fig.)* unterhöhlen, -graben, -minieren, *(lay mines)* Minen verlegen, verminen, *(work in a mine)* in einem Bergwerk arbeiten;
~ **coal** Kohlengrube ausbeuten; ~ **the entrance of a harbo(u)r** Hafeneinfahrt verminen; ~ **the foundation of a house** Haus unterspülen;
to be engaged in working ~s Bergbau treiben; **to exploit a** ~ Bergwerk in Betrieb nehmen; **to go down a** ~ in eine Grube einfahren; **to inspect a** ~ Grube befahren; **to lay ~s** Minen legen; **to man a** ~ Grube mit Arbeitern belegen; **to shut down a** ~ Grube auflassen; **to spring (touch off) a** ~ Mine auslösen; **to sweep ~s** Minen räumen; **to work a** ~ **at a profit** Bergwerk mit Gewinn betreiben; **to work in the ~s** Grubenarbeiter sein, im Bergwerk arbeiten;
~ **barrier** Minensperre; ~ **car** Grubenwagen, Hund; ~ **chamber** Sprengkammer; ~ **clearance** Minenräumung; ~ **closing** Grubenstillegung; ~ **crater** Sprengtrichter; ~ **detector** Minensuchgerät; ~ **dump** Grubenhalde; ~ **explosion** Grubenexplosion; ~ **fan** Grubenventilator; ~ **field** Minenfeld, -gebiet; ~ **fire** Grubenbrand; ~ **foreman** Obersteiger; ~ **gallery** Minenstollen; ~ **gas** Grubengas, schlagende Wetter; ~ **layer** Minenleger; ~ **laying** Verminen; **~-laying vessel** Minenverleger; ~ **operation** Schachtbetrieb; ~ **operator** Bergbauindustrieller; ~ **owner** Zechenbesitzer, Bergbauindustrieller; ~ **safety** Grubensicherheit; ~ **shutdown** Grubenschließung, -stillegung; ~ **survey** Markscheidung; ~ **surveyor** Markscheider; ~ **sweeper** Minenräumboot, Minensucher, Minensuchboot; ~ **sweeping** Minenräumung; **~-sweeping fleet** Minensuchboote; ~ **tubbing** Grubenverschalung; ~ **ventilation** Grubenbewetterung; ~ **viewer** Berginspektor, Bergwerksaufseher; ~ **warfare** Grubenkrieg.
min(e)able abbaufähig.
mined vermint;
to be ~ von einer Mine getroffen werden;
~ **area** Minenfeld, -sperrgebiet.
miner Bergknappe, Grubenarbeiter, Kumpel;
~s' benefit (provident) fund Knappschaftskasse; **~s' insurance** Knappschaftsversicherung; **~'s lamp** Grubenlampe; **~s' union** Knappschaftsverband.
mineral Mineral, Grubengut;
to win ~s Mineralien abbauen;
~ **claim** Bergbaukonzession; ~ **coal** Steinkohle; ~ **deposit** Mineralvorkommen, Erzlagerstätte; **to work** ~ **deposits** Mineralvorkommen ausbeuten; ~ **district** Bergbaugebiet; ~ **extraction** Gewinnung von Bodenschätzen; ~ **lands** bergbaufähiges Land; ~ **lease** Pacht eines Bergwerkrechtes; ~ **lode** Erzader; ~ **oil** Erd-, Mineralöl, Petroleum; **~-oil industry** Mineralölwirtschaft; **~-oil processing** Mineralölverarbeitung; **~-oil tax** Mineralölsteuer; ~ **pitch** Asphalt; ~ **resources** Mineralölvorkommen, Bodenschätze; ~ **right** Bergregal, -baufreiheit, Abbaurecht; ~ **rights duty** *(Br.)* Bergregal-, Bergwerksteuer; ~ **royalty** Bergregal; ~ **servitude** Bergbaugerechtigkeit; ~ **spring** Heilbrunnen, Mineralquelle; ~ **vein** Erzader; ~ **water** Mineralwasser, Sprudel.
mingle *(v.)* sich vermischen (vereinigen);
~ **with the crowd** sich unter die Menge begeben, *(fig.)* gesellschaftlich verkehren.
mingled vermischt;
with ~ feelings mit gemischten Gefühlen.
mini | -boom, consumption-led von der Konsumseite ausgelöste Minikonjunktur; **~-car** Kleinstwagen; **to receive a ~-injection**

of reflation erneute Mini-Injektionsspritze bekommen; **~-price** Minipreis; **~-recession** Minirezession; **~-recovery** Minibelebung; **~-revival** Miniaufschwung.
miniature | camera Kleinbildkamera; ~ **copy** Verkleinerung; ~ **film** Kleinbildfilm; ~ **railway** Kleinbahn; ~ **replica** Miniaturausgabe.
minibus Kleinbus;
volunteer-run ~ **service** auf freiwilliger Basis betriebener Kleinomnibusdienst.
minicab Kleintaxi.
minimal minimal, mindest;
~ **amount** Mindestbetrag; ~ **damage** Bagatellschaden; **to carry** ~ **supplies of foreign notes** nur in sehr begrenztem Umfang ausländische Sorten zur Verfügung halten; ~ **value** Mindestwert.
minimization Reduzierung auf ein Minimum, Bagatellisierung.
minimize *(v.)* auf ein Minimum bringen, bagatellisieren, als geringfügig darstellen;
~ **an accident** Unfall herunterspielen; ~ **the danger of a task** Gefahr einer Aufgabe verharmlosen; ~ **its exposure to currency fluctuations** Abhängigkeit von Devisenschwankungen auf ein Minimum begrenzen; ~ **a loss** Schaden mindern.
minimizing of losses Schadensminderung.
minimum Minimum, Mindestmaß, -betrag, *(meteorology)* Tief[druckgebiet];
exemption ~ *(taxation)* Mindestfreibetrag; **legal** ~ *(taxation)* gesetzlich zulässiger Mindestsatz, *(wages)* gesetzlicher Mindestlohn; **shifting** ~ automatisch angepaßte Mindestleistung; ~ **of age** Mindestalter; ~ **of capital** Mindestkapital; ~ **of existence** Existenzminimum; ~ **of losses** minimale Verluste; **to stand at a** ~ *(stock exchange)* sehr niedrig stehen;
~ *(a.)* minimal, mindest;
~ **age** Mindestalter; ~ **altitude** Mindesthöhe; ~ **amount [of subscription]** Mindest[zeichnungs]betrag; **to require a** ~ **balance** Unterhaltung eines Mindestguthabens verlangen; ~ **balance charges** Mindestsaldogebühren; ~ **benefit** Mindestunterstützungssatz; ~ **bill of lading charge** Mindest-, Minimalfracht; ~ **block** Minimalklischee; ~ **call pay** Mindestlohn für nur stundenweise Tätigkeit; ~ **capital** Mindestkapital; ~ **carload weight** *(US)* Mindeststückgutgewicht; ~ **cash payment** Mindestbarzahlung; ~ **cash reserve** Pflichtreserve; ~ **charge** *(carrier)* Mindestsatz, *(post)* Mindestgebühr; **guaranteed** ~ **circulation** Mindestauflage; ~ **claim** Mindestforderung; ~ **commission rate** Mindestprovisionssatz; ~ **cost** Mindestkosten; ~ **demand** Mindestbedarf; ~ **deposit** Mindesteinlage, -anzahlung; ~ **downpayment** *(US)* Mindestanzahlung; ~ **economic size** wirtschaftliche Mindestgröße; ~ **expectation** Mindesterwartung; ~ **fee** Mindestgebühr; ~ **figure** Mindestzahl; ~ **food needs** Mindestbedarf an Nahrungsmitteln; ~ **freight** Mindestfracht; ~ **hourly rates of pay** Mindeststundenlöhne; ~ **housing need** Mindestwohnungsbedarf; ~ **import price** *(EC)* Mindesteinfuhrpreis; ~ **income** Mindesteinkommen; ~ **income figure** Mindesteinkommensziffer; ~ **income statement content** Mindestumfang einer Einkommensteuererklärung; ~ **initial subscription** *(investment fund)* Mindestbeteiligung beim Ersterwerb; ~ **interest rate** Mindestzinssatz; ~ **inventory** Mindestbestand; ~ **investment** Mindesteinlage; ~ **job rate** Mindestakkordsatz; ~ **lending rate** *(Br.) (Bank of England)* Mindestausleihungs-, -diskontsatz; ~ **liabilities** Mindestverpflichtungen; ~ **liability** Haftpflichtmindestgrenze; **basic** ~ **limit of liability** Mindestgrenze für Haftungsschäden; ~ **limit** Mindestgrenze; ~ **linage** *(advertisement)* Mindestgröße; ~ **load** geringste Belastung; ~ **maintenance** notwendiger Lebensunterhalt; ~ **margin requirements** Mindestdeckung; ~ **number** Mindest[an]zahl; ~ **output** Mindestproduktion, *(el.)* Leistungsminimum; ~ **paid-in capital** *(US)* Mindestkapital; ~ **pay** Mindestverdienst; ~ **penalty** Mindeststrafe; ~ **pension age** Mindestalter zum Rentenbezug, Mindestrentenalter; ~ **period** Mindestzeitraum; ~ **period of employment** Mindestbeschäftigungszeit; **statutory** ~ **period of notice** gesetzliche Mindestkündigungsfrist; ~ **piece rate** Mindeststücklohntarif; ~ **plant rate** betrieblicher Mindestlohn; ~ **point values** Mindestpunktwerte; ~ **premium** *(insurance)* Minimaltarif; ~ **price** Mindestsatz, *(stock exchange)* Mindestkurs, Mindest-, niedrigster (minimaler) Preis; **to prescribe** ~ **prices** Mindestverkaufspreise für den Einzelhandel festlegen (vorschreiben); ~ **price system** *(EC)* Mindestpreisregelung; ~ **purchase** Mindestbezug; **commercial** ~ **quantity** handelsübliche Mindestmenge; ~ **rate** Mindestsatz, -preis, Minimalsatz, *(carrier)* Mindesttarif, *(foreign exchange)* Mindestkurs, *(insurance)* Mindestprämie, *(wages)* Mindestlohnsatz; ~ **guaranteed rate** garantierter Mindestlohnsatz; ~

ratio Mindestverhältnis; ~ **rent** Mindestpacht; ~ **rental period** Mindestmietzeit; ~ **requirements** Mindesterfordernisse; **maintained ~ resale price** gebundener Preis auf der Stufe des Endverbrauchers; ~ **reserve** *(US, banking)* Mindestreserve; ~ **reserve ratio** *(US)* Mindestreservensatz ~ **reserve requirements** *(US)* erforderliche Mindestreserven, Mindestreservenerfordernisse; **to increase the ~ reserve requirements** *(US)* Mindestreserven bei der Bundesnotenbank erhöhen; **maintained ~ retail price** Mindestwiederverkaufspreis; ~ **return** Mindestertrag, *(film)* Mindesteinspielergebnisse; ~ **royalty** Mindesttantieme; ~ **salary** Mindestgehalt; ~ **speed** Mindestgeschwindigkeit; ~ **standard** Mindesteinheitssätze; **to live below the ~ standard** Existenzminimum unterschreiten; ~ **standard reduction** *(taxation)* feststehender Mindestfreibetrag; ~**standard rates** Mindesteinheitssätze; ~ **subscription** Minimalzeichnungsbetrag; ~ **subsistence level** existenznotwendiger Lebensunterhalt; ~ **supply** Mindestvorrat, -versorgung; ~ **tariff** Minimaltarif; ~ **taxation** Mindestbesteuerung, Steuermindestsatz; ~ **temperature** Mindesttemperatur; ~ **terms and period of an insurance** Mindestversicherungsleistung; ~ **terms' order** *(wage council)* tariflich festgelegte Arbeitnehmerschutzbestimmungen; ~ **term penalty** Mindeststrafe; ~ **time** Mindestzeit; ~ **time rate** Mindestzeitlohntarif; ~ **value** Minimal-, Mindestwert; ~ **wage** Mindestlohn; **guaranteed ~ wage for all trades** garantierter absoluter Mindestlohn; ~ **weekly budget** wöchentliches Existenzminimum; ~ **weight** Mindestgewicht; ~ **width** Mindestbreite; ~ **workweek** wöchentliche Mindestarbeitszeit; ~ **yield** Mindestertrag.

mining Grubenbetrieb, Bergbau, Förderung;
open-cast ~ Tagebau; **coal** ~ Kohlenbergbau; **subsurface** ~ Untertagebau;
~ **academy** Bergbauakademie; ~ **accident** Gruben-, Zechenunfall; ~ **accountant** Schichtmeister; ~ **area** Grubendistrikt, [Bergbau]revier, Bergbaugebiet; ~ **board** Grubenvorstand; ~ **bond** Bergwerksobligation; ~ **claim** Mutung, Schürfrecht; ~ **company** Zechen-, Bergwerksgesellschaft; ~ **concern** Bergwerks-, Montagenunternehmen; ~ **concession** Mutungsrecht; ~ **disaster** Bergwerksunglück; ~ **district** Bergbaubezirk, -gebiet; ~ **engineer** Bergbauingenieur; ~ **expert** Bergbausachverständiger; ~ **franchise** Abbaukonzession; ~ **industrialist** Bergbauindustrieller; ~ **industry** Montanindustrie; **to insulate the ~ industry against the interplay of market forces** Bergbau den Gesetzen der Marktwirtschaft entziehen; ~ **interests** Bergwerksinteressen; ~ **law** Bergrecht; ~ **lease** Bergwerkspacht; ~ **licence** Bergbaukonzession, Mutungsrecht; ~ **location** Inbesitznahme einer Schürfstelle; ~ **losses** Abbauverluste; ~ **market** Montanmarkt; ~ **operations** Abbauverfahren; ~ **partnership** *(US)* Bergbaugenossenschaft, Gewerkschaft; ~ **and foundry plant** Bergwerks- und Hüttenanlage; ~ **property** Bergbauvermögen; ~ **register** Berggrundbuch; ~ **rent** Pachtzins für Bergwerksrechte; ~ **right** Abbaurecht; ~ **royalty** Bergregal; ~ **securities** Montanwerte; ~ **share (stock,** *Br.)* Grubenanteil, Bergwerks-, Montanaktie, Kux, Bergwerksanteil; ~ **ticket day** *(Br.)* Abrechnungstag für Montanwerte; ~ **timber** Grubenholz; ~ **venture** Bergwerksunternehmen; ~ **works** Bergwerksbetrieb.

minion Günstling, Favorit, *(print.)* Mignon, Kolonel;
double ~ Mittelschrift;
~ **of the law** Gerichtsvollzieher.

minister Minister, *(diplomatics)* diplomatischer Vertreter, Gesandter, *(ministerial officer)* Vollzugsbeamter, Gerichtsvollzieher, *(priest)* Geistlicher;
acting ~ amtierender Minister; **cabinet** ~ *(Br.)* Kabinettsmitglied; **career** ~ Berufsdiplomat; **conjoint** ~ Ministerkollege; **defence** ~ *(Br.)* Verteidigungsminister; **departmental** ~ Fachminister; **environmental** ~ Minister für Umweltfragen; **farm** ~ Landwirtschaftsminister; **foreign** ~ Botschafter; **[Deputy] Foreign** ~ [stellvertretender] Außenminister; **former** ~ bisheriger Minister; **junior** ~ parlamentarischer Staatssekretär, Staatsminister; **late** ~ früherer Minister; ~ **plenipotentiary and extraordinary** außerordentlicher und bevollmächtigter Gesandter; **Prime** ~ Premierminister, Ministerpräsident; **public** ~ *(US)* ranghöherer diplomatischer Vertreter; **social service** ~ Sozialminister; **transportation** ~ *(US)* Verkehrsminister.

Minister | of Foreign Affairs Minister für auswärtige Angelegenheiten; ~ **of Agriculture, Fisheries and Food** *(Br.)* Ernährungs-, Landwirtschaftsminister; ~ **for Air** Luftfahrtminister; ~ **of Aviation Supply** *(Br.)* Luftfahrtminister; ~ **of the Crown** *(Br.)* Minister; ~ **of Culture** Kultusminister; ~ **of Defence** *(Br.)* Verteidigungsminister; ~ **for the Department of the Environment** *(Br.)* Umweltminister, Minister für Umweltschutz; ~ **difficult**

to get at schwer ansprechbarer Minister; ~ **of Economics (Economic Affairs)** *(Br.)* Wirtschaftsminister; ~ **of Education** Kultus-, Erziehungsminister; ~ **of Employment** *(Br.)* Arbeitsminister; ~ **of Environment** *(Br.)* Minister für Fragen des Umweltschutzes; ~ **of External Affairs** *(Australia)* Außenminister; ~ **of Finance** Finanzminister; ~ **of Health** *(Br.)* Gesundheitsminister; ~ **of Housing and Local Government** *(Br.)* Wohnungsbauminister, Minister für Wohnungsbau und Kommunalverwaltung; ~ **of Justice** Justizminister; ~ **of Labour** *(Br.)* Arbeitsminister; ~ **of Manpower** *(Canada)* Einwanderungsminister; ~ **of Mining** *(Australia)* Bergbauminister; ~ **for Overseas Development** Minister für die Entwicklung der Überseegebiete; ~ **of Pensions** *(Br.)* Minister für Pensionen und Renten; ~ **of Pensions and National Insurance** *(Br.)* Renten und Sozialminister; ~ **without Portfolio** Minister ohne Geschäftsbereich; ~ **for Post and Telecommunications** *(Br.)* Minister für Post- und Fernmeldewesen; ~ **of Power** *(Br.)* Minister für Energiewirtschaft; ~ **of Production** *(US)* Produktionsminister; ~ **of Science and Technology** *(Br.)* Forschungsminister; ~ **of Shipping and Transport** *(Australia)* Verkehrsminister; ~ **of Social Security** *(Br.)* Sozialminister; ~ **for Sport** *(Br.)* Sportminister; ~ **of State** Staatsminister; **senior ~ of State** erster Staatsminister; ~ **of State for Industries** Minister für Staatsbetriebe; ~ **of State for Defence** *(Br.)* Verteidigungsminister; ~ **of Supply** *(Br.)* Versorgungsminister; ~ **of Transport** *(Br.)* Verkehrsminister; ~ **of Works** *(Br.)* Minister für öffentliche Bauten;
~ *(v.)* **to s. one's needs** für jds. Bedürfnisse sorgen;
to impeach a ~ Minister unter Anklage stellen; **to indemnify a ~** Minister von der Beschuldigung der Überschreitung seiner Befugnisse freisprechen; **to remove a ~ from office** Minister entlassen; **to unseat a ~** Minister stürzen;
~**counsellor** Gesandter; ~**'s portfolio** Ministerressort; ~ **resident** *(diplomacy)* Ministerresident.

ministerial *(Br.)* ministeriell, verwaltungsmäßig, amtlich, weisungsgebunden, *(subservient)* untergeordnet;
~ **act** Ministerialverfügung; ~ **appointment** Ministerialstellung; ~ **approach** ministerielle Zustimmung; ~ **benches** *(Br.)* Regierungs-, Ministerbank; ~ **bill** Regierungsvorlage; **in his ~ capacity** in seiner Eigenschaft als Minister; ~ **committee** Ministerausschuß; ~ **Council** Ministerrat; ~ **duties** ministerielle Aufgaben; ~ **duty** Amtspflicht; ~ **functions** vollziehende Funktionen, Ministerialtätigkeit, ministerielle Tätigkeit; **on a [at] ~ level** auf Ministerebene; ~ **meeting** Kabinettssitzung; ~ **office** Ministerstelle, -amt; **to attain ~ office** Ministeramt erhalten; **to pass up a ~ office** Ministerium ablehnen; ~ **officer (official)** Verwaltungsbeamter; ~ **order** *(Br.)* Ministerialerlaß, Verordnung; ~ **post** Ministeramt, Ministerposten; ~ **powers** ministerielle Vollmachten; ~ **responsibility** *(Br.)* Ministerverantwortung; ~ **salary** Ministergehalt; ~ **services** weisungsgebundene Tätigkeit; ~ **session** Tagung der Minister; ~ **statement** Verlautbarung eines Ministers; ~ **trust** weisungsgebundene Treuhandverwaltung.

ministerialist Regierungsanhänger.

ministry Ministerium, Regierung, *(diplomacy)* Amt eines Gesandten, *(governmental department)* Regierungsabteilung, *(ministerial term)* Amtsdauer eines Ministers, *(office)* Ministerposten, -amt, Ressort eines Ministers, *(priest)* Priesteramt.

Ministry, Air *(Br.)* Luftfahrtministerium; **executive** ~ *(Br.)* Ministerialbürokratie; **Prime** ~ Ministerpräsidentschaft;
~ **of Agriculture, Fisheries and Food** *(Br.)* Landwirtschaftsministerium; ~ **of Arts and Culture** Kultusministerium; ~ **of Aviation** Luftfahrtministerium; ~ **of Defence** *(Br.)* Verteidigungsministerium; ~ **of Education** *(Br.)* Kultusministerium; ~ **of the Environment** *(Br.)* Umweltministerium; ~ **of Finance** Finanzministerium; ~ **of Food** Ernährungsministerium; ~ **of Foreign Affairs** Ministerium für auswärtige Angelegenheiten, Auswärtiges Amt; ~ **of Fuel and Power** *(Br.)* Energieministerium; ~ **of Health** *(Br.)* Gesundheitsministerium; ~ **of Housing and Local Government** *(Br.)* Wohnungsbauministerium; ~ **of Information** Informationsministerium; ~ **of Internal Affairs** Innenministerium; ~ **of Justice** Justizministerium; ~ **of Labour** *(Br.)* Arbeitsministerium; ~ **of Local Government and Development** *(Br.)* Ministerium für Gemeindeverwaltung und Erschließung; ~ **of Marine** Marineministerium; ~ **of National Insurance** *(Br.)* Sozialministerium; ~ **of Oil** Ölministerium; ~ **of Fuel and Power** *(Br.)* Energieministerium; ~ **of Public Buildings and Works** *(Br.)* Ministerium für Wohnungsbau; ~ **of Social Security** *(Br.)* Sozialministerium; ~ **of Supply** *(Br.)* Versorgungsministerium; ~ **of Technology** *(Br., abolished 1970)* [etwa] Forschungsministerium; ~ **of Town and Country Planning** *(Br.)* Städtebauministerium, Wiederaufbauministerium; ~ **of**

Transport [and Aviation] *(Br.)* Verkehrsministerium; ~ **of Public Building and Works** *(Br.)* Ministerium für öffentliche Bauten;
to be called to the ~ ins Ministerium berufen werden; **to be given a** ~ Ministerium zugeteilt erhalten; **to form a** ~ Ministerium übernehmen;
~ **official** Ministeriumsvertreter, Ministerialbeamter.

minor minderjähriges Kind, Minderjähriger [über 7 Jahre], *(school, US)* Nebenfach, *(Scot.)* Heranwachsender;
~ *(a.)* unmündig, minderjährig, *(school, US)* nebensächlich, *(small)* unbedeutend, geringfügig, klein[er];
~ *(v.)* **in** *(US)* im Nebenfach studieren;
~ **accident** unbedeutender Unfall; ~ **amendment** unwesentlicher Abänderungsvorschlag; ~ **character** Nebenfigur; ~ **coin** *(US)* Scheidemünze (5 Cent-, 1 Centstück); ~ **coinage profit fund** *(US)* Gewinn[fonds] aus der Prägung von Scheidemünzen; ~ **crime** Vergehen; ~ **defects** geringfügige Mängel, unbedeutende Einzelheiten; ~ **expenses** kleine Ausgaben; ~ **fact** *(law of evidence)* untergeordnete Beweistatsache; ~ **group** Untergruppe; ~ **injuries** geringfügige Verletzung; **of** ~ **interest** von untergeordnetem Interesse; ~ **issue** Nebenfrage; ~ **loss** *(insurance)* Bagatell-, Kleinschaden; ~ **point** Nebensache; ~ **repairs** kleinere (geringfügige) Reparaturen; ~ **subject** *(US)* Nebenfach.

minorities problem Minderheitsfrage.

minority Minorität, Minderheit, -zahl, *(state of being a minor)* Minderjährigkeit, Unmündigkeit;
blocking ~ Sperrminorität; **dissenting** ~ überstimmte Minderheit; **legal** ~ Minderjährigkeit; **linguistic** ~ Sprachminderheit;
to be in a ~ in der Minderheit sein; **to freeze out a** ~ Minderheit überstimmen; **to oppress a** ~ Minderheit unterdrücken; **to present a substantial** ~ gewichtige Minderheit darstellen; **to quell a** ~ Minderheit unterdrücken;
~ **applicant** Bewerber einer Minderheit; ~ **government** Minderheitsregierung; ~ **group** Minderheitengruppe; ~ **hiring** Einstellung von Minderheitsangehörigen; ~ **holder** *(Br.)* Minoritätsaktionär; ~ **holdings** Minderheitsbeteiligung, -paket; ~ **interests** *(balance sheet)* Ausgleichsposten für Anteile im Fremdbesitz; ~ **interest in income** *(balance sheet)* konzernfremden Gesellschaften zustehender Gewinn; ~ **interest in losses** *(balance sheet)* auf konzernfremde Gesellschaften entfallender Verlust; ~ **member** Angehöriger einer Minderheit; ~ **opinion** Rechtsauffassung (Ansicht) der Minderheit; ~ **owner** Minderheitsaktionär; ~ **problem** Minderheitenfrage; ~ **report** Bericht der Minderheit; ~ **rights** Rechte der Minderheit; ~ **safeguards** Schutzbestimmungen für die Minderheit; ~ **share** Minderheitsbeteiligung; ~ **shareholder** *(Br.)* Minderheitsaktionär; ~ **shareholding** *(Br.)* Minderheitsbeteiligung; ~ **stock participation** *(US)* Minoritäts-, Minderheitsaktienbeteiligung; ~ **stockholder** *(US)* Minoritätsaktionär; ~ **support** Unterstützung der Minderheiten; ~ **treaty** Minderheitenvertrag; ~ **vote** Stimmenminderheit.

mint Münze, Münzamt, -anstalt, -stätte, *(fig.)* Fundgrube;
~ **of money** *(coll.)* sehr viel Geld;
~ *(v.)* prägen, münzen;
~ **a word** Wort prägen;
to be worth a ~ **of money** steinreich sein; **to spend a** ~ **of money** Vermögen ausgeben;
~ *(a.)* funkelnagelneu, *(book, stamp)* unbeschädigt;
in ~ **condition** *(of coins)* funkelnagelneu, unbeschädigt, gut erhalten; ~ **mark** Münzzeichen; ~**-master** Leiter des Münzamtes; ~ **par** Münzpari; ~ **par of bullion** *(US, price of gold)* Gegenwert eines Gewichtes Feingold; ~ **par of exchange** feste Wechselparität; ~ **parity** Münzparität; ~ **price** Münzpreis, -wert; ~ **ratio** Münzfuß, *(US)* gesetzlich festgelegtes Gewichtsverhältnis der Gold- zu Silbermünzen; ~ **remedy** *(US)* Toleranz; ~ **stamp** Münzgepräge; ~ **tie** Münzparität.

mintage Ausprägung, Ausmünzung, *(cost of coinage)* Prägegebühr.

minting Münzprägung;
~ **charges** Prägegebühren; ~ **press** Prägepresse.

minus weniger, abzüglich.

minute Minute, *(Br., notes)* Notiz, Konzept, Entwurf, Denkschrift, Memorandum, Exposé, Bericht, *(protocol)* Protokolleintragung, *(rough draft)* Entwurf, Konzept, Notiz;
to the ~ genau, pünktlich; **up to the** ~ hypermodern, mit der neuesten Mode schritthaltend;
treasury ~**s** Verlautbarung des Finanzministeriums;
~**s of the proceedings** Verhandlungsprotokoll;
~ *(v.)* entwerfen, aufsetzen, *(make a draft)* Entwurf anfertigen, *(enter in the minutes)* protokollieren;

~ **s. th. down** Aktenvermerk anfertigen; ~ **a meeting** in einer Sitzung Protokoll führen;
to arrive to (on) the minute mit dem Glockenschlag ankommen; **to make a** ~ **of s. th.** Aktenvermerk anfertigen;
~ **account** spezifizierte Rechnung; ~ **book** Protokollbuch, *(general meeting)* Protokoll [von Aktionärsversammlungen und Vorstandssitzungen]; **to enter in the** ~ **book** protokollieren; ~ **current** *(el.)* Schwachstrom; ~ **description** detaillierte Beschreibung; ~ **difference** feiner Unterschied; **15** ~**s drive from the airport** 15 Autominuten vom Flugplatz; ~ **examination** minutiöse Untersuchung; ~ **guns** Notschütze; ~ **hand** Minutenzeiger; ~ **movie** *(US)* einminütiger Werbefilm, Kurzfilm; ~ **report** detaillierter Bericht; **a** ~**'s rest** kurze Ruhepause; **a** ~**'s walk** Minutenentfernung; ~ **writing** Protokollabfassung.

minutes Niederschrift, Sitzungsbericht, Protokolleintrag, [Verhandlungs]protokoll, -buch;
agreed ~ *(law of nations)* vereinbarte Niederschrift; **board** ~ Vorstandsprotokoll; **corporate** ~ Hauptversammlungsprotokoll einer Aktiengesellschaft; **specimen** ~ Protokollmuster;
~ **of board meetings (the board of directors)** Protokoll der Vorstandssitzung; ~ **of a case** Prozeßakten; ~ **of corporate meetings** Hauptversammlungsprotokoll; ~ **as evidence** Beweiskraft eines Protokolls; ~ **of a meeting** Sitzungsbericht, Sitzungsprotokoll; ~ **of the proceedings** Verhandlungsprotokoll; ~ **of resolution** Beschlußprotokoll;
to adopt the ~ **of the last meeting** Protokoll der letzten Sitzung bestätigen; **to approve the** ~ Protokoll genehmigen; **to attach to the** ~ dem Sitzungsprotokoll beifügen; **to confirm the** ~ **of the last meeting** vorhergehendes Sitzungsprotokoll bestätigen; **to draft (draw up) the** ~ Protokoll (aufnehmen); **to enter in the** ~ im Protokoll vermerken; **to keep (take) the** ~ Protokoll führen (abfassen); **to read and confirm the** ~ **of the preceding meeting** Protokoll der vorhergehenden Sitzung verlesen und genehmigen; **to sign** ~ Protokoll abzeichnen; **to take** ~ **of a conversation** von einer Unterredung eine Niederschrift anfertigen; **to tick off the** ~ Minuten verstreichen lassen; **to vote for amendment of the** ~ für eine Protokolländerung stimmen; **to vote for approval of the** ~ dem Sitzungsbericht zustimmen.

minuteman *(US)* Bürgerwehr.

miracle Wunder[werk];
to a ~ überraschend gut;
to promise ~**s** goldene Berge versprechen; **to work** ~**s** Wunder wirken;
~ **worker** Wundertäter.

mirage Luftspiegelung, Fata Morgana, *(fig.)* Täuschung, Luftbild.

mire Schlamm, Sumpf, *(fig.)* Klemme, Patsche, Verlegenheit;
~ *(v.)* in den Schlamm fahren, *(fig.)* in Schwierigkeiten bringen;
to be deep in the ~ tief in der Tinte sitzen; **to drag s. one's name through the** ~ jds. Namen in den Dreck ziehen;
to be ~**d in** steckenbleiben in.

mirror Spiegel, Reflektor, Rückstrahler, Vorbild, Muster;
internally adjustable ~ innen verstellbarer Außenspiegel; **concave** ~ Hohlspiegel; **distorting** ~ Zerrspiegel; **driving** ~ Rückspiegel; **external** ~ *(car)* Außenspiegel;
to be the ~ **of fashion** wie aus dem Modeheft geschnitten sein; **to hold up a** ~ **to one's contemporaries** Spiegelbild seiner Zeitgenossen sein;
~ **finish** Hochglanz; ~ **image** Spiegelbild; ~**-inverted** seitenverkehrt; ~**-inverted image** seitenverkehrte Abbildung; ~ **sight** Spiegelvisier; ~ **landing system** Spiegellandesystem; ~ **writing** Spiegelschrift.

mirth Fröhlichkeit, Frohsinn;
loud ~ **of the guests** Ausgelassenheit der Gäste.

misaddress *(v.)* falsch adressieren, an die falsche Addresse richten.

misadventure Unglücksfall, Unfall.

misadvise *(v.)* falsch (schlecht) beraten.

misallege *(v.)* falsch zitieren.

misalliance Mesalliance.

misanthrope Menschenfeind.

misapplication Unterschlagung, Untreue;
~ **of funds** Veruntreuung von Geldern.

misapply *(v.)* falsch anwenden, *(abuse)* zu unerlaubten Zwecken (widerrechtlich) verwenden;
~ **funds** Gelder unterschlagen; ~ **public money** öffentliche Gelder veruntreuen.

misapprehension Mißverständnis, Irrtum;
~ **of facts** Verkennung der Tatsachen;
to labo(u)r under a ~ sich in einem Irrtum befinden.

misappropriate *(v.)* (appropriate improperly) unrechtmäßig (widerrechtlich) verwenden, veruntreuen, unterschlagen, *(devote to wrong purpose)* [Kapital] fehlleiten;
~ **the society's funds** Vereinsgelder unterschlagen.

misappropriated capital fehlgeleitetes Kapital, [Kapital]fehlinvestition.

misappropriation *(appropriation for improper purpose)* unrechtmäßige Verwendung, Entwendung, Veruntreuung, Unterschlagung, *(wrong appropriation)* [Kapital]fehlleitung, Mißwirtschaft;
~ **of public funds** Unterschlagung öffentlicher Gelder, Amtsunterschlagung; ~ **of trademarks** Warenzeichenverletzung.

misbehavio(u)r schlechtes Benehmen, schlechte Führung, *(law)* ungebührliches Benehmen.

misbegotten unehelich;
~ **plan** hundsgemeine Absicht.

misbehave *(v.)* sich schlecht (unpassend) benehmen.

misbill *(v.)* falschen Lieferschein ausstellen.

misbilling Ausstellung eines falschen Lieferscheines.

misbrand *(v.)* Falschbezeichnung.

misbranding of commodities mißbräuchliche Bezeichnung (Falschbezeichnung) von Waren als Markenartikel.

miscalculate *(v.)* falsch berechnen (kalkulieren), sich verrechnen.

miscalculation falsche Berechnung, Fehlkalkulation, Rechen-, Kalkulationsfehler.

miscarriage *(delivery)* Fehlgeburt, *(failure)* Fehlschlagen, Mißlingen, Scheitern, *(mismanagement)* fahrlässige Geschäftsführung, *(contract law)* Fehlverhalten, *(of a letter)* Verlorengehen, Fehlleitung, Irrläufer, *(shipment)* Versandfehler;
~ **of goods** Verlustsendung; ~ **of justice** Fehlurteil, Justizirrtum, Rechtsbeugung.

miscarry *(v.)* schlecht ausfallen, *(letter)* verlorengehen, fehlgeleitet werden, *(plan)* scheitern, fehlschlagen, *(woman)* Fehlgeburt haben.

miscast *(v.)* *(theater)* unpassend besetzten.

miscasting Zählfehler, Fehlrechnung, Prüfirrtum, *(theater)* Fehlbesetzung, unpassende Rollenverteilung.

miscegenation Rassenmischung.

miscellanea Sammlung vermischter Gegenstände.

miscellaneous *(newspaper)* Verschiedenes, Vermischtes, Sonstiges;
~ *(a.)* verschieden[artig], *(mixed)* gemischt;
~ **assets** *(balance sheet)* verschiedene Anlagegüter; ~ **collections of goods** gemischte Warensendung; ~ **column** *(newspaper)* Spalte Verschiedenes; ~ **expense** *(income statement)* Nebenausgaben; ~ **goods** Sammelgut; ~ **income** *(balance sheet)* vermischte Einkünfte, verschiedene Erträge; ~ **investments** *(balance sheet)* verschiedene Beteiligungen; ~ **items** *(catalog(ue))* Verschiedenes; ~ **market** Markt für verschiedene Wertpapiere; ~ **revenues** *(balance sheet)* sonstige Einkünfte.

miscellanies *(newspaper)* Verschiedenes.

miscellany vermischte Aufsätze, Sammelband.

mischance Mißgeschick, unglücklicher Zufall;
by ~ unglücklicherweise.

mischarge fehlerhafte Anklage.

mischief Unglück, Schaden, *(law)* Übelstand;
out of pure ~ aus reiner Bosheit;
criminal ~ *(US)* strafbare Sachbeschädigung; **malicious** ~ *(US)* böswillige Sachbeschädigung; **public** ~ grober Unfug;
to be full of ~ immer auf Dummheiten aus sein; **to be bent on** ~ Böses im Schilde führen; **to do much** ~ **to shipping** der Schiffahrt schweren Schaden zufügen; **to get into** ~ etw. anstellen; **to make** ~ **between** Zwietracht säen; **to play** ~ **with s. th.** etw. auf den Kopf stellen; **to remedy a** ~ Mißstand beseitigen; **to work great** ~ unselige Leidenschaften hervorrufen;
~ **maker** Störenfried; ~ **making** Intrigieren, Hetzen.

misclassify *(v.)* *(mil.)* in die falsche Geheimhaltungsstufe einordnen.

miscomputation Fehlkalkulation, falsche Berechnung.

miscompute *(v.)* falsch berechnen.

misconceive *(v.)* mißverstehen, falsch auffassen;
~ **one's duty** falsche Auffassung von seinen Pflichten haben.

misconcieved capital project Fehlinvestition.

misconception irrige Meinung, falsche Vorstellung.

misconduct schlechtes Benehmen, Fehlverhalten, Ungebühr, *(arbitrator)* Verfehlen, *(married couple)* ehewidriges Verhalten, *(mil.)* schlechte Führung, *(official)* Verletzung der Amtspflicht, Amtspflichtverletzung, *(servant)* ungehöriges (ordnungswidriges) Verhalten;
gross ~ schwere Verfehlung; **professional** ~ standeswidriges Verhalten; **wilful** ~ schwere Verfehlung;

wilful ~ **on the part of the agent** schuldhaftes Verhalten des Handelsvertreters; ~ **of management** schlechte Geschäftsführung; ~ **in office by a public officer or employee** *(US)* Amtsdelikt, -pflichtverletzung; ~ **of the tenant** unzumutbares Verhalten des Mieters;
~ *(v.)* schlecht verwalten;
~ **o. s.** sich schlecht benehmen; ~ **one's business affairs** seine geschäftlichen Angelegenheiten schlecht führen.

miscontruable doppeldeutig, mißdeutbar.

misconstruction falsche Auslegung.

misconstruance fehlerhafte Auslegung.

misconstrue *(v.)* falsch auslegen.

miscorrect *(v.)* falsch verbessern.

miscount falsche Zählung, Rechenfehler;
~ *(v.)* sich verrechnen, sich verzählen, falsch kalkulieren;
~ **votes at an election** Wahlstimmen falsch auszählen.

miscredit, to cast ~ **on s. th.** etw. zweifelhaft erscheinen lassen.

miscue *(v.)* *(theater)* Auftritt verpassen.

misdate falsches Datum;
~ *(v.)* falsch datieren.

misdating falsche Datumsangabe.

misdeed Übeltat.

misdeliver *(v.)* falsch beliefern.

misdelivery ordnungswidrige Lieferung, Fehllieferung, *(carrier)* falsche Ablieferung.

misdemean *(v.)* sich vergehen.

misdemeanant [Misse]täter, Straffälliger, Täter, Delinquent.

misdemeano(u)r Vergehen, Übertretung;
petty ~ *(US)* Übertretung;
~ **in office** Amtsvergehen, -delikt;
to commit (make o. s. guilty of) a ~ sich eines Verbrechens schuldig machen.

misdescription ungenaue Beschreibung, *(contract)* falsche Angaben.

misdirect falsch unterrichten, *(letters)* unrichtig (falsch) adressieren, fehlleiten;
~ **one's abilities** nicht den richtigen Gebrauch von seinen Fähigkeiten machen; ~ **capital** Kapitalfehlleitung vornehmen; ~ **a jury** Geschworene falsch belehren.

misdirected falsch adressiert, fehlgeleitet;
~ **charity** falsch angebrachte Wohltätigkeit; ~ **demand** Bedarfsfehlentwicklung; **national** ~ **investments** volkswirtschaftliche Fehlinvestitionen.

misdirection *(letters)* falsche Adresse (Adressierung);
~ **of capital** Kapitalfehlleitung; ~ **of funds** unberechtigter Mitteleinsatz; ~ **of a jury** unrichtige Rechtsbelehrung von Geschworenen; ~ **of a letter** Fehlleitung eines Briefes.

misdoing Missetat, Vergehen;
~s **of advertising** Reklameauswüchse.

mise Prozeßauslagen, -kosten;
~ **money** Konzessionsgebühr.

misemploy *(v.)* falsch anwenden;
~ **one's money** sein Geld falsch anlegen (investieren); ~ **one's time** seine Zeit vergeuden.

misemployment falsche Verwendung, Mißbrauch, *(money)* Fehlinvestition, -anlage.

misenter *(v.)* falsch eintragen (buchen).

misentry falscher Eintrag, falsche (unrichtige) Buchung, Falschbuchung.

miser Geizhalz, -kragen, Filz.

miserable elend, jämmerlich;
to make s. one's life ~ jem. ein elendes Dasein bereiten (das Leben zur Hölle machen);
~ **dwelling** jämmerliche Unterkunft; ~ **journey** mühsame Reise; ~ **lives of refugees** kümmerliche Flüchtlingsexistenzen; ~ **salary** lächerliches Gehalt; ~ **speech** miserable Rede; ~ **sum** unbedeutender Betrag.

miserably underpaid jämmerlich unterbezahlt.

misery Elend, Not;
abject (deepest) ~ drückende Not;
to live in ~ **and want** in jämmerlichen Verhältnissen leben; **to put s. o. out of his** ~ jds. Leiden ein Ende bereiten.

misestimate falsche Schätzung, Fehlkalkulation.

misestimation Fehlschätzung.

misfeasance *(contract)* nachlässige Vertragsausführung, *(director)* Untreue, *(injurious exercise of powers)* Ermessensmißbrauch, -überschreitung, *(negligence)* nachlässige Ausführung, *(trespass)* unerlaubte Handlung, Übertretung, Delikt, *(officer)* Amtsvergehen, pflichtwidrige Handlung;
to take ~ **proceedings** Verfahren wegen Amtsmißbrauchs einleiten.

misfire *(motor)* Fehlzündung;
~ *(v.)* fehlzünden, aussetzen.
misfit nicht passendes Stück, mißratene Arbeit;
to be a ~ Versager sein.
misfortune Unglücksfall;
~ **never comes singly** ein Unglück kommt selten allein.
misgiving böse Vorahnung.
misgovern *(v.)* schlecht regieren (verwalten), mißwirtschaften.
misgovernment schlechte Verwaltung, Mißwirtschaft.
misgovernor schlechter Verwalter.
misguidance Irreführung, Verleitung, schlechte Beratung.
misguide *(v.)* schlecht beeinflussen (beraten);
misguided moment schwacher Augenblick.
mishandle *(v.)* fehlerhaft bearbeiten, falsch handhaben, verkorksen.
mishap Unfall, *(car)* [Auto]panne.
misinform *(v.)* falsch berichten (informieren);
~ **against s. o.** falsch gegen j. aussagen.
misinformed falsch unterrichtet (informiert).
misinformation falsche Auskunft, unrichtige Berichterstattung, Fehlinformation.
misinvestment Fehlinvestition.
misinterpret *(v.)* falsch auslegen (erklären).
misinterpretion falsche Auslegung (Information), Mißdeutung, Fehlauslegung.
misjoinder | **of action** unzulässige Klageverbindung; ~ **of inventor** irrtümliche Angabe eines Miterfinders; ~ **of parties** unzulässige Streitgenossenschaft.
misjudge *(v.)* **s. one's motives** jds. Motive verkennen.
misjudgment Fehlurteil.
mislaid verlegt;
~ **property** abhandengekommene Sache.
mislay *(v.)* **a document** Urkunde verlegen.
mislead *(v.)* fehlleiten, *(give wrong impression)* täuschen, irreführen;
~ **s. o. as to one's intentions** j. über seine Absichten täuschen.
misleading | **advertisement** irreführende (täuschende) Werbung; ~ **indication** irreführende Bezeichnung; ~ **instruction** *(jury)* irreführende Belehrung; ~ **statement** *(financial statement)* irreführende Angaben.
mismanage *(v.)* schlecht verwalten (wirtschaften).
mismanagement Mißwirtschaft, schlechte Verwaltung (Geschäfts-, Betriebsführung);
criminal ~ strafbare unsaubere Geschäftsführung.
mismarriage Mesalliance.
mishmash *(sl.)* Mischmasch.
mismatch Fehlanpassung.
misname *(v.)* falsch bezeichnen.
misnomer unrichtige Namensangabe, *(law)* Namensirrtum.
misplace *(v.)* **the decimal point** Komma falsch setzen.
misplaced am unrechten Ort;
~ **advertising** falsch angesetzte Werbung.
misplay *(US)* falsches Spiel.
misplead *(v.)* falsch plädieren.
mispleading fehlerhafter Schriftsatz, falsches Plädoyer.
misprint Satz-, Setzfehler, Druckfehler, *(imprinted sheet)* Fehldruck;
~ *(v.)* fehl-, verdrucken.
misprision *(maladministration)* Vernachlässigung einer Amtspflicht, Amtsunterschlagung, *(clerical error)* Protokollfehler, *(contempt against the sovereign)* Majestätsbeleidigung;
negative ~ pflichtwidrige Unterlassung einer Anzeige; **positive** ~ Amtsunterschlagung;
~ **of felony** Verheimlichung eines Verbrechens; ~ **of treason** Nichtanzeige von Hochverrat.
mispronounce falsch aussprechen.
mispronunciation falsche Aussprache.
misquotation falsches Zitat.
misquote *(v.)* falsch zitieren.
misread *(v.)* *(law)* falsch auslegen.
misreading falsche Urkundenverlesung.
misrecital *(deed)* falsche Präambel.
misreckon *(v.)* falsch rechnen.
misreckoning falsche Rechnung (Kalkulation).
misrendering falsche Übersetzung, Übersetzungsfehler.
misreport falscher (ungenauer) Bericht.
misrepresent *(v.)* falsch darstellen, unrichtig angeben, *(act counter)* Auftraggeber nicht gehörig vertreten;
~ **fraudulently** falsche Tatsachen vorspiegeln; **fraudulently** ~ **one's financial condition** betrügerische Darstellung seiner finanziellen Verhältnisse abgeben.

misrepresentation falsche Darstellung (Angaben bei Vertragsabschluß), unrichtige Tatsachenerklärung;
false (fraudulent) ~ Vorspiegelung falscher Tatsachen, arglistige Täuschung; **innocent** ~ unbeabsichtigte Falschdarstellung; **material** ~ *(insurance)* absichtliches Verschweigen von für die Versicherungsgesellschaft bedeutsamen Tatsachen; **negligent** ~ fahrlässige Unrichtigkeit; **wil(l)ful** ~ arglistige Täuschung, Betrug;
~ **of facts** Falschdarstellung, Tatsachenverdrehung; ~ **of a representative** unrichtige Vertretung des Auftraggebers.
misrouted | **document** Irrläufer; ~ **freight** fehlgeleitete Sendung.
misrule Mißwirtschaft, -regierung.
miss Verpassen, Versäumnis;
lucky ~ geglücktes Entkommen;
~ *(v.)* [ver]fehlen, versäumen, *(train)* verpassen;
~ **an accident** mit knapper Not einem Unfall entgehen; ~ **one's aim** sein Ziel verfehlen; ~ **an appointment** Verabredung nicht einhalten; ~ **the boat** Chance verpassen; ~ **the bus** Anschluß (Chance, günstige Gelegenheit) verpassen; ~ **one's chance** günstige Gelegenheit verpassen; ~ **one's entrance** *(actor)* seinen Auftritt verpassen; ~ **one's footing** stolpern; ~ **one's holiday** um seinen Urlaub kommen; ~ **a lesson** Unterrichtsstunde versäumen; ~ **out s. th.** Gelegenheit verpassen; ~ **out the fish course** Fischgericht weglassen; ~ **out a line** *(print.)* Zeile übersehen (auslassen); ~ **one's mark** sein Planziel nicht erreichen; ~ **the market** sich eine Verkaufsmöglichkeit entgehen lassen; ~ **the true meaning of a text** wahren Sinn eines Textes nicht erkennen; ~ **the right moment** richtigen Zeitpunkt verpassen; ~ **one's opportunity** sich eine Gelegenheit entgehen lassen; ~ **the point** das Wesentliche nicht begreifen; ~ **the point of a joke** Pointe eines Witzes nicht erfassen; ~ **one's way** sich verlaufen;
to be no great ~ entbehrlich sein; **to give s. th. a** ~ einer Sache aus dem Wege gehen.
missed | **approach** Fehlanflug; ~ **discount** nicht in Anspruch genommener Rabatt, Skontoverlust; ~ **profit** entgangener Gewinn.
missile *(mil.)* Geschoß, *(rocket)* Flugkörper, Fernlenkgeschoß, Lenkwaffe, Raketenwaffe;
anti-ballistic ~ *(US)* Antiraketen-Rakete; **guided** ~ ferngesteuerte Rakete, Fernlenkwaffe; **helicopter-borne antitank** ~ vom Hubschrauber abgefeuerte Tankabwehrrakete; **intercontinental ballistic** ~ Interkontinentalrakete; **land-based** ~ Bodenrakete; **medium-range** ~ Mittelstreckenrakete; **short-range** ~ Kurzstreckenrakete; **submarine-launched ballistic** ~ Rakete auf U-Bootbasis; **surface-to-air** ~ Bodenluftrakete;
to guide a ~ **to its target** Rakete ins Ziel steuern;
~ **age** Zeitalter der Raketenwaffen; ~ **base** Raketenabschußstelle; ~ **launching** Raketenabschuß, -feuerung; ~ **movements** Raketenverschiebungen; ~ **silo** Raketensilo; ~ **site** Raketenabschußstelle; **safeguard** ~ **system** Raketenabwehrsystem; ~ **testing centre** Raketenprüfgelände.
missing abgängig, fehlend, abwesend, *(mil.)* vermißt;
to be ~ fehlen, vermißt werden; **to be reported** ~ *(mil.)* als vermißt gemeldet werden;
~ **amount** Fehlbetrag; ~ **goods** fehlende Ware; ~ **items** verlorene Postsendungen; ~ **link** fehlendes Glied; ~ **person** Verschollener; ~ **ship** überfälliges Schiff; ~ **word** *(print.)* Auslassung, Leiche.
mission [Sonder]delegation, *(airplane)* Feindflug, Einsatz, *(commission)* Auftrag, *(dipl.)* diplomatische Mission, ständige Gesandtschaft, Botschaft, *(mar., mil.)* Einsatz-, Kampfauftrag, *(missionary work)* Mission[stätigkeit], *(permanent foreign embassy, US)* ständige Vertretung im Ausland, *(personnel)* Gesandtschaftspersonal;
on special ~ in besonderer Mission, in besonderem Auftrag;
domestic ~ innere Mission; **foreign** ~ auswärtige Vertretung; **goodwill** ~ Mission des guten Willens; **historical** ~ historische Aufgabe; **home** ~ innere Mission; **military** ~ Militärmission; **permanent** ~ ständige Mission; **special** ~ Sonderauftrag, -mission; **trade** ~ Handelsdelegation, -mission;
~ **of inquiry** Untersuchungsausschuß; ~ **in life** Lebensaufgabe; **to be sent on a** ~ **to s. o.** zu jem. entsandt werden; **to complete one's** ~ **successfully** seine Mission erfolgreich beenden; **to perform a** ~ Aufträge durchführen; **to withdraw a** ~ ausländische Vertretung aufheben;
~ **furniture** massive Möbel; ~ **head** Missionschef; ~ **staff** Missionsangehörige.
missionary Missionar;
~ **field** Missionsgebiet; ~ **salesman** Werbeschulungsleiter; ~ **society** Missionsgesellschaft; ~ **work** Missionstätigkeit; ~ **worker** *(sl.)* angeheuerter Streikbrecher; ~ **zeal** Bekehrungseifer.

misspell *(v.)* falsch schreiben (buchstabieren).
misspelling Rechtschreibe-, orthographischer Fehler.
misspend *(v.)* **money** Geld falsch ausgeben.
misspent youth vertane Jugend.
misstate *(v.)* falsch angeben, unrichtig darstellen.
misstatement falsche Angaben, Falschdarstellung;
~ **of facts** falsche Sachdarstellung; ~ **in prospectus** falsche Angaben im Subskriptionsanzeiger (im Börsenprospekt).
misstep Fehltritt, *(fig.)* Mißgriff.
mist [feuchter] Nebel, *(US)* Sprühregen;
~ *(v.)* **over** *(mirror)* sich beschlagen;
to be in a ~ ganz verdutzt sein; **to be lost in the** ~ **of time** durch die Zeit verloren gegangen sein; **to see things through a** ~ Schwierigkeiten voraussehen.
mistake Fehler, Mißgriff, *(error)* Irrtum, *(law)* Geschäftsirrtum, *(unintentional wrong act)* Versehen, *(wrong apprehension)* Mißverständnis;
by ~ irrtümlich, aus Versehen, versehentlich;
bad ~ grober Irrtum; **clerical** ~ Schreibfehler; **common** ~ allgemein verbreiteter Irrtum; **fatal** ~ verhängnisvoller Irrtum; **fundamental** ~ grundlegender Fehler; **grammatical** ~ grammatischer Fehler; **honest** ~ entschuldbarer Irrtum; **mutual** ~ beidseitiger Irrtum, beiderseitiges Versehen; **operative** ~ beachtlicher Irrtum, *(law of contract)* Irrtum, der die Vertragsentstehung verhindert; **slight** ~ kleiner Fehler; **spelling** ~ orthographischer Fehler, Rechtschreibungsfehler; **typographical** ~ Druckfehler; **unilateral** ~ einseitiger Irrtum;
~ **in calculation** Rechen-, Kalkulationsfehler; ~ **as to the character of a person** Irrtum über eine wesentliche Eigenschaft einer Person; ~ **as to the existence of the subject matter** Irrtum über die Geschäftsgrundlage; ~ **in the expression of true agreement** Irrtum über die rechtliche Bedeutung einer abgegebenen Willenserklärung; ~ **of fact** Tatsachenirrtum; ~ **as to a fact fundamental to the entire agreement** Irrtum über eine für den ganzen Vertrag wesentliche Tatsache; **common** ~ **as to a fact fundamental to the agreement** Irrtum von fundamentaler Bedeutung für den Vertragsabschluß; ~ **in the figures** Rechenfehler; ~ **in the inducement** *(US)* Motivirrtum; ~ **of judgment** Fehlbeurteilung, -urteil; ~ **in labelling** Auszeichnungsfehler; ~ **of law** Rechtsirrtum; ~ **as to the nature of the document signed** Irrtum über die Rechtsnatur der unterschriebenen Urkunde; ~ **as to the nature of the subject matter** Irrtum im Beweggrund, Motivirrtum; ~ **by the offerer in expressing his intentions** Irrtum bei der Formulierung der Vertragsofferte; ~ **common to both partners** Irrtum beider Vertragsparteien, beidseitiger Irrtum; **unilateral** ~ **as to the identity of the person contracted** Identitätsirrtum; **mutual** ~ **as to the identity of the subject matter of the contract** beidseitiger Irrtum über den Vertragsgegenstand; ~ **as to the quality of the subject matter** Irrtum über wesentliche Eigenschaften; **fundamental** ~ **as to the tenor of words** Irrtum über den Wortlaut einer Erklärung; ~ **in transcription** Übertragungsfehler; ~ **in translation** Übersetzungsfehler;
~ *(v.)* verwechseln, verkennen, *(misunderstand)* mißverstehen;
~ **s. o. for somebody else** j. verwechseln; ~ **one's way** sich verlaufen;
to acknowledge one's ~ seinen Fehler zugeben (eingestehen); **to correct a** ~ Fehler beseitigen; **to detect a** ~ Fehler entdecken; **to labo(u)r under a** ~ sich im Irrtum befinden; **to make a** ~ Fehler begehen; **to make a** ~ **in calculation (reckoning)** falsch addieren, sich verrechnen; **to take s. one's umbrella in** ~ **for one's own** aus Versehen einen fremden Schirm mitnehmen.
mistaken irrtümlich, falsch;
to be ~ sich irren;
~ **appointment** Fehlbesetzung; ~ **identity** Irrtum über die Person, Personen-, Identitätsverwechslung; ~ **investment** Fehlinvestition; ~ **kindness** unangebrachte Freundlichkeit; ~ **opinion** irrtümliche Meinung; ~ **party** im Irrtum befangene Vertragspartei; ~ **statement** irrtümliche Erklärung.
Mister Big *(sl.)* Drahtzieher im Hintergrund.
mistranslate *(v.)* falsch übersetzen.
mistranslation falsche Übersetzung.
mistransportation in shorthand fehlerhafte Stenogrammübertragung.
mistreat *(v.)* mißhandeln.
mistreatment Mißhandlung.
mistress Herrin, Gebieterin, *(expert)* Expertin, *(housewife)* Hausfrau, *(school, Br.)* Lehrerin, *(kept woman)* Mätresse.
mistrial fehlerhaftes Gerichtsverfahren, *(jury, US)* ergebnisloses Schwurgerichtsverfahren;
to rule a ~ Fehlurteil verkünden.

mistrust fehlendes Vertrauen, Mißtrauen.
misty dunstig, nebelig.
misunderstand *(v.)* falsch verstehen, mißverstehen.
misunderstanding Mißverständnis;
to clear up a ~ Mißverständnis bereinigen (beseitigen).
misusage Mißhandlung.
misuse falsche Anwendung, mißbräuchliche Verwendung, Mißbrauch;
~ **of authority** Mißbrauch der Amtsgewalt, Amtsmißbrauch; ~ **of a flag** Flaggenmißbrauch; **fraudulent** ~ **of funds** Unterschlagung; ~ **of official positions** Mißbrauch politischer Positionen; ~ **of a patent** Patentmißbrauch; ~ **of power** Vollmachtsmißbrauch; ~ **of public funds** Unterschlagung öffentlicher Gelder; ~ **of slot machines** Automatenmißbrauch; ~ **of words** Wortverwechslung;
~ *(v.)* **a term** falschen Begriff verwenden.
misuser Rechtsmißbrauch.
mite Scherflein, Deut, Heller;
the widow's ~ kleine Witwenspende;
to give one's ~ **for a good cause** sein Scherflein für eine gute Sache beitragen; **to offer a** ~ **of comfort** etw. Trost spenden.
mitigate *(v.)* mildern, abschwächen;
~ **one's damage** seinen Schaden mindern; ~ **a penalty** Strafe mildern.
mitigating circumstances (factors) mildernde Umstände.
mitigation Milderung;
~ **of damages (loss)** Herabsetzung des Schadensbetrages; ~ **of punishment** Strafmilderung; ~ **of a tax** Steuermilderung;
to consider in ~ strafmildernd berücksichtigen; **to plead in** ~ für Strafmilderung plädieren.
mitt camp *(sl.)* Wahrsagerzelt.
mitten Fausthandschuh;
to get the ~ *(coll.)* Korb bekommen, abgewiesen werden.
mittimus *(coll.)* blauer Brief, Amtsentlassung, *(criminal law, US)* Hafteinweisung, -befehl, *(writ for removing of records)* Aktenversandanweisung;
~ *(v.)* *(Br.)* ins Gefängnis einweisen.
mix *(fight, sl.)* Keilerei, Rauferei, *(muddle, coll.)* Durcheinander, *(social gathering, sl.)* gesellschaftliche Veranstaltung;
ancient ~ altbekannte Mischung;
~ *(v.)* vermischen;
~ **with s. o.** sich mit jem. vertragen; ~ **into s. one's business** *(US)* sich in jds. Angelegenheiten einmischen; ~ **business with pleasure** das Angenehme mit dem Nützlichen verbinden; ~ **with the crowd** sich mit dem Volk gemein machen; ~ **in politics** sich politisch betätigen; ~ **a salad** Salat anrichten; ~ **with the best society** in der besten Gesellschaft verkehren; ~ **up** *(fig.)* verquicken, durcheinanderbringen; **not** ~ **well** schlecht mit den Leuten auskommen.
mix-up Durcheinander, Wirrwarr, *(melee)* Handgemenge, Schlägerei.
mixed ge-, vermischt, *(aviation)* erste Klasse und Touristenklasse kombiniert, *(muddled)* beschwipst, *(science)* angewandt;
~ **up with a gang** mit einer Bande kooperierend;
to be ~ geteilter Meinung sein; **to be** ~ **up in an affair** in eine Sache (Affäre) verwickelt sein;
~ **account** gemischtes Konto, Mischkonto, *(brokerage accounting)* Kundenkonto für kurz- und langfristige Dispositionen; ~ **action** schuldrechtliche und zugleich dingliche Klage; ~ **assortment** gemischtes Sortiment; ~ **bag** *(fam.)* reichlich gemischte Angelegenheit; ~ **bathing** Familienbad; ~ **blood** Mischling; ~ **cargo** *(Br.)* gemischte Ladung, Stückgutladung, -sendung, Stückgüter; ~ **cargo rate** *(Br.)* Stückguttarif; ~ **carload** *(US)* gemischte Ladung, Stückgutsendung; ~ **carload rate** *(US)* Stückguttarif; ~ **collateral** *(US)* Sicherheit durch Hinterlegung verschiedenartiger Effekten; ~ **commission** gemischter Ausschuß; ~ **company** gemischte Gesellschaft; ~ **contract** gemischter Vertrag; ~ **economy** gemischte Wirtschaftsform, -ordnung; ~ **enterprise** gemischtwirtschaftliches Unternehmen; ~ **estate** *(US)* Erbpacht, -baurecht auf 99 Jahre; ~ **feelings** gemischte Gefühle; ~ **forest** Mischwald; ~ **fund** *(investment company)* gemischter Fonds; ~ **goods** gemischte Warensendung; ~ **ice** gemischtes Eis; ~ **government** gemischte Staatsform; ~ **income** Einkünfte aus selbständiger und nichtselbständiger Arbeit; ~ **insurance company** Versicherungsgesellschaft mit Gewinnbeteiligung; ~ **larcency** schwerer Diebstahl; ~ **life assurance** *(Br.)* gemischte Lebensversicherung, Lebensversicherung auf Erlebens- und Todesfall; ~ **loan** durch Lombardierung verschiedengemischter Wertpapiere gesicherter Kredit; ~ **marriage** Mischehe; ~ **ownership property** gemischtwirtschaftliches Unternehmen; ~ **policy** gemischte Schiffsversicherung, *(Br.)*

Zeit- und Reiseversicherung; ~ **price** Mischpreis; ~ **property** Mischeigentum; ~ **race** Mischvolk; **to accord a ~ reception** geteilten Beifall spenden; ~ **sample** gemischte Stichprobe; ~ **school** *(Br.)* Schule für beide Geschlechter, Gemeinschaftsschule; ~ **shipment** gemischte Sendung; ~ **space units** *(advertising)* verschiedene Anzeigengrößen; ~ **tariff** kombinierter Zolltarif; ~ **train** Zug mit angehängten Güterwagen.

mixer Mischpult, *(kitchen)* Küchenmaschine, *(share, coll.)* Aktie mit hoher Rendite;
concrete ~ Betonmischer; **good ~** guter Gesellschafter.

mixing│table Regiepult;
~ **of trust money** Vermischung treuhänderisch gehaltener Geldbeträge.

mixture Gemisch, Mischung, *(print.)* gemischter Satz.

mizzle Nieselregen;
~ *(v.)* nieseln, fein regnen.

moat Burg-, Stadtgraben.

mob Pöbel, -haufe, Zusammenrottung, *(safecracker, sl.)* Geldschrankknacker;
the swell ~ die Unterwelt;
~ *(v.)* sich zusammenrotten, in einer Rotte angreifen;
to form (gather into) a ~ sich zusammenrotten; **to join the ~** sich erniedrigen (mit dem Pöbel einlassen);
~ **law** Lynchjustiz; ~ **oratory** Hetzrede; ~ **psychology** Massenpsychologie; ~ **rule** Pöbelherrschaft.

mobbed überfüllt;
~ **by teenagers** von Jugendlichen belagert (umschwärmt);
to be ~ by the crowd vom Pöbel attackiert werden.

mobbing and rioting *(Scot.)* Landfriedensbruch.

mobile beweglich, *(mil.)* sofort verlegbar (verschiebbar);
barely ~ kaum fahrtüchtig;
~ **gangway** fahrbare Treppe; ~ **home** Wohnwagen, -mobil; ~ **home compound** Wohnwagenabstellplatz; ~ **home manufacturing** Herstellung transportabler Häuser; ~ **home park** Parkanlage für transportable Häuser; ~ **home plant** Fertigungsbetrieb für transportable Häuser; ~ **home site** Abstellplatz für ein transportables Haus; ~ **library** *(Br.)* Auto-, Wanderbücherei; ~ **patrol** Funk-, Verkehrsstreife; ~ **people** ständig auf Achse befindliche Leute; ~ **radio station** bewegliche Funkstelle; ~ **radiotelephone scheme** Verkehrsfunknetz; ~ **selling unit** ambulante Verkaufseinrichtung; ~ **shop** fahrbare Verkaufsstelle, Verkaufswagen; ~ **unit** fahrbarer Relaissender, Übertragungswagen; ~ **voter** nicht parteigebundener Wähler; ~ **warfare** Bewegungskrieg.

mobility *(mil.)* leichte Beweglichkeit, Mobilität.
geographical ~ gesamtwirtschaftliche Mobilität;
~ **of labo(u)r** Freizügigkeit der Arbeitskräfte;
~ **allowance** Mobilitätszuschuß; ~ **bonus** Mobilitätsprämie.

mobilizable mobilisierbar, realisierbar.

mobilization Mobilisierung, Einsatz, *(converting of real estate)* Veräußerung von Grundbesitz, *(mil.)* Mobilmachung, Aufgebot;
economic (industrial) ~ Mobilisierung der Wirtschaft; **partial ~** Teilmobilmachung;
~ **of funds** Flüssigmachen von Kapital;
~ **day** Mobilmachungstag; ~ **order** Mobilmachungsbefehl.

mobilize *(v.)* *(funds)* flüssigmachen, *(mil.)* mobilmachen.

mobocracy Pöbelherrschaft.

mobsman, mobster Gangster.

mock Spott, Verhöhnung, *(faking)* Nachahmung, Fälschung;
to [make a ~ of] s. o. j. zum Gespött machen;
~ *(a.)* scheinbar nachgemacht, falsch, unecht;
~ **attack** *(mil.)* Scheinangriff; ~ **auction** Scheinauktion; ~ **battle** Scheingefecht; ~ **bidder** Scheinbieter; ~ **election** Scheinwahl; ~ **purchase** Scheinkauf; ~ **trial** Scheinverfahren, -prozeß.

mockery *(fig.)* Zerrbild, *(theater)* Possenspiel, Farce, *(trial)* Farce.

mockup Verkaufs-, Lehr-, Anschauungsmodell.

modal durch die Verhältnisse bedingt;
~ **will** mit Ausführungen über die Vollstreckung versehenes Testament.

modalities Modalitäten [der Vertragserfüllung];
~ **of payment** Zahlungsmodalitäten.

modality Ausführungsart, Modalität.

mode Art und Weise, Verfahren, Methode, *(statistics)* häufigster (dichtester) Wert, *(style of fashion)* Mode;
~ **of appointment** Bestallungsverfahren; ~ **of conveyance** Versendungs-, Beförderungsart; ~ **of election** Wahlmodus; ~ **of employment** Beschäftigungsart; ~ **of frequency function** Extrempunkt einer Häufigkeitsfunktion; ~ **of government**

Regierungsart; ~ **of life (living)** Lebensweise; ~ **of operations** Wirkungsweise; ~ **of packing** Verpackungsart; ~ **of payment** Zahlungsweise; ~ **of proceeding** Verfahrensmethode; ~ **of process** Herstellungsverfahren; ~ **of speaking** Redeweise; ~ **of transfer** Übertragungsweise; ~ **of working** Bearbeitungsverfahren;
to be all the ~ ganz modern sein.

model *(car)* Bauart, Typ, Konstruktion, *(design)* Entwurf, Schablone, *(exemplary piece)* Muster[stück], *(exhibition)* Ausstellungsstück, Verkaufsmodell, *(fashion)* Mannequin, *(paragon)* Vorbild, *(pattern)* Vorlage, Muster, *(representation)* Modell;
on the ~ of nach dem Muster von;
deluxe ~ Luxusmodell; **demonstrator ~** Vorführmodell; **economy ~** billiges Modell; **full-size ~** unverkleinertes Modell; **the latest Paris ~s** letzte Pariser Modelle; **market ~** Modellfall; **previous year's ~** Vorjahresmodell; **scale ~** maßstabsgetreues Modell; **cigarette-pack-size ~** Modell in der Größe einer Zigarettenpackung; **sports ~** Sportwagen; **three-bedroom ~** Haus mit drei Schlafzimmern; **top-of-the-line ~** Spitzenmodell; **working ~** Arbeitsmodell, -muster;
~ **of self-control** Muster von Selbstbeherrschung; ~ **of virtue** Ausbund der Tugend;
~ *(v.)* *(fashion)* als Vorführdame fungieren, *(form)* formen, bilden nach, modellieren;
~ **a political constitution** Verfassung aufsetzen;
~ *(a.)* vorbildlich, musterhaft;
~ **act** *(US)* Mustergesetz; ~ **agreement** Manteltarifabkommen; ~ **aircraft (airplane)** Modellflugzeug; ~ **behavio(u)r** musterhaftes Betragen; ~ **boy** Musterknabe; ~ **business letter** Geschäftsbriefmuster; ~ **city** Modell-, Musterstadt; ~ **community** Mustergemeinde; ~ **convention** Musterabkommen; ~ **dwelling** Muster-, Modellhaus; ~ **enterprise** Musterbetrieb; ~ **farm** landwirtschaftlicher Musterbetrieb; ~ **house** Modell-, Musterhaus; ~ **husband** Mustergatte; ~ **letter** Briefmuster; ~ **mobile home** transportables Modellhaus; ~ **plant** Musterbetrieb; ~ **procedure** Bestverfahren; ~ **release** *(photo)* Freigabeerklärung; ~ **room** Modellsalon; ~ **school** Musterschule; ~ **set of articles** Mustersatzung; ~ **socialist** Muster von einem Sozialisten; ~ **stock** Spezialsortiment; ~ **stock plan** Musterkollektionssystem; ~ **tank** Versuchstank; ~ **T Ford** *(coll., US)* vorsintflutliche Einrichtung, veraltete Sache, veraltetes Modell; ~ **town** Musterstadt; ~ **train** Modellzug; ~ **workshop** Musterbetrieb.

moderate *(politics)* Gemäßigter;
~ *(a.)* *(claim, income)* bescheiden, *(opinion)* gemäßigt, *(prices)* billig, niedrig, mäßig;
~ *(v.)* mäßigen, mildern, *(preside)* führen, leiten;
~ **an assembly** einer Versammlung präsidieren; ~ **one's claims (demands)** seine Forderungen ermäßigen; ~ **a public meeting** öffentliche Versammlung leiten;
to be ~ in one's demands mäßige Forderungen stellen;
~**ly large audience** ziemlich große Zuhörerschaft; ~ **breeze** mäßige Brise; ~ **capacities** durchschnittliche Begabung ~ **income** bescheidenes Einkommen; ~ **language** gemäßigte Sprache; ~ **party** gemäßigte Partei; ~ **political views** gemäßigte politische Ansichten; ~**-priced** billig, preiswert; ~**-priced room** Hotelzimmer zu einem annehmbaren Preis; **to demand a ~ ransom** tragbares Lösegeld fordern; ~**-sized** in Mittelgröße; ~**-sized house** mittelgroßes Haus; ~ **weather** mildes Wetter.

moderateness *(claim)* Angemessenheit, *(quality)* Mittelmäßigkeit, *(prices)* Billigkeit.

moderating influence mäßigender Einfluß.

moderation Mäßigung, Maßhalten.

moderator *(arbiter)* Schiedsrichter, Vermittler, *(broadcasting)* Moderator, *(machine)* Ölzuflußregler, *(nonpartisan officer)* neutraler Vorsitzender, *(panel discussion)* unparteiischer Diskussionsleiter.

modern Mensch mit modernen Anschauungen, *(data processing)* [Daten]übertragungsgerät, *(print.)* moderne Antiqua;
~ *(a.)* modern, neuzeitlich;
with all ~ conveniences mit allem Komfort; ~ **English** Neuenglisch; ~ **history** neuere Geschichte; ~ **house** modernes Haus; ~ **language** lebende Sprache; ~ **languages** Neuphilologie; ~ **methods** neuere Richtung; ~ **school** *(Br.)* Realabteilung; ~ **times** Neuzeit; ~ **writer** moderner Schriftsteller.

modernism moderne Ansichten.

modernity, streamlined fortschrittliche Modernität.

modernization Modernisierung;
~ **loan** Modernisierungskredit; ~ **process** Modernisierungsprozeß; ~ **program(me)** Modernisierungsprogramm; ~ **project** Modernisierungsvorhaben; ~ **requirements** Modernisierungsbedürfnisse.

modernize *(v.)* modernisieren;
~ **a building** Gebäude mit technischen Neuerungen versehen.

modest bescheiden, anspruchslos;
to be ~ about one's achievements seine Tätigkeit nicht überbewerten; **to be ~ in one's requirements** bescheidene Ansprüche stellen;
~ **fortune** bescheidenes Vermögen; **to live in a ~ little house** in einem bescheidenen kleinen Haus wohnen.

modicum | of effort Mindestmaß an Anstrengung; ~ **of truth** Körnchen Wahrheit;
to live in a very small ~ in bescheidensten Verhältnissen leben;
to make a ~ of sense wenig sinnvoll sein.

modifiable änderungsfähig.

modification [teilweise] Abänderung, Modifikation, *(limitation)* Einschränkung, Umstellung;
subject to ~s Änderungen vorbehalten;
~ **of articles of association** Satzungsänderung; ~ **of the constitution** Verfassungsänderung; ~ **of a design** Musterabänderung; ~ **of the terms of a contract** Änderung der Vertragsbedingungen; **to make some ~s** einige Änderungen vornehmen; **to make ~s in a program(me)** Programmänderung vornehmen.

modified union shop gewerkschaftspflichtiger Betrieb mit Beschränkung auf neue Betriebsmitglieder.

modify *(v.)* [teilweise] abändern, umstellen, *(restrict)* einschränken;
~ **one's demands** seine Forderungen mäßigen; ~ **the whole structure of society** gesamte Gesellschaft umstrukturieren.

modish dress modischer Anzug.

modular housing vorfabrizierte Wohnungseinheiten.

modulate *(v.)* abstufen, modulieren, regulieren.

modulation Abstimmung, Regulierung, *(wireless)* Modulation.

module Kapsel, Modul.

modus Art und Weise, Modus, *(acquisition of property)* direkter Besitzerwerb;
~ **of an indictment** Verbrechensschilderung.

mogul gewichtige Persönlichkeit, Magnat;
~ **locomotive** *(US)* Personen- und Güterzuglokomotive.

moieties, to hold by *(joint tenants)* hälftigen Anteil haben.

moiety Halbteil, Hälfte.

moil Schinderei, Plackerei.

moist from ink druckfeucht.

mold *(US)* Schablone, Form, *(crumbling earth)* Ackerkrume, lockere Erde, *(matrix)* Matrize;
cast in the same ~ *(fig.)* aus demselben Holz geschnitzt;
~ *(v.)* formen, gießen, modellieren.

molder *(US)* Former, Gießer, *(print.)* Mustergalvano;
~ *(v.)* **away** vermodern.

molding *(US)* **of the corporate image** Gestaltung des Firmengesichts.

mole *(in harbo(u)r)* Mole, Hafendamm.

molecule Molekül.

molehill *(fig.)* Kleinigkeit;
to make a mountain out of a ~ aus einer Mücke einen Elefanten machen.

molest *(v.)* belästigen.

molestation Belästigung, *(law)* Besitzstörung.

mollifying remarks abschwächende Bemerkungen.

monzer *(sl.)* Mäzen.

moment Augenblick, Moment, *(importance)* Bedeutung, Tragweite, Wichtigkeit;
under the impulse of the ~ einer ersten Anregung folgend.

momentum of sales *(US)* Warenumsatz.

monarch Monarch, Herrscher.

monarchist Monarchist.

monarchy absolute unbeschränkte Monarchie;
constitutional (limited) ~ konstitutionelle Monarchie; **despotic ~** absolute Monarchie; **elective ~** Wahlmonarchie; **hereditary ~** Erbmonarchie.

Monday, Black *(sl.)* erster Schultag; **St. ~** *(Br.)* blauer Montag;
to take ~ off, to keep Saint ~ *(Br.)* blauen Montag machen.

monetarily weak währungsschwach.

monetarist Geldtheoretiker.

monetary geldlich, finanziell, monetär;
~ **aggregate** Geldgesamtbestand; ^ **Agreement** Währungsabkommen; ~ **anarchy** Währungsanarchie; ~ **area** Währungsgebiet; ~ **arrangements** Gelddisposition; ~ **authorities** Währungsbehörden, -instanzen; **International ^ Authorities** Weltwährungsbehörde; ~ **base** Zentralbankgeldmenge; ~ **body** Währungsorgan; ~ **brake** monetäre Bremse; ~ **capital** Geldkapital; ~ **claim** Geldforderung; ~ **collapse** Währungszusammenbruch; ^ **Commission** Währungsausschuß, -kommis-

sion; **National ^ Committee** Währungsausschuß; ~ **conference** Währungskonferenz; ~ **constitution** Währungsverfassung; ~ **contraction** Einschränkung der Geldmenge; ~ **contribution** Geldbeitrag; ~ **convention** Münzkonvention, Währungsabkommen; ~ **cooperation** Zusammenarbeit (Kooperation) auf dem Währungsgebiet; ~ **correction** Geldwertkorrektur, Wertsicherungssystem durch Indexkoppelung; ~ **council** Währungsbeirat; ~ **crisis** Währungskrise; ~ **curbs** Drosselung des Geldangebots; ~ **difficulties** Finanz-, Währungsschwierigkeiten; ~ **disaster** Währungskatastrophe; ~ **ease** Geldmarkterleichterungen; ~ **economics** Geldwirtschaft; ~ **equation** Geldausgleich; ~ **expansion** Geldausweitung; ~ **flows** Geldströme; ~ **fluctuation** Geldwertschwankungen; **International ^ Fund** Welt-, Internationaler Währungsfonds; ~ **gain** Währungsgewinn, -schnitt; ~ **gold** Münzgold; ~ **grant** Geldbeihilfe; ~ **growth rate** Zuwachsrate der Geldmenge; ~ **holdings** Geldbestand; ~ **indemnity** Geldabfindung; ~ **inflation** Geldinflation; ~ **influences** Währungseinflüsse; ~ **leaders** Währungskapazitäten; ~ **loss** Währungsverlust; ~ **market turmoil** große Unruhe am Geldmarkt; ~ **matters** Geldangelegenheiten, -wesen; ~ **measures** währungspolitische Maßnahmen; ~ **nature** Geldcharakter; **to provide fully to the increasing ~ needs** zunehmenden Geldbedarf hundertprozentig decken; ~ **official** Währungsführer; ~ **order** Währungsordnung; ~ **organization** Finanzgruppe; **to hold to restrictive ~ policies** harte Geldmarktpolitik betreiben; ~ **policy** Währungsfragen, -politik, geldpolitischer Kurs, Geldpolitik; **countercyclical ~ policy** monetäre Konjunkturpolitik; **Federal Reserve ^ Policy** *(US)* Geldmarktpolitik der Bundesnotenbank; **to carry out the ~ policy of a country** erforderliche währungspolitische Maßnahmen treffen; **to relax ~ policy** geldmarktpolitische Erleichterungen zulassen; **to shift ~ policy** geldmarktpolitische Änderungen vornehmen; ~ **policy devices** geldpolitische Maßnahmen; ~ **policy instruments** Geldmarktinstrumentarium; ~ **powers** *(US)* Währungskompetenz; ~ **pressure** Geldknappheit; ~ **proceeds of assets of the estate** *(US)* Summenvermächtnis; ~ **reform** Neuordnung des Geldwesens, Geld-, Währungsreform, Geldneuordnung; ~ **rehabilitation** Währungssanierung; ~ **relationship** Valutaverhältnis; ~ **relaxation** monetäre Auflockerungsmaßnahmen; ~ **reserve** *(Federal Reserve Bank, US)* Währungsreserve; ~ **restraint** monetäre Beschränkungsmaßnahmen, Geldknappung; ~ **restrictiveness** Geldrestriktion; ~ **restriction** monetäre Beschränkungsmaßnahmen, Geldknappung; ~ **reward** finanzielle Vergütung, Geldvergütung, -belohnung; ~ **scarcity** Geldmarktverknappung; ~ **scene** Währungsgebiet; **to tighten the ~ screws** Geldschraube fester anziehen; ~ **seminar** Währungsseminar; **to handle the ~ side** sich um die geldpolitische Aufgabe kümmern; ~ **situation** Währungslage; ~ **sovereignty** Währungshoheit; **in the ~ sphere** in geldwirtschaftlicher Hinsicht; ~ **stability** Geld-, Währungsstabilität; ~ **stabilization** Währungsstabilisierung; ~ **standard** Münzfuß, [Münz]standard, Währungsstandard, -einheit; ~ **statistics** Währungsstatistik; ~ **stock** *(US)* gesamter Geldbestand [eines Landes]; ~ **strain** Anspannung des Geldmarktes; ~ **structure** Geldverfassung, -gefüge, -struktur; ~ **supply** Geldbedarf; ~ **system** Geld-, Währungssystem; **international ~ system** internationales Währungssystem; ~ **techniques** währungspolitische Maßnahmen; ~ **and fiscal techniques** Geldmarktinstrumentarium; ~ **techniques at the government's disposal** geldmarkttechnische Möglichkeiten der Regierung; ~ **technocrat** Geldtechnokrat; ~ **theory** Geldtheorie; ~ **tightness** Geldverknappung; **to throw over the ~ traces** Geldmarktbeschränkungen über Bord werfen; ~ **transaction** Geldtransaktion; ~ **turmoil** Währungsaufruhr; ~ **union** Währungsunion; ~ **unit** Geld-, Währungseinheit; ~ **variable** währungspolitische Größe; ~ **wealth** Geldvermögen; ~ **wealth formation** Geldvermögensbildung.

monetization Ausmünzung, Münzprägung;
~ **of the debt** *(US)* Erhöhung des Zahlungsmittelumlaufs.

monetize *(v.)* *(coin)* [zu Gold] ausprägen, *(give standard value to)* Münzfuß festsetzen, *(legalize as money)* zum gesetzlichen Zahlungsmittel machen.

money Geld[sorte], Münze, *(amount of ~)* Geldbetrag, *(legal tender)* Zahlungsmittel, *(wealth)* Reichtum, Vermögen;
at a heavy cost of ~ unter schweren Geldopfern; **for ~** gegen Barzahlung, *(stock exchange)* netto Kasse; **for ready ~, for ~ out of hand** gegen bar; ~ **down** gegen bar; **in place of ~** an Zahlungs Statt; **in the ~** *(sl.)* bei Kasse; **ready ~ only** nur gegen Barzahlung; **for neither love nor ~** nicht für Geld und gute Worte; **pressed for ~** in Geldverlegenheit; **scant of ~** nur mit wenig Geld versehen; **short of ~** schlecht (knapp) bei Kasse; **worth the ~** preiswert, -würdig;

active ~ lebhafter Geldmarkt; ~ **advanced** ausgelegtes Geld, Vorschuß; **atonement** ~ Buße, Bußgeld, Reugeld, *(restoration)* Wiedergutmachung; **back** ~ Garantie für Rückvergütung bei Nichtgefallen; **bad** ~ Falschgeld; **bank** ~ *(US)* Buch, Giralgeld; **bargain** ~ Drauf-, An-, Handgeld; **barren** ~ totes Kapital; **base** *(Br.)* **(bogus)** ~ falsches Geld, Falschgeld; **black** ~ schwarzes Geld; **blood** ~ Kopf-, Blutgeld; **boarding** ~ Kostgeld; **boot** ~ Draufgabe; **borrowed** ~ geliehenes Geld, Fremd-, Leihgeld, Fremdmittel; **bottomry** ~ Bodmereigelder; **broken** ~ Kleingeld; **call** ~ *(US)* tägliches Geld, Geld auf Abruf, Tagesgeld; **cash** ~ *(US)* bares Geld; **caution** ~ Kaution; **cheap** ~ billiges Geld; **close** ~ knappes (teures) Geld; **coined** ~ Hartgeld; ~ **coming in** eingehende Gelder; **commodity** ~ *(US)* Indexwährung; **condemnation** ~ Entschädigungsbeitrag; **conduct** ~ *(witness)* Reisekosten; **conscience** ~ *(income tax)* nachgezahlte Einkommensteuer, Reugeld; **consideration** ~ Gegenwert in Geld, Entschädigung, *(shares, Br.)* Effektenstempel; **consigned** ~ anvertrautes Geld, Depositengelder; **consolidated** ~ Festgeld; **convertible** ~ konvertierbares Geld; **corporation** ~ Firmenvermögen; **counterfeit** ~ Falschgeld, falsches Geld; **covered** ~ *(US)* gedecktes Papiergeld; **credit** ~ Giralgeld; **current** ~ Kurantgeld, umlaufendes (kursierendes, im Verkehr befindliches) Geld, Landeswährung; **day-to-day** ~ *(Br.)* tägliches Geld, Geld auf tägliche Kündigung, Tagesgeld; **dear** ~ knappes (teures) Geld; **demand** ~ tägliches Geld, Tagesgeld; **deposit** ~ *(Br.)* Depositengelder, Buch-, Giralgeld; **deposited** ~ Hinterlegungssumme; **dispatch** ~ Vergütung für schnelle Entladung; **door** ~ Eintrittsgeld; ~ **down** *(sl.)* bares Geld; **dry** ~ bares Geld; ~ **due** ausstehendes Geld, Geldforderung; **earnest** ~ An-, Handgeld; **easier** ~ leichteres Geld; **easily earned** ~ leicht verdientes Geld; **easy** ~ billiges Geld, *(condition of money market)* flüssiger Geldmarkt; **easy-terms** ~ billiges Geld; **effective** ~ umlaufendes Geld; **emergency** ~ Notgeld; **entrance** ~ Eintrittsgeld; **even** ~ gerade passendes Geld, *(betting)* keine Annahme; **excess** ~ Geldüberhang; ~ **expended** verbrauchte Mittel; **facultative** ~ fakultatives Geld; **fiat** *(US)* **(fiduciary)** ~ ungedeckte Banknoten, Buch-, Giralgeld; **floating** ~ verfügbare Gelder; **foreign** ~ ausländische Zahlungsmittel; **forfeit** ~ Reugeld; **fractional** ~ Wechsel-, Kleingeld; **fugitive** ~ Fluchtgeld; **gate** ~ Eintritts-, Einlaßgeld; **good** ~ richtiges (echtes) Geld; ~ **had and received** [etwa] ungerechtfertigte Bereicherung; **happy** ~ für Vergnügungszwecke vorgesehener Geldbetrag; **hard** ~ frei konvertierbares Geld, *(US)* Münze, Hart-, Metallgeld; **hard-earned** ~ mühsam verdientes Geld; **head** ~ Kopfgeld; **hot** ~ heißes Geld, Fluchtgeld; **hush** ~ Bestechungs-, Schweigegeld; **immobilized** ~ festgelegtes Geld; **imprest** ~ Handgeld; ~ **invested** angelegtes Geld, Geschäftseinlage; **key** ~ *(Br.)* Mietvorauszahlung, Abstandsgeld, -zahlung; **lawful** ~ *(US)* gesetzliches Zahlungsmittel; ~ **left over** überzähliges Geld; ~ **lent** *(pleading)* wegen Darlehns; **light** ~ billiges Geld; **locked-up** ~ *(Br.)* fest angelegtes Geld; **lodging** ~ Zimmermiete; **long-term** ~ langfristiges Geld; ~ **made** mittels Zwangsvollstreckung eingetriebenes Geld; **mortgage** ~ Hypothekenvaluta; **near** ~ *(US)* geldähnliche Forderungen (Werte), leicht liquidierbare Einlagen; **night** ~ *(Br.)* kurzfristige Bankdarlehen an Wechselmakler; **nonsecured** ~ Geldbetrag ohne Sicherheiten; **nonstandard** ~ irreguläres Geld; **occupation** ~ Besatzungsgeld; **odd** ~ restliches Geld; **one-year** ~ Jahresgeld; **option** ~ Reugeld; **outstanding** ~ Geldforderung; **owing** ~ geschuldeter Betrag, Schuld, Außenstände; ~ **owing to us** *(balance sheet)* Guthaben; ~ **paid in** Geldeinlage, -eingang; ~ **paid out** Auszahlung; **paper** ~ Papiergeld; ~ **payable** *(balance of payment, US)* Zahlungsverpflichtung; ~ **payable periodically** regelmäßig zahlbare Beträge; ~ **paying no interest** brachliegendes Kapital; **pin** ~ Nadelgeld; **pocket** ~ Taschengeld; **possession** ~ *(Br.)* Verwahrungsgebühr für zwangsvollstreckte Gegenstände; **postal** ~ postalisch überwiesenes Geld; ~ **pouring in** eingehende Gelder; **premium** ~ Prämiengeld; **present** ~ bares Geld; **press** ~ Handgeld; **prize** ~ Prisengeld; **proper** ~ Zentralbankgeld; **public** ~s öffentliche Gelder (Mittel), Staatsmittel; **purchase** ~ Kaufpreis, -geld; **quasi** ~ *(US)* geldähnliche Forderungen; **ready** ~ Bargeld, flüssige[s] Geld[er] (Mittel); **real** ~ Gold-, Silbermünzen; ~ **receivable** *(balance of payment, US)* eingehende Gelder, Zahlungseingänge; ~ **received** Geldeingänge; ~ **received and expended** vereinnahmtes und verausgabtes Geld; **redemption** ~ Tilgungsbetrag; **regular** ~ *(US)* ziemlich festes Tagesgeld; **rent** ~ Pachtzins, -geld; **representative** ~ Papiergeld; **requisite** ~ Geldbedarf, notwendige Summe; ~ **safely invested** sicher angelegtes Geld; **salvage** ~ Bergelohn; **scrip** ~ *(US)* Schwundgeld; **secured** ~ gesicherte Geldforderung; **seed** ~ Starthilfe, Anfangskapital; **short-[term]** ~ kurzfri-

stiges Darlehen; **silver** ~ Silbergeld, -münzen; **small** ~ Kleingeld; **smart** ~ *(exemplary damages)* über den verursachten Schaden hinausgehende Entschädigungssumme, Schmerzensgeld, *(for release from engagement)* Reu-, Abstandsgeld; **soft** ~ *(US sl.)* Papiergeld; **sound** ~ gesunde Währung; **spare** ~ Erspartes, erübrigtes Geld; **spent** ~ aufgebrauchtes Geld; **stable** ~ Geld mit gleichbleibendem Wert; **stake** ~ Einsatz, Wettgebühr; **stall** ~ Standgeld; **standard** ~ vollwichtige Münze, Währungsgeld; **sterling** ~ vollwertiges Geld; **store-of-value** ~ wertbeständiges Geld; **straggling** ~ *(mil.)* Geldstrafe für unerlaubte Abwesenheit; **string-free** ~ ohne Auflagen zur Verfügung gestellte Geldbeträge; **substitute** ~ Zahlungssurrogat; **surplus** ~ überflüssiges Geld, *(foreclosure proceedings)* im Zwangsversteigerungsverfahren erzielter Überschuß; **table** ~ [Dienst]aufwandsentschädigung; **telegraphic** ~ telegrafisch überwiesenes Geld, telegrafische Überweisung; **three-months** ~ Vierteljahresgeld; ~ **thrown away** weggeworfenes Geld; **tied-up** ~ fest angelegtes Geld; **tight** ~ teures Geld, Geldknappheit; **till** ~ Geld in der Ladenkasse, Handgeld, -kasse, *(banking)* Kassenbestand; **time** ~ Festgeld, langfristiges Börsengeld (angelegtes Geld); **token** ~ Papiergeld, -währung; **trust** ~ Hinterlegungsgelder, Treuhand-, Stiftungsgelder, Mündelgeld, Depositeneinlagen, -gelder; **unemployed** ~ nicht angelegtes Kapital; **wasted** ~ herausgeworfenes Geld; **weekly** ~ Wochengeld; **white** ~ Silbergeld, *(counterfeit)* Falschgeld;

bills and ~ *(stock exchange)* Brief und Geld; ~ **in account** *(Br.)* Buch-, Giralgeld; ~ **of account** Rechnungsmünze, Landeswährung; ~ **on account** Guthaben; ~ **paid on account of costs** Gerichtskostenvorschuß; ~ **in the bank** Bankguthaben; ~ **at (on) call** Gelder auf Abruf, täglich fälliges Geld, Tagesgeld; ~ **at call and short notice** *(Br.)* Tagesgeld, kurzfristige Geldmarktkredite; **total** ~ **in circulation** Geld-, Zahlungsmittelumlauf; ~ **withdrawn from circulation** aus dem Verkehr gezogenes Geld; ~ **for the monthly clearance** Ultimogeld; **the** ~ **at my command** die mir zur Verfügung stehenden Mittel; ~ **paid into court** bei Gericht hinterlegtes Geld; ~ **on current account** täglich fälliges Geld; ~ **that is no longer current** ungültiges Geld; ~ **put by for a rainy day** Sparpfennig; ~ **on deposit** Gelddepot, Depositen, Bankguthaben; ~ **on deposit account** *(Br.)* auf einem Sparkonto angelegtes Geld; ~ **refunded in full** restlos zurückgezahltes Geld; ~ **for fuel supplied** Bezahlung von Benzinlieferungen; ~ **on hand** jederzeit verfügbares (verfügbare) Geld(er); ~ **lying idle** brachliegendes Geld, totes Kapital; ~ **paying no interest** brachliegendes Kapital; ~ **for jam** *(Br., sl.)* guter Profit für wenig Mühe, leicht verdientes Geld; ~ **of necessity** Notgeld; ~ **for old rope** leicht verdientes Geld; ~ **on short notice** kurzfristige Gelder, kurzfristig kündbares Geld; ~ **no object** Geld spielt keine Rolle; ~ **owing to us** uns zustehender Betrag; ~ **in plenty** viel Geld; ~s **provided by Parliament** *(Br.)* parlamentarisch bewilligte Mittel; ~ **in the post** (mail, *US*) unterwegs befindliche Gelder; ~ **put by for a rainy day** Sparpfennig; ~ **put up** angelegtes Geld; ~ **refunded in full** restlos zurückgezahltes Geld; ~ **at short notice** kurzfristig kündbare Einlagen, täglich fälliges Geld; ~ **held on trust** treuhänderisch verwahrtes Geld, anvertrautes Geld;

to advance ~ Geld vorschießen (vorstrecken); **to advance** ~ **on securities** Wertpapiere lombardieren; **to aid s. o. with** ~ jem. mit Geld aushelfen; **to appropriate** ~ Geld seiner Zweckbestimmung zuführen; **to ask for** ~ um Geld bitten; **to ask for more** ~ **for defence** Erhöhung des Verteidigungsetats beantragen; **to assist with** ~ mit Geld unterstützen; **to back s. o. with** ~ j. finanziell unterstützen; **to be about to relax** ~ geldmarktpolitische Erleichterungen in Erwägung ziehen; **to be after (out for)** ~ auf Geld aus sein; **to be coining** ~ Dukatenesel sein; **to be flush of** ~ reichlich mit Mitteln versehen (gut bei Kasse, bei Gelde) sein; **to be flush with new bonus** ~ durch Prämiengelder flüssig sein; **to be very flush with one's** ~ sorglos mit seinem Geld umgehen; **to be hard set to find** ~ in großer Geldverlegenheit sein; **to be hard up for** ~ kaum Geld haben; **to be in the** ~ *(competitor)* Gewinner sein; **to be lawful** ~ *(US)* Gültigkeit haben; **to be liberal with** ~ in Geldangelegenheiten großzügig sein; **to be made of** ~ aus lauter Geld bestehen; **to be very neat with one's** ~ mit seinem Geld geizen; **to be open-handed with** ~ mit Geld freigebig sein; **to be pressed for** ~ **from all quarters** von allen Seiten um Geld angegangen werden; **to be pushed for** ~ in Geldverlegenheit (-schwierigkeiten) sein; **to be rolling in** ~ im Gelde schwimmen (ersticken); **to be short of** ~ knapp bei Kasse (Gelde) sein, geringe Geldmittel zur Verfügung haben; **to be simply coining** ~ enorm viel Geld verdienen, Geld scheffeln; **to be about to relax** ~ geldmarktpolitische Erleichterungen in

Erwägung ziehen; **to be worth ~** sein Geld wert sein; **to bestow one's ~ wisely** sein Geld klug anlegen; **to borrow ~** Geld aufnehmen (leihen); **to bring in big ~** das große Geld bringen; **to bucket ~** im Geld schwimmen; **to call in ~** Kapital kündigen; **to change ~** Geld wechseln; **to coin ~** Geld scheffeln; **to collect the ~ for the newspaper once a month** Zeitungsgeld monatlich kassieren; **to come into ~** zu Geld kommen, Erbschaft machen; **to come into the big ~** plötzlich zu viel Geld kommen; **to come into one's own ~** Verfügungsgewalt über sein Geld bekommen; **to contribute ~** Geld zuschießen; **to convert into ~** zu Geld machen, realisieren, versilbern; **to convert ~ to one's own use** Geld unterschlagen; **to cost a great deal of ~** schweres Geld kosten; **to cost a packet of ~** Haufen Geld kosten; **to count ~ before s. o.** jem. Geld vorzählen; **to create ~** Geld schöpfen, Geldschöpfung vornehmen; **to cut down ~ for the arts** finanzielle Zuwendungen für künstlerische Belange kürzen; **to deposit ~ with a bank** Geld bei einer Bank einzahlen; **to disburse ~** Geld verauslagen; **to divert ~** Geld abzweigen; **to do s. th. for ~** etw. aus Geldgründen tun; **to draw ~** Geld abheben; **to draw on s. o. for ~** j. um Geld angehen; **to drop a lot of ~** sehr viel Geld verlieren; **to earn big (heavy) ~** viel (schweres) Geld verdienen; **to earn a lot of ~ in one coup** auf einen Schlag viel Geld verdienen; **to ease ~ free** Geld flüssig machen; **to elicit ~ from s. o.** Geld aus jem. herausholen; **to embark ~** Geld hineinstecken, Kapital anlegen; **to favo(u)r easier ~** sich für Erleichterungen des Geldmarktverkehrs einsetzen; **to feel the need of ~** nicht genügend Geld haben; **to feel no qualms about borrowing ~ from friends** bei Freunden hemmungslos Geld pumpen; **to finance ~ away** Geld beiseiteschaffen; **to finance with short-term ~** mit kurzfristigen Geldmitteln finanzieren; **to find the ~** Geld beschaffen, Kosten aufbringen; **to find the ~ for an undertaking** Geld für ein Unternehmen auftreiben; **to fleece s. o. of all his ~** j. um sein ganzes Geld betrügen; **to fling one's ~ about** mit dem Geld nur so um sich werfen (schmeißen); **to fritter away one's ~** sein Geld verpulvern; (verplempern); **to furnish ~** Geld beschaffen; **to get along with little ~** mit wenig Geld auskommen; **to get fat off s. one's ~** sich an jem. fett machen; **to get one's ~ back** sein Geld zurückbekommen; **to get ~ out of s. o.** Geld aus jem. herausholen; **to get rid of one's ~** sein Geld loswerden; **to get good value for one's ~** sein Geld gut angelegt haben; **to get one's ~'s worth** für sein Geld etw. [Gleichwertiges] bekommen; **to give ~ to the bank for safekeeping** sein Geld einer Bank anvertrauen; **to give s. o. a run for his ~** jem. für sein Geld etw. bieten; **to go in for ~** viel Geld zu verdienen suchen; **to go through all one's ~** sein ganzes Geld ausgeben; **to grant ~** Geld (Mittel) bewilligen; **to handle large sums of ~** große Geldbeträge verwalten; **to have ~ in the funds** (Br.) Geld in Staatspapieren angelegt haben; **to have ~ lodged with s. o.** Geld bei jem. stehen haben; **to have ~ on one** Geld bei sich haben; **to have ~ in the bank** Geld auf der Bank [liegen] haben; **to have ~ to burn (blow)** Geld wie Heu haben; **to have ~ in a business** an einem Unternehmen beteiligt sein; **to have a little ~ in reserve** kleine Geldreserve haben; **to have lots of ~** scheffelweise Geld haben; **to have ~ owing** Außenstände haben; **to have ~ of one's own** eigenes Vermögen haben; **to have one's pockets full of ~** seine Taschen voller Geld haben; **to have ~ put by** Geld zurückgelegt haben; **to have the ~ required** über die erforderlichen Mittel verfügen; **to have a pot of ~** Unmenge Geld haben, steinreich sein; **to have a run for one's ~** etw. für sein Geld geboten bekommen; **to have scads of ~** Geld wie Heu (Mist) haben; **to have ~ in sufficiency** genügend Geld haben; **not to have any ~ on one** kein Geld bei sich haben; **to hold the ~ in dispute independently** im Streit befangene Geldbeträge auf neutralen Konten führen; **to hold ~ to the order of s. o.** Geld zu jds. Verfügung halten; **to husband one's ~** sparsam mit seinem Geld umgehen (wirtschaften); **to invest one's ~ to good account** sein Geld gut anlegen; **to invest one's ~ in stocks and shares** sein Geld in Aktien anlegen; **to jockey s. o. out of all his ~** j. um sein ganzes Geld betrügen; **to keep s. o. in ~** j. mit Geld versehen; **keep ~ at a bank** Geld bei einer Bank stehen haben; **to keep the odd ~** restliches Geld behalten; **to keep s. o. out of ~** j. mit der Bezahlung hinhalten, jem. sein Geld vorenthalten; **to keep s. o. short of ~** j. knapphalten; **to lay out one's ~ to advantage** sein Geld vorteilhaft anlegen; **to lay out one's ~ profitably** sein Geld nutzbringend anlegen; **to leave all one's ~ to charity** sein gesamtes Vermögen wohltätigen Zwecken hinterlassen; **to lend ~ on interest** Geld auf Zinsen ausleihen; **to lend ~ on mortgage** Hypothekendarlehn gewähren; **to lend ~ on security** Geld gegen Sicherheiten ausleihen; **to let one's ~ lie idle** sein Geld nicht arbeiten lassen; **to let s. o. whistle for his ~** j. um sein Geld betteln lassen; **to live on little ~** mit wenig Geld auskom-

men; **to lodge ~ with s. o.** Geld bei jem. hinterlegen; **to lodge ~ in the bank** Geld bei der Bank deponieren; **to look after one's ~** seine paar Groschen zusammenhalten; **to loosen the lid on tight ~** Geldmarktverknappung beseitigen; **to lose ~ on s. th.** bei etw. draufzahlen; **to make ~** Geld verdienen; **to make (play) ducks and drakes of (with) one's ~** (sl.) sein ganzes Geld verprassen, mit dem Geld nur so um sich schmeißen; **to make off with the ~** mit der Kasse durchbrennen; **to make out the ~** Geld herbeischaffen; **to make ~ out of s. th.** Geld aus etw. herausschlagen; **to make ~ hand over fist** schnell Geld verdienen; **to make piles of ~** schöne Stange Geld verdienen; **to make bad use of one's ~** sein Geld schlecht anlegen; **to manage one's ~ more effectively** aus seinem Geld mehr machen; **to mark up call ~** (US) Satz für tägliches Geld heraufsetzen; **to marry ~** Geldheirat eingehen, nach Geld heiraten; **to misspend ~** Geld falsch anlegen; **to mobilize ~** Geld flüssigmachen; **to obtain ~ by fraud** sich Geld durch Betrug verschaffen; **to offer s. o. ~** jem. Geld anbieten; **to owe ~** Geld schulden; **to part with one's ~** sich verausgaben; **to part s. o. from his ~** j. um sein Geld erleichtern; **to part with all one's ~** sein ganzes Geld hergeben; **to pay ~ into an account** Geld auf ein Konto einzahlen; **to place ~ on deposit** Geld fest anlegen; **to place ~ in savings accounts** Geld auf Sparkonten anlegen; **to pay in German ~** in deutschem Geld zahlen; **to pay ~ down (in ready ~)** bar [auf den Tisch des Hauses] bezahlen; **to place ~ on interest** Geld auf Zinsen ausleihen; **to play for ~** ums Geld spielen; **to pocket ~** Geld einstreichen (einstecken); **to press for ~** Geld erpressen; **to procure ~** Geld aufbringen; **to pump ~ into a country** Geld in ein Land hineinpumpen; **to pump s. o. for ~** (fam.) j. anpumpen; **to put ~ by** Geld auf die hohe Kante legen; **to put ~ into a bank** Geld bei einer Bank einzahlen; **to put ~ into circulation** Geld unter die Leute bringen; **to put a good deal of ~ aside** schönes Stück Geld zurücklegen; **to put ~ into houses** sein Geld in Hausbesitz anlegen; **to put ~ into land** Geld in Grundbesitz investieren; **to put ~ out** Geld unterbringen (anlegen); **to put out ~ at interest** Geld verzinslich anlegen (auf Zinsen ausleihen); **to put up the ~ for an undertaking** Geld für ein Unternehmen aufbringen; **to put ~ to good use** Geld vernünftig anlegen; **to raise ~** Geld aufnehmen; **to raise any ~ requisite** erforderlichen Kredit aufnehmen; **to raise ~ on the security of the assets** Geld gegen Verpfändung der Anlagenwerte aufnehmen; **to rake together a little ~** ein bißchen Geld zusammenkratzen; **to receive ~** Geld vereinnahmen; **to recover one's ~** sein Geld zurückbekommen; **to refund ~** Geld zurückerstatten; **to relieve s. o. of his ~** j. um sein Geld bringen; **to remit ~** Geld überweisen, Geld anweisen; **to remit ~ home each month** monatlich Geld nach Hause schicken; **to replace stolen ~** gestohlenes Geld ersetzen; **to require ~** Geld kosten; **to reserve ~ for unforeseen contingencies** Geld für unvorhergesehene Ereignisse zurücklegen; **to run into ~** ins Geld gehen; **to rush s. o. for ~** j. eilig um Geld bitten; **to scare up ~** Geld auftreiben; **to scatter ~ broadcast** mit dem Geld nur so um sich werfen (schmeißen); **to scramble for ~** sich um Geld balgen; **to scramble up ~** Geld zusammenkratzen; **not to see the colo(u)r of one's ~ from s. o.** keinen Pfennig Geld von jem. zurückbekommen; **to shell out one's ~** sein Geld auf den Tisch legen; **to shove ~ into one's pocket** sich die Taschen voller Geld stopfen; **to sink ~ in an annuity** sein Geld in Rentenwerten anlegen; **to sink all one's ~ into the concern** sein ganzes Geld ins Geschäft stecken; **to spend ~** Geld ausgeben; **to spend ~ on s. o.** Geld für j. aufwenden; **to spend one's ~ on books** sein Geld zum Ankauf von Büchern verwenden; **to spend ~ with a free hand** Geld leicht ausgeben; **to spend lots of ~** eine Menge Geld ausgeben; **to spend one's ~ for no purpose** sein Geld umsonst ausgeben; **to spend ~ like water (without stint)** Geld mit vollen Händen ausgeben; **to spill ~** Geld ausspucken; **to spring ~** (Br., coll.) Geld locker machen; **to squeeze ~ out of s. o.** jem. Geld abknöpfen; **to stink of ~** (sl.) nach Geld stinken; **to stint s. o. for ~** jem. Geld abknöpfen; **to stretch one's ~** mit Mark und Pfennig rechnen; **to take ~ from the till** Geld aus der Ladenkasse nehmen; **to take ~ out of a fund** Geldbetrag aus einem Fonds entnehmen; **to take up ~ at the bank** Bankkredit aufnehmen; **to talk s. o. out of his ~** jem. sein Geld abschwatzen; **to tell one's ~** (US) sein Geld zählen; **to throw one's ~ about** sein Geld verschleudern; **to throw ~ about like dirt** mit dem Geld nur so um sich werfen; **to throw one's ~ away** unnützen Aufwand treiben; **to throw away one's ~ for nothing** sein Geld für nichts und wieder nichts ausgeben; **to throw ~ down the drain** Geld zum Fenster hinauswerfen; **to throw good ~ after bad** (fam.) gutes Geld schlechtem Geld nachwerfen; **to touch for ~** anpumpen; **to transfer ~** Geld überweisen; **to transfer ~ by**

cable telegrafisch Geld überweisen; **to trifle away one's ~** Geld vergeuden; **to turn into ~** in Geld umsetzen, zu Geld machen; **to turn one's ~ three times a year** sein Kapital dreimal im Jahr umsetzen; **to use public ~ only for legitimate purposes** öffentliche Gelder bestimmungsgemäß ausgeben; **to venture ~ in speculation** Geld spekulativ anlegen; **to want [to get] one's ~ back** sein Geld zurückverlangen; **to waste ~** Geld durchbringen; **to withdraw ~** Geld abheben; **to worm ~ out of s. o.** Geld aus jem. herauskitzeln;
there is ~ in it damit kann man viel Geld verdienen;
black ~ account Schwarzgeldkonto; **~ act** Finanzgesetz; **~ affairs** Geldangelegenheiten; **~ agency** Geldinstitut; **~ agent** Geldwechsler, *(banker)* Bankier; **~ allowance** Barvergütung, Geldzuschuß; **~ amount** Geldbetrag; **~ article** Nachrichten über den Geldmarkt, Geldmarktbericht; **ready-~ article** Barartikel; **~-back guarantee** Geldrückgabezusicherung; **~ bargain (business)** Effektivgeschäft; **~ bill** *(parl.)* Finanzvorlage, Steuergesetzantrag; **~ bote** Geldstrafe; **~ box** Sammel-, Sparbüchse; **~ broker** Geldvermittler, -makler; **~ bug** *(US sl.)* Geldprotz; **ready-~ business** Kassageschäft; **~ capital** Geldkapital; **~ center** *(US)* **(centre,** *Br.***)** Geld-, Finanzzentrum; **~-changer** Geldwechsler; **~-changer's business** Wechselstube; **~ changing** Geldwechseln; **~ chest** Geldkassette, -schrank; **~ circulation** Geldumlauf; **to reflect easier ~ circumstances** erleichterte Geldmarktbedingungen aufweisen; **~ claim** Zahlungsanspruch, Geldforderung; **~ clause** *(Br., parl.)* Geldbewilligungsklausel; **~ compensation** Geldentschädigung; **~ concerns** Geldangelegenheiten; **~ condemnation** gerichtlich festgesetzte Geldentschädigung; **~ costs** Geld[beschaffungskosten]; **~ credit system** Geldkreditsystem; **~ crisis** Geldkrise; **~ damage** finanzieller Schaden, geldliche Einbuße; **~ dealer** Geldwechsler; **~ dealings** Geldgeschäfte; **~ debt** Geldschuld; **~ demand** Geldbedarf; **~ desk** *(New York stock exchange)* Maklerstand für Tagesgeld; **~ difficulties** Geldnot, -schwierigkeiten; **~ drawer** Geldschublade, Ladenkasse; **~ earnings** Gelderlös; **~-earning** Geld verdienend; **~ economy** Geldwirtschaft; **~ embargo** Geldausfuhrverbot; **~ equivalent** Gegenwert in Geld; **~ expert** Währungsspezialist, -fachmann; **~ gap** Finanzierungslücke; **~ getter** Geldjäger; **~ gift** Geldspende, -geschenk; **~ grant** Geldbewilligung; **~ growth** Geldzuwachs, -zunahme; **~-guzzling** viel Geld verschlingend; **~ hoarder** Geldhorter; **~ holdings** Geldbestände; **~ income** Geldeinkommen; **~ indemnity** Geldentschädigung; **~ inflation** Geldinflation; **~ inflows** Geldzufluß; **~ interest** Geldverzinsung; **~ interests** Finanzwelt; **to have no ~ interest in a concern** finanziell an einem Unternehmen nicht beteiligt sein; **~ investment** Geldanlage; **~ jobber** *(Br.)* Geldhändler, -maker; **~ land** testamentarisch zum Ankauf in einem Land vorgesehenes Geld; **~ lent and lodged book** *(Br.)* Kontokorrentbuch; **~ letter** *(US)* Geld-, Wertbrief; **~ loan** Kassendarlehn; **~ loser** Verlustträger, -betrieb; **~-losing operation** Verlustgeschäft, -betrieb; **~-mad** geldsüchtig; **~-making** *(a.)* Geldverdiener; **~-making** Geldverdienen, -erwerb, gewinnbringend, einträglich; **~ management** Finanz-, Vermögensverwaltung; **~ management operation** Vermögenstransaktion; **~ manager** Vermögensverwalter; **professional ~ manager** Geldfachmann.
money market Geldmarkt;
active ~ lebhafter Geldmarkt; **parallel ~** grauer Wertpapiermarkt, Parallelmarkt; **two-tier ~** gespaltener Geldmarkt;
~ and capital market Kreditmarkt;
to be a creditor in the ~ auf dem Geldmarkt aktiv sein; **to place pressure on the ~** Druck auf den Geldmarkt ausüben; **to produce a ripple effect on the ~** geldmarktpolitische Konsequenzen auslösen; **to tap the ~ heavily** Geldmarkt stark in Anspruch nehmen; **to tempt investors out of the ~ into bonds** Geldmarktanleger zum Rentenkauf verführen;
~ business Geldmarktgeschäft; **~ conditions** Geldmarktbedingungen; **~ control** Geldregulierung; **~ indebtedness** Geldmarktverschuldung; **~ instruments** Geldmarktinstrumentarium; **~ operations (transactions)** Geldmarktgeschäfte; **~ paper** Geldmarktpapier; **~ rates** Geldmarktsätze; **~ regulations** Geldmarktvorschriften; **under its ~ regulating arrangements** im Rahmen der Geldmarktregulierung; **~ report** Börsenbericht; **~ securities** Geldmarktpapiere; **~ situation** Geldmarktlage.
money matters Geldsachen, -angelegenheiten; **to handle one's day-to-day ~ matters** seinen täglichen Geldverkehr abwickeln; **~ means** Geldmittel; **to begin its new ~-minded balancing act** seine geldmarktbedingten Balanzierungskünste wieder aufnehmen; **~ motive** Geldmotiv.
money order *(Br.)* *(M.O.)* Zahlungs-, Geld-, Postanweisung, Geldüberweisung durch die Post;

bank ~ Bankanweisung; **cable ~** Kabelanweisung; **domestic postal ~** Inlandspostanweisung; **express ~** *(US)* telegrafische Geldanweisung; **foreign (international) postal ~** Auslandspostanweisung; **postal ~** *(US)* Geldüberweisung durch die Post, Postanweisung; **service ~** gebührenfreie Postanweisung; **telegraph[ic] ~** telegrafische Postanweisung; **trade charge ~** *(Br.)* Nachnahmepostanweisung;
~ telegram telegrafische Geldüberweisung.
money output monetär bewertete Produktionsmenge; **~ panic** Währungspanik; **~ parcel** Geldpaket, -rolle; **~ payment** Barzahlung; **~ payments** Geldrente; **~ penalty** Geldstrafe; **~ pinch** [zeitweilige] Geldknappheit; **~ pool** *(US)* in Krisenzeiten für Börsenmakler gebildetes Bankenkonsortium; **~ post** *(US)* Maklerstand [für tägliches Geld an der New Yorker Börse]; **~ power** Geldmacht; **~-proof** unbestechlich; **~ rate** Geldmarktsatz, Geldkurs; **easy ~ rates** leichte Geldmarktsätze; **to continue their turn towards ease in ~ rates** Tendenz in der Politik der Geldmarkterleichterungen fortsetzen; **~ relief** Geldentschädigung, -unterstützung; **~ request** Geldanforderung; **~ reserve** Geldreserve; **~ restrictiveness** restriktive Geldpolitik; **~ sale** Barverkauf; **~ saver** wirtschaftlicher Artikel; **~ scarcity** Geldknappheit, -verknappung; **~ shortage** Geldverknappung; **~ spinner** *(coll.)* [etwa] Dukatenesel; **~ squeeze** [zeitweilige] Geldklemme; **tight ~ squeeze** angespannte Finanzlage; **~ standard** Währungs[standard]; **~ starvation** Geldaushungerung; **~ stock** *(US)* gesamter Geldbestand [eines Landes]; **~ stock policy** Geldmengenpolitik; **~ stringency** *(US)* Geldknappheit, -mangel; **~ substitute** Geld-, Zahlungssurrogat; **~ supply** Geldbedarf, -versorgung, -vorrat; **effective ~ supply** tatsächlich verfügbares Geld; **to keep an iron grip on the ~ supply** Geldversorgung im eisernen Griff halten; **to leak damaging into a country's internal ~ supply** inländische Geldversorgung gefährlich aufblähen; **~-supply economist** Geldtheoretiker; **~-supply expansion multiplier** Kreditschöpfungsmultiplikator; **~-supply figures** statistische Angaben (statistisches Material) über die Geldversorgung; **~-supply growth** wachsender Geldbedarf, verbesserte Geldversorgung, Geldbedarfszuwachs; **to turn off the ~-supply tap** Geldhahn zudrehen; **~-supply target** Geldbedarfssollziffer; **~-supply trend** Geldbedarfsentwicklung; **independent ~ system** Freigeldsystem; **~ taker** Kassierer; **to turn on the ~ tap** Geldhahn auf drehen; **~ teller** Geldzähler, Kassierer; **~ theorist** Geldtheoretiker; **~ tightness** Geldknappheit; **~ transaction** Geld-, Effektivgeschäft; **~ transactions** Geldverkehr; **~ and capital transactions** Geld- und Kapitalverkehr; **~ transfer** Geldüberweisung; **~ transfers** Zahlungsverkehr; **~ transmission** Geldüberweisung; **to shake the ~ tree** finanzielle Zuwendungen hereinholen; **~ troubles** Geldschwierigkeiten, -sorgen; **~ trust** *(US)* Bankenkonzentration; **~ turnover** Geldumsatz; **~ value** Gestehungs-, Geldwert, *(stock exchange)* Kurswert; **~ vault** *(US)* Kassenschrank; **~ veil** Geldschleier; **~ wage** Geld-, Nominal-, Barlohn; **~ winner** geschäftlicher Erfolg; **~'s worth** Geldeswert; **to get one's ~'s worth** etw. für sein Geld bekommen;
~ [is] no object *(advertisement)* auf Geld wird nicht gesehen.
moneyage Münzgerechtigkeit.
moneybag Geldbeutel, *(rich person)* Geldprotz, -sack.
moneyed pekuniär, finanziell, *(wealthy)* mit Geld versehen, reich, vermögend;
~ aristocracy Geldaristokratie, -adel; **~ assistance** finanzielle Hilfe; **~ capital** flüssiges Anlagekapital, liquide Vermögenswerte, Kapitalvermögen; **~ classes** besitzende Klassen; **~ corporation** *(US)* Bank- und Versicherungsgesellschaft, Kapitalgesellschaft; **~ influence** finanzieller Einfluß; **~ interests** finanzielles Interesse, finanzielle Belange, *(capitalist)* Kapital[isten], Finanzwelt, Hochfinanz; **~ man** wohlhabender (begüterter) Mann, Kapitalist; **~ people** reiche Leute, Geldleute, Kapitalisten; **~ resources** Geldquellen.
moneygrubber Geizkragen.
moneygrubbing geldgierig.
moneylender gewerbsmäßiger Geldgeber, -verleiher;
to entangle o. s. with~s sich mit Geldverleihern einlassen;
⌂ Act *(Br.)* Kreditwesengesetz; **to register o. s. under the ⌂ Act** *(Br.)* Kreditgewerbe anmelden.
moneylending gewerbsmäßiger Geldverleih, Kreditgewerbe;
~ agreement Kreditvertrag; **~ company** Geldinstitut.
moneyless mittellos, ohne Geld.
moneymonger Geldverleiher, *(usurer)* Wucherer.
moneymongering Geldverleih, -handel.
moneysaving wirtschaftlich.
monger Händler, Krämer;
~ *(v.)* handeln, Geschäfte machen mit.

mongrel Bastard, Mischling;
~ **race** Mischrasse.

monition Mahnung, *(Admiralty Law)* [Vor]ladung;
general ~ Ladung aller am Verfahren beteiligten Personen.

monitor Warnzeichen, Warnung, *(broadcasting)* Monitor, *(mar.)* Feuerlöschboot, *(person employed to monitor)* Abhörer, *(schoolboy)* aufsichtführender Schüler, Klassenordner, *(tel.)* Abhörgerät, -anlage, *(television)* Fernsehkontrollbild;
~ *(v.)* Nachrichtenverbindungen überwachen, *(tel.)* ab-, mithören, *(radio television)* Sendequalität überwachen;
~ **a call** Radiodurchsage überwachen; ~ **a circuit** in eine Leitung eintreten;
~ **jack** Mithör-, Überwachungsklinke; ~ **room** Abhörraum; ~ **screen** Kontrollschirm.

monitoring Funk-, Rundfunküberwachung, *(recording)* Aufzeichnungskontrolle;
~ **booth** *(film)* Abhörbox; ~ **committee** Überwachungsausschuß; ~ **desk** Mischpult; ~ **device** Abhörvorrichtung; ~ **key** *(tel.)* Mithörtaste; ~ **operator** Tonmeister; ~ **picture** *(television)* Kontrollbild; ~ **procedure** Überwachungsverfahren; ~ **receiver** *(television)* Kontrollempfänger; ~ **station** Abhör-, Überwachungsstelle; ~ **system** Überwachungsanlagen.

monitory|item *(balance sheet)* Merkposten; ~ **letter** Mahnschreiben; **to write a ~ letter** brieflich mahnen; ~ **system** Überwachungs-, Abhörsystem.

monk Mönch, *(print., Br.)* Schmierstelle, Kleks.

monkey *(Br., sl.)* 500 Pfund, *(mining)* Wetterschacht;
~ *(v.)* Schabernack treiben;
~ **about with s. th.** mit etw. herumfummeln; ~ **about with tools** an Geräten herumhantieren;
to get one's ~ up fuchtig werden; **to put s. one's ~ up** j. auf die Palme bringen;
~ **act** Sensationsschau; ~ **business** fauler Zauber, Schwindelgeschäft, Affentheater; ~ **time** *(sl.)* Sommerzeit; ~ **tricks** Affenkommödie, Mätzchen; ~ **wrench** Universalschraubenschlüssel; **to throw a ~ wrench into the machinery** *(US)* etw. durcheinanderbringen.

monochrome einfarbig.

monocrat Alleinherrscher.

monocratic autokratisch.

monogamy Einehe.

monograph Einzeldarstellung, Monographie.

monometallism Monometallismus, Einzelwährung.

monoplane Eindecker.

monopolies and merger|commission *(Br.)* Kartellaufsichtsbehörde; ~ **and Restrictive Practices Act** *(Br.)* Kartellgesetz.

monopolism Monopolwirtschaft.

monopolist Monopolist, Monopolbesitzer, Alleinhändler.

monopolistic monopolartig, monopolistisch, marktbeherrschend;
semi-~ monopolähnlich;
~ **agreement** Monopolabkommen; **to discourage ~ business practices** monopolistische Geschäftsmethoden bekämpfen; **of ~ character** monopolartig, -ähnlich; ~ **competition** monopolistischer Wettbewerb; ~ **control** monopolistische Beherrschung, Monopolkontrolle; ~ **enterprise** Monopol, marktbeherrschendes Unternehmen; ~ **exploitation** monopolistische Ausbeutung; ~ **industry** Monopolindustrie; ~ **position (situation)** Monopolstellung; ~ **power** wirtschaftliche Machtstellung, Monopolmacht; ~ **price** Monopolpreis; **to split a ~ structure** Monopolstellung beseitigen; ~ **tendencies** monopolistische Tendenzen; ~ **use of a patent** Ausschließlichkeitsnutzung eines Patents; ~ **wages** Monopollöhne.

monopolization Monopolisierung.

monopolize *(v.)* monopolisieren, Monopol besitzen, allein beherrschen, *(engross)* an sich reißen;
~ **a business** Monopolstellung haben; ~ **the conversation** das große Wort führen; ~ **a meeting** Gesprächsführung in einer Sitzung an sich reißen.

monopolized industry Monopolindustrie.

monopoly ausschließliche Gewerbeberechtigung, Monopol[stellung], Ausschließlichkeits-, Alleinherstellungsrecht, *(company having ~)* marktbeherrschendes Unternehmen, *(sale)* Alleinverkauf, -vertriebsrecht;
promotive of ~ *(US)* monopolfördernd;
absolute ~ absolutes Monopol; **artificial ~** gesetzliches Monopol; **beneficial ~** verbraucherfreundliche Monopolstellung; **buyer's ~** Nachfragemonopol; **commercial ~** Handelsmonopol; **complete ~** hundertprozentiges Monopol; **discriminating ~** diskriminierende Ausnutzung einer Monopolstellung; **export ~** Ausfuhrmonopol; **fiscal ~** Staats-, Finanzmonopol;

global ~ Weltmonopol; **government ~** Staatsmonopol, Regie; **import ~** Einfuhrmonopol; **internal ~** Binnenmonopol; **manufacturing ~** Produktions-, Fabrikationsmonopol; **market ~** Marktbeherrschung; **natural ~** natürliches Monopol; **note-issuing ~** Banknotenmonopol; **outright ~** vollständiges Monopol; **partial ~** Teilmonopol; **patent ~** Monopolpatent; **production ~** Fabrikations-, Produktionsmonopol; **public consumption ~** staatliches Verbrauchermonopol; **special privilege ~** gesetzliches Monopol; **spirits ~** Branntweinmonopol; **state ~** Staatsmonopol; **state-buying ~** staatliches Einkaufsmonopol; **trade ~** Handelsmonopol; **foreign-trade ~** Außenhandelsmonopol;
~ **in the issue of bank notes** Banknotenmonopol; ~ **of learning** Bildungsmonopol; ~ **of opinion** Meinungsmonopol; ~ **of production** Produktionsmonopol; ~ **of foreign trade** Außenhandelsmonopol;
to break up a ~ Monopol auflösen; **to enforce a ~** Monopol ausüben; **to establish a ~** Monopol errichten; **to foster a ~** Monopol errichten; **to grant a ~** Monopol verleihen; **to have the ~ of (on, US) s. th.** Monopol von etw. haben; **to hold a ~** Monopolstellung innehaben; **to pass beyond the boundaries of the ~** Monopolgrenze überschreiten;
~ **agreement** *(Br.)* Monopolabsprache, Kartell; ~ **capitalism** Monopolkapitalismus; ~ **charge** Kartellklage, -verfahren; ~ **committee** Kartellaufsichtsamt; ~ **enterprise** marktbeherrschendes Unternehmen, Monopolunternehmen; ~ **income** Monopolrente; ~ **intent** Monopolisierungsabsicht; ~ **issue** Monopolfrage; ~ **position** Monopolstellung; ~ **power** Monopolmacht; ~ **price** Monopolpreis; ~ **privilege** Monopolrecht; ~ **problem** Monopol-, Kartellproblem; ~ **profits** Monopolgewinne, -erträge; ~ **rent** Monopolgewinn, -rente; ~ **revenue** Monopolrente; ~ **right** gewerbliches Schutzrecht, Ausschließlichkeitsrecht; **to infringe ~ rights** Ausschließlichkeitsrechte verletzen; ~ **rôle** Monopolrolle; ~ **status** Monopolstellung; ~ **system of foreign trade** Außenhandelsmonopol; ~ **tax** Monopolabgabe; ~ **value** Monopolverkaufswert; ~ **wealth** Monopolvermögen.

monotony of work Monotonie im Arbeitsprozeß.

monopsony Nachfragemonopol.

monorail Einschienenbahn;
~ **connections** Einschienenbahnverbindungen.

monotype [Letterguß]setzmaschine, Monotype;
~ **composition** Monotypesatz.

monster Mißgeburt, Monster.

montage Foto-, Bildmontage.

month Monat;
at three ~s' date drei Monate dato; **by the ~** monatlich; **early in the ~** zum Monatsanfang; **of last ~** vorigen Monats; **twice a ~** halbmonatlich; **within a ~** binnen Monatsfrist;
calendar ~ Kalendermonat; **current ~** laufender Monat; **this ~** im laufenden Monat;
~ **of electioneering** Wahlmonat; ~ **under examination** Berichtsmonat; ~ **under report (review)** Berichtsmonat; **corresponding ~ of the previous year** Vorjahrsmonat; **a ~ of Sundays** eine ewig lange Zeit;
to ask £ 100 a ~ as rent Monatsmiete von 100 Pfund verlangen; **to be heard next ~** *(law case)* nächsten Monat anstehen; **to fall due next ~** nächsten Monat fällig werden; **to hire by the ~** monatlich mieten; **to owe for three ~s rent** seit einem Vierteljahr die Miete schuldig bleiben; **to pay by the ~** monatlich bezahlen; **to send goods every ~** monatlich liefern; **to settle up at the end of the ~** am Monatsende bezahlen;
to employ s. o. on a ~-to-~ basis j. monatlich anstellen; **a ~'s credit** monatlich eingeräumter Kredit; **three ~s' draft** Dreimonatspapier; **one ~ loan** Monatsgeld; **three ~s' money** Vierteljahresgeld; **subject to a ~'s notice** mit monatlicher Kündigung; **one ~'s notice** Kündigungsfrist von einem Monat; **to give a ~'s notice** zum nächsten Ersten kündigen; ~ **order** *(US)* für einen Monat geltender Börsenauftrag; **a ~'s pay** Monatsgehalt; **to receive one's ~'s pay** sein monatliches Gehalt bekommen; **a ~'s supply** Monatsbedarf; **this ~'s trading** letzter Monatsumsatz.

monthly Monatsschrift, monatlich erscheinende Zeitschrift;
~ *(a.)* monatlich;
~ **account** monatliche Rechnung, Monatsrechnung; ~ **accruals** Ultimofälligkeiten; ~ **allowance** *(student)* Monatswechsel; ~ **average** Monatsdurchschnitt; ~ **balance sheet** Monatsbilanz, monatlicher Bilanzbogen; ~ **instal(l)ment** Monatsrate; ~ **labo(u)r summary** monatliche Lohnübersicht; ~ **magazine** Monatszeitschrift; ~ **mean** Monatsmittel; ~ **pay** Monatsgehalt; ~ **payment** monatliche Zahlung; ~ **preceding** *(advertising)* Anzeigenschluß einen Monat vor Erscheinen; ~ **production**

Monatsproduktion; ~ **profit** Monatsverdienst; ~ **publication** monatlich erscheinende Veröffentlichung; ~ **reconciliation** monatliche [Konten]abstimmung; ~ **rental** Monatsmiete; ~ **report** Monatsbericht; ~ **report of the labo(u)r force** monatliche Meldung über den Beschäftigungsstand; ~ **requirements** Monats-, Ultimobedarf; ~ **return** *(Br.)* Monatsausweis; ~ **return ticket** Monatskarte; ~ **review** Monatsbericht; ~ **salary** Monatsgehalt; ~ **season ticket** Monats[zeit]karte; ~ **settlement** Monatsabschluß, Ultimoabrechnung; ~ **statement [of account]** Monatsausweis, -aufstellung, -abschluß, -bericht; ~ **tenancy** monatlich kündbares Mietverhältnis; ~ **wages** monatlich gezahlte Löhne.

monument [Bau]denkmal, Grabstein, *(stone)* Vermessungspunkt, Grenz-, Markstein.

monumental | inscription Grabinschrift; ~ **operation** Massenveranstaltung.

mood Stimmung, Laune;
   in the ~ to write zum Schreiben aufgelegt;
   mercurial ~s wechselnde Stimmungen;
   ~ **of the market** Marktlage, Börsenstimmung;
   to be in sunny ~ *(stock market)* sich ganz aufgeschlossen zeigen; **to be in the ~ to refuse point blank** zu einer glatten Absage neigen; **to be in the ~ to work** arbeitslustig (arbeitswillig) sein; **to be a man of ~s** launenhaft veranlagt (Stimmungsmensch) sein; **to catch s. o. in one of his good ~s** j. erwischen, wenn er guter Laune ist; **to have ~s** Stimmungen unterworfen sein, launenhaft sein;
   ~ **swing** *(US)* Stimmungsumschwung.

moody index *(US)* Weltpreisindex für Stapelware.

moon Mond;
   once in a blue ~ einmal im Jahrhundert;
   cry for the ~, to ask for the ~ and stars nach Unmöglichem verlangen; **to promise s. o. the ~ and stars** jem. das Blaue vom Himmel versprechen; **to shoot the ~** bei Nacht und Nebel ausrücken;
   ~ **landing** Mondlandung; ~ **shot** Raketenstart zum Mond.

moonlight Mondschein;
   ~ **flit[ting]** *(renter, sl.)* Ausziehen bei Nacht und Nebel; ~ **walk** Mondscheinspaziergang.

moonlighter *(US coll.)* Doppelverdiener.

moonlighting *(US coll.)* Ausübung einer Nebenbeschäftigung.

moonshine *(fig.)* Unsinn, Gefasel, *(sl.)* Fusel, geschmuggelter Schnaps;
   to talk ~ Unsinn reden;
   ~ *(a.)* *(fig.)* leer, nichtig, *(sl.)* geschmuggelt.

moonshiner *(US sl.)* Schwarzbrenner, Branntweinschmuggler.

moor Moor;
   ~ **a ship** Schiff vertäuen (festmachen);
   to be ~ed festgemacht liegen.

moorage Liegeplatz[gebühr];
   ~ **mast** Ankermast.

mooring Verankerung, Vertäuung;
   ~ **buoy** Hafen-, Vertäuungsboje, Festmacheboje; ~ **dues** Liegeplatzgebühren.

moot *(Br.)* Diskussion theoretisch möglicher Rechtsfälle;
   ~ *(v.)* zur Diskussion stellen;
   ~ *(a.)* umstritten, strittig;
   ~ **case** hypothetischer Fall; ~ **point** strittiger Punkt, noch offene Frage; ~ **question** juristisches Problem.

mop Scheuer-, Wischlappen;
   Mrs. ⌐ *(fam.)* Putzfrau;
   ~ *(v.)* säubern, abwischen.

mop up *(v.)* aufräumen, *(mil.)* säubern;
   ~ **an area** feindliches Gebiet durchkämmen; ~ **arrears of work** Arbeitsrückstände aufarbeiten; ~ **the floor with s. o.** mit jem. Schlitten fahren; ~ **a mess** Durcheinander wieder in Ordnung bringen; ~ **profits** dicke Gewinne einstreichen; ~ **the trenches** Schützengräben aufrollen; ~ **unemployment by means of export growth** der Arbeitslosigkeit mit Exportsteigerungen zu Leibe rücken.

moral Moral;
   contrary to good ~s gegen die guten Sitten verstoßend;
   ~**s** Sittenlehre, Ethik;
   loose ~s lockere Sitten; **professional ~s** Standesethik;
   ~ **of a story** Moral einer Geschichte;
   to draw the ~ of an experience Moral einer Geschichte ziehen; **to improve the ~s of a country** allgemeines sittliches Bewußtsein anheben; **to undermine ~s** Moral zersetzen;
   ~ *(a.)* moralisch, sittlich, charakterlich;
   ~ **act** gute Tat; ~ **action** willkürliche Handlung; ~ **certainty** an Sicherheit grenzende Wahrscheinlichkeit, moralische Gewiß-

heit; **of good ~ character** charakterlich einwandfrei; ~ **conduct** moralische Verhaltensweise; ~ **consideration** moralische Verpflichtung; ~ **conviction** moralische Überzeugung; ~ **courage** Zivilcourage; **to be in ~ danger** sittlich gefährdet sein; ~ **duress** moralischer Druck; ~ **evidence** Wahrscheinlichkeitsbeweis; ~ **faculty** moralisches Urteilsvermögen, Sittlichkeitsgefühl; ~ **force** sittliche Kraft; ~ **fraud** vollendeter Betrug; ~ **hazard** *(insurance)* Risiko falscher Angaben des Versicherten, subjektives Risiko; ~ **imperative** moralischer Imperativ; ~ **incentive** moralischer Anreiz; ~ **insanity** moralischer Defekt, krankhafte Hemmungslosigkeit; ~ **law** Sittengesetz; **to live a ~ life** einwandfreies Leben führen; ~ **man** Mann mit moralischen Grundsätzen; ~ **necessity** sittliche Notwendigkeit; ~ **obligation** moralische Verpflichtung, Anstandspflicht; **to feel a ~ obligation** sich moralisch verpflichtet fühlen; ~ **outrage** moralische Empörung; ~ **philosophy** Moralphilosophie; ~ **pressure** moralischer Druck; ~ **principles** moralische Grundsätze; ~ **question** Frage der Moral; ~ **rearmament** moralische Wiederaufrüstung; ~ **right** moralisches Recht; ~ **science** Sittenlehre, Ethik; ~ **sense** Sittlichkeitsgefühl; **to act against the ~ sentiment of the community** gegen die guten Sitten verstoßen; **to raise the ~ standard of the community** allgemeines Sittlichkeitsgefühl anheben; ~ **suasion** gütliches Zureden, *(cyclical policy)* Maßhalteappell, Seelenmassage; ~ **support** moralische Unterstützung; ~ **turpitude** moralische Verworfenheit; ~ **value** moralischer Wert; ~ **victory** moralischer Sieg; ~ **virtues** moralische Tugenden; ~ **whitewashing** moralische Schönfärberei.

morale Moral, geistige Verfassung;
   ~ **of the army** Kampfmoral des Heeres; **failing ~ of the enemy** nachlassender Kampfgeist des Feindes; ~ **at work** Betriebs-, Arbeitsmoral;
   to boost the ~ Arbeitsmoral heben; **to build ~** zur Moral beitragen;
   ~**-boosting** Durchhalteappell.

moralism Moralpredigt.

moralist Sittenlehrer, Moralist.

morality sittliches Verhalten, Moral, Ethik;
   commercial ~ kaufmännische Berufsehre.

moralization moralische Auslegung, Moralpredigt.

moralize *(v.)* moralische Betrachtungen anstellen, moralisieren.

morally moralisch, von einem moralischen Standpunkt;
   ~ **bound** moralisch verpflichtet; ~ **firm** innerlich gefestigt.

moratorium, moratory Moratorium, Zahlungsaufschub, Stillhalteabkommen;
   ~ **on debt** Schuldenmoratorium; ~ **on immigration** Einwanderungsstopp; ~ **on prices (in price increase)** Preismoratorium;
   to grant a ~ Moratorium gewähren.

moratory loan Moratoriumsanleihe.

morbid krankhaft, pathologisch.

morbidity Kränklichkeit, *(sickness rate)* Prozentsatz der Kranken, Erkrankungsziffer.

morgue *(US)* Leichenhalle, -schauhaus, *(journalism, US)* [Zeitungs]archiv.

moribund Todgeweihter.

morning Morgen, Vormittag;
   the ~ after [the night before] Kater;
   ~ **call** Höflichkeits-, Vormittagsbesuch; ~ **dress** Konferenzanzug; **early ~ edition** Morgenausgabe; ~ **gift** Morgengabe; ~ **glass** Frühschoppen; ~ **loan** *(US)* Tagesgeld für Makler; ~ **mail** *(US)* Morgenpost; ~ **news** *(broadcasting)* Frühnachrichten; ~ **paper** Morgenblatt, -zeitung; ~ **performance** Matinée; ~ **post** *(Br.)* Morgenpost; ~ **room** *(hotel)* Frühstückszimmer; ~ **session** Vormittagssitzung; ~ **shift** Frühschicht; ~ **train** Vormittagszug; ~ **watch** *(mar.)* Morgenwache.

moron Schwachsinniger, Trottel.

Morris Plan Bank *(US)* Kleinkreditbank.

morse | code Morsealphabet; ~ **telegraph** Morsetelegraph.

morsel [Lecker]bissen.

mortal sterblich, *(coll.)* endlos, totlangweilig;
   ~ **agony** Todeskampf, Agonie; ~ **disease** tödliche Krankheit; ~ **enemies** Todfeinde; ~ **fear** Todesangst; ~ **hour** Todesstunde; ~ **hurry** Mordseile; ~ **offence** tödliche Beleidigung; ~ **power** Menschenkraft; ~ **remains** sterbliche Überreste (Hülle), Leiche; ~ **struggle** erbitterter Kampf; **of no ~ use** absolut zwecklos.

mortality Sterblichkeit[sziffer], Sterbehäufigkeit, *(asset)* Lebensdauer;
   actual ~ *(insurance)* eingetretene Sterblichkeit; **heavy (high) ~** hohe Sterblichkeitsziffer; **infant ~** Säuglingssterblichkeit; **low ~** niedrige Sterblichkeitsziffer;
   low-~ area Gebiet mit niedriger Sterblichkeit; ~ **control** Sterblichkeitskontrolle; ~ **curve** Sterblichkeitskurve; ~ **rate** Sterb-

lichkeitsziffer; ~ **ratio** Sterblichkeitsquotient; ~ **reduction** Rückgang der Sterblichkeitsziffer; ~ **risk** Sterblichkeitsrisiko; ~ **statistics** Sterbestatistik; ~ **table** Sterbetafel, Sterblichkeitstabelle.

mortar *(mar.)* Lebensrettungskanone.

mortgage *(act of conveying as security)* hypothekarische Belastung, *(estate of land)* Grundpfandrecht, -schuld, Hypothek, hypothekarische Sicherheit, *(deed)* Hypothekenbrief, *(security for payment)* Pfandurkunde, -recht;

by way of a ~ hypothekarisch; **covered by a** ~ hypothekarisch belastet; **on** ~ hypothekarisch; **secured by** ~s durch Grundpfandrechte gesichert;

adjustment ~ Hypothek zur Sicherung von Inhaberschuldverschreibungen; **aggregate** ~ Gesamthypothek; **aircraft** ~ Pfandrecht an einem Luftfahrzeug; **amortization** ~ Amortisationshypothek; **blanket** ~ Global-, Gesamt-, Generalhypothek; **bulk** ~ *(US)* Verpfändung ganzer Bestände; **chattel** ~ Mobiliarverpfändung, [etwa] Sicherungsübereignung; **closed** ~ dem Betrag nach unveränderliche Hypothek, Festgeldhypothek; **closed-end** ~ von der Höhe der Forderung und dem Umfang des belasteten Grundstücks unabhängige Hypothek; **collective** ~ Gesamthypothek; **common-law** ~ gewöhnliche Hypothek; **completed** ~ ordnungsgemäß bestellte Hypothek; **consolidated** ~ *(US)* Gesamthypothek; **construction** ~ Bau[geld]hypothek; **contributory** ~ für mehrere Gläubiger bestellte Hypothek; **conventional** ~ Sicherungshypothek; **corporate** ~ von einer Aktiengesellschaft aufgenommene Hypothek; **cutthroat** ~ Hypothek zu mörderischen Bedingungen; **defaulted** ~ notleidende Hypothek, verfallene Hypothek; **development** ~ Hypothek zur Erschließung von Baugelände; **discharged** ~ gelöschte Hypothek; **distress-sale** ~ Zwangshypothek; **distressed** ~ gepfändete Hypothekforderung; **dry** ~ [etwa] Grundschuld; **equitable** ~ hypothekenähnliches Sicherungsrecht; **farm** ~ Hypothek auf landwirtschaftlichem Grundbesitz; **first** ~ *(Br.)* erste (erststellige, erstrangige, bevorrechtigte) Hypothek, Ersthypothek; **fixed** ~ Festgeldhypothek; **fleet** ~ Pfandrecht auf alle Flugzeuge eines Unternehmens; **floating** ~ Globalverpfändung; **foreclosed** ~ verfallene Hypothek; **general** ~ Global-, Gesamthypothek; **government-backed** ~ Hypothekenzusage mit Staatsgarantie; **house** ~ Eigenheimhypothek; **index-linked** ~ mit Indexklauseln ausgestattete Hypothek; **instal(l)ment** ~ Tilgungs-, Amortisationshypothek; **insured** ~ mit einer Lebensversicherung gekoppelte Hypothek; **judicial** ~ *(Louisiana)* gerichtlich entstandenes Pfandrecht, Zwangshypothek; **junior** ~ *(US)* nachrangige (im Range nachgehende) Hypothek; **leasehold** ~ Verpfändung eines Pachtgrundstücks; **legal** ~ *(Br.)* kraft Gesetzes entstandene Hypothek, *(shares)* Aktienverpfändung durch Registereintragung; **limited open-end** ~ bis zum Höchstbetrag in Anspruch genommene Belastung; **low-start** ~ Hypothek mit Tilgungsstreckung; **maximum** ~ Höchstbetragshypothek; **open** ~ nicht voll valutierte Hypothek; **option** ~ Landesdarlehn mit Grundbuchsicherung, grundbuchlich gesicherte verbilligte Hypothek; **ordinary** ~ Verkehrshypothek; ~s **outstanding** hypothekarische Verpflichtungen; **overlying** ~ nachstellige (nachrangige) Hypothek; **owner's** ~ [etwa] Eigentümergrundschuld; **paid off** ~ abgelöste Hypothek; **participating** ~ mehreren Gläubigern zustehende Hypothek; **party** ~ treuhänderisch hinterlegter Hypothekenbrief [von Gesamtgläubigern]; ~s **payable** *(general ledger, US)* hypothekarische Verpflichtungen, Hypothekenschulden; **prior** ~ vorrangige Hypothek; **private-housing** ~ Eigenheimhypothek; **puisne** ~ *(Land Charges Act, Br.)* nicht grundbuchlich registrierte, gesetzlich entstandene Hypothek, nachrangige Hypothek; **purchase-money** ~ Restkaufgeldhypothek; **real-estate** ~ *(US)* Grundstückshypothek; ~ **receivables** *(balance sheet, US)* hypothekarisch gesicherte Forderungen, Hypothekenforderungen; **recorded** ~ *(US)* Buchhypothek; **prior-recorded** ~ *(US)* im Range vorgehende Hypothek; **refunding** ~ Ablösungshypothek; **repayment** ~ Abzahlungs-, Ratenhypothek; **residential** ~ Eigenheim-, Wohnungsbauhypothek; **revalorized** ~ aufgewertete Hypothek; **running-account** ~ *(Br.)* Höchstbetragshypothek; **second** ~ zweitrangige Hypothek, Zweithypothek; **senior** ~ *(US)* im Rang vorgehende (bevorrechtigte) Hypothek; **[preferred] ship** ~ *(US)* [vorrangige] Schiffshypothek; **standing** ~ Festhypothek; **subsequent** ~ nachrangige Hypothek; **tacit** ~ *(Louisiana)* kraft Gesetzes entstandene [Sicherungs]hypothek; **technical** ~ formgerecht bestellte Hypothek; **terminable** ~ Amortisationshypothek; **third** ~ drittrangige Hypothek; **trust** ~ Sicherungshypothek; **ultra-vires** ~ satzungsmäßig nicht gedeckte Hypothek; **underlying** ~ Vorrangshypothek; **unified** ~ Einheitshypothek; **unlimited** ~

offene Hypothek; **unregistered** ~ *(Br.)* [etwa] Briefhypothek; **Welch** ~ Nutzpfand;

~ **on the currency** Währungshypothek; ~ **by deposit of title deeds** Hypothekenbestellung durch Hinterlegung von Eigentumsurkunden; ~ **of goods** [etwa] Sicherungsübereignung; ~ **of an equitable interest** Verpfändung eines obligatorischen Anspruchs; ~ **of land** Grundstücksbelastung, Grundpfandrecht; ~ **on leasehold property** Verpfändung eines Pachtgrundstücks; ~ **on real estate** Grundpfandrecht, Grundstückshypothek; ~ **repayable in a lump sum** Kündigungshypothek; ~ **of shares** Aktienverpfändung, Sicherungsübereignung von Kapitalanteilen; ~ **over ships** Schiffshypothek; ~ **for a fixed sum** Festgeldhypothek;

~ *(v.) (personal property)* verpfänden, *(real estate)* hypothekarisch belasten, Hypothek bestellen;

~ **o. s. to a clause** sich einer Bestimmung unterwerfen; ~ **one's happiness** *(fam.)* sein Glück versuchen; ~ **one's house** sein Haus hypothekarisch belasten; ~ **a piece of real estate** Grundstück hypothekarisch belasten; ~ **one's reputation** seinen guten Ruf riskieren;

to assume a ~ Hypothek [unter Anrechnung auf den Kaufpreis] übernehmen; **to be in** ~ verpfändet sein; **to borrow on** ~ **by deposit of title deeds** *(Br.)* Hypothek gegen Hinterlegung von Eigentumsurkunden aufnehmen, Geld gegen hypothekarische Sicherheit aufnehmen; **to call in a** ~ Hypothek kündigen; **to clear [off] a** ~ Hypothek tilgen (zurückzahlen); **to close a** ~ Hypothek für verfallen erklären; **to complete a** ~ Hypothek bestellen; **to cover by a** ~ hypothekarisch sicherstellen; **to create (deliver) a** ~ Pfandrecht (Hypothek) bestellen; **to default on one's** ~ mit der Verzinsung und Amortisation seiner Hypothek in Verzug geraten; **to discharge a** ~ Hypothek löschen; **to effect a** ~ **with a building society** Bausparhypothek aufnehmen; **to encumber with a** ~ mit einer Hypothek (hypothekarisch) belasten; **to execute a** ~ aus einer Hypothek zwangsvollstrecken; **to extinguish a** ~ Hypothek amortisieren (tilgen); **to foreclose a** ~ Hypothek für verfallen erklären (kündigen), *(US)* aus einer Hypothek die Zwangsvollstreckung betreiben; **to give in** ~ verpfänden; **to have a** ~ **recorded in the office of the register of deeds** *(US)* Hypothek in das Grundbuch eintragen lassen; **to hold a** ~ Hypothekengläubiger (Pfandgläubiger) sein; **to issue a** ~ Hypothekendarlehn aufnehmen; **to lend on** ~ auf eine Hypothek leihen, Hypothekendarlehn gewähren; **to pay off a** ~ Hypothek ablösen (tilgen, zurückzahlen); **to pay off the first** ~ erste Hypothek ablösen; **to place a** ~ **on a property** Hypothek auf einem Grundstück eintragen lassen; **to pool** ~s Hypotheken vereinigen; **to raise a** ~ **on a house** Hypothek auf ein Haus aufnehmen, Haus beleihen; **to record a** ~ *(US)* Hypothek eintragen; **to redeem a** ~ Hypothek ablösen (tilgen); **to register a** ~ *(Br.)* Hypothek [im Grundbuch] eintragen; **to register a** ~ **at the port of registry** *(Br.)* Schiffshypothek beim Heimathafen registrieren; **to release a** ~ Hypothek im Grundbuch löschen lassen; **to repay a** ~ Hypothek tilgen; **to satisfy a** ~ Hypothek ablösen (tilgen, zurückzahlen); **to secure a debt by** ~ Schuld hypothekarisch sicherstellen; **to tack** ~s Hypotheken verschiedenen Ranges zusammenschreiben; **to take a** ~ Hypothek aufnehmen; **to take over a** ~ Hypothek übernehmen; **to wipe off a** ~ Hypothek tilgen (zurückzahlen);

~ **account** Hypothekenkonto; ~ **advance** Hypothekarkredit; ~ **agreement** Hypothekendarlehnsvertrag; ~ **amortization** Hypothekentilgung, Amortisation einer Hypothek; ~ **assignment** Hypothekenabtretung; ~ **assistance** Hypothekenbeschaffung; ~ **bank** Hypothekenbank; ~ **bank business** Hypothekenbankgeschäft; **long-term** ~ **bank lendings** langfristige Ausleihungen im Hypothekenbankgeschäft; ~ **bond** hypothekarisch gesicherte Schuldverschreibung, Pfandbrief; **first** ~ **bonds** durch erststellige Hypothek gesicherte Pfandbriefe; **total** ~ **bonds outstanding** Pfandbriefumlauf; ~ **broker** Hypothekenmakler; ~ **broking** Hypothekenvermittlung; ~ **business** Hypothekengeschäft; ~ **buying** Hypothekenanlagen, -käufe; ~ **caution** Hypothekenvormerkung; ~ **certificate** Hypothekenbrief, -urkunde; ~ **charge** *(Br.)* hypothekarische Belastung, Hypothekenbelastung; ~ **claim** hypothekarisch gesicherte Forderung; **[junior]** ~ **claim** [nachstehende] Hypothekenforderung; ~ **company** Hypothekenbank; ~ **contract** Hypothekenbestellung, Bestellung einer Hypothek; ~ **creditor** Hypothekengläubiger; ~ **debenture** *(Br.)* hypothekarisch gesicherte [Grund]schuldverschreibung, Hypothekenpfandbrief; ~ **debenture stockholder** *(Br.)* Hypothekenpfandbriefinhaber; ~ **debt** hypothekarisch gesicherte Forderung, hypothekarische Belastung, Hypothekenschuld; ~ **debtor** Hypothekenschuldner; ~ **deed** Verpfändungsurkunde, *(real estate)* Hypothekenbrief, -schein, -urkunde; ~ **department** Hypothekenabteilung; ~ **endorsement scheme** Hypothekengewährung gegen Abtretung einer Versicherung für den Erlebensfall; ~ **facility** Hypothekenangebot; ~ **finance (financing)** Hypothekenfinazierung; ~ **foreclosure** (US) Zwangsvollstreckung aus einer Hypothek; ~ **foreclosure suit** (US) Zwangsvollstreckungsverfahren; ~ **form** Hypothekenformular; ~ **guarantee** Hypothekenzusage; ~ **guaranty insurance** Hypothekengarantieversicherung; ~ **guaranty policy** Hypothekenzusageversicherung; ~ **indebtedness** Hypothekenverschuldung; ~ **instrument** Verpfändungsurkunde; ~ **insurance company** Hypothekenversicherungsanstalt; ~ **interest** Hypothekenzinsen, *(fire insurance)* Versicherungsinteresse des Hypothekengläubigers; ~ **interest payments** Hypothekenzinszahlungen; ~ **interest rate** Hypothekenzinssatz; maximum ~ **interest rate** Hypothekenhöchstzins; ~ **interest relief** für Hypothekenzinszahlungen gewährte Steuervergünstigung; ~ **investments** Hypothekengeschäft; first ~ **investments** Anlagen in Ersthypotheken; ~ **lender** Hypothekengeldgeber; ~ **lending** Hypothekenausleihungen; ~ **lending institution** Hypothekenbankinstitut; ~ **liability** Hypothekenschuld; ~ **lien** Grundpfandrecht; ~ **loan** Hypothekendarlehn, Hypothekarkredit, hypothekarisch gesichertes Darlehn; first ~ **loan** erststelliger Hypothekarkredit; ~ **loan and investment company** (US) Hypothekenbank, Bodenkreditinstitut; ~ **loan application** Antrag auf Gewährung eines Hypothekendarlehns; ~ **loss** Hypothekenausfall; ~ **market** Hypothekenmarkt; to force-feed ~ **markets with big budget surpluses** Hypothekenmärkte verstärkt mit Etatüberschüssen anreichern; ~ **money** Hypothekenvaluta; ~ **moratorium** Hypothekenmoratorium; ~ **note** hypothekarisch gesicherte Schuldurkunde, Hypothekenbrief; ~ **obligation** hypothekarische Verpflichtung; ~ **papers** Hypothekenwerte; ~ **participation certificate** Hypothekenpfandbrief; ~ **payment** Hypothekenrückzahlung, -tilgung; ~ **payment delinquency** nicht eingehaltene Hypothekenrate; ~ **period** Laufzeit einer Hypothek; ~ **pool** Hypothekenfonds; ~ **rates** Hypotheken[zins]sätze; ~ **recording office** (US) Hypothekenregister; ~ **redemption insurance** für Hypothekenrückzahlung abgeschlossene Lebensversicherung; ~ **registry** (US) Hypothekenregister; ~ **repayment** Hypothekenrückzahlung, -tilgung; ~ **sales** Hypothekenabschlüsse; to introduce a low-start ~ **scheme** Hypothekenfinanzierung mit Tilgungsstreckung vermitteln; ~ **security** hypothekarische Sicherheit; ~ **service** Hypothekenbereitstellung; ~ **subsidy scheme** Hypothekensubventionierungssystem; **option ~ system** Gewährung verbilligter Landesdarlehn mit Grundbuchsicherung; ~ **tax relief** Steuerbegünstigung für gezahlte Hypothekenzinsen; ~ **term** (Br.) Laufzeit einer Hypothek; ~ **transaction** Hypothekargeschäft, Hypothekenvertrag; ~ **underwriting agency** (US) Hypothekengarantiekasse.

mortgageable pfändbar, hypothekisierbar, hypothekarisch belastbar, hypothekenfähig.

mortgaged verpfändet, hypothekarisch belastet; ~ **property** belasteter Grundbesitz, verpfändetes Vermögen.

mortgagee Pfandgläubiger, -inhaber, *(real estate)* Grundpfand-, Hypothekengläubiger; **equitable** ~ hypothekenähnlicher Pfandgläubiger; **legal** ~ erststelliger Hypothekengläubiger; **prior** ~ im Rang vorgehender Hypothekengläubiger; **subsequent (subordinate)** ~ im Rang nachgehender (nachstehender) Hypothekengläubiger; ~ **of land** Hypothekengläubiger; ~ **in possession** Pfandgläubiger im Besitz des Pfandstücks; ~ **clause** *(fire insurance)* Hypothekenklausel; ~ **endorsement** Abtretung des Versicherungsanspruches an den Hypothekengläubiger.

mortgager, mortgagor Sicherungsgeber, Verpfänder, Pfand-, Hypothekenschuldner; **original** ~ ursprünglicher Hypothekenschuldner.

mortician (US) Leichenbestatter.

mortification Demütigung, Kränkung, *(Scot.)* Übergang auf die tote Hand.

mortify *(v.)* demütigen, kränken; ~ **land for a charitable purpose** *(Scot.)* Grundvermögen der öffentlichen Hand zu wohltätigen Zwecken überlassen.

mortise *(print.)* ausgeklinktes Klischee; ~ **lock** Steckschloß.

mortmain [Grundstücksüberlassung an die] tote Hand, unveräußerliches Gut; **in** ~ unveräußerlich, im Vermögen der toten Hand; ~ *(v.)* an die tote Hand veräußern.

mortuary (Br.) Leichenhalle; ~ **dividend** *(insurance, US)* Todesfalldividende; ~ **rites** Bestattungsgebräuche; ~ **table** *(insurance, US)* Sterblichkeitstabelle.

mosaic *(aviation)* Reihenbild.

mosquito | boat *(craft) (mar.)* Schnellboot; ~ **net** Moskitonetz.

mossback (US) Reaktionär, Spießer.

most-favo(u)red nation | clause Meistbegünstigungsklausel; ~ **policy** Präferenzpolitik; ~ **principle** Meistbegünstigungsprinzip; ~ **rate** Meistbegünstigungssatz; ~ **status** Meistbegünstigungsstellung; ~ **tariff** Meistbegünstigungstarif; ~ **treatment** Meistbegünstigung.

most profitable purchase Artikel mit größter Gewinnspanne.

motel (US) Motel, Kraftfahrerhotel.

mothball Mottenkugel, *(grid, sl.)* Streber, Büffler; **in** ~**s** *(mil.)* eingemottet; ~ *(v.) (mil.)* einmotten; **to put into the** ~**s** in die Mottenkiste verbannen; **to take out of** ~**s in a jiffy** in kürzester Zeit bei Bedarf wieder einsetzen.

mother Mutter, Ahnfrau, *(fig.)* Quelle, Ursprung, *(religious house)* Äbtissin, Oberin; **expectant** ~ werdende Mutter; **working** ~**s** berufstätige Ehefrauen; ~**-in-law** Schwiegermutter; ~ *(v.)* bemuttern, wie eine Mutter sorgen, *(adopt)* an Kindes Statt annehmen, *(book)* Urheberschaft anerkennen; ~ **a novel on s. o.** jem. einen Roman zuschreiben; ~**s' aid (allowance, compensation)** Sozialrente für bedürftige Mütter mit minderjährigen Kindern; ~ **country** Mutterland; ~'s **Day** Muttertag; ~ **ditch** (US) Hauptkanal; ~ **gate** Hauptförderstrecke; ~'s **help** Haustochter; ~ **lode** Hauptflöz; ~**s' pension** Sozialrente für bedürftige Mütter mit minderjährigen Kindern; ~ **ship** (Br.) Mutterschiff; ~ **tongue** Muttersprache; ~ **wit** Mutterwitz.

motherhood Mutterschaft.

Mothering Sunday (Br.) Muttertag.

motif Leitgedanke, Motiv.

motion Bewegung, Gang, *(machine)* Antrieb, *(proposal)* Antrag; **in** ~ *(vehicle)* in Fahrt befindlich; **of one's own** ~ aus eigenem Antrieb; **abandoned** ~ zurückgezogener Antrag; **adjournment** ~ Vertagungsantrag; **cross** ~ Gegenantrag; **dilatory** ~ *(parl.)* Obstruktions-, Verzögerungsantrag; **dropped** ~ zurückgezogener Antrag; **formal** ~ Formalantrag, Verfahrensantrag; **no-confidence** ~ *(parl.)* Mißtrauensantrag; **next business** ~ Antrag auf Behandlung des nächsten Tagesordnungspunktes; **original** ~ ursprünglicher Antrag; **parliamentary** ~ im Parlament eingebrachter Antrag; **previous-question** ~ Antrag auf Übergang zur Tagesordnung; **privileged** ~ *(parl.)* Dringlichkeitsantrag; **procedural** ~ Verfahrensantrag, *(parl.)* Geschäftsordnungsantrag; **special** ~ Antrag, über den nur in mündlicher Verhandlung entschieden werden kann; **substantive** ~ Antrag zur Sache; ~ **for adjournment (to adjourn)** Vertagungsantrag, *(law court)* Antrag auf Einstellung des Verfahrens; ~ **to amend a** ~ Abänderungsantrag; ~ **on appeal** Antrag in der Berufungsinstanz; ~ **in arrest of judgment** Antrag auf Einstellung des Verfahrens; ~ **to set aside judgment** Aussetzungsantrag; ~ **of censure** *(parl.)* Mißtrauensantrag; ~ **of course** mündliche Verhandlung zu entscheidender Antrag; ~ **in court** Klageantrag; ~ **for decree** Antrag auf gerichtliche Entscheidung (Terminanberaumung); ~ **for dismissal** Antrag auf Klageabweisung; ~ **in error** Verfahrensrüge; ~ **for judgment** (Br.) Klagesachantrag; ~ **denied on the law** (US) rechtlich unbegründeter abgewiesener Antrag; ~ **of no confidence** *(parl.)* Mißtrauensantrag; ~ **having priority** vorrangig zu behandelnder Antrag; ~ **for reargument** (US) Antrag auf erneute Verhandlung; ~ **down for today** heute eingebrachter Antrag; ~ **for a new trial** Antrag auf Wiederaufnahme des Verfahrens; ~ **of urgency** Dringlichkeitsantrag; **to abandon a** ~ Antrag zurückziehen; **to accept a** ~ **undebated** Antrag ohne Debatte annehmen; **to adopt a** ~ **by a large majority** Antrag mit großer Mehrheit annehmen; **to bring forward a** ~ Antrag einbringen (stellen); **to carry a** ~ Antrag annehmen; **to defeat (deny) a** ~ Antrag überstimmen (ablehnen); **to dismiss a** ~ Antrag ablehnen; **to dispose of a** ~ Antrag erledigen; **to drop a** ~ Antrag zurückziehen; **to file a** ~ Antrag stellen; **to go through the** ~**s** sich einer Pflichtübung unterziehen, leeres Ritual durchspielen; **to grant a** ~ einem Antrag stattgeben; **to hear a** ~ über einen Antrag verhandeln; **to lay a** ~ **on the table** (US) Antrag auf unbestimmte Zeit zurückstellen; **to make a** ~ Antrag stellen; **to oppose a** ~ sich gegen einen Antrag aussprechen; **to present (propose, put down) a** ~ **of nonconfidence** Mißtrauensantrag einbringen; **to propose (put) a** ~ Antrag einbringen (stellen), beantragen; **to put a** ~ **for adjournment** Antrag auf Vertagung (Vertagungsantrag) stel-

len; **to put a ~ to the vote** Antrag zur Abstimmung bringen; **to put into ~** in Gang bringen; **to reject a ~** Antrag ablehnen; **to resist a ~** Antragsgegner sein; **to second a ~** Antrag unterstützen; **to set in ~** in Gang bringen; **to shelve a ~** *(Br.)* Antrag zurückstellen; **to speak against the ~** Gegenantrag unterstützen; **to speak for (support) the ~** Antrag unterstützen; **to submit a ~ in writing** Antrag schriftlich einbringen; **to table a ~** Antrag einbringen; **to take a ~ from the table** Antrag zur Debatte stellen; **to throw out a ~** Antrag ablehnen; **to vote down a ~** Antrag ablehnen; **to watch s. one's ~s** jds. Schritte im Auge behalten; **to withdraw a ~** Antrag zurückstellen;
~ **analysis** Bewegungsstudie.

motion picture *(US)* Film[werk];
~**s** Filmerzeugnisse;
to get into ~s ins Filmgeschäft einsteigen;
~ **business** Filmgeschäft, -branche; **to be in the ~ business** beim Film (in der Filmbranche) sein; ~ **camera** Filmkamera, Aufnahmeapparat; ~ **company** Filmgesellschaft; ~ **director** Filmaufnahmeleiter; ~ **industry** Filmindustrie, -wesen; ~ **producer** Filmproduzent; ~ **production** Filmproduktion; ~ **projector** Filmprojektor, -vorführapparat; ~ **sets** Filmbauten; ~ **star** Filmstar; ~ **studio** Filmatelier, -studio; ~ **title** Filmtitel.

motion|sickness See-, Luft-, Autokrankheit; ~ **study** Zeit-, Bewegungsstudie.

motivate *(v.)* Gründe vorbringen, begründen, motivieren;
~ **politically** politisch motivieren.

motivation Begründung, Motivierung, Motivation.

motivational research Motivforschung.

motive Ursache, Beweggrund, Motiv;
base ~s niedrige Beweggründe; **buying ~** Kaufmotiv; **economic ~s** wirtschaftliche Beweggründe; **ulterior ~s** tiefere Beweggründe;
~ **to prefer** Begünstigungsmotiv;
to be actuated by low and selfish ~s von niedrigen und selbstsüchtigen Beweggründen angetrieben sein;
~ **power** Antriebskraft; ~ **transport** Fortbewegungsmittel.

motor [Verbrennungs]motor, *(motorcar)* Kraftwagen, Motorfahrzeug, Automobil;
~**s** *(stock exchange, Br.)* Automobilwerte, Autoaktien;
auxiliary ~ Hilfsmotor; **electric ~** Elektromotor;
~ *(v.)* in einem Kraftfahrzeug fahren;
~ **s. o. home** j. mit dem Auto nach Hause bringen; ~ **through a town** durch eine Stadt fahren;
~ **accident** Autounfall, Kraftfahrzeugunfall; ~ **accident casualties** duch Autounfälle entstandene Verluste; ~ **ambulance** Krankenwagen, Ambulanz; ~**-assisted** mit Hilfsmotor; ~ **bandit** Autogangster; ~ **bicycle** *(bike, fam.)* Motorrad; ~**-body sheet** Autoblech; ~ **bus** Omnibus; **to be in the ~ business** in der Autobranche sein; ~ **camp** *(US)* Auto-, Campingplatz; ~ **car** *(Br.)* Kraftwagen, Auto; ~ **car badly dented in a collision** *(Br.)* bei einem Zusammenstoß schwer beschädigtes Kraftfahrzeug; ~ **car manufacturer** *(Br.)* Kraftfahrzeugbetrieb; ~ **caravan** Autoanhänger; **electric ~ carriage** Draisine; ~ **carrier** Lastwagentransportunternehmen, Spediteur; ~**-carrier industry** Lastkraftwagen-, Speditionsgeschäft; ~ **cavalcade** Autokolonne; ~ **claims** Ansprüche aus einer Kraftfahrzeugversicherung; ~ **coach** Omnibus für Fernfahrten, Reisebus; ~ **company** Autofirma; ~ **concern** Automobilkonzern; ~ **court** *(US)* Motel; ~ **dealer** Auto-, Kraftfahrzeughändler; ~ **drive** Motorantrieb; ~ **engine** Motor; ~ **engineer** Kraftfahrzeugingenieur; ~ **exhibition** Autoausstellung; ~ **fitter** Autoschlosser, -mechaniker; ~ **fuel** Treibstoff, Brennstoff; ~ **generator** Generator; ~ **group** *(stock exchange)* Markt für Automobilwerte; ~ **home rental program(me)** Verleihsystem für bewegliche Wohnungseinheiten; ~ **hood** Motorhaube; ~ **industry** *(Br.)* Kraftfahrzeug-, Auto[mobil]industrie; ~ **insurance** *(Br.)* Auto-, Kraftfahrzeugversicherung; **to carry a public liability ~ insurance** *(Br.)* Autohaftpflichtversicherung unterhalten; ~ **insurance premium** *(Br.)* Kraftfahrzeugversicherungsprämie; ~ **insurance rates** *(Br.)* Kraftfahrzeugversicherungssätze; ~ **insurers** Kraftfahrzeugversicherungsgesellschaft; ~ **insurers' bureau** *(Br.)* Kraftfahrzeugversicherungsstelle für Schadensausgleich ungedeckter Haftungsfälle; ~ **launch** *(Br.)* Motorbarkasse, -boot; ~ **manager** Leiter der Kraftfahrzeugversicherungsabteilung; ~ **manufacturer** Autofabrikant, -produzent, Automobilhersteller; ~ **mechanic** Autoschlosser, -mechaniker; ~ **oil** Motorenöl; ~ **policy** Kraftfahrzeugpolice; ~ **pool** *(mil.)* Fahrbereitschaft; ~ **power** Motorleistung; ~ **race** Autorennen; ~ **renewal** Erneuerung einer Kraftfahrzeugversicherung; ~ **repairs** Autoreparatur; **to decline certain types of ~ risk** bestimmte Versicherungsarten von Kraftfahrzeugen ablehnen; ~ **road** Auto-,

Schnellstraße; ~ **saw** Motorsäge; ~ **school** Fahrschule; ~ **scooter** Motorroller; ~ **shares (stocks,** *US)* Automobilwerte; ~ **ship** Motorschiff; ~ **show** *(Br.)* Autoausstellung; ~ **spirit** Benzin; ~ **starter** Anlasser; ~ **tariff** Kraftfahrzeugversicherungstarif; ~**-tax receipts** Kraftfahrzeugsteueraufkommen; ~ **torpedo boat** Schnellboot; ~ **tractor** Zugmaschine, Traktor, Schlepper; ~ **trade** Kraftfahrzeughandel, -gewerbe; ~ **trader** Autohändler; ~ **traffic** Kraftfahrzeug-, Autoverkehr; ~ **traffic management** Verkehrsregelung; ~ **transport** Lastwagentransport; ~ **transport agency** Kraftverkehrsunternehmen; ~ **transportation insurance** *(US)* Kraftverkehrs-, Kraftfahrzeugversicherung; ~ **truck** *(US)* Lastkraftwagen; ~ **truck transit** *(US)* Lastwagentransport; ~ **van** *(Br.)* Liefer-, kleiner Lastwagen; ~ **van expenses** *(Br.)* Lieferwagenunkosten, Unterhaltungskosten eines Kleinlastwagens.

motor vehicle Kraftfahrzeug;
to operate a ~ *(US)* Kraftfahrzeug führen; **to register a ~** Kraftfahrzeug anmelden; **to own a ~** Kraftfahrzeughalter sein; ~ **accessories** Autozubehörteile; ~ **acquisition** Kraftfahrzeugerwerb; ~ **driver** Kraftfahrzeugführer; ~ **duty** *(Br.)* Kraftfahrzeugsteuer; ~ **engine** Kraftfahrzeugmotor; ~ **insurance** Kraftfahrzeugversicherung; ~ **insurance business** Kraftfahrzeugversicherungswesen; ~ **liability insurance** Kraftfahrzeughaftpflichtversicherung; ~ **licence** Kraftfahrzeugzulassung; ~ **passenger insurance** *(Br.)* Auto-, Kraftfahrzeug-, Insassenversicherung; ~ **owner** Kraftfahrzeughalter; ~ **ownership** Kraftfahrzeugbestand; ~ **production** Automobilproduktion; ~ **registration** Kraftfahrzeuganmeldung; ~ **registration certificate** *(US)* Kraftfahrzeugbrief, -schein; ~ **repair shop** Kraftfahrzeugreparaturwerkstätte; ~ **speed limit** Höchstgeschwindigkeit für Kraftfahrzeuge; ~ **tax** *(US)* Auto-, Kraftfahrzeugsteuer; ~ **traffic** Kraftfahrzeugverkehr.

motor|vessel Motorschiff; ~ **wear** Motorabnutzung.

motorbike Motorrad;
~ **maker** Motorradfabrikant.

motorboat Motorboot.

motorbus Autobus, Omnibus;
~ **line** Omnibus-, Autobuslinie.

motorcab Taxi, Taxe, Autodroschke.

motorcade *(US)* Autokolonne, -korso.

motorcar *(US)* Auto, Automobil, Kraftfahrzeug, -wagen;
private ~ Personenkraftwagen;
~ **accident** Autounfall; ~ **credit** Autokredit; ~ **dealer** Autohändler; ~ **industry** Kraftfahrzeug-, Auto[mobil]industrie; ~ **insurance** Auto[haftpflicht]-, Kraftfahrzeugversicherung; ~ **production** Auto[mobil]produktion ; ~ **sales** Autoverkauf; ~ **spares** Autoersatzteile; ~ **tyre** Autoreifen.

motorcycle Motorrad;
~ **helmet** Sturzhelm; ~ **plant** Motorradfabrik; ~ **track** Motorradpiste.

motorcyclist Motorradfahrer.

motordrome Autorennstrecke.

motorhome motorisierter Wohnwagen.

motoring Kraftfahrsport, -wesen;
safe ~ sicheres Autofahren;
~ **center** *(US)* **(centre,** *Br.)* Touristenzentrum; ~ **conditions** Straßenzustand; ~ **fine** *(Br.)* Knöllchen, gebührenpflichtige Verwarnung; ~ **guide** Autoreiseführer; ~ **offence** *(Br.)* Verkehrsübertretung, -delikt; ~ **organization** Automobilclub; ~ **public** Autofahrer; ~ **report on road conditions** Straßenzustandsbericht.

motorist Kraft-, Autofahrer, Automobilist;
hit-and-run ~ unfallflüchtiger Fahrer; **lower risk ~** geringeres Risiko darstellender Autofahrer; **private car ~** Privatwagenbesitzer.

motorization Motorisierung.

motorize *(v.)* motorisieren.

motorized motorisiert;
~ **agriculture** mechanisierte Landwirtschaft.

motorless flight Segelflug.

motorman Straßenbahnführer.

motorteria Autowaschanstalt.

motorway *(Br.)* Schnellstraße, Autobahn;
~ **construction** *(Br.)* Autobahnbau; ~ **extension** *(Br.)* Autobahnausbau; ~ **feeder road** *(Br.)* Autobahnzubringer; ~ **metrification** *(Br.)* Umstellung der Autobahnschilder auf das metrische System; **20 ~ minutes** *(Br.)* 20 Autobahnminuten Fahrt; ~ **ring road** *(Br.)* Autobahnring; **near ~ standard** *(Br.)* autobahnähnliche Qualität; ~ **system** *(Br.)* Autobahnnetz; ~ **traffic** *(Br.)* Autobahnverkehr.

motorwayification board *(Br.)* Autobahnbauamt.

motto Wahlspruch, Motto.
mould *(Br.)* Schablone, Form, *(Br., sl.)* Torpedo, Aal;
cast in the same ~ aus demselben Holz geschnitzt, vom gleichen Kaliber;
~ *(v.)* matern, formen;
to squirt a ~ Torpedo abschießen.
mouldy *(fig.)* antiquiert, altmodisch.
mound Erdwall, Damm;
~s of paper Berge von Papier, Papierflut.
mount Aufziehleinwand, -karton;
~ *(v.)* (assemble parts) montieren, zusammenbauen, *(bill)* betragen;
~ to *(prices)* ansteigen bis; **~ guards** Posten aufstellen; **~ jewels in gold** Juwelen in Gold fassen; **~ an offensive** Angriff vortragen, Offensive starten; **~ stamps** Briefmarken einkleben; **~ the throne** Thron besteigen; **~ troops** Truppen beritten machen; **~ up *(prices)*** steigen; **~ up to** sich belaufen auf.
mountain | of debts Schuldenberg; **~ of difficulties** Haufen von Schwierigkeiten;
to make a ~ out of a molehill aus einer Mücke einen Elefanten machen;
~ adventurer leichtsinniger Bergsteiger; **~ barometer** Höhenbarometer; **~ center *(US)* (centre, *Br.*)** Bergwachtstation; **~ chain** Gebirgskette; **~ climate** Höhenklima; **~ guide** Bergführer; **~ pass** Bergpaß; **~ railway** Gebirgsbahn; **~ range** Gebirgskette; **~ retreat** Ruhesitz in den Bergen; **~ sickness** Höhenkrankheit; **on the ~ side** am Berghang gelegen; **~ slide** Bergsturz; **~ troops** Gebirgstruppen; **~ wave** Föhnwelle.
mountaineer Hochtourist, Bergsteiger.
mountaineering Hochtouristik, Bergsteigerei.
mountainous | country Gebirgsland; **~ district** Gebirgsgegend.
mountebank Marktschreier.
mounted montiert, *(photo)* aufgezogen, *(precious stone)* gefaßt;
~ on metal auf Bleifuß;
~ police berittene Polizei.
mounting *(mil.)* Lafette, *(placing in position)* Aufstellung, Montierung, Montage, Installation;
~ frame Montagerahmen.
mourn *(v.)* Trauerkleidung anlegen.
mourner Leidtragender.
mourning Trauer[kleidung];
national ~ Staats-, Nationaltrauer;
to come out of ~ Trauer ablegen; **to go into ~** Trauer anlegen;
~ apparel Trauerkleidung; **~ band** Trauerflor; **~ coach** Trauerwagen; **~ paper** Kondolenzpapier; **~ period** Trauerzeit; **~ time** Trauerzeit.
mousehole Mauseloch.
mousetrap Mausefalle, *(inferior theater, sl.)* mieser Nachtklub.
mouth Mund, *(harbo(u)r)* Ein-, Ausfahrt, *(river)* Mündung;
by word of ~ in mündlicher Form; **down in the ~** niedergeschlagen, bedrückt;
to give ~ to one's thoughts seinen Gedanken Ausdruck verleihen; **to keep one's ~ shut** *(coll.)* Mund halten; **to laugh on the wrong side of one's ~** jammern, klagen; **to make a poor ~** Armut vorschützen; **to make s. one's ~ water** jem. den Mund wässerig machen; **to put s. th. into s. one's ~** jem. etw. in den Mund legen; **~-filling** bombastisch, geschwollen.
mouthful *(sl.)* unbedeutende Bemerkung, Nichtigkeit.
mouthpiece Sprachrohr, *(fig.)* Wortführer, *(law court sl.)* Strafverteidiger.
movable fahrbar;
~ estate bewegliches Vermögen, Habe; **~ feast** bewegliches Fest; **~ goods (property)** bewegliches Vermögen, Mobilien, Fahrnis, Mobiliarvermögen; **~ property *(US)*** bewegliches Vermögen, Mobilien, Mobiliarvermögen, beweglicher Nachlaß; **~ property of a bankrupt** Konkursmasse.
movables Mobiliar[vermögen], Mobilien, bewegliches Vermögen, Fahrnis;
~ and immovables bewegliches und unbewegliches Vermögen.
move *(moving)* Umzug, *(step)* Maßnahme, Schritt, Aktion;
on the ~ auf dem Marsch; **always on the ~** immer unterwegs;
a clever ~ kluger Schachzug;
~ into a dwelling Beziehen einer Wohnung; **~ towards settling a strike** Schritte zur Streikbeendigung;
~ *(v.)* sich bewegen, *(change residence)* weg-, ver-, umziehen, seinen Wohnsitz verändern, *(consideration of contract)* übergehen, *(prefer, sl.)* in Vorschlag bringen, beantragen, Antrag stellen, *(request)* ersuchen;
~ s. o. jds. Umzug übernehmen;
~ about freely Freizügigkeit genießen; **~ about in the country** im Lande herumziehen; **~ that the case be adjourned** Vertagung

beantragen, Vertagungsantrag stellen; **~ an affidavit *(US)*** Antrag mit eidesstattlicher Erklärung untermauern; **~ an amendment** Abänderungsantrag einbringen; **~ briskly ahead *(prices)*** rasch steigen, stark anziehen; **~ away** fortziehen; **~ away from** abrücken von; **~ back to the pavement** auf den Bürgersteig zurückdrängen; **~ backward *(economy)*** zurückgehen, nachlassen; **~ a censure *(parl.)*** Tadelsantrag stellen; **~ closure *(parl.)*** Antrag auf Schluß der Debatte stellen; **~ dirt *(railroad use)*** Kohlen schaufeln; **~ down[wards] *(prices)*** zurückgehen, sich abwärts bewegen; **~ for** beantragen, Antrag stellen; **~ into the country** aufs Land ziehen; **~ into a flat** Wohnung beziehen; **~ heaven and earth** Himmel und Hölle in Bewegung setzen; **~ forward *(troops)*** vorrücken; **not ~ hand or foot** keinen Finger rühren; **~ into a new high *(prices)*** neuen Höchststand erreichen; **~ higher** steigen; **~ house** umziehen; **~ into a house** Haus beziehen, in ein Haus einziehen; **~ into s. one's house** bei jem. einziehen; **~ in** einziehen, *(film)* einschwenken; **~ s. th. indoors** etw. nach innen verlegen; **~ in on s. o.** sich jem. mit Vorschlägen nähern; **~ s. o. very little** j. kaum (nur schwach) beeindrucken; **~ into new rooms** neue Wohnung beziehen; **~ one's lodgings** seine Wohnung wechseln; **~ in a matter** Initiative in einer Angelegenheit ergreifen; **~ off *(train)*** abfahren, *(troops)* abrücken, abziehen, sich in Marsch setzen; **~ an official** Beamten versetzen; **~ out of a flat** aus einer Wohnung ausziehen; **~ for papers in the House of Lords *(Br.)*** Debatte im Oberhaus beantragen; **~ s. o. to pity** jds. Mitleid erregen; **~ at a snail's pace** sich im Schneckentempo fortbewegen; **~ to another seat** seinen Platz wechseln; **~ to another place** nach auswärts ziehen; **~ the previous question *(parl.)*** Antrag auf Behandlung der Tagesordnung stellen; **~ the rejection of a bill** Antrag auf Ablehnung einer Vorlage stellen; **~ a resolution** Entschließung (Resolution) einbringen; **~ slowly** langsam vorankommen, *(fig.)* sich langsam entwickeln; **~ in the best society** sich in den besten Gesellschaftskreisen bewegen; **~ through the streets *(procession)*** sich durch die Straßen bewegen; **~ towards its end** sich dem Ende nähern; **~ troops** Truppen verlegen; **~ troops to the front** Truppen an die Front werfen; **~ up *(prices)*** sich aufwärts bewegen, fester werden, steigen, anziehen, *(school)* versetzen; **~ up sharply** scharf anziehen; **~ sharply on little business** trotz kleiner Umsätze scharf anziehen; **~ up three points** um drei Punkte steigen; **~ up a trifle** etw. anziehen; **~ one's stores downtown *(US)*** seinen Laden ins Stadtzentrum verlegen; **~ violently *(stock exchange)*** heftig reagieren; **~ a vote** Antrag einbringen; **~ in one's most tactful way** mit größter Vorsicht und größtem Takt operieren;
~ that the debate be adjourned Vertagung der Debatte beantragen; **~ that the meeting be adjourned** Vertagung beantragen; **~ that the meeting postpone consideration of the subject** Antrag auf Zurückstellung der Sacherörterung stellen; **~ that the question be now put** Antrag auf Schluß der Debatte und Abstimmung stellen;
to arise from an internal career development ~ auf innerbetriebliche laufbahnbedingte Versetzungen zurückzuführen sein; **to be on the ~** im Einziehen (Ausziehen) begriffen (beim Umzug) sein; **to be always on the ~** kein Sitzfleisch haben; **to be up to every ~** *(fam.)* alle Tricks beherrschen; **to get the crowd to ~ on** Menge zum Weitergehen auffordern; **to make a ~** aufbrechen; **to make a (the) first ~** ersten Schritt tun.
moved, if ~ return to sender falls verzogen, zurück an den Absender;
~ by secret motives von geheimen Beweggründen bestimmt;
to ask to be ~ um seine Versetzung einkommen; **to be much ~ by the news** von Nachrichten sehr betroffen sein; **to be easily ~ to tears** nahe am Wasser gebaut sein; **to be ~ up *(pupil)*** versetzt werden.
movement Bewegung, *(machine)* Lauf, *(market activity)* Umsatz, *(mil.)* Truppenbewegung, *(stock exchange, sl.)* Kursbewegung, *(tendency)* Bestrebung, Tendenz, Richtung;
~s Schritte, Maßnahmen;
capital ~ Kapitalbewegung, -verkehr; **downward ~ *(stock exchange)*** Abwärtsbewegung, rückläufige Bewegung, Fallen, Rückgang; **free ~** Freizügigkeit; **grassroots political ~ *(US)*** volksverbundene politische Bewegung; **labo(u)r ~** Arbeiterbewegung; **little ~ *(stock market)*** wenig Bewegung; **no ~ *(stock exchange)*** ohne Umsatz; **popular ~** Volksbewegung; **retrograde ~ *(stock exchange)*** rückläufige Bewegung; **social ~** soziale Bewegung; **underground ~** Untergrund-, Widerstandsbewegung; **unitary ~** Einheitsbewegung; **upward ~** Steigen, Anziehen, Aufwärtsbewegung;
~ of an army Truppenbewegungen; **free ~ of capital *(EC)*** freier Kapitalverkehr; **~ of commodities** Warenverkehr, Warenbe-

wegung; ~ **in demand** Nachfrageverlagerung; ~ **in [exchange] rates** [Wechsel]kursschwankungen; ~ **of freight (goods)** Waren-, Güterverkehr; **mid-year** ~ **of funds** Kapitalbewegungen zum Halbjahresultimo; **free** ~ **of goods** *(EC)* freier Warenverkehr; **free** ~ **of labo(u)r** freie Wahl des Arbeitsplatzes; ~ **of persons** Personenverkehr; ~ **of prices** Kurs-, Preisbewegung, -entwicklung; **free** ~ **of services** freier Dienstleistungsverkehr; **not much** ~ **in oil shares** geringe Umsätze in Ölaktien; ~ **of ships** Schiffsbewegungen; ~ **to abolish slavery** Feldzug zur Abschaffung der Sklaverei; **upward** ~ **of stocks** Anziehen der Aktienkurse; ~ **of a wag(g)on** Waggonverschiebung; **free** ~ **of workers** *(EC)* Freizügigkeit der Arbeitnehmer;
to be in the ~ mit der Zeit gehen; **to lack** ~ *(novel)* langweilig (ohne Handlung) sein; **to study a criminal's** ~s Verbrecher beobachten lassen.

mover Antragsteller, *(of household goods, US)* Fuhrunternehmer, Möbelspediteur;
prime ~ Hauptbetreiber;
to be the prime ~ **of an enterprise** Haupttriebfeder (Seele) eines Unternehmens sein.

movie *(US)* Filmstreifen;
~s Kino-, Lichtspielhaus, *(performance)* Filmvorführung;
free in-house ~ kostenlose Filmvorführung im Hotel; **full-length** ~ abendfüllender Film; **rerun** ~ wieder aufgeführter Film; **wide-screen** ~ Breitwandfilm;
~ **in the round** dreidimensionaler Film;
to go to the ~s ins Kino (in den Kintop) gehen;
~ **admission price** Kinoeintrittspreis; ~ **advertisement** Kinoreklame, Filmwerbung; ~ **actor** Filmschauspieler; ~ **audience** Kinopublikum; ~ **business** Filmgeschäft; ~ **camera** [Schmal]filmkamera; ~ **cartridge** Filmkassette; ~ **company** Filmgesellschaft; ~ **film clip** Standfoto; ~ **financing** Filmfinanzierung; ~-**goer** Kinobesucher; ~-**goers** Filmpublikum; ~ **house** Lichtspiel-, Filmtheater; ~ **magazine** Filmzeitschrift; ~ **man** Kameramann, Vorführer; ~ **mogul** Filmboss; ~ **performance** Filmvorführung; ~ **picture advertising** Filmwerbung; ~ **program(me)** Filmprogramm; ~ **projector** Filmprojektor; ~ **public** Filmpublikum; ~ **star** Filmstar; ~ **theater** Kino, Lichtspielhaus.

moviedom Filmwirtschaft, -industrie.
movieland Traumland.
moviemaker *(US)* Filmproduzent, -hersteller.
moviemaking *(US)* Filmherstellung, -produktion.
moving Umzug, *(transfer of official)* Versetzung;
~ **back** Zurückdrängung; ~ **forward** *(mil.)* Vorrücken; ~ **in** Bezug; ~ **into a new flat** Einzug in eine neue Wohnung; ~ **off** *(mil.)* Abrücken, Abmarsch; ~ **out** Ausziehen, Auszug;
~ **for an argument** Antrag auf mündliche Verhandlung;
~ *(a.)* bewegend, rührend, *(article)* gut verkäuflich;
not ~ *(article)* schlecht verkäuflich;
to be ~ **up** *(prices)* aufwärts gehen, anziehen;
~ **allowance** *(US)* Umzugsgeld, -beihilfe; ~ **average** gleitender Durchschnitt; ~ **cause** Beweggrund; ~ **company** *(US)* Möbelspediteur; ~ **day** Umzugstag; **to take care of the** ~ **details** sich um den gesamten Umzug kümmern; ~ **expenses** Umzugskosten; ~ **insurance** Umzugsversicherung; ~ **man** *(US)* Umzugsspediteur, Packer; ~ **papers** Urkunden zur Unterstützung eines Antrages (Schriftsatzes); ~ **party** Antragsteller; ~ **picture** Film; ~-**picture advertising** Filmwerbung; ~-**picture rights** Filmrechte; ~ **power** treibende Kraft; ~ **speech** bewegende Ansprache; ~ **staircase (stairway)** Rolltreppe; ~ **train** fahrender Zug; ~ **van** *(US)* Möbelwagen; ~ **violation** *(US)* Verkehrsdelikt.

muck Mist, Dung, *(money)* Mammon, *(nasty mess)* Schund, Mist;
~ *(v.)* misten, düngen, *(sl.)* verpfuschen, vermasseln, verkorksen;
~ **about** *(v.)* *(Br., sl.)* sich herumtreiben; ~ **out** ausmisten; ~ **up** *(coll.)* besudeln, beschmutzen, *(sl.)* verpfuschen, vermanschen; ~ **up a job** *(fam.)* Arbeit verpfuschen;
to be all in a ~ von oben bis unten bespritzt sein; **to be in a** ~ **of a sweat** *(fam.)* im Schweiß gebadet sein; **to make a** ~ **of s. th.** *(coll.)* etw. verpfuschen;
~ **heap** Misthaufen; ~ **rake** Mistgabel.

mucker Reinfall;
to come a ~ reinfallen.

muckrake *(v.)* *(fig.)* im Schmutz herumrühren, *(US sl.)* Korruptionsfälle aufspüren und politisch ausnutzen.

muckraker Schnüffler, Skandalkolporteur.
muckworm Geizhals, Knicker.
mud Schlamm, Morast, *(radio use, sl.)* undeutliches Funksignal, *(vilest part)* Abschaum;

to bathe a patient in ~ einem Kranken ein Schlammbad verabfolgen; **to be all over** ~ völlig verschmutzt sein; **to get stuck in the** ~ im Schlamm stecken bleiben; **to sling (throw)** ~ **at s. o.** Rufmord an jem. begehen;
~ **bath** Moor-, Schlammbad; ~ **cure** Schlammkur; ~ **floor** Lehmboden; ~ **hut** Lehmhütte.

muddle Durcheinander;
~ **and waste of government departments** bürokratisches Durcheinander und staatliche Überorganisation;
~ *(v.)* durcheinanderbringen;
~ **account books** Buchführung durcheinanderbringen; ~ **away a fortune** Vermögen durchbringen; ~ **s. one's life** Unruhe in jds. Leben bringen; ~ **away one's opportunities** seine Chancen vertun; ~ **on** draufloswirtschaften, weiterwursteln; ~ **one's papers** seine Papiere durcheinanderbringen; ~ **a scheme completely** Plan völlig durcheinanderbringen; ~ **through** sich durchwursteln; ~ **things up** verschiedene Sachen durcheinanderwerfen;
to be in a ~ völlig durcheinander sein; **to get into a** ~ in Verwirrung geraten; **to make a** ~ **of an affair** Angelegenheit völlig durcheinanderbringen;
~ **head** Wirrkopf.

muddy schlammig, schmutzig, beschmiert, *(colo(u)r)* verschwommen, *(fig.)* verworren, unklar;
~ **ideas** konfuse Ideen; ~ **road** schmutzige Straße; ~ **terminology** verschwommene Terminologie.

mudguard *(Br.)* Kotflügel, Schutzblech.
mudhole Schlammloch.
mudslinger *(coll.)* Rufmörder.
mudslinging *(coll.)* Verleumdung, Rufmordbegehung.
muff Muff, *(fig., coll.)* tölpelhaftes Benehmen.
muffled up in thick furs in dicken Pelzen vermummt.
muffler Auspufftopf, *(silencer, US)* Schalldämpfer.
mug Kanne, Krug, *(Br., dupe)* Tölpel, Einfaltspinsel, *(swot, Br.)* Büffler, Streber
~ *(v.)* *(criminal)* Verbrecher photographieren, *(US sl.)* ausrauben, Raubüberfall durchführen;
~ **up for an examination** für ein Examen büffeln (ochsen); ~ **up a subject** sich in einem Fach einpauken;
~ **shot** *(sl.)* Porträtaufnahme [eines Verbrechers].

mugging *(fam.)* Raubüberfall.
muggy days feuchtes Wetter.
mugwump *(party politics)* unzuverlässiges Parteimitglied, *(politics)* Unabhängiger, Einzelgänger, *(v.i.p., US)* hohes Tier, wichtige Person.

mugwumpery *(US sl.)* *(party politics)* Unzuverlässigkeit, *(politics)* Einzelgängertum.

mulct Geldstrafe, Buße;
~ *(v.)* **s. o. in £ 50** j. zu fünfzig Pfund Geldstrafe verurteilen; ~ **s. o. of s. th.** j. um etw. erleichtern.

mule Maulesel, *(pony, sl.)* Eselsbrücke, Klatsche, *(stubborn person, coll.)* Dickkopf, störrischer Mensch, *(technical)* Schlepper, Traktor;
~ **skinner** *(US)* Maultiertreiber; ~ **track** Saumpfad.

multi-industry experience Erfahrungen in mehreren Industriezweigen
multiaxle drive Mehrachsenantrieb.
multibreak *(el.)* Serienschalter.
multicolo(u)r mehrfarbig;
~ **advertising** Mehrfarbenabdruck.
multicolumn journal Mehrspaltenjournal.
multicorporate enterprise *(US)* Konzern.
multicraft union Fachgewerkschaft für mehrere Spezialberufe.
multicylindered mehrzylindrig.
multidisciplinary team aus mehreren Fakultäten zusammengesetzte Ausbildungsmannschaft.
multidivision vielschichtig;
~ **corporation** *(US)* regional verstreute Gesellschaft.
multiemployer bargaining Tarifverhandlungen auf Verbandsebene.
multiengined mehrmotorig.
multifamily dwelling Mehrfamilienhaus.
multifarious *(lawsuit)* verschiedene ungleichartige Ansprüche verbindend;
~ **duties** verschiedenartige Aufgaben.
multifariousness *(law)* unzulässige Klagenverbindung.
multigraph *(print.)* Vervielfältigungsapparat;
~ *(v.)* vervielfältigen.
multilateral vielseitig, *(agreement)* multilateral, mehrseitig;
~ **agreement** *(international law)* multilaterales Abkommen; ~ **clearing** multilaterales Clearing; ~ **clearing system** multilateraler Verrechnungsverkehr; ~ **disarmament** multilaterale Abrü-

stung; ~ **system of payments** multilaterales Zahlungssystem; ~
trade multilateraler Handel; ~ **treatment** multilaterales Verfahren; ~ **treaty** mehrseitiges Abkommen.
multilevel | circulation pattern mehrstöckige Verkehrsanord-
nung; ~ **government** vielschichtige Verwaltungsmethoden.
multiline telephone number *(US)* Sammelnummer.
multilinear tariff für mehrere Linien geltender Eisenbahntarif.
multilingual mehrsprachig.
multilith Rotaprint.
multimillionaire Multimillionär.
multinational multinational, vielstaatlich;
  to go ~ sich weltweit orientieren;
  ~ **company** multinationales Unternehmen; ~ **merger** multinationale Fusion; ~ **state** Nationalitätenstaat.
multiopoly freie Unternehmerwirtschaft.
multipack Mehrstückpackung.
multipart freight bill Frachtrechnung in mehrfacher Ausfertigung.
multipartite *(law of nations)* multilateral.
multiparty | coalition Mehrparteienregierung; ~ **pluralism** Mehr-
parteienpluralismus; ~ **system** Mehrparteiensystem.
multiphase mehrphasig;
  ~ **current** Mehrphasenstrom.
multiplace *(aeroplane)* mehrsitzig.
multiplane fighter Mehrfachkampfflugzeug.
multiple *(Br.)* Filialunternehmen, -betrieb, Kettenladen, *(el.)*
Parallelschaltung;
  in ~ parallel geschaltet;
  price earnings ~ Kurs-Ertragsmultiplikator;
  ~ *(a.)* vielfach, mehrfach, mannigfaltig, *(el.)* parallel;
  ~ **basing point system** *(US)* kollektive Frachtsatzberechnung,
  Preisortsystem; ~ **certificate** *(US)* Globalaktie; ~ **chain** Filialunternehmen im Einzelhandel; ~ **choice questions** *(opinion research, US)* Auswahlfragen; ~ **classification** Mehrfachklassifi-
  zierung; ~ **cropping** mehrfache Bebauung; ~ **currency** multiple
  (gespaltene) Wechselkurse; ~**-currency bonds** *(US)* Obligationen, deren Kapitalbetrag und Zinsen in Währungen verschiedener Länder zahlbar sind; ~**-currency system** Devisenver-
  rechnungssystem; ~**-delivery contract** Sukzessivlieferungsvertrag; ~**-disk clutch** Mehrscheibenkupplung; ~ **dwelling**
  Mietsgebäude, -haus; ~ **exchange rates** multiple (gespaltene)
  Wechselkurse; ~ **expansion of credit** Mehrfachausnutzung
  eines Kredits; ~**-family dwelling** Mehrfamilienhaus; ~ **firm**
  (Br.) Kettenladen; ~ **image** *(television)* Mehrfachbild; ~ **insertion rate** Sonderpreis für Daueranzeigen; ~ **interests** vielseitige
  Interessen; ~ **jack panel** *(tel.)* Vielfachklinke; ~ **lease** Mietvertrag über mehrere Wohneinheiten; ~ **lines of credit** gleichzei-
  tige Kreditlinie bei mehreren Kreditinstituten; ~**-line system of
  insurance** System der Zulassung aller Versicherungsarten bei
  einer Gesellschaft, Mehrfachversicherung; ~ **listing** *(US)*
  Anhandgeben von Grundstücken an mehrere Makler; ~ **loading** Verladung mehrerer Stückgutladungen; ~ **management**
  (US) System der mehrfachen Führungsgremien, mehrstufiges
  Betriebsführung; ~ **licensing** Mehrfachlizenzen; ~ **national**
  Mehrstaatler; ~ **party system** Mehrparteiensystem; ~ **piecework
  system** Stücklohnverfahren; ~ **price** Mengenrabattpreis;
  ~ **product firm** diversifiziertes Unternehmen, Firma mit breitgestreutem Produktionsprogramm; ~ **production** Serienherstellung; ~**-purpose cooperation** Universalgenossenschaft; ~
  rate system System multipler (gespaltener) Wechselkurse; ~
  ride traffic Zeitkartenverkehr; ~ **seizure** mehrfache Pfändung;
  ~ **share** Mehrstimmrechtsaktie; ~**-shift operation** Schichtbetrieb; ~ **shop** *(Br.)* Kettenladen, -unternehmen, Massenfilialbetrieb; ~ **stage sales tax** Mehrphasenumsatzsteuer; ~ **stock** *(US)*
  Mehrstimmrechtsaktie; ~ **store** *(Br.)* Kettenladen; ~ **store enterprise** *(US)* Kettenunternehmen; ~ **survey** Mehrthemenbefra-
  gung; ~ **switch** *(el.)* Mehrfach-, Vielfachschalter; ~ **tariff**
  Mehrfachzoll; ~ **tariff system** für mehrere Linien geltendes
  Tarifsystem; ~ **taxation** mehrfache Besteuerung, Mehrfachbesteuerung; ~ **telegram** vervielfältigtes Telegramm; ~ **tenure**
  gemeinsamer Grundbesitz; ~ **unit housing** Mehrzweckbauten;
  ~**-unit item** Mehrstückpackung; ~**-unit train** Mehrfach-Schienenbus;
  ~ **independently targetable reentry vehicle** Mehrfachspreng-
  köpfe mit voneinander unabhängiger Steuerung; ~ **voting**
  mehrfache Stimmrechtsausübung; ~ **voting share** Mehrstimmrechtsaktie; ~ **warhead** mehrfacher Atomsprengkopf.
multiplex | operation Mehrfachbetrieb; ~ **telegraphy** Mehrfach-
telegraphie.
multiplicable multiplizierbar.
multiplication Vervielfältigung, Multiplikation.
multiplication table Einmaleins.

multiplicity | of action *(suits)* Einbringung verschiedener Klagen
über einen Streitgegenstand; ~ **of small city states** Vielzahl
kleiner Stadtstaaten.
multiplier Vervielfältiger, Multiplikator;
  ~ **effect** Multiplikationswirkung, -effekt.
multiply *(v.)* vermehren, vervielfältigen.
multiplying glass Vergrößerungsglas.
multipurpose | aircraft Mehrzweckflugzeug; ~ **joint authority**
Mehrzweckverband; ~ **weapon** Mehrzweckwaffe.
multiracial country Staat mit mehreren Rassen.
multirange receiver Allwellenempfänger.
multiroute vielstreckig.
multistage mehrstufig;
  ~ **interview** Mehrstufenbefragung; ~ **rocket** mehrstufige
  Rakete, Mehrstufenrakete; ~ **sampling** mehrphasige Auswahl;
  ~ **survey** mehrstufige Untersuchung; **cumulative ~ system**
  (taxation) Mehrphasensteuer; ~ **tax** All-, Mehrphasensteuer.
multistor(e)y mehrstöckig;
  ~ **car park (garage)** Parkhochhaus, Hochgarage.
multitude Masse, Menge.
multiway plug Viel-, Mehrfachstecker.
mum Stille, Schweigen;
  ~ *(v.)* Mummenschanz treiben;
  to keep ~ on political matters in politischen Fragen Zurückhaltung zeigen.
mumming play Mummenschanz.
mummy Mumie;
  to beat s. o. to a ~ j. grün und blau schlagen.
mundane weltlich, irdisch.
municipal gemeindeeigen, gemeindlich, kommunal, städtisch,
(relating to a state) innerstaatlich, national;
  ~**s** Kommunalschuldverschreibungen, -anleihen;
  ~ **accounting** kommunales Rechnungswesen; ~ **accountant**
  Stadtkämmerer; ~ **action** kommunale Gewaltenausübung; ~
  administration Stadt-, Kommunalverwaltung; ~ **affairs**
  Gemeinde-, Kommunalangelegenheiten; ~ **aid** kommunale
  Unterstützung, Gemeindezuschuß, finanzielle Unterstützung
  durch die kommunalen Stellen; ~ **assembly** Stadtratssitzung;
  ~ **authorities** Kommunalbehörden, Stadtverwaltung, -rat,
  Gemeinde; ~ **bank** Kommunalbank; ~ **board** Gemeinderat,
  Magistrat; ~ **bonds** *(US)* kommunale Schuldverschreibungen,
  Kommunalanleihe, -obligationen, Kommunalschuldverschreibung; ~ **negotiable bond** Kommunalschuldschein; ~
  bond market Markt für Kommunalanleihen; ~ **border** Stadt-
  grenze; ~ **borough** [etwa] kreisangehörige Stadt; ~ **budget**
  Gemeinde-, Kommunalhaushalt; ~ **buildings** Kommunal-,
  städtische Gebäude; ~ **charter** *(US)* Gemeindeordnung, -sat-
  zung, Ortsstatut; ~ **compensation** *(US)* Konzessionsabgabe;
  ~ **corporation** Selbstverwaltungskörper, Stadtverwaltung,
  (US) Stadtgemeinde, Gemeindeverband; **quasi-~ corporation**
  selbstverwaltungsähnliche Körperschaft; ~ **council** Gemein-
  de-, Stadtrat; ~ **councillor** Stadtverordneter, Ratsherr; ~ **court**
  Amts-, Stadtgericht; ~ **credit** Kommunalkredit; ~ **debts**
  Gemeinde-, Kommunalschulden; ~ **default** Zahlungsunfähigkeit einer Gemeinde; ~ **district** Kommunal-, Stadtbezirk; ~
  domicile Inlandswohnsitz; ~ **elections** *(US)* Gemeinde-, Kommunalwahlen; ~ **employee** Kommunalbediensteter, Gemein-
  deangestellter; ~ **enterprise** städtisches Unternehmen, Kommunalbetrieb; ~ **expansion** Erweiterung der Kommunalbefug-
  nisse; ~ **expenses** Kommunalausgaben; ~ **finances** Kommunalfinanzen; ~ **functions** Kommunalveranstaltungen; ~ **government** *(US)* Kommunal-, Stadtverwaltung; ~ **indebtedness**
  Kommunalverschuldung; ~ **instrument of indebtedness** Kommunalschuldschein; ~ **issue** Kommunalemission; ~ **law** innerstaatliches Recht, *(US)* Kommunalrecht; ~ **lien** städtische
  Reallast; ~ **loan** Kommunalanleihe; ~ **market** Markt für Kommunalpapiere; **tax-exempt ~ market** Markt für steuerfreie
  Kommunalwerte; ~ **office** städtisches Amt, Gemeindeamt; ~
  officer *(US)* Kommunalbeamter, städtischer Beamter; ~ **ordinance** *(US)* Gemeindestatut, -verordnung, städtische Verordnung; ~ **paper** Kommunalobligation; ~ **polling** Kommunalwahl; ~ **property** Gemeinde-, Kommunalvermögen; ~
  purposes kommunale (öffentliche) Zwecke; ~ **rates** *(Br.)*
  Gemeindesteuer, Kommunal-, Stadtabgaben; ~ **reform**
  Reform des Kommunalwesens; ~ **savings bank** städtische
  Sparkasse, Stadtsparkasse, Kommunalkreditinstitut; ~ **seat**
  Gemeinderatssitz; ~ **securities** Kommunalanleihen; ~ **services**
  städtische Einrichtungen (Dienstleistungsbetriebe); ~ **stock**
  (Br.) Kommunalobligation; ~ **structure** Kommunalstruktur; ~
  support Kommunalunterstützung; ~ **taxes** *(US)* städtische
  Abgaben, Kommunal-, Gemeindeabgaben, -steuern; ~ **town**

Stadt mit Selbstverwaltung; ~ **trading** gemeindliche Gewerbe-tätigkeit, Gemeindewirtschaft; ~ **transit** städtischer Verkehr; ~ **treasurer** *(Br.)* Stadtkämmerer; ~ **undertaking** Kommunal-betrieb; ~ **utility** kommunaler Versorgungsbetrieb; ~ **warrant** kommunale Zahlungsanweisung, Kommunalschuldschein; ~ **worker** Gemeinde-, Kommunalarbeiter.

municipalism städtische Selbstverwaltung, *(devotion to one's own municipality)* Lokalpatriotismus.

municipalist Lokalpatriot.

municipality Stadtverwaltung, Stadtgemeinde als Selbstver-waltungsbezirk, Magistrat, Stadtbehörde.

municipalization Vergesellschaftung, Eingemeindung, Überfüh-rung in städtischen Besitz.

municipalize *(v.)* vergesellschaften, eingemeinden, in Kommu-nalverwaltung (städtischen Besitz) überführen, kommuna-lisieren.

municipally owned im Kommunaleigentum.

muniment Rechtstitel;
~ **of title** Grundstücksurkunde;
~ **room** Archiv.

munitions Kriegsmaterial, -vorräte, Munition;
~ **of war** Kriegsmaterial;
~ **factory** Munitions-, Rüstungsfabrik; ~ **industry** Rüstungsin-dustrie; ~ **shortage** knappe Munitionsvorräte; ~ **work** Rüstungsbetrieb.

mural | painting Wandmalerei; ~ **tablet** Gedenktafel.

murder Mord[fall], Ermordung;
on charge of ~ unter Mordanklage;
attempted ~ Mordversuch, -anschlag; **felony** ~ *(US)* Körper-verletzung mit tödlichem Ausgang; **hired** ~ bezahlter Mord; **judicial** ~ Justizmord; **premeditated** ~ vorsätzlicher Mord; **ritual** ~ Ritualmord;
~ **in the first degree** *(US)* Mord; ~ **in the second degree** *(US)* Totschlag; ~ **by poison** Giftmord; ~ **attended with robbery** Raubmord;
~ *(v.)* [er]morden;
~ **a language** Sprache verhunzen, radebrechen; ~ **time** Zeit totschlagen;
to be declared guilty of ~ wegen Mordes verurteilt werden; **to come near to** ~ fast einem Mord gleichkommen; **to commit a** ~ Mord begehen; **to cry blue** ~ *(coll.)* Zeter und Mordio (wie am Spieß) schreien; **to get away with** ~ *(sl.)* gerade noch mit einem blauen Auge davonkommen; **to lie under suspicion of** ~ unter Mordverdacht stehen; **to meditate** ~ mit Mordgedanken umge-hen; **to try s. o. for** ~ Mordprozeß gegen j. durchführen;
~ **charge** Mordanklage; ~ **hunt** Jagd nach dem Mörder; ~ **mystery** Krimi[nalfall]; ~ **suspect** Mordverdächtiger; ~ **trial** Mordprozeß; ~ **weapon** Mordwaffe.

murderer Mörder;
to hire a ~ Mörder dingen.

murdering Ermordung.

murderous | attempt Mordversuch; ~ **intent** Mordabsicht; ~ **plot** Mordverschwörung, -anschlag; ~ **war** mörderischer Krieg; ~ **weapon** Mordwaffe.

murky fog dichter (undurchdringlicher) Nebel.

murmur Gemurmel;
~ *(v.)* **against new taxes** sich über neue Steuern beklagen;
to pay higher taxes without a ~ höhere Steuern ohne Ein-spruchserhebung zahlen; **to swallow it without a** ~ wider-spruchslos hinnehmen.

muscle Muskel[kraft], *(sl.)* Muskelprotz;
~ *(v.) (US coll.)* sich rückhaltslos vorwärtsdrängen;
~ **in** *(sl.)* sich seinen Beuteanteil gewaltsam sichern; ~ **out of a movement** aus einer Organisation ausschließen;
to flex one' ~**s** *(fig.)* seine Muskeln spielen lassen; **to give financial** ~ finanzielle Basis verstärken; **to have enough** ~ über genügend Durchsetzungsvermögen verfügen; **not to move a** ~ mit keiner Wimper zucken; **to show one's** ~ seine Stärke zeigen; **to use more political** ~**s** im stärkeren Maße politisch beeinflussen.

museum Museum;
art ~ Museum der Schönen Künste; **industrial** ~ Gewerbe-museum;
~ **catalog(ue)** Museumskatalog; ~ **explosion** Hausse im Museumsbau; ~ **guide** Museumsführer; ~ **piece** Museums-stück.

mush *(sl.)* sentimentales Geschwätz.

mushroom Pilz, *(upstart)* Emporkömmling;
~ *(v.)* **into a production order** lawinenartigen Produktionsauf-trag auslösen; ~ **up** *(US)* aus dem Boden schießen;
to shoot (spring up) like ~**s** wie Pilze hervorschießen.

~ **desk lamp** Pilzlampe; ~ **enterprise** Spekulationsbetrieb; ~ **fame** Eintagsruhm; ~ **growth** rapides Wachstum; ~ **growth of a suburb** pilzartiges Anwachsen einer Vorstadt; ~ **town** pilzartig gewachsene Stadt.

mushy gefühlsduselig, sentimental;
~ **sentimentality** Gefühlsduselei.

music Musik, Tonkunst, *(musical composition)* Musikstück, Komposition;
dance ~ Tanzmusik; **orchestral** ~ Orchestermusik; ~ **of the birds** Gesang der Vögel;
to face the ~ Suppe auslöffeln, die man sich eingebrockt hat; **to make fine** ~ **together** gut miteinander harmonisieren; **to play from** ~ vom Blatt spielen;
~ **book** Notenheft, -buch; ~ **box** *(US)* Spieldose; ~ **case** Noten-schrank; ~ **company** Musikverlag; ~ **drama** Musikdrama; ~ **hall** Konzerthalle, *(Br.)* Varieté[theater]; ~ **house** Musikalien-handlung; **popular** ~ **program(me)** volkstümliches Musikpro-gramm; ~ **stand** Notenständer; ~ **stool** Klavierstuhl.

musical Musical;
~ *(a.)* musikalisch, melodisch, harmonisch;
~ **art** Tonkunst; ~ **box** *(Br.)* Spieldose; ~ **comedy** musikalisches Lustspiel, Musikal; ~ **composition** Komposition, Musikwerk; ~ **evening** musikalische Abendunterhaltung, Privatkonzert; ~ **film** Musikfilm; ~ **instrument** Musikinstrument; ~ **pro-gram(me)** Musiksendung; ~ **segment** Musikstück; ~ **tabloid** Kurzoperette; ~ **watch** Metronom.

musician Musiker.

must Muß, Unerläßlichkeit;
an absolute ~ Notwendigkeit;
~ *(a.)* unbedingt, absolut;
~ **legislation** *(US)* unerläßlich notwendige Gesetze; ~ **reading** Zwangs-, Pflichtlektüre; ~ **restriction** unerläßliche Ein-schränkung.

muster *(mil.)* Antreten zum Appell, Musterung, *(samples)* Musterkollektion;
~ *(v.)* zustande-, zuwegebringen, versammeln, zusammen-treiben;
~ **a two-third majority** Zweidrittelmehrheit auf die Beine bringen;
~ **in** *(mil., US)* zum Wehrdienst einziehen; ~ **out** *(US)* aus dem Wehrdienst entlassen; ~ **up all one's courage** allen Mut zusam-mennehmen; ~ **up all one's strength** seine ganze Kraft anspannen;
to pass ~ gemustert (für tauglich erklärt) werden, *(fig.)* Zustim-mung finden; **to take** ~ **of troops** Parade abnehmen;
~ **book** *(mil.)* Stammrollenbuch; ~ **parade** Paradeabnahme; ~ **roll** *(mil.)* Muster-, Stammrolle, *(ship)* Schiffsmusterrolle.

mutation of libel Klageänderung.

mute stumm;
~ **as a fish** stumm wie ein Fisch;
to stand ~ *(criminal law, Br.)* Aussage verweigern.

mutilate verstümmeln.

mutilated bank note beschädigter Geldschein.

mutilation schwere Körperverletzung, Verstümmelung, *(cheque)* Beschädigung, *(of coins)* Münzverschlechterung.

mutineer Meuterer;
~ *(v.)* meutern.

mutinous behavi(o)ur aufrührerisches Verhalten.

mutiny Meuterei;
~ *(v.)* meutern;
to be guilty of ~ der Meuterei schuldig sein; **to institute a** ~ Meuterei anstiften.

mutton, dead as mausetot;
to cut ~ **with s. o.** jds. Gastfreundschaft genießen; **to return to one's** ~ seinen Schäfchenbrocken wieder aufnehmen.

mutual gegen-, wechselseitig, austauschbar;
~ **accounts** Kontokorrentverhältnis; ~ **affection** gegenseitige Zuneigung; ~ **affray** Zweikampf; ~ **agreement** gegenseitiges Einvernehmen; ~ **aid** gegenseitige Hilfsaktion (Hilfeleistung); ~ **aid plan** Hilfsabkommen auf Gegenseitigkeit; ~ **arrangement** gegenseitiges Einvernehmen; ~ **assent** *(law of contract)* Eini-gung; ~ **assistance treaty** Beistandspakt; ~ **assurance** Versiche-rung der Gegenseitigkeit; ~ **assurance company** *(Br.)* Versicherungsverein auf Gegenseitigkeit; ~ **Balanced Force Reduction** *(MBFR)* wechselseitiges ausgewogener Truppenab-bau; ~ **benefit association** Wohltätigkeitsverein auf Gegensei-tigkeit; ~ **benefit society** *(US)* Gegenseitigkeitsverein; ~ **building association** Baugenossenschaft; ~ **company** Versiche-rungsverein auf Gegenseitigkeit; ~ **consent** beiderseitiges Ein-verständnis; **by** ~ **consent** in gegenseitiger Übereinkunft; ~ **consideration** Gegenleistung; ~ **contract** synallagmatischer

(gegenseitiger) Vertrag; ~ **corporation** Gegenseitigkeitsgesellschaft; ~ **covenants** gegenseitige Verpflichtungen; ~ **credits** gegenseitige Gutschriften; ~ **currency account** gegenseitiges Währungskonto; ~ **dealings** wechselseitiger Geschäftsverkehr; ~ **defence agreement** Abkommen über gegenseitige Verteidigungshilfe; ~ **demands** gegenseitige Forderungen; ~ **enterprise** Genossenschaftsunternehmen; ~ **fund** *(US)* Kapitalanlage-, Investmentgesellschaft; **insurance-run** ~ **fund** von einer Versicherungsgesellschaft verwaltete Investmentgesellschaft; **top-performing** ~ **funds** Spitzenreiter unter den Investmentfonds; ~ **fund brokerage** Provisionsgeschäfte einer Kapitalanlagegesellschaft; ~ **fund contractual plan** Investmentvertragssystem; ~ **fund industry** Kapitalanlage-, Investmentwesen; ~ **fund insurance package** mit einer Lebensversicherung gekoppeltes Investmentzertifikat; ~ **gable** *(Scot.)* Trenn-, Brandmauer; ~ **guarantee** gegenseitiges Garantieversprechen; ~ **improvement society** Fortbildungsverein; ~ **indebtedness** doppelseitiges Schuldverhältnis; ~ **indemnity insurance** Schadensversicherung auf Gegenseitigkeit; ~ **insurance** Versicherung auf Gegenseitigkeit; ~ **insurance company** Versicherungsverein auf Gegenseitigkeit; ~ **interest** gegenseitiges Interesse; ~ **loan association** *(US)* Bausparkasse auf Gegenseitigkeit; ~ **loan society** Kreditgenossenschaft; ~ **office** *(Br.)* Versicherungsgesellschaft auf Gegenseitigkeit; ~ **principle** *(law of nations)* Gegenseitigkeitsprinzip; **to arrange a transaction on** ~ **principles** Geschäft auf der Grundlage der Gegensei-

tigkeit vorbereiten; ~ **promise** Gegenseitigkeitsverpflichtung; ~ **relief association** Unterstützungskasse auf Gegenseitigkeit; ~ **reserve company** Versicherungs- und Sparverein; ~ **savings bank** *(US)* genossenschaftsähnliche Sparkasse; ~ **Security Agency** *(US)* Amt für gegenseitige Sicherheit; **on** ~ **terms** auf Gegenseitigkeit; ~ **testament** *(US)* gegenseitiges (Berliner) Testament; ~ **trust** *(US)* Gemeinschaftsfonds; ~ **wall** *(Scot.)* Trennmauer; ~ **will** *(US)* gegenseitiges (Berliner) Testament.

mutuality Gegenseitigkeit, Reziprozität.

mutualize *(v.)* Gegenseitigkeitsverhältnis schaffen.

muzzle Maulkorb;
~ *(v.)* knebeln, mundtot machen.

muzzling of the press Knebelung der Presse.

myrmidon skrupeloser Gefolgsmann, Häscher;
~ **of the law** Scherge des Gerichts.

mystery Geheimnis[krämerei], Heimlichtuerei;
to be wrapped in ~ von Geheimnissen umgeben sein;
~ **novel** Kriminal-, Detektivroman; ~ **ship** U-Bootfalle; ~ **train** Fahrt ins Blaue.

mystic schleierhaft, rätselhaft, *(law, US)* versiegelt, geheim;
~ **testament** *(Scot.)* notarielles Testament.

mystical wealth sagenhafter Reichtum.

mystification Irreführung, Täuschung, Mystifikation.

mystified, to be vor einem Rätsel stehen.

mystify *(v.)* hinters Licht führen, irreführen.

myth Mythos, Sage.

N

nab *(coll.)* Polizist, Detektiv;
~ *(v.) (coll.)* schnappen, erwischen.
nabbed by the police von der Polizei erwischt (geschnappt).
nabob Krösus.
nacelle Luftschiffgondel.
nack *(sl.)* Spion.
nadir *(fig.)* Tiefpunkt, -stand.
nag *(v.)* nörgeln, meckern;
~ **at s. o.** an jem. herumnörgeln.
nagger Nörgelfritze.
nagging Meckern, Nörgeln.
nail Nagel;
hard as ~**s** stahlhart, voller Energie, in guter Verfassung; **on the** ~ auf der Stelle, sofort, *(problem)* brennend, von unmittelbarem Interesse; **right as** ~**s** ganz richtig; **to the** ~ vollendet, vollkommen;
~ **in my coffin** Nagel zu meinem Sarg;
~ *(v.)* annageln, *(sl.)* schnappen, verhaften, festhalten;
~ **s. o. down to his promise** j. auf sein Versprechen festnageln; ~ **one's eyes on s. th.** *(fam.)* etw. mit den Augen fixieren; ~ **a lie to the counter (barn door)** j. mit einer Lüge festnageln, Sachverhalt aufdecken; ~ **down a criminal** Verbrecher zur Strecke bringen; ~ **down an enormous amount of money** enormen Geldbetrag fest anlegen; ~ **one's colo(u)rs to the mast** sich in einer Sache festlegen; ~ **together (up)** zusammennageln; ~ **up a notice on a wall** Mitteilung an die Wand anschlagen;
to drive a ~ **in s. one's coffin** Nagel zu jds. Sarg sein; **to drive the** ~ **home** Sache zum guten Ende bringen; **to fight tooth and** ~ alle Kräfte für den Sieg einsetzen; **to hit the** ~ **[right] on the head** Nagel auf den Kopf treffen; **to pay on the** ~ bar (pünktlich) bezahlen.
nailed | to the ground wie an den Erdboden festgenagelt; ~**-up drama** zusammengebasteltes Drama.
nailer großartiger Kerl;
to be a ~ **at it** etw. asshaft beherrschen; **to work like a** ~ wie besessen arbeiten.
nailing *(sl.)* prima, famos, glänzend;
~ **good time** märchenhafte Zeit.
naked schutz-, wehrlos, *(oil)* lose, *(uncertified)* nicht bestätigt;
~ **of all provisions** bar jeder Vorräte;
~ **authority** unentgeltlich ausgeübte Vollmacht; **to believe s. one's** ~ **assertion** jds. Zusicherung blindlings glauben; ~ **bond** einseitige Verpflichtung; ~ **confession** glattes Eingeständnis; ~ **contract** einseitiger (nicht bindender, unverbindlicher) Vertrag; ~ **debenture** *(Br.)* ungesicherte Schuldverschreibung; ~ **deposit** unentgeltliche Verwahrung; ~ **facts** nackte Tatsachen; ~ **field** Brachfeld; **to fight with** ~ **fists** mit den bloßen Fäusten kämpfen; **to reveal one's** ~ **heart** aus seinem Herzen keine Mördergrube machen; ~ **possession** tatsächlicher Besitz [ohne Rechtsanspruch]; ~ **reserve** *(Federal Reserve Bank, US)* besondere Rücklage; ~ **trust** Treuhandstellung ohne besonderen Aufgabenbereich; ~ **truth** ungeschminkte Wahrheit.
nakedness Schutz-, Wehrlosigkeit;
to reveal the crime in all its ~ Verbrechen ungeschminkt offenbaren.
namby-pamby geziert, affektiert.
name Name, Bezeichnung, Benennung, *(family)* Familie, Sippe, *(influential person, sl.)* einflußreiche Persönlichkeit, *(reputation)* Ruf, Renommee;
by ~ namentlich; **by the** ~ **of** namens, unter dem Namen von; **in** ~ **only** nur dem Namen nach; **in the** ~ **and behalf of** im Namen und im Auftrag von; **in the** ~ **of the law** im Namen des Gesetzes; **in one's own** ~ **and on one's account** in eigenem Namen und für eigene Rechnung; **to one's** ~ eigen;
assumed ~ angenommener Name, Deckname, Pseudonym; **bad** ~ schlechter Ruf; **business** ~ [Handels]firma, Firmenname; **brand** ~ Markenname; **Christian** ~ Tauf-, Ruf-, Vorname; **code** ~ Deckname; **collective** ~ Sammelname, -begriff; **commercial** ~ Handelsbezeichnung; **corporate** ~ *(US)* handelsgerichtlich eingetragener Name, Firmenname; **distinctive** ~ *(US)* Markenname; **family** ~ Familienname; **fancy** ~ erfundener Name; **feigned** ~ angenommener Name; **fictitious** ~ Deckname, Pseudonym; **first** ~ *(US)* Vorname; **first-class** ~ *(bill of exchange)* erstklassige Adresse; **full** ~ Vor- und Zuname; **given** ~ Ruf-, Taufname; **insulting** ~**s** Beschimpfungen; **last** ~ *(US)* Familienname; **maiden** ~ Mädchenname; **misleading** ~ irreführende Bezeichnung; **pen** ~ Schriftstellername; **prime** ~ *(bill*

of exchange) erstklassige Adresse; **proprietary** ~ gesetzlich geschützter Name; **registered** ~ handelsgerichtlich eingetragener Firmenname; **trade** ~ Firma, Firmenname, Firmen-, Geschäfts-, Handelsbezeichnung; **trademark** ~ Markenname; ~ **of an account** Kontobezeichnung; ~ **of the bearer** Name des Inhabers; **great** ~**s of our century** berühmte Persönlichkeiten unseres Jahrhunderts; ~ **of a company** *(Br.)* Firmenname, handelsgerichtlich eingetragener Name einer Gesellschaft; ~ **and description** Angaben zur Person, Personalien; ~ **in lights clauses** Bestimmungen über übertarifliche Vergütung; ~ **of a maker** Name des Ausstellers; ~ **of a place** Ortsname; ~**s of those present** Anwesenheitsliste; ~ **of a ship** Wahlspruch eines Schiffes;
~ *(v.) (call)* [be]nennen, Namen geben, *(designate)* namhaft machen, benennen, *(determine)* festlegen, bestimmen, *(parliament, Br.)* zur Ordnung rufen, Ordnungsruf erteilen;
~ **a day** Tag bestimmen; ~ **the day (a day for the wedding)** Hochzeitstag festsetzen; ~ **s. o. to an office** j. für ein Amt vorschlagen; ~ **a price** Preis benennen (festsetzen); ~ **the source of one's information** seine Informationsquelle nennen (aufdecken);
to act in one's own ~ im eigenen Namen handeln; **to assume a** ~ Namen annehmen, sich einen Namen beilegen; **to be in s. one's** ~ *(share)* auf jds. Namen eingetragen sein; **to be made out in the** ~ **of the holder** auf den Inhaber lauten; **to bear a** ~ Namen führen; **to book a ticket in the** ~ **of s. o.** Fahrkarte auf jds. Namen bestellen; **to call s. o.** ~**s** j. mit Schimpfworten belegen; **to carry on the business under one's** ~ Geschäft unter seinem Namen führen; **to change the** ~ **of a ship** Schiff umtaufen; **to check off** ~**s on a list** Namen auf einer Liste abhaken; **to defend one's good** ~ seinen guten Ruf wahren; **to enter one's** ~ sich eintragen; **to fill in one's** ~ **on an official form** seinen Namen in ein Formular einsetzen; **to give a dog a bad** ~ **and hang him** j. wegen einer Missetat ein für allemal verurteilen; **to give in one's** ~ auf einer Liste eintragen; **to give a new** ~ **to a street** Straße umbenennen; **to give up using one's** ~ seinen Namen ablegen; **to go under the** ~ **of** unter dem Namen laufen; **to have a bad** ~ schlechten Ruf genießen; **to have s. th. to one's** ~ etw. aufzuweisen haben; **to have one's** ~ **in the Gazette** für bankrott erklärt werden; **to have one's** ~ **up** im Ruf stehen; **to have a** ~ **for honesty** als anständig gelten; **to have the** ~ **of a miser** im Geruch eines Geizhalses stehen; **to have a** ~ **for good workmanship** für gute Arbeit (Ausführung) bekannt sein; **to have a great** ~ **in one's field** Berühmtheit (Kapazität) in seinem Fach sein; **not to have a penny to one's** ~ keinen Pfennig Geld mehr besitzen; **to inquire s. one's** ~ j. nach seinem Namen fragen; **to inscribe the** ~ **of shareholders (stockholders, US)** Namensaktionäre registrieren; **to keep one's** ~ **on the books** seine Mitgliedschaft beibehalten; **to know s. o. by** ~ j. namentlich kennen; **to lend one's** ~ **an enterprise** seinen guten Namen für ein Unternehmen zur Verfügung stellen; **to make a** ~ **for o. s.** sich einen [guten] Namen machen; **to mention by** ~ namentlich erwähnen; **to pass a** ~ *(Br.)* Effektenabrechnung erteilen; **to place a** ~ **in case of need on a draft** Namen als Notadresse auf einen Wechsel setzen; **to put one's** ~ **down** kandidieren; **to put a tick against a** ~ Namen auf einer Liste abhaken; **to refer to s. o. by** ~ j. namentlich erwähnen; **to send in one's** ~ sich anmelden lassen; **to set one's** ~ **to a document** Urkunde unterschreiben (unterfertigen); **to stain s. one's** ~ jds. Namen beschmutzen; **to stand in the** ~ **of s. o.** *(motion)* in jds. Namen eingebracht sein; **to strike s. one's** ~ **off a list** jds. Namen auf einer Liste streichen; **to sue in one's corporate** ~ unter seinem handelsgerichtlichen Namen klagen; **to supply** ~**s of prospects** *(US)* Anschriften potentieller Kunden liefern; **to take s. one's** ~ **and address** sich mit jem. verabreden, *(police)* j. aufschreiben; **to take a** ~ **off the books** Namen von der Mitgliederliste streichen; **to take one's** ~ **off the books** seine Mitgliedschaft aufgeben, *(university, Br.)* sich exmatrikulieren lassen; **to take s. one's** ~ **in vain** jds. Namen mißbrauchen; **to write one's** ~ **in full** seinen Vor- und Nachnamen aufschreiben; **to write one's** ~ **in the space indicated** seinen Namen an die freigelassene Stelle setzen;
~ **badge** Namensschild; ~ **block** *(advertising)* Markenwortbild; ~ **brand** Markenartikel; ~ **day** Namenstag, *(stock exchange, Br.)* Abrechnungs-, Skontierungstag; ~**-dropper** Eindrucksschinder; ~**-dropping** Eindruckschinden; ~ **part** *(theater)* Titel-

rolle; ~ **plate** Türschild, *(motor)* Namens-, Firmenschild; ~ **son** Namensvetter; ~ **supplier** Adressenlieferant; ~ **tape** eingewebtes Wäschezeichen; ~ **test** Namenstest.

nameboard Namensschild.

named genannt, erwähnt;
   last ~ letztgenannt; **positively** ~ ausdrücklich benannt; ~ **above** obengenannt;
   not to be ~ **in the same breath with his brother** *(fam.)* mit seinem Bruder nicht im gleichen Atemzug genannt werden können; **to be** ~ **for the directorship** zum Direktor vorgeschlagen worden sein;
   ~ **policy** Seepolice mit Angabe des befördernden Schiffes.

naming of a member *(parl., Br.)* Erteilung eines Ordnungsrufes.

nameless unbekannt, obskur, *(illegitimate)* unehelich, illegitim.

namesake Namensvetter.

naming Namhaftmachung, Benennung;
   ~ **a member** *(parl,. Br.)* Erteilung eines Ordnungsrufes.

nap Nickerchen;
   to go ~ *(fig.)* alles auf eine Karte setzen, höchstes Risiko eingehen; **to have (take) a** ~ Nickerchen machen;
   ~ **hand** *(fig.)* gute Gewinnaussichten.

napkin Serviette;
   to lay s. th. up in a ~ etw. ungenutzt lassen.

nark *(sl.)* Polizeispitzel, Denunziant;
   ~ *(v.)* spionieren, bespitzeln.

narcotic Betäubungsmittel, Rauschgift, *(person)* Rauschgiftsüchtiger;
   ~ **addict** *(US)* Rauschgiftsüchtiger; ~ **Division** Rauschgiftabteilung; ~ **drugs** Rauschgift; ~ **ring** Rauschgiftbande; ~ **speech** einschläfernde Rede; ~**s smuggling** Rauschgiftschmuggel; ~**s traffic** Rauschgifthandel.

narrate *(v.)* berichten.

narratio *(lat.)* Klagebegründung.

narration Erzählung, Geschichte;
   ~ **of an entry** Wortlaut einer Buchung.

narrative *(conveyancing, Scot.)* Beurkundung;
   ~ **form** *(balance sheet)* Berichtsform.

narrator Erzähler, *(broadcasting)* Sprecher.

narrow enge Stelle, Meerenge, *(US)* Engpaß;
   ~ *(a.)* eng, *(straitened)* knapp, beschränkt;
   ~ *(v.)* knapper werden, *(road)* sich verengen, schmäler werden; ~ **down** sich beschränken; ~ **down s. one's power** jds. Vollmacht beschränken; ~ **profit margin** Gewinnspanne einengen; ~ **the search down to two men** Nachforschungen auf zwei Personen einengen;
   within ~ **bounds** in engen Grenzen; ~ **circle of friends** kleiner Freundeskreis; ~ **circumstances** *(coll.)* beschränkte Verhältnisse; **to live in** ~ **circumstances** *(fam.)* sich sehr einschränken müssen, in bescheidenen Verhältnissen leben; ~ **construction** enge Auslegung; **to have a** ~ **escape** gerade noch (mit knapper Mühe) davonkommen; ~ **film** Schmalfilm; ~ **fortune** kleines Vermögen; ~-**gauge** schmalspurig; ~-**gauge film** Schmalfilm; ~-**gauge railway** Schmalspurbahn; ~-**gauged** schmalspurig; ~ **goods** Kurz-, Bandwaren; ~ **investigations** genaue Nachforschungen; ~ **majority** knappe Mehrheit; **to win an election with a** ~ **margin** Wahl mit geringer Umsatz, enger Markt, *(stock exchange)* flauer Markt, beschränkte Verkaufsmöglichkeiten; **to have a** ~ **market** *(stock exchange)* wenig gehandelt werden; ~ **means** knappe Mittel; ~-**minded** geistig beschränkt, engstirnig, borniert; ~-**mindedness** Beschränktheit, Borniertheit, Engstirnigkeit; ~ **profit margin** schmale Verdienstspanne; ~ **sales area** stark eingegrenztes Verkaufsgebiet; ~ **search** sorgfältige Überprüfung; **to have a** ~ **shave (squeak)** *(coll.)* mit knapper Not davonkommen; **in** ~ **straits** in Geldverlegenheit.

narrowly eng, beschränkt;
   ~ *(v.)* **miss being run over** um ein Haar überfahren werden; **to construe a clause** ~ Klausel eng auslegen; **to look** ~ **into an affair** Sache genau untersuchen.

narrowing of profit margins Einengung der Gewinnchancen.

narrowness of the market Marktenge; ~ **of mind** geistige Beschränktheit.

nasty accident böser Unfall; ~ **corner** gefährliche Straßenecke; ~ **fellow** unangenehmer Kerl; ~ **sea** gefährliche See.

natality Geburtenziffer.

nation Nation, Volk, Land;
   throughout the ~ im ganzen Land;
   civilized ~ Kulturvolk; **commercial** ~ Handelsvolk; **creditor** ~ Gläubigerland; **debtor** ~ Schuldnerland; **divided** ~ geteiltes Land; **friendly** ~ befreundeter Staat; **host** ~ Gastgeberland; **industrial** ~ Industriestaat; **maritime** ~ Seefahrervolk; **member**

~ **Mitgliedstaat; mercantile** ~ handeltreibende Nation; **neighbo(u)ring** ~ Nachbarvolk; **neutral** ~ neutraler Staat; **riparian** ~ Anliegerstaat; **trading** ~ Handelsvolk, -nation; **uncommitted** ~ bündnisfreies Land;
   most-favo[u]red ~ **clause** Meistbegünstigungsklausel; ~ **state** Nationalstaat; ~-**wide** allgemein, sich auf das ganze Land erstreckend, überregional; ~-**wide advertisement** überregionale Werbung; ~-**wide movement** Volksbewegung; **to find a** ~-**wide response** im ganzen Volk Widerhall finden.

national Inländer, Staatsangehöriger;
   foreign ~ ausländischer Staatsangehöriger;
   ~ *(a.)* national, staatlich, inländisch, *(EC)* einzelstaatlich, *(patriotic)* vaterländisch, patriotisch, *(US)* bundesstaatlich, gesamtamerikanisch;
   ~ **accounts** volkswirtschaftliche Gesamtrechnung; ~ **accounts budget** National-, Staatsbudget; ~ **accounting** volkswirtschaftliche Gesamtrechnung; ~ **advertising** *(US)* überregionale Werbung; ~ **Aeronautics and Space Administration (NASA)** *(US)* Bundesluft- und Raumfahrtbehörde; ~ **Advisory Council on Education for Industry and Commerce** *(Br.)* Beratungsausschuß in Berufungsfragen; ~ **agricultural credit corporation** *(US)* Kreditinstitut zur Vergabe von Krediten an die Landwirtschaft; ~ **anthem** Nationalhymne; ~ **Arbitration Tribunal** *(Br.)* Zwangsschiedsgericht [in Kriegszeiten]; ~ **archive** Staatsarchiv; ~ **Assembly** Nationalversammlung; ~ **assistance** *(Br.)* staatliche Fürsorge, Sozialhilfe, Fürsorgeunterstützung; **to be in receipt of** ~ **assistance** *(Br.)* Sozialhilfe beziehen; ~ **Assistance Act** *(Br.)* Sozialhilfegesetz; ~ **Assistance Board** *(Br.)* Staatliche Fürsorge, Sozialamt; ~ **Assistance Grant** *(Br.)* Sozialzuschuß; ~ **assistance rate** Sozialhilfesatz.

National Association of Credit Men *(US)* Auskunftei der Kreditinstitute; ~ **of Estate Agents** [etwa] Bundesverband der Immobilienmakler; ~ **of Investment Clubs** *(Br.)* Verband britischer Kapitalanlagegesellschaften; ~ **of Savings Banks** *(US)* Sparkassenverband; ~ **of Parish Councils** *(Br.)* Gemeindetag, -verband; ~ **of Securities Dealers** *(US)* Börsenmaklerverband; ~ **of Securities Dealers Automated Quotation System (NSDAQ)** automatisches Kurswiedergabesystem des amerikanischen Börsenmaklerverbandes.

national attachment Nationalgefühl; ~ **bank** *(US)* Nationalbank, Staats-, Landesbank; ~ **bank circulation** *(US)* Banknotenumlauf der Nationalbanken; ~ **bank tax** *(US)* Notenbanksteuer; ~ **banking association** *(US)* Bankiersvereinigung; ~ **banking system** *(US)* Nationalbankwesen; ~ **bankruptcy** Staatsbankrott; ~ **Bankruptcy Act** *(US)* Konkursordnung; ~ **Board of Fire Underwriters** *(US)* Feuerversicherungsverband; ~ **Board for Prices and Incomes** *(Br.)* Preisüberwachungsstelle; ~ **boundary** Staats-, Landesgrenze; ~ **brands** *(US)* überall bekannte Qualitätserzeugnisse, Schutzmarken mit breiter Verkehrsgeltung; ~ **budget** *(US)* Bundeshaushalt, Staatsbudget; ~ **Bureau of Economic Research** *(US)* Statistisches Bundesamt; ~ **Bureau economist** Konjunkturpolitiker; **to reduce** ~ **capacity** Kapazitäten der einzelnen Länder reduzieren; ~ **capital spending** volkswirtschaftlicher Kapitalaufwand; ~ **certificate** staatliche Bescheinigung, Staatsdiplom; ~ **character** Volkscharakter; ~ **church** Staatskirche; ~ **Coal Board** *(Br.)* Staatliche Kohlenbehörde; ~ **colo(u)rs** Nationalfarben, -flagge; ~ **commision (committee)** Landesgruppe; ~ **conscious** nationalbewußt; ~ **consciousness** Nationalbewußtsein; ~ **convention** *(US)* Bundesparteitag; ~ **costume** Landestracht; ~ **council** Nationalrat; ~ **Credit Corporation** *(US)* Auffangsinstitut für notleidende Kreditinstitute; ~ **currency** Landeswährung; ~ **custom** Landessitte; ~ **debt** Staatsschuld, öffentliche Schuld; **external** ~ **debt** äußere Staatsschuld; **internal** ~ **debt** innere Staatsschuld; **to manage the** ~ **debt** Bundesschuldenverwaltung leiten; **to repudiate the** ~ **debt** Staatsschuld nicht anerkennen; ~ **Debt Commissioner** *(Br.)* [etwa] Bundesschuldenverwaltung; ~ **debt interest** Verzinsung der Staatsschuld; ~ **Debt Register** Staatsschuldbuch; ~ **defense (defence, Br.)** Landesverteidigung; ~ **defence contribution** *(Br.)* Aufrüstungsabgabe; ~ **defense premises** *(US)* Verteidigungsanlagen; ~ **Defense Research Council** *(US)* Bundesforschungsrat; ~ **development bonds** *(Br.)* 5%ige Staatsanleihe; ~ **diploma** Staatsdiplom; ~ **dividend** Volks-, Nationaleinkommen; ~ **domain** Staatsvermögen; ~ **domicile** Inlandswohnsitz; ~ **dress** Landestracht; ~ **economic accounting** volkswirtschaftliche Gesamtrechnung; ~ **Economic Development Council** *(Br.)* [etwa] Bundeswirtschaftsrat; ~ **economic planning** [etwa] volkswirtschaftliche Planung, Planwirtschaft; ~ **economy** Staats-, Volkswirtschaft, Nationalökonomie; ~ **emblem** Hoheitszeichen; ~ **emergency** Staatsnotstand; ~ **emergency council** zentrale Notstandsbehörde; ~ **ensign** Nationalflagge; ~ **enterprise** Staatsbetrieb, staatliches Unternehmen; ℓ **Enterprise Board** *(Br.)* staatliche Unternehmensverwaltung, Holdinggesellschaft, Ministerialabteilung für Staatsbetriebe; ℓ **Executive Committee** Parteivorstand; ~ **expenditure** Staatsausgaben; ~ **family allowance** staatliche Familienbeihilfe; ℓ **Farmers Union** *(Br.)* Bauernverband; ℓ **Federation of Employers** *(Br.)* Arbeitgeberverband; ~ **finance** Staatsfinanzen; ~ **flag** National-, Landesflagge; ~ **fund** National-, Staatsfonds; ~ **funeral** *(US)* Staatsbegräbnis.

National Giro *(Br.)* Postscheck;
  for use by ~ *(Br.)* mit Postschecküberweisung;
  ~ **Account** *(Br.)* Postscheckkonto; ~ **Centre** *(Br.)* zentrales Postscheckamt; ~ **Office** *(Br.)* Postscheckamt; ~ **Service** *(Br.)* Postscheckdienst; ~ **System** *(Br.)* Postscheckwesen.

National Girobank services *(Br.)* Postscheckdienst.

national | government *(US)* Bundesregierung; ℓ **and Local Government Officers' Association** [etwa] Angestelltengewerkschaft; ℓ **Graphical Union** *(Br.)* [etwa] IG Druck und Papier; ℓ **Guard** *(US)* Nationalgarde, Miliz; ~ **hatred** Nationalhaß; ~ **health** Volksgesundheit; ~ **health contribution** *(Br.)* Krankenkassenbeitrag; ℓ **Health Insurance** *(Br.)* staatliche Krankenversicherung; ℓ **Health Service** *(Br.)* staatlicher Gesundheitsdienst; ℓ **Health Service Contribution** *(Br.)* Krankenkassenbeitrag; ℓ **Health Service employee** *(Br.)* Angestellter des staatlichen Gesundheitsdienstes; ℓ **Health Service Employees' contribution** *(Br.)* Arbeitnehmeranteil zur Krankenkasse; ~ **holiday** gesetzlicher Feiertag; ~ **home** Heimstätte; ℓ **House-Building Council Scheme** *(Br.)* System des sozialen Wohnungsbaus; ℓ **Housing Act** *(US)* Wohnungsbaugesetz; ℓ **Housing Agency** *(US)* Wohnungsbaubehörde; ~ **identity** nationales Selbstverständnis.

national income Sozialprodukt, National-, Volkseinkommen;
  gross ~ Bruttosozialprodukt; **net** ~ Nettosozialprodukt;
  ~ **by distributive shares** *(US)* Volkseinkommen nach Einkommensarten;
  ~ **accounts (accounting)** volkswirtschaftliche Gesamtrechnung; ~ **policy** Konjunkturmaßnahmen auf dem Gebiet der Einkommenspolitik; ~ **statistics** Sozialstatistik.

National | Industrial Conference Board *(US)* Spitzenverband amerikanischer Arbeitgeber; ~ **Industrial Injuries Act** *(Br.)* Sozialversicherungsgesetz; ~ **Industrial Recovery Act** *(US)* Gesetz über den Wiederaufbau der Wirtschaft; ~ **Industrial Relations Court** *(Br.)* Schiedsgericht in Arbeitsstreitigkeiten, Schiedsgerichtshof für Arbeitnehmerfragen; ℓ **insolvency** Staatsbankrott; ~ **Institute of Economic and Social Research** *(Br.)* Konjunkturinstitut; ℓ **institution** Staatseinrichtung.

national insurance Sozialversicherung;
  ℓ **Act** *(Br.)* Sozialversicherungsgesetz; ℓ **Advisory Committee** *(Br.)* Beratungsausschuß für Sozialversicherungsfragen; ~ **benefits** *(Br.)* Sozialversicherungsleistungen; ~ **card** *(Br.)* Sozialversicherungskarte; **to stamp s. one's** ~ **card** Sozialversicherungsbeiträge für j. abführen; ~ **cheque** *(Br.)* Sozialversicherungszahlung; ℓ **Commissioner** *(Br.)* Sozialversicherungsaufsichtsamt; ~ **contribution** *(Br.)* Beiträge zur Sozialversicherung, Sozialversicherungsbeitrag; ~ **contributor** *(Br.)* Sozialversicherungspflichtiger; ~ **dependency benefits** *(Br.)* Sozialversicherungszuschläge für Kinder; ~ **fund** *(Br.)* Sozialversicherungsstock; ~ **institution** *(Br.)* Sozialversicherungsträger; ~ **legislation** *(Br.)* Sozialversicherungsgesetzgebung; ~ **recipient** *(Br.)* Sozialversicherungsempfänger; ~ **regulations** *(Br.)* Sozialversicherungsbestimmungen; ~ **standard** ~ **retirement pension** *(Br.)* übliche Sozialversicherungsrente; ~ **scheme** *(Br.)* Sozialversicherungssystem, -wesen; ~ **stamp** *(Br.)* Sozialversicherungsmarke; ~ **widow's allowance** Witwenrente.

national | interest Staatsinteresse; **to be on balance expedient in the** ~ **interest** das Staatsinteresse hinreichend gewährleisten; ~ **interurban road programme** *(Br.)* [etwa] Ausbauplan für das Bundesfernstraßennetz; ~ **joint council** *(Br.)* Arbeitgeber-Arbeitnehmergremium der öffentlichen Hand; ℓ **Labor Relations Act** *(US)* Gesetz über das Recht gewerkschaftlicher Koalition; ℓ **Labor Relations Board** *(US)* Bundesamt zur Regelung der Beziehungen zwischen Arbeitgebern und Arbeitnehmern; ~ **language** Mutter-, Landessprache; ~ **law** innerstaatliches Recht, Landesrecht, *(EC)* einzelstaatliches Recht; ~ **legislation** innerstaatliche Gesetzgebung, *(US)* bundesstaatliche Gesetzgebung; ~ **loan** Staatsanleihe; ~ **media** überregionale Werbeträger; ℓ **Mediation Board** *(US)* Bundesschlichtungsausschuß; ~ **monetary commission** Währungsausschuß; ~ **monopoly** Staatsmonopol; ~ **monument** Nationaldenkmal; ~ **mourning** Landestrauer; ℓ **Office** *(US)* zentrale Steuerbe-

hörde; ~ **opinion poll** Meinungsumfrage; ~ **organization** *(US)* Bundesorganisation; ~ **output** volkswirtschaftliche Gesamtproduktion; ~ **park** *(US)* Naturschutzgebiet, Nationalpark; ~ **plan** *(Br.)* Wirtschaftsförderungsprogramm; ℓ **Ports Council** *(Br.)* staatliche Hafenbehörde; ~ **press** überregionale Presse; ~ **print run** Inlandsauflage; ~ **product** *(Br.)* Sozialprodukt; **gross** ~ **product** Bruttosozialprodukt; **net** ~ **product** Nettosozialprodukt; ~ **product account** Sozialproduktrechnung; **gross** ~ **product figures** Bruttosozialproduktziffern; ~ **productivity increase** Sozialproduktzuwachs; ~ **property** National-, Volksvermögen, Staatseigentum; ℓ **Research Development Corporation** *(Br.)* Forschungsrat; ℓ **Research Council** *(US)* Forschungsrat; ~ **resident** Inländer; ~ **revenue** *(US)* National-, Volkseinkommen, Staatseinkünfte; ~ **safety** nationale Sicherheit; ℓ **Safety Council** *(US)* Verkehrssicherheitsrat; ~ **savings** *(Br.)* Sparwesen; ~ **savings bank** *(Br.)* Postsparkasse; ~ **savings bank account** *(Br.)* Postsparkonto; ℓ **Savings Bank Ordinary Account Book** *(Br.)* Sparkassenbuch; ~ **savings certificate** *(Br.)* Sparkassengutschein, -bon; ~ **savings gift tokens** *(Br.)* Geschenkprämien für Sparkassengutscheine; ~ **savings stamps** *(Br.)* Spargutmarken; ℓ **Savings Stock Register** *(Br.)* Register englischer Staatspapiere; ℓ **Science Foundation** *(US)* Bundesbehörde zur Förderung der Grundlagenforschung; ~ **security** nationale Sicherheit, Staatssicherheit; **to imperil** ~ **security** Staatssicherheit gefährden; ℓ **Security Council** *(US)* Sicherheitsausschuß; ~ **service** *(Br.)* Wehr-, Militärdienst; ~ **solidarity** nationale Solidarität; ~ **state** Nationalstaat; ~ **status** Staatsangehörigkeit, Nationalität; ℓ **Tax Association** *(US)* Verband der Steuerzahler; ~ **tendencies** nationale Strömungen; ~ **territory** Staatsgebiet; ~ **theatre** Theater mit Staatszuschuß; ~ **treasury** Staatsschatz; ~ **treatment** Inländerbehandlung; ℓ **Trust** *(Br.)* Nationalstiftung [zur Erhaltung kulturbedeutsamer Bauten]; ~ **union** Zentralverband, *(US)* Gewerkschaftsverband; ℓ **Union of Journalists** *(Br.)* Journalistengewerkschaft; ℓ **Union of manufacturers** *(Br.)* [etwa] Arbeitgeberverband; ℓ **Union of mineworkers** *(US)* Bergarbeitergewerkschaft; ℓ **Union of Railwaymen** *(Br.)* Eisenbahnergewerkschaft; ℓ **Union of Students** *(Br.)* Fachverband der britischen Studenschaften; ~ **unity government** nationale Einheitsregierung; ℓ **Wages Board** *(Br.)* Staatliches Lohnschlichtungsamt; ~ **waters** Binnengewässer; ~ **wealth** Volksvermögen.

nationalism Nationalgefühl, Nationalismus.

nationality Staatsangehörigkeit, Volkszugehörigkeit, Nationalität, *(national attachment)* Nationalgefühl, *(commodity)* Ursprung;
  without a ~ staatenlos;
  acquired ~ erworbene Staatsangehörigkeit; **dual** ~ Doppelstaatsangehörigkeit; **original** ~ ursprüngliche Staatsangehörigkeit;
  ~ **at birth** durch Geburt erworbene Staatsangehörigkeit;
  to acquire ~ Staatsangehörigkeit erwerben; **to deprive s. o. of his** ~ jem. die Staatsangehörigkeit aberkennen; **to opt for a** ~ für eine Staatsangehörigkeit optieren; **to renounce one's** ~ auf seine Staatsangehörigkeit verzichten;
  ~ **law** *(airplane)* Staatsangehörigkeitsgesetz; ~ **mark** *(airplane)* Hoheitszeichen; ~ **plate** nationales Kennzeichen; **to place** ~ **restrictions on its members** Staatsangehörigkeitsbeschränkungen für Mitglieder festsetzen.

nationalization *(Br.)* Nationalisierung, Verstaatlichung, Sozialisierung, Einverleibung, *(act of nationalizing)* Naturalisierung, Einbürgerung;
  ℓ **Act** *(Br.)* Verstaatlichungsgesetz; ~ **indemnity** *(Br.)* Sozialisierungsentschädigung; ~ **mark** *(airplane)* Staatszugehörigkeitszeichen; ~ **plan** *(Br.)* Verstaatlichungsabsicht; ~ **threat** drohende Verstaatlichung.

nationalize *(v.)* *(Br.)* verstaatlichen, nationalisieren, sozialisieren;
  ~ **o. s.** sich naturalisieren;
  ~ **the coal mines** *(Br.)* Bergbau verstaatlichen; ~ **a holiday** Feiertag zum Nationalfeiertag machen; ~ **the steel industry** *(Br.)* Stahlindustrie verstaatlichen.

nationalized, to become nationalisiert werden;
  ~ **industries** *(Br.)* verstaatlichte Industriezweige; ~ **industry committee** *(Br.)* Sozialisierungsausschuß; ~ **undertaking** *(Br.)* Staatsbetrieb.

nationalizer Verstaatlicher.

nationalty Nationaleigentum.

native Inländer, Landeskind, Einheimischer;
  ~**s** einheimische Bevölkerung;
  to be a ~ **of a town** aus einer Stadt stammen; **to go** ~ verwildern, *(US sl.)* sich völlig akklimatisieren;

~ *(a.)* einheimisch, inländisch, *(inherent)* angeboren, *(mineral)* natürlich vorkommend;
~ ability natürliche Veranlagung; **~-born** im Inland geboren; **~-born citizen** *(US)* gebürtiger Amerikaner; **~ charm** angeborene Liebenswürdigkeit; **~ country** Vater-, Heimat-, Geburtsland; **~ customs** Eingeborenenbräuche; **to behave with ~ ease** sich völlig ungezwungen benehmen; **~ gifts** geistige Anlagen; **~ gold** gediegenes Gold; **~ industry** einheimische Industrie; **~ labo(u)r** einheimische Arbeitskräfte; **~ land** Heimatland; **~ language** Muttersprache; **~ place** Heimat-, Geburtsort; **~ population** einheimische Bevölkerung; **~ port** Heimathafen; **~ product** Landeserzeugnis; **~ quarter** Eingeborenenviertel; **~ rising** Eingeborenenaufstand; **~ settlement** Eingeborenensiedlung; **my ~ shore** mein Heimatland; **~ tongue** Muttersprache; **~ town** Heimatstadt, Vaterstadt; **~ tribe** Eingeborenenstamm.

nativism *(US)* Begünstigung der Einheimischen, Inländerbegünstigung.

natural Naturgenie, *(idiot)* Schwachsinniger, Idiot;
to be a ~ for a job für einen Beruf wie geschaffen sein;
~ *(a.)* natürlich, auf natürlichen Instinkten beruhend, *(not artificial)* unbearbeitet, im Naturzustand;
~ advantages naturgegebene Vorteile; **~ affection** natürliche Zuneigung; **~-born** von Geburt; **~-born American citizen** gebürtiger Amerikaner; **~-born subject** *(Br.)* britischer Staatsangehöriger kraft Geburt; **~ boundary** natürliche Grenze; **~ business year** normales Geschäftsjahr; **~ child** natürliches (eheliches) Kind; **~ day** Kalendertag; **to die a ~ death** eines natürlichen Todes sterben; **~ disaster** Naturkatastrophe; **~ disaster coverage** Versicherungsschutz gegen Naturkatastrophen; **~ domicile** ursprünglicher Wohnort; **~ economy** Naturalwirtschaft; **~ drying** Lufttrocknung; **~ equity** [etwa] gesundes Rechtsempfinden; **~ event** Naturereignis; **~ fool** Schwachsinniger von Geburt; **~ fruits** Bodenfrüchte; **~ gas** Erdgas; **~ gas industry** Erdgasindustrie; **~ gift** natürliche Begabung; **~ guardian** sorgeberechtigter Elternteil; **~ heir** in gerader Linie verwandter Erbberechtigter; **~ history** Naturgeschichte; **~ idiot** von Geburt Schwachsinniger; **~ increase** natürliches Bevölkerungswachstum; **~ infancy** Kindesalter [bis 7 Jahre]; **~ interest rate** originärer Zins; **~ law** Naturrecht; **~ life** Erdenleben; **during his ~ life** auf Lebenszeit; **to be a ~ linguist** angeborene Sprachbegabung haben; **~ loss** natürlicher Schwund; **~ marketing area** natürliches Absatzgebiet; **~ milk shed** natürliches Milchversorgungsgebiet; **~ monopoly** natürliches Monopol; **~ monument** Naturdenkmal; **~ object of testator's bounty** gesetzlich vorgesehener Erbberechtigter; **~ obligation** Naturalobligation; **~ orator** geborener Redner; **~ person** natürliche Person; **~ possession** tatsächlicher Besitz; **~ premium** *(life insurance)* von Jahr zu Jahr ansteigende Lebensversicherungsprämie; **~ presumption** natürliche Schlußfolgerung; **~ price** durchschnittlicher Marktpreis; **~ product** Rohprodukt; **~ reserve** Naturschutzgebiet; **~ resources** Bodenschätze; **~ rights** originäre Rechte, Naturrechte; **~ science** Naturwissenschaft; **~ selection** natürliche Zuchtwahl; **~ size** natürliche Größe; **~ son** natürlicher Sohn; **in the ~ state** im Naturzustand; **~ steel** Rohstahl; **~ succession** gesetzliche Erbfolge; **to have a ~ tendency to do s. th.** ausgesprochene Neigung für etw. haben; **~ vibration** Eigenschwingung; **~ wastage** üblicher Abgang an Arbeitskräften; **~ waste** üblicher Verschleiß.

naturalization Einbürgerung, Naturalisierung;
collective ~ Kollektiveinbürgerung;
to be admitted to citizenship by ~ *(US)* eingebürgert (naturalisiert) werden; **to be eligible for ~** *(US)* Einbürgerungsvoraussetzungen erfüllen; **to petition for ~** *(US)* Einbürgerungsantrag stellen.

naturalization papers Einbürgerungsurkunde;
to take out ~ *(US)* sich einbürgern lassen.

naturalize *(v.)* naturalisieren, einbürgern;
~ immigrants into a country Einwanderern die Staatsbürgerschaft verleihen.

naturalized British subject eingebürgerter Engländer; **~ citizen** *(US)* eingebürgerter Ausländer.

nature Natur, Beschaffenheit, *(person)* Wesen, Art, Veranlagung;
by its very ~ aus seiner ureigensten Natur heraus; **in the ~ of a trial** nach Art eines Verhörs; **true to ~** wirklichkeitstreu; **honest ~** ehrliche Haut; **human ~** menschliche Natur; **general ~ of business** allgemeiner Geschäftszweck; **~ of contents** Inhaltsbeschreibung; **~ of employment** Beschäftigungsart; **~ of pension** Pensionsart;
to be of a happy ~ glückliches Naturell haben; **to be of a protracted ~** *(negotiations)* sich in die Länge ziehen; **to be in the**

~ of a threat einer Drohung nahekommen; **to pay one's debt to ~** sterben;
it is in the ~ of things es liegt in der Natur der Dinge;
~ boy *(sl.)* Naturbursche; **≗ Conservancy** *(Br.)* Naturschutzamt; **~ reserve** Naturschutzgebiet; **~ worship** Naturanbetung.

naught Null, *(fig.)* Mißerfolg, Untergang, Verderb;
to add a ~ Null anhängen; **to bring s. one's plans to ~** jds. Pläne vereiteln; **to care ~ for s. th.** an etw. überhaupt kein Interesse haben; **to come to ~** nichts daraus werden; **to get a ~** null Fehler machen; **to set advice at ~** Ratschlag in den Wind schlagen; **to set the law at ~** Gesetz mißachten.

nausea Seekrankheit;
to be filled with ~ mit Abscheu erfüllt sein; **to be overcome with ~** seekrank werden; **to be sated to ~ with travelling** das Reisen bis oben hin stehen haben.

nauseating food ekelerregende Nahrungsmittel.

nautical nautisch;
~ almanac nautisches Jahrbuch; **~ assessor** amtlich bestellter Schiffssachverständiger; **~ chart** Seekarte; **~ custom** Seebrauch; **~ matters** Seefahrtsangelegenheiten; **~ mile** Seemeile; **~ school** Seefahrtsschule; **~ term** Marineausdruck; **~ yarn** *(fam.)* Seemannsgarn.

naval seemännisch;
~ academy Marineakademie, Navigationsschule; **~ action** Seegefecht; **~ agreement** Flottenabkommen; **~ air arm** Marineluftwaffe; **~ air station** Marinefliegerstützpunkt; **~ airplane** Marineflugzeug; **~ architect** Marineingenieur; **~ architecture** Kriegsschiffbau; **~ artillery** Schiffsartillerie; **~ attaché** Marineattaché; **~ auxiliary** *(US)* Hilfsfahrzeug; **~ aviation** Marinefliegerei, -flugwesen; **~ base** Flottenstützpunkt; **~ battle** Seeschlacht, -gefecht; **~ blockade** See-, Hafenblockade; **~ board** Marineamt; **~ brigade** Marinebrigade; **~ code** Signalbuch; **~ college** Seekriegsschule; **~ construction** Schiffsbau; **~ constructor** *(US)* Schiffbaufachmann; **~ court** Seeamt, Schiffahrtsgericht; **~-court martial** Flottengericht; **~ docks** Marinewerft; **~ engagement** Seegefecht; **~ engineer** Marine-, Schiffsbauingenieur; **~ engineering** Schiffbautechnik; **~ estimates** Marineetat; **~ forces** Seestreitkräfte, Kriegsflotte; **~ gun** Schiffsgeschütz; **~ intelligence** Marinenachrichtendienst; **~ manoeuvres (maneuvers, US)** Flottenmanöver; **~ officer** *(US)* höherer Zollbeamter, *(mar.)* Marineoffizier; **~ port** Kriegshafen; **~ power** Seemacht; **~ review** Flottenparade; **~ ship** Kriegsschiff; **~ ship repair yard** Marinewerft; **~ stores** Schiffsvorräte; **~ station** Flottenstützpunkt; **~ supremacy** Seeherrschaft; **~ treaty** Flottenvertrag; **~ unit** Flotteneinheit; **~ vessel** Marinefahrzeug; **~ warfare** Seekriegführung.

navicert Geleit-, Blockadefreischein, Warenpaß.

navigable schiffbar, *(airship)* lenkbar;
~ by sea-going vessels für Hochseeschiffe befahrbar; **in ~ condition** *(ship)* in seetüchtigem Zustand; **~ river or stream** schiffbarer Fluß; **~ road** Wasserstraße; **~ waters** schiffbare Gewässer.

navigate *(v.)* beschiffen, befahren, *(airplane)* durchfliegen;
~ a bill through Parliament Gesetzvorlage durchs Parlament durchsteuern; **~ a ship** Schiff steuern.

navigating officer Navigationsoffizier; **~ room** Navigationsraum.

navigation Schiffahrt, Seefahrt, *(seamanship)* Navigation, Ortung, Navigationskunde;
aerial ~ Luftschiffahrt; **coastal ~** Küstenschiffahrt; **commercial ~** Handelsschiffahrt; **high-seas ~** Hochseeschiffahrt; **inland ~** Binnenschiffahrt; **line ~** Linienschiffahrt; **maritime ~** Seeschiffahrt; **occasional ~** Trampschiffahrt; **regular ~** Linienschiffahrt; **river ~** Flußschiffahrt;
to obstruct ~ Schiffahrt behindern;
≗ Act *(Br.)* Schiffahrtsgesetz; **~ agreement** Schiffahrtsabkommen; **~ channel** Fahrwasser; **~ company** Schiffahrtsgesellschaft; **steamship ~ company** Dampfschiffahrtsgesellschaft; **~ dues** Schiffsabgaben; **~ guide** Bake; **~ head** Schiffbarkeitsgrenze; **~ law** Schiffahrtsgesetz; **~ light** *(airplane)* Positionslichter; **~ officer** Navigationsoffizier; **~ route** Schiffahrtsstraße; **~ school** Seemannsschule; **~ servitude** Benutzungsrecht öffentlicher Gewässer.

navigational aid Navigationshilfe; **~ chart** Navigationskarte; **~ gear** nautische Ausrüstung.

navigator Schiffer, See-, Steuermann, *(airplane)* Beobachter, *(US)* Navigationsoffizier.

navvy *(Br.)* Kanal-, Erd-, Streckenarbeiter, *(sl.)* Tiefbauarbeiter.

navy Kriegsmarine, Flotte, *(merchant marine)* Handelsmarine;
to join the ~ in die Marine eintreten; **to serve in the ~** bei der Marine dienen;

~ bill *(Br.)* vom Marineministerium ausgestellter Wechsel; ⸰ **Board** *(Br.)* Admiralität; **~ certificate** Seegeleitschein; ⸰ **Department** *(US)* Marineministerium, -amt; **~ estimates** Flottenvorlage, Marinehaushalt; **~ list** *(Br.)* Rangliste; **~ league** Flottenverein; **~ pay** Wehrsold; **~ pension** Ruhegeld für Marineangehörige; ⸰ **Register** *(US)* [halbjährliches] Schiffsverzeichnis; **~ yard** Marinewerft, Reparaturdock.

near nahe gelegen, *(fam.)* verwandt, vertraut, *(narrow)* sparsam, in beschränkten Verhältnissen, *(roughly, coll.)* annähernd, nahezu;
~ by nahe gelegen;
as ~ as one can remember soweit man sich zu erinnern vermag;
not ~ly so good keineswegs so gut;
~ completion fast fertig; **~ the town** in der Nähe der Stadt;
to be ~ at hand kurz bevorstehen; **to be very ~ with one's money** mit seinem Geld sehr sparsam umgehen (geizen); **to come ~ to** sich ungefähr belaufen; **to come ~ to murder** fast einem Mord gleichkommen; **to come ~ being knocked down by the bus** beinahe vom Omnibus überfahren worden sein; **to have ~ at hand** jederzeit greifbar haben; **to keep as ~ as possible to the prices quoted** sich weitgehend an die festgesetzten Preise halten; **to live ~** sparsam leben; **to live ~ by** ganz in der Nähe wohnen; **to pay calls ~ at hand** Besuche in der Nachbarschaft absolvieren; **to stand ~** dicht dabeistehen;
~ beer *(US)* bierähnliches Getränk; **to reach ~ collapse** *(traffic)* beinahe zusammenbrechen; **~ copy** genaue Abschrift; **~ delivery** kurzfristige Lieferung; **~-dictatorial** diktaturähnlich; ⸰ **East** Naher Osten, *(US)* Nahost- und Balkanstaaten; **~ escape** knappes Entkommen (Entrinnen); **~-fatal** nahezu tödlich; **~ friend** intimer Freund; **~ future** nahe Zukunft; **~ leather** Imitationsleder; **a ~ miss** knappverfehltes Ziel, fast ein Erfolg; **~ money** *(US)* geldähnliche Forderungen, leicht liquidierbare Einlagen, Aktiva hoher Liquiditätsstufe; **~-monopoly** monopolähnlich; **~ relation** naher Verwandter; **~ relatives** engere Verwandte; **~ side** eigene Fahrbahnhälfte; **a ~ thing** knappes Entkommen; **~-term effect** kurzfristiger Effekt; **~ translation** wortgetreue Übersetzung.

nearby dwelling nahegelegene Wohnung.

nearest, one's ~ of kin nächste Blutsverwandte; **~ port** nächster Hafen; **~ price** genauester Preis; **to go by the ~ road** kürzesten Weg fahren.

nearness Nähe, *(parsimony)* Knauserigkeit, Knickerei;
~ to market Marktnähe; **~ of relationship** nahe Verwandtschaft; **~ of translation** Genauigkeit einer Übersetzung; **~ to water supply** nahegelegene Wasserversorgung.

neat Rindvieh;
~ (a.) ordentlich, sauber, reinlich, gepflegt, *(style)* geschmackvoll, von schlichter Eleganz, *(undiluted)* unverdünnt, *(weight)* rein, netto;
as ~ as a new pin blitzsauber;
to be ~ with one's hands geschickt sein;
~ answer kluge Antwort; **~ balance** Reinbilanz; **~ cattle** Rinder; **~ desk** sorgfältig aufgeräumter Schreibtisch; **~ dress** geschmackvolle Kleidung; **~ figure** gute Figur; **~ handwriting** saubere Handschrift; **~ house** Kuhstall; **~ little speech** hübsche kleine Rede; **~ work** sorgfältige Arbeit.

neatness Sauberkeit, Gefälligkeit, schlichte Eleganz, *(pleading)* knappe Darstellung.

nebulous wolkig, nebelig, *(fig.)* unklar, verschwommen.

necessaries Bedarfsartikel, -gegenstände, *(livelihood)* notwendiger Lebensbedarf, -bedürfnisse, lebensnotwendige Dinge;
printing ~ Bedarfsartikel für Buchdruckereien; **strict ~** dringendster Lebensbedarf; **travel ~** Reiseartikel;
~ of life Lebensbedürfnisse, lebensnotwendiger Bedarf; **bare ~ of life** notdürftiger Unterhalt;
to be liable only for ~ vertraglich nur für den notwendigen Lebensunterhalt haften; **to meet the ~ of life** Lebensbedürfnisse befriedigen; **to pledge the husband's credit for ~** *(Br.)* [etwa] Schlüsselgewalt ausüben; **to procure the bare ~** Existenzminimum sicherstellen.

necessarily notwendigerweise.

necessary notwendiger Unterhalt;
~ (a.) notwendig, nötig, erforderlich, *(involuntary)* notgedrungen, unfreiwillig, gezwungen;
if [it should prove] ~ gegebenenfalls; **rendered ~ by circumstances** durch die Umstände bedingt; **~ and convenient** erforderlich und zweckmäßig;
not to do more than is absolutely ~ nur das unbedingt Notwendige tun; **to make it ~** es erforderlich machen; **to stay no longer than is absolutely ~** seinen Aufenthalt auf das unbedingt Notwendige beschränken;

to make all ~ arrangements alles Erforderliche veranlassen; **~ article** Bedarfsartikel; **~ compliments** übliche Komplimente; **~ condition** notwendige Bedingung; **~ consequence** unvermeidliche Folge; **~ damages** Ersatz für die gesamten Schadensfolgen; **~ deposit** Aufbewahrung aus Geschäftsführung ohne Auftrag; **~ domicile** gesetzlich erforderlicher Wohnsitz; **~ expenditure** notwendige Ausgaben **~ implication** zwingende Auslegung; **~ injury** *(Wrongful Death Statute)* Vermögensschaden; **~ interference** unvermeidbare Einmischung; **~ intromission** unfreiwillige Geschäftsführung ohne Auftrag; **~ part** unentbehrlicher Bestandteil; **~ parties** notwendige Streitgenossen; **to have the ~ qualifications for a post** den Erfordernissen einer Stellung Genüge leisten; **~ repairs** *(ship)* unentbehrliche Reparaturen; **to take the ~ steps** erforderliche Schritte (Maßnahmen) veranlassen; **~ way** Notweg.

necessitate *(v.)* erfordern, notwendig machen;
~ action Eingreifen erforderlich machen; **~ borrowing money** Geldaufnahme unumgänglich machen.

necessitation Nötigung, Zwang.

necessities lebensnotwendige Güter;
bare ~ of life lebensnotwendiger Bedarf, notdürftiger Unterhalt, Existenzminimum.

necessitous notgedrungen, *(destitute)* bedürftig, notleidend, ärmlich;
~ circumstances Unterhaltsbedürfnisse, dürftige Verhältnisse; **~ selling** Notverkäufe.

necessity Notwendigkeit, Zwang, Zwangslage, Unumgänglichkeit, Bedürfnis, *(indigency)* äußerste Not, Notlage, -stand;
in case of ~ im Notfall; **of ~** notwendigerweise; **dire ~** dringende Notwendigkeit; **logical ~** logische Folge; **public ~** öffentliches Bedürfnis; **vital ~** Lebensnotwendigkeit; **to be in ~** in einer Notlage sein, bittere Not leiden; **to be under the ~** es notwendig finden; **to be under the ~ of doing s. th.** zu etw. gezwungen sein; **to bow to ~** sich dem Zwang der Verhältnisse fügen; **to do s. th. out of ~** etw. der Not gehorchend tun; **to lay (put) s. o. under the ~** j. in eine Zwangslage versetzen; **to make a virtue of ~** aus der Not eine Tugend machen;
~ is the mother of invention Not macht erfinderisch; **~ knows no law** Not kennt kein Gebot.

neck Genick, *(geography)* Landzunge, *(print.)* Konus;
in the ~ of unmittelbar nach;
~ and ~ Kopf an Kopf; **~ of a bottle** Flaschenhals; **~ and crop** *(fam.)* mit Haut und Haaren, ganz und gar, mit Stumpf und Stiel (Sack und Pack); **narrow ~ of land** enge Landzunge; **~ or nothing** alles oder nichts, auf Biegen und Brechen; **~ of the woods** *(US coll.)* Nachbarschaft;
to be a millstone round s. one's ~ all his life jem. sein ganzes Leben lang wie ein Mühlstein am Halse hängen; **to be out on one's ~** *(coll.)* rausgeworfen werden, seinen Posten verlieren; **to be up to one's ~ in s. th.** bis zum Hals in etw. stecken; **to be up to the ~ in [one's] work** tief in seiner Arbeit stecken; **to break one's ~** sich das Genick brechen; **to break the ~ of a task** Hauptteil einer Arbeit hinter sich bringen; **to breathe down s. one's ~** jem. im Genick sitzen; **to catch (get) it in the ~** *(sl.)* böse Erfahrungen machen, eins aufs Dach bekommen, gefeuert werden; **to crane one's ~** sich den Hals verrenken; **to finish ~ and ~** Kopf an Kopf durchs Ziel gehen; **to have the ~ to ask for a loan** *(sl.)* so dreist sein, um ein Darlehen zu bitten; **to keep ~ and ~ with the printers** *(fam.)* Druckerei immer rechtzeitig beliefern; **to lose by a ~** um Haaresbreite verlieren; **to risk one's ~** sein Leben riskieren; **to save one's ~** sein Gesicht [be]wahren, aus der Patsche kommen; **to stick one's ~ out** *(sl.)* sich zu weit vorwagen, es herausfordern; **to throw s. o. out ~ and crop** j. achtkantig hinausschmeißen; **to win by a ~** um eine Nasenlänge gewinnen.

necktie party *(US sl.)* Lynchjustiz durch Hängen.

necropsy Obduktion.

need *(destitution)* Not[stand], -lage, Bedrängnis, Bedürftigkeit, *(necessity)* dringende Notwendigkeit, Bedürfnis, *(requirement)* Bedarf, Nachfrage, *(want)* Mangel;
for one's own ~s für den Eigenbedarf; **in ~ of assistance** hilfsbedürftig, *(Br.)* fürsorgebedürftig; **in case of ~** notfalls, erforderlichenfalls; **in ~ of repair** reparaturbedürftig;
~s Erfordernisse;
anticipated ~ voraussichtlicher Bedarf; **borrowing ~s** Kreditbedarf; **civilian ~s** Bedürfnisse des zivilen Sektors; **consumer ~s** Verbraucherbedürfnisse; **few ~s** geringe Bedürfnisse; **local ~s** örtliche Bedürfnisse; **monetary ~s** Geldbedarf; **one's personal ~s** seine persönlichen Bedürfnisse; **present ~s** augenblickliche Bedürfnisse; **public ~s** öffentlicher Bedarf; **spot ~s** örtliche Bedürfnisse; **urgent ~** dringender Bedarf;

647 negligibility

~ **for capital** Kapitalbedarf; ~ **to communicate** Mitteilungsbedürfnis; ~ **to cover** Deckungserfordernis; ~ **for foreign exchange** Devisenbedarf; ~ **for liquidity** Liquiditätsbedürfnis; ~ **for men and material** Menschen- und Materialbedarf; ~ **of money** Geldbedarf; ~ **for security** Sicherheitsbedürfnis;
~ *(v.)* benötigen, brauchen, Bedarf haben [an];
~ **some explanation** der Erklärung bedürfen; ~ **tactful handling** mit großem Takt behandelt werden müssen; ~ **a lot of asking** Haufen Fragen aufwerfen; ~ **a rest** der Ruhe bedürfen;
to aim at the ~s of a customer auf die Wünsche eines Kunden abstellen; **to be in ~ of s. th.** etw. dringend brauchen; **to be in great ~** in sehr bedrängten Verhältnissen leben; **to be a great ~ for a book** als Buch dringend benötigt werden; **to examine the ~ for granting a licence** Bedarfsfrage bei Erteilung einer Konzession prüfen; **to feel the ~ of money** nicht genügend Geld haben; **to fill a crying ~** empfindliche Lücke schließen; **to meet the ~s** Bedarf decken, den Bedürfnissen entsprechen; **to meet the ~s of trade** Bedarf des Handels decken; **to provide for the ~s** Bedürfnisse befriedigen; **to provide fully for the increasing monetary ~s** zunehmenden Geldbedarf hundertprozentig decken; **to satisfy one's ~s** seine Bedürfnisse befriedigen; **to supply the ~s of s. o.** für jds. Bedürfnisse sorgen; **to tackle the urgent ~s of the economy** sich mit den vordringlichsten Wirtschaftsaufgaben beschäftigen; **to tailor to s. one's specific ~s** auf jds. bestimmte Bedürfnisse abstellen; **to take account of the ~s** den Bedürfnissen Rechnung tragen;
~s **test** *(Br.)* Bedürftigkeitsnachweis.
needful *(sl.)* nötiges Kleingeld, nötige Moneten;
~ *(a.)* notwendig, erforderlich, unerläßlich;
to supply the ~ das notwendige Geld herbeischaffen.
neediness Bedürftigkeit.
needle Grammophonnadel, *(sl.)* Spritze;
as sharp as a ~ äußerst schlagfertig; **on the ~** *(sl.)* rauschgiftsüchtig; **the ~** *(sl.)* Anfall von Nervosität;
~ *(v.)* Handarbeiten machen, *(fig.)* aufziehen, necken, sticheln; ~ **a speech with humo(u)r** Rede mit Humor würzen; ~ **one's way through** sich durchschlängeln;
to give s. o. the ~ jem. auf die Nerven gehen; **to look for a ~ in a bundle of hay (in a hay stack)** Nadel im Heuhaufen suchen; **to sit on pins and ~s** wie auf glühenden Kohlen sitzen.
needless work sinnlose Arbeit.
needlewoman Näherin.
needlework Näharbeit, Stickerei.
needy bedürftig, mittellos, arm;
to be in ~ circumstances in dürftigen Verhältnissen leben; ~ **family** unterstützungsbedürftige Familie.
negate *(v.)* für null und nichtig erklären, annullieren;
~ **a warranty** Haftung ablehnen.
negation *(law)* Nichtigerklärung, Annullierung;
oral ~ mündliche Ablehnung.
negative *(el.)* negativer Pol, *(math.)* Minuszeichen, *(photo)* Negativ, *(veto)* Einspruch, Veto;
enlarged ~ Negativvergrößerung;
~ *(v.)* verwerfen, ablehnen, *(v./i.)* entgegenstehen;
~ **an appeal** Berufung verwerfen; ~ **a bill** Gesetzesvorschlag ablehnen; ~ **a defence under the statute of limitations** einem Verjährungseinwand entgegenstehen; ~ **a liability** Haftpflicht ausschließen;
to answer in the ~ verneinen; **to argue in the ~** sich dagegen aussprechen;
~ *(a.)* verneinend, negativ, *(US)* defaitistisch;
~ **answer** abschlägiger Bescheid; **to maintain a ~ attitude** bei seiner ablehnenden Haltung bleiben; ~ **averment** formelles Bestreiten, negatorische Einrede; ~ **balance** Minussaldo; **to have a ~ cast** unangenehme Vorzeichen haben; ~ **clause** Negativklausel; ~ **clearance** *(antitrust law, US, EC)* Einspruchsrücknahme; ~ **condition** vertraglich ausbedungene Unterlassung, Negativbedingung; ~ **conductor** *(el.)* Minusleitung; ~ **covenant** Unterlassungsverpflichtung; ~ **earned surplus** Kapitalschmälerungen; ~ **easement** negative (auf eine Unterlassung gerichtete) Grunddienstbarkeit; ~ **economic growth rate** rückläufige Wachstumsrate; ~ **evidence** Negativbeweis; ~ **goodwill** Fusionsüberschuß; ~ **income tax** negative Einkommensteuer; ~ **injunction** gerichtliches Verbot; ~ **investment** Desinvestition; ~ **plate** Negativklischee; ~ **pole** *(el.)* Minuspol; ~ **prescription** Ersitzung; ~ **reply** Absage; ~ **report** Fehlanzeige; ~ **response** *(marketing)* negative Reaktion; ~ **savings** Vermögensaufzehrung; ~ **servitude** negative Dienstbarkeit; ~ **sign** Minuszeichen; ~ **taxes** negative Steuern; ~ **term** Unterlassensbestimmung; ~ **trade balance** Passivsaldo im Außenhandel, passive Handelsbilanz; ~ **vote** Neinstimme.

negatory verneinend, ablehnend.
neglect Versäumnis, Unterlassung, Vernachlässigung, *(law)* Fahrlässigkeit;
culpable ~ schuldhaftes Unterlassen; **wilful ~** *(husband)* vorsätzliche Unterhaltsverletzung;
~ **of business** Geschäftsvernachlässigung; ~ **of children** Kindervernachlässigung; ~ **of one's duties** Dienstvernachlässigung, pflichtwidriges Unterlassen, Dienstvergehen; ~ **of proper precautions** Unterlassung der erforderlichen Vorsichtsmaßregeln; ~ **to provide maintenance** Verletzung (Vernachlässigung) der Unterhaltspflicht; **wil(l)ful ~ to provide reasonable maintenance** *(Br.)* vorsätzliche Verletzung der Unterhaltspflicht;
~ *(v.)* unterlassen, versäumen, vernachlässigen, nicht sorgen;
~ **one's business** sich nicht um sein Geschäft kümmern; ~ **to pay one's debts** seine Schulden nicht bezahlen; **utterly ~ one's family** seine Familie der Gefahr des Notstands aussetzen; ~ **the odd pence** *(coll.)* Pfennige verachten; ~ **an opportunity** Chance versäumen; ~ **a precaution** Vorsichtsmaßnahme außer Acht lassen; ~ **one's studies** sein Studium vernachlässigen;
to be in the state of ~ verwahrlost sein; **to die in total ~** völlig verwahrlost sterben; **to leave one's children in utter ~** seine Kinder ohne jede Hilfe zurücklassen; **to suffer from ~** *(cattle)* nicht versorgt sein, *(machine)* nicht gewartet werden; **to treat an offer with ~** Angebot unbeachtet lassen.
neglected *(in little demand)* wenig gefragt, vernachlässigt;
~ **minor** vernachlässigter Minderjähriger; ~ **wife** verlassene Ehefrau.
neglectful nachlässig;
to be ~ of one's appearance sein äußeres Erscheinungsbild vernachlässigen; **to be ~ of one's interests** seine Interessen nicht wahrnehmen.
negligence Nachlässigkeit, *(law)* Fahrlässigkeit, *(road user)* achtloses (fahrlässiges) Verhalten;
by ~ fahrlässig;
actionable ~ zum Schadensersatz verpflichtende Fahrlässigkeit; **collateral ~** Haftung für die Fahrlässigkeit des Erfüllungsgehilfen; **comparative ~** *(US)* Mitverschulden; **concurring (contributory,** *Br.)* mitwirkendes (konkurrierendes) Verschulden, schuldhafte Nichtabwendung einer bekannten Gefahr; **crash ~** grobe Fahrlässigkeit; **criminal ~** strafbares (strafrechtliches) Verschulden; **culpable ~** Außerachtlassen der im Verkehr erforderlichen Sorgfalt; **gross ~** grobe Fahrlässigkeit, Leichtfertigkeit; **hazardous ~** Leichtfertigkeit; **imputed ~** zu vertretende Fahrlässigkeit; **legal ~** Außerachtlassen der gesetzlich vorgeschriebenen Sorgfalt; **mutual contributory ~** beiderseitiges Mitverschulden; **ordinary ~** *(US)* gewöhnliche (leichte) Fahrlässigkeit, Mangel der im Verkehr erforderlichen Sorgfalt; **passive ~** *(US)* fahrlässiges Unterlassen; **slight ~** *(US)* leichte (geringe) Fahrlässigkeit; **statutory ~** *(US)* Verletzung der gesetzlich vorgeschriebenen Sorgfalt; **wanton (willful) ~** *(US)* bewußte (grobe) Fahrlässigkeit (Leichtfertigkeit);
~ **in contract** fahrlässiger Vertragsabschluß; ~ **without fault** reine Fahrlässigkeit; ~ **in law** Verletzung der gesetzlich erforderlichen Sorgfaltspflicht, zum Schadenersatz verpflichtende Fahrlässigkeit; ~ **per se** *(US)* Fahrlässigkeitshaftung ohne Nachweis der Schuld, gesetzlich vermutete Fahrlässigkeit; ~ **in tort** fahrlässig begangene unerlaubte Handlung;
to attribute the servant's ~ to the master Dienstherrn für das Verschulden des Erfüllungsgehilfen haftbar machen; **to be chargeable with ~** sich dem Vorwurf der Fahrlässigkeit ausgesetzt haben; **to be due to s. one's ~** auf jds. Fahrlässigkeit zurückzuführen sein; **to constitute ~** Tatbestand der Fahrlässigkeit erfüllen; **to have been guilty of ~** notwendige Sorgfalt außer Acht gelassen haben; **to sue for professional ~** wegen Außerachtlassung der im Berufsleben erforderlichen Sorgfalt verklagen;
~ **case** Fall von Fahrlässigkeit; ~ **clause** Freizeichnungsklausel; ~ **complaints** Beschwerden über fahrlässiges Verhalten.
negligent nachlässig, fahrlässig, *(debtor)* säumig, *(road user)* unachtsam;
grossly ~ grob fahrlässig;
to be ~ of one's duties pflichtvergessen sein; **to be ~ in one's supervision** seine Aufsicht mangelhaft ausüben; **to be ~ of traffic rules** sich um Verkehrsbestimmungen einfach nicht kümmern; **to be ~ in one's work** seine Arbeit vernachlässigen;
~ **act** fahrlässige Handlung; ~ **care** fahrlässige Handlung; ~ **escape** fahrlässiges Entweichenlassen; ~ **homicide** *(US)* fahrlässige Tötung; ~ **offence** fahrlässige Straftat; ~ **violation of statute** fahrlässige Verletzung eines Gesetzes.
negligently done schlampig erledigt.
negligibility Geringfügigkeit.

negligible geringfügig.

negotiability Verhandlungs-, Aushandelbarkeit, *(bankability)* Bank-, Börsenfähigkeit, *(endorsability)* Begeb-, Indossierbarkeit, Begebungsfähigkeit, *(marketability)* Verkehrsfähigkeit, *(realizability)* Verwertbarkeit, *(salability)* Verkäuflich-, Umsetzbarkeit, *(transferability)* Übertragbarkeit.

negotiable verhandlungsfähig, aushandelbar, *(bankable)* börsen-, bankfähig, *(endorsable)* indossierfähig, begebbar, begebungs-, umlauffähig, durch Indossament übertragbar, *(marketable)* verkehrsfähig, *(realizable)* verwertbar, *(salable)* umsetzbar, veräußerlich;

not ~ nicht übertragbar, nur zur Verrechnung; **quasi-~** quasi-übertragbar;

~ **without endorsement** einfach übertragbar; ~ **on the stock exchange** börsenfähig;

~ **bill** durch Indossament übertragbarer Wechsel; ~ **bill of lading** Orderfrachtbrief; ~ **character** Verkehrs-, Begebungsfähigkeit; ~ **cheque** girierfähiger Scheck; ~ **document** begebbares Wert-, Order-, Inhaberpapier jeder Art; ~ **instrument** begebbares Wertpapier, auf Zahlung von Geld gerichtetes Order- und Inhaberpapier; **quasi-~ instrument** unechtes Orderpapier; ~ **instruments** Effekten; **Uniform ~ Instruments Act** *(US)* Wertpapiergesetz; ~ **kind of property** übertragbare Vermögenswerte; ~ **note** begebbarer eigener Wechsel, Solawechsel; ~ **paper** begebbares Wertpapier; ~ **quality** Eigenschaft der Begebbarkeit; ~ **securities** durch Indossament übertragbare Wertpapiere; ~ **warehouse receipt** Orderlagerschein; ~ **words** Begebbarkeits-, Orderklausel.

negotiate *(v.) (bill)* begeben, unterbringen, negoziieren, übertragen, *(conclude a contract)* zustandebringen, abschließen, *(confer with)* ver-, aus-, unterhandeln, in Unterhandlung stehen mit, *(exports)* Dokumentengeschäft tätigen, *(sell)* umsetzen, verkaufen, verhandeln;

difficult to ~ *(bill of exchange)* schwer unterzubringen;

~ **back** zurückgeben; ~ **a bill of exchange** Wechsel begeben; ~ **en bloc** globale Tarifverhandlungen führen; ~ **a contract** Vertrag aushandeln; ~ **a contract in exhausting detail** Vertrag bis zu den kleinsten Kleinigkeiten aushandeln; ~ **a documentary credit** Dokumentengeschäft tätigen; ~ **a corner** *(car)* gut um eine Ecke herumkommen; ~ **a curve** *(car)* Kurve nehmen; ~ **by delivery only** formlos übertragen; ~ **a difficult road** mit dem Bau einer schwierigen Straße fertig werden; ~ **a draft** Tratte ankaufen; ~ **with the employers about wage claims** Lohnverhandlungen mit den Arbeitgebern führen; ~ **further** weiterbegeben; ~ **a loan** Anleihe unterbringen (begeben); ~ **for peace** in Friedensverhandlungen eintreten; ~ **for new premises** in Mietverhandlungen stehen; ~ **a price** Preis aushandeln; ~ **for the purchase of a house** über den Ankauf eines Hauses verhandeln; ~ **a sale** Verkauf abschließen (zum Abschluß bringen, tätigen); ~ **on better terms** günstigere Verhandlungsposition haben; ~ **for some time** schon geraume Zeit in Verhandlungen stehen; ~ **a transaction** Geschäft vermitteln (zustandebringen); ~ **a treaty** Vertrag aushandeln.

negotiated wage vereinbarter Tariflohn.

negotiating Aushandeln, Verhandeln;

to be ~ **with s. o.** mit jem. in Verhandlungen stehen; **to have been** ~ **for some time** seit einiger Zeit in Unterhandlungen stehen;

~ **atmosphere** Verhandlungsatmosphäre, -klima; ~ **bank** negoziierende Bank; ~ **bluff** Verhandlungstrick; ~ **committee** Verhandlungsausschuß; **to slam shut the** ~ **door** Verhandlungstür zuschlagen; ~ **group** Verhandlungsgruppe; ~ **package** Verhandlungsgegenstand; **joint** ~ **panel** gemeinsames Verhandlungsgremium; ~ **partner** Verhandlungspartner; ~ **party** Verhandlungspartner; ~ **plan** Verhandlungsplan; ~ **power** starke Verhandlungsposition, -stärke, -vollmacht; ~ **rights** Verhandlungsvollmacht; **to run out of** ~ **room** keinerlei Verhandlungsspielraum mehr haben; ~ **route** Verhandlungsweg; ~ **success** Verhandlunsgerfolg; ~ **table** Verhandlungstisch; ~ **tactics** Verhandlungstaktik; ~ **team** Verhandlungsdelegation.

negotiation *(conclusion of contract)* Vertragsabschluß, *(conference)* Unter-, Verhandlung, *(documentary credit)* Beteiligung an einem Dokumentengeschäft, *(issue)* Begebung, Übertragung, Unterbringung, Negoziierung;

by ~ im Verhandlungswege; **open to** ~**s** zu Verhandlungen bereit, verhandlungsbereit; **pending** ~**s** während der Verhandlungen; **under** ~ in Verhandlung;

backstage ~**s** hinter den Kulissen geführte Verhandlungen; **complicated** ~**s** schwierige Verhandlungen; **contract** ~**s** Vertragsverhandlungen; **commercial** ~**s** Handelsbesprechungen; **cut-and-dried** ~**s** intensiv vorbereitete Verhandlungen; **dead-**

locked ~**s** festgefahrene Verhandlungen; **detailed** ~**s** Einzelbesprechungen; **forthcoming** ~**s** bevorstehende Verhandlungen; **further** ~ Weiterbegebung; **pending** ~**s** schwebende Verhandlungen; **preliminary** ~**s** Vorverhandlungen; **private (secret)** ~**s** Geheimverhandlungen; **tariff** ~**s** Zollverhandlungen; **top-level** ~**s** Verhandlungen auf höchster Ebene; **trade** ~**s** Wirtschaftsverhandlungen; **union** ~**s** Verhandlungen mit den Gewerkschaften;

~**s for an armistice** Waffenstillstandsverhandlungen; ~ **of a bill of exchange** Begebung eines Wechsels (einer Anleihe), Wechselbegebung; ~ **at (on) call** Schluß auf Abruf; **further** ~ **of a check** Weiterbegebung eines Schecks; ~ **of a commercial paper** Diskontierung einer Dokumententratte; ~ **of a draft** Trattenankauf; ~**s for an entry** Beitrittsverhandlungen; ~**s hitherto** bisherige Verhandlungen; ~ **of a loan** Übernahme einer Anleihe, Anleiheübernahme; ~**s in progress** schwebende Verhandlungen; ~ **for time** Zeit-, Lieferungsgeschäft; ~ **for a treaty** Vertragsverhandlungen;

to aid ~**s** Verhandlungen unterstützen; **to be in** ~**s** mit jem. in Verhandlung stehen; **to be open for** ~**s** zu Unterhandlungen bereit (verhandlungsbereit) sein; **to be open to** ~**s at national level** zu bundesweiten Verhandlungen bereit sein; **to break off** ~**s** Unterhandlungen abbrechen; **to bring** ~**s to a satisfactory conclusion** Verhandlungen zu einem erfolgreichen Abschluß bringen; **to call s. o. in on the** ~**s** j. in die Verhandlungen einschalten; **to carry on (conduct)** ~**s** Verhandlungen fortführen (leiten); **to carry on** ~**s for a settlement** Vergleichsverhandlungen führen; **to carry out** ~**s on a selective product-by-product basis** Zollverhandlungen über einzeln ausgewählte Waren führen; **to continue** ~**s** Verhandlungen fortsetzen; **to cut off** ~**s** Verhandlungen abbrechen; **to enter into** ~ **with s. o.** in Unterhandlungen mit jem. eintreten; **to initiate** ~**s** Verhandlungen einleiten; **to open** ~**s with s. o.** Verhandlungen mit jem. aufnehmen; **to resume** ~**s** Verhandlungen wiederaufnehmen; **to set** ~**s on foot** Verhandlungen eröffnen; **to set** ~**s in motion** Verhandlungen in Gang bringen; **to settle by** ~ im Verhandlungswege regeln; **to speak for** ~**s** sich für Verhandlungen aussprechen; **to start** ~**s** Verhandlungen eröffnen (beginnen); **to take up** ~**s** Verhandlungen aufnehmen; **to terminate** ~ Verhandlungen zum Abschluß bringen;

~ **basis** Verhandlungsbasis; ~ **credit** Negoziierungs-, Trattenankaufskredit; ~ **group** Verhandlungsdelegation; ~ **package** Verhandlungspaket; ~ **price** *(underwriting)* Übernahmekurs, -preis; ~ **table** Verhandlungstisch.

negotiator Verhandlungsführer, Unterhändler, *(broker)* Makler, *(mediator)* Vermittler;

industry ~ Verhandlungspartner auf Seiten der Industrie; **union** ~ Verhandlungsmitglied der Gewerkschaft.

negotiorium gestio *(lat.)* Geschäftsführung ohne Auftrag.

neighbo(u)r Nachbar, Anlieger, -wohner;

next-door ~**s** unmittelbare Nachbarn; **vexatious** ~ leidiger (streitsüchtiger) Nachbar;

~ **at dinner** Tischnachbar;

~ *(v.)* benachbart sein, in der Nachbarschaft wohnen;

~ **on an estate** an ein Grundstück grenzen;

to be on friendly terms with one's ~**s** gutnachbarliche Beziehungen unterhalten; **to have good** ~**s** angenehme Nachbarn haben; **to think small of one's** ~**s** auf seine Nachbarn herabsehen; **to walk s. o. over to the** ~**s' house** j. zum Nachbarn begleiten;

to stop a ~**'s light** einem Nachbarn die Aussicht verbauen; **good-**~ **policy** Politik der guten Nachbarschaft; ~ **state** Nachbarstaat.

neighbo(u)rhood Nachbarschaft, *(district)* Stadtgegend, -viertel, -bezirk, [Um]gegend, Wohngegend;

in the ~ **of** *(US)* etwa in der Größenordnung von; **in the** ~ **of a town** im Bereich einer Stadt;

fashionable ~ vornehme Wohngegend; **good** ~ *(state)* gute Nachbarschaft; **high-risk** ~ hoch versicherte Gegend; **low-income** ~ niedrige Einkommensgegend; **tough** ~ verrufene Gegend; **wealthy** ~ reiches Stadtviertel;

~ **of a noisy airport** nahe Belegenheit eines lauten Flugplatzes; **to be in a good** ~ in einer guten Wohngegend leben; **to live in the immediate** ~ in unmittelbarer Nähe leben; **to live in the** ~ **of London** in einem Ort in der Nähe von London leben; **to lose a sum in the** ~ **of $ 1000** *(US)* etwa tausend Dollar verlieren;

~ **bank branch** *(US)* Depositenkasse; ~ **center** Neben-, Sekundärzentrum, Stadtteil; ~ **conditions** Nachbarschaftsverhältnisse; ~ **improvements** Anliegerbeiträge; ~ **lot** *(premises)* Nachbargrundstück; ~ **nation** Nachbarland; ~ **parish** Nachbardorf; ~ **shop** Geschäft mit Produkten des täglichen Bedarfs.

neighbo(u)ring benachbart, umliegend, angrenzend;
~ **community** Nachbargemeinde; ~ **country** *(nation)* Nachbarland; ~ **house** Nachbarhaus; ~ **peasant** Anrainer; ~ **property** Nachbargrundstück; ~ **right** verwandtes Schutzrecht; ~ **state** Nachbarstaat; ~ **village** Nachbardorf.

neighbo(u)rliness, good *(pol.)* gute Nachbarschaft, gutnachbarliche Beziehungen.

neighbo(u)rly gutnachbarlich;
to act in a ~ fashion gutnachbarlich handeln; ~ **intercourse** nachbarlicher Verkehr.

neither party keine der Parteien.

neologism Wortneuschöpfung.

neon|lamp Neonlampe; ~ **light** *(advertisement)* Neonlicht; ~ **light advertising** Leuchtreklame; ~ **sign** Neonlichtwerbung; ~ **tube** Neonlampe, -röhre.

nepotism Vetternwirtschaft.

nerve *(fig.)* Energie, Selbstbeherrschung, *(coll., cheeck)* Unverfrorenheit, Unverschämtheit, Frechheit;
~**s of a country** Nervenstränge eines Landes;
~ *(v.)* **o. s.** sich aufraffen; ~ **o. s. to make a speech** sich zu einer Rede entschließen (aufraffen); ~ **o. s. to a task** sich eine Aufgabe zutrauen;
to be all ~s reines Nervenbündel sein; **to be in a state of ~s** äußerst nervös sein; **to get on s. one's ~s** jem. auf die Nerven gehen; **to get up the ~** den Mut aufbringen; **to have the ~ to do s. th.** unverschämt genug sein, etw. zu tun; **to have one's ~s frayed at both ends** ein Nervenbündel sein; **to have iron ~ (~s of steel)** *(fam.)* eiserne Nerven haben; **to lose one's ~s** seine Nerven (Beherrschung) verlieren; **to regain one's ~** seine Selbstsicherheit wiederfinden; **to strain every ~** alle nur möglichen Anstrengungen unternehmen; **to touch a sensitive ~ in s. o.** j. an einer empfindlichen Stelle treffen;
~ **case** Nervenleidender; ~ **center** *(fig.)* Befehlszentrum, -zentrale; ~ **food** Nervennahrung; ~ **gas** Nervengas; ~ **patient** Nervenleidender.

nervous|attack Nervenkrise; ~ **breakdown** Nervenzusammenbruch; ~ **exhaustion** nervöse Erschöpfung; ~ **system** Nervensystem, -kostüm; ~ **twitch** Nervenbündel.

nervy *(sl.)* dreist, keck.

nest Nest, *(fig.)* behagliche Wohnung, Nest, *(hiding)* Schlupfwinkel, Versteck, *(serial)* Serie;
~ **of crime** Schlupfwinkel von Verbrechern; ~ **of ore** Erznest; ~ **of pirates** Piratenschlupfwinkel; ~ **of vice** Lasterhöhle;
~ *(v.)* sich einnisten (niederlassen);
to feather one's ~ sein Schäfchen ins Trockene bringen; **to foul one's own ~** das eigene Nest beschmutzen; **to stir up a hornet's ~** in ein Wespennest stechen;
~ **egg** Sparpfennig, Notgroschen; **to build up a financial ~ egg somewhere abroad** finanzielle Reserven irgendwo im Ausland anlegen.

nestle *(v.)* unterbringen, mit einer Behausung versehen;
~ **down in an armchair** es sich in einem Lehnstuhl behaglich machen.

nestling *(fig.)* Nesthäkchen.

net Netz, *(advertising)* Agenturnetto, *(net income)* Reingewinn, -ertrag, Nettoeinkommen, *(math.)* Koordinatennetz;
marketing ~ Einkaufsnetz; **mosquito ~** Moskitonetz; **road ~** Straßennetz;
~ **in advance** Nettokasse im Voraus;
~ *(v.) (to gain as ~ profit)* Reingewinn erzielen, netto verdienen, *(to yield as ~ profit)* Reingewinn abwerfen, netto erbringen;
~ **£ 400** vierhundert Pfund Reingewinn erzielen; ~ **off cash or securities against the income tax accrual** Bargeld oder Wertpapiere mit Einkommensteuerforderungen verrechnen; ~ **out** *(banking)* saldieren;
~ *(a.)* netto, rein, nach allen Abzügen, frei von Bezügen;
~ **of tax** steuerfrei; ~ **of tax relief** Netto vor Steuerermäßigung; **to cast a ~** Netz auswerfen; **to pay ~** netto bezahlen; **to walk into the ~** jem. ins Netz gehen;
~ **amount** Rein-, Nettobetrag; ~ **annual value** jährlicher Nettoertragswert; ~ **assets** Reinvermögen; ~ **asset position** *(US)* Vermögensbilanz; ~ **asset value** *(investment fund)* Liquidations-, Inventarwert; ~ **avails** *(discounted note)* Diskonterlös, *(US)* Nettoerlös, Gegenwert; ~ **spendable weekly average** für den wöchentlichen Lebensunterhalt zur Verfügung stehender Lohnanteil; ~ **balance** Reinüberschuß, -erlös, Nettosaldo, -bilanz, -betrag; ~ **barter terms of trade** Nettoaustauschverhältnis; ~ **bonded debt** reine Anleiheschuld, *(municipal accounting, US)* Schuldscheinverpflichtungen; ~ **beneficiary** per Saldo Begünstigter; ~ **book agreement** Rabattvereinbarung zwischen Verlagen und dem Sortimenter; ~ **book amount** wertberichtigtes Anlagevermögen; ~ **book system** Rabattsystem für preisgebundene Bücher; ~ **book value** Buchwert nach Vornahme von Abschreibungen; ~ **capital exports** Nettokapitalexport; ~ **capital gain** Nettokapitalwert; ~ **capital imports** Nettokapitalimport; ~ **cash** netto Kasse, bar ohne Abzug, Nettopreis; ~ **cash in advance** Nettokasse im voraus; ~ **cashflow** Abschreibungen plus nicht ausgeschüttete Gewinne; ~ **change** reiner Kursunterschied; ~ **change in business inventories** *(national income accounting)* Nettobestandsveränderung, bereinigte Inventarveränderung; ~ **change in working capital** Nettobestandsveränderung des Betriebskapitals; ~ **commission** Nettoprovision; ~ **cost** Grund-, Nettopreis, Selbstkostenpreis; ~ **cost of purchase** Nettobezugskosten; ~ **credit balance** Nettokreditsaldo; ~ **creditor [limit] position** *(currency policy)* Nettoüberschußposition; ~ **current assets** Betriebskapital; ~ **debt** Nettoverbindlichkeiten, *(municipal accounting, US)* fundierte und schwebende Schulden abzüglich des Tilgungsfonds; ~ **dividend** Nettodividende; ~ **domestic product** Nettosozialprodukt zu Faktorpreisen; ~ **earnings** Nettoverdienst, -erträge, -einkünfte, Reinverdienst, Effektivlohn; ~ **earnings of management** Unternehmerreingewinn; ~ **earnings rule** Nettoertragswertberechnung; ~ **estate** reiner Nachlaß nach Auszahlung aller Legate; ~ **expenditure** Nettoaufwand; ~ **exports** Außenbeitrag, Nettoexport; ~ **financial investment** Finanzierungssaldo; ~ **flow** Nettoleistung; ~ **freight** Nettofracht; ~ **gain** Rein-, Nettogewinn; ~ **gifts** *(taxation)* steuerfreie Schenkungsbeträge; ~ **holdings** Nettobestände, -guthaben; ~ **income** Nettoeinkommen, Reinertrag, (Nettoverbindlichkeiten); **surtax ~ income** *(US)* Nettoeinkommen nach Abzug der Steuerfreibeträge; ~ **income from abroad** Nettoeinkünfte aus dem Ausland, Nettoauslandseinkünfte; ~ **income after taxes** Nettoeinkommen (Nettoerträge) nach Steuern; ~ **income for the year** Jahreseinkommen; ~ **increase** Nettoerhöhung; ~ **indebtedness** echte Verschuldung, Reinverschuldung; ~ **interest** Nettozins; ~ **interest return** Nettoverzinsung; ~ **investment** reiner Investitionsaufwand nach Abschreibungen, Nettoinvestition; ~ **investment income** Nettoanlageeinkommen; ~ **investment spending** Nettoinvestitionsausgaben; ~ **invoice price** Nettorechnungswert; ~ **level annual premium** Nettobetrag der auf die Versicherung entfallenden Prämie; ~ **liabilities** reine Schulden (Nettoverbindlichkeiten) nach Abzug der flüssigen Aktiva; ~ **line** *(insurance)* Höchstgrenze des Selbstbehalts; ~ **liquidity** Nettoliquidität; ~ **load** Nutzlast; ~ **loss** Netto-, Reinverlust; ~ **margin** Nettogewinnspanne; ~ **merchantable production** verkaufsfähige Nettoförderung; ~ **national product** Nettosozialprodukt; ~ **nonoperating profit** betriebsfremder Reinertrag; ~ **off** *(market report)* Reinertrag geringer als im Vorjahr; ~ **operating deficit** Nettobetriebsverlust; ~ **operating income** Nettobetriebseinnahmen; ~ **operating profit** Betriebseinkommen; ~ **output** Nettoproduktionswert; ~ **paid circulation** tatsächlich abgesetzte [Zeitungs]auflage; ~ **payment** Nettoausschüttung; ~ **position on services** *(US)* Dienstleistungsbilanz; ~ **premium** kostendeckende Prämie, Nettoprämie; ~ **present-value method** Kapitalwertmethode; ~ **price** Nettopreis; ~ **private domestic investment** private Nettoinlandsinvestitionen; ~ **proceeds** Reinertrag, -gewinn, Nettoertrag, -erlös, barer Ertrag; ~ **product** Nettoprodukt; **marginal ~ product** Nettogrenzprodukt; ~ **profit[s]** Reinerlös, -gewinn, Nettogewinn; ~ **profit including balance** Reingewinn einschließlich Vortrag; ~ **profit from operation (operating profit)** Betriebsreingewinn; ~ **profit on sales** Nettoverkaufserlös; ~ **profits to ~ worth ratio** *(US)* Verhältnis des Reingewinns zum Eigenkapital; **full ~ program(me)** Sendergruppenprogramm; ~ **production rate** Nettoproduktionsziffer; ~ **purchase** Nettoeinkaufspreis; ~ **quick assets** Betriebskapital; ~ **rate of interest** Nettozinssatz; ~ **rate of tax** *(Br.)* vom Finanzamt zurückzuerstattende Kapitalertragssteuer; ~ **real estate** Grundstückswert nach Abschreibung; ~ **real rate of return** Nettorenditesatz; ~ **realizable value** *(Br.)* realisierbarer Verkaufswert; ~ **receipts** Nettoeingänge, -einkommen, -einnahmen; ~ **receipts surplus** Betriebsüberschuß; ~ **reduction** Nettoabzug; ~ **relevant distribution** Nettoausschüttung; ~ **rent** Grundrente; ~ **rental** Nettomiete, -pacht; ~ **reproduction rate** Nettoreproduktionsrate; ~ **reserve** Nettoreserve; ~ **rest** reiner Überschuß; ~ **result** *(US)* Nettoergebnis, Bilanz; ~ **result of overall economic activity** *(US)* Bilanz der gesamten Volkswirtschaft; ~ **retention** *(reinsurance)* Selbstbehalt; ~ **returns** Nettoumsatz, *(banking)* Nettoausweis, *(of a bond)* Nettoertrag, Rendite, Verzinsung; ~ **revenues** Reineinnahme; ~ **revenue expenditure** Nettoaufwand für Investitionen; ~ **sales** *(US)* Nettoverkaufserlös, Netto-, Reinumsatz;

certified ~ **sale** *(newspaper)* beglaubigter Nettoverkauf; ~ **salvage** Reinerlös des Abbruchwertes; ~ **savings** Nettoersparnisse; ~ **social benefit** volkswirtschaftlicher Wert; ~ **surplus** *(US)* zwecks Rückstellung auf Reservekonto verfügbarer Gewinn, Reingewinn [nach Ausschüttung der Dividende]; ~ **tare** reine Tara; ~ **tax liability** Nettosteuerschuld; ~ **ton** Nettoregistertonne; ~ **tonnage** Nettoregistertonnage, -raumgehalt; ~ **unduplicated audience** *(advertising)* Nettoreichweite; ~ **valuation** *(insurance)* Bewertung nach dem Nettowert der Prämien; ~ **value** Nettowert, *(life insurance)* Deckungskapital, Prämienreserve; ~ **value added** *(national accounting)* Mehrwert, Wertschöpfung; ~ **value of shares** Nettoinventarwert von Anteilen; ~ **realizable value** *(Br.)* realisierbarer Verkaufserlös; ~ **weight** *(US)* Netto-, Rein-, Eigen-, Trockengewicht; ~ **working capital** *(US)* Differenz zwischen Umlaufvermögen und kurzfristigen Verbindlichkeiten, Betriebskapital; ~ **worth** reiner Wert, Nettowert, *(stockholder, US)* Nettoanteil, Eigenkapital einer Gesellschaft; **corporate** ~ **worth** *(US)* Eigenkapital einer Gesellschaft; ~ **yield** Rein-, Nettoertrag, effektive Rendite (Verzinsung); ~ **yield effective** *(securities)* effektive Verzinsung, Rendite.

netted, to have reinen Gewinn ergeben haben.

netting transactions among the clients *(banking)* Direktgeschäfte zwischen Bankkunden.

nettle *(v.) (fig.)* ärgern, reizen;
to grasp the ~ Stier bei den Hörnern packen.

network Netz, Verflechtung, *(advertising)* Stellennetz, *(broadcasting)* Sendernetz, -gruppe, Rundfunksendernetz, *(el.)* Leitungs-, Verteilernetz, *(system of lines)* Eisenbahn-, Kanal-, Lichtnetz, *(technique)* Netzplan, *(television)* Fernsehprogramm;
basic ~ Sendergruppe; **global** ~ weltumfassendes Netz; **far-flung** ~ weitgespanntes Netz; **highway** ~ Straßennetz; **television** ~ *(US)* privates Fernsehsystem;
~ **of agents** Agentenring; ~ **of air routes** Flugverkehrsnetz; ~ **of branches** Geschäftsstellennetz, Filialnetz, Branchennetz; ~ **of canals** Kanalsystem; ~ **of dealers** Händler-, Absatznetz; ~ **of falsehoods** Netz von Intrigen; ~ **of highways** Fernstraßennetz; ~ **of influence** Machtverflechtung; ~ **of motorways** *(Br.)* Autobahnnetz; ~ **of railways** Eisenbahnnetz; **interlacing** ~ **of roads** zusammenhängendes Straßensystem; ~ **of sprinkler valves** Rohrnetz mit Wasserbrausen; ~ **of terrorists** Terroristenbande; ~ **of treaties** Vertragsnetz; ~ **of underground pipes** unter der Erde verlegtes weitverzweigtes Röhrennetz;
to broadcast on state ~s über alle öffentlichen Sender verbreiten; **to sell through a** ~ **of 550 dealers** über ein Netz von 550 Vertragshändlern verkaufen;
~ **affiliate** Ortssender; ~ **clearance bureau** *(US)* Selbstkontrollinstitut der Funkwerbung; ~ **commentator** Fernsehkommentator; ~ **distribution** Nachrichtenverteilernetz; ~ **prime time** *(television)* Hauptsendezeit einer Fernsehgruppe; ~ **technique** Netzplantechnik; ~ **television** Fernsehsendergruppe.

neutral Neutraler, Parteiloser, Unparteiischer, *(international politics)* neutraler Staat;
~ *(v.)* neutral, parteilos, *(gear)* im Leerlauf, *(politics)* überparteilich;
to be ~ **as regards distributed and retained profits** einbehaltene und ausgeschüttete Gewinne steuerneutral behandeln; **to put the lever into** ~ in den Leerlauf schalten; **to remain** ~ sich zu keiner Partei schlagen, neutral bleiben, *(state)* Neutralität bewahren; **to slip the gear into** ~ Gang in Leerlaufstellung bringen;
to maintain a ~ **attitude** sich neutral verhalten; ~ **countries** neutrales Ausland; ~ **gear** Leerlauf[gang]; ~ **ground** neutraler Boden; ~ **money** Indexwährung; ~ **nation** neutraler Staat, neutrales Land; ~ **position** Nullstellung, *(gear)* Leerlauf; ~ **property** im Eigentum neutraler Staatsangehöriger stehendes Vermögen; ~ **rate of interest** Gleichgewichtszins; ~ **ship** neutrales Schiff; ~ **state** neutraler Staat; ~ **status** Neutralität; ~ **territory** neutrales Gebiet; ~ **waters** neutrale Gewässer; ~ **wire** *(el.)* Nulleiter.

neutralism Neutralismus, Neutralitätspolitik, Politik der Blockfreiheit.

neutralist Neutralist, Neutraler, Neutralitätspolitiker.

neutralistic neutralistisch.

neutrality Neutralität, Parteilosigkeit, Unparteilichkeit, *(politics)* neutraler Staat, Zugehörigkeit zu einem neutralen Staat;
armed ~ bewaffnete Neutralität; **benevolent** ~ wohlwollende Neutralität; **friendly** ~ wohlwollende Neutralität; **permanent** ~ ständige (ewige) Neutralität; **unconditional** ~ unbedingte Neutralität; **voluntary** ~ freiwillige Neutralität;

~ **of a port** neutraler Hafen;
to infract (violate) ~ Neutralität verletzen; **to respect** ~ Neutralität anerkennen;
~ **agreement** Neutralitätsabkommen; ~ **laws** *(US)* Neutralitätsgesetze; ~ **legislation** Neutralitätsgesetzgebung; ~ **proclamation** *(US)* Neutralitätserklärung.

neutralization Neutralisierung, Neutralitätserklärung, *(mil.)* Niederhaltung, Lahmlegung;
~ **fire** Niederkämpfungsfeuer.

neutralize *(v.)* neutralisieren, *(mil.)* niederkämpfen, *(politics)* für neutral erklären.

neutralized zone neutralisierte Zone.

never-never *(sl., Br.)* Stottern, Abzahlen;
~ **land** Wolkenkuckucksheim, Phantasieland.

new neu, *(book)* soeben erschienen, *(newly elected)* neugewählt, neuernannt, *(linguistic)* neu, noch nicht gebräuchlich;
brand ~ fabrikneu; **of** ~ *(Scot.)* vollkommen neues Verfahren; ~ **for old** *(insurance)* neu für alt; ~ **from school** frisch von der Universität; ~ **and useful** *(patent law)* gewerblich verwertbar, Neuheit;
to allow the deduction of one third ~ **for old upon the balance** Drittel für Neuwertleistung abziehen; **to be** ~ **to business** ohne Geschäftserfahrung sein; **to be** ~ **to a town** neu zugezogen sein; **to do s. th. up like** ~ etw. wieder ganz auf neu machen; **to find something** ~ auf etw. Neues stoßen;
~ **acquisition** Neuerwerbung; ~ **assets** *(executor)* nach Ablauf der Verjährungsfristen dem Nachlaß zufallende Vermögenswerte; **to be wholly** ~ **ball-game** etw. ganz Neues sein; ~ **birth** Wiedergeburt, Regeneration; **to elect a** ~ **board** Neuwahl des Aufsichtsrats vornehmen; ~ **book department** Sortimentsabteilung; ~-**born** neu geboren; ~-**born passion** neu entdeckte Leidenschaft; ~ **boy** neu eingetretener Schüler; ~ **bread** frisches Brot; ~ **building** Neubau; ~-**built** neu errichtet (gebaut); ~ **business** Neugeschäft; ~-**business commission** Abschlußprovision; ~-**business department** *(US)* Akquisitionsabteilung [einer Bank]; ~ **car** Neuwagen; ~-**car registration** Neuzulassung von Kraftfahrzeugen; ~-**car sales** Neuwagengeschäft; ~-**car shortage** Neuwagenknappheit; ~-**car warranty** Neuwagengarantie; ~ **cause of action** neue klagebegründende Tatsachen; ~ **chum** *(Australia, sl.)* Einwanderer, *(sl.)* unerfahrener Neuling; ~ **coinage** Neuprägung; ~-**coined word** neugeprägtes Wort; ~-**come** soeben angekommen; ~ **company** Neugesellschaft; **in** ~ **condition** wie neu; ~ **construction** Neubau; ~ **course** Neuorientierng; ~ **deal** *(US)* Neubeginn; ~ **departure** *(politics)* Neuorientierung; ~ **draft** neuer Entwurf; ~ **edition** Neuauflage; **to call a** ~ **election** Neuwahlen ansetzen (ausschreiben); ~ **entrant** Neuzugang; ~ **entrants** Firmenneugründungen; ~ **establishment** Geschäftsneugründung; ~-**fallen snow** frisch gefallener Schnee; ~ **fashion** neue Mode; ~-**est fashion** letzte Modeneuheit; ~-**fashioned** neu eingeführt; ~ **financing** Neu-, Erstfinanzierung; ~ **frontiers** *(fig.)* Neuland; ~ **generation** Nachwuchs; ~ **ground** Neuland; **to break** ~ **ground** Neuland betreten; ~ **hats department** Neuernennungsliste; ~ **high** neuer Höchststand, -kurs; ~ **hire** *(US) (labour force)* Neuling; ~ **hiring** *(US)* Neueinstellung; ~ **home starts** Neubauten; ~ **impression** Wiederabdruck; ⌾ **International Economic Order** *(UNO)* Neue Weltwirtschaftsordnung; ~ **issue** Neuemission; ~ **issue market** Markt für Neuemissionen; ~ **land** *(US)* Neuland, unbebautes Land; **to turn over a** ~ **leaf** neuen Anfang machen, neues Leben anfangen; **the** ~ **learning** moderne Wissenschaft; **to lead a** ~ **life** neues Leben beginnen; **the** ⌾ **Look** neue Linie, *(politics)* die neue Perspektive; ~ **man** Emporkömmling; **to feel a** ~ **man** sich wie neugeboren fühlen; **to make a** ~ **man of s. o.** ganz anderen Menschen aus jem. machen; ~ **matter** *(pleading)* neuer Sachvortrag; ~ **member of parliament** erstmalig ins Parlament gewählter Kandidat; ~-**model** *(v.)* umformen; ~ **orders** Neuabschlüsse, -aufträge; **the** ~ **poor** verschämte Arme; ~ **practicality** neue Sachlichkeit; ~ **president** neuer Präsident; ~-**product introduction** Einführung neuer Artikel; ~ **promise** Schuldanerkenntnis; ~ **publications** neu erschienene Bücher, Neuerscheinungen; **to jump into** ~ **purchases** sich auf Neuerwerbungen stürzen; ~ **registration** Neueintragung; ~[**ly**] **rich** Neureicher; ~-**rich** neureich; ~-**rich snobbery** neureiches Protzentum; **to add five** ~ **rooms to a house** fünf Zimmer anbauen; ~ **shares** *(stocks, US)* junge Aktien; ~ **trial** Wiederaufnahmeverfahren; ~ **tilt to an old song** neuer Version einer alten Geschichte; ~ **town** *(Br.)* Satellitenstadt; ~-**tyred** neu bereift; ~ **tricks** Neuerungen; ~ **version** Neufassung; ~ **woman** emanzipierte Frau; **the** ⌾ **Worlds** Nord- und Südamerika; ~-**year card** Neujahrskarte; ~-**year's greetings** Neujahrsglückwünsche; ⌾ **Year's Day** Neujahrstag; ⌾ **Year's Message** Neujahrsansprache.

New York|Curb Exchange New Yorker Freiverkehrsbörse; ~ **equivalent** New Yorker Parität; ~ **exchange** *(funds)* Auszahlung New York.

newcomer Fremdling, Neuling, *(marketing)* Außenseiter; **to be a ~ in the community** neu zugezogen sein; **to be a ~ to a subject** auf einem Gebiet noch Neuling sein.

newfangled neumodisch, hypermodern; ~ **ideas about education** neumodische Erziehungsmethoden.

newly|discovered evidence neuentdecktes Beweismaterial; ~ **married couple** Hochzeitspaar.

news Kunde, Neuigkeit, Nachrichten; **broadcast ~** Rundfunknachrichten; **business ~** geschäftliche Nachrichten, Handels-, Wirtschafts-, Börsennachrichten; **city ~** *(Br.)* Wirtschaftsnachrichten; **commercial ~** Börsen-, Handelsteil; **chief ~** wichtigste Nachrichten; **cold ~** bedrückende Nachrichten; **disturbing ~** beunruhigende Nachrichten; **false ~** falsche Nachrichten; **financial ~** Börsennachrichten, Nachrichten aus dem Finanzleben; **foreign ~** Auslandsnachrichten; **heartening ~** beruhigende Nachrichten; **[very] latest ~** neueste Nachricht[en], letzte Meldungen; **local ~** Lokalteil; **official ~** amtliche Verlautbarung; **redhot ~** allerneueste (sensationelle) Nachrichten; **stale ~** abgestandene Neuigkeiten; **startling ~** alarmierende Nachrichten; **stop-press ~** *(Br.)* allerletzte (nach Redaktionsschluß einlaufende) Nachrichten; **~ in brief** Nachrichten in Kurzfassung, Kurznachrichten; **~ hot from the press** allerneueste Nachrichten; **to angle ~** Nachrichten aufmachen; **to be in the ~** in der Öffentlichkeit von sich reden machen, in der Öffentlichkeit notiert werden; **to break an item of ~** Nachricht veröffentlichen; **to break the ~ to s. o.** jem. eine [schlechte] Nachricht übermitteln; **to be all the ~** neueste Neuigkeit sein; **to be apparently ~ to s. o.** offenbar völlig neu für j. sein; **to be eager for ~** ungeduldig auf Nachrichten warten; **to be stunned by the ~** von den Nachrichten wie gelähmt sein; **to carry ~** Nachrichten bringen; **to circulate false ~** falsche Nachrichten verbreiten, Falschmeldung verbreiten; **to discount ~** Nachrichten bei der Kursfestsetzung berücksichtigen; **to disperse ~** Nachrichten verbreiten; **to edit ~ for the public** Nachrichten aufmachen (frisieren); **to exercise censorship over ~** Nachrichten zensieren; **to feature a piece of ~** Nachricht aufmachen; **to filter ~** *(mil.)* Nachrichten auswerten; **to flash ~ across the world by radio** Nachrichten ausstrahlen; **to forge ~** falsche Nachrichten aufbringen; **to get the ~ across** Nachrichten unter die Leute bringen; **to have ~ from s. o.** Nachricht von jem. haben; **to manufacture ~** Neuigkeiten fabrizieren; **to pick up ~** Neuigkeiten auftreiben; **to prepare s. o. for bad ~** j. auf schlechte Nachricht vorbereiten; **to publish ~ with all reserve** Nachrichten mit allem Vorbehalt veröffentlichen; **to publish ~ without vouching for its accuracy** Nachrichten ohne Nachprüfung veröffentlichen; **to read the ~** Nachrichten durchgeben; **to shrug off bad ~** von schlechten Nachrichten keine Notiz nehmen; **to slant ~** Nachrichten aufmachen; **to spread ~** Nachrichten verbreiten; **to tell the ~** Neuigkeit bekanntgeben; ~ **advertisement** Zeitungsannonce, Pressedienst, Nachrichtenbüro, Zeitungsverkaufsstelle; ~ **agency** Pressedienst, Nachrichtenbüro, Zeitungsverkaufsstelle; ~ **agent** Presseagent, *(newsdealer)* Zeitungsverkäufer; ~ **analyst** [Nachrichten]kommentator; ~ **blackout** Nachrichtensperre; ~ **broadcasting** Nachrichtensendung; ~ **bulletin** Nachrichtensendung; ~ **bureau** Nachrichtenbüro; ~ **business** *(coll.)* Nachrichtenmedien; ~ **butcher** *(US)* Süßigkeiten- und Zeitungsverkäufer; ~ **cameraman** Bildberichterstatter; ~ **capital** Nachrichtenweltstadt; ~ **censorship** Pressezensur; ~ **cinema** Aktualitätenkino; ~ **commentary** Nachrichtenkommentar; ~ **commentator** Rundfunkkommentator; ~ **conference** Pressekonferenz; ~ **corps** akkreditierte Journalisten; ~ **coverage** Informationsbereich; ~-**crammed** mit Neuigkeiten vollgestopft; ~ **dealer** *(US)* Zeitungshändler, -verkäufer; **to buy at the ~ dealer** *(US)* am Zeitungskiosk kaufen; ~ **department** Nachrichtenabteilung; ~ **desk** Redakteur von Dienst; ~ **editor** Chef vom Dienst; ~ **flash** *(US)* Kurznachricht; ~ **film** Wochenschau; ~ **gathering machine** Nachrichtenbeschaffungssystem; ~ **hawk** *(US)* Zeitungsverkäufer; ~ **headlines** Nachrichten in Kurzfassung, Nachrichtenübersicht; ~ **house** *(Br.)* Zeitungsdruckerei; ~ **item** Nachrichtenmeldung, Zeitungsnotiz; ~ **items** Nachrichten[sendung], Kurznachrichten; ~ **lag** Informationslücke; ~ **leak** gezielte Indiskretion; ~ **magazine** Nachrichtenmagazin; ~ **management (manipulation)** Manipulation von Nachrichten; ~ **media** Nachrichtenmedia, -mittel; ~ **monitoring** Nachrichtenüberwachung; ~ **outfit** Nachrichtenagentur; ~ **outlet** Nachrichtenstelle; ~ **photographer** Bildberichterstatter; ~ **picture** Bildreportage; ~ **program(me)** Nachrichtensendung; ~ **release**

Freigabe einer Zeitungsmeldung, Pressenotiz; ~ **reporter** Zeitungskorrespondent; ~ **reporting abilities** Berichterstattungsmöglichkeiten; ~-**scrammed** mit Neuigkeiten vollgestopft; ~ **service** Nachrichtendienst; **industrial ~ service** Nachrichten aus dem Wirtschaftsleben; ~ **show** Nachrichtensendung; ~ **slip** Nachrichtenstreifen; ~ **stall** *(Br.)* Zeitungskiosk, -stand; ~ **stock** Rotationspapier; ~ **story** aktueller Text; ~ **summary** Nachrichten in Kurzfassung; ~ **syndicate** Zeitungs-, Pressesyndikat, Nachrichtenbüro; ~ **theatre** Aktualitätenkino; ~ **typist** Pressestenograph; ~ **value** Neuigkeitswert; ~ **vendor** Zeitungsverkäufer, -händler; ~-**wire network** Nachrichtennetz; ~ **writer** Journalist.

newsbill *(Br.)* Nachrichtenmagazin, Bulletin.

newsboard *(Br.)* Aushang, Schwarzes Brett.

newsboy Zeitungsverkäufer, -träger.

newscast Nachrichtensendung.

newscaster Nachrichtensprecher.

newscasting Nachrichtensendung.

newsie Zeitungsjunge.

newsletter internes Rundschreiben, Informationsblatt.

newsman Zeitungsbesitzer, *(journalist)* Journalist, *(newsdealer)* Zeitungsverkäufer.

newsmonger Neuigkeitskrämer.

newspaper Zeitung, Journal, Blatt; **afternoon ~** Nachmittagszeitung; **antigovernment ~** regierungsfeindliche Zeitung; **baled ~s** gebündelte Zeitungen; **commercial ~** Börsenblatt, Wirtschaftszeitung; **daily ~** Tageszeitung; **financial ~** Börsenblatt; **German-language ~** deutschsprachige Zeitung; **home-town ~** Stadtanzeiger; **local ~** Lokalzeitung; **morning ~** Morgenzeitung; **right-wing ~** rechtseingestellte Zeitung; **widely read ~** weit verbreitete Zeitung; **weekly ~** Wochenzeitung, -blatt, -zeitschrift, wöchentlich erscheinende Zeitung; ~ **having many advertisements** Anzeigenblatt; ~ **sent by air** Luftpostzeitungsgut; ~ **with a wide circulation** weitverbreitete Zeitung; ~**s and periodicals** Zeitungen und Zeitschriften; ~**s of every shade** Zeitungen aller Schattierungen; **to advertise in a ~** in einer Zeitung inserieren; **to attack in a ~** in der Zeitung angreifen; **to be on a ~** bei einer Zeitung beschäftigt sein, einer Redaktion angehören; **to be stated in the ~** in der Zeitung gestanden haben; **to discontinue a ~** Zeitung abbestellen; **to do a ~ round** Zeitung austragen; **to edit a ~** Zeitung herausgeben; **to establish a ~** Zeitung gründen; **to file an item of information to a ~** einer Zeitung eine Nachricht zukommen lassen; **to insert (put) in a ~** in eine Zeitung einrücken, inserieren; **to open a ~** Zeitung aufschlagen; **to print [off] a ~** Zeitung drucken; **to read in the ~** in der Zeitung lesen; **to scan a ~** Zeitung durchblättern; **to subscribe to** *(US)* **(take in,** *Br.)* **a ~** Zeitung halten (beziehen, abonnieren); **to suspend a ~** Herausgabe einer Zeitung vorübergehend untersagen; **to syndicate a ~** zu einem Zeitungskonzern zusammenschließen; **to unfold a ~** Zeitung entfalten; ~ **account** Zeitungsbericht; ~ **advertisement** Zeitungsannonce, -inserat; ~ **advertising** Zeitungs-, Inseratenwerbung; ~ **announcement** Pressenotiz; ~ **article** Presse-, Zeitungsartikel; **to contribute ~ articles** Zeitungsartikel beisteuern; ~ **attention** Zeitungsinteresse; ~ **audience** Zeitungsleser; ~-**audience measurement** Messung des Leserverhaltens; ~ **circulation** Zeitungsauflage; ~ **clipper** *(US)* Ausschnittbüro; ~ **clipping** *(US)* Zeitungsausschnitt; ~ **column** Zeitungsspalte; ~ **columnist** Kolumnenschreiber; ~ **competition** Zeitungsausschreibung; ~ **copy** Zeitungstext; ~ **correspondent** [Zeitungs]korrespondent, Berichterstatter; ~ **cutting** Zeitungsausschnitt; ~ **delivery** Zeitungszustelldienst, -austragen; ~ **dispatch office** Zeitungsexpedition; ~ **editor** [Zeitungs]redakteur; ~ **graveyard** Anzeigenfriedhof; ~ **group** Zeitungskonzern; ~ **heading** Zeitungskopf; ~ **headline** Zeitungs-, Titelüberschrift; ~ **hoax** Zeitungsente; ~ **industry** Zeitungsindustrie, -wirtschaft; ~ **insurance** Abonnentenversicherung; ~ **interview** Zeitungsinterview; ~ **leak** Zeitungsindiskretion; ~ **magnate** Zeitungskönig; **to call for the ~ money** Zeitungsgeld einziehen; ~ **office** Annoncenannahme; ~ **owner** Zeitungsbesitzer, -verleger; ~ **real-estate pages** Immobilienteil einer Zeitung, Grundstücksnachrichten; ~ **plant** Zeitungsbetrieb; ~ **post** *(Br.)* Zeitungen und Zeitschriften, Zeitungsdrucksachen; ~ **press** Nachrichtenpresse, Informationsblätter; ~ **production** Herstellung einer Zeitung; ~ **proprietor** Zeitungsbesitzer; ~ **publisher** *(US)* Zeitungsverleger; ~ **rack** Zeitungsablage, -ständer; ~ **rates** Drucksachentarif für Zeitungen; ~ **reader** Zeitungsleser; ~ **real-estate pages** Immobilienteil einer Zeitung, Grundstücksnachrichten; ~ **report** Zeitungs-, Pressebericht; ~ **reporter** Berichterstatter; **to pay the**

travelling expenses of a ~ reporter Reisekosten eines Journalisten übernehmen; **~ reporting** Berichterstattung für eine Zeitung; **~ representative** *(advertising)* Anzeigenvertreter; **~ size** Zeitungsformat; **~ slot machine** Zeitungsautomat; **° Society** *(Br.)* Zeitungsverlegerverband; **~ space** *(advertising)* Anzeigenraum; **large ~ space user** bedeutender Anzeigenkunde; **~ stake** Zeitungsbeteiligung; **~ strike** Zeitungsstreik; **~ style** Zeitungsstil; **~ subscription** [Zeitungs]abonnement; **~ supplement** Zeitungsbeilage; **~ syndicate** Nachrichtenbüro, -agentur; **~ vendor** Zeitungsverkäufer; **~ woman** Journalistin; **~ work** Zeitungsdruck; **~ wrapper** Kreuz-, Streifband, Streifbandzeitung; **~ writing** Zeitungsstil.

newspaperdom Presse.

newspaperman *(dealer)* Zeitungsverkäufer, -händler, *(owner)* Zeitungsbesitzer, *(writer)* Journalist.

newsprint Rotations-, Zeitungspapier; **~ paper** Zeitungspapier; **~ screen** Zeitungsraster.

newsprinting Zeitungswesen.

newsreel Wochenschau; **speed-up ~** Nachrichtensendung im Zeitraffertempo; **~ company** Wochenschaugesellschaft.

newsroom Lesezimmer, *(agency, broadcasting, television station)* Nachrichtenzentrale, *(library)* Zeitschriftenzimmer, *(kiosk, US)* Zeitungskiosk, -laden, -verkaufsstelle.

newssheet kleines Nachrichtenblatt.

newsstand *(US)* Zeitungsstand, Kiosk; **to be off ~s** am Kiosk nicht zu haben sein; **~ distribution** *(US)* Kioskabsatz; **~ sales** Einzel-, Kioskverkauf, über den Kioskhandel laufender Teil einer Auflage.

newsworthiness nachrichtenmäßige Bedeutung.

newsworthy berichtenswert, von Interesse für den Zeitungsleser.

newsy *(US)* Zeitungsjunge.

next künftig, folgend, *(US sl.)* informiert, im Bilde; **~ on the agenda** nächster Tagesordnungspunkt; **~ to no evidence** fast kein Beweis; **~ to impossible** fast unmöglich; **~ of kin** nächste An-, Blutsverwandte; **~ to nothing** fast gar nichts; **~ to reading matter** *(advertising)* textanschließende Anzeige; **to get ~ to o. s.** *(sl.)* sich über seine Unbeliebtheit klar werden; **~ devisee** Testamentserbe; **~ door** im Nebenhaus, nebenan; **~-door neighbo(u)rs** allernächste Nachbarn; **to live ~ door** in der allernächsten Nähe leben, nebenan wohnen; **to be continued in our ~ edition** Fortsetzung folgt; **~ entitled** Nächstberufener; **~ friend** *(minor)* Prozeßbeistand eines Minderjährigen, Prozeßvertreter; **~ larger size** nächsthöhere Größe; **with the ~ mail** postwendend; **the ~ man** der erste Beste.

nexus Zusammenhang, Verbindung, Komplex; **~ of interest** Verflechtung von Interessen.

nib Schreibfeder.

nibble Bissen, Happen; **~** *(v.)* [Löhne] herabsetzen; **~ at one's food** mit langen Zähnen essen, im Essen herumstochern; **~ at an offer** an einem Angebot herumkritteln.

nice *(coll.)* liebenswürdig, freundlich, hübsch, *(scrupulous)* genau, gewissenhaft, sorgfältig; **~ and easy** sehr leicht; **to be ~ to s. o.** jem. freundlich begegnen, j. nett behandeln; **to be ~ in the choice of words** seine Worte vorsichtig wählen; **not to be ~ about the means** in der Wahl seiner Mittel nicht zimperlich sein; **~ affair** kitzlige Angelegenheit; **~ chap** *(Br.)* netter Kerl; **~ distinction** feiner Unterschied; **~ guy** *(US)* netter Kerl; **~ judgment** kritisches Urteil; **to be in a ~ mess** in der Patsche sitzen; **~ point of law** schwierige Rechtsfrage; **~ question** heikle Frage; **~ shades of meaning** feine Bedeutungsnuancen; **~ state of affairs** schöne Bescherung; **~ little sum** hübscher Betrag; **to say ~ things to s. o.** jem. Liebenswürdigkeiten sagen.

nicely fein, nett; **to be doing ~** *(patient)* sich gut erholen; **to do s. o. ~** *(sl.)* j. schön hereinlegen; **to talk ~ to s. o.** jem. gute Worte geben; **~ prepared meal** hübsch angerichtete Mahlzeit.

niceties, financial finanztechnische Feinheiten; **~ of life** Annehmlichkeiten des Lebens; **~ in politics** peinliche Befolgung aller Gepflogenheiten des politischen Lebens; **not to stand upon ~** es nicht so genau nehmen, nicht so pingelig sein.

nicety Nuance, Feinheit, *(subtility)* Spitzfindigkeit, Kritik; **to a ~** bis aufs Haar; **~ of criticism** spitzfindige Kritik; **~ of judgment** Urteilsschärfe.

niche Nische, *(fig.)* Versteck, Zufluchtsort; **~** *(v.)* *(fig.)* verbergen; **to fill a ~ of its own** besonderen Platz einnehmen; **to find the**

right ~ for o. s. sein Leben so einrichten wie man will; **to have a ~ in the temple of fame** Ehrenplatz in der Ruhmeshalle einnehmen.

nick Kerbe, Einschnitt, *(print.)* Signaturrinne, *(sl.)* Kittchen; **in the ~ of time** zum rechten Augenblick; **~** *(v.)* *(sl.)* hereinlegen, neppen; **~ a bank** *(sl.)* Bank ausrauben; **~ the time** richtigen Zeitpunkt abpassen.

nickel Nickel, *(US)* Fünfcentstück; **not worth a plugged ~** *(US)* keinen Pfifferling wert.

nickname Spitzname.

nifty *(US sl.)* Retourkutsche; **~** *(a.)* *(US sl.)* schick, fesch.

niggard Geizhals, Filz.

nigger *(vulgar)* Neger, Nigger; **~ in the woodpile** böse Absicht, versteckter Nachteil; **to work like a ~** wie ein Sklave arbeiten.

niggle *(v.)* pedantisch sein, herumtüfteln.

niggling zu detailliert.

night, in the silence of the in nächtlicher Stille; **open all ~** die ganze Nacht geöffnet; **first (opening) ~** *(US)* Premiere; **the servants' ~ out** freier Abend der Hausangestellten; **to be accustomed to late ~s** Nachtvogel sein; **to have a ~ out (off)** Abend frei haben; **to make a ~ of it** sich die ganze Nacht um die Ohren schlagen; **to sleep the whole ~ through** ganze Nacht durchschlafen; **to stay over ~** übernachten; **to travel by ~** nachts reisen; **to turn ~ into day** Nacht zum Tage machen; **to work day and ~** Tag und Nacht arbeiten; **~ attack** *(mil.)* Nachtangriff; **~ attire** Nachtgewand; **~ bell** Nachtglocke; **~ bird** *(fig.)* Nachtvogel; **~-blind** nachtblind; **~ call** Nachtzeitgespräch, nächtlicher Anruf; **~ cellar** *(Br.)* Kellerlokal; **~ charge** Nachttarif; **~ club** Nachtklub, -lokal; **~ depository** Nachttresor; **~ duty** Nachtdienst; **~ editor** Schlußredakteur; **~ effect** Dämmerungswirkung; **~ employment** Nachtarbeit; **~ exposure** Nachtaufnahme; **~ fighter** Nachtjäger; **late ~ final** Nachtausgabe; **~ flight** Nachtflug; **~-fly** *(v.)* bei Nacht fliegen; **~ flying** Nachtflug; **~ lamp** Nachtlampe; **~ letter[gram]** *(US)* Brieftelegramm; **~ life** Nachtleben; **~ light** Nachtlicht; **~'s lodging** nächtliche Unterbringung, Nachtquartier, -lager; **~ magistrate** Polizeibeamter mit Nachtdienstfunktionen; **~ mail** Nachtpost; **~ man** der Arbeiter der Nachtschicht; **~ number** *(tel.)* Nachtanschluß; **~ performance** Nachtvorstellung; **~ porter** *(hotel)* Nachtportier; **~ rate** Nachtgebühr, -tarif; **~ safe** Nachttresor; **~ safe deposit** Außen-, Spätschalter; **~ school** Fortbildungsschule, Abendkursus, [etwa] Volkshochschule; **~ service** Nachtdienst; **~ shelter** Obdachlosen-, Nachtasyl; **~ shift** Nachtschicht, -arbeit; **~-shift bonus** Nachtschichtvergütung; **~ spot** Nachtlokal; **~-stop** *(v.)* nachts zwischenlanden; **~ tariff** Nachttarif; **~ time** Nachtzeit; **~ tourist** Nachtreisender; **~ train** Abendzug; **~ vision** nächtliche Vision; **~ watch** Nachtwache; **~ watchman** Nachtwächter.

nightcap kleiner Schlaf-, Nachttrunk, Schlummertrunk, Betthupferl.

nighterie *(sl.)* Nachtklub.

nightingale *(sl.)* Spitzel, Denunziant.

nightly performance Abendvorstellung.

nightmare Albdruck, Alptraum, Schreckgespenst.

nightwork Nachtarbeit; **~ premium** Nachtarbeiterzuschlag.

nighttime Nachtzeit; **~ program(me)** Nachtprogramm; **to fly ~ sorties** Nachteinsätze fliegen.

nightwork premium Nachtarbeitszuschlag.

nil Null, Nichts; **~ growth rate** Nullwachstumsrate.

nimble hurtig, flink, *(fig.)* geistig beweglich, schnell auffassend; **~ thinker** Mensch mit schnellem Reaktionsvermögen.

nimbostratus Regenwolkendecke.

nimbus Nimbus, Ruhm.

niminy-pimininess Geziertheit, Affektiertheit.

niminy-piminy geziert, affektiert, etepetete.

nincompoop Trottel.

nine, to be dressed up to the ~s aufgedonnert (piekfein) gekleidet sein; **a ~-days wonder** kurzlebige Berühmtheit; **in the ~ holes** *(US)* in Schwierigkeiten; **~ times out of ten** im allgemeinen.

nineteen to the dozen, to talk das Blaue vom Himmel herunterreden.

ninety days loan[s] Dreimonatsgeld.

ninny Tölpel, Trottel, Gimpel.

nip *(plants)* Frostbrand, -beschädigung;
  ~ *(v.) (plants)* vernichten, beschädigen, *(sl.)* flitzen;
  ~ **in the bud** im Keim ersticken; ~ **in and out of the traffic** sich zwischen den Fahrzeugen hindurchzwängen.

nipped | by the frost vom Frost beschädigt; ~ **by ice** vom Eis eingeschlossen.

nipper | s *(coll.)* Handschellen;
  ticket ~ Fahrkartenzange.

nitwit Dummkopf.

nix *(US)* unbestellbare Postsendung, *(sl.)* nichts;
  to grub for ~ umsonst essen; **to work for** ~ umsonst arbeiten.

no Absage, Weigerung, *(parl.)* Gegenstimme;
  the ayes and ~**es** Stimmen für und wider;
  to be ~ **more** nicht mehr existieren; **not to take** ~ **for an answer** Absage nicht entgegennehmen;
  ~ **a/c** *(account)* kein Konto; ~**-account** *(US dial)* wertloser Mensch, unbedeutend; ~ **admittance** Eintritt verboten; ~ **admittance except on business** nur für Geschäftsleute; ~ **advice** mangels Avis zurück; ~ **agents** *(house sale, Br.)* Makler verbeten; ~ **arrival**, ~ **sale** bei Nichteintreffen kein Kaufzwang; ~ **bargain** *(sl.)* unbedeutende Erscheinung; ~ **bill** *(grand jury)* Verfahren eingestellt, *(sl.)* Gewerkschaftsgegner; ~ **cards** *(funeral)* statt Karten; ~ **change given** Geld abgezählt bereithalten; ~**-claim bonus** *(Br.)* Bonus, Prämiennachlaß bei Schadensfreiheit, Schadensfreiheitsrabatt; ~**-confidence motion** Mißtrauensantrag; ~ **costs** Kostenaufhebung; ~ **date** *(catalog(ue))* ohne Jahresangabe; ~ **end of money** sehr viel Geld; ~ **end of a good time** herrliche Zeit; ~ **expense to be incurred** ohne Kosten; ~**-fault insurance plan** Gewährung von Entschädigung ohne Untersuchung der Unfallursache; ~ **flowers** Blumenspenden verbeten; ~ **funds** *(cheque)* keine Deckung; ~**-good** Taugenichts; ~ **goods** *(Br.)* Pfändungsversuch erfolglos; ~ **goods exchange** Umtausch nicht gestattet; ~ **great shakes** *(coll.)* gerade keine Leuchte; ~ **guarantee** ohne Gewähr; **to wing away from the** ~**-hands attitude** sich aus der Politik völliger Untätigkeit lösen; ~ **flies on s. o.** nicht zu beanstanden bei jem.; ~ **kidding** stimmt das auch?; ~ **letting clause** Mietverbotsklausel; ~ **liability whatever** unter Ausschluß jeder Haftung; ~**-load** Leerlauf; ~**-man's land** umstrittenes Gebiet, *(mil.)* Niemandsland; **by** ~ **means** durchaus nicht; **and** ~ **mistake** ohne Zweifel, sicherlich; ~**-nonsense** sachlich; ~ **orders** *(Br.)* kein Auftrag; ~ **par** ohne Nennwert; ~**-par value stock** *(US)* nennwertlose Aktie, Aktie ohne Nennwert; ~ **parking** Parken verboten; ~**-profits employer** Grenzarbeitgeber; ~ **protest** *(bill of exchange)* ohne Protest; ~**-purpose loan** nicht zweckgebundener Kredit; ~**-quarter man** schonungslos Vorgehender; ~ **recourse** völliger Haftungsausschluß; ~ **reduction** feste Preise; ~ **sale** kein Umsatz; ~ **salvage charge** Haftungsausschluß für Bergungskosten; ~**-show** *(US sl.)* beim Abflug nicht erschienener Fluggast, nicht ausgenutzte Platzbuchung; ~ **small matter** keine Kleinigkeit; ~ **smoking** Rauchen verboten; ~**-strike agreement** Streikenthaltungsabkommen; ~**-strike clause** Streikverbotsklausel; ~ **thoroughfare** Durchfahrt verboten; ~ **through road** Sackgasse; **in** ~ **time** ziemlich schnell; **to invoke the** ~**-vote procedure** Abstimmung verhindern; ~**-work** Faulenzen, Flanieren.

nob of the first water *(sl.)* ganz hohes Tier.

Nobel | Foundation Nobelstiftung; ~ **laureate** Nobelpreisträger; ~ **prize** Nobelpreis; ~ **prize winner** Nobelpreisträger.

nobelist Nobelpreisträger.

nobility Adel;
  landed ~ Landadel;
  ~ **of mind** vornehme Gesinnung; ~ **of soul** Seelengröße;
  to marry into the ~ in Adelskreise einheiraten.

noble Edelmann, Adliger;
  ~ *(a.)* adlig, edel, vornehm;
  to be of ~ **birth** vornehmer Abkunft sein; ~ **building** imposantes Gebäude; ~ **mind** vornehmer Charakter; **to do things on a** ~ **scale** besondere Größenausmaße anlegen; ~ **sentiments** edle Gefühle.

nobleman Edelmann, Adliger.

nobody unbedeutende Person, Niemand;
  a simple ~ eine glatte Null;
  to be ~ nichts zu sagen haben; **to be** ~ **in particular** ganz gewöhnlicher Mensch sein; **to knew s. o. when he was** ~ j. gekannt haben bevor er berühmt wurde; **to treat s. o. as a mere** ~ j. wie den letzten Dreck behandeln;
  ~**'s business** worum sich niemand kümmert.

noctanter Vollstreckung in der Nacht.

nod Kopfnicken, Wink;
  ~ *(v.)* **off** einnicken; ~ **approval** *(one's assent)* zustimmend nicken;

to get the ~ eingestellt werden, den Job bekommen; **to give s. o. a** ~ jem. zunicken; **to give one's** ~ **of approval** zustimmend nicken;
  Homer sometimes ~**s** selbst Homer schläft gelegentlich.

nodal | point Brenn-, Knotenpunkt; ~ **region** Ballungsgebiet.

nodding | acquaintance flüchtige (oberflächliche) Bekanntschaft;
  to be on ~ **terms with s. o.** j. nur vom Grüßen kennen.

noddle *(sl.)* Birne, Schädel;
  to be cracked in the ~ nicht richtig im Oberstübchen sein.

noes Neinstimmen.

noise Geräusch, Lärm, *(tel.)* Rauschen, *(fig.)* Aufsehen, Krach, *(bad news, sl.)* schlechte Nachrichten;
  big ~ *(sl.)* hohes Tier; **disturbing** ~ ruhestörender Lärm;
  ~ *(v.)* **abroad** bekanntwerden lassen, herumtratschen;
  to make a ~ **about s. th.** Aufheben um etw. machen, Krach schlagen; **to make a** ~ **in the world** Aufsehen in der ganzen Welt erregen;
  ~ **abatement** Lärmverminderung, -bekämpfung; ~ **abatement zone** Lärmschutzbereich; ~ **control** Lärmbekämpfung; ~ **eliminator** Entstörungsvorrichtung; ~ **level** Geräusch-, Lärmpegel; ~ **pollution** Lärmbelästigung, -belastung; ~ **prevention** Lärmbekämpfung; ~ **reduction** Schallminderung; ~ **restrictions** Geräuschauflagen; **to develop effective** ~ **standards acceptable to the courts** für die Gerichte annehmbare Geräuschnormen entwickeln; ~ **suppression** Störschutz.

noiseless geräuscharm;
  ~ **typewriter** geräuschlose Schreibmaschine.

noisemaker Ruhestörer.

noisemaking Störung, Ruhestörung.

noisy | advertising Werberummel; ~ **engine** lautgehender Motor; ~ **street** laute Straße.

nolle prosequi *(US)* Klagerücknahme, *(prosecutor)* Einstellung des Verfahrens, Verfahrenseinstellung;
  ~ *(v.)* Anklage niederschlagen.

nolo contendere *(lat.)* Schuldigerklärung.

nomadic life Nomadenleben.

nomenclature Bezeichnungsweise, Nomenklatur, *(register)* Namenregister, -verzeichnis, Fachsprache, Terminologie, *(tariff)* Tarifschema, -nomenklatur.

nominal nur dem Namen nach, nominal, nominell;
  ~ **account** Erfolgskonto, *(Br.)* Sachkonto, totes Konto; ~ **amount** Nominal-, Nennbetrag, Nominal-, Nennwert; ~ **assets** *(US)* Buchwerte; ~ **balance** Sollbestand; ~ **capital** *(Br.)* Grund-, Gründungs-, Stammkapital, *(corporation)* autorisiertes Aktienkapital, *(US)* geringfügiges Kapital, Nominalkapital; ~ **consideration** *(Br.)* formale Gegenleistung; ~ **damages** der Form halber festgesetzter geringer (nomineller) Schadenersatz; ~ **defendant** notwendiger Streitgenosse; ~ **exchange** nomineller Umrechnungskurs; ~ **fine** nominelle (unbedeutende) Geldstrafe; **to be the** ~ **head** nur dem Namen nach der Chef sein; ~ **hours** nach dem Tarif vorgesehene Arbeitszeit, Nominalarbeitsstunden; ~ **income** Nominaleinkommen, Proformabezüge; ~ **interest** Nominalzinssatz, Normalverzinsung, nominelle Beteiligung; ~ **list of shareholders** *(Br.)* Namensverzeichnis der Aktionäre, Aktionärsverzeichnis; ~ **market** *(stock exchange)* fast umsatzlose Börse; ~ **par** Nenn-, Nominalwert; ~ **parity** Nennwertparität; ~ **partner** Scheingesellschafter; ~ **party** Streitgenosse ohne Prozeßinteresse; ~ **plaintiff** Kläger in Prozeßstandschaft; ~ **price** Nominalpreis, *(stock exchange)* nomineller Kurs; ~ **quotation** genannte Notierung, Notiz ohne Umsätze; ~ **rank** Titularrang; ~ **rate of interest** Nominalzinssatz; ~ **register** Namensverzeichnis; ~ **rent** sehr geringe Miete; ~ **roll** *(mil.)* Namenverzeichnis; ~ **ruler of a country** nur dem Namen nach Herrscher; ~ **share** *(Br.)* Strohaktie; ~ **stock** Gründungs-, Stammkapital; ~ **sum** pro forma angesetzter [sehr niedriger] Betrag; ~ **value** Nominal-, Nennwert, *(US)* Erinnerungswert; ~ **wages** Nominallohn, -einkommen, symbolische Entlohnung; ~ **workweek** Normalarbeitswoche; ~ **yield** Nominalverzinsung.

nominate *(v.)* ernennen, bestallen, berufen, *(propose)* namhaft machen, aufstellen, vorschlagen, nominieren;
  ~ **an arbitrator** Schiedrichter vorschlagen; ~ **a beneficiary** *(life insurance)* Begünstigten einsetzen; ~ **a candidate** Kandidaten aufstellen; ~ **a new director** Vorstandsmitglied ernennen; ~ **an executor of a will** Testamentsvollstrecker einsetzen; ~ **a man for the Presidency** Präsidentschaftskandidaten benennen; ~ **s. o. for mayor** j. zum Kandidaten für das Amt des Bürgermeisters nominieren; ~ **s. o. for a post** j. für eine Position vorschlagen.

nominating | candidates Anwärter-, Kandidatennominierung; ~ **convention** Nominierungskonvent; ~ **time** Ernennungstermin.

nomination Er-, Benennung, Bestallung, Namhaftmachung, Nominierung, Aufstellung;
direct ~ direkte Wahl; **fresh** ~ erstmalige Kandidatenaufstellung;
~ **for an appointment** Ernennungsvorschlag; ~ **of beneficiary** *(life insurance)* Einsetzung eines Begünstigten; ~ **of a candidate** Kandidatenaufstellung;
to be in ~ als Kandidat aufgestellt sein; **to make a** ~ **from the floor** Kandidaten im Plenum vorschlagen; **to put in** ~ ernennen; **to ratify s. one's** ~ jds. Nominierung bestätigen;
~**s committee** Ernennungsausschuß; ~ **paper** [etwa] Wahlvorschlagsliste einer parteifreien Wählergemeinschaft; ~ **petition** Wahlvorschlagliste; ~ **policy** Versicherungspolice mit unwiderruflicher Bezugsberechtigung.
nominative │ candidate vorgeschlagener Kandidat; ~ **shares** Namensaktien.
nominee *(candidate)* Kandidat, vorgeschlagener Bewerber, *(life insurance)* Begünstigter, *(man of straw)* vorgeschobene Person, Strohmann, *(proxy)* Bevollmächtigter, *(recipient of annuity, grant)* Leibrenten-, Zuschußempfänger;
company's ~ Firmenbevollmächtigter;
~**s of a bank** *(Br.)* Treuhandagentur für den Effektentransfer; ~ **company** Strohmanngesellschaft; ~ **shareholder (stockholder, US)** als Aktionär vorgeschobener Strohmann; ~ **shareholdings (stockholdings, US)** auf den Namen von Strohmännern lautende Aktienbeteiligungen.
non-U *(Br.)* plebeisch, nicht vornehm.
non │ compos mentis *(lat.)* nicht zurechnungsfähig, unzurechnungsfähig, zurechnungsunfähig, geisteskrank; ~ **liquet** *(lat.)* unschlüssig, unklar.
nonability Geschäftsunfähigkeit, *(to sue)* [Einrede der] Prozeßunfähigkeit.
nonacceptance *(of a bill)* Akzeptverweigerung, Nichtakzeptierung, -annahme, *(of goods)* Annahmeverweigerung, Nichtannahme;
for ~ mangels Annahme zurück.
nonaccess *(matrimonial cause)* Nichtbeiwohnung.
nonaccidental nicht zufällig.
nonacknowledgement Nichtanerkennung.
nonaction Unterlassung.
nonactionable nicht einklagbar.
nonadmission Zulassungsverweigerung, Nichtzulassung;
~ **of the public** Ausschluß der Öffentlichkeit.
nonadmitted assets *(insurance accounting)* ungeeignete Deckungsmittel.
nonage Minderjährigkeit, Unmündigkeit;
to be in one's ~ minderjährig sein.
nonaged *(US)* minderjährig.
nonagreement Nichteinigung;
~ **country** Nichtvertragsstaat.
nonaggression pact (treaty) Nichtangriffspakt, Gewaltverzichtsabkommen.
nonagricultural │ establishment nichtlandwirtschaftlicher Betrieb; ~ **working force** nicht in der Landwirtschaft tätige Arbeitskräfte.
nonalcoholic beverages alkoholfreie Getränke.
nonalienation Nichtveräußerung.
nonaligned block-, bündnisfrei, neutral;
~ **nation** blockfreier (bündnisfreier) Staat.
nonalignment *(politics)* Ungebundenheit, Bündnislosigkeit, Blockfreiheit.
nonancestral estate frei erworbenes Grundstück.
nonappealable nicht rechtsmittelfähig, rechtskräftig.
nonappearance *(lawcourt)* Nichterscheinen, -einlassung.
nonappearing abwesend [bei Gericht].
nonapplicability Nichtanwendbarkeit.
nonapprentice Praktikant.
nonapproval Nichtgenehmigung, Ablehnung.
nonarrival *(train)* Ausbleiben.
nonassented bonds (securities, stocks) am Sanierungsverfahren nicht beteiligte Obligationen (Wertpapiere, Aktien).
nonassessable nicht steuerpflichtig, abgaben-, steuerfrei;
~ **stock** *(US)* nicht nachschußpflichtige (nachzahlungsfreie, voll eingezahlte) Aktie.
nonassignable nicht übertragbar.
nonassumpsit Einrede mangelnder Verpflichtung.
nonattendance Abwesenheit, Nichterscheinen, Aus-, Fernbleiben.
nonattendant Nichterschienener.
nonattributable *(income)* nicht zurechenbar.
nonavailability Unabkömmlichkeit.

nonavailable unabkömmlich.
nonaviation business nicht zur Flugzeugindustrie gehörige Geschäftssparte.
nonbailable ohne Kautionsverpflichtung.
nonbank │ customers Nichtbanken-Kundschaft; ~ **place** Banknebenplatz.
nonbanker Nichtbankier.
nonbanking │ business bankfremdes Geschäft; ~ **interests** bankfremde Interessen; ~ **venture** bankfremdes Risiko.
nonbasic │ commodities kriegsunwichtige Agrarprodukte; ~ **income** Nahbedarfseinkommen.
nonbelligerence Nichtkriegsführung.
nonbelligerent nicht kriegführend.
nonbroadcasting hours sendefreie Zeiten.
nonbusiness geschäftsunkundig;
~ **days** *(Br.)* Sonn- und Feiertage.
noncalendered matt.
noncallable nicht stornierbar;
~ **bond** nicht vorzeitig kündbare Schuldverschreibung.
noncash bargeldlos;
~ **charges** unbare Belastungen.
noncharitable nicht gemeinnützig.
nonclaim zu spät geltend gemachter (verjährter) Anspruch, verwirktes Klagerecht.
nonclearing │ countries Länder ohne Verrechnungsabkommen; ~ **house stocks** nicht durch die Clearingsvereinigung lieferbare Aktien.
noncognoscenti Laien.
noncollection policy Konkursversicherungspolice.
noncollegiate *(course)* nicht an ein Universitätsstudium heranreichend.
noncombatant Nichtkämpfer, Nichtkombattant;
~**s** Zivilbevölkerung.
noncommercial nicht kommerziell (gewerblich, auf Gewinn gerichtet);
~ **enterprise** nicht gewerbliches (gemeinnütziges) Unternehmen; ~ **quantities** nicht zum Handel geeignete Warenmengen; ~ **trade** landwirtschaftliches Gewerbe.
noncommissioned nicht bevollmächtigt, *(mil.)* in einer nicht ausgewiesenen Stelle;
~ **officer** Unteroffizier.
noncommittal Unverbindlichkeit, freie Hand, Neutralität;
~ *(a.)* sich nicht festlegend, unverbindlich.
noncommitted *(politics)* blockfrei, neutral, bündnisfrei;
~ **state** blockfreier Staat.
noncommutable investment nicht ablösbare Kapitalanlagen.
noncompetence Unzuständigkeit.
noncompeting nicht konkurrierend;
~ **groups** nicht konkurrierende Gruppen.
noncompetitive bid nicht wettbewerbskonformes Angebot.
noncompletion Nichtfertigstellung.
noncompliance Nichtbefolgung, -einhaltung, Zuwiderhandlung.
noncompulsory clauses fakultative Bestimmungen.
nonconcurrence Nichtübereinstimmung.
nonconcurrent policies verschiedenartige das gleiche Versicherungsinteresse deckende Policen.
nonconfidence Mißtrauensvotum;
to pass a ~ **motion** Mißtrauensvotum annehmen.
nonconfirming use *(zoning statute)* genehmigte abweichende Bebauungsweise.
nonconductor *(el.)* Nichtleiter.
nonconformism Nonkonformismus.
nonconformist Nonkonformist, *(Br.)* Dissenter.
nonconsent Nichtzustimmung.
nonconsolidated *(balance sheet)* nicht konsolidiert.
noncontent Auftragsgegner.
noncontentious nicht streitig;
~ **business** freiwillige Gerichtsbarkeit; ~ **easement** vorrübergehende Dienstbarkeit.
noncontestable nicht anfechtbar;
~ **clause** *(insurance)* Unanfechtbarkeitsklausel.
noncontingent │ claims bedingte Forderungen; ~ **preference stock** *(Br.)* kumulative Vorzugsaktie.
noncontracting states Nichtvertragsstaaten.
noncontractual liability außervertragliche Haftung.
noncontribution clause *(fire insurance)* Vergünstigungsklausel allein für die Ersthypothek.
noncontributory nicht beitragspflichtig, beitragsfrei;
~ **pension** beitragsfreie Betriebspension; ~ **pension plan** beitragsfreies Pensionssystem.
noncontroversial nicht umstritten, unpolemisch.

noncounty borough Kreisstadt, kreisangehörige Stadt.
noncultivation Brachliegenlassen.
noncumulative nicht kumulativ, *(dividend)* ohne Nachzahlungsverpflichtung;
~ **dividend** gewöhnliche Dividende; ~ **preferred stock** Vorzugsaktie ohne Nachbezugsrecht.
nondeclaration Nichtabgabe einer Erklärung.
nondelegable nicht übertragbar.
nondeducted unabgerechnet.
nondeductible *(income tax)* nicht abzugsfähig.
nondelivery Nicht[aus]lieferung, -ausfolgung, -erfüllung, *(mail)* Nichtbestellung;
in case of ~ **return to sender** falls nicht zustellbar zurück an Absender.
nondepartmental minister Minister ohne Geschäftsbereich.
nondeployment *(nuclear weapon)* Nichtstationierung.
nondescript nicht klassifizierbar, *(labo(u)r market)* arbeitsunfähig, invalide;
to be ~ nirgendwohin gehören.
nondescriptive marks nicht einwandfrei unterscheidbare Warenzeichen.
nondetachable *(coupon)* untrennbar;
~ **facilities** im Handel unverwendbare Einbauten.
nondirection *(of jurors)* fehlende Rechtsbelehrung.
nondisclosure Nichtoffenbarung, -angabe, Verschweigen, *(insurance law)* Verletzung der vertraglichen Anzeigepflicht;
material ~ Verschweigen wesentlicher Tatsachen;
~ **of material facts** Verschweigen wesentlicher Tatsachen.
nondiscretionary trust *(Br.)* Investmentfonds mit strengen Anlagevorschriften.
nondiscrimination *(customs)* Gleichbehandlung.
nondiscriminatory treatment *(customs)* Nichtdiskriminierung.
nondisposable capital gesetzliche Rücklage.
nondistributed profit unverteilter Gewinn.
nondistrictive marks nicht einwandfrei unterscheidbare Warenzeichen.
nondistributable funds nicht zur Ausschüttung gelangende Geldbeträge.
nondiversified company *(US)* Kapitalanlagegesellschaft ohne Anlagenstreuung.
nondrawn profit nicht entnommener Gewinn.
nondumping certificate Dumpingfreistellungsbescheinigung.
nondurable consumer goods kurzlebige Verbrauchsgüter.
nondutiable abgaben-, zollfrei.
nondwelling facilities nicht für Wohnzwecke bestimmte Anlagen.
nonedgelined *(road)* ohne Fahrbahnbegrenzungslinie.
noneffective unwirksam, *(mil.)* dienstuntauglich, -unfähig.
nonefficient *(mil.)* nicht genügend ausgebildet.
noneligible nicht wählbar (zulassungsfähig).
nonemployed erwerbs-, arbeitslos;
~ **person** Nichtbeschäftigter, Erwerbsloser.
nonenforceability Nichteinklagbarkeit, -vollstreckbarkeit, Rechtsschutzversagung.
nonenforceable nicht einklagbar.
nonentity Nichtexistenz, *(fig.)* unbedeutende Person, Null.
nonessentials, nonessential elements Nebensächlichkeiten, unwesentliche (fakultative) Bestandteile, *(goods)* nicht lebenswichtige Güter.
nonexclusive nicht ausschließlich;
~ **licence** einfache Lizenz.
nonexecution Nichtdurch-, -ausführung.
nonexempt pfändbar, *(customs)* zollpflichtig.
nonexistence Nichtbestehen, Abwesenheit.
nonexistent nicht vorhanden.
nonexpendable | trust fund Thesaurierungsfonds; ~ **supplies** *(mil.)* Gebrauchsgüter.
nonexpert Nichtfachmann, Laie.
nonexportation *(US)* Exportverweigerung.
nonextant nicht vorliegend.
nonextradition Nichtauslieferung.
nonfactor costs nicht faktorbezogene Kosten.
nonfading *(colo(u)r)* farbecht, *(wireless set)* schwundfrei.
nonfeasance pflichtwidrige Unterlassung, Nichterfüllung.
nonferrous | industry Nichteisenmetallindustrie; ~ **metals** Nichteisenmetalle.
nonfiction book Sachbuch.
nonfinancial public enterprise nicht mit Finanzierungsaufgaben befaßter Staatsbetrieb.
nonfoods Einzelhandelsartikel außerhalb des Nahrungsmittelsektors.

nonforfeitable nicht pfändbar.
nonforfeiting *(life insurance)* der Anspruchswirkung nicht unterworfen.
nonforfeiture Unverfallbarkeit;
~ **provisions** *(insurance)* obligatorische Rückkaufsbestimmungen; ~ **value** *(insurance)* Rückkaufswert.
nonfraternization Fraternisierungsverbot.
nonfreezing kältebeständig.
nonfulfilment Nichterfüllung.
nongovernmental nichtstaatlich, -amtlich.
nongraded products unsortierte Ware.
nonhalation plate *(photo)* lichthoffreie Platte.
nonhero, to make a ~ **of s. o.** j. ausplazieren.
nonincome charges einkommensunabhängige Belastung.
nonindependent unselbständig.
nonindustrial activities nichtindustrielle Wirtschaftszweige.
noninsurance Nichtversicherung.
noninsured nicht versichert.
nonintercourse *(states)* Verweigerung zwischenstaatlichen Wirtschaftslebens.
noninterest-bearing zinslos, unverzinslich;
~ **securities** unverzinsliche Werte.
noninterference, nonintervention Nichteinmischung;
~ **pact** Nichteinmischungspakt; ~ **policy** Nichteinmischungspolitik.
noninvolvement Nicht-Engagement.
nonissuable plea prozeßhindernde Einrede.
nonitinerant trade stehendes Gewerbe.
nonjoinder Nichtbeitritt bei Streitverkündung.
nonjudicial day *(lawcourt)* sitzungsfreier Tag.
nonjuror Eidesverweigerer.
nonjury case nicht vor ein Geschworenengericht gehörende Strafsache.
nonledger assets in der Bilanz nicht aufgeführte Anlagegüter, nicht buchungsfähige Wirtschaftsgüter.
nonlegal ungesetzlich;
in legal and ~ **matters** gerichtlich und außergerichtlich.
nonleviable unpfändbar.
nonliability Haftungsausschluß, Nichthaftung, *(taxation)* Nichtbestehen einer Steuerpflicht.
nonliable mit Ausschluß der Haftung.
nonlicensed ohne Schankkonzession.
nonliquid illiquide;
~ **position** Illiquidität.
nonliquidity nicht vorhandene Liquidität, Illiquidität.
nonlisting *(stock exchange, US)* Nichtzulassung zur amtlichen Notierung.
nonlitigious nicht streitig, außergerichtlich;
~ **business** Angelegenheiten der freiwilligen Gerichtsbarkeit.
nonmailable *(US)* nicht durch die Post versandfähig, vom Postversand ausgeschlossen.
nonmanufactured nicht in Serie hergestellt.
nonmarket forces marktunfähige Einflußgrößen.
nonmarketable securities nicht verkehrsfähige (begebbare) Wertpapiere.
nonmedical policy Lebensversicherungspolice ohne ärztliche Untersuchung.
nonmember Nichtmitglied;
~ **bank** *(US)* nicht dem Federal-Reserve-System angeschlossene Bank; ~ **countries** *(EC)* Drittländer; ~ **government** Nichtmitgliedsregierung; ~ **state** Nichtmitgliedsstaat.
nonmembership Nichtmitgliedschaft.
nonmercantile nicht kaufmännisch.
nonmerchantable title nicht rechtsmängelfreies Liegenschaftsrecht.
nonmetered mail *(US)* nicht durch Freistempler freigemachte Post.
nonmobile troops nicht motorisierte Truppen.
nonmonetary advantages in Geldwert nicht ausdrückbare Vorteile; ~ **advantages and disadvantages** Vorzüge und Nachteile eines Arbeitsplatzes.
nonmotorist Nichtautofahrer.
nonnational Ausländer;
~ **resident** *(US)* Wohnsitzberechtigter, *(Exchange Control Act, Br.)* Devisenausländer.
nonnavigable nicht schiffbar.
nonnegotiability Unübertragbarkeit;
~ **notice** Sperrvermerk.
nonnegotiable nicht begebbar, unübertragbar;
~ **bill** Rektawechsel; ~ **check** *(US)* **(cheque,** *Br.)* Rektascheck, nicht übertragbarer Verrechnungsscheck.

nonnotice Nichtanzeige, -benachrichtigung.

nonnotification Nichtbenachrichtigung;
to operate on a ~ basis Forderungsabtretung in stiller Form vornehmen; **~ plan** Forderungsabtretung in stiller Form.

nonobligatory nicht obligatorisch;
~ spending *(EC)* in den Römischen Verträgen nicht festgelegte Ausgaben.

nonobservance Nichtbeachtung, -befolgung, -erfüllung.

nonoccupational berufsfremd, nicht berufsmäßig;
~ accident Nichtberufsunfall.

nonofficer untergeordneter Angestellter.

nonofficial *(US)* Nichtbeamter.
~ *(a.)* nichtamtlich, inoffiziell;
~ report offiziöser Bericht.

nonoperating nicht in Betrieb, außerbetrieblich, betriebsfremd;
~ company verpachtete Gesellschaft; **~ expense** betriebsfremder Aufwand, Erlösschmälerungen; **~ factory** stillgelegte Fabrik, stillgelegter Betrieb; **~ income** betriebsfremde Erträgnisse; **~ items** betriebsfremde Posten; **~ property** stillgelegter Betrieb; **~ revenue** *(balance sheet)* betriebsfremder Ertrag, nicht aus dem Geschäftsbereich stammende sonstige Erträgnisse.

nonowner Nichteigentümer.

nonownership liability insurance Autohaftpflichtversicherung für Unfälle von Erfüllungsgehilfen.

nonpareil *(print.)* Nonpareilleschrift.

nonparticipating *(life insurance)* ohne Gewinnbeteiligung;
~ countries *(ECU)* Nichtmitgliedsstaaten; **~ employments** *(Br.)* Beschäftigungszweige mit eigener Altersversorgung; **~ insurance** nicht gewinnbeteiligte Versicherung; **~ policy** Lebensversicherungspolice ohne Gewinnbeteiligung; **~ preferred stock** *(US)* nicht zu einer zusätzlichen Dividende berechtigende Vorzugsaktie; **~ state** Nichtteilnehmerstaat.

nonparticipation Nichtbeteiligung;
~ policy nicht gewinnberechtigte Lebensversicherungspolice.

nonpartisan überparteilich, unparteiisch, keiner Partei angehörend.

nonpartner Nichtteilhaber.

nonparty überparteilich, parteilos;
~ bill von allen Parteien eingebrachter Gesetzesentwurf; **~ council** parteilose Ratsversammlung; **~ spirit** überparteiliche Einstellung.

nonpayment Zahlungsverweigerung, Nichtzahlung, Nichteinlösung, -erfüllung, Verlust, Ausfall;
returned for ~ mangels Zahlung zurück.

nonpecuniary costs and benefits immaterielle Kosten und Erträge.

nonperformance Nichterfüllung, Unterlassung.

nonperishable nicht verderblich.

nonpermanent member nichtständiges Mitglied.

nonpiecework bonus plan Gruppenprämiensystem.

nonpinking *(fuel)* klopffest.

nonplace völlig obskurer Ort.

nonplacer Mißtrauensvotum;
~ *(v.)* Vorschlag ablehnen.

nonplus *(Br.)* Klemme, Nichtweiterkönnen;
~ *(v.)* total überraschen, in die Enge treiben;
to be brought to a ~ wie der Ochs am Berge stehen, völlig verdutzt sein.

nonpolitical unpolitisch.

nonpolluting industries umweltfreundliche Gewerbezweige.

nonpractising nicht ausübend.

nonprepayment Nichtfrankierung.

nonpresentment Nichtvorlage.

nonprice competition außerpreislicher Wettbewerb.

nonprivileged nichtbevorrechtigt.

nonproduction stillgelegte Produktion, *(nonpresentment)* Nichtvorzeigung, -vorlage;
~bonus Prämie für Produktionsstillegung.

nonproductive unproduktiv;
~ department Hilfskostenstelle; **~ expense** Generalunkosten; **~ labo(u)r** Gemeinkostenlohn; **~ material** Gemeinkosten, Hilfsmaterial.

nonproductiveness Unproduktivität.

nonprofessional nicht berufsmäßig (fachmännisch).

nonprofit nicht auf Gewinn gerichtet, gemeinnützig;
~ agreement Gewinnausschließungsvereinbarung; **~ hospital** gemeinnütziges Krankenhaus; **~-making** nicht auf Gewinn gerichtet; **~-making corporation (enterprise)** gemeinnütziges Unternehmen; **~ organization** Organisation ohne Erwerbscharakter.

nonproliferation agreement Atomsperrvertrag.

nonpromotion Nichtbeförderung.

nonproprietary rights nicht aus dem Eigentum hergeleitete Rechte.

nonproprietor Nichteigentümer.

nonprospectus company *(Br.)* durch Simultangründung entstandene Gesellschaft.

nonprovable claim nicht nachweisbare Forderung.

nonprovided *(school)* nicht aus öffentlichen Mitteln unterstützt.

nonqualification mangelnde Qualifikation.

nonquality mangelnde Qualität.

nonquota nicht am Kontingent beteiligt, nicht kontingentiert;
~ goods nicht kontingentierte Waren; **~ immigrant** *(US)* außerhalb des Kontingents Eingewanderter; **~ imports** kontingentfreie Einfuhren.

nonquotation *(of stocks)* Nichtzulassung zur amtlichen Notierung, Kursstreichung.

nonratification Nichtgenehmigung.

nonrationed goods nicht bewirtschaftete Waren.

nonrebuttable unwiderlegbar.

nonrecognition Nichtanerkennung.

nonrecourse loans *(US)* nicht einseitig aufkündbare Farmerkredite.

nonrecurrent einmalig, nicht wiederkehrend.

nonrecurring | charges (expenses) einmalige Ausgaben; **~ income** *(Br.)* außergewöhnliche Erträge.

nonredeemable unkündbar.

nonregistration Nichteintragung, unterlassene Registrierung.

nonreimbursable nicht erstattungsfähig.

nonremovable nicht absetzbar.

nonremunerative nicht ertragreich.

nonrenewal Nichterneuerung.

nonrenounceable nicht verzichtbar, unverzichtbar.

nonrepair Nichtausführung vereinbarter Reparaturen, schlechter Erhaltungszustand.

nonresidence Nichtvorhandensein eines Wohnsitzes, Nichtansässigkeit, *(foreign exchange)* Ausländereigenschaft.

nonresident *(exchange control)* nicht in England (USA) ansässige Person, Devisenausländer, Nichtansässiger, Gebietsfremder;
~ *(a.) (member)* nicht ortsgebunden, im Ausland ansässig, nicht ortsansässig, auswärtig;
~ account Ausländer-, Auslandskonto ; **~ alien** im Ausland Ansässiger, Ausländer; **~ beneficiary** begünstigter Devisenausländer; **~ citizen** *(US)* Staatsbürger mit Wohnsitz im Ausland; **~ company** *(Br.)* Gesellschaft ohne Hauptgeschäftssitz in England; **~ convertibility** Ausländerkonvertierbarkeit, *(Br.)* Freikonvertierbarkeit für das englische Pfund; **~ corporation** *(US)* Gesellschaft ohne Geschäftssitz in USA; **~ person** Nichtansässiger, Devisenausländer, Gebietsfremder; **~ sources** ausländische Devisenquellen; **~ stockholder** *(US)* auswärtiger Aktionär; **~ subsidiary** *(US)* Auslandstochter; **~ tax** Steuer für Devisenausländer; **~ taxpayer** beschränkt Steuerpflichtiger; **~ tuition** *(US)* Studiengebühr für Nichtansässige.

nonresidential nicht ansässig, auswärtig, gebietsfremd;
~ building outlay Aufwand der gewerblichen Wirtschaft für Bauleistungen; **~ investment** *(construction)* Bürobauvorhaben.

nonresistance blinder Gehorsam.

nonresistant widerstandslos.

nonrespondent *(interview)* abgelehnte Antwort.

nonresponse Nichtbeantwortung.

nonretroactivity Nichtrückwirkung.

nonreturnable nicht zurückzahlbar, *(package)* verloren;
~ bottle Einwegflasche; **~ package (packing)** verlorene Verpackung, Einwegpackung.

nonrevenue | freight kostenlos beförderte Eigenmaterialien; **~ receipts** *(governmental accounting)* Einnahmen im außerordentlichen Etat.

nonreversible keine Berufung zulassend, formell, rechtskräftig.

nonriparian state Nichtanliegerstaat.

nonrivalry in consumption Ausschluß der Konsumentenkonkurrenz.

nonroutine business besondere Tagesordnungspunkte.

nonsampling error systematischer Umfragefehler.

nonsane unzurechnungsfähig;
~ memory Unzurechnungsfähigkeit.

nonscheduled *(US)* nicht fahrplanmäßig;
to fly on a ~ trip Chartermaschine benutzen.

nonself-governing territories Gebiete ohne Selbstregierung.

nonsense Unsinn, dummes Zeug;
to make ~ *(passage)* keinen Sinn ergeben; **to take (have) no ~** sich nichts gefallen lassen; **to talk ~** dummes Zeug reden.

nonsignatory government Nichtunterzeichnerregierung.
nonsigner *(price maintenance, US)* Nichtunterzeichner der Preisbindungsbestimmungen.
nonsked business *(US)* Charterfluggeschäft.
nonskidding rutschfest, -sicher, mit Gleitschutzprofil versehen.
nonsmoker *(railway)* Nichtraucherabteil.
nonsmoking Nichtraucher.
nonsolvency Zahlungsunfähigkeit, Insolvenz.
nonsolvent zahlungsunfähig, insolvent.
nonspecie nicht in Hartgeld einlösbar.
nonspecific factors of production nicht spezialisierte Produktionsfaktoren, jederzeit auswechselbare Produktionsfaktoren.
nonspinning *(airplane)* trudelsicher.
nonstandard nicht der allgemein anerkannten Norm entsprechend.
nonstock | corporation *(US)* nicht auf Gewinn gerichtete Gesellschaft mit beschränkter Haftung; ~ **banking corporation** *(US)* nicht in der Form der AG betriebene Bankgesellschaft; ~ **moneyed corporation** *(US)* Genossenschaftskasse.
nonstop *(plane, Br.)* ohne Zwischenlandung, *(train)* durchgehend;
    to fly ~ Direktflug durchführen; **to get** ~ **to A** Direktverbindung nach A erhalten;
    ~ **cinema** Aktualitätenkino mit fortlaufendem Programm; ~ **flight** Flug ohne Zwischenlandung; ~ **journey** Reise ohne Unterbrechung; ~ **performance** Dauervorstellung; ~ **train** durchgehender Zug.
nonstrategic goods nicht kriegswichtige Waren.
nonstriker Nichtstreiker, Streikbrecher.
nonsubscribe *(v.)* nicht beziehen.
nonsubscription Nichtbezug.
nonsuit Prozeßbeendigung;
    involuntary ~ Klageabweisung; **voluntary** ~ Klagerücknahme;
    ~ *(v.)* mit der Klage abweisen;
    to direct a ~ Klageabweisungsantrag stellen.
nonsupport *(US)* Verletzung (Nichterfüllung) der Unterhaltspflicht.
nontariff fehlender Tarif;
    ~ **barriers** nicht tarifgebundene Handelshindernisse; **to ease** ~ **barriers** auf Zolldisparitäten beruhende Handelsschranken abbauen.
nontax revenue nicht aus Steuern herrührende Staatseinnahmen.
nontaxability Steuerfreiheit.
nontaxable steuerfrei, nicht steuerpflichtig;
    ~ **income** steuerbefreites Einkommen.
nontaxed nicht steuerpflichtig.
nonterm sitzungsfreie Zeit, Gerichtsferien.
nontrader Nichtkaufmann.
nontrading nicht kaufmännisch tätig;
    ~ **firm** nicht Handel treibende Firma; ~ **partnership** Personalgesellschaft, Sozietät.
nontransfer Nichtübertragung.
nontransferable nicht übertragbar.
nonunion gewerkschaftlich nicht organisiert;
    to go ~ *(US)* ohne Gewerkschaftsvermittlung handeln; ~ **country** *(Br.)* nicht dem Weltpostverein angehöriges Land; ~ **labo(u)r** nicht gewerkschaftlich organisierte Arbeiter; ~ **shop** *(US)* gewerkschaftsfreier Betrieb; ~ **worker** Nichtgewerkschaftler.
nonunionism Gewerkschaftsgegnerschaft.
nonunionist nicht organisierter Arbeiter, Gewerkschaftsgegner.
nonusage, nonuser Nichtausübung, -gebrauch;
    ~ **of a patent** unterlassene Patentausnutzung.
nonutility mangelnde Verwertbarkeit.
nonvalidating stamp *(US)* Entwertungsstempel.
nonvalue bill Gefälligkeitswechsel, -akzept.
nonvoter Nichtwähler.
nonvoting nicht stimmberechtigt;
    ~ **share** *(Br.)* stimmrechtslose Aktie.
nonwage demands lohnfremde Forderungen.
nonwaiver agreement *(fire insurance)* Vereinbarung über den Vorbehalt aller Rechte.
nonwarranty Haftungsausschluß;
    ~ **clause** Freizeichnungs-, Haftungsausschlußklausel, Ausschluß der Sachmängelhaftung.
nonwork journey private Fahrt.
nonworking wife nicht mitarbeitende Ehefrau.
nook Schlupfwinkel, Versteck;
    ~ **of land** Stück Land;
    to search for s. th. in every ~ **and corner (cranny)** in jedem Winkel nach etw. suchen, alle Ecken und Enden absuchen.

noon | edition Mittagsausgabe; ~ **rest** Mittagsruhe.
noontide, noontime Mittagszeit.
noose *(fig.)* Fallstrick;
    to put one's head into a ~ in die Falle gehen; **to put one's head in the marriage** ~ sich ins Ehejoch begeben; **to slip one's head out of the hangman's** ~ mit knapper Not dem Galgen entgehen.
noplaceville *(sl.)* Provinzstadt, Nest.
norm Norm, Regel, Richtschnur, *(pattern)* Muster, *(production)* Produktionsstandard, *(school)* Durchschnittsleistung;
    to become the ~ Allgemeingut werden; **to fulfil one's** ~ seine Norm erfüllen; **to set the workers a** ~ Arbeitern eine Norm auferlegen.
normal Normalstand, normaler Zustand;
    beyond the ~ über das Normalmaß hinaus;
    ~ *(a.)* normal, durchschnittlich, vorschriftsmäßig, mustergültig;
    to be incidental to the ~ **activity of a business** im Rahmen des üblichen Geschäftsverkehrs liegen; ~ **capacity** Normalkapazität; ~ **channels** Dienst-, Instanzenweg; ~ **consumer** Normalverbraucher; ~ **cost** durchschnittlich niedrigste Produktionskosten; ~ **deviation** Normalabweichung; ~ **distribution** Normalverteilung; ~ **distribution curve** Normalverteilungskurve; ~ **error curve** normale Fehlerkurve; ~ **flight** Normalflug; ~ **loss** natürlicher Schwund; ~ **mind** durchschnittliche Geistesverfassung; ~ **operations** normaler Aufgabenkreis; ~ **operator** *(US)* Durchschnitts-, Normalarbeiter; ~ **output** Normalerzeugnis; ~ **pension** Normalpension; ~ **performance** Normalleistung; ~ **price** Gleichgewichtspreis; ~ **profit** Mindestunternehmergewinn; ~ **return** Normalverzinsung; ~ **school** Lehrerbildungsanstalt, -seminar; ~ **speed** Betriebsdrehzahl; ~ **status** Normalstatus; ~ **tax** *(income tax, US)* Basissteuer; ~ **value** Normalwert; ~ **view** *(law)* Verkehrsanschauung; ~ **worker** Normalarbeiter; ~ **working day** Normalarbeitstag.
normalization Normalisierungsprozeß;
    ~ **of diplomatic relations** Normalisierung der diplomatischen Beziehungen.
normalize *(v.)* normalisieren;
    ~ **diplomatic relations** diplomatische Beziehungen normalisieren.
normally im Regel-, Normalfall, in der Regel.
normative effect *(collective agreement)* normative Bestimmungen.
North Atlantic | Council Nordatlantikrat; ~ **Treaty** Atlantikpakt; ~ **Treaty Organization** *(NATO)* Nordatlantische Verteidigungsgemeinschaft.
North-South dialogue Nord-Süd-Dialog.
northern lights Nordlicht.
nose *(airplane)* Kanzel, *(ship)* Bug, *(Br., tea)* Aroma, *(nark, sl.)* Polizeispitzel;
    as plain as the ~ **on one's face** so klar wie Kloßbrühe; **by a** ~ um eine Nasenlänge; **[right] under s. one's** ~ direkt vor jds. Augen; ~ **of wax** fügsamer Mensch;
    ~ *(v.)* seine Nase in anderer Leute Angelegenheiten stecken, *(nark, sl.)* Polizeispitzel sein;
    ~ **about the village** im Dorf herumstolzieren; ~ **around** herumspionieren, schnüffeln; ~-**dive** *(prices)* stürzen, rapide fallen; ~-**down** im Steilflug niedergehen; ~ **into other people's affairs** seine Nase in fremder Leute Tasche stecken; ~ **out** herauskommen, austüfteln, *(sl.)* um eine Nasenlänge gewinnen; ~ **out economic truth** konjunkturelle Tatsachen ans Tageslicht bringen; ~ **out a scandal** Skandal aufdecken; ~ **over** *(plane)* sich [bei der Landung] überschlagen; ~ **up** *(airplane)* hochziehen; ~ **its way slowly through the ice** *(ship)* seinen Weg langsam durch das Eis nehmen; ~ **one's way through the traffic** vorsichtig durch den Verkehr steuern;
    to be on the ~ *(sl., US)* allen Anforderungen entsprechen; **to bite s. one's** ~ **off** jem. eine scharfe Antwort erteilen; **to count the** ~**s** Zahl der voraussichtlichen Jastimmen zählen; **to cut off one's** ~ **to spite one's face** sich ins Fleisch schneiden; **to follow one's** ~ immer der Nase nach gehen, *(fig.)* seinem Instinkt folgen; **to get up s. one's** ~ jem. eine Nase drehen; **to go on under one's** ~ sich direkt vor jds. Augen abspielen; **to have a good** ~ *(coll.)* einen Riecher haben; **to have a** ~ **round** sich im Städtchen etw. umsehen; **to have a** ~ **for scandal** Skandalgeschichten wittern; **to keep one's** ~ **clean** *(US)* sich eine reine Weste bewahren; **to keep one's** ~ **to the grindstone** in der Tretmühle sein; **to keep s. one's** ~ **to the grindstone** j. stramm arbeiten lassen; **to lead s. o. by the** ~ j. an der Nase herumführen; **to look down one's** ~ **at s. o.** auf j. herabsehen; **to look down one's** ~ **at s. th.** herablassend auf etw. blicken; **to make a long** ~ **at s. o.** jem. eine lange Nase machen; **to pay through the** ~

Apothekerpreise zahlen, sich neppen lassen; **to pull s. one's ~** j. zurechtweisen; **to poke (put, thrust) one's ~ into s. one's business** seine Nase in fremder Leute Taschen stecken; **to put s. one's ~ out of joint** jem. einen bösen Streich spielen (jds. Selbstgefühl verletzen), *(fig.)* jds. Pläne zum Scheitern bringen; **to rub ~s with s. o.** mit jem. intim befreundet sein; **to rumple one's ~** seine Nase rümpfen; **to screw (turn) up one's ~ at s. th.** über etw. die Nase rümpfen; **to snap s. one's ~ off** jem. eine scharfe Antwort erteilen, j. anranzen; **to speak through the ~** durch die Nase sprechen; **to tell the ~s** Zahl der Anwesenden (voraussichtliche Jastimmen) feststellen; **to turn up one's ~ at s. th.** über etw. die Nase rümpfen;

~-bag *(fig.)* Mittagessen in der Tüte, *(horse)* Freßbeutel; **to put on the ~ bag** *(sl.)* während der Arbeit schnell etw. futtern; ~ **cone** Raketenspitze; ~ **dive** Sturzflug, *(prices)* Preissturz, *(stock exchange)* Kurssturz; ~ **heaviness** Kopflastigkeit; **~-heavy** kopflastig; ~ **landing wheel** Buglanderad.

noser Spitzel.
nosing Ausladung;
~ **of a staircase** Treppenkante;
to have a gift for ~ things out über einen guten Spürsinn verfügen.
nostro | accounts Nostrokonten; ~ **balance** Nostroguthaben; ~ **liabilities** Nostroverpflichtungen.
nostrum Patentrezept.
nosy Parker *(fam.)* Geschaftlhuber.
not | to be on delivery *(stock exchange)* nicht lieferbar sein; ~ **to be had** *(market report)* fehlt; ~ **to be noted** *(Br.)* **(protested)** ohne Protest;
~ **accountable** nicht rechnungslegungspflichtig; ~ **assignable** nicht übertragbar; ~ **binding offer** freibleibendes Angebot; ~ **dry behind the ears** noch nicht ganz trocken hinter den Ohren; ~ **exceeding** nicht höher als; ~ **guilty** nicht schuldig, unschuldig; ~ **later than** spätestens; ~ **less than** wenigstens, mindestens; ~ **negotiable** nicht übertragbar; ~ **to order** Rektaklausel; ~ **paying** unrentabel; ~ **possessed** nicht im Besitz; ~ **proven** *(Scot.)* nicht nachgewiesen; ~ **provided for** keine Deckung; ~ **satisfied** *(sheriff)* fruchtlos gepfändet; ~ **a soul** keine Menschenseele; ~ **subject to call** nicht vorzeitig kündbar; ~ **sufficient (funds) (n. s.)** keine Deckung; ~ **transferable** nicht übertragbar (begebbar).
notability wichtige Persönlichkeit, Standesperson.
notable | artist hervorragender Künstler; ~ **difference** bemerkenswerter Unterschied; ~ **event** denkwürdiges Ereignis; ~ **speaker** bedeutender Redner.
notables Honaratioren.
notarial notariell, vor einem Notar;
~ **act** Notariatshandlung; ~ **act of hono(u)r** *(bill of exchange)* notariell beurkundeter Ehreneintritt; ~ **attestation** notarielle Beglaubigung; ~ **certificate** notarielle Bescheinigung, Notariatsbescheinigung; ~ **charges (expenses)** Notariatsgebühren, -kosten; ~ **charges not to be incurred** *(bill of exchange)* ohne Kosten; ~ **deed** Notariatsakt, -urkunde, -urteil; ~ **document** Notariatsurkunde; ~ **office** Notariatsbüro; ~ **protest certificate** *(US)* Protesturkunde; ~ **seal** Notariatssiegel; ~ **separation** *(Dutch law)* notariell abgesprochene eheliche Trennung; ~ **service** Notariatstätigkeit; ~ **style** Notariatsstil; ~ **ticket** *(bill of exchange)* Notariatsgebühren; ~ **will** notariell (vor einem Notar) errichtetes Testament.
notariate Notariat.
notarize *(v.)* in notarieller Form abschließen, *(attest)* notariell bestätigen (beglaubigen);
~ **an income tax declaration** Einkommensteuererklärung in notarieller Form abgeben.
notarized copy notariell beglaubigte Abschrift.
notary, [public] Notar;
before a ~ in notarieller Form; **certified (attested) by a ~** notariell beglaubigt;
to be concluded before a ~ in notarieller Form abgeschlossen werden; **to draw up before a ~** notariell abschließen; **to strike a ~ off the roll** *(Br.)* Notariatsbefugnis entziehen;
~'s clerk Notariatsangestellter; **~'s fees** Notariatsgebühren; **~'s office** Notariatskanzlei; ~ **seal** Notariatssiegel.
notation Aufzeichnung, Notierung, Vermerk;
~ **on a bill of exchange** Protestvermerk;
to make ~ on the record in den Büchern einen Vermerk machen.
notch Kerbe, Einschnitt;
~ *(v.)* **up record profits** Rekordgewinne verzeichnen.
note Notiz, Vermerk, Aufzeichnung, *(account)* Nota, Rechnung, *(bank-note)* Banknote, Kassenschein, *(brief comment)* Anmer-

kung, *(brief writing)* Billet, Briefchen, Zettelchen, schriftliche Mitteilung, *(concise statement)* Aktenauszug, *(knowledge)* Kenntnis, Kunde, Nachricht, *(official communication)* amtliche Note, diplomatische Mitteilung, *(print.)* Anmerkung, Bemerkung, Interpunktionszeichen, *(promissory note)* Schuldschein, eigener Wechsel, Solawechsel;
as per ~ laut Nota (Rechnung); **of ~** bemerkenswert; **nothing of ~** nichts von Bedeutung; **please ~** zur Beachtung; **worthy of ~** beachtenswert;
~s Papiergeld, *(balance sheet)* Bilanzerläuterungen, *(debenture stock, US)* mittelfristige ungesicherte Schuldverschreibungen, *(law review, US)* Anmerkungen zu Gerichtsentscheidungen, *(s. th. taken down)* Aufzeichnungen;
accommodation ~ Gefälligkeitswechsel; **advance ~** Vorschußanweisung; **advice ~** Benachrichtigung, [Versand]anzeige; **bank ~** *(Br.)* Banknote; **bibliographical ~** bibliographisches Verzeichnis; **biographical ~s** biographische Mitteilungen, Lebensabriß; **bond ~** Zollbegleit-, -vormerkschein; **bought and sold (broker's) ~** Schlußschein; **cancelled ~s** entwertete Kassenscheine; **circular ~** Zirkular-, Reisekreditbrief; **cognovit ~** *(US)* schriftliche Schuldanerkenntnis, eigener Wechsel mit Unterwerfungsklausel; **collateral ~** *(US)* durch Verpfändung von Sicherheiten gedeckter Schuldschein; **collective ~** *(dipl.)* Kollektivnote; **commission ~** Provisionsgutschrift; **confidential ~** vertrauliche Note; **confirmation ~** Auftrags-, Vertragsbestätigung, Bestätigungsschreiben; **consignment ~** Versandanzeige; **counterfeit ~** Falschgeldnote; **country ~** *(Br.)* Regionalwechsel; **covering ~** *(fire insurance)* vorläufige Deckungszusage; **credit ~** Gutschriftsanzeige; **currency ~** Kassenschein, *(Br.)* englischer Schatzschein im 1. Weltkrieg; **customs ~** Zollvormerkschein; **customhouse ~** Zollrechnung, -schein; ~ **debit** Belastungs-, Lastschriftanzeige; **delivery ~** Lieferschein; **demand ~** Sichtpapier, *(dunning)* Mahnschreiben, *(taxation, Br.)* Steuerbescheid; **diplomatic ~** diplomatische Note; **discount ~** Diskontgutschrift; **discounted ~** diskontierter Wechsel; **dispatch ~** Versandanzeige, Verladeschein, *(bordereau)* Stückeverzeichnis, *(foreign parcel)* Paketkarte; **domiciliated promissory ~** domizilierter trockener Wechsel; **doubtful ~s and accounts** *(balance sheet, US)* dubiose Forderungen; **dud ~** falsche Banknote; **past due ~** überfälliger Schuldschein; **fascinating ~s** spannende Streiflichter; **foot ~** Fußnote; **fiduciary ~** *(Br.)* ungedeckte Banknote; **foreign ~** ausländische Banknote, *(bill of exchange)* ausländischer Wechsel; **foreign coins and ~s** Sorten; **freight ~** Frachtnota, -rechnung; **head ~s** *(decision)* Leitsätze; **identical ~** *(dipl.)* Mantelnote; **inland ~** inländischer eigener Wechsel; **iron-clad ~** erstklassig abgesicherter Schuldschein; **jerque ~** *(Br.)* Zolleinfuhrbescheinigung; **joint and several ~** *(US)* gesamtschuldneriches Zahlungsversprechen; **joint promissory ~** solidarischer trockener Wechsel; **judgment ~** *(US)* Schuldschein mit Unterwerfungsklausel, Unterwerfungsschuldschein; **low-value ~s** kleine Geldscheine; **marginal ~** Anmerkung, Randglosse; **mortgage ~** Hypothekenbrief, Hypothekenschein; **multilated ~** beschädigter Geldschein; **negotiable ~** Solawechsel; **official ~** Amtsbescheid; **past due ~** überfälliger Wechsel, überfälliger Schuldschein; **parallel ~s** *(dipl.)* gleichlautende Noten; **~s payable** *(balance sheet, US)* fällige Wechsel, Wechselschulden, -verbindlichkeiten, Kreditoren aus Wechseln, Verbindlichkeiten aus der Ausstellung eigener Wechsel; **pendant ~** beigefügter Kommentar; **promissory ~** schriftliches Schuldversprechen, Promesse, Schuldschein, *(bill of exchange)* Solawechsel, eigener (trockener) Wechsel; **prompt ~** Warennote; **~s receivable** *(balance sheet, US)* Wechselforderungen, Bestand an (Debitoren aus) Wechseln, Besitzwechseln, Schuldscheinen und Akzepten; **receivable discounted ~** vorzeitig diskontierter Wechsel; **receiving ~** Versandanzeige; **renewed ~** verlängerter Schuldschein; **sales ~** *(broker)* Schuldschein; **secured ~** durch Sicherheiten gedeckter Schuldschein; **shipping ~** Warenbegleitschein, *(Br.)* Verzeichnis der versandten Waren, Lade-, Anlieferungs-, Frachtannahmeschein; **short ~s** *(US)* kurzfristige Schuldscheine; **shorthand ~s** stenografische Aufzeichnungen; **stock ~** *(US)* durch Lombardierung von Wertpapieren gesicherter Schuldschein; **straight ~** *(US)* auf den Namen ausgestelltes Papier; **test ~** Einführungsvermerk; **title-retaining ~** schriftlicher Eigentumsvorbehalt; **trade ~s receivable** *(US)* Kundenwechsel; **treasury ~** *(US)* Schatzschein, -anweisung, Kassenschein; **urgent ~** Dringlichkeitsvermerk; **unsecured ~** ungesicherter Schuldschein; ~ **verbale** *(dipl.)* Verbalnote;
doubtful ~s and accounts *(balance sheet, US)* dubiose Forderungen, Dubiose; ~ **on an agreement** Vertragskommentierung; ~ **of allowance** *(Br.)* Mitteilung der Rechtsmittelzulassung; **~s**

due to banks Wechselverpflichtungen gegenüber Banken; ~ **of blocking** Sperrvermerk; ~ **of box-office receipts** Einnahmeaufstellung einer Vorverkaufskasse; ~**s and small change** Banknoten und Kleingeld; ~ **of charges** *(Br.)* Gebühren-, Spesen-, Kostenrechnung; ~**s in circulation** umlaufende Banknoten, [Bank]notenumlauf; **foreign** ~**s and coins** Sorten; ~ **in conformity with** gleichlautende Vormerkung; ~ **of disbursements** Auslagenrechnung, -nota; ~ **of entry** Eintragungsvermerk; ~ **of exchange** Kursblatt, -zettel; ~ **of exclamation** Ausrufungszeichen; ~ **of expenses** *(Br.)* Spesen-, Auslagenrechnung; ~ **of fees** Gebührenrechnung; ~ **of hand** *(Br.)* eigener (trockener) Wechsel, *(promissory note)* Hand-, Schuldschein, abstraktes Schuldanerkenntnis; ~ **of interrogation** Fragezeichen; ~ **of issue** *(law court, US)* Mitteilung der Terminfestsetzung; ~**s written in (on) the margin** Marginalien; ~ **or memorandum** *(statute of frauds)* kurze Vertragsniederschrift; ~ **of prepayment** Frankovermerk; ~ **of protest** *(bill of exchange)* Vormerkung zum Protest, *(dipl.)* Protestnote; ~ **of purchase** Kassenzettel; ~ **in reply** *(dipl.)* Antwortnote; ~ **of sale** Verkaufsvertrag; ~ **of self-satisfaction** Anzeichen von Genugtuung; ~ **of specie** Sortenverzeichnis; ~ **of tension** Spannungsanzeichen; ~ **of thanks** kurzer Dankbrief; ~ **of travelling expenses** *(Br.)* Reisekosten-, Spesenabrechnung; **critical** ~**s on a work** kritische Bemerkungen über ein Werk;

~ *(v.)* Kenntnis nehmen, beachten, bemerken, *(write down)* notieren, aufschreiben, vermerken;
~ **a bill (draft)** Wechselprotest erheben, Wechsel protestieren; ~ **in conformity with** gleichlautend buchen; ~ **down** notieren, aufzeichnen, vermerken, vormerken, *(debit)* anschreiben, belasten, buchen; ~ **down every word** jedes Wort mitschreiben; ~ **s. th. as a fact** etw. als Tatsache feststellen; ~ **a misprint** Druckfehler feststellen; ~ **an order** Auftrag vormerken; ~ **prices** Preise angeben; ~ **a protest** *(notary)* Wechsel mit Protestvermerk versehen; ~ **a right on the record** Recht vormerken; ~ **a statement** Erklärung zur Kenntnis nehmen;
to change one's ~ seinen Ton ändern; **to collect on a** ~ Wechsel zur Zahlung vorlegen; **to compare** ~**s** Gedanken austauschen; **to deliver a** ~ *(dipl.)* Note überreichen; **to exchange** ~**s** *(dipl.)* Noten austauschen; **to forge a bank** ~ Banknote fälschen; **to go over one's** ~**s** seine Notizen durchgehen; **to hit the right** ~ richtigen Ton treffen; **to issue [bank]** ~**s** Banknoten ausgeben; **to keep** ~**s** sich Notizen machen; **to make a** ~ vermerken, notieren, aufschreiben; **to make good on a** ~ Wechsel einlösen; **to put a** ~ **on the bulletin board** Mitteilung am schwarzen Brett anschlagen; **to receive a** ~ Anweisung bestätigen; **to refer to one's** ~**s** seine Notizen konsultieren; **to refuse to accept a** ~ Annahme einer Note verweigern; **to receive a** ~ Anweisung erhalten; **to reject a** ~ Note zurückweisen; **to retain some** ~**s** Notizen aufheben; **to send s. o. a** ~ jem. ein paar Zeilen schreiben; **to set down** ~**s** Notizen niederschreiben **to shuffle one's** ~**s** mit seinen Aufzeichnungen herumhantieren; **to sound the** ~ **of war** vom Krieg sprechen; **to speak from (with)** ~**s** anhand von Aufzeichnungen sprechen; **to speak without** ~**s** völlig frei sprechen; **to strike (sound) a false** ~ *(fig.)* falschen Ton anschlagen; **to strike a querulous** ~ seiner Stimme einen leicht nörgelnden Ton geben; **to strike the right** ~ richtigen Ton anschlagen; **to take** ~ **of** beachten, berücksichtigen; **to take [down]** ~**s of s. th.** sich über etw. Notizen machen; **to take** ~ **of a declaration** Erklärung zur Kenntnis nehmen; **to take a** ~ **of s. th. in one's pocket book** sich etw. in seinem Notizbuch notieren; **to take lecture** ~**s** Vorlesung mitschreiben; **to take** ~ **of an address** sich eine Adresse notieren; **to take** ~ **of a declaration** von einer Erklärung Kenntnis nehmen; **to take good** ~**s on a lecture** Vorlesung ausführlich mitschreiben; **to utter forged** ~**s** Falschgeld in Umlauf setzen; **to withdraw bank** ~**s** *(Br.)* Banknoten einziehen; **to write** ~**s on a text** Text kommentieren; **to write a** ~ **of excuse for s. o.** jem. eine Entschuldigung schreiben;
~ **bank** Notenbank; ~ **broker** *(US)* Diskont-, Wechselmakler, -händler; ~ **brokerage** *(US)* Wechselhandel, -geschäft; ~ **and coin circulation** Bargeldumlauf; ~ **collection** Wechselinkasso; ~ **cover** Notendeckung; ~ **forger** Banknotenfälscher; ~ **form** Notiz in Kurzform; **to sum up in** ~ **form** Notizen in Kurzform zusammenfassen; ~ **issue** *(Br.)* Notenkontingent, Banknotenausgabe; **fiduciary** ~ **issue** *(Br.)* ungedeckte Notenausgabe; ~**-issuing privilege** *(Br.)* Banknotenprivileg; ~ **journal** Wechselbuch; ~ **maker** *(US)* Wechselaussteller; ~ **market** Schuldscheinmarkt; ~**-pad** Notizbuch; ~ **paper** Briefpapier, -bogen, Schreibpapier; ~ **paper and envelopes to match** Briefpapier und dazupassende Umschläge; ~**-paper heading** Briefkopf; **to record on** ~~**paper** schriftlich festhalten; ~~**-paying system** Wechselverrechnungssystem; ~ **press** Banknotendruckerei; ~

register *(Br.)* Konto der von einer Notenbank ausgegebenen Banknoten, *(US)* Wechselbuch; ~ **return** *(Br.)* Banknotenausweis; ~**s scandal** Wechselfälschungsskandal; ~ **shaver** *(US)* wucherischer Diskontmakler; ~ **size** *(letter)* Kleinformat; ~ **taking** Anfertigen von Notizen; ~**-taking system** Aufzeichnungssystem; ~ **teller** *(banking, US)* Inkassobeamter; ~ **tickler** *(US)* Wechselverfallbuch.

notebook Heft, Merk-, Notizbuch, Kladde, Stenoblock, *(bookkeeping)* Wechselbuch.

notecase Brief-, Geldscheintasche.

noted [amtlich] notiert;
~ **before the official hours** vorbörslich; ~ **below** unten erwähnt; ~ **for protest** *(bill of exchange)* zum Protest vorgemerkt;
to cause a bill to be ~ Wechsel zu Protest gehen lassen; **to have a bill** ~ Wechsel protestieren lassen, Protest erheben.

noteholder Schuldscheininhaber.

nothing Kleinigkeit, Nichts, *(coll.)* keine Spur;
for ~ ohne Entgelt, gratis; **next to** ~ fast nichts;
~ **to it** unrentabel; ~ **of note** nichts von Bedeutung; ~ **to make a song about** nichts Welterschütterndes; ~ **to speak of** nicht der Rede wert; ~ **to write home about** völlig unbedeutend;
airy ~**s** Bagatellen; **a few** ~**s** nichtssagende Redensarten;
~ **doing** *(stock exchange)* kein Umsatz; ~ **offered** *(market report)* fehlt;
to be ~ **to s. o.** j. ganz kalt lassen; **to be** ~ **like as good as his earlier book** Vergleich mit seinem früheren Buch in keiner Weise aushalten; **to beat s. o. all to** ~ j. an den Bettelstab bringen; **to come to** ~ nichts erbringen, erfolglos bleiben; **to fade away to** ~ *(colo(u)r)* völlig verblassen; **to go for** ~ nichts erbracht haben; **to have** ~ **to do with s. o.** mit jem. nichts zu tun haben; **to have** ~ **of one's own** kein eigenes Vermögen besitzen; **to make** ~ **of s. th.** nicht viel Wesens von etw. machen; **to reduce an army to total** ~ Armee völlig vernichten; **to think** ~ **of** nichts Besonderes dabei finden;
there was ~ **else for it** es ließ sich nicht umgehen;
~ **interesting in the newspaper** nichts Interessantes in der Zeitung.

notice *(attention)* Aufmerksamkeit, Beachtung, Beobachtung, Wahrnehmung, Kenntnisnahme, *(bill of exchange)* Notanzeige, *(instruction)* Anordnung, Unterweisung, Vorschrift, *(intimation)* Nachricht, Anzeige, Ankündigung, Benachrichtigung, Benachrichtigungszettel, Mitteilung, *(in newspaper)* Notiz, Anzeige, Bericht, *(knowledge of facts)* Kenntnis, Kennenmüssen, *(note)* Vermerk, *(patent)* Anmeldung, *(public advertisement)* [öffentliche] Bekanntmachung, Verlautbarung, *(report)* Bericht[erstattung], *(review)* Besprechung, Rezension, *(tel.)* *(warning)* Warnung, Kündigung;
at a moment's ~ jederzeit kündbar; **at short** ~ kurzfristig kündbar; **at a very short** ~ in kürzester Frist; **by special** ~ durch besondere Mitteilung; **subject to** ~ kündbar; **subject to three months'** ~ mit vierteljährlicher Kündigung; **subject to change without** ~ freibleibend; **subject to** ~ **on either side** mit gegenseitiger Kündbarkeit; **till further** ~ bis auf weiteres; **without [given]** ohne Kündigungsfrist (vorherige Benachrichtigung), fristlos, *(purchaser)* gutgläubig; **without previous** ~ ohne vorherige Mitteilung; **without giving the requisite** ~ ohne Einhaltung der vorgeschriebenen Kündigungsfrist;
actual ~ tatsächliche Kenntnis, *(Br.)* zurechenbare Kenntnis; **arbitrary** ~ willkürliche Kündigung; **assessment** ~ Steuerbescheid; **calling-forward** ~ Warenabruf; **church** ~**s** kirchliche Nachrichten; **constructive** ~ schuldhafte Nichtkenntnis, fahrlässige Unkenntnis, zurechenbare Kenntnis, Kennenmüssen; **correct** ~ angemessene Kündigungsfrist; **defective** ~ Zustellungsmangel; **due** ~ rechtzeitige (ordnungsgemäße) Kündigung; **expiration** ~ Benachrichtigung über einen Fristablauf; **express** ~ ausdrückliche Mitteilung; **a fortnight's** ~ 14tägige Kündigung; **general** ~ *(director)* Mitteilung über mögliche Interessenskollision; **immediate** ~ *(insurance policy)* unverzügliche Anzeige [eines Versicherungsfalles], Schadensanzeige; **implied** ~ vermutete Kenntnis; **imputed** ~ zurechenbare Kenntnis [des Stellvertreters]; **insufficient** ~ unzureichende Kündigungsfrist; **judicial (jurisdiction)** ~ eigene Kenntnis des Gerichts, gerichtsnotorisch; **lawful** ~ ordnungsgemäße Kündigung; **legal** ~ gesetzlich vorgeschriebene Kündigungsfrist; **long** ~ frühzeitig erfolgte Kündigung; **monthly (one, a month's)** ~ monatliche Kündigung[sfrist]; **obituary** ~ Todesanzeige; **official** ~ Amtskenntnis; **peremptory** ~ zwingende Anordnung; **personal** ~ unmittelbar persönliche Empfängerbenachrichtigung; **presumptive** ~ vermutete Kenntnis; **previous** ~ Voranzeige, -ankündigung; **proper** ~ ordnungsgemäße Kündigung; **public** ~ öffentliche Bekanntmachung, Aufruf; **reading** ~

redaktionelle Anzeige; **reasonable ~** angemessene Kündigungsfrist; **seven days' ~** wöchentliche Kündigung; **shorter ~**
abgekürzte Ladungsfrist; **special ~** *(general meeting)* besondere Einberufung, qualifizierte Ladungsfrist; **statutory ~**
gesetzliche Kündigungsfrist; **stop ~** *(to shareholders)* Vorpfändung; **sufficient ~** ausreichender Kündigungsgrund; **third-
party ~** Streitverkündung, Intervention, Beteiligung Dritter
am Rechtsstreit; **two weeks' ~** vierzehntägige Kündigung; **one
week's ~** wöchentliche Kündigungsfrist; **withdrawal ~** Kündigung zur Rückzahlung; **written ~** schriftliche Kündigung
(Anzeige);
~ **of abandonment** Abandonerklärung; ~ **of acceptance** Annahmeerklärung; ~ **of accident** Unfallmeldung; ~ **of action** Klage-
androhung; ~ **of admission** *(Br.)* schriftliche Aufforderung an
den Beklagten, Tatsachen anzuerkennen; ~ **to admit** Aufforderung zur Urkundenanerkennung; ~ **in advance** Voranzeige,
-anmeldung; ~ **by advertisement in the press** öffentliche Zustellung; ~ **of allowance** Benutzungsermächtigung; ~ **of appeal**
Berufungsschrift[satz]; ~ **of appearance** gerichtliche Vorladung; ~ **of arrival** Eingangsbestätigung; ~ **of assessment** Steuerbescheid, *(company)* Gewinnfeststellungsbescheid; ~ **of
amended assessment** Steueränderungsbescheid; ~ **of assignment** Abtretungsbenachrichtigung; ~ **of birth** Geburtsanzeige;
~ **of call** Einzahlungsaufforderung; ~ **of cancellation** Kündigung[sbenachrichtigung], Rücktritt; ~ **of a second charge on a
security** Benachrichtigung über die Nachhaftung einer gestellten Sicherheit; ~ **of a claim** *(insurance)* Schadensanzeige,
-meldung; ~ **of coding** *(Br.)* Zusammenstellung der gesetzlich
gewährten Einkommenssteuerfreibeträge; ~ **of confirmation**
Bestätigungsvermerk; ~ **of consignment** Versandanzeige; ~ **of
death** Todesanzeige; ~ **by a debtor** Schuldnermitteilung; **formal ~ to the debtor** förmliche Schuldnerbenachrichtigung; ~ **of
default** Anzeige der Nichterfüllung, Inverzugsetzung; ~ **of
defects** Mängelrüge, -anzeige; ~ **of deficiency** *(income tax, US)*
Mitteilung über festgestellte Unrichtigkeiten; ~ **of delivery**
Empfangsbestätigung, Zustellungsurkunde; ~ **of denial**
Ablehnungsbescheid; ~ **of denunciation of a convention** Kündigung eines Abkommens; ~ **of departure** *(international law)*
polizeiliche Abmeldung; ~ **of deposit** *(Br.)* Hinterlegungsbe-
scheid; ~ **of discharge** Kündigungsmitteilung; ~ **of dishono(u)r**
Anzeige der Akzept-, Annahmeverweigerung [eines Wech-
sels], Notifikation, Notanzeige; ~ **of dismissal** Kündigungsmitteilung, Entlassungsbescheid; ~ **of distribution** Ausschüt-
tungsbenachrichtigung; ~ **of dividend** Dividendenankündi-
gung; ~ **of drawing for redemption** Bekanntmachung über die
Auslosung zur Rückzahlung [von Wertpapieren]; ~ **of engagement** Verlobungsanzeige; ~ **of error** Berichtigungsanzeige; ~ **to
admit evidence** *(Br.)* Aufforderung zur Vorlage von Beweismaterial; ~ **of exemption** *(taxation)* Freistellungsbescheid; ~ **of
foreclosure** Pfandverfallsankündigung; ~ **of incumbrances**
Belastungsmitteilung; ~ **of intention** *(US)* Antrag auf Erteilung
einer Bankkonzession; ~ **of issue** Benachrichtigung über die
Terminfestsetzung; ~ **of judgment** Mitteilung über den Ver-
kündungstermin; ~ **in the land register** *(Br.)* Grundbuchver-
merk; ~ **by a landlord** Kündigung des Vermieters; ~ **to leave**
Kündigung; ~ **of lien** Benachrichtigung von der Geltendmachung des Zurückbehaltungsrechts; ~ **in lieu of distringas** *(garnishee)* Vorpfändungsbenachrichtigung, *(to shareholders)*
Vorpfändung von Kapitalrechten; ~ **in lieu of service** Ersatzzustellung; ~ **of loss** Verlustanzeige, *(insurance)* Schadensmeldung, -anzeige; ~ **of marriage** Heiratsanzeige; ~ **of measures to
be taken** Ankündigung der zu ergreifenden Maßnahmen; ~ **of a
meeting** Einberufung einer Versammlung, Einberufungsschreiben, Sitzungsbenachrichtigung, *(company)* Einberufung
der (Ladung zur) Hauptversammlung; ~ **to members** Benachrichtigung von Aktionären; ~ **of motion** *(law)* Klageandro-
hung, Schriftsatzzustellung, *(parl.)* Initiativantrag; ~ **of
opposition** *(patent law)* Einspruchseinlegung; ~ **to pay** Zahlungsaufforderung; ~ **of payment in** Hinterlegungsbenachrich-
tigung; ~ **to perform a contract** Aufforderung zur Vertragserfüllung; ~ **to plead** Einlassungsfrist zwecks Vermeidung eines
Versäumnisurteils; **written ~ of postponement** schriftliche Rang-
rücktrittseinwilligung; ~ **to proceed** Zustellung eines Schriftsatzes zur Fortsetzung des Verfahrens; ~ **to produce**
Aufforderung zur Vorlage von beweiserheblichen Urkunden;
~ **of intended prosecution** Unterrichtung über ein beabsichtig-
tes Strafverfahren; ~ **of protest** *(notary, US)* Protestbenach-
richtigung; ~ **by publication** öffentliche Bekanntmachung; ~ **of
new publications** Verlagsankündigung; ~ **to quit** Mietkündigung, Kündigung des Pacht-, Mietverhältnisses; ~ **of readiness**
Benachrichtigung über die Ladebereitschaft; ~ **of receipt** Emp-

fangsbescheinigung, Rückschein; ~ **of redemption** *(loan)*
Anleihekündigung, *(mortgage)* Hypothekenkündigung, *(securities)* Bekanntmachung über die Einlösung und Tilgung von
Wertpapieren; ~ **of reference** *(Restrictive Practice Court, Br.)*
Klagebenachrichtigung; ~ **of registration** *(Registrar of Companies)* Registrierungsmitteilung; ~ **of rejection** Ablehnungsbescheid; ~ **of removal** Anzeige über die erfolgte Geschäftsverlegung; ~ **of renunciation** Verzichtsanzeige, -erklärung; ~ **of
rescission** Anzeige des Vertragsrücktritts; ~ **of revocation**
Widerrufsanzeige, Rücktrittsmitteilung; ~ **of revocation in
writing** schriftliche Widerrufserklärung, -anzeige; ~ **of rights**
Bezugsmitteilung; ~ **of sales by auction** Auktionsankündigung; ~ **of satisfaction** *(charges)* Mitteilung über aufgehobene
Belastungen; ~ **to be given on both sides** Kündigungsfrist für
beide Seiten; ~ **of a storm** Sturmwarnung; ~ **of suspension of
payments** Benachrichtigung über die Zahlungseinstellung; **formal ~ to terminate one's engagement** offizielles Kündigungsschreiben; ~ **of termination of employment** Kündigung des
Dienstverhältnisses; ~ **of termination of treaty** Vertragsaufkündigung, Kündigung eines Vertrages; ~ **to third party** Streitverkündung, Nebenintervention; ~ **to treat** Aufforderung zu
Verhandlungen über einen Zwangsverkauf; ~ **of trial** *(US)*
Ladung zur mündlichen Verhandlung; ~ **to vacate** Kündigung
des Mietverhältnisses; ~ **of withdrawal** Kündigungsbenachrichtigung, *(securities)* Kündigung von Wertpapieren, Kündi-
gungsnachricht, *(society)* Austrittsanzeige; **written ~ of
withdrawal** Kündigungsschreiben, schriftliche Rücktrittser-
klärung; ~ **of withdrawal of credit** Kreditkündigung; ~ **of withdrawal of funds** Kündigung von Einlagen, Einlagenkündigung;
~ **of writ of summons** Klageschriftzustellung ins Ausland; ~ **in
writing** schriftliche Mitteilung (Kündigung);
~ *(v.) (law)* benachrichtigen;
~ **a book** Buch rezensieren (besprechen); ~ **s. one's services** *(in a
speech)* jds. Verdienste würdigen; ~ **s. o. in the crowd** j. in der
Menschenmenge erspähen;
to acquire for value without ~ gutgläubig gegen Entgelt erwerben; **to attract ~** sich bemerkbar machen; **to be beneath ~** nicht
der Aufmerksamkeit wert sein; **to be deemed to have ~** als
informiert gelten, kennen müssen; **to be given ~ of** Kenntnis
erlangen; **to be on ~** *(US)* Kenntnis haben; **to be given special ~**
besonders berücksichtigt werden; **to be under six months' ~**
halbjährlich kündbar sein; **to be under ~ to leave (quit)** gekündigt sein; **to be put on ~** auf Rechte Dritter aufmerksam
gemacht werden; **to bring o. s. into ~** sich ins rechte Licht
setzen; **to bring s. th. to s. one's ~** jem. etw. zur Kenntnis
bringen; **to come [in]to ~** *(author)* allmählich bekannt werden;
to come under s. one's ~ jem. bekanntwerden; **to constitute ~ to
the insurance company** Voraussetzung einer Versicherungsanzeige erfüllen; **to dismiss s. o. without ~** j. sofort (fristlos)
entlassen; **to do s. th. at short ~** etw. kurzfristig tun; **to escape ~**
unbeobachtet bleiben; **to fill ~ of opposition** *(patent law, US)*
Patenteinspruch einlegen; **to give ~** [Mieter] kündigen; **to give
s. o. ~ of s. th.** j. von etw. benachrichtigen; **to give due ~**
formgerecht mitteilen, ordnungsgemäß kündigen; **to give ~ of
an amendment** Abänderungsvorschlag einbringen; **to give ~ of
appeal** Einlegung der Berufung ankündigen; **to give ~ of approach** *(car)* sein Kommen ankündigen; **to give ~ to the authorities** Behörden unterrichten; **to give ~ of cancellation of the insurance policy** Versicherung kündigen, Versicherungsvertrag
kündigen; **to give ~ of claims** Versicherungsschaden (Versicherungsforderung) anmelden; **to give ~ in accordance with the
contract** vertragsgemäß kündigen; **to give ~ to the debtor**
Schuldner mahnen; **to give ~ of dishono(u)r** Notanzeige erstatten; **to give ~ of distraint** Arrestbeschluß verkünden, Pfändungsbeschluß zustellen; **to give ~ to an employee** einem
Angestellten kündigen; **to give ~ to one's employer** seinem
Arbeitgeber kündigen; **to give one's employer ~ that one intends
to leave** seinem Arbeitgeber von seiner Kündigungsabsicht
Kenntnis geben; **to give ~ of cancellation of the insurance policy**
Versicherung kündigen; **to give ~ of a meeting of creditors**
Gläubigerversammlung einberufen; **to give s. o. a month's ~**
jem. mit einer Frist von einem Monat kündigen; **to give six
months' ~** Frist von sechs Monaten setzen; **to give official ~ of
s. th.** etw. amtlich feststellen; **to give out a ~** Bekanntmachung
erlassen; **to give ~ of a patent** Patent anmelden; **to give prompt
~** umgehend benachrichtigen; **to give ~ of a question** Interpellation einbringen; **to give a tenant ~ to quit** einem Mieter die
Kündigung zustellen (kündigen); **to give ~ to a third person**
(US) jem. den Streit verkünden; **to give s. o. ~ of one's intentions** j. von seinen Absichten in Kenntnis setzen; **to give s. o.
short ~** j. spät benachrichtigen, j. in Verlegenheit bringen,

(tenant) j. kurzfristig kündigen; **to give six weeks'** ~ sechswöchige Kündigungsfrist einhalten; **to give ~ of one's withdrawal** seinen Austritt erklären; **to give ~ of withdrawal of bonds** Obligationen zur Rückzahlung anmelden; **to give in one's** ~ seine Kündigung einreichen; **to give eight clear working days** ~ acht Werktage vorher kündigen; **to give ~ in writing** schriftlich benachrichtigen; **to have** ~ Kenntnis haben; **to have ~ to quit** gekündigt sein; **to leave without** ~ Kündigungsfrist nicht einhalten; **to have to leave at half an hour's** ~ binnen einer halben Stunde abreisen müssen; **to have never taken any ~ of it** sich nie darum gekümmert haben; **to make a public** ~ öffentlich bekanntgeben; **to observe the period of** ~ Kündigungsfrist einhalten; **to pin up a** ~ Bekanntmachung anschlagen; **to postpone a** ~ Kündigung hinausschieben; **to put a ~ in the papers** Annonce in die Zeitung setzen (einrücken); **to put up a** ~ Bekanntmachung anschlagen (anheften); **to receive** ~ Kenntnis erlangen, *(to quit)* seine Entlassung erhalten; **to receive no particular** ~ keine besondere Beachtung erfahren, kein besonderes Interesse hervorrufen; **to receive two months ~ to quit** mit zweimonatlicher Frist gekündigt werden; **to replace s. o. without a moment's** ~ j. stehenden Fußes entlassen; **to rise to** ~ Bekanntheitsgrad erzielen; **to send s. o. a second** ~ jem. eine zweite Mahnung zukommen lassen, j. erneut verwarnen; **to serve ~ on s. o.** j. gerichtlich vorladen; **to serve an appropriate counter** ~ zu einer Mietkündigung ordnungsgemäß Stellung nehmen; **to serve ~ in lieu of distringas** Wertpapierrechte verpfänden; **to serve ~ of mortgage** vorgehenden Hypothekengläubiger von einer nachrangigen Eintragung unterrichten; **to serve ~ upon a servant** Dienstboten (Hausangestellten) kündigen; **to serve ~ upon a tenant** einem Mieter die Kündigung zustellen; **to serve out one's ~ with s. o.** bis zum Ende des Kündigungstermins bleiben; **to sit up and take ~** *(fam.)* aufhorchen, Interesse zeigen; **to stick up a** ~ Bekanntmachung anschlagen; **to take ~ of** zur Kenntnis nehmen; **to take no ~ of** nicht beachten, ignorieren; **to take no ~ of an objection** Einspruch nicht beachten; **to take not the least** ~ überhaupt nicht reagieren; **to terminate employment without** ~ fristlos kündigen; **to waive** ~ auf Einhaltung der Kündigungsfrist verzichten; **to waive ~ of dishono(u)r** auf Notanzeige verzichten; **to work out a written** ~ bis zum Ende der Kündigungsfrist arbeiten; ~ **board** *(Br.)* Schwarzes Brett, Aushang, Anschlagtafel; ~ **paper** Sitzungsprogramm; ~ **period** Kündigungsfrist; ~ **plate** *(letter box)* Stundenplatte.

noticeable bemerkenswert, auffällig.

notifiable anzeige-, meldepflichtig, der Meldepflicht unterliegend; ~ **disease** meldepflichtige Seuche.

notification *(advertisement)* [Werbe]anzeige, *(citation)* Ladung[s-schreiben], Vorladung, *(giving public notice)* Bekanntmachung, Mitteilung, *(information)* Benachrichtigung, Anzeige, Mitteilung, *(law of nations)* Notifizierung, Notifikation, *(railway)* Eingangsmitteilung; **emergency action** ~ Ankündigung des Ausnahmezustands; **official** ~ amtliche Bekanntmachung; ~ **of an accident** Unfallanzeige, -meldung; ~ **of birth** Geburtsanmeldung; ~ **of change** Änderungsanzeige; ~ **of claim** *(insurance)* Schadensanzeige; ~ **to the contrary** gegenteilige Mitteilung; ~ **of death** Todesfallanzeige; ~ **of defects** Mängelrüge, -anzeige; ~ **of goods despatched** Versandbenachrichtigung; ~ **of liquidation** Abwicklungsmitteilung; ~ **of loss** *(insurance)* Verlust-, Schadensanzeige; ~ **of the police** Benachrichtigung der Polizei; ~ **of protest** Protestanzeige; ~ **of residence** Aufenthaltsanzeige; ~ **of signatures** Unterschriftsbenachrichtigung; **to address the** ~ **to** Mitteilung richten an; **on a** ~ **basis** im Notifizierungswege; **to operate on a** ~ **basis** Forderungsabtretung offenlegen; ~ **form** Benachrichtigungsformular; ~ **orders** Meldevorschriften; ~ **regulations** Meldebestimmungen; ~ **type of a loan** Kreditgewährung mit offengelegter Forderungsabtretung.

notify *(v.) (give public notice)* bekanntgeben, -machen, *(give official notice)* amtlich mitteilen (bekanntgeben), zur Kenntnis geben, *(inform)* benachrichtigen, anzeigen, Nachricht geben; ~ **the authorities** Behörden verständigen; ~ **a birth** Geburt beim Standesamt anmelden; ~ **a claim** Anspruch anmelden; ~ **s. o. of the day of one's visit** j. von seinem beabsichtigten Besuch verständigen; ~ **a death** Todesfall anzeigen; ~ **s. o. of a decision** jem. ein Urteil zustellen; ~ **a defect** Mängelrüge vornehmen; ~ **the parties** Parteien vorladen; ~ **the police of s. th.** Polizei von etw. unterrichten, etw. bei der Polizei anzeigen; ~ **the police of a loss** Verlustanzeige bei der Polizei abgeben; ~ **protest** Protest aufnehmen lassen.

notifying | bank avisierende Bank; ~ **clause** Notadresse.

noting Feststellung, *(advertising)* Leserprozentsatz, der eine Anzeige gesehen hat, *(notary)* Beurkundungsvermerk; ~ **of bill** notarieller Wechselvermerk über erfolglose Wechselvorlage; ~ **brief** Beweiserhebungsanweisung; ~ **slip (ticket,** *Br.*) [Wechsel]protesturkunde.

notion Einfall, Begriff, Gedanke, Idee, Vorstellung, *(inclination)* Neigung, Absicht, Lust; **according to ~s received** nach herkömmlichen Begriffen; ~**s** *(US)* kleine Modeartikel, Galanteriewaren; **clear-cut ~s** abgegrenzte Begriffe; **preconceived** ~ vorgefaßte Meinung; **to explode a** ~ Vorstellung widerlegen; **to fall into the** ~ auf den Gedanken kommen; **to form a true ~ of s. th.** sich einen richtigen Begriff machen; **to have no ~ of time** keinen Zeitbegriff haben; **not to have the vaguest ~ of s. th.** nicht die leiseste Ahnung von etw. haben; **to seize on a** ~ Idee aufgreifen.

notional begrifflich, rein gedanklich, *(visionary)* imaginär, eingebildet; ~ **income** *(income tax, Br.)* fiktives Einkommen, Nutzungswert der eigengenutzten Wohnung im Einfamilienhaus; ~ **man** *(US)* Phantast; ~ **premium** imaginäre Abstandssumme; ~ **possession** offenkundiger Besitz.

notorious offenkundig, notorisch; ~ **criminal** berüchtigter Verbrecher; ~ **insolvency** stadtbekannte Zahlungsunfähigkeit; ~ **swindler** notorischer Schwindler.

notour bankrupt *(Scot.)* offenkundiger Bankrott.

notwithstanding ungeachtet, unbeschadet, in Abweichung, ohne Rücksicht, nichtsdestoweniger; ~ **the objections** trotz der Einwände; ~ **anything in the foregoing provisions** ohne Rücksicht auf etwa anderslautende Bestimmungen; ~ **our remonstrances** ungeachtet unserer Proteste.

nought Null; **to bring to** ~ ruinieren; **to come to** ~ mißlingen, fehlschlagen, zunichtewerden; **to set at** ~ *(fig.)* in den Wind schlagen.

noun *(grammar)* Gegenstandswort; **common** ~ Gattungswort; **proper** ~ Eigenname.

nourish *(v.)* ernähren, *(fig.)* unterstützen, -halten; ~ *(v.)* **a feeling** Gefühl hegen.

nourishing power Nährkraft.

nourishment Nahrung, Ernährung; **to take** ~ Nahrung zu sich nehmen.

nouveauté *(US)* Neuheit.

novation Schuldübernahme, *(substitution of new obligation)* Novation.

novel Roman, *(law)* Novelle, Nachtragsgesetz; **adventure** ~ Abenteurroman; **detective** ~ Kriminalroman; **historical** ~ historischer Roman; **short** ~ Kurzroman; **sophisticated** ~ Roman für gehobene Ansprüche; **standard** ~ klassischer Roman; **straight** ~ gewöhnlicher Roman; ~ **in instal(l)ments** Fortsetzungsroman; **to overdraw characters in a** ~ lebensfremde Romanfiguren darstellen; **to read like a** ~ wie ein Roman anmuten; ~ *(a.) (law)* novellistisch, ergänzend, *(patent)* neu, neuartig; ~ **assignment** *(US)* zusätzliche Klagebegründung; ~ **feature** Neuheitsmerkmal; ~ **method** neuartiges Verfahren; ~ **writer** Romanschriftsteller.

novelette *(Br.)* Groschenroman, Schnulze.

novelist Romanauthor, Romanier.

novelization Darstellung in Romanform; ~ **of successful films** nachträgliche Romanfassung erfolgreicher Filme.

novelize *(v.)* in Romanform darstellen.

novelties Neuheiten, neueingeführte Artikel, Modeartikel.

novelty *(patent law)* Neuheit, *(trade)* Werbegeschenkartikel; ~ **of surroundings** ungewohnte Umgebung; **to constitute a bar as to** ~ neuheitsschädlich sein; **to negate the** ~ Neuheit verneinen; ~ **advertising** Werbung durch Verteilung von Geschenkartikeln, Warenprobenverteilung; ~ **item** Neuheit, Schlager; ~ **search** *(patent)* Neuheitsprüfung.

novice Schüler, Anfänger, Neuling.

now zum gegenwärtigen Zeitpunkt, *(last will)* zum Todeszeitpunkt.

noxious gesundheitsschädlich, übelriechend; ~ **air** *(law)* Immissionen; ~ **trade** Gewerbe belästigender Art.

nozzle Düse.

nub of a matter *(US)* Kern einer Sache.

nubile heiratsfähig.

nubility Ehe-, Heiratsfähigkeit.

nuclear mit Atom angetrieben, atomgetrieben;
~ **age** Atomzeitalter; ~ **aircraft** atomgetriebenes Flugzeug; ~ **arms** Atomwaffen; ~ **arms control** Begrenzung der atomaren Rüstung; ~ **attack** Atombombenangriff; ~ **bomb** Atombombe; ~ **burial ground** Atomdeponie; ~ **chain reaction** nukleare Kettenreaktion; ~ **damage** nuklearer Schaden; ~ **defence** Kernwaffen-, Nuklearverteidigung; ~ **deterrent** nukleare Abschreckung; ~ **disarmament** nukleare Abrüstung; ~ **disintegration** Kernzerfall; ~ **division** Kernteilung; ~ **energy** Kernenergie; ~ **energy plant** Atommeiler; **to put on the** ~ **escalator** zur Ausweitung des Atomkriegs zwingen; ~ **explosive** nuklearer Sprengsatz; ~ **facilities** Nuklear-, Atomanlagen; ~ **factory** Atommeiler; ~ **fission** Kernspaltung, Atomzertrümmerung, -spaltung; ~ **fission bomb** Atombombe; ~-**free zone** atomwaffenfreie Zone; ~ **force** Atomstreitmacht; ~ **fuel** Kernbrennstoff; ~ **fusion** Kernfusion; ~ **guarantee** Atomgarantieversprechen; ~ **industry** Kernindustrie; ~ **inspection** nukleare Überwachung; ~ **parity** nukleares Gleichgewicht; ~ **physics** Atomphysik; ~ **policy** Nuklear-, Atompolitik; ~ **power** Atommacht; ~ **power park** Kernkraftanlage; ~ **power plant** Atommeiler; ~ **power reactor** Atomreaktor; ~ **power station** Kernreaktoranlage, Atomkraftwerk; ~-**powered** atomangetrieben; ~-**powered ship** Schiff mit Atomantrieb; **limited** ~ **reaction** (mil.) begrenzte nukleare Vergeltung; ~ **reactor** Atomreaktor; ~ **research** Kern-, Atomforschung; ~ **sharing** nukleare Mitbestimmung; ~ **site** Kernenergieanlage; ~ **stalemate** Atompatt; ~ **station** Atomwerk; ~ **submarine** Atom-U-Boot; ~ **state** Nuklearmacht; ~ **strike** Atomschlag; ~ **strike force** Atomstreitmacht; ~ **test** Atom-, Kernwaffenversuch; ~ **terror balance** Gleichgewicht des atomaren Schreckens; ~-**tipped missile** Rakete mit Atomsprengkopf; ~ **transmutation** Kernumwandlung; ~ **warfare** Atomkrieg[sführung]; ~ **warhead** Atomsprengkopf; ~ **waste** Atommüll; ~ **waste disposal** Atommüllbeseitigung; ~ **waste reprocessing** Wiederaufbereitungsanlage für Atommüll; ~ **weapons** Atom-, Kernwaffen; ~ **weapon deal** Atomwaffenabkommen; ~ **weapon test** Atomwaffenversuch; ~ **weapons stock** Atomwaffenlager.

nucleus Kern, Mittelpunkt;
atomic ~ Atomkern;
~ **of an affair** Hauptsache (Kern) einer Angelegenheit; ~ **of a library** Grundstock einer Bibliothek; ~ **of a party** Kern einer Partei;
to gather round a ~ sich um einen Mittelpunkt versammeln;
~ **crew** (ship) Stammpersonal.

nude nackt, bloß, (law) ohne Gegenleistung, ungültig, nichtig;
~ **contract** einseitiger nicht bindender Vertrag; ~ **fact** nackte Tatsache; ~ **matter** Behauptung ohne Beweisantritt.

nudge Andeutung, Wink;
~ (v.) **30%** sich 30% nähern; ~ **s. o.** jem. einen Wink geben.

nudism Freikörperkultur.

nudist camp Nudistenlager.

nugatory unwirksam, gegenstandslos.

nugget Goldklumpen.

nuisance Ärgernis, Mißstand, Belästigung, Beeinträchtigung, Unfug, Skandal, (damage to neighbo(u)ring property) schädliche Einwirkung auf Nachbargrundstücke, Immissionen, Polizeiwidrigkeit, Unzuträglichkeit, Besitzstörung, (person) Quälgeist, lästiger Mitmensch, Pest;
actionable ~ rechtserhebliche Störung; **attractive** ~ (US) Gefahrenquelle für Kinder; **civil** ~ Besitzstörung; **common** ~ grober Unfug, öffentliches Ärgernis; **continuing (permanent)** ~ anhaltende Belästigung, Dauerbelästigung; **private** ~ Besitzstörung, nachbarliche Belästigung, verbotene Eigenmacht; **public** ~ öffentliches Ärgernis, grober Unfug, Störung der öffentlichen Sicherheit und Ordnung; **trivial** ~ unbedeutende Belästigung;
~ **at law (per se)** rechtswidrige Störung; ~ **in fact** aufgrund der Belegenheit störendes Bauwerk;
to abate a ~ Mißstand beseitigen (abstellen); **to be a** ~ **to s. o.** jem. lästig werden; **commit no** ~! Verunreinigung verboten!; **to make o. s. a** ~ **to one's neighbo(u)rs** seinen Nachbarn belästigen;
~ **abatement assessment** (US) Sonderabgabe für Schutt- und Müllbeseitigung; ~ **costs** Ausgleich für Nervenbelastung; ~ **industries** störende Industrien, Emissionsbetriebe; ~ **lawsuit** Mißbrauchsklage; ~ **settlement** Abfindungsvergleich, Vergleich zur Vermeidung des Rechtsweges wegen eines unsicheren Haftpflichtanspruchs; ~ **tax** unwirtschaftliche Steuer; ~ **value** Ablösungswert.

null (invalid) nichtig, ungültig, unwirksam, null, (amounting to nothing) gehaltlos, nichtssagend;

~ **and void** null und nichtig;
to declare ~ **and void** für null und nichtig erklären; **to render** ~ **and void** annullieren.

nulla bona (lat.) keine Pfandobjekte, Unpfändbarkeitsbescheinigung.

nullification Annullierung, Nichtig[keits], Ungültig[keits]erklärung, Ungültigmachung.

nullify (v.) für nichtig erklären, ungültig machen, annullieren;
~ **an obligation** Verpflichtung aufheben; ~ **a patent** Patent für nichtig erklären lassen; ~ **all rate and position protections** (advertising) alle Rabattvorteile und Vorzugsplazierungen aufheben.

nullity (invalidity) Nichtigkeit, Ungültigkeit;
~ **of marriage** Ehenichtigkeit;
to declare an act a ~ Nichtigkeitsurteil erlassen; **to shrink to a** ~ (army) keinerlei Kampfkraft mehr haben;
~ **appeal** Nichtigkeitsbeschwerde; ~ **suit** (marriage) Anfechtungs-, Nichtigkeitsverfahren, -klage, Eheaufhebungsklage, Klage auf Feststellung der Nichtigkeit, Klage auf Nichtigkeitserklärung.

number [An]zahl, Ziffer, Haus-, Zimmer-, Telefonnummer, (copy) Exemplar, (issue) Ausgabe, Heft, Nummer, (part delivery of a book) [Teil]lieferung;
in great ~s in großer Anzahl; **in round** ~s in runder Zahl; **on a** ~ **of counts** aus verschiedenen Gründen; **without** ~ zahllos; ~s Menge, Schar, Anzahl, viele;
admissible ~s zulässige Zahlen; **average** ~ Durchschnittszahl; **back** ~ Ladenhüter, (newspaper) altes [Zeitungs]exemplar, (person) verstaubte Erscheinung; **broken** ~ Bruch[zahl]; **calculated** ~ Sollbestand; **call** ~ (tel.) Rufnummer; **cardinal** ~ Grundzahl; **chassis** ~ Fahrgestellnummer; **check** ~ Kontrollnummer; **Christmas** ~ Weihnachtsausgabe; **code** ~ Kennziffer, -zahl, (post) Postleitzahl; **collective** ~ (tel.) Sammelnummer; **composite** ~ zusammengesetzte Zahl; **cubic** ~ Kubikzahl; **consecutive** ~s fortlaufende Zahlen; **current** ~ (newspaper) heutige Ausgabe; **dead** ~ unbenutzte Zahl; **dealer's licence** ~ (car) rote Nummer; **drawing** ~ gezogene Nummer; **drawn** ~ Auslosungsnummer; ~ **engaged** (tel.) besetzt; **even** ~ gerade Zahl; **ex-directory** ~ (tel.) Geheimnummer; **file** ~ Aktenzeichen; **fractional** ~ Bruchzahl; **greater** ~ Mehrzahl; **house** ~ Hausnummer; **index** ~ Indexzahl; **invoice** ~ Rechnungsnummer; **lottery** ~ Losnummer; **maximum** ~ Höchstzahl; **mean** ~ Durchschnittszahl; **odd** ~ ungerade Zahl, (magazine) vereinzelte Zeitschrift; ~ **one** das eigene Ich; **one-digit** ~ einstellige Zahl; **opposite** ~ Gegenspieler, Kollege; **ordinal** ~ Ordnungszahl; **outside** ~ (tel.) Außenanschluß; **page** ~ Seitenzahl; **plural** ~ Mehrzahl; **postal district** ~ Zahl des Postzustellbezirks; **postal zone** ~ Postleitzahl; **red** ~s (interest) Zinszahlen; **reference** ~ Aktenzeichen; **registered (registration)** ~ Eintragungs-, Registriernummer, (car) polizeiliches Kennzeichen; **rounded** ~ abgerundete Zahl; **road** ~ Bundesstraßennummer; **running** ~ laufende Zahl; **serial** ~ Serien-, Fabrik-, laufende Nummer; **singular** ~ Einzahl; **statistical code** ~ Nummer des statistischen Warenverzeichnisses; **supply** ~ Bestellnummer; **telephone** ~ Telefonnummer; **ticket** ~ Losnummr; **toll-free** ~ gebührenfreier Telefonanruf; **total** ~ Gesamtzahl; **unlisted** ~ (US) Geheimnummer; **wrong** ~ falsche Telefonnummer; **zip** ~ (US) Postleitzahl;
~ **of calls** verschiedene Besuche; ~ **of a car** polizeiliches Kennzeichen; ~ **of a check** (US) (cheque, Br.) Schecknummer; ~ **of children** Kinderzahl; ~ **of employees** Personalstand; ~ **of entry** Buchungsnummer; ~ **of incidence** Verbreitungsziffer; ~ **of inhabitants** Einwohnerzahl; ~ **of lines** Zeilenzahl; ~ **of pages** Seitenzahl; ~ **of participants** Teilnehmerzahl; ~ **of a patent** Patentnummer; **large** ~ **of people** viele Menschen; ~ **of people present** Zahl der Anwesenden; ~ **of periods** Anzahl von Zinsperioden; ~ **of persons** Kopfzahl; ~ **of persons employed** Beschäftigtenzahl; ~ **of picture elements** (television) Bildpunktzahl; ~ **of population** Volkszahl, Kopfzahl der Bevölkerung; ~ **of revolutions** Dreh-, Tourenzahl; ~ **of transaction** Handelsmenge; ~ **of units** Stückzahl; ~ **of votes recorded** abgegebene Stimmenzahl; [sufficient] ~ **of votes** [genügende] Stimmenzahl;
~ (v.) (add) zusammenzählen, aufrechnen, (to amount to) sich beziffern auf, (assign a number) numerieren, (count) zählen;
~ **50.000** (army) 50.000 Mann stark sein; ~ **among** rechnen unter; ~ **among s. one's friends** zu jds. Freunden zählen; ~ **consecutively** [fort]laufend numerieren; ~ **pages** paginieren;
to appear in ~s lieferungsweise (in Teillieferungen) erscheinen; **to assign a** ~ Nummer zuweisen; **to be a back** ~ sehr altmodisch sein, antiquiert denken; **to be good at** ~s gut rechnen können; **to be present in great** ~s zahlreich anwesend sein; **to buy a**

periodical by the ~ Zeitschrift einzeln kaufen; **to dial a ~** [Telefon]nummer wählen; **to exceed in** ~s zahlenmäßig übertreffen; **to give the ~** Nummer angeben; **to have s. one's ~** j. durchschaut haben; **to have the advantage of (in)** ~s zahlenmäßig überlegen sein; **to look after ~ one** auf seinen eigenen Vorteil bedacht sein; **to make up the ~** um die Zahl vollzumachen; **to mark with** ~s beziffern; **to raise to full ~** komplettieren; **to stamp the ~ of an engine** Motorzahl einprägen; **to swell the ~ of subscribers** Subskriptionsliste erweitern; **to take s. one's ~** jds. Telefonnummer aufschreiben, *(fam.)* jds. Wert einschätzen; **to take care of ~ one** nur auf seinen Vorteil sehen; **to take a car's ~** Auto polizeilich anmelden; **to win by** ~s seinen Sieg seiner Übermacht verdanken;

box ~ ad *(US)* Schließfachnummerninserat; **~s game** illegales Zahlenlotto; **~ one hit** Spitzenschlager; **~-one guideline** Leitgrundsatz; **~ plate** *(car)* Nummernschild; **~s pool** Zahlenlotto; **~-two level** Stellvertreterebene; **~-two man** zweiter Mann; **~ system** Zahlensystem.

numbered numeriert;
consecutively ~ fortlaufend numeriert;
~ account Nummernkonto.

numbering Numerierung, Nummernbezeichnung, Bezifferung;
consecutive ~ fortlaufende Numerierung;
~ stamp Zahlennumerierungsstempel.

numerable zählbar.

numeral language Ziffernsprache.

numerate *(v.)* aufzählen.

numeration *(numbering)* Zählung, Zählen, Rechnen, *(designation by numbers)* Numerierung;
decimal ~ Dezimalsystem.

numerative system Zahlensystem.

numerator Zählvorrichtung, -werk.

numerical numerisch, zahlenmäßig;
~ equation Zahlengleichung; **~ example** Zahlenbeispiel; **~ majority** zahlenmäßige Mehrheit; **~ note** *(US)* Nummernaufgabe, Stückeverzeichnis; **~ order** Zahlenfolge; **~ quantity** Zahlengröße; **~ statement** Zahlenaufstellung; **~ support** zahlenmäßiger Rückhalt; **~ symbol** Zahlensymbol; **~ value** Zahlenwert.

numerous zahlreich;
~ assembly große Versammlung;
~ly attended stark besucht.

numismatics Numismatik, Münzkunde.

nun Nonne;
~ buoy Klappboje.

nunciature Nuntiatur.

nuncio Nuntius.

nuncupation mündliche testamentarische Verfügung.

nuncupative will mündliche, vor Zeugen abgegebene letztwillige Verfügung, mündliches Testament.

nuptial ehelich;
~ ceremony Trauungsfeierlichkeit; **~ chamber** Brautgemach; **~ day** Hochzeitstag.

nurse [Kranken]schwester, Krankenpflegerin;
assistant ~ Hilfsschwester; **district ~** Gemeindeschwester; **head ~** Oberschwester; **practical ~** *(US)* Krankenschwester; **registered ~** *(US)* staatlich geprüfte Krankenschwester; **state-registered ~** *(Br.)* staatlich geprüfte Krankenschwester; **trained ~** geprüfte Kinderschwester;
~ on duty diensthabende Schwester;
~ *(v.)* warten, pflegen, pfleglich behandeln, vorsichtig umgehen;
~ an account *(Br.)* faules Konto versuchsweise sanieren; **~ s. o. back to health** j. gesund pflegen; **~ a business** sich um ein Geschäft besonders kümmern; **~ the capital market** Kapitalmarkt pfleglich behandeln; **~ a cold** Erkältung auskurieren,

Schnupfen auskurieren; **~ a connexion (connection)** Verbindung (Beziehung) pflegen; **~ one's constituency** sich um seinen Wahlkreis kümmern; **~ feelings of revenge** Rachegefühle hegen; **~ the fire** Feuer schüren; **~ an infant industry** neugegründeten Industriezweig fördern; **~ a plant** Betrieb umsichtig leiten; **~ one's public** etw. für seine Popularität tun; **~ resources** Mittel sorgfältig verwalten; **~ one's voice** seine Stimme schonen;
to have a lot of unsalable stock to ~ unverkäufliches Lager am Hals haben; **to put a child out to ~** Kind in Pflege geben;
~ child Pflegekind; **~s' union** Schwesternverband.

nursed in luxury im Luxus aufgewachsen.

nursery Kinderstube, *(day school)* Kindertagesstätte, Kinderkrippe, *(fig.)* fördernde Beschäftigung, *(horticulture)* Baumschule;
day ~ Kindergarten; **night ~** Kinderschlafsaal; **resident ~** Säuglingsheim;
~ of young trees Schonung;
~ garden Baumschule; **~ governess** Kinderfräulein; **~ rhyme** Kindervers, -lied; **~ school** Kindergarten; **~ slope** Übungshang, Idiotenhügel; **~ tale** Ammenmärchen.

nursing Krankenpflegeberuf, Pflege;
careful ~ sorgfältige Pflege; **rough ~** schlechte Pflege;
~ of an account *(Br.)* versuchsweise Sanierung eines faulen Kontos;
to take up ~ as a career Schwesternberuf ergreifen;
~ benefit Stillgeld; **~ care** Krankenpflege; **~ home** Privatklinik, Sanatorium; **~ infant** Säugling, Brustkind; **~ mother** stillende Mutter, *(fig.)* Adoptivmutter; **~ plant** Setzling; **~ profession** Schwesternberuf; **~ staff** *(hospital)* Pflegepersonal; **during the ~ time** in der Stillzeit.

nursling Säugling, Schützling, Liebling.

nurture Nahrung, Ernährung;
~ of the mind geistige Nahrung.

nut Nuß, *(coal)* Nußkohle, *(fig.)* schwieriges Problem, Schwierigkeit, *(smartly dressed person)* Stutzer, Geck, *(US sl.)* Pinkepinke, *(techn.)* [Schrauben]mutter;
as sweet as a ~ wie aus dem Ei gepellt; **not for ~s** *(sl.)* überhaupt nicht; **off one's ~** *(sl.)* verrückt; **on the ~** *(US sl.)* pleite abgebrannt; **tough ~** *(coll.)* schwierige Person;
~s and bolts praktische Details; **a hard ~ to crack** *(fig.)* harte Nuß;
to be ~s *(sl.)* verrückt sein; **to be dead ~s on s. o.** total in j. verschossen sein; **to be ~s about films** Kinonarr sein; **to go off one's ~** *(sl.)* verrückt werden; **to have a ~ to crack with s. o.** mit jem. ein Hühnchen zu rupfen haben; **to have experience of the ~s and bolts in development** sich in Entwicklungsfragen gründlich auskennen;
~ college (factory, house) *(sl.)* Klappsmühle.

nutrition Ernährung;
~ expert Ernährungsfachmann; **~ level** Ernährungsniveau; **~ science** Ernährungswissenschaft.

nutritional|crisis Nahrungsmittelkrise; **~ deficiency** Unterernährung; **~ excellence** Nährwert; **~ status** Ernährungszustand.

nutritionist Ernährungsfachmann.

nutritive value Nährwert.

nutshell Nußschale;
in a ~ in aller Kürze, kurz gesagt;
~ *(v.)* in gedrängter Form berichten;
to put it in a ~ in wenigen Worten zusammenfassen.

nutty *(sl.)* verrückt, bekloppt;
~ idea Schnapsidee.

Nylies *(New York Life Assurance Companies)* New Yorker Lebensversicherungsgesellschaften.

nylon Nylon;
~ process Nylonprintverfahren.

O

oaf Einfaltspinsel.

oar, to be chained to the ~**s** schwer schuften müssen; **to have an** ~ **in every man's boat** sich überall einmischen; **to lie on one's** ~**s** auf der faulen Haut liegen, untätig sein; **to put in one's** ~ *(coll.)* seinen Senf dazugeben; **to rest on one's** ~ sich auf seinen Lorbeeren ausruhen; **to shove an** ~ **in** *(coll.)* sich unberufen einmengen.

oasis Oase.

oat Hafer;
to be off one's ~ sich indisponiert fühlen; **to feel one's** ~ sich wichtig fühlen (aufspielen); **to sow one's wild** ~ sich die Hörner abstoßen;
~ **opera** *(sl.)* Wildwestfilm, Western.

oater *(sl.)* Wildwestfilm, Westen.

oath Eid, Schwur;
by (on, upon, under) ~ unter Eid, eidlich; **in lieu of an** ~ an Eides Statt;
assertory ~ *(US)* Beteuerung durch Eid, eidesstattliche Erklärung; **coronation** ~ Krönungseid; **corporal** ~ feierlicher Eid, Bibeleid; **decisive (decisory)** ~ *(civil law)* zugeschobener Eid, Parteieid; **extrajudicial** ~ außergerichtlicher Eid; **false** ~ Meineid; **gospel** ~ Eid auf die Bibel; **judicial** ~ vor Gericht abgelegter Eid; **loyalty** ~ *(US)* Treueeid; **official** ~ *(Br.)* Amts-, Diensteid; **parliamentary** ~ *(Br.)* von Parlamentsmitgliedern geleisteter Eid; **poor debtor's** ~ Offenbarungseid; **promissory** ~ Verfassungs-, Verpflichtungseid; **qualified** ~ *(Scot.)* eingeschränkter Eid; **solemn** ~ feierliche Eidesleistung, feierlicher Eid; **suppletory** ~ Parteieid; **voluntary** ~ Parteieid;
~ **for administrators** *(Br.)* Nachlaßverwaltereid; ~ **of allegiance** Amts-, Treueeid; ~ **of calumny** *(civil law)* eidliche Redlichkeitserklärung; ~ **of disclosure** *(US)* Offenbarungseid; ~ **of entry** *(customs)* eidesstattliche Eingangserklärung; ~ **of evidence** Beteuerung unter Eid, eidesstattliche Erklärung; ~ **in litem** Prozeß-, Parteieid; ~ **of manifestation** *(US)* Offenbarungseid; ~ **of office** *(US)* Amts-, Diensteid; ~ **in supplement** vom Gericht auferlegter Eid; ~ **of supremacy** Treueeid;
to administer an ~ **to s. o.** jem. vereidigen, jem. den Eid abnehmen; **to affirm under** ~ eidesstattlich (an Eides Statt) versichern; **to be on one's** ~ eidlich (durch einen Eid) gebunden; **to bind s. o. by** ~ j. eidlich verpflichten; **to break one's** ~ seinen Eid brechen; **to confirm by** ~ eidlich erhärten; **to declare s. th. [up]on** ~ eidlich aussagen; **to examine on** ~ eidlich vernehmen; **to execute an** ~ Eid ablegen; **to impose an** ~ Eid auferlegen; **to make an** ~ Eid leisten (schwören); **to make** ~ **upon average** Verklarung ablegen; **to make** ~ **and depose** eidliche Zeugenaussage machen; **to make a statement on** ~ Erklärung unter Eid abgeben; **to put s. o. on his** ~ jem. einen Eid zuschieben (auferlegen); **to refuse to take the** ~ Eid verweigern; **to release (relieve) s. o. from his** ~ jem. seines Eides entbinden; **to swear (take) an** ~ Eid schwören (leisten); **to take the** ~ **of s. o.** j. eidlich verpflichten; **to tender an** ~ Eid abnehmen; **to tender back an** ~ **to s. o.** jem. den Eid zurückschieben; **to testify under** ~ unter Eid aussagen; **to violate one's** ~ seinen Eid brechen;
~**-bound** eidlich verpflichtet; ~ **breaking** Eidbruch; ~**-taking ceremony** Vereidigung.

oathmaker Eidesleister.

oathworthiness Eidesfähigkeit, -mündigkeit.

oathworthy eidesfähig, -mündig.

obedience Gehorsam, Gesetzestreue;
in ~ **to your orders** entsprechend Ihren Anordnungen;
implicit ~ unbedingter Gehorsam; **servile** ~ sklavischer Gehorsam; **unquestioning** ~ blinder Gehorsam;
to compel ~ **from s. o.** Gehorsam von jem. verlangen; **to enforce** ~ **to the law** dem Gesetz Respekt verschaffen; **to reduce s. o. to** ~ *(fam.)* j. zum Gehorsam zwingen.

obedient ergeben, unterwürfig;
your ~ **servant** Ihr sehr ergebener.

obeissance Ehrerbietung.

obey | *(v.)* **the dictates of one's conscience** seinem Gewissen folgen; ~ **the helms** *(ship)* dem Ruder gehorchen; ~ **the law** Gesetze befolgen; ~ **orders** Anordnungen Folge leisten; ~ **a summons** einer Vorladung Folge leisten.

obit Beerdigungsfeier.

obiter dictum beiläufige Bemerkung.

obituary notice Nachruf [in der Zeitung], Todesanzeige.

object Gegenstand, Sache, Ding, *(aim)* Ziel, Zweck, *(tax)* [Steuer]objekt;

money no ~ Geld spielt keine Rolle; **salary no** ~ *(advertisement)* Gehalt Nebensache; **time is no** ~ *(ad.)* Zeit spielt keine Rolle; **with no** ~ **in life** ohne Lebensziel; **with the** ~ **of gain** in gewinnsüchtiger Absicht;
ancillary ~ Nebenzweck; **convincing** ~ *(trial)* Beweisstück; ~ **found** Fundgegenstand, -sache; **immediate** ~ Nahziel; **main** ~ *(company)* Hauptgewerbezweck;
~ **of an action** Klagegegenstand; ~ **of admiration** Gegenstand der Bewunderung; ~**s of art** Kunstgegenstände; ~**s of a company (enterprise)** Gesellschafts-, Betriebszweck, Gegenstand eines Unternehmens; ~ **of exchange** Tauschobjekt; ~ **belonging to the inheritance** Nachlaßgegenstand; ~ **of a letter** Zweck eines Briefes, Briefzweck; ~ **in life** Lebensziel; ~ **of pity** Gegenstand des Mitleids; ~ **of purchase** Kaufgegenstand; ~ **of a statute** Satzungszweck; ~ **of supply** Liefergegenstand; ~ **of value** Wertgegenstand;
~ *(v.)* beanstanden, Einspruch erheben, Einwendungen machen, einwenden, vorbringen, protestieren;
~ **s. th. to a proposal** etw. gegen einen Vorschlag einzuwenden haben; ~ **to the reduction of share capital** einer Kapitalherabsetzung nicht zustimmen; ~ **in strong language** heftig widersprechen; ~ **to a witness** Zeugen ablehnen; ~ **that s. o. is too young for a position** j. für eine Position als zu jung erachten;
to attain one's ~ seinen Zweck erreichen; **to fail in one's** ~ sein Ziel nicht erreichen; **to make it one's** ~ sich etw. angelegen sein lassen; **to succeed in one's** ~ sein Ziel erreichen; **to value each** ~ jeden Gegenstand einzeln abschätzen; **to wander about without any** ~ ziellos umherstreifen; **to work with the** ~ **of earning fame** auf seinen Ruhm bedacht sein;
~ **classification** Ausgabengruppierung nach Art der Gegenleistung; ~**s clause** Gewerbezweckklausel, Gesellschaftszweckbestimmung; ~ **drawing** Zeichnen nach Modellen; ~ **found** Fundgegenstand; ~ **lessons (teaching)** Anschauungsunterricht.

objected beanstandet.

objection Einspruch, Beanstandung, Einwand, Einwendung, Reklamation, Hindernisgrund, *(dislike)* Abneigung;
immaterial ~ unerheblicher Einwand; **justifiable** ~ berechtigter Einwand; **overruled** ~ dem Einwand wird nicht stattgegeben; **pettifogging** ~**s** schikanöse Einwendungen; **preliminary** ~ prozeßhindernder Einwand; **technical** ~ formeller Einwand; **chief** ~ **to s. o.** Haupteinwand gegen j.; ~ **to an arbitrator** Ablehnung eines Schiedsrichters; ~ **to election** Wahleinspruch; ~ **to the jurisdiction** Einrede der Unzuständigkeit; ~ **to a juror** Ablehnung eines Geschworenen; ~ **to payment** Zahlungseinwand; ~ **in point of law** Bestreiten der Schlüssigkeit der Klage; ~ **to a witness** Zeugenablehnung;
to allow an ~ einem Einwand stattgeben; **to brush aside an** ~ Einspruch übergehen; **to disallow an** ~ Einspruch verwerfen; **to face down all** ~ alle Einwände überkommen; **to file an** ~ **to a bankrupt's discharge** Einspruch gegen die Entlastung eines Gemeinschuldners einlegen; **to foreclose an** ~ Einwand übergehen; **to have no** ~**s** nichts einzuwenden haben; **to have strong** ~ **to s. o.** starke Bedenken gegen j. haben; **to ignore an** ~ Einwand nicht anerkennen; **to lodge an** ~ Einspruch erheben (einlegen); **to make an** ~ Widerspruch erheben; **to make no** ~ keine Einwendungen erheben; **to obviate s. one's** ~**s** jds. Einwänden zuvorkommen; **to offer** ~ *(dipl.)* Einspruch erheben; **to offer no reasons for** ~**s** zu Beanstandungen keinen Anlaß geben; **to overrule an** ~ Einspruch zurückweisen; **to preclude** ~**s** Einwände vorwegnehmen; **to raise an** ~ beanstanden, einwenden, Einwendungen erheben; **to refute an** ~ Einwand widerlegen; **to start an** ~ Einwendungen machen; **to sustain an** ~ einem Einwand stattgeben; **to take** ~ Protest erheben, beanstanden; **to take no notice of an** ~ Einspruch nicht beachten; **to uphold an** ~ einem Einspruch stattgeben; **to withdraw an** ~ Einspruch zurückziehen.

objectionable zu beanstanden, nicht einwandfrei;
~ **conduct** anstößiges Betragen; **to use** ~ **language** anstößige Ausdrücke benutzen; **most** ~ **person** schwer zu ertragender Mensch.

objective Ziel[setzung], Zweck, *(mil.)* Operationsziel, Gefechtauftrag, *(traveller)* Reiseziel;
primary ~ Hauptziel;
~ *(a.)* sachlich, gegenständlich, objektiv;
~ **function** Zielfunktion; ~ **method** induktive Methode; ~ **point** *(mil.)* Operationsziel; ~ **value** Schätzwert.

objectiveness Objektivität, Sachlichkeit.

objectivism *(art)* Realismus.

objectivist Objektivist, *(art)* Realist.

objector Gegner, Opponent, Einspruchserheber;
 conscientious ~ Kriegsdienstverweigerer.

oblations *(Br.)* Zahlungen an die Kirche.

obligate *(v.)* verpflichten.

obligated balance *(government accounting)* ausgegebene, jedoch noch nicht angewiesene Haushaltsmittel.

obligation *(bond)* Verpflichtungsschein, Schuldschein, -verschreibung, Obligation, *(liability)* Verbindlichkeit, Verpflichtung, [Schuld]verpflichtung, Bindung, Obliegenheit;
 of ~ unumgänglich, obligatorisch; **no** ~ unverbindlich; **without** ~ unverbindlich, freibleibend;
 absolute ~ unabdingbare (zwingende) Verpflichtung; **accessory** ~ Nebenverpflichtung, -leistung; **alternative (conjunctive)** ~ Alternativverpflichtung; **bond** ~ Anleiheschuld; **business** ~ Geschäftsverbindlichkeit; **cash** ~ Barverpflichtung; **cautionary** ~ Eventualverpflichtung; **civil** ~ einklagbare (schuldrechtliche) Verpflichtung, Rechtspflicht; **conditional** ~ bedingte Verpflichtung; **continuing** ~ Dauerverpflichtung; **contract[ual]** ~ Vertragspflicht; **determinate** ~ Speziesschuld; **direct** ~ direkte (unmittelbare) Verpflichtung; **divisible** ~ Verpflichtung zu einer teilbaren Leistung; **equitable** ~ auf Billigkeitsrecht beruhende Verpflichtung; **express** ~ ausdrücklich festgelegte Verpflichtung; **financial** ~ finanzielle Verpflichtung, Zahlungsverpflichtung; **general** ~ allgemeine Verpflichtung; **guarantee** ~ Garantieverpflichtung; **heritable** ~ vererbliches Schuldverhältnis; **imperfect** ~ Naturalobligation, nicht einklagbare Verpflichtung; **implied** ~ stillschweigende Verpflichtung; ~ **incumbed on s. o.** jem. obliegende Pflicht; ~s **incurred** *(governmental accounting)* Gesamtheit der Haushaltsbewilligungen; **indeterminate** ~ Gattungsschuld; **indivisible** ~ Verpflichtung zu einer unteilbaren Leistung; **interest-bearing** ~s *(US)* verzinsliche Schuldverschreibungen; **joint** ~ Gesamtverpflichtung; **joint and several** ~ *(US)* gesamtschuldnerische Verpflichtung; **legal** ~ Rechtspflicht; **long-term** ~ langfristige Verbindlichkeit; **moral** ~ moralische Verpflichtung, Anstandspflicht; **mortgage** ~ Hypothekenschuld; **natural** ~ nicht einklagbare Verpflichtung, Naturalobligation; **obediential** ~ Obliegenheit; **outstanding** ~s *(government accounting)* bewilligte, jedoch noch nicht ausgegebene Haushaltsmittel; **part[ial]** ~ Teilschuldverhältnis; **pecuniary** ~ finanzielle Verpflichtung; **penal** ~ durch Konventionalstrafklausel verstärkte Verpflichtung; **perfect** ~ juristisch durchsetzbare Verpflichtung; **personal** ~ persönliche Verpflichtung; **primary** ~ hauptsächliche Vertragspflicht; **primitive** ~ Hauptverpflichtung; **principal** ~ Hauptverbindlichkeit, -schuld; **prospective** ~ in Zukunft anfallende Verpflichtung; **pure** ~ unbedingte Verpflichtung; **real** ~ dingliche Verpflichtung; **rigid** ~ harte Verpflichtung; **secondary** ~ Nebenpflicht; **several** ~ unabhängige Verpflichtung; **short-time (-term)** ~s kurzfristige Verbindlichkeiten; **simple** ~ unabhängige Verpflichtung; **single** ~ Leistungsversprechen; **solidary** ~ Solidarverpflichtung; **specific** ~ Speziesschuld; **statutory** ~ gesetzliche Verpflichtung; **tax-free** ~s steuerfreie Obligationen; **tenant's** ~s Mieterpflichten; **valid** ~ rechtsgültige Verbindlichkeit;
 ~ **to accept the goods** Abnahmeverpflichtung; ~ **to buy** Kaufzwang, -verpflichtung; ~ **under a contract** vertragliche Verpflichtung, Vertragsleistung, -pflicht; **legal** ~ **of convertibility** gesetzliche Einlösungspflicht; ~ **to deliver** Lieferverpflichtung, -pflicht; ~ **to disclose** Anzeigepflicht bei Versicherungsabschluß, Auskunftspflicht; ~ **to extradite** Auslieferungspflicht; ~s **of good citizenship** [Staats]bürgerpflichten; ~ **of guaranty** Bürgschaftsverpflichtung; ~ **to give information** Auskunftspflicht; ~s **of a landlord** Vermieterpflichten; ~s **incident to life in the diplomatic service** mit dem im diplomatischen Beruf verbundene Verpflichtungen; ~ **to maintain** Unterhaltspflicht; ~ **to pay** Obligo, Zahlungsverpflichtung; ~ **to pay alimony** *(US)* Unterhaltspflicht; ~ **to pay rent, rates and taxes** Pacht-, Abgaben- und Steuerpflicht; ~ **to perform** Erfüllungsverpflichtung; ~ **to provide packing** Verpackungsauflage; ~ **to register** Registrierungspflicht; ~ **to repair** Reparaturverpflichtung; ~ **to repay** Rückerstattungspflicht; ~ **to repurchase** Rücknahmeverpflichtung; ~ **in respect of maintenance** Unterhaltspflicht; ~ **of debt service** Schuldentilgungsverpflichtung; **legal** ~ **to support** gesetzliche Unterhaltspflicht; ~ **pursuant to a treaty** Verpflichtungen aus einem Vertrag, Vertragspflichten; ~ **not to commit waste** Verpflichtung, sich der Substanzverringerung zu enthalten;
 to assume ~s Verbindlichkeiten (Verpflichtungen) übernehmen; **to back out of an** ~ sich einer Verpflichtung entziehen; **to**

be under an ~ **to s. o.** jem. verpflichtet sein; **to be under a great** ~ **to s. o.** jem. großen Dank schuldig sein; **to be under** ~ **to pay alimony** unterhaltspflichtig sein; **to cancel an** ~ Engagement lösen; **to carry out one's** ~s seine Verpflichtungen erfüllen; **to contract o. s. out of an** ~ sich einer Verpflichtung durch Vertragsabschluß entziehen; **to discharge one's** ~s seinen Verpflichtungen nachkommen; **to discharge s. o. from an** ~ j. aus einer Verpflichtung entlassen; **to elude an** ~ sich einer Verpflichtung entziehen; **to enter into an** ~ Verpflichtung eingehen; **to enter into pecuniary** ~s finanzielle Verpflichtungen übernehmen; **to evade one's legal** ~s **to support** sich seiner Unterhaltspflicht entziehen; **to extinguish an** ~ Schuldverhältnis zum Erlöschen bringen; **to fail to meet one's** ~s seinen Verpflichtungen nicht nachkommen; **to fasten an** ~ **on s. o.** jem. eine Verpflichtung auferlegen; **to fulfil(l) one's** ~s **under a contract of sale** seinen Verpflichtungen als Verkäufer vertragsgemäß nachkommen; **to impair the** ~ **of a contract** in vertragliche Rechte eingreifen; **to impose an** ~ Verpflichtung auferlegen; **to incur an** ~ Verpflichtung eingehen; **to infringe an** ~ einer Verpflichtung nicht nachkommen; **to lay s. o. under an** ~ jem. eine Verpflichtung auferlegen; **to lie under an** ~ verpflichtet sein **to meet one's** ~s seinen Verbindlichkeiten (Zahlungsverpflichtungen) nachkommen; **to meet one's contract** ~s seinen Verpflichtungen vertragsgemäß nachkommen; **to obtain a release from an** ~ aus einer Verpflichtung entlassen werden; **to put** ~s **on the market in large blocks** Obligationen in großen Paketen auf den Markt bringen; **to put under an** ~ verpflichten; **to redeem an** ~ Verpflichtung erfüllen; **to release s. o. from an** ~ j. aus einer Verpflichtung entlassen; **to remain under an** ~ **to s. o.** jem. weiterhin verpflichtet sein; **to repay an** ~ sich revanchieren; **to repudiate financial** ~s sich finanziellen Verpflichtungen entziehen; **to satisfy an** ~ einer Verpflichtung nachkommen; **to throw s. o. under an** ~ jem. eine Verpflichtung auferlegen.

obligator *(US)* Schuldner, Verpflichteter.

obligatory obligatorisch, bindend, zwingend, rechtsverbindlich, vorgeschrieben, unabdingbar;
 to make it ~ **upon s. o.** jem. die Verpflichtung auferlegen;
 ~ **agreement** bindende Abmachung; ~ **disposition** Mußvorschrift; ~ **insurance** Pflichtversicherung; ~ **investment** Pflichteinlage; ~ **maturity** *(US)* zwangsmäßige Fälligkeit; ~ **pact** obligatorischer Vertrag; ~ **registration** polizeiliche Meldepflicht; ~ **rights** obligatorische Ansprüche; ~ **scope of a contract** obligatorischer Charakter eines Vertrages; ~ **writing** bindende schriftliche Verpflichtung, Schuldschein.

oblige *(v.)* *(bind)* verpflichten, binden, *(compel)* zwingen, nötigen, *(civil law)* sich strafbar machen;
 ~ **o. s.** sich verpflichten (binden); ~ **s. o.** jem. gefällig sein (eine Gefälligkeit erweisen); ~ **s. o. with a check** *(US)* (cheque, *Br.*) jem. einen Scheck ausstellen; ~ **a friend** einem Freund einen Gefallen erweisen;
 full particulars will ~ nähere Auskunft erwünscht.

obliged verpflichtet, *(gratified)* verbunden, dankbar;
 to be ~ haftbar (verantwortlich) sein; **to be** ~ **to s. o.** Verbindlichkeiten gegenüber jem. haben; **to be statutorily** ~ gesetzlich verpflichtet sein; **to be** ~ **to sell one's house** sein Haus verkaufen müssen.

obligee Gläubiger, Forderungsberechtigter, *(bonds)* Obligationsgläubiger.

obliging entgegenkommend, gefällig, kulant, verbindlich, willfährig;
 to be ~ Entgegenkommen zeigen, entgegenkommen;
 ~ **neighbo(u)rs** hilfsbereite Nachbarn.

obligingness Gefälligkeit, Entgegenkommen, Kulanz, Zuvorkommenheit.

obligor Schuldner, Verpflichteter, *(bonds)* Obligationsschuldner;
 joint ~ Mitschuldner; **primary** ~ *(US)* selbstschuldnerischer Bürge;
 ~ **company** Schuldnergesellschaft, Schuldnerin.

oblique| accusation versteckte Anschuldigung; ~ **aerial photograph** *(mil.)* Schrägluftaufnahme; ~ **hint** verstohlener Wink; ~ **stroke** Schrägstrich; **to achieve s. th. by** ~ **ways** etw. auf Schleichwegen (indirekt) erreichen.

obliterate *(v.)* ausstreichen, -löschen, *(stamp)* entwerten, abstempeln;
 ~ **the writing of a check** Scheck durch Streichungen ungültig machen.

obliterated passage *(newspaper)* Zensurstelle.

obliterating stamp Entwertungsstempel.

obliteration Ausstreichung, Auslöschung, *(of stamps)* Abstempelung, Entwertung.

oblivion Vergessenheit, *(pol.)* Straferlaß, Gnadenerweis;
  to rescue from ~ der Vergessenheit entreißen; **to sink (subside) into** ~ in Vergessenheit geraten.
oblong size Längsformat.
obloquy Verleumdung, Schmähung, Vorwurf;
  held up to public ~ der öffentlichen Verachtung preisgegeben;
  to cast ~ **upon s. o.** jem. Schlechtes nachsagen; **to fall into** ~ in Verruf geraten; **to heap** ~ **upon s. o.** j. mit Schmähungen überschütten.
obnoxious Anstoß erregend, anstößig, anrüchig;
  ~ **conduct** anstößiges Betragen; ~ **statesman** verhaßter Politiker.
obreption Erlangung durch Betrug.
obscene unanständig, unzüchtig, obszön;
  to talk ~**ly** Obszönitäten sagen;
  ~ **book or paper** pornographische Veröffentlichung; ~ **literature** Schundliteratur; ~ **publication** pornographische Veröffentlichung.
obscenity Obszönität.
obscure unverständlich, unklar, *(photo)* unscharf;
  ~ *(v.)* **the understanding** unverständlich machen; ~ **the view of the driver** Gesichtsfeld des Fahrers behindern;
  ~ **corner** unübersichtliche Straßenecke; **to live an** ~ **life** zurückgezogen leben; ~ **locality** gänzlich unbekannter Ort; **to be of** ~ **origin** unbekannter Herkunft sein; ~ **retreat** unbedeutendes Nest; ~ **style** unverständlicher Stil; ~ **view** schlechte Sicht.
obscurity Unverständlichkeit, Unklarheit;
  to lapse into ~ der Vergessenheit anheimfallen; **to retire into** ~ sich vom öffentlichen Leben zurückziehen; **to spring from** ~ aus dem Unbekannten kommen.
obsequies feierliche Bestattung, Leichenbegängnis, Trauerfeierlichkeiten.
obsequious untertänig, unterwürfig, willfährig.
observable change bemerkenswerte Veränderung.
observance Einhaltung, Beobachtung, Befolgung, *(custom)* Herkommen, Brauch, *(rule)* Regel, Vorschrift;
  with due ~ **of** unter gebührender Beachtung von;
  strict ~ genaue Einhaltung;
  ~ **of a contract** Vertragstreue; ~ **of duties** Pflichterfüllung; ~ **of the laws** Einhaltung (Befolgung) der Gesetze; ~ **of a time limit** Fristeinhaltung;
  to maintain the customary ~**s** vorgeschriebene Riten einhalten.
observant | **of contract** vertragstreu;
  to be ~ **of s. th.** etw. befolgen; **to be very** ~ **of forms** sehr auf Formen halten; **to be always** ~ **of one's duties** stets sehr pflichtbewußt sein.
observation Befolgung, Einhaltung, *(market, US)* Marktbeobachtung, *(remark)* Bemerkung, *(teacher)* Klassenaufsicht;
  for your ~ zu Ihrer Stellungnahme;
  behavio(u)r ~ Verhaltensforschung; **final** ~ Schlußbemerkung; **purchase** ~ Beobachtung der Kaufgewohnheiten;
  ~ **of the enemy** Feindbeobachtung; ~ **of the ground** Geländeüberwachung;
  to escape ~ der Beobachtung entgehen; **to keep s. o. under** ~ j. beobachten lassen; **to publish one's** ~**s** seine Untersuchungsergebnisse veröffentlichen; **to work an** ~ *(mar.)* Länge und Breite ausrechnen;
  ~ **balloon** Fesselballon; ~ **basket** *(balloon)* Beobachtungskorb; ~ **car** Aussichtswagen; ~ **center** *(juvenile offender)* Beobachtungszentrum; ~ **deck** Zuschauerterrasse; ~ **form** *(time study)* Beobachtungsposten; ~ **period** Beobachtungszeitraum; ~ **port** *(tank)* Sehklappe; ~ **post** *(mil.)* Beobachtungsposten; ~ **sample** beobachtete Bevölkerungsgruppe; ~ **tower** Aussichtsturm, Beobachtungswarte; ~ **train** *(US)* gläserner Zug, Aussichtszug; ~ **ward** Beobachtungsstation.
observational technique *(marketing)* Beobachtungsmethode.
observatory Observatorium, Wetter-, Sternwarte.
observe *(v.)* einhalten, befolgen, beobachten;
  ~ **an anniversary** Jubiläum begehen; ~ **the articles of association** Gesellschaftsstatuten einhalten; ~ **a birthday** Geburtstag feiern; ~ **care** Sorgfalt anwenden; ~ **a condition** Bedingung erfüllen; ~ **a law** Gesetz befolgen; ~ **moderation in what one says** sich gemäßigt ausdrücken; ~ **the enemy's movements** feindliche Bewegungen beobachten; ~ **the period of notice** Kündigungsfrist einhalten; ~ **the proprieties** Form (Anstandsregeln) bewahren; ~ **the provisions of an act** Gesetzesbestimmungen befolgen; ~ **a rule** Regel beachten; ~ **silence** Schweigen bewahren; ~ **the time limit** Frist einhalten.
observer Beobachter, *(airplane)* Luftspäher;
  ~**s** Beobachterdelegation;
  expert ~**s** erfahrene Beobachter;

strict ~ **of etiquette** überzeugter Anhänger der Etikette; ~ **of the United Nations** Beobachter der Vereinten Nationen;
  to admit ~**s** Beobachter zulassen;
  ~ **status** Beobachterstatus.
observing mind gute Beobachtungsgabe.
obsessed | **with an idea** von einer Idee besessen; ~ **by fear of unemployment** von der Zwangsvorstellung befallen, arbeitslos zu werden.
obsession Verbohrtheit, Verranntheit, fixe Idee, *(med.)* Verfolgungswahnsinn, Zwangsvorstellung.
obsignatory ratifizierend und bestätigend.
obsolescence Unbrauchbarkeit, Überalterung [von Einrichtungen], *(wear and tear)* Abschreibungsursache;
  industry ~ industrielle Überalterung; **planned** ~ geplante Überalterung, absichtliches Altmodischwerden;
  ~ **of seasonal goods** Überfälligkeit von Saisonwaren; ~ **of stock** Lagerüberalterung;
  ~ **allowance** Bewertungsfreibetrag bei Ersatzanschaffungen; ~ **method** veraltetes Produktionsverfahren.
obsolescent veraltet.
obsolete veraltet, überholt, außer Gebrauch, nicht mehr gültig, *(worn out)* abgenutzt, verbraucht;
  to grow ~ überholt (veraltet) sein;
  ~ **inscription** nicht mehr lesbare Inschrift; ~ **law** nicht mehr angewendetes, aber formell noch nicht aufgehobenes Gesetz; ~ **securities** *(US)* aufgerufene und ungültig gemachte Wertpapiere; ~ **textbook** überholter Kommentar; ~ **theory** überholte Theorie.
obsoletism veraltete Redewendung.
obstacle Hindernis;
  ~**s to planning** Planungshindernisse; ~**s to registration** Eintragungshindernisse; ~**s to world peace** Hindernisse auf dem Wege zu einem Weltfriedenszustand;
  to be an ~ entgegenstehen; **to prove an** ~ **to s. one's promotion** jds. Beförderung im Wege stehen; **to put** ~**s in s. one's way** jem. Schwierigkeiten machen; **to remove (smooth away) an** ~ Hindernis beseitigen.
obstetrician Geburtshelfer.
obstinate halsstarrig;
  ~ **cold** hartnäckige Erkältung; ~ **desertion** böswilliges Verlassen; ~ **disease** hartnäckige Krankheit; ~ **resistance to an attack** entschlossener Widerstand.
obstruct *(v.)* blockieren, hemmen, hindern, verhindern, nicht durchlassen, versperren, *(pol.)* Obstruktion treiben, verschleppen;
  ~ **another car** fremdes Fahrzeug im Verkehr behindern; ~ **an easement** Ausübung einer Dienstbarkeit verhindern; ~ **s. o. in the execution of his duty** j. an der Ausübung seiner Pflichten hindern; ~ **governmental operations** *(US)* Regierungsmaßnahmen behindern; ~ **a highway** Straße blockieren (versperren); ~ **s. one's movements** jds. Freizügigkeit behindern; ~ **navigation** Schiffahrt behindern; ~ **an officer** *(US)* **(constable, Br.)** performing his duties Widerstand gegen die Staatsgewalt leisten; ~ **the police in the execution of their duties** Widerstand gegen polizeiliche Anordnungen leisten; ~ **proceedings of bankruptcy** Konkursverschleppung begehen; ~ **the proceedings of legislature** Parlamentsnötigung begehen; ~ **process** Zwangsvollstreckung (Zustellung) vereiteln; ~ **the progress of a bill through the House of Commons** Verabschiedung eines Gesetzentwurfes im Parlament verschleppen (aufhalten), Durchlauf eines Gesetzantrages im Unterhaus blockieren; ~ **the street** Straße verstopfen; ~ **the traffic** Verkehr behindern; ~ **the view** Sicht nehmen, Aussicht verbauen.
obstructing | **governmental operations** *(US)* Behinderung von Regierungsmaßnahmen; ~ **highways** Verkehrsbehinderung auf öffentlichen Straßen; ~ **justice** Behinderung der Rechtspflege; ~ **an officer** *(US)* **(constable, Br., the police)** performing his (in the execution of its) duties Widerstand gegen die Staatsgewalt (polizeiliche Anordnungen); ~ **proceedings of bankruptcy** Konkursverschleppung; ~ **proceedings of legislature** Parlamentsnötigung; ~ **process** Zustellungvereitelung, Vollstreckungsbehinderung, Vereitelung der Zwangsvollstreckung; ~ **the recruiting or enlistment** *(Espionage Act, US)* Behinderung der Erfassung zum Wehrdienst.
obstruction Hindernis, Behinderung, Versperrung, Verstopfung, Hemmnis, *(parl.)* Verschleppung, Quertreiberei, Obstruktion;
  ~ **of bankruptcy** Konkursverschleppung; ~ **of another car** Verkehrsbehinderung eines fremden Fahrzeugs; ~ **of an easement** verhinderte Ausübung einer Grunddienstbarkeit; ~ **of the highway** Behinderung des Straßenverkehrs, Straßenblockierung, -sperre; ~ **on the line (road)** Verkehrshindernis; ~ **of**

members Abgeordnetennötigung; ~ **to navigation** Behinderung der Schiffahrt; ~ **of a police officer in the execution of his duties** Widerstand gegen die Staatsgewalt; ~ **of polling** Behinderung in der Ausübung des Wahlrechts; **wilful** ~ **of traffic** vorsätzliche Verkehrsbehinderung;
  to be guilty of ~ sich wegen einer Verkehrsbehinderung strafbar machen; **to cause an** ~ Verkehr behindern; **to practise** ~ Obstruktion[spolitik] betreiben, verschleppen;
  ~ **guard** Schienenräumer.
obstructionism Verschleppung[spolitik], Obstruktionspolitik.
obstructionist Verschleppungstaktiker, Quertreiber, Obstruktionspolitiker.
obstructive Obstruktionspolitiker;
  ~ (*a.*) verstopfend, verschleppend;
  to be ~ **to s. one's plans** jds. Plänen im Wege stehen (hinderlich sein);
  ~ **measures** Obstruktionsmethoden.
obtain (*v.*) erhalten, erlangen, erwirken, bekommen, (*procure*) sich beschaffen (verschaffen), beziehen, auftreiben, (*stock exchange*) erzielen, erreichen;
  ~ **acceptance** Akzept einholen; ~ **an adjournment** Aufschub erlangen; ~ **an advance of money** Vorschuß erhalten; ~ **s. one's appointment to a post** jds. Ernennung für eine Stellung durchsetzen; ~ **by artifice** erschleichen; ~ **s. one's confidence** jds. Vertrauen erlangen; ~ **the contract** Zuschlag (Auftrag) erhalten; ~ **the copyright** Urheberrecht erwerben; ~ **credit by fraud** Kreditbetrug begehen; ~ **in some districts** (*custom*) sich in einigen Landstrichen halten; ~ **by fraud** betrügerisch (unter Vorspiegelung falscher Tatsachen) erlangen; ~ **goods** Waren beziehen; ~ **goods straight from the factory** Waren direkt von der Fabrik (mit Beziehungen) kaufen; ~ **information** Informationen erhalten; ~ **a judgment against s. o.** Urteil gegen j. erwirken; ~ **by labo(u)r** erarbeiten; ~ **lawfully** rechtmäßig erwerben; ~ **legal force** Rechtskraft erlangen; ~ **a loan of money by application** beantragtes Darlehen erhalten; ~ **a measure of economic independence** ein bißchen nebenher verdienen; ~ **money by false pretences** Kreditbetrug begehen; ~ **a month's leave** Monat Urlaub bekommen; ~ **nothing** (*creditor*) leer ausgehen; ~ **one's object** sein Ziel erreichen; ~ **an offer** Angebot einholen; ~ **an order** Auftrag erhalten (buchen); ~ **permission** Erlaubnis (Genehmigung) erhalten; ~ **first place** ersten Preis in einem Wettbewerb bekommen; ~ **a position** Stellung bekommen; ~ **a price** Preis erzielen; ~ **property by false pretences** Vermögensvorteil durch Betrug erlangen; ~ **provisions** Vorräte bekommen; ~ **from the publisher** direkt vom Verlag beziehen; ~ **redress from s. o.** Regreß gegen jem. nehmen; ~ **a week's leave** Woche Urlaub bekommen;
  to be easy (difficult) to ~ leicht (schwer) erhältlich sein.
obtainable erhältlich, beziehbar;
  ~ **on the market** an der Börse gehandelt; ~ **on order** gegen Bestellung erhältlich; ~ **at par** zum Nennwert erhältlich; ~ **from all stockists** in allen einschlägigen Geschäften zu haben;
  to be ~ (*stock exchange*) gehandelt werden.
obtained, details can be ~ **from** Näheres zu erfahren von (bei).
obtaining|by fraud the consent of creditors betrügerische Erschleichung der Gläubigerzustimmung; ~ **credit by fraud (money by false pretences)** Kreditbetrug; ~ **property by false representation** Vermögenserschleichung mittels vorsätzlicher Täuschung.
obtainment Erwerb.
obtrude (*v.*) **o. s. upon s. o.** sich jem. aufdrängen.
obtrusion of one's opinions on others Aufdrängen seiner Meinung.
obverse (*coin*) Vorder-, Bildseite.
obviate (*v.*) **objections** Einwänden zuvorkommen.
obviation Vorbeugung, Verhinderung.
obvious offenbar, -sichtlich, augenscheinlich, deutlich, klar;
  to be ~ auf der Hand liegen; **to be most** ~ am meisten ins Auge fallen;
  ~ **advantage** offensichtlicher Vorteil; ~ **danger** ohne weiteres erkennbare Gefahr; ~ **risk** (*accident insurance*) klar erkennbares Risiko; ~ **thing to do** das Naheliegende.
occasion (*incident*) Vorfall, Fall, (*incidental cause*) Anlaß, Ursache, Grund, (*need*) Bedarf, (*opportunity*) Gelegenheit;
  as ~ **may require** nach Bedarf; **on all** ~s bei jeder Gelegenheit; **for the** ~ eigens zu diesem Zweck; **if the** ~ **(should the** ~**) arise** gegebenenfalls; **on the** ~ **of** anläßlich; **on great** ~s bei gewichtigem Anlaß; **on particular** ~s in Einzelfällen; **on this particular** ~ aufgrund dieses besonderen Anlasses; **on a privileged** ~ in Wahrnehmung berechtigter Interessen; **when** ~ **serves** bei passender Gelegenheit; **on the** ~ **of his death** gelegentlich seines Todes; **when the** ~ **shows** bei passender Gelegenheit;

ceremonial ~ förmlicher Anlaß; **great** ~ großes Ereignis; **special** ~ besonderer Anlaß, besondere Gelegenheit;
  ~ **for complaint** Beschwerdegrund; ~ **for a family gathering** Anlaß zu einem Familientreffen; **no** ~ **to intervene** kein Grund zum Eingreifen; **one of the rare** ~s einer der seltenen Augenblicke;
  ~ (*v.*) verursachen, veranlassen;
  ~ **emotion** Emotionen hervorrufen; ~ **a rising** Aufruhr hervorrufen;
  to be the ~ **of s. th.** Anstoß für etw. geben; **to celebrate the** ~ Ereignis feiern; **to dress as befits the** ~ sich den Umständen entsprechend anziehen; **to give** ~ **to s. th.** Anstoß zu etw. geben; **to give** ~ **to an outburst of popular indignation** Anlaß zur öffentlichen Entrüstung geben; **to have no** ~ **for s. one's help** jds. Hilfe nicht benötigen; **to rise to the** ~ sich einer Lage (Situation) gewachsen zeigen.
occasional bei besonderer Gelegenheit, gelegentlich, (*casual*) zufällig;
  ~ **absence** gelegentliche Abwesenheit; ~ **cause** auslösende Ursache; ~ **contraband** bedingte (relative) Konterbande; ~ **fits** gelegentliche Anfälle; ~ **gift** Gelegenheitsgeschenk; ~ **hand** Gelegenheitsarbeiter; ~ **labo(u)r** Gelegenheitsarbeit; ~ **licence** (*Br.*) bechränkte Schankkonzession; ~ **poem** Gelegenheitsgedicht; ~ **purchase** Gelegenheitskauf; ~ **reader** gelegentlicher Leser; ~ **valet** Lohndiener; ~ **visit** Gelegenheitsbesuch; ~ **writer** Gelegenheitsschriftsteller.
Occident Abendland.
occidental abendländisch, westlich.
occupancy Besitz, Innehaben, Gewahrsam, (*fire insurance*) vorgesehene Benutzung, (*law of nations*) Okkupation, (*taking possession*) Besitzergreifung, Aneignung, (*time of occupancy*) Besitzdauer;
  during his ~ **of the post** solange er die Stelle innehatte;
  immediate ~ (*ad*) Einzug sofort, sofort beziehbar; **transient** ~ vorübergehende Benutzung;
  ~ **of space** Inanspruchnahme von Raum;
  to run at 90% ~ zu 90% vermietet sein;
  ~ **charge** Benutzungsgebühr; ~ **expenses** Hausinstandhaltungskosten; ~ **tax** Besitzsteuer.
occupant Besitzer, Inhaber, Bewohner, Insasse, (*of unowned property*) Besitzergreifer;
  special ~ treuhänderisch besitzender Erbe;
  ~ **of an insured car** Mitfahrer eines versicherten Fahrzeugs; ~s **of a house** Hausbewohner; ~ **of an office** Amtsinhaber; ~ **of a post** Stelleninhaber; ~ **of a vehicle** Fahrzeuginsasse.
occupation (*business*) Geschäft, Gewerbe, (*calling*) Beruf, (*employment*) Beschäftigung, Berufsarbeit, -tätigkeit, -leben, berufliche Tätigkeit, (*house*) Beziehen, Bezug, Bewohnen, (*law of nations*) Okkupation, Besatzung, Besetzung, (*taking possession*) Besitzergreifung, (*tenure*) Besitz, Innehabung;
  as a regular (permanent) ~ hauptberuflich; **as a secondary** ~ im Nebenberuf, nebenberuflich; **by** ~ von Beruf; **fit for** ~ bewohnbar; **without** ~ berufs-, beschäftigungslos; **without a permanent** ~ ohne feste Beschäftigung;
  actual ~ tatsächliche Besitzergreifung, tatsächlicher Gewahrsam; **agricultural** ~ Tätigkeit in der Landwirtschaft, landwirtschaftlicher Beruf; **belligerent** ~ kriegerische Besetzung; **business** ~ berufliche Beschäftigung, Berufstätigkeit; **casual** ~ gelegentlich ausgeübter Beruf, Gelegenheitsbeschäftigung; **chief** ~ Hauptberuf, -beschäftigung; **clerical** ~ Bürotätigkeit; **commercial** ~ Handelstätigkeit; **dangerous** ~ gefährlicher Beruf; **disease-breeding** ~ Berufskrankheiten auslösende Beschäftigung; **dull** ~ langweilige Tätigkeit; ~ **entry** Anfangsberuf; **female** ~ Frauenarbeit; **gainful** ~ Erwerbstätigkeit; **godforsaken** ~ ausgefallener Beruf; **hazardous** ~ gefährlicher Beruf; **immediate** ~ Sofortbezug, sofort beziehbar; **industrial** ~ Beschäftigung in der Industrie; **intellectual** ~ geistiger Beruf; **light** ~ leichte Beschäftigung; **minor** ~ Nebenberuf, -beschäftigung; **no** ~ ohne Beschäftigung; **pacific** ~ friedliche Besetzung; **paid** ~ unselbständige Erwerbstätigkeit; **paramount** ~ (*taxation*) überwiegende Beschäftigung; **peaceful** ~ friedliche Besetzung; **principal** ~ Haupttätigkeit, -beruf; **professional** ~ freier Beruf, freiberufliche Tätigkeit; **public** ~ Tätigkeit im Dienst der Öffentlichkeit; **regular** ~ normale (regelmäßige) Beschäftigung; **remunerative** ~ gewinnbringende (einträgliche) Beschäftigung; **skilled** ~ Beruf mit Fachausbildung; **soulless** ~ geisttötende Beschäftigung; **usual** ~ gewöhnliche Beschäftigung;
  ~ **for o. s.** Eigennutzung; ~ **of business premises** Benutzung eines Geschäftslokals; ~ **on completion** Besitzergreifung bei Vertragsbeendigung; ~ **of enemy territory** Besetzung feindli-

chen Gebiets; ~ **of a house** Bewohnen eines Hauses; ~ **outside of office work** nebenberufliche Tätigkeit; ~ **of land** Inbesitznahme eines Grundstücks; ~ **of a professional nature** freiberufliche Tätigkeit, selbständige Arbeit; ~ **of realty** Besitzerlangung;

to be in a reserved ~ kriegswichtigen Beruf ausüben; **to be in ~ of a house** Haus bewohnen, Hausbewohner sein; **to choose an** ~ Berufswahl treffen; **to enter into ~ of premises** Betriebsgrundstück in Besitz nehmen; **to give s. o.** ~ j. beschäftigen; **to go about one's lawful** ~ seiner geregelten Beschäftigung nachgehen; **to have no heart in one's** ~ an seinem Beruf keine Freude haben; **to look for an** ~ **suited to one's abilities** sich nach einer geeigneten Beschäftigung umsehen; **to pursue a gainful** ~ Erwerbstätigkeit ausüben; **to put down one's** ~ seinen Beruf angeben, Berufsbezeichnung eintragen;

~ **authorities** Besatzungsbehörden; ~ **bridge** Privatbrücke; ~ **census** Berufszählung; ~ **costs** Besatzungskosten; ~ **damages** Besatzungsschaden; ~ **forces** Besatzungstruppen, -mächte; ~ **franchise** Stimmrecht der Grundstücksbesitzer; ~ **group** Berufsgruppe; ~ **lease** mit der Berufsausübung verbundene Pacht; ~ **licence** Weidepacht; ~ **money** Besatzungsgeld; ~ **power** Besatzungsmacht; ~ **records** Besatzungsunterlagen; ~ **road** (Br.) Zufahrts-, Privatstraße, -weg; ~ **stamps** von einer Besatzungsarmee herausgegebene Briefmarken; ~ **statute** Besatzungsstatut; ~ **tax** Gewerbesteuer; ~ **troops** Besatzungstruppen, -armee; **to keep ~ troops in a country** einem Land Besatzung auferlegen; ~ **zone** Besatzungsgebiet, -zone.

occupational zum Beruf gehörig, beruflich;

~ **accident** Berufsunfall; ~ **census** Berufszählung; ~ **center** (US) **(centre,** Br.) Beschäftigungs-, Berufszentrum; ~ **category** Berufsgruppe; ~ **characteristic checklist** Berufskatalog; ~ **choice** Berufswahl; ~ **class** Berufsgruppe, -klasse; ~ **classification** Berufsgliederung, -zugehörigkeit, (magazine) Berufsanalyse der Bezieher; ~ **competence** berufliche Eignung; ~ **decision** Berufswahl; ~ **deferment** berufliche Unabkömmlichkeit; ~ **description** Berufsbezeichnung; ~ **disease** (Br.) Gewerbe-, Berufskrankheit; ~ **distribution** Berufsgliederung, -zusammensetzung; ~ **duties** (insured person) Berufsaufgaben, berufliche Tätigkeit; ~ **efficiency** berufliche Tüchtigkeit, berufliche Leistungsfähigkeit; ~ **families** verwandte Berufe; ~ **fatigue** Überarbeitung; ~ **forces** Besatzungstruppen, -macht; ~ **goal** Berufsziel; ~ **group** Berufsgruppe, -verband; ~ **grouping** Berufskategorie; ~ **hazard** betriebliche Unfallgefährdung, Berufsrisiko, -gefahr; ~ **illness** beruflich bedingte Krankheit, Berufskrankheit; ~ **immobility** (labo(u)rer) nicht vorhandene Umsetzfähigkeit; ~ **index** Berufsgruppenindex; ~ **injury** Berufsunfall; ~ **interest** Berufsinteresse; ~ **jargon** Fachjargon; ~ **level** Berufsniveau; ~ **mobility** (labo(u)rer) Umsetzfähigkeit; ~ **mobility of workers** Umsetzfähigkeit, berufsbedingte Arbeitskräftemobilität; ~ **mortality** Berufssterblichkeit; ~ **name** Berufsbezeichnung; ~ **neurosis** Berufsneurose; ~ **opportunities** Berufsmöglichkeiten; ~ **pension** Betriebspension, betriebliches Ruhegehalt, -geld; ~ **pension scheme** betriebliche Pensionskasse, betriebliche Altersversorgung; ~ **pyramid** Berufspyramide; ~ **rate** Berufstarif; ~ **representation** Berufsvertretung; ~ **resettlement (retraining)** [Berufs]umschulung; ~ **risk** Berufsrisiko; ~ **scheme** (Br.) berufliche Altersversorgung; ~ **shift** Berufswechsel; ~ **statistics** Berufsstatistik; ~ **therapist** Facharzt für Berufskrankheiten; ~ **therapy** Beschäftigungstherapie; ~ **title** Berufsbezeichnung; ~ **training** berufliche Ausbildung, Berufs-, Fachausbildung; **to have had ~ training in** einem Beruf ausgebildet sein; ~ **union** Berufsgewerkschaft; ~ **wage** Branchentariflohn; ~ **wear and tear** berufsbedingte Körperschäden.

occupied beschäftigt, ausgelastet, (hospital) belegt, (seat) besetzt, belegt;

fully ~ (enterprise) vollbeschäftigt; **gainfully** ~ einträglich beschäftigt;

~ **at night** nachts bewohnt; ~ **rent-free** kostenlos bewohnt;

to be ~ in translating a novel mit der Übersetzung eines Romans beschäftigt sein; **to keep one's mind** ~ seinen Geist beschäftigen;

~ **house** bewohntes Haus; ~ **population** werktätige Bevölkerung; ~ **zone** Besatzungszone.

occupier Besitzer, Inhaber, (owner or tenant) Wohnungsinhaber, Grundstückseigentümer, Hausbewohner, (of ownerless land) Besitzergreifer;

contiguous ~ Anlieger;

~ **of a factory** Fabrikbesitzer; ~ **of premises** Grundstückseigentümer; ~ **of a shop** Ladeninhaber;

~'s **liability** Grundstückshaftung.

occupy (v.) (o. s.) sich beschäftigen, (s. o.) j. beschäftigen, (invest) Kapital investieren, (lodge) bewohnen, (mil.) besetzen, (possess) besitzen, innehaben, (take possession) Besitz ergreifen;

~ **an appartment** Wohnung besitzen; ~ **a dual capacity** mit sich selbst kontrahieren; ~ **the chair** Vorsitz führen (innehaben), präsidieren; ~ **the enemy's capital** feindliche Hauptstadt besetzen (einnehmen); ~ **the ground floor** Erdgeschoß bewohnen; ~ **three hours** drei Stunden beanspruchen; ~ **a house** Haus bewohnen; ~ **an office** Amt bekleiden; ~ **a post** Stellung innehaben; ~ **a high position in society** gesellschaftlich einen hohen Rang einnehmen; ~ **an important position** bedeutsamen Posten bekleiden; ~ **a seat** Sitz belegen; ~ **too much space** zuviel Platz beanspruchen; ~ **a suite of rooms** Zimmerflucht bewohnen; ~ **one's time** seine Zeit verwenden.

occupying power Besatzungsmacht.

occur (v.) vorkommen, sich ereignen, eintreten, stattfinden, (loss) entstehen;

should the case ~ gegebenen-, eintretendenfalls.

occurrence Vorkommnis, Ereignis, Vorfall, -gang, Begebenheit;

on the ~ **of death** im Todesfall;

singular ~ singuläres Ereignis; **unfortunate** ~ unglückliches Ereignis;

~ **of the event insured against** Versicherungsfall; ~ **of gold** Goldvorkommen; ~ **of loss** Versicherungsfall;

to be of frequent ~ häufig vorkommen.

ocean Ozean, Meer, See;

~ **of complaints** Flut von Beschwerden; ~**s of money** (fam.) Säcke voller Geld; ~**s of room** (sl.) unendlich viel Platz;

to cross the ~ über das große Wasser fahren;

~ **bill of lading** Seekonnossement, Seefrachtbrief; ~ **carrier** Seehafenspediteur; ~**-carrying trade** Hochseeschiffahrt; ~ **chart** Meereskarte; ~ **current** Meeresströmung; ~ **floor** Meeresboden, -grund; ~ **freight** Seefracht; ~ **freight broker** Hochseeschiffsmakler; ~ **freight rate** Transatlantikfrachtsatz; ~**-going fleet** Hochseeflotte; ~**-going liner (steamer)** Ozean-, Überseedampfer; ~**-going tug** Hochseeschlepper; ~ **greyhound** Schnelldampfer; ~ **lane** Schiffahrtsroute; ~ **liner** Passagierdampfer; ~ **manifest** (US) Ladungsverzeichnis; ~ **marine insurance** (US) Überseeversicherung; ~ **palace** Luxusdampfer; ~ **shipment** Überseetransport; **packed for** ~ **shipment** seeverpackt; ~ **shipping** Hochseeschiffahrt, Atlantikfrachtverkehr; ~ **steamer** Ozeandampfer; ~ **trade** (US) Überseehandel; ~ **traffic** Überseehandel; ~ **transport** (US) Überseetransport; ~ **voyage** Ozean-, Seereise; ~ **weather ship** Wetterschiff.

octane Oktan;

high-~ mit hoher Oktanzahl;

~ **number** Oktanzahl, Klopffestigkeitsgrad.

octavo Oktavformat;

large ~ Großoktav;

~ **volume** Oktavband.

octopoid industry dezentralisierter Großbetrieb.

ocular | demonstration sichtbarer Beweis; ~ **estimate** Augenmaß; ~ **inspection** Augenschein; ~ **proof** sichtbarer Beweis, Augenscheinbeweis; ~ **witness** (US) Augenzeuge.

odd seltsam, merkwürdig, sonderbar, (left over) überzählig, (numbers) ungerade, (single) einzeln, gelegentlich, (uneven) ungleich;

40 ~ einige vierzig;

~**-come shortly** bald kommender Tag; ~**-come shorts** Überreste, Abfälle; ~ **day** Schalttag; ~ **hand** Ersatzmann; ~ **jobs** Gelegenheitsaufträge, -arbeiten; ~ **linage unit** nicht reguläre Zeileneinheit.

odd lot ungerade Menge, Restpartie, (auction sale) Auktionsposten, (stock exchange) gebrochener Börsenschluß (weniger als 100 Aktien oder weniger als 1000 Obligationen), (US) nicht offiziell an der Börse gehandelte Abschnitte;

to buy shares in ~**s** Aktien in ungewöhnlich geringen Mengen erwerben;

~ **broker (dealer,** US) Makler in kleinen Effektenabschnitten; ~ **business** (US) Geschäfte (Handel) in kleinen Effektenabschnitten; ~ **trading** (US) Handel in kleinen Effektenabschnitten.

odd | man Ersatzmann, (holder of casting vote) Inhaber der entscheidenden Stimme, (occasional worker) Gelegenheitsarbeiter; ~ **money** restliches Geld; **to keep the** ~ **money** restliches Geld behalten; **to make up the** ~ **money** Summe vollmachen; ~ **months** Monate mit 31 Tagen; ~ **numbers** vereinzelte Nummern einer Zeitschrift; **200** ~ **pages** etw. über 200 Seiten; ~ **piece** Einzelstück; ~ **set** unvollständiger Satz; ~ **size** nicht gängige Größe; **some** ~ **stamps** kein vollständiger Satz; **at** ~ **times** unregelmäßig; ~ **volume** überzähliger Band.

oddments Reste, Abfälle, Überbleibsel, Einzelstücke, Ramschwaren, übriggebliebene Waren, *(print.)* Titelei;
remnants and ~ Reste und Gelegenheitskäufe;
~ market *(book trade)* Ramschmarkt.

odds *(advantage)* Überlegenheit, Vorteil, *(equalizing allowance)* Vorgabe, *(betting)* Wettkurs, *(chance)* Möglichkeit, Gelegenheit, [Gewinn]chance, *(difference)* Unterschied, *(inequality)* Ungleichheit, Verschiedenheit;
at ~ with im Streit (uneins) mit; **over the United Kingdom ~** höher als der englische Inlandpreis;
~ and ends allerlei Kleinigkeiten, Reste, Abfälle, Krimskrams;
to be at ~ with s. o. sich mit jem. streiten; **to fight against heavy ~** mit einem großen Handikap fertig werden müssen; **to give s. o. ~** jem. etw. vorgeben; **to lay long ~** größeren Einsatz machen; **to perform against the ~ in all the wrong areas** mit den Unwägbarkeiten aller Märkte fertig werden müssen; **to reduce the ~** Wettquoten herabsetzen; **to set at ~s** gegeneinander hetzen; **to supply ~** Nachteile vergüten;
~-on aussichtsreich, mit guter Gewinnchance.

oddball *(sl.)* Exzentriker.

odium Makel, Odium;
to bring s. o. into ~ j. verhaßt machen.

odometer Entfernungsmesser, Kilometerzähler.

odo(u)r Geruch, *(fig.)* Ruf;
in bad ~ with the authorities auf Kriegsfuß mit den Behörden;
to be in good ~ with s. o. gut bei jem. angeschrieben sein; **to be in ill ~ with s. o.** bei jem. in schlechtem Ruf stehen; **to die in the ~ of sanctity** im Geruch eines Heiligen sterben.

off *(away)* entfernt, weg, *(concert)* abgesagt, ausgefallen, *(dish in restaurant)* ausgegangen, nicht mehr da, *(el.)* abgeschaltet, außer Betrieb, *(engagement)* aufgelöst, *(mar.)* vom Land ab, *(market)* in einer Flaute, flau, lustlos, *(quality)* minderwertig, von schlechter Qualität, *(sold out)* ausgegangen, *(theater)* hinter der Bühne;
afternoon ~ freier Nachmittag; **badly ~** schlecht dran; **better ~** bessergestellt; **comfortably ~** wohl situiert; **dividend ~** ausschließlich Dividende; **right (straight) ~** sofort, augenblicklich; **slightly ~** *(meat)* leicht angegangen; **some way ~** etw. entfernt; **well ~** in guten Verhältnissen, gut situiert;
~ colo(u)r indisponiert; **~ the cuff** ohne Manuskript, frei; **~ duty** dienstfrei; **~ one's feed** *(sl.)* appetitlos; **~ its feet** *(print.)* schiefstehend; **~ one's head** *(sl.)* verrückt, durchgedreht; **~ limits** *(US)* Zutritt verboten, beschlagnahmefrei; **~-line** abgeschaltet, *(data processing)* nicht an die Zentrale gekoppelt; **~ the line** nicht im Gewahrsam der Bahn; **~ the map** *(coll.)* weit abgelegen, *(sl.)* nicht mehr existierend; **~ the mark** unbeachtlich, irrelevant; **~ and on** in Intervallen, von Zeit zu Zeit; **~ the point** nicht zur Sache gehörig, belanglos; **~ the record** nicht zur Veröffentlichung bestimmt, inoffiziell; **~ schedule** *(US)* außerfahrplanmäßig; **~ shade** nicht ganz dem Farbmuster entsprechend; **~ smoking** nicht mehr rauchen; **~-stage** hinter der Szene; **~ standard** abweichend von der üblichen Qualität; **~-street** Nebenstraße; **~ the streets** abseits der Straße; **~ the beaten track** abgelegen;
to arrange to take two days ~ sich zwei Tage frei machen; **to allow 2 per cent ~ for ready money** 2% Skonto bei Barzahlung gewähren; **to be ~** *(sl.)* abgeschaltet sein, *(commodities)* ausgegangen sein; **to be ~ one's feed** keinen Appetit haben; **to be badly (poorly) ~** in ärmlichen Verhältnissen leben; **to be badly ~ for tools** dringend neue Werkzeuge benötigen; **to be cut ~ in a telephone conversation** in einem Telefongespräch unterbrochen werden; **to be ~ the point** weitab vom Thema liegen; **to be ~ three points** *(stock exchange)* drei Punkte tiefer liegen; **to be ~ to London** nach London unterwegs sein; **to be ~ with s. o.** mit jem. nichts mehr zu tun haben; **to be a little ~** ein bißchen verrückt sein; **to be on and ~ with s. th.** nur nach Laune arbeiten; **to be right ~ it** *(sl.)* faseln, dummes Zeug reden; **to be standing ~ the road** außerhalb der Straße abgestellt sein; **to be well ~** in guten Verhältnissen leben; **to be worse ~** noch schlechter dran sein; **to be ~ smoking** nicht mehr rauchen; **to borrow money ~ a friend** Geld von einem Freund leihen; **to declare ~** rückgängig machen; **to finish ~ a job** Arbeit fertigstellen; **to get one's stock ~** seinen Vorrat loswerden; **to give the staff a day ~** dem Personal (der Belegschaft) einen Tag frei geben; **to go ~ duty** Dienst beenden; **to have time ~** über freie Zeit verfügen; **to offer goods at 10% ~ the regular price** Waren mit einem 10%igen Abschlag vom Normalpreis anbieten; **to pay ~ one's debts** seine Schulden bezahlen; **to rain on and ~ all day** hin und wieder regnen; **to sell ~** ausverkaufen; **to take 3% ~ the price** 3% Skonto gewähren; **to take a matter ~ s. one's hands** jem. die Verantwortung in einer Sache abnehmen; **to take s. th. ~ the**

price Preisnachlaß gewähren; **to take an afternoon ~** sich einen Nachmittag frei nehmen; **to turn ~ the radio** Rundfunkgerät abschalten; **to wander ~ the point** vom Thema abkommen (abschweifen); **to work at it ~ and on** mit Unterbrechungen arbeiten;
~ base *(sl.)* dreist, zudringlich; **~-beat** unkonventionell; **~-beat advertising** ausgefallene Reklame; **~-beat role** außergewöhnliche Funktion; **~ board** Rückseite; **~-board market** *(US)* Markt für amtlich nicht notierte Werte; **~-board securities** *(US)* amtlich nicht notierte Werte; **~-board trading** *(US)* Handel in amtlich nicht notierten Werten; **~-brand** nicht markengebunden; **~-cast** abgetane Sache; **~ chance** schwache Möglichkeit, geringe Chance; **to be on the ~ chance** fast keine Chance haben; **~ charges** abzurechnende Kosten; **~ colo(u)r** nicht in Ordnung, indisponiert; **for ~ consumption** *(alcoholics, Br.)* zum Mitnehmen; **~ day** freier Tag; **~ duty** dienstfrei, nicht im Dienst; **to leave a lot of spare ~-duty time on s. one's hands** jem. viel Freizeit lassen; **~-going crop** Ernte auf dem Halm; **~ issue** untergeordnete Nebenfrage; **~-the-job accident** Unfall außerhalb der Arbeitszeit; **~-the-job activities** Freizeitbeschäftigung; **~-licence** *(Br.)* Schankrecht (Schankausschank) über die Straße, Wein- und Spirituosengeschäft; **~-load** *(v.)* **passengers** Reisende aussteigen lassen; **~-loading** *(South Africa)* Entladung; **~-peak** außerhalb der Spitzenbelastung; **~ peak hours** Zeiten geringer Belastung, verkehrsschwache Stunden; **to provide ~-peak services to isolated villages** Fahrgelegenheit zu abgelegenen Plätzen außerhalb der Spitzenzeit des Verkehrs sicherstellen; **~-peak tariff** Nachtstromtarif; **to be on the ~ point** *(US)* auf dem Holzweg sein; **~ position** Ausschaltstellung; **~ print** Separat-, Sonderdruck; **~-reckoning** Abzug; **~-the-cuff response** aus dem Ärmel geschüttelte Antwort; **~-road vehicle** Geländefahrzeug; **~-season** stille (tote) Saison (Zeit), Vor- und Nachsaison; **~-season buy** Erwerb in der verkaufsarmen Zeit; **~-season fares** Tarif außerhalb der Saison; **~-side** *(bookkeeping)* Rückseite; **~-street parking** Parken auf Nebenstraßen; **~-street unloading** Abladen am Hintereingang; **~-time** Freizeit; **~ work** unbeschäftigt; **~ year** Fehljahr, *(US)* kein Präsidentenwahljahr; **in ~ years** in nicht so guten Jahren.

offal *(fig.)* Schund, Auswurf, *(rubbish)* Abfall.

offence, offense *(US)* *(affront)* Ärgernis, Anstoß, *(mil.)* Angriff, Aggression, *(punishable act)* Vergehen, Verstoß, strafbare Handlung, Straftat, Übertretung, Delikt, Gesetzesverletzung, Zuwiderhandlung;
in case of a fresh ~ im Wiederholungsfall; **in case of a second ~** im Rückfall;
capital ~ Kapitalverbrechen; **~ charged with** zur Last gelegte Handlung; **coinage ~** Münzvergehen; **~ committed** vollendete Straftat; **continuing ~** Dauerstraftat; **criminal ~** strafbare Handlung; **currency ~** Devisenvergehen; **customs ~** Zollvergehen; **disciplinary ~** Dienst-, Disziplinarvergehen; **economic ~** Wirtschaftsverbrechen; **first ~** Straftat eines Ersttäters; **fiscal ~** Zollhinterziehung; **hit-and-run ~** Fahrerflucht; **indictable ~** *(Br.)* schweres Vergehen, Schwurgerichtssache; **juvenile ~** Jugendstraftat; **matrimonial ~** ehewidriges Verhalten, Ehewidrigkeit; **minor ~** geringfügiges Vergehen, Bagatelldelikt; **motoring ~** *(Br.)* Verkehrsübertretung, -delikt; **pecuniary ~** mit Geldstrafe belegte Übertretung; **petty ~** *(Br.)* Übertretung, *(US)* Straftat mit geringer Strafandrohung; **police ~** Übertretung von Polizeivorschriften; **political ~** politische Straftat, Verstoß gegen die öffentliche Ordnung; **punishable ~** strafbare Handlung; **revenue ~** Steuerdelikt, -straftat, Zolldelikt; **same ~** bereits abgeurteilte Straftat; **second ~** Rückfallvergehen; **statutory ~** strafbare Handlung; **summary ~** *(Br.)* Bagatellsache; **tax ~** Übertretung von Steuerbestimmungen, Steuerdelikt; **trifling ~** Bagatelldelikt;
criminal ~ under bankruptcy law Konkursdelikt; **~ against decency** Anstandsverstoß; **~ against the law** Gesetzesverstoß; **~ against good manners** schlechtes Benehmen, gesellschaftliche Entgleisung; **~ against the neighbo(u)rhood** Belästigung der Nachbarschaft; **~ against a person** körperlicher Angriff; **against property** Eigentumsvergehen; **~s against public order** *(US)* Erregung eines öffentlichen Ärgernisses; **~ against property** *(US)* Eigentumsvergehen; **~ against a Revenue Statute** Steuerdelikt; **~ under the Road Traffic Acts** Ordnungswidrigkeit gegen das Straßenverkehrsgesetz, Verkehrsvergehen, -delikt;
to admit an ~ Straftat eingestehen; **to be quick to take ~** leicht beleidigt sein; **to cause ~ to s. o.** j. kränken, jem. Kränkungen zufügen; **to commit an ~ against the law** Gesetzübertretung (Straftat) begehen, sich vergehen; **to commit an ~ against s. one's rights** jds. Rechte beeinträchtigen (verletzen); **to commit**

an ~ **against good taste** gegen den guten Geschmack verstoßen; **to constitute an** ~ strafbare Handlung darstellen; **to give** ~ Anstoß erregen, beleidigen, ärgern; **to give no** ~ keinen Angriffspunkt bieten; **to mean no** ~ j. nicht verletzen wollen; **to report an** ~ Straftat anzeigen; **to take** ~ Anstoß nehmen, beleidigt sein; **to take** ~ **at the slightest thing** sofort beleidigt sein.

offend (v.) verletzen, beleidigen, (law) verstoßen, zuwiderhandeln, sich vergehen;

~ **against decency** Anstandsgefühl verletzen; ~ **the eye** Beleidigung für das Auge darstellen; ~ **against grammar** Grammatikfehler machen; ~ **against the law of courtesy** gegen die Gesetze der Höflichkeit verstoßen; ~ **against good manners** schlechtes Benehmen darstellen; ~ **morals** gegen die Moralgesetze verstoßen; ~ **public policy** gegen die guten Sitten verstoßen; ~ **one's sense of justice** sein Gerechtigkeitsgefühl verletzen; ~ **against tradition** gegen die Tradition verstoßen.

offended, easily leicht (sofort) beleidigt;
in an ~ **tone of voice** mit beleidigter Stimme.

offender Gesetzesübertreter, [Misse]täter, Straftäter;
chief ~ Haupttäter; **first** ~ Ersttäter, nicht Vorbestrafter; **habitual persistent** ~ (Br.) Gewohnheitsverbrecher; **juvenile (youthful)** ~ jugendlicher Straftäter; **petty** ~ (US) Übertreter; **political** ~ politischer Verbrecher; **second** ~ (US) rückfälliger Täter, Rückfälliger, Rückfalltäter;
to be a hardened ~ hartgesottener Verbrecher sein;
First ⚥s **Act** Ersttätergesetz.

offense (US) → **offence.**

offensive (mil.) Offensive, Angriff[shandlung];
major ~ Großoffensive; **peace** ~ Friedensoffensive; ~ **of détente** Entspannungsoffensive;
to take the ~ Offensive ergreifen;
~ (a.) verletzend, beleidigend, anstößig, Ärgernis erregend, (aggressive) angreifend, offensiv;
to be ~ **to s. o.** j. beleidigen; **to mount an** ~ Offensive starten; **to throttle an** ~ Offensive abwürgen;
~ **alliance** Angriffsbündnis; ~ **answer** beleidigende Antwort; **to give an** ~ **answer** grob antworten; ~ **and defensive arms** Angriffs- und Verteidigungswaffen; ~ **conduct** ungehöriges Benehmen; ~ **language** Beschimpfungen; ~ **and defensive league** Angriffs- und Verteidigungsbündnis; ~ **strike** Angriffs-, Kampfstreik; **in an** ~ **tone** in einem beleidigenden Ton; ~ **trade** (Br.) Anstoß erregendes Gewerbe, belästigender Gewerbebetrieb; ~ **war** Angriffskrieg; ~ **weapon** Angriffswaffe; ~ **words** ungehörige Worte.

offer Offerte, Angebot, Vorschlag, Anerbieten, Vertrags-, Verkaufsangebot, (bid) gebotener Preis, (stock exchange) Angebot, Brief;
according to (as per) ~ offertegemäß; **at the best possible** ~ bestens; **on** ~ verkäuflich, zu verkaufen, zum Kauf angeboten, im Angebot, (stock exchange) Brief, angeboten;
abundant ~s reichhaltiges Angebot; **attractive** ~ reizvolles Angebot; **best** ~ Meist-, Höchstgebot; **binding** ~ festes Angebot, Festangebot, verbindliche Offerte; **not binding** ~ freibleibendes Angebot; **bona-fide** ~ solides Angebot; **buried** ~ in einer Anzeige verstecktes Angebot; **cabled** ~ Kabelangebot; **cash** ~ Bargebot; **combination** ~ gekoppeltes Angebot; **compatible** ~ vergleichbares Angebot; **comprehensive** ~ umfassendes Angebot; **compromise** ~ Vergleichsvorschlag; **contractor's** ~ Lieferangebot, Submission; **definitive** ~ festes Angebot; **exceptional** ~ Vorzugsangebot; **few** ~s (stock exchange) spärliches Angebot; **firm** ~ festes Angebot, Festangebot, verbindende Offerte; **flat** ~ (US) freibleibende (unverbindliche) Offerte; **free** ~ freibleibendes Angebot; **freight** ~ Angebot am Frachtenmarkt; **general** ~ Auslobung, öffentliches Angebot; **hidden** ~ verstecktes Angebot; **higher** ~ höheres Angebot; **highest** ~ Höchstgebot; **implied** ~ stillschweigendes Angebot; **industrial** ~ kaufmännisches Angebot; **liberal** ~ großzügiges Angebot; **noncompetitive** ~ nicht wettbewerbskonformes Angebot; **open** ~ freibleibendes Angebot, freibleibende Offerte; **original** ~ ursprüngliches Angebot; **positive** ~ festes Angebot; **preferential (preference)** ~ Vorzugsangebot; **sample[d]** ~ bemustertes Angebot; **special** ~ Sonder-, Vorzugsangebot; **standing** ~ gleichbleibendes Angebot; **subscription** ~ Zeichnungsaufforderung, Einladung zur Zeichnung, Subskriptionsangebot; **take-over** ~ Übernahmeangebot; **telegraphic** ~ telegrafisches Angebot, Drahtofferte; **tempting** ~ bestechendes (verlockendes) Angebot; **unconditional** ~ vorbehaltsloses Angebot; **valid** ~ gültige Offerte; **verbal** ~ mündliches Angebot; **voluntary** ~ unverlangtes Angebot, spontanes Angebot;
~ **and acceptance** Angebot und Annahme; ~ **of amends** (Br.) Angebot der Wiedergutmachung, Schadensersatzvorschlag; ~

of appointment Stellenangebot; ~ **of assistance** Unterstützungsangebot; ~ **in blank** Blankooferte; ~ **to buy** Kaufgesuch, -offerte; ~ **without commitment** unverbindliche (freibleibende) Offerte; ~ **of compromise** Vergleichsvorschlag, -angebot; ~ **for delivery** Lieferangebot, -offerte; ~ **of employment** Stellenangebot; ~ **without engagement** freibleibende (unverbindliche) Offerte, freibleibendes Angebot; ~ **of help** Hilfsangebot; ~ **of indemnity** Garantieangebot; ~ **of marriage** Heiratsantrag; ~ **of mediation** Schlichtungsvorschlag, Vermittlungsvorschlag, -angebot; ~ **without obligation** freibleibendes Angebot; ~ **by preference** Vorzugsangebot; ~ **to the public** öffentliches Angebot, Auslobung; ~ **of purchase** Kaufofferte; ~ **to repair goods** Reparaturangebot; ~ **to resign** angebotene Demission; ~ **of security [for an individual]** Bürgschaftsangebot; ~ **to sell (for sale)** Verkaufsangebot, -offerte; ~ **to sell property** Grundstücksofferte; ~ **of service** Geschäftsempfehlung; ~ **subject to prior sale (subject unsold)** freibleibendes Angebot, Zwischenverkauf vorbehalten; ~ **for subscription** Zeichnungsangebot; ~ **of suretyship** Bürgschaftsangebot; ~ **made to the world at large** an die Allgemeinheit gerichtetes Angebot, Auslobung;
~ (v.) (propose) anbieten, Angebot machen, offerieren, (express readiness) sich erbieten;
~ **s. th. to s. o.** jem. etw. antragen; ~ **an apology** seine Entschuldigung anbieten; ~ **assistance** Hilfsangebot machen; ~ **bail** Sicherheit anbieten; ~ **bills for discount** Wechsel zum Diskont einreichen; ~ **o. s. as candidate** kandidieren, sich als Kandidat in Vorschlag bringen; ~ **as a compromise** Vergleichsangebot machen; ~ **without engagement** unverbindlich offerieren; ~ **English as one of one's foreign languages** Englisch als fremdsprachliches Prüfungsfach wählen; ~ **an excuse** Entschuldigung vorbringen; ~ **firm** fest anbieten (offerieren); ~ **one's flank to the enemy** dem Feind eine offene Flanke zeigen; ~ **goods at 15 per cent off the regular price** Waren 15% unter Preis anbieten; ~ **goods for sale** Waren zum Verkauf anbieten; ~ **guarantee** (Br.) Bürgschaft leisten, Delkredere stehen; ~ **one's hand** seine Hand ausstrecken; ~ **s. o. a house for $ 40.000** jem ein Haus zum Preis von 40.000 Dollar anbieten; ~ **a job** Stellung anbieten; ~ **a loan** Kreditofferte machen; ~ **s. o. money** jem. Geld anbieten; ~ **an opinion** Meinung äußern, Stellungnahme vorbringen; ~ **a plea** Einrede erheben; ~ **o. s. for a post** sich für eine Stellung in Vorschlag bringen; ~ **a price** bieten, Preisangebot machen; ~ **no prospects** (job) aussichtslos sein; ~ **a remark** Bemerkung machen; ~ **[no] resistance** [keinen] Widerstand leisten; ~ **a resolution** Resolutionsentwurf vorlegen; ~ **a reward** Belohnung aussetzen; ~ **a salary** Gehaltsangebot machen; ~ **for sale** zum Verkauf anbieten, offerieren, feilbieten; ~ **one's services to s. o.** jem. seine Dienste anbieten; ~ **new shares to the holders of old ones** den Inhabern alter Aktien neue Aktien anbieten; ~ **to strike s. o.** Hand gegen j. erheben; ~ **for subscription** zur Zeichnung auflegen; ~ **a suggestion** Vorschlag machen; ~ **violence to s. o.** jem. mit Gewalt drohen;
to accept an ~ Angebot annehmen; **to avail o. s. of an** ~ von einem Angebot Gebrauch machen, einem Angebot nähertreten; **to be open to an** ~ Angebot entgegennehmen, auf Preisangebote warten; **to close with an** ~ Angebot annehmen; **to communicate an** ~ Angebot übermitteln; **to decline an** ~ Angebot ablehnen; **to decline an** ~ **as it stands** augenblickliches Angebot ablehnen; **to embrace s. one's** ~ jds. Angebot annehmen; **to entertain an** ~ einem Angebot nähertreten; **to hold an** ~ **open** Angebot aufrechterhalten; **to improve on s. one's** ~ sich jds. Angebot zunutze machen; **to invite an** ~ zur Abgabe eines Angebots auffordern; **to make an** ~ Offerte abgeben, offerieren; **to make a firm** ~ fest an die Hand geben; **to make an** ~ **orally** mündliches Angebot machen; **to make an** ~ **in writing** schriftliches Angebot machen; **to rebut s. one's** ~ jds. Angebot zurückweisen; **to refuse an** ~ Angebot ablehnen; **to reject an** ~ Angebot ablehnen (ausschlagen); **to revoke an** ~ Angebot zurückziehen; **to set aside an** ~ Angebot ablehnen; **to snatch at an** ~ Angebot schnellstens (sofort) annehmen; **to stick on an** ~ auf einem Angebot sitzenbleiben; **to submit** ~s Angebote unterbreiten, Offerten vorlegen; **to take an** ~ Bestellung annehmen; **to vary the terms of an** ~ Angebotsbedingungen abändern; **to withdraw an** ~ Angebot zurückziehen;
~ **price** Angebotspreis, (investment certificate) Ausgabepreis, Ausgabekurs, (stock exchange) Briefkurs.

offered, freely stark angeboten, **nothing** ~ (market report) fehlt; **position** ~ Angebot am Arbeitsmarkt, angebotene Stelle; ~ **down** (US) unter der letzten Notierung angeboten; ~ **firm** fest angeboten; ~ **subject to prior sale** Zwischenverkauf vorbehalten.

offeree Angebotsadressat, Empfänger eines Angebots.

offerer, offeror Anbieter;

highest ~ Höchst-, Meistbietender; **no ~s** *(auction)* ohne Angebote.

offering Angebot, Anerbieten, *(church)* Kollekte;

~s *(stock exchange, US)* Material, Angebot;

ample ~s reichhaltiges Angebot; **few ~s** spärliches Angebot; **peace** ~ Friedensangebot; **unfilled jobs** ~ Angebot (Ausschreibung) offener Stellen;

~ of bribes Bestechungsversuch;

~ **book (list)** *(stockbroker)* Angebotsbuch; ~ **date** Verkaufstermin; ~ **price** Submissions-, Angebotspreis, *(investment trust)* Ausgabe-, Verkaufspreis; ~ **sheet** *(US)* Angebotsliste einer Bank für den Verkauf von Effektenemissionen.

offertory *(church)* Geldopfer, Almosen.

offhand spontan, unvorbereitet, auf der Stelle, aus dem Stegreif (Handgelenk);

to be ~ about s. th. nicht viel Aufhebens von etw. machen; **to speak** ~ ohne Manuskript (unvorbereitet, frei, aus dem Stegreif) reden;

in an ~ manner nur ganz beiläufig; **to treat s. o. in an ~ manner** j. lässig behandeln; ~ **remarks** unüberlegte Bemerkungen; ~ **sale** freihändiger Verkauf; ~ **speech** völlig unvorbereitete Rede, Stegreifrede.

offhanded *(off the cuff)* aus dem Stegreif.

offhandedness Lässigkeit.

office *(branch)* Zweigniederlassung, *(bureau)* Büro, Geschäftszimmer, Kanzlei, Geschäftsstelle, Amtszimmer, -raum, Kontor, *(duty)* Aufgabe, Funktion, Dienst, *(governmental agency)* Amt, Dienststelle, Behörde, *(governmental office)* Amtszimmer, -gebäude, *(life insurance company, Br.)* Versicherungsgesellschaft, *(Ministry, Br.)* Ministerium, *(official position)* Amt, amtliche Stellung, Amtstätigkeit, Posten, *(profession)* Geschäft, Beruf, *(religion)* Gottesdienst[ordnung], *(seat)* Sitz, *(service)* Dienst, *(sl.)* Wink, Tip, *(solicitor, Br.)* Anwaltskanzlei, -büro, *(staff)* Büropersonal;

before taking ~ vor dem Amtsantritt; **in virtue of his** ~ kraft seines Amtes; **on accepting** ~ bei Amtsübernahme; **through the good ~s of a friend** durch die gütige Vermittlung eines Freundes; **upon entering into** ~ bei Amts-, Dienstantritt;

~s Büro-, Geschäftsräume, *(branches)* Zweigstellen, *(outbuildings, Br.)* Nebengebäude, Wirtschaftsräume;

advisory ~ Beratungsstelle; **audit** ~ Rechnungshof; **billeting** ~ Quartieramt; **booking** ~ Fahrkartenschalter, Vorverkauf[s-kasse-, stelle]; ~ **box** Schalter, [Theater]kasse; **branch** ~ Filialbüro, Filiale, Außen-, Neben-, Zweigstelle, Niederlassung; **burdensome** ~ schweres Amt; **business** ~ kaufmännisches Büro; **cash** ~ Kasse; **central** ~ Hauptbüro, -geschäftsstelle, Zentrale, Zentralbüro; **chief** ~ Hauptbüro; **civil** ~ Zivildienststelle; **clearing** ~ Abrechnungsstelle; **competent** ~ zuständige Stelle; **complaints** ~ Büro für Reklamationen, Beschwerdestelle; **county** ~ Grafschaftsamt; **court's** ~ Geschäftsstelle [des Gerichts]; **director's** ~ Direktion; **dispatching** ~ Abfertigungsstelle; **distributing** ~ *(post office)* Verteiler-, Postverteilungsstelle; **district** ~ *(US)* Bezirksbüro, -agentur [einer Bank]; **drawing** ~ technisches Büro, Konstruktionsbüro; **emigration** ~ Auswandererbüro; **Excise** ☖ Regieverwaltung; **executive** ~ leitende Dienststelle; **field** ~ Außenstelle; **fire [insurance]** ~ *(Br.)* Feuerversicherungsgesellschaft; **fiscal** ~ Finanzamt; **Foreign** ☖ *(Br.)* Auswärtiges Amt; **forwarding** ~ Versand-, Expeditionsabteilung; ~ **found** *(jury, Br.)* Befund; **freight** ~ Frachtbüro; **general** ~ Zentralbüro, Zentrale; **general post** ~ Hauptpostamt; **General Registry** ☖ *(Br.)* Standesamt; **good ~s** Freundschaftsdienst; **government** ~ Regierungsstelle, öffentliches Amt, *(Br.)* Ministerium, *(building)* Regierungsgebäude; **head** ~ Hauptgeschäftsstelle; ~ **held** bekleidetes Amt; **Home** ☖ *(Br.)* Ministerium des Inneren, Innenministerium; **honorary** ~ Ehrenamt; **incompatible ~s** nicht gleichzeitig zu bekleidende Ämter; **inland revenue** ~ *(Br.)* Steuerbehörde, Finanzamt; **inquiry** ~ Informations-, Auskunftsbüro, -stelle; **insurance** ~ *(Br.)* Versicherungsbüro, -anstalt, -gesellschaft; **intelligence** ~ Auskunftsstelle; **issuing** ~ Ausgabestelle; **international labo(u)r** ~ internationales Arbeitsamt; **judicial** ~ richterliches Amt; **land** ~ *(Br.)* Grundbuchamt; **lawyer's** ~ Anwaltsbüro, -kanzlei; **legal-aid** ~ Rechtsberatungsstelle; **life** ~ *(Br.)* Lebensversicherungsanstalt; **little domestic ~s** kleine häusliche Verrichtungen; **local** ~ örtliche Niederlassung; **lost-property** ~ Fundbüro; **lucrative** ~ einträgliche Pfründe; **luggage** ~ *(Br.)* Gepäckannahme, -aufbewahrung; **main** ~ *(US)* Hauptstelle, -geschäftsstelle, -verwaltung, -niederlassung, Zentrale; **manager's** ~ Direktion; **metropolitan** ~ Stadtbüro; **military** ~ mili-

tärische Dienststelle; **ministerial** ~ Ministeramt, -stelle, nachgeordnete (weisungsgebundene) Behörde, Verwaltungsstelle; **notary's** ~ Notariatsbüro; **open-plan** ~ Großraumbüro, Büro nach dem Raumgliederungssystem; **our London** ~ unser Büro in London; **parcel** ~ Paketpostamt; **passport** ~ Paßstelle; **patent** ~ Patentamt; **pawnbroker's** ~ Leihamt, -haus; **pay** ~ Zahlmeisterei; **paying** ~ Zahlstelle; **payroll** ~ Lohnbüro; **permanent** ~ ständiges Büro; **police** ~ Polizeipräsidium; **political** ~ politische Amtsstelle; **porter's** ~ Portiersloge; **post** ~ Postamt; **principal** ~ Hauptsitz einer Firma, Hauptgeschäftsstelle, Zentrale; **private** ~ Privatbüro, -kontor; **public** ~ öffentliches Amt, Staatsamt; **rating** ~ Prämienberechtigungsstelle; **real-estate** ~ Immobilienbüro; **receiving** ~ [Paket]annahmestelle; **reception** ~ Empfangsbüro; **record** ~ Gerichtskanzlei; **Public Record** ☖ *(Br.)* Staatsarchiv; **recruiting** ~ Rekrutierungsbüro; **main regional** ~ Kopffiliale; **registered** ~ Firmensitz, *(of a company)* eingetragener Geschäftssitz; **registry** ~ Stellenvermittlungsbüro; **revenue** ~ Staatskasse; **salaried** ~ besoldetes Amt; **secretary's** ~ Sekretariat; **shipping** ~ *(US)* Versand-, Speditionsbüro; **statutory** ~ *(US)* Büroadresse; **sub-~** Zweigstelle, -büro; **subsidiary** ~ nachgeordnete Dienststelle; **superintendent's** ~ Betriebsbüro; **tax** ~ Finanzamt; **telegraph** ~ Telegrafenamt; **ticket** ~ Fahrkartenschalter; **vacant** ~ freie Stelle; **vital statistics** ~ *(US)* Standesamt; **war** ~ Kriegsministerium;

~, factory and other buildings Geschäfts-, Fabrik- und andere Bauten;

~ **of auditors** Revisorenamt; ☖ **of Business Economics** *(US)* Statistisches Bundesamt; ☖ **of Censorship** Zensurbehörde; ~ **of a chairman** Amt des Vorsitzenden, Präsidentenamt; ☖ **of the Chancellor of the Exchequer** *(Br.)* Finanzministerium; **~s of a court** Amtsräume eines Gerichts; **receiver's** ~ **for the customs** Zollabfertigungsstelle; **~s for the dead** Totenmesse; ~ **of delivery** Zustellungspostamt; ~ **of destination** Bestimmungspostamt; ~ **of director** Vorstandsposten; ~ **of dispatch** Abfertigungsstelle, *(post office)* Abgangs-, Aufgabeamt; ☖ **of Education** *(US)* Unterrichtsministerium; ☖ **of Emergency Preparedness** *(US)* Technische Nothilfe; ~ **for fair trading** *(Br.)* Preisbindungsstelle, Kartellamtsbehörde; ~ **of hono(u)r** Ehrenamt; ~ **of host** Gastgeberfunktion; ~ **of issue** *(post office, Br.)* Ausgabestelle; ~ **of a judge** Richteramt; ☖ **of the Land Registry** *(Br.)* Grundbuchamt; ~ **for life** lebenslängliches Amt; ~ **of management and budget** *(US)* Haushalt- und Verwaltungsbüro, Haushaltsbehörde; ~ **of origin** Aufgabepostamt; ~ **of payment** *(Br.)* Zahl-, Auszahlungsstelle, -postamt; ~ **of posting** *(Br.)* Aufgabepostamt; ☖ **of the President** *(US)* Präsidialkanzlei; ☖ **of Price Administration** *(US)* Preisprüfungsamt; ~ **of Price Stabilization** Preisausgleichsamt; ~ **of the registrar of deeds** *(US)* Grundbuch[amt]; ~ **for reservation of seats** Platzkartenschalter; ~ **of science and technological policy** *(US)* Dienststelle für wissenschaftliche und technologische Entwicklungen; ~ **of trustee** Treuhänderamt; ~ **on wage and price stability** *(US)* Lohn- und Preisüberwachungsstelle; ~ **of fair trading** Preisbindungsamt; ☖ **of Works** Gebäudeunterhaltungsbehörde;

to accede to an ~ Amt antreten; **to accept** ~ Amt annehmen; **to act in virtue of one's** ~ in amtlicher Eigenschaft handeln (tätig werden); **to aim at** ~ Ministerium anstreben; **to apply at the** ~ sich im Büro melden; **to appoint s. o. to an office** j. in ein Amt berufen; **to assign s. o. to an** ~ j. einer Dienststelle zuteilen; **to assume an** ~ Amt übernehmen; **to be ambitious of** ~ Ministerium anstreben; **to be called to** ~ ins Ministerium berufen werden; **to be in** ~ im Amte sein, amtieren, [öffentliches] Amt bekleiden, *(political party)* an der Macht (am Ruder) sein, in der Regierung sitzen; **to be firmly in** ~ fest im Sattel sitzen; **to be in** ~ **on good behavio(u)r** Amt auf Bewährung innehaben; **to be out of** ~ *(political party)* in der Opposiiton sein, nicht mehr Regierungschef sein; **to be in charge of an** ~ einem Amt vorstehen; **to be in charge of an** ~ **pro tempore** Amt zeitweilig innehaben; **to be swept back into** ~ wieder zum Regierungschef gewählt werden; **to be working in an** ~ Büroarbeit verrichten; **to bear an** ~ Amt innehaben; **to bring an** ~ **up to date** Büro modernisieren; **to cease to hold** ~ aus dem Amt ausscheiden; **to cling onto** ~ sich an sein Amt klammern; **to come into** ~ *(Br.)* Amt antreten (übernehmen), *(minister)* Ministerium übernehmen, *(party)* zur Macht kommen; **to continue in one's** ~ in seinem Amt verbleiben; **to depose from** ~ des Amtes entheben; **to deprive s. o. of his** ~ j. seines Amtes entheben; **to divest o. s. of an** ~ von einem Amt zurücktreten; **to do s. o. a good** ~ jem. einen guten Dienst leisten; **to ease out of** ~ aus dem Amt verdrängen; **to elect to an** ~ in ein Amt wählen; **to entor upon** ~ Amt (Stellung) antreten; **to establish s. o. in an** ~ j. in ein Amt einführen; **to execute an** ~ Amt verwalten (ausüben); **to extend the term of** ~ Amtszeit verlängern; **to give s. o. the** ~ *(sl.)* jem. einen Tip geben; **to go to the** ~ ins Geschäft gehen; **to hold an** ~ Amt innehaben (bekleiden); **to hold all the** ~**s of a club** alle Klubämter auf sich vereinigen; **to hold a plurality of** ~**s** mehrere Ämter auf sich vereinigen; **to institute s. o. in an** ~ j. in ein Amt einsetzen; **to invest s. o. with an** ~ j. mit einem Amt bekleiden; **to lay down an** ~ von seinem Amt zurücktreten; **to leave** ~ demissionieren; **to locate a new** ~ neues Büro errichten; **to look in at the** ~ kurz im Büro hereinschauen; **to maintain an** ~ Büro unterhalten; **to maintain s. o. in** ~ j. im Amt belassen; **to name s. o. to an** ~ j. für ein Amt vorschlagen; **to offer one's good** ~**s** seine guten Dienste anbieten; **to operate own** ~**s throughout the world** eigene Büros in der ganzen Welt unterhalten; **to oust a rival from** ~ Konkurrenten aus einer Stellung verdrängen; **to perform the** ~ **of secretary** im Sekretariat tätig (Sekretär[in]) sein; **to perform the last** ~**s for s. o.** jem. die letzten Ehren erweisen; **to recall s. o. to an** ~ j. wieder in ein Amt berufen; **to relieve s. o. of his** ~ j. seines Amtes entheben, j. aus einem Amt entlassen; **to relinquish** ~ Amt abgeben; **to remain in** ~ im Amt bleiben; **to remove from** ~ aus dem Dienst entlassen; **to falsely represent o. s. to be a person holding** ~ **under Her Majesty** *(Br.)* Amtsanmaßung begehen; **to resign one's** ~ von seinem Amt zurücktreten, sein Amt niederlegen; **to retain s. o. in his** ~ jem. in seinem Amt belassen; **to run for an** ~ *(US)* sich um eine Stellung bewerben, sich als Kandidat aufstellen lassen; **to serve in an** ~ Amt ausfüllen; **to share an** ~ **with s. o.** Bürogemeinschaft mit jem. unterhalten; **to staff an** ~ Büropersonal engagieren; **to stand for an** ~ kandidieren; **to strip s. o. of his** ~ j. seines Amtes entsetzen (entkleiden); **to succeed to s. one's** ~ jem. im Amt nachfolgen; **to suspend s. o. from an** ~ j. seines Amtes vorläufig entheben, Beamten suspendieren; **to take** ~ Amt antreten (übernehmen), *(minister)* Ministerium übernehmen; **to take** ~**s** Büroräume mieten; **to take the** ~ *(sl.)* Tip befolgen; **to sweep a party back into** ~ Partei wieder an die Macht bringen; **to undertake an** ~ Amt übernehmen; **to vacate an** ~ aus dem Amt ausscheiden; **to work in an** ~ im Büro arbeiten, Büroangestellter sein;

~ **accommodation** Büroräume, -gebäude, -unterbringung; ⌐, **Shops and Railway Premises Act** *(Br.)* Gesetz zur Bereitstellung sicherer Arbeitsräume; ~ **allowance** Aufwandsentschädigung; ~ **appliances** Bürobedarfsartikel, -ausstattung; **[actual]** ~ **area** Büro[nutz]fläche; **pleasant** ~ **atmosphere** angenehmes Betriebsklima; ~ **automation** Automatisierung der Büroarbeit; ~ **bearer** Stellen-, Amtsinhaber, -träger, Amtsperson, Funktionär; ~ **block** Bürogebäude; ~ **bomb** Kassenknüller; ~ **book** amtliches Register; ~ **books** Geschäftsbücher; ~ **boy** Laufbursche, -junge, Bürodiener, -gehilfe; ~ **boy** *(v.)* Laufjunge sein; ~ **building** Bürohaus, -gebäude, Geschäftsgebäude, Bürobauten; ~ **building boom** Bürobautenkonjunktur; ~ **building tenant** Mieter eines Bürogebäudes; ~ **burglary insurance** gewerbliche Einbruchsversicherung; ~ **call** *(doctor)* Konsultation in der Praxis, Praxisaufsuche; ~ **car** Dienst-, Behördenfahrzeug; ~ **car park** Behördenparkplatz; ~ **chair** Bürostuhl; **to come under** ~ **charges** zu den Bürokosten gehören; ~ **circular** Dienstanweisung; ~ **clerk** Büroangestellter, Kontorist, Handlungsgehilfe; ~ **construction** Büroneubauten; ~ **copy** *(Br.)* beglaubigte Abschrift einer Urkunde, amtlich erteilte Abschrift (Ausfertigung); ~ **copy of the land register** *(Br.)* Grundbuchauszug; ~ **copy probe** *(Br.)* Abschrift eines Testamentsvollstreckerzeugnisses; ~ **day** Arbeitstag; ⌐ **Development Permit** *(Br.)* Genehmigungsbescheid für die Errichtung neuer Bürogewerbeflächen; ~ **equipment** Büroausstattung, -einrichtung, *(balance sheet)* Betriebs- und Geschäftsausstattung; ~~-**equipment firm** Bürobedarfsfirma; ~~-**equipment market** Büroartikelmarkt; ~ **executive** *(US)* leitender Angestellter; ~ **expense** Geschäfts-, Bürounkosten; ~ **extension** *(tel.)* Geschäftsanschluß; ~ **files** Geschäftsunterlagen; ~ **fittings** Büroeinrichtung; ~ **floor space** Büronutz[ungs]fläche; ~ **fixtures** Büroinventar; ~ **floater** *(US)* globale Versicherung der Büroeinrichtung; ~ **force** Bürokräfte, -personal; ~ **furnishing[s]** Büroeinrichtung; ~ **furniture** Büromöbel, -einrichtung; ~ **furniture and equipment** *(balance sheet)* Betriebs- und Geschäftsausstattung; ~ **girl** Büro-, Laufmädchen; ~ **glut** Überangebot an Büroräumen; ~ **gossip** Büroklatsch; ~ **grant** *(Br.)* Auflassung von Amts wegen; ~ **hands** *(US)* Büropersonal; ~ **host** Gastgeber im Büro; ~ **hours** Dienst-, Geschäfts-, Bürostunden, Geschäftszeit; **to correlate** ~ **hours** Amtsstunden angleichen; ~ **hunter** *(US)* Posten-, Stellenjäger; ~ **hunting** *(US)* Ämterskandal, Stellenjägerei; ~ **jobbing** Ämterhandel; ~ **keeper** Bürovorsteher; ~ **lawyer** *(US)* beratender Anwalt; ~ **layout** Büroausstattung; ~ **machine** Büro-

maschine; ~ **management** Büroleitung, -verwaltung, -organisation; ~ **management people** *(US)* leitende Angestellte; ~ **manager** leitender Angestellter, Büroleiter, -vorsteher; ~ **model** Bürogerät; ~ **operating** Bürobetrieb; ~~-**operating costs** Geschäfts-, Bürounkosten; ~ **organization** Büroorganisation; ~ **overheads** generelle Bürounkosten; ~ **paper** *(US)* Finanzierungswechsel; ~ **personnel** [Büro]personal; ~ **planner** Büroraumgestalter; ~ **planning** Bürogestaltung; ~ **politics** Machenschaften im Betrieb; ~ **practice** *(US)* Bürotätigkeit, *(chamber practice)* beratende Anwaltstätigkeit, anwaltliche Beratungspraxis; ~ **premises** Geschäftsgrundstück, -räume, Büroräume; ~ **premium** *(insurance, Br.)* Bruttoprämie einschließlich Verwaltungskostenzuschlag; ~ **procedure** Bürobetrieb; **general** ~ **procedure** allgemeiner Geschäftsgang; ~ **rent** Büromiete; ~ **requirements** Bürobedarf; ~ **requisites** Bürobedürfnisse; **to furnish** ~ **rooms** Büroraum zur Verfügung stellen; ~ **routine** gewöhnliche Büroarbeit, Geschäftsbetrieb, -praxis; **to be familiar with all** ~ **routine** mit allen Büroarbeiten vertraut sein; ~ **salaries** Angestellten-, Bürogehälter; ~ **seeker** *(US)* Postenjäger; ~~-**seeking politician** ämtersüchtiger (Ministerium anstrebender) Politiker; ~ **services** Bürotätigkeit; ~ **space** Büroraum; **unlet** ~ **space** unvermietete Büroräume; ~ **staff** Büropersonal; ~ **stamp book** Portokasse; ~ **stationery** Bürobedarf, -material; ~ **supplies** Bürobedarfsartikel; ~ **telephone** Büroanschluß; ~ **theft** Bürodiebstahl; ~ **tower** Bürohochhaus; ~ **typewriter** Büroschreibmaschine; ~ **typist** Bürostenotypist; ~ **use** Benutzung als Geschäftsraum, *(magazine)* Eigenverbrauch; **for** ~ **use** für Bürozwecke; ~ **wall** Bürowand; ~ **work** Bürotätigkeit, -arbeit, Innendienst; ~ **worker** Büroangestellter, -kraft.

officeholder *(US)* Amts-, Stelleninhaber, Amtsperson, Funktionär, Beamter.

officeholding *(US)* Staatsdienst.

officer *(administration)* Beamter, Angestellter, *(club)* Vorstandsmitglied, *(company)* leitender Angestellter, Direktor, *(mil.)* Offizier, *(police)* Polizist, Polizeibeamter, *(of society)* Funktionär;

while an ~ in dienstlicher Eigenschaft;

~**s** Vorstand;

administrative ~ Verwaltungsbeamter; **assignments** ~ Beamter der Personalabteilung; **bank** ~ Bankbeamter; **cabinet** ~ *(US)* Minister; **chief** ~ leitender Beamter; **civil** ~ *(US)* Verwaltungsbeamter, Staatsbediensteter; **clerical** ~ *(Br.)* Beamter des mittleren Dienstes; **chief** ~ *(county)* leitender Bediensteter; **control** ~ Aufsichtsbeamter; **corporate** ~ *(US)* leitender Angestellter [einer Aktiengesellschaft]; **customs** ~ Zollbeamter; **customhouse** ~ Zollbeamter; **commanding** ~ Befehlshaber, Kommandeur; **commissioner** ~ Offizier; **deck** ~ Deckoffizier; **duty** ~ *(mil.)* Offizier vom Dienst; **engine** ~ technischer Offizier; **established** ~ planmäßiger Beamter, Planstelleninhaber; **excise** ~ *(Br.)* Akziseneinnehmer; **executive** ~ *(US)* Vollzugsorgan, ausführendes Organ, Beamter (Angestellter) in leitender Stellung; **chief executive** ~ *(US)* Präsident eines Unternehmens; **field** ~ Außenbeamter; **first** ~ *(mar.)* erster Offizier; **fiscal** ~ Finanz-, Steuerbeamter; **foreign-service** ~ Beamter des Auswärtigen Dienstes; **forest** ~ Forstbeamter, Förster; **general** ~ *(mil.)* Offizier im Generalsrang; **governmental** ~ Regierungs-, Staatsbeamter; **local government** ~ *(Br.)* Kommunalbeamter; **group chief** ~ *(local government, Br.)* Dezernatsleiter; **half-pay** ~ zur Disposition gestellter Offizier; **health** ~ Beamter des Gesundheitsdienstes; **higher executive** ~ höherer Beamter; **immigration** ~ Einwanderungsbeamter; **incoming** ~ neu eintretender Beamter; **inferior** ~ untergeordneter Beamter; **investigating** ~ Ermittlungsbeamter; **judicial** ~ Justiz-, Gerichtsbeamter; **law** ~ *(legal)* Justizbeamter; **liaison** ~ Verbindungsoffizier; **local government** ~ *(Br.)* Kommunalbeamter; **medical** ~ Amtsarzt; **military** ~ Berufsoffizier; **ministerial** ~ Verwaltungsbeamter; **municipal** ~ *(US)* Kommunalbeamter; **naval** ~ Marineoffizier; **noncommissioned** ~ Unteroffizier; **orderly** ~ diensthabender Offizier; **peace** ~ Polizeibeamter; **permanent** ~ festangestellter Beamter; **perpetual** ~ unabsetzbarer Beamter; **highly placed** ~ hochgestellter Beamter; **police** ~ Polizeibeamter, Polizist; **preventive** ~ Zollfahndungsbeamter; **professional** ~ *(US)* Berufsoffizier; **public** ~ Staatsbeamter, Beamter im öffentlichen Dienst, *(stock banking company, Br.)* Justiziar; **quarantine** ~ Quarantänebeamter; **regimental** ~ Truppenoffizier; **regular** ~ Berufsoffizier; **relieving** ~ *(Br.)* Fürsorgebeamter, Sozialfürsorger; **reserve** ~ Reserveoffizier; **retired** ~ pensionierter Offizier; **returning** ~ *(Br.)* Wahlleiter; **revenue** ~ *(US)* Finanz-, Steuerbeamter; **second-ranking** ~ zweithöchster Beamter; **senior** ~ *(US)* leitender (rangältester) Angestellter; **senior and semi-senior level** ~**s** Angestellte im gehobenen und mittleren

Dienst; **serving** ~ aktiver Offizier; **sheriff's** ~ Gerichtsvollzieher; **staff** ~ Berater des Vorstands, Betriebsberater, *(mil.)* Stabsoffizier; **subordinate** ~ mittlerer Beamter, Subalternbeamter; **taxing** ~ Kostenfestsetzungsbeamter; **top-ranking** ~ leitender Beamter; **unestablished** ~ außerplanmäßiger Beamter; ~ **of a bank** leitender Bankangestellter; ~ **of the board** Vorstandsmitglied; ~ **in charge** Sachbearbeiter, zuständiger (beauftragter) Beamter, *(mil.)* Offizier vom Dienst; ~ **commanding a garrison** Standortältester; ~ **of a company (corporation,** US) [etwa] Vorstandsmitglied; [**single-managing**] ~ **of a corporation** [geschäftsführendes] Vorstandsmitglied; **~s and crew** Offiziere und Mannschaft; **paid** ~ **of a council** Kommunalbediensteter; ~ **in default** säumiges Vorstandsmitglied; ~ **on duty** diensthabender Offizier; ~ **de facto** faktischer Amtsinhaber; ~ **of Health** *(Br.)* Beamter des Gesundheitsdienstes; **medical** ~ **of health** Kreisarzt; ~ **of an insurance company** Versicherungsangestellter; ~ **de jure** festangestellter Staatsbeamter; ~ **of justice (of the law)** Justizbeamter, -angestellter; ~ **on the active list** aktiver Offizier; **~s and men** Offiziere und Soldaten; ~ **authorized to sign** mit Unterschriftsbefugnissen ausgestatteter Beamter; ~ **of a society** Vorstandsmitglied eines Vereins, **~s of a society** Vereinsvorstand; **~s and staff** leitende Angestelle und sonstiges Personal; ~ **of a state** höherer Staatsbeamter, Minister; ~ **authorized to take acknowledg(e)ment of deeds** Urkundsbeamter der Geschäftsstelle;

to hold two ~s in a corporation *(US)* zwei Vorstandsmitglieder haben; **to prefer an** ~ Offizier befördern; **to retire an** ~ **from the active list** aus der Liste der aktiven Offiziere streichen;

~'s commissioner *(mil.)* Offizierspatent; ~ **group** Offiziersgruppe; **~s' mess** Offiziersmesse, -kasino; **~s' training corps** Kriegsschule.

official Beamter, Angestellter, Funktionär;

administrative (administration) ~ Verwaltungsbeamter; **bank** ~ Bankbeamter; **city** ~ städtischer Beamter, Angestellter bei der Stadt; **court** ~ Gerichtsbeamter; **customs** ~ Zollbeamter; **ex** ~ abgegangener Beamter; **government[al]** ~ Regierungs-, Staatsbeamter; **high** ~ hoher Beamter; **high-administrative** ~ höherer Ministerialbeamter; **high-ranking** ~ höherer Beamter; **higher** ~ höherer Beamter; **higher-echelon** ~ Beamter des gehobenen Dienstes; **higher-grade** ~ höherer Beamter; **inactive** ~ untätiger Beamter; **key** ~ Beamter in einer Schlüsselposition; **key state** ~ erster Staatsdiener; **local public** ~ Kommunalbeamter; **minor** ~ untergeordneter (mittlerer) Beamter; **petty** ~ kleiner Beamter; **police** ~ Polizeibeamter; **policy-making** ~ Beamter in leitender Stellung; **post-office** ~ Postbeamter; **railway** ~ Eisenbahnbeamter; **top[-ranking]** ~ Spitzenkraft; **senior** ~ leitender Mitarbeiter; **senior [departmental]** ~ höherer [Ministerial]beamter; **supervisory (supervising)** ~ Aufsichtsbeamter; **tax** ~ Steuerbeamter; **trade union** ~ Gewerkschaftsfunktionär; **veteran** ~ im Dienst ergrauter Beamter;

~ **in charge** zuständiger Beamter, Sachbearbeiter; ~ **of the day** *(mil.)* Offizier vom Dienst; ~ **of whom residence is required** Beamter mit Residenzpflicht;

to axe a number of ~s radikalen Beamtenabbau durchführen; **to displace a government** ~ Staatsbeamten ablösen; **to move an** ~ Beamten versetzen; **to remove an** ~ Beamten absetzen; **to second an** ~ Beamten vorübergehend abstellen; **to supersede an** ~ Beamten ablösen;

~ *(a.)* behördlich, amtlich, amtsüblich, offiziell, dienstlich, *(authorized)* bevollmächtigt;
demi- ~ halbamtlich; **not** ~ offiziös; **quasi-~** halbamtlich; **semi-** ~ inoffiziös, halbamtlich;

~ **act** Amtshandlung; ~ **announcement** amtliche Verlautbarung; ~ **assignee [in bankruptcy]** behördlich bestellter Konkursverwalter; **to receive** ~ **attentions** amtlicherseits Beachtung finden; ~ **attire** Amtstracht; ~ **authorization** amtliche Genehmigung; ~ **bond** Kaution eines Staatsbeamten; ~ **business** dienstliche Angelegenheit, Dienstsache; ° **Business** *(US)* Dienstpost; **on** ~ **business** dienstlich; **to travel on** ~ **business** dienstlich unterwegs sein; ~ **business day** Börsentag; ~ **call** *(tel.)* Dienstgespräch; ~ **capacity** amtliche Funktion; **in one's** ~ **capacity** dienstlich, amtlich, in amtlicher Eigenschaft; **to act in one's** ~ **capacity** in amtlicher Eigenschaft tätig werden; ~ **career** Amtslaufbahn; ~ **ceremony** feierlicher Staatsakt; ~ **channels** Instanzen-, Dienstweg; ~ **character** Amtscharakter; ~ **communication** dienstliche Mitteilung; ~ **corruption** Ämterkorruption; ~ **denial** amtliches Dementi; ~ **description** Amtsbezeichnung; ~ **dinner** offizielles Essen; ~ **document** öffentliche Urkunde; ~ **duty** Dienstobliegenheit, Amts-, Dienstpflicht; ~ **emoluments** Dienstbezüge; ~ **exchange rate** amtlicher Wechsel-, Umrechnungskurs; ~ **family** *(US)* Präsidentenkabi-

nett; ~ **fees** amtliche Gebühren; ~ **figures** amtliche Zahlen; ~ **financing account** Devisenbilanz; ~ **function** Amts-, Diensthandlung; ~ **gazette** *(US)* Staatsanzeiger, Gesetz-, Amtsblatt; ° **Gazette of the European Communities** Amtsblatt der Europäischen Gemeinschaften; ~ **guide** amtlicher [Reise]führer; ~ **hours** Geschäfts-, Dienst-, Bürozeit, Amts-, Dienststunden, Öffnungszeiten, *(stock market)* Börsenstunden, -zeit; **after** ~ **hours** nach Börsenschluß; **before** ~ **hours** vorbörslich; ~ **inquiry** amtliche Untersuchung, amtliche Ermittlungen; ~ **instructions** Dienstvorschriften; ~ **journey** Dienstreise; ~ **language** Amtssprache; ~ **letter** amtliches Schreiben; ~ **list** *(stock exchange, Br.)* Liste der zum Börsenhandel zugelassenen Werte, amtliches Börsenblatt; ~ **listing** *(US)* offizielle Zulassung zum Börsenhandel; ~ **listing notice** *(stock exchange, US)* Zulassungsbescheid; ~ **machinery** Behördenapparat; ~ **mail** *(US)* Dienstpost; ~ **matter** dienstliche Angelegenheit, Dienstsache; ~ **messenger** Amts-, Kanzleibote; ~ **misconduct** Disziplinarvergehen; ~ **news** amtliche Mitteilungen; ~ **nomenclature** amtliche Bezeichnung; ~ **notice** amtliche Bekanntmachung, Amtsbescheid; ~ **oath** *(Br.)* Dienst-, Amtseid; ~ **opening** offizielle Eröffnung; ~ **organ** amtliches Organ; ~ **paid** *(Br.)* portofrei; ~ **position** amtliche Stellung, Beamtenstellung; ~ **powers** Amtsgewalt; ~ **price list** amtlicher Kurszettel; ~ **publication** amtliche Bekanntmachung; ~ **publicity bureau** Werbestelle; **from** ~ **quarters** von amtlicher Stelle; ~ **quotation** offizielle (amtliche) [Kurs]notierung; ~ **rate of discount** Bankdiskont, Diskontsatz; ~ **rate of exchange** amtlicher Umrechnungskurs; ~ **receiver** *(Br.)* behördlich bestellter [vorläufiger] Konkurs-, Zwangsverwalter, Sequester; ~ **record** amtliches Protokoll; ~ **records** amtliche Unterlagen; ~ **referee** Sachverständiger; ° **Register** *(US)* Gesetz-,Amtsblatt; ~ **regulations** Dienstvorschriften; ~ **religion** Staatsreligion; ~ **report** amtlicher Bericht, amtliche Meldung; ~ **representative** bevollmächtigter Vertreter; ~ **residence** Dienst-, Amtssitz; ~ **responsibility** Amtshaftung; ~ **seal** Dienst-, Amtssiegel; ~ **secrecy** Amtsverschwiegenheit; ~ **secret** Dienst-, Staats-, Amtsgeheimnis; **to hold an** ~ **situation** öffentliches Amt bekleiden; ~ **solicitor** *(court of chancery, Br.)* Amtspfleger; ~ **source** amtliche Quelle; ~ **spokesman** Pressesprecher; ~ **statement** amtliche Erklärung; **without any** ~ **status** ohne offiziellen Auftrag; **to be written in an** ~ **style** als Amtsschreiben abgefaßt sein; ~ **title** Amtsbezeichnung; ~ **tour (trip)** Dienstreise; ~ **trustee of charity lands** *(Br.)* Beamter des Stiftungsaufsichtsamtes; ~ **uniform** Dienstanzug; ~ **use only** nur für den Dienstgebrauch; ~ **valuation** zollamtliche Bezeichnung; ~ **version** amtliche Darstellung; ~ **wisdom** Amtsweisheit; ~ **year** Geschäftsjahr.

officialdom Beamtentum, -stand, -schaft, Bürokratie.
officialese Kanzlei-, Behördendeutsch, Amtssprache.
officiality amtlicher Charakter.
officialism Beamtentum, *(red tapism)* Bürokratismus, Amtsschimmel, Paragraphenreiterei.
officiality amtlicher Charakter.
officialize *(v.)* amtlich tätig werden, reglementieren.
officially von Amts wegen.
officialty Amtsbereich.
officiary amtlich, offiziell.
officiate *(v.)* amtieren, Amt versehen, Dienst verrichten, fungieren;
~ **as chairman** präsidieren, als Vorsitzender amtieren; ~ **as host** Gastgeber sein; ~ **as host at a dinner party** als Gastgeber bei einem Abendessen fungieren; ~ **at a marriage** Traugottesdienst abhalten.
officiation Amtswaltung.
officio, ex *(lat.)* von Amts wegen.
officious halbamtlich, offiziös, *(volunteering)* dienstbeflissen, übereifrig, zudringlich;
~ **will** Testament zugunsten der gesetzlichen Erben.
officiousness Dienstbeflissenheit, *(diplomatics)* offiziöses Gehaben, *(volunteering)* übertriebene Geschäftigkeit;
to smack of ~ *(letter)* nach Amtsdeutsch riechen.
offing, in the in einiger Zeit bevorstehend.
offish reserviert, zurückhaltend.
offprint Sonder-, Separatdruck.
offscourings of humanity Abschaum der Menschheit.
offset Gegenposten, -rechnung, -forderungen, Ausgleich, Ver-, Aufrechnung, Kompensation;
printed by ~ im Offsetverfahren gedruckt;
~s of savings Ersparnisverwendung;
~ *(v.)* aufwiegen, *(compensate, US)* kompensieren, ver-, aufrechnen, in Gegenrechnung bringen, ausgleichen, *(print.)* im Offsetverfahren drucken;

~ **against a claim** mit einem Anspruch aufrechnen; ~ **earlier losses** frühere Verluste ausgleichen, Verlustausgleich herbeiführen; ~ **the effects** die Wirkungen ausgleichen; ~ **the publisher's costs** Druckkostenrechnung decken, Deckungsauflage sicherstellen; ~ **a small salary by living economically** bescheidenes Gehalt durch sparsame Lebensweise kompensieren; **to be available for** ~ zur Verrechnung zur Verfügung stehen; **to be an** ~ **to a fault** Fehler ausgleichen;

~ **account** Verrechnungs-, Wertberichtigungs-, Gegenkonto; ~ **agreement** *(foreign exchange)* Verrechnungs-, Devisenausgleichsabkommen; ~ **allowance** Ausgleichsabzug; ~ **country** dem Verrechnungsabkommen angeschlossenes Land; ~ **credit** Verrechnungskredit; ~ **dollar** Verrechnungsdollar; ~ **lithography** Offsetdruck; ~ **paper** Umdruckpapier; ~ **payments** Devisenausgleichszahlungen; ~ **press** Offsetpresse; ~ **printing** Offsetdruck; ~ **printing inks** Offsetdruckfarben; ~ **process** *(print.)* Offsetverfahren; ~ **sheet** Durchschußbogen; ~ **transparency** Offsetfilm.

offsetting | **entry** Storno-, Änderungs-, Gegenbuchung; ~ **transaction** Verrechnungs-, Kompensationsgeschäft.

offshoot Seitenzweig, -linie, Abkömmling, *(branch)* Ableger, *(organization)* Unterorganisation;
all the ~**s of this policy** alle Nebenauswirkungen dieser Politik.

offshore vor der Küste gelegen, *(US)* im Ausland getätigt, *(wind)* ablandig;
~ **breeze** Landwind; ~ **currencies** *(US)* auswärtige (ausländische) Währungen; ~ **fields** in Küstennähe gelegene Ölfelder; ~ **fisheries** Tiefseefischerei; ~ **fund** *(US)* Kapitalanlagegesellschaft mit steuerfreiem Auslandssitz; ~ **mutual fund** *(US)* im Ausland vertriebener Investmentfonds; ~ **investment vehicle** *(US)* Medium für Auslandsinvestitionen; ~ **location** Auslandsbelegenheit; ~ **marshalling yard** ausländische Verteilerstelle; ~ **oil development** Erschließung küstennaher Ölvorkommen; ~ **order** *(US)* Auslands-, Rüstungs[hilfs]auftrag; ~ **purchases** *(US)* Auslandskäufe von Kriegsmaterial; ~ **real-estate fund** *(US)* im Ausland vertriebener Immobilienfonds; ~ **reserves** *(US)* Auslandsrücklagen; ~ **trade** *(US)* Auslandsgeschäft; ~ **waters** Küstengewässer; ~ **wind** Landwind.

offspring Abkommen, Nachkommen[schaft], Leibeserbe, Nachkömmling, Abkömmling.

offstage hinter der Bühne.

offtake *(deduction)* Abzug, *(purchase)* [Waren]einkauf.

oil Öl, Erd-, Mineralöl, Petroleum;
long in ~**s** mit hohem Ölgehalt;
~**s** *(stock exchange)* Erdölwerte;
animal ~ Knochen-, Tieröl; **burning** ~ Verbrennungsöl; **crude** ~ Erdöl; **engine** ~ Maschinenöl; **heating** ~ Heizöl; **imported** ~ Erdöleinfuhren, -importe; **lubricating** ~ Schmieröl; **machine** ~ Schmieröl; **mineral** ~ Erdöl; **vegetable** ~ pflanzliches Öl;
~ **and vinegar** wie Feuer und Wasser;
~ *(v.)* einölen, -fetten, mit Öl schmieren;
s. one's palm *(fam.)* j. schmieren (bestechen); ~ **the tongue** glattzüngig reden; ~ **the wheels** Karren schmieren;
to add ~ **to the fire (flames)** Öl aufs Feuer gießen; **to be heavy on** ~ *(engine)* viel Öl verbrauchen; **to burn the midnight** ~ bis spät in die Nacht arbeiten; **to consume a lot of** ~ *(car)* viel Öl verbrauchen; **to discharge** ~ Öl ablassen; **to give s. o. a little strap** ~ jem. eine Tracht Prügel verabreichen; **to paint in** ~**s** mit Ölfarben malen; **to pour** ~ **on the flames** Öl ins Feuer gießen; **to pour** ~ **on troubled waters** aufgeregte Gemüter beruhigen; **to prospect for** ~ nach Öl bohren; **to smell of [midnight]** ~ sehr nach Nachtarbeit riechen; **to strike** ~ auf ein Öllager (auf Erdöl) stoßen, *(fig.)* fündig werden, sehr erfolgreich sein, Glück haben; **to take** ~ **to extinguish water** Öl aufs Feuer gießen;
~ **affluence** Erdölüberfluß; ~ **barrel** Ölfaß; ~ **basin** [Erd]ölvorkommen; ~-**bearing** ölhaltig; ~ **burner** Ölbrenner; ~ **burning** Ölfeuerung; ~ **cake** Ölkuchen; ~ **cellar** Ölkeller; ~ **colo(u)r** Ölfarbe; ~ **company** Ölgesellschaft; ~ **concession** Erdölkonzession; ~ **consumer** *(car)* Ölverbraucher; ~-**consuming nation** Ölverbraucherland; ~ **consumption** Ölverbrauch; ~ **consumption test** Ölverbrauchstest; ~ **countries** Erdölländer; **to recycle the** ~ **countries' surplus into the world economy** Überschüsse der Erdölländer in den weltwirtschaftlichen Kreislauf zurückschleusen; ~ **crisis** Ölkrise; ~ **deficit** Erdöldefizit; ~ **demand** Erdölbedarf; ~ **deposit** Erdöllagerstätte, -vorkommen; ~ **derrick** Bohrturm; ~ **dipstick** Ölpeilstab; ~ **discovery** Erdölfund; ~ **exploration** Erdölbohrungen; ~ **export** Ölexport; ~ **exporter** Ölexportland, Ölausfuhrland; ~ **exporters** erdölexportierende Länder; ~-**exporting country** Erdölausfuhrland; ~ **facilities** Ölverwertungsanlagen; ~ **facility** *(International Monetary*

Funds) Erdölfazilitäten; ~ **field** Erdölfeld, -vorkommen; ~ **fuel** Heizöl; ~ **funds** Ölgelder; ~ **gauge** Ölstandsmesser; ~ **glut** überdimensionale Erdölangebote; ~ **heater** Ölheizung, -ofen; ~ **imports** Erdöleinfuhren, Öleinfuhr, -import; ~ **import quota** Öleinfuhrquote; ~ **industry** Erdölindustrie; ~ **interest(s)** Ölinteressen; ~ **lamp** Petroleumlampe; ~ **level** *(car)* Ölstand; ~ **market** Erdölmarkt; ~ **merchant** Ölhändler; ~ **ministry** Ölministerium; ~ **money** aus der Erdölindustrie stammende Mittel; **state** ~ **monopoly** staatliches Ölmonopol, Ölmonopol des Staates; ~ **occurrence** Erdölvorkommen; ~ **painting** Ölgemälde; ~ **pan** *(car)* Ölwanne; ~ **pipeline** Ölleitung; ~ **platform** Förderplattform, Bohrinsel; ~ **policy** Erdölpolitik; ~ **price** [Erd]ölpreis; **frozen** ~ **price** eingefrorener Erdölpreis; **Opec-fixed** ~ **price** von der Opec festgelegter Erdölpreis; ~ **price hike (increase)** Ölpreissteigerung, -anstieg, Ölpreiserhöhung; ~ **producer** Erdölproduzent; ~-**producing countries** Erdölförderländer; ~-**producing state** Erdölland; ~ **production** Erdölgewinnung, -förderung; ~ **prospector** Erdölsucher; ~ **pump** Ölpumpe; ~ **refining** Ölraffinierung; ~ **refining plant (refinery)** Ölraffinerie; ~ **reserves** Erdölreserven; ~ **reservoir** Ölvorkommen; ~ **rig** Bohrturm; ~ **rights** Erdölkonzession; ~ **sanctions** Ölboykott; ~ **sands** Ölsände; ~ **shares (stocks,** US**)** Ölaktien; ~ **shortage** Erdölverknappung; ~ **slick** Öllache, Ölfladen, -schlick, ausgelaufene Ölschicht, Ölteppich; ~ **spill** Öllache, Ölverseuchung; **to turn on the** ~ **spigot** Ölproduktion steigern; ~ **spring** Mineralölquelle; ~ **supply** Öllieferung, -zufuhr; ~ **surplus land** Erdölüberschußland; ~ **tank** Öltank; ~ **tanker** Tanker; ~ **tax revenue** Erdölsteuereinkünfte; ~ **territory** Erdölgebiet; ~ **varnish** Leinölfirnis; ~ **well** Ölbohrung, -quelle.

oilcan Ölkanister, *(sl.)* Versager.

oiler [Öl]tanker, *(oilcan)* Ölkanister.

oilhole Schmierloch.

oilman Unternehmen in der Ölbranche, Ölhändler, -produzent, *(US)* Delikateßwarenhändler.

oilproof ölundurchlässig, ölbeständig.

oilskin Ölanzug, -kleidung.

oilstove Ölofen.

ointment Salbe.

okay *(print., US)* Imprimatur;
~ *(v.) (US)* annehmen, gutheißen;
~ **a purchase** *(US)* Ankauf genehmigen;
~ *(a.)* gut, genehmigt, *(print., US)* druckreif;
~ **with corrections** nach Korrektur druckreif.

okie *(US sl.)* Wanderarbeiter.

old alt, altersschwach, *(long-standing)* althergebracht, lange bestehend, *(paper)* abgenutzt, vergilbt, *(past)* früher, vergangen, *(weakened from age)* verkalkt;
as ~ **as Adam (the hills)** ur-, steinalt, so alt wie Methusalem; ~ **and young** Alt und Jung, jedermann;
to be ~ **in crime** abgefeimter Verbrecher sein; **to be** ~ **in diplomacy** über langjährige diplomatische Erfahrungen verfügen; **to be** ~ **in sin** alter Sünder sein;
~-**acquainted** einander seit langem bekannt; **to cast off the** ~ **Adam** alte Unsitten aufgeben.

old age hohes Alter, Greisenalter,
to be saving for one's ~ für sein Alter zurücklegen; **to die at a good** ~ im hohen Alter sterben; **to live to an** ~ hohes Alter erreichen; **to make provision for** ~ Altersvorsorge treffen.

old-age | **annuity** Alters-, Invalidenrente; ~ **assets** Altguthaben; ~ **assistance** *(US)* Altershilfe, -unterstützung; ~ **benefit** *(US)* Altersversorgung; ~ **benefit taxes** *(US)* Sozialabgaben für die Arbeiterrentenversicherung; ~ **exemption** *(US)* Altersfreibetrag; ~-**exemption limit** *(US)* Altersfreibetragsgrenze; ~ **insurance** *(US)* Renten-, Altersversicherung; ~ **insurance benefits** *(social security,* US*)* Altersrente; ~ **pension** *(Br.)* Altersversorgung, Alters-, Invalidenrente; ᵉ **Pensions Act** *(Br.)* Altersversorgungsgesetz; ~ **pension fund** Altersversorgungskasse, -versicherung; ~ **pension insurance** *(Br.)* Rentenversicherung; ~ **pension scheme** *(US)* Altersversorgungskasse; ~ **pensioner** Bezieher einer staatlichen Altersrente, Rentner; ~ **pensioners' club** Seniorenverein; ~ **provisions** Bestimmungen über die Altersversicherung; ~ **security** Altersversicherung; ᵉ **Superannuation Act** *(US)* Altersversorgungsgesetz; ~ **survivor's and disability insurance** *(US)* Sozial-, Alters- und Hinterbliebenenversorgung.

old, the ~ **army game** *(sl.)* die übliche Schwindelei; ~ **bachelor** eingefleischter Junggeselle; ~ **boy** *(fam.)* alter Junge, altes Haus; ~ **buffer** *(fam.)* Schafskopf; ~ **campaigner** Veteran; ~ **civil servant** pensionierter Beamter; ~ **clothes** abgetragene Kleider; ~-**clothes shop** Altwarengeschäft; ~ **clothesman** Trödler; ~ **countries** seit langem besiedelte Länder; ~ **country** *(immi-*

grant) Heimatland; ~ **crock** ausgedientes Fahrzeug; ~ **customs** alte Sitte, althergebrachte Gewohnheiten; ~ **debt** Schuld älteren Datums; ~ **dodge** alter Trick; ~ **egg** *(Br., sl.)* altes Haus, alter Schwede; ~**-established firm** alteingesessene Firma; ~ **family** alteingesessene Familie; ~**-fashioned** altmodisch, veraltet; ~**-fashioned child** altkluges Kind; ~**-fashioned servant** Diener aus der alten Zeit; ~ **firm** frühere Firma; ~**-fogyish** verknöchert, verkalkt; ~ **fogy** *(sl.)* alter Knacker; ~ **fogydom** Verkalktheit; ~ **frump** alte Schachtel; **the** ~ **gentleman** der Teufel; ~ **gold** Altgold; **to travel over** ~ **ground** sich auf bekanntem Gelände bewegen; ~ **hand** alter Hase; ~ **hand at work** erfahrener Routinier; **to be an** ~ **hand at it** große Berufserfahrungen in etw. haben; ~ **Harry** Teufel; ~**-hat** *(fam.)* ein alter Hut sein; ~ **head** *(sl.)* leitender Angestellter; **to have an** ~ **head on young shoulders** altklug sein; **to put an** ~ **head on young shoulders** Altersweisheit von der Jugend verlangen; ~ **horse** *(fig.)* alter Haudegen; ~ **lady** meine Alte; ⌷ **Lady of Threadneedle Street** Bank von England; ~**-line** konservativ, traditionell; ~**-line life insurance** normale Todesfallversicherung; ~**-line rails** *(US)* erstklassige Eisenbahnwerte; ~ **maid** alte Jungfer, altjüngferliche Person; ~**-maidish** altjüngferlich; ~ **man** der Alte, Vater, *(boss)* Chef, Direktor; **to call up** ~ **memories** alte Erinnerungen wachrufen; ~ **moon** abnehmender Mond; ~ **name** altbekannter Name; **to collect** ~ **newspapers for salvage** Altpapiersammlung durchführen; ~ **offender** alter Sünder; ~ **parts of a town** Altstadt; ~ **people's home** Altersheim, Pflegeheim; ~ **pupil** alter Schulfreund; ~ **salt** *(mar.)* alter Seebär; ~**-school** altmodisch; ~ **school tie** alter Zopf, Traditionsgebundenheit; ~**-standing** altrenommiert; ~**-standing debt** Schuld älteren Datums; ~ **stock** Ladenhüter; **to have a high** ~ **time** sich köstlich amüsieren; ~ **timer** altmodische Person, rückständischer (altmodischer) Fachmann, *(expert)* erfahrener Fachmann; **the good** ~ **times** die gute alte Zeit; ~ **top** *(sl.)* altes Haus, alter Knabe; ~ **wives' tales** Ammenmärchen; ~ **womanish** sehr umständlich; ~**-womanish maid** alte Jungfer; ~**-world cottage** altertümliches Landhaus; ~ **year** vergangenes Jahr.

oligarchy Oligarchie.

oligopolistic market von wenigen Abnehmern bestimmter Markt.

oligopoly Oligopol, Preiskontrolle;
~ **price** Oligopolpreis.

olographic testament eigenhändig geschriebenes Testament.

Olympic Games Olympische Spiele, Olympiade.

omen Vorzeichen, Omen;
to take s. th. as a good ~ etw. als gutes Vorzeichen werten.

ominous schicksalsschwer, bedeutungsvoll;
~ **silence** ominöse Stille, unheilvolles Schweigen.

omission Wegfall, *(noninclusion)* Auslassung, Übergehung, Wegfall, *(nonperformance)* Versäumnis, Unterlassung, *(print.)* Leiche;
acts and ~**s** Handlungen und Unterlassungen, Untätigbleiben;
errors and ~**s excepted** Irrtümer und Auslassungen vorbehalten;
~ **of important contents** Weglassung wesentlicher Inhaltsteile;
~ **of date** fehlendes Datum; ~ **to send notice** versäumte Benachrichtigung;
to supply an ~ nachtragen, Ergänzungen vornehmen.

omit *(v.)* *(fail)* versäumen, weg-, unterlassen, *(leave out)* auslassen;
~ **a dividend** Dividende ausfallen lassen; ~ **an opportunity** Chance fahren lassen; ~ **to do a piece of work** überhaupt nichts tun.

omnibus Omnibus, [Auto]bus, *(intelligence test)* Intelligenzprüfung, *(general public)* Allgemeinheit, *(publication)* Anthologie, *(waiter's assistant, coll.)* Kellnergehilfe;
railway ~ Schienenbus;
to go by (take the) ~ mit dem Omnibus fahren;
~ *(a.)* allgemein, umfassend, global;
~ **account** *(Br.)* Sammelkonto; ~ **act** Mantel-, Rahmengesetz; ~ **bar** *(el.)* Sammelschiene; ~ **bill** Mantelgesetz; ~ **bill of lading** Sammelkonnossement; ~ **book** Almanach, Anthologie; ~ **box** *(theatre)* Proszeniumsloge; ~ **charge** Globalbelastung; ~ **claim** *(Br.)* zusammenfassender Anspruch; ~ **clause** General-, Sammelklausel, *(automobile insurance, US)* Vertreter des Fahrzeughalters deckende Versicherungsklausel; ~ **credit** *(Br.)* Warenkredit; ~ **deposit** Girosammeldepot; ~ **driver** Busfahrer; ~ **driving** Omnibusfahren, -lenken; ~ **injunction** *(US)* uneingeschränkter Gerichtsbefehl; ~ **order** Sammelbestellung; ~ **party** Sammelpartei; ~ **policy** *(warehouse)* Einheitsversicherung; ~ **proprietor** Omnibusbesitzer; ~ **resolution** globale Beschlußfas-

sung; ~ **route** Omnibuslinie; ~ **service** Omnibusverkehr; ~ **train** *(Br.)* Personen-, Bummelzug; ~ **volume** Sammelband; ~ **wire** *(el.)* Sammelleitung.

omnium *(finance, Br.)* Gesamtwert einer fundierten öffentlichen Anleihe.

on *(US sl.)* im Bilde;
~ **and off** hin und wieder;
to have a drink ~ **s. o.** auf jds. Kosten einen nehmen;
~ **campus** auf dem Universitätsgelände gelegen; ~**-carrier** übernehmender Spediteur, Weiterbeförderer; ~**-the-job accident** Betriebs-, Arbeitsunfall; ~**-licence** *(Br.)* Schankkonzession im eigenen Betrieb; ~**-position** Einschaltstellung; ~**-sale date** Verkaufstermin; ~**-shore wind** Seewind.

once | **in a blue moon** *(fam.)* alle Jubeljahre einmal; ~ **in jeopardy** Grundsatz der einmaligen Bestrafung.

once-off payment einmalige Sofortzahlung.

once-over *(US sl.)* flüchtige Überprüfung;
to give the ~ flüchtig prüfen; **to give a stranger the** ~ Fremden mit einem Blick abschätzen.

oncoming | **generation** kommende Generation; ~ **pedestrian** entgegenkommender Fußgänger; ~ **shift** antretende Arbeitsschicht; ~ **traffic** Gegenverkehr; ~ **winter** bevorstehender Winter.

oncost *(Br.)* Gemein-, Regiekosten, allgemeine Handlungsunkosten, Kostenzuschlag.

one | **for the books** großartige Leistung; ~ **of the crowd** ein Mann aus dem Volke; ~ **in the eye** Denkzettel; ~ **at a time** Stück für Stück; ~ **for the road** Satteltrunk; ~ **too many** ein Schluck zu viel;
to be at ~ **with s. o.** mit jem. einer Meinung sein; **to be** ~ **of the family** zur Familie gehören; **to be always thinking of number** ~ immer nur an sich (seine eigenen Interessen) denken; **to be** ~ **up on s. o.** jem. voraus sein; **to call at a pub for a quick** ~ sich schnell einen in der Kneipe genehmigen; **to give s. o.** ~ **on the nose** *(fam.)* jem. eins auf die Nase geben; **to have** ~ **on the house** Freibier erhalten; **to take care of number** ~ nur auf seinen Vorteil sehen;
~**-arm pint** *(sl.)* billiger Ausschank; ~**-armed bandit** *(US)* Spielautomat; ~**-circuit set** Einkreisempfänger; ~**-cylinder** einzylindrig; ~**-column wide** einspaltig; ~**-crop system** Monokultur; ~**-day loan** *(US)* Vierundzwanzigstundenkredit, Tagesgeld; ~**-digit number** einstellige Zahl; ~**-family house** Einfamilienhaus; ~ **foot in the grave** mit einem Fuß schon im Grabe; ~ **gallus** *(US sl.)* Bagatelle; ~**-horse** einspännig, *(US coll.)* bedürftig, zweitrangig; ~**-horse town** Provinznest, *(coll., US)* unbedeutendes Nest, kleine Provinzstadt; ~**-hour** einstündig; ~**-knob tuning** Einknopfbedienung; ~**-line** einzeilig; ~**-line business (shop)** Spezial-, Fachgeschäft; **as** ~ **man** wie ein Mann; ~ **man in a hundred** Einer unter Hunderten; ~ **man or collegiate** *(US)* *(committee)* direktorial oder kollegial; ~**-man business (firm, US)** Einmannbetrieb, Einzelunternehmen, -firma; ~**-man company** Einmanngesellschaft; ~**-man job** Einzelbeschäftigung; ~**-man leadership** Einmannführung; ~**-man outfit** Einmannbetrieb; ~**-man service** Einmannbetrieb; **a** ~**-man show** Einmannbetrieb; ~**-name paper** *(US)* Papier mit nur einer Unterschrift; ~**-night stand** *(US)* einmaliges Gastspiel; ~**-off** einzeln angefertigter Artikel; ~**-off production** Sonderanfertigung, Auftragsproduktion; ~ **and only** jds. Schatz; ~**-party dictatorship** Einparteienherrschaft; ~**-party state** Einparteienstaat; ~ **person,** ~ **vote** allgemeines gleiches Wahlrecht; ~ **piece** einteilig; ~**-point rise** Erhöhung um einen Punkt; ~**-price** Festpreis; ~**-price article** Einheitspreisware, -artikel; ~**-price policy** Festpreisverkaufspolitik; ~**-price store** Einheitspreisgeschäft; ~**-room school house** Zwergschule; ~ **shot** Geschichte ohne Fortsetzung; ~**-serving size** Portionspackung; ~**-shot** *(story)* Geschichte ohne Fortsetzung; ~**-shot** *(a.)* einmalig; ~**-shot bill** einmaliges Gesetz; ~**-shot camera** Einbelichtungs-, Spaltbildkamera; ~**-shot promotion** Stoßaktion; ~**-shot whodunit** *(broadcasting)* Kriminalstück ohne Fortsetzungen; ~**-side account of a quarrel** einseitige Darstellung einer Auseinandersetzung; ~**-sided** einseitig, voreingenommen, parteiisch; ~**-sided contract** einseitiger Vertrag; ~**-sided judgment** parteiisches Urteil; ~**-sided notice** einseitige Kündigung; ~**-sided street** nur auf einer Seite bebaute Straße; ~**-stop shopping** Einkauf (alles) unter einem Dach [im Supermarkt]; ~**-stage tax** Einphasensteuer; ~**-storey house** einstöckiges Haus; ~**-storeyed (storied)** einstöckig; **for** ~ **thing** zunächst einmal; ~**-third page** Drittelseite; ~**-thousand hour clause** *(part-time employee)* Höchststundenzahl in 26 Arbeitswochen; ~**-time** ehemalig; ~**-time purchaser** Laufkunde; ~**-time rate** Anzeigentarif für Einzelinsertion ohne Rabatt, Einmalta-

rif; **~-track mind** Fachidiot; **~-track railway** eingleisige Bahn; **~-trip container** *(US)* Wegwerf-, Einwegbehälter, verlorene Verpackung; **~-trip product** *(US)* Einwegerzeugnis; **~-way** einbahnig, *(fare, US)* einfach, nur für die Hinfahrt; **~-way only** *(Br.)* Einbahnstraße; **~-way package** Einweg-, Wegwerfpackung; **~-way rental** *(rent-a-car)* Einwegmiete; **~-way street** Einbahnstraße; **~-way switch** Einwegschalter; **~-way ticket** *(US)* einfache Fahrkarte; **~-way traffic** einspuriger Verkehr, Einbahnverkehr.

oner *(coll.)* Eins, Einer, *(sl.)* Könner, Kanone, *(thing, sl.)* Mordsding.

onerous drückend, lästig, *(law)* einseitig verpflichtend;
~ **cause** angemessene Gegenleistung; ~ **clause** lästige Bedingung; ~ **contract** entgeltlicher Vertrag; ~ **deed** *(Scot.)* Urkunde über ein entgeltliches Rechtsgeschäft; ~ **duties** lästige Pflichten; ~ **gift** mit Auflagen verbundenes Geschenk; ~ **goods** unwirtschaftliche Güter; ~ **obligation** schwer zu erfüllende Verpflichtung; ~ **property** belastetes Grundstück; ~ **provisions** vertragliche Grundstückslasten; ~ **task** schwierige Aufgabe; ~ **title** entgeltlich erworbenes Eigentum.

onion Lauch, Zwiebel;
off one's ~ meschugge, aus dem Häuschen, ein bißchen verrückt;
to know one's ~s *(sl.)* sich in der Welt auskennen.

onionskin Luftpostpapier, *(typewriter)* Durchschlagpapier.

onlooker Zuschauer, Unbeteiligter.

onrush Vorstoß.

onset *(mil.)* Attacke, Angriff, Sturm;
at the first ~ gleich beim ersten Anlauf;
~ **of a disease** Beginn einer Krankheit; ~ **of a strike** Streikbeginn;
to withstand the ~ of the enemy den feindlichen Angriffen Stand halten.

onshore landwärts;
~ **oil** Erdöl im Küstenvorland; ~ **oil fields** Küstenölfelder; ~ **wind** auflandiger Wind.

onslaught Angriff, Ansturm, Überfall;
~ **of the years** Last der Jahre;
to make a savage ~ on the Prime Minister heftigen Angriff gegen den Premierminister richten.

onus of proof Beweislast;
to discharge the ~ Beweis erbringen.

onward *(course)* vorwärts gerichtet;
~ **course** Kurs nach vorn; ~ **march of ideas** Vormarsch von Ideen; **for ~ transmission** zur Weiterleitung.

oodles of money Geld wie Heu (Mist).

oom-pah-pah Bumsmusik.

ooze langsamer Abfluß, Sickern;
~ *(v.)* herumflanieren;
~ **away** dahinschwinden; ~ **out** *(secret)* durchsickern.

oozing out of a secret Durchsickern eines Geheimnisses.

oozy bottom *(mar.)* Schlickgrund.

open offene See, freier Himmel;
in the ~ im Freien;
the ~ die Öffentlichkeit;
~ *(a.)* offen, offenstehend, *(book)* aufgeschlagen, *(drugstore)* dienstbereit, *(exhibition)* geöffnet, *(patent)* ersichtlich, offensichtlich, *(public)* für alle geöffnet, öffentlich zugänglich, *(undecided)* noch nicht entschieden, *(unsettled)* offenstehend, *(visible)* sichtbar;
~ **all night** ganze Nacht geöffnet; ~ **day and night** Tag und Nacht geöffnet; ~ **to** zugänglich; [**not**] ~ **to bribery** [un]bestechlich; ~ **to buy** Einkaufsbudget für bestimmten Zeitraum; ~ **to discussion** diskussionsfähig; ~ **to improvement** verbesserungsfähig, verbesserungsbedürftig; ~ **to any reasonable offer** jedem vernünftigen Angebot zugänglich; ~ **to the public** für den öffentlichen Verkehr freigegeben, der Öffentlichkeit zugänglich; ~ **to the public on weekdays only** nur an Wochentagen zu besichtigen; ~ **to question** bestreitbar, anfechtbar; ~ **to residents only** frei für Anlieger; ~ **round the clock** ganztägig geöffnet; ~ **for signature** unterschriftsreif; ~ **for subscription** zur Zeichnung aufgelegt; **not** ~ **on Sunday** Sonntags geschlossen; ~ **to temptation** gegen Versuchungen nicht gefeit; ~ **to traffic** für den öffentlichen Verkehr freigegeben; ~ **and unbuilt upon** unbebaut; ~ **throughout the year** ganzjährig geöffnet;
~ *(v.)* öffnen, aufmachen, -schließen, *(go on the road)* auf Tournee gehen, *(shop)* Betrieb aufnehmen, *(theatre)* Spielzeit eröffnet, *(to traffic)* [dem Verkehr] übergeben;
~ **o. s. to s. o.** sich jem. eröffnen; ~ **an account** Konto einrichten; ~ **an account with the bank to the (in) favo(u)r of s. o.** Konto bei einer Bank zu jds. Gunsten eröffnen; ~ **an account in s.**

one's name Konto für j. errichten; ~ **active** *(stocks)* von Anfang an gefragt sein; ~ **the ball** den Reigen eröffnen; ~ **bids** Versteigerung fortsetzen; ~ **a new branch** neue Filiale eröffnen; ~ **the budget** Haushaltsvoranschlag vorlegen; ~ **a business** Geschäft eröffnen; ~ **a case** in die Verhandlung eintreten; ~ **at ten o'clock** um zehn Uhr eröffnen; ~ **a commission** Ausschußtätigkeit beginnen; ~ **with a compliment** mit einem Kompliment beginnen; ~ **the convention for signature** Abkommen zur Unterzeichnung auflegen; ~ **a correspondence** Briefwechsel beginnen; ~ **up a country to trade** Land für den Handel erschließen; ~ **a court** Sitzung eröffnen; ~ **a credit** Kredit (Akkreditiv) eröffnen; ~ **a crossing** *(Br.)* gekreuzten Scheck in einen Barscheck abändern, Scheckkreuzung rückgängig machen; ~ **a debate** Diskussion eröffnen; ~ **a default** *(US)* Wiedereinsetzung nach Versäumnisurteil bewilligen; ~ **a deposition** schriftliche Zeugenaussage vor Gericht verlesen; ~ **one's designs** seine Absichten mitteilen; ~ **directly on to the street** direkt auf die Straße herausführen; ~ **at a slight discount** *(stock exchange)* leicht abgeschwächt eröffnen; ~ **a discussion** in eine Diskussion eintreten; ~ **the door to abuses** Tür für Mißbräuche öffnen; ~ **the door to more imports** größere Einfuhrmengen hereinlassen; ~ **the door to s. th.** einer Sache Tür und Tor öffnen; ~ **one's eyes** große Augen machen; ~ **s. one's eyes** jem. die Augen öffnen; ~ **a factory** Fabrik in Betrieb nehmen; ~ **fire** *(mil.)* das Feuer eröffnen; ~ **firm** *(stock exchange)* fest eröffnen; ~ **flat** *(stock exchange)* anfangs flau sein; ~ **one's heart to s. o.** jem. sein Herz ausschütten; ~ **a highway** Verkehrsweg zur öffentlichen Benutzung freigeben; ~ **irregularly** *(stock exchange)* uneinheitlich eröffnen; ~ **a judgment** Verhandlung wiederaufnehmen; ~ **a letter of credit** Akkreditiv eröffnen; ~ **a line for traffic** Bahnlinie dem Verkehr übergeben; ~ **a loan** Kreditkonto einrichten, Kredit eröffnen; ~ **the mail** *(US)* Post öffnen; ~ **into the main road** in die Hauptstraße einmünden; ~ **new markets** neue Märkte erschließen; ~ **a public meeting** öffentliche Versammlung eröffnen; ~ **one's mind to s. o.** jem. seine Gedanken mitteilen; ~ **a mine** Bergwerk erschließen; ~ **one's mouth** *(fig.)* etw. ausplaudern; ~ **negotiations** Verhandlungen einleiten; ~ **new prospects to s. o.** jem. neue Möglichkeiten erschließen; ~ **a newspaper** Zeitung aufschlagen; ~ **out** *(motor)* Vollgas geben; ~ **out to s. o.** sich jem. eröffnen; ~ **out a folding map** zusammenklappbare Karte aufschlagen; ~ **a parcel** Paket aufmachen; ~ **a park to the public** Park für die öffentliche Benutzung freigeben; ~ **Parliament** *(Br.)* Parlament eröffnen; ~ **a patent to the public** *(US)* Patent zwangsweise für alle zur Verfügung stellen; ~ **the pleadings** mit dem Plädoyer beginnen; ~ **the proceedings** Verfahren eröffnen; ~ **to the public** dem Publikum zur Besichtigung freigeben, der Allgemeinheit zugänglich machen; ~ **quietly** *(stock exchange)* ruhig eröffnen; ~ **a road** Straße für den öffentlichen Verkehr freigeben; ~ **a rule** Verfahren nach Aufhebung eines Beschlusses fortsetzen; ~ **one's shop** seinen Laden öffnen (aufmachen); ~ **steady** *(stock exchange)* fest eröffnen; **not** ~ **on Sunday** Sonntags geschlossen bleiben; ~ **a text** Text auslegen; ~ **a trade** Gewerbe beginnen; ~ **undeveloped land** Baugelände erschließen; ~ **up** Gelände erschließen, *(car)* Geschwindigkeit erhöhen, *(fig., sl.)* voll aufdrehen, *(market)* erschließen; ~ **up one's own account** auf eigene Rechnung arbeiten; ~ **up business relations** in Geschäftsverbindung treten; ~ **up an old case** Verfahren wiederaufnehmen; ~ **up a coal mine** Bergwerk erschließen; ~ **up a country to trade** Land dem Handel erschließen; ~ **up in a new country** in einem fremden Land von vorn anfangen; ~ **up a new road to traffic** neue Straße dem Verkehr eröffnen (erschließen); ~ **up to the tourist trade** für den Fremdenverkehr erschließen; ~ **up a new territory for trade** neues Absatzgebiet erschließen; ~ **a way through the crowd** sich einen Weg durch die Menge bahnen; ~ **a will** Testament eröffnen;
to be ~ offen stehen, freistehen, *(book of condolence)* aufliegen; **to be ~ with s. o.** ganz offen zu jem. sein; **to be ~ to advice** Rat annehmen, Ratschlägen zugänglich sein; **to be ~ to all** jedermann zugänglich sein; **to be ~ to conviction** mit sich reden lassen; **to be ~ to dispute** anfechtbar sein; **to be ~ to s. o. to object** jem. freistehen, zu widersprechen; **to be ~ to objection** Widerspruch herausfordern; **to be ~ to an offer** Angebot in Betracht ziehen; **to be ~ to prejudices** Vorurteilen ausgesetzt sein; **to be still ~** noch unbesetzt sein; **to be tried in ~ court** öffentlich verhandelt werden; **to burst the door ~** Tür aufbrechen; **to come out into the ~ with one's plans** seine Pläne öffentlich bekanntgeben; **to hold ~ an offer** Angebot aufrechterhalten; **to keep one's account ~ at a bank** Bankkonto unterhalten; **to keep a day ~** sich einen Tag frei halten; **to keep a job ~** Stellung offen halten; **to keep a shop ~** Laden (Geschäft) offen

halten; **to lay ~** klarlegen, aufdecken; **to lay o. s. ~ to calumny** der Verleumdung Tür und Tor öffnen; **to lay o. s. ~ to criticism** sich der Kritik aussetzen; **to lay o. s. open to ridicule** sich lächerlich machen; **to leave a matter ~** Angelegenheit noch nicht entscheiden; **to sleep in the ~** im Freien schlafen; **to stand ~** offen stehen;

~ **account** (US) laufendes Konto, laufende Rechnung, Kontokorrentkonto, (not yet settled) offenstehende Rechnung; **to have an ~ account** in laufender Rechnung stehen; **to grant ~-account facilities** (terms) Kontokorrentbedingungen gewähren; **in the ~ air** im Freien.

open-air Imbißstand im Freien;

~ **cinema** (Br.) Freilichtkino; ~ **cure** Freiluftkur; ~ **market** Wochenmarkt; ~ **meeting** Versammlung unter freiem Himmel; ~ **performance** Freilichtaufführung; ~ **plants** Gartenpflanzen; ~ **restaurant** Gartenrestaurant; ~ **school** Freiluftschule; ~ **site** Freigelände; ~ **swimming pool** Freibad; ~ **temperature** Außentemperatur; ~ **theatre** Freilichtbühne.

open, to receive s. o. ~-armed j. mit offenen Armen aufnehmen; **~-armed reception** herzlicher Empfang; ~ **arrest** einfacher Arrest; ~ **assembly** öffentliche Versammlung; ~ **boat** Boot ohne Verdeck; **to read s. o. like an ~ book** in jem. wie in einem offenen Buch lesen; ~ **book account** (US) laufende Rechnung; ~ **book credit** laufender Buchkredit; ~ **bulk** noch unverpackte Massenware; **~-to-buy allowance** (US) freie Einkaufsgrenze [im Einzelhandel]; ~ **car** Kabriolet; ~ **championship** Amateurmeisterschaften; ~ **character** freimütiger Charakter; ~ **charge account** offener Buchkredit; ~ **charter** noch nicht genehmigte Konzession; ~ **check** (US) (cheque, Br.) Barscheck, offener Scheck; ~ **circuit** (el.) offener Stromkreis; **~-circuit television** öffentliches Fernsehen; ~ **city** (mil.) offene Stadt; ~ **claim** (insurance) noch nicht entschiedener Versicherungsanspruch; ~ **competition** freier Wettbewerb; ~ **contest** Preisausschreiben; ~ **contract** Grundsatzvereinbarung; ~ **country** flaches Land, offenes Gelände; ~ **court** öffentliche Gerichtsversammlung; **in ~ court** in öffentlicher Sitzung; **to be tried in ~ court** öffentlich verhandelt werden; **to pronounce judgment in ~ court** Urteil öffentlich verkünden; ~ **cover** General-, Pauschalversicherung; ~ **credit** (US) offener (laufender) Kredit, Blanko-, Kontokorrentkredit, (Br.) nicht dokumentierter Trassierungskredit; ~ **day** freier Tag; ~ **day mining** Tagebau; ~ **display** offen ausgelegte Ware; ~ **door** freier Eintritt, (economic policy) freier Zugang für den Handel; **~-door** frei zugänglich; **to force an ~ door** (fam.) offene Türen einrennen; **to keep ~ door** gastfrei sein, gastfreies Haus führen; **~-door invitation** Tag der offenen Tür; **~-door policy** Politik der offenen Tür; **~-doored** gastfreundlich; **with ~ ears** aufmerksam; ~ **end** Briefhülle mit Schmalrandklappe; **~-end** unbestimmt hoch, ohne feste Grenze, (investment company) mit nicht begrenzter Zahl auszugebender Anteile.

open-end | account (depreciation method) offener Bestand; ~ **agreement** (employee's compensation) unbefristete Entschädigungsvereinbarung; ~ **bonds** (US) hypothekarische Schuldverschreibungen; ~ **commercial** Werbefilm mit eingeblendeten Händleradressen; ~ **contract** unbefristeter Lieferungsvertrag; ~ **fund** (US) Investmentfonds mit beliebiger Emissionshöhe; ~ **investment company** (US) Kapitalanlagegesellschaft mit der Höhe nach unbegrenztem Investmentfonds; ~ **mortgage** nicht voll valutierte Hypothek; ~ **transcription** Standardwerbeprogramm; ~ **wage contract** Tarifvertrag mit Lohngleitklausel.

open | -ended commitment, to make an sich offen zu einer Verpflichtung bekennen; **~-ended question** frei beantwortbare Frage; ~ **felling** Lichtung; ~ **fields** Gemeinschaftsfelder; **~-field system** Dreifelderwirtschaft; ~ **force** nackte Gewalt; ~ **fracture** (med.) komplizierter Bruch; ~ **grave** offenes Grab; ~ **ground** Freigelände; **with ~ hands** freigebig; **to have an ~ hand** offene Hand haben; **to give ~-handedly** mit offenen Händen (freigebig) geben; **~-handedness** Freigebigkeit; **~-hearted** aufrichtig, offenherzig; **~-hearth furnace** Siemens-Martin Ofen; ~ **hostilities** offene Feindseligkeiten; ~ **house** Gastfreundschaft; **to keep ~ house** sehr gastfrei sein; ~ **ice** fahrbares Eis; ~ **indent** Auslandsauftrag mit freier Einkaufsmöglichkeit; ~ **insolvency** Nichteröffnung des Konkursverfahrens mangels Masse; ~ **items** offenstehende Beträge; ~ **item system** offene-Posten Buchführung; ~ **lecture** öffentliche Vorlesung; ~ **letter** offener Brief; ~ **licence** Rahmenlizenz; ~ **lot** Eckgrundstück.

open market offener (freier) Markt, Freiverkehr, Offenmarkt;

to grant to the publisher on an ~ basis dem Verleger überall Verkaufsmöglichkeiten gewähren; ~ **committee** Offenmarktausschuß; ~ **credit** Schuldscheindarlehn; ~ **loan** Offenmarktkredit; ~ **operations** Offenmarktgeschäfte, Transaktionen am offenen Markt; ~ **paper** Schuldscheindarlehnsurkunde; ~ **papers** im Freiverkehr gehandelte Werte; ~ **policy** Offenmarktpolitik der Notenbank; ~ **price** freier Marktpreis; ~ **purchases** Käufe am offenen Markt; ~ **rates** Geldsätze am offenen Markt, freier Kapitalmarktzins; ~ **rent** verkehrsübliche Miete; ~ **sales** Verkäufe am offenen Markt, Offenmarktverkäufe; ~ **transactions** Offenmarktgeschäfte; ~ **valuation** Bewertung des Verkehrswerts; ~ **value** Verkehrswert.

open | matter (print.) weit durchschossener (lichter) Satz; ~ **meadows** Gemeinschaftsweide; **to keep an ~ mind on s. th.** keine vorgefaßte Meinung haben; **to be ~-minded on a subject** Thema völlig unvoreingenommen angehen; ~ **mine** im Tagebau betriebenes Bergwerk; ~ **mortgage** nicht voll valutierte Hypothek; ~ **mortgage clause** Ermächtigung zum Einzug der Versicherungssumme; **to stand with ~ mouth before s. th.** völlig überrascht sein; **~-mouthed** maßlos überrascht, gaffend; ~ **order** (US) bis zum Widerruf gültiger Auftrag, (troops) offene Schlachtordnung; ~ **pattern** ungeschütztes Muster; ~ **pit** Tagebau; **~-plan office** Großraumbüro; ~ **policy** (insurance, Br.) laufende Police, Pauschalversicherungspolice; ~ **policy terms** Generalpolicenbestimmungen; ~ **population** geringe Bevölkerungsdichte; ~ **port** Freihafen; ~ **position** unbesetzte Stelle; ~ **price** vor Verkaufsbeginn der Konkurrenz bekanntgegebener Preis, Preis freibleibend; ~ **price agreement** Preisinformationsabrede; **~-price association** (US) Preismeldestelle; **~-price system** (US) Preismelde-, Preisinformationskartell; ~ **pricing** Preisaustausch zwischen Konkurrenten; ~ **primary** (US) Wahlkandidatenaufstellung; ~ **purchases** Käufe am offenen Markt; ~ **question** unentscheidene Frage; ~ **rate** (advertising) Anzeigengrundpreis; ~ **rates** (US) Geldsätze am offenen Markt; ~ **river** schiffbarer Fluß; ~ **road** allgemein zugängliche Straße; ~ **roadstead** offene Reede; ~ **sale** öffentliche Versteigerung; ~ **sales** Verkäufe am offenen Markt; ~ **scandal** öffentlicher Skandal; ~ **scholarship** (Br.) jedermann zugängliches Stipendium; ~ **sea** freies Meer, Hochsee, hohe See; ~ **season** Jagdzeit; ~ **secret** offenes Geheimnis; ~ **sesame** Zauberformel; ~ **session** öffentliche Sitzung; ~ **shop** (US) nicht gewerkschaftspflichtiger Betrieb; **~-and-shut case** (US) abgemachte Sache; ~ **side** Briefhülle mit Briefbandklappe; ~ **sitting** öffentliche Sitzung; ~ **skies** (fig.) nicht geheim zu halten, gegenseitige Luftinspektion (Luftüberwachung); ~ **spaces** freier Platz, (Br.) unbebautes Gelände; **~-space area** Freiflächen und Grünanlagen; **~-space planning** Grünflächenplanung; **~-spaced setting** perlender Satz; ~ **stock** ständig vorrätige Ware; ~ **terms** offenes Zahlungsziel; ~ **time rate** (US) Anzeigengrundpreis; **~-top** (US) ohne Verdeck, offen; ~ **town** unbefestigte Stadt, (sl.) liberale Stadt; ~ **track** freie Strecke; ~ **trade** noch nicht abgeschlossenes Spekulationsgeschäft; ~ **trial** öffentliche Verhandlung; ~ **type** Konturschrift; ~ **union** (US) Gewerkschaft, die jeden Arbeiter als Mitglied aufnimmt; ~ **university** Fernuniversität; **~-use area** ungenutztes Freigelände; ~ **verdict** (jury) Todesfeststellung ohne Angabe des Grundes; ~ **warfare** Bewegungskrieg; ~ **water** schiffbares (eisfreies) Gewässer; ~ **winter** frostfreier Winter; **~-worked** (mining) im Tagebau; ~ **working** (mining) Tagebau.

opencast im Tagebau ausgebeutet;

~ **coal** im Tagebau gewonnene Kohle; ~ **mining** Tagebau; ~ **production** Übertageförderung; ~ **working** Tagebau.

opened up (US) mit voll laufendem Motor.

opener Eröffnungsmasche, (cotton machine) Reißwolf, (sport) Eröffnungsspiel;

can ~ Büchsenöffner; **planned ~** Anfangsplan; **tin ~** (Br.) Büchsenöffner;

~-upper (sl.) einleitendes Musikstück.

opening Öffnung, Durchfahrt, Durchlaß, Lücke, Bresche, (of account) Errichtung, Eröffnung, (counsel for the plaintiff) Sachvortrag des Klägers, (forest, US) Lichtung, (letter) Briefanfang, (opportunity) Gelegenheit, günstige Aussicht, Chance, (plant) Inbetriebsetzung, -nahme, (position) freie Stelle, (sales) Absatzmöglichkeit, (stock exchange) Eröffnung, (theater) Eröffnungsvorstellung, Erstaufführung;

at the ~ (stock exchange) bei Börsenbeginn;

active ~ (stock exchange) lebhafte Eröffnung; **formal ~** feierliche Eröffnung; **immediate ~** sofort zu besetzende Stelle; **long-winded ~** langatmige Einleitung; **new store ~** Eröffnung eines neuen Ladens; **split (wide, US) ~** (stock exchange) Eröffnungsnotierung mit weit abweichenden Kursen; **Sunday ~** Offenhalten am Sonntag; **unfilled jobs ~** Angebot offener Stellen;

~ **of an account** Einrichtung eines Kontos, Kontoeröffnung; ~ **in an advertising agency** freie Stelle in einem Werbebüro; ~ **in a bank** freie Stelle bei einer Bank; ~ **of a book** Buchanfang; ~ **for**

business gute Geschäftsmöglichkeiten; **~ of a business** Geschäftseröffnung; **~ of a case** Eröffnung der Verhandlung; **~ of the courts** Wiederbeginn des Gerichtsbetriebs; **~ of credit** Krediteröffnung; **~ a crossing** *(Br.)* Abänderung eines gekreuzten Schecks in einen Barscheck durch den Aussteller; **~ in a hedge** Lücke in einer Hecke; **~ of a hotel** Hoteleröffnung; **~ to the left** *(pol.)* Öffnung nach links; **~ of a letter of credit** Eröffnung eines Akkreditivs, Akkreditiveröffnung; **attractive ~s on managerial levels** Aufstiegschancen in der Betriebshierarchie; **~ of negotiations** Eröffnung (Beginn) von Verhandlungen, Verhandlungsbeginn; **~ of Parliament** Parlamentseröffnung; **~ of a speech** Einleitung einer Rede; **~ of a new street** Fertigstellung einer neuen Straße; **~ for subscription** Auflegung zur Zeichnung; **~ of a tent** Zeltöffnung; **~ for trade** Handelschance; **~ up** *(making accessible)* Auf-, Erschließung; **~ of a will** Testamentseröffnung; **fine ~ for a young man** gute Berufsaussichten für einen jungen Mann;

to find an ~ Stellung (Wirkungskreis) finden; **to turn weak after a firm ~** *(stock exchange)* nach fester Eröffnung schwach werden; **to wait for an ~** auf eine Gelegenheit warten, *(railway)* auf das Abfahrtssignal warten;

~ (a.) einleitend;

~ address Eröffnungsansprache; **~ announcement** *(television)* Kopfansage; **~ balance [sheet]** Anfangsbestand, Eröffnungsbilanz; **~ bank** Akkreditiv ausstellende Bank; **~ bid** Eröffnungsangebot; **~ capital** Grund-, Stamm-, Anfangskapital; **~ case** *(lawyer)* Eröffnungsvortrag; **~ ceremony** Eröffnungsfeier[lichkeit]; **~ date** Submissionstermin; **~ day of the session** erster Sitzungstag; **~ discussion** einleitende Besprechung; **~ entry** erste Buchung, Eröffnungs-, Anfangsbuchung; **~ hours** Eröffnungszeit; **~ inventory** Anfangsbestand, Eröffnungsinventar; **~ night** Eröffnungsvorstellung, Premiere; **~-night audience** Premierenpublikum; **~ paragraph** Einleitungssatz; **~ premium** Anfangsprämie; **~ price (quotation, rate)** Eröffnungs-, Einführungs-, Anfangskurs, erster Kurs, Eröffnungspreis; **~ remarks** Einführungsworte; **~ round** Eröffnungsrunde; **~ season** kommende Saison; **~ session** *(parl.)* Eröffnungssitzung; **formal ~ sitting** feierliche Eröffnungssitzung; **~ speech** Eingangs-, Eröffnungsansprache; **~ statement** einleitende Erklärung, Eröffnungsansprache; **~ statement of counsel** *(for jury)* Tatbestandserläuterung des Verteidigers; **~ stock** Eröffnungsbestand, Anfangsinventar; **~ talks** einleitende Besprechungen; **~ time** Eröffnungszeit; **~ year** Eröffnungsjahr.

openjaw *(air travel)* Rundflugkarte mit variablem Endflugplatz.

openly in aller Öffentlichkeit (Offenheit).

openwork *(mining)* Tagebau.

opera Oper, *(building)* Opernhaus, Oper, *(libretto)* Operntext, Libretto, *(performance)* Opernaufführung;

comic ~ komische Oper;

~ cloak Abendmantel; **~ glass** Opernglas; **~ house** Opernhaus; **~ season** Opernsaison.

operate *(v.)* *(be in action)* funktionieren, arbeiten, laufen, in Betrieb (Tätigkeit) sein, *(bring out)* bewirken, *(handle)* handhaben, betätigen, *(have desired effect)* wirken, sich auswirken, *(law)* Anwendung finden, *(machine)* bedienen, betreiben, in Betrieb nehmen, *(manage, US)* verwalten, führen, leiten, betreiben, tätig sein, *(medicine)* operieren, *(mil.)* operieren, militärische Bewegungen durchführen, *(speculate, coll.)* spekulieren, handeln, *(stock exchange)* operieren;

~ (v.) on s. o. j. operieren; **~ on AC** mit Wechselstrom laufen; **~ as** Wirkung haben als; **~ an account** Konto unterhalten; **~ for one's own account** in eigener Regie (auf eigene Rechnung) betreiben; **~ to s. one's advantage** jem. zum Vorteil gereichen, *(tax)* sich zu jds. Vorteil auswirken; **~ an airline** Luftverkehrsunternehmen betreiben; **~ s. one's automobile** *(US)* jds. Auto benutzen; **~ on batteries** elektrisch fahren; **~ a brake** Bremse betätigen; **~ a business** Geschäft betreiben; **~ above capacity** überlasten; **~ at below two thirds of capacity** nur zwei Drittel der Betriebskapazität ausnutzen; **~ at close to capacity** Kapazität fast ausfahren; **~ a car** Auto fahren; **~ against one's client** gegen die Interessen seines Kunden handeln; **~ a coal mine** Bergwerk betreiben; **~ on alternating current** mit Wechselstrom arbeiten; **~ day and night** *(machinery)* Tag und Nacht (durchgehend) laufen; **~ at a deficit** mit Verlust arbeiten; **~ to s. one's disadvantage** sich gegen j. auswirken; **~ economically** sparsam wirtschaften, wirtschaftlich arbeiten; **~ on the exchange** an der Börse spekulieren; **~ a factory** Fabrik betreiben (besitzen); **~ for a fall** *(stock exchange)* auf Baisse spekulieren, fixen; **~ from the first of April** vom 1. April ab gelten; **~ personally on a high level** auf höherer Ebene persönlich tätig werden; **~ the lift** Aufzug bedienen; **~ at a loss** mit Verlust

arbeiten; **~ a motor vehicle** *(US)* Kraftfahrzeug führen; **~ a network of depots** umfangreiche Lager unterhalten; **~ at night** nachts betreiben; **~ offices** Zweigstellen unterhalten; **~ 7% below its potentiality** 7% unterhalb der Kapazitätsgrenze laufen; **~ at a profit (profitably)** Gewinn erzielen, mit Gewinn betreiben; **~ against the public interest** sich gegen das öffentliche Interesse richten; **~ quickly** schnelle Wirkung zeigen; **~ a railroad** *(US)* Eisenbahnlinie betreiben; **~ at a rate of 85% capacity** zu 85% ausgelastet sein; **~ a relay** Relais ansprechen lassen; **~ by remote control** fernsteuern, -betätigen; **~ for a rise** *(stock exchange)* auf Hausse spekulieren; **~ on a large scale** *(mil.)* großräumig operieren; **~ on a drastically reduced scale** Betrieb in stark verkleinertem Umfang weiterführen; **~ within the settling period** kulissieren; **~ with skill** geschickt vorgehen; **~ in global spread** weltweite Unternehmungen betreiben; **~ in stocks** agiotieren; **~ at full strength** voll beschäftigt sein; **~ an undertaking** *(US)* Unternehmen betreiben; **~ to bring on a war** Kriegsausbruch bewirken; **~ on a shorter wave length** mit reduzierter Kraft arbeiten; **~ a state-wide system of branches** Filialen im ganzen Land unterhalten; **~ world-wide** in der ganzen Welt tätig sein;

safe to ~ betriebssicher.

operated betrieben;

commercially ~ auf kommerzieller Basis betrieben; **power-~** durch Maschinenkraft betrieben; **state-~** staatlich betrieben;

~ by electricity elektrisch betrieben;

to be ~ on operiert werden.

operatic | music Opernmusik; **~ singer** Opernsinger.

operating *(machine)* Betreiben, Betrieb;

smooth ~ reibungsloses Funktionieren;

~ of sleeping cars Schlafwagenbetrieb; **~ on a large scale** *(mil.)* militärische Operationen in großem Ausmaß; **~ of a motor vehicle** *(US)* Führen eines Kraftfahrzeugs;

to be ~ im Betrieb sein, arbeiten; **to be ~ at a high level** voll beschäftigt sein; **to be ~ at a loss** mit Verlust arbeiten;

~ (a.) in Betrieb [befindlich], betrieblich;

~ ability Betriebsfähigkeit; **~ account** Betriebskonto; **~ accounts** Betriebsbuchführung; **~ activities** Betriebstätigkeit; **~ area** Betriebsgebiet; **~ assets** Betriebsvermögen; **~ authority** Vollmacht für die Betriebsleitung; **~ budget** Betriebsvoranschlag; **~ bye-law** Betriebssatzung; **~ cash reserve** Betriebsmittelrücklage; **~ charges** *(balance sheet)* Betriebskosten; **~ chart** Arbeitsplan; **~ circuit** *(el.)* Arbeitsstromkreis; **~ company** *(US)* Betriebs[kapital]gesellschaft, *(transport)* Transportunternehmen; **~ competence** Betriebskapazität; **~ concern** laufendes Unternehmen; **~ concession** Betriebskonzession; **~ condition** betriebsfähiger Zustand, Betriebsfähigkeit, -zustand; **in ~ conditions** Betriebsbedingungen; **in ~ condition** in betriebsfähigem Zustand; **~ cost** Betriebsunkosten; **general ~ costs** Betriebsgemeinkosten, *(airplane)* Flugunterhaltungskosten; **~ cost ratio** Betriebskostensatz; **~ cycle** Betriebszyklus; **~ data** Betriebsdaten; **~ decision** Betriebsentscheidung; **~ deficit** Betriebsfehlbetrag, -defizit; **~ department** *(railway)* Betriebsabteilung; **~ dummy** Scheinunternehmen; **~ earnings** Betriebseinnahmen; **~ earnings figures** Betriebsergebniszahlen; **~ efficiency** betriebliche Leistungsfähigkeit, Betriebsleistung, Wirtschaftlichkeit; **~ employees** *(railway)* Betriebspersonal; **~ engineer** Betriebsingenieur; **~ equipment** Betriebseinrichtung; **~ executive** Betriebsfachmann; **~ expenses** betriebliche Aufwendungen, Geschäfts-, Betriebs[un]kosten, -aufwand; **~ experience** Betriebserfahrung; **~ factors** Betriebsfaktoren; **~ figures** Betriebskennzahlen; **~ fleet** Kraftfahrzeugpark; **~ fund** Betriebsmittel, -kapital; **~ income** Betriebseinnahmen, Geschäftserträge; **~ instructions** Bedienungs-, Betriebsanweisung, -vorschriften; **~ ledger** Betriebskonto; **~ leverage** Hebelwirkung der Fixkosten; **~ loss** Betriebsverlust; **~ manager** Betriebsleiter; **~ method** Betriebsweise, Arbeitsmethode; **~ officer** leitender Angestellter; **~ performance income statement** Betriebsergebnisrechnung; **~ period** Betriebsdauer, -zeitraum; **~ permission** Betriebserlaubnis; **to assign ~ personnel** Betriebspersonal einsetzen (abstellen); **~ planning** Betriebsplanung; **~ practices** Betriebsmethoden; **~ principles** Geschäftsgrundlagen; **~ problem** Betriebsproblem; **~ procedure** Betriebsverfahren, Fertigungsmethode; **net ~ profit** *(US)* Betriebsreingewinn; **~ property** *(US)* arbeitender Betrieb; **~ rate** Beschäftigungsgrad; **~ ratio** *(US)* Betriebskoeffizient, -zahl; **~ regulations** *(railway)* Fahrdienstvorschriften; **~ report** Betriebs-, Geschäftsbericht; **~ requirements** Betriebsbedürfnisse, -anforderungen; **~ reserve** Betriebsmittelrücklage; **~ result** Abschluß-, Betriebsergebnis; **~ revenue** Betriebseinnahmen; **~ room** Operationssaal; **~ rule** Betriebsvorschrift; **~ staff** *(US)*

Belegschaft, Betriebspersonal; ~ **standpoint** Betriebsstandpunkt; ~ **statement** *(US)* Erfolgs-, Betriebsbilanz, Gewinn- und Verlust-, Betriebsergebnis-, Betriebsabrechnung, -aufstellung; ~ **subsidiary** Betriebsgesellschaft; ~ **supplies** Hilfs- und Betriebsstoffe; ~ **surgeon** behandelnder Chirurg; ~ **surplus** Betriebsüberschuß, -gewinn; ~ **system** *(data processing)* Betriebssystem; ~ **table** Operationstisch; ~ **tax** Betriebssteuer; ~ **theatre** Operationsraum; ~ **time** Arbeitszeit, *(el.)* Schaltzeit; ~ **unit** Betriebseinheit; ~ **voltage** *(el.)* Betriebsspannung; ~ **year** Betriebsjahr.

operation *(business activity)* [Geschäfts]tätigkeit, *(efficacy)* Wirksamkeit, Wirkung, Geltung, *(enterprise)* Unternehmen, Geschäft, Betrieb, *(machine)* Betrieb, Inbetriebsetzung, Bedienung, Handhabung, Betreiben, Bewegung, Gang, *(management)* Leitung, Betrieb, *(medicine)* operativer (chirurgischer) Eingriff, Operation, *(mil.)* Operation, Kampfhandlung, Einsatz, Unternehmen, *(plant)* Betrieb, *(process)* Verfahren, Arbeits[vor]gang, -prozeß, Arbeitsausführung, *(transaction)* [finanzielle] Transaktion;

by ~ of kraft; **by ~ of law** kraft Gesetzes; **in ~** in Betrieb; **in full ~** vollbeschäftigt, *(machine)* in vollem Betrieb (Einsatz); **ready for ~** betriebsfertig, -bereit; **reliable in ~** betriebssicher; ~**s** Geschäftstätigkeit, *(plant)* Arbeitsvorgänge;

airborne (air-landed, *US)* ~ Luftlandeunternehmen; **associated ~s** verwandte Arbeitsphasen; **authorized ~** Betriebsgenehmigung; **automatic ~** *(tel.)* Selbstwählverkehr; **banking ~s** Bankgeschäfte, -transaktionen; **bearish ~** *(US)* Baissespekulation, Blankoabgabe; **building ~s** Bauarbeiten, -vorhaben; **cash ~** Kassageschäft; **chemical ~** chemischer Prozeß; **combined ~s** *(mil.)* Zusammenarbeit; **commercial ~** geschäftliche Unternehmung; **continuous ~** Tag- und Nachtbetrieb, durchgehender Betrieb, *(business concern)* Geschäftstätigkeit; **credit ~s** Kreditgeschäfte; **criminal ~** Abtreibungseingriff; **current ~** laufender Betrieb; **day-to-day ~** Tagesablauf; **economic[al] ~** wirtschaftliche Betriebsführung, Wirtschaftlichkeit, rentabler (sparsamer) Betrieb; **financial ~** Finanztransaktion; **forward ~** Zeit-, Termingeschäft, Terminhandel; **high-speed ~** *(railway)* Schnellverkehr; **insurance ~s** Versicherungsgeschäfte; **intercompany ~s** Verrechnungs-, Konzerngeschäfte; **landing ~** Landungsunternehmen; **limited ~** beschränkte Wirkung; **machining ~** Arbeitsvorgang; **major ~** *(med.)* größere (gefährliche) Operation; **manufacturing ~** Fabrikationsbetrieb; **marketing ~s** absatzwirtschaftliche Maßnahmen; **minor ~** *(med.)* harmlose Operation; **nuisance ~** *(mil.)* Störeinsatz; **plant ~s** Betriebsverfahren; **profitable ~** Gewinnbetrieb; **progressive ~** Fließarbeit; **scheduled ~** *(US)* fahrplanmäßiger Betrieb; **single-shift ~** *(US)* Einzelschichtbetrieb; **stock ~s** *(stock exchange)* Börsengeschäfte, -transaktionen; **thriving ~** florierendes Unternehmen; **trading ~** Tauschgeschäft; **uninterrupted ~** störungsfreier Betrieb; **wholly-owned ~** im Allgemeineigentum stehender Betrieb;

~ **for own account** Nostrotransaktion; ~ **of an aircraft** Betrieb eines Luftfahrzeugs; ~ **for appendicitis** Blinddarmoperation; ~ **of a business** Betrieb eines Geschäftes, Geschäftsbetrieb; **governmental ~ of business** Regierungsbetrieb, Regieunternehmen; ~ **of a company** Leitung einer Gesellschaft; ~ **of a convention** Anwendung eines Abkommens; ~ **of facilities** Ausnutzung von Anlagen; ~ **in futures** *(stock exchange)* Termingeschäft; **partial ~ of an industry** Teilleitung eines Industriebetriebs; ~ **of postal service** Unterhaltung des Postverkehrs; ~ **of a railway (railroad,** *US)* Betrieb einer Eisenbahnlinie; ~ **of rule** Regelanwendung; ~ **of a school** *(US)* Leitung einer Schule; ~ **of a ship** Betrieb eines Schiffes; ~**s to smooth the market** marktglättende Transaktionen; ~ **on the stock exchange** Börsentransaktion, -geschäft; ~ **of a tax table** Anwendung einer Steuertabelle; ~ **of thinking** Denkvorgang; ~ **of a treaty** Geltungsbereich eines Vertrages;

to be in ~ *(factory, service)* in Betrieb sein, funktionieren, *(law)* gelten, in Kraft sein; **to be in active ~** in Betrieb sein; **to be no longer in ~** *(law)* keine Geltung mehr haben; **to be out of ~** außer Betrieb sein; **to begin ~s** in Betrieb gehen, Geschäftstätigkeit aufnehmen; **to bring a decree into ~** Verordnung zur Anwendung bringen; **to cease ~s** Betrieb (Geschäftstätigkeit) einstellen; **to come into ~** in Gang kommen, *(law)* in Kraft treten, wirksam werden; **to commence ~s** in Betrieb nehmen; **to exclude from the ~ of the constitution** Verfassungsrecht aufheben; **to expend ~s** Betrieb ausdehnen; **to go into ~** in Betrieb genommen werden; **to perform an ~** chirurgischen Eingriff vornehmen; **to put into ~** in Betrieb setzen, [Betrieb] anlaufen lassen; **to put the law into ~ in all its rigo(u)r** Gesetz mit aller Strenge anwenden; **to put out of ~** außer Betrieb setzen; **to set in**

~ **in Betrieb setzen; to slim down ~s** Geschäftsvolumen verringern; **to suspend ~s** Geschäftstätigkeit einstellen; **to suspend the ~ of a law** Gesetz vorübergehend außer Kraft setzen; **to undergo an ~** sich einer Operation unterziehen;

~ **analysis** Betriebsanalyse, Arbeitsstudie, -analyse; ~ **analysis chart** Bewertungsformblatt; ~ **audit** Unternehmensbewertung; ~ **card** Arbeitskarte; ~ **center** Bedienungszentrale; **joint ~ center** *(US)* **(centre,** *Br.)* gemeinsamer Führungsstab; ~ **costs** Betriebskosten; ~**s crisis** Betriebskrise; ~ **cycle** Arbeitszyklus; ~ **department** Führungsstab; ~ **job card** Arbeits-, Auftragsabrechnungskarte; ~**s manager** *(US)* Betriebsleiter; ~ **order** *(mil.)* Einsatzbefehl; ~ **plan** Bearbeitungsplan, [maschineller] Arbeitsplan; ~ **policy** Unternehmenspolitik; ~**s research** *(US)* Entscheidungs-, Verfahrens-, Unternehmensforschung, Optimalplanung; ~**s research analyst** *(US)* Betriebsingenieur für Datenanlagen; ~**s room** *(mil.)* Kommandozentrale; ~**s section** *(mil.)* Operationsabteilung; ~ **sheets** Betriebsabrechnungsbogen; ~ **staff** *(company, mil.)* Führungs-, Operationsstab; ~ **supervision** Betriebsüberwachung.

operational betrieblich, betriebsbedingt, -technisch, innerorganisatorisch, *(airliner)* einsatz-, betriebsbereit, *(mil.)* einsatzfähig;

~ **accounting** Betriebsabrechnung; ~ **area** Einsatzgebiet; ~ **auditing** Prüfung der Arbeitsabläufe, Überprüfung der Betriebstätigkeit; ~ **base** *(mil.)* Aufmarschgebiet; ~ **blindness** Betriebsblindheit; ~ **control** Betriebskontrolle; ~ **costs** Betriebs[un]kosten; ~ **credit** Betriebsmittelkredit; ~ **deficiencies** betriebliche Verlustquellen; ~ **deficit** Betriebsdefizit; ~ **difficulties** Betriebsschwierigkeiten; ~ **directive** Einsatzanweisung; ~ **duties** *(mil.)* Frontdienst; ~ **efficiency** Betriebswirksamkeit; ~ **expenditure** Betriebsaufwand; ~ **fatigue** Kampfmüdigkeit, Kriegsneurose; ~ **game** Unternehmensplanspiel; ~ **gearing** Hebelwirkung der Fixkosten; ~ **hazard** Betriebsrisiko; ~ **headquarters** Führungsstab; ~ **height** *(airplane)* Einsatzflughöhe; **at ~ level** beim tatsächlichen Einsatz; ~ **loss** Betriebsverlust; ~ **management** Spitze der Betriebsführung; **to be heavy on ~ management experience** erhebliche Erfahrungen in der zentralen Leitung von Unternehmungen haben; ~ **method** Arbeitsmethode; ~ **mission** *(mil.)* Einsatz; ~ **network** Betriebsnetz; ~ **objective** Operationsziel; ~ **plan** Feldzugsplan; ~ **planning** betriebliche Planung, Betriebsplanung; ~ **problem** Betriebsproblem; ~ **procedure** Betriebsablauf; ~ **profit** Betriebsgewinn; ~ **profitability** Rentabilität eines Unternehmens; ~ **rate of revolutions** Betriebsdrehzahl; ~ **readiness** Einsatzbereitschaft; ~ **requirements** betriebliche Erfordernisse, Betriebserfordernisse; ~ **research** *(Br.)* Entscheidungs-, Verfahrens-, Unternehmensforschung; ~ **risk** Betriebsrisiko; ~ **safety precautions** Betriebsschutz; ~ **setup** Betriebsschema; ~ **staff** Belegschaft; ~ **stage** Betriebsabschnitt; ~ **technique** Betriebstechnik; ~ **test** Funktionsprüfung; ~ **training** einsatzmäßige Ausbildung; ~ **zone** *(mil.)* Kriegs-, Sperrgebiet.

operationally | **fit** einsatzbereit; ~ **necessary** betriebsnotwendig.

operative *(artisan)* Handwerker, *(co-operator)* Mitarbeiter, *(detective, US)* Agent, Detektiv, *(machinist)* Mechaniker, Maschinist, *(mill hand)* [Fabrik]arbeiter, *(US)* Angestellter; **building ~** Bauarbeiter; **skilled ~** Facharbeiter;

~ *(a.)* *(having effect)* [rechts]wirksam, gültig, *(mil.)* operativ, *(in operation)* tätig, in Betrieb, betrieblich, betriebsfähig, *(practical)* praktisch, *(working)* arbeitend, beschäftigt, tätig; **no longer ~** nicht mehr gültig;

to be ~ gelten, Gültigkeit haben; **to become ~** in Kraft treten, wirksam werden; **to make ~** in Kraft treten lassen; **to make a decree ~** Verordnung anwenden;

~ **characteristics** Arbeitsweise; ~ **class** Arbeiterklasse; ~ **clause** *(insurance)* Bestimmung des Versicherungsumfangs; ~ **dose** wirksame Dosis; ~ **effect** Wirksamkeit; ~ **facts** *(US)* Tatbestandsmerkmale; ~ **machinery** im Betrieb befindliche Maschinenanlagen; ~ **mistake** beachtlicher Irrtum; ~ **part of an act** wesentlicher Teil eines Gesetzes; ~ **penalty** wirksame Strafe; ~ **point** springender Punkt; ~ **position** Arbeitslage; ~ **provisions** *(judgment)* Urteilstenor, -formel; ~ **side of an industry** industrielle Fabrikationsstätten; ~ **technique** *(med.)* Operationstechnik; ~ **treatment** chirurgische Behandlung; ~ **words** *(deed)* rechtsgestaltende Worte.

operator *(charming boy, sl.)* Salonlöwe, *(machine)* Bedienungspersonal, *(manager, US)* Unternehmer, Betriebsführer, -leiter, Produzent, *(med.)* operierender Arzt, Operateur, *(stock exchange)* Börsenspekulant, *(tel.)* Telefonist[in], Telefonfräulein, Vermittlung, Zentrale, *(worker)* Arbeiter;

~**s** Bedienungspersonal, *(data processing)* Datenverarbeitungspersonal;

advertising ~ Werbeflächenpächter im öffentlichen Dienst; **big-time ~** *(sl.)* Salonlöwe; **black-market ~** Schwarzhändler; **chief ~** Telefonzentrale; **crane ~** Kranführer; **engine ~** Maschinist; **franchise ~** Pächter von Werbeflächen; **gasoline-station ~** Tankstellenbesitzer; **linotype ~** Linotypsetzer; **long-distance ~** *(tel.)* Fernanmeldung, -amt; **low-cost ~** mit geringen Selbstkosten arbeitender Hersteller (Produzent); **market ~** [berufsmäßiger] Spekulant; **radio ~** Funker; **telegraph ~** Telegrafenbeamter; **telephone ~** Telefonist; **wireless telegraph ~** Funker; **private ~ in civil aviation** private Flugzeuggesellschaft; **~ of a car** *(US)* Fahrzeugführer; **~s for the fall** Baissepartei, -clique; **~s for a rise** Haussepartei, -spekulanten; **~ of a motor vehicle** *(US)* Kraftfahrzeugführer;

to be a purely intuitive ~ sich weitgehend auf seine Intuition verlassen; **to call the ~** *(tel.)* Zentrale anrufen;

~'s licence *(US)* Führerschein, *(carrier)* Speditionskonzession.

operetta Operette.

opinion Meinung, Ansicht, Stellungnahme, *(auditor)* Testat, *(discretion)* Ermessen, *(judgment)* Entscheidungsgründe, Urteilsbegründung, *(legal expert, Br.)* Rechtsgutachten, *(statement by expert)* Gutachten;

at the bar of public ~ vor den Schranken der öffentlichen Meinung; **in my ~** meines Erachtens; **in my poor ~** nach meiner unmaßgeblichen Meinung; **in the ~ of experts** nach Ansicht (Meinung) der Sachverständigen;

advisory ~ Sachverständigen-, Rechtsgutachten; **attorney's ~** anwaltliches Gutachten; **bias(s)ed ~** Vorurteil; **clashing ~s** widerstreitende Meinungen; **common ~** allgemeine Meinung; **concurring ~** *(US)* in der Begründung zustimmende Meinung, zustimmendes Votum; **counsel's ~** *(Br.)* Rechtsgutachten; **current ~** weit verbreitete Meinung; **dissenting (dissentient) ~** *(US)* abweichende Meinung, Minderheitsvotum; **divided ~** geteilte Auffassung; **draft ~** Gutachtenentwurf; **expert ~** Sachverständigengutachten; **extreme ~s** radikale Ansichten; **widely held ~** weitverbreitete Auffassung; **individual ~** Privatmeinung; **jarring ~s** widerstreitende Meinungen; **judicial ~** Auffassung des Gerichts; **just ~** vernünftige Auffassung; **lawyer's ~** anwaltliches Gutachten; **legal ~** Rechtsgutachten; **local financial ~s** örtliche Finanzkreise; **majority ~** *(US)* Mehrheitsvotum; **medical ~** ärztliches Gutachten; **mere ~** bloße Meinungsäußerung; **minority ~** Ansicht (Auffassung) der Minderheit; **outside ~** Meinung eines Außenstehenden; **political ~** politische Überzeugung (Ansichten); **prejudiced ~** vorgefaßte Meinung; **public ~** öffentliche Meinung; **received ~** allgemeine (herrschende) Meinung; **separate ~** abweichende Meinung, *(law court)* gesonderte Urteilsbegründung; **settled ~** feste Meinung; **undivided ~** einhellige Meinung;

~ of counsel Rechtsgutachten; **~ of the court** Urteilsbegründung; **~ of a medical expert** Gutachten eines medizinischen Sachverständigen; **~ of the people** öffentliche Meinung; **~ of official quarters** maßgebliche Meinung; **~ of a witness** Meinungsäußerung eines Zeugen;

to act up to one's ~ seiner Überzeugung entsprechend handeln; **to advance an ~** Ansicht äußern, Meinung vorbringen; **to agree with s. one's ~** sich jds. Ansicht anschließen (zu eigen machen); **to alter one's ~ radically** seine Meinung gründlich ändern; **to ask for an ~** Stellungnahme einholen; **to ask s. one's ~** sich von jem. beraten lassen; **to be of the ~** Standpunkt vertreten; **to be entitled to one's ~** Recht auf eigene Meinung haben; **to be divided in ~** geteilter Meinung sein; **to be entirely of s. one's ~** jds. Ansicht völlig teilen; **to be a reflex of public ~** öffentliche Meinung widerspiegeln; **to bias the ~ of the people** öffentliche Meinung beeinflussen; **to change one's ~** seine Meinung ändern; **to deliver an ~** Meinung äußern, *(expert)* Gutachten erstatten, sich gutachtlich äußern; **to differ in ~** anderer Meinung sein; **to dissent from s. one's ~** abweichende Meinung vertreten; **to endorse an ~** gleicher Meinung sein, sich einer Auffassung anschließen; **to excite public ~** öffentliche Meinung erregen; **to express an ~** Stellungnahme abgeben; **to express one's ~ in favo(u)r of a proposition** sich für einen Vorschlag aussprechen; **to fall in with s. one's ~** jds. Meinung beitreten; **to fall in s. one's good ~** an Ansehen bei jem. verlieren; **to form an ~** sich eine Meinung bilden; **to gauge public ~** öffentliche Meinung abschätzen; **to give an expert ~** Gutachten abgeben; **to give way to s. one's ~** sich jds. Meinung anschließen; **to have the courage of one's ~** zu seiner Meinung stehen, Zivilcourage haben; **to have a favo(u)rable ~ of s. o.** gute Meinung von jem. haben; **to have no ~ of s. th.** sich noch keine Meinung gebildet haben; **to have a high ~ of s. o.** große Stücke auf j. halten; **to have a low (poor) ~ of s. o.** von jem. nicht viel halten; **to have no settled ~s** noch keine feste Meinung haben;

to hold an ~ Ansicht vertreten; **to line up public ~** Übereinstimmung in der öffentlichen Meinung herbeiführen; **to maintain an ~** Meinung verfechten; **to manufacture public ~** öffentliche Meinung künstlich beeinflussen; **to obtain an ~** Gutachten einholen; **to offer an ~** Stellungnahme vorbringen; **to pin one's ~ on s. one's sleeve** sich von jds. Meinung abhängig machen; **to place o. s. in opposition to public ~** sich in Gegensatz zur öffentlichen Meinung bringen; **to put forward an ~** seine Meinung äußern; **to render an ~** Gutachten erstatten; **to reverse one's ~** seine Meinung völlig ändern; **to seek the ~ of an expert** Experten (Sachverständigen) konsultieren; **to share s. one's ~** jds. Meinung teilen; **to take up current ~s** sich die augenblicklichen Ansichten zu eigen machen; **to take counsel's ~** Gutachten einholen; **to voice an ~** Ansicht äußern;

public ~ analyst Meinungsforscher; **~ book** *(Br.)* Auskunftsbuch [zur Eintragung von Auskünften über Kunden]; **~ evidence** Sachverständigengutachten; **~ former** Meinungsbildner; **~ leader** meinungsbildende Persönlichkeit, Meinungsbildner; **~ leading** Meinungsbildung; **~ list** *(Br.)* Kundenauskunftbuch; **~ poll (survey, test)** Meinungsbefragung, -untersuchung; **national ~ poll** umfassende Meinungsumfrage; **to outstrip all other politicians in ~ poll ratings** in der Gunst der öffentlichen Meinungsbefragung allen anderen Politikern den Rang ablaufen; **~ rating** Meinungsbewertung; **public ~ research** Meinungsforschung; **~ research corporation** Meinungsumfrageinstitut; **~ scale** Meinungsskala; **~ survey** Meinungsumfrage; **~ test** Erforschung der öffentlichen Meinung.

opinionaire *(US)* Fragebogen für die Meinungsforschung, Umfragebogen.

opponent Antragsgegner, [Prozeß]gegner, Opponent, Gegenseite, -partei;

~ on principle grundsätzlicher Gegner.

opportune opportun, gelegen, günstig, passend;

~ moment günstiger Zeitpunkt; **~ speech** zeitgerechte Rede.

opportunism Opportunismus.

opportunist Opportunist, Konjunkturritter.

opportunistic opportunistisch.

opportunity [günstige] Gelegenheit, Chance, günstiger Zeitpunkt, Möglichkeit;

at the first ~ bei der ersten Gelegenheit; **should the ~ arise** gegebenenfalls;

business ~ geschäftliche Möglichkeit; **employment ~** Beschäftigungsmöglichkeit; **golden ~** glänzende Gelegenheit; **good ~** günstige Gelegenheit; **lost ~** verpaßte Gelegenheit; **once-in-a lifetime ~** einmalige Gelegenheit; **payoff ~** reelle Chance;

~ for advancement (to advance) Aufstiegsmöglichkeit; **~ to buy** Kaufgelegenheit, Einkaufsmöglichkeit; **~ for depreciation** Abschreibungsmöglichkeit; **~ for employment** Beschäftigungsmöglichkeit; **~ for fraud** Betrugsmöglichkeit; **~ for gain** Gewinnchance; **~ for growth** Aufstiegsmöglichkeit; **~ for promotion** Beförderungschance; **~ to rationalize** Rationalisierungsmöglichkeit; **~ for roll-over contacts** laufende Kontaktmöglichkeiten; **~ for savings** [Steuer]sparmöglichkeit; **~ for work** Arbeitsgelegenheit;

to afford s. o. the ~ jem. die Gelegenheit verschaffen; **to avail o. s. of an ~** Gelegenheit beim Schopf ergreifen; **to bide one's ~** auf eine Gelegenheit warten; **to have good ~ to come into contact with all sorts of people** gute Kontaktmöglichkeiten mit allen nur möglichen Leuten haben; **to leap at an ~** Gelegenheit beim Schopf ergreifen; **to make the most of an ~** Gelegenheit ausnutzen, Chance wahrnehmen; **to miss (let slip) an ~** sich eine Chance entgehen lassen; **to muddle away one's ~** seine Chance vertun; **to profit by an ~** Gelegenheit benutzen; **to provide an ~ for s. o.** jem. eine Gelegenheit verschaffen; **to seize (take) an ~** günstige Gelegenheit ergreifen (wahrnehmen); **to take what ~ is presented** jede sich bietende Möglichkeit wahrnehmen; **to throw away an ~** sich eine Chance entgehen lassen; **~ advertising** gelegentliche Werbung; **~ chart** Beförderungstabelle; **~ costs** alternative Kosten, Opportunitäts-, Wartekosten; **~ reasons** Opportunitätsdenken.

oppose *(v.)* entgegentreten, opponieren, ablehnend gegenüberstehen, entgegentreten, Widerstand leisten, *(debtor)* Widerspruch erheben;

~ an action Einspruch erheben; **~ advantages and disadvantages** Vor- und Nachteile gegenüberstellen; **~ an application** *(patent law)* gegen eine Anmeldung Einspruch einlegen; **~ a bill** Gesetzesvorschlag bekämpfen; **~ a bill on the floor** gegen einen Gesetzentwurf im Plenum sprechen; **~ the divorce** der Scheidung widersprechen; **~ the government** in Opposition zur Regierung stehen; **~ a marriage** einer Heirat seine Zustimmung versagen; **~ a motion** sich gegen einen Antrag aussprechen; ~ **s. one's plans** sich jds. Plänen widersetzen; ~ **a rigorous resistance to the enemy** dem Feind heftigen Widerstand leisten; ~ **s. one's plans** sich jds. Plänen widersetzen; ~ **a scheme** einem Plan widersprechen.

opposed gegensätzlich, entgegengesetzt, feindlich;
to be ~ to all reason jeder Vernunft Hohn sprechen.

opposer Gegner, Widersacher, Opponent, *(patent law, US)* Erheber eines Patentwiderspruchs.

opposing gegnerisch, opponierend;
~ **benches** Reihen der Opposition; ~ **counsel** gegnerischer Anwalt; **to go on ~ course** Gegenkurs einschlagen; ~ **effect** gegenteilige Wirkung; ~ **number** Gegenspieler, Kollege; ~ **opinion** gegenteilige Ansicht; ~ **party** Antragsgegner, Prozeßgegner, Gegenpartei.

opposite Gegenteil, *(reverse)* umgekehrt, entgegengesetzt;
~ *(a.)* gegenüberliegend, -stehend;
house ~ gegenüberliegendes Haus;
to play ~ X *(film)* Gegenspieler für X sein; **to sit ~ to s. o.** jem. gegenübersitzen;
to go on (take) an ~ course Gegenkurs einschlagen, entgegengesetzten Kurs einschlagen; **to pass a ship on an ~ course** Schiff auf einem Gegenkurs passieren; **in the ~ direction** im entgegengesetzter Richtung; ~ **opinion** gegenteilige Ansicht; **on the ~ page** auf der gegenüberliegenden Buchseite; ~ **pole** Gegenpol; **the ~ sex** das andere Geschlecht; ~ **side** Gegenseite; ~ **side of the road** andere Straßenseite.

opposition Widerstand, Gegensatz, *(bankruptcy proceedings)* verweigerte Entlastung, Entlastungsverweigerung, *(parl.)* Opposition, *(patent law)* Patenteinspruch, -anfechtung, *(trademark)* Widerspruch;
left-wing ~ Linksopposition; **Her Majesty's most loyal ~** *(Br.)* Oppositionspartei; **right-wing ~** Rechtsopposition;
~ **to a patent** Patentanfechtung;
to be in ~ zuwiderlaufen, entgegenstehen, *(parl.)* in der Opposition sein; **to break down all ~** jeden Widerstand brechen; **to defect to the ~** zur Opposition hinüberwechseln; **to encounter ~** auf Widerstand stoßen; **to find o. s. in ~ to one's friends** mit seinen Freunden geteilter Meinung sein; **to go into ~** in Opposition treten; **to meet with a stiff ~** auf heftigen Widerstand stoßen; **to meet with strong ~ all along the front** an allen Frontabschnitten heftigem Widerstand begegnen; **to offer ~** opponieren, Widerstand leisten; **to offer a determined ~ to a measure** einer Maßnahme entschiedenen Widerstand entgegensetzen; **to place o. s. in ~ to public opinion** sich in Gegensatz zur öffentlichen Meinung bringen; **to pre-silence the ~** Opposition vorher beruhigen; **to recede from one's ~** *(US)* oppositionelle Haltung im Kongreß aufgeben; **to reject the ~** *(patent law)* Einspruch zurückweisen; **to roll up ~** Opposition hervorrufen; **to run into a solid ~** starke Oppositionskräfte mobilisieren; **to start in ~ to s. o.** Konkurrenzgeschäft eröffnen;
~ **benches** *(parl.)* Opposition; ~ **camp** Oppositionslager; ~ **campaign** Wahlfeldzug der Opposition; ~ **circles** Oppositionskreise; **to preempt ~ demands** Forderungen der Opposition vorwegnehmen; ~ **fee** *(patent law)* Einspruchsgebühr; ~ **group** Oppositionsgruppe; ~ **leader** Oppositionsführer; ~ **league** Gegenkoalition; ~ **left** oppositionelle Linke; ~ **meeting** Protestversammlung; ~ **[news]paper** Oppositionszeitung, -blatt; ~ **party** Oppositionspartei; ~ **party majority** Oppositionsmehrheit; ~ **politician** Oppositionspolitiker; ~ **press** Oppositionspresse; ~ **proceedings** *(patent law, US)* Einspruchsverfahren.

oppositional oppositionell, regierungsfeindlich.

oppositionist Mitglied der Opposition.

oppress *(v.)* unterdrücken, tyrannisieren.

oppression Unterdrückung, *(US)* Mißbrauch der Amtsgewalt, Amtsmißbrauch;
official ~ *(US)* Nötigung im Amt, Mißbrauch der Amtsgewalt; ~ **of minorities** Vergewaltigung der Minderheit.

oppressive *(rigorous)* unbillig, hart, drückend, heiß;
~ **law** ungerechtes Gesetz; **in an ~ manner** auf tyrannisierende Art und Weise; ~ **ruler** Tyrann; ~ **taxes** drückende Steuern.

oppressor Unterdrücker, Tyrann, *(public officer, US)* Amtsmißbrauch ausübender Beamter.

opt *(v.)* optieren, sich entscheiden, stimmen, wählen;
~ **for early retirement** sich zur freiwilligen Pensionierung entschließen; ~ **for a nationality** für eine Staatsangehörigkeit optieren; ~ **out** auf sein Optionsrecht verzichten.

optant *(pol.)* Optant.

optation Option.

optical | illusion optische Täuschung; ~ **industry** optische Industrie; ~ **instruments** optische Instrumente; ~ **range finder** optischer Entfernungsmesser.

optimal | pattern of production optimale Produktions- und Handelsstruktur; ~ **quantity of money** optimale Geldmenge; ~ **size** optimale Betriebsgröße.

optimalization Optimalisierung.

optimism on profits Gewinnoptimierung.

optimum Bestfall, -wert, Optimum;
~ **capacity** Höchstleistungsfähigkeit, -kapazität; ~ **conditions** günstigste Bedingungen; ~ **firm** Optimalbetrieb; ~ **level** Höchstniveau; ~ **pattern of production** optimale Struktur von Produktion und Handel; ~ **population** optimal günstige Bevölkerungsgröße, Bevölkerungsoptimum; ~ **rating** Höchstbewertung; ~ **result** Bestresultat; ~ **size** Optimalgröße; ~ **size firm** optimale Betriebsgröße; ~ **statistics** beste statistische Meßzahl; ~ **test** bestmöglicher Test.

opting | out *(International Monetary Fund)* Möglichkeit der Nichtteilnahme; ~ **person** Optant.

option *(choice)* freie Wahl, Wahlmöglichkeit, Entscheidungsfreiheit, Alternative, *(contract law, Br.)* Prämie, *(insurance)* Wahlrecht hinsichtlich der Auszahlungsmodalitäten, *(put and call)* Börsentermingeschäft, Terminhandel, *(real estate)* Vorverkaufsrecht, *(stock exchange)* Option[srecht], Wahlrecht;
at one's ~ nach Wahl; **at buyer's ~** *(cash operation)* Lieferung nach Käufers Wahl; **on the exercise of an ~** aufgrund der Ausübung eines Bezugsrechtes;
buyer's ~ Kaufoption, Vorprämie, **buyer's ~ to double** *(stock exchange)* Nochgeschäft in Käufers Wahl; **call ~** Kauf-, Bezugsoption, Vorprämie[ngeschäft]; **compound ~** Doppelprämie[ngeschäft]; **double ~** Termineinkauf und -verkauf; **first ~** Vorhand [beim Kauf]; ~ **forward** *(Br.)* Optionsgeschäft in Termindevisen; **joint ~** gemeinsam ausgeübte Option; **local ~** *(Br.)* Ortsabstimmung (Ortsentscheid) über eine Schankkonzession; **put ~** Rückprämie[ngeschäft]; **seller's ~** Verkaufsoption, Rückprämie; **seller's ~ to double** Nochgeschäft in Verkäufers Wahl; **settlement ~** Option zur Festlegung der Auszahlung von Lebensversicherungsraten; **single ~** einfaches Prämiengeschäft; **stock ~** *(US)* Aktienbezugsrecht; **traded ~s** gehandelte Optionen; **unexercised ~** nicht ausgeübtes Optionsrecht;
~ **for call** Vorprämiengeschäft; ~ **to double** Nochgeschäft; ~ **of exchange** Umtausch-, Austauschrecht; ~ **to extend** Verlängerungsoption; ~ **of a fine** Wahlrecht einer Geldstrafe; ~ **of nationality** Staatsangehörigkeitsoption; ~ **of (to) purchase** Vorkaufsrecht, [An]kaufsoption; ~ **to purchase land** Vorkaufsrecht beim Erwerb von Grundbesitz; ~ **to put** Käufers Wahl, Option; ~ **of redemption** Rückkaufsrecht; ~ **to sell** Verkaufsoption; ~ **to subscribe to new shares (on new stock, US)** Bezugsrecht auf junge Aktien;
~ *(v.)* Optionsrecht (Vorkaufsrecht) einräumen;
to abandon an ~ Optionsrecht nicht ausüben (aufgeben); **to ask for an ~ on the film rights of a book** an den Filmrechten eines Buches interessiert sein; **to be left to s. one's ~** jem. freigestellt sein; **to be renewable at the ~ of the tenant** nach Ausübung einer Option seitens des Verpächters verlängerbar sein; **to buy an ~ on stock** Bezugsrecht kaufen; **to buy a call ~** Vorprämie kaufen; **to call an ~** *(Br.)* Prämiengeschäft eingehen; **to deal in ~s** *(Br.)* Prämiengeschäfte (Optionsgeschäfte) machen; **to declare ~s** *(Br.)* Prämien erklären; **to exercise one's ~** sein Optionsrecht ausüben; **to give an ~** an die Hand geben; **to give s. o. the ~ of participating** jem. die Teilnahme (Beteiligung) freistellen; **to grant an ~** Optionsrecht einräumen; **to have an ~ on a piece of land** Grundstücksvorkaufsrecht haben (besitzen); **to have no ~ but** keine andere Wahl haben; **to keep one's ~ open** sich noch nicht festlegen; **to leave to s. one's ~** jem. freistellen, in jds. Belieben stellen; **to let one's ~ slide** seine Option verfallen lassen; **to make one's ~** seine Wahl treffen; **to renounce an ~** Option aufgeben; **to rent a building with the ~ of purchase** Haus mit Vorkaufsrecht mieten; **to reserve an ~ to acquire** sich ein Vorkaufsrecht vorbehalten; **to take an ~ on all the future works of an author** Ausschließlichkeitsvertrag mit einem Autor abschliessen; **to take up an ~** Kaufoption (Bezugsrecht) ausüben;
~ **agreement** Bezugsrechtsvereinbarung; ~ **bond** Optionsanleihe, Bezugsrechtsobligation; ~ **business** Terminhandel, Distanz-, Options-, Prämiengeschäft, -handel; ~ **buyer** Prämienkäufer; ~ **certificate to bearer** Inhaberzertifikat; ~ **clause** Optionsklausel; ~ **contract** *(Br.)* Vertrag über den Abschluß eines Prämiengeschäftes; ~ **day** *(Br.)* [Prämien]erklärungstag; ~ **deal** *(Br.)* Prämiengeschäft; ~ **deal for the call** Vorprämiengeschäft; ~ **deal for the put** Rückprämiengeschäft; ~ **dealer** Prämienhändler; ~ **dealings** Options-, Prämien-, Termingeschäfte; ~ **department** Terminabteilung; ~ **exchange** Options-

börse; ~ **exercise** Optionsausübung; **~s market** *(Br.)* Termin-, Prämienmarkt; ~ **money** *(Br.)* Prämiengeld, Prämie; ~ **mortgage** grundbuchlich gesichertes Landesdarlehn; ~ **operator** Prämienspekulant; ~ **order** Auftrag auf Abruf; ~ **payment** Optionszahlung; ~ **period** Optionsfrist, -zeit; ~ **price** Prämienkurs; ~ **rates** *(Br.)* Prämiensätze; **to stipulate an ~ right** Optionsrecht vereinbaren; ~ **stock** *(Br.)* Prämienwerte; ~ **trader** Options-, Terminhändler; ~ **trading** Optionshandel, Termingeschäfte; ~ **writer** Terminhändler.

optional *(US)* Wahlfach;
~ *(a.)* freigestellt, fakultativ, beliebig, wahlfrei, -weise, nicht pflichtgemäß;
~ **at extra cost** auf Wunsch gegen besondere Berechnung; ~ **with the buyer** nach Käufers Wahl;
to be ~ with s. o. in jds. Belieben stehen; **to leave it ~ with s. o.** *(US)* es jem. freistellen;
~ **bargain** Prämiengeschäft; ~ **bonds** *(US)* jederzeit kündbare Obligationen, Optionsanleihe; ~ **clause** Fakultativ-, Optionsklausel; ~ **dividend** Dividende in bar oder in Form einer Gratisaktie; ~ **equipment** *(car)* Extra-, Sonderausstattung; ~ **extras** Zubehör bei Bedarf, *(car)* besondere Ausstattungswünsche; ~ **insurance** fakultative Versicherung; ~ **modes of settlement** *(insurance)* Wahlrecht beim Empfang der Versicherungsleistung; ~ **money** Prämie; ~ **order** Auftrag auf Abruf; ~ **price** Prämienkurs; ~ **provisions** durch Parteivereinbarung abgeänderte (dispositive) Vorschriften; ~ **retirement** Pensionierung auf eigenen Wunsch; ~ **right** Wahl-, Optionsrecht; ~ **standard provision** *(insurance)* verzichtbare Standardbestimmung; ~ **studies** fakultative Studienfächer; ~ **subject** Wahl-, fakultatives Fach; ~ **writ** Aufforderung zur Klageeinlassung.

optionee Optionsberechtigter.

optioner Optionsgewährer, -geber.

opulent sehr vermögend, begütert;
~ **society** Überschußgesellschaft.

oracle *(fig.)* Prophezeiung, unklare Aussage, *(person)* unfehlbare Autorität, Prophet;
to work the ~ *(Br.)* schieben, auf krummen Wegen zum Ziel kommen, hinter den Kulissen agieren.

oracular utterance orakelhafte Äußerungen.

oral mündliches Examen;
~ *(a.)* mündlich;
~ **agreement** mündliche Vereinbarung; ~ **contract** mündlich abgeschlossener Vertrag; ~ **evidence** mündliche Zeugenvernehmung; ~ **examination** mündliche Prüfung; ~ **interview** mündliche Befragung; ~ **partnership** auf mündlicher Vereinbarung beruhende Gesellschaft; ~ **pleading** mündliche Verhandlung; ~ **report** mündlicher Bericht; ~ **teacher** Taubstummenlehrer; **for ~ use** *(med.)* zum innerlichen Gebrauch; ~ **vaccine** Schluckimpfstoff.

orally in mündlicher Form.

orange, squeezed *(fig.)* ausgequetschte Zitrone.

oration Ansprache, offizielle Rede;
[in]direct ~ [in]direkte Rede; **funeral ~** Grabrede.

orator Redner, Sprecher, *(law of equity, US)* Kläger;
public ~ *(Br.)* Universitätssprecher;
to throw out an ~ Redner aus dem Konzept bringen.

oratorial | contest Rednerwettbewerb; **to rise to ~ heights** rednerische Glanzleistung vollbringen.

oratory Rhetorik;
forensic ~ forensische Beredsamkeit;
~ *(a.)* rhetorisch.

orb *(planet)* Einflußgebiet.

orbit *(spaceship)* Kreis-, Umlaufbahn, *(sphere of power)* Machtsphäre, Einflußbereich, Einführungsbereich, -sphäre;
fixed ~ feste Umlaufbahn;
~ *(v.)* Umlaufbahn beschreiben, *(airplane)* auf der Wartebahn fliegen, *(spaceship)* Erde umkreisen;
to blast into ~ in eine Erdumlaufbahn katapultieren; **to bring within the ~ of taxation** Besteuerungsvoraussetzungen schaffen; **to park in a low ~** in eine niedrige Umlaufbahn bringen; **to put into ~** auf eine Umlaufbahn schießen.

orbital | bombing Kreisbahnraketensystem; ~ **distance** Erdentfernung; ~ **ferry** Raumfähre; ~ **flight** Erdumkreisung; ~ **parking space** Erdkreisparkraum.

orbiting auf einer Erdumlaufbahn;
~ **laboratory** Raumfahrtstation; ~ **platform** Weltraumstation; ~ **road** ringförmige Umgehungsstraße; ~ **satellite** Weltraumsatellit.

orchestra Orchester, *(stalls)* erstes Parkett; Orchestersitz;
symphony ~ Symphonie-Orchester;
~ **stall** Sperrsitz.

orchestral | accompaniment Orchesterbegleitung; ~ **performance** Orchestervorstellung.

ordain *(v.)* bestimmen, ver-, anordnen.

ordeal | by fire *(fig.)* Feuerprobe; ~ **in the press** mit der Presse zu bestehende Zerreißprobe;
to go through a terrible ~ schreckliche Zerreißprobe bestehen müssen.

order Ordnung, *(commission)* Auftrag, Bestellung, Order, Kommission, *(court)* gerichtliche Anordnung (Verfügung), *(decree, Br.)* Verfügung, Erlaß, Gebot, Rechtsverordnung, *(direction)* Ver-, Anordnung, [An]weisung, Befehl, Bestimmung, *(honorary distinction)* Orden, Ordenszeichen, *(entry permit, Br.)* Freikarte, Einlaßschein, *(ling.)* Satzstellung, Wortfolge, *(mil.)* vorschriftsmäßige Uniform und Ausrüstung, *(parl.)* Geschäftsordnung, *(order to pay)* Zahlungsanweisung, Order, *(proceedings)* Verfahrensweise, -regel, *(rank)* Art, Sorte, Klasse, Grad, Rang, Reihen-, Rangfolge, *(social status)* Stand, Rang[ordnung], Rangstufe, Gesellschaftsschicht, *(statistics)* Anordnung, *(established succession)* [Reihen]folge, Ordnung, *(Supreme Court, Br.)* Verfahrensregel;
~! ~! *(parl.)* zur Tagesordnung!;
according to your ~ gemäß Ihrer Bestellung; **against ~** auf Bestellung; **as per ~** laut Bestellung; **awaiting your ~s** Ihrer Aufträge gewärtig; **by ~** *(commerce)* laut Auftrag, *(state)* auf Befehl (Anweisung), befehlsgemäß, im Auftrag; **by joint ~** auf gemeinsame Anweisung; **by special ~** *(Br.)* mit besonderem Einlaßschein; **by my ~s** auf meine Veranlassung; **by ~ and for account of** im Auftrag und auf Rechnung von; **by ~ of the court** auf Anordnung des Gerichts; **by ~ of the government** im Staatsauftrag (Auftrag der Regierung); **by ~ of a third party** im Auftrag eines Dritten; **contrary to ~** ordnungswidrig, den Bestimmungen zuwider; **in ~** in der richtigen Reihenfolge, *(parl.)* in Übereinstimmung mit der Geschäftsordnung, zulässig; **in alphabetical ~** in alphabetischer Reihenfolge; **in bad ~** in schlechtem Zustand; **in the ~ of** in der Größenordnung von; **in chronological ~** in zeitlicher Reihenfolge; **in first-rate ~** in erstklassigem Zustand; **in good working ~** in Ordnung, in gutem Zustand; **in good ~ and well conditioned** gut und wohlerhalten; **in marching ~** in Marschordnung; **in numerical ~** nach Nummern geordnet; **in open ~** *(mil.)* in geöffneter Ordnung; **in running ~** betriebsfertig; **in short ~** *(US)* sofort, sogleich; **in working ~** betriebsfähig; **in ~ to balance our account** zum Ausgleich unseres Kontos; **in ~ of merit** dem Range nach; **in ~ of size** der Größe nach [geordnet]; **made to ~** auf Bestellung angefertigt; **made out to ~** an Order ausgestellt; **obtainable on ~** gegen Bestellung erhältlich; **of the first ~** erstklassig; **of a high ~** von hohem Rang; **on ~** in Auftrag gegeben, auf Bestellung, bestellt; **on the ~ of** auf Anordnung (Befehl) von; **on placing the ~** bei Bestellung; **out of ~** *(defective)* nicht betriebsfähig, defekt, kaputt, *(parl.)* nicht in der richtigen Reihenfolge, im Widerspruch zur Geschäftsordnung, unzulässig; **overwhelmed with ~s** mit Aufträgen überhäuft; **owing to lack of ~s** mangels Auftragseingängen; **payable to ~** zahlbar an Order, an Order lautend; **per ~** laut Auftrag, nach Maß; **per ~ of date** chronologisch; **subject to your ~** entsprechend (gemäß) Ihrem Auftrag; **to ~** auf Bestellung, auftragsgemäß, *(check)* an Order, *(mil.)* befehlsgemäß; **to the ~ of** an die Order; **to our own ~** an unsere eigene Order; **under the ~ of** unter dem Befehl von; **until further ~s** bis auf weitere Anweisungen (Bestellungen); **when placing an ~** bei Auftragserteilung;
~s Auftragseingang;
additional ~ zusätzliche Bestellung, Nachbestellung; **adjudication ~** Konkurseröffnungsbeschluß; **administrative ~** Verwaltungsverfügung; **adoption ~** Adoptionsbeschluß; **advance ~** Vorausbestellung; **affiliation ~** Vaterschafts-, Unterhaltsurteil; **attachment ~** Anordnung der Zwangsvollstreckung Beschlagnahmeverfügung, Arrestbefehl; **back ~** rückständiger Auftrag, Auftragsrückstand, -polster, noch ausstehende Restlieferung; **bankruptcy ~** Beschluß über die Eröffnung des Konkursverfahrens; **bastardy ~** *(US)* Unterhaltsurteil; **battle ~** Schlachtordnung; **big-ticket ~** *(stock exchange)* Großauftrag **big ~s** Massenaufträge, massierte Bestellungen; **binding ~** verbindliche Bestellung; **blank ~** Blankoauftrag; **blanket ~** Blankoauftrag; **~s booked** Auftragsbestand, -eingänge; **buying ~** Kaufvertrag; **cable ~** telegrafische Bestellung, Kabelauftrag; **good until cancelled ~** auf Widerruf gültiger Auftrag; **capitalistic ~** kapitalistische Wirtschaftsordnung; **carte blanche ~** Blankoauftrag; **cease-and-desist ~** Unterlassungsverfügung; **charging ~** vorläufiges Verfügungsverbot, Beschlagnahmeverfügung; **chronological ~** chronologische Reihenfolge; **conditional ~** freibleibender Auftrag; **considerable ~**

bedeutende Bestellungen; **~ contained therein** darin enthaltener Auftrag; **continental ~** *(Br.)* Festlandsauftrag; **contingent ~** gekoppelter Auftrag; **covering ~** Deckungsauftrag, -order; **crossed ~** Selbsteintrittsangebot; **curfew ~** Polizeistundenverordnung; **custom ~** Auftragsfertigung; **day ~** nur einen Tag gültiger Börsenauftrag; **decretal ~** einstweilige Anordnung; **delivery ~** Lieferanweisung, Lager-, Lieferschein; **departmental ~** ministerielle Verfügung (Anweisung), ministerieller Erlaß; **deportation ~** Ausweisungsbefehl; **direction ~** *(labo(u)r exchange)* arbeitsamtliche Zuweisung; **disbursing ~** Auszahlungsverfügung; **discretionary ~** unbeschränkter Auftrag; **dispatch ~** Versand-, Speditionsauftrag; **dissolution ~** Liquidationsanordnung; **dividend ~** Dividendenauszahlungsanweisung [des Aktionärs]; **domestic ~** Inlandsauftrag; **emergency ~** *(US)* Ausführungsbestimmung, Durchführungsverordnung; **executive ~** *(US)* Ausführungsbestimmung, Durchführungsverordnung; **export ~** Exportauftrag; **Export Goods Control** ⚲ *(Br.)* Kontrollverfügung für Exportwaren; **expulsion ~** Ausweisungsbefehl; **filled ~s** erledigte (ausgeführte) Aufträge; **final ~** Schlußverfügung; **firm ~** feste Bestellung, fester Auftrag; **forward ~** Kaufauftrag [im Termingeschäft]; **four-day ~** Vollzugsfrist von vier Tagen; **further ~s** weitere Aufträge; **future ~s** zukünftige Aufträge; **garnishee ~** Pfändungs- und Überweisungsbeschluß; **general ~s** *(law court)* Verfahrensanweisungen; **good ~** limitierter Börsenauftrag; **good-until-cancelled ~** bis zum Widerruf gültiger Auftrag; **government ~** Staatsauftrag; **heavy ~s** umfangreiche (große) Aufträge; **higher ~s** höhere Stände; **holy ~s** Priesterweihe; **home-market ~** Inlandsauftrag; **housing ~** Bauauftrag; **huge ~** umfangreicher Auftrag; **implement ~** Durchführungsverordnung; **incoming ~s** eingehende Aufträge, Bestell-, Auftragseingang; **individual ~** Einzelauftrag; **induction ~** *(US)* Gestellungsbefehl; **industrial ~** Wirtschaftssystem; **initial ~** Anfangsbestellung; **instalment ~** Anordnung von Ratenzahlungen; **interim ~** Zwischenverfügung, vorläufige Anordnung; **interlocutory ~** Zwischenverfügung; **judicial ~** richterliche Verfügung, Gerichtsbeschluß; **landing ~** *(Br.)* Zollpassierschein; **large ~** Großauftrag, *(fig.)* schwierige Aufgabe; **a large ~** *(fam.)* viel verlangt; **lawful ~** *(employ)* vertragsgemäße Anweisung; **limited ~** limitierte (begrenzte) Order, limitierter Börsenauftrag; **long ~** Verkaufsauftrag über eigene Aktien; **lost ~** stornierter Auftrag; **lower ~s** *(society)* niedrigere Gesellschaftsschichten; **mail ~** *(US)* Auftrag durch die Post; **make-and-take ~** Abrufauftrag; **maintenance ~** *(Br.)* Unterhaltsurteil; **marching ~s** Marschbefehl; **market ~** *(US)* unlimitierter Börsenauftrag, Bestens-Order; **matched ~s** *(US)* gekoppelte Börsenaufträge; **matrimonial ~** *(Br.)* Anordnung des Getrenntlebens; **the military ~** Soldatenstand; **ministerial ~** Ministerialerlaß, -verfügung; **monastic ~** Mönchsorden; **money ~** *(Br.)* Zahlungs-, Postanweisung [bis zu £ 40], Geldüberweisung durch die Post; **foreign (international) money ~** Auslandspostanweisung; **money-losing ~** Verlustauftrag, -geschäft; **new ~s** Neuaufträge; **new ~s received** Auftragseingänge; **~ nisi** vorläufiger Gerichtsbeschluß; **no ~s** keine Aufträge; **off-the shelf ~s** Bestellungen auf Abruf, Abrufauftrag; **offshore ~s** *(US)* Auslands-, Rüstungshilfsaufträge; **open ~** unlimitierte (bis auf Widerruf gültige) Order, *(mil.)* geöffnete Ordnung; **option ~** Auftrag auf Abruf; **oral ~** mündliche Bestellung; **outstanding ~s** unerledigte Aufträge; **own ~** eigene Order; **peremptory ~** berufungsunfähige gerichtliche Verfügung; **periodical ~** periodischer Auftrag; **permanent ~** Dauerauftrag; **pickup ~** Auslieferungsanweisung; **positive ~** ausdrücklicher Befehl; **postal ~** *(Br.)* Postanweisung; **postal money ~** *(US)* Postanweisung [für kleinere Beträge]; **post-office ~** *(Br.)* Geldüberweisung durch die Post, Postanweisung [bis £ 40]; **procedural ~** Verfahrensbeschluß; **production ~** Produktionsauftrag; **provisional ~** *(Br.)* einstweilige Anordnung, Ausnahme-, Notverordnung; **purchasing (purchase) ~** Kaufvertrag, Bestellung; **~s received** Auftragseingang; **receiving ~** *(Br.)* Konkurseröffnungsbeschluß, offener Arrest; **reception ~** Entmündigungsbeschluß; **regimental ~s** Regimentsbefehl; **release ~** Freilassungsbeschluß; **renewal ~** Erneuerungsauftrag; **repeat ~** Nachbestellung; **requisition ~** *(house)* Beschlagnahmebefehl; **reserve ~s** zurückgehaltene Aufträge; **restraining ~** *(Br.)* Verfügungsverbot; **routing ~** Anordnung eines Leitwegs; **rush ~** vordringlicher Auftrag, dringende Bestellung, Eilauftrag; **sailing ~s** Auslaufbefehl; **sealed ~s** Geheimbefehl; **second ~** Nachbestellung; **selling ~** Verkaufsauftrag; **service ~** Betriebsauftrag; **short ~** *(restaurant)* Schnellgericht; **social ~** Gesellschaftsordnung; **speaking ~** Erläuterungsbeschluß; **special ~** Sonderauftrag, *(Br.)* Verordnung mit Gesetzeskraft; **specific ~** Sonderauftrag; **standing ~** laufender Auftrag, lau-

fende Bestellung, Dauerauftrag; **standing ~s** [amtliche] Regeln, Bestimmungen; **statutory ~** *(Br.)* Anordnung mit Gesetzeskraft, Verwaltungs-, Rechtsverordnung, *(parl.)* Geschäftsordnung; **stock-exchange ~** Börsenauftrag; **stocking-up ~** Lagerauftrag; **stop ~** *(broker)* Auftragsstop; **stop-[loss] ~** bei Erreichung eines bestimmten Kurses wirksam werdende Bestens-Order; **stop-payment ~** Auszahlungssperre; **strict ~** ausdrückliche (genaue) Anweisung; **strike ~** Streikbefehl; **supervision ~** *(liquidation)* Überwachungsverfügung, *(police, Br.)* Anordnung der Polizeiaufsicht; **supplementary ~** Nachbestellung; **tall ~** starke Zumutung; **telephone ~** telefonisch aufgegebene Bestellung; **trial ~** Probeauftrag; **unconditional ~** unwiderruflich erteilter Zahlungsauftrag; **unfilled ~s** unerledigte Aufträge, Auftragsüberhang; **union benefit ~** von der Gewerkschaft ausgehandelte Unterstützung; **unlimited ~** unlimitierter Auftrag, unlimitierte Order; **urgent ~** Eilbestellung; **verbal ~** mündlich aufgegebene Bestellung, mündliche Anweisung; **vesting ~** gerichtliche Besitzeinweisung; **walking ~s** *(mil.)* Marschbefehl; **week ~** Börsenauftrag auf Wochenfrist; **working ~** betriebsfähiger Zustand; **written ~** schriftliche Bestellung;

law and ~ öffentliche Ordnung und Sicherheit;

~ from abroad Auslandsautrag; **~ for an account** Anordnung der Rechnungslegung, Rechnungslegungsbeschluß, *(stock exchange)* Terminauftrag; **~ of adjudication** Beschluß über die Eröffnung des Konkursverfahrens; **~ of administration** Reihenfolge der Regelung von Nachlaßverbindlichkeiten, Verteilungsanordnung; **~ in advance** Vorausbestellung; **~ appointing receiver [in bankruptcy]** *(US)* Konkurseröffnungsbeschluß; **~ to arbitrate** Schlichtungsverfügung; **~ of attachment** Forderungspfändung, Pfändungsbeschluß; **~ on a bank** Überweisungsauftrag; **standing ~ on a bank** Dauerauftrag an eine Bank; **~ of battle** Kampfgliederung, Kräfteverteilung; **~ at best** Bestensauftrag; **~s on the book** gebuchte Aufträge; **~s for the building industry** Nachfrage nach Bauleistungen; **~ of business** *(parl.)* Tagesordnung; **~ of capital seniority** Priorität der Kapitalkonten; **~ to clear** Einlösungsauftrag; **~s completed and still in work** abgewickelte und noch laufende Aufträge; **~ for collection** Inkassoauftrag; **~s to come** erwartete Aufträge; **~ of commitment** Einweisungsanordnung; **~ for costs** Kostenentscheidung; **~ in council** *(Br.)* königlicher Erlaß, Rechtsverordnung, Kabinettverfügung; **~ from within the country** Inlandsauftrag; **~ of the court** gerichtliche Verfügung, Gerichtsbeschluß; **~ to cover** Deckungsorder, -auftrag; **~ of the day,** *(mil.)* Tagesbefehl, *(parl.)* festgelegte Tagesordnung; **~ of delivery** Lieferauftrag; **~ for delivery** Auslieferungsanweisung; **~ of discharge** *(Br.)* (for discharge, *US*) [of bankrupt] Aufhebung des Konkursverfahrens, Rehabilitierungs-, Konkursaufhebungsbeschluß; **~ discharging a trustee** Entlastungsverfügung eines Treuhänders; **~ and disposition** *(bankruptcy, Br.)* Besitz und scheinbares Eigentum; **~ of distribution** *(debtors)* Prioritätsordnung; **statutory ~ of distribution** gesetzliche Erbfolge; **~ for the enforcement** Vollstreckungsklausel; **~ of filiation** Unterhalts-, Vaterschaftsurteil; **~ for foreclosure** *(Br.)* Ausschlußurteil, Pfandverfallsbeschluß; **~ for futures** Terminlieferungsauftrag; **~ for goods** Warenauftrag, -bestellung; **~s on hand** vorliegende Aufträge, Auftragsbestand; **~ of liquidity** Liquiditätspriorität; **~ of magnitude** Größenordnung; **~ of march** *(mil.)* Marschordnung; **~ of merit rating** Reihenfolge der Wichtigkeit, Rangfolge, *(advertising)* Anzeigeneinstufung nach dem Webetext, Methode zur Feststellung der Werbewirkung, *(honorary distinction)* Verdienstorden; **~ to negotiate** Negoziierungsauftrag; **~ to pay (for payment)** Zahlungsanweisung, -aufforderung; **conditional ~ to pay** bedingte Zahlungsanweisung; **~ to pay costs** Kostenentscheidung, -urteil; **~s payable at foreign banks** Anweisungen auf auswärtige Plätze; **~ to stop payment** Auftrag zur Zahlungseinstellung; **~s placed by letter** schriftlich erteilte Aufträge; **~s placed by telephone** telefonisch erteilte Aufträge; **~ for possession** *(Br.)* gerichtlicher Räumungsbeschluß; **~ of precedence** Rangfolge, -ordnung, Vorzugsanordnung; **~ of preference** Vorzugsanordnung; **~ of presentation** Reihenfolge der Aufführung von Bilanzposten; **~ of priority** Prioritätenrangfolge; **~ to purchase** Kaufauftrag, -order; **~ to quit** *(Br.)* Räumungsbeschluß; **~ of rank** Rangordnung; **~ of reference** Verweisungsbeschluß, *(committee)* Aufgabengebiet; **~ of registrations** Reihenfolge der Eintragungen; **~ of reinsurance** Rückversicherungsauftrag; **~ for the release from prison** Haftentlassungsanordnung; **~ for remittance** Überweisungsauftrag; **~ of removal** Ausweisungsbefehl, Ortsverweisung; **~ to sell** Verkaufsauftrag, -order; **~ for sequence** zeitliche Reihenfolge; **~ of sequestration** Beschlagnahmeanordnung, -beschluß; ~ **for the settlement** *(stock exchange, Br.)* Terminauftrag; ~ **to show cause** Aufforderung zur Klagebegründung; ~ **of speaking** Rednerfolge; ~ **of speech** Rednerfolge; ~ **of succession** Erbfolgeordnung; ~ **to tax costs** Kostenurteil; ~ **valid today** Tagesauftrag; ~ **of validation** prozeßleitende Verfügung; ~ **to view** Besichtigungserlaubnis; **negotiated** ~ **of withdrawal** *(US)* Abhebungsvoraussetzung; ~ **in writing** schriftliche Verfügung;

~ *(v.)* *(commission)* bestellen, Auftrag aufgeben, in Auftrag geben, *(direct)* befehlen, regeln, anordnen, -weisen, verfügen, *(put in order)* regeln, ordnen, gliedern;

~ **an account to be blocked** Konto sperren lassen; ~ **one's affairs** seine Angelegenheiten in Ordnung bringen; ~ **in advance (beforehand)** vor[aus]bestellen; ~ **again** nachbestellen; ~ **away** *(criminal)* abführen; ~ **back** zurückbeordern; ~ **by cable** telegrafisch bestellen; ~ **by telephone** telefonisch bestellen; ~ **s. o. back to his post** j. auf seinen Posten zurückbeordern; ~ **a cab** Taxi bestellen; ~ **the car** Auto vorfahren lassen; ~ **s. o. a change of air** jem. Luftveränderung anordnen; ~ **to bear the costs** Kosten auferlegen; ~ **s. o. out of the country** jds. Ausweisung veranlassen; ~ **s. th. for dinner** etw. zum Mittagessen bestellen; ~ **and direct** durch Beschluß anordnen; ~ **expressly** ausdrücklich anordnen; ~ **to the front** an die Front beordern; ~ **goods** Waren bestellen; ~ **goods from London** Warenbestellung für London aufgeben; ~ **goods through a representative** Waren über einen Vertreter bestellen; ~ **goods from the sample** laut Muster bestellen; ~ **s. o. to be hanged** zum Tode durch Erhängen verurteilen; ~ **s. o. home** j. zurückrufen; ~ **s. o. out of one's house** j. aus seinem Haus weisen; ~ **an inquiry** Untersuchung veranlassen; ~ **large quantities** große Aufträge erteilen; ~ **one's life according to strict rules** strenge Richtlinien für seine Lebensführung festlegen; ~ **lunch for 1.30** Mittagessen um (auf) 13.30 Uhr bestellen; ~ **orally** mündlich bestellen; ~ **the removal of disorderly persons** ungehörige Besucher aus dem Sitzungssaal weisen lassen; ~ **a player off the field** Spieler vom Platz verweisen; ~ **the retreat** Rückzug anordnen; ~ **out of the room** aus dem Zimmer weisen; ~ **silence** um Ruhe bitten; ~ **one's supplies for the season** seinen Bedarf für die kommende Saison decken; ~ **in supplies** Vorräte bestellen; ~ **s. o. suspended** j. vom Dienst suspendieren; ~ **a taxi** Taxi bestellen; ~ **on preferential terms** mit Vorzugsbedingungen bestellen; ~ **out troops** Truppen aufbieten; ~ **by wire** telegrafisch bestellen; **to acknowledge an** ~ Annahme einer Bestellung bestätigen; **to act in compliance with one's** ~**s** auftragsgemäß handeln; **to act (go, run) contrary to s. one's** ~**s** gegen jds. Anordnungen handeln; **to act upon an** ~ Auftrag ausführen; **to apply to the court for an** ~ **of discharge** Aufhebung des Konkursverfahrens beantragen; **to arrange in alphabetical** ~ alphabetisch anordnen; **to arrange in chronological** ~ chronologisch anordnen; **to arrange in** ~ **of value** wertmäßig anordnen; **to arrange things in one's own** ~ eigenmächtige Anordnungen treffen; **to attend to an** ~ Auftrag erledigen (ausführen); **to be behind on** ~**s** mit den Aufträgen im Rückstand sein; **to be favo(u)red with an** ~ Auftrag erhalten; **to be in** ~ *(accounts)* stimmen, *(passport)* vollgültig sein; **to be in apple-ple** ~ in bester Ordnung (in Butter) sein; **to be arranged in alphabetical** ~ alphabetisch angeordnet sein; **to be in holy** ~**s** dem geistlichen Stand angehören; **to be in good working** ~ voll betriebsfähig (in betriebsfähigem Zustand) sein, gut funktionieren; **to be of a high** ~ auf hoher Stufe stehen; **to be made out to** ~ an Order lauten; **to be on** ~ bestellt sein (in Auftrag gegeben, mit Aufträgen versehen sein; **to be out of** ~ defekt sein, *(lift)* ausgefallen sein; **to be the** ~ **of the day** an der Tagesordnung sein, zur Tagesordnung gehören; **to be under sailing** ~**s** Marschbefehl erhalten haben; **to be under** ~**s to leave** Abreisetermin erhalten haben; **to be called to** ~ Ordnungsruf erhalten; **to be wearing all one's** ~**s** alle seine Orden tragen; **to book an** ~ Bestellung aufnehmen (annehmen, buchen); **to call for** ~**s** Bestellungen einholen; **to call to** ~ zur Ordnung rufen, Ordnungsruf erteilen; **to call a meeting to** ~ *(US)* Versammlung eröffnen; **to cancel an** ~ abbestellen, Bestellung rückgängig machen, Auftrag annullieren (stornieren); **to canvass** ~**s** Aufträge hereinholen; **to carry out** ~**s** Weisungen (Vorschriften) ausführen, Auftrag erledigen; **to carry out an** ~ **to the letter** Auftrag buchstabengetreu ausführen; **to come to** ~ in die Tagesordnung eintreten, zur Tagesordnung übergehen; **to comply with an** ~ Verfügung befolgen; **to confirm an** ~ **in writing** Bestellung schriftlich bestätigen; **to countermand an** ~ Bestellung widerrufen; **to deal with an** ~ Auftrag bearbeiten (ausführen); **to deal with an** ~ **as one of special urgency** Auftrag als vordringlich behandeln; **to decline an** ~ Bestellung (Auftrag) ablehnen; **to discharge an** ~ Verfü-

gung aufheben; **to effect an** ~ Auftrag ausführen; **to enforce** ~ *(parl.)* auf parlamentarischen Spielregeln bestehen; **to enter up s. one's** ~ jds. Auftrag buchen; **to execute an** ~ Auftrag ausführen; **to execute an** ~ **to the best advantage** Auftrag bestens ausführen; **to execute an** ~ **in every detail** Auftrag in allen Punkten ausführen (erledigen); **to execute all** ~**s in strict rotation** Aufträge in der Reihenfolge des Eingangs erledigen; **to fail to comply with the court's** ~**s** Anordnungen des Gerichts mißachten; **to fill an** ~ *(US)* Aufrag ausführen (erledigen); **to get out of** ~ in Unordnung geraten, *(machine)* nicht mehr funktionieren; **to give** ~**s for the work to be started** Fabrik in Betrieb setzen lassen; **to give a buying (selling)** ~ zum Kauf (Verkauf) aufgeben; **to give an** ~ Auftrag erteilen, Bestellung machen (aufgeben), bestellen; **to give** ~**s** Anordnungen erlassen, Verfügung treffen; **to give an administrative** ~ Verwaltungsverfügung erlassen; **to give one's best attention to an** ~ Auftrag bestens ausführen; **to give s. o. the** ~ **of the boot** jem. feuern; **to give a tradesman an** ~ **for goods** Warenauftrag an einen Händler erteilen; **to handle** ~**s** Aufträge bearbeiten; **to personally handle an** ~ sich persönlich um die Auftragserledigung kümmern; **to have an** ~ als Lieferauftrag vorliegen haben; **to hold money to s. one's** ~ Geld zu jds. Verfügung halten; **to hold to the buyer's** ~ zur Verfügung des Käufers halten; **to ignore an** ~ Anordnung nicht beachten; **to issue an** ~ Verfügung (Anordnung) erlassen; **to keep** ~ für Ruhe und Ordnung sorgen; **to keep in** ~ in Ordnung halten, beaufsichtigen; **to keep** ~ **in a class room** für Ordnung in einer Schulklasse sorgen; **to keep pace with the rush of** ~**s** Auftragseingänge zügig erledigen; **to lag behind incoming** ~**s** hinter dem Auftragseingang herhinken; **to leave one's affairs in perfect** ~ sein Haus wohlbestallt zurücklassen; **to mail in one's** ~ *(US)* postalisch Aufrag erteilen; **to make an** ~ Verfügung (Anordnung) erlassen; **to make to** ~ nach Bestellung anfertigen; **to make a bill payable to** ~ Wechsel an Order ausstellen; **to make an** ~ **for conditional discharge** Strafe zur Bewährung aussetzen; **to make a subsequent** ~ nachbestellen; **to make an** ~ **prohibiting a public procession** Demonstration[szug] verbieten; **to make an** ~ **vacating a registration** Sperrvermerksbeschluß erlassen; **to make up an** ~ Auftrag zusammenstellen; **to make an** ~ **for the winding up** Liquidationsbeschluß erlassen, *(Br.)* Konkurseröffnungsbeschluß erlassen; **to meet all** ~**s in strict rotation** alle Aufträge in der Reihenfolge des Eingangs erledigen; **to note an** ~ von einem Auftrag Vormerkung nehmen; **to obtain an** ~ Gerichtsbeschluß erwirken; **to obtain an** ~ **of possession** *(Br.)* Räumungsurteil erwirken; **to pass (proceed) to the** ~ **of the day** zur Tagesordnung übergehen; **to pay to s. one's** ~ an jds. Order zahlen; **to place an** ~ in Auftrag geben, Auftrag erteilen; **to place an** ~ **direct** Auftrag unmittelbar erteilen; **to place an** ~ **with a firm** Artikel bei einer Firma bestellen; **to place an** ~ **at once** sofort bestellen; **to preserve the** ~ **of business** Tagesordnung einhalten; **to proceed to the** ~ **of the day** zur Tagesordnung übergehen; **to process an order** Bestellung bearbeiten; **to put one's affairs in** ~ sein Testament machen; **to put goods on** ~ Warenbestellung aufgeben; **to put everything out of** ~ riesiges Durcheinander anrichten; **to put high in one's** ~ **of priority** hohen Dringlichkeitswert zuerkennen; **to put in** ~ in Ordnung bringen; **to put a machine out of** ~ Maschine kaputtmachen; **to put a room in** ~ Zimmer aufräumen; **to quash the** ~ **of an inferior court** Verfügung eines untergeordneten Gerichts aufheben; **to raise a point of** ~ auf die Tagesordnung setzen; **to refuse an** ~ Bestellung ablehnen; **to release an** ~ Auftrag erteilen; **to remand an** ~ Auftrag zurücknehmen; **to renew an** ~ nachbestellen; **to repeat an** ~ Bestellung erneuern; **to restore peace and** ~ öffentliche Ordnung wiederherstellen; **to revoke an** ~ Auftrag rückgängig machen (stornieren), Aufträge kassieren; **to rise to** ~ *(parl.)* zur Geschäftsordnung sprechen; **to rule a question out of** ~ Frage als nicht zur Tagesordnung gehörig bezeichnen; **to secure an** ~ Auftrag erhalten (buchen); **to send an** ~ **by letter** Auftrag brieflich erteilen; **to send for** ~**s** Aufträge erbitten, Bestellungen entgegennehmen; **to set in** ~ ordnen; **to set one's house in** ~ seinen Nachlaß regeln; **to set aside an** ~ Beschluß aufheben; **to set up a new** ~ neues Herrschaftssystem begründen; **to share an** ~ **on a 50:50 basis** an einem Auftrag hälftig beteiligt sein; **to shift** ~**s** Aufträge verlagern; **to signal an** ~ Befehl übermitteln; **to solicit** ~**s** sich um Aufträge bemühen, Aufträge sammeln; **to space** ~**s** Aufträge verteilen; **to take an** ~ Bestellung annehmen; **to take holy** ~**s** in den geistlichen Stand eintreten; **to take** ~**s only from s. o.** sich nur nach jds. Anweisungen richten; **to transmit an** ~ Auftrag übermitteln; **to undertake** ~**s** Aufträge annehmen; **to withdraw an** ~ Auftrag stornieren (entziehen);

~-**acceptance form** Bestellaufnahmeformular; ~-**acceptance slip** (*bookseller*) Aufnahmezettel; ~ **backlog** Auftragsbestand; ~ **bill of exchange** Orderpapier, -wechsel; ~ **bill of lading** Orderfrachtbrief, -konnossement; ~ **blank** Beschlußformular, (*US*) Bestellschein, -zettel, Auftragsformular; ~ **bonds** Orderschuldverschreibungen; ~ **book** Bestell-, Auftragsbuch, -liste, (*mil.*) Parolebuch, (*parl., Br.*) Liste angemeldeter Anträge; **lengthening** ~ **books** wachsender Auftragsbestand; ~ **book figures** Auftragszahlen; ~-**book sheet** Bestellbuchblatt; ~ **card** Bestell-, Auftragskarte; ~ **card-index** Bestellkartei; ~ **checker** Auftragsprüfer; ~ **checking** Auftragsprüfung; ~ **cheque** (*Br.*) Orderscheck; ~ **clause** Orderklausel; ~ **and disposition clause** (*bankrupt*) Eigentumsvermutungsklausel; ~ **clerk** Auftragsbuchhalter; **standing** ~**s committee** Geschäftsordnungsausschuß; ~ **date** Auftragsdatum; ~ **department** Auftragsabteilung; ~ **entry** Auftragseingang; ~ **filling** Auftragserledigung; ~ **flow** Auftragszugang, -strom; ~ **form** Auftragsformular, -schein, Bestellschein, -zettel, -formular; **combination sales-**~-**shipper invoice form** kombiniertes Auftrags- und Versandrechnungsformular; **postcard** ~ **form** vorgedruckte Auftragspostkarte; **purchase** ~ **form** Bestellformular; ~ **handling** Auftragsbearbeitung; ~ **index** Auftragsindex; ~ **instrument** Orderpapier; ~ **intake** Auftragseingang; ~-**letter** Bestellbrief; ~ **level** Auftragshöhe; ~ **list** Bestelliste; ~ **number** Kommissions-, Bestellnummer; ~ **paper** (*US*) Orderpapier, (*parl.*) Tages-, Sitzungsprogramm, schriftliche Tagesordnung; ~ **picture** Auftragsbild, -lage; ~ **placing** Auftragsvergabe; ~ **position** Auftragslage; ~ **processing** Auftragsbearbeitung; ~ **processing system** Auftragsbearbeitungssystem; **economic** ~ **quantity** wirtschaftliche Auftragsgröße; ~-**of-merit rating** Vergleichsindex eines Werbewirksamkeitstests; ~ **service** Bestelldienst, Auftragserledigung; ~ **sheet (slip)** Auftragsschein, Auftrags-, Bestellformular, -zettel; ~ **statistic** Anordnungsmaßzahl; ~ **taker** Auftragskassierer; **electronic** ~ **transmission** elektronische Bestellübermittlung.

ordered, as wie bestellt, laut Bestellung, auftragsgemäß;
it is hereby ~ **and adjudged** hiermit wird zu Recht erkannt;
to be ~ **abroad** auf eine Auslandsreise geschickt werden; **to be** ~ **to pay costs** zu den Kosten verurteilt werden.

ordering Bestellung;
when ~ bei Auftragserteilung (Vergabe von Aufträgen);
timed ~ terminierte Bestellungen;
~ **in advance** Vorausbestellung; ~ **in salesroom** Bestellung im Verkaufsraum; **requirement-related** ~ **of stock** bedarfsgerechte Lagerbestellung;
to be fond of ~ **people about** Leute gern herumkommandieren;
~ **activity** Auftragstätigkeit; ~ **department** Bestellabteilung; **to switch to a hand to mouth** ~ **pace** Auftragserteilung nur im Bedarfsfall vornehmen; ~ **references** Bestellhinweise.

orderly Krankenwärter, -pfleger, (*mil.*) Ordonnanz, (*street cleaner, Br.*) Straßenkehrer;
hospital ~ Feldlazarettgehilfe, Sanitätsunteroffizier;
~ (*a.*) ordentlich, (*regular*) ordnungs-, regelmäßig, (*mil.*) diensthabend, -tuend, im Dienst;
to be very ~ sehr methodisch vorgehen;
~ **arrangement** systematische Anordnung; ~ **behavio(u)r** ordnungsgemäßes Verhalten; ~ **bin** (*Br.*) Müllkasten; ~ **book** (*mil.*) Befehls-, Parolebuch; ~ **citizen** friedlicher Bürger; ~ **crowd** friedliche Menge; ~ **desk** aufgeräumter Schreibtisch; **to be on** ~ **duty** Ordonnanzdienst haben; **to be arranged in an** ~ **fashion** methodisch geordnet sein; ~ **housewife** methodisch arbeitende Hausfrau; ~ **officer** diensthabender Offizier, Ordonnanzoffizier, Offizier vom Dienst; ~ **retreat** geordneter Rückzug; ~ **room** (*mil.*) Schreibstube, Geschäftszimmer.

ordinal succession (*math.*) Reihenfolge.

ordinance [Magistrats]verordnung, Verfügung, Erlaß;
municipal ~ (*US*) Gemeindesatzung, -verfassung, -ordnung, städtische Verordnung; **police** ~ Polizeiverordnung; **traffic** ~ Verkehrsvorschrift;
~ **of the forest** (*Br.*) Forstgesetz;
to issue (pass) an ~ Verordnung erlassen (verabschieden).

ordinaries (*Br.*) Stammaktien;
participating preferred ~ zusätzlich gewinnbeteiligte Vorzugsaktien.

ordinary (*employment*) ständiges Dienst- und Anstellungsverhältnis, (*judge*) ordentlicher Richter, (*meal*) gewöhnliche Mahlzeit, Alltagskost, (*probate court, US*) Nachlaßrichter, (*tavern*) fester Mittagstisch;
in ~ von Amts wegen; **out of the** ~ ungewöhnlich;
merely ~ (*US*) nur Hausmannskost;
to be laid up in ~ (*ship*) außer Dienst gestellt werden;

~ (*a.*) (*customary*) gebräuchlich, herkömmlich, gewöhnlich, normal, (*judicial procedure*) ordentlich, (*ex officio*) von Amts wegen, (*salaried*) fest angestellt, (*usual*) gewöhnlich, üblich;
~ **account** normales Konto; ~ **agent** ständiger Vertreter; ~ **ambassador** ordentlicher Gesandter; ~ **amount of business** üblicher Geschäftsumfang; ~ **annuity** nachschüssige Rente; ~ **bill** normale (übliche) Rechnung; ~ **bill of exchange** Handelswechsel; ~ **budget** ordentlicher Haushalt; ~ **business** normaler Geschäftsgang, (*general meeting*) übliche Tagesordnung, (*life insurance*) Prämienzahlung mittels weit auseinanderliegender Zeiträume; ~ **calling** ständige Arbeitsverrichtung; ~ **capital** Stammkapital; ~ **care** im Verkehr übliche Sorgfalt; ~ **conveyance** außergerichtliche Auflassung; ~ **course of business** normaler Geschäftsgang; ~ **course of post** normale Postbeförderung und Zustellung; **to act in the** ~ **course of the partnership** sich im Rahmen der üblichen Gesellschaftertätigkeit halten; ~ **court** (*US*) ordentliches Gericht; ~ **creditor** Massegläubiger; ~ **unsecured creditor** einfacher Massegläubiger; ~ **dangers incident to employment** Berufsrisiko; **an** ~ **day's work** normale Tagesleistung; ~ **dealings** gewöhnliche Zahlungsbedingungen; ~ **debts** Buch-, Masseschulden; ~ **department** (*savings bank*) Abteilung für jederzeit kündbar angelegte Spargelder; ~ **depreciation** normale Abschreibung, Normalabschreibung; ~ **diligence** verkehrsübliche Sorgfalt; ~ **dividend** Stammdividende; ~ **domestic arrangements** (*Br.*) gewöhnliche eheliche Haushalts- und Lebensgemeinschaft; ~ **expenses** (*municipal business*) notwendige Ausgaben; ~ **face** Alltagsgesicht; ~ **handling** (*railway*) normale Abfertigung; ~ **hazards of occupation** übliches Berufsrisiko; ~ **income** Normaleinkommen; ~ **inspection** (*railroad*) übliche Prüfung bei der Abfertigung; ~ **endowment insurance** abgekürzte Lebensversicherung; ~ **life insurance** (*US*) (*assurance, Br.*) Lebensversicherung auf den Todesfall, Großlebensversicherung; ~ **interest** Zinsen auf Basis von 360 Tagen; ~ **income** Normaleinkommen; ~ **job** irgendeine Beschäftigung; ~ **kerosene** markenübliches Kerosin; **very** ~ **kind of man** (*sl.*) Dutzendversicherung; ~ **man in the street** kleiner Mann auf der Straße; ~ **meeting** (*Br.*) ordentliche Hauptversammlung; ~ **member** ordentliches Mitglied; ~ **mortal** gewöhnlicher Sterblicher; ~ **mortgage** Verkehrshypothek; ~ **neglect** Mangel der im Verkehr erforderlichen Sorgfalt; ~ **negligence** (*US*) leichte Fahrlässigkeit; ~ **partner** (*Br.*) Komplementär; ~ **partnership** (*Br.*) offene Handelsgesellschaft; ~ **people** das Volk, Normalverbraucher; ~ **[prudent] person** normaler Durchschnittsmensch; ~ **policy** (*life insurance*) Normalpolice; ~ **position** (*advertising*) Plazierung ohne Berücksichtigung von Sonderwünschen; ~ **preferred share** (*Br.*) gewöhnliche Vorzugsaktie; ~ **proceedings** ordentliches Verfahren; ~ **quality** durchschnittliche Qualität; ~ **rate** normales Porto; ~ **reader** Durchschnittsleser; ~ **receipts** (*US*) ordentliche Staatseinnahmen; ~ **rent** wirtschaftliche Rente; ~ **repairs** normal (üblicherweise) anfallende Reparaturen, Erhaltungs- und Schönheitsreparaturen; ~ **residence** gewöhnlicher Aufenthaltsort, Steuerwohnsitz; ~ **resolution** Beschluß mit einfacher Stimmenmehrheit; ~ **risk** gewöhnliches Berufsrisiko; ~ **scale of remuneration** üblicher Gehaltsrahmen; ~ **seaman** Leichtmatrose; ~ **services** (*administrator*) ordnungsgemäße Nachlaßabwicklung; ~ **session** ordentliche Sitzungsperiode; ~ **share** (*Br.*) Stammaktie; ~ **share capital** (*Br.*) Stammkapital; ~ **shareholder** (*Br.*) Stammaktionär; ~ **skill in an art** handelsübliche (handwerkliche) Geschicklichkeit; ~ **stock** (*Br.*) auf das Stammkapital lautende Wertpapiere; ~ **stockholder** (*US*) Stammaktionär; ~ **telegram** gewöhnliches Telegramm; ~ **tourist** gewöhnlicher Tourist; ~ **train** fahrplanmäßiger Zug; ~ **travel** verkehrsübliche Straßenbenutzung; ~ **treaty** (*law of nations*) rechtsgeschäftlicher Vertrag; ~ **unsecured debts** einfache Masseschulden; ~ **use** gewöhnlicher Gebrauch; **in the** ~ **way** üblicherweise; ~ **written law** gesetztes Recht.

ordnance (*mil.*) Ausrüstung, Waffen, Artillerie, Feldzeugwesen;
♀ **Department** (*US*) Zeug-, Waffenamt; ~ **depot** (*mil.*) Materialdepot, Arsenal; ~ **map** (*US*) Generalstabskarte; ~ **office** Zeugamt; ~ **officer** Waffenoffizier; ~ **park** Feldzeugpark; ♀ **Survey** (*Br.*) amtliche Landaufnahme, -vermessung.

ore, low-grade geringwertiges Erz.

organ Orgel, (*instrument*) Werkzeug, Instrument, Hilfsmittel, Organ, (*intermediary*) Vermittler, (*newspaper*) Sprachrohr, Organ;
through the government ~ durch behördliche Äußerungen;
administrative ~ Verwaltungsorgan; **house** ~ (*US*) Betriebszeitung; **official** ~ offizielles Organ; **party** ~ Parteiorgan; **principal** ~ (*UNO*) Hauptorgan; **street** ~ Leierkasten; **subsidiary** ~ Hilfsorgan; **theater** ~ Kinoorgel;

~ **of communication** Verbindungsglied; ~ **of corporation** Verbandsblatt; ~ **of the editor** Organ des Herausgebers; ~ **of government** Regierungsorgan; ~ **of public opinion** Organ der öffentlichen Meinung; ~ **of the party** Parteiorgan; **~s of the United Nations** Organe der Vereinten Nationen;

~ **company** *(US)* Organgesellschaft; ~ **grinder** Leierkastenmann.

organic organisiert, systematisch, *(constitutional)* organisch, verfassungsrechtlich, -mäßig, konstitutionell;

~ **act** *(politics, US)* Grundgesetz, Gründungsstatut; ~ **chemistry** organische Chemie; ~ **disease** organische Krankheit; ~ **law** Verfassungs-, Grundgesetz; ~ **whole** organisches Ganzes.

organism Organismus, Struktur;

social ~ soziales Gefüge.

organizable organisierbar.

organization *(company)* Betrieb, Firma, *(framing)* Gliederung, Einrichtung, *(organized body)* organisierter Zusammenschluß, Organisation, Vereinigung, Verband, Körperschaft, *(organizing)* Gestaltung, Einrichtung, Bildung, Organisierung, *(politics)* Parteiorganisation, *(of undertaking)* Gründung, Bildung; **without an ~ behind** ohne jeden Rückhalt;

administrative ~ Verwaltungsapparat; **affiliated** ~s angeschlossene Verbände; **business** ~ Geschäftsgründung, Organisation eines Unternehmens; **business** ~s Unternehmensformen des Handelsrechts; **central** ~ Zentralorganisation; **charity** ~ Fürsorge-, Wohlfahrtsorganisation, -verband; **Common Market** ~ Marktordnung der Europäischen Gemeinschaft; **compulsory** ~ Organisationszwang; **cover** ~ Deckorganisation; **criminal** ~ Verbrecherorganisation; **denominational** ~ konfessionell gebundene Organisation; **United Nations Educational Scientific and Cultural** ~ **(UNESCO)** Organisation der Vereinten Nationen für Erziehung, Wissenschaft und Kultur; **faulty** ~ Organisationsfehler; **head** ~ Spitzenverband; **industrial** ~ Industrieverband; **informal** ~ lose Organisationsform; **labo(u)r** ~ Arbeiter-, Gewerkschaftsorganisation; **marketing** ~ Absatzorganisation; **nongovernment** ~ nichtstaatliche Organisation; **nonprofit** ~ gemeinnützige Einrichtung; **personnel** ~ Personalverwaltung; **professional** ~ berufsständische Vertretung, Berufsverband; **retail sales** ~ Einzelhandelsverkaufsorganisation; **scalar** ~ Linienorganisation; **self-regulatory** ~ Verband mit eigenen Kontrollfunktionen; **shadow** ~ Deckorganisation; **smalltime** ~ unwichtiger Verband; **standard** ~ Einheitsorganisation; **subsidiary** ~ Unterorganisation; **technical** ~ Fachorganisation, -verband; **tentative** ~ vorläufige Organisation; **top-head (top-heavy)** ~ kopflastige Verwaltung; **trade** ~ Handelsorganisation, Wirtschaftsverband; **two-tier** ~ zweistufige Organisation; **welfare** ~s soziale Einrichtungen; **worldwide** ~ Weltorganisation; **youth** ~ Jugendorganisation;

~ **of African Unity** Organisation für die Einheit Afrikas; ~ **of business** Firmen-, Geschäftsgründung; ~ **of businessmen** Wirtschaftsorganisation, -verband; ~ **of a club** Vereinsgründung; ~ **of corporation** *(US)* Gründungsgeschäft; ~ **of European Economic Cooperation (OEEC)** Europäische Organisation für wirtschaftliche Zusammenarbeit und Entwicklung, Europäischer Wirtschaftsrat; ~ **of employers** *(Br.)* Arbeitnehmerorganisation; ~ **of a government** Regierungsbildung; ~ **of hospitals** Gründung von Krankenhäusern; ~ **of labo(u)r** Arbeitsteilung; ~ **for the Maintenance of Supplies** *(Br.)* Technische Nothilfe; ~ **of Petroleum Exporting Countries (OPEC)** Verband der erdölexportierenden Länder; ~ **of American States (OAS)** Organisation der amerikanischen Staaten; ~ **of workers** *(Br.)* Arbeitnehmerorganisation; ~ **for standardization** Normenausschuß; ~ **of troops** Truppengliederung;

to call an ~ into existence Organisation ins Leben rufen; **to hold the reins of an ~** organisatorische Leitung haben; **to infiltrate an ~** Organisation unterwandern; **to join an ~** einer Organisation beitreten; **to pass through an ~** Sanierungsphase durchlaufen; **to set up an ~** Organisation gründen;

~ **arrangement** Organisationsplan; ~ **certificate** *(US)* Gründungs-, Konzessionsurkunde [einer Bank]; ~ **chart** Organisationsplan, -schema; **top-heavy** ~ **chart** kopflastiger Stellenbesetzungsplan; ~ **cost** *(US)* Gründungskosten; ~ **development** betriebliche Entwicklung; ~ **diagram** Organisationsschaubild; ~ **expenses** *(US)* Gründungsaufwand; ~ **files** Gründungsakten; ~ **fund** Organisationsfonds; **shop** ~ **law** *(US)* Betriebsverfassungsgesetz; ~ **library** Verbandsarchiv; ~ **meeting** *(US)* Gründungsversammlung; ~ **positioning** Organisationsplanung; ~ **program(me)** Organisationsprogramm; ~ **status** Status der Gesellschaft; ~ **tax** *(US)* Gründungssteuer.

organizational organisatorisch;

~ **ability** Organisationstalent; **to put an idea into effective** ~

action Idee praktisch und wirksam zur Anwendung bringen; ~ **arrangement** Organisationsschema; ~ **changes** organisatorische Veränderungen; ~ **chart** Organisationsschema, -struktur; **to preserve the ~ fabric of human society** Aufrechterhaltung der Regierungstätigkeit und der öffentlichen Ordnung sicherstellen; ~ **form** Organisationsform; ~ **grounds** organisatorische Gründe; ~ **ineffectiveness** Organisationsmängel, -fehler; ~ **issue** Organisationsaufgabe; ~ **machinery** Organisationsapparat; ~ **matters** Organisationsfragen; ~ **picketing** organisierte Streikposten; ~ **realignment** organistorische Sanierungsmaßnahmen; ~ **setup** Organisationsschema, -aufbau; ~ **specialist** Organisationsfachmann; ~ **structure** Organisationsschema, -aufbau; ~ **talent** Organisationstalent; ~ **unity** organisatorische Einheit.

organize *(v.)* organisieren, gründen, veranstalten, *(arrange)* arrangieren, einrichten, gestalten, bilden, *(systemize)* in ein System bringen, systematisieren, *(unionize)* gewerkschaftlich organisieren;

~ **a corporation** *(US)* Aktiengesellschaft gründen; ~ **a demonstration** Demonstration veranstalten; ~ **an expedition** Expedition zusammenstellen; ~ **a factory** Arbeiter und Angestellte einer Fabrik organisieren; ~ **a fair** Messe aufziehen (veranstalten); ~ **a government** Regierung bilden; ~ **a partnership** Teilhaberschaft begründen; ~ **a political party** Partei gründen; ~ **into a trade union** gewerkschaftlich erfassen; ~ **one's work** seine Arbeit systematisieren.

organized organisiert;

highly ~ forms of life hoch organisierte Lebensformen; ~ **labo(u)r** gewerkschaftlich organisierte Arbeitnehmer; ~ **market** Interessenzusammenschluß zwecks einheitlicher Verkaufspolitik, Punktmarkt.

organizer Organisator, Ordner, *(corporation)* [Gesellschafts]-gründer, gründendes Mitglied;

born ~ geborener Organisator.

organizing Organisierung;

~ *(a.)* organisatorisch;

~ **ability** organisatorische Fähigkeit, Organisationstalent; ~ **committee** *(US)* Gründungsausschuß; ~ **genius** Organisationstalent.

orgy Orgie, Saufgelage;

to be in an ~ of spending die Spendierhosen anhaben.

orient Orient, östliche Länder;

~ *(v.)* ausrichten, orientieren;

~ **o. s.** sich unterrichten; ~ **one's ideas to new conditions** seine Ideen der neuen Lage anpassen;

~ **pearl** Orientperle.

oriental orientalisch, morgenländisch;

~ **civilization** orientalische Kultur; ~ **luxury** orientalischer Luxus; ~ **rug** Perserteppich.

orientate *(v.)* orientieren;

~ **o. s.** sich orientieren.

orientation Orientierung, Lagebestimmung, *(new employee)* Arbeitsplatzeinweisung.

oriented ausgerichtet, orientiert, intensiv;

ethnically ~ nach Volksgruppen.

origin Ursprung, Quelle, *(of goods)* Provenienz, Herkunft;

of foreign ~ ausländischer Herkunft; **of humble** ~ aus kleinen Verhältnissen; **of Latin** ~ lateinischen Ursprungs; **regional** ~ örtliche Herkunft; ~ **of a quarrel** Entstehung eines Streites; **to be of noble** ~ vornehmer Abstammung sein; **to trace an event to its** ~ Ereignis bis zu seinem Ursprung zurückverfolgen; ~ **brand** Herkunftsbezeichnung.

original Urschrift, Urtext, Original, Erstanfertigung, Vorlage, *(person)* Original, Unikum;

in the ~ im Urtext, urschriftlich;

single ~ nur einmal vorhandene Urkunde;

to copy s. th. from the ~ vom Original Abschrift nehmen; **to keep close to the** ~ sich eng an das Original halten; **to read a book in the** ~ Buch im Urtext lesen;

~ *(a.)* ursprünglich, original;

~ **acquisition** Ersterwerb; ~ **advertisement (advertising)** Einführungswerbung; ~ **agreement** ursprüngliche Vereinbarung; ~ **aims of an association** ursprüngliche Gesellschaftsziele; ~ **application** *(patent law)* Erstanmeldung; ~ **appointment** *(civil servant)* Probeanstellung; ~ **assets** Anfangskapital, -vermögen; ~ **bill** erstmalig vorgetragener Rechtsfall, *(US)* Original-, Primawechsel; ~ **binding** Originaleinband; ~ **block** Originalklischee; ~ **capital** *(US)* Gründungs-, Anfangs-, Stamm-, Grundkapital; ~ **charter** Erstkonzession; ~ **check** *(US)* Originalscheck; ~ **contract** Hauptvertrag; ~ **contractor**

Hauptlieferant; ~ **conveyance** Entstehung eines Grundstücksrechtes; ~ **cost** *(outlay for assets)* Selbst-, Anschaffungs-, Erwerbskosten, Ankaufwert, *(public utility accounting)* Herstellungs-, Gründungsaufwand; ~ **data** Originalunterlagen; ~ **design** eigener Entwurf; ~ **document** Originalurkunde; ~ **edition** Original-, Erstausgabe; ~ **entry** Grundbuchung; ~ **equipment** *(car)* Erstausstattung; ~ **estate** originäres Eigentum; ~ **evidence** originäres Beweismaterial; ~ **frustration** *(contract)* ursprüngliche Unmöglichkeit; ~ **goods** freie Naturgüter; ~ **inhabitants** Ureinwohner; ~ **inventor** *(patent law)* eigentlicher Erfinder; ~ **inventory** Anfangswarenbestand; ~ **investment** Anfangs-, Gründungskapital, *(partner)* Ersteinlage; ~ **invoice** Originalrechnung, -faktura; ~ **issue stock** Gründeraktien; ~ **jurisdiction** Zuständigkeit in erster Instanz, erstinstanzliche Gerichtsbarkeit; **to have ~ jurisdiction** erstinstanzlich tätig sein; ~ **literary work** originäres Schriftwerk; ~ **manuscript** Originalmanuskript, -handschrift; ~ **meaning** Grundbedeutung; ~ **media** Urbelege; ~ **member of a club** Gründungsmitglied eines Vereins; ~ **nationality** ursprüngliche Staatsangehörigkeit; ~ **offer** ursprüngliches Angebot; ~ **package** Originalverpackung; ~ **patent** Haupt-, Stammpatent; ~ **period** *(statistics)* Wertungszeit; ~ **plan** ursprünglicher Plan; ~ **policy** Haupt-, Originalpolice; ~ **price** Anschaffungs-, Einkaufspreis; ~ **process** Klage nebst Ladung; ~ **purchase** Ersterwerb; ~ **purchaser** Ersterwerber; ~ **receipt** Originalquittung; ~ **share** *(Br.)* Stammaktie; ~ **stock** Stammkapital, *(share, US)* Stammaktie; ~ **issue stock** Gründeraktien; ~ **subscriber** Ersterwerber; ~ **syndicate** *(US)* Übernahmekonsortium; ~ **text** Urtext; ~ **thinker** selbständiger Denker; ~ **title** Originalwerk; **to give an ~ touch to one's writings** sehr originell schreiben; ~ **user** Erstbenutzer; ~ **value** Neu-, Anschaffungswert; ~ **value date** Originalvaluta; ~ **vein** Hauptader; ~ **vote** Urabstimmung; ~ **way of advertising** neuartige Werbemethode; ~ **will** Originaltestament; ~ **wrapping** Originalverpackung; ~ **writ** Klagezustellung.

originate *(v./t.)* Anstoß geben, ins Leben rufen, hervorbringen, schaffen, *(v./i.)* seinen Ursprung (seine Ursache) haben; ~ **from a common ancestor** von einem gemeinsamen Vorfahren abstammen; ~ **from a country** aus einem Lande stammen; ~ **with the government** *(plan)* von der Regierung ausgehen; ~ **an industry** Industriezweig begründen; ~ **in a misunderstanding** seinen Ausgang von einem Mißverständnis nehmen; ~ **a reform** Reformbewegung ins Leben rufen; ~ **in the rivalry of two tribes** aus der Gegnerschaft zweier Stämme herrühren.

originating | **bank** Akkreditivbank; ~ **motion** verfahrensleitender Antrag; ~ **notice** Klageschrift; ~ **point** Abgangsort; ~ **summons** Ladung zur Hauptverhandlung.

origination Entstehung, Ursprung, Anfang, *(invention)* Erfindung.

originator Urheber, Schöpfer, Gründer, *(inventor)* Erfinder.

ornament Ornament, *(print.)* Vignette, *(railroad use, sl.)* Bahnhofsvorsteher; **radiator ~** Kühlerverzierung; ~ **of one's profession** Zierde seines Berufsstandes; **to be an ~ to a circle** *(fam.)* einem Zirkel zur Zierde gereichen.

ornamental dekorativ; ~ **borders** Schmuckleiste; ~ **grounds** Parkanlagen; ~ **letter** Zierbuchstabe; ~ **plants** Zierpflanzen.

orometer Höhenbarometer.

orphan Waise, Waisenkind; **war ~** Kriegswaise; ~ **asylum** Waisenhaus, ~ **chamber** *(Dutch law)* Vormundschaftsgericht; ~ **child** Waisenkind; ~**s' court** *(Delaware, Maryland, Pennsylvania, New Jersey)* Vormundschafts- und Nachlaßgericht; ~ **master** Vormundschaftsrichter; ~**'s pension** Waisenrente.

orphanage Waisenhaus.

orphaned boy Waisenknabe.

orthography Rechtschreibung, Orthographie.

oscillate *(v.)* *(fig.)* hin- und herschwanken.

oscillation *(fig.)* Unschlüssigkeit, Schwanken.

ossified übertrieben konventionell, verknöchert.

ossify auf übertrieben konventionell machen.

ostensible angeblich, scheinbar, vorgeschoben, vorgeblich, anscheinend; ~ **agency** Vertretung ohne Vertretungsmacht; ~ **agent** Vertreter ohne Vertretungsmacht; ~ **authority** scheinbar erteilte Vollmacht, Anscheinsvollmacht; ~ **partner** gesellschaftsähnlich Beteiligter, Scheingesellschafter; ~ **purpose** angeblicher Zweck; ~ **reasons** plausible Gründe.

ostentation Zurschaustellung.

ostracism soziale Ächtung, Scherbengericht.

ostracize *(v.)* gesellschaftlich ächten, verbannen.

ostrich policy Vogelstrauß-Politik.

other verschieden, sonstig, zusätzlich; ~ **assets** *(balance sheet)* sonstige Aktiva; **any ~ business** *(agenda)* Verschiedenes; ~ **charges** *(balance sheet)* sonstiger Aufwand; ~ **deductions** neutraler Aufwand; ~ **deposits** *(Bank of England)* Nichtbankeinlagen; ~ **evidence** weiteres Beweismaterial; ~ **income** *(balance sheet)* sonstige Erträge; ~ **investment [securities]** *(balance sheet)* diverse (sonstige) Anlagewerte; ~ **liabilities** *(balance sheet)* sonstige Verpflichtungen; ~ **party** Gegenkontrahent; ~ **payments** *(balance sheet)* sonstige Ausgaben; ~ **receipts** *(balance sheet)* sonstige Einkünfte; ~ **revenue** *(balance sheet)* sonstige Erträge; ~ **side** Gegenseite; ~ **world** Jenseits.

otherwise engaged anderweitig beschäftigt.

ounce Unze, *(fig.)* Körnchen, Fünkchen; **by the ~** nach dem Gewicht; ~ **of common sense** Funken gesunden Menschenverstandes.

oust *(v.)* *(eject)* aus dem Besitz zwangsweise entfernen, Zwangsräumung durchführen, exmittieren, *(from office)* eines Amtes entheben; ~ **the jurisdiction of a court** ordentliche Gerichtsbarkeit (Rechtsweg) ausschließen; ~ **from the market** vom Markt verdrängen; ~ **a rival from office** Konkurrenten aus der Firma verdrängen.

ouster Entfernung aus dem Amt, Besitzvertreibung, -vorenthaltung, Entsetzung, *(from office)* Amtsenthebung, *(tenant)* Exmittierung, Zwangsräumung; ~ **of jurisdiction** Ausschluß des Rechtsweges.

out Ausgeschiedener, *(print.)* Auslassung, Leiche, *(protecting angle)* Vorsprung, *(unharmonious relationship, US)* gespanntes Verhältnis, *(short vacation, coll.)* Kurzurlaub, *(coll., way out)* Ausweg, Schlupfloch; **at ~s** *(US)* im gespannten Verhältnis; ~**s** ausstehende Forderungen, Außenstände., *(parl., Br.)* Opposition[smitglieder]; **ins and ~s** Einzelheiten, Feinheiten; **ins and ~s of a street** Windungen einer Straße; ~**s in overtime** zurückgehende Überstundenzeiten; **the ins and ~s** *(pol.)* Regierung und Opposition; ~ *(a.)* auswärts, außerhalb, nicht zu Hause, ausgezogen, *(book)* ausgeliehen, *(extraordinary)* außergewöhnlich, *(let)* vermietet, verpachtet, *(mil.)* im Felde, *(of office)* nicht mehr im Amt, außer Dienst, *(party)* nicht mehr am Ruder, *(published)* veröffentlicht, amtlich ausgegeben, *(servant)* als Hausangestellte beschäftigt, *(social life)* in die Gesellschaft eingeführt, *(used up)* verbraucht, alle, *(of works)* erwerbs-, arbeitslos; **all ~** *(car)* mit Höchstgeschwindigkeit; **not yet ~** *(book)* noch nicht erschienen, *(girl)* noch nicht gesellschaftsfähig; **Sunday ~** freier Sonntag; ~ **and about** wieder auf den Beinen; ~ **and away** bei weitem, mit großem Abstand; ~ **on bail** gegen Bürgschaft freigelassen; ~ **of benefit** Versicherungsschutz vorübergehend aufgehoben; ~ **of bond** außerhalb des Zollverschlusses, vom unverzollten Lager; ~ **of bounds** *(Br.)* Betreten (Zutritt) verboten; ~ **of cash** nicht bei Kasse; ~ **of control** außer Kontrolle; ~ **of court** außergerichtlich, *(plaintiff)* ohne Aktivlegitimation; ~ **of danger** außer Gefahr; ~**-of-date** unmodern, veraltet, *(Br., cheque)* Einlösungsfrist abgelaufen; ~**-of-date plant** veraltete Betriebseinrichtungen; ~**-of-doors** im Freien, *(Br.)* außerparlamentarisch; ~ **at elbows** abgetragen, schäbig; ~ **of employment** arbeitslos; ~ **of my estate** aus meinem Nachlaß; ~**-of-fashion** aus der Mode gekommen, veraltet, unmodern; ~ **on one's feet** *(fig.)* schwer angeschlagen, erledigt; ~**-of-focus** unscharf; ~ **of force** ungültig; ~**-of-hand** außer Kontrolle, aus dem Stegreif; ~ **of health** gebrechlich; ~ **and home** hin und zurück; ~ **of the housekeeping money** vom Haushaltsgeld; ~ **at interest** auf Zinsen ausgeliehen, verzinslich ausgeliehen; ~ **of joint** aus den Fugen; ~**-of-line** vom Üblichen abweichend, *(of order)* außer Betrieb; ~ **and ~** vollkommen, ganz und gar, durch und durch; ~**-of-place** deplaciert; ~**-of-pocket** in bar bezahlt, Geld dabei verloren; ~ **of print** vergriffen; ~ **of one's own purse** aus der eigenen Tasche, auf eigene Kosten; ~**-of-reach** unzugänglich; ~ **of repair** in schlechtem Erhaltungszustand; ~**-of-school** außerschulisch; ~**-of-season** zur Unzeit; ~ **of a situation** ohne Stellung, arbeitslos; ~ **of the state** außerhalb der Staatsgrenzen; ~**-of-stock** nicht am Lager (vorrätig); ~ **of term** zwischen den Sitzungen, in den Gerichtsferien; ~ **of time** *(ship)* überfällig; ~**-of-town** außerhalb gelegen, auswärtig, *(away)* abwesend, verreist; ~ **of trim** *(cargo)* schlecht gestaut; ~ **of use** außer Gebrauch, veraltet; ~-of-vogue veraltet, überholt, unmodern; ~ of the way abgelegen; ~ of wedlock unehelich; ~ of work erwerbs-, arbeitslos;

~ (v.) hinauswerfen, vertreiben;

~ with a story mit einer Geschichte herausrücken;
to arrive ~ from sea seewärts einlaufen; to be ~ weggegangen (nicht im Büro) sein, (book) veröffentlicht sein, (compositor, print.) kein Manuskript mehr haben, (copyright, lease) abgelaufen sein, (gas) nicht brennen (an sein), (library) ausgeliehen sein, (not in office) nicht [mehr] im Amt sein, (political party) nicht am Ruder (an der Macht) sein, (secret) bekanntgeworden (enthüllt, ruchbar) sein, (on strike) streiken, (tide) niedrig sein, (traveller) auf Tour (Achse) sein, (troops) aufgeboten sein, (warrant) erlassen sein, (watch) ungenau gehen; to be ~ after s. o. nach j. recherchieren; to be at ~s with s. o. (US) sich mit jem. nicht vertragen (in der Wolle haben); to be $ 10 ~ um 10 Dollar ärmer sein; to be ~ of s. th. etw. nicht mehr vorrätig haben; to be ~ and about again wieder auf dem Damm sein; to be ~ on account of illness wegen Krankheit der Arbeit fernbleiben; to be ~ in one's account sich verrechnet haben; to be ~ again erneut streiken; to be ~ against s. o. (warrant) gegen j. erlassen sein; to be ~ of all keinen Pfennig mehr besitzen, mittellos sein; to be ~ of an article Artikel nicht mehr führen (auf Lager haben); to be ~ for s. one's blood j. auf den Kieker haben; to be ~ on business geschäftlich unterwegs sein; to be ~ of the whole business sich im Geschäft nicht mehr auskennen; to be ~ in one's calculation sich verrechnet haben; to be ~ for compliments nach Komplimenten fischen; to be ~ of the country im Ausland sein; to be settled ~ of court außergerichtlich erledigt werden; to be ~ for curios auf Antiquitätenjagd sein; to be $ 100 ~ hundert Dollar Verluste haben; to be down and ~ heruntergekommen sein; to be far ~ mächtig auf dem Holzweg sein; to be ~ at interest verzinslich angelegt sein; to be ~ of it nicht mit dabei (abgehängt) sein; to be ~ upon a lease verpachtet sein; to be ~ of line (US) aus dem Rahmen fallen; to be ~ to capture a market Absatzgebiet erobern wollen; to be ~ of money by s. th. bei einer Sache Geld verlieren; to be ~ for money aufs Geld aus sein; to be ~ of order gestört sein; to be ~ of petrol kein Benzin mehr haben; to be ~ of the question nicht in Frage kommen; to be ~ in one's reckoning sich verrechnet haben; to be all ~ for reform überzeugter Reformpolitiker sein; not to be ~ to reform the world kein Weltverbesserer sein; to be ~ with a story mit einer Geschichte herausrücken; to be ~ for a long time schon lange aus der Mode sein; to bring ~ the meaning of a paragraph Sinn eines Paragraphen verdeutlichen; to cheat s. o. ~ of his money j. um sein Geld betrügen; to dine ~ außerhalb (auswärts) essen; to drive ~ Main Street Hauptstraße entlang hinausfahren; to fall ~ of work arbeitslos werden; to fit ~ ausrüsten, -staffieren; to frighten s. o. ~ of his wits j. zu Tode ängstigen; to get the cart ~ of the ditch Wagen aus dem Dreck ziehen; to get money ~ of s. o. Geld aus jem. herausholen; to go ~ in den Streik treten, streiken; to go ~ viel ausgehen; to go all ~ for s. th. alle Anstrengungen für etw. unternehmen; to go in at one door and ~ at the other zur einer Tür hereingehen und zur anderen herauskommen; to go ~ for a walk Spaziergang machen; to have one day ~ a week einen Tag in der Woche frei haben; to have an evening ~ Abend auswärts verbringen, abends ausgehen; to have a night ~ (fam.) nächtliche Prassereien genießen; to have one's sleep ~ sich richtig ausschlafen; to hear s. o. ~ j. bis zum Ende anhören; to insure ~ and home hin- und rückversichern; to keep s. o. ~ of money j. mit der Bezahlung hinhalten; to leave s. o. an ~ jem. einen Ausweg lassen; to live ~ in the country auf dem Land leben; to live ~ of town nicht in der Stadt wohnen; to live ~ of the world sich völlig zurückgezogen haben; to make an ~ (print.) beim Setzen etw. auslassen; to oppose s. th. ~ and ~ sich einer Sache mit allem Fasern seines Herzens widersetzen; to pay for s. th. ~ of the housekeeping money etw. vom Haushaltsgeld bezahlen; to sleep ~ (servant) außerhalb wohnen; to steam ~ with all lights ~ völlig abgedunkelt fahren; to take s. o. ~ j. [zum Essen] ausführen, j. zu etw. einladen; to tell s. o. straight ~ jem. etw. geradeheraus sagen; to turn s. o. ~ of the house j. herauswerfen;

~-and-outer (sl.) Hundertprozentiger, Waschechter; ~ basket Ausgangskörbchen; ~ benefit (pay) Arbeitslosenunterstützung; ~-and-out bourgeois typischer Spießbürger; ~ [clearing]book (Br.) Buch über die zur Verrechnung abgegebenen Schecks; ~-clearing (bank, Br.) insgesamt an andere Verrechnungsstellen gesandte Schecks; ~-of-date methods veraltete Methoden; ~ group (sociology) Fremdgruppe; ~-of-hospital expenses außerhalb der Klinik angefallene Krankenkosten; ~-of-line rate übertariflicher Lohn; ~-of-pocket

expenses tatsächliche Auslagen, Barauslagen; ~-of-pocket loss rule Schadensersatz für Mehraufwendungen; ~-of-school activities außerschulische Veranstaltungen; ~-of-stock items ausgegangene Artikel; ~ of time (ship) überfällig; ~-of-town bill (US) Distanzwechsel; ~-of-town check (US) auswärtiger Scheck; ~-of-town collections (US) auswärtige Inkassi; ~-of-town items (US) Abschnitte auf auswärtige Plätze; ~-of-town point (banking) Nebenplatz; ~-and-~ nationalist uneinsichtiger Nationalist; ~-and-~ republican überzeugter Republikaner; ~-and-~ rogue abgefeimter Schurke; ~ and home voyage Hin- und Rückreise; ~-of-the-way items of knowledge unbekannte Wissensgebiete; ~-of-the-way spot gottverlassenes Nest.

outbalance (v.) überwiegen.

outbargain (v.) übervorteilen.

outbearing (techn.) Außenlager.

outbid (v.) überbieten, mehr bieten, übersteigern;
~ s. o. in generosity j. an Großzügigkeit übertreffen.

outbidder (US) Mehrbietender.

outbidding höheres Gebot, Mehrgebot.

outboard motor Außenbordmotor.

outbound (ship) auslaufend, nach dem Ausland bestimmt, auf der Ausreise befindlich;
~ transportation Ausgangsfracht.

outboundary (US) äußerste Grenze.

outbreak Ausbruch;
~ of an epidemic Epedemieausbruch; ~ of fire Feuerausbruch; ~ of hostilities Ausbruch von Feindseligkeiten; ~ of war Kriegsausbruch.

outbuilding Nebengebäude, Anbau[ten].

outburst Ausbruch.

outcarry (v.) ausführen, exportieren.

outcast Ausgestoßener, Verbannter, Vertriebener;
social ~ Asozialer;
~ (a.) ausgestoßen, verbannt, vertrieben;
~ misery elendes Leben in der Verbannung.

outcaste Kastenloser;
~ (v.) aus einer Kaste ausstoßen.

outclass (v.) weit übertreffen.

outclearance (mar.) Ausklarieren.

outclearing (Br.) Scheckaußenstände.

outcollege extern.

outcome Ergebnis, Folge;
~ of a division Abstimmungsergebnis; ~ of the election Wahlergebnis; ~ of one's labo(u)r Arbeitsergebnis.

outcrop zutage tretende Schicht;
~ (v.) erscheinen, zutagetreten.

outcry Aufschrei, Entrüstungsschrei, (auction) Auktion;
to raise an ~ against s. o. seiner Entrüstung über j. Luft machen.

outdated veraltet;
to be ~ by events von den Ereignissen überholt sein.

outdistance (v.) (fig.) überflügeln, ausstechen.

outdo (v.) s. o. in kindness j. an Freundlichkeit übertreffen.

outdoor draußen, im Freien, außer Haus, (parl. Br.) außerparlamentarisch;
~ advertising Außenwerbung, Plakat-, Straßenreklame, Werbung am Verkehrsstrom; ~ advertising firm Plakatunternehmen; ~ aerial Außenantenne; ~ apprentice nicht bei seinem Lehrherrn wohnender Lehrling; ~ display Außenwerbung; ~ garments Straßenkleidung; ~ job Außenarbeit; ~ labo(u)r Außenarbeit; to lead an ~ life Leben im Freien führen; ~ lighting Außenbeleuchtung; ~ media Medien der Außenwerbung; ~ photo Außenaufnahme; ~ relief (Br.) Sozialhilfe, Fürsorgeunterstützung; to apply for ~ relief Sozialhilfe beantragen; ~ scenes Außenaufnahmen; ~ service Außendienst; ~ sign Außenschild; ~ sports event Sportveranstaltung im Freien; ~ staff im Außendienst tätiges Personal; ~ station Außenstation; ~ work Außenarbeit.

outdoorman im Freien Beschäftigter.

outdweller Vorstadtbewohner.

outer | bar (Br.) jüngere Anwälte; ~ door Haus-, Wohnungstür; ~ form (print.) Schöndruck; ~ harbo(u)r Außenhafen; ~ hull äußerer Schiffskörper; ~ ring of sympathisers Sympathisantenkreis; ~ space Weltraum; ~ space law Weltraumrecht; ~ station Außenbahnhof; ~ suburb Stadtrandsiedlung; ~ world Außenwelt.

outerwear Oberbekleidung.

outface (v.) a situation einer Lage Herr werden.

outfall (river) Mündung.

outfit Ausrüstung, -stattung, Einrichtung, Apparat, (costs) Ausstattungskosten, (dipl.) Repräsentationsgelder, (mil., US)

Truppenteil, *(plant)* Betrieb, Unternehmen, *(ship)* Schiffausstattung, *(shop)* Laden, *(tourism)* Gruppe, Reisegesellschaft, *(US)* Personenkreis, Gesellschaft;
   bridal ~ Aussteuer; **camping ~** Zeltausrüstung; **cooking ~** Küchengeräte; **first-aid ~** Verbandskasten; **repair[ing] ~** Reparaturausrüstung; **tropical ~** Ausstattung für die Tropen, Tropenausrüstung; **the whole ~** der ganze Kram (Laden);
   ~ of tools Werkzeugkasten;
   ~ *(v.)* ausrüsten, -statten;
   ~ allowance *(mil.)* Einkleidungszuschuß, Kleidergeld.
outfitter Ausstatter, Einrichtungshändler, *(haberdashery)* Modegeschäft, *(tourism)* Lieferant von Ausrüstungsgegenständen;
   electrical ~ Elektrogroßhändler; **gentlemen's ~** Herrenausstatter.
outfitting Ausstattung, -rüstung;
   ~ department Ausstattungsabteilung; **~ shop** Modegeschäft.
outflank *(v.)* umfassen, überflügeln;
   ~ the enemy Feind umgehen.
outflanking movement Umgehungsmanöver.
outflow *(investment trust)* Mittelrückfluß;
   foreign exchange ~ Devisenabgänge;
   ~ of capital Kapitalabfluß; **~ of cash** Kassenabgänge; **~ of funds** Mittelabfluß, Guthabenabgang; **~ of gold bullion** Goldabfluß;
   to slow down the sterling ~ Pfundabgänge drosseln; **to turn the ~ of money into a flood** Geldabfluß zu einer Flut anschwellen lassen.
outgeneral *(v.)* an Organisationstalent alles übertreffen.
outgo *(Br.)* Aufwendungen, Ausgaben.
outgoing|s Aufwendungen, Ausgaben;
   ~ *(a.)* abgehend, abtretend, ausscheidend;
   ~ administration (ministry) demissionierende Regierung; **~ boat** abfahrendes (abgehendes) Schiff; **~ freight** Ausgangsfracht; **~ goods** Warenausgänge; **~ long-distance call** abgehendes Ferngespräch; **~ mail** Postauslauf; **~ officeholder** ausscheidender Amtsinhaber; **~ partner** ausscheidender Teilhaber (Gesellschafter); **~ ship** auslaufendes Schiff; **~ stocks** Ausgänge; **~ tenant** ausziehender Mieter (Pächter); **~ tide** zurückgehende Flut; **~ train** abfahrender Zug.
outgrow *(v.)* herauswachsen;
   ~ a habit Gewohnheit ablegen; **~ a prejudice** Vorurteil überwinden.
outgrowth *(mil.)* vorgeschobener Posten, Feldwache.
outhector *(v.)* durch befehlshaberisches Auftreten einschüchtern.
outhouse Wirtschafts-, Seiten-, Nebengebäude, *(US)* Außenklosett.
outing Ausflug;
   factory ~ Betriebsausflug;
   day's ~ in a car Tagesausflug mit dem Wagen;
   to go for an ~ on Sunday Sonntagsausflug machen.
outland Grenzland;
   ~ bill *(Br.)* im Außenhandel gebrauchter Wechsel.
outlander Ausländer.
outlandish ausländisch, fremdartig.
outlaw Geächteter, Bandit, Gewohnheitsverbrecher;
   ~ *(v.)* rechtsunwirksam machen, der Rechtskraft berauben, *(US)* für verjährt erklären;
   ~ s. o. j. für vogelfrei erklären; **~ a debt** Schuld verjähren lassen; **~ war** Krieg ächten;
   ~ strike von der Gewerkschaft nicht anerkannter (wilder) Streik.
outlawed|claim *(US)* verjährter Anspruch; **~ obligation** verjährte Forderung.
outlawry Gesetzesmißachtung, *(criminal)* Rechtlosigkeit, *(non-enforciability, US)* Nichteinklagbarkeit, -erklärung;
   ~ of war Kriegsächtung.
outlay Ausgaben, -lagen, [Kosten]aufwand;
   with no considerable ~ ohne großen Kostenaufwand;
   cash ~ Barauslagen; **first (initial) ~** Anschaffungskosten; **professional ~s** *(income tax)* Werbungskosten; **total ~** Gesamtaufwand, -kosten;
   ~ on (for) armaments Rüstungsausgaben; **~ for inventory** Lageraufwand; **large ~ on scientific research** großer Kapitalaufwand für Forschungsarbeiten;
   ~ *(v.)* [Geld] auslegen, ausgeben;
   to make ~s of money *(US)* Geld auslegen; **to recover one's ~** *(US)* seine Auslagen zurückerhalten;
   ~ cost Kostenauslagen; **~ curve** Auslagenkurve; **~ growth** Ausgabenzunahme; **~ taxes** indirekte Steuern, Ausgabensteuern.

outlearn *(v.)* perfekt (erschöpfend) erlernen.
outlet Ausgang, *(bulk buyer)* Großabnehmer, *(el.)* Anschlußstelle, -punkt, *(fig.)* Betätigungsfeld, Ventil, *(market)* Absatzfeld, -gebiet, -möglichkeit, -markt, *(retail)* Verkaufs-, Vertriebsstelle, Markt, *(stand)* Kiosk;
   cash ~ Kassamarkt; **non-giro ~s** nicht am Postscheckverkehr beteiligte Stellen; **water ~** Wasserabfluß;
   ~ for one's energies Ventil für überschüssige Kräfte; **~ for export trade** Auslandsmarkt; **~ to the sea** Zugang zum Meer; **to find an ~ for one's emotions** seinen Gefühlen Luft machen; **to provide an ~ for the smoke** Rauchabzug vorsehen; **to seek an ~ for one's creative instinct** Betätigungsfeld für seine kreative Anlagen suchen;
   ~ box *(el.)* Steck-, Anschlußdose; **~ pipe** Ableitungsrohr; **~ store** Resteladen; **~ valve** Auslaufventil.
outline Skizze, Umriß, Überblick, Entwurf, *(advertisement)* skizzierte Grundkonzeption, *(arrangement)* Anlage, Gliederung, *(print.)* Konturschrift, *(sketch)* Umriß, Grundriß, Profil;
   in ~ skizziert, in Konturzeichnung;
   ~s Umrisse, Hauptzüge, -linien;
   elegant ~ of a car elegante Konturen eines Wagens; **~ of economic history** Grundriß (Leitfaden) der Wirtschaftsgeschichte; **~ for a lecture** Vortragsentwurf; **main ~s of a scheme** Grundzüge eines Planes;
   ~ *(v.)* entwerfen, skizzieren, Übersicht (Überblick) geben, umreißen, in großen Zügen (in Umrissen) darstellen;
   ~ a scheme Plan skizzieren;
   ~ agreement Rahmenvereinbarung; **~ map** Übersichtskarte; **~ specification** Einstellungsbedingungen.
outlined sich abhebend (abzeichnend);
   to be ~ against sich als Silhouette abheben.
outlive *(v.)* überleben, -dauern.
outliver Überlebender.
outlodging außerhalb des College wohnend.
outlook Aussichten, Vorschau, *(view)* Ansicht, Auffassung, Standpunkt;
   business ~ Konjunktur-, Geschäftsaussichten; **economic ~** Konjunkturaussichten, Wirtschaftsvorschau, Konjunkturprognose; **further ~** *(weather forecast)* weitere Aussichten; **political ~** politische Aussichten;
   ~ for the economy Konjunkturaussichten, -prognose; **~ in Europe** allgemeine Lage in Europa; **~ on life** Einstellung dem Leben gegenüber, Weltanschauung; **~ for peace** Friedensaussichten; **~ for stocks** Aktienaussichten; **bright ~ for trade** günstige Handelsaussichten;
   to be on the ~ for s. th. nach etw. Ausschau halten; **to broaden the ~** Horizont erweitern; **to have a melancholic ~ on life** Leben melancholisch betrachten; **to have a narrow ~ on life** engen Horizont haben.
outlying außerhalb gelegen, abgelegen, außenliegend;
   ~ building Nebengebäude; **~ considerations** nebensächliche Überlegungen; **~ districts** entlegene Gebiete; **~ farm buildings** landwirtschaftliche Nebengebäude; **~ quarter** abgelegenes Viertel; **~ village** abgelegenes Dorf.
outmanoeuvre *(v.)* durch geschicktes Manövrieren überlisten.
outmoded aus der Mode gekommen, unmodern, veraltet;
   ~ views überholte Ansichten.
outnumber *(v.)* zahlenmäßig überlegen sein, an Zahl übertreffen.
outnumbered in der Minderheit.
outpace *(v.)* überholen.
outpatient ambulant behandelter Patient;
   to treat s. o. as an ~ j. ambulant behandeln;
   ~ clinic ambulante Klinik; **private ~ consultation** private ambulante Behandlung; **~s' department** Krankenhausabteilung für ambulante Patienten, Ambulanz; **~ treatment** ambulante Behandlung.
outpay *(v.)* überreichlich bezahlen.
outpayment Auszahlung.
outpensioner alleinwohnender Unterstützungsempfänger.
outperform *(v.)* leistungsmäßig übertreffen;
   ~ the market überdurchschnittliche Börsenergebnisse zeitigen.
outplacement Beratung beim Positionswechsel.
outpoll *(v.)* bei der Wahl schlagen.
outport an die Flußmündung vorverlegter Seehafen, Außenhafen.
outporter *(Br.)* Dienstmann.
outportion austeilen, verteilen.
outpost *(fig.)* Vorposten, *(mil.)* vorgeschobene Stellung, Vor-, Außenposten;
   backward ~ rückständiger Außenposten;
   ~ of freedom Bollwerk der Freiheit.

output *(machine)* Leistung[sfähigkeit], *(mine)* Ausbeute, Förderung, *(program(m)ing)* Ausgangswert, *(quantity produced)* Produktion, Produktionsleistung-, menge, -ziffer, -ertrag, Ausstoß, Ertrag, *(working capacity)* Arbeitsleistung, -ertrag;
annual ~ Jahreserzeugung, -produktion; **automobile** ~ Autoproduktion; **average** ~ Durchschnittsproduktion; **daily (day's)** ~ Tagesleistung, -produktion; **the country's** ~ volkswirtschaftliche Gesamtleistung; **domestic** ~ Inlandserzeugung; **effective** ~ Nutzleistung; **hourly** ~ Stundenleistung; **increased** ~ Mehrproduktion; **industrial** ~ Industrieerzeugung, -produktion, Produktionsstand; **individual** ~ Einzelleistung; **literary** ~ literarische Produktion; **man-hour** ~ Ausstoß pro Arbeitsstunde; **maximum** ~ Höchst-, Maximalleistung, -produktion; **minimum** ~ Mindestproduktion; **normal** ~ Normalleistung; **peak** ~ Höchstleistung; **per-man-shift** ~ *(mining)* Schichtleistung; **power** ~ *(sl.)* Leistungsabgabe; **real** ~ effektive Produktionsziffer; **reduced** ~ Minderleistung; **total** ~ Gesamtertrag, -produktion; **world** ~ Weltproduktion; **last year's** ~ Vorjahresproduktion;
~ **of cars** Autoproduktion; ~ **of coal** Kohlenförderung; ~ **of open-cut coal** Tagebauförderung; ~ **of a colliery** Förderung eines Kohlenbergwerks; ~ **of goods** Güterausstoß; ~ **of high export potential** Produktion mit großen Exportmöglichkeiten; ~ **per hour** Stundenleistung; **coal** ~ **per man per day** tägliche Kohlenförderung pro Kopf; ~ **of mine** Grubenförderung; **standard** ~ **per shift** normale Schichtleistung; ~ **of the staff** Leistung des Personals; ~ **of crude steel** Rohstahlproduktion; ~ **of openhearth steel** Produktion von Siemens-Martin-Stahl; ~ **in volume** mengenmäßige Erzeugnung, Produktionsmenge; **literary** ~ **of the year** literarisches Jahresergebnis; **to cut back** ~ Ausstoß verringern; **to increase the** ~ Förderung steigern; **to keep to the** ~ **40 - 50% of budgeted levels for the past two years** zu einer um 40 - 50% verkürzter Produktionsleistung im Rahmen der Planung der letzten beiden Jahre führen; **to match** ~ **to the absorption capacities** Förderung den Absatzmöglichkeiten anpassen; **to reduce the** ~ Ausstoß verringern; **to up its** ~ seinen Ausstoß steigern;
~ **bonus** Produktionsprämie; ~ **capacity** Produktionskapazität, *(machine)* Stückleistung; ~ **cost** Produktionskosten; ~ **contribution** Beitrag zur Produktionssteigerung; ~ **cut** Produktionseinschränkung; ~ **data** *(data processing)* Ausgabedaten; ~ **evaluation** Leistungsermittlung; ~ **figures** Produktions-, Ausstoß-, Leistungszahlen; ~ **gap** Deflationslücke; ~ **growth** Produktionszunahme; ~ **method of calculating depreciation** auf dem Umfang der Anlagenausnutzung beruhende Abschreibungsmethode; ~ **potential** Produktionspotential; ~ **price** Verkaufspreis; ~ **quota** Förderungskontingent; ~ **rate** Ausstoßziffer; ~ **restriction** Produktions-, Erzeugungsbeschränkung; ~ **target** Produktionsziel; ~ **tax** *(Br.)* Bruttomehrwertsteuer.

outputter *(US)* Erzeuger, Produzent.

outrage Freveltat, Verbrechen, Gewalttat, Gewalttätigkeit;
~s Ausschreitungen;
anti-semitic ~s antisemitische Ausschreitungen; **bomb** ~ Bombenanschlag;
~ **upon decency** *(morals, US)* grobe Verletzung des Anstands; ~ **upon justice** Vergewaltigung der Gerechtigkeit;
~ *(v.)* sich vergehen, freveln, mißhandeln;
~ **common sense** *(fam.)* gegen den gesunden Menschenverstand verstoßen; ~ **all decency** Anstandsgefühl verletzen; ~ **s. one's feelings** jds. Gefühle mit Füßen treten; ~ **public opinion** öffentliche Meinung außer Rand und Band bringen;
to commit ~s Ausschreitungen (Greueltaten) begehen;

outrageous frevelhaft, verbrecherisch;
~ **behavio(u)r** empörendes Benehmen; ~ **conduct** unerhörtes Verhalten; ~ **heat** gräßliche Hitze; ~ **injustice** flagrante Ungerechtigkeit; ~ **insult** schändliche Beleidigung; ~ **price** unverschämter Preis; ~ **statement** unerhörte Erklärung.

outrageously expensive exorbitant teuer.

outrageousness of a price exorbitanter Preis.

outrank *(v.)* im Rang übertreffen, *(bankruptcy)* im Range vorgehen.

outrelief *(Br.)* Sozialhilfe.

outride *(v.)* **one's pursuers** seinen Verfolgern davonreiten.

outrider *(police, Br.)* Eskortefahrer.

outright völlig, gänzlich, total, ohne Vorbehalt, vorbehaltslos, *(on the spot)* sofort;
to buy ~ *(US)* gegen sofortige Lieferung (per Kasse) kaufen; **to buy a house** ~ Kaufpreis für ein Haus in bar erlegen; **to buy rights** ~ Gesamtrechte erwerben; **to give one's opinion** ~ offen seine Meinung sagen; **to kill s. o.** ~ j. auf der Stelle töten; **to own**

~ volles Eigentumsrecht besitzen; **to pay s. o.** ~ j. voll auszahlen; **to refuse** ~ glatt (rundweg) ablehnen; **to sell** ~ in Bausch und Bogen verkaufen;
~ **acceptance** vorbehaltslose Annahme; ~ **course** direkter Weg; ~ **denial** glattes Dementi; ~ **expenses** Gesamtausgaben; ~ **forward** *(Br.)* Devisentermingeschäft mit vereinbartem Erfüllungstag; ~ **gift** bedingungslose Zuwendung; ~ **gold-value guarantee** volle Geldwertgarantie; ~ **loss** totaler Verlust; ~ **owner** Volleigentümer; ~ **payment** vollständige Auszahlung; ~ **purchase** *(bookseller)* Festbezug; ~ **rate of exchange** Termindevisensatz; ~ **refusal** glatte Weigerung; ~ **sale** fester Verkaufsabschluß, Abschluß zu einem festen Verkaufspreis.

outrival *(v.)* übertreffen, ausstechen.

outrun *(v.)* übersteigen, -treffen;
~ **the constable** sich verschulden, sich in Schulden stürzen, über seine Verhältnisse leben; ~ **one's credit** seinen Kredit überschreiten; ~ **the facts** Tatsachen übertreffen; ~ **one's income** über seine Verhältnisse leben; ~ **increases in productivity** Produktivitätszunahme wettmachen; ~ **the market average** Börsendurchschnittswerte übertreffen; ~ **punishment** der Strafe entgehen.

outsample Ausfallmuster.

outsea Hochsee.

outsell *(v.)* *(obtain higher price, US)* teurer verkaufen, *(exceed in amount of sales)* mehr verkaufen.

outsentry *(mil.)* Vorposten.

outset Anfang, Beginn;
at the ~ **of his career** zu Beginn seiner Laufbahn; **from the** ~ gleich von Anfang an;
to get bogged down at the very ~ in den ersten Ansätzen steckenbleiben.

outshine *(v.)* in den Schatten stellen.

outside Außenwelt, *(appearance)* Außenseite, äußere Erscheinung, *(bus, Br.)* Außensitz, *(passenger)* Außenpassagier;
at the ~ höchstens;
~ *(a.)* außerhalb, außenstehend, *(of college)* außerakademisch, *(extreme)* äußerst, *(illegitimate, sl.)* unehelich, *(sideline)* außerberuflich;
~ **the conference** am Rande der Konferenz; ~ **of the fence** jenseits des Zauns; ~ **one's official functions** außerdienstlich; **to be** ~ **of s. one's circle of friends** nicht zu jds. Freundeskreis gehören; **to be little used** ~ **a business letter** fast nur in Geschäftsbriefen üblich sein; **not to be able to get** ~ **one's pudding** *(sl.)* nicht aus seiner Haut herauskönnen; **to be controlled by influence from** ~ von außen beeinflußt werden; **to come from** ~ von auswärts kommen; **to cost $ 10 at the** ~ höchstens zehn Dollar kosten; **to get** ~ **of a good dinner** *(sl.)* sich ein erstklassiges Abendessen einverleiben; **to go** ~ **the evidence** über das Beweismaterial hinausgehen; **to go** ~ **one's range** *(artist)* sich außerhalb seines Metiers betätigen; **to have no occupation** ~ **of one's office work** keiner Nebenbeschäftigung nachgehen; **to judge s. th. from the** ~ nach Äußerlichkeiten urteilen; **to lie** ~ **the scope of one's address** außerhalb von jds. Aufgabenkreis liegen; **to stay for a week at the** ~ höchstens eine Woche bleiben;
~ **activities** außerberufliche Beschäftigung; ~ **agent** Außenvertreter; ~ **appearance** äußere Erscheinung; ~ **artist** *(advertising)* freier Mitarbeiter; ~ **bank** keinem Clearingsystem angeschlossene Bank; ~ **bleed** *(ad)* Außenanschnitt; ~ **board** *(US)* [etwa] Verwaltungsrat; ~ **bookmaker** freier Buchmacher; ~ **broadcast** Sendung außerhalb des Studios; ~ **broker** freier (nicht zur Börse zugelassener) Makler, Winkelmakler; ~ **broking** freie Maklertätigkeit, Betätigung als Winkelmakler; ~ **call** auswärtiges Telefongespräch; ~ **capital** betriebsfremde Mittel, Fremdkapital; ~ **chance** entfernte Möglichkeit; ~ **collector** Inkassostelle; ~ **countries** *(EC)* Drittländer; ~ **director** *(US)* freier Berater des Vorstandes; ~ **economist** wirtschaftlicher Berater; ~ **estimate** möglichst genaue Schätzung; ~ **financing** Fremdfinanzierung; ~ **funds** fremde Mittel, Fremdmittel, -kapital; ~ **help** zusätzliche Arbeitskräfte; ~ **influences** äußere Einflüsse; ~ **interest** außerhalb des eigentlichen Studiums liegendes Interesse, besondere Interessensgebiete; ~ **labo(u)r** Außenarbeit; ~ **loan** amtlich nicht notierte (im Freiverkehr gehandelte) Anleihe; ~ **man** Außenseiter; ~ **market** Freiverkehr[smarkt]; ~ **measurements** Außenmaße; ~ **opinion** Meinung eines Außenstehenden; ~ **person** Außenstehender; ~ **position** *(ad)* Außenspalte; ~ **prices** Höchstpreise; **to quote the** ~ **prices** äußerste Preise angeben; **in** ~ **quarters** in Kreisen außerhalb der Firma; ~ **repairs** Außenreparaturen; ~ **resources** Fremdmittel; ~ **role** Außenseiterrolle; ~ **seat** Außensitz, *(bus)* Platz im Oberstock; ~ **securities** Freiverkehrswerte; ~

service Fremdleistung; ~ **station** Außenstation; ~ **tender** *(Br.)* Schatzwechselofferte von regionalen und ausländischen Börsen; ~ **training** außerbetriebliche Ausbildung; ~ **transactions** *(stock exchange)* Freiverkehrsumsätze; ~ **user** *(industrial library)* außerbetrieblicher Benutzer; ~ **work** Außenarbeit; ~ **worker** Heimarbeiter; ~ **world** Außenwelt.

outsider Außenseiter, -stehender, Nichtfachmann, *(nonmember)* Nichtmitglied, *(nonofficial, US)* Nichtbeamter, *(price maintenance)* an Preisabsprachen nicht gebundener Betrieb, *(shipping company)* außerhalb der Konferenz fahrendes Unternehmen, *(social life)* nicht gesellschaftsfähige Person, *(stock exchange)* Freiverkehrsmakler, Coulissier;
  rank ~ krasser Außenseiter.
outsight Beobachtungsgabe.
outsit *(v.)* länger in einer Sitzung sein;
  ~ **the other guests** länger als die anderen Gäste bleiben.
outsize Übergröße.
outskirt Weichbild, *(subject)* Randgebiet, Peripherie;
  ~s of society Halbwelt, Lebewelt; ~ **of a town** Stadtrand[bezirk].
outsmart *(US)* an Schlauheit übertreffen.
outsold ausverkauft.
outspeed *(v.)* an Geschwindigkeit übertreffen.
outspent völlig erschöpft.
outspoken offen, geradezu;
  to be ~ offen reden, sehr direkt sein;
  ~ **criticism** unverblümte Kritik.
outspread *(v.)* sich ausbreiten (ausdehnen).
outstand *(v.)* prominent sein;
  ~ **an assault** einem Angriff widerstehen.
outstander außenstehender Posten.
outstanding | s unbeglichene Rechnungen, ausstehende Gelder, Außenstände;
  ~ *(a.)* prominent, hervorstechend, -ragend, *(unsettled)* aus-, offenstehend, rückständig, fällig, *(work)* noch nicht erledigt, unerledigt;
  longest ~ am längsten fällig;
  to have a good deal of work ~ erhebliche Arbeitsrückstände haben; **to leave** ~ ausstehen lassen;
  ~ **accounts** offene (ausstehende) Rechnungen, Außenstände; ~ **achievement** hervorragende Leistung; ~ **bonds** ausstehende Schuldverschreibungen; ~ **capital stock** *(US)* ausgegebenes Aktienkapital; ~ **check** *(US)* **(cheque,** *Br.)* zur Einlösung noch nicht vorgelegter Scheck; ~ **coupons** notleidende Zinsscheine; ~ **crop** Ernte auf dem Halm; ~ **debts** ausstehende Forderungen, Rückstände, [Aktiv]außenstände; **to assign** ~ **debts** Außenstände abtreten; ~ **event** herausragendes Ereignis; ~ **fact** feststehende Tatsache; ~ **features of a landscape** hervorstehende Landschaftsmerkmale; ~ **features of a race** hervorragende Rassemerkmale; ~ **interest** unbezahlte Aktivzinsen, Zinsrückstände; ~ **liabilities** ausstehende Verbindlichkeiten; ~ **matter** unerledigte Angelegenheit; ~ **money** ausstehendes Geld; ~ **notes** Wechselumlauf; ~ **order** unerledigter Auftrag; ~ **payment** ausstehende Zahlung; ~ **personality** prominente Persönlichkeit; ~ **premium** Prämienrückstand; ~ **securities** ausgegebene Obligationen und Aktien; ~ **shares** **(stocks,** *US)* Aktien in Publikumsbesitz; ~ **term** restliche Pachtzeit; ~ **title** besseres Recht.
outstation Außenstelle [einer Behörde], *(mil.)* Hilfs-, Außenstation.
outstay *(v.)* **one's welcome** zu lange bleiben.
outstep *(v.)* **the truth** übertreiben.
outstrip *(v.)* überflügeln;
  ~ **the supply** Angebot übersteigen.
outsweepings Kehrricht.
outtalk *(v.)* in Grund und Boden reden.
outtrade *(v.)* umsatzmäßig überflügeln.
outturn *(US)* Ertrag, Produktion, Ausstoß;
  ~ **sample** Ausfallmuster.
outvalue *(v.)* an Wert übertreffen.
outvote *(v.)* durch Stimmenmehrheit besiegen, überstimmen;
  to find o. s. ~d in der Minorität bleiben.
outvoter *(Br.)* Brief-, Stimmschein-, Wahlscheinwähler.
outwall Außenmauer.
outward *(Br.)* Außenbezirk, *(hospital)* Außenstation;
  ~ *(a.)* nach außen, auswärts, äußerlich;
  ~ **and inward** hin und zurück;
  licence ~ Ausfuhrlizenz;
  to clear ~ Schiff ausklarieren, bei der Ausfahrt verzollen; **to travel** ~ **via N** auf der Ausreise über N fahren;
  ~ **appearance** *(goods)* äußere Aufmachung; **for** ~ **application**

zur äußerlichen Anwendung; ~ **bill of lading** Exportkonnossement; **~-bound** auf der Ausreise (Ausfahrt) ins Ausland begriffen; ~ **bounder** ausfahrendes Schiff; ~ **cargo (freight,** *Br.)* abgehende (ausgehende) Ladung, Hinfracht, Fracht; ~ **fee** Postversandgebühr; ~ **half** Fahrkartenabschnitt für die Hinfahrt; ~ **journey** *(Br.)* Aus-, Hinreise; ~ **mail department** *(US)* Postversandabteilung, Expedition; ~ **manifest** Zollausfuhrerklärung; ~ **passage** Ausfahrt; ~ **road** aus der Stadt hinausführende Straße, Ausfallstraße; ~ **room** nach außen gelegenes Zimmer, Außenzimmer; ~ **ticket** Fahrkarte für die Ausreise; ~ **trade** Ausfuhrhandel; ~ **voyage** Ausreise.
outwear *(v.)* abnutzen.
outweigh *(v.)* mehr wiegen als, *(exceed in worth)* übertreffen.
outwit *(v.)* an Schlauheit übertreffen;
  ~ **the police** Polizei überlisten.
outwork Heimarbeit, *(mil.)* Außenwerk, vorgeschobene Befestigung.
outworker Heimarbeiter.
outworn ideas abgedroschene Gedanken.
oval office *(US)* Amtszimmer des Präsidenten.
ovation Ovation, Huldigung;
  standing ~ Ovation im Stehen.
over Überschuß, Mehrbetrag, *(special copy)* Extraexemplar, *(radio, tel.)* Ende;
  ~s *(weight)* Mehrgewicht;
  cash shorts and ~s *(US)* Kassenüberschüsse und Fehlbeträge; ~ **in the cash** *(US)* Kassenüberschuß; ~ **and next matter** *(advertising)* unmittelbar über und neben dem Rand plazierte Anzeige; ~ **and short account** *(US)* Ausgleichs-, Kassen-, Differenzkonto; **~s and shorts** *(US)* Konto zur vorläufigen Verbuchung unklarer Posten;
  ~ *(a.)* überschüssig, -zählig, mehr, weiter;
  ~ **a barrel** in einer Kompromißsituation; ~ **and above** extra, darüberhinaus;
  to be all ~ **s. o.** *(sl.)* an jem. einen Narren gefressen haben; **to get** ~ **it** darüber hinwegkommen; **to get tips** ~ **and above their wages** zusätzliche Trinkgelder erhalten; **to go** ~ *(article)* ankommen; **to go** ~ **to the enemy** zum Feind überlaufen; **to recover** ~ *(US)* Regreß nehmen; **to warn s. o.** ~ **and** ~ **again** j. immer wieder verwarnen;
  ~ **copies** überschüssige Exemplare; ~ **spot** *(Br.)* Report.
over-the-counter *(US)* freihändig, im Freihandel verkauft, *(unofficial)* außerbörslich;
  ~ **business (trade)** *(US)* Schalterverkehr, außerbörslicher Effektenhandel; ~ **market** *(US)* Handel mit nicht zum offiziellen Börsenverkehr zugelassenen Wertpapieren, Freiverkehr, Telefonhandel, *(Br.)* Wertpapiergeschäft am Bankschalter; ~ **receipts** Tageslosung; ~ **sale** *(unlisted securities, US)* Verkauf im Freiverkehr, Freihandverkauf.
over-the-window requirements *(US)* Anforderungen im Schalterverkehr.
overabound *(v.)* im Überschuß vorhanden sein.
overabsorbed | charges zu hoch angesetzte Gesamtkosten; ~ **overhead** Gemeinkostenüberdeckung.
overabundance Überfluß.
overact *(v.)* Rolle überspielen.
overactivity übermäßige Aktivität.
overage *(US)* [Waren]überschuß;
  ~ **of cash** *(US)* Kassenüberschuß;
  ~ *(a.)* älter als der Durchschnitt.
overagio *(Br.)* Extraprämie, -aufgeld.
overall *(Br.)* Schutzanzug, Arbeits-, Hauskleid;
  ~ *(a.)* total, global, gesamt, pauschal, einschließlich, umfassend;
  ~ **balance of payment** Gesamtzahlungsbilanz, globale Zahlungsbilanz; ~ **budget** Gesamtetat; ~ **conditions** Gesamtbedingungen; ~ **consumption** Gesamtverbrauch eines Produkts; ~ **costs** Gesamtkosten; ~ **economic demand** gesamtwirtschaftliche Nachfrage; ~ **economic potential** gesamtwirtschaftliche Leistungsfähigkeit; ~ **economics (economy)** Gesamtwirtschaft; ~ **effect** Gesamtwirkung; ~ **efficiency** Gesamtleistung; ~ **elasticity of supply** volkswirtschaftliche Angebotselastizität; ~ **engagement** Gesamtobligo; ~ **estimate** Gesamtschätzung; ~ **examination** Generalüberholug, Gesamtrevision; ~ **goal** Gesamtziel; ~ **increase** Anstieg auf der ganzen Linie, Gesamtsteigerung; ~ **increase of prices** generelle Preiserhöhung; ~ **index** Gesamtnachweis, -index; ~ **length** Gesamtlänge; ~ **level** Gesamtniveau; ~ **limitation** *(income tax, US)* Anrechnung im Ausland insgesamt gezahlter Steuern; ~ **loss** Gesamtverlust; ~ **measurements of a room** Gesamtdimensionen eines Zimmers; ~ **picture** Bild der Gesamtlage, Gesamtbild; ~ **plan** Gesamt-

plan; ~ **position** Gesamtposition; ~ **profit** Gesamtgewinn; ~ **profitibility** Unternehmensrentabilität; ~ **quota** Global-, Gesamtkontingent; ~ **rate** Pauschalsatz; ~ **report** Gesamtbericht; ~ **result** Gesamtergebnis; ~ **risk** Gesamtrisiko; ~ **settlement** Gesamtregelung, vollständige Regelung; ~ **statement** *(US)* Bilanz; ~ **study** Globaluntersuchung; **to shore up the ~ surplus** Globalüberschuß anreichern; ~ **survey** Gesamtübersicht; ~ **tendency** generelle Tendenz; ~ **trade balance** gesamte Handelsbilanz; ~ **unemployment** Gesamtarbeitslosigkeit; ~ **view** Gesamtüberblick.

overassess *(v.)* hoch veranlagen.

overassessment zu hohe [Steuer]einschätzung, -veranlagung.

overawe *(v.)* s. o. into submission j. komplett einschüchtern.

overbalance Überschuß, -gewicht;
~ **of exports** Exportüberschuß;
~ *(v.)* überwiegen.

overbank *(v.)* zu stark in die Kurve gehen.

overbearance herrisches Auftreten, Anmaßung.

overbearing arrogant, hochmütig.

overbid Mehrgebot;
~ *(v.)* überbieten, -steigern.

overboard über Bord;
~ *(v.) (sl.)* sich übermäßig begeistern;
to be washed ~ über Bord gespült werden; **to go ~** über Bord gehen, *(fig.)* sich übermäßig begeistern (vor Begeisterung überschlagen); **to throw a scheme ~** Plan völlig aufgeben.

overbought market *(US)* wegen spekulativer Ankäufe nicht mehr aufnahmefähiger Markt.

overbridge *(v.)* überbrücken.

overbuild *(v.)* überbauen, zu dicht bebauen.

overbuilt | with bungalows mit Bungalows bebaut; ~ **part of a town** zu dicht bebauter Stadtteil.

overburden Überlastung;
~ *(v.)* überlasten, -laden.

overburdened with grief von Kummer überwältigt.

overbusy überbeschäftigt.

overbuy *(v.)* zu teuer kaufen, *(buy too much)* zuviel kaufen.

overcapacity Überkapazität.

overcapitalization Überkapitalisierung.

overcapitalize *(v.)* überkapitalisieren, *(corporation)* zu hohen Nennwert für das Stammkapital angeben.

overcapitalized überkapitalisiert.

overcare übertriebene Sorgfalt.

overcarriage zu weit beförderte Ladung.

overcast Bewölkung;
~ **sky** bedeckter Himmel.

overcaution übertriebene Vorsicht.

overcautiously, to act übervorsichtig handeln.

overcertification Ausstellung eines Überziehungsschecks, *(US)* Bestätigung eines ungedeckten Schecks.

overcertify *(v.) (US)* ungedeckten Scheck bestätigen.

overcharge Mehrbelastung, Überforderung, -teuerung, zuviel berechneter Betrag, *(overloading)* Überladen, zu hohe Belastung, *(public utility)* überhöhter Tarif;
fraudulent ~ betrügerische Übervorteilung;
~ **of freight** zuviel berechnete Fracht;
~ *(v.)* zuviel fordern (anrechnen, belasten), überfordern, Überpreis verlangen, *(overload)* überladen, -lasten;
~ **s. o.** einen zu hohen Preis (zuviel) berechnen, jem. übervorteilen; ~ **on an account** zu hoch in Rechnung stellen; ~ **an electric circuit** Stromkreis überlasten; ~ **a description with detail** Darstellung mit Einzelheiten überladen; ~ **goods** zu hohen Preis für eine Lieferung verlangen;
to make an ~ on s. th. etw. zu teuer verkaufen.

overcharged prices übersetzte Preise.

overcharging Gebührenerhöhung.

overcheck *(US)* Überziehungsscheck;
~ *(v.)* [Konto] überziehen.

overclaim Rückzahlungsanspruch wegen Überforderung.

overclassify *(v.) (mil.)* in zu hohe Geheimhaltungsbestimmungen einstufen.

overclimb *(v.)* überziehen.

overclothes Oberbekleidung.

overcoat Überzieher, Mantel.

overcome *(v.) | dangers* Gefahren bestehen; ~ **the enemy** Feind überwältigen; ~ **a bad habit** schlechte Angewohnheit loswerden; ~ **an obstacle** Hindernis überwinden; ~ **s. one's resistance** jds. Widerstand brechen;
to be ~ by emotion von seinen Gefühlen überwältigt werden.

overcommitment finanzielle Leistungsfähigkeit übersteigende Verpflichtungen, *(pol.)* zu starke politische Bindung.

overcompensation Überkompensation.

overconfidence übermäßiges Vertrauen.

overconservative übertrieben konservativ.

overcorrect überkorrekt.

overcovered, to be überversichert sein.

overcredit *(v.)* zuviel gutschreiben, überkreditieren.

overcritical überkritisch.

overcrop *(v.)* Raubbau betreiben.

overcrowd *(v.)* übersetzen, überfüllen;
~ **a room** Zimmer überladen.

overcrowded *(premises)* überbelegt;
~ **bus** vollgestopfter Omnibus; ~ **conditions** beengte Wohnverhältnisse; ~ **labo(u)r market** Überangebot an Arbeitskräften; ~ **profession** übersetzter (überfüllter) Berufszweig; ~ **region** Ballungsgebiet; ~ **train** überfüllter Zug.

overcrowding Übersetztsein, *(apartment)* Überbelegtsein, -belegung;
~ **of large cities** Menschenansammlung in den Großstädten.

overdevelop *(v.) (photo)* überentwickeln.

overdischarge *(el.)* Überbelastung.

overdiscount *(v.)* **the market** *(US)* erwartete Hausse am Markt überschätzen.

overdo *(v.)* übertreiben, zu weit treiben;
~ **o. s.** sich überanstrengen; ~ **it** Bogen überspannen; ~ **one's part in a play** seine Rolle zu stark ausspielen.

overdoctored mit Ärzten übersetzt.

overdose Überdosis;
~ *(v.)* überdosieren.

overdraft überzogener Betrag, Kontoüberziehung, *(bank)* Rückbuchung eines überzogenen Betrages;
bank ~ Banküberziehung; **hard-core ~** laufende Kontoüberziehung; **static ~s** Dauerüberziehungen;
~ **of credit** Kreditüberziehung, -überschreitung; ~ **on current account** überzogenes Kontokorrentkonto;
to ask the banker for an ~ um Einräumung eines Überziehungskredites einkommen; **to have an ~** sein Konto überzogen haben; **to run up ~s** Konto lautend überziehen;
~ **commission (fee)** Überziehungsprovision; ~ **credit** Dispositionskredit; ~ **facilities** Überziehungsmöglichkeiten; **to grant a firm ~ facilities** einer Firma Kreditfazilitäten zur Verfügung stellen; ~ **facility** Überziehungsmöglichkeit; ~ **finance** Überziehungsfinanzierung; ~ **interest** Überziehungszinsen; **agreed ~ limit** vereinbarte Überziehungsgrenze; ~ **privilege** Überziehungsrecht; ~ **rate** Zinssatz für überzogene Konten.

overdraw übermäßiger Absatz;
~ *(v.)* **one's account (the badger, Br.)** sein Konto (seinen Kredit) überziehen, -schreiten; ~ **characters in a novel** lebensfremde Romanfiguren darstellen.

overdrawer Kontoüberzieher.

overdrawing Kontoüberziehung;
~ **of a credit** Kreditüberziehung, -überschreitung.

overdrawn, to be ~ at the bank bei der Bank im Debet sein; **to be ~ to the extent of £ 100** bis zu einer Höhe von 100 Pfund überzogen haben, Debetsaldo in Höhe von 100 Pfund aufweisen;
~ **account** überzogenes Konto, Kontoüberzug.

overdress *(v.)* sich zu elegant anziehen.

overdrive *(car)* Fern-, Autobahn-, Schnellgang;
~ *(v.)* bis zur Erschöpfung schinden.

overdriven übertourt.

overdue überfällig, *(in arrears)* rückständig, *(bill)* notleidend, verfallen, *(train)* überfällig;
when ~ *(bill)* nach Verfall;
to be ~ *(debt)* ausstehen, *(train)* Verspätung haben, sich verspäten;
~ **amount** rückständiger Betrag; ~ **bill** *(Br.)* überfälliger Wechsel; ~ **interest** Verzugszinsen, rückständige Zinsen; ~ **payments** fällige (rückständige) Zahlungen; ~ **premium** Prämienrückstand; ~ **reform** längst fällige Reform.

overemployment Überbeschäftigung.

overenter *(v.)* zu hoch deklarieren.

overentry zu hohe Zollangabe.

overestimate *(balance sheet)* Überbewertung;
~ *(v.) (balance sheet)* überbewerten, zu hoch einschätzen (ansetzen);
~ **one's own importance** sich selbst etw. weismachen wollen; ~ **by very large margins** sehr stark überschätzen.

overestimation Überschätzung, Überbewertung.

overexert *(v.)* **o. s.** sich überanstrengen.

overexertion Überanstrengung.

overexpansion übermäßige Ausweitung;
~ **of credit** Kreditüberspannung.

overexpose *(v.)* überbelichten.

overexposure Überbelichtung.

overextend *(v.)* **o. s.** sich übernehmen.

overextended account *(US)* ungenügend gedecktes Konto.

overextension *(condition of business)* angespannte Lage (Überschuldung) eines Betriebes;
~ **of banking credits** Ausweitung von Bankkrediten.

overfamiliar, to be ~ with s. o. jem. zu sehr auf die Bude rücken.

overfatigue Übermüdung.

overflights unerlaubtes Überfliegen.

overflood *(v.)* überschwemmen, -fluten.

overflow Überschwemmung, -flutung, Flut, *(abundance)* Überschuß, -fluß;
~ **of a library** nicht mehr unterzubringende Bibliothek; ~ **of population** Bevölkerungsüberschuß;
~ *(v.)* überschwemmen;
~ **its bank** über die Ufer treten; ~ **the barriers** Schranken durchbrechen; ~ **with riches** unermeßlich reich sein;
~ **basin** Überlaufbehälter; ~ **drain** Überlaufkanal; ~ **meeting** Parallelversammlung; ~ **traffic** nicht mehr zu bewältigender Verkehr; ~ **valve** Überlaufventil.

overflowing überlaufend;
~ **harvest** überreiche Ernte; ~ **house** ausverkaufte Vorstellung; ~ **kindness** übergroße Güte.

overfly *(v.)* überfliegen.

overflying rights Überfliegungsrechte.

overfree in one's conduct sich allzusehr gehen lassend.

overfreight Überfracht, -gewicht, *(railroad)* Gütersendung ohne Frachtbegleitschein, Verladung ohne Frachtbrief;
~ *(v.)* überbefrachten.

overful employment Überbeschäftigung.

overgild *(v.)* vergolden.

overgovern *(v.)* zu strengen Einschränkungen unterwerfen.

overgrow *(v.)* **o. s.** zu schnell wachsen.

overgrown überwuchert.

overhang *(inventory)* Überhang;
~ *(v.)* überhängen;
~ **the market** Markt erdrücken.

overhanging | branches Überhang; ~ **danger** drohende Gefahr.

overhaul Überprüfung, -holung, gründliche Untersuchung (Revision), *(car)* Generalüberholung;
collective ~ Generalüberholung; **major** ~ umfassende Überholung;
~ *(v.)* überholen, reparieren, *(accounts)* erneut prüfen, genau überprüfen;
~ **a cargo boat** Frachtschiff überholen; ~ **the engine of a car** Motor generalüberholen; ~ **stock** Lager abschreiben; ~ **thoroughly** gründlich überholen;
to need a drastic ~ gründlich überholt werden müssen; **to subject a machine to a careful** ~ Maschine einer sorgfältigen Überholung unterziehen;
~ **works** Überholungsarbeiten; ~ **workshop** Reparaturwerkstätte.

overhauled durchuntersucht;
to be ~ sich gründlich untersuchen lassen;
~ **car** überholtes Auto.

overhauling, complete Generalüberholung;
~ **of stock** Lagerabschreibung.

overhead(s) fortlaufende (fixe) Kosten, Fest-, Fix-, Betriebs-, Gemeinkosten, Generalunkosten;
factory ~ fixe (feste) Kosten, Fertigungsgemeinkosten; **idle** ~ potentielle Produktivität; **large** ~ *(US)* hohe Unkosten; **overabsorbed** ~ Gemeinkostenüberdeckung;
~ *(a.)* im Stockwerk darüber, *(average)* durchschnittlich;
~ **in debt** bis über die Ohren verschuldet;
to live ~ im Stockwerk darüber wohnen;
factory ~ **account** Betriebs-, Fertigungsgemeinkostenkonto; ~ **allocation** Aufteilung der Generalunkosten; ~ **antenna** Hochantenne; ~ **cable** Freileitungs-, Luftkabel; ~ **charges (costs, expenses)** Handlungs-, General-, allgemeine Unkosten, Fest-, Fix-, Regiekosten; ~ **charges account** Fertigungsgemein-, Handlungsunkostenkonto; ~ **company** Dachgesellschaft; ~ **control** zentrale Kontrolle; **[factory]** ~ **costs (expenses)** Fertigungsgemeinkosten; ~ **distribution** Gemeinkostenumlage; ~ **items** Generalunkostenposten; ~ **lights** Deckenbeleuchtung; ~ **line** oberirdische Leitung, Frei-, Oberleitung; ~ **organization** Dachorganisation; ~ **price** Pauschal-, Gesamtpreis; ~ **railway** *(Br.)* Hochbahn; ~ **rate** Gemeinkosten, Unkostenanteil, -satz, -zuschlag; ~ **statement** Gesamtübersicht; ~ **supply** Überangebot; ~ **variance** Gemeinkostenabweichung; ~ **way** Überführung.

overheap *(v.)* überhäufen.

overhear *(v.)* Gespräch belauschen.

overheat *(v.)* überheizen;
~ **the economy** Konjunktur überhitzen.

overheated economy überhitzte Konjunktur.

overheating the boom Konjunkturüberhitzung.

overhoused in zu großen Räumlichkeiten wohnend.

overimportation übermäßige Einfuhr.

overindebtedness Überschuldung.

overindulge *(v.)* **in wine** zu viel Wein trinken.

overinsurance Überversicherung.

overinsure *(v.)* überversichern.

overinsured zu hoch versichert, überversichert.

overinvest *(v.)* zu hohe Investitionen vornehmen, überinvestieren.

overinvestment Überinvestition;
~ **in inventories** übermäßige Kapitalinvestitionen in Warenbeständen; ~**s in receivables** übermäßige Kapitalinvestierungen in Debitoren.

overinvoice *(v.)* **imports** überhöhte Einfuhrrechnungen ausstellen.

overinvoicing of imports Ausstellung überhöhter Einfuhrrechnungen.

overissue Mehrausgabe, Überemission, unzulässig hohe Ausgabe;
~ **of currency notes** Anspannung des Notenumlaufs, Papiergeldinflation;
~ *(v.)* überemissionieren.

overknee boots Kniestiefel.

overlabo(u)r *(v.)* überarbeiten, -anstrengen.

overlaid with gold mit Gold überzogen.

overland über Land, auf dem Landwege;
~ **links** Überlandverbindungen; ~ **mail** Überlandpost; ~ **route** Überlandweg; ~ **transport** Überlandverkehr.

overlap Überschneiden, -schneidung, -lappung;
~ **of basis periods** Überschneidung von Veranlagungsräumen; ~ **of insurances** sich überschneidende Versicherungsansprüche; ~ **of taxing authority** Besteuerungsrechtsüberschneidung;
~ *(v.)* überlappen, sich überschneiden, sich decken.

overlapping Überschneidung;
~ **circulation** *(advertising)* überlappende Streuung; ~ **lectures** sich zeitlich überschneidende Vorlesungen; ~ **situation** *(advertising)* überschneidendes Streuungsgebiet.

overlay Überkleber, *(print.)* Zurichtung, Zurichtebogen, Auflageblatt;
~ **of gold** Goldauflage;
~ *(v.) (print)* zurichten.

overleaf umseitig, auf umstehender Seite.

overlive *(v.)* überleben, mit dem Leben davonkommen.

overload Übergewicht, -lastung, zu hohes Gewicht;
~ *(v.)* überladen, -lasten, zu hohen Belastungen aussetzen.

overloaded zu stark belastet, überladen, -lastig;
~ **economy** Volkswirtschaft mit zurückgestauter Inflation.

overlook Aussichtspunkt, *(slip)* Versehen, Unterlassung;
~ *(v.)* übersehen, -lesen, *(control)* überwachen, beaufsichtigen;
~ **a printer's error** Druckfehler übersehen; ~ **a fault** über einen Fehler hinwegsehen; ~ **s. one's services** j. nicht entsprechend [seinen Fähigkeiten] bezahlen.

overlooker *(Br.)* Aufseher.

overlord *(cabinet)* Überminister.

overlordship Schirmherrschaft.

overlying | bond durch nachstellige Hypothek gesicherte Schuldverschreibung; ~ **mortgage** *(US)* nachstellige Hypothek.

overman Vorarbeiter, Aufseher, *(mining)* Steiger;
~ *(v.)* **a ship** Schiff zu stark bemannen.

overmanning Überbesetzung mit Arbeitskräften;
to cut ~ personelle Überbesetzung abbauen.

overmeasure Übermaß.

overmuch homework zuviel Schularbeiten.

overnice distinctions übertriebene Unterscheidungen.

overnight während der Nacht;
to become famous ~ über Nacht berühmt werden; **to make preparations** ~ nächtliche Vorbereitungen treffen; **to stay** ~ über Nacht bleiben;
~ **borrowing** Tagesgeldaufnahme; ~ **case** Handkoffer; ~ **charge** Nachtzuschlag; ~ **guests** *(hotel)* einmalige Übernachtungen; ~ **journey** nächtliche Reise; ~ **loan** *(US)* innerhalb 24 Stunden rückzahlbarer Kredit, Tagesgeld; ~ **market** Markt für Tagesgeld, Tagesgeldmarkt; ~ **money** *(Br.)* kurzfristiges Maklerdarlehn; ~ **stay** Übernachtung; ~ **stop** nächtliche Unterbrechung, *(airplane)* Nachtlandung; ~ **telegram(me)** Brieftelegramm.

overpaid workman überbezahlter (zu hoch bezahlter) Arbeiter.
overparticular überpenibel.
overpass kreuzungsfreie Überführung.
overpay *(v.)* überbezahlen, zu teuer bezahlen, zu reichlich entschädigen.
overpayment Überzahlung, *(account)* Überziehung;
~ **of tax** Steuerüberzahlung.
overpeopled übervölkert.
overpicture *(v.)* übertriebenes Bild zeichnen.
overplus Überschuß, Mehrbetrag;
~ **of a great fortune** Rest eines großen Vermögens.
overpopulated übervölkert.
overpopulation Überbevölkerung.
overpower *(v.)* überwältigen, bezwingen.
overpowered | **by the police** von der Polizei überwältigt;
to be ~ by the news von den Nachrichten überwältigt sein.
overpressure Überdruck.
overprice Überpreis, übertrieben hoher Preis;
~ *(v.)* zu hohen Preis verlangen.
overprint Überdruck;
~ *(v.)* überdrucken, *(photo)* beim Kopieren überbelichten, *(print too many)* zu große Auflage drucken.
overprize *(v.)* überbewerten.
overproduce *(v.)* zuviel produzieren.
overproduction Überproduktion.
overproportion Übergröße.
overpurchase zu teuerer Einkauf;
~ *(v.)* zu viel kaufen.
overrate zu hohe Veranlagung;
~ *(v.)* zu hoch schätzen (werten), überschätzen, *(for rating purposes)* zu hoch veranlagen;
~ **s. one's abilities** jds. Fähigkeiten zu hoch einschätzen; ~ **one's strength** seine Kräfte überschätzen.
overrated book überbewertetes Buch.
overreact *(v.)* überempfindlich reagieren.
overreach *(v.)* überragen, *(cheat)* übervorteilen;
~ **one's purpose** über sein Ziel hinausschießen; ~ **one's resources and finances** seine finanziellen Mittel überstrapazieren.
overreaching Übervorteilung;
~ **of interests** *(legal estate)* Anspruchsvorrang;
~ **clause** *(resettlement)* Erfassungsklausel, *(trustee)* Erstreckungsklausel; ~ **conveyance** *(Br.)* lastenfreie Auflassung.
overreach *(v.)* **o. s.** sich übernehmen.
overread *(v.)* zu viel lesen.
overrent *(v.)* zu teuer vermieten, zu hohen Pachtzins verlangen.
override *(managerial personnel)* Tantieme;
~ *(v.)* beiseite schieben, sich rücksichtslos darüber hinwegsetzen, *(annul)* für ungültig erklären, außer Kraft setzen, *(storm)* überstehen;
~ **one's advisers** sich über seine Berater hinwegsetzen; ~ **arguments** Einwände zurückweisen; ~ **s. one's claims** sich über jds. Ansprüche hinwegsetzen; ~ **one's commission** seine Vollmachten überschreiten; ~ **all other considerations** alle anderen Überlegungen unwichtig erscheinen lassen; ~ **a decision** frühere Entscheidung umstoßen; ~ **any forms or conditions referred to by the buyer** alle Bedingungen des Käufers ausschließen; ~ **a veto** Einspruch übergehen, Veto überstimmen; ~ **s. one's wishes** jds. Wünsche beiseiteschieben.
overrider *(Br.)* Emissionshaus.
overriding vorrangig, erstrangig;
~ **charges** nicht erstattungsfähige Anwaltskosten; ~ **clause** Aufhebungsklausel; ~ **commission business**, *Br.)* dem Generalvertreter verbleibender Provisionsanteil, Gebietsprovision, *(underwriting)* Superprovision des Konsortialführers; ~ **importance** überragende Bedeutung; ~ **interests** *(Br.) (land registry)* nicht eintragungspflichtige Grundstücke (Grundstücksrechte); ~ **principle** beherrschender Grundsatz; ~ **responsibility** Gesamtverantwortlichkeit; ~ **royalty** *(petroleum industry)* Tantiemenanteil.
overrule *(v.)* abweisen, nicht stattgeben, außer Kraft setzen;
~ **s. o.** jds. Entscheidung wieder aufheben; ~ **an application** Antrag ablehnen; ~ **an argument** Argument zurückweisen; ~ **a claim** Anspruch nicht anerkennen; ~ **a lower court** Entscheidung der unteren Instanz aufheben; ~ **a previous decision** frühere Entscheidung umstoßen, von einer Vorentscheidung abweichen; ~ **one's own holdings** *(US)* von seinen eigenen Entscheidungen abgehen; ~ **objections** Einwände (Einsprüche) zurückweisen; ~ **an obligation** Einspruch zurückweisen; ~ **a plea** Einrede zurückweisen (verwerfen); ~ **a precedent** Vorentscheidung nicht akzeptieren; ~ **a proposal** Vorschlag verwerfen.

overruled *(antitrust law, US)* nicht anerkannt;
~ **by the majority** von der Mehrheit überstimmt, majorisiert.
overruling decision aufhebende Entscheidung.
overrun Überschuß, -hang, *(books)* Remittenden, *(fig.)* Überschwemmung;
~**s** *(US)* Extra-, Mehrkosten, Kostenüberschreitung;
~ *(v.)* überschwemmen, -fluten, *(print.)* umbrechen, *(subject)* flüchtig berühren, *(tourists)* scharenweise einfallen, überlaufen;
~ **a book** Buch überfliegen; ~ **the constable** *(fam.)* über seine Verhältnisse leben; ~ **the contents of a book** Buch durchblättern; ~ **a country** in ein Land einfallen, *(idea)* im Lande um sich greifen, sich im Lande breitmachen; ~ **a signal** Signal überfahren; ~ **the allotted time** *(broadcast)* Sendezeit überziehen; ~ **the time allowed** *(speaker)* Redezeit überschreiten;
~ **by enemy troops** vom Feind besetzt; ~ **with weeds** vom Unkraut überwuchert;
to be ~ with tourists von Touristen überlaufen sein.
overrunning clutch Freilaufkupplung.
oversample zu große Stichprobe.
oversaturation with advertising Werbemüdigkeit.
oversaving übermäßige Spartätigkeit.
oversea(s) Übersee;
~ *(a.)* überseeisch, im Ausland;
to go ~ nach Übersee gehen, Überseereise machen;
~ **advertising** Auslandswerbung; ~ **agency** Überseevertretung; ~ **aid** Auslands-, Überseehilfe; **tax-free ~ allowance** steuerfreier Überseezuschlag; ~ **assets** überseeische Vermögenswerte; ~ **assignment** Auslandsposten, -verwendung; ~ **bank** Überseebank; ~ **branch** überseeische Filiale, Auslandsfiliale; ~ **broadcast program(me)** überseeisches Rundfunkprogramm; ~ **business** Überseehandel, -geschäft, überseeisches Geschäft; ~ **buyer** Auslandskunde, Kunde aus Übersee; ~ **call** *(Br.)* Auslandsgespräch; ~ **commerce** Überseehandel; ~ **company** *(Br.)* ausländische Gesellschaft mit Niederlassung in England; ~ **contract** Auslandsvertrag; ~ **countries** Überseeländer, Ausland; ~ **customers** Überseekundschaft; ~ **debt** Auslandsschulden; ~ **demands** Überseebedarf; ~ **edition** Überseeausgabe; ~ **exhibition** Überseeausstellung; ~ **expedition** Übersee-Expedition; ~ **goods** Auslandssendungen; ~ **holder of dollars** überseeischer Dollarbesitzer; ~ **income** Auslandseinkommen; ~ **interests** überseeische Interessen; ~ **investment** Auslandsinvestitionen; ~ **journey** Überseereise; ~ **loan** Überseedarlehn; ~ **mail** *(Br.)* Auslandspost; ~ **market** überseeischer Markt, Überseemarkt; ~ **negotiations** Auslandsverhandlungen; ~ **order** Überseeauftrag; ~ **orders** Bestellungen aus Übersee; ~ **ordinary money order** Auslandspostanweisung; ~ **operations** Überseeverkehr; ~ **post** Auslandsposten, *(post office)* Auslandspost; ~ **parcel rate** Auslandspaketgebühr; ~ **possessions** überseeische Gebiete; ~ **postage rates** *(Br.)* Auslandsporto, Auslandsposttarif; ~ **prices** Überseepreise; ~ **Private Investment Corporation** *(US)* Entwicklungsgesellschaft; ~ **producer** Überseeproduzent; ~ **report** Überseebericht; ~ **sales** Auslandsumsätze, Umsätze im Überseegeschäft; ~ **spending** Auslandsausgaben, -investitionen; ~ **territories** überseeische Hoheitsgebiete; ~ **trade** Überseehandel, -geschäft; ~ **trade service** Außenhandelsorganisation; ~ **trade corporation** *(Br.)* steuerlich begünstigte Auslandsgesellschaft mit Geschäftssitz in England; ~ **transport** Überseeverkehr; ~ **travel** Auslands-, Überseereisen; ~ **vessel** Überseeschiff; ~ **visitors** Besucher aus Übersee.
oversee *(v.)* **work** Arbeiten beaufsichtigen.
overseer Vorarbeiter, Aufseher, *(building trade)* Polier, *(public officer)* Inspektor, *(print.)* Faktor;
~ **of customs** Zollinspektor; ~**s of highways** Straßenbauamt; ~ **of the machine room** Schriftsetzer; ~**s of the poor** *(Br.)* Sozialamt; ~ **of a port** Hafenmeister.
overseership Meister-, Vorarbeiterstelle, Aufseheramt.
oversell *(v.)* in zu großen Mengen (mehr als man liefern kann) verkaufen, *(stock exchange)* über den Bestand verkaufen.
overselling übertriebene Verkaufspolitik.
overset *(print.)* Stehsatz;
~ *(v.)* umstürzen, -kippen, *(fig.)* durcheinanderbringen, in Verwirrung stürzen, *(print.)* zu breit setzen, zu viel Satz herstellen.
overshadow *(v.)* in den Schatten stellen, überschatten.
overshoe Überschuh, Gummischuh.
overshoot *(airplane)* Hinausschießen über die Landemarke;
~ *(v.)* übertreiben, zu weit gehen;
~ **the mark** über das Ziel hinausschießen, zuviel behaupten; ~ **the runway** über die Landebahn hinausschießen; ~ **the truth** Wahrheit strapazieren.

overside überbord, über Schiffsseite;
  to discharge cargo ~ Fracht auf Leichter entladen;
  ~ clause Überbordauslieferungsklausel; **~ delivery** Überbordauslieferung.
oversight *(negligence)* Flüchtigkeitsfehler, Versehen, *(omission)* Übersehen, *(supervision)* Aufsicht, Überwachung;
  by an ~ aus Versehen; **under the ~** unter der Aufsicht;
  ~ powers Aufsichts-, Überwachungsfunktionen.
oversimplification zu große Vereinfachung.
oversize Übergröße;
  ~ in tyres Reifenübergröße.
overslaugh *(Br.)* Abkommandierung zu einem höheren Kommando;
  ~ *(v.) (mil., Br.)* abkommandieren.
oversleep *(v.)* verschlafen.
oversleeve Ärmelschoner.
oversold market *(US)* infolge von Baisseverkäufen überlasteter (bei fallenden Kursen nicht mehr aufnahmefähiger) Markt.
oversolicitude übergroße Ängstlichkeit.
overspeculation Überspekulation.
overspeed gear Geschwindigkeitsregler, Ausschaltvorrichtung bei Übergeschwindigkeit.
overspend *(v.)* zuviel ausgeben, über seine Verhältnisse leben.
overspill [population] Bevölkerungsüberschuß;
  ~ area Entlastungsgebiet; **~ relief** *(taxation)* Ermäßigung für im Ausland gezahlte überhöhte Steuersätze.
overspread *(v.)* o. s. sich ausbreiten.
overstaffed personell überbesetzt;
  to be ~ zuviel Personal haben, mit Personal überbesetzt sein;
  ~ civil service überbesetzter Verwaltungsapparat.
overstaffing Überbesetzung mit Arbeitskräften.
overstate *(v.)* übertreiben, zu hoch angeben, zu stark auftragen, *(balance sheet)* überbewerten;
  ~ one's case eigene Sache übertreiben, zu stark auftragen.
overstated zu hoch angegeben.
overstatement Übertreibung.
overstay *(v.)* Zeit überschreiten;
  ~ one's leave seine Urlaubszeit überschreiten; **~ one's market** *(US)* richtigen Zeitpunkt zum Verkauf verpassen; **~ one's welcome** seine Besuchszeit überschreiten, zu lange bleiben.
overstep | *(v.)* **one's authority** seine Vollmachten überschreiten; **~ the limits of one's contractual duties** außerhalb seiner Vertragsverpflichtungen tätig werden.
overstock Überfluß, -vorrat, zu großes Lager, *(shares)* über das genehmigte Aktienkapital hinaus ausgegebene Aktien;
  ~ *(v.)* zu viel auf Lager haben; **~ with goods** übermäßig (über den Bedarf) mit Waren eindecken; **~ the market** Markt überschwemmen; **~ a shop** zuviel Waren einlagern.
overstocked zu hoch eingedeckt, mit Vorräten überhäuft;
  to be ~ zu großes Lager führen.
overstocking Überbevorratung.
overstrain | *(v.)* **one's conscience** sein Gewissen strapazieren; **~ the economy** Wirtschaft überfordern; **~ o. s. with working** sich überarbeiten (übernehmen).
overstrung nervlich überlastet.
overstudy übermäßiges Studium.
overstuffed mit tiefen Polstern überzogen.
oversubscribe *(v.)* [Anleihe] überzeichnen.
oversubscribed überzeichnet.
oversubscription Überzeichnung.
oversupply Überangebot, *(EC)* Überschuß;
  ~ *(v.)* überreichlich versehen.
overt offenkundig, offenbar;
  market ~ offener Markt;
  ~ act objektiver Tatbestand; **~ hostility** offene Feindseligkeit; **~ word** unmißverständliches Wort.
overtake *(v.)* einholen, *(car)* überholen;
  ~ arrears of work Rückstände aufarbeiten; **~ the boom** Konjunktur überhitzen; **~ improperly** unvorschriftsmäßig überholen; **~ on the left** links überholen; **~ other cars on the road** andere Wagen auf der Straße überholen; **~ a string of cars** Wagenkolonne überholen.
overtaken | **by disater** vom Unglück befallen; **~ by a storm** von einem Sturm überrascht; **~ by surprise** überrascht.
overtaking Überholen;
  no ~ Überhol[ungs]verbot;
  ~ of the boom Konjunkturüberhitzung; **~ prohibited** Überholen verboten.
overtask *(v.)* überfordern;
  ~ one's strength sich zuviel zumuten.
overtax *(v.)* übersteuern, zu hoch besteuern;

~ s. one's patience jds. Geduld zu sehr strapazieren; **~ one's strength** sich zuviel zumuten.
overtaxation übermäßige steuerliche Belastung, Übersteuerung;
  ~ by inflation inflationsbedingte Übersteuerung.
overthrow Umsturz;
  ~ of the government Regierungssturz;
  ~ *(v.)* umstoßen, stürzen;
  ~ the government Regierung stürzen.
overthrower Umstürzler.
overtime Überstunden, -schicht, *(overtime pay)* Überstundenzuschlag;
  compulsory ~ Pflicht-, Zwangsüberstunden; **~ worked** geleistete Überstunden;
  ~ *(v.) (photo)* überbelichten;
  to be paid extra for ~ Überstundengeld erhalten; **to be on (make, work) ~** Überstunden machen; **to employ on ~** Überstunden machen lassen; **to pay for ~** Überstunden abgelten;
  ~ allowance Überstundenvergütung; **~ authorization** Überstundengenehmigung; **~ ban** Überstundenverbot; **~ bonus (compensation)** Mehrarbeitszuschlag, Überstundengelder; **~ employment** Überschreitung der betrieblichen Arbeitszeit; **~ hours** Überstundenzeit; **~ pay** Überstundenbezahlung, -lohn, Mehrarbeitszuschlag; **~ payments** Überstundengelder; **~ premium** Überstundenzuschlag; **~ rate** Überstundenlohn, -satz; **~ rate of time and a half** anderthalbfacher Tarifsatz für Überstunden; **~ request** *(customs officers)* Überstundengesuch, -forderung; **~ session** verlängerte Sitzung; **~ wage** Überstundenlohn.
overtail Überanstrengung, -arbeitswut.
overtonnage zuviel vorhandener Schiffsraum.
overtower *(v.)* überragen.
overtrade *(v.) (buy goods beyond one's uses, US)* über die zur Verfügung stehenden Geldmittel hinaus kaufen, sich absatzmäßig übernehmen, *(stock exchange)* ohne kapitalmäßige Deckung spekulieren.
overtrading übermäßiger Kreditkauf, übermäßige Absatzausweitung, Liquiditätsschwierigkeiten wegen zu hoher Lagerhaltung, *(stock exchange)* übermäßige Spekulation.
overture Annäherungsversuch, *(music)* Ouvertüre, Vorspiel, Eröffnung, *(offer)* Angebot, Vorschlag;
  peace ~ Friedensangebot, -vorschlag;
  ~ *(v.)* vorschlagen, beantragen.
overturn Umstürzen, Umfallen, *(US)* Umsatz;
  ~ *(v.)* umstürzen, -kippen, umstoßen.
overvaluation Überbewertung, -schätzung.
overvalue *(v.)* zu hoch ansetzen, überbewerten, -schätzen.
overvalued überbewertet;
  ~ currency überbewertete Währung.
overvote *(v.)* überstimmen.
overwatched übernächtigt.
overwear *(v.)* abtragen.
overweight zu hohes Gewicht, Mehr-, Übergewicht;
  ~ *(v.)* überlasten, *(statistics)* zu großes Gewicht beilegen;
  ~ baggage *(US)* *(luggage, Br.)* Gepäck mit Übergewicht, Übergewicht.
overweighted überlastet, -laden;
  ~ with packages mit Paketen überladen.
overwhelm *(v.)* überschütten, -häufen, *(fig.)* überwältigen, -mannen;
  ~ the enemy Feind überwältigen; **~ with questions** mit Fragen überschütten.
overwhelmed | **by the flood** von der Flut zerstört; **~ with orders** mit Aufträgen überhäuft; **~ with work** mit Arbeit überlastet;
  to be ~ at the news von den Nachrichten überwältigt sein.
overwhelming | **majority** überwältigende Mehrheit; **~ victory** überwältigender Sieg.
overwork *(overtime)* Überstunden, *(excessive work)* Überarbeitung, -anstrengung;
  ~ *(v.)* überanstrengen;
  ~ o. s. sich überarbeiten; **~ s. o.** j. mit Arbeit überladen.
overwrap Umverpackung.
overwrite *(general agent)* Superprovision;
  ~ *(v.)* Vielschreiber sein, sich ausschreiben, *(pay to general agent)* Superprovision zahlen.
overzeal Übereifer.
owe *(v.)* schulden, schuldig sein;
  ~ s. o. £ 10 jem. 10 Pfund schulden; **~ allegiance to s. o.** jem. Gehorsam schulden; **~ a great deal to s. o.** jem. sehr viel verdanken; **~ for one's house** noch Schulden auf seinem Haus haben; **~ one's life** sein Leben verdanken; **~ for three months'**

rent seit drei Monaten die Miete schuldig bleiben; ~ **it to one's reputation** es seinem Namen schuldig sein; ~ **respect to one's father** seinem Vater Respekt schulden.

owing geschuldet, schuldig, offenstehend;

amount ~ ausstehender Betrag; **rent** ~ Mietrückstand; **large sums still** ~ noch ausstehende große Beträge;

~ **to circumstances** umständehalber; ~ **to the expenses** aufgrund der Kosten; ~ **to subsidiaries** *(balance sheet)* Verpflichtungen gegenüber Tochtergesellschaften;

to be ~ noch offenstehen; **to be** ~ **to s. one's carelessness** jds. Sorglosigkeit zuzuschreiben sein; **to have money** ~ Geld ausstehen haben; **to pay all that is** ~ alle Schulden bezahlen.

owelty | **of exchange** Wertausgleich bei Grundstückstausch; ~ **of partition** Wertausgleich bei Naturalteilung.

own eigen, selbst;

of its ~ von sich aus; **on one's** ~ selbständig, unabhängig, eigenständig;

~ *(v.)* besitzen, innehaben, zu eigen (Eigentum) haben, Eigentümer sein, *(recognize)* einräumen, anerkennen;

~ **s. th.** im Besitz einer Sache sein; ~ **o. s. beaten** sich geschlagen geben; ~ **beneficially** nießbrauchberechtigt sein; ~ **a child** Vaterschaft eines Kindes anerkennen; ~ **a claim against s. o.** *(US)* obligatorischen Anspruch gegen j. haben; ~ **that a claim is justified** Forderung als berechtigt anerkennen; ~ **one's faults** seine Fehler zugeben; ~ **the force of an argument** sich einer Beweisführung beugen; ~ **as heir** als Erben anerkennen; ~ **a house jointly** Haus gemeinsam besitzen; ~ **land** Grund und Boden besitzen, Grundeigentümer sein; ~ **a life estate** lebenslänglichen Nießbrauch haben; ~ **a motor vehicle** Kraftfahrzeughalter sein; ~ **subsidiaries outright** Tochtergesellschften hundertprozentig besitzen; ~ **o. s. supporter of reforms** sich selbst als reformfreudig bezeichnen; ~ **up** mit der Sprache herausrücken; ~ **up to a crime** Verbrechen eingestehen;

to be [working] on one's ~ selbständig sein; **to be left on one's** ~ sich selbst überlassen bleiben; **to claim one's** ~ sein Eigentum herausverlangen; **to come into one's** ~ seinen rechtmäßigen Besitz erlangen, *(fig.)* sich durchsetzen; **to do s. th. entirely on one's** ~ etw. im Alleingang unternehmen; **to do well enough on one's** ~ ganz gut allein zurechtkommen; **to have a car of one's** ~ seinen eigenen Wagen fahren; **to have a copy of one's** ~ Durchschlag erhalten haben; **to have a flavo(u)r all its** ~ ganz besonderen Geschmack haben; **to have a house of one's** ~ eigenes Haus besitzen; **to have money of one's** ~ eigenes Geld haben (Vermögen besitzen); **to have no resources of one's** ~ über kein eigenes Vermögen verfügen; **to hold one's** ~ seine Stellung behaupten, *(patient)* sich wacker halten; **to hold one's** ~ **in competitive markets** sich wettbewerbsmäßig (auf dem Markt) durchsetzen; **to live on one's** ~ allein leben; **to stand on one's** ~ freistehend sein; **to work on one's** ~ auf eigene Rechnung arbeiten;

~ **acceptance** eigenes Akzept; **of one's** ~ **accord** aus eigenem Entschluß; **on one's** ~ **account** *(fig.)* aus eigener Kraft; **of one's** ~ **account** aus eigenem Entschluß; **for one's** ~ **account** für eigene Rechnung; **to be in business on one's** ~ **account** sein eigenes Geschäft haben, selbständig sein; ~ **brand** Eigen-, Hausmarke; ~ **brother** leiblicher Bruder; **one's** ~ **business** Eigengeschäft; ~ **capital** Eigenkapital; ~ **consumption** Eigenverbrauch; ~ **costs** Selbstkosten; **at one's** ~ **expense** auf eigene Rechnung; ~ **financing** Eigenfinanzierung; ~ **funds** Eigenmittel; **by one's** ~ **hand** eigenhändig; **to write s. th. in one's** ~ **hand** etw. eigenhändig schreiben; ~ **home** Eigenheim; ~ **house** eigenes Haus; ~ **insurance** Selbstversicherung; ~ **insurer** Selbstversicherer; ~ **make** eigenes Fabrikat, Eigenfabrikat; **to be one's** ~ **man (master)** sein eigener Herr (unabhängig, selbständig) sein; ~ **money** eigenes Geld; **under one's** ~ **name** im eigenen Namen; ~ **production** Eigenproduktion; ~ **resources** Eigenmittel; ~ **retail store** betriebseigener [Verkaufs]laden; **to have s. th. in one's** ~ **right** selbst Vermögen besitzen; **to possess in one's** ~ **right** als Eigentümer besitzen; ~ **risk** *(insurance)* Selbstbehalt; **at one's** ~ **risk** auf eigene Gefahr; **to do one's** ~ **thing** etw. aus eigenem Antrieb tun, tun, was einem gefällt.

owned im Eigentum, gehörig, gehörend;

employer- ~ im Eigentum des Arbeitgebers; **family-** ~ im Familienbesitz; **foreign-** ~ in ausländischem Besitz (Eigentum im öffentlichen Besitz); **government-** ~ im Staatseigentum, in Staatsbesitz; **independently** ~ im Alleineigentum stehend; **jointly** ~ im gemeinsamen Eigentum (Besitz); **privately** ~ im Privatbesitz; **publicly** ~, **state-** ~ im Staatseigentum (Staatsbesitz);

~ **by the parish** gemeindeeigen;

to be ~ **by s. o.** in jds. Eigentum stehen; **to be jointly** ~ im gemeinsamen Eigentum stehen; **to be partially** ~ **by foreign capital** teilweise in ausländischem Eigentum stehen; **to be principally** ~ **by foreign capital** überwiegend in ausländischem Besitz sein; **to be** ~ **by the state** dem Staat gehören; ~ **capital** Eigenkapital.

owner Besitzer, Eigentümer, Eigner, [Rechts]inhaber, Berechtigter, *(entrepreneur)* Unternehmer, *(shipowner)* Reeder; ~**s** Reederei;

absolute ~ unumschränkter Eigentümer; **abutting (adjoining)** ~ Besitzer des Nachbargrundstückes; **apartment house** ~ Mietshausbesitzer; **beneficial** ~ Nießbrauchberechtigter, Nutznießer; **bona-fide** ~ gutgläubiger Besitzer (Eigentümer); **builder** ~ Bauherr; **co-** ~ Miteigentümer; **common** ~ Miteigentümer; **de facto** ~ tatsächlicher Besitzer; **dominant** ~ Eigentümer des herrschenden Grundstücks; **equitable** ~ wirtschaftlicher Eigentümer; **estate** ~ Grundstückseigentümer; **exclusive** ~ alleiniger Besitzer; **factory** ~ Fabrikbesitzer; **former** ~ früherer Inhaber; **general** ~ Volleigentümer; **house** ~ Hausbesitzer, -eigentümer; **joint** ~ Miteigentümer, -besitzer; **land** ~ Grundbesitzer, -eigentümer; **lawful** ~ rechtmäßiger Inhaber (Eigentümer); **legal** ~ formeller (treuhänderischer) Eigentümer; **life** ~ lebenslänglicher Eigentümer; **limited** ~ Nießbrauchberechtigter; **managing** ~ Korrespondenzreeder; **reasonally minded** ~ vernünftig denkender Eigentümer; **outright** ~ Volleigentümer; **part** ~ Bruchteilseigentümer; **person not the** ~ Nichteigentümer; **policy** ~ Versicherungsnehmer; **present** ~ gegenwärtiger Besitzer (Eigentümer); **previous** ~ Vorbesitzer, -eigentümer; **property** ~ Grundstückseigentümer; **real** ~ wirklicher Eigentümer; **real-estate** ~ Grundstückseigentümer; **record** ~ *(stock)* registrierter Eigentümer; **registered** ~ eingetragener Eigentümer; **reputed** ~ vermutlicher Eigentümer; **rightful** ~ rechtmäßiger Eigentümer; **riparian** ~ Flußanlieger; **servient** ~ Eigentümer des belasteten Grundstücks; **severalty** ~**s** Bruchteilseigentümer; **sole** ~ Alleineigentümer; **sole and unconditional** ~ *(fire insurance)* alleinverfügungsberechtigter Eigentümer; **special** ~ vorübergehender Eigentümer; **store** ~ *(US)* Ladenbesitzer, -inhaber; **subsequent** ~ Besitznachfolger; **trademark** ~ Warenzeicheninhaber; **true** ~ rechtmäßiger (wirklicher) Eigentümer;

~ **and charterer** Reeder und Verfrachter;

~ **of a banking account** Bankkontoinhaber; ~ **of an automobile** Kraftfahrzeughalter; ~ **of a building** Gebäudeeigentümer; ~ **of a business** Geschäftsinhaber; ~ **of a car** Kraftfahrzeughalter; ~ **and charterer** Ver- und Befrachter; ~ **of an estate** Gutsbesitzer; ~ **of large estates** Großgrundbesitzer; ~ **of a factory** Fabrikbesitzer; ~ **in fee simple** unbeschränkter Grundstückseigentümer; ~ **of a firm** Firmeninhaber, Geschäftsinhaber; ~ **of the goods** Wareneigentümer; ~ **of a house** Hauseigentümer, -besitzer; ~ **of land** Grund[stücks]eigentümer, -besitzer; ~ **of a motor vehicle** Kraftfahrzeughalter; ~ **of a patent** Patentinhaber; ~ **of premises** Grundstückseigentümer; ~ **of real estate (property)** Grund[stücks]eigentümer; ~ **of a rent charge** *(Br.)* Erbzinsberechtigter; ~ **of a registered trademark** Schutzmarken-, Warenzeicheninhaber; ~ **of shares** *(Br.)* Aktienbesitzer; ~ **of securities** Depotinhaber; ~ **of a ship** Schiffsreeder; **joint** ~ **of a ship** Mitreeder; ~ **for the time being** derzeitiger Eigentümer; ~ **of a trademark** Warenzeicheninhaber;

to indemnify the ~ **of property taken for public use** enteigneten Eigentümer entschädigen; **to return to its original** ~ zum ursprünglichen Eigentümer zurückkehren; **to return property to its rightful** ~ dem rechtmäßigen Eigentümer zurückgeben; **to take as true** ~ **goods out of the bankrupt's possession** sein Eigentum aus dem Konkurs aussondern;

~-**driver** Selbst-, Herrenfahrer; ~-**farmer** selbständiger Landwirt; ~ **occupation** *(house)* Eigennutzung; ~-**occupied** vom Eigentümer bewohnt, eigengenutzt; ~-**occupied dwelling** Eigentumswohnung; ~-**occupied house** *(Br.)* Eigenheim; ~-**occupied housing** Eigenheimbesitz; ~-**occupied property** vom Eigentümer bewohntes Haus; ~-**occupier** Eigenheimbesitzer; ~-**operated farm** landwirtschaftlicher Eigenbetrieb; ~-**operator** *(agriculture)* Eigenbetrieb; ~'**s public liability insurance** Eigentümerhaftpflichtversicherung; **at** ~ **risk** auf eigene Gefahr, *(carriage of goods)* Gefahr beim Absender; **to park at the** ~'**s risk** auf eigene Gefahr parken; ~-**user** Eigentumsbenutzer.

ownerless dog herrenloser Hund.

ownership Eigentum, Eigentumsrecht, -verhältnis, Besitz;

under new ~ unter neuer Leitung;

absolute ~ unumschränktes (absolutes) Eigentumsrecht; **bare** ~ bloßes Eigentumsrecht; **collective** ~ Kollektiveigentum; **common** ~ Miteigentum; **corporate** ~ Firmen-, Gesellschaftseigentum; **equitable** ~ wirtschaftliches Eigentum; **exclusive** ~ Alleineigentum; **foreign** ~ Auslandsbesitz; **full** ~ Allein-, Volleigentum; **imperfect** ~ belastetes Eigentum; **industrial** ~ Besitz der Produktionsmittel; **joint** ~ Eigentum zur gesamten Hand, Gesamthandeigentum; **legal** ~ juristisches Eigentum; **limited** ~ beschränktes Eigentum; **part** ~ Bruchteilseigentum; **perfect** ~ lastenfreies (unbelastetes) Eigentum; **private** ~ System des Privateigentums; **public** ~ Staatseigentum; **record** ~ grundbuchlich nachgewiesenes Eigentumsverhältnis; **reputed** ~ vermutliches (augenscheinliches) Eigentum, Eigentumsvermutung; **restricted** ~ zeitlich beschränktes Eigentum; **social** ~ soziales Eigentum; **special** ~ beschränktes Eigentum; **state** ~ *(US)* Staatseigentum; **stock** ~ Aktienbesitz, Gesellschaftsanteil; **uncertain** ~ ungeklärtes Eigentumsverhältnis; **unlimited** ~ unbeschränktes Eigentum;

~ **in common** Gemeinschaftseigentum; ~ **in fee** *(US)* unbeschränktes Eigentum; **public** ~ **of industry** verstaatlichte Industrie; ~ **of land** Grundeigentum, Grundbesitz; ~ **of the sea** Seeherrschaft; ~ **of stock** Aktienbesitz; ~ **of wealth** Vermögensbesitz;

to acquire ~ Eigentum erwerben; **to be under foreign** ~ von ausländischem Kapital kontrolliert werden; **to be under public**
~ in öffentlichem Eigentum stehen, der öffentlichen Hand gehören; **to dispute s. one's** ~ jem. den Besitz einer Sache streitig machen, jds. Eigentumsrecht bestreiten; **to pass into** ~ in das Eigentum übergeben; **to retain** ~ **in one's policy** Begünstigter bleiben; **to retain the** ~ **of one's property** Eigentum an seinem Grundstück behalten; **to transfer** ~ Eigentum übertragen;

~ **capital** Eigenkapital; ~ **combination** *(US)* Konzern; ~ **distribution** Eigentumsverteilung; ~ **interest** Kapital-, Gesellschaftsanteil; **to exercise** ~ **power** Eigentumsrechte ausüben; ~ **purchase** Eigentumserwerb; ~ **representation** Vertretung der Anteilseignerseite; ~ **representative** Vertreter der Anteilseigner; ~ **securities** Dividendenpapiere; ~ **share** Eigentumsanteil, Kapitalbeteiligung; ~ **tally** Eigentumsmarke.

oxygen mask Sauerstoffmaske.

oyer gerichtliche Untersuchung.

oyster *(profitable business, US)* vorteilhafte Sache;
to be as close as an ~ völlig zugeknöpfter Mensch sein.

ozalide Blaupause.

ozone *(fig.)* belebender Einfluß;
~ **concentration** Ozongehalt; ~ **layer** Ozonschicht.

ozoner Auto-, Freiluftkino.

P

pabulum, mental geistige Nahrung.
pac *(stock exchange, Br.)* Stellagegeschäft.
pace Schritt, Tempo, Leistung, *(film story)* Schwung, *(work)* Geschwindigkeit;
at a great ~ sehr schnell; **off the** ~ *(sl.)* zweiter;
~ **for** ~ Schritt vor Schritt;
sluggish ~ **of business** konjunkturelle Flautebewegung; ~ **of business activity** Konjunkturtempo; ~ **of expansion** Expansionstempo; ~ **of investment** Investitionstempo;
~ *(v.) (fig.)* lenken, zügeln;
~ **s. o.** jds. Schrittmacher sein; ~ **the general increase of living cost** der allgemeinen Preiserhöhung vorangehen, preistreibend für die Lebenshaltungskosten sein; ~ **the market** Schrittmacher abgeben; ~ **off a distance** Entfernung abschreiten; ~ **the station platform** auf dem Bahnsteig hin und her laufen, Bahnsteig entlangmarschieren; ~ **up and down the room** im Zimmer auf und ab gehen;
to gather ~ an Geschwindigkeit zunehmen; **to go the** ~**s** Geld mit vollen Händen ausgeben; **to hit the** ~ flott leben; **to keep** ~ Schritt halten; **to keep** ~ **with modern invention** mit der modernen Entwicklung Schritt halten; **to put s. o. through his** ~**s** j. auf Herz und Nieren prüfen; **to set the** ~ Tempo angeben; **to stand the** ~ Tempo durchhalten; **to step up the** ~ **of stockbuilding** lagerzyklisch aktiver werden, Lagerzyklus positiv beeinflussen.
pacemaker Schrittmacher;
~**s in public opinion** meinungsbildende Persönlichkeiten; ~ **of European unity** Schrittmacher der europäischen Einheit.
Pacific Stiller (Pazifischer) Ozean;
~ *(a.)* friedlich, *(geographical)* pazifisch;
~ **blockade** *(international law)* Friedensblockade; ~ **Islands** Pazifische Inseln; ~ **nature** friedfertige Natur; ~ **Ocean** Stiller Ozean, Pazifik; ~ **policy** Friedenspolitik.
pacification Beruhigung, Befriedigung, Beschwichtigung.
pacificator Friedensstifter.
pacifism Pazifismus.
pacifist Pazifist.
pacify *(v.)* befrieden, beschwichtigen.
pacing the general increase of prices Vorlauf vor der allgemeinen Preiserhöhung.
pack *(bale)* Ballen, *(bundle)* Bündel, *(conservation)* Konservierungsmethode, *(mil.)* Marschgepäck, *(parcel)* Paket, Packen, Verpackungseinheit, *(quantity)* Haufen, Menge, *(submarine)* Rudel, *(total of tinned production)* Konservenproduktion;
loose or in ~**s** lose oder verpackt;
the moneyed ~ die Stinkreichen;
~ **of cigarettes** Zigarettenpackung; ~ **of films** Filmpack; ~ **of hounds** Meute; ~ **of lies** Haufen von Lügen, lauter Lügen; ~ **of nonsense** *(sl.)* Haufen Dummheiten; ~ **of thieves** Diebesbande;
~ *(v.)* [ver]packen, einpacken, *(load)* bepacken, *(tin)* konservieren, eindosen;
~ **the bag in the dick(e)y of a car** Gepäck auf dem Rücksitz eines Autos verstauen; ~ **a carriage with passengers** Eisenbahnwaggon vollstopfen; ~ **a child off to bed** Kind zu Bett bringen (ins Bett verpacken); ~ **into a cinema** sich in ein Kino drängeln; ~ **down hard** *(snow)* sich zusammenballen; ~ **easily** sich leicht verpacken lassen; ~ **in** *(sl.)* aufgeben, Leine ziehen; ~ **it in** *(sl.)* seine Chancen wahrnehmen; ~ **a jury** Geschworenenbank aus parteilichen Geschworenen zusammenstellen; ~ **a meeting** große Anzahl von Anhängern in eine Versammlung dirigieren; ~ **s. o. off** jem. eine Abfuhr erteilen, j. schnellstens loswerden; ~ **out** auspacken, *(ship)* abladen; ~ **people into an already overcrowded bus** Menschen in einen schon überfüllten Bus hineinpferchen; ~ **a revolver** *(US sl.)* Revolver bei sich tragen; ~ **round the speaker** sich um den Redner scharen; ~ **the trunks** Koffer packen; ~ **up** verladen, aufladen, *(aircraft's engine, sl.)* aussetzen, stottern, *(fam.)* kaputt gehen, *(finish work)* zu arbeiten aufhören, *(go away)* sein Bündel schnüren, seine Sachen packen, die Bude zumachen; ~ **up again** umpacken; ~ **up one's things** seine Sachen packen; ~ **up one's wares** seine Waren in Ballen verpacken;
to be one of the family ~ zur Familie gehören;
~ **animal** Pack-, Tragtier; ~ **drill** *(mil.)* Strafexerzieren in Gefechtsausrüstung; ~ **film** Filmpack; ~ **goods** Ballengüter; ~ **horse** Packpferd; ~ **ice** Packeis; ~ **mule** Packesel; ~**-rat** *(sl.)* kleiner Gauner; ~ **road** Maultierpfad; ~ **sheet** Packleinwand; ~ **train** *(US)* Tragtierkolonne; ~ **twine** Bindfaden, Packzwirn.
package *(advertising issue)* Werbematerial für Händler, *(advertising in transit vehicle)* Linienabschluß, *(assembling)* Einbauteil, Anlage, *(bale, US)* [Waren]ballen, Kollo, Gebinde, *(bargaining)* Tarifabschluß, *(broadcasting)* Originalprogramm, *(building trade)* zur Aufstellung fertige Baueinheit, *(bundle)* Bündel, *(charge for packing)* Packerlohn, *(manner of packing)* Verpackungsart, *(money, sl.)* Haufen Geld, *(negotiations)* Verhandlungspaket, *(number of program, US)* Programmnummer, *(packing)* Verpacken, Verpackung, Emballage, *(packing material)* Verpackung, Emballage, *(parcel, US)* Paket, Packung, Pack[en], Fracht-, Versandstück, *(program(me)) in allen Einzelheiten ausgearbeitetes Programm, (radio, television)* pauschal verkaufte fertige Sendung;
loose or in ~**s** lose oder verpackt; **in** ~**s** packweise, in Gebinden;
including (inclusive of) ~ einschließlich Verpackung;
Christmas ~ *(US)* Weihnachtspaket; **collect-on-delivery** ~ *(US)* **(cash-on-delivery,** *Br.***)**Nachnahmepaket; **considered** ~ zusammenhängendes Paket; **cost-saving** ~ *(airline)* kostensparender Linienabschluß; **dual-usage** ~ wiederverwendbare Packung; **executive pay** ~ umfassendes Vergütungsangebot für Führungskräfte; **expendable** ~ verlorene Packung; **export** ~ *(US)* Ausfuhrkolli; **express** ~ *(US)* Eilpaket; **kaleidoscopic** ~ Packung mit Bildfolge; **negotiating** ~ Verhandlungsgegenstand; **original** ~ Originalverpackung, Paket üblicher Art und Größe; **overall** ~ gesamtes Verhandlungsangebot; **re-use** ~ wiederverwendbare Verpackung; **reform** ~ Bündel von Reformvorschlägen; **registered** ~ Einschreibpaket; **restrictive** ~ Restriktionsbündel; **secondary-usage** ~ weiterverwendbare Verpackung; **settlement** ~ neuer Tarifabschluß; **special** ~ Sonderverpackung;
~ **of goods** Warensendung; ~ **of monetary relief** ganzes Bündel geldmarkterleichternder Maßnahmen; **comprehensive** ~ **of services** umfassendes Dienstleistungsangebot;
~ **is not allowed for** Verpackung wird berechnet; ~ **is not charged for** Verpackung nicht berechnet;
~ *(v.)* verpacken, in Pakete packen;
~ **transportation services for its customers** seinen Kunden den ganzen Fächer einer Speditionsfirma anbieten; ~ **votes** Wahlstimmen verschieben;
to bid for the whole ~ als Interessent für das gesamte Fertigungsprogramm auftreten; **to make up in** ~**s** in Bündeln packen; **to put numbers on** ~**s** Pakete numerieren; **to send a** ~ **collect** *(US)* Paket per Nachnahme schicken;
~ **advertising** Versandwerbung; ~ **band premium** Gutschein in Form eines um die Ware gewickelten Streifens; ~ **car** Waggon für Stückgutladungen; **total** ~ **contracting** Beschaffungsvergabe mit von Anfang an festgelegten Pauschalpreisen; ~ **conveyor** [Versand]behälter; ~ **deal** Kopplungsgeschäft, *(negotiations)* Gesamtvereinbarung, Pauschalarrangement, Verhandlungspaket; ~ **design** Verpackungsmuster; ~ **food** Fertiggericht; ~ **freight** *(US)* Stückgutsendungen, -fracht; ~ **goods** gepackte Ware, Versandgeschäftsartikel; ~ **goods commercial** Fernsehsendung für Versandartikel; ~ **holiday** Pauschalferienreise; ~ **insert** *(air carrier)* Linienabschlüsse, *(packing, US)* Packungsbeilage, -beileger; ~ **library** *(US)* Wanderbibliothek; ~ **licensing** *(patent law)* Zusammenfassung von Lizenzen; ~ **offer** Kopplungsangebot, -geschäft; ~ **policy** Sammelpolice; ~ **price** *(tourism)* Abonnements-, Pauschalreise; **easy-to-pay** ~ **price** bequem zu begleichender Kombinationspreis; **total** ~ **procurement** *(defense industry)* Beschaffungsauftrag mit von vornherein festgelegten Preisen; ~ **settlement** gebündeltes Übereinkommen; ~ **size** Paketgröße; ~ **size standards** Verpackungsnormen; ~ **store** *(US)* Alkoholverkauf nur außerhalb des Ladens; ~ **tour** Pauschalreise; ~ **tourism** Pauschalreisesystem.
packaged verpackt;
to be ~ **off** Pauschalreise unternehmen; **to have s. th. securely** ~ etw. sicher unter Kontrolle haben;
~ **goods** abgepackte Ware; ~ **groceries** abgepackte Lebensmittel; ~ **tour** *(US)* Pauschalreise.
packaging [Ver]packen, Verpackung, Aufmachung, *(advertising)* Linienabschlüsse, *(material)* Verpackungsmaterial;
fancy ~ Luxuspackung;
~ **of votes** Wahlstimmenverschiebung;
~ **classifications** Verpackungsrichtlinien; ~ **consultant** Verpackungsspezialist; ~ **costs** Verpackungskosten; ~ **department** Verpackungsabteilung; ~ **engineer** *(US)* Verpackungsfach-

mann; ~ **engineering** *(US)* Verpackungstechnik; ~ **material** *(US)* Verpackungsmaterial; ~ **policy** Ausstattungspolitik; ~ **regulations** Verpackungsbestimmungen; ~ **requirements** Verpackungserfordernisse; ~ **slip** Packzettel; ~ **test** Verpackungstest.

packcloth Packtuch, -leinwand.

packed *(train)* gerammelt voll;
  falsely ~ mit unzulässiger Beimischung verpackt; **mixed** ~ verschiedene Qualitäten enthaltend;
  ~ **to the door** *(bus)* voll besetzt; ~ **by the dozen** dutzendweise verpackt; ~ **for exportation by sea** seemäßig verpackt; ~ **like herrings in a box (sardines in a tin)** wie Heringe in einer Büchse zusammengepfercht; ~ **for railway transport** bahnmäßig verpackt; ~ **as usual in trade** handelsüblich verpackt; ~ **up** *(aircraft engine, sl.)* ausgefallen;
  to be ~ and more than ~ restlos überfüllt sein;
  ~ **house** zum Bersten volles Haus; ~ **lunch** Frühstückspaket; ~ **meeting** überfüllte Versammlung; ~ **parcel** Sammelpaket, Stückgutsendung; ~ **train** überfüllter Zug.

packer [Ver]packer, Lader, *(machine)* Packmaschine, *(wholesale dealer, US)* [Fleisch]konservenhersteller;
  ~'s **wages** Packerlohn.

packery Versandabteilung, Verpackungsraum.

packet Pack[en], *(Br.)* kleines Paket, Päckchen, *(Br., sl.)* ziemlicher Haufen Geld, *(fig.)* kleine Menge, *(shipping)* Post-, Paketboot;
  postal ~ *(Br.)* Postpaket; **registered** ~ *(Br.)* Einschreibepaket; **small** ~ *(Br.)* Päckchen; **surprise** ~ *(Br.)* Überraschungspäckchen;
  ~ **of books** Büchersendung, -paket; ~ **of cigarettes** *(Br.)* Zigarettenpäckchen; ~ **of letters** Bündel (Stoß) Briefe; ~ **of money** Haufen Geld, Geldbündel;
  ~ *(v.)* zu einem Paket verpacken;
  to catch (get, stop) a ~ *(mil. sl.)* ziemlich schwer verwundet werden; **to earn a** ~ Haufen Geld verdienen; **to make a** ~ *(fam.)* sich gesundstoßen; **to sell s. o. a** ~ *(coll.)* j. für dumm verkaufen; **to stop a** ~ schwer verwundet werden;
  ~ **boat** Postdampfer, Paketboot; ~ **day** Versandtag; ~ **line** Postbootroute; **small** ~ **rates** *(Br.)* Päckchengebühren; ~ **ship (vessel)** Postschiff, -boot, Paketboot.

packhouse Packhaus, -hof, Lagerhaus, *(US)* Konservenfabrik.

packing [Ver]packen, Einpacken, Verpackung, *(conservation)* Konservierung, *(material)* Pack-, Verpackungsmaterial;
  ~ **extra** Verpackung wird besonders berechnet; ~ **included** einschließlich Verpackung; ~ **not included** Verpackung nicht inbegriffen; **inclusive of** ~ einschließlich Verpackung; **no charge is made for** ~ Verpackung wird nicht berechnet; ~ **to be returned** Verpackung zurücksenden; **without** ~ netto;
  bad ~ schlechter Verpackungszustand; **customary** ~ handelsübliche Verpackung; **deceptive** ~ Mogelpackung; **defective** ~ mangelhafte Verpackung; **external** ~ äußere Verpackung; **faulty** ~ fehlerhafte Verpackung; **improper** ~ unsachgemäße Verpackung; **insufficient** ~ mangelhafte Verpackung; **internal** ~ Innenverpackung; **nonreturnable** ~ Verpackung zum Wegwerfen, verlorene Verpackung; ~ **ordered** vorschriftsmäßige Verpackung; **original** ~ Original-, Fabrikverpackung; **outer** ~ äußere Verpackung; **overtime** ~ Überschreitung der Packzeit; **poor** ~ schlechter Verpackungszustand; **seaworthy** ~ seetüchtige (seefeste) Verpackung, Seeverpackung; **waterproof** ~ wasserdichte Verpackung;
  ~ **at cost** Verpackung zum Selbstkostenpreis; ~ **for export** Überseeverpackung; ~ **of jury** betrügerische (parteiische) Zusammenstellung eines Geschworenengerichts;
  not to allow for ~ Verpackung wird berechnet; **to be ~ into the cinemas on a wet day** sich an einem Regentag in die Kinos drängeln; **to be sent** ~ schwere Abfuhr erleiden; **to do one's** ~ *(coll.)* packen; **to send s. o.** ~ jem. eine Abfuhr verpassen, j. schnellstens loswerden;
  ~ **agent** Verpacker; ~ **box** Packkiste; ~ **cardboard** Packkarton; ~ **case** Pappkarton, -kiste, Packkiste; **empty** ~ **case** Leerkiste; ~ **charges (costs)** Verpackungskosten; ~ **cloth** Packleinwand; ~ **company (house, plant)** *(US)* Konservenfabrik; ~ **credit** *(Br.)* Versandbereitstellungskredit; ~ **department** Verpackungsabteilung, Packerei; ~ **house** Warenlager, *(factory, US)* Großschlächterei, Konservenfabrik; ~ **industry** *(US)* Konservenindustrie; ~ **instructions** Versand-, Verpackungsanweisung; ~ **list** Pack-, Versandliste; ~ **material** Verpackungsmaterial; ~ **note** Versand-, Packliste; ~ **officer** *(Br.)* Zollkontrolleur; ~ **paper** Packleinwand, -papier; ~ **plant** Verpackungsbetrieb, *(US)* Konservenfabrik; ~ **press** Bündelpresse; ~ **regulations** Verpackungsbestimmungen; ~ **ring** Dichtungsring; ~ **room**

Packraum; ~ **sheet** Packleinwand, -papier; ~ **slip** Packzettel; ~ **ticket** Packzettel; ~ **trade** *(US)* Konservenindustrie; ~ **wage** Packerlohn.

packman Hausierer.

packsack Rucksack.

packsaddle Saum-, Packsattel.

packthread Bindfaden.

packway Saumpfad.

pact Pakt, Abkommen, Vertrag;
  mutual assistance ~ Beistandspakt; **nude** ~ einseitig verpflichtender Vertrag; **obligatory** ~ formlose obligatorische Vereinbarung, schuldrechtlich bedeutungslose Erklärung; **peace** ~ Friedenspakt;
  ~ **of mutual assistance** Beistandspakt; ~ **of nonaggression** Nichtangriffspakt;
  to make a ~ Pakt schließen; **to make a suicide** ~ beschließen, gemeinsam aus dem Leben zu scheiden.

paction *(international law)* sofort erfüllbare Vereinbarung.

pactional vereinbart.

pad Papier-, Notizblock, *(automobile licence plate)* Nummernschild, *(cushion)* Polster, *(rockets)* Start-, Abschußrampe, *(for rubber stamps)* Stempelkissen, *(sl.)* Opiumhöhle, *(tempory bed, sl.)* Bleibe;
  inking ~ Anfeuchter; **launching** ~ *(for rockets)* Abschußstelle; **porter's carrying** ~ Tragekissen des Gepäckträgers; **stamp** ~ Stempelkissen **writing** ~ Brief-, Schreibblock;
  ~ *(v.)* polstern, wattieren, *(travel)* trampen;
  ~ **it home** auf Schusters Rappen nach Hause kommen; ~ **a speech** Rede aufbauschen;
  ~ **room** *(sl.)* Opiumhöhle.

padded shoulders wattierte Schultern.

padder Straßenräuber.

paddle Paddel, *(steamer)* Schaufel;
  ~ *(v.)* *(US)* verprügeln, verbleuen;
  ~ **one's own canoe** sich auf sich selbst verlassen (aus eigener Kraft durchs Leben schlagen), es allein schaffen;
  ~ **steamer** Raddampfer.

paddling pool Planschbecken.

paddy, to put s. o. in a *(sl.)* j. auf die Palme bringen;
  ~ **waggon** *(US)* Grüne Minna.

padhouse Bleibe.

padlock Vorhängeschloß;
  ~ *(v.)* mit Vorhängeschloß versehen, *(US)* behördlich schließen.

padrone *(restaurant)* Wirt, *(for worker, US)* Stellenvermittler.

page Seite, Blatt, *(boy)* Page, *(chronic)* Bericht, Chronik, *(print.)* Kolumne, ganzseitige Schriftseite;
  by ~s kolumnenweise; **first-~** *(US)* auf der ersten Seite;
  advertising ~ Anzeigenseite; **airport** ~ Ausrufanlage auf dem Flugplatz; **black and white advertising** ~ Schwarzweißseite; **bleed** ~ *(ad)* [druck]angeschnittene Seite; **front** ~ Vorder-, Titelseite; **full** ~ ganze Seite; **intervening** ~s dazwischenliegende Seiten; **left-hand** ~ Rückseite; **200 odd** ~s etw. über 200 Seiten; **right-hand** ~ Vorderseite; **title** ~ Titelseite; **white** ~ leere Seite; **whole** ~ ganze Seite; **closely written** ~s eng beschriebene Seiten;
  ~s **of advertising** Anzeigen-, Reklameteil; ~ **of two columns** zweispaltige Seite;
  ~ *(v.)* mit Seitenzahlen versehen, paginieren;
  ~ **s. o.** j. [durch Lautsprecher] ausrufen; ~ **through a book** *(US)* in einem Buch blättern; ~ **the documents** Unterlagen durchnumerieren;
  to hold down a corner in a ~ Eselsohr in eine Seite machen; **to hold 4 typewritten** ~s 4 Schreibmaschinenseiten umfassen; **to jump off the** ~ besonders ins Auge springen; **to place a** ~ **in a magazine** Seite in einer Zeitschrift belegen; **to turn down a** ~ **in a book** Blatt in einem Buch einschlagen;
  ~ **boy** Laufbursche; ~ **depth** Satzspiegel; ~ **dominance** seitenbeherrschende Anzeige; ~ **layout** Seiten-Layout; ~ **number** Seitenzahl, *(sl.)* Leitartikel; ~ **proof** Seitenabzug; ~ **rate** Seitenpreis, -tarif; **full** ~ **rate** voller Seitenpreis; **one-time black-and-white** ~ **rate** Anzeigenpreis für eine Schwarzweißseite; ~ **size** Seitenformat.

pageant Festspiel.

pager Paginierer.

paginal seitenweise;
  ~ **references** Seitenverweise; ~ **reprint** seitenweiser Nachdruck.

paginate *(v.)* paginieren, mit Seitenzahlen versehen.

paging Paginierung, Seitenbezeichnung, Seitenumbruch, *(loudspeaker)* Ausrufenlassen;
  loudspeaker ~ **device** Lautsprecheranlage.

pagoda Pagoda, Tempel;
  to shake the ~ *(India)* schnell zu Geld kommen.
paid bezahlt, *(on receipted bill)* Zahlung erhalten, bezahlt;
  ~ in eingezahlt; **not to be ~ for** unbezahlbar; **when ~** nach
  Eingang;
  carriage ~ frachtfrei; **duty [not] ~ [un]**verzollt; **fully ~** voll
  eingezahlt; **highly ~** hoch (teuer) bezahlt; **low ~** gering bezahlt;
  partly ~ teilweise bezahlt; **postage ~** frei[gemacht]; **~ quarterly**
  in vierteljährlichen Raten; **reply ~** Rückantwort bezahlt; **well-
  ~** gut bezahlt;
  ~ into the bank bei der Bank einbezahlt; **~ out of capital** aus
  dem Kapital gezahlt; **~ for** bezahlt, vergütet; **~ for in cash** in
  bar bezahlt; **~ in full** voll bezahlt;
  to be adequately ~ anständiges Gehalt beziehen; **to be ~ back**
  rückzahlbar sein; **to be ~ on Fridays** Freitags gelöhnt werden;
  to be ~ monthly monatlich bezahlt werden; **to be ~ by the
  quarter** vierteljährlich bezahlt werden; **to be ~ by sender** vom
  Absender bezahlt werden; **to be ~ out in cash by the postman**
  Geld durch Zahlkarte überwiesen erhalten; **to be ~ out of the
  town funds** auf der städtischen Lohnliste stehen; **to be ~ without
  deduction of income tax** einkommensteuerfrei ausbezahlt werden; **to get ~** sich bezahlen lassen; **to make o. s. (itself) ~** sich
  bezahlt machen; **to put ~ to s. th.** *(sl.)* einer Sache ein Ende
  setzen;
  ~ announcement *(advertising)* bezahlte Werbeankündigung; **~
  attorney** engagierter Anwalt; **~ check** *(US)* (**cheque,** *Br.*) eingelöster Scheck; **~ circulation** abgesetzte Auflage; **~ holiday** *(Br.)*
  bezahlter Urlaub; **~ labo(u)r** bezahlte Arbeitskräfte, Lohnarbeit; **~ mortgage** abgelöste Hypothek; **~ office** besoldetes Amt;
  ~-on charges *(Br.)* Auslagen; **~ sick leave** bezahlter Krankenur-
  laub; **badly ~ situation** schlecht bezahlte Stellung; **~ subscriber**
  Subskribent, der mindestens 50% des Bezugspreises bezahlt
  hat; **~ vacation** *(US)* bezahlter Urlaub; **~ work** bezahlte
  Lohnarbeit.
paid-in eingezahlt;
  ~ capital eingezahltes Kapital, Einlagekapital; **~ surplus**
  (accounting, US) Agiocrlös, *(profit, US)* nicht entnommener
  Gewinn.
paid-off|creditor abgefundener Gläubiger; **~ mortgage** abge-
  löste Hypothek.
paid out ausbezahlt, ausgezahlt;
  ~ dividends ausgeschüttete Dividenden.
paid up abgezahlt, abgetragen, *(capital)* voll eingezahlt;
  ~ addition *(life insurance)* Verwendung des Prämienerlöses zur
  Erhöhung der Versicherungssumme, Summenzuwachs [durch
  stehengelassene Prämie]; **~ capital** voll eingezahltes Kapital,
  (corporation) eingezahltes Grundkapital; **~ debt** abgetragene
  Schuld; **~ insurance** prämienfreie [Lebens]versicherung; **~
  membership** zahlende Mitglieder; **~ policy** voll eingezahlte
  Police; **fully ~ shares (stocks,** *US)* eingezahltes Aktienkapital,
  (in a cooperative society) Geschäftsguthaben; **~ value** *(life
  insurance)* Rückkaufs-, Umwandlungswert.
pail Eimer, Kübel.
pain Schmerz, Leid, Kummer;
  upon ~ of bei Strafe von; **under ~ of death** bei Todesstrafe;
  ~ in the neck Nervensäge; **mental ~ and suffering** psychische
  Leiden;
  to be at ~s sich Mühe geben (anstrengen); **to give s. o. ~** jem.
  Schmerzen bereiten; **to give s. o. a ~ in the neck** jem. auf die
  Nerven gehen; **to have a ~ in one's little finger** ein Wehwehchen
  haben; **to have nothing for one's ~s** praktisch umsonst arbeiten;
  to spare no ~s sich jede nur erdenkliche Mühe geben; **to take
  great ~s to please one's employer** sich große Mühe geben, um
  seinen Arbeitgeber zufriedenzustellen; **to work hard and get
  very little for all one's ~** für harte Arbeit und Mühewaltung
  kümmerlich entlohnt werden;
  ~ killer schmerzlindernde Tablette, Schmerztablette.
painful schmerzhaft;
  to produce a ~ expression peinlich wirken.
painstaker gewissenhafter Mensch.
painstaking sorgfältig, gewissenhaft, rührig.
paint Farbe, Malerarbeiten, *(varnish)* Farbe, Schminke;
  as fresh as ~ *(coll.)* frisch wie ein Fisch;
  wet ~! frisch gestrichen;
  ~ in oils Ölmalerei;
  ~ (v.) [aus]malen, [an]streichen, *(fig.)* schildern, beschreiben;
  ~ black in schwarzen Farben schildern (malen); **~ everything in
  rosy colo(u)rs** alles in rosigen Farben schildern; **~ one's face**
  sich schminken; **~ the Forth Bridge** Sysiphusaufgabe zu erledigen haben; **~ a house** Haus anstreichen; **~ the scenery for a play**
  Theaterkulissen malen; **~ shutters** Fensterläden streichen; **~**

the town red *(sl.)* Stadt auf den Kopf stellen, auf eine Sauftour
  gehen (die Pauke hauen); **~ in water-colours** in Wasserfarben
  malen;
  ~ and varnish industry Farbenindustrie; **~ sprayer** Spritzpistole; **~ work** Anstrich, Malerarbeiten.
paintbox Tuschkasten.
paintbrush Pinsel.
painted gestrichen, bemalt, *(disguised)* gefärbt, tendenziös, verfälscht, *(sl.)* vom Radar erfaßt.
painter [Kunst]maler, Anstreicher;
  landscape ~ Landschaftsmaler; **master ~** Malermeister; **portrait ~** Portraitist; **scene ~** Kulissenmaler;
  to cut the ~ *(fig.)* sich selbständig machen; **to cut one's ~**
  (colony) sich vom Mutterland lösen.
painting Malen, Malerei, *(picture)* Gemälde, *(paintwork)*
  Malerarbeiten;
  ~ the town red *(sl.)* Sauftour.
pair Paar, *(mining)* Kameradschaft;
  ~ of binoculars Feldstecher; **~ of compasses** Zirkel; **~ of glasses
  (spectacles)** Brille;
  ~ (v.) off paarweise anordnen, *(parliament)* beiderseitig einer
  Sitzung fernbleiben; **~ off with a shop girl** *(coll.)* Ladenmädchen heiraten.
paired comparison Paarvergleich.
pairing off *(parliament)* vereinbarte gegenseitige Abwesenheit.
pais Geschworene;
  in ~ vor ein Schwurgericht gehörig, *(assurance)* außergerichtlich.
pal *(coll.)* Kumpel, Spezi, *(sl.)* Kumpan, Spießgeselle;
  ~ (v.) up freundschaftlich verkehren, Freundschaft schließen;
  to make a ~ of s. o. jds. Kumpel sein.
palace Palast, Schloß, Palais, *(gaudy establishment)* Vergnügungslokal;
  the ~ einflußreiche Hofbeamte;
  ~ of justice Justizpalast;
  ~ car *(US)* Salonwagen; **~ coup** Palastrevolte; **~ guard** Palastwache, *(fig.)* Präsidentenclique; **~ hotel** Palasthotel; **~ revolution** Palastrevolution.
paladin Paladin, Beschützer.
palate *(fig.)* Geschmack, Gefallen;
  to have a good ~ for wines Weinkenner sein.
palatial, on ~ lines im pompösen Rahmen.
palaver Unterredung, Geschwätz.
pale *(fig.)* begrenztes Gebiet;
  beyond the ~ jenseits der Grenzen des Erlaubten, gesellschaftlich nicht akzeptabel; **outside the ~ of civilization** fern aller
  Zivilisation; **within the ~ of the Church** im Schoße der Kirche.
paling Latten-, Staketenzaun.
palisade Pallisade.
pall Sarg-, Leichentuch;
  ~ of smoke Rauchwolke;
  ~ (v.) keinen Reiz mehr ausüben, langweilig (zuwider) werden;
  ~ upon most of the listeners auf den größten Teil der Zuschauer
  ermüdend wirken.
pallbearer Sargträger.
pallet Palette.
palliate *(v.)* lindern, *(fig.)* bemänteln, beschönigen.
palliation Linderung, *(fig.)* Bemäntelung, Beschönigung.
palliative Schmerzlinderungsmittel.
palm Handfläche, -teller, *(fig.)* Siegespalme, *(mil.)* Ordensspange;
  ~ of martyrdom Krone des Märtyrertums;
  ~ (v.) *(Br.)* schmieren, spicken, bestechen, *(US sl.)* klauen,
  stehlen, *(conceal, sl.)* vor der Konkurrenz verbergen;
  ~ s. th. off on s. o. jem. etw. aufschwindeln (aufdrängen,
  anhängen, andrehen); **~ off s. th. as a genuine article** als Markenartikel andrehen; **~ off a bad coin on s. o.** Falschgeld
  betrügerisch in Umlauf (in den Verkehr) bringen, jem. ein
  falsches Geldstück andrehen; **~ off old stock on a client** einem
  Stammkunden Lagerreste (Ladenhüter) aufschwatzen;
  to bear (carry off) the ~ Sieg davontragen; **to have an itching ~**
  offene Hand haben; **to have (hold) s. o. in the ~ of one's hand** j.
  völlig in der Hand haben; **to yield the ~ to s. o.** sich geschlagen
  geben;
  ~ frond Ordensspange; **~ grease** *(sl.)* Bestechungsgeld; **~ greas-
  ing** *(sl.)* Bestechung; **~ oil** *(sl.)* Schmier-, Bestechungsgelder.
palming off *(US)* unerlaubter Wettbewerb.
palpable offensichtlich.
palter *(v.)* knickern, schachern;
  ~ with s. o. about s. th. mit jem. um etw. feilschen; **~ with a
  question** Frage nicht ernst nehmen.

palterer Betrüger.
paltry unbedeutend, gering, armselig, wertlos;
~ **debts** Bagatellschulden; ~ **excuse** fadenscheinige Entschuldigung; ~ **two shillings** lumpige zwei Schillinge; ~ **sum** Schand-, Spottgeld.
pamper *(v.)* verzärteln, verhätscheln.
pamphlet Flugblatt, -schrift, Streitschrift, Pamphlet, Broschüre, Prospekt, *(newspaper)* kurzer Artikel;
~ *(v.)* Flugschriften herausgeben;
~ **copy** broschierte Ausgabe; ~ **laws** *(Pensylvania)* halbjährige Gesetzessammlung.
pamphleteer Flugblattverfasser.
pan Pfanne, Ziegel, *(fragment of ice)* treibende Eisscholle, *(pair of scales)* Waagschale, *(panel, Br.)* Wandplatte, *(US sl.)* negative (scharfe) Kritik;
on the ~ *(sl.)* auf dem Präsentierteller; **out of the frying** ~ **into the fire** vom Regen in die Traufe;
warming ~ Wärmflasche, Bettwärmer;
~ *(v.) (film camera)* schwenken, fahren, verschieben, *(US coll.)* herunterreißen, zusammenstauchen, scharf kritisieren;
~ **out** *(US sl.)* sich auszahlen, Ertrag bringen, ergiebig sein, *(US coll.)* bekommen, kriegen; ~ **out gold** Gold auswaschen; ~ **out as a new kind of religion** sich zu einer Ersatzreligion entwickeln; **not** ~ **out well** nichts einbringen;
~-**jerker** *(sl.)* Restaurantangestellter; ~ **shot** *(film)* Schwenk.
Pan American Union Panamerikanische Union.
panache Angabe, Prahlerei.
pancake *(airplane)* Durchsack-, Bumslandung;
~ *(v.)* durchsacken lassen;
~ **ice** Scheibeneis, dünne Eisscholle; ~ **landing** Durchsacklandung; ~ **turner** *(sl.)* Diskjockey.
pancaking *(airplane)* Geschwindigkeitsverlust, Überziehen.
pandemonium Riesenspektakel, Höllenlärm.
pander[er] Kuppler;
~ *(v.)* Kuppelei treiben;
~ **to s. one's ambition** jds. Ergeiz anstacheln; ~ **to the public interest in crime** dem öffentlichen Interesse für Verbrechen Vorschub leisten.
pandering, panderism Kuppelei.
panel Ausschuß, Forum, Gremium, geschlossener Personenkreis, *(advertisement)* Kästchen, *(airship)* Stoffbahn, *(architecture)* Paneel, Täfelung, *(bookbinding)* Titelfeld, *(el.)* Schaltkasten, -tafel, *(health service, Br.)* Kassenarztliste, *(instruments)* Armaturen-, Instrumentenbrett, *(jurors)* Geschworenenliste, *(persons reviewed)* befragter Personenkreis, Befragtengruppe, *(photo)* Hochformat, *(prisoner at the bar, Scot.)* Angeklagter, *(wing of airplane)* Verkleidung[sblech];
on the ~ *(Br.)* als Kassenarzt zugelassen;
advisory ~ beratender Ausschuß; **presidentially appointed** ~ vom Präsidenten eingesetzter Ausschuß; **blue-ribbon** ~ besonders zusammengestellter Ausschuß; **complaints** ~ Beschwerdestelle, -ausschuß; **educational** ~ Erziehungsausschuß; **electoral** ~ Wählerschaft;
~ **of arbitrators** Schiedsrichterausschuß, -gremium; ~ **of consumers** Verbraucherausschuß; ~ **of experts** Expertengremium, -gruppe, Fachausschuß, Gutachterkommission, Sachverständigenausschuß; ~ **of jurors** Geschworenenliste; ~ **of physicians** Ärztegremium; ~ **of reporters** Reportergruppe; ~ **of trade unions** Gewerkschaftsausschuß;
to be on the ~ auf der Liste stehen, *(committee group)* in einem Ausschuß sitzen, *(health service, Br.)* als Kassenarzt zugelassen sein; **to place patients on a doctor's** ~ *(Br.)* Patienten einem für die Kasse zugelassenen Arzt überweisen; **to serve as a** ~ Ausschußfunktionen wahrnehmen;
~ **board** Parkettbrett, *(el.)* Schalttafel; ~ **chairman** Ausschußvorsitzender; ~ **dentist** *(Br.)* Kassenzahnarzt; ~ **discussion** *(US)* Podiums-, Forumsdiskussion, Gruppengespräch, öffentliche Diskussion; ~ **doctor** *(Br.)* Kassenarzt; ~ **envelope** Fensterbriefumschlag; ~ **heating** Flächen-, Wandheizung; ~ **house** *(US)* Bordell; ~ **meeting** *(US)* Zusammenkunft ausgewählter Diskussionsmitglieder, Diskussionsveranstaltung; ~ **member** *(US)* Diskussionsteilnehmer, *(committee)* Ausschußmitglied; ~ **patient** *(Br.)* Kassenpatient; ~ **patient treatment** *(Br.)* kassenärztliche Behandlung; ~ **practice** *(Br.)* Kassen[arzt]praxis; ~ **report** Ausschußbericht; ~ **show** fernsehübertragene Diskussion; ~ **solicitor** Vertrauensanwalt; ~ **switch** *(tel.)* Stangenwähler; ~ **system** *(Br.)* Kassenarztsystem, *(UNO)* Lizenzsystem [für Vertreterauswahl]; **to be working under the** ~ **system** *(Br.)* zur Kassenpraxis zugelassen sein.
panelist Forums-, Diskussionsteilnehmer, *(broadcasting)* Teilnehmer bei einem Quizprogramm.

panelize *(v.)* an einer Fernsehdiskussion teilnehmen.
panellation Einsetzung der Geschworenen.
panelled walls getäfelte Wände.
panelling Täfelung, Holzverkleidung.
panelwork Fachwerk.
pang stechender Schmerz;
death ~s Todesqualen;
~s **of conscience** Gewissensbisse; ~s **of hunger** nagender Hunger;
~-**wangle** *(v.) (sl.)* sich nicht unterkriegen lassen.
panhandle *(territory, US)* Korridor, Entenschnabel;
~ *(v.) (US sl.)* schnorren, fechten, betteln.
panhandler *(US sl.)* Schnorrer, Bettler.
panic Panik, Angstpsychose, *(stock exchange)* Börsenpanik, Kurssturz, Deroute;
~ *(v.)* in Panik versetzen, *(US theater, sl.)* animieren, in Stimmung bringen, rasanten Beifall erzielen;
to spread a ~ Panik verbreiten;
to hit the ~ **button** in absolute Panik geraten; **to push the** ~ **button** *(sl.)* übermenschliche Leistungen verlangen; ~ **buying** Angstkäufe; ~ **fear** panikartige Angst; ~ **haste** blinde Hast; ~ **ice** loses Küsteneis; ~ **price** Angstpreis; ~-**proof** krisenfest; ~ **purchases** Hortungskäufe; ~ **seat** *(pilot)* Schleudersitz; ~ **selling** Angstverkäufe; ~-**stricken** von Panik erfaßt.
panicmonger Panik-, Gerüchtemacher.
panicky panikartig, überängstlich;
~ **article** alarmierender Zeitungsartikel; ~ **measures** panikartige Maßnahmen; ~ **rumo(u)rs** alarmierende Gerüchte.
panorama Rundblick, -sicht, Panorama, *(fig.)* vollständiger Überblick;
~ **equipment** *(radar)* Rundsuchgerät; ~ **view** Panoramablick; ~ **windshield** *(car, US)* Panorama-, Vollsichtscheibe.
panoramic camera Panoramakamera.
pantechnicon Möbelspeicher, *(Br.)* Möbelwagen;
~ **van** *(Br.)* Möbelwagen.
pantelegraph Bildtelegraf.
papal päpstlich;
~ **election** Papstwahl.
paper Papier, Pappe, *(balance sheet)* kurzfristiger Schuldtitel, *(bill)* Wechsel, *(counterfeit money)* Falschgeld, *(document)* Dokument, Urkunde, Schriftstück, *(lecture)* wissenschaftlicher Vortrag, Abhandlung, Vorlesung, *(money)* Papiergeld, Banknote, *(negotiable instrument)* Wertpapier, Urkunde, Schriftstück, *(newspaper)* Zeitung, *(report)* Bericht, *(school)* Klassenarbeit, *(stock exchange)* Brief, *(theater, sl.)* Freikarte, -platz, *(travel(l)er)* Paß, *(university)* Examensaufgabe, Arbeit, Klausur, schriftliche Prüfung, Prüfungsarbeit;
on ~ schriftlich, *(fig.)* theoretisch, in der Theorie;
~s Urkunden, Dokumente, Schriftstücke, amtliche Unterlagen, *(for identification)* Ausweis-, Beglaubigungs-, Legitimationspapiere;
absorbent ~ Saugpapier; **accommodation** ~ Gefälligkeitswechsel, -akzept; **answering** ~ Verteidigungsschrift; **art** ~ Kunstdruckpapier; **ballot** ~ Wahl-, Stimmzettel; **bank[able]** ~ bankfähiges Papier, Bankakzept, -wechsel; **best** ~ erstklassiger Wechsel; **Bible** ~ Bibel-, Dünndruckpapier; **black-edged** ~ Papier mit Trauerrand; **blank** ~ Blankopapier, *(fig.)* unbeschriebenes Blatt; **blotting** ~ Löschpapier; **blueprint** ~ Pauspapier; **bond** ~ Papier für den Druck von Obligationen; **bright-colo(u)red** ~ Buntpapier; **bromide** ~ *(photo)* Gelatinepapier; **brown** ~ Packpapier; **business** ~ Handelswechsel; **cap** ~ Tüten-, Packpapier; **carbon** ~ Kohlepapier; **cartridge** ~ Linienpapier; **cattle** ~ durch Verpfändung von Vieh gesicherter Wechsel; **cloth-mounted** ~ Leinen[papier]; **coated** ~ Kunstdruckpapier; **coated or enameled** ~ gestrichenes Papier; **commercial** ~ Waren-, Handelswechsel, Wechselmaterial; **commodity** ~ Warenwechsel; **convertible** ~ [in Gold] einlösbares Papiergeld; **corporation** ~ *(US)* begebbares Papier; **court** ~s Gerichtsakten; **daily** ~ Tageszeitung; **defunct** ~ eingegangene Zeitung; **demand** ~ *(US)* Sichtpapier, -wechsel; **double-name** ~ Wechsel mit zwei Unterschriften; **drawing** ~ Zeichenpapier; **dubious** ~ Papier von zweifelhaftem Wert, unsicherer Wechsel; **eligible** ~ *(US)* [zentral]bankfähiger Wechsel; **evening** ~ Abendblatt, -zeitung; **examination** ~ schriftliche Prüfungsaufgabe; **fashion** ~ Modejournal; **filed** ~ Eingabe; **filigreed** ~ Wasserzeichenpapier; **filter** ~ Filterpapier; **financial** ~ Handels-, Börsenblatt; **fine (first-class)** ~ erstklassiger Wechsel; **foreign note** ~ Übersee-, Luftpostpapier; **glass** ~ Glaspapier; **glazed** ~ satiniertes (glattes) Papier; **good** ~ feiner Wechsel; **government** ~s Staatspapiere, -anleihe; **grained** ~ gekörntes Papier; **gutter** ~ Revolverblatt, Schund-, Schmutz-

blatt; **handmade** ~ handgeschöpftes Büttenpapier; **history** ~ historischer Aufsatz; **identification** ~s Beglaubigungspapiere; **illustrated** ~ Illustrierte; **inconvertible** ~ nicht einlösbares Papiergeld; **ineligible** ~ *(US)* nicht diskontfähiges Papier; **key (leading)** ~ führende Zeitung; **laid** ~ geripptes (gestreiftes) Papier, *(notes)* Wertzeichenpapier; **letter** ~ Briefpapier; **long-dated** ~ langfristiger Wechsel; **lost** ~ verlegte Urkunde; **machine-finished** ~ maschinenglattes Papier; **manifold** ~ Vervielfältigungspapier; **manila** ~ festes Packpapier; **mat** ~ mattes Papier; **mercantile** ~ Warenwechsel; **mourning** ~ Trauerpapier; **moving** ~ Urkunden zur Unterstützung eines Antrags; **negotiable** ~ begebbares (durch Indossament übertragenes) Papier; **noneligible** ~ *(US)* nicht zentralbankfähiger Wechsel; **note** ~ Banknotenpapier; **official** ~s amtliche Unterlagen (Schriftstücke); **one-name** ~ *(US)* Wechsel mit nur einer Unterschrift; **packing** ~ Packpapier; **parliamentary** ~s Informationsmaterial für Abgeordnete; **petition** ~ Stempelpapier; **photocopying** ~ Lichtpauspapier; **plotting** ~ Zeichenpapier; **printed** ~s Drucksachen; **printing** ~ Druckpapier; **purchased** ~ *(US)* per Kasse gekauftes Papier; **good-quality** ~ Qualitätspapier; **the most widely read** ~ meistgelesene Zeitung; **right-wing** ~ rechtseingestellte Zeitung; **roofing** ~ Dachpappe; **ruled** ~ liniertes Papier; **second-rate** ~ zweitklassiges Papier; **self-liquidating** ~ kurzfristiges Papier; **sensitized** ~ lichtempfindliches Papier; **shiny** ~ glattes Papier; **ship's** ~s Schiffspapiere; **shipping** ~s *(US)* Versandpapiere; **short** ~ kurzfristiger Wechsel; **short[-sighted]** ~ kurzfristiger Wechsel; **silk** ~ Seidenpapier; **silver** ~ Staniol-, Silberpapier; **single-name** ~ Wechsel mit nur einer Unterschrift; **sized** ~ geleimtes Papier; **smooth** ~ glattes Papier; **special** ~ *(law court)* Liste von Sonderterminen; **stamped** ~ Stempelpapier; **state** ~s Staatspapiere; **street** ~ *(US)* kurzfristiger durch Makler verkaufter Schuldschein; **Sunday** ~ Sonntagszeitung; **test** ~ Klausurarbeit, *(Br.)* Zulassungsprüfung; **testamentary** ~ Testament, letztwillige Verfügung [ohne gesetzliche Formerfordernisse]; **third-class** ~ Wechsel dritter Güte; **three-months** ~ Dreimonatsakzept; **time** ~ Wechsel mit fester Laufzeit; **tissue** ~ Seidenpapier; **today's** ~s die heutigen Zeitungen; **toilet** ~ Toilettenpapier; **tracing** ~ Pauspapier; **trade** ~ Fachzeitschrift, Verbandsorgan, *(bill of exchange)* Handels-, Kunden-, Warenwechsel; **transfer** ~ *(Br.)* Umdruck-, Überdruckpapier; **two-name** ~ *(US)* Wechsel mit zwei Unterschriften; **typewriting** ~ Schreibmaschinenpapier; **unglazed** ~ mattes Papier; **unsized** ~ ungeleimtes Papier; **unstamped** ~ ungestempeltes Papier; **voting** ~ Stimmzettel; **walking** ~s *(US sl.)* Entlassungspapiere; **wall** ~ Tapete; **waste** ~ Abfall-, Ausschuß-, Makulaturpapier; **waxed** ~ wasserdichtes Papier; **weekly** ~ Wochenzeitung, -blatt; **white** ~ unbeschriebenes Papier, *(politics)* Weißbuch; **wood-content** ~ holzhaltiges Papier; **wood-free** ~ holzfreies Papier; **working** ~s Arbeitspapiere; **wrapping** ~ Packpapier;

~s **on appeal** *(US)* Berufungsakten; ~s **in the case** Prozeßunterlagen; ~ **of cases (causes)** *(Br.)* Sitzungsliste; ~s **of a business concern** Geschäftsunterlagen; ~s **under censorship** zensierte Zeitungen; ~ **of world-wide circulation** Weltblatt; ~ **on currency reform** Abhandlung über die Währungsreform; ~ **of direction** *(label)* Adreßkarte; ~s **opposed to the government** regierungsfeindliche Presse; ~ **just on the line** gerade noch durchgehende Examensarbeit; ~ **deprived of news** schlecht informierte Zeitung; ~s **with various periods to run** Papiere mit verschiedenen Verfallzeiten; ~s **and periodicals** Zeitungen und Zeitschriften; ~ **read before a society** vor einer wissenschaftlichen Vereinigung gehaltener Vortrag; ~ **in reels** Papier in Ballen; ~ **signed in blank** Blankopapier; ~ **of no standing** unangesehenes Blatt, wenig angesehene Zeitung;

~ *(v.)* in Papier einwickeln, *(put down in writing)* schriftlich niederlegen, *(theater, sl.)* Freikarten verteilen;
~ **a room** Zimmer tapezieren; ~ **up** *(bookbinding)* Vorsatzpapier einkleben; ~ **a theater for an opening night** *(sl.)* Theater durch Freikartenverteilung für eine Premiere füllen;
to be in the ~s in der Zeitung stehen; **to be a good scheme on** ~ theoretisch ein guter Plan sein; **to commit to** ~ zu Papier bringen; **to crumple** ~ Papier zusammenknüllen; **to do a** ~ Klausur schreiben; **to examine** ~s Akten einsehen; **to explain s. th. on** ~ etw. schriftlich darlegen; **to figure in the** ~s von der Presse erwähnt werden; **to fix one's thoughts to** ~ seine Gedanken zu Papier bringen; **to fold in** ~ in Papier einwickeln (einschlagen); **to forage among** ~s Papiere durchwühlen; **to get into the** ~s Pressestoff liefern; **to hand** ~s **to one's solicitor** seinem Anwalt Unterlagen zuleiten; **to have one's** ~s **viséd** Visum erhalten; **to insert in a** ~ in eine Zeitung setzen; **to make the** ~s Titelnachricht abgeben; **to move for** ~s *(parliament)* Vorlage

der Unterlagen eines Falles beantragen; **to own stock in a** ~ *(US fam.)* an einer Zeitung beteiligt sein; **to peddle one's** ~s *(sl.)* um seinen eigenen Dreck kümmern; **to pin** ~s **together** Papiere zusammenheften; **to produce one's** ~s sich ausweisen; **to put one's** ~s **in** *(sl.)* sich bei einer Universität einschreiben; **to put pen to** ~ zur Feder greifen; **to read a** ~ Vorlesung (Vortrag) halten; **to ruffle** ~ Papier zusammenknüllen; **to send in one's** ~s seinen Abschied nehmen; **to sit for a** ~ Klausur schreiben; **to spoil a sheet of** ~ Blatt Papier verschreiben; **to subscribe to a** ~ Zeitung halten; **to suppress a** ~ Zeitung beschlagnahmen (verbieten); **to take in a** ~ *(Br.)* Zeitung abonnieren (halten); **to write a** ~ *(school)* Klassenaufsatz schreiben, *(university)* Klausur schreiben; **to wrap up in** ~ in Papier einschlagen (einwickeln); **to write in the** ~s journalistisch tätig sein;

~ **assets** Papierwerte; ~ **bag** Papierbeutel, -tüte; ~ **basis** Papierwährung, -valuta; ~ **bid** Übernahmeangebot durch Abgabe eigener Aktien; ~ **bill** Zeitungsgeld; ~ **blockade** nicht effektiv gewordene Blockade; ~ **book** Aktenzusammenstellung, Formularbuch; ~-**bound book** broschiertes Buch; ~ **box** Karton, Pappschachtel; ~ **chase** Schnitzeljagd; **to increase** ~ **circulation** Notenumlauf steigern; ~ **city** Reißbrettstadt; ~ **clip** Büro-, Briefklammer; ~ **credit** offener Wechselkredit; ~ **currency** *(circulation)* Banknotenumlauf, *(money)* Papiergeld, Banknoten, *(standard)* Papierwährung; ~ **cutter (cutting machine)** Papierschneidemaschine; ~ **days** Verhandlungs-, Sitzungstage; ~ **debts** Wechselschulden; ~ **dollar** Papierdollar; ~ **exchanges** Papiervaluten; ~ **factory** Papierfabrik; ~ **fastener** Musterklammer; ~ **gold** *(coll.)* Sonderziehungsrechte; ~ **hanger** Tapezierer; ~ **hanging** Tapezieren, *(sl.)* Scheckfälscher; ~ **hangings** Tapeten; ~ **holdings** Wechselbestand; ~ **house** *(sl.)* aus vielen Freikarteninhabern bestehendes Theaterpublikum; ~ **industry** Papierindustrie; ~ **knife** Briefaufschneider; ~ **maker** Papiermacher; ~ **manufacturing** Papierfabrikation; ~ **mill** Papierfabrik.

paper money Papiergeld, Banknoten, Scheine;
~ **expansion** Papiergeldausweitung; ~ **inflation** Papiergeldinflation.

paper | **office** *(Br.)* Staatsarchiv; ~ **profit** unrealisierter (rechnerischer) Gewinn, *(inflation)* Scheingewinne; ~ **punch** Locher; ~ **pusher** *(sl.)* Falschgeldverbreiter; ~ **rags** Lumpen, Hadern; ~ **rate** *(railroad)* nur auf dem Papier stehender (überhöhter) Tarif; ~ **route** *(US)* Strecke des Zeitungsverkäufers; ~ **scissors** Papierschere; ~ **seal** Verschlußmarke; ~ **standard** Papierwährung; ~ **strength** *(mil.)* Sollstärke; ~ **surplus** Papiergewinne; ~ **tape** Lochstreifen; ~ **tiger** *(politics)* Papiertiger; ~ **tissue** Papiertaschentuch; ~ **title** nur auf dem Papier bestehendes Eigentumsrecht; ~ **trade** Papierindustrie; ~ **value** Papiervaluta; ~ **war** Pressekrieg; ~ **warfare** Papierkrieg, *(journalism)* Pressefehde, -krieg; ~ **wedding** erster Hochzeitstag; ~ **work** *(administration work)* schriftliche Arbeiten, Schreibarbeit, Büroarbeiten, *(solicitor)* Aktendurchsicht; **to be good at** ~ **work** mit allen Verwaltungsaufgaben bestens vertraut sein; ~ **works** Papierfabrik.

paperback broschiertes Buch, Taschenbuch, Taschenausgabe; ~ **book** *(US)* Volksausgabe.
paperboard Pappe, Pappdeckel.
paperboy Zeitungsjunge.
papering Tapezieren.
paperweight Briefbeschwerer, *(railroad, sl.)* Fahrkartenverkäufer.
papoose *(sl.)* Nichtgewerkschaftler.
pappy guy *(sl.)* Vorarbeiter.
par *(equality)* Gleichwertigkeit, Ebenbürtigkeit, *(face value)* Pari, Nennwert, *(newspaper)* kurzer Zeitungsartikel;
above (below) ~ über (unter) Pari (dem Nennwert); **at** ~ al pari, zum Nennwert; **on a** ~ *(Br.)* durchschnittlich, im Durchschnitt, *(with s. o.)* auf gleicher Ebene; **repayable at** ~ al pari zurückzahlbar;
face ~ Nennbetrag; **issue** ~ Emissionskurs; **nominal** ~ Nominalwert;
~ **of exchange** Wechselpari[tät], Parikurs; **mint** ~ **of exchange** Münzpari; ~ **of stocks** Effektenparität;
~ *(v.)* gleichwertig machen;
to be above ~ über Pari stehen; **to be at** ~ [auf] Pari stehen, *(profit and loss)* sich die Waage halten; **to be on a** ~ **with** gleich (ebenbürtig) sein; **to be up to** ~ gesundheitlich auf der Höhe sein; **to fall below** ~ unter Pari sinken; **to feel below** ~ *(fam.)* sich nicht ganz wohl fühlen; **to issue at** ~ zum Nennwert ausgeben; **to pass at** ~ zu Pari umlaufen; **to place at** ~ Pari begeben; **to put on a** ~ **with** gleichstellen; **to receive at** ~ zu Pari nehmen; **to run (stand) at** ~ Pari stehen;

~ clearance (US) Clearing zu Pariwert; **~ collection** Inkasso zum Pariwert; **~ collection of checks** (US) Inkasso von Schecks zum Pariwert ohne Abzug der Spesen; **~ emission** Pari-Emission; **~ exchange rate** (International Monetary Fund) Wechselkurssatz; **~ line** (of stock) Aktienmittelwert; **~ list** (US) Pariliste, Paritätstabelle; **~ point** (US) Pariplatz; **~ redemption system** Parieinlösungssystem; **~ remittance** (US) Überweisung eines Schecks zum Parikurs, Nettoüberweisung; **~ value** Pari-, Nennwert, Parität; **~ value of currencies** Währungsparität; **~ value stock** (US) Nennwertaktie; **no ~ value share** (Br.) (stock, US) nennwertlose Aktie, Quotenaktie.

paraborne fallschirmgelandet.

parabrake (v.) **an airplane** Flugzeug durch einen Heckfallschirm abbremsen.

parachronism Zeitberechnungsfehler.

parachute Fallschirm;
~ (v.) am Fallschirm abspringen;
~ **boat** Einmanngummi-, Fallschirmboot; **~ detachment** Fallschirmeinheit; **~ flare** Leuchtbombe, Christbaum; **~ jumper** Fallschirmspringer; **~ light** Leuchtfallschirm; **~ mine** Luftmine; **~ troops** Fallschirmtruppen.

parachuter Fallschirmjäger, -springer.

parachutism Fallschirmabsprung.

parachutist Fallschirmspringer, -jäger.

parade Aufmarsch, (assembly of promenaders) Gruppe von Spaziergängern, (mil.) [Truppen]parade, (public walk, Br.) Promenade, (pompous show) Zurschaustellen, Vorführung; **off ~** im Privatleben; **on ~** in der Öffentlichkeit;
celebration ~ Festaufmarsch; **fashion ~** Modeschau; **identification ~** (witnesses) Gegenüberstellung; **mannequin ~** Modeschau; **police ~** Polizeiparade; **political ~** Demonstrationszug; **program(me) ~** (broadcast) Programmvorschau;
~ (v.) vorbeimarschieren, Umzug veranstalten, durch die Straßen ziehen, (demonstrate) zur Schau stellen, vorführen;
~ one's whole family in the park mit der ganzen Familie im Park herumstolzieren; **~ one's knowledge** mit seinen Kenntnissen protzen, sein Wissen zur Schau stellen; **~ on the pier in full dress** (fam.) in voller Kriegsbemalung auf der Mole aufkreuzen; **~ through the streets** durch die ganze Stadt marschieren; **~ a false title** sich mit einem falschen Titel schmücken;
to be on public ~ für alle sichtbar sein; **to make a ~ of one's apparel** mit seinen Kleidern Staat machen; **to make a ~ of one's misery** sein Elend zur Schau tragen;
~ ground Paradeplatz; **~ poster** Außenwerbung an öffentlichen Verkehrsmitteln; **~ shed** (police, sl.) Vorführraum [zur Täteridentifizierung].

paradise Paradies, siebenter Himmel;
Ethiopian ~ (theater, sl.) Olymp;
to live in a Fool's ~ im Schlaraffenland leben.

paradrop (v.) mit dem Fallschirm absetzen.

paragon Muster, Vorbild, (diamond) hundertkarätiger Solitär, (print.) Schriftgrad;
~ of virtue Tugendbold.

paragraph Abschnitt, Absatz, Paragraph, (newspaper) kurzer Artikel, Notiz;
fresh (new) ~ neuer Absatz; **loose ~s** einzelne Paragraphen; **personal ~** Glosse; **sub-~** Unterabschnitt;
~ by ~ absatzweise;
~ (v.) in Paragraphen einteilen, (journalism) kurzen Zeitungsartikel schreiben;
to begin a new ~ Absatz machen, Zeile absetzen, neuen Absatz beginnen;
~ mark Absatz-, Paragraphenzeichen; **personal ~ writer** Glossenschreiber.

paragrapher Leitartikler, (US) Kurzartikelschreiber.

paragraphical abgesetzt, in Absätze eingeteilt.

paragraphist (Br.) Kurzartikelschreiber.

parakite (aviation) Fallschirmdrachen.

parallel Parallele, Parallelität, Ähnlichkeit;
~ of latitude Breitenkreis;
~ (a.) parallel, gleichgerichtet, -laufend;
~ (v.) **the railway** parallel zur Eisenbahn verlaufen;
to draw a ~ Parallele ziehen; **to run ~ with s. th.** mit etw. parallel laufen;
~ conscious business behavio(u)r (antitrust law, US) bewußt gleichlaufendes Geschäftsverhalten; **~ case** Parallelfall; **~ connection** (el.) Nebeneinander-, Parallelschaltung; **~ credit market** Parallelmarkt; **~ negotiations** Parallelverhandlungen; **~ passage** gleichlautende Stelle; **~ posting** gleichlautende Buchung; **~ rate of exchange** inoffizieller Wechselkurs; **~ standards** Parallel-, Doppelwährung.

paralysation Lahmlegung, Lähmung.

paralyse (v.) paralysieren, (traffic) lahmlegen.

parameter (fig.) vorauszusetzende Entwicklung.

paramilitary paramilitärisch, militärähnlich.

paramount an der Spitze stehend, vorrangig, überragend;
to be ~ with s. o. jem. über alles gehen;
~ chief oberster Chef; **~ equity** stärkerer Billigkeitsanspruch; **of ~ importance** von allergrößter Bedeutung; **~ necessity** überragende Notwendigkeit; **~ title** (real property) älteres Recht.

paramountcy Vorrangstellung.

paraph Paraphe;
~ (v.) paraphieren, mit seinen Initialen abzeichnen.

paraphernal property, Zubehör, Gerät, (property) eingebrachtes Gut, Sondervermögen (Vorbehaltsgut) der Ehefrau.

paraphrase Umschreibung [mit anderen Worten], Textinterpretation, freie Wiedergabe;
~ (v.) durch Worte umschreiben;
~ a text Text frei wiedergeben;
~ poster (US) Außenwerbung an öffentlichen Verkehrsmitteln.

parasite Schmarotzer, Parasit.

paraspotter Fallschirmjäger mit Zielobjektauftrag.

paratroops Fallschirmtruppen.

parcel (bundle) Bündel, Ballen, (conveyancing) Grundstücksbeschreibung, (of goods) Posten, Partie, Menge, Los, Ware, (luggage) Gepäckstück, (package) [Post]paket, Versandstück, (piece of land) [Grundstücks]parzelle, Stück Land, (packet, US) Päckchen;
by (in) ~s in kleinen Posten, stückweise, (post) als Paketpost; **~s** Stückgüter, (description of property) Grundstücksbeschreibung;
air mail ~ Luftpostpaket; **cash-on-delivery (collect on delivery, US) (C.O.D.) ~** Nachnahmepaket; **express ~** Eilpaket; **insured ~** (Br.) Wertpaket; **numbered ~** Wertpaket; **large ~s** große Partien; **packed ~** Stückgut, Stückgutsendung; **postal ~** Postpaket; **registered ~** (US) Einschreibepäckchen; **sealed ~** Wertpaket; **special-handling ~** Schnellpaket; **uninsured ~** gewöhnliches (unversichertes) Paket;
part and ~ wesentlicher Bestandteil;
~ to be called for postlagerndes Paket; **~s awaiting delivery** noch nicht zugestellte Sendungen; **~ of diamonds** Brillantenkollektion; **~ of goods** Warenpartie; **~ of land** Grundstücksparzelle; **~ of lies** lauter Lügen; **part and ~ of another piece** wesentlicher Bestandteil eines anderen Grundstücks; **~ of shares** Aktienpaket;
~ (v.) Paket packen, (cut up into lots) abteilen, parzellieren;
~ estates out to small family farmers große Landgüter parzellieren und auf Bauernfamilien übertragen; **~ a customer's purchases** Einkäufe eines Kunden einpacken; **~ into farms** in Güter aufteilen; **~ goods** Waren in Partien aufteilen; **~ an inheritance** Erbschaftsverteilung (Auseinandersetzung) vornehmen; **~ land into smallholdings** Land (Großgrundbesitz) parzellieren; **~ out** ab-, aufteilen, (bankruptcy) aussondern, (real estate) parzellieren; **~ up a consignment of books** Büchersendung zusammenstellen;
to assemble two ~s of land zwei Grundstücksparzellen zusammenschreiben; **to direct a ~ correctly** Paket ordnungsgemäß beschriften; **to do up in ~s** einpacken; **to do up (lot out) goods in ~s** Waren in Partien aufteilen; **to make a ~** Paket packen; **to pay the carriage for a ~** Paket frankieren; **to reinstate the value of a ~** Paketwert ersetzen; **to roll up a ~** Paket packen; **to send a ~ [by] express** als Eilpaket aufgeben; **to slice up large ~s of land** große Grundstücksflächen parzellieren; **to take ~s to the post** Pakete zur Post bringen; **to win a ~** (sl.) Haufen Geld gewinnen;
~ bill Paketeingangszettel; **~ book** Gepäckbuch; **~ carrier** Paketwagen; **~s carriage** Paketzustellung; **~ cartage** (Br.) Paketzustellung; **~ cartage service** (Br.) Paketzustelldienst; **~s clerk** Fakturist; **~ delivery** Paketzustellung, -ausgabe; **~ delivery company** Paketfahrtgesellschaft; **~ delivery service** Paketzustellungsdienst; **~ express company** Paketexpreßgesellschaft; **~-gilt** teilweise vergoldet; **~ goods** Stückgüter; **~ lift** Warenaufzug; **~ mailing form** Paketkarte; **~ office** (US) Paketannahme- und ausgabestelle, (cloakroom, Br.) Gepäckabfertigung, -aufbewahrung; **~ package** (US) Postpaket; **~ paper** Paketpapier.

parcel post Paketpost, -sendung;
by ~ als Paket; **by insured ~** (Br.) als Wertpaket;
foreign ~ Paketpost ins Ausland;
to send s. th. by ~ etw. als Postpaket schicken (Paket aufgeben).

parcel-post als [Post]paket;
~ **insurance** Paketversicherung; ~ **office** *(US)* Paketannahmestelle; ~ **rates** Paketposttarif, -sätze; ~ **service** Paketpostdienst; ~ **shipment** Paketversand; ~ **stamp** Paketpostbriefmarke, -gebühr; ~ **system** Paketpostwesen; ~ **window** Paketschalter.

parcel | postage Paketporto; ~**s rate** Paketgebühr; ~ **receipt** Paketempfangsschein; ~ **room** *(Br.)* Handgepäckaufbewahrung; ~ **service** *(Br.)* Paketpostdienst; **to be sent by the air ~ service** als Luftpostpaket verschickt werden; **to pull the ~ service into profit** Paketpostdienst in die Gewinnzone bringen; **to use the inland ~ service** per Paketpost schicken; ~ **shipment** Muster-ohne-Wert-Sendung; ~ **sticker** Paketaufklebeadresse; ~ **traffic** Paketverkehr; ~ **van** *(Br.)* Paketpostwagen; ~ **windows** Paketschalter.

parcellation Parzellierung.

parcelled gesondert, einzeln, parzelliert.

parcel(l)ing [out] Teilung, Parzellierung;
~ **of land into smallholdings** Grundstücksparzellierung; ~ **machine** Verpackungsmaschine.

parcenary Gesamthandseigentum, *(inheritance)* Eigentum der Erbengemeinschaft, *(partnership)* Teilhaberschaft.

parcener *(heir)* Miterbe, *(owner)* Miteigentümer.

parchment Pergament, Gerichtsurkunde;
~ **paper** Pergamentpapier.

pardon Verzeihung, *(release from penalty)* Begnadigung, Straferlaß;
absolute ~ unbeschränkte Begnadigung; **conditional** ~ bedingter Straferlaß; **full** ~ volle Begnadigung; **general** ~ Amnestie; **partial** ~ teilweiser Straferlaß;
~ *(v.)* begnadigen, amnestieren;
~ **s. o.** jem. das Leben schenken; ~ **s. o. an offence** jem. eine Beleidigung verzeihen;
to be granted a ~ begnadigt werden; **to deny a** ~ Begnadigung ablehnen; **to grant s. o.** ~ jem. Verzeihung gewähren; **to issue a general** ~ Amnestie erlassen; **to receive** ~ begnadigt werden.

pardoned person Begnadigter.

pare *(v.)* **[down]** verringern, be-, einschränken;
~ **expenditures** Kosteneinsparung vornehmen; ~ **margins to the bank** Gewinnmargen auf ein Minimum reduzieren; ~ **to the quick** empfindlich kränken; ~ **the work force** Belegschaft verringern, Belegschaftsabbau herbeiführen.

parent Elternteil, *(ancestor)* Vorfahr, Ahn, Stammvater, *(fig.)* Ursprung, Quelle, *(guardian)* Vormund, *(person standing in loco parentis)* Erziehungsberechtigter;
adoptive ~**s** Adoptiveltern; **foster** ~**s** Pflegeeltern;
~**-in-law** angeheirateter Elternteil; ~**s and relations** Eltern und Verwandte;
~ *(a.)* elterlich;
~**s' assembly** Elternversammlung; ~ **bank** Gründer-, Stammbank; ~ **body** Muttergesellschaft; ~ **company (concern, corporation, enterprise, establishment)** Mutter-, Dach-, Holding-, Gründergesellschaft, Stammhaus; ~ **country** Vaterland; ~**s' evening** Elternabend; ~ **house** Stammhaus; ~**s' insurance benefit** *(social insurance, US)* Hinterbliebenenrente; ~ **organization** Dachorganisation; ~ **plane** Abschußflugzeug; ~ **plant** Stammwerk, -betrieb; ~ **population** *(statistics)* Ausgangsgesamtheit; ~ **ship** Unterseebootbegleitschiff; ~ **store** Hauptgeschäft, Stammhaus; ~**-subsidiary relationship** *(US)* Mutter-Tochter-verhältnis; ~**-teacher association** Elternbeirat; ~ **union** Ober-, Dachgewerkschaft; ~ **unit** *(mil.)* Stammeinheit, -truppenteil.

parentage Abstammung, Abkunft;
of unknown ~ unbekannter Abstammung;
mixed ~ Mischehe.

parental elterlich, väterlich;
~ **authority (power, US)** elterliche Gewalt; ~ **care** elterliche Fürsorge; **to lack** ~ **care** von den Eltern nicht versorgt werden; ~ **contribution** elterlicher Wechsel; ~ **duties** elterliche Pflichten; ~ **neglect** Vernachlässigung der elterlichen Pflichten.

parenthesis Paranthese, eingeklammerte Stelle, Einschub;
to put in ~ einklammern.

parenthesize *(v.)* einklammern.

parenthood Elterschaft.

pari passu gleichrangig, *(creditors)* gleichberechtigt, mit gleichen Quoten;
to rank as ~ Gleichrang haben, gleichrangig sein; **to rank** ~ **with new shares issue** mit neuen Aktien gleichberechtigt sein; ~ **bonds** gleichrangige Obligationen.

pariah Entrechteter, Paria.

paring | of employment Beschäftigungsrückgang; ~ **a program(me)** Programmkürzung, -beschneidung;
~**-down committee** Einsparungsausschuß.

Paris Club Zehnergruppe.

parish *(Br.)* Gemeinde[bezirk], *(country, US)* Kreis, *(religion)* Kirchspiel, Pfarrbezirk, [Kirchen]gemeinde;
on the ~ auf Fürsorgeunterstützung (Sozialhilfe) angewiesen;
civil ~ *(Br.)* Gemeinde-, Selbstverwaltungskörper; **district** ~ Gemeindebezirk; **highway** ~ Fernstraßenbezirk; **land-tax** ~ *(Br.)* Grundsteuerbehörde; **new** ~ Fürsorgebereich; **poor-law** ~ *(Br.)* Sozialamt, Fürsorgebehörde, -verband;
to be (go) on the ~ Sozialhilfe (Fürsorgeunterstützung) beziehen; **to be thrown upon the** ~ auf Fürsorgeunterstützung angewiesen sein; **to come on the** ~ unterhaltsbedürftig (Sozialhilfeempfänger) werden, von der Wohltätigkeit der Gemeinde leben; **to fall upon the** ~ der Gemeinde auf der Tasche liegen;
~ **apprentice** *(Br.)* Fürsorge-, Gemeindelehrling; ~ **authority** Kirchen-, Gemeindebehörde; ~ **book** Einwohnermeldekartei; ~ **boy** Findelkind; ~ **church** örtliche Kirchengemeinde; ~ **clerk** *(Br.)* Gemeindeschreiber, -sekretär, *(church)* Küster; ~ **constable** Gemeindepolizist; ~ **council** *(Br.)* Gemeinderat, -vertretung; ~ **councillor** *(Br.)* Gemeinderatsmitglied; ~ **court** *(Louisiana)* Nachlaßgericht; ~ **house** Gemeindehaus; ~ **magazine** Gemeindeblättchen; ~ **meeting** *(Br.)* Stadtrats-, Gemeindeversammlung, -sitzung; ~ **nurse** Gemeindeschwester; ~ **office** *(Br.)* Kirchenvorstand; ~ **officer** Gemeindepolizist, *(church warden, Br.)* Gemeindebeamter; ~ **priest** Gemeindepfarrer; ~ **property** gemeindeeigenes Grundstück; ~**-pump gossip** Lokaltratsch; ~**-pump politics** Kirchturmspolitik; ~ **record** Kirchenarchiv; ~ **register** Einwohnermeldeamt, -kartei, *(church)* Kirchenregister, -buch; ~ **relief** *(Br.)* Sozialhilfe, Fürsorgeunterstützung; ~ **road** Landstraße; ~ **school** Gemeindeschule; ~ **welfare** Gemeindepflege.

parishioner *(Br.)* Gemeindemitglied.

paritor Gerichtsdiener.

parity Parität, Parikurs, Pariwert, Umrechnungskurs, *(equality)* Gleichheit;
at ~ paritätisch; **at the** ~ **of** zum Umrechnungskurs von; **at** ~ **of prices** bei Gleichheit der Preise;
commercial ~ *(US)* Handelsparität; **dollar** ~ Dollarparität; **gold** ~ Goldparität; **mint** ~ Münzparität; **nominal** ~ Nennwertparität; **peacetime** ~ Friedensparität; **purchasing-power** ~ Kaufkraftparität;
~ **of a currency** Währungsparität; ~ **of exchange** Wechsel-, Kursparität; ~ **of pay** gleiche Bezahlung; ~ **of reasoning** Analogieschluß; ~ **of stocks** Effektenparität; ~ **of value** *(gold)* Umwechslungspreis; ~ **of votes** Stimmengleichheit;
to be (stand) at a ~ pari stehen; **to bring back to** ~ **with each other** gegenseitige Parität wiederherstellen; **to crawl one's** ~ seine Währungsparität langsam ändern;
~ **change** Wechselkursänderung; ~ **clause** Paritätsklausel; ~ **payments** Auszahlungen zum Parikurs; ~ **point** Paritätspunkt; ~ **price** Paritäts-, Parikurs; **at the** ~ **rate** zum mittleren Kurs; ~ **representation** paritätische Interessensvertretung; ~ **representation of shareholders and workers to the supervisory board** paritätische Vertretung von Aktionären und Arbeitnehmern im Aufsichtsrat; ~ **rights** Paritätsrechte; ~ **shift** Paritätsveränderung; ~ **structure** Paritätsgefüge; ~ **table** Paritätstabelle.

park Park[anlagen], städtische Anlagen, *(reserved area)* Naturschutzgebiet, *(mil.)* Kraftfahrzeugpark;
car ~ *(Br.)* Parkplatz; **mobile home** ~ Parkanlage für Wohnmobile; **multi-storey car** ~ Parkhochhaus; **national** ~ Natur-, Landschaftsschutzgebiet, Nationalpark;
~ *(v.) (car)* parken, abstellen, *(mil.)* deponieren, lagern;
~ **o. s. on s. o.** *(fam.)* sich bei jem. einnisten; ~ **one's baggage** *(US) (luggage, Br.)* **at the station** sein Gepäck beim Bahnhof lassen; ~ **in a confined space** sich in eine Parklücke einrangieren;
to double-~ neben einem abgestellten Fahrzeug parken; **to open a** ~ **to the public** Park zur öffentlichen Benutzung freigeben;
car-~ **attendant** *(Br.)* Park[platz]wächter; ~ **bench** Parkbank; ~**s department** Gartenbauamt; ~ **development** Parkerschließung; ~ **keeper** Parkwächter; ~ **lands** Parkanlagen.

parking Parken, *(strip of turf, US)* Grünstreifen;
no ~ **except for residents** Parken nur für Anlieger;
curb ~ Parken neben dem Gehsteig; **disk** ~ Parkscheibensystem; **fringe** ~ Parken außerhalb der Ladenstadt; **fringe-area** ~ Parkrandgebiete; **monthly** ~ monatliche Parkgebühr; **no** ~ Parkverbot; **on-street** ~ Parken auf der Straße; **overtime** ~ Überschreiten der Parkzeit; **prohibited** ~ Parken verboten; **roof-top** ~ überdachte Parkmöglichkeit; **street** ~ Parken auf der Straße; **underground** ~ Parken in einer Tiefgarage; **unilateral** ~ auf eine Seite beschränktes Parken;

~ **in dangerous position** Parken im Parkverbot;
to provide for ~ Parkmöglichkeit schaffen;
~ **area** Parkzone; **no-~ area** Parkverbotsgebiet; ~ **attendant** Parkwächter; ~ **ban** Parkverbot; ~ **bay** reservierter Parkplatz; ~ **brake** Handbremse; ~ **building** Parkhaus; ~ **charges** Parkgebühren; ~ **controls** Parkbestimmungen; ~ **demand** Parkbedürfnisse; ~ **disk** Parkscheibe; ~ **facilities** Parkmöglichkeiten; ~ **fee** Parkgebühr; ~ **fine** Verkehrsstrafe, gebührenpflichtige Verwarnung wegen falschen Parkens, Strafzettel für falsches Parken; ~ **garage** *(US)* Hochhausgarage; ~ **light** Standlicht, Parklicht; ~ **limitation** beschränkte Parkmöglichkeiten; ~ **lot** *(US)* Parkplatz, -möglichkeit; **free** ~ **lot** kostenlose Parkmöglichkeiten; **guaranteed** ~ **lot** *(US)* bewachter Parkplatz; ~ **meter** Parkuhr; **~-meter violation** Parkzeitüberschreitung; **~-meter zone** Parkuhrbereich; ~ **offence** Parkvergehen; ~ **orbit** *(spaceship)* vorübergehende Umlaufbahn; **[public]** ~ **place** [öffentlicher] Parkplatz; ~ **policy** Parkplatzpolitik; ~ **regulations** Parkplatzvorschriften; ~ **restraint** eingeschränkte Parkmöglichkeiten; ~ **site** *(Br.)* Parkplatz; ~ **slot** Parkuhr; ~ **space** Parkplatz; **to preempt a** ~ **space** sich einen Parkplatz sichern; ~ **spot** Parkplatz, -möglichkeit; ~ **ticket** Parkzettel, *(US)* Strafzettel für ordnungswidriges Parken, gebührenpflichtige Verwarnung wegen falschen Parkens; ~ **time** Parkzeit; **low-cost night ~-time** ~ billige Parkmöglichkeiten während der Nachtzeit; ~ **violation** Verstoß gegen die Parkbestimmungen; **no-~ zone** Parkverbotsgebiet.

parkway Autobahnseitenstreifen, *(US)* Promenade, Allee, Grünstreifen.

parlance Redeweise, Sprache;
in legal ~ in der Sprache der Juristen, juristisch ausgedrückt; **commercial** ~ Geschäftssprache; **common** ~ Umgangssprache; **to adopt the common** ~ sich vulgär ausdrücken.

parlay erneuter Gewinneinsatz;
~ *(v.)* nutzbringend verwenden, *(US)* auswerten, Kapital aus etw. schlagen.

parley Verhandlung, Unterhandlung, Konferenz, Besprechung, Debatte, *(mil.)* Waffenstillstandsverhandlungen;
~ *(v.)* **with** in Unterhandlungen stehen mit, verhandeln, unterhandeln;
~ **with the rebels** mit den Aufrührern verhandeln;
to hold a ~ über einen Waffenstillstand verhandeln.

Parliament Parlament, Abgeordnetenkammer, *(Br.)* Unterhaus;
accountable to ~ dem Parlament verantwortlich (rechenschaftspflichtig);
rubberstamp ~ Parlament von Jasagern;
to adjourn ~ Parlament vertagen; **to be defeated in** ~ durch das Parlament gestürzt werden; **to be up before** ~ dem Parlament vorliegen; **to contest for a seat in** ~ sich um einen Parlamentssitz bewerben; **to convoke** ~ Parlament einberufen; **to dissolve** ~ Parlament auflösen; **to enter** ~ Parlamentsmitglied werden; **to get into** ~ ins Parlament gewählt werden; **to go into** ~ Abgeordneter werden; **to have a seat in** ~ Abgeordneter sein; **to hold** ~ Parlament einberufen; **to meet the** ~ sich dem Parlament stellen; **to open** ~ Parlament eröffnen; **to prorogue** ~ Parlament vertagen; **to redistribute the seats in** ~ Parlamentssitze neu verteilen; **to return to** ~ ins Parlament schicken (wählen); **to run for** ~ für das Parlament kandidieren; **to sit in** ~ dem Parlament angehören, Abgeordneter sein; **to stand for** ~ *(Br.)* für das Unterhaus kandidieren, sich um einen Abgeordnetensitz bemühen; **to summon** ~ Parlament einberufen;
♀ **Act** *(Br.)* Parlamentsgesetz; ~ **house** Parlamentsgebäude; ~ **rapporteur** Berichterstatter des Parlaments; ~ **roll** Parlamentsprotokoll.

parliamentarian Parlamentarier, Parlamentsanhänger, Abgeordneter;
~ *(a.)* parlamentarisch.

parliamentarianism parlamentarisches Regierungssystem, Parlamentarismus.

parliamentary parlamentarisch, *(enacted by Parliament)* vom Parlament beschlossen;
~ **act** Parlamentsbeschluß; ~ **agent** *(Br.)* parlamentarischer Vertreter [für Privatvorlagen]; **to give** ~ **airing** im Parlament voll unterstützen; **to announce in a** ~ **answer** im Parlament bekanntgeben; ~ **appeal** Zustimmung des Parlaments; ~ **borough** *(Br.)* Wahlkreis, Parlamentsbezirk; ~ **candidate** Parlaments-, Unterhauskandidat; ♀ **Commissioner for Administration** *(Br.)* Ombudsmann; ~ **committee** parlamentarischer Ausschuß, Unterhaus-, Parlamentsausschuß; ~ **control** Kontrolle durch das Parlament; ~ **debate** Parlamentsdebatte, parlamentarische Beratung; ~ **debates** *(Br.)* gedruckte Parlamentsberichte; ~ **defeat** parlamentarische Niederlage;

delegate Parlamentsmitglied; ~ **deliberations** parlamentarische Beratungen; ~ **election** Parlamentswahlen, Abgeordnetenwahl; ~ **eloquence** parlamentarische Beredsamkeit; **to get lost in a** ~ **fog** im Parlament verwischt werden; ~ **franchise** *(Br.)* allgemeines Wahlrecht; ~ **government** parlamentarische Regierung; ~ **grant** Bewilligung durch das Parlament; ~ **group** Fraktion; **old ~ hand** alterfahrener Parlamentarier; ~ **immunity** parlamentarische Immunität, Abgeordnetenimmunität; ~ **institutions** parlamentarische Einrichtungen; ~ **language** parlamentarische Sprache (Ausdrucksweise); ~ **law** parlamentarische Geschäftsordnung; ~ **leader of a party** Fraktionsführer, -vorsitzender; ~ **mandate** Parlamentsmandat; ~ **motion** im Parlament eingebrachter Antrag, Parlamentsantrag; ~ **oratory** parlamentarische Beredsamkeit; ~ **order** Parlamentsbeschluß, Legislaturperiode; ~ **papers** Informationsmaterial für Abgeordnete; ~ **party** Fraktion; ~ **pay** Abgeordnetenbezüge, Diäten; ~ **powers** parlamentarische Genehmigung; ~ **practice** Parlamentsbrauch; ~ **privilege** [Abgeordneten]immunität; ~ **proceeding** Parlamentssitzung; ~ **procedure** parlamentarisches Verfahren; ~ **question** parlamentarische Anfrage; ~ **regime** parlamentarisches Regierungssystem; **little-notice** ~ **reply** wenig beachtete Beantwortung einer parlamentarischen Anfrage; ~ **rule** Parlamentsherrschaft; ~ **seat** Abgeordnetensitz; ♀ **Private Secretary** *(Br.)* parlamentarischer Staatssekretär; ~ **session** *(Br.)* Sitzung (Tagung) des Parlaments; ~ **speech** Parlamentsrede; ~ **state** parlamentarisch regierter Staat; ~ **summary** Sitzungsprotokoll des Parlaments; ~ **system** Parlamentarismus; ~ **system of government** parlamentarische Regierungsform; ~ **taxes** vom Parlament eingezogene Steuern; ~ **train** *(Br.)* Personenzug [mit billigem Fahrpreis]; ♀ **Undersecretary** *(Br.)* parlamentarischer Staatssekretär; ~ **vote** Parlamentsabstimmung.

parlo(u)r Empfangs-, Wohnzimmer, *(inn)* Klub-, Gesellschaftszimmer, *(practitioner)* Sprechzimmer, *(US)* Geschäftsraum;
photographer's ~ fotografisches Atelier;
~ **boarder** bevorrechtigter Internatsschüler; ~ **car** *(US)* Salonwagen; ~ **furniture** Wohnzimmermöbel; ~ **house** *(sl.)* Bordell; ~ **pink** *(sl.)* Salonbolschewist; ~ **radical** Salonbolschewist; ~ **snake** *(sl.)* Salonlöwe; ~ **tricks** *(fam.)* gesellschaftliche Talente.

parlo(u)rmaid Stubenmädchen.

parochial gemeindlich, dörflich, *(fig.)* eng, beschränkt, provinzlerisch;
~ **boundaries** regionale Grenzen, Gemeindegrenzen; ~ **business** Gemeindeangelegenheit; ~ **charity** gemeindebezogene Fürsorge; ~ **council** *(Br.)* Kirchenvorstand; ~ **officer** Gemeindebeamter; ~ **outlook** beschränkter Gesichtskreis; ~ **point of view** enger Horizont (Gesichtskreis); ~ **politics** Kirchturmpolitik; ~ **rates** Gemeindeabgaben; ~ **relief** Gemeindefürsorge; ~ **school** Gemeindeschule, konfessionelle Schule; ~ **spirit** provinzlerische Einstellung.

parochialism Spießigkeit, provinzielle Deutungsweise, *(pol.)* Lokalpatriotismus.

parol Plädoyer, *(oral declaration)* mündliche Erklärung;
by ~ aufgrund mündlicher Vereinbarung;
~ *(a.)* mündlich, *(uncertified)* unbeglaubigt, formlos;
~ **agreement** formloser Vertrag; ~ **arrest** während der Sitzung erlassener Haftbefehl; ~ **contract** mündliche Vereinbarung; ~ **evidence** mündliche Beweiserhebung; ~ **lease** mündlich abgeschlossener Miet-, Pachtvertrag.

parole bedingte Strafaussetzung (Haftentlassung), Bewährungshilfe, *(mil.)* Kennwort;
~ **of hono(u)r** *(mil.)* Ehrenwort;
~ *(v.)* *(prisoner)* bedingt entlassen;
to be on ~ auf Ehrenwort (bedingt) freigelassen sein; **to be allowed out on** ~ Strafurlaub erhalten; **to be eligible for** ~ Voraussetzungen der Bewährungshilfe erfüllen, zur Bewährung anstehen; **to be released on** ~ bedingt entlassen werden; **to break one's** ~ sein Ehrenwort brechen; **to deny** ~ Bewährungshilfe versagen; **to put s. o. on** ~ j. bedingt entlassen, jds. Strafe auf Bewährung aussetzen; **to revoke the** ~ bedingte Entlassung widerrufen;
~ *(a.)* *(US)* bedingt entlassen;
~ **administration** Bewährungshelfer; ~ **board** Bewährungshilfeausschuß; **to delegate more** ~ **decisions to local review committees** Entscheidungen über Aussetzung der Strafe zur Bewährung örtlichen Prüfungsausschüssen überlassen; ~ **eligibility** Voraussetzungen für die bedingte Entlassung; ~ **officer** Bewährungshelfer; ~ **supervision** Bewährungsaufsicht; ~ **term** Bewährungszeit.

parolee *(US)* bedingt (auf Bewährung) Entlassener.

parquet *(theater, US)* Parkett, Sperrsitz.

parricide Vatermord, *(treason)* Landesverrat.

parsimony Knauserei.

parson Pfarrer, Geistlicher.

parsonage Pfarrhaus.

part Teil, Stück, *(of book issued at intervals)* Lieferung, *(duty)* Amt, Aufgabe, *(of a loan)* Tranche, Teilbetrag, *(location)* Gegend, *(share)* Anteil, Bestandteil, Partie, *(side)* Seite, Partei; **for the most ~** meistens; **for my ~** von meiner Seite aus, von mir aus, was mich betrifft; **in ~** teilweise, zum Teil, auf Abschlag; **in ~s** auszugsweise; **in the early ~ of the week** am Wochenanfang; **in equal ~s** zu gleichen Teilen; **in foreign ~s** im Ausland; **in whole or in ~s** ganz oder teilweise; **of the first ~** erstgenannt; **on the ~ of** seitens;

accusatory ~ Aufführung der Straftaten in einer Anklageschrift; **blind ~** unbedruckter Teil; **component (constituent) ~s** Bau-, Bestandteile; **essential ~** wesentlicher Teil; **integral ~** wesentlicher Bestandteil; **leading ~** führende Rolle; **machine ~** Maschinenteil, -element; **orchestra ~s** Orchestermelodie; **~s replaced** ausgewechselte Teile; **single ~s** einzelne Stücke, Einzelteile; **small ~s** *(theater)* kleine Rollen; **spare ~** Ersatzteil; **~ by ~** Stück für Stück; **the funny ~ about it is** das Komische daran ist; **~ and parcel** wesentlicher Bestandteil; **~ and pertinent** *(Scot.)* Grundstückszubehör;

~ of a business Teilbetrieb; **appreciable ~ of commerce** *(antitrust law, US)* notwendiger Marktanteil; **~ in a conference** Rolle auf einer Konferenz; **substantive ~s of a contract** wesentliche Vertragsbestimmungen; **later ~ of the evening** späterer Abend; **~ of house to let** Haus teilweise zu vermieten; **~ of income** Einkommensanteil; **greater ~ of inhabitants** Mehrzahl der Bevölkerung; **greater ~ of the population** Bevölkerungsmehrheit; **~s of speech** Satzteile;

~ (v.) teilen, einteilen, zerteilen, trennen; **~ with s. th** etw. aufgeben, sich von etw. trennen; **~ with one's child** sich von einem Kind trennen; **~ company** verschiedener Ansicht sein, *(travel differently)* sich trennen; **~ the crowd** Menschenmenge zerstreuen; **~ good friends** sich als gute Freunde trennen; **~ with one's money** mit dem Geld herausrücken, sein Scheckbuch zücken; **not to like to ~ with one's money** sich von seinem Geld schwer trennen können; **~ with a property** Vermögensanteil aufgeben; **~ with a right** Recht veräußern;

to act a ~ *(theater)* Rolle spielen; **to act one's ~ well** seine Rolle glänzend spielen; **to appear in ~s** *(books)* in Lieferungen erscheinen, *(novel)* in Fortsetzungen erscheinen; **not to be bad in ~s** teilweise ganz gut sein; **to be ~ of s. one's functions** zu jds. Aufgaben gehören; **to be composed of three ~s** sich in drei Absätze gliedern; **to be ~ of the inventory** zum Inventar gehören; **to be ~ of s. one's official duties** zu jds. Dienstobliegenheiten gehören; **to be the ~ of parents** zu den elterlichen Aufgaben gehören; **to be issued in weekly ~s** in wöchentlichen Lieferungen (wöchentlich) erscheinen; **to be a man of ~s** fähiger Kopf sein; **to be ~ and parcel of s. th.** wesentlichen Bestandteil bilden (abgeben); **to be a stranger in these ~s** sich in dieser Gegend nicht auskennen; **to break down into six ~s** in sechs Teile gliedern; **to contribute in ~ to the expense of production** Produktionskosten teilweise übernehmen; **to divide into three ~s** in drei Abschnitte gliedern; **to do one's ~** das Seinige (seine Schuldigkeit) tun; **to form a ~** Teil bilden; **to form a ~ of the German Republic** zur Bundesrepublik Deutschland gehören; **to give off ~s** Teile reprivatisieren; **to have a ~ in s. th.** an etw. teilhaben; **to have no ~ in s. th.** an etw. unbeteiligt sein; **to have no ~ in a plot** nicht zu den Verschwörern gehören; **to have neither ~ nor lot in it** weder interessiert noch beteiligt sein; **to have only a small ~ in the events** an den Ereignissen nur geringfügig beteiligt sein; **to keep back ~ of the price** Teil des Preises zurückhalten; **to issue in fortnightly ~s** alle 14 Tage eine Lieferung herausbringen, 14tägig liefern; **to make a payment in ~** Abschlagszahlung leisten; **to pay in ~s** Teilzahlungen leisten; **to play a ~** sich verstellen, Theater spielen; **to play a ~ in the business** an einer Sache beteiligt sein; **to play the hero's ~** Heldenrolle in einem Stück spielen; **to take ~** teilnehmen an, partizipieren; **to take s. one's ~** *(take ~ with s. o.)* sich auf jds. Seite stellen, zu jem. stehen, jds. Partei ergreifen, jem. die Stange halten; **to take ~ in an action** *(mil.)* an einem Gefecht teilnehmen; **to take ~ in a discussion** sich an einer Diskussion beteiligen; **to take s. th. in good ~** etw. gut aufnehmen; **to take no ~ in it** unbeteiligt (uninteressiert) sein; **to take a job in ~s** Werk in Lieferungen abnehmen; **to take ~ in the rescue work** sich an den Rettungsarbeiten beteiligen; **to take an active ~ in an undertaking** großen Anteil an einer Sache haben; **to take one's ~ in a work** sich an einer Arbeit beteiligen;

~ III accommodation *(National Assistance Act, Br.)* Unterbringung im Altersheim; **~ cargo** Teilfracht; **~-charter** Teilcharter; **~ damage** Teilschaden; **~ delivery** Teillieferung; **~s depot** Ersatzteillager; **~ disposal** Teilveräußerung; **~ interest** Teilanspruch; **~ interest in a patent** Patentanteil; **~ loads** Stückgüter; **~-load traffic** Stückgutverkehr; **~-machined** teilweise maschinell hergestellt; **~ number** Ersatzteilnummer; **~ owner** Teil-, Miteigentümer, *(shipping)* Mitreeder, Schiffspartner; **~ ownership** Teil-, Miteigentum, *(ship)* Partenreederei; **~-paid stock** *(US)* teilweise eingezahltes Aktienkapital; **~ payment** Teil-, Raten-, Abschlagszahlung; **in ~ payment** auf Abschlag *(Raten)*; **in ~ payment of the outstanding balance** zur teilweisen Begleichung des noch ausstehenden Betrags; **~ payment on account** Akontozahlung eines Teilbetrags; **to make a ~ payment** teilweise bezahlen, Teilzahlung leisten; **~-payment terms** Teilzahlungsbedingungen; **~ performance** Teilerfüllung, -leistung; **~ short-age** Ersatzteilknappheit; **~s supply** Ersatzteilversorgung.

part time verkürzte Arbeitszeit; **to be on (be employed) ~** nicht ganztägig beschäftigt sein, kurzarbeiten.

part-time nebenberuflich; **on a ~ basis** auf Zeitarbeitsgrundlage; **~ commitment** Teilzeitbeschäftigung; **~ day release** Halbtagsbeurlaubung; **~ employee** nicht ganztägig beschäftigter Angestellter, Teilzeitbeschäftigter, Kurzarbeiter; **~ employment** Kurzarbeit, Halbtags-, Teilzeitbeschäftigung; **~ factory earnings** Halbtagsverdienst durch Fabrikarbeit; **~ job** Halbtagsstelle, nebenberufliche Beschäftigung; **~ member** nichtselbständiges Mitglied; **~-time poet** Gelegenheitsdichter; **~ school** Fortbildungsschule; **~ student** Student auf Zeit; **~ vacancy** angebotene Teilzeitbeschäftigung; **~ work** Kurz-, Halbtags-, Teilzeitarbeit; **~ worker** Kurzarbeiter, Teilzeit-, Halbtagskraft.

part | timer Aushilfs-, Kurzarbeiter, Halbtagskraft; **~ truckload** *(Br.)* Teilwaggonladung; **~ warrant** *(warehouse)* Teillagerschein.

partable teilbar.

partake *(v.)* teilnehmen, teilhaben, sich beteiligen; **~ freely of the bottle** der Flasche eifrig zusprechen; **~ of insolence** Zeichen von Unverschämtheit sein; **~ at a meal** an einem Essen teilnehmen; **~ of the profits** am Gewinn teilnehmen, gewinnbeteiligt sein.

partaker Teilnehmer, Teilhaber.

parte, ex Antragsteller.

parterre Baugelände, *(theater)* Parkett.

Parthian shot *(fig.)* scharfe Bemerkung beim Weggehen.

partial *(biassed)* voreingenommen, parteiisch, einseitig, befangen, unsachlich, *(incomplete)* teilweise, partiell; **to be ~ to s. o.** Schwäche für j. haben; **to be ~ to s. th.** Vorliebe für etw. haben; **to be too ~ to the bottle** dem Alkohol zu sehr zusprechen;

~ acceptance Teilakzept; **~ account** *(executor)* Teilabrechnung; **~ agreement** Teilabkommen; **~ amount** Teilbetrag; **~ assignment** Teilabtretung; **~ audit** Teilrevision; **~ average** besondere (einfache) Havarie; **~ award** parteiischer Schiedsspruch; **~ board** halbe Pension; **~ bond** *(Br.)* Teilschuldschein, -schuldverschreibung; **~ breach** teilweiser Vertragsbruch; **~ cessation** *(business)* Teilstillegung; **~ damage to goods** Teilschaden; **~ data** Teilerhebung; **~ debenture** Teilschuldverschreibung; **~ delivery** Teillieferung; **~ dependence** *(workmen's compensation)* Abhängigkeitsgrad [vom Arbeitslohn]; **~ disability** Teilinvalidität; **~ endorsement** Teilindossament; **~ equilibrium** partielles Gleichgewicht; **~ eviction** Teilräumung; **~ evidence** Teilbeweis; **~ execution** Teilausführung; **~ freighting** Teilbefrachtung; **~ incapacity** Teilinvalidität; **~ indemnification** Teilentschädigung; **~ insanity** zeitweilige krankhafte Störung der Geistestätigkeit; **~ judge** voreingenommener Richter; **~ loss** *(marine insurance)* Teilschaden, -verlust; **~ mobilization** Teilmobilmachung; **~ monopoly** unvollständiges Monopol; **~ offer** Teilofferte; **~ payment** Abschlags-, Raten-, Teilzahlung; **~ payment of debts** Schuldenregelung im Vereinbarungswege; **~-payment plan** Abzahlungsplan; **~ repayment** Teilrückzahlung; **~ replacement** Teilersatz; **~ reverse** Teilstorno; **~ sale** Partieverkauf; **~ self-service** Tempoladen; **~ shipment** *(US)* Teilsendung, -lieferung; **~ statement** einseitige Behauptung; **~ success** Teilerfolg; **~ succession** Teilrechtsnachfolge; **~ unemployment** partielle Arbeitslosigkeit; **~ unemployment benefit** Teilarbeitslosenunterstützung; **~ verdict** Teilurteil; **~ withdrawal** Teilabhebung.

partiality Voreingenommenheit, Parteilichkeit, *(judge)* Befangenheit;

~ for one's children Schwäche den eigenen Kindern gegenüber; **to have a ~ for the bottle** der Flasche frönen; **to plead ~** sich für befangen erklären.

partially insured teilversichert.

partible lands teilbarer Grundbesitz.

participant Teilhaber, -nehmer, Beteiligter;

special drawing rights **~** (International Monetary Fund) Teilnehmerland;

~ in a conference Konferenzteilnehmer; **~ of a meeting** Sitzungsteilnehmer.

participate (v.) Anteil haben, teilnehmen, (have share) teilhaben, beteiligt sein an, (share in profits) gewinnbeteiligt sein;

~ in a business sich an einem Geschäft beteiligen; **~ in committing an offence** an einer strafbaren Handlung beteiligt sein; **~ in the conversation** sich am Gespräch beteiligen; **~ in a discussion** an einer Diskussion teilnehmen; **~ in an estate** Gesamthandseigentümer sein, Grundstück gemeinsam besitzen; **~ in a loss** am Verlust beteiligt sein; **~ in a plot** sich an einer Verschwörung beteiligen, zu den Verschworenen gehören; **~ equally in the profits** gleichen Gewinnanteil haben.

participating [gewinn]berechtigt, -beteiligt;

to be not ~ unbeteiligt sein;

~ bonds (US) Obligationen mit Gewinnbeteiligungsrecht, Gewinnschuldverschreibungen, Vorzugsobligationen; **~ capital stock** (US) mit zusätzlicher Dividendenberechtigung ausgestattetes Aktienkapital, (liquidation) am Liquidationsgewinn beteiligte Vorzugsaktien; **~ carrier** Teilhaberspedition; **~ certificate** Genußschein; **~ company** beteiligte Gesellschaft; **~ contract** (insurance law) Gewinnbeteiligungsvertrag; **~ dividend** Vorzugsdividende; **~ government** Teilnehmerregierung; **~ guarantee** Bietungsgarantie; **~ insurance** gewinnbeteiligte Versicherung; **~ insurance policy** Police mit Gewinnbeteiligung, gewinnbeteiligte Versicherungspolice; **~ mortgage** mehreren Gläubigern zustehende Hypothek; **~ policy** gewinnbeteiligte Versicherungspolice; **~ preference shares** (Br.) (preferred stock, US) mit zusätzlicher Dividendenberechtigung ausgestattete Vorzugsaktien; **~ program(me)** Publikumsbeteiligung, (advertising) Gemeinschaftswerbung in Funk und Fernsehen; **~ receipt** Anteilschein; **~ rights** Genuß-, Gewinnbeteiligung[srechte]; **~ state** Teilnehmerstaat.

participation Mitwirkung, Teilnahme, (banking) Konsortialbeteiligung, (profit sharing) Gewinn-, Mit-, Kapital-, Konsortialbeteiligung, (taking part in a company) kommanditistische Beteiligung, Teilhaberschaft;

~s Anteile;

electoral ~ Wahlbeteiligung; **financial ~** finanzielle Beteiligung, Kapitalbeteiligung; **government ~** staatliche Beteiligung; **grass-roots ~** breit verankerte Mitbestimmung; **immediate ~** unmittelbare Gewinnbeteiligung; **industrial ~** Industriebeteiligung; **nominal ~** formale Beteiligung; **underwriting ~** Konsortialbeteiligung; **worker ~** (Br.) [Arbeiter]mitbestimmung, Mitbestimmung im Betrieb;

~ in a business Geschäfts-, Konsortialbeteiligung; **~ in dividends** Dividendenberechtigung; **~ in earnings (surplus)** [Rein-]gewinnbeteiligung; **~ in an enterprise** Beteiligung an einem Unternehmen; **~ in the management** (worker) Mitbestimmung im Betrieb; **~ in a meeting** Versammlungsteilnahme, Teilnahme an einer Sitzung (Versammlung); **~ in profits** Gewinnbeteiligung; **~ in a syndicate** Konsortialbeteiligung;

to take up a financial ~ sich kapitalmäßig beteiligen;

~ account Beteiligungs-, Konsortialkonto; **~ agreement** Mitbestimmungsvereinbarung, Gewinnbeteiligungsvereinbarung; **~ certificate** (US) Anteilschein, Teilobligation; **~ clause** Allbeteiligungsklausel; **~ council** Mitbestimmungsbeirat; **immediate ~ guarantee** Garantie für unmittelbare Gewinnbeteiligung; **~ loan** (US) Konsortialkredit; **~ plan** Mitbestimmungssystem; **~ rate** Erwerbstätigenquote; **~ share** Anteilschein; **~ show** Fernsehübertragung mit Beteiligung des Publikums.

participator Teilnehmer, Teilhaber.

particle Teilchen, Stückchen, (fig.) Spur, Fünkchen;

~s of dust Staubteilchen; **no ~ of truth** auch nicht ein Körnchen Wahrheit.

particular Einzelheit, besonderer Umstand;

in a material ~ in einem wesentlichen Punkt;

~s (details) Einzelheiten, nähere Angaben, Umstände, (of person) Angaben zur Person, Personalien;

without entering into ~s ohne in Details einzutreten;

full ~s eingehender Bericht, detaillierte Angaben, genaue Einzelheiten; **a London ~** (fam.) typischer Londoner Nebel; **personal ~s** Personenbeschreibung, -angaben;

~s of an account einzelne Abrechnungsposten; **~s of breaches**

and objections (patent law, Br.) detaillierte Angaben der Patentverletzung; **~s of a car** Autosteckbrief; **~s of a criminal charge** Einzelheiten der Anklage, Anklagepunkte; **~s of a claim** Klagevorbringen; **~s of an entry** Buchungsangaben; **~s of options** Optionsvorzugsrechte; **~s of pleadings** (Br.) Einzelheiten der Schriftsätze; **~s on a postmark** Besonderheiten des Poststempels; **~s of a risk** Gefahrenmerkmale; **~s of sale** (auction sale) detaillierte Objektbeschreibung;

~ (a.) besonders, einzeln, speziell, individuell, örtlich, (law) dem Besitzer nur beschränkt gehörend;

to ask for full (further) ~s nähere Einzelheiten erfragen (Angaben erbitten); **to ask s. o. for ~s about s. o.** j. um Auskunft über einen Dritten bitten; **to be ~ about one's dress** auf seine Kleidung größten Wert legen; **to be ~ about one's food** an seinem Essen herummäkeln; **to be ~ as regards one's choice of friends** in der Auswahl seiner Freunde äußerst wählerisch sein; **to be very ~ about having things done methodically** an alles äußerst methodisch herangehen; **to be ~ on points of hono(u)r** in Ehrensachen sehr penibel sein; **not to be ~ to a few pounds** es auf ein paar Mark nicht ankommen lassen; **to enter into ~s** auf Einzelheiten eingehen; **to execute an order in every ~** Auftrag in jedem Punkt ausführen; **to furnish ~s** Einzelheiten mitteilen; **to give full ~s** Sache in allen Details darlegen; **to go into ~s** detaillierten Bericht geben, ins einzelne (in Einzelheiten) gehen; **to have nothing ~ to do** nichts Besonderes vorhaben; **to take down s. one's ~s** jds. Personalien aufnehmen;

full and ~ account eingehender Bericht; **~ average** kleine (besondere) Havarie, Teilhavarie; **~ branch** besonderer Geschäftszweig; **to call on ~ business** aus besonderem Anlaß kommen; **to take no ~ care over doing s. th.** etw. nicht besonders sorgfältig erledigen; **~ case** Einzel-, Sonderfall; **~ circumstances** besondere Umstände; **~ costs** direkte Kosten; **~ custom** Ortsgebrauch; **~ description** ausführliche Beschreibung; **to have a ~ dislike for s. o.** j. absolut nicht leiden können; **~ equilibrium** partielles Gleichgewicht; **~ estate** lebenslängliches Nießbrauchrecht; **~ friend** intimer (enger) Freund; **~ fund** besonders bezeichneter Vermögensfonds; **~ legacy** Sondervermächtnis; **~ lien** Pfandrecht an einem bestimmten Gegenstand; **~ malice** Rachedurst; **~ object** bestimmtes Objekt; **~ partnership** Gelegenheitsgesellschaft, (US) Handelsgesellschaft zur Durchführung einer besonderen Transaktion; **to fasten an article to a ~ person** jem. Bestimmten einen Artikel zuschreiben; **~ power** Sonder-, Spezialvollmacht; **to leave for no ~ reason** ohne besonderen Grund weggehen; **~ risk** Risiko in einem Sonderfall; **~ statement** substantiierte Klage; **to take ~ trouble** sich besondere Mühe geben.

particularism Partikularismus, Kleinstaaterei.

particularist Partikularist, Lokalpatriot.

particularity (pleading) hinreichende Substantiierung.

particularization Einzelaufführung, Spezifizierung.

particularize (v.) auf Einzelheiten eingehen, im einzelnen darstellen, detailliert ausführen, eingehend darlegen, spezifizieren.

parties | belligerent am Krieg Beteiligte; **~ concerned** die Beteiligten; **contending ~** Prozeßparteien; **~ contracting** vertragsschließende Parteien (Teile), Kontrahenten; **~ indispensable** notwendige Streitgenossen; **~ interested** Interessenten; **~ jointly and severally liable** Gesamtschuldner; **~ primarily liable** (on commercial papers) unmittelbar Wechselverpflichtete; **necessary ~** notwendige Streitgenossen;

~ to the agreement vertragsschließende Teile, Vertragspartner; **~ to a bill** Wechselparteien, -kontrahenten; **~ to a case** Prozeßbeteiligte; **prior ~ to a bill** Wechselvorgänger; **~ to a dispute** streitende Parteien; **~ in interest** Konkursgläubiger; **~ and privies** unmittelbare Vertragsparteien;

to notify the ~ Parteien vorladen; **to temporize between ~** zwischen den Parteien lavieren.

parting Abschied, Abreise;

to be at the ~ of the ways sich an einer Wegegabelung (einem Scheideweg) befinden;

~ injunctions Anweisungen beim Abschied; **~ visit** Abschiedsbesuch, (dipl.) Abschiedsaudienz; **~ words** Abschiedsworte.

partisan Anhänger, Parteigänger, (mil.) Freischärler, Partisan;

~s Gefolgschaft;

~ of the present government Regierungsanhänger; **~ of peace** Friedenskämpfer;

~ (a.) parteigängerisch;

narrowly ~ parteigebunden;

~ charge Parteianklage; **~ fight** Parteistreit; **~ movement** Partisanenbewegung; **~ politics** Parteipolitik; **~ politician** Parteipolitiker; **~ speech** Parteirede; **to act in a ~ spirit** Parteidisziplin wahren.

partisanship Anhängerschaft, *(pol.)* Parteigängertum, Partei-, Vetternwirtschaft, Cliquenwesen.

partition Teilung, Aufteilung, *(car)* Trennscheibe, *(real estate)* Grundstücksteilung;
brick ~ Ziegeltrennwand; **glass ~** *(car)* Trennscheibe; **internal ~** Zwischenwand; **provisional ~** vorläufige Nachlaßteilung; **distribution and ~** *(US)* Verteilung des beweglichen und unbeweglichen Nachlasses, Erbauseinandersetzung;
~ of a farm Parzellierung eines Gutshofs; **~ of a succession** *(Br.)* Erbauseinandersetzung;
~ *(v.)* ver-, aufteilen, *(parcel)* parzellieren;
~ an estate among the heirs Erbschaft zur Verteilung bringen, Auseinandersetzung vornehmen; **~ off a room** Zimmer abteilen;
~ plan Parzellierungsplan; **~ treaty** Teilungsvertrag; **~ wall** Brandmauer.

partly teilweise, zum Teil;
wholly or ~ ganz oder teilweise;
~ by force, ~ by persuasion teils mittels Gewalt, teils aufgrund Überredung;
to be ~ depreciated teilabgeschrieben sein;
~ paid stock *(US)* teilweise eingezahltes Aktienkapital.

partner Beteiligter, Teilnehmer, *(in partnership)* Teilhaber, Gesellschafter, Kompagnon, Partner, Sozius;
active (acting) ~ geschäftsführender Teilhaber (Gesellschafter), Komplementär; **apparent ~** Scheingesellschafter; **associated ~** unbeschränkt haftender Teilhaber; **chief ~** Hauptgesellschafter; **continuing ~** verbleibender (das Gesellschaftsverhältnis fortsetzender) Teilhaber; **contracting ~** Vertragspartner; **deceased ~** verstorbener Teilhaber (Gesellschafter); **dormant ~** stiller Teilhaber (Gesellschafter); **floor ~** *(US)* Teilhaber einer Maklerfirma; **general ~** persönlich haftender Gesellschafter (Teilhaber), Komplementär; **individual ~** Einzelgesellschafter; **holding-out ~** Scheingesellschafter; **inactive ~** nichttätiger (nicht geschäftsführender) Gesellschafter; **incoming ~** neueintretender Gesellschafter (Teilhaber); **infant ~** minderjähriger Gesellschafter; **junior ~** jüngerer Teilhaber, Juniorchef; **latent ~** stiller Teilhaber; **limited ~** beschränkt haftender Teilhaber (Gesellschafter), Kommanditist; **liquidating ~** Liquidator, abwickelnder Teilhaber; **managing ~** geschäftsführender Gesellschafter, Geschäftsführer, Seniorchef; **marital ~** Ehegatte; **nominal ~** Scheingesellschafter; **ordinary ~** *(Br.)* persönlich haftender Teilhaber; **ostensible ~** gesellschaftsähnlicher Teilhaber, Scheingesellschafter, vorgeschobener Gesellschafter; **outgoing ~** ausscheidender Gesellschafter; **past ~** ausgeschiedener Gesellschafter; **quasi ~** Scheingesellschafter; **responsible ~** persönlich (unbeschränkt) haftender Teilhaber (Gesellschafter); **retired ~** ausgeschiedener Gesellschafter; **retiring ~** ausscheidender Gesellschafter; **secret ~** stiller Teilhaber (Gesellschafter); **senior ~** Hauptgesellschafter, Seniorchef; **silent (sleeping) ~** stiller (nicht geschäftsführender) Gesellschafter; **solvent ~** vom Konkurs nicht betroffener Teilhaber (Gesellschafter); **special ~** beschränkt haftender Teilhaber, Kommanditist; **state-run ~** staatlicher Teilhaber; **subordinate ~** *(Br.)* nicht persönlich haftender Gesellschafter; **trade ~** Handelsvertragspartner; **surviving ~** das Gesellschaftsverhältnis fortsetzender (überlebender) Teilhaber; **unlimited ~** persönlich haftender Gesellschafter, Komplementär; **withdrawing ~** ausscheidender Gesellschafter; **working ~** tätiger Teilhaber, geschäftsführender Gesellschafter;
~ in business Mitgesellschafter, Geschäftspartner; **~ in crime** Komplice, Mittäter; **~ in default** zahlungsunfähiger Teilhaber; **~ in life** Lebensgefährte; **~ at table** Tischnachbar, -herr;
~ *(v.)* sich assoziieren, Partner sein;
to admit as ~ als Teilhaber aufnehmen; **to be a ~** teilhaben; **to be personally liable as a ~** als Gesellschafter persönlich haften; **to become a ~** sich liieren; **to become ~ in a firm** als Teilhaber in eine Firma eintreten, sich ins Geschäft einsteigen, Gesellschafter werden; **to buy out a ~** Teilhaber abfinden; **to connect o. s. as ~ with a house** als Teilhaber in eine Firma eintreten; **to enter a firm as ~** als Teilhaber in eine Firma eintreten; **to hold s. o. out as ~** j. als Gesellschafter ausgeben; **to introduce as ~** als Gesellschafter aufnehmen; **to join a firm as ~** Gesellschafter werden, als Teilhaber eintreten; **to take in a ~** Teilhaber aufnehmen; **~-like stake** unternehmerähnliches Interesse; **~ trustee** geschäftsbevollmächtigter Partner.

partner's authority Gesellschaftervollmacht; **~ capital** Einlagekapital; **~ country** Vertragsland; **~ duties** Gesellschafterpflichten; **~ interest (share)** Gesellschafteranteil, -beteiligung; **~ rights** Gesellschafterrechte; **~ salary** Teilhabervergütung.

partnership *(articles)* Gesellschaftsvertrag, *(business association)* [offene] Handels-, Personengesellschaft, Sozietät[svertrag], *(participation)* Teilhaber-, Partnerschaft, Mitbeteiligung, *(relationship)* Gesellschaftsverhältnis;
with a view to ~ mit der Aussicht späterer Beteiligung;
commercial ~ Handelsgesellschaft; **dormant ~** stille Teilhaberschaft; **general ~** offene Handelsgesellschaft [mit unbeschränkter Haftpflicht]; **industrial ~** *(US)* Gewinnbeteiligung der Arbeitnehmer; **leonine ~** leoninische Gesellschaft; **limited ~** Kommanditgesellschaft; **mercantile ~** *(US)* Handelsgesellschaft; **mining ~** *(US)* Bergwerksgesellschaft; **nontrading ~** Personalgesellschaft, Sozietät; **oral ~** auf mündlicher Vereinbarung beruhende Teilhaberschaft; **ordinary ~** *(US)* offene Handelsgesellschaft; **particular ~** *(US)* Gelegenheitsgesellschaft; **private ~** Gesellschaft mit nicht mehr als 50 Beteiligten; **quasi ~** Scheingesellschaft; **secret ~ (silent, US, sleeping, Br.)** stille Beteiligung; **special ~** Handelsgesellschaft zwecks Durchführung einer besonderen Transaktion, Gelegenheitsgesellschaft; **trading ~** Handelsgesellschaft; **universal ~** Gesellschaft mit Einbringung des Gesamtvermögens aller Gesellschafter; **unlimited ~** *(US)* [etwa] BGB-Gesellschaft, Gesellschaft des bürgerlichen Rechts; **~ wanted** *(advertisement)* Teilhaber gesucht;
~ in commendam stille Gesellschaft; **~ in crime** Komplizenschaft; **~ by estoppel** *(Br.)* Gesellschaft kraft Rechtsscheins; **~ limited by shares** Kommanditgesellschaft; **~ in syndicate** Konsortialbeteiligung; **~ at will** jederzeit kündbare Gesellschaft, [etwa] Gesellschaft des bürgerlichen Rechts;
to be in ~ with s. o. mit jem. assoziiert sein; **to be admitted into a ~** in eine Gesellschaft aufgenommen werden; **to bring one's skill into a ~** seine Arbeitskraft in eine Gesellschaft einbringen; **to carry on a ~** Gesellschaftsverhältnis fortsetzen; **to create a ~** Gesellschaftsverhältnis begründen; **to dissolve a ~** Gesellschaft auflösen, sich trennen; **to enter into ~ with s. o.** sich mit jem. assoziieren; **to establish a ~** Gesellschaft gründen; **to give s. o. a ~ in business** einen Geschäftsanteil überlassen; **to hold the property in trust for a ~** als Treuhänder von Grundvermögen einer OHG fungieren; **to join a ~** als Teilhaber eintreten (aufgenommen werden); **to leave a ~** als Teilhaber ausscheiden; **to organize a ~** Teilhaberschaft[sverhältnis] begründen; **to retire from a ~** als Teilhaber ausscheiden; **to take into ~** zum Teilhaber machen (nehmen), als Teilhaber aufnehmen; **to take up a ~ in a venture** sich an einem Unternehmen beteiligen; **to treat a ~ as a continuing business** Handelsgesellschaft als fortgeführt behandeln; **to withdraw from a ~** als Teilhaber (Gesellschafter) ausscheiden, Gesellschaftsverhältnis beenden;
~ account Gesellschafts-, Firmenkonto; **~ accounts** Firmenbuchführung; **~ Act** *(Br.)* Gesetz über die offenen Handelsgesellschaften; **Limited ~ Act** *(Br.)* Gesetz über Kommanditgesellschaften; **~ affairs** Gesellschaftsangelegenheiten; **~ agreement** Gesellschafter-, Teilhabervertrag, Gesellschaftervereinbarung; **~ articles** Gesellschaftssatzung, -vertrag; **~ assessment** Steuerveranlagung einer Handelsgesellschaft; **~ assets** Gesellschaftsvermögen; **~ assurance** *(Br.)* Teilhaberversicherung; **~ bankruptcy** Gesellschafts-, Firmenkonkurs; **~ books** Geschäftsbücher einer OHG; **within the scope of the ~ business** im Rahmen der Gesellschaftstätigkeit; **~ capital** Gesellschaftskapital; **~ claim** Gesellschaftsanspruch, -forderung; **~ concerns** Gesellschaftsangelegenheiten; **~ contract** Gesellschaftervertrag; **~ creditor** Firmen-, Gesellschaftsgläubiger; **~ debts** Firmenschulden, Gesellschaftsschulden; **~ deed** Sozietäts-, Gesellschaftsvertrag; **~ estate** Gesellschafts-, Firmenvermögen; **~ firm** Gesellschaft; **~ funds** Gesellschaftskapital; **~ goods** Gesellschaftsvermögen; **~ income** Firmeneinkommen, Einkünfte (Erträge) einer Handelsgesellschaft; **~ insurance** Teilhaberversicherung; **~ interest** Firmen-, Gesellschaftsanteil; **limited ~ interest** Beteiligung an einer Kommanditgesellschaft, Kommanditanteil; **~ land** Firmengrundstück; **~ law** Gesellschaftsrecht; **~ to reach ~ level** sich als Teilhaber qualifizieren; **~ liability** Firmenhaftung; **~ loss** Firmen-, Gesellschaftsverlust; **~ name** Firmenname; **~ obligations** Firmen-, Gesellschaftsverpflichtungen; **~ personalty** Mobiliarvermögen einer Gesellschaft; **~ profit** Gesellschaftsgewinn; **~ property** Firmen-, Gesellschaftseigentum, -vermögen; **~ purpose** Gesellschaftszweck; **~ realty** Grundbesitz einer Gesellschaft; **~ registration** Eintragung einer Gesellschaft im Handelsregister; **to withdraw from ~ registration** Gesellschaft im Handelsregister löschen lassen; **~ relation** Teilhaber-, Partnerschaftsverhältnis; **~ share** Gesellschaftsanteil; **~ stock** Gesellschaftskapital, -vermögen; **~ transaction** Gesellschaftstransaktion.

party Partei, *(to an action)* [Prozeß]partei, *(to a contract)* [Vertrags]partei, -partner, Kontrahent, *(mil.)* Abteilung, Kommando, *(participant)* Teilhaber, Interessent, beteiligte Person, Beteiligter, *(pol.)* politische Partei, *(social life)* Gesellschaft, Party, Einladung;
for account of a third ~ zugunsten eines Dritten; **by order of a third ~** im Auftrag eines Dritten;
accommodated ~ Begünstigter; **advance ~** *(mil.)* Vorauskommando; **adverse ~** Prozeßgegner; **aggrieved ~** unterlegene (beschwerte, benachteiligte) Partei; **~ appealing** Berufskläger; **benefited ~** Bereicherter; **birthday ~** Geburtstagsfest, -feier; **~ chargeable** kostenpflichtige Partei; **cold-meat ~** *(sl.)* Leichenbegängnis; **Communist[ic] ♀** kommunistische Partei; **competent ~** Sachverständiger; **~ concerned** Betroffener, Interessent, Beteiligter; **Conservative ♀** *(Br.)* Konservative Partei; **contracting ~** vertragsschließender Teil, Kontrahent; **countersigning ~** Gegenzeichnender; **dancing ~** Abendgesellschaft mit Tanz; **defeated ~** unterlegene Partei; **Democratic ♀** *(US)* demokratische Partei; **dinner ~** Abendgesellschaft, Dinner; **~ entitled** Berechtigter; **evening ~** Abendgesellschaft; **extreme ~** radikale Partei; **extreme left ~** Partei der äußersten Linken; **fatigue ~** Arbeitskommando; **firing ~** Hinrichtungskommando; **fringe ~** Splitterpartei; **garden ~** Gartenfest; **governing ~** an der Macht befindliche Partei; **guilty ~** *(divorce suit)* schuldiger Teil; **hen ~** *(coll.)* Damenkränzchen; **house ~** geselliges Zusammensein über mehrere Tage; **immediate ~** *(bill of exchange)* unmittelbar Beteiligter; **injured ~** Verletzter, Beschädigter; **innocent ~** gutgläubiger Dritter; **interested ~** Beteiligter, Interessent; **intervening ~** Nebenintervenient; **Labou(u)r ♀** *(Br.)* Labour(Arbeiter)-Partei; **landing ~** *(Br.)* Kommandounternehmen, Landungstrupp; **left-wing ~** Linkspartei; **liable ~** Schuldner, Verpflichteter; **Liberal ♀** *(Br.)* liberale Partei; **litigant ~** Prozeßpartei; **losing ~** unterliegende Partei; **the middle ~** Mitte; **moderate ~** gemäßigte Partei; **moving ~** Antragsteller; **necktie ~** *(sl.)* Lynchjustiz; **nominal ~** Streitgenosse ohne eigenes Prozeßinteresse; **nondefaulting ~** vertragstreue Partei; **offended ~** beleidigter Teil, Beleidigter; **opposing ~** Prozeßgegner; **opposition ~** Oppositionspartei; **~ ordering** Auftraggeber; **other ~** Gegenkontrahent; **petitioning ~** antragstellende Partei; **pleasure ~** Ausflugsgesellschaft; **political ~** [politische] Partei; **~ presenting** Präsentant [eines Wechsels]; **prevailing ~** obsiegende Partei; **primary ~** Hauptschuldner; **prior ~** Wechselvormann; **private ~** geschlossene Gesellschaft; **prosecuting ~** Kläger; **real ~** aktiv legitimierte Partei; **receiving ~** Empfänger; **remote ~** *(bill of exchange)* mittelbar Beteiligter; **Republican ♀** *(US)* Republikanische Partei; **rescue ~** Bergungs-, Rettungsmannschaft; **right-wing ~** Rechtspartei; **ruling ~** an der Macht befindliche Partei; **search ~** Suchtrupp; **small ~** kleine Feier; **socialist ~** sozialistische Partei; **storming ~** *(mil.)* Sturmtrupp, -kolonne; **successful ~** obsiegende Partei; **~ sued** Beklagter; **~ suing** Kläger; **surviving ~** *(life insurance)* überlebender Teil; **tea ~** Tee-Einladung; **third ~** nicht beteiligte Partei, Dritter; **unsuccessful ~** unterlegene Partei; **winning ~** obsiegende Partei; **working ~** Arbeitsgruppe; **wronged ~** Geschädigter, Verletzter;
~ to an action Prozeßpartei; **~ to an agreement** Vertragsteilnehmer, -partner, -partei; **~ in breach** vertragsbrüchige Partei; **~ to a bill of exchange** Wechselverpflichteter, -beteiligter; **~ to a case** Prozeßpartei; **~ to be charged** Beklagter; **~ entitled to a claim** Anspruchsberechtigter; **~ to a conspiracy** Teilnehmer einer Verschwörung, Mitverschwörer; **~ to a contract** vertragsschließende (vertraglich verpflichtete) Partei, Kontrahent; **~ liable for cost** Kostenschuldner; **~ in default** nicht erschienene (im Verzug befindliche, säumige) Partei; **~ to a dispute** Prozeßpartei; **~ at fault in an accident** Unfallschuldiger; **~ of holidaymakers** Touristengruppe; **~ in interest** Konkursbeteiligter; **real ~ in interest** *(US)* wirkliche Prozeßpartei; **~ to a lawsuit** Prozeßpartei; **~ of the first part** erstgenannte Partei; **~ and ~** die streitenden Parteien; **~ in power** an der Macht befindliche Partei, Regierungspartei; **~ liable to recourse** Regreßschuldner; **~ entitled to service** Empfangsberechtigter; **torn by internal strife** durch innere Streitigkeiten zerrissene Partei; **~ to a suit** *(US)* Prozeßpartei; **~ to surrender** Herausgabeverpflichteter;
to accede to a ~ einer Partei beitreten; **to ban a ~** Partei verbieten; **to be affiliated to a ~** einer Partei als Mitglied angehören; **to be a natural governing ~** wie selbstverständlich an der Regierung sein; **to be one of the ~** dazugehören; **to become ~ to an action** sich an einem Prozeß beteiligen; **to become ~ to an agreement** einem Vertrag beitreten, an einem Vertrag beteiligt sein; **to become [a] third ~ to an agreement**

Nebenintervenient werden; **to become a ~ to a crime** Komplice eines Verbrechens werden; **to belong to s. one's ~** *(fam.)* auf jds. Seite stehen; **to constitute o. s. a ~** Partei bilden (gründen); **to deposit a sum in the hands of a third** Summe bei einem Treuhänder hinterlegen; **to desert a ~** Partei verlassen; **to escort a ~** Reisegesellschaft begleiten; **to follow the Conservative ♀** konservatives Parteimitglied sein; **to form a ~** Partei gründen; **to get up a shooting ~** Jagdgesellschaft zusammenstellen; **to give a ~** gesellschaftlichen Empfang veranstalten, Fest geben; **to give one's vote to a ~** Partei wählen; **to have a ~ to dinner** Gäste zum Abendbrot haben; **to join a ~** in eine Partei eintreten, einer Partei beitreten; **to join s. one's ~** sich um jds. Fahne scharen; **to make one of the ~** sich einer Gesellschaft anschließen; **to make up a ~** sich zu einer Partei zusammenschließen; **to make s. o. a ~ to an undertaking** j. an einem Unternehmen beteiligen, j. als Teilhaber aufnehmen; **to organize a political ~** politische Partei gründen; **to purge from a ~** aus einer Partei ausschließen; **to put public interest before ~** Parteiinteressen dem öffentlichen Wohl unterordnen; **to rat a ~** Partei im Stich lassen; **to rejoin a ~** sich wieder einer Partei anschließen; **to resign (withdraw) from a ~** aus einer Partei austreten; **to split a ~ on a question** in einer Frage in einer Partei verschiedener Meinung sein; **to support a political ~** Partei finanziell unterstützen; **to win s. o. to one's ~** j. für seine Sache gewinnen;
~ accessories Parteiutensilien; **~ activist** hauptamtliches Parteimitglied; **~ adviser** parteiinterner Berater; **~ affiliation** Parteiverbundenheit, -zugehörigkeit; **~ alignment** Parteigruppierung; **~ appeal** Parteiappell; **~ archive** Parteiarchiv; **~ assembly** Parteitag, -versammlung; **~ autonomy** Parteiautonomie; **~ backing** Parteiunterstützung; **~ badge** Parteiabzeichen; **~ ballot** Parteiabstimmung; **~ boss** Parteichef; **~ boy** Gesellschaftslöwe; **~ business** Parteigeschäfte; **to make ~ capital** als Partei aus einer Sache Kapital schlagen; **~ caucus** Parteikongreß, -tag; **~ chairman** Parteivorsitzender; **~ chief** *(US)* Parteiführer; **~ clash** Parteikonflikt; **~ coalition** Koalitionspartei; **~ colo(u)r** Parteizugehörigkeit; **~ conference** Sonderparteitag; **~ considerations** Parteirücksichten; **~ constitution** Parteistatuten; **~ control** Parteikontrolle; **~ convention** *(US)* Parteikongreß, -tag; **~ and ~ costs** *(law case)* erstattungsfähige Kosten; **~ council** Parteiversammlung; **third-~ creditor (beneficiary)** Begünstigter eines Vertrages zugunsten Dritter; **~ discipline** *(Br.)* Fraktions-, Parteidisziplin; **to modify the ~ dissidents** aufrührerische Geister der Partei besänftigen; **~ domination** Parteiherrschaft; **~ dress** Gesellschaftsanzug; **~ dues** Parteibeiträge; **~ emblem** Parteiabzeichen; **~ executives** Parteivorstand; **~ follower** Parteiangehöriger; **~ friend** Parteifreund; **~ functions** Parteiaufgaben; **~ funds** Parteikasse; **~ headquarters** Parteizentrale; **~ henchman** opportunistischer Parteianhänger; **~ hierarchy** Parteiherrschaft, -hierarchie; **third-~ [indemnity] insurance** Haftpflichtversicherung; **~ labels** Parteidogmen; **to run under a ~'s label** sich für ein Parteiemblem entscheiden; **~ leader** Parteiführer; **~ leaders** Parteiführung; **~ leadership** Parteiführung; **to run for ~ leadership** sich um das Amt des Parteivorsitzenden bewerben; **~ line** *(pol.)* Parteilinie, -kurs, -grundsätze, Generallinie einer Partei, offizielles Parteiprogramm, *(tel.)* Sammelanschlußnummer; **across ~ lines** über Parteigrenzen hinweg; **to cross the ~ line in making appointments** *(US)* bei Ernennungen auch Mitglieder anderer Parteien berücksichtigen; **to cut across ~ lines** quer durch die Parteien gehen; **to follow the ~ line** sich an die Parteigrundsätze halten, sich der Parteidisziplin fügen, linientreu sein; **~-line vote** Abstimmung unter Fraktionszwang; **~ liner** linientreues Parteimitglied; **~ list** Kandidatenliste; **~ list system** Listensystem; **~ machine[ry]** *(US)* Parteiapparat; **~ man** Parteigänger, -mann, treues Parteimitglied; **~ manager** Parteigeschäftsführer; **~ meeting** Parteiversammlung; **enrolled ~ member** eingeschriebenes Parteimitglied, -angehöriger, -genosse; **~ official** *(US)* Parteifuntionär, Mitglied des Parteivorstands; **~ organ** Parteiblatt, -organ; **~ organization** Parteiorganisation; **~ platform** Parteiprogramm; **~ policy document** Parteipapier; **~-policymaker** Parteiprogrammatiker; **~ politics** Parteipolitik; **~-political** parteipolitisch; **~ political reason** parteipolitischer Grund; **~ politician** Parteipolitiker; **~ poll** Parteiumfrage; **~ pooper** *(sl.)* zuerst aufbrechender Gast; **~ post** Parteiposten; **~ president** Parteivorsitzender; **to desert ~ principles** gegen Parteigrundsätze verstoßen; **~ professional** Parteifunktionär; **~ program(me)** Parteiprogramm; **~ quarrels** innere Auseinandersetzungen einer Partei, Parteigezänk; **~ rally** Parteiversammlung; **~ reorganization** Reorganisation einer Partei; **~ resolution** Fraktionsbeschluß; **~ revolt** Parteirevolte; **third-~**

risk Regreßrisiko; ~ **rival** Parteirivale; **to follow the ~ roll book** sich dem Fraktionszwang fügen; ~ **rule** Parteiherrschaft; ~ **secretariat** Parteisekretariat; ~ **slogan** Parteiparole; ~ **spirit** Parteibegeisterung; **to lack the ~ spirit** nicht genügend Begeisterung für seine Partei aufbringen; ~ **split** Parteispaltung; ~ **support** Parteiunterstützung; ~ **strategist** Parteistratege; ~ **system** Parteiensystem; **multiple ~ system** Mehrparteiensystem; ~ **ticket** *(pol.)* Empfehlungsbrief der Partei für einen Kandidaten, *(railway)* Sammelfahrschein, Gruppenfahrkarte; **to have the ~ ticket** offizieller Parteikandidat sein; ~ **transactions** Parteigeschäfte; ~ **treasurer** Schatzmeister einer Partei; ~ **truce** politischer Burgfriede; ~ **unity** Einheit der Partei, Parteieinheit; ~ **wall** Trenn-, Brandmauer; ~ **warfare** Parteistreitigkeiten; ~'**s weight** Bedeutung einer Partei; ~ **whip** *(Br.)* Einpeitscher, *(US)* politischer Druck; **to be under the ~ whip** durch Stimmenzwang gebunden sein; **lower-ranking ~ workers** einfache Parteimitarbeiter.

parvenu Emporkömmling, Neureicher, Parvenü.

pass *(identification card)* Personalausweis, Ausweiskarte, *(mil., US)* Urlaubsschein, *(opening)* [Eng]paß, Durchgang, *(permission to ~)* Paß, Grenz-,Erlaubnis-, Passierschein, Ausweis, Geleitbrief, *(free ticket)* Freifahrkarte, *(railroad, US)* Dauerkarte, Jahresbillet, *(short leave, US)* Kurzurlaub, *(university)* bestandenes Examen;

on ~ *(soldier)* auf Urlaub;

bus ~ Omnibuszulassungskarte; **customhouse ~** Zollbegleitschein; **free ~** *(mil.)* Urlaubsschein, *(railway)* Dauer-, Freifahrschein, *(theater)* Freikarte; **frontier ~** Grenzschein; **international travelling ~** Carnet; **labo(u)r ~** Arbeitserlaubnis; **narrow ~** Engpaß, Durchfahrt; **police ~** Polizeiausweis; **sea ~** Schiffspaß; **strange ~** kritische Lage; **transit ~** Passierschein, Durchfahrterlaubnis; **visitor's ~** *(prison)* Besuchererlaubnis;

~ *(v.)* passieren, *(adopt bill)* durchbringen, annehmen, verabschieden, votieren, *(approve)* genehmigen, *(bookkeeping)* eintragen, buchen, *(coins)* gültig sein, Kurs haben, *(convey)* Eigentum übertragen, *(correspondence)* hin und hergehen, *(event)* sich ereignen, eintreten, *(fashion)* kommen und gehen, unmodern werden, *(leave out)* überschlagen, unerwähnt lassen, keine Notiz nehmen, *(to be rendered in legal procedure)* rechtskräftig machen, gesetzliche Kraft verleihen, *(receive approval)* angenommen werden, durchgehen, *(risk)* übergehen, *(take no notice)* unerwähnt lassen, keine Notiz nehmen, *(time)* verstreichen, vorübergehen, *(vehicle)* vorbeifahren, überholen;

~ **an account** Rechnung genehmigen; ~ **to s. one's account** jem. in Rechnung stellen; ~ **an item to the current account** *(Br.)* Posten verbuchen; ~ **an act** Gesetz verabschieden; ~ **along** *(price)* abwälzen; ~ **an amendment** Abänderungsantrag annehmen; ~ **an amount to the credit of s. o.** jem. einen Betrag gutschreiben; ~ **an amount to the debit of s. o.** j. mit einem Betrag belasten; ~ **one's approbation** seine Zustimmung erteilen; ~ **away** dahinschwinden, vorübergehen, *(empire)* zugrundegehen; ~ **away in one's sleep** im Schlaf sterben; ~ **the baby** *(US)* Verantwortung abschieben; ~ **belief** *(story)* unglaubwürdig sein; ~ **beyond** vorüberschreiten; ~ **a bill** trassieren, *(parl.)* Gesetz verabschieden; ~ **a bill (draft) on** trassieren auf; ~ **into the books** buchen, eintragen; ~ **the border** Grenze überschreiten; ~ **the buck** *(US)* jem. die Verantwortung (den schwarzen Peter) zuschieben; ~ **by** defilieren, *(time)* vergehen; ~ **a candidate** Prüfling bestehen lassen; ~ **the censor** von der Zensur durchgehen lassen; ~ **the chair** Vorsitz abgeben; ~ **the channel** Kanal passieren; ~ **a check** *(US)* **(cheque,** *Br.)* Scheck einlösen; ~ **in one's checks** seine Spielmarken eintauschen; **to ~ a forged cheque (check,** *US)* gefälschten Scheck in Verkehr bringen; ~ **in certain circles** in bestimmten Kreisen geduldet sein; ~ **close to the village** *(road)* nahe am Dorfe vorbeiführen; ~ **forged coins** Falschgeld in Umlauf bringen; ~ **s. one's comprehension** über jds. Begriffe (Verstand, Horizont) gehen; ~ **in conformity** gleichlautend buchen; ~ **costs on** Unkosten abwälzen; ~ **on rising cost without becoming uncompetitive** gestiegene Kosten ohne Verschlechterung der Wettbewerbssituation weitergeben; ~ **automatically on fuel cost increases to customers** Treibstoffkostenerhöhungen automatisch auf die Verbraucher abwälzen; ~ **to s. one's credit** jem. gutschreiben; ~ **a criticism on s. th.** etw. kritisieren (seiner Kritik unterziehen); ~ **to the Crown as goods vacated** *(Br.)* als herrenloser Nachlaß dem Staat zufallen; ~ **current** allgemein gültig sein; ~ **the customs** Zoll passieren, zollamtlich abgefertigt werden; ~ **a customs entry** Zollerklärung abgeben, zur Verzollung deklarieren; ~ **a few pleasant days with s. o.** ein paar angenehme Tage mit jem. verbringen; ~ **on death** beim Todesfall übergehen; ~ **to s. one's**

debit j. belasten (debitieren); ~ **a decision** Entscheidung fällen; ~ **by deed** urkundlich übertragen werden; ~ **over the details** Einzelheiten übergehen; ~ **on one's discoveries to one's employer** seinem Arbeitgeber alle Betriebserfindungen zur Verfügung stellen; ~ **a dividend** *(US)* Dividende ausfallen lassen; ~ **down the ranks** *(mil.)* Front abschreiten; ~ **an entry** Eintragung machen, Buchung vornehmen; ~ **[through] an examination** Prüfung (Examen) bestehen; ~ **for** gelten als; ~ **each other frequently in the streets** sich häufig in der Straße treffen; ~ **into other hands** in andere Hände übergehen; ~ **the hat round** Geldsammlung veranstalten; ~ **to s. one's heirs** auf jds. Erben übergehen; ~ **the House of Commons** *(bill, Br.)* im Unterhaus angenommen werden; ~ **increased labo(u)r costs on to consumers** erhöhte Lohnkosten auf die Verbraucher abwälzen; ~ **an invoice** Rechnung gutheißen; ~ **an item to an account** Posten auf ein Konto verbuchen; ~ **an item of expenditure** Spesenrechnung genehmigen; ~ **judgment** Urteil fällen; ~ **a judgment for the plaintiff in a suit** Urteil zugunsten des Klägers erlassen; ~ **into law** zum Gesetz werden, Gesetzeskraft erhalten; ~ **for a liberal** für liberal gehalten werden; ~ **one's life in review** sein Leben im Geist Revue passieren lassen; ~ **off one's goods as those of another make** *(US)* seine Waren unter falschem Warenzeichen vertreiben; ~ **a measure through a committee** Ausschußresolution herbeiführen; ~ **for military service** für wehrdiensttauglich erklären; ~ **counterfeit money** Falschgeld in Umlauf setzen; ~ **a motion** [Gesetz]antrag annehmen; ~ **muster** Probe bestehen, für tauglich befunden werden, *(fig.)* Zustimmung finden; ~ **a name** *(stock exchange, London)* Abrechnungszettel zustellen; ~ **by the name of** unter dem Namen laufen (bekannt sein); ~ **into nothingness** der Vergessenheit anheimfallen; ~ **one's oath** sein Wort verpfänden; ~ **off** *(agitation)* sich legen; ~ **o. s. off as a doctor** sich als Arzt ausgeben; ~ **s. th. off as a joke** etw. als Witz hinstellen; ~ **off an awkward situation** unangenehme Situation überspielen; ~ **off well (smoothly)** glatt (gut) verlaufen; ~ **on** abwälzen, weitergeben, -leiten; ~ **s. th. on s. o.** jem. etw. aufhalsen; ~ **s. th. on to one's neighbo(u)r** dem Nachbarn weitergeben; ~ **on to a new subject** zu einem neuen Thema übergehen; ~ **on a warning to s. o.** jem. eine Warnung zukommen lassen; ~ **s. th. on to s. o.** etw. an jem. weiterleiten; ~ **on rising cost without becoming uncompetitive** gestiegene Kosten ohne Verschlechterung der Wettbewerbssituation weitergeben; ~ **on an order to s. o.** jem. eine Verfügung zustellen; ~ **an opinion** Meinung abgeben (äußern); ~ **out** *(pupil)* abgehen, *(US sl.)* in Ohnmacht fallen, ohnmächtig werden, umkippen; ~ **out highest** besten Abschluß machen; ~ **up an opportunity** Gelegenheit vorübergehen lassen; ~ **the oral** mündliche Prüfung bestehen; ~ **to the order of the day** zur Tagesordnung übergehen; ~ **over** auslassen; ~ **over an affront** Beleidigung übersehen; ~ **over in a ferry** in einer Fähre übersetzen; ~ **over s. one's land** jds. Grundstück betreten; ~ **over an obstacle** Hindernis überwinden; ~ **over in silence** mit Stillschweigen übergehen; ~ **into the ownership** als Eigentum übertragen; ~ **at par** zu Pari umlaufen; ~ **by Parliament** Vorlage im Gesetz durchlassen; ~ **into s. one's possession** in jds. Besitz übergehen; ~ **off quietly** *(meeting)* ruhig verlaufen; ~ **remarks on s. th.** Bemerkungen über etw. machen, etw. kommentieren; ~ **a resolution** Resolution (Entschließung) annehmen, Beschluß fassen; ~ **for rich** für reich gehalten werden; ~ **a river** Fluß überqueren; ~ **round to all the members of the family** bei allen Familienmitgliedern zirkulieren; ~ **by sale** *(title of goods)* beim Verkauf übergehen; ~ **the seal** durch das Staatssiegel beglaubigt werden; ~ **the Senate** *(US)* im Senat angenommen werden; ~ **sentence** Urteil verkünden, Strafurteil fällen; ~ **sentence on the accused** Angeklagten verurteilen; ~ **a station** Bahnhof durchfahren; ~ **a statute** Gesetz verabschieden; ~ **on a tax to s. o.** Steuer auf jem. abwälzen; ~ **a test** sich einem Test mit Erfolg unterziehen.

pass through | a country Land bereisen; ~ **a crisis** Krise durchlaufen, -machen; ~ **several hands** durch mehrere Hände gehen; ~ **the journal** Journal durchlaufen; ~ **hard times** schwierige Zeiten durchmachen; ~ **s. one's head** jem. durch den Kopf gehen; ~ **heavy trials** schwere Prüfungen zu bestehen haben.

pass | the time of the day with s. o. *(coll.)* sich mit jem. im Vorbeigehen unterhalten; ~ **a title** Eigentum übertragen; ~ **to** *(change hands)* in jds. Besitz übergehen, fallen an; ~ **a transfer** *(Br.)* Übertrag machen; ~ **troops in review** Truppenparade abnehmen; ~ **up** *(US sl.)* ablehnen, zurückweisen, *(student, sl.)* Mindestvorlesungszahl belegen; ~ **up a chance** Gelegenheit ungenutzt verstreichen lassen; ~ **up a ministerial office** Ministerium ablehnen; ~ **a vote of confidence** Vertrauen[svotum] aussprechen; ~ **one's word** sein Wort verpfänden;

to be on ~ *(mil.)* auf Kurzurlaub sein; **to be at a desperate ~** lebensgefährlich erkrankt sein; **to be waiting for the postman to ~** auf die Post warten; **to bring to ~** bewirken; **to come to ~** eintreten, geschehen; **to get a bare ~** gerade noch bestehen; **to get a ~ in an examination** Examen befriedigend bestehen; **to have come to a pretty ~** sich zugespitzt haben; **to have come to a sad ~** sich unglücklich entwickelt haben; **to hold the ~** Stellung halten, *(fig.)* für eine Sache eintreten; **to let ~** gelten lassen; **to let the appointed time ~** Frist verstreichen lassen; **to make a ~ to a woman** *(sl.)* Annäherungsversuche unternehmen; **to obtain a ~** Prüfung bestehen; **to sell the ~** *(fig.)* Sache verpfeifen;

do not ~ Überholen verboten;

~ book *(Br.)* Zollscheinheft; **~ check** *(US)* Passierschein, Eintrittskarte, Kontermarke; **~ degree** *(Br.)* unterster akademischer Grad, Diplom ohne besondere Auszeichnung; **~ duty** Durchgangszoll; **~ examination** *(Br.)* Universitätsschlußexamen; **~ office** Passierscheinstelle; **~-out check** *(theatre, Br.)* Kontermarke; **~ sheet** Grenzübertrittsschein für Kraftfahrzeuge, *(Br.)* Kontoauszug.

passable *(money)* gültig, gangbar, *(river)* schiffbar, *(road)* begehbar, befahrbar, passierbar;

~ by vehicles befahrbar;

~ knowledge of English annehmbare englische Sprachkenntnisse.

passably goods ziemlich gut.

passage *(Br.)* Durchgang, [Haus]flur, Korridor, Gang, *(airplane)* Flugreise, *(book)* [Text]stelle, Belegstelle, Passage, *(channel)* Fahrwasser, Kanal, *(crossing)* Überfahrt, Durchfahrt, Passage, *(easement)* freier Durchgang, *(fare)* Fahr-, Überfahrtsgeld, *(gallery)* Strecke, *(money)* Fahrgeld, -preis, *(negotiation)* Verhandlung, *(parl.)* Annahme [eines Gesetzes], Verabschiedung, *(river)* Furt, *(road)* Straße, Verbindungsgang, -straße, *(technics)* Durchlaß, -tritt, *(transit)* Durchreise, -fahrt, [Waren]transit, *(transition)* Übergang, *(voyage)* Seereise, -fahrt; -straße;

by ~ of time durch Zeitablauf; **on ~** unterwegs; **on his ~ home** auf seiner Heimreise;

~s Vertraulichkeiten;

air ~ Flug[reise]; **assisted ~** Reise-, Fahrgeldzuschuß; **covered ~** überdeckter Gang; **innocent ~** *(law of nations)* friedliche Durchfahrt; **melodic ~** *(music)* Notenfolge; **narrow ~** enge Durchfahrt; **no ~** Durchfahrt verboten; **nominated ~** *(Australia)* bezahlte Überfahrt für Einwanderer; **priority ~** vorrangiges Durchfahrtsrecht; **quick ~** schnelle Überfahrt; **rough ~** stürmische Überfahrt; **selected ~s** ausgewählte Stellen; **simple ~** *(law of nations)* bloße Durchfahrt; **smooth ~** ruhige Überfahrt; **underground ~** unterirdischer Gang;

~ of air Luftzufuhr; **~ of arms** Auseinandersetzung, Waffengang; **~ of a bill** Verabschiedung (Annahme) einer Gesetzesvorlage; **most touching ~s of a book** rührendste Szenen eines Buches; **~ through the canal** Durchfahrt durch den Kanal, Kanaldurchfahrt; **~ of confidence** Austausch verkäuflicher Nachrichten; **~ of current** Stromdurchgang; **~ of a front** Frontdurchgang; **~ of time** Zeitablauf; **~ of title** Eigentumsübergang;

~ (v.) Rededuell austragen;

to amend a ~ in a book Buchpassage abändern; **to book one's ~** seine Schiffskarte (Flugkarte) lösen; **to force a ~ through a crowd** sich einen Weg durch die Menge erzwingen; **to have angry ~s with an opponent in a debate** schweren Zusammenstoß mit einem Diskussionsteilnehmer haben; **to have a bad ~** schlechte Überfahrt haben; **to misquote a ~** Stelle falsch anführen; **to pay for one's ~** seine Überfahrt bezahlen; **to reword a ~** Passus neu formulieren; **to take one's ~ to New York** sich nach New York einschiffen; **to translate a ~ into English** Textstelle ins Englische übertragen; **to work one's ~** seine Überfahrt abarbeiten;

~ bird Zugvogel; **~ boat** Fährboot; **~ broker** *(Br.)* Auswanderungsagent; **~ contract** Beförderungsvertrag; **~ money** Überfahrtsgeld, Schiffspassagekosten.

passageway Durchgang, Korridor, Passage.

passbook *(Br.)* Konto[gegen]-, Sparkassen-, Einzahlungsbuch, *(customs, Br.)* Zollscheinheft, *(dealer)* Anschreibebuch, *(savings account)* Sparbuch;

customs ~ Carnet; **deposit ~** Sparkassenbuch;

~ entries Sparbucheintragungen; **~ register** Verzeichnis einer Bank über die von ihr ausgegebenen Kontobücher; **~ savings** Kontobuchersparnisse, Sparleistungen.

passe-partout Papprahmen, Klebestreifen, *(master key)* Hauptschlüssel;

~ frame Wechselrahmen.

passé veraltet, altmodisch.

passed *(bill)* verabschiedet, *(candidate)* mit Erfolg geprüft;

~ by the censor von der Zensur freigegeben; **~ without a dissentient voice** einstimmig angenommen;

to be ~ zur Genehmigung vorlegen; **to have ~ the chair** schon Präsident gewesen sein;

~ dividend *(US)* ausgefallene Dividende.

passenger Passagier, Reisender, Fahrgast, *(airplane)* Fluggast, *(incompetent member, sl.)* Schmarotzer;

aircraft ~ Fluggast; **cabin ~** Kajütenpassagier; **fellow ~** Mitreisender; **first-class ~** Passagier (Reisender) erster Klasse; **deck ~** Deckpassagier; **foot ~** Fußgänger; **full-fare paying ~** *(US)* vollen Flugpreis zahlender Linienfluggast; **individual ~** Einzelreisender; **public transit ~** Benutzer öffentlicher Verkehrsmittel; **regular ~** Dauerfahrgast; **revenue ~** zahlender Passagier; **regularly scheduled ~** *(US)* Fluggast einer Linienmaschine; **ship's ~** Schiffspassagier; **short-distance ~** Nahverkehrsteilnehmer; **steerage ~** Passagier dritter Klasse (der Touristenklasse), Zwischendeckpassagier; **through ~** Durchreisender; **tourist ~** Passagier der Touristenklasse;

~ in a car Mitfahrender;

to drop a ~ Fahrgast absetzen; **to offload ~s** Reisende aussteigen lassen; **to put down ~s** Fluggäste (Schiffsreisende) absetzen; **to seat a ~** Fluggast unterbringen; **to shepherd ~s to an airline** Passagiere zum Flugzeug geleiten; **to ship ~s** Passagiere (Flugreisende) befördern; **to take on (up) ~s** Schiffsreisende (Fluggäste) aufnehmen; **to transfer ~s from one class to another** Reisende in eine andere Klasse überwechseln lassen;

~ accident insurance Insassenunfallversicherung; **~ accommodation** Passagierräume; **~ account** Passagierverkehrskonto; **~ agent** *(tourist office, US)* Reiseagent, *(railroad, US)* Schalterbeamter; **~ aircraft** Passagierflugzeug; **~'s baggage** *(US)* Reisegepäck; **~ boarding** Passagiereinschiffung; **~ boat** Personendampfer; **~ cabin** Fluggastkabine; **~ capacity** Fluggastkapazität; **~ car** *(US)* *(carriage, Br.)* Personenwagen; **~ car production** *(US)* Personenwagenherstellung; **~ car registration** *(US)* Zulassung von Personenkraftwagen; **~ certificate** Zulassung zur Personenbeförderung; **~ check-in** Fluggastannahme; **~ coach** Personenwagen; **~ contract** Fahrtvertrag, Personenbeförderungsvertrag; **~ density** Passagierverkehrsdichte; **~ depot** *(US)* Personenbahnhof; **~ duty** Fahrkartensteuer; **~ elevator** *(US)* Personenaufzug; **~ fare** Personenfahrpreis; **~ goods** Passagiergut; **~ handling** Fluggastbetreuung; **~ kilometer (kilometre, Br.)** Personenkilometer, *(airplane)* Fluggastkilometer; **~ list** Passagierliste; **~ locomotive** *(US)* Personenzuglokomotive; **~'s luggage** *(Br.)* Reisegepäck, *(airplane)* Fluggepäck; **~ manager** Verkehrsdienstleiter; **~ mil(e)age** Beförderungsziffern; **~ plane** Verkehrsflugzeug; **~ railway carriage** *(Br.)* Personenwagen; **~ rates** Personentarif; **~ record** Passagierliste; **~ requirements** Fluggastbedürfnisse; **~ reservation** Flugreservierung; **~ revenue** Einkünfte aus dem Passagierverkehr; **~ seat** Beifahrersitz; **~ service** Passagier-, Personenbeförderung, -verkehr; **short-distance ~ service** Nahverkehrsbetrieb; **~ service charge** Fluggastgebühr; **~ ship** Fahrgastschiff; **~ space** Fahrgastraum; **~ station** Personenbahnhof; **~ steamer** Passagierdampfer; **~ tariff** Personen-, Beförderungstarif; **~ ticket** Fahrkarte, -schein, *(airplane)* Flugkarte, -schein, *(ship)* Schiffskarte; **~ traffic** Passagier-, Personenverkehr; **commutation ~ traffic** *(US)* Zeitkartenverkehr; **~ train** Personenzug; **by ~ train** als Eilgut; **to forward a box by ~ train** Kiste mit der Bahn schicken; **~-train service** Personenzugverkehr; **~ vessel** Personenfahrzeug.

passer-by Vorübergehender, Passant.

passing Durchgang, Furt, Paß, *(car, US)* Überholen, *(resolution)* Annahme, Verabschiedung;

in ~ im Vorbeigehen, beiläufig;

improper ~ falsches Überholen; **no ~** *(US)* Überholverbot;

~ away Versterben; **~ of a bill** Verabschiedung einer Gesetzesvorlage; **~ counterfeit money** Inumlaufsetzen von Falschgeld; **~ of a dividend** *(US)* Dividendenausfall; **~ off one's goods as those of another make** *(US)* Kennzeichenmißbrauch; **~ of a judgment** Urteilsverkündung; **~ on of an order** Weitergabe eines Auftrags; **~ to the order of the day** Übergang zur Tagesordnung; **~ of property** Eigentumsübergang; **~ of a resolution** Annahme (Verabschiedung) einer Resolution, Annahme einer Entschließung, Resolutionsannahme; **~ of risk** *(conveyance)* Gefahrübergang, *(insurance)* Risikoabwälzung; **~ through** Durchkommen, -wandern; **~ of title** Eigentumsübergang;

to be ~ through auf der Durchfahrt sein;

~ (a.) vorüber-, durchgehend, *(examination)* genügend, befriedigend;

~ bell Sterbe-, Totenglocke; **~ cyclist** vorbeifahrender Radfahrer; **~ events** Tagesereignisse, Aktualitäten; **~ grade** *(US)* befriedigende Note; **~ history** Zeitgeschichte; **~-off action** *(US)* Klage wegen unlauteren Wettbewerbs; **~-out ceremony** *(students)* Abschiedsfeier; **~-out list** Liste der Schulabgänger; **~ place** *(railway)* Ausweichstelle; **~ ticket** *(canal, Br.)* Zollquittung; **~ traveller** Durchreisender; **~ whim** seltsamer Einfall; **~ years** dahinschwindende Jahre.

passion Leidenschaft, heftige Gemütsbewegung, Zorn;
in the heat of ~ im Affekt;
~ for music Vorliebe für Musik; **~ for work** Arbeitswut; **to be filled with ~ for s. o.** große Schwäche für j. haben; **to fly into a ~** äußerst wütend werden, in Zorn geraten; **to have a ~ for painting** begeisterter Maler sein; **to put s. o. into a ~** j. in Wut bringen;
~ pit *(sl.)* Autokino; **~ Week** Passionswoche.

passiontide Passionszeit.

passive zurückhaltend, passiv, *(economics)* still, untätig, *(interest)* nicht zinstragend, unverzinslich;
~ bond unverzinsliche Schuldverschreibung; **~ commerce** Passivhandel; **~ debt** unverzinsliche Schuld; **~ obedience** passiver Widerstand; **~ resistance** passiver Widerstand; **~ resister** Widerstandskämpfer; **~ spectator** untätiger Zuschauer; **~ title** Passivlegitimation; **~ trade** Passiv-, Einfuhrhandel; **~ trade balance** *(US)* passive Handelsbilanz; **~ trust** Treuhand ohne Verwaltungsfunktion; **~ voice** *(Gr.)* Passivum.

passivism Teilnahmslosigkeit, Passivität.

passkey Hauptschlüssel, Drücker.

passman *(university)* Durchschnittskandidat.

passout *(theatre)* Kontermarke.

passover system *(antitrust law, US)* Finanzausgleich zwischen einzelnen Händlern.

passport Reisepaß, *(international law)* Schiffspaß, Geleitschein, *(maritime law)* Seepaß, *(licence to pass goods)* Erlaubnisschein, *(US)* Passierschein;
collective ~ Sammelpaß; **diplomatic ~** Diplomatenpaß; **hard-to-get ~** schwer zu erlangender Paß; **official ~** Amtspaß; **ship's ~** Seepaß; **valid ~** gültiger Paß;
~ (v.) mit einem Paß versehen;
to amend a ~ Paß abändern; **to apply for a ~** Paß beantragen; **to deprive s. o. of his ~** jem. den Reisepaß entziehen; **to examine a ~** Paß prüfen, Paßrevision durchführen; **to extend a ~** Paß verlängern; **to forge a ~** Paßfälschung begehen; **to issue a ~** Paß ausstellen (ausgeben); **to make out a ~ for s. o.** Reisepaß für j. ausstellen; **to make false statements for procuring a ~** falsche Angaben zur Erlangung eines Passes machen; **to renew a ~** Paß verlängern; **to show a ~** Paß vorzeigen; **to stamp a ~** Paß abstempeln; **to take out a ~** sich einen Paß verschaffen;
money is a ~ to everything Geld öffnet alle Türen;
~ application Paßantrag; **~ application form** Paßantragsformular; **~ control** Paßkontrolle; **~ division** Paßabteilung; **~ fee** Paß[ausstellungs]gebühr; **~ forgery** Paßfälschung; **~ formalities** Paßförmlichkeiten; **~ holder** Paßinhaber, -besitzer, -eigentümer; **~ inspection** Paßkontrolle; **~ provisions** Paßbestimmungen; **~ office** Paßstelle; **~ officer** Paßbeamter; **~ people** Beamter der Paßkontrolle; **~ photograph** Paßfoto; **to withhold tentatively ~ privileges** Paß vorübergehend außer Kraft setzen; **~ provisions** Paßbestimmungen; **~ requirement** Paßzwang; **~ system** Paßwesen.

passway Engpaß.

password Kennwort, Losung, Parole.

past verflossen, abgelaufen, ehemalig;
~ due überfällig;
to be ~ caring what happens an den Ereignissen seiner Umwelt nicht mehr teilnehmen;
~ bill überfälliger Wechsel; **~ consideration** bereits erbrachte Gegenleistung; **~ cure** unheilbar; **~-due interest** Verzugszinsen; **~ generations** vergangene Generationen; **~ history** *(coll.)* olle Kamellen; **~ president** früherer Präsident; **~ tense** *(gr.)* Vergangenheit; **~ year** vergangenes Jahr.

paste Klebstoff, Kleister;
to be of another ~ von ganz anderem Schlag sein;
~ (v.) up a placard Plakat aufkleben; **~ the notice up on the wall** Bekanntmachung an die Wand kleben;
~-on-label Aufklebeadresse; **~ up** Schrift-, Bildmontage; **~ water** *(bookbinding)* dünner Kleister.

pasteboard Pappe, Pappdeckel, Karton, *(sl.)* Eintritts-, Fahr-, Visitenkarte;
~ binding Pappband.

pastedown *(bookbinding)* Vorsatz.

pasting *(bookbinding)* Klebstoff.

pastoral ländlich, idyllisch, *(religion)* seelsorgerisch;
~ letter Hirtenbrief.

pastry Backwerk, Konditorware;
~ cook Konditor.

pasturage Weiderecht.

pasture Weide[land], Trift;
common ~ Weiderecht;
~ (v.) weiden, grasen;
~ one's sheep on the village common seine Schafe auf dem Dorfanger weiden lassen;
to put out to ~ auf die Weide treiben.

pastureland, high alpine Hochgebirgsalm.

pat Schlag, Klaps;
~ on the back *(Br.)* lobender Zuspruch, Eloge;
~ (v.) o. s. on the back sich beweihräuchern; **~ s. o. on the shoulder** jem. auf die Schulter klopfen;
~ (a.) prompt, parat, bereit;
to give s. o. a ~ on the back jem. Elogen sagen; **to have it down ~** etw. wie am Schnürchen können; **to have one's excuse ~** Entschuldigung parat halten; **to stand ~** bei seinem Entschluß bleiben.

patch Flicken, *(book)* Stück, Stelle, Abschnitt, *(of land)* Stückchen Land, *(mar.)* kleine Eisscholle;
in ~es stellenweise;
~es of fog Nebelfetzen; **not a ~ on** nicht im Entferntesten so gut; **~ of blue sky** Stückchen blauer Himmel;
~ (v.) a motorcycle Motorrad zurechtflicken; **~ off** abblättern; **~ together** zusammenflicken; **~ up** zusammenstoppeln;
to be good in ~es *(book)* stellenweise gut sein; **to strike a bad ~** Pechsträhne haben.

patched-up | motor cycle zusammengeflicktes Motorrad; **~ peace** zusammengestoppelter Friede; **~ quarrel** mühsam beigelegter Streit.

patcher Stümper, Pfuscher.

patchery Flickarbeit.

patchword Flickwort.

patchwork zusammengestückeltes Flick-, Stückwerk;
~ peace zusammengestoppelter Friede.

patchy *(book)* ungleich geschrieben, zusammengestoppelt;
to be ~ Flickwerk sein.

patent Patent[urkunde], *(letters patent)* Privileg, Freibrief, Bestallung, *(licence)* Konzession, *(territory, US)* Landgewährung;
covered by a ~ patentrechtlich geschützt, patentgeschützt;
additional ~ *(Br.)* Zusatzpatent; **~ alive** bestehender Patentschutz; **~ applied for** angemeldetes Patent; **~ barred** verweigerte Patenterteilung; **basic ~** grundlegendes Patent; **blanket ~** umfassendes Patent; **blocking-off ~** Sperrpatent; **clean ~** einwandfreies Patent; **complete ~** endgültiges Patent; **confirmation ~** Bestätigungspatent; **conflicting ~** strittiges Patent; **defective ~** mangelhaftes Patent; **design ~** *(US)* Gebrauchs-, Geschmacksmuster; **device ~** Vorrichtungspatent; **earlier ~** früher eingereichtes Patent; **expired ~** abgelaufenes (erloschenes) Patent; **fencing-in ~** Einkreisungspatent; **improvement ~** Verbesserungs-, Vervollkommnungspatent; **independent ~** Hauptpatent; **interfering ~** Kollisionspatent; **~ issued** erteiltes Patent; **joint ~** Gemeinschaftspatent; **land ~** *(US)* Landzuweisung; **lapsed ~** abgelaufenes (verfallenes) Patent; **later-dated ~** Nachpatent; **letters ~** Erfindungs-, Patenturkunde; **litigious ~** strittiges Patent; **main ~** Hauptpatent; **master ~** Grundpatent; **mate's ~s** Schifferpatent für kleine Fahrt; **original ~** Haupt-, Stammpatent; **~ pending** angemeldetes Patent; **petty ~** *(US)* Gebrauchsmuster; **pioneer ~** Stammpatent, bahnbrechendes (grundlegendes) Patent; **prior ~** älteres Patent, Vorzugspatent; **process ~** Verfahrenspatent; **reissue ~** Abänderungspatent; **related ~** Bezugspatent; **secret ~** Geheimpatent; **shotgun ~** *(US)* Wegelagererpatent; **single ~** Einzelpatent; **subsequent ~** jüngeres Patent, Nachpatent; **~ sued upon** angefochtenes Patent; **supplemental ~** Zusatzpatent; **unexpired ~** noch nicht abgelaufenes Patent; **universal ~** Weltpatent; **utility ~** *(US)* Verwertungspatent; **valid ~** gültiges Patent;
~ of addition *(Br.)* Zusatzpatent; **~ in force** gültiges Patent; **~ of gentility** *(fam.)* Zeichen von Liebenswürdigkeit; **~ of improvement** Verbesserungs-, Vervollkommnungspatent; **~ for invention** Erfindungspatent; **~ of nobility** *(Br.)* Adelsbrief;
~ (v.) (grant a patent) patentieren, Patent erteilen, *(take out a patent)* Patent nehmen, sich etw. patentieren lassen;
~ an invention Erfindung zum Patent anmelden;
to abandon a ~ Patent verfallen lassen, auf ein Patent verzichten; **to acquire a ~ compulsorily** Patent enteignen; **to annul a ~** Patent für null und nichtig erklären; **to apply for a ~** Patent

anmelden; **to assign a** ~ **Patent** übertragen; **to attack a** ~ Patent anfechten; **to base a** ~ **on a discovery** Patent auf eine Erfindung stützen; **to be entitled to a** ~ auf ein Patent Anspruch haben; **to be put up for a** ~ zum Patent angemeldet sein; **to cancel a** ~ Patent im Register löschen; **to circumvent a** ~ Patent umgehen; **to defeat the right to a** ~ Patentanspruch zu Fall bringen; **to derive benefits from a** ~ Patenteinkünfte haben; **to drop a** ~ Patent [ver]fallen lassen; **to exploit a** ~ Patent verwerten; **to extend [the terms of] a** ~ Patentfrist verlängern; **to file an application for a** ~ **abroad** Patentanmeldung im Ausland einreichen, Auslandspatent anmelden; **to form a sound basis for a** ~ Patentgrundlage abgeben; **to give notice of a** ~ Patent anmelden; **to grant a** ~ patentieren, Patent erteilen; **to hold a** ~ Patent besitzen; **to infringe a** ~ Patent verletzen; **to invalidate a** ~ Patentanspruch verwirken; **to issue a** ~ Patent ausstellen (erteilen); **to keep a** ~ **alive** Patent in Geltung erhalten; **to lodge an opposition to a** ~ Patentwiderspruch anmelden; **to maintain a** ~ **in force** Patentanspruch aufrechterhalten; **to obtain a** ~ Patent [zugesprochen] erhalten; **to oppose a** ~ Patent anfechten; **to put up for a** ~ Patent anmelden; **to reduce a** ~ **to practice** Patent praktisch verwerten; **to refuse a** ~ Patent versagen, Patenterteilung ablehnen; **to reissue a** ~ *(US)* Patentschrift neu ausgeben; **to revoke a** ~ Patentrechtsanspruch aufheben, Patent für nichtig erklären; **to seek a** ~ um ein Patent einkommen; **to shelve a** ~ Patent ungenutzt lassen; **to sue s. o. for infringement of a** ~ Patentklage gegen j. erheben; **to surrender a** ~ Patent aufgeben; **to take out a** ~ Patent erhalten, sich patentieren lassen; **to take out a** ~ **to protect a new invention** Erfindung patentieren lassen, Patent auf eine Erfindung nehmen; **to withhold the grant of a** ~ Patent versagen; **to work a** ~ Patent ausüben (verwerten);

~ *(a.) (manifest)* offenkundig, offensichtlich, *(patented)* gesetzlich geschützt, patentiert, *(privileged)* mit offiziellen Privilegien ausgestattet;

℠ **Act** *(Br.)* Patentgesetz; ~ **administration department** Patentverwaltungsabteilung; ~ **advantage** offensichtlicher Vorteil; ~ **advertising** Patentberühmung; **chartered** ~ **agent** *(Br.)* zugelassener Patentanwalt; ~ **ambiguity** *(law)* offener Dissens; ~ **annuity** Patentjahresgebühr; ~ **appeal** Patenteinspruch; ℠ **Appeal Tribunal** *(Br.)* Patentberufungsgericht; ~ **applicant** Patentanmelder; ~ **application** Patentanmeldung; ~ **appointment** Patentsachbearbeiterstelle; ~ **article** Markenartikel; ~ **assignment** Abtretung von Patentrechten; ~ **attorney** *(US)* Patentanwalt; ~ **award** Patentgutachten; ~ **bar** *(US)* Patentanwaltschaft; ~ **broker** Patentmakler; ~ **business** Patentschutzverfahren, -streit; ~ **case** Patentfall, -angelegenheit; ~ **charges** Patentkosten; ~ **claim** Patentanspruch; **to assert a** ~ **claim** Patentanspruch verteidigen; ℠ **Compensation Board** *(US)* Patententschädigungsamt; ~ **convention** Patentvereinbarung; ~ **and established crime** nachgewiesenes Verbrechen; ~ **defect** offensichtlicher Fehler, offener Mangel; ~ **defects** Patentmängel; ~ **department** Patentabteilung; ~ **description** Patentbeschreibung; ~ **device** Patentvorrichtung; ~ **document** öffentliche Urkunde; ~ **drawing** Patentzeichnung; ~ **engineer** Patentspezialist; ~ **examiner** Patentprüfer; ~ **exchange contract** Patentaustauschvertrag; ~ **exploitation** Patentverwertung, -ausübung; ~ **facts** feststehende Tatsachen; ~ **fee** patentamtliche Gebühr, Patentgebühr; ~ **filing** Patentschrift; ~ **foods** Markennahrungsmittel; ~ **fuel** Presskohle; ~ **goods** Markenartikel; ~ **holder** Patentbesitzer, -inhaber; ~ **infringement** Patentverletzung; ~ **infringement proceedings** Patentverletzungsverfahren; ~ **insides** nur einseitig bedruckte Zeitungsblätter für Lokalnachrichten; ~ **invention** Patenterfindung; ~ **law** Patentrecht; ~ **laws** Patentgesetzgebung; ~ **law amendment** Patentänderungsgesetz; ~ **law firm** Patentanwaltskanzlei, -büro; ~ **lawyer** Patentanwalt; ~ **leather** Lackleder; ~ **legislation** Patentgesetzgebung; ~ **licence** Patentlizenz; ~ **licence agreement** Patentlizenzabkommen; ~ **licensing** Patentvergabe; ~**'s life** Patentdauer; ~ **litigation** Patentstreit; ~ **marking** Patentkennzeichnung; ~ **matter** Patentangelegenheit; ~ **medicine** warenzeichenrechtlich geschütztes Arzneimittel; ~ **misuse** Patentmißbrauch; ~ **monopoly** Monopolpatent; ~ **number** Patentnummer; ~ **offence** feststehendes Verbrechen; ~ **office** Patentamt; **International** ℠ **Office at the Hague** Internationales Patentamt; **to deposit at (lodge with) the** ~ **office** beim Patentamt niederlegen; **to be recognized to practise before the** ℠ **Office** *(US)* als Anwalt beim Patentamt zugelassen sein; ~ **office journal** Patentblatt; ~**-office procedure** Patentverfahren; ~ **owner** Patentinhaber, -besitzer; ~ **pool** *(US)* Patentkartell; ~ **property** Patentbesitz; ~ **recipe** Patentrezept; ~ **reform** Reform der Patentgesetzgebung; ~ **register** *(US)* Patentrolle; ~**-related**

work patentähnliche Tätigkeit; ~ **right** Erfinder-, Patentrecht, Patentanspruch; **to infringe on a** ~ **right** Patentrecht verletzen; **to observe** ~ **rights** Patentschutz gewähren; **to remove** ~ **rights** Patentrechte aufheben; ~**-right dealer** Patentmakler; ~ **rolls** *(Br.)* Patentregister, -rolle; ~ **royalty** Patentgebühr; ~ **royalties received** vereinnahmte Patenterträge; ℠ **Rules** *(Br.)* (℠ **Rules of Practice,** *US*) patentamtliche Vorschriften, Ausführungsbestimmungen zum Patentgesetz; ~ **situation** Patentlage; ~ **solicitor** Patentanwalt; ~ **specification** Patentbeschreibung, -schrift; ~ **suit** Patentstreit, -prozeß; ~ **system** Patentwesen; ~ **tax** Patentsteuer; ~ **value** Patentwert; **to have a** ~ **way of doing s. th.** *(fam.)* Patentverfahren für etw. haben.

patentable patentierbar, patentfähig;
  ~ **invention** patentfähige Erfindung.

patented durch Patent (patentrechtlich) geschützt, patentiert, gesetzlich geschützt;
  ~ **article** patentiertes Erzeugnis, Patentgegenstand, Markenartikel; ~ **process** patentiertes Verfahren; **to be manufactured by a** ~ **process** nach einem Patentverfahren hergestellt sein; ~ **product** patentiertes Erzeugnis.

patentee Patentinhaber, -träger;
  former (prior) ~ Patentvorgänger, früherer Patentinhaber; **intended** ~ Patentanmelder; **joint** ~ Patentmitinhaber; **sole** ~ alleiniger Patentinhaber.

patentor Patentgeber, -verleiher.

paterfamilias Familienoberhaupt.

paternal|authority väterliche (elterliche) Gewalt; ~ **care** väterliche Fürsorge; ~ **power** väterliche Gewalt; ~ **property** väterliches Vermögen; ~ **side** Abstammung auf der Vaterseite.

paternalism väterliche Fürsorge, *(plant)* paternalistische Betriebsführung.

paternity Vaterschaft, *(fig.)* Urheberschaft;
  ~ **unknown** unbekannter Abstammung;
  to acknowledge the ~ **of a child** Vaterschaft eines Kindes anerkennen; **to admit the** ~ **of a book** sich als Autor eines Buches bekennen; **to deny** ~ Vaterschaft ableugnen; **to determine s. one's** ~ jds. Vaterschaft feststellen;
  ~ **case** *(US)* Vaterschaftsprozeß; ~ **suit** *(US)* Vaterschaftsprozeß; ~ **test** *(US)* Vaterschaftsfeststellung, Blutgruppenuntersuchung.

paternoster Paternoster.

path Weg, Pfad;
  beaten ~ ausgetretener Pfad; **cycle** ~ Radfahrweg; **marked-out** ~ bezeichneter Wanderweg; ~ **of current** Stromweg; ~ **of duty** Weg der Pflicht; ~ **of economy** Volkswirtschaftstrend, Konjunkturverlauf; ~ **of a storm** Bahn eines Sturms;
  to cross s. one's ~ jds. Weg kreuzen; **to follow the** ~ **of glory** nach Ruhm dürsten.

patience Geduld, Ausdauer, Langmut;
  ~ **of Job** unendliche Geduld;
  ~ *(v.)* Geduld üben;
  to be out of ~ **with s. o.** über j. aufgebracht sein; **to exhaust s. one's** ~ jds. Geduld erschöpfen; **to get out of** ~ seine Geduld verlieren; **to have no** ~ **with s. o.** j. nicht ausstehen können; **to possess one's soul in** ~ sich in Geduld üben; **to tax (try) s. one's** ~ jds. Geduld strapazieren.

pathfinder *(fig.)* Bahnbrecher, *(US, police)* Polizeispitzel.

patient Kranker, Patient, *(Br.)* Geisteskranker;
  to discharge a ~ Patienten entlassen; **to visit one's** ~**s** seine Patienten besuchen;
  ~ *(a.)* geduldig, nachsichtig, diszipliniert;
  to be ~ **of adversity** Schicksalsschläge geduldig hinnehmen; **to be** ~ **of misery** Beleidigungen geduldig ertragen; **to be** ~ **of two interpretations** zwei Auslegungen zulassen.

patio Licht-, Innenhof.

patrial *(Br.)* mit Staatsangehörigkeitsrechten ausgestattet.

patriarch Patriarch.

patriarchal patriarchalisch.

patrician Patrizier, Mensch von Kultur;
  ~**s** Patriziertum;
  ~ *(fig.)* aristokratisch, aus gutem Hause.

patrimonial ererbt.

patrimony väterliches Erbteil.

patriot Patriot.

patriotic patriotisch;
  ~ **stock** *(Br.)* an Devisenausländer zu Kriegszeiten ausgegebene steuerfreie Wertpapiere.

patriotism Patriotismus, Vaterlandsliebe.

patrol Runde, *(mil.)* Patrouille, Späh-, Stoßtrupp, *(police)* [Polizei]streife;

Automobile Association *(A.A.)* ⚥ [etwa] Streifenfahrzeug des ADAC; **coast** ~ Küstenwache; **police** ~ Polizeistreife;
~ *(v.)* patrouillieren, Streife gehen, Runde machen;
~ **the line** Seegebiet laufend überwachen; ~ **the parks** städtische Anlagen schützen; ~ **the streets** Streifendienst auf den Straßen durchführen;
to be (go) on ~ seine Runde gehen, auf Streife sein, abpatrouillieren; **to maintain a constant air** ~ Luftraum laufend überwachen;
~ **boat** Vorpostenboot; ~ **car** Streifenwagen; ~ **craft** Vorpostenboot; ~ **flight** Patrouillenflug; ~ **force** Funkstreifeneinsatzkräfte; ~ **leader** Streifen-, Patrouillenführer; ~ **mission** Patrouillenflug; ~ **seaplane** Patrouillenflugzeug der Marine; **ice** ~ **service** Eiswachdienst; ~ **vessel** Küstenwachboot; ~ **waggon** *(protective association, Br.)* patrouillierendes Auto, *(US)* Gefängnis-, Gefangenentransportwagen, Grüne Minna.
patrolman *(US)* Polizist im Streifendienst, Streifengänger, -polizist;
~ **of the AA** *(Br.)* [etwa] Mechaniker des ADAC;
~ **vessel** Küstenwachboot.
patron *(arch.)* Atelierleiter, *(protector)* Förderer, Gönner, Mäzen, Schutzherr, Schirmherr, Wohltäter, *(restaurant)* Stammgast, *(of ship)* Schiffsherr, *(in private school)* Förderer, *(shop)* Stammkunde, Klient, *(theater)* Besucher;
for ~**s only** Parken nur für Kunden;
hospital's ~ Krankenhausmäzen; **regular** ~ Stammkunde;
~ **of the fine arts** Förderer der schönen Künste; ~**s of the drama** Theaterpublikum;
~ *(v.)* unterstützen, fördern;
~ **saint** Schutzheiliger.
patronage Wohlwollen, Gunst, Patronage, Protektion, Gönnerschaft, Mäzenatentum, Schirmherrschaft, *(financial subsistence)* Unterstützung, *(pol., US)* Stellenvergabe, Ernennungsrecht, Ämterpatronage, *(shop, coll.)* Kundschaft, Besucherkreis, Klientele, regelmäßige Einkäufer;
under the ~ **of the mayor** unter den Auspizien (der Schirmherrschaft) des Bürgermeisters;
state ~ Schirmherrschaft durch die Regierung;
to confer one's ~ **upon an undertaking** einem Unternehmen seine Unterstützung angedeihen lassen; **to extend one's** ~ **to s. o.** jem. seine Gunst gewähren; **to have a select** ~ vornehme Kundschaft haben;
~ **discount** *(US)* Rabatt für Stammkunden, Treuerabatt; ~ **dividend** *(US)* Rabattmarke, Rückvergütung; ~ **refund** *(US)* Kundenrabatt; ~ **secretary** *(Br.)* Parlamentssekretär des Premierministers; ~ **system** Vetternwirtschaft.
patronization Unterstützung, regelmäßiger Besuch.
patronize *(v.)* [als Kunde (häufig)] besuchen, *(other countries)* gönnerhaft behandeln, *(favo(u)r)* begünstigen, protektionieren, fördern, unterstützen, *(restaurant)* Stammgast sein;
~ **a cinema** Kino frequentieren.
patronizer Gönner, Förderer, Wohltäter, *(client)* regelmäßiger Kunde, Stammkunde, *(restaurant)* Stammgast.
patronizing gönnerhaft;
~ **air** Gönnermiene.
patter Geplapper, *(street vendor)* marktschreierisches Anpreisen;
thieves' ~ Gaunersprache, Rotwelsch;
~ *(v.)* plappern, schwatzen.
pattern *(coinage)* Probemodell, *(excellent example)* Muster[exemplar], *(model)* Muster, Modell, Vorlage, Schema, Schablone, *(sample)* Warenprobe, *(structure)* Struktur, Gefüge, *(technics)* Gußmodell;
according to ~ nach Muster (Probe), mustergetreu; **as per** ~ **enclosed** laut beiliegender Qualitätsprobe; **by** ~ nach Muster;
behavio(u)r ~ Verhaltensweise; **dress (paper)** ~ Schnittmuster; **dressmaker's** ~ Schnittmuster, *(pattern)* gewohntes Verfahren; **frost** ~ Eisblumenmuster; **historical** ~ historische Gesetzmäßigkeiten; **holding** ~ *(airplane)* Warteschleife; **landing** ~ *(airplane)* Platzrunde; **open** ~ ungeschütztes Muster; **reference** ~ Ausfallmuster; **registered** ~ Gebrauchsmuster; **repeated** ~ wiederkehrendes Muster; **set** ~ festes Schema; **standard** ~ Einheitsmuster; **uniform** ~ einheitliches Modell;
~ **of benefit** Versorgungsmodell; ~ **of consumption** Verbrauchsstruktur einer Ware; ~ **of financial consumption** Endnachfragestruktur; ~ **of education** Bildungsstruktur; ~ **of expenditure** Ausgabengestaltung, -struktur; ~ **of forces** Kräftebild; ~ **of interrogation** Befragungsschema, -instruktionen; ~ **of investment** Investitionsschema; **familiar** ~ **of life** vertraute Lebensgewohnheit; **new** ~**s of family life** neue Formen des Familienlebens; ~ **of organization** Organisationsschema, -typ;

~ **of roses** *(wallpaper)* Rosenmuster; ~ **of trade** Handelsstrom, -struktur; ~ **of working** Arbeitsrezept;
~ *(v.)* bemustern, mit Mustern versehen, *(copy)* nachbilden, kopieren;
~ **on** ausrichten nach; ~ **s. one's conduct** sich ein Beispiel an jem. nehmen;
to arrange ~**s** Muster zusammenstellen; **to be a** ~ **of virtue** Ausbund der Tugend sein; **to be according to an established** ~ übliche Verfahrensregeln einhalten; **to be essentially of the same** ~ *(novels)* gleichen Aufbau aufweisen; **not to be up to** ~ dem Muster nicht entsprechen; **to call off a holding** ~ *(airplane)* von einer Wartebahn abrufen; **to change the demand** ~ Umstrukturierung der Nachfrage hervorrufen; **to circle on a landing** ~ *(airplane)* Platzrunde fliegen, Landeschleife ziehen; **to correspond to** ~ dem Muster entsprechen; **to decide on a** ~ sich auf ein Muster festlegen; **to have a look at the** ~**s** Muster einsehen; **to put on a holding** ~ *(airplane)* auf Wartebahn schicken; **to reshape business** ~**s** Modellformen in der Wirtschaft umgestalten; **to take s. o. as a** ~ sich j. als Beispiel wählen; **to wait on with** ~**s** Muster vorführen; **to work from a** ~ nacharbeiten, nach einem Muster arbeiten;
~ **agreement** Modellabkommen, -tarif; ~ **articles** Massenware; ~**bomb** *(v.)* mit einem Bombenteppich belegen; ~ **bombing** Flächenbombardierung; ~ **book** Musterbuch; ~ **card** Musterkarte; ~ **design** Probemodell, Schablone; ~ **designer** Modellzeichner; ~ **drawer** Muster-, Modellzeichner; ~ **maker** Modellmacher, -schlosser; ~ **making** Modellanfertigung, -bau; ~ **man** Musterreisender; ~ **painting** *(mil.)* Tarnanstrich; ~ **parcel** Mustersendung; ~ **plate** Maternklischee; **by** ~ **post** als Muster ohne Wert; ~ **pupil** Musterschüler; ~ **reference** Ausfallmuster, Warenprobe; ~ **shop** Modellwerkstätte; ~ **son** Mustersohn; ~ **and practice suit** Musterprozeß; ~ **wife** perfekte Ehefrau.
patterned gemustert;
large-~ mit großem Muster, großgemustert;
~ **sample** Probestück, schematische Stichprobenauswahl.
paucity | **of money** Geldmangel; ~ **of news** kaum neue Nachrichten; ~ **of words** Wortarmut.
pauper Armer, *(US)* Unterstützungsempfänger, *(suitor, US)* im Armenrecht klagende Partei;
~ *(v.)* bettelarm machen;
~ **asylum** Obdachlosen-, Armenasyl; ~ **burial** Armenbegräbnis; ~ **children** Bettelkinder; ~ **costs** *(US)* Armenrechtskosten; ~ **grave** Armengrab; ~ **legislation** Armengesetzgebung; ~ **petition** *(US)* Armenrechtsantrag; ~ **relief** Armenunterstützung; ~**'s right** *(US)* Armenrecht.
pauperis, to sue in forma *(US)* im Armenrecht klagen;
to petition for leave ~ Antrag auf Erteilung des Armenrechts stellen.
pauperage Dauerarmut.
pauperism Verarmung, Massenarmut.
pauperization totale Verarmung;
~ **theory** Verelendungstheorie.
pauperize *(v.)* bettelarm (zum Wohlfahrtsempfänger) machen.
pause Pause, Unterbrechung, Zögern, *(print.)* Gedankenstrich, *(rest)* Betriebs-, Ruhepause, *(shift)* Schicht;
~ **to take breath** Atempause; ~ **in the conversation** Gesprächspause, -stille;
~ *(v.)* stehenbleiben, pausieren;
~ **at the door** sich kurz an der Tür aufhalten; ~ **at every shop window** bei jeder Schaufensterauslage stehenbleiben;
to make a ~ pausieren, innehalten;
~ **dots** Auslassungspunkte.
pave *(v.)* pflastern;
~ **the way** *(fig.)* Weg bereiten (bahnen); ~ **the way to fame for s. o.** Ruhmesweg für j. vorbereiten.
paved | **with good intentions** mit guten Vorsätzen gepflastert;
~ **road** Pflasterstraße.
pavement Straßenpflaster, *(Br.)* Bürgersteig, Trottoir, Fußweg, -steig, *(US)* gepflasterte Straße, Fahrbahn, *(interior floor)* Fußboden;
marble ~ Marmorfußboden;
to be on the ~ *(fam.)* in Sicherheit sein;
~ **artist** Pflastermaler; ~ **cafe** Boulevardrestaurant.
pavilion Pavillon, Gartenhäuschen, *(exhibition)* Ausstellungszelt, -gebäude, -pavillon.
paving Straßenpflaster;
~ **of streets** Straßendecke;
~ **rate** Straßenunkostenbeitrag; ~ **stone** Pflasterstein; ~ **tile** Fliese, Kachel.
paw Pfote, Tatze, *(coll.)* Klaue, schlechte Handschrift.

pawl Sperrklinke.

pawn Pfand[stück], Pfandgegenstand, -objekt, -sache, Faustpfand, *(bailment of goods)* Verpfändung, *(figurehead)* Strohmann, Marionette;
by ~ pfandweise; **in (at) ~** verpfändet;
~ (v.) versetzen, verpfänden, zum Pfand setzen, *(Br., securities)* lombardieren;
~ one's hono(u)r seine Ehre verpfänden; **~ one's life** sein Leben einsetzen;
to advance money on ~s gegen Pfandbestellung vorschießen; **to be in ~** beim Pfandleiher sein; **to deliver for ~** verpfänden; **to give in ~** verpfänden; **to hold in ~** als Pfand behalten; **to keep in ~** Pfand halten; **to lend on ~s** Darlehn gegen Pfandbestellung gewähren; **to put in ~** verpfänden, ins Leihhaus (Pfandhaus) tragen, versetzen; **to redeem a ~** Pfand auslösen; **to take in ~** zum Pfand nehmen; **to take out of ~** Pfand einlösen;
~ money Pfandgebühr; **~ office** Pfandleihanstalt; **~ taking** Pfandnahme; **~ ticket** Pfandschein.

pawnable versetzbar, verpfändbar, *(stocks)* lombardfähig.

pawnage Verpfändung.

pawnbroker Pfand[ver]leiher, -hausbesitzer;
~ Act *(Br.)* Pfandleihgesetz; **~'s business (shop)** Pfandleihe, Leihhaus, -amt.

pawnbrokery, pawnbroking Pfandleihgeschäft, -leihe.

pawned|bill of exchange verpfändeter Wechsel; **~ object** Pfandsache, -gegenstand; **~ stock** *(Br.)* [bei einer Bank] lombardierte Wertpapiere.

pawnee Pfandnehmer, -gläubiger.

pawner (pawnor) Pfandleiher, -schuldner, -geber, Verpfänder.

pawning Pfandbestellung, Verpfändung, *(securities)* Lombardierung.

pawnshop Pfand-, Leihhaus, Pflandleihanstalt.

pay *(mil.)* Besoldung, Wehrsold, *(payment)* Bezahlung, *(remuneration)* Entgelt, Vergütung, Entschädigung, *(reward)* Belohnung, *(salary)* Gehalt, Dotierung, *(ship)* Heuer, *(wages)* [Arbeits]lohn, Löhnung, Sold, Besoldung, Entlohnung;
in the ~ of beschäftigt (angestellt) bei; **in the ~ of the enemy** vom Gegner als Spion bezahlt; **more to ~** nicht genügend frankiert; **without ~** unbezahlt;
active service ~ Wehrsold; **additional ~** Gehaltsaufbesserung, -zulage, Geldzuschuß; **back ~** Gehalts-, Lohnrückstand, *(US)* Gehaltsnachzahlung; **basic ~** Grundgehalt, -lohn; **building trades ~** Löhne im Baugewerbe; **call-back ~** zusätzliche Vergütung für außerplanmäßige Arbeit; **civil service ~** Beamtengehalt; **deadheading ~** Wegegeld; **disablement ~** Auszahlung der Invalidenrente; **dismissal ~** Entlassungsabfindung, -ausgleich, Entschädigungssumme; **not enough ~** unzureichende Bezahlung; **equal ~** gleiche Entlohnung; **extra ~** Zulage, Lohnzuschlag; **final ~** *(pension scheme)* auf das letzte Gehalt abgestellte Rentenzahlung; **full ~** volles Gehalt; **gross ~** Bruttogehalt, -bezüge; **half ~** Wartegeld; **holiday ~** doppelte Entlohnung für Arbeit an gesetzlichen Feiertagen; **insufficient ~** ungenügende Bezahlung; **leave ~** Urlaubsbezahlung, -geld; **longevity ~** altersbedingte Gehaltserhöhung; **lost ~** Lohnausfall; **make-up ~** *(US)* Akkordzuschlag; **military ~** Wehrsold; **minimum call ~** *(US)* Mindestlohn für nur stundenweise Tätigkeit; **monthly ~** Monatsgehalt; **one year's ~** ein Jahresgehalt; **overdue ~** rückständiges Gehalt; **overtime ~** Überstundenzuschlag; **public sector ~** Entlohnung im Bereich der öffentlichen Hand; **regular ~** Grundgehalt; **retired ~** *(mil.)* Pension; **retirement ~** Pension[szahlung]; **severance ~** Entlassungsabfindung; **sick ~** Krankengeld; **strike ~** Streiklohn, -geld; **takehome ~** Nettogehalt, *(profit taken)* mitgenommener Gewinn; **taxfree ~** lohnsteuerfreies Gehalt; **taxable ~** lohnsteuerpflichtiges Gehalt; **weekly take-home ~** wöchentlicher Nettolohn; **unemployed ~** Arbeitslosenunterstützung; **weekly ~** Wochenlohn; **~ in advance** Vorschußzahlung; **ordinary ~ and allowance** *(mil.)* Sold und Kostgeld; **~ by the day** Tageslohn; **~ after stoppage** *(Br.)* Nettogehalt; **~ before stoppage** *(Br.)* Bruttogehalt; **~ in lieu of vacation** Urlaubsabgeltung; **equal ~ for equal work** gleicher Lohn für gleiche Arbeit;
~ (v.) zahlen, Zahlung leisten, *(debt)* bezahlen, begleichen, befriedigen, *(reward)* belohnen, *(salary)* [aus]zahlen, *(yield)* sich rentieren, Gewinn abwerfen, sich bezahlt machen;
~ an account Rechnung bezahlen (begleichen); **~ money into an account** Geld auf ein Konto einzahlen; **~ on account** a conto zahlen, anzahlen, Anzahlung leisten; **~ in addition** nachzahlen; **~ an additional amount (sum)** Geld nachschießen; **~ in advance (by anticipation)** im voraus bezahlen, (entrichten), Vorauszahlung leisten, vorausbezahlen, pränumerando (vor Fälligkeit, im voraus) zahlen; **~ the rent annually in advance** Jahresmiete

im voraus bezahlen; **~ alimony** Unterhalt zahlen; **~ an amount in full** Betrag in voller Höhe bezahlen; **~ s. o. an annuity** jem. eine Rente zahlen; **~ attention** Aufmerksamkeit schenken (zuwenden), beachten; **~ away** auszahlen; **~ back** zurück[be-]zahlen, zurückerstatten, Schulden abdecken; **~ s. o. back in his own coin** jem. mit gleicher Münze zurückzahlen; **~ back its loan from the ship's charter earnings** Finanzierungsanleihe mit Chartereinnahmen zurückzahlen; **~ the balance** Unterschiedsbetrag (Rest) begleichen; **~ through a bank** Geld durch die Bank überweisen; **~ into the bank** bei der Bank einzahlen; **~ beforehand** pränumerando zahlen, vorauszahlen; **~ a bill** Zeche bezahlen, Rechnung begleichen, *(of exchange)* Wechsel einlösen; **~ by means of a bill** mit einem Wechsel bezahlen; **~ a call on s. o.** jem. einen Besuch abstatten; **~ a [further] call on shares** Teilzahlung (geforderte Einlage) auf Aktien leisten; **~ the carriage** Transport bezahlen; **~ cash [down]** bar bezahlen, in bar entrichten, Barzahlung leisten; **~ in hard cash** in klingender Münze zahlen; **~ an extra charge** Zuschlag bezahlen; **~ by check** *(US)* (cheque, *Br.*) per Scheck bezahlen, Scheck einlösen; **~ s. one in his own coin** jem. in gleicher Münze zurückzahlen; **~ compensation** Entschädigung (Abfindung) gewähren (leisten, zahlen), Schadensersatz leisten; **~ compliments** Komplimente machen; **~ one's compliments to s. o.** jem. einen Höflichkeitsbesuch abstatten; **~ one's contribution** seinen Beitrag zahlen; **~ the costs** Kosten tragen; **~ into court** bei Gericht hinterlegen; **~ one's creditors in full** seine Gläubiger voll befriedigen; **~ damages** Schadensersatz leisten; **~ on the date agreed** fristgemäß bezahlen; **~ one's debts** seine Schulden bezahlen (begleichen); **~ one's debts to the last penny** seine Schulden auf Heller und Pfennig bezahlen; **~ on delivery** bei Lieferung zahlen; **~ a deposit** Anzahlung leisten, anzahlen, *(guarantee)* Kaution leisten (stellen); **~ a deposit on goods** Draufgeld für eine Lieferung zahlen; **~ the devil** etw. teuer bezahlen müssen; **~ a dividend** Dividende ausschütten; **~ a dividend out of capital** Dividende vom Kapital zahlen; **~ on the dot** ganz pünktlich bezahlen; **~ double the price** doppelten Preis bezahlen; **~ down** bar [be]zahlen, *(downpayment)* Anzahlung leisten; **~ duty** Zoll bezahlen, verzollen; **~ employer's national insurance contribution** Sozialversicherungsanteil zahlen; **~ the expenses** für die Kosten aufkommen; **~ extra** nachbezahlen; **~ extra duty** Steuerzuschlag bezahlen; **~ extra postage** Strafporto zahlen; **~ the fare** für die Fahrt bezahlen; **~ the full fare** vollen Fahrpreis bezahlen; **~ a fee to s. o.** jem. honorieren, jem. ein Honorar bezahlen; **~ the fiddler** *(US sl.)* berappen, blechen, Zeche bezahlen; **~ a fine** Geldstrafe bezahlen; **~ one's footing** seinen Einstand bezahlen.

pay (v.) for bezahlen, Kosten tragen, entgelten, aufkommen für, *(costs)* sich rentieren;
~ dearly one's experience seine Erfahrungen teuer bezahlen müssen, teures Lehrgeld zahlen; **~ dearly one's happiness** sein Glück teuer bezahlen; **~ dearly one's whistle** sich sein Hobby etw. kosten lassen; **~ one's folly** Opfer seiner Dummheit sein; **~ itself** sich bezahlt machen; **~ up to the hilt** schrecklich für seine Fehler büßen müssen; **~ s. o.** *(restaurant)* j. einladen; **~ a domestic help** Haushaltshilfe entlohnen; **~ hono(u)r** als Intervenient zahlen; **~ too much s. th.** etw. überzahlen; **~ s. o. at the pictures** j. zum Kino einladen; **~ s. one's schooling** für jds. Ausbildung aufkommen; **~ services** Dienst belohnen, Dienstleistungen honorieren; **~ the value of s. one's services** jds. Verdiensten entsprechend honorieren; **~ a trip** Reise bezahlen; **~ s. o. his trouble** j. für seine Bemühungen entschädigen.

pay (v.) in full voll begleichen (bezahlen), restlos bezahlen; **~ or by instal(l)ment** im ganzen oder in Raten zahlen; **~ as you go** aus laufenden Erträgen bezahlen; **~ half the cost** Kosten zur Hälfte (hälftig) tragen; **~ handsomely** anständig bezahlen; **~ home** heimzahlen, vergelten; **~ homage to s. o.** jem. Ehre erweisen; **~ due hono(u)r to a draft** Wechsel honorieren; **~ s. o. by the hour** j. stundenweise bezahlen.

pay in (v.) einzahlen;
~ an amount as a deposit Betrag als Deckung einzahlen; **~ a check** *(US)* (cheque, *Br.*) Scheck einlösen; **~ for credit** zur Gutschrift einzahlen; **~ to a fund** zu einem Fonds beisteuern; **~ monthly instal(l)ments** in Monatsraten bezahlen, monatliche Teilzahlungen leisten; **~ kind** in Naturalien (Sachwerten) bezahlen; **~ the lump** im ganzen bezahlen; **~ money** Einzahlung vornehmen; **~ part** teilweise bezahlen, auf Abschlag zahlen; **~ an equal sum** Einlage in gleicher Höhe machen.

pay interest on s. th. etw. verzinsen.

pay into (v.) einlegen;
~ an account auf ein Konto einzahlen; **~ the bank** bei einer Bank einzahlen; **~ court** Geld bei Gericht hinterlegen.

pay *(v.)* | **little heed** wenig beachten; ~ **before maturity** vorausbezahlen, vor Fälligkeit bezahlen; ~ **by two methods of trading** auf zwei Usi bezahlen; ~ **ready money** prompt bezahlen; ~ **through the nose** Wucherpreis (Apothekerpreise) bezahlen.

pay off *(v.)* ausbezahlen, abgelten, *(pay in full)* tilgen, [vollständig] ab[be]zahlen, *(sl.)* abwimmeln, *(workers)* auszahlen, entlohnen;

~ **s. o. for s. th.** es jem. heimzahlen, Revanche nehmen; ~ **bonds** Obligationen einlösen; ~ **one's creditors** seine Gläubiger voll befriedigen; ~ **the crew** Mannschaft abmustern (entlassen); ~ **one's debts** seine Schulden abbezahlen (abtragen); ~ **an employee** *(US)* Angestellten ausbezahlen; ~ **a loan** Darlehn zurückzahlen; ~ **a mortgage** Hypothek amortisieren (ablösen, zurückzahlen); ~ **in increased profits** sich in Gewinnerhöhungen niederschlagen; ~ **old scores** alte Schulden (Rechnungen) bezahlen (begleichen); ~ **shares** Aktien zurückkaufen (einziehen); ~ **the ship's head** Schiff leewärts steuern.

pay *(v.)* | **on the nail** auf der Stelle (sofort) bezahlen; ~ **to the order of s. o.** an jds. Order zahlen.

pay out *(v.)* auszahlen;

~ **s. o.** j. abfinden; ~ **s. o. for s. th.** es jem. heimzahlen, Revanche nehmen; ~ **the balance** Restbetrag auszahlen; ~ **in part** Teilzahlung leisten; ~ **60% of profit to shareholders** 60% der Erträgnisse an die Aktionäre ausschütten; ~ **s. o.'s share** jem. seinen Gewinnanteil auszahlen; ~ **large sums of money** große Geldbeträge ausgeben; ~ **s. th. under a policy** Ansprüche aufgrund einer vorhandenen Versicherung abdecken; ~ **s. o. for his tricks** sich bei jem. für seine unanständige Handlungsweise revanchieren; ~ **the wages** Löhne auszahlen, löhnen.

pay *(v.)* | **over the counter** am Schalter aus[be]zahlen; ~ **one's passage** seine Überfahrt zahlen; ~ **the penalty of a crime** Verbrechen sühnen; ~ **the piper** Unkosten tragen; ~ **s. o. a hundred pounds to hold his tongue** jem. 100 Pfund Schweigegeld zahlen; ~ **in the long run** sich längerfristig gesehen auszahlen; ~ **s. o. from of one's own pocket** j. aus der eigenen Tasche bezahlen; ~ **extra postage** Strafporto zahlen; ~ **on presentation** bei Vorlage zahlen; ~ **promptly** pünktlich bezahlen; ~ **punctually** pünktlich zahlen; ~ **according to the quality of the work** Lohn nach der Leistung bemessen; ~ **ready money** in bar bezahlen; ~ **on receipt** postnumerando (bei Erhalt) bezahlen; ~ **the rent annually in advance** Jahresmiete im voraus bezahlen; ~ **one's final (last) respects to s. o.** jem. die letzten Ehren erweisen; ~ **reverence to s. o.** jem. Ehrerbietung erweisen; ~ **scot and lot** auf Heller und Pfennig bezahlen; ~ **self** *(cheque)* zahlen Sie an mich; ~ **the shot** Kosten tragen; ~ **one's own shot** seinen Anteil an der Rechnung bezahlen; ~ **on the spot** [in] bar bezahlen; ~ **a sum of money into the court** Geld bei Gericht hinterlegen; ~ **a sum by way of indemnification** jem. etw. im Entschädigungswege zahlen; ~ **taxes** Steuern abführen; ~ **DM 1.000,- in taxes** DM 1.000,- an Steuern zahlen; ~ **upon tender of shipping documents** *(US)* bei Eingang der Versandpapiere bezahlen; ~ **on time** pünktlich zahlen; ~ **top prices** Höchstpreise zahlen; ~ **of the town funds** aus dem städtischen Etat bezahlen; ~ **twice as much** doppelt soviel bezahlen

pay *(v.)* **up** voll bezahlen, tilgen, *(shares)* voll einzahlen;

~ **one's debts** seine Schulden abzahlen, sich von seinen Schulden befreien; ~ **shares** Aktien voll einzahlen.

pay *(v.)* | **one's own upkeep and conservation** sich aus Eigenmitteln selbst erhalten können; ~ **s. o. a visit** jem. einen Besuch abstatten; ~ **wages** Gehalt geben, Lohn zahlen; ~ **one's way** seinen Verbindlichkeiten nachkommen, sich vor Schulden bewahren, auf seine Kosten kommen, genug verdienen, genug zum Lebensunterhalt verdienen, sein Auskommen [ohne Zuschuß] haben, für seinen Lebensunterhalt aufkommen können; ~ **one's own way** für sich selbst bezahlen; ~ **by way of compensation** als Abstand (Abfindung) zahlen; ~ **its own way in ten years** sich in zehn Jahren rentieren; ~ **by the week** wochenweise entlohnen, wöchentlich zahlen; ~ **well** guten Ertrag abwerfen, sich gut rentieren, viel eintragen, *(wages)* gute Gehälter zahlen;

to be in s. one's ~ bei jem angestellt sein; **to be in the ~ of the enemy** gegen sein eigenes Land spionieren, für den Gegner arbeiten; **to be a good ~** *(US)* guter Zahler sein, gute Zahlungsmoral haben; **to be unable to ~** zahlungsunfähig sein; **to draw one's ~** Sold beziehen; **to get an increase in ~** Lohnerhöhung bekommen; **to increase ~** Lohnerhöhung vornehmen; **to keep s. o. in one's ~** jem. Lohn und Brot geben; **to receive one's ~** sein Gehalt bekommen; **to stick out for higher ~** auf höherem Lohn bestehen; **to withhold so much out of s. one's ~** soundsoviel von jds. Lohn einbehalten;

~ *(a.)* gewinnbringend, ertragreich, profitabel;

~ **account** Lohnkonto; ~ **agreement** Lohnabkommen; ~ **bargaining** Lohnverhandlungen; ~ **bargaining structure** Tarifverhandlungsstruktur; ~ **bed** *(hospital, Br.)* privat bezahltes Bett; ~ **bill** Gehalts-, Lohnliste, *(Br.)* Kassen-, Zahlungsanweisung; ~**Board** *(Br.)* Richtlinienausschuß für Lohn- und Gehaltsfragen; ~ **book** *(mil.)* Soldbuch; ~ **boost** Gehaltsanstieg; **upper ~ brackets** höhere Besoldungsgruppen (Gehaltsstufen); ~ **ceiling** Lohnplafond; ~ **check** *(US)* **(cheque,** *Br.***)** Lohn-, Gehaltsscheck; ~ **claim** Lohn-, Gehaltsforderung; ~ **clerk** Lohnbuchhalter, *(mil.)* Rechnungsführer, Zahlmeistergehilfe; ~ **code** Lohnschlüssel, -kode; **6 £ ~ code** *(Br.)* Lohnerhöhungsbegrenzung auf 6 Pfund; ~ **code numbers** *(Br.)* Lohnsteuerkennziffern; ~ **control** Tarifbegrenzung, Lohntarifüberwachung; ~ **credit** Gehaltsgutschrift; ~ **curb** Lohnbremse, -einschränkung; ~ **cut** Lohn-, Gehaltskürzung; **to roll back the ~ cuts** Gehaltskürzungen rückgängig machen; ~ **date** Auszahlungstermin, Zahltag; ~ **desk** Kasse[nschalter]; ~ **differential** Lohnunterschied, -gefälle; ~ **dirt** *(gold mining)* abbauwürdiges Gestein; ~ **discrimination** Gehaltsdiskriminierung; ~ **dispute** Lohnstreitigkeit; ~ **envelope** Lohntüte; ~-**envelope advertising** Lohntütenwerbung; ~ **gap** Gehaltsunterschied; ~ **gate** Drehkreuz [für Fußgänger]; ~ **grade (group)** Besoldungsgruppe; ~ **guest** Pensionär; ~ **guidelines** lohnpolitische Richtlinien, Lohnrichtlinien, -leitlinien; ~ **hospital** Privatkrankenhaus; ~-**in slip** Einzahlungsbeleg; ~ **increase** Gehaltserhöhung, -steigerung, Lohnerhöhung, Besoldungsverbesserung; ~-**increase procedure** Gehaltssteigerungsverfahren; ~-**increase program(me)** Gehaltserhöhungsprogramm; ~ **item** kostenvergütete Position; ~ **jump** starker Gehaltsanstieg; ~ **level** *(US)* Gehälter-, Lohnniveau, Gehaltsstufe; ~ **list** Lohnliste; ~ **load** *(US)* Lohnkostenanteil, Belastung durch Lohnkosten, *(plane, ship)* Nutzlast; ~ **negotiations** Lohnverhandlungen; ~-**off** *(sl.)* Lohnzahlung, *(payday)* Löhnungstag, *(film)* wirksamer Schlußteil, *(instalment)* letzte Rate; ~-**off period** *(US)* Tilgungszeitraum, Kapitalrückflußdauer; ~-**off stage** Gewinnschwelle; ~ **offer** Lohn-, Tarifangebot, Gehaltsvorschlag; ~ **office** Kasse, Zahlstelle, Lohnbüro, Schalter; **central ~ office** Hauptkasse; ~ **ore** ertragsreiches Erz; ~ **pacesetter** Lohnschrittmacher; ~ **package** gebündeltes Lohnangebot; ~ **packet** Lohntüte; ~ **pact** Lohnabkommen; ~ **parade** *(mil.)* Löhnungsappell; ~ **pause** *(Br.)* Lohnpause, Lohn- und Gehaltsstopp; ~ **period** Lohn-, Gehaltsperiode; ~ **phone** *(tel., US)* Münzfernsprecher; ~ **plan** *(US)* Besoldungsordnung; ~ **policy** Lohnpolitik, Tarifpolitik; **new ~ policy** *(Br.)* Politik der Einkommensbeschränkung; **public-sector ~ policy** Lohnpolitik im öffentlichen Bereich; ~ **policy carrot** lohnpolitische Bestechungsmaßnahme; ~ **policy guidelines** lohnpolitische Richtlinien; ~ **raise** *(US)* Lohn-, Gehaltserhöhung; **effective ~ rate** tatsächliches Gehalt; **master ~ record** Lohnkonto; ~ **reduction** Lohnherabsetzung; ~ **restraint** zurückhaltende Lohnforderungen; ~ **restraint policy** Politik zurückhaltender Tarifabschlüsse; ~ **research system** *(civil service, Br.)* System der Analyse von Beamtengehältern; ~ **review body** *(Br.)* Lohnprüfungsstelle; ~ **rise** *(Br.)* Gehaltserhöhung; ~ **round** Lohnrunde; ~ **scale** *(US)* Lohntabelle, Gehaltsskala; ~ **schedule** Gehalts-, Lohntabelle; ~ **seniority** *(US)* Besoldungsdienstalter; ~ **settlement** Lohnregelung, -abkommen, Tarifabschluß; **to keep ~ settlement down to within the 10% margin** Tarifabschlüsse im Rahmen einer zehnprozentigen Steigerung halten; ~ **sheet** *(Br.)* Gehälter, -Lohn-, Auszahlungsliste; ~ **slip** Lohnzettel, -abrechnung; ~ **squeeze** Lohndruck; ~ **stabilization** Gehälterstabilisierung; ~ **station** *(US)* Münzfernsprecher, Fernsprechkabine, -automat, -häuschen; ~ **structure** Lohn-, Gehaltsgefüge; **to rationalize its ~ structure** sein Lohngefüge rationalisieren; ~ **supplement** Gehaltszuschlag, -zulage; ~ **supplements** zusätzliche Gehaltsregelungen; **incentive ~ system** Akkordlohnsystem; **new ~ system** neues Lohntarifsystem; **free ~ table** *(Br.)* Tabelle lohnsteuerfreier Beträge; ~ **target** Lohnerhöhungsgrenze; ~ **telephone** Münzfernsprecher; ~ **ticket** Zahlungsanweisung; ~ **toilet** Münztoilette, -klo; ~ **voucher** *(Br.)* Zahlungs-, Kassenanweisung.

pay-as-you | -**earn** *(PAYE)* *(Br.)* Lohnsteuereinbehaltung, -abzug; ~-**earn income tax** *(Br.)* Lohnsteuer; ~-**earn principle** Quellenabzugsverfahren; ~-**earn system** *(Br.)* Lohnsteuerabzugsverfahren; ~-**go system** *(US)* Quellenbesteuerung, Lohnsteuereinbehaltungsverfahren; ~ **go tax** *(US)* Lohn-, Quellensteuer; ~ **go tax system** *(US)* Lohnsteuereinbehaltungs-, -abzugsverfahren; ~-**see television** Münzfernsehen; ~-**use principle** Finanzierung von Ausgabenspitzen langfristiger Projekte durch Anleihen.

payability Fälligkeit, Zahlbarkeit.

payable | s *(US)* Verbindlichkeiten, Kreditoren;
~s **to affiliates** *(balance sheet)* Verbindlichkeiten gegenüber verbundenen Unternehmern; ~s **to suppliers** *(balance sheet)* Warenlieferungen;
~ *(a.)* zahlbar, bezahlbar, begleichbar, zu zahlen, *(due)* fällig, schuldig, *(profitable)* rentabel, ertragreich, gewinnbringend, lohnend;
not ~ nicht tilgbar;
accounts ~ *(balance sheet)* Passiva, Buchschulden, Verbindlichkeiten; **bill ~** verfallener Wechsel; **bills ~** *(balance sheet)* Wechselverbindlichkeiten; **coupons ~ at the ... bank** Zahlstelle für Kupons ist die ... Bank; **mortgages ~** Hypothekenschulden; **pay deductions** *(Br.)* fällige Lohnsteuerabzüge;
~ **abroad** im Ausland zahlbar; ~ **at address to payee** am Wohnsitz des Empfängers zahlbar; ~ **in advance** im voraus (pränumerando) zahlbar, vorauszahlbar; ~ **afterwards** postnumerando zahlbar; ~ **annually** jährlich zahlbar; ~ **on application** zahlbar bei Antragstellung (Bestellung); ~ **by banks abroad** bei ausländischen Banken zahlbar; ~ **at the X-bank** bei der X-Bank zahlbar; ~ **to bearer** zahlbar an Überbringer (Inhaber), auf den Inhaber (Überbringer) lautend; ~ **in cash** bar zu zahlen; ~ **only through the clearinghouse** nur zur Verrechnung; ~ **at our counters** an unseren Schaltern zahlbar; ~ **in currency** in Devisen zahlbar; ~ **on delivery** bei Lieferung zahlbar; ~ **on demand** zahlbar bei Anforderung, ohne vorherige Benachrichtigung zahlbar, täglich fällig, *(bill)* bei Verlangen (bei Sicht) zahlbar; ~ **when due** bei Fälligkeit zahlbar; ~ **with exchange** *(US)* zahlbar zuzüglich Einzugsspesen; ~ **at expiration** bei Verfall zahlbar; ~ **as per indorsement** *(Br.)* zahlbar zu den im Indossament vermerkten Umrechnungskurs; ~ **later** postnumerando zahlbar; ~ **at maturity** bei Fälligkeit (Verfall) zahlbar; ~ **in monthly instal(l)ments** monatlich abzahlbar, in monatlichen Raten zahlbar; ~ **with Mr. X** bei Herrn X zahlbar; ~ **to order** an Order (auf den Namen) lautend; ~ **on presentation** bei Vorlage (Sicht) zahlbar; ~ **on the 15th prox.** am 15. n. M. fällig; ~ **quarterly** vierteljährlich zahlbar; ~ **on receipt** zahlbar bei Erhalt (Empfang); ~ **at the collecting bank's selling rate for sight drafts on London** zahlbar zum Verkaufskurs der einziehenden Bank für Sichtwechsel auf London; ~ **after sight** nach Sicht zahlbar; ~ **at sight** bei Sicht (Vorlage) zahlbar; ~ **upon submission of proof of identity** zahlbar gegen Vorlage des Personalausweises; ~ **to suppliers** *(balance sheet)* Warenlieferungen; ~ **against surrender of shipping documents** zahlbar gegen Aushändigung der Begleitpapiere; ~ **by the tenant** vom Mieter (Pächter) zu bezahlen;
to be ~ from *(interest)* laufen vom; **to be ~ on the 15th prox.** am 15. des nächsten Monats fällig sein; **to declare ~** für zahlbar erklären; **to make ~** domizilieren, zahlbar stellen; **to make a bill ~ to s. o.** Wechsel an jds. Order ausstellen; **to make a cheque** *(Br.)* **(check, US) ~ to bearer** Scheck auf den Überbringer ausstellen; **to make an expense ~ out of public funds** Summe zur Zahlung aus der Staatskasse anweisen; **to make ~ by a third party** bei einem Dritten zahlbar stellen;
bills ~ book *(journal)* Wechselverfallsbuch; **~ coding guide** *(Br.)* Lohnsteuerkennzifferhinweis.

payback | method Investitionsabzahlungsberechnung; ~ **period** *(US)* Kapitalrückflußdauer.

paybox *(Br.)* Kasse, Schalter.

payday Zahltag, *(bill)* Erfüllungstag, *(stock exchange, Br.)* Lieferungs-, Liquidations-, Abrechnungs-, Zahltag, Ablieferungstermin, *(workers)* Löhnungstag;
to make a ~ *(sl.)* Fischzug machen.

paye code *(Br.)* Lohnsteuerkennziffer;
to operate ~ on the remaining net pay *(Br.)* Lohnsteuersätze auf das verbliebene Nettogehalt anwenden.

payee Zahlungsempfänger, -berechtigter, *(bill)* Wechselinhaber, -nehmer, Remittent;
alternative ~s wahlweise Remittenten; **fictitious ~** fingierter Remittent; **a/c ~ only** nur zur Gutschrift [des Kontoinhabers]; ~ **of an addressed bill** Domizilitat; ~ **of a bill of exchange** Wechselnehmer, Remittent; ~ **of a check** *(US)* **(cheque, Br.)** Scheckempfänger.

payer [Ein]zahler, Auszahlender, *(bill of exchange)* Trassat, Bezogener, Zahlungsverpflichteter;
dilatory (slow, tardy, US) ~ säumiger Zahler (Schuldner); **prompt ~** pünktlicher Zahler; **tax ~** Steuerzahler;
~ **of a bill of exchange** Trassat, Bezogener; ~ **of contango** Reportgeber; ~ **for hono(u)r** *(bill of exchange)* Ehrenzahler, Honorant;
~ **bank** zahlende Bank; ~ **benefit** *(insurance, US)* Prämienbefreiung bei Tod oder Invalidität.

paying Zahlung, Zahlen;
~ **back** Rückzahlung; ~ **in** Einzahlung; ~ **off** Abtragung, -zahlung, Tilgung, *(mortgage)* Amortisation, *(US)* Auszahlung; ~ **off one's creditors** Gläubigerbefriedigung, -abfindung; ~ **off a mortgage** Hypothekentilgung; ~ **off shares** Aktieneinziehung; ~ **out** Auszahlung, *(partner)* Abfindung; ~ **up** Abzahlung, volle Bezahlung;
~ *(a.)* einträglich, ertragreich, einbringlich, lohnend, rentabel, gewinnabwerfend, -bringend, lukrativ, sich bezahlt machend, zahlend;
not ~ unrentabel;
to be ~ viel einbringen; **to be slow in ~** langsam zahlen, schlechte Zahlungsmoral haben; **to default in ~ a note** mit der Bezahlung eines Wechsels in Verzug geraten; **to keep on ~ out small sums** immer alles verpfuschen;
~ **agent** [Kupon]zahlstelle; **to indicate as ~ agent** als Zahlstelle angeben; ~ **bank[er]** auszahlende Bank; **cash (specie)-~ bank** barzahlende (beauftragte) Bank; ~ **business** rentables Geschäft; **to put a business on a ~ basis** Rentabilität eines Geschäftes sicherstellen; **to put its relationship on a ~ basis** seine Beziehungen finanziell untermauern; ~ **boarder** Kostgänger; ~ **concern** einträgliches Geschäft, rentables Unternehmen; ~ **counter** Auszahlungsschalter; ~ **cashier** Auszahlungsbeamter; ~ **department** Kassenabteilung für Auszahlungen; ~ **guest** Feriengast, Pensionär; **to take ~ guests** Gäste gegen Bezahlung aufnehmen; ~ **habits** Zahlungsgepflogenheiten.

paying-in | book *(Br.)* Einzahlungsbuch; ~ **form** Einzahlungsformular; ~ **slip** *(Br.)* Einzahlungsbeleg, -schein.

paying | investment gewinnbringende Anlage; ~ **load** Nutzlast, *(pay load, US)* Lohnkostenanteil, Belastung durch Lohnkosten und Gehälter; ~ **member** zahlendes Mitglied; ~ **office** Zahl-, Auszahlungsstelle, Kasse; ~-**out post office** Auszahlungspostamt; ~ **officer** Lohnbuchhalter; ~ **quantities** gewinnbringende Mengen; ~ **teller** *(US)* Kassierer für Auszahlungen, erster Kassierer; ~ **teller's department** *(US)* Auszahlungskasse; ~ **up** Schuldenabzahlung.

payload *(enterprise, US)* Lohnkostenanteil, Belastung durch Lohnkosten und Gehälter, *(plane, ship)* Nutzlast.

paymaster Kassierer für Auszahlungen, *(mil.)* Zahlmeister;
assistant ~ stellvertretender Kassierer; ~ **general** *(Br.)* Generalzahlmeister [des englischen Schatzamtes];
~ **robbery insurance** Versicherung gegen Lohngeldberaubung.

paymastership Zahlmeisterstelle.

payment *(bill, cheque)* Einlösung, *(creditor)* Befriedigung, *(of debt)* Begleichung, Abtragung, *(paying)* [Be]zahlung, Ein-, Auszahlung, Zahlungsleistung, Entrichtung, Entgelt, *(paying method)* Zahlungsweise, *(wages)* Entlohnung, Lohn, Löhnung, Vergütung;
against ~ gegen Bezahlung, entgeltlich; **in ~ of our account** zum Ausgleich unserer Rechnung; **as ~** zahlungshalber; **as ~ for** zum Ausgleich für; **as ~ for your services** als Entgelt (Vergütung) für Ihre Dienste; **by easy ~s** unter Zahlungserleichterungen; **in lieu of ~** an Zahlungs Statt; **in default of ~** mangels Zahlung; **failing ~** mangels Zahlung; **for want of ~** mangels Zahlung; **in consideration of the ~ of a sum** gegen Zahlung eines Betrages; **on ~** nach Eingang, gegen Bezahlung (Erlegung); **on ~ of costs** unter Auferlegung der Kosten; ~ **provided** vorbehaltlich der Zahlung; **reserving due ~** vorbehaltlich des richtigen Eingangs; **subject to ~** gegen Entgelt; **upon ~ of charges** gegen Zahlung der Gebühren; **without ~** kostenlos, gratis, unentgeltlich, umsonst;
~**s** Zahlungsverkehr;
additional ~ nachträgliche Zahlung, Nachschuß, Nach-, Zuschlags-, Zuzahlung; **advance ~** Vorauszahlung, Zahlung vor Fälligkeit; **anticipated ~** *(US)* Vorausbezahlung, Zahlung vor Fälligkeit; **back ~** Nachzahlung; ~ **back** Bankanweisung; **benefit ~** Unterstützungszahlung; **cash [down] ~** Barzahlung, *(banking)* Kassenauszahlungen; **cashless ~** *(US)* bargeldlose Zahlung; **clean ~** Bezahlung gegen offene Rechnung; **commutation ~** Abfindung; **composition ~** Abfindungszahlung; **compulsory ~** erzwungene Zahlung; ~ **countermanded** widerrufene Zahlung, Zahlung gesperrt; **current ~s** laufende Zahlungen; **declined ~** Zahlungsverweigerung; **deferred ~** *(US)* aufgeschobene Zahlung, Abschlags-, Ratenzahlung; **delayed ~** verspätete Zahlung; **delinquent ~s** nicht geleistete Zahlungen, Zahlungsrückstände; **dividend ~** Dividendenzahlung; **dilatory ~** langsame Bezahlung; **direct ~** endgültige Zahlung; **down ~** Anzahlung; **due ~** fällige Zahlung; **easy ~s** Abzahlung in bequemen Raten, Zahlungserleichterungen; **equalization ~** Ausgleichszahlung; **ex gratia ~** Gratifikation, *(third-party insurance)* freiwillige Entschädigungsleistung, Zahlung ohne

Anerkennung einer Rechtspflicht; **extra** ~ außerordentliche Zahlung, Zuschlags-, Nachzahlung; **feigned** ~ Scheinzahlung; **fictitious** ~ fingierte Zahlung; **final** ~ Rest-, Abschlußzahlung, Restquote; **fortnightly** ~ Halbmonatszahlung; **fresh** ~ Nachschuß[zahlung]; **full** ~ Vollbezahlung; **further** ~s nachträgliche Zahlungen; **general** ~s allgemeiner Zahlungsverkehr; **immediate** ~ sofortige Zahlung; **indefinite** ~ allgemeine Schuldenrückzahlung; **initial** ~ erste Zahlung, Anzahlung; **international** ~s internationaler Zahlungsverkehr; **inward** ~ *(bookkeeping)* Eingänge; **irregular** ~s unpünktliche (unregelmäßige) Zahlungen; **large** ~s große Zahlungen; **loss** ~ Auszahlung der Schadenssumme; **lump-sum** ~ Pauschalzahlung, -abfindung; **money** ~s Geldrente; **monthly** ~s monatliche Zahlungen; **all-in-one monthly** ~ monatliche Gesamtzahlung; **multilateral** ~ multilaterale Zahlung; **outright** ~ vollständige Bezahlung; **outstanding** ~ Zahlungsrückstand; **outward** ~ *(bookkeeping)* Ausgänge; **overdue** ~ überfällige Zahlung; **overtime** ~s Überstundengelder; **parity** ~s [Aus]zahlungen zum Parikurs; **part** ~ Teil-, Raten-, Abschlagszahlung; **partial** ~ Teilzahlung; **pension** ~ Pensionszahlung; **periodical** ~s laufend anfallende (periodische) Zahlungen, wiederkehrende Zahlungen, Geldrente; **preferential** ~ bevorrechtigte (bevorzugte) Gläubigerbefriedigung; **preferred** ~ bevorrechtigte Gläubigerbefriedigung; **premium** ~ Prämienleistung, -zahlung; **principal** ~s Zahlungen aus dem Kapital; **progress** ~ proratarische (anteilige) Bezahlung; **prompt** ~ sofortige (schnelle) Bezahlung; **pro-rata** ~ anteilige Zahlung, quotenmäßige Befriedigung; **quarterly** ~s Zahlungen am Vierteljahresultimo, Quartalszahlung; ~ **received** Betrag erhalten; ~s **received** Eingänge, eingegangene Zahlungen; ~ **refused** verweigerte Zahlung; **regular** ~s laufende Zahlungen, Geldrente; **relief** ~ Entlohnung für Notstandsarbeiten; **rental** ~ Mietzahlung; **restitution** ~s Wiedergutmachungsleistungen; **retroactive** ~ Zahlung mit rückwirkender Kraft; **revolving** ~s regelmäßig wiederkehrende (revolvierende) Zahlungen; **short** ~ sofortige (unvollständige) Bezahlung; **single** ~ einmalige Zahlung; ~ **stopped** eingestellte Zahlung; **subsequent** ~ Nachzahlung; **supplementary** ~ Nachschuß, Nachzahlung, *(relief)* Zusatzunterstützung; **tax** ~ Steuerzahlung; **tax-free** ~ steuerfreie Zahlung; **token** ~ Anerkenntniszahlung; **transitional** ~ Übergangszahlung; **voluntary** ~ freiwillige Zahlung des [Gemein]schuldners; **wage** ~ Lohnzahlung;

~ **into an account** Einzahlung auf ein Konto; ~ **on account** abschlägige Zahlung, An-, Abschlags-, Akontozahlung, Anzahlungssumme; ~ **on account of costs** Kostenvorschuß; ~s **on account received** erhaltene Anzahlungen; ~ **per account** Saldozahlung; ~ **for admission** Eintrittsgeld; ~ **in advance (by anticipation)** Voraus, Vorschuß, Pränumerandozahlung; ~s **made under a separation agreement** Zahlungen aufgrund einer Trennungsvereinbarung; ~ **in arrears** rückständige Zahlung, Nach-, Nachtrags-, Rückstandszahlung; ~ **of the balance** Restzahlung; ~ **of benefits** Sozialunterstützung; ~ **by way of a bill** Zahlung durch Wechsel; ~ **of a bill** Wechseleinlösung; ~ **for breakage** Refaktie; ~ **of calls** Einzahlung auf abgerufene Kapitalanteile; ~ **of calls in advance** Vorauszahlung auf Kapitalanteile; ~ **of a capital nature** kapitalähnliche Zahlung; ~ **in cash** Barzahlung, -ausschüttung, Zahlung gegen Kasse, Entlohnung in bar; ~s **within the charge** Zahlungen mit dem Recht der Steuereinbehaltungen; ~ **to charity** Zahlungen für wohltätige Zwecke; ~ **by check** *(US)* (**cheque,** *Br.*) Scheckzahlung; ~ **of a cheque under advice** *(Br.)* Scheckeinlösung im Lastschriftkassoverfahren; ~ **of a commission** Provisionszahlung; ~ **on completion of purchase** Zahlung bei Kaufabschluß; ~ **of contributions** Beitragszahlung, -leistung; ~ **over the counter** Schalterauszahlung; ~s **due from foreign countries** internationaler Zahlungsverkehr; ~ **in due course** ordnungsgemäße Zahlung, *(bill of exchange)* Wechseleinlösung bei Fälligkeit; ~ **into court** Hinterlegung bei Gericht, Einzahlung bei Gericht (in die Gerichtskasse); ~ **of creditor** Gläubigerauszahlung, -befriedigung; ~ **of secured creditors** *(US)* Befriedigung absonderungsberechtigter Gläubiger; ~ **of unsecured creditors** Befriedigung von Masseglläubigern; ~ **of creditors on account** Akontozahlungen an Gläubiger; ~ **under deed of covenant** Zahlungen aufgrund vertraglich eingegangener Verpflichtungen; ~ **due on death** Sterbegeld; ~ **of debts** Schuldenbezahlung, -begleichung; ~ **under deed of covenant** Zahlungen aufgrund vertraglich eingegangener Verpflichtungen; ~ **on delivery** Zahlung bei Lieferung, Lieferung gegen bar (Nachnahme); ~ **must be made upon delivery of the goods** Zahlung bei Eingang der Waren; ~ **on demand** Zahlung bei Wechselvorlage; ~ **of dividends** Dividendenzahlung, -ausschüttung, *(out of a bankrupt's*

estate) Abschlagsverteilung; ~ **of dues** Beitragszahlung; ~ **of duty** Steuerzahlung, *(customs)* Verzollung; ~ **against documents** Zahlung gegen Aushändigung der [Verschiffungs]dokumente; ~s **for the European Community** Leistungen für die Europäische Gemeinschaft; ~ **in excess** Überzahlung; ~ **in excess of standard rates** übertarifliche Lohnzahlungen (Leistungen); ~ **of a fee** Gebührenbegleichung, -entrichtung; ~ **in full** vollständige [Aus]zahlung, Voll[ein]zahlung; ~ **in full on allotment** Volleinzahlung einer repartierten Zuteilung; ~ **in goods** Bezahlung in Waren; ~ **in holder's own giro account** Einzahlung auf das eigene Postscheckkonto; ~ **for hono(u)r** Ehreneintritt, Subventionszahlung; ~ **for hono(u)r supra protest** Ehrenzahlung nach Protest; ~ **during illness** Gehaltsfortzahlung im Krankheitsfall; ~-**in** Einzahlungen; ~ **by instal(l)ments** Abschlags-, Ratenzahlung; ~ **of interest** Verzinsung, Zinsendienst, Zinszahlung; ~ **by intervention** Interventionszahlung; ~ **on invoice** Bezahlung bei Rechnungsvorlage; ~ **in kind** Sach-, Naturalleistung, -entlohnung, Sachbezüge, -zuwendung, Entlohnung in Sachwerten; ~ **during leave** Urlaubsgeld; ~ **by letter** briefliche Auszahlung; ~ **is in the mail** Zahlung erfolgt gleichzeitig per Post; ~ **in lieu of vacation** Urlaubsabgeltung; ~s **for maintenance** Unterhaltszahlungen; ~ **over and above** außertarifliches Gehalt; ~ **in part** Teil-, Abschlagszahlung; ~ **on behalf of a third party** Zahlung zugunsten eines Dritten, Interventionszahlung; **[regular]** ~ **of premiums** [laufende] Prämienzahlung; ~ **pro rata** quotenmäßige Befriedigung; ~ **of rent in advance** Mietvorauszahlung; ~ **supra protest** Ehren-, Interventionszahlung; ~ **in ready money** Barzahlung; ~ **of remainder** Restzahlung; ~ **of rent[al]** Begleichung der Miete, Mietzahlung; ~ **of rent in advance** Mietvorauszahlung; ~ **of reparations** Reparationsleistungen; ~ **on request** Zahlung auf Verlangen; ~ **on reserve** Zahlung unter Vorbehalt; ~ **by result** Stück-, Leistungs-, Erfolgslohn; ~ **of royalties** Tantiemenvergütung; ~ **of salaries** Gehaltszahlung; ~ **for shares** Einzahlung auf Aktien; ~ **to suppliers** Lieferantenzahlungen; ~ **conditional to survival** *(life insurance)* Auszahlung nur im Erlebensfall; ~ **of taxes** Steuerzahlung; ~ **in due time** fristgemäße Zahlung; ~ **of wages** Lohnabrechnung; ~ **by way of a bill** Zahlung durch Wechsel; ~s **over and above of wage scale** übertarifliche Bezahlung; ~ **as you feel inclined** Zahlung nach Belieben;

to accept ~ Zahlung annehmen; **to accept in** ~ in Zahlung nehmen; **to agree on a date for the** ~ Zeitpunkt für die Zahlung (Zahlungstermin) vereinbaren; **to anticipate** ~ Zahlung vor Fälligkeit leisten; **to apply to the** ~ **of a debt** Geld für die Bezahlung (Begleichung) von Schulden verwenden; **to apply a** ~ **to a particular debt** Zahlung zur Begleichung einer bestimmten Schuld bestimmen; **to apply** ~s **for the reduction of interest** Zahlung zur Verkürzung von Zinsrückständen verwenden; **to assess for additional** ~s zu zusätzlichen Zahlungen heranziehen; **to be admitted in** ~ gesetzliches Zahlungsmittel sein; **to be behind (in arrears) with one's** ~s mit seinen Zahlungen im Rückstand sein; **to be exact (punctual, prompt) in one's** ~s seinen Zahlungsverpflichtungen pünktlich nachkommen; **to be slow in** ~ schlechter Zahler sein, schlechte Zahlungsmoral haben; **to call for additional** ~ Nachschuß einfordern; **to cease** ~s Zahlungen einstellen; **to claim** ~ Zahlung verlangen; **to compel** ~ Zahlung erzwingen; **to countermand a** ~ Zahlungsauftrag stornieren; **to decline** ~ [Be]zahlung ablehnen; **to default on one's** ~s mit den Zahlungen in Verzug kommen, mit der Zahlung im Rückstand bleiben; **to defer** ~ Zahlung aufschieben, später zahlen; **to delay [in making]** ~ mit der Zahlung in Verzug sein; **to delay intra-group** ~s konzerninterne Zahlungen zeitlich verschieben; **to deliver in** ~ in Zahlung geben; **to demand** ~ zur Zahlung auffordern; **to demand prompt** ~ auf sofortiger Bezahlung bestehen; **to effect** ~ Zahlung leisten; **to elude** ~ sich einer Bezahlung entziehen; **to enforce** ~ **by legal proceedings** Zahlung gerichtlich beitreiben; **to evade** ~ sich einer Zahlungsverpflichtung entziehen; **to exact** ~s Zahlungen ein-, beitreiben; **to extend the time of** ~ Zahlungsfrist verlängern; **to fall behind with one's** ~s mit seinen Zahlungen in Rückstand geraten; **to give an order to stop** ~ Auftrag zur Zahlungssperre geben; **to grant a delay in** ~ Zahlungsaufschub gewähren; **to insist on** ~ auf Bezahlung bestehen; **to keep up one's** ~s seine Zahlungsverpflichtungen einhalten; **to keep international** ~s **in balance** Zahlungsbilanzen im Gleichgewicht halten; **to lodge for** ~ zur Zahlung hereingeben; **to make** ~ Zahlung leisten; **to make** ~s **on account** Akontozahlungen leisten; **to make an additional (further)** ~ nachzahlen, Nachzahlung leisten; **to make** ~ **in advance** pränumerando (im voraus) bezahlen; **to make a subsequent** ~ nachbezahlen; **to make a**

supplementary ~ nachschießen; **to make ~s for customers** Zahlungsaufträge von Kunden durchführen; **to make ~s under deduction of tax** Steuerbeträge bei der Auszahlung einbehalten; **to make ~ without deduction of tax** Lohn ohne Steuerabzüge (lohnsteuerfrei) auszahlen, keine Lohnsteuerabzüge einbehalten; **to meet the ~s** Ratenzahlungen (Zahlungsverpflichtungen) einhalten; **to miss a ~ on one's home** mit einer Hypothekenrate in Verzug kommen; **to obtain an extension of time for ~** Verlängerung der Zahlungsfrist erhalten; **to offer as ~ in** Zahlung geben; **to pass an account for ~** Etattitel zur Zahlung anweisen; **to postpone ~** Zahlung aufschieben; **to present a bill for ~** Wechsel zur Zahlung vorlegen; **to present a check (US) (cheque, Br.) for~** Scheck zur Einlösung vorlegen; **to procure ~** Inkasso besorgen; **to provide ~** für Deckung sorgen; **to put off a ~** mit einer Zahlung aufhören; **to receipt a ~** Zahlung bescheinigen; **to receive ~s** Zahlungen entgegennehmen; **to receive in ~** in Zahlung nehmen; **to record a ~ on the reverse side of a letter of credit** Zahlung auf der Rückseite eines Kreditbriefes notieren; **to refuse ~** Zahlung verweigern; **to release goods against ~** Waren gegen Zahlung freigeben; **to request ~** zur Zahlung auffordern; **to require ~ on delivery** Zahlung Zug um Zug verlangen (vereinbaren); **to resume ~s** Zahlungen wiederaufnehmen; **to secure ~** Zahlung sicherstellen; **to settle ~s in pounds** Zahlungen in Pfund vornehmen; **to space ~s over several years** Zahlungen auf mehrere Jahre verteilen; **to specify application of one's ~** Zahlungsaufforderung belegen; **to stand surety for the ~ of a sum** für den Eingang eines Betrages bürgen; **to stipulate ~s in gold** Zahlungen auf Goldbasis vereinbaren; **to stipulate that ~ should be quarterly** vierteljährliche Zahlungen vereinbaren; **to stop (suspend) ~s** Zahlungen vorübergehend einstellen; **to stop ~ of a cheque** Scheckauszahlung sperren; **to sue for ~** Betrag einklagen; **to take in (as) ~** an Zahlungs Statt annehmen; **to take in part ~** als Teilzahlung annehmen; **to terminate a ~** mit der Zahlung aufhören; **to transgress ~** Zahlungstermin nicht einhalten; **to withhold ~** Zahlung vorenthalten;

~-of-Wages-Act (Br.) Gesetz über bargeldlose Entlohnung; **~ agreement** Zahlungsabkommen, -regelung; **~ arrangement** Zahlungsregelung; **~ balance** Zahlungsbilanz; **~s balance discipline** Zahlungsbilanzdisziplin; **~ bill** zur Zahlung vorzulegender Wechsel, Dokumentenwechsel; **~ conditions** Zahlungsbedingungen; **~s deficit** Zahlungsbilanzdefizit; **~s gap** Zahlungsbilanzlücke; **~ guarantee** Zahlungsgarantie; **~ imbalance** Zahlungsunausgeglichenheit; **~ instructions** Zahlungsanweisungen; **~ moratorium** Zahlungsmoratorium; **~ order** Auszahlungsanweisung, Zahlungsauftrag; **~s outlook** Zahlungsaussichten; **~ pattern** Zahlungsstruktur; **~ performance** Zahlungsgebaren; **~ period** Zahlungsfrist; **~ plan** Zahlungsplan; **~ sheet (Br.)** Lohn-, Gehälterliste; **~ side** Ausgabenseite; **~ surplus** Zahlungsbilanzüberschuß; **~ system** Zahlungsverkehr; **~ terms** Zahlungsbedingungen; **~ transactions** Zahlungsverkehr; **~ troubles** Zahlungsschwierigkeiten; **~ voucher** Zahlungsanweisung.

payoff Lohnzahlung, *(sl.)* Bestechung;
political ~ to an interest group politische Abfindungsleistung an eine Interessentengruppe;
~ (a.) ausschlaggebend, *(remunerative)* rentabel, lohnend; **~ opportunities** reelle Chancen; **~ period (US)** Kapitalrückflußdauer; **~ scandal** Bestechungsskandal; **~ stage** Ertragsschwelle.

payola *(sl.)* Bestechungs-, Schmiergelder, *(broadcasting, US)* bestochene Rundfunksendung.

payor Zahlungspflichtiger, *(bill of exchange)* Wechselbezogener; **~ bank (US)** zahlende Bank.

payout Auszahlung;
lump-sum ~ Abfindungszahlung;
~ period Kapitalrückflußdauer, Abschreibungszeitraum eines Investitionsbetrags; **~ variations** verschiedene Auszahlungsmöglichkeiten.

payroll Lohnliste, Gehaltsverzeichnis, Gehälterliste, *(for individual employee)* Lohnkonto, *(US)* Lohn- und Gehaltsabrechnung;
on the ~ (US) angestellt, im Angestelltenverhältnis;
~s (balance sheet, US) Löhne und Gehälter;
accrued ~s (balance sheet, US) fällige Löhne und Gehälter; **daily ~** tägliche Lohnsumme; **government ~** staatliche Lohnaufwendungen; **weekly ~** wöchentliche Lohnliste;
to be off the ~ (US) arbeitslos (entlassen) sein; **to be on the ~ (US)** auf der Lohnliste stehen, beschäftigt sein; **to be no longer on s. one's ~ (US)** nicht mehr bei jem. beschäftigt sein; **to cut the ~ by 10%** zehnprozentige Lohnkürzung durchführen; **to**

have a huge ~ Riesensumme an Löhnen zahlen müssen; **to increase the weekly ~** wöchentliche Lohnkosten erhöhen; **to make out a ~** Gehalts-, Lohnliste aufstellen; **to throw s. o. off the ~** j. nicht mehr auf der Lohnliste führen; **to pad a ~** überhöhte Lohnkosten berechnen;
~ account (US) Gehalts-, Lohnkonto; **~ accounting** Lohnbuchhaltung, Lohn- und Gehaltsabrechnung; **~ audit (US)** Revision der Lohnbuchhaltung; **~ book (US)** Lohnliste; **~ clearing account (US)** Lohnverrechnungskonto; **~ clerk (US)** Lohnbuchhalter; **~ data** Gehaltsangaben; **~ deductions (US)** Lohnsteuerabzüge; **~ deductions plan (US)** Lohnsteuerabzugsverfahren; **~ department (US)** Lohnbüro, Gehalts-, Lohnabteilung; **~ disbursement** Lohn-, Gehaltsauszahlung; **~ distribution** Lohnkostenaufteilung; **~ division (US)** Lohnabteilung; **~ employment** lohnsteuerpflichtiger Beruf; **~ file (US)** Lohnkartei; **~ fund** Gehälterfonds; **~ journal** Lohnrechnung, -buchführung; **~ period** Lohn-, Gehaltsperiode, Lohnzahlungszeitraum; **~ procedure** Lohnlistenverfahren; **~ records (US)** Lohnsteuerunterlagen, Lohnabrechnungen; **~s serving** *(banking)* Gehaltsauszahlung; **~ sheet (US)** Lohn- und Gehaltsliste; **~ summary** Lohnübersicht; **~ system (US)** Lohnsteuerverfahren; **~ tax (US)** Lohnsummensteuer, Arbeitgeberbeiträge zur Sozialversicherung; **~ variance** Lohnabweichung; **~ voucher (US)** Lohnzettel, -auszahlungsbeleg; **~ work** Lohnabrechnung.

payroller (US) Gehalts-, Lohnempfänger.

pea Erbse;
as easy as shelling ~s kinderleicht; **as like as two ~s** wie ein Ei dem anderen gleichen;
~ coal Erbskohle; **~-shooter** *(airforce, sl.)* Kampfflugzeug; **~ soup** Erbsensuppe, *(thick fog, sl.)* Waschküche.

peace Friede, *(state of public tranquillity)* Landfrieden, öffentliche Sicherheit und Ordnung;
at ~ im Friedenszustand; **deep in ~** im tiefsten Frieden; **for the sake of ~ and quietness** um des lieben Friedens willen;
brief ~ kurze Friedenszeit; **collective ~** Kollektivfrieden; **dictated ~** Diktatfrieden, Friedensdiktat; **enduring ~** dauerhafter Frieden; **hono(u)rable ~** ehrenvoller Frieden; **industrial ~** Arbeitsfrieden; **lasting ~** dauerhafter Frieden; **public ~** öffentliche Ruhe und Ordnung, Landfriede; **unbroken ~** ununterbrochener Friede;
~ with hono(u)r ehrenvoller Friede; **~ to his memory** Friede seiner Asche; **~ by negotiation** Verhandlungsfrieden; **~ at any price** Friede um jeden Preis; **public ~ and quiet** öffentliche Ruhe und Sicherheit; **~ and quietude** öffentliche Ruhe und Ordnung; **~ of the state** öffentliche Ruhe und Sicherheit;
to be at ~ with the neighbo(u)ring countries mit seinen Nachbarländern in Frieden leben; **to be sworn of the ~ (Br.)** zum Friedensrichter ernannt werden; **to break the ~** öffentliche Sicherheit und Ordnung stören, Aufruhr anzetteln; **to bring ~ to a country** einem Land Frieden bringen; **to consolidate the ~** Frieden festigen; **to disturb the ~** Aufruhr anzetteln, öffentliche Sicherheit und Ordnung stören; **to endanger the ~** Frieden gefährden; **to ensure ~** Frieden gewährleisten; **to establish ~** Frieden stiften; **to give s. o. no ~** jem. keine Ruhe lassen; **to hold one's ~** Schweigen bewahren; **to keep the ~** Frieden aufrechterhalten, öffentliche Sicherheit bewahren; **to leave s. o. in ~** j. in Ruhe lassen; **to make one's ~** Streit beilegen, sich versöhnen; **to make ~ with a country** Frieden mit einem Land schließen; **to negotiate for ~** Friedensverhandlungen führen; **to preserve ~** Frieden bewahren; **to restore ~** Frieden wiederherstellen; **to strengthen ~** Frieden festigen; **to threaten the ~** Frieden gefährden; **to treat for ~** wegen des Friedens verhandeln, Friedensverhandlungen führen; **to violate the ~** Landfriedensbruch begehen;
~ accord Friedensabsprache; **to make a tentative ~ approach** Friedensfühler ausstrecken; **~ bid** Friedensangebot; **~ camp** Friedenslager; **~ conference** Friedenskonferenz; **~ Corps (US)** Friedenskorps; **~ delegation** Friedensabordnung; **~ drive** Friedensfeldzug; **~ economy** Friedenswirtschaft; **~ efforts** Friedensbemühungen; **~ establishment (mil.)** Friedensstärke; **to put out ~ feelers** Friedensfühler ausstrecken; **~ footing (mil.)** Friedensstärke; **~ initiative** Friedensinitiative; **~-loving** friedliebend; **~ mission** Friedensmission; **~ movement** Friedensbewegung; **~ negotiations** Friedensverhandlungen; **~ offensive** Friedensoffensive; **~ offer** Friedensangebot; **~ offering** Friedensangebot; **~ officer** Schutzpolizist, Sicherheits-, Polizeibeamter; **~ operations** Friedensaktion; **~ overture** Friedensangebot; **~ pact** Friedenspakt; **~ plan** Friedensplan; **~ preliminaries** Vorfriedensvertrag; **~ program(me)** Friedensprogramm; **~ rally** Friedensresolution; **~ search** Friedensbe-

mühungen; ~ **settlement** Friedensregelung; ~ **society** Friedens-
gesellschaft; ~ **talk** Friedensgespräch; ~ **terms** Friedensbedingungen; ~ **treaty** Friedensvertrag.

peaceable friedlich, friedliebend, unangefochten;
~ **possession** ungestörter Besitz.

peacebreaker Friedensbrecher.

peacebreaking Friedensbruch, Störung der öffentlichen Sicherheit und Ordnung.

peaceful| application of atomic energy Anwendung der Atom-
energie für friedliche Zwecke; ~ **change** friedliche Veränderung;
~ **death** friedlicher Tod; ~ **evening** friedlicher Abend; ~ **nation**
friedliebende Nation; ~ **penetration** friedliche Durchdringung;
~ **picketing** nicht aggressiv durchgeführtes Streikpostenstehen; ~ **policy** Friedenspolitik; ~ **settlement** gütliche Beilegung;
~ **solution** friedliche Lösung; ~ **use of atomic energy** friedliche
Nutzung der Atomenergie.

peacekeeping| force Friedenstruppen; ~ **operation** Friedensak-
tion; ~ **role** Rolle des Friedensstifters.

peacemaker Friedensstifter.

peacetime Friedenszeit;
~ **(a.)** friedensmäßig;
~ **application** Friedensverwendung; ~ **budget** Friedensetat; ~
consumption Friedensverbrauch, -bedarf; ~ **economy** Friedenswirtschaft; ~ **figures** Friedenszahlen; ~ **needs** Friedensbedarf; ~ **operation** Friedensbetrieb; ~ **parity** Friedensparität; ~
production Friedensproduktion; ~ **requirements** Friedensbedarf.

peach *(sl.)* prima Sache;
~ **of a fellow** ein Prachtskerl; **a** ~ **of a hat** Gedicht von einem
Hut;
~ **(v.) (sl.)** verpfeifen, denunzieren.

peachy *(sl.)* prima, fabelhaft.

peak höchster Stand, Gipfel, Höchstpunkt, *(fig.)* Höhepunkt,
(el., traffic) Hauptbelastung, Stoßzeit, *(peak price)* Höchst-,
Maximalpreis;
post-war ~ Nachkriegshöchststand;
~ **of the demand** Spitzenbedarf; ~ **of production** Produktionshöchststand;
~ **(v.)** Höchststand erreichen;
~ **at 4%** in der Spitze vier Prozent erreichen; ~ **in the first
quarter** Höchstsätze im ersten Vierteljahr erreichen;
to be off only slightly from their ~ knapp unter der Spitzenposition liegen; **to be past one's** ~ Höhepunkt seiner Laufbahn
überschritten haben; **to break through its previous March** ~
erstmals den Höchststand vom März wieder überschreiten; **to
have reached its** ~ in voller Blüte stehen; **to reach the** ~ Höchststand erreichen;
~ **advance requirements** Spitzenkreditbedürfnis; ~ **capacity**
Höchstleistungsgrenze; ~ **capitalism** Hochkapitalismus; ~
construction season Hochbausaison; **to cope with** ~ **consumption** Maßnahmen gegen den Höchstverbrauch treffen; ~ **cost of
borrowing** teuerste Form der Kreditaufnahme; ~ **demand** Spitzenbedarf; off-~ **flights** gering belegte Flugzeiten, flugarme
Zeiten; ~ **hours** Spitzenbelastung, Stoßzeit, Hauptgeschäftszeit; ~ **hours of traffic** Verkehrsspitze, verkehrsreiche Stunden, Hauptverkehrszeit, -stunden; ~**-hour traffic** Verkehrsstoß; ~ **industry's hours** Zeiten größter Belastung in der
Industrie, Spitzenbelastungszeit; **to have its** ~ **hours in the
evening** abends am stärksten belastet sein; ~ **investment** Schei-
telpunkt der Investitionsanstrengungen; ~ **level** Höhepunkt,
Höchststand, höchster Stand, Rekordgröße; **to reach** ~ **levels**
(stock exchange) Höchstkurse erzielen; ~ **load** Maximalbelastung, *(electricity)* Spitzen-, Höchst-, Hauptbelastung, *(work)*
Arbeitshäufung, Belastungsspitze; ~ **output** Spitzenleistung,
Produktionsmaximum, Höchstproduktion; ~ **performance**
Spitzen-, Gipfelleistung; off-~ **periods** Zeiten geringerer Belastung; ~ **price** Höchstpreis, -kurs; **to handle the seasonal** ~
problem mit dem Problem der saisonalen Spitzenbelastung
fertig werden; ~ **sales** Spitzenverkaufszahlen; ~ **sales period**
Hauptgeschäftszeit; ~ **season** Hochsaison, Hauptverkaufszeit;
~ **time** konjunktureller Wellenberg, Hochkonjunktur, *(traffic)*
Hauptverkehrs-, Stoßzeit, Verkehrsspitze; ~ **traffic** Spitzenverkehr; ~ **value** Spitzen-, Höchstwert; ~ **wage** Spitzen-,
Höchstlohn; ~ **year** Spitzenjahr; ~ **yield** Ertragsspitze.

peanut *(person, US)* unbedeutender Mensch;
~**s** *(small profit, sl.)* kleiner Profit;
to have to work for ~**s** *(sl.)* für einen Apfel und ein Ei arbeiten;
~ **gallery** *(theater, sl.)* Olymp; ~ **politician** *(US sl.)* unbedeutender Politiker; ~ **politics** *(US fam.)* Kirchturmspolitik.

pearl Perle, *(fig.)* Köstliches, Zierde, Krone, *(print.)* Perlschrift;
to cast ~**s before swine** Perlen vor die Säue werfen;

~ **diver (fisher)** Perlenfischer, *(restaurant, sl.)* Tellerwäscher; ~
necklace Perlenhalsband, -kette.

peasant Bauer, Landwirt, *(labo(u)rer)* Landarbeiter;
~ **holding** bäuerlicher Grundbesitz; ~ **labo(u)r** landwirtschaftliche Arbeitskräfte; ~ **property holding** Bauernhof; ~ **proprietor** Landwirt, kleinbäuerlicher Grundbesitzer.

peasantry Landvolk, Bauerntum.

peasouper dichter gelber Nebel.

peat coal Torfkohle.

pebble Kieselstein;
to be not the only ~ **on the beach** keineswegs unersetzlich sein.

peck Menge, Haufen, *(Br., sl.)* Futter;
~ **of troubles** Haufen Sorgen;
~ **(v.)** hacken, *(Br., coll.)* futtern;
~ **at s. o.** an jem. herumnörgeln, auf jem. herumhacken; ~ **at
one's dinner** in seinem Essen herumstochern; ~ **down a wall**
Wand niederreißen; ~ **up the ground** Boden aufhacken.

pecker *(sl.)* Mut, Courage;
to keep up one's ~ sich nicht kleinkriegen (unterkriegen) lassen,
Kopf hoch halten.

pecking order *(fig.)* Gesellschaftshierarchie, durch Titelsucht
bestimmte Gesellschaftsordnung.

peculate *(v.) (law)* [öffentliche Gelder] unterschlagen, veruntreuen, sich Unterschlagungen zuschulden kommen lassen.

peculation [Amts]unterschlagung, -schleif, Veruntreuung öffentlicher Mittel.

pecular Veruntreuer, Defraudant.

peculiar Vorrecht, Privileg, Prärogative *(private interest)*
Privatinteresse;
~ **(a.)** besonders, eigentümlich, *(coll.)* verdreht, komisch;
to be a little ~ etw. sonderlich sein; **to be** ~ **in one's dress** sich
extravagant anziehen;
~ **characteristics** *(antitrust law, US)* besondere Eigenschaften;
to be of ~ **interest** besonderes Interesse hervorrufen; **God's** ~
people *(religion)* das auserwählte Volk; **to have one's own** ~
reason seine ganz besonderen Gründe haben.

peculiarities, special *(pass)* besondere Kennzeichen;
~ **of speech** Sprachangewohnheiten.

peculiarity besonderes Merkmal, Besonderheit.

pecuniary geldlich, finanziell, pekuniär;
~ **advantage** materieller Vorteil, Vermögensvorteil; ~ **affairs**
Geldangelegenheiten; ~ **aid** geldliche (finanzielle) Unterstützung; ~ **assets** Vermögenswerte; ~ **assistance** finanzielle Hilfe;
~ **benefit** geldlicher Vorteil, Vermögensvorteil; ~ **causes** vermögensrechtliche Streitigkeiten; ~ **circumstances** Vermögensverhältnisse, -lage, finanzielle Lage; ~ **claim** Geldforderung; ~
compensation Geldentschädigung; ~ **condition** von geldwerter
Art; ~ **consideration** Äquivalent in Geld; ~ **damage** Vermögensschaden; ~ **demand** Geldforderung; ~ **detriment** Vermögensnachteil; ~ **difficulty (embarrassment)** Geldverlegenheit,
-klemme, -sorgen; **for** ~ **gain** in gewinnsüchtiger Absicht,
zwecks Erlangung eines Vermögensvorteils; ~ **interest** finanzielle Belange (Interesse); ~ **investment** Vermögensanlage; ~
legacy Geldvermächtnis; ~ **liability** finanzielle Verbindlichkeit; ~ **loss** finanzieller Schaden, Vermögensverlust, -schaden,
finanzieller Verlust; ~ **obligations** finanzielle Verpflichtungen;
~ **offence** mit Geldstrafe belegte Übertretung; ~ **penalty** Geldstrafe; ~ **prejudice** Vermögensnachteil; ~ **present** Geldgeschenk; ~ **property** bares Vermögen; ~ **punishment** Geldstrafe;
~ **requirements** Geldbedarf; ~ **resources** Geldquellen, -mittel,
finanzielle Mittel (Möglichkeiten); ~ **return** pekuniär bewerte-
ter Ertrag; ~ **reward** [Geld]belohnung; **for** ~ **reward** gegen
Entgelt; ~ **satisfaction** finanzielle Abfindung, Geldentschädigung; ~ **wants** finanzielle Bedürfnisse.

pecuniosity Wohlhabenheit.

pecunious wohlhabend, reich.

pedal Pedal, Trittbrett, Fußhebel;
brake ~ Bremspedal;
~ **brake** Fußbremse; ~ **control** Fußschaltung; ~ **cyclist**
Radfahrer.

pedant Pedant.

peddle *(v.)* Hausierhandel treiben, hausieren, Wandergewerbe
(Reisegewerbe) betreiben, *(US)* verkloppen, *(be busy about
trifles)* sich mit Kleinigkeiten abgeben;
~ **through its branch offices** durch das eigene Filialnetz vertreiben; ~ **gossip** herumtratschen; ~ **without a licence** ohne Gewerbeschein tätig sein; ~ **out** *(sl.)* alte (getragene) Sachen an den
Altwarenhändler verkaufen; ~ **it out** *(loan)* in kleineren Beträgen abgeben; ~ **one's papers** *(US sl.)* sich um seine eigenen
Angelegenheiten kümmern; ~ **scandals** *(fam.)* Skandale kolportieren; ~ **away one's time** seine Zeit verplempern.

peddled on the pavement auf dem Bürgersteig zum Verkauf ausgelegt.

peddler *(US)* Hausierer, fliegender Händler, Reise-, Wandergewerbetreibender, *(railroad, sl.)* Bummel-, Vorortzug; **~'s French** Kauderwelsch; **~'s licence** *(US)* Wandergewerbe, Hausierschein.

peddlery *(US)* Hausiergeschäft, -handel, Reise-, Wandergewerbe.

peddling ambulantes Gewerbe, Hausierhandel, Reise-, Wandergewerbe;
~ *(a.)* unbedeutend, wertlos, nichtig;
~ details Kleinigkeitskrämerei.

pedestal Sockel, Postament, Piedestal, *(fig.)* Grundlage, Basis;
to set s. o. on a ~ j. vergöttern;
~ writing table Diplomatenschreibtisch.

pedestrian Spazier-, Fußgänger;
oncoming ~ entgegenkommender Fußgänger; **solitary ~** einzelner Fußgänger;
~ *(a.)* zu Fuß, *(fig.)* prosaisch, ohne Schwung, uninteressant;
to knock down a ~ Fußgänger um-, an-, überfahren;
~ crossing Fußgängerüberweg, Straßenübergang; **~ crossing light** Fußgängerampel; **~ crossing regulation** Regelung des Fußgängerverkehrs; **~ island** Fußgängerreservoir; **~ journey** Reise auf Schusters Rappen; **~ lines** Übergang für Fußgänger; **~ mall** Fußgängerpromenade; **~ platform** Fußgängergehweg; **~ precinct** Fußgängerbereich; **~ street** Fußgängerweg; **~ subway** Fußgängerunterführung; **~ traffic** Passanten-, Fußgängerverkehr; **~ work** langweilige Tätigkeit; **~ zone** Fußgängerbereich; **car-free ~ zone** Fußgängerzone.

pedestrianize *(v.)* zu Fuß gehen, für Fußgänger anlegen.

pedigree Stammbaum, Ahnentafel;
~ race Zuchtrasse.

pedlar *(Br.)* fliegender Händler, Hausierer, Wander-, Reisegewerbetreibender;
~'s certificate *(Br.)* (licence, *US*) Wandergewerbeschein.

pedlary *(Br.)* Reise-, Wandergewerbe, Hausierhandel, Hausierer.

peel *(print.)* Aufhängekreuz;
~ *(v.)* **off** *(mil.)* ausscheren, *(wall paper)* abgehen, sich ablösen.

peeler *(Br., sl.)* Polyp, *(stripper, sl.)* Schönheitstänzerin.

peep *(door)* Guckloch;
at ~ of day bei Tagesanbruch;
~ of the scenery Blick auf die Landschaft;
~ *(v.)* **through a keyhole** durch ein Schlüsselloch gucken; **~ out a secret** Geheimnis ausspionieren;
to have a ~ through the window kurzen Blick aus dem Fenster werfen;
~ hole Guckloch.

peeper Schnüffler, Spion, *(coll.)* Guckloch.

peepie-creepie *(sl., US)* tragbares Funksprechgerät.

Peeping Tom heimlicher Beobachter.

peer Ebenbürtiger, Gleichrangiger, *(mate)* Kamerad, Kollege, *(nobleman, Br.)* Adliger, Mitglied des Oberhauses, Peer;
without a ~ unvergleichlich;
life ~ *(Br.)* lebenslängliches Oberhausmitglied; **one's ~s** Seinesgleichen;
to be the ~ of Vergleich aushalten;
~ group Gleichaltrigengruppe.

peerage Hochadel, Adelsstand;
to be raised to the ~ in den Adelsstand erhoben werden.

peg Stöpsel, Pflock, *(journalism)* Aufhänger, *(surveying)* Markierungs-, Absteckpflock, *(stock exchange)* Kurs-, Marktunterstützung;
off the ~ von der Stange [gekauft]; **on the ~** *(US sl.)* mit erlaubter Geschwindigkeit, *(US, army, sl.)* eingebuchtet;
adjustable ~ fallweise veränderte Parität; **clothes ~** Wäscheklammer; **crawling ~** *(US)* Stufenflexibilität; **discretionary crawling ~** ermessensmäßig vorgenommene [vorsichtige] Kursstützung (Wechselkursänderung); **hat ~** Hutständer;
~ to hang a claim on Vorwand für eine Forderung; **~ to hang a grievance on** Aufhänger für eine Beschwerde; **a square ~ in a round hole** zu kleine Schuhnummer für eine Position;
~ *(v.)* mit Pflöcken versehen, *(drink, Br., sl.)* süffeln, *(journalism)* aufhängen, als Aufhänger benutzen, *(laundry)* festklammern, *(price)* [Kurs] stützen, stabilisieren;
~ away drauflosarbeiten, unverdrossen arbeiten, schuften; **~ the exchange** Wechselkurs stabilisieren; **~ their exchange rates at par** Wechselkurse in der festgelegten Währungsparität halten; **~ the highway** Landstraße entlangtrotten; **~ the market** Kursstützungen durchführen; **~ out** Land abstecken, *(Br., sl.)* aufgeben, es aufstecken, abkratzen, sterben; **~ out a claim**

Mutung abstecken; **~ out one's claim** seine Ansprüche vorbringen; **~ out a line** Linie festlegen; **~ out the ground plan** Grundriß abstecken; **~ the pound** Pfund stützen; **~ a price** Preis stützen, Preisstützung vornehmen; **~ one's production** sein Arbeitspensum schaffen; **~ the value of the pound to the dollar** Kurs des Pfundes an den Dollar anhängen; **~ the wages at** Löhne stoppen bei;
to be a square ~ in a round hole für eine Position völlig ungeeignet sein, fehl am Platze sein; **to buy a suit of clothes off the ~** Anzug von der Stange kaufen; **to come down a ~** einige Pflöcke zurückstecken; **to mix o. s. a stiff ~** sich einen steifen Grog machen; **to put s. o. on the ~** *(mil., sl.)* j. beim Vorgesetzten anzeigen; **not to stir a ~** *(sl.)* keinen Finger rühren; **to take s. o. down a ~ or two** jem. einen Dämpfer aufsetzen (eins auf den Hut geben);
~ ladder Sprossenleiter; **~ leg** Holzbein; **~ switch** *(el.)* Umschalter; **adjustable ~ system** *(US)* System der fallweise veränderten Wechselkurse; **crawling ~ system** *(US)* Stufenflexibilitätssystem.

pegged mit Pflöcken befestigt;
~ down with regulations in seiner Bewegungsfreiheit durch Bestimmungen eingeschränkt; **~ out** *(US)* ruiniert;
to be ~ *(mil.)* eines Vergehens angeklagt (bezichtigt) sein; **to be ~ down to one's work** an seine Arbeit gefesselt sein;
~ exchange rates künstlich gehaltene (festgelegte) Wechselkurse; **~ market** *(US)* gestützte Börsenkurse; **~ price** subventionierter Preis, Stützpreis, *(stock exchange)* künstlich gehaltener (stabilisierter) Kurs, Stützkurs.

pegging *(market, price)* Kurs-, Preisstützung;
~ away Drauflosarbeiten; **~ the exchange** Kursstützung, Wechselkursstabilisierung; **~ of prices** Preisstabilisierung; **wage-~ efforts** Lohnstabilisierungsbemühungen; **~ operations** [Kurs]interventionen.

pejoration Verschlechterung, *(Scot.)* Wertminderung.

pell-mell wie Kraut und Rüben.

pelt Schlag, Wurf;
at full ~ so schnell als möglich;
~ *(v.)* **s. o. with abuses** j. maßlos beschimpfen; **~ s. o. with invitations** j. mit Einladungen überschütten; **~ s. o. with mud** j. mit Dreck bewerfen; **~ s. o. with questions** j. mit Fragen bombardieren (durchlöchern).

pen Feder, *(enclosure)* Pferch, Verschlag, *(prison)* Gefängniszelle, *(sl.)* Kittchen, *(writer)* Schriftstellerei;
drawing ~ Zeichenfeder; **fountain ~** Füllfeder; **ready ~** gewandte Feder; **writing ~** Schreibfeder;
~ and ink Schreibzeug;
~ *(v.)* aufschreiben;
~ o. s. up in one's office sich in sein Büro zurückziehen;
to have a facile ~ gewandte Feder haben; **to have a scathing ~** scharfe Feder führen; **to make one's living by one's (the) ~** sich als Schriftsteller seinen Lebensunterhalt verdienen; **to put (set) one's ~ to paper** zur Feder greifen;
~ desk set Füllhalterständer; **~-and-ink** Federzeichnung; **~ friend** Brieffreund[schaft]; **~ name** Schriftstellername, Pseudonym; **~ pusher** *(sl.)* Federfuchser, Bürohengst; **~ shop** Schreibwarengeschäft; **~-and-ink sketch** Federzeichnung.

penal strafrechtlich, strafbar;
to be ~ to the work-shy sich für Arbeitsscheue nachträglich auswirken;
~ act strafbare Handlung, Straftat; **~ action** Strafverfahren, -prozeß; **~ administration** Strafvollzugsbehörde; **~ bond** Vereinbarung einer Konventionalstrafe; **~ clause** *(contract)* Strafklausel, -bestimmung; **~ code** Strafgesetzbuch; **~ colony** Verbrecher-, Strafkolonie; **~ duty** Strafzoll; **~ establishment (institution)** Straf[vollzugs]anstalt; **~ interest** *(US)* Verzugszinsen; **~ law** Strafrecht; **~ legislation** Strafgesetzgebung; **~ liability** *(US)* Strafmündigkeit; **~ neglect** strafbare Unterlassung; **~ offence** strafbare Handlung, Straftat; **~ proceedings** Strafverfahren; **~ prosecution** Strafverfolgung; **~ provision** Strafbestimmung; **~ rate** Kampfzoll; **~ reform** Strafrechtsform; **~ servitude** *(Br.)* Zwangsarbeit, Zuchthaus; **~ servitude for life** *(Br.)* lebenslängliche Zuchthausstrafe; **~ settlement** Verbrecher-, Strafkolonie; **~ statute** Strafgesetz, -bestimmung; **~ suit** *(US)* Strafverfahren, -prozeß; **~ sum** Reugeld, Konventionalstrafe; **~ time** Strafzeit.

penalize *(v.)* in Strafe nehmen, mit einer Strafe belegen.

penalization Bestrafung.

penalties *(balance sheet, US)* Gesamtbetrag betrieblicher Sozialaufwendungen.

penalty Strafe, *(fine)* Geldstrafe, -buße, *(for nonfulfilment of contract)* Vertrags-, Konventionalstrafe;

under ~ of bei Strafe von; **forbidden under ~ of death** bei Todesstrafe verboten;

criminal ~ Geldstrafe; **customs ~** Zollstrafe; **death ~** (US) Todesstrafe; **fiscal ~** Steuerstrafe; **heavy ~** schwere (hohe) Strafe; **increased ~** verschärfte Strafe; **light ~** leichte Strafe; **maximum ~** Höchststrafe; **operative ~** wirksame Strafe; **pecuniary ~** Geldstrafe; **slight ~** geringfügige Strafe; **stern ~** strenge Strafe; **substituted ~** Ersatzstrafe;

~ for delay (default) Verzugsstrafe; **~ of imprisonment** Gefängnisstrafe; **extreme ~ of the law** Todesstrafe; **~ for nonperformance of a contract** Konventional-, Vertragsstrafe bei Nichterfüllung; **~ of progress** Nachteile (Tribut) des Fortschritts;

to be subject to ~ strafbar sein; **to carry a ~** mit Strafe bedroht sein, Bestrafung nach sich ziehen; **to impose (inflict) a ~** Strafe verhängen; **to incur a ~** sich strafbar machen, straffällig werden; **to make o. s. liable to a ~** sich strafbar machen; **to mitigate a ~** Strafe mildern; **to pay** (fig.) Tribut zollen, benachteiligt werden; **to pay the ~ of fame** mit den Auswirkungen seines Ruhms fertig werden müssen; **to pay the ~ of one's foolishness** Folgen seiner Dummheit zu tragen haben; **to relax a ~** Strafe mildern; **to remit a ~** Strafe erlassen;

~ area (football) Strafraum; **motorist's ~ chart** Straftabelle für Verkehrsübertretungen; **~ clause** Strafklausel, -bestimmung, Festsetzung einer Vertragsstrafe; **~ envelope** (US) Briefumschlag frei durch Ablösung, frankierter Dienstumschlag; **fixed ~ notice** gebührenpflichtige Verwarnung; **~ postage** Strafporto; **~ provisions** Strafbestimmungen; **~ rate** (US, insurance) Zusatztarif, Gefahrenzulage, (tax) Straftarif; **~ tariff** Zusatztarif.

pence rates (Br.) in Penny notierte Devisenkurse.

pencil Zeichen-, Farb-, Bleistift, (fig.) Zeichenkunst;

with a fine ~ so billig als möglich;

carbon ~ Durchschreibestift; **colo(u)red ~** Farbstift; **eyebrow ~** Augenbrauenstift; **indelible ~** Tintenstift; **propelling ~** Drehstift;

~ of light Lichtbündel, Lichtkegel;

~ (v.) malen, zeichnen, entwerfen;

to have a bold ~ kühnen Pinselstrich führen;

~ box Federkasten; **~ drawing** Bleistiftzeichnung; **~ holder** Bleistiftverlängerer; **~ sharpener** Bleistiftspitzer; **~ sketch** Bleistiftzeichnung; **~ tray** Bleistiftschale.

pend (v.) schweben, in der Schwebe sein.

pendant (book) Anhang;

to form a ~ Gegenstück bilden.

pendency Schweben, Schwebezeit, Unentschiedenheit, (suit) Anhängigsein, Rechtshängigkeit.

pendent (law) in der Schwebe, anhängig;

~ notes beigefügter Kommentar; **~ rocks** überhängendes Gestein.

pendente lite (lat.) in einem schwebenden Verfahren.

pendicle (Scot., law) Teil einer Parzelle.

pending (suit) anhängig, schwebend, rechtshängig, (undecided) schwebend, unentschieden;

~ his acceptance of the offer solange, bis er das Angebot angenommen hat; **~ the action** solange der Prozeß schwebt; **~ appeal** noch nicht rechtskräftig; **~ arrangement** bis zur Erledigung; **~ in court** rechtshängig; **~ a decision of the court** solange die gerichtliche Entscheidung aussteht, während der Rechtshängigkeit; **~ delivery** bis zur Ablieferung; **~ these discussions** während der anstehenden Diskussion; **~ instructions** vorbehaltlich andersartiger Weisungen; **~ at law** rechtshängig; **~ negotiations** während des Schwebens der Verhandlungen; **~ further news** bis zum Eintreffen weiterer Nachrichten;

to be ~ (lawsuit) schweben, in der Schwebe sein, im Gange (anhängig) sein;

~ action schwebender (anhängiger) Prozeß; **~ application** (patent law) schwebende Anmeldung; **~ charges** vorliegende Anklagen; **~ debts** schwebende Schulden; **~ delivery** bis zur Ablieferung; **~ files** Unerledigtes; **~ lawsuit** schwebender Prozeß; **~ litigations** anhängige Prozesse; **~ operations** schwebende Transaktionen; **~ proceedings** schwebende Gerichtsverfahren, anhängige Strafsachen; **~ risks** laufende Versicherungsrisiken; **~ suit** anhängiger (schwebender) Prozeß.

pendulate (v.) pendeln, (fig.) Schwankungen unterworfen sein, schwanken.

pendulation Schwanken.

pendulum Pendel, (fig.) Pendelbewegung;

~ of public opinion schwankende öffentliche Meinung.

penetralia (fig.) Privatleben, Intimsphäre.

penetrant durchdringend, scharfsinnig.

penetrate (v.) durchdringen, eindringen;

~ armo(u)r Panzerung durchdringen; **~ a building** (smell) Gebäude durchziehen; **~ into a country** in ein Land einsickern; **~ s. one's disguise** jds. Maske durchschauen; **~ through the enemy's lines** feindliche Linien durchdringen; **~ s. one's heart with pity** jds. Herz mit Mitleid erfüllen; **~ a market** sich auf einem Absatzmarkt durchsetzen; **~ s. one's mind** jds. Geist erleuchten; **~ the plot against o. s.** Verschwörung gegen sich ergründen; **~ into a secret** Geheimnis ergründen.

penetrating odo(u)r durchdringender Geruch.

penetration Eindringen, (advertisement) Durchdringungsvermögen, (sharp discernment) durchdringender Verstand, Scharfsinn;

economic ~ wirtschaftliche Durchdringung; **peaceful ~** (pol.) friedliche Durchdringung;

to develop its initial ~ of the primary Eurobond market seine ersten Einsichten in die Geschäfte des Euroanleihemarktes weiter vertiefen.

penguin (airplane) Übungsflugzeug, (airforce use) Schreibtischbulle.

peninsula Halbinsel.

penitence Reue, Zerknirschung.

penitent reuig, bußfertig, zerknirscht.

penitentiary (US) Gefängnis, Zuchthaus, Strafanstalt, (Br.) Besserungsanstalt;

~ letter Entschuldigungsbrief; **~ offence** (US) zuchthauswürdiges Verbrechen; **~ system** Gefängnissystem.

penknife Federmesser.

penman Schriftsteller, (forger, sl.) Fälscher.

penmanship Schriftstellerei, schriftstellerische Leistung.

penmaster erfolgreicher Schriftsteller.

pennant Stander, Wimpel.

pennies, my few meine paar Groschen;

to think of ~ mit dem Pfennig rechnen.

penniless vermögens-, mittellos, arm;

to leave s. o. ~ j. völlig mittellos zurücklassen.

pennon Wimpel, Standarte.

penny (Br.) Penny, (fig.) Heller, Kleinigkeit, (US) Eincentstück;

to the last ~ bis zum letzten Heller;

pretty ~ hübsche Sümmchen; **no paternoster no ~** umsonst ist der Tod; **a ~ for your thoughts** wenn ich nur wüßte was Sie denken; **in for a ~, in for a pound** wer A sagt, muß auch B sagen; **to be a bad ~** unangenehmes Subjekt sein; **to be a ready ~** leichten Verdienst abgeben; **not to be a ~ the wiser** um keinen Deut klüger sein; **to come back like a bad ~** immer wieder zurückkommen; **to come in for a pretty ~** hübsches (beträchtliches) Vermögen erben; **to cost a pretty ~** schönes Stück Geld kosten; **to have not a ~ to bless o. s. with** keinen roten Heller haben, völlig auf dem Trockenen sitzen; **to know how to turn a ~** sein Geschäft verstehen; **to look at every ~** twice jeden Pfennig zweimal umdrehen; **to make a pretty ~ out of s. th.** an einer Sache ein schönes Stück Geld verdienen; **to pay to the last ~** auf Heller und Pfennig bezahlen; **to save every ~ one can** jeden nur möglichen Groschen sparen; **to spend a ~** (coll.) WC benutzen; **to turn an honest ~** sein Geld auf anständige Art und Weise (ehrlich) verdienen; **to want the ~ and the bun** auf zwei Hochzeiten tanzen wollen.

penny-a-line nach der Zeile (schlecht) bezahlt, (fig.) minderwertig, billig;

~ (v/i) Zeilen schinden, als schlecht bezahlter Berichterstatter arbeiten.

penny-a-liner (Br.) nach der Zeile bezahlter Journalist, Zeilenschinder, Vielschreiber.

penny-a-linism Zeilenschinderei.

penny|catch-~ article Pfennigartikel; **~ bank** (Br.) Sparkasse, Sparkassenannahmestelle; **~ deposit** Pfennigsparen; **~ dreadful** (Br.) Schauer-, Hintertreppenroman; **~ fee** Hungerlohn; **~ horrible** (Br.) Groschenheft; **~-in-the-slot** automatisch; **~-in-the-slot machine** Groschen-, Verkaufsautomat; **~ magazine** Boulevardblatt; **~ mail** Geldrente; **~ pincher** Pfennigfuchser; **to be a self-proclaimed ~ pincher** sich selbst als Pfennigfuchser bezeichnen; **~ pinching** (sl.) knauserig; **~ post** gewöhnliche Briefpost; **~ press** Boulevardpresse; **~ rent** Geldrente, (income) Einkommen; **~ saver** Sparer; **~ stocks** (US) Kleinaktien; **~-wise** sparsam in Kleinigkeiten; **~-wise and pound foolish** knickerig bei Kleinigkeiten und verschwenderisch im Großen; **~ wisdom** Pfennigfuchserei;

the ~'s dropped der Groschen ist gefallen.

pennyweight (sl.) Juwelen, Schmuck.

pennyworth (bargain) wohlfeiler Kauf, gutes Geschäft;

bad ~ schlechtes Geschäft;

not a ~ of food in the house nicht mal ein Stück trockenes Brot zu Hause;

not to be the height of six ~ of coppers Dreikäsehoch sein; **to find s. th. a good ~** gutes Geschäft machen; **to have no mighty ~ of s. th.** keinen bedeutenden Gewinn aus etw. ziehen.

penological kriminalkundlich.

penology Kriminalstrafkunde, Strafrechtslehre, -vollzugswissenschaft.

pension Pension, Rente, Ruhegehalt, -geld, *(allowance)* Zehr-, Kostgeld, *(board and lodging)* Pension, Fremdenheim, *(boarding school)* Pensionat, Internat, *(employee's insurance portion)* Pensionsanteil des Arbeitnehmers, *(university, Br.)* Gebühren;

entitled to (eligible for) a ~ pensionsberechtigt, -fähig, versorgungsberechtigt, ruhegehaltsberechtigt;

~s Versorgungsbezüge;

assistance ~ *(Br.)* Bedürftigkeitsrente; **basic flat-rate ~** pauschale Grundrente; **company ~** Betriebspension; **contributory ~** beitragspflichtige Pension; **director's ~** Altersbezüge eines Vorstandsmitgliedes; **disability ~** Invaliden-, Kriegsversehrtenrente; **earnings-related ~** Indexrente; **earnings-related additional ~** bruttolohnbezogene Zusatzrente; **employee ~** Angestelltenpension; **in-bank ~s** Bankruhezahlungen; **life ~** lebenslängliche Rente, Pension auf Lebenszeit; **lump-sum ~** festgesetzte Pensionszahlung; **mother's ~** *(US)* Rente für Mutter und Kind; **noncontributory ~** beitragsfreie Pension (Rente); **nontaxable ~** steuerfreie Rente; **normal ~** Normalpension; **old-age ~** *(Br.)* Alters-, Invalidenrente, Altersversorgung; **~s paid** Pensionszahlungen, Ruhegeldleistungen; **portable ~** übertragbarer Pensionsanspruch; **public-service ~** Staatspension; **retiring (retirement) ~** Ruhegehalt, *(Br.)* Altersrente; **basic national insurance retirement ~** *(Br.)* Mindestrente der Sozialversicherung, Sozialrente; **satisfactory ~** auskömmliche Pension; **social security ~** Sozialversicherungsrente; **state ~** Staatspension; **state retirement ~** staatliche Altersrente; **supplementary ~** Zusatzrente, -versorgung; **survivor's ~** Hinterbliebenenrente; **war ~** Kriegs-, Hinterbliebenenrente; **widow's ~** Witwenrente, -pension, geld;

~s and assistances Aufwendungen für Altersversorgungen und Unterstützung; **~ charged on an income** auf das Einkommen angerechnete Pension; **~ for injury at work** Betriebsunfallrente; **~ for life** lebenslängliche Pension, Lebensrente;

~ *(v.)* pensionieren, in den Ruhestand versetzen, Ruhegehalt gewähren, *(v./i.)* in Pension sein;

~ s. o. off jem. ein Ruhegehalt gewähren, j. mit Pension verabschieden (in den Ruhestand versetzen), j. pensionieren, jem. seinen Abschied bewilligen;

to apply for retirement (to be retired) on a ~ um seine Pensionierung einkommen; **to be awarded a ~** Pension (Ruhegehalt) erhalten (beziehen); **to be discharged with a ~** entlassen und pensioniert werden; **to be entitled to a ~** Pensionsberechtigung (Ruhegehaltsansprüche) haben, pensionsberechtigt sein; **to be ~ed off** in den Pensionsstand treten; **to begin receiving a ~** rentenberechtigt sein; **to cancel s. one's ~** jem. die Pension entziehen; **to carry a ~** zu einer Pension berechtigen, Pensionsberechtigung gewähren; **to claim a ~ by virtue of one's long military service** Pensionsansprüche unter Berücksichtigung der langjährigen Militärdienstzeit stellen; **to draw a ~** Pension (Rente) beziehen; **to forfeit the right to a ~** Ruhegehaltsansprüche verlieren; **to go on a ~** in den Ruhestand treten, sich pensionieren lassen; **to go to the Post Office to draw one's ~** sich bei der Post seine Rente auszahlen lassen; **to grant a ~ to s. o.** jem. eine Pension zahlen; **to have one's ~ inflation-proofed** inflationssichere Pension erhalten; **to have a ~ on two-thirds salary** Grundpension in Höhe von zwei Dritteln des Gehaltes beziehen; **to live in ~** in einer Pension wohnen; **to live on a ~** von seiner Pension (Rente) leben; **to make a ~ for s. o.** jem. eine Pension aussetzen; **to pay only 2% for an inflation-proofed (index-related, -linked) noncontributory ~** lediglich 2% zu einer sonst beitragsfreien und inflationssicheren Pension beitragen; **to put up the rate of a ~** Pension (Ruhegehalt) erhöhen; **to qualify for a ~** Voraussetzungen für die Gewährung einer Pension (Pensionsvoraussetzungen) erfüllen; **to rate a ~** Pensionshöhe festsetzen; **to receive a ~** Pension bekommen; **to retire on a ~** pensioniert werden, in Pension gehen, sich pensionieren lassen, in den Ruhestand treten; **to revalue a ~ post-retirement in line with prices** Rente nach Ausscheiden aus dem Berufsleben laufend dem Preisniveau anpassen; **to revalue a ~ pre-retirement in line with earnings** Rente während der Beschäftigungszeit laufend dem Bruttolohn anpassen; **to settle a ~** Ruhegehalt aussetzen; **to struggle along on a ~** mit einer

Pension auskommen müssen; **to supplement one's ~** zu seiner Pension hinzuverdienen; **to suppress s. one's ~** jem. seine Pension vorenthalten; **to take away a ~ from s. o.** jem. keine Pension mehr zahlen;

~ account Pensionskasse; **Old-Age ~s Act** *(Br.)* Altersversorgungsgesetz; **~s administration and development** Verwaltung und Förderung des Pensionsfonds; **~ age** pensionsfähiges (rentenberechtigtes) Alter, Pensionsalter; **to be over ~ age** renten-, pensionsberechtigt sein; **~ Appeal Tribunal** *(Br.)* Sozialgericht; **~ augmentation** Renten-, Pensionserhöhung; **~ benefit** Rentenleistung, Pensionszahlung; **~ Benefit Guaranty Corporation** *(US)* Aufsichtsamt für das Pensionskassenwesen; **~ board** Pensionsausschuß; **occupational ~ board** Aufsichtsamt für betriebliche Pensionskassen; **~ burden** Pensionsverpflichtungen; **~ claim** Pensionsanspruch; **~ committee** Pensionsausschuß; **~ contribution** Pensionszuschuß; **~ costs** Pensionslasten; **~ credit** Pensionsgutschrift; **~ deficit** Defizit der Pensionskasse; **~ expectancy** Pensionsanwartschaft; **~ fund** Pensionskasse, -fonds, Versorgungsträger; **employees' ~ fund** Pensionskasse für Betriebsangehörige; **legally independent ~ fund** rechtlich selbständige Versorgungskasse; **occupational ~ fund** berufliche Pensionskasse; **staff ~ fund** *(Br.)* betriebliche Pensionskasse, -fonds; **Old-Age ~ Fund** Altersversorgungskasse; **~ reserve fund** Rücklagen für Pensionsverpflichtungen; **to diversify ~ funds into other companies' shares** Vermögen einer Pensionskasse in Aktien einer anderen Gesellschaft anlegen; **to levy 100 $ a year for the ~ fund** Jahresbeitrag von 100 Dollar für die Pensionskasse erheben; **~ fund assets** Vermögen einer Pensionskasse; **~ fund's holding** Beteiligungen einer Pensionskasse; **~-fund manager** Treuhänder eines Pensionsfonds; **~ fund money** von einer Pensionskasse verwaltete Mittel; **~ improvements** Verbesserung der Pensionsleistungen (Ruhegehaltsbezüge); **~ income** Versorgungs-, Ruhegehaltsbezüge; **~ increase** Pensions-, Ruhegehaltserhöhung; **~ increment** Pensionserhöhung, Rentensteigerungsbetrag; **old-age ~ insurance** Alters-, Ruhegeld-, Rentenversicherung; **government ~ insurance program(me)** staatlicher Altersversicherungsplan; **~ law** Pensionsordnung; **~ level** Rentenniveau; **old-age ~ management company** Ruhegeldverwaltungsgesellschaft; **~ obligations** Ruhegeld-, Pensionsverpflichtungen; **~ office** Versorgungsamt; **graduated ~ part** *(national insurance, Br.)* gestaffelter Rentenanteil; **~ payment** Pensionszahlung, -leistung, Versorgungsleistung, Rentenzahlung, -leistung, Ruhegeldleistung; **~ payments** *(balance sheet)* Ruhegehalt-, Versorgungsbezüge, Pensionszuschüsse, Rentenleistungen; **~ portfolio** Effektenportefeuille eines Pensionsfonds.

pension plan Pensionssystem, -ordnung, [Alters]versorgungswerk, Pensionskasse, Ruhegeldordnung;

company-financed ~ beitragsfreies (allein vom Unternehmer finanziertes) Pensionssystem; **contributory ~** beitragspflichtige Pensionskasse; **definite benefit ~** Pensionssystem mit feststehenden Lohnsätzen, gehaltsgebundenes Pensionssystem; **graduated ~** abgestuftes Sozialrentensystem; **group annuity ~** Gruppenrentenversicherungssystem; **joint annuity survivor ~** Pensionssystem mit Zahlung von Überlebensrenten; **noncontributory ~** beitragsfreie Pensionskasse; **self-administrated ~** betriebliche Pensionskasse; **trust agreement ~** außerbetriebliche Pensionskasse; **vested ~** unentziehbarer Ruhegeldanspruch;

to fund a ~ Pensionsfonds (Pensionskasse) errichten;

~ retirement age Pensionierungsalter nach der Pensionsordnung; **~ trust fund** Treuhandvermögen eines Altersversorgungswerkes, Pensionserfüllungskasse.

pension | policy holder Rentenversicherungsberechtigter; **personal ~ with profits policy** private gewinnbeteiligte Rentenversicherungspolice; **~ pool** *(US)* Pensionskasse mehrerer Industriebetriebe; **~ portfolio** Effektenportefeuille eines Pensionsfonds; **~ rates** Ruhegehalts-, Pensionssätze; **~ reserve** Pensionsrückstellung, Rückstellung für Ruhegeldverpflichtungen; **~ right** Ruhegehaltsanspruch, Pensionsberechtigung; **to cancel the ~ rights** Ruhegehaltsansprüche aberkennen; **~ scheme** Altersversorgungswerk; **additional ~ scheme** zusätzliche Altersversorgung; **contracted out ~ scheme** nicht an der staatlichen Altersversorgung partizipierende Pensionskasse; **graduated ~ scheme** Rentensystem mit proportionalen Beiträgen und Leistungen; **occupational ~ scheme** betriebliche Altersversorgung, Ruhegeldordnung; **self-administrated ~ scheme** betriebliche Altersversorgung; **state ~ scheme** staatliche Altersversorgung; **to be a participant in a ~ scheme** pensionsberechtigt sein; **~ scheme arrangement** Pensionsvereinbarung; **~ settlement** Pensionsvereinbarung; **~s system**

Renten-, Altersversorgungs-, Pensionssystem; **to belong to a ~ system** Ansprüche an die betriebliche Altersversorgung haben, Pensionskassenmitglied sein; ~ **trust** Pensions- [und Unterstützungs]kasse; **to make contributions to the ~ trust** Beiträge zur Pensionskasse leisten; ~ **unit** versicherungspflichtige Renteneinheit; ~ **warrants** Auszahlungsermächtigungen für Pensionen.

pensionable ruhegehalts-, pensionsfähig, -berechtigt;
~ **age** pensionsfähiges Alter, Renten-, Versorgungs-, Pensionsalter; **to offer employment on a ~ basis** pensionsberechtigte Stellung anbieten; ~ **earnings** auf die Pension anrechnungsfähige Einkünfte; ~ **emoluments** Pensions-, Versorgungs-, Ruhegehaltsbezüge; ~ **employment** pensionsberechtigte Stellung; ~ **pay** ruhegehaltsfähiger Lohnanteil; ~ **post** pensionsberechtigte Stellung.

pensionary *(Br.)* Pensionär, Ruhegehaltsempfänger, *(v.i.p.)* hohes Tier;
~ **on the government** pensionierter Beamter;
~ *(a.)* pensioniert, im Ruhestand, *(consisting of a pension)* in einer Pension bestehend, *(hired)* gedungen, bezahlt; ~ **provisions** Pensionsbestimmungen; ~ **spy** bezahlter Spion.

pensioned | off mit Pension verabschiedet;
to be ~ off pensioniert, in den Ruhestand versetzt; **to be ~ on the government** staatliche Pension beziehen.

pensioner Pensionär, Rentner, Ruhegehalts-, Renten-, Versorgungs-, Pensionsempfänger, *(boarding house)* Pensionsgast, *(boarding school)* Internatszögling;
army ~ pensionierter Soldat, Invalide; **civil ~** Invalide; **old-age ~** Bezieher einer Altersversorgung, Rentner; **retired ~** Rentner; **state ~** Staatspensionär, -rentner;
to be s. one's ~ in jds. Solde stehen;
~ **delegate** Pensionärsvertreter.

pensioning | off Pensionierung; ~ **warrant** Pensionszusicherungsschein.

pensum *(school)* Strafarbeit.

pent-road gesperrte Straße, Sackgasse.

pent-up | demand Nachholbedarf; ~ **inflation** gesteuerte Inflation.

penthouse Dachwohnung in einem Hochhaus.

penurious arm, geizig, filzig.

penury Mangel, Knappheit, Armut.

people Menschen, Leute, Einwohner, Bevölkerung, Volk, *(family)* Angehörige, Familie, Vorfahren;
among his own ~ im Kreise seiner Familie;
colo(u)red ~ Farbige; **the common ~** das gemeine Volk; **country ~** Landbevölkerung; **English-speaking ~** englisch sprechende Nationen; **exposed ~** werblich erreichbarer Personenkreis; **fashionable ~** Modewelt; **literary ~** Literaten; **middle-class ~** Mittelstandsschicht; **moneyed ~** wohlhabende Leute; **most ~** die meisten Menschen; **my ~** meine Familie; **the ~ responsible** die Verantwortlichen; **simple ~** kleine Leute; **town ~** Stadtbevölkerung; **village ~** Dorfbewohner; **young ~** junge Leute; **employer and his ~** Arbeitgeber und seine Arbeitnehmer;
~ **affected by the crisis** von der Krise betroffene Bevölkerungsschichten; ~ **of importance** wichtige Persönlichkeiten; ~ **down the ladder** untere Dienstgrade; **the ~ at large** die Masse des Volkes; ~ **of name** renommierte Leute; ~ **outside the profession** Leute, die nicht vom Fach sind; ~ **from the provinces** Provinzler; ~ **of all ranks** Menschen aus allen Schichten; ~ **of spirit** Menschen mit Energie; ~ **in the village** Dorfbevölkerung;
~ *(v.)* besiedeln, bevölkern;
to be one of those ~ who ... zu den Leuten gehören, die ...; **to go to the ~** Neuwahlen abhalten; **to inform one's ~** seine Angehörigen benachrichtigen; **to keep a ~ down by force** Volk unterdrücken; **to reside in the ~** *(power)* beim Volk liegen;
~**'s democracy** Volksdemokratie; ~**'s front** *(pol.)* Volksfront; ~**'s Republic** Volksrepublik.

peopled bevölkert;
densely ~ dicht bevölkert;
to become ~ besiedelt werden, sich bevölkern.

pep Energie, Elan, Schwung, Mumm;
full of ~ energiegeladen;
~ *(v.)* anfeuern, energisch betreiben;
~ **it up** Druck dahinter machen; ~ **up the economy** Wirtschaft ankurbeln; ~ **up a story** Geschichte interessanter machen;
to have ~ Mumm haben; **to lack ~** *(book)* keinen Schwung haben; **to put some ~ into s. o.** j. auf Schwung bringen; **to put ~ back into the investment trust sector** Anlagebereitschaft der Kapitalanlagegesellschaften animieren; **to take the ~ out of s. th.** einer Sache den Elan nehmen;
~ **rally** *(sl.)* Propagandaveranstaltung; ~ **talk** aufmunternde Worte, moralische Aufrichtung.

pepper *(v.)* *(fig.)* bepfeffern, bombardieren;
~ **s. o. with abuse** j. gehörig ausschimpfen; ~ **the enemy with machine-gun fire** Feind mit Maschinengewehrsalven eindecken; ~ **with questions** mit Fragen überhäufen; ~ **a speech with classic quotations** klassische Zitate in eine Rede einfließen lassen.

peppercorn rent nominelle Rente.

per, as ~ account rendered laut erhaltener (ausgestellter) Rechnung; ~ **advance** im voraus; ~ **advice** laut Anzeige; ~ **autre vie** auf die Lebensdauer eines Dritten; ~ **aversionem** *(lat.)* Pauschalkauf; ~ **annum** jährlich; ~ **bearer** durch Überbringer; ~ **capita** pro Kopf der Bevölkerung; ~ **capita quota** Kopfbetrag; ~ **capita sales** *(turnover)* Pro-Kopf-Umsatz; ~ **cent** Prozent, vom Hundert; ~ **contra** als Gegenbuchung eintragen; ~ **curiam** von Amtswegen; ~ **diem** pro Tag, täglich; ~**-diem allowance** *(US)* Tagegeld, Diäten; ~ **mille** pro Tausend, promille; ~ **misadventure** durch Unglücksfall; ~ **post** durch die Post; ~ **procuration** *(p.p.)* per Prokura, als Bevollmächtigter; ~ **quod** *(lat.)* aufgrund besonderer Tatumstände; ~ **rail** per Achse, mit der Bahn; ~ **sample** nach Probe; ~ **se** *(lat.)* für sich allein; ~ **stirpes** *(law of inheritance)* nach Stämmen; ~ **year** jährlich.

perambulate *(v.)* durchwandern, bereisen;
~ **the parish** Gemeinde besichtigen.

perambulation Besichtigungsreise, Grenzbegehung, *(law)* Gerichtssprengel.

perambulator Grenzbegeher, *(Br.)* Kinderwagen.

percent vom Hundert, Prozent;
~ *(a.)* prozentig;
~**s** festverzinsliche Wertpapiere;
to have one's money in seven ~s sein Geld in siebenprozentigen Wertpapieren angelegt haben.

percentable in Prozenten auszudrücken.

perceivable risk übersehbares Risiko.

percentage Prozent[satz], Anteilsgebühr, *(allowance)* Tantieme, *(commission)* Provision, *(content)* [Prozent]gehalt, -satz, *(of earned income)* Gewinnbeteiligung, -anteil, *(share)* [An]teil;
expressed as a ~ prozentual ausgedrückt;
average ~ Durchschnittsprozentsatz; **certain ~** sicherer Gewinn; **commission ~** Provisionsanteil; ~ **contract** vertraglich ausgehandelter Provisionssatz; **director's ~** Vorstandstantieme; **lowest ~** *(mining)* Mindestgehalt; **mark-up ~** Bruttogewinnsatz; **statutory ~** gesetzliche Verzinsung, gesetzlicher Zinsfuß, -satz;
~ **of alcohol** Alkoholanteil, -prozentsatz; ~ **of capital** Kapitalanteil; ~ **of cost** Kostenprozentsatz; ~ **of distribution** Verteilungsschlüssel; **disquietingly high ~ of errors** beunruhigend hoher Fehlerprozentsatz; ~ **of gold** Goldgehalt; ~ **of the retail or net price** Prozentsatz vom Laden- oder Nettopreis; ~ **of the incentive rate** Leistungslohnanteil; ~ **of income** Einkommensprozentsatz; ~ **of increase** prozentuale Zunahme; ~ **on profit** Anteil am Geschäftsgewinn, Gewinnanteil; **director's ~ of profit** Vorstandstantieme; ~ **of recovery** *(US)* Konkursquote; ~ **of rejects** Ausschußquote; ~ **of sales** Umsatzprovision; ~ **of silver** Silbergehalt; ~ **of voting** Wahlbeteiligung;
to allow a ~ on all transactions Umsatzprovision gewähren; **to get a good ~ in one's outlay** fast alle Spesen ersetzt bekommen; **to yield a ~** Prozente abwerfen;
on a ~ basis gegen Prozente; ~ **depletion** *(income tax)* für Substanzvermögen zugelassener Abschreibungssatz; ~ **distribution** *(statistics)* Prozentverteilung, *(board)* Tantiemeverteilung; **fixed ~ fee** fester Provisionssatz; ~ **figures** Prozentsätze; ~ **increase** prozentualer Anstieg, Prozentzunahme; ~ **lease** Umsatzpacht; **fixed ~ method** gleichmäßige Abschreibung vom Buchwert; ~**-of-sales method** *(advertising budget)* Prozent- oder Kostensatzmethode; ~ **premium** Prämienprozentsatz, Anteilsprämie; ~ **rate** Prozentsatz; ~ **requirements** Mehrheitserfordernisse; ~ **shop** *(US)* Unternehmen mit festgelegter Mindestzahl an Gewerkschaftsmitgliedern; ~ **statement** vergleichende Betriebsbilanz; ~ **tare** Bruttotara; ~ **worker** *(sl.)* Profitgeier.

percentaged prozentual, in Prozenten [ausgedrückt].

percentil Hundertstelstelle.

percentual prozentual.

perception Wahrnehmung;
subliminal ~ unterschwellige Wahrnehmung;
~ **of crops** Besitzergreifung der Ernte.

perch *(fig.)* feste Stellung, *(measuring)* Meßstange;
~ *(v.)* s. o. **at the top of the house** j. auf der obersten Etage unterbringen;
to knock s. o. off his ~ j. von seinem hohen Roß herunterstoßen.

percolate *(v.)* filtern, filtrieren, *(motor car)* kochen.

percolator Kaffeemaschine.
percussion Stoß, Erschütterung;
~ **cap** Sprengkapsel.
perdition verderben, Ruin.
perdurable immerwährend.
peremption klageabweisendes Prozeßurteil.
peremptory *(law)* zwingend, endgültig, unbedingt, peremptorisch;
~ **assertion** unwiderlegbare Behauptung; ~ **challenge** *(jurors)* Ablehnung ohne Gründe; ~ **day** unaufschiebbarer Verhandlungstermin; ~ **defense (defence,** *Br.*) peremptorischer Einwand, Klageleugnung, klageleugnender Einwand; ~ **exception** rechtsvernichtende Einrede; ~ **mandamus** unanfechtbare gerichtliche Verfügung; ~ **necessity** unbedingte Notwendigkeit; ~ **nonsuit** zwingende Klageabweisung; ~ **order** keine Berufung zulassende gerichtliche Verfügung; ~ **paper** Liste unerledigter Fälle; ~ **plea** *(US)* peremptorische Einrede; ~ **provision** Muß-, zwingende Vorschrift; ~ **rule** zwingende Vorschrift; ~ **term** *(US)* Notfrist; ~ **writ** *(US)* persönliche Vorladung.
perennial dauernd, beständig, immerwährend;
~ **debater** Dauerredner.
perfect vollendet, -kommen, *(title)* voll rechtsgültig, durchsetzbar, *(versed)* bewandert, gründlich unterrichtet;
word-~ rollenfest;
~ **in the performance of one's duties** unübertroffen in seiner Pflichterfüllung;
~ *(v.) (print.)* auf beiden Seiten bedrucken;
~ **o. s. in** sich in etw. vervollkommnen; ~ **an invention** Erfindung auf den neuesten Stand bringen; **to be** ~ **in everything** alles meisterhaft beherrschen; **to have one's lessons** ~ seine Aufgaben am Schnürchen können;
~**-attestation clause** *(last will)* Vollständigkeitsklausel; ~ **competition** *(US)* uneingeschränkter Wettbewerb; ~ **condition** mangelfreier Zustand; ~ **idiot** unheilbarer Geisteskranker; ~ **instrument** eingetragene Urkunde; ~ **knowledge of a market** vollkommene Markttransparenz; **to have a** ~ **knowledge of s. th.** umfassende Kenntnisse von etw. haben; ~ **machine** vollendete Erfindung; ~ **manners** vollendete Manieren; ~ **market** homogener Markt; ~ **monopoly** absolutes Monopol; ~ **nonsense** reiner Unsinn; ~ **obligation** juristisch durchsetzbare Verpflichtung; ~ **ownership** lastenfreies Eigentum; ~ **specimen** Musterbeispiel; ~ **stranger** völliger Fremder; ~ **trust** rechtsgültig errichtete Stiftung, detailliert festgelegtes Treuhandverhältnis; ~ **type of the old aristocrat** vollendeter Vertreter der alten Aristokratie; **word-~** rollenfest; ~ **usufruct** uneingeschränkter Nießbrauch.
perfected vollendet;
to have been ~ *(claim)* entstanden sein.
perfection Perfektion, Reife, *(process of perfecting)* Fertigstellung, Vervollkommnung;
~ **to** meisterhaft, vortrefflich;
~**s** Fertigkeiten;
~ **itself** absolute Perfektion;
~ **of details** Fertigstellung von Einzelheiten;
to be the ~ **of kindness** vollendete Güte sein; **to bring to** ~ vervollkommnen; **to do s. th. to** ~ etw. vollendet beherrschen.
perfectly, to know s. th. umfassende Kenntnisse auf einem Gebiet haben.
perfidious heimtückisch, treulos, verräterisch.
perfidy Heimtücke.
perforate *(v.)* lochen, perforieren;
~ *(a.)* durchlöchert, gelocht.
perforated sheet of postage stamps perforierter Briefmarkenbogen.
perforating machine Bohrmaschine.
perforation Durchlochung, Perforierung.
perforator Lochzange, Locher.
perform | *(v.) (do)* leisten, erfüllen, *(execute)* ausführen, verrichten, vollziehen, bewerkstelligen, *(present)* aufführen, produzieren, spielen;
~ **a barred obligation** verjährte Leistung erbringen; ~**-certain conditions** bestimmte Bedingungen erfüllen; ~ **a contract** Vertrag erfüllen; ~ **the duties of one's office** sein Amt versehen; ~ **one's duty** seine Pflicht tun; ~ **in the public interest** im öffentlichen Interesse liegen; ~ **one's obligations** seinen Verpflichtungen nachkommen; ~ **the part of the host** Rolle des Gastgebers übernehmen; ~ **in a play** Rolle in einem Theaterstück spielen; ~ **a promise** Versprechen halten; ~ **quarantine** Quarantäne machen; ~ **satisfactorily** *(car)* zufriedenstellend laufen; ~ **useful work** nützliche Arbeit leisten; ~ **well** *(machine)* gut laufen.

performable aus-, durchführbar, *(play)* aufführbar.
performance *(carrying out)* Erfüllung, Durchführung, Leistung, *(execution)* Ausführung, Verrichtung, Bewerkstelligung, *(investment trust)* Geschäftsgebaren, *(theater)* Vorführung, Veranstaltung, Aufführung, *(thing done)* Leistung, Werk;
in lieu of ~ an Erfüllungs Statt;
afternoon ~ Nachmittagsvorstellung; **aircraft** ~ fliegerische Leistung; **best** ~ Höchstleistung, erstklassige Darbietung; **brilliant** ~ Glanzstück; **cancelled** ~ ausgefallene Veranstaltung; **charity** ~ Wohltätigkeitsveranstaltung; **collateral** ~ Nebenleistung; **comparative** ~ vergleichbare Leistungsfähigkeit; **consumer's actual car-buying** Verbraucheraufwendungen für Autoanschaffungen; **contemporaneous** ~ Erfüllung Zug um Zug; **continuous** ~ *(cinema)* durchgehende Vorstellung, Dauervorstellung; **defective** ~ mangelhafte Erfüllung; **divisible** ~ teilbare Leistung; **evening** ~ Abendvorstellung; **economic** ~ wirtschaftliche Leistungsfähigkeit; **executive** ~ Leistungen einer Führungskraft; **extra** ~ Sonderleistung; **faithful** ~ vertragstreue Erfüllung; **farewell** ~ Abschiedsvorstellung; **finished** ~ abgerundete Leistung; **first** ~ Premiere; **glittering debut** ~ glanzvolle schauspielerische Leistung; **ideal** ~ Optimalleistung; **increased** ~ Mehrleistung, Leistungssteigerung; **indivisible** ~ unteilbare Leistung; **musical** ~ musikalische Vorführung; **no** ~ **to-night** Vorstellung fällt heute aus; **normal** ~ normale Leistung; **part** ~ Teilerfüllung, teilweise Erfüllung; **peak** ~ Höchstleistung; **personnel** ~ betriebliche Leistungen, Leistungen des Personals; **property-creating** ~ vermögenswirksame Leistung; **simultaneous** ~ Erfüllung Zug um Zug; **specific** ~ effektive (vertragsgemäße) Erfüllung, Vertragserfüllung, Naturalherstellung, -erfüllung, Realleistung; **substantial** ~ im wesentlichen vertragstreue Erfüllung; **substituted** ~ Ersatzleistung, -vornahme; **well-attended** ~ gutbesuchte Ausstellung;
~ **in aid of the poor** Wohltätigkeitsveranstaltung; ~ **of a contract** Vertragserfüllung; **faithful** ~ **of contract** vertragstreue Erfüllung; ~ **of a duty** Pflichterfüllung, -leistung; ~ **of earnings** Gewinnentwicklung; ~ **of functions** Durchführung von Aufgaben; ~ **in kind** Sach-, Naturalleistung; ~ **in money** Geldleistung; ~ **of profit** Gewinnentwicklung; ~ **of a promise** Einhaltung eines Versprechens; ~ **in public** öffentliche Aufführung; ~ **under service conditions** Betriebsleistung;
~ **begins at 8 o'clock** Beginn der Vorstellung 8 Uhr; **to drive on contractor** ~ größere Leistungen von den Lieferanten fordern; **to effect** ~ Leistung bewirken; **to get behind with the** ~ **of the contract** mit den Vertragsleistungen in Verzug geraten; **to give an uneven** ~ *(stock exchange)* unruhiges Bild abgeben; **to have a run of one hundred** ~**s** hundert Aufführungen erlebt haben; **to make** ~ **impossible** Nichterfüllung zu vertreten haben; **to offer** ~ Leistungen anbieten; **to put up a good** ~ gute Leistung erbringen; **to refuse** ~ Leistung verweigern; **to tender** ~ Leistung andienen, Leistungserfüllung anbieten; **to sue for specific** ~ auf Erfüllung klagen; **to turn in another strong** ~ *(stock exchange)* erneuten Auftrieb erhalten; **to turn in stellar** ~ *(stock exchange)* raketenartigen Auftrieb erfahren;
~ **appraisal** Leistungsbeurteilung, -bewertung; ~ **bond** Leistungsversprechen, *(US)* Submissions-, Gewährleistungs-, Bietungsgarantie; ~ **bonus** Leistungsprämie; ~ **budget** Istetat; ~ **chart** Leistungsdiagramm, -übersicht; ~ **data** Leistungsangaben; ~ **efficiency** Leistungsgrad; ~ **evaluation** Leistungsbewertung; ~ **factor** Leistungsfaktor; ~ **fund** *(investment trust)* Wachstumsfonds; ~ **graph** Leistungskurve; ~ **guarantee** *(Br.)* Liefergarantie; ~ **indicator** Planerfüllungsindikator; ~ **level** Leistungsgrad, -soll, -niveau; ~ **possibilities** Leistungsmöglichkeiten; ~ **qualifications** Leistungsqualität; ~ **rating** Leistungsnote, -bewertung, -beurteilung; ~ **rating factor** Leistungsfaktor; ~ **rating scale** Leistungsbeurteilungsskala; ~ **report** Leistungsbericht; ~ **review** Leistungsüberprüfung; ~ **rights** *(theatre)* Aufführungs-, Vorführungsrechte; ~ **standard** Leistungsstandard; ~ **table** Leistungstabelle, -übersicht; ~ **test** Leistungsprüfung; ~ **standard time** Normalausführungszeit.
performer Erfolgsunternehmen, *(stock exchange)* Erfolgsaktie, *(theatre)* ausübender Künstler, Spieler;
to be principle ~ Hauptrolle spielen.
performing | **animal** dressiertes Tier; ~ **rights** Aufführungsrechte;
~ **Rights Society** *(Br.)* [etwa] GEMA.
perfunctory inspection oberflächliche Überprüfung.
periculum in mora *(lat.)* Gefahr im Verzug.
peril Risiko, Gefahr;
at one's (your) ~ auf eigene (Ihre) Gefahr; **at the** ~ **of** bei Vermeidung von;
excepted ~**s** Freizeichnung für Schäden; **extraneous** ~ *(insur-*

ance) Sondergefahr; **imminent** ~ drohende (akute) Gefahr; **home-owner's multiple** ~ mehrere Gefahren des Wohnungsinhabers; **~s insured against** versicherte Gefahren; **marine (maritime)** ~ Seetransportgefahr;

~s **of the lakes** *(US)* Schiffahrtsgefahren auf den großen Seen; ~ **of one's life** Todesgefahr; ~s **of the ocean (sea)** Seegefahren, Gefahren der See; ~s **of the streets** Transportgefahren im Straßenverkehr; ~ **of transportation** Transportrisiko; ~s **of war** Kriegsrisiko;

to be in ~ **of one's life** in Lebensgefahr schweben; **to do s. th. at one's own** ~ etw. auf eigene Gefahr tun; **to thrust o. s. into** ~ sich Hals über Kopf in Gefahr begeben;

excepted ~ **clause** *(law of insurance)* Freizeichnungsklausel; ~ **point** *(customs duty, US)* kritischer Punkt, kritische Schwelle.

perilous gefährlich.

period *(break)* Pause, Absatz, *(lecture)* Vorlesungsdauer, *(portion of time)* Laufzeit, Zeit[abschnitt], Zeitraum, -dauer, Periode, Phase, *(school)* Unterrichtsstunde, *(sport)* Spielzeit, *(term)* Frist;

at an early ~ in früher Zeit; **at dated** ~s **of time** in regelmäßigen Zeitabständen; **during certain** ~s **of life** in bestimmten Lebensabschnitten; **for a** ~ für einige Zeit; **for a** ~ auf die Dauer von; **for a fixed** ~ auf eine bestimmte Zeit; **within a reasonable** ~ innerhalb einer angemessenen Frist; **within a** ~ **of one month from the date of requirement** binnen eines Monats nach Antragstellung;

accounting ~ Rechnungsabschnitt; **additional** ~ Nachfrist; **after-war** ~ Nachkriegszeit; **apprehensive** ~ Periode erhöhter Gefahr; **assessment** ~ Veranlagungszeitraum; **basic** ~ *(International Monetary Fund)* Zuteilungsperiode; **break-in** ~ Einarbeitungszeit; **busy** ~ verkehrsstarke Zeit, Hauptgeschäftsstunden; **comparable** ~ Vergleichszeitraum; **contractual** ~ vertragliche Laufzeit, Vertragsdauer; **copyright** ~ Schutzfrist; **covered** ~ Berichtszeitraum; **credit** ~ Laufzeit eines Kredits; **lengthening delivery** ~s länger werdende Lieferfristen; **equated** ~ Durchschnittslaufzeit; **filing** ~ *(patent)* Anmeldefrist; **fiscal** ~ Steuerabschnitt; **given** ~ Berichtsperiode, -zeitraum; **glacial** ~ Eiszeit; **guarantee** ~ Garantiefrist; **intervening** ~ Übergangszeit; **inventory** ~ Inventarfrist; **legislative** ~ Legislaturperiode; **limitation** ~ Verjährungsfrist; **one-year** ~ Jahresfrist; **operating** ~ Betriebsdauer; **policy** ~ Laufzeit einer Police; **postwar transitional** ~ Nachkriegsübergangszeit; **preceding** ~ *(taxation)* vorhergehendes Veranlagungsjahr; **probationary** ~ Probezeit, *(criminal law)* Bewährungsfrist; **qualifying** ~ Probezeit; **quarantine** ~ Quarantänezeit; **rest** ~ Arbeits-, Ruhepause; **retention** ~ Aufbewahrungszeit; **return** ~ *(statistics)* Periode der Wiederkehr; **settling-in** ~ Eingewöhnungszeit; **specific** ~ vereinbarte Frist; **subscription** ~ Bezugsdauer, *(shares)* Zeichnungsfrist; **tender** ~ Einreichungs-, Bewerbungsfrist; **testing** ~ Probe-, Versuchszeit; **three-month** ~ Zeitraum von drei Monaten; **transitional (transitory)** ~ Übergangszeit, -periode; **waiting** ~ Wartezeit, *(insurance)* Karenzzeit; **well-rounded** ~s schön gedrechselte Phrasen; **working** ~ Arbeitszeit, Betriebszeitraum, -periode;

~ **of an account** Rechnungsperiode; ~ **of adjustment** Angleichungsperiode, Anpassungszeitraum; ~ **of vocational (professional) adjustment** Einarbeitungszeit; ~ **for appeal** Rechtsmittel-, Berufungsfrist; ~ **of appointment** Amtsdauer; ~ **of apprenticeship** Lehr-, Lehrlingszeit; ~ **of assessment** Veranlagungszeitraum; ~ **under audit** Prüfungsabschnitt; ~ **of availability of a ticket** Gültigkeitsdauer einer Fahrkarte; ~ **of benefit** Leistungsdauer; ~ **of buoyancy** Hausseperiode; ~ **allowed for carriage** Beförderungsfrist; ~ **of circulation** Umlaufzeit; ~ **of civilization** Kulturepoche; ~ **for claims** Mängelrügefrist; ~ **of computation** Berechnungszeitraum; ~ **of possible conception** Empfängniszeit; ~ **of construction** Bauzeit; ~ **of copyright** Schutzfrist; ~ **of coverage** *(insurance)* Deckungszeit; ~ **of a credit** Laufzeit eines Kredits; ~ **set for declaration** Anmeldefrist, -zeit; ~ **of decline in economic activity** abgeschwächte Konjunkturphase; ~ **for delivery** Lieferzeit; ~ **of depression** Depressionsphase; ~ **of development** Entwicklungszeitraum; ~ **of disability** Dauer der Arbeitsunfähigkeit; ~ **of a disease** Krankheitsphase; ~ **of embargo** Sperrfrist; **[minimum]** ~ **of employment** [Mindest]beschäftigungszeit, -dauer, Betriebszugehörigkeit; **different** ~s **of employment** verschiedene Beschäftigungszeiten; ~ **of engagement** Anstellungszeitraum; ~ **of enjoyment** Nutzungsdauer; ~ **of erection** Bauperiode, -zeit; ~ **of exchange** Umtauschfrist; ~ **of exposure** *(photo)* Belichtungszeit; ~ **of extension** Stundungs-, Verlängerungsfrist; ~ **set for filing** *(patent law)* Anmeldefrist, Gnadenfrist; ~ **of prolonged growth** lange Wachstumsperiode;

~ **of guarantee** Garantiezeit, -frist; ~ **of implementation** Durchführungszeitraum; ~ **of imprisonment** Dauer einer Freiheitsstrafe; ~ **of incubation** Inkubationszeit; ~ **of inflation** Inflationszeit; ~ **of insurance** Versicherungsdauer; ~ **of interruption of employment** unterbrochene Beschäftigungsdauer; ~ **of investment** Anlagezeitraum; ~ **of lease** Miet-, Pachtdauer, Pacht-, Mietzeit; ~ **of a licence** Lizenzdauer; ~ **of limitation** Verjährungs-, Ausschluß-, Klagefrist; **statutory** ~ **of limitation** gesetzliche Verjährungsfrist; ~ **of a loan** Anleihelaufzeit; ~ **of lucidity** *(insane person)* lichter Intervall; **lesson** ~ **of 45 minutes** Unterrichtsstunde von 45 Minuten; ~ **of a month** Monatsfrist; ~ **of three months** dreimonatige Frist, Vierteljahresfrist; ~ **of nonnegotiability** *(securities)* Sperrfrist; ~ **of notice** Benachrichtigungs-, Ladungs-, Kündigungsfrist; ~ **for objection** Einspruchsfrist; ~ **of office** Amtsdauer; ~ **for entering an opposition** *(patent law)* Einspruchsfrist; ~ **of overdraft** Überziehungszeitraum; ~ **of performance** Ausführungsfrist; ~ **covered by the policy** gedeckte Zeitspanne; ~ **of prescription** *(real estate)* Ersitzungs-, Verjährungsfrist; ~ **of probation** Probezeit, *(criminal law)* Bewährungsfrist; ~ **of production** Herstellungs-, Produktions-, Arbeitszeit; ~ **of general prosperity** Hochkonjunktur; ~ **of quiet after the election** Ruhepause nach den Wahlen; ~ **of recession** Rezessionszeit, Abschwungphase; ~ **of redemption** Amortisationsdauer; ~ **of repayment** Tilgungsfrist; ~ **under review** Berichtszeitraum; ~ **to run** Laufzeit; ~ **of dull sales** Absatzflaute; ~ **of service** Dienstzeit; ~ **of shipment** Ladezeit, Verladungsfrist; ~ **of sluggishness** Flautezeit; ~ **of stagnation** Stagnationszeit; ~ **of proposed stay** beabsichtigte Aufenthaltsdauer; ~ **of stoppage** Sperrzeit; ~ **of subscription** Bezugs-, Subskriptionsdauer; ~ **under survey** *(statistics)* Erhebungszeitraum; ~ **of time** Zeitraum, Frist; ~ **of training** Ausbildungszeit; ~ **of transition** Übergangszeit, -periode; ~ **of transport** Beförderungsdauer; ~ **of usefulness** Nutzungsdauer; ~ **of validity** Gültigkeitsdauer, *(guarantee)* Gewährleistungsfrist; ~ **of waiting** Warte-, Karenzzeit; ~ **subsequent to the war** Nachkriegsperiode; ~ **of warranty** Gewährleistungsfrist; **twenty teaching** ~s **a week** zwanzig Unterrichtsstunden in der Woche; ~ **of last year** Vorjahresfrist;

to be protected for a ~ **of 21 years** *(patent law)* während der nächsten 21 Jahre patentrechtlich geschützt sein; **to be subject to a** ~ **of limitation of 4 years** in vier Jahren verjähren; **to compute a** ~ Frist berechnen; **to discharge a liability within the agreed** ~ Schuld innerhalb der vereinbarten Zeit zurückzahlen; **to extend a** ~ Frist verlängern; **to fix a** ~ Frist setzen; **to shorten a** ~ Frist abkürzen;

~ **costume** Tracht einer bestimmten Epoche; **peak** ~ **demand** Spitzenzeitbedarf; ~ **ends** Ende des Betriebsabschnitts; ~ **furniture** Möbel aus der Zeit, Stilmöbel; ~ **piece** Museumsstück; **current** ~ **taxation** laufendes Veranlagungsjahr.

periodic | accounting Abrechnung in regelmäßigen Abständen; ~ **audit** laufend durchgeführte Revision; ~ **average inventory plan** Bewertung des Vorratsvermögens zu Durchschnittspreisen; ~ **charges (cost, expense)** wiederkehrende Aufwendungen; ~ **dues** laufende Beiträge; ~ **payment** laufend anfallende Zahlungen; ~ **reports** laufende Berichte; ~ **statement** Periodenbilanz.

periodical Magazin, [periodische] Zeitschrift; **monthly** ~ Monatszeitschrift; **weekly** ~ Wochenzeitschrift; ~s **and works published in continued parts** Fortsetzungswerke; ~ *(a.)* regelmäßig wiederkehrend, in regelmäßigen Abständen, periodisch, *(publication)* fortlaufend erscheinend; ~ **advertising** Zeitschriftenwerbung; ~ **contribution** regelmäßiger Beitrag; ~ **meeting** regelmäßige Zusammenkunft; ~ **newspaper** Zeitschrift; ~ **payments** regelmäßig wiederkehrende Zahlungen; ~ **payments of interest** laufende Zinszahlungen; ~ **reports** Berichtsreihe; ~ **tenancy** festgelegte Pachtzeit.

periodicalist Zeitschriftenverleger, -herausgeber.

periscope Sehrohr, Periskop, *(mil.)* Geländespiegel.

perish *(v.)* umkommen, zugrunde gehen, untergehen; ~ **by cold** erfrieren; ~ **by drowning** ertrinken; ~ **in an earthquake** bei einem Erdbeben umkommen; ~ **by hunger** verhungern; ~ **by its own mistakes** über die eigenen Fehler stürzen; ~ **tyres** Reifen zerstören.

perishability *(food)* Verderblichkeit, *(goods)* Kurzlebigkeit.

perishable *(food)* leicht verderblich, *(goods)* kurzlebig; ~s leicht verderbliche Ware, kurzlebige Verbrauchsgüter; ~ **cargo** verderbliche Ladung; ~ **commodities** Verbrauchsgüter; ~ **goods** leicht verderbliche Waren; ~ **consumer goods** kurzlebige Konsumgüter; **of** ~ **nature** dem Verderb ausgesetzt, leicht verderblich; ~ **tool** Verschleißwerkzeug; ~ **traffic** Handel in leicht verderblichen Waren.

perishableness *(food)* leichte Verderblichkeit.
perished goods verdorbene Waren.
perjure *(v.)* o. s. Meineid leisten (schwören), meineidig werden.
perjured meineidig;
~ **evidence** meineidige Zeugenaussage.
perjurer Meineidiger.
perjury Meineid, Eidbruch;
to commit ~ Meineid leisten, falschen Eid schwören.
perk *(v.)* auf dem hohen Roß sitzen;
~ **it** *(US)* sich brüsten; ~ **up** aufmöbeln, *(orders)* hereinkommen; ~ **up one's ears** seine Ohren spitzen.
perks *(Br., sl.)* Nebeneinnahme, -verdienst, *(sl.)* freiwillige Sozialleistungen.
perm *(Br., sl.)* Dauerwelle.
permanency Dauerzustand, Bestand, *(permanent position)* Dauerstellung.
permanent dauernd, [be]ständig, fest, *(for life)* auf Lebenszeit, lebenslänglich, *(mil.)* ortsfest, *(population)* bodenständig, seßhaft, ortsansässig;
~ **abode** ständiger Aufenthaltsort, Wohnsitz; ~ **address** ständige Adresse; ~ **advisory board** ständiger Beirat; ~ **alimony** lebenslängliche Unterhaltsrente; ~ **appointment (assignment)** feste Anstellung, Dauerstellung; ~ **assembly** ständige Versammlung; ~ **assets** *(accounting)* Anlagevermögen; ~ **body** ständiges Organ; ⸢ **Boundary Commission** *(Br.)* ständige Wahlkreiskommission; ~ **building and loan association** Bausparkasse mit ständiger Aktienausgabe; ~ **building society** *(Australia)* Bausparkasse; ~ **camp** *(mil.)* festes Lager; ~ **capital** Anlagekapital; ~ **committee** ständiger Ausschuß; ⸢ **Court of Arbitration** Haager Schiedsgerichtshof; ⸢ **Court of International Justice** Weltgerichtshof; ~ **debt** fundierte konsolidierte Schuld; ~ **disability** dauernde Arbeitsunfähigkeit, Vollinvalidität; ~ **partial disability insurance** Arbeiterrentenversicherung für begrenzte Erwerbsfähigkeit; ~ **echo** *(radar)* Festzeichen; ~ **effect** Dauerwirkung; ~ **emplacement** *(mil.)* ortsfeste Stellung; ~ **employee** Festangestellter; ~ **employment** Dauerstellung, feste Anstellung; ~ **establishment** Betriebsstätte; ~ **files** Archivunterlagen; ~ **fund** eiserner Bestand; ~ **holdings** Daueranlagen; ~ **income** festes Einkommen, ständige Einkünfte, Dauereinkommen; ~ **institution** feststehende Einrichtung; ⸢ **Insurance Fund** *(banking, US)* Einlagenversicherungsfonds; ~ **life insurance** jährlich kündbare Lebensversicherungspolice; ~ **investment** langfristige Kapitalanlage, Daueranlage; ~ **labo(u)r** ständige Arbeitskräfte; ~ **medium** feste Währung; ~ **member** ständiges Mitglied; ~ **neutrality** ewige Neutralität; ~ **office** ständiges Büro; ~ **order** Dauerauftrag; ~ **portfolio** *(securities)* Dauerbesitz, -anlage; ~ **position (post)** Dauerstellung, -arbeitsplatz; ~ **poster** Dauerplakat; ~ **power of attorney** Dauervollmacht; ~ **president** auf Lebenszeit gewählter Präsident; ~ **regulation** Dauerregelung; ~ **representative** ständiger Vertreter; ~ **residence** ständiger Wohnsitz; ~ **secretary** *(politics, Br.)* ständiger Staatssekretär; ~ **staff** ständiges Personal; ~ **stock** eiserner Bestand; ~ **tenant** Dauermieter; ~ **unemployment** Dauerarbeitslosigkeit; ~ **wave** Dauerwelle; ~ **way** *(Br.)* Bahnkörper, -oberbau; ~**-wayman** Gleisbegeher.
permanently, to be ~ **appointed** fest angestellt sein; **to be** ~ **attached to a firm** Dauerstellung in einer Firma haben.
permeate *(v.)* durchdringen, durchsickern;
~ **among the people** sich im Lande verbreiten.
permillage Promille, Tausendsatz.
permissible zulässig, erlaubt, fakultativ;
~ **clearance** zulässiger Spielraum; ~ **deviation** Toleranz; ~ **dose** zulässige [Strahlen]dosis; ~ **expenses** *(taxation)* abzugsfähige Unkosten; ~ **load** Höchstbelastung; ~ **margin of fluctuation** zulässige Fluktuationsbreite.
permission Erlaubnis[schein], Genehmigung, Zulassung, Bewilligung, Gestattung;
after ~ nach vorheriger Genehmigung; **by special** ~ mit besonderer Genehmigung; **subject to** ~ genehmigungsbedürftig; **with kind** ~ mit freundlicher Genehmigung; **without** ~ unbefugt;
blanket ~ *(US)* generelle Erlaubnis; **express** ~ ausdrückliche Genehmigung; **general** ~ generelle Erlaubnis; **government** ~ *(Br.)* behördliche Genehmigung, staatliche Erlaubnis; **owner's** ~ Erlaubnis des Eigentümers;
~ **by authorities** behördliche Genehmigung; ~ **for building** Bauerlaubnis, -genehmigung; ~ **to deal on the stock exchange** Börsenzulassung, -genehmigung; ~ **to develop** Erschließungsgenehmigung; ~ **to dispose of a body** Exhumierungserlaubnis; ~ **to print** Druckerlaubnis; **written** ~ **to reside** schriftliche Aufenthaltserlaubnis; ~ **to transact business** Gewerbegenehmigung; ~ **in writing** schriftliche Erlaubnis;

to accord ~ **to transact business** Gewerbelizenz erteilen; **to apply for a** ~ um Genehmigung einkommen; **to give** ~ genehmigen, erlauben; **to grant** ~ Genehmigung (Erlaubnis) erteilen.
permissive zulässig, erlaubt, statthaft;
~ **legislation** Ermessensgesetzgebung; ~ **power** Ermessensvollmacht; ~ **provision** Kannvorschrift; ~ **society** äußerst freizügige Gesellschaft, alles tolerierende (tolerante) Gesellschaft; ~ **use** gestatteter Gebrauch; ~ **wage-adjustment clause** genehmigte Lebenshaltungskostenklausel; ~ **waste** Vernachlässigung notwendiger Gebäudereparaturen.
permissiveness Auslegungsspielraum.
permit Erlaubnis, Genehmigung, Gestattung, *(customs)* Zollgeleit-, Zollfreischein, -abfertigungsschein, Ausfuhrerlaubnis, *(to enter)* Durchlaß-, Passierschein, -zettel, *(licence, Br.)* Lizenz, Zulassung, Zulassungsschein, Konzession, *(for rationed goods)* Bezugsschein;
building ~ *(US)* baupolizeiliche Genehmigung, Baubewilligung, -genehmigung; **customs** ~ Zollabfertigungs-, Zollfreischein; **customhouse** ~ Zollabfertigungsschein; **discharging** ~ Löscherlaubnis; **entry** ~ Einreisebewilligung, -erlaubnis, -genehmigung; **exit** ~ Ausreisebewilligung, -genehmigung; **export** ~ Ausfuhrgenehmigung, -erlaubnis, -deklaration, Exportgenehmigung; **fishing** ~ *(US)* Fischereischein; **government** ~ staatliche Genehmigung; **hunting** ~ *(US)* Jagdschein; **import** ~ Einfuhrerlaubnis; **labo(u)r** ~ Arbeitsbewilligung, -genehmigung; **landing** ~ Landeerlaubnis; **leaving** ~ polizeiliche Abmeldebescheinigung; **loading** ~ [Ver]ladeerlaubnis; **omnibus** ~ generelle (allgemeine) Erlaubnis; **production** ~ Produktionserlaubnis; **purchase (purchasing)** ~ Warenbezugsschein; **residence** ~ Aufenthaltsgenehmigung; **special** ~ Ausnahme-, Sondergenehmigung; **stay** ~ Aufenthaltsgenehmigung; **transit** ~ Durchfuhrbescheinigung, -genehmigung, Transitbewilligung; **visitor's** ~ kurzfristige Aufenthaltserlaubnis; **working** ~ Arbeitserlaubnis; **written** ~ Genehmigungsurkunde;
~ **for home and consumption** Zollfreischein für im Land verbleibende Waren; ~ **of transit** Transitschein;
~ *(v.)* zulassen, erlauben, genehmigen, gestatten;
~ **an appeal** Berufung zulassen; ~ **one's car to be used** sein Auto zur Verfügung stellen; ~ **of no delay** keine Verzögerung zulassen; ~ **no reply** keine Antwort gestatten; ~ **to visit the works** Betriebsbesichtigung gestatten;
to extend a ~ Erlaubnisschein verlängern; **to issue a** ~ Erlaubnis ausstellen; **to take out a** ~ sich eine Erlaubnis geben (etw. genehmigen) lassen; **to withdraw a** ~ Genehmigung widerrufen;
~ **card** *(trade union)* gewerkschaftlicher Erlaubnisschein als Nichtorganisierter vorübergehend im gewerkschaftspflichtigen Betrieb zu arbeiten; ~ **holder** Berechtigter, Inhaber eines Berechtigungsscheins; **priority** ~ **holder** Bezugsscheinbesitzer; ~**-issuing locality** Konzessionsbereich; ~ **number** Zulassungsnummer; ~ **requirements** Genehmigungsvoraussetzung, Voraussetzungen für die Genehmigung; ~ **system** Genehmigungssystem.
permitted gestattet, genehmigt, zugelassen;
~ **by law** gesetzlich zulässig;
to be ~ **to sit for an examination** zu einer Prüfung zugelassen werden; **to be** ~ **to visit the works** Fabrikanlagen besichtigen dürfen;
~ **hours** *(Br.)* Konzessionszeit, Schankstunden.
permittee Berechtigter, Lizenzinhaber.
permutation Umschwung, Veränderung, *(law)* Tauschhandel, -geschäft;
~ **lock** Vexierschloß.
pernicious verderblich, nachteilig, schädlich;
~ **to the welfare of society** gesellschaftsfeindlich;
~ **disease** bösartige Krankheit; ~ **drug** gefährliche Droge.
perorate *(v.)* Rede abschließen, zum Schluß kommen.
peroration zusammenfassender Schluß einer Rede.
perpendicular Lot, *(Br., sl.)* stehend eingenommener Imbiß.
perpetrate *(v.)* begehen, verüben;
~ **an anachronism** sich eines Anchronismus schuldig machen; ~ **a breach of good taste** gegen den guten Geschmack verstoßen; ~ **a crime** Verbrechen verüben; ~ **a fraud on the court** Gericht irreführen.
perpetration of a crime Begehung (Verübung) eines Verbrechens.
perpetrator Täter, Verbrecher.
perpetual fort-, immerwährend, unaufhörlich, dauernd, *(annuity)* unablösbar, unkündbar, unbefristet, ewig;
~ **annuity** ewige (unkündbare) Rente; ~ **bond** unkündbare

Anleihe, Rentenanleihe; ~ **calendar** ewiger (immerwährender) Kalender, Dauerkalender; ~ **chatter** unentwegtes Geschwätz; ~ **complaint** Dauerbeschwerde; ~ **debentures** unkündbare Schuldverschreibungen; ~ **injunction** Unterlassungsurteil; ~ **inventory** *(US)* buchmäßig laufend geführtes Inventar, Buchinventur; ~ **inventory card** *(US)* laufende Bestandskarte; ~ **inventory file** *(US)* laufende Bestandskartei; ~ **lease** unkündbare Pacht; ~ **neutrality** ewige Neutralität; ~ **officer** unabsetzbarer Beamter; ~ **screw** Schraube ohne Ende; ~ **statute** zeitlich unbeschränktes Gesetz; ~ **succession** fortwährender Bestand, Dauerbestand; ~ **trust** auf unbegrenzte Zeit errichtete Stiftung, Dauertreuhandverwaltung.

perpetuate *(v.)* **evidence** Aussage zur Beweissicherung aufnehmen.

perpetuating testimony Beweissicherung.

perpetuity Dauerzustand, *(inalienableness rule)* Unveräußerlichkeitsverfügung, *(perpetual annuity)* immerwährende (ewige) Rente, *(perpetual possession)* zeitlich unbegrenzter Besitz;
in ~ auf unbegrenzte Zeit;
~ **period** Rentenbezugsdauer, *(real estate)* Unveräußerlichkeitszeitraum; ~ **rule** Fideikommißverbot.

perplex *(v.)* Verwirrung stiften;
~ **s. o. with questions** j. mit Fragen verblüffen.

perquisite Verdienst, Einkommen, *(gratuity)* Sondervergütung, Trinkgeld, *(law)* Selbsterworbenes;
~**s** *(Br.)* Nebenverdienst, -bezüge, -einkünfte, Sachbezüge, Sporteln, *(US)* Selbsterworbenes;
~**s of trade** Handelsverdienst;
⚖ **and Accumulations Act** *(Br.)* Gesetz gegen längerfristige erbrechtliche Bindungen.

perquisition Haus-, Durchsuchung.

perquisitor Ersterwerber.

perron Freitreppe.

persecute *(v.)* verfolgen, drangsalieren;
~ **with requests for subscriptions** mit Bezugsaufforderungen belästigen.

persecuted [person] Verfolgter.

persecution Verfolgung;
to live through ~ **and exile** Verfolgung und Verbannung erfahren; **to suffer cruel** ~**s** schrecklichen Verfolgungen ausgesetzt sein;
~ **mania** Verfolgungswahnsinn.

persecutor Verfolger.

perseverance Beharrlichkeit, Ausdauer.

persevere *(v.)* *(in debate)* nicht nachgeben;
~ **in one's studies** sein Studium fortsetzen.

Persian carpet Perserteppich.

persist *(v.)* ausharren, hartnäckig bestehen;
~ **in most areas** *(fog)* sich weitgehend halten; ~ **in a demand** auf einer Forderung bestehen; ~ **in going on** hartnäckig fortdauern; ~ **in one's opinion** bei seiner Meinung bleiben; ~ **in saying** bei seiner Behauptung bleiben.

persistent anhaltend, beharrlich, beständig;
~ **attacks of malaria** immer wiederkehrende Malariaanfälle; ~ **demand** hartnäckige Forderung; ~ **inflation** schleichende Inflation; ~ **offender** Gewohnheitsverbrecher.

person Person, Einzelwesen, Individuum, *(theater)* Rolle, Gestalt;
in ~ persönlich, selbst; **without exception of** ~**s** ohne Ansehen der Person;
accountable ~ Rechnungsleger, -pflichtiger; **aggrieved** ~ Beschwerter, Geschädigter; ~ **appearing** Erschienener; ~ **arrested** Untersuchungsgefangener; ~ **artificial** juristische Person, Körperschaft; **assisted** ~ *(Br.)* Armenrechtskläger; **authorized** ~ Berechtigter; **average** ~ Durchschnittsmensch; ~ **carried over** *(Br.)* Reportgeber; ~ **carrying over** Reportnehmer; ~ **cashing** Inkassobeamter; ~ **charged** Beschuldigter; ~ **concerned** Betroffener; **confidential** ~ Vertrauensperson; ~ **convicted** Vorbestrafter, Verurteilter; **dead** ~ Toter, Getöteter; **detained** ~ Inhaftierter; ~ **disabled** Invalide; ~ **displaced** Vertriebener, Ausgewiesener, Flüchtling, Verschleppter, *(labo(u)rer)* Zwangsarbeiter; ~ **distrained** Vollstreckungsschuldner; ~ **domiciled here** Wohnsitzberechtigter; **drowned** ~ Ertrunkener; **drowning** ~ Ertrinkender; **drunken** ~ Betrunkener; ~ **employed** Arbeitnehmer; ~ **entitled** Anspruchsberechtigter; **entrepreneurially-oriented** ~ unternehmerisch eingestellte Persönlichkeit; **fictitious** ~ juristische Person; ~ **imprisoned** Straf-, Untersuchungsgefangener; ~ **injured** Geschädigter, Benachteiligter, *(accident)* Verletzter; **insane** ~ Geisteskranker; ~ **insured** Versicherter; ~**s interested** beteiligte Personen, Interessenten; ~ **international** Völkerrechtssubjekt; ~ **involved** Beteiligter,

Verwickelter; **irresponsible** ~ Unzurechnungsfähiger; **juridical (juristic)** ~ juristische Person; **legal** ~ juristische Person; ~ **duly licensed** Konzessionsinhaber; ~ **murdered** Ermordeter; **natural** ~ natürliche Person; ~ **notified** Streitverkündeter; **physical** ~ natürliche Person; **private** ~ Privatperson; **reasonable and prudent** ~ verständig und umsichtig handelnde Person; **reporting** ~ Anzeigeerstatter; ~**s reviewed** befragter Personenkreis; **the said** ~**s** die genannten Personen; **sick** ~ Kranker; **single** ~ Einzelperson; **stateless** ~ Staatenloser; **third** ~ Dritter; **unauthorized** ~ Unbefugter, Unberechtigter; **undesirable** ~ unerwünschter Ausländer; **some unknown** ~ unbekannter Täter; **wanted** ~ Gesuchter, gesuchter Verbrecher, jemand auf der Fahndungsliste; **young** ~ Jugendlicher;
~ **of full age and capacity** Volljähriger und Geschäftsfähiger; ~ **needing care and attention** Pflegebedürftiger; ~ **under arrest** Festgenommener; ~ **of mixed blood** Mischling; ~ **of unblemished character** unbescholtene Person; ~ **in charge** Verwahrer, Verwalter, *(carriage)* Fahrer; ~ **making a complaint** Beschwerdeführer; ~ **of great consequence** einflußreiche Persönlichkeit; ~ **remanded in custody** Untersuchungshäftling, -gefangener; ~**s of influence in the world of art** maßgebende Persönlichkeiten in der Kunstwelt; ~ **under disability** beschränkt Geschäftsfähiger, Geschäftsunfähiger; ~ **of distinction** distinguierte Persönlichkeit; **first** ~ **to file** *(patent law)* erster Einreichender; ~ **detained for hearing** *(US)* Untersuchungsgefangener; ~ **of incidence** Anspruchsschuldner; ~ **of inheritance** Erbschaftsgläubiger; ~ **of private (independent) means** Rentier, finanziell Unabhängiger; ~ **of unsound mind** Geisteskranker; ~ **without nationality** Staatenloser; ~ **non grata** *(dipl.)* unerwünschte Person; ~ **authorized to give notice** Zustellungsberechtigter; ~ **giving notice** *(US)* Streikverkündender; ~ **holding office under her Majesty** *(Br.)* Staatsbediensteter; ~ **of prominence** bedeutende Persönlichkeit; ~ **of ordinary prudence** normaler Durchschnittsmensch; ~**s of the best quality** Personen höheren Ranges; ~ **of rank** hochgestellte Persönlichkeit, Standesperson; ~ **resident in a territory** Gebietsansässiger; ~ **not resident in a territory** Gebietsfremder; ~ **who serves** Zusteller; ~**s of standing** Honoratioren; ~ **suffering duty** Steuerbelasteter; ~ **under suspicion** Tatverdächtiger; ~ **liable for tax** Steuerpflichtiger; ~ **who is not the owner** Nichteigentümer;
to act in ~ persönlich auftreten; **to appear in** ~ persönlich erscheinen; **to be delivered to the addressee in** ~ persönlich zustellen; **to be present at a meeting in** ~ an einer Versammlung persönlich teilnehmen; **to be no respector of** ~**s** keinen Respekt vor Persönlichkeiten haben; **to be treated by law as a** ~ **in his (her) own right** rechtlich als Träger von Rechten und Pflichten gelten;
wanted-~ **file** Fahndungsbuch.

personable gutaussehend, *(law)* rechts-, prozeßfähig.

personableness gute Erscheinung, *(law)* Rechts-, Prozeßfähigkeit.

personage Standesperson, Persönlichkeit;
elevated ~ hochgestellte Persönlichkeit.

personal *(law)* beweglicher Gegenstand, *(newspaper item, US)* Personalnotiz;
~**s** *(newspaper, US)* Persönliches;
~ *(a.)* *(claim)* obligatorisch, *(private)* privat, vertraulich, *(property)* persönlich, beweglich;
purely ~ höchstpersönlich;
to become ~ anzüglich werden;
~ **access to children** *(divorced)* persönlicher Verkehr mit den Kindern; ~ **accident insurance** private Unfallversicherung gegen Personenschäden; ~ **account** Personal-, Kundenkonto, *(private account)* laufendes Konto, Privatkonto; ~ **account charges** Gebühren für ein Privatkonto; ~ **accounting** Privatbuchhaltung; ~ **action** Leistungsklage; ~ **allowance** *(employee)* persönliche Freizeit, *(income tax, Br.)* persönlicher Steuerfreibetrag, abzugsfähiger Betrag; ~ **analysis** Persönlichkeitsanalyse; ~ **announcement** Familienanzeige; **to make a** ~ **application** sich persönlich bewerben; ~ **articles** persönliche Gebrauchsartikel; ~ **assets** *(bankrupt)* Privatvermögen des Gemeinschuldners, *(deceased person)* beweglicher Nachlaß; ~ **attendance required** *(advertisement)* persönliche Vorstellung erwünscht; ~ **baggage** *(US)* Handgepäck; ~ **benefit** persönlicher Vorteil; ~ **business** Privatangelegenheit, persönliche Angelegenheit; ~ **call** *(tel., Br.)* Gespräch mit Voranmeldung; **to make a** ~ **call** persönlichen Besuch abstatten; **in one's** ~ **capacity** als Privatperson, persönlich; ~ **card** Personalausweis; ~ **characteristics** besondere Eigenschaften; ~ **chattels** *(Br.)* Kleidungsstücke, Hab und Gut, Hausrat; ~ **cheque service** *(Br.)* vereinfachter Scheckdienst; ~ **column** *(newspaper)* Briefkasten; ~ **consump-**

tion privater Verbrauch, Privatverbrauch; ~ **contract** privatrechtlicher Vertrag mit dem Gemeinschuldner; ~ **contribution to social insurance** *(US)* Arbeitnehmeranteil zur Sozialversicherung; ~ **covenant** schuldrechtlicher Vertrag; ~ **credit** persönlicher Kredit, Personalkredit; ~ **danger** *(insurance company)* Personenschaden; ~ **data** Angaben zur Person, Personalien; ~ **data and testimonials** Bewerbungsunterlagen; ~ **demand** persönliche Zahlungsaufforderung; ~ **disability** auf eine bestimmte Person beschränktes Unvermögen; ~ **drawings** Privatentnahmen; ~ **earnings** Einkünfte aus freiberuflicher Tätigkeit; ~ **effects** Mobiliarvermögen, Privateigentum, persönliche Effekten (Gebrauchsgegenstände); ~ **equitations** persönliche Beobachtungsfehler; ~ **estate** Mobiliarvermögen, bewegliches Eigentum (Vermögen); ~ **exemption** *(taxation, US)* persönlicher Steuerfreibetrag; ~ **expense** *(worker)* Eigenaufwand für Geräte und Bekleidung; ~ **explanation** *(parl.)* persönliche Erklärung; ~ **exports** *(Br.)* Waren für den persönlichen Verbrauch; ~ **favo(u)r** persönlicher Gefallen; ~ **files** Personal-, Handakten; ~ **finance company** *(US)* Finanzierungsgesellschaft für Kleinkredite, Kundenkreditgesellschaft; ~ **franchise** Verleihung der Rechtspersönlichkeit; ~ **history form** Personalbogen; ~ **holdup insurance** Versicherung gegen Raubüberfall; ~ **income** Privateinkommen; ~ **income tax** *(US)* Einkommensteuer; ~ **injury** Personenschaden, Körperverletzung; ~ **injury policy** Personenschadenversicherungspolice; ~ **insurance** Individual-, Personenversicherung; ~ **interview** mündliches Interview; ~ **inviolability** *(dipl.)* persönliche Unverletzbarkeit; ~ **judgment** Leistungsurteil; ~ **jurisdiction** *(law of nations)* Personalhoheit; ~ **knowledge** eigene Kenntnis; ~ **labo(u)r** eigene Arbeit; ~ **ledger** Privatkontenbuch; ~ **letter** vertraulicher Brief; ~ **letter in business** persönlich gehaltener Geschäftsbrief; ~ **liability** persönliche Haftung; ~ **liability insurance** Privathaftpflichtversicherung; ~ **liberty** persönliche Freiheit; ~ **loan** Personalkredit; **to obtain a ~ loan upon application** auf Antrag einen Personalkredit erhalten; ~ **loan broker** *(US)* Makler für Personalkredite; ~ **loan company** *(US)* Abzahlungsfinanzierungsgesellschaft; ~ **loan department** Personalkreditabteilung; ~ **luggage** *(Br.)* Handgepäck; ~ **matter** Privatangelegenheit; ~ **name** Personenname; **one's ~ needs** persönliche Bedürfnisse; ~ **notice** unmittelbare persönliche Empfängerbenachrichtigung; ~ **obligation** persönliche Verpflichtung, persönliches Schuldverhältnis; ~ **opinion** persönliche Meinung; ~ **property** Privateigentum, -vermögen, Mobiliarvermögen, *(deceased person)* beweglicher Nachlaß; ~ **property tax** *(US)* Vermögenssteuer auf bewegliches Eigentum; ~ **qualifications** persönliche Voraussetzungen; ~ **record** Personalbogen; ~ **relations** persönliche Beziehungen; ~ **relief** *(income tax, Br.)* persönlicher Freibetrag; ~ **remarks** anzügliche Bemerkungen; **to make ~ remarks** persönlich werden; ~ **replevin** Haftprüfungsverfahren; ~ **representative** persönlicher Referent, *(estate)* Nachlaßverwalter, Testamentsvollstrecker; ~ **requirements** Eigenbedarf; ~ **rights** Individualrechte, Bürgerrechte; ~ **ring** persönliche Note; ~ **salesmanship** Verkaufsgewandtheit, -kunst; ~ **sector** Haushaltssektor; ~ **security** persönliche Sicherheit; ~ **securities** Namenspapiere; ~ **selling** Verkauf mit persönlichem Einsatz; ~ **service** *(law)* persönliche Zustellung; ~ **service business** *(US)* Dienstleistungsgewerbe; ~ **service corporation** *(US)* Dienstleistungsbetrieb; ~ **servitude** persönliche Dienstbarkeit; ~ **share** Namensaktie; ~ **shopper** Auftragskäufer; ~ **sovereignty** Personalhoheit; **to put one's ~ stamp on a company** einem Unternehmen seinen Persönlichkeitsstempel aufdrücken; ~ **status** Familien-, Personenstand; ~ **statute** Personalstatut; ~ **style** persönlicher Lebensstil; ~ **tax** Kopfsteuer, Steuer auf das bewegliche Vermögen, zusammengezogene Einkommensteuer- und Ergänzungsabgabe; ~ **ties** persönliche Bindungen; ~ **tithes** Zehntabgabe vom Gewerbeertrag; ~ **tort** unerlaubte Handlung; **to give a ~ touch to s. th.** einer Sache eine persönliche Note geben; ~ **trust** *(US)* Treuhandverwaltung für bestimmte Begünstigte; ~ **union** Personalunion; ~ **use** *(lease)* Eigenbedarf; **for ~ use** zum persönlichen Gebrauch; ~ **warranty** persönlich übernommene Bürgschaft; ~ **worth** Liebhaberwert.

personals bewegliches Gut, persönliche Habe.

personalia Personalien, Personenangaben, Angaben zur Person, *(concerns)* Privatangelegenheiten.

personalist Verfasser biographischer Artikel.

personalities | of the stage and screen persönliche Vertrautheit mit dem Theater- und Fernsehleben;
to take to ~ persönlich werden.

personality [Eigen]persönlichkeit, *(magnetic personal quality)* Individualität, Ausstrahlung;

dissociate ~ gespaltene Persönlichkeit; **enterprising ~** unternehmerische Persönlichkeit; **legal ~** Rechtspersönlichkeit; **multiple ~** Doppelpersönlichkeit; **outstanding ~** bedeutende Persönlichkeit; **pleasing ~** Mensch mit verbindlichen Umgangsformen; **split ~** gespaltene Persönlichkeit; **strong ~** starke Persönlichkeit;
to have international ~ Völkerrechtspersönlichkeit haben; **to make one's ~ felt** sich Geltung verschaffen (durchsetzen); **to capitalize on one's ~ assets** aus seinen Persönlichkeitswerten Kapital schlagen; **to prove a ~** sich positiv für die Beurteilung einer Persönlichkeit auswirken; ~ **cult** Personenkult; ~ **impact** persönliche Ausstrahlung; ~ **rating** *(US)* Persönlichkeitsbeurteilung.

personalization Personifizierung.

personalize *(v.)* personifizieren, typisieren, illustrieren;
~ **the spirit of one's age** typischer Vertreter des Zeitgeistes sein.

personalized, less weniger ich-bezogen.

personally persönlich, eigenhändig;
~ **conducted tour** Ferienreise mit eigenem Reisebegleiter; ~ **liable** persönlich haftbar.

personalty Mobiliarvermögen, bewegliches Vermögen, persönliches (bewegliches) Eigentum, Privateigentum;
quasi ~ Zubehör;
to convert realty in ~ Grundvermögen realisieren.

personate personifizieren, *(theater)* Rolle spielen;
~ **s. o.** sich für j. ausgeben;
falsely ~ for s. o. sich fälschlich für j. ausgeben.

personation, false Vorgeben einer falschen Persönlichkeit, Personenstandsfälschung, Identitätstäuschung.

personification Personifizierung, Verkörperung;
~ **of selfishness** verkörperte Selbstsucht.

personify *(v.)* personifizieren.

personnel Personal, Belegschaft, Betriebsangehörige, Mitarbeiter, *(ship)* Besatzung, Mannschaft;
administrative ~ Verwaltungspersonal; **efficient ~** geschultes Personal; **executive ~** Führungskräfte, leitende Angestellte; **flying ~** fliegendes Personal; **office ~** Büropersonal, -kräfte; **operating ~** Belegschaft; **sales ~** Verkaufspersonal; **skilled (specialized, trained) ~** geschultes Personal; **technical ~** Fachkräfte;
~ **laid down in the agreement** vereinbarte Personalstärke;
to recruit ~ *(US)* Personal einstellen;
~ **accounting** Lohn- und Gehaltsbuchhaltung, Personalbuchhaltung; ~ **administration** Personalverwaltung; ~ **assistant** Personalsachbearbeiter; ~ **audit** Überprüfung der Personalpolitik; ~ **bomb** Bombe für lebende Ziele; ~ **budget** Personalausgaben; ~ **carrier** Truppentransporter, Mannschaftstransporter; **armo(u)red ~ carrier** gepanzerter Mannschaftswagen; ~ **changes** Personalveränderungen; ~ **chart** Stellenbesetzungsplan; ~ **chief** Personalchef; ~ **controller** Personalleiter; ~ **costs** Personalausgaben; **additional ~ costs** Personalzusatzkosten; **outside ~ costs** Fremdpersonalkosten; ~ **counsellor** Personalberater, Berater des Personalchefs; ~ **cutback** Personalkürzungen, -abbau, Belegschaftsabbau; ~ **data** Personalausgaben; ~ **department** Personalabteilung, -büro; ~ **development** Mitarbeiterförderung; ~ **difficulties** Personalschwierigkeiten; ~ **director** Personalchef, Leiter der Personalabteilung; ~ **division** *(US)* Personalabteilung, -büro; ~ **expenses** Personalaufwendungen, -kosten; ~ **files (folders)** Personalakten, -blatt; ~ **form** Personalbogen; ~ **functions** Personalaufgaben; ~ **inventory** Personalbestandskontrolle; ~ **management** Personalführung, -verwaltung; ~ **manager** Personalchef, -leiter; ~ **matters** Personalangelegenheiten; ~ **mobility** Belegschaftsfluktuation; ~ **needs** Personalbedürfnisse; ~ **office** Personalbüro; ~ **officer** Personalchef, -abteilungsleiter, -sachbearbeiter; ~ **organization** Personalverwaltung, Organisation des Personalwesens, Personalorganisation; ~ **performance** betriebliche Leistungen; ~ **periodical** Betriebszeitschrift; ~ **policy** Personalpolitik; ~ **problems** Personalfragen, -probleme; ~ **program(me)** Personalprogramm; ~ **rating** Personalbeurteilung; ~ **records** Personalunterlagen, -akten; ~ **relations** Arbeitgeber-Arbeitnehmerbeziehungen; ~ **requirements** Personalbedarf; ~ **review** Personalbeurteilung; ~ **service** *(US)* [soziale] Betriebsfürsorge; ~ **shakeup** personelle Umbesetzungen; ~ **shift** personelle Versetzungen, Personalumbau, -umsetzung; ~ **specialist** Personalfachmann, spezialisierter Personalberater; ~ **statute** Personalstatut; ~ **strength** personelle Ausstattung, Stärke der Belegschaft, Belegschaftsstärke; ~ **technician** Personalbearbeiter; ~ **transfer** Versetzungen innerhalb des Betriebs, innerbetriebliche Umsetzungen (Versetzungen).

perspective Perspektive, *(fig.)* Ausblick, Perspektive;
aerial ~ Perspektive aus der Luft;
~ **from below** Froschperspektive;
to have no ~ Dinge nicht in ihrer relativen Bedeutung sehen; **to see a matter in its right** ~ *(fam.)* Sache in den richtigen Dimensionen sehen.

persuade *(v.)* überreden, -zeugen, dazubringen;
~ **s. o.** seine Überredungskunst bei jem. spielen lassen; ~ **s. o. not to do s. th.** jem. abreden, etw. zu tun; ~ **s. o. out of his plan** j. von einem Plan abbringen; ~ **s. o. of the truth of one's statement** j. von der Wahrheit seiner Erklärung überzeugen.

persuader Überreder, *(sl.)* Revolver, Waffe.

persuasion *(religion)* Glaubensrichtung;
moral ~ moralische Beeinflussung;
to be both of the same ~ der gleichen Religionsgemeinschaft angehören.

persuasive|advertising stark überzogene Werbung; ~ **authority** nicht bindender Präzedenzfall; ~ **force** Überzeugungskraft; ~ **power** Überredungskunst.

pertain *(v.)* angehören, betreffen;
not to ~ **to s. one's office** nicht jds. Amtes sein.

pertaining dazugehörig, betreffend.

pertinency Angemessenheit.

pertinent sach-, zweckdienlich, einschlägig, zur Sache gehörig;
~ **to the matter in hand** zur vorliegenden Sache passend;
to be ~ **to** Bezug haben auf; **not to be** ~ **to the subject** nicht zum Thema gehören;
~ **data** sachdienliche Angaben, entsprechende Unterlagen; ~ **information** sachdienliche Mitteilungen; ~ **literature** einschlägige Literatur; ~ **reply** sachdienliche Antwort.

pertinents Zubehör.

perturb *(v.)* beunruhigen.

perturbation Beunruhigung, Bestürzung;
to show some ~ sich einigermaßen beunruhigt zeigen.

perturbing rumo(u)rs beunruhigende Gerüchte.

perusal Durchsicht, Einsichtnahme, Durchlesen, Prüfung;
for ~ zur Einsichtnahme; **for your kind** ~ zur gefälligen Durchsicht;
~ **of documents** Urkundenüberprüfung;
to give s. th. a careful ~ etw. einer genauen Durchsicht unterziehen, etw. sorgfältig überprüfen.

peruse *(v.)* durchlesen, -sehen, überfliegen;
~ **an account** Rechnung durchgehen; ~ **a book** Buch sorgfältig lesen; ~ **title deeds** Eigentumsurkunden überprüfen.

pervade *(v.)* durchdringen.

pervasive influence immer gegenwärtiger Einfluß.

perverse verderbt, böse, schlecht;
~ **verdict** *(jury)* auf falscher Rechtsbelehrung fußendes Urteil.

perversion Perversion, *(of true meaning)* Entstellung;
~ **of justice** Rechtsbeugung; ~ **of the truth** Verdrehung der Wahrheit.

pervert *(v.) (corrupt)* verderben, *(misinterpret)* [Sinn] verkehren, verdrehen, entstellen;
~ **the course of justice** Rechtsbeugung begehen.

pervious to light lichtdurchlässig.

pest Seuche, Pest, *(fig.)* lästiger Mensch;
~**s** Ungeziefer;
garden ~ Gartenplage;
~ **of corruption** Korruptionsseuche;
~ **control** Schädlingsbekämpfung; ~ **destruction agent** Schädlingsbekämpfungsmittel; ~ **hole** Seuchenherd; ~ **house** Aussätzigenspital, Seuchenlazarett.

pester *(v.)* belästigen, beunruhigen;
~ **s. o.** jem. in den Ohren liegen; ~ **s. o. for money** j. anpumpen; ~ **s. o. with questions** j. mit Fragen bedrängen; ~ **s. o. with requests of help** j. mit Hilfsanforderungen belästigen.

pestering child lästiges Kind.

pesticide blitz konzentrierte Schädlingsbekämpfungsaktion.

pet Haustier, Lieblingstier, *(fit of ill humo(u)r)* Verdruß, schlechte Laune;
in a ~ schlecht gelaunt;
mother's ~ Mutters Liebling (Schoßkind);
~ **of fortune** Glückskind;
~ *(v.)* **a child** Kind verzärteln;
to be a ~ **of society** gesellschaftlich überall begehrt werden; **to make a** ~ **of an animal** Tier verhätscheln; **to take** ~ **at s. th.** etw. übelnehmen;
~ **aversion** besondere Abneigung; ~ **name** Kose-, Spitzname; **to be a** ~ **peeve for s. o.** rotes Tuch für j. sein; ~ **pupil** Lieblingsschüler; ~ **shop** Tierhandlung; **to be on one's** ~ **subject again** schon wieder über sein Lieblingsthema reden.

petard Feuerwerkskörper, Kanonenschlag;
to be hoist with one's own ~ den eigenen Ränken zum Opfer fallen.

pete|box *(sl.)* Safe; ~**man** *(sl.)* Geldschrankknacker.

Peter, blue Abfahrtssignal;
~ *(v.)* **out** allmählich aufhören;
to rob ~ **to pay Paul** ein Loch aufreißen, um ein anderes zuzustopfen.

petit|jury Geschworenenbank; ~ **larceny** leichter Diebstahl.

petition [schriftliches] Gesuch, Antrag, Eingabe, Petition, Ansuchen, Bitte, Bittschrift, *(complaint, US)* Klageschrift, Antrag;
by way of a ~ auf dem Petitionswege;
collective ~ gemeinsam eingebrachtes Gesuch; **creditor's** ~ Konkurseröffnungsantrag eines Gläubigers; **cross** ~ Gegenantrag, -klage; **debtor's** ~ Konkurseröffnungsantrag des Gemeinschuldners; **election** ~ *(Br.)* Wahlprotest, -anfechtungsklage; **voluntary** ~ *(US)* Konkursanmeldung [durch den Gemeinschuldner]; **winding-up** ~ Abwicklungs-, Auflösungs-, Liquidationsantrag;
~ **for adjudication** von den Gläubigern gestellter Konkurseröffnungsantrag; ~ **of appeal** *(Br.)* Berufungsantrag; ~ **for arrangement** Vergleichsantrag; ~ **in bankruptcy** Antrag auf Konkurseröffnung, Konkurseröffnungsantrag, -begehren, -anmeldung; ~ **for clemency** Gnadengesuch; ~ **for discharge [of bankrupt]** *(US)* Antrag auf Aufhebung des Konkursverfahrens; ~ **for dissolution** *(company)* Auflösungsantrag; ~ **for divorce** Antrag auf Ehescheidung, Scheidungsklage; ~ **in error** *(US)* Wiederaufnahmeantrag; ~ **in lunacy** Entmündigungsantrag; ~ **for mercy** Gnadengesuch; ~ **for naturalization** *(US)* Einbürgerungsantrag; ~ **for pardon** Gnadengesuch; ~ **for reorganization** *(US)* Vergleichs-, Sanierungsantrag; ~ **a reprieve** Begnadigungsgesuch; ~ **for respite** Fristverlängerungsgesuch; ~ **against the return** Wahlprotest, -anfechtung; ~ **for review** *(of judgment)* Nachprüfungsantrag; ~ **of right** *(Br.)* Klageschrift gegen die Krone; ~ **for sequestration** Beschlagnahmeantrag; ~ **to wind up** Liquidationsantrag; ~ **for a writ of habeas corpus** Beantragung eines Haftprüfungstermins;
~ *(v.)* Eingabe, Petition einreichen, ersuchen, nachsuchen, beantragen, bitten;
~ **for s. th.** um etw. nachsuchen (ansuchen); ~ **the court to do s. th.** Antrag bei Gericht stellen; ~ **for divorce** Scheidungsklage einreichen, auf Scheidung klagen; ~ **for leave to sue in forma pauperis** *(US)* Armenrechtsgesuch stellen, Armenrecht beantragen; ~ **the mayor** Eingabe beim Bürgermeisteramt einreichen; ~ **for mercy (a reprieve)** Begnadigungsgesuch einreichen; ~ **for the winding up** Liquidationsverfahren beantragen;
to act favo(u)rably on a ~ einem Antrag entsprechen; **to dismiss a** ~ [Konkurs]antrag zurückweisen (ablehnen); **to dismiss a** ~ **on cause that the assets will be exhausted by costs** Konkursantrag mangels Masse abweisen; **to draw up a** ~ Bittschrift aufsetzen; **to enter a** ~ Gesuch bei Gericht einreichen; **to file a** ~ Antrag (Gesuch, Klage) einreichen, Eingabe machen, *(debtor)* Konkurseröffnung beantragen; **to file an involuntary** ~ Zwangskonkurs beantragen; **to file one's** ~ **in bankruptcy** Antrag auf Konkurseröffnung stellen, Einleitung eines Konkursverfahrens beantragen; **to file a** ~ **in voluntary bankruptcy** *(US)* Konkurs anmelden; **to file a** ~ **for a receiving order in bankruptcy** Antrag auf Erlaß eines Konkurseröffnungsbeschlusses stellen; **to file a** ~ **for divorce** Scheidungsklage einreichen; **to get up a** ~ Unterschriften für etw. zusammenstellen; **to grant a** ~ einer Eingabe stattgeben; **to hear a** ~ Gesuch entgegennehmen; **to make a** ~ Bittschrift einreichen; **to present a** ~ **against s. o.** Konkurseröffnung gegen j. beantragen; **to present a** ~ **for composition** Konkursvergleich vorschlagen; **to receive a** ~ Gesuch entgegennehmen; **to refuse a** ~ Gesuch (Eingabe) ablehnen; **to urge a** ~ Petition überreichen.

petitioner Gesuch-, Antragsteller, Bittsteller, *(Br.)* Scheidungskläger;
female ~ Antragstellerin.

petitioning|creditor betreibender Konkursgläubiger; ~ **party** antragstellende Partei, Antragsteller.

petitory action *(Scot.)* Eigentumsklage, Klage auf Herausgabe des Eigentums.

petrify *(v.)* bestürzen, lähmen.

petrochemical industries petrochemische Industrie.

petrol *(Br.)* Benzin, Sprit, Treibstoff, Kraftstoff;
lead ~ bleihaltiges Benzin; **2 star** ~ Normalbenzin; **4 star** ~ Super[kraftstoff], Superbenzin; **high-grade** ~ Qualitätsbenzin; **high-octane** ~ klopffestes Benzin; **low-grade** ~ minderwertiges Benzin;
~ *(v.)* auftanken;

to be short of ~ kein Benzin mehr haben; **to fill up with** ~ tanken, Benzin nachfüllen; **to run on** ~ mit Benzin fahren;
~ **allowance** Benzinzuteilung; ~ **can** Benzinkanister; ~ **consumption** Benzinverbrauch; ~ **economy** sparsamer Benzinverbrauch; ~ **engine** Benzin-, Vergasermotor; ~ **filter** Benzinfilter; ~ **gauge** Benzinstandsanzeiger, -uhr; ~ **level** Benzinstand; ~ **lighter** Benzinfeuerzeug; ~ **motor** Vergaser, Benzinmotor; ~ **pipe** Kraftstoffleitung; ~ **price** Benzinpreis; ~ **pump** Benzinpumpe; ~ **ration** Benzin-, Kraftstoffzuteilung; **basic** ~ **ration** Benzinnormalzuteilung; ~ **ration coupon** Benzinmarke; ~ **rationing** Benzinrationierung; ~ **shortage** Benzinknappheit; ~ **station** Tankstelle; **to stop at the next** ~ **station** an der nächsten Tankstelle halten; ~-**station attendant** Tank[stellen]wärter, Tankwart; ~ **store** Benzinlager; ~ **tank** Benzintank; ~ **tap** Benzinhahn; ~ **tax** Benzinsteuer; ~ **tax increase** Benzinsteuererhöhung.

petroleum Petroleum, Erdöl;
~ **cartel** Erdölkartell; ~ **industry** Erdölindustrie; ~ **production** Erdölgewinnung; ~ **refinery** [Erd]ölraffinerie; ~ **revenue tax** Erdöleinnahmensteuer; ~ **waste** Ölabflüsse.

petticoat Unterrock, *(el.)* Isolierglocke, *(fig.)* Weibsbild, weibliches Wesen;
in ~ in einer Frauenrolle;
to be always after a ~ Schürzenjäger sein; **to have known s. o. since he was in** ~**s** j. von Kindesbeinen an kennen;
~ **government** Weiberregiment; **to be under** ~ **government** unter dem Pantoffel stehen; ~ **insulator** Glockenisolator.

petties verschiedene (kleine) Spesen.

pettifoggery Kleinigkeitskrämerei, Rabulismus, *(law)* Advokatenkniff, Rechtsverdrehung.

pettifogging schikanös, *(law)* rechtsverdrehend;
~ **lawyer** Winkeladvokat; ~ **objections** schikanöse Einwendungen; ~ **shyster** Rechtsverdreher, skrupelloser Winkeladvokat.

pettifogulize *(v.)* auf Kleinigkeiten herumreiten.

petty geringfügig, unbedeutend, klein;
~ **affairs** Bagatellsachen; ~ **amounts** geringfügige Beträge, kleine Ausgaben; ~ **animosities** unbedeutende Animositäten; ~ **average** Vergütung für kleinere Reiseunkosten eines Schiffes; ~ **book** Portokassenbuch; ~ **case** Bagatellsache.

petty cash kleine Ausgaben, geringfügige Beträge, Bagatellbeträge, kleine Bar-, Portokasse;
~ **account** Kassakonto; ~ **book** kleines Kassenbuch, Portokassenbuch; ~ **fund** Portokassenfonds; ~ **voucher** Kassen-, Barzahlungsbeleg.

petty cashier Portokassenführer; ~ **cause** Bagatellsache; ~ **charges (expenses)** kleine Spesen, Portospesen; ~ **constable** örtlicher Polizeichef; ~ **damage** Bagatellschaden; ~ **dealer** unbedeutender Händler, Kleinhändler; ~ **debts** Läpper-, Bagatellschulden; ~ **details** unwesentliche Einzelheiten; ~ **farmer** Kleinlandwirt; ~ **faults** unbedeutende (geringfügige) Fehler; ~ **form** *(Br.)* unterste Schulklasse; ~ **goods** Kurzwaren; ~ **journal** Kladde; ~ **jury** *(US)* Geschworenengericht; ~ **larceny** *(US)* Mundraub; ~-**minded** kleinlich; ~-**mindedness** Kleinlichkeit; ~ **offense** *(US)* **(offence,** *Br.)* Übertretung; ~ **officer** mittlerer Beamter, *(mar.)* Maat, *(mil.)* Unteroffizier; **the** ~ **officers** die unteren Dienstgrade; ~ **patent** *(US)* Gebrauchsmuster; ~ **prince** Duodezfürst; ~ **regulations** engstirnige Bestimmungen; ~ **school** Kleinkinderschule; ~ **sessions** *(Br.)* Verhandlungen vor dem Friedensrichter; ~ **shopkeeper (trader)** kleiner Geschäftsmann; ~ **theft** Mundraub; ~ **troubles** geringfügige Schwierigkeiten; ~ **wares** Kurzwaren.

phantasm Phantom, Trugbild, Halluzination.

phantasmagoria Blendwerk, Trugbild.

phantom Phantom, Gespenst, Trugbild, *(payroll, sl.)* Lohnsteuerpflichtiger mit falschem Namen;
~ **of authority** Scheinautorität; ~ **of a king** Schattenkönig; ~ **appreciation** Wertsteigerung nur buchmäßig existierenden Aktienbesitzes; ~ **circuit** *(el.)* Simultanleitung, Viererkreis; ~ **ship** Geisterschiff, fliegender Holländer; ~ **stocks** *(US)* nur buchmäßig gutgeschriebene Aktien; ~ **stock deal** *(US)* nur buchmäßig erfaßtes Aktiengeschäft; ~ **stock plan** *(US)* nur zu Verrechnungszwecken vorgenommene Aktiengutschriften; ~ **trade** Kleingewerbe; ~ **trader** Kleingewerbetreibender.

pharmaceutical s Apothekerwaren;
~ **industry** pharmazeutische Industrie.

pharmacopoeia amtliche Arzneimittelliste.

pharmacist Apotheker.

pharmacy Arzneimittelkunde, *(dispensary)* Apotheke.

phase Stadium, Entwicklungsstufe, Phase, Stufe, Etappe;
in a strike's early ~ beim Streikbeginn, in der ersten Streikphase;

passing ~ abklingende Phase, Übergangsphase; **recession** ~ Rezessionsphase;
~ **of adjustment** Anpassungsreaktion; ~**s of a man's career** berufliche Entwicklungsstadien; ~ **of development** Entwicklungsstadium; ~ **of history** geschichtliches Entwicklungsstadium; **all** ~**s of operations** gesamter Operationsablauf; **alternating** ~**s of the cyclical trend** konjunkturelle Wechselphasen; **critical** ~ **of an illness** kritisches Stadium einer Krankheit; **political** ~ **of a problem** politischer Aspekt einer Frage;
~ *(v.)* in Phasen einteilen, *(el.)* synchronisieren;
~ **out** abwickeln, auslaufen, Produktion einstellen; ~ **out low-margin products** Erzeugnisse mit niedriger Gewinnspanne produktionsmäßig auslaufen lassen; ~ **out an exemption** Steuerfreibetrag nicht mehr gewähren; ~ **out a project** Projekt auslaufen lassen; ~ **out subsidies** Vergabe weiterer Investitionen beenden; ~ **out a tax** Steuer in Etappen abschaffen; ~ **out tax allowances** Steuervergünstigungen auslaufen lassen; ~ **in tariff reductions** Zollsenkungen synchronisieren;
to be in ~ phasengleich sein; **to be out of** ~ **with the national economy** mit der allgemeinen Entwicklung der Volkswirtschaft nicht Schritt halten; **to enter upon a new** ~ **of one's life** neuen Lebensabschnitt beginnen;
~ **adjustment** Phasenangleichung; **three-**~ **current** Drehstrom; ~ **difference** Phasenunterschied; ~ **distortion** Phasenverzerrung; ~ **line** *(mil.)* Zwischenziel; ~-**out** Auslaufen, Produktionseinstellung; ~ **recorder** Phasenschreiber.

phasing-in of tariff reduction Synchronisierung von Zollsenkungen.

phasing out Auslaufen.

pheeze *(v.)* **for a fraternity** *(sl.)* für eine Verbindung keilen.

phenomenon Phänomen, Erscheinung;
~ **of nature** Naturerscheinung.

philanthropic | al activities Wohlfahrtstätigkeit; ~ **institutions** philanthropische Einrichtungen.

philatetic sales counter Philatelieschalter.

philatelist Briefmarkensammler.

philately Philatelie.

philistine Spießbürger, *(politics)* Reaktionär.

philistinism Spießbürgertum.

philosophy | of business Wirtschaftsphilosophie; ~ **of law** Rechtsphilosophie.

phone *(coll.)* Telefon, Fernsprecher;
~ *(v.)* telefonieren, anrufen, Ferngespräch führen;
to answer the ~ Telefongespräch abnehmen; **to be on the** ~ Telefonanschluß haben; **not to be on the** ~ kein Telefon besitzen, telefonisch nicht erreichbar sein; **to call s. o. to the** ~ j. an den Apparat rufen;
~ **booth** *(US)* Fernsprechstelle, Münzfernsprecher; ~ **company** Telefongesellschaft; ~-**in program(me)** jederzeitige telefonische Erreichbarkeit; **to operate over ordinary** ~ **lines** normale Fernsprechleitungen benutzen; ~ **rate** Fernsprechgebühr; **global** ~ **service** Weltfernsprechdienst; ~-**wide register** Telefon-, Fernsprechbuch.

phonetic writing Lautschrift.

phonogram Lautzeichen, *(grammophone record)* Schallplatte, *(message)* zugesprochenes Telegramm.

phonograph Plattenspieler, Grammophon;
~ **needle** Grammophonnadel.

phonography Stenografie, Kurzschrift.

phonopost Sprechbrief.

phonotype phonetisches Schriftzeichen.

phony *(US sl.)* fauler Kunde, fauler Zauber, unsicherer Kantonist, *(imitation)* Schwindel, Fälschung, fauler Zauber;
~ *(a.)* gefälscht, unecht, fingiert, *(US sl.)* windig, faul, nicht koscher;
~ *(v.)* **up** *(form)* falsch ausfüllen;
to throw s. o. a ~ **line** *(US)* jem. etw. weißmachen wollen; ~ **war** Sitzkrieg.

photo Foto[grafie];
~ *(v.)* fotografieren, knipsen;
~ **equipment** Fotoausrüstung; ~-**offset** Lichtsatz; ~-**offset composing system** Lichtsatzverfahren.

photocell Photozelle.

photochromy Farbphotographie.

photochronograph Zeitlupenaufnahme.

photocomposing machine Lichtsetzmaschine.

photocomposition Lichtsatz.

photocopied fotokopiert.

photocopier Fotokopiergerät.

photocopy Fotokopie, Lichtpause, Ablichtung;
certified ~ beglaubigte Fotokopie.

photocopying machine Fotokopiergerät.
photodrama tragischer Film.
photoelectric│cell Selenzelle; ~ **meter** elektrischer Belichtungsmesser.
photoengrave *(v.) (print.)* [fotografisches] Klischee herstellen.
photoengraving Klischeeherstellung, Autotypie.
photofinishing Fotolaborarbeiten.
photoflash lamp Blitzlicht.
photoflood lamp Photolampe.
photogelatine Foto-, Lichtdruck;
~ **process** Lichtdruckverfahren.
photogenic fotogen.
photogrammetry Lichtbildauswertung.
photograph Fotografie, Lichtbildaufnahme;
passport ~ Paßfoto;
~ *(v.)* fotografieren;
~ **s. o. side-face** j. im Profil aufnehmen;
to have one's ~ **taken** fotografiert werden.
photographer Fotograf;
amateur ~ Amateurfotograf; **press** ~ Bildberichterstatter,
-reporter.
photographic fotografisch, *(fig.)* mechanisch kopierend;
~ **album** Fotoalbum; ~ **apparatus** Fotoapparat; ~ **copy** Fotokopie; ~ **facilities** Fotoeinrichtungen; ~ **goods** Fotoartikel; ~
goods shop Fotogeschäft; ~ **library** Film-, Diabibliothek; ~
paper Abzugspapier; ~ **periodical** Fotozeitschrift; ~ **printing**
Lichtdruck.
photographical fotografisch.
photography Fotografie;
air ~ Luftbildaufnahmen; **colo(u)r** ~ Farbfotografie;
to go in for ~ Photograph werden.
photogravure Kupfertiefdruck.
photointerpreter Bildauswerter.
photojournalist Bildjournalist.
photomap Luftbildkarte.
photomechanical fotomechanisch.
photomicrograph Mikrofotografie.
photomontage Fotomontage.
photomural Riesenvergrößerung.
photon Photon, Lichtquant.
photoplay Verfilmung eines Theaterstücks.
photoprint Fotokopie.
photoprocess fotomechanisches Druckverfahren.
photoradiogramm Funkbild.
photoreconnaissance Aufklärungsflug zu Bildaufnahme-
zwecken.
photoretouch *(v.)* retuschieren.
photosensitive lichtempfindlich.
photostat Fotokopie, Ablichtung, *(apparatus)* Fotokopiergerät;
~ *(v.)* fotokopieren.
photostatic copy *(US)* Fotokopie.
phototelegram Bildtelegramm.
phototelegraph *(v.)* Bildtelegramm absenden, bildtelegrafisch
übermitteln;
~ **service** Bildübermittlungsdienst.
phototelegraphic bildtelegrafisch.
phototelegraphy Bildtelegrafie.
phototype Lichtdruck[platte].
phototypographic im Lichtsatz hergestellt.
phototypography Lichtsatz.
phrase Redensart, Redewendung;
in a ~ kurz gesagt; **in simple** ~ ohne Umschweife;
empty ~s nichtssagende Redensarten; **set** ~s feststehende
Redewendungen; **stock** ~ feste Redensart; **well-worn** ~s abgedroschene Redensarten;
~ **of civility** Höflichkeitsfloskel;
~ *(v.)* in Worte fassen, ausdrücken;
~ **carefully** sorgfältig formulieren;
to learn some polite ~s einige Höflichkeitsphrasen erlernen;
~ **book** Sammlung von Redewendungen; **to be a** ~**-maker** Phrasendrescher sein.
phrasemonger Phrasendrescherei.
phrasemongering Phrasendrescherei.
phraseological phraseologisch.
phraseology Ausdrucksweise, Wortlaut, Phraseologie, Sammlung von Redewendungen.
physic Arznei[mittel].
physical natürlich, wirklich, körperlich, physisch, *(concerned
with natural science)* naturwissenschaftlich;
~ **assets** Sachanlagevermögen; ~ **capacity** körperliche Leistungsfähigkeit; ~ **comfort** Wohlbefinden; ~ **compulsion** kör-

perlicher Zwang; ~ **condition** Aggregatzustand; ~ **contact**
Berührung; ~ **control** direkte Steuerung von Produktion und
Verbrauch, Bewirtschaftungsmaßnahmen; ~ **damage** materieller Schaden; ~ **defect** körperliches Gebrechen; ~ **depreciation** auf Grund natürlicher Abnutzung erforderliche Abschreibung, Gebrauchsabschreibung; ~ **description** Sachbe-
zeichnung; ~ **destruction of armaments** Verschrottung von
Rüstungsmaterial; ~ **disability** Arbeits-, Erwerbsunfähigkeit;
~ **distribution** Verteilung durch den Handel; ~ **education** Lei-
beserziehung; ~ **equation** Bewegungsablauf; ~ **exercises** Gymnastik; ~ **fact** sinnlich wahrnehmbare Tatsache; ~ **fitness**
körperliche Tauglichkeit; ~ **force** physische (unmittelbare)
Gewalt; ~ **geography** physikalische Geographie; ~ **impossibility** faktische Unmöglichkeit; ~ **injury** Körperverletzung; ~
inventory tatsächlich aufgenommenes Inventar, körperliche
Bestandsaufnahme; ~ **life** *(machine)* technische Nutzungsdauer; ~ **necessity** physische Zwangslage; ~ **output** mengenmäßiger Ausstoß; ~ **person** natürliche Person; ~ **possession**
unmittelbarer Besitz; ~ **regionalization** naturräumliche Gliederung; ~ **resources** Sachwerte; ~ **science** Physik, Naturwissenschaft; ~ **shape** körperliche Verfassung; ~ **strength** Körper-
kraft; ~ **turnover** mengenmäßiger Umsatz; ~ **valuation**
Erneuerungskostenberechnung; ~ **value** Erneuerungswert; ~
variance Leistungsgradabweichung.
physically│disabled Versehrter, Invalide; ~ **handicapped** kör-
perbehindert.
physician Doktor, Arzt, Heilpraktiker, *(intern)* Internist;
resident ~ Krankenhausarzt;
~ **in attendance** Bereitschaftsarzt; ~ **to a hospital** Krankenhausarzt; ~ **in ordinary** Leibarzt; ~ **of the soul** Seelenarzt;
~'s **prescription** ärztliches Rezept.
pica *(print.)* Cicero.
picaroon Plünderer, Räuber.
picayune Bagatelle, Kleinigkeit, *(person)* Null;
not worth a ~ keinen roten Heller wert;
~ **business** unbedeutendes Geschäft.
pick Auswahl, Auslese, *(crop)* Ernte, *(instrument)* Kreuz-, Spitz-
hacke, *(print.)* Spieß;
daily ~ Tagesernte;
~ **of the army** Elite der Armee; ~ **of the bunch (basket)** das Beste
von allem; ~ **of land** schmale Grundstücksecke;
~ *(v.)* auswählen, -suchen, *(pilfer)* Taschendiebstähle begehen,
klauen, *(use pointed instrument)* mit der Pike arbeiten;
~ **apart** scharf kritisieren, herunterreißen; ~ **at s. o.** an jem.
herumnörgeln; ~ **a bit** Happen essen; ~ **a bone with** Streit mit
jem. austragen; ~ **s. one's brains** jds. geistiges Eigentum stehlen,
plagiieren; ~ **and choose** sehr sorgfältig auswählen; **not to** ~
and choose nicht lange wählen; ~ **a hole in s. one's coat (jacket)**
an jem. etw. auszusetzen haben; ~ **one's company** sich seine
Gesellschaft sorgfältig aussuchen; ~ **the least deserving candidate** ungeeignetsten Kandidaten aussuchen; ~ **at one's food** an
seinem Essen herumstochern; ~ **holes in** s. o. j. bekritteln; ~
holes in s. th. etw. kritisieren; ~ **holes in an argument** Beweisführung durchlöchern; ~ **a hole in s. one's reputation** jds. guten Ruf
ankratzen; ~ **a lock** Schloß mit dem Dietrich öffnen; ~ **off**
abpflücken, abreißen, *(mil.)* einzeln abschießen; ~ **out** *(select)*
aussuchen, wählen; ~ **out the good from the bad** Spreu vom
Weizen trennen; ~ **out the meaning of a passage** Sinn einer
Textstelle herausfinden (enträtseln); ~ **out one's friends in a
crowd** seine Freunde in der Menge ausmachen; ~ **out a plane**
(searchlight) Flugzeug mit dem Scheinwerfer erfassen; ~ **s.
one's pocket** jem. die Taschen ausräumen; ~ **s. one's purse** j. um
seinen Geldbeutel erleichtern; ~ **a quarrel** Streit provozieren
(vom Zaun brechen); ~ **rags** Lumpen sammeln; ~ **the rest of the
commission** letzte Ausschußmitglieder wählen; ~ **and steal**
klauen; ~ **one's steps** sich bedachtsam einen Weg suchen; ~ **a
theory to pieces** Theorie zerpflücken; ~ **the liberal vote apart**
Stimmenanteil der liberalen Wähler abschmelzen; ~ **one's way**
sich durchlavieren; ~ **a winner** auf den Sieger setzen; ~ **one's
words** seine Worte sorgfältig wählen.
pick up *(v.) (acquire)* erwerben, auftreiben, aufheben, *(convalesce)* sich erholen, *(criminal)* ergreifen, hopsnehmen, *(earn)*
verdienen, *(market)* sich erholen (beleben), *(motor)* auf Touren kommen, *(passengers)* aufnehmen, *(prostitute)* ansprechen, *(radio signal)* auffangen, *(sales)* steigen, zunehmen,
(scrape acquaintance) bekannt werden mit;
~ **s. o.** j. abholen; ~ **upon s. o.** *(coll.)* mit seinem Überholmanöver vorankommen; ~ **on s. th.** etw. nachholen; ~ **acquaintance
with s. o.** jds. Bekanntschaft machen; ~ **an anchor** Anker
aufnehmen (hochziehen); ~ **again** *(business)* sich erholen; ~ **a
bargain** gutes Geschäft machen; ~ **a bargain at an auction**

Gelegenheitskauf auf einer Auktion machen; ~ **bargains** *(stock exchange)* Gewinne mitnehmen; ~ **bits of information** einzelne Informationen aufschnappen; ~ **a broadcasting station** Sender hereinbekommen; ~ **a new business** Neugeschäfte abschließen; ~ **cheap** billig erstehen; ~ **enemy planes by searchlights** Feindflugzeuge mit Scheinwerfern erfassen; ~ **a habit** sich etw. angewöhnen; ~ **s. o. at his house** j. zu Hause abholen; ~ **a knowledge of English** englische Sprachkenntnisse erwerben; ~ **s. th. along the line** etw. nebenbei lernen; ~ **a language** Fremdsprache leicht aufschnappen; ~ **a livelihood** seinen Lebensunterhalt finden; ~ **the mistakes in a work** Fehler in einer Arbeit heraussuchen; ~ **news** Neuigkeiten erfahren (aufgabeln); ~ **an old painting** altes Gemälde aufgabeln; ~ **one's parcels** seine Pakete aufnehmen; ~ **a part of the costs** Kosten teilweise auffangen; ~ **for a pittance** für ein Butterbrot bekommen; ~ **profit** Gewinn machen; ~ **by radar installations** radarmäßig erfassen; ~ **route 51** der Bundesstrasse 51 folgen; ~ **scraps of knowledge** Bruchstücke von Wissen aufschnappen; ~ **a shipwrecked crew** Besatzung eines gestrandeten Schiffes aufnehmen (retten); ~ **for a song** *(sl.)* spottbillig kaufen; ~ **speed** auf Touren kommen; ~ **spirit** sich zusammenraffen; ~ **s. o. up sharply** unverblümt mit jem. umgehen; ~ **on the street** auf der Straße kennen lernen; ~ **strength** *(market)* widerstandsfähig werden, *(person)* sich erholen; ~ **a telegraph cable** Telefonkabel an Bord nehmen; ~ **the thread of a discussion** Faden der Unterhaltung wiederaufnehmen; ~ **with s. o.** jds. Bekanntschaft machen.

pick, to have a bone (crow) to ~ with s. o. mit jem. ein Hühnchen zu rupfen haben.

pick|-a-back plane Huckepackflugzeug; ~ **and shovel man** Tiefbauarbeiter; **~-me-up** *(fig.)* Stärkung[sgetränk]; **~-off** *(US)* abnehmbar, montierbar.

pickage Messestandsgebühr.

picked ausgewählt, ausgesucht;
~ **out** *(employee)* außer der Reihe ausgewählt, -gesucht; **to be ~ up by** aufgefrischt werden; **to be ~ up by the police** von der Polizei aufgegriffen werden; **to keep things ~-up** nichts herumliegen lassen;
~ **sample** entnommene Stichprobe.

picker Dietrich;
~-up Spediteur; **~-upper** *(sl.)* Autofahrer der Anhalter mitnimmt.

pickery *(Scot. law)* Munddiebstahl.

picket Zaunlatte, *(during strike)* Streikposten, -wache;
alignment ~ Absteckpfahl; **fire** ~ Feuerwache; **outlying** ~ *(mil.)* Vorposten, Feldwache; **police** ~ Polizeistreife;
~ *(v.)* einzäunen, *(mil.)* durch Vorposten sichern, *(as a picket)* Streikposten stehen, *(beset with pickets)* durch Streikposten absperren, Streikposten aufstellen, *(post pickets)* Streikposten aufstellen;
~ **a factory** Streikposten vor einer Fabrik aufstellen; **to place strikers on** ~ Streikposten aufstellen; **to throw out ~s** *(mil.)* Vorposten aufstellen;
~ **assignment** Streikposteneinteilung; ~ **boat** *(mil.)* Wach-, Vorpostenboot; **to place strikers on** ~ **duty** Streikposten aufstellen; ~ **fence** Lattenzaun; ~ **line** Streikpostenlinie, -kette, -sperre; **to cross the** ~ **line** als Arbeitswilliger durch die Streikpostenlinie gehen; **to throw a** ~ **line** Streikposten aufstellen; **to stand on (walk) the** ~ **lines** Streikposten beziehen; ~ **pin** *(US)* Weidepflock.

picketeer *(US)* Streikposten.

picketing Aufstellen von Streikposten;
cross ~ Streikpostenaufstellung durch zwei Gewerkschaften; **mass** ~ großes Streikpostenaufgebot; **organizational** ~ organisierte Streikposten; **peaceful** ~ nicht aggressiv durchgeführtes Streikpostenstehen; **secondary** ~ *(US)* betriebsfremde Streikposten, Streikposten von Betriebsfremden; **unlawful** ~ widerrechtliche Behinderung durch Streikposten, unerlaubtes Streikpostenstehen, Gewaltstreik;
~ **conduct** Streikverhalten; ~ **row** Streikpostenkette.

picking|and stealing Klauen; ~ **pockets** Taschendiebstahl; ~ **up of the wounded** Aufnahme der Verwundeten;
to be ~ **up again** *(market)* sich wieder erholen;
to have a ~ **choice** vollkommene Auswahl haben.

pickings Nebeneinkünfte, Beiseitegebrachtes;
~ **out of one's office** Sporteln; **~s and stealings** nicht koschere Nebeneinkünfte;
to make one's ~s out of the housekeeping money beim Wirtschaftsgeld Überschüsse machen.

pickle saure Gurke, *(piece of land)* von Hecken umschlossenes Kleingrundstück, *(troublesome person, coll.)* Früchtchen;

sad (sorrow) ~ Patsche;
to be in a ~ in der Klemme sitzen; **to be three ~s shy of a barrel** nicht alle beisammen haben.

picklock Nachschlüssel, Dietrich.

pickpocket Taschendieb.

pickup *(acceleration)* Anzugs-, Startvermögen, *(chance acquaintance)* Reise-, Zufalls-, Straßenbekanntschaft, *(bargain)* Gelegenheitskauf, *(broadcasting)* Aufnahme- und Übertragungseinrichtung, *(collecting)* Abholung, *(small commercial body)* Liefer-, Kleinlastwagen, *(el.)* Schalldose, *(impromptu, US sl.)* Improvisiertes, *(mil.)* Meldesammelstelle, *(recession, US sl.)* Konjunkturerholung, Auftriebstendenz, Wiederanstieg, *(record player)* Tonabnehmer, *(free ride, sl.)* Mitnehmen im Auto, *(television)* Abtastgerät;
casual ~ Zufallsbekanntschaft; **magnetic** ~ Tonabnehmer mit Magnetsystem; **phonograph** ~ Tonabnehmer; **remote** ~ *(broadcasting)* Außenübertragung; **smart** ~ rasches (rasantes) Anzugsvermögen; **television** ~ Fernsehaufnahme;
gradual ~ **in industrial activity** leichter Konjunkturanstieg, allmähliche Geschäftsbelebung; ~ **in employment** Beschäftigungsanstieg; ~ **of publishers' enclosures** Abholung von Verlegerbeischlüssen; ~ **in filings** Antragszunahme; ~ **in orders** Auftragszunahme, -erholung; ~ **in profits** bessere Gewinnentwicklung; ~ **of suspects** Verhaftung von Verdächtigen;
~ **camera** Aufnahmekamera; ~ **camper** schnelles Campingfahrzeug; ~ **cartridge** Tonabnehmerkopf; ~ **method** Selbstausbildungsverfahren; ~ **order** Auslieferungsanweisung; ~ **performance** *(antenna)* Aufnahmefähigkeit; ~ **and delivery service** Abhol- und Zustelldienst; ~ **transmitter** Aufnahmemikrofon; ~ **truck** *(US)* schneller Lkw, Kleinlastwagen, Abholfahrzeug.

picnic Picknick;
no ~ kein Zuckerlecken, keine leichte Sache;
~ **basket** Picknickkorb; **to take a** ~ **lunch** Mittagessen auf dem Picknick zu sich nehmen.

picknicker Picknickteilnehmer.

picknicky behelfsmäßig.

pictogram *(statistics)* Bildstatistik, figürliche Darstellung.

pictographic inscription Bilderschrift.

pictorial illustrierte Zeitung, Illustrierte;
~ *(a.)* malerisch;
~ **advertising** Bildwerbung.

picture Bild, Abbildung, *(description)* Schilderung, *(imagination)* geistiges Bild, Vorstellung, *(photo)* Photo, Aufnahme, *(television)* Fernsehbild;
in the ~ im Bilde; **not in the** ~ ungelegen; **quite out of the** ~ ohne Belang;
~s *(fam.)* Kintopp;
blood ~ Blutbild; **clinical** ~ Krankheitsbild, Befund; **colo(u)red** ~ Buntbild; **employment possibilities** ~ Bild über die Beschäftigungsmöglichkeiten; **feature-length** ~ abendfüllender Spielfilm; **jobless** ~ Bild des Arbeitslosenmarktes; **living ~s** *(theatre)* lebende Bilder; **mental** ~ Vorstellungsbild; **motion** ~ Film, Kino; **overall** ~ Bild der Gesamtlage; **rosier** ~ günstiges Bild; **rounded** ~ abgerundetes Bild; **slow-motion** ~ Zeitlupenaufnahme; **sound** ~ Tonfilm; **television** ~ Fernsehbild; **word** ~ bildhafte Schilderung;
~s of current events Aktualitäten-, Wochenschau;
~ *(v.)* abbilden, darstellen, *(fig.)* sich im Geist ausmalen, *(shoot a film)* filmen;
~ **an incident** Ereignis auf einem Gemälde festhalten;
to be in the ~ auf dem Laufenden (im Bilde) sein; **to be the** ~ **of one's father** seinem Vater sprechend ähnlich sehen, Ebenbild seines Vaters sein; **to be the very** ~ **of health** vor Gesundheit strotzen, wie das blühende Leben aussehen; **to be a** ~ **of misery** wie ein Häufchen Elend aussehen; **to be out of the** ~ nicht im Bilde sein; **to break into ~s** zum Film gehen; **to build up an on-the-spot ~** sich an Ort und Stelle im Bild machen; **to come into the** ~ in Erscheinung treten; **to come to a true** ~ sich ein klares Bild machen; **to draw a faithful** ~ **of s. th.** getreues Bild von etw. geben; **to draw a rapid** ~ **of s. th.** etw. in großen Zügen darstellen; **to form a** ~ **of s. th.** sich ein Bild von etw. machen; **to get the** ~ Sache begreifen; **to go to the ~s** *(Br.)* ins Kino gehen; **to paint a** ~ Bild malen; **to put s. o. in the** ~ *(fam.)* j. ins Bild setzen; **to sit for one's** ~ sich malen lassen; **to transmit ~s** bildsenden;
~ **advertisement** Lichtspielhauswerbung; ~ **book** Bilderbuch; **motion** ~ **camera** Aufnahmeapparat; ~ **disk** Bildplatte; ~ **distortion** *(television)* Bildverzerrung; **~s editor** Bildredakteur; ~ **frame** Bilderrahmen; ~ **frequency** Bildfrequenz; ~ **gallery** Gemäldegalerie, *(police, sl.)* Verbrecheralbum; ~ **goer** Kino-

gänger, -besucher; ~ **house** Lichtspieltheater; ~ **line standard** *(television)* Zeilenzahl; ~ **maker** Filmproduzent; ~ **marriage** Bilderbuchheirat; ~ **molding** *(US)* **(moulding,** *Br.***)** Bilderleiste; ~ **palace** Filmpalast, Schauburg, Lichtspieltheater; ~ **phone** Bildtelefon; ~ **plane** Bildfläche; ~ **play** Film; ~ **postcard** Ansichtspostkarte; ~ **probe** Bildtest; ~ **puzzle** Vexierbild, Bilderrätsel; ~ **resolution** *(television)* Bildschärfe; ~ **restorer** [Gemälde]restaurateur; ~ **screen** Bildschirm; ~**-screen text** Bildschirmtext; ~ **service** Bilderdienst; ~ **show** Filmvorführung; ~ **story** Bildbericht; ~ **taker** *(US sl.)* Streifenpolizist mit Radargerät; ~**-taking lens** Bildlinse; ~ **telegraphy** Bildfunk; ~ **theater** Kino, Lichtspiel-, Filmtheater; ~ **trademark** Bildwarenzeichen, -marke; ~ **transmission** Bildfunk, -übertragung; ~ **transmitter** Fernsehbildsender; ~ **tube** Bildröhre; ~ **window** großes Aussichtsfenster.

picturedom Filmwelt.

picturedrome Lichtspieltheater.

picturephone Fernsehtelefon.

picturesque malerisch, pittoresk.

picturization *(US)* Verfilmung.

picturize *(US)* verfilmen.

piddle *(v.)* sich mit Kleinigkeiten abgeben, seine Zeit vertrödeln.

pidgin *(Br., coll.)* Sache, Angelegenheit.

pie Kuchen, Pastete, *(easy task, sl.)* Spaziergang, *(fig.)* Durcheinander, Wirrwarr, *(politics, US sl.)* Protektion, Bestechung, *(print.)* Zwiebelfisch;
~ **in the sky** goldene Berge, leere Versprechungen;
~ *(v.)* durcheinanderbringen;
to be as easy as ~ *(sl.)* Kinderspiel (kinderleicht) sein; **to have a finger in the** ~ seine Finger im Spiel haben, mitmischen;
~ **card** *(sl.)* Gewerkschaftsausweis; ~ **chart** Kreisdiagramm; ~ **counter** *(sl.)* Futterkrippe; ~ **hunter** *(sl.)* Pöstchenjäger; ~ **wagon** *(US sl.)* Grüne Minna.

piece Stück, Teil, *(land)* Stück Land, Grundstück, *(financial interest, sl.)* Beteiligung, Kuchenanteil, *(simple lunch, US)* einfaches Mittagessen, *(school, US)* Vortragstück, *(theater)* Bühnenstück, *(workpiece)* Werkstück, Stück Arbeit;
a (by the) ~ pro (per) Stück, stückweise; **all of one** ~ alle aus einem Stück; **all to** ~**s** *(fam.)* ganz erledigt, bankrott; **in** ~**s** in Scherben, kaputt; **of a** ~ von derselben Art, *(undivided)* aus einem Stück; **sold only by the** ~ nur im Stück verkauft;
~ **by** ~ Stück für Stück, stückweise;
chatty ~ salopp geschriebener informeller Artikel; **pocket** ~ Glückspfennig; **a pretty** ~ *(sl.)* hübsches Weibsbild; **five-shilling** ~ Fünfschillingstück;
~ **of advice** Ratschlag; ~ **out of a book** Lesestück aus einem Buch, Buchstelle; ~ **of business** Geschäftsangelegenheit; **risky** ~ **of business** gewagte Spekulation; **nice** ~ **of change** *(sl.)* schönes Stück Geld; **finest** ~**s of a collection** schönste Stücke einer Sammlung; ~ **of cotton cloth** Ballen Baumwollstoff; **each** ~ **for a dollar** jedes Stück für einen Dollar; ~ **of evidence** Beweisstück; ~ **of extravagance** extravagantes Stück; ~ **of furniture** Möbelstück; ~ **of gold** Goldstück; ~ **of ground** Baugrundstück, -parzelle; ~ **of impertinence** unverschämtes Stück; ~ **of information** Information; **flagrant** ~**s of injustice** Fälle flagranter Ungerechtigkeit; ~ **of land** Grundstück, Stück Land, Parzelle; ~ **of good luck** Glücksfall, glücklicher Zufall; ~ **of ill luck** unglücklicher Zufall; ~ **of luggage** *(Br.)* Gepäckstück; ~ **of money** Geldstück; ~ **of news** Neuigkeit; **various** ~**s of news** verschiedene Nachrichten; ~ **of paper** Blatt Papier; ~ **of property** Vermögensgegenstand; ~ **de resistance** Hauptgericht, -sache, Glanzstück; ~ **of silver** Silbermünze; ~ **of wallpaper** Rolle Tapeten; ~ **of wine** Faß Wein; **excellent** ~ **of work** hervorragende Arbeit[sleistung];
~ *(v.)* ausbessern, flicken, Stück ansetzen, stückeln;
~ **s. o. off** *(sl.)* j. bestechen; ~ **out** vervollständigen, ergänzen; ~ **together odds and ends of cloth** Kleiderreste zusammenstückeln; ~ **together facts** Tatsachenmaterial zusammenstellen; ~ **up** Beute verteilen;
to be all of a ~ alle vom gleichen Kaliber sein; **to be of a** ~ **with the furniture** *(hangings)* mit den Möbeln farblich übereinstimmen; **to be paid by the** ~ Stücklohn erhalten; **to break to** ~**s** kaputtgehen; **to break a** ~ **of news to s. o.** jem. eine Nachricht schonend beibringen; **to come to** ~**s** zermürbt werden; **to complete (finish) a** ~ **of work** Arbeit fertigmachen; **to fall to** ~**s** in Scherben gehen, kaputtgehen, zerbrechen; **to give s. o. a good** ~ **of advice** j. gut beraten; **to give s. o. a** ~ **of one's mind** jem. gehörig die Meinung sagen; **to go to** ~**s** völlig durchdrehen; **to have three** ~**s of luggage** drei Gepäckstücke haben; **to have a** ~ **of news at first hand** Nachricht aus erster Hand haben; **to help s. o. to pick up the** ~**s** jem. wieder auf die Beine helfen; **to know s.**

th. **all to** ~**s** *(US)* etw. wie seine Hosentasche kennen; **to pay workmen by the** ~ Arbeiter im Akkord (Stücklohn) bezahlen; **to pick s. o. to** ~**s** j. herunterputzen, -machen; **to pull an author to** ~**s** Autor in Grund und Boden verreißen; **to say one's** ~ Stück rezitieren; **to sell goods by the** ~ Waren stückweise verkaufen; **to speak one's** ~ offen seine Meinung sagen, aus seinem Herzen keine Mördergrube machen; **to take to** ~**s** zerlegen, auseinandernehmen, abmontieren; **to tear to** ~**s** in Stücke reißen; **to tear an argument to** ~**s** Argument zerpflücken; **to work by the** ~ im Akkord (Stücklohn) arbeiten;
~ **broker** Restehändler; ~ **cost** Stückkosten; ~ **goods** nach dem Stück verkaufte [Textil]waren, Stückgüter, Meter-, Schnittwaren; ~ **labo(u)r** Stück-, Akkordarbeit; ~ **list** Stückliste; ~ **market** *(Br.)* Stückgutmarkt; ~ **master** *(Br.)* Akkordlohnvermittler; ~ **number** Stückzahl; ~ **price** Stückpreis, -akkord; ~ **price system** *(prison work)* Akkordsystem, Stücklohnverfahren.

piece rate Stücklohn-, Akkordlohnsatz;
group ~ Gruppenakkordlohn.

piece-rate│bonus Akkordlohnzuschlag, -prämie; ~ **earnings** Akkordverdienst; ~ **formula** Akkordlohnformel; ~ **plan (system)** Prämienlohn-, Akkordsystem; ~ **ticket** Akkordlohnschein; ~ **wages** Akkord-, Stücklohn; ~ **work** Akkordarbeit.

piece│scale Stücklohn-, Akkordlohnordnung; ~ **wage** Akkord-, Gedinge-, Stücklohn.

piecemeal stückweise, Stück für Stück;
to buy only ~ nur stückweise einkaufen;
~ **contracts** Einzelaufträge; **to work on a** ~ **plan** ohne Plan und Überlegung arbeiten; ~ **price fixing** *(US)* Preisfestsetzung von Fall zu Fall.

piecework Arbeit im Akkord, Akkord-, Stücklohn-, Gedingearbeit, *(print.)* Paketsatz;
high ~ progressiver Leistungslohn;
~ **with base guarantee** Akkordlohn mit garantiertem Mindestbetrag;
to do ~ im Akkord arbeiten (stehen); **to pay by the** ~ im Akkord bezahlen; **to put s. o. on** ~ j. im Akkord (Stücklohn) beschäftigen; **to work by the** ~ im Akkord arbeiten;
~ **bonus** Akkordzuschlag; ~ **contract** Akkordvertrag; ~ **earnings** Gesamtverdienst bei Anwendung des Prämienlohnsystems, Akkordverdienstlohn, Stücklohnverdienst; ~ **employee** Akkordarbeiter; ~ **pay** Akkord-, Stücklohn; ~ **pay rate** Akkordtariflohn; **non-**~ **bonus plan** nicht akkordmäßiger Leistungslohn; ~ **rate** Akkordrichtsatz; **multiple** ~ **system** Akkordlohnsystem.

pieceworker Akkord-, Stückarbeiter.

piecing together [Zusammen]stückelung.

pied-à-terre vorübergehende Unterkunft, Absteigequartier.

pier Hafendamm, Lösch-, Landungsplatz, Landungssteg, Mole, Kai;
floating ~ schwimmende Landungsbrücke; **landing** ~ Landungsplatz;
~ **glass** großer Wandspiegel.

pierage Hafen-, Kaigebühren, Kai-, Ufergeld.

pierce *(v.)* durchbohren, -löchern;
~ **the darkness** Finsternis durchdringen; ~ **the enemy's lines** feindliche Linien durchbrechen; ~ **s. o. to the head** *(fam.)* j. auf Herz und Nieren prüfen; ~ **the mystery** Geheimnis durchschauen; ~ **s. o. through and through** j. mit seinen Augen durchbohren.

piercing│cold schneidende Kälte; ~ **pain** stechender Schmerz; ~ **shriek** gellender Schrei; ~ **wind** durchdringender Wind.

piffle Unsinn, Quatsch;
~ *(v.)* quatschen, faseln.

pig Schwein, *(metal)* Roheisen, *(print., Br., sl.)* Buchdrucker, *(stool pigeon, sl.)* Polizeispitzel;
please the ~ wenn alles klappt;
sucking ~ Spanferkel;
~ **on pork** *(Br.)* Wechsel auf die eigene Niederlassung;
to buy a ~ **in a poke** Katze im Sack kaufen; **to bring one's** ~**s to a pretty (the wrong) market** aufs falsche Pferd setzen; **to carry** ~ **to market** Geschäft machen wollen; **to look at one another like stuck** ~**s** sich ganz verdutzt ansehen; **to make a** ~ **of o. s.** Vielfraß sein;
~ **bed** Gießbett; ~ **breeding** Schweinezucht; ~ **farm** Schweinezucht; ~ **iron** Roh-, Masseleisen; ~**'s whisper** Flüstern, Zischeln, Geheimniskrämerei;
~**s might fly** es geschehen noch Zeichen und Wunder.

pigeon Taube, *(deadhead, sl.)* Gimpel, Einfaltspinsel, *(professional gambler, sl.)* Berufsspieler, *(special position)* verantwortliche Sonderstellung;

carrier (homing) ~ Brieftaube;
~ *(v.) (sl.)* mogeln, übers Ohr hauen, rupfen;
  to pluck a ~ einen Dummen übers Ohr hauen.
pigeongram Brieftaubennachricht.
pigeonhole [Brief]fach, Ablagefach, Zettelkasten;
~ *(v.)* ablegen, in ein Fach legen, *(classify)* einordnen, klassifizieren, *(for future consideration)* zurückstellen, auf die lange Bank schieben, auf Eis legen;
~ **facts** Tatsache einordnen; ~ **files** Akten ablegen; ~ **a report for future consideration** Bericht auf später zurückstellen.
piggery Schweinemästerei, -züchterei.
piggy Ferkel;
~ **bank** Sparschwein; ~**-bank factor** Geldhortungsfaktor.
piggyback|export scheme Huckepackausfuhrsystem; ~ **[rail] service** Huckepackverkehr.
piggly-wiggly-store *(US)* Lebensmittelautomat.
pigheaded borniert, stur.
pignorative contract Pfandvertrag.
pignus *(lat.)* Pfand.
pike *(US coll.)* Zollschranke, Schlagbaum;
~ *(v.)* **along** seinen Weg machen; ~ **off** abhauen.
pikeman Zolleinnehmer.
piker *(miser, sl.)* Filz, Geizkragen, *(shirker, US sl.)* Drückeberger, *(speculator, US sl.)* kleiner Spekulant, *(tramp)* Stromer, Tippelbruder.
pile Stapel, Stoß, Packen, Haufen, *(el.)* Säule, *(group of buildings)* Gebäudekomplex, *(pillar)* Pfahl, [Eisen]pfeiler, *(textiles)* Velours, Samt, Plüsch;
atomic ~ Atommeiler, Reaktor; **funeral** ~ Scheiterhaufen;
~ **of arms** Gewehrpyramide; ~ **of books** Stapel Bücher, Bücherstapel; ~ **of correspondence** Stoß (Stapel) von Briefen; ~ **of documents** Aktenstoß; ~ **of money** Haufen Geld; ~ **of newspapers** Stapel Zeitungen; ~ **of ore** Erzhalde; ~ **of good sense** Portion gesunden Menschenverstands; ~ **of wood** Holzstoß;
~ *(v.)* Pfähle einrammen, *(store up)* aufstapeln, -schichten;
~ **on the agony** *(coll.)* in einer Wunde unnötig herumwühlen; ~ **more coal on** Kohlen nachlegen; ~ **it on** *(coll.)* ganz schön übertreiben; ~ **on the expense** Unkosten anwachsen lassen; ~ **up** *(airplane)* abstürzen, Bruch machen, *(mar., sl.)* Schiff auflaufen lassen, *(motor vehicle)* zusammenstoßen, *(work)* über den Kopf wachsen, *(v./i.)* sich ansammeln (aufhäufen), aufspeichern, -stapeln, -schichten, *(v./i., mar.)* stranden, auflaufen; ~ **up debts** Schulden anhäufen; ~ **a table with dishes** Tisch mit Gerichten überladen; ~ **up planks** Bretter aufklaftern;
to have a ~ **of money** Geld wie Heu haben; **to make one's** ~ sein Glück machen; **to make a** ~ **of money** Stange Geld verdienen; **to strengthen with** ~**s** mit Pfählen abstützen, unterpfählen;
~ **driver** Ramme; ~ **dwelling** Pfahlbau; ~ **fabric** Samtstoff; ~ **up** *(car)* Massenkarambolage, Kettenunfall; ~ **work** Pfahlbau.
pilework Pfahlwerk.
pilfer *(v.)* klauen, filzen, mausen.
pilferage Plünderung, *(modern use)* Mundraub, Notdiebstahl;
~ **hazard** Plünderungsrisiko.
pilferer Langfinger.
pilfering Klauen.
pilgrim Pilger, Wallfahrer;
~ **route** Pilgerstraße.
pilgrimage Wallfahrt.
piling up of demand Nachfragestau.
pill Pille, *(chronic complainer, sl.)* Meckerziege, *(cigarette, sl.)* Stäbchen, *(mil., sl.)* blaue Bohne, Ei, Koffer;
bitter ~ *(fig.)* bittere Pille;
a ~ **to cure an earthquake** Tropfen auf dem heißen Stein;
~ *(v.)* Pille verschreiben, *(mil., sl.)* beschießen, *(sl.)* [bei der Wahl] durchfallen lassen;
to swallow the ~ bittere Pille schlucken; **to take a** ~ Pille nehmen.
pillage Plünderung, Brandschatzung;
~ *(v.)* [aus]plündern, brandschatzen.
pillager Plünderer.
pillar Pfeiler, *(fig.)* Säule, Hauptstütze, *(techn.)* Träger, Stütze, Support;
the ~**s of Hercules** die Säulen des Herkules; ~ **of the Liberal Party** die Säulen der Liberalen; ~ **of smoke** Rauchsäule; ~**s of wisdom** Säulen der Weisheit;
~ *(v.)* durch Pfeiler oder Säulen stützen;
to run from ~ **to post** von Pontius zu Pilatus laufen;
~ **box** *(Br.)* Briefkasten; **board and** ~ **work** Strecken- und Pfeilerbau.
pillbox Pillenschachtel, *(army use)* Bunker, Unterstand, *(car, sl.)* Straßenfloh.

pillion Soziussitz;
  to ride (seat) on a ~ auf dem Soziussitz mitfahren;
~ **passenger (rider)** Bei-, Soziusfahrer; ~ **seat** Beifahrer-, Soziussitz.
pillory Pranger;
  to put s. o. in the ~ j. in den Pranger stellen.
pillow, to consult one's etw. überschlafen.
pilot *(airplane)* Flugzeugführer, Pilot, Flieger, *(compass)* Kompaßregulierer, *(fig.)* Wegweiser, Berater, *(railroad, US)* Schienenräumer, *(ship)* Lotse;
airline ~ Flugzeugkapitän, -kommandant; **branch** ~ amtlich angestellter Lotse; **chief** ~ Oberlotse; **co-**~ zweiter Flugzeugführer; **coast** ~ Küstenlotse; **compulsory** ~ Zwangslotse; **dock** ~ Hafenpilot; **in-shore** ~ Küstenlotse; **licensed** ~ seeamtlich befähigter Lotse, geprüfter Pilot; **master** ~ Lotseninspektor; **second** ~ Kopilot; **sky** ~ geprüfter Pilot; **truck** ~ Lkw-Beifahrer;
~ **in command** *(US)* Flugzeugkommandant;
~ *(v.)* lotsen, steuern, *(plane)* führen;
~ **a bill through the Congress** Gesetzesvorlage durch den Kongreß manövrieren; ~ **a ship through a channel (canal)** Schiff durch den Kanal lotsen;
to drop a ~ Lotsen von Bord gehen lassen, *(fig.)* sich von einem unbequemen Berater trennen; **to license a** ~ Pilotenprüfung abnehmen; **to take a** ~ **on board** Lotsen an Bord nehmen;
~ **balloon** Versuchsballon; ~ **beam** Leitstrahl; ~ **boat** Lotsenboot; ~ **bridge** Kommandobrücke; ~ **biscuit** Schiffszwieback; ~ **census** Probezählung; ~ **cloth** Marinetuch; ~**'s cockpit** Führerkanzel; ~ **company** federführende Gesellschaft; ~ **craft (cutter)** Lotsenboot; ~ **engine** Leerfahrt-, Vorlokomotive; ~ **experiment** Vorversuch; ~ **flag** Lotsenflagge; ~ **instructor** Fluglehrer; ~ **jack** Lotsenflagge; ~ **jacket** Schifferjacke; ~ **lamp** Kontrollampe; ~ **length** Versuchsstrecke; ~**'s licence** Lotsenschein, *(plane)* Piloten-, Flugzeugführerschein; ~ **light** Sparbrenner; ~ **lot** Null-, Versuchsserie; ~ **office** Lotsenamt, -büro; ~ **officer** *(Br.)* Fliegerleutnant; ~ **parachute** Auszieh-, Hilfsfallschirm; ~ **plant** Versuchsbetrieb, -anlage, Musterbetrieb; ~ **product** *(EC)* Leiterzeugnis; ~ **production** Prototyp-, Versuchsproduktion; ~ **program(me)** Versuchsprogramm; ~ **project** Versuchsprojekt; ~ **relay** Steuer-, Kontrollrelais; **on a** ~ **scale** auf Versuchsbasis; ~ **scheme** Versuchsprojekt; ~ **series** Versuchsserie(n); ~ **service** Lotsendienst; ~ **ship** Lotsenfahrzeug; ~ **stage** Entwicklungsstadium; ~ **strike** Pilotenstreik; ~ **study** [Leit]studie, *(opinion poll)* Probeerhebung, -befragung, Vor-, Probetest; ~ **survey** Leitstudie, *(statistics)* Probeerhebung, -untersuchung, Stichprobe; ~ **test** Probeuntersuchung; ~ **train** *(mil.)* Vorzug; ~ **trainee** Flugschüler.
pilotage Auslotsung, *(compensation)* Lotsengebühr, *(fig.)* Leitung, Führung, *(pilot's office)* Lotsenbüro;
coastal ~ Lotsendienst an der Küste; **compulsory** ~ Lotsenzwang; **free** ~ Lotsenfreiheit; ~ **inwards (outwards)** Lotsengebühr beim Einlaufen (Auslaufen);
~ **authority** Lotsenbehörde, -amt; ~ **district** Lotsenbereich; ~ **dues** Lotsengebühren; ~ **waters** Lotsenstrecke, -revier.
pilothouse Brücken-, Ruderhaus.
pilotless aircraft unbemanntes Flugzeug.
pimp Zuhälter.
pin Bolzen, Zapfen, Nadel, *(coll.)* Kleinigkeit, Bagatelle, *(instance of pinning)* Kribbeln, *(surveying)* Pflock;
neat as a new ~ funkelnagelneu; **not worth a** ~ keinen Pfifferling wert; **on a jolly** ~ in gehobener Stimmung;
clothes ~ *(US)* Wäscheklammer; **fraternity** ~ Verbindungsabzeichen; **safety** ~ Sicherheitsnadel; **scarf** ~ Krawattennadel;
~**s and needles** *(fig.)* Kribbeln;
~ *(v.)* feststecken, -machen;
~ **an accusation on s. o.** jem. eine strafbare Handlung anhängen; ~ **down** genau herausfinden; ~ **down the enemy** *(mil.)* Feind fesseln; ~ **s. o. down on his promise** j. auf sein Versprechen festnageln; ~ **s. o. down to what he said** j. auf eine Aussage festlegen; ~ **one's hopes on s. o.** seine Hoffnung auf j. setzen; ~ **one's opinions on s. one's sleeves** sich von jds. Meinung abhängig machen; ~ **one's opponent down to a point** seinen Gegner auf einen Punkt festnageln; ~ **papers together** Papier zusammenheften; ~ **up a notice** Bekanntmachung anschlagen; ~ **s. o. against the wall** j. an die Wand drücken; ~ **a witness down to facts** Zeugen zwingen, sich an die Tatsachen zu halten;
to be quick on one's ~**s** flink auf den Beinen sein; **not to care a** ~ sich einen Dreck um etw. kümmern; **to knock s. o. off his** ~**s** j. total umschmeißen, *(coll.)* j. umstoßen (zu Fall bringen, aus der Fasson bringen); **to pull the** ~**s** *(sl.)* Laden hinschmeißen; **to sit on** ~**s and needles** wie auf Kohlen sitzen;

~ **boy** Kegeljunge; ~ **money** *(daughter)* Nadelgeld, *(outworker)* Heimarbeiterlohn, *(seasonal worker)* Saisonarbeiterverdienst.
pin-striped mit Nadelstreifen.
pincer|s Kneif-, Beißzange;
~ **movement** *(mil.)* Zangenbewegung.
pinch kritischer Augenblick, Klemme, Notlage, *(apprehension, sl.)* Festnahme, *(stock exchange)* plötzliche Kurssteigerung, *(organize, coll.)* Klauen, Mausen;
if it comes to the ~ im Alleräußersten; **at** *(Br.)* **(on,** *US)* **a** ~ im Notfall; **with a** ~ **of salt** *(fig.)* mit Vorbehalt;
money ~ zeitweilige Geldknappheit;
~ **of hunger** quälender Hunger; ~ **of poverty** drückende Armut; ~ **on profits** Erlösdruck;
~ *(v.)* zusammenpressen, -quetschen, *(apprehend, sl.)* verhaften, festnehmen, *(narrow)* beengen, einengen, -pferchen, *(stint)* geizen, knausern, *(US sl.)* klauen, erleichtern;
~ **o. s.** sich auf das Nötigste beschränken; ~ **s. o.** j. in die Enge treiben (am Kragen kriegen); ~ **the blossom** Blüten abfrieren lassen; ~ **one's fingers in the doorway** sich die Finger in der Tür einklemmen; ~ **s. o. for food** j. auf schmale Kost setzen; ~ **money out of s. o.** jem. Geld abknöpfen (Geld aus der Tasche ziehen); **to have to** ~ **and scrape** jeden Pfennig zusammenkratzen müssen; ~ **and scrape for one's children** seiner Kinder wegen sich alles vom Munde absparen;
to be under the ~ **of necessity** unter dem Zwang der Verhältnisse stehen; **to come to a** ~ zum Äußersten kommen; **to feel the** ~ von der Depression betroffen werden; **to feel the** ~ **of poverty** in drückender Armut leben; **to know where the shoe** ~**es** wissen, wo der Schuh drückt;
~ **hitter** *(US)* Ersatzmann.
pinched im Druck, in Bedrängnis;
to be ~ in Bedrängnis sein, darben, *(stock exchange)* plötzlich zu Deckungskäufen gezwungen sein; **to be** ~ **with cold** durchfroren sein; **to be** ~ **for money** in finanzielle Schwierigkeiten geraten sein, knapp dran (bei Kasse) sein; **to be** ~ **for poverty** bettelarm sein; **to be** ~ **for time** wenig Zeit haben, zeitknapp sein;
~ **circumstances** beschränkte Verhältnisse; ~ **face** abgehärmtes Gesicht.
pincher *(sl.)* Langfinger.
pinchfist Geizkragen, -hals, Knauserer.
pinching| cold schneidende (beißende) Kälte; ~ **parsimony** Knauserei; ~ **want** drückende Not.
pinchpenny *(Br.)* Pfennigfuchser.
pinhead Stecknadelkopf, *(fig.)* Kleinigkeit, Geringfügigkeit.
pinhead-sized stecknadelkopfgroß.
pinhole camera Lochkamera.
pine| *(v.)* **[away]** verschmachten; ~ **away with grief** vor Gram (Kummer) vergehen; ~ **after news** auf Neuigkeiten aus sein.
pining for home heimwehkrank.
pinion box Getriebekasten.
pink Stutzer, *(US)* Salonbolschewist, rosarot Angehauchter, *(driving right, sl.)* Fahrerlaubnis, *(peak)* Musterbeispiel, Krone, Gipfel;
~ **of courtesy** äußerste Höflichkeit; ~ **of elegance** das Eleganteste vom Eleganten; ~ **of fashion** allerneueste Mode; ~ **of perfection** höchste Vollendung; ~ **of politeness** Ausbund (Gipfel) von Höflichkeit;
~ *(a.)* *(US sl.)* kommunistisch angehaucht;
~ *(v.)* *(engine)* klopfen;
to be in the ~ **of condition** in erstklassiger Kondition (Hochform) sein; **to be the** ~ **of politeness** Höflichkeit in Person sein;
balance of payments ~ **book** *(Br.)* Rosabuch über die monatliche Zahlungsbilanzsituation; ~ **slip** *(sl.)* Entlassungspapiere; ~ **socialism** gemäßigter Sozialismus; ~ **tea** *(US)* feudale Gesellschaft, in gehobenem Kreis; ~ **zone** *(London)* absolute Parkverbotszone.
Pinkerton, pinkie Privatdetektiv.
pinnacle Bergspitze, Gipfel, *(fig.)* Höhepunkt, Gipfel, Spitze;
at the ~ **of one's fame** auf dem Höhepunkt seines Ruhms; **ice** ~ Gletscherspalte; **snow** ~ Schneewächte.
pinockle season *(garment industry, sl.)* Nachsaison, tote Zeit.
pinpoint Kleinigkeit;
~ *(v.)* haargenau festlegen, *(mil.)* Zielwurf durchführen; ~ **the location of a radio operator** Standort eines Funkers anpeilen; ~ **a target** gezielten Bombenabwurf durchführen; **to turn down the gas to a** ~ Gas auf Sparflamme stellen;
~ **bombing** gezielter Bombenabwurf; ~ **flame** Sparflamme; ~**-the-downtown survey** Konjunkturabschwung mit Argusaugen notierende Übersicht; ~ **target** Punktziel.
pinprick *(fig.)* Stichelei.

pinup Illustriertenphoto, schick;
~ **[girl]** Illustriertenschönheit.
pint halber Liter;
~**-sized** Dreikäsehoch.
pioneer Pionier, Bahnbrecher, Wegbereiter, Schrittmacher, Avangardist, *(mil.)* Angehöriger eines Vorauskommandos;
~ *(v.)* bahnbrechend (Schrittmacher) sein, bahnbrechend wirken, Pionierarbeit leisten;
~ **broadcasting station** erste Rundfunkstation; ~ **patent** Stammpatent, grundlegendes Patent; **to do** ~ **work** bahnbrechend sein, bahnbrechende Arbeit leisten.
pioneering| job Pioniertätigkeit; ~ **service** Pionierdienst.
pious| effort gutgemeinter Versuch; ~ **fraud** frommer Betrug; ~ **wish** frommer Wunsch.
pip *(Br., sl.)* schlechte Laune, Depressionsanfall, *(radar)* Leuchtfleck, Impuls, Blip, *(remarkable person, sl.)* toller Kerl, *(time signal)* hoher Ton, Zeitton, Piepsen;
~ *(v.)* *(blackball, sl., Br.)* durchfallen lassen, *(fig.)* in die Tasche stecken;
to give s. o. the ~ jem. auf die Nerven gehen; **to have the** ~**s** *(sl.)* Depressionen haben.
pipe Rohr, Röhre, *(business conversation, sl.)* Geschäftsgespräch, *(mar.)* Bootsmannspfeife, *(music)* Blasinstrument, *(smoking)* Pfeife, *(plain sailing, sl.)* klarer Fall, *(easy task, sl.)* kleine Fische;
in a feeble ~ mit schwacher Stimme;
ascending ~ Steigrohr; **drainage** ~ Dränagerohr; **gas** ~ Gasrohr; **flexible** ~ Schlauch; **rain[-water]** ~ Dachrinne; **steel-lined** ~ Stahlmantelrohr; **supply** ~ Versorgungsleitung; **water** ~ Wasserrohr;
~ *(v.)* Rohrleitung legen, *(inform, sl.)* singen;
~ **away** *(mar.)* unter Deck schieben; ~ **down** *(coll.)* Mund halten; ~ **all hands on deck** Mannschaft auf dem Deck zusammenrufen; ~ **off** *(sl.)* sich bei der Polizei beschweren; ~ **s. o. off** *(sl.)* j. auf die schwarze Liste setzen; ~ **the oil to the refinery** Öl durch eine Rohrleitung zur Raffinerie pumpen; ~ **a victim** *(sl.)* Opfer beobachten;
to clear one's ~ sich räuspern; **to dance to s. one's** ~ nach jds. Pfeife tanzen; **to hit the** ~ *(sl.)* Marijuana rauchen; **to lay** ~**s** Rohrleitung verlegen; **to put s. th. into one's** ~ **and smoke it** *(coll.)* versuchen, mit etw. fertig zu werden; **to smoke the** ~ **of peace with s. o.** Friedenspfeife mit jem. rauchen;
~ **clip** Rohrschelle; ~ **course** *(sl.)* Anfängerkursus; ~ **dream** verrückte Idee, Chimäre, Luftschloß, Hirngespenst; ~ **failure** Rohrbruch; ~ **joint** Rohrkupplung; ~ **plant** Röhrenwerk; ~ **requirements** Röhrenbedarf.
pipeclay *(v.)* *(fig.)* in Ordnung bringen.
pipelayer Rohrverleger.
pipeline Rohrleitung, *(fig.)* geheime Informationsquelle;
in the ~ auf dem Transport, unterwegs, *(fig.)* im Vorbereitungsstadium;
coal slurry ~ Rohrleitung zum Transport pulverisierter Kohle;
to be in the ~ im Vorstadium sein;
~ **break** Rohrleitungsbruch; ~ **engineering** Rohrleitungsbau; ~ **fault** Rohrleitungsbruch; ~ **route** Rohrleitungsverlauf; ~ **system** Rohrleitungssystem; ~ **tariff** Rohrleitungstarif.
pipeliner Rohrverleger.
piper, to pay the Zeche bezahlen; **to pay the** ~ **and call the tune** Unternehmen finanzieren und dafür das Sagen haben.
piping Rohrleitungskonstruktion.
piracy Seeräuberei, Piraterie, *(infringement of copyright)* unerlaubter Nachdruck (Raubdruck), Plagiat, *(patent)* Patentverletzung;
air ~ Luftpiraterie; **design** ~ sklavische Nachahmung; **labo(u)r** ~ Abwerbung von Arbeitskräften; **literary** ~ Plagiat;
~ **of an invention** Diebstahl einer Erfindung;
to commit a ~ Piratenakt begehen, *(fig.)* Plagiat (Raubdruck) begehen.
pirate Seeräuber, *(omnibus, Br., coll.)* behördlich nicht zugelassener Omnibus, *(omnibus driver, Br., coll.)* Schwarzfahrer, *(patent law)* Verletzer eines Patentrechts, *(plagiarist)* Plagiator, *(printing)* Raubdrucker, *(ship)* Kaper-, Piratenschiff;
radio (wireless) ~ Schwarzhörer;
~ *(v.)* Piratenakt begehen, Seeräuberei betreiben, *(print illegally)* unbefugt nachdrucken, Raubdruck begehen, *(plagiarize)* Plagiat begehen, sich am geistigen Eigentum Dritter vergehen, *(workers)* abwerben;
~ **a copyright** Urheberrecht verletzen; ~ **designs** Gebrauchsmuster kopieren; ~ **labo(u)rers into other jobs** Arbeitskräfte abwerben; ~ **a trademark** Warenzeichen nachahmen; ~ **a wave length** Wellenlänge absorbieren;

~ broadcasting station Piratensender; **~ bus** *(Br., coll.)* behördlich nicht zugelassener Omnibus; **~ version** ungenehmigter Nachdruck, Raubdruck.

piratic unerlaubt nachgedruckt;
~ edition Raubdruck; **~ printer** Nachdrucker.

pirating Plagiat, *(of workers)* Personalabwerbung.

piscary Fischereirecht, *(fishing place)* Fischgrund, -fangstelle, -revier.

piscatorial für die Fischerei bestimmt.

pisciculture Fischzucht.

pisciculturist Fischzüchter.

pistol Pistole;
air ~ Luftpistole; **cap ~** Spielzeugpistole; **duelling ~s** Duellpistolen;
~ shot Pistolenschuß; **within ~ shot** in Pistolenschußweite.

piston Kolben;
~ displacement Hubraum; **~ engine** Kolbenmotor; **~ valve** Kolbenventil.

pit Grube, Loch, *(agriculture)* Miete, *(coal pit)* Kohlenbergwerk, Zeche, Grube, *(commodity exchange, US)* Maklerstand für den Handel bestimmter Warengattungen, Produktenbörse, *(fig.)* [Fall]grube, Falle, *(mining)* Schacht, *(motor racing)* Box, *(stalls, Br.)* zweites Parkett, Parterre;
down the ~ unter Tage;
coal ~ Kohlenbergwerk; **grain ~** Getreidebörse; **orchestra ~** Orchesterversenkung; **refuse ~** Müllgrube; **repair ~** *(car)* Grube; **wheat ~** *(US)* Weizenbörse;
~ of hell Abgrund der Hölle; **~ with a poor safety record** Zeche mit hohen Betriebsunfallquoten;
~ (v.) *(agriculture)* einmieten;
~ against one another als Konkurrenz gegenüberstellen; **~ one's strength against a rival** seine Kräfte mit einem Gegner messen;
to dig a ~ for s. o. *(fam.)* jem. eine Falle stellen;
~ boss Vorarbeiter; **~ box** *(Br.)* Parterreloge; **~ closure** Zechenstillegung; **~ coal** Steinkohle; **~ coal mining** Steinkohlenbergbau; **~-head ballot** Schachtabstimmung; **~ hand** Grubenarbeiter; **~-head stocks** Kohlenhalde, Haldenbestände; **~-head price** Zechen-, Grubenpreis; **~-head worker** Übertagearbeiter; **~ incentive deal** Leistungsabkommen für Zechenarbeiter; **~ prop** Grubenstempel; **~ saw** Schrotsäge; **~ talk** Bergarbeitersprache; **~ trader** *(US)* selbständiger Produktenmakler.

pitch Pech, Bitumen, *(accoustics)* Tonhöhe, *(caravans)* fester Wohnwagenplatz, *(mining)* Baufeld, *(peak)* Höhepunkt, Gipfel, *(sales talk, sl.)* Überredungskünste, *(street trade, Br.)* Verkaufsstelle, Stand [eines Straßenhändlers], *(wares for sale)* angebotene Warenmenge, Warenangebot;
as dark as ~ pechschwarz; **at the lowest ~ of one's fortune** am Tiefpunkt von jds. Mißgeschick; **on the ~** *(sl.)* hinter dem Gelde her;
common black ~ Schiffspech; **mineral ~** Asphalt; **wheat ~** *(US)* Weizenbörse; **wild ~** Vorstoß auf Geratewohl;
~ of greatness Gipfel des Ruhms; **~ of proficiency** Leistungshöchststufe; **~ and toss** Kopf oder Wappen;
~ (v.) Verkaufsstand aufschlagen, *(sell news, sl.)* Neuigkeiten verkaufen, *(ship)* stampfen, *(offer for sale)* zum Verkauf anbieten;
~ one's aspirations too high seine Erwartungen zu hoch spannen; **~ a camp** Lager aufschlagen; **~ a large consignment** große Warenpartie verkaufen; **~ an estimate too low** zu niedrige Schätzung vornehmen; **~ upon an expediency** auf einen Notbehelf verfallen; **~ hay** Heu aufstaken; **~ in** *(US)* sich tüchtig ins Zeug legen, kräftig mitmachen; **~ a ladder against a building** Leiter an eine Hauswand anlegen; **~ one's hopes too high** seine Hoffnung zu hoch schrauben; **~ upon the most suitable man for a job** durch Zufall auf den geeignetsten Mann stoßen; **~ out a drunkard** Besoffenen vor die Tür setzen; **~ a ship** Schiff teeren; **~ a slope** Böschung mit Steinen bepacken; **~ a speech on** Rede abstimmen auf; **~ it straight to s. o.** jem. die Wahrheit sagen; **~ it strong** ganz schön auftragen; **~ upon** aufschlagen; **~ into the work** sich tüchtig an die Arbeit machen; **~ a yarn** *(fig.)* ein Garn spinnen, Geschichten erzählen;
to excite s. one's interests to the highest ~ jds. Neugier auf das Höchste erregen; **to fly a high ~** *(sl.)* sich hoch hinaufschwingen; **to fly at a higher ~ than s. o.** j. überrunden (übertreffen), jem. den Rang ablaufen; **to give the orchestra the ~** dem Orchester den Ton angeben; **to play ~ and toss with s. th.** leichtfertig mit etw. umgehen; **to provoke s. o. to the highest ~ of resentment** j. aufs Äußerste provozieren; **to queer s. one's ~** jds. Pläne stören, jem. in die Quere kommen (ins Handwerk pfuschen);

to shout at the ~ of one's voice mit höchster Stimmstärke rufen; **~ angle** Steigungswinkel; **~ chain** Eimerkette; **~ level** Ton-, Stimmlage.

pitched|battle offene Feldschlacht; **high-~ roof** steiles Dach; **~ work** Steinpackung.

pitchfork Heu-, Mistgabel;
~ (v.) s. o. into a position j. in eine Stellung lancieren; **~ troops into battle** Truppen in die Schlacht werfen.

pitching *(goods)* Ausstellung, Feilhaltung, *(ship)* Stampfen;
~ a tent Zeltaufstellung.

pitchman *(US coll.)* Straßenhändler, *(television, sl.)* Fernsehwerber.

pitfall Falle, Fallgrube, *(fig.)* Fußangel;
~s of the law *(fam.)* Fallstricke des Gesetzes.

pitman Bergmann, -arbeiter, Kumpel, Gruben-, Schacht-, Zechenarbeiter.

pittance kleine Summe, *(meagre wage)* Hungerlohn;
to work all day for a mere ~ für ein Butterbrot (einen Apfel und ein Ei) arbeiten.

pitwood Grubenholz.

pity Mitleid, Erbarmen;
for ~'s sake um Himmels willen;
to excite public ~ öffentliches Mitleid erregen.

pivot Zapfen, Stift, *(fig.)* Angel-, Mittelpunkt;
the ~ on which the whole question turns der Punkt, um den sich die ganze Frage dreht;
~ (v.) a question on a fact Frage an einer Tatsache aufhängen;
~ bearing Zapfenlager; **~ hole** Zapfenloch.

pivotal lebenswichtig, zentral;
~ industry Schlüsselindustrie; **~ point** Angelpunkt; **~ position** Schlüsselstellung; **~ question** lebenswichtige Frage; **~ role** Schlüsselrolle; **~ trades** Schlüsselgewerbe.

pix *(sl.)* Filmindustrie.

placard Plakat, Anschlag[zettel];
~ (v.) durch Anschlag bekanntgeben, *(wall)* plakatieren, mit Plakaten bekleben;
to post a ~ Plakat anschlagen.

placarder *(US)* Plakatkleber.

placarding Anschlag, Aushang.

placate *(v.)* befriedigen, beruhigen, beschwichtigen, besänftigen, *(US)* durch Schmiergelder günstig stimmen.

placation Besänftigung, Beschwichtigung.

placatory mission Versöhnungsmission.

place Ort, Ortschaft, Platz, Stelle, *(employment)* [An]stellung, Amt, *(location)* Örtlichkeit, *(mil.)* fester Platz, Festung, *(passage)* Stelle, *(residence)* Wohnort, Wohnung, *(restaurant)* Gaststätte, Lokal;
all over the ~ überall verstreut; **at this ~** am hiesigen Platz; **customary in a ~** ortsüblich; **from this ~** ab hier; **in ~** *(minister)* im Amt (Staatsdienst); **in his ~** an seiner Stelle; **in ~ of** an Stelle von; **in ~s** stellenweise; **in the first ~** an erster Stelle; **of several ~s** mehrstellig; **out of a ~** stellenlos, *(unsuitable)* nicht angebracht; **without ~** außer Dienst;
burial ~ Beerdigungsort, Begräbnisstätte; **celebrated ~** berühmter Ort; **confidential ~** Vertrauensstellung; **find ~** Fundort; **fortified ~** befestigter Platz; **highest ~** höchste Stelle; **interesting ~** interessante Stelle; **issuing ~** Ausstellungsort; **landing ~** Anlegestelle, Landeplatz; **loading ~** Verladeort; **manufacturing ~** Herstellungsort, Fabrikationsstätte; **market ~** Markt[platz]; **meeting ~** Treffpunkt; **native ~** Heimat-, Geburtsort; **open ~** freier Platz; **permanent ~** Dauerstellung; **polling ~** Wahllokal; **populous ~** größere Ortschaft; **public ~** allgemein zugänglicher Ort; **shipping ~** Verladungs-, Versandort; **small ~** Nest; **watering ~** Badeort; **working ~** Arbeitsstätte, -platz;
~ of abode Wohnsitz; **~ of accident** Unfallort; **~ of amusement** öffentliche Vergnügungsstätte; **~ of arbitration** Sitz des Schiedsgerichts; **~ of arrival** Ankunftsort; **~ of assembly** Treffpunkt; **~ to begin** Ausgangspunkt; **~ of birth** Geburtsort; **~ of business** Geschäftssitz, gewerbliche Niederlassung; **fixed ~ of business** feste Geschäftseinrichtung; **principal ~ of business** Hauptniederlassung; **~ of call** Anlaufhafen; **~ of coinage** Prägeort; **~ of consignment** Versendungsort; **~ of contract** Gerichtsstand des Erfüllungsortes; **~ as provided in the contract** vertraglich vereinbarter Ort; **nice ~ in the country** hübscher Landsitz; **~ of custody** Verwahrungsort; **~ of decimal** Dezimalstelle; **~ of delivery** Lieferungs-, Erfüllungsort; **~ of departure** Abgangsort; **~ of deposit** Hinterlegungsort, -stelle; **~ of destination** Bestimmungsort; **~ of discharge** Ausladeort, Löschungsplatz; **~ of dispatch** Aufgabestation; **~ of distraining** Pfändungsort; **~ of employment** Arbeitsplatz, -stätte; **~ of

permanent employment Dauerarbeitsplatz; ~ of entry Zollhafen; ~ of exchange Wechselplatz; ~ of execution Richt-, Hinrichtungsstätte; ~ of hearing Verhandlungsort; ~ of hiding Zufluchtsort, Versteck; ~ of incorporation Geschäftssitz; ~ of interest Sehenswürdigkeit; ~ of issue Ausgabe-, Ausstellungsort; ~ of loading Verladeort; ~ of loss Schadensort, -stelle; ~ of management Sitz der Geschäftsleitung, Verwaltungssitze; ~ of manufacture Fabrikationsort, -stätte, Herstellungsort; ~ of meeting Versammlungs-, Tagungsort, Treffpunkt; ~ of the same name gleichnamiger Ort; ~ of origin Urprungsort; ~ of payment Zahlungsort; ~ of performance Erfüllungsort; ~ of presentment Vorlageort; ~ of protest Protestort; ~ of purchase Einkaufsort; ~ of refuge Zufluchtsort; ~ of residence Wohnort; established (settled) ~ of residence fester Wohnsitz; ~ of shipment [Ver]ladestelle, Versandort; ~ of strength (mil.) fester Platz; ~ and time Ort und Zeit; ~ of tort Tatort; ~ of transmission Löschungshafen; ~ of transshipment Umschlagplatz; ~ of unloading Ausladeplatz; ~ of work Arbeitsplatz, -stelle, -stätte; ~ of worship Gotteshaus;

~ (v.) (arrange) anordnen, (dispose goods) liefern, (into a home) unterbringen, (invest) investieren, Investition vornehmen, anlegen, (loan) plazieren, unterbringen, absetzen, (put in office) anstellen, (put in place) stellen, legen, setzen, (find situation for) unterbringen;

~ s. o. j. identifizieren; ~ to s. one's account jem. in Rechnung stellen, auf jds. Rechnung setzen, j. belasten; ~ to new account auf neue Rechnung vortragen; ~ on the agenda auf die Tagesordnung setzen; ~ an amount to s. one's credit jem. [einen Betrag] gutschreiben; ~ under arrest verhaften; ~ on board an Bord verbringen; ~ bonds Obligationen unterbringen; ~ a book with a publisher Verlagsvertrag über ein Buch abschließen; ~ a call Telefongespräch anmelden; ~ in a category einstufen; ~ a child under s. one's care Kind in jds. Obhut geben, jem. ein Kind anvertrauen; ~ s. o. in command jem. Befehlsgewalt übertragen; ~ confidence in s. o. Vertrauen in j. setzen (zu jem. haben); ~ a contract Auftrag vergeben; ~ to s. one's credit in a bank auf jds. Bankkonto übertragen; ~ to s. one's debit jds. Konto belasten; ~ on the file zu den Akten (in Vormerkung) nehmen, vormerken; ~ on the same footing gleichstellen; ~ funds (Br.) Auslagegeld zurückbekommen; ~ goods Ware absetzen; ~ goods at the buyer's disposal Ware für den Käufer bereitstellen; ~ under guardianship unter Vormundschaft stellen; ~ s. th. into the hands of s. o. jem. etw. zur Bearbeitung übergeben; ~ one's fate in s. one's hands sein Schicksal in jds. Hände legen; ~ a matter in other hands Angelegenheit einem Dritten übertragen; ~ a matter into the hands of a lawyer Fall einem Anwalt übertragen; ~ a manuscript not later than the tenth century Entstehungszeit eines Manuskriptes in das frühe zehnte Jahrhundert legen; ~ an insurance Versicherung abschließen; ~ an issue Emission unterbringen; ~ s. o. on the retired list Offizier verabschieden; ~ a loan at 98% Anleihe zum Kurs von 98% unterbringen; ~ money on interest Geld zinsbringend anlegen; ~ a name in case of need on a draft Namen als Notadresse auf einen Wechsel setzen; ~ s. o. in one's office j. bei sich [im Büro] unterbringen; ~ an order Auftrag erteilen (vergeben); ~ an order direct Auftrag unmittelbar erteilen; ~ an order for an article with a firm Artikel bei einer Firma bestellen (in Auftrag geben); ~ an order for books Bücherauftrag erteilen; ~ o. s. under s. one's orders Anweisungen von jem. entgegennehmen; ~ s. o. out (US) j. unterbringen; ~ a page in a magazine Seite in einer Zeitschrift belegen; ~ o. s. under s. one's power sich jem. auf Gnade und Ungnade übergeben; ~ pressure on the money market Druck auf dem Geldmarkt verursachen (ausüben); ~ s. o. on probation jem. Bewährungsfrist zubilligen; ~ on record aktenkundig machen, zu den Akten nehmen, schriftlich festhalten; ~ to the reserve der Rücklage überweisen; ~ a restriction on a power Vollmacht einschränken; ~ one's seal on a document Urkunde mit seinem Siegel versehen; ~ o. s. at s. one's service jem. seine Dienste zur Verfügung stellen; ~ shares Aktien unterbringen (plazieren); ~ a stop on a check Scheck sperren lassen; ~ a sum against Summe validieren; ~ a sum at the disposal of s. o. jem. einen Geldbetrag zur Verfügung stellen; ~ surplus stock überschüssige Ware loswerden; ~ in war bonds in Kriegsanleihe anlegen; ~ in a warehouse auf einem Speicher unterbringen; ~ a work Arbeit zuweisen; ~ workers Arbeiter unterbringen; ~ among the great writers unter die großen Schriftsteller einreihen;

to attain to a high ~ hohen Rang einnehmen; to be s. one's ~ jds. Aufgabe sein; to be in a ~ Stelle [als Hausangestellter] haben; to be difficult to ~ schwer einzurangieren (zu beurteilen) sein; to be out of ~ (remarks) nicht am Platze (angebracht) sein; not

to be able ~ s. o. j. sich an j. nicht erinnern können; to be a difficult man ~ schwer zu beurteilen sein; to be looking for a little ~ that is not too expensive nach einem nicht zu teuren Nest Umschau halten; not to be quite in ~ nicht ganz angemessen sein; to book a ~ sich einen Platz reservieren lassen; to calculate to five ~s of decimals auf fünf Dezimalstellen ausrechnen; to change ~s with s. o. Plätze mit jem. tauschen; to click into ~ einrasten; to come from my ~ aus meinem Ort stammen; to continue at a ~ an einem Ort bleiben; to feel out of ~ sich deplaziert fühlen; to fill s. one's ~ jds. Stelle einnehmen; to find one's ~ sich zurechtfinden; to give ~ to s. o. von. jem ersetzt werden; to give ~ to a ship einem Schiff einen Hafenplatz zuweisen; to go ~s verschiedene Vergnügungsstätten aufsuchen; to go to ~s and see things Touristenreise machen; to have a ~ to stay without cost unentgeltlich übernachten können; to have everything in its ~ alles an Ort und Stelle haben; to have found a ~ in history in die Geschichte eingegangen sein; to hold the first ~ erste Stelle einnehmen; to keep one's ~ Distanz wahren; to keep a ~ Platz freihalten; to keep s. o. in his ~ j. auf Abstand halten; to know one's ~ (fig.) Abstand zu wahren wissen, sich Zurückhaltung auferlegen; to know the ~ Lokalverhältnisse kennen; to lay a ~ Gedeck auflegen; to look [sadly] out of ~ ganz verdattert aussehen; to move from ~ to ~ dauernd umziehen; to own a fine ~ schönes Anwesen haben; to point off ~s Stellen abstreichen; to post in a conspicuous ~ an gut sichtbarer Stelle anschlagen; to put o. s. in s. one's ~ sich in jds. Lage versetzen; to put s. o. in his ~ j. zurechtweisen; to put one's finger on the bad ~ seinen Finger auf die offene Wunde legen; to resume one's ~ seinen Platz wieder einnehmen; to return a book to its ~ Buch wieder einrangieren; to show s. o. his ~ j. zu seinem Platz führen; to swop (swap) ~s with s. o. Platz mit jem. tauschen; to supply s. one's ~ für j. einspringen, an jds. Stelle treten; to take ~ passieren, sich ereignen, steigen, stattfinden; to take s. one's ~ [at a duty] jds. Stelle einnehmen, für j. einspringen, an jds. Stelle einrücken; to take ~ without disorder ohne Zwischenfälle verlaufen; to take one's ~ in a queue sich [in eine Warteschlange] einreihen; to take a prominent ~ bedeutende Stelle innehaben; to take second ~ zweiten Platz belegen; ~ bet Platzwette; ~ card Platz-, Tischkarte; ~ holder Angestellter, Platzhalter; ~ hunter Stellenjäger; ~ hunting Ämterjagd; ~ mat Telleruntersatz, Platzgedeck; ~ name Ortsname, (at table) Tischkarte; ~ seeker Stellungssuchender.

placed untergebracht, plaziert;
~ on short time als Kurzarbeiter beschäftigt.
placeman (Br.) Futterkrippenpolitiker, Pöstcheninhaber.
placemanship (Br.) Futterkrippenwirtschaft.
placement Unterbringung, (employees) Arbeitseinsatz, -einstellung, (investment) Investition, Anlage, (securities, US) Plazierung, Placement, Unterbringung;

actual ~ (railway car) tatsächliche Bereitstellung; constructive ~ (railway car) mittelbare Bereitstellung; direct ~ (securities) Direktunterbringung, -plazierung; job ~ (US) Stellenvermittlung;

~ of capital Kapitalanlage; ~ of funds Kapitalverwendung; appropriate ~ of labo(u)r sinnvolle Verwendung (richtige Verteilung) von Arbeitskräften;

~ agency (US) Arbeits-, Stellenvermittlung; ~ agent (US) Stellenvermittler; ~ bureau (US) Arbeitseinsatzbüro, Berufsberatungsstelle; government ~ center (US) staatliche Stellenvermittlung; ~ climate Plazierungsklima; ~ concept Plazierungskonzept; ~ consulter (US) Berufsberater; ~ facilities Stellenvermittlungsmöglichkeiten; private ~ market privater Kapitalmarkt; ~ officer (US) Berufsberater, Stellenvermittler; ~ service (US) Berufsberatungs-, Stellenvermittlungsdienst; ~ specialist (US) Berufsberater.
placemongering Ämterhandel.
placer (superficial deposit) Mineralvorkommen;
~ claim Schürfanspruch.
placet Plazet, Zustimmung.
placeta (US) Plätzchen, Gärtchen.
placing (issue, shares) Plazierung, Anlage, Anlegen;
investment ~ Anlageinvestitionen;
~ of an advertisement (advertising) Anzeigenaufgabe, -plazierung; ~ on board Anbordverbringung; ~ of children in foster homes Unterbringung von Kindern in Pflegeheimen; ~ a contract Auftragsvergabe; ~ of a contract by tender Verdingung; ~ of employees Unterbringung von Arbeitskräften; ~ of a loan Anleiheplazierung, -unterbringung; ~ of an order Auftragserteilung, Aufgabe einer Bestellung; ~ in a position Unterbringung; ~ of a poster Plakatanschlag; ~ of securities with the public Effektenplazierung; ~ of shares Aktienplazierung;

to participate in the ~ of an issue an der Unterbringung einer Emission beteiligt sein;

~ broker Versicherungsmakler; **~ potential** Plazierungskraft; **~ power** Plazierungskraft; **~ price** Einführungspreis.

plagiarism Nachahmung, Plagiat;

to commit ~ geistigen Diebstahl (Plagiat) begehen.

plagiarist Plagiator.

plagiarize *(v.)* Plagiat begehen.

plague Seuche, Pest, *(fig.)* Heimsuchung, Geißel, Strafe, *(nuisance, coll.)* Quälgeist;

~ *(v.)* belästigen, stören, quälen;

~ s. one's life out jem. das Leben vergiften (zur Hölle machen);

~ s. o. with questions j. mit Fragen belästigen;

~ bacillus Pestbazillus; **~ spot of a city** Schandfleck einer Stadt.

plaguer Quälgeist.

plaguy *(coll.)* verflixt, verteufelt.

plain Ebene, Flachland;

~ *(a.)* eben, *(easy)* einfach, unkompliziert, *(without lines)* unliniert, *(ore)* rein, unverfälscht, *(simple)* unscheinbar, schlicht, schmucklos, ungemustert;

as ~ as ~ can be, as ~ as daylight sonnenklar; **as ~ as pikestaff** *(fam.)* so klar wie Kloßbrühe; **as ~ as print** so klar wie dicke Tinte;

to be ~ with s. o. mit jem. ganz offen reden; **to be ~ on the evidence** aufgrund der Beweiserhebung feststehen; **to make ~** ebnen; **to make s. th. ~ to s. o.** jem. etw. klar machen; **to make one's meaning perfectly ~** keinen Zweifel an seiner Einstellung lassen;

~ answer klare Antwort; **~ bond** ungesicherter Schuldschein; **~ chart** *(mil.)* Plankarte; **~ clothes** Zivilanzug; **in ~ clothes** in Zivil; **~-clothes man** *(policeman)* Polizist in Zivil, Kriminalbeamter, Detektiv; **~ cooking** bürgerliche Küche; **~ country** flaches Land; **~ country folk** einfache Dorfbewohner; **under ~ cover** unauffällig; **~ dealing** lauteres (reelles) Geschäftsgebaren; **~-dealing man** offener und loyaler Mensch; **s. one's ~ duty** selbstverständliche Pflicht; **~ fare** Hausmannskost; **to be marked in ~ figures** *(goods)* unmißverständlich ausgezeichnet sein; **~ folly** heller Wahnsinn; **~ food** einfache Ernährung; **~ furniture** einfache Möbel; **~ language** *(telegram)* unverschlüsselter Text; **in ~ language** ohne Umschweife, klipp und klar, *(telegram)* unverschlüsselt; **to use ~ language** unverblümt sprechen; **~ living** schlichte Lebensweise; **~ paper** unliniertes Papier, *(photo)* mattes Papier; **~ postcard** gewöhnliche Postkarte; **~ sailing** einfache Angelegenheit, klare Sache; **~ speaking** Aufrichtigkeit, Offenheit; **to be a ~-spoken man** kein Blatt vor den Mund nehmen; **~ talk** unverblümte Redeweise; **to explain s. th. in ~ and precise terms** etw. deutlich und präzise erklären; **to tell the ~ truth** die reine Wahrheit sagen; **to live in a ~ way** einfaches Leben führen; **~ work** Weißnäherei.

plainsman Flachlandbewohner.

plaint Klage, Klageschrift.

plaintiff Kläger, Prozeßführer;

for the ~ klägerischerseits;

infant ~ minderjähriger Kläger; **joint ~** Nebenkläger; **use ~** Interessent (Drittbegünstigter) einer Klage;

~ in appeal Berufungskläger; **~ in error** *(US)* Revisionskläger; **to appear as ~** als Kläger auftreten; **to appear for the ~** als Prozeßbevollmächtigter auftreten; **to call the ~** Kläger aufrufen; **to find for the ~** antragsgemäß erkennen, dem Klagebegehren stattgeben; **to nonsuit the ~** Kläger mit seiner Klage abweisen; **to reside with the ~** dem Kläger obliegen; **to stipulate with the ~** mit dem Kläger ein Abkommen treffen;

~ company Klägerin; **~'s counsel** Anwalt (Prozeßbevollmächtigter) des Klägers;

plan *(arrangement)* Anordnung, System, Plan, Projekt, Programm, Grundriß, *(design)* Entwurf, Anlage, Zeichnung, *(intention)* Vorhaben, Absicht, *(method)* Verfahren, Weg, Vorgehen, Methode;

according to ~ programmgemäß;

backstage ~ hinter den Kulissen ausgeheckter Plan; **development ~** Bebauungs-, Bauleitplan; **employee-benefit ~** System betrieblicher Sozialzulagen; **end-state ~** Zielplan; **felling ~** Abholzungsplan; **financing ~** Finanzierungsplan; **five-year ~** Fünfjahresplan; **full cost-of-living escalator ~** System mit vollwirksamer Preisgleitklausel für Lebenshaltungskosten; **general ~** Übersichtsplan; **good ~** gute Idee; **ground ~** Grundriß; **instal(l)ment ~** Abzahlungssystem; **investment ~** Investitionsvorhaben; **mature ~** ausgereifter Plan; **medical ~** Krankenversicherungsschutz; **national health insurance ~** *(Br.)* Kassenarztsystem; **organized ~** fester Plan; **pension ~** Altersversorgungswerk, Pensionskasse; **preliminary ~** Vorprojekt;

production ~ Fabrikations-, Produktionsprogramm; **share-the-work ~** *(US)* Kurzarbeitsvereinbarung; **stretch ~** Plan in großen Umrissen;

~ of accumulation Kapitalansammlungssystem; **~ of action** Schlachtplan; **~ of arrangement** Vergleichsvorschlag; **~ of attack** Angriffsplan; **~ of building** Bauplan; **~ of distribution** Absatz-, Verkaufs-, Vertriebssystem; **~s in embryo** noch im Anfangsstadium begriffene Pläne; **~ for expansion** Erweiterungsprojekt; **~ of a house** Gebäudeplan; **~ of the installation** Lage-, Übersichtsplan; **~ of interrogation** Befragungsschema; **~ for a merger** Fusionsprojekt; **~ of mobilization** Mobilmachungsplan; **~ liable to modification** abänderungsfähiger Plan; **~ of operations** Feldzugs-, Operationsplan; **~ of readjustment** Sanierungsprogramm, -plan; **~ of redemption** Amortisationsplan; **~ of reorganization** Sanierungsprogramm, -plan; **~ for a settlement** Vergleichsvorschlag; **~ of site** Übersichts-, Lageplan; **~ to encourage thrift** Sparanreizsystem; **~ for zoning** *(US)* Bebauungs-, Flächennutzungsplan;

~ *(v.)* planen, entwerfen, ausarbeiten, projektieren;

~ s. th. etw. vorhaben; **~ everything ahead** alles im voraus festlegen; **~ out a military campaign** Feldzug ausarbeiten (planen), Feldzugspläne entwerfen; **~ a piece of work** sich eine Arbeit vornehmen; **~ a city** Flächennutzungsplan aufstellen; **~ out one's time** seine Zeit verplanen; **~ together to kill s. o.** gemeinsamen Mordplan ausarbeiten; **~ a scheme** Projekt ausarbeiten;

to abide by a ~ sich an einen Plan halten; **to act with no concerted ~** ohne festen Plan handeln; **to adhere to a ~** einem Plan treu bleiben; **to alter one's ~s** seine Pläne ändern; **to be covered in a ~** in einem Plan enthalten sein; **to come out into the open with one's ~s** seine Pläne bekanntmachen; **to draw a ~** Plan ausarbeiten; **to execute a ~** Plan ausführen (durchführen); **to follow no preconcerted ~** keinem festen Plan folgen, nicht nach einem festen System vorgehen; **to form a new ~** neuen Plan entwerfen; **to get a ~ under way** Projekt in Gang bringen; **to go according to ~** planmäßig verlaufen; **to go ahead with one's ~s** seine Pläne verwirklichen; **to have no fixed ~s** keine festen Pläne haben; **to incorporate suggestions in a ~** Anregungen in einem Entwurf verarbeiten; **to interfere with s. one's ~s** jds. Pläne durchkreuzen, jds. Pläne stören; **to make one's ~s for the next day** morgigen Tagesablauf festlegen; **to make ~s for the future** Zukunftspläne machen; **to make ~s for the holidays** Ferien-, Urlaubspläne machen; **to modify a ~** Plan abändern (modifizieren); **to oppose s. one's ~s** sich jds. Plänen widersetzen; **to propose a ~** Plan vorlegen; **to remain below ~** Produktionsziel nicht erreichen; **to show one's ~s** seine Pläne erläutern; **to table a ~** Grundriß aufnehmen; **to thwart (upset) a ~** Plan vereiteln; **to trace out the ~ of a house** Grundriß eines Hauses entwerfen; **to unfold one's ~s to s. o.** jem. seine Pläne entwickeln; **to work on a piecemeal ~** ohne Plan und Überlegung arbeiten; **to work out the ~ of a speech** Entwurf einer Rede anfertigen;

~s board *(advertising agency)* Planungsstab; **~ review** Planüberprüfung.

plane *(airplane, coll.)* Flugzeug, Ebene, Fläche, *(consciousness)* Bewußtseinsebene, *(fig.)* Niveau, Sphäre, *(level of development)* Entwicklungsstadium, *(mining)* Förderstrecke, *(tool)* Kerbel, *(wing)* Tragfläche;

on the same ~ auf dem gleichen Niveau; **on a higher social ~** auf höherer gesellschaftlicher Ebene; **on the upward ~** *(fig.)* ansteigend, im Anstieg; **on a wider ~** auf umfassender Ebene;

chartered ~ Charterflugzeug; **high-performance ~** hochleistungsfähiges Flugzeug; **hijacked ~** entführtes (gekapertes) Flugzeug; **idle ~** nicht eingesetztes Flugzeug; **inclined ~** schiefe Ebene; **mail ~** Postflugzeug; **pilotless ~** automatisch gesteuertes Flugzeug; **propeller ~** Propellerflugzeug; **special ~** Sonderflugzeug; **tail-steering ~** schwanzgesteuertes Flugzeug; **waiting ~** bereitstehendes Flugzeug;

high ~ of intelligence hohes Intelligenzniveau;

~ *(v.)* hobeln, glätten, planieren, *(print.)* bestoßen;

~ away abhobeln; **~ away the irregularities** Unregelmäßigkeiten abschleifen; **~ down** heruntergehen; **~ s. th. smooth** etw. glatthobeln;

to allow a ~ into revenue service Flugzeug für Linienverkehr freigeben; **to bank a ~** Flugzeug in Schräglage bringen; **to be on the same ~ as a savage** auf dem Niveau eines Wilden stehen; **to board (enter) a ~** Flugzeug besteigen; **to [bring] down a ~** Flugzeug abschießen; **to catch a ~** Flugzeuganschluß (Anschlußflugzeug) erreichen; **to ground a ~** einem Flugzeug Startverbot erteilen; **to shoot down a ~** Flugzeug abschießen; **to take a ~** hinfliegen, Flugzeug nehmen;

~ **angle** Flächenwinkel; ~ **bit** Hobeleisen; ~ **connection** Flugzeuganschluß, Anschlußflugzeug; ~ **crash** Flugzeugunfall, -absturz, -unglück; ~ **fare** Flugpreis; ~ **geometry** Planimetrie; ~ **reservation** Flugplatzreservierung; ~ **table** Meßtisch; ~ **trip** Flugreise; ~ **trip home** Rückflug; **main ~ unit** Tragwerk.

planeload Flugzeugladung.

planer Hobel[maschine], *(print.)* Klopfbrett.

planet Planet.

planing Planieren, Hobeln;
~ **bench** Hobelbank.

plank Bohle, Planke, Diele, Brett, *(ship)* Schiffsplanke, *(US)* Programmpunkt, Wahlversprechen;
~ **in the party platform** Artikel des Parteiprogramms;
~ *(v.)* mit Bohlen (Brettern) belegen;
~ **down the ready** *(fam.)* Bargeld auf den Tisch legen (knallen);
to walk the ~ *(fig.)* gehen müssen;
~ **bed** *(prison)* Pritsche; ~ **bottom** Dielenboden; ~ **floor** Bretterboden; ~ **revetment** Bretterverkleidung; ~ **way** Bohlenweg.

planking Verschalung;
roof ~ Dachverschalung.

planned planmäßig, dirigistisch;
to be being ~ in der Planung sein;
~ **economy** Planwirtschaft; ~ **labo(u)r** Arbeitslenkung; ~ **location of industry** gelenkte Industrieansiedlung; ~ **obsolescence** geplante Überalterung, geplanter Verschleiß; ~ **parenthood** Familienplanung.

planner [Betriebs]planer, Plänemacher;
city ~ Stadtplaner; **long-range** ~ für langfristige Planungen eingesetzter Mitarbeiter.

planning Planung, Ausarbeitung, *(goods)* Bewirtschaftung, *(land)* Erschließung;
artistic ~ künstlerische Gestaltung; **bad** ~ Fehlplanung; **basic** ~ grundlegende Planung; **business** ~ betriebliche Planung; **city** ~ *(US)* Stadtplanung, -bebauungsplan, Aufstellung eines Flächennutzungsplanes; **corporate** ~ kommunale Entwicklungsplanung; **economic** ~ Wirtschaftsplanung; **estate** ~ Nachlaßregelung, -vorsorge; **family** ~ Familienplanung; **hospital** ~ Planungen für den Krankenhausbau; **local** ~ Kommunalplanung; **long-range** ~ langfristige Planung, Planung auf lange Sicht; **overall** ~ Gesamtplanung; **physical** ~ *(US)* Umwelt- und Bauleitplanung; **private** ~ industrielle Zukunftsplanung; **product-line** ~ Planung der Produktionsgebiete; **productive** ~ erfolgreiche Planung; **program(me)** ~ Programmplanung, -festlegung; **regional** ~ Regionalplanung, Landesplanung; **sector** ~ Fachplanung; **short-range** ~ kurzfristige Planung; **town** ~ *(Br.)* Aufstellung eines Flächennutzungsplanes; **traffic (transport, transportation,** *US)* ~ Verkehrsplanung;
~ **of a factory** Fabrikplanung; ~ **of industry** Industrieplanung; ~ **of work** Einteilung der Arbeit;
to accomplish ~ Planung durchführen; **to be in on the** ~ an den Planungsarbeiten beteiligt sein;
~ **activity** Planungstätigkeit; ~ **agency** Planungsbehörde, -stelle; **governmental** ~ **agency** staatliches Planungsbüro; ~ **agreement** *(Br.)* Planungsvereinbarung, Investitionsabsprache; ~ **area** Planungsgebiet, -raum; **local** ~ **authority** kommunale Planungsbehörde; ~ **board** Planungsstelle, -amt, -stab, -instanz; **Economic** ⌂ **Board** *(Br.)* Landesplanungsbehörde; ~ **commission (committee)** Planungsausschuß, **Economic** ⌂ **Council** *(Br.)* Landesplanungsrat; ~ **consultant** Planungssachverständiger; ~ **department** Planungsabteilung, Betriebsbüro; ~ **division** Planungsabteilung; ~ **efforts** Planungsbestrebungen; ~ **engineer** Fertigungsplaner, Arbeitsvorbereiter; ~ **function** Planungsaufgabe; ~ **fund** Erschließungsfonds; ~ **job** Planungsaufgabe; ~ **legislation** *(Br.)* Gesetzgebung für die regionale Erschließung; ~ **measures** dirigistische Maßnahmen; ~ **methods** Planungssystem; ⌂ **Minister** *(Br.)* Planungsminister; ~ **office** Lenkungsstelle; ~ **official (officer)** Planungsbeamter, Stadtplaner; ~ **permission** *(Br.)* Erschließungs- und Bauentwicklungserlaubnis, Baugenehmigung; ~ **principles** Planungsgrundsätze; ~ **process** Planungsverfahren; ~ **program(me)** Planungsprogramm; ⌂**-Programming Budgeting System** Verfahren eines integrierten Planungs-, Programmierungs- und Haushaltssystems; **[economic]** ~ **region** *(Br.)* Planungsgebiet, -region; ~ **scheme** Planungsvorhaben, Projekt; ~ **sector** Planungsbereich; ~ **session** Planungssitzung; ~ **staff** Planungs-, Arbeitsstab; **to pass the** ~ **stage** über das Entwurfsstadium hinausgelangen; **to be in the** ~ **stage** im Entwurf sein; ~ **study** Planstudie; ~ **target** Entwicklungsziel; ~ **unit** Planungseinheit.

planograph Flachdruck.

planography Flachdruckverfahren.

plant Pflanze, Steckling, Setzling, *(factory)* [Werk-, Betriebs-, Fabrik]anlage, Fabrik, Gewerbebetrieb, Betriebsstätte, *(cache, sl.)* Hehler, Hehlerware, *(criminal law, Br., sl.)* Unterwanderer, Spion, [Polizei]spitzel, *(fig.)* geistiges Rüstzeug, *(machinery)* technische Anlage, Maschinenanlage, Betriebsinventar, Gerätschaften, *(railway)* Betriebsmaterial, *(swindling plot, sl.)* fauler Zauber, abgekartete Sache, ausgemachter Schwindel, Schwindelunternehmen;
alternating current ~ Wechselstromanlage; **armaments** ~ *(Br.)* Rüstungsbetrieb, -fabrik; **assembly** ~ Montagewerk; **fully automated** ~ vollautomatisiertes Werk; **bicycle** ~ Fahrradfabrik; **branch** ~ Filialbetrieb; **colliery** ~ Anlage einer Steinkohlenzeche; **competing** ~ Konkurrenzbetrieb; **only partially depreciated** ~ nur teilweise abgeschriebene Betriebsanlage; **electric** ~ elektrische Anlage; **newly established** ~ neu in Betrieb genommene Anlage; **finishing** ~ Veredelungsbetrieb; **government-furnished** ~ staatlich ausgerüsteter Fabrikbetrieb; **government-operated** ~ Staatsbetrieb; **high-cost** ~ kapitalintensiver Betrieb; **idle** ~ stilliegende Betriebsanlage; **indoor pot** ~ Topfpflanze; **industrial** ~ Industrieanlage; **lighting** ~ Licht-, Beleuchtungsanlage; **limited-capacity** ~ Betrieb mit begrenzter Kapazität; **low-cost** ~ billig arbeitender Betrieb; **low-wage** ~ Betrieb mit niedrigem Lohnniveau; **manufacturing** ~ Fabrikations-, Herstellungsbetrieb; **middle-sized** ~ mittelgroßer Betrieb; **model** ~ Musterbetrieb; **movable** ~ beweglicher Maschinenpark; **out-of-date** ~ veraltete Betriebseinrichtung; **pilot** ~ Versuchsbetrieb; **poster** ~ Plakatanschlagsunternehmen; **power** ~ Kraftwerk, *(airplane)* Triebwerk, *(car)* Motor und Getriebe; **regular** ~ abgekartete Sache; **small** ~ Kleinbetrieb; **subsidiary** ~ Nebenanlage; **waggon-way** ~ Förderbahn;
~ **under construction** Anlagen im Bau; ~ **and equipment** *(balance sheet)* Betriebseinrichtung und Ausstattung, Maschinen und Einrichtungen; ~ **and machinery** *(balance sheet)* Betriebseinrichtung und Maschinen; ~ **for motorists** Autofalle; ~ **in process of conversion** Umstellungsbetrieb; ~ **working with a deficit** Verlustbetrieb;
~ *(v.)* anbauen, pflanzen, *(colonize)* besiedeln, ansiedeln, kolonisieren, *(establish)* anlegen, errichten, gründen, *(manipulate, sl.)* aushecken, manipulieren, arrangieren;
~ **a bomb in an airplane** Bombe in ein Flugzeug einschmuggeln; ~ **a field with corn** Getreide anpflanzen; ~ **o. s. in front of s. o.** sich vor jem. aufpflanzen; ~ **stolen goods on s. o.** jem. Hehlerware andrehen; ~ **an idea in s. one's mind** jem. eine Idee einpflanzen; ~ **land with fruit trees** Obstgarten anlegen; ~ **a manuscript with a publisher** Buch bei einem Verlag unterbringen; ~ **a sentry before the door** Wachposten vor einer Tür aufstellen; ~ **the surplus population abroad** überschüssige Bevölkerung in Übersee ansiedeln;
to expand its ~ Anlagen erweitern; **to move a ~ to another locality** Betrieb verlagern, Betriebsverlagerung durchführen; **to obtain a firm ~ on the ground** festen Fuß fassen; **to pluck up a** ~ Fabrik demontieren; **to run a** ~ Betrieb leiten; **to take a ~** sich postieren;
~ **account** Anlagekonto; ~ **addition** Betriebserweiterung; ~ **agreement** Betriebsvereinbarung; ~ **assets** Betriebsanlagewerte; ~ **bargaining** betriebliches Tarifwesen; ~ **bargaining problems** betriebliche Tarifprobleme; ~ **blindness** Betriebsblindheit; ~ **breeding** Pflanzenzucht; ~ **capacity** betriebliche Leistungsfähigkeit, Betriebskapazität; **idle** ~ **capacity** betriebliche Reservekapazität; ~ **closing (closure)** Betriebsschließung, -einstellung; ~ **committee (council,** *US)* Betriebsrat; ~ **community** Betriebsgemeinschaft; ~ **conditions** Betriebsverhältnisse; ~ **construction costs** Kosten für Betriebsbauten; ~ **controller** Betriebsrevisor; ~ **costs** Betriebsunkosten; ~ **deficiency** Betriebsverlust, -fehlbetrag; ~ **efficiency** betriebliche Leistungsfähigkeit; ~ **equipment** maschinelle Anlagen; ~ **estimates** Betriebsbudget; ~ **expansion** Fabrik-, Betriebsausweitung, -erweiterung; ~ **expansion program(me)** betriebliches Ausbauprogramm; ~ **extension** Betriebsvergrößerung, -erweiterung; ~ **facilities** Betriebseinrichtungen, Fabrikationsanlagen; ~ **fund** *(institutional accounting)* Betriebserweiterungsfonds; ~ **gate** Fabriktor; ~ **grounds** Fabrik-, Betriebsgelände; ~ **improvements** Betriebsverbesserungen; ~ **inspection** Betriebsaufsicht; ~ **inventory** Betriebsinventar; ~ **investment** Betriebsinvestitionen; ~ **job** Fabrikposten, Arbeitsplatz in der Fabrik; ~ **layout** Planung von Produktionsstätten, betriebliche Anlagenplanung, Fabrik-, Betriebsanlage; ~ **leasing** Vermietung (Verpachtung) von Industrieanlagen, [Industrie]anlagenvermietung; ~ **ledger** Betriebshauptbuch, Betriebsanlagebuch, Inventarverzeichnis; ~ **location** Fabriklage, Betriebsbelegenheit; ~ **magazine** Betriebszeitschrift; ~ **maintenance** *(US)*

Werkserhaltung; ~ **management** *(US)* Betriebsführung, -leitung, Fabrik-, Werksleitung; ~ **manager** *(US)* Werks-, Betriebs-, Fabrikleiter, Betriebsführer; ~ **operations** Betriebsverfahren; ~ **physician** Betriebsarzt; ~ **premises** Fabrikgebäude; ~ **processing** Werksveredelung; ~ **productivity** betriebliche Produktivität; ~ **program(me)** Produktionsprogramm; ~ **protection** Pflanzenschutz; ~ **rationalization** Betriebsrationalisierung; ~ **records** Betriebsunterlagen; ~ **regulations** Betriebsvorschriften; ~ **rehabilitation** Wiederaufbau des Betriebs; ~ **rules** Betriebsrichtlinien, -anweisung; ~ **security** *(US)* Werkschutz; ~ **shopper** Einkäufer für die Betriebsmitglieder; ~ **shutdown** Betriebsschließung, -einstellung, Fabrikschließung; ~ **site** Betriebsgrundstück, -gelände, Fabrikgelände, -grundstück; ~ **space** Betriebsgelände; ~ **superintendent** *(US)* Betriebsdirektor, -leiter; ~ **supervision** Betriebskontrolle, -überwachung; ~ **tour** Betriebsbesichtigung; ~ **training** innerbetriebliche Ausbildung, Ausbildung am Arbeitsplatz; ~ **unemployment benefit** vom Betrieb gezahlte Arbeitslosenunterstützung; ~ **utilization** Betriebsausnutzung, Ausnutzung der Betriebskapazität; ~ **utilization factor** Betriebsausnutzungsfaktor; ~ **value** Betriebswert; ~ **visit** Betriebsbesichtigung; ~**-wide burden rate** Gemeinkostenzuschlag; ~**-wide shutdowns** umfassende Betriebsstillegungen.

plantation Plantage, Anpflanzung, *(fig.)* Gründung, Stiftung.

plaster Pflaster, *(coating)* Verputz, Mörtel, *(tail)* Schatten, Verfolger, *(US sl.)* Eindollarnote;
adhesive (sticking) ~ Heftpflaster;
~ **for all sores** *(fam.)* Allheilmittel für alle Sorgen; ~ **of Paris** Stuck;
~ *(v.)* Pflaster anlegen, *(placard)* mit Plakaten belegen;
~ **a house** *(sl.)* Haus hypothekisieren; ~ **an old trunk with hotel labels** alten Koffer mit Hotelaufklebern bepflastern; ~ **over** verputzen; ~ **s. o. with praise** j. mit Lobsprüchen überschütten;
~ **bandage** Gipsverband.

plastered *(sl.)* betrunken;
~ **with advertisements** mit Reklame übersät; ~ **with decorations** mit Auszeichnungen bepflastert.

plastic | s Kunststoff;
~ *(a.) (fig.)* plastisch, anschaulich, bildend;
~ **bag** Plastiktüte, -beutel; ~ **block** Kunstharzklischee; ~ **film** Kunststoffolie; ~**s industry** Kunststoffindustrie; ~ **materials** Kunststoffe; ~ **mind** bildungsfähiger Verstand; ~ **operation** plastische Operation; ~**-processing industry** kunststoffverarbeitende Industrie; ~ **products** Kunststofferzeugnisse; ~ **raincoat** synthetischer Regenmantel; ~ **surgery** plastische Chirurgie.

plat Katasterplan, *(plot of land)* kleines Stück Land;
~ *(v.) (land)* in einen Grundplan aufnehmen;
~ **book** Grundbuch.

plate Teller, *(Br.)* goldenes (silbernes) Besteck (Geschirr), *(company)* Namens-, Firmenschild, *(course)* Gang, *(photography)* Platte, *(print.)* Druckstock, -platte, *(restaurant, US)* Gedeck, *(sport)* Pokal;
British ~ Neusilber; **door** ~ Türschild; **etched** ~ Radierung; **finger** ~ *(tel.)* Wählscheibe; **identification** ~ Erkennungszeichen; **licence** ~ *(car, US)* Nummern-, Kennzeichenschild; **name** ~ Firmen-, Namenschild; **number** ~ Kennzeichen-, Nummernschild; **roof** ~ Mauerlatte; **steel** ~ Stahl-, Panzerplatte; **tin** ~ Blech;
~ *(v.)* mit Platten belegen, *(print.)* Druckplatten herstellen;
to have enough on one's ~ mehr als genug zu tun haben; **to have more pressing things on one's** ~ wichtigere Dinge zu tun haben; ~ **armo(u)r** Plattenpanzerung; ~ **basket** *(Br.)* Besteckkorb; ~ **carrier** Speiseaufzug; ~ **glass** Tafelglas, Spiegelglas; ~**-glass insurance** Glasversicherung; ~ **iron** Walzeisen, -blech; ~ **lights** *(car)* Kennzeichenbeleuchtung; ~ **paper** Kupferdruckpapier; ~ **printing** Kupferdruck; ~ **rack** Geschirrablage, -trockner.

plateau Hochebene, Plateau, flache Stelle, *(plaquette)* Plakette;
to reach an 8 - 10% ~ **next year** *(inflation)* sich auf 8 - 10% im nächsten Jahr stabilisieren.

plateholder *(photo)* Kassette.

plated versilbert, vergoldet.

platelayer Schienenleger, Streckenarbeiter.

platelaying Verlegung von Bahnschienen, Schienenverlegung.

platform Bahnsteig, *(aeronautics)* Abschußbühne, *(depot)* Bühne, *(oil field)* Bohrinsel, *(party, US)* Grundsatzerklärung, politischer Standpunkt, Parteiprogramm, parteipolitische Grundsätze, Wahlplattform, *(place for public discussion)* Forum, *(outer space)* Raumstation, *(for speaker)* Podium, Rednerbühne, Plattform, Podest, *(staircase)* Treppenabsatz, *(supporters of movement, Br.)* Anhänger;

arrival ~ Ankunftsbahnsteig; **common** ~ gemeinsame Basis; **departure** ~ Abfahrtsbahnsteig; **election** ~ Wahlprogramm; **end** ~ Kopfbahnsteig; **flying-off** ~ Abflugdeck; **goods** ~ Güterabladeplatz; **loading** ~ Verladebahnsteig; **mass-media** ~ Rednerbühne in einer Massenveranstaltung; **party** ~ Parteiprogramm; **raised** ~ erhöhte Tribüne; **traffic policeman's raised** ~ erhöhter Stand eines Verkehrsschutzmannes, Verkehrspodest; **travelling** ~ Schiebebühne; **unloading** ~ Abladeplatz; **entrance** ~ **of a bus** Fahrkartenverkauf im Omnibus;
~ *(v.)* auf eine Rednerbühne stellen, *(v./tr.)* von einem Podium aus sprechen;
to come in at ~ **4** auf Gleis (Bahnsteig) 4 einlaufen; **to erect a** ~ Tribüne errichten; **to leave from a** ~ von einem Bahnsteig abgehen; **to speak from a broader national** ~ mit einem breiteren Programm vor die Öffentlichkeit treten; **to walk up and down the station** ~ auf dem Bahnsteig auf und ab laufen;
~ **barrier** Bahnsteigsperre; ~ **car** *(US)* **(carriage)** offener Güterwagen; ~ **desk** Abflugdeck; ~ **representations** Verkaufsdarbietungen auf einer Tribüne; ~ **speech** grundsätzliche Rede; ~ **ticket** Bahnsteigkarte; ~ **waggon** offener Güterwagen.

platformer öffentlicher Redner.

plating Verschönerung, Versilberung, Vergoldung.

platitude Gemeinplatz, Plattitüde.

platitudinarian Phrasendrescher.

platoon *(mil.)* Zug, *(police)* Polizeiaufgebot;
in ~**s** zugweise;
~ **school** Gruppenschule.

platter *(US)* Servierplatte, *(radio, television, sl.)* Aufzeichnung, *(record, sl.)* Schallplatte.

platting of subdivision Grundplanaufteilung.

plaudit Beifall, Beifallsklatschen;
~ **of the audience** Publikumserfolg.

plausibility Glaubwürdigkeit.

plausible glaubhaft, plausibel;
~ **story** nicht unwahrscheinliche Geschichte.

play Spiel, Erholung, Zeitvertreib, *(drama)* Schauspiel, Vorstellung, Vorführung, *(gambling)* Glücksspiel, *(gearing)* toter Gang, *(labo(u)r)* Arbeitseinstellung, Feiern, Ferien, Nichtstun, *(rope)* Bewegungsfreiheit, Spielraum;
at the ~ im Theater; **in full** ~ in vollem Gang; **out of mere** ~ aus reiner Spielerei;
child's ~ kinderleichte Sache, Kinderspiel; **fair** ~ ehrliches Verfahren; **foul** ~ *(fig.)* Verrat; **free** ~ Spielraum;
~ **of colo(u)rs** Farbenspiel; **lively** ~ **of fantasy** lebhafte Phantasie; ~ **of forces** Spiel der Kräfte; ~ **in progress** Stehgreifschauspiel; ~ **upon words** Wortspiel;
~ *(v.)* spielen, Glücksspieler sein, *(theater)* Bühnenstücke aufführen, Theater spielen;
~ **on s. o.** j. aufziehen; ~ **with s. o.** mit jem. am gleichen Strang ziehen; ~ **with s. one's affections** mit jds. Gefühlen Schindluder treiben; ~ **into one another** ineinanderarbeiten; ~ **around** *(sl.)* seine Beschäftigung nicht ernst nehmen; ~ **around the compass** in allen Kompaßrichtungen suchen; ~ **away** vergeuden, verschleudern; ~ **away a fortune** Vermögen verspielen; ~ **back** *(record)* abspielen; ~ **ball** zusammenarbeiten, mitmachen; ~ **to empty benches** vor leeren Bänken spielen; ~ **booty** sich verstellen, um einen Vorteil zu erzielen; ~ **cards** Karten spielen; ~ **one's cards ill** ungeschickt vorgehen; ~ **one's cards well** geschickt verhandeln, seine Chance nutzen; ~ **cases** auf Nummer Sicher gehen; ~ **the larger cities** Vorstellungen in den größeren Städten geben; ~ **it cool** nicht nervös werden, ganz ruhig bleiben, eiskalt sein; ~ **within a cylinder** sich in einem Zylinder bewegen; ~ **the deuce with s. o.** Teufelsspiel mit jem. treiben; ~ **double or quits** *(fam.)* alles auf eine Karte setzen; ~ **down** in den Hintergrund rücken; ~ **down to the crowd** an den Masseninstinkt appellieren; ~ **down an issue** Problem verniedlichen; ~ **down rumo(u)rs** Gerüchte herunterspielen; ~ **down a piece of news** Nachricht herunterspielen; ~ **the dozens** *(sl.)* das eigene Nest beschmutzen; ~ **ducks and drakes with one's money** mit seinem Geld nur so um sich schmeißen; ~ **both ends against the middle** lachender Dritter sein; ~ **fair** sich anständig aufführen; ~ **s. o. false** falsches Spiel mit jem. treiben; ~ **fast and loose with father's money** leichtsinnig mit Vaters Geld umgehen; ~ **on s. one's feelings** mit jds. Gefühlen Schindluder treiben; ~ **second fiddle** *(fig.)* zweite Geige spielen; ~ **in a film** in einem Film mitspielen; ~ **with fire** mit dem Feuer spielen; ~ **the fool** Narrenpossen treiben; ~ **foul** unredlich handeln; ~ **to the gallery** an den Masseninstinkt appellieren; ~ **the game** sich anständig benehmen, sich an den ungeschriebenen Ehrenkodex halten, gut verlieren können; ~ **games with** *(sl.)* einen gegen den anderen ausspielen; **not** ~ **the game according to set rules**

sich nicht nach den Spielregeln richten; ~ **a safe game** auf Nummer Sicher gehen; ~ **the gentleman** sich vornehm gerieren; ~ **the guns on s. th.** Feuer auf etw. dirigieren; ~ **a lone hand on s. th.** auf eigene Faust vorgehen; ~ **into the hands of s. o.** jem. in die Hände arbeiten; ~ **into one another's hand** sich einander in die Hände spielen; ~ **hard** mit harten Bandagen arbeiten; ~ **havoc with** völlig durcheinanderbringen, sich verheerend auswirken; ~ **with one's health** seine Gesundheit aufs Spiel setzen; ~ **heavily upon the sight** Augen überanstrengen; ~ **hell and tommy with s. o.** jem. die Hölle heiß machen; ~ **high** mit hohem Einsatz spielen; ~ **hookey** *(US)* sich drücken, Schule schwänzen; ~ **a hose on fire** Wasserschlauch auf das Feuer richten; ~ **to full houses** volle Häuser haben; ~ **with the idea** mit der Idee spielen; ~ **the innocent** den Unschuldigen spielen; ~ **a joke on s. o.** sich einen Scherz mit jem. erlauben; ~ **for keeps** um Geld spielen; ~ **a good knife and fork** tüchtig essen, starker Esser sein; ~ **least in sight** *(fig.)* immer ausweichen; ~ **colo(u)red lights on a fountain** Springbrunnen bunt anstrahlen; ~ **loosely** Schelmereien begehen; ~ **it too low** Scherz zu weit treiben; ~ **it low on s. o.** j. ganz gemein ausnehmen, j. in gemeiner Weise ausnutzen; ~ **for love** um die Ehre spielen; ~ **the man** sich mannhaft betragen; ~ **the market** an der Börse spekulieren; ~ **the stock market** an der Börse (auf dem Aktienmarkt) spielen; ~ **for money** um Geld spielen; ~ **off s. o.** sein Spiel mit jem. treiben; ~ **one off against the other** einen gegen den anderen ausspielen; ~ **off a draw (tie)** unentschieden bleiben; ~ **off fireworks** Feuerwerk abbrennen; ~ **off graces** seine Reize spielen lassen; ~ **out** Rolle ausspielen; ~ **a part** eine Rolle spielen; ~ **one's part well** erfolgreich sein; ~ **at politics** sich politisch betätigen, politische Drähte ziehen; ~ **possum** sich tot stellen; ~ **pranks** Streich verüben; ~ **the races** beim Pferderennen wetten; ~ **for safety** auf Nummer sicher gehen, kein Risiko eingehen; ~ **the old soldier** sich krank stellen; ~ **the sovereign** *(US sl.)* Stimmenfang betreiben; ~ **a searchlight on a road** Straße mit dem Scheinwerfer ausleuchten; ~ **for high stakes** hoch (um hohe Einsätze) spielen; ~ **in a theater** im Theater auftreten; ~ **for time** Zeit zu gewinnen suchen; ~ **with edged tools** mit dem Feuer spielen; ~ **a tragedy** Tragödie aufführen; ~ **s. o. a trick** j. hereinlegen; ~ **tricks with s. one's tools** jds. Werkzeuge mißbrauchen; ~ **truant** Schule schwänzen; ~ **one's trump card** seine Trumpfkarte ausspielen; ~ **up** *(fig.)* hochspielen, in den Vordergrund rücken; ~ **s. o. up** jem. einen Streich spielen, j. auf den Arm nehmen; ~ **up to one's boss** seinem Vorgesetzten schmeicheln; ~ **up a piece of news** Nachricht groß aufmachen (in großer Aufmachung bringen); ~ **on the velvet** *(US)* ganzen Gewinn aufs Spiel setzen; ~ **with s. o.** j. zum Besten haben; ~ **upon words** Wortspiel machen;
to allow full (free) ~ to a th. einer Sache freien Lauf lassen; **to allow full ~ to one's curiosity** seiner Neugier die Zügel schießen lassen; **to ban a ~** Theaterstück verbieten; **to be in full ~** in vollem Betrieb sein; **to bring into ~** in Gang bringen; **to bring power into ~** Macht zur Geltung bringen; **to come into ~** in Betrieb gehen; **to give a ~** Theaterstück vorführen; **to give s. o. fair ~** j. anständig behandeln; **to give free ~ to one's fancy** seine Phantasie sich voll entfalten lassen; **to give full ~** Spielraum lassen; **to give full ~ to one's imagination** seiner Einbildung Raum geben; **to go to the ~s** ins Theater gehen; **to have ~ (machine)** Spiel haben; **not to have sufficient ~** nicht genügend Spiel haben; **to make good ~** sich gehörig anstrengen; **to put into ~** in Gang bringen; **to put s. o. out of his ~** jem. aus der Fassung bringen; **to see fair ~** für ein ehrliches Spiel sorgen; **to tailor a ~ for the audience** Theaterstück auf den Geschmack des Publikums abstellen;
to be a ~ actor Schau abziehen; ~ **area** Spielplatz; ~ **bus** Spielomnibus; ~ **craftsman** *(film theater)* Produzent; ~ **date** *(advertising)* Ausstrahlungstermin; ~ **debt** Spielschuld; ~ **doctor** Textbuchrevisor; ~ **group** Kleinkinderspielgruppe; ~ **money** Spielgeld.
playable bühnengerecht, -reif, aufführbar.
playback erneutes Abspielen, Rückspielen, Playback;
~ **unit** Rückspieleinrichtung.
playbill Theaterzettel.
playbook Textbuch.
playboy Playboy, Lebemann.
playday schulfreier Tag, *(workers, Br.)* arbeitsfreier Tag.
played out erschöpft, *(sl.)* pleite, *(entertainment)* aus der Mode;
to be ~ seine Vitalität verloren haben.
player [Glücks]spieler, *(theater)* Schauspieler;
foul ~ Betrüger; **record ~** Plattenspieler.
playfellow Spielkamerad.
playgoer Theaterbesucher.

playground [Kinder]spielplatz, *(school)* Schulhof.
playhouse Schauspielhaus.
playing *(theater)* Rolleninterpretation;
to be ~ at politics sich zum Zeitvertreib mit Politik beschäftigen;
~ **card** Spielkarte; ~ **field** Spielplatz; ~ **machine** Abspielgerät; ~ **the market** *(coll.)* Spekulationstätigkeit.
playlet kurzes Schauspiel.
playmate Spielkamerad.
plaything Spielzeug.
playtime Spiel-, Freizeit.
plaza öffentlicher Platz.
plea [dringende] Bitte, Gesuch, *(common-law practice)* Klagevorbringen, Sacheinwand, [sachliche] Einwendung, *(demurrer)* [Prozeß]einwand, -wendung, -rede, Einspruch, Klageerwiderung, -beantwortung, *(excuse)* Rechtfertigung;
on the ~ of illness aus Krankheitsgründen; **under the ~ that** unter dem Vorwand, daß;
affirmative ~ rechtsvernichtende Einwendung; **available ~** schlüssiger Einwand; **bad ~** schikanöser Einwand; **common ~s** bürgerliche Rechtsstreitigkeiten; **counter ~** Gegeneinwand; **defendants ' ~** Klageerwiderung, -beantwortung; **dilatory ~** *(US)* dilatorische (aufschiebende) Einrede; **double ~** Einwendung der unzulässigen Anspruchshäufung; **false ~** Verzögerungsmanöver, Scheineinrede; **foreign ~** Einwand der Unzuständigkeit; **frivolous ~** Einwand der Schikane; **jurisdictional ~** Einrede der Unzuständigkeit; **negative ~** entscheidendes Bestreiten eines Klagepunktes, negatorische Einrede, Bestreiten eines Prozeßpunktes; **peremptory ~s** *(US)* peremptorische Einrede; **pure ~** mit Gegenforderungen begründete Einrede; **rolled-up ~** *(action for defamation)* gestaffelte Einwendungen; **sham ~** schikanöses Gegenvorbringen, Verzögerungsmanöver; **special ~** substantiiertes Gegenvorbringen, prozeßhindernde Einrede, neue Einrede; **supplemental ~** zusätzliche Einwendung;
~ **in abatement** *(US)* Nichtigkeitseinrede, Einrede eines Prozeßmangels (der Unzuständigkeit), prozessuale Einrede; ~ **in bar** *(US)* prozeßhindernde (peremptorische) Einrede, Klageabweisungsantrag; ~ **of the Baby Act** *(US)* Einwand der Minderjährigkeit; ~ **for clemency** Gnadengesuch; ~ **for fair comment** Einrede sachlicher Kritik; ~ **of confession and avoidance** *(US)* Einrede des erledigten Klageanspruchs; ~ **of autrefois convict** Einrede der rechtskräftig entschiedenen Sache; ~ **of the crown** *(Br.)* Strafverfahren; ~ **of debt** schuldrechtliches Verfahren; **incidental ~ of defence** *(Br.)* **(defense, US)** Verteidigungseinwand; ~ **of demurrer** Leugnen des Klagegrundes, Bestreiten der Schlüssigkeit; ~ **in discharge** Einrede des erfüllten Vertrages, Einrede der Erfüllung des Klageanspruchs; ~ **of guilty** Schuldgeständnis; ~ **of infancy** Einwand der Minderjährigkeit; ~ **of insanity** Einrede der Unzurechnungsfähigkeit; ~ **of the general issue** Zurückweisung der gesamten Klagebehauptungen; ~ **as to jurisdiction** Einwand der Unzuständigkeit; ~ **of res judicata** Einrede der Rechtskraft (der rechtskräftig entschiedenen Sache); ~ **of justification** Rechtfertigungsvorbringen unter Anerbieten des Wahrheitsbeweises; ~ **of lapse of time** Einrede der Verjährung; ~ **for mercy** Gnadengesuch; ~ **of necessity** Notwehreinwand; ~ **of nole contendere** Abgabe einer Erklärung des Nichtbestreitens; ~ **of nullity** Nichtigkeitsbeschwerde; ~ **of superior order** *(law of nations)* Einrede des höheren Befehls; ~ **of payment** Einwand der geleisteten Zahlung; ~ **of the privilege** *(US)* Geltendmachung des Zeugnisverweigerungsrechts; ~ **in reconvention** Gegenvorbringen, Einrede der Aufrechnung; ~ **of release** Einwand des späteren Verzichts; ~s **in short by consent** abgesprochenes abgekürztes Gegenvorbringen;
to enter (put forward) a ~ of insanity Unzurechnungsfähigkeit einwenden; **to enter (put in) a ~ in bar of trial** Einwand der Unzuständigkeit erheben; **to make a ~ against** Einspruch erheben gegen; **to make a ~ against the general issue** Klagebehauptung (gesamtes Klagevorbringen) bestreiten; **to make a ~ for s. th.** sich für etw. einsetzen; **to present a ~** Einwand vorbringen; **to put in a ~** Einrede vorbringen; **to put in a ~ of alienism** Einwand der Ausländereigenschaft erheben; **to put in a ~ in bar of trial** Unzuständigkeit des Gerichts behaupten; **to put in a ~ of forgery** Echtheit bestreiten; **to put up a ~ of impossibility** es für unmöglich erklären, *(law)* Unmöglichkeit der Leistung einwenden; **to raise a ~ of non est factum** Einwand der Nichterrichtung einer Urkunde erheben; **to submit the ~ that ...** einwenden, daß ...; **to urge ~ of necessity** Notwendigkeit vorschützen;
~ **side** *(law court)* Zivilprozeßabteilung.

plead *(v.)* *(address court)* vortragen, plädieren, verhandeln, Sache vertreten, *(allege as plea)* als Klageerwiderung vortragen, einwenden, Einwand vorbringen, geltend machen, sich berufen;
~ **for s. o.** j. verteidigen; ~ **with s. o. for s. o.** sich für j. bei einem anderen einsetzen (verwenden);
~ **the Baby Act** *(US)* sich auf Minderjährigkeit berufen, Einwand der Minderjährigkeit erheben; ~ **at the bar** vor Gericht auftreten (plädieren); ~ **a case** Fall vertreten (vortragen); ~ **the case of the old-age pensioners** sich für die Rentner einsetzen; ~ **one's case well** seine Sache gut vertreten; ~ **one's cause** sich selbst vertreten; ~ **s. one's cause** j. verteidigen; ~ **as a defence** Einrede vorbringen; ~ **a demurrer** Klagegrund leugnen; ~ **one's good faith** sich auf seinen guten Glauben berufen; ~ **fatigue** Müdigkeit vorschützen; ~ **a five** *(sl.)* vollkommen uninteressiert sein; ~ **guilty** sich schuldig bekennen, seine Tat zugeben; ~ **not guilty** seine Schuld leugnen, seine Unschuld beteuern, sich für unschuldig erklären; ~ **one's ignorance** sich mit Unwissenheit entschuldigen, Unwissenheit vorschützen; ~ **ignorance of the law** Rechtsunkenntnis vorschützen; ~ **the inexperience of youth** jugendliche Unerfahrenheit vorschützen; ~ **infancy** Einwand der Minderjährigkeit erheben; ~ **insanity** Einwand der Unzurechnungsfähigkeit erheben; ~ **instanter** unverzüglich vortragen; ~ **issuably** für die Entscheidung wesentliche Dinge vortragen; ~ **lapse of time** Einrede des Fristablaufs vorbringen; ~ **for mercy** um Gnade bitten; ~ **to the merits** materiellrechtlich vortragen; ~ **over** weiterhin nur ganz allgemein bestreiten; ~ **postal delay** sich auf verspätete Zustellung berufen; ~ **poverty** Einwand der Mittellosigkeit vorbringen, Bedürftigkeit einwenden; ~ **a statute** sich auf eine gesetzliche Vorschrift berufen; ~ **the Statute of Limitations** Einrede der Verjährung geltend machen, sich auf Verjährung berufen;
to get a lawyer to ~ **one's cause (case)** sich durch einen Anwalt vor Gericht vertreten lassen.

pleadable vertretbar, zu vertreten, triftig.

pleader [Prozeß]anwalt, Prozeßbevollmächtigter, Verteidiger;
special ~ beratender Anwalt.

pleading *(oral advocacy of a cause in court)* Parteivortrag vor Gericht, Klageantrag, Plädoyer, *(preparing written statements)* Abfassung der Schriftsätze;
~s *(written statements of party, Br.)* schriftliches Parteivorbringen, -ausführungen, vorbereitende Schriftsätze, Handakten;
articulated ~ substantiiertes Vorbringen; **colo(u)rable** ~ Gegenvorbringen; **common-law** ~ Zivilprozeß; **double** ~ Anspruchshäufung; **oral** ~ mündlicher Vortrag, Plädoyer; **special** ~ qualifizierte Klageleugnung;
~ **the Baby Act** *(US)* Berufung auf Minderjährigkeit; ~ **to the charge** Einlassung auf die Anklage;
to abridge a ~ Schriftsatz zusammenstreichen; **to amend a** ~ Klageantrag abändern; **to deliver ~s** Schriftsätze einreichen; **to draw ~s** Schriftsatz aufsetzen; **to file ~s** Schriftsätze einreichen; **to withdraw a** ~ Klageantrag zurückziehen.

pleasant angenehm, wohltuend, freundlich;
to be ~ to deal with leicht zu nehmen sein; **to combine the ~ with the useful** das Angenehme mit dem Nützlichen verbinden; **to keep things ~** für gute Stimmung sorgen; **to make o. s. ~** es sich bequem machen; **to make o. s. very ~** sich äußerst nützlich machen; **to make o. s. ~ to visitors** Gäste freundlich aufnehmen;
~ **breeze** sanfte Brise; ~ **day** schöner Tag; ~ **news** erfreuliche Nachrichten; **to make a ~ reading** sich bequem lesen lassen, angenehme Lektüre darstellen; ~ **society** charmante Gesellschaft; ~ **surprise** angenehme Überraschung.

please *(v.)* Freude bereiten, gefallen, zusagen, zufriedenstellen;
only to ~ you nur aus Gefälligkeit für Sie;
~ **o. s.** seine Wünsche befriedigen; ~ **s. o. greatly** jem. große Freude bereiten; ~ **the public** den Wünschen der Öffentlichkeit Rechnung tragen;
to be hard to ~ schwer zufriedenzustellen sein.

pleased befriedigt, zufrieden, glücklich;
to be anything but ~ ziemlich verärgert sein; **to be ~ to do s. th.** etw. gern tun; **to be easily ~** leicht zufriedenzustellen sein; **to be ~ at the news** Nachrichten erfreut zur Kenntnis nehmen; **to be as ~ as Punch** sich wie ein Schneekönig freuen; **to be very well ~ with o. s.** mit sich selbst äußerst zufrieden sein.

pleasing gefällig, entgegenkommend;
~ **countenance** angenehme Umgangsformen; ~ **figure** wohltuende Erscheinung.

pleasure Vergnügen, Amüsement, *(discretion)* Gutdünken, Belieben, Wahl, *(grace)* Gefallen, Gefälligkeit;

at ~ nach Belieben; **at the** ~ **of the owner** widerruflich; **for the** ~ **of it** weil es Spaß macht; **looking forward to the** ~ **of your instructions** in Erwartung Ihres geschätzten Auftrags;
~ *(v.)* seine Freude (sein Vergnügen) haben, *(coll.)* blau machen;
to cruise for ~ Vergnügungsfahrt unternehmen; **to do s. o. a** ~ jem. eine Gefälligkeit erweisen; **to hold office during Her Majesty's** ~ *(Br.)* (**at the** ~ **of the President,** *US)* jederzeit kündbar sein; **to make known one's** ~ seinen Willen kundtun; **to postpone s. th. to one's** ~ etw. beliebig lange aufschieben können; **to request the** ~ **of s. one's company** sich die Ehre geben, j. einzuladen; **to serve at the** ~ **of the board** an Vorstandsweisungen gebunden sein; **to stay at one's** ~ solange bleiben, wie man will; **to travel for** ~ Vergnügungsreise unternehmen;
~ **boat** Ausflugs-, Vergnügungsdampfer; ~ **boating** Wassersport; ~ **cruising** Vergnügungsfahrt; ~ **grounds** *(Br.)* Anlage, Erholungsgelände, -flächen, Vergnügungspark; ~ **house** Vergnügungslokal; ~ **lover** vergnügungssüchtiger Mensch, Genußmensch; **~-loving** vergnügungssüchtig; ~ **resort** Ausflugs-, Erholungsort; ~ **seeker** Vergnügungsreisender; **~-seeking** vergnügungssüchtig; ~ **spot** Ausflugsort; ~ **train** Ausflugszug; ~ **trip (travel)** Vergnügungsreise, Ausflug.

pleasuring, to go bummeln gehen.

pleb *(coll.)* Plebejer.

plebeian plebejisch, pöbelhaft, gemein;
to speak with a ~ **accent** mit einem gewöhnlichen Akzent sprechen.

plebiscitary | area Abstimmungsgebiet; ~ **vote** Volksabstimmung.

plebiscite Volksabstimmung, -entscheid, Plebiszit;
to approve by ~ durch Volksabstimmung billigen; **to hold a** ~ Volksabstimmung durchführen; **to submit to a** ~ einer Volksabstimmung unterbreiten;
to put the ~ **label on the outcome** dem Ergebnis den Charakter einer Volksabstimmung beimessen.

pledge *(article pledged)* Pfand[gegenstand], [Faust]pfand, *(contract of pledge)* Verpfändungsvertrag, *(fraternity, college, sl.)* Eintrittsverpflichtung, *(guaranty)* Bürgschaft, *(promise)* Versicherung, Zusicherung, Unterpfand, Garantie, *(state of being pledged)* Verpfändung;
as a ~ als Pfand; **by way of** ~ pfandweise; **in** ~ verpfändet; **in** ~ **of good faith** zur Beglaubigung der Echtheit; **under** ~ **of secrecy** unter dem Siegel der Verschwiegenheit;
the ~ Enthaltsamkeitsverpflichtung, -gelübde;
chattel ~ Mobiliarpfand; **dead** ~ Faustpfand; **documentary** ~ Dokumentenpfand; **forfeited** ~ verfallenes Pfand; **living** ~ Grundstücksverpfändung bis zur Schuldentilgung durch den laufenden Ertrag; **price** ~ Verpflichtung zur Preisstabilität; **unlawful** ~ widerrechtliche Verpfändung; **unredeemed** ~ nicht ausgelöster Pfand;
~ **of aid** feste Hilfszusage; ~ **of friendship** Zeichen der Freundschaft; ~ **of goods** Warenverpfändung; ~ **of personal property** Verpfändung beweglichen Eigentums; **~s to restore** *(foreign attachment, Br.)* Bürgengestellung vor Pfändung; ~ **of securities** Verpfändung von Sicherheiten; ~ **of stocks** Aktienverpfändung;
~ *(v.)* versetzen, verpfänden, Pfand bestellen, *(engage)* verpflichten;
~ **o. s. for s. th.** sich zu etw. verpflichten, für etw. einstehen; ~ **the bride and bridegroom** auf das Wohl des Brautpaars trinken; ~ **the credit** für die Kreditwürdigkeit einstehen; ~ **one's hearers to secrecy** seine Zuhörer zum Stillschweigen verpflichten; ~ **one's hono(u)r** sich ehrenwörtlich verpflichten; ~ **her husband's credit for necessaries** *(Br.)* im Rahmen der Schlüsselgewalt handeln, Schlüsselgewalt ausüben; ~ **one's property** sein Vermögen als Sicherheit stellen; ~ **securities with a bank for payment of a loan** Effekten bei einer Bank lombardieren lassen; ~ **as security** sicherheitshalber übereignen; ~ **a student for a fraternity** *(sl.)* Studenten für eine Verbindung keilen; ~ **one's support** sich zur Unterstützung verpflichten; ~ **one's word** sein Ehrenwort geben (verpfänden);
to accept as ~ als Pfand annehmen; **to be in** ~ verpfändet sein; **to be lying in** ~ *(goods)* verpfändet sein; **to create a** ~ Pfandrecht begründen; **to enforce the** ~ **by selling** durch Pfandverkauf verwerten; **to hold in** ~ als Pfand halten (besitzen); **to hold property as a** ~ Pfandhalter sein; **to leave for a** ~ als Pfand lassen; **to make good on a** ~ Versprechen einhalten; **to put in** ~ verpfänden; **to realize a** ~ Pfand verwerten; **to redeem a** ~ Pfand einlösen; **to sign the** ~ schriftlich dem Alkohol entsagen, sich zur Enthaltsamkeit verpflichten; **to take in** ~ in Pfand nehmen; **to take out of** ~ Pfand auslösen;

~ **card** Verpflichtungserklärung; ~**-free** pfandfrei; ~ **keeper** Pfandhalter; ~ **taker** Pfandnehmer.

pledgeable verpfändbar.

pledged verpfändet, zur Sicherheit gestellt;
~ **as security** sicherheitsübereignet;
to be ~ **to secrecy** zur Verschwiegenheit verpflichtet werden;
~ **article** Pfandobjekt; **to recover a** ~ **article** Pfand[gegenstand] einlösen; ~ **assets** Pfandsicherheit; ~ **chattels** verpfändete Gegenstände; ~ **merchandise** sicherungsübereignete Waren; ~ **property** Pfand[gut], Pfandobjekt, -sache; **to levy against the** ~ **property** Vollstreckung in den Pfandgegenstand betreiben; ~ **securities** lombardierte (beliehene) Effekten; ~ **thing** verpfändeter Gegenstand, Pfandstück.

pledgee Pfandnehmer, -inhaber, -gläubiger.

pledger Verpfänder, Pfandschuldner, Pfandgeber.

pledging Verpfändung, Pfandbestellung;
~ **of securities** Lombardierung von Wertpapieren, Effektenlombardierung.

pledgor (US) Pfandgeber, Schuldner, Verpfänder;
~**'s creditor** Pfandgläubiger.

plenary vollständig, umfassend, (licence, US) uneingeschränkt;
~ **action** (US) Klage im ordentlichen Verfahren; ~ **assembly** Voll-, Plenarsitzung, -versammlung; ~ **confession** umfassendes Geständnis; ~ **licence** uneingeschränkte Erlaubnis; ~ **meeting** Vollversammlung; ~ **powers** umfassende (unumschränkte) Vollmacht; ~ **session** Plenarsitzung, Plenum; ~ **suit** streng formales Verfahren.

plene | administravit Einrede der Dürftigkeit des Nachlasses; ~ **computavit** Einrede der erfolgten Rechnungslegung.

plenipotentiary [General]bevollmächtigter, (diplomacy) bevollmächtigter Vertreter (Gesandter, Minister), [Sonder]bevollmächtigter;
~ (a.) unbeschränkt, absolut, bevollmächtigt.

plentitude of power Machtfülle.

plentiful reichlich, im Überfluß;
~ **supply** überreichliches Angebot.

plenty (abundance) Fülle, Überfluß, Menge, (wealth) Reichtum;
~ **of money** viel Geld; ~ **of time** viel Zeit; ~ **of times** (coll.) viele Male, sehr oft;
to arrive in ~ **of time** völlig rechtzeitig eintreffen; **to have** ~ **of s. th.** mit etw. reichlich versehen sein, etw. in Hülle und Fülle haben; **to have** ~ **of courage** sehr mutig sein; **to have** ~ **to live upon** gut von seinem Vermögen leben können; **to live in** ~ in Überfluß leben; **to live in peace and** ~ wie im Schlaraffenland leben.

plenum Plenum, Vollversammlung.

pliable leicht beeinflußbar, geschmeidig;
~ **character** nachgiebiger Charakter.

pliancy Geschmeidigkeit;
~ **rule** Kurvenlineal.

pliers Kneif-, Drahtzange.

plight Zustand, [unangenehme] Lage, Misere;
in a wretched ~ in trauriger Verfassung;
hopeless ~ hoffnungslose Lage;
to be in a ~ in der Klemme (Patsche, Tinte) sitzen.

plimsoll line Ladelinie.

plod (v.) mühsam gehen;
~ **along** entlangtrotten, sich dahinschleichen, (fig.) sich abschuften; ~ **along through life** im Leben tüchtig schuften müssen; ~ **away at a dull task** sich mit einer langweiligen Arbeit abmühen (abquälen); ~ **on a problem** sich mit einem Problem herumquälen.

plodder harter Arbeiter, Arbeitstier, Büffler.

plodding Plackerei, Schufterei.

plombé [amtlich] plombiert.

plot (drama) Handlung, (land) Grundstück, Parzelle, Bauplatz, -grundstück, (novel) Handlung, Fabel, (radar) Position, Standort, (secret plan) Verschwörung, Komplott, Anschlag, geheimer Plan;
assassination ~ geplantes Attentat; **building** ~ Baugrundstück, -platz, -parzelle; **communistic** ~**s** kommunistische Verschwörungen; **consolidated** ~ abgesteckter Baugrund; **subordinate** ~ unbedeutende Intrige; **vegetable** ~ Gemüseecke;
~ **of unbuilt ground** unbebautes Grundstück; ~ **to overthrow the government** Verschwörung zum Sturz der Regierung; ~ **of land** Grundstück, Parzelle;
~ (v.) einzeichnen, -tragen, Diagramm zeichnen, (land, US) in Parzellen aufteilen, (plan secretly) heimlich planen, anzetteln, sich verschwören, Verschwörung planen;
~ **aircraft movement by radar** Flugzeugbewegungen auf dem Radarschirm erfassen; ~ **a curve** Kurve graphisch darstellen; ~

with s. o. against the government sich an einer Verschwörung gegen die Regierung beteiligen; ~ **out a line** trassieren, Baufluchtlinie abstecken; ~ **a mutiny** Meuterei anzetteln;
to be concerned in a ~ in eine Verschwörung verwickelt sein; **to defeat (foil, frustrate) a** ~ Anschlag vereiteln; **to devise (hatch, lay) a** ~ Komplott anzetteln (schmieden); **to discover a** ~ Verschwörung aufdecken; **to smoke out a** ~ Verschwörung wittern; **to spring a** ~ Komplott aufdecken; **to take part in a** ~ sich an einer Verschwörung beteiligen; **to unravel a** ~ Knoten lösen; **to weave a** ~ Komplott schmieden.

plottage im Wert gestiegene Parzellenfläche;
~ **increment** (US) Wertsteigerung bei Zusammenlegung; ~ **value** (property) lagemäßig gestiegener Wert.

plotter Planzeichner, (data processing) unrichtig gesteuertes Zeichengerät, (secret plan) Verschwörer, Ränkeschmied, Anstifter.

plotless (drama) handlungsarm.

plotting Planzeichnen, (secret plan) Verschwörung, Komplott;
~ **paper** Zeichenpapier; ~ **scale** Zeichenmaßstab.

plough, plow (US) Pflug, (examination) Mißerfolg;
~ (v.) pflügen, ackern;
~ **into s. th.** voll auf etw. auffahren; ~ **a lonely furrow** allein seinen Weg gehen, Arbeit ganz allein machen; ~ **back the profits (one's earnings) of a business** Erträge nicht entnehmen und wieder im Geschäft anlegen, Geschäftsgewinn sofort wieder anlegen; ~ **half the candidates** (sl.) Hälfte der Prüflinge durchfallen lassen; ~ **the sand** nutzlose Arbeit verrichten; ~ **through s. th.** etw. durchackern; ~ **through a dull textbook** sich durch ein langweiliges Lehrbuch quälen; ~ **one's way through the mud** sich durch den Schlamm einen Weg bahnen;
to put one's hand to the ~ an die Arbeit gehen, Hand ans Werk legen.

plough-bote Holzentnahmerecht.

ploughing (plowing, US) Pflügen, Ackern;
~ **back of earnings (profits)** Gewinnrückstellung, nicht entnommener Gewinn, Nichtausschüttung (Wiederanlage, Reinvestierung) von Erträgen, Gewinnthesaurierung, Selbstfinanzierung.

plowland (US) **ploughland** (Br.) anbaufähiges Land, Ackerland.

ploughtail, to be at the Landarbeit verrichten.

ploy Kriegslist, Notlüge, (Scot.) Beschäftigung, Tätigkeit.

pluck Schneid;
~ (v.) (university, Br., sl.) durchrasseln, -fallen;
~ **s. o. j.** ausnehmen; ~ **a crow** Auseinandersetzung bereinigen; ~ **out** (fig.) vertilgen, ausrotten; ~ **up courage** seinen ganzen Mut zusammennehmen;
to be ~**ed** (Br., sl.) in einer Prüfung durchrasseln.

plug Pflock, (advertising) [Rundfunk]reklamesendung, unbezahlte Werbebotschaft, (book, sl.) Ladenhüter, (el.) Stöpsel, Stecker, (labo(u)rer, sl.) ungelernter Arbeiter, (recommendation, coll.) Befürwortung, Empfehlung, (slow-selling goods, US) unmoderner Artikel, (drudging student) Büffler, (tooth) Plombe, (WC) Spülvorrichtung;
old ~ alter Plunder; **safety** ~ Sicherungsstöpsel; **spark** (US) **(sparking,** Br.) ~ Zündkerze; **three-pin** ~ dreiteiliger Stecker;
~ (v.) (coll.) befürworten, empfehlen, (broadcasting) wiederholt Rundfunkwerbung betreiben, (plod away, coll.) schuften, sich abplacken, (tooth) plombieren;
~ **away at** hart an einer Sache arbeiten; ~ **s. one's plans** jds. Pläne zunichtemachen; ~ **the radio in** Rundfunkgerät anschließen; ~ **a new song** (commercial broadcasting) Rundfunkwerbung für einen neuen Schlager betreiben; ~ **in a wireless set** Rundfunkgerät anschließen;
to pull the ~ (sl.) Unterstützung einstellen;
~ **box** Steckdose, -kontakt; ~ **contact** Steckkontakt; ~ **hat** (US sl.) Zylinderhut, Angströhre; ~**-in apparatus** Steckervorrichtung; ~**-ugly** (US sl.) Straßenlümmel.

plugboard (el.) Schalttafel.

plugged line verstopfte Leitung.

plugger Arbeitstier.

plum (best part) das Beste, Rosine, (desirable post, coll.) begehrenswerte Stellung, (100.000 £, sl.) 100.000 englische Pfund, (melon, US sl.) Gratisaktie, Sonderdividende.

plumb Lot, Senkblei;
out of ~ aus dem Lot;
~ (v.) plombieren, verlöten, (house) Installationsarbeiten durchführen, Klempnerarbeit verrichten, (fig.) sondieren, (mar.) ausloten;
~ (a.) lotrecht, senkrecht, (US coll.) total, komplett;
~ **crazy** (US sl.) total verrückt, plemplem; ~ **nonsense** (coll.) glatter Unsinn.

plumber Klempner, Installateur, Rohrverleger;
~'s **shop** Klempner-, Installateurwerkstatt.
plumbery Klempner-, Installationsarbeit, *(shop)* Klempnerei, Installationswerkstatt.
plumbing Gas-, Wasserleitung, *(plumbery)* Installations-, Klempnerarbeit;
indoor ~ Installationsanlage.
plume Feder;
in borrowed ~s mit fremden Federn;
~ **of cloud** Wolkenstreifen; ~ **of smoke** Rauchfahne;
~ *(v.)* o. s. sich mit etw. brüsten;
to win the ~ Sieg davontragen.
plummet Lot, Senkblei, *(fig.)* Bleigewicht;
~ *(v.) (stock market)* fallen, stürzen;
~ **in s. one's esteem** plötzlich in jds. Achtung sinken.
plump Plumps, heftiger Fall;
~ *(v.) (utter opinion)* unverblümt sagen, mit seiner Meinung herausplatzen, *(pol.)* kumulieren;
~ **o. s. into an armchair** sich in einen Sessel pflanzen; ~ **for a course of action** *(fam.)* sich auf eine bestimmte Handlungsweise festlegen; ~ **down a suitcase** Koffer absetzen; ~ **for a candidate** *(coll.)* alle Stimmen einem Kandidaten geben; ~ **out a remark** Bemerkung fallen lassen;
to give s. o. a ~ **no for an answer** jem. eine glatte Absage erteilen;
~ *(a.)* pummelig, rund, *(fig.)* ansehnlich, reichlich, *(coll.)* ohne Umschweife, unverblümt;
~ **fee** fettes Honorar; ~ **lie** plumpe Lüge.
plumper *(pol.)* kumulativ abgegebene Stimme.
plunder Plünderung, Raub, Kriegsbeute, *(junk, US coll.)* Kram, Plunder, *(sl.)* Rebbach, ergaunerter Gewinn;
~ *(v.)* [aus]plündern, brandschatzen;
~ **the citizens of a conquered town** eroberte Stadt brandschatzen; ~ **a palace of its treasures** Palastschätze plündern;
to live by ~ vom Plündern leben.
plunderage Unterschlagung von Schiffsgut.
plunderer Plünderer.
plunge Sturz, *(fig.)* waghalsiges Unternehmen, *(stock exchange)* plötzlicher Kurssturz;
~ **in sterling** Pfundsturz;
~ *(v.)* sich stürzen, *(sl.)* waghalsig spekulieren;
~ **[downward]** *(of prices)* plötzlich fallen, stürzen; ~ **ahead with** im Angriff nehmen; ~ **into an argument** heftige Auseinandersetzung beginnen; ~ **into business** sich in die Arbeit stürzen; ~ **a country into war** Land in einen Krieg stürzen; ~ **into debt** sich in Schulden stürzen; ~ **headlong into a description** hastige Beschreibung geben; ~ **s. o. into despair** j. in Verzweiflung stürzen; ~ **one's hand into one's pockets** seine Hände in die Tasche stecken; ~ **private industry into pitifully low earnings** Erträge der Privatwirtschaft enorm zurückgehen lassen; ~ **a nation into debt** Staat total verschulden; ~ **into the room** ins Zimmer stürzen;
to take the ~ entscheidenden Entschluß fassen, wichtigen Schritt tun, den Rubikon überschreiten.
plunged into debt völlig verschuldet; ~ **into poverty** völlig verarmt.
plunger waghalsiger Spekulant, Hasardeur.
plunk Plumps, Fall, *(US coll.)* Dollar;
~ *(v.)* **a coin on the floor** Münze fallen lassen; ~ **down** *(sl.)* blechen, berappen.
plural Mehrzahl, Plural;
~ *(a.)* mehrfach;
~ **marriage** Polygamie; ~ **society** pluralistische Gesellschaft; ~ **tenure** gemeinsamer Besitz; ~ **vote** Pluralwahl-, Mehrstimmenrecht; ~ **voter** in mehreren Wahlbezirken gleichzeitig aufgestellter Kandidat, Listenführer; ~ **voting** Abstimmung nach dem Mehrstimmenwahlrecht.
pluralism Ämterhäufung.
plurality Mehrzahl, *(benefits)* Ämterhäufung, *(pol., US)* relative Stimmenmehrheit;
~ **of votes** Stimmenmehrheit;
to hold a ~ **of offices** mehrere Ämter auf sich vereinigen.
plus Pluszeichen;
~ *(a.)* plus, zuzüglich, *(el.)* positiv;
~ **angle** Plusseite; ~ **factor** Gewinnfaktor; **to be in the $ 3000** ~ **range** in der Preislage von 3000 Dollar aufwärts liegen; **on the** ~ **side of the account** auf der Aktivseite; ~ **sign** Pluszeichen, positives An-, Vorzeichen; ~ **value** Mehrbetrag, Wertzuwachs.
plush Plüsch;
~ *(v.) (sl.)* luxuriöses Leben führen;
~ *(a.)* luxuriös, feudal.

plushery *(sl.)* Luxushotel, feudaler Klub.
plute *(sl.)* Plutokrat.
plutocracy Geldherrschaft, -aristokratie, -adel, Plutokratie.
plutocrat Plutokrat, Kapitalist.
plutocratic plutokratisch.
pluvious policy Regenversicherungspolice.
ply *(tendency)* Richtung, Neigung, Hang;
~ *(v.)* handhaben, umgehen, *(ferry)* Fährdienst versehen, verkehren, *(mar.)* aufkreuzen, lavieren, *(work hard)* unermüdlich arbeiten;
~ **s. o. with drinks** j. zum Trinken nötigen; ~ **for hire** *(taxi driver, Br.)* auf Kunden warten, auf Fahrgastsuche herumfahren; ~ **s. o. with questions** mit Fragen auf j. eindringen; ~ **the river** *(ferry)* auf dem Fluß verkehren; ~ **a trade** Handwerk betreiben;
to take one's ~ Richtung einnehmen.
plying for hire *(taxi)* Herumfahren auf Fahrgastsuche.
plywood Sperrholz.
pneumatic | brake Druckluftbremse; ~ **dispatch** Rohrpost; ~ **drill** Preßluftbohrer; ~ **hammer** Preßlufthammer; ~ **post** *(Br.)* Rohrpost; ~ **pump** Luftpumpe; ~ **tube items** Rohrpostsendungen; ~ **tyre** Luftreifen.
poach *(v.)* wildern, *(take unfair advantage)* in jds. Geschäftsbereich eindringen;
~ **employees** *(coll.)* Angestellte abwerben; ~ **on a neighbo(u)r's land** auf fremdem Gebiet wildern; ~ **on s. one's preserve** jem. ins Gehege kommen.
poacher Wilderer, Wilddieb, *(trade, sl.)* Branchenfremdling.
poaching Wildern, Jagdfrevel;
inter-union ~ Mitgliederabwerbung zwischen Gewerkschaften;
~ **of staff** *(coll.)* Abwerbung von Belegschaftsangehörigen;
to go out ~ wildern, Wilderei betreiben; **to go out** ~ **on a neighbo(u)r's land** in jds. Revier wildern.
pocket Tasche, *(for money)* Geldbeutel, -sack, -vorrat, *(mil.)* Kessel, *(mining)* Erz-, Goldnest, *(punched card system)* Ablagefach;
out of one's own ~ aus der eigenen Tasche;
air ~ Luftloch, Fallbö; **coat** ~ Manteltasche; **empty** ~ armer Schlucker; **timeless** ~ zeitlose Enklave; **waistcoat** ~ Westentasche;
~s **under the eyes** Tränensäcke; ~s **full of money** Taschen voller Geld; ~s **of unemployment** Gebiete mit hoher Arbeitslosigkeit; ~s **of resistance** *(mil.)* Widerstandsnester;
~ *(sl.)* unhaltbare Lage;
~ *(v.)* einstecken, in die Tasche stecken, *(mil.)* einkesseln, *(politics, US)* Gesetzvorlage ohne Unterzeichnung zurückhalten, *(take fraudulently)* sich unrechtmäßig aneignen, einheimsen;
~ **a borough** *(Br.)* Wahlkreis kontrollieren; ~ **cash** Geld einkassieren; ~ **half of the profits (takings)** Hälfte des Gewinns kassieren; ~ **an insult** Beleidigung einstecken; ~ **the money** Geld einstecken; ~ **one's pride** klein beigeben, etw. herunterschlucken; ~ **a profit** unberechtigten Gewinn einstecken; ~ **up wrongs** Unrecht stillschweigend hinnehmen;
to be in ~ gut bei Kasse sein; **to be £ 10 in** ~ 10 Pfund profitieren; **to be always in s. one's** ~s jem. immer am Halse hängen; **to be out of** ~ Verluste haben, sein Geld nicht hereinbekommen; **to be hundreds of dollars out of** ~ **each year** jedes Jahr Hunderte von Dollars zusetzen; **to be within the** ~ **of s. o.** im Bereich der finanziellen Möglichkeiten von jem. liegen; **to have s. o. in one's** ~ j. in seiner Gewalt (in der Tasche) haben; **to have empty** ~s kein Geld mehr haben; **to line one's** ~s sich bereichern (die Taschen füllen), schwer Geld verdienen, in die eigene Tasche arbeiten; **to pay s. o. from one's own** ~ j. von sich aus (mit privaten Mitteln, aus eigener Tasche) bezahlen; **to pick s. one's** ~s jem. die Taschen ausräumen; **to put s. o. in one's** ~ j. in die Tasche stecken, mit jem. spielend fertig werden; **to put one's hand in one's** ~s zur Geldausgabe bereit sein, tief in die Tasche greifen; **to put one's pride in one's** ~ klein beigeben; **to reach deeper into one's** ~s tiefer in die Tasche greifen; **to suffer in one's** ~ jem. an den Geldbeutel gehen; **to zip one's** ~s **tighter** seinen Geldbeutel noch fester zuhalten;
~ **adding machine** Kleinaddiermaschine; ~ **agreement** Nebenabrede; ~ **almanac** Taschenkalender; ~ **battleship** Westentaschenkreuzer; ~ **borough** *(Br.)* kontrollierter Wahlkreis; ~ **calculator** Taschenrechner; ~ **camera** Kleinbildkamera; ~ **computer** Taschenrechner; ~ **dictionary** kleines Lexikon, Taschenwörterbuch; ~ **edition** Taschenausgabe; **out-of-**~ **expenses** *(Br.)* bare Auslagen, Spesen; ~ **guide** Führer im Taschenbuchformat; ~~**handkerchief lawn** kleiner Rasenplatz;

~ **judgment** vollstreckbare Schuldverschreibung; ~ **knife** Taschenmesser; ~ **lamp** Taschenlampe; ~ **lighter** Taschenfeuerzeug; ~ **money** Taschengeld; **to suffer in one's** ~ **money** finanzielle Verluste erleiden; ~ **picking** Taschendiebstahl; ~ **piece** Heck-, Glückspfennig; ~ **pistol** kleiner Revolver, Taschenpistole, *(humo(u)r)* Reiseflasche; ~**-size[d]** [in] Taschenformat; ~**-size-camera** Kleinbildkamera; ~**-size machine** Maschine im Taschenformat; ~ **veto** *(politics, US)* Zurückhaltung (Verzögerung) eines Gesetzentwurfes; ~ **volume** Taschenbuch[ausgabe].

pocketbook Taschenausgabe, -buch, *(notebook)* Notizbuch, *(wallet, US)* Geldbeutel, -täschchen, Brieftasche; **taken out of the public** ~ mit öffentlichen Mitteln finanziert; **average** ~ Normaleinkommen, Durchschnittsgeldbeutel; ~ **battle** Kampf um den Geldbeutel; ~ **edition** Taschenbuchausgabe.

pocketful of money Taschen voller Geld.

podium Podest, Podium.

pogey, pogy *(sl.)* Altersheim.

pogrom Pogrom.

poinding *(Scot.)* Pfändung, Zwangsvollstreckung; **personal** ~Mobiliarpfändung; **real** ~ *(land)* Zwangsverwaltung; ~ **of the ground** Zwangsverwaltung.

point Punkt, Stelle, Ort, *(agenda)* Punkt, Einzel-, Teilfrage, *(el.)* Stecker, *(gas)* Gasanschluß, *(hint)* Hinweis, Tip, *(land)* Vorgebirge, Landspitze, Kap, *(peak)* Gipfel-, Höhe-, Grenzpunkt, *(ration coupon)* Punkt, *(scale)* Grad, *(stock exchange)* Punkt, Einheit bei Kursschwankungen, *(subject matter)* fraglicher Gegenstand, *(of view)* Gesichts-, Standpunkt, Argument, Ansicht; **almost to the** ~ **of parody** in beinahe parodistischer Weise; **at all** ~s vollinhaltlich; **at the** ~ **of death** an der Schwelle des Todes; **at the** ~ **of the sword** mit Gewalt; **from the historian's** ~ **of view** aus der Sicht des Historikers; **in all** ~s vollinhaltlich; **beside the** ~ nicht zur Sache gehörig, abwegig, unangebracht; **from a political** ~ **of view** politisch gesehen; **in** ~ **of** hinsichtlich; **in** ~ **of fact** in tatsächlicher Hinsicht, tatsächlich; **in** ~ **of intelligence** was die Intelligenz anbelangt; **not to the** ~ nicht zur Sache gehörig; **off the** ~ nicht zur Sache gehörig, weitab vom Thema; **on a** ~ **of order** zur Tagesordnung; **to the** ~ zutreffend, sachdienlich, zur Sache gehörig; **up to a** ~ bis zu einem gewissen Grade; ~s Weiche; **basing** ~ *(long-distance rates)* Knotenpunkt, *(price determination)* Ausgangspunkt; **boiling** ~ Siedepunkt; **bullion** ~ Goldpunkt; **business turning** ~ konjunktureller Wendepunkt; **chief** ~ Hauptpunkt; **contrary** ~ gegenteiliges Argument; **dead** ~ toter Punkt; **decimal** ~ Dezimalstelle; **discussion** ~ Diskussionsgegenstand; **freezing** ~ Gefrierpunkt; **gold** ~ Goldausfuhrpunkt; **handing-over** ~ Übergabeort; **main** ~ Hauptsache; **main negotiating** ~s Hauptverhandlungspunkte; **melting** ~ Schmelzpunkt; **minor** ~ Nebensache; **moot** ~ strittiger Punkt; **nodal** ~ Knotenpunkt; **out-of-town** ~ *(banking)* Nebenplatz; **peril** ~ kritischer Punkt; ~ **reserved** *(trial)* Entscheidung unter Vorbehalt; **set-down** ~ vereinbarte Haltestelle; **sore** ~ wunder Punkt; **starting** ~ Ausgangspunkt; **strategic** ~ strategisch wichtiger Punkt; **strong** ~ starke Seite; **not s. one's strong** ~ nicht gerade jds. Stärke; **subtle** ~ heikler Punkt; **telling** ~ bezeichnender Zug; **tender** ~ wunder Punkt; **the** ~ der springende Punkt; **unloading** ~ Entladestelle; **weak** ~ schwache Stelle, schwacher Punkt; **working** ~ *(mining)* Ort; **stage** ~s **of a bus route** Anfang- und Endstelle einer Omnibustour, -route; **turning** ~ **in s. one's career** Wendepunkt in jds. Laufbahn; ~ **of claim** *(Br.)* Klageschrift; ~s **of comparison** Vergleichspunkte; ~ **of conscience** Gewissensfrage; ~ **of control** Kontrollpunkt; ~ **of culmination** Kultimationspunkt; ~s **of defence** *(Br.)* Klagebeantwortung; ~ **of delivery** Lieferort; ~ **of departure** Ausgangspunkt; ~ **of destination** Bestimmungsort; ~s **of difference** offen gebliebene Punkte; ~ **of dispatch** Versandstation; ~ **of entry** Zoll-, Eingangshafen, Grenzübergangsstelle; ~ **of exclamation** Ausrufungszeichen; ~ **of an exercise** Sinn eines Verfahrens; ~ **of an exhibition** Anziehungspunkt einer Ausstellung; ~ **of exit** Ausfahrt; ~ **of fact** Tatfrage; **highest** ~ **of glory** Gipfelpunkt des Ruhms; ~ **of hono(u)r** Ehrensache; ~ **of impact** Aufschlagspunkt; ~ **of intersection** Schnittpunkt; ~ **of interest** interessante Frage; ~ **at issue** Streitfrage, Kernpunkt, strittiger Punkt, entscheidende Frage; ~ **of a joke** Pointe eines Witzes; ~ **of land** Landzunge; ~ **of law** Rechtsfrage; ~s **from letters** zusammengefaßte Korrespondenzberichte, Auszüge aus Leserbriefen; **shady** ~ **in s. one's life**

dunkler Punkt in jds. Leben; ~ **of loading** Verladeort; ~ **of order** Verfahrensfrage; ~ **of origin** *(US)* Herkunfts-, Ursprungsort, Versandort, -station; ~ **by** ~ Punkt für Punkt; ~ **of procedure** Verfahrensfragen; ~s **of protocol** Protokollfragen; ~ **of purchase** Einkaufsort; ~ **of reshipment** Rückladeort; ~ **of no return** *(airplane)* Gefahrenmitte, Umkehrgrenzpunkt; ~ **of sale** Verkaufsort; ~ **of shipment** Versandort; ~ **of a story** Pointe einer Geschichte; ~ **of time** Zeitpunkt; **converging** ~s **of traffic** Brennpunkt des Verkehrs; ~ **of view** Gesichts-, Standpunkt, Argument, Ansicht, Meinung; **banking** ~ **of view** banktechnischer Gesichtspunkt; ~s **on which we agreed to differ** Punkte, über die wir uns nicht einigen konnten; **seven** ~s **below zero** 7 Grad unter Null;

~ *(v.)* mit Interpunktionszeichen versehen, *(stress)* unterstreichen, betonen; ~ **to s. o. as the culprit** j. als den Täter erscheinen lassen; ~ **into a direction** in eine Richtung zeigen; ~ **one's finger at s. o.** mit dem Finger auf j. zeigen; ~ **to s. one's guilt** auf jds. Schuld hinweisen; ~ **to a happy issue of the negotiations** auf einen glücklichen Ausgang der Verhandlungen hindeuten; ~ **to the north** *(needle of compass)* nach Norden zeigen; ~ **out** hinweisen auf, erklären, klarmachen, verdeutlichen, bemerken; ~ **out s. o. as a capable man** j. als fähigen Mann bezeichnen; ~ **out to s. o. his duty** j. auf seine Pflicht hinweisen; ~ **out to s. o. the folly of his conduct** jem. das Törichte seines Verhaltens klarmachen; ~ **s. o. out as guilty** j. als schuldig erscheinen lassen; ~ **out the matter of chief interest** Wichtigkeit einer Angelegenheit hervorheben; ~ **out a mistake** Fehler anzeigen; ~ **off places** Stellen abstreichen; ~ **a pencil** Bleistift spitzen; ~ **a rifle at s. o.** mit dem Gewehr auf j. anlegen; ~ **to the south** *(house)* nach Süden liegen; ~ **up** aufzeigen, unterstreichen;

to alter the course two ~s **to the west** Kurs zwei Punkte nach Westen abändern; **to answer to the** ~ zur Sache sprechen; **to be at the** ~ **of death** an der Schwelle des Todes stehen; **to be beside the** ~ am Kern der Sache (am Thema) vorbeigehen; **to be on the** ~ **of departure** im Begriff stehen, abzureisen; **to be half a** ~ **less** einen halben Punkt niedriger stehen; **to be on the** ~ **of getting married** kurz vor der Hochzeit stehen; **to be off three** ~s *(stock exchange)* drei Punkte niedriger liegen; **to be on** ~s **of Karten erhältlich (bewirtschaftet) sein; to be on the** ~ **of leaving** im Aufbruch begriffen sein; **to be right in every** ~ auf der ganzen Linie im Recht sein; **to be stronger in** ~ **of numbers** zahlenmäßig überlegen sein; **to be at such at** ~ **that** so weit gediehen sein, daß; **to beat s. o. on** ~s j. nach Punkten schlagen; **to carry one's** ~ seine Ansicht durchsetzen, sein Ziel erreichen; **to catch s. one's** ~ jds. Argumentation begreifen; **to come to the** ~ zur [Haupt]sache kommen; **to concede a** ~ in einem Punkt nachgeben; **to confine one's remarks to specific** ~s sich nur zu bestimmten Punkten äußern; **to consider s. th. from all** ~s **of view** etw. von allen Gesichtspunkten aus betrachten; **to decline 5** ~s um 5 Punkte nachgeben, 5 Punkte fallen; **to discuss a** ~ *(agenda)* Punkt erledigen; **to discuss from** ~ **to** ~ Punkt für Punkt durchgehen; **to drive home a** ~ mit Nachdruck darauf hinweisen; **to drop two** ~s um zwei Punkte zurückgehen; **to forge ahead 13** ~s **to 567** um 13 Punkte auf 567 steigen; **to gain one's** ~s sich mit seiner Ansicht durchsetzen; **to get totally off the** ~ völlig vom Thema abkommen; **to get to the** ~ auf das Hauptthema kommen; **to give a case in** ~ im Beispiel erläutern; **to give** ~ **to an argument** Beweisführung unterstützen; **to give** ~ **to one's words** seinen Worten Nachdruck verleihen; **to go on** ~s bewirtschaftet (rationiert) sein; **to go back to a** ~ auf einen Punkt zurückkommen; **to go up several** ~s *(cost of living)* um mehrere Punkte steigen; **to have one's good** ~s über Qualitäten verfügen; **to keep to the** ~ sachlich bleiben; **to labo(u)r a** ~ auf einen strittigen Punkt ausführlich eingehen; **to lack** ~ *(remarks)* wirkungslos bleiben; **to maintain one's** ~ seinen Standpunkt behaupten; **to make a** ~ **of** ausdrücklich feststellen; **to make one's** ~ sein Anliegen unterstreichen; **to make a** ~ **of doing** es sich angelegen sein lassen; **to make s. th. a** ~ **of hono(u)r** etw. als Ehrensache betrachten; **to miss the whole** ~ Sache völlig mißverstehen; **to miss the** ~ **of a joke** Pointe eines Witzes nicht begreifen; **to pin one's opponent down to a** ~ seinen Gegner auf einen Punkt festnageln; **not to put too fine a** ~ **on it** sich nicht gerade sehr gewählt ausdrücken; **to push ahead about ten** ~s etwa um zehn Punkte steigen; **to raise a** ~ **of order** das Wort zur Geschäftsordnung verlangen, Einwendungen gegen die Tagesordnung erheben; **to release on** ~s *(rationing)* auf Punkte freigeben; **to restrict one's matter to two** ~s sich auf zwei Punkte beschränken; **to rise a** ~ *(stock exchange)* um einen Punkt steigen; **to set up in eight-** ~ **Times** aus der acht-Punkt Times setzen; **to score a** ~ sich mit einem Argument

durchsetzen; **to sell on ~s** auf Punkte verkaufen; **to speak to the ~** zur Sache sprechen; **to speak on a ~ of order** zur Tagesordnung sprechen; **to stick to the ~** bei der Sache bleiben; **to stress a ~** auf einen Punkt Nachdruck (Gewicht) legen; **to stretch a ~** Zugeständnis machen; **to take the ~ out of an anecdote** einer Anekdote die Pointe nehmen; **to treat a few ~s in a report separately** einzelne Punkte in einem Bericht gesondert behandeln; **to wander from the ~** vom Thema abkommen; **to yield a ~ to s. o.** jem. in einem Punkt nachgeben;
~-of-purchase advertising Werbung an der Verkaufsstelle; **~ alphabet** Blindenschrift; **~-blank** klipp und klar, schnurstracks, geradezu, schlankweg, ohne Umschweife; **to fire ~-blank at s. o.** direkt auf j. schießen; **to refuse ~-blank** glatt ablehnen; **~-blank refusal** glatte Ablehnung; **~-of-purchase display** Verkaufsförderungsmittel; **~ duty** *(police, Br.)* Verkehrsdienst; **~ estimation** Punktwertung; **~-free** punktfrei; **~-head** *(sl.)* Nichteingeweihte; **~ plan** *(employee rating)* Punktsystem; **~ policeman** *(Br.)* Verkehrsschutzmann; **~-to-~ race** Geländerennen; **~ rail** Mittelschiene; **~ rating system** Punktbewertungssystem; **~ rationing** Rationierung von Produktgruppen; **~ rise** Punktanstieg; **~ score** Punktwert; **~ system** *(print.)* Punktsystem, *(job evaluation)* Punktbewertungssystem, *(rationing)* Rationierung nach dem Punktsystem; **basing ~ system** *(US)* Frachtausgangspunktsystem, Preisberechnungsverfahren auf einheitlicher Frachtbasis; **to sell under the ~ system** auf Punkte verkaufen; **~s value** Punktwert; **~ wage system** Punktlohnsystem.

pointed zutreffend, deutlich, *(style)* pointiert;
~ roof Spitzdach; **~ style** *(architecture)* gotischer Stil.

pointer Zeiger, *(US)* Fingerzeig, Tip, Hinweis.

pointsman *(Br.)* Verkehrsschutzmann, -polizist, *(railway)* Weichensteller.

poise Gleichgewicht, *(balance of mind)* Ausgeglichenheit, *(suspense)* Schwebe, Unentschiedenheit;
to hang at ~ sich in der Schwebe befinden; **to restore the ~ of mind** seelisches Gleichgewicht wiederherstellen.

poised ausbalanciert, abgewogen.

poison Gift[trank], *(fig.)* negativer (zersetzender) Einfluß;
rat ~ Rattengift; **slow ~** schleichendes Gift;
~ for killing weeds Unkrautvertilgungsmittel;
~ (v.) vergiften, *(fig.)* zersetzen;
~ one's hand sich die Hand infizieren; **~ s. one's mind against s. o.** j. gegen einen Dritten negativ beeinflussen; **~ one's whole life** jds. ganzes Leben ruinieren;
to administer ~ Gift beibringen; **to commit suicide by taking ~** sich vergiften; **to give s. o. a dose of ~** jem. Gift verabreichen;
~ gas Giftgas, Kampfstoff; **~ pen** Verfasser anonymer Briefe;
~-pen letter anonymer Brief.

poisoner Giftmörder.

poisoning Vergiftung, Giftmord;
blood ~ Blutvergiftung.

poisonous giftig, *(fig.)* zersetzend, verderblich.

poisson distribution Gesetz der seltenen Ereignisse.

poke Stoß, Puff, *(US)* Trödler, träger Mensch, *(wallet, sl.)* Brieftasche;
~ (v.) *(fig.)* herumschnüffeln, spionieren;
~ about herumtrödeln, bummeln; **~ about in every corner** in allen Ecken herumsuchen; **~ into other people's business** sich in anderer Leute Sachen einmischen; **~ a fire** Feuer schüren; **~ fun at s. o.** sich über j. lustig machen; **~ one's head round the corner** um die Ecke gucken; **~ one's head out of the window** seinen Kopf aus dem Fenster stecken; **~ one's nose into s. one's affairs** seine Nase in jds. Angelegenheiten stecken; **~ and pry** herumspionieren, -schnüffeln; **~ o. s. up** sich verkriechen; **to buy a pig in a ~** eine Katze im Sack (unbesehen) kaufen; **to give s. o. a ~ in the ribs** jem. einen Rippenstoß geben;
~-out *(sl.)* Mahlzeit am Lagerfeuer.

poker Feuer-, Schürhaken, *(beadle, Br., sl.)* Pedell, *(spectre, US coll.)* Popanz, Schreckgespenst.

poky little room enges kleines Zimmer.

polar | circle Polarkreis; **~ front** Polarfront; **~ lights** Polarlicht; **~ region** Polarregion.

polarity Polarität.

polarize *(v.)* polarisieren.

pole Stange, Stab, Pfosten, Pfahl, *(fig.)* Gegenpol, Extrem, *(geography)* Pol, *(flag)* Fahnenmast;
up the ~ *(sl.)* aufgeschmissen;
boundary ~ Grenzpfosten; **curtain ~** Vorhangsstange; **North ⚲** Nordpol; **positive ~** *(el.)* positiver Pol; **South ⚲** Südpol; **telegraph ~** Telegraphenstange; **tent ~** Zeltpflock;
~ of attraction Anziehungspunkt.

~ (v.) *(student, sl.)* büffeln;
to be still ~s apart *(at negotiations)* noch meilenweit auseinander sein, *(diametral)* entgegengesetzt sein; **to be up the ~** *(sl.)* in der Klemme sitzen;
~ star Polarstern, *(fig.)* Leitstern.

police Polizei[truppe], *(control and regulation of a community)* öffentliche Ordnung, *(government department)* Polizeibehörde, -verwaltung, *(mil., US)* Ordnungs-, Reinigungsdienst;
wanted by the ~ steckbrieflich gesucht, auf der Fahndungsliste;
air ~ Luftpolizei; **border ~** Grenzpolizei; **city ~** Gemeindepolizei; **civil ~** Ordnungspolizei; **detective ~** Kriminalpolizei; **extra ~** besondere (zusätzliche) Polizeikräfte; **harbo(u)r ~** Hafenpolizei; **local ~** Ortspolizeibehörde; **military ~** Militärpolizei, Feldgendarmerie; **motorized ~** motorisierte Polizei; **mounted ~** berittene Polizei; **naval ~** Strompolizei; **political ~** *(US)* politische Polizei, Geheim-, Staatspolizei; **private ~** Wach- und Schließgesellschaft; **railway ~** *(Br.)* Bahnpolizei; **riot ~** Bereitschaftspolizei; **river ~** Strom-, Flußpolizei; **rural ~** Gendarmerie; **secret ~** *(Br.)* Geheimpolizei; **security ~** Sicherheitspolizei; **special ~** Wachdienst;
~ of the port Hafenpolizei;
~ (v.) polizeilich beaufsichtigen (überwachen), schützen;
~ a camp *(US)* Lager aufräumen (säubern); **~ a city** Polizeikräfte in einer Stadt stationieren; **~ a country** Land unter Polizeigewalt halten; **~ price increases** Preisanstiege überwachen; **~ a strip of land** Polizeirechte in einem Gebiet ausüben; **~ the world** Weltpolizei spielen;
to ask the ~ for help Polizeihilfe in Anspruch nehmen; **to give o. s. up to the ~** *(criminal)* sich stellen; **to give s. o. in charge of the ~** j. der Polizei übergeben; **to guide ~ by radio telephone** Polizei durch Sprechfunk führen; **to hand over to the ~** den Polizeibehörden übergeben; **to have the ~ on its tail** Polizei direkt auf den Fersen haben; **to hide from the ~** sich den Nachforschungen der Polizei entziehen; **to notify the ~** Polizei benachrichtigen; **to register with the ~** sich polizeilich anmelden; **to report to the ~** sich der Polizei stellen; **to report an offence to the ~** der Polizei eine Straftat melden; **to serve in the ~** Polizeibeamter sein;
~ action Polizeiaktion; **to court tough ~ action** rücksichtsloses polizeiliches Einschreiten herausfordern; **~ administration** Polizeiverwaltung; **~ agent** Polizeispitzel; **~ alarm** Alarmanlage; **to be in the hands of ~ authorities** in Polizeigewahrsam sein; **~ authority** Polizeibehörde, -verwaltung; **~ badge** Polizeiabzeichen; **~ baton** *(Br.)* Gummi-, Polizeiknüppel; **~ beat** Polizeistreife; **~ blotter** *(US)* Dienstbuch, Polizeibericht; **~ boat** Polizeiboot; **~ bodyguard** Polizeischutz; **~ business** Polizeiangelegenheit; **~ cadets** polizeiliche Nachwuchskräfte; **~ car** Polizeiauto, Funkstreife; **~ chief** *(US)* Polizeichef, Polizeipräsident; **~ commissioner** *(US)* Polizeipräsident; **~ constable** Polizist, Schutzmann; **~ contingent** Polizeikontingent; **~ control** Polizeikontrolle; **to break through a ~ cordon** Polizeikordon durchbrechen; **~ court** [etwa] Schnellgericht; **to end up in a ~ court** auf der Polizeiwache landen; **~ custody** Polizeigewahrsam; **in ~ custody** in polizeilichem Gewahrsam; **~ department** Polizeidezernat, -behörde; **~ detachment** Polizeiaufgebot; **~ detective** Kriminalbeamter; **~ detention** polizeiliche Verwahrung; **~ division** Polizeidistrikt; **~ document** polizeiliches Vernehmungsprotokoll; **~ dog** Dienst-, Polizeihund; **~ duties** polizeiliche Aufgaben; **~ duty** Polizeidienst; **~ escort** polizeiliche Bedeckung (Begleitmannschaft), Polizeieskorte; **~ failure** polizeiliches Versagen; **~ force** Polizeiapparat, -kräfte, -truppe; **international ~ force** internationale Polizeitruppe; **uniformed ~ force** uniformierte Polizeikräfte; **~ form** [polizeiliches] Anmeldeformular; **~ gazette** Fahndungsblatt; **~ headquarters** Polizeipräsidium, -direktion, Hauptwache; **~ helicopter** Polizeihubschrauber; **~ inspector** *(Br.)* Polizeiinspektor, -kommissar; **~ intelligence** Nachrichten aus dem Gerichtsleben; **~ interrogation** polizeiliche Vernehmung; **~ investigations** polizeiliche Untersuchung; **to concentrate ~ investigations** polizeiliche Nachforschungen konzentrieren; **~ jury** *(Louisiana)* Gemeinderat; **~ judge** *(US)* Schnellrichter; **~ justice** Polizei-, Schnellrichter; **~ lantern** Blendlaterne; **~ line** polizeiliche Absperrkette; **~ magistrate** *(US)* Schnellrichter; **~ matron** Polizeibeamtin; **~ matter** Sache für die Polizei, Polizeiangelegenheit; **~ morgue** Polizeiarchiv; **~ offence** *(US)* Übertretung; **~ office** *(Br.)* Polizeipräsidium; **~ officer (official)** Polizist, Polizeibeamter; **~ officer controlling traffic** Verkehrspolizist; **~ official** Polizeibeamter; **~ operation** Polizeiaktion; **~ ordinance** Polizeiverfügung, polizeiliche Anordnung; **~ organization** Polizeiorganisation; **~ pass** Polizeiausweis; **~ patrol** Verkehrs-, Polizeistreife; **~ picket** Polizeipatrouille, -streife; **~**

powers polizeiliche Vollmachten, Polizeigewalt, Polizeibefugnisse, -hoheit; ~ **protection** Polizeischutz; ~ **questioning** Polizeiverhör; ~ **radio** Polizeifunk; ~ **raid** polizeiliche Razzia; ~ **record** Polizei-, Strafregister; **to have a ~ record** Vorstrafen haben; ~ **regulations** polizeiliche Bestimmungen (Vorschriften), Polizeiverfügung, -verordnung; **contrary to ~ regulations** polizeiwidrig; ~ **reinforcement** polizeiliche Verstärkung, Verstärkung der Polizeikräfte; ~ **sergeant** Polizeiwachtmeister; ~ **service** Polizeifunktionen; ~ **services** Polizeiapparat; ~ **squad** Polizeiabteilung; ~ **state** Polizeistaat, totalitärer Staat; ~ **station** [Polizei]revier, -kommissariat, Wache; ~ **station open day and night** Tag und Nacht geöffnete Polizeistation; **to dial the ~ station** Überfallkommando anrufen; **to report to the ~ station** sich bei der Polizei melden; **to take s. o. to the ~ station** j. auf die Polizeiwache mitnehmen; ~ **strike** Streik von Polizeibeamten; ~ **supervision** *(Br.)* Polizeiaufsicht; ~ **surveillance** polizeiliche Überwachung; **to be under ~ surveillance** unter polizeilicher Aufsicht stehen, polizeilich überwacht werden; ~ **swoop** Überrumpelung durch die Polizei; ~ **task** polizeiliches Aufgabengebiet; ~ **trap** Autofalle; ~ **troops** Polizeitruppen, -mannschaften; ~ **unit** Polizeieinheit; ~ **use** Polizeizweck; ~ **van** Überfallwagen; ~ **visit** polizeiliche Durchsuchung; ~ **waggon** Überfallwagen; ~ **war** Polizeikrieg; ~ **warning** polizeiliche Auflage; ~ **weapons** Waffen der Polizei; ~ **whistle** Trillerpfeife; ~ **work** polizeiliche Tätigkeit.

policeman Schutzmann, Polizist;
mounted ~ berittener Polizist; **patrolling** ~ Polizeistreife; **river** ~ Flußpolizist; **rural** ~ Landgendarm; **traffic** ~ Verkehrspolizist.

policewoman Polizeibeamtin, Polizistin.

policies Richtlinien;
free enterprise ~ freie Unternehmergrundsätze; **major** ~ Grundsatzfragen; **nonconcurrent** ~ mehrere verschiedenartige, dasselbe Versicherungsinteresse abdeckende Policen; **political** ~ allgemeinpolitische Gründe;
~ **of a business** Geschäftspolitik; ~ **of expansion** Expansionspolitik

policing Aufrechterhaltung von Ruhe und Ordnung.

policy [Regierungs]methode, [politisches] Verfahren, Taktik, Politik, *(investment fund)* Geschäftspolitik, *(lotto, US)* Zahlenlotto, *(science of government)* Regierungskunst, Staatswissenschaft, *(insurance)* Versicherungsschein, [-]police, *(shrewdness)* Durchtriebenheit, Gerissenheit;
against public ~ sittenwidrig; **as per copy of** ~ **annexed** laut beigeschlossener Police; **contrary to public** ~ ordnungswidrig; **for reasons of** ~ aus politischen Gründen;
accident ~ Unfallpolice; **activist** ~ bewegliche Politik; **accident only** ~ *(motor insurance, Br.)* reine Sachschadenversicherung; **additional** ~ Nachtrags-, Zusatzpolice; **agreed value** ~ Versicherungspolice mit frei vereinbartem Wert; **all-risks** ~ *(car)* Universalversicherungspolice; **ambiguous** ~ undurchsichtige (doppelsinnige) Politik; **annual** ~ Jahrespolice; **antedated** ~ auf den Tag der Antragstellung rückdatierte Police; **anti-recession** ~ Politik der Konjunkturbelebung; **assessable** ~ nachschußpflichtige Police; **automobile** ~*(US)* Kraftfahrzeugpolice; **bearer** ~ Inhaberpolice; **blank** ~ Blankopolice, Policenformular; **blanket** ~ *(US)* Pauschalpolice; **block** ~ Generalpolice, laufende Police; **building risk** ~ *(ship)* Bauunternehmerhaftpflichtversicherung; **burglary** ~ Einbruchsdiebstahlpolice; **business** ~ Betriebs-, Geschäftspolitik, -methode; **buy-American** ~ Kaufbindungspolitik; **cargo** ~ Frachtpolice; **cheap-money** ~ Politik des billigen Geldes, Liquiditätspolitik; **colonial** ~ Kolonialpolitik; **combined** ~ kombinierte Versicherung; **commercial** ~ Handelspolitik, *(insurance)* ausschließliche Police für Berufstätige; **compound** ~ *(US)* Pauschalpolice; **comprehensive** ~ Pauschalpolice; **convertible term** ~ umwandelbare Lebensversicherungspolice; **coordinated** ~ einheitliche (koordinierte) Politik; **cyclical** ~ Konjunkturpolitik; **declaration** ~ *(US)* Feuerversicherungspolice mit laufender Wertangabepflicht; **declared** ~ *(marine insurance)* offene Police, Generalpolice, Police ohne Wertangabe; **defence** ~ Verteidigungspolitik; **deferred annuity** ~ Police über eine aufgeschobene Rentenversicherung; **deflationary** ~ Deflationspolitik; **deliberate** ~ besonnene (gezielte) Politik; **depreciation** ~ Abschreibungspolitik; **diversification** ~ Politik der Risikoverteilung; **deeply divisive** ~ spaltungsgefährdete Politik; **domestic** ~ Innenpolitik; **do-nothing** ~ Politik des Untätigseins; **economic** ~ Wirtschaftspolitik; **endowment assurance** ~ *(Br.)* abgekürzte Lebensversicherungspolice; **exchange-rate** ~ Wechselkurspolitik; **expired** ~ abgelaufene Versicherungspolice; **extended term** ~ prolongierte Versicherungspolice; **Fabian** ~

Verzögerungspolitik; **family income** ~ Familienvorsorgeversicherung; **financial (fiscal)** ~ Finanz-, Steuerpolitik; **fire-insurance** ~ Feuerversicherungspolice; **fleet** ~ Kraftfahrzeugsammelversicherungsschein; **floater** ~ Pauschalversicherung für verschiedene Transportgefahren; **floating** ~ offene Police, *(fire insurance)* Pauschalversicherungsschein für alle im Gebäude vorhandenen Gegenstände, Generalpolice; **foreign** ~ auswärtige Politik; **free** ~ prämienfreie Police; **freight** ~ Frachtpolice; **general** ~ allgemeine Richtlinie; **general accident** ~ allgemeine Unfallversicherungspolice; **general liability** ~ allgemeine Haftpflichtpolice; **get-tough** ~ Politik der Härte; **go-it-alone** ~ auf eigene Faust betriebene Politik; **good neighbo(u)r** ~ freundnachbarliche Beziehungen; **group** ~ Sammelpolice; **guaranteed dividend** ~ Versicherung mit Gewinnbeteiligungsgarantie; **hands-off** ~ hemdsärmelige Politik, Nichteinmischungspolitik; **high-level** ~ Politik auf höchster Ebene; **householder's (houseowner's)** ~ kombinierte Hausratversicherung; **hull** ~ Schiffskaskoversicherungspolice; **income** ~ Rentenversicherungspolice zugunsten eines Dritten [nach dem Tode des Versicherungsnehmers]; **incomes** ~ *(Br.)* Einkommenspolitik; **individual** ~ Einzelpolice; **industrial life** ~ Kleinlebensversicherungspolice; **industrial location** ~ Standortpolitik; **inflationary** ~ Inflationspolitik; **instal(l)ment** ~ Police über eine in Teilbeträgen zahlbare Versicherungssumme; **insurance** ~ Versicherungspolice; **jeweller's block** ~ Juwelentransportpolice; **joint life** ~ Police über eine Überlebensversicherung; **labo(u)r** ~ Arbeitsmarktpolitik; **lapsed** ~ verfallene Police; **last survivor** ~ auf den Letztlebenden ausgestellte Versicherungspolice; **liability** ~ Haftpflichtversicherungspolice; **life** ~ Lebensversicherungspolice; **limited** ~ Police mit beschränktem Risiko; **limited-payment** ~ Versicherung mit begrenzter Prämienzahlung; **limited-payment life** ~ Lebensversicherungspolice mit abgekürzter Prämienzahlung, abgekürzte Lebensversicherungspolice; **long-range** ~ Politik auf lange Sicht; **managerial** ~ Unternehmenspolitik; **marine insurance** ~ Seeversicherungspolice; **maritime** ~ Seeversicherungspolice; **master** ~ *(life insurance)* Haupt-, Rahmenpolice; **mixed** ~ *(marine insurance)* Zeit- und Reiseversicherungspolice; **moderate** ~ gemäßigte Politik; **monetary** ~ Währungspolitik; **motor** ~ Kraftfahrzeug-, Autoversicherung; **named** ~ Namenspolice, Seepolice mit Angabe des zu befördernden Schiffes; **nonassessable** ~ *(US)* nachschußfreie Versicherungspolice; **noncancellable** ~ unkündbare Lebensversicherung; **nonmedical** ~ Lebensversicherung ohne amtliche Untersuchung; **nonparticipating** ~ nicht gewinnberechtigte (gewinnbeteiligte) Police; **open** ~ *(Br.)* offene (laufende) Police, Pauschalpolice, Police ohne Wertangabe; **open-door** ~ Politik der offenen Tür; **ordinary life** ~ Lebensversicherungspolice mit gleichbleibenden Prämien, normale Lebensversicherungspolice; **ordinary with profits** ~ gewinnberechtigte Normalpolice; **original** ~ Hauptpolice; **ostrich** ~ Vogelstrauß-Politik; **pacific** ~ Friedenspolitik; **package** ~ Sammelpolice; **paid-up** ~ prämienfreie Versicherung; **fully paid-up** ~ prämienfreie Versicherung; **participating** ~ Versicherung mit Gewinnbeteiligung, gewinnberechtigte Police; **participating life** ~ Lebensversicherungspolice mit Gewinnbeteiligung; **peaceful** ~ Friedenspolitik; **permanent sickness** ~ unbegrenzte Versicherung im Krankheitsfall; **pluvious** ~ Regenversicherungspolice; **population** ~ Bevölkerungspolitik; **portion** ~ Aussteuerpolice; **pricing** ~ Preispolitik; **with profits** ~ gewinnbeteiligte Lebensversicherungspolice; **without profits** ~ nicht gewinnbeteiligte Lebensversicherungspolice; **public** ~ Gemeinwohl, Staatsraison, öffentliches Interesse; **registered** ~ auf den Namen ausgestellte Police; **renewable term** ~ erneuerungsfähige Lebensversicherungspolice; **rental value** ~ Mietausfallversicherung; **reporting** ~ *(US)* aufgrund periodisch zu erstattender Wertangaben ausgestellte Feuerversicherungspolice; **return premium** ~ Prämienrückgewährversicherung; **scheduled** ~ gegliederte Versicherungspolice; **scorched-earth** ~ Politik der verbrannten Erde; **short-period** ~ Versicherungspolice unterhalb der Dauer eines Jahres; **short-term automobile-and-hospitalization** ~ *(US)* kurzfristige Auto- und Krankenhausversicherung; **single** ~ Einzelpolice; **social** ~ Sozialpolitik; **sound** ~ **throughout** durch und durch vernünftige Politik; **specific** ~ Einzelversicherungspolice; **standard** ~ Einheits-, Normalfeuerpolice; **standing** ~ laufende Police, Einheitspolice; **standpat** ~ reaktionäre Politik; **stock** ~ Lagerversicherungspolice; **stock declaration** ~ Lagerversicherung mit [vierteljähriger] Bestandsmeldung; **stock [rate]** ~ Lebensversicherungspolice ohne Gewinnbeteiligung; **straight (whole) life** ~ Versicherungspolice auf den Todesfall; **subsequent** ~ Nachtragspolice; **supplementary** ~ Zusatz-, Nachtragspolice; **survivorship annuity** ~ Rentenversicherungspolice zugunsten eines überlebenden Dritten; **tariff** ~ Zollpolitik; **term** ~ zeitlich befristete Lebensversicherungspolice; **round** ~ **throughout** durch und durch vernünftige Politik; **time** ~ zeitlich befristete Police, Zeitpolice; **tourist** ~ Reiseversicherungspolice; **tourist floater** ~ Reisegepäckversicherung; **trade** ~ Handelspolitik; **trader's combined** ~ kombinierte Betriebsversicherung; **transportation** ~ Verkehrspolitik; **unlimited** ~ Pauschalversicherungspolice; **unvalued** ~ Pauschalpolice, *(Br.)* Police ohne Wertangabe; **value** ~ Police auf eine bestimmte Summe; **valued** ~ *(marine insurance)* taxierte Police, Police mit Wertangabe, *(fire insurance)* Wert-, Summenversicherungspolice; **voyage** ~ Reiseversicherungspolice, *(marine insurance)* Seeversicherungspolice für eine bestimmte Ladung; **wage** ~ Lohnpolitik; **wage-freezing and price-lowering** ~ Lohnstopp- und Preissenkungspolitik; **wager** ~ Versicherung mit Wettcharakter; **whole life** ~ Lebensversicherung auf den Todesfall; **won't-touch** ~ abstinente Politik, Politik der Untätigkeit;

~ **of alliances** Bündnispolitik; **paid-up** ~ **of a reduced amount** prämienfreie Versicherungspolice mit gekürzter Versicherungssumme; ~ **of appeasement** Beschwichtigungspolitik; ~ **of assurance** *(Br.)* Versicherungspolice; ~ **of attrition** Zermürbungspolitik; ~ **to bearer** Inhaberpolice; **general** ~ **of the business** allgemeine Geschäftspolitik; ~ **of compromise** Politik des Ausgleichs, Kompromißpolitik; ~ **of no compromise** unnachgiebige Politik; ~ **of containment** Eindämmungspolitik; ~ **of diversification** System der Anlagenstreuung; ~ **of the drift** Politik des sich Treibenlassens; ~ **of active ease** Liquiditätspolitik; ~ **of economy** Sparpolitik; ~ **of encirclement** Einkreisungspolitik; ~ **of expansion** Expansionspolitik; ~ **of expediency** Verlegenheitspolitik; ~ **of force** Gewaltpolitik; ~ **of the present government** Politik der gegenwärtigen Regierung; ~ **of gradualism** Politik der kleinen Schritte; ~ **of inaction** Politik des Gewährenlassens; ~ **of insurance** Versicherungsschein, Police; ~ **of insurance against fatal accidents** Unfalltodversicherungspolice; ~ **of marine insurance** Seeversicherungspolice; ~ **based on an inventory and value** mit einem sachverständig geschätzten Inventar gekoppelte Versicherungspolice; ~ **of the law** *(US)* Gesetzeszweck, gesetzgeberische Absicht; ~ **of money supply** Geldmengenpolitik; ~ **of neutrality** Neutralitätspolitik; ~ **of nonintervention** Nichteinmischungspolitik; ~ **of obstruction** Obstruktionspolitik; ~ **of the open door** Politik der offenen Tür; ~ **to order** Orderpolice; ~ **of pinpricks** Politik der Nadelstiche; ~ **for prices and income** Einkommens- und Preispolitik; ~ **for productivity** Produktivitätspolitik; ~ **of rapprochement** Annäherungspolitik; ~ **of repression** Unterdrückungspolitik; ~ **of restraint** zurückhaltende Politik; ~ **of restraint in sales** nicht aggressive Verkaufspolitik; ~ **of retrenchment** Einsparungspolitik; ~ **of the middle road** Politik der Mitte; ~ **of scuttle** Politik der Unentschlossenheit, unentschlossene Politik; ~ **of suppression** Unterdrückungspolitik; ~ **of mutual understanding** Verständigungspolitik; ~ **of wait and see** abwartende Politik; **to adopt a** ~ Verfahrensweise einführen; **to adopt a ca'canny** ~ Obstruktionspolitik betreiben; **to adopt a new** ~ neuen Kurs einschlagen; **to adopt a tough** ~ harte Linie in der Politik verfolgen; **to amend a** ~ Police ergänzen; **to be answerable for** ~ *(minister)* politische Verantwortung tragen; **to cancel a** ~ Versicherung aufheben; **to deem it** ~ es für diplomatisch halten; **to define a common** ~ gemeinsame Politik festlegen; **to drop a** ~ Versicherung aufheben; **to effect a** ~ Police ausfertigen; **to find one's** ~ **vindicated** seine Politik bestätigt finden; **to fix one's** ~ seine Politik orientieren; **to follow a** ~ Politik verfolgen; **to implement a** ~ seiner Politik die Treue halten; **to inaugurate a new** ~ neue Politik einleiten; **to issue a** ~ Police ausfertigen; **to keep the** ~ **in force** Versicherung aufrechterhalten; **to lend money on a** ~ Police beleihen; **to always make s. th. one's** ~ sich etw. zur festen Regel machen; **to maintain a** ~ an einer Politik festhalten; **to pursue a certain** ~ bestimmte Politik verfolgen; **to reinstate a lapsed** ~ abgelaufene Versicherung wieder aufleben lassen; **to renew a** ~ Police erneuern; **to revise one's** ~ seine Politik revidieren; **to speak in support of one's** ~ sich für jds. Politik aussprechen; **to stand for a** ~ Politik unterstützen; **to take out a** ~ sich versichern lassen, Versicherungsvertrag abschließen, Police nehmen;

~ **adviser** politischer Berater; ~ **alternatives** politische Alternativen; ~ **book** Policenbuch, -register; ~ **borrowing** Policenbeleihung; ~ **broker** Versicherungsmakler, -agent; ~ **committee** Richtlinienausschuß, Ausschuß für Geschäftspolitik; ~ **conditions** Versicherungsbedingungen; ~ **contract** Versicherungsvertrag; ~ **decision** Entscheidung von politischer Tragweite; ~ **differences** politische Meinungsverschiedenheiten; ~ **directive**

politische Direktive; ~ **discussion** Grundsatzbesprechung; ~ **dividend** Beitragsrückerstattung; ~ **document** *(company)* schriftlich niedergelegte Geschäftspolitik, *(insurance)* Versicherungsurkunde, -schein, Policenform; ~ **drafting** Policenausfertigung; ~ **duty** Versicherungssteuer; ~ **excess** Selbstbehalt; ~ **exclusion of contribution** Ausschluß der Ausgleichspflicht des Versicherers; ~ **factors** politische Faktoren; ~ **form** Policenformular, -vordruck; ~ **formulation** Festlegung der Firmenpolitik, geschäftspolitische Aussage; ~ **franchise** *(insurance business)* Selbstbeteiligung bei Bagatellschäden; ~ **guidelines** politische Richtlinien; ~ **inception** Versicherungsbeginn; **basic** ~ **issues** politische Grundsatzfragen; ~ **initiatives** politische Initiativen; ~ **information at corporate level** Verdeutlichung der Geschäftspolitik auf Vorstandsebene; ~ **lines** politisches Programm; **general** ~ **line** politische Grundrichtung; ~ **loan** Policenbeleihung, -darlehen, Beleihung einer Versicherung; ~ **manual** Leitfaden der Geschäftspolitik; ~ **meeting** geschäftspolitische Tagung; ~ **modification** Policenänderung; ~ **money** ausgezahlte Versicherungssumme; ~ **number** Policennummer; ~ **owner** Versicherungsnehmer; ~ **period** Laufzeit einer Police, Policendauer; ~ **playing** *(US)* Lottospielen; ~ **premium** Versicherungsprämie; ~ **prescription** politisches Rezept; ~ **proof of interest** *(marine insurance)* als Nachweis des Anspruchs genügt die Police; ~ **provisions** Versicherungsbestimmungen; ~ **racket** *(US)* illegales Zahlenlotto; ~ **researcher** politischer Meinungsforscher; ~ **reserves** Schadensreserven; ~ **restraint** politische Zurückhaltung; ~ **shift** politische Richtungsänderung; ~ **shop** *(US)* Lottoannahmestelle; ~ **signing office** Policenausstellungsbüro; ~ **simulation** wirtschaftspolitische Simulation, Simulation an Modellen; ~ **slip** *(US)* Wettkarte, Lottoschein; ~ **speech** Richtlinienrede; ~ **stance** politische Haltung; ~ **statement** *(US)* politische Willenserklärung, Grundsatzprogramm, -erklärung; ~ **switch** politische Umstellung, Änderung der Politik; ~ **ticket** *(US)* Lottoschein; ~ **value** Versicherungswert; ~ **variations** Policenänderung, -abwandlung; ~ **year** Versicherungsjahr.

policyholder Versicherungsnehmer, Policeninhaber.
policymaker of business führende Persönlichkeit des Wirtschaftslebens.
policymaking grundsätzliche Geschäftsentscheidungen;
~ *(a.)* richtungsweisend;
~ **cluster** politische Beratergruppe; ~ **official** *(US)* Beamter in leitender Stellung; ~ **procedure** entscheidender Arbeitsprozeß.
polish *(fig.)* Schliff, Politur, Glanzmittel;
boot ~ Schuhwichse, -creme; **floor** ~ Bohnerwachs; **furniture** ~ Möbelpolitur; **high** ~ Hochglanz; **shoe** ~ Schuhwichse, -creme;
~ *(v.)* abschleifen, polieren, verfeinern;
~ **off** *(knock out, sl.)* erledigen, beseitigen, *(meal, sl.)* verputzen; ~ **off arrears of correspondence** Briefschulden aufarbeiten (wegputzen); ~ **up** aufpolieren; ~ **up one's French** sein Französisch auffrischen (auf Hochglanz bringen); ~ **up a piece of work** einer Arbeit den letzten Schliff geben; ~ **up one's style** seinen Stil verbessern;
to give s. th. a ~ etw. polieren; **to lack** ~ keinen Schliff haben; **to lose its** ~ seinen Glanz verlieren; **to put a certain** ~ **on s. o.** j. anlernen.
polished glatt, glänzend, poliert;
less-than-highly ~ nicht gerade glänzend;
~ **gentleman** eleganter Herr; ~ **manners** tadellose Manieren; ~ **style** verbesserter Stil.
polisher Polierer, Schleifer, *(s. th. used in polishing)* Poliermittel, *(bookbinding)* Glättzahn.
polishing Glätten, Schleifen, Polieren;
~ **wax** Bohnerwachs.
politbureau Politbüro.
polite höflich, galant, *(refined)* vornehm, gebildet;
to be exquisitely ~ sich von äußerster Höflichkeit zeigen; **to do the** ~ *(fam.)* sich galant aufspielen, auf vornehm machen;
~ **arts** schöne Künste; ~ **learning** schöne Wissenschaften; ~ **letter** höflicher Brief; ~ **society** feine Gesellschaft.
politechnic Polytechnikum.
politic [staats]klug, geschickt, diplomatisch;
body ~ Staatsgebilde;
political politisch, staatsmännisch, *(civic)* staatsbürgerlich, *(party politics)* parteipolitisch;
~ **action** politische Maßnahme; ~ **activity** politische Tätigkeit; ~ **agitator** Volksaufwiegler; ~ **antenna** Spitzengefühl eines Politikers; ~ **ascendancy** politisches Übergewicht; ~ **aspects** politische Aspekte; ~ **asylum** politisches Asyl; ~ **attitude** politische Einstellung (Haltung); ~ **bargaining power** politische Verhandlungsstärke; ~ **belief** politisches Bekenntnis; ☌ **Bureau**

Politbüro; ~ **calm** politische Flaute; ~ **campaign** Wahlfeldzug; **for** ~ **campaign use** für Wahlfeldzugzwecke; **to make** ~ **capital by** politisches Kapital schlagen; ~ **card** politische Karte; ~ **change** politischer Umschwung; ~ **circles** politische Kreise; ~ **clout** politische Schlagkraft; ~ **committee** Wahl-, Wählervereinigung; ~ **consolidation** politische Konsolidierung; ~ **consultant** politischer Berater; ~ **conviction** politische Gesinnung (Überzeugung); ~ **corporation** Gebietskörperschaft; **to follow a** ~ **course** klug (geschickt) vorgehen; ~ **crisis** politische Krise; ~ **currents** politische Strömungen; ~ **detainee** politischer Häftling, politischer Gefangener; ~ **dispute** politischer Streitfall; ~ **disturbance** politische Unruhen, Landfriedensbruch; ~ **economist** Volkswirt, Nationalökonom; ~ **economy** Volkswirtschaft, Nationalökonomie, Volkswirtschaftslehre; ~ **education** politische Schulung; ~ **endorsement** politische Unterstützung; ~ **expediency** politische Zweckmäßigkeit; **to put the least** ~ **face on s. th.** etw. möglichst weit entfernt von der Politik ansiedeln; ~ **figures** bedeutsame Politiker; ~ **free-for-all** offener Kandidatenwettbewerb; ~ **freedom** staatsbürgerliche Freiheit; ~ **fund** *(trade union)* politischer Fonds, Sonderfonds; ~ **gathering** politische Versammlung; ~ **geography** politische Geographie; ~ **goal** politisches Ziel; **on** ~ **grounds** aus politischen Gründen; ~ **horizon** politischer Horizont; ~ **incrimination** politische Belastung; ~ **integration** politische Integrierung; ~ **jobber** politischer Schacher; ~ **law** Staatsrecht; ~ **liberties** politische Freiheiten (Grundrechte); ~ **maxim** Staatsgrundsatz, -maxime; ~ **meeting** politische Versammlung; ~ **mistake** falsche politische Entscheidung; ~ **motive** politische Beweggründe (Motive); **to have** ~ **muscles** starke politische Kräfte mobilisieren; ~ **observer** politischer Beobachter; ~ **offence** Verstoß gegen die öffentliche Ordnung, politisches Vergehen; ~ **offender** politischer Verbrecher; ~ **office** politische Stellung; ~ **opinion** politische Ansicht; ~ **opponent** politischer Gegner; ~ **organization** politische Organisation; ~ **panel** politischer Ausschuß; ~ **party** politische Partei; ~ **party system** Parteisystem; ~ **plane** politische Ebene; **to win** ~ **points** sich politisch profilieren; ~ **prisoner** Staatsgefangener, Häftling; **for** ~ **purposes** für politische Zwecke; ~ **questions** politische Probleme; **for** ~ **reasons** aus politischen Gründen; ~ **refugee** politischer Flüchtling; **to make a** ~ **retreat** politischen Rückzieher machen; ~ **rights** staatsbürgerliche Rechte; ~ **science** Staatswissenschaft, Politologie; ~**-scientific** staatswissenschaftlich; ~ **scientist** Staatswissenschaftler, Politologe; **on the** ~ **side** auf dem politischen Sektor; ~ **situation** politische Konstellation (Lage); **to display (deploy) one's best** ~ **skills** seine politische Begabung effektvoll einzusetzen wissen; ~ **subdivision** *(US)* politisch nachgeordnete Behörde, Gebietskörperschaft; ~ **thaw** [politisches] Tauwetter; ~ **tension** politische Spannung; ~ **uniform** Parteiuniform; ~ **union** politischer Zusammenschluß; **moderate** ~ **views** gemäßigte politische Ansichten; ~ **wilderness** politische Wüste.

politically in politischer Hinsicht;
~ **clear** unbelastet; ~**-minded** politisch interessiert.

politician Politiker, Staatsmann;
influential ~ aufschlußreicher Politiker; **mere** ~ reiner Geschäftemacher; **office-seeking** ~ ämtersüchtiger Politiker; **party** ~ Parteipolitiker; **radical** ~ radikaler Politiker; **rising** ~ kommender Politiker, Politiker mit Zukunft; **serious** ~ ernstzunehmender Politiker; **shrewd** ~ gewitzter Politiker; **tricky** ~ durchtriebener Politker; **two-bit** ~ bestechlicher Politiker.

politicitation *(civil law)* noch nicht angenommenes Angebot.

politicize *(v.)* politisieren, sich politisch betätigen.

politicking *(US)* Wahlkampftechnik.

politico *(sl.)* machthungriger Politiker;
~**-economical** wirtschaftspolitisch; ~**-social** sozialpolitisch.

politics Politik, politisches Leben, Staatswissenschaft, -kunde, Staatskunst, -führung, *(intrigue, US)* politische Machenschaften;
in the field of ~**s** auf politischem Gebiet;
domestic ~ *(US)* Innenpolitik; **foreign** ~ auswärtige Politik, Außenpolitik; **internal** ~ Innenpolitik; **local** ~ Gemeinde-, Lokalpolitik; **partisan** ~ Parteipolitik; **party** ~ Parteipolitik; **power** ~ Machtpolitik; **practical** ~**s** Realpolitik; **right-wing** ~ rechteingestellte Politik;
to argue in ~ politisch verschiedener Meinung sein; **to be engaged in** ~ politisch tätig sein, sich mit Politik befassen; **to be interested in** ~ sich mit Politik abgeben; **not to be practical** ~ nicht durchführbar sein; **to be injected forcefully into international** ~ in die internationale Politik katapultiert werden; **to dabble in** ~**s** politisieren; **to deal in** ~ sich politisch betätigen; **to engage in** ~**s** sich auf die Politik werfen; **to enter** ~

Politiker werden; **to get mixed up in** ~ politisch involviert werden; **to go into** ~ Politiker werden; **to launch into** ~**s** in die Politik einsteigen; **to mix in** ~**s** sich politisch interessieren (betätigen); **to play** ~ zweifelhafte Manipulationen durchführen; **to run on** ~**s** *(conversation)* sich um Politik drehen; **to study** ~ staatswissenschaftliches Studium ergreifen; **to take a hand (an interest) in** ~ sich politisch betätigen; **to take no great interest in** ~**s** sich kaum für Politik interessieren; **to talk** ~ politisieren, über Politik reden, über Politik sprechen, sich politisch unterhalten.

polity Politik, Verfahren, *(constitution)* Regierungsform, politische Ordnung, Verfassung, *(community of persons)* Gemeinwesen.

poll *(inquiry)* Umfrage, Stichprobenerhebung, *(list of electors)* Liste der Wahlberechtigten, Wählerliste, *(polling place)* Wahlort, -lokal, *(result of votes)* Wahlergebnis, *(scrutiny)* Stimmenzählung, *(voting)* Abstimmung, Stimmabgabe, Wählen, Wahl, *(votes registered)* Stimmenzahl, Wahlbeteiligung;
at the opening of the ~ bei Eröffnung der Wahllokale; **per** ~ pro Kopf;
~**s** *(US)* Wahllokal, -urne;
constituency ~ Wahlkreisergebnis; **deed** ~ einseitig verpflichtende Urkunde; **gallup** ~ Gallupumfrage; **heavy** ~ hohe Wahlbeteiligung; **light** ~ schwache Wahlbeteiligung; **popularity** ~ Beliebtheitsumfrage; **national opinion** ~ umfassende Meinungsumfrage; **public opinion** ~ öffentliche Meinungsbefragung, -umfrage; **social issue** ~ Sozialumfrage; **small** ~ geringe (schlechte) Wahlbeteiligung;
~ *(v.)* wählen, abstimmen, seine Stimme abgeben, *(ascertain opinion)* befragen, um Stellungnahme ersuchen, *(jurors)* Geschworene nach Befragung auswählen, *(enter in register)* [namentlich] registrieren, in eine Wahlliste eintragen, *(get voters)* Wahlstimmen auf sich vereinigen, Wählerstimmen erhalten, *(US sl.)* sich in die Wählerliste eintragen;
~ **for a candidate** Kandidaten wählen; ~ **all adult citizens** alle Wahlberechtigten erfassen; ~ **a country on a question** Bevölkerung in einer Angelegenheit befragen; ~ **as much as 25% of the vote** 25% der abgegebenen Stimmen bei einer Wahl erzielen; ~ **heavily** großen Wahlsieg erringen; ~ **a hundred votes** hundert Stimmen erhalten; ~ **the jurors** *(US)* Geschworene einzeln befragen; ~ **a majority of votes cast** Mehrheit der abgegebenen Stimmen erhalten;
to be at the bottom of the ~ wenigste Stimmen erhalten haben; **to be defeated at the** ~**s** Wahlniederlage erleiden; **to be successful at the** ~**s** aus den Wahlen als Sieger hervorgehen; **to conduct a** ~ Meinungsbefragung durchführen; **to declare the** ~ Wahlergebnis bekanntgeben; **to defeat at the** ~**s** Wahlsieg erringen; **to demand a** ~ Volksabstimmung verlangen, *(company meeting)* schriftliche Abstimmung nach Kapitalanteilen verlangen; **to exclude s. o. from the** ~ jem. das [passive] Wahlrecht nehmen; **to go to the** ~**s** zur Wahl[urne] gehen, abstimmen, seine Stimme abgeben, wählen; **to head the** ~ die meisten Wahlstimmen haben; **to release a** ~ Meinungsumfrage veröffentlichen; **to return the result of the** ~ Wahlergebnis veröffentlichen; **to take a** ~ Meinungsumfrage veranstalten;
~**-money** Kopfgeld; ~ **ratings** Umfrageergebnisse; ~ **suffrage** allgemeines Wahlrecht; ~ **tax** Bürger-, Kopfsteuer; ~ **vote** *(meeting)* Stimmenzählung, schriftliche Abstimmung.

pollable wahlberechtigt, wählbar.

pollbook Wahl-, Wählerliste.

pollee *(US)* Befragter.

poller Wahlhelfer.

polling Wahl-, Wahlakt, -handlung, -beteiligung, Wählen, *(ballot)* Wahlgang, -vorgang, *(data processing)* Datenabruf;
~ **the jury** Einzelbefragung der Geschworenen; ~ **over half the votes** Erringung von mehr als der Hälfte der Wahlstimmen;
~ **agent** Wahlagent; ~ **booth** Wahlzelle; ~ **clerk** Wahlbeisitzer, -protokollführer, Abstimmungsleiter; ~ **day** Wahltag; ~ **district** Wahlbezirk; ~ **list** Abstimmungs-, Wahlliste; ~ **place (station)** Wahllokal.

pollist Meinungsbefrager.

pollster *(US)* Fragesteller, Meinungsforscher.

polltaker *(US)* Meinungsforscher.

pollutants Schadstoffe.

pollute *(v.)* verschmutzen, verunreinigen.

polluted water verschmutztes Wasser.

polluter Schmutzbetrieb.

pollution, environment Umweltverschmutzung;
~ **of the air** Luftverschmutzung, -verunreinigung, -verpestung; ~ **of rivers** Verschmutzung der Flüsse, Flußverschmutzung; ~ **of the sea** Verschmutzung der See, Meeresverschmutzung;

~ control Umwelt-, Verschmutzungskontrolle; **~ control tax credits** *(US)* Steuerfreibeträge für Umweltschutzmaßnahmen; **~ damage** Verschmutzungs-, Verunreinigungsschaden; **~ issue** Verschmutzungsproblem; **~ protection** Immissionsschutz; **to meet ~ standards** den Anforderungen des Umweltschutzes entsprechen.

polly plane Lautsprecherflugzeug.

polycentrism Polizentrismus.

polygamy Vielehe, strafbare Bigamie.

polyglot sprachkundig.

polygraph Vervielfältigungsapparat.

polyphase current Drehstrom.

polytechnic *(London)* technische Fachschule.

pomp Prunk, Pomp, Pracht, Gepränge;
~ and circumstance Prachtentfaltung;
~ of State Opening of Parliament bei der Parlamentseröffnung entfalteter Prunk;
to escort s. o. with great ~ großen Bahnhof für j. veranstalten; **to like ~** prunksüchtig sein; **to renounce the ~s and vanities of this wicked world** der Pracht und der Eitelkeit dieser sündigen Welt entsagen.

pompous | man großspurig auftretender Mann; **~ official** aufgeblasener Beamter; **~ language** schwülstige (überladene) Sprache; **~ style** pompöser Stil.

pond Teich, Weiher, *(sl.)* Atlantik, der große Teich;
private ~ Privatweiher.

ponder *(v.)* nachgrübeln, -denken;
~ one's words seine Worte sorgfältig wägen.

pondering silence nachdenkliches Schweigen.

ponderosity Gewichtigkeit, Schwerfälligkeit.

ponderous style umständlicher Stil.

pontage Brückengebühr, -zoll.

pontifical päpstlich;
~ airs feierliche Allüren; **º State** Kirchenstaat.

pontificate *(v.)* dozieren, dozierend vortragen.

pontoon bridge Schiffsbrücke.

pontooneer *(mil.)* Brückenbaupionier.

pony Pony, *(book)* Miniaturausgabe, *(car)* Kleinauto, *(school, US)* Eselsbrücke, Klatsche;
~ *(v.)* *(US)* Klatsche benutzen;
~ up berappen, blechen;
to ride a ~ *(sl.)* Klatsche benutzen;
~ edition Ausgabe in Miniformat, Miniaturausgabe; **~ engine** *(US)* Rangierlokomotive; **~ truck** *(railway)* Laufwagen.

pooch *(sl.)* Ansichtskartenladen.

poodle-father *(sl.)* Gigolo.

pooh-pooh *(v.)* geringschätzig behandeln, Nase rümpfen.

pool Interessengemeinschaft, -verband, *(arrangement between companies)* Kartell, Ring, Pool, Vereinigung, Unternehmenszusammenschluß, *(body of water)* Teich, Weiher, *(common fund)* gemeinsamer Fonds, *(International Monetary Fund)* Währungsreserve, *(races)* Toto, Totalisator, *(traffic agreement)* Verkehrsverband;
~s Lotto, *(shipping business)* Gewinnabrechnungsgemeinschaften, -verteilungskartell;
bear (bull) ~ Spekulantengruppe zur Herbeiführung einer Baisse (Hausse); **blind ~** unbeschränkte Vollmacht des Geschäftsführers einer Interessengemeinschaft; **buffer ~** Ausgleichspool; **closed ~** Patentgemeinschaft, Patentvergabe nur an bestimmte Außenseiter; **football ~s** [Fußball]toto; **money ~** *(US)* in Krisenzeiten für Makler gebildeter Fonds, Kapitalbereitstellungsgemeinschaft, in Krisenzeiten operierende Bankengruppe; **gross-money ~** *(traffic)* Gewinnbeteiligungskartell; **net-money receipts ~** Reingewinnbeteiligungsvertrag; **passenger ~** Gewinnabrechnungsgemeinschaft im Passagierverkehr; **patent ~** Patentmonopol; **press ~** Journalistenkontingent; **purchasing ~** Einkaufsgemeinschaft; **railway ~** Eisenbahnkartell; **secretarial (typing) ~** Gemeinschaftssekretariat, Schreibsaal; **swimming ~** Schwimmbecken, -bassin; **tonnage ~** Gewinnabrechnungsgemeinschaft im Frachtverkehr; **wagering ~** Wettgemeinschaft;
~ of blood Blutlache; **~ of expenditure** Zusammenfassung der Ausgaben, zusammengefaßter Aufwand; **~ of liquidity** Liquiditätsfonds; **~ of technical power** Zusammenstellung von Fachkräften; **~ of mortgages** Hypothekenfonds; **~ on the road** Straßenpfütze;
~ *(v.)* zusammenwerfen, *(coordinate)* zusammenfassen, koordinieren, vereinigen, *(form a pool)* einer Interessengemeinschaft unterwerfen, Kartell bilden, kartellieren, zusammenschließen, *(share profits)* [Gewinne] teilen, poolen, *(throw in common fund)* Kräfte (Material) gemeinsam einsetzen;

~ efforts Kräfte gemeinsam einsetzen; **~ expenses** sich an den Kosten schlüsselmäßig beteiligen, Unkosten aufschlüsseln; **~ funds** Gelder zusammenlegen (zusammenschießen); **~ mortgages** Hypotheken vereinigen (zusammenschreiben); **~ orders** Aufträge zusammenfassen (poolen, kartellisieren); **~ patents** Patente zusammenwerfen; **~ the profits** Gewinne teilen; **~ one's resources** sein Geld zusammenwerfen; **~ one's savings** seine Ersparnisse zusammentun; **~ traffic** gemeinsame Verkehrspolitik betreiben;
to lie in a ~ of blood im Blut schwimmen; **to win a fortune from (on) the ~s** beim Toto ein Vermögen machen;
º s Betting Act Lottogesetz; **~ car service** Sammelladungsspedition; **~ cost** zusammengefaßte Unkosten; **~ coupon** Totoschein; **~ filler** Lottospieler; **~ interests** Kartellanteile; **~ photo** *(journalism)* Gemeinschaftsfoto; **~ seller** Lottoverkäufer; **~ selling** Verkauf im Rahmen eines Kartells; **~ support** Stützungskäufe der Poolbeteiligten; **~ ticket** Lottoschein.

pooled fund gemeinsames Kapital, Gemeinschaftskapital.

pooling Kartellisierung, Poolbildung, Poolung;
~ of accounts Kontenzusammenlegung; **~ of efforts** gemeinsamer Einsatz von Kräften, gemeinsamer Kräfteeinsatz; **~ of freight** *(US)* Frachtenverrechnungsabkommen; **~ of interests** Interessenvereinigung, -gemeinschaft; **~ of mortgages** Hypothekenvereinigung, -zusammenlegung, -zusammenschreibung; **~ of profits** Gewinnteilung, -poolung, *(in restraint of trade, US)* wettbewerbsbeschränkende Absprache; **~ of risk** Risikoverteilung [innerhalb eines Unternehmens]; **~ of votes** Stimmenvereinigung;
~ agreement (contract) Poolvertrag, Kartellabkommen, Arbeits-, Interessengemeinschaft, *(transport services)* Verkehrsverbandsvertrag.

poolroom *(US)* Wettlokal, -büro, Lottoannahmestelle.

poop *(information, sl.)* Information aus sicherer Quelle, *(ship)* Heck;
~ deck erhöhtes Achterdeck; **~ light** Hecklicht; **~ sheet** Aufklärungsprospekt, *(sl.)* detaillierte Anweisungen.

poor schwach, schlecht, ärmlich, arm, besitzlos, kümmerlich, elend, *(business)* ungünstig, *(debtor)* arm, mittellos, *(needy)* [unterstützungs]bedürftig, *(profit)* dürftig, mager, schlecht, *(without reserves)* schlecht fundiert, ohne [Geld]reserven, *(soil)* unergiebig, mager;
~ as a church mouse *(Job's cat, US)* so arm wie eine Kirchenmaus; **~ and needy** bedürftig;
the ~ die Besitzlosen; **the new ~** verschämte Arme;
to be ~ at mathematics schlechter Mathematiker sein; **to become ~er in ideas** ideenarm werden; **to collect for the ~** für die Armen sammeln; **to grind the faces of the ~** die Armen aussaugen; **to help the ~** Arme unterstützen; **to render aid to the ~** Not der Armen lindern;
~ attendance schwacher Besuch; **~ box** Opferstock; **~ breakfast** dürftiges Frühstück; **~ business** schlechtes Geschäft; **~ cattle** mageres Vieh; **to have but a ~ chance of success** nur geringe Erfolgsaussichten haben; **~ coal** Magerkohle; **~ creature** klägliches Geschöpf; **~ crop** schlechte Ernte; **~ debtor** pfändungsfreier Schuldner; **~ debtor's oath** *(US)* Offenbarungseid; **~ dress** ärmliche Kleidung; **~ driver** schlechter (unzuverlässiger) Fahrer; **~ excuse** schwache (dürftige) Entschuldigung; **~ fare** magere (knappe) Kost; **~ farm** *(US)* Armensiedlung; **to cut a ~ figure** jämmerliche Figur abgeben; **to make up one's mind on ~ grounds** sich eine wenig fundierte Meinung bilden; **~ harvest** schlechte Ernte; **in ~ health** in schlechtem Gesundheitszustand; **~ ten days' holiday** Urlaub von ganzen zehn Tagen; **~ investment** schlechte (ungünstige) Kapitalanlage.

poor-law *(Br.)* Fürsorgerecht, Armengesetzgebung;
~ administration öffentliches Fürsorgewesen; **~ board** Fürsorgebehörde; **~ guardian** Fürsorgebeamter; **~ matters** Armenrechtssachen; **~ litigant** *(US)* Armenrechtskläger, Partei im Armenrecht; **~ management relief** öffentliche Fürsorge, Armenfürsorge, -pflege, Wohlfahrtspflege; **~s' roll** *(Scot.)* Prozeßliste der Armenrechtsfälle; **~ union** Fürsorgeverband.

poor | litigant *(US)* Armenrechtskläger, Partei im Armenrecht; **~-looking house** verwahrlost aussehendes Haus; **~ lookout** schlechte Aussichten; **~ man** Armer; **~ management** schlechte Geschäftsführung; **~ mark** *(school)* schlechte Noten; **~ market** schwacher Markt, schleppender Warenabsatz; **~ memory** schlechtes Gedächtnis; **~ mixture** *(car)* schlechtes Benzingemisch; **to have had a ~ night** schlecht geschlafen haben; **in my ~ opinion** meiner unmaßgeblichen Meinung nach; **to have a ~ opinion of s. o.** wenig von jem. halten, schlechte Meinung von jem. haben; **~ orator** schlechter Redner; **~ person** Partei im Armenrecht, Armenrechtskläger; **~ person's certificate**

Armenrechtszeugnis; ~ **prisoner** *(Br.)* mittelloser Häftling, Armenrechtsberechtigter; ~ **prospects** schlechte Aussichten; ~ **quality** schlechte (nicht ausreichende) Qualität; **~-quality goods** Waren geringer Qualität; ~ **quarter** Armenviertel; ~ **rate** Armenabgabe; **to give s. o. a ~ reception** jem. einen kümmerlichen Empfang bereiten; ~ **relations** bedürftige Angehörige; ~ **relief** *(Br.)* Armenfürsorge, -pflege, Wohlfahrtsunterstützung, Sozialhilfe; ~ **result** mageres Ergebnis; ~ **soil** unergiebiger (magerer, dürrer) Boden; **~-spirited** feige, erbärmlich; **to have ~ students in a year** diesmal unterdurchschnittlich begabte Studenten in einem Semester haben; **to sell ~ stuff** kümmerliches Zeug verkaufen; ~ **supply** jämmerliches Angebot; ~ **trash** *(US)* weißes Gesindel.

poorer|classes ärmere Volksschichten;
to be the ~ by a thousand pounds tausend Pfund verloren haben.

poorhouse Armenhaus.

poorly dürftig, armselig, *(coll.)* unpäßlich, kränklich;
to be ~ off in dürftigen Verhältnissen leben; **to be looking very ~** sehr schlecht aussehen; **to be rather ~ this morning** *(coll.)* sich heute gar nicht wohl fühlen; **to think ~ of s. th.** nicht viel von etw. halten;
~ **cushioned seat** schlecht gepolsterter Sitz; ~ **furnished room** dürftig möbliertes Zimmer; ~ **gifted** schwach begabt; ~ **lighted streets** schlecht beleuchtete Straßen.

poormaster *(US, local)* Sozialpfleger.

poorness Armut.

pop Knall, Pfiff, Schuß, *(champagne, coll.)* Schampus, *(popular song)* Schlager, Schnulze;
in ~ *(Br., sl.)* versetzt, auf der Pfandleihe;
~ **of a cork** Korkenknall;
~ *(v.)* plötzlich erscheinen (auftauchen), flitzen, *(US)* mit der Sprache herausrücken, *(Br., sl.)* versetzen, verpfänden;
~ **away** schnell wegstecken; ~ **a cork** Korken knallen lassen; ~ **down to the country** Landpartie machen; ~ **down one's ideas to paper** seine Gedanken schnell zu Papier bringen; ~ **one's head out of the window** Kopf zum Fenster hinausstecken; ~ **in** hereinschauen, auf einen Sprung vorbeikommen; ~ **in and out** laufend zu Besuch da sein; ~ **into one's clothes** schnell in die Kleider schlüpfen; ~ **s. th. into a drawer** etw. in eine Schublade stopfen; ~ **off** abhauen, sich aus dem Staub machen; ~ **over to the grocer's** schnell zum Kolonialwarenhändler laufen; ~ **a peter** *(sl.)* Safe knacken; ~ **the question** *(coll.)* Heiratsantrag machen; ~ **round** vorbeikommen; ~ **up** plötzlich aufkreuzen, aus dem Boden schießen; ~ **up to town** von der Stadt einen kurzen Besuch abstatten; ~ **one's watch** *(Br., sl.)* seine Uhr verpfänden;
to go ~ knallen, platzen;
~ **bottle** *(sl.)* kümmerliche Kamera; ~ **car** *(US sl.)* Draisine; **~-and-mom shop** Tante Emma Laden.

pope Papst.

popping the question Heiratsantrag.

poppycock *(US coll.)* dummes Zeug, Quatsch, Unsinn.

populace, populacy Plebs, Hinz und Kunz.

popular volkstümlich, populär, *(having general currency)* allgemein, weit verbreitet;
to be ~ with s. o. gute Nummer bei jem. haben; **to be ~ with the neighbo(u)rs** sich mit seinen Nachbarn gut stehen;
~ **action** öffentliche Klage; ~ **appeal** Volkstümlichkeit; ~ **article** zugkräftiger Artikel; ~ **book** volkstümliches Buch, Volksbuch; ~ **concert** Konzert zu volkstümlichen Preisen; ~ **discontent** allgemeine Unzufriedenheit; ~ **edition** Volksausgabe; ~ **election** allgemeine Wahl; ~ **error** weit verbreiteter Irrtum; ~ **event** beliebtes Sportereignis; ~ **film star** Filmstar; **to build up a ~ following** seine Anhängerschaft in der großen Masse suchen; ~ **front** *(pol.)* Volksfront; **~-front alliance** Volksfrontbündnis; ~ **government** Volksherrschaft; ~ **hero** Volksheld; ~ **initiative** *(Switzerland)* Volksbegehren; ~ **insurrection** Volksaufstand; ~ **leader** Volksführer; ~ **lecture** volkstümliche Vorlesung; ~ **newspaper** Volksblatt; ~ **papers** Boulevardpresse; ~ **party** Volkspartei; ~ **phrase** volkstümliche Redewendung; ~ **press** Massenpresse, -blätter; ~ **price** volkstümlicher Preis; **~-priced** zu volkstümlichen Preisen; ~ **priced car** billiges Auto; ~ **science** Popularwissenschaft; ~ **sense** laienhafte Bedeutung; ~ **song** bekannter Schlager; ~ **sovereignty** Volkssouveränität; ~ **tumult** Volksaufruhr; ~ **tune** Schlager; ~ **verdict** Volksmeinung; ~ **voice** Stimme des Volkes; ~ **writer** Volksschriftsteller.

popularity Beliebtheit, Popularität, Volksgunst;
mounting ~ steigende Popularität;
to gain in ~ volkstümlich werden; **to ride on a wave of ~** von einer Woge der Volksgunst getragen werden;

to send s. o. soaring in the ~ charts jem. in den Volkstümlichkeitstabellen Auftrieb geben; ~ **contest** *(US)* Beliebtheitswettbewerb; ~ **poll** *(US)* Beliebtheitsumfrage; **to top the personal ~ poll** Beliebtheitsliste anführen; ~ **test** Beliebtheitswettbewerb.

popularization Popularisierung.

popularize *(v.)* popularisieren.

populate *(v.)* besiedeln, bevölkern.

populated, densely (sparsely) dicht (schwach) bevölkert.

population Bevölkerung, Einwohnerzahl, Einwohnerschaft, *(statistics)* Gesamtzahl, Grundgesamtheit, statistische Masse;
autochthonous ~ bodenständige Bevölkerung; **civilian ~** Zivilbevölkerung; **constituent ~** wahlberechtigte Bevölkerung; **dense ~** dichte Bevölkerung; **dependent ~** unterhaltsabhängiger Bevölkerungsteil; **dissident ~s** andersdeutende Bevölkerungsteile; **employed ~** arbeitende (berufstätige) Bevölkerung; **floating ~** fluktuierende Bevölkerung, nicht seßhafter Bevölkerungsteil, schwankende Bevölkerungsziffer; **foreign ~** fremdländischer Bevölkerungsanteil; **frontier ~** Grenzbevölkerung; **home ~** einheimische Bevölkerung; **labo(u)ring ~** arbeitende Bevölkerung; **local ~** einheimische Bevölkerung; **married ~** verheirateter Bevölkerungsanteil; **native ~** einheimische Bevölkerung; **nonnormal ~** *(statistics)* nicht normal verteilte Bevölkerung; **occupied ~** werktätige (berufstätige) Bevölkerung; **open ~** geringe Bevölkerungsdichte; **permanent ~** ortsansässige Bevölkerung, Wohnbevölkerung; **rural ~** Landbevölkerung; **settled ~** seßhafte Bevölkerung; **small ~** geringe Bevölkerungszahl; **sparse ~** geringe Bevölkerungsdichte; **stationary ~** stationäre Bevölkerung, gleichbleibende Bevölkerungszahl; **surplus ~** Bevölkerungsüberschuß; **total ~** absolute Bevölkerung, Gesamtzahl; **urban ~** Stadtbevölkerung; **voting ~** wahlberechtigte Bevölkerung; **voting-age ~** wahlberechtigter Bevölkerungsanteil; **world ~** Weltbevölkerung; **working-class ~** werktätige (berufstätige) Bevölkerung;
to project to the entire ~ auf die Gesamtbevölkerung umrechnen;
~ **bomb** Bevölkerungsbombe; ~ **boom** starke Bevölkerungszunahme; ~ **bulge** geburtenstarke Jahrgänge; **teenage ~ bulge** geburtenstarker Jahrgang Jugendlicher; ~ **census** Volkszählung; ~ **changes** Bevölkerungsumschichtungen; **net ~ charge** Bevölkerungsbilanz; ~ **class** Bevölkerungsgruppe; ~ **curve** Bevölkerungskurve; ~ **decline** Bevölkerungsrückgang; ~ **density** Bevölkerungsdichte; ~ **explosion** *(UN)* Bevölkerungs-, Geburtenexplosion; ~ **figure** Bevölkerungszahl; ~ **forecast** Bevölkerungsprognose; ~ **growth** Bevölkerungswachstum, -zunahme; **zero ~ growth** eingefrorene Bevölkerungszunahme; ~ **growth rate** Bevölkerungszuwachsrate; ~ **increase** Bevölkerungszuwachs; ~ **limitation** Begrenzung des Bevölkerungszuwachses; ~ **mobility** Bevölkerungsmobilität, -bewegung; ~ **movement** Bevölkerungsbewegung; ~ **needs** Bevölkerungsbedürfnisse; ~ **overspill** abgewanderter Bevölkerungsteil; ~ **policy** Bevölkerungspolitik, bevölkerungspolitische Maßnahmen; ~ **pressure** Bevölkerungsdruck; ~ **problem** Bevölkerungsproblem; ~ **projection** Bevölkerungsprognose; ~ **pyramid** Alterspyramide; ~ **redistribution** Umverteilung der Bevölkerung; ~ **register** Einwohnermeldeamt; ~ **sampling** Bevölkerungsstichprobe; ~ **shift** Bevölkerungsverschiebung; ~ **stabilization** Stabilisierung der Bevölkerungszunahme; ~ **statistics** Bevölkerungsstatistik; ~ **stratum** Bevölkerungsschicht; ~ **structure** Bevölkerungsstruktur; ~ **supply** Versorgung der Bevölkerung; ~ **target** Zielgröße der Bevölkerung; ~ **theory** Bevölkerungskunde, -theorie; ~ **tide** Bevölkerungstrom; ~ **transfer** Bevölkerungsaustausch; ~ **trend** Bevölkerungsentwicklung.

populational bevölkerungspolitisch.

populous dicht bevölkert.

populousness Bevölkerungsdichte.

porcelain Porzellan;
~ **glass** Milchglas.

porch *(US)* überdachter Vorbau, Portal, *(US)* Veranda;
~ **climber** *(sl.)* Einsteigdieb, Fassadenkletterer, Klettermaxe.

pore Pore;
through every ~ am ganzen Körper;
~ *(v.)* **one's eyes out** sich die Augen verderben; ~ **over** eifrig studieren; ~ **over one's books** über seinen Büchern sitzen; ~ **over a letter** über einem Brief brüten; ~ **upon a problem** sich mit einem Problem beschäftigen.

pork *(politics, US)* fette Beute;
~ **barrel** *(US sl.)* politisch bedingte Staatszuschüsse; **~-chopper** *(sl.)* Pöstchenjäger.

pornographic pornografisch, obszön.

pornography Pornografie, Schmutzliteratur.

port [See]hafen, Flughafen, *(opening in a ship)* Ladeluke, -pforte, *(left side of ship)* Backbord[seite];

approved ~ zugelassener Hafen; ~ **arrived from** letzter Verladehafen; **artificial** ~ künstlicher Hafen; **bonded** ~ Hafen mit Zollager; **cargo** ~ Ladeluke, Stückpforte; **city** ~ Stadttor; **close** ~ *(Br.)* innerer Hafen, Binnenhafen; **coaling** ~ Kohlenhafen; **commercial** ~ Handelshafen; **deep-water** ~ Hochseehafen; **discharging** ~ Entladehafen, Löschplatz; **domestic** ~ Inlandshafen; **emergency** ~ Nothafen; **final** ~ Endhafen; **foreign** ~ Auslandshafen; **free** ~ Freihafen; **home** ~ Heimathafen; **ice-free** ~ eisfreier Hafen; **import** ~ Einfuhrhafen; **inner (inland)** ~ Binnenhafen; **intermediate** ~ Zwischenhafen; **inward** ~ Einfuhrhafen; **loading** ~ Verladehafen; **maritime** ~ Seehafen; **natural** ~ natürlicher Hafen; **naval** ~ Kriegshafen; **observation** ~ *(cinema)* Beobachtungsfenster; **outer** ~ äußerer Hafen, Vorhafen; **poop** ~ *(ship)* Heckfenster; **river** ~ Flußhafen; **sea** ~ Seehafen; **shipping** ~ Ausfuhr-, Versandhafen; **trading** ~ Handelshafen; **unequipped** ~ gesperrter Hafen;

~ **of anchorage** Nothafen; ~ **of arrival** Ankunftshafen; ~ **of call** Anlauf-, Order-, Anlegehafen, *(airplane)* Anflughafen; ~ **of clearance** Abgangs-, [Zoll]abfertigungshafen; ~ **of commission** Heimathafen; ~ **of delivery** Liefer-, Entladehafen, -platz; ~ **of departure** Abgangs-, Abfahrtshafen, *(airplane)* Abflughafen; ~ **of destination** Bestimmungshafen; ~ **of discharge** Löschhafen, -ort, Entladeplatz, -hafen; ~ **of disembarkation** Ausschiffungshafen; ~ **of distress** Nothafen; ~ **of embarkation** Einschiffungs-, Ausgangshafen; ~ **of entry** Eingangs-, Zollabfertigungshafen; ~ **of exportation** Ausfuhrhafen; ~ **of import** Einfuhrhafen; ~ **of lading** Ladehafen; ~ **of landing** Landungshafen; ~ **of loading** Verlade-, Versandhafen; ~ **of refuge** Nothafen; ~ **of registry** Heimathafen, -ort; ~ **of sailing** Abfahrts-, Abgangshafen; ~ **of shipment** Versand-, Verlade-, Verschiffungshafen; ~ **of transit** Transithafen; ~ **of transshipment** Umlade-, Umschlaghafen;

to be held up in ~ **with engine troubles** mit Maschinenschaden im Hafen festliegen; **to blockade a** ~ Hafen sperren; **to call at a** ~ Hafen anlaufen, *(airplane)* Flughafen anfliegen; **to clear a** ~ aus einem Hafen auslaufen; **to close a** ~ Hafen sperren (schließen); **to come into** ~ in den Hafen einlaufen; **to come safe to** ~ sein Ziel erreichen; **to drop into (enter) a** ~ in einen Hafen einlaufen; **to exclude from a** ~ Hafenzugang verwehren; **to leave** ~ auslaufen; **to make (put in)** ~ Hafen anlaufen, in einen Hafen einlaufen, auf einen Hafen zuhalten; **to reach** ~ Hafen erreichen, in den Hafen gelangen; **to reach safely** sicher in den Hafen einlaufen; **to run out of a** ~ aus einem Hafen auslaufen; **to shut up a** ~ Hafen sperren;

~ **administration** Hafenverwaltung, -amt; ~-**admiral** *(Br.)* Hafenkommandant; ~-**admiral's office** *(Br.)* Hafenkommandantur; ~ **area** Hafengebiet; ~ **authority** Hafenbehörde; **to report to the** ~ **authority** sich beim Hafenamt melden; ~ **bar** Sandbank, Untiefe; ~ **bill of lading** Hafenkonnossement; ~ **call** Hafenbesuch; ~ **captain** Hafenkapitän; ~ **charges (dues)** Hafengebühren; ~ **construction site** Hafenanlagen; ~ **development** Hafenausbau; ~ **engine** Backbordmotor; ~ **entrance** Hafeneinfahrt; ~ **equalization** Frachtbasis; ~ **equipment** Hafenanlagen; ~ **facilities** Hafenanlagen; ~-**greve** Hafenmeister; ~ **improvement** Hafenausbau; ~ **installations** Hafenanlagen; ~ **interests** Hafeninteressen; ~ **operation** Hafenbetrieb; ~ **operators' association** Hafenbetriebsgesellschaft; ~ **plane** *(airplane)* linke Tragfläche; ~ **reeve** Hafenmeister; ~ **regulations** Hafenordnung; ~ **risk** *(marine insurance)* Hafenrisiko, -gefahr; ~ **risk insurance** Versicherung des Hafenrisikos; ~ **sanitary authority** Hafengesundheitsbehörde; ~ **side** Backbordseite; ~ **station** Hafenbahnhof; ~ **toll** *(US)* Hafengebühren; ~ **warden** *(US)* Hafenaufseher, -meister.

portable transportabel, tragbar;
~ **pension** übertragbarer Pensionsanspruch; ~ **radio set** Kofferradio; ~ **typewriter** Reiseschreibmaschine.

portage *(freight)* Ladung, Fracht, *(transporting)* Transport, *(charge for transportation)* Transport-, Frachtkosten, Rollgeld, Zustellgebühr.

portal-to-portal pay *(miners, US)* Lohnvergütung für den Anmarschweg zum Arbeitsplatz.

porter Portier, Pförtner, *(Pullman, US)* Steward, Schlafwagenschaffner, *(harbo(u)r)* Hafenarbeiter, *(station)* [Gepäck]träger, Dienstmann;
bank ~ Kassen-, Bankbote; **hotel** ~ Hotelportier; **luggage** ~ *(Br.)* Gepäckträger; **market** ~ Lastträger; **ticket** ~ Bahnsteigschaffner, *(Br.)* Gepäckträger;
~ **of bad news** Überbringer schlechter Nachrichten;
to swear like a ~ wie ein Landsknecht fluchen.

porter's | fee Gepäckträgergebühr; ~ **lodge** Portierloge.

porterage Botenlohn, *(luggage)* [Gepäck]trägerlohn, *(parcel, telegram)* Zustellgebühr.

porterhouse *(US)* Bierrestaurant, -lokal.

portfolio *(list of investment)* Effektenbestand, [Wertpapier]-portefeuille, *(map)* Aktentasche, -koffer, Mappe, *(minister)* Geschäftsbereich, Portefeuille, Ressort;

business ~ *(building society)* Vertragsbestand; **commercial** ~ Bestand an Handelsbeteiligungen; **direct** ~ Direktinvestitionen; **diversified** ~ gestreutes Effektenportefeuille; **insurance** ~ Versicherungsbestand; **investment** ~ Wertpapierportefeuille, -bestand; **minister's** ~ ministerieller Geschäftsbereich, Ministerressort; **pension** ~ Portefeuille eines Pensionsfonds; **security** ~ Wertpapierportefeuille; **shadow** ~ *(Br.)* Portefeuille (Ressort) im Schattenkabinett;

balanced ~ **of assets** ausgewogen angelegtes Effektenvermögen; ~ **of a bank** Bankenportefeuille; ~ **of bills** Bestand an Wechseln, Wechselportefeuille, -bestand; ~ **of investments (securities)** Wertpapierportefeuille, Effektenguthaben, -depot; ~ **of shares** Aktienportefeuille;

to be without ~ kein besonderes Ressort haben; **to resign one's** ~ sein Ministerium abgeben;

~ **bill** Portefeuillewechsel; ~ **buying** Anlagekäufe; ~ **changes** Anlageveränderung im Effektenportefeuille; ~ **deal** Portefeuillegeschäft; ~ **description** *(investment fund)* Wertpapieraufstellung; ~ **investment** Kapitalanlage in Wertpapieren; ~ **management** Effektenverwaltung [eines Investmenttrusts]; ~ **manager** Vermögens-, Effektenverwalter; ~ **selection** *(investment company)* Anlagenauswahl, optimale Zusammenstellung eines Wertpapierdepots; ~ **switch** Effektenaustausch.

porthole Bullauge.

portico Vorbau, Säulen-, Arkadengang.

portion Teil, Stück, *(block of shares)* Tranche, *(dowry)* Mitgift, Heiratsgut, Aussteuer, *(of food)* Portion, *(inheritance)* Erb[an]-teil, *(lot)* Los, Schicksal, *(share)* Anteil, Quote, Portion;
in equal ~s zu gleichen Teilen;
aggressive ~ *(investment trust, US)* risikoreichere Effektenanlage; **available** ~ verfügbarer Anteil; **defensive** ~ *(investment trust, US)* risikoärmere Effektenanlage; **disposable** ~ pflichtteilsfreier Nachlaßteil; **legal** ~ Pflichtteil, gesetzliches Erbteil; **marital** ~ *(Louisiana)* Pflichtteilsanspruch der Ehefrau; **marriage** ~ Aussteuer, Mitgift; **maturing** ~ fällige Tranche; **prorata** ~ anteiliger Betrag; **statutory** ~ *(US)* gesetzliches Erbteil, Pflichtteil; **through** ~ *(railway)* Durchgangswagen; **unexpended** ~ nicht abgehobener Betrag;

separate ~ **on a child** Abfindung eines Kindes auf Lebenszeit; ~ **of claim** Forderungsteilbetrag; ~ **of cost** Kostenanteil; **unused** ~ **of credit** offener Kreditbetrag; ~ **of the gain** Gewinnanteil; **accruing to each heir** jedem Erben zukommender Anteil, Erbanwachs; ~ **of income** Einkommensanteil; ~ **of inheritance** Erbanteil; **unsold** ~ **of an issue** unverkaufte Emissionsspitze; ~ **of a loan** Tranche (Abschnitt) einer Anleihe; ~ **of proceeds** Erlös-, Ertragsanteil; ~ **of profits** Gewinnanteil; ~ **of property** Vermögensteil, -stück; ~ **of shares** Aktienpaket;

~ *(v.)* ein-, ver-, zuteilen, *(dowry)* aussteuern, -statten; ~ **to the eldest son** *(estate)* auf den ältesten Sohn übergehen, dem ältesten Sohn zufallen; ~ **off** aussteuern, -statten; ~ **out** auf-, zuteilen;

to raise ~s **for children** Abfindungszahlungen an Kinder leisten; **to settle a separate** ~ **on a child** Kind zu Lebzeiten abfinden;

~-**debts** Schulden aus einer Pflichtteilsvereinbarung; ~ **policy** Aussteuerpolice.

portioner Anteilsberechtigter.

portionist Anteilsempfänger.

portmanteau *(Br.)* [lederner] Handkoffer.

portrait, to take s. one's j. porträtieren lassen;
~ **lens** Porträtlinse; ~ **painter** Porträtmaler.

pose, without unaffektiert;
mere ~ reines Theater;
~ *(v.)* **for an artist** einem Künstler Modell stehen; ~ **as a hero** sich als Held aufspielen; ~ **a play to** s. o. jem. ein Stück zuschreiben; ~ **no problem** kein Problem darstellen.

posh *(fam.)* fesch, schick.

position *(advertising)* Plazierung, *(airplane)* Standort, *(financial condition)* finanzielle Verfassung, *(employment)* Anstellung, Stelle, Stellung, Platz, Posten, Position, *(mil.)* Verteidigungsstellung, *(point of view)* Standpunkt, *(post office)* [Post]schalter, *(rank)* Position, Stellung, *(ship)* Besteck, Position, Schiffsort, *(situation)* Stand, Lage, Stellung, Position, *(tariff)* Tarifnummer;

~ **as per ...** Stand vom ...; **in a high ~** in einer hohen Position; **of good ~** in guten Verhältnissen; **out of ~** deplaziert; **advance ~** *(mil.)* vorgeschobene Stellung; **advanced ~** gehobene [Dienst]stellung; **advantageous ~** günstige Stellung; **awkward ~** schwierige (verzwickte) Lage; **~s available** Stellenangebot; **balance-of-payments ~** Zahlungsbilanzposition; **bear ~** Baisseposition; **bull ~** Hausseposition; **business ~** berufliche Stellung; **career ~** beruflich bedeutsame Stellung, berufliche Erfolgsposition; **cash ~** Kassenlage, -stand; **~ closed** *(post office)* hier keine Abfertigung, Schalter geschlossen; **commanding ~** beherrschende Stellung; **competitive ~** Konkurrenzfähigkeit, Wettbewerbslage; **creditor ~** Gläubigerstellung; **critical ~** kritische Lage; **current ~** *(bank)* Liquiditätslage; **debtor ~** Schuldnerstellung; **developable ~** ausbaufähige Stellung; **elevated ~** gehobenere Stellung; **exceptional ~** Ausnahme-, Sonderstellung; **exchange ~** Devisenlage; **executive ~** leitende Stellung; **factual ~** Sachlage; **fiduciary ~** Vertrauensstellung, -position; **financial ~** Vermögens-, Finanzlage; **food ~** Ernährungslage; **fortified ~** befestigte Stellung; **full ~** *(US)* Vorzugsplazierung; **geographical ~** geographische Lage; **good ~** gute Stellung; **guaranteed ~** *(advertising)* garantierte Plazierung; **healthy ~** gesunde Lage; **high-paying ~** hochbezahlte Stellung; **honorary ~** ehrenamtliche Tätigkeit, Ehrenamt; **inferior ~** untergeordnete Stellung; **intermediate ~** Zwischenstellung; **January ~** *(trading in futures)* Januarposition; **key ~** leitende Stellung, Schlüsselstellung; **leading ~** leitende Stellung; **legal ~** Rechtslage, -stellung; **long ~s** Positionen der Haussepartei; **look-see ~** abwartende Haltung; **lower ~** untergeordnete Stellung; **lucrative ~** lukrativer Posten; **management ~** leitende Stellung; **managerial ~** leitende Stellung; **~s offered** Stellenangebot; **official ~** amtliche Eigenschaft; **ordinary ~** *(advertising)* Plazierung ohne Berücksichtigung von Sonderwünschen; **permanent ~** Dauer-, Lebensstellung, feste Stellung; **policy-making ~** leitende Stellung; **preferred ~** *(advertising)* Sonderplazierung; **prescribed ~** *(advertising)* Plazierungsvorschrift; **quasi-official ~** beamtenähnliche Stellung; **quick ~** *(of a business)* Flüssigkeit (Liquidität) eines Unternehmens; **reference ~** Bezugsposition; **responsible ~** verantwortliche Stellung; **salaried ~** besoldete Stellung; **senior ~** leitende Stellung; **ship's ~** Schiffsposition; **short ~** Baisseposition; **social ~** gesellschaftliche Stellung; **sound ~** gesunde Finanzverhältnisse; **special ~** Sonderstellung, *(advertising)* besondere Plazierung; **stated ~** *(advertisement)* vorgeschriebene Plazierung; **strategic ~** strategische Lage; **subordinate ~** untergeordnete Stellung; **supervisory ~** Aufsichtstätigkeit; **taxation ~** steuerliche Lage; **top ~** Spitzenstellung; **top-right ~** *(advertising)* Plazierung oben rechts; **unpaid ~** ehrenamtliche Tätigkeit, Ehrenamt; **vacant ~** unbesetzte Stelle; **well-established ~** angesehene Stellung; **well-paid ~** gut dotierte Stellung;

~ **of account** Kontostand; ~ **of an advertisement** Plazierung einer Anzeige; ~ **of affairs** Stand der Dinge; ~ **of authority** verantwortungsvolle Stellung; **customer's ~ at the bank** Kundenbeurteilung durch die Bank; ~ **in the cabinet** Kabinettsposition, -sitz; **relative ~ within the organizational chart** Stellung in der Betriebshierarchie; ~ **in class** *(school)* Klassenplatz; ~ **of community leadership** führende Stellung in der Gemeinde; ~ **of constraint** Zwangslage; ~ **at the end of the year** Stand am Jahresende; ~ **of a firm** Finanzlage einer Firma; ~ **in the Fund** *(International Monetary Fund)* Position gegenüber dem Weltwährungsfonds; ~ **in industry** Industriestellung; ~ **of influence** einflußreiche Position; ~ **in law** Rechtsstellung; ~ **of life** Lebensstellung; ~ **of priority** Vorrangstellung; ~ **on the promotion roster** Rangstelle; ~ **with good prospects** ausbaufähige Stellung; ~ **of responsibility** verantwortliche Stellung; **[low] ~ in society** [unbedeutende] gesellschaftliche Stellung; ~ **of trust** Vertrauensposten, -stellung; **great ~ in the world** Weltstellung; ~ **(v.)** *(mil.)* stationieren;

~ **s. o.** j. an den richtigen Platz stellen;

to accept a ~ Stellung annehmen; **to adopt a definite ~ on a question** seine Stellung zu einer Frage beziehen; **to apply for a ~** sich um eine Stellung bewerben, für einen Posten kandidieren; **to assure s. one's ~** jds. Stellung festigen; **to be in a ~** in der Lage sein; **to be equal to a ~** einem Posten gewachsen sein; **to be in an established ~** in Amt und Würde sein; **to be in a good ~** gute Stelle haben; **to be the only possible man for a ~** als einziger für eine Position in Frage kommen; **to be in a solid ~** sich in einer guten Ausgangslage befinden; **to be in a strong ~** starke Position haben; **to be in a subordinate ~** in abhängiger Stellung sein; **to be promoted to a better ~** in eine höhere Stelle aufrücken; **to bring a gun to the firing ~** Geschütz in Stellung bringen; **to build**

up a sizable ~ in stocks *(US)* beträchtliches Aktienpaket zusammenkaufen; **to change one's ~** seine Stellung wechseln; **to consolidate a ~** Stellung ausbauen; **to define one's ~** seinen Standpunkt darlegen; **to develop an influential ~ in the market** sich branchenmäßig durchsetzen, in der Branche anerkannt sein; **to drop into a ~** gute Stellung erlangen; **to establish o. s. in a secure ~** sich in einer Stellung verankern; **to fall from one's ~** seine Stellung verlieren; **to fill a ~** Posten besetzen, Stelle bekleiden, Platz ausfüllen; **to find the ~** *(ship)* orten; **to fix a ship's ~** Position eines Schiffes bestimmen; **to gain a ~** sich eine Stellung schaffen; **to get a good ~ in the Civil Service** *(Br.)* guten Beamtenposten bekommen; **to get a ~ in the government service** als Beamter angestellt werden; **to give up a ~** Stellung aufgeben; **to have a first-rate ~** erstklassige Stellung haben; **to hold a ~** Amt bekleiden, Stellung innehaben; **to hold one's ~** sich in seiner Stelle behaupten; **to hold a ~ all its own** Klasse für sich darstellen; **to hold a good ~ in a class** unter den Klassenbesten sein; **to hold a high-level ~** führende Stellung einnehmen; **to hold a ~ of management responsibility in business** im Wirtschaftsleben eine verantwortungsreiche Stellung haben; **to imagine o. s. in another's ~** sich in jds. Lage versetzen können; **to improve one's ~** vorwärtskommen; **to jockey for a ~** sich mit allen Mitteln um eine Position bemühen; **to land s. o. in an awkward ~** j. in eine schiefe Lage bringen; **to leave one's ~** seine Stellung aufgeben; **to lose one's ~** seine Stellung verlieren; **to lose one's ~ as a Great Power** seine Großmachtstellung verlieren (einbüßen); **to maintain one's ~** seinen Platz behaupten; **to maintain s. o. in his ~** j. in seiner Position belassen; **to maintain a ~ in sound stocks** auf guten Werten sitzen bleiben; **to manoeuvre for ~** sich in eine günstige Ausgangslage bringen; **to move to a ~ of greater responsibility** verantwortungsvolleren Posten bekommen; **to move up to an executive ~** in eine führende Stellung gelangen; **to occupy a ~** Funktion ausüben; **to occupy a humble ~** bescheidene Stellung einnehmen; **to occupy a prominent ~** an führender Stelle stehen; **to occupy a ~ of highest power** allergrößte Machtbefugnisse innehaben; **to overstay a ~** Engagement durchhalten; **to owe one's ~ to influence** seine Stellung seinen Beziehungen verdanken; **to put o. s. in s. one's ~** sich in jds. Lage versetzen; **to retain one's ~** seine Stellung behalten; **to rise to a better ~** in eine höhere Stelle aufrücken; **to run for a ~** sich um einen Posten bewerben; **to show a stronger ~** gesündere finanzielle Verfassung erkennen lassen; **to state the ~ desired** gewünschte Position angeben; **to storm the enemy's ~** feindliche Stellung erstürmen; **to strengthen one's ~** seine Stellung befestigen; **to take a ~** Stellung annehmen; **to take a ~ on a question** zu einer Frage Stellung nehmen; **to take up a ~** Standpunkt vertreten, *(begin working)* seinen Dienst (seine Stellung) antreten; **to wind up to a top policy ~** höchstmögliche Position erreichen; **to work o. s. into a good ~** sich hocharbeiten;

~ **bookkeeping** *(securities market)* Liste der eingegangenen Verpflichtungen; ~ **charge** Plazierungsaufschlag; ~ **closing** *(stock exchange)* Glattstellung; ~ **costs** Plazierungskosten; ~ **finder** Funkortungsgerät; ~ **finding** Funkortung, Ortsbestimmung; ~ **lights** *(airplane)* Positionslichter; ~ **mark** Markierung; ~ **paper** Positionspapier, schriftlich festgehaltene Ansicht, *(electioneering)* Wahlprogramm [eines Abgeordneten]; ~ **report** *(plane)* Standortmeldung; ~ **sheet** *(foreign exchange dealings)* Devisenposition, -status.

positioning, fixed vereinbarte Plazierung.

positive *(photo)* Positiv;

~ *(a.)* sicher, bestimmt, feststehend, unumstößlich, positiv, *(coll.)* ausgemacht, komplett, total, vollkommen, *(el.)* positiv, *(self-assured)* selbstherrlich, -sicher;

to be ~ genau wissen; **to be ~ about s. th.** einer Sache völlig sicher sein;

~ **answer** zustimmende Antwort; ~ **asseveration** uneingeschränkte Versicherung; ~ **condition** an den Eintritt eines Ereignisses geknüpfte Bedingung; ~ **confirmation** vorbehaltlose Bestätigung; **to be a ~ crime** wirklich verbrecherisch sein; ~ **discrepancy** *(testimonials)* absoluter Widerspruch; ~ **easement** unbeschränkte Grunddienstbarkeit; ~ **electrode** Anode; ~ **evidence** endgültiger (eindeutiger) Beweis; ~ **fact** feststehende Tatsache; ~ **fool** absoluter Dummkopf, kompletter Narr; ~ **fraud** arglistige Täuschung; ~ **help** praktische Hilfe; **to give s. o. ~ instructions** jem. ganz klare Anweisungen geben; ~ **knowledge** sichere Kenntnis; ~ **law** Satzungsrecht; ~ **list** *(export, US)* Verbotsliste; ~ **miracle** absolutes Wunder; **to be a ~ nuisance** wahres Ärgernis sein; ~ **offer** festes Angebot; ~ **order** ausdrückliche Anweisung; ~ **prescription** Eigentumserwerb durch Ersitzung; ~ **proof** voller Beweis, sicherer (unumstößlicher) Beweis; ~ **servitude** positive Dienstbarkeit; ~ **sign**

Pluszeichen; ~ **statement** positive Zeugenaussage; ~ **suggestion** konstruktive Anregung; ~ **turn of mind** positive Lebenseinstellung; ~ **wrong** vorsätzlich begangenes Unrecht.

positivism positive Lebenseinstellung.

posse Möglichkeit, *(detachment)* Schar, Menge, Truppe, *(police)* Polizeiaufgebot;
~ **of twenty police** zwanzigköpfige Polizeieinheit;
to be in ~ möglich sein;
~ **comitatus** *(lat.)* Landsturm.

possess *(v.)* besitzen, im Besitz (Gewahrsam) haben, innehaben, im Bésitz einer Sache sein;
~ **o. s. of a th.** etw. in Besitz nehmen, sich etw. aneignen; ~ **s. o. with an idea** j. mit einer Idee behelligen; ~ **s. o. with indignation** j. mit Unwillen erfüllen; ~ **jointly** gemeinsam besitzen; ~ **a language** Sprache beherrschen; ~ **certain rights** bestimmte Rechte innehaben; ~ **in one's own rights** als Eigentümer besitzen; ~ **one's soul in patience** sich in Geduld fassen (üben); ~ **a great value** sehr wertvoll sein.

possessed im Besitz, *(self-possessed)* selbstsicher;
like all ~ *(US)* wie verrückt, wie besessen;
~ **of fear** von Furcht beherrscht; ~ **of land** im Besitz von Ländereien;
to be ~ **with an idea** von einer Idee besessen sein; **to be** ~ **of a quality** mit einer Eigenschaft ausgestattet sein; **to become** ~ **of** Besitz erlangen.

possession Innehabung, Sachherrschaft, *(thing possessed)* Besitzgegenstand, Besitz[tum], Besitzung, *(self-control)* Selbstbeherrschung;
in ~ **of a passport** im Besitz eines Passes; **in full** ~ **of the facts** bei voller Kenntnis der Tatsachen; **in full** ~ **of his faculties** im Vollbesitz seiner geistigen Kräfte; **with immediate** ~ *(house)* sofort bezugsfähig;
~**s** Güter, Besitzungen, Liegenschaften;
actual ~ tatsächlicher (unmittelbarer) Besitz; **adverse** ~ fehlerhafter Besitz, [Besitz durch] Ersitzung; **apparent** ~ Besitz kraft rechtlicher Vermutung, Besitzvermutung; **civil** ~ fiktiver Besitz; **colonial** ~ Kolonialbesitz; **concurrent** ~ gemeinsamer Besitz; **constructive** ~ mittelbarer Besitz; **continuous** ~ Dauerbesitz; **corporeal** ~ unmittelbarer Besitz, tatsächliche Besitzergreifung; **derivative** ~ Besitz aufgrund eines Besitzmittlungsverhältnisses; **exclusive** ~ ausschließlicher Besitz, Alleinbesitz; **de facto** ~ tatsächlicher Besitz; **faulty** ~ widerrechtlicher Besitz; **foreign** ~**s** auswärtige Besitzungen, *(income tax, Br.)* Vermögensgegenstände im Ausland; **hostile** ~ widerrechtlicher Besitz; **joint** ~ Mitbesitz; **lawful** ~ rechtmäßiger Besitz; **naked** ~ tatsächlicher Besitz [ohne Rechtsanspruch]; **natural** ~ unmittelbare Sachherrschaft; **notorious** ~ offenkundiger Besitz; **open** ~ *(real property)* offene Besitznahme; ~**s overseas** überseeische Besitzungen; **peaceable** ~ ungestörter Besitz; **personal** ~ tatsächlicher (unmittelbarer) Besitz; **my personal** ~ mein persönlicher Besitz; **physical** ~ unmittelbarer Besitz; **proprietary** ~ Eigenbesitz; **quasi** ~ besitzähnliches Verhältnis; **quiet** ~ ungestörtes Besitzrecht; **scrambling** ~ eigenmächtig erworbener Besitz; **self-**~ Selbstbeherrschung, -sicherheit; **vacant** ~ verlassenes Grundstück (Haus), bezugsfertiges Haus; **valued** ~ wertvoller Besitz;
~**s in expectation** zu erwartendes Erbteil; **illegal** ~ **of fire arms** unerlaubter Besitz von Handfeuerwaffen; ~ **of property** Vermögensbesitz; **unlawful** ~ **of an official stamp** unberechtigter Besitz eines behördlichen Stempels; **unauthorized** ~ **of weapons** unerlaubter Waffenbesitz;
to acquire by adverse ~ ersitzen; **to be in** ~ **of s. th.** im Besitz einer Sache sein, Sache besitzen; **to be in adverse** ~ fehlerhaft besitzen; **to be in the full** ~ **of one's senses** voll verantwortlich sein; **to be in** ~ **of a large fortune** großes Vermögen besitzen; **to be in the** ~ **of a family** im Familienbesitz sein; **to be in** ~ **of the House** *(pol.)* in einer Sitzung das Wort haben; **to be in** ~ **of pledges** durch Sicherheiten gedeckt sein; **to be let with immediate** ~ bezugsfertig vermietet werden; **to be restored to** ~ wieder in den Besitz eingesetzt werden; **to come into** ~ **of a fortune** Vermögen erben; **to come into** ~ **of an estate (inheritance)** Besitz (Erbschaft) antreten; **to deliver a** ~ Besitz verlassen (räumen); **to dispute the** ~ **of the ground** Besitzverhältnisse bestreiten; **to enjoy quiet** ~ von ungestörtem Besitz[genuß] sein; **to enter into** ~ **of an estate** Erbschaft antreten; **to gain** ~ **of s. th.** Besitzrecht an einer Sache erwerben; **to get** ~ **of s. th.** sich in den Besitz von etw. setzen; **to have s. th. in one's** ~ etw. in seinem Besitz haben; **to hold** ~ **under colo(u)r of title** Besitzrecht aufgrund behaupteten Rechtstitels ausüben; **to interfere with s. one's** ~ j. im Besitz stören; **to keep papers in one's** ~ Urkunden verwahren; **to maintain** ~ *(tenant)* nicht ausziehen;

to part with ~ Besitz aufgeben; **to pass into the** ~ **of ...** in den Beistz von ... übergehen; **to put s. o. in** ~ **of an inheritance** j. in eine Erbschaft einweisen; **to regain** ~ **of s. th.** wieder in den Besitz einer Sache gelangen; **to remain in** ~ *(Br.)* im Besitz der Mietwohnung bleiben; **to remain in** ~ **of the business** Geschäfte weiterführen dürfen; **to remain in** ~ **of the field** Feld behaupten; **to render up** ~ Besitz zurückgeben; **to restore to** ~ wieder in den Besitz einsetzen; **to resume** ~ Besitz wiedererlangen; **to resume** ~ **of one's domicile** seinen Wohnsitz erneut begründen; **to retain** ~ Besitz ausüben, *(tenant)* nicht ausziehen; **to retain** ~ **of the goods** unmittelbarer Besitzer der Ware bleiben; **to seize actual** ~ unmittelbar Besitz erlangen; **to sell off one's** ~**s** seinen Besitz abstoßen; **to sue for** ~ *(Br.)* auf Räumung klagen; **to surrender** ~ Besitz aufgeben; **to take** ~ **[of]** in Besitz nehmen, Besitz ergreifen; **to take** ~ **of an estate** Besitz (Erbschaft) antreten; **to take** ~ **of a house** in ein Haus einziehen; **to transfer** ~ Besitz verschaffen; **to vest in** ~ in Besitz übergehen;
~ **money** *(Br.)* Verwahrungsgebühr für zwangsvollstreckte Gegenstände; ~ **order** *(Br.)* Räumungsbeschluß; ~ **proceedings** *(Br.)* Räumungsverfahren.

possessive|**nature** einnehmendes Wesen; ~ **right** Besitzrecht.

possessor Besitzer, Inhaber;
actual ~ tatsächlicher (unmittelbarer) Besitzer; **adverse** ~ unberechtigter Besitzer, Ersitzer; **bona-fide** ~ gutgläubiger Besitzer; **legal** ~ rechtmäßiger Besitzer; **mala-fide** ~ bösgläubiger Besitzer; **naked** ~ tatsächlicher Besitzer [ohne Rechtsanspruch]; **proprietory** ~ Eigenbesitzer;
~ **of a driving licence** *(Br.)* Führerscheininhaber;
to be the ~ **of a large fortune** im Besitz eines großen Vermögens sein;
~**'s agent** Besitzdiener.

possessorship Besitz.

possessory besitzrechtlich, besitzend, possessorisch;
~ **action** *(US)* Besitzstörungsklage, possessorische Klage; ~ **claim** Besitzanspruch, -anrecht; ~ **interest** Besitzanspruch; ~ **judgment** besitzbestätigendes Urteil; ~ **lien** Besitzpfandrecht; ~ **lord** Grundherr, -besitzer; ~ **right** Besitzanspruch, -recht; ~ **title** Besitztitel, -recht.

possibilities, unlimited unbegrenzte Möglichkeiten;
~ **of fraud** Betrugsmöglichkeiten;
to allow for all (foresee) ~ alle Möglichkeiten einkalkulieren (Eventualitäten berücksichtigen); **to have** ~ Chancen haben; **to see great** ~ **in a scheme** große Erfolgschancen für einen Plan sehen.

possibility Möglichkeit, Zulässigkeit;
not by any ~ keinesfalls; **within the range of** ~ im Rahmen des Möglichen;
bare (naked, rare) ~ *(interest in real estate)* nur eine Chance; **near (ordinary)** ~ nähere Anwartschaft; **extraordinary (remote)** ~ entfernte Möglichkeit;
~ **of confusion** Verwechslungsmöglichkeit; ~ **to exist** Lebensmöglichkeit, Existenzchance; ~ **coupled with an interest** Anwartschaft; ~ **of severe penalties** Aussicht auf schwere Bestrafung; ~ **on a** ~ entfernte Anwartschaft; **long-term** ~ **of return** *(bookseller)* langfristige Rückgabemöglichkeit; ~ **of reverter** mögliches Heimfallrecht;
to consider the ~ **of an event** möglichen Eintritt eines Ereignisses erwägen; **to rule out a** ~ Möglichkeit ausschließen.

possible|**s** *(US)* Siebensachen;
~ *(a.)* möglich, durchführbar, eventuell, *(coll.)* in Frage kommend, erträglich;
as early as ~ so früh wie möglich; **least** ~ geringstmöglich; ~ **of performance** erfüllbar;
to do one's ~ sein Möglichstes tun; **to make** ~ ermöglichen; **to insure against** ~ **accidents** gegen eventuelle Unfälle versichern; **to give all** ~ **details** alle nur möglichen Einzelheiten mitteilen; ~ **event** Eventualität; **to be the only** ~ **man for a position** als Einziger für eine Stellung in Frage kommen; **to be quite** ~ **people** annehmbare Leute sein; **to be insured against all** ~ **risk** voll versichert sein; ~ **use** Benutzungsmöglichkeit; **to live in the simplest** ~ **way** alltereinfachsten Lebenszuschnitt haben.

possum, to play Krankheit vorschützen.

post Posten, Pfahl, Stange, Ständer, Säule, *(dipl.)* Einsatzort, Auslandsposten, *(employment)* Amt, Stelle, [An]stellung, Posten, *(item)* Rechnungsposten, *(letter box, Br.)* Post-, Briefkasten, *(message)* Botschaft, Nachricht, *(mil.)* Posten[dienst], Wache, Standort, Garnison, Platz, *(mining)* Streckenpfeiler, *(post office, Br.)* Post[amt], *(postal delivery)* Postzustellung, *(postal matters, Br.)* Postsendungen, -sachen, Post, *(stock exchange, US)* Makler-, Börsenstand, *(trading settlement)* Handelsniederlassung;

by ~ per Post; **by return of (earliest)** ~ *(Br.)* mit umgehender Post, postwendend; **by to-day's** ~ mit der heutigen Post; **from pillar to** ~ von Pontius zu Pilatus; **if delivered by** ~ *(Br.)* bei Postbezug;

advanced ~ *(mil.)* vorgeschobener Posten, Vorposten; **air** ~ *(Br.)* Luftpost; **bank** ~ Briefpapier mit Gewicht von 5 1/2 bis 10 Pfund per Ries; **belated** ~ verspätete Nachricht; **book** ~ *(Br.)* Drucksachenpost; **boundary** ~ Grenzpfahl; **confidential** ~ Vertrauensposten; **direction** ~ Wegweiser; **door** ~ Türpfosten; **established** ~ Planstelle; **finger** ~ Wegweiser; **first** ~ *(mil.)* erste Wache; **first-aid** ~ Unfallstation; **general** ~ ortsübliche Postzustellung, *(Br.)* Früh-, Morgenpost; **goal** ~ Zielposten; **half-penny** ~ *(Br.)* Drucksachen; **halfpenny packet** ~ *(Br.)* Päckchenpost; **holiday** ~ Ferienbeschäftigung; **incoming** ~ Posteingang; **judicial** ~ Richteramt; **last** ~ *(mil. Br.)* Zapfenstreich; **lamp** ~ Laternenstange; **late-fee** ~ *(Br.)* letzte Zustellung; **letter** ~ *(Br.)* Briefpost; **mile** ~ Meilenstein; **military** ~ *(Br.)* Feldpost; **morning** ~ *(Br.)* Morgenpost; **newspaper** ~ *(Br.)* Drucksachenpost; **nurse's** ~ Wache einer Krankenschwester; **outgoing** ~ *(Br.)* abgehende Post, Postausgang; **parcel** ~ *(Br.)* Paketpost; **penny** ~ *(Br.)* normales Briefporto; **permanent** ~ Dauerstellung; **pigeon** ~ *(Br.)* Brieftaubenpost; **pneumatic** ~ *(Br.)* Rohrpost; **remunerative** ~ einträglicher Posten; **steering** ~ *(car)* Steuersäule; **today's** ~ *(Br.)* heutige Post; **trading** ~ Handelsniederlassung;

~ **of authority** einflußreiche Stellung; **general** ~ **in the Cabinet** Kabinetts-, Regierungsumbildung; ~ **of commanding importance** ausschlaggebende Stellung; ~ **of confidence (trust)** Vertrauensstellung; **good** ~ **in the Civil Service** gute Beamtenstellung; ~ **of great responsibility** sehr verantwortungsreicher Posten; ~ **of a secretary** Sekretärsposten, *&* **and Telecommunications** *(Br.)* Post- und Fernmeldeministerium; ~ **still unapplied for** ohne Bewerber gebliebene Ausschreibung;

~ *(v.) (appoint to post)* ernennen, abkommandieren, *(enter in a list)* [Namen] in eine Liste eintragen, *(examinee, Br.)* auf die Liste der Durchgefallenen setzen, *(letter, Br.)* aufgeben, zur Post geben, auf der Post aufliefern, mit der Post befördern (senden), *(mil.)* aufstellen, postieren, *(publish)* anschlagen, öffentlich bekanntgeben, *(publish name of ship)* Schiff als verloren erklären, *(transfer to ledger)* [ins Hauptbuch] übertragen, eintragen, [ver]buchen, *(forbid trespassers, US)* [durch Verbotstafeln] vor unbefugtem Zutritt schützen;

~ **no bills!** Zettelankleben verboten; ~ **an airliner as missing** Verlust eines Flugzeugs bekanntgeben; ~ **an announcement on the notice board** Hinweis am Schwarzen Brett anbringen; ~ **bills** Zettel ankleben; ~ **charges to customer's account** Belastungsanzeigen auf einem Kundenkonto verbuchen; ~ **at the counter** *(Br.)* am Schalter aufgeben; ~ **s. o. as a coward** j. als Feigling anprangern; ~ **an entry** Buchung vornehmen; ~ **each entry singly** jeden Posten einzeln verbuchen; ~ **forward** vor-, übertragen, transportieren; ~ **gains** Gewinne verzeichnen; ~ **an item** Posten verbuchen; ~ **a journal into the ledger** Buchung in das Hauptbuch übertragen; ~ **a letter** *(Br.)* Brief einwerfen; ~ **s. o. for nonpayment of his dues** bei jem. die Bezahlung der Mitgliedsbeiträge anmahnen; ~ **in a conspicuous place** an gut sichtbarer Stelle anschlagen; ~ **sentinels** Wachen (Wachposten) aufstellen; ~ **a ship as missing** Schiff als verloren bekanntgeben; ~ **a wall with placards** Wand plakatieren.

post up anschlagen, aushängen, *(bookkeeping)* übertragen, *(keep informed, US)* auf dem laufenden halten;

~ **o. s. up on a matter** sich in einer Frage auf den neuesten Stand bringen; ~ **an account** Konto abschließen; ~ **the books** Bücher à jour bringen; ~ **export sales** Exportumsätze nachbuchen; ~ **an item from the ledger** Posten im Hauptbuch verbuchen; ~ **the ledger** Hauptbuch vollständig nachtragen (nachbuchen); ~ **on a wall** an eine Mauer anschlagen.

post, to advertise a Stelle ausschreiben; **to apply for a** ~ sich um ein Amt (eine Stellung) bewerben; **to be on** ~ *(mil.)* Posten stehen; **to be dismissed from one's** ~ aus dem Dienst entlassen werden; **to be first past the** ~ als Sieger hervorgehen; **to be given a** ~ **as general manager** zum Generaldirektor ernannt werden; **to be shorn of one's** ~ seines Amtes entkleidet werden; **to be on the wrong side of the** ~ *(fam.)* sich völlig verrannt haben; **to deal with one's** ~ *(Br.)* seine Post erledigen; **to dispatch (forward, send) by** ~ *(Br.)* mit der Post senden (schicken); **to fill up a** ~ Stelle besetzen, Amt innehaben; **to go through one's** ~ *(Br.)* seine Post erledigen; **to hold a permanent** ~ in beamteter Stellung sein; **to miss the** ~ *(Br.)* abgehende Post verpassen; **to open one's** ~ *(Br.)* seine Post öffnen; **to remain at one's** ~ auf seinem Posten bleiben; **to reply by return of** ~ *(Br.)* umgehend antworten; **to send by** ~ *(Br.)* mit der Post schicken; **to sound the last** ~ Ehrensalut schießen; **to staff overseas** ~**s** Stabspersonal ausländischer Vertretungen darstellen; **to stay like a** ~ wie angenagelt dastehen; **to take a** ~ Stelle annehmen; **to take** ~ **in the rear** hinter die Front Aufstellung nehmen; **to take a letter to the** ~ *(Br.)* Brief zur Post bringen (geben); **to take up one's** ~ seine Stellung antreten; **to undertake a** ~ Stelle übernehmen;

~**-act** Nachtat; ~ **audit** Rechnungsprüfung; ~ **bag** *(Br.)* Postbeutel; ~ **bill** [Post]begleit-, Ladezettel; ~ **boat** *(Br.)* Postschiff, Post-, Paketdampfer; ~ **check** Kontrolle nach Erscheinen, nachträgliche Analyse; ~ **coach** Postkutsche; ~**-commitment hearing** *(US)* Verfahren nach Einweisung in eine Heilanstalt; ~**-date** *(v.)* nachdatieren; ~**-dated check** nachdatierter Scheck; ~ **day** *(Br.)* Posttag, *(London exchange)* Treffen der Händler ausländischer Wechsel; **general** ~ **delivery** ~ *(Br.)* erste Zustellung; ~ **directory** *(Br.)* Postadreßbuch; ~ **dispatcher** Expedient; ~ **distributing office** Postverteilungsstelle; ~ **doctoral fellow** *(US)* Akademiker; ~**-doctoral standard** *(US)* mit Doktorabschluß; ~ **endorsement** Nachindossament; ~**-entry** Nachtragsbuchung, *(duty)* Nachverzollung; *&* **Exchange** *(US)* Soldatenkaufhaus, Marketenderei; ~**-free** *(Br.)* portofrei; ~ **graduate** *(US)* Doktorand; ~ **hole** Pfostenloch; ~ **horn** Posthorn; ~ **horse** Postpferd; ~ **hours** *(Br.)* Schalterstunden; ~ **interview recall test** Erinnerungstest nach einer Werbeaktion; ~ **line** Postbootroute; ~ **meridiem** *(p. m.)* nachmittags; ~**-mortem** Leichenschau, Totenuntersuchung, Obduktion, *(fig.)* Manöverkritik; **to hold a** ~ **mortem** Leichenschau abhalten; ~**-mortem costs** nachkalkulierte Kosten; ~**-mortem examination** Autopsie; ~ **notes** Bankanleihe; ~**-nuptial** nachehelich; ~**-nuptial settlement** Ehevertrag nach der Eheschließung; ~ **obit bond** *(Br.)* beim Tode eines Dritten fällig werdender Schuldschein.

post office Post[amt], Poststelle, *(administration, Br.)* Postverwaltung;

branch ~ Zweigpostamt; **distributing** ~ Verteiler[post]amt; **district** ~ Bezirkspostamt; **general** ~ Hauptpostamt; **General** *&* *(Br.)* Oberpostdirektion; **head** ~ Hauptpostamt; **issuing** ~ Ausstellungspostamt; **paying** ~ Auszahlungspostamt; **railway** ~ Bahnpostamt; **separating** ~ Verteiler[post]amt; **special** ~ Sonderpostamt; **sub** ~ *(Br.)* Postnebenstelle; **travelling** ~ *(T.P.O.)* Bahnpost[amt];

to be paid in cash at ~**s** bar von der Post ausgezahlt werden; **to go to the** ~ zur Post (zum Postamt) gehen; **to keep one's savings in the** ~ Postspparguthaben besitzen;

~ *(a.)* postalisch; *&* **Act** *(Br.)* Gesetz über das Postwesen, Postgesetz; ~ **address** *(US)* Postanschrift, Zustellungsadresse; ~ **advance** Postlaufakkreditiv, Postvorschuß; ~ **assistant** Postgehilfe; ~ **box** Briefabholfach, Post[schließ]fach; ~ **building** Postgebäude; ~ **car** Postwagen, -auto; ~ **clerk** Postbeamter; ~ **counter** Postschalter; ~ **Department** *(US)* Postministerium; ~ **directory** Postadressbuch; *&* **Giro** Postscheckwesen; ~ **giro system** Postscheckverkehr; *&* **Guide** *(Br.)* Posthandbuch, Postgebührenheft; ~ **hours** Schalterstunden; ~ **list** Postversandliste; ~ **money order** *(US)* Zahlungs-, Postanweisung; ~**'s monopoly** Monopolstellung der Post; ~ **national giro** *(Br.)* Postscheckverkehr; ~ **newspaper-charge regulations** Postzeitungsgebührenordnung; ~ **newspaper list** Postzeitungsliste; ~ **official** Postbeamter; ~ **order** *(Br.)* Zahlungs-, Postanweisung, Gebührenüberweisung durch die Post; ~ **pension fund** Pensionskasse der Post; ~ **philatelic bureau** *(Br.)* Postversandstelle für Sammlermarken; ~ **receipt** Post[einlieferungs]schein, -quittung, Einschreibequittung; ~ **reform** Reform des Postwesens; ~ **register** *(Br., till 1969)* Verzeichnis der durch die Post beziehbaren kapitalerwerbsteuerfreien Papiere; ~ **regulation** *(Br.)* Postordnung.

post office savings bank *(Br.)* Postsparkasse;

~ **account** Postsparkonto; *&* **Act** *(Br.)* Postsparkassengesetz; ~ **business** Postsparkassengeschäft; ~ **fund** *(Br.)* Postsparkassenvermögen; ~ **interest** *(Br.)* Zinsen von einem Postsparkassenbuch; *&* **Regulations** *(Br.)* Bestimmungen über das Postspar[kassen]wesen.

post office savings | book *(Br.)* Postsparbuch; ~ **deposits** *(Br.)* Postspareinlagen; ~ **service** *(Br.)* Postsparkassenverkehr.

post office | servant *(Br.)* Postangestellter; ~ **sorter** Postsortierer; ~ **user** Postkunde; ~ **worker** Postangestellter.

post | official Postbeamter; ~**-prandial** nach dem Essen; ~**-primary education** höheres Schulwesen; ~ **remittance** *(Br.)* Postüberweisung; **bank** ~ **remittance** *(Br.)* Postüberweisung im Bankauftrage; ~ **road** Poststraße; ~ **route** Postroute; ~**-scoring** *(film)* spätere Synchronisation; ~**-season** Nachsaison; ~ **town** Paketverteilungsstelle.

postage Porto[gebühr], Briefporto, Portospesen;
~ **free, free of** ~ freigemacht, portofrei, franko; ~ **included** einschließlich Porto; **liable (subject) to** ~ portopflichtig; ~ **paid** portofrei, postfrei, freigemacht, franko; ~ **unpaid** unfrankiert, nicht freigemacht;
additional ~ Portozuschlag, Nachgebühr; **book** ~ Drucksachenporto; ~ **due** Strafporto, Nachgebühr; **excess** ~ Nachgebühr, Strafporto; **extra** ~ Portozuschlag, Straf-, Nachporto; **inland** ~ Inlandsporto; **ordinary** ~ einfaches Porto; **overseas** ~ *(Br.)* Auslandsporto; **return** ~ Rück[sende]porto; **return** ~ **guaranteed** Rücksendeporto trägt der Empfänger; **statement** ~ Porto für Kontoauszüge; **underpaid** ~ ungenügende Freimachung, nicht genügend frankiert;
~ **to be collected** unter Portonachnahme; ~ **refunded by way of free copies** *(book trade)* Portoersatz durch Freiexemplare; ~ **by weight** Gewichtsporto;
~ **will be paid by licensee** Gebühr zahlt Empfänger;
to be exempt from ~ Portofreiheit genießen; **to charge the** ~ **to the customer** dem Kunden Portogebühren in Rechnung stellen; **to pay the** ~ Brief freimachen (frankieren); **to reimburse for** ~ **incurred** Portoauslagen vergüten;
~ **account** Portorechnung; ~ **book** Porto[kassen]buch; ~ **charges** *(US)* Portokosten; **special handling** ~ **charge** *(US)* Eilzustellgebühr; ~ **compensation** Portoerstattung, -ausgleich; ~ **cost** Portounkosten; **to refund the** ~ **cost** Portospesen zurückvergüten; ~**-due stamp** *(philately)* Nachportomarke; ~ **envelope** *(US)* Freiumschlag; ~ **expenses** Portoauslagen, -spesen; ~ **meter [machine]** *(US)* Frankiermaschine, Freistempler; ~ **rates** *(Br.)* Portogebühren, Postgebühren, -tarif; **overseas** ~ **rates** *(Br.)* Auslandsporto; ~ **and postal revenue** Portoeinnahmen; ~ **stamp** Briefmarke, Postwertzeichen; ~ **stamp rates** Portogebühren.

postal *(fam., US)* Postkarte;
~ *(a.)* postalisch;
~ **address** Postanschrift; ~ **advertising reply** *(Br.)* Werbeantwort; ~ **agency** Postagentur; ~ **arrangements** postalische Einrichtungen; ~ **authorities** Postbehörde, -verwaltung; ~ **ballot** Briefwahl; ~ **building** Postamt, -gebäude; ~ **business** Postverkehr; ~ **car** *(US)* Bahnpostwagen, Postwaggon; ~ **card** *(US)* Postkarte; ~ **cash order** Postnachnahme; ~ **censorship** Brief-, Postzensur; ~ **charges** Postgebühren; ~ **check** *(US)* **(cheque,** *Br.)* Postscheck; **to cash a** ~ **cheque** *(Br.)* Postscheck einlösen; **to draw a** ~ **cheque** *(Br.)* Postscheck ausstellen; ~ **check account** *(US)* Postscheckkonto; ~ **cheque account** *(Br.)* Postscheckkonto, -guthaben; ~ **cheque system** *(Br.)* Postschecksystem; ~ **clerk** Postangestellter, -beamter, *(US)* Bahnpostangestellter; ~ **code** *(Br.)* Postleitzahl; ~ **code system** *(Br.)* Postleitzahlwesen; ~ **collection** Briefkastenleerung, Geldeinziehung durch die Post; ~ **collection order** *(US)* Einziehungs-, Postauftrag; ~ **communication** Postverkehr, -verbindung; ~ **convention** Postabkommen, -konvention; ~ **currency** Briefmarkenwährung; ~ **deficit** Defizit der Post; ~ **delay** verspätete Zustellung; ~ **delivery** Postzustellung, -beförderung, -bezug, Bestellung; ~ **delivery van** Postauto; ~ **delivery zone** *(US)* Postzustellbezirk; ~ **directory** [Post]adreßbuch; ~ **district** postalischer Bezirk, Zustellbezirk; ~ **district number** Nummer des Postzustellbezirks; ~ **employee** Postbeamter, -angestellter; ~ **establishment** Postanstalt; ~ **expenses** Portokosten, -spesen; ~ **fees** Postgebühren; ~ **giro** *(Br.)* Postscheck; ~ **giro office** *(Br.)* Postscheckamt; ~ **giro system** *(Br.)* Postscheckwesen, -dienst, -verkehr; ~ **guide** Posthandbuch; ~ **increase** Erhöhung der Postgebühren, Portoanstieg; ~ **information** Auskunft in Postangelegenheiten; ~ **inspector** Postinspektor; ~ **items** Postsachen; ~ **lot** Postgewicht; ~ **manual** Posthandbuch; ~ **matter** Brief- und Paketpost; ~ **matters** Postsachen, -wesen; ~ **money order** *(US)* Postanweisung; ~ **newspaper material** Postzeitungsgut; ~**newspaper service** *(US)* Postzeitungsordnung; ~ **note** *(Canada, US)* Zahlungs-, Postanweisung; ~ **number** Postleitzahl; ~ **official** Postbeamter; ~ **order** *(Br.)* Postanweisung [für kleinere Beträge], Geldüberweisung durch die Post; ~ **packet** *(Br.)* Postpaket, -sendung; ~ **plant** Postbetrieb; ~ **principle** *(US)* Postprivileg; ~ **rates** Post-, Portogebühren, Posttarif; ~ **rates within Britain** Inlandsporto; ~ **receipt** Posteinlieferungsschein, -abschnitt, -quittung; ~ **reform** Postreform, ⍻ **Reform Act** *(US)* Postreformgesetz; ~ **regulations** postalische Bestimmungen, Postordnung; ~ **room** Postabfertigungsstelle.

postal savings Ersparnisse auf dem Postsparkassenbuch, Postsparguthaben;
~ **account** *(US)* Postspar[kassen]konto, -guthaben; ~ **bank** *(US)* Postsparkasse; ~ **bond** *(US)* Postsparkassenschuldverschreibung; ~ **book** *(US)* Postsparkassenbuch; ~ **certificate** *(US)* Postsparkarte, Postsparkassenquittung, Postscheckguthabenbescheinigung; ~ **deposit** *(US)* Postspareinlage; ~ **depository** *(US)* Postsparkasse; ~ **fund** *(US)* Vermögen der Postsparkasse, Postsparkassenvermögen; ~ **office** *(US)* Postsparkasse; ~ **service** Postsparkassendienst, -verkehr; ~ **stamp** *(US)* Postsparmarke; ~ **system** *(US)* Postsparkassenwesen.

postal│section Postdezernat; ~ **sector** Postbezirk; ~ **service** Postverkehr, -dienst, -zustellung; **army** ~ **service** Feldpostdienst; **technical** ~ **service** Postbetriebsdienst; **US** ⍻ **Service** amerikanische Bundespost; **to improve the** ~ **services** postalische Einrichtungen (Dienstleistungen der Post) verbessern; **to suspend** ~ **services** Postverkehr einstellen; **to use the inland** ~ **service** sich der postalischen Einrichtungen (Dienstleistungen der Post) bedienen; ~ **situation** postalische Verhältnisse; ~ **staff** Postangestellte, *(company)* Versandpersonal; ~ **cancellation stamp** Postentwertungsstempel; ~ **station** *(US)* Postnebenstelle; ~ **strike** Postarbeiterstreik; ~ **subscription rate** Postbezugspreis; ~ **system** Postwesen; ~ **tariff** *(US)* Postgebühren, -tarif; ~ **survey** postalische Umfrage, Umfrage auf dem Postwege; ~ **system** Postwesen; ~ **trade** Postversandwesen, -geschäft; ~ **trade union** Postarbeitergewerkschaft; ~ **traffic** Postverkehr; ~ **transfer** Postscheküberweisung; ~ **transport** Beförderung durch die Post, Postbeförderung; ~ **transport contractor** Postunternehmer; ~ **tube** Versandrolle; ~ **union** Postarbeitergewerkschaft; **Universal** ⍻ **Union** Weltpostverein; **self-service** ~ **unit** betriebseigenes Postamt; ~ **user** Postbenutzer; ~ **weight** Postgewicht; ~ **worker** Postangestellter, -arbeiter; ~ **wrapper** Streif-, Kreuzband; ~ **wrapping** Paketverpackung; ~ **zone number** Postleitzahl; ~ **zoning system** Postleitzahlsystem.

postalization Gebührenvereinheitlichung.

postbox Briefkasten.

postboy Briefträger, -bote.

postcard *(Br.)* Postkarte, *(US)* Postkarte ohne Marke;
foreign ~ Welt-, Auslandspostkarte; **picture** ~ Ansichts[post]karte; **plain** ~ *(Br.)* gewöhnliche Postkarte; **ready-printed** ~ *(Br.)* vorgedruckte Postkarte; **reply-paid** ~ *(Br.)* Postkarte mit Rückantwort;
~ **automatic supply** *(Br.)* Postkartenautomat; ~ **order form** vorgedruckte Auftragspostkarte.

postcheque *(Br.)* Postscheck.

postclosing balance sheet berichtigte Bilanz.

postcode *(Br.)* Postleitzahl;
~ **system** *(Br.)* Postleitzahlsystem.

postdate späteres Datum;
~ *(v.)* später datieren, nachdatieren.

poste restante *(Br.)* Abteilung für postlagernde Sendungen, Postaufbewahrungsstelle;
~ *(a.)* postlagernd.

posted gebucht, *(well-informed)* unterrichtet;
well ~ gut unterrichtet;
to be ~ *(examinee, Br.)* nicht bestanden haben, durchgefallen sein; **to be** ~ **home** nach Hause versetzt werden; **to be** ~ **as missing** *(ship)* als vermißt gemeldet werden; **to be** ~ **to a unit** zu einer Einheit versetzt werden; **to be** ~ **up in recent affairs** immer über alle Neuigkeiten im Bilde sein; **to keep s. o.** ~ **[on]** jem. auf dem laufenden halten;
best- ~ **correspondent** *(US)* bestinformierter Journalist; ~ **price** Listenpreis; ~ **property** *(US)* Besitz mit verbotenem Zugang; ~ **rate** *(US)* Briefkurs für ausländische Valuta; ~ **waters** Privatgewässer.

postentry *(bookkeeping)* nachträgliche [Ver]buchung, nachträglicher Eintrag, *(customs)* Nachdeklaration, -verzollung;
to pass a ~ *(customs)* Nachverzollung durchführen.

poster [Laden]plakat, Anschlagzettel, *(courier)* Kurier, Eilbote;
advertising ~ Reklameplakat; **bill** ~ Zettelankleber; **floor-to-ceiling** ~ stockwerkgroßes Plakat; **glaring** ~ grellfarbiges Plakat; **permanent** ~ Dauerplakat; **picture** ~ farbiges Plakat; **screaming** ~ grellfarbiges Plakat; **time** ~ Aushängefahrplan; **torn** ~ beschädigtes Plakat;
~ **advertising** Bogenanschlag-, Plakatwerbung; ~ **artist** Plakatgestalter; ~ **boarding** *(Br.)* Anschlagtafel; ~ **colo(u)r** Plakatfarbe; ~ **design** Plakatentwurf; ~ **display** Plakatwerbung; ~ **hoarding** Anschlagtafel, -zaun; ~ **panel** Plakat-, Anschlagtafel, Werbefläche; ~ **pillar** Anschlag-, Litfaßsäule; ~ **plant** Bogenanschlagsunternehmen; ~ **showing** *(advertising)* Anschlagstellenblock; ~ **site** Anschlagstelle, -tafel, -säule.

posterity Nachwelt, Nachkommenschaft;
to leave a large ~ zahlreiche Nachkommen haben.

postfactum nachträgliche Handlung.

postgraduate Promovierter, Jungakademiker;
~ *(a.)* nach beendigter Studienzeit;
~ **course** Doktorandenstudium; ~ **course in economics** Volkswirtschaftskursus für Jungakademiker; ~ **fellowship** Doktorandenstipendium; ~ **work** wissenschaftliche Arbeiten nach der Promovierung.
posthaste in großer Eile, schnellstens.
posthumous *(literary work)* nachgelassen, nach dem Tode des Verfassers veröffentlicht;
~ **child** nach dem Tode des Vaters geborenes Kind; ~ **work** nachgelassenes Werk.
posthouse Poststation.
posting *(advertisement)* Anschlag[werbung], Plakatierung, *(bookkeeping)* Übertragung in das Hauptbuch, *(dipl.)* Auslandsposten, *(entering)* Eintragung, [Ver]buchen, Verbuchung, *(letter, Br.)* Aufgabe bei der Post, Posteinlieferung, -aufgabe, Auflieferung, Absendung, *(mil.)* Abkommandierung, Ernennung;
fly ~ wilder Anschlag; **free** ~ Gratisplakat; **ledger** ~s Übertragung ins Hauptbuch, Hauptbucheintragung; **machine** ~ maschinelle Buchung; **parallel** ~ Parallel-, Übertragungsbuchung;
~ **of items** *(Br.)* Einlieferung von Postsendungen;
~ **bill** Anschlagzettel, Plakat; ~ **machine** Buchungsmaschine; ~ **medium** Buchungsunterlage; ~ **operation** Buchungsverfahren, -vorgang; ~ **period** Kontoübertragungszeitraum; ~ **reference** Parellelbuchungsbeleg, Übertragungshinweis; ~ **time** postalische Abfertigungszeiten; ~ **time advice leaflet** Broschüre über postalische Abfertigungszeiten.
postman *(Br.)* Briefträger, Brief-, Postbote;
rural ~ Landzusteller;
~ **of the walk** Revierbriefträger.
postmark Datum-, Tages-, Entwertungs-, Poststempel;
~ *(v.)* Post abstempeln;
~ **cancellation** Postentwertungsstempel.
postmarked the 20th mit dem Poststempel vom 20. versehen.
postmarking stamp Entwertungsstempel.
postmaster Postamtsvorsteher, Posthalter;
⌂ General *(US)* Postminister; **⌂ Generalship** *(US)* Postministerium.
postmastership Postmeisterstelle.
postpaid portofrei, Porto bezahlt, frankiert;
to send ~ frankieren, freimachen.
postponable aufschiebbar.
postpone *(v.)* auf-, verschieben, zurückstellen, anstehen lassen, vertagen, *(mortgage)* Rangrücktritt gewähren;
~ **an answer to a request** Beantwortung eines Gesuchs zurückstellen; ~ **a burial** Begräbnis verschieben; ~ **a charge** mit einer Belastung im Range rücken; ~ **consideration of a subject** Sacherörterung zurückstellen; ~ **a date** Termin verlegen; ~ **a hearing** Verhandlung vertagen; ~ **a journey** Reise aufschieben; ~ **a matter for a week** Sache für eine Woche zurückstellen; ~ **a meeting** Versammlung vertagen; ~ **payment of an amount** Überweisung eines Geldbetrages verzögern.
postponed | case vertagte Verhandlung; ~ **trial** aufgeschobenes Verfahren.
postponement Aufschub, Verschiebung, Zurückstellung, Befristung, Stundung, Vertagung;
~ **of charge** Rangrücktritt einer Belastung; ~ **of expense** verzögerte Aufwandsregelung; ~ **of national service** *(Br.)* Zurückstellung vom Wehrdienst; ~ **of payment** Hinausschieben von Zahlungen, Moratorium; ~ **of priority** Rangrücktritt; ~ **of trial** Vertagung (Verlegung) der Verhandlung.
postprandial speech Rede nach Tisch.
postscript *(P. S.)* Nachschrift, -trag;
by way of a ~ als Nachtrag.
postulant Antragsteller.
postulate | (v.) to be free seine Freiheit fordern; ~ **one's wishes** seine Wünsche formulieren.
postulation Forderung, Postulat.
posture Haltung, *(fig.)* theatralische Positur, *(situation)* Lage, Situation;
in the present ~ **of public affairs** bei dem augenblicklichen Stand der öffentlichen Angelegenheiten; **in a sitting** ~ in sitzender Stellung;
~ *(v.)* sich in Positur setzen;
to assume an easy ~ legere Haltung annehmen;
~ **chair** Schreibmaschinenstuhl mit Rückenstütze; ~ **statement** Absichtserklärung.
postwar Nachkriegs....;
~ **boom** Nachkriegskonjunktur; ~ **capitalism** Nachkriegskapi-

talismus; ~ **conference** Nachkriegskonferenz; ~ **credit** *(Br.)* Zwangsanleihe; ~ **demands** Nachkriegsbedürfnisse; ~ **development** Nachkriegsentwicklung; ~ **economic aid** nach dem Krieg gewährte Wirtschaftshilfe; ~ **economic recovery** wirtschaftliche Wiederbelebung der Nachkriegszeit; ~ **economy** Nachkriegswirtschaft; ~ **epoch** Nachkriegsepoche; ~ **era** Nachkriegszeit; ~ **issue** Nachkriegsaufgabe; ~ **job** Nachkriegsstellung; ~ **landscape** Nachkriegslandschaft; ~ **peak** Nachkriegshöchststand; ~ **period** Nachkriegszeit; ~ **planning** Nachkriegsplanung; ~ **potentialities** Nachkriegsmöglichkeiten; ~ **recession** Rezession der Nachkriegswirtschaft; ~ **rehabilitation** Wiederaufbau in der Nachkriegszeit; ~ **transitorial period** Übergangswirtschaft der Nachkriegszeit.
pot Topf, Kanne, *(Br.)* stimulierende Droge, *(Br., sl.)* favorisiertes Rennpferd, *(railroad, sl.)* Lokomotive;
big ~ *(fam.)* großes Tier, bedeutende Persönlichkeit; **coffee** ~ Kaffeekanne; **flower** ~ Blumentopf; **jam** ~ Marmeladentopf;
big ~ **in the business world** Wirtschaftsboss; ~s **of money** Haufen (viel) Geld, Heidengeld;
to cost a ~ **of money** schweres Geld kosten; **to drop a** ~ **of money** einen Haufen Geld verlieren; **to go to** ~ *(sl.)* vor die Hunde gehen, *(fam.)* in die Brüche gehen, *(country)* abwirtschaften; **to have** ~s **of money** Geld wie Mist (Heu) haben, enorm reich (ein Krösus) sein; **to keep the** ~ **boiling** Sache in Gang halten, *(livelihood)* sein Leben fristen; **to make a** ~ **of money** Haufen Geld verdienen, Großverdiener sein; **to make** ~s **and pans of one's property** sein Geld verjubeln (Vermögen durchbringen);
~ **companion** Zechkumpane; **to take** ~-**luck with s. o.** mit jds. Essen vorlieb nehmen; ~-**shot** niederträchtiger Angriff; **to take a** ~-**shot at s. o.** j. in gemeiner Weise attackieren; ~ **test** *(sl.)* unerwartetes Examen; ~-**valo(u)r** angetrunkener Mut; ~-**walloper** *(sl.)* Tellerwäscher.
potato Kartoffel;
quite the ~ *(sl.)* genau das Richtige;
not to be quite the ~ nicht gerade das Richtige sein; **to drop s. th. like a hot** ~ etw. wie eine heiße Kartoffel fallen lassen; **to think o. s. no small** ~ sehr von sich eingenommen sein;
~ **trap** *(sl.)* große Klappe.
potboiler aus reinem Erwerbssinn veröffentlichtes Buch, *(fig.)* reine Erwerbsquelle.
potboy Bierkellner.
potent stark, mächtig;
to be judged most ~ für am wirkungsvollsten gehalten werden.
potentate Machthaber, Herrscher.
potential Potential, Möglichkeit, Kapazität, Hilfsquellen;
economic ~ Wirtschaftspotential; **military** ~ militärisches Potential; **war-making** ~ Kriegspotential; **working** ~ Arbeitskräftepotential, -reserven;
~ **for growth** Wachstumsmöglichkeit;
to prove one's ~ seine Leistungsfähigkeit unter Beweis stellen;
~ *(a.)* denkbar, möglich, potentiell;
~ **buyer** Kaufinteressent, potentieller Käufer; ~ **customer** möglicher (voraussichtlicher) Kunde; ~ **demand** potentieller Bedarf; ~ **earnings** geschätzte Verdienstmöglichkeiten; ~ **market** potentieller Markt, Absatzmöglichkeiten, -chance, mengenmäßiger Absatzspielraum; **to be a** ~ **murderer** fähig sein, einen Mord zu begehen; ~ **output** potentieller Ausstoß einer Volkswirtschaft; ~ **resources** latente Hilfsquellen; ~ **sales** Umsatz-, Absatzchancen; ~ **stock** Emissionsreserve.
potestative condition Postestativbedingung.
pothead *(el.)* Kabelendverschluß.
pothole Schlagloch;
~ *(v.) (Br., coll.)* Höhlen erforschen;
to be strewn with ~s mit Schlaglöchern übersät sein.
potholer *(Br.)* Höhlenforscher.
pothouse Schenke, Kneipe, Wirtshaus;
~ **manners** Benehmen wie in der Kneipe.
potter Töpfer;
~ *(v.)* herumlungern, -pfuschen;
~ **about in the garden** im Garten herumwerkeln; ~ **away one's time** seine Zeit vertrödeln.
pottery Steingut, Keramik, Töpferwaren;
~ **industry** keramische Industrie.
potty *(sl.)* närrisch, *(coll.)* kinderleicht;
to be ~ **about s. o.** ganz verrückt nach jem. sein;
~ **little jobs** unbedeutende Beschäftigungen.
pouch Beutel, Sack, Tasche, *(postman)* Postbeutel, *(Br., sl.)* Geldgeschenk;
diplomatic ~ Kuriergepäck, -post; **tobacco** ~ Tabakbeutel;
~ *(v.)* sich aneignen, in die Tasche stecken, *(coll.)* Trinkgeld geben.

poultry Geflügel;
~ **culture (raising)** Geflügelzucht; ~ **farm** Geflügelfarm; ~
husbandry Geflügelwirtschaft, -zucht; ~ **keeper** Geflügelhal-
ter; ~ **keeping** Geflügelhaltung; ~ **shop** Geflügelladen; ~ **show**
Geflügelausstellung.
poultryman Geflügelzüchter.
pounce Satz, Sprung;
~ *(v.)* **into a room** ins Zimmer stürzen;
~ **paper** Pauspapier.
pound Stoß, Schlag, *(Br.)* Pfund Sterling, *(for cattle)* Pferch,
Pfandstall, *(dungeon)* Gefängnis, Kerker, *(hopeless situation)*
Falle, Klemme, ausweglose Situation, *(weight)* Pfund;
by the ~ pfundweise;
car ~ Wagenpark; **forward** ~ Terminpfund; **overt** ~ nicht
eingefriedetes Grundstück;
~ *(v.)* zertrümmern, zermalmen, *(impound)* pfänden, *(plod)*
schuften, schwer arbeiten, *(ship)* stampfen;
~ **the asphalt** *(US fam.)* Plaster treten; ~ **the books** *(sl.)* eifrig
studieren; ~ **on a door** an eine Tür hämmern; ~ **the ear** *(US sl.)*
sich aufs Ohr gelegt haben; ~ **out a letter on the typewriter** Brief
auf der Schreibmaschine herunterhauen; ~ **the permanent** *(sl.)*
alle Straßen nach einer Beschäftigung abklappern; ~ **along a**
road Straße herunterlaufen; ~ **on the rocks** *(ship)* an den Felsen
zerschellen; ~ **sense into s. o.** jem. Vernunft beibringen;
to pay ten shillings in the ~ Konkurs anmelden; **to pay twenty**
shillings in the ~ seine Schulden auf Heller und Pfennig bezahlen; **to have one's** ~ **of flesh** unbarmherzig auf seiner Forderung
bestehen;
~ **breach** Arrest-, Pfandbruch; ~ **lock** *(river)* Wehr; ~ **net**
Fischnetz; ~ **note** Pfundnote; ~ **strengthening** Pfunderholung.
poundage nach dem Gewicht erhobener Zoll, *(fig.)* Zentnerlast,
(postal order, Br.) Gebühr, *(paid as wages)* Tantieme, *(stray*
cattle) Einlösegebühr;
sheriff's ~ *(Br.)* Zwangsvollstreckungsgebühren.
pounding *(mil.)* Beschuß, *(ship)* Stampfen;
to take a ~ unter schwerem Beschuß stehen.
pour | in *(v.)* hereinströmen, in großen Mengen eingehen;
~ **on the coal** *(sl.)* aufs Gas treten; ~ **cold water on s. one's ideas**
auf jds. Begeisterung abkühlend wirken, skeptisch auf jds.
Ideen reagieren; ~ **comfort into s. one's heart** jds. Herzem Trost
spenden; ~ **down** *(rain)* in Strömen fallen, stark regnen, schütten; ~ **down blessings on s. o.** j. mit Glücksgütern überschütten;
~ **oil on troubled water** Streit schlichten, die Gemüter beruhigen; ~ **it on** *(sl.)* sich völlig konzentrieren; ~ **into a town** in eine
Stadt strömen, eine Stadt überfluten.
pour out *(v.)* | **one's indignation on s. o.** seiner Verachtung jem.
gegenüber Laut geben; ~ **tale of misfortune** seine Unglücks-
schichte herausprudeln; ~ **one's thanks** seiner Dankbarkeit
voller Beschämung Ausdruck verleihen; ~ **of the theatre** aus
dem Theater strömen; ~ **threats** Drohungen ausstoßen; ~ **a**
torrent of abuse Strom von Flüchen vom Stapel lassen; ~ **one's**
troubles seinem Herzen Luft machen.
pour *(v.)* | **one's sorrows into s. one's heart** *(fam.)* seine Sorgen bei
jem. abladen; ~ **itself into the sea** sich ins Meer ergießen;
it never rains but it ~**s** ein Unglück kommt selten allein.
pourboire Trinkgeld.
pouring rain Platzregen.
poverty Armut, Bedürftigkeit, Mangel, Not, Besitz-, Mittellosigkeit;
abject ~ äußerste Armut;
~ **of blood** Blutarmut; ~ **of ideas** Ideenarmut; ~ **of invention**
(patent) mangelnde Erfindungshöhe; ~ **of soil** Unergiebigkeit
des Bodens, Bodenarmut; ~ **in vitamins** Vitaminmangel;
to be reduced to ~ verarmt sein; **to die in abject** ~ völlig verarmt
sterben; **to fall into** ~ in Armut geraten; **to live in** ~ in ärmlichen
Verhältnissen leben, Mangel leiden;
~ **affidavit** *(US)* Mittellosigkeitseid; ~ **area** Armutsgebiet; ~
law Armenrecht; ⌾ **Law Centre** *(US)* Armenrechtsberatungs-
stelle; ~ **level** Bedürftigkeitsgrad; **below** ~ **level** unter dem
Existenzminimum; **to be (live) below the** ~ **line** Mindestein-
kommensgrenze (Existenzminimum) unterschreiten; ~ **relief**
Wohlfahrtsunterstützung, Sozialhilfe; ~ **specialist** Armen-
rechtsspezialist; ~**-striken home** armselige Behausung; ~ **trap**
Lähmung der Arbeitsbereitschaft durch Fürsorgeleistungen.
powder Pulver, Staub;
black (miner's) ~ Sprengpulver; **face** ~ Gesichtspuder;
not to be worth ~ **and shot** *(coll.)* keinen Schuß Pulver Wert
sein; **to keep one's** ~ **dry** auf der Hut sein; **to take a** ~ *(sl.)*
Zechprellerei begehen;
~ **bag** Puderbeutel; ~ **box** Puderdose; ~ **magazine** *(mil.)* Pulver-
magazin; ~ **room** *(US)* Damentoilette.

powdery snow Pulverschnee.
power *(ability to act)* Macht, *(authority)* Vollmacht, Berechtigung, Befugnis, Ermächtigung, *(capacity)* Vermögen, Fähigkeit, *(capacity of engine)* Leistung, *(competency)* Zurechnungsfähigkeit, *(drive)* Antriebskraft, Motor, *(energy)* Kraft,
Energie, *(electric power)* [Kraft]strom, *(mathematics)* Potenz,
(mental strength) Gewalt, Herrschaft, *(state)* Land Staat,
Regierung, Macht;
as far as it lies in my ~ soweit es in meiner Macht liegt; **by virtue**
of ~ **of attorney** laut Vollmacht; **in** ~ *(in office)* im Amt [befind-
lich], *(political party)* an der Macht; **outside the** ~**s** *(corporation)* außerhalb des ordnungsgemäßen Geschäftsbereichs; **to**
the utmost of my ~ mit allen meinen Kräften; **within s. one's** ~**s**
im Rahmen seiner Vertretungsvollmacht;
~**s** Machtbefugnisse;
absolute ~ unumschränkte Macht; **administrative** ~ ausübende
Gewalt, Exekutive; **antiinflationary** ~**s** antiinflationistische
Vollmachten; **appendant (appurtenant)** ~ mit einem Grundbesitz gekoppelte Verfügungsmacht; **attractive** ~ Anziehungskraft; **bargaining** ~ *(trade union)* Tarifabschlußvollmacht;
belligerent ~ kriegsführende Macht; **bond** ~ Vollmacht zur
Übertragung von Schuldverschreibungen; **borrowing** ~ *(director)* Kreditaufnahmebefugnis; **brain** ~ Verstandskräfte; **buying**
~ Kaufkraft; **collateral** ~ einfache Vollmacht; **collecting** ~
Inkassovollmacht; **collective** ~ Gesamtvollmacht; **competitive**
~ Konkurrenzfähigkeit; **constituent** ~ verfassungsgebende
Gewalt; **Continental (European)** ⌾**s** Kontinentalmächte; **contracting** ~**s** vertragsschließende Mächte; **contractual** ~ Vertragsfähigkeit; **corporate** ~**s** *(US)* satzungsmäßige Gesellschaftsbefugnisse; **delegated** ~ Ermächtigung; **delivery** ~
Lieferfähigkeit; **derived** ~**s** abgeleitete Vollmachten; **detaining**
~ Gewahrsamsmacht; **disciplinary** ~ Disziplinarbefugnis; **discretionary** ~ Ermessensbefugnis, *(judge)* richterliche Machtvollkommenheit; **disposing** ~ Verfügungsgewalt, -befugnis;
earning ~ Ertragsfähigkeit; **economic** ~ wirtschaftliche Machtstellung, Wirtschaftspotential, -macht; **electric** ~ elektrischer
Strom; **emergency** ~**s** Ermächtigung zur Anwendung außerordentlicher Maßnahmen, Notverordnungsbefugnis; **enumer-
ated** ~**s** *(US)* gesetzlich festgelegte Machtbefugnisse; **executive**
~ vollziehende Gewalt, Exekutive; **exclusive** ~ *(estate)* ausschließliches Verfügungsrecht; **express** ~ ausdrücklich erteilte
Vollmacht; **extended** ~ verlängerte Vollmacht; **financial** ~
Finanzkraft, finanzielle Leistungsfähigkeit; **foreign** ~ auswärtige Macht; **full** ~**s** unbeschränkte Befugnisse, [General]voll-
macht; **general** ~ Generalvollmacht; **governmental** ~ Staatsgewalt; **Great** ⌾ Großmacht; **hybrid** ~ ungleichartige
Vollmacht; **hydroelectric** ~ Wasserkraftstrom; **implied** ~ stillschweigend erteilte (implizierte) Vollmacht, (zuerkannte)
abgeleitete Befugnisse; **inherent** ~**s** originäre Befugnisse; **great**
intellectual ~ große Intelligenz; **judicative** ~ Urteilskraft; **judicial** ~ richterliche Gewalt; **large** ~**s** umfangreiche Vollmachten; **legal** ~ gesetzliche Vollmacht; **legislative** ~ gesetzgeberische Initiative, Legislative; **lending** ~ Ausleihungsbefugnis; **maritime** ~ Seemacht; **mental** ~**s** Geisteskräfte; **military**
~ Militärmacht; **ministerial** ~ *(conveyancing, Br.)* Veräuße-
rungsbefugnisse; **naked** ~ einfache (unentgeltlich ausgeübte)
Vollmacht; **naval** ~ Seemacht; **nuclear** ~ Atomkraft; **occupying**
~ Besatzungsmacht; **official** ~**s** Amtsgewalt; **parental** ~ elterliche Gewalt; **particular** ~ Sondervollmacht; **placing** ~ Plazierungskraft; **plenary** ~ unumschränkte Vollmachten; **police** ~
Polizeigewalt; **productive** ~ Produktionskraft, Leistungsfähigkeit; **protecting** ~ Schutzmacht; **purchasing** ~ Kaufkraft; **revisory** ~**s** Überprüfungsrecht, -befugnis; **sea** ~ Seemacht; **senatorial**
~**s** Vollmacht des Senats; **signatory** ~**s** Signatar-
mächte; **simply collateral** ~ reine Vollmacht; **sovereign** ~
Hoheitsgewalt, -recht, hoheitsrechtliche Funktionen; **special**
~ Einzel-, Spezial-, Sondervollmacht; **spending** ~ Ausgabener-
mächtigung, -befugnis; **staying** ~ Widerstandskraft; **substitute**
~ Untervollmacht; **supreme** ~ oberste Staatsgewalt; **treaty-
making** ~**s** Zuständigkeit für völkerrechtliche Vertragsabschlüsse; **tax[ing]** ~ Besteuerungsrecht; **trustee's** ~ Vollmacht
eines Treuhänders; **unlimited** ~[**s**] unumschränkte Vollmacht,
Blankovollmacht; **vesting** ~**s** Beschlagnahmerecht; **voting** ~
Stimmrecht; **water** ~ Wasserkraft; **will** ~ Willenskraft; **world** ~
Weltmacht;
the ~**s that be** maßgebliche Stellen, Obrigkeit; ~ **to operate on**
an account Kontovollmacht, Verfügungsberechtigung über
ein Konto; ~ **to accumulate** *(trustee)* Thesaurierungsbefugnis;
~ **of advancement** *(trustee)* Aussteuerbefugnis; ~ **of an agent**
Vertretungsbefugnis; ~ **of alienation** Veräußerungsbefugnis; ~
to amend Abänderungsbefugnis; ~ **of appointing new trustees**

Ernennungsbefugnis weiterer Vermögensverwalter; **~ of appointment** Ernennungsbefugnis, Bestallungs-, Designationsrecht, *(administrator)* Bestimmung des Begünstigten, *(estate)* Nachlaßeinsetzung.

power of attorney Handlungs-, Vertretungsvollmacht, notarielle Vollmacht, Vollmachtsurkunde, *(lawsuit)* Prozeßvollmacht; **as per ~** laut Vollmacht;

authorized ~ beglaubigte Vollmacht; **general (full) ~** Blanko-, Generalvollmacht; **joint ~** Kollektivprokura; **permanent ~** Dauervollmacht; **specific ~** Einzel-, Sondervollmacht; **terminated ~** erloschene Vollmacht.

power│of avoidance Anfechtungsbefugnis, Anfechtungsrecht, -möglichkeit; **~ to borrow [money]** Kreditaufnahmebefugnis; **statutory ~ to borrow** satzungsgemäß gestattete Kreditaufnahmebefugnis; **~ to collect** Inkassovollmacht, -befugnis, Einziehungsbefugnis; **~ of command** Befehlsgewalt; **~ of committal** *(debtor's Act, Br.)* Inhaftierungsvollmacht; **~ of a committee** Ausschußvollmachten; **~ to compete** Konkurrenzstärke; **~ of concentration** Konzentrationsvermögen; **~ of Congress** *(US)* Machtbefugnisse des Kongresses; **~ of consolidation** *(mortgages)* Hypothekenvereinigungsanspruch; **~ to consume** Konsumkraft [einer Zielgruppe]; **~ to contract** Vertragsfähigkeit, Vertrags-, Abschlußvollmacht; **~ to control** Überwachungsbefugnis; **definite ~s of a court** einem Gericht zugewiesene Befugnisse; **~s of darkness** Mächte der Finsternis; **~ of decision** Entscheidungsbefugnis; **~ to delegate** Vollmachtsübertragung; **~s of deliberation** Beratungsbefugnisse; **~ of direction of labo(u)r** Vollmacht für den Arbeitskräfteeinsatz; **~ of discretion** Ermessensfreiheit, -befugnis; **~ of disposal** Verfügungsbefugnis, Dispositionsrecht; **~ of disposition** Verfügungsmacht; **limited ~ to bind a firm** beschränkte Handlungsvollmacht; **~ to indorse** Indossamentsvollmacht; **~ of initiative** Initiativvorrecht; **~ coupled with an interest** [etwa] Vollmacht unter Einschluß des Selbstkontrahierens; **~ of investment** Anlagebefugnis; **~ of the keys** Hausrecht; **~ of the law** Gesetzeskraft; **~ of life and death** Macht über Tod und Leben; **~ of a liquidator** Vertretungsvollmacht eines Abwicklers; **~ of maintenance** *(trustee)* Unterhaltsbefugnis; **~ supplied by a motor** von einem Motor gelieferte Kraft; **~ in the nature of a trust** treuhandähnliche Vollmachtstellung; **~ to negotiate** Verhandlungsvollmacht, *(negotiable instrument)* Begebungsrecht; **~ of pardon** Begnadigungsrecht; **~ of people** ein Haufen Menschen; **~s of the Prime Minister** Vollmachten des Ministerpräsidenten; **~ of the purse** *(US, Congress)* Zweckbestimmungsbefugnis; **~ of redemption** Rückkaufsrecht; **~ to reject** Abnahmeverweigerungsrecht; **~ of removal** Abberufungsrecht; **~ to represent** Vertretungsbefugnis; **~ of resistance** Widerstandskraft; **~ of revocation (to revoke)** Widerrufsrecht, Widerrufsbefugnis; **~ of sale** Verkaufsvollmacht, Veräußerungsbefugnis; **~ to sign** Unterschriftsvollmacht, -befugnis; **~ of suasion** Überzeugungskraft, Überredungsgabe; **~ of substitution** Delegationsbefugnis, Untervollmacht; **~ to sue and to be sued** aktive und passive Prozeßvollmacht; **~ of suggestion** Suggestions-, Überzeugungskraft; **~ of tax** Besteuerungsrecht; **~ of testation** Testierfähigkeit; **general ~ to transact business** Geschäftsabschlußvollmacht; **~ per unit of displacement** Hubraumleistung; **~ to use a casting vote** Ermächtigung zur Abgabe der entscheidenden Stimme; **~ of visitation** Befugnisse des Kurators einer Stiftung; **more ~ to your elbow** *(coll.)* viel Erfolg!;

~ *(v.)* **up** aufladen;

to act in excess of one's ~ seine Befugnisse (Vollmacht) überschreiten; **to act with full ~** alle Vollmachten haben; **to ascend to ~** Macht ergreifen; **to ask for ~s to conclude peace** Vorlage der Friedensbevollmächtigung fordern; **to assume ~** Macht übernehmen; **to be in ~** *(political party)* an der Macht (Regierung, am Ruder) sein; **not to be within s. one's ~s** außerhalb jds. Möglichkeiten sein; **to be a ~ in the land** Macht in einem Lande darstellen; **to be at the height of one's ~** im Zenit seiner Macht stehen; **to bestow (grant) ~ of attorney** Vollmacht erteilen; **to bring ~ into play** Macht zur Geltung bringen; **to bring a town under its ~** Stadt in seine Gewalt bringen; **to come [in]to ~** zur Macht kommen (gelangen), Macht (Regierung) übernehmen; **to confer ~s [of attorney] on s. o.** jem. Vollmacht erteilen, j. bevollmächtigen; **to continue in ~** an der Macht bleiben; **to cut down the ~** Motor drosseln; **to define s. one's ~** jds. Vollmacht abgrenzen, **to delegate one's ~** seine Vollmacht (Machtbefugnisse) delegieren (übertragen); **to discharge the ~s** Machtbefugnisse ausüben; **to do s. o. a ~ of good** jem. mächtig gut tun; **to do a ~ of work** Berge von Arbeit bewältigen; **to exchange ~s** Vollmachten austauschen; **to exercise ~** Macht ausüben; **to exercise one's ~ [of attorney]** Gebrauch von seiner

Vollmacht machen; **to exceed one's ~s** seine Vollmacht (Machtbefugnisse) überschreiten; **to execute a ~ of attorney** Vollmacht ausstellen; **to exercise one's ~ of attorney** Gebrauch von seiner Vollmacht machen; **to exercise the ~ of the purse** *(Br.)* seine Zuständigkeiten bei der Mittelszuweisung voll ausschöpfen; **to exercise ~s entirely at will** Vollmacht ganz nach Ermessen ausüben; **to extend one's ~s** seine Machtbefugnisse überschreiten; **to fall into s. one's ~** in jds. Machtbereich fallen (geraten); **to float s. o. into ~** j. an die Macht bringen; **to furnish s. o. with full ~** jem. Generalvollmacht erteilen; **to give s. o. ~ of attorney** j. zum Bevollmächtigten einsetzen; **to give s. o. discretionary ~s** jem. unumschränkte Vollmachten erteilen; **to go beyond one's ~s** seine Vollmacht überschreiten; **to have a general ~ to dispose of the property** [etwa] befreiter Vorerbe sein; **to have absolute ~** unumschränkt herrschen; **to have large ~s of initiative** sehr initiativ sein; **to have reached the zenith of one's ~** auf dem Gipfel der Macht stehen; **to have sole ~** allein befugt sein; **to have no ~s over s. o.** keinen Einfluß auf j. haben; **to have no ~ to bind a company** Gesellschaft nicht verpflichten können; **to hold ~ of attorney of s. o.** von jem. bevollmächtigt (jds. Bevollmächtigter) sein, Vollmacht von jem. erhalten haben; **to invest s. o. with full ~s** jem. Generalvollmacht erteilen; **to lose the ~ of holding one's audience** seine Zuhörer nicht mehr zu fesseln vermögen; **to make a ~ of money** *(fam.)* enorm viel Geld verdienen; **to outline a ~ in a mandate** Vollmachtsumfang einer Weisung genau festlegen; **to place o. s. in s. one's ~** sich jem. auf Gnade und Ungnade ausliefern; **to prescribe ~s** Befugnisse festlegen; **to produce a ~ of attorney** seine Vollmacht vorlegen; **to remain in ~** an der Macht (am Ruder) bleiben; **to restrain ~s** Befugnisse einschränken; **to restrict s. one's ~** jds. Vollmacht beschränken; **to return to ~** Macht erneut (wieder) übernehmen; **to revoke a ~** Vollmacht widerrufen; **to seize ~** Macht an sich reißen (ergreifen); **to strain one's ~s** seine Befugnisse überschreiten; **to strip totally of any ~** vollständig entmachten; **to survive in ~** an der Macht bleiben; **to take ~ in a coup** mittels eines Staatsstreiches zur Macht gelangen; **to tax one's ~ too much** sich zuviel übernehmen; **to throw out of ~** Regierung stürzen; **to vest in s. o. under the deed of a trust** Treuhänder mit Vollmachten ausstatten; **to work the engine at half ~** Maschine nur mit halber Kraft fahren;

Special ~s Act *(Ireland)* Notstandsgesetz; **~ allocation** Energiezuteilung; **~ amplifier** *(radio)* Endverstärker; **~-assisted steering wheel** Servolenkung; **~ base** Machtbasis; **~ blackout** Stromausfall; **~ brake** *(car)* Servobremse; **~ breakdown** *(line failure)* Netzausfall; **~ cable** Starkstromkabel; **irrevocable ~ of attorney clause** unwiderrufliche Vollmachtsklausel; **~ circuit** Starkstromkreis; **~ commission** Energiekommission; **electric ~ company** Elektrizitätsgesellschaft; **~ consumption** Energie-, Stromverbrauch; **~ current** Starkstrom; **~ cut** Stromsperre, -abschaltung; **~ demand** Energiebedarf; **~ dive** *(airplane)* Vollgassturzflug; **~-dive** *(v.)* Sturzflug machen; **~ drill** elektrische Bohrmaschine; **~ drive** Kraftantrieb; **~-driven** motorgetrieben, *(fig.)* machtbesessen; **~ economy** Energiewirtschaft; **~ failure** Stromausfall; **~ gas** Verbrennungsgas; **~ generation** Stromerzeugung; **~ glider** Motorsegler; **electric ~ industry** Energiewirtschaft; **~ installation** Kraftbetrieb; **~ instrument** Machtinstrument; **~ interruption insurance** Stromunterbrechungsversicherung; **~ line** Überland-, Elektrizitäts-, Starkstromleitung; **~ load** Strom-, Netzbelastung; **~ loading** *(plane)* Leistungsbelastung; **~ loss** Energieverlust; **~ off** *(technics)* Leerlauf; **~-operated** durch Maschinenkraft betrieben; **~ output** Nenn-, Stromleistung, Leistungsabgabe, *(motor)* Hubleistung; **~ pack** *(radio)* Netzanschlußgerät; **[electric] ~ plant** Elektrizitäts-, Kraftwerk, Energiewirtschaftsunternehmen; **~ politics** Machtpolitik; **~ press** Presse; **~ production** Energieproduktion, -leistung; **~-propelled vehicle** Kraftfahrzeug; **~ rationing** Stromeinschränkung; **~ reactor** Leistungsreaktor; **~ requirements** Strom-, Energiebedarf; **~ sharing** Gewalteinteilung, Machtbeteiligung; **~ shift** Machtverlagerung; **~ shortage** Energieknappheit; **~-sharing agreement** Vereinbarung über geteilte Machtausübung; **~ shovel** Löffelbagger; **~ shutdown** Stromsperre; **~ source** Kraftquelle; **~ station** Elektrizitäts-, Kraftwerk; **hydroelectric ~ station** Wasserkraftwerk; **nuclear ~ station** Atomkraftwerk; **~ steering** *(car)* Servolenkung; **~ stroke** Arbeits-, Krafthub; **[electric] ~ supply** Stromversorgung, -abgabe, Energieversorgung; **~ supply connection** Kraftanschluß; **~ supply industry** Energiewirtschaft; **~ transformer** Netztransformator; **~ transmission** Energieübertragung; **~ tube** Senderöhre; **~ unit** *(airplane)* Triebwerk; **~ vacuum** Machtvakuum; **~ window** *(car)* automatisch versenkbares Fenster; **~ works** Elektrizitätswerk.

powerboat Motorboot.
powered *(motor)* angetrieben;
  high-~ car hochtouriger Wagen; **high-~ salesman** hochqualifizierter Verkäufer.
powerful wirksam, kräftig, leistungsfähig, *(influential)* einflußreich, bedeutend;
  ~ arguments überzeugende Argumente; **~ engine** starker Motor;
  ~ lot of money eine Masse Geld.
powerhouse Maschinenhaus, *(power station)* Elektrizitätswerk, *(fig.)* Energiebündel;
  spiritual ~ geistiges Krafteigentum.
powerless machtlos, *(space shuttle)* antriebslos;
  to be ~ to resist keinen Widerstand leisten können, nicht widerstandsfähig sein.
practicability Durchführbarkeit, praktische Brauchbarkeit, Tunlichkeit.
practicable *(feasable)* tunlich, praktisch, anwendbar, *(road)* fahr-, gangbar, *(serviceable)* brauchbar;
  administratively ~ verwaltungstechnisch durchführbar;
  ~ agriculture praktische Landwirtschaft; **~ aim** erreichbares Ziel; **~ method** anwendbare Methode.
practicableness Durchführbarkeit, Gangbarkeit.
practical praktisch, brauchbar, tunlich, *(applicable)* praktisch anwendbar, zweckmäßig, nützlich, *(labouring)* werktätig;
  ~ application praktische Anwendung; **to have ~ control of** praktisch die Kontrolle ausüben; **to overcome the ~ difficulties of a scheme** Schwierigkeiten eines Planes bei der Umsetzung in die Praxis bewältigen; **~ experience** praktische Anwendung; **to play a ~ joke on s. o.** jem. einen Streich spielen; **~ knowledge** auf Erfahrung beruhende Kenntnis, praktische Kenntnise; **~ mechanics** Maschinenlehre; **~ men** Männer der Praxis; **~ method** nützliche (brauchbar) Methode; **to appeal to ~ minds** praktisch eingestellten Menschen gefallen; **~ nurse** ausgebildete Krankenschwester; **~ politician** Berufspolitiker; **~ proposal** praktischer Vorschlag; **for all ~ purposes** in praktischer Hinsicht, für die Zwecke der Praxis; **~ suggestion** zweckmäßiger Vorschlag; **~ tradesman** Geschäftstätiger; **in ~ terms** effektiv gesehen; **with ~ unanimity** nahezu einstimmig; **of no ~ value** praktisch wertlos.
practice *(custom)* Brauch, Gewohnheit, *(repeated exercise)* ständige Übung, Praxis, *(intrigue)* Machenschaften, Umtriebe, Intrigen, Ränkespiel, *(working method)* Arbeitsweise, Verfahren, *(legal procedure)* Verfahren[sregel], Gerichtsverfahren, Rechtsgang, *(profession)* Praxis, Berufsausübung, *(commercial usage)* Usance;
  in ~ in der Praxis; **out of ~** aus der Übung;
  ~s Gepflogenheiten, Verhaltensweise, Praktiken, *(cartel)* Geschäftspraktiken;
  administrative ~s Verwaltungspraktiken; **Annual ℒs** *(Br.)* Sammlung von Prozeßvorschriften; **banking ~** Bankusancen; **business ~s** *(cartel law)* Geschäftspraktiken; **deceptive business ~s** *(US)* unlautere Machenschaften; **commercial ~** Handelsbrauch; **common ~** allgemein übliches Verfahren; **concerted ~s** *(cartel law)* aufeinander abgestimmte Verhaltensweise, Gruppendisziplin; **corrupt ~** Durchstechereien, Korruption, *(election)* Wahlbestechung; **court ~** Praxis der Gerichte; **electoral ~s** Wahlpraktiken; **established ~** *(law court)* ständige Rechtsprechung; **illegal ~s** *(Br.)* verbotene Wahlkampfmethoden; **improper ~s** unsaubere (unlautere) Geschäftsmethoden; **large ~** große Praxis; **law ~** Anwaltspraxis; **legal ~** Anwaltspraxis; **lucrative ~** lukrative Praxis; **restrictive ~s** *(cartel)* aufeinander abgestimmte wettbewerbsbeschränkende Verhaltensweise, Gruppendisziplin; **sharp ~** Schiebung, unlautere (dunkle) Machenschaften; **shop ~** Geschäftsübung, -gebrauch; **solicitor's ~** Anwaltspraxis; **target ~** *(mil.)* Übungsschießen; **trade ~s** Handelspraktiken;
  ~ of banking Bankusancen, Bankpraxis; **~ of closing shop on Sundays** Sonntagsruhe im Geschäftsleben; **~ to the contrary** entgegenstehender Brauch; **~ of the courts** ständige Rechtsprechung; **~ of law** anwaltliche Praxis, Ausübung des Anwaltsberufes; **unauthorized ~ of law** unerlaubte Rechtsberatung; **~ of medicine** ärztliche Tätigkeit; **~ of merchants** Handelsgebrauch; **~ of profession** Berufsausübung; **~ makes perfect** Übung macht den Meister.
practice **(practise**, *Br.*) *(v.)* betreiben, Beruf ausüben, *(doctor)* praktizieren, Praxis ausüben;
  ~ as an attorney *(US)* **(at the bar**, *Br.*) als Anwalt (anwaltlich) tätig sein, Anwaltsberuf ausüben;
  ~ bribery bestechen; **~ in a court** als Anwalt vor Gericht auftreten; **~ upon s. one's credulity** jds. Leichtgläubigkeit aus-

nutzen; **~ deceit on s. o.** Finten jem. gegenüber gebrauchen; **~ a fraud on the court** Gericht täuschen; **~ one's French on s. o.** seine französischen Sprachkenntnisse bei jem. ausprobieren; **~ journalism** sich journalistisch betätigen; **~ law** Anwaltspraxis (Anwaltsberuf) ausüben; **~ medicine** Arztpraxis haben; **~ on the piano** Klavier üben; **~ politeness** sich in Höflichkeit üben; **~ what one preaches** praktisches Beispiel geben; **to ~ the same profession** gleichen Beruf ausüben; **~ early rising** gewöhnlich (aus Gewohnheit) früh aufstehen.
practice, to be in Praxis haben, praktizieren; **to be no longer in ~** seine Praxis nicht mehr ausüben; **to be normal ~** üblich sein; **to be out of ~** aus der Übung sein; **to buy a ~** Praxis erwerben; **to carry on a ~** Praxis ausüben; **to have a large ~** große Kanzlei haben; **to make it one's ~** es sich zur Gewohnheit machen; **to make a ~ of cheating at examinations** bei Examensarbeiten grundsätzlich betrügen; **to put into ~** praktisch durchführen, in die Tat setzen; **to put a principle into ~** Prinzip in die Praxis umsetzen; **to reduce to ~** praktisch anwenden, *(invention)* Nachweis der praktischen Verwertbarkeit führen; **to retire from a ~** Praxis aufgeben; **to sell one's ~** seine Praxis verkaufen; **to take over a ~** Praxis übernehmen; **to take years of ~** jahrelange Erfahrung (benötigen) erfordern; **to work in ~** praktisch funktionieren; **to work up a ~ as physician** sich eine Praxis schaffen;
  Civil ℒ Act *(US)* Zivilprozeßordnung; **~ administration** Praxisverwaltung; **~ allowance** *(health insurance)* Praxisvergütung; **~ firing** *(mil.)* Übungsschießen; **~ rules** Verfahrensvorschriften; **~ ship** Schulschiff.
practiced (practised, *Br.*) geübt, erfahren, routiniert;
  ~ organization of a paper erfahrener Zeitungsapparat.
practician Berufsausübender, Praktiker.
practicing (practising, *Br.*)**| certificate** Anwaltsbestellung, Zulassungsurkunde; **~ lawyer** praktizierender Anwalt; **~ premises** Praxisräume.
practitioner freiberuflich Tätiger, Berufstätiger, *(expert)* Fachmann;
  general ~ Doktor, praktischer Arzt; **legal ~** Rechtsberater, Jurist; **tax ~** *(Br.)* Steuerberater.
praecipe Vollstreckungsauftrag.
praise Lob[preisung];
  ~ over the left *(sl.)* das Gegenteil von Lob;
  to be beyond all ~ über jedes Lob erhaben sein; **to be chary of ~** selten Lob spenden; **to be loud in one's ~ of s. o.** laute Loblieder auf j. singen; **to be warm in s. one's ~** jem. Elogen sagen; **to break into ~ for s. o.** in Lobpreisungen ausbrechen; **not to be given to ~** ungern schmeicheln; **to sound one's own ~s** sich selbst beweihräuchern; **to sound the ~s of s. o.** j. wie einen Schellenkönig (über den grünen Klee) loben; **to speak in ~ of s. o.** j. lobend erwähnen; **to win high ~s** hohes Lob erhalten.
pram *(Br., sl.)* Kinderwagen.
prang *(Br., sl.)* Bruchlandung;
  ~ *(v.)* bruchlanden, Bruchlandung machen.
prate *(v.)* plappern, schwatzen;
  ~ about a subject of which one knows nothing über ein Thema quatschen, von dem man nichts versteht.
pratique *(mar.)* Verkehrserlaubnis;
  to admit to ~ Verkehrserlaubnis erteilen.
praxis Praxis, Gepflogenheit.
pray *(v.)* bitten, ersuchen;
  ~ s. o. to show mercy j. um Gnade anflehen.
prayer Gebet;
  ~ of process Klagebegehren, -antrag; **~ for rain** Bitte um Regen;
  to have not a ~ *(sl.)* keine Chance haben;
  ~ rug Gebetsteppich.
preacquaint *(v.)* **s. o. with the facts** j. mit den Tatsachen vorher bekanntmachen.
preacquaintance vorherige Kenntnis.
preacquisition| losses Geschäftsverluste vor Konzerneingliederung; **~ profits** Gesellschaftsgewinne vor Konzerneingliederung.
preadmission vorherige Zulassung.
preadmonition vorherige Warnung.
preach *(v.)* predigen, Predigt halten;
  ~ down s. th. gegen etw. losziehen; **~ s. o. a sermon** jem. eine Moralpredigt halten; **~ up equality** für die Gleichheit eintreten; **~ glad tidings** herrliche Zeiten vorhersagen.
preamble Präambel, Vorrede, Vorwort;
  ~ of a decree Begründung einer Verordnung;
  ~ *(v.)* Präambel schreiben.
preannouncement Vorankündigung.

preappointment vorläufige Ernennung.
prearrange *(v.)* vorher vereinbaren (absprechen).
prearrangement vorherige Abmachung.
preassessment Vorausschätzung;
~ **of a loss** Vorausvereinbarung eines pauschalierten Schadensersatzes.
preaudience Vortrittsrecht.
preaudit Vorprüfung, *(disbursing officer)* Prüfung der Auszahlungsbelege.
prebend Pfründe.
prebendary Pfründeinhaber.
precalculate *(v.)* vorausberechnen.
precalculation Vorausberechnung.
precarious unsicher, gefährdet, prekär, schwankend, *(law)* [jederzeit] widerruflich;
~ **assumption** fragwürdige (schlecht begründete) Annahme; ~ **circumstances** besorgniserregende Umstände; ~ **fortune** gefährdetes Vermögen; ~ **life** gefahrenreiches Leben; ~ **livelihood** unsicherer Lebensunterhalt; ~ **living** unsichere Erwerbsquelle; **to make a** ~ **living** unsichere Existenz haben; ~ **loan** jederzeit kündbares Darlehn; ~ **popularity** schwankende Volksgunst; ~ **possession** jederzeit entziehbarer Besitz; ~ **privileges** unsichere Privilegien; ~ **right** widerruflich übertragenes Recht; ~ **situation** mißliche (bedenkliche) Lage; ~ **state of health** unstabiler Gesundheitszustand; ~ **trade** *(international law)* geduldeter Handel neutraler Staaten; **to enjoy the** ~ **use of s. th.** etw. widerruflich benutzen dürfen.
precast *(concrete)* vorfabriziert.
precatory ersuchend, empfehlend;
~ **clause** *(last will)* letzte Bitte; ~ **expressions** letztwillige Formulierungen; ~ **words** letztwillige Bitte.
precaution Vorsichtsmaßregel, Vorkehrung;
as a ~ vorsichtshalber; **by way of** ~ als Vorsichtsmaßnahme; **airraid** ~**s** Luftschutz; **ample** ~**s** umfangreiche Vorkehrungen; ~**s against fire** Brandverhütung;
to neglect ~**s** Vorsichtsmaßnahmen außer Acht lassen; **to take** ~**s** Sicherheitsmaßnahmen treffen, vorbauen; **to use every** ~ sehr vorsichtig handeln.
precautionary vorbeugend;
~ **demand** Geldnachfrage aus Vorsorgegründen; ~ **measures** Vorbeugungs-, Vorsichtsmaßnahmen; ~ **motive** *(Keynes)* Vorsorgemotiv, *(cash management)* Vorsichtsmotiv; ~ **signal** Warnsignal.
precede *(v.)* Vorrang (Vortritt) haben, voraus-, vorangehen;
~ **a lecture with a few words** einem Vortrag ein paar Worte vorausschicken; ~ **the storm** dem Sturm vorausgehen.
preceded | **by a reception** durch einen Empfang eingeleitet; ~ **by a teacher** vom Lehrer geführt.
precedence Vortritt, Rangordnung, *(creditors)* Vorrang, Vorrecht, Priorität;
ceremonial ~ protokollarische Rangordnung;
to contend for ~ **with s. o.** mit jem. über Rangfragen streiten; **to have** ~ *(bankruptcy law)* vorgehen, bevorrechtigt sein; **to take** ~ Vortritt (Vorrang) haben; **to take** ~ **over all others** allen anderen vorangehen; **to take s. th. as** ~ etw. als Präzedenzfall betrachten; **to yield** ~ **to s. o.** jem. den Vortritt lassen; ~ **question** Präzedenzfrage.
precedent Präzedenzfall, Grundsatzentscheidung, Präjudiz;
without ~ noch nicht dagewesen, *(law court)* noch nicht höchstrichterlich entschieden;
binding ~ bindender Präzedenzfall; **persuasive** ~ nicht bindende Entscheidung;
~ *(a.)* vor[an]gehend, vorhergehend;
condition ~ aufschiebende Bedingung;
~**s of a case** Rechtsprechung zu einem Fall;
to cite a ~ Präzedenzfall anführen; **to constitute a** ~ Präzedenzfall bilden; **to overrule a** ~ sich über einen Präzedenzfall hinwegsetzen; **to quote a** ~ Präzedenzfall anführen; **to set a** ~ Präzedenzfall schaffen; **to take s. th. as a** ~ etw. als Präzedenzfall betrachten;
~ **book** Formularbuch.
precedential case Präzedenzfall.
preceding vorhergehend;
~ **article** vorhergehender Absatz; ~ **indorser** Vor[der]mann; ~ **judgment** Zwischenurteil; ~ **speaker** Vorredner; ~ **year** Vorjahr.
precept Regel, Richtschnur, *(authority)* Vorschrift, Verordnung, amtliche Anweisung, *(election)* Wahlerlaubnisschein, *(law)* gerichtliche Anordnung, Gerichtsbefehl, *(taxation)* Steuerveranlagung, Umlagebescheid.
precepting authority *(Br.)* Steuererhebungsstelle.

preceptor Schulleiter.
preceptorate Lehramt, -stelle.
precinct eingefriedeter Bezirk, *(boundary)* Grenze, *(district)* [Amts]bezirk, Polizeibezirk, *(inviolable space)* Bannmeile;
within the ~**s of** innerhalb der Grenzen; **within the sacred** ~**s** im Kirchenbereich; **within the** ~ **of a city** im Weichbild einer Stadt; ~**s** Umgebung, Bereich;
election ~ *(US)* Wahlkreis; **magisterial** ~ *(US)* örtlicher Zuständigkeitsbereich; **pedestrian** ~ Fußgängerbereich; **shopping** ~ Geschäftsgegend;
~ **captain** *(party, US)* Wahlkreisleiter; ~ **worker** *(US)* Wahlhelfer.
precious wertvoll, kostbar, *(coll.)* reichlich;
to take ~ **good care of s. th.** sich ganz besonders um etw. kümmern; **to leave s. o.** ~ **little to do** jem. verflixt wenig übrig lassen; **to care** ~ **little** sich fast gar nicht darum kümmern; ~ **little hope** fast gar keine Hoffnung mehr; **to have** ~ **little money left** kaum mehr Geld übrig haben; ~ **metal** Edelmetall; **to make a** ~ **mess of s. th.** etw. ganz schön durcheinanderbringen; ~ **pronunciation** gezierte Aussprache; ~ **rascal** Erzschurke; ~ **sampling** gezielte Stichprobe; **to cost a** ~ **sight** ganz schön teuer sein; **to think a** ~ **sight too much of o. s.** ganz schön auf sich eingebildet sein; ~ **stone** Edelstein.
precipe Weisung an den Rechtspfleger.
precipice Klippe, jäher Abgrund, *(fig.)* kritische Lage;
to rescue s. o. from the edge of the ~ j. vom Abgrund zurückreißen.
precipitance Überstürzung, Hast;
with utmost ~ mit äußerster Eile.
precipitate *(v.)* *(meteorology)* Niederschlag bilden, *(urge)* heraufbeschwören, herbeiführen;
~ **themselves** *(news)* sich überstürzen; ~ **into an abyss** in einen Abgrund stürzen; ~ **a country into a war** Land in einen Krieg stürzen; ~ **a crisis** Krise hervorrufen; ~ **a journey** Abreise beschleunigen; ~ **s. one's ruin** jds. Ruin beschleunigen;
~ *(a.)* jählings, steil abfallend;
to be too ~ **in declaring war** überstürzte Kriegserklärung abgeben;
~ **illness** unerwartete Krankheit; ~ **retreat** hastiger Rückzug.
precipitated flight überstürzte Flucht.
precipitation Sturz, *(fig.)* Überstürzung, Hast, *(meteorology)* Niederschlag;
annual ~ Jahresniederschlag; **to act with** ~ überstürzt handeln.
précis gedrängte Darstellung, kurze Zusammenfassung;
~ **of a set of documents** Aktenauszug;
to make a ~ **of an affair** Analyse einer Angelegenheit fertigen.
precise deutlich, klarumrissen, *(minutely exact)* pedantisch, übergenau;
~ **amount** genauer Betrag; ~ **answer** präzise Antwort; ~ **definition** genaue Definition; ~ **moment of departure** genauer Abfahrtstermin; **very** ~ **gentleman** distinguierter Herr; ~ **moment** richtiger Augenblick; ~ **order** präzise Anweisung; ~ **statement** Präzisierung.
precision Präzision, Genauigkeit;
~ **adjustment** Feineinstellung, ~ **bombing** gezielte Bombenabwürfe, Zielwurf; ~ **engineering** feinmechanische Industrie; **high-**~ **engineering** Präzisionstechnik, Feinmechanik; ~ **and optical goods** Feinmechanik und Optik; ~ **instrument** Präzisionsinstrument; ~ **landing** Ziellandung; ~ **mechanics** Feinmechanik; ~ **tool** Präzisionswerkzeug; ~ **toolmaker** Feinmechaniker.
preclosing trial balance Probebilanz.
preclude *(v.)* ausschließen;
~ **from an allotment** von der Zuteilung [bei der Aktienemission] ausschließen; ~ **all doubts** alle Zweifel beseitigen; **in order to** ~ **any misunderstanding** um jedes Mißverständnis auszuschließen; ~ **objections** Einwände vorwegnehmen; ~ **recovery by suit** gerichtliche Schadensforderung ausschließen.
preclusion Ausschließung, Ausschluß;
~ **clause** Ausschließungsklausel.
precode erste Verschlüsselungsstufe.
precocious child frühreifes (altkluges) Kind.
precognition *(Scot.)* Voruntersuchung.
precognosce *(Scot.)* Voruntersuchung.
preconceived | **idea** Vorurteil; ~ **opinion** vorgefaßte Meinung.
preconcert *(v.)* vorher verabreden.
preconcerted abgekartet;
to follow no ~ **plan** ohne festen Plan vorgehen.
precondition Vorbedingung;
~ *(v.)* vorweg behandeln.
precollection letter *(US)* letzte Mahnung.

preconcert vorherige Absprache.
preconsideration vorherige Überlegung.
preconstruction time Bauvorbereitungszeit.
precontract vorherige Vereinbarung, Vorvertrag, *(marriage)* vertragliches Eheversprechen;
~ *(v.)* Vorvertrag abschließen.
precool *(v.)* vorkühlen.
precursor Vorbote, Vorläufer, *(in office)* Amtsvorgänger.
precursory remarks vorausgehende Bemerkungen.
precut house Fertighaus.
predate *(newspaper)* vordatierte Ausgabe;
~ *(v.)* zurückdatieren;
~ **orders** Bestellungen vorziehen.
predacious | animal Raubtier; ~ **instinct** Raubtierinstinkt.
predating of order Vorziehen einer Bestellung.
predatory plündernd, räuberisch;
~ **animal** Raubtier; ~ **band** Räuberbande; ~ **exploitation** Raubbau; ~ **incursion** räuberischer Einfall; ~ **practices** rücksichtslose Wettbewerbsmethoden; ~ **price cutting** ruinöse Preisunterbietung; ~ **price differential** *(US)* gezielte Kampfpreise.
predecease *(v.)* vorher sterben, vorversterben.
predeceased Vorverstorbener.
predecessor | in interest Rechtsvorgänger; ~ **in office** [Amts]vorgänger; ~ **in title** vorheriger Eigentümer, Voreigentümer, Rechtsvorgänger;
~ **company** Vorgesellschaft, Geschäftsvorgänger[in].
predestination Vorherbestimmung, Prädestination.
predetermine *(v.)* vorher beschließen, festsetzen;
~ **the cost of a building** Baukostenvoranschlag machen.
predetermined costs vorkalkulierte Kosten.
predicament gefährliche (mißliche) Lage;
to be in an awkward ~ sich in einer scheußlichen Lage befinden; **to be in the same** ~ gleichfalls in der Tinte sitzen.
predicate Titel;
~ *(v.)* begründen, stützen;
~ **the goodness of a motive** sich auf seine guten Absichten berufen.
predict *(v.)* prophezeien, weissagen, vorhersagen;
~ **future developments** zukünftige Entwicklungen voraussagen; ~ **a good harvest** auf eine gute Ernte schließen lassen; ~ **that there will be an earthquake** Erdbeben (prophezeien) voraussagen.
predicted cost Standard-, Normalkosten.
prediction Vorhersage;
to throw a ~ **off** Vorhersage über den Haufen werfen; ~ **interval** Voraussagespanne, Prognosekorridor.
predispose *(v.)* vorher anordnen, im voraus verfügen;
~ **consumption** Verbrauch steigern.
predisposed | to illness krankheitsanfällig;
to be ~ **in s. one's favo(u)r** geneigt sein, j. zu bevorzugen.
predominance Vorherrschaft, Übergewicht.
predominant überwiegend, vorherrschend.
predominate *(v.)* vorherrschen, überlegen sein.
pre-election Vorwahl;
~ **paralysis** politische Untätigkeit in der Vorwahlzeit; ~ **promise** Wahlversprechen.
pre-eminent überragend, hervorragend;
to be ~ **above all one's rivals** alle Konkurrenten ausstechen.
pre-eminence, economic wirtschaftliche Vorrangstellung.
pre-empt *(v.) (obtain right of pre-emption)* Vorkaufsrecht erwerben, *(obtain by pre-emption)* durch Ausübung des Vorkaufsrechtes erwerben;
~ **an idea** Idee mit Beschlag belegen; ~ **a parking space** sich einen Parkplatz sichern.
pre-emptible vorkaufspflichtig.
pre-emption Vorkauf[srecht], *(law of nations)* Ankauf einer Prise, *(stockholder, US)* Bezugsrecht;
clause of ~ *(Scot.)* Vormerkung;
to obtain by ~ im Wege des Vorkaufsrechtes erwerben; **to settle upon land subject to** ~ *(US)* Grundstück mit Vorkaufsberechtigung besitzen;
~ **claimant** Vorkaufsberechtigter; ~ **clause** *(company law)* Vorkaufsklausel; ~ **entry** Ausübung des Vorkaufsrechtes; ~ **price** Vorkaufspreis; ~ **right** Vorkaufsrecht.
pre-emptioner Vorkaufs-, Vormerkungsberechtigter.
pre-emptive | priorities absolute Prioritäten; ~ **right** Vorkaufsrecht, *(stockholder, US)* Bezugsrecht.
pre-emptor Vorkaufsberechtigter, Vorkäufer.
pre-engage *(v.)* vorausbestellen.
pre-engaged vorher verabredet.
pre-engagement vorher eingegangene frühere Verpflichtung.

pre-estimate Kostenvoranschlag;
~ **of a damage** Vorausberechnung eines Schadens; ~ **of loss** Verlustvorausschätzung.
pre-examination Voruntersuchung.
pre-examine *(v.)* vorher vernehmen, voruntersuchen.
pre-existing bisherig.
prefab *(Br., coll.)* Fertighaus;
~ *(a.)* vorfabriziert.
prefabricate *(v.)* [Hausteile] fabrikmäßig herstellen, vorfabrizieren, genormte Hausteile vorfertigen.
prefabricated vorgefertigt;
~ **house** Fertighaus; ~ **housing module** vorgefertigte Wohneinheit; ~ **part** Fertigteil; ~ **units** Fertighausteile.
prefabrication serienmäßige Vorfertigung, fabrikmäßige [Häuser]teilanfertigung;
prefabricator Fertighausbetrieb.
preface Vorwort, Vorrede, Einleitung, Geleitwort;
~ *(v.)* einleitende Worte sprechen (schreiben);
~ **a crisis** eine Krise voraussagen; ~ **one's remarks with an anecdote** seine Ausführungen mit einer Anekdote beginnen;
to write a ~ **to a book** Vorwort für ein Buch schreiben.
prefatory Vorbemerkung;
~ **remarks** einleitende Bemerkungen, Vorrede.
prefect Präfekt, Statthalter, *(school, Br.)* Vertrauensschüler, Ordner;
~'s **court** *(New Mexiko)* Nachlaßgericht.
prefecture Präfektur.
prefectural office Präfektur.
prefer *(v.)* bevorzugen, vorziehen, Vorzug geben, lieber tun, *(creditors)* bevorzugt befriedigen, *(promote)* befördern;
~ **an accusation against s. o.** j. anklagen, Anklage gegen j. erheben; ~ **a bill of indictment** Anklage erheben; ~ **a charge against a motorist** Autofahrer bei der Polizei anzeigen; ~ **claims against s. o.** Ansprüche gegen jem. erheben; ~ **a complaint** Beschwerde vorbringen; ~ **one creditor over others** Gläubiger bevorzugen, sich der Gläubigerbevorzugung schuldig machen; ~ **to go without rather than pay so dearly for it** lieber auf etw. verzichten als einen so hohen Preis dafür zu zahlen; ~ **an officer** Offizier befördern; ~ **a petition** Gesuch einreichen; ~ **to a higher post** befördern; ~ **a suit** Klage einreichen.
preferable vorzugsweise, *(law)* bevorzugt zu befriedigen, bevorrechtigt;
to be ~ **to establish a guarantee fund** besser (lieber) einen Garantiefonds errichten.
preference Bevorzugung, Vorrang, Vorzug, *(in bankruptcy)* Vorrang, vorzugsweise Befriedigung, Bevorrechtigung, [Gläubiger-, Konkurs]vorrecht, *(claim)* Vorzugs-, Prioritätsrecht, *(customs, Br.)* Meistbegünstigung[starif], Präferenz, *(preference share, Br.)* Vorzugsaktie, *(trade)* Begünstigung, Bevorzugung, Priorität, Vorzugsbehandlung;
by ~ vorzugsweise;
~**s** *(stock exchange)* Vorzugsaktien;
Commonwealth ~ *(Br.)* Vorzugszollsystem im Commonwealth; **consumer** ~ Bevorzugung durch den Verbraucher; **fraudulent** ~ *(in bankruptcy)* Gläubigerbegünstigung; **Imperial** ~ *(Br.)* Bevorzugung der Empirestaaten, Vorzugszoll, Meistbegünstigung; **recoverable** ~ Aussonderungsrecht; **revealed** ~ bekundete Präferenz; **tariff** ~**s** Zollpräferenzen; **undue** ~ ungerechte Bevorzugung, *(bankruptcy)* Gläubigerbegünstigung; **voluntary** ~ beabsichtigte Gläubigerbegünstigung;
~ **as to assets** *(dissolution of company)* Vorzugsbehandlung im Falle einer Liquidation; ~ **of creditors** Gläubigerbegünstigung; ~ **as to dividends** Dividendenbevorrechtigung; ~ **in liquidation** Liquidationsvorrecht;
to be entitled to ~ Anspruch auf bevorzugte Befriedigung haben; **to be given** ~ bevorzugt sein; **to enjoy** ~ bevorzugt behandelt werden; **to give a** ~ einem [Gläubiger] vorzugsweise Befriedigung gewähren; **to give s. th. the** ~ **over another** eine Sache einer anderen vorziehen; **to enjoy no** ~**s** keine Vergünstigungen genießen; **to receive a** ~ Vorzugsstellung erhalten; **to take** ~ vorrangig behandelt werden;
~ **area** Zollvorzugs-, Präferenzgebiet; ~ **bonds** *(Br.)* Prioritätsobligationen, Prioritäten; ~ **claim** bevorrechtigte (privilegierte) Forderung; ~ **dividend** *(Br.)* Vorzugsdividende; ~ **freight** *(US)* zu Vorzugsbedingungen beförderte Fracht, Vorzugsfracht; ~ **income** steuerlich begünstigte Einkünfte; ~ **income bonds** *(US)* Prioritätsobligationen, Prioritäten; ~ **issue** Vorzugsausgabe; ~ **items** *(taxation)* steuerlich begünstigte Posten; ~ **legacy** Vorausvermächtnis; **to bequeath s. th. as a legacy** als Vorausvermächtnis zuwenden; ~ **loan** Vorrechts-, Prioritätsanleihe; ~ **margin** Präferenzspanne; ~ **offer** Vor-

zugs-, Sonderangebot; **founder's ~ rights** Gründerrechte; ~ **scale** Nutzenskala; **~ shares** *(Br.)* Prioritäts-, Vorzugsaktien; **convertible ~ shares** *(Br.)* mit Umtauschberechtigung ausgestattete Vorzugsaktien; **cumulative ~ shares** *(Br.)* nachzugsberechtigte Vorzugsaktien; **nonparticipating ~ shares** *(Br.)* nicht zu einer zusätzlichen Dividende berechtigte Vorzugsaktien; **nonvoting ~ shares** *(Br.)* stimmrechtslose Vorzugsaktien; **participating ~ shares** *(Br.)* Vorzugsaktien mit zusätzlicher Dividendenberechtigung; **redeemable ~ shares** *(Br.)* rückkaufbare Vorzugsaktien; **~ share certificate** *(Br.)* Vorzugsaktienzertifikat; **~ shareholder** *(Br.)* Vorzugsaktionär; **~ stock** *(US)* Prioritäts-, Vorzugsaktien; **~ stockholder** *(US)* Vorzugsaktionär; **~ voting** Vorwahl.

preferential mit einem Vorzugsrecht ausgestattet, bevorzugt, bevorrechtigt;
to treat a creditor's claim as ~ Gläubigerforderung absondern; **~ arrangement** *(GATT)* Präferenzabmachung, -regelung; **~ quantitative arrangement** mengenmäßige Präferenzregelung; **~ assignment** Vermögensübertragung auf die Konkursgläubiger; **~ ballot** Vorwahl; **~ benefit** *(US)* Voraus-, Vorwegentnahme; **~ claim** bevorrechtigte Forderung, Vorzugsrecht, Absonderungsanspruch; **to give a matter ~ consideration** Angelegenheit bevorzugt behandeln; **~ creditor** *(Br.)* bevorrechtigter (absonderungsberechtigter) Gläubiger, Vorzugsgläubiger; **~ debt** *(Br.)* bevorrechtigte [Konkurs]forderung; **~ discount rate** Vorzugsdiskontsatz; **~ dividend** *(Br.)* Vorzugsdividende; **~ dockets** Liste vorrangig angesetzter Gerichtstermine; **~ duty** Vorzugs-, Präferenzzoll; **~ fee for book-trade order forms** Vorzugsgebühr für Bestellformulare des Buchhandels; **~ hiring** *(US)* bevorzugte Einstellung von Gewerkschaftsmitgliedern; **~ loan** *(Br.)* Prioritätsanleihe; **~ offer** Vorzugs-, Sonderangebot; **~ payment** *(bankruptcy proceedings, Br.)* bevorrechtigte Gläubigerbefriedigung; **~ position** Vorzugsstellung; **~ price** Vorzugspreis; **~ priority** Vorzugsrangfolge; **~ rate** *(custom)* Präferenzzollsatz, Vorzugstarif; **~ right** *(Br.)* Absonderungs-, Vorzugsrecht; **~ share** *(Br.)* Vorzugs-, Prioritätsaktie, **~ shareholder** *(Br.)* Vorzugsaktionär; **~ shop** *(union, US)* Betrieb, der Gewerkschaftsmitglieder bei der Einstellung bevorzugt; **~ stocks** *(US)* Vorzugs-, Prioritätsaktien; **~ tariff** Präferenz-, Vorzugszoll, -tarif, *(Br.)* Meistbegünstigungstarif; **~ tariff area** Zollvorzugsgebiet; **~ terms** Vorzugsbedingungen; **~ trade agreement** Präferenzabkommen; **~ treatment** bevorzugte Behandlung, Bevorzugung, Vorzugsbehandlung, *(bankruptcy)* abgesonderte Befriedigung, Absonderung; **to be given ~ treatment** bevorrechtigte Behandlung erfahren, *(bankruptcy)* Absonderung vornehmen können; **to enjoy ~ treatment** *(customs)* Präferenz genießen; **~ voting** Präferenzwahl, Vorzugswahlsystem; **~ voting rights** Vorzugsstimmrecht.

preferentialism *(trade relations)* Präferenzsystem.

preferment Bevorzugung, *(pre-emption)* Vorkaufsrecht, *(promotion)* Beförderung, Ernennung;
~ to take a benefice Einsetzung in eine Pfründe;
to calculate on ~ mit einer Beförderung rechnen.

preferred mit einem Vorteil ausgestattet, bevorzugt, bevorrechtigt;
to be ~ to an office für ein Amt vorgeschlagen werden;
~ bonds Prioritätsobligationen; **~ capital stock** *(US)* aus Vorzugsaktien bestehendes Kapital; **~ claim** Vorzugsanspruch, bevorrechtigte Konkursforderung; **~ creditor** *(US)* bevorrechtigter [Konkurs]gläubiger; **~ debt** *(US)* bevorrechtigte [Konkurs]forderung; **~ dividend** *(US)* Vorzugsdividende; **~ payment** *(US)* bevorrechtigte Gläubigerbefriedigung; **~ position** Vorzugsstellung, *(advertising)* Vorzugsplatz, bevorzugte Plazierung, Sonderplazierung; **~ risks** Sonderversicherungstarif; **~ risk plan** *(US)* Schadensfreiheitsrabatt; **~ share** *(Br.)* Prioritäts-, Vorzugsaktie; **~ ordinary shares** *(Br.)* bevorzugte Stammaktien; **~ stocks** *(US)* Vorzugsaktien, Prioritäten; **adjustment ~ stocks** *(US)* im Sanierungsverfahren ausgegebene Vorzugsaktien; **convertible ~ stocks** *(US)* konvertierbare Vorzugsaktien, Vorzugsaktien mit Umtauschrecht; **cumulated ~ stock** *(US)* zusätzliche Vorzugsaktien; **cumulative ~ stock** *(US)* Vorzugsaktien mit Dividendennachzahlungsverpflichtung; **first ~ stocks** *(US)* Prioritätsaktien erster Emission; **nonassessable ~ stocks** *(US)* nicht nachschußpflichtige Vorzugsaktien; **noncumulative ~ stocks** *(US)* Vorzugsaktien ohne Dividendennachzahlungsverpflichtung; **nonparticipating ~ stock** *(US)* nicht zu einer zusätzlichen Dividende berechtigende Vorzugsaktie; **participating ~** *(US)* mit zusätzlicher Dividendenbevorrechtigung ausgestattete Vorzugsaktie; **second ~ stock** *(US)* Vorzugsaktien zweiter Klasse; **~ stockholder** *(US)* Vorzugsaktionär.

prefinance *(v.)* vorfinanzieren.
prefinancing Vorfinanzierung.
prefix Vorsilbe, *(title)* Titel;
~ *(v.)* voranstellen;
~ a new paragraph neuen Absatz einfügen;
call ~ *(tel.)* Vorwählnummer, -ziffer.
pregnancy Schwangerschaft;
~ test Schwangerschaftstest.
pregnant schwanger, *(fig.)* fruchtbar, [ideen]reich;
~ in ideas voller Ideen, schöpferisch; **~ with meaning** bedeutungsvoll;
to be ~ with consequences Folgen zeitigen;
~ mind einfallsreicher Geist.
preignition Frühzündung.
prejudge *(v.)* ohne vorherige Prüfung urteilen, zu früh urteilen.
prejudgment Vorurteil, *(pre-examination)* Voruntersuchung, *(judge)* Befangenheit.
prejudication Präzedenzfall, *(preceding judgment)* Zwischenurteil.
prejudice *(bias)* Vorurteil, Voreingenommenheit, *(detriment)* Beeinträchtigung, [Rechts]nachteil, Schaden, *(judge)* Befangenheit;
to the ~ of zum Schaden von; **with ~** mit materieller Rechtskraft; **without ~** ohne Schaden, ohne Obligo (Verbindlichkeit), ohne Anerkennung einer Rechtspflicht; **without ~ to any claim** ohne Beeinträchtigung (unbeschadet) irgendwelcher Ansprüche;
class ~ Standesvorurteil; **ingrained ~** tief eingewurzeltes Vorurteil; **racial ~** Rassenvorurteil; **strong ~** ausgeprägtes Vorurteil;
~s prevailing in this country hierzulande herrschende Vorurteile;
~ *(v.)* *(bias)* mit Vorurteil erfüllen, voreingenommen sein, voreilig urteilen, *(court)* ohne vorherige Prüfung verurteilen, *(damage)* schaden, schädigen, Abbruch tun, abträglich sein, *(impair)* benachteiligen, beeinträchtigen;
~ s. o. against s. o. j. gegen einen anderen beeinflussen; **~ one's claims** seinen Ansprüchen Abbruch tun; **~ the due course of justice** gerichtliches Verfahren behindern; **~ a decision** Entscheidung beeinflussen; **~ s. o. in favo(u)r of s. o.** j. zugunsten eines Dritten einnehmen; **~ s. o. in favo(u)r of s. th.** j. für etw. einnehmen; **~ s. one's interests** jds. Interessen beeinträchtigen; **~ s. one's rights** jds. Rechte beeinträchtigen; **~ a fair trial** schwebendes Verfahren beeinträchtigen;
to be of ~ to s. one's interests jds. Interessen abträglich sein; **to get the better of one's ~s** sich von seinen Vorurteilen frei machen; **to have a ~ against s. o.** Vorurteil gegen j. haben; **to have a ~ in favo(u)r of modern music** Anhänger moderner Musik sein, moderne Musik bevorzugen; **to hold no ~** kein Vorurteil haben; **to outgrow a ~** Vorurteil überwinden; **to work on s. one's ~s** jds. Vorurteile in Rechnung stellen.
prejudiced voreingenommen, *(judge)* befangen;
to be ~ Partei sein; **to be ~ against s. o.** gegen j. voreingenommen sein; **to be ~ in favo(u)r of s. o.** für j. eingenommen sein; **to be deeply ~ in favo(u)r of s. th.** leidenschaftlich für etw. eingenommen sein;
~ opinion vorgefaßte Meinung.
prejudicial schädlich, nachteilig;
to be ~ to s. one's interests sich nachteilig auf jds. Interessen auswirken; **to effect ~ly** nachteilig beeinflussen;
~ error schwerwiegender Verfahrensirrtum.
prelanding operations Vorbereitungen zu einem Landungsunternehmen.
prelect *(v.)* Vorlesungen halten.
prelection öffentliche Vorlesung.
preliminaries erste Schritte, Vorverhandlungen, Präliminarien;
~ to a negotiation Vorverhandlungen; **~ of peace** Präliminarfriede.
preliminary Einleitung, *(examination, US)* Zwischenexamen;
~ *(a.)* vorläufig, vorbereitend, einleitend, *(in advance)* im voraus;
~ to the mountains dem Gebirge vorgelagert;
~ act *(admiralty practice, Br.)* Kollisionsurkunde; **~ advice** Voravis, -anzeige; **~ agreement** vorläufiges Abkommen, Vorvereinbarung; **~ announcement** Voranzeige; **~ answer** vorläufiger Bescheid, Vorbescheid; **~ application blank** Personalfragebogen; **~ articles of a treaty** einleitende Bestimmungen (Präliminarien) eines Vertrages; **~ audit** Vorprüfung; **~ balance sheet** Vorbilanz; **~ calculation** Vorausberechnung, Vorkalkulation, -anschlag; **~ considerations** Vorüberlegungen; **~ consultations** Vorbereitungsgespräche, Vorkonferenz;

~ **contract** Vorvereinbarung, Vorvertrag; ~ **cost** *(US)* Gründungs- und Organisationskosten; ~ **costing** Vorkosten; ~ **decision** Vorentscheid, -abentscheidung; ~ **discussion** Vorbesprechung; ~ **draft** Vorentwurf; ~ **dressing** Notverband; ~ **edition** Vorausausgabe; ~ **election** Vorwahl; ~ **enquiries** Vorprüfung; ~ **estimate** Vorausschätzung, Kostenvoranschlag; ~ **examination** Vor-, Aufnahmeprüfung, *(bankruptcy proceedings, Br.)* Schuldnervernehmung, *(patent and criminal law)* Voruntersuchung, *(statistics)* Vorerhebungen; ~ **expenses** *(company, Br.)* Gründungskosten; ~ **and issue expenses** *(balance sheet, Br.)* Gründungs- und Unterparikosten; ~ **financing** Vorfinanzierung; ~ **findings** Voruntersuchungen; ~ **hearing** Voruntersuchung, -verhandlung; ~ **injunction** *(US)* einstweilige Verfügung; ~ **inquiry** gerichtliche Voruntersuchung; ~ **instructions** Einführungsunterricht; ~ **investigation** Voruntersuchung; ~ **measures** vorläufige (vorbereitende) Maßnahmen, *(Court of Justice)* prozeßleitende Verfügungen; ~ **negotiations** Vorverhandlungen; ~ **notice** Vorausbenachrichtigung; ~ **plan** Vorentwurf; ~ **proceedings** Vorverfahren; ~ **products** Vorprodukte; ~ **proof** *(insurance)* erster Schadensnachweis; ~ **question** Vorfrage; ~ **remarks** einleitende Bemerkungen, Vorbemerkungen; ~ **repayments** vorzeitige Rückzahlung; ~ **report** Vorbericht; ~ **ruling** *(EC)* Vorabentscheidung; ~ **scheme** Vorentwurf; **at the** ~ **stage** im Vorfeld; ~ **steps for an establishment** der Gründung vorausgehende Schritte; ~ **talks** Vorbesprechungen; ~ **treatment** Vorbehandlung; ~ **treaty** Vorvertrag; ~ **trial** Ausscheidungskampf; ~ **work** Vor[bereitungs]arbeiten.

prelude Einleitung, einleitende Maßnahmen, Auftakt; ~ **to the battle** Vorspiel zur Schlacht; ~ **to a conference** Auftakt einer Konferenz; ~ *(v.)* einleiten, Auftakt sein.

premature vorzeitig, verfrüht; ~ **birth** vorzeitige Geburt, Frühgeburt; ~ **decision** voreilige Entscheidung; ~ **repayment** vorzeitige Rückzahlung; ~ **report** Vorbericht; ~ **retirement** vorzeitige Pensionierung.

premeditate *(v.)* überlegen, planen.

premeditated mit Vorbedacht; ~ **design** Vorbedacht, Tatvorsatz; ~ **insolence** einkalkulierte Unverschämtheit; ~ **murder** vorsätzlicher Mord.

premeditation Überlegung, Vorbedacht.

premeeting preparations Sitzungsvorbereitungen.

premerger notification *(US)* vorausgehende Fusionsmitteilung.

premier *(Br.)* Ministerpräsident, Premierminister.

première Ur-, Erstaufführung, Premiere; ~ *(v.)* Premiere geben.

premilitary vormilitärisch.

premise Vordersatz, Prämisse, Voraussetzung; ~ *(v.)* Vorbemerkung machen, vorausschicken.

premises dazugehöriger Grund und Boden, [Betriebs]grundstück, Haus und Nebengebäude, Anwesen, Örtlichkeit, Geschäftsräume, -lokal, Betriebsgrundstück, Räumlichkeiten, *(contract law)* vorerwähnte Punkte, Vorstehendes, *(conveyancing)* das oben erwähnte Grundstück, *(document)* Einleitungssätze, *(insurance law)* versicherter Gegenstand, *(stating part of a bill)* Sachverhaltsschilderung, Rubrum; **in consideration of these** ~ *(pleading)* in Berücksichtigung des Sachvortrags; **off the** ~ außerhalb des Lokals; **on the** ~ im Lokal, *(plant)* im Betrieb, an Ort und Stelle; **on these** ~**s** an Ort und Stelle, auf dem Grundstück; **bank** ~ Bankgebäude; **business** ~ Geschäftsgrundstück, -lokal, -räume; **company** ~ Betriebsgrundstück, Verwaltungsgebäude; **decontrolled** ~ [etwa] im weißen Kreis gelegene (nicht mehr bewirtschaftete) Wohnung; **demised** ~ Miet-, Pachtgrundstück, Mieträume; **extensive** ~ ausgedehnte Geschäftsräume; **exhibition** ~ Ausstellungsräume; **factory** ~ Fabrikgrundstück, -gebäude; ~ **insured** *(fire insurance)* versicherte Gegenstände; **licensed** ~ *(Br.)* Lokal mit Schankkonzession, Schanklokal, Gaststätte; **mortgaged** ~ hypothekisiertes Grundstück; **neighbo(u)ring** ~ Nachbargrundstück; **open-air** ~ im Freien gelegene Betriebsstätte; **residential** ~ Wohngebäude, -grundstück; **shop** ~ Ladenräume; ~ **of an airport** Flughafengebäude; ~ **owned by the Crown** *(Br.)* Staatsgebäude; ~ **of the employer** Arbeitsstätte; ~ **required for landlord or a member of his family** *(Br.)* Wohnräume mit nachgewiesenem Eigenbedarf; ~ **of a mission** Botschaftsgelände; ~ **badly in need of repair** reparaturbedürftige Geschäftsräume; **to be consumed on the** ~ zum Verzehr im Lokal bestimmt sein; **to enter** ~ Grundstück betreten; **to transfer to new** ~ in neue Geschäftsräume verlegen; **to visit the** ~ Lokal durchsuchen; ~ **account** Grundstücks-, Liegenschaftskonto.

premium *(agio)* [Wechsel]agio, Aufgeld, Zuschlag, *(apprenticeship)* Lehrgeld, *(bonus)* Bonus, Prämie, *(bounty)* Zuschuß, *(dividend)* Extradividende, *(fee for instruction)* Ausbildungshonorar, *(insurance)* Versicherungsprämie, Beitrag, *(object offered free)* Zugabe[artikel], *(special offer)* Gratis-, Sonder-, Vorzugsangebot, *(renting a house)* bezahlter Abstand, Abstandssumme, verlorener Zuschuß, *(reward)* Prämie, Preis, Belohnung, Anreiz, *(shop)* Rabattmarke, *(stock exchange)* Agio, Aufgeld, Prämie, Reugeld, *(trading in futures)* Kursaufschwung, Report, *(wages)* Extralohn;

at a ~ über Pari, *(fig.)* hoch im Kurs; **free of** ~ *(insurance)* prämienfrei;

additional ~ zusätzliche Prämie, Zuschlags-, Ergänzungsprämie, Prämienzuschlag; **advance** ~ Vorauszahlungsprämie; **advanced** ~ veranlagte Versicherungsprämie; **advertising** ~ Zugabeartikel; **annual** ~ Jahresprämie; **average** ~ Durchschnittsprämie; **bleed** ~ *(advertising)* Anschnittszuschlag; **call** ~ *(trading in futures)* Vorprämie; **compound** ~ Doppelprämie; **constant** ~ anstehendes Agio; **continuity** ~ Zugabewerbung in Sammelform; **current** ~ Folgeprämie; **deferred** ~ noch nicht fällige Prämie; **double-option** ~ zweischneidige Prämie; ~ **due** ausstehende Prämie, Sollprämie; ~ **earned** Prämieneinkommen; **exchange** ~ Aufgeld, Agio; **export** ~ Ausfuhrprämie; **extra** ~ Sonder-, Zusatzprämie; **first** ~ Erstprämie; **fixed** ~ feste Prämie; **flat rate** ~ Pauschalprämie; **fluctuating** ~ veränderliches Agio; **gold** ~ Goldagio; **gross** ~ Bruttoprämie; **high** ~ hohe Prämie; **incentive** ~ Gratiskupon; **initial** ~ Anfangsprämie; **insurance** ~ Versicherungprämie; **level** ~ gleichbleibende Prämie; **limited** ~ abgekürzte Prämienzahlung; **long** ~ hohe Prämie; **mail-in** ~ *(US)* Zugabe gegen eingesandten Kupon; **minimum** ~ Mindestprämie; **monthly** ~ Monatsprämie; **natural** ~ Mindestprämie zur Fortsetzung der Versicherung; **net** ~ kostendeckende Prämie, Nettoprämie; **office** ~ Bruttoprämie einschließlich Verwaltungskostenzuschlag; **opening** ~ erste Prämie; **outstanding** ~s Prämienrückstände; **pure** ~ Nettoprämie; **put** ~ *(trading in futures)* Rückprämie; **quarterly** ~ Vierteljahresprämie; **renewal** ~ *(insurance)* Erneuerungs-, Folgeprämie; **return** ~ rückvergütete Prämie, Rückgabeprämie; **risk** ~ Risikoprämie; **self-liquidating** ~ Warenprobe zum Selbstkostenpreis; **semi-annual** ~ Halbjahresprämie; **share** ~ Emissionsagio; **short** ~ niedrige Prämie; **single** ~ Einmalprämie; **sliding-scale** ~ gleitende Prämie; **step-rate** ~ progressive Prämie; **stipulated** ~ ausbedungene Prämie; **stock** ~ *(life insurance)* Gewinnbeteiligung; **supplementary** ~ Zuschlags-, Zusatzprämie; **tabular** ~ Tarifprämie; **total** ~ Gesamtprämie; **unearned** ~ *(life insurance)* noch nicht verdiente Prämie; **uniform** ~ *(life insurance)* Einheitsprämie;

~ **of apprenticeship** Lehrgeld, Ausbildungskosten; ~ **in arrears** Prämienrückstände; ~ **for the call** *(trading in futures)* Vorprämie[ngeschäft]; ~ **on capital increase** Agio aus Kapitalerhöhung; **high-risk** ~ **on capital investment** hohe Risikoprämie bei Anlageinvestitionen; ~ **on capital stock** Emissionsagio; ~ **for good conduct** Prämie für gute Führung; ~ **in course of collection** im Einzug befindliche Prämie; ~ **of the dollar over the franc** Dollaragio gegenüber dem Franken; ~ **on exchange** Wechselagio, Aufgeld; ~ **for export** Exportbonus; ~ **on gold** Goldagio; ~ **paid for insurance** Versicherungsprämie; ~ **on a lease** Agio bei Auslösung einer Kaution; ~ **for [single] option to put** Rückprämie[ngeschäft]; ~ **for double option (spread,** *US)* Stellgeld; ~ **out and home** Versicherungsprämie für Hin- und Rückreise; ~ **payable on redemption** Rückprämie, Anleiheagio; ~ **qualifying for relief** *(Br.)* steuerbegünstigte Versicherungsprämie; ~ **received on the issue of new shares** Emissionsagio; **to arrange a** ~ Prämie vereinbaren **to assess a** ~ Prämie festsetzen; **to be at a** ~ über Pari (Nennwert) stehen, *(in high esteem)* sehr gesucht (geschätzt) sein; **to buy at a** ~ über Pari kaufen; **to command a** ~ Agio genießen; **to fix a** ~ Prämie festsetzen; **to pay a** ~ **to an agent** Provision an einen Vertreter zahlen; **to pay** ~s **to date** Versicherungsprämie fortzahlen; **to pay a** ~ **with an insurance company** Prämie an eine Versicherung zahlen; **to place a** ~ **on s. th.** Preis (Belohnung) für etw. aussetzen; **to put a** ~ **on s. th.** Preis (Belohnung) für etw. aussetzen; **to put a** ~ **on laziness** Faulheit belohnen; **to put a** ~ **on business dishonesty** steuerliche Unehrlichkeit belohnen; **to raise the** ~ Prämie erhöhen; **to reduce a** ~ Prämie herabsetzen; **to refund a** ~ Prämie zurückerstatten; **to reward with a** ~ prämiieren; **to sell at a** ~ über Pari stehen, *(v./t.)* mit Gewinn (Aufpreis) verkaufen; **to yield a** ~ Prämie abwerfen;

~ **bargain** Prämiengeschäft; ~ **bond** Prämien-, Anreizschein; ~ **bonds** *(Br.)* Prämienanleihe, -lose, -obligationen, Agiopapiere; ~ **bonus** Prämienlohn; ~ **bonus system** Prämien-, Leistungslohnsystem, Prämiensystem für eingesparte Arbeitsstunden;

boost Prämienerhöhung; ~ **brand** Markenerzeugnis hoher Qualität; ~ **catalog(ue)** Preis-, Prämienverzeichnis; ~ **computation** Prämienberechnung; ~ **costs** Prämienaufwendungen; ~ **deposit** Prämieneinzahlung; ~ **dodge** *(fam.)* Prämienschwindel; ~ **drawing** Prämienziehung; ~ **due date** [Prämien]fälligkeitstag; ~ **earnings** Prämieneinnahmen; ~ **funds** Prämienmittel, -erträge, -einnahmen; ~ **hunter** Kursspekulant; ~ **hunting** Börsenspiel, Agiogeschäft, Agiotage; ~ **income** Prämieneinnahme, -aufkommen; **net** ~ **income** *(life insurance)* Prämienüberschüsse; ~ **increase** Prämienerhöhung; ~ **instal(l)ment** Prämienrate; **low** ~ **insurance** Versicherung mit ermäßigten Prämiensätzen; **single** ~ **insurance** Lebensversicherung gegen Zahlung einer Einmalprämie; ~ **loan** Prämienanleihe; ~ **money** Prämiengeld; ~ **note** Prämienrechnung; ~ **offer** *(US)* Verkauf mit Zugaben, Zugabenangebot; **dealer** ~ **offer** Zugabeangebot für Händler; ~ **overtime** Überstundenzuschlag; ~ **pay** *(US)* Prämie, Überstundengeld, Sondervergütung, Lohnzulage; ~**paying period** Prämienzahlungskredit; ~ **payment** Prämienleistung, -zahlung; ~ **plan** Prämien[lohn]system; **return** ~ **policy** Prämienrückgewährpolice; ~ **product** Zugabeprodukt; ~ **promotion** Zugabewesen; ~ **rate** Prämiensatz, -tarif für Vorzugsplazierung; **to quote a** ~ **rate for a risk** Prämiensatz für ein Versicherungsrisiko festsetzen; ~ **rebate** Prämienrabatt, Beitragsermäßigung; ~ **receipt** Prämienquittung; ~ **reduction** Prämienermäßigung; ~ **reminder** *(insurance company)* Mahnschreiben; **unearned** ~ **reserve** *(insurance)* Prämienreserve, -übertrag, Deckungskapital; ~ **reserve fund** Deckungsstock; ~ **savings bond** Prämienbon, *(Br.)* Sparprämienobligation, -brief; **short-period** ~ **scales** erhöhte Prämiensätze für Versicherungen unter einem Jahr; ~ **selling** Zugabewesen; ~ **statement** Beitrags-, Prämienabrechnung; ~ **stock** Deckungsstock; ~ **system** Prämien[lohn]system; ~ **tax** Versicherungssteuer; ~ **token** Prämien-, Gutschein; ♻ **Treasury Bond** *(US)* Prämienschatzanweisung, Babybond; ♻ **Trust Fund** *(Lloyds)* treuhänderisch verwalteter Prämienfonds; ~ **wage** Prämienlohn; ~ **wage system** Prämienlohnsystem.

premonition vorherige Warnung.
prender Entnahmewahl.
prenotification Vorausbenachrichtigung.
preoccupation vorherige Inbesitznahme;
  without ~ unbeeinflußt.
preoccupy *(v.)* vollständig in Anspruch nehmen.
preordain *(v.)* vorher annehmen.
preordained vorher festgelegt.
prep *(fam.)* Hausaufgabe, -arbeit;
  to do one's ~ seine Aufgaben machen;
  ~ **book** Aufgabenbuch; ~ **school** Vorbereitungsschule.
prepacking Vorverpackung.
prepaid vorausbezahlt, *(post)* frankiert, freigemacht, portofrei;
  carriage ~ frachtfrei;
  ~ **assets** *(balance sheet)* transitorische Posten; ~ **expense** *(balance sheet)* transitorische Posten, aktive Rechnungsabgrenzungsposten, vorausbezahlte Aufwendungen; ~ **freight** vorausbezahlte Fracht; ~ **income** *(balance sheet)* transitorische Passiva, im voraus eingegangene Erträge; ~ **letter** frankierter Brief; ~ **notice** Freivermerk; ~ **reply** Freiantwort, [Rück]antwort bezahlt; ~ **telegram** Rückworttelegramm; ~ **wage plan** Lohnvorauszahlungssystem für vorübergehend Arbeitslose.
preoccupation, major Hauptbeschäftigung.
preparation Vorbereitung, *(criminal law)* Vorbereitungshandlung, *(document)* Abfassung, *(readiness)* Bereitschaft, Vorbereitetsein, *(school)* Hausaufgabe, -arbeit, *(preliminary study, Br.)* Studien-, Vorbereitungszeit, *(treatment for preservation)* Imprägnierung, Haftbarmachung;
  alimentary ~ Nährpräparat; **budgetary** ~s Etatvorbereitungen; **commercial** ~ handelsübliches Präparat; **food** ~ Nahrungsmittelzubereitung; **general** ~s allgemeine Vorbereitungen; **large** ~s umfassende Vorbereitungen; **pharmaceutical** ~ Arzneimittel; **warlike** ~ Kriegsvorbereitungen;
  ~ **of a budget** Etatvorbereitung, -aufstellung; ~ **of a document for execution** Herstellung einer vollstreckbaren Ausfertigung; ~ **of drugs** Arzneimittelbereitung; **customary** ~ **of goods** handelsübliche Herrichtung der Ware; ~ **of a form** Ausfüllung eines Formulars; ~s **for a journey** Reisevorbereitungen; ~ **of ores** Erzaufbereitung; ~ **for teaching** Unterrichtsvorbereitung; ~ **of troops for battle** Truppenbereitstellung; ~s **for a voyage** Reisevorbereitungen; ~s **for war** Kriegsvorbereitungen;
  to be in ~ in Vorbereitung sein; **to be in good** ~ **for war** umfassende Kriegsvorbereitungen getroffen haben; **to do one's** ~s Hausaufgaben machen; **to do s. th. with no** ~ etw. völlig unvorbereitet tun; **to make** ~s Anstalten treffen; **to make** ~s for

a journey (voyage) Reisevorbereitungen treffen; **to make** ~s **for a meal** Essen vorbereiten;
  ~ **expense** *(factory)* Aufwand vor Produktionsaufnahme; ~ **unit cost** Vorbereitungskosten je Einheit.
preparative *(mil.)* Hornsignal.
preparatory vorbereitend, in Vorbereitung befindlich;
  ~ **to leaving** abfahrtsbereit;
  ~ **committee** vorbereitender Ausschuß; ~ **course** Vorbereitungskursus; ~ **measures** vorbereitende Maßnahmen; ~ **period** Vorbereitungszeit, *(insurance)* Wartezeit; ~ **school** *(Br.)* Vorbereitungsschule; ~ **student** Student im Vorbereitungsdienst; ~ **training** Vorbereitungsdienst; ~ **work** Vorbereitungsarbeiten, *(plant)* Fertigungsvorbereitung.
prepare *(v.)* *(document)* ausstellen, abfassen, *(fill out)* ausfüllen, *(fit out)* ausrüsten, *(make preparation)* vorbereiten, *(make ready)* fertigstellen, -machen, anfertigen, vorbereiten, zurichten;
  ~ **o. s.** sich vorbereiten; ~ **the balance sheet** Bilanz aufstellen; ~ **the budget** Haushaltsplan aufstellen; ~ **a contract** Vertrag aufsetzen; ~ **for departure** seine Abreise vorbereiten; ~ **the dinner** Essen fertigmachen; ~ **draft rules** Verfügungsentwürfe ausarbeiten; ~ **the estimates** Etat aufstellen; ~ **an expedition** Expedition ausrüsten; ~ **one's lessons** seine Schularbeiten machen; ~ **a meal** Mahlzeit zubereiten; ~ **s. o. for bad news** j. auf eine schlechte Nachricht vorbereiten; ~ **a surprise for s. o.** jem. eine Überraschung bereiten; ~ **troops for action** Truppen zum Gefecht bereitstellen; ~ **for war** zum Krieg rüsten, Kriegsvorbereitungen treffen; ~ **the way for negotiations** Weg für Verhandlungen ebnen.
prepared bereit, vorbereitet, fertig, *(made ready by special treatment)* präpariert;
  not ~ **for guests** nicht auf Gäste eingestellt; ~ **for war** für den Krieg gerüstet ~ **to deliver** lieferbereit; ~ **to take a risk** risikofreudig;
  to be ~ **to** in der Lage sein zu, vorbereitet sein auf, *(willing to)* gewillt sein; **to be** ~ **for anything** mit allem rechnen, auf alles gefaßt sein; **to be** ~ **to be coolly received** mit einem kühlen Empfang rechnen; **to be** ~ **to supply goods** lieferbereit sein;
  well- ~ **dish** hübsch angerichtete Schüssel; ~ **foodstuffs** Waren der Lebensmittelindustrie; ~ **speech** vorbereitete Rede.
preparedness for war Verteidigungs-, Kriegsbereitschaft.
preparer of poison Giftmischer.
preparing, before vor Ausfüllung.
prepay | s *(balance sheet, US)* Anzahlungen an Lieferanten;
  previous ~s *(railway)* [monatlich] vorausbezahlte Frachtsätze; ~ *(v.)* vorausbezahlen, vor Fälligkeit bezahlen, im voraus *(pränumerando, vor Fälligkeit)* bezahlen, *(post)* freimachen, frankieren;
  ~ **a reply to a telegram** Rückantwort eines Telegramms (telegrafische Rückantwort) vorausbezahlen.
prepayable vorauszahlbar, im voraus zahlbar.
prepayment Anzahlung, Voraus-, Pränumerandozahlung, vorzeitige Rückzahlung, *(post)* Freimachung, Frankierung, *(rent-a-car)* Baranzahlung;
  without ~ unfrankiert, unfrei, nicht freigemacht;
  ~s *(balance sheet)* Anzahlungen bei Lieferanten;
  compulsory ~ Freimachungszwang; **insufficient** ~ ungenügende Frankierung;
  ~s **for capital additions** *(balance sheet, US)* Anzahlungen für Neuanlagen; ~ **of interest** Zinsvorauszahlungen; ~ **of postage** Freimachung, Frankierung; ~ **of rent** Mietvorauszahlung; ~ **of taxes** Steuervorauszahlungen;
  ~ **clause** Vorfälligkeitsklausel; ~ **facility** Vorauszahlungsmöglichkeiten; ~ **fee** Freimachungsgebühr; ~ **plan** *(wage-hour law, US)* Überstundenvorauszahlungsschema; ~ **table** Anzahlungstabelle.
prepense vorbedacht, -sätzlich;
  with malice ~ in böswilliger Absicht.
preponderance Übergewicht;
  ~ **of evidence** überwiegendes Beweismaterial.
preponderant überwiegend, vorwiegend.
preponderate *(v.)* Übergewicht haben;
  ~ **in favo(u)r of s. o.** sich zu jds. Gunsten neigen; ~ **in voting** Stimmenübergewicht haben.
prepossess *(v.)* vorher in Besitz nehmen, *(place)* vorher einnehmen;
  ~ **s. o. towards compulsory education** j. für die allgemeine Schulpflicht einnehmen; ~ **s. o. with a notion** jem. eine Meinung beibringen.
prepossessed voreingenommen;
  ~ **in favo(u)r** günstig beeindruckt.

prepossessing anziehend, einnehmend;
~ **person** sympathischer Mensch.
prepossession vorgefaßte Meinung, Voreingenommenheit.
prepossessor früherer Besitzer, Vorbesitzer.
preprandial vor dem Mittagessen.
preprint Anzeigenvorabdruck, Andruck.
preprocess cost Rohstoffbeschaffungskosten.
preproduction|costs Vorverfahrenskosten; ~ **model** Herstellungsmuster.
preproducts Vorprodukte, -erzeugnisse.
preprofessional vorberuflich.
preprogram(me) *(v.)* vorprogrammieren.
prepromote *(v.)* außer der Reihe befördern.
prepromotion Beförderung außer der Reihe.
prepublication price Subskriptionspreis.
precord *(v.) (broadcasting)* auf Dose nehmen.
prerecorded *(broadcasting)* auf Dose, sendefertig;
~ **broadcast** Bandaufnahme; ~ **tape** Konserve, vorweg aufgenommenes Band.
prerelease showing of a film Filmvorführung vor der Premiere.
prerequisite Grund-, Vorbedingung, [erste] Voraussetzung, *(school)* erforderlicher Grundkurs;
~ **for claim** Anspruchsvoraussetzung; ~ **for development** Entwicklungsvoraussetzung; ~ **of entrance** Eintrittsvoraussetzungen; ~ **for insurance** Versicherungsvoraussetzung;
to create the ~s Voraussetzungen schaffen.
preretail *(v.)* **an order** Kleinhandelspreis bereits bei der Bestellung festsetzen.
prerogative Vorrecht, Privilegium, Prärogative;
royal ~ königliches Hoheitsrecht;
~ **of a legislature** Vorrecht eines Parlaments; ~ **of pardon** *(Br.)* Begnadigungsrecht;
to invest with a ~ Vorrecht verleihen;
~ **court** *(Br.)* Nachlaßgericht; ~ **law** königliches Vorrecht; ~ **officer** *(Br.)* Nachlaßrichter; ~ **writ** Freilassungsanordnung, *(US)* außerordentliches Rechtsmittel.
preschool|age vorschulpflichtiges Alter; ~ **center** Vorschulzentrum; ~ **child** noch nicht schulpflichtiges Kind; ~ **education** vorschulische Erziehung, Vorschulerziehung.
preschooler noch nicht schulpflichtiges Kind.
prescind *(v.)* absondern, abstrahieren.
prescribable ersitzungsfähig.
prescribe *(v.) (lay down)* vorschreiben, vorsehen, verordnen, *(become invalid through lapse of time)* verjähren, *(med.)* verschreiben, *(outlaw by prescription)* durch Verjährung ungültig machen, *(assert a title to)* Ersitzungsrecht geltend machen;
~ *(v.)* **for s. o.** j. ärztlich behandeln; ~ **s. th. for a complaint** etw. gegen Beschwerden verschreiben; ~ **powers** Vollmacht festlegen; ~ **regulations** Vorschriften erlassen; ~ **to (for) a right** Recht ersitzen; ~ **in twenty years** in zwanzig Jahren verjähren.
prescribed, as nach Vorschrift, vorschriftsmäßig;
~ **by law** gesetzlich bestimmt, vom Gesetz vorgeschrieben;
to be ~ durch Verjährung ungültig werden;
~ **industrial disease** *(Br.)* Berufskrankheit; ~ **form** vorgeschriebenes Formblatt; **within a** ~ **period** fristgemäß; ~ **position** *(advertisement)* vorgeschriebene Plazierung; ~ **rate** vorgeschriebener Satz; ~ **task** vorgeschriebene Aufgabe; ~ **text books** vorgeschriebene Lehrbücher; **in the** ~ **time** in der hierfür vorgesehenen Zeit.
prescript Vorschrift, Anordnung.
prescription *(prescribing)* Vorschrift, Verordnung, *(recipe)* ärztliche Verordnung, Rezept, *(acquisition of title by long usage)* Ersitzung, Verjährung;
barred by ~ verjährt; **to** ~ nach Vorschrift;
acquisitive ~ Ersitzung; **extinctive** ~ Verjährung; **negative** ~ Verjährung; **positive** ~ Ersitzung;
~ **of a bill of exchange** Wechselverjährung;
to acquire by ~ ersitzen; **to bar** ~ Verjährung ausschließen; **to become invalid by** ~ verjähren; **to claim a right by** ~ Recht aufgrund von Ersitzung beanspruchen; **to dispense a** ~ Rezept ausstellen; **to extend a term of** ~ Verjährung unterbrechen; **to fill a doctor's (make a)** ~ Rezept ausstellen; **to plead** ~ Verjährungseinwand erheben, Verjährung geltend machen; **to take one's** ~ seine Arznei einnehmen; **to write out a** ~ **for s. o.** Rezept für j. ausstellen;
 Act *(Br.)* Verordnung über die Änderung der Verjährungsfristen; ~ **book** Rezeptbuch; ~ **charge** Rezeptgebühr; **Pricing Authority** *(Br.)* Überwachungsbehörde für Rezeptgebühren.
prescriptive verordnend, *(law)* auf Verjährung beruhend, durch Verjährung erworben, ersessen;

~ **debt** verjährte Schuld; ~ **law** Gewohnheitsrecht; ~ **place** Stammplatz; ~ **right** ersessenes Recht, durch Ersitzung erworbenes Recht, Gewohnheitsrecht; ~ **title** durch Ersitzung erworbenes Eigentum.
preselect *(v.)* vorwählen.
preselection *(tel.)* Vorwahl.
preselector *(tel.)* Vorwähler.
presell *(v.)* Verkaufsförderung vor dem Marktabsatz vornehmen.
preselling Vorverkauf eines Produkts.
presence Gegenwart, Dasein, *(appearance)* Auftreten, Aussehen, Gestalt, *(attendance)* Anwesenheit, Vorhandensein, *(Br.)* Audienz;
in the ~ **of danger** angesichts der Gefahr; **in** ~ **of an officer** *(offence)* in Sichtweite eines Beamten; **in the** ~ **of witnesses** vor Zeugen;
~ **abroad** Auslandspräsenz; **actual** ~ physische Anwesenheit; **constructive** ~ indirekte Präsenz;
~ **of the court** *(contempt of court)* Wahrnehmungsbereich des Gerichtes; ~ **of mind** Geistesgegenwart; ~ **of testator** Hörweite des Testierenden;
to be admitted to the ~ zur Audienz zugelassen werden; **to be lacking in personal** ~ im Aussehen zu wünschen übrig lassen; **to come to the** ~ Audienz erhalten; **to have a good** ~ über ein gutes Aussehen verfügen; **to lose in** ~ an Wirksamkeit verlieren; **to lose one's** ~ **of mind** aus der Fasson geraten; **to retire backward out of the** ~ sich rückwärts aus einer Audienz zurückziehen;
~ **chamber** *(room) (Br.)* Audienz-, Empfangs-, Thronsaal.
present Geschenk, Gabe, Gratifikation;
~s Dokument, [vorliegendes] Schriftstück;
birthday ~ Geburtstagsgeschenk; **going-away** ~ Abschiedsgeschenk;
~ **in return** Gegengeschenk;
~ *(a.)* anwesend, zugegen, gegenwärtig, präsent, *(current)* laufend, *(being dealt with)* vorliegend, *(existing now)* gegenwärtig, heutig;
at ~ gegenwärtig, augenblicklich, im Augenblick; **by the** ~s beigefügt, hierdurch; **by these** ~s hiermit, auf Grund vorliegender Urkunde; **for the** ~ vorderhand, vorläufig, einstweilen; **up to the** ~ bis dato;
those ~ *(US)* Anwesende, Teilnehmer;
~ *(v.) (bill)* vorlegen, präsentieren, *(broadcast)* bringen, *(lay a charge)* Anklage erheben, Anzeige erstatten, anzeigen, *(introduce)* vorstellen, *(show)* zeigen, darbieten, *(submit)* über-, einreichen, vorlegen, unterbreiten, eingeben, *(theater)* aufführen, vorführen;
~ **o. s. to s. o.** sich bei jem. vorstellen, sich mit jem. bekanntmachen; ~ **s. o. with s. th.** jem. etw. schenken; ~ **for acceptance** zur Aufnahme (zum Akzept) vorlegen; ~ **accounts** Rechnungen vorlegen; ~ **again** *(cheque)* wieder vorlegen; ~ **a lamentable appearance** jämmerlichen Anblick bieten; ~ **o. s. by appointment** sich bei jem. zum festgesetzten Termin einfinden; ~ **a balance of $ 100 to your credit** Saldo von 100 Dollar zu Ihren Gunsten ausweisen; ~ **a bill** Gesetzentwurf einbringen; ~ **a bill for acceptance** Wechsel zur Annahme vorlegen; ~ **a bill for payment** Wechsel zur Einlösung vorlegen; ~ **a candidate** j. als Kandidaten aufstellen; ~ **a case** Fall vor Gericht vertreten; ~ **a certificate** Bescheinigung vorlegen; ~ **a check** *(US)* **(cheque,** *Br.)* **to the bank** Scheck bei der Bank einreichen; ~ **a claim** Forderung bei Gericht anmelden; ~ **for collection** zum Inkasso vorlegen; ~ **one's compliments** sich empfehlen lassen; ~ **coupons** Kupons einreichen; ~ **difficulties** Schwierigkeiten bereiten; ~ **a document** Urkunde vorlegen; ~ **an envoy to the king** Gesandten dem König vorstellen; ~ **for evidence** Beweismittel beibringen; ~ **o. s. for an examination** sich für eine Prüfung melden (einem Examen unterziehen); ~ **some interesting features** einige interessante Merkmale aufweisen; ~ **a bold front to the world** einer schwierigen Situation entschlossen begegnen; ~ **one's greetings** seine Grüße übermitteln; ~ **o. s. at a friend's house** sich im Hause eines Freundes sehen lassen; ~ **itself in a new light** sich in neuem Licht darstellen; ~ **a memorial** Denkschrift vorlegen; ~ **a message** Botschaft überbringen; ~ **a motion** Antrag stellen, beantragen; ~ **s. o. with a motor car** jem. ein Auto anbieten; ~ **for payment** zur Zahlung vorliegen; ~ **a petition** Gesuch einreichen; ~ **a petition to the governor** dem Gouverneur eine Bittschrift überreichen; ~ **a very rosy picture** Lage äußerst rosig darstellen; ~ **a pistol at s. one's head** Pistole auf jds. Kopf richten; ~ **a plan to a meeting** einer Versammlung einen Vorschlag unterbreiten; ~ **a play** Theaterstück aufführen; ~ **a plea** Einwand vorbringen (erheben); ~ **one's regards** Grüße übermitteln; ~ **a fine spectacle to the eyes** wahre Augen-

weide sein; ~ **o. s. for trial** persönlich zur Verhandlung erscheinen; ~ **a village with a bus shelter** Unterstellungsmöglichkeit bei der Omnibushaltestelle im Dorf schaffen; ~ **vouchers** Belege einreichen;

to be ~ **at** teilnehmen an, anwesend sein bei; **to be** ~ **at a ceremony** an einer Feierlichkeit teilnehmen; **to be enough for the** ~ im Augenblick genügen; **to be** ~ **to s. one's mind** jem. vor Augen stehen; **to decline a** ~ Geschenk zurückweisen; **to make s. o. a** ~ **of s. th.** jem. etw. zum Geschenk machen;

know all men by these ~**s** hiermit wird allen kundgetan;

~ **agreement** dieses Abkommen; ~ **cabinet** gegenwärtige Regierung; ~ **capital** tatsächlich eingezahltes Kapital; ~ **case** vorliegender Fall; ~ **company** die Anwesenden; ~ **conveyance** sofort gültige Eigentumsübertragung; ~ **day** heutiger Tag, heute; ~**-day significance** gegenwärtige Bedeutung; ~ **enjoyment** gegenwärtiger Besitz und Nutznießung; ~ **estate** gegenwärtiges Vermögen; ~ **fashion** geltende Mode; ~ **government** gegenwärtige Regierung; **a very** ~ **help in trouble** im Notfall stets zur Verfügung; ~ **interest** Recht auf sofortige Inbesitznahme; ~ **market** effektiver Markt; ~ **money** bares Geld; ~ **needs** gegenwärtiger Bedarf; ~ **price** Tagespreis; **at** ~ **prices** *(stock market)* bei dem gegenwärtigen Kursstand; ~ **and future property** gegenwärtiges und zukünftiges Vermögen; ~ **state of affairs** gegenwärtige Lage; ~ **study** vorliegende Studie; ~ **time** Gegenwart; ~ **value (worth)** gegenwärtiger Wert, Bar-, Tages-, Gegenwarts-, Zeitwert, *(annuity)* Kapitalwert; ~ **volume** vorliegender Band; ~ **year** laufendes Jahr.

presentable annehmbar, vorzeigbar, stattlich;

in ~ **form** in präsentabler Form.

presentation *(advertising)* Aufmachung, Markenausstattung, *(advertising agency)* Vorlage eines Werbeplanes, Werbeplanvorlage, *(bill of exchange)* Präsentierung, Vorlegung, Vorlage, *(book)* Aufmachung, *(of a case)* Darstellung, *(donation)* Schenkung, [feierliche] Überreichung, -gabe, *(film)* Darbietung, feierliche Vorstellung, Vor-, Aufführung, *(introduction)* Vorstellung, *(submitting)* Eingabe, Präsentation, Überreichung;

on (upon) ~ gegen Vorlage, bei Vorzeigung; **payable on** ~ bei Sicht zahlbar; **upon** ~ **of the invoice** bei Rechnungsvorlage;

personal ~ persönliche Vorstellung; **special** ~ besondere Wechselvorlage;

~ **for acceptance** Einreichung (Vorlage) zum Akzept; ~ **of accounts** Rechnungslegung; ~ **of the annual balance sheet** Vorlage des Jahresabschlusses; ~ **of claim** Anspruchserhebung; ~ **of documents** Einreichung von Dokumenten, Dokumentenvorlage; ~ **of a motion** Antragstellung; ~ **of a petition** Einreichung eines Konkursantrages; ~ **of a petition for winding up** Einreichung eines Liquidationsantrages; ~ **of a new play** Aufführung eines neuen Theaterstücks; ~ **of proof** Beweisantritt; **to be payable on** ~ bei Vorlage zahlbar werden; **to mature upon** ~ bei Sicht fällig werden;

~ **ceremony** feierliche Vorstellung; ~ **copy** Dedikations-, Gratis-, Pflichtexemplar, *(book inscribed by the author)* Widmungsexemplar, *(publisher)* Freiexemplar; ~ **draft** *(US)* Sichtwechsel; ~ **form** Vorlageformular; ~ **pack** Geschenkpackung.

presented, when bei Vorlage.

presentee Schenkungsempfänger, *(Br.)* bei Hofe vorgestellte Person.

presenter *(of a bill)* Vorzeiger.

presentiment Vorahnung.

presentment Darstellung, Wiedergabe, *(bill of exchange)* Vorlegung, *(criminal practice)* Anklageschrift, *(criminal practice, US)* Anklage vor dem Schwurgericht, *(theater)* Darstellung, Vor-, Aufführung;

good ~ rechtsgültige Wechselvorlage; **pre-**~ vorzeitige Vorlage; **special** ~ Anklageschrift;

~ **for acceptance** Vorlage zur Annahme (zum Akzept), Akzeptvorlage; ~ **of a bill of exchange** Wechselvorlage; ~ **of a case** Darstellung eines Falles; ~ **for payment** Vorlage zur Einlösung (Zahlung); ~ **through the Post Office** Wechselvorlage durch die Post.

preservable konservierbar.

preservation Bewahrung, Konservierung, Erhaltung;

in good ~ *(picture)* in gut erhaltenem Zustand; **in an excellent state of** ~ in sehr gutem Zustand;

self-~ Selbsterhaltung;

~ **of capital** Kapitalsicherung; ~ **of land for public benefit** Widmung eines Grundstücks zur öffentlichen Sache; ~ **of life** Lebenshaltung; ~ **of peace** Bewahrung (Erhaltung) des Friedens; ~ **of public order** Aufrechterhaltung der öffentlichen Ruhe und Ordnung; ~ **of order of business** Einhaltung der

Tagesordnung; ~ **of testimony** Beweissicherung; ~ **from improper use** Bewahrung vor Mißgebrauch;

to be listed for ~ unter Denkmalschutz sein;

~ **order** Gebäudeerhaltungsauflage.

preservative Konservierungsmittel.

preservatory *(Br.)* Heim für gefallene Mädchen.

preserve *(Br.)* Gehege, Reservat, Wildpark, Revier, *(fig.)* Sondergebiet, -interesse, Monopol;

~**s** Eingemachtes, Konserven;

game ~ Wildreservat, Jagdgehege, Wildpark;

~ *(v.)* [auf]bewahren, erhalten, konservieren;

~ **appearances** das Dekorum wahren; ~ **one's composure** Haltung bewahren; ~ **the estate** Nachlaß sichern; ~ **fruits** Obst einkochen (einmachen); ~ **game** Wild hegen; ~ **peace** Frieden bewahren; ~ **records** Akten aufbewahren; ~ **recourse** Regreß wahren; ~ **rights** Rechte wahren; ~ **traces** Spuren sichern; ~ **certain traditions** gewisse Traditionen beibehalten;

to poach (trespas) on s. one's ~ jem. ins Gehege kommen, sich in jds. Sachgebiet einmischen;

~ **jar** Weckglas.

preserved, well ~ gut erhalten;

~ **food** Konserven; ~ **meat** Büchsenfleisch, Fleischkonserven; ~**-meat factory** Fleischkonservenfabrik; ~ **work** vorgetane Arbeit.

preserver *(Br.)* Wildhüter, Heger.

preserving | **of traces** Spurensicherung;

~ **jar** Konservenglas; ~ **traces** Spurensicherung.

preside *(v.)* | **over** Vorsitz haben (führen), vorsitzen, präsidieren; ~ **over a business** Geschäft führen; ~ **at a meeting** Sitzung leiten, bei einer Versammlung den Vorsitz haben.

presided over geleitet von.

presidence *(term of office)* Amtsdauer.

presidency Vorsitz, Präsidium, *(state)* Präsidentschaft, Präsidentenstelle, -amt;

under the ~ **of** unter dem Vorsitz von;

to assume the ~ Vorsitz übernehmen; **to run (stand) for the** ~ *(US)* für die Präsidentschaft kandidieren.

president Präsident, Vorsitzender, *(of corporation)* Generaldirektor, Vorsitzender des Vorstandes, Vorstandsvorsitzender, *(politics, US)* Präsident, *(university, US)* Rektor;

acting ~ amtierender Präsident; ~**-designate** designierter Präsident; ~**-elect** *(US)* gewählter (noch nicht eingeführter) Präsident; **managing** ~ geschäftsführender Präsident; **permanent** ~ auf Lebenszeit gewählter Präsident; **vice** ~ stellvertretender Vorsitzender, Vizepräsident; **executive vice** ~ geschäftsführender Vorsitzender, *(US)* stellvertretender Generaldirektor;

~ **of the assembly** Parlamentspräsident; ⚲ **of the Board of Education** *(Br.)* Unterrichtsminister; ⚲ **of the Board of Trade** *(Br.)* Handelsminister; ~ **of a limited company** *(US)* Generaldirektor einer Aktiengesellschaft; **Lord** ⚲ **of the Council** *(Br.)* Präsident des Geheimen Staatsrates; ~ **of a trade union** Generalsekretär einer Gewerkschaft; ⚲ **of the United States** Präsident der Vereinigten Staaten von Nordamerika;

to be elected ~ zum Präsidenten gewählt werden; **to consent to being** ~ Präsidentenwahl annehmen;

~ **judge** Gerichtspräsident.

presidential präsidial;

~ **address** Ansprache des Präsidenten; ~ **campaign** *(US)* Wahlkampf für die Präsidentschaft; ~ **candidate** Präsidentschaftskandidate; ~ **chair** Präsidentenstuhl; ~ **democracy** Präsidialdemokratie; ~ **election** Präsidentschafts-, Präsidentenwahl; ~ **electors** *(US)* Wahlmänner; ~ **judge** Vorsitzender; ~ **letter** *(US)* Brief des Vorstandes; ~ **message** *(US)* Botschaft des Präsidenten; ~ **nomination** Ernennung zum Präsidentschaftskandidaten; ~ **nominee** Präsidentschaftskandidat; ~ **primary** *(US)* Vorwahl zur Präsidentennominierung; ~ **prospect** Präsidentenanwärter; ~ **succession** *(US)* Präsidentennachfolge; ~ **suite** Präsidentensuite; ~ **system** *(US)* Präsidialsystem, -demokratie; ~ **term** Dauer der Präsidentschaft, Amtsperiode des Präsidenten; ~ **trip** Präsidentenreise; ~ **year** Präsidentschaftsjahr.

presidentship Präsidentschaft, Präsidentenstelle.

presiding | **at a meeting** Versammlungs-, Sitzungsleitung;

~ *(a.)* vorsitzführend, präsidierend;

~ **examiner** Prüfungsvorsitzender; ~ **judge** Gerichtspräsident, Vorsitzender; ~ **officer** *(Br.)* Wahlvorsitzender, -vorsteher.

presidium *(communist countries)* Präsidium.

press *(of affairs)* Hast, Drang, *(crowd)* Masse, Menge, *(newspaper)* Presse, Zeitungswesen, Journalismus, *(newspaper writers as a class)* Journalisten, Zeitungsschreiber, *(printing plant)* Druckerei, Druckanstalt;

„~" „gut zum Druck";

before going to ~ vor Redaktionsschluß (der Drucklegung); **fresh from the** ~ eben aus der Presse; **got up by the** ~ von den Zeitungen aufgebauscht; **in the** ~ im Druck; **in the** ~ **of the fight** in der Hitze des Gefechtes; **in the thick of the** ~ in der Menge eingekeilt; **lost in the** ~ in der Masse untergegangen; **off the** ~ gedruckt; **ready for** ~ druckfertig, -reif; **through the medium of the** ~ durch die Presse;

bad ~ schlechte Presse; **baling** ~ Ballenpresse; **the cheaper** ~ Boulevardzeitungen; **big city** ~ Großstadtpresse; **coining** ~ Münzprägemaschine; **computerized** ~ vollautomatisierte Druck- und Setzmaschine; **copying** ~ Kopierpresse; **corrupt** ~ bestechliche Presse; **forging** ~ Falschgeldwerkstatt; **gallery** ~ Abziehpresse; **German-language** ~ deutschsprachige Presse; **gutter** ~ Asphaltpresse, Skandalblätter, -presse, Journaille; **hydraulic** ~ hydraulische Presse, Wasserdruckpumpe; **kept** ~ bezahlte Presse; **letter** ~ Kopierpresse; **local** ~ Lokalblätter, -zeitungen, örtliche Presseorgane; **national** ~ inländische Prese; **penny** ~ Groschenblatt, Boulevardpresse; **printing** ~ Druckerpresse; **regional** ~ Regionalzeitungen; **reptile** ~ gedungene Presse; **rotary** ~ Rotationspresse; **screw** ~ Prägepresse; **stamping** ~ Stanzpresse; **technical** ~ Fachpresse; **yellow** ~ sensationslüsterne Blätter, Sensationspresse;

~ **of business** Drang der Geschäfte, Geschäftsandrang; ~ **forward of an army** Vormarsch eines Heeres; **the** ~ **of modern life** fieberhafte Tätigkeit des modernen Lebens;

~ (v.) pressen, drängen, bedrängen, betreiben, zusetzen, drücken;

~ **one's advantage** seinen Vorteil rücksichtslos wahrnehmen; ~ **ahead with s. th.** Sache vorantreiben; ~ **for an answer** auf Antwort dringen; ~ **an attack** entschlossenen Angriff führen; ~ **back** (enemy) zurückdrängen; ~ **the bricks** (US sl.) in der Stadt herumlungern; ~ **one's case** seine Sache nachdrücklich betreiben; ~ **a claim** auf einer Forderung bestehen; ~ **s. o. for a debt** von jem. dringend die Rückzahlung einer Schuld verlangen; ~ **for a decision to be made** auf eine Entscheidung drängen; ~ **down the accelerator** Gaspedal herunterdrücken; ~ **down heavily** (tax) sich drückend bemerkbar machen; ~ **the enemy hard** Feind heftig bedrängen; ~ **a gift [up]on s. o.** (fam.) jem. ein Geschenk aufdrängen; ~ **s. o. hard** j. hart bedrängen, jem. auf die Bude rücken; ~ **heavily upon s. o.** jem. wie eine schwere Last auf der Seele liegen; ~ **for an inquiry into a question** auf Untersuchung einer Frage drängen; ~ **the juice out of a lemon** Zitrone auspressen; ~ **money on s. o.** jem. Geld aufnötigen; ~ **s. o. for money** von jem. Geld erpressen; ~ **one's opinion on s. o.** seine Meinung oktroyieren; ~ **for payment** auf Zahlung drängen (bestehen), Zahlung dringend anmahnen; ~ **the pedal down** Gaspedal durchtreten; ~ **one's point** seine Ansicht durchsetzen; ~ **into a useful purpose** für einen nützlichen Zweck verwenden; ~ **into service** einsetzen, verwenden, benutzen; ~ **s. o. into service** sich jds. Dienste versichern; ~ **a suit** Anzug bügeln; ~ **heavily on the tradesmen** (tax) schwer auf der Geschäftswelt lasten; ~ **s. one's words too far** jds. Worte zu weit auslegen; ~ **on with one's work** seine Arbeit vorantreiben;

[not] to be available for the ~ sich der Presse [nicht] stellen; **to be by the** ~ gedruckt werden; **to be favo(u)rably noticed in the** ~ gute Aufnahme in der Presse finden; **to come from the** ~ gerade ausgedruckt sein; **to correct the** ~ Korrekturfahnen lesen; **to fight one's way through the** ~ sich durch die Menge drängen; **to figure in the** ~ in den Zeitungen erwähnt werden; **to gag the** ~ Presse mundtot machen; **to go to** ~ in Druck gehen, gedruckt werden; **to have a good** ~ gute Kritiken bekommen, gut aufgenommen werden; **to leak s. th. into the** ~ absichtliche Indiskretion begehen, in die Presse lancieren, etw. der Presse (den Zeitungen) zuspielen; **to liaise with the** ~ mit der Presse ständig Verbindung halten; **to muzzle the** ~ Presse knebeln; **to pass a proof for** ~ Korrekturen zum Satz geben; **to read for** ~ Korrekturfahnen lesen; **to receive a good** ~ gute Presse haben; **to release a statement to the** ~ Presseverlautbarung herausgeben; **to roll off the** ~es Druckmaschinen verlassen; **to see a work through the** ~ Drucklegung eines Buches überwachen; **to send to** ~ in Druck tun; **to sign for** ~ für druckfähig erklären, Imprimatur erteilen; **to subsidize the** ~ Presse subventionieren; **to suppress the** ~ freie Presse unterdrücken; **to write for the** ~ sich journalistisch betätigen, für Zeitungen schreiben; **to write a statement for the** ~ Presseerklärung verfassen;

~ **activities** Pressetätigkeit; ~ **advertisement** Zeitungsanzeige; ~ **advertising** Anzeigenwerbung; ~ **agency** Nachrichtenagentur, -büro, Pressebüro; ~ **agent** (theatre, US) Werbechef; ~ **amalgamation court** Untersuchungsausschuß für Pressekonzentrationen; ~ **announcement** Zeitungsanzeige; ~ **archives** Pressearchiv; ~ **arrangement** Presseabkommen; ~ **assistant**

Pressemitarbeiter; ~ **association** Journalistenvereinigung, Presseverband; ~ **attaché** Presseattaché; ~ **attention** Presseinteresse; ~ **bill** Pressegesetz; ~ **box** Presseloge; ~ **briefing** Presseinformation, -unterrichtung, -konferenz; ~ **bureau** Pressebüro; ~ **button** Druckknopf; ~**button war** Druckknopfkrieg; ~ **campaign** Pressekampagne; ~ **censorship** Pressezensur; ~ **center** Pressezentrum; ~ **charter** Presseverfassung, -gesetz; ~ **clipping** (US) Zeitungsausschnitt; ~ **clipping bureau** (US) Ausschnittsbüro; ~ **club** Presseclub; ~ **code** journalistischer Ehrenkodex; ~ **comments** Pressestimmen, Stimmen der Presse; ~ **commentary** Pressekommentar; ~ **communications** Pressemitteilungen, -nachrichten; ~ **conference** Pressekonferenz, -besprechung; **off-the-record** ~ **conference** Pressekonferenz ohne besonderen Anlaß, vertrauliches Pressegespräch; **live televised** ~ **conference** durchs Fernsehen übertragene Pressekonferenz; ~ **contingent** ausgewählte Journalistengruppe, Pressekontingent; ~ **controversy** Pressepolemik, -kontroverse; ~ **copy** Presse-, Besprechungsexemplar, Durchschlag herstellen; ~ **corrector** Korrektor, Korrekturenleser; ~ **correspondent** Berichterstatter, Korrespondent; ~ **council** Presserat; ~ **coverage** Pressebetreuung, Berichterstattung in der Presse; ~ **credentials** Journalistenausweis; ~ **cutting** (Br.) Zeitungsausschnitt; ~ **cutting agency** (Br.) [Zeitungs]ausschnittsdienst; ~ **date** (day) Redaktionsschluß; ~ **department** Presseabteilung, -büro; ~ **disclosure** Presseenthüllung; ~ **distortions** entstellte Presseberichte; ~ **entourage** begleitende Pressegruppe; ~ **Establishment** konservative Presse; ~ **facilities** Presseeinrichtungen; ~ **gallery** (parl., Br.) Pressetribüne; ~ **guide** Pressekatalog; ~ **interview** Presse-, Zeitungsinterview; ~ **iron** Bügel-, Plätteisen; ~ **item** Zeitungsnotiz; ~ **junket** Journalistenreise; ~ **key** (el.) Drucktaste; ~ **kit** Journalisten-, Pressemappe; ~ **law** Pressegesetz; ~ **list** Presse-, Journalistenliste; ~ **lord** Zeitungskönig; ~ **luncheon** Journalistenfrühstück; ~ **mapping agency** Lesezirkeldienst; ~ **mark** Bibliothekszeichen; ~ **material** Pressematerial; ~ **matter** druckfähige Sache; ~ **message** Pressetelegramm; ~ **money** Handgeld; **stop-**~ **news** letzte Nachrichten; ~ **note** Pressenotiz; ~ **notice** Presseankündigung, -notiz; ~ **office** Presseamt, -stelle; ~ **officer** Pressereferent, -chef, Leiter der Pressestelle, Kontaktmann zur Presse; ~ **orientation** Presseunterrichtung; ~ **photo** Pressefoto; ~ **photographer** Pressefotograf, Bildberichterstatter; ~ **preview** Pressevorschau; ~ **program(me)** Presseprogramm; ~ **proof** druckfertiger Korrekturbogen, Maschinenkorrektur, letzte Korrektur; ~ **proprietor** Zeitungsbesitzer; ~ **publicity** Pressewerbung; ~ **query** Zeitungsrückfrage; ~ **quotations** Pressezitate, -stimmen; ~ **reader** Korrektor; **hostile** ~ **reception** negative Aufnahme in der Presse; ~ **relations** Presseverbindungen; ~ **relations counsel** (officer) Kontaktmann zur Presse, Leiter der Presseabteilung, Pressechef; ~ **release** freigegebenes Pressematerial, -mitteilung, -verlautbarung; ~ **report** Pressebericht, Zeitungsmeldung; ~ **representative** Pressevertreter; ~ **review** Presseschau; ~ **revise** druckfertiger Korrekturbogen, Maschinenkorrektur, Umbruchkorrekturbogen; ~ **service** Presseagentur, -dienst; **to buy** ~ **space** Anzeigenteil kaufen; ~ **statement** Presseerklärung; ~ **stone** Setzstein; ~ **telegram** Pressetelegramm; ~ **tycoon** Pressezar; ~ **view** (exhibition) Vorbesichtigung durch die Presse; ~ **watch-dog group** Selbstkontrolle der Presse.

pressboard Presspan.

pressed | by one's creditors von seinen Gläubigern bedrängt; ~ **for funds** (money) geldknapp, in Geldverlegenheit; ~ **for space** raumknapp, beengt; ~ **for time** zeitknapp;

to be hard ~ hart bedrängt werden; **to be** ~ **for time** unter Zeitdruck stehen;

presser (printer) Drucker.

pressgang Zwangsrekrutierte;

~ (v.) **minimal support** minimale Unterstützung erzielen.

pressing Stanzen, (papermaking) Satinieren, Glätten, (record) Preßplatte, Plattendruck;

~ **of one's point** hartnäckiges Bestehen auf einem Punkt; ~ **seamen** Zwangsanheuerung von Matrosen;

~ (a.) eilig, dringend;

to be ~ **against the barriers** gegen die Absperrungen drängen; **to be** ~ **for a decision to be made** auf eine Entscheidung drängen; **to require** ~ Druck nötig haben; **not to need much** ~ keines besonderen Drängens bedürfen;

~ **board** (bookmaking) Preßbrett; ~ **business** dringende Geschäfte; ~ **case** dringender Fall; ~ **danger** drohende Gefahr; ~ **debt** drückende Schuld; ~ **invitation** eilige Einladung; ~ **matter** dringende Angelegenheit; ~ **necessity** dringende Notwendigkeit; ~ **need** drückende Not; **to attend to the most** ~ **thing first** Dringendes zuerst erledigen.

pressman *(printer)* Drucker, *(journalist, Br.)* Berichterstatter, Korrespondent, Reporter.

pressmark Signatur, *(library)* Bibliotheksnummer, -zeichen; ~ *(v.)* mit einer Bibliotheksnummer versehen.

pressroom Maschinensaal, Druckerei.

pressure Drängen, Druck[anwendung], *(el.)* Spannung;
under the ~ **of poverty** in drückender Armut;
blood ~ Blutdruck; **economic** ~ wirtschaftlicher Druck; **financial** ~ finanzielle Schwierigkeiten; **high** ~ *(meteorol.)* Hochdruck; **inflationary** ~ Inflationsdruck; **low** ~ Niederdruck, *(meteorol.)* Tiefdruck; **monetary** ~ Geldknappheit, -mangel; **moral** ~ moralischer Druck; **peaceful** ~ Sanktionsmaßnahmen; **tyre** ~ Reifendruck; **union** ~ von den Gewerkschaften ausgeübter Druck; **water** ~ Wasserdruck; **wind** ~ Winddruck; ~ **of the atmosphere** atmosphärischer Druck; ~ **of axle** *(car)* Achsdruck; ~ **of business** Geschäftsanspannung, Drang der Geschäfte; ~ **of the button** Knopfdruck; ~ **to buy** Kaufzwang; ~ **of circumstances** Druck der Verhältnisse; ~ **of conscience** Gewissensnot; ~ **of costs** Kostendruck; ~ **of demand** Nachfragedruck, -sog; ~ **on the labo(u)r market** Anspannung des Arbeitsmarktes, Arbeitsmarktanspannung; ~ **of liquidity** Liquiditätsdruck, -anspannung; ~ **for money** Geldknappheit; ~ **of the money market** Versteifung des Geldmarkts; ~ **on money supply** erschwerte Geldmarktversorgung; ~ **of necessity** dringende Notwendigkeit; ~ **to perform** Leistungsdruck; ~ **of the price** Druck der Preise, Preisdruck, *(stock exchange)* Kursdruck; ~ **of increasing prices** Teuerungsdruck; ~ **of taxation** Steuerdruck, -belastung; ~ **of time** Zeitdruck; ~ **on wages** Lohndruck, -belastung; ~ **of work** Arbeitsandrang;
to act under ~ unter Zwang (Druck) handeln; **to be free of election-eve** ~ nicht dem Druck der öffentlichen Meinung vor den Wahlen ausgesetzt sein; **to be under** ~ unter Druck stehen, *(stock exchange)* gedrückt liegen, stark angespannt sein; **to be under selling** ~ unter Verkaufsdruck liegen; **to be under** ~ **of poverty** von der Armut bedrängt sein; **to bring** ~ **to bear upon s. o. j.** unter Druck setzen, Druck auf j. ausüben, Druckmittel bei jem. ausüben; **to ease seasonal** ~s für Druckausgleich saisoneller Schwankungen sorgen; **to exert** ~ Druck ausüben; **to give way to** ~ dem Druck nachgeben; **to know the** ~ **of poverty** Armut kennengelernt haben; **to place** ~ **on the money market** Druck auf den Geldmarkt ausüben (verursachen); **to put** ~ **on the management** Vorstand unter Druck setzen; **to remain under heavy** ~ weiterhin stark gedrückt liegen; **to suffer from high blood** ~ unter hohem Blutdruck leiden; **to work at high** ~ mit Hochdruck arbeiten; **to yield to the** ~ **of public opinion** dem Druck der öffentlichen Meinung nachgeben;
~ **altitude** Barometerdruck; ~ **bargaining** unter Streikdruck stehende Tarifverhandlungen; ~ **boiler** Druckkessel; ~ **cabin** *(airplane)* Luftdruckkabine; ~ **chamber** Druckkammer; ~ **cooker** Schnellkocher, Schnellkochtopf; ~ **drop** Druckabfall; ~ **gauge** Druckanzeiger, Manometer; ~ **gauge reading** Manometerstand; ~ **group** Interessenverband, -gruppe; ~ **group policy** Interessenpolitik; ~ **map** Luftdruckkarte; ~ **pattern** Druckverteilung; ~-**proof** *(cabin)* druckfest; ~ **pump** Druckpumpe; ~ **suit** Überdruckanzug; ~ **tank** Druckbehälter; ~ **variations** Luftdruckschwankungen.

prestable *(Scot.)* zahlbar.

pressurize *(v.)* druckdicht halten.

pressurized *(cabin)* klimatisiert;
~ **cabin** Druckkabine.

presswork *(journalism)* Berichterstattung, Journalismus, *(product of a printing press)* Druckarbeiten.

pressworker Berichterstatter, Journalist.

prest Handgeld;
to give in ~ als Handgeld geben;
~ **money** *(ship)* Handgeld.

prestabilization debts Schulden vor der Währungsreform.

prestige Ansehen, Einfluß, Prestige;
international ~ **of a country** Geltung eines Landes in der Welt; **to commit one's** ~ sich prestigemäßig festlegen; **to mean loss of** ~ Prestigeverlust bedeuten; **to ruin the** ~ **of a country** Prestige eines Landes ruinieren;
~ **advertising** Image-, Prestige-, Repräsentations-, Sympathiewerbung; ~ **bias** *(opinion poll)* auf Prestigegründen beruhende falsche Antwort; ~ **building** Prestigegewinn; ~-**conscious** prestigeempfindlich; ~ **magazine campaign** Publizitätskampagne; ~ **merchandise** Prestigeartikel; ~ **publication** repräsentative Veröffentlichung; ~ **value** Repräsentationswert.

presume *(v.)* vermuten, annehmen, schließen, unterstellen, *(dare)* sich herausnehmen (vermessen, erdreisten), wagen, *(law)* als wahr annehmen;

~**upon a short acquaintance** kurze Bekanntschaft dreist ausnutzen; ~ **conclusively** schlüssig unterstellen; ~ **a fact from another** eine Tatsache aus einer anderen abschließen; ~ **s. o. innocent** j. für unschuldig halten; ~ **s. one's kindness** jds. Gutmütigkeit mißbrauchen; ~ **on one's wealth** sich aufgrund seines Reichtums vermessen.

presumption Annahme, Vermutung, Unterstellung, *(law)* Präsumption, Vermutung;
on the ~ in der Annahme;
absolute ~ unwiderlegbare Rechtsvermutung; **artificial** ~ gesetzliche Vermutung; **conclusive** ~ unwiderlegbare Rechtsvermutung; **disputable** ~ widerlegbare Vermutung; **false** ~ falsche Vermutung; **inconclusive** ~ widerlegbare Rechtsvermutung; **irrebuttable** ~ unwiderlegbare Rechtsvermutung; **legal** ~ Rechtsvermutung; **mixed** ~ tatsächliche und gesetzliche Vermutung; **natural** ~ natürliche Folgerung; **nonrebuttable** ~ unwiderlegbare Vermutung; **prima facie** ~ Primafacievoraussetzung; **rebuttable** ~ widerlegbare Vermutung; **refutable** ~ widerlegbare Rechtsvermutung; **violent** ~ zwingender Schluß; ~ **of advancement** *(Br.)* Erbvorausvermutung, Schenkungsvermutung; ~ **of confiscation** *(restriction law)* Entziehungsvermutung; ~ **of death** Todesvermutung, Verschollenheit; ~ **of fact** Tatsachenvermutung; ~ **in favo(u)r of s. o.** Unterstellung zu jds. Gunsten; ~ **of gifts** Schenkungsvermutung; ~ **of innocence** Vermutung im Zweifel zugunsten des Angeklagten; **general** ~ **of law** Rechtsvermutung, gesetzliche Vermutung; ~ **of ownership** Eigentumsvermutung; ~ **of paternity** Vaterschaftsvermutung; ~ **of survival (survivorship)** *(life insurance)* Überlebensvermutung; ~ **of title** Eigentumsvermutung; **strong** ~ **against the truth of the news** Gründe die stark gegen die Wahrheit von Nachrichten sprechen; ~ **of a trust** Vermutung einer Treuhandregelung; ~ **of value** Vermutung der entgeltlichen Übertragung;
to raise a ~ Vermutung begründen; **to rebut a** ~ Vermutung widerlegen (entkraften).

presumptive vermutlich, mutmaßlich;
~ **damages** erlittenen Schaden übersteigender Schadenersatzanspruch, Bußgeld; ~ **death** Todesvermutung; ~ **evidence** Indizienbeweis; **heir** ~ mutmaßlicher Erbe; ~ **loss** *(ship)* Schiffsverschollenheit; ~ **proof** Wahrscheinlichkeitsbeweis; ~ **title** präsumptiver Besitztitel.

presuppose *(v.)* zur Voraussetzung haben, voraussetzen;
~ **long years of study** *(calling)* langjähriges Studium bedingen.

presupposition Voraussetzung.

pretax vor Steuer;
to narrow ~ **differentials** vorsteuerliches Lohngefälle einebnen; ~ **income** Einkommen vor Abzug der Steuern; ~ **profit** Gewinn vor Steuern.

preteens die jüngeren Jahrgänge.

pretence, pretense *(claim)* Anspruch, Anforderung, *(pretext)* Vorwand, Scheingrund, *(false reason)* Vorspiegelung;
under the ~ unter dem Vorwand;
false ~s Vorspiegelung falscher Tatsachen;
to do s. th. under the ~ **of patriotism** Vaterlandsliebe vorschützen; **to do s. th. under the** ~ **of friendship** etw. unter dem Vorwand eines Freundschaftsdienstes tun; **to force one's way in under false** ~ sich mit Lug und Trug Eingang verschaffen; **to make no** ~ **to** keinen Anspruch erheben auf; **to obtain s. th. under false** ~s sich etw. durch betrügerische Angaben verschaffen; **to obtain credit by false** ~ Kreditbetrug begehen.

pretend *(v.)* Anspruch erheben, *(feign)* vorgeben, vortäuschen, heucheln, simulieren, fälschlich behaupten;
~ **to be very busy** voll ausgelastet zu sein heucheln; ~ **to be a doctor** sich als Arzt ausgeben; ~ **ignorance** Unkenntnis vorschützen; ~ **sickness (to be ill)** Krankheit vorschützen (simulieren); ~ **to the throne** Ansprüche auf den Thron erheben.

pretended angeblich, vorgeblich, vorgetäuscht;
~ **title to land** angebliches Grundstückseigentum.

pretender rechtmäßiger Inhaber, *(claimant to a throne)* Thronbewerber.

pretendership Thronbewerbung.

pretensed right (title) Herausgabeanspruch des Nichtbesitzers.

pretension Anspruch, Forderung;
baseless ~s grundlose (unberechtigte) Forderungen; **territorial** ~s territoriale Ansprüche, angemaßte Gebietsansprüche;
to have social ~s gesellschaftlichen Ehrgeiz haben;
to have no higher ~ nicht nach Höherem streben; **to have** ~s **to be considered a scholar** als Wissenschaftler gewertet werden wollen; **to have** ~ **to literary taste** literarische Ansprüche stellen; **to make** ~s **to expert knowledge on a subject** Fachkenntnisse auf einem Gebiet in Anspruch nehmen.

pretentious anspruchsvoll, prätentiös;
    to speak in a ~ language hochtrabende Worte gebrauchen; **~ man** Snob; **~ style** gespreizter Stil.

preterition *(of heir)* Übergehung.

pretermission *(offspring, US)* Übergehen bei der letztwilligen Verfügung.

pretermit *(heir, US)* übergehen.

pretermitted heir *(US)* übergangener Erbe.

pretest *(advertising)* Werbewertprüfung, *(interview)* Probebefragung, -test.

pretext Ausrede, Ausflucht, Vorwand, *(international law)* berechtigter Grund;
    under the ~ of consulting his lawyer unter dem Vorwand sich von seinem Anwalt beraten zu lassen;
    to find a ~ for refusing Ausrede für eine Absage erfinden; **~** *(v.)* **sickness** Krankheit vorschützen.

pretorium *(Scot.)* Gerichtsgebäude.

pretrial|detention *(US)* Untersuchungshaft; **~ hearing** Voruntersuchung; **~ procedure** *(US)* Vorverfahren.

pretties schöne Sachen, Schmucksachen, *(US)* Krimskrams.

pretty hübsch, liebenswürdig, *(coll.)* ganz schön, beträchtlich, *(finial)* geziert, gespreizt;
    sitting ~ *(coll.)* gut gerüstet;
    as ~ as a picture so schön wie gemalt; **~ nearly the same** fast das Gleiche;
    to be ~ much alike sich ziemlich ähneln; **to be ~ sick about it** Schnauze von etw. voll haben; **to fill one's glass to the ~** sein Glas bis zum Rand füllen; **to sit ~** fein heraus sein;
    ~ mess schöne Geschichte; **~ penny** hübsches Sümmchen; **to cost a ~ penny** schöne Stange Geld kosten; **to make ~ speeches** Artigkeiten sagen; **~ state of affairs** ganz schönes Durcheinander; **to play a ~ trick upon s. o.** j. ganz schön hereinlegen.

prevail *(v.)* vorherrschen, maßgebend, (wirksam, ausschlaggebend) sein, Ausschlag geben, *(prove superior)* Oberhand gewinnen, sich durchsetzen;
    ~ upon o. s. es übers Herz bringen; **~ upon s. o. to consent** jem. seine Zustimmung abringen; **~ on s. o. to do s. th.** j. dazu bringen, etw. zu tun; **~ over an enemy** Oberhand über einen Feind behalten; **~ upon s. o. to lend s. o. £ 50** jem. überreden, einem 50 Pfund zu leihen.

prevailing *(predominating)* vorherrschend, maßgeblich, üblich, *(price)* gangbar, handelsüblich;
    under the ~ circumstances unter den gegebenen Umständen; **~ fashion** herrschende Mode; **~ opinion** herrschende Meinung, *(US)* **party** obsiegende Partei; **~ price** gegenwärtiger Preis, Marktpreis; **~ rate** geltender Lohntarif; **~ tone** *(stock exchange)* Grundton, -stimmung, -tendenz; **~ wind** üblicher Wind.

prevalence Vorherrschen, Verbreitung, Übergewicht, -handnehmen;
    ~ of bribery verbreitete Bestechlichkeit; **~ of murder** Überhandnehmen von Mordfällen; **~ of typhus in a place** Überhandnehmen von Typhusfällen in einem Ort.

prevalent vorherrschend, überwiegend, verbreitet;
    to be ~ verbreitet sein, grassieren;
    ~ fashion geltende Mode; **~ idea on a question** allgemein vertretene Ansicht zu einer Frage; **~ opinion** allgemeine Meinung.

prevaricate *(v.)* unwahre Angaben machen, Wahrheit verdrehen, Ausflüchte gebrauchen, *(collude)* mit der Gegenpartei ins Einvernehmen treten, Parteivorrat begehen, *(law)* Amtspflicht verletzen;
    ~ a crime Verbrechen verheimlichen.

prevarication Winkelzug, Verdrehen der Wahrheit, Tatsachenverdrehung, *(collusion)* Parteiverrat, *(officer)* Amtspflichtverletzung, -vergehen, Dienstwidrigkeit.

prevaricator Rechts-, Wortverdreher.

prevent *(v.)* vermeiden, verhindern, verhüten, zuvorkommen;
    ~ s. o. [from] doing s. th. j. an etw. hindern; **~ an accident** Unfall verhüten; **~ the exercise of a right** Rechtsausübung verhindern; **~ the murderer from being lynched** Lynchmord verhindern.

prevented verhindert, ferngehalten;
    to be unavoidably ~ from doing s. th. absolut verhindert sein; **to have been ~ by a previous engagement from taking the chair** infolge einer früheren Verabredung an der Übernahme des Vorsitzes verhindert sein.

preventer Vorbeugungs-, Schutzmaßnahme.

prevention Verhinderung, Vermeidung, Verhütung, Hintertreibung, *(med.)* Vorbeugung, Prophylaxe;
    in case of ~ im Verhinderungsfall;
    claim ~ Verhinderung des Entstehens von Ersatzansprüchen; **rust ~** Rostschutz;

~ of accidents Unfallverhütung; **~ of competition** Wettbewerbsbehinderung; **~ of crime** Verbrechensverhütung; **~ of disease** Krankheitsverhütung; **~ of enjoyment** *(possession)* Besitzstörung; **~ of hardships** Vermeidung von Härtefällen; **~ of labo(u)r accidents** Arbeiterunfallverhütung, -unfallschutz; **~ of loss** Schadensverhütung; **~ of performance** Verhinderung der Vertragserfüllung; **~ of war** Kriegsverhütung;
    to take measures for the ~ of diseases Vorkehrungen gegen den Ausbruch von Krankheiten treffen;
    ♀ **of Crimes Act** Vorbeugegesetz gegen Gewohnheitsverbrecher; ♀ **of Fraud Act** *(Br.)* Gesetz zur Verhütung von Kapitalanlagenbetrug.

preventive Vorbeugungs-, Schutzmittel;
    ~ *(a.)* vorbeugend, verhütend, präventiv;
    ~ custody *(Br.)* Sicherungsverwahrung; **~ injunction** Verbotsverfügung; **rust ~** Rostschutzmittel; **~ investigation** *(Br.)* Zollfahndung; **~ justice** Maßnahmen gegen Gewohnheitsverbrecher; **~ maintenance** *(plant)* vorbeugende Instandhaltung, Vorsorgemaßnahmen zur Werkserhaltung; **~ measures** vorbeugende Maßnahmen, Schutz-, Vorsichts-, Abwehrmaßnahmen; **~ medicine** Gesundheitsvorsorge, -pflege; **~ officer** *(Br.)* Beamter des Zollfahndungsdienstes, Zollfahndungsbeamter; **~ preparation** Vorbeugungsmittel; **~ protection** Schutzhaft; **~ service** *(Br.)* Zollgrenz-, Küstenschutz-, Zollfahndungsdienst; **~ treatment** Präventivbehandlung; **~ vaccination** Schutzimpfung; **~ war** Präventivkrieg.

preventively vorbeugend, sicherheitshalber.

preview Filmvorführung vor der Uraufführung.

previous vorig, vorhergehend, früher;
    too ~ voreilig;
    to be rather ~ in forming a plan voreiligen Plan fassen;
    ~ application *(patent law)* Voranmeldung; **~ approval** vorherige Zustimmung; **~ arrangements** vorausgegangene Vereinbarungen; **~ career** bisherige Tätigkeit; **our ~ communications** unsere früheren Briefe (Vorkorrespondenz); **~ conviction** Vorstrafe; **~ day** *(stock exchange)* letzter Notierungstag; **~ decision** frühere Entscheidung; **~ endorser** Vor[der]mann; **~ engagement** anderweitige (frühere) Verabredung; **~ examination** Vorexamen, Zulassungsprüfung; **to have ~ experience** Vorkenntnisse haben; **~ holder** früherer Inhaber, Vorbesitzer, Vordermann; **~ illness** *(insurance)* altes Leiden; **~ month** Vormonat; **~ notice** Vorankündigung; **on a ~ occasion** bei früherer Gelegenheit; **~ payment** Vorschußzahlung; **~ question** *(parl.)* Antrag auf Schluß der Debatte; **to move the ~ question** Übergang zur Tagesordnung beantragen; **~ quotation** letzte Notierung; **~ speaker** Vorredner; **~ year** Vorjahr.

previously|convicted vorbestraft; **as ~ mentioned** wie oben erwähnt.

prevocational training Berufsschulausbildung.

prevue *(film, US)* Vorschau.

prewar vor dem Krieg;
    ~ compromise Vorkriegsvergleich; **~ days** Vorkriegszeit; **~ debts** Vorkriegsschulden; **~ era** Vorkriegszeit; **~ export** Vorkriegsausfuhr; **~ goods** Waren aus der Vorkriegszeit; **~ holdings** Vorkriegsbeteiligungen; **~ level** Vorkriegsstand; **~ loan** Vorkriegsanleihe; **~ performance** Vorkriegsleistung; **~ period** Vorkriegszeit; **~ position** Vorkriegsposition; **~ price** Friedens-, Vorkriegspreis; **~ price level** Vorkriegspreisniveau; **~ principles** Vorkriegsgepflogenheiten; **~ purchasing power** Vorkriegskaufkraft; **~ rent** Friedens-, Vorkriegsmiete; **~ standard of profits** Vorkriegsgewinnstandard; **~ value** Vorkriegswert.

prey *(fig.)* Opfer, Beute;
    ~ *(v.)* auf Raub (Beute) ausgehen; **~ on s. one's mind** jds. Sache belasten, an jds. Herzen nagen; **~ upon the poor** die Armen ausbeuten;
    to be an easy ~ to s. o. eine leichte Beute für j. darstellen; **to fall a ~ to circumstances** Opfer der Verhältnisse werden; **to fall a ~ to temptations** seinen Versuchungen erliegen.

preyer *(fig.)* Ausbeuter.

price Preis, Kauf-, Marktpreis, *(award offered for apprehension)* Kopfpreis, *(bribe)* Bestechungsgeld, -summe, *(consideration)* Entgelt, Gegenleistung, *(cost)* Kosten, *(reward)* Lohn, Belohnung, *(stock exchange)* Kurs[wert], *(value)* Wert, Schätzung;
    above ~ unschätzbar; **according to the ~** nach Maßgabe des Preises; **adjusted for ~** preisbereinigt; **at all ~s** in jeder Preislage; **at any ~** um jeden (zu jedem) Preis; **not at any ~** um keinen Preis der Welt; **at constant ~s** preisbereinigt; **at the lowest ~** bei billigster Berechnung; **at present ~s** bei den gegenwärtigen Kursen; **not at any ~** um nichts in der Welt, um keinen Preis; **at the ~ of** *(stock exchange)* zum Kurs von; **at the best ~** *(stock exchange)* bestens, bestmöglich; **at current market**

~s *(stock exchange)* zum Tageskurs; **at the established** ~ zum amtlich festgesetzten Preis; **at the given** ~ zum festgesetzten Preis; **at half** ~ zum halben Preis; **at a higher** ~ zu erhöhten Preisen; **at a low** ~ billig; **at one** ~ zu festem Preis; **all at one** ~ zum Einheitspreis; **all at one** ~**, a dollar** jedes Stück für einen Dollar; ~s **dropping off** *(stock exchange)* bei sinkenden (weichenden) Kursen; **at present** ~s *(stock exchange)* bei dem heutigen Kursstand; **at a reduced** ~ mit Preisnachlaß, zu herabgesetztem (zurückgesetztem) Preis, herabgesetzt; **at 1980 survey** ~s nach der letztgreifbaren Statistik des Jahres 1980, auf der Grundlage der Preise im Jahre 1980; **at the understood** ~ zum vereinbarten Preis; **beyond** ~ unbezahlbar; **by declining** ~s bei sinkenden Preisen, *(stock exchange)* bei sinkenden Kursen; **for half the** ~ zum halben Preis; **of great** ~ von hohem Wert; **under** ~ unter [dem Selbstkosten]preis; **within the limits of this** ~ in derselben Preislage; **without** ~ unschätzbar; ~ **is no object** der Preis spielt keine Rolle;

~ **absorbing freight** Frachtkosten inbegriffen; **acceptable** ~ annehmbarer Preis; **actual** ~ tatsächlich erzielter Preis, Markt-, Tagespreis; **additional** ~ Preisaufschlag, Auf-, Mehrpreis; **adequate** ~ angemessener Preis; **adjustable** ~ gestaffelter Preis, Staffelpreis; **administered** ~ amtlich festgesetzter (bewirtschafteter) Preis; **advanced** ~ erhöhter (angehobener) Preis (Kurs); **advancing** ~s steigende Preise; **advertised** ~ *(newspaper)* Bezugspreis; **agreed** ~**, agreed upon** vereinbarter (abgesprochener) Preis; **agricultural** ~s Preise landwirtschaftlicher Erzeugnisse; **allround** ~ allgemein gültiger Preis, Preis in Bausch und Bogen, Pauschal-, Gesamtpreis; **approved** ~ genehmigter Preis; **arbitrary** ~ willkürlicher Preis; ~ **asked** geforderter Preis, *(stock exchange)* Briefkurs; **asking** ~ Preiserwartung, Angebotspreis; **attractive** ~ vorteilhafter (anziehender) Preis; **auction** ~ Auktionspreis; **average** ~ Durchschnittspreis, mittlerer Preis, *(stock exchange)* Kursdurchschnitt, Durchschnittskurs; **average cost** ~ Durchschnittsgestehungspreis; **bargain** ~ Vorzugs-, Ausverkaufpreis; **base (basic)** ~ Basis-, Grundpreis; **basing point** ~ Zielpreis; **best** ~ höchst erzielbarer Preis; **bid** ~ gebotener Preis, *(stock exchange)* Geldkurs; **bidding** ~ erstes Gegenangebot; **blanket** ~ Einheits-, Pauschalpreis; **booming** ~s haussierende Kurse; **boomtime** ~s Preis in Zeiten der Hochkonjunktur; **bottom** ~ niedrigster (äußerster) Preis, *(stock exchange)* niedrigster Kurs; **budget** ~ billiger Preis; **bulk** ~ Pauschalpreis; **buoyant** ~s hochschnellende Kurse; **buy-back** ~ Rückkaufspreis; **buying** ~ Einkaufspreis; **call** ~ Vorprämienkurs; **cash** ~ Bar-, Kassapreis, Preis bei Barzahlung, *(stock exchange)* Kassakurs; **catalog(ue)** ~ Katalog-, Versandhaus, Listenpreis; **ceiling** ~ [amtlicher] Höchstpreis; **not-to-exceed ceiling** ~ unüberschreitbarer Höchstpreis; **center-spread** ~ *(advertising)* Preis für eine doppelseitige Anzeige in Heftmitte; **certain** ~ durchschnittlicher Marktpreis, *(foreign exchange)* fester Umrechnungskurs; **charge** ~ gewöhnlicher Preis; **city** ~ *(stock exchange)* Börsenkurs; **class** ~ überhöhter, von Kunden akzeptierter Preis; **close** ~ scharf (äußerst) kalkulierter Preis, *(stock exchange)* um Bruchteile differierender Kurs; **closing** ~ *(stock exchange)* Schlußkurs, -notierung; **closing bid and asked** ~ Geld- und Briefkurs; **commercial** ~ echter Preis; **commodity** ~ Warenpreis; **common** ~ gewöhnlicher Preis; **competitive (competitor's)** ~ konkurrenzfähiger Preis, Wettbewerbs-, Konkurrenzpreis; **highly concessional** ~ sehr günstiger Preis; **conditional** ~ ausbedungener Preis; **consecutively quoted** ~s laufende Kursnotierungen; **construction** ~s Baukosten; **consumer** ~ Verbraucherpreis; **contract (contracted)** ~ Vertragspreis, vertraglich vereinbarter Preis, Lieferpreis; **controlled** ~ gebundener (amtlich festgesetzter) Preis, Stopppreis; **cost** ~ Selbstkosten-, Anschaffungs-, Einkaufs-, Einstandspreis, Herstellungskosten; **cost-plus** ~ Selbstkostenpreis plus vereinbartem Zuschlag; **curb [market]** ~ außergewöhnlicher Kurs, Freiverkehrskurs; **current** ~ üblicher (laufender, jetziger, gegenwärtiger) Handelspreis, Tagespreis; **current bid** ~ *(investment certificate)* Rücknahmepreis; **cushioning** ~ Stützpreis; **customary** ~ gewöhnlicher (ortsüblicher) Preis; **cut** ~ herabgesetzter (erniedrigter) Preis; ~ **cut very fine** scharf kalkulierter Preis; **cut-rate** ~ Schleuder-, Reklamepreis; **cutthroat** ~ mörderischer Preis, Schleuderpreis der Konkurrenz; **cutting** ~ Schleuderpreis; **declining** ~s fallende Kurse (Preise); **deferred-payment** ~ *(US)* Preis bei Ratenzahlung, Abzahlungspreis; **delivered** ~ Bezugs-, Lieferpreis; **delivered-in** ~ Preis frei Haus; **depressed** ~s gedrückte Kurse; **differential** ~ Staffelpreis; **discount** ~ Preis für Wiederverkäufer, Wiederverkaufspreis; **diverging** ~ abweichender Preis; **domestic** ~ Inlandspreis; **dropping** ~s fallende Preise, *(stock exchange)* Kursrückgang; **dumping** ~ Dumping-

preis; **early-bird** ~ Reklame-, Einführungspreis; **elastic** ~s bewegliche (nachgebende) Preise; **enhanced** ~ erhöhter Preis; **equalization** ~ Ausgleichskurs; **equilibrium** ~ Wettbewerbspreis; **equity** ~s Kurse von Dividendenwerten; **escalation** ~ gleitender Preis; **established** ~s eingependelte Preise; **estimated** ~ Schätzungspreis, -wert; **exceptional** ~ Sonder-, Ausnahme-, Vorzugspreis; **exaggerated** ~ übersetzter Preis; **excess[ive]** ~ Überpreis; **exercise** ~ Kurs im Zeitpunkt der Optionsausübung; **exhaust** ~ *(forward deal)* Sicherungsvorschuß erschöpfender Preis; **exorbitant (extortionate)** ~ stark überhöhter (exorbitanter) Preis, Wucherpreis; **expected** ~ Preisvorschlag; **fabulous** ~ unerhörter Preis; **factory** ~ Erzeuger-, Fabrikpreis, Preis ab Fabrik; **factory-gate** ~ Preis ab Fabrik (Werk); **fair** ~ angemessener (reeller) Preis; **fair market** ~ marktgerechter Preis, Normalpreis; **fairly good** ~ leidlicher Preis; **falling** ~ sinkender Preis; **fancy** ~ Phantasie-, Liebhaberpreis, Affektionswert; **farm** ~s Preis landwirtschaftlicher Erzeugnisse, Agrarpreise; **FAS** ~ Preis incl. sämtlicher Kosten bis zum Schiff; **favo(u)rable** ~ günstiger Preis; **final** ~ Endpreis; **firm** ~s stabile Preise, *(stock exchange)* feste Kurse; **first** ~ Ankaufs-, Einkaufs-, Anschaffungspreis; **fixed** ~ gebundener Preis, Festpreis, fester Preis (Satz, Kurs); **fixed contract** ~ vertraglich festgesetzter Preis; **flat** ~ Pauschal-, Sammel-, Einheitspreis; **flexible** ~s bewegliche Preise; **floor** ~ Mindestpreis; **fluctuating** ~s schwankende Preise (Kurse); **foreign** ~ Auslandspreis; **forward** ~ Preis für künftige Lieferungen, *(stock exchange, Br.)* Kurs für Termingeschäfte, Terminkurs; **free** ~ ungebundener (unabhängiger) Preis, empfohlener Ladenpreis, unverbindliche Preisempfehlung; **free at frontier** ~ *(EC)* Preis frei Grenze; **free market** ~ *(stock exchange)* Freiverkehrskurs; **frozen** ~ gestoppter (eingefrorener) Preis, Stopppreis; **full** ~ voller (nicht herabgesetzter) Preis; **full economic** ~ nicht subventionierter Preis; **futures** ~ *(US)* Terminkurs; **giveaway** ~ Schleuderpreis; **going-** ~ augenblicklich gültiger (geltender) Preis; **going-market** ~ gängiger Marktpreis; **going-to-press** ~s letzte Kursnotierung; **gold** ~ Goldpreis; **graduated** ~ gestaffelter Preis, Staffelpreis; **gross** ~ Bruttopreis; **guaranteed** ~ Garantiepreis; **guide** ~ *(EC)* Orientierungspreis; **guiding** ~ Richtpreis; **half** ~ halber Preis; **high** ~ hoher Preis[stand]; **ruinously high** ~ mörderischer Preis; **highflying** ~ hochgestochener Preis; **higher** ~ Mehrpreis; **highest** ~ Best-, Höchstpreis, *(stock exchange)* Höchstkurs; **hire-purchase** ~ *(Br.)* Abzahlungspreis, Preis bei Abzahlung; **home-market** ~ Inlandspreis; **huge** ~ enormer Preis; **in-bond** ~ Preis für unverzollte Ware im Zollager; **inclusive** ~ Pauschalpreis; **increased** ~ erhöhter Preis, Preiserhöhung; **increasing** ~s steigende Preise; **industrial** ~ Fabrikpreis; **industrial share** ~s Notierungen für Industriewerte; **industry-wide** ~ in der ganzen Industrie geltender Preis; **inflated** ~s künstlich überhöhte Preise; **inflationary** ~s inflationistische Preise; **inofficial** ~ *(stock exchange)* außerbörslicher Kurs, Freiverkehrskurs; **internal** ~ interner Verrechnungspreis; **inventory** ~ Inventurpreis; **invoice[d]** ~ auf der Rechnung angegebener (fakturierter) Preis, Rechnungsbetrag, Fakturenpreis; **issue** ~ Ausgabe-, Emissionskurs; **keener** ~ konkurrenzfähiger Preis; **kerb[-stone]** ~ *(Br.)* nachbörslicher Kurs, Freiverkehrskurs; **key** ~ marktentscheidender Preis; **knockdown** ~ Reklamepreis, äußerster Preis, *(auction)* Taxe; **knockout** ~ Schleuderpreis; **land** ~ Boden-, Grundstückspreis; **landed** ~ Preis frei Bestimmungshafen; **last** ~ letzter Kurs, letzte Börsennotierung; **latest** ~ Tagespreis; **limited** ~ limitierter Preis, Preislimit, *(stock exchange)* limitierter Kurs, Kurslimit; **listed** ~ *(US)* notierte Kurse; **list[ing]** ~ Katalog-, Listenpreis; **loco** ~ Lokopreis; **long** ~ hoher Preis; **losing** ~ nicht die Selbstkosten deckender Preis; **loss-making** ~ Verlustpreis; **low** ~ niedriger Preis (Kurs); **lowest possible** ~ äußerster (niedrigster) Preis, Mindestpreis, *(stock exchange)* niedrigster Kurs; **lump-sum** ~ Global-, Pauschalpreis; **in-the-mail** ~ Preis frei Haus; **maintained** ~s gebundene Preise; **making-up** ~ äquivalenter Preis, *(Br.)* Abrechnungs-, Lieferungs-, Verrechnungs-, Liquidationskurs; **managed (manipulated)** ~ manipulierter (gesteuerter, künstlich beeinflußter) Preis, *(stock exchange)* manipulierter Kurs; **manufacturer's [sales] (manufacturing)** ~ Fabrik-, Herstellungspreis; **marked** ~ ausgezeichneter Preis; **marked-down** ~ herabgesetzter Preis; **marked-up** ~ heraufgesetzter Preis; **market** ~ augenblicklicher (handelsüblicher) Preis, Tages-, Marktpreis, *(auditing, US)* Wiederbeschaffungswert, *(stock exchange)* Tages-, Börsenkurs; **maximum** ~ obere Preisgrenze, *(stock exchange)* Höchstkurs; **maximum [selling]** ~ Höchst[verkaufs]preis; **maximum wholesale** ~ Großhandelshöchstpreis; **medium** ~ Mittelkurs; **middle [market]** ~ Mittelkurs; **minimum** ~ niedrigster Preis, Mindest[verkaufs]preis,

Mindestpreisgrenze, *(stock exchange)* Mindestkurs; **minimum resale ~** in der zweiten Hand gebundener Preis, Mindestwiederverkaufspreis; **moderate ~** mäßiger (billiger, ziviler, bescheidener) Preis; **monopoly ~** Monopolpreis; **natural ~** durchschnittlicher Marktpreis; **~s nearest** genauester Preis; **~s negotiated** *(stock exchange)* bezahlt; **net ~** Nettopreis; **nominal ~** theoretischer Preis, Nominalpreis, -kurs; **normal ~** Normalpreis; **obligopoly ~** Obligopreis; **~ obtained** tatsächlich erzielter Preis; **off-season ~** Preis außerhalb der Saison; **~ offer[ed]** angebotener Preis, *(stock exchange)* Briefkurs; **open ~** vor Verkaufsbeginn von der Konkurrenz bekanntgegebener Preis; **open-market ~** freier Marktpreis; **opening ~** *(stock exchange)* erster Kurs, Anfangs-, Eröffnungskurs; **option ~s** Prämiensätze; **operative ~** verbindlicher Preis; **original ~** Anschaffungs-, Einkaufspreis; **outrageous ~** unverschämter Preis; **~s outsoaring the wages** über das Lohnniveau emporschnellende Preise; **overcharged ~** übersetzter Preis; **overhead ~** Herstellungs- und Generalunkosten deckender Preis; **overseas ~s** Überseepreise; **~ paid** Kaufpreis bezahlt; **parity ~** Parikurs; **paying ~** lohnender (lukrativer) Preis; **peak ~** Höchstpreis, *(stock exchange)* Höchstkurs; **pegged ~** Stützungspreis, gestützter Preis, *(stock exchange)* gestützter Kurs; **pithead ~** Preis ab Schacht; **popular ~** volkstümlicher Preis; **posted ~** Listenpreis, *(oil industry)* Preis; **preemption ~** Vorkaufspreis; **preferential ~** Vorzugspreis; **premium ~** Überseepreis; **present ~** Tagespreis, -kurs; **prevailing ~** geltender (üblicher) Preis, Tagespreis; **previous ~** vorheriger Preis; **prewar ~** Vorkriegs-, Friedenspreis; **private ~** Sonder-, Spezial-, Vorzugspreis; **producer ~** Erzeuger-, Herstellerpreis; **product ~s** Preis der Erzeugnisse; **profitable ~** wirtschaftlicher Preis; **prohibitive ~** unerschwinglicher Preis; **property ~** *(Br.)* Grundstückspreis; **public ~** Ladenpreis; **publication ~** Verlagspreis; **purchase ~** Einkaufspreis, Kauf-, Erwerbs-, Anschaffungspreis; **put ~** Rückprämienkurs; **put-up ~** heraufgesetzter Preis, *(auction)* geringstes Gebot, Mindestgebot; **put and call ~** Stellagekurs; **quantity ~** Mengenpreis; **quoted ~** angegebener (angebotener) Preis, Preisangebot; **~s quoted** notierter Kurs, Kursnotierung; **consecutively quoted ~** fortlaufend notierte Kurse; **rate-card ~** Preis lt. gültigem Anzeigentarif; **raw-material ~** Rohmaterialaufwand; **real ~** effektiver (echter) Preis; **real-estate ~** Grundstückspreis; **reasonable ~** mäßiger (angemessener, ziviler) Preis; **receding ~** fallender Preis; **receding ~s** *(stock exchange)* fallende Kurse, Kursrückgang; **recommended ~** empfohlener Preis, Richtpreis; **noncommittal recommended ~** unverbindliche Preisempfehlung; **record ~** Rekordpreis; **reduced ~** gesunkener (herabgesetzter, ermäßigter, erniedrigter) Preis, Minderpreis; **reference ~** empfohlener Preis; **regular ~** regulärer Preis, Normalpreis; **remunerative ~** lohnender Preis; **replacement ~** Wiederbeschaffungskosten; **resale ~** Wiederverkaufspreis; **fixed resale ~** gebundener Preis; **reservation ~** Mindestverkaufspreis; **reserve ~** *(auction)* Preislimit, unteres Versteigerungslimit; **reserved ~** Wiederverkaufspreis, *(auction)* Mindestgebot; **retail ~** Kleinverkaufs-, Einzelhandels-, Kleinhandelspreis; **retail ceiling ~** Einzelhandels-, Verbraucherhöchstpreis; **retroactive ~s** weichende Kurse; **retrograde ~s** rückläufige Preise (Kurse); **ridiculously low ~** Spottgeld; **rigid ~** starrer (unelastischer) Preis; **rising ~** steigender Preis; **rock-bottom ~** allerniedrigster (äußerst kalkulierter) Preis, niedrigstes Preisangebot; **rocketing ~** raketenartig ansteigende Preise; **rollback ~** *(US)* auf den Höchstpreis zurückgesetzter Preis; **ruinous ~** Verlust-, Schleuderpreis; **ruling ~** laufender (geltender) handelsüblicher Preis, Tages-, Marktpreis; **sagging ~s** nachgebende Preise (Kurse), Kursrückgang, -rückschlag; **sales ~** Verkaufspreis; **scarcity ~** Knappheitskurs; **secondhand ~** Preis zweiter Hand, *(car)* Gebrauchtwagenpreis; **selling ~** Laden-, Verkaufspreis; **set ~** fester Preis, Festpreis; **settled ~** aus-, abgemachter (festgesetzter) Preis; **settling ~** Liquidationspreis, *(stock exchange)* Abrechnungskurs; **~s shaded for quantities** Mengentarifpreise; **share ~** Aktienkurs; **short ~** reduzierter (ermäßigter) Preis; **sidewalk ~** *(US)* nicht amtlicher Kurs, Freiverkehrskurs; **skyrocketing ~** *(US)* Phantasiepreis; **slackening ~s** nachgebende (drückende) Kurse; **sliding-scale ~s** gleitende Preise, Staffelpreise; **smart ~** ganz schöner Preis; **soaring ~s** in die Höhe schnellende (steigende) Preise, *(stock exchange)* rasch steigende (davonlaufende) Kurse; **special ~** Sonder-, Ausnahme-, Vorzugspreis; **speculative ~** spekulativer Kurs (Preis); **spot ~** Preis für greifbare Mengen, Lokopreis, *(stock exchange)* Kassakurs; **stable ~s** stabile Preise; **standard ~** Einheits-, Normalpreis; **standardized ~** genormter Preis; **standing ~** fester Preis; **starting ~** Einsatzpreis; **stated ~** festgesetzter Preis; **at-station ~** Preis ab

Versandbahnhof; **stationary ~** stabiler Preis; **steady ~s** feste (stabile) Preise; **steep ~** unverschämter Preis; **sticky ~** *(US)* stabiler Preis; **stiff ~s** überhöhte Preise, Apothekerpreise; **stipulated ~** vereinbarter Preis; **stock ~** *(US)* Aktienkurs; **stop ~** gestoppter Preis, Stoppreis; **street ~s** *(Br.)* nachbörsliche Kurse, *(curb market)* Freiverkehrskurse; **sub-marginal ~** unterschwelliger Preis; **subscription ~** Subskriptions-, Bezugspreis; **subsidized ~** subventionierter Preis; **suggested ~** empfohlener Richtpreis; **support[ed] ~** subventionierter Preis, Stützpreis; **barely supported ~** knapp aufrechterhaltener Kurs; **take-over ~** Übernahmepreis; **tape ~** telegrafische Kurse; **target ~** abänderungsfähiger Grundpreis; **terminal ~** *(Br.)* Preis für die letzte Lieferung; **time ~** Abzahlungspreis, Preis bei Ratenzahlung; **today's ~** Tagespreis, -kurs; **top ~** Höchstpreis; **trade ~** Wiederverkäufer-, Händler-, Großhandels-, Engrospreis; **turbulent ~s** Preisturbulenz; **two-way ~** *(Br.)* doppelter Kurs; **uncompetitive ~** nicht konkurrenzfähiger Preis; **underrated ~** zu geringer Preis; **uniform ~** Einheitspreis; **uniform delivered ~** *(US)* vom Lieferort unabhängiger Preis, Einheitsversandpreis; **unlimited ~** unbeschränkter Preis; **unreasonable ~** unangemessener Preis; **unit ~** Stück-, Einheitspreis; **upset ~** *(foreclosure proceedings)* Anschlags-, Einsatzpreis, Mindestgebot; **exwarehouse ~** Preis ab Speicher; **varying ~s** schwankende Preise (Kurse); **weak ~** schwacher Preis; **wholesale ~** Großhandels-, Engrospreis; **wide ~s** stark divergierende Preise, große Preisunterschiede, *(stock exchange)* Kurse mit großer Spanne zwischen Geld- und Briefkurs, starke Kursunterschiede; **world ~** Weltmarktpreis; **wretched ~** Schleuderpreis; **zone ~** *(US)* Zonenpreis;

~ for the account *(Br.)* Terminkurs; **~ of adjudication** Zuschlagspreis, Höchstgebot; **~ subject to adjustment** gleitender Preis, Gleitpreis; **~ of admission** Eintrittspreis; **~s subject to alterations** unverbindliche Preise; **~ agreed upon by arrangement** vertraglich vereinbarter Preis; **~ by arrangement of the authorities** amtlich festgesetzter Preis; **~ of call** Vorprämienkurs; **~ calculated in accordance with the terms of the Agreement of Trust** von der Kapitalanlagegesellschaft festgelegter Rücknahmepreis; **~ for cash** Bar-, Kassapreis, *(stock exchange)* Kassakurs; **~ subject to change without notice** freibleibend, Preisänderung vorbehalten; **~s without commitment** unverbindliches Preisangebot; **~ to be considered** zugrunde zu legender Preis; **~ to consumer** Verbraucher-, Endpreis; **~ to the ultimate consumer** Endverbraucherpreis; **~ covering the costs of production** kostendeckender Preis; **~ for delivery** Terminpreis; **~ of delivery** Liefer-, Bezugspreis; **~ of the dinner exclusive of wine** Preis des trockenen Gedecks; **~ ex dock** Preis frei verzollt; **~ by the dozen** Dutzendpreis; **~s without engagement** unverbindliches Preisangebot, Preise freibleibend; **~ of exchange** Aufgeld; **~ fixed by the government** Festpreis; **~s of foodstuffs** Lebensmittelpreise; **~ for forward (future) delivery** Terminpreis; **~s of goods** Warenpreise; **~ of industrial goods** Industriegüterpreise; **~ after hours** nachbörslicher Kurs; **~ of issue** Zeichnungs-, Ausgabe-, Emissionskurs; **~ of labo(u)r** Wert der Arbeit; **~ in the lump** Pauschalpreis; **~s laid down by the manufacturer** vom Hersteller festgesetzte Verkaufspreise; **~ on the free market** Freiverkehrskurs; **~ of material** Baustoffpreis, Materialkosten; **~ is a matter for negotiation** Preis ist Verhandlungssache; **~ of money** Diskontsatz, Kapitalmarktzins; **~ of option** Prämienkurs; **high ~ to pay for peace** hoher Preis für die Erhaltung des Friedens; **~s at peacetime level** friedensmäßige Preise, Friedenspreise; **~ inclusive of postage and packing** Preis einschließlich Porto und Verpackung; **~s suited to the average pocketbook** erschwingliche Preise; **~ of products** Fabrikatspreis; **~ of production** Herstellungskosten zuzüglich Normalgewinnzuschlag; **~ paid for progress** für den Fortschritt gezahlter Preis; **~ of put** Rückprämienkurs; **~s shaded for quantities** Mengentarifpreise; **~ of redemption** Ablösungsbetrag, Tilgungskurs, *(investment fund)* Rücknahmepreis; **~ of securities** Effektenkurs; **~ for the settlement** *(Br.)* Terminkurs; **~ of shares** Börsen-, Aktienkurs; **~ at station** Preis frei Station; **~ ex store** Preis bei sofortiger Lieferung; **~s quoted in tenders** in verbindlichen Angeboten abgegebene Preise; **~ per unit** Stückpreis; **~ of units** *(Br.)* Zertifikatspreis; **~s exclusive vat** Preise für Vorsteuerabzugsberechtigte; **~s inclusive vat** Preise für Endverbraucher inkl. Mehrwertsteuer (Mwst); **~s outsoaring the wages** über das Lohnniveau emporschnellende Preise; **~ at works** Preis ab Werk (Fabrik), Fabrikpreis;

~ *(v.) (appraise)* abschätzen, bewerten, *(fix price)* Preis festsetzen (ansetzen), mit einem Preis (Preisangebot) versehen, *(inquire a price, coll.)* nach dem Preis fragen;

~ **goods** Waren auszeichnen; ~ **s. th. high** etw. hoch bewerten; ~ **low** niedrig bewerten (auszeichnen); ~ **o. s. out of the market** sich durch überhöhte Preise (überzogene Preispolitik) dem Markt entfremden, wettbewerbsunfähig werden; ~ **one's service freely** seine Dienstleistungsgebühr unabhängig festsetzen; **to abate a** ~ Preis nachlassen (herabsetzen); **to adjust** ~s Preise angleichen; **to administer a** ~ Richtpreis festsetzen; **to advance the** ~ Preis (Kurs) erhöhen; **to advance in** ~ im Preis (Kurs) steigern; **to affect** ~s Preise beeinflussen; **to agree about (upon) a** ~ Preis vereinbaren (einvernehmlich festsetzen), Preisvereinbarung treffen; **to allow a reduced** ~ jem. einen Preisabschlag einräumen; **to approximate** ~s **progressively** (EC) Preise schrittweise angleichen; **to arrive at a** ~ Preis kalkulieren (berechnen, ermitteln); **to ascertain a** ~ Preis festsetzen; **to ask a** ~ Preis fordern (verlangen); **to ask about the** ~ sich nach dem Preis (Markt) erkundigen; **to ask moderate** ~s niedrige Preise berechnen; **to bang** ~s Preise drücken; **to be affected by a fall in** ~s von einem Preisrückgang betroffen werden; **to be marked by a decline of** ~s im Zeichen der Baisse stehen; **to be moving neck and neck with** ~s sich Kopf an Kopf mit der Preisentwicklung bewegen; **to be subject to a condition as to the** ~ der Preisbindung unterliegen; **to be willing to pay a** ~ mit einem Preis einverstanden sein; **to bear too high a** ~ zu hoch zu stehen kommen; **to beat down a** ~ Preis herunterhandeln; **to bid a fair** ~ angemessenen Preis bieten; **to bid up the** ~ Preis in die Höhe steigern; **to bid up the** ~s **higher** Preise weiter in die Höhe treiben; **to boost** ~s Preise hinauftreiben; **to bring down the** ~ Preis herunterdrücken; **to buttress a** ~ Preis (Kurs) stützen; **to calculate a** ~ Preis berechnen (kalkulieren), Preiskalkulation vornehmen; **to carry the** ~s **to a low level** Kurse auf einen neuen Tiefstand bringen; **to charge s. o. a** ~ jem. einen Preis abverlangen; **to charge the old** ~ alten Preis berechnen; **to chop** ~s Preise stark herabsetzen; **to command a high** ~ hoch im Preis stehen; **to consent to a reduction in** ~ in eine Preisherabsetzung einwilligen; **not to consider the** ~ nicht auf den Preis sehen; **to control a** ~ Preis regulieren; **to cut a** ~ Preis ermäßigen (herabsetzen), abbauen; **to cut** ~s Preise verderben; **to cut s. one's** ~s j. preislich (im Preise) unterbieten; **to cut down a** ~ Preis herabsetzen (ermäßigen); **to cut** ~s **to the minimum** Preise schärfstens kalkulieren; **to cut down** ~s **on the quiet** Preise stillschweigend herabsetzen; **to decline in** ~ im Preise niedriger werden; **to demand a** ~ Preis verlangen; **to depress the** ~s Kurse drücken; **to determine a** ~ Preis bestimmen; **to drive down a** ~ Preis herunterbringen; **to drive up the** ~s Preise in die Höhe treiben; **to enhance in** ~ im Preis steigen; **to establish a** ~ Preis amtlich festsetzen; **to establish minimum** ~s Mindestpreise für den Einzelhandel festlegen; **to establish a** ~ **at a low level** Preis sehr vorsichtig kalkulieren; **to experience a rise in** ~s Preiserhöhung erfahren, (stock exchange) im Kurs steigen; **to fall in** ~ im Kurs (Preis) fallen; **to fetch a** ~ Gewinn erzielen; **to fetch huge** ~s enorme Gewinne erzielen; **to fix a** ~ Preis (Kurs) bestimmen (festsetzen); **to flatten** ~s Preise abflachen, (stock exchange) Kurse abschwächen; **to force down a** ~ Preis herunterdrücken, Kurs drücken; **to force up** ~s Preise hinauftreiben, (stock exchange) Kurs in die Höhe treiben; **to freeze** ~s (US) Preise auf einer amtlich festgesetzten Höhe halten, Preisstop durchführen; **to gear** ~s **to formulas based on government** ~ **indexes** Preise entprechend dem amtlichen Preisindex festsetzen; **to get a good** ~ zu einem guten Preis verkaufen; **to get a** ~ **reduced** Preis herunterhandeln; **to give a long** ~ teuer kaufen (bezahlen); **to go down in** ~ im Kurs fallen; **to go into a** ~ Preis bestimmen (ausmachen); **to go up in** ~ sich verteuern, im Preis (Kurs) steigen; **to haggle over the** ~ um den Preis feilschen; **to hammer down a** ~ **of shares** Aktienkurs herunterdrücken; **to have one's** ~ (person) bestechlich sein; **to have a high** ~ hohen Preis haben; **to have the most stable** ~ preisstabilstes Land sein; **to hold back on** ~s bestehende Preise beibehalten; **to hold down** ~s Preise niedrig halten; **to hold the line on** ~s Preise stabil halten; **to improve the** ~ Kurs hinaufsetzen; **to increase** ~s Preise anheben; **to increase in** ~ im Preis (Kurs) steigen; **to influence** ~s Einfluß auf die Preise ausüben; **to inquire about the** ~ nach dem Preis fragen, sich nach dem Preis erkundigen; **to jack** ~s Preise anheben; **to jump [up]** ~s Preise sprunghaft erhöhen (herauftreiben); **to keep** ~s **down** Preise niedrig halten, Preissteigerung vermeiden; **to keep** ~s **on an even level** Preise stabil halten; **to keep** ~s **up** Preise hoch halten; **to knock off the** ~ vom Preis abziehen; **to let go under** ~ unter dem Preis losschlagen; **to level up** ~s Preise hinaufschrauben; **to limit a** ~ Preislimit einhalten; **to limit to a** ~ an einen Preis binden; **to list** ~s (US) Kurse börsenmäßig feststellen (notieren); **to lower a** ~ verbilligen, Preis reduzieren (senken); **to maintain** ~s Preise

halten; **to maintain fixed resale** ~s Preisbindung der zweiten Hand beibehalten; **to make a** ~ Preis festsetzen; **to make an allowance upon (a reduction in) the** ~ vom Preis nachlassen, Preisabschlag gewähren; **to meet the requirements of a competitive** ~ preisgünstig liegen; **to muffle one's forecast on** ~s abgeschwächte Preisentwicklungsprognose abgeben; **to name a** ~ Preis festsetzen (nennen, berechnen); **to negotiate a** ~ Preis vereinbaren (aushandeln), über einen Preis verhandeln; **to negotiate** ~s **on block trades** besondere Kurse für Aktienpakete aushandeln; **to obtain a** ~ Preis realisieren; **to obtain s. th. at a ransom** ~ etw. zu einem exorbitanten Preis bekommen; **to offer a** ~ Preisangebot machen; **to pay a heavy** ~ mit Geld aufwiegen; **to pay top** ~s Höchstpreise zahlen; **to peg** ~s Preise stützen, (stock exchange) Kurse stützen; **to prescribe minimum** ~s Mindestverkaufspreise für den Einzelhandel vorschreiben; **to push up the** ~ Preis hochtreiben, (stock exchange) Kurs in die Höhe treiben; **to put a** ~ **on s. one's head** Belohnung für jds. Ergreifung aussetzen; **to put up** ~s Preise erhöhen; **to put a crimp in** ~s Preise durcheinanderbringen; **to pyramid a** ~ Preise immer weiter erhöhen; **to quote a** ~ Kurs notieren, Preis festsetzen (angeben); **to quote** ~s **conditionally** Preise freibleibend aufgeben; **to quote** ~s **ex-dividend** Kurse ausschließlich Dividende notieren; **to quote a lower** ~ niedriges Preisangebot stellen; **to quote the outside** ~s äußerste Preise angeben; **to raise a** ~ Preis erhöhen; **to raise the level of** ~s Preisniveau anheben; **to reach a** ~ Preis erzielen; **to realize a** ~ Preis erzielen; **to recommend a** ~ Preisempfehlung aussprechen; **to reduce a** ~ verbilligen, Preis abbauen (ermäßigen), mit dem Preis heruntergehen; **to refund the purchase** ~ Kaufpreis zurückerstatten; **to remain stationary at yesterday's** ~ sich auf dem gestrigen Kurs halten (behaupten); **to ring up the** ~ an der Ladenkasse den Preis notieren; **to roll back** ~s (US) Preis durch Subventionsmaßnahmen senken; **to run down** ~s Preise drücken; **to sag in** ~ im Preis (Kurs) fallen; **to screw up** ~s Preise hochschrauben; **to secure higher** ~s bessere Preise erzielen; **to sell s. th. above the established** ~ etw. über Preis (zu höherem als dem amtlich festgesetzten Preis) verkaufen; **to sell below** ~ unter Wert verkaufen; **to sell at a low** ~ **and recoup o. s. by large sales** ermäßigte Preise durch große Umsätze wettmachen; **to sell goods subject to a condition as to the** ~ Ware mit Preisbindungsklausel verkaufen; **to sell under cost** ~ unter dem Selbstkostenpreis abgeben; **to sell under list** ~ unter dem Listenpreis verkaufen; **to sell a house at a good** ~ guten Preis für ein Haus erzielen; **to sell at reduced** ~s zu ermäßigten Preisen verkaufen; **to send down a** ~ Preis herunterdrücken; **to send up a** ~ Preise hinaufschrauben, (stock exchange) Kurse hochtreiben; **to set a** ~ **on an article** Preis für etw. festsetzen (eines Artikels festlegen); **to set a** ~ **on s. one's head** Belohnung für jds. Ergreifung aussetzen; **to set a high** ~ **on s. th.** einer Sache großen Wert beimessen; **to settle on a** ~ Preis ausmachen (absprechen); **to shade** ~s Preise herabsetzen; **to slash** ~s Preise stark ermäßigen (herabsetzen); **to squeeze down a** ~ Preis herunterdrücken; **to stabilize** ~s Preise stabilisieren; **to stick to** ~s auf Preise halten; **to stick to the fixed** ~ Limit einhalten; **to straighten out foundered** ~s Preisverzerrungen ausgleichen; **to suggest a** ~ Preis empfehlen; **to support a** ~ Preis (Kurs) stützen; **to take so much off a** ~ so und soviel vom Preis nachlassen; **to undercut s. one's** ~s jds. Preise unterbieten; **to valorize a** ~ Preis stützen; ~s **are advancing** Kurse ziehen an; ~s **are on the decline** Kurse fallen (geben nach); ~s **are easing off** Kurse bröckeln ab; ~ **are firm** Kurse sind fest; ~ **are going up** Kurse steigen (ziehen an); ~s **are hardening** Kurse ziehen an; ~s **are improving** Kurse bessern sich; ~ **are a shade lower** Kurse liegen eine Kleinigkeit niedriger; ~ **become firmer** Kurse werden fest; ~s **continue stable** Kurse bleiben stabil; ~s **crumble [off]** Kurse bröckeln ab; ~s **have advanced** Kurse sind gestiegen; ~s **have eased [off]** Kurse sind abgeschwächt (abgebröckelt); ~s **have dropped (gone down)** Kurse sind gefallen; ~s **have gone up** Kurse sind gestiegen; ~s **have hardened** Kurse zogen an; ~s **have improved** Kurse liegen gebessert; ~s **have jumped** Kurse gingen sprunghaft in die Höhe; ~s **have increased** Preise steigen; ~ **have receded** Kurse sind zurückgegangen; ~ **have remained unchanged** Kurse sind unverändert; ~ **is no object** der Preis spielt keine Rolle; ~s **recovered their old level** Kurse erreichten das frühere Niveau; ~s **remain steady** Kurse halten sich; ~s **remain unchanged** Kurse liegen unverändert; ~s **rise sharply** Preise (Kurse) ziehen heftig an; ~s **show a downward tendency** Kurse zeigen eine rückläufige Bewegung;
~ **abatement** Preisnachlaß, -ermäßigung; ~ **acceleration** beschleunigter Preisanstieg; **Resale** ~ **Act** (Br.) Preisbindungsgesetz; ~ **and Incomes Act** (Br., 1965) Preis- und Lohngesetz; ~

action Preismaßnahme, -aktion, *(stock exchange)* Kursverhalten; ~ **adjustment** Preisausgleich, -angleichung, -anpassung, *(stock exchange)* Kurskorrektur; ≗ **Adjustment Board** *(US)* Preisausgleichsstelle; ~ **adjustment levy** *(EC)* Abschöpfungsbetrag; ~ **administration** *(US)* Preislenkung [durch Richtpreise], -überwachung; ≗ **Administrator** *(US)* Preiskommissar; ~ **advance** Preis-, Kurssteigerung, Preis-, Kurserhöhung, Kursanstieg; ~ **advantage** Preisvorteil, preislicher Vorteil; ~ **advertising** Werbung mit [niedrigen] Preisen; ~ **agreement** Preiskonvention, -vereinbarung, -abrede, -absprache; **resale ~ agreement** Preisbindungsabkommen, -absprache; ~ **allowance** Preisnachlaß; ~ **alteration** Neufestsetzung eines Verkaufspreises, Preisänderung; ~ **announcement** Preisankündigung; ~ **appeal** preislicher Anreiz, Kaufanreiz durch einen besonders günstigen Preis; ~ **announcement** Preisankündigung; ~ **area** Preisgebiet, *(special product)* Preisspanne; ~ **arrangement** Preisvereinbarung; ~ **arrangement scheme** Preisbindungsvereinbarung, Preisbindung der zweiten Hand; ~ **atmosphere** Preisklima; ~ **association** Preiskartell; **open ~ association** *(US)* Preismeldestelle; ~ **authority** Preisbehörde; ~ **average** Preisdurchschnitt; ~ **barometer** Preisbarometer; ~ **barrier** Preisgrenze; ~ **base** Preissockel; ~ **basis** Preisgrundlage, -basis; ~ **behavio(u)r** Preisverhalten; ~ **board** Preistafel; ≗ **and Income Board** *(Br.)* Preis- und Lohnbehörde; ~ **boost** *(fam.)* Preissteigerung, -erhöhung, -treiberei; ~**-bound** preisgebunden; ~ **bracket** Preislage; ~ **break** Preisnachlaß; ~ **calculation** Preiskalkulation, -bildung, -berechnung, *(stock exchange)* Kursberechnung; ~ **carousel** Preiskarusell; ~ **cartel** Preiskartell; ~ **catalog(ue)** Preisliste, -katalog, -verzeichnis; ~ **ceilings** festgesetzte Preisobergrenze, Höchstpreis; ~ **change** Neufestsetzung (Berichtigung) eines [Verkaufs]preises; ~ **changes** Preisberichtigungen, Preis-, Kursänderungen; ~ **change slip** Preisänderungsmitteilung; ~ **climb** Preisanstieg; ~ **code** *(Br.)* staatliches Preisabkommen, -ordnung, -kode; ~ **collapse** Preiszusammenbruch, -verfall, *(stock exchange)* Kurszusammenbruch; ~ **combination** Preiskartell, Preisabsprache für eine Produktfamilie; ≗ **Commission** *(Br.)* Preisüberwachungsstelle; ≗ **Commission Act** *(Br.)* Preisüberwachungsgesetz; ~ **commission report** *(Br.)* Preisüberwachungsbericht; ~ **commitments** Preiszusagen; ~ **comparison** Preisvergleich; ~ **competition** Preiskonkurrenz, -wettbewerb; ~**-competitive** preislich konkurrenzfähig; ~ **competitiveness** preisliche Wettbewerbsfähigkeit, Wettbewerbsfähigkeit auf dem Preisgebiet; ~ **concession** Gewährung preislicher Vorteile, Preiszugeständnis, -konzession; **off-season ~ concessions** außerhalb der Saison gewährte Preisnachlässe; ~ **condition** Preisbestimmung, -bedingung, -festlegung; ~ **conditions** Preisklima; ~**-conscious** preisbewußt; ~ **consciousness** Preisbewußtsein; ~ **continuity** Preisstabilität; **fixed ~ contract** Festpreisvereinbarung; **fixed ~ contracts with provision for redetermination of ~** *(US)* Festpreisaufträge mit Neufestsetzungsklausel des Preises; **straight-fixed-~ contracts** *(US)* Aufträge zu regulärem Festpreis; ~ **control** Preisüberwachung; **administration ~ control** staatliche Preiskontrolle, -überwachung, -bindung; ≗ **Control Board** *(US)* Preisüberwachungsstelle, -behörde; ~**-controlled** preisgebunden; ~**-controlled articles** der Preisüberwachung unterliegende Waren; ~**-controlled economy** kontrollierte Wirtschaft; ~ **convention** Preisabkommen, -vereinbarung; ~ **crisis** Preiskrise; ~ **curb** Preisdrosselung; ~**s current** Preisliste, -bericht, -verzeichnis; ~ **cushioning** Abfangen von Kursschwankungen; ~ **cut** Preisherabsetzung, -ermäßigung, -senkung, -kürzung, -abbau; ~ **cutter** billiger anbietende Firma, Preisunterbieter, Schleuderfirma; ~ **cutting** erhebliche Preissenkung, -unterbietung, -schleuderei, -drückerei, -dumpingaktion; ~**-cutting** preissenkend; ~**-cutting move** Preissenkungsaktion; ~**-cutting program(me)** Preissenkungsprogramm; ~**-cutting scheme** Preisunterbietungssystem, -plan; **to lead the ~-cutting wave** Preisbrechergruppe anführen; ~ **data** Preisunterlagen, -angaben; ~**-deciding** preisbestimmend, -entscheidend, -beherrschend; ~ **decline** Preisverfall, *(stock exchange)* Kursabfall; ~ **decontrol** Aufhebung (Abbau) der Preisüberwachungsvorschriften, Freigabe der Preise, Preisfreigabe; ~ **decrease** Preisherabsetzung; ~ **deduction** Preisnachlaß, -abschlag; ~ **deflation** Preisdeflation; ~ **deflator** preislicher Deflationsfaktor; ~ **determinants** Preisbildungsfaktoren; ~ **determination** Festsetzung eines Preises, Preisbestimmung, -stellung, -festsetzung, *(stock exchange)* Kursbildung; ~**-determining** preisbestimmend; ~ **development** Preisentwicklung; ~ **difference** Preisunterschied, -differenz, *(stock exchange)* Kursdifferenz; **to split the ~ difference** strittigen Preisunterschied teilen; ~ **differential** Preisunterschied,

-differenzierung, -gefälle; ~ **differentiation** Preisunterscheidung; ~ **dip** Preisrückgang; ~ **discrimination** *(US)* preislich unterschiedliche Behandlung, Preisdiskriminierung; **unfair ~ discrimination** *(US)* unlautere Preisunterbietung; ~ **distortion** Preisverzerrung; ~ **drop** Preisverfall, *(stock exchange)* Kursrückgang; ~**-earnings multiple** Kursertragsmultiplikator; ~**-earnings ratio** Kurs-Ertragsverhältnis; ~ **effect** Preisauswirkungen; ~ **elasticity** Preiselastizität; ~ **elasticity of demand** Preiselastizität der Nachfrage; ~ **element** Preisbestandteil; ~**-enhancing** preisauftriebsfördernd, -treibend; ~ **equalization** Preisausgleich; ~ **equation** Preisgleichung; ~ **equilibrium** Preisausgleich, -gleichgewicht; ~ **equivalent** Preisäquivalent; ~ **escalator** automatischer Preisausgleich; ~ **estimate** Preiskalkulation; ~ **examiner** Preisprüfer; ~ **expectancy** Preiserwartung, *(moving picture business)* kalkulierte Mindesteinnahmen, erwarteter Einspielerlös; ~ **expectations** Preiserwartungen; **commodity ~ explosion** Explosion der Warenpreise; ~ **factor** Preisfaktor; ~ **fall** Preisrückgang, *(stock exchange)* Kursrückgang; ~ **figures** Preisziffern; ~ **firmness** Festigkeit der Preise; ~**-fixed** preisgebunden, -gestoppt; ~**-fixed merchandise** Produkt mit gebundenem Preis; ~ **fixing** Preisfestsetzung, -limitierung, -bestimmung, -bindung, staatliche -regelung, *(cartel law)* Preisabsprache, -vereinbarung; **piecemeal ~ fixing** Preisfestsetzung von Fall zu Fall; **resale ~ fixing** *(Canada)* Preisbindung der zweiten Hand; ~**-fixing** preisbestimmend, -bindend; ~**-fixing agreement** Preiskonvention, -vereinbarung, -abrede, -kartell; ~**-fixing committee** *(US)* Preisfestsetzungsausschuß; ~**-fixing conspiracy** Preisverschwörung; **vertical ~-fixing contract** vertikale Preisvereinbarung, vertikale Preisbindung; ~**-fixing meeting** Preiskonferenz; ~**-fixing restrictions** preiseinschränkende Bestimmungen; ~**-fixing rules** *(EC)* Preisfestsetzungsbestimmungen; ~ **flexibility** Anpassungsfähigkeit der Preise, Preisflexibilität; ~ **floor** Preisuntergrenze, -minimum; ~ **floor law** *(US)* Gesetz zur Festlegung von Mindestpreisen; ~ **fluctuations** Preisschwankungen, -fluktuationen, Fluktuieren der Preise, *(stock exchange)* Kursschwankungen, -ausschläge; **to be subject to ~ fluctuations** Preisschwankungen (Kursschwankungen) unterliegen; ~ **formation** Preisbemessung, -bildung, -gestaltung; ~ **formula** Preisformel; ~ **formulation** Berechnungsmethode für bestehende Preise; ~ **freedom** freiheitliche Preisgestaltung; ~ **freeze** Einfrieren der Preise, Preisstopp; ~ **front** Preisfront; ~ **gain** Preisgewinn; **stock ~ gain** Kursgewinn; ~ **gap** Preisgefälle, -lücke; ~ **government** Preissteuerung; ~ **guarantee** Preisgarantie; ~ **guidelines** Preisrichtlinien; ~ **hike** *(fam.)* Preiserhöhung, -anstieg; ~ **implications** Preisfolgewirkungen; ~ **improvement** Preiserhöhung, -steigerung, *(stock exchange)* Kursverbesserung; ~ **increase (increment)** Preisanhebung, -erhöhung, steigerung, -anstieg, -auftrieb, *(stock exchange)* Kurserhöhung; **general ~ increase** globale Preiserhöhung, Teuerung; **to curb the ~ increase** Preisauftrieb bremsen; **to delay ~ increases as long as possible** Preiserhöhungen solange wie möglich vermeiden; **to police the ~ increase** Preisanstieg überwachen; ~ **increase rate** Preissteigerungsrate; ~ **index** Preisindex, -meßzahl; **cost-of-living ~ index** Lebenshaltungsindex; **cost-of-living consumer ~ index** Verbraucherpreisindex; **retail ~ index** Einzelhandelspreisindex; **weighted ~ index** gewogener Preisindex; **wholesale ~ index** Großhandelspreisindex; ~ **index of exports** Ausfuhrpreisindex; ~ **index of imports** Einfuhrpreisindex; ~**-index escalator** gleitendes Preisindexsystem; ~ **index figure of materials** Materialkostenindex; ~ **index number** Preisindexzahl; ~ **indication** Richtpreis; ~ **indicator** Preisindikator; ~**-induced** preisbedingt; ~**-inelastic** preisunelastisch; ~ **inflation** Preisaufblähung, -inflation, -auftrieb; ~ **influences** Preiseinflüsse; ~ **inquiry** Preisanfrage; ~ **inspection** Preisprüfung, -überwachung; ~ **inspector** Preisprüfer; ~ **intervention** Preisintervention, *(stock exchange)* Kursintervention; ~ **jump** plötzlicher Preisanstieg; ~ **label** Preisschild, -zettel, Etikett; ~ **leader** *(US)* Preisführer; ~ **leadership** *(US)* Preisführerschaft, -stellung; ~ **legislation** Preisgesetzgebung; ~ **level** Preishöhe, -niveau, -stand, *(stock exchange)* Kursniveau; **unwarranted ~ level** Kursanomalie; **wholesale ~ level** Großhandelspreisniveau; **to carry to higher ~ levels** zu neuen Kurssteigerungen führen; **fixed-~ lifting** Festpreisaufhebung; ~ **limit** Preisgrenze, -limit, -begrenzung; ~ **line** *(US)* Einheitspreis; **fixed ~ line** preisgebundene Artikel.

price list Preisverzeichnis, -liste, -katalog, Katalog mit Preisangabe, *(stock exchange)* Kurszettel;

daily ~ Tageskurszettel; **illustrated ~** Bilderkatalog, illustrierte Preisliste; **market ~** Marktbericht;

to post up a ~ Preistafel aushängen.

price | loss *(stock exchange)* Kursverlust, -rückgang; ~ **lowering** preissenkend; **~-maintained goods** preisgebundene Waren, preisgestützte Erzeugnisse.

price maintenance Preisbindung [für Markenartikel]; **resale (retail)** ~ Preisbindung der zweiten Hand; ~ **agreement** Preisbindungsabsprache; ~ **law** Preisbindungsverordnung.

price | -maintained articles (goods, commodities, products) Produkte mit stabilen (gestützten) Preisen, preisgebundene Waren, ~ **making** Preisfestsetzung, -bildung; **~-making function** Preisbildungsfunktion; ~ **margin** Preisspanne; ~ **mark[ing]** Preiszettel, -angabe, -auszeichnung; **~-market mechanism** Marktpreismechanismus; ~ **marking** Preisauszeichnung; ~ **mechanism** Preismechanismus; ~ **merry-go-round** Preiskarussel; ~ **method** *(US)* Stück-, Akkordlohnsystem; ~ **mirror** Preisspiegel; ~ **moderation** Preiszurückhaltung; ~ **modification** Preisänderung; ~ **moratorium** Preismoratorium; ~ **movement** Preisbewegung, -entwicklung, *(stock exchange)* Kursbewegung, -entwicklung; **to be in a downward ~ movement** abwärts gerichtete Kursbewegung haben; **to be in a sidewise ~ movement** weder steigen noch fallen; ~ **number** Preisindexziffer; **to release from the fixed-~ obligations** aus der Preisbindung herausnehmen; ~ **obstacle** Preishindernis; ~ **offer** Preisangebot; ~ **oscillations** Preis-, Kursschwankungen; ~ **outlook** Preiserwartungen, -aussichten; **~-output policy** kombinierte Produktions- und Preispolitik; ~ **pattern** Preisschema; ~ **pause** Preispause, Pause in der Preisbewegung; **high-~ period** Preiskonjunktur; **[open-]** ~ **piracy** Preispiraterie; ~ **plateau** Preisplattform; ~ **pledge** Verpflichtung zur Preisstabilität; ~ **policy** Preispolitik; ~ **and Income Policy** *(Br.)* Preis- und Lohnpolitik; ~ **poster** Preisständer; ~ **producer** Preisverursacher; ~ **protection** Preisschutz; ~ **publication** Preisauszeichnung; ~ **push** Preisschub; ~ **quotation** Preisangabe, -notierung, *(stock exchange)* Kursfestsetzung, -notierung, -stellung; **excessive ~ quotation** Preisüberhöhung; ~ **raising** Preiserhöhung; **~-raising** preissteigernd, -treibend; **~-raising factors** preiserhöhende (preistreibende) Faktoren; **~-raising tendency** preissteigernde Tendenz, Preisauftrieb; ~ **rally** Hausse; ~ **range** Preisskala, -lage, -spanne, *(stock exchange)* Kursspanne; **medium ~ range** mittlere Preislage; **to carry the full ~ range** Erzeugnisse aller Preisklassen führen; ~ **ratio** Preisrelation, *(corporation, US)* Bewertungsmaßstab; ~ **recession** rückläufige Preistendenz, Preis-, Kursrückgang; ~ **recommendations** Preisempfehlungen; ~ **record** Höchstpreise; ~ **recovery** Preisanstieg, Erholung der Kurse; **~-reducing** preissenkend; ~ **reduction** Preisherabsetzung, -senkung, -rückgang, -nachlaß, -verbilligung; ~ **regulations** Preislenkung, -regelung, -regulierung, -vorschrift, *(stock exchange)* Kursregulierung; **maximum ~ regulations** Höchstpreisbestimmungen; ~ **relationship** Preisverhältnis, -relation; ~ **relative** Preismeßziffer; ~ **relief** Preisstützung; ~ **relief measures** Preisstützungsmaßnahmen; ~ **reserve** Preisvorbehalt; ~ **resistance** Preiswiderstand, Widerstandfähigkeit der Preise; ~ **responsibility** Preisverantwortung; ~ **restraint** zurückhaltende Preispolitik; **~-restraint cooperation** gemeinsame Preiszurückhaltung; ~ **review** Preisüberprüfug; **government ~ review** Preisüberprüfung durch staatliche Stellen; ~ **review system** Preisüberwachungssystem; ~ **review team** Preisüberwachungsgruppe; ~ **rigidity** Preisstarre, eingefrorene Preise; ~ **ring** Preis-, Verkaufskartell, Verkäuferring, *(stock exchange)* Börsenkonsortium; ~ **rise** Preis-, Kostensteigerung; **well publicised ~ rise** in der Öffentlichkeit gut vorbereitete Preiserhöhung; ~ **rise out of proportion** *(stock exchange)* überproportionale Kurssteigerung; **to hold ~ rise to low level** nur geringfügige Preissteigerungen zulassen; **~-rising tendency** Preiserhöhungstendenz; ~ **risk** Kursrisiko; ~ **rollback** *(US)* staatliche Preissenkungsaktion; ~ **rules** Preisvorschriften; **~-ruling** preisbestimmend, -entscheidend, -beherrschend; ~ **scale** Preisskala; ~ **schedule** Preisliste; ~ **scheme** Preisabsprache; ~ **scissors** Preisschere; ~ **searcher** Preisfixierer; ~ **setback** Kursrückgang, -schlag; ~ **setter** Preisführer; ~ **setting** Preisführerschaft; ~ **shading** Preisnachlaß aus Konkurrenzgründen; ~ **signal** Preissignal; ~ **situation** Preissituation, -verhältnisse; ~ **slashing** Preisschleuderei; ~ **slowdown** verlangsamter Preisanstieg, rückläufige Preiskonjunktur; ~ **slump** Preis-, Kurssturz; **to ride out the ~ slump** plötzliche Kursstürze überstehen; ~ **spectrum** Preisspektrum; ~ **speed-up** plötzlicher Preisanstieg; ~ **spiral** Preisspirale; ~ **split** Preisspaltung; ~ **spread** *(US)* Preisspanne, -unterschied, *(stock exchange)* Kursdifferenz; ~ **stability** Preis-, Geldwert, Preisbeständigkeit, konstante Preise; ~ **stabilization** Kurs-, Preisstabilisierung, Stabilisierung der Preise (Kurse); ~ **stabilization**

agreement Preisstabilisierungsabkommen; ~ **stabilization pact** Preisstabilisierungsabkommen; ~ **stabilization program(me)** Preisstabilisierungsprogramm; **~-stabilizing** preisstabilisierend; ~ **standard** Verrechnungspreis; ~ **statistics** Preisstatistik; ~ **stop** Preisstopp; **one-~ store** Einheitspreisgeschäft; ~ **strength** Kurshöhe; ~ **sticker** Preisschild; ~ **structure** Preisgefüge, *(stock exchange)* Kursgefüge; **stable ~ structure** festes Preisgefüge; **wage-~ structure** Lohn-, Preisgefüge; ~ **subsidy** Subvention von Preisen, Preissubvention; ~ **supervision** Preisüberwachung; ~ **supplement** Mehrpreis.

price support Kurs-, Preisstützung, *(agriculture)* Interventionspreissystem, *(US)* staatliche Stützung der Landwirtschaftspreise; ~ **activities** Preisstützungsmaßnahmen; ~ **level** Preisstützungsstufe; ~ **period** Kursstützungsperiode; ~ **scheme** Preisstützungsaktion.

price | -supporting program(me) Preisstützungsprogramm; ~ **surveillance** Preisaufsicht, -überwachung; ~ **swing** Kursumschwung; ~ **switchback** Zickzackkurve der Preisbewegungen; ~ **system** Preisfestsetzungswesen; **delivered ~ system** *(US)* Kalkulations-, Preisbindungssystem; **differential ~ system** Preisdifferenzierungssystem; **free ~ system** freie Marktwirtschaft; **open ~ system** Preisinformationssystem; ~ **tag** Preismarke, -schild, -etikett, -zettel, Auszeichnungszettel; **~-tagged** preislich ausgezeichnet; ~ **theorist** Preistheoretiker; ~ **ticket** *(US)* Preiszettel, -etikett, -schild; **to pin on a ~ ticket** Preisetikett feststecken; **~-tight situation** angespannte Preissituation; ~ **trend** Preistendenz, -entwicklung; **declining ~ trend** rückläufige Preis-, Kursentwicklung; ~ **turn** Preiswende; ~ **undercutting** Preisunterbietung; ~ **understandings** Preisvereinbarungen; ~ **uptrend** Preisauftrieb; ~ **variance** Preisabänderung, -abweichung; ~ **variation clause** Preisgleitklausel; ~ **volatility** Preisunbeständigkeit; **~-wage spiral** Preis-Lohn-Spirale; ~ **war** Preiskrieg, -kampf; ~ **weakness** Abschwächung der Preise, Preisabschwächung, *(stock exchange)* Kursabschwächung; ~ **weapon** Preiswaffe; ~ **yield basis** Kurs-Gewinnrendite.

priced | at mit Preisen (Preisangabe) versehen, preislich ausgezeichnet; **budget-~** *(US)* preisgünstig; **completely ~** schärfstens kalkuliert; **economy-~** vergleichsweise preisgünstig; **high-~** hochbewertet, teuer; **low-~** niedrig bewertet, billig, in niedriger Preislage; **medium-~** in mittlerer Preislage; **moderately ~** preiswert; **thrift-~** *(US)* preisgünstig; **to be ~ at $ 2** zum Preis von 2 Dollar verkauft werden; **to be clearly ~** *(goods)* sorgfältig ausgezeichnet sein; **to be competitively ~** im Preis konkurrenzfähig sein; **to be fully ~** vollauf bezahlt sein; **to be ~ right** preislich richtig liegen; ~ **catalog(ue)** Preiskatalog, -liste, verzeichnis; **medium-~ field** mittleres Preisgebiet.

priceless unschätzbar.

pricer Preiskalkulator, *(Br.)* Preisprüfer.

pricing *(calculation of prices)* Preiskalkulation, -feststellung, -festlegung, -bestimmung, -bildung, -festsetzung, -auszeichnung, *(estimate)* Bewertung, Schätzung; **area ~** Preisfestsetzung nach Zonengebieten, regionale Preisdifferenzierung; **cost-based ~** kostenorientierte Preisbildung; **cost-plus ~** Preiskalkulation durch Gewinnaufschlag auf die Herstellungskosten; **dual ~** Doppelpreissystem; **flat ~** pauschalierte Preisbestimmung; **full-cost ~** Preiskalkulation incl. Risikofaktor und Gemeinkosten; **return-on-capital ~** von der Kapitalverzinsung ausgehende Preisbestimmung; **zone ~** *(freightage, US)* Preisfestsetzung nach Zonengebieten, regionale Preisdifferenzierung; ~ **in code** verdeckte Preisauszeichnung; ~ **out of the market** Marktentfremdung; ~ **of requisitions** Kostenfestsetzung bei Materialanforderungen; ~ *(a.)* preisbestimmend; ~ **arrangement** Preisabrede; ~ **decision** Preisentscheidung; ~ **factors** preisbestimmende Faktoren; ~ **formula** Preisberechnungsmethode; ~ **lines** Preisrichtlinien; ~ **mechanism** Preisbildungsmechanismus; ~ **method** Preisberechnungsmethode, -gestaltung; ~ **philosophy** Preisphilosophie; **to become the leader in established ~ policies** Preisführerschaft übernehmen; ~ **policy** Preispolitik; ~ **and regulations policy** Preisregulierungspolitik; ~ **policy formulation** Entwicklung der Preispolitik; ~ **practices** Kalkulationsverfahren; ~ **process** Preismechanismus; ~ **regulations** Preisfestlegungen; ~ **rules** Preisfestsetzungsrichtlinien; ~ **schedule** Preisbestimmungs-, Kalkulationstabelle; ~ **system** Preisbildungs-, Kalkulationssystem; **basing-point ~ system** System der differenzierten Preisfestsetzung bei verschiedenen Auslieferungsstellen.

prick spitzer Gegenstand, Stich;
  pin ~ *(fig.)* Nadelstich;
  ~s of conscience (remorse) Gewissensbisse;
  ~ *(v.)* durchstechen, lochen, *(fig.)* plagen, quälen;
  ~ off names on a list Namen auf einer Liste abstreichen; **~ off a ship's position on the chart** Schiffskurs auf der Karte abstecken;
  ~ out a pattern Schnittmuster ausradeln; **~ up one's ears** seine Ohren spitzen; **~ up items** Posten abstreichen; **~ a sheriff** *(Br.)* Sheriff ernennen;
  to feel the ~s of conscience sich von seinem Gewissen beunruhigt fühlen; **to kick against the ~** wider den Stachel löcken.
pricking Punktieren, Lochen;
  ~ for sheriff *(Br.)* Ernennung des Sheriffs;
  ~ note Warenempfangs-, Ausfuhrversandliste.
pricky heikel, knifflig, wählerisch, penibel.
pricy teuer, kostspielig;
  to deem ~ in political coinage sich in politischer Münze auszahlen.
pride Stolz, Überheblichkeit, Hochmut, *(fig.)* Blüte, beste Zeit;
  in the ~ of manhood im besten Mannesalter; **puffed up with ~** vor Stolz platzend;
  false ~ falscher Stolz;
  ~ of ownership Besitzerstolz; **~ of rank** Standesbewußtsein; **~ of the season** beste Jahreszeit;
  ~ *(v.)* o. s. on s. th. sich mit etw. brüsten;
  to be eaten up with ~ vor Stolz platzen; **to cast ~ to the winds** seinen Stolz fahren lassen; **to take an empty ~ in s. th.** blasiert sein; **to take ~ in one's knowledge** sich mit seinen Kenntnissen brüsten; **to take ~ in one's work** stolz auf seine Arbeit sein; **to wound s. one's ~** jds. Stolz verletzen;
  ~ will have (goes before) a fall Hochmut kommt vor dem Fall.
priest Geistlicher, Priester;
  parish ~ Gemeindepfarrer.
prig Snob, Tugendbold.
priggery Dünkel.
priggish eingebildet, affektiert.
prim pedantisch, geziert, affektiert, gekünstelt, gedrechselt;
  ~ *(v.)* o. s. up geziert tun; **~ up a room** Zimmer peinlichst genau aufräumen.
prima *(print., Br.)* erstes Wort einer neuen Seite.
prima facie | case glaubhaft gemachter Sachverhalt; **to establish a ~ case** Sachverhalt glaubhaft machen; **~ evidence** glaubhafter Beweis, Glaubhaftmachung, Anscheinsbeweis; **to be ~ evidence** öffentlichen Glauben genießen; **~ presumption** Primafacievoraussetzung.
primacy Vorrang, Primat.
primage Frachtzuschlag, Primgeld.
primarily liable unmittelbar (selbstschuldnerisch) haftbar.
primary Hauptsache, Wichtigstes, *(US el.)* Hauptleitung;
  ~ *(a.)* *(chief)* hauptsächlich, wichtigst, in erster Linie, primär, *(fundamental)* elementar, grundlegend, *(original)* ursprünglich, zuerst, anfänglich;
  ~ account Hauptbuchkonto; **~ aim** Hauptzweck; **~ allegation** *(pleading)* Hauptbegründung; **~ appeal** *(advertising)* Hauptblickfang; **~ assembly** Urwählerversammlung; **~ beneficiary** Hauptnutznießer, Erstbegünstigter; **~ benefit** *(social insurance)* Grundrente; **~ benefit formula** Grundrentenformel; **~ bill** Primawechsel; **~ boycott** unmittelbarer Boykott; **~ business** erste (wichtigste) Aufgabe, Hauptangelegenheit; **~ circuit** *(el.)* Primärstromkreis; **~ claim** Hauptanspruch; **~ colo(u)r** Primärfarbe; **~ commodities** Grund-, Rohstoffe; **~ component** Grundbestandteil; **~ concern** Hauptanliegen; **~ contract** Hauptvertrag; **~ conveyance** Auflassung; **~ cost** effektive Kosten; **~ customer** Hauptkunde; **~ data** Primärdaten; **~ demand** vordringlicher Bedarf; **~ deposits** *(US)* effektive (durch Einzahlung entstandene) Einlagen; **~ discount** echter Skonto; **~ disposal of the soil** Erstvergabe von Land; **~ duty** vorrangige Aufgabe; **~ education** *(Br.)* Grundschulausbildung; **~ election** *(US)* Vorwahl; **~ energy consumption** Primärenergieverbrauch; **~ evidence** Beweismaterial erster Ordnung; **~ examiner** *(patent law, US)* Vorprüfer; **~ export** primärer Export; **~ factors** Hauptfaktoren; **~ factor of production** ursprünglicher Produktionsfaktor; **~ franchise** *(US)* Grundtalent; **~ fuel** Primärenergie; **~ grades** *(US)* Grundschulstufen; **~ group** *(sociology)* Primärgruppe; **of ~ importance** von höchster Wichtigkeit; **~ income** Primäreinkommen; **~ industries** Grundstoffindustrie; **~ input** primäre Aufwendungen; **~ instruction** Volksschulunterricht; **~ insurance amount** maßgeblicher Versicherungsbetrag, *(pension scheme, US)* Grundrente; **~ insurance benefit** Erstbegünstigung; **~ language** gesprochene Sprache; **~ liability** direkte (unmittelbare) Haftung, selbst-

schuldnerische Haftung; **~ liquidity** liquide Mittel erster Ordnung; **~ market** *(US)* Richtwerte setzender Rohstoffmarkt, *(Eurobond Market)* Vormarkt für erstklassige Wertpapiere; **~ materials** Rohstoffe; **~ matter** Urstoff; **~ meaning of a word** Grundbedeutung eines Wortes; **~ meeting** Urwählerversammlung; **~ money** originäres Geld; **~ obligation** *(US)* Hauptverbindlichkeit, *(bill of exchange)* primäre Haftung; **~ obligor** *(US)* selbstschuldnerischer Bürge, *(bill of exchange)* Erstverpflichteter; **~ party** Hauptschuldner; **~ planet** Hauptplanet; **~ point** *(US)* Hauptumschlagplatz für landwirtschaftliche Erzeugnisse; **~ powers** Grundvollmachten; **~ producer** Urerzeuger, Rohstoffproduzent, -land; **~ products** Grund-, Rohstoffe; **~ production** Primärgüter-, Urproduktion, Rohstofferzeugung; **~ purpose** Hauptzweck; **~ quality** Haupteigenschaft; **~ readership** hauptsächlicher Leserstamm; **~ receipts** *(US)* Tageszufuhren für die Hauptgetreidemärkte; **~ reserve** *(banking)* Primär-, Kassenreserve; **~ responsibility** *(antitrust law, US)* Hauptverantwortung; **~ risk** *(EC)* hohes Investitionsrisiko; **~ road** Landstraße erster Ordnung; **~ rocks** Urgestein; **~ sampling** Einheit der ersten Auswahlstufe; **~ sampling units** erste Auswahlstufe bei der Erhebung; **~ scholar** Grund-, Volksschüler; **~ school** Grund-, Volksschule; **~ school teacher** Volksschullehrer; **~ sector** Urproduktion; **~ shipments** *(US)* Tagesverschiffung von den Hauptgetreidemärkten; **~ stress** *(ling.)* Hauptakzent; **~ trend** *(stock market)* Grundtendenz; **~ unit** Einheit der ersten Auswahlstufe; **~ vaccination** Erstimpfung.
prime Primasorte, auserlesene Qualität, Spitzenqualität, *(fig.)* Blüte, Lebenskraft, *(stock exchange)* Prämie;
  in the ~ of youth in der Blüte des Lebens;
  ~ of the day Morgendämmerung; **~ of perfection** Gipfel der Vollendung; **~ of the year** Frühling;
  ~ *(v.)* in Betrieb setzen, *(engine)* Kraftstoff einspritzen, *(fig.)* informieren, instruieren;
  ~ s. o. *(sl.)* j. bestechen, *(cram)* j. einpauken; **~ s. o. with beer** j. mit Bier vollaufen lassen; **~ with facts** Tatsachenmaterial zur Verfügung stellen; **~ the pump** *(US)* Wirtschaft ankurbeln; **~ s. o. with a speech** jem. einbleuen, er sagen soll; **~ a witness** *(lawyer)* Zeugen genauestens unterrichten (präparieren);
  to be past one's ~ die besten Jahre hinter sich haben; **to be in the ~ of one's career** in der Blütezeit seiner Laufbahn stehen;
  ~ *(a.)* prima, vorzüglich, erstklassig, ausgezeichnet, *(original)* ursprünglich;
  ~ banker's acceptances *(US)* Prima-, Privatdiskonten; **~ bill** *(US)* prima (erstklassige) Wechsel; **~ bond** erstklassige Obligation; **~ candidate** Hauptanwärter; **~ condition** vorzüglicher Zustand; **~ conductor** *(el.)* Hauptleiter; **~ contract** Generalunternehmervertrag; **~ contractor** Hauptlieferant, Generalunternehmer; **~ cost** *(cost price)* Selbstkosten-, Gestehungspreis, Gestehungskosten, *(purchase price)* Einkaufspreis, Anschaffungskosten, -wert, *(US)* Einzelkosten; **to sell at ~ cost** zum Einkaufspreis (Selbstkostenpreis) verkaufen; **~ cost burden rate** Gemeinkostenzuschlagsatz auf Basis der Einzelkosten; **~ election** *(goods)* erste Wahl; **~ entry** vorläufige Zolldeklaration; **of ~ importance** von höchster Wichtigkeit; **~ investment** erstklassige Kapitalanlage; **~ market area** Hauptabsatzgebiet; **~ Minister** Premierminister, Ministerpräsident; **~ ministry** Ministerpräsidentschaft; **~ motive** Hauptmotiv; **~ mover** *(fig.)* treibende Kraft, Triebfeder; **to be the ~ mover of an enterprise** Haupttriebfeder eines Unternehmens sein; **~ necessity** dringende Notwendigkeit; **~ number** Primzahl; **~ paper** erstklassiges Wertpapier; **~ quality** Primasorte, vorzügliche (erstklassige) Qualität; **~ [lending] rate** *(US)* Bankzinssatz für erstklassige Firmen, Eckkredit-, Vorzugs-, Leitzinssatz; **~ formula-established rate** *(US)* festgelegter Leitzinssatz; **~ reason** Hauptgrund; **~ suspect** Hauptverdächtiger; **~ target** Hauptziel; **~ time** *(broadcasting, television)* Hauptsendezeit, -fernsehzeit; **~ trade bill** *(US)* erstklassiger Handelswechsel; **~ value** Spitzenwert.
primed instruiert;
  ~ by a lawyer *(witness)* von einem Anwalt präpariert;
  to be well ~ with information über erstklassige Informationen verfügen; **to be well ~ with liquor** *(coll.)* total betrunken sein.
primer Elementarbuch, Fibel, ABC-Buch, *(fig.)* Leitfaden;
  great ~ *(print.)* anderthalb Cicero; **long ~** *(print.)* Garmondschrift;
  ~ pump Einspritzpumpe.
priming *(engine)* Einspritzung;
  ~ the pump *(US)* Ankurbelung der Wirtschaft;
  ~ coat Grundanstrich; **~ colo(u)r** Grundierfarbe; **~ pump** Einspritzpumpe; **~ valve** *(boiler)* Sicherheitsventil.

primitive anfänglich, frühest, *(not civilized)* unziviliziert, primitiv, auf niedriger Kulturstufe stehend;
~ **colo(u)r** Primärfarbe; ~ **weapons** primitive Waffen.
primness Förmlichkeit, Geziertheit.
primogenital right Erstgeburtsrecht.
primogeniture Erstgeburtsrecht.
primrose path Pfad der Freude.
prince Fürst, Herrscher;
merchant ~ Wirtschaftsführer;
~ **of the blood** *(Br.)* Prinz von königlichem Geblüt;
~ **consort** Prinzgemahl; ~ **regent** Prinzregent.
princedom Fürstentum.
princely | gift königliches Geschenk; **to treat s. o. in a** ~ **manner** j. fürstlich bewirten.
principal *(capital)* Kapital, Kapitaleinlage, -summe, Hauptsumme, Grundkapital, *(chief)* Chef, Leiter, *(civil service)* Ministerialbeamter, *(criminal law)* Haupttäter, Anführer, Rädelsführer, *(employer of agent)* Auftrag-, Vollmachtgeber, *(estate)* Masse, *(leader in action)* Hauptperson, *(person primarily liable)* Hauptschuldner, *(presiding officer)* Präsident, Vorsitzender, *(principal matter)* Hauptsache, -angelegenheit, *(proprietor)* Unternehmer, Geschäfts-, Firmeninhaber, Geschäftsherr, *(school)* Vorsteher, Rektor, Direktor, *(superior)* Vorgesetzter, Dienstherr, Chef, *(theater)* Hauptdarsteller;
only ~s will be dealt with *(newspaper)* Vermittler verbeten;
foreign ~ ausländischer Arbeitgeber; **senior** ~ *(Br.)* höherer Ministerialbeamter; **undisclosed** ~ ungenannter (verdeckter) Auftraggeber; **vice** ~ Geschäftsführer;
~ **and agent** Aufraggeber und Auftragnehmer, Vollmachtgeber und -nehmer, Stellvertretung; ~ **and charges** volle Summe einer Forderung, Kapital und Spesen; ~ **of a debate** Hauptdiskussionsredner; ~ **in the first degree** Mittäter; ~ **in the second degree** *(US)* Tatgehilfe, Beihelfer; ~ **of a firm** Firmeninhaber; ~ **of the house** Vorstand eines Anwaltsvereins; ~ **and interest** Kapital nebst Zinsen; ~ **with interest accrued** Kapital samt aufgelaufenen Zinsen; ~ **of a loan** Kapitalbetrag einer Anleihe; ~ **and surety** Bürgschaftsverhältnis;
to be liable as a ~ selbstschuldnerisch (unmittelbar) haften; **to be punished as** ~ wie der Haupttäter bestraft werden; **to consult one's** ~ sich mit seinem Auftraggeber besprechen; **to draw out all one's** ~ gesamtes Kapital aufbrauchen; **to make incursions into (invade,** *US)* **the** ~ Kapital angreifen; **to inform the** ~ **immediately** Geschäftsherrn sofort verständigen;
~ *(a.)* hauptsächlich, zum Kapital gehörig;
~ **activity** Haupttätigkeit; ~ **actor** Rädelsführer, Anführer, *(theatre)* Hauptdarsteller; ~ **agent** Generalvertreter; ~**-agent relationship** Vertreterverhältnis; ~ **agreement** Hauptabkommen; ~ **amount** Kapitalbetrag; ~ **amount of the loan** Anleihebetrag; ~ **area of consumption** Hauptverbrauchergebiet; ~ **argument** Hauptbeweisgrund; ~ **beneficiary** Haupt-, Erstbegünstigter; ~ **challenge** *(jurors)* Ablehnung wegen Befangenheit; ~ **city** Hauptstadt; ~ **claim** Hauptforderung; ~ **clause** *(Br.)* Hauptsatz; ~ **clerk** *(ministry)* Obersekretär; ~ **consumer** Hauptverbraucher, -zielgruppe der Verbraucher; ~ **contract** Hauptvertrag; ~ **creditor** Hauptgläubiger; ~ **debt** Hauptschuld; ~ **debtor** Hauptschuldner; **to discuss a** ~ **debtor** Hauptschuldner ausklagen; ~ **defect** Hauptmangel; ~ **endorser** Erstgirant; ~ **establishment (firm, house)** Zentrale, Hauptniederlassung, Stammhaus; ~ **events in s. one's life** Hauptvorkommnisse in jds. Leben; ~ **fact** entscheidende Tatsache; ~ **features of a program(me)** Höhepunkt eines Programms; ~ **establishment (firm, house)** Zentrale, Stammhaus; ~ **food** Hauptnahrungsmittel; ~ **income** Haupteinkommen; ~ **market** Hauptabsatzgebiet; ~ **matter** Wesentliches, Hauptsache; ~ **member** Hauptträger; ~ **men of a city** Spitzen der Stadt; ~ **moneys** Kapitalbetrag; ~ **note** hypothekarisch gesicherter Schuldschein; ~ **object** Hauptziel; ~ **obligation** Hauptverbindlichkeit; ~ **occupation** Hauptbeschäftigung; ~ **office** Hauptgeschäftsstelle, Zentrale; ~ **official** Hauptfunktionär; ~ **organs** *(UNO)* Hauptorgane; ~ **owner** Hauptinhaber, *(shipping)* Hauptreeder; ~ **part** Hauptteil, *(theatre)* Hauptrolle; ~ **payments** Zahlungen aus dem Kapital; **to be the** ~ **performer** Hauptrolle spielen; ~ **place of business** Haupt[geschäfts]sitz, Hauptniederlassung; ~ **rafter** Haupt-, Stützbalken; ~ **register** *(trademarks)* Hauptregister; ~ **shareholder (stockholder,** *US)* Großaktionär; ~ **speaker** Hauptredner; ~ **subject matter** Hauptverhandlungsgegenstand; ~ **sum** Kapitalbetrag, Gesamtsumme, *(accident insurance)* Kapitalabfindung, ~ **surety** Hauptbürge; ~ **town** Hauptstadt; ~ **underwriter** Erstversicherer; ~ **value** Kapitalwert, *(Br.)* gemeiner Wert; ~ **vein** *(mining)* Hauptader; ~ **witness** Hauptzeuge; ~ **work** Hauptarbeit.

principality Fürstentum.
principally grundsätzlich, im Prinzip.
principalship *(school)* Direktorposten, *(university)* Rektorat.
principle Grundgedanke, -regel, -satz, Prinzip, *(chem.)* Grundbestandteil;
on ~ grundsätzlich, prinzipiell;
economy-of-effort ~ Wirtschaftlichkeitsprinzip; **good accounting** ~s *(US)* Grundsätze ordnungsgemäßer Buchführung und Bilanzierung; **first** ~s Grundprinzipien; **guiding** ~ Leitgedanke, -satz; **leading** ~ Haupt-, Leitgrundsatz; **legal** ~ Rechtsgrundsatz; **let-alone** ~ Grundsatz der freien Wirtschaft; **most-favo(u)red-nation** ~ Meistbegünstigungsprinzip; **overall** ~ Bruttoprinzip; **overriding** ~ beherrschender Grundsatz; **generally recognized** ~ allgemein anerkannter Grundsatz; **rigid** ~s strenge Grundsätze; **settled** ~s festgelegte Rechtsgrundsätze; **strong** ~s feste Grundsätze;
~s **of accounting** Buchführungsmethoden, Prüfungs-, Revisionsgrundsätze; ~ **of free association** freies Vereinigungsrecht; ~s **of bookkeeping** Grundbegriffe der Buchführung; ~s **of causality** Gesetz von Ursache und Wirkung, Kausalitätsprinzip; ~s **of the economy** Grundsätze der Wirtschaftsordnung; ~s **of political economy** volkswirtschaftliche Theorie; ~ **of efficiency** Leistungsprinzip; ~ **of equality** Gleichheitsgrundsatz; ~ **of exemption** Ausnahmeprinzip; ~s **of interpretation** Auslegungsgrundsätze; **established** ~s **of law** bestehende Rechtsgrundlage; ~s **of international law** völkerrechtliche Grundsätze; ~ **of limited liability** Haftungsbeschränkungsgrundsatz; ~ **of life** Lebensprinzip; ~s **of limitation** Verjährungsregeln; ~s **of navigation** Grundregeln der Schiffahrt; ~s **of prescription** Verjährungsregeln; ~ **of relativity** *(Einstein)* Relativitätstheorie; ~ **of self-determination** Selbstbestimmungsprinzip; ~s **of selling** Verkaufsrichtlinien; ~ **of settlement** Vergleichsgrundlage; ~ **of substitution** Substitutionsprinzip; ~ **of taxation** Steuerprinzip;
to be the ~ **of good government** zur Richtschnur guter Verwaltung gehören; **to deviate from a** ~ von einem Grundsatz abgehen; **to lay down a** ~ Grundsatz aufstellen; **to have cast-iron** ~s eiserne Grundsätze haben; **to live up to one's** ~s an seinen Grundsätzen festhalten, seinen Prinzipien treu bleiben; **to make a** ~ **of** etw. zum Prinzip machen; **to refuse on** ~ sich grundsätzlich weigern, grundsätzlich dagegen sein; **to sit tight on one's** ~s auf seinen Prinzipien herumreiten; **to stick to one's** ~s an seinen Grundsätzen festhalten; **to work on the same** ~ nach dem gleichen Prinzip arbeiten;
~ **debate** Grundsatzdebatte.
print Druck, *(form)* Modell, Stanze, *(lithography)* Lithographie, Radierung, Kupferstich, *(mould)* Druckstock, *(newspaper)* Zeitung, *(plate)* Abklatsch, Abguß, *(photo)* Abzug, Kopie, Ablichtung, *(printed characters)* Druckbuchstaben, -schrift, *(printed edition)* Druckauflage, *(printed goods)* Druckwaren, *(printed matter, US)* gedruckte Veröffentlichung, Gedrucktes, Druckschrift, *(proof)* Abdruck, *(textiles)* Druckmuster;
in ~ im Druck, erschienen, gedruckt vorliegend, *(at hand)* vorrätig, auf Lager; **in cold** ~ schwarz auf weiß; **in small** ~ kleingedruckt; **not yet in** ~ noch nicht vorrätig (auf Lager); **out of** ~ vergriffen; **out of** ~, **reprint planned** vergriffen, Neuauflage vorgesehen;
~**blotted** ~ durchgeschlagener Druck; **blue** ~ Lichtpause; **clear** ~ klarer Druck; **contact** ~ Kontaktstreifen; **colo(u)red** ~ Farbdruck; **daily** ~s *(US)* Tageszeitungen; **finger** ~s Fingerabdrücke; **glossy** ~ Hochglanzabzug, Abzug auf Kunstdruckpapier; **large** ~ großer Druck; **mat** ~ Mattkopie; **separate** ~ Sonderabzug; **small** ~ kleiner Druck; **the** ~s *(US)* die Presse; **weekly** ~s Filmkopie;
~ **of one's education on one's character** Stempel seiner Erziehung auf den Charakter; ~ **of a film** Filmkopie; ~ **of a seal in wax** Wachsabdruck; ~s **of a wheel** Radspuren;
~ *(v.)* [ab]drucken, eindrucken, drucken, *(be printing)* drucken, sich im Druck befinden, *(cause to be printed)* in Druck geben, drucken lassen, *(photography)* kopieren, *(publish)* verlegen, veröffentlichen, *(stamp)* Stempel aufdrücken, *(work as printer)* Drucker sein, *(write in typographical characters)* in Druckbuchstaben schreiben;
~ **to** andrucken; ~ **s. o.** *(sl.)* jem. die Fingerabdrücke abnehmen; ~ **an address** Adresse in Druckschrift schreiben; ~ **badly** schlechte Abzüge liefern; ~ **in bold type** durch fetten Druck hervorheben; ~ **one's footsteps on the sand** seine Fußspuren im Sand hinterlassen; ~ **in italics** kursiv drucken; ~ **one's lectures** seine Vorlesungen in Buchform erscheinen lassen; ~ **themselves on the memory** *(incidents)* sich dem Gedächtnis einprägen; ~ **s. th. on s. one's mind** jem. etw. einprägen; ~ **full of monks** sehr

unsauber drucken; ~ **one's name** seinen Namen in Druckbuchstaben (Druckschrift) schreiben; ~ **off** abziehen, kopieren; ~ **[off] a newspaper** Zeitung drucken; ~ **a seal on wax** Wachsabdruck machen; ~ **waste** makulieren;

to **appear in** ~ im Druck erscheinen; **to be in** ~ gedruckt vorliegen, erhältlich sein, *(on sale)* im Buchhandel sein; **to like to see o. s. in** ~ sich gern gedruckt sehen; **to okay to** ~ *(US)* für druckfertig erklären; **to put into** ~ in Druck geben; **to put into the public** ~s in die öffentlichen Blätter einrücken; **to rush into** ~ beschleunigt verlegen, unüberlegt veröffentlichen; **to take a** ~ **from a negative** Abzug machen;

~ **advertising** Werbung in gedruckten Medien; ~ **cloth** Druckstoff; ~ **cutter** Formschneider; ~ **hand** Druckbuchstaben; ~ **order** Druckauftrag; ~**-out time** Ausdruckszeit; **blue** ~ **paper** Pauspapier; ~ **room** *(museum)* graphische Sammlungen; ~ **run** Druckauflage; ~ **seller** Graphikhändler; ~ **shop** Graphikhandlung; ~ **union** Gewerkschaft Druck und Papier, Druckergewerkschaft.

printable druckfähig, *(worth being printed)* wert, veröffentlicht zu werden.

printed gedruckt, *(phot.)* kopiert;
~ **in double columns** zweispaltig gedruckt; ~ **in three languages** in dreisprachigem Text; ~ **off** *(book)* ausgedruckt;
~ **application form** gedrucktes Antragsformular; ~ **clause** vorgedruckte Klausel; ~ **and mixed consignment** Postwurfsendung; ~ **description** *(patent law)* Patentschrift; ~ **document** Druckschrift; ~ **exchange** Kurszettel; ~ **form** Vordruck, Formular; ~ **form of receipt** Quittungsformular; ~ **goods** bedruckte Stoffe; ~ **matter (paper,** *Br.***)** Drucksache, -schrift; ~ **page** Druckseite; ~ **paper conditions** *(Br.)* Bestimmungen über den Versand von Standarddrucksachen; ~ **paper rate** *(Br.)* Drucksachentarif, -gebühr, -porto; ~ **papers reduced rate** Drucksache zu ermäßigter Gebühr; ~ **publication** *(patent law)* druckschriftliche Veröffentlichung; ~ **wallpaper** bedruckte Tapeten.

printer Drucker, Druckereibesitzer, *(copying apparatus)* Kopierapparat, *(establishment)* Druckereibetrieb, *(printing telegraph)* Fernschreiber, *(terminal)* Klarschreiber;
direct ~ direkte Fernschreibverbindung; **page** ~ Blattschreiber; **public** ~ *(US)* Leiter der Regierungsdruckerei; **wheel** ~ Typenraddrucker; **wire** ~ Matrixdrucker;
~ **and publisher** Drucker und Verleger;
~**'s devil** Druckereigehilfe, Mitarbeiter; ~**'s error** Druckfehler; ~**'s flourish** Vignette; ~**'s flower** Schmuckleiste; ~**'s gauge** Kolumnen-, Zeilenmaß; ~**'s imprint** Impressum; ~**'s ink** Druckerschwärze, Druckfarbe; ~**'s licence** Druckerlaubnis; ~**'s mark** Druckerzeichen; ~**'s proof** Hauskorrektur; ~**'s reader** Korrektor.

printery *(US)* Druckerei.

printing Drucken, Drucklegung, Buchdruck, Gedrucktes, *(amount printed)* Auflageziffer, *(phot.)* Abziehen, Kopieren;
in course of ~ im Druck;
anastatic ~ anastatischer Druck; **cutwork** ~ Illustrationsdruck; **hard-cover** ~ fest eingebundenes Buch; **immense** ~ sehr hohe Druckauflage; **intaglio** ~ Tiefdruck; **job** ~ kleinere Druckarbeiten; **level** ~ Flachdruck; **public** ~ Druck im Staatsauftrag; **relief** ~ Hochdruck; **rotary** ~ Rotationsdruck; **silkscreen** ~ Sieb[schablonen]druck; **surface** ~ Flachdruck;
to be ~ im Druck sein, drucken; **to go into** ~ ins Druckereigeschäft einsteigen; **to start** ~ mit den Druckarbeiten beginnen; **to supervise the** ~ Druck überwachen;
~ **block** Druckform, Klischee; ~ **charges (costs, expenses)** Druckkosten; ~ **craft** graphischer Beruf; ~ **delay** Druckverzögerung; ~ **equipment** Maschinenpark einer Druckerei; ~ **error** Druckfehler; ~ **establishment** Druckerei, graphischer Betrieb, typografische Anstalt; ~ **estimate** Druckkostenvoranschlag; ~ **fee** Drucklegungsgebühr; ~ **frame** *(photo)* Kopierrahmen; ~ **house** typografische Anstalt, Druckerei; ~**-in** Hineinkopieren; ~ **industry** Druckereigewerbe; ~ **ink** Druckerschwärze; ~ **machine** *(Br.)* Schnellpresse; **cylinder** ~ **machine** Rotationspresse; **copper-plate** ~ **machine** Kupfertiefdruckmaschine; ~ **machinery** Maschinenpark einer Druckerei; ~ **method** Druckverfahren; ~ **office** Druckerei; **lithographic** ~ **office** lithografische Anstalt; ~ **order** Druckauftrag; ~**-out paper** Kopierpapier; ~ **paper** Druckpapier; **thin** ~ **paper** Dünndruckpapier; ~ **paper for copper engravings** Kupfertiefdruckpapier; ~ **plant** Druckerei[betrieb]; ~ **plate** Druckplatte; **stereotype, electrotype and nylon** ~ **plates for relief prints** Stereo-, Galvano- und Nylonprintverfahren für den Hochdruck; ~ **press** Druckerpresse; ~ **process** Druck-, Kopierverfahren; ~ **requisites** Bedarfsartikel für Buchdruckereien; ~ **shop** *(US)* Druckerei,

typografische Anstalt; ~ **space** Satzspiegel; ~ **telegraph** Fernschreiber; ~ **trade** Druckergewerbe, graphisches Gewerbe; ~ **type** Buchdruckletter; ~ **worker** Drucker, Setzer; ~ **works** Druckerei.

printline Druckzeile.

printout *(computer)* ausgedruckter Datenstreifen.

printscript Druckschrift.

printworks Tapetendruckerei.

prior früher, älter, vorher-, vorausgehend, vorrangberechtigt;
~ **to his appointment** vor seiner Ernennung; ~ **to deduction of taxes** vor [Abzug der] Steuern, brutto; ~ **to my departure** vor meiner Abreise; ~ **to any discussions** bevor wir in die Diskussion eintreten; ~ **to maturity** vor Fälligkeit;
~ **applicant** *(patent law)* früherer Anmelder, Voranmelder; ~ **application** *(patent law)* Voranmeldung; ~ **approval** vorherige Genehmigung; ~**art** *(patent law)* Stand der Technik; ~ **charge** vorrangiger Anspruch; ~ **charges** *(company)* Vorbelastungen, vorhergehende Ansprüche, *(balance sheet)* Anleihezinsen und Vorzugsdividenden; ~ **claim** älterer Anspruch, bevorrechtigte Forderung, *(patent law)* Prioritätsanspruch; **to give a** ~ **claim** bevorrechtigen; **to have a** ~ **claim** bevorrechtigt sein; ~ **creditor** bevorrechtigter Gläubiger; ~ **education** Vorbildung; **to carry** ~ **encumbrances** Vorlasten haben; ~ **endorser** Vormann; ~ **engagement** frühere Vereinbarung; ~ **holder** früherer Inhaber, besitzer; ~ **indorser** Vormann; ~ **invention** *(patent law)* ältere Erfindung; ~ **inventor** Ersterfinder; ~ **judgment** früheres Urteil; ~ **lien** älteres (dem Range nach vorgehendes) Pfandrecht; ~ **lien bonds** *(US)* durch Vorrangshypothek abgesicherte Obligationen, Prioritätsobligationen; ~ **mortgage** vorgehende (vorrangige) Hypothek; ~ **obligation** ältere Verpflichtung; ~ **preference (preferred,** *US***) stock** Sondervorzugsaktien; ~ **publication** *(patent law, US)* druckschriftliche Veröffentlichung; ~ **printed publication** *(patent law, US)* druckschriftliche Veröffentlichung; **of** ~ **rank** vorrangig; **to grant** ~ **rank** Vorrang einräumen; ~ **redemption** vorzeitige Tilgung; ~ **right** Vor[zugs]recht; **subject to** ~ **sale** Zwischenverkauf vorbehalten; ~ **taxable year** vorangehendes Steuerjahr; ~ **use** Vorbenutzungsfall; ~ **user** Vorbenutzer; ~ **year** Vorjahr; ~ **year charges** vorjährige Belastungen.

priorities, discretionary Prioritäten mit Ermessensspielraum; **preemptive** ~ absolute Prioritäten;
to be low on the ~ am Ende der Dringlichkeitsliste stehen; **to get top** ~ höchste Dringlichkeitsstufe erhalten; **to reorder** ~ Prioritätenliste neu zusammenstellen; **to shake up** ~ Prioritäten in Frage stellen.

priority *(bankruptcy)* Rangfolge, *(order that takes priority)* Dringlichkeitsauftrag, *(preference)* Dringlichkeit, Priorität, Vorzug[srecht], Vorrecht, Vorrang, *(urgency)* Dringlichkeitsstufe;
according to ~ dem Range nach; **of top** ~ von höchster Dringlichkeit; **with** ~ **over** mit Vorrang vor;
absolute ~ unabdingbares Vorrecht; **convention** ~ Verbandspriorität; **head-of-the-line** ~ relative Priorität; **top** ~ höchste Dringlichkeitsstufe; **union** ~ *(dipl.)* Unionsvorrang;
~ **of birth** Erstgeburt, -recht, Primogenitur; ~ **of a claim** Vorrang (Vorgehen) eines Anspruchs; ~ **of creditors** Gläubigervorrang, Rangordnung der Gläubiger; ~ **of date** zeitlicher Vorrang; ~ **of debts** Rangfolge von Forderungen; ~ **of invention** Erfindungspriorität; ~ **of liens** Rangordnung von Pfandrechten; ~ **of a mortgage** Hypothekenvorrang; ~ **in the payment of debts** Vorzugsbefriedigung; ~ **of rank** Vorrang;
to be given ~ bevorzugt abgefertigt werden; **to claim** ~ **for an application** *(patent law)* Erstanmeldung beanspruchen; **to come under** ~ zur ersten Dringlichkeitsstufe gehören; **to distribute according to** ~ *(proceeds of sale)* rangentsprechend ausgeschüttet werden; **to enjoy** ~ Priorität genießen; **to establish** ~ über Dringlichkeitsfragen entscheiden; **to give** ~ Vorrang einräumen, bevorzugt behandeln (abfertigen); **to give high** ~ als besonders dringlich behandeln; **to give** ~ **to an order** Bestellung vorziehen; **to give top** ~ **in the allocation** hinsichtlich der Zuteilung höchste Dringlichkeitsstufe zuerkennen; **to have first** ~ Vorrang genießen, vordringlich behandelt werden; **to have low** ~ kaum als vorrangig angesehen werden; **to have** ~ **over s. o.** jem. im Rang vorgehen (gegenüber bevorrechtigt sein); **to have** ~ **over s. o. in one's claim on mortgaged property** jem. im Grundbuch vorgehen; **to have the highest** ~ höchste Dringlichkeitsstufe besitzen; **to lose** ~ Rangverlust erleiden; **to promote with** ~ bevorzugt befördern; **to raise s. th. into first** ~ einer Sache absoluten Vorrang einräumen; **to rank in** ~ Vorrang haben; **to take** ~ Vorrang haben; **to take advantage of the** ~ **of previous application** *(patent law)* Priorität einer vorhergehenden Anmeldung in Anspruch nehmen;

~ **area** Vorrangsgebiet; ~ **attention** vordringliche Behandlung; ~ **bonds** Prioritätsobligationen, Prioritäten; ~ **call** *(tel.)* dringendes Gespräch, Vorranggespräch; ~ **caution** Rangvormerkung; ~ **claim** Prioritätsanspruch; **to receive** ~ **consideration** bevorzugt behandelt (abgefertigt) werden; ~ **date** *(patent law)* Prioritätstermin, -tag; ~ **delivery** Vorzugslieferung; ~ **documents** *(patent law)* Prioritätsbelege; ~ **fee** Gebühr für bevorzugte Abfertigung; ~ **holder** Vorzugsberechtigter, Bevorrechtigter; ~ **permit holder** Inhaber einer Vorzugsberechtigung; ~ **job** Schlüsselberuf; ~ **lane** Bushaltelinie; ~ **list** Vorrang-, Vorzugs-, Dringlichkeitsliste; ~ **message** dringende Meldung; ~ **notice** *(real estate law, Br.)* [Auflassungs]vormerkung; ~ **period** *(patent law)* Prioritätsfrist; ~ **rating** Festsetzung der Dringlichkeit; ~ **redemption** vorzeitige Tilgung; ~ **right** Prioritäts-, Vorzugsrecht; ~ **sale** *(securities)* Prioritätsverkauf; ~ **share** *(Br.)* Prioritäts-, Vorzugsaktie; ~ **system** Bewirtschaftungssystem; ~ **table** Prioritätsliste; ~ **task** vordringliche Aufgabe; ~ **telegram** dringendes Telegramm; ~ **treatment** Vorrangbehandlung.

prison Haft-, Straf-, Gefangenenanstalt, Gefängnis, *(building)* Gefängnisgebäude, *(imprisonment)* Inhaftierung;
convict ~ Strafgefängnis; **remand** ~ Untersuchungsgefängnis; **state** ~ *(US)* Staatsgefängnis, Zuchthaus;
~ **without walls** offenes Gefängnis;
~ *(v.)* gefangensetzen, -halten;
to be in ~ im Gefängnis sitzen; **to be kept three months in** ~ **awaiting trial** dreimonatige Untersuchungshaft absitzen; **to be released from** ~ aus dem Gefängnis entlassen werden; **to break out of** ~ aus dem Gefängnis ausbrechen; **to commit s. o. to** ~ Haftanordnung erlassen; **to condemn to** ~ auf Gefängnis erkennen; **to discharge from** ~ aus dem Gefängnis entlassen; **to endorse noncustodial alternatives to** ~ sich für nicht die Freiheit beschränkende Strafalternativen aussprechen; **to escape from** ~ aus dem Gefängnis entkommen; **to go to** ~ ins Gefängnis kommen; **to languish in** ~ im Gefängnis schmachten; **to order s. one's release from** ~ jds. Haftentlassung anordnen; **to put s. o. in** ~ j. ins Gefängnis stecken (werfen); **to recommit to** ~ wieder verhaften, für einen Gefangenen erneute Haft anordnen; **to release from** ~ aus dem Gefängnis entlassen; **to send s. o. to** ~ j. ins Gefängnis einweisen; **to sit in** ~ im Gefängnis sitzen; **to take off to** ~ ins Gefängnis abführen; **to throw s. o. into** ~ j. ins Gefängnis werfen;
~ **bounds** *(imprisoned debtor)* Gefängnisbereich; ~ **breach (breaking)** Gefängnisausbruch; ~ **breaker** entsprungener Häftling, Ausbrecher; ~ **breakout** Gefängnisausbruch; ~ **building** Gefängnisanstalt; ~ **camp** Gefangenenlager; ~ **cell** Gefängniszelle; ~ **clinic** Gefängniskrankenhaus; ~ **commissioners** Gefängnisbehörde; ~ **director** Gefängnisdirektor; ~ **editor** Sitzredakteur; ~ **escape** Gefangenenausbruch; ~ **fee** Haftgeld; ~ **functions** Gefängnisaufgaben; ~ **garb** Gefängniskleidung; ~ **governor** *(Br.)* Gefängnisdirektor; ~ **hospital** Gefängniskrankenhaus; ~ **house** Gefängnis, Haftanstalt; ~ **inmate** Gefängnisinsasse, Sträfling; ~ **labo(u)r** Gefangenenarbeit; ~**-made goods** durch Gefangene hergestellte Artikel; ~ **officer** Gefängnisbeamter; ~ **parol board** Bewährungsausschuß für Strafgefangene; ~ **population** im Gefängnis einsitzender Bevölkerungsteil; ~ **production** Herstellung durch Gefangene; ~ **psychosis** Haftpsychose; ~ **record** Vorstrafenregister; ~ **reform** Gefängnisreform; ~ **riot** Gefangenenaufstand, Gefängnisrevolte; **split-level** ~ **sentence** *(Br.)* aufgegliederte Gefängnisstrafe; **to suspend a** ~ **sentence** Gefängnisstrafe zur Bewährung aussetzen; **to undergo a** ~ **sentence** Gefängnisstrafe verbüßen; ~ **system** Strafvollzugssystem; ~ **terms** Gefängnisstrafe; ~ **train** Gefangenenzug; ~ **uniform** Gefängniskleidung; ~ **van** *(Br.)* Gefängniswagen, Grüne Minna; ~ **ward** Gefängnisabteilung; ~ **warden** *(US)* Gefängnisaufseher, -wärter; ~ **welfare** Gefangenenfürsorge; ~ **work** Gefangenenarbeit; ~ **workshop** Gefängniswerkstatt; ~ **yard** Gefängnishof.

prisoner Gefangener, Sträfling, Häftling;
close ~ streng bewachter Gefangener; **detention-without-trial** ~ nicht vor Gericht gestellter Untersuchungsgefangener; **fellow** ~ Mithäftling, -gefangener, Zellengenosse; **general** ~ *(US)* in Strafhaft einsitzender Soldat; **maximum security** ~ Gefangener mit dem höchsten Sicherheitsrisiko; **political** ~ politischer Häftling; **remand** ~ *(Br.)* Untersuchungsgefangener; **state** ~ Staatsgefangener; **young** ~ jugendlicher Häftling;
~ **at the bar** Angeklagter in der Hauptverhandlung; ~ **on remand** *(Br.)* Untersuchungsgefangener; ~ **under sentence** Strafgefangener; ~ **of state** politischer Gefangener, Staatsgefangener; ~ **on trial** inhaftierter Angeklagter; ~ **of war** Kriegsgefangener;

to bail a ~ Haftentlassung eines Gefangenen erwirken; **to be a** ~ **to one's bed** an sein Bett gefesselt sein; **to be a** ~ **of war** in Gefangenschaft sein; **to be held** ~ gefangengehalten werden; **to be taken** ~ in Gefangenschaft geraten; **to chain a** ~ Gefangenen fesseln; **to commit a** ~ **for trial** Gefangenen in Untersuchungshaft nehmen; **to free a** ~ Gefangenen freilassen; **to give o. s. up as a** ~ sich gefangennehmen lassen; **to harbo(u)r an escaped** ~ einem entsprungenen Sträfling Unterschlupf gewähren; **to hold s. o.** ~ j. gefangenhalten; **to keep a** ~ gefangenhalten; **to lock up a** ~ Gefangenen einsperren; **to produce a** ~ Untersuchungsgefangenen vorführen; **to put a** ~ **on parole** Gefangenen bedingt entlassen; **to release a** ~ Gefangenen freilassen; **to remand a** ~ **on bail** Gefangenen gegen Kautionsgestellung aus der Haft entlassen; **to remove a** ~ Gefangenen abführen; **to surrender a** ~ Gefangenen überstellen; **to take s. o.** ~ j. gefangennehmen;
Dischargeds' ⚯ **Act** *(Br.)* Gefangenenfürsorgeverein; ~ **camp** Kriegsgefangenenlager; ~**'s statement** Gefangenenaussage; ~**-of-war status** Kriegsgefangenenstatus.

privacy Zurückgezogenheit, Vertraulichkeit, Intimsphäre, private Sphäre, Eigenleben, *(private matter)* Privatangelegenheit, *(secrecy)* Geheimhaltung;
in strict ~ streng vertraulich;
~ **of one's house** Privatsphäre des eigenen Hauses;
to be married in strict ~ heimlich getraut werden; **to disturb s. one's** ~ Eingriff in jds. Intimsphäre vornehmen; **to intrude on** ~ sich in Privatsachen einmischen; **to invade s. one's** ~ jds. Intimsphäre verletzen; **to live in** ~ zurückgezogen leben;
~ **scrambler** *(tel.)* Verschlüsselungsmaschine.

private *(mil.)* gemeiner (gewöhnlicher) Soldat, Mannschaftsdienstgrad;
~**s** *(sl.)* teure Privathäuser;
„~" „Eintritt verboten";
in ~ unter vier Augen, *(court)* nicht öffentlich;
~ *(a.)* privat, im Privatleben, persönlich, *(not known)* vertraulich, nicht öffentlich, nicht für die Öffentlichkeit bestimmt, *(out of court)* außergerichtlich, *(secluded)* zurückgezogen, abgeschlossen, *(secret)* geheim, heimlich, verborgen, *(unofficial)* nicht amtlich, außerdienstlich, -geschäftlich;
~ **and confidential** streng vertraulich;
to be very ~ **about one's affairs** in eigenen Angelegenheiten sehr reserviert sein; **to dine in** ~ Essen im Kreis der Familie einnehmen; **to go** ~ *(company)* in ein Privatunternehmen umgewandelt werden; **to hear a case in** ~ Fall als Einzelrichter verhandeln; **to keep** ~ verheimlichen, geheimhalten; **to mark a letter** ~ Brief als persönlich kennzeichnen; **to sit in** ~ nicht öffentliche Sitzung abhalten; **to talk to s. o. in** ~ mit jem. eine persönliche Unterredung führen, j. unter vier Augen sprechen;
~ **account** Privatguthaben, *(secret fund)* Geheimkonto; ~ **accountant** *(US)* betriebseigener Revisor, unselbständiger Wirtschaftsprüfer; ⚯ **Act of Parliament** *(Br.)* Privatgesetz [für eine Körperschaft]; ~ **address** Privatanschrift; ~ **advantage** Gewinnstreben; ~ **affairs** persönliche Angelegenheiten, Privatangelegenheiten; ~ **agent** Vertrauensmann, persönlicher Vertreter; ~ **arrangement** gütlicher (außergerichtlicher) Vergleich, gütliche Einigung; ~ **assets** Privatvermögen; ~ **attorney** Bevollmächtigter, Beauftragter; **to be received in** ~ **audience** in Privataudienz empfangen werden; ~ **bank** Privatbank[haus]; ~ **banker** Privatbankier; ~ **banking account** persönliches Bankkonto; **to sell by** ~ **bargain** unter der Hand verkaufen; ~ **bathroom** *(hotel)* eigenes Bad; ~ **bay** Privatbucht, -strand; ~ **bill** *(parl.)* privater Gesetzentwurf; ~ **bill of exchange** Kundenwechsel; ~ **bill office** *(Br.)* Parlamentsbüro für private Gesetzentwürfe; ~ **boarding house** Privatpension; ~ **bonds** Industrieobligationen; ~ **books** Geheimbücher; ~ **boundary** Privatgrenze; ~ **box** Abhol-, Schließfach; ~ **branch exchange** *(tel.)* Hauszentrale, -vermittlung; ~ **brand** Haus-, Händler-, Eigenmarke; ~ **bridge** Privatbrücke; ~ **building** private Bautätigkeit; ~ **bus** reservierter Omnibus; ~ **business** Privatwirtschaft; **to enter** ~ **business** in die Wirtschaft gehen; **to interfere with** ~ **business** in die Privatwirtschaft eingreifen; **to do s. th. in a** ~ **capacity** etw. als Privatmann (nicht amtlich) unternehmen; ~ **capital** Privatvermögen; ~ **capitalism** Privatkapitalismus; ~ **car** eigener Wagen, *(railroad, US)* vorbestellter Eisenbahnwaggon; ~ **car[riage]** Sonderanfertigung; ~ **car comprehensive policy** Privathaftpflichtpolice; ~ **carrier** Gelegenheitsspediteur; **through** ~ **channels** aus vertraulicher Quelle; ~ **charity** private Wohltätigkeit; ~ **chattel scheme** *(Br.)* Kriegsentschädigung für bewegliches Vermögen; ~ **citizen** einfacher Bürger, Privatmann; ~ **clothes** Zivilanzug, -kleidung; ~ **commercial station** Privatsender; ~ **communication** private Mitteilung; ~ **company** *(Br.)* auf höchstens 50 Mitglieder beschränkte Aktienge-

sellschaft, Personengesellschaft, [etwa] Gesellschaft mit beschränkter Haftung; ~ **concern** Privatangelegenheit; ~ **consumption** privater Konsum, Selbst-, Eigenverbrauch; ~ **contract** Privatabkommen; **by** ~ **contract** freihändig; ~ **conversation** vertrauliche Unterredung, Gespräch unter vier Augen; ~ **corporation** *(US)* Gesellschaft des bürgerlichen Rechts; ~ **correspondence** Privatkorrespondenz; ~ **cost** private Unkosten, Privatausgaben, individuelle Kosten; ~ **customer** Privatkunde; ~ **dance** Ball nur für geladene Gäste; ~ **debts** persönliche Schulden, Privatschulden; ~ **deposit** privates Guthaben; ~ **detective** Privatdetektiv; ~ **discount rate** Privatdiskontsatz; ~ **devotion** Hausandacht; ~ **document** Privaturkunde; ~ **door** Privateingang; ~ **dwelling** eigene Wohnung, Privatwohnung; ~ **dwelling house** Eigenheim; **to be for s. one's** ~ **ear** als vertrauliche Information für j. bestimmt sein; ~ **economic power** privatwirtschaftliche Machtstellung; ~ **education** Privaterziehung; ~ **ends** Privatzwecke; ~ **enterprise** privatwirtschaftliche Aktivität, Privatinitiative; ~ **enterprise system** Privatwirtschaft, freie Wirtschaft; ~ **entrance** Privateingang; ~ **establishment** Privatbetrieb; ~ **examination** Vernehmung durch den Einzelrichter; ~ **expenses** persönliche Ausgaben; ~ **eye** *(sl.)* Privatdetektiv; ~ **files** Privatakten; ~ **firm** Privatfirma, -unternehmen, Einzel-, Handelsfirma; ~ **gentleman** Privatmann, Rentier, Rentner; **to pass into** ~ **hands** in Privathand übergehen; ~ **home** Privatquartier; ~ **hotel** Fremdenheim; ~ **house** Privathaus; **at my** ~ **house** bei mir zu Hause; ~ **household** Privathaushalt; ~ **income** Privateinkommen; ~ **individual** Privatperson, -mann; **to act merely as a** ~ **individual** als Privatperson handeln; ~ **industry** Privatwirtschaft; ~ **information** vertrauliche Informationen (Mitteilung); ~ **initiative** persönliche Initiative; ~ **insurance** Privatversicherung; ~ **insurer** Selbstversicherer; ~ **interest** eigenes Interesse; ~ **international law** internationales Privatrecht; ~ **interpretation** individuelle Auslegung; ~ **interview** persönliche Zusammenkunft; ~ **investor** privater Anleger; ~ **judgment** Recht der persönlichen Meinungsbildung; ~ **labelling** Ausstattung mit Eigenmarken; ~ **law** Privat-, Zivilrecht; ~ **ledger** *(Br.)* Geheimbuch, -konto; ~ **lessons** Privatunterricht; ~ **letter** persönlicher (vertraulicher) Brief; ~ **liability** persönliche Haftung; ~ **library** Privatbibliothek; ~ **life** Privatleben; **to retire into** ~ **life** sich ins Privatleben zurückziehen; ~ **limited company** *(Br.)* Gesellschaft mit beschränkter Haftung; ~ **line** *(tel.)* Privatanschluß; ~ **line car** *(US)* vorbestellter Waggon; ~ **management** Unternehmertum; ~ **means** Privatvermögen, private Mittel, Eigenmittel; **to live on** ~ **means** von seinem Vermögen leben; ~ **meeting** nicht öffentliche Sitzung; ~ **member** Einzelmitglied; ~ **member of the House of Commons** *(Br.)* einfacher Abgeordneter des Unterhauses, Parlamentsmitglied ohne Regierungsfunktion; ~ **money** Privateinkünfte; ~ **motives** persönliche Motive; ~ **motor car** Privatfahrzeug; ~ **negotiations** geheime Verhandlungen; ~ **net product** Nettosozialprodukt zu Faktorpreisen; ~ **news** vertrauliche Mitteilung; ~ **nuisance** verbotene Eigenmacht; ~ **offering** Absatz an Private; ~ **office** Privatkontor, -büro; **in my** ~ **opinion** nach meiner persönlichen Meinung; ~ **ownership of the means of production** Privateigentum an den Produktionsmitteln; ~ **papers** Privatpapiere; ~ **party** geschlossene Gesellschaft; ~ **patient** Privatpatient; ~ **performance** *(theatre)* geschlossene Vorstellung (Veranstaltung); ~ **person** Privatperson; ~ **placement of securities** *(US)* Wertpapierverkäufe an Private; ~ **placing** *(Br.)* direkte Effektenplazierung; ~ **plans** nicht für die Öffentlichkeit bestimmte Pläne; ~ **pond** persönlicher Fischteich; ~ **practice** Privatpraxis; ~ **press** nicht öffentlich erscheinende Zeitung; ~ **property** Privatvermögen, -eigentum, -grundstück, persönliches Vermögen; **to take** ~ **property for public use** Privatgrundstücke für öffentliche Zwecke enteignen; ~ **proprietor** Privatunternehmer; ~ **prosecutor** Anzeigender einer Straftat; ~ **quarters** Privatwohnung; ~ **railway company** *(Br.)* Privatbahn; ~ **rate of discount** *(Br.)* Diskontsatz der Geschäftsbanken; ~ **rent** Miete für eine frei finanzierte Wohnung; ~ **reasons** private Gründe; ~ **residence** Privatwohnung; ~ **road** nicht öffentlicher Weg, Privatstraße, -weg; ~ **room** *(hotel)* reserviertes Besprechungszimmer; ~ **sale** freihändiger Verkauf, Privatverkauf; **at** ~ **sale** unter der Hand verkauft; ~ **school** Privatschule; ~ **schoolmaster** Direktor einer Privatschule; ~ **secretary** Privatsekretär[in]; ~ **sector [of the economy]** Privatwirtschaft; ~ **sector companies** privatwirtschaftliche Unternehmen; ~ **sector current bank accounts** Giroguthaben der Wirtschaft; ~ **siding** Werksanschluß; ~ **situation** Privatverhältnisse; ~ **soldier** gemeiner Soldat; ~ **spending** Privatausgaben; ~ **sphere** Intimsphäre; ~ **staircase** Hintertreppe; ~ **station** privater Sender; ~ **statute** für bestimmte Personen

erlassenes Gesetz; ~ **street** Privatstraße; ~ **study** Sonderstudium; ~ **talk** Gespräch unter vier Augen; ~ **teacher (tutor)** Privat-, Hauslehrer; ~ **theater (theatre,** *Br.)* Liebhabertheater; ~ **theatricals** Theateraufführungen im Familienkreis; ~ **trade** Eigenhandel; ~ **trader** selbständiger Unternehmer; ~ **treaty** freihändiger Verkauf; **to sell by** ~ **treaty** freihändig verkaufen; ~ **trust** Familienstiftung, Treuhandverwaltung für bestimmte Begünstigte; ~ **trust funds** von einer Bank verwaltetes Privatvermögen; ~ **underwriter** *(US)* Einzelversicherungsunternehmen; ~ **undertaking** Privatbetrieb, -unternehmen; **for** ~ **use** nur zum eigenen Gebrauch (Privatgebrauch); **reserved for** ~ **use** für persönliche Zwecke reserviert, nur zum eigenen Gebrauch; ~ **view** Besichtigung durch geladene Gäste; ~ **want** individuelles Bedürfnis; ~ **water** Privatgewässer; ~ **way** Nachbarweg; ~ **wedding** Trauung im kleinsten Kreis; ~ **wharf** Privatpier; ~ **wire house** *(US)* Börsenmitglied mit eigenen Fernschreibleitungen zu Filialen; ~ **wrong** unerlaubte Handlung.

privateer Kaperschiff;
~ *(v.)* kapern;
~ **practice** Kaperwesen.

privateering Kaperwesen;
to fit out a ship for ~ Kaperschiff ausstatten; **to go** ~ Kaperei betreiben, Kapern.

privately privat, als Privateigentum, vertraulich, freihändig, unter der Hand;
~ **operated** im Privatbereich; ~ **owned** im Privatbesitz (Privateigentum); ~ **printed** als Manuskript gedruckt, im Privatdruck erschienen; ~ **sold** Verkauf nur an Private;
to benefit ~ **from s. th.** bei etw. persönlich profitieren; **to hear s. th.** ~ etw. vertraulich erfahren; **to sell** ~ unter der Hand verkaufen; **to settle s. th.** ~ etw. intern regeln; **to speak to s. o.** ~ j. unter vier Augen sprechen;
~ **owned enterprise (establishment, undertaking)** Privatbetrieb, privates Unternehmen.

privateness Privatleben.

privation Wegnahme, Entziehung, Entzug, *(depriving of office)* Absetzung, Amtsenthebung, *(destitution)* Entbehrung, Not;
~**s of war** Entbehrungen der Kriegszeit;
to live in ~ entbehrungsreiches Leben führen; **to suffer many small** ~**s** sich zahlreiche Entbehrungen auferlegen müssen; **to undergo severe** ~**s** große Not leiden.

privies gemeinschaftlich Beteiligte, Genossen;
~ **of blood** Blutsverwandte; ~ **in law** notwendige Streitgenossen;
~ **in respect to contract** Vertragsbeteiligte.

privilege *(advantage)* [Vor]zugs-, Sonderrecht, Vergünstigung, Privileg, *(bankruptcy)* Konkurs-, Gläubigervorrecht, *(franchise)* Gerechtsame, Nutzungsrecht, *(immunity)* Immunität, Indemnität, *(legal nonrestraint)* Rechtfertigungsgrund, *(marine insurance)* Frachtzuschlag, *(primage)* Prisengeld, *(stock exchange, US)* Spekulations-, Prämien-, Stell-, Zeitgeschäft, Stellage, *(witness)* Zeugnisverweigerungsrecht;
absolute ~ *(defamation)* absoluter Rechtfertigungsgrund, *(statement made in legislative debates)* uneingeschränktes Immunitätsrecht, absolute Immunität; **circulation** ~ Notenbankprivileg; **commercial** ~ Konzession, Gewerbeberechtigung; **conditional** ~ *(defamation)* bedingter Rechtfertigungsgrund, *(statement made in legislative debates)* bedingtes Immunitätsrecht, bedingte Immunität; **diplomatic** ~ diplomatische Immunität; **exclusive** ~ ausschließliches Patentrecht; **executive** ~ Amtsprivileg des amerikanischen Präsidenten; **financial** ~ Finanzhoheit; **intercorporate** ~ Schachtelprivileg; **judicial** ~ richterliche Immunität; **monopoly** ~ Monopolrecht; **note-issuing** ~ Notenbankprivileg; **legal professional** ~ anwaltliches Aussageverweigerungsrecht; **parliamentary** ~ parlamentarische [Abgeordneten]immunität; **personal** ~ persönliches Vorrecht; **qualified** ~ *(defamation)* nur bedingt anerkannter Rechtfertigungsgrund, eingeschränkte Immunität; **real** ~ *(Br.)* grundstücksgekoppelte Konzession; **reciprocal** ~**s** gegenseitig eingeräumte Vorrechte; **Royal** ~ Regal; **special** ~ Sondervorrecht; **statutory** ~ gesetzlich begründete Immunität; **subscription** ~ Bezugs-, Subskriptionsrecht; **tax** ~ steuerliche Vergünstigung, Steuerbegünstigung;
~ **of age** Altersvorrecht; ~ **from arrest** persönliche Immunität; ~ **in bankruptcy** Konkursvorrecht; ~ **of birth** Erstgeburtsrecht; ~ **of operating a business** Gewerbeberechtigung; ~**s of citizens** Bürgerrechte; ~ **of communications** Verkehrsprivileg; ~ **of a consul** konsularische Privilegien; ~ **of fishing** Fischereigerechtigkeit; ~ **of freedom from arrest** persönliche Immunität; ~ **of the house** Parlamentsvorrecht; ~**s and immunities** *(US)* verfassungsrechtlich geschützte Grundrechte; ~**s of the nobility**

Adelsprivilegien; ~ **of note issue** Notenbankprivileg; ~ **of Parliament** *(Br.)* [Abgeordneten]immunität; ~ **of printing a book** Druckerlaubnis; ~ **by reason of occasion** *(Br.)* Wahrnehmung berechtigter Interessen; ~ **of self-defence** *(US)* Notwehr[recht]; ~ **of transit** *(railway)* Umladerecht; ~ **of voting** Wahlrecht; ~ **of witness** Zeugnisverweigerungsrecht; ~ **of the writ of habeas corpus** Anspruch auf Anordnung eines Haftprüfungstermins;
~ *(v.)* bevorzugen, bevorzugt behandeln, bevorrechtigen, privilegieren, mit Privilegien ausstatten;
~ **from arrest** persönliche Immunität gewähren; ~ **legislators from arrest** Mitgliedern gesetzgebender Versammlungen Immunität gewähren;
to abridge ~s of the citizens verfassungsmäßig garantierte Privilegien beschränken; **to accord a ~** Vorrecht einräumen; **to claim a ~** Vorrecht beanspruchen; **to curtail s. one's ~s** jds. Vorrechte (Privilegien) einschränken; **to enjoy ~s** Vorrechte (Vorzüge) genießen; **to grant ~s** Vorrecht gewähren, *(licence)* Konzession erteilen; **to have the ~ of being admitted** zur Zulassung berechtigt sein; **to hold special ~s** besondere Vorrechte genießen; **to invade s. one's ~s** in jds. Vorrechte eingreifen; **to retrench ~s** Vorrechte (Privilegien) aufheben; **to stretch a ~** Vorrecht mißbrauchen; **to surrender a ~** auf ein Vorrecht verzichten; **to waive a ~** *(witness)* auf das Zeugnisverweigerungsrecht verzichten;
~ **broker** *(US)* Spezialitäten-, Prämienmakler; ~ **cab** *(Br.)* Bahnhofsdroschke; ~ **tax** *(US)* Konzessionsabgabe, -gebühr.

privileged bevorrechtigt, mit besonderen Vorrechten ausgestattet, privilegiert, *(banker, doctor, lawyer)* unter das Berufsgeheimnis fallend, in Wahrnehmung berechtigter Interessen handelnd, *(immunity)* geschützt, unter die Immunität fallen;
~ **from discovery** nicht vorlagepflichtig; ~ **from distress** nicht pfändbar, unpfändbar; ~ **from production** nicht vorlagepflichtig;
to be ~ Vorrechte genießen, bevorrechtigt sein, Vorzug haben; **to be ~ from disclosure** nicht der Offenlegungspflicht unterliegen;
~ **claim** bevorrechtigte [Konkurs]forderung, ~ **classes** privilegierte Stände; ~ **communications** *(confidential communication)* der Schweigepflicht unterliegende vertrauliche Mitteilung, Berufsgeheimnis, *(libel action)* der Rechtsverfolgung entzogene Äußerung, *(parl., Br.)* Äußerung in Wahrnehmung berechtigter Interessen; ~ **creditor** bevorrechtigter Gläubiger; ~ **debt** bevorrechtigte Konkursforderung; ~ **deed** *(Scot.)* formfreies Testament; ~ **document** vertrauliche Urkunde; **legal ~ evidence** *(US)* dem Zeugnisverweigerungsrecht unterliegende Aussage; **a ~ few** ein paar Auserwählte; ~ **issues** bereinigte Emissionen; ~ **motion** *(parl.)* Dringlichkeitsantrag; ~ **occasion** *(Br.)* Erklärung in Wahrnehmung berechtigter Interessen; ~ **person** Bevorrechtigter, Priviligierter; ~ **place** Asylort; **to have a ~ position** bevorzugte Stellung einnehmen; ~ **report** gesetzlich genehmigter Bericht über ein Gerichtsverfahren; ~ **share** *(Br.)* Vorzugsaktie; ~ **shareholder** *(Br.)* Vorzugsaktionär; ~ **statement** *(parl.)* Äußerung im Rahmen der Immunität; **to make a statement on a ~ occasion** *(Br.)* Erklärung in Wahrnehmung berechtigter Interessen abgeben; ~ **stock** *(US)* Vorzugsaktie; ~ **stockholder** *(US)* Vorzugsaktionär; ~ **vessel** vorfahrtberechtigtes Schiff; ~ **witness** aussageverweigerungsberechtigter Zeuge.

privity *(knowledge shared)* Mitwissen, Mitwisserschaft, Eingeweihtsein, *(participation in interest)* Interessengemeinschaft, *(legal relation)* gemeinsame Rechtsbeziehung, *(mutual relationship to same rights)* Rechtsgemeinschaft, *(trusteeship)* Treueverhältnis;
with his ~ and consent mit seinem Wissen und Willen;
~ **of blood** Verwandschaftsverhältnis; ~ **of contract** vertragliche Bindung, unmittelbares Vertragsverhältnis, vertragliches Treueverhältnis; ~ **in deed** vertragliche Verpflichtung (Rechtsbeziehung); ~ **of estate** Erbengemeinschaft, *(tenancy)* Pacht-, Mietverhältnis; ~ **of knowledge** Mitwisserschaft, Kenntnis; ~ **in law** Rechtsverpflichtung; ~ **of law** [etwa] Vertragsprinzip; ~ **of lease** Pachtverhältnis;
to enter into ~ vertragliche Bindungen eingehen, in Rechtsbeziehungen eintreten.

privy Beteiligter, Mitwisser;
~ **to a fraud** Betrugsbeteiligter;
to be ~ to eingeweiht sein; **to be ~ to an act** an einer Handlung teilnehmen; **to be made ~ to it** ins Vertrauen gezogen werden; **to have ~ of a plot** von einer Verschwörung Kenntnis haben; **to make ~** ins Vertrauen ziehen;
~ *(a.)* eingeweiht, vertraulich, *(criminal law)* mitschuldig, mitbeteiligt;

~ **chamber** Geheimkabinett; ~ **Council** *(Br.)* Kron-, Staatsrat; ~ **Council(l)or** *(Br.)* Mitglied des Geheimen Staatsrates; ~ **purse** *(Br.)* Zivilliste, königliche Privatschatulle; ~ **seal** *(Br.)* Geheimsiegel; ~ **signet** *(Br.)* königliches Handsiegel; ~ **token** gefälschter Gegenstand.

prize *(competition)* Preis, Prämie, *(lottery)* Treffer, [Lotterie]gewinn, *(ship)* aufgebrachtes Schiff, Prise, Kriegsbeute, Konfiskationsgut;
consolation ~ Trostpreis; **first (grand, great, highest) ~** großes Los, Hauptgewinn; **lawful ~** gute Prise; **lottery ~** Lotteriegewinn; **Nobel ~** Nobelpreis;
~**s of a profession** höchste Stellung in einer Berufssparte; ~ **of war** Kriegsprise;
~ *(v.)* *(appraise)* schätzen, taxieren, *(force with a lever)* aufstemmen, *(value highly)* hochschätzen, *(vessel)* als Prise aufbringen;
~ **a box open** Kiste aufbrechen; ~ **a lid up** Deckel hochstemmen;
to award a ~ Preis zuerkennen, prämieren; **to be awarded a ~ for good conduct** für gute Führung ausgezeichnet werden; **to bring the ~ into port** Prise in den Hafen einbringen; **to carry away the first ~** ersten Preis davontragen; **to condemn as lawful ~** als gute Prise erklären; **to distinguish with a ~** mit einem Preis auszeichnen; **to distribute (present) the ~s** Preise verteilen; **to draw a ~ in a lottery** Lotteriegewinn machen; **to draw the first ~** großes Los gewinnen; **to exhibit a ~** Stipendium ausschreiben; **to gain a ~** Preis gewinnen; **to make ~ of a ship** Schiff als Prise aufbringen (wegnehmen), Schiff kapern; **to offer a ~** Preis aussetzen; **to put a ~ on** Prämie aussetzen; **not to qualify for a ~** bei der Preisverteilung ausscheiden müssen; **to win a ~** Preis gewinnen;
~ *(a.)* preiswürdig, erstklassig, *(having been awarded a ~)* preisgekrönt, prämiert;
~ **bounty** Prisengeld; ~ **catch** begehenswertes Objekt; ~ **cattle** preisgekröntes Vieh; ~ **causes** Prisensachen; ~ **commission** *(naval court)* Prisenabteilung; ~ **competition (contest)** Preisausschreiben; ~ **court** Prisengericht; ~ **crew** Prisenkommando; **to put a ~ crew on board a vessel** einem Prisenkommando ein Schiff übergeben; ~ **distribution** Preisverteilung; ~ **draw** Verlosung, Auslosung, Prämienziehung; ~ **drawing** Prämienziehung, Aus-, Verlosung; ~ **essay** preisgekrönter Aufsatz; ~ **fellow** *(Br.)* Inhaber einer akademischen Auszeichnung; ~ **fight** öffentlicher Boxkampf; ~ **fighter** Berufsboxer; ~ **fund** Auslosungs-, Prämienfonds; ~ **giving** Prisenverteilung; ~ **goods** Prisengut; ~ **law** Prisenrecht; ~ **list** Gewinnliste, *(marine law)* Liste der Prisenberechtigten; ~ **master** Prisenoffizier; ~ **medal** Medaille; ~ **medallist** Inhaber einer Preismedaille, Medaillenträger, -besitzer; ~ **money** ausgeloster Betrag, *(navy)* Prisengeld; ~ **packet** Überraschungspäckchen; ~ **plum** *(fig.)* dicke Rosine; ~ **possessions** wertvolle Besitzgegenstände; ~ **question** Preisfrage; ~ **ring** Ring, *(fig.)* Wettkampf; ~ **salvage** Rettungsgeld des neuen Nehmers; ~ **scholarship** Freiplatz, -stelle; **to draw a ~-winning ticket** Gewinnlos ziehen; ~ **system** Prämien[lohn]system; ~ **winner** Los-, Preisgewinner, Preisträger; ~**-winning** preisgekrönt.

prizeholder Preisträger.

prizeman Preisträger, *(scholarship)* Freistelleninhaber.

prizer Abschätzer, Taxierer.

prizetaker Preisgewinner.

prizeworthy preiswürdig, erstklassig.

pro Profi, *(parl.)* Jastimme, *(probationer, sl.)* Bewährungsanwärter;
~ **and con** *(evidence)* Für und Wider; ~ **confesso** *(bill in equity)* zugestanden;
~**-British** englandfreundlich; ~**-government** regierungsfreundlich; ~ **rata** prorata; ~ **tempore** provisorisch; ~**-union** gewerkschaftsfreundlich.

proagriculture *(US)* für die Landwirtschaft eingestellt, agrarfreundlich.

probability Wahrscheinlichkeit;
in all ~ höchstwahrscheinlich; **with utmost ~** mit an Sicherheit grenzender Wahrscheinlichkeit;
conditional ~ bedingte Wahrscheinlichkeit; **posterior ~** statistische Wahrscheinlichkeit;
~ **of damage** Schadenswahrscheinlichkeit; ~ **of life** Lebenswahrscheinlichkeit, -erwartung; ~ **of loss** Schadenswahrscheinlichkeit; ~ **of survival** *(life assurance)* Erlebenswahrscheinlichkeit;
~ **calculus** Wahrscheinlichkeitsrechnung; ~ **sample** zufallsgesteuerte Stichprobenauswahl, Wahrscheinlichkeitsstichprobe; ~ **sampling** Wahrscheinlichkeitsauswahl.

probable wahrscheinlicher Kandidat, *(aero., mil.)* wahrscheinlicher Abschuß;
~ *(a.)* wahrscheinlich, mutmaßlich, vermutlich, einleuchtend;
~ **author** vermutlicher Verfasser; ~ **cause** ausreichender Grund, *(criminal)* dringender Tatverdacht; ~ **consequence** adäquate Folge; **to reckon the** ~ **costs** sich die voraussichtlich entstehenden Kosten ausrechnen; ~ **date of arrival** mutmaßlicher (voraussichtlicher) Ankunftstag; ~ **duration of life** wahrscheinliche Lebensdauer; ~ **error** *(statistics)* Wahrscheinlichkeitsfehler, wahrscheinlicher Fehler statistischer Mittelwerte; ~ **events** wahrscheinlich eintretende Ereignisse; ~ **evidence** Wahrscheinlichkeitsbeweis; ~ **future payments** *(workmen's compensation act)* voraussichtliche zukünftige Leistungen; ~ **ground** voraussichtlich vorhandener Klagegrund; ~ **life** *(life insurance)* mutmaßliche Lebensdauer; ~ **plot** mutmaßliches Attentat; ~ **reasoning** Wahrscheinlichkeitsbeweisführung; ~ **winner** voraussichtlicher Sieger.

probate *(proving a will)* gerichtliche Testamentsbestätigung und Erbscheinerteilung, *(verified copy of will)* beglaubigte Testamentsabschrift, Erblegitimation;
~ **denied** verweigerte Testamentsbestätigung; **facsimile** ~ wortgetreue Testamentsbestätigung; **office copy** ~ *(Br.)* Abschrift eines gerichtlich erteilten Testamentsvollstreckerzeugnisses;
~ **in common form** *(Br.)* einfache Testamentsbestätigung; ~ **of an estate** Nachlaßfeststellung; ~ **of a will** Testamentseröffnung, [etwa] Erbscheinsverfahren; ~ **in solemn form** *(Br.)* rechtskräftige Testamentsbestätigung, Erbscheinerteilung nach Durchführung eines Gerichtsverfahrens;
~ *(v.)* gerichtlich bestätigen;
~ **a paper as a will** Urkunde als rechtsgültiges Testament bestätigen; ~ **a will** Testament gerichtlich bestätigen lassen; **to admit to** ~ Testament zwecks Erbscheinerteilung vorlegen; **to grant** ~ **of a will** Testament bestätigen, Erbschein erteilen; **to obtain a** ~ gerichtliche Testamentsbestätigung bewirken; **to take out** ~ **of a will** [etwa] sich einen Erbschein erteilen lassen; ~ **action** Testamentssache, Nachlaßverfahren; ~ **bond** Testamentsvollstreckerkaution; ~ **book** *(bank)* Nachlaßunterlagen; ~ **code** Testamentsabschrift; ~ **court** *(US)* Nachlaßgericht; ~ **court judge** *(US)* Nachlaßrichter; ~ **court registry** *(Br.)* Geschäftsstelle des Nachlaßgerichts; ~ **division** *(Br.)* Nachlaßgericht; ~ **duty** *(Br.)* Erbschaftssteuer [auf bewegliches Vermögen]; ~ **homestead** *(US)* aus dem Nachlaß ausgegliedertes Eigenheim, Pflichtteilseigenheim; ~ **judge** *(US)* Nachlaßrichter; ~ **jurisdiction** Zuständigkeit in Nachlaßsachen; ~ **matters** Nachlaßsachen; ~ **Office** Geschäftsstelle des Nachlaßgerichts; ~ **proceeding** Nachlaßverfahren; **district** ~ **registry** *(Br.)* Geschäftsstelle des Nachlaßgerichts; **noncontentious** ~ **rules** *(Br.)* Vorschriften über die Abwicklung von Nachlässen im Rahmen der freiwilligen Gerichtsbarkeit; ~ **valuation** Nachlaßbewertung; ~ **value** Nachlaßwert eines einzelnen Gegenstandes.

probation Probe, Eignungsprüfung, *(criminal)* Bewährung[sfrist], bedingte Strafaussetzung, Strafaussetzung zur (Strafe mit) Bewährung, *(time of probate)* Probe[zeit];
on ~ auf Probe, widerruflich, *(criminal)* unter Zubilligung von Bewährungsfrist, auf Bewährung;
~ **of three months** dreimonatige Probezeit;
to be [employed] on ~ auf Probe angestellt sein, seine Probezeit abmachen; **to be placed on** ~ Bewährungsfrist bekommen; **to bind a sentence over on** ~ Strafe zur Bewährung aussetzen; **to break the terms of** ~ den Bewährungsauflagen zuwiderhandeln; **to engage s. o. for two years on** ~ jem. mit einer zweijährigen Probezeit einstellen; **to get three years on** ~ drei Jahre Gefängnis mit Bewährung erhalten; **to grant suspension on** ~ Strafaufschub zur Bewährung zubilligen; **to place (release) s. o. on** ~ jem. Bewährungsfrist zubilligen, j. auf Bewährung freilassen; **to suspend a sentence on** ~ Strafe zur Bewährung aussetzen; ~ **appointment** Probeanstellung; ~ **officer** *(US)* Bewährungshelfer, *(for moral welfare of infants)* Fürsorgebeamter; ~ **order** Bewährungsurteil; **to make a** ~ **order** auf Strafaussetzung zur Bewährung erkennen; ~ **period** Bewährungsfrist, Probezeit; ~ **service** *(US)* Bewährungshilfe; ~ **system** Bewährungssystem; ~ **year** Probejahr.

probationary auf Probe angestellt, *(criminal)* bedingt freigelassen, auf Bewährung entlassen;
~ **appointment** Probeanstellung; ~ **arrangement** Probe[dienst-]zeit; ~ **employee** probeweise beschäftigter Angestellter; ~ **employment** Probebeschäftigung, -anstellung; ~ **period** Probezeit, *(criminal)* Bewährungsfrist; ~ **rate** während der Probezeit gezahlter Lohn, Probeentlohnung, -gehalt; ~ **term** Bewährungs-, Probezeit.

probationer auf Probe Angestellter, provisorisch angestellter Beamter, *(candidate for membership)* Anwärter, Probekandidat, *(criminal)* bedingt Freigelassener, *(fig.)* Neuling;
~ **for higher grade** *(civil service)* Anwärter für den höheren Dienst;
to qualify as ~ **for a post** Anwartschaft auf eine Stelle erwerben.

probationership Prüfungs-, Lehrzeit.

probative *(law of evidence)* beweiskräftig;
~ **experience** Prüfung; ~ **facts** beweiserhebliche Tatsachen; ~ **force** Beweiskraft; ~ **value** Beweiswert.

probatory *(US)* als Beweis dienend;
~ **force** *(US)* Beweiskraft; ~ **term** *(US)* Frist zur Beweiserbringung.

probe *(explorative examination, US)* Untersuchung, *(fig.)* Sondierung, Prüfung, *(med.)* Sonde, *(space traffic)* [Raum]sonde;
lunar ~ Mondrakete;
legislative ~ **of banking practices** Bankenquete;
~ *(v.)* gründlich prüfen, sondieren;
~ **s. one's official conduct** jds. dienstliches Verhalten untersuchen; ~ **deep into a matter** einer Angelegenheit auf den Grund gehen; ~ **the evidence** Beweismaterial gründlich durchleuchten; ~ **into a scandal** Hintergründe eines Skandals aufdecken; ~ **into the subconscious mind** in das Unterbewußtsein eindringen.

probity Redlichkeit, Rechtschaffenheit.

problem schwierige Aufgabe, Problem, *(fig.)* Rätsel;
balance-of-payment ~ Zahlungsbilanzproblem; **diversification** ~s Probleme der Anlagenstreuung; **frontier** ~ Grenzfrage; **housing** ~ Wohnungsnot; **management** ~s Geschäftsführungsprobleme; **tactical** ~ *(mil.)* taktisches Thema; **timing** ~ Frage der richtigen Zeitwahl; **vital** ~ entscheidendes Problem;
~s **for discussion** Diskussionsfragen; ~ **of liquidity** Liquiditätsproblem; ~ **of particular urgency** besonderes Dringlichkeitsproblem; ~ **of taxes** Steuerfrage;
to be facing a ~ sich vor ein Problem gestellt sehen; **to be a real** ~ **to s. o.** echtes Problem für j. darstellen; **to escape from** ~s Problemen aus dem Wege gehen; **to grapple with (get down to) a** ~ sich mit einem Problem auseinandersetzen; **to link a** ~ *(US)* Problem meistern; **to roll a** ~ **round in one's head** Problem wälzen; **to run into bushy** ~s in ein Problemdickicht geraten; **to solve a** ~ **between the departments concerned** Problem zusammen mit den zuständigen Abteilungen lösen; **to wade into a** ~ Problem angehen; **to work out a** ~ mit einem Problem fertig werden; **to worry out a** ~ Problem nicht loslassen; ~ **child** schwieriges Kind; ~ **play** *(theatre)* Problemstück.

probusiness *(US)* wirtschaftsfreundlich eingestellt.

procedural verfahrensrechtlich, -mäßig, prozessual;
~ **bias** *(statistics)* systematischer Erhebungsfehler; ~ **committee** Verfahrensausschuß; ~ **contract** Vertrag, der den Prozeßweg nicht ausschließt; **to iron out** ~ **difficulties** verfahrensrechtliche Schwierigkeiten beseitigen; ~ **grounds** Verfahrensgründe; ~ **improvements** verfahrenstechnische Verbesserungen; ~ **innovations** Verfahrenserneuerungen; ~ **law** formelles Recht, Verfahrensrecht; ~ **machinery** Verfahrensmechanismus; ~ **manoeuvre** Verfahrensmanöver; ~ **matter** Verfahrensfrage, -angelegenheit; ~ **motion** *(parl.)* Antrag zur Geschäftsordnung; ~ **order** Verfahrensbeschluß; ~ **provisions** Verfahrensvorschriften; ~ **question** Verfahrensfrage; ~ **requirements** Verfahrenserfordernisse; **to comply with** ~ **requirements** Verfahrensvorschriften erfüllen; ~ **rules** prozessuale Vorschriften, Prozeß-, Verfahrensordnung; ~ **tactics** Verfahrenstaktik; ~ **wrangling** Verfahrensstreitigkeiten.

procedure Verfahrens[art], Verfahrensregeln, -methode, Vorgehen, Procedere, Verhalten, Handlungsweise, *(management)* Verfahrensordnung, *(proceedings)* Prozeß, *(process of production)* Arbeitsprozeß, -ablauf, *(transaction)* Transaktion;
accounting ~ Revisionsverfahren; **administrative** ~ Verwaltungsverfahren; **appellate** ~ Rechtsmittelverfahren; **arbitration** ~ schiedsgerichtliches Verfahren, Schiedsverfahren; **auditing** ~ Prüfungs-, Revisionsverfahren; **budget** ~ Verfahren bei der Aufstellung des Haushalts; **census** ~ statistisches Verfahren; **civil** ~ Zivilprozeß, Verfahren in Zivilsachen; **contentious** ~ *(dipl.)* Verfahren zur Regelung eines Streitfalls; **the correct** ~ vernünftige Lebensweise; **criminal** ~ Strafverfahren, -prozeß; **declassification** ~ Verfahren zur Freigabe von Geheimmaterial; **electoral** ~ Wahlverfahren; **established** ~ bewährtes Verfahren; **grievance** ~ Schlichtungsverfahren; **informal and speedy** ~ formloser und schneller Verfahrensablauf; **legal** ~ Gerichtsverfahren; **legislative** ~ Gesetzgebungsverfahren; **operating** ~ Herstellungs-, Betriebsverfahren; **parliamentary** ~ parlamentarisches Verfahren; **routine** ~ [all-

gemein] übliches Verfahren; **tariff** ~ Zolltarifverfahren; **tax** ~ Steuerrechtsverfahren; **trademark** ~ Verfahren in Warenzeichenangelegenheiten; **uniform** ~ einheitlich festgelegtes Verfahren; **usual** ~ übliches Verfahren; **voting** ~ Abstimmungsverfahren;

~ **on appeal** *(taxation)* Einspruchsverfahren; ~ **by arbitration** Schiedsgerichtsverfahren; ~ **of assessment** Veranlagungsverfahren; ~ **in bankruptcy** Konkursverfahren; **usual** ~ **at committee meetings** übliches Ausschußverfahren; ~ **of a court** Gerichtsverfahren; ~ **of court martial** Kriegsgerichtsverfahren; ~ **of execution** Vollstreckungsverfahren; **arbitration** ~ **governing disputed firings** Schiedsverfahren wegen strittiger Arbeiterentlassungen; ~ **by foreclosure** Zwangsvollstreckungsverfahren; ~ **in obtaining a patent** Patentverfahren; ~ **of reorganization** Sanierungsverfahren; ~ **on taking a poll** Abstimmungsverfahren; ~ **before trial** Vor-, Ermittlungsverfahren;

to argue about ~ über Verfahrensfragen streiten; **to carry out a** ~ Verfahrensmodus anwenden; **to reverse a** ~ Verfahren ändern, umgekehrtes Verfahren wählen; **to stop arguing about [questions of]** ~ Debatte über Verfahrensfragen beenden;

~ **Act** *(US)* Verfahrensordnung; ~ **agreement** Verfahrensvereinbarung, -regelung.

proceed *(v.)* fortsetzen, fortfahren, weitermachen, *(adopt course of action)* verfahren, vorgehen, *(originate)* herrühren, entspringen, *(conduct legal procedure)* gerichtlich vorgehen, Verfahren einleiten, *(play)* weiter gehen, *(university, Br.)* akademischen Grad erlangen, promovieren;

~ **against s. o.** gegen j. [gerichtlich] vorgehen, j. verklagen, Prozeßverfahren gegen j. einleiten; ~ **with s. th.** etw. in Angriff nehmen (durchführen); ~ **to the agenda** zur Tagesordnung schreiten; ~ **with an application** Antrag bearbeiten; ~ **to the attack** zum Angriff übergehen; ~ **to blows** zu einer Schlägerei kommen; ~ **to business** zur Sache kommen, an die Arbeit gehen; ~ **to the next business** zum nächsten Punkt der Tagesordnung übergehen; ~ **cautiously** vorsichtig vorgehen; ~ **to the degree of M.A.** *(Br.)* Magistertitel erwerben (erlangen); ~ **to the dining room** zum Essen gehen; ~ **to the election** zur Wahl schreiten; ~ **on the footing that it is true** als wahr unterstellen; ~ **with the lesson** Unterricht fortsetzen; ~ **to the next item on the agenda** nächsten Punkt auf der Tagesordnung behandeln; ~ **on one's journey** seine Reise fortsetzen; ~ **from most noble principles** in äußerst noblen Grundsätzen fundiert sein; ~ **to the order of the day** zur Tagesordnung übergehen; ~ **ex parte** auf Antrag einer Partei verhandeln; ~ **at a moderate speed** langsam fahren; ~ **with one's speech** in seiner Rede fortfahren; ~ **towards the town** auf die Stadt vorrücken; ~ **by stages** schrittweise vorgehen; ~ **to another subject** Thema wechseln; ~ **with the trial** Verhandlung fortsetzen; ~ **to violence** sich zu Tätlichkeiten hinreißen lassen; ~ **to a vote** zur Abstimmung schreiten; ~ **on the voyage** *(ship)* Fahrt fortsetzen; ~ **from war** Kriegsfolgeerscheinung sein; ~ **on one's way** seinen Weg fortsetzen; ~ **with one's work** mit seiner Arbeit fortfahren;

to pay as the work ~**s** entsprechend dem Arbeitsfortschritt bezahlen.

proceeding *(act)* Handlung, Maßnahme, Vorgehen, *(action in law)* Prozeßverfahren, *(ship)* Weiterfahrt;

~**s** Verfahren, Gerichtsverhandlung, *(criminal procedure)* Untersuchungsakten, *(deliberations)* Beratungen, *(records of meeting)* Sitzungsberichte, -protokoll, *(steps taken in legal action)* Verhandlungen;

administrative ~**s** Verwaltungsverfahren; **bankruptcy** ~**s** Konkursverfahren; **cancellation** ~**s** *(securities)* Aufgebotsverfahren; **civil** ~**s** zivilrechtliches Verfahren, Verfahren in Zivilsachen, Zivilprozeß; **collateral** ~ Nebenverfahren; **collection** ~**s** Inkassoverfahren; **commission** ~**s** Ausschußverhandlungen; **composition** ~**s** Vergleichsverfahren, -verhandlungen; **conciliatory** ~ Güteverfahren; **condemnation** ~**s** Entschädigungsverfahren; **costly** ~ kostspieliges Verfahren; **court** ~**s** gerichtliches Verfahren; **criminal** ~ Strafverfahren; **disciplinary** ~**s** Disziplinarverfahren; **divorce** ~**s** Ehescheidungsverfahren; **eminent domain** ~**s** *(US)* Enteignungsverfahren; **earlier** ~**s** frühere Prozesse; **executory** ~ *(Louisiana)* Vollstreckbarkeitsverfahren; **extradition** ~**s** Auslieferungsverfahren; **foreclosure** ~ *(US)* Zwangsvollstreckungsverfahren; **high-handed** ~ aufgeblasene Art und Weise, großkotziges Auftreten; **illegal** ~ unerlaubte Transaktion; **immigration** ~**s** Einwanderungsverfahren; **improper legal** ~ unzuständiges Gerichtsverfahren; ~**s instituted** anhängig gemachtes Verfahren; **interference** ~ *(patent law)* Verfahren zur Feststellung der Prioritätsrechte, Anfechtungsverfahren, Prioritätsstreit; **interlocutory** ~**s** Vor-,

Inzidentfeststellungsverfahren; **irregular** ~**s** unter Formfehlern leidendes Verfahren; **judicial** ~ Prozeß-, Rechts-, Gerichtsverfahren; **legal** ~**s** Gerichtsverfahren, gerichtliches Verfahren, Prozeß; **lengthy** ~ langwieriges Verfahren; **liquidation** ~**s** Abwicklungs-, Liquidationsverfahren; **opposition** ~**s** *(patent law)* Einspruchsverfahren; **ordinary** ~**s** ordentliches Verfahren; **pending** ~**s** schwebendes Gerichtsverfahren; **preliminary** ~**s** Ermittlungs-, Vorverfahren; **price-fixing** ~**s** Preisbindungsverfahren; **sharp** ~**s** unanständige Manöver; **special** ~ Sonderverfahren; **statutory** ~ gesetzlich vorgeschriebenes Verfahren; **summary** ~ summarisches Verfahren, Schnellverfahren; **supplementary** ~ *(US)* Verfahren zur Offenlegung der Vermögensverhältnisse; **written** ~ Verhandlungsprotokoll, -bericht, Sitzungsbericht;

~ **to appeal** Revisionsverfahren, Berufungsverfahren; ~**s in bankruptcy** Konkursverfahren; ~**s in civil cases** Verfahren in Zivilsachen; ~ **in error** Verfahren in der Berufungsinstanz, Revisions-, Rechtsmittelverfahren; ~**s at law** Gerichtsverfahren; ~**s at the meeting** Sitzungsberichte; **suspicious** ~**s in committee meetings** verdächtiges Verhalten bei Ausschußsitzungen; ~**s for libel or slander** Beleidigungs- oder Verleumdungsverfahren; ~**s at a general meeting** Hauptversammlungsverlauf; ~**s of attaching property** Pfändungsverfahren; ~ **in rem** *(lat.)* dingliche Rechtsstreitigkeit; ~**s of a society** Abhandlungen einer Gesellschaft; ~ **of the Royal Society** Protokolle der Königlichen Gesellschaft; ~**s in tort** Verfahren wegen unerlaubter Handlung;

to accelerate ~**s** Verfahren beschleunigen; **to annul judicial** ~**s** Gerichtsverfahren für ungültig erklären; **to authorize legal** ~**s** gerichtliches Verfahren ermöglichen; **to carry on legal** ~**s** gerichtliches Verfahren durchführen; **to conduct the** ~**s** Diskussion leiten; **to conduct legal** ~**s** Gerichtsweg beschreiten, prozessieren; **to conduct the** ~**s in winding up of a company** Abwicklungsverfahren einer Gesellschaft leiten; **to declare** ~**s at an end** Sitzung für beendet erklären; **to file Chapter TEN** ~**s** *(US)* Vergleichsverfahren beantragen; **to institute legal** ~**s against s. o.** gegen j. gerichtlich vorgehen, Gerichtsverfahren gegen j. anstrengen; **to object to the regularity of the** ~**s** Rechtsgültigkeit des Verfahrens bestreiten; **to order** ~**s to be taken against s. o.** Verfahren gegen j. einleiten; **to publish the commission's** ~**s** Ausschußprotokoll veröffentlichen; **to record** ~**s of a court** Gerichtsverfahren protokollieren; **to regularize the** ~**s** ordnungsgemäßes Verfahren sicherstellen; **to review the** ~**s** Verfahren überprüfen; **to squash** ~**s** Verfahren niederschlagen; **to start legal** ~**s against s. o.** gerichtliches Verfahren gegen j. einleiten; **to suspend (stay) the** ~**s** gerichtliches Verfahren aussetzen; **to take judicial** ~**s against s. o.** Gerichtsverfahren gegen j. anstrengen, j. verklagen, gegen j. gerichtlich vorgehen (einen Prozeß anstrengen), Sache gegen j. anhängig machen; **to take legal** ~**s for ejectment** Räumungsklage erheben; **to take [legal]** ~**s for the recovery of a debt** Forderung einklagen;

to be ~ vorankommen; **to be** ~ **as usual** normal verlaufen.

proceeds Erlös, Ertrag, Einnahmen, Einkünfte, Eingänge (von Zahlungen), Gewinn, *(of bills)* Diskonterlös, *(of cheque)* Gegenwert;

actual ~ Isteinnahme; **annual** ~ Jahresertrag; **business** ~ Geschäftseinnahmen; **cash** ~ Barerlös; **entire** ~ Gesamtertrag; **factory** ~ Produktionserlös; **foreign-exchange** ~ Devisenerlös, -einnahmen; **gross** ~ Brutto-, Rohertrag; **interest** ~ Zinserträge; **missed** ~ entgangene Erträge; **net** ~ Netto-, Reinertrag, Nettoerlös; **quantity** ~ Mengenertrag; **realization** ~ Verkaufserlös; **short** ~ Mindererlös; **total** ~ Gesamterlös, -ertrag; **working** ~ Betriebsertrag;

~ **of an auction** Versteigerungserlös; ~ **from capital** Kapitalerträge; ~ **of a cargo** *(insurance)* durch den Verkauf der Hinfracht erworbene Rückfracht; ~ **in cash** Barerlös; ~ **to go to local charities** für örtliche Wohltätigkeitseinrichtungen bestimmte Erträge; ~ **of collection** Inkassobeträge; ~ **of a distress** Pfändungserlös; ~ **from exports** Exporterlös; ~ **of an issue** Anleiheerlös; ~ **of a liquidation** Liquidationserlös; ~ **of policies** Policenerlös; ~ **of sale** Veräußerungs-, Verkaufserlös; ~ **from the sale of subscription rights** Bezugsrechtserlöse; ~ **from utilization of waste material** Erlöse aus Abfallverwertung; **to credit the** ~ **of an account** Konto mit dem Gegenwert erkennen; **to distribute the** ~**s** Erlös verteilen; **to hold the** ~ **at disposal of Messrs ...** Gegenwert zur Verfügung der Firma ... halten; **to place the** ~ **to the credit of s. o.** Gegenwert jem. gutschreiben; **to remit the** ~ Gegenwert anschaffen.

procès verbal Sitzungsbericht, Protokoll.

process *(action of law)* Rechtsstreit, Prozeß, gerichtliches Verfahren, Gerichtsverfahren, *(course)* Fortgang, Fortschreiten,

Lauf, *(course of action)* Vorgang, Ablauf, Verfahren, *(judicial writ)* gerichtliche (prozeßleitende) Verfügung, *(method of production)* Ablauf, Arbeitsprozeß, -stufe, -gang, Verfahren, Verfahrensweise, [Verfahrens]methode, *(photo)* Übereinanderkopieren, *(print.)* fotomechanische Klischeeherstellung, *(summons)* [Vor]ladung;

during the ~ of dismantling während der Demontagearbeiten; **during the ~ of removal** während des Umzugs; **in ~** in der Herstellung; **in ~ of completion** in der Verarbeitung begriffen; **in ~ of construction** im Bau [begriffen]; **in ~ of development** in der Entwicklung begriffen; **in ~ of time** im Lauf (Verlauf) der Zeit;

adjustment ~ Anpassungsverfahren; **changing ~** Umstellungsprozeß; **compulsory ~** Zwangsverfahren; **equalizing ~** Ausgleichsverfahren; **executory ~** Vollstreckungsverfahren; **final ~** Vollstreckungsklausel; **finishing ~** Veredelungsverfahren; **first ~** erste Instanz; **industrial ~** industrielles Herstellungsverfahren; **inspection ~** Prüfungsverfahren; **irregular ~** ungültiges (fehlerhaftes, unter Formfehlern leidendes) Verfahren; **judicial ~** gerichtliches Verfahren, *(criminal case)* Klagemitteilung, Anklageerhebung; **lawful (legal) ~** gerichtliches Verfahren, Rechtsverfahren; **lengthy ~** langwieriges Verfahren; **managerial ~** Entwicklung zum Unternehmer; **manufacturing (production) ~** Produktionsprozeß, Herstellungsverfahren; **mechanical ~** mechanisches Verfahren; **mental ~** Denkvorgang; **mesne ~** *(US)* Zwischenverfahren; **operating ~** Arbeitsverfahren; **original ~** Klage nebst Ladung, Vorladungsbeschluß; **patentable ~** patentfähiges Verfahren; **regular ~** ordentliches (rechtmäßiges) Verfahren; **screening ~** Prüfungsverfahren; **secret ~** Geheimverfahren; **shortened ~** abgekürztes Verfahren; **slow ~** langsamer Vorgang; **special ~** Spezialverfahren; **summary ~** summarisches Verfahren, Schnellverfahren; **trustee ~** Forderungspfändungsverfahren; **verbal ~** mündliches Verfahren; **void ~** nichtiges Verfahren; **working ~** Arbeitsverfahren;

~ of automation Automatisierungsprozeß; **~ of accommodation** Anpassungsverfahren; **~ of bankruptcy** Konkursverfahren; **~ of combustion** Verbrennungsprozeß; **~ of concentration** Konzentrationsprozeß; **~ of disintegration** Disintegrationsprozeß; **~ of dismantling** Demontageverfahren; **~ of distraint** Zwangsvollstreckungsverfahren; **~ of distribution** Verteilungsprozeß; **~ of expansion** Expansionsprozeß; **~ of growth** Wachstumsprozeß; **~ of industrialization** Industrialisierungsprozeß; **~ of integration** Integrationsvorgang, Konzentrationsprozeß; **~ of interpleader** Eigentumsfeststellungsklage; **~ of law** Rechtsweg; **due ~ of law** ordentliches (rechtsstaatliches) Gerichtsverfahren; **~ of legislation** Gesetzgebungsverfahren; **[industrial] ~ of manufacture** [industrielles] Herstellungsverfahren, Fertigungsverfahren, Produktionsprozeß; **~ of the mind** Denkvorgang; **~ of negotiations** Verhandlungsdauer; **~ of recovery** Wiedergewinnungsverfahren; **~ of registration** Registrierungsverfahren; **~ of reunification** Wiedervereinigungsprozeß; **~ in tax proceedings** Verfahren in Steuersachen; **~ of thought** Denkprozeß; **~ of transformation** Umwandlungsprozeß; **~ of transition** Übergangsprozeß;

~ (v.) *(finish)* veredeln, weiterverarbeiten, *(food)* haltbar machen, *(law)* vorladen, gerichtlich belangen (vorgehen), *(photo)* fotomechanisch herstellen, *(office practice)* [Brief] mechanisch herstellen, vervielfältigen, *(raw material)* behandeln, ver-, bearbeiten, einem Verfahren unterwerfen, *(textiles)* imprägnieren;

~ s. o. j. gerichtlich belangen, *(US)* j. durchschleusen (abfertigen); **~ against s. o.** Verfahren gegen jem. in Gang bringen; **~ a case** Fall bearbeiten; **~ data** Daten (statistisches Material) aufbereiten; **~ in** anlernen; **~ into** verarbeiten; **~ orders** Aufträge bearbeiten; **~ out** für einen Berufswechsel vorbereiten; **~ new recruits** *(US)* neu angeworbene Arbeitskräfte anlernen; **~ s. o. for a particular situation** j. besonders ausbilden; **to be in ~** im Gange sein; **to be in ~ of manufacture** sich in Arbeit (in der Herstellung) befinden; **to be in ~ of being reorganized** sich in einem Umwandlungsprozeß befinden; **to be in ~ of removal** umziehen; **to be responsible for the ~ of winding up** für das Abwicklungsverfahren verantwortlich sein; **to hasten the ~** Ablauf der Dinge beschleunigen; **to serve a ~ on s. o.** j. gerichtlich vorladen, jem. eine gerichtliche Verfügung (Vorladung) zustellen; **to undergo a ~ of concentration** sich einem Konzentrationsprozeß unterwerfen;

~ (a.) nach besonderen Verfahren behandelt; **~ account** Fabrikationskonto; **~ accounting** Divisionskalkulation; **~ application** *(patent law)* Anmeldung eines Verfahrens; **~ block** photomechanisches Klischee; **~ chart** Arbeitsablaufdiagramm; **~ control** Fertigungs-, Qualitätskontrolle; **~ costing** Berechnung der Produktionskosten, Kostenrechnung für Serienfertigung; **~ costs** Verarbeitungskosten; **~ cost system** Kostenrechnung für Serienfertigung (Massenfertigung); **~ engineering** Verfahrenstechnik, Fertigungsvorbereitung; **~ -engraving** photomechanische Klischeeherstellung; **~ letters** vervielfältigte Briefe; **~ model** Ablaufmodell; **~ patent** Verfahrenspatent; **~ plate** Mehrfarbenklischee; **~ printing** Vier-, Mehrfarbendruck; **~ roll** Prozeßregister; **~ server** Zustellungsbeamter, Zusteller.

processed│foods verarbeitete Nahrungsmittel; **~ products** Veredelungserzeugnisse.

processer, processor Weiterarbeiter;
~ of commodities Verarbeitungsbetrieb.

processing Be-, [Weiter]verarbeitung, Veredelung;
contract ~ Lohnveredelung; **data ~** Datenverarbeitung; **food ~** Lebensmittelverarbeitung; **textile ~** Imprägnierung;
~ in bond Zollveredelung; **~ of a complaint** Beschwerdeerledigung; **~ under a job contract** Lohnveredelung;
~ center *(US)* **(centre,** *Br.***)** Verarbeitungszentrum; **~ company** Weiterverarbeitungsbetrieb; **~ cost** Fabrikations-, Herstellungskosten; **~ country** Veredelungsland; **~ department** Veredelungs-, Verarbeitungsabteilung; **~ enterprise** Verarbeitungs-, Veredelungsbetrieb; **~ expenses** Verarbeitungs-, Veredelungskosten; **~ fee** Bearbeitungsgebühr; **~ industry** verarbeitende Industrie, Veredelungsindustrie; **food ~ industry** Lebensmittelindustrie; **~ permit** Verarbeitungsgenehmigung; **end-~ plant** Verarbeitungs-, Veredelungsbetrieb, Aufarbeitungsanlage; **~ prescription** Verarbeitungsvorschrift; **~ product** Weiterverarbeitungsprodukt; **~ prohibition** Verarbeitungsverbot; **~ restriction** Verarbeitungsbeschränkung; **~ stage** Veredelungs-, Verarbeitungsstufe, Fertigungsphase; **~ tax** *(US)* Veredelungs-, Verarbeitungssteuer; **~ traffic** Veredelungsverkehr.

procession feierlicher Umzug, Prozession;
funeral ~ Leichen-, Trauerzug;
~ (v.) Prozession veranstalten, Umzug durchführen;
to go in a ~ Prozession durchführen, Umzug veranstalten; **to re-route a ~** Demontrationszug umleiten; **to veto a ~** Umzug verbieten; **to walk in ~ through the streets** Umzug durch die Stadt durchführen, Prozession veranstalten.

processioning Grenzbegehung.

prozessionist Umzugs-, Prozessionsteilnehmer.

processor Weiterverarbeiter, Veredeler.

processual prozessual[istisch].

proclaim *(v.)* öffentlich bekanntgeben (verkünden), proklamieren, kundgeben, Aufruf erlassen, *(interdict a strike)* Streik durch Regierungsbeschluß verbieten, *(mil.)* Ausnahmezustand verhängen;
~ the banns Verlobte aufbieten; **~ a district** Bezirk unter Quarantäne stellen, Ausnahmezustand über ein Gebiet verhängen; **~ emperor** zum Kaiser ausrufen; **~ a public holiday** zum öffentlichen Feiertag erklären; **~ from the housetops** an die große Glocke hängen, öffentlich verkünden; **~ martial law** Standrecht verhängen; **~ a meeting** Versammlung verbieten; **~ a republic** Republik ausrufen; **~ a strike** Streik durch Regierungsbeschluß verbieten; **~ a man a traitor** j. zum Verräter erklären; **~ war** Kriegszustand erklären.

proclaimer Ausrufer.

proclamation *(law)* An-, Verkündigung, öffentliche Bekanntmachung, Aufruf, feierliche Kundgebung, Proklamation;
by public ~ im Wege öffentlicher Bekanntmachung;
~ of martial law Verhängung des Standrechts; **~ of the Republic** Ausrufung der Republik;
to issue a ~ Proklamation (Aufruf) ergehen lassen; **to make ~ of s. th.** etw. unter die Leute bringen; **to make s. th. known by public ~** etw. öffentlich bekanntmachen.

proclivity Hang, Veranlagung.

procrastinate *(v.)* verzögern, zaudern;
~ in every emergency in jedem Notfall verzögernd wirken.

procrastination Verzögerung, Aufschub.

procrastinator Zögerer, Zauderer.

proctor *(Admiralty Court)* Anwalt vor Gerichten der freiwilligen Gerichtsbarkeit, *(procurator)* Sachwalter, Bevollmächtigter, *(school, US)* Aufsicht, *(university, Br.)* Proktor, Universitätsrichter;
~ (v.) Aufsicht führen;
~ at an examination Examenskandidaten beaufsichtigen;
~'s dog (man) *(university, Br., sl.)* Pedell.

proctoring *(US)* Beaufsichtigung.

proctorize *(v.)* maßregeln, Verweis erteilen.

procurable erhältlich, erlangbar.
procuracy Vollmachtsurkunde.
procuration *(brokerage fee)* Maklergebühr, *(instrument)* Vollmachtsurkunde, *(delegation of authority)* [etwa] Prokura, Bevollmächtigung, *(indorsing a bill of exchange)* Vollmacht, *(procurement)* Beschaffung, Versorgung, *(sexual offence)* Kuppelei;
per ~ (per proc.) in Vertretung (Vollmacht);
branch ~ [etwa] Filialprokura; **express ~** ausdrücklich erteilte Vollmacht; **implied ~** stillschweigend erteilte Vollmacht; **joint ~** [etwa] Gesamthandlungsvollmacht, -prokura; **single (sole) ~** Einzelhandlungsvollmacht; **tacit ~** stillschweigend erteilte Vollmacht;
~ of a loan Anleihebeschaffung;
to act by ~ als Bevollmächtigter (in Vollmacht) handeln; **to cancel ~** Vollmacht (Prokura) entziehen; **to confer (give) ~** Vollmacht (Prokura) erteilen; **to hold ~** [etwa] Prokura haben; **to indorse a bill by ~** Wechsel in Vollmacht unterschreiben; **to sign by (per) ~** [etwa] per Prokura zeichnen;
~ fee (money) Maklerprovision für Kreditvermittlung; **~ officer** Anforderungsbeamter; **~ signature** [etwa] Unterschrift per Prokura.
procurator *(US)* [Prozeß]bevollmächtigter, Rechtskonsulent;
~ fiscal *(Scot.)* Staatsanwalt; **~ litis** Prozeßvertreter; **~ in rem suam** selbstkontrahierender Stellvertreter.
procuratory Vollmachtsauftrag.
procure *(v.)* besorgen, beibringen, beschaffen, verschaffen, vermitteln, erlangen, herbeischaffen, *(criminal law)* verkuppeln, Kuppelei betreiben;
~ acceptance Akzept einholen; **~ capital** Kapital[interessenten] beschaffen; **~ s. o. to break his contract** j. zum Vertragsbruch verleiten; **~ s. one's death by poison** j. durch Gift beseitigen; **~ documents** Unterlagen beibringen; **~ employment** Arbeit verschaffen; **~ evidence** Beweise erbringen; **~ funds** Kapital[interessenten] beschaffen; **~ goods** Waren beziehen; **~ a loan** Darlehn beschaffen; **~ judgment** Urteil erwirken; **~ money** Geld beschaffen; **~ a patent** Patent erwerben.
procurement Beschaffung, Besorgung, Beibringung, Erlangung, Erwerbung, Vermittlung;
defence ~ *(mil.)* Beschaffungswesen; **government ~** staatliches Beschaffungswesen;
~ of capital Kapitalbeschaffung; **~ of documents** Beibringung von Unterlagen; **~ of foreign exchange** Devisenbeschaffung; **~ of funds** Beschaffung von Mitteln, Geldbeschaffung, Mittelaufbringung; **~ of goods** Warenbezug; **~ of a judgment** Erwirkung eines Urteils; **~ of a loan** Darlehnsbeschaffung, -vermittlung, Anleihevermittlung; **~ of merchandise** Warenbeschaffung; **~ of a patent** Patenterwerb;
~ agency *(US)* Beschaffungsstelle, -amt; **~ authorization** Beschaffungsermächtigung; **~ budget** Arbeitsbeschaffungsetat; **normal ~ channels** normaler Beschaffungsweg; **~ contract** Beschaffungsvertrag; **~ division** Beschaffungsabteilung; **~ office** Beschaffungsstelle; **~ officer** Beschaffungsbeamter; **government ~ policy** beschaffungspolitische Maßnahmen des Staates; **~ transactions** Besorgungsgeschäfte; **~ tying** Beschaffungsbindung.
procurer Beschaffer, Besorger, Vermittler, *(criminal law)* Kuppler.
procuring Beschaffung, Vermittlung;
~ breach of contract Verleitung zum Vertragsbruch;
~ agency Beschaffungsbehörde; **~ cause** unmittelbare Ursache.
prod Ahle, *(fig.)* Ansporn;
~ *(v.)* s. o. on j. auf Trapp bringen; **~ s. one's memory** jds. Gedächtnis nachhelfen.
prodigal Verschwender, wegen Verschwendungssucht Entmündigter;
~ *(a.)* verschwenderisch;
~ administration verschwendungssüchtige Verwaltung;
to be ~ of s. th. verschwenderisch mit etw. umgehen; **to give ~ly to charity** seine Wohltätigkeit übertreiben.
prodigality Verschwendungssucht.
prodigious sum of money ungeheurer Geldbetrag.
prodigy Wunder[tat];
infant ~ Wunderkind;
~ of learning Wunder an Gelehrsamkeit.
prodition Verrat.
proditor Verräter.
produce *(product)* Erzeugnis, Produkt, *(agricultural product)* landwirtschaftliches Erzeugnis, *(yield)* Ertrag, Gewinn, Ausbeute;

agricultural ~ landwirtschaftliche Erzeugnisse; **colonial ~** Kolonialwaren; **daily ~** Tagesleistung; **excess ~** Überschußerzeugnis; **farm ~** landwirtschaftliche Erzeugnisse; **foreign ~** ausländisches Erzeugnis; **garden ~** Gartenerzeugnisse; **gross ~** Rohertrag; **home (inland) ~** inländische Bodenerzeugnisse, einheimische (eigene) Erzeugnisse; **natural ~** Bodenerzeugnisse; **net ~** Reinertrag, -gewinn; **raw ~** Rohmaterial, Rohstoffe; **surplus ~** Überschußprodukt;
~ of the country Landesprodukte; **~ of an invention** Früchte einer Erfindung; **~ of soil** Bodenertrag; **~ of 5 years' work** Ergebnis fünfjähriger Arbeit;
~ *(v.)* (for broadcasting) [für den Funk] bearbeiten, *(effect)* bewirken, schaffen, *(farming)* Ertrag bringen (liefern), erzeugen, *(film)* produzieren, *(manufacture)* [Güter] erzeugen, herstellen, ausstoßen, produzieren, fabrizieren, fertigen, *(theater)* einstudieren, aufführen, *(yield)* einbringen, abwerfen;
~ accounts for inspection Bücher zur Revision vorlegen; **~ an actress** Schauspielerin herausbringen; **~ an after-effect** nachwirken, Nachwirkung erzielen; **~ an alibi** Alibi beibringen; **~ one's authority** seine Vollmacht vorlegen; **~ a book** Buch veröffentlichen; **~ a certificate** Bescheinigung vorlegen; **~ heavy crops** reiche Ernten einbringen; **~ documents** Urkunden als Beweis[material] vorlegen; **~ evidence** Beweismittel vorlegen, Beweis antreten; **~ mainly for export** in der Hauptsache für den Export anfertigen (herstellen); **~ at an economic figure** rentabel produzieren; **~ goods by machinery** Produkte maschinell herstellen; **~ interest** Zinsen tragen; **~ an invention** Erfindungsgegenstand herstellen; **~ one's passport** seinen Paß vorzeigen; **~ a photograph** Fotografie machen; **~ a new play** neues Stück aufführen; **~ a power of attorney** Vollmacht vorlegen; **~ a prisoner** Untersuchungsgefangenen vorführen; **~ profit** Gewinn abwerfen (einbringen); **~ the proofs of a statement** Beweise für eine Aussage liefern; **~ a large quantity of fruit** zahlreiche Früchte tragen; **~ reasons** Gründe anführen; **~ a sensation** Sensation hervorrufen (auslösen); **~ a spark** *(el.)* Funken auslösen; **~ one's railway ticket at the station [upon request]** seine Fahrkarte bei der Sperre [auf Verlangen] vorzeigen; **~ a witness** Zeugen beibringen;
~ advance Produktionskredit; **~ broker** Produkten-, Warenmakler; **~ business** Produktenhandel; **~ dealer** Waren-, Produktenhändler; **~ exchange** Waren-, Produktenbörse; **~ facilities** Warenkreditfazilitäten; **~ loan** Warenkredit; **~ market** Produkten-, Warenmarkt; **wholesale ~ market** Großhandelsmarkt; **~ merchant** Produktenhändler; **~ middleman** Produktenmakler; **~ trade** Produktenhandel.
producer Hersteller, Erzeuger, Produzent, Herstellerfirma, *(broadcasting)* Rundfunkbearbeiter, Sendeleiter, *(film, Br.)* Filmproduzent, -regisseur, Spielleiter;
domestic ~ inländischer Erzeuger; **diversified ~** Herstellungsbetrieb mit breitem Produktionsprogramm; **executive ~** Produktionsleiter; **gas ~** Generator; **high-cost ~** mit hohen Kosten arbeitender Produzent, teurer Herstellungsbetrieb; **industrial ~** Industrieller; **inland ~** Inlandserzeuger; **low-cost ~** billiger Herstellungsbetrieb; **marginal ~** Betrieb an der Grenze der Rentabilität; **primary ~** Urerzeuger; **small-lot ~** Kleinserienerzeuger;
~ advertising Herstellerwerbung; **~ association** Produzentenverband; **~'s brand** Herstellermarke; **~'s capital** Produktionsgüter; **~ cartel** Produktionskartell; **~'s contract** Erzeugervertrag; **~ cooperative (society, Br.)** Erzeuger-, Produktivgenossenschaft, landwirtschaftliche Absatzgenossenschaft; **~ costs** Gestehungskosten; **~'s cost price** Erzeugungs-, Herstellungspreis; **~'s country** Hersteller-, Erzeugerland; **~'s credit** Produzentenkredit; **~'s direction** Regieanweisung; **~ display** Herstellerauslage; **~'s durable equipment** Ausrüstungsinvestitionen; **~ gas** Generatorengas; **~ goods** Produktionsgüter, -mittel; **~ goods industry** Produktionsgüterindustrie; **~'s liability insurance** *(US)* Gewährleistungsversicherung des Produzenten; **~'s mark** Herstellermarke; **~ organization** Erzeugerverband; **~ power** Produktionskapazität; **~ price** Produzenten-, Erzeugerpreis; **~'s rent** Unternehmergewinn, Produzentenrendite; **~'s risk** Erzeugerrisiko; **~ society** *(Br.)* Absatzgenossenschaft; **~ stage** Erzeugerstufe; **~'s surplus** Hersteller-, Unternehmergewinn.
producibility Herstellbarkeit.
producible herstell-, produzierbar.
producing Herstellung, Produktion;
~ for stock Lageranfertigung;
~ *(a.)* produzierend, herstellend;
~ area Produktionsgebiet; **raw-material ~ area** Rohstoffgebiet; **~ capacity** Produktions-, Leistungsfähigkeit; **~ cause**

(broker's commission) unmittelbare Ursache; ~ **center** *(US)* **(centre,** *Br.)* Herstellungsstätte, Produktionszentrum; ~ **country** Herstellungs-, Produktionsland; ~ **facilities** Produktions-, Fabrikationsanlagen; **to expand one's** ~ **facilities** seine Produktionskapazität erweitern; ~ **factory** Erzeugungs-, Produktionsstätte; ~ **industries** erzeugende Industrie, Produktionswirtschaft; ~ **interests** Produktionsinteressen; ~ **power** Produktionskapazität, -leistung; ~ **unit** Produkt[ions]einheit, Produktionsstätte.

product Erzeugnis, Produkt, Fabrikat, Artikel, Ware, *(result)* Ergebnis, Frucht;

~**s** *(Br.) (interest)* Zinszahlen, -nummern;

advertised ~ Reklame-, Werbeartikel; **agricultural** ~**s** landwirtschaftliche Erzeugnisse; **basic** ~**s** Grundprodukte; **best** ~ bestes Fabrikat; **black** ~**s** *(interest, Br.)* schwarze [Zins]nummern; **by-**~ Nebenerzeugnis, -produkt; **chief** ~ Hauptprodukt; **colonial** ~**s** Kolonialprodukte, -waren; **credit** ~**s** *(Br.)* Habenzinsnummern; **debit** ~**s** *(Br.)* Sollzinsnummern; **domestic** ~ unser eigenes Erzeugnis; **established** ~ gut (im Markt) eingeführter Artikel; **factory** ~ gewerbliches Erzeugnis; **farm** ~**s** landwirtschaftliche Erzeugnisse; **faulty** ~ Fehlprodukt; **final** ~ Endprodukt, -erzeugnis; **finished** ~**s** fertige Erzeugnisse, Fertigerzeugnisse, -waren; **half-finished** ~**s** Halbfabrikate; **foreign** ~ **[-made]** ~**s** ausländische Erzeugnisse; **hard-to-move** ~ schwer zu verkaufendes Erzeugnis, schwer absetzbare Ware; **high-quality** ~**s** hochqualifizierte Produkte (Erzeugnisse), Produkte des gehobenen Bedarfs, Qualitätserzeugnisse, -produkte; **highly perishable** ~**s** leicht verderbliche Waren; **home** ~**s** inländische Erzeugnisse; **horticultural** ~**s** Gartenbauerzeugnisse; **industrial** ~**s** Industrieerzeugnisse, -produkte; **inferior** ~ minderwertige Ware; **inland** ~ einheimisches Fabrikat; **intermediary (intermediate)** ~ Zwischenprodukt; **joint** ~**s** Verbundprodukte; **light** ~**s** Erzeugnisse der Leichtindustrie; **literary** ~ literarisches Erzeugnis; **machine-made** ~**s** maschinell hergestellte Erzeugnisse; **manufactured** ~**s** gewerbliche Erzeugnisse; **misbranded** ~**s** mit falschen Warenzeichen versehene Erzeugnisse; **national** ~ Sozialprodukt, volkswirtschaftliche Produktionsleistung; **[total] gross national** ~ Bruttosozialprodukt; **natural** ~ Früchte einer Sache; **net** ~ Reingewinn; **nondefence** ~**s** nichtstrategische Erzeugnisse; **nongraded** ~ nicht sortierte Artikel; **nonprice-maintained** ~**s** nicht preisstabile Produkte; **price-maintained** ~**s** Artikel (Erzeugnisse) mit stabilen Preisen, preisstabile Erzeugnisse; **patented** ~ patentiertes Erzeugnis; **primary** ~**s** Grund-, Rohstoffe; **processing** ~**s** Weiterverarbeitungserzeugnisse; **profit-yielding** ~ Erfolgsträger; **raw** ~ Rohprodukt; **red** ~ *(bookkeeping)* rote Zahlen; **residual** ~ Abfall-, Nebenprodukt; **responsive** ~**s** vom Einkommen des Durchschnittsverbrauchers abhängige Erzeugnisse; **rival** ~ Konkurrenzerzeugnis, -fabrikat; **secondary** ~ Nebenprodukt; **semifabricated (-finished)** ~**s** Halbfabrikate, -fertigwaren; **sophisticated** ~ hochqualifiziertes Produkt (Erzeugnis); **spinoff** ~**s** anfallende Nebenprodukte; **standardized** ~ Standarderzeugnisse; **staple** ~ Hauptartikel, -produkt; **substitute** ~ Ersatzerzeugnis; **surplus** ~ Produktionsüberschuß; **throwaway** ~**s** weggeworfene Erzeugnisse, Wegwerfartikel; **tying** ~ gekoppeltes Produkt; **waste** ~ Abfallprodukt;

~ **of one's brain** Schöpfungen seines Geistes, geistiges Produkt; ~ **of a country** Erzeugnisse eines Landes, Landeserzeugnisse, -produkte; ~**s of one's labo(u)r** Früchte seiner Arbeit; ~**s on lease** vermietete Erzeugnisse; ~**s of agricultural levies** Abschöpfungsbeitrag auf Agrareinfuhren; ~ **of foreign make** ausländische Artikel; ~ **for further processing** Vorerzeugnis; ~**s of the season** Früchte der Saison; ~ **available to sell** zum Verkauf bereitstehende Erzeugnisse, Vertriebslagerbestände; ~ **difficult to sell** schwer abzusetzende Artikel;

to market ~**s** Erzeugnisse absetzen; **to showcase new** ~**s** neue Produkte vorführen;

~ **acceptance** Warenaufnahme; ~ **advertising** produktbezogene Werbung; ~ **analysis** Warenanalyse, -kunde; ~ **base** Produktenbasis; **to carry out negotiations on a selective** ~~**-by basis** Verhandlungen über einzeln ausgewählte Waren führen; ~ **budget** Produktetat; ~ **category** Produktkategorie, -einteilung; ~ **choice** Produktauswahl; ~ **class** Produktgruppe; ~ **control** Fertigungsüberwachung; ~ **cost** Herstellungs-, Produktionskosten, -aufwand; ~ **cost accounting** Erzeugniskalkulation; ~ **cost card** Vorkalkulationskarte; ~ **designer** Produktgestalter, Designer; ~ **development** Fortentwicklung einzelner Erzeugnisse; ~ **differentiation** Produktdifferenzierung; ~ **diversification** reichhaltiges Produktionsprogramm, Produktionsbreite; **to shift** ~ **emphasis** Produktionsschwerpunkt verlagern; ~ **endorsement** Produktaussage; ~ **engineer**

(US) Fertigungsingenieur, -konstrukteur; ~ **engineering** *(US)* produktionsreife Abschlußarbeiten, Fertigungstechnik; ~ **exposure** Produktbekanntmachung; ~ **family** Gruppe ähnlicher Erzeugnisse; ~ **features** Produkteigenschaften; ~ **grouping** Produktbündel; ~ **history** Entwicklung eines Produkts im Markt; ~ **information** Produktenkenntnis, Information über ein Erzeugnis; ~ **liability** Produzentenhaftung; ~ **liability claim** auf Produzentenhaftung gegründete Schadenersatzforderung; ~ **liability insurance** Gewährleistungsversicherung gegen aus Produzentenhaftung herrührende Schäden; ~ **liability premium** Versicherungsprämie für Produzentenhaftung; ~ **liability settlement** zur Abwendung von Produzentenhaftungsansprüchen getroffene Regelung; ~ **life cycle** Entwicklungskurve eines Produkts; ~ **line** Produktionszweig, Produkt-, Erzeugnisgruppe; ~ **lines** Sortiment; **broadly diversified** ~ **lines** breit gestreutes Warensortiment; **principle** ~ **line** Hauptproduktion; **to round up its** ~ **line** Fertigungsprogramm abrunden; ~ **line extension** Sortimentsausweitung; ~ **line margin** Branchenhandelsspanne; ~ **line planning** Planung der Produktionsgebiete; ~ **line simplification** Sortimentsverkleinerung, -vereinfachung; ~ **line strategy** langfristige Planung der Produktionsgebiete; ~ **manager** Verkaufsförderer, Markenbetreuer; ~ **managing** Markenbetreuung; ~ **material** Informationsmaterial für einzelne Erzeugnisse; ~ **mix** *(US)* gemischtes Produktionsprogramm, [Fertigungs]sortiment; ~ **personality** Profil eines Produktes; ~ **planning** Marktreifgestaltung, Produktplanung; ~ **policy** Herstellungspolitik; **farm-**~ **prices** landwirtschaftliche Erzeugerpreise; ~ **promotion** auf ein bestimmtes Produkt abgestellte Verkaufsförderung; ~ **public liability insurance** Betriebshaftpflichtversicherung; ~ **publicity** Aufklärungswerbung für ein Produkt; ~ **quality** Qualität eines Erzeugnisses, Produktionsqualität; ~ **research** Marktforschung für ein neues Erzeugnis; ~ **sales breakdown** Umsatzaufschlüsselung; ~ **sharing** Deputatenentlohnung; ~ **simplification** Fertigungsvereinfachung; ~ **specification** Produktbeschreibung; ~ **split** Produktionsaufteilung; **finished** ~ **stage** Fabrikationsreife; ~ **standards** Warennormen; ~ **test[ing]** Testen eines Produkts, Waren-, Produktionstest; ~ **timing** Terminplanung für die Markteinführung; ~ **training** Produkteinführung; ~ **warranty** Mängelgewähr.

production Hervorbringen, Herstellung, Erzeugung, Ausstoß, Fertigung, Fabrikation, Produzieren, Produktion, *(broadcasting)* Rundfunk-, Fernsehproduktion, *(of documents)* Vorlage, -legung, Beibringung, Beweismaterial, *(film)* Regie, Produktion, *(mining)* Förderleistung, *(print.)* Herstellung der Druckunterlagen, *(theater)* Auf-, Vorführung, Inszenierung, *(works of mental creation)* geistiges Erzeugnis, Werk;

ready to go into ~ fertigungs-, produktionsreif;

agricultural ~ Erzeugung landwirtschaftlicher Produkte; **annual** ~ Jahresproduktion, -erzeugung; **armaments** ~ Rüstungsproduktion; **average** ~ Durchschnittserzeugung, -produktion; **big-diameter pipe** ~ Großrohrproduktion; **budgeted** ~ geplante Produktion, Produktionsplanung; **changeover** ~ vorübergehende Produktion; **commercial** ~ handelsübliche Fertigung; **constant** ~ fortlaufende Erzeugung; **contracting** ~ schrumpfende Produktion; **copyrighted** ~**s** *(US)* urheberrechtlich (patentamtlich) geschützte Produktion (Veröffentlichung); **current** ~ laufende Produktion; **curtailed** ~ gedrosselte (verminderte) Produktion; **domestic** ~ Eigenerzeugung, inländische Produktionleistung, Inlandsproduktion; **dwindling** ~ Produktionsabnahme; **ebbing** ~ abnehmende Produktion; **economic** ~ gewerbliche Produktion, industrielle Erzeugung, Industrieproduktion; **excessive** ~ Überproduktion; **factory** ~ gewerbliche Produktion; **falling** ~ rückläufige Produktion, Produktionrückgang; **farm** ~ landwirtschaftliche Erzeugung; **flow** ~ Fließarbeit, -bandfertigung; **full** ~ volle Produktion; **full-capacity** ~ hundertprozentig ausgenutzte Produktionskapazität; **genuine** ~ wirkliche Produktion; **high-cost** ~ mit hohen Selbstkosten arbeitende Industrie, teure Produktion; **home** ~ Eigenerzeugung, inländische Produktionsleistung; **increased** ~ Produktionssteigerung; **indirect** ~ mittelbare Produktion; **individual** ~ Einzelanfertigung; **industrial** ~ industrielle Produktion, Industrieproduktion; **initial** ~ Anfangsproduktion, erste Produktionsergebnisse; **large-scale** ~ Massenfertigung, -produktion, Großserienproduktion, -herstellung; **line** ~ Produktion am laufenden Band; **literary** ~ literarische Erzeugnisse; **lot** ~ Massenherstellung, -produktion; **low-cost** ~ mit niedrigen Unkosten (niedrigen Selbstkosten) arbeitende Industrie; **machine** ~ maschinelle Herstellung; **marginal** ~ innerhalb der Rentabilität liegende Produktion, Produktion an der Kostengrenze; **mass** ~ fabrik-

mäßige (serienmäßige) Herstellung, Massenherstellung, -produktion; **moving-band** ~ Produktion am laufenden Band; **peacetime** ~ Friedensproduktion; **primary** ~ Lebensmittel- und Rohstofferzeugung; **quantity** ~ Massenherstellung, -produktion; **record** ~ Rekordproduktion; **seasonal** ~ saisonbedingte Produktionstätigkeit, Saisonproduktion; **secondary** ~ Produktion des sekundären Sektors; **serial (series)** ~ Reihenanfertigung, Serienherstellung; **settled** ~ stetige Produktion; **soft goods** ~ Produktion schnell verbrauchbarer Güter; **speculative** ~ Produktion vor Auftragseingang; **standard** ~ Normal-[arbeits]leistung; **standardized** ~ genormte Produktion, Herstellung am laufenden Band; **steady** ~ gleichmäßige Produktion; **surplus** ~ Überproduktion; **total** ~ Gesamtproduktion; **volume** ~ serienmäßige Herstellung, Massenerzeugung, -produktion; **war** ~ Rüstungsproduktion; **wartime** ~ Kriegsproduktion; **wholesale** ~ großbetriebliche Produktion; **world** ~ Weltproduktion; **yearly** ~ Jahresproduktion;
~ **of armaments** Rüstungsproduktion; ~ **of balance sheets** Vorlage von Bilanzen, Bilanzvorlage; ~ **of books** Vorlage der Geschäftsbücher; ~ **of the brain** Hirngespinst; ~ **in bulk** Massenherstellung, -produktion; ~ **for commerce** (US) Erzeugung für den Handel; ~ **of crops** Erntehervorbringung; ~ **of current** Stromerzeugung; ~ **of documents** Urkundenvorlage; ~ **of forged documents** Vorlage falscher Urkunden; ~ **of electricity** Elektrizitätserzeugung; ~ **of evidence** Erbringen von Beweisen, Beweisvorbringen, -antritt; ~ **of gold** Goldgewinnung, -produktion; ~ **of goods** Gütererzeugung; ~ **of manufactured goods** Herstellung von Massengütern; ~ **of hardware** Herstellung von Eisen-, Blech- und Metallwaren; ~ **of income** Einkommensbildung; ~ **of nature** Naturprodukte; ~ **of a prisoner** Vorführung eines Untersuchungsgefangenen; ~ **of services** Erzeugung von Dienstleistungen; ~ **of the soil** Naturprodukte; ~ **for stock** Vorrats-, Lageranfertigung; ~ **of suit** Klageformel; ~ **of a witness** Beibringung eines Zeugen; **his early ~s as a writer** seine ersten literarischen Arbeiten;
to be in ~ (film) gerade gedreht werden; **to be in good** ~ genügend hergestellt werden; **to be no longer in** ~ nicht mehr hergestellt werden, ausgelaufen sein; **to be in process of** ~ in der Herstellung begriffen (in Produktion) sein; **to broaden its line of** ~ Produktionsprogramm erweitern; **to check** ~ Produktion einschränken; **to contribute a part of the expense of** ~ Produktionskosten teilweise übernehmen; **to convert** ~ Produktion umstellen; **to crank up** ~ Produktion ankurbeln; **to curb (curtail)** ~ Produktion drosseln, Erzeugung beschränken; **to cut** ~ Produktion einschränken (drosseln), Produktionsdrosselung vornehmen; **to diversify** ~ Produktionsprogramm auffächern; **to encourage** ~ Produktionssteigerung hervorrufen; **to form the bulk of** ~ wesentlichen Teil der Produktion ausmachen; **to gear** ~ Produktion anpassen; **to gear up** ~ Produktion hochtreiben; **to gear** ~ **to the capacity of a plant** Produktionskapazität voll ausfahren; **to go into** ~ (new factory) Produktion aufnehmen; **to have the exclusive rights in a** ~ alleinige Herstellungsrechte haben; **to hive off** ~ Produktionsaufträge in einem fremden Werk herstellen lassen; **to increase** ~ Förderung (Produktion) steigern, Fabrikation erhöhen, Produktionssteigerung herbeiführen; **to increase** ~ **by better methods** Produktionsausstoß durch bessere Fertigungsmethoden steigern; **to operate at full** ~ mit voller Kapazität arbeiten; **to put into** ~ in die Fabrikation geben; **to put the brake (a check) on** ~ Produktion abstoppen; **to raise** ~ **to a maximum** Produktion auf den Höchststand bringen; **to reduce** ~ Produktion verringern; **to reschedule** ~ neue Produktionseinteilung vornehmen; **to restrict** ~ Produktion einschränken (drosseln); **to round off one's** ~ sein Produktionsprogramm abrunden; **to rush into** ~ sofort mit der Produktion beginnen, Produktionsbeginn sofort aufnehmen; **to satisfy** ~ (law) Beweismaterial vorlegen; **to scale** ~ Produktion programmieren; **to schedule** ~ Produktionsablauf festlegen; **to slash** ~ Produktion einschränken, Produktionskürzung vornehmen; **to start full** ~ mit der Serienproduktion beginnen; **to speed (step) up** ~ Produktion steigern (erhöhen), Produktionsausstoß erhöhen; **to stimulate** ~ Produktion anregen; **to sublet part of its** ~ Produktionsaufträge teilweise bei Fremdbetrieben unterbringen; **to tailor** ~ **to demand** Produktion der Nachfrage anpassen; **to trim excess** ~ Produktionsüberschüsse beseitigen;
~ **account** Fabrikations-, Herstellungs-, Produktionskonto; ~ **activity** Produktionstätigkeit; **civilian** ~ **administration** (US) Produktionslenkung des zivilen Bedarfs; ~ **agents** Produktionsfaktoren; ~ **aim** Produktionsziel; ~ **allocation program(me)** (US) kriegsbedingte Produktionslenkung; ~ **apparatus** Produktionsapparat; ~ **area** Erzeugungs-, Produktions-

gebiet; ~ **assistant** (publisher) Hersteller; ~ **average** Produktionsdurchschnitt; ~ **bonus** (US) Produktions-, Leistungsprämie, Erfolgsanteil; ~ **breakdown** Zusammenbruch der Produktion; ~ **budget** Produktionsplan, -etat, -programm; ~ **capacity** Ertrags-, Leistungsfähigkeit, Mengenleistung, Erzeugungskraft, Produktionskapazität, Produktionsleistung[sfähigkeit], Fabrikations-, Förderkapazität; ~ **capital** Produktivkapital; ~ **car** Serienwagen; **to set** ~ **ceilings** Produktionshöchstgrenzen festlegen; ~ **center** (US) (centre, Br.) Fertigungs[haupt]stelle, Produktionszentrum; ~ **certificate** Typenbescheinigung des Herstellers; ~ **chief** Produktionsleiter; ~ **coefficient** Produktions-, Vorleistungskoeffizient; ~ **combination** Produktionskartell; ~ **committee** Produktionsausschuß; ~ **contract** Produktionsauftrag, -vertrag; ~ **control** Produktionskontrolle, -lenkung, -steuerung, -beschränkung, Fabrikationskontrolle, Fertigungskontrolle, Fertigungssteuerung, -überwachung; ~ **controller** Produktionsüberwacher; ~ **cooperative** Produktionsgenossenschaft; ~ **cost** Gewinnungs-, Herstellungs-, Gestehungskosten, Produktionsaufwand, -kosten; ~ **credit** Produktivkredit; ~ **credit association** (US) landwirtschaftliche Kreditgenossenschaft; ~ **credit corporation** Produktivkreditgenossenschaft; ~ **crusade** Produktionskreuzzug; ~ **curve** Produktionskurve; ~ **cut** Produktionseinschränkung, -kürzung, Drosselung der Produktion; ~ **cutback** Produktionsdrosselung, -kürzung; ~ **cycle** Produktionskreislauf; ~ **date** Produktionstermin; ~ **decision** Produktionsentscheidung; ~ **decline** Produktionsrückgang; ~ **decrease** Produktionsrückgang; ~ **delay** Produktionsverzögerung; ~ **department** Fertigungs-, Herstellungs-, Fabrikationsabteilung; ~ **difficulties** Produktionsschwierigkeiten; ~ **director** (broadcasting) Sendeleiter; ~ **disincentive** Produktionsabschreckung; ~ **diversions** Produktionsbereich; ~ **division** Produktions-, Herstellungs-, Fertigungsabteilung; **to sell** ~ **divisions to raise cash** einzelne Fertigungszweige zum Zweck der Liquiditätsverbesserung aufgeben; ~ **engineer** Fertigungs-, Betriebsingenieur; ~ **engineering** Fertigungs-, Betriebstechnik, Fertigungsvorbereitung; ~ **enterprise** Fabrikationsstätte; ~ **equipment** Produktionsausstattung, Betriebseinrichtung; **high-~ equipment** Höchstleistungseinrichtung; ~ **expertise** Produktionsgutachten; ~ **facilities** Produktionsanlagen, -stätten, Fabrikationsanlagen; **to expand one's ~ facilities** Produktionskapazität erweitern; ~ **factors** Produktions-, Elementarfaktoren; ~ **figures** Ausstoß-, Produktionszahlen, Förderziffern; ~ **financing** Produktionsfinanzierung; ~ **flow** Fertigungs-, Produktionsablauf; ~ **force** Belegschaft; ~ **function** Produktionsaufgabe, -funktion; ~ **goal** Produktionsziel; **to fall short of** ~ **goal** Produktionsziel nicht erreichen; ~ **goods** Produktionsgüter, -mittel; ~ **goods industry** Produktionsgüterindustrie; ~ **grant** (Br.) Produktionsprämie; ~ **increase** Produktionssteigerung, -zunahme; ~ **index** Produktionsindex, -kennziffer; ~ **indifference curve** Produktionskapazitätskurve; ~ **job** Fertigungsberuf; ~ **level** Produktionsstand; ~ **limit figure** Produktionshöchstziffer; ~ **line** Förder-, Transport-, Fließband, Fertigungsstraße, Arbeitsstrecke; **empty ~ line** auftragsloser Fertigungszweig; **to halt ~ lines** einzelne Produktionszweige stillegen; ~ **load** Auslastung der Fertigungsanlagen; ~ **loss** Produktionsverlust, -ausfall; ~ **machinery** Produktionsanlage; **mechanical ~ man** Produktionsfachmann; ~ **management** Produktionssteuerung, -lenkung, Führung des Fertigungsbereichs; ~ **manager** Betriebs-, Fertigungs-, Fabrikations-, Herstellungs-, Produktionsleiter, Direktor der Produktionsabteilung, (publishing) Herstellungsleiter; ~ **method** Produktionsmethode, -verfahren, Herstellungsart, -verfahren; **cost-saving ~ methods** kostensparende Produktionsmethoden; ~ **model** Fertigungsmodell; ~ **monopoly** Erzeuger-, Fabrikations-, Produktionsmonopol; ~ **network** Produktionsapparat; ~ **office** Fertigungsbüro; ~ **operations** Produktionsablauf; ~ **optimum** Produktionsoptimum; ~ **order** Fertigungs-, Produktions-, Fabrikationsauftrag; **to mushroom in ~ orders** lawinenartige Produktionsaufträge auslösen; ~**-oriented** produktionsorientiert; ~ **outlook** Produktionsvorschau; ~ **overhead charges** Fertigungsgemeinkosten; ~ **part** Fertigungsteil; ~ **pause** Produktionspause; ~ **permit** Produktionserlaubnis, Fabrikationsgenehmigung; ~ **period** Fabrikationsdauer; ~ **picture** Produktionsbild; ~ **plan** Produktionsprogramm, -plan, -disposition, Fabrikations-, Fertigungsplan, Fabrikationsprogramm; ~ **planning** Fertigungs-, Produktionsplanung, Produktionssteuerung, Auftragsplanung und -steuerung; ~ **plant** Produktionsanlage, Fertigungsstätte; **to build up ~ plants abroad** ausländische Produktionsstätten errichten; ~ **policy** Produktionspolitik; ~ **potential** Produktionspotential;

~ prescriptions Herstellungs-, Fabrikations-, Produktionsvorschriften; ~ **price** Fabrikations-, Herstellungspreis; ~ **process** Produktionsgang, -prozeß, Herstellungsverfahren, -prozeß; ~ **program(me)** Fertigungs-, Produktionsprogramm, -dispositionen; ~ **prohibition** Fabrikations-, Herstellungsverbot; ~ **quota** Produktions-, Erzeugungsquote, Produktionskontingent; ~ **rate** Produktionstempo, -leistung; ~ **rationalization** rationalisiertes Produktionsverfahren; **all-time** ~ **record** Produktionshöchststand, -spitze; ~ **report** Produktionsbericht; ~ **return** Produktionsübersicht; **to have the exclusive** ~ **rights** alleinige Produktionsrechte haben; ~ **run** Produktionsablauf, -verlauf; ~ **schedule** Produktions-, Herstellungsprogramm, -plan, Produktionsziel; ~ **scheduler** *(US)* Produktionsprogrammierer; ~ **scheduling** *(US)* Produktionsprogrammierung, Fertigungsplanung; ~ **scheme** Produktionsplan, Erzeugungsvorhaben; ~ **slowdown** Produktionsverlangsamung; ~ **slump** Produktionsabfall; ~ **staff** Produktionsstab; ~ **standard of workers** durchschnittliche Leistungsfähigkeit der Arbeiter; ~ **statement** Produktionsbilanz; ~ **step** Produktionsstufe; ~ **supervision** Produktionsüberwachung; ~ **supervisor** Produktionsleiter; ~ **surplus** Produktionsüberschuß; ~ **system** Herstellungs-, Fabrikationssystem; ~ **target** Produktionsziel; ~ **technique** Produktions-, Herstellungsverfahren; ~ **time** Herstellungsdauer, Produktions-, Stück-, Fertigungszeit; **individual** ~ **time** Stückzeit; ~ **total** Gesamtproduktion; ~ **transfer** *(US)* aus Betriebsgründen erfolgende Versetzung, innerbetriebliche Umsetzung von Arbeitskräften; ~ **unit** Produktionseinheit, -stelle, Fertigungsgruppe, -einheit; ~ **value** Produktions-, Herstellungswert; ~ **volume** Produktionsvolumen, -umfang, -stand; **to keep the** ~ **wheels humming** Produktion in Gang halten; ~ **worker** Industriearbeiter; ~ **workers** in der Produktion Beschäftigte.

productive leistungsfähig, produzierend, *(creative)* schöpferisch, kreativ, ideenreich, fruchtbar, *(tending to produce exchangeable value)* produktiv, werteschaffend, *(yielding in abundance)* ertragreich, ertragsfähig, ergiebig, fruchtbar; **to be** ~ erzeugen; **to be** ~ **only of quarrels** lediglich Streitigkeiten hervorrufen;
~ **ability** Produktionsfähigkeit; ~ **activity** Fabrikationstätigkeit, *(yielding activity)* gewinnbringende Tätigkeit; ~ **apparatus** Produktionsapparat; ~ **assets** werbende Aktiva; ~ **bed** *(mining, US)* abbauwürdige Lagerstätte; ~ **burden center** *(US)* **(centre,** *Br.)* Fertigungskostenstelle; ~ **capacity** Leistungsfähigkeit, Produktivität, Produktionspotential, -fähigkeit, -kapazität, Mengenleistung; **national** ~ **capacity** Sozialproduktvolumen; ~ **capital** arbeitendes (gewinnbringendes) Kapital, Produktivkapital; ~ **cooperative society** Produktivgenossenschaft; ~ **cooperation** Produktionsgenossenschaft; ~ **department** Herstellungs-, Produktionsabteilung; ~ **efficiency** Leistungsfähigkeit [eines Betriebes], [betriebliche] Leistungs-, Produktionsfähigkeit, Produktivität; ~ **efforts** Produktionsanstrengungen; ~ **energy** Produktionskraft; ~ **enterprise** ertragbringendes Unternehmen; ~ **equipment** Produktions-, Fabrikationseinrichtungen, Produktionsmittel; ~ **establishment** Fabrikations-, Produktionsstätte; **home-based** ~ **expansion** im Inland vorgenommene Produktionsausweitung; ~ **expenses (expenditure)** werbende Ausgaben; ~ **experience** Fabrikationserfahrung; ~ **facilities** Produktionsmöglichkeiten, Produktionseinrichtungen; ~ **factor** Produktionsfaktor; ~ **function** produktive Aufgabe; ~ **industry** Produktionsmittelindustrie; ~ **investments** werteschaffende Anlagen; ~ **labo(u)r** Fertigungslöhne, produktive Löhne; ~ **machinery** Produktionsanlagen; ~ **mine** Ausbeutezeche; ~ **-motivated basic premium** vermögenspolitisch motivierte Sockelprämie; ~ **occupation** Produktionstätigkeit; ~ **period of an author** schöpferische Phase eines Schriftstellers; ~ **potential** volkswirtschaftliches Produktionspotential; ~ **power** betriebliche Leistungsfähigkeit; ~ **power of the soil** Fruchtbarkeit des Bodens; ~ **process** Herstellungs-, Produktionsprozeß, -vorgang; ~ **productionsvermögen;** ~ **purpose** Produktivitätszweck; ~ **resource** Produktivkraft; ~ **resources** nutzbare Reserven, Produktionsmittel, -möglichkeiten; ~ **service** Faktor-, Produktivleistung; ~ **soil** ergiebiger (ertragreicher) Boden; ~ **technique** Herstellungsverfahren, -prozeß; ~ **trading society** Produktivgenossenschaft; ~ **undertaking** Produktionsunternehmen, -betrieb; ~ **unit** Produktionsstätte; ~ **value** Herstellungswert; ~ **wages** produktive Löhne, Fertigungslöhne; ~ **weakening** Produktionsabschwächung.

productively in gewinnbringender Weise.

productivity Ertragsfähigkeit, Ergiebigkeit, wirtschaftliche Leistungsfähigkeit, Produktivität, *(writer)* Ideenreichtum;

increased ~ erhöhte Produktivität, Produktivitätszunahme; **labo(u)r** ~ Arbeitsleistung; **long-time** ~ Dauerertragsfähigkeit; **marginal** ~ Produktivitätsgrenze, Grenzproduktivität; **plant** ~ betriebliche Produktivität;
~ **of an enterprise** finanzielle Leistungsfähigkeit eines Unternehmens;
to increase ~ Produktivität erhöhen, Produktivitätsgrad steigern; **to return to** ~ Produktivitätszunahme wettmachen;
~ **agreement** *(Br.)* Produktivitätsvereinbarung, -abkommen; ~ **bargaining** am Produktivitätszuwachs orientierte Tarifvereinbarung; ~ **boost** Produktivitätssteigerung; ~**-boosting machinery** produktivitätssteigernder Maschinenpark; ~ **curve** Ertragskurve; ~ **deal** *(Br.)* Produktivitätsabkommen; **self-financing** ~ **deal** *(Br.)* an die Produktivität gekoppelte und sich selbst finanzierende Lohnvereinbarung; ~ **differential** Produktivitätsgefälle; ~ **drive** Produktivitätsfeldzug; ~ **gain** Produktivitätszuwachs, -gewinn, -fortschritt; ~ **growth** Produktivitätswachstum; ~ **hike** Produktivitätssteigerung; ~ **improvements** Produktivitätsverbesserungen; ~ **incentive system** Anreizsystem zur Produktivitätssteigerung; ~ **increase** Produktivitätszuwachs; **to turn in the best** ~ **performance** erstklassige Produktivitätsergebnisse aufweisen; ~ **rise (raise,** *US)* Produktivitätssteigerung; **to settle for rises based on a** ~ **rate** Tariferhöhungen auf Produktivitätszunahmesätze abstellen; ~**-related pay hike** produktivitätsgekoppelter Lohnanstieg; ~ **showing** Produktivitätsbild; ~ **standards** Produktivitätsnormen; ~ **surge** rasanter Produktivitätsanstieg; ~ **team** Produktivitätsberatung; **marginal** ~ **theory** Grenzproduktivitätstheorie; ~ **theory of interest** Produktivitätstheorie des Zinses; ~ **trend** Produktivitätsentwicklung; ~ **value** Produktivitätswert; ~ **wages** auf die Produktivität abgestellte Löhne.

profanation Entweihung.

profane weltlich, profan;
~ *(v.)* entheiligen, entweihen;
~ **building** Profanbau; ~ **language** Lästern; ~ **literature** weltliche Literatur; ~ **word** Blasphemie.

profanity Gotteslästerung.

profess *(v.)* als Beruf ausüben, *(avow)* öffentlich erklären, *(Br.)* dozieren, als Professor lehren, *(be expert)* Fachwissen haben, Fachgebiet beherrschen;
~ **Christianity** sich zum christlichen Glauben bekennen; ~ **o. s.** **a communist** sich zum Kommunismus bekennen; ~ **a great esteem for s. o.** große Verehrung für j. erkennen lassen; ~ **to be an expert on a subject** sich auf einem Gebiet als Fachmann ausgeben; ~ **an interest in s. one's future** sich an jds. Zukunft interessiert zeigen; ~ **law** Jurist sein; ~ **loyalty** Loyalitätserklärung vortäuschen; ~ **principles which one does not practise** Prinzipien vertreten, die man selbst nicht praktiziert; ~ **to purchase** sich anheischig machen zu kaufen; ~ **o. s. in an order** Ordensgelübde ablegen; ~ **o. s. to be a social reformer** sich für Sozialreformen aussprechen; ~ **o. s. satisfied** sich für befriedigt erklären; ~ **extreme sorrow** übergroße Trauer zur Schau tragen.

professed offenkundig;
~ **Christian** Bekenntnischrist; ~ **excuse** Ausrede, Vorwand; ~ **friendship** Scheinfreundschaft; **self-**~ **hero** Maulheld; **to be a** ~ **spy** Spionagehandwerk betreiben; ~ **woman-hater** erklärter Weiberfeind.

profession *(collective body)* Berufsschicht, -stand, *(learned* ~*)* freier (akademischer) Beruf, freiberufliche Tätigkeit, *(vocation)* Beruf[szweig], Erwerbszweig, Gewerbe, Berufsleben;
by ~ von Beruf; **in my** ~ in meinem Fach; **without** ~ beschäftigungslos;
the ~**s** akademische Berufe, *(colleagues)* [Berufs]kollegen;
commercial ~ Kaufmannsstand, -beruf; **crowded** ~ überfüllter (übersetzter) Beruf; **learned** ~**s** akademische Berufe; **legal** ~ Anwaltsberuf, -stand; **liberal** ~ freier Beruf; **main** ~ Haupterwerbszweig; **military** ~ Soldatenberuf; **sedentary** ~ sitzende Tätigkeit; **theatrical** ~ Bühnenlaufbahn;
~ **of accounting** Wirtschaftsprüfer-, Buchprüferberuf; ~ **of arms** Soldatenberuf; ~ **of business** Beruf; ~ **of faith** Treuebekenntnis; ~ **of friendship** Freundschaftsbeteuerung; ~ **of journalism** Journalistenberuf; ~ **of letters** Schriftstellerberuf; ~ **of loyalty** Loyalitätserklärung; ~ **of medicine** Arztberuf; ~ **of teaching** Lehrerberuf; ~ **of vocation** *(income tax, Br.)* freie oder sonstige selbständige Berufe;
to arise from the exercise of a ~ **or employment** *(income tax)* aus freiberuflicher oder unselbständiger Tätigkeit stammen; **to attach little faith to s. one's** ~ **of esteem** jds. Wertschätzungserklärungen geringen Glauben schenken; **to be a lawyer by** ~ Anwaltsberuf ausüben; **to be skilled in one's** ~ sein Fach verste-

hen; **to be trained in a** ~ Berufsausbildung genossen haben; **to be without any particular** ~ keinem bestimmten Beruf nachgehen, ohne festen Beruf sein; **to belong to the** ~ *(fam.)* zum Theater gehören; **to carry on a** ~ Beruf ausüben; **to change one's** ~ seinen Beruf wechseln; **to enter a** ~ Beruf ergreifen; **to enter the legal** ~ Jurist werden; **to exercise a** ~ Beruf ausüben; **to follow one's** ~ seinem Beruf nachgehen; **to go in for (take up) a** ~ Beruf ergreifen, in einen freien Beruf gehen; **to have not stated one's** ~ ohne Berufsangabe sein; **to take up the military** ~ militärische Laufbahn einschlagen.

professional Berufsangehöriger, *(expert)* sachverständiger Berater, Fachmann, -arbeiter, *(sport)* Profi, *(stock exchange)* Berufsspekulant, *(university man)* Geisteswissenschaftler, Akademiker, Geistes-, Kopfarbeiter;
full-time ~ ganztägig tätiger Freiberufler;
~ **of high calibre and potential** hochqualifizierter und überzeugender Fachmann;
~ *(a.)* beruflich, fachlich, berufsmäßig, *(expert)* fachmännisch, -gemäß, *(liberal profession)* freiberuflich tätig, akademisch, *(making a profession)* berufsmäßig;
to turn ~ *(sport)* Berufsspieler (Profi) werden;
~ **activity** [frei]berufliche Tätigkeit, Berufstätigkeit; **to take** ~ **advice from s. o.** j. beruflich in Anspruch nehmen, sich von jem. fachmännisch beraten lassen; ~ **agency** Berufsorganisation, -vertretung; ~ **agitator** professioneller Unruhestifter; ~ **aptitude** berufliche Eignung; ~ **army** Berufsarmee, -heer; ~ **association** Berufsverband, -vereinigung; ~ **attainment** Berufseignung; ~ **audit** Prüfung durch einen selbständigen Wirtschaftsprüfer; ~ **auditor** selbständiger Wirtschaftsprüfer; ~ **background** beruflicher Werdegang, berufliche Entwicklung; ~ **beauty** Filmschönheit; ~ **body** Berufsverband, Fachgremium, Berufskörperschaft; ~ **business** Berufstätigkeit; **to be of** ~ **caliber** sich für einen Beruf besonders eignen; ~ **capacity** berufliche Eigenschaft; ~ **career** berufliche Laufbahn; ~ **character** berufliche Eigenschaft; ~ **charges** Gebühren für freiberufliche Beratung; ~ **chart** Fachtabelle; ~ **classes** höhere Berufsstände, Angehörige freier Berufe; ~ **classification** Berufszugehörigkeit; ~ **clothes** Berufskleidung; ~ **colleague** Berufskollege; ~ **conduct** standesgemäßes Verhalten; ~ **confidence** Berufsgeheimnis; ~ **consul** Berufskonsul; ~ **consultant** Berufsberater; ~ **contacts** berufliche Kontakte; ~ **corporation** Berufsgenossenschaft; ~ **criminal** Berufsverbrecher, Profi; ~ **customs** Gewerbeusancen; ~ **dictionary** Fachwörterbuch; ~ **diplomatist** Karrierediplomat; ~ **discretion** Schweigepflicht, Berufsgeheimnis; ~ **division** berufliche Gliederung; ~ **driver** Berufsfahrer; ~ **duty** Berufspflicht; ~ **earnings** Einkünfte aus freiberuflicher Tätigkeit; ~ **education** Berufs-, Fachausbildung, Berufserziehung; ~ **employee** akademisch vorgebildeter Bediensteter; ~ **employment** berufliche Tätigkeit, Berufstätigkeit; ~ **engineer** Diplomingenieur; ~ **ethics** Berufsmoral, -ethos, Standespflichten; ~ **etiquette** Standesehre, -regeln; ~ **examination** Fachprüfung; ~ **exertion** Berufsausübung; ~ **expenditure** *(income tax statement)* Werbungskosten; ~ **experience** Berufserfahrung; ~ **fee** [Sachverständigen]honorar; ~ **fellow** Stipendiat; ~ **firm** Fachunternehmen; ~ **group** Berufs-, Fachgruppe; ~ **goal** Berufsziel; ~ **government** Berufsbeamtentum; ~ **growth** berufliche Entwicklung; ~ **hono(u)r** Standesehre, Berufsethos; ~ **injury** Berufsschaden; ~ **institution** Berufsverband; ~ **insurance** Berufshaftpflichtversicherung; ~ **investor** berufsmäßiger Kapitalanleger; ~ **idiosyncrasy** charakteristische Ausdrucksweise; ~ **jealousy** Konkurrenzneid; ~ **job** fachmännische Arbeit; ~ **journal** Fachzeitschrift; ~ **judge** Berufsrichter; ~ **killer** Berufsmörder; ~ **liability** Unternehmerhaftpflicht; ~ **life** Berufsleben; ~ **magazine** Fachzeitschrift, -blatt; ~ **man** freiberuflich Tätiger, Angehöriger eines freien Berufs, Intellektueller, Fachmann, *(scientist)* Akademiker, geistig Schaffender, Gelehrter, Geistesarbeiter; ~ **management** fachmännische (fachkundige) Leitung; **to demand** ~ **management standards** ausgebildete Führungskräfte erfordern; **in a** ~ **manner** fachmännisch; ~ **minded** berufsinteressiert; ~ **name** Künstlername; **of a** ~ **nature** einschlägig, ins Berufsfach schlagend; ~ **obligation** Berufspflicht; ~ **organization** berufsständische Vertretung, Berufsverband; ~ **outlays** *(income tax statement)* Werbungskosten; ~ **partnership** Berufsgemeinschaft, -genossenschaft, Sozietät; ~ **people** Angehörige der freien Berufe; ~ **player** *(sport)* Berufsspieler; ~ **politician** Berufspolitiker; ~ **practice** Berufserfahrung, -ausübung, -praxis, *(lawyers)* Sozietät; ~ **pride** Berufsdünkel; ~ **privilege** berufliches Aussageverweigerungsrecht; ~ **problem** Berufsfrage, -problem; ~ **promoter** gewerbsmäßiger Gründer [von Gesellschaften]; ~ **prospects** Berufsaussichten; ~ **qualification**

berufliche Qualifikation, Berufseignung, fachliche Eignung; ~ **qualifications in economics** nachgewiesene wirtschaftswissenschaftliche Befähigungen; **to receive top** ~ **recognition** höchste Anerkennung innerhalb der maßgebenden Berufskreise erwerben; ~ **record** beruflicher Werdegang; ~ **representation** Berufsvertretung; ~ **reputation** berufliches Ansehen; ~ **risk indemnity insurance** *(Br.)* Berufshaftpflichtversicherung; ~ **school** Berufs-, Fachschule; ~ **schooling** Berufsausbildung; ~ **secrecy** berufliche Schweigepflicht; ~ **secret** Berufsgeheimnis; ~ **service** freier Beruf; ~ **services** freiberufliche Dienstleistungen; ~ **skill** Berufserfahrung, Fachvirtuosität; ~ **society** Berufsverband; ~ **soldier** Berufssoldat; ~ **speculator** *(US)* berufsmäßiger Spekulant; **to be a** ~ **spy** Spionagehandwerk Ausübender; ~ **staff** Expertenstab; ~ **standards** berufsethische Grundsätze; **to maintain high** ~ **standards** auf hohe ethische Grundsätze bei der Berufsausübung bedacht sein; ~ **status** berufliche Stellung; ~ **studies** Fachstudium; ~ **subject** Berufsthema, fachmännisches Thema; ~ **tax** Gewerbesteuer; ~ **traders** *(stock exchange)* Berufshandel, Kulisse; ~ **training** Fachstudium, berufliche Ausbildung, Berufs-, Fachausbildung; **extended** ~ **training** berufliche Weiterbildung; ~ **union** Berufsverband; ~ **user** beruflicher Benutzer; **in a** ~ **way** berufsmäßig, professionell, als Broterwerb; ~ **woman** berufstätige Frau; ~ **work** Berufstätigkeit; ~ **worker** freiberufliche Arbeitskraft, Berufstätiger; ~ **world** Berufswelt; ~ **wrong** Berufsschaden.

professionalism Berufs- Fachausübung, *(experts)* Experten, Spezialistentum, *(solidarity)* Berufssolidarität.

professionalize *(v.)* berufsmäßig ausüben, zum Gewerbe machen;
~ **sport** Sport zum Beruf erheben.

professionally|trained beruflich ausgebildet, mit Berufsausbildung;
to act ~ in Ausübung seines Berufes handeln; **to consult s. o.** ~ j. beruflich in Anspruch nehmen.

professor Professor, Ordinarius, Hochschullehrer, *(coll.)* Lehrmeister, Fachmann, *(teacher, US)* Lehrer;
associate (adjunct) ~ *(US)* außerordentlicher Professor; **assistant** ~ Dozent; **exchange** ~ Austauschprofessor; **extraordinary** ~ außerordentlicher Professor; **full** ~ ordentlicher Professor, Ordinarius; **ordinary** ~ ordentlicher Professor, Honorarprofessor; **visiting** ~ Gastprofessor;
~ **of languages** Sprachlehrer; ~ **in ordinary** ordentlicher Professor;
to be a ~ Professur innehaben;
~'s **chair** Lehrstuhl, Professur.

professordom, mad wissenschaftliche Übergeschnapptheit.

professorial professorenhaft;
~ **appointment** Ernennung zum Professor; ~ **chair** Lehrstuhl, Professur; ~ **duties** Pflichten (Aufgaben) eines Professors; **to be within the** ~ **range** im professorialen Bereich liegen; ~ **socialist** Kathedersozialist.

professoriate Professorenschaft.

professorship Lehrstuhl, Professur;
endowed ~ gestiftete Professur; **full** ~ ordentliche Professur, Ordinariat;
to accept a ~ Berufung annehmen; **to be appointed to a** ~ Professur (Professorenstelle, Ruf als Professor) erhalten, auf einen Lehrstuhl berufen werden; **to refuse a** ~ Berufung ablehnen.

proffer|of peace Friedensangebot;
~ *(v.)* anbieten, andienen.

proficiency Fertigkeit, Tüchtigkeit, Leistungsvermögen, -fähigkeit;
~ **in Latin** gute Leistungen in Latein;
to attain a [stage of] ~ Leistungsstand erreichen;
~ **pay** Leistungszulage; **to pass a** ~ **test** Vorprüfung bestehen.

proficient tüchtig, leistungsfähig, *(advanced)* fortgeschritten;
to be ~ **in bookkeeping** versierter Buchhalter sein.

profile Profil, Seitenansicht, *(short biography)* Kurzbiographie, *(short sketch)* kurze Übersicht;
~ *(v.)* Kurzbiographien schreiben;
~ **iron** Profileisen.

profit *(advantage)* Nutzen, Vorteil, Genuß, *(arising from land)* Rente, Ertrag, Nutzung, *(balance sheet)* Gewinnanteil, *(gain)* Gewinn, Erträgnis, Erlös, Verdienst, Profit, Rendite;
at a ~ mit Gewinn; **on joint** ~ **and loss** auf gemeinschaftlichen Gewinn und Verlust gerichtet; **with** ~ *(insurance)* mit Gewinnbeteiligung; **with an eye to** ~ aus Gewinnsucht; **with a view to** ~ auf Gewinn gerichtet, in gewinnsüchtiger Absicht;
~s *(insurance)* Gewinnanteile, *(law)* Früchte;

accumulated ~s angesammelte Gewinne, Gewinnvortrag; **actual** ~ tatsächlich erzielter Gewinn, Effektivgewinn; **additional** ~ Nebengewinn; **adjusted** ~ steuerlich bereinigter (berichtigter) Gewinn; **aggregate** ~ Gesamterlös; **annual** ~ Jahresgewinn, -ertrag; **anticipated** ~ erwarteter (erhoffter) Gewinn, Gewinnerwartung; **apparent** ~ Scheingewinn; **appendant** ~ gesetzlich zugerechneter Gewinn; ~ **appurtenant** vertraglich zugerechneter Gewinn; **assessable** ~ steuerpflichtiger Gewinn; **attributable** ~ zurechenbarer Gewinn, zustehender Gewinn; **available** ~ verfügbarer Gewinn; **back** ~s rückständige Gewinne; **book** ~ buchmäßiger Gewinn, Buchgewinn; **business** ~ Unternehmergewinn, Geschäftsgewinn, Gewinn aus Unternehmerbetrieb, Gewerbeertrag; **capital** ~ Kapitalgewinn, Veräußerungsgewinn aus Investitionsgütern; **casual** ~ gelegentlicher Gewinn, Gelegenheitsgewinn; **clear (clean)** ~ glattes Geschäft, Netto-, Reingewinn, -ertrag, -erlös; **commercial** ~s Einkünfte aus Gewerbebetrieb, gewerblicher Gewinn; **company** ~ Gesellschaftsgewinn, -ergebnis; **contingent** ~ eventueller Gewinn; **decent** ~ stattlicher Gewinn; **deferred** ~ vorweggenommener Gewinn, als antizipatives Passivum gebuchter Ertragsposten; **departmental** ~ auf die Abteilungen aufgeschlüsselter Gewinn; **differential** ~ Differenzialrente; **disposable** ~ Bilanzgewinn; **distributed** ~ ausgeschütteter Gewinn; **easy** ~ müheloser Gewinn; **excess** ~s Mehr-, Übergewinn, überschießender Gewinn; **exchange** ~ Kursgewinn; **extra** ~s außerordentliche Erträge; **extraneous** ~ Konjunkturgewinn; **extraordinary** ~s außerordentliche Erträge; **fair** ~ angemessener Gewinn; **fat** ~ fetter (dicker) Gewinn; **gambling** ~ Spielgewinn; **gross** ~ Roh-, Bruttogewinn, -ertrag; **growing** ~ steigender Gewinn; **handsome** ~ stattlicher Gewinn; **hidden** ~s versteckte Gewinne; **honest** ~ ehrlicher Gewinn; **illicit** ~s unerlaubte Gewinne; **illusory** ~ Scheingewinn; **imaginary** ~ Scheingewinn; **incidental** ~ unmittelbarer Nutzen, Nebengewinn; **industrial** ~ Einkünfte aus Gewerbebetrieb, Gewerbeertrag; **inflation-generated** ~ inflationsbedingter Gewinn; **intercompany** ~s Konzernerlöse; **investment** ~ (balance sheet) Erträgnisse aus Beteiligungen; ~ **left** stehengebliebener Gewinn; **lost** ~ Gewinnausfall, entgangener Gewinn; ~ **made** erzielter Gewinn; **manufacturing** ~ Fabrikationsgewinn; **marginal** ~ Grenzertrag, -nutzen, Rentabilitätsschwelle; **mesne** ~s (Br.) zwischenzeitliche Nutzungen, unrechtmäßig gezogene Grundstücksfrüchte; **minimum** ~ Gewinnminimum; **missed** ~ entgangener Gewinn; **monopoly** ~s Monopolerträgnisse; **monthly** ~ Monatsverdienst; **net** ~ reiner Überschuß, Reingewinn, Nettogewinn, -ertrag; **net trading** ~ Geschäftsreinertrag; **nondrawn** ~ nicht entnommener Gewinn; **nonoperating** ~ betriebsfremder Ertrag; **nonrecurring** ~s außerordentliche Erträge; **normal** ~ Durchschnittsgewinn; **operating** ~ Betriebsgewinn, Gewinn aus der Hauptbetriebstätigkeit, betriebsbedingter Ertrag, gewerblicher Gewinn, Gewerbeertrag; **optimum** ~ optimaler Gewinn; **overall** ~ Gesamterlös; **paper** ~ rechnerischer (noch nicht realisierter) Gewinn, Buchgewinn, spekulative Gewinnerwartungen; **pretax** ~ Gewinn vor Berücksichtigung der Steuern; ~ **ploughed (plowed, US) back** nicht entnommener (stehengelassener) Gewinn; **prospective** ~ zu erwartender Gewinn; **pure** ~ Unternehmerreingewinn; **realized (secured)** ~ erzielter (realisierter) Gewinn; ~ **retained** thesaurierter Gewinn; **sales** ~s Gewinne aus Veräußerungen, Veräußerungserlöse; **secret** ~ versteckter Gewinn; ~ **set aside** abgezweigter Gewinn; **shave-off** ~ verkürzter Gewinn, Ertragseinbuße; **shrivel(l)ing** ~s schwindende Gewinne, Erlösrückgang; **slight** ~ mäßiger Gewinn; **small** ~ geringer Verdienst; **soaring** ~s rapid ansteigende Gewinne; **speculative** ~ Spekulationsgewinn; **surplus** ~s überschießender Gewinn, Gewinnüberschuß, Reingewinn; **artificially swollen** ~s künstlich aufgeblähte Gewinne; **after-tax** ~ Erträge nach Steuern, Gewinne nach Abzug der Steuern; **taxable** ~ steuerpflichtiger (zu versteuernder) Gewinn; **taxed** ~ versteuerter Gewinn; **trading** ~ Betriebs-, Geschäftsgewinn; **unapplied** ~s nicht verwendeter (ausgeschütteter) Gewinn; **unappropriated** ~ (US) für die Dividendenausschüttung verfügbarer (nicht ausgeschütteter) Gewinn, unverteilter Reingewinn, thesaurierter Gewinn; **undistributed net** ~ (Br.) unverteilter Reingewinn; **undivided** ~s unausgeschütteter (unverteilter) Gewinn; **unlawful** ~s Gewinne aus einem nicht genehmigten Gewerbe; **unrealized** ~ stehengelassener Gewinn, nicht realisierter Gewinn; **unwithdrawn** ~ nicht entnommener Gewinn, Entnahmeverzicht; **war** ~ Kriegsgewinn; **windfall** ~ unerwarteter Gewinn, Zufallsgewinn; **winding-up** ~ Liquidationserlös; **yearly** ~ Jahresertrag;
net ~ **available for appropriation** zur Ausschüttung zur Verfü-

gung stehender Nettoertrag; ~s **on the sale of fixed assets** Gewinne aus dem Verkauf von Anlagegütern, realisierte Verkaufserlöse aus dem Anlagevermögen; ~s **of the business** Geschäfts-, Betriebsgewinn; ~s **of (from) capital** Kapitalerträge; ~s **prior to consolidation** Gewinn vor der Fusionierung, Vorgründungsgewinn; ~ **in common** gemeinsame Nutzung fremder Grundstücke; ~s **chargeable to corporation tax** der Körperschaftssteuer unterworfene Gewinne, körperschaftssteuerpflichtige Gewinne; ~ **before depreciation** Ertrag vor Vornahme der Abschreibungen; ~ **available for dividend** Bilanzgewinn; **undivided** ~s **at end of year** unverteilte Jahresschlußgewinne; ~s **on an estate** Grundstücksrendite; ~s **on exchange** Kursgewinne; **projected net** ~ **expected to be earned over the period of advance** während der Darlehnszeit erwartete Nettoeinnahmen; ~ **of the group** Konzerngewinn; ~ **on investment** Gewinn aus Kapitalanlagen, Kapitalerlös; ~ **and loss** Gewinn und Verlust; ~ **from operations** (US) Unternehmergewinn; [net] ~ **from (on) operations** (US) Betriebs[rein]-, Nettobetriebsgewinn; ~ **due from participations** Erträgnisse aus Beteiligungen; ~ **from patents and secret processes** (balance sheet, US) Gewinne aus Monopolen, Monopolerlöse; ~ à **prendre** Holz-, Gras-, Torfgerechtigkeit; ~s **of profession or vocation** freiberufliche Einkünfte, Einkünfte aus freiberuflicher Tätigkeit; ~ à **rendre** Nutzungen; ~ **retained and added to reserve** den Rücklagen zugeführte Gewinn; ~ **on sale** Veräußerungserlös; ~ **gross** ~ **on sales** Umsatz-, Warenrohgewinn, Bruttoerlös; ~ **on sale of motor car** beim Autoverkauf erzielter Gewinn; ~ **attributable to shareholders** für die Aktionäre zur Verfügung stehender Gewinn; ~ **issuing from stocks** Aktienrendite; ~s **before taxation** Ertrag vor Abzug der Steuern; **attributable** ~ **before taxation** steuerpflichtiger Gewinn; ~ **after tax** Gewinn nach Steuern; ~ **before tax** Gewinn vor Steuern, Vorsteuergewinn; ~s **brought within the charge of tax** der Steuerpflicht unterliegende Gewinne; ~s **from trade or business** Einkünfte aus Gewerbebetrieb, Gewerbeeinkünfte; ~ **on a transaction** Erlös einer Transaktion; ~ **per unit** Erlös pro Verkaufseinheit; ~s **arising during a winding up** im Liquidationszeitraum entstandene Gewinne; ~ **derivable from work** aus Arbeit zu erwirtschaftender Gewinn; ~ **for the year** Jahresgewinn; ~ **brought forward from previous year** Gewinnvortrag aus dem Vorjahr;
~ (v.) nützen, von Vorteil sein, Nutzen bringen, Vorteil (Nutzen) ziehen, profitieren;
~ **by s. one's advice** sich jds. Ratschlag bestens dienen lassen; ~ **by a bargain** bei einem Geschäft profitieren; ~ **by experience** aus Erfahrung lernen; ~ **nothing** nichts einbringen; ~ **by an opportunity** Gelegenheit nutzen; ~ **from reading a book** Buch mit Gewinn lesen; ~ **by the tendency** Kurstendenz ausnutzen; **to allocate the** ~ **among the employees** Gewinn unter die Angestellten verteilen; **to apportion part of the** ~s **to a particular tax year** Gewinnanteile steuerlich auf ein bestimmtes Jahr aufteilen; **to ascertain the** ~ Gewinn feststellen; **to attribute** ~s Gewinne steuerlich zurechnen; **to bring in** ~ nutzbringend sein, Gewinn abwerfen; **to bring in good** ~s reichen Ertrag einbringen; **to capitalize** ~s Gewinne aktivieren; **to clear a** ~ Reingewinn erzielen; **to compute** ~s Gewinne einkalkulieren; **to conceal** ~s Gewinne verschleiern; **to cut into** ~s Gewinnmarge beschneiden; **to derive a** ~ **from s. th.** Nutzen aus etw. ziehen; **to determine the** ~ Gewinn feststellen (ermitteln); **to distribute** ~s Gewinne verteilen; **to divide** ~s Gewinne ausschütten; **to do s. th. for** ~ etw. gewerbsmäßig betreiben; **to draw** ~s Gewinne erzielen; **to eat up one's** ~s seine Gewinne aufzehren; **to exhibit large** ~s große Gewinne vorweisen; **to extract no unusual** ~ **from s. th.** keinen bedeutenden Gewinn aus etw. ziehen; **to gain** ~ **from one's studies** von seinen Studien profitieren; **to get back into** ~ Gewinnschwelle wieder erreichen; **to get only a small** ~ **for one's money** nur geringen Nutzen aus etw. ziehen; **to have produced zero** ~ **to date** bisher noch keinen Gewinn gemacht haben; **to have taken a course with** ~ Nutzen aus einem Kursus gezogen haben; **to hold down** ~s Gewinne niedrig halten; **to hurt** ~s Gewinne nachteilig beeinflussen; **to improve away one's** ~s seine Gewinne aufzehren; **to increase one's** ~s seinen Ertrag steigern; **to leave a** ~ Nutzen (Gewinn) abwerfen (bringen); **to lock in the** ~ Gewinn kassieren; **to lock up** ~ Gewinn nicht ausschütten; **to make a** ~ verdienen; **to make a** ~ **out of s. th.** Nutzen aus etw. ziehen (herauswirtschaften); **to make a good** ~ **out of a transaction** an einem Geschäft verdienen, Gewinn aus einem Geschäft ziehen, Transaktion mit Gewinn abschließen; **to make huge** ~s schwer verdienen, riesige Gewinne erzielen; **to make illicit** ~s unerlaubte Gewinne einstreichen; **to make a** ~ **of a shilling on every article sold** beim Verkauf jedes Stücks einen

Shilling verdienen; **to mop** ~s hohe Gewinne kassieren; **to operate at a** ~ mit Gewinn arbeiten; **to partake in** ~s am Gewinn teilnehmen; **to participate in the** ~ Gewinnanteil haben; **to place the** ~s **to s. one's account** jds. Konto mit dem Erlös erkennen; **to plow (plough,** *Br.***)** **back** ~s **into research** Gewinnrücklagen für Forschungszwecke einsetzen; **to prorate** ~s Gewinne anteilsmäßig aufteilen; **to put down to** ~ **and loss** in die Erfolgsrechnung einsetzen; **to realize a** ~ Gewinn erzielen; **to reap a** ~ Gewinn einstreichen; **to render a** ~ Nutzen abwerfen; **to repatriate** ~s Gewinne transferieren; **to retain** ~s **for expansion** thesaurierte Gewinne für Investitionen verwenden; **to run for** ~ auf Renditebasis betreiben; **to secure** ~s Gewinne erzielen, *(stock exchange)* Gewinne mitnehmen; **to sell at a** ~ mit Gewinn verkaufen; **to share in** ~s am Gewinn beteiligt sein, Gewinnanteil haben; **to shove up** ~s Gewinnchancen verbessern; **to show a** ~ Gewinn, Ertrag aufweisen (bringen); **to show a good** ~ ertragreich sein; **to siphon (skim) off** ~s Gewinn abschöpfen, Gewinnabschöpfung vornehmen; **to split the** ~s Gewinne untereinander aufteilen; **to study s. th. to one's** ~ bei der Beschäftigung einer Sache profitieren; **to take** ~s Gewinne realisieren, Gewinne mitnehmen; **to trim** ~s Gewinne beschneiden; **to turn s. th. to** ~ aus etw. Nutzen ziehen; **to turn to one's** ~ sich zunutze machen; **to turn a healthy** ~ angemessene Gewinne erzielen; **to work a mine at a** ~ Bergwerk mit Gewinn betreiben; **to yield fair** ~s angemessene Gewinne abwerfen; **to yield a** ~ **over the book value** den Buchwert übersteigenden Erlös abwerfen;

~ **account** Gewinnkonto, Gewinn-, Erfolgsrechnung; ~ **and loss account (statement)** Gewinn- und Verlust-, Erfolgsrechnung; ~ **and loss accounts** Erfolgskonten; ~ **and loss summary account** Gewinn- und Verlustsammelkonto; **to pass to** ~ **and loss account** auf Gewinn- und Verlustkonto buchen; ~ **agreement (arrangement)** Gewinn[beteiligungs]vereinbarung, -vertrag; ~ **amount** Gewinnbetrag; ~ **analysis** Ertragsanalyse; ~ **balance** Gewinn nach Vortrag, Gewinnsaldo, -überschuß; ~ **basis** Gewinnbasis; ~-**bearing** gewinnträchtig; ~ **builder** gewinnförderndes Element; **net** ~ **calculation** Reineinnahmenschätzung; ~ **carryforward** Gewinnvortrag; ~ **center** Erfolgsbereich eines Unternehmens; ~-**centered** gewinnorientiert; ~ **chance** Gewinnchance; ~ **claims** Gewinnanspruch; ~ **commission** Erfolgsprovision; ~ **contribution** Deckungsbeitrag, Bruttogewinn; **to turn the** ~ **corner** Gewinnschwelle überschreiten; ~ **costs** Ertragsaufwand; ~ **decline** Gewinnrückgang; ~ **development** Gewinnentwicklung; **to show considerable** ~ **diminutions** beträchtlichen Ertragsrückgang aufweisen; ~ **dip** Erlös-, Gewinnrückgang; ~ **distribution** Gewinnverteilung; **hidden** ~ **distribution** versteckte Gewinnausschüttung; **mandatory** ~ **distributions under agreement** *(balance sheet)* an konzernfremde Gesellschaften abgeführter Gewinn; ~ **drop** Gewinnabfall, -rückgang; **excess** ~s **duty** *(Br.)* Mehrgewinnsteuer; ~ **earner** Gewinnträger, -faktor; ~ **earning** rentabel, gewinnbringend; ~-**earning capacity** Ertragsfähigkeit, Rentabilität; ~-**earning possibilities** Ertragschancen; ~ **erosion** Gewinnerosion; ~ **expectations** Gewinnaussichten, -erwartungen; ~ **and loss expenses** Handlungsunkosten; ~ **explosion** Gewinnexplosion; ~ **figures** Gewinnzahlen, -ziffern; **interim** ~ **figures** zwischenzeitliche Ertragswerte; ~ **forecast** Gewinnprognose, Ertragsvorschau; ~ **forward** Gewinnvortrag; **minor coinage** ~ **fund** *(US)* Gewinn aus Prägung von Scheidemünzen; ~ **goals** Gewinnabsichten; ~ **growth** Gewinnzuwachs; ~ **guarantee** Gewinngarantie; ~-**guaranteeing contract** Gewinngarantievertrag; ~ **improvement** Erlös-, Ertrags-, Gewinnverbesserung; ~ **incentive** Gewinnmotiv; ~ **insurance** Gewinnausfallversicherung, Gewinnverlustversicherung; ~ **maker** Ertrags-, Erlös-, Gewinnfaktor; ~ **making** Gewinnerzielung; ~-**making** auf Gewinn gerichtet, gewinnbringend; ~-**making ability** Gewinneigenschaft; ~ **margin** Verdienst-, Gewinn-, Erlösspanne, Gewinnmarge, *(limit)* Ertragsgrenze; ~ **maximation** Gewinnmaximierung; ~ **motive** Gewinnmotiv, -streben, -prinzip; ~ **opportunity** Gewinnmöglichkeit, -chance; ~ **orientation** Profit-, Gewinnorientierung; ~ **outlook** Ertrags-, Gewinnaussichten; ~ **picture** Ertragsbild; ~ **pinch** Erlös-, Gewinnverknappung; ~ **planning** Gewinnmaximierung, -planung; **long-range** ~ **planning** langfristige Erfolgsplanung; ~ **pooling** Gewinnpooling, -teilung; ~-**pooling agreement** Gewinngemeinschaft; ~ **potential** Gewinnpotential; ~ **potentiality** Gewinnmöglichkeit; ~-**producing** gewinnbringend, einträglich, ertragreich; ~ **projection** Gewinnvorschau, -projektion; ~ **prospects** Gewinnaussichten; ~ **ratio** Gewinnverhältnis, -quote; ~ **record** Rekordhöhe der Gewinne; ~-**reducing** erlös-, ertrags-, gewinnmindernd; ~ **responsibility** Renditever-

antwortung; ~ **review** Ertragsprüfung; ~s **rise** Gewinnsteigerung; **with** ~s **scheme** *(life insurance)* mit Gewinnbeteiligung; ~ **seeking** Gewinnstreben; ~-**seeking** auf Gewinn gerichtet; ~-**seeking motive** Gewinnmotiv; ~ **share** Anteil am Gewinn, Erlös-, Gewinnanteil.

profit sharing Beteiligung am Gewinn, Erfolgs-, Ertragsbeteiligung, *(employees)* Gewinnbeteiligung, Partnerschaft, Lohnkorrektur;

deferred ~ aufgeschobene Gewinnbeteiligung; **employee** ~ Gewinnbeteiligung des Arbeitnehmer; ~ **and loss sharing** Gewinn- und Verlustbeteiligung;

~ **by the workmen** Arbeitergewinnbeteiligung;

~ **agreement (arrangement)** Gewinnbeteiligungsvertrag, -vereinbarung; ~ **bond** *(US)* Schuldverschreibung mit Gewinnbeteiligung, Gewinnobligation; ~ **employee** gewinnbeteiligter Arbeitnehmer; ~ **fund** Gewinnbeteiligungsfonds; ~ **goals** Gewinnbeteiligungsziele; ~ **payment in cash** Barauszahlung aus einer Gewinnbeteiligungsvereinbarung; **to set up a** ~ **plan** Gewinnbeteiligungsvertrag abschließen; ~ **and loss sharing ratio** Gewinn- und Verlustbeteiligungsschlüssel; ~ **scheme** Gewinnbeteiligungsplan; **to initiate (start) a** ~ **scheme** Gewinnbeteiligung einführen (ins Leben rufen); ~ **sharing trust** Investmentfonds; ~ **system** Erfolgsanteilsystem.

profit|shrinkage Gewinnschrumpfung; ~ **situation** Erlös-, Ertragsanlage, -situation; ~ **slide** rasanter Gewinnrückgang; ~ **slump** Erlös-, Gewinneinbruch; ~ **squeeze** Verminderung der Gewinnspanne, Gewinnrückgang, Gewinnverdeckung, -druck; ~s **system** kapitalistisches System; ~ **taker** Nutznießer; ~ **taking** *(stock exchange)* Gewinnsicherung, -mitnahme, -realisierung; ~-**taking sales** Realisierungsverkäufe, Gewinnmitnahmen; ~ **target** Gewinnplanziel; ~s **tax** *(Br.)* Ertrags-, Gewinnsteuer; **excess**-~s **tax** *(US)* Mehrgewinnsteuer, Kriegssteuer; **undistributed** ~s **tax** Steuer auf stehengelassenem Gewinn; ~ **transfer** Gewinnabführung; ~ **trend** Gewinnentwicklung, -trend; ~ **variables** *(US)* veränderliche Gewinnfaktoren (Gewinngrößen); ~-**yielding** ertragreich.

profitability Wirtschaftlichkeit, Einträglichkeit, Rentabilität; ~ **of net worth** Rentabilität des Eigenkapitals; ~ **graph** Rentabilitätsdiagramm; ~ **index of stock held** Rentabilitätsziffer des Warenlagers; ~ **level** Gewinnschwelle; ~ **ratio** *(US)* Gewinn je Kapitaleinheit; ~ **trend** Erlös-, Ertragstendenz.

profitable *(yielding gain)* gewinnbringend, gewinn-, ertragreich, einbringlich, einträglich, wirtschaftlich, rentabel, rentierlich, *(useful)* vorteilhaft, nützlich;

mutually ~ für beide Teile vorteilhaft;

to be ~ [sich] rentieren; **to be** ~ **for all** sich für alle auszahlen; **to find a transaction** ~ Nutzen aus einem Geschäft ziehen; **to stay** ~ Gewinnposition beibehalten;

~ **advice** nützlicher Ratschlag; ~ **basis** Gewinnschwelle; **to be on a** ~ **basis** Gewinnschwelle überschritten haben, mit Gewinn arbeiten; ~ **business** einträgliches (rentables) Geschäft; ~ **earner** Gewinnträger; ~ **employment** einträgliche Beschäftigung; ~ **enterprise** rentabler Betrieb, lebensfähiges Unternehmen; ~ **investment** lohnende (gewinnbringende) Anlage, rentable Kapitalanlage; ~ **operation** Gewinnbetrieb; ~ **profession** einträglicher Beruf; **to put a company on the more** ~ **road** Firma gewinnträchtiger machen; ~ **speculation** vorteilhaftes Spekulationsgeschäft; **to put on a** ~ **track** ertragsfähig machen, Rendite erwirtschaften; ~ **trade** einträgliches Gewerbe.

profitableness Wirtschaftlichkeit, Rentabilität.

profitably mit Gewinn, vorteilhaft;

to lay out one's money ~ sein Geld nutzbringend anlegen; **to study** ~ mit Erfolg studieren; **to use one's time** ~ seine Zeit nutzbringend verwerten.

profiteer Geschäftemacher, Schieber, Schwarzhändler, Profitgeier, -jäger, Wucherer;

war ~ Kriegsgewinnler;

~ *(v.)* Schiebergeschäfte machen, schieben.

profiteering Geschäftemacherei, Preistreiberei, Wuchergeschäfte, Schiebung, Schiebertum;

~ **in land** überhohe Spekulationsgewinne im Immobilienhandel;

~ **Act** *(Br.)* Gesetz zur Kontrolle der Geschäftsbücher; ~ **job** Schiebergeschäft.

profitless ohne Nutzen;

to be engaged in a ~ **task** umsonst arbeiten.

profitmonger Wucherer, Profitjäger.

profitmongering wucherisch.

profligacy unsittlicher Lebenswandel, Lasterhaftigkeit, Verworfenheit, *(squandermania)* Verschwendungssucht.

profligate *(v.)* **one's inheritance** sein ganzes Erbteil durchbringen.

proforma Proforma, zum Schein, *(product)* voraussichtlicher Verkauf;
~ **account** Proformarechnung, fingierte Verkaufsrechnung; ~ **account sales** zum Kalkulationsvergleich vorgenommener Proformaabschluß; ~ **balance sheet** fiktive Bilanz; ~ **bill** Keller-, Gefälligkeits-, Proformawechsel; ~ **invoice** fingierte Rechnung, Proformarechnung; ~ **purchase** Scheinkauf, Proformageschäft; ~ **receipt** Scheinquittung; ~ **sale** Scheinverkauf, ~ **statement** fiktive Bilanz; ~ **transaction** Proforma-, Scheingeschäft.

profound inhaltsschwer, profund;
~ **arguments** durchdachte Argumente; ~ **book** tiefschürfendes Buch; ~ **interest** tiefgreifendes Interesse; ~ **knowledge** tiefschürfende Kenntnisse, profundes Wissen; ~ **learning** umfassendes Wissen; ~ **respect** größte Hochachtung; ~ **thinker** tiefgründiger Denker.

profundity of knowledge tiefgründiges Wissen.

profuse freigiebig, verschwenderisch, großzügig;
to be ~ **in one's apologies** sich vielmals bedanken; **to be** ~ **in one's praise** überreichliches Lob spenden;
~ **expenditure** übermäßige (verschwenderische) Ausgabenwirtschaft; ~ **gratitude** überfließende Dankbarkeit; **to give with a** ~ **hand** überreichlich spenden.

profusely | illustrated reichhaltig (üppig) illustriert;
to praise s. o. ~ j. überschwenglich loben.

profusion Verschwendung, Vergeudung, Luxus;
to make promises in ~ freigiebig überall Versprechungen machen.

progency Ab-, Nachkommen[schaft], *(fig.)* Frucht, Produkt, Ergebnis;
~ **of war** Kriegsfolgen, Früchte des Krieges.

progenitor [geistiger] Ahne, Vorläufer.

progeniture Nachkommenschaft.

prognosis Prognose, Vorausschätzung, -schau, Vorhersage;
to give a very serious ~ sehr ernste Prognose stellen.

prognostic Vorhersage, Prophezeiung;
advisory ~ prognostische Dispositionsberatung;
~ **of development** Entwicklungsvorhersage; ~ **of failure** Fehlervoraussage.

prognosticate *(v.)* vorhersagen, prognostizieren.

prognostication Vorhersage, Vorschau;
~**s into the future** Zukunftsprognosen; ~**s of war** Kriegsvorzeichen.

prognosticator Konjunkturprognostiker.

program(me) Programm, Plan, *(broadcasting)* Rundfunkprogramm, Sendung, Sendefolge, *(festival)* Festprogramm, *(pol.)* Parteiprogramm, *(schedule of work)* Arbeitsplan, *(theatre)* Spielplan;
aid ~ Hilfsprogramm; **bread-and-butter** ~ wirklichkeitsnahes Programm; **broadcast** ~ Rundfunkprogramm; **comprehensive** ~ umfassendes Programm; **cooperative** ~ *(advertising)* Gemeinschaftswerbesendung; **crash** ~ Sofortprogramm; **electioneering** ~ Wahlprogramm; **executive development** ~ Programm für die Weiterbildung von Führungskräften; **financial** ~ Finanzplan; **full-length** ~ abendfüllendes Programm; **high-rated** ~ beliebtes Fernsehprogramm; **housing** ~ Wohnungsbauprogramm; **low-cost housing** ~ Plan für die Beschaffung billiger Wohnungen (von Sozialwohnungen); **ladies'** ~ Damenprogramm; **legislative** ~ Gesetzgebungsprogramm; **manufacturing** ~ Produktionsprogramm; **opposite** ~ *(broadcasting)* Kontrast-, Konkurrenzprogramm; **overall compensation** ~ umfassendes System zusätzlicher Vergünstigungen; **overseas broadcast** ~ überseeisches Rundfunkprogramm; **party** ~ Parteiprogramm; **planned** ~ geplantes Programm; **political** ~ politisches Programm; **production** ~ Produktionsprogramm, -plan; **radio** ~ *(US)* Rundfunkprogramm; **recorded** ~ auf Tonband (Dose) aufgenommenes Programm; **recreational** ~ Freizeit-, Erholungsprogramm; **relief** ~ Hilfsplan, -programm; **working** ~ Arbeitsplan, -programm;
~ **for achievement** Förderungsprogramm; ~ **for action** Aktionsprogramm; ~ **for coverage** Betreuungsprogramm; ~ **of personal development** persönlicher Fortbildungsplan; ~ **of the government** Regierungsprogramm; ~ **of investment** Investitionsprogramm, -vorhaben; ~ **of a meeting** Sitzungsprogramm; ~ **of research** Forschungsprogramm;
~ *(v.)* Programm gestalten (aufstellen), *(computer)* programmieren;
to adhere strictly to a ~ sich streng an ein Programm halten; **to arrange a** ~ Programm gestalten; **to be thrown in the** ~ ins Programm eingestellt werden; **to draw up a** ~ Arbeitsplan

(Programm) aufstellen; **to outline one's** ~ sein Programm skizzieren (umreißen); **to record a television** ~ **from the air** Fernsehprogramm auf Band aufnehmen; **to spare a** ~ **from meat-axe cuts** scharfe Einsparungsmaßnahmen eines Programms verhindern; **to watch a television** ~ Fernsehprogramm anschauen;
~ **advertising** Theater-, Kinowerbung; ~ **analysis** Programmanalyse, *(television)* Programmanalysegerät; ~ **announcement** Programmansage; ~ **budget** Istetat; ~ **description** Programmbeschreibung; ~ **director** Programmdirektor, Sendeleiter; ~ **flow** Programmablaufplan; ~ **evaluation and review technique** Projektfortschrittsplanung; ~ **management** Programmdirektion; ~ **music** Programmusik; ~ **picture** Nebenfilm; ~ **planner** Programmhersteller, *(television)* Fernsehproduzent; ~ **parade** *(broadcast)* Programmvorschau; ~ **producer** Programmhersteller; **to hold the lead in** ~ **ratings** führende Stellung bei Hörerbefragungen einnehmen; ~ **seller** Programmverkäufer.

programmatic programmatisch.

programmed instruction programmiertes Lehrmaterial.

programmer Programmgestalter, *(computer)* Programmierer;
television ~ Fernsehproduzent.

program(m)ing Programmgestaltung, *(computer)* Programmierung;
[non]linear ~ [nicht] lineare Programmierung.

progress *(onward course)* Fortgang, Verlauf, Entwicklung, *(expedition)* Expedition, Reise, Tour, *(improvement)* Verbesserung, Fortschritt, Weiterentwicklung;
in ~ im Werden; **in full** ~ in vollem Gange; **in** ~ **of time** im Laufe der Zeit;
~ **achieved** erzielter Fortschritt; **company** ~ Entwicklung eines Unternehmens; **economic** ~ wirtschaftlicher Aufschwung; **engineering** ~ technischer Fortschritt; **good** ~ Gedeihen, Vorankommen; **marked** ~ merklicher Fortschritt; **personal** ~ persönliche Entwicklung; **technological** ~ technologischer Fortschritt;
~ **achieved in respect of a matter** in einer Angelegenheit erzielter Fortschritt; ~ **of an army** Vorrücken einer Armee; ~ **of business** Konjunkturverbesserung; ~ **in civilization** Fortschritt der Zivilisation; ~ **of a disease** Überhandnehmen einer Krankheit; ~ **of economics** wirtschaftliche Fortschritte; ~ **of events** Gang der Ereignisse; ~ **of thought** Gedankenentwicklung; ~ **of title** *(Scot., law)* Eigentumsurkundenkette;
~ *(v.)* *(career)* Fortschritte machen, vorankommen, sich weiterentwickeln, beruflich vorwärtskommen;
~ **by leaps and bounds** glänzend vorankommen; ~ **towards completion** seiner Vollendung entgegengehen; ~ **towards a place** auf einen Platz vorrücken; ~ **steadily** langsam aber sicher vorankommen; ~ **with one's studies** mit seinem Studium vorankommen; ~ **for some time** sich noch einige Zeit hinziehen; **to be in** ~ im Gange sein; **to be making** ~ vom Fleck kommen; **to bring about a better** ~ **of representation** seine Repräsentationspflichten verstärkt wahrnehmen; **to gauge the** ~ **made** Fortschritte abschätzen; **to make** ~ Fortschritte machen, guten Fortgang (Verlauf) nehmen, *(negotiations)* vom Fleck kommen; **to make astonishing** ~ erstaunliche Fortschritte machen; **to be making good** ~ *(patient)* sich erholen; **to make great** ~ gut vorankommen; **to make little** ~ **in a fog** wegen Nebels nur langsam vorankommen; **to make rapid** ~ *(disease)* schnell um sich greifen; **to make slow** ~ langsam fortschreiten; **to make** ~ **in one's studies** mit seinen Arbeiten vorankommen; **to report** ~ über Fortschritte berichten; **to stop** ~ Fortschritt aufhalten;
~ **billing** *(US)* Fakturierung von Halbfabrikaten; ~ **certificate** Arbeitsfortschrittsbescheinigung; ~ **chart** Entwicklungsdiagramm; ~ **chaser (clerk)** Ablaufsplaner; ~ **control** Arbeitskontrolle; ~ **payment** proratarische Bezahlung; ~ **report** Arbeitsfortschrittsbericht, Tätigkeitsbericht, *(on employee)* Beurteilung [eines Probeangestellten]; ~ **sharing** Erfolgsbeteiligung am Produktivitätszuwachs; ~ **test** Klausur für Fortgeschrittene.

progression Fortschreiten, Progression, Steigerung, Stufenfolge, *(lapse of time)* Verlauf, *(taxation)* Staffelung;
arithmetical ~ arithmetische Progression; **geometrical** ~ geometrische Progression;
~ **wages** gestaffelte Löhne.

progressionist Fortschrittler.

progressive fortschrittlich eingestellter Mensch, Fortschrittler;
~ *(a.)* modern, fortschrittlich, schrittweise, *(person)* fortschrittlich eingestellt, *(tax)* progressiv, gestaffelt;
to be ~ Fortschrittsanhänger sein;
~ **advance** ständiger Fortschritt; ~ **approximation** *(EG)* schrittweise Angleichung; ~ **assembly** Fließbandmontage; ~ **disease** zunehmende (progressive) Krankheit; ~ **education** fortschritt-

liche Erziehungsmethoden; **~-minded** fortschrittlich gesinnt; **~ movement** Vorwärtsbewegung; **~ numbers** laufende Nummern; **~ operations** Fließbandarbeit; **~ organization** fortschrittliches Unternehmen; **~ party** *(US)* Fortschrittspartei; **~ policy** progressive Politik; **~ political party** fortschrittlich eingestellte Partei; **~ proof** Farbandruck; **~ rate** Staffelsatz, *(interest)* progressiver Zinssatz; **~ rates of taxation** Staffelung der (gestaffelte) Steuersätze; **~ rent** Miete mit automatischer Steigerungsklausel; **~ removal of restrictions** stufenweiser Abbau von Beschränkungen; **~ scale of tax rates** progressiver Steuertarif; **by ~ stages** stufenweise; **~ step** Schritt nach vorn; **~ tax** nach oben gestaffelte (progressive) Steuer, Progressionssteuer; **~ taxation** progressive Besteuerung, **~ tendencies** fortschrittliche Strömungen; **~ wages** mit der Produktion steigende Löhne; **~ wage rate** Progressivlohn.

progressivity of taxation progressive Besteuerung.
prohibit *(v.)* verbieten, untersagen.
prohibited verboten, untersagt, unzulässig;
  ~ area Sperrzone, -gebiet; **~ articles** Schmuggelware, Konterbande; **~ class of risks** nicht versicherbare Risiken; **~ degrees** verbotene Verwandtschaftsgrade; **~ goods** Schmuggelware, Konterbande; **~ list** Verbotsliste; **~ punishment** unzulässige Bestrafung; **~ risk** *(insurance)* nicht versicherungsfähiges Interesse; **~ aerial space** Luftsperrgebiet; **~ transaction** verbotenes (unzulässiges) Rechtsgeschäft; **~ transport** Beförderungsverbot; **~ zone** Sperr-, Grenzgebiet, Verbotszone.
prohibition Untersagung, *(US)* [Alkohol]verbot, Prohibition;
  in favo(u)r of ~ *(US)* prohibitionsfreundlich;
  export ~ Ausfuhrverbot; **marriage ~** Eheverbot; **statutory ~** gesetzliches Verbot;
  ~ to deliver Auslieferungs-, Lieferverbot; **~ of employment** Beschäftigungsverbot; **~ of exports** Export-, Ausfuhrverbot; **~ of frontier traffic** Grenzsperre; **~ of imports** Einfuhrverbot; **~ of interest** Zinsverbot; **~ of issue** Emissionssperre; **~ from sailing** Abfahrverbot; **~ to sell** Veräußerungsverbot; **~ of trade** Handelsverbot;
  to ignore a ~ Verbot nicht achten; **to impose a ~** Verbot erlassen;
  ~ laws *(US)* Prohibitionsgesetz; **~ notice** Verbotshinweis; **~ sign** Verbotszeichen.
prohibitionism Schutzzollsystem.
prohibitionist Schutzzöllner, *(US)* Alkoholgegner;
  ~ country Land mit Alkoholverbot.
prohibitive verhindernd, verbietend, untersagend, vorbeugend;
  ~ cost untragbare Kosten; **~ duty** Schutz-, Prohibitiv-, Sperrzoll; **~ price** unerschwinglicher Preis; **~ system** Schutzzoll-, Prohibitivsystem; **~ tax** prohibitive Steuer.
prohibitory|law Verbotsgesetz; **~ legislation** Verbotsgesetzgebung.
project Projekt, Plan, Entwurf, Vorhaben, *(research work)* Forschungsunternehmen, *(school, US)* Planaufgabe;
  development ~ Entwicklungsvorhaben; **final ~** endgültiger Entwurf; **financed ~** finanziertes Vorhaben; **financial ~** Finanzprojekt; **high-technology ~** technologisch aufwendiges Projekt; **hush ~** Geheimprojekt; **ill-fated ~** unter einem Unglücksstern stehendes Projekt; **industrial ~** Wirtschaftsprojekt; **investment ~** Investitionsvorhaben, -projekt; **joint ~** gemeinsames Projekt; **preliminary ~** Vorentwurf; **specific ~** bestimmtes Vorhaben;
  ~ now in agitation (under discussion) zur Diskussion stehendes Projekt; **~ in the planning stage** in der Planung befindliches Projekt; **~ supported by taxes** aus Steuern finanziertes Projekt;
  ~ *(v.)* entwerfen, planen, vorhaben, erwägen, *(be busy, US coll.)* eifrig mit einem Plan beschäftigt sein, *(imagine)* sich bildhaft vorstellen, *(v/i)* vorspringen, vorragen;
  ~ adequately *(broadcasting programme)* angemessen wiedergeben; **~ a beam of light on s. th.** Lichtstrahlbündel auf etw. richten; **~ beyond the building line** Baufluchtlinie überschreiten; **~ one's feelings into** seine Gefühle übertragen auf; **~ a journey** Reise planen; **~ a missile into space** Geschoß in den Weltraum befördern; **~ o. s. into the past** sich in die Vergangenheit zurückversetzen; **~ a plan** Plan entwerfen; **~ a picture on a screen** Bild auf die Leinwand werfen; **~ a new railway line** neue Eisenbahnlinie projektieren; **~ a shadow** Schatten werfen; **~ o. s. into the world of tomorrow** sich in die Welt von morgen versetzen;
  to carry out (engineer) a ~ Projekt durchführen; **to engage in a ~** Vorhaben in Angriff nehmen; **to sell s. o. a ~** jem. ein Projekt schmackhaft machen; **to upset a ~** Projekt zu Fall bringen; **to withdraw from a political ~** sich aus einem politischen Unternehmen zurückziehen;

~ agreement Projektabkommen; **~ analyst** Projektberater; **~ appraisal** Projektbewertung; **~ control** Projektkontrolle, -steuerung; **~ engineer** Projektingenieur; **~ evaluation** Projektbewertung; **~ execution** Projektdurchführung; **~ financing** Projektfinanzierung; **~ funds** Projektmittel; **~ identification** Projektauswahl; **~ leader** Projektleiter; **~ management** Projektleitung, Planung, Organisation, Durchführung und Kontrolle eines Projekts; **~ manager** Projektleiter; **~ officer** Projektbearbeiter; **~ performance** Projektdurchführung; **~ report** Projektbericht; **~ team** Projektgruppe; **~ tying** Projekt-, Zweckbindung.
projected financial statement zukünftiger Finanzstatus.
projectile Geschoß, Projektile.
projection Planung, Planen, *(photo)* Vorführung, Projektion, *(prognosis)* Vorhersage, Prognose, *(sample)* Ergebnisübertragung auf die Gesamtheit;
  Mercator's ~ Merkators Kartenprojektion;
  ~ of profit Gewinnplanung, -projektion; **~ of a new railway line (railroad, US)** Projektierung einer neuen Eisenbahnlinie;
  ~ apparatus Vorführ-, Projektionsapparat; **~ booth** Vorführkabine; **~ error** Prognosefehler; **~ machine** Projektions-, Vorführgerät; **~ room** Vorführraum; **~ screen** Projektions-, Bildwand; **~ system** Projektionsvorrichtung.
projectionist Filmvorführer, *(television)* Fernsehmechaniker.
projector Gründer, *(photo)* Bildwerfer, Projektionsapparat, *(swindler)* Spekulant;
  cinema ~ Vorführ[ungs]apparat, Filmvorführanlage; **floodlight ~** Flutlichtscheinwerfer; **picture ~** Bildwerfer.
prolabor *(US)* gewerkschaftsfreundlich.
proletarian Proletarier;
  ~ (a.) proletarisch.
proletariat Proletariat.
proliferation starke Vermehrung, Verbreitung, *(politics)* Weitergabe von Atomwaffen.
prolific author fruchtbarer Schriftsteller.
prolix weitschweifig, umständlich.
prolixity *(pleadings)* Weitschweifigkeit.
prolocutor Wortführer, Sprecher.
prologue Einleitung, Vorwort, Prolog.
prolong *(v.)* verlängern, *(bill of exchange)* prolongieren, Fälligkeit hinausschieben;
  ~ one's leave seinen Urlaub verlängern; **~ a visit** Besuchsdauer ausdehnen.
prolongation [Frist]verlängerung,, Aufschub, *(allonge)* Verlängerungsstück, *(bill of exchange)* Prolongation, Prolongierung;
  ~ of an agreement Vertragsverlängerung; **~ of a bill** Wechselprolongation; **~ of a meeting** Sitzungsverlängerung; **~ of payment** Stundung, Zahlungsaufschub; **~ of time** Nachfrist, Terminverlängerung;
  ~ agreement Verlängerungsabkommen; **business ~** Prolongationsgeschäft; **~ clause** *(marine insurance)* Verlängerungsklausel.
prolusion kurze Abhandlung.
promenade Spaziergang, *(public walk)* Promenade, *(college ball, US)* Studentenball;
  ~ deck Promenadendeck.
prominence Prominenz, Berühmtheiten;
  to come into ~ in den Vordergrund treten, prominent werden; **to give ~ to an idea** Idee hervorheben.
prominent prominent, berühmt;
  to play a ~ part in civic life im Leben der Stadt eine prominente Rolle spielen; **~ playgoers** Abonnentenpublikum; **~ position** bedeutsame Stellung.
promiscuous unterschiedslos, buntgewürfelt;
  ~ charges diverse Kosten; **~ friendship** leichtfertig geschlossene Freundschaft; **~ hospitality** Gastfreundschaft gegenüber jedermann; **~ sexual intercourse** Promiskuität; **~ standards** schwankende Wertmaßstäbe.
promise Versprechen, Zusage, Zusicherung;
  under ~ of secrecy unter dem Siegel der Verschwiegenheit; **absolute ~** absolutes Versprechen; **bare ~** abstraktes Schuldversprechen; **binding ~** bindende Zusage; **conditional ~** bedingtes Versprechen; **contractual ~** Vertragszusage; **election ~** Wahlversprechen; **express ~** ausdrückliches Versprechen; **fictitious ~** unterstellte Verpflichtung; **gratuitous ~** Versprechen ohne Gegenleistung; **joint ~** Gesamthandsverpflichtung; **mutual ~** Gegenseitigkeitsverpflichtung; **naked ~** abstraktes Schuldversprechen; **new ~** Schuldanerkenntnis; **parol ~** mündliches Versprechen, mündliche Zusage; **solemn ~** ehrenwörtliches Versprechen; **unlawful ~** unsittliches Versprechen;

~ to finance Finanzierungszusage; **~ to make a gift** Schenkungsversprechen; **~ of guarantee or suretyship** Bürgschaftsvertrag; **~ of help** Unterstützungs-, Hilfszusage; **~ of a loan** Darlehnszusage; **~ of marriage** Heiratsversprechen; **~ to pay [the debt of another]** Zahlungsversprechen; **~ of reward** Auslobung; **~ under seal** [etwa] notarielles Versprechen; **unconditional ~ in writing** unbedingtes schriftliches Versprechen;
~ (v.) versprechen, sich verpflichten, zusagen, *(reward)* Belohnung aussetzen;
~ to come auf eine Einladung hin zusagen; **~ an immediate safety** Schutz zusichern; **~ well** zu den besten Hoffnungen berechtigen;
to carry out (deliver) a ~ Versprechen erfüllen; **to feed s. o. with empty ~s** j. mit leeren Versprechungen hinhalten; **to give a solemn ~** hoch und heilig versprechen; **not to show much ~** keine guten Resultate aufweisen.
promisee Versprechungsempfänger.
promising vielversprechend, verheißungsvoll, günstig;
to look ~ sich gut anlassen, *(harvest)* gut stehen;
~ market erfolgversprechender Absatzmarkt; **to be in a ~ state** guten Ausgang erwarten lassen; **~ undertaking** erfolgversprechendes Unternehmen.
promisor Versprechensgeber.
promissory note Schuldschein, schriftliches Versprechen, *(bill of exchange)* eigener (trockener) Wechsel, Eigen-, Solawechsel, Eigenakzept, Promesse;
joint ~ Gesamtschuldschein; **joint and several ~** gesamtschuldnerischer Solarwechsel;
~ made out to bearer Inhaberwechsel; **~ made out to order** Ordertratte; **~ payable on demand** Sichttratte.
promote *(v.) (advance to higher position)* befördern, *(advertise, US)* Reklame machen, anpreisen, propagieren, *(float)* gründen, *(support)* fördern, unterstützen, begünstigen, befürworten, vorantreiben;
~ a bill in Parliament Gesetzentwurf initiieren; **~ a new business company** *(Br.)* neue Gesellschaft gründen; **~ good feelings between ...** Beziehungen zwischen ... fördern; **~ s. o. to an office** j. in eine Stellung aufrücken lassen; **~ with priority** bevorzugt befördern; **~ a pupil to a higher class** Schüler in eine höhere Klasse versetzen; **~ the sale** Verkauf fördern; **~ a scheme** Plan unterstützen; **~ s. o. from the shadows** völlig unbekannten Kandidaten fördern.
promoted gefördert, befördert;
to be ~ nachrücken, avancieren, in eine höhere Rangstufe befördert werden; **to be about to be ~** zur Beförderung anstehen; **to be ~ over s. one's head** vor jem. befördert werden; **to be ~ in order of age** nach Dienstjahren befördert werden; **to be preferentially ~** bevorzugt befördert werden; **to be ~ to a higher rank** in einen höheren Rang befördert werden; **to be ~ by selection** außer der Reihe befördert werden; **to be ~ by seniority** nach Dienstjahren befördert werden.
promoter *(furtherer)* Förderer, Gönner, *(of joint stock company)* Gründer, *(organizer)* Organisator, Veranstalter;
company ~ Firmengründer;
~ of a company Firmen-, Gesellschaftsgründer; **~ of a meeting** Veranstalter einer Versammlung; **~ for the occasion** Veranstalter;
~'s expenses Gründungsaufwand, -kosten; **~'s shares (stocks, US)** Gründeraktien.
promoterism Gründungsschwindel.
promoting Aufstellen von Kandidaten;
~ from within Besetzung leitender Stellen aus dem eigenen Bereich (Betrieb);
~ syndicate *(Br.)* Gründerkonsortium.
promotion *(advertising, US)* Reklame, Werbung, Propagierung, *(furtherance)* Unterstützung, Begünstigung, Befürwortung, Förderung, Hebung, *(marketing)* Verkaufsförderung, *(to higher rank)* Beförderung, *(of joint stock company)* Gründung;
~s Werbezwecke;
given adequate ~ bei angemessener Verkaufsförderung;
business ~ wirtschaftliche Förderung; **continuity ~** *(US)* Verkaufsförderung von Sammelartikeln; **corporate ~** betriebliche Förderung; **direct-mail ~** *(US)* Werbung durch Postversand; **executive ~** Beförderung von Führungskräften; **export ~** Exportförderung; **government ~** staatliche Förderung; **in-class ~** Beförderung in eine höhere Gehaltsstufe; **instore ~** *(US)* im Laden betriebene Verkaufsförderung; **lineal ~** Beförderung der Reihe nach; **product ~** auf einen bestimmten Artikel abgestellte Verkaufsförderung; **sales ~** Verkaufswerbung, -förderung; **special ~s** *(retail trade)* Sonderveranstaltungen; **volume incentive ~** mengenmäßige Leistungsförderung;

~ of companies Gründungsgeschäft; **~ of employment** Arbeitsbeschaffung; **~ of exports** Ausfuhrförderung; **~ of imports** Importförderung; **~ of industries** Förderung der Wirtschaft; **~ of investments** Investitionsförderung; **~ to an office** Amtseinsetzung; **~ of prospective managers** Nachwuchsförderung; **~ of science** Förderung der Wissenschaften; **~ by selection** Beförderung außer der Reihe; **~ by seniority** Beförderung nach dem Dienstalter; **~ of tourism (tourist traffic)** Fremdenverkehrsförderung; **~ of trade** Wirtschaftsförderung;
to be in line of (on one's, down for) ~ in der Beförderung an der Reihe sein, zur Beförderung anstehen; **to forward s. o. for a ~** j. für eine Beförderung eingeben; **to get one's ~** befördert werden; **to mark out for ~** zur Beförderung vorsehen; **to merit ~** Förderung verdienen; **to urge one's ~** auf seine Beförderung hinarbeiten; **to win ~** befördert werden;
~ allowance *(US)* Reklamenachlaß, Werberabatt; **sales-~ budget** Verkaufsförderungsetat; **sales-~ campaign** *(US)* Verkaufsförderungsplan; **~ and advertising costs** *(US)* Werbungskosten; **~ department** *(US)* Werbeabteilung; **~ exercise** *(US)* Werbeaktion; **~ expense** Gründungskosten, -aufwand; **~ gimmick** *(US)* Werbegag; **~ list** Beförderungsliste; **~ manager** *(US)* Werbeleiter; **~ matter** *(US)* Verkaufsförderungs-, Werbematerial; **~ money** *(Br.)* Gründungsaufwand, -kosten, Finanzierungskosten; **~ plan** Beförderungsplan; **~ practice** Beförderungsverfahren; **~ roster** Beförderungsliste, -plan; **sales-~ technique** *(US)* Verkaufsförderungsverfahren; **~ shares (stock, US)** Gründeraktien.
promotional fördernd, *(US)* werbend;
~ activity Förderungsmaßnahmen; **~ arrangements** Beförderungsbestimmungen; **~ chart** Beförderungstabelle; **~ examination** Aufstiegsprüfung; **~ expenses** *(US)* Werbungskosten, Werbeaufwand; **~ idea** *(US)* verkaufsfördernde Idee; **~ literature** *(US)* Werbematerial; **~ material** *(US)* Werbematerial, *(personnel)* Beförderungsunterlagen; **~ measures** Förderungsmaßnahmen; **~ opportunity** Aufstiegsmöglichkeit; **~ policy** Beförderungspolitik; **~ program(me)** Beförderungsplan, -programm; **~ push** energische Förderungsmaßnahmen; **~ rise** *(Br.) (raise, US)* Gehaltsaufbesserung bei einer Beförderung; **~ roster** Beförderungsliste; **~ selling** Werbeverkäufe; **~ status** Beförderungsaussichten; **~ support** *(US)* verkaufsfördernde Maßnahmen; **~ system** Beförderungswesen, -system; **~ value** *(US)* Werbewert.
promotive fördernd, begünstigend;
~ of monopoly *(US)* monopolfördernd.
prompt *(theater)* Souflieren, *(time limit)* Ziel, Zahlungsfrist, Kaufvertrag mit Zahlungsziel;
at a ~ of three months mit einer Frist von drei Monaten, drei Monate Ziel, mit Dreimonatsziel;
~s *(Br.)* sofort lieferbare Ware;
~ (a.) (immediate) baldmöglichst, prompt, unverzüglich, sofort, *(payment)* bar, *(punctual)* pünktlich, prompt;
~ to volunteer hilfsbereit;
~ (v.) s. o. with an answer jem. eine Antwort suggerieren; **~ to riot** zum Aufruhr antreiben; **~ a witness** Zeugen beeinflussen;
to take ~ action Sofortmaßnahmen einleiten; **~ answer** umgehende Antwort; **~ attention to an order** sofortige Auftragserledigung; **~ box** *(theater)* Souffleurkasten; **for ~ cash** gegen Barzahlung (sofortige Kasse); **~ day** *(London, stock exchange)* Abrechnungstag; **~ decision** sofortige Entscheidung; **~ delivery** Lieferung innerhalb kürzester Frist, sofortige Lieferung; **~ forwarding** sofortiger Versand; **~ note** Mahnzettel, Verkaufsnota, Schlußschein mit Lieferfristangabe; **~ payer** pünktlicher Zahler; **~ payment** pünktliche (prompte) Zahlung; **~ reply** sofortige (schnelle, prompte, schlagfertige) Antwort; **~ service** prompte Bedienung; **~ shipment** sofortiger Versand.
promptbook *(theater)* Text-, Soufflierbuch.
prompting, on the ~ of auf Veranlassung von.
promptitude, promptness Bereitwilligkeit *(in payment)* Promptheit, Pünktlichkeit.
promptly sofort;
to arrive ~ auf die Minute pünktlich sein; **to deal ~ with** sofort erledigen; **to pay ~** pünktlicher Zahler sein, pünktlich zahlen.
promulgate *(v.)* [Gesetz] verkünden, öffentlich bekanntgeben, veröffentlichen.
promptness of delivery pünkliche Lieferung.
promulgation öffentliche Bekanntmachung, Verkündigung, [Gesetz]veröffentlichung.
prone *(fig.)* geneigt, empfänglich, anfällig veranlagt;
~ to accidents unfallanfällig; **~ to crisis** krisenanfällig; **~ to a disease** krankheitsanfällig; **~ to superstition** abergläubisch;
to become more ~ to settle abschlußbereiter werden.

proneness|to crisis Krisenanfälligkeit; ~ **to speculate** Spekulationssucht.

pronounce *(v.)* verkünden, aussprechen, *(sentence, award)* fällen; ~ **an acquittal** Freispruch verkünden; ~ **against s. o.** sich gegen j. äußern; ~ **upon s. th.** Erklärung über etw. abgeben; ~ **a judgment** Urteil verkünden; ~ **for (in favo(u)r of) a proposal** Vorschlag befürworten; ~ **a sentence of death** auf Todesstrafe erkennen, Todesurteil fällen; ~ **the signature to be a forgery** Unterschrift für gefälscht erklären; ~ **on a subject** in einer Sache entscheiden.

pronounced *(tendency)* deutlich erkennbar; ~ **improvement** sichtliche Besserung; **to have very ~ views** sehr bestimmte (dezidierte) Ansichten haben.

pronouncement Verkündigung, Proklamation, *(declaration)* Erklärung; ~ **of judgment** Urteilsverkündung.

pronunciation, incorrect fehlerhafte Aussprache.

proof Nachweis, Beweis, Beweismittel, -grund, *(bankruptcy)* Nachweis, *(photo)* Probebild, -abzug, *(print.)* Korrekturbogen, -fahne, Probeabdruck, Andruck, *(test)* Erprobung, Probe; **as ~** als Beweis; **failing (in the absence of) ~** in Ermangelung von Beweisen; **in ~ of delivery** zum Nachweis der Lieferung; **in ~ of his claim** zum Nachweis seines Anspruchs; **[not] capable of ~** [nicht] beweiskräftig; **~s** *(documentary evidence)* Beweismittel; **accessory ~** Nebenbeweis; **affirmative ~** überzeugender Beweis; **author's ~** Autorenkorrektur; **brush ~** *(print.)* Bürstenabzug; **cast-iron ~** schlagender Beweis; **clean ~** *(print.)* Revisionsbogen; **conclusive ~** schlüssiger (zwingender) Beweis; **convincing ~** überzeugender Beweis; **copy ~** Korrekturabzug; **badly corrected ~** schlechte Korrekturen; **documentary ~** urkundliches Beweismaterial, Urkundenbeweis; **double ~** *(bankruptcy)* doppelte Anmeldung einer Forderung; **final ~** letzter Korrekturabzug; **first ~** *(print.)* erste Korrektur, Vorkorrektur, Fahnenabzug; **formal ~** formeller Beweis; **foul ~** schlechter Abzug; **full ~** vollgültiger Beweis; **galley ~** Druckfahne; **half ~** Anscheinsbeweis; **legal ~** Rechtsnachweis; **machine ~** Maschinenabzug; **negative ~** negativer Beweis; **open-letter ~** *(print.)* Abzug mit offener (voller) Schrift; **policy ~** Nachweis durch Police allein; **positive ~** endgültiger (voller) Beweis; **preliminary ~** *(insurance)* erster Schadensnachweis; **press ~** druckfertiger Korrekturbogen; **progressive ~** Farbandruck, -satzskala; **revised ~** verbesserte Korrektur, Probeabzug für die zweite Korrektur, zweiter Korrekturbogen; **satisfactory ~** hinreichende Glaubhaftmachung; **signed ~** signierter Abzug; **slip ~** Fahnenabzug, -korrektur; **specious (sham) ~** Scheinbeweis; **stereotyped ~** Plattenabzug; **striking ~** schriftlicher Beweis; ~ **of ability** Befähigungsnachweis; ~ **of authenticity** Echtheitsbeweis; ~ **of authority** Nachweis der Vertretungsbefugnis; ~ **in bankruptcy** Forderungsnachweis, -anmeldung [im Konkursverfahren]; ~ **of a claim** Anspruchsbegründung, Anspruchsnachweis, *(bankruptcy)* Forderungsanmeldung, -nachweis; ~ **of competency** Befähigungsnachweis; ~ **to the contrary** Gegenbeweis; ~ **of conveyance** Beförderungsnachweis; ~ **of death** Todesnachweis, Nachweis des Ablebens; ~ **of a debt** Forderungsnachweis, Anmeldung im Konkursverfahren; ~ **for dividend** *(bankruptcy proceedings)* Nachweis der Konkursquotenberechtigung; ~ **by documentary evidence (of documents)** urkundlicher Beweis, Urkundenbeweis; ~ **beyond any reasonable doubt** keinen Zweifel lassender Beweis; ~ **by the evidence of witnesses** Zeugenbeweis, schriftliche Zeugenaussage; ~ **evident or presumption great** *(accused)* dringender Tatverdacht; **clear ~ of guilt** klarer Schuldbeweis; ~ **of one's identity** Legitimation, Personalausweis, Nämlichkeitszeugnis, Identitätsnachweis; ~ **of indebtedness** Schuldtitel; ~ **of insolvency** Nachweis der Zahlungsunfähigkeit, Überschuldungsnachweis; ~ **of loss** Schadensnachweis, *(fire insurance)* Schadensanzeige; ~ **of nationality** Nachweis der Staatsangehörigkeit; ~ **of need** Bedürftigkeitsnachweis; ~ **of origin** Herkunftsnachweis; ~ **of performance** Leistungsnachweis; ~ **of qualification** Befähigungsnachweis; ~ **of a right** Rechtsnachweis, Feststellung eines Rechts; ~ **of service** Zustellungsnachweis; ~ **of spirits** Feststellung des Alkoholgehalts; ~ **for voting** *(bankruptcy proceedings)* Nachweis der Stimmberechtigung; ~ **of a will** Testamentseröffnung, Bestätigung der Gültigkeit eines Testaments; ~ **of a witness** *(solicitor, Br.)* schriftliche Niederlegung der geplanten Zeugenaussage;

~ *(a.)* gewappnet, gefeit, sicher, *(drink)* normalstark, *(evidence)* stichhaltig;

~ **against bribes (corruption)** unbestechlich; ~ **against bullets** kugelsicher;

to admit of an easy ~ sich leicht beweisen lassen; **to be put to strict ~** klar beweisen müssen; **to challenge a ~** es auf die Probe ankommen lassen; **to furnish ~** Beweise liefern; **to give ~ of s. th.** etw. unter Beweis stellen, Nachweis führen; **to give ~ of one's nationality** seine Nationalität nachweisen; **to lead ~** *(Scot.)* Beweis antreten; **to lodge a ~** [of debt] **in bankruptcy** zur Konkurstabelle anmelden, Nachweis einer Forderung erbringen, [Konkurs]forderung anmelden; **to offer ~** Beweise anbieten; **to pass the ~s for press** Druckerlaubnis erteilen; **to pay s. o. a sum upon submission of ~ of identity** jem. gegen Vorlage seines Personalausweises einen Betrag auszahlen; **to produce ~ to the contrary** Gegenbeweis führen; **to produce documents in ~ of a claim** Dokumente zum Beweis seiner Ansprüche vorlegen; **to pull a ~** Abzug machen, Korrekturabzug anfertigen, andrücken; **to read the ~s** Korrekturen besorgen (lesen); **to require ~s of a statement** Beweise für eine Behauptung verlangen; **to show ~** nachweisen; **to stand a ~** Probe bestehen; **to take ~s in galley** Satz in Fahnen abziehen; **to turn in a ~ of debt** Konkursforderung anmelden; **to work off a ~** Korrekturabzug anfertigen, andrücken;

~ **coin** Probemünze; ~**-correct** Korrekturen lesen; ~ **correction** Korrekturenbesorgung; ~ **drive** Probefahrt; ~ **impression** *(print.)* Probeabzug; **bullet-~ jacket** kugelsichere Weste; ~ **leaf** Korrekturabzug; ~ **load** Probebelastung; ~ **print** Revisionsbogen; ~ **puller** Fahnenabzieher; ~ **sheet (slip)** Korrekturbogen, Probeabzug, -druck, Druckfahne; ~ **value** *(bankruptcy proceedings)* Wert einer nachgewiesenen Konkursforderung.

proofread *(v.)* Korrekturen lesen.

proofreader Korrekturenleser, Korrektor; ~**'s mark** Korrekturzeichen.

proofreading Korrekturenlesen.

proofroom Korrektorensaal.

prop [Stütz]pfahl, *(fig.)* Halt, Stütze; ~ **of his parents** Stütze seiner Eltern.

propaganda propagandistische Tätigkeit, Propaganda, *(contemptuous)* Lügenpropaganda, *(scheme of propagation)* Propagandaplan, *(publicity)* Reklame, Werbetätigkeit, Werbung; **atrocity ~** Greuelpropaganda; **belligerent ~** Kriegspropaganda;

~ **of the enemy** Feindpropaganda; ~ **by government departments for better driving** staatliche Aufklärungsaktion für die Verkehrssicherheit; **to make ~** Propagandatrommel rühren, werben; **to serve as good ~** gute Reklame abgeben; **to set up ~ for s. th.** Propaganda (Reklame) für etw. machen; **for ~ advantages** aus Reklamegründen; ~ **apparatus** Propagandaapparat; ~ **balloon** Werbeballon; ~ **barrage** Werbehindernis; ~ **broadcast** Werbesendung; **to make ~ capital out of s. th.** Kapital aus etw. schlagen; ~ **efforts** Werbeanstrengungen; **to harvest a ~ feast** reichlich Propaganda aus etw. schlagen; ~ **film** Propaganda-, Werbefilm; ~ **leaflet** Werbeprospekt; ~ **offensive** Werbeoffensive, Propagandaoffensive; ~ **organization** Propagandaorganisation, -unternehmen; ~ **play** Propagandastück; ~ **purpose** Propagandazweck; ~ **value** Propagandawert; ~ **week** Reklame-, Werbewoche; ~ **writings** Reklameschriften.

propagandism Propagandawesen, propagandistische Tätigkeit.

propagandist Propagandist.

propagandize *(v.)* sich mit Propaganda beschäftigen, propagandieren.

propagate *(v.)* propagieren, verbreiten; ~ **news** Nachrichten verbreiten.

propagation Verbreitung, Propagierung.

propagator Propagandist.

propelled angetrieben.

propeller Luftschraube, Propeller; ~**-driven** mit Schraubenantrieb.

propelling pencil Drehstift.

propensity Neigung, Hang; ~ **to buy (purchase)** Kauflust, -bereitschaft; ~ **to consume** Konsumfreudigkeit, -neigung; ~ **to exaggerate** Übertreibungssucht; ~ **to export** Exportneigung; ~ **to invest** Anlagebereitschaft, Investitionsfreudigkeit, -neigung; ~ **to save** Sparbereitschaft, -freudigkeit; ~ **to spend** Ausgabeneigung, -bereitschaft; **to have a ~ for getting into debt** zum Schuldenmachen neigen.

proper richtig, passend, angemessen, geeignet, *(correct)* sach-, ordnungsgemäß, *(due)* gebührend, *(coll., Br.)* anständig, gehörig, richtig, *(competent)* maßgebend, zuständig, *(decent)* anständig, schicklich, korrekt;

~ **to certain regions** in bestimmten Gebieten auftretend; **to be ~ for an occasion** der Gelegenheit angemessen sein; ~ **accounts** buchhalterisch richtige Abrechnung; ~ **independent advice** unabhängiger fachmännischer Rat; **to be of a ~ age to sign** unterschriftsberechtigt sein; **not a very ~ attitude** nicht gerade das richtige Verhalten; ~ **authority** zuständige Behörde; ~ **behavio(u)r** ordentliches Benehmen; ~ **care** hinreichende Sorgfalt; **through the ~ channels** auf dem Dienstwege; ~ **clothes (dress)** korrekte Kleidung; **to paint s. o. in his ~ colo(u)rs** j. im wahren Licht schildern; **in ~ condition** in ordnungsgemäßem Zustand; ~ **custody** ordnungsgemäße Aufbewahrung; ~ **evidence** zugelassene Beweismittel; **in the ~ form** formgerecht; ~ **fraction** gewöhnlicher Bruch; ~ **interpretation** richtige Auslegung; ~ **law** zuständiges Gesetz; ~ **lodging** angemessene Unterbringung; ~ **lookout** *(motorist)* vernünftige Fahrweise; ~ **meaning** eigentliche Bedeutung; **to use only ~ means** nur einwandfreie Mittel anwenden; ~ **measures** geeignete Maßnahmen; **to be in a ~ mess** ganz schön durcheinander sein; ~ **name** Eigenname; **due and ~ notice** ordnungsgemäß zugestellte Kündigung; ~ **party** richtige Prozeßpartei; ~ **and convenient place** geeignete Stelle; **to apply to the ~ quarters** sich an die richtige Adresse wenden; **at the ~ rate** zum Tarifsatz; ~ **receipt** ordnungsgemäße (rechtsgültige) Quittung; **to take action at the ~ season** zum richtigen Zeitpunkt handeln; **in the ~ sense** im eigentlichen Sinn; **to be the ~ sort of man** genau der Richtige sein; ~ **state of affairs** geordnete Zustände; ~ **state of repair** ordnungsgemäßer Erhaltungszustand; ~ **surroundings** passende Umgebung; **at the ~ time** zeitgerecht; ~ **usage** sachgemäße Behandlung; **to put s. th. to its ~ use** etw. sachgemäß verwenden.

properly ordnungsgemäß;
~ **speaking** streng genommen;
to behave ~ sich anständig benehmen.

propertied begütert;
~ **classes** begüterte Kreise, besitzende Klassen.

properties Liegenschaften, Immobilien;
nonoperating ~ stillgelegte Betriebe; **onerous ~** belastetes (beschwertes) Vermögen.

property *(fortune)* Habe, Gut, Güter, Vermögen[sgegenstand], Vermögenswert, *(inn)* Lokal, Gaststätte, *(ownership)* Eigentum[srecht], *(piece of ~)* Grundstück, Stück Land, *(quality)* Eigenschaft, Eigentümlichkeit, Beschaffenheit, *(real estate)* Grundbesitz, -vermögen, Besitz[tum], Immobilien;
of handsome ~ bemittelt; **in (on) one's own ~** auf eigenem Grund und Boden;
abandoned ~ herrenloses Eigentum; **absolute ~** absolutes (unbeschränktes) Eigentum; **adjoining ~** Nachbargrundstück, angrenzendes Grundstück; **affected ~** entzogene Vermögenswerte; **after-acquired ~** später erworbenes Vermögen, *(wife)* nach der Heirat erworbenes Eigentum, nach der Eheschließung erworbenes Vermögen; **aggregate ~** Gesamteigentum, -vermögen; **alien ~** feindliches Vermögen, Ausländervermögen; **bailed ~** hinterlegte Vermögensstücke; **beneficial ~** Nießbrauch; **blocked ~** gesperrtes Vermögen; **built-on ~** bebautes Grundstück; **business ~** Geschäftsgrundstück; **cash ~** Barvermögen; **charged ~** belastetes Grundstück; **child's ~** Kindesvermögen; **collective ~** Gemeinschaftsvermögen; **commercial ~** gewerblich genutzter Grundbesitz; **common ~** Gesamtgut, gemeinsames Vermögen, *(municipal corporation)* Gemeindeeigentum, Gemeingut; **community ~** Gemeinschaftseigentum, *(US)* Güter-, Errungenschaftsgemeinschaft; **condemned ~** *(US)* enteignetes Grundstück; **confiscated ~** beschlagnahmtes Vermögen; **corporate ~** Eigentum der Gesellschaft, Gesellschaftsvermögen; **country ~** Landbesitz, -gut; **crown ~** *(Br.)* fiskalisches Eigentum, Staatsvermögen; **cultural ~** Kulturgüter; **debtor's ~** Schuldnervermögen; **depreciable ~** abschreibungsfähige Vermögenswerte; **disclaimed ~** herrenloses (verlassenes) Grundstück; **distrainable ~** massefreies Vermögen; **distributable ~** für die Gläubiger zur Verfügung stehendes Vermögen; **dotal ~** eingebrachtes Gut der Ehefrau; **downtown ~** *(US)* zentral gelegenes Grundstück; **dutiable ~** steuerpflichtiges Vermögen; **encumbered ~** belastetes Grundstück; **enemy ~** Feindvermögen; **enemy-controlled ~** vom Feind beschlagnahmtes Vermögen; **entailed ~** unveräußerlicher Grundbesitz; ~ **escheated** heimgefallenes Gut; **estate ~** Gutsbesitz; **exempt ~** unpfändbare Gegenstände, *(bankruptcy)* konkursfreies Eigentum; **external (foreign) ~** Auslandsvermögen; **factory ~** Betriebs-, Fabrikgrundstück; **family ~** Familienvermögen; **foreign-owned ~** im Eigentum eines Ausländers stehendes Vermögen, ausländisches Eigentum, Ausländervermögen; **freehold ~** Grundbesitz; **funded ~** in Effekten (Staats-

papieren) angelegtes Vermögen, Kapitalvermögen; **future-acquired ~** zukünftiges Vermögen; **general ~** unbeschränktes Eigentum; **government ~** fiskalisches Eigentum, Staatseigentum; **hot ~** heiß begehrtes Anlageprojekt; **house ~** Wohngrundstück; **identifiable ~** feststellbare Vermögensgegenstände; **immovable ~** *(US)* unbewegliches Vermögen, Liegenschaften, Immobilien; **improved ~** bebautes (erschlossenes) Grundstück; **income-producing ~** ertragabwerfendes (zinstragendes) Vermögen (Kapital); **incorporeal ~** immaterielle Vermögenswerte; **individual ~** persönliches Vermögen [eines Gesellschafters]; **industrial ~** Fabrik-, Industriegrundstück, gewerblich genutztes Grundstück, gewerbliches Eigentum; **intangible ~** immaterielle Vermögenswerte; **intellectual ~** geistiges Eigentum; **joint ~** Gesamthandseigentum, Gütergemeinschaft; **landed ~** Grundeigentum, -vermögen, unbewegliches Vermögen, Grundbesitz, Liegenschaften, Immobilien, Immobilienvermögen; **leased ~** verpachtetes Grundstück, Pachtgrundstück, Mietsache; **leasehold ~** [Erb]pachtgrundstück; ~ **left** Nachlaß, Hinterlassenschaft; ~ **let** vermietete Gebäude, verpachtete Grundstücke; ~ **let commercially** gewerbsmäßig verpachtetes Grundstück; **literary ~** geistiges Eigentum, Urheberrecht; **similarly located ~** Grundstück in gleicher Lage, ähnlich gelegenes Grundstück; **lost ~** Fundgegenstände, -sachen; **married woman's ~** Vermögen der Ehefrau; **maternal ~** mütterliches Vermögen; **no ~ worth mentioning** kein nennenswertes Vermögen; **mixed ~** bewegliches und unbewegliches Vermögen, Mischeigentum; **mortgaged ~** hypothekarisch belastetes Grundstück; **movable ~** *(US)* Fahrnis, bewegliche Habe, bewegliches Vermögen, Mobilien; **municipal ~** städtisches Eigentum, gemeindeeigenes Grundstück, Gemeindeeigentum, -vermögen; **national ~** Staats-, Volkseigentum, Nationalvermögen; **neutral ~** im Eigentum neutraler Staatsangehöriger befindliches Vermögen; **nondistributable ~** für die Gläubiger nicht zur Verfügung stehendes Vermögen; **nonessential ~** zufälliges Merkmal; **original ~** Anfangsvermögen; **own ~** eigenes Vermögen, Sondergut; **paraphernal ~** Zubehör, Gerät, *(wife)* eingebrachtes Gut, Vorbehaltsgut; **paternal ~** väterliches Vermögen; **pecuniary ~** bares Vermögen; **personal ~** bewegliches Vermögen (Eigentum), persönliches Eigentum, Mobiliarvermögen, Mobilien, *(inheritance)* beweglicher Nachlaß; **pledged ~** Pfandgut, -objekt, -sache, verpfändete Vermögensstücke; **present and future ~** gegenwärtiges und zukünftiges Vermögen; **private ~** Privateigentum, -vermögen; **public ~** Allgemeingut, öffentliches Eigentum, Staatseigentum; **qualified ~** zeitlich beschränktes Eigentumsrecht; **railway (railroad, US) ~** Bahneigentum; **real ~** unbeweglicher Nachlaß, Grund[stücks]eigentum, Grundbesitz, Immobilien[vermögen], Liegenschaften; **remaining ~** verbleibendes Vermögen, Restvermögen; **requisitioned ~** beschlagnahmtes Vermögen; **reserved ~** *(Br.)* Rückstellung für Abschreibungen; **residential ~** Wohngrundstück; **residuary ~** Nachlaß nach Zahlung aller Verbindlichkeiten; **restituted ~** rückerstatteter Vermögensgegenstand; **restricted ~** zweckgebundenes Vermögen, Zweckvermögen; **salvaged ~** gerettetes Vermögen; **separate ~** Sondervermögen, *(wife)* eingebrachtes Gut der Ehefrau, abgesondertes Vermögen, Vorbehaltsgut; **settled ~** *(Br.)* erbrechtlich gebundener Besitz, erbrechtlich gebundenes Sondervermögen; **shifting ~** *(insurance)* veränderliches Gut; **sizable ~** ansehnliches Vermögen; **slum ~** im Sanierungsgebiet gelegenes Grundstück; **small ~** Kleinlandbesitz; **special ~** beschränktes Eigentum, Sondervermögen, Fremdbesitz; **state ~** öffentliches Eigentum, Staatseigentum; **stolen ~** Diebesware; **store ~** *(US)* Laden-, Geschäftsgrundstück; **stranded ~** Strandgut; **tangible ~** greifbare Vermögenswerte; **aggregate taxable ~** steuerpflichtiges Gesamtvermögen; **territorial ~** Territorial-, Staatshoheitsgebiet; **top-quality office ~** Bürogrundstück in Spitzenlage; **trust ~** Treuhandvermögen; **unattachable ~** konkursfreies (pfändungsfreies) Vermögen; **undivided ~** Eigentum zur gesamten Hand; **vacant ~** nicht genutztes Grundstück, leerstehendes Haus; **void ~** leerstehendes Wohngrundstück; **waterfront ~** Ufergrundstück;
~ **acquired after adjudication** vom Gemeinschuldner nach Konkurseröffnung erworbenes Vermögen; ~ **acquired by fraud** unrechtmäßig erworbenes Vermögen; ~ **acquired during the marriage** während der Ehe erworbenes Vermögen, Errungenschaft; ~ **of another** *(US)* fremdes Eigentum, fremde Sache; ~ **lodged with a bank** bei einer Bank deponiertes Vermögen; ~ **of a bankrupt** Konkursmasse; ~ **of a capital nature** Kapitalvermögen; ~ **of a corporation** *(city)* städtisches Eigentum; ~ **charged as security for a debt** als Kreditsicherheit dienendes Grundstück; ~ **of a debtor** Konkursmasse, Schuldnervermögen; ~ **to**

be declared anmeldepflichtiges Vermögen; ~ **exempt from distribution in bankruptcy** konkursfreies Vermögen; ~ **and effects** Vermögen; ~**, plant and equipment** *(balance sheet, US)* Grundstücke und Gebäude, Maschinen und maschinelle Anlagen, Sachanlagen; ~ **exempt from estate duty** erbschaftssteuerfreies Vermögen; ~ **liable to estate duty** erbschaftssteuerpflichtiges Vermögen; ~ **in expectancy** Anwartschaftsvermögen; ~ **in the goods** Eigentum an den Waren; ~ **with the instalment option** Erbschaftssteuerraten unterliegendes Nachlaßvermögen; ~ **without the instalment option** sofort erbschaftssteuerpflichtiges Vermögen; ~ **in land** Grundvermögen, Grundbesitz; ~ **of material** Werkstoffeigenschaft; ~ **available for payment of debts** zur Schuldenbegleichung zur Verfügung stehendes Vermögen; ~ **to be reported** anmeldepflichtiges Vermögen; **small ~ for sale** *(ad, US)* kleines Grundstück zu verkaufen; ~ **listed for sale** *(US)* zum Verkauf gestelltes Grundstück; ~ **charged as security for a debt** als Kreditsicherheit dienendes Grundstück; ~ **held in fee simple** unbeschränkt vererbliches Grundeigentum; ~ **of state** *(US)* Staatseigentum; **no ~ worth mentioning** kein nennenswertes Vermögen; **to act as a trustee for one's** ~ jds. Vermögen verwalten; **to acquire** ~ Eigentum erwerben; **to alienate** ~ Vermögen veräußern; **to assess a** ~ **[for taxation]** Vermögen [steuerlich] bewerten; **to assign** ~ Vermögen übertragen; **to be s. one's** ~ j. zu Eigentum gehören; **to be common** ~ allgemein bekannt sein; **to be entire master of one's** ~ völlig frei über sein Vermögen verfügen können; **to be free with other people's** ~ mit fremdem Geld leichtsinnig umgehen; **to be generous with other people's** ~ großzügig mit fremdem Geld umgehen; **to be liable to the extent of one's** ~ mit seinem ganzen Vermögen haften; **to bring one's** ~ **into the commercial estate** sein Eigentum in die Gemeinschaft einbringen; **to charge** ~ Eigentum belasten; **to class as** ~ **transferred under fraudulent preference** unter vom Konkursgläubiger hinterzogene Vermögenswerte einrangieren; **to come into** ~ Besitz erben; **to come into a little** ~ kleines Vermögen erben; **to convert** ~ sich unberechtigt Eigentum aneignen; **to convey** ~ [Grundstücks]eigentum übertragen; **to cut s. o. out from one's** ~ j. von einem Vermögensanteil ausschließen; **to declare** ~ Vermögen anmelden; **to define** ~ Eigentum kennzeichnen; **to devise** ~ Vermögen vermachen; **to dispose of** ~ als Eigentümer verfügen; **to divide one's** ~ **among one's heirs** sein Vermögen unter seinen Erben verteilen; **to encumber** ~ Grundstück belasten; **to enter upon** ~ Vermögen in Besitz nehmen; **to get a** ~ **free from all encumbrances** Grundstück lastenfrei erwerben; **to have** ~ **in land** Land besitzen; **to have a** ~ **100% rented at all times** Haus ganzjährig vermietet haben; **to have a small** ~ **in the country** kleines Haus auf dem Land besitzen, etw. Grundbesitz haben; **to hold** ~ Eigentum haben (besitzen), Eigentümer sein; **to infringe on s. one's** ~ jds. Eigentum verletzen; **to keep a** ~ **fully insured** ausreichenden Versicherungsschutz für ein Grundstück unterhalten; **to lease** ~ Grundstück verpachten; **to leave** ~ **to one's wife for life with remainder to one's children** Ehefrau als Vorerben einsetzen; **to let off a** ~ **as a whole** Grundstück pauschal verpachten; **to let s. o. occupy a** ~ **without charging him for rent** j. mietfrei wohnen lassen; **to levy on the entire** ~ Vollstreckung in das gesamte Vermögen betreiben; **to locate the lines of a** ~ *(US)* Grundstücksgrenzen festsetzen; **to part with a** ~ Vermögensteil aufgeben; **to pledge one's** ~ sein Vermögen als Sicherheit stellen; **to price a** ~ Verkaufspreis für ein Grundstück festsetzen; **to purchase** ~ **with money to be advanced by a bank** Grundstückserwerb mittels Bankkredit finanzieren; **to put** ~ **into a trust** Vermögen einer Treuhandverwaltung unterstellen; **to put one's** ~ **under the control of a trustee in bankruptcy** sein Vermögen auf den Konkursverwalter übertragen; **to rate s. one's** ~ **at £ 1000 per annum** 1000 Pfund Vermögenssteuer für j. festsetzen; **to realize one's** ~ sein Vermögen flüssig machen; **to reinvest** ~ Eigentum zurückübertragen; **to remain the** ~ **of the seller** im Eigentum des Lieferanten verbleiben; **to remove** ~ *(bankrupt)* Vermögensstücke beiseite schaffen; **to renounce one's** ~ auf sein Vermögen verzichten; **to report** ~ Vermögen anmelden; **to reserve the right of** ~ sich das Eigentum vorbehalten; **to restore confiscated** ~ beschlagnahmtes Vermögen zurückgeben; **to retain the** ~ **in one's estate** Eigentum am Grundstück behalten; **to revest** ~ Eigentum wieder in Besitz nehmen; **to seize** ~ Vermögen beschlagnahmen; **to serve s. o. heir to a** ~ j. in den Besitz einer Erbschaft setzen; **to settle all one's** ~ **on one's wife** seiner Frau sein ganzes Vermögen hinterlassen; **to slice a piece** ~ Grundstückskomplex aufteilen; **to steal public** ~ Diebstahl an öffentlichem Eigentum begehen; **to survey a** ~ Grundstück ausmessen; **to take the** ~ **over** Eigentum übernehmen; **to take charge of s. one's** ~ jds. Vermögen beschlagnahmen; **to take private** ~ **for public use** Privatgrundstücke für öffentliche Zwecke enteignen; **to throw a** ~ **into business use** Grundstück für die Errichtung von Geschäftshäusern freigeben; **to transfer** ~ Vermögen übertragen; **to transmit one's** ~ **by will** sein Vermögen testamentarisch vermachen; **to trench upon s. one's** ~ jds. Eigentumsrechte beeinträchtigen; **to use a** ~ **for residential purposes only** Anwesen nur für Wohnzwecke nutzen; **to vest** ~ **in s. o.** Vermögen auf j. übertragen; **to write down** ~ Grundstück abschreiben;

~ **account** Sach-, Immobilien-, Anlagenkonto; ~ **accountability** Rechnungslegungsfrist für Grundbesitz; ~ **accounting** Anlagenbuchhaltung; ~ **accounting department** Anlagenbuchhaltung; **Married Woman's** ⌐ **Act** *(Br.)* Gesetz über die Verfügungsgewalt der Ehefrau über eingebrachtes Gut; ~ **assets** Vermögenswerte; ~ **balance** Vermögensbilanz; ~ **bombing** Bombenanbringung in Gebäuden; ~ **boom** Hausse auf dem Immobilienmarkt; ~ **brief** Grundstückspapiere; ~ **business** Immobiliengeschäft; ~ **capital** in Wertpapieren angelegtes Kapital; ~ **carve-up** Grundstücksaufsplitterung; ~ **company** Grundstücks-, Immobiliengesellschaft; ~ **conglomerate** Grundstückskonzern; ~ **control** Vermögensaufsicht, -kontrolle; ~ **corporation** Immobiliengesellschaft; ~ **cost record cards** Anlagenkartei; ~ **crime** *(US)* Eigentumsdelikt; **alien** ~ **custodian** *(US)* ausländische Vermögensverwaltung; ~ **damage** Sach-, Vermögensschaden; ~ **damage [liability] insurance** Sachschadenversicherung; ~ **deal** Grundstücksgeschäft; ~ **dealing** Grundstücks-, Bodenverkauf; ~ **dealing company** Immobiliengeschäft; ~ **and share-dealing company** Immobilienfonds; ~ **deed** Besitzurkunde; ~ **depreciation** Grundstücksabschreibung; ~ **developer** Immobilienmakler; ~ **development** Grundstückserschließung, Urbanisation; ~ **development costs** [Grundstücks]erschließungskosten; ~ **dividend** Dividende in Gestalt von Gratisaktien anderer Aktiengesellschaften, Sachwertdividende; ~ **finance consultant** Vermögensberater; ~ **holder** Eigentümer, Vermögensbesitzer; ~ **holdings** Vermögenswerte; ~ **income** Bruttoeinkommen aus Vermögen, Einkünfte aus Land- und Forstbesitz; ~ **increment tax** Wertzuwachssteuer; ~ **insurance** Sachversicherung; ~ **insurance market** Sachversicherungsmarkt; ~ **insurance stocks** Sachversicherungsaktien; ~ **interest** Vermögensanteil; ~ **investments** Anlagevermögen; ~ **investment company** Immobiliengesellschaft; ~ **investment market** Immobilienmarkt; ~ **investment opportunities** Anlagechancen im Immobilienbereich; ~ **issue form** Materialausgabeschein; ~ **law** Sachenrecht, *(US)* Liegenschaftsrecht; ~ **lawyer** Grundstücksspezialist, auf Immobilien spezialisierter Anwalt; ~ **ledger** Anlagen-, Grundstücks-, Betriebshauptbuch; ~ **levy** Vermögensabgabe; ~ **loss** Vermögensverlust, -schaden; ~ **maintenance** Gebäudeunterhaltung; ~ **man (master)** *(theater)* Requisiteur; ~ **management** Grundstücks-, Vermögens-, Anlagen-, Hausverwaltung; ~ **manager** Immobilien-, Grundstücks-, Hausverwalter; ~ **market** *(Br.)* Immobilien-, Grundstücksmarkt; **lost-~ office** Fundbüro; ~ **outfit** Immobilienfirma; ~ **owner** Vermögensträger, Haus-, Grundstückseigentümer, Haus-, Vermögensbesitzer; ~ **owners' association** Hausbesitzerverband; ~ **portfolio** Grundstücksportefeuille; ~ **price** *(Br.)* Grundstückspreis; ~ **provisions** Eigentumsbestimmungen; ~ **purchase** Grundstückskauf; ~ **qualification** Vermögens-, Eigentumsnachweis; ~ **rarity** einmaliges Grundstück; ~ **record** Liegenschaftsverzeichnis; ~ **register** *(Br.)* [etwa] Abteilung 1 des Grundbuchs; ~ **rents** Miet-, Pachteinkünfte; **found-~ report** Liste gefundener Gegenstände; ~ **reserve** Vermögensreserve; ~ **returns** Rücklieferungen der Kundschaft; ~ **right** Eigentumsrecht, -anspruch, Vermögensrecht; ~ **room** *(law court)* Asservatenraum, *(theater)* Requisitenkammer; ~ **sale** Grundstücksverkauf; ~ **settlement** Vermögensregelung; ~ **speculation** Grundstücksspekulation; ~ **speculator** Grundstücks-, Immobilienspekulant; ~ **statement** Vermögensaufstellung, -erklärung, -rechnung; ~ **structure** Eigentumsgefüge; ~ **sword** Theaterdegen; ~ **tax** *(Br.)* Vermögensbesteuerung, Grund- und Gebäude-, Besitzsteuer, *(US)* Vermögenssteuer; ~ **tax, general** ~ **tax** *(US)* Grundsteuer; ~ **tax assessment** Grundsteuerveranlagung; ~ **tax payable** *(US)* fällige Vermögenssteuer; ~ **tax receipt** *(US)* Vermögenssteuerbescheinigung; ~ **taxation** *(US)* Vermögensbesteuerung; ~ **tort** Vermögensschaden; ~ **value** *(Br.)* Grundstückswert, Besitz-, Eigentums-, Vermögenswert, *(real estate)* Gebäudewert, Grundstückswert; ~ **valuation** Vermögensbewertung; **to be widely respected in the** ~ **world** im Immobilienhandel einen guten Ruf genießen; **to bring** ~ **yields down** Immobilienrenditen verkürzen.

prophet Prophet, *(fig.)* Vorkämpfer, Fürsprecher;
weather ~ Wetterprophet;
~ of evil Unglücksprophet, Schwarzseher; **~ of socialism** Fürsprecher des Sozialismus.
propine *(Scot.)* Trinkgeld.
proponent *(Br.)* Antragsteller, *(last will, US)* präsumptiver Testamentserbe.
proportion *(part)* [An]teil, Verhältnis, Proportion, *(math.)* Verhältnisgleichung, Dreisatzrechnung, *(ratio)* Verhältnisziffer, Proportion;
in ~ to anteils-, verhältnismäßig, im Verhältnis, proratarisch; **out of all ~** in keinem Verhältnis stehend; **in due ~** im angemessenen Verhältnis; **in the ~ of one new share to every two old shares held** im Verhältnis 1 : 2 von neuen zu alten Aktien; **of gigantic ~s** von gewaltigen Ausmaßen; **out of ~** unverhältnismäßig, nicht im Verhältnis;
average ~ Durchschnittsanteil; **relative ~s** *(quantity)* Mengenverhältnis, *(size)* Größenverhältnis, Proportionen; **stated ~** fester (bestimmter) Anteil;
~ of costs Kostenanteil; **~ of liability** Haftpflichtanteil; **~ of the net load to the gross load** Verhältnis der Netto- zur Bruttobelastung; **~ of loss** Verlustanteil; **~ of profit** Gewinnanteil; **~ of property** Vermögensanteil; **~ of reserves to liabilities** Verhältnis der Reserven zu den Verbindlichkeiten;
~ *(v.)* anteilmäßig verteilen (bemessen), in ein [richtiges] Verhältnis bringen, anpassen;
~ one's expenses to one's income seine Ausgaben dem Einkommen anpassen;
to allow imports in ~ to exports Einfuhren nur im Verhältnis zu Exporten zulassen; **to be out of ~ to one's income** zum Einkommen in keinem Verhältnis stehen; **to bear no ~** in keinem Verhältnis stehen; **to build up an export of substantial ~s** erhebliches Exportgeschäft aufziehen; **to divide expenses in equal ~s** Unkosten umlegen; **to do one's ~ of a work** seinen Anteil bewältigen; **to have an eye for ~s** Augenmaß haben; **to lose all sense of ~** jedes Größenmaß überschreiten, erschreckende Dimensionen annehmen; **to pay one's ~ of the expenses** seinen Unkostenanteil übernehmen.
proportional proportional, anteils-, verhältnismäßig, entsprechend;
~ allotment Quote; **~ assessment** anteilsmäßige Veranlagung; **~ ballot** Verhältniswahl; **~ distribution of goods** mengenmäßige Güterverteilung; **~ frequency** *(statistics)* proportionale Häufigkeit; **~ rate** *(railroad)* Distanztarif; **~ representation [in voting]** Verhältniswahl; **~ representation system** Verhältniswahlsystem; **~ scale** Proportionalsystem; **~ schedule of tax rates** proportionaler Steuertarif; **~ share** Quote, Proportionalsatz, verhältnismäßiger Anteil; **~ tax system** proportionales Steuersystem; **~ taxation** Proportionalbesteuerung; **~ vote** Proportional-, Verhältniswahl.
proportionalism Verhältniswahlsystem.
proportionate anteilig, anteils-, verhältnismäßig, angemessen im richtigen Verhältnis;
~ charge Anteilsgebühr; **~ share** anteilmäßige Befriedigung; **to claim one's ~ share** seinen vollen Anteil beanspruchen.
proposal Vorschlag, Antrag, *(insurance)* Versicherungsantrag, *(marriage offer)* Heiratsangebot, *(trade)* Lieferungsangebot;
administrative ~ Vorschlag der Verwaltungsstellen; **alternative ~** Alternativ-, Gegenvorschlag; **committee's ~** Ausschußvorschlag; **counter ~** Gegenantrag; **draft ~** Vorschlagsentwurf; **farreaching ~s** weitgehende Vorschläge; **inadmissible ~** unannehmbarer Vorschlag; **~s received** eingegangene Anträge; **sealed ~** verschlossenes Angebot; **tax-cut ~** Steuersenkungsvorschlag;
~ for amendment [Ab]änderungsvorschlag; **~ of autonomy** Autonomievorschlag; **~ for a composition** Vergleichsvorschlag; **~ of insurance** Versicherungsantrag; **~ of marriage** Heiratsantrag; **~ of a motion** Einbringung eines Antrags, Antragsstellung; **~ for peace** Friedensvorschlag, -angebot; **~ for a settlement** Vergleichsvorschlag; **~ for a subscription** Subskriptionsangebot; **~s for increasing trade between two countries** Vorschläge für die Ausweitung des Handels zwischen zwei Staaten;
to accept a ~ Antrag annehmen; **to accept a ~ with unanimous approval** Vorschlag einstimmig gutheißen; **to adopt a ~** Vorschlag zustimmen; **to approve a ~** einem Vorschlag zustimmen; **to bottle up a ~** Vorschlag zu Fall bringen; **to enter a ~** Vorschlag einreichen; **to entertain a ~** Vorschlag in Erwägung ziehen; **to initiate a ~** Vorschlag machen; **to kill a ~** Vorschlag scheitern lassen; **to make a ~** Vorschlag machen; **to overrule a ~** Vorschlag verwerfen; **to place ~s before s. o.** jem. Vorschläge

unterbreiten; **to pronounce o. s. in favo(u)r of a ~** sich zugunsten eines Vorschlags aussprechen; **to put forward a ~** Vorschlag machen; **to put a ~ to the board** Vorschlag dem Vorstand zuleiten; **to receive a ~ favo(u)rably** Vorschlag günstig aufnehmen; **to reject (refuse) a ~** Vorschlag ablehnen; **to submit ~s** Vorschläge unterbreiten; **to think a ~ over** sich einen Vorschlag durch den Kopf gehen lassen;
~ bond Bietungsgarantie; **~ form** Antragsformular, *(insurance)* Policenformular.
propose *(v.)* vorschlagen, Vorschlag machen, in Vorschlag bringen, *(marriage)* Heiratsantrag machen, *(for membership)* zur Mitgliedschaft vorschlagen, *(motion)* Antrag stellen, beantragen, einbringen, *(toast)* Trinkspruch ausbringen;
~ a candidate Kandidaten vorschlagen (aufstellen, benennen); **~ s. o. for chairman** j. als Vorsitzenden vorschlagen; **~ a course of action** Handlungsmaxime vorschlagen; **~ a dividend** Dividende in Vorschlag bringen; **~ s. one's health** auf jds. Gesundheit anstoßen; **~ to an insurance company** Versicherungsantrag stellen; **~ marriage** Heiratsantrag machen; **~ a motion** Antrag stellen (einbringen); **~ a resolution** Resolution (Entschließungsantrag) einbringen; **~ an early start** frühe Abreise vorschlagen; **~ terms of a settlement** Vergleichsvorschlag machen; **~ a vote of censure** *(parl.)* Mißtrauensvotum einbringen; **~ a vote of thanks** Dankadresse beantragen.
proposed| amendment Abänderungsvorschlag; **~ budget** Haushaltsvorschlag; **~ distribution of profits** Gewinnverteilungsvorschlag.
proposer [of a motion] Antragsteller.
proposition Vorschlag, Antrag, *(offer)* Kauf-, Verkaufsobjekt, Angebot, *(plan)* Plan, *(project involving some action, coll.)* Sache, Geschichte, Problem, Angelegenheit;
business ~ geschäftlicher Vorschlag; **easy ~** kleine Fische, Kleinigkeit; **mining ~** Bergwerksunternehmen; **practical ~** praktisch durchführbare Aufgabe; **tough ~** schwierige Angelegenheit, schwieriger Fall;
to accept a ~ Vorschlag annehmen; **to come out strongly for a ~** Vorschlag kräftig unterstützen.
propound *(v.)* [Frage] vorlegen, vorbringen, unterbreiten;
~ for admission zur Aufnahme vorschlagen; **~ a will** *(executor)* Antrag auf Anerkennung eines Testaments stellen.
propounding a will Antragstellung auf Bestätigung eines Testaments.
proprietary Besitzstand, *(landed estate)* Grundstückseigentum, *(ownership)* Eigentumsrecht, *(proprietor)* Eigentümer, Besitzer;
landed ~ Grundbesitzer; **peasant ~** landwirtschaftlicher Besitz; **~** *(a.)* eigentümlich, eigentumsartig, -ähnlich, einem Besitzer gehörig, vermögensrechtlich, *(patented)* patentrechtlich geschützt, vermögensrechtlich;
~ account Eigenkapitalkonto, *(governmental accounting)* Haushaltskonto; **~ articles** patentierte Artikel, Monopolartikel, *(branded goods, US)* Markenartikel; **~ assurance** Prämienversicherung; **~ capital** Eigenkapital; **~ classes** besitzende Klassen; **~ club** Subskriptionsverein; **~ company** *(US)* kontrollierende Gesellschaft, Holdinggesellschaft, *(land-leasing company, Br.)* Grundstückgesellschaft, *(privately owned company, Br.)* Gesellschaft des bürgerlichen Rechts; **~ designation** geschützte Bezeichnung; **~ duties** *(municipality)* nichtkommunaler Aufgabenbereich; **~ establishment** Gemeindeschule; **~ food** *(US)* Markennahrungsmittel; **~ fund** Grundstücksfonds; **~ goods** *(US)* Markenartikel; **~ governments** autonome Verwaltungseinheiten; **~ industrial process** patentiertes (geschütztes) Herstellungsverfahren; **~ insurance** *(Br.)* Prämienversicherung; **~ insurance company** *(Br.)* Prämienversicherungsgesellschaft; **~ interest** Eigentums-, Vermögensrecht; **~ lease** Hauptmiet-, -pachtvertrag; **~ medicines** *(US)* gesetzlich geschützte Arzneimittel; **~ name** gesetzlich geschützter Name; **~ possession** Eigenbesitz; **~ possessor** Eigenbesitzer; **~ right** Eigentumsrecht; **to reserve one's ~ rights** Eigentumsvorbehalt machen, sich das Eigentum vorbehalten; **~ share** Aktienanteil.
proprieties korrektes Verhalten, Anstandsformen, Formen des Anstands;
conventional ~ Konventionen;
to observe the ~ Höflichkeitsformen wahren; **to offend against the ~** gegen die Anstandsregeln verstoßen.
proprietor *(holder)* Berechtigter, Inhaber, *(owner)* Eigner, Eigentümer, *(possessor)* Besitzer;
former ~ früherer Besitzer; **individual ~** *(US)* Einzelunternehmer; **joint ~** Miteigentümer; **landed ~** Grundeigentümer, -besitzer; **peasant ~** Kleinlandwirt; **private ~** Privateigentümer; **registered ~** eingetragener Gebrauchsmusterinhaber, *(land

registry, Br.) eingetragener Grundstückseigentümer; **riparian** ~ Uferanlieger; **single (sole,** *US***)** ~ Alleineigentümer, -inhaber, Einzelfirma, -unternehmer;

~ **of a bank** Bankinhaber, -herr; ~ **of a business** Geschäfts-, Firmeninhaber; ~ **of a commercial establishment** Handelsherr, Prinzipal, Geschäftsinhaber; ~ **of a firm** Firmenbesitzer, -inhaber; ~ **of a hotel** Hotelbesitzer, Hotelier; ~ **of a patent** Patentinhaber; ~ **of a shop** Ladenbesitzer; ~s **in a joint-stock company** *(Br.)* Aktionäre; ~ **of a trademark** Warenzeicheninhaber; ~ **in a trading company** Gesellschafter einer Handelsgesellschaft;

to apply to be registered as ~ Grundbucheintragung als Eigentümer beantragen;

~'s **capital** Eigenkapital; ~'s **capital account** Kapitalkonto; ~'s **drawings** Einnahmen des Firmeninhabers; ~ **income** Vermögenseinkünfte; ~'s **stake** Eigenkapital.

proprietorial|attitude Unternehmerhaltung, -einstellung; ~ **outlook** Unternehmeransicht.

proprietorship Eigentumsrecht, Eigenbesitz, Eigentum, *(balance sheet, US)* Eigenkapital;

corporate ~ *(US)* Reinvermögen einer Aktiengesellschaft; **individual** ~ *(US)* Einzelfirma, -unternehmen; **single** ~ *(US)* Einzelfirma, -unternehmen; **sole** ~ *(US)* Einzelinhaberschaft, *(ownership)* alleiniges Besitzrecht (Eigentumsrecht); **total** ~ *(US)* Gesamteigenkapital;

~ **account** Kapitalkonto; ~ **register** Eigentumsregister, *(land register, Br.)* Eigentumsverzeichnis.

propriety Anstand, Schicklichkeit;

to persuade s. o. of the ~ **of resigning** j. dazu bringen, aus Anstandsgründen zurückzutreten; **to play** ~ Anstandswauwau spielen; **to question the** ~ **of granting a request** Zweckmäßigkeit der Genehmigung eines Gesuches bezweifeln.

props *(theater)* Requisiten.

propter affectum *(lat.)* wegen Besorgnis der Befangenheit.

propulsion Antrieb[skraft], *(fig.)* Antrieb, Drang; **jet** ~ Düsenantrieb.

prorata *(lat.)* verhältnismäßig, anteilmäßig, proratarisch;

~ **apportionment** anteilsmäßige Aufteilung; **on a** ~ **basis** anteilsmäßig; ~ **contribution** anteilsmäßiger Beitrag; ~ **distribution** anteilsmäßige Verteilung, *(group policy)* anteilige Deckung; ~ **freight** Distanzfracht; ~ **premium** verdienter Prämienanteil; ~ **rate** anteilige Prämie; ~ **share** verhältnismäßiger Anteil.

proratable *(US)* anteilsmäßig.

prorate *(v.)* nach Verhältnis berechnen, *(assess, US)* anteilsmäßig veranlagen, nach einem bestimmten Schlüssel aufteilen, umlegen, aufschlüsseln;

~ **an amount** Betrag verhältnismäßig aufteilen; ~ **profits** Gewinne aufschlüsseln; ~ **the sale over a three-year period** Verkaufserlös über einen Dreijahreszeitraum verteilen.

prorated expenses *(US)* Schlüsselgemeinkosten.

proration *(US)* anteilsmäßige Aufteilung.

prorogate *(v.) (parl., Br.)* vertagen.

prorogated jurisdiction *(Scot.)* vereinbarte Einzelrichterzuständigkeit.

prorogation *(parl., Br.)* Vertagung [bis zur nächsten Sitzungsperiode].

prorogue *(parl.)* vertagen.

proscribe *(v.)* verbannen, proskribieren, ächten, für vogelfrei erklären.

proscription Ächtung, Proskription.

proscriptive tribunal Proskriptionsgericht.

prose Prosa, ungebundene Rede, *(matter-of-factness)* Alltäglichkeit, Nüchternheit, *(school, Br.)* Übersetzung.

prosecute *(v.)* belangen, verfolgen, betreiben, *(criminal law)* strafrechtlich verfolgen, anklagen, *(follow to the end)* weiterführen, *(at law)* als Kläger auftreten, Verfahren betreiben;

~ **s. o.** j. gerichtlich verfolgen (belangen); ~ **an action** Prozeß betreiben (durchführen); ~ **an application** *(patent law)* Anmeldung durchführen; ~ **a claim** Anspruch verfolgen, Forderung einklagen; ~ **a company** Gesellschaft verklagen; ~ **for exceeding the speed limit** wegen Überschreitung der Geschwindigkeitsgrenze belangen; ~ **an inquiry** Untersuchung durchführen; ~ **an investigation** Untersuchung bis zum Ende durchführen; ~ **a journey with the utmost dispatch** Reise mit größter Beschleunigung fortsetzen; ~ **one's practice of law** Anwaltskanzlei besitzen; ~ **one's studies** seinem Studium obliegen; ~ **a trade** einem Gewerbe nachgehen.

prosecuting|attorney *(US)* Anklagevertreter, Staatsanwalt; ~ **officer** *(US)* Strafverfolgungsbeamter; ~ **party** klagende (das Verfahren betreibende) Partei; ~ **witness** Belastungszeuge.

prosecution Fortsetzung, Verfolgung, Durchführung, Betreiben, *(of claim)* Einklagen einer Forderung, *(criminal law)* Strafverfolgung, Anklageerhebung, -vertretung, -behörde;

in ~ **of his duties** in Erfüllung seiner Pflichten; **liable to** ~ strafbar;

criminal ~ strafrechtliche Verfolgung, strafrechtliches Verfahren; **the** ~ Anklagebehörde; **malicious** ~ böswillige Rechtsverfolgung, wissentlich falsche Anschuldigung, Prozeßmißbrauch; **pending** ~ anhängiges Strafverfahren;

~ **of an action** Rechtsverfolgung;

to authorize ~ Strafverfolgung veranlassen; **to avoid** ~ sich der Strafverfolgung entziehen; **to bar the initiation of** ~ Strafverfolgung unterbrechen; **to discharge from** ~ außer Verfolgung setzen; **to make o. s. liable to** ~ sich strafbar machen, strafbare Handlung begehen; **to put a** ~ **under way** Strafverfolgung einleiten; **to result in** ~ Strafverfahren nach sich ziehen; **to start a** ~ **against s. o.** strafrechtlich gegen j. vorgehen, Strafverfolgung gegen j. einleiten; **to stifle** ~ Strafverfolgung niederschlagen; **to withdraw a** ~ Strafverfahren einstellen;

~ **witness** Belastungszeuge.

prosecutor Vertreter der Anklage, Ankläger, *(complainant)* Kläger;

on the part of the ~ anklägerischerseits;

army ~ Militärstaatsanwalt; **federal** ~ Bundesanwalt; **private** ~ Privatkläger; **public** ~ Staatsanwalt, öffentlicher Ankläger, Anklagevertreter; **special** ~ Sonderankläger;

~ **of the pleas** *(New Jersey)* Generalstaatsanwalt.

prospect Aussicht, Erwartung, *(consumer, US)* potentieller Verbraucher (Käufer), voraussichtlicher Kunde, Reflektant, *(mining claim)* Schürfrecht, -stelle, Mineralvorkommen, Mutung, *(politics)* möglicher Bewerber (Kandidat), Interessent, *(view)* Aussicht, Blick, Fernsicht;

with little ~ **of finding a job** mit nur geringen Arbeitsplatzaussichten;

bright ~s glänzende Aussichten; **cyclical** ~s Konjunkturaussichten; **dull** ~s trostlose Aussichten; **future** ~s Zukunftsaussichten; **sales** ~ *(US)* möglicher Kunde; **short-term** ~s Aussichten auf kurze Sicht;

no ~ **of agreement** keine Hoffnung auf eine Vereinbarung; ~s **of compromise** Kompromißchancen; ~s **of economy** wirtschaftliche Aussichten, Konjunkturaussichten; ~ **of future events** Vorschau auf künftige Ereignisse; ~ **of growing rate** vorausschaubare Zuwachsrate; ~ **of the harvest** Ernteaussichten; ~s **of life** Lebensaussichten; ~s **of the market** Konjunkturaussichten; ~s **of partnership** Teilhaberchancen; ~s **of success** Erfolgschancen, Erfolgsaussichten; **future** ~s **of an undertaking** Zukunftsaussichten eines Unternehmens;

~ *(v.)* durchforschen, *(mining)* schürfen, prospektieren, [Bergwerk] versuchsweise ausbeuten;

~ **a district** Gegend auf das Vorhandensein von Mineralvorkommen untersuchen; ~ **for gold** nach Gold schürfen; ~ **for oil** nach Öl bohren; ~ **well** *(mine)* gute Schürfergebnisse versprechen;

to be a good ~ **for any young girl** erstklassige Partie abgeben; **to have fair** ~s gute Aussichten haben; **to have good** ~s Erbschaftsaussichten haben; **to have in** ~ in Aussicht haben; **to have nothing in** ~ keine Stellung in Aussicht haben; **to have fine** ~s **before o. s.** große Zukunft haben; **to have a job in** ~ Stellung in Aussicht haben; **to hold out bright** ~s goldene Berge versprechen; **to hold out the** ~s **of a new flat** neue Wohnung in Aussicht stellen; **to hold out any immediate** ~s etw. direkt in Aussicht stellen; **to injure one's** ~s seiner Karriere schaden; **to lure s. o. with bright** ~s jem. die Zukunft in schillernden Farben malen; **to offer good** ~s aussichtsreich sein; **to open up a new** ~ **to s. o.** jem. völlig neue Berufsaussichten eröffnen;

~ **tower** Aussichtsturm.

prospecting Schürfen, Prospektierung;

~ **for gold** Goldsuchen;

~ **activities** Schürfvorhaben; ~ **contract** Schürfvertrag; ~ **licence** Schürfrecht, -erlaubnis; ~ **operation** Schürfbetrieb; ~ **party** *(US)* Schürfgesellschaft; ~ **shaft** Probeschacht, Schürfschacht.

prospective in Aussicht stehend, voraussichtlich, erwartet, zukünftig, *(forward looking)* vorwärtsschauend, *(law)* nicht rückwirkend;

~ **advantage** erwarteter (voraussichtlicher) Vorteil; ~ **beneficiary** Anwartschaftsberechtigter; ~ **buyer** potentieller Käufer, Kaufinteressent, -reflektant, -anwärter; ~ **client** potentieller Kunde; ~ **consumer** *(US)* potentieller Verbraucher; ~ **customer** voraussichtlicher (möglicher) Kunde; ~ **damage** *(US)* mittelbarer Schaden, entgangener Gewinn; ~ **damages** Ersatz für zukünftigen Schaden; ~ **insurer** Versicherungsanwärter, Versicherungskunde; ~ **investors** anlagesuchendes Publikum; ~ **legislation** zukünftige Gesetzgebung; ~ **majority** erwartete Mehrheit; ~ **managers** Führungsnachwuchs; ~ **mother** werdende Mutter; ~ **obligation** in der Zukunft anfallende Verpflichtung; ~ **professor** angehender Professor; ~ **purchaser** potentieller Käufer, Interessent; ~ **ruling** *(US)* zukünftig abweichende Rechtssprechung; ~ **son-in-law** zukünftiger Schwiegersohn; ~ **subscriber** potentieller Zeichner.

prospector *(mining)* Schürfer, Goldsucher, Prospektor, *(stock exchange, sl.)* Spekulant;
   oil ~ Ölsucher.

prospectus gedruckter Plan, Prospekt, Werbeblatt, -schrift, Ankündigung, Voranzeige, *(of a new company)* Subskriptionsanzeige, Börsenprospekt, Zeichnungsangebot, *(price list)* Preisliste, *(private school)* Unterrichtsprogramm;
   ~es **sold here** Prospekte hier erhältlich;
   to issue a ~ Börsenprospekt herausgeben; **to send out a** ~ Prospekt versenden, Prospektversand durchführen;
   ~ **company** *(Br.)* Gesellschaft mit Börsenprospekt, Gründungsgesellschaft; ~ **cover** Prospektumschlag; ~ **liability** Prospekthaftung; ~ **method** Prospektzwang, Kapitalaufbringung mittels Börsenprospektes.

prosper *(v.)* blühen, gedeihen, florieren.

prosperity Wohlstand, Gedeihen, Blütezeit, Aufschwung, Prosperität, Hochkonjunktur;
   circumstantial ~ wirtschaftlicher Wohlstand; **commercial** ~ blühender Handel; **vastly increased** ~ enorm gestiegener Wohlstand; **national** ~ Volkswohlstand; **peak** ~ Hochkonjunktur; **specious** ~ Scheinblüte, -konjunktur;
   to live in ~ Wohlstandsleben führen;
   ~ **era** wirtschaftliche Blütezeit; ~ **index** Wohlstandsindex; ~ **phase** Konjunkturperiode.

prosperous erfolgreich, gut gehend, blühend, wohlhabend;
   ~ **business (enterprise)** erfolgreiches (gut gehendes) Unternehmen; ~ **winds** günstige Winde; ~ **year** erfolgreiches Jahr, Erfolgsjahr.

prostitute Prostituierte;
   ~ *(v.)* **o. s.** sich prostituieren (verkaufen); ~ **one's energies** seine Kräfte vergeuden; ~ **one's hono(u)r** seine Ehre verlieren.

prostitution gewerbsmäßige Unzucht, Prostitution.

prostrate *(v.)* unterwerfen, niederzwingen;
   ~ **o. s. before s. o.** sich vor jem. demütigen;
   ~ *(a.)* erschöpft, hinfällig, kraftlos;
   ~ **country** zugrundegerichtetes Land.

prostrated with grief vom Gram gebeugt.

prostration Niederwerfung, Unterwerfung, *(physical condition)* Erschöpfung, *(fig.)* Niedergeschlagenheit;
   heat ~ Hitzschlag.

protect *(v.)* schützen, wahren, abschirmen, protegieren, *(bill)* honorieren, *(by imposition of duties)* durch Erhebung von Schutzzöllen schützen, *(technics)* abschreiben, abschirmen;
   ~ **a bill at maturity** Wechsel bei Verfall einlösen; ~ **o. s. from the cold** sich gegen die Kälte schützen; ~ **o. s. from danger** sich gegen eine Gefahr schützen; ~ **s. one's interests** jds. Interessen wahrnehmen; ~ **domestic products from foreign competition by trade barriers** einheimische Erzeugnisse durch Zollschranken vor ausländischer Konkurrenz schützen; ~ **an estate** Nachlaß sichern; ~ **public health** Maßnahmen zum Schutz der öffentlichen Gesundheit treffen; ~ **a signature** Aussteller durch Ehreneintritt stützen; ~ **a tenant** Mieterschutzbestimmungen anwenden; ~ **a tenant against eviction** einem Mieter Räumungsschutz gewähren; ~ **a train** Zugfahrt absichern; ~ **s. th. from the weather** vor Wetterunbilden schützen.

protected | **by copyright** urheberrechtlich geschützt; ~ **by law** gesetzlich geschützt; ~ **by letters patent** patentrechtlich geschützt;
   ~ **area** Naturschutzgebiet; ~ **articles** durch Einfuhrzölle geschützte Waren; ~ **children** zur Adoption vorgesehene Kinder; ~ **industries** *(US)* durch Zollschranken geschützte Industriezweige; ~ **person** Protegierter, Schützling; **British ~ person** britischer Staatsangehöriger; ~ **profit stop** *(US)* limitierte Verkaufsorder; ~ **transactions** unter Konkursanfechtung fallende Geschäfte.

protecting | **duty** Schutzzoll; ~ **power** Schutzmacht; ~ **prince** Schutzherr; ~ **state** Schutzmacht, -staat; ~ **varnish** Deckanstrich; ~ **wall** Schutzmauer.

protection Schutz, Schirm, Protektion, *(bribe, sl.)* an die Polizei gezahltes Bestechungsgeld, *(economy)* Schutzzollpolitik, -system, *(bill of exchange)* [Wechsel]honorierung, *(insurance)* Versicherungsschutz, *(marine)* Schutz-, Geleitbrief, *(mercan-*

tile law, US) Schutzbrief, *(public commercial law)* Schutzzoll;
   under the ~ of the law unter dem Schutz des Gesetzes;
   airraid ~ Luftschutz; **call** ~ Kündigungsschutz; **environmental** ~ Umweltschutz; **fire** ~ Feuerschutz; **functional** ~ Schutz der internationalen Beziehungen; **legal** ~ Rechtsschutz; **quality** ~ Güteschutz; **statutory** ~ *(collecting bank)* Freizeichnung der Inkassobank; **tariff** ~ Schutzzollsystem; **trademark** ~ Warenzeichenschutz;
   ~ **against accidents** Unfallschutz; ~ **for bankers** Rechtsschutz für Banken; **double** ~ **of body-shell against corrosion** doppelter Korrosionsschutz der Gesamtkarosserie; ~ **of children** Kinderschutz; ~ **against the cold** Kälteschutz; ~ **by copyright** Urheberrechtsschutz; ~ **of creditors** *(bankruptcy)* Gläubigerschutz; ~ **of cultural goods** Kulturgüterschutz; ~ **of registered designs** *(Br.)* Geschmacksmusterschutz; ~ **of an estate** Vermögens-, Nachlaßsicherung; ~ **and indemnity** Schiffs-, Reederhaftpflicht; ~ **against inflation** Inflationsschutzmaßnahmen; ~ **of industrial property** gewerblicher Rechtsschutz; ~ **of interests** Wahrnehmung von Interessen; ~ **of inventions** Gebrauchsmusterschutz; ~ **of investors** Anlegerschutz; ~ **of labo(u)r** Arbeiterschutz; ~ **of the law** gleicher Schutz durch die Gesetzte; ~ **of minorities** Minderheitenschutz; ~ **by patent** Patentschutz; ~ **of property** Eigentumsschutz; ~ **of third parties acting in good faith** Schutz gutgläubiger Dritter; ~ **from the sun** Schutz gegen die Sonne; ~ **of trademarks** Warenzeichenschutz;
   to afford ~ *(patent)* Schutz gewähren; **to claim the** ~ **of the Rent Acts** *(Br.)* Mieterschutzrechte in Anspruch nehmen; **to claim the** ~ **of the Cheques Act** *(Br.)* am vereinbarten Scheck- und Lastschriftinkasso teilnehmen; **to claim the** ~ **of the law** Schutz der Gesetze anrufen; **to erect a** ~ **against the wind** Windblende errichten; **to extend one's** ~ **to a young author** einem jungen Autor seine Gönnerschaft zuwenden; **to fall outside the** ~ **of the statutory and common laws relating to safety** nicht den Arbeiterschutzgesetzen unterliegen; **to find (meet with) due** ~ *(bill)* akzeptiert (honoriert) werden; **to give a draft due** ~ Tratte akzeptieren (honorieren); **to need** ~ **against the weather** gegen Wetterunbilden geschützt werden müssen; **to provide** ~ **from harm** gegen Unbill schützen; **to show due** ~ **to a draft** Tratte honorieren; **to travel under the** ~ **of soldiers** unter militärischer Bewachung reisen;
   ⌃ **of Depositors Act** *(Br.)* Depotgesetz; ⌃ **of Inventions Act** Gebrauchsmustergesetz; ~ **duty** Wachdienst; ~ **gang** Erpresserbande; ~ **and indemnity insurance** Schiffshaftpflichtversicherung; ~ **money** Geldaufwendungen für den persönlichen Schutz, *(US)* Bestechungsgelder, erpreßtes Geld; ~ **order** *(Br.)* Beschluß über die Aussetzung des Verfahrens zugunsten eines durch die Kriegsverhältnisse in Liquidation geratenen Schuldners, *(divorce court, Br.)* einstweilige Anordnung zum Schutz des Vorbehaltsguts der Ehefrau; ~ **racket** Erpressung unter Gewaltandrohung; ~ **society** Gläubigerschutzverband.

protectionism Schutzzollsystem, -politik, Protektionismus, Protektionswirtschaft;
   to edge towards ~ sich immer mehr dem Protektionismus zuwenden; **to keep** ~ **at bay** Protektionismus in Schach halten.

protectionist Schutzzöllner, Schutzzollpolitiker;
   ~ *(a.)* schutzzöllnerisch, protektionistisch;
   ~ **activities** protektionistische Maßnahmen; ~ **congress** protektionistisch eingestellter Kongreß; ~ **partner** schutzzöllnerisch eingestellter Anhänger; ~ **sentiment** wachsender Protektionismus; **to resist the** ~ **side** protektionistischen Einflüsterungen widerstehen.

protective schützend, *(tariff)* schutzzöllnerisch;
   ~ **agreement** Schutzzollabkommen; ~ **aspect** *(tariff)* Schutzwirkung; ~ **association** Schutzvereinigung; ~ **belt** Schutzgürtel; **to put in** ~ **claims** Forderungen zunächst lediglich zur Wahrung von Rechtsansprüchen erheben; ~ **clause** Freizeichnungs-, Schutzklausel; ~ **clothing** Schutzkleidung; ~ **committee** Gläubigerausschuß; ~ **deck** *(ship)* Panzerdeck; ~ **department** *(fire insurance)* Feuerschutzabteilung; ~ **detention** Schutzhaft; ~ **duty** Schutzzoll; ~ **food** vitaminreiche Lebensmittel (Nahrung); ~ **labor legislation** *(US)* Arbeitsschutzgesetzgebung; ~ **measures** Abwehr-, Schutzmaßnahmen; ~ **paint** Schutzfarbe; ~ **rights** Schutzrechte; ~ **system** Schutzzollsystem, -politik; ~ **[customs] tariff** Abwehrzoll, Schutzzoll[tarif]; ~ **trade measures** handelspolitische Schutzmaßnahmen; ~ **troops** Schutztruppen; ~ **trust** *(Br.)* Treuhandfonds auf Lebenszeit, Unterstützungs-, Unterhaltsfonds; ~ **umbrellas** *(fig.)* Schutzmaßnahmen.

protector Schirmherr, Schutzherr, Mäzen, Protektor, *(law of nations)* Schutzmacht, Protektor;
   ~ **of a settlement** Vollstrecker eines Treuhandverhältnisses.

protectoral schutzherrlich.

protectorate geschützter Staat, Schutzgebiet, Protektorat.

protectorship Schutz-, Schirmherrschaft.

protégé Schützling, Schutzbefohlener, Protegee.

protest Verwahrung, Einspruch, Widerspruch, Protest, Reklamation, *(bill of exchange)* Wechselprotest[urkunde], *(parl., Br.)* Minderheitsprotest, *(solemn declaration)* feierliche Erklärung, Beteuerung;

as a ~ zum (als) Protest; **in the absence of** ~ mangels Protest; **no** ~ *(bill)* ohne Kosten; **supra** ~ nach Protest; **under** ~ unter Vorbehalt; ~ **waived** ohne Protest (Kosten);

due ~ rechtzeitiger Protest; **extended** ~ *(navigation)* Seeprotest, Verklarung; **forward** ~ voreiliger Protest; **householder's** ~ *(bill of exchange)* [etwa] Wand-, Abwesenheitsprotest; **past due** ~ zu spät erhobener Protest; **public** ~ öffentlicher Protest; **retarded** ~ verspäteter Protest; **sharp** ~ scharfer Protest; **ship's** ~ See-, Havarieattest, Verklarung; **vigorous** ~s nachdrückliche Protestaktionen;

~ **of intervention** Interventionsprotest; ~ **of a bill for nonacceptance** Wechselprotest wegen Nichtabnahme; ~ **for nonpayment** Protest mangels Zahlung; ~ **for better security** Wechselprotest zwecks weiterer Sicherheiten [bei Zahlungsunfähigkeit des Akzeptanten]; **general** ~ **of the people** allgemeine Protestbewegung; ~ **of the shipmaster** Verklarung, Seeprotest; ~ **in writing** schriftlicher Vorbehalt;

~ *(v.)* Einspruch (Protest, Verwahrung) erheben, einwenden, protestieren;

~ **against** vorstellig werden wegen; ~ **against an appointment** gegen eine Ernennung sein Veto einlegen; ~ **a bill** Wechselprotest einlegen; ~ **a bill for better security** Wechsel zwecks weiterer Sicherheitengestellung zu Protest gehen lassen; ~ **a bill for nonacceptance** Wechsel mangels Annahme protestieren; ~ **a bill for nonpayment** Wechsel mangels Zahlung protestieren; ~ **one's good faith** versichern, in gutem Glauben gehandelt zu haben; ~ **to a government** Verwahrung (Protest) bei einer Regierung einlegen; ~ **one's innocence** seine Schuldlosigkeit beteuern; ~ **against a measure** gegen getroffene Maßnahmen protestieren; ~ **that one has never been near the scene of a crime** beteuern, nie in der Nähe des Tatorts gewesen zu sein; ~ **a witness** *(US)* Zeugen ablehnen, gegen einen Zeugen Einspruch einlegen;

to accept under ~ unter Vorbehalt annehmen; **to act under** ~ gegen Gewaltanwendung protestieren, unter Zwang handeln; **to bring forth** ~ Proteste hervorrufen; **to defer (delay) the** ~ Protest hinausschieben; **to draw up a** ~ Protest aufnehmen; **to enter a** ~ formellen Protest (Einspruch, Einwendungen) erheben (einlegen), Verwahrung einlegen; **to enter a** ~ **in case of damage** Verklarung über die Beschädigung eines Schiffes einlegen; **to extend** ~ Verklarung einlegen; **to give rise to** ~s zu Protesten Anlaß geben; **to give way without** ~ keine Einwendungen mehr erheben; **to go to** ~ zu Protest gehen; **to join in a** ~ sich einem Proteststreik anschließen; **to leave a meeting under** ~ Sitzung unter Protest verlassen; **to lodge a** ~ Verwahrung einlegen, Protest erheben; **to make a** ~ Verwahrung einlegen, Protest erheben; **to make a written** ~ schriftlichen Einspruch einlegen; **to note (notify) a** ~ Protest aufnehmen [lassen]; **to pass a resolution of** ~ Protest beschließen; **to pay a bill under** ~ Wechsel unter Protesterhebung einlösen; **to pay a tax demand under** ~ Steuerforderung unter Einlegung eines Einspruchs zahlen; **to raise a** ~ Einspruch einlegen; **to raise a strong** ~ scharfen Protest erheben; **to receive** ~ Einsprüche entgegennehmen; **to return under** ~ mit Protest zurückgehen lassen; **to ride over all** ~s sich über alle Proteste hinwegsetzen; **to spark** ~ Proteste auslösen;

~ **activities** Protestaktion; ~ **certificate** Protesturkunde; ~ **charges (expenses, fees)** Protestkosten, -spesen; ~ **demonstration** Protestdemonstration; ~ **march** Protest-, Demonstrationsmarsch; ~ **meeting** Protestversammlung; ~ **strike** Proteststreik.

protestant *(a.)* evangelisch, protestantisch;

to bring up in the ~ **faith** protestantisch erziehen.

protestation Protesterhebung, feierliche Versicherung.

protested *(bill of exchange)* zu Protest gegangen;

~ **for nonacceptance** mangels Annahme protestiert; ~ **for nonpayment** mangels Zahlung protestiert;

to be ~ **at once** sofort zu Protest gehen; **to have a bill** ~ Wechsel protestieren lassen; **to return a bill** ~ Wechsel unter Protest zurückgehen lassen;

~ **check** *(US)* **(cheque,** *Br.)* protestierter Scheck.

protesting *(bill of exchange)* Protestaufnahme.

protestor Protestierender, Protesterhebender, -gläubiger.

protocol Verhandlungs-, Sitzungsbericht, Niederschrift, Protokoll, *(international agreement, US)* Staatsvertrag, Zusatzvertrag, -protokoll, *(body of formulas)* protokollarische Verhaltungsregeln, *(diplomatic document)* einleitende Floskeln, Einleitungsformeln, *(labo(u)r dispute)* Beilegung von Streitigkeiten;

according to ~ protokollgemäß;

additional ~ Zusatzprotokoll; **final** ~ Schlußprotokoll; **secret** ~ Geheimprotokoll; **supplementary** ~ Zusatzprotokoll; ~ **of amendment** Veränderungsprotokoll; ~ **of extension** Verlängerungsprotokoll; ~ **of interpretation** Auslegungsprotokoll; ~ **of ratification** Protokoll über den Austausch von Ratifikationsurkunden;

~ *(v.)* protokollieren, Protokoll aufnehmen (abfassen, ausgeben);

to be according to ~ den protokollarischen Bestimmungen genügen; **to break the rules of** ~ gegen das Protokoll verstoßen; **to draw up a** ~ Verhandlungsprotokoll aufsetzen, Protokoll aufnehmen; **to issue a** ~ Protokoll ausgeben; **to record in** ~ zu Protokoll nehmen, Protokoll führen; **to state in a** ~ protokollarisch festhalten;

~ **chef** Protokollchef; ~ **greeting** übliche protokollarische Grußadresse; ~ **section** Protokollabteilung; ~ **service** Tätigkeit des Protokolls.

protocolary protokollgemäß, protokollarisch.

protocolist *(US)* Protokollführer.

protocolization Protokollierung.

protocolize *(v.)* Protokoll aufsetzen, protokollieren, Verhandlung aufnehmen.

prototype erstes Muster[exemplar], Modell, Prototyp, Ausgangsbaumuster, Erstausführung;

~ **aircraft** Probeflugzeug; ~ **contract** Muster-, Modellvertrag; ~ **production** Musterproduktion.

protract *(v.)* in die Länge ziehen, hinziehen, hinaus-, verzögern; ~ **a lawsuit** Prozeß verschleppen.

protracted, to be sich verzögern;

~ **debate** langwierige Debatte; ~ **loss** lang anhaltender Schaden; ~ **visit** verlängerter Besuch.

protraction Hinausziehen, Verzögerung, Verschleppung;

~ **of a debate** Verlängerung einer Debatte; ~ **of a lawsuit** Prozeßverschleppung.

proud stolz, dünkelhaft, eingebildet, *(river)* angeschwollen;

purse-~ auf seinen Reichtum eingebildet.

provability Beweisbarkeit.

provable be-, nachweisbar;

~ **claim** anmeldefähige Konkursforderung; ~ **debt** nachweisbare Forderung;

to have been admitted ~ **in bankruptcy** als Konkursforderung anerkannt sein.

provableness Beweisbarkeit.

prove *(v.) (attest)* beglaubigen, beurkunden, *(bankruptcy)* [Forderung im Konkursverfahren] geltend machen, *(demonstrate)* unter Beweis stellen, Nachweis führen, be-, nachweisen, *(print.)* Probeabzug machen, *(put to the test)* prüfen, erproben, *(turn out)* sich erweisen (herausstellen);

~ **o. s.** sich bewähren; ~ **s. o. still alive** Nachweis für jds. am-Leben-Gebliebensein bilden; ~ **to be true** sich als wahr erweisen, sich bestätigen; ~ **one's case** seine Klage vorbringen, unter Beweis stellen; ~ **a claim in bankruptcy** Konkursforderung anmelden; ~ **the contrary** das Gegenteil beweisen; ~ **correct** sich bestätigen, Bestätigung finden, sich als richtig herausstellen; ~ **one's damage** seinen Schaden nachweisen; ~ **surrender the security and** ~ **the whole debt** *(secured creditor)* auf Sicherheitenverwertung verzichten und den Gesamtbetrag als Konkursforderung anmelden; ~ **a debt in liquidation** Forderung im Gesellschaftskonkurs nachweisen; ~ **beyond doubt** unwiderlegbar beweisen; ~ **against the estate** Konkursforderung (Forderung gegen die Konkursmasse) anmelden; ~ **by facts** faktisch beweisen, mit Tatsachen untermauern; ~ **false** sich nicht bestätigen (als falsch herausstellen); ~ **to be a forgery** sich als Fälschung herausstellen; ~ **s. th. to be genuine** Echtheitsbeweis für etw. antreten; ~ **s. one's guilt** jds. Schuld nachweisen; ~ **one's identity** sich legitimieren (ausweisen), seine Identität nachweisen; ~ **ownership** Besitznachweis erbringen; ~ **to the satisfaction of the court** dem Gericht glaubhaft machen; ~ **a sum** Betrag verifizieren; ~ **unequal to one's tasks** sich seiner Aufgabe nicht gewachsen zeigen; ~ **up** *(US)* gesetzliche Erfordernisse als erfüllt nachweisen; ~ **up on a concession** *(US)* Konzessionserfordernisse erfüllen; ~ **useful** sich als nützlich beweisen; ~ **useless** sich als unbrauchbar herausstellen; ~ **a will** Gültigkeit eines Testaments bestätigen lassen; **~ that the defamatory words were true in substance and in fact** Wahrheitsgehalt für beleidigende Äußerungen antreten.

proved bewiesen, erwiesen, *(tested)* bewährt, erprobt;
after being ~ nach erfolgter Glaubhaftmachung; **clearly ~** klar erwiesen;
to be ~ by adversity von Schicksalsschlägen heimgesucht sein; **to have ~ correct** sich als richtig erwiesen haben; **to have a will ~** Testament durch das Nachlaßgericht eröffnen lassen;
~ damages festgestellter Schadensersatzanspruch; **~ debt** festgestellte [Konkurs]forderung; **~ remedy** bewährtes Mittel; **~ will** als gültig anerkanntes Testament.

proven erwiesen, bewiesen, nachgewiesen;
not ~ *(Scot.)* Schuldbeweis nicht erbracht;
~ territory ölträchtiges Land.

provenance Herkunft, Provenienz.

proverb Sprichwort;
to be a ~ for meanness sprichwörtlicher Geizkragen sein.

proverbial sprichwörtlich;
to be ~ for zum Sprichwort geworden sein.

provide *(v.)* beschaffen, [be]liefern, [mit]besorgen, bereitstellen, sorgen, Vorsorge treffen, versorgen, *(law)* bestimmen, festsetzen, vorsehen, *(money)* anweisen, anschaffen, bereitstellen.

provide against *(v.)* verhindern, unmöglich machen, Vorsorge treffen;
~ accidents Unfallverhütungsmaßnahmen treffen; **~ a coal shortage** sich gegen eine Kohlenknappheit eindecken; **~ a danger** sich vor einer Gefahr schützen.

provide for *(v.)* vorsehen, in Rechnung stellen;
~ s. o. für jds. Lebensunterhalt sorgen; **~ a bill** Deckung für einen Wechsel anschaffen; **~ an emergency** für einen Notfall Vorsorge treffen; **~ the entertainment of our visitors** für das Amüsement unserer Gäste Vorsorge treffen; **~ an eventuality** für einen Notfall Vorsorge treffen; **~ everything** nichts in seinen Vorkehrungen vergessen; **~ the expenses against the suit** Gerichtskosten abdecken; **~ a large family** große Familie unterhalten; **~ maintenance s. o.** für jds. Unterhalt sorgen; **~ the needs** Bedürfnisse befriedigen; **~ urgent needs** für Notfälle bereitstellen; **~ an opportunity for s. o.** jem. eine Gelegenheit verschaffen; **~ payment** Deckung anschaffen, für Zahlung (Deckung, Anschaffung) sorgen; **~ security** Sicherheit leisten; **~ deferred taxes** Rückstellungen für Steuervorauszahlungen bilden; **~ the necessary transport** notwendige Transportmittel bereitstellen.

provide with *(v.)* versehen (beliefern, ausstatten) mit;
~ o. s. sich eindecken; **~ a bill acceptance** Wechsel mit Akzept versehen; **~ s. o. cover** j. mit Deckung versehen, jem. Deckung anschaffen.

provide|employment Arbeit beschaffen, beschäftigen; **~ an exit** Notausgang vorsehen; **~ funds** Deckung anschaffen; **~ funds for payment of interest** Mittel für den Zinsendienst bereitstellen; **~ matter for a newspaper** Zeitungsnachricht abgeben; **~ matter for gossip** Klatschspalten füllen; **~ payment** Deckung anschaffen; **~ security** Kaution stellen; **~ a time limit** Frist vorsehen; **~ in one's will** in seinem Testament bestimmen.

provided vorbehaltlich, vorgesehen, vorgeschrieben, vertragsvereinbarungsgemäß, *(furnished)* ausgestattet, versorgt, versehen;
as hereinafter ~ gemäß nachstehender Bestimmungen; **not ~ for** keine Deckung; **not otherwise ~** nicht anderweitig vorsehen; **save as otherwise ~** mit Ausnahme gegenteiliger Bestimmungen;
~ that vorausgesetzt daß, unter der Bedingung (Voraussetzung);
~ by the articles of the association in den Satzungen der Gesellschaft vorgesehen, satzungsgemäß; **~ for in the budget** in den Etat eingestellt, im Etat vorgesehen, eingeplant; **as ~ in the contract** wie vertraglich vereinbart; **~ for all eventualities** für alle Eventualitäten gerüstet; **~ with funds** mit Mitteln versehen, gedeckt; **~ funds permit** solange die Mittel reichen; **~ by law** gesetzlich vorgesehen; **~ due payment** [rechtzeitiger] Empfang vorbehalten; **~ by statute** gesetzlich vorgesehen;
to be ~ for versorgt sein; **to be ~ by law** gesetzlich vorgesehen sein; **to be well ~ with capital** kapitalkräftig sein;
~ school *(Br.)* Gemeindeschule, städtische Schule.

providence Vorsorge, Voraussicht, *(thrift)* Sparsamkeit;
by a special ~ durch eine besondere Fügung;
~ society Unfallversicherungsgesellschaft.

provident *(exercising foresight)* vorausschauend, vor-, fürsorglich, *(thrifty)* sparsam, haushälterisch;
~ association *(Br.)* private Krankenkasse; **~ bank** Sparkasse;

benefit Fürsorgeunterstützung; **~ care** Vor-, Fürsorge; **~ company** Wirtschaftsgenossenschaft; **~ fund** Unterstützungskasse, Hilfskasse, Fürsorge-, Pensions-, Unterstützungsfonds; **miner's ~ fund** Knappschaftskasse; **~ fund for the staff** Unterstützungsfonds für die Belegschaft, Belegschaftsfonds; **~ fund scheme** Pensionskassenwesen; **~ reserve** Sonderrücklage, -stellung; **~ reserve fund** außerordentliche Rücklage; **~ scheme** Hilfsaktion; **~ society** *(Br.)* Versicherungs-, Wohlfahrts-, Unterstützungsverein [auf Gegenseitigkeit]; **industrial and ~ society** *(Br.)* Erwerbs- und Wirtschaftsgenossenschaft.

providential schicksalhaft.

providently vorsorglich.

provider Ernährer, Fürsorger, *(supplier)* Versorger, Lieferant;
good ~ *(coll.)* treusorgender Vater; **lion's ~** gemeiner Kriecher; **universal ~s** *(Br.)* Gemischtwarenhandlung, Waren-, Kaufhaus.

province Provinz, *(branch of learning)* [Wissens]gebiet, Fach, *(region)* Gebiet, Landstrich, Gegend, *(sphere of action)* Geschäftskreis, Bereich, Feld, -gebiet, Beruf, Wirkungskreis, Aufgabenbereich, Tätigkeits-, Arbeitsgebiet, *(scope of office)* Amts-, Geltungsbereich, Ressort;
in the ~s in der Provinz; **within the ~ of** innerhalb des Aufgabenbereichs;
~ of the jury Aufgabe der Geschworenen;
to be s. one's ~ in jds. Bereich fallen; **not to be within s. one's ~** nicht in jds. Gebiet fallen (Fach schlagen); **to come (fall) within s. one's ~** zu jds. Aufgabenbereich gehören; **to fall outside the ~ of science** nicht in den Bereich der Wissenschaft gehören; **to tour the ~s** *(theater)* in der Provinz gastieren.

provincial Provinzler, Kleinstädter;
~ (a.) aus der Provinz, provinziell, regional, *(narrow)* provinziell, kleinstädtisch, spießbürgerlich;
~ agency Regional-, Provinzvertretung; **~ attitude of mind** provinzielle Einstellung; **~ authorities** Provinzbehörden; **~ bank** Regionalbank; **~ center** *(US)* **(centre, Br.)** Provinzzentrum; **~ city** Provinzstadt; **~ clearing** *(Br.)* regionaler Verrechnungsverkehr; **~ daily** regionale Tageszeitung; **~ election** Wahlen in der Provinz, Provinzwahlen; **~ exchange** *(Br.)* Regionalbörse; **~ government** Provinzregierung; **~ interests** beschränkte Interessen; **~ market** *(Br.)* Regionalbörse; **~ newspapers (press)** Regionalpresse, -zeitungen; **~ taxes** Provinzialabgaben; **~ town** Provinzstadt; **~ university** Landesuniversität.

provincialism Provinzlertum, Provinzialismus, *(parochialism)* Lokalpatriotismus, Kirchtumspolitik.

provincialize *(v.)* provinzlerischen Charakter geben.

proving Erprobung, Prüfen, *(law)* Beweisführung;
~ of debts Forderungsnachweis; **~ of identity** Legitimationsprüfung; **~ of steam boilers** Dampfkesselerprobung; **~ of the tenor** Inhaltsnachweis einer verlorengegangenen Urkunde; **~ a will** Testamentseröffnung;
to be ~ unproductive sich als wirtschaftlicher Fehlschlag erweisen;
~ ground Prüffeld, Versuchsgelände.

provision Vorkehrung, Maßnahme, Vorsorge, *(balance sheet)* Rückstellung, Rücklage, *(clause)* Klausel, Vorschrift, *(insurance)* Reserve, *(previous preparation)* Vorsorge, Anstalt, *(proviso)* Bestimmung, Klausel, Vorbehalt, Bedingung, *(remittance)* Übermachung, Bereitstellung, Deckung, *(stipulation)* Bestimmung, Verordnung, Vorschrift, Verfügung, *(supply)* Eindeckung, Beschaffung, Versorgung, Vorrat;
after ~ for contingencies nach Rückstellungen für unvorhergesehene Ausgaben; **in accordance with the ~s of the agreement** gemäß den vertraglichen Bestimmungen; **not withstanding any ~s to the contrary** ungeachtet entgegenstehender Bestimmungen; **till further ~s** bis auf weitere Verfügung; **under the usual ~s** unter üblichem Vorbehalt;
~s Lebensmittel, Proviant, Nahrungsmittel, *(reserve, Br.)* Rückstellungen und Wertberichtigungen;
additional ~s Zusatzbestimmungen; **adequate ~** genügende Vorsorge; **anti-avoiding ~s** Bestimmungen gegen den Mißbrauch von Steuervergünstigungen; **bad-debt ~s** *(US)* Rückstellungen für faule Kunden; **canned ~s** Konserven; **capital gains (loss) ~s** Bestimmungen über die steuerliche Behandlung von Kapitalgewinnen (Kapitalverlusten); **concluding ~s** Schlußbestimmungen; **constitutional ~s** Verfassungsbestimmungen; **doubtful-debt ~s** *(Br.)* Rückstellung für zweifelhafte Schulden (Dubiose); **exemption ~s** Ausnahme-, Befreiungsbestimmungen; **family ~** *(Br.)* Fürsorge für die Familie; **final ~s** Schlußbestimmungen; **fiscal ~s** steuerrechtliche Bestimmungen (Vorschriften); **general ~s** allgemeine Bestimmungen; **implementing ~s** Ausführungsbestimmungen; **legal ~s** gesetzli-

che Bestimmungen, Gesetzesbestimmungen; **liberal** ~s reiche Vorräte; **long-term** ~s langfristige Rückstellungen; **major** ~s hauptsächliche Bestimmungen; **nonforfeiture** ~s Bestimmungen über die Aufrechterhaltung der Versicherungsansprüche bei Verfall (Rückkauf) der Police; **old-age** ~s Altersvorsorge; **optional** ~s dispositive (durch Parteivereinbarungen abgeänderte) Vorschriften; **penal** ~ Strafklausel, -bestimmung; **pension[ary]** ~s Pensionsbestimmungen; **peremptory** ~ Mußvorschrift, zwingende Vorschrift; **permissive** ~ Kannbestimmung; **redemption** ~s Einlösungsbestimmungen; **relevant** ~s einschlägige Bestimmungen (Vorschriften); **restrictive** ~s einschränkende Bestimmungen; ~s **running out** ausgehende Vorräte; **special** ~s Sonderbestimmungen; **standard** ~s *(insurance)* allgemeine Versicherungsbedingungen; **statutory** ~s gesetzliche Bestimmungen (Vorschriften); **supplementary** ~s Ergänzungsbestimmungen; **tax-law** ~s steuerrechtliche Bestimmungen, Steuerbestimmungen;

~ **for doubtful accounts** *(Br.)* Rückstellung für faule Kunden (Dubiose); ~ **against s. th.** Vorsorge gegen etw.; ~ **for old age** Altersvorsorge; **formal** ~s **of an agreement** protokollarische Vertragsbestimmungen; ~s **of arbitration** Schiedsgerichtsbestimmungen; ~s **as to audits** Revisionsbestimmungen; ~s **of a bill** Gesetzesbestimmungen; ~s **of the bill of lading** Konnossementsbedingungen; ~ **for building repairs** Gebäudereparaturrücklage; ~ **of capital** Kapitalbeschaffung, -bereitstellung, -disposition; ~ **and issue of coins** Münzprägung und Münzausgabe; ~ **for contingencies** Rückstellung für unvorhergesehene Ausgaben (Eventualverbindlichkeiten); **[clear-cut]** ~s **of a contract** [glasklare] Vertragsbestimmungen; ~ **to the contrary** gegenteilige Bestimmungen; ~s **of a convention** Bestimmungen einer Konvention; **specific** ~s **against particular debts** Sonderrückstellungen für einzeln ausgewiesene Schulden; ~ **for depreciation** Rückstellungen für Abschreibungen (Wertminderung), Entwertungsrücklage; ~ **for depreciation of investments** Kapitalentwertungsrücklage; ~s **for dissolution** Auflösungsbestimmungen; ~ **for the education of one's children** Vorsorge für eine gute Ausbildung seiner Kinder; ~ **of equipment** Bereitstellung von Arbeitsgerät; ~ **in execution of a law** Durchführungsbestimmung; ~ **of funds** Kapitalbeschaffung, Deckung; ~ **for the future** Vorsorge für die Zukunft; ~ **of housing** Bereitstellung von Wohnungen; ~ **of information for credit purposes** Beschaffung von Kreditunterlagen; ~s **of an insurance policy** Bestimmungen einer Versicherungspolice, Versicherungsbestimmungen; ~ **for inventory reserve** Rückstellung für Inventarauffüllung; ~ **of a law** Gesetzesbestimmung; ~s **in the lease** Pachtvertragsbestimmungen; ~s **of the Limitation Act** *(Br.)* Verjährungsbestimmungen; **statutory** ~s **for liquidation** gesetzliche Liquidationsbestimmungen; ~s **for possible loan losses** Rückstellungen für Kreditausfälle; ~ **for outstanding losses** *(insurance)* Schadensreserve; ~s **of the memorandum** Satzungsbestimmungen; ~s **as to notice and procedure at general meetings** Bestimmungen über die Einberufung und Abhaltung von Hauptversammlungen; ~ **of the necessities of life** Fürsorge für die Lebensbedürfnisse; ~ **for obsolescence** Rückstellung für Überaltung; ~s **for pensions** Pensionsrückstellungen; ~ **for renewals** *(Br.)* Rückstellung für Ersatzbeschaffung; ~ **for deferred repairs and renewals** Rückstellungen für Reparaturen und Erneuerungen; ~ **of rent** Mietgeld; ~ **for replacement of inventories** *(US)* Rückstellung für die Auffüllung des Lagerbestandes; ~ **for retirement** Altersvorsorge; ~ **of services** Dienstleistungsangebot; ~ **for taxation on unrealized surpluses** Steuerrückstellung für nicht entnommene Gewinne; ~ **for taxes** Steuerrückstellung; ~s **of a will** Testamentsbestimmungen; ~ **of work** Beschäftigungspflicht;

~ *(v.)* mit Proviant (Lebensmitteln) versehen, verproviantieren;

~ **a ship for a voyage** Schiff für eine Reise verproviantieren; **to abolish** ~s Bestimmungen aufgeben; **to apply a** ~ Bestimmung anwenden; **to break into** ~s Vorräte anbrechen; **to come within the** ~s **of an act (a law)** unter die Bestimmungen eines Gesetzes (die gesetzlichen Bestimmungen) fallen; **to commandeer** ~s Vorräte beschlagnahmen; **to condemn defective** ~s schlecht gewordene Lebensmittel beschlagnahmen; **to cut off** ~s Lebensmittelzufuhr abschneiden; **to implement the** ~s **of a convention** Bestimmungen eines Abkommens in Kraft setzen; **to issue** ~s Lebensmittel ausgeben; **to issue a** ~ **of meat** Fleischportion ausgeben; **to lay in a store of** ~s Vorratslager anlegen; **to make** ~ versorgen, ernähren, *(mil.)* verproviantieren; **to make** ~s Anstalten (Vorkehrungen) treffen, *(balance sheet)* Rückstellung bilden (vornehmen), Reserven anlegen; **to make** ~ **for s. o.** jem. eine Pension aussetzen; **to make no** ~ **for a case**

of this kind *(law)* keine Bestimmungen für einen derartigen Fall getroffen haben; **to make** ~s **for one's old age** Vorkehrungen für sein Alter (Altervorsorgebestimmungen) treffen; **to make** ~s **for one's clothing** seinen Bedarf an Kleidungsstücken decken; **to make** ~ **for cover of a bill** Deckung für einen Wechsel anschaffen, für die Deckung eines Wechsels sorgen; **to make** ~s **for one's family** für die Zukunft seiner Familie sorgen; **to make** ~s **for the future** seine Zukunft sicherstellen; **to make a special** ~ **about s. th.** besondere Vorsorge für etw. treffen; **to make proper** ~ **for the pension liabilities** ausreichende Rückstellungen für Pensionsverpflichtungen vornehmen; **to make** ~ **for taxation** für Steuern zurückstellen, Steuerrückstellung vornehmen; **to make** ~s **for deferred tax compulsory** Rückstellungen für herausgeschobene Steuerzahlungen zur Pflicht machen; **to retain a** ~ Bestimmung beibehalten; **to run short of** ~s nicht genügend Lebensmittel haben; **to supply with** ~s verproviantieren; **to touch** ~s Vorräte angreifen;

wholesale ~ **business** Lebensmittelgroßhandel; ~ **dealer (merchant)** Kolonialwaren-, Feinkost-, Lebensmittelhändler; ~s **industry** Nahrungsmittelindustrie; ~ **room** *(ship)* Proviantkammer.

provisional *(philately)* vorläufige Briefmarke;

~ *(a.)* vorläufig, provisorisch, zeit-, einstweilig, kommissarisch, interimistisch;

~ **account** vorläufiges Konto; ~ **agenda** vorläufige Tagesordnung; ~ **application** *(patent law)* vorläufige Anmeldung; ~ **arrangement** vorläufige (einstweilige) Anordnung, Provisorium; **to make a** ~ **arrangement** vorläufige Vereinbarung treffen; ~ **arrest** vorläufige Festnahme; ~ **bill** Interimswechsel; ~ **bond** Zwischen-, Interimsschein; ~ **booking** provisorischer (vorläufiger) Abschluß, Vorratsbuchhaltung; ~ **certificate** Zwischen-, Interimsschein; ~ **committee** vorübergehend eingesetzter Ausschuß; ~ **contract** vorläufiger Vertrag; ~ **court** *(US)* Sondergericht; ~ **cover** vorläufige Deckungszusage; ~ **decision** Vorbescheid; ~ **duties** einstweilige Funktionen; ~ **government** provisorische Regierung, Interimsregierung; ~ **invoice** vorläufige Rechnung; ~ **injunction** Zwischenverfügung; ~ **judgment** vorläufiges Urteil, Vorbehaltsurteil; ~ **law** Übergangsgesetz; ~ **order** *(Br.)* einstweilige Verfügung [durch eine Provinzbehörde], Ausnahme-, Notverordnung; ~ **receipt** Interims-, Zwischenquittung; ~ **regulations** Übergangsbestimmungen; ~ **remedy** vorläufiger Rechtsbehelf, einstweilige Anordnung; ~ **scrip** Zwischen-, Interimsschein; ~ **seizure** *(Louisiana)* Arrest, Beschlagnahme; ~ **specification** *(patent law)* vorläufige Beschreibung; ~ **treaty** vorläufiger Vertrag; ~ **volume** Interimsband.

provisionality provisorischer Charakter.

provisionally einstweilig, vorläufig, als vorläufige Maßnahme, bis auf weiteres;

appointed ~ provisorisch ernannt;

to sign an agreement ~ Abkommen mit Vorbehalt unterzeichnen.

provisioner Lebensmittellieferant, -händler.

provisioning *(mil.)* Versorgung.

proviso Bedingung, Klausel, einschränkende Bestimmung, *(conditional stipulation)* Vorbehalt[sklausel], Modalität;

subject to this ~ vorbehaltlich der nachfolgenden Bestimmung; **under the** ~ unter dem Vorbehalt; **with [a]** ~ vorbehaltlich, unter der Bedingung; **with (under) the usual** ~ unter üblichem Vorbehalt (u. ü. V.);

~ **in case of war** Kriegsklausel; ~ **for redemption** Rückzahlungsklausel, Einlösungsvorbehalt;

to act under the ~ unter Vorbehalt handeln; **to make it a** ~ Vorbehalt (zur Bedingung) machen;

~ **clause** Vorbehaltsklausel.

provisory vorläufig, einstweilen, provisorisch;

~ **care** Für-, Vorsorge.

provocation Herausforderung, Provokation, *(anger)* Verärgerung, Ärger, *(occasion)* Anlaß, Veranlassung;

at (on) the slightest ~ beim geringsten Anlaß; **without any** ~ ohne jede Veranlassung;

calculated ~ beabsichtigte Provokation;

wilful ~ **of public disorder** Anstiftung öffentlicher Unruhen;

to act (do) s. th. under ~ zu etw. provoziert worden sein, aufgrund von Provokationen handeln.

provocative aufreizend, provozierend;

~ **remarks** herausfordernde Bemerkungen.

provoke *(v.)* herausfordern, provozieren;

~ **a controversy** Auseinandersetzung provozieren; ~ **s. o. beyond endurance** j. bis zum Äußersten reizen; ~ **s. o. out of inertia** j. aus seiner Trägheit reißen; ~ **pity** Mitleid hervorrufen.

provoking│a difficulty Herausforderung von Auseinandersetzungen;
~ **speeches** herausfordernde (provozierende) Reden.
provost *(Cambridge)* Collegeleiter, *(mil.)* Kriegsrichter, *(Scot.)* Vorsteher, *(university, US)* hoher Verwaltungsbeamter;
~ **court** Kriegsgericht; ~ **guard** Militärpolizei; ~ **Marshal** Feldjägerkommandant.
prowl Herumstreunen;
~ *(v.)* herumlungern, -streunen, *(sl.)* nach Waffen abtasten;
~ **about the streets** in den Straßen herumlungern;
to be on the ~ auf der Lauer liegen; **to be forever on the** ~ richtiges Landstreicherleben führen; **to go on the** ~ auf Beute aus sein; **to have extra patrols on the** ~ zusätzliche Streifenwagen eingesetzt haben;
~ **car** *(US)* Streifenwagen.
prowler Landstreicher, Herumtreiber, Strauchdieb.
prowling Herumlungern.
proxies, to solicit *(US)* sich um Stimmrechtsvollmachten bemühen.
proximate in der Nähe liegend, benachbart, *(direct)* unmittelbar, direkt;
~ **to the river** am Fluß gelegen;
~ **cause** unmittelbare Ursache; ~ **consequence or result** unmittelbare Folge; ~ **damages** Ersatz des unmittelbaren Schadens; ~ **houses** unmittelbar danebenstehende Häuser.
proximity Nähe, Nachbarschaft, nahe Lage;
in close ~ in nächster Nähe von; **in the** ~ **of a town** in Stadtnähe; ~ **to a bank** Banknähe; ~ **of blood** nahe Verwandtschaft, Blutsverwandtschaft; ~ **of two estates** benachbarte Lage zweier Güter; ~ **to the market** Marktnähe; ~ **to power** bequemer Zugang zu Energiequellen; ~ **to the station** Bahnhofsnähe; ~ **to transportation** Verkehrsnähe, nahe Verkehrsbelegenheit.
proximo (prox.) nächsten Monat.
proxy [Handlungs]vollmacht, Stellvertretung, *(agency)* Geschäftsbesorgung, *(ballot, US)* Wahlgang, *(document)* Vollmachtsurkunde, *(for meeting of shareholders)* Stimmrechtsermächtigung, -vollmacht, Depotstimmrecht, *(procurator)* Anwalt, Mandator, *(representative)* Rechts-, Stellvertreter, Bevollmächtigter, Berechtigter, bevollmächtigter Vertreter, Geschäftsträger;
by ~ in Vollmacht ([Stell]vertretung);
general ~ Generalvollmacht; **irrevocable** ~ *(shareholders' meeting, Br.)* unwiderruflich erteilte Vollmacht; **special** ~ Ermessensvollmacht, *(general meeting)* auf eine Hauptversammlung begrenzte Stimmrechtsermächtigung, begrenztes Depotstimmrecht; **two-way** ~ auf zwei Personen ausgestellte Stimmrechtsermächtigung;
to act as ~ sich das Stimmrecht übertragen lassen; **to appear by** ~ als Stellvertreter fungieren; **to appoint (authorize) a** ~ sich vertreten lassen, Bevollmächtigten bestellen, jem. Vollmacht erteilen; **to make s. o. one's** ~ j. zu seinem Bevollmächtigten ernennen (bestimmen); **to produce one's** ~ seine Vollmacht vorlegen; **to reject a** ~ Vollmacht zurückweisen; **to revoke a** ~ Vollmacht widerrufen; **to send a** ~ sich vertreten lassen, Vertreter entsenden; **to send in** ~ **against (in favo(u)r)** *(shareholders' meeting)* sein Stimmrecht durch einen Bevollmächtigten dagegen (dafür) ausüben lassen; **to sign by** ~ in Vollmacht unterschreiben; **to stand** ~ **for s. o.** als Stellvertreter für j. fungieren; **to vote by** ~ sich bei der Abstimmung vertreten lassen, durch einen Bevollmächtigten abstimmen;
~ **card** *(annual meeting)* Stimmrechtskarte; ~ **contest (fight,** **US)** Stimmrechtskampf; ~ **form** Vollmachtsformular, *(general meeting)* [Depot]stimmrechtsformular; **two-way** ~ **form** Stimmenrechtsermächtigung ohne Stimmrechtsbindung; **to deposit a** ~ **form** Stimmrechtsformular hinterlegen; ~ **giver** Vollmachtsgeber, Stimmenrechtsaussteller; ~ **paper** Stimmrechtsurkunde, -vollmacht; ~ **power** Depotstimmrechtsermächtigung; ~ **rights** Depotstimmrecht; ~ **signature** Unterschrift als Stellvertreter; ~ **solicitation** *(US)* Bewerbung um Stimmrechtsvollmachten; ~ **statement** Vollmachtsanweisung, -schreiben, *(shareholders)* Aktionärsinformation; ~ **vote** *(US)* in Stellvertretung abgegebene Wahlstimme; ~ **voting** Stimmrechtsausübung durch Stellvertretung, Vollmachtsstimmrecht; ~**-wedded** ferngetraut.
proxyholder Stellvertreter eines Aktionärs, Stimmbevollmächtigter.
prudence Besonnenheit, Umsicht, Klugheit, *(law)* Vorsicht, Sorgfalt;
ordinary ~ im Verkehr erforderliche Sorgfalt.
prudent umsichtig, besonnen, klug, haushälterisch;
to be reasonably ~ **in circumstances where one is** im branchenüblichen Verkehr erforderliche Sorgfalt walten lassen;

~ **business man** umsichtiger Kaufmann; ~ **housekeeper** umsichtige Haushälterin; ~ **husband** bedachter Ehemann; ~ **investment** ordnungsgemäß vorgenommene Kapitalanlage; ~ **man** einsichtiger (vorsichtig denkender) Mensch.
prudential│s kluge Erwägungen;
~ **affairs** *(municipality)* Wohnungsbaumaßnahmen; ~ **committee** *(US)* Beratungs-, Verwaltungsausschuß, Beirat; ~ **insurance** Volksversicherung; ~ **motives** vernünftige Motive; **for** ~ **reasons** aus Gründen praktischer Überlegung.
prune *(aeronautics, sl.)* Bruchpilot;
~ *(v.)* **away all flourishes** alle unnötigen Schnörkel streichen; ~ **budget requests** Haushaltsanforderungen beschneiden; ~ **an essay** Aufsatz von unnützem Ballast befreien;
to talk ~s and prisms affektiert reden.
pry Naseweis;
~ *(v.)* spähen, *(break open)* aufbrechen, -stemmen;
~ **into another's affairs** seine Nase in anderer Leute Angelegenheiten stecken; ~ **a door open** Tür aufbrechen; ~ **out** ausfindig machen; ~ **a secret out of s. o.** jem. ein Geheimnis entlocken.
pseudograph gefälschte Schrift.
pseudonym Deckname, Pseudonym.
psyche *(v.)* **out** psychologisch überlisten.
psyched up ausgeflippt.
psychiatric│disorder Gemütskrankheit; ~ **social work** Sozialfürsorge für Nervenkranke.
psychiatrist Psychiater, Nervenarzt.
psychoanalyst Psychoanalytiker.
psychoanalyse *(v.)* psychoanalytisch behandeln.
psychological│breaking point *(income taxation)* psychologischer Schockpunkt; ~ **impact** psychologische Wirkung; ~ **moment** psychologisch richtiger Moment; ~ **torture** psychologische Folter; ~ **warfare** psychologische Kriegsführung.
psychology, crowd Massenpsychologie; **industrial** ~ Wirtschaftspsychologie;
~ **of advertising** Werbepsychologie.
pub *(Br.)* Kneipe, Schänke, Schankwirtschaft, Wirtshaus;
to go round to the ~ in die Kneipe an der Ecke gehen;
~ *(v.)* **-crawl** *(fam.)* Sauftour machen.
puberty Pubertät, *(civil law)* heiratsfähiges Alter.
public Öffentlichkeit, Allgemeinheit, *(audience)* Zuschauer, Publikum;
in ~ in aller Öffentlichkeit; **open to the** ~ der Öffentlichkeit zugänglich;
the general ~ die Öffentlichkeit; **general investing** ~ das anlageinteressierte (anlagesuchende) Publikum; **notary** ~ Notar; **reading** ~ Lesegemeinde; **theatergoing** ~ Theaterpublikum; **wider** ~ breiteres Publikum;
~ **at large** breitere Öffentlichkeit;
~ *(a.)* allgemein, öffentlich [bekannt], offenkundig, *(opposed to private)* staatsbürgerlich, staatlich, *(serving as official)* im öffentlichen Dienst stehend;
to announce to the ~ öffentlich bekanntgeben; **to appeal to a large** ~ *(book)* großes Lesepublikum haben; **to appear in** ~ an die Öffentlichkeit treten; **to be dangerous to the** ~ Gefahr für die öffentliche Sicherheit darstellen; **to be rising in the estimation of the** ~ in der Öffentlichkeit zunehmend positiv aufgenommen werden; **to become** ~ bekannt werden; **to bring before the** ~ der Öffentlichkeit übergeben, vor die Öffentlichkeit bringen; **to exclude the general** ~ *(law court)* Öffentlichkeit ausschließen; **to go** ~ *(company)* in eine öffentlich-rechtliche Gesellschaftsform umwandeln, öffentliche Rechtsform annehmen, in eine AG umwandeln; **to keep from the** ~ vor der Öffentlichkeit verbergen; **to make** ~ bekanntmachen; **to make known to the** ~ öffentlich bekanntgeben, an die Öffentlichkeit bringen; **to make the balance sheet** ~ Bilanz veröffentlichen; **to open to the** ~ *(patent law, US)* der Öffentlichkeit zwangsweise zur Verfügung stellen; **to reach the** ~ in die Öffentlichkeit dringen; **to sell the** ~ **on s. th.** in der Öffentlichkeit anpreisen; **to show o. s. in** ~ sich in der Öffentlichkeit sehen lassen;
~ **acceptance** positive Aufnahme in der Öffentlichkeit; ~ **accommodations** öffentliche Einrichtungen; ~ **account** *(Br.)* Staatskonto, Konto für staatliche Gelder; ~ **accounts** öffentliches Rechnungswesen, Staatshaushalt; ~ **accounts committee (PAC)** *(Br.)* Rechnungsprüfungsausschuß; ~ **account system** Gefangenenarbeitswesen; ~ **accountancy** *(US)* Wirtschaftsprüfungswesen; **[certified]** ~ **accountant** *(US)* Bücherrevisor, Wirtschaftsprüfer; ~ **accounting** Wirtschafts-, Jahresabschlußprüfung; ~ **acknowledgement of paternity** Vaterschaftsanerkennung; ~ **act** Öffentlichkeit interessierende Angelegenheit; ~ **address system** Lautsprecheranlage; ~ **administration**

Regie, öffentliche Verwaltung; ~ **administrator** *(US)* gerichtlich bestellter Nachlaßverwalter; ~ **affairs** Staatsangelegenheiten; ~ **agent** Beauftragter der öffentlichen Hand, Staatsbeauftragter; ~ **analyst** *(Br.)* öffentlich bestellter chemischer Prüfer; ~ **announcement** öffentliche Bekanntmachung (Ankündigung, Verlautbarung); **by** ~ **announcement** im Wege öffentlicher Bekanntmachung; ~ **appearance** Auftreten in der Öffentlichkeit; **to make a** ~ **appearance** vor die Öffentlichkeit treten; ~ **appointment** öffentliches Amt, Staats[an]stellung; ~ **approval rating** *(US)* Beliebtheitsprozentzahl; ~ **assistance** *(US)* Sozialhilfe, Fürsorgeunterstützung; ~ **assistance benefits** *(US)* Leistungen der Sozialhilfe; ~ **assistance committee** *(US)* Sozialhilfeausschuß; ~ **assistance policy** *(US)* Fürsorge-, Sozialhilfepolitik; **to be put on** ~ **assistance rolls** *(US)* Wohlfahrtsempfänger werden, der sozialen Fürsorge anheimfallen; ~ **attitude** Einstellung der Öffentlichkeit; ~ **attorney** *(US)* Staatsanwalt; ~ **auction** öffentliche Versteigerung; ~ **auditor** öffentlicher Bücherrevisor; ~ **authorities** öffentliche Hand (Stellen), Behörden; ~ **bill** Regierungsvorlage; ~ **blockade** völkerrechtlich ratifizierte Blockade; ~ **body** öffentlichrechtliche Körperschaft, Anstalt des öffentlichen Rechts, öffentlicher Rechtsträger; ~ **bonds** *(US)* Staatsanleihe, -schuldverschreibungen; ~ **book** öffentliches Register; ~ **boundary** natürliche Grenze; ~ **budgeting** Staatshaushaltsführung; ~ **building** öffentliches Gebäude; ~ **burden** *(Scot.)* Grundstückslast; ~ **business** Staatsbetrieb, Unternehmen der öffentlichen Hand; ~ **business administration** Verwaltung öffentlich-rechtlicher Betriebe; ~ **call** *(US)* Kursfestsetzung im Wege des Zurufs; ~ **call box** *(Br.)* öffentliche Fernsprechzelle; ~ **calling** Tätigkeit im Dienst der Öffentlichkeit; ~ **capacity** Gemeinnützigkeit; ~ **capital expenditure** Investitionen der öffentlichen Hand; ~ **carrier of passengers** Personenbeförderungsunternehmen; ~ **chapel** Gemeindekapelle; ~ **character** Persönlichkeit des öffentlichen Lebens; ~ **charges** öffentliche Lasten (Abgaben); ~ **charity** öffentliche Wohlfahrt; ~ **clock pillar** Normaluhrsäule; ~ **company** *(Br.)* Aktiengesellschaft; ~ **concern** öffentliche Belange; ~ **confidence** Vertrauen der Öffentlichkeit; - **consumption monopoly** staatliches Verbrauchermonopol; ~ **contract** Staatsauftrag; ~ **convenience** öffentliche Bedürfnisanstalt; ~ **corporation** *(municipal corporation) (Br.)* Körperschaft des öffentlichen Rechts, öffentlich-rechtliche Körperschaft, Wirtschaftsunternehmen der öffentlichen Hand, Magistrat; ~ **cost** Staatskosten; ~ **correspondence** öffentlicher Nachrichtenaustausch; ~ **credit** öffentlicher Kredit, Staatskredit; ~ **creditor** Staatsgläubiger; ~ **debt** *(US)* Staatsschuld, öffentliche Schuld; **new** ~ **debt** *(US)* staatliche Neuverschuldung; **to offend** ~ **decency** öffentliches Ärgernis erregen; ~ **defender** *(US)* Offizial-, Pflichtverteidiger; ~ **deposits** *(Br.)* aus öffentlichen Geldern bestehende Einlagen [bei der Bank von England], Zentralbankguthaben der öffentlichen Hände; ~ **depository** öffentliche Gelder verwaltendes Kreditinstitut; ~ **disaster** nationale Katastrophe; ~ **document** öffentlichrechtliche Urkunde; ~ **domain** staatlicher Grundbesitz, Staatsländereien, -domäne; ~ **easement** öffentlichrechtliche Grunddienstbarkeit; ~ **economist** Nationalökonom; ~ **economy** Volkswirtschaftslehre, Nationalökonomie; ~ **education** öffentliches Schulwesen; ~ **elementary school** *(Br.)* staatlich geförderte Schule ohne Religionsunterschied; ~ **employee** Staatsangestellter; ~ **employment** Staatsdienst, öffentlicher Dienst; ~ **employment office (service)** Arbeitsvermittlung[sbüro]; ~ **enemy** *(US)* Volks-, Staatsfeind; ~ **enquiry** öffentliche Untersuchung; ~ **enterprise** staatliches Unternehmen, Staatsbetrieb; ~ **entertainer** Veranstalter; ~ **examination** öffentliche Anhörung, *(bankruptcy proceedings)* Prüfungstermin; ~ **expenditures** Ausgaben der öffentlichen Hände; ~ **expenditure estimate** Staatsausgabenvoranschlag; **at the** ~ **expense** auf Kosten des Steuerzahlers, auf Staatskosten; **to be large in the** ~ **eye** in der Öffentlichkeit viel in Erscheinung treten; ~ **facilities** öffentliche (gemeinnützige) Einrichtungen; **to fall from** ~ **favo(u)r** in der Öffentlichkeit unbeliebt werden (nicht mehr beliebt sein); ~ **ferry** öffentliche Fähre; ~ **festival** Volksfest; ~ **figure** Persönlichkeit des öffentlichen Lebens; ~ **finances** öffentliches Finanzwesen, staatliche Finanzwirtschaft; ~ **function** amtliche Stellung; ~ **functionary** Staatsbeamter; ~ **fund** Publikumsfonds; ~ **funds** *(Br.)* öffentliche Gelder, *(government securities, Br.)* Staatspapiere; ~ **gallery** Publikums-, Zuschauertribüne; ~ **good** Gemeinwohl; ~ **grant** Konzessions-, Lizenzerteilung; ~ **grin** Lächeln für die Öffentlichkeit; ~ **health** Volksgesundheit, öffentliche Gesundheitspflege; ~ **health center** *(US)* Gesundheitsamt; ℮ **Health Service** *(US)* öffentliche Gesundheitspflege, staatlicher Gesundheitsdienst; ~ **hearing** öffentliche

Anhörung (Sitzung); **to grill at** ~ **hearings** bei öffentlichen Anhörungen äußerst hart anfassen; ~ **highway** öffentlicher Verkehrsweg, Landstraße; ~ **holiday** gesetzlicher Feiertag (Ruhetag); ~ **hospital** mit öffentlichen Mitteln unterhaltenes Krankenhaus; ~ **house** *(Br.)* Gaststätte, konzessionierter Alkoholausschank, Schankwirtschaft, Kneipe; **to catch the** ~ **imagination** in der Öffentlichkeit Anklang finden; ~ **importance** Bedeutung für die Allgemeinheit; ~ **indecency** *(US)* unanständiges Benehmen in der Öffentlichkeit; ~ **inquiry** *(Br.)* amtliche Untersuchung; ~ **institution** gemeinnütziges Unternehmen, öffentlich-rechtliche Einrichtung (Anstalt); ~ **interest** öffentliches Interesse, öffentliche Belange; **to enlist** ~ **interest in a matter** Öffentlichkeit für etw. interessieren; **to lie in the** ~ **interest** im öffentlichen Interesse liegen; **to serve the** ~ **interest** öffentlichem Interesse dienen; ~ **investments** Investitionen der öffentlichen Hand; ~ **issue** öffentliche Aufforderung zur Aktienzeichnung; **to be a matter of** ~ **knowledge** allgemein bekannt sein; ~ **land** *(US)* Staatsdomäne; ~ **laundry** Waschsalon; ~ **lavatory** öffentliche Bedürfnisanstalt; ~ **law** öffentliches Recht, Staatsrecht; **under** ~ **law** öffentlichrechtlich; ~ **lecture** Universitätsvorlesung, öffentlicher Vortrag; ~ **ledger** Hauptbuch; ~ **lending right** gebührenpflichtiges Ausleihungsrecht; ~ **liability insurance** Haftpflichtversicherung; ~ **liability motor insurance** Kraftfahrzeughaftpflichtversicherung; ~ **librarian** staatlich geprüfter Bibliothekar; ~ **library** Stadtbücherei, -bibliothek, Volksbibliothek; ~ **life** Leben in der Öffentlichkeit; **to enter** ~ **life** in der Öffentlichkeit bekannt werden, sich öffentlichen Belangen widmen; ~ **limited company** *(Br.)* [etwa] Aktiengesellschaft; **to be in the** ~ **line** *(coll., Br.)* im Gaststättengewerbe tätig sein; ~ **loan** Staatsanleihe, öffentliche Anleihe, öffentlicher Kredit; ~ **man** Mann der Öffentlichkeit, *(cabinet)* Kabinettsmitglied; ~ **market** öffentlicher Markt; ~ **means** öffentliche Mittel; ~ **meeting** öffentliche Versammlung (Tagung); ℮ **Meeting Act** *(Br.)* Versammlungsgesetz; ~ **mind** Bewußtsein der Öffentlichkeit; ~**minded** auf das Gemeinwohl bedacht, gemeinnützig; ~**mindedness** Gemeinnützigkeit; ~ **minister** *(Br.)* höherer Diplomat; ~ **mischief** grober Unfug; ~ **money** öffentliche Mittel, Steuergelder; **to be light with** ~ **money** mit Steuergeldern äußerst leichtsinnig umgehen; ~ **mood** Stimmung in der Öffentlichkeit; **to offend against** ~ **morals** gegen das allgemeine Sittlichkeitsempfinden verstoßen; ~ **necessity** öffentliches Bedürfnis; ~ **notice** öffentliche Bekanntmachung; ~ **nuisance** öffentliches Ärgernis; ~ **occupation** Tätigkeit im Dienst der Öffentlichkeit; ~ **offence** strafbare Handlung; ~ **offerings** Börseneinführung, öffentliche Aufforderung zur Zeichnung von Effekten; ~ **office** Staatsanstellung, -amt, Amtsstelle; **to hold a** ~ **office** öffentliches Amt bekleiden; ~ **officer** Staatsbeamter, *(corporation)* Direktor einer AG; ~ **official bond** Kaution eines Staatstreuhänders.

public opinion öffentliche Meinung;
to carry ~ **with one** die Öffentlichkeit hinter sich haben; **to create a** ~ **favo(u)rable** günstige Aufnahme in der Öffentlichkeit finden; **to exploit** ~ sich die öffentliche Meinung dienstbar machen; **to sway** ~ öffentliche Meinung beeinflussen;
~ **analyst** Meinungsforscher; ~ **poll** Meinungsbefragung, -umfrage, demoskopische Untersuchung, Umfrage zur Erforschung der öffentlichen Meinung; ~ **poll rating** Bewertungsnote nach einer Meinungsumfrage; ~ **research** Meinungsforschung, Demoskopie; ~ **survey** Meinungsbefragung.

public│orator *(university, Br.)* Sprecher; ~ **order** öffentliche Sicherheit und Ordnung; ℮ **Order Act** *(Br.)* Gesetz zur Aufrechterhaltung von Ruhe und Ordnung, Versammlungsgesetz; ~ **order members** *(options exchange)* Mitglieder auswärtiger Börsen, die für Unternehmen der öffentlichen Hand tätig sind; ~ **outcry** öffentliche Versteigerung; ~ **overhead capital** Suprastruktur; ~ **ownership** Staatseigentum, *(municipal accounting)* Kommunalbesitz, Gemeindeeigentum; ~ **papers** öffentliche Blätter; ~ **parks** Parkanlagen, öffentliche Anlagen; ~ **parking place** öffentlicher Parkplatz; ~ **part** *(land)* der Öffentlichkeit zugänglicher Teil; **without** ~ **participation** ohne die Öffentlichkeit zu befragen; ~ **passage** Durchfahrtsrecht auf öffentlichen Gewässern; ~ **peace** öffentliche Ruhe und Sicherheit, Landfrieden; ~ **pension** Staatspension; ~ **person** Repräsentant eines souveränen Staates; ~ **place** allgemein zugänglicher Ort, öffentlicher Platz; ~ **policy** öffentliche Belange, öffentliches Interesse, Gemeinwohl; **contrary to** ~ **policy** gegen das öffentliche Interesse; ~ **pond** *(New England)* größeres Gewässer; ~ **porter** Gepäckträger; ~ **power district** Stromversorgungsbezirk; ~ **price** Ladenpreis; ~ **printer** *(US)* Leiter der Staatsdruckerei; ~ **printing** *(US)* Staatsdruckerei; ~ **prints** öffentliche

Blätter; ~ **prior use** *(patent laws)* offenkundige Vorbenutzung; ~ **procession** öffentlicher Umzug, Demonstration[szug]; ~ **project** öffentliches Bauvorhaben; ~ **property** Staatseigentum, -besitz, Eigentum der öffentlichen Hand; ~ **prosecution** Strafverfolgung; ~ **prosecutor** Staatsanwalt; ~ **purpose** gemeinnütziges Werk, Gemeinbedarf; ~ **purse** Staatssäckel; ~ **record** *(Br.)* öffentlich aufbewahrte Urkunde, Staatsurkunde, *(politics)* politische Vergangenheit; ⚓ **Records Office** Staatsarchiv; ~ **recording official** Urkundenbeamter; ~ **regulation** Staatsaufsicht, staatliche Beaufsichtigung.

public relations öffentliche Meinungspflege, Kontaktpflege, Öffentlichkeitsarbeit, Vertrauenswerbung;
~ **adviser** Berater in Fragen der Öffentlichkeitsarbeit; ~ **campaign** Aufklärungsfeldzug; ~ **consultant (counsellor)** Berater in Fragen der Öffentlichkeitsarbeit; ~ **director** Vorstandsmitglied für Öffentlichkeitsfragen; ~ **executive** Sachbearbeiter für Öffentlichkeitsfragen; ~ **firm** Agentur für Öffentlichkeitsfragen; ~ **manager** Leiter der PR-Abteilung, PR-Chef; ~ **officer** Sachbearbeiter für Öffentlichkeitsfragen, PR-, Pressechef; ~ **practitioner** erfahrener PR-Mann; ~ **setup** Arbeitsstab für Öffentlichkeitsfragen; ~ **society** Public-Relationsgesellschaft; ~ **stunt** Reklamemasche; ~ **support** Unterstützung durch Öffentlichkeitsarbeit; ~ **work** Öffentlichkeitsarbeit.

public | relief *(Br.)* öffentliche Fürsorge; ~ **requirements** öffentlicher Bedarf; ~ **revenue** Staatseinkünfte, Einkünfte der öffentlichen Hand; ~ **reward** Auslobung; ~ **rights** Rechte der Allgemeinheit, Bürgerrechte und -pflichten; ~ **right of way** öffentliches Wegerecht; ~ **river** öffentlicher Wasserweg; ~ **road** Landstraße; ~ **road administration** *(US)* Straßenverwaltung durch den Staat; ~ **rooms** Empfangs-, Gesellschaftsräume; ~ **safety** öffentliche Sicherheit; ~ **sale** Auktion, öffentliche Versteigerung; ~ **sanction** Betätigung durch die Öffentlichkeit; ~ **school** *(Br.)* reich dotierte Privatschule mit Internat, *(US)* städtische Schule, Volks-, Gemeindeschule, *(Br.)* Privatschule, höhere Mittelschule mit Alumnat; ~ **seal** Staatssiegel.

public sector öffentlicher Bereich;
in the ~ im Bereich der öffentlichen Hand;
~ **of the economy** öffentlicher Sektor der Wirtschaft;
~ **borrower** Kreditkunde der öffentlichen Hand; ~ **borrowings** Verschuldung der öffentlichen Hand; ~ **borrowing requirements** Kreditbedarf der öffentlichen Hand; ~ **building** öffentlicher Bausektor; ~ **deficit** Defizit der öffentlichen Hand; **tight ~ employment policy** sehr zurückhaltende beschäftigungspolitische Maßnahmen der öffentlichen Hand; ~ **investment** Investitionen der öffentlichen Hand; ~ **investment orders** Investitionsaufträge der öffentlichen Hand; ~ **manpower** im öffentlichen Bereich tätige Arbeitskräfte; ~ **onslaught** heftige Angriffe im öffentlichen Bereich; ~ **pay claims** Lohnforderungen im Bereich der öffentlichen Hand; ~ **pay control** Überwachung der Tarifpolitik im öffentlichen Bereich; ~ **pay settlements** Tarifvereinbarungen im öffentlichen Bereich; ~ **strike** Staatsstreik, Streik der öffentlichen Bediensteten; ~ **undertaking** Unternehmen der öffentlichen Hand.

public | securities Staatspapiere, -obligationen, Obligationen der öffentlichen Hand; ~ **servant** Staatsbeamter, Beamter im öffentlichen Dienst, Staatsangestellter; ~ **servants' trade union** Gewerkschaft öffentlicher Dienste.

public service *(US)* Staatsdienst, öffentlicher Dienst, *(business of supplying utilities, US)* Bereitstellung gemeinnütziger Betriebsmittel (von Versorgungseinrichtungen);
~**s** Dienstleistungssektor;
major ~ wesentlicher Beitrag für die Öffentlichkeit;
to train for ~ *(US)* sich auf den Staatsdienst vorbereiten;
~ **commission** *(US)* Aufsichtsbehörde für öffentliche Versorgungsbetriebe; ~ **company (corporation, enterprise, US)** öffentlicher Versorgungs-, gemeinnütziger Betrieb; ~ **union** Gewerkschaft im öffentlichen Dienst Beschäftigter; ~ **vehicle** öffentliches Verkehrsmittel.

public | sewer Hauptkanal; ~ **speaker** Sprecher; ~ **speaking** öffentliche Aussprache; ~ **spending** Staatsausgaben; ~ **spending on the social services** öffentlicher Sozialaufwand; ~ **spending control** Ausgabenkontrolle der öffentlichen Hand; ~ **spending cuts** Staatsausgabenkürzung; ~ **spending plan** Ausgabenprogramm der öffentlichen Hand; ~ **spirit** Gemeinsinn, Patriotismus; ~**-spirited** auf das Gemeinwohl bedacht, um das Gemeinwohl besorgt, patriotisch; **to show o. s. ~-spirited** seinen Bürgersinn unter Beweis stellen; ~ **square** öffentlicher Platz; ~ **statement** öffentliche Erklärung; ~ **statute** allgemeines Gesetz; ~ **stocks** Obligationen der öffentlichen Hand, Staatsanleihen; ~ **store** öffentliches Vorratslager, *(customs)* Zollniederlage; ~ **supply undertaking** öffentliches Versorgungsunter-

nehmen; ~ **taking of private property** Enteignung; ~ **taxes** öffentliche Abgaben; ~ **telephone** Münzfernsprecher; ~ **tender** Ausschreibung; ~ **thoroughfare** öffentlicher Durchgang (Weg); ~ **trading body** öffentlich-rechtliches Handelsunternehmen, Staatshandelsbetrieb; ~ **transport** öffentliches Verkehrswesen; **by ~ transport** mit öffentlichen Verkehrsmitteln; ~ **transport undertaking** öffentliches Verkehrsunternehmen; ~ **trial** öffentliche Verhandlung; ~ **trust** gemeinnützige (öffentlich-rechtliche) Stiftung; ~ **trustee** *(Br.)* gemeinnütziges Stiftungsamt, *(US)* staatliche Treuhandstelle, staatlich eingesetzter Treuhänder; ⚓ **Trustee Act** *(Br.)* Hinterlegungsverordnung; ⚓ **Trustee Office** *(Br.)* öffentliche Hinterlegungsstelle; ~ **undertaking** öffentlicher Betrieb, Staatsbetrieb; ~ **use** *(US)* Verwendung im öffentlichen Interesse; ~ **use proceedings** *(patent laws, US)* Einspruchsverfahren; ~ **utilities** Stadtwerke, Verkehrs- und Versorgungsbetriebe, Versorgungswirtschaft, Stadtwerke, *(US)* Verkehrsunternehmen, *(stock exchange, US)* Versorgungswerte.

public utility [öffentlicher] Versorgungsbetrieb, *(US)* Verkehrsunternehmen;
~ **agency** *(US)* Versorgungsbetrieb; ~ **bonds** Obligationen der Versorgungsbetriebe, Versorgungswerte; ~ **common stocks** *(US)* Stammaktien gemeinnütziger Unternehmen; ~ **company (corporation, establishment, undertaking)** Gemeinde-, öffentlicher Versorgungsbetrieb, Versorgungsunternehmen, *(US)* Verkehrsunternehmen; ~ **field** Gebiet der öffentlichen Versorgungsbetriebe; ~ **shares (stocks)** Tarif-, Versorgungswerte; ~ **society (undertaking)** Versorgungsunternehmen.

public | vehicle öffentliches Verkehrsmittel; ~ **verdict** öffentlich verkündetes Geschworenenurteil; ~ **vessel** Staatsschiff; ~ **want** öffentliches Bedürfnis; ~ **war** Völkerkrieg; ~ **warehouse** *(US)* [öffentlicher] Speicher; ~ **waters** schiffbare Gewässer; ~ **way** öffentlicher Weg, Landstraße; ~ **weal** Allgemeinwohl; ~ **weigher** Wiegemeister; ~ **welfare** öffentliche Wohlfahrt, Sozialhilfe; ~ **works** öffentliche Arbeiten (Bauten); ⚓ **Works Administration** *(US)* Arbeitsbeschaffungsbehörde; ⚓ **Works Committee** *(US)* Arbeitsbeschaffungsausschuß; ~ **works expenditure** für Arbeitsbeschaffungsaufgaben eingesetzte Mittel; ~ **works loan board** *(Br.)* Finanzierungsstelle für Kommunalinvestitionen; ~ **works program** *(US)* Arbeitsbeschaffungsprogramm; ~ **works project** *(US)* Arbeitsbeschaffungsprojekt; ~ **works and wages system** *(US)* Gefangenenarbeit für Aufgaben im öffentlichen Interesse; ~ **worship** öffentlicher Gottesdienst; ~ **wrong** strafbare Handlung.

publican *(Br.)* Gastwirt.

publication Veröffentlichung, öffentliche Bekanntmachung, Kenntnisgabe, Kundgabe, *(book)* Veröffentlichung, Erscheinen, Publikation, Druckschrift, Herausgabe, *(law of libel)* Verbreitung, *(law of wills)* Erklärung des letzten Willens, *(that which is published)* herausgegebenes Werk, Presseerzeugnis, Verlagsartikel, -werk, -objekt, Organ, *(summons)* öffentliche Zustellung, Aufgebotsverfahren;
for favo(u)r of ~ in your columns mit der Bitte um Veröffentlichung in Ihrer Zeitung;
annual ~ Jahresschrift; **business ~** Wirtschaftswerbung; **class ~** exklusive Veröffentlichung; **consumer ~** Verbraucher-, Publikationszeitschrift; **copyrighted ~** urheberrechtlich geschützte Ausgabe; **daily ~** tägliches Erscheinen; **external ~** außerbetriebliche Veröffentlichung; **governmental ~** amtliche Veröffentlichung; **industrial ~** wirtschaftliche Veröffentlichung; **legal ~** rechtswirksame Veröffentlichung; **memorial ~** Festschrift; **monthly ~** Monatsschrift; **new ~** Neuerscheinung; **obscene ~** pornographische Veröffentlichung; **official ~** amtliche Bekanntmachung; **printed ~** öffentliche Druckschrift, druckschriftliche Veröffentlichung; **prior ~** Vorveröffentlichung; **quarterly ~** Vierteljahreszeitschrift; **serial ~** Veröffentlichung in Fortsetzungen; **top ~** führendes Organ, Veröffentlichung ersten Ranges; **trade ~** geschäftliche Bekanntmachung; **undue ~** unzulässige Veröffentlichung; **weekly ~** Wochenschrift;
~ **of the banns** Aufbietung eines Brautpaares; ~ **of the balance sheet** Bilanzveröffentlichung; ~ **of books** Bücherveröffentlichung; ~ **of a libel** Verbreitung einer verleumderischen Behauptung; ~ **of rates** Tarifveröffentlichung; ~ **of a report** Herausgabe eines Berichts;
to announce the ~ of a book Buchankündigung vornehmen, Buch anzeigen; **to cease ~** Erscheinen einstellen; **to constitute legal ~** durch die Veröffentlichung rechtswirksam werden; **to limp into ~** endlich veröffentlicht werden; **to read a book on first ~** Buch gleich bei Erscheinen lesen; **to resume ~** *(newspaper)* Erscheinen wiederaufnehmen, wiedererscheinen; **to schedule the ~ for November** Publikation für November vor-

sehen; **to subscribe for a** ~ Publikation im voraus bestellen; **to suppress a** ~ Veröffentlichung untersagen; **to suspend a** ~ Publikation vorübergehend einstellen;

~ **date** Veröffentlichungs-, Erscheinungsdatum, -termin; ~ **division** Presseabteilung; ~ **fee** Bekanntmachungsgebühr; ~ **goal** geplantes Erscheinungsdatum; ~ **issue date** Veröffentlichungs-, Ausgabedatum; ~ **price** *(bookshop)* Ladenpreis; ~ **schedule** Erscheinungsweise; ~**'s standards** Niveau einer Zeitschrift.

publicism Publizistik, Journalismus.

publicist Schriftsteller, Publizist, Journalist, *(international law)* Völkerrechtler, *(publicity agent)* Werbefachmann.

publicistic publizistisch.

publicity Öffentlichkeit, *(advertising)* Reklame, Propaganda, Werbung, Werbewesen, -tätigkeit, *(attention gained)* starker Widerhall in der Öffentlichkeit, Publizität, *(public relations)* Öffentlichkeitsarbeit;

in the full blaze of ~ im vollen Rampenlicht;

broadcast ~ Rundfunkwerbung; **export** ~ Exportwerbung; **outdoor** ~ Straßenreklame;

~ **from the air** Luftwerbung; ~ **of a scandal** Offenkundigkeit eines Skandals; ~ **on television** Fernsehpublizität;

to attract ~ Aufsehen erregen; **to avoid** ~ Publizität vermeiden; **to create favo(u)rable** ~ positive Reaktionen in der Öffentlichkeit auslösen; **to give s. th.** ~ etw. allgemein bekanntgeben; **to give a new book wider** ~ großangelegte Werbung für ein neues Buch veranstalten; **to live one's life in the full blaze of** ~ sein ganzes Leben im Scheinwerferlicht der Öffentlichkeit stehen; **to restore** ~ *(law court)* Öffentlichkeit wiederherstellen; **to seek** ~ bekannt werden wollen;

~ **agency** Werbeagentur; ~ **agent** freiberuflicher Mittler für werbliche Informationen, Werbungsmittler; ~ **bureau** Anzeigenannahmestelle, Werbebüro; ~ **campaign** Werbefeldzug, -aktion; **to conduct a** ~ **campaign** Werbefeldzug durchführen; ~ **costs** Plazierungskosten für werbliche Informationen; ~ **department** Propaganda-, Werbeabteilung; **Foreign** ~ **Department** Propagandabteilung des Foreign Office; ~ **director** Werbeleiter, Leiter der Werbeabteilung; ~ **document** Werbeschrift; ~ **editor** für den Anzeigenteil verantwortlicher Redakteur; ~ **effort** Werbekampagne; ~ **expenses** Werbekosten, -aufwand; ~ **expert** Werbefachmann; ~ **fund** Propagandafonds; ~ **gag** Werbemasche; **to put o. s. through all the** ~ **hops** *(sl.)* sich durch die Mühlen des Presserummels drehen lassen; ~ **kit** Werbemappe; ~ **man** Werbefachmann, -berater; ~ **manager** Werbeleiter; ~ **material** Werbe-, Prospektmaterial; ~ **medium** Informationskanal; ~ **method** Werbemethode; ~ **office** Werbebüro; ~ **officer** Sachbearbeiter für Öffentlichkeitsfragen; ~ **program(me)** Werbeprogramm; ~ **purpose** Werbezweck; ~ **representative** Werbemanager, -leiter; ~ **sign** Reklameschild; ~ **spokesman** autorisierter Sprecher; ~ **stunt** Werbefeldzug, Reklametrommel; ~ **technique** Werbetechnik.

publicly | demanded von der Öffentlichkeit gefordert; ~ **owned** staatseigen, im öffentlichen Eigentum;

to announce ~ öffentlich bekanntgeben; **to appear** ~ vor der Öffentlichkeit treten; **to be** ~ **owned** im öffentlichen Eigentum stehen;

~ **owned corporation (enterprise)** *(US)* staatliche Gesellschaft, Staatsbetrieb, Unternehmen der öffentlichen Hand.

publicize *(v.)* öffentlich bekanntmachen, publizieren, *(advertise)* Reklame machen, werben, Werbung betreiben.

publicized, highly öffentlich herausgestellt.

publicness öffentlicher Charakter.

publish *(v.)* *(book trade)* herausgeben, verlegen, publizieren, veröffentlichen, *(intentionally exhibit libellous matter)* ehrenrührige Dinge verbreiten, *(promulgate)* öffentlich bekanntgeben;

~ **the banns of marriage** [Heirats]aufgebot bestellen; ~ **a book** Buch drucken (verlegen, veröffentlichen); ~ **a book under one's own name** Buch unter seinem eigenen Namen erscheinen lassen; ~ **comment on cases pending** in ein laufendes Verfahren eingreifen; ~ **counterfeit money** Falschgeld in Umlauf setzen; ~ **a decree** Verordnung erlassen; ~ **the news** Neuigkeit bekanntgeben; ~ **news without vouching for its accuracy** Nachrichten ohne Nachprüfung veröffentlichen; ~ **a newspaper** Zeitung herausgeben; ~ **a report** Meldung veröffentlichen; ~ **a scandal** Skandal öffentlich bekanntmachen; ~ **a selection** Werke im Auswahl herausbringen.

publishable publizierbar, für eine Veröffentlichung geeignet.

published veröffentlicht, erschienen;

just ~ soeben erschienen; **not yet** ~, **order noted** noch nicht erschienen, Bestellung ist vorgemerkt;

~ **by** herausgegeben von; ~ **by the author** im Selbstverlag des Verfassers; **as soon as** ~ sofort nach Erscheinen;

to be ~ veröffentlicht werden, erscheinen, herauskommen; **to be** ~ **in instalments (parts)** in Lieferungen erscheinen; **to be** ~ **in no particular order** in ungezwungener Folge erscheinen; **to be** ~ **shortly** demnächst (in Kürze) erscheinen; **to be** ~ **weekly** wöchentlich erscheinen;

~ **price** Ladenpreis; ~ **works** erschienene Werke.

publisher [Zeitungs]verleger, Herausgeber, *(book trade)* Verlagsbuchhändler, -anstalt, Verlag;

to place a book with a ~ Verlagsvertrag über ein Buch abschließen;

~**'s binding** Verlegereinband; ~**'s brochure** Verlegerbroschur; ~**'s calculation** Verlagskalkulation; ~**'s catalog(ue)** Verlagskatalog; ~**'s delivery agency (department)** Verlagsauslieferung; ~**'s encashment agency** Verlegerinkassostelle; ~**'s imprint** Druckortangabe; ~**'s overheads** Verlagsgemeinkosten; ~**'s profit** Verlagsgewinn; ~**'s representative** Verlagsrepräsentant, -vertreter; ~**'s statement** *(advertising)* geprüfte Auflagenmeldung, -bestätigung.

publishing Veröffentlichung, Herausgabe, Verlegertätigkeit;

to keep ~ weiterhin erscheinen; **to start out in** ~ Verlag gründen;

~ **agreement** Verlagsvertrag; ~ **bookseller** Verlagsbuchhändler; ~ **business** Verlagsbuchhandel, -geschäft; ~ **concern** Verlagskonzern; ~ **cost (expenses)** Veröffentlichungskosten; ~ **firm** Verlag, Verlagshaus; ~ **formula** Veröffentlichungsdevise; ~ **house** Verlagsbuchhandlung, Verlag; ~ **price** Laden-, Verkaufspreis eines Buches; ~ **profit** Verlagsgewinn; **to set** ~ **records** Auflagenrekorde aufstellen; ~ **trade** Verlagsbuchhandel, -geschäft, -wesen.

pudding | heart Feigling; ~**-proof** narrensicher.

puddle Pfütze, Lache, *(fig.)* Durcheinander, Wirrwarr;

~ **jumper** *(sl.)* Bummelzug, Klapperkasten.

puff Windstoß, Hauch, *(quack, Br.)* marktschreierische (unerlaubte) Reklame, überzogene Werbung, unreelle Anpreisung, *(book review)* lobhudelnde Kritik;

~ *(v.)* schnaufen, keuchen, *(advertise)* marktschreierisch anpreisen, *(auction)* Scheinangebot abgeben;

~ **o. s. up** sich aufblasen; ~ **out of the station** *(train)* aus der Station dampfen; ~ **up goods** Warenpreis in die Höhe treiben; ~ **box** Puderdose.

puffed außer Atem;

~ **up with pride** stolzgebläht.

puffer Marktschreier, *(auction)* Scheinbieter [für den Grundeigentümer], Preistreiber.

puffery *(Br.)* übertriebene Reklame.

puffing Aufbauschung, -blähung, *(Br.)* übertriebene Anpreisung, Marktschreierei, *(auction)* Abgabe von Scheingeboten, *(prices)* Preistreiberei;

harmless ~ *(Br.)* überzogene Werbung;

~ **advertisement** marktschreierische Reklame.

pug *(Br.)* Verschublokomotive.

puisne *(judge)* Beisitzer;

~ *(a.)* nachgeboren, jünger, *(rank)* rangjünger, nachstehend; ~ **mortgage** *(Br.)* nachstehende (nachrangige) Hypothek.

pull Zug, Ruck, *(influence, sl.)* Macht, politischer Einfluß, Protektion, gute Beziehungen, *(print.)* Probeabzug, Andruck, letzte Fahne, *(sale)* Verkaufsanreiz, -wirkung, Zugkraft, *(spoils)* Schiebung;

bell ~ Glockenzug;

~ **of demand** Nachfragesog; **inflation-induced** ~ **of imports** inflatorisch bedingter Einfuhrsog; ~ **of twenty tons** Zugkraft von zwanzig Tonnen;

~ *(v.)* ziehen, Zug haben, *(use one's influence)* seinen Einfluß geltend machen, seine Beziehungen spielen lassen, *(police, sl.)* Razzia veranstalten, *(print.)* abziehen, bedrucken;

~ **about** unsanft behandeln; ~ **back** sich einschränken, *(date earlier)* zurückdatieren, *(film)* rückblenden, *(give a setback)* zurückwerfen; ~ **the ball** klingeln, läuten; ~ **a boat** Boot rudern; ~ **caps** streiten; ~ **in the cash** Außenstände eintreiben; ~ **the chestnuts out of the fire** die Kastanien aus dem Feuer holen; ~ **custom** *(US)* Kundschaft anziehen; ~ **devil, ~ baker** jeden sein Äußerstes tun lasen; ~ **down** herunterziehen, -reißen, *(sl.)* wöchentlich verdienen; ~ **down a building** Gebäude (Haus) abreißen; ~ **down the prices of stocks** Aktienkurse herunterdrücken; ~ **in one's expenses** Kosten sparen (reduzieren); ~ **a face** Grimassen schneiden; ~ **one's forelock** respektvoll grüßen; ~ **heavily** *(engine)* schwer gehen; ~ **in** *(arrest, sl)* verhaften; ~ **in one's horns** seinen Unmut zügeln; ~ **the job** *(sl.)* ein Ding drehen; ~ **into a layby** auf einem Rastplatz halten; ~ **s.**

one's leg jem. etw. weismachen wollen, jem. auf den Arm nehmen, jem. einen Streich spielen; ~ **to the left** *(car)* nach links ziehen; ~ **the levers** Schalthebel ziehen; ~ **a lone oar** *(fig.)* seinen Weg ganz allein gehen; ~ **off** Erfolg haben, zuwegebringen, schaffen, bewirken, *(print.)* abziehen; ~ **off a crime** *(sl.)* Verbrechen begehen; ~ **off some good things at the races** einige erfolgreiche Wetten abschließen; ~ **off a parachute** Fallschirm lösen; ~ **off a good speculation** erfolgreiche Spekulation durchführen; ~ **off twenty tons** Zugkraft von zwanzig Tonnen haben; ~ **s. th. on s. o.** *(coll.)* j. mit etw. hereinlegen; ~ **on the trigger** abdrücken; ~ **out** *(US)* sich entfernen, fortgehen; ~ **out one's cheque book** sein Scheckbuch zücken; ~ **the government out of the mess** Regierung aus der Krise heraussteuern; ~ **s. o. out of a hole** *(fam.)* jem. aus der Klemme helfen; ~ **out from behind a lorry** *(driver)* zum Überholmanöver hinter einem Lastwagen ansetzen; ~ **out of the station** *(train)* aus dem Bahnhof herausfahren; ~ **out of unprofitable waggonload service** vom unrentierlichen Sammellastzugsverkehr abgehen; ~ **over to the side of the road** auf die Straßenseite fahren; ~ **to pieces** *(fig.)* in Stücke reißen, verreißen, heruntermachen; ~ **s. o. to pieces** an jem. kein gutes Haar lassen; ~ **s. one's proposal to pieces** jds. Vorschlag zerpflücken; ~ **the plane of the ground** Flugzeug starten; ~ **rank** *(sl.)* seine gesellschaftliche Stellung ausnutzen; ~ **round in the country** sich auf dem Lande erholen; ~ **strings** *(sl.)* hinter den Kulissen agieren; ~ **s. one's teeth** *(fig.)* jem. die Zähne ziehen; ~ **through** erfolgreich durchführen, *(patient)* durchkommen; ~ **s. o. through** j. aus einer Schwierigkeit heraushelfen; ~ **together** zusammenhalten; ~ **o. s. together** sich zusammenreißen; ~ **the trigger** abdrücken; ~ **up** *(chairman)* Verweis erteilen; ~ **up s. o.** *(police)* j. schnappen; ~ **up the brake** Bremse anziehen; ~ **up at the kerb** am Bürgersteig anhalten; ~ **up short** plötzlich anhalten; ~ **up stakes** *(US coll.)* umziehen; ~ **o. s. upright** sich hochrappeln; ~ **one's weight** *(fig.)* seinen Teil beitragen; ~ **well together** gut zusammenarbeiten; ~ **wires** seine Beziehungen spielen lassen; ~ **the wool over s. one's eyes** *(US)* jem. Sand in die Augen streuen; ~ **a yarn** *(fam.)* Garn spinnen; **to be a heavy ~ upon s. one's purse** jem. teuer zu stehen kommen; **to have an extra ~** *(candidate)* über besondere Meriten verfügen; **to have a ~ over s. o.** j. in seiner Hand haben; **to have a strong ~ with s. o.** großen Einfluß auf j. ausüben; **to secure an office through one's ~** Stellung durch Beziehungen bekommen; ~ **bell** Zugglocke; ~ **box** *(el.)* Auschlußkasten; **~-off of a parachute** Lösen eines Fallschirms; **~-out** Faltblatt, *(airplane)* Hochziehen, *(book)* ausklappare Seite; **~-out supplement** *(magazine)* herausnehmbare Beilage; ~ **switch** *(el.)* Zugschalter; **~-through** Gewehrreiniger; **~-up** *(Br.)* Halteplatz, *(car)* Anhalten, Stehenbleiben.

pulled up by the police von der Polizei festgenommen, ausgehoben.

puller *(sl.)* Zugartikel, zugkräftiger Artikel, Schlager; **~-in** *(US)* Anreißer, Kundenfänger.

pulley Flaschenzug.

pulling | to pieces *(article, book)* Verriß; ~ **boat** Ruderboot; ~ **power** Anziehungskraft.

Pullman | car *(US)* Schlafwagen; ~ **express** D-Zug-Waggon.

pulp *(US)* minderwertige Zeitschrift, Schundroman, *(mining)* gewaschenes Erz, *(papermaking)* Papierbrei, Ganzzeug; ~ *(v.)* zermalmen, zu Brei machen, *(printed matter)* einstampfen; **to be reduced to a ~** *(fig.)* völlig erledigt sein; **to reduce to ~** windelweich schlagen; ~ **magazine** Schundzeitschrift.

pulpit Kanzel; ~ **orator** Kanzelredner; ~ **oratory** Kanzelpredigt.

pulsate *(v.)* pulsieren, vibrieren; ~ **with excitement** vor Erregung zittern.

pulsator Kläger.

pulse Puls; **to feel s. one's ~** *(fig.)* jem. auf den Zahn fühlen; **to feel the ~ of the electorate** Stimmung der Wählerschaft ausfindig machen; **to keep a finger on the ~ of business activity day by day** Geschäftstätigkeit Tag für Tag genauestens überwachen.

pulverize *(v.)* zermalmen, pulverisieren, völlig vernichten.

pump Pumpe, *(fig.)* Ausfragen, -holen; ~ **on** *(dial.)* auf Pump; **bicycle ~** Fahrradpumpe; **bilge ~** Lenzpumpe; **gear ~** Getriebepumpe; **hand ~** Handpumpe; **lift and force ~** Saug- und Druckpresse; **piston ~** Kolbenpumpe; ~ *(v.)* pumpen; ~ **s. o.** bei jem. auf den Busch klopfen; ~ **abuses upon s. o.** j. mit Verwünschungen überschütten; ~ **economic aid into a country** einem Land Wirtschaftshilfe gewähren; ~ **aid loans and guarantees into the steel works** der Stahlindustrie mit generellen Hilfszusagen, Anleihen und Staatsgarantien Mittel zuführen; ~ **air into a tyre** Reifen aufpumpen; ~ **one's brains for ideas** sich den Kopf zerbrechen; ~ **facts into the heads of dull pupils** gelangweilten Schülern Tatsachenwissen eintrichtern; ~ **information out of s. o.** Nachrichten aus jem. herausholen; ~ **knowledge into a candidate** einem Prüfling Wissen einbleuen; ~ **s. o. for money** j. um Geld anpumpen; ~ **money into** Geld hineinpumpen; ~ **out** *(fig.)* auspumpen, erschöpfen; ~ **out a boat** Boot auspumpen; ~ **a secret out of s. o.** *(fam.)* jem. ein Geheimnis entreißen; ~ **up one's bike** *(fam.)* sein Fahrrad aufpumpen; ~ **for some form of wage restraint** sich halbwegs um Zurückhaltung bei Lohnforderungen bemühen; ~ **a well dry** Brunnen leerpumpen; **to work a ~** Pumpe betätigen; ~ **brake** Pumpenbremse; ~ **house** Pumpenhaus; ~ **lever** Pumpenhebel; ~ **price for petrol** Benzinabgabepreis; ~ **priming** *(US)* Starthilfe, konjunkturelle Initialzündung, Ankurbelung der Wirtschaft durch Staatsaufträge; **~-priming credit** *(US)* Ankurbelungskredit; **~-priming program** *(US)* Konjunkturprogramm; ~ **room** Pumpenhaus, *(spa)* Trinkhalle.

pumped out erschöpft, ausgepumpt.

pumping Pumpen; ~ **in foreign aid** Gewährung von Auslandshilfe; ~ **out** Auspumpen; ~ **up** Aufpumpen; ~ **engine** Dampfpumpe; ~ **plant** Pumpwerk; ~ **station** Pumpstation.

pumpkin *(US coll.)* hohes Tier.

pun *(v.)* **upon a word** Wortspiel machen.

punch Punch, *(die)* Prägestempel, *(fig.)* Durchschlagskraft, Schwung, *(perforator)* Stanze, *(sl.)* improvisierte Party; **as proud as ~** stolz wie ein Zinshahn; ~ *(v.)* **a bus ticket** Omnibusfahrkarte lochen; ~ **one's card** *(worker)* seine Karte stechen; **to pull one's ~es** seine Kräfte zurückhalten; **to write with ~** schwungvoll schreiben; ~ **card** Hollerith-, Lochkarte; **~-card society** nur in Schablonen denkende Gesellschaft; ~ **line** Pointe, Knalleffekt; ~ **pliers** Lochzange.

punched card Hollerith-, Lochkarte; ~ **experience** Lochkartenerfahrung; ~ **machine** Lochkartenmaschine; ~ **method (system)** Lochkartenverfahren.

punched tape Lochstreifen.

puncheon Prägestempel.

puncher Locher.

punctilio heikler Punkt; ~ **of hono(u)r** Ehrenpunkt; **to stand upon ~s** es mit Protokollfragen übergenau nehmen.

punctilious pedantisch, förmlich; **to be ~ on the point of hono(u)r** in Ehrensachen peinlich genau sein.

punctiliousness Förmlichkeit, pedantische Genauigkeit; **to act with extreme ~ towards one another** einander genau dem Protokoll entsprechend behandeln.

punctual prompt, pünktlich, rechtzeitig; **as ~ as the clock** pünktlich wie die Uhr; ~ **in the performance of one's duties** prompt in der Erfüllung seiner Pflichten; ~ **to the minute** auf die Minute pünktlich; **to be ~ in one's payment** seine Zahlungstermine einhalten (pünktlich erledigen); **to be ~ in the payment of one's rent** seine Miete pünktlich bezahlen; **to meet ~ly** seinen Verpflichtungen pünktlich nachkommen; ~ **payment** pünktliche Zahlung.

punctuality Pünktlichkeit; ~ **in carrying out one's duties** Genauigkeit bei der Erledigung seiner Aufgaben; **to have a name for ~** für seine Pünktlichkeit bekannt sein.

punctuate *(v.)* Interpunktionszeichen setzen; ~ **a speech with cheers** Rede mit Beifallsrufen unterbrechen; ~ **one's sentences with thumps on the table** seine Meinung mit Schlägen auf den Tisch unterstreichen.

punctuation Zeichensetzung, Interpunktion; **close ~** strikte Zeichensetzung; **open ~** großzügige Zeichensetzung.

puncture Reifenpanne, *(el.)* Durchschlag; ~ *(v.)* Reifenpanne haben; ~ **proof** *(tyre)* nagel-, pannensicher.

punctured verletzt.

pundit Experte, Weiser; **~s of public opinion** Auguren der öffentlichen Meinung.

punish *(v.)* bestrafen, Strafe auferlegen;
~ **s. one's cellar** in jds. Weinkeller tüchtig aufräumen; ~ **s. o. corporally** j. züchtigen; ~ **a crime with death** Verbrechen mit dem Tode bestrafen; ~ **the engine** Motor zu sehr strapazieren; ~ **with a fine** mit einer Geldstrafe belegen; ~ **a tower** *(mil.)* einer Stadt Kriegskontributionen auferlegen.

punishable straffällig, -würdig;
~ **by a fine** mit Geldstrafe zu bestrafen; ~ **by law** gesetzlich strafbar;
~ **act** strafbare Handlung.

punishing work Strafarbeit.

punishment Bestrafung, Strafe, *(coll.)* grobe Behandlung, Zurichten;
adequate ~ angemessene Bestrafung; **arbitrary** ~ Strafe nach freiem Ermessen; **capital** ~ Todesstrafe; **collective** ~ Kollektivstrafe; **corporal** ~ Züchtigung, Prügelstrafe; **cruel and unusual** ~ grausame Bestrafung; **cumulative** ~ erhöhte Bestrafung von Rückfalltätern; **disciplinary** ~ Disziplinarstrafe; **exemplary** ~ abschreckende Bestrafung; **infamous** ~ Zuchthausstrafe; **lawful** ~ gesetzlich zulässige Strafe; **lenient** ~ milde Bestrafung; **light** ~ leichte Bestrafung; **maximum** ~ Höchststrafe; **minimum** ~ Mindeststrafe; **severe** ~ schwere Strafe; **summary** ~ *(mil.)* Disziplinarstrafe;
to be brought to ~ **for one's crimes** der gerechten Strafe für seine Verbrechen entgegensehen; **to evade** ~ sich der Bestrafung entziehen; **to incur a** ~ sich strafbar machen; **to inflict** ~ bestrafen, Bestrafung auferlegen; **to inflict severe** ~**s on criminals** Verbrecher hart bestrafen; **to make the** ~ **fit the crime** adäquate Strafe verhängen; **to stand one's** ~ **like a man** seine Bestrafung mannhaft hinnehmen.

punitive strafend;
to take ~ **action** Strafaktion unternehmen; ~ **damages** *(US)* Bußgeld, Buße, erlittenen Schaden übersteigender Schadensersatz; ~ **detention** *(Br.)* Jugendarrest; ~ **expedition** Strafexpedition; ~ **law** Strafgesetz; ~ **measures** Strafmaßnahmen; ~ **power** *(state)* Strafgewalt; ~ **statute** Strafgesetz.

punk *(criminal, sl.)* kleiner Gauner, *(motion picture, sl.)* unerfahrener Kameragehilfe, *(touchwood, US)* Zunderholz, *(trash, sl.)* Plunder, Schund;
~ *(v.) (US sl.)* Laufburschen machen;
~ **out** sein Versprechen zurücknehmen;
~ *(a.) (sl.)* miserabel, zum Davonlaufen;
to have an absolutely ~ **evening** *(sl.)* tödlich langweiligen Abend verbringen; **to talk a lot of** ~ Haufen Dummheiten von sich geben.

punt *(Br.)* flachgehendes Flußboot;
~ *(v.)* Wetten, *(gambling)* gegen die Bank spielen.

punter Börsenspekulant.

pup, conceited eingebildeter Jüngling;
to sell s. o. a ~ jem. etw. aufschwatzen;
~ **tent** Einmannzelt.

pupil Schüler, *(civil law)* Minderjähriger, *(ward)* Mündel;
beginning ~ Schulanfänger; **nonresident** ~ Externer; **resident** ~ Interner; **secondary school** ~ Mittelschüler;
to bring forward a ~ Schüler fördern; **to keep a** ~ **in** Schüler mit Arrest bestrafen; **to retard a** ~ Schüler nicht fördern; **to take** ~**s** Schüler annehmen.

pupilage Minderjährigkeit, Mündelstand;
to be still in its ~ *(industry)* noch in den Kinderschuhen stecken.

pupilarity *(Scot.)* Kindheitsalter.

pupilize *(v.)* Privatstunden geben.

puppet [Draht]puppe, *(fig.)* Werkzeug, Handlanger;
~ **on a string** Marionette;
~ **government** Marionettenregierung; ~ **show** Marionettenspiel; **to pull the** ~ **strings** Marionetten dirigieren; ~ **union** *(US)* Betriebsgewerkschaft.

puppy eingebildeter Laffe;
~ **love** erste Liebe.

puppyhood Jugendjahre.

purchasable käuflich, ankaufsfähig, erwerbbar, *(penal)* korrupt.

purchase Kauf, Kaufen, An-, Einkauf, *(acquisition)* Erwerb, Erwerbung, Be-, Anschaffung, Bezug, *(position of influence)* Machtstellung, einflußreiche Position, *(of property)* Grundstückserwerb, *(annual return from land)* Jahresertrag;
by ~ käuflich, durch Kauf; **at thirty years'** ~ zum Dreißigfachen des Jahresertrages; **at the time of** ~ beim Kaufabschluß;
by way of ~ kaufweise;
~**s** *(balance sheet)* Wareneingänge;
advance ~ Vorratseinkauf; **bona-fide** ~ gutgläubiger Erwerb; **bulk** ~ Massen-, Mengen-, Großeinkauf; **bull** ~ Kauf auf

Hausse; **cash** ~ Barkauf, Kauf gegen bar; **compulsory** ~ *(Br.)* Enteignung; **conditional** ~ bedingter Erwerb; **cover[ing]** ~ Deckungskauf; **credit** ~ Kreditkauf; **fictitious** ~ Scheinkauf; **firm** ~ Festkauf; ~ **forward** Terminkauf, Kauf auf Zeit (Lieferung); **future** ~ *(US)* Terminkauf; **heavy** ~**s** bedeutende Käufe; **hire** ~ *(Br.)* Abzahlungskauf, -geschäft; **innocent** ~ gutgläubiger Erwerb; **large** ~**s** Großeinkauf; **lump-sum** ~ Kauf in Bausch und Bogen; **material** ~**s** Materialeinkäufe; **mock** ~ Scheinkauf; **occasional** ~**s** spekulative Käufe, Meinungs-, Spekulationskauf; **open-market** ~ Käufe am offenen Markt; **outright** ~ fester Kaufabschluß, *(bank)* Übernahme auf dem Konsortialwege, *(bookseller)* Festbezug, *(US)* Kauf gegen sofortige Lieferung; **proforma** ~ Scheinkauf; **quantity** ~ Großeinkauf; **quasi-**~ kaufähnliches Rechtsgeschäft; **ready-money** ~ Barkauf; **sham** ~ fingierter Kauf; **short** ~ *(US)* Kauf auf Baisse; **specific** ~ Spezifikationskauf; **speculation (speculative)** ~**s** spekulative Käufe, Meinungs-, Spekulationskauf; **ten-years'** ~ zehnfacher Jahresertragswert; **trade** ~ Handelskauf; **volume** ~ Mengen-, Massen-, Großeinkauf; **wholesale** ~ Engros-, Pauschalkauf;
~ **for acceptance** Kauf gegen Akzept; ~ **for the account** *(Br.)* Terminkauf; ~ **on account** Kauf auf Kredit ([feste] Rechnung); ~ **of account receivables** *(US)* Forderungsaufkauf; ~ **on approval** Kauf auf Probe; ~ **of art** Ankauf von Kunstgegenständen; ~ **in auction** Ersteigerung; ~ **of a building** Hauskauf; ~ **in bulk** Messen-, Mengen-, Großeinkauf; ~ **of a business** Geschäftserwerb; ~ **of a car** Autokauf, -anschaffung; ~ **for cash** Barkauf, Kauf gegen bar, *(stock exchange)* Kassakauf; ~ **on commission** Kommissionskauf, -bezug; ~ **on credit** Kauf auf Ziel, Kreditkauf; ~ **for daily delivery** Kauf gegen sofortige Lieferung; ~ **for future delivery** *(US)* Lieferungs-, Terminkauf; ~ **by description** Gattungskauf; ~ **of foreign currency** Devisenerwerb; ~ **of gold** Goldankauf; ~ **of certain definite goods** Spezieskauf; ~ **of goods in replacement** Deckungskauf; ~ **of goods and services** Bezug von Gütern und Dienstleistungen; ~ **of a home** Eigenheimerwerb; ~ **subject to inspection** Kauf zur Ansicht (Probe); ~ **of investment securities** Ankauf von Wertpapieren; ~ **of land** Grundstückserwerb, Grunderwerb; ~ **and liquidation** *(savings bank)* Totalliquidation; ~ **in the lump** Kauf in Bausch und Bogen; ~ **of materials** Materialeinkauf; ~ **of merchandise on credit** Warenbezug auf Kredit; ~ **in the name of another** Erwerb in fremdem Namen; ~ **of office** Ämterkauf; ~**s on the open market** Käufe am offenen Markt; ~ **at option** Prämienkauf; ~ **of participation** Beteiligungserwerb; ~ **of a patent** Patenterwerb; ~ **of real estate** Grundstückskauf; ~ **of a reversion** Erwerb eines Heimfallrechts (Anwartschaftsrechtes); ~ **with right to exchange** *(bookseller)* Bezug mit Umtauschrecht; **outright** ~ **with right to return** *(bookseller)* Kommissionsbezug, fest mit Remissionsrecht; ~ **and sale** Einkauf und Verkauf; ~ **according to (by) sample (pattern)** Kauf nach Probe; ~ **of securities** Effektenerwerb; ~ **of shares** Aktienerwerb; ~ **for the settlement** *(Br.)* Terminkauf; **conditional** ~ **and settlement** Bedingtbezug und Bedingtabrechnung; ~ **on speculation** Ankauf zu Spekulationszwecken, Meinungs-, Spekulationskauf; ~ **on the deferred payment system** *(US)* Abzahlungskauf; ~ **on term** Kauf auf Lieferung; ~ **on trial** Kauf zur Probe mit Rückgaberecht; ~ **for value without notice** gutgläubiger Erwerb; ~ **of a van** Lastkraftwagenankauf;
~ *(v.) (acquire)* erstehen, [käuflich] erwerben, *(buy)* kaufen, ab-, an-, einkaufen, anschaffen;
~ **on account (credit)** auf Rechnung kaufen; ~ **at auction** ersteigern; ~ **for cash** gegen bar kaufen; ~ **compulsorily** *(Br.)* enteignen; ~ **a flat to let for holiday purposes** Eigentumswohnung zur Vermietung an Feriengäste erwerben; ~ **forward** auf Termin (Lieferung) kaufen; ~ **freedom with one's blood** sein Leben für die Freiheit einsetzen; ~ **for future delivery** *(US)* auf Lieferung (Termin) kaufen; ~ **goods** Waren beziehen; ~ **at first hand** aus erster Hand kaufen; ~ **the sole interest in a business** Geschäft voll übernehmen; ~ **in the open market** am offenen Markt kaufen; ~ **a portion of a new issue** Konsortialanteil einer Anleihe übernehmen; ~ **at secondhand** antiquarisch erwerben; ~ **for transshipment** zur Weiterausfuhr kaufen; ~ **for value** käuflich erwerben; ~ **wholesale** engros (im Großhandel, in Bausch und Bogen) kaufen;
to acquire by ~ käuflich erwerben; **to cancel a** ~ Kauf rückgängig machen; **to conclude a** ~ Kauf tätigen; **to fill one's car with one's** ~**s** seine Einkäufe im Auto verstauen; **to finance a** ~ **of property** Grundstückskauf finanzieren; **to get a** ~ gutes Geschäft tätigen; **to have some** ~**s to make** einige Besorgungen zu erledigen haben (machen müssen); **to live on one's** ~ einträgliche Beschäftigung haben; **to make a** ~ Kauf tätigen; **to make one's** ~**s on a cash basis** seine Einkäufe bar bezahlen; **to nego-**

tiate for the ~ of a house über den Ankauf eines Hauses verhandeln; to okay a ~ *(US)* Ankauf genehmigen; to profess to ~ sich anheischig machen zu kaufen; to repudiate a ~ vom Kauf[vertrag] zurücktreten; to secure a ~ gutes Geschäft tätigen; to sell at thirty years ~ für den dreißigfachen Pachtertrag verkaufen; to withdraw from a ~ vom Kauf zurücktreten; ~s account Wareneingangskonto, -rechnung, Einkaufsrechnung; hire-~ agreement *(Br.)* Abzahlungsvertrag; ~ and sale agreement *(US)* Grundstückskaufvertrag; ~ agreement form Kaufvertragsvordruck; ~ allowance Preisnachlässe; ~ annuity Restkaufgeldrente; ~ area Einkaufsgebiet; ~ book Wareneingangsbuch; ~ budget Einkaufsbudget; ~ commitment *(issue of securities)* Konsortialprovision; ~ commitments *(balance sheet)* Konsortialverpflichtungen; ~ consideration Kaufentgelt, -wert; ~ contract Kaufvertrag, *(stock exchange)* Schlußnote; ~ costs Bezugskosten; ~ cost of real estate Grunderwerbskosten; ~ date Bestellungstermin; ~ decision Kaufentscheidung; ~ decision aid Entscheidungshilfe beim Einkauf; ~ deed Kaufvertrag, -urkunde; ~ diary Einkaufszettel; ~ discount Einkaufsrabatt; ~ form *(stock market)* Kaufauftrag; ~ fund Ankaufsfonds; ~ group *(issue of securities, US)* Konsortium; ~ intention Kaufabsicht; ~ invoice Einkaufsrechnung; ~ journal Wareneingangsbuch, Einkaufsjournal; ~ ledger *(accounting)* Kreditorenbuch.

purchase money Kaufpreis, -summe, -geld, Anschaffungskosten; ~ allowance Kaufgeldminderung, -nachlaß; ~ bonds Kaufgeldobligationen; ~ chattel mortgage *(US)* Sicherungseigentum; ~ financing Kaufgeldfinanzierung; ~ loan Warenbeschaffungskredit, Restkaufgelddarlehen; ~ mortgage *(US)* Restkaufgeldhypothek; ~ obligations Kaufgeldverpflichtungen; ~ security interest *(US)* zur Abdeckung des Kaufpreises bestelltes Sicherungsrecht.

purchase|notice Bedarfsmeldung; prior ~ obligation Vorkaufsrecht; ~ observation Beobachtung der Kaufgewohnheiten; ~ offer Kaufangebot; ~ order Kunden-, Kaufauftrag, Bestellung; ~ order form Bestellformular; ~ order number Bestellnummer; ~ pattern Käuferverhalten; ~ planning richtige Einkaufsdisposition; ~ preference list *(stock exchange)* Liste bevorzugter Werte; ~ permit Bezugschein, -genehmigung; ~ price Ankaufs-, Anschaffungs-, Erwerbs-, Kaufpreis, Kaufsumme; to abate the ~ price Kaufpreis herabsetzen; to refund the ~ price Kaufpreis zurückerstatten; ~ privilege Vorkaufsrecht; ~ proceeds Kauferlös; ~ proposition Verkaufsargumentation; ~ quota Einkaufskontingent; ~ record Einkaufsbeleg; ~ register Kreditorenjournal; ~ requisition Bedarfsmeldung, Lageranforderung, Kaufanweisung; ~ requisition number Bestellnummer; ~ returns Einkaufsretouren, Warenrücksendungen; ~ returns account Retourenkonto; ~ returns book (journal) Retourenjournal, Rückwarenbuch; ~ syndicate *(issue of securities)* [Emissions]konsortium; ~ tax *(US)* Umsatzsteuer auf Güter des gehobenen Bedarfs, Einphasenwarenumsatzsteuer; to be exempted from ~ tax *(Br.)* erwerbssteuerfrei sein; ~ tender Einkaufsangebot; ~ terms Kaufbestimmungen; ~ trial Abnahmeprüfung; ~ value Einkaufswert; ~ voucher Einkaufsbeleg.

purchased|paper *(US)* per Kasse gekauftes Papier; dearly ~ victory teuer erkaufter Sieg.

purchaser An-, Einkäufer, Erwerber, Abnehmer, Kunde, Bezieher, *(auction)* Ersteigerer, *(securities)* Konsortialmitglied; failing a ~ in Ermangelung eines Käufers; bona-fide ~ gutgläubiger Erwerber; chief ~ Haupteinkäufer; conditional ~ Vorbehaltskäufer; defrauded ~ betrogener Käufer; first ~ Ersterwerber; full-price ~ Normalkäufer; individual ~ Einzelabnehmer; innocent ~ gutgläubiger Erwerber; intending (prospective) ~ [Kauf]reflektant, Kauflustiger, -interessent; male fide ~ bösgläubiger Erwerber; marginal ~ unschlüssiger Käufer; one-time ~ Laufkunde; original ~ Ersterwerber; ~ of a bill Käufer eines Wechsels; ~ in bad faith bösgläubiger Erwerber; ~ in good faith gutgläubiger Erwerber; ~ of land Grundstückskäufer; ~ of a note Käufer eines Wechsels, Wechselankäufer; ~ of property Grundstückserwerber; prospective ~s of technical textbooks Fachbuchinteressenten; innocent ~ for value (without notice) gutgläubiger entgeltlicher Erwerber; to debit a ~ Käufer für verkaufte Waren belasten; to find (meet with) ~s Abnehmer finden.

purchasing Kauf[en], Einkauf, Ankauf, Erwerb, *(procurement)* Beschaffung; centralized ~ zentraler Einkauf; direct ~ Direkteinkauf, -bezug; joint ~ Gemeinschaftseinkauf; ~ of assets Anlagenkauf; ~ on credit Kreditkauf;

~ agency Einkaufsgesellschaft; ~ agent Einkaufssachbearbeiter, Einkäufer, *(independent middleman)* Zwischenhändler, *(purchasing department)* Leiter der Einkaufsabteilung, Einkaufsleiter; ~ association Einkaufsgenossenschaft, -verband; cooperative ~ association Einkaufs-, Bezugsgenossenschaft; ~ behavio(u)r Einkaufsverhalten; ~ broker Warenmakler; ~ business Einkaufsgeschäft; ~ cartel Abnehmerkartell; ~ combine Einkaufsgemeinschaft; ~ commission (committee) Einkaufskommission; ~ company Käuferin; ~ cooperative Einkaufsgenossenschaft; ~ costs Bezugs-, Warenbeschaffungskosten; ~ country Abnahmeland, Käuferland; ~ decision *(advertising business)* Ankaufsentscheidung; ~ department Einkaufsabteilung; ~ frequency Einkaufshäufigkeit; ~ functions Aufgaben des Einkaufs; ~ group Einkaufsgemeinschaft; ~ high Käuferhausse; ~ influence Kaufbeeinflussung; ~ level Stufen des Beschaffungsprozesses; ~ manager Einkaufsleiter; ~ motive Kaufmotiv; ~ office Einkaufsbüro; ~ officer Einkaufsleiter, Einkäufer; ~ order Kaufauftrag, Bestellung; ~ party Käufer[in], Erwerber[in]; ~ pattern Einkaufsverfahren; ~ permit Einkaufsgenehmigung, Bezugsschein; ~ pool Einkaufsgemeinschaft.

purchasing power Kaufkraft; excessive ~ Kaufkraftüberhang; prewar ~ Vorkriegskaufkraft; real ~ effektive Kaufkraft; ~ of money Kaufkraft des Geldes; ~ of the population Massenkaufkraft; to decline in ~ an Kaufkraft verlieren; ~ index Kaufkraftindex; ~ parity Kaufkraftparität; ~ parity theory Kaufkraftparitätstheorie; to skim off ~ surplus überschüssige Kaufkraft abschöpfen.

purchasing|rate Ankaufspreis; ~ responsibilty Verantwortung in Einkaufsfragen; ~ syndicate Emissionskonsortium; ~ value Einkaufswert; ~ value of money Anschaffungs-, Kaufkraftwert.

pure unverfälscht, rein, makellos, *(gold)* massiv; ~ accident unvorhergesehener Unfall, bloßer Zufall; ~ alcohol unverfälschter (reiner) Alkohol; ~ charity gemeinnützige Einrichtung; ~ competition *(US)* freier Wettbewerb, vollkommene Konkurrenz; ~ debt *(Scot.)* fällige Forderung; ~ economics reine Volkswirtschaftslehre; ~ endowment insurance Kapitalversicherung auf den Erlebensfall; ~ gold pures Gold, Feingold; ~ interest Nettozinssatz; ~ and simple laziness glatte Faulheit; out of ~ malice aus reiner Bosheit; ~ mischief nichts als Unglück; ~ monopoly homogenes Monopol; ~ nonsense glatter Unsinn; ~ obligation unbedingte Verpflichtung; ~ political economy Volkswirtschaftstheorie; ~ premium Nettoprämie; ~ public good spezifisch öffentliches Gut; ~ profit Unternehmerreingewinn; ~ recall Werbeerinnerung ohne Gedächtnisstützen; ~ science reine Wissenschaft; ~ theory of international trade Außenwirtschaftstheorie; ~ thoughts unschuldige Gedanken; ~ and simple truth einfache und reine Wahrheit; ~ waste of time glatter Zeitverlust; ~ water sauberes Wasser.

purgation *(exoneration of a crime)* Rechtfertigung.
purgatory Fegefeuer.
purge Verfolgung, Säuberung; political ~ Säuberungsaktion, -welle; ~ *(v.)* säubern, reinigen, *(party politics)* aus der Partei ausschließen; ~ o. s. *(fig.)* sich reinwaschen; ~ away wegwaschen; ~ o. s. of a charge sich vor Gericht rechtfertigen, sich gegen eine Anklage behaupten; ~ one's contempt sich für ein ungebührliches Verhalten entschuldigen; ~ the finances of a country Finanzen eines Landes in Ordnung bringen; ~ an offence Verbrechen sühnen; ~ o. s. from a suspicion sich von einem Verdacht reinigen.

purged of partial counsel vom Verdacht der Zeugenbeeinflussung befreit.
purging a tort Rechtfertigung einer unerlaubten Handlung.
purify *(v.)* raffinieren.
purist Pedant, Genauigkeitskrämer.
purlieu *(fig.)* Jagdgründe; ~s *(outlying district)* Außen-, Nachbarbezirk; to keep within one's ~s in seinen Grenzen bleiben.
purloin *(v.)* stehlen.
purloiner Dieb.
purpart Teileigentum.
purparty *(estate)* Auseinandersetzungsanteil.
purple Purpur; born in the ~ in einem hohen Rang geboren; ~ *(a.)* bombastisch, *(style)* effektvoll, brillant;

~ **airway** *(Br.)* Flugroute einer königlichen Maschine; ~ **passage** Glanzstelle; ~ **sunset** farbenprächtiger Sonnenuntergang.

purport erklärte Absicht, *(document)* Bedeutung, Sinn, Inhalt, *(tenor)* Wortlaut;

~ **of a letter** Sinn (Aufgabe) eines Briefes;

~ *(v.)* anscheinend besagen, bedeuten;

~ **to be an autobiography** Eindruck einer Autobiographie erwecken; ~ **to be a lawyer** sich als Anwalt ausgeben; ~ **to be a police officer** sich als Polizeibeamter ausgeben, den Polizisten spielen.

purporting des Inhalts, besagend.

purpose Absicht, Vorhaben, Entschluß, Wille, Zweck[bestimmung];

for advertising ~s zu Werbezwecken; **for all practical** ~s praktisch gesehen; **for commercial** ~s zu Gewerbezwecken; **for fraudulent** ~s zu betrügerischen Zwecken; **for illustration** ~s zwecks Erläuterung; **for the** ~ **of this agreement** im Sinne dieses Abkommens; **for the** ~ **of gain** zur Gewinnerzielung; **for the** ~ **of negotiation** für Begegnungszwecke; **for the** ~ **of trade** zu Gewerbezwecken; **of set** ~ für einen bestimmten Zweck, *(law)* vorsätzlich; **on** ~ absichtlich, vorsätzlich; **to little** ~ mit geringer Wirkung; **to no** ~ umsonst, vergeblich, ohne Erfolg; **to the** ~ zweckdienlich, -bewußt; **with honesty of** ~ in ehrlicher Absicht; **weak of** ~ ohne Entschlußkraft;

additional ~ Nebenabsicht; **business** ~ Geschäftszweck; **charitable** ~ wohltätiger Zweck; **common** ~ gemeinsame Absicht; **farming** ~s landwirtschaftliche Zwecke; **intended** ~ beabsichtigter Zweck; **fundamental national** ~ erstes nationales Anliegen; **normal** ~ normaler Gebrauchszweck; **public** ~ gemeinnütziges Werk;

~ **of agency** Vollmachtszweck; ~ **of auditing** Prüfungszweck; **frustrated fundamental** ~ **of a contract** fortgefallene Vertragsgrundlage; ~ **of a loan** Darlehenszweck; ~ **of a meeting** Versammlungszweck; ~ **of redemption** Tilgungszweck; ~ **of use** Benutzungszweck;

~ *(v.)* beabsichtigen, vorhaben;

~ **a further attempt** weiteren Versuch unternehmen; **to achieve one's** ~ sein Ziel erreichen; **to answer the** ~ zweckentsprechend sein, dem Zweck entsprechen; **to be to little** ~ kaum Erfolg haben; **to be used for a specific** ~ für eine Sonderverwendung bestimmt sein; **to be used for various** ~s mehreren Zwecken dienen; **to come for this** ~ eigens zu diesem Zweck kommen; **to do s. th. on** ~ etw. mit voller Absicht (vorsätzlich) tun; **to form a commission for the** ~ **of investigation** Untersuchungskommission bilden; **to have a strong** ~ sich ernsthaft vornehmen; **to intervene to little** ~ mit seiner Intervention fast nichts erreichen; **to serve two** ~s zwei Zwecken dienen; **to speak to the** ~ zur Sache sprechen; **to spend one's money for no** ~ sein Geld umsonst ausgeben; **to suit s. one's** ~ jem. in den Kram passen; **to talk to no** ~ in die Luft reden; **to turn to good** ~ nutzbringend verwenden; **to work to good** ~ mit Erfolg arbeiten; **special-** ~ **buildings** Zweckbauten; **to be** ~-**directed** auf ein Ziel abgestimmt sein; ~ **novel** Tendenzroman; **general-** ~ **waggon** Mehrzweckwaggon.

purposely vorsätzlich.

purposive zweckbewußt;

~ **sampling** stichprobenartig durchgeführte Marktforschung.

purse Börse, [Geld]beutel, Portemonnaie, *(finance)* Hilfsmittel, -quellen, *(prize)* Belohnung, *(sum collected)* gesammeltes Geld, Geldsammlung, -geschenk, *(sum of money)* Geld[summe], Mittel, Fonds;

common ~ gemeinsame Kasse; **heavy (long)** ~ wohlgespickte (volle) Börse; **ill-lined** ~ leeres Portemonnaie; **a light** ~ magerer Geldbeutel, Armut; **privy** ~ *(Br.)* königliche Privatschatulle; **public** ~ öffentliche Gelder (Mittel), Staatsschatz, -säckel; **to be beyond one's** ~ etw. nicht erschwingen können; **to drain s. one's** ~ jds. Geldbeutel leeren, j. ausnehmen; **to ease s. one's** ~ *(fig.)* jds. Portemonnaie erleichtern; **to have a common** ~ gemeinsame Kasse machen; **to have a well-lined** ~ mit Geld reichlich versehen sein; **not to know the length of s. one's** ~ über jds. finanzielle Möglichkeiten nicht Bescheid wissen; **to live within one's** ~ seinen Verhältnissen entsprechend leben; **to make (put) up a** ~ Geld zu einem bestimmten Zweck sammeln; **to unstring one's** ~ seinen Geldbeutel zücken; **to win the** ~ Geldpreis gewinnen;

joint ~ **agreement** *(Br.)* Gewinnabrechnungsgemeinschaft für Verkehrseinnahmen; ~ **bearer** Kassenwart, Säckelmeister; ~ **pride** Geldstolz; ~**proud** protzig; ~ **snatcher** *(US)* Taschendieb; ~ **snatching** Beutelschneiderei; **to command the** ~ **strings** über den Geldbeutel verfügen; **to grip one's** ~ **strings tightly** sein Portemonnaie festhalten; **to hand over the** ~ **strings** Geld-

verwaltung übertragen; **to hold the** ~ **strings tightly** das Portemonnaie haben, über den Geldbeutel verfügen; **to loosen the** ~ **strings** in die Tasche greifen; **to tighten the** ~ **strings** Daumen auf den Geldbeutel halten, Ausgabenwirtschaft einschränken.

purser *(mil.)* Zahlmeister.

pursuance Ausführung, Fortführung, Verfolgung;

in ~ **of** auf Grund von; **in** ~ **of this decree** in Anwendung dieser Verordnung; **in** ~ **of an order** auftragsgemäß; **in** ~ **of truth** auf der Suche nach Wahrheit; **in** ~ **of my vocation** in Ausübung meines Berufes;

~ **of a plan** Weiterverfolgung eines Planes.

pursuant gemäß, zufolge, übereinstimmend;

~ **to the contract** vertragsgemäß; ~ **to your instructions** gemäß Ihren Instruktionen, weisungsgemäß; ~ **to the statute** nach dem Gesetz.

pursue *(v.)* *(continue)* fortführen, -setzen, weiterführen, betreiben, ausüben, *(chase)* verfolgen, *(prosecute, Scot. law)* strafrechtlich verfolgen;

~ **s. o. j.** verfolgen; ~ **advice** Ratschlag befolgen; ~ **one's business** seinen Geschäften (seinem Beruf) nachgehen; ~ **a realistic course** realistischen Kurs einschlagen; ~ **one's duties** seine Aufgabe erledigen; ~ **a fugitive from justice** einem flüchtigen Verbrecher nachsetzen; ~ **game** Jagd ausüben; ~ **a goal** Ziel verfolgen; ~ **an inquiry** Nachforschungen anstellen; ~ **a line of conduct** bestimmte Linie einhalten; ~ **an occupation** einer Tätigkeit nachgehen, Beruf ausüben; ~ **one's legal remedies** von seinen Rechtsmitteln Gebrauch machen, Rechtsmittel in Anspruch nehmen; ~ **one's studies to an end** sein Studium abschließen; ~ **one's studies after leaving school** sein Studium nach der Schulentlassung fortsetzen; ~ **a trade** Gewerbe betreiben, gewerbliche Tätigkeit ausüben.

pursued | by misfortune vom Unglück verfolgt; ~ **by remorse** vom Gewissen gepeinigt.

pursuer Verfolger, *(Scot.)* Kläger.

pursuit *(carrying into effect)* Durchführung, Verfolgung, *(occupation)* Betätigung, Beschäftigung, Ausübung, Beruf, Tätigkeit;

~s Studien, Arbeiten;

commercial (mercantile) ~s kaufmännische Betätigung; **favo(u)rite** ~ Lieblingsbeschäftigung; **fresh** ~ sofortige Verfolgung; **hot** ~ *(law of nations)* Verfolgungsrecht; **literary** ~s literarische Interessen; **professional** ~ berufliche Betätigung;

~ **of game** Jagdausübung; ~ **of happiness** Jagd nach dem Glück, *(constitutional law)* Persönlichkeitsentfaltung; ~ **of knowledge** Wissensdrang, Streben nach Wissen; ~ **of a murderer** Verfolgung eines Mörders; ~ **of office** Sucht nach Machtpositionen; ~ **of profit** Gewinnstreben; ~ **of a scheme** Betreiben eines Planes; ~ **of a trade** Gewerbeausübung; **to be in** ~ **of s. o.** j. verfolgen, jem. nachsetzen; **to engage in scientific** ~s sich für eine wissenschaftliche Laufbahn entscheiden; **to take up the** ~ Verfolgung aufnehmen;

~ **pilot** Jagdflieger; ~ **plane** Jagdflugzeug; ~ **squadron** Jagdstaffel.

purvey *(v.)* versorgen, [Lebensmittel] liefern, [Vorräte] anschaffen;

~ **for s. o.** für jds. Bedürfnisse sorgen; ~ **for the army** für das Heer liefern, Heereslieferant sein; ~ **meat to one's customers** seine Kundschaft mit Fleisch beliefern.

purveyance Anschaffung, Lieferung.

purveyor [Lebens]mittellieferant;

~ **to the Royal Household** *(Br.)* Hoflieferant.

purview Wirkungskreis, Aufgabengebiet, Betätigungs-, Tätigkeitsfeld, Ressort, *(body of statute)* gesetzgeberische Absicht, *(horizon)* Blickfeld, Horizont, Gesichtskreis, *(law)* Geltungsbereich;

within the ~ innerhalb der Zuständigkeit liegend;

~ **of a legislative body** Aufgabenbereich eines Gesetzgebungskörpers;

to be outside the ~ **of an inquiry** außerhalb des Untersuchungsauftrags liegen; **to come (lie) within the** ~ **of s. o.** innerhalb jds. Aufgabenbereichs liegen; **to come within the** ~ **of the Home Office** *(Br.)* im Bereich des Innenministeriums liegen; **to come within the** ~ **of a law** in den Geltungsbereich eines Gesetzes fallen.

push Schub, Stoß, *(pep)* Unternehmungsgeist, Energie, Elan, Schwung, Tatkraft, *(extreme case)* äußerster Fall, Notfall, *(vigorous effort)* neue Anstrengung, Bemühung, *(gang of thieves, sl.)* Diebesbande, *(influence)* Protektion, Beziehungen, *(mil.)* Vorstoß, [Groß]offensive;

at a ~ im kritischen Augenblick, im Notfall; **at the first** ~ auf den ersten Anhieb; **until it comes to the** ~ wenn Not am Mann ist; **when it comes to the** ~ wenn es zum Äußersten kommt; **upward** ~ **on costs** Kostenauftrieb; ~ **of demand** Nachfragedruck; ~ **(v.)** stoßen, **(counterfeit money, sl.)** Falschgeld in den Verkehr setzen, **(promote)** fördern, Reklame machen, propagieren, **(work hard)** schuften, sich tüchtig ins Zeug legen (sehr anstrengen), energisch betreiben;

~ **ahead about six points** etwa sechs Punkte gewinnen; ~ **one's advantage** seinen Vorteil wahrzunehmen wissen; ~ **one's affairs** seine Angelegenheiten voranzutreiben; ~ **s . o. around** j. herumkommandieren; ~ **back the crowd (police)** Menge zurückdrängen; ~ **the boat out (fam.)** Sache lancieren; ~ **one's business** sein Geschäft voranbringen, energische Verkaufsanstrengungen unternehmen; ~ **a button** Knopf drücken; ~ **one's claims** sein Recht in Anspruch nehmen; ~ **to completion** energisch der Vollendung zuführen; ~ **one's conquests** seine Eroberungen ausdehnen; ~ **one's demands** seine Ansprüche durchsetzen; ~ **on to one's destination** seine Reise zum Bestimmungsort fortsetzen; ~ **a door open** Tür aufstoßen; ~ **s. th. too far** etw. zu weit treiben; ~ **one's fortune** sein Glück machen wollen; ~ **forward (mil.)** vorgehen, vorstoßen; ~ **o. s. forward** Aufmerksamkeit auf sich lenken; ~ **forward to the attack** Offensive ergreifen; ~ **goods** Waren aufdrängen; ~ **s. one's hand** j. schwer unter Druck setzen; ~ **hard for s. th.** sich energisch für etw. einsetzen; ~ **one's way into a job** sich in eine Stellung hineindrängeln; ~ **off (coll.)** sich auf den Weg machen, **(goods, coll.)** losschlagen, abstoßen, [Lager] räumen; ~ **open** aufstoßen; ~ **s. o. for payment** j. mit der Rückzahlung bedrängen; ~ **a pen (sl.)** Federfuchser (Bürohengst) sein; ~ **one's products** für seine Erzeugnisse werben, ~ **on a pupil** Schüler fördern; ~ **s. th. into the shadow** etw. ganz in den Hintergrund drängen; ~ **shares (stock exchange, Br.)** Schwindelaktien an der Börse unterbringen; ~ **a matter through** Sache zu Ende bringen; ~ **up (prices)** hinauf-, in die Höhe treiben, hinaufschrauben; ~ **up a scheme** Projekt vorantreiben; ~ **one's wares** seine Waren absetzen; ~ **one's way through the crowd** sich einen Weg durch die Menge bahnen; ~ **one's way into a meeting** sich gewaltsam Zugang zu einer Versammlung verschaffen; ~ **one's way into a job** sich mit List und Tücke eine Stellung besorgen; ~ **on with one's work** seine Arbeit zu Ende bringen; **to act from an inner** ~ aus innerem Antrieb handeln; **to bring to the last** ~ zum Äußersten treiben; **to get the** ~ **(Br., sl.)** hinausfliegen, herausgeschmissen werden; **to get a job by** ~ seine Position reiner Protektion verdanken; **to give s. o. the** ~ **(Br., sl.)** j. hinausschmeißen; **to give s. o. a helping** ~ j. protektionieren; **to have enough** ~ **to succeed as a salesman** über die notwendige Durchsetzungskraft als Verkäufer verfügen; **to have plenty of** ~ über genügend Elan verfügen; **to make a** ~ sich energisch anstrengen; **to make a** ~ **to get home** sich beeilen, nach Hause zu kommen; **to make a** ~ **to finish a job** sich zur Beendigung einer Arbeit aufraffen; **to make a** ~ **on the western front** an der Westfront angreifen;

~ **bicycle** einfaches Fahrrad; ~ **button** Druckknopf; ~**-button** automatisch, durch einen Druckknopf auslösbar, vom Schaltbrett aus; **to adjust electrically by** ~**-button (car seat)** sich elektrisch einstellen lassen; ~**-button access** Druckknopfzugang; ~**-button dialling (tel.)** Drucktastenwahl; ~**-button operation** Drucktastenbedienung; ~**-button radio** Knopfdruckradio; ~**-button switching** Druckknopfschaltung; ~**-button timing** Drucktasteneinteilung; ~**-button tuning** Drucktasteneinteilung; ~**-button warfare** Druckknopfkrieg; ~**-button way** Patentlösung; ~**-chair** Sportkinderwagen; ~ **cyclist (fam.)** Fahrradfahrer; ~**-off (coll.)** Anfang; **to give a club** ~**-off** Vereinsgründung hintertreiben; ~ **money** Verkäuferprämie für Absatz von Ladenhütern; ~ **pencil** Druckstift; ~**-pram (Br., coll.)** Kinderwagen; ~**-pull circuit** Gegentaktschaltung.

pushed | for time zeitknapp;
to be ~ **for an answer** zu einer Antwort gedrängt werden; **to be** ~ **for money** in Geldverlegenheit sein.
pusher Draufgänger Schieber, **(swot, coll.)** Streber;
share ~ **(Br.)** Aktienschwindler;
~ **airplane** Flugzeug mit Druckschraube; ~ **barge** Schubschiff.
pushing unverschämt;
~ **on the work** Arbeitsbeschleunigung;
to be ~ **with strangers** sich Fremden unangemeldet aufdrängen; ~ **man** Emporkömmling.
pushover (sl.) leicht zu überzeugender Zeitgenosse, **(trifle)** Kinderspiel, Kleinigkeit;
to be a ~ **for that sort of advertising** auf diese Art von Reklame leicht hereinfallen.
pushpin Bildernagel.

pussy Kätzchen, Muschi;
poor ~ **in the public pavement** öffentlich geprügelter Hund.
pussyfoot | s Schleicher, Leisetreter, **(Br., sl.)** Abstinenzler, Alkoholgegner;
~ **(v.) (US sl.)** sich ja nicht festlegen, sich um eine Meinungsäußerung herumdrücken;
~ **(a.) (Br., sl.)** abstinenzlerisch, **(US sl.)** sich nicht festlegend.
pussyfooting leisetreterisch.
put (stock exchange) Rückprämie, Verkaufsoption;
~ **and call** Stellagegeschäft, Geschäft auf Geben und Nehmen, Terminkauf, -handel; ~ **of more** Nach[lieferungs]geschäft, Nochgeschäft auf Geben (in Verkäufers Wahl); ~**s and refusals (Br.)** Termingeschäfte;
~ **(v.)** stellen, setzen, **(option money)** geben, liefern;
~ **an amount in the expenditure** Betrag im Soll buchen; ~ **an amount in the receipts** Betrag im Haben buchen; ~ **a shore an Land bringen**; ~ **the bee (bite) on s. o. (US sl.)** j. anpumpen; ~ **a bee in s. one's bonnet (Br.)** jem. einen Floh ins Ohr setzen; ~ **it bluntly** ungeschminkt sagen; ~ **one's cards on the table** seine Karten auf den Tisch legen; ~ **o. s. under s. one's care** sich in jds. Obhut begeben; ~ **the cart before the horse** Pferd beim Schwanz aufzäumen; ~ **a case very well** Fall völlig klarstellen; ~ **a curb on s. one's passions** j. an die Kandare nehmen; ~ **it differently** es anders formulieren; ~ **a good face on** das Beste aus einer Sache machen; ~ **s. o. in fear of his life** jem. Todesängste einjagen; ~ **a field under wheat** Feld mit Weizen bestellen; ~ **the finger on s. o.** j. anschwärzen; ~ **the finishing touches to** einer Sache den letzten Schliff geben; ~ **a flea in s. one's ear (US sl.)** jem. einen Floh ins Ohr setzen; ~ **one's hand in one's pocket** für wohltätige Zwecke stiften; ~ **s. o. in a hole (coll.)** j. in Schwierigkeiten bringen; ~ **hono(u)r before riches** seine Ehre höher stellen als Reichtum; ~ **a horse to the cart** Pferd anspannen; ~ **one's initials** abzeichnen; ~ **o. s. in a good light** sich ins rechte Licht setzen; ~ **things in a clearer light** Dinge deutlicher darstellen; ~ **a man on extra fatigue (mil.)** j. strafexerzieren lassen; ~ **a matter in the hands of a solicitor** Angelegenheit einem Rechtsanwalt übertragen; ~ **numbers on packages** Pakete numerieren; ~ **it otherwise** es anders ausdrücken; **not** ~ **it past s. o.** jem. etw. zutrauen; ~ **s. o. in his place** j. auf den ihm zustehenden Platz verweisen; ~ **a play on the stage** Stück aufführen; ~ **a population at 2 millions** Bevölkerung auf 2 Millionen schätzen; ~ **one's shoulder to the wheel** sich tüchtig ins Zeug legen; ~ **it that way** es so ausdrücken; ~ **things in such a way** Dinge so darstellen.
put (v.) about | o. s. sich plagen; ~ **a rumo(u)r** Gerücht in Umlauf setzen (verbreiten); ~ **a ship** neuen Kurs einschlagen.
put (v.) across klarmachen;
~ **a business deal** Geschäft erfolgreich abschließen; ~ **a play** mit einem Theaterstück ankommen.
put (v.) against entgegenstellen;
~ **a tick against s. one's name** jds. Name auf einer Liste abhaken.
put (v.) aside beiseite legen (stellen), weglegen, aufsparen, **(sl.)** versetzen;
~ **a book aside** zu lesen aufhören; ~ **a good deal of money aside** schönes Stück Geld zurücklegen; ~ **one's work aside** Arbeit beenden.
put (v.) at (US local) pausenlos schwätzen;
~ **a stock a certain price** Aktien zu einem zugesicherten Festpreis liefern; ~ **s. one's income at $ 4000 a year** jds. Einkommen auf jährlich 4000 Dollar schätzen.
put (v.) away wegtun, beiseiteschaffen, **(do in, sl.)** umbringen, aus dem Wege räumen, **(jail, sl.)** einlochen, **(pop, sl.)** verpfänden, versetzen;
~ **s. o.** j. in eine Anstalt verbringen; ~ **for one's old age** Geld für seine alten Tage zurücklegen; ~ **one's books** seine Bücher weglegen; ~ **all ideas** alle Hoffnungen begraben.
put (v.) back wiederherstellen, in den ursprünglichen Zustand zurückversetzen, **(ship)** um-, zurückkehren;
~ **the efforts of the reformers** Bemühungen der Reformer zunichtemachen; ~ **a minute hand** Uhrzeiger zurückstellen; ~ **to harbo(u)r** in den Hafen zurückkehren; ~ **production** Produktion zurückwerfen; ~ **a pupil** Schüler zurückstellen lassen; ~ **a reference book back on the shelf** Nachschlagewerk ins Regal zurückstellen.
put (v.) by einbringen, **(money)** zurücklegen, beiseitelegen;
~ **for the future** für später zurücklegen;
to have money to ~ Geld zurücklegen können.
put (v.) down aufschreiben, eintragen, niederschreiben, **(airplane)** landen;
~ **o. s. down** sich eintragen; ~ **to s. th.** auf etw. zurückführen; ~ **s. o. down for s. th.** für etw. vormerken; ~ **to s. one's account**

jem. in Rechnung stellen; ~ **to a customer's account** *(Br.)* für einen Kunden anschreiben; ~ **the goods down to s. one's account** Einkäufe auf jds. Rechnung setzen; ~ **an address** Adresse notieren; ~ **on the agenda** auf die Tagesordnung setzen; ~ **on the airport in time** rechtzeitig landen; ~ **bore holes** *(mining)* Bohrlöcher anbringen; ~ **a buoy** Boje auslegen; ~ **s. o. at the corner** j. an der Ecke aussteigen lassen; ~ **s. o. down for $ 20** jds. Namen in eine Subskriptionsliste mit 20 Dollar eintragen; ~ **s. o. as an Englishman** j. für einen Engländer halten; ~ **one's expenditure** seine Ausgabenwirtschaft einschränken; ~ **a heckler at a meeting** Unruhestifter auf einer Versammlung zum Schweigen bringen; ~ **it down to s. one's inexperience** etw. auf jds. Unerfahrenheit zurückführen; ~ **the money** Geld auf den Tisch legen, bar zahlen; ~ **one's name** sich [in eine Liste] eintragen; ~ **passengers** Fahrgäste absetzen; ~ **to profit and loss** in die Ergebnisrechnung einsetzen; ~ **a rebellion** Aufruhr niederschlagen; ~ **s. one's success down to luck** jds. Erfolge seinem Glück zuschreiben; ~ **on time** rechtzeitig landen; ~ **in writing** nieder-, aufschreiben.

put *(v.)* **forth** *(propose)* vorschlagen, *(ship)* auslaufen;
~ **a new book** neues Buch herausbringen.

put *(v.)* **forward** unterbreiten, vorbringen, zur Debatte stellen;
~ **o. s. forward** sich in den Vordergrund schieben; ~ **an argument** Argument vorbringen; ~ **o. s. forward as a candidate** sich für einen Posten bewerben; ~ **a claim** Anspruch auf etw. erheben; ~ **s. o. forward for a decoration** j. für eine Auszeichnung vorschlagen; ~ **o. s. forward as a wealthy man** sich selbst als wohlhabend bezeichnen; ~ **a list of candidates** Kandidatenliste aufstellen; ~ **reasons** Gründe vorbringen; ~ **a new theory** neue Theorie aufstellen; ~ **a word** ein Wort mitsprechen.

put *(v.)* **in** einfügen, einschieben, *(in bank)* einlegen, *(employ)* an-, einstellen, *(file)* vorlegen, einreichen, *(ship)* einlaufen;
~ **action** in Gang (Betrieb) setzen; ~ **an advertisement** Annonce in die Zeitung einrücken lassen, in der Zeitung inserieren; ~ **an appearance** einer Ladung Folge leisten; ~ **bail** Kaution stellen; ~ **a bailiff** Bürgen stellen; ~ **a caretaker** Hausmeister einstellen; ~ **a catalog(ue)** in einen Katalog aufnehmen; ~ **a caveat** Vormerkung eintragen lassen; ~ **two cents** *(sl.)* ungefragt seine Meinung äußern; ~ **charge of a case** mit der Bearbeitung eines Falles beauftragen; ~ **a claim for damages** Schadenersatzanspruch stellen; ~ **commission** in Dienst stellen; ~ **court** bei Gericht einreichen; ~ **a crimp in prices** *(US sl.)* Preise durcheinander bringen; ~ **default** in Verzug setzen; ~ **a distress** Zwangsvollstreckung betreiben; ~ **a document** Dokument vorlegen, Urkundenbeweis antreten; ~ **for an election** als Kandidat auftreten; ~ **evidence** als Beweis vorbringen; ~ **s. o. for an examination** j. zu einer Prüfung anmelden; ~ **an hour reading newspapers** Stunde mit Zeitunglesen verbringen; ~ **an extra hour's work** Überstunde machen; ~ **funds** mit Deckung versehen; ~ **hold** in Haft nehmen; ~ **for a job** sich um eine Stellung bewerben; ~ **for three days leave** um einen dreitägigen Urlaub einkommen; ~ **mind** erinnern; ~ **motion** in Gang setzen; ~ **s. one's oar** jem. nicht erbetene Ratschläge erteilen; ~ **operation** in Betrieb setzen; ~ **one's papers in** *(sl.)* sich bei der Universität einschreiben; ~ **pawn** verpfänden; ~ **a plan** Plan vorlegen; ~ **a plea for forgery** Einwand der Fälschung erheben, Echtheit bestreiten; ~ **at a port** in den Hafen einlaufen; ~ **s. o. for the position of cashier** j. zum Schatzmeister vorschlagen; ~ **possession** jem. Besitz verschaffen; ~ **for a post** sich um eine Stellung bewerben; ~ **practice** praktisch anwenden; ~ **print** drucken lassen; ~ **prison** ins Gefängnis werfen; ~ **repair** in einwandfreien Zustand versetzen; ~ **for repairs** *(ship)* zu Reparaturarbeiten einlaufen; ~ **requisition** in Anspruch nehmen; ~ **store** einlagern; ~ **suit** Klage einreichen; ~ **one's term of military service** seiner Wehrpflicht genügen; ~ **the time** sich Zeit mit etw. lassen; ~ **one's time reading** seine Zeit lesend verbringen; ~ **a trade** in die Lehre (zur Ausbildung) geben; ~ **a child in ward** Kind unter Vormundschaft stellen; ~ **s. o. in the right way** j. auf den rechten Weg bringen; ~ **a good word for s. o.** gutes Wort für j. einlegen, sich für j. verwenden; ~ **an hour's work before breakfast** vor dem Frühstück eine Arbeitsstunde einlegen.

put *(v.)* **into** Geld einschießen;
~ **capital into a business** Geld in ein Geschäft stecken; ~ **circulation** in Umlauf setzen; ~ **commission** *(ship)* in Dienst stellen; ~ **effect by administrative action** im Verwaltungswege zur Durchführung bringen; ~ **force** in Kraft setzen; ~ **French** ins Französische übertragen; ~ **s. one's hands** eine Sache zur Erledigung übertragen, Angelegenheit in jds. Hände legen; ~ **harbo(u)r** in den Hafen einlaufen; ~ **o. s. into s. one's head** jem. die Regelung seiner Probleme überlassen; ~ **the market** auf den Markt (in den Verkehr) bringen; ~ **money into a bank** Geld bei einer Bank anlegen, Geld bei einer Bank einzahlen, Geld auf die Bank legen; ~ **money into houses** Hausbesitz als Daueranlage erwerben; ~ **one's money into land** sein Vermögen in Grundstücken (Immobilien) anlegen; ~ **money into an undertaking** Geld in ein Geschäft stecken; ~ **operation** in Betrieb nehmen; ~ **the laws into operation** Gesetze zur Anwendung bringen; ~ **a satellite into orbit round the earth** Satelliten in eine Erdumlaufbahn schießen; ~ **port** in den Hafen einlaufen; ~ **a port for stores** Hafen zur Verproviantierung anlaufen; ~ **s. o. virtually into a poverty trap** auf die Sozialhilfebasis herunterdrücken; ~ **practice** in die Praxis umsetzen, verwirklichen; ~ **one's system** sich einverleiben; ~ **writing** schriftlich abfassen.

put *(v.)* **off** auf-, ver-, hinausschieben, anstehen lassen, auf die lange Bank schieben, *(coll.)* aus der Fassung bringen, *(forged money)* in Umlauf setzen, *(goods)* an den Mann bringen, losschlagen, *(ship)* auslaufen;
~ **s. o. off** j. vor den Kopf stoßen, j. abschreiben; ~ **a case for a week** Verhandlung eine Woche vertagen; ~ **one's creditors** seine Gläubiger hinhalten; ~ **a dun with an instalment** Gläubiger mit einer Ratenzahlung beruhigen; ~ **s. th. upon s. o.** jem. etw. andrehen; ~ **everybody off by one's lordly airs** alle Leute mit seiner Aufgeblasenheit vor den Kopf stoßen; ~ **s. o. off with an excuse** j. einer Entschuldigung besänftigen; ~ **a counterfeit note** Falschgeld in den Verkehr bringen; ~ **one's guests** Einladung zurückziehen; ~ **the mask** seine Maske fallen lassen; ~ **a meeting** Sitzung verlegen; ~ **a payment** mit einer Zahlung aufhören; ~ **from the pier** vom Landungssteg ablegen; ~ **s. o. off his plans** j. von seinem Vorhaben abbringen; ~ **s. o. off with vague promises** j. mit leeren Versprechungen hinhalten; ~ **from the shore** Küste verlassen; ~ **things** sich mit seinen Gläubigern auf gewisse Termine einigen; ~ **until next week** bis zur nächsten Woche verschieben.

put *(v.)* **on** einführen, *(clothes)* anziehen, *(sum)* aufschlagen;
~ **airs** sich aufblasen; ~ **an air of innocence** unschuldige Miene aufsetzen; ~ **an (a new) article on the market** Ware auf dem Markt anbieten, neuen Artikel lancieren; ~ **one's best bib and tucker** seinen Sonntagsstaat anlegen; ~ **the books in die Bücher aufnehmen; ~ **the brake** Bremse anziehen; ~ **more coaches** zusätzliche Waggons anhängen; ~ **a dinner jacket** Smoking anziehen; ~ **a dish** Gericht auftragen; ~ **the dog** prahlen, sich brüsten (großtun); ~ **the file** zu den Akten nehmen; ~ **goods on order** Waren bestellen; ~ **the grammophone** Grammophon anstellen; ~ **the grill** *(sl.)* einem scharfen Verhör unterziehen; ~ **half pay** auf Wartegeld setzen; ~ **the invalid** Krankheit simulieren; ~ **it on** übertreiben, sich aufspielen; ~ **it on during the holiday season** während der Ferienzeit höhere Preise verlangen; ~ **s. o. onto a job** jem. eine Stellung verschaffen; ~ **onto the market** auf den Markt bringen; ~ **numbers on packages** Pakete numerieren; ~ **s. o. on his oath** jem. den Eid zuschieben; ~ **a par with** gleichstellen mit; ~ **a play on again** Stück wieder aufführen; ~ **a price on each article** jeden Artikel einzeln auszeichnen; ~ **s. th. onto the price** etw. auf den Preis aufstellen; ~ **a price on a painting** Wert eines Gemäldes abschätzen; ~ **a new service on line** neues Zugpaar auf einer Strecke einsetzen; ~ **s. th. special on** etw. Besonderes auf die Beine stellen; ~ **full speed** mit höchster Geschwindigkeit fahren; ~ **the spot** *(US)* ans Messer liefern; ~ **s. o. on the stand** *(US)* j. als Zeugen vernehmen; ~ **a tax on s. th.** etw. besteuern; ~ **one's thinking cap** gründlich über etw. nachdenken; ~ **extra trains** Sonderzüge einsetzen; ~ **trial** vor Gericht stellen; ~ **no value on s. one's advice** jds. Ratschlag keinerlei Wert beimessen; ~ **weight** zunehmen.

put *(v.)* **out** verdingen, *(dismiss)* entlassen, herauswerfen;
~ **s. o. out** j. aus dem Text bringen; ~ **o. s. out for s. o.** sich für j. engagieren; ~ **s. o. out of action** j. außer Gefecht setzen; ~ **to apprentice** in die Lehre (Ausbildung) geben; ~ **1000 bales of goods weekly** wöchentlich 1000 Warenballen produzieren; ~ **a boat** Boot aussetzen; ~ **of court** jds. Aussage umstoßen; ~ **of face** beschämen, verwirren; ~ **a fire** Feuer löschen; ~ **one's flags** flaggen, Flagge aushängen; ~ **funds** Mittel investieren; ~ **the gas** Gas abstellen; ~ **to graze** auf die Weide stellen; ~ **at interest** verzinslich anlegen; ~ **lines out to dry** Wäsche zum Trocknen aushängen; ~ **money** Geld anlegen; ~ **an open tender** öffentlich ausschreiben; ~ **of operation** außer Betrieb setzen; ~ **s. o. out of the room** j. hinauswerfen; ~ **a pamphlet** Flugblatt (Flugschrift) herausbringen; ~ **at 5 per cent** zu 5% anlegen; ~ **repairs** Reparaturen nach außen vergeben; ~ **to sea** in See stechen; ~ **all one's strength** sich völlig verausgaben; ~ **the washing** Wäsche weggeben; ~ **of the way** umbringen, umlegen; ~ **o. s. out of the way** sich selbst in Schwierigkeiten bringen; ~ **work in Submission** vergeben;
to be ~ with s. o. über j. verärgert sein.

put *(v.)* **over** vertagen, *(do in, sl.)* umbringen, umlegen, *(sl.)* ankommen, durchsetzen, *(explain)* verständlich machen, erklären, *(postpone cause in court)* vertagen;

~ **o. s. over** beim Publikum Ankratz finden; ~ **a policy** für eine Politik Verständnis gewinnen; ~ **s. o. over the river** j. über den Fluß bringen.

put *(v.)* **through** ausführen, durchführen, *(tel.)* Verbindung herstellen;

~ **s. o. through to s. o.** j. mit einem anderen telefonisch verbinden; ~ **s. o. through it** j. auf Herz und Nieren prüfen, j. durch die Mangel drehen; ~ **a business deal** Geschäft zu einem erfolgreichen Abschluß bringen; ~ **s. o. through an examination** j. durch eine Prüfung bringen; ~ **s. o. through a severe examination** j. einem strengen Verhör unterziehen (unterwerfen); ~ **a measure of legislation** gesetzliche Maßnahmen durchführen; ~ **s. o. through the mill** j. in eine harte Schule schicken, j. durch die Mangel drehen; ~ **at once** *(tel.)* sofort durchstellen; ~ **s. o. through an ordeal** j. auf die Feuerprobe stellen; ~ **s. o. through his paces** sich j. gründlich vornehmen; ~ **one's pen through a word** Wort durchstreichen.

put *(v.)* **to** *(horse)* anspannen;

~ **s. o. to it** es jem. schwer machen; ~ **account** in Rechnung stellen, berechnen; ~ **good account** verwerten; ~ **a child to a nurse** Kind einer Amme anvertrauen; ~ **s. o. to death** j. umbringen; ~ **the enemy to flight** Feind in die Flucht schlagen; ~ **great expense** große Unkosten verursachen; ~ **s. o. to great inconvenience** jem. große Unbequemlichkeiten bereiten; ~ **an end to one's life** Selbstmord begehen; ~ **land** sich an Land begeben; ~ **the money to good use** Geld vernünftig anlegen; ~ **s. o. to a lot of trouble** jem. einen Haufen von Schwierigkeiten bereiten; ~ **a proposal to the board** Vorschlag dem Vorstand zuleiten; ~ **a question to the vote** Frage zur Abstimmung stellen, über eine Frage abstimmen lassen; ~ **s. o. to ransom** j. gegen Lösegeld festhalten; ~ **a resolution to the meeting** Resolutionsentwurf einer Versammlung vorlegen; ~ **sale** zum Verkauf bringen; ~ **the question** foltern; ~ **a question to s. o.** jem. eine Frage vorlegen; ~ **right** in Ordnung bringen; ~ **sea** in See stechen; ~ **one's signature to a document** Urkunde unterzeichnen; ~ **one's signature to a will** Testament unterzeichnen; ~ **large sums to reserve** große Rückstellungen machen (vornehmen); ~ **silence** Redeverbot auferlegen; ~ **a stand** anhalten; ~ **s. o. to the torture** j. der Folter unterwerfen; ~ **s. o. to a trade** j. ein Handwerk erlernen lassen; ~ **s. o. to a lot of trouble** jem. einen Haufen von Schwierigkeiten bereiten; ~ **one's trumps** j. zur Anwendung seines letzten Mittels zwingen; ~ **s. th. to a good cause** etw. nutzbringend verwenden; ~ **one's thoughts together** sich konzentrieren; ~ **the vote** zur Abstimmung bringen; ~ **wages** zur Dienstbotentätigkeit verdammen; ~ **s. o. to work** j. an die Arbeit bringen.

put *(v.)* **together** vereinigen, zusammenstellen, -setzen;

~ **one's heads together** miteinander beratschlagen; ~ **a machine together** Maschine zusammenbauen; ~ **a few things together in a handbag** ein paar Sachen in seinen Koffer stopfen; ~ **two and two together** zwei und zwei zusammenzählen, seine Schlüsse ziehen, kombinieren.

put *(v.)* **under** | **s. one's care** in jds. Obhut geben; ~ **contribution** Kontributionen auferlegen; ~ **the screw** Repressionen aussetzen; ~ **s. o. under tutelage** j. entmündigen (unter Vormundschaft stellen).

put *(v.)* **up** *(umbrella)* aufspannen, *(increase)* erhöhen, heraufsetzen, (Aktien) übernehmen, *(at a hotel)* übernachten [in], *(placard)* anschlagen, *(parl.)* als Kandidat auftreten, kandidieren, *(stand)* aufstellen, errichten, *(wrap up)* einpacken;

~ **s. o.** j. aufnehmen, jem. Unterkunft gewähren; ~ **with s. th.** sich mit etw. abfinden, etw. in Kauf nehmen; ~ **for A** sich in A um einen Parlamentssitz bewerben; ~ **with an affront** Beleidigung einstecken; ~ **for auction** zur Versteigerung bringen; ~ **goods in a carton** Waren in einem Karton einpacken; ~ **in barrels** in Fässern verpacken; ~ **as a candidate** als Kandidaten aufstellen; ~ **£ 10.000 capital** Kapital von 10.000 Pfund aufbringen; ~ **s. o. up for a club** j. als Vereinsmitglied vorschlagen; ~ **s. o. up to a crime** j. zu einem Verbrechen anstiften; ~ **with bad fare** mit einem kümmerlichen Essen vorliebnehmen; ~ **a flag** Flagge setzen; ~ **funds** Geld (Mittel) aufbringen; ~ **goods to (for) auction** Waren zur Auktion geben; ~ **at a hotel** in einem Hotel absteigen; ~ **a house up** Haus zum Verkauf annoncieren; ~ **at an inn for the night** für eine Nacht in einem Gasthof absteigen; ~ **a job** *(sl.)* Komplott schmieden; ~ **money** Geld aufbringen; ~ **the money for an undertaking** Geld für ein Unternehmen zur Verfügung stellen; ~ **s. o. up to the news** jem. eine Nachricht mitteilen; ~ **a notice** Bekanntmachung anschlagen;

~ **for parliament** für das Parlament kandidieren; ~ **a petition** Gesuch einreichen; ~ **a play** Theaterstück aufführen; ~ **s. o. up for the position as secretary** j. zum Schriftführer vorschlagen; ~ **a price** Preiserhöhung vornehmen, Preis heraufsetzen; ~ **the rate of pension** Rentenerhöhung vornehmen; ~ **the rate of tax** Steuersatz anheben; ~ **the rent by 20 £ a week** Miete (Mietpreis) um 20 Pfund wöchentlich heraufsetzen; ~ **for sale** zum Verkauf anbieten; ~ **for a seat** sich um einen Parlamentssitz bewerben; ~ **the new secretary up to her duties** neue Sekretärin einweisen; ~ **for the secretaryship** sich als Kandidat für das Amt des Sekretärs zur Verfügung stellen; ~ **the shutters** Laden (Geschäft) schließen, *(fig.)* Laden dicht machen; ~ **a tax** Steuer heraufsetzen; ~ **a tent** Zelt aufschlagen; ~ **travellers** Reisende unterbringen; ~ **with** sich abfinden, dulden, ruhig hinnehmen; ~ **a yarn** *(sl.)* ein Garn spinnen; ~ **a vessel for freight** Schiff zur Verladung vormerken; ~ **for the weekend** übers Wochenende unterbringen.

put, to be ~ **up** *(stock exchange)* aufgerufen werden, *(patent)* zum Patent angemeldet sein; **to be hard** ~ **to pay one's debts** sich mit der Schuldenabzahlung schwer tun.

put and call option Verkaufsoption, Rück-, Lieferungsprämie.

put-off Verschiebung, Vertagung;

~ **price** Rückprämienkurs.

put premium Rückprämie;

~ **operation (transaction)** Rückprämiengeschäft.

put-up *(Br., coll.)* Nachtquartier;

~ **job** aufgelegter Schwindel, abgekartete Sache; ~ **price** *(auction)* Taxpreis.

put-you-up Bettcouch.

putative mutmaßlich, vermeintlich;

~ **father** angeblicher Vater; ~ **marriage** Putativehe.

putback Mißerfolg, Rückschlag.

putting | **away** Weg-, Beiseitelegen; ~ **back** Wegstellen; ~ **by** Zurücklegen; ~ **down a buoy** Bojenauslegung; ~ **forward of a document** Einreichung einer Urkunde; ~ **forward a new theory** Aufstellung einer neuen Theorie; ~ **in** *(advertisement)* Insertion, *(of document)* Vorlage; ~**-in of an advertisement** Einrücken einer Anzeige; ~**-in of an article** Plazierung eines Zeitungsartikels; ~**-in of a bail** Gestellung eines Bürgen; ~**-in of a candidate** Aufstellung eines Kandidaten; ~**-in of a document** Vorlage einer Urkunde, Antritt eines Urkundenbeweises; ~ **in hotchpot** Ausgleichung, Kollation, Erbausgleich; ~ **into force** Inkraftsetzung; ~ **into operation** Inbetriebsetzung; ~ **off** Verschiebung, Vertagung; ~**-on of more coaches** Anhängung zusätzlicher Waggons; ~**-on of a play** Aufführung eines Stückes; ~**-on of prices** Preiserhöhung; ~**-out system** Heimarbeit; ~ **the question** *(parl., Br.)* Fragestellung; ~ **up** Unterbringung; ~ **up a candidate** Kandidatenaufstellung; ~**-up of funds** Kapitalaufbringung; ~ **up a petition** Einreichung einer Bittschrift; ~**-up of prices** Preiserhöhung.

putt-putt *(coll.)* Außenbordmotor.

putter | **-off** *(sl.)* Zögerer, Zauderei; ~ **of a question** Fragesteller.

puzzle Rätsel, *(embarrassment)* Verwirrung, Verlegenheit;

crossword ~ Kreuzworträtsel; **jig-saw** ~ Zusammensetzspiel; **pictorial** ~ Bilderrätsel;

~ *(v.)* vor ein Rätsel stellen, durcheinanderbringen, komplizieren;

~ **one's brains** sich den Kopf zerbrechen; ~ **out** Lösung eines Rätsels finden; ~ **s. o. with a question** j. mit einer Frage in Verlegenheit setzen;

to be in a ~ verwirrt sein;

~ **corner** *(newspaper)* Rätselecke; ~ **lock** Vexierschloß, Buchstabenschloß.

puzzled | **air** verlegenen Miene;

to be ~ **what to do next** nicht wissen, was man zuerst tun soll.

puzzlehead Wirrkopf.

puzzler Rätsel, *(addict to solving puzzles)* passionierter Rätsellöser.

puzzling | **one's brains** Kopfzerbrechen;

~ *(a.)* rätselhaft.

PX *(US)* Marketenderei.

pylon Hochspannungsmast, *(airfield)* Orientierungsturm.

pyramid *(advertisement)* pyramidenförmige Anordnung, *(stock exchange)* ständig zunehmender Börsengewinn;

~ *(v.)* pyramidenförmig aufhäufeln, *(monopoly position)* verschachteln, Unternehmen durch Holdinggesellschaften beherrschen, *(stock exchange, US)* [Aufträge] zu Spekulationszwecken sich häufen lassen;

~ **prices** Preise immer weiter erhöhen; ~ **reserves** Rücklagen anhäufen;

~ **climber** Gipfelstürmer; ~ **display** Auslagen in Pyramidenform; ~ **scheme** sofortige Wiederanlage von Spekulationsgewinnen; ~ **selling** [Verkauf nach dem] Schneeballsystem, Schneeballverkaufssystem, Beschäftigung von Untervertretern.

pyramidal fashion, in pyramidenförmig.

pyramided structure Verschachtelungsstruktur.

pyramiding Verschachtelung, *(market, US)* Benutzung noch nicht realisierter Gewinne zu neuen Spekulationen, *(monopoly position)* finanzielle Monopolstellung, Unternehmensbeherrschung durch Holdinggesellschaften; ~ **of reserves** Reservenanhäufung; ~ **business** Schachteltransaktion; ~ **technique** Verschachtelungstechnik; ~ **transaction** Gewinnanlagegeschäft.

pyromania Brandstiftungstrieb.

pyrotechnical feuerwerkartig, *(fig.)* brillant.

pyrotechnics Feuerwerk, *(stock exchange, US)* heftige Kursbewegungen.

pyrotechnist Feuerwerker.

pyrric victory Phyrrussieg.

Q

Q. T., on the unter der Hand.
Qu department *(Br.)* Quartiermeisterabteilung.
quack Kurpfuscher, Quacksalber, Scharlatan;
~ *(v.)* marktschreierisch anpreisen, sich als Scharlatan
aufführen;
~ **doctor** Quacksalber; ~ **remedy** Arzneimittel eines
Kurpfuschers.
quackery Marktschreierei, Schwindel.
quackish marktschreierisch.
quadder *(newspaper)* Füller.
quadrangle Innenhof.
quadrangular operation in exchange vierseitiges Devisengeschäft.
quadrilingual viersprachig.
quadrillion *(US)* Billiarde.
quadripartite agreement Viermächteabkommen.
quadruplicate vierfache Ausfertigung;
~ **copies** vierfach vorhandene Kopien.
quagmire Klemme, Patsche.
quaint | costume malerisches Gewand; ~ **idea** drollige Idee; ~ **tale**
wunderliche Geschichte.
quake *(v.) (earth)* zittern, beben;
~ **in one's shoes** vor Angst zittern, Herz in der Hose haben.
qualifiable bestimmbar, qualifizierbar.
qualification *(act of qualifying)* [erforderliche] Befähigung, persönliche Begabung, [berufliche] Eignung, Berufseignung,
Fähigkeit, Qualifikation, *(classification)* Bezeichnung, Klassifizierung, *(of corporate director)* Pflichtaktienkapital eines
Vorstandsmitgliedes, Aktienkaution, *(modification)* Einschränkung, Modifikation, Verklausulierung, *(requisite)*
Erfordernis, [Vor]bedingung, Voraussetzung, *(restriction)*
Einschränkung, Vorbehalt;
subject to ~s Änderungen vorbehalten; **with the ~** mit der
Einschränkung; **with certain ~s** beziehungsweise; **without any**
~ ohne jede Einschränkung;
full ~ Vollberechtigung; **legal ~** juristische Befähigung; **necessary ~** erforderliche Befähigung; **professional ~s** fachliche
Qualifikationen, Befähigung für einen akademischen Beruf;
property ~ Eigentums-, Vermögensnachweis; **registrable ~s**
Immatrikulationserfordernisse; **no ~s required** kein Befähigungsnachweis erforderlich;
~ **benefit** Leistungsvoraussetzung, Unterstützungsvoraussetzung; ~ **of citizenship** Voraussetzung für den Erwerb der
Bürgerrechte; ~ **for dividend** Dividendenberechtigung; ~ **for
election** Wahlberechtigung; **~s for an examination** *(US)* Prüfungsvoraussetzungen; **~s for membership [of a club]** Mitgliedschaftsvoraussetzungen; **~s for naturalization** *(Br.)* Einbürgerungsbedingungen; ~ **of an offer** Einschränkung eines
Angebots; **~s for a public office** Vorbedingung (Befähigung)
für ein öffentliches Amt, Beamteneigenschaften; **to hold the
office of a judge** Befähigung zum Richteramt; ~ **for pension**
Pensionsberechtigung; ~ **of a privilege** Vorrechtsbeschränkung; ~ **in shares** Aktienkaution; ~ **to vote** Wahlberechtigung;
to accept without ~ vorbehaltslos annehmen; **to bring one's ~s
with o. s.** seine Papiere (Unterlagen) mitbringen; **to contain ~s**
(auditors' certificate) Einschränkungen enthalten; **to have the
necessary ~s [for a post]** den gestellten Anforderungen [für
Besetzung eines Postens] genügen; **to hold the ~s** [berufliche]
Voraussetzungen erfüllen; **to hold a professional ~ in accountancy** fachliche Qualifikationen auf dem Gebiet des Rechnungswesens mit sich bringen; **to make only one ~** nur eine
Abänderung vornehmen; **to possess professional or technical
~s** beruflichen oder fachlichen Befähigungsnachweis erbringen können;
~ **card** Personalbogen, Eignungskarte; ~ **form** Bewerbungsformular; ~ **rating** *(US)* Eigenschaftsbeurteilung; ~ **requirements**
Berechtigungserfordernisse; ~ **shares** *(Br.)* Pflicht-, Qualifikationsaktien; ~ **test** Eignungsprüfung.
qualificatory einschränkend.
qualified *(authorized)* autorisiert, befugt, berechtigt, *(eligible)*
berechtigt, *(fit)* qualifiziert, geeignet, befähigt, beschaffen,
tauglich, *(balance sheet approval)* eingeschränkt, mit Einschränkungen, *(limited)* bedingt, eingeschränkt, beschränkt,
modifiziert;
fully ~ voll befähigt; **ill ~** nicht geeignet (qualifiziert); **not ~**
unfähig, ungeeignet; **well ~** gut qualifiziert;
~ **to inherit** erbberechtigt; ~ **to list** *(shares)* börsenfähig; ~ **for a
post** anstellungsberechtigt; ~ **as to time** zeitlich beschränkt;

to be ~ to do s. th. Ermächtigung für etw. haben; **to be ~ in one's
subject** fachlich qualifiziert sein; **to be ~ to speak** *(fam.)* ein
Wort mitzureden haben; **to be badly ~ for a task** für eine
Aufgabe schlecht ausgerüstet sein; **to be ~ to teach English**
englischen Sprachunterricht erteilen dürfen; **to be ~ to vote**
wahlstimmberechtigt sein, Wahlrecht besitzen; **to consider o. s.**
~ sich für berechtigt halten; **to practise medicine without being
~** ärztliche Praxis ohne Approbation ausüben;
~ **acceptance** Annahme unter Vorbehalt, bedingte Annahme,
(bill of exchange) bedingtes (eingeschränktes) Akzept; **to give a
scheme one's ~ approval** einem Plan nur bedingt zustimmen; ~
certificate *(auditing)* eingeschränkter Prüfungsbericht, eingeschränkter Bestätigungsvermerk; ~ **conversion** *(law)* beschränkte Umdeutungsmöglichkeit eines Rechtsgeschäftes; ~
doctor zugelassener Arzt; ~ **elector** Wahlberechtigter; ~ **estate**
auflösend bedingtes Nießbrauchsrecht; ~ **expert** amtlich
bestellter Sachverständiger; ~ **indorsement** Giro ohne Verbindlichkeit, eingeschränktes Indossament, Indossament
ohne Obligo; ~ **investments** *(investment company, US)* zulässige Kapitalanlagen; ~ **majority** qualifizierte Mehrheit; ~
medical practitioner approbierter Arzt; **to give a ~ no** bedingte
Absage erteilen, auf Grund einzelner Bestimmungen ablehnen; ~ **oath** beschränkter Eid; ~ **operator** qualifizierter Arbeiter; ~ **person** berechtigte Person, Fachkraft; ~ **pilot**
zugelassener Pilot; ~ **plan** *(trust, US)* steuerlich begünstigter
Gewinnbeteiligungs- oder Pensionsplan; ~ **privilege** *(defamation)* bedingter Rechtfertigungsgrund; ~ **procedure** *(US)*
Zulassungsverfahren; ~ **property** [zeitlich] beschränktes
Eigentum; ~ **report** *(auditing)* einschränkender Prüfungsbericht; ~ **reserve** Wertberichtigungsreserve; ~ **sale** Konditionskauf; ~ **seaman** Maat; **in a ~ sense** mit Einschränkungen; **to
entrust the working of an undertaking to a ~ staff** Unternehmensführung einem Stab von Fachleuten übertragen (qualifizierten Mitarbeiterstab anvertrauen); ~ **test** Eignungsprüfung;
~ **title** Anwartschafts-, beschränktes Eigentumsrecht; ~ **voter**
Wahlberechtigter; ~ **worker** Facharbeiter, Spezialist.
qualify *(v.) (authorize)* autorisieren, qualifizieren, *(entitle)*
berechtigen, *(to be fit)* sich eignen, Befähigung besitzen, befähigt sein, *(to make fit)* qualifizieren, befähigen, *(to prove fit)*
seine Befähigung nachweisen, sich qualifizieren, Voraussetzungen [einer Bewerbung] erfüllen, *(modify)* einschränken,
modifizieren, *(official, US)* Diensteid leisten;
~ **o. s.** sich durch eine Prüfung qualifizieren;
~ **for the appointment as auditor** zum Revisor geeignet sein; ~
as an aviator Pilotenprüfung ablegen; ~ **for the bar** Voraussetzungen für die Anwaltszulassung erfüllen; ~ **for capital allowances** als steuerlich zulässige Abschreibung anerkannt sein;
~ **as a captain** Kapitänspatent besitzen; ~ **a certificate** *(auditor)*
nur einen eingeschränkten Prüfungsvermerk erteilen; ~ **for
citizenship** Voraussetzungen für die Staatsangehörigkeit erfüllen; ~ **a claim** Forderung substantiieren; ~ **for dividend** dividendenberechtigt sein; ~ **as a doctor** ärztliche Approbation
besitzen; ~ **for the election** *(US)* den Wahlvoraussetzungen
genügen; ~ **for an examination** Prüfungsvoraussetzungen
erfüllen; ~ **[o. s.] for (to hold) a job** berufliche Voraussetzungen
erfüllen, sich für einen Posten qualifizieren; ~ **as a judge** Befähigung zum Richteramt haben; ~ **for medicine** Medizin studieren; ~ **for an office** nötige Voraussetzungen für ein Amt
nachweisen; ~ **for a pension** für die Pensionierung reif sein, zur
Pensionierung anstehen; ~ **for a pension under national insurance** rentenberechtigt sein; ~ **for a civil-service position** Befähigung für den Staatsdienst erfüllen; ~ **s. o. for relief** j. zum
Empfang einer Unterstützung berechtigen; ~ **for reduced-rate
relief** Nachlaß verkürzter Steuersätze in Anspruch nehmen
können; ~ **for double-taxation relief** Vergünstigungen des
Doppelbesteuerungsabkommens genießen; ~ **a security for
sale to the public [with the Securities and Exchange Commission, US]** Wertpapier zur Börsenzulassung anmelden, Börsenzulassung für ein Wertpapier beantragen; ~ **as a solicitor** *(Br.)*
als Rechtsanwalt zugelassen werden; ~ **a statement** einschränkende Erklärung abgeben; ~ **a stock issue** *(US)* Emissionsgenehmigung besitzen; ~ **the terms of a will by means of a clause**
Testamentsbedingungen verklausulieren; ~ **s. o. as a toady** j.
als Speichellecker bezeichnen; ~ **for unemployment insurance**
Voraussetzungen für die Arbeitslosenunterstützung erfüllen;
~ **as a university lector** sich habilitieren; ~ **for the vote** den
Wahlvoraussetzungen Genüge leisten.

qualifying | agreement *(Br.)* Lombardschein; ~ **beneficiaries** begünstigter Personenkreis; ~ **certificate** Befähigungsnachweis; ~ **conditions** einschränkende Bestimmungen; ~ **date** Stichtag für die Wahlberechtigung; ~ **examination** Eignungsprüfung; **to pass the ~ examination of the Chartered Insurance Institute** *(Br.)* sein Abschlußexamen als Versicherungskaufmann bestehen; ~ **experience** nachgewiesene Erfahrungen, Befähigungsnachweis; ~ **grounds** Ausscheidungsgründe; ~ **period** Anwartschaftszeit [in der Sozialversicherung], Warte-, Karenzzeit; ~ **period of service** auf die Pension anrechnungsfähige (anwartschaftsberechtigte) Dienstzeit; ~ **reserve** Wertberichtigung; ~ **round** Ausscheidungsgründe; ~ **service** anwartschaftsfähige Dienstzeit; ~ **shares** *(US)* [nach den Statuten] vorgeschriebener Aktienbesitz, Pflichtaktien; ~ **statement** berichtigende Erklärung.

qualitative qualitativ, der Güte nach;
~ **analysis** qualitative Analyse; ~ **credit restrictions** *(treasury directive)* einzelne, gezielte Kreditrestriktionen; ~ **data** qualitative Angaben; ~ **interview** *(market research)* Tiefeninterview, informelles Interview.

qualities, intellectual geistige Eigenschaften; **managerial ~** Führungs-, Unternehmereigenschaften;
~ **of character** Charaktereigenschaften; ~ **of merchandise** Warenqualität; ~ **required for a post** geforderte berufliche Eigenschaften; **fighting ~ of a ship** Kampfkraft eines Schiffes; **to have many good ~** über viele gute Eigenschaften verfügen; **to manufacture goods in various ~** Waren verschiedenster Qualität herstellen.

quality *(degree of excellence)* Güte, Qualität, Wert, Beschaffenheit, *(faculty)* Eigenschaft, Fähigkeit, *(grade)* Gütegrad, Sorte, Marke, *(kind)* Gattung, Art;
in ~ gütemäßig; **of first (prime) ~** feinster Sorte, von bester Qualität; **of high ~** von guter Qualität; **of ordinary ~** von durchschnittlicher Qualität; **of special ~** extrafein; **of superior ~** von vorzüglicher Beschaffenheit; **of top ~** von erstklassiger Qualität; **of uniform kind and ~** von gleichmäßiger Art und Güte; **varying in ~** von ungleicher Güte;
accidental ~ zufällige Eigenschaft; **agreed ~** vereinbarte Qualität; **average ~** Durchschnittsqualität; **bottom ~** schlechteste Qualität; **choice ~** erste (ausgesuchte) Qualität; **choicest ~** feinste Sorte; **commercial ~** Handelswert [einer Ware], Handelsqualität; **concrete (definitive) ~** bestimmte Qualität; **well conditioned ~** gut abgelagerte Qualität; **current ~** gängige Qualität; **essential ~** notwendige Eigenschaft; **fair ~** gute Qualität; **fair average ~** Durchschnittsqualität; ~ **falling short** minderwertige Qualität; **first-class (rate) ~** erstklassige (prima) Ware (Marke); **good ~** Qualitätsware; **guaranteed ~** zugesicherte Eigenschaft; **heating ~** Heizkraft; **inferior ~** unterwertige (minderwertige) Güte, Minderwertigkeit, geringere (abfallende) Qualität (Sorte); **lowest ~** schlechteste Qualität; **medium (middling) ~** Mittelsorte, Mittel-, Sekundaqualität; **merchantable ~** Ware mittlerer Art und Güte, marktgängige Qualität; **good middling ~** gute Mittelsorte; **next ~** nächstbeste Sorte; **poor ~** schlechte (nicht ausreichende) Qualität, minderwertige Güte; **prime ~** auserlesene Qualität; **promised ~** zugesicherte Eigenschaft (Qualität); ~ **rated** gewertete Eigenschaft; **required ~** erforderliche Qualität; **second-class ~** zweite Qualität; **secondary ~** Nebeneigenschaft; **standard ~** durchschnittliche Güte, Durchschnittsqualität; **sterling ~** hervorragende Eigenschaft, allererste Qualität; **stipulated ~** ausbedungene Qualität; **superior ~** vorzügliche Qualität, Bonität; **supervisory ~** Aufsichtsstellung; **top[-grade] ~** erstklassige Qualität; **uniform ~** Standardware; **unsatisfactory ~** unzureichende Qualität; **warranted ~** zugesicherte Eigenschaft;
~ **will tell in the end** Qualität setzt sich durch;
like grade and ~ gleiche Beschaffenheit und Güte;
~ **of audience** Leserschaftsqualität; ~ **of commodities** Handelswert einer Ware; **good merchantable ~ and condition** gute Qualität (handelsübliche Güte) und Beschaffenheit; ~ **of estate** Umfang der Eigentumsrechte; ~ **of goods** Warenqualität; ~ **of land** Bodenbeschaffenheit, Bonität; ~ **of life** Lebensqualität; ~ **of prints** Druckausfall; ~ **as per sample** Qualität laut Muster; ~ **not up to standard** schlechtere Qualität; ~ **of work** Arbeitsqualität;
to act in the ~ of an agent als Vertreter handeln; **to aim at ~** Qualitätsleistungen anstreben; **to be of inferior ~** untergeordneten Wert haben; **to check ~** Qualitätsprüfung vornehmen; **to correspond in ~ with the sample** mit der vorgezeigten Probe in der Qualität übereinstimmen; **to enrich (heighten) a ~** Qualität steigern; **to give a taste of one's ~** zeigen, was man kann; **to have the ~ of inspiring confidence** Vertrauen ausstrahlen; **to seek size**

rather than ~ mehr auf Quantität als auf Qualität gehen; **to stock only one ~** nur eine Sorte führen; **to upgrade ~** Qualität steigern; **to vary in ~** qualitativ verschieden ausfallen;
~ **area** Güteklasse; ~ **assurance** Qualitätszusicherung; ~ **assurance analysis** Qualitätskontrolle; ~ **car** Wagen für gehobenere Ansprüche; ~ **categories** Güteklassen; ~ **characteristic** Güteeigenschaft; ~ **circulation** Qualitätsauflage; ~ **complaint** Qualitätsrüge; ~ **conformance** Qualitätsübereinstimmung; **statistical ~ control** Qualitätskontrolle, statistische Güteüberwachung; **to subpoena a company's records on ~ control** Fabrik auf Vorlage ihrer Unterlagen über Qualitätskontrolle verklagen; ~**-control practice** Qualitätskontrollverfahren; ~ **description** Güte-, Qualitätsbezeichnung; ~ **designation** Qualitäts-, Gütebestimmung; ~ **factor** Gütefaktor; ~ **film** gehaltvoller Film; ~ **goods** Qualitätswaren; **high-~ goods** Güter des gehobeneren Bedarfs; **medium-~ goods** Waren mittlerer Qualität (Art) und Güte; **poor-~ goods** Waren von schlechter Qualität, minderwertige Erzeugnisse; ~ **grade** Qualitätssorte-, stufe; ~ **hotel** Hotel für Anspruchsvolle (gehobenere Ansprüche); ~ **increment** Qualitätszuwachs; ~ **inspection** *(Br.)* Abnahmeprüfung; ~ **inspector** *(Br.)* Abnahmebeamter; ~ **label** Gütezeichen; ~ **language** gewählte Sprache; **[acceptable] ~ level** [toleriertes] Qualitätsniveau; **average outgoing ~ level** durchschnittliches Qualitätsniveau der Leistungen der Lieferanten; ~ **mark** Gütezeichen; ~ **market** Qualitätsmarkt; ~ **markup** Güteaufpreis; ~ **merchandise** Qualitätsware; ~ **performance** Qualitätsleistung; ~ **picture** Qualitätsbild; **high-~ product** Qualitätserzeugnis; ~ **protection** Qualitätsschutz, Güteschutz; **average-~ protection** Gewährleistung der Durchschnittsqualität; ~ **range** Qualitätslage; ~ **rating** Qualitätsbeurteilung; ~ **rules** Qualitätsvorschriften; ~ **specification** *(Br.)* Güte-, Abnahmevorschriften; ~ **stabilization** *(US)* Preisbindung der zweiten Hand; ~ **standards** Qualitätsnormen; ~ **test** Abnahme-, Qualitätsprüfung; ~ **warranty** Bürgschaft für Qualität, Garantieverpflichtung; ~ **workmanship** Qualitätsarbeit.

qualm Bedenken, Skrupel;
~**s of conscience** Gewissensbisse; ~**s of economy** Anwandlungen von Sparsamkeit;
to feel no ~s about borrowing money from friends bei Freunden hemmungslos Geld pumpen; **to have ~s of conscience** einen Moralischen haben; **to have no ~s about doing s. th.** keinerlei Skrupel bei einer Tätigkeit empfinden.

quandaries, on-the-job berufliche Schwierigkeiten.

quandary Verlegenheit, Schwierigkeit;
to be in a ~ sich in einem Dilemma befinden.

quantal response Ja-Nein-Reaktion.

quantiles *(statistics)* Häufigkeitsstufen.

quantitative mengenmäßig, der Menge nach, quantitativ;
~ **analysis** quantitative Analyse; ~ **control** Mengenkontrolle; ~ **credit restrictions** *(treasury directive, Br.)* generelle Kreditrestriktionen; ~ **data** quantitative Angaben; ~ **economics** Makroökonomik; ~ **forecasting** Intervallprognose; ~ **index** Mengenindex; ~ **interview** vorher im einzelnen festgelegtes Interview; ~ **market tendencies** Mengenkonjunktur; ~ **ratio** Mengenverhältnis; ~ **regulations** Mengenvorschriften; ~ **restrictions** mengenmäßige Beschränkungen; ~ **sales** Mengenkonjunktur; ~ **survey** tabellenmäßig zu erfassendes Untersuchungsergebnis.

quantities große Mengen;
in large ~ in Massen, massenweise;
noncommercial ~ nicht zum Handel geeignete Mengen;
~ **of rain** erheblicher Niederschlag;
to buy things in large ~ Mengeneinkäufe tätigen; **to order large ~** Großaufträge erteilen; **to survey a building for ~** *(Br.)* Baukostenkalkulation durchführen, Baukostenvoranschlag machen; **to take out the ~** erforderlichen Erdaushub vornehmen.

quantity Quantität, Quantum, *(great amount)* Menge, Masse, *(law)* Zeitdauer;
average ~ Durchschnittsmenge, Pauschquantum; **consumer ~** Verbrauchsmenge; ~ **delivered** Liefermenge; ~ **demanded** Mengennachfrage; ~ **issued** *(inventory)* Abgang; **large (vast) ~** Unmasse; **minimum commercial ~** handelsübliche Mindestmenge; **negligible ~** übersehbare Größe; **numerical ~** Zahlengröße; ~ **ordered** bestellte Menge; ~ **permitted** *(customs)* zollfreie Menge; ~ **received** *(inventory)* Zugang; **small ~** geringe Menge; ~ **sold** Absatzmenge; ~ **supplied** angebotene Menge; **unknown ~** unbekannte Größe; **unpredictable ~** schwer abzuschätzende Persönlichkeit; **wrong ~** unrichtige Menge;
~ **of goods** Warenmenge; ~ **of heat** Wärmemenge; ~ **of money** Geldmenge; ~ **of production** Produktionsmenge; ~ **of sales** Absatzmenge; **great ~ of work** gewaltige Menge Arbeit;

~ **adjuster** Mengenanpasser; ~ **buyer** Großabnehmer, Grossist, Masseneinkäufer; ~ **buying** Mengen-, Großabnahme, Massenankauf; ~ **contract** Gattungskauf; ~ **control** Mengenregulierung; ~ **description** Mengenbezeichnung; ~ **deviation** Mengenabweichung; ~ **discount** Ermäßigung bei Mengenabnahme, Großhandels-, Mengenrabatt; ~ **equation** Verkehrs-, Quantitätsgleichung, Währungsausgleich; ~ **index** Mengenindex; ~ **manufacturing** Massenherstellung, -erzeugung, Serienproduktion; ~ **mark** Mengenangabe; ~ **order** Mengenauftrag; ~ **price** Mengenpreis; ~ **proceeds** Mengenerlös; ~ **production** Massen-, Mengenherstellung, Massenproduktion; ~ **purchase** Großhandelseinkauf, -abnahme; ~ **rate** Mengen, Grossistentarif, Mengenrabatt; ~ **rebate** Großhandels-, Mengenrabatt; ~ **reduction** Mengennachlaß, -rabatt; ~ **relative** *(statistics)* Mengen-, Meßziffer; ~ **restrictions** Mengenbeschränkungen; ~ **scale** Mengenstaffel; ~ **standard** Mengenvorgabe; ~ **surveying** Baukosten-, Preiskalkulation; ~ **surveyor** *(Br.)* Preiskalkulator, Bausachverständiger; ~ **theory of money** Quantitätstheorie des Geldes; ~ **turnover** mengenmäßiger Umsatz, Mengenumsatz; ~ **variance** Mengenabweichung.

quantum Menge, Betrag, Quantum;
~ **of damages** Höhe des zuerkannten Schadens, Schadensersatzbetrag; ~ **of forces** *(mil.)* Iststärke; ~ **of relief** Steueranrechnungsbetrag;
~ **index** Mengenindex; ~ **meruit** angemessene Teillohnvergütung; ~ **meruit claim** Forderung auf angemessene Vergütung; ~ **theory** Quantentheorie.

quarantine Quarantäne[station], *(isolation hospital)* Infektionskrankenhaus, *(restraint)* Isolierung, Absonderung, Quarantänemaßnahmen, *(widow, US)* 40-Tage-Hausrecht;
~ **of observation** Beobachtungsquarantäne;
~ *(v.)* unter Quarantäne stellen, Quarantäne verhängen (auferlegen), isolieren;
~ **a country** Staat politisch und wirtschaftlich völlig isolieren;
~ **a war** Krieg lokalisieren;
to be in ~ Quarantäne machen; **to be out of** ~ Quarantäne hinter sich haben; **to be subject to** ~ Quarantäne halten müssen; **to discharge from** ~ aus der Quarantäne entlassen; **to go into** ~ in Quarantäne gehen; **to perform one's** ~ Quarantäne durchmachen; **to put under** ~ in Quarantäne legen; **to remain in** ~ in Quarantäne liegen; **to remove the** ~ Quarantäne aufheben; **to ride at** ~ Quarantäne halten; **to take off the** ~ Quarantäne aufheben;
~ **certificate** Gesundheitszeugnis; ~ **expenses** Quarantänegelder; ~ **flag** Quarantäneflagge; ~ **harbo(u)r** Quarantänehafen; ~ **inspection** Quarantäneprüfung; ~ **officer** Quarantänebeamter; ~ **period** Quarantänezeit; ~ **regulations** Quarantänevorschriften, -bestimmungen; **to break the** ~ **regulations** Quarantänevorschriften verletzen; ~ **risk** Quarantänerisiko; ~ **service** Quarantänedienst; ~ **station** Quarantänestation.

quarrel Streit[igkeit], Zank, Hader;
in a good ~ in gerechter Sache;
~ *(v.)* **with one's bread and butter** seinen eigenen Interessen schaden, sich selbst im Licht stehen; ~ **with each other** miteinander streiten; ~ **with one's lot** mit seinem Schicksal hadern; ~ **with one's tools** an seinem Werkzeug etw. auszusetzen haben;
to be always fighting other people's ~s jedermann zu seinem Recht zu helfen trachten; **to find** ~ **over a straw** sich um einen Strohhalm zanken; **to have no** ~ **against s. o.** sich über j. nicht beklagen können; **to make up their** ~ ihren Streit beenden; **to pick a** ~ Streit vom Zaun brechen; **to try to pick a** ~ **with s. o.** Streit mit jem. suchen.

quarry Steinbruch, *(fig.)* Fundgrube;
~ *(v.)* im Steinbruch arbeiten;
~ **among old documents** in alten Dokumenten wühlen; ~ **information from books** Informationen aus Büchern gewinnen; ~ **treasures from old books** Schätze aus alten Büchern heben.

quart Flüssigkeitsmaß von 1/4 Gallone (1,136 Liter).

quarter Viertel, *(college, US)* Studienquartal, *(dollar, US)* Vierteldollar, *(mar.)* Posten, *(mil.)* Pardon, Schonung, *(region)* Gegend, Landesteil, *(source)* Quelle, Stelle, Seite, *(of town)* Stadtviertel, -bezirk, *(of year)* Vierteljahr, Quartal;
at close ~s in allernächster Nähe, *(crowded)* eng zusammengepfercht; **every (by the)** ~ quartalsweise, vierteljährlich; **for** ~ **the price** für ein Viertel des Preises; **from authoritative** ~s von maßgebender Seite; **from official** ~s von amtlichen Stellen; **from a safe** ~ aus sicherer Quelle; **in diplomatic** ~s in diplomatischen Kreisen; **in higher** ~s höheren Orts; **in informed** ~s in unterrichteten Kreisen; **in responsible** ~s an zuständiger Stelle; ~s *(lodging)* Quartier, Logis, Unterkunft, Wohnung, Aufenthalt, *(billets)* Unterkunft, Quartier;

business ~ Geschäftsgegend, -viertel; **calendar** ~ Kalendervierteljahr; **Chinese** ~ Chinesenviertel; **close** ~s beschränkte Wohnverhältnisse; **crew's** ~s Mannschaftsquartier; **emigrants'** ~s Auswandererlogis; **excellent** ~s hervorragende Unterkunft; **financial** ~s Finanzkreise; **free** ~s Freiquartier; **general** ~s *(mar.)* Klarmachen zum Gefecht; **half** ~ Quartalsmedio; **industrial** ~ Industriegegend; **living** ~s Quartier, Appartment, größere Wohnung; **manufacturing** ~ Industrie, Fabrikviertel, -gegend, Industrieviertel; **poor** ~ Armenviertel; **present** ~ laufender Termin; **private** ~s Privatwohnung; **proper** ~ zuständige Stelle; **residential** ~ Wohnviertel, -bezirk, -gegend; **slum** ~ Elends- Barackenviertel; **well-informed** ~s eingeweihte Kreise; **winter** ~s *(mil.)* Winterlager;
a bad ~ **of an hour** eine böse (unangenehme) Viertelstunde; **the four** ~s **of the globe** die vier Himmelsrichtungen; ~s **in kind** freie Unterkunft; ~ **of a year** Vierteljahr, einundneunzig Tage;
~ *(v.)* vierteilen, *(take one's abode)* vorübergehend Aufenthalt nehmen, wohnen, leben, *(mil.)* einquartieren, mit Einquartierung belegen, *(v./i.)* einquartiert sein;
~ **o. s. on s. o.** sich bei jem. einquartieren; ~ **troops on the villagers** Truppe in Bürgerquartieren unterbringen;
to apply to the proper ~ sich an die zuständige Stelle wenden; **to arrive from all** ~s von überall herkommen; **to ask for** ~ um Gnade bitten; **to be paid by the** ~ vierteljährlich bezahlt werden; **not to be a** ~ **as good as it should be** nicht halb so gut sein, wie es sollte; **to be confined to one's** ~s Stubenarrest haben; **to be pressed for money from all** ~s von allen Leuten um Geld angegangen werden; **to be rumo(u)red in certain** ~s in bestimmten Stellen gerüchtweise verlauten; **to beat to** ~s Mannschaft auf ihre Posten rufen, *(mar.)* klar zum Gefecht blasen; **to buy s. th. at the (a)** ~ **of the price** etwas für ein Viertel des Wertes kaufen; **to change one's** ~s andere Wohnung nehmen, umziehen; **to cry for** ~ um Gnade flehen; **to find excellent** ~s **at an inn** in einem Gasthof sehr gut unterkommen; **to find no favo(u)r in the highest** ~s oberen Orts ungünstig aufgenommen werden; **to flock in from all** ~s aus allen Gegenden zusammenströmen; **to give fair** ~ Nachsicht üben; **to go into winter** ~s Winterquartier beziehen; **to have to expect no help from that** ~ von dieser Stelle auf keinen Pfennig hoffen können (keinen Pfennig zu erwarten haben); **to have free** ~s umsonst wohnen; **to have received news from other** ~s Nachrichten von anderer Stelle haben; **to have one's** ~ **on the second floor** im zweiten Stock wohnen; **not to have a** ~ **the pleasure as s. o. else** sich längst nicht so gut wie alle anderen amüsieren; **to hear it from all** ~s überall hören; **to live in close** ~s in bedrängten Verhältnissen leben; **to owe several** ~s' **rent** mehrere Mietraten schuldig sein; **to pay one's rent at the end of each** ~ seine Miete vierteljährlich postnumerando zahlen; **to receive** ~ begnadigt werden; **to receive news from another** ~ zusätzliche Informationen erhalten; **to remove to other** ~s umquartieren; **to return to** ~s *(mil.)* in die Kaserne einrücken; **to run from all** ~s von überall angelaufen kommen; **to shift one's** ~s umziehen, andere Wohnung nehmen; **to take up one's** ~ sein Quartier aufschlagen; **to take up** ~s **with s. o.** mit jem. zusammenziehen (zusammenwohnen), sich bei jem. einquartieren; **to travel in every** ~ **of the globe** ganze Welt bereisen;
~s **allowance** Beköstigungsgeld; ~ **bell** Viertelstundenglocke; ~ **bill** Quartalsabrechnung, *(mar.)* Schiffsrolle; ~ **binding** Halbfranzband; ~**-breed** Mestize; ~ **chest of tea** Kiste Tee; ~ **day** Quartalstag, Zinstag, Termin, *(mil.)* Zahl-, Löhnungstag; ~**-deck** *(mar.)* Achterdeck, *(fig.)* Offiziere; ~ **dollar** *(US)* Vierteldollar; ~ **earnings** Vierteljahreserträgnisse; ~ **final** Viertelfinale; ~ **guard** *(Br.)* Lagerwache; ~ **gunner** *(mar.)* Geschützführer; ~ **hour** Viertelstunde; **to strike the** ~ **hours** viertelstündlich schlagen; ~'s **instalment** Vierteljahresrate; ~ **light** *(car)* Rückfenster; ~ **page** *(advertising)* Viertelseite; ~'s **payment** Quartalszahlung; ~**-phase** *(el.)* zweiphasig; ~ **plate** *(photo)* Platte; ~'s **rent** Quartalsmiete; ~**-sales** *(estate, New York)* Kaufpreiserstattung eines Viertels bei Weiterverkauf; ~ **seal** *(Scot.)* Nebensiegel; ~ **section** 1/4 Planquadrat; ~ **sessions** *(Br.)* vierteljährlich abgehaltene Sitzungen für kleinere Straffälle; ~ **stock** *(US)* Viertelsaktie, mit nur 1/4 des Pariwertes gehandelte Aktie; ~ **sheet** *(Br.)* Pferdedecke; ~**-yearly instal(l)-ment** vierteljährliche Ratenzahlung.

quarterage Quartals-, Vierteljahreszahlung, *(mil.)* Quartier, Unterkunft.

quarterback *(v.) (sl.)* Sache organisieren.

quartered beherbergt, untergebracht, *(mil.)* einquartiert;
to be ~ **upon s. o.** bei jem. im Quartier liegen.

quartering *(billeting)* [Zwangs]einquartierung, *(lodging assigned)* Logis, Quartier, Unterkunft;
~ **of troops** Verteilung von Truppenquartieren.

quarterly *(paper)* Vierteljahreszeitschrift;
~ *(a.)* quartalsweise, vierteljährlich;
to be paid ~ vierteljährlich bezahlt werden;
~ **account** Quartalsrechnung; ~ **accounts** vierteljährlicher Rechnungsabschluß; ~ **allowance** Quartalsgeld; ~ **bulletin** *(Bank of England)* Vierteljahresbericht; ~ **disbursement** Quartalszahlung, Zahlung am Vierteljahresultimo; ~ **dividend** Vierteljahresdividende; ~ **figures** Vierteljahreszahlen; ~ **magazine** Vierteljahreszeitschrift; ~ **payment** vierteljährliche Zahlung, Vierteljahresrate, Quartalszahlung; ~ **period** Quartal; ~ **salary** Vierteljahresgehalt; ~ **settlement** Abwicklung der Quartalsverbindlichkeiten; ~ **statement** Quartals-, Vierteljahresbericht, vierteljährlicher Bericht; ~ **subscription** Vierteljahresabonnement; ~ **trade accounts** vierteljährliche Abschlüsse.
quartermaster *(marine)* Steuermannsmaat, *(mil.)* Quartiermeister;
~ **general** Generalquartiermeister.
quarto Quartformat.
quartz clock Quarzuhr.
quash *(v.)* aufheben, annullieren, niederschlagen, ungültig machen, kassieren;
~ **a conviction** Schuldspruch (Strafurteil) aufheben; ~ **a decision** Entscheidung aufheben; ~ **an indictment** Eröffnung des Hauptverfahrens ablehnen, Verfahren einstellen; ~ **a judgment on a point of law** Urteil aus Rechtsgründen aufheben; ~ **the order of the inferior court** Verfügung des unteren Gerichts aufheben; ~ **proceedings** Verfahren niederschlagen (einstellen); ~ **a rebellion** Aufstand niederschlagen; ~ **a verdict** Strafurteil kassieren.
quashing Annullierung, Aufhebung, Niederschlagung;
~ **of a judgment** Urteilsaufhebung.
quasi scheinbar, gewissermaßen, gleichsam, ähnlich, quasi;
~ **agreement** vertragsähnliche Vereinbarung, *(antitrust law, US)* aufeinander abgestimmtes Verhalten, Gruppendisziplin; ~-**colonial** kolonialähnlich; ~-**contract** vertragsähnliche Verpflichtung, vertragsähnliches Schuldverhältnis; ~-**contractual** vertragsähnlich; ~-**contractual right** vertragsähnliches Recht; ~ **corporation** Selbstverwaltungsorganisation; ~ **crime** Ordnungswidrigkeit; ~ **delict** fahrlässige unerlaubte Handlung; ~-**deposit** verwahrungsähnliches Verhältnis; ~ **derelict** wrackähnlicher Zustand; ~-**diplomatic** diplomatenähnlich; ~ **easement** dienstbarkeitsähnliches Recht; ~ **entail** fideikommißähnliche Nachlaßbindung; ~ **expert** halber Sachverständiger; ~-**governmental corporation** halbstaatliche Einrichtung; ~ **judicial** richterähnlich; ~-**legislative** gesetzgebungsähnlich; ~ **military organization** halbmilitärische Organisation; ~-**municipal bonds** *(US)* nicht vollwertige Kommunalanleihe; ~ **municipal corporation** gemischtwirtschaftlicher Versorgungsbetrieb; ~-**official** halbamtlich; ~-**official position** beamtenähnliche Stellung; ~ **partner** *(US)* Scheingesellschafter; ~ **partnership association** Vorvereinigung, Gesellschaft vor Eintragung; ~ **personalty** zum beweglichen Vermögen gehörende Grundstücksbestandteile; ~ **possession** besitzähnliches Verhältnis; ~-**private good** meritorisches Gut; ~ **prosperity** Scheinkonjunktur; ~-**public company** Gesellschaft mit öffentlich-rechtlichen Befugnissen, *(corporation US)* gemischtwirtschaftliches Unternehmen, gemischter Versorgungs-, Regiebetrieb; ~ **purchase** aus den Umständen zu entnehmende Kaufabsicht; ~ **realty** Grundstückszubehör; ~-**rent** *(Marshall)* Produzentenrente, temporärer Unternehmergewinn; ~ **tenant at sufferance** geduldeter Gewahrsamsinhaber (Unterpächter); ~ **tort** deliktsähnliche Haftung; ~-**trust character** konzernähnlicher Charakter; ~ **trustee** Treuhänderhaftung bei Unterschlagung; ~ **usufruct** nießbrauchähnliches Verhältnis; ~ **war** kriegsähnlicher Zustand.
quay Schiffslandeplatz, Anlegestelle, Kai;
alongside the ~ längsseits Kai; **ex** ~ ab Kai; **ex** ~ **duties unpaid** ab Kai unverzollt;
legal ~ Zollkai;
to discharge at the ~ am Kai löschen;
~ **dues** Kaigebühren; ~ **receipt** Kai-Empfangsschein; ~ **rent** Kailagergeld; ~-**side worker** Hafen-, Dockarbeiter.
quayage Anlegegebühren, Kaigeld, -gebühren, Landungszoll.
Queen's|award of industry von der Königin verliehener Industriepreis; ~ **counsel** *(Br.)* Kronanwalt; ~ **enemies** durch Feindeinwirkung entstandener Schaden; ~ **English** *(Br.)* reines Englisch; ~ **evidence** belastendes Beweismaterial; ~ **prison** Schuldnergefängnis; **the** ~ **speech** Parlamentseröffnungsrede.
queer *(US)* Falschgeld, Blüten;
~ *(a.)* *(counterfeit, sl.)* gefälscht, nachgemacht, wertlos, *(suspicious, coll.)* fragwürdig, zweifelhaft, *(tight, sl.)* besoffen;

~ *(v.)* *(sl.)* verkorksen;
~ **s. one's pitch** j. etw. vermasseln;
to feel ~ **all over** sich ganz (völlig) benommen fühlen;
~ **bill** fauler Wechsel; ~ **character** fragwürdiger Charakter; ~ **fellow** komischer Kauz; ~ **maker** *(sl.)* Falschmünzer; ~ **notion** seltsame Vorstellung; ~ **story** seltsame Geschichte; **to be in** ~ **street** *(sl.)* in Geldschwierigkeiten sein, in der Tinte sitzen; ~ **transaction** verdächtiges (faules) Geschäft; ~ **way of talking** sonderbare Art zu reden.
quell *(v.)* **a revolt** Aufstand niederschlagen.
quench *(v.)* auslöschen;
~ **s. one's enthousiasm** abkühlend auf jds. Begeisterung reagieren; ~ **steel** Stahl abschrecken.
querulous nörgelsüchtig;
~ **person** Querulant; **in a** ~ **tone** in mürrischem Ton.
query Monitum, Rückfrage, Erkundigung, *(print.)* Fragezeichen;
~ *(v.)* Rückfrage halten, monieren, beanstanden, in Frage stellen;
~ **s. one's instructions** jds. Anweisungen in Zweifel ziehen; ~ **the items of an account** Rechnungsposten beanstanden; ~ **a vote** Abstimmung beanstanden;
to make a ~ monieren, Rückfrage halten; **to make a** ~ **to s. o.** *(fam.)* jem. einen fragenden Blick zuwerfen; **to raise a** ~ Einwand erheben; **to settle a** ~ Zweifel beseitigen.
quest Suche, Streben, *(search)* Untersuchung;
~ **for food** Nahrungssuche; ~ **for gold** Goldsuche; ~ **for independence** Unabhängigkeitsforderung.
question [Streit]frage, Streitpunkt, *(interrogation)* gerichtliche Untersuchung, Vernehmung, Verhör, *(request for information, parl.)* kleine Anfrage, Interpellation;
~**!** *(at meeting)* zur Sache!;
in ~ fraglich; **open to** ~ zweifelhaft; **out of the** ~ vollkommen ausgeschlossen;
academic ~ rein akademische Frage; **cabinet** ~ Kabinettsfrage; **categorical** ~ mit Ja oder Nein zu beantwortende Frage; **closed-end** - Frage mit vorgegebener Antwortmöglichkeit; **common** ~ gewöhnliche Folter; **cross** ~ Kreuzfrage; **a much debated** ~ große Streitfrage; **economic** ~ Wirtschaftsproblem; **federal** ~ *(US)* nach Bundesrecht zu entscheidende Frage; **hypothetical** ~ hypothetische Frage; **incidental** ~ Zwischenfrage; **indirect (oblique)** ~ indirekte Frage; **interlocking** ~ korrespondierende Frage; **judicial** ~ zu entscheidende Frage; **key** ~ entscheidende Frage; **labo(u)r** ~ Arbeiterfrage; **leading** ~ Suggestivfrage; **legal** ~ Rechtsfrage; **live** ~ aktuelle Frage; **moral** ~ Frage der Moral; **nice** ~ heikle Frage; **open-ended** ~ Kommentarfrage; **pending (unsettled)** ~ schwebende Angelegenheit; **political** ~ politische Frage; **probing** ~ Testfrage; **procedural** ~ Verfahrensfrage; **recurring** ~ immer wieder auftretende Frage; **social** ~ soziale Frage; **supplementary** ~ Zusatzfrage; **technical** ~ verfahrensrechtliche Frage; **64thousand dollar** ~ Gretchenfrage; ~ **thrown in** Zwischenfrage; **vexed** ~ strittige Frage; **vital** ~ Lebensfrage;
~ **of adjournment** Vertagungsfrage; ~ **of apprenticeship** Lehrlingsausbildungsproblem; ~ **of common concern** Frage von allgemeinem Interesse; ~ **of construction** Auslegungsfrage; ~ **of costs** Kostenfrage; ~ **relating to craft** Berufsproblem; ~**s of currency** Währungsfragen; ~**s of the day** Tagesfragen; ~ **under debate (discussion)** zur Diskussion anstehende Frage; ~ **in dispute** strittige Frage, Streitfrage; ~ **of establishment** Niederlassungsfrage; ~ **of fact** Tatfrage; ~ **from the floor** Zuhörerfrage; ~ **of form** Formsache; ~ **of minor interest** Frage von zweitrangiger Bedeutung, zweitrangige Frage; ~**s of present interest** aktuelle Fragen; ~**s of public interest** Fragen von öffentlichem Interesse (von allgemeiner Bedeutung); ~ **of interpretation** Auslegungsfrage; ~ **of law** Rechtsfrage; ~ **of life and death** Sache auf Leben oder Tod; ~ **of merit** Sachfrage; ~ **of money** Geldfrage; ~ **that is on the nail** anstehende Frage; ~ **of privilege** Zuständigkeitsfrage; ~ **of routine** Routinefrage; ~ **of substance** Frage von Bedeutung; ~ **of time** Zeitfrage;
~ *(v.)* zur Debatte stellen, diskutieren, *(examine by queries)* [Zeugen be]fragen, verhören, vernehmen;
~ **a candidate** Kandidaten prüfen; ~ **the computation of an account** Kontoabrechnung nicht anerkennen; ~ **an election** Wahl anfechten; ~ **the honesty of s. o.** Ehrlichkeit in Frage stellen; ~ **a right** [Rechts]anspruch bestreiten; ~ **the stars** die Sterne befragen; ~ **s. one's veracity** jds. Glaubwürdigkeit in Frage stellen; ~ **a witness** Zeugen befragen (vernehmen);
to address a ~ *(parl.)* Anfrage richten; **to allow s. one's claim without** ~ jds. Forderung widerspruchslos anerkennen; **to answer the** ~**s** Prüfungsaufgaben schriftlich beantworten; **to ask s.**

o. a ~ *(parl.)* j. interpellieren; **to ask a lot of ~s** Haufen von Fragen stellen; **to be all ~s** neugierig sein; **to be beside the ~** nicht zur Sache gehören; **to be calling for the ~** Schluß der Debatte verlangen; **to be at issue on a ~** Frage diskutieren; **to be out of the ~** nicht in Frage kommen; **to beg the ~** dem wahren Sachverhalt ausweichen; **to blink a ~** einer Frage ausweichen; **to broach a ~** Frage anschneiden; **to bump into s. o. with a ~** j. mit einer Frage überrumpeln; **to call in ~** zur Rechenschaft (in Zweifel) ziehen, *(police)* einem Verhör unterwerfen; **to call s. one's statement in ~** jds. Erklärungen in Zweifel ziehen; **to come into ~** *(fam.)* aufs Tapet kommen; **to deviate (digress) from the ~** vom Thema abschweifen; **to evade a ~** einer Frage ausweichen; **to give notice of a ~** Interpellation einbringen; **to go further into a ~** tiefer in eine Frage eindringen; **to have a ~ placed on the agenda** Frage auf die Tagesordnung setzen lassen; **to interrupt the debate with a ~** während der Debatte eine Frage stellen; **to launch an inquiry on a ~** Untersuchungsausschuß zur Lösung einer Frage einsetzen; **to leave a ~ in the cold** Frage ausklammern; **to leave a ~ undecided** Frage offenlassen; **to maintain an open mind to a ~** einer Frage aufgeschlossen gegenüberstehen; **to move the previous ~** *(parl.)* Übergang zur Tagesordnung beantragen; **to obey without ~** widerspruchslos gehorchen; **to overwhelm with ~s** mit Fragen überschütten; **to ply s. o. with ~s** mit Fragen in j. dringen; **to pop the ~** Heiratsantrag machen; **to postpone a ~ until later in the meeting** Frage auf einen späteren Zeitpunkt der Sitzung zurückstellen; **to put the ~** *(parl.)* zur Abstimmung schreiten, Antrag zur Abstimmung stellen; **to put s. o. a ~** jem. eine Frage stellen; **to put a man to the ~** j. der Folter unterwerfen; **to raise a ~** Frage ventilieren, anschneiden, aufwerfen; **to resolve a ~** Frage entscheiden; **to restate a ~** Frage neu formulieren; **to rule a ~ out of order** Frage als nicht zur Tagesordnung gehörig behandeln; **to rule that a ~ is out of order** *(law court)* Frage nicht zulassen; **to settle a ~** Frage entscheiden; **to shirk the ~** sich der Beantwortung einer Frage entziehen, sich vor der Beantwortung einer Frage drücken; **to sit on a ~** sich mit einer Frage beschäftigen; **to state a ~** Frage aufwerfen; **to submit a ~ to the court** dem Gericht einen Streitfall vorlegen; **to table a ~** parlamentarische Anfrage schriftlich einbringen; **to throw out a ~** Frage aufwerfen; **to view a ~ from all sides** Frage von allen Seiten beleuchten;

to be ~ed by the police von der Polizei verhört werden; **~ and answer session** Frage- und Antworttreffen; **~ form** Fragebogen; **~ mark** Fragezeichen; **~ master** Quizmaster; **~ period** *(parl., US)* Fragestunde; **~ time** *(Br.)* Fragestunde.

questionable fragwürdig, bedenklich, *(at issue)* streitig, strittig; **~ assertion** fragwürdige Behauptung; **~ privilege** zweifelhaftes Privileg.

questioner Fragesteller.

questioning Verhör; **after prolonged ~** nach intensiver Befragung; **~ an election** Wahlanfechtung.

questionist *(Harvard)* Prüfungskandidat.

questionnaire, questionary Fragebogen; **census ~** statistischer Fragebogen; **job ~** beruflicher Fragebogen; **mail ~** brieflicher Fragebogen; **to fill in a ~** Fragebogen ausfüllen; **~ survey** Umfrage anhand von Fragebogen.

quetch *(v.)* herumnörgeln.

queue *(file of persons)* Schlange, Reihe; **bread ~** für Brot Anstehende; **~ of applicants** Schlange von Bewerbern, Bewerberschlange; **~ of cars** Fahrzeug-, Autoschlange; **~ (v.) up** *(Br.)* Schlange stehen (bilden), in einer Reihe anstehen, sich anstellen; **~ up to buy tickets** *(Br.)* sich für Fahrkarten anstellen; **to form (stand in) a ~** Schlange stehen; **to jump the ~** etw. außer der Reihe erhalten; **~ jumper** Kolonnenspringer.

queuing | line Warteschlange; **~ model** Warteschlangenmodell; **~ theory** Warteschlangentheorie.

quia timet | injunction vorbeugende Unterlassungsverfügung; **~ proceedings** vorbeugendes Unterlassungsverfahren.

quibble Wortklauberei, Spitzfindigkeit; **~ (v.)** herumreden, Ausflüchte machen, Haarspalterei betreiben.

quick Kern, Wesentliches; **to the ~** durch Mark und Bein, durch und durch; **the ~ and the dead** die Lebenden und die Toten; **~ (a.)** schnell reagierend, sofort, prompt, fix, *(in business)* geschäftsgewandt, aktiv, *(fire)* gut brennend;

~ to answer back rasch in der Replik, schlagfertig; **~ of belief** leichtgläubig; **~ with child** schwanger; **~ at figures** gut im Rechnen; **~ as lightning** blitzschnell; **~ to make up one's mind** schnell entschlossen;

to be a ~ one auf Draht sein; **to be ~ of sale** sich gut verkaufen; **to be touched to the ~** bis ins Mark getroffen sein; **to be ~ of understanding** intelligent sein; **to be ~ on the uptake** rasche Auffassungsgabe haben; **to sting s. o. to the ~** j. tödlich beleidigen; **to wish to get rich ~** schnell reich werden wollen;

~ answer prompte Antwort; **~ ash** Flugasche; **~ assets** leicht realisierbare Aktivposten, *(balance sheet, US)* flüssige (liquide) Anlagen, Aktiva hoher Liquiditätsstufe; **~-assets ratio** *(US)* Flüssigkeitsverhältnis, Liquiditätsgrad; **~-break switch** Schnellschalter; **~-change gear** *(car)* Schnellgang; **~ ear** feines Gehör; **~ eye** scharfes Auge; **~-fire** Schnellfeuer; **~-fire release** sofortige Freilassung; **~ firer** Schnellfeuergeschütz; **~-firing gun** Schnellfeuergeschütz; **~ fix** Patentlösung, Schnelllösung; **~-freeze** *(v.)* tiefkühlen; **~-freeze goods** Lebensmittel dem Tiefkühlverfahren unterziehen; **~ freezing** Tiefkühlverfahren; **~-frozen food** tiefgekühlte Nahrungsmittel; **~ growth** schnelles Wachstum; **~ hedge** lebende Hecke; **~ items** schnell realisierbare (äußerst liquide) Bilanzposten; **~ liabilities** kurzfristig rückzahlbare Schulden; **~-lunch bar (counter)** Imbißstube, Schnellrestaurant; **~ luncheon** Schnellgericht; **to have a ~ meal** einen Happen essen; **~-motion camera** Zeitrafferkamera; **~-motion picture** Zeitrafferaufnahme; **to have just time for a ~ one** gerade Zeit haben einen zu nehmen; **~ over** *(sl.)* flüchtige Prüfung; **at a ~ pace** in schnellem Tempo; **~ ratio** Liquiditäts-, Flüssigkeitsverhältnis; **~ recovery** rasche Erholung (Gesundung); **~ restaurant** Schnellimbißstätte; **~ returns** schneller Umsatz; **~ succession relief** Steuernachlaß bei schneller Todesfolge nachlaßsteuerpflichtigen Vermögens; **to have a ~ temper** heißblütig sein; **~ time** *(mil.)* schnelles Marschtempo; **~ train** Schnellzug; **~ way of doing** rasche Erledigung; **to find ~ ways of doing s. th.** rasch zu seinem Ziel kommen; **to have ~ wits** schlagfertig sein; **~ workman** flotter Arbeiter.

quicken beschleunigen, *(make more lively)* Auftrieb geben, beleben; **~ the animation** Phantasie anregen.

quickening *(medical jurisprudence)* erste Kindesbewegungen im Mutterleib.

quickie *(advertising)* kurzer Werbespot, *(article cheaply produced)* Ramschware, *(film, sl.)* billiger (schnell zusammengestoppelter) Film; **~ strike** von den Gewerkschaften nicht genehmigter (wilder) Streik, Kurzstreik.

quickly, to go off reißenden Absatz finden, sich sehr gut verkaufen.

quickness Schnelligkeit, geistige Beweglichkeit; **~ of mind** rasche Auffassungsgabe; **~ of temper** Heißblütigkeit.

quicksand Triebsand.

quicksilver Quecksilber, *(fig.)* lebhaftes Temperament.

quid *(Br., sl.)* Pfund Sterling; **~ pro quo** *(lat.)* Gegenleistung, Äquivalent; **to be ~s in** *(fam.)* großen Vorteil haben.

quiet Ruhe, Stille, *(fig.)* Ausgeglichenheit; **on the ~** im Stillen, klammheimlich; **~ (a.)** ruhig, friedlich, ausgeglichen, *(secluded)* abgeschlossen, zurückgezogen, *(stock exchange)* lustlos, still, ruhig, flau; **~ (v.)** beruhigen, besänftigen, *(law)* Beeinträchtigung beseitigen; **~ down after political disturbances** nach den politischen Verwirrungen zur Ruhe kommen; **~ hysteria** Hysterie dämpfen; **~ s. one's suspicious** jds. Verdacht verstummen lassen; **~ a tumult** Aufstand unterdrücken (beenden);

to be as ~ as a mouse mucksmäuschenstill sein; **to be very ~** *(market)* sehr ruhig liegen; **to do s. th. on the ~** etw. klammheimlich erledigen; **to enjoy perfect peace and ~** vollkommene Ruhe genießen; **to keep ~** sich ruhig verhalten; **to keep a child ~** Kind ruhig halten; **to live in peace and ~** friedliches Leben führen; **to tell s. o. s. th. on the ~** jem. etw. vertraulich erzählen; **~ dig** versteckte Bemerkung; **to have a ~ dig at s. o.** diskrete Andeutung über j. machen; **~ dinner party** formlose Abendgesellschaft; **~ enjoyment** ungestörter Genuß (Besitz); **to lead a ~ life** ruhiges Leben führen; **to live a ~ life in the country** zurückgezogen auf dem Lande leben; **~ nook** stiller Winkel; **~ period** *(telephone)* Sprechpause; **to harbo(u)r ~ resentment** seinen Groll verbergen; **~ running of a machine** geräuschloser Lauf einer Maschine; **~ title proceedings** Eigentumsfeststellungsverfahren; **~ waters** stilles Gewässer; **to live in a ~ way** bescheidenen Lebensstil haben; **~ wedding** intime Hochzeitsfeier.

quietus Gnadenstoß, *(debts)* restlose Schuldentilgung, General-quittung, *(discharge from office)* Entlassung, *(law, Br.)* Freispruch, *(some states in USA)* Treuhänderentlastung;
to give s. o. his ~ jem. den Gnadenstoß geben, j. endgültig außer Gefecht setzen; **to give a ~ to a rumo(u)r** Gerücht endgültig verstummen lassen.

quiff *(sl.)* Moos, Moneten.

quill | driver Schreiberling, Federfuchser; ~ **driving** Federfuchserei, Schmiererei.

quilt Steppdecke;
~ *(v.)* **money into s. th.** Geld in etw. einnähen.

quinquennial fünfjährig;
~ **valuation** *(Br.)* alle fünf Jahre erfolgende Einheitswertfeststellung.

quintal Doppelzentner.

quintuplicate fünffach.

quip geistreiche Bemerkung;
~**s and cranks** Scherze und Streiche.

quire *(print.)* Buch (24 Bogen).

quirk Eigentümlichkeit, Verschrobenheit.

quirky lawyer gerissener Anwalt.

quisling Verräter, Kollaborateur.

quit ungenehmigte Arbeitsabwesenheit;
~ *(a.)* frei, befreit;
~ **of charges** spesenfrei, nach Abzug der Kosten;
~ *(v.)* *(give up)* aufgeben, verzichten, *(leave)* gehen, verlassen, ausziehen, räumen, *(pay back)* zurückzahlen, begleichen;
~ **business** sich vom Geschäft zurückziehen; ~ **cost** Unkosten bezahlen; ~ **an employment** Stellung (Beschäftigung) aufgeben; ~ **one's job** *(US)* seine Stelle aufgeben, kündigen; ~ **office** sein Amt niederlegen; ~ **the premises** *(tenant)* Grundstück (Wohnung) räumen, ausziehen; ~ **the ranks** fahnenflüchtig werden, desertieren; ~ **scores** Konto ausgleichen; ~ **the service** Dienst quittieren; ~ **five years earlier than required** fünf Jahre vorzeitig in Pension gehen; ~ **work** Arbeit einstellen;
to be ~ for a fine mit einer Geldstrafe wegkommen; **to be ~ of a trouble** Sorge los sein; **to give notice to ~** Mieter kündigen; **to have notice to ~** gekündigt sein;
~ **rate** Kündigungsprozentsatz.

quitclaim Verzicht[leistung], Anspruchsverzicht, *(conveyance, US)* Auflassungsurkunde;
~ **deed** Auflassungs-, Grundstückskaufvertrag.

quits, to be ~ with s. o. quitt mit jem. sein.

quittance Bezahlung, Quittung.

quitter *(US)* Arbeitsunlustiger, Drückeberger.

quitting clause *(US)* Dienstschlußklausel.

quiz Denksportaufgabe, Quiz, *(coaching, US)* Einpauken, *(college, coll.)* Kurzprüfung;
~ *(v.)* *(US)* einpauken;
~ **master** Quizmaster; ~ **program(me)** Quizsendung.

quo warranto Klage wegen Amtsanmaßung.

quod *(sl.)* Loch, Kittchen.

quoin *(print.)* Schließkeil, Druckform schließen.

quondam friend ehemaliger Freund.

quorum beschlußfähige [Mitglieder]zahl, Beschlußfähigkeit;
directors' ~ beschlußfähiger Vorstand; **disinterested ~** durch Eigeninteressen nicht verhinderte Beschlußfähigkeit; **incompetent ~** nicht ordnungsgemäß besetztes Beschlußgremium; **valid ~** ausreichende Beschlußfähigkeit;
~ **of directors** beschlußfähiger Vorstand;
to ascertain that there is a ~ Beschlußfähigkeit feststellen; **to be counted in a ~** bei der Beschlußfähigkeit mitgezählt werden; **to break a ~** Beschlußunfähigkeit herbeiführen; **to constitute (form) a ~** Beschlußfähigkeit herbeiführen, beschlußfähig sein; **not to count towards a ~** auf die Beschlußfähigkeit ohne Einfluß sein; **to fix the ~** Bestimmungen über die Beschlußfähigkeit festlegen; **to have a ~** beschlußfähig sein; **to have ceased to constitute a ~** beschlußunfähig geworden sein; **to lack a ~** beschlußunfähig (nicht beschlußfähig) sein; **to maintain a ~** Beschlußfähigkeit aufrecht erhalten; **to muster a ~** beschlußfähige Mehrheit zustandebringen;
~ **call** Einberufung des Plenums.

quota *(allocation)* Kontingent, Quote, *(bankruptcy)* [Konkurs]quote, -dividende, *(contribution)* Beitrag, *(delivery, US)* Liefersoll, *(immigration, US)* Einwanderungskontingent, -quote, *(share)* [Verhältnis]anteil, Rechnungs-, verhältnismäßiger Anteil, prozentuale Beteiligung, Beteiligungsverhältnis, [Teil]quantum;
subject to a ~ kontingentiert;
applicable ~ in Frage kommendes Kontingent; **basic ~** Grundkontingent; **building ~** Baukontingent; **buying ~** Einkaufskon-

tingent; **electoral ~** Wahlkontingent; **exhausted ~** erschöpftes Kontingent; **export ~** Export-, Ausfuhrquote; **foreign-exchange ~** Devisenkontingent; **full ~** volle Zuteilung; **immigration ~** Einwanderungskontingent; **import ~** Einfuhrkontingent, -quote; **initial export ~** Ausfuhrausgangskontingent; **legislated ~** gesetzlich festgesetztes Kontingent; **mandatory ~** Zwangskontingent; **marketing ~** Absatzkontingent; **maximum ~** Höchstkontingent; **overall ~** Globalkontingent; **overall import ~** Gesamteinfuhrquote; **production ~** Produktionsquote; **purchase ~** Einkaufskontingent; **provided for ~** vorgesehene Quote; **sales ~** Absatz-, Verkaufskontingent; **tariff-rate ~** Zollkontingent; **taxable ~** steuerpflichtige Dividende; **territory ~** regionales Verkaufskontingent; **yearly ~** Jahreskontingent;
~ **of advertising to editorial** Relation von Anzeigen zum Text; ~ **per capita** Kopfquote; ~ **of immigrants** *(US)* Einwanderungsquote, -kontingent; ~ **of production** Produktionsquote; ~ **of profits** Gewinnanteil; **full ~ of troops** voller Truppenkontingent;
~ *(v.)* Kontingent aufteilen;
to allocate export ~s Export kontingentieren; **to allow unfilled ~s to carry into next year** unausgenutzte Quoten ins nächste Jahr übertragen lassen; **to apportion (assign) a ~** Quote zuteilen; **to apportion ~s for import** Einfuhrkontingente festsetzen; **to contribute one's ~** seinen Anteil bezahlen, seine Quote übernehmen; **to dispose of a ~** über ein Kontingent verfügen; **to exceed a ~** Kontingent überziehen; **to fix a ~** Kontingent (Quote) festsetzen, kontingentieren, zuteilen; **to increase (raise) a ~** Kontingent (Quote) erhöhen; **to reduce a ~** Kontingent kürzen; **to stay within the ~ voluntarily agreed** sich innerhalb der freiwilligen Quotenvereinbarung bewegen; **to use up a ~** Kontingent erschöpfen;
~ **accountancy** Quotenabrechnung; ~ **admission** Zulassungsquote; ~ **agent** Kontingentträger; ~ **agreement** Kontingentsvereinbarung; ~ **bargaining** Quotenaushandlung; ~ **basis** Kontingentierungsgrundlage; - **bill** Kontingentierungsgesetz; ~ **country** *(immigration policy, US)* Kontingentsland; ~ **cuts** Kontingentkürzungen; ~ **goods** kontingentierte (bewirtschaftete) Waren; ~ **immigrant** *(US)* Einwanderer im Rahmen der Quotenzuteilung; ~ **imports** kontingentierte Einfuhren; ~ **increase** Quotenerhöhung, -aufstockung, *(International Monetary Fund)* Quotenaufstockung; ~ **law** *(US)* Einwanderungsgesetz; ~ **litis** *(US)* Erfolgshonorar; ~ **restriction** Kontingentsbeschränkung, Kontingentierung; ~ **sample** *(population)* proportionaler Bevölkerungsausschnitt, *(statistics)* Quotenstichprobe, -auswahl, Stichprobenanalyse; ~ **sampling** Quotenauswahlverfahren; ~ **selection** Quotenauswahl; ~ **share** Kontingentsanteil, *(reinsurance)* Quote; ~ **share reinsurance** Quotenrückversicherung; ~ **share treaty** *(reinsurance)* Quotenvertrag; ~ **system** Kontingentierungs-, Zuteilungssystem; ~ **treaty** *(reinsurance)* Schadensbeteiligungs-, Quotenvertrag; ~ **wall** Kontingentsmauer.

quotabl | e *(stocks)* notierbar;
to be ~y higher etw. höher stehen;
~**e book** druckfähiges Buch.

quotation Anführung, Zitierung, zitierte Stelle, Beweis, Belegstelle, Zitat, *(naming of prices)* Preisangabe, -anschlag, -ansatz, -notierung, -stellung, Offerte, *(print.)* Steg, *(stock exchange)* [Kurs]notierung, Kursnotiz, Börsennotierung, Effektenkurs, -notiz, Kurs[meldung];
at the present ~ zum gegenwärtigen Kurs; **below ~** unter Kurswert; **under today's ~** unter Tagespreis; **without official ~** ohne Kurs;
~**s** gehandelte Kurse;
above ~ obiger Preis; **actual ~** effektiver Kurs; **asked ~** Briefkurs, -notierung; **average ~** Durchschnittsnotierung; **bid ~s** Geldkurs; **cabled ~** Kabelpreis; **cash ~** Kassakurs; **closing ~** Schlußnotierung; **competitive ~** wettbewerbsfähiges Preisangebot; **consecutive ~** variable Notierung; **current ~** Tageskurs; **daily ~s** Kursbericht, -blatt; **demand ~** Geldnotiz; **dollar ~** Dollarnotierung; **exaggerated ~** übersteigerter Kurs; **exchange ~** Börsennotierung; **final ~** Schlußnotierung, -kurs; **flat ~** *(US)* Kursnotierung ohne Zinsberücksichtigung; **fluctuating ~** schwankender Kurs; **foreign exchange ~** Devisennotierung; **highest ~** höchster Kurs; **latest ~** zuletzt notierter Kurs, Tagespreis; **lowest ~** niedrigster Kurs; **market ~** Kurs-, Börsennotierung; **nominal ~** Notiz ohne Umsätze; **noon ~** mittägliche Notierungen; **official ~** amtliche Notierung, amtlicher Kurs, Börsenbericht, -blatt; **opening ~** erste Notierung, Eröffnungskurs; **previous ~** letzte Notierung; **price ~** Preisangabe, *(stock exchange)* Kursnotierung; **regular ~** einheitliche Notierung;

share ~s *(Br.)* Aktiennotierung; **split** ~ uneinheitliche Notierung; **spot** ~ Preis bei sofortiger Lieferung; **standard** ~ Einheitskurs; **stock** ~ Aktiennotierung, Effektenkurs; **stock-exchange** ~ Börsenkurs, Kursangabe; **tabulated** ~ tabellarisch angeordnete Preisstellung; **telegraphic [exchange]** ~ Kurstelegramm, Drahtangabe; **today's** ~ heutige Notierung; **uniform** ~ Einheitskurs; **unit** ~ Stücknotiz; **verbatim** ~ wörtliches Zitat; **weakened** ~ abgeschwächte Kurse; **wholesale** ~s Großhandelsnotierung; **word-for-word** ~ wörtliches Zitat;

~ **of one's authorities (authority)** Quellenangabe; ~ **of a case** Berufung auf eine Entscheidung; ~ **of the day** Tageskurs, -notierung; ~s **for forward delivery** Terminnotierungen; ~ **of [foreign] exchange [rates]** Devisen-, Valutanotierungen; ~s **of freight rates** Frachtkursnotierung, -notiz; ~s **for futures** Terminnotierung; ~ **of a loan** Anleihenotierung, Anleihekurs; ~ **on a foreign market** Auslandsnotierung; ~ **without obligation** freibleibendes Angebot; ~ **in per cent** *(shares)* Prozentnotiz; ~s **for plant** Betriebserrichtungskosten; ~ **of a price** Preisangabe; ~ **of prices** Kursnotierung; ~ **of shares** Aktiennotierung; ~ **of specie** Geldkurszettel; ~ **of stocks** *(US)* Aktiennotierung; **latest** ~s **from the stock exchange** letzte Kursnotierung; ~ **on the stock market** Börsenkurs, -notierung;

to admit for ~ **on the stock exchange** zur Börsennotierung zulassen; **to apply for official** ~ *(Br.)* Zulassung zur Börse beantragen; **to ask for a** ~ Angebot verlangen; **to be admitted for** ~ **on the stock exchange** zum Handel an der Börse zugelassen werden; **to display** ~s **for each security** Effektenkurs jeder Gesellschaft widerspiegeln; **to give a** ~ **for building a house** Hausbaukosten berechnen, Kostenvoranschlag für einen Hausbau vornehmen; **to pepper a speech with** ~s Rede mit Zitaten würzen; **to suspend the** ~ Kursnotierung aussetzen; **to use** ~s **in a speech** Zitate in einer Rede anbringen;

~ **board** Kurstafel; ~ **committee** *(London)* Börsenzulassungsausschuß; ~ **form** direkte Redeform; **to bolster the** ~ **level** Kursniveau aufblähen; ~ **marks** Anführungsstriche; **to put a word in** ~ **marks** Wort in Anführungsstriche setzen; ~ **service** Kursübermittlungsdienst; **automatic** ~ **service** automatische Börsennotierungen; ~ **ticker** *(US)* Börsenfernschreiber.

quotational quotenmäßig.
quote Preisangebot, *(citation)* Zitat;
~ *(v.) (cite)* anführen, zitieren, *(state price)* Preise angeben, ansetzen, berechnen, *(stock exchange)* Kurse börsenmäßig feststellen, notieren, quotieren, Kurs feststellen;
~ **s. th.** sich auf etw. berufen; ~ **as authority** als Quelle angeben; ~ **from a book** Stelle aus einem Buch zitieren; ~ **a case** Entscheidung (Präzedenzfall) anführen; ~ **from a case** aus einer Entscheidung zitieren; ~ **an instance** Beispiel anführen; ~ **literally** wörtlich zitieren; ~ **a number in reply to a letter** bei der Briefantwort eine Chiffre angeben; ~ **at par** pari notieren; ~ **a precedent** sich auf einen Präzedenzfall berufen; ~ **a price** Preisangebot machen, Preis quotieren, *(stock exchange)* Kurs notieren; ~ **a lower price** niedriges Preisangebot stellen; ~ **references** Referenzen angeben; ~ **on the stock exchange** zur Börsennotierung zulassen; ~ **verbatim** wörtlich zitieren.
quoted verzeichnet;
~ **above** oben angeführt; **at the price** ~ zu dem verzeichneten Preis; **not** ~ ohne Kurs, nicht notierend, keinen Kurs habend; **officially** ~ amtlich notiert;
~ **at foot** unten notiert; ~ **on exchange** börsengängig;
to be ~ **at** notieren (im Kurs stehen) mit; **to be** ~ **consecutively** fortlaufend notiert werden; **to be** ~ **on the stock exchange** amtlich notiert (an der Börse gehandelt) werden; **to be** ~ **higher [im Kurs]** gestiegen sein; **to be** ~ **officially** amtlich notiert werden, zur Notierung kommen;
~ **company** Gesellschaft deren Aktien an der Börse gehandelt werden; ~ **investment at costs** *(balance sheet, Br.)* börsengängige Wertpapiere zum Anschaffungskurs; ~ **list** *(Br.)* amtlicher Kurszettel; ~ **price** angegebener (angebotener) Preis, Preisangebot, *(stock exchange)* notierter Kurs, Kursnotierung; **consecutively** ~ **prices** laufende Kursnotierung; ~ **securities** börsengängige Wertpapiere, notierte Werte; ~ **shares (stocks, US)** zur Börsennotierung zugelassene (notierte) Aktien; ~ **value** Kurswert.
quotient Quotient;
election ~ Wahlquotient.
quotum Anteil.

R

rabbit food *(sl.)* Rohkost.
rabbitfoot *(sl.)* ausgebrochener Gefangener.
rabble Pöbel, Mob;
~ **rouser** Volksaufwiegler, Agitator, Demagoge; ~ **rousing** aufhetzerische Reden, Volksaufwiegelung.
race Rasse, Völkerstamm, *(career)* Laufbahn, *(sport)* [Wett]rennen, -lauf;
of noble ~ vornehmer Herkunft;
armament ~ Rüstungswettlauf; **human** ~ Menschengeschlecht; **motor** ~ Autorennen;
~ **to regroup** Umgruppierungswettlauf; ~ **of glory** ruhmvolle Laufbahn; ~ **of politicians** Kaste der Politiker; ~ **for presidency** Wettlauf um die Präsidentschaft; ~ **against time** Wettlauf mit der Zeit;
~ *(v.)* *(engine)* durchdrehen lassen;
~ **a bill through parliament** Gesetzentwurf durch das Parlament durchpeitschen; ~ **one's car against a tree** mit dem Auto gegen einen Baum fahren; ~ **s. o. through examinations** j. durch Prüfungen durchhetzen;
to be in a ~ **against the election clock** im Wettlauf mit dem Wahltermin liegen; **to count s. o. out of the** ~ j. nicht mehr zum engeren Favoritenkreis zählen;
~ **boat** Rennboot; ~ **card** Rennprogramm; ~ **circuit** Rennstrecke; ~~**conscious** rassenbewußt; ~ **course** Rennbahn, -platz; ~ **difference** Rassenunterschied; ~ **driver** Rennfahrer; ~ **hatred** Rassenhaß; ~ **problem** Rassenfrage; ~ **Relations Act** *(Br.)* Gesetz gegen unterschiedliche Behandlung aus Rassengründen, Einwanderungsgesetz; ~ **riot** Rassenkrawall; ~ **suicide** Rassenselbstmord; ~~**betting tax** Wettgewinn-, Rennwettsteuer; ~ **track** Rennbahn; ~~**track operator** Buchmacher; ~~**type statute** *(land register, US)* Eintragungssystem nach zeitlichen Präferenzen; ~~**way** künstlicher Kanal.
racer Rennfahrzeug, Rennfahrer.
racial|barriers Rassenschranken; ~ **complex** Rassenkomplex; ~ **conflict** Rassenkampf; ~ **discrimination** Rassendiskriminierung; ~ **dissention** Rassenzwiestreit; ~ **distinction** Rassenunterschied; ~ **equity** Rassengleichheit; ~ **hatred** Rassenhaß; ~ **hostility** Rassenfeindschaft; ~ **intolerance** Unduldsamkeit in Rassenfragen; ~ **issue** Rassenfrage; ~ **minority** rassische Minderheit; ~ **mixing** Rassenvermischung; ~ **outbreak** Ausbruch von Rassenunruhen; ~ **persecution** Rassenverfolgung; ~ **policy** Rassenpolitik; ~ **prejudice** Rassenvorurteil; ~ **problem** Rassenfrage; ~ **segregation (separation)** Rassentrennung; ~ **troubles** Rassenunruhen; ~ **unrest** Rassenunruhen.
racialist Rassenfanatiker.
racialism *(US)* übertriebenes Rassenbewußtsein, Rassendiskriminierung, -verfolgung.
racing|boat *(Br.)* Rennboot; ~ **car** Rennwagen; ~ **motorist** Rennfahrer; ~ **tip** Wett-Tip; ~ **track** Autorennbahn.
racism Rassenfanatismus.
racist *(US)* Rassenfanatiker, Rassenpolitiker.
rack Gestell, Ständer, Verkaufsständer, *(print.)* Setzregal, *(railway)* Gepäcknetz, -ablage;
on the ~ auf die Folter gespannt;
baggage ~ *(US)* Gepäcknetz, -ablage; **clothes** ~ Kleiderständer; **newspaper** ~ Zeitungsständer; **unloading** ~ Abladeplatz;
~ **of pamphlets** Gestell für Broschüren;
~ *(v.)* **one's brains** sich den Kopf zerbrechen;
to buy a suit off the ~ Anzug von der Stange kaufen; **to go to** ~ **and ruin** völlig zugrundegehen; **to live at** ~ **and manger** in Saus und Braus leben; **to put on the** ~ auf die Folter spannen;
~ **folder** Werbefaltblatt für Spezialauslagen; ~ **jobber** *(US)* Regalgroßhändler, Großlieferant eines Kaufhofs; ~ **railway** Zahnradbahn.
racket *(confused noise)* Radau, Spektakel, Krach, *(line of business, sl.)* Geschäftszweig, Fach, *(criminal organization)* Verbrecherbande, *(sharp practices, coll.)* Schiebung, Schiebergeschäft, Betrügerei, Geschäftemacherei, dunkle Machenschaften, *(trick, US sl.)* Dreh, Masche, *(social whirl)* Vergnügungstaumel, Rummel, gesellschaftlicher Trubel, ausgelassene Veranstaltung, Betrieb;
alimony ~ Unterhaltsbetrug; **blackmail** ~ *(US)* Erpressertrick; **the fortune telling** ~ Wahrsagergewerbe;
to be in the ~ vom Bau sein; **to be in on the** ~ *(sl.)* mit unter einer Decke stecken; **to be lonely in the midst of a** ~ auf einer großen Veranstaltung völlig verloren sein; **to give a** ~ **once a year** einmal im Jahr eine Gesellschaft geben; **to hate the** ~ **of a city**

Großstadtgetriebe hassen; **to kick up no end of a** ~ unwahrscheinlichen Krach machen; **to make a** ~ **at election time** Wahlrummel veranstalten; **to stand the** ~ *(coll.)* Prüfung bestehen, durchkommen; **to work a** ~ Betrügereien begehen;
~ **jawing** *(sl.)* leichte Konversation.
racketeer *(US)* Schieber, unsauberer Geschäftemacher, *(blackmailer)* Erpresser, Gangster.
racketeering *(US)* [gewissenlose] Geschäftemacherei, *(blackmailing)* Gangsterunwesen, Erpressergeschäft.
rackrent *(Br.)* jahresübliche Miete, *(Ireland)* unerschwingliche Miete, Wuchermiete;
~ *(v.)* *(Ireland)* mit übermäßiger Miete belasten.
rackrenter *(Ireland)* überforderter Mieter.
radar Funkmeßgerät, Radar;
to follow the flight of an aircraft by ~ Flugzeug auf dem Radarschirm verfolgen;
~ **aircraft** Radarflugzeug; ~ **bearing** Funkpeilung; ~ **installation** Radaranlage; ~~**ridden** vollgepfropft mit Radaranlagen; ~ **screen** Radarschirm; ~ **speedmeter** Verkehrsradar, Radarfalle; ~ **station** Radarstation; ~ **trap** Radarfalle.
radiation Strahlung;
~ **dose** Strahlendosis; ~ **hazard** Strahlengefährdung; ~ **injury** Strahlenschaden; ~ **level** Strahlungsdosis; ~ **protection** Strahlenschutz; **enhanced** ~ **weapon** verstärkte Strahlungswaffe.
radiator *(car)* Kühler;
~ **grill** Kühlerschutzgitter; ~ **shell** Kühlerhaube.
radical [Links]radikaler;
~ *(a.)* grundlegend, *(pol.)* radikal;
to undergo a ~ **change** sich von Grund auf ändern; ~ **error** fundamentaler Fehler; ~ **measures** drastische Maßnahmen; ~ **party** radikale Partei; ~ **politician** radikaler Politiker; ~ **reform** gründliche Reform.
radicalism Radikalismus.
radio Hörfunk, Rundfunk, Radio, *(apparatus)* Rundfunkgerät, -empfänger, *(wireless telegraphy)* Funk;
broadcast by ~ über den Rundfunk gesendet; **by** ~ durch Sprechfunk; **on the** ~ im Rundfunk; **over the** ~ durch den Rundfunk;
jam-resistant ~ gegen Funkstörungen unempfindliches Funkgerät, entstörtes Rundfunkgerät; **mobile** ~ fahrbarer Sender; **short-wave** ~ Kurzwellenempfänger; **state-run** ~ Staatsrundfunk; **wired** ~ *(US)* Drahtfunk;
~ **and television** Funk und Fernsehen;
~ *(v.)* senden, durch Rundfunk übertragen (durchgeben), *(wire)* Funkmeldung durchgeben;
~ **an urgent appeal** Hilferuf ausstrahlen;
to buy a new ~ neues Rundfunkgerät kaufen; **to send a message by** ~ Funkspruch schicken; **to talk over the** ~ im Rundfunk sprechen;
~ *(a.)* *(US)* drahtlos;
~ **adaptation** Funkfassung, -bearbeitung; ~ **address** Rundfunkansprache; ~ **advertiser** Rundfunkwerbung betreibende Firma; ~ **advertising** Rundfunkreklame, -werbung, Hörfunkwerbung; ~ **announcement** Rundfunkdurchsage; ~ **audience** Rundfunkhörerschaft; ~ **beacon** Peilfunksender, Funkbake; ~ **beam** Richtstrahl, Funkstrahl, -bake; ~ **bearing** Funkpeilung; ~ **booking office** Hörfunkbuchungsbüro; ~ **broadcast** Rundfunksendung, -übertragung; ~ **broadcaster** Rundfunksender; ~ **car** Funkwagen; ~ **channel** Funkkanal; ~ **circuit** Rundfunkfrequenz; ~ **combination clock** Radiouhr; ~ **communication** Funkverbindung; ~ **compass** Peilfunkempfänger, Funkpeiler; ~ **contact** Funkkontakt; **to be in** ~ **contact** durch Funk miteinander in Verbindung stehen, Funkkontakt haben; ~ **control** *(US)* Funksteuerung; ~~**control** *(v.)* funksteuern; ~~**controlled boat** Fernlenkboot; ~~**direction finding** Funkortung; ~ **drama** Hörspiel; ~ **engineer** Rundfunktechniker; ~ **engineering** Funktechnik; ~ **equipment** Rundfunkgerät; ~~**equipped** mit Funksprechanlage ausgestattet; ~ **frequency** Trägerfrequenz; ~ **hookup** Ringsendung; ~ **installation** Funkanlage; ~ **intelligence** Funkaufklärung; ~ **interference** Funkstörung; ~ **jammer** Störsender; ~ **jamming** Störsendung; ~ **journalist** Rundfunkjournalist; ~ **landing beam** Gleit-, Landungsstrahl; ~ **licence** Funkerlaubnis; ~ **link** Funksprechverbindung; ~ **listener** Rundfunkhörer; ~ **lottery** Funklotterie; ~ **marker** Funkbake, Anflugbake; ~ **message** Funkspruch; ~ **navigation** Funkortung; ~ **network** Funknetz; ~ **newsreel** *(Br.)* Nachrichtensendung; ~ **operator** Funker; ~ **patrol car** Funkstreifenwagen; ~

periodical Funkzeitschrift; ~ **picture** Funkbild; **to sponsor a ~ program(me)** Finanzierung eines Rundfunkprogramms übernehmen; ~-**range beacon** Richtfunkfeuer, Leitstrahlbake; ~ **receiver** Rundfunkgerät, -empfänger; ~ **relay** Funkübertragung; ~ **script** Rundfunkmanuskript; ~ **serial** Hörfolge; ~ **set** Rundfunkempfänger, -gerät; **call-in ~ show** Rundfunkveranstaltung mit Telefonanfragen; ~ **speech** Rundfunkansprache; ~ **spot** kurze Werbedurchsage; ~ **station** Rundfunksender, -station; ~ **tax** Rundfunkgebühr; ~ **taxi** Funktaxi; ~ **telephone** Funktelephon, Funksprechgerät; ~ **time** Rundfunkzeit; ~ **tower** Funkturm; ~ **transmitter** Rundfunksender; **space-borne ~ transmitter** Weltraumsender; ~ **volume** Radiolautstärke; ~ **wave** Funkwelle.
radioactive│contamination radioaktive Verseuchung; ~ **losses** radioaktive Schäden; ~ **warfare** radioaktive Kriegsführung; ~ **waste** Atommüll; ~ **waste material** Atommüll.
radioactivity Radioaktivität.
radiogram Funktelegramm, -meldung.
radiogramophone Musiktruhe.
radiograph Röntgenaufnahme, -bild.
radiolocate *(v.)* Flugzeug mit Radar anpeilen.
radiolocation Radarpeilung, Funkortung, Echolotung.
radiolocator Funkortungsgerät.
radiophotograph Funkbild.
radiophotography Bildfunk.
radiosonde Radiosonde, Wettermeßinstrument mit funkentelegraphischer Fernübertragung.
radiotelegram Funktelegramm.
radiotelegraph *(v.)* Funktelegramm senden.
radiotelegraphist Funker.
radiotelegraphy Funktelegraphie, -sprechverkehr, drahtlose Telegraphie.
radiotelephone Funksprechgerät;
~ *(v.)* funktelefonisch übermitteln;
~ **conversation** Funkgespräch.
radiotelephony drahtlose Telegraphie, Funksprechverkehr.
radiovision Funkfernsehen, drahtloses Fernsehen.
radius Radius, Umkreis, *(fig.)* Wirkungskreis, Einflußzone;
~ **of action** Aktionsradius; ~ **of activity** Tätigkeitsbereich;
flying ~ of an airplane Flugradius eines Flugzeugs;
~ **clause** *(trainee)* Verpflichtungsklausel.
raffle *(lottery)* Ausspielung, Verlosung, Tombola, *(stock exchange)* Auslosung von Wertpapieren;
~ *(v.)* an einer Tombola teilnehmen, auf einer Tombola verlosen, *(stock exchange)* [Wertpapiere] verlosen;
~ **a motor scooter** Motorroller verlosen; ~ **off** Tombola verlosen.
raft Floß.
rag Lumpen, Fetzen, *(newspaper)* Skandal-, Schundblatt;
no ~ of evidence nicht der Fetzen eines Beweises;
~**, tag and bobtail** Krethi und Plethi;
~ *(v.)* abkanzeln, herunterputzen;
~ **and bone dealer** *(Br.)* Lumpensammler; ~ **fair** Trödelmarkt; ~ **money** *(US)* entwertetes Papiergeld; ~ **trade** Lumpenhandel.
rage Wut, *(fashion)* große Mode;
martial ~ Kriegstaumel;
~ **for collecting things** Sammelwut;
to be all the ~ sehr gefragt sein.
ragged│bonds *(US)* Obligationen mit abgetrennten, noch nicht fälligen Kupons; ~ **copy** Flattersatz.
ragpaper Haderpapier.
raid Streifzug, Einfall, [bewaffneter] Überfall, *(police)* Polizeistreife, Razzia, *(prices)* Druck, *(stock exchange)* Kursdruck;
bank ~ Banküberfall, -raub; **police ~** [Polizei]razzia;
~ **on a bank** Banküberfall; ~ **on the reserves** Angreifen der Reserven;
~ *(v.)* überfallen, Überfall machen, *(pirate members)* [Mitglieder] abwerben, *(plunder)* plündern, *(police)* Razzia durchführen;
~ **a country** Land überfallen; ~ **a house** Razzia in einem Haus durchführen; ~ **the market** Kurse durch Verkäufe drücken; ~ **the labo(u)r market** Arbeitsmarkt leerpumpen; ~ **the reserves** Reserven angreifen; ~ **a rival organization** Arbeitskräfte von einem Konkurrenzbetrieb abwerben;
to make a ~ Razzia durchführen; **to make a ~ into a country** in ein Land einfallen; **to make a ~ upon the enemy's camp** feindliches Lager überfallen; **to undertake plundering ~s** Raubzüge durchführen.
raider Räuber, *(mil.)* Kommandounternehmen, *(police)* Razziateilnehmer;
~**s past signal** Entwarnung.

raiding *(police)* Razziadurchführung, *(trade union, US)* Mitgliederabwerbung;
~ **aircraft** Feindflugzeug; ~ **party** Polizeistreife.
rail Geländer, Brüstung, *(railway)* Schiene, *(ship)* Reling;
by ~ per [Eisen]bahn; **ex ~** ab Bahnhof; **free on ~** frei Waggon (Bahn); **off the ~s** entgleist, *(fig.)* durcheinander, in Unordnung;
~**s** *(shares)* Eisenbahnaktien, -werte;
~ *(v.)* mit der Eisenbahn fahren, *(convey by rail)* mit der [Eisen]bahn befördern;
~ **goods** Waren mit der Eisenbahn befördern;
to forward by ~ mit der Bahn befördern; **to go by ~** mit der Bahn fahren; **to go off the ~s** auf die schiefe Bahn geraten; **to run off the ~s** entgleisen; **to send by ~** mit der Bahn schicken; **to travel by ~** mit der Eisenbahn fahren;
~ **bonds** *(US)* Eisenbahnobligationen; ~ **car** [Eisenbahn]waggon, *(self-propelled car)* Schienenfahrzeug, Triebwagen; **gasoline ~ car** Kesselwagen; ~-**car leasing** Waggonmiete; ~-**car plant** Waggonfabrik; ~ **carriage** Bahntransport; ~ **charges** Eisenbahnfrachtkosten; ~ **closure** Stillegung einer Eisenbahnstrecke; **high-speed ~ corridor** Eisenbahnschnellweg; ~ **equities** Eisenbahnobligationen; ~ **facilities** Gleisanlagen; ~ **freight** [Eisen]bahnfracht; ~ **freight rate** [Eisenbahn]frachttarif; ~ **freight revenue** Frachteinnahmen; ~ **freight tariff** Bahnfrachtsätze, Güterfrachttarif; ~ **freight traffic** Güterfrachtverkehr; ~ **joint** Schienenstoß; ~ **journey** Bahnfahrt; ~ **line** Eisenbahnlinie; ~ **link** Bahnverbindung; ~ **motor [coach]** Triebwagen; ~ **passenger** Bahnbenutzer; ~ **piggyback** Huckepackverkehr; ~ **police** Bahnpolizei; **by an all-~ route** ausschließlich mit der Bahn; ~ **speed** Eisenbahngeschwindigkeit; ~ **tariff** Güterfrachttarif; ~ **and water terminal** Güterumschlagstelle, Umschlagplatz; ~ **ticket** Eisenbahnfahrkarte; ~ **tie-up** Eisenbahnstillegung; ~ **traffic** Schienen-, Eisenbahnverkehr; ~ **traffic trust** Schienenkartell; ~ **traffic vehicle** Schienenfahrzeug; ~ **transit system** Eisenbahndurchgangsverkehr; ~ **transport** Bahntransport; ~ **transportation insurance** *(US)* Bahntransportversicherung; ~ **or bus travel** Bahn- oder Busverbindungen; **long-distance ~ travel** Eisenbahnfahrt über eine weite Entfernung; ~ **trip** *(coll.)* Bahnfahrt.
railhead *(mil.)* Kopfstation.
railroad *(US)* Eisenbahn, *(railway line)* Eisenbahnlinie, Schienenweg;
~**s** *(shares)* Eisenbahnwerte, -aktien;
branch ~ Nebenbahn, -strecke; **elevated ~** Hochbahn;
~ *(v.)* mit der Eisenbahn befördern (fahren), *(work for the railroad)* bei der Eisenbahn arbeiten;
~ **s. o.** *(sl.)* j. ohne Verfahren einbuchten; ~ **a bill through Congress** Gesetz im Kongreß durchpeitschen; ~ **a country** Eisenbahnen in einem Land bauen;
~ **accident** Eisenbahnunglück; ~ **agreement** Eisenbahnabkommen; ~ **bill of lading** Bahnfrachtbrief; ~ **bonds** Eisenbahnobligationen; ~ **bridge** Eisenbahnbrücke; ~ **brotherhood** Eisenbahnergewerkschaft; ~ **bulletin** Streckenplakat; ~ **car** Eisenbahnwaggon; ~ **gasoline car** Kesselwagen; ~ **carloading** Bahnfrachtsendung; ~ **carrier** bahnamtlicher Spediteur, Bahnspediteur; ~ **cartage agent** bahnamtlicher Rollfuhrunternehmer; ~ **center** Eisenbahnzentrum; ~ **charges** Gütertarif; ~ **company** Eisenbahngesellschaft; ~ **crossing** Bahnübergang; ~ **division** Eisenbahnabteilung; ~ **earnings** [Eisenbahn]betriebseinnahmen; ~ **employee** Eisenbahnbeamter, Bahnangestellter; ~ **engineer** Eisenbahntechniker; ~ **equipment** Eisenbahnzubehör, -ausrüstungsteile; ~ **equipment bond** Schuldverschreibung einer Finanzierungsgesellschaft für Eisenbahnbedarf; ~ **executive** höherer Bahnbeamter; ~ **fare** [Eisenbahn]fahrpreis; ~ **freight** Bahnfracht; ~ **freight car** [Eisenbahn]waggon, Güterwagen; ~ **freight line** Güterverkehrslinie; ~ **freight rates** Gütertarif; ~ **freight service** Eisenbahn-, Güterfrachtverkehr; ~ **freight transportation** [Eisenbahn]frachtverkehr; ~ **industry** Waggonindustrie; ~ **junction** Eisenbahnknotenpunkt; ~ **labo(u)r board** staatliches Eisenbahnschlichtungsamt; ~ **line** Eisenbahnlinie, -strecke; ~ **matters** Eisenbahnwesen; ~ **merger** Fusion von Eisenbahnlinien; ~ **net** Eisenbahnnetz; ~ **operation** *(US)* Eisenbahnbetrieb; ~ **passenger car** Personenwagen, -waggon; ~ **property** Bahneigentum; ~ **rates** Eisenbahntarif; ~ **relief fund** Eisenbahnunterstützungsfonds; ~ **route** Eisenbahnstrecke, -linie; ~ **routing** Streckenführung einer Bahn; ~ **service** Eisenbahnbetrieb; ~ **shares** Eisenbahnaktien; ~ **showing** Bahnplakat; ~ **sickness** Reisekrankheit; ~ **siding** Abstell-, Anschlußgleis; **free ~ station** Bahnhof, Bahnstation; **free ~ station of consignee** *(US)* frei Bahnstation des Empfängers; **nearest ~ station** *(US)* Zielbahnhof; ~-**station telegram** Bahntelegramm;

~ **stocks** Eisenbahnwerte, -aktien; ~ **strike** Eisenbahnstreik; ~ **system** Schienennetz; ~ **ticket** [Eisenbahn]fahrkarte; ~ **track** Eisenbahngleis; ~ **tracks** Gleisanlage; ~ **train** [Eisenbahn]zug; ~ **trunk line** Haupt[eisenbahn]linie; ~ **worker** Eisenbahnarbeiter.

railroader (US) Eisenbahn[angestellt]er.

railroading (US) Eisenbahnbau, -wesen; ~ **history** Eisenbahngeschichte.

railroadman (US) Eisenbahner.

railway (Br.) Eisenbahn, Schienenweg, (branch line) Neben-, Lokalbahn;
~**s** (stock exchange) Eisenbahnwerte;
arterial ~ Hauptstrecke; **branch** ~ Nebenlinie, Zweigbahn; **circular** ~ Ring-, Gürtelbahn; **defunct** ~ stillgelegte Bahn; **district** ~ Vorort-, Lokalbahn; **double-track** ~ zweigleisige Eisenbahnlinie; **electric street** ~ elektrische Straßenbahn, Elektrische; **factory** ~ Schlepp-, Werkbahn; **government** ~ Staatsbahn; **harbo(u)r** ~ Hafenbahn; **high-speed** ~ Schnellbahn; **industrial** ~ Betriebsbahn; **interurban** ~ S-, Stadtbahn; **junction** ~ Verbindungsbahn; **light** ~ Klein-, Nebenbahn; **local** ~ Lokalbahn; **multiple-line** ~ mehrgleisige Bahn; **narrow-gauge** ~ Kleinbahn; **overhead** ~ Hochbahn; **single-line** ~ eingleisige Bahn; **standard-gauge** ~ Normalspurbahn; **street** ~ Straßenbahn; **suburban** ~ Vorortbahn; **transcontinental** ~ Überland[eisen]bahn; **trunk** ~ Hauptstrecke;
~ (v.) mit der Eisenbahn fahren;
to build a new ~ neue Eisenbahnlinie anlegen; **to work on the** ~ bei der Eisenbahn arbeiten;
~ **accident** Eisenbahnunglück; ~ **advertising** Eisenbahnwerbung; ~ **advice** Eisenbahnavis; ~ **assets** Eisenbahnwerte; ~ **authorities** Eisenbahndienststelle, Eisenbahnverwaltung; ~ **bill of lading** Bahnfrachtbrief; **British** ⚏ **Board** Hauptverwaltung der englischen Eisenbahn; ~ **bonds** Eisenbahnobligationen; ~ **bookstall** Bahnhofsbuchhandlung; ~ **bridge** Eisenbahnbrücke; ~ **brotherhood** Eisenbahnergewerkschaft; ~ **building** Bahnhofsgebäude; ~ **car** Triebwagen; ~ **carman** Lokomotivführer; ~ **carriage** Eisenbahn-, Personenwagen, (transport) Bahnfracht; ~ **clerk** Bahnangestellter; ~**-collecting vehicle** bahnamtliches Zubringerfahrzeug; ⚏ **Commissioners** (Br.) Bahnaufsichtsamt; ~ **committee** Eisenbahnverwaltungsrat; ~ **communication** Eisenbahnverkehr; ~ **company (corporation)** Eisenbahngesellschaft; ~ **compartment** Eisenbahnabteil; ~ **concession** [Eisen]bahnkonzession; ~ **connection** Eisenbahnverbindung; ~ **consignment note** Bahnfrachtbrief; ~ **contractor** Eisenbahnunternehmer; ~ **crossing** [Eisen]bahnübergang; ~ **debentures** Eisenbahnobligationen; ~**s' deficit** Eisenbahndefizit; ~ **delivery** Bahnzustellung; ~ **depot** Bahnhof; ~ **diagram** Eisenbahnkarte; ~ **discriminations** unerlaubte Tarifvergünstigungen; ~ **dispatch office** Bahnabfertigung; ~ **earnings** [Eisenbahn]betriebseinnahmen; ~ **employee** Bahnangestellter; ~ **employees' department** Spitzenverband der Eisenbahnarbeiter; ~ **engineer** Eisenbahningenieur; ~ **equipment** Bahneinrichtungen, Eisenbahnanlagen; ⚏ **Executive** Eisenbahnverwaltung; ~ **express** Expreß-, Eilgut; ~ **express agency** [Eisen]bahnspedition, bahnamtlicher Spediteur; ~ **express business** Eilgutverkehr; ~ **facilities** [Eisen]bahnanlagen; ~ **fare** [Eisenbahn]fahrpreis; ~ **freight** [Eisenbahn]fracht; ~ **freight charges (rates)** [Eisenbahn]frachttarif; ~ **gauge** Spur, Eisenbahnspur; ~ **goods manager** Lademeister; ~ **goods traffic** [Eisenbahn]güterverkehr; ~ **guard** Zugschaffner; ~ **guide** [Eisenbahn]kursbuch; ~ **hopper** Selbstentlader; ~ **hotel** Eisenbahnhotel; ~ **journey** Bahnfahrt; ~ **junction** Eisenbahnknotenpunkt; ~ **level crossing** schienengleicher Bahnübergang; ~ **line** Eisenbahnlinie, -streckenführung, Bahnstrecke; **to operate a** ~**line** Eisenbahnlinie betreiben; ~ **loan** [Eisen]bahnanleihe; ~ **mail service** Bahnpostdienst; ~ **man** Eisenbahner; ~ **map** Eisenbahnübersichtskarte; ~ **market** (stock exchange) Markt für Eisenbahnwerte; ~ **matters** Eisenbahnwesen; ~ **network** Eisenbahnnetz; ~ **novel** Reiselektüre; ~ **official (officer)** Beamter der Eisenbahn, Bahnbeamter; ~ **officials** Zugpersonal; ~ **parcels** Bahnfrachtgut; ~ **parcels service** Bahnfrachtdienst; ~ **passenger duty** Beförderungsteuer; ~ **passenger insurance** Eisenbahnunfallversicherung; ~ **passenger transportation** [Eisenbahn]personenverkehr; ~ **platform** Bahnsteig; ~ **police** Bahnpolizei; ~ **port** Eisenbahnhafen; ~ **porter** Gepäckträger; ~ **premises** Bahngrundstück, -gebäude; ~ **property** Bahneigentum; ~ **rates** [Eisen]bahntarif; ~ **rates tribunal** Tarifbehörde; ~ **regulations** Bahnvorschriften; ~ **route** Bahnstrecke, -linie; ~ **scrip** Interimsschein einer Eisenbahnaktie; ~ **securities** Eisenbahnpapiere, -werte; ~ **services** Bahnbetrieb; ~ **share** Eisenbahnaktie; ~ **shareholder** Inhaber von Eisenbahnaktien; ~ **sickness** Reise-,

Eisenbahnkrankheit; **at** ~ **speed** blitzschnell; ~ **station** Bahnstation, Stationsgebäude, Bahnhof; **light-** ~ **station** Kleinbahnhof; **nearest** ~ **station** Zielbahnhof; **free** ~ **station consignee** frei Bahnstation des Empfängers; ~**-station office** Bahnpostamt; ~ **stocks** Eisenbahnwerte; ~ **strike** Eisenbahnerstreik; ~ **subsidies** Eisenbahnsubventionen; ~ **supplier** Eisenbahnzulieferer; ~ **system** Eisenbahn-, Schienennetz; **to reduce the** ~ **system to chaos** chaotische Zustände im Eisenbahnbetrieb hervorrufen; ~ **tariff** [Bahn]frachttarif; ~ **terminal** Kopfbahnhof; ~ **ticket** [Eisenbahn]fahrkarte; ~ **track** Eisenbahngleis; ~ **traffic** Bahnverkehr; ~ **traffic regulations** Eisenbahnverkehrsordnung; ~ **transport** Bahntransport; ⚏ **Travel Office** Reise-, Verkehrsbüro; ~ **travel(l)er** Reisender; ~ **undertaking** Eisenbahnbetrieb; ~ **union** Eisenbahnergewerkschaft; ~ **waggon** Eisenbahnwaggon; ~ **working** Bahnbetrieb.

rain Regen;
come ~ **or shine** bei jedem Wetter;
~ **of congratulations** Flut von Glückwünschen;
~ (v.) **cats and dogs** wie mit Kannen gießen, Bindfaden regnen; ~ **area** Regengebiet; ~ **check** (run of the house, US) ständige Einladung, (US) Einlaßkarte für Ersatzveranstaltung; ~ **frequency** Regenhäufigkeit; ~ **glass** Barometer; ~ **insurance** Regenversicherung; ~ **maker** Regenmacher; ~ **spell** Regenperiode; ~ **squall** Regenbö; ~**-water** Regenwasser.

rainfall Niederschlagsmenge;
~ **intensity** Regendichte.

rainy day Notzeiten;
~**s** Regentage;
to put away for a ~ für schlechte Zeiten sparen, Notgroschen zurücklegen.

rainy season Regenzeit.

raise (US) Lohn-, Gehaltserhöhung, -aufbesserung, -verbesserung;
tax-free ~ steuerfreie Gehaltserhöhung;
~ **in salary (wages)** Gehalts-, Lohnerhöhung, Gehaltsaufbesserung, -verbesserung;
~ (v.) (claim) stellen, geltend machen, (increase) anheben, erhöhen, in die Höhe treiben, steigern;
~ **an action** Prozeß anhängig machen; ~ **an army** Heer aufstellen; ~ **the bank rate** Diskontsatz erhöhen; ~ **a blockade** Blockade aufheben; ~ **a building** Gebäude aufstocken; ~ **capital** Kapital aufnehmen (aufbringen); ~ **additional capital for new plant facilities** Kapitalerhöhung zwecks Durchführung von Betriebserweiterungen vornehmen; ~ **cash** Geld aufbringen (auftreiben); ~ **cattle** Vieh züchten; ~ **a check** (US) (cheque, Br.) Scheckziffern in betrügerischer Absicht erhöhen; ~ **children** (US) Kinder erziehen; ~ **a claim under a guarantee** Garantieansprüche stellen (geltend machen); ~ **a collection** Sammlung veranstalten; ~ **a credit** Kredit aufnehmen; ~ **the discount [rate]** Diskont[satz] erhöhen; ~ **the dividend** Dividendenerhöhung vornehmen; ~ **a doubt** Bedenken erheben; ~ **a dust** (fig.) Staub aufwirbeln; ~ **an embargo** Embargo (Beschlagnahme) aufheben; ~ **a great estate out of small profits** aus kleinen Gewinnen ein großes Vermögen machen; ~ **exports** Ausfuhr steigern; ~ **a family** Familie ernähren; ~ **a fine** Strafe verschärfen; ~ **a fund** Fonds errichten; ~ **funds** Geldmittel beschaffen; ~ **funds for a holiday** Ferienfonds schaffen; ~ **funds by subscription** Geld durch Zeichnung aufbringen; ~ **one's glass to s. o.** jem. zutrinken; ~ **hell** Aufruhr hervorrufen; ~ **a house two storeys** Haus um zwei Stockwerke erhöhen; ~ **an injunction** einstweilige Verfügung aufheben; ~ **the interest from 7 per cent to 8 per cent** Zinsfuß von 7% auf 8% erhöhen; ~ **an issue** Frage aufwerfen, Thema anschneiden, (pleadings) Rechtsstreit entstehen lassen; ~ **the land next morning** (ship) Land am nächsten Tag erreichen; ~ **the level of prices** Preisniveau anheben; ~ **the lid** (sl.) Beschränkungen aufheben; ~ **the limit** Limit erhöhen; ~ **a loan** Anleihe (Darlehn) aufnehmen; ~ **a matter** Angelegenheit zur Sprache bringen; ~ **money** Geld auftreiben (beschaffen, aufnehmen); ~ **money on an estate** Geld (Hypothek) auf ein Grundstück aufnehmen; ~ **money for an industry** Industriezweig mit Kapital ausstatten; ~ **money for a new undertaking** Geld für ein neues Unternehmen bereitstellen; ~ **a monument** Denkmal errichten; ~ **a mortgage** Hypothek aufnehmen; ~ **an objection** Einspruch (Einwand) erheben; ~ **no objection** keinen Widerspruch hervorrufen; ~ **s. o. to the peerage** j. zum Lord machen; ~ **a point of order** Punkt für die Tagesordnung vorschlagen; ~ **a presumption** Vermutung entstehen lassen; ~ **prices** Preise erhöhen, verteuern; ~ **production to a maximum** Produktion auf den Höchststand bringen; ~ **a protest** Protest erheben; ~ **a question** Frage anschneiden (aufwerfen), Frage zur Sprache bringen; ~ **s. o. to a higher rank** j. in

einen höheren Rang erheben (im Rang erhöhen); ~ **slightly the current rate of spending** Umfang der vorgesehenen Investitionen leicht vergrößern; ~ **the rent** Mieterhöhung vornehmen; ~ **one's reputation** seinen Ruf verbessern; ~ **s. one's reputation** jds. Stellung festigen; ~ **revenue** Steuer (Abgaben) erheben; ~ **the salary** Gehalt erhöhen (aufbessern); ~ **a sunken ship** gesunkenes Schiff heben; ~ **a siege** Belagerung aufheben; ~ **a soldier from the ranks** einfachen Soldaten zum Offizier machen; ~ **the standard of revolt** einer Revolte zum Sieg verhelfen; ~ **a subject** Thema zur Sprache bringen (anschneiden); ~ **a tariff** Tariferhöhung (Steuererhöhung) vornehmen; ~ **a tax** Steuer erhöhen; ~ **to the throne** auf den Thron erheben; ~ **the top** *(securities)* Höchstkurs heraufsetzen; ~ **the town** Stadt in Aufruhr versetzen; ~ **troops** Truppen ausheben; ~ **the value of the franc** Franken aufwerten; ~ **the wages** Löhne erhöhen; ~ **the wind** *(sl.)* sich das nötige Geld verschaffen;
to get a ~ *(US)* Gehaltsaufbesserung erfahren; **to make a ~ of a hundred dollars** *(US)* hundert Dollar aufbringen.
raised|bill *(US)* durch Werterhöhung gefälschter Wechsel; ~ **check** *(US)* durch Erhöhung des Betrages gefälschter Scheck; ~ **letters** erhabene Buchstaben.
raiser, curtain *(journalism)* Vorbericht, Vorspann, *(theater)* Vorspiel; **morale ~** *(mil.)* Maßnahmen zur Verbesserung der Kampfmoral.
raising *(capital)* Aufnahme, *(prices)* Erhöhung, Steigerung;
~ **an action** *(Scot.)* Anstrengung eines Prozesses, Klageerhebung; ~ **of personal allowances** Erhöhung der persönlichen Steuerfreibeträge; ~ **of the bank rate** Diskonterhöhung; ~ **of capital** Kapitalaufbringung, -aufnahme; ~ **of a claim** Geltendmachung eines Anspruchs; ~ **of credit** Kreditaufnahme; ~ **of the necessary funds** Beschaffung der benötigten Geldmittel; ~ **of a loan** Anleiheaufnahme; ~ **of money** Geldaufbringung; ~ **of a mortgage on an estate** hypothekarische Beleihung eines Grundstücks; ~ **an objection** Einlegung eines Widerspruchs, Vorbringen eines Einspruchs; ~ **of portions** Aufbringung von Abfindungszahlungen; ~ **of portions for younger children** Pflichtteilsfestsetzung für jüngere Geschwister; ~ **of postal** *(Br.)* **(postage, US) rates** Portoerhöhung; ~ **of prices** Preiserhöhung, -anhebung; ~ **a promise** Begründung eines Versprechens; ~ **of railway rates** *(Br.)* Erhöhung der Eisenbahntarife; ~ **of rents** Mietsteigerung; ~ **of revenues** Steueranhebung; ~ **of salaries** Gehaltserhöhung, -aufbesserung; ~ **of the school-leaving age** Heraufsetzung des Schulentlassungsalters; ~ **a use** Begründung eines Nutzungsrechtes;
to organize the ~ of funds for charitable purposes Geldsammlung für Wohltätigkeitszwecke veranstalten.
rake *(croupier)* Rechen, *(US)* Provision, Gewinnbeteiligung;
as thin as a ~ *(sl.)* spindeldürr;
~ *(v.)* **s. o. over the coals** j. tüchtig herunterputzen; ~ **about among old documents** in alten Urkunden herumkramen; ~ **in profits** Gewinne scheffeln; ~ **through old manuscripts** alte Unterlagen durchsehen; ~ **one's memory** sein Gedächtnis durchkämmen; ~ **together wealth** Vermögen zusammenscharren; ~ **up old grievances** alte Beschwerden von neuem vorbringen; ~ **up old quarrels** alte Streitereien wieder ausgraben;
~**-off** *(US sl.)* betrügerischer Gewinnanteil, unberechtigte Provision; **to have a ~-off on s. th.** Profit aus etw. ziehen.
raker *(sl.)* Bombensache, Mordsding.
rally *(car owners)* Rally, *(meeting, US)* Tagung, Treffen, Zusammenkunft, Massenversammlung, *(recovery of strength)* Kräftigung, *(stock exchange)* [schnelle] Erholung, [Preis]aufschwung;
election ~ Wahlversammlung; **party ~** Parteitag; **peace ~** Friedensresolution; **political ~** politische Versammlung; **price ~** Kurserholung;
~ *(v.)* versammeln, *(prices)* anziehen, sich erholen (verbessern, verstärken);
~ **briskly** stark anziehen; ~ **to a cause** sich einer Sache anschließen; ~ **from an illness** sich von einer Krankheit erholen; ~ **round s. o.** sich um j. scharen; ~ **one's strength** wieder zu Kräften kommen; ~ **to the support of the Minister** sich zur Unterstützung um den Minister scharen;
to hold a ~ Versammlung abhalten;
~ **juncture** Krisensituation im Börsenaufschwung.
rallying cry Schlagwort, Parole; ~ **point** Sammelpunkt, -platz; ~ **sign** *(mil.)* Zeichen zum Sammeln.
ram Rammbock;
~ *(v.)* *(coach)* einpauken;
~ **a submarine** Unterseeboot rammen; ~ **one's clothes into a suitcase** seine Kleidung in einen Koffer stopfen; ~ **down s. one's throat** jem. etw. aufdrängen; ~ **through** durchpauken.

ramble Ausflug, Wanderung, Bummel;
~ *(v.)* vom Thema abschweifen;
~ **about the city** durch die Stadt bummeln;
to go for a country ~ Landpartie machen, Ausflug aufs Land unternehmen.
rambler Wanderer.
rambling mansion weiträumiges Gutshaus.
ramification Verzweigung, Verästelung, *(company)* Zweiggesellschaft;
~**s of a plot** Verzweigungen einer Verschwörung; **widespread** ~**s of trade** weitverzweigte Handelsorganisation.
ramify *(v.)* sich verzweigen.
ramp Rampe, *(usury, Br., sl.)* Preistreiberei, Geldschneiderei;
aircraft ~ Landetreppe; **furnished flat ~s** *(Br., sl.)* Preistreibereien bei möblierten Wohnungen;
~ *(v.)* *(Br., sl.)* schröpfen;
~ **agent** Flugspeditionsvertreter; ~ **boat** *(mil.)* Landungsfahrzeug.
rampancy Überhandnehmen.
rampant, to be überhandnehmen, um sich greifen.
rampart [Festungs]wall.
ramshackle kaputt, funktionsunfähig;
~ **old bus** ausgedienter alter Omnibus; ~ **empire** abgewirtschaftetes Imperium; ~ **house** baufälliges Haus, Bruchbude.
ranch *(US)* landwirtschaftlicher Betrieb, [Zucht]farm.
rancher Farmer, Viehzüchter.
random Zufall;
(a.) aufs Geratewohl, zufällig;
to drop bombs at ~ Bomben ziellos abwerfen; **to talk at ~** in den Tag hinein reden;
~ **access** *(computer)* Direktzugriff; ~ **distribution** Zufallsverteilung; ~ **error** Zufallsfehler; ~ **guess** bloße Vermutung; ~ **order** Zufallsanordnung; ~ **purchase** Mengenkauf ohne Besichtigung; ~ **sample** Stichprobe; ~ **sample selection** Stichprobenauswahl; ~ **sampling** Stichprobenerhebung; ~ **sampling numbers** *(statistics)* Zufallszahlen; ~ **selection** Zufallsauswahl; ~ **shot** Schuß ins Blaue; ~ **start** Zufallsanfangszahl; ~ **test** Stichprobe; ~ **thought** flüchtiger Gedanke.
randomization methodische Marktuntersuchung.
range *(bot., zool.)* Verbreitungsgebiet, *(collection)* Sammlung, Kollektion, *(country district, US)* Stadtbezirk mit einer Ausdehnung bis zehn km, *(grazing grounds, US)* ausgedehnte Weideflächen, *(limits of variation)* Spielraum, äußere Grenze, *(mil.)* Schießplatz, *(music)* Ton-, Stimmumfang, *(port)* Reihe frachtgleicher Häfen, *(production)* Programm, *(sphere)* Raum, Gebiet, Spannweite, Bereich, Fächer, Umfang, Aktionsradius, Wirkungskreis, -gebiet, Reichweite, *(statistics)* Streuungs-, Toleranzbereich, *(stock exchange)* Schwanken der Kurse, Schwankung, *(cooking stove)* Gas-, Küchen-, Elektroherd;
at close ~ aus geringer Entfernung; **at a ~ of 8 miles** im Umkreis von 12 Kilometern; **in the ~ of politics** auf politischem Gebiet; **within the ~ of possibility** im Bereich des Möglichen; **within the ~ of vision** in Sichtweite;
comprehensive ~ gute Auswahl; **lowest ~** unterste Klassen; **price ~** Preisbewegung, -bildung, *(stock exchange)* Kursbewegung, -bildung; **rate ~** Lohnspanne; **salary ~** Gehaltsklasse, -spanne, -rahmen; **wide ~** breiter Fächer;
~ **of action** Tätigkeits-, Aktionsbereich; ~ **of activities** Betätigungsfeld; ~ **of application** Anwendungsbereich, -gebiet; **the whole ~ of articles in stock** alle einschlägigen Artikel, ganzes Sortiment; **generous ~ of benefits** großzügiges Angebot von Sondervergütungen; ~ **for cable transfers** Satz für Kabelauszahlungen; ~ **of capacity** *(engine)* Leistungsbereich; **narrow ~ of choice** kleine Auswahl; ~ **of colo(u)rs** Farbskala; **wide ~ of colo(u)rs** große Auswahl in Farben; ~ **of customers** Kundenkreis; ~ **of dispersion** Streuungsbreite; ~ **of earnings to be affected** betroffene Einkommensgruppen; ~ **of experience** Reichtum an Erfahrung; **maximum ~ of permitted fluctuations** höchstzugelassene Bandbreite der Wechselkurse; ~ **of goods** Produktangebot; **large ~ of goods offered** breiter Fächer von Warenangeboten; ~ **of income** Einkommensbereich; **wide ~ of items** großes Warenangebot; ~ **of knowledge** Wissensbereich; ~ **of models** Musterkollektion; ~ **of mountains** Gebirgskette; ~ **of patterns** Musterkollektion; ~ **of prices** Preisskala, -klasse, -lage, -spanne; ~ **of products** Produktionsrahmen, Umfang des Fertigungsprogramms; **full ~ of samples** vollständige Musterkollektion; ~ **of services** Dienstleistungsangebot; **whole ~ of services** Dienstleistungsbündel; **full ~ of banking and financial services** breite Palette von Dienstleistungen auf dem Bank- und Finanzierungsgebiet; **annual ~ of temperature** jährliche

Temperaturschwankungen; ~ **of thought** Ideenkreis; **wide ~ of topics** breiter Themenkreis; ~ **of validity** Gültigkeitsbereich; ~ **of a voice** Stimmumfang;

~ *(v.) (place in specified order)* einrangieren, -ordnen, -reihen, in Reihen aufstellen, klassifizieren, *(print.)* zurichten, ausgleichen, *(stock exchange)* schwanken, sich bewegen;

~ **o. s.** sich rangieren, seine Verhältnisse ordnen; ~ **o. s. with s. o.** zu jem. halten; ~ **among** im gleichen Rang stehen; ~ **between 10 and 20** zwischen 10 und 20 schwanken; ~ **the coast** Küste entlangfahren; ~ **east and west** von Osten nach Westen verlaufen; ~ **o. s. with the enemy** zum Feind halten; ~ **far and wide** viele Themen beherrschen; ~ **from 5 to 10 marks** *(prices)* zwischen 5 und 10 Mark liegen; ~ **over a wide field** großes Gebiet erfassen; ~ **with the street** in Straßenfront stehen; ~ **themselves along the route of the procession** sich entlang des Prozessionsweges aufstellen; ~ **widely** vielseitig sein; ~ **with** im gleichen Rang stehen, rangieren; ~ **with the great writers** zu den großen Schriftstellern zählen;

to be outside s. one's ~ nicht zu jds. Fachbereich gehören; **to continue in a narrow** ~ sich weiter in engen Grenzen halten; **to have a wide** ~ **of goods** über ein großes Sortiment verfügen; **to hold the widest possible** ~ **of stock** größtmögliches Sortiment anbieten; **to move in a narrow** ~ geringe Kursschwankungen aufweisen; **to slide below a trading** ~ **anchored in a special plateau** vorher festgelegte Kursmarke unterschreiten;

~ **cattle** Weidevieh; ~ **finder** *(photo)* Entfernungsmesser; **long-~ gun** Fernkampfgeschütz; ~ **land** Viehzuchtgebiet; **narrower-~ part** *(trust fund, Br.)* eingeschränkterer Anlagenteil; **wider-~ part** *(trust fund, Br.)* weniger weisungsgebundener Anlagenteil; ~ **pole** *(surveying)* Fluchtstab.

ranger *(Br.)* Forstamtmann, -aufseher, Jagdaufseher, *(rocketry, US)* Mondsonde, *(police, US)* berittener Polizist.

rank *(formation)* Ordnung, Formation, Aufstellung, *(line)* Linie, Reihe, Kette, *(mil.)* Charge, Rang, Dienstgrad, Glied, *(order of precedence)* Rang[ordnung], *(position in life)* Rang, Klasse, Stand, Dienstgrad, -rang, [soziale] Stellung, Schicht, Würde, *(statistics)* Rangordnungsnummer;

in ~ **and file** in Reih und Glied; **of all** ~**s and classes** aus allen Schichten der Gesellschaft; **of equal** ~ gleichrangig; **of high** ~ hochgestellt; **of prior** ~ im Range vorgehend, rangbesser, vorrangig; **of second** ~ zweitrangig; **of subsequent** ~ nachrangig; **with** ~ **equal to** im gleichen Range mit;

~**s** *(mil.)* Mannschaften, Mannschaftsstand; **cab** ~ *(Br.)* Taxistand, -haltestelle; **civil** ~ Zivilistenstand; **honorary** ~ ehrenhalber verliehener Rang; **managerial** ~**s** betriebliche Rangordnung; **prior** ~ älterer Rang, Priorität; **service** ~ Dienstgrad; **taxi** ~ *(Br.)* Taxistand;

~ **of cabs** *(Br.)* Droschken-, Taxihalteplatz, -stand; ~ **and fashion** vornehme Gesellschaft; ~ **and file** Unteroffiziere und Mannschaften, *(fig.)* die breite Masse, die gewöhnlich Sterblichen; ~ **and file of a party** Fußvolk einer Partei; ~ **of general** Generalsrang; ~**s of middle management** Schicht der gehobenen Angestellten; ~ **of mortgage** Hypothekenrang; ~ **of workers** Heer der Arbeiter;

~ *(v.)* bevorrechtigt sein, *(have priority, US)* höheren Rang einnehmen, Vortritt haben, *(range in a class)* einordnen, einreichen, klassifizieren, rangieren, *(bankruptcy proceedings)* als forderungsberechtigt aufgeführt werden, bevorrechtigt sein; ~ **after** im Range nachstehen (nachfolgen); ~ **alike** gleichen Rang haben; ~ **before** Vorrang haben, im Rang vorgehen; ~ **as a citizen** Bürgerrechte besitzen; ~ **a creditor** Rangordnung eines Gläubigers bestimmen; ~ **as creditor** als Gläubiger Anspruch erheben; ~ **as a preferential creditor** Stellung eines Vorzugsgläubigers einnehmen; ~ **as preferred debt** als bevorrechtigte Konkursforderung behandelt werden; ~ **for the July dividends** *(Br.)* schon im Juli an der Dividendenausschüttung teilnehmen; ~ **equally** *(debts of a bankruptcy)* gleichen Rang haben, gleichrangig sein; ~ **first** ersten Rang einnehmen, erstrangig sein; ~ **first in dividend rights** *(Br.)* dividendenbevorrechtigt sein; ~ **high** hohe Stellung einnehmen; ~ **high in public favo(u)r** großes Ansehen in der Öffentlichkeit genießen; ~ **off** abmarschieren; ~ **in the order of issue** in der Rangordnung dem Ausgabedatum unterliegen; ~ **pari passu with** *(bankruptcy)* gleichrangig sein; ~ **pari passu with new shares issue** mit neuen Aktien gleichberechtigt sein; ~ **past** vorbeimarschieren; ~ **for pension** pensionsberechtigt sein; ~ **among the Great Powers** zu den Großmächten zählen; ~ **as preferential** Vorrang haben; ~ **next to the President** gleich nach dem Präsidenten kommen; ~ **in priority** Vorrang (Priorität) haben; ~ **s. o. among the great statesman** j. zu den großen Staatsmännern zählen (rechnen); ~ **with s. o.** gleichen Rang wie ein anderer haben;

to be a person of high ~ Standesperson sein; **to be in the** ~**s of the unemployed** zu der Schar der Arbeitslosen (dem Arbeitslosenheer) gehören; **to be promoted to the** ~ **of captain** zum Hauptmann befördert werden; **to be reduced to the** ~**s** degradiert werden; **to break through the enemy's** ~ **and files** feindliche Aufstellungen durchbrechen; **to close one's** ~**s behind s. o.** jem. Rückendeckung geben; **to fall into the second** ~ zweitrangig werden; **to form into** ~ *(crowd)* sich formieren; **to grant prior** ~ Vorrang einräumen; **to hold a** ~ Charge bekleiden; **to hold a high** ~ hohen Rang bekleiden; **to hold the** ~ **of major** Majorsrang bekleiden; **to join the** ~**s** ins Heer eintreten; **to pass down the** ~**s** Front abschreiten; **to pull** ~ *(sl.)* seine gesellschaftliche Stellung ausnutzen; **to quit the** ~**s** desertieren; **to reduce to the** ~**s** *(mil.)* degradieren; **to rise from the** ~**s** von der Pike auf dienen; **to serve in the** ~**s** als gemeiner Soldat dienen; **to stand in the first** ~ an erster Stelle stehen; **to take high** ~ *(Br.)* hoch gewertet werden; **to take** ~ **with s. o.** mit jem. gleichrangig sein, in gleichem Rang mit jem. stehen; **to take the taxi at the head of the** ~ *(Br.)* erstes Taxi an der Haltestelle nehmen; **to thin the** ~**s** Reihen lichten;

~ *(a.) (soil)* üppig, fruchtbar, fett; ~ **climate** abscheuliches Klima; ~**-and-file union member** einfaches Gewerkschaftsmitglied; ~ **land** fruchtbarer Boden; ~ **language** unanständige Worte; ~ **nonsense** völliger Unsinn; ~ **order** *(employees)* Rangordnung; ~ **order statistics** Rangordnungsmeßzahlen; ~ **prejudice** Klassenvorurteil; ~ **swindle** Erzschwindel; ~ **treason** regelrechter Verrat.

ranker *(mil.)* aus dem Mannsschaftsstand hervorgegangener Offizier.

ranking Rangeinteilung, -verhältnis, -folge, -ordnung, *(marshalling of creditors)* Vorrang, Priorität;

job ~ berufliche Rangordnung;

~ **of assets** Rangfolge von Konkursgegenständen; ~ **of claims** Rangordnung der Ansprüche; ~ **of a creditor** Gläubigerrang; ~ **of liens** Rangordnung von Pfandrechten; ~ **of mortgages** Hypothekenrang, Rangordnung der Hypotheken;

~ *(a.) (US)* führend;

~ **for dividend** dividendenberechtigt;

equally ~ **creditor** gleichrangiger Gläubiger; ~ **member** *(US)* rangältestes Kongreßmitglied; ~ **officer** *(US)* ranghöchster Offizier.

ransack *(v.)* durchsuchen, *(pillage)* [aus]plündern;

~ **one's conscience** sein Gewissen erforschen; ~ **a dictionary to find just the right word** Wörterbuch nach dem richtigen Wort durchforschen; ~ **one's pockets** seine Taschen durchsuchen.

ransom Lösegeld, Loskauf;

a king's ~ große Summe;

~ **of cargo** Auslösung der Ladung;

~ *(v.)* Lösegeld verlangen, *(redeem from captivity)* loskaufen; **to exact a** ~ **from s. o.** Lösegeld von jem. erpressen; **to hold s. o. to** ~ j. bis zur Zahlung eines Lösegeldes festhalten;

~ **bill (bond)** *(captured ship)* Lösegeldverpflichtung; ~ **demand** Lösegeldforderung; ~ **money** Lösegeld; ~ **price** Wucherpreis; **to obtain s. th. at a** ~ **price** etw. zu einem exorbitanten Preis bekommen.

rap Deut, Pfifferling;

not worth a ~ keinen Pfifferling wert; ~ **on the knuckles** *(Br.)* Verweis; **to hang a** ~ **on s. o.** jem. einen Strick daraus drehen.

rape Vergewaltigung;

statutory ~ Vergewaltigung einer Minderjährigen; ~ **of the forest** Forstfrevel; ~ **reeve** *(Br.)* Bezirksschulze.

rapid *(film)* hochempfindlich, *(quick)* schnell, rasch;

~ **depreciation** Schnellabschreibung; ~ **cross examination** Schnellverhör; ~ **mass transport** Schnelltransport von Massengütern; ~ **transit from city to city** *(US)* Nahschnellverkehr; ~ **transit bond** *(US)* Schnellverkehrsobligation; ~ **transit line** *(US)* Nahschnellverkehrslinie; ~ **transit railroad** *(US)* Schnellbahn; ~ **transit system** *(US)* Nahschnellverkehrswesen; ~ **writing** Schnellschreiben.

rapidly, to be taken up schnell vergriffen sein; **to decline** ~ *(prices)* schnell sinken;

~ **flowing river** reißenden Fluß.

rapine Plünderung, Raub.

rapport Beziehung, Verhältnis;

for better ~ zum harmonischen Ausgleich;

to bring o. s. into closer ~ **with one's environment** engeres Verhältnis zu seiner Umgebung zustandebringen; **to come in** ~ **with s. o.** Beziehungen mit jem. aufnehmen.

rapporteur Berichterstatter.

rapprochement Fühlungnahme, Herstellung freundschaftlicher Beziehungen, Annäherung;
~ between two states Annäherung zweier Staaten;
to seek a ~ Annäherungsversuche machen.

rare commodity Seltenheitsgut.

raree show Straßenvorführung.

rascal Schurke, Gauner, Halunke.

rash of accidents epidemieartige Unfallhäufung.

raster (television) Raster.

rasure ausradierte Stelle.

rat (freshman, sl) Erstsemester, (informer, sl.) Denunziant, (mil.) Überläufer, (pol.) Verräter, Abtrünniger, Überläufer, (printer, sl.) Drucker ohne Gewerkschaftsausweis, (strike) Streikbrecher;
~ (v.) (politician) umfallen, überlaufen, zur Gegenseite übergehen, seine Partei im Stich lassen, (strike) Streik brechen;
~ s. o. j. verpfeifen;
to be like a ~ in a hole wie die Ratte in der Falle sitzen; to look like a drowned ~ miserabel aussehen; to see ~s (sl.) weiße Mäuse sehen; to smell a ~ Lunte (den Braten) riechen;
~ pack (sl.) jugendliche Bande; ~ race (airplane) Hintereinanderfliegen, (politics, sl.) Statuskampf, Pöstchenjägerei, erbarmungsloser Konkurrenzkampf.

rata, pro (lat.) verhältnismäßig, anteilig, proratarisch;
to contribute ~ seinen verhältnismäßigen Anteil beitragen.

ratability Abschätzbarkeit, (customs) Zollpflichtigkeit, (municipal tax, Br.) Abgaben-, Kommunalsteuerpflicht, Umlagepflicht.

ratable verhältnis-, anteilsmäßig, (estimable) abschätzbar, bewertungsfähig, (liable to customs duty) zollpflichtig, (municipal tax, Br.) umlage-, kommunalsteuer-, abgabepflichtig;
~ estate (property) (Br.) steuerpflichtiges Grundstück; ~ freight Distanzfracht; ~ property (Br.) steuerpflichtiger Grundbesitz; ~ share Verhältnisanteil; ~ value (Br.) steuerbarer Wert, Veranlagungs-, Steuermeßwert; ~ value of a house (Br.) Veranlagungswert eines Hauses.

ratal (Br.) Kommunalsteuersatz, Steuermeßbetrag, Veranlagungswert.

ratched effect (consumption) Trägheitseffekt.

rate (advertising) Anzeigenpreis, (amount) Betrag, (broadcasting) Minutenpreis, (public charge) Gebühr, Leistungsentgelt, (customs) Zollsatz, Tarif, (electricity, gas, US) Abgabepreis, Tarif, (estimate) Preis, Veranschlagung, Anschlag, Berechnung, Taxe, Preisansatz, Wert, (degree) Grad, (insurance) Prämiensatz, (marine insurance) Risikoklasse, (post) Gebührenbetrag, Porto[satz], Posttarif, (proportion) Maß[stab], Verhältnis[ziffer], (quota) Quote, (railway) fester Satz, Frachtsatz, Tarif, (ratepayer) Kommunalabgabe, (share) [verhältnismäßiger] Anteil, Rate, (ship) Rang, Klasse, (stock exchange) Kurs, Preis[stand], (velocity) Geschwindigkeit, (wages) Lohnsatz;
all the same ~ zum gleichen Preis; at any ~ (in any case) auf jeden Fall, (price) zu jedem Preis; at the ~ zum Preise (Kurse, Satze) von, (proportion) im Verhältnis von; at the best possible ~ bestens, bestmöglich; at a cheap (low) ~ wohlfeil, billig, preiswert; at the current ~ of exchange zum gegenwärtigen Kurs (Tageskurs); at a dear (high) ~ teuer; at an easy ~ ohne große Unkosten; at an exponential ~ in geometrischer Progression; at a favo(u)rable ~ zu besonders günstigem Kurs; at a favo(u)rable ~ of interest zinsgünstig; at a fearful ~ in einem erschreckenden Ausmaß; at a firm ~ zu festem Preis; at a fixed ~ zu einem bestimmten (festen) Satz; at a great ~ mit großer Geschwindigkeit; at a high ~ zu hohen Zinsen; at the highest ~ of exchange zum höchsten Kurse; at a low ~ of interest zinsgünstig; at a lower ~ zu ermäßigtem Preis; at a modified ~ zu einer herabgesetzten Preis; at the most favo(u)rable ~ zum günstigsten Kurs; at a ~ of 4 per cent zu einem [Zins]satz von 4%; at the best possible ~ zum günstigsten Satz; at the present ~ of consumption beim augenblicklichen Verbrauch; at the proper ~ zum Tarifsatz; at the ~ [of exchange] quoted zum verzeichneten Kurs; at a reduced ~ zu ermäßigter Gebühr, zu einem ermäßigten Satz; at a slow ~ in langsamem Tempo;
~s (municipal taxes, Br.) Gemeindeabgaben, Gemeinde-, Kommunalsteuern, -abgaben, Umlage, (tariff) Tarif;
first-~ erster Klasse, erstklassig; second-~ zweitrangig; third-~ von minderwertiger Qualität;
activity ~ Erwerbsquote; actual ~s besondere [nachgewiesene] Bankspesen; currently adjusted ~ fortlaufender Kurs; advanced ~ erhöhter Frachtsatz (Tarif); advertising ~ (Br.) Anzeigentarif, -preisliste; all-commodity ~ Stückgütertarif; alternative ~ wechselweise in Ansatz gebrachter Tarif; annual ~

(insurance) Jahresprämie; any-quantity ~ (US) von der Mengeneinheit unabhängiger Tarif; applicable ~ gültiger Frachtsatz, (taxation) anwendbarer Steuersatz; appropriate ~ entsprechende Gebühr; ~ asked Briefkurs; authorized ~ genehmigter (zulässiger) Tarif; average ~ Durchschnittssatz, (stock exchange) Mittel-, Durchschnittskurs; average earned ~ Durchschnittsverdienst; bank ~ (US) Diskont[satz]; base (basic) ~ (carrier) Grundtarif, -gebühr, (corporation tax, Br.) einheitlicher Grundtarif, (wages) Ecklohntarif; basing ~ Ausgangsfrachtsatz; beneficial ~s kostendeckende Leistungsabgaben; berth ~ (maritime traffic) Stückguttarif; birth ~ Geburtenziffer; blanket ~ (insurance, US) Pauschaltarif, -satz, (long-distance traffic, US) Sammeltarif; block ~ (el.) degressiv gestaffelter Tarif; borough ~s (Br.) Gemeindeabgaben, -umlagen; bulk-supply ~ Mengentarif; buying ~ Ankaufs-, Geldkurs; cable ~ Kabelkurs, Kabelsatz; call-money ~ Satz für täglich fälliges Geld, Satz für Tagesgeld; cargo ~ Gesamttonnagesatz; carload ~ (US) Waggonfrachtsatz; cash ~ Scheckkurs, (stock exchange) Kassakurs; central ~ (European snake) Leitkurs; charge ~ (el., US) Grundgebühr nebst Verbrauchstarif; church ~ (Br.) Kirchensteuer; circulation ~ Auflageziffer; class ~ Grundgehalt, -tarif, (freight) Gruppen-, Sammel-, Sondertarif, (insurance) Tarifprämie; class A ~ (broadcast commercial) höchste Preisgruppe; clearing ~ Verrechnungskurs; clock-card ~ (wage earner) garantierter Stundenlohn; closing ~ Schlußkurs; yesterday's closing ~s gestrige Schlußnotierung; 4-colo(u)r ~ (advertising) Preis für vierfarbige Anzeigen; combination ~ (advertising) kombinierter Anzeigenrichtsatz, Kombinationstarif, (railway) Durchgangsfrachtsatz, -tarif; combination mileage and ~ prorate (US) kombinierter Frachttarif; combination through ~ kombinierter Durchgangsfrachtsatz; combined ~ (advertising) kombinierter Tarif; commission ~ Provisions-, Kommissionssatz; commodity ~s (airliner, US) Vorzugstarif, (US) Diskontsatz für Dokumententratten; common labo(u)r ~ Tariflohn für ungelernte Arbeiter; comparable ~ Vergleichstarif; composite ~ Durchschnittssatz; composition ~ Vergleichsquote; contango ~ Report-, Deportkurs; continental ~s (Br.) Sorten und Devisenkurse auf europäischen Plätzen; contribution ~ Beitragssatz; cost-per-thousand ~ (advertising) Tausenderpreis; county ~ (Br.) Kommunal-, Bezirks-, Kreisumlage; coupled ~ (Br.) gekoppelter Tarif; current ~ Tageskurs; currently adjusted ~ fortlaufender Kurs; customs ~ Zollsatz; daily ~ Tagessatz; day ~ Tagessatz, -kurs; death ~ Sterblichkeitsziffer; deferred ~ verbilligter Tarif für später zugestellte Telegramme; demand ~ (el., US) Höchstverbrauchertarif; deposit ~ Habenzinssatz; differential ~s gestaffelter Tarif, Staffeltarif, unterschiedliche Frachtsätze, Ausnahmefrachtsätze; discount ~ Diskont[satz]; distance ~ Distanzfrachttarif, (car) Kilometersatz; dividend ~s Dividendensätze; divorce ~ Scheidungsziffer; dollar ~ Dollarkurs; domestic ~s Inlandspostgebühren; double ~ doppelte Gebühr; dropping ~ rückläufige Kurse; education ~ Schulgeld; effective ~ Effektivzins, (Br.) Höchstbetrag der Steuer, Steuerhöchstbetrag; electric ~ (US) Strompreis, -tarif; entrance ~ (US) Anfangsgehalt, -lohn; equitable ~ (insurance) gerechte Prämie; established ~ fester Kurs; exceptional ~ Ausnahmetarif; exchange ~ Wechsel-, Devisen-, Umrechnungskurs; exorbitant ~ übersetzter Tarif; experience ~ (workmen's compensation insurance) Erfahrungsrichtsatz; factory overhead ~ Fertigungsgemeinkostensatz; fair ~ annehmbarer Preis; falling ~ fallender Kurs; favo(u)rable ~ günstiger Kurs; federal funds ~ (US) Tageskurs für Staatsanleihen; first ~ erste Qualität, (stock exchange) Anfangskurs; fixed ~ fester Kurs, Festkurs, feste Valuta; flat ~ Pauschal-, Einheitspreis, -satz, -tarif, (advertising) Anzeigenfestpreis, (el., US) Einheits-, Kleinabnehmertarif; flat-car ~ (US) Waggonfrachtsatz; flat mil(e)age ~ Kilometerpauschale; fluctuating ~ schwankender Kurs; fluctuating market ~ (US) veränderlicher Kurs; foreign ~ Auslandsporto; forward ~ Terminkurs; forward exchange ~ Devisenterminkurs; free ~ freier Devisenkurs; freight ~s Frachtrate, -satz, -gebühren, Gütertarif, Seefrachtsatz; freight-of-all-kinds ~s gleichmäßiger Frachttarif; full ~ voller Fahrpreis, volle Gebühr, (customs) allgemeiner Zolltarif; futures ~ (US) Kurs für Termingeschäfte; gas ~ (US) Gastarif; general ~s (Br.) allgemeine Kommunalabgaben, Allgemeintarif; graduated ~ gestaffelter Satz, Staffeltarif; ground ~ (railway) Grundtarif; group ~ (long-distance traffic) Sammeltarif; growth ~ Zuwachs-, Wachstumsrate; guaranteed ~ garantiertes Grundgehalt; half ~ halber Fahrpreis (Tarif); harbo(u)r ~s Hafengebühren; high ~ hoher Satz; highway ~s Straßenabgabe; hourly ~ Stundenlohnsatz; income-tax ~ Einkommensteuersatz; individual ~ Einzelprämie; initial ~

Anfangssatz, -prämie; **inland** ~ *(postage, Br.)* Inlandsporto; **insurance** ~ Versicherungsprämie; **interest** ~ Zinssatz, -fuß; **interior** ~ *(shipping)* Übergangstarif; **interstate** ~ *(US)* Frachtsatz zwischen Einzelstaaten; **introductory** ~ Einführungstarif; **job** ~ Tarifgruppe, Akkordrichtsatz; **joint** ~s Verbundstarif, *(railway)* kombinierter Frachttarif, Sammeltarif; **joint combination** ~s *(railway)* kombinierter Sammeltarif; **judgment** ~ *(fire insurance, US)* nach eigenem Ermessen festgesetzte Prämie, Selbsteinschätzung; **key** ~ *(banking, Br.)* Leitzinssatz, *(insurance)* nach Gefahrenklassen eingeteilte Grundprämie; **last-age** ~s Löschungsgebühren; **lawful** ~ gesetzlich zulässiger Tarif; **legal** ~ *(interest)* gesetzlicher Zinsfuß, *(railway)* gesetzlich anerkannter Tarif; **less-than-carload** *(LCL)* ~s *(US)* Stückguttarif; **less-than-truckload** ~ *(US)* Stückguttarif; **letter** ~ *(Br.)* Briefporto; **life** ~ gesamte Lebensversicherungsprämie; **line** ~ Mindesttarifsatz; **liner's** ~s Frachtraten nach regulären Bedingungen, Frachtraten nach den Bedingungen des Linienverkehrs; **loan** ~ durchschnittlicher Handelskredit-, Darlehnszinssatz; **local** ~s ortsübliche Sätze, *(advertising)* Anzeigentarif für ortsansässige Firmen, *(shipping)* Ortstarif, *(taxation, Br.)* Gemeindeabgaben, Kommunalsteuer, -abgabe; **Lombard** ~ Lombardzinssatz; **long-term interest** ~s Sätze für langfristiges Geld; **loose** ~ überdurchschnittlich hoher Lohn; **low** ~ niedriger Kurs (Satz); **lowest [possible]** ~ Mindestpreis, -satz, äußerst reduzierter Preis; **lump-sum** ~ Pauschalsatz; **marine** ~ Prämiensatz der Seetransportversicherung; **market** ~ Marktpreis, *(Br., discount rate)* Diskontsatz, *(stock exchange)* amtlicher Kurs, Kurswert, Börsenkurs; **marriage** ~ Zahl der Eheschließungen, Heiratsziffer; **maximum** ~ Höchstsatz, -preis, *(carrier)* Höchsttarif, *(insurance)* Höchstprämie, *(stock exchange)* Höchstkurs; **merit** ~ *(insurance)* besonders festgesetzte Versicherungsprämie; **meter** ~ *(el., US)* Tarif nach normalem Verbrauch; **mil(e)age** ~ *(car)* Kilometersatz, -tarif, *(railway)* Differenzfrachtsatz; **minimum** ~ Mindestpreis, -satz, *(employee)* Mindestlohn, *(freight)* Mindesttarif, *(insurance)* Mindestprämie, *(stock exchange)* Mindestkurs; **minimum lending** ~ *(Br.)* Mindestdiskontsatz; **minimum piece** ~ Mindeststücklohntarif; **minimum plant** ~ betrieblicher Mindestlohn; **minimum time** ~ Mindestzeitlohntarif; **mixed cargo** ~ *(Br.)* Stückguttarif; **mixed carload** ~ *(US)* Stückguttarif; **money** ~ Geldkurs; **money market** ~ Geldmarktsatz; **mortality** ~ Sterblichkeit[sziffer]; **mortgage** ~ Hypothekenzinssatz; **multiple** ~s multiple Wechselkurse; **municipal** ~s *(Br.)* Kommunalumlage, -abgabe; **net U. K.** ~ *(Br.)* Nettosteuersatz nach Anrechnung der Doppelsteuer; **newspaper** ~ Zeitungsporto; **nominal** ~ einem Wertpapier aufgedruckter Zinssatz; **normal commercial** ~ handelsüblicher Satz; **occupational** ~ üblicher Stundenlohn; **official** ~ behördlich genehmigter Frachttarif, *(stock exchange)* amtlicher Kurs; **one-time** ~ *(advertising)* Seitenpreis, Einmaltarif, Anzeigentarif für Einzelinsertionen ohne Rabatt; **one-time black-and-white** ~ Anzeigenpreis für eine Schwarz-Weißseite; **onerous** ~s nicht kostendeckende Leistungsabgaben; **opening** ~ Eröffnungs-, Anfangskurs; **open-market** ~s *(US)* Geldsätze am offenen Markt, Offenmarktsätze; **option** ~ *(Br.)* Prämiensatz; **page** ~ Seitenpreis; **ordinary** ~ normales Porto; **overtime** ~ Überstundenlohn, -satz; **overtime** ~ **of time and a half** anderthalbfacher Tarifsatz für Überstunden; **paper** ~ *(railway)* nur auf dem Papier stehender (überhöhter) Tarif; **parcels** ~ Paketgebühr; **parish** ~ *(Br.)* Kommunalabgabe; **part-time** ~ Lohn für nicht ganztägig beschäftigte Arbeitskräfte; **passenger** ~s Personentarif; **piece** ~ Stücklohn-, Akkordsatz; **poor** ~ Armenumlage; **postage** ~s *(Br.)* Porto-, Postgebühren, Posttarif; **postal** ~s Porto[gebühr]; **posted** ~ übliche Bankspesen; **preferential** ~s *(customs)* Vorzugssatz, -tarif; **premium** ~ Prämiensatz; **prevailing** ~ *(US)* Mindestlohn für Arbeiter bei öffentlichen Bauvorhaben; **previous** ~ bisheriger (letzter) Preis; **prime** ~ *(banking, US)* Leitzinssatz; **private** ~ *(Br.)* Privatdiskontsatz; **probationary** ~ Anfangsgehalt, -lohn; **production** ~ Produktionsleistung; **proportional** ~ *(railway)* Distanztarif; **public utility** ~s Gebührnisse öffentlicher Betriebe; **quantity** ~ Grossisten-, Mengentarif; **railroad** *(US)* **(railway, Br.)** ~s Eisenbahntarif[sätze]; **railroad freight** ~s *(US)* Gütertarif; **reasonable** ~ angemessener Frachtsatz; **rediscount** ~ *(US)* Diskontsatz; **reduced** ~ *(Br.)* ermäßigter Tarif; **regular** ~ feste Valuta, *(railway)* Normaltarif, *(wages)* Normallohn, -gehalt; **released** ~ *(US)* ermäßigter Tarif bei beschränkter Haftpflicht des Spediteurs; **remnant** ~ *(advertising)* verbilligter Anzeigenpreis; **remunerative** ~s kostendeckende Leistungsentgelte; **renewal** ~ Prolongationssatz; **reshipping** ~ Distanztarif; **returned-shipment** ~ *(US)* verbilligter Frachtsatz für Leergut; **river** ~ Flußfrachtsatz; **ruling**

~ bestehender Kurs; **runaway** ~ überdurchschnittlich hoher Lohn, überhöhter Akkordsatz; **salary** ~ Angestelltengehalt; **sample** ~ Tarif für Mustersendungen; **saving** ~ Sparquote; **scale** ~ *(Br.)* Staffeltarif; **schedule** ~ Tarifprämie; **seasonable** ~ *(railway)* Saisontarif [für bestimmte Waren]; **selling** ~ Verkaufs-, Briefkurs; **short** ~ *(advertising)* ermäßigter Tarif, *(fire insurance)* Versicherungsprämie für einen Zeitraum unter einem Jahr; **short-period** ~ *(insurance)* erhöhte Prämiensätze für Versicherungen unter einem Jahr; **sight** ~ Satz für Sichtwechsel; **single** ~ Einheitslohn; **small companies** ~ *(Br.)* verkürzter Steuersatz für Klein- und Mittelbetriebe; **special** ~ Zweckabgabe, *(preferential* ~*)* Vorzugssatz, -tarif; **special** ~s *(railway)* Ausnahmetarif; **specific** ~ *(insurance)* Sondertarif, *(statistics)* spezifische Verhältnisziffer; **spot** ~ Platzkurs, *(freight)* Frachttarif für Expressversand, *(stock exchange)* Kassakurs; **standard** ~ Einheits-, Normalsatz, *(advertising)* Standard-, Grundtarif, *(stock exchange)* Normalkurs, *(taxation, Br.)* [Steuer]normalsatz, *(wages)* Tariflohnsatz; **standard** ~ **per mile** Kilometersatz, -preis; **standard time** ~ Normalstundentarif; **standard wage** ~ Einheitstarif, Tariflohnsatz; **starting** ~ *(US)* Anfangsgehalt, -lohn; **state-approved** ~ staatlich genehmigter Tarif; **step** ~ stufenförmiger Satz, *(el., US)* Verbrauchstarif; **straight-line** ~ *(el., US)* vom Verbrauch unabhängiger Tarif, *(depreciation, US)* linearer Abschreibungssatz; **straight piece** ~ reiner Stücklohn; **subminimum** ~ untertariflicher Lohn; **subscription** ~ Abonnements-, Subskriptionspreis; **substandard** ~ unterdurchschnittlicher Lohnsatz für behinderte Arbeiter; **supplementary** ~ Zuschlag; **tapering** ~s Staffeltarif; **tariff** ~ *(customs)* Zollsatz, *(insurance)* Tarifprämie; **tax** ~ Veranlagungssatz, Steuersatz; **telegram** ~ Wortgebühr; **telephone** ~ *(US)* Telefongebühr, -tarif; **temporary** ~ Sonderlohnsatz; **through** ~ *(Br.)* Frachtsatz für Ladungen unter 50 kg, *(US)* Durchgangstarif; **time** ~ *(US)* Zeitlohn, *(advertising)* Serienrabatt innerhalb eines Jahres; **today's** ~ Tageskurs, Marktpreis; **tonnage** ~ Tonnenlohn; **town** ~s städtische Abgaben; **transient** ~ Anzeigentarif für Einzelinsertion ohne Rabatt; **transit** ~ verbilligter Frachttarif für Durchgangsgüter, Transittarif; **transportation** ~ Frachtsatz, -tarif; **trial** ~ Probegehalt; **two-charge** ~ *(el.)* gemischter Stromtarif, Grundgebühr und Verbrauchstarif; **uncertain** ~ veränderliche Valuta; **unchanged** ~s unveränderte Preise; **uniform** ~ Einheitsgebühr, -tarif; **union** ~ Tariflohn, Mindestlohnsatz; **usual** ~ üblicher Wechselkurs; **wage** ~ Lohntarif, -satz; **water** ~s *(Br.)* Wassergeld;

~s **and taxes** *(Br.)* Kommunalabgaben und Staatssteuern; ~ **of absenteeism** Abwesenheitsquote; ~ **of advance** Steigerungsbetrag; ~ **for advances on securities** Lombardsatz; ~**-in-aid** *(Br.)* kommunale Ausgleichsumlage; ~ **of ascent** *(airplane)* Steiggeschwindigkeit; ~ **of assessment** Veranlagungs-, Hebesatz, Steuersatz, Bewertungsmaßstab; ~s **of benefits** *(social insurance)* Unterstützungssätze, Leistungshöhe; **increased** ~s **of child benefits** erhöhte Kindergeldsätze; ~ **of building** Bautempo; ~ **per cable transfer** Satz für Kabelauszahlung; ~ **per car-mile** Kilometersatz; ~ **of carriage** Beförderungstarif; ~ **per cent** Kurs in Prozenten; ~ **to be charged for commission** Provisionsgebühr; **good** ~ **of climb** *(airplane)* gute Steigfähigkeit; ~ **of commission** Provisionssatz; ~ **of compensation** Kompensationskurs; ~ **of consideration** Prämiensatz; ~ **of consumption** Verbrauchssatz, -rate, Verbrauchszahlen; ~ **of contango** Prolongationsgebühr, Reportsatz; ~s **of contribution** Beitragssätze; ~ **of conversion** Konversionssatz, Umrechnungskurs; ~ **of corporation tax** Körperschaftssteuersatz; **letter postage** ~ **to foreign countries** *(Br.)* Auslandsbriefporto; ~ **of customs duties** Zolltarifsatz; ~ **of the day** *(stock exchange)* Tageskurs, -notierung; ~ **for day-to-day money** Tagesgeldsatz; ~ **for delivery** Löschquantum; ~ **of depreciation** Abschreibungssatz; ~ **of discount** Diskontsatz; ~ **of duty** *(Br.)* Steuer-, Zollsatz; **preferential** ~ **of duty** *(Br.)* Zollvorzugssatz, Präferenzzoll; **ad valorem** ~ **of duty** *(Br.)* Wertzollsatz; ~ **of emigration** Abwanderungsrate; ~ **of erection** Montagesatz; ~ **of estate duty** *(Br.)* Erbschaftssteuersätze, -tarif.

rate of exchange Kursstand, -verhältnis, *(agio)* Agio, *(bill of exchange)* Wechsel-, Devisen-, Valuta-, Umrechnungskurs;

at a favo(u)rable ~ zu besonders günstigem Kurs;

arbitrated ~ ermittelter Arbitrageumrechnungskurs; **forced** ~ Zwangskurs; **official fixed** ~ amtlicher Wechselkurs; **present** ~ gegenwärtige Valuta.

rate | of economy Konjunkturmaßstab; ~ **of expansion** Zuwachs-, Expansionsrate; ~ **of extraction** Förderungsquantum; ~ **of fare** Fahrpreis, Eisenbahntarif; ~ **of fluctuation** Fluktuationsrate; ~s **in force** geltende Tarife; ~ **of gain** Gewinnrate; **going** ~

on gilts *(Br.)* gegenwärtige Rendite mündelsicherer Wertpapiere; ~ **of gold** Goldkurs; ~ **for goods finished in transit** einheitlicher Tarif für während des Transports verarbeitete Ware; ~ **of growth** Zuwachs-, Wachstumsrate; ~ **of economic growth** Wachstumsrate des Sozialprodukts; ~ **of income growth** Einkommenszuwachsrate; ~ **of income tax** Einkommenssteuersatz; **highest marginal ~ of income tax** höchster Einkommenssteuersatz; ~ **of increase** Steigerungsbetrag, -satz, Zuwachsrate; ~ **of increment** Zuwachssatz; ~ **of inflation** Inflationsrate; ~ **of insurance** Versicherungsprämie, Prämiensatz; ~ **of interbank loans** Zinssatz für von Banken aufgenommene Gelder, Tagesgeldsatz.

rate of interest Zinsfuß, -satz, *(participation)* Beteiligungsquote; **attractive ~s** anziehende Zinssätze; **contract ~s** vertraglich ausbedungene Zinssätze; **effective ~** effektive Verzinsung; **high ~** hoher Zinsfuß; **legal ~** gesetzlicher Zinsfuß; **sliding ~** gleitender Zinsfuß; **stipulated ~** vereinbarter Zinssatz; **~ on mortgage loans** Hypothekenzinssatz.

rate | of investment Investitionsrate, -grad; ~ **of issue** Ausgabe-, Emissionskurs; ~ **for the job** Lohnkosten für die einzelne Arbeitsverrichtung; ~ **of levy** *(EC)* Abschöpfungsbetrag; ~ **of living** Lebensstandard; ~ **for loans on collateral** Lombardsatz; ~ **of mail transfer** *(US)* Satz für briefliche Auszahlung; ~ **of the market** Platzkurs; **special ~s including free mil(e)age** Pauschaltarif inkl. aller gefahrenen Kilometer; **~s for money on loan** *(banking)* Geldsätze; ~ **of money growth** Geldzuwachsrate; ~ **of mortality** Sterblichkeitsziffer, -rate; **~s obtained at today's market** heute erzielte Börsenkurse; ~ **of operations** Betriebsvolumen; ~ **of option** *(Br.)* Prämiensatz; ~ **of output** Ausstoßziffer; **actual ~ of output** Ist-Ausstoß; ~ **of pay** Lohnsatz, -tarif; **flat ~ of pay** Tarifgehalt; **hourly ~ of pay** Stundenlohnsatz; ~ **of pension** Pensionshöhe; **weekly ~ of pension** wöchentliche Rentenzahlung; ~ **of performance** Leistungsziffer; **annual ~ of population increase** jährlicher Bevölkerungszuwachs; **percentage ~ of population growth per annum** jährlicher Bevölkerungszuwachs in Prozenten; ~ **of portion** Beteiligungsquote; ~ **of postage** Portosatz; **~s of postage** Posttarif, -gebühren; ~ **of premium** Prämiensatz; ~ **of price increase (rise)** Preissteigerungsrate, Rate des Preisanstiegs; ~ **for printed matter** Drucksachenporto; ~ **of private saving** privater Sparprozentsatz; **~s of production** Produktionshöhe, -ziffern; **increased ~ of production of a machine** erhöhte Produktionsleistung einer Maschine; ~ **of productivity** Produktivitätsrate; ~ **of profit** Gewinnsatz, Gewinnrate; ~ **of progression** Progressionssatz; **annual ~s of property tax** jährliche Vermögenssteuersätze; ~ **of redemption** Rückzahlungs-, Einlösungskurs, Tilgungsrate; **~s of relief** *(income tax, Br.)* ermäßigte Steuersätze; ~ **of remuneration** Tarifentgelt, Vergütungstarif; **lower ~ of remuneration** niedrigeres Arbeitsentgelt; ~ **of repayment** Tilgungsrate; ~ **of return** *(US)* Kapitalverzinsung; **fixed ~ of return** feste Rendite; **highest ~ of return on investment** *(US)* höchste Investitionsrendite; **low ~ of return** geringe Rendite; **real post-tax ~ of return on money** nach Steuerzahlungen tatsächlich erzielte Geldrendite; ~ **of settlement** Abrechnungs-, Kompensationskurs; ~ **of shares** Aktienkurs; ~ **of shipping** Frachttarif; ~ **of stock building** Lageraufüllungsprozentsatz; ~ **of stock turnover** Lagerumschlagsgeschwindigkeit; ~ **of stockshedding** Lagerabbaurate, -satz; ~ **of stowage** Stauerlohn; ~ **of subscription** Bezugspreis, Abonnementsgebühr, *(stock exchange)* Zeichnungskurs; **reduced ~ of tax** verkürzter Steuersatz; ~ **of taxation** Steuersatz; **maximal ~ of taxation** Spitzensteuersatz; **progressive ~s of taxation** Staffelung der (gestaffelte) Steuersätze; **~s and taxes** *(Br.)* Kommunal- und Staatssteuern; ~ **of turnover** Umsatzziffer, -geschwindigkeit, Umschlagsgeschwindigkeit, *(employees)* Fluktuationsquote; ~ **of unemployment** Arbeitslosenprozentsatz, Arbeitslosenquote; **seasonable adjusted ~ of unemployment** saisonbedinger Arbeitslosenprozentsatz; **full ~ of unemployment benefit** höchste Arbeitslosenunterstützung; **higher ~ of vat** höherer Mehrwertsteuersatz; ~ **of wages** Lohnsatz, -tarif; ~ **of waste** Schwundsatz; ~ **of wear and tear** Abnutzungssatz; ~ **of withdrawal** Entnahmesatz; **~ at which the franc has been established** Stützungskurs des Franken;

~ *(v.) (appraise)* [ab]schätzen, [be]werten, bemessen, berechnen, taxieren, *(assess, Br.)* einschätzen, einstufen, besteuern, veranlagen, zur Kommunalabgabe heranziehen, *(employees)* beurteilen, *(range)* bestimmten Wert haben, rangieren, *(ship goods, US)* Waren zu einem bestimmten Frachtsatz versenden; ~ **s. o.** j. nach seinen Fähigkeiten beurteilen, *(assess)* j. zu einer Umlage heranziehen; ~ **s. o. up** *(insurance)* j. höher (in eine höhere Prämiengruppe) einstufen;

~ **a building for insurance purposes** Gebäude für die Versicherung schätzen lassen; ~ **a coin** Münze taxieren; ~ **s. one's fortune at $ 400.000** jds. Vermögen auf 400.000 Dollar taxieren; ~ **among one's friends** zu seinen Freunden zählen; ~ **goods** *(US)* Waren zu einem bestimmten Frachtsatz versenden; ~ **heavily** kräftig besteuern; ~ **s. o. high** j. hoch einschätzen; ~ **high in** hohe Quote haben; ~ **as hospitable** für gastfreundlich halten; ~ **a pension** Pensionshöhe festsetzen; ~ **s. one's performance** jds. Leistung bewerten; ~ **on points** nach Punkten bewerten; ~ **s. one's property at £ 100 per annum** 100 £ Vermögenssteuer für j. festsetzen; ~ **a ship** Schiff klassifizieren; ~ **the tare** Tara berechnen; ~ **up** höher versichern, in eine höhere Prämienstufe einstufen;

to accord s. o. favo(u)rable ~s jem. einen günstigen Tarif zugestehen (einräumen); **to advance the ~** Kurs heraufsetzen; **to apply a ~ of five per cent** Satz von 5% in Anrechnung bringen; **to be increasing at a fearful ~** beängstigend zunehmen; **to be quoted at the ~ of ...** zum Kurs von ... notiert werden; **to be subject to preferentially low ~s of tax** Steuervorzugssätzen unterliegen; **to become liable for ~s as occupier** als Grundstücksbesitzer für Kommunalabgaben erfaßbar sein; **to buy things at a ~ of 8 $ a hundred** hundert Stück zum Preis von je acht Dollar kaufen; **to cover a ~** Kurs sichern; **to cut ~s** Gebühren senken; **to cut the ~ of discount** Diskont herabsetzen; **to enjoy a fast ~ of growth** hohe Zuwachsrate haben; **to fix ~s** *(stock exchange)* Kurse (Preise) festsetzen, *(tariff policy)* tarifieren; **to hedge a ~** Kurs sichern; **to improve (the) ~** Kurs heraufsetzen; **to lay a ~ on a building** Hauszinssteuer erheben; **to levy a ~** *(Br.)* Kommunalabgabe erheben; **to live at the ~ of 9000 $ a year** 9000 Dollar im Jahr ausgeben; **to lose at the ~ of ten pounds a week** wöchentlich 10 Pfund zusetzen; **to lower the ~** Kurs herabsetzen; **to mark the ~ down** Satz herabsetzen; **to pay s. o. at the ~ of 4 dollars an hour** jem. einen Stundenlohn von 4 Dollar zahlen; **to put up the ~ of a pension** Pension erhöhen; **to quote ~s** Kurse angeben; **to quote a ~ for an open policy** Prämiensatz für eine Generalversicherung mitteilen; **to reduce ~s** Umlagen herabsetzen; **to reduce the discount** *(Br.)* **(rediscount, US) ~** Bankdiskont (Diskontsatz) herabsetzen; **to sell s. th. at a reasonable ~** etw. zu einem vernünftigen Preis verkaufen; **to settle for rises based on a productivity ~** Tariferhöhungen auf Produktivitätszunahmen abstellen; **to take the ~** Geld aufnehmen; **to travel at a ~ of 60 miles an hour** mit einer Geschwindigkeit von 100 Stundenkilometern fahren; **to trim slightly the current ~ of spending** Umfang der vorhergesehenen Investitionen leicht verringern; **to value at a high ~** *(US)* hoch bewerten (veranschlagen); **to value at a low ~** *(US)* niedrig einschätzen;

~ **adjustment** Prämienregulierung; **excessive basic ~ adjustment** *(income tax, Br.)* Steuerausgleich für fälschlich mit Sätzen des unteren Proportionalbereichs besteuerte Einkünfte; ~ **aid** *(Br.)* kommunale Unterstützung; **~-aided** *(Br.)* mit gemeindlicher (kommunaler) Unterstützung, gemeindeabgabenbegünstigt; **~-aided person** *(Br.)* Unterstützungsempfänger; ~ **announcement** Preisankündigung, *(advertising)* Mitteilung über die Anzeigentarife, Anzeigenpreisliste; ~ **association** Tarifgemeinschaft; ~ **base** Richtsatz; **advertising ~ base** Anzeigenrichtsatz; **circulation ~ base** auf der Auflagenhöhe beruhende Anzeigenpreisliste; ~ **basis** Frachtberechnungsgrundlage; ~ **book** Steuerrolle, Umlagenregister, *(advertising)* Zeitungskatalog, Nachschlagewerk, *(freight)* Tarifbuch, Preisliste, *(municipal corporation, Br.)* Umlageregister; **wage ~ bracket** Tariflohngruppe; **~-of-return calculation** Renditekalkulation; ~ **card** *(advertising, US)* Preistafel, Anzeigentarif, -preisliste, Tarif, Annoncenpreisstaffel, Inseratenpreisliste; ~ **case** Tarifstreik; ~ **change** Tarif-, Prämienänderung; ~ **check** Überprüfung von Frachtrechnungen; ~ **class** *(broadcasting)* Tarifklasse; ~ **collection** Umlagenerhebung; ~ **collector** Gemeindesteuereinnehmer; ~ **collector's office** Stadtsteueramt; ~ **competition** Prämienkonkurrenz; ~ **cut** Tarifkürzung; ~ **cutting** Fracht-, Tarifermäßigung, -herabsetzung, -senkung, -unterbietung, Anwendung der Akkordschere, *(shipping)* Frachtunterbietung, *(wages, US)* Lohnkürzung; **~-cutting** verbilligend; ~ **decrease** Tarifverbilligung; ~ **deficiency grants (payments)** *(Br.)* Ausgleichsleistungen an finanzschwache Gemeinden, Zuweisungen im vertikalen Finanzbereich; ~ **demand** Kommunalabgabenanforderung; ~ **deregulation** Tariffreigabe; ~ **differential** Tarifgefälle; ~ **discrimination** diskriminierender Listenpreis, Tarifdiskriminierung; ~ **factors** Tariffaktoren; ~ **filing** Tarifklage; ~ **fixer** Tarifbehörde; ~ **fixing** *(US)* Kursfestsetzung, *(piece wage)* Akkordberechnung; **~-fixing** kursbestimmend, *(freight)* tarifbestimmend; **to live a**

~-free life kommunalabgabenfrei wohnen; **~ of return function** Kapitalverzinsungsfunktion; **general ~ fund** *(Br.)* kommunales Sondervermögen; **~ guarantee (guaranty)** Kursgarantie, -sicherung; **~ hike** Gebühren-, Tariferhöhung; **~ holder** *(advertising)* Komplettierungsanzeige, Rabattkunde, -schinder, *(US)* laufende kleine Anzeigen, Dauerinserat; **~ increase** Gebühren-, Tariferhöhung; **~ level** *(insurance)* Prämienhöhe; **~ limit** *(mail, US)* Höchstgewicht; **~ maker** Tarifberechner, Gebührenfestsetzer; **~ making** Gebührenfestsetzung, *(insurance)* Prämienfestsetzung, *(wages)* Tarifberechnung, -bildung.

rate-making tarifbestimmend;

~ association Tarifverband; **~ body** *(US)* Tarifbehörde; **~ margin** Kursspielraum, Kursmarge; **~ method** Tarif-, Prämienbildung, -festsetzungsmethode.

rate|notification *(tel.)* Gebührenansage; **~-paying** steuerumlagezahlend; **~ policy** Tarifpolitik; **~ of time preference** Zeitpräferenzrate; **~ protection** Gebührenschutz; **for ~ purposes** zu Tarifzwecken; **~-raising** tariferhöhend; **~ range** Tarifspanne; **~ rebate** *(low incomes, Br.)* Ermäßigung der Kommunalabgaben; **~s receipt** *(Br.)* Kommunalabgabenquittung; **~ reduction** Tarifkürzung, -ermäßigung, *(municipal accounting, Br.)* Umlageermäßigung; **~-regulating** tarifbestimmend; **~ regulation** *(insurance industry)* *(US)* Festlegung des Höchsttarifs; **~ scale** *(US)* gestaffelter Frachttarif, Staffel-, Zonentarif; **~ schedule** Anteilsaufstellung; **advertising ~ schedule** Anzeigentarif; **~ setting** *(US)* Lohnfestsetzung, Tarifbestimmung, *(time study)* Vorgabezeitermittlung; **joint ~ setting** *(US)* Lohnfestsetzung durch Betriebsführung und Betriebsrat; **~-setting** tarifbestimmend; **temporary ~ sheet** zur Zeit gültige Anzeigenpreisliste; **~ structure** Kursgefüge; **~ support grant** *(Br.)* Staatszuschuß an die Kommunen, kommunale Finanzausgleichszuweisung, Schlüsselzuweisung; **~ supporting** Kursstützung; **~ tariff** *(carrier)* Speditionssatz; **first-~ teacher** erstklassiger Lehrer; **~ treatment** Tarifbehandlung, -regelung; **~ war** *(US)* Tarifkrieg, -kampf, Preiskampf.

rat(e)ability [Ab]schätzbarkeit, *(customs)* Zollpflichtigkeit, *(municipal tax)* Abgaben-, Kommunalsteuerpflicht, *(tax)* Umlagepflicht.

rat(e)able *(Br.)* verhältnismäßig, anteilmäßig, *(customs)* zollpflichtig, *(estimable)* [ab]schätzbar, *(municipal tax)* veranlagungspflichtig, abgaben-, kommunalsteuerpflichtig, *(tax)* taxierbar, besteuerbar, umlagepflichtig;

~ property der Besteuerung unterliegendes Vermögen, *(Br.)* steuerpflichtiger Grundbesitz; **~ value** *(Br.)* steuerbarer Wert, Einheitswert.

rated eingeschätzt, klassifiziert, *(municipal taxation)* gemeindesteuerpflichtig;

to be highly (heavily) ~ hoch besteuert sein; **to be ~ for insurance purposes** zu Versicherungszwecken geschätzt werden; **to be ~ of the best managed companies** zu den Unternehmen mit dem besten Vorstand gehören;

~ tax Reparationssteuer; **~ value of property** Mietertragswert eines Grundstückes.

ratee *(US)* Prüfling [in einer Leistungsprüfung].

rateless von der Umlagepflicht befreit.

ratepayer *(Br.)* Kommunalsteuerpflichtiger, umlagepflichtiger Grundbesitzer, Gemeindeabgabenpflichtiger, -steuerzahler, Anlagenzahler;

~ in arrears rückständiger Kommunalabgabenpflichtiger.

ratepaying umlage-, kommunalsteuerpflichtig.

rater Taxator, Schätzer, *(US)* [Leistungs]prüfer, Beurteilender;

a first ~ Schiff erster Klasse.

ratification *(consent)* Genehmigung, Bestätigung, Anerkennung, *(pol.)* Ratifizierung, Ratifikation, Heilung;

express ~ ausdrückliche Zustimmung; **implied ~** stillschweigende Zustimmung;

~ made after full age als Volljähriger vorgenommene Genehmigung; **~ of directors' acts** Entlastung des Vorstands, Vorstandsentlastung; **~ of executive committee's acts** Entlastung des Aufsichtsrats; **~ of an authorized signature** nachträgliche Anerkennung einer berechtigten Unterschriftsleistung; **to deposit the ~** Ratifikationsurkunde hinterlegen;

~ clause Genehmigungsklausel.

ratifier Ratifizierender.

ratify *(v.)* *(confirm)* bestätigen, ratifizieren, *(consent)* genehmigen, übereinkommen, anerkennen;

~ a contract einem Vertrag zustimmen, Vertrag bestätigen (unterzeichnen); **~ the governor's nomination** Ernennung des Gouverneurs bestätigen; **~ a sale made under power of attorney** einem vom bevollmächtigten Vertreter getätigten Verkauf zustimmen; **~ a treaty** Vertrag ratifizieren.

ratifying bestätigend.

rating *(amount fixed, Br.)* [Steuer]satz, zu zahlende Steuer, Gemeindesteuerbetrag, -abgabe, städtische[r] Umlage[betrag], Beitragsbemessung, *(appraisal)* Bemessung, Bewertung, Einschätzung, [Ab]schätzung, Taxieren, Taxierung, *(assessment, Br.)* [Steuer]einschätzung, Veranlagung, Heranziehung zu einer Umlage (Kommunalabgabe), kommunale Besteuerung, Umlagenerhebung, *(banking)* Krediteinschätzung, Bonitätsprüfung, *(broadcasting)* Hörerbefragung [über Beliebtheit von Sendungen], *(class)* Klasse, Kategorie, *(collection of rates, Br.)* Heranziehung zu Kommunalabgaben, Umlagenerhebung, *(financial standing)* finanzielle Stellung, *(fixing of rates)* Tarifierung, Tariffestsetzung, *(insurance business)* Prämienfestsetzung, *(mar., Br.)* Rang eines Matrosen, *(performance of machine)* Leistung, *(position)* Rang, finanzielle Stellung [eines Unternehmers], *(railway)* Tarif, *(ranging)* Klassifizierung, Klasseneinteilung nach Rangklassen;

~s *(US, stock exchange)* Effektenbewertung, *(television)* Einschaltquote, Einschaltziffern;

A ~ erste Anlagen; **capital ~** *(US)* finanzielle Bewertung, Kapitalbewertung; **class ~** *(railway)* Tarifeinstufung; **classification ~** Tarifeinstufung; **competitive ~** Festsetzung von Konkurrenztarifen; **continuous ~** *(machine)* Dauerbelastung; **credit ~** *(US)* Einschätzung der Kreditfähigkeit, Bonitätsprüfung; **efficiency ~** Leistungsbeurteilung, -analyse; **employee ~** *(US)* Beurteilung der Arbeitnehmer, Angestellteneinstufung; **experience ~** *(US)* Leistungsbeurteilung, -einstufung; **individual ~** *(insurance)* Prämienanpassung an das konkrete Risiko; **job ~** *(US)* Arbeitsbewertung; **merit ~** *(US)* Leistungsbeurteilung, -bewertung; **mutual ~** *(US)* gegenseitige Beurteilung [von Betriebsangehörigen]; **performance ~** *(US)* Leistungsbeurteilung; **qualification ~** *(US)* Eigenschaftsbeurteilung; **railway ~** Festsetzung der Eisenbahntarife; **service ~** *(US)* Leistungsanalyse; **special ~** *(US)* Kreditauskunft; **treasury ~** *(car)* Steuerleistung;

officers and ~s *(ship)* Offiziere und Unteroffiziere; **~ of the entire mortgage pattern** Abschätzung zwecks hypothekarischer Beleihung; **~ by points** punktuelle Bewertung; **~ of premium** Prämienberechnung; **~ of supervisors** Leistungsanalyse von Vorgesetzten; **~ of warehouses** Festsetzung von Feuerversicherungsprämien für öffentliche Speicher;

~ Act *(Br.)* Gemeindeumlagegesetz; **~ and Valuation Act** *(Br.)* Gesetz über die Neufestsetzung von Einheitswerten; **~ agreement** Tarifvereinbarung; **~ appeal** Einspruch gegen zu hohe Einschätzung [des Firmenwertes]; **~ area** *(Br.)* kommunaler Steuer-, Veranlagungs-, Umlagenbezirk; **~ area** *(insurance business)* Versicherungs[tarif]bezirk; **~ assessment** Einschätzung der Kreditfähigkeit, *(Br.)* Steuer-, [insbesondere] Firmenveranlagung; **~ authority** *(Br.)* kommunale Steuerbehörde, Umlagebehörde; **~ book** *(US)* Sammelauskunfts-, Bewertungsbuch, Unterlagen einer Kreditauskunftei; **~ bureau** Prämien-, Tarifbüro, *(insurance business)* Zweckverband; **~ column** Tarifrubrik; **~ committee** *(assessment, Br.)* Bewertungsausschuß, *(employees)* Beurteilungsausschuß; **~ engineer** Prämiensachverständiger; **~ error** Beurteilungsfehler; **~ firm** Unternehmen zur Feststellung von Einschaltquoten; **~ flop** vom Publikum abgewertetes Fernsehprogramm; **~ form** Beurteilungsformular; **~ freedom** *(insurance business)* Tariffreiheit; **~ measures** Festsetzung der Prämienhöhe; **~ method** *(insurance business)* Prämienfestsetzungsmethode; **~ office** Prämienberechnungsstelle; **~ period** Beurteilungszeitraum für [Gehaltseinstufungen]; **experience ~ plan** aufgrund von Erfahrungen aufgestelltes Prämienschema; **~ point** Bewertungspunkt; **~ procedure** [Gehalts]einstufungsverfahren; **~ program(me)** Beurteilungsprogramm für Gehaltseinstufung; **~ reform** Abgabenreform; **to claim ~-relief** *(Br.)* Vergünstigung bei der Festsetzung der Kommunalabgabe beantragen; **~ scale** Schätz-, Beurteilungsskala; **~ system** *(employees)* Leistungswesen, *(fire insurance)* Prämienfestsetzungssystem, *(freight)* Tarifsystem, *(municipal undertaking)* Gemeindeabgabensystem; **~ table** *(securities, US)* Bewertungstabelle; **~ up** Festsetzung höherer Prämien; **~ valuation** *(Br.)* Grundsteuereinschätzung.

ratio Verhältnis[zahl], Proportion, Verteilungsschlüssel, Koeffizient, Quotient, *(balance sheet)* Wertverhältnis;

in the ~ of im Verhältnis von; **in equal ~** verhältnismäßig; **in inverse ~** im umgekehrten Verhältnis;

bond-stock ~ Renditeverhältnis; **capital structure ~** Kapitalstrukturverhältnis; **capital turnover ~** Kapitalumsatzverhältnis; **cash position ~** Kassenstandskoeffizient; **clearing ~** Verrechnungsschlüssel; **collection ~** Forderungsumschlagzif-

fer; **cover ~** *(bank notes)* Deckungsverhältnis; **current [position]** ~ Verhältnis zwischen Umlaufvermögen und kurzfristigen Schulden, Flüssigkeitsverhältnis (Liquiditätsstatus) eines Unternehmens; **distribution ~** Verteilungsschlüssel; **electoral ~** Wahlkoeffizient; **equity ~** Verhältnis der Aktiva zum Eigenkapital, Eigenkapitalquote, -koeffizient; **expense ~** Aufwendungsquote, Unkostensatz; **financial ~** Verhältnis der finanziellen Mittel; **fixed ~** festes Verteilungsverhältnis; **gross profit ~** Rohgewinnquotient; **inventory turnover ~** Umschlagshäufigkeit der Vorräte; **investment ~** Investitionsquote; **liabilities to worth ~** Verhältnis sämtlicher Verbindlichkeiten zum Eigenkapital; **liquidity ~** *(banking)* Liquiditätskoeffizient, -quote; **loss ~** *(insurance)* Schadensquote; **minimum ~** Mindestverhältnis; **operating ~** Betriebs[wirtschaftlichkeits]koeffizient; **price-earnings ~** Kurs-Gewinnverhältnis; **profit ~** Gewinnverhältnis; **reserve ~** *(US)* Flüssigkeitskoeffizient (Liquiditätsspielraum) der Federal-Reserve-Banken; **rule-of-thumb ~** über den Daumen gepeilter Verteilungsschlüssel; **turnover ~** Umschlagshäufigkeit der Vorräte; **working-capital ~** Betriebskapitalverhältnis;
~ **of allotment** Zuteilungsquote; ~ **of components** Mischungsverhältnis; ~ **of current assets to total liabilities** Verhältnis der flüssigen Aktiva zu den gesamten Verbindlichkeiten; ~ **between supply and demand** Verhältnis zwischen Angebot und Nachfrage; **average ~ of depreciation** durchschnittliches Abschreibungsverhältnis; ~ **of distribution** Verteilungsschlüssel; ~ **of exchange** Wechselparität; ~ **of indebtedness to net capital** Verschuldungskoeffizient; **high ~ of old people** hoher Prozentsatz alter Leute; ~ **of sales to receivables** Kontoumsatz; **military ~ of strength** militärisches Kräfteverhältnis; **60 - 40 ~ of text to advertising** Verhältnis von 60% Text zu 40% Anzeigenraum; ~ **of wages and salaries to national product** Lohnquote; ~ **of working expenses** Betriebskostenkoeffizient; **to contain a high ~ of old people** größtenteils aus alten Leuten bestehen;
~ **analysis** Analyse der Bilanzverhältniszahlen, Bilanzanalyse, Bilanzuntersuchung; ~ **chart** Verhältnistabelle; ~ **delay study** Zeithäufigkeitsstudie, Multimomentverfahren; ~ **figure** Verhältniszahl; **common ~ positions** vergleichbare Verhältnispositionen; ~ **scale** Verhältnismaßstab.
ration Ration, *(mil.)* Verpflegungssatz, Tagesration, Portion, *(rationing)* Zuteilung;
off the ~ unrationiert, nicht bewirtschaftet, marken-, punktfrei;
~s Nahrungsmittel, Verpflegung;
basic ~ Normalzuteilung, **basic petrol ~** Benzinnormalzuteilung; **C ~** eiserne Ration von 3.500 Kalorien; **daily ~** Tagesration; **emergency ~** eiserne Ration; **extra ~** Sonderzuteilung; **food ~** Lebensmittelzuteilung; **iron ~** eiserne Ration; **monthly ~** monatliche Zuteilung; **travel ~s** Reiseproviant;
~ *(v.)* *(control)* rationieren, in Rationen zuteilen, der Zwangsbewirtschaftung unterwerfen, [zwangs]bewirtschaften, *(currency)* kontingentieren, *(mil.)* verpflegen;
~ **an army** Armee verpflegen; ~ **[out] bread** Brot rationieren; **to be on short ~** mit gekürzten Rationen auskommen müssen; **to dispense ~s** Rationen ausgeben; **to draw ~s** Rationen beziehen; **to live on lean ~s** mit verkürzten Rationen auskommen müssen; **to put on [short] ~s** auf [knappe] Rationen setzen; **to slash rations** Rationen kürzen; **to shorten a ~** Ration kürzen; **to take s. th. off the ~** Rationierung für etw. aufheben;
~ **board** Kartenstelle; ~ **book** Lebensmittel-, Zuteilungskarte; **~-book holder** Karteninhaber; ~ **card** Lebensmittel-, Rationierungs-, Zuteilungskarte, Bezugsschein; **~-card agency** Karten-, Zuteilungsstelle; ~ **coupon** Lebensmittelkartenabschnitt; ~ **cut** Rations-, Zuteilungskürzung; **~-free** markenfrei; ~ **money** Verpflegungsgeld; ~ **period** Karten-, Zuteilungsperiode; ~ **rates** Rationssätze; ~ **strength** *(mil.)* Verpflegungsstärke; ~ **ticket** Lebensmittelkarte.
rational rational, zweckmäßig, *(able to reason)* vernünftig, verständig;
~ **argument** Vernunftgrund; ~ **behavio(u)r** *(economic theory)* vernünftiges Verhalten; ~ **doubts** begründete Zweifel; ~ **dress** Reformkleidung; ~ **employment** rationelle Ausnutzung; ~ **explanation** vernünftige Erklärung; ~ **sales** rationelles Verkaufsargument.
rationalism Rationalismus.
rationalist Rationalist.
rationalistic rationalistisch.
rationalization Rationalisierung, Wirtschaftlichkeit, wirtschaftliche Vereinfachung;
industrial ~ betriebswirtschaftliche Rationalisierung;

~ **advantage** Rationalisierungsvorteil; ~ **boom** Rationalisierungskonjunktur; ~ **efforts** Rationalisierungsanstrengungen; ~ **measures** Rationalisierungsmaßnahmen; **for ~ purposes** zu Rationalisierungszwecken.
rationalize *(v.)* rationalisieren.
rationed rationiert, [zwangs]bewirtschaftet, karten-, bezugsscheinpflichtig;
~ **goods** bewirtschaftete Güter; ~ **item** rationierter Artikel.
rationing Rationierung, Zuteilung, Kontingentierung, Bewirtschaftung, Zwangswirtschaft;
food ~ Rationierung von Lebensmitteln;
~ **of consumption** Verbrauchsregelung; ~ **of credit** Kreditkontingentierung; ~ **of foreign exchange** Devisenbewirtschaftung, -zwangswirtschaft;
~ **arrangements** Rationierungsmaßnahmen, Maßnahmen zur Warenbewirtschaftung; ~ **card** Zuteilungskarte; **~-card agency** Karten-, Zuteilungsstelle; ~ **program(me)** Bewirtschaftungsprogramm; ~ **regulations** Rationierungsvorschriften; ~ **scheme** Bewirtschaftungsplan; ~ **system** Rationierungssystem; -wesen, Bewirtschaftungssystem.
ratten *(Br., sl.)* an der Arbeit hindern, Sabotage treiben, sabotieren, *(unionism, Br., sl.)* zum Gewerkschaftsbeitritt nötigen.
rattener *(Br.)* Saboteur.
rattening *(Br., sl.)* Arbeitsbehinderung, Sabotage.
ratter politischer Überläufer, Deserteur, Saboteur.
rattery Parteiverrat.
ratting *(pol.)* Umfall.
rattle *(sl.)* leeres Geschwätz, Gerede;
~ *(v.)* rattern, klappern;
~ **the begging bowl** mit der Sammelbüchse klappern; ~ **a bill through the house** *(Br.)* Gesetz durchpeitschen;
~ **trap** Klapperkasten, -kiste.
rattlebrain Hohlkopf.
rattler *(car)* Klapperkiste, *(railway, sl.)* Güterschnellzug, *(stunner, sl.)* tolle Sache.
rattling | rate tolle Geschwindigkeit; ~ **good speech** glänzende Rede; ~ **time** herrliche Zeit; ~ **trade** florierendes Geschäft.
rave *(v.)* phantasieren, *(sl.)* sich begeistert äußern, *(storm)* toben, wüten, heulen.
ravine Schlucht.
ravish vergewaltigen.
ravisher Notzuchttäter.
ravishment Vergewaltigung, Notzucht.
raw *(land, US)* unkultiviert, unbebaut, *(not manufactured)* roh, unbe-, unverarbeitet, *(untrained)* unerfahren, ungeschult, ohne [jede] Praxis;
~ **or processed** unbearbeitet oder bearbeitet;
to touch s. o. on the ~ j. an seiner empfindlichen Stelle treffen; ~ **data** Primärmaterial; ~ **deal** unfaire (rüde) Behandlung; **to get a ~ deal** unfair behandelt werden; ~ **fruits** frisches Obst; ~ **goods** Warenladungsgut.
raw material Rohmaterial, -stoff, Werkstoff, Ausgangsmaterial; **duty-free ~** zollfreier Rohstoff; **~s used** Rohstoffverbrauch; **~s and supplies** *(balance sheet)* Roh-, Hilfs- und Betriebsstoffe; **to be lacking entirely in ~** über keinerlei Rohstoffbasis verfügen; **to meet the requirements of ~** Rohstoffbedarf decken.
raw-material | board Rohstoffausschuß; ~ **content** Rohstoffgehalt; ~ **imports** Rohstoffeinfuhren; ~ **inventory** Rohstofflager; ~ **market** Rohstoffmarkt; ~ **producing area** Rohstoffgebiet; ~ **producing country** Rohstoffland; ~ **purchases** Rohstoffeinkäufe; ~ **requirements** Rohstoffbedarf; ~ **shortage** Rohstoffknappheit; ~ **supply** Rohstoffversorgung.
raw | produce (products) Rohprodukte, -stoffe; ~ **silk** Rohseide; ~ **state** Ursprungszustand.
ray | of hope Hoffnungsschimmer; ~ **of truth** Körnchen Wahrheit.
rayon Kunstseide.
raze *(v.)* ausradieren.
razed by earthquake von einem Erdbeben dem Erdboden gleichgemacht.
razon bomb ferngesteuerte Bombe.
razor's edge *(fig.)* kritische Lage;
to be on a ~ auf des Messers Schneide stehen.
razzia Razzia.
razzle Bummel, Saufgelage;
~-dazzle *(sl.)* Kuddelmuddel;
to go on a ~ auf den Bummel gehen.
re *(lat.) (law)* in Sachen, gegen, *(letterhead)* bezüglich, betreffs, wegen;
in ~ X versus Y in Sachen X gegen Y.
reacceleration of growth erneute Wachstumsbeschleunigung.

reaccount *(bill of exchange)* Rückrechnung.
reaccuse *(v.)* wieder (erneut) anklagen.
reach Trag-, Reichweite, Bereich, *(canal)* Kanalabschnitt, *(extension)* Spielraum, Ausdehnung, Bereich, *(influence)* Einflußbereich, -sphäre, *(mental capacity)* Fassungskraft, Leistungsfähigkeit;
> **as far as the eye can ~** so weit das Auge reicht; **beyond the ~ of accident** unfallsicher; **out of s. one's ~** unerschwinglich; **within the ~ of all** jedermann zugänglich; **within easy ~ of the station** in Bahnhofsnähe; **within the ~ of a small purse** erschwinglich; **higher (upper) ~es** höhere Stellen;
> **~** *(v.)* erreichen, erlangen, *(amount)* ausmachen, sich belaufen, *(goods)* eintreffen, *(influence)* beeinflussen, *(print.)* [Neuauflage] erleben;
> **~ s. o.** j. ansprechen, *(come to)* bei jem. eintreffen; **~ the age limit** Altersgrenze erreichen; **~ an agreement** Vereinbarung treffen (erzielen), zu einer Verständigung gelangen; **not ~ a case** Fall nicht umfassen (einschließen); **~ ten editions** zehn Auflagen erleben; **~ the end of the chapter** Kapitel beenden; **~ high** nach Hohem streben; **~ one's majority** volljährig werden; **~ out to** Verbindung herstellen; **~ port** in einen Hafen einlaufen; **~ a high price** hohen Preis erzielen; **~ the second reading** *(bill)* zur zweiten Lesung anstehen; **~ an understanding** Vereinbarung (Verständigung) erzielen;
> **to be beyond ~ of human aid** jenseits menschlicher Hilfe sein; **to be within the ~ of s. one's pocket** im Rahmen von jds. finanziellen Möglichkeiten liegen; **to come within ~** in greifbare Nähe rücken; **to have within ~** in Reichweite haben; **to put s. th. out of s. one's ~** etw. jds. Zugriff entziehen.
reach-me-down Anzug von der Stange;
> **~s** Konfektionskleidung, -ware, Kleider von der Stange;
> **~** *(a.)* zum Gebrauch fertig, billig, *(clothes)* konfektioniert.
reacquire *(v.)* wiedererlangen, zurückerwerben.
reacquired capital stock Portefeuille eigener Aktien.
reacquirer Rückerwerber.
reacquisition Wiedererlangung, -erwerb, Rückerwerb.
react *(v.)* rück-, entgegenwirken, reagieren, wieder aufführen, *(stock exchange)* weichen;
> **~ to applause** auf Beifall reagieren; **~ markedly lower** *(stock exchange)* mit erheblich niedrigeren Notierungen einsetzen; **~ on each other** sich gegenseitig beeinflussen; **~ with shock** Schockwirkung zeigen; **~ against a political system** Reaktionen gegen ein politisches System zeigen; **~ to kind treatment** auf freundliche Behandlung ansprechen.
reaction Reaktion, Rück-, Gegenwirkung, *(mil.)* Gegenstoß, *(pol.)* reaktionäre Bewegung, Reaktion, Rückschritt, Gegenbewegung, *(response)* Stellungnahme, *(stock exchange)* Umschwung, Rückschlag, -gang, rückwertige Bewegung;
> **mixed ~** geteilte Reaktion; **sharp ~** *(stock exchange)* scharfer Rückschlag;
> **~ of cost on prices** Kostenreaktion auf die Preise; **~ to a piece of news** Reaktion auf eine Nachricht; **~s of a policy** politische Auswirkungen; **~ in prices** Preis-, Kursrückgang; **~ to a proposal** Reaktion auf einen Vorschlag; **~ on the stock market** Rückwirkung auf den Effektenmarkt;
> **to suffer a slight ~** leichten [Kurs]rückgang erleiden;
> **~ period (time)** Schrecksekunde.
reactionary Reaktionär;
> **prototypical ~** Prototyp des Reaktionärs;
> **~** *(a.)* reaktionär, *(stock exchange)* rückgängig;
> **~ blimp** Erzreaktionär.
reactionist Reaktionär.
reactivate *(v.)* wieder in Gang setzen.
reactivation Wiederingangsetzung.
reactor Kernreaktor;
> **~ site** Kernreaktorgelände.
read Lesung, *(period of reading)* Lesezeit, -pause;
> **~** *(v.)* lesen, *(run)* lauten, *(university)* Vorlesung halten;
> **~ again** nachlesen; **~ aloud** vorlesen; **~ out the agenda** Tagesordnung verlesen; **~ for the bar** Rechtswissenschaften (Jura) studieren, sich für den Anwaltsberuf vorbereiten; **~ a bill for the third time** Gesetz in dritter Lesung behandeln; **~ s. o. like a book** j. völlig durchschauen; **~ through a contract** Vertrag genau durchlesen; **~ for a degree** sich auf eine Universitätsprüfung vorbereiten; **~ in depth** in Ruhe lesen; **~ a discourse** Vorlesung halten; **~ for one's examination** sich auf sein Examen vorbereiten; **~ fluently** flüssig (ohne Stocken) lesen; **~ o. s. into a language** sich in eine Sprache einlesen; **~ law** Jura studieren; **~ a lecture** Vorlesung (Vortrag) halten; **~ s. o. a lesson** sich j. tüchtig vornehmen; **~ a letter aloud** Brief laut vorlesen; **~ between the lines** zwischen den Zeilen lesen; **~**

differently in the manuscript im Manuskript anders lauten; **~ the meter** Zähler ablesen; **~ the minutes** Protokoll verlesen; **~ in the newspaper** in der Zeitung lesen; **~ off** ablesen; **~ out** vor-, ablesen; **~ s. o. out of a party** j. aus einer Partei ausstoßen; **~ over a copy with the original** Abschrift mit dem Original vergleichen; **~ s. one's palm** jem. aus der Hand wahrsagen; **~ a paper** Vortrag halten; **~ for the press** Preßrevision lesen; **~ proofs** Korrekturen lesen; **~ a report [to the meeting]** Bericht zur Verlesung bringen; **~ a riddle** Rätsel lösen; **~ while one runs** sofort Bescheid wissen; **~ into a sentence what is not there** falschen Sinn aus einer Passage herauslesen; **~ shorthand notes** stenografische Aufzeichnungen verstehen; **~ silence as consent** Schweigen als Zustimmung auslegen; **~ smoothly** sich glatt lesen; **~ a statement as an insult** Feststellung als Beleidigung auffassen; **~ up a subject** sich über ein Fachgebiet informieren, sich mit einem Thema vertraut machen; **~ too much into a text** zuviel in einen Text hineinlesen; **~ through** durchlesen; **~ to A** *(ticket)* bis A gelten; **~ for the first time** *(parl.)* erste Lesung vornehmen; **~ traffic signs** Verkehrszeichen verstehen; **~ like a translation** wie eine Übersetzung klingen; **~ both ways** *(clause)* sich so und so auslegen lassen; **~ well** sich gut lesen lassen; **~ out a will** Testament eröffnen;
> **~** *(a.)* gelesen;
> **~, agreed and signed** vorgelesen, genehmigt und unterschrieben; **~ most** *(readership analysis)* das meiste gelesen;
> **to be well ~** sehr belesen sein; **to be ~ for the first time** *(bill)* erste Lesung erfahren; **to have a good ~ in the train** in der Eisenbahn Zeit zum Lesen finden; **to have a short ~** kurze Lesepause einschalten; **to take the minutes as ~** Sitzungsprotokoll ohne Verlesung genehmigen;
> **most-~ book** meist gelesenes Buch; **well-~ person** gebildeter Mensch.
readable handwriting gut lesbare Handschrift.
readdress *(v.)* [Brief] umadressieren, nachsenden.
reader Leser, *(elementary book)* Lese-, Lehrbuch, Fibel, *(lecturer)* Lektor, *(print.)* Korrektor, *(sl.)* Wandergewerbeschein, *(university, Br.)* Dozent, außerordentlicher Professor, Extraordinarius;
> **the ~s** Leserschaft, -kreis, Publikum;
> **editorial ~** wissenschaftlicher Korrektor; **the gentle ~** der geneigte Leser; **publisher's ~** Verlagslektor;
> **~ in English** englischer Lektor, Lektor für Englisch; **~ in law** *(Br.)* Professor der Rechte;
> **to be a hard ~** eifrig seinem Studium obliegen;
> **~ advertisement** Textanzeige, redaktionelle Anzeige; **~ circulation** tatsächliche Leser, wirkliche Auflagenhöhe; **~ confidence** Leserwohlwollen; **~ feedback score** Leserecho; **~ interest research** Leserforschung; **~'s mark** Korrekturzeichen; **~'s proof** Korrekturbogen; **~ service** innerbetrieblicher Ausschnittsdienst; **~ traffic** Leserprozentsatz.
readership Vorlesungsamt, *(lectorship)* Dozentenstelle, Dozentur, *(newspaper)* Leserkreis, -zirkel, -schaft, *(print.)* Korrektorstelle, *(university, Br.)* Extraordinariat;
> **steady ~** Stammleserschaft; **upper-income ~** Leserschaft der höheren Einkommensklasse;
> **~ of four million** vier Millionen Leser;
> **~ analysis** Leseranalyse, -umfrage; **~ chart** Leserschaftstabelle; **~ figures** Leserschaftsziffern, -zahlen; **~ ratings** Ergebnisse einer Leserumfrage; **~ research** Leserumfrage; **~ survey** Leser[schafts]analyse; **~ test** Leserschaftskontrolle.
readily marketable staples *(US)* sofort realisierbares Lager.
readiness Bereitschaft, *(promptness)* Geneigtheit, Schnelligkeit, Pünktlichkeit;
> **in ~** bereit;
> **~ to change** Veränderungswünsche; **~ to commit** *(US)* Engagementsbereitschaft; **~ for delivery (to deliver)** Lieferbereitschaft; **~ to help others** Hilfsbereitschaft; **~ to invest** Anlageneigung, Investitionsbereitschaft; **~ of mind** Geistesgegenwart, schnelle Auffassungsgabe; **~ to pay** Zahlungsbereitschaft; **~ in payment** pünktliche Bezahlung; **~ to accept a proposal** Bereitwilligkeit, einen Vorschlag anzunehmen; **~ for service** Einsatzbereitschaft; **~ of speech** Redefertigkeit, Beredtsamkeit; **~ for war** Kriegsbereitschaft;
> **to have everything in ~ for an early start** alle Vorbereitungen für einen sofortigen Aufbruch getroffen haben;
> **~ clause** Fertigstellungsklausel.
reading Lesen, Verlesung, *(interpretation)* Lesart, Deutung, Auslegung, *(knowledge)* Belesenheit, *(lecture)* Vorlesung, *(matter which is read)* Lesestoff, Lektüre, *(parl.)* Lesung [eines Gesetzes], *(recital)* Rezitation, Vorlesen, *(thermometer)* Ablesung;

advanced ~ Lektüre für Fortgeschrittene; **basic** ~ Grundlektüre, grundlegende Bücher; **different** ~ verschiedene Lesart, Variante; **first** ~ *(parl.)* erste Lesung; **proof** ~ Korrekturlesen; **reverse** ~ seitenverkehrt; **right** ~ seitenrichtig; **systematic** ~ systematische Lesetätigkeit; **wide** ~ Belesenheit;
~ **of the balance sheet** Bilanzlesen; ~ **of a bill** Beratung eines Gesetzes; ~ **of a clause in an agreement** Auslegung einer Vertragsklausel; ~ **of the copy** Vorkorrektur; ~s **from Dickens** Beiträge von Dickens; ~ **the minutes** Protokollverlesung, Verlesen des Protokolls; ~ **of a will** Testamentseröffnung, Eröffnung eines Testaments;
to be a man of wide ~ umfassende Bildung haben; **to be rejected in the third** ~ *(bill)* bei der dritten Lesung abgelehnt werden; **to consider a bill in second** ~ Gesetzesvorlage in der zweiten Lesung prüfen; **to give a** ~ Vorlesung halten; **to give a second** ~ **for a bill** Gesetz in zweiter Lesung beraten; **to give a bill its third** ~ Gesetz in der dritten Lesung beschließen; **to make good** ~ lesenswert sein;
~ **book** Lehrbuch; ~ **circle** Lesezirkel; ~ **day** Lesetag; ~ **desk** Lesepult; ~ **ease** Stilflüssigkeit; ~ **glass** Vergrößerungsglas; ~ **habits** Lesegewohnheiten; ~ **lamp** Leselampe; ~ **light** Leselicht; ~ **light switch** Leselichtschalter; ~ **list** Leseliste, Zusammenstellung von Lesestoff; ~ **machine** Lesemaschine, -gerät; ~ **matter** Lesestoff, *(newspaper)* redaktioneller Teil; ~ **notice** redaktionell aufgemachte Anzeige, Textanzeige im redaktionellen Teil; ~ **play** Vorlesestück; ~ **practice** Leseübung; ~ **program(me)** Leseplan; ~ **public** Leserpublikum; ~ **room** Lesezimmer, *(printing)* Korrektorensaal; ~ **skill** Lesemethode; ~ **society** Lesekreis; ~ **station** *(punch-card system)* Abfühlstation; ~ **time** Lesezeit.
readjourn *(v.)* erneut vertagen.
readjournment erneute Vertagung, Wiedervertagung.
readjust *(v.)* wieder in Ordnung bringen, neuordnen, *(company)* sanieren;
~ **the accounts** Konten in Ordnung (Übereinstimmung) bringen; ~ **the exchange rates** Wechselkurse anpassen.
readjustment Wiederanpassung, -herstellung, *(of business enterprise)* [wirtschaftliche] Sanierung, *(reorientation)* Neuausrichtung, -ordnung, -regelung, Neuorientierung, Reorganisation; **debt** ~ Schuldenregelung;
~ **of capital stock** Berichtigung des Aktienkapitals; ~ **of exchange rates** Neuanpassung der Wechselkurse; ~ **of priorities** Neuverteilung von Vorzugsaktien;
~ **measures** Sanierungsmaßnahmen; ~ **phase** Sanierungszeitraum; ~ **report** Sanierungsbericht.
readmission, readmittance Wiederzulassung.
readmit *(v.)* wieder zulassen.
ready, the Moneten, Bargeld, Kasse;
~ *(a.)* bereit, *(available)* [gebrauchs]fertig, greifbar, verfügbar, einsatzbereit, fertig, *(market)* aufnahmefähig, geneigt, *(money)* flüssig, bar, *(on the spot)* prompt;
~**for collection** abhol-, abrufbereit; ~ **for delivery** auf Abruf lieferbar, Lieferung sofort; ~ **to discharge** löschbereit; ~ **for dispatch** versandbereit; ~ **to drive** fahrbereit; ~ **for hearing** *(case)* verhandlungsreif; ~ **for the journey** reisefertig; ~ **for loading** ladebereit; ~ **to march** marschfertig; ~ **to move in** bezugsfertig; ~ **for occupancy** bezugsfertig; ~ **for printing** druckreif; ~ **to take responsibility** verantwortungsfreudig; ~ **to sail** abreisefertig; ~ **for sea** seeklar; ~ **for shipment** versandfertig; ~ **to shoot** *(camera)* aufnahmebereit; ~ **to spend** ausgabefreudig; ~ **to start** startbereit, reisefertig; ~ **to take off** *(airplane)* einsatzbereit, startbereit, -klar, flugklar; ~ **for use** gebrauchsfertig; ~ **to be voted on** beschlußreif; ~**-to-wear** *(Br.)* konfektioniert; ~ **and willing** handlungsbereit und verfügungsberechtigt; ~ **for working** betriebsfertig;
tickets ~! Fahrkarten bereithalten!
to be ~ bereitstehen; **to be** ~ **in apprehension** rasche Auffassungsgabe besitzen; **to be always** ~ **to help** immer (jederzeit) hilfsbereit sein; **to be well supplied with the** ~ *(fam.)* mit Bargeld wohlversehen sein; **to get** ~ sich vorbereiten; **to get** ~ **for a journey** sich für eine Reise fertigmachen; **to lie** ~ in Bereitschaft liegen;
to have always a ~ **answer** nie um eine Antwort verlegen sein, auf alles eine Antwort wissen; ~**assets** verfügbare Vermögenswerte; ~ **cable** Platzkurs; ~ **capital** Umlaufkapital, -vermögen; ~ **cash** Barzahlung, -geld, sofortige Kasse; ~ **consent** prompte Zustimmung; **to buy food** ~**-cooked** vorgekochte Lebensmittel einkaufen.
ready-made [zum Gebrauch] fertig, gebrauchsfertig, *(clothes)* konfektioniert, von der Stange, *(fig.)* einfallslos, konventionell, *(imitated)* nachgemacht;

~**-clothes** Konfektionsartikel, -ware; **to come to a subject with** ~ **ideas** mit vorgefaßter Meinung an ein Thema herangehen; ~ **furniture** Katalogmöbel; ~ **shop** Konfektionsgeschäft; ~ **suit** Anzug von der Stange, Konfektionsware, -anzug.
ready market aufnahmefähiger Markt, schneller Absatz;
to find (meet with) a ~ gut gehen, leicht (schnellen) Absatz finden.
ready money Bargeld, bares Geld;
for ~ in bar; **without** ~ bargeldlos;
to pay ~ in bar bezahlen.
ready-money | **article** Barartikel; ~ **business** Kassageschäft; ~ **purchase** Bargeschäft.
ready | **pen** gewandte Feder; ~ **reckoner** Rechen-, Zinstabelle; ~ **reply** prompte Antwort; ~ **room** *(airport)* Bereitschaftsraum; ~ **sale** leichter (schneller) Absatz; **to find a** ~ **sale** gut gehen, schnell Absatz finden; ~**-to-serve dish** Fertiggericht; ~**-to-wear clothes** *(Br.)* Konfektionskleidung; ~**-to-wear department** Konfektionswarenabteilung; ~**-to-wear textile firm** Fertigkleidungsbetrieb; ~ **wit** schnelle Auffassungsgabe; ~ **workman** flotter Arbeiter; ~ **writer** rasch arbeitender Schriftsteller.
reaffirm *(v.)* erneut bestätigen.
reafforest *(v.)* wieder aufforsten.
reafforested wieder aufgeforstet.
real tatsächlich, real, wirklich, effektiv, *(genuine)* nicht gefälscht, echt, *(law)* dinglich, unbeweglich, sachlich;
~ **account** Bestands-, Sachkonto; ~ **action** dingliche Klage; ~ **amount** Istbestand; ~ **analysis** güterwirtschaftliche Analyse; ~ **assets** *(law)* Immobiliarvermögen, Liegenschaften, *(deceased)* unbewegliches Vermögen, unbeweglicher Nachlaß; **a** ~ **bash** *(US sl.)* Riesenfête; ~ **bill** *(Br.)* echter Wechsel; ~ **burden** *(Scot.)* Grundstücksbelastung, Reallast; ~ **capital** Sachkapital, in Grundstücken angelegtes Kapital; ~ **chattels** Rechte an einem Grundstück; ~ **contract** dinglicher Vertrag, *(US)* Liegenschaftsvertrag; ~ **costs** alternative Kosten, Warte-, Grundkosten; ~ **covenant** Grundstücksvertrag; ~ **earnings** Realeinkommen, -lohn;
real estate unbewegliches Vermögen, Immobilien, Immobiliarvermögen, Grundstück[seigentum], Grundeigentum, Liegenschaften, Grundbesitz, Grund und Boden, *(balance sheet)* unbebaute und bebaute Grundstücke, *(deceased)* Immobiliarnachlaß;
developed ~ bebautes Grundstück; **farm** ~ landwirtschaftliches Grundstück; **improved** ~ im Wert gestiegenes Grundstück; **industrial** ~ gewerblich genutztes Grundstück; **institutionally owned** ~s Grundstücke im Besitz von Kapitalsammelstellen; **mortgaged** ~ [hypothekarisch] belastetes Grundstück; **ordinary** ~ freies Grundeigentum; **net** ~ Grundstückswert nach Abschreibungen;
~ **and buildings** *(balance sheet)* Grundstücke und Gebäude;
to mortgage a piece of ~ Grundstück hypothekarisch belasten; **to trade in** ~ Grundstücks-, Immobilienmakler sein.
real-estate | **account** Grundstückskonto, Liegenschaftskonto; ~ **activities** Immobilientätigkeit; ~ **advertising** Grundstücksreklame; ~ **agency** *(US)* Immobilienbüro; ~ **agent** *(US)* Grundstücks-, Immobilienmakler; ~ **appraisal** Grundstücksschätzung; ~ **appreciation** Grundwertsteigerung; ~ **assets** Immobiliarnachlaß; ~ **bank** Bodenkreditbank; ~ **board** Maklerverband; ~ **bonds** *(US)* Grundstücksobligationen, Grundpfandbriefe, Obligationen eines Immobilienfonds; ~ **broker** *(US)* Immobilien-, Grundstücksmakler; **to list with (place in the hands of) a** ~ **broker** einem Grundstücksmakler an die Hand geben; ~ **brokerage** *(US)* [Grundstücks]maklergebühr; ~ **business** Immobiliengeschäft; ~ **closing** Unterzeichnung des Grundstückskaufvertrages; ~ **column** *(newspaper)* Immobilien-, Grundstücksmarkt; ~ **company (corporation, US)** Terrain-, Immobiliengesellschaft; ~ **consultant** Grundstücksvermittler; ~ **credit** Immobiliarkredit; ~ **deal** Grundstückgeschäft; ~ **dealer** Grundstücksmakler, Immobilienhändler; ~ **dealing** Grundstücksgeschäft; ~ **depreciation** Grundstücksabschreibung; ~ **depreciation fund** Grundbesitzentwertungsfonds; ~ **developer** Grundstücks-, Baulanderschließungsgesellschaft; ~ **development project** Erschließungsvorhaben; ~ **exchange** Grundstücktausch; ~ **field** Grundstückswesen; ~ **finance** Grundstücksfinanzen; ~ **financing** Grundstücksfinanzierung; ~ **firm** Immobiliengeschäft, Terraingesellschaft; ~ **foreclosure** Zwangsversteigerung; **offshore** ~ **fund** *(US)* im Ausland betriebener Immobilienfonds; ~ **holdings** Immobilienbesitz; ~ **[holding] corporation** Grundstücksgesellschaft; ~ **interest** Grundstücksrecht; ~ **interests** Grundstücksinteressen; ~ **investment** Anlage in Grundstücken, Grundstücksanlage, Investitionen im Immobilien-

sektor; ~ **investment counsellor** Immobilienanlageberater; ~ **investment trust** Immobilien-, Immobiliarinvestmentfonds; ~ **investor** Kapitalanleger in Grundstücken; ~ **law** Immobilien-, Grundstücksrecht; ~ **lawyer** *(US)* auf Immobilien (Grundstücksrecht) spezialisierter Anwalt; ~ **levy** Grundbesitzabgabe; ~ **loan** hypothekarisch gesicherter Kredit, Real-, Hypothekenkredit; ~ **manager** Grundstücksverwalter; ~ **map** Grundbuchblatt; ~ **market** *(US)* Grundstücks-, Immobilienmarkt; ~ **marketing** *(US)* Grundstücksgeschäft; ~ **matters** Grundstücksangelegenheiten; ~ **mortgage** *(US)* [Grundstücks]hypothek; ~ **mortgage note** Hypothekenpfandbrief; ~ **offering** Grundstücksangebot; ~ **office** Immobilien-, Maklerbüro; ~ **operator** *(US)* Grundstücksmakler; ~ **owner** Grundstückseigentümer, -besitzer; ~ **pages** Immobilienteil einer Zeitung; ~ **picture** Grundstücksbeschreibung; ~ **price** *(US)* Grundstückspreis; ~ **project** Grundstücksprojekt; ~ **records** Grundstücksurkunden, Grundbuchpapiere; ~ **recording** *(US)* Grundbucheintragung; ~ **recording office** *(US)* Grundbuchamt; ~ **register** *(US)* Grundbuch; ~ **and equivalent rights** *(balance sheet)* Grundstücke und grundstücksgleiche Rechte; ~ **salesman** *(US)* Grundstücksagent, -makler, Immobilienmakler; ~ **section** *(newspaper)* Grundstücks-, Immobilienmarkt; ~ **securities** Grundstückswerte; ~ **selling** Grundstücksverkauf; ~ **subject** Grundstücksangelegenheit; ~ **syndicate** Terraingesellschaft; ~ **tax** *(US)* Grundsteuer; ~ **transactions** Immobilienhandel, Grundstückstransaktionen; ~ **transfer** Grundstücksübertragung; ~ **trust** Terraingesellschaft; ~ **utility** Nutzungswert eines Grundstücks; ~ **value** Grundstückswert; ~ **venture** Grundstücks-, Bodenspekulation.

real | evidence tatsächliche Beweisführung, Augenschein; ~ **exchange** bezahlter (gemachter) Kurs; ~ **flows** Güterströme; ~ **gold** reines (echtes) Gold; ~ **growth** reales Wachstum; ~ **head of a business** eigentlicher Kopf eines Unternehmens; ~ **income** wirkliches Einkommen, Realeinkommen; ~ **after-tax income** Realeinkommen nach Steuern; ~ **personal disposable income** frei verfügbares Realeinkommen; ~ **injury** Körperverletzung; ~ **interest rate** reale Verzinsung; ~ **investment** Sachanlage, -investition; ~ **issue** echter Klagegrund; ~ **law** Sachenrecht; **manager of a business** eigentlicher Geschäftsführer; ~ **money** klingende Münze, *(cash)* Bargeld, *(coin, US)* Metallgeld; ~ **obligation** dingliche Verpflichtung, Realleistung; ~ **offer** effektives Angebot; ~ **outlays** Realausgaben; ~ **party** aktiv legitimierte Partei; ~ **price** effektiver Preis; ~ **property** Grundstückseigentum, Grundbesitz; ~ **property investment** Grundstücksinvestition; ~ **property law** Immobilien-, Grundstücksrecht; ~ **property purchases** Immobilienerwerb; ~ **purchasing power** effektive Kaufkraft; ~ **reasons** wirkliche Gründe; ~ **receipts** tatsächliche Einkünfte, Isteinnahme; ~ **representative** Liegenschaftsnachlaßverwalter, *(heir)* Immobiliarerbe; ~ **resources** Güter- und Dienstleistungen; ~ **return on investment** reale Kapitalverzinsung; ~ **right** dingliches Recht; ~ **security** *(US)* Grundpfand, hypothekarische (dingliche) Sicherheit; ~ **servitude** *(US)* Grunddienstbarkeit; ~ **shares (stock, US)** tatsächlicher Bestand, Istbestand, effektiv im Besitz befindliche Aktien; ~ **state of affairs** tatsächliche Sachlage; ~ **statute** Realstatut; ~ **take-home pay** wirklicher Nettolohn; ~ **tare** Nettotara; ~ **tax** Realsteuer; ~ **term** preisbereinigte Größe; ~ **things** unbewegliche Sachen, Immobilien; ~ **time** *(data processing)* Real-, Echtzeit; ~ **union** Realunion; ~ **value** effektiver (wirklicher) Wert, Sach-, Real-, Effektivwert; ~ **wages** Reallohn; ~ **wrong** widerrechtliche Grundstücksentziehung.

realign *(v.)* anpassen, [Politik] neu ausrichten (orientieren).

realignment *(policy)* Anpassung, Neuorientierung.

realism of intellect realistisches Denken.

realistic politics Realpolitik.

reality Wirklichkeit, Sachlichkeit;
~ **of consent** *(law)* tatsächliche Einigung;
to describe with extraordinary ~ außerordentlich realistisch schildern; **to tailor to** ~ der Realität anpassen.

realizability Realisierbarkeit, Verwertbarkeit.

realizable ausführbar, *(convertible into capital)* kapitalisierbar, *(salable)* verkäuflich, umsetzbar, *(utilizable)* verwertbar, realisierbar;
~ **at short notice** kurzfristig realisierbar;
~ **assets** effektiver Bestand, Effektivbestand; ~ **stock** börsengängige Papiere.

realization *(converting into capital)* Kapitalisierung, *(converting into fact)* Verwirklichung, Realisierung, Erfüllung, Durchsetzung *(converting into money)* Flüssigmachung, Liquidation, Versilberung, *(evening up)* Glattstellung, Flüssigwerden, *(sale)* Verkauf *(utilization)* Verwertung;

compulsory ~ Zwangsglattstellung; **current** ~ laufende Liquidation; **revenue** ~ Gewinnrealisierung; **usual weekend** ~s übliche Glattstellungen am Wochenende;
~ **of a pledge** Pfandverwertung; ~ **of profit** Gewinnrealisierung, -mitnahme; ~ **of a project** Durchführung eines Vorhabens; ~ **of properties** Verwertung von Sicherheiten; ~ **of securities** Verwertung von Sicherheiten, Sicherheitenverwertung;
~ **[and liquidation] account** Glattstellungs-, Realisations-, Liquidationskonto; ~ **clause** Verwertungsklausel; ~ **figures** Liquidationspreise; ~ **order** Glattstellungsauftrag; ~ **price** Liquidations-, Verkaufspreis; ~ **proceeds** Verwertungserlös; ~ **sale** Verkaufsrealisation, Glattstellungsverkauf; ~ **[and liquidation] statement** Konkurs[abwicklungs]bilanz; ~ **value** Liquidations-, Realisationswert.

realize *(v.) (convert into capital)* kapitalisieren, *(convert into fact)* in die Wirklichkeit umsetzen, verwirklichen, *(convert into money)* flüssig- (zu Geld) machen, in Geld umsetzen, realisieren, verwerten, versilbern, erlösen, *(even up)* glattstellen, aktivieren, *(perform)* leisten, *(sell)* verkaufen, veräußern, unterbringen, *(understand)* zur Feststellung gelangen;
~ **one's ambitions** seine ehrgeizigen Pläne verwirklichen; ~ **assets** Vermögenswerte flüssigmachen; ~ **bonds at short notice** Obligationen kurzfristig flüssigmachen; ~ **at book value** Buchwerte bei der Verwertung erzielen; ~ **the debtor's property** Schuldnervermögen versilbern; ~ **goods** Waren verwerten; ~ **a patent** Patent verwerten; ~ **a pledge** Pfand verwerten; ~ **a [high] price** [hohen] Preis erzielen; ~ **profit from s. th.** Nutzen aus etw. ziehen; ~ **profits** Gewinne realisieren; ~ **large profits** große Gewinne erzielen; ~ **a project** Vorhaben durchführen; ~ **a scheme** Plan verwirklichen; ~ **shares** Aktien veräußern.

realized profit (revenue) realisierter Gewinn.

realizing Realisierung, Glattstellung;
~ **order** Glattstellungsauftrag; ~ **sale** Verkaufsrealisation, Glattstellung[sverkauf];
~ **a scheme** Plan verwirklichen; ~ **shares** Aktien veräußern.

reallocate *(v.) (land)* umlegen, neu verteilen (zuteilen);
~ **import quotas** Einfuhrkontingente neu zuteilen; ~ **workers** Arbeitskräfte umsetzen.

reallocation Neuverteilung-, zuteilung, *(land)* Umlegung;
~ **of import quotas** Neuzuteilung von Einfuhrkontingenten; ~ **of labo(u)r** Umsetzung (Umplazierung, Umverteilung) von Arbeitskräften.

reallot *(v.)* repartieren.

reallotment Repartierung.

realm Königreich, *(fig.)* Bereich, Gebiet;
in the ~ **of fiction** im Bereich der Fabel; **within the** ~ im Inland.

realtor *(US)* Realitäten-, Immobilien-, Grundstücksmakler.

realty Grundbesitz, -eigentum, -vermögen, Immobilien, Liegenschaften;
partnership ~ Grundbesitz einer Gesellschaft; **quasi** ~ Grundstückszubehör;
to convert ~ **into personalty** unbewegliches in bewegliches Vermögen umwandeln, Grundbesitz realisieren;
~ **company** *(US)* Grundstücksgesellschaft; ~ **rates** Grundsteuersatz; ~ **transfer tax** *(US)* Grunderwerbssteuer.

ream Ries Papier.

reanimate *(v.)* **trade** Handel wieder beleben.

reanimation of trade Wiederbelebung des Handels.

reap *(v.)* **lasting benefits** dauernde Vorteile gewinnen; ~ **the corn** Getreide ernten; ~ **a field** Feld abernten; ~ **profits** Gewinne realisieren; ~ **a great success** großen Erfolg zeitigen; ~ **in terms of substantially increased profits** in wesentlich erhöhten Gewinnen abkassieren; ~ **where one has not sown** ernten, wo man nicht gesät hat.

reappear *(v.)* wiedererscheinen.

reapplication erneuter Antrag, erneutes Gesuch.

reappoint *(v.)* wieder ernennen (anstellen);
~ **the retiring treasurer** bisherigen Schatzmeister bestätigen.

reappointment Wiederernennung, -anstellung, -einstellung.

reappraisal Neubewertung;
~ **of our relations with China** Überprüfung unserer chinesischen Beziehungen.

reappraise *(v.)* überprüfen, neubewerten.

reappraiser Zollwertüberprüfer.

rear Rückseite, Hintergrund, *(house)* Rück-, Hinterseite, *(mil.)* Nachtrab, -hut, *(Br., sl.)* Lokus, Latrine;
at the ~ **of the house** hinter dem Haus; **at the** ~ **of the train** am Zugende; **from the** ~ *(parl.)* von den hinteren Sitzreihen;
~ **of the house** rückwärtiger Teil eines Hauses;
~ *(v.)* aufziehen;

~ **a family** Familie großziehen; ~ **a monument** Denkmal errichten;
to be at the ~ **of a building** im rückwärtigen Gebäudeteil liegen;
to hang on s. one's jem. auf dem Fuße folgen;
~ **admiral** Konteradmiral; ~ **axle** Hinterachse; ~ **communications** rückwärtige Verbindungen; ~ **door** Hintertür; ~ **drive** Hinterachsenantrieb; ~ **echelon** *(mil.)* rückwärtiger Stab; ~-**end collision** Auffahrunfall; ~-**engined** mit Heckmotor; ~ **entrance** Hintereingang; ~ **guard** Nachhut; ~-**guard action** Nachhutgefecht; ~ **lamp** *(car)* Rücklampe, -licht; ~ **fog lamp** Nebelschlußleuchte; ~ **lights** Rücklicht; ~ **screen projection** im Studio gedrehte Außenaufnahme; ~ **suspension** Hinterradaufhängung; ~-**view mirror** Rückspiegel; **heated** ~ **window** beheizte Heckscheibe.

rearguard *(mil.)* Nachhut;
~ **action** Nachhutgefecht.

reargue *(v.)* *(law court)* erneut verhandeln.

rearing Aufzucht.

rearm *(v.)* wiederbewaffnen, aufrüsten.

rearmament Wiederaufrüstung;
~ **boom** Rüstungskonjunktur; **international** ~ **economy** Weltaufrüstungswirtschaft.

rearrange *(v.)* neu anordnen, umordnen, -gruppieren.

rearrangement Neuordnung, Umwandlung, -gruppierung;
~ **of business** Änderung der Tagesordnung; ~ **of debts** Schuldenregelung; ~ **of a time-table** Fahrplanänderung;
~ **expenses** innerbetriebliche Umzugskosten.

rearrest *(v.)* erneut verhaften.

reason [Beweis]grund, Ursache, *(mental faculties)* Vernunft, Verstand, *(motive)* Beweggrund, Motiv;
by ~ **of** auf Grund von; **by** ~ **of age** aus Altersgründen; **for no** ~ **at all** für nichts und wieder nichts; **for a particular** ~ aus gegebener Veranlassung; **for** ~**s of state** aus Gründen der Staatsraison; **from** ~**s of policy** aus Gründen der Klugheit;
~**s** *(law court)* Urteilsgründe;
the above ~**s** die oben aufgeführten Gründe; ~**s adduced** Begründung eines Urteils; **compelling** ~**s** zwingende Gründe; **important** ~ gewichtiger Grund; **main** ~ Hauptgrund; **overriding** ~ ausschlaggebender Grund; **serious** ~**s** schwerwiegende Gründe; **sound** ~ stichhaltiger Grund; **sufficient** ~ hinreichender Grund;
~**s for an appeal** Berufungsbegründung; ~ **of arrest** Haftgrund; ~ **to believe** Grund zur Annahme; ~**s for deportation** Ausweisungsgründe; ~ **for a dismissal** Entlassungs-, Kündigungsgrund; [**sufficient**] ~ **for dismissal** [ausreichender] Entlassungsgrund; ~**s for judgment** Urteilsgründe; ~ **of state** Staatsraison;
~ *(v.)* schließen, schlußfolgern, urteilen;
~ **s. o. into a sensible course of action** j. zu einer vernünftigen Handlungsweise bringen;
to apply ~ **to** Vernunft walten lassen; **to be deprived of one's** ~ seines Verstandes beraubt sein; **to bring s. o. to** ~ j. zu Verstand bringen; **to complain with** [**good**] ~ Grund zur Beschwerde haben; **to cost a sum out of all** ~ völlig unsinnigen Preis kosten; **to give the** ~**s for a judgment** Urteil begründen; **to give specific** ~**s** im einzelnen belegen; **to listen to** ~ Vernunft annehmen; **to lose one's** ~ verrückt werden, durchdrehen; **to state the** ~**s for an appeal** Berufung begründen; **to state one's** ~**s for a decision** Begründung für eine Entscheidung angeben;
~-**why advertising** Aufklärungswerbung; ~-**why copy** rationell argumentierender Werbetext.

reasonability *(price)* Angemessenheit.

reasonable vernünftig, *(current)* gangbar, *(fair)* angemessen, annehmbar, gerechtfertigt, solide, reel, *(moderate)* mäßig, billig;
to be ~ **in one's demands** vernünftige Forderungen stellen;
~ **access** *(to children)* angemessene Besuchsregelung; ~ **act** zumutbare Tätigkeit; ~ **aids** angemessene Dienste; ~ **care and diligence** im Verkehr erforderliche Sorgfalt; ~ **care and skill** im Berufsleben erforderliche Sorgfalt; ~ **cause** triftiger Grund; ~ **and probable cause** hinreichender (dringender) Tatverdacht; ~ **cause to believe a debtor insolvent** ausreichender Verdacht für das Vorliegen von Zahlungsunfähigkeit eines Schuldners; **with** ~ **certainty** mit ausreichender Bestimmtheit, mit hinreichender Sicherheit; **fair and** ~ **compensation** angemessene Vergütung; **fair and** ~ **contract** Vertrag mit angemessenen Gegenleistungen; ~ **creature** menschliches Lebewesen; ~ **demand** billige Forderung; ~ **doubt** begründeter Zweifel; ~ **exchangeability** *(antitrust law, US)* Austauschbarkeit nach vernünftigen Grundsätzen; ~ **excuse** ausreichende Entschuldigung; ~ **expenses** angemessene Auslagen; ~ **grounds for**

suspicion hinreichende Verdachtsgründe; ~ **hour** zumutbare Tageszeit; ~ **length of time** angemessener Zeitraum; ~ **man** normaler Durchschnittsmensch; **fair and** ~ **market value** Verkehrswert; ~ **notice** ausreichende (angemessene) Kündigungsfrist; ~ **offer** vernünftiges Angebot; ~ **part** *(Br.)* Pflichtteil der Witwe und der Kinder; ~ **period of time** angemessene Frist; ~ **price** angemessener (annehmbarer, mäßiger) Preis; ~ **skill** durchschnittliche Fähigkeit; ~ **terms** annehmbare Bedingungen; ~ **time** angemessene Frist; **fair and** ~ **toll** angemessene Marktabgabe; ~ **value** entsprechender Gegenwert; **fair and** ~ **value** angemessener Wert, Verkehrswert; ~ **wear and tear** übliche Abnutzung.

reasonableness Vernünftigkeit, Angemessenheit, Sachgemäßheit;
~ **of prices** Mäßigkeit (Angemessenheit) der Preise.

reasoned decision mit Gründen versehene Entscheidung.

reasoning Argumentation, Schlußfolgerung, Begründung, Beweisführung.

reassemble *(v.)* wieder zusammenbauen.

reassess *(v.)* nochmals abschätzen (besteuern), neu veranlagen, *(revalorize)* aufwerten, *(securities)* bereinigen.

reassessment Neuveranlagung, *(revalorization)* Aufwertung, *(securities)* Bereinigung;
~ **of real property** Neufestsetzung des Einheitswertes; ~ **of taxes** Berichtigungsveranlagung.

reassign *(v.)* wiederabtreten, zurückübertragen.

reassignment Rückübertragung, Wiederabtretung.

reassurance erneute Bestätigung, *(reinsurance)* Rückversicherung.

reassure *(v.)* rückversichern.

reassurer Rückversicherer.

reattachment wiederholte Pfändung.

rebased, periodically der Inflationsentwicklung laufend angepaßt.

rebate [Preis]nachlaß, -ermäßigung, Rabatt, Abzug, Abstrich, Herabminderung, *(banking)* Bonifikation, *(drawback)* Rückzoll, *(insurance)* Provisionsbeteiligung durch den Versicherungsmakler, *(interest)* Zins-, Rückvergütung;
less ~ abzüglich Rabatt; **on** ~ auf Rabatt;
a 25 per cent ~ Rabatt von 25%, 25%iger Rabatt; **dealer's** ~ Händlernachlaß, -rabatt; **deferred** ~ Frachtrabatt für regelmäßige Verlader; **freight** ~ Frachtnachlaß; **quantity** ~ Mengenrabatt; **special** ~ Vorzugsrabatt; **tax** ~ Steuernachlaß, -erstattung;
~ **on the bills (items) not due** Wechseldiskontabzug; ~ **for book retail trade** Rabatt für den Bucheinzelhandel; ~ **of freight** Frachtnachlaß; ~ **of income tax** Einkommensteuernachlaß; ~ **of interest** Zinsermäßigung, -vergütung; ~ **for simultaneous purchase of ...** Rabatt bei gleichzeitigem Bezug von ...; ~ **on sales** Verkaufsrabatt;
~ *(v.)* Nachlaß gewähren, Rabatt zugestehen, Preis ermäßigen, *(shipping)* Frachtrabatt gewähren;
to allow a ~ **on an account** Rechnungsnachlaß gewähren; **to grant a** ~ Abzug (Rabatt) gewähren; **to take up a bill under** ~ Wechsel vor Fälligkeit bezahlen;
~ **certificate** Steuergutschein; ~ **system** [Fracht]rabattsystem.

rebated acceptance *(US)* vor Fälligkeit bezahltes Akzept.

rebel Aufrührer, Aufständischer, Rebell;
~ **in the home** widerspenstiges Kind;
~ *(v.)* rebellieren, sich empören, Aufstand proben;
~ **against the government** sich gegen die Regierung auflehnen;
~ **forces** Aufrührer, Aufständische; ~ **government** Rebellenregierung; ~ **group** Gruppe von Rebellen, Rebellengruppe.

rebellion Aufstand, Aufruhr, Empörung, Rebellion;
to rise in ~ sich empören, im Aufstand sein; **to work up a** ~ Aufstand anzetteln.

rebellious aufrührerisch, aufständisch, *(illness)* hartnäckig;
~ **assembly** *(Br.)* Zusammenrottung; ~ **boy** widerspenstiger Junge; ~ **subjects** aufsässige Untertanen; ~ **troops** Truppen im Aufruhr.

rebind *(v.)* **a book** Buch neu einbinden.

rebirth Wiedergeburt.

rebook *(v.)* umbuchen.

rebooking Umbuchung.

reborrow *(v.)* erneut borgen.

rebound *(stock exchange)* [heftiger] Umschwung;
~ *(v.)* **from the war** sich vom Krieg erholen.

rebroadcast Wiederholungssendung, *(relay transmission)* Relaisübertragung, Ballsendung;
~ *(v.)* Sendung wiederholen, *(relay)* durch Relaisstationen übertragen.

rebuff abschlägige Antwort, Zurückweisung;
~ *(v.)* zurückweisen, abschlägige Antwort erteilen, abschlägig bescheiden;
to get (meet with) a ~ abschlägigen Bescheid erhalten, Zurückweisung erfahren.

rebuild *(v.)* wiederaufbauen, -herstellen, umbauen;
~ **a house** Haus wieder aufbauen; ~ **liquidity** Liquidität verbessern; ~ **inadequate reserves** unzureichende Reserven anreichern.

rebuilding *(house)* Wiederaufbau, Umbau;
~ **of liquidity** Liquiditätsverbesserung; ~ **of premises** Wiederaufbau eines Anwesens; ~ **of stocks** Vorratsaufstockung.

rebuilt typewriter wieder zusammengesetzte Schreibmaschine.

rebuke scharfer Verweis;
~ *(v.)* **a subordinate** einem Untergebenen einen scharfen Verweis erteilen.

rebus Bilderrätsel.

rebut *(v.)* Gegenbeweis führen, durch Beweis widerlegen;
~ **an equity** Anspruch zu Fall bringen; ~ **s. one's offer** jds. Angebot zurückweisen; ~ **a presumption** Vermutung entkräften.

rebuttable widerlegbar;
~ **presumption** Rechtsvermutung, widerlegbare Vermutung.

rebuttal *(US)* [Widerlegung durch] Gegenbeweis, Entkräftung;
~ **of a presumption** Widerlegung einer Vermutung;
to file a ~ **with a court** Zurückweisung einer Klage bei Gericht beantragen.

rebutter *(law)* Quadruplik.

rebutting evidence Gegenbeweis.

rebuy *(v.)* zurück-, wiederkaufen, eindecken.

recalcitrant unbotmäßig, widerspenstig, ungehorsam.

recalculation erneute Berechnung.

recall Rückruf, Zurückberufung, *(cancellation)* Widerruf, *(credit)* [Auf]kündigung, *(dipl., US)* vorzeitige Abberufung, Zurückberufung, *(obligations)* Aufruf, *(publisher)* Rückruf;
~ **of an ambassador** Zurückberufung (Abberufung) eines Botschafters; ~ **of qualified items** *(book trade)* Rückruf von Konditionsgut; ~ **for redemption** Aufforderung zur Rückzahlung;
~ *(v.)* zurückrufen, (Kapital, Kredit, Anleihe) [auf]kündigen, *(cancel)* widerrufen, aufheben;
~ **an ambassador** Botschafter zurückberufen; ~ **from circulation** aus dem Verkehr ziehen, außer Kurs setzen, einziehen; ~ **a decree** Verordnung zurückziehen; ~ **an envoy** Gesandten zurückbeordern; ~ **goods** Waren abrufen; ~ **a judgment** Urteil aufheben; ~ **s. o. to life** j. wiederbeleben; ~ **a loan** Darlehen kündigen; ~ **s. o. to an office** j. wieder in ein Amt berufen; ~ **one's schooldays** sich an seine Schulzeit erinnern; ~ **troops from the front** Truppen aus der Frontlinie herausnehmen; ~ **a wire** Telegramm widerrufen; ~ **a witness** Zeugen erneut vernehmen lassen;
to sound the ~ zum Rückzug blasen;
~ **campaign** Abberufungsfeldzug; ~ **election** Abstimmung zum Zweck der Abberufung; ~ **method** Erinnerungstestmethode; ~ **test** Erinnerungs-, Gedächtnistest; **aided-** **test** Gedächtnistest unter Zuhilfenahme von Gedächtnisstützen; **pure (unaided)** ~ **test** reiner Gedächtnistest; ~ **vote** Abberufungsabstimmung.

recallable *(judgment)* annullierbar.

recalled, until bis auf Widerruf.

recant *(v.)* **a former declaration** frühere Erklärung widerrufen.

recantation Widerruf;
forced ~ erzwungener Widerruf.

recapitalization Neufinanzierung, Neukapitalisierung, Kapitalberichtigung;
~ **of business** [Geschäfts]sanierung;
~ **surplus** *(US)* aus Kapitalherabsetzungen entstandener Gewinn.

recapitalize *(v.)* kapitalisieren, neufinanzieren, sanieren, Kapital berichtigen.

recapitulate *(v.)* zusammenfassen, rekapitulieren.

recapitulation Zusammenfassung;
~ **sheet** Sammelbogen [für Materialausgabe oder Löhne].

recaption Wiederinbesitznahme, *(prisoner)* erneute Verhaftung.

recapture *(confiscation, US)* Enteignung, *(international law)* erneute Beschlagnahme, Wiederaufbringung, *(mil.)* Zurückeroberung;
~ **of excess depreciation upon sale of property** Wegfall von Sonderabschreibungen (besonders gewährten Steuervorteilen) bei Grundstücksverkäufen;
~ *(v.)* erneut beschlagnahmen, *(railroad accounting, US)* mehr als den vereinbarten Gewinnanteil entnehmen, *(prize)* erneut zur Prise erklären;

~ **clause** Rückforderungsklausel, *(railroad accounting, US)* Gewinnabführungsklausel.

recartelization Rückverflechtung.

recast *(book)* Umänderung, *(theater)* neue Besetzung;
~ *(v.)* *(account)* [Konto] überprüfen, *(cast anew)* umändern, *(calculate anew)* durchrechnen, *(theater)* umbesetzen;
~ **a chapter** Kapitel umschreiben; ~ **a paragraph** Absatz neu fassen; ~ **a play** Stück neu besetzen; ~ **a sentence** Urteil abändern.

recede Abstandnehmen, *(decline in value)* Wertminderung, *(prices)* Rückgang, Weichen;
~ *(v.)* [im Wert] zurück-, heruntergehen, sinken, *(cede back)* zurückübertragen, *(desist)* Abstand nehmen, abstehen, *(politics, US)* oppositionelle Haltung im Kongreß aufgeben, *(prices)* weichen, nachgeben;
~ **from an amendment** von einem Abänderungsgesetz Abstand nehmen; ~ **from a contract** von einem Vertrag zurücktreten; ~ **from a demand** auf eine Forderung verzichten, seine Forderung aufgeben; ~ **fractionally** *(stock exchange)* abbröckeln; ~ **from an opinion** ablehnende Meinung ändern; ~ **a point** *(shares)* um einen Punkt nachgeben; ~ **from one's position** seinen Rücktritt erklären; ~ **from sanctions** Sanktionen fallen lassen; ~ **conquered territory** erobertes Gebiet zurückgeben.

receding prices fallende Preise, *(stock exchange)* weichende (nachgebende) Kurse.

receipt *(bill)* Rechnung, Quittung, Kassenbon, *(of letter)* Empfang, Erhalt, Inempfangnahme, *(luggage)* Aufgabeschein, *(receiving)* Annahme, *(scrip)* Interimsanleiheschein, *(voucher)* Quittung, Beleg, Abnahme-, Empfangs-, Übernahmeschein, Empfangsbescheinigung, -bestätigung;
against ~ gegen Quittung; **as per** ~ **enclosed** laut beiliegender Quittung; **in** ~ **of your favo(u)r** *(letter)* im Besitz Ihres geschätzten Schreibens; **on** ~ gegen Quittung, nach Eingang; **on** ~ **of** gegen Einsendung von, bei (nach) Empfang; **on** ~ **of the draft** bei Eingang des Wechsels; **on** ~ **of the news** beim Eintreffen der Nachrichten;
~**s** *(goods)* eingehende Waren, *(market)* Vorräte, *(money received)* eingehende Gelder, Einnahmen, Einkünfte, Eingang, Ertrag;
accountable ~ Buchungs-, Rechnungsbeleg, Quittungsbescheinigung; **actual** ~**s** Ist-, Effektiveinnahme; **annual** ~**s** Jahresertrag; **application** ~ *(shares, Br.)* Zeichnungsbescheinigung; ~**s not assessable** nicht veranlagungspflichtige Einnahmen; **bank** ~ Depotschein; **binding** ~ *(insurance)* Deckungszusage; **box-office** ~**s** Kasseneinnahmen; **cash** ~**s** Kasseneingang; **clean** ~ vorbehaltlose Quittung; **conditional** ~ *(insurance)* Deckungszusage; **current** ~**s** laufende Einnahmen *(US, balance sheet)* Umlaufvermögen; **customhouse** ~ Zollquittung; **daily** ~**s** tägliche Eingänge, Tageseinnahme; **delivery** ~ Lieferschein; **dock** ~ Dock-, Kaiempfangsschein; **double (duplicate)** ~ doppelte Quittung, Quittungsduplikat; **double ~ good for single** doppelt für einfach gültige Quittung; **effectual** ~ rechtsgültige Quittung; **excess** ~ Mehreinnahmen; **formal** ~ förmliche Quittung; ~ **given** quittiert; **gross** ~**s** Bruttoeinnahme[n], Rohertrag; **interest** ~**s** Zinseingänge; **interim** ~ vorläufige Quittung, Zwischenquittung; **luggage** ~**s** *(Br.)* Gepäckschein; **mate's** ~ Steuermannsempfangsschein; **net** ~ Nettoeinkommen, -eingang, -einnahme[n], Betriebsüberschüsse, *(tax)* Nettosteueraufkommen; **nonnegotiable warehouse** ~ Rektalagerschein; **nonrecurrent** ~ einmalige Erträge; **official** ~ amtliche Empfangsbescheinigung; **other** ~**s** *(balance sheet)* sonstige Einnahmen; **petty-cash** ~ Eingangsbeleg der Portokasse; **post-cessation** ~ Einnahmen nach Einstellung eines Gewerbebetriebes; **post-office** ~ Posteinlieferungsschein; **postal** ~ Posteinlieferungsschein; **provisional** ~ Interims-, Zwischenquittung; **renewal** ~ Erneuerungsschein; **return** ~ *(post)* Rück-, Empfangsschein; **ship's** ~ Schiffsempfangsschein; ~ **not signed** Quittung ohne Unterschrift; **smaller** ~**s** Mindereinnahmen; **sundry** ~**s** *(balance sheet)* verschiedene Einnahmen; **stamped** ~ gestempelte Quittung; **supposed** ~**s** Solleinnahmen; **tax** ~**s** Steueraufkommen; **temporary** ~ Zwischenquittung, Zwischen-, Interimsschein, vorläufige Empfangsbescheinigung; **total** ~**s** Gesamterlös, -eingänge, -einnahme; **trust** ~ *(US)* *(certificate of deposit)* Hinterlegungsschein; **valid** ~ rechtsgültige Quittung; **warehouse** ~ Lagerschein; **yearly** ~**s** Jahreseinnahmen;
~ **for the balance** Schlußquittung; ~ **in blank** unausgefüllte Quittung, Blankoquittung; ~ **with consideration for payment stated** Quittung mit Angabe des Zahlungsgrundes; ~**s from customers** Eingänge von Kunden; ~**s of the day** Tageskasse; ~ **of delivery** Aushändigungs-, Rück-, Ablieferungsschein; ~ **of deposit** Depot[hinterlegungs]schein, Einzahlungsbescheini-

gung; ~ **in full discharge** Schluß-, Ausgleichsquittung; ~ **in duplicate** doppelt ausgefertigter Empfangsschein; **~s and expenditures (expenses)** Einnahmen und Ausgaben[buch]; ~ **in due form** ordnungsgemäße Quittung; ~ **in full** Pauschal-, Ausgleichs-, Generalquittung; ~ **for goods** Warenempfangsbestätigung; ~ **for loan** Darlehnsquittung; ~ **of money** Geldempfang; ~ **of a capital nature** kapitalähnliche Einkünfte; ~ **of an income nature** einkommensähnliche Einkünfte; **~s on the increase** steigende Einnahmen; ~ **of an order** Auftragseingang, -empfang, -erhalt; ~ **that is not in order** unvollständige Quittung; ~ **in part** Teilquittung; **~s and payments** Ein- und Auszahlungen; ~ **for payment** Zahlungsquittung; **~s as per profit and loss account** Erträge gemäß Gewinn- und Verlustrechnung; **current ~s from securities** laufende Erträge aus Wertpapieren;
~ *(v.)* Quittung ausstellen, quittieren, mit Quittungsstempel versehen;
~ **a bill** Rechnung quittieren, [Geld]empfang bescheinigen; ~ **a hotel bill** Quittungsstempel auf eine Hotelrechnung setzen; ~ **in full** Generalquittung ausstellen;
to acknowledge [the] ~ Empfang bestätigen (anzeigen); **to acknowledge [the]** ~ **of a letter** Briefeingang (Eingang) eines Briefes) bestätigen; **to be in** ~ **of** im Besitz sein von; **to be in [the]** ~ **of a good income** gutes Einkommen haben; **to be in** ~ **of DM 20.000,- a year** Jahreseinkommen von 20.000 DM haben; **to count the ~s** Kasse schließen; **to enter as** ~ als Einnahme buchen; **to get a** ~ **for money spent** Spesenzettel erhalten; **to give (make out) a** ~ Quittung ausstellen, Empfang schriftlich bescheinigen; **to give** ~ **in full** per Saldo quittieren; **to pay [up]on** ~ bei Empfang (postnumerando) zahlen; **to put one's** ~ **on** quittieren; **to sign a** ~ Empfangsbescheinigung ausstellen; **to take** ~ **of** in Empfang nehmen;
please acknowledge ~ um Bestätigung des Empfangs wird gebeten;
~ **book** Einnahme-, Quittungsbuch; ~ **card** Quittungskarte; ~ **declaration** Empfangsbestätigung; ~ **form** Empfangs-, Quittungsformular; ~ **holder** Lagerscheininhaber; ~ **number** Eingangsnummer; ~ **side** Einnahmeseite; ~ **stamp** Eingangs-, Empfangs-, Bezahlt-, Quittungsstempel, -marke; ~ **tax** Einnahmen-, Umsatzsteuer; ~ **voucher** Empfangsbescheinigung.

receipted bill of exchange quittierter Wechsel.
receiptor Quittungsaussteller, *(bailee)* Aufbewahrer beschlagnahmten Eigentums.
receivable ausstehend, offen, noch als Eingang zu erwarten, auf Zahlung wartend, zu zahlen, *(admissible)* zulässig;
~s *(balance sheet, US)* Forderungen, Außenstände, Debitoren [aus Buch-, Kunden-, Wechselforderungen, Schuldscheinen]; **accounts** ~ *(US)* Debitoren aus Buchforderungen, Außenstände, ausstehende Rechnungen; **aging** ~ **accounts** *(US)* Debitorenaufstellung nach Fälligkeiten, nach Fälligkeiten sortierte Außenstände; **deferred accounts** ~ *(US)* künftig fällige Forderungen; **accounts** ~ **discounted** *(US)* abgetretene Außenstände, zedierter Debitorenbestand; **other accounts** ~ *(balance sheet, US)* sonstige Forderungen; **past-due accounts** ~ *(US)* überfällige Debitoren; **pledged accounts** ~ *(US)* abgetretene Außenstände; **trade accounts** ~ *(balance sheet, US)* Forderungen an Kunden [aufgrund von Warenforderungen]; **account ~s less reserve** *(US)* Buchschulden abzüglich Rückstellungen; **accruals** ~ *(US)* entstandene Forderungen; **bills** ~ *(US)* Wechselforderungen, Rimessen; **bond subscription ~s** *(US)* Debitoren aus Schuldverschreibungen; **contingent ~s** *(US)* bedingte Forderungen; **current ~s** *(balance sheet, US)* Umlaufvermögen; **extended ~s** *(US)* überfällige Kundenforderungen; **long-term ~s** *(US)* langfristige Debitoren; **mortgages** ~ *(US)* Hypothekenforderungen; **notes** ~ *(US)* Wechselforderungen, Bestand an Wechseln, Schuldscheinen und Akzepten; **outstanding ~s** *(US)* ausstehende Forderungen; **period-end ~s** *(US)* Forderungen am Ende eines Rechnungsabschnittes; **trade acceptances** ~ *(US)* ausstehende Handelsakzepte; **uncollectable ~s** langfristige Forderungen;
~s from customers *(balance sheet, US)* Forderungen an Kunden, Kundenforderungen; **~s and payables** *(US)* Forderungen und Verbindlichkeiten;
to be ~ als gesetzliches Zahlungsmittel gelten; **to be** ~ **in evidence** als Beweismittel zugelassen sein;
accrued ~ **accounts** *(US)* entstandene, aber noch nicht fällige Forderungen; ~ **assets** ausstehende Guthaben; ~ **interest** Zinsaußenstände; ~ **item** debitorischer (ausstehender) Posten; **accounts** ~ **loan** *(US)* Debitorenkredit; **to flag the** ~ **records** *(US)* Debitorenbuchhaltung mit einem Alarmsystem

ausstatten; **accounts** ~ **statement** *(US)* Debitorenauszug; **~s turnover** *(US)* Umschlagsgeschwindigkeit der Forderungen, Forderungsumschlagsziffer.
receive *(v.)* annehmen, empfangen, in Empfang nehmen, entgegennehmen, erhalten, *(evidence)* zulassen, *(money)* einnehmen, vereinnahmen;
~ **in advance** vorausempfangen; ~ **approval** Genehmigung erhalten; ~ **a benefit in kind** Sachbezüge erhalten; ~ **a bribe** sich bestechen lassen; ~ **s. o. into a charge** jem. ein Amt übertragen; ~ **DM 100,- clear** 100,- DM auf die Hand bekommen; ~ **for collection** zum Inkasso übernehmen; ~ **a complaint** Beschwerde entgegennehmen; ~ **upon credit** auf Kredit erhalten; ~ **a distinction** Auszeichnung erhalten; ~ **dividends** Dividenden beziehen; ~ **in evidence** als Beweismittel zulassen; ~ **in exchange** eintauschen; ~ **s. o. into one's family** j. in seine Familie aufnehmen; ~ **goods** Waren in Empfang nehmen (hereinbekommen); ~ **stolen goods** als Hehler fungieren, Hehlerware verheimlichen, Hehlerei begehen; ~ **information** Auskunft erhalten; ~ **a legacy** Vermächtnisnehmer sein; ~ **a letter** Brief erhalten; ~ **a loan back** Kredit zurückgezahlt bekommen; ~ **a foreign minister** Beglaubigungsschreiben eines Gesandten entgegennehmen; ~ **money** Geld vereinnahmen; ~ **[the] news** Nachrichten hören; ~ **one's notice** gekündigt werden; ~ **an order** Auftrag entgegennehmen; ~ **a pardon** begnadigt werden; ~ **a petition** Gesuch entgegennehmen; ~ **a proposal favo(u)rably** Vorschlag günstig aufnehmen; ~ **a refusal** Ablehnung erfahren; ~ **a report** *(parl.)* Ausschußbericht entgegennehmen; ~ **a salary** Gehaltsempfänger sein, Gehalt beziehen; ~ **a sentence** bestraft werden; ~ **a summons** vorgeladen werden; ~ **a telegram** Telegramm erhalten; ~ **visitors** Besucher empfangen; ~ **a warm welcome** herzlich willkommen geheißen werden;
to be open to ~ **guests** für Gäste bereitstehen.
received [Zahlung] erhalten, empfangen, *(generally accepted)* authentisch, echt;
cash ~ Betrag bar erhalten; **duly** ~ richtig erhalten; **value** ~ *(bill of exchange)* Wert empfangen; **when** ~ nach Empfang (Erhalt); ~ **on account** in Gegenrechnung empfangen, als Akontozahlung erhalten; ~ **for shipment** zur Beförderung übernommen; ~ **with thanks** dankend erhalten;
to be ~ *(money)* eingehen; **to be** ~ **in audience** in Audienz empfangen werden; **to have been well** ~ **throughout the country** allenthalben wohlwollend aufgenommen worden sein; **to be** ~ **without deduction of income tax** einkommenssteuerfrei vereinnahmt werden;
~ **doctrine** *(law)* herrschende Meinung; **payment** ~ Betrag erhalten, bezahlt; ~ **stamp** Quittungs-, Eingangsstempel; ~ **text** authentischer Text; ~ **version** gültige Fassung; ~ **view** allgemeine Ansicht.
receiver Empfänger, Adressat, Übernehmer, *(bankruptcy, US)* Konkurs-, Masseverwalter, *(court officer)* Rechtspfleger der Hinterlegungsstelle, *(for person with mental defect, Br.)* Pfleger, *(estate)* Nachlaßkonkursverwalter, *(money)* Einnehmer, *(official liquidator, Br.)* [amtlich bestellter] Liquidator, Zwangsverwalter, *(shipping business)* Ladungsempfänger, *(tel.)* Telefonhörer, Hörmuschel, *(teller)* Kassierer, *(trustee)* Treuhänder, Sachwalter, behördlich bestellter Verwalter, Vermögensverwalter, *(wholesale marketing)* Aufkäufer, *(wireless)* Empfangsgerät, Empfänger;
ancillary ~ Gehilfe eines Konkursverwalters mit Wohnsitz im Staat des Konkursvermögens; **emergency** ~ Notempfänger; **official** ~ *(Br.)* behördlich bestellter (amtlicher) Konkursverwalter, Sequester; ~ **pendente lite** Prozeßpfleger; **radio** ~ Rundfunkempfänger; **television** ~ Fernsehgerät, Fernseher;
givers and ~s *(stock exchange)* Geber und Nehmer;
~ **appointed by the bank** von der Bank bestellter Liquidator; ~ **in bankruptcy** Konkursverwalter [im Zwangskonkurs]; ~ **under a floating charge** aufgrund einer Globalverpfändung eingesetzter Sequester; ~ **of customs** Zolleinnehmer; ~ **in equity** Zwangsverwalter; ~ **by way of equitable execution** *(Br.)* Zwangsverwalter, für die Durchführung eines Zwangsvollstreckungsbeschlusses bestellter Verwalter; ~ **of goods** Konsignator, Warenempfänger; ~ **of an indemnity** Entschädiger; ~ **of a loan** Darlehnsnehmer; ~ **of stolen property** Hehler; ~ **general of the public revenue** *(Br.)* Obersteuereinnehmer; ~ **and manager** *(Br.)* Vermögensverwalter mit Geschäftsführungsbefugnis; ~ **pendente lite** Sequester [während der Prozeßdauer]; **~s and triers of petitions** *(parl.)* Petitionsausschuß; ~ **of stolen property** Hehler; ~ **of taxes** *(US)* Steuereinnehmer; ~ **of wreck** *(US)* Strandvogt;

to appoint a ~ for the bankrupt's estate Konkursverwalter bestellen; **to lift the ~** Hörer abnehmen; **to petition for the appointment of a ~** *(US)* Antrag auf Geschäftsaufsicht stellen; **to replace the ~** Telefonhörer auflegen; **to take off the ~** Telefonhörer abheben;

at ~'s account zu Lasten des Empfängers; **~'s authority** Vollmacht eines Pflegers (Verwalters); **~'s bond** Konkursverwalterkaution; **~'s certificate** [Zwangs]versteigerungsvermerk, Beschlagnahmeverfügung; **~'s certificates (notes, US)** von einem Konkursverwalter ausgegebene Obligationen; **~ country** *(International Monetary Fund)* Empfängerland; **~'s expense** Konkursverwaltergebühren; **~'s office** Hebestelle, Steueramt; **~ general's office** *(Br.)* Hauptsteueramt; **~'s office for the customs** Zollabfertigungsstelle; **official ~'s report** Konkursverwalterbericht; **~ rest** *(tel.)* Gabel.

receivership Vermögensverwaltung, *(bankruptcy, US)* Zwangs-, Konkursverwaltung, Geschäftsaufsicht, *(lunatic, Br.)* Pflegschaft, Vermögenspflegschaft, *(taxation)* Amt des Steuereinnehmers;

under ~ in Konkurs;

official ~ vorläufige Konkursverwaltung; **temporary ~** Geschäftsaufsicht, Sequestration; **to be put under ~** unter Geschäftsaufsicht gestellt werden; **to go into ~** bankrott werden, Konkurs machen; **to make application for ~** Antrag auf Geschäftsaufsicht stellen; **to put a corporation under ~** Gesellschaft unter Geschäftsaufsicht stellen; **to steer near ~** auf den Konkurs zusteuern.

receiving An-, Abnahme, Empfangnahme, *(department)* Warenannahme[stelle], *(wireless set)* Empfang;

~ a bribe passive Bestechung; **~ of goods** Warenannahme; **~ stolen goods** gewerbsmäßige Hehlerei; **~ an order** Entgegennahme eines Auftrags;

to do the ~ Kassierer sein, kassieren;

~ box Briefkasten; **~ cashier** Kassierer am Einzahlungsschalter; **~ clerk** *(US)* Abnahmebeamter; **~ counter** Briefannahmestelle; **~ division (department)** Warenempfangs-, Warenannahmeabteilung; **~ house** Brief- und Paketannahmestelle, *(goods, Br.)* Auslieferungslager; **to leave the ~ line** offiziell empfangen worden sein; **~ nation** Empfängerland; **~ note** Lade-, Versandschein, Versandanzeige; **~ office** Annahmestelle, *(mail)* Empfangspostamt; **~ order** *(Br.)* Veräußerungsverbot, vorläufiger Konkurseröffnungsbeschluß, Sequestration, offener Arrest; **to petition the court to make a ~ order** Antrag auf Konkurseröffnung stellen; **~ place** Empfangsort; **~ report** Wareneingangsmeldung; **~ room** Empfangsraum, *(goods)* Wareneingangsstelle, -annahme; **~ set** Empfangsgerät, Empfänger; **~ sheet** Warenannahmeschein; **~ ship** Ausbildungsschiff; **~ slip** Wareneingangsschein; **~ state** Empfangsstaat; **~ station** Empfangsstation, *(telegraph)* Empfänger; **~ teller** Kassierer am Einzahlungsschalter; **~ ticket** Warenempfangsschein.

recense *(v.)* durchsehen, revidieren.

recension Prüfung, Durchsicht, *(revised text)* revidierte Ausgabe.

recent kürzlich geschehen;

to be ~ *(news)* neuesten Datums sein;

~ acquaintance neueste Bekanntschaft; **~ events** noch nicht lange zurückliegende Ereignisse; **~ news** neueste Nachrichten.

recentralization Rezentralisierung.

recentralize *(v.)* rezentralisieren.

reception *(acceptance)* Inempfangnahme, *(admission)* Zulassung, Aufnahme [in einen Verein], *(bill)* An-, Aufnahme, *(hospital)* Aufnahme, *(formal party)* [offizieller] Empfang, Gratulationskur, *(radio)* Empfang;

civic ~ Empfang durch die Stadtverwaltung; **cocktail ~** Cocktailempfang; **farewell ~** Abschiedsempfang; **formal ~** offizieller (feierlicher) Empfang; **friendly ~** freundschaftliche Aufnahme; **poor ~** *(wireless set)* schlechter Empfang; **radio ~** Rundfunkempfang; **rousing ~** rauschender Empfang; **sourspirited ~** unfreundliche Aufnahme; **wedding ~** Hochzeitsempfang;

~ of deposits Annahme von Einlagen; **~ of evidence** Entgegennahme von Beweisen, Beweiserhebung; **~ of guests** Aufnahme von Gästen; **~ without interference** störungsfreier Empfang; **~ of a letter** Empfang eines Briefes; **~ of a television program(me)** Qualität eines Fernsehprogramms;

to give (hold) a ~ Empfang abhalten; **to give s. o. a cordial ~** jem. einen herzlichen Empfang bereiten; **to give a speech a hostile ~** Rede ungünstig aufnehmen; **to give weekly ~s** Jour fix abhalten; **to have a favo(u)rable ~** günstige Aufnahme finden; **to meet with a cool (win a cold) ~** kühle Aufnahme finden, kühl aufgenommen werden.

~ area Auffang-, Aufnahmegebiet, *(hotel)* Empfangshalle; **~ area for refugees** Auffangsgebiet für Flüchtlinge; **~ camp** Auffang-, Aufnahmelager; **~ center (centre, Br.)** Aufnahmezentrum, Obdachlosenasyl, -heim, *(child offenders)* Jugendbewahranstalt [für Kinder unter 15 Jahren], *(New York)* Gefängnis; **~ clerk** Empfangschef; **~ committee** Empfangskomitee; **~ desk** Empfang[sbüro]; **~ hall** Empfangshalle; **~ institute** Irren-, Nervenheilanstalt; **~ office** *(hotel)* Empfang[sbüro], *(hospital)* Aufnahme; **~ order** *(Br.)* Entmündigungsbeschluß, Einweisung in eine Heil- und Pflegeanstalt; **~ room** Empfangsraum, -salon, *(hotel)* Gesellschaftsraum, -zimmer, *(office)* Wartezimmer.

receptionist Empfang, Empfangschef, -dame, *(doctor)* Sprechstundenhilfe.

receptive aufnahmebereit, -fähig, rezeptiv.

receptiveness of the market Aufnahmefähigkeit des Marktes.

receptivity *(market)* Aufnahmebereitschaft.

recess *(break)* [Arbeits]pause, Sitzungspause, Unterbrechung, *(of the court, US)* Gerichtsferien, *(parl.)* Ferien, *(retreat)* stiller Winkel, Unterschlupf, *(room)* Nische, *(school, US)* Ferien;

~ of parliament Parlamentsferien;

~ (v.) sich vertagen;

~ for an hour Sitzung für eine Stunde unterbrechen;

to be in ~ Sitzung unterbrechen, *(parl.)* in den Ferien sein; **to rise for ~** *(parl.)* Parlamentsferien beginnen; **to take a ~** Sitzungspause einlegen, *(school)* Ferien geben;

~ appointment (constitution, (US) Ferienberufungsrecht; **~ bed** [in die Wand] zusammenklappbares Bett; **~ committee** *(parl.)* Ferienausschuß.

recession [Preis-, Kurs]rückgang, Rückschlag, *(cyclical movement)* Rezession, [leichter] Konjunkturrückgang, -rückschlag, -flaute, Abschwung, rückläufige Entwicklung, Wirtschaftsrückgang, -flaute, *(insurance)* Rückabtretung, *(weather)* Abzug;

vulnerable to ~ rezessionsempfindlich;

business ~ wirtschaftlicher Rückschlag, Geschäftsrückgang; **economic ~** Wirtschaftsrezession; **far-reaching ~** tiefgreifende Rezession; **full-fledged ~** gesamte Wirtschaft erfassende Rezession; **initial violent ~** anfängliches starkes Nachgeben [der Kurse]; **material ~** beträchtlicher [Kurs]rückgang; **post-oil-crisis ~** der Ölkrise folgende Rezession; **trade ~** wirtschaftlicher Rückschlag, Konjunkturrückgang;

~ in business (of business activity) Konjunkturrückgang, -flaute; **~ in profits** Gewinnrezession; **~ of conquered territory** Rückgabe eroberten Gebiets;

to be in a deep ~ in einer tiefen Rezession stecken; **to buck the ~** *(US)* sich mit allen Mitteln gegen die Rezession stemmen; **to come out of a ~** Rezession gerade hinter sich gebracht haben; **to head into ~** Rezessionsperiode ansteuern; **to steer out of a ~** aus einer Rezession herausführen; **to topple into a severe ~** in eine heftige Rezession stürzen;

~-borne rezessionsgesteuert; **~-clouded** unter einem bedeckten Rezessionshimmel; **~ fear** Rezessionsangst, -befürchtungen; **~ gap** Rezessionsloch, -lücke; **~-induced** rezessionsbedingt; **to be still at a ~ level** noch immer Rezessionszeiten entsprechen, immer noch auf der Rezessionssohle verharren; **~ money** Abstandsgeld; **~ period** Rezessionszeit, -phase; **anti-~ policy** Politik der Konjunkturbelebung; **~-proof** rezessionsunempfindlich; **to put a ~ tag on a period** Zeitraum als Rezession definieren, einer Wirtschaftsepoche den Rezessionsstempel aufdrücken; **~ times** Rezessionszeit; **~ trough** Rezessionsmulde, Rezessionstief, Konjunkturmulde; **~ year** Jahr wirtschaftlichen Rückgangs.

recessional *(business)* rückläufig, rezessionsbedingt.

recessionary trend rückläufige Konjunkturbewegung.

recharge *(battery)* Nachladen, *(mil.)* Gegenangriff;

~ (v.) (mil.) von neuem angreifen;

~ a battery Batterie aufladen.

recharter Weiterbefrachtung, Unterfrachtvertrag;

~ (v.) wiederverfrachten, weiterverfrachten.

recidivism *(criminal)* Rückfall, -fälligkeit.

recidivist Gewohnheits-, Rückfalltäter;

~ (a.) rückfällig.

recidivous rückfällig.

recipe Rezept;

~ book Buch für Kochrezepte.

recipiendary akzeptierter Kandidat.

recipient Empfänger, Empfangsberechtigter, *(benefited party)* Bedachter;

authorized ~ Empfangsberechtigter, *(law)* Zustellungsbevollmächtigter;

~ **of an allowance** Zuschuß-, Zuteilungs-, Kostgeldempfänger;
~ **of dividends** Dividendenberechtigter; ~ **of a favo(u)r** Begünstigter; ~ **of a gift** Schenkungsempfänger; ~ **of income** Einkommensempfänger; ~ **of a payment** Zahlungsempfänger; ~ **of a pension** Pensions-, Ruhegehaltsempfänger; ~ **of relief** Fürsorge-, Sozialhilfeempfänger; ~ **of services** Leistungsempfänger; ~ **of unemployment relief** Arbeitslosenunterstützungsempfänger;
~ **country** Empfängerland; ~**'s screen** Empfängerbildschirm.

reciprocal wechsel-, gegenseitig, beiderseits, entsprechend;
~ **contract** gegenseitiger Vertrag; ~ **debt** Gegenschuld; ~ **demand** reziproke Nachfrage; ~ **exchange** *(US)* Gegenseitigkeitsverein; ~ **insurance** *(US)* Versicherung auf Gegenseitigkeit; ~ **privileges** wechselseitig eingeräumte Vorrechte; ~ **protection of investments** *(law of nations)* gegenseitiger Schutz von Kapitalanlagen; ~ **relationship** Gegenbeziehung; ~ **service** Gegendienst; ~ **trade agreement** Gegenseitigkeitsabkommen, Handelsabkommen mit Meistbegünstigungsklausel; **to grant** ~ **treatment** Gegenseitigkeit gewähren; ~ **understanding** Gegenseitigkeitsvereinbarung; ~ **will** [etwa] Berliner Testament.

reciprocate *(v.) (return service)* Gegendienst leisten;
~ **an entry** Posten übereinstimmend vortragen;
glad to ~ **in similar kind** zu Gegendiensten jederzeit bereit.

reciprocating engine Kolbenmotor.

reciprocation of courtesies Austausch von Höflichkeiten.

reciprocity Gegenseitigkeit;
on a basis of (based on) ~ auf Gegenseitigkeit beruhend; **subject to** ~ unter Voraussetzung der Gegenseitigkeit;
~ **in trade** Gegenseitigkeit der Zolltarife;
~ **clause (stipulation)** Gegenseitigkeitsklausel; ~ **dealings** Gegenseitigkeitsgeschäfte; ~ **principle** Gegenseitigkeitsprinzip; ~ **treaty** Gegenseitigkeitsvertrag.

recission Vertragsaufhebung.

recital *(detailed account)* Schilderung, Darstellung, eingehender Bericht, *(concert)* Konzertabend, *(contract)* Bestimmung, Feststellung, *(pleading)* einleitende Sachdarstellung, *(preamble)* Einleitungsworte, einleitender Teil, Präambel;
~ **of debts** Schuldenverzeichnis; ~ **of facts** Darstellung des Sachverhalts;
~ **clause** *(policy form)* Präambel.

recite vortragen;
~ *(v.)* **facts** Darstellung des Sachverhalts geben; ~ **one's grievances** seine Beschwerden einzeln aufzählen.

reciter Vorleser, -tragender.

reckless rücksichtslos, sorglos, leichtfertig, *(law)* grob fahrlässig;
~ **conduct** unverantwortliche Handlungsweise; ~ **disregard of rights of others** *(automobile law)* grob fahrlässige Mißachtung der Rechte anderer Verkehrsteilnehmer; ~ **driver** rücksichtsloser Autofahrer; ~ **driving** rücksichtslose Fahrweise; ~ **endangering of s. o.** *(US)* leichtfertige Gefährdung Dritter; ~ **spender** unüberlegter Geldausgeber.

recklessness Rücksichtslosigkeit, Leichtfertigkeit, *(law)* grobe Fahrlässigkeit.

reckon *(v.) (compute)* berechnen, kalkulieren, *(count)* rechnen, zählen, *(include in computation)* anrechnen, in Ansatz bringen;
~ **a business generally as prosperous** Geschäftsbranche generell für gewinnträchtig halten; ~ **on s. one's coming** mit jds. Erscheinen rechnen; ~ **the cost of a holiday** Kostenaufwand eines Urlaubs ausrechnen; ~ **the cost of an undertaking** Kostenaufwand eines Unternehmens kalkulieren; ~ **with a danger** Gefahr in Rechnung stellen; ~ **on human foolishness** sich auf die menschliche Dummheit verlassen; ~ **s. o. one's friend** j. zu seinen Freunden zählen; ~ **in one's head** im Kopf ausrechnen; ~ **upon s. one's help** auf jds. Hilfe zählen; ~ **without one's host** Rechnung ohne den Wirt machen; ~ **in** einrechnen; ~ **in the cost of a taxi** Kosten einer Taxifahrt mit einkalkulieren; ~ **one's total indebtedness** sich über den Umfang seiner Schulden klarwerden; ~ **among the leaders** zu den Führern gerechnet werden; ~ **s. o. the richest man hereabouts** j. für den reichsten Mann in der Gegend halten; ~ **over** durchrechnen, prüfen; ~ **over again** nachrechnen; ~ **rent in the cost of living** Mietanteil in die Lebenshaltungskosten mit einbeziehen; ~ **the size of an audience** Zuhörerzahl schätzen; ~ **the size of one's total indebtedness** seine Gesamtverschuldung überschlagen; ~ **up** *(Br.)* Kasse machen, *(cast up)* zusammenrechnen, -zählen, addieren, *(set off)* aufrechnen, verrechnen; ~ **up the bill** Rechnung addieren; ~ **up one's losses** Verlustbilanz aufstellen; ~ **upon s. th.** auf etw. rechnen, sich auf etw. verlassen.

reckoned | **in the aggregate (all together)** im ganzen gerechnet; ~ **in cash** in bar gerechnet; ~ **in the majority in value** der wertmäßigen Stimmenmehrheit entsprechend;

to be ~ **among the leaders** zu den führenden Persönlichkeiten gezählt werden.

reckoner [Be]rechner;
ready ~ Umrechnungs-, Zinstabelle.

reckoning *(computing)* [Be]rechnung, *(counting)* Rechnung, Rechnen, Zählen, Zählung, *(inn)* Rechnung, Zeche, *(ship)* Besteck;
by my ~ meiner Berechnung nach; **without** ~ **the travel(l)ing expenses** Reisespesen ungerechnet;
dead ~ *(ship)* gegißte Berechnung;
to be out of one's ~ sich verrechnet haben; **to include in the** ~ mit einrechnen; **to pay the** ~ Rechnung begleichen; **to work out the ship's** ~ Besteck berechnen (nehmen);
day of ~ Abrechnungstag.

reclaim Rückforderung, *(technics)* Regenerierung;
~ *(v.)* zurückfordern, beanspruchen, herausverlangen, reklamieren, *(agriculture)* kulturfähig (urbar) machen, kultivieren, dem Meer abgewinnen, *(appeal, Scot.)* Berufung einlegen, *(technics)* regenerieren;
~ **against** protestieren (auftreten) gegen; ~ **s. o. to a sense of his duty** j. auf den Weg der Pflicht zurückführen.

reclaimable [ver]besserungsfähig, *(land)* kulturfähig.

reclaimant *(law)* Beschwerdeführer.

reclaimed | **animals** Haustiere; ~ **drunkard** entwöhnter Trinker; ~ **rubber** regenerierter Gummi.

reclaiming | **bill** *(Scot.)* Berufungsschrift; ~ **days** Berufungsfrist.

reclamation *(agriculture)* Urbarmachung, *(banking)* Differenzbetrag [in der Scheckverrechnung], *(protest)* Reklamation, Beschwerde, Einspruch, Einwand, Mängelrüge, Rückforderung, *(rectification, US)* Richtigstellung;
land ~ Urbarmachung von Grund und Boden, Neulandgewinnung;
~ **of land** Neulandgewinnung;
⌀ **Act** *(US)* Urbarmachungsgesetz; ~ **district** Kulturbezirk; ~ **proceedings** *(US)* Aussonderungsverfahren; ~ **project** Landgewinnungsprojekt; ~ **water** *(US)* aus Bewässerungsvorhaben gewonnenes Wasser.

reclassification Neueinstufung, -einteilung, -gruppierung.

reclassify *(v.)* neu einstufen, umgruppieren.

recluse Zurückgezogener, Klausner, Einsiedler.

reclusion Zurückgezogenheit, Einsiedlerleben, *(punishment)* Einzelhaft, *(Louisiana)* Zuchthausstrafe.

recoal *(v.)* Kohlenvorrat ergänzen, Kohlen bunkern.

recognition *(advertising)* Anzeigenwiedererkennung, *(claim)* Anerkennung, *(confirmation)* Genehmigung, Bestätigung, *(international law)* Anerkennung der Unabhängigkeit, *(parl., US)* Worterteilung, *(ratification)* Ratifizierung;
in ~ **of s. one's services** in Anerkennung von jds. Diensten;
de-facto ~ De-facto-, faktische Anerkennung; **de-jure** ~ De-jure- (endgültige) Anerkennung; **professional** ~ professionelle Anerkennung; **union** ~ Anerkennung einer Gewerkschaft;
~ **of belligerence** Anerkennung als kriegsführende Macht; ~ **of the border** Anerkennung der Grenze; ~ **of a new state** völkerrechtliche Anerkennung eines Staates;
to receive top professional ~ Aufmerksamkeit innerhalb der maßgebenden Berufskreise erregen; **to win** ~ *(artist)* sich durchsetzen;
~ **dispute** *(trade union)* Streit über die Anerkennung einer Gewerkschaft; ~ **lag** Erkennungsverzögerung; ~ **light** *(airplane)* Kennlicht; ~ **mark** Kennzeichen; ~ **order** Anerkennungsverfügung; ~ **procedure** Anerkennungsverfahren; ~ **process** Anerkennungsverfahren; ~ **test** *(advertising)* Erinnerungs-, Wiedererkennungstest.

recognizable anerkennungsfähig.

recognizance [Schuld]anerkenntnis, Schuldschein, *(sum liable to forfeiture)* Kaution, Sicherheitsleistung;
on one's own ~ ohne Kaution;
to enter into ~ Anerkenntnis vor Gericht abgeben, Kaution stellen; **to sign a** ~ **to accept affiliation responsibilities** Unterhaltsverpflichtung schriftlich anerkennen.

recognize *(v.)* [Schuld] anerkennen, *(law court)* sich vor Gericht schriftlich verpflichten, *(international law)* Unabhängigkeit anerkennen;
~ **an old acquaintance** alten Bekannten erkennen; ~ **a natural child** Vaterschaft anerkennen; ~ **a claim** Anspruch anerkennen; ~ **a consul** Konsul anerkennen; ~ **a defeat** sich geschlagen geben; ~ **a government** Regierung völkerrechtlich anerkennen; ~ **a government as a belligerent** Staat als kriegsführende Partei anerkennen; ~ **s. o. as lawful heir** j. als rechtmäßigen Erben anerkennen; ~ **one's lack of qualification(s)** seine mangelnde Eignung für eine Stellung zugeben; ~ **a member** *(US)* einem

Abgeordneten das Wort erteilen; ~ **an obligation** Verpflichtung anerkennen; ~ **s. one's services** jds. Verdienste würdigen; ~ **a state** Staat anerkennen;
to refuse to ~ **one's signature** seine Unterschrift nicht anerkennen.

recognized anerkannt;
~ **by law** rechtlich anerkannt;
to be ~ **to practise before the Patent Office** (US) als Patentanwalt zugelassen sein;
~ **agent** anerkannter (zugelassener) Vertreter; ~ **holiday** gesetzlich geschützter Feiertag; ~ **merchant** Gewerbesteuerpflichtiger; ~ **stock exchange** staatlich anerkannte Börse.

recognizee Schuldscheinnehmer.

recognizor Schuldscheinaussteller.

recoin (v.) umprägen, wiederprägen.

recoinage Umprägung.

recollection Erinnerungsvermögen, Gedächtnis;
to the best of my ~ soweit meine Erinnerung reicht;
~**s** Erinnerungen;
~**s of one's childhood** Kindheitserinnerungen.

recolonization Wiederbesiedlung.

recolonize (v.) wiederbesiedeln.

recommence (v.) (statute of limitations) wieder zu laufen beginnen.

recommend (v.) vorschlagen, empfehlen, befürworten;
~ **the amount of dividends** Dividendenempfehlung haben; ~ **a candidate for a post** Kandidaten vorschlagen; ~ **to s. one's care** jem. anvertrauen; ~ **caution** zur Vorsicht raten; ~ **a child to s. one's care** Kind jds. Fürsorge anempfehlen; ~ **customers** Kunden überweisen; ~ **s. o. highly** j. besonders empfehlen; ~ **s. o. kindly** schöne Grüße von jem. ausrichten; ~ **a price** als [Richt]preis empfehlen; ~ **strongly (warmly)** dringend (warm) empfehlen.

recommendable empfehlenswert.

recommendation Befürwortung, Empfehlung, Vorschlag, Anpreisung, Einführung [von Personen], (proposed agreement) Einigungsvorschlag;
upon the ~ **of** auf Veranlassung (Empfehlung) von; **with a favo(u)rable** ~ befürwortend;
cordial ~ angelegentliche Empfehlung;
~**s of the commission** Ausschußempfehlungen; ~ **of a committee** Ausschußempfehlung; ~ **of a price** Richtpreisempfehlung; **to attend s. one's** ~**s** jds. Ratschläge beachten; **to buy s. th. on the** ~ **of a friend** auf Empfehlung eines Freundes erwerben; **to make a** ~ Empfehlung aussprechen; **to speak in** ~ **of s. o.** sich für j. einsetzen; **to write on s. one's** ~ auf jds. Empfehlung schreiben.

recommendatory empfehlend;
~ **letters** Einführungsschreiben.

recommended price empfohlener Preis, Richtpreis, unverbindliche Preisempfehlung.

recommission (v.) (mil.) reaktivieren.

recommit | (v.) [an eine Kommission] zurückverweisen;
~ **a bill** Gesetzentwurf an einen Ausschuß zurückverweisen; ~ **a prisoner to prison** Haftfortdauer für einen Gefangenen anordnen; ~ **a ship** Schiff wieder in Dienst stellen; ~ **temporarily** vorübergehende Haft anordnen.

recommitment (recommittal) Rückverweisung, (prisoner) erneute Verhaftung (Haftanordnung);
~ **of a bill** Zurückverweisung eines Gesetzentwurfes.

recompense (amends) Entgelt, Ersatz, Entschädigung, (reward) Belohnung, Vergeltung;
as ~ **for your trouble** für Ihre Mühewaltung;
~ (v.) (make amends) erstatten, ersetzen, entschädigen, Ersatz leisten, wiedergutmachen, (reward) belohnen;
~ **s. o. for a loss** j. für einen erlittenen Verlust entschädigen; ~ **s. o. for his trouble** j. für seine Bemühungen entschädigen;
to receive a ~ **for one's services** Vergütung für seine Mühewaltung erlangen; **to work without** ~ ehrenamtlich tätig sein.

recompose (v.) (print.) neu setzen.

recomposition Umbildung, -gruppierung, (print.) Neusatz.

recompute (v.) erneut berechnen.

reconcentrate (v.) wieder konzentrieren, rückverflechten.

reconcentration [Re]konzentration, Rückverflechtung.

reconcilable vereinbar.

reconcile (v.) [sich] aussöhnen, (accounts) abstimmen, in Übereinstimmung bringen, postenweise vergleichen, kollationieren, (harmonize) in Einklang bringen;
~ **o. s. to s. th.** sich mit etw. abfinden; ~ **with the facts of the case** mit den Tatsachen eines Falles in Übereinstimmung bringen; ~ **o. s. to one's work** seine Arbeit liebgewinnen;

to have to ~ **o. s. to a life of poverty** sich mit ärmlichen Verhältnissen abfinden müssen.

reconciled (account) abgestimmt.

reconcilement Schlichtung, Beilegung, (accounts) [Konten]abstimmung, Kollationierung;
~ **of bank statement** (Br.) Anerkenntnis des Rechnungsabschlusses (Bankauszugs).

reconciliation Vereinbarung, Beilegung, Schlichtung, (married couple) Wiederaussöhnung;
~ **of [bank] accounts** Kontenabstimmung; ~ **of cash** Kassenabstimmung; ~ **of surplus** Gewinnberichtigung;
to bring about a ~ Aussöhnung zustande bringen;
~ **account** Berichtigungskonto; ~ **agreement** Schlichtungsvereinbarung; ~ **date** (banking) Abstimmungstermin; ~ **statement** Saldenanerkenntnis.

recondite tiefgründig;
~ **book** schwer verständliches Buch.

recondition (v.) überholen, aufarbeiten, (reeducate) umschulen.

reconditioned automobile generalüberholtes Auto.

reconditioning Wiederinstandsetzung, [General]überholung, Aufarbeitung, (reeducation) Umschulung;
~ **charge** Instandsetzungskosten.

reconduction (lease) Erneuerung des Pachtverhältnisses.

reconfirm (v.) **a reservation** Buchung bestätigen.

reconfirmation | **of a reservation** Buchungsbestätigung;
~ **notice** (airplane) Buchungsbestätigung.

reconnaissance (mil.) Aufklärung;
~ **in force** gewaltsame Aufklärung;
to make a ~ Gelände sondieren; **to make a** ~ **of the work to be done** die zu erledigende Arbeit vorher im einzelnen feststellen;
~ **aircraft** Fernaufklärer; ~ **drone** ferngesteuertes Aufklärungsflugzeug; ~ **plane** Aufklärungsflugzeug, ~ **satellite** Aufklärungssatellit.

reconnect (v.) Anschluß wiederherstellen.

reconnoitre (v.) **the grounds** (mil.) Gelände aufklären.

reconsider (v.) nochmals erwägen, nachprüfen, Entscheidung überprüfen, (parl.) nochmals beraten;
~ **a motion** (parl.) Antrag erneut debattieren.

reconsideration nochmalige Erwägung (Beratung);
~ **of a claim** Nachprüfung einer Forderung;
to give ~ erneut überprüfen.

reconsign (v.) Waren an neue Adresse weitersenden, (new address) umleiten, umadressieren.

reconsignment Zurücksendung, nochmalige Sendung, (new address) Umadressierung, Weiterleitung.

reconstitute (v.) wiederherstellen, (mil.) erneut aufstellen.

reconstitution Wiederherstellung, Wiedereinsetzung, -herstellung.

reconstruct (v.) neu (wieder) aufbauen, umbauen, reorganisieren, sanieren;
~ **a company** (Br.) Gesellschaft durch Umgründung sanieren;
~ **a crime** Verbrechen rekonstruieren.

reconstruction (house) Um-, Wiederaufbau, (patent law) Neuherstellung, (reestablishment) Neugründung, (reorganization, Br.) Wiederaufbau, Reorganisation, Sanierung;
economic (industrial) ~ Wiederaufbau der Wirtschaft; **educational** ~ Schulreform;
~ **of a company** (Br.) Reorganisation eines Unternehmens, Sanierungsumgründung; ~ **of a crime** Rekonstruktion eines Verbrechens; ~ **and reorganization** (Br.) Sanierungsumgründung; ~ **of works** Wiederaufbau eines Gewerbebetriebs, Wiedererrichtung gewerblicher Anlagen;
~ **credit** Aufbaukredit, Ankurbelungskredit; ~ Finance Corporation (US) Wiederaufbaubank, Kreditanstalt für Wiederaufbau; ~ **loan** Wiederaufbauanleihe; -kredit; ~ **program(me)** Reorganisations-, Wiederaufbauprogramm; ~ **program(me)** Wiederaufbauprogramm; ~ **proposal** Sanierungsvorschlag.

reconvene (v.) (parl.) wieder zusammentreten;
~ **a conference** Konferenz erneut einberufen.

reconvention (law) Gegen-, Widerklage.

reconventional demand Vorbringen von Gegenforderungen, Aufforderung zur Widerklage.

reconversion [Rück]umwandlung, Umstellung, (plant) Wiederumstellung;
~ **of industry** Umstellung der Wirtschaft auf Friedensproduktion; ~ **of stock** Aktienumwandlung;
~ **difficulties** Umstellungsschwierigkeiten; ~ **investment** für die Betriebsumstellung erforderliche Kapitalien.

reconvert (v.) umstellen, umwandeln;
~ **industry** Wirtschaft wieder auf Friedensproduktion umstellen; ~ **shares** Aktien umwandeln.

reconvey *(v.)* zurückübertragen, rückübereignen.

reconveyance Rückübertragung, -übereignung; **~ under seal** notarielle Rückübertragung; **~ price** Rückübertragungspreis.

reconviction erneute Verurteilung.

record *(disk)* [Schall]platte, [Ton]band, *(document)* Urkunde, Dokument, Akte, Aktenstück, *(minutes)* Aufzeichnung, Protokoll, Niederschrift, *(passbook)* Kontobuch, *(peak performance)* Höchst-, Spitzenleistung, Rekord, *(person's past)* politische Vergangenheit, Werdegang, Vorleben, Ruf, Leumund, *(piece of evidence)* Zeugnis, Beweisstück, Beleg, Unterlage, *(register)* Tabelle, Register, Liste, Verzeichnis, *(written report)* schriftlicher Bericht, Aufzeichnung, Registrierung, *(Scot.)* Klagebeantwortung, -begründung, *(witness)* Zeuge, Zeugnis;

for the ~ für das Protokoll; **for want of ~** mangels Eintragung; **of ~** amtlich beurkundet, gerichtlich eingetragen; **off the ~** *(US)* inoffiziell, außerhalb des Protokolls, nicht zur Veröffentlichung bestimmt; **on ~** schriftlich niedergelegt, protokolliert, registriert; **on the ~** nach Aktenlage; **with a proven ~ of success** mit nachweisbaren Erfolgen; **struck out (stricken,** *US*) **from the ~** aus dem Protokoll gestrichen;

~s Aufzeichnungen, Geschäftsunterlagen, Akten, *(archive)* Archiv, *(form)* Regelnachweis auf Vordrucken, *(legal proceedings)* Prozeßakten, *(statistical table)* Zahlenübersicht; **accounting ~s** Buchungsbelege, -unterlage; **bad ~** schlechter Ruf (Leumund); **business ~s** [Geschäfts]bücher; **case ~** Prozeß-, Gerichtsakte; **cash ~** Kassenbeleg; **clean ~** einwandfreie Vergangenheit; **consumption ~** Rekordverbrauch; **criminal ~** Vorstrafenregister, -verzeichnis; **departmental ~** Abteilungsbericht; **deposit ~s** Depotunterlagen; **expense ~** Spesenabrechnung; **false ~** gefälschte Lohnliste; **final ~** authentische Urkunde; **good ~** guter Ruf; **high ~** Höchstkurs, -preis; **inventory ~** Inventarverzeichnis; **judicial ~s** *(US)* Prozeß-, Gerichtsakten; **land ~s** *(US)* Grundstücksregister; **official ~** anerkannter Rekord; **old ~s** Registratur, Archiv; **our ~s** unsere Aufzeichnungen; **payroll ~s** *(US)* Lohnsteuerunterlagen, -abrechnungen; **personal ~** Lebenslauf; **plant ~s** Betriebsunterlagen; **police ~** Vorstrafenregister; **previous ~** bisheriger Rekord; **private ~** private Urkunde; **profit ~** Rekordhöhe der Gewinne; **progressive ~s** laufend geführte Aufzeichnungen; **property ~** Liegenschaftsverzeichnis; **public ~** öffentliche Urkunde, *(law court)* gerichtliches Protokoll; **Public ~s** *(Br.)* Staatsarchiv; **accounts receivable ~s** *(US)* Aufzeichnungen der Kundenbuchhaltung; **service ~** *(mil.)* Führungszeugnis; **shorter ~** kürzere Dienstzeit; **stenographic ~** stenographische Niederschrift; **subsidiary ~s** Hilfsaufzeichnungen; **supporting ~s** Buchungsbelege; **top-selling ~s** Favoriten im Schallplattengeschäft; **trial ~** Sitzungsprotokoll; **written ~** Niederschrift;

books and ~s Bücher und Geschäftspapiere; **~ of attendance** Anwesenheitsliste; **~s of a bank** Bankbelege; **~ of contributions** *(national insurance, Br.)* anerkennungsfähige Beitragszeit; **~ by way of conveyance** Auflassungsurkunde; **~ of prior convictions** *(US)* Vorstrafenregister; **~s of a corporation** *(US)* Unterlagen einer Gesellschaft, Firmenarchiv; **~ of the court** Sitzungsprotokoll; **~ of evidence** Beweisprotokoll; **~ of interrogation** Vernehmungsprotokoll; **~ of names** Namensverzeichnis; **~ of nisi prius** *(Br.)* Prozeß, Gerichtsakte; **~ in office** während der Regierungszeit erzielte Erfolge; **~ of original entry** Grundbuchung; **~s of the past** Zeugnisse der Vergangenheit; **~ of patent rights** Patentregister; **~ of payment** Zahlungsnachweis; **~ of the proceedings** Sitzungsbericht, -protokoll; **~ of release** Entlassungsbericht; **~ of reliability** Zuverlässigkeitsrekord; **~ of road accidents** Unfallstatistik; **~ of school attendance** Aufzeichnungen über den Schulbesuch; **longest ~ of service** längste Dienstzeit; **official ~s of a society** Veröffentlichungen einer Gesellschaft; **~ of success** Erfolgsnachweis; **~s of a law suit** *(US)* Prozeßakten; **~ of a trial** Sitzungsprotokoll;

~ *(v.) (in book)* buchen, eintragen, *(in minutes)* beurkunden, protokollieren, Protokoll führen, aufzeichnen, *(phonograph)* auf Schallplatte (Tonband) aufnehmen, *(prove with documents)* urkundlich belegen, *(put down in writing)* aufzeichnen, verzeichnen, ver-, vormerken, registrieren, in ein Register eintragen;

~ a deed *(US)* Grundstücksübertragungsurkunde registrieren, Rechtsgeschäft beurkunden; **~ gains** Gewinne verzeichnen; **~ no mention** keine Eintragung enthalten; **~ in the minutes** im Protokoll vermerken; **~ a mortgage** *(US)* Hypothek eintragen; **~ a payment on the reverse side of a letter of credit** Zahlung auf der Rückseite eines Kreditbriefes notieren; **~ the proceedings**

~ of a court Gerichtsverfahren protokollieren; **~ the requirements** Bedarf schriftlich angeben; **~ a speech** Rede aufnehmen, Tonband besprechen, Rede auf Band sprechen; **~ television program(me)s off the air** Fernsehprogramme auf Band aufnehmen; **~ one's voice** aufs Band sprechen; **~ one's vote** wählen; **~ a wireless program(me)** Rundfunkprogramm auf Band aufnehmen;

to appear on the ~ aktenmäßig feststehen; **to be incorporated in the ~s** aktenmäßig festgehalten sein; **to be off the ~** nicht zur Veröffentlichung freigegeben sein; **to be a matter of public ~** öffentlich bekannt sein; **to be required to keep full ~s** zur vollständigen Buchführung verpflichtet (buchführender Einkommenssteuerpflichtiger) sein; **to be shown only as a ~** nur als Merkposten bestehen; **to bear ~** Zeugnis ablegen; **to bear ~ of s. one's conduct** jem. als Referenz zur Verfügung stehen; **to beat a ~** Rekord brechen; **to call in ~s** Akten anfordern; **to cancel a ~ in the real-estate register** *(US)* Eintragung im Grundbuch löschen; **to consult ~s** Akten heranziehen, in den Akten nachschlagen; **to decide on the ~s** auf Grund der Akten entscheiden; **to draw up a ~** Protokoll aufnehmen; **to enter the ~** ins Protokoll aufnehmen, vermerken, *(Scot.)* registriert werden; **to enter a document into the ~s** Urkunde zu den Akten nehmen; **to equal a ~** Rekord einstellen; **to establish new high ~s** neue Höchstkurse erreichen; **to examine old ~s** alte Akten durchsehen; **to go on ~** *(US)* zu Protokoll genommen werden, Stellungnahme zu Protokoll geben; **to go into s. one's ~s** in jds. Akten vermerkt werden; **to go on ~ as a free trader** sich für den Freihandel aussprechen; **to have a bad ~** schlechten Ruf haben, *(airline)* viele Unfälle erlitten haben; **to have a bad health ~** oft krank gewesen sein; **to have a clean ~** nicht vorbestraft sein; **to have a good ~** *(employee)* gut beurteilt werden; **to have an hono(u)rable ~ of service** sich im Dienst ausgezeichnet haben; **to have established a successful and financial sound ~ in its industry** branchenmäßig erfolgreich und finanziell gesund sein; **to hold the ~** Rekord halten; **to keep the ~s** Archiv führen (leiten); **to keep a ~ of s. th.** Buch über etw. führen; **to keep a ~ of road accidents** Unfallstatistik führen; **to keep one's ~s** Unterlagen aufbewahren; **to keep a ~ of one's expenses** Spesenbelege sammeln; **to keep ~s of the proceedings** Verhandlungsprotokoll führen; **to leave on ~** protokollieren lassen; **to link up ~s** Akten zusammenheften; **to lodge ~s** Urkunden deponieren; **to lower a ~** Rekord drücken; **to maintain ~s** Bücher führen; **to make a matter of public ~** etw. öffentlich bekanntmachen; **to make notation on the ~s** in den Büchern einen Vermerk machen; **to pass ~s to another department** Akten an eine andere Behörde abgeben; **to place on ~** aktenkundig machen, zu Protokoll geben, amtlich protokollieren (registrieren) lassen, zu den Akten geben (nehmen); **to preserve ~s** Akten aufbewahren; **to put s. o. on ~** j. festnageln; **to put s. th. on ~** etw. offiziell erklären, etw. in die Akten eintragen; **to put the ~ straight** Tatsachen ins rechte Licht setzen; **to put a resolution on ~** Antrag auf die Tagesordnung setzen; **to read in the ~** für das Protokoll verlesen; **to search old ~s** in alten Urkunden forschen; **to set up a ~** Rekord aufstellen; **to speak off the ~** nicht für die Öffentlichkeit bestimmte Bemerkungen machen, sich vertraulich äußern; **to stand on ~** im Protokoll vermerkt sein; **to take a ~** sich Aufzeichnungen machen; **to take down on ~** protokollieren; **to travel out of the ~** *(fam.)* außerhalb der Tagesordnung sprechen;

~ *(a.) (US)* noch nicht überboten;

~ attendance Rekordbesuch; **~ book** Protokollbuch; **~ breaking sales** Rekordabsatzziffern; **~ cabinet** Plattenarchiv; **~ card** *(US)* Karteikarte; **~ changer** Plattenwechsler; **~ commission** Urkundenkommission; **~ company** Schallplattenfirma; **~ date [for payment of dividend]** *(day, US)* Dividendentermin; **~s department** Erkennungsdienst, *(US)* Registratur; **~ destruction** Akteneinstampfung; **~ figures** Rekordziffern, -zahlen; **~ high** Rekordhöhe; **~ ink** Kanzleitinte; **~ inventory** Buchinventur; **~ keeping** Unterlagenführung, Archivierung; **~ level** Rekordhöhe; **to climb to ~ levels** Rekordhöhen erreichen; **~ low** *(stock exchange)* Rekordtiefstand; **~ majority** Rekordmehrheit; **~ office** *(Br.)* [Gerichts]kanzlei, Archiv, *(US)* Grundbuchamt; **[Public] ~ Office** *(Br.)* [Englisches] Staatsarchiv; **~ office copy** beglaubigte Abschrift aus dem Staatsarchiv; **~ orders** Rekordaufträge; **~ output** Rekordproduktion; **~ owner of stock** registrierter Aktienbesitzer; **to run a ~ pace** Rekordergebnisse zeitigen; **~ peak** Rekordhöhe; **~ performance** Best-, Höchst-, Rekordleistung, auf Schallplatte (Tonband) festgehaltene Interpretation; **~ player** Grammophonapparat, Plattenspieler; **~ prices** Rekordpreise; **~ production** Rekordproduktion; **~ profit** Rekordgewinn; **~ rack** Plattenständer; **~ rate** Rekord-,

Höchstsatz; **to enter at close to ~ rates** nahezu Höchstsätze erreichen; **to pour in at ~ rates** Höchstsätze erzielen; **~ sales** Spitzenumsatz; **~ savings volume** Rekordsparleistung; **~ sheet** *(US)* Aktenblatt; **~ sleeve** Schallplattenhülle; **~ surplus** Rekordüberschuß; **~ time** Rekordzeit; **~ traffic** Meldeverkehr.

recordable eintragungs-, registrierfähig, aufzeichenbar.

recordare *(US, justice of the peace)* Vorlagebeschluß.

recordation Eintragung, Registrierung.

recorded protokollarisch, registriert, *(on tape)* [auf Band] aufgenommen;

~ **broadcast** Übertragung vom Band; ~ **delivery** *(Br.)* Posteinlieferungsschein; ~ **program(me)** auf Tonband aufgenommenes Rundfunkprogramm; ~ **tape** besprochenes (bespieltes) Band; **~time value** *(rating)* festgelegter Zeitfaktor.

recorder Registrator, Archivar, Registerführer, *(court official)* Gerichtsschreiber, Protokollführer, Urkundsbeamter, *(criminal court, US)* Strafrichter, *(el.)* Zähler, *(magistrate, US)* Polizei-, Schnell-, Einzelrichter, *(meeting)* Protokollant, Verhandlungs-, Protokollführer, *(real estate, US)* Grundbuchbeamter, *(recording apparatus)* Registrierapparat, Tonwiedergabegerät, Bandgerät;

tape ~ Tonbandgerät;

~ **of deeds** *(US)* Urkundbeamter der Geschäftsstelle, Geschäftsstellenleiter, Grundbuchbeamter.

recording *(US)* Registrierung, Eintragung, Protokollierung, Protokollaufnahme, Aufzeichnung;

tape ~ Tonbandaufnahme;

~ **of accidents** Unfallstatistik; ~ **of deeds (documents)** Urkundenbeglaubigung; ~ **of evidence** Protokollaufnahme; ~ **of a mortgage** *(US)* Hypothekeneintragung; ~ **of title** Grundbucheintragung;

to do a ~ Schallplattenaufnahme machen;

~ **act** Eintragungsvorgang; ~ **Act** *(US)* Gesetz über amtlich zu führende Register; ~ **apparatus** Registrierapparat, Bandgerät; ~ **clerk** Protokollführer; ~ **company** Schallplattenfirma; ~ **consent** *(US)* Eintragungsbewilligung; ~ **fees** *(US)* Eintragungsgebühren, -kosten; ~ **machine** Bandgerät; ~ **medium** Buchungsbeleg; ~ **method** Aufzeichnungsmethode; ~ **office** *(US)* [etwa] Grundbuchamt; ~ **officer** *(US)* Grundbuchbeamter; ~ **official** Gerichtsschreiber, Urkundsbeamter; ~ **program(me)** auf Dose genommenes Rundfunkprogramm; ~ **requirements** *(US)* Eintragungserfordernisse; ~ **routine** Buchungsgang, Eintragungsverlauf; ~ **secretary** Urkundsbeamter, Schrift-, Protokollführer; ~ **session** Schallplattenaufnahme; ~ **stencil** Wachsmatrize; ~ **studio** Aufnahmestudio; ~ **system** Abhöranlage, *(filing)* Ablagesystem, *(land registry, US)* Eintragungssystem; **one-hour ~ time** einstündige [Ab]spieldauer; ~ **van** Aufnahmewagen.

recount Nachzählen, *(votes)* Über-, Nachprüfung;

~ *(v.)* nachrechnen, -zählen, *(give account)* Bericht erstatten;

~ **the votes** Stimmen überprüfen;

to demand a ~ Stimmenüberprüfung verlangen.

recoup *(v.) (cross action)* Schadenersatz im Wege der Gegenklage erhalten, *(deduct)* Abzüge machen, einbehalten, abrechnen, abziehen, *(price, US)* mindern, *(recompense)* ersetzen, Ersatz leisten, entschädigen, schadlos halten, *(recover)* vollständig wiedereinbringen, *(yield)* einbringen, ergeben, abwerfen;

~ **o. s.** sich schadlos halten; **the increasing cost of labo(u)r by raising one's prices** gestiegenen Lohnkostenanteil durch Preiserhöhungen auffangen; ~ **one's disbursements** seine Auslagen wieder hereinbekommen (erstattet bekommen); ~ **o. s. for an injury** j. schadenersatzpflichtig machen, Regreß bei jem. nehmen; ~ **a loss** Verlust ausgleichen; ~ **one's losses in gaining on the stock market** Verluste durch Börsenspekulation wieder hereinholen;

to sell at a low price and ~ o. s. by large sales Preisermäßigung durch große Umsätze wettmachen.

recoupment Entschädigung, Schadloshaltung, *(recovery)* Wiedereinbringung, *(retention)* Ein-, Zurückbehaltung, Aufrechnungsrecht, *(US)* Minderung.

recourse Entschädigung, Schadloshaltung, Ersatzanspruch, [Regreß]recht, -anspruch, Rekurs, Rückgriff;

liable to ~ regreßpflichtig; **with ~** mit Rückgriff (Regreß, Obligo); **without ~** *(bill of exchange)* ohne Regreß (Obligo); **without ~ to public funds** ohne Inanspruchnahme öffentlicher Mittel;

~ **to the capital market** Inanspruchnahme des Kapitalmarktes; ~ **to a credit** Kreditinanspruchnahme; ~ **to the endorser** Rückgriff auf den Indossanten; ~ **of guarantee** Kautionsregreß; ~ **to public money** Beanspruchung öffentlicher Mittel; ~ **to a prior party** Sprungregreß;

~ *(v.)* Rückgriff (Regreß) nehmen;

to be liable to ~ regreßpflichtig sein; **to have ~ against s. o.** j. regreßpflichtig machen, sich an j. halten, Regreß bei j. nehmen; **to have ~ to arbitration** Schiedsgericht anrufen; **to have ~ to a book** Buch konsultieren; **to have ~ to the capital market** Kapitalmarkt in Anspruch nehmen; **to have ~ against the preceding party** sich an den Vordermann halten; **to have ~ to the endorser of a note** sich beim Giranten erholen; **to have ~ to foul means** zu unredlichen Mitteln greifen; **to have ~ to law** Rechtsweg beschreiten; **to have ~ to public money** öffentliche Mittel beanspruchen; **to preserve ~** Regreßrecht wahren; **to reserve the right of ~** sich Regreßansprüche vorbehalten; **to seek ~** Regreßansprüche stellen;

~ **agreement** Regreßvereinbarung; ~ **basis** Rückgriffsmöglichkeit.

recover *(v.) (bankruptcy)* aussondern, *(collect)* einziehen, eintreiben, beitreiben, *(get back)* wiederbekommen, -erlangen, -erhalten, -finden, zurückerlangen, *(make up for)* wiedereinbringen, -gutmachen, *(market)* sich [wieder] erholen, wieder steigen, ansteigen, anziehen, sich wiederbeleben, *(mil.)* zurückerobern, *(repossess)* wieder in Besitz nehmen, *(salvage)* retten, *(secure compensation)* sich schadlos halten, Regreß nehmen, Ersatz erhalten, sich Ersatz verschaffen;

~ **an amount** Betrag einziehen; ~ **a lost article** verlorenen Gegenstand zurückbekommen; ~ **a pledged article** Pfand einlösen; ~ **one's authority** seine Autorität wiedergewinnen; ~ **average** Ersatz für Havarie erhalten; ~ **the body of a drowned man** Ertrunkenen bergen; ~ **by-products from coal** Kohlenebenprodukte gewinnen; ~ **the coupon** Kuponabschlag einbringen; ~ **one's credit** wieder zu Ansehen gelangen; ~ **damages from s. o.** von jem. Schadenersatz erhalten, von jem. entschädigt werden; ~ **debts** Schulden bei-, eintreiben; ~ **one's disbursements** seine Auslagen vergütet bekommen; ~ **from the effects of a war** sich von den Kriegsauswirkungen erholen; ~ **the expenses** Ausgaben wiedereinbringen, sich für den Betrag seiner Spesen erholen; ~ **one's properly incurred expenses** gerechtfertigte Spesen erstattet bekommen; ~ **after a business failure** finanziellen Zusammenbruch überstehen; ~ **financially** sich finanziell erholen; ~ **a fine** Geldstrafe beitreiben; ~ **one's fallen fortune** sein verlorenes Vermögen wiederbekommen; ~ **from an illness** sich von einer Krankheit erholen; ~ **a judgment** *(US)* Urteil erwirken; ~ **judgment against the defendant** *(US)* Urteil gegen den Beklagten erwirken; ~ **land in ejectment of a real action** mit seiner Räumungsklage durchdringen; ~ **land from the sea** dem Meer Land abgewinnen; ~ **in one's lawsuit** seinen Prozeß gewinnen; ~ **the old level** *(prices)* alten Kursstand (altes Niveau) wieder erreichen; ~ **one's losses** seine Verluste ersetzt bekommen, sich schadlos halten, *(stock market)* Kursverluste wieder ausgleichen; ~ **a lost advantage** wieder die Oberhand bekommen; ~ **a lost article** verlorenen Gegenstand zurückbekommen; ~ **one's money** sein Geld zurückbekommen; ~ **money advanced** Vorschußzahlungen (Vorschüsse) zurückbekommen; ~ **over** *(US)* bei einem Dritten Regreß nehmen; ~ **possession by law** Besitz wiedererlangen; ~ **by-products from coal** Kohlenebenprodukte gewinnen; ~ **after a business setback** sich von einem geschäftlichen Rückschlag erholen; ~ **sharply** *(stock exchange)* kräftig anziehen; ~ **shipwrecked goods** Güter aus einem verunglückten Schiff bergen; ~ **smartly** *(stock market)* kräftig anziehen; ~ **one's strength** wieder zu Kräften kommen; ~ **in one's suit** *(US)* seinen Prozeß gewinnen; ~ **lost time** verlorene Zeit aufholen; ~ **title** sein Eigentum wiedererlangen.

recoverable ein-, beitreibbar, einziehbar, *(bankruptcy)* aussonderungsfähig, *(expenses)* erstattungsfähig, *(redeemable)* ablöslich;

~ **by law** einklagbar;

~ **costs** Kostenrückstand, *(governmental accounting)* Kostenauslage; ~ **debt** beitreibbare Schuld; ~ **loss** ersetzbarer Verlust.

recoverableness Eintreibbarkeit, Wiedererlangbarkeit, *(bankruptcy)* Aussonderungsfähigkeit.

recoveree Regreßpflichtiger.

recoverer Regreßnehmer.

recovering charges Inkassospesen, Einziehungskosten.

recovery Zurück-, Wiedererlangung, -erhaltung, *(cyclical)* Aufschwung, Erholung, *(debt)* Beitreibung, Einziehung, *(illness)* Gesundung, Wiedergenesung, Besserung, *(recuperation)* Rückgewinnung, *(lawsuit)* Prozeßgewinn, *(US)* Eingang einer bereits als Verlust gebuchten Forderung, *(salvage)* Bergung, Rettung, *(stock exchange)* Erholung, Wiederbelebung, Anziehen, Anstieg, Festigung der Börse, Geschäftsbelebung;

past ~ unwiederbringlich verloren; **by way of ~** auf dem Regreßwege.

common ~ [etwa] Auflassungsverfahren; **consumer-led** ~ konsumbedingte Konjunkturerholung; **day-trip** ~ Tageserholung; **economic** ~ Konjunktur-, Wirtschaftsbelebung, Konjunkturanstieg; **export-led** ~ ausfuhrbestimmter Konjunkturaufschwung; **final** ~ *(US)* obsiegendes Endurteil, Prozeßgewinn in letzter Instanz; **financial** ~ finanzielle Gesundung (Erholung), Sanierung; **industrial** ~ Konjunktur-, Wirtschaftsbelebung; **postwar economic** ~ Wiederbelebung der Nachkriegszeit; **quick** ~ rasche Erholung; **total** ~ Gesamtausbeute; **trade** ~ Wiederbelebung des Handels, Konjunktur-, Wirtschaftsbelebung; **world economic** ~ Erholung der Weltwirtschaft;

restrained ~ **in economic activity** gezügeltes Wiederanlaufen der Konjunktur; ~ **of amounts outstanding** Eintreibung (Einkassierung) von Außenständen; ~ **of a lost article** Wiedererlangung einer verlorenen Sache; ~ **in business** Konjunktur-, Geschäftsbelebung; ~ **of by-products** Gewinnung von Nebenprodukten; ~ **of capital** Kapitaldeckung; ~ **of international credit** Wiederherstellung des internationalen Vertrauens; ~ **of damages** Erlangung von Schadensersatz, Schadensersatzerlangung; ~ **of outstanding debts** [gerichtliche] Eintreibung (Einkassierung) ausstehender Schulden; ~ **of fines** Beitreibung von Geldstrafen; ~ **in housing** Wiederbelebung des Wohnungsbaumarktes; ~ **of land** Wiedererlangung eines Grundstückes; ~ **at law** gesetzliche Wiedererlangung; ~ **of maintenance** Geltendmachung des Unterhaltsanspruchs; ~ **of the market** Festigung des Marktes, Kurserholung; ~ **of money** Geldeintreibung, -einziehung; ~ **of payment made by mistake** Wiedereingang einer versehentlich geleisteten Zahlung; ~ **of prices** Ansteigen der Preise, Preisanstieg, *(stock exchange)* Erholung der Kurse, Kurserholung, erneuter Kursanstieg; ~ **in profits** Ertragsbesserung; ~ **of property** Wiedererlangung des Eigentums; ~ **of the stock market** Börsenerholung; ~ **of stolen goods** Wiedererlangung gestohlener Gegenstände; ~ **of title** Wiedererlangung des Eigentums; ~ **of trade** Wiederbelebung des Handels; ~ **of waste** Abfallverwertung;

to be past ~ hoffnungslos darniederliegen; **to experience a** ~ *(market)* sich [wieder] erholen; **to seek** ~ Regreß nehmen; **to share in a subsequent** ~ *(stock exchange)* an einer nachfolgenden Erholung teilhaben;

~ **charges** Einziehungskosten, -spesen; ~ **exclusion** Steuerfreibetrag für Dubiose; ~ **means** Wiederaufbaumittel; ~ **measures** Wiederaufbaumaßnahmen; ~ **party** Abschleppkommando; **[economic]** ~ **program(m)e** [wirtschaftliches] Wiederaufbauprogramm; **European** ⌂ **Program(me) (ERP)** Europäisches Wiederaufbauprogramm; ~ **prospects** Aufschwungsaussichten; ~ **right** Schadenersatzanspruch; ~ **task** Rettungsoperation; **to move farther along the** ~ **track** konjunkturelle Fortschritte machen; ~ **value** Ausschlachtungswert; ~ **vehicle** Abschleppwagen.

recreate *(v.)* ausspannen, sich erholen.

recreation Ausspannen, Erholung, Arbeitsruhe, Freizeit[gestaltung];
~ **area** Urlaubs-, Freizeits-, Erholungsgebiet; ~ **boom** Urlaubskonjunktur; ~ **center** *(US)* **(centre,** *Br.)* Erholungsstätte; ~ **director** Freizeitleiter, -gestalter; ~ **facilities** Erholungseinrichtungen, -anlagen, Freizeiteinrichtungen; ~ **field** Freizeitwesen; ~ **ground** Erholungsstätte, Spiel-, Sportplatz; ~ **guidance** Freizeitberatung; ~ **market** Freizeitindustrie; ~ **room** Aufenthaltsraum; ~ **site** Freizeits-, Erholungsgelände; ~ **time** Erholungspause, -zeit, Ruhepause.

recreational | activities Freizeitbeschäftigung, -gestaltung; ~ **amenities** gute Erholungsmöglichkeiten; ~ **area** Freizeitgelände; ~ **area for half day** Naherholungsgebiet; ~ **club** Freizeitklub; ~ **equipment** Freizeitgeräte; ~ **facilities** Erholungsmöglichkeiten; ~ **procedure** Berichtigungsverfahren; ~ **program(me)** betriebliches Freizeitprogramm; **sceneric and property** Landschafts- und Freizeitgelände; ~ **space** *(hotel)* Gesellschaftsräume; ~ **value** Freizeit-, Erholungswert; ~ **vehicle** Urlaubs-, Hobbyfahrzeug, Freizeitfahrzeug.

recreative erholsam, entspannend, unterhaltend.

recredited wiedergutbracht.

recriminate *(v.) (divorce suit)* Gegenbeschuldigungen vorbringen.

recrimination *(divorce suit, US)* Gegenbeschuldigung, -klage.

recroom *(coll.)* Aufenthaltsraum.

recrudesce *(v.)* wieder aufflackern.

recrudescence Wiederaufleben, Rückfall;
~ **of civil disorder** Wiederausbruch (Wiederaufflackern) öffentlicher Unruhen.

recruit Rekrut, *(laborer)* neu angeworbene Arbeitskraft, *(new member)* neues Vereinsmitglied, *(novice)* Anfänger, Neuling;

raw ~ blutiger Anfänger;
~**s to engineering** Ingenieursnachwuchs;

~ *(v.) (crew)* anheuern, *(labo(u)r)* anwerben, anstellen, einstellen, unter Vertrag nehmen, *(mil.)* ausheben, einziehen, rekrutieren, *(recover)* sich erholen, *(replenish)* wieder auffüllen, erneuern;

~ **afresh** neu verpflichten; ~ **an army by a new draft** Armee duch Neuaushebungen auffüllen; ~ **on campus** Arbeitskräfte (Nachwuchskräfte) direkt von der Universität wegengagieren; ~ **easily** *(mil.)* sich leicht wieder rekrutieren; ~ **one's health** seine Gesundheit wiederherstellen, sich erholen; ~ **labo(u)r** Arbeitskräfte einstellen; ~ **a new political party from the middle classes** neue Partei aus dem Reservoir des Mittelstandes bilden; ~ **one's strength** wieder zu Kräften kommen; ~ **supplies** Lager auffüllen, *(mil.)* Nachschub sicherstellen;
to beat up for ~s Werbetrommel rühren; **to gain a few** ~**s to one's party** seiner Partei einige neue Anhänger zuführen.

recruital gesundheitliche Wiederherstellung.

recruited, to be ~ **from** sich ergänzen aus; **to be** ~ **from the middle classes** *(party)* seine Anhänger im Mittelstand haben.

recruiter *(mil.)* Anwerber, Werbeoffizier, *(plant)* Beschaffer (Anwerber) von Arbeitskräften, Einstellungsleiter.

recruiting *(labo(u)r)* personelle Ergänzung, Einstellung [von Arbeitern], *(mil.)* Rekrutierung, Anwerbung;
executive ~ Anwerbung von Führungskräften; **personnel** ~ Personalbeschaffung; **university** ~ Anwerbung auf der Hochschule;
~ **and replacement** *(mil.)* Ersatzwesen;
~ **administration** *(mil.)* Wehrersatzverwaltung; ~ **agent** *(US)* Arbeitsvermittlungsstelle; ~ **attempt** Anstellungsversuch; ~ **campaign** Anwerbe-, Rekrutierungsfeldzug; ~ **district** *(mil.)* Ersatzbezirk; ~ **drive** Anwerbefeldzug; ~ **firm** Anwerbe-, Rekrutierungsbüro; ~ **gang** Einstellungsgruppe; ~ **ground** Rekrutierungsgelände, Werbegebiet, *(supply area)* Versorgungsquelle; ~ **methods** Einstellungsmethoden; ~ **office** Anstellungs-, Rekrutierungsbüro, *(mil.)* Ersatzdienststelle; **local** ~ **office** Wehrersatzkommando; ~ **officer** *(mil.)* Werbeoffizier; ~ **season** Anwerbe-, Einstellungszeit; **motorized** ~ **squad** motorisiertes Einstellungsbüro; ~ **staff** Einstellungsstab, -personal; ~ **technique** Anwerbetechnik.

recruitment *(labo(u)r)* Anstellung (Einstellung) von Arbeitskräften, *(mil.)* Anheuerung, Rekrutierung;
~ **of apprentices** Lehrlingsanwerbung; ~ **of labo(u)r** Einstellung von Arbeitskräften, Arbeitskräfteanwerbung; ~ **of staff** Personaleinstellung;
~ **ban** Einstellungsverbot; ~ **campaign** Einstellungskampagne; ~ **committee** Anstellungskommission; ~ **obligations** Neueinstellungszusagen; ~ **policy** Einstellungspolitik; ~ **practices** Ein-, Anstellungsmethoden; ~ **process** Einstellungsverfahren; ~ **program(me)** Ein-, Anstellungs-, Anwerbungsprogramm; ~ **sources** Arbeitskräftereservoir; ~ **technique** An-, Einstellungsverfahren.

rectifiable berichtigungsfähig, korrigierbar.

rectification Richtigstellung, Berichtigung, [Fehler]verbesserung, Korrektur, Bereinigung, *(instrument)* richtige Einstellung, [Null]eichung;
~ **of an account** Ansatzberichtigung; ~ **of boundaries** Grenzkorrektur, -bereinigung; ~ **of capital stock** Kapitalberichtigung; ~ **of a contract** *(Br.)* Vertragskorrektur; ~ **of an entry** Buchungskorrektur; ~ **of an error** Berichtigung eines Irrtums, Fehlerberichtigung; ~ **of a price** Preisberichtigung; ~ **of the register** Berichtigung des Grundbuchs, Register-, Grundbuchberichtigung.

rectified korrigiert, berichtigt, bereinigt;
~ **balance sheet** Berichtigungsbilanz.

rectify *(v.)* berichtigen, richtigstellen, verbessern, korrigieren, bereinigen;
~ **abuses** Mißbräuche abschaffen (abstellen); ~ **entries** Eintragungen abändern (berichtigen); ~ **an error** Irrtum korrigieren; ~ **a method** Methode verbessern; ~ **a register** Register bereinigen; ~ **a statement** Aussage richtigstellen.

rectifying | entry Berichtigungsbuchung; ~ **letter** Berichtigungsschreiben.

rectitude comparative *(divorce suit, US)* Abwägung des beiderseitigen Verschuldens.

rector Pfarrer, *(university)* Präsident.

rectory Pfarrei.

recultivation Rekultivierung.

recuperate *(v.)* sich [finanziell] wieder erholen, wieder auf die Beine kommen;
~ **a loss** sich für einen Verlust schadlos halten.

recuperation Erholung, Wiederherstellung;
economic ~ wirtschaftliche Erholung, Konjunkturbelebung;
~ **of health** Gesundung; ~ **of prices** Preis-, Kurserholung; ~ **of waste** Abfallverwertung.

recur (v.) sich wiederholen, wieder (periodisch) auftreten;
~ **to the mind** ins Gedächtnis zurückkommen; ~ **periodically** periodisch auftreten; ~ **to a former subject** auf ein Gesprächsthema zurückkommen.

recurrence Zurückkommen [im Gespräch], (illness) Wiederkehr, -auftauchen.

recurrent wiederkehrend, periodisch auftretend;
~ **expenses** regelmäßig wiederkehrende Ausgaben.

recurring | cost (US) laufende Geschäftskosten; ~ **disease** wiederkehrende Krankheit; ~ **question** immer wieder auftauchende Frage.

recusation (strange heir) Erbausschlagung, (judge) Ablehnung wegen Befangenheit.

recuse (v.) **a judge** Richter wegen Befangenheit ablehnen.

recycle (v.) regenerieren, (finance) Öldollar international (beim Kunden) wieder anlegen, (refuse) Müll aufbereiten;
~ **aid** Förderungsmittel revolvierend einsetzen; ~ **money** rückschleusen, in den Kreislauf zurückführen; ~ **petrodollars** Öldollarüberschüsse erneut anlegen; ~ **refuse** Abfälle verwerten, Müll aufbereiten.

recycling Rückschleusung, (international financing) Rückführung (Wiederanlage) von Geldmitteln, (waste) Abfall-, Wiederverwertung;
~ **of petrodollars** Wiederanlage von Öldollarströmen; ~ **of refuse** Müllaufbereitung;
~ **facilities** Wiederanlagemöglichkeiten; ~ **fund** Wiederanlagefonds; ~ **job** Wiederanlageaufgabe; ~ **plan** Wiederanlageplan.

red (balance sheet) Schulden-, Debetseite, (loss, US coll.) Verlust, Defizit, Schulden, (politics) Revolutionär, Anarchist, Kommunist, Bolschewist, Roter, Marxist;
in the ~ (US coll.) in den roten Zahlen;
to be in the ~ Verluste haben, im Debet sein; **to be still in the** ~ noch nicht über den Berg sein; **to be still operating in the** ~ weiter mit roten Zahlen arbeiten; **to be wound up in the** ~ mit Verlust liquidiert werden; **to climb (get, come) out of the** ~ aus den roten Zahlen herauskommen, Gewinn erzielen; **to go into the** ~ in die Verlustzone geraten; **to go heavily into the** ~ schwere [finanzielle] Verluste erleiden; **to paint the town** ~ Stadt auf den Kopf stellen; **to plunge deeper in the** ~ immer tiefer in Defizit geraten; **to run in the** ~ in die roten Zahlen geraten, mit Verlust arbeiten; **to see** ~ rot sehen; **to wind up in the** ~ mit Verlust liquidiert werden;
~ (a.) rot, (map, Br.) Britisch, (revolutionary) rot, anarchistisch, revolutionär, bolschewistisch, kommunistisch, marxistisch;
⚹ **Air Force** Rote Luftflotte; ~ **apple** (sl.) Nichtgewerkschaftler; ⚹ **Army** Rote Armee; ~-**bait** (v.) (US sl.) als kommunistisch schikanieren; ~ **baiting** (US sl.) Kommunistenverfolgung; ~ **ball** (sl.) Schnellzug; ~ **battle** blutige Schlacht; ⚹ **Book** (Br.) Adelskalender, (politics) Rotbuch; ~ **carpet** roter Teppich, Staatsempfang, großer Bahnhof; ~-**carpet** (v.) für j. einen großen Bahnhof veranstalten; **to lay (roll) out the** ~ **carpet** roten Teppich auslegen, Staatsempfang geben; **to give a visiting notability a** ~-**carpet reception** für einen berühmten Gast den roten Teppich auslegen; ~-**carpet treatment** großer Bahnhof, Empfang mit allen Ehren; ~ **clause** (letter of credit) Vorschußklausel; ⚹ **Cross** Rotes Kreuz; ~ **ensign** (Br.) Handelsflagge; ~-**faced** verlegen; ~ **figures** (balance sheet) rote Zahlen, Verlustzahlen; ~ **flag** (pol.) rote Fahne, (railway, roads) Signal-, Warnflagge; **with** ~ **hands** mit blutbefleckten Händen; ~-**handed** auf frischer Tat, in flagranti; **to be caught** ~-**handed** auf frischer Tat ergriffen werden; ~ **hat** Kardinalshut; ~ **herring** Ablenkungsmanöver, Finte, (securities issue, US) Vorankündigung eines Emissionsprospektes; **to draw a** ~ **herring across the trail** Ablenkungsmanöver durchführen; ~-**herring prospectus** (US) Vorankündigung einer Emission, vorläufiger Börseneinführungsprospekt; ~-**hot** heftig diskutiert; ~-**hot enthusiasm** wilde Begeisterung; ~-**hot news** allerneueste Nachrichten; ~-**hot news journal** (sl.) Skandalblatt mit heißen Nachrichten; **to cope with** ~ **ink** (US) mit dem Defizit fertig werden; **to fall into** ~ **ink** (US) in die Verlustzone geraten; **to run (spurt)** ~ **ink** (US) plötzlich in die roten Zahlen (Verlustzone) geraten; **to show** ~ **ink** (US) rote Zahlen (Verluste) aufweisen; ~-**ink entry** (US) Verlusteintragung; **to raise the accumulated** ~-**ink figures** (US) schon bestehendes Defizit erhöhen; ~ **interest** Sollzinsen; ~-**letter** (v.) rot ankreuzen; ~-**letter day** Glücks-, Fest-, Feiertag; ~ **light** rotes Licht, Gefahrensignal; ~-**light s.**

o. (v.) (sl.) j. aus dem Zug stoßen; **to cross against the** ~ **light** bei Rot die Straße überqueren; **to see the** ~ **light** Katastrophe vorausahnen; ~-**light district** Prostituiertengegend, Bordellviertel; ~ **numbers** Soll-, Zinszahlen; ~ **one** (sl.) glänzender Geschäftstag; ~ **pencil** Rotstift; ~ **rag** (fig.) rotes Tuch; ~ **rag to a bull** rotes Tuch für einen Bullen; **to act like a** ~ **rag to a bull** wie ein rotes Tuch wirken; **to be a** ~ **rag to s. o.** wie ein rotes Tuch auf j. wirken; **all-**~ **route** (Br.) Hauptverbindungslinie; ~ **tape** Bürokratismus, Amtsschimmel; ~ **tape in government office** Ämterbürokratie; **to be fond of** ~ **tape** Amtsschimmel reiten; ~-**tape** bürokratisch; ~ **tapism** Beamtenwirtschaft, Paragraphenreiterei, Bürokratismus; ~-**tapist** Bürokrat.

redcap (sl., Br.) Militärpolizist, (US) Gepäckträger.

reddendum (agreement) Zahlungs-, Vorbehaltsklausel.

redecorate (v.) neu dekorieren.

redecoration Neudekorierung.

redeem (v.) (amortize) amortisieren, (buy off) zurückzahlen, ablösen, tilgen, (make amends) Schadenersatz leisten, entschädigen, wiedergutmachen, ausgleichen, (pledged goods) [wieder] einlösen, zurückkaufen, auslösen;
~ **an annuity** Rente ablösen; ~ **bank notes** Banknoten einlösen; ~ **a bill** Wechsel honorieren (einlösen); ~ **a bond** Schuldverschreibung tilgen; ~ **bonds by drawing** Pfandbriefe zur Rückzahlung auslosen; ~ **a debt** Schuld abtragen (tilgen); ~ **a debenture** Schuldverschreibung tilgen; ~ **an error** Fehler gutmachen; ~ **at an interest date** zu einem Zinstermin ablösen; ~ **a legacy** Vermächtnis widerrufen; ~ **a loan** Darlehn tilgen; ~ **a mortgage** Hypothek tilgen (ablösen); ~ **an obligation** Verpflichtung erfüllen; ~ **paper money** Papiergeld einlösen; ~ **a pledge** Pfand einlösen; ~ **by purchase** zurückkaufen; ~ **one's rights** seine Rechte wiedererlangen; ~ **a security** (trustee) Sicherheit zurückkaufen; ~ **a slave** Sklaven freikaufen; ~ **a pawned watch** verpfändete Uhr einlösen.

redeemability Abzahlbarkeit, Ab-, Einlösbarkeit, Tilgbarkeit, (annuities) Ablösbarkeit.

redeemable (to be amortized) tilg-, amortisierbar, (loan) kündbar, (recoverable) ablöslich, auslösbar, (securities) rückzahlbar, (treasury bonds) auslösbar;
not ~ unkündbar;
~ **in advance** vorzeitig tilgbar; ~ **at par** zum Nennwert einlösbar; ~ **on demand** auf Verlangen einzulösen; ~ **in gold** in Gold zurückzahlbar;
~ **annuity** ablösbare Rente, Ablösungsrente; ~ **bonds** auslösbare (kündbare) Obligationen, Amortisationsschuld; ~ **charge** rückzahlbare Belastung; ~ **currency** Papiergeld mit Silber- oder Goldumtauschrecht; ~ **debentures** rückkaufbare (kündbare) Obligationen; ~ **feature** Kündigungsrecht; ~ **loan** Tilgungsdarlehen; ~ **preference shares** (Br.) rückkaufbare Vorzugsaktien; ~ **right** Heimfall-, Ablösungsrecht; ~ **security** Wertpapier mit vereinbartem Einlösungstermin; ~ **stock** rückkaufbare Werte; ~ **preferred stock** (US) rückkaufbare Vorzugsaktie.

redeemableness, redeemability Tilg-, Ablös-, Auslos-, Einlösbarkeit.

redeemed getilgt, amortisiert;
~ **by lot** zur Rückzahlung ausgelost.

redeeming feature Ausgleichsmoment.

redeliver (v.) rückliefern, zurückgeben, [zu]rückerstatten.

redelivery Rückgabe, Rücklieferung, -sendung, Rückerstattung;
~ **bond** Kautionsstellung bei der Zwangsvollstreckung.

redemand Rückforderung;
~ (v.) zurückfordern, (capital) kündigen.

redemise Rückübertragung;
~ (v.) wieder überlassen, zurückübertragen, -auflassen.

redemption (amortization) Amortisierung, Tilgung, (coupon) Gutscheineinlösung, (investment trust) Rückzahlung von Investmentanteilen, (of pledge) Aus-, [Wieder]einlösung, (repayment) Rückzahlung, Ablösung, (repurchase) Rück-, Wiederkauf, (shares) Einziehung;
subject to ~ tilgbar, kündbar;
anticipated ~ vorzeitiger Rückkauf; **loan** ~ Anleiheablösung, -tilgung; **mandatory** ~ Einlösung vor Verfall; **previous (priority)** ~ vorzeitige Tilgung (Einlösung); **solicited** ~ vertraglich vereinbarte Ablösung; **voluntary** ~ Pfandfreigabe;
~ **of an annuity** Rentenablösung; ~ **of bank notes** Einlösung von Banknoten; ~ **of bonds** Tilgung von Schuldverschreibungen, Pfandbriefauslosung; ~ **before due date** Rückzahlung vor Fälligkeit; ~ **of debts** Schuldtilgung; ~ **in gold** Rückzahlung in Gold; ~ **of land tax** (Br.) Grundsteuerablösung; ~ **of a legacy** Rücknahme eines Vermächtnisses, Vermächtniswiderruf; ~ **of a loan** Dar-

lehnstilgung, Anleiheablösung, -tilgung; ~ **at maturity** Einlösung bei Verfall; ~ **before maturity of noncallable bonds** frühzeitige Tilgung unkündbarer Schuldverschreibungen; ~ **before maturity under a call provision** vorzeitige Tilgung bei vorher vereinbarter Kündigungsmöglichkeit; ~ **of a mortgage** Hypothekentilgung, -rückzahlung; ~ **at par** Einlösung zum Nennwert; ~ **of pledge** Pfandeinlösung; ~ **of prisoners of war** Kriegsgefangenenentlassung; ~ **of a promise** Einlösung eines Versprechens; ~ **of shares (stocks, US)** Aktienrückkauf [durch die Gesellschaft]; ~ **of slums** Beseitigung von Elendsgebieten; ~ **of units** Rückerwerb von Investmentzertifikaten;
to become a member of a society by ~ sich in eine Gesellschaft einkaufen; **to call for** ~ zur Einlösung aufrufen; **to draw for** ~ zur Einlösung auslosen; **to join a society by** ~ sich in einen Verein einkaufen;
~ **account** Tilgungs-, Amortisationskonto; ~ **action** Klage auf Rückgabe der Pfandsache; ~ **agent** *(US)* Mitglied einer Clearingvereinigung, das mit Nichtmitgliedern im Clearingverkehr steht; ~ **agreement** Tilgungsvereinbarung; ~ **bonds** neufundierte Obligationen, Ablösungsschuldverschreibungen; ~ **capital** Ablösungsbetrag; ~ **charge** Tilgungsgebühr, *(investment fund)* Rücknahmespesen; ~ **check** *(US)* Verrechnungsscheck für Ausgleichsbeträge; ~ **clause** Tilgungs-, Einlösungsklausel; ~ **cost** *(investment trust)* Verkaufsspesen; ~ **date** Rückzahlungs-, Ablösungs-, Tilgungs-, Einlösungstermin; ~ **expenditure** Amortisationsausgaben; ~ **feature** Einlösungsform; ~ **fee** Einlösungskosten; ~**-free** tilgungsfrei; ~ **fund** Ablösungs-, [Schulden]tilgungs-, Amortisationsfonds, Tilgungsstock; ~ **instal(l)ment** Tilgungsquote, -rate; ~ **loan** Tilgungs-, Ablösungsanleihe, Abgeltungsdarlehen; ~ **money** Tilgungs-, Abgeltungsbetrag; ~ **mortgage** Amortisationshypothek; ~ **office** Tilgungs-, Einlösungs-, Amortisationskasse; ~ **payment** Ablösungszahlung, Tilgungsleistung; ~ **period** Tilgungsdauer; ~ **plan** Schuldentilgungsplan; ~ **premium** Amortisationsprämie, Rückzahlungsprämie, Ablösungsprämie, Agio; ~ **price** Rückzahlungspreis, Ablösungsbetrag, -summe, Einlösungs-, Tilgungskurs, *(investment fund)* Rücknahmepreis; ~ **proceedings** Einlösungsverfahren; ~ **provisions** Ablösungs-, Einlösungs-, Amortisationsbestimmungen; ~ **rate** Tilgungskurs, -quote, Amortisationssatz; ~ **record** Tilgungsprotokoll; ~ **reserve** Tilgungsrücklage; **capital** ~ **reserve fund** *(Br.)* Rücklage zum Rückkauf von Vorzugsaktien; ~ **right** Ablösungsrecht, Auslosungsrecht; ~ **sum** Abgeltungsbetrag, Ablösungssumme; ~ **table** Amortisations-, Ablösungszeitplan, Tilgungsplan; ~ **value** Rückkaufs-, Rückzahlungs-, Ablösungs-, Tilgungswert; ~ **voucher** Einlösungsschein; ~ **warrant** Einlösungsabschnitt; ~ **yield** Aktienrendite.
redemptory price Lösegeld.
redeploy *(v.)* umgruppieren, umstrukturieren, *(mil.)* verlegen, verschieben, auf einem anderen Kriegsschauplatz einsetzen;
~ **the assets of a company** Vermögenswerte eines Unternehmens anderweitig einsetzen; ~ **the labo(u)r force** Arbeitskräfte umgruppieren; ~ **proceeds** Erträge erneut anlegen; ~ **a wasting capital asset** brachliegende Kapitalanlagen anderweitig einsetzen.
redeployment Umstrukturierung, *(labo(u)r)* Umgruppierung (Umsetzung) von Arbeitskräften, *(mil.)* anderweitiger Einsatz, [Truppen]verschiebung, Verlegung;
~ **of the assets of a company** anderweitiger Einsatz der Vermögenswerte einer Gesellschaft; ~ **of proceeds** Wiederanlage von Erträgen.
redeposit Wiedereinzahlung;
~ *(v.)* wieder einzahlen.
redevelop *(v.)* baulich neu gestalten, *(photo)* nachentwickeln, *(urban district)* sanieren.
redevelopment bauliche Neugestaltung, *(city)* Sanierung;
~ **areas** städtische Sanierungsgebiete; ~ **plan** *(city)* Sanierungsplan.
redhibition *(US) (sales contract)* Wandlung;
to give rise to a ~ zur Wandlung berechtigen, Wandlungsrecht begründen.
redhibitory *(US)* zur Rückgängigmachung eines Kaufes (Wandlung) berechtigend;
~ **action** *(US)* Wandlungsklage; **to maintain a** ~ **action** *(US)* auf Wandlung klagen; ~ **clues** *(US)* zur Wandlung berechtigende Mängel; ~ **defect (vice)** *(US)* Gewährleistungsmangel, Wandlungsfehler; ~ **suit** *(US)* Wandlungsverfahren.
rediffusion *(radio)* Wiederholungssendung.
redintegrate *(v.)* wiederherstellen;
~ **s. o. in his possession** j. in seinen Besitz wiedereinsetzen.
redintegration Wiedereinsetzung in den Besitz.

redirect *(v.) (letter)* umadressieren, nachschicken, -senden;
~ **capital** Kapitalströme umlenken; ~ **examination** *(US)* nochmalige Vernehmung nach dem Kreuzverhör.
redirection *(of letters)* Nachsendung, Umadressierung;
~ **of capital** Kapitalumlenkung.
rediscount Rediskont, *(US)* Diskont;
eligible for ~ rediskontfähig, *(US)* diskontfähig;
~ *(v.)* rediskontieren, *(US)* diskontieren;
~ **credit** Rediskontkredit, *(US)* Diskontkredit; ~ **facility** *(Br.)* Rediskontfähigkeit, *(US)* Diskontfähigkeit; ~ **market** *(US)* Diskontmarkt; ~ **policy** Rediskontpolitik, *(US)* Diskontpolitik; ~ **quota** Rediskontkontingent, *(US)* Diskontkontingent; ~ **rate** Rediskontsatz, *(US)* Diskontsatz; **to cut (lower, reduce) the** ~ **rate** *(US)* Diskontsatz (Bankdiskont) herabsetzen; **to raise the** ~ **rate** *(US)* Diskontsatz erhöhen; ~ **rate change** *(US)* Diskontänderung.
rediscountable rediskontierbar, *(US)* diskontierbar;
~ **at the federal bank** zentral-, bundesbankfähig;
~ **bill** rediskontierbarer Wechsel.
rediscounting *(Br.)* Rediskontierung, *(US)* Diskontierung.
redistribute *(v.)* neu verteilen, aufteilen, umverteilen;
~ **income** Einkommensumverteilung vornehmen; ~ **throughout the company** über das ganze Unternehmen verteilt einsetzen; ~ **seats in Parliament** Parlamentssitze neu verteilen.
redistribution Um-, Neuverteilung;
~ **of electoral districts** Neueinteilung der Wahlkreise; ~ **of income** Einkommensumschichtung, -umverteilung, Einkommensneuverteilung; ~ **of loss** Schadensumschichtung, -abwälzung; ~ **of seats in Parliament** Neuverteilung der Parlamentssitze.
redivide *(v.)* neu aufteilen.
redivision Neuaufteilung.
redistrict *(v.) (US)* in neue Wahlbezirke einteilen.
redistriction of Congressional districts *(US)* Neueinteilung der Wahlbezirke.
redline *(v.) (sl.)* in der Soldliste streichen.
redo *(v.)* nochmals tun.
redoing erneute Erledigung.
redouble *(v.)* ~ **one's efforts** seine Anstrengungen verdoppeln.
redound *(v.)* **to s. one's advantage** sich zu jds. Vorteil auswirken.
redraft neuer (zweiter) Entwurf, Umformulierung, *(return draft)* Rückwechsel, Rikambio[wechsel];
~ *(v.)* umformulieren, neuen Entwurf machen, neufassen;
~ **charges** Rückwechselspesen.
redrafting neuer Entwurf, Neufassung.
redraw | *(v.)* **upon** Rückwechsel ziehen, zurücktrassieren;
to draw and ~ **bills** Wechselreiterei treiben.
redress *(act of redeeming)* Abhilfe, Abstellung, Beseitigung eines Übelstandes, *(amends)* Entschädigung, Wiedergutmachung;
legal ~ Rechtshilfe, -schutz;
~ **of grievances** Abstellung von Übelständen;
~ *(v.)* Abhilfe schaffen, abstellen;
~ **an airplane** Flugzeug in die normale Fluglage zurückbringen; ~ **the balance of trade** Handelsbilanz ausgleichen; ~ **an error** Fehler beseitigen; ~ **grievances** Beschwerden (Mißstände, Übelstände) abstellen; ~ **injuries** Schäden beseitigen;
to get no ~ **for one's losses** unentschädigt bleiben, für seine Verluste keine Entschädigung erhalten; **to have one's** ~ **against s. o.** sich an j. halten, bei jem. Regreß nehmen; **to obtain** ~ **from s. o.** gegen j. Regreß nehmen.
redressable abstellbar.
redressing the balance of trade Ausgleich der Handelsbilanz.
reduce *(v.) (abate)* ermäßigen, ab-, nachlassen, verbilligen, *(bring in possession)* in Besitz bringen, *(diminish in value)* herab-, heruntersetzen, reduzieren, herunterdrücken, senken, herabsetzen, *(impair)* [ver]mindern, *(mil.)* unterwerfen, *(retrench)* abbauen, verringern, *(Scot.)* annullieren;
~ **the assessment on a building** Gebäude niedriger bewerten; ~ **the bank rate** Diskontsatz senken; ~ **the barriers** Handelsschranken abbauen; ~ **a business by one half** Geschäft um die Hälfte verkleinern; ~ **the capital** *(Br.)* Grundkapital herabsetzen; ~ **the capital stock** *(US)* Grundkapital herabsetzen; ~ **a claim** Forderung reduzieren; ~ **to classes** klassifizieren; ~ **consumption** Verbrauch einschränken; ~ **costs** Unkosten verringern, Kosten senken; ~ **debts** Schulden abbauen; ~ **to a common denominator** auf einen Generalnenner bringen; ~ **to distress** in Not bringen; ~ **the customs duties** Zollsätze herabsetzen; ~ **the establishment** Personalabbau durchführen; ~ **expenses** Ausgaben einschränken (reduzieren), Unkosten senken; ~ **a fee** Gebühr ermäßigen; ~ **forces** Arbeitskräfte abbauen, *(mil.)* Truppen vermindern; ~ **to a form** auf eine

Form bringen; ~ **by half** um die Hälfte ermäßigen; ~ **imports** Einfuhr beschränken; ~ **land to public use** Land für öffentliche Zwecke enteignen; ~ **money** Devisen umrechnen; ~ **a number of officials** Personal vermindern; ~ **an officer to the ranks** Offizier degradieren; ~ **the output** Produktion drosseln; ~ **an overdraft** Kontoüberziehung zurückführen; ~ **into possession** Besitz erlangen; ~ **pounds to francs** Pfunde in Franken umrechnen; ~ **s. o. to poverty** j. an den Bettelstab bringen; ~ **to practice** praktisch anwenden; ~ **pressure** Druck vermindern; ~ **the price of an article** Preis eines Erzeugnisses herabsetzen; ~ **the principal amount on a mortgage** Hypothekendarlehn durch Tilgungsleistungen abtragen; ~ **pro rata** nach dem Verhältnis der Beträge kürzen; ~ **rebels to submission** Aufrührer unterwerfen; ~ **one's reliance on defence (defense, US) contracts** sich aus dem Rüstungsgeschäft teilweise zurückziehen; ~ **the share capital** Grundkapital herabsetzen, Kapitalherabsetzung vornehmen; ~ **the speed** Geschwindigkeit herabsetzen; ~ **the staff** Personal einsparen (abbauen); ~ **a statement to its simplest form** Erklärung auf den einfachsten Nenner bringen; ~ **to a system** in ein System bringen; ~ **tariffs** Zölle abbauen; ~ **a tax** Steuer herabsetzen; ~ **the tax on a house** Grundsteuer ermäßigen; ~ **to simple terms** auf eine kurze Formel bringen; ~ **a theory into practice** Theorie praktisch anwenden; ~ **a town to ashes** Stadt einäschern; ~ **trade barriers** Handelsschranken abbauen; ~ **in value** einer Wertverminderung ausgesetzt sein, entwerten; ~ **a will** einem Testament richterliche Anerkennung versagen; ~ **to writing** zu Papier bringen, schriftlich niederlegen (fixieren).

reduced herabgesetzt, ermäßigt;
and ~ *(capital stock, Br.)* und herabgesetzt, mit herabgesetztem Kapital;
~ **to the ranks** *(mil.)* degradiert;
to be ~ **to judgment** *(US)* urteilsmäßig festgestellt sein; ~ **annuity** verkürzte Rente; ~ **assessment** niedrige Bewertung (Veranlagung); ~ **capital** herabgesetztes Kapital; **in** ~ **circumstances** in beschränkten Verhältnissen, heruntergekommen, verarmt; **at a** ~ **fare** zu ermäßigtem Fahrpreis; **at a** ~ **fee** für ein mäßiges Honorar; ~ **goods** Ausverkaufsware; ~ **liquidity** Liquiditätsbeengung; ~ **price** ermäßigter (herabgesetzter, verbilligter) Preis; **to sell at a** ~ **price** mit Abschlag verkaufen; ~ **rate** ermäßigter Tarif (Satz), ermäßigte Gebühr, *(advertising)* ermäßigter Anzeigenpreis; ~**-rate relief** *(Br.)* gestaffelte Steuerermäßigung; ~**-rate ticket** *(Br.)* verbilligte Fahrkarte; **in a** ~ **state** geschwächt.

reducible herabsetzbar, reduzierbar.

reducing|-balance form Gewinn- und Verlustrechnung in Staffelform; ~**-balance method** degressive Abschreibung; ~ **form** übliches Einkommensformular; ~**-fraction method of calculating depreciation** Abschreibungsmethode mit fallenden Quoten; **to compute on the** ~ **instalment basis** nach der Abschreibungsmethode mit fallenden Quoten berechnen.

reduction *(abatement)* Abschlag, Abzug, [Preis]nachlaß, -ermäßigung, Rabatt, *(conversion)* Umwandlung, Wandlung, *(decreasing)* Reduzierung, Einschränkung, Herab-, Heruntersetzung, Abbau, *(diminution)* Verkleinerung, Kürzung, *(of foreign exchange)* [Devisen]umrechnung, *(impairment)* [Verminderung, Entwertung, *(restoration)* Zurückführung, *(retrenchment)* Abbau, *(waste)* Abgang, Schwund;
without ~ ohne Abschlag;
customs ~ Zollsenkung; **dividend** ~ Dividendenrückgang; **freight** ~ Frachtermäßigung, -senkung; **great** ~ starke Ermäßigung; **import** ~ Einfuhrrückgang; **inventory** ~ Lagerabbau; **no** ~**s** feste Preise; **price** ~ Preissenkung, Preisermäßigung, -abbau, -senkung; **retail** ~ Herabsetzung des Kleinhandelspreises; **stock** ~ Abbau der Bestände; **tariff** ~ Abbau der Zölle; **tax** ~ Steuererleichterung, -ermäßigung, -nachlaß; **wage** ~ Lohnsenkung, -abbau;
~ **in acreage** Verringerung der Anbaufläche; ~ **in the bank rate** Diskontsenkung; ~ **of barriers of trade** Abbau der Handelsschranken; ~ **of capacity** Kapazitätsreduzierung; ~ **of capital** *(Br.)* Herabsetzung des Grundkapitals, Kapitalherabsetzung, -zusammenlegung; ~ **of capital stock** *(US)* Herabsetzung des Grundkapitals, Kapitalherabsetzung, -zusammenlegung, Zusammenlegung von Aktien; ~ **of charges** Gebührenherabsetzung; ~ **of a claim** Anspruchskürzung; ~ **for children** Kinderermäßigung; ~ **of competition** Wettbewerbsbeschränkung; ~ **of consumption** Konsumverzicht; ~ **of damage** Schadensminderung; ~ **in the damages** Herabsetzung des Schadenersatzes; ~ **of data** Konzentration des statistischen Materials; ~ **of debts** Schuldenabbau; ~ **in the discount rate** Herabsetzung des Diskontsatzes, Diskontherabsetzung, -ermäßigung; ~ **of dividends** Dividendenkürzung, -herabset-

zung; ~ **of duty** Steuerermäßigung, -herabsetzung, -verkürzung, *(customs)* Senkung der Zollsätze; ~ **of earning capacity** Minderung der Erwerbsfähigkeit, Erwerbsminderung; ~ **of employment** Sinken der Beschäftigungszahl; ~ **in estate** Nachlaßverkürzung [zu Steuerzwecken]; ~ **of expenses** Kosteneinsparung, -verringerung; ~ **of an expression** Vereinfachung eines Ausdrucks; ~ **in fares** Flug-, Fahrpreisermäßigung, -senkung; ~ **of forces** Truppenverminderung; ~ **in the freight rate** Frachtermäßigung, -senkung; ~ **of fees** Gebührenermäßigung; ~ **to a lower grade** *(US)* Rangverlust, Degradierung; ~ **of hazard** Risikoherabsetzung; ~ **in hours of work** Arbeitszeitverkürzung; ~ **of indebtedness** Schuldenabbau; ~ **in inflation** Inflationsrückgang; ~ **of the interest [rate]** Zinsherabsetzung, -senkung; ~ **of 5% on all lines** fünfprozentige Preisherabsetzung für das ganze Sortiment; ~ **in current liabilities** Rückführung der kurzfristigen Verbindlichkeiten; ~ **in liquidity** Liquiditätsverknappung, -abbau, -verringerung; ~ **of a loan account** Abbau eines Kreditkontos; ~ **of losses** Verlustreduzierung, -minderung; ~ **of membership** Rückgang der Mitgliederzahl, Mitgliederrückgang; ~ **in the minimum reserves** Mindestreservensenkung; ~ **of money** [Geld]umrechnung; ~ **in mortality** Rückgang der Sterblichkeit; ~ **of output** Drosselung der Produktion; ~ **of an overdraft** Zurückführung einer Kontoüberziehung; ~ **of old paper** Papiereinstampfung; ~ **into possession** Besitzerlangung; ~ **to practice** *(invention)* praktische Verwertung; ~ **of premises account** Abschreibungen auf Verwaltungsgebäude; ~ **in prices** Preisermäßigung, -abbau; **sweeping** ~**s in prices** weitgehende Preissenkungen; ~ **of principal** Kapitaltilgung; ~ **in proceeds** Ertragsrückgang; ~ **in rank** *(Br.)* Rangverlust, Degradierung; ~ **in rate** Tarifermäßigung, Tarif-, Frachtsenkung; ~ **of rates** *(Br.)* Kommunalsteuersenkung; ~ **in the rate of duty** Zollsenkung; ~ **in the rediscount rate** *(US)* Diskontherabsetzung; ~ **of rent** Mietsenkung; ~ **in reserves** Reservenauflösung, Auflösung von Rücklagen; ~ **in revenue[s]** Einnahmen, Ertragsrückgang; ~ **for round trips** Rundreiseverbilligung; ~ **of salary** Gehaltsabzug, -senkung, -abbau, -kürzung; ~ **of share capital** *(Br.)* Zusammenlegung (Herabsetzung) des Aktienkapitals, Kapitalherabsetzung, -zusammenlegung; ~ **of sentence** Strafnachlaß; ~ **in staff** Personalabbau, -verringerung; ~ **of stock** Lagerabbau; ~ **in stock valuation** Bewertungsabschlag; ~ **of tariffs** Tarifermäßigung, -senkung, *(customs)* Abbau der Zölle; ~ **of taxes (taxation)** Steuererleichterung, -ermäßigung, -senkung; ~ **in the tax credit rate** Herabsetzung der Steuerfreibetragssätze; ~ **of trade barriers** Abbau der Handelsschranken; ~ **in train schedules** Fahrplaneinschränkung; ~ **of the trust property into possession** Besitzerlangung des Treuhandvermögens; ~ **in turnover** Minderumsatz; ~ **in value** Wertrückgang, -herabsetzung, -minderung, Entwertung; ~ **in the gold value** Goldwertschwund; ~ **of wages** Lohnsenkung, -kürzung; ~ **of working hours** Arbeitszeitverkürzung; ~ **in yield** Ertragsrückgang;
to allow a ~ Ermäßigung (Rabatt) gewähren; **to be in for a sharp** ~ für eine scharfe Kürzung vorgesehen sein; **to claim a** ~ **of assessment** Neubewertung verlangen; **to fund** ~**s in income tax** Einkommensteuerherabsetzungen finanzieren; **to give s. o. a** ~ **of 15 per cent** jem. eine Bonifikation von 15% gewähren; **to grant (make) a** ~ Preisermäßigung eintreten lassen; **to make a** ~ **of 15 per cent** 15% Rabatt gewähren; **to sell at a** ~ mit Rabatt verkaufen;
~ **formula** Umrechnungsformel; ~ **improbation** *(Scot.)* Klage auf Anfechtung einer gefälschten Urkunde; ~ **works** Müllverwertungsanlage.

redundancy Übermaß, Überschuß, *(labo(u)r)* Überschuß an Arbeitskräften, Stellenlosigkeit, *(pleadings)* Weitschweifigkeit;
~ **of workers** Überangebot an [nicht benötigten] Arbeitskräften;
to be selected for ~ **on arbitrary basis** *(Br.)* willkürlich zur Entlassung bei Überangebot von Arbeitskräften vorgesehen werden;
private ~ **agreement** *(Br.)* betriebliche Abfindungsvereinbarung; ~ **cheque** *(Br.)* Abfindungsscheck; ~ **fund** *(Br.)* Arbeitgeberfonds für soziale Abfindungen; ~ **fund contribution** *(unemployment insurance, Br.)* Arbeitslosenhilfe beim Überangebot von Arbeitskräften; ~ **insurance** *(Br.)* soziale Abfindungsleistungen; ~ **legislation** *(Br.)* Gesetzgebung zur Regelung von Sozialabfindungen; ~ **notice** *(Br.)* Stellenaufkündigungsmitteilung; ~ **pay** *(Br.)* soziale Abfindung im Kündigungsfall, Entlassungsabfindung, Übergangshilfe; ~ **payment** *(Br.)* Abfindungszahlung bei Stillegungen, Entlassungsabfindung, soziale Abfindung im Kündigungsfall; ℗ **Payments**

Act *(Br.)* Gesetz zur Regelung von Entlassungsabfindungen, Sozialabfindungsgesetz; ~ **payment fund** *(Br.)* Entschädigungsfonds für freigesetzte Arbeitskräfte; ~ **payments scheme** *(Br.)* Regelung im Fall von Sozialabfindungen; ~ **payment system** *(Br.)* Abfindungswesen bei Entlassungen; ~ **rebate** *(Br.)* Steuerfreibetrag für Sozialabfindungen; **private** ~ **scheme** *(Br.)* betriebliche Abfindungsregelung.

redundant überschüssig, -flüssig, -zählig, *(at pleading)* weitschweifig;
to become ~ nicht mehr gebraucht werden; **to have been made** ~ **by economic factors** seinen Arbeitsplatz aufgrund ökonomischer Entwicklungen verloren haben; **to make s. o.** ~ **j. als nicht mehr benötigt entlassen;
~ **capital** Kapitalüberschuß; ~ **employee** überflüssig gewordener Arbeitnehmer; ~ **labo(u)r** überzählige Arbeitskräfte, Arbeitskräfteüberschuß; **to first reinstate** ~ **workers** als erste wieder früher entlassene Arbeitskräfte einstellen.

reduplication Verdopplung.

reed Schiff[rohr];
broken ~ *(fig.)* unzuverlässiger Mensch, schwankendes Rohr; **to lean on a** ~ sich auf eine unzuverlässige Person verlassen.

reedify *(v.)* wieder aufbauen.

reedit *(v.)* neu herausgeben.

reedition Neuausgabe.

reeducate *(v.)* umschulen, umerziehen.

reeducation Umschulung, Umerziehung;
~ **camp** Umschulungslager.

reef Flöz;
~ *(v.)* **one's sails** *(fig.)* sich einschränken, kurztreten; **to take in a** ~ kürzer treten, *(economics)* Kürzungen vornehmen, *(fig.)* vorsichtig vorgehen, kurztreten.

reefer *(railroad, sl.)* Kühlwaggon.

reel *(film)* Filmstreifen, -rolle, -spule;
right off the ~ *(fig.)* hintereinander, ohne Pause; ~ *(v.)* **off a list of names** Namensliste herunterrasseln; **to transcribe from s. one's** ~ jds. Tonbanddiktat in die Schreibmaschine übertragen.

reelect *(v.)* wiederwählen;
not to ~ abwählen.

reelected, overwhelmingly mit überwältigender Mehrheit wiedergewählt.

reelection Wiederwahl;
eligible for ~ wiederwählbar; **to plan to seek** ~ seine Wiederwahl betreiben; **to run for** ~ sich zur Wiederwahl stellen; **to stand for** ~ **in rotation** sich turnusmäßig zur Wiederwahl stellen;
~ **committee** Wiederwahlausschuß.

reeler *(sl.)* Sauftour.

reeligible wiederwählbar.

reembark *(v.)* sich wieder einschiffen.

reembarkation Wiedereinschiffung.

reemploy *(v.)* wiedereinstellen, -beschäftigen, -anstellen.

reemployment Wiedereinstellung, -beschäftigung, *(market)* Belebung des Arbeitsmarktes, Arbeitsmarktbelebung.

reenact *(v.)* wieder in Kraft setzen, *(theater)* neu inszenieren.

reenactment neue Verordnung, *(theater)* Neuinszenierung.

reengage *(v.)* wiederanstellen.

reengagement Wiederanstellung, -einstellung, *(theater)* Neuengagement;
~ **recommendation** *(industrial tribunal)* Wiedereinstellungsempfehlung.

reenlist *(v.)* wiedereinstellen, *(mil.)* wieder eintreten;
~ **s. one's services** jds. Dienste wieder in Anspruch nehmen.

reenlistment Wiederanstellung, -einstellung, verwendung.

reenter *(v.)* wieder eintragen;
~ **an employment** Stellung wiederannehmen; ~ **an examination** sich erneut zu einer Prüfung melden; ~ **s. one's services** wieder in jds. Dienste treten; ~ **upon** wieder in Besitz nehmen.

reentrance Wiedereintritt.

reentry *(law)* Wiederinbesitznahme [eines Grundstücks], *(satellite)* Wiedereintritt.

reequip *(v.)* *(industry)* Industrie neu ausrüsten (ausstatten).

reequipment Neuausstattung.

reestablish *(v.)* wiederherstellen, *(reappoint)* wiedereinsetzen;
~ **one's affairs** sich sanieren; ~ **the currency** Währung stabilisieren; ~ **a firm's credit** Kredit eines Unternehmens wiederherstellen; ~ **a fund** Fonds auffüllen; ~ **the parity** Währungsparität neu festlegen; ~ **s. o. in his possession** j. in seinen Besitz wiedereinsetzen; ~ **diplomatic relations** diplomatische Beziehungen wiederherstellen; ~ **s. o. in his rights** j. wieder in seine Rechte einsetzen.

reestablishment Sanierung, Wiederherstellung, -einsetzung;
~ **of currency** Stabilisierung der Währung, Währungssanierung; ~ **of a fund** Fondsauffüllung; ~ **of parity** Neufestsetzung der Währungsparität.

reeve *(Canada)* Gemeindevorsteher.

reexamination Nachprüfung, nochmalige Prüfung;
~ **of a witness** Gegenkreuzverhör eines Zeugen.

reexamine *(v.)* nochmals prüfen, nachprüfen;
~ **a witness** Zeugen in ein Gegenkreuzverhör nehmen.

reexchange *(Br.)* Wechselprotestunkosten im Ausland, Devisenverlust.

reexport | **s** wieder ausgeführte Ware[n];
~ *(v.)* wieder ausführen.

reexport[ation] Wiederausfuhr;
~ **prohibition** Wiederausfuhrverbot; ~ **trade** Wiederausfuhrhandel.

ref. Aktenzeichen, Bezug.

reface *(v.)* [Haus]fassade erneuern.

refection Erfrischung, Imbiß, *(civil law)* Wiederherstellung, Reparatur.

refer *(v.)* verweisen, *(mention as a reference)* sich berufen;
~ **to acceptor** an den Akzeptanten zurück; ~ **to drawer** an den Aussteller zurück;
~ **to an act** sich auf ein Gesetz berufen; ~ **a dispute to arbitration** Streitfall einem Schiedsgericht vorlegen; ~ **to an authority** sich auf eine Quelle berufen; ~ **back to** zurückverweisen an; ~ **back a recommendation to the committee** Empfehlung an den Ausschuß zurückverweisen; ~ **to the board** Vorstand ansprechen; ~ **a case** Sache (Rechtsstreit) abgeben; ~ **a check (cheque,** *Br.)* **to the drawer** Scheck an den Aussteller zurückgeben; ~ **to one's colleague** sich auf seinen Kollegen berufen; ~ **to a committee** an einen Ausschuß verweisen; ~ **to a dictionary** in einem Wörterbuch nachschlagen; ~ **a dispute to the United Nations** Streitigkeit der UNO zur Entscheidung vorlegen; ~ **to a document** sich auf eine Urkunde beziehen; ~ **to a document as proof** Urkunde zum Beweis heranziehen; ~ **to a former employer** letzten Arbeitgeber als Referenz angeben; ~ **to an encyclopaedia** im Lexikon nachschlagen; ~ **to a footnote** auf eine Fußnote verweisen; ~ **s. o. to the manager** j. zum Betriebsleiter bestellen; ~ **to a matter again** auf eine Sache noch einmal zurückkommen; ~ **to one's notes** seine Aufzeichnungen konsultieren (Notizen zu Rate ziehen); ~ **to a passage** Stelle zitieren; ~ **a question to s. one's decision** jem. eine Frage zur Entscheidung vorlegen; ~ **a request to s. o.** jem. ein Gesuch vorlegen; ~ **s. o. to the secretary** j. an die Sekretärin verweisen; ~ **to s. one's statement** sich auf jds. Aussage berufen; ~ **one's success to good teaching** seinen Erfolg auf eine gute Ausbildung zurückführen.

referee *(arbitrator, US)* Schiedsrichter, *(in court)* Berichterstatter, Einzelrichter, *(expert)* gerichtlicher Sachverständiger, *(informant)* Auskunftgeber, Gewährsmann, *(parl.)* Referent;
official ~ *(Br.)* beauftragter Richter, Einzelrichter; **special** ~ vereinbarter Schiedsrichter, Sonderrichter;
~ **in bankruptcy** *(US)* Konkursrichter; ~ **in case of need** Notadressat.

reference *(act of referring)* Anspielung, Bezugnahme, Hinweis, Verweisung, *(book)* Belegstelle, *(competence)* Zuständigkeit, *(decision by referee)* Sachverständigenentscheidung, *(dictating)* Zeichen, *(law court)* Vorlage einer Rechtsfrage, *(letter)* Empfehlungsschreiben, *(person giving information)* Referenz, Auskunftgeber, Gewährsmann, *(record)* Beleg, Empfehlung, Unterlage, *(reference mark)* Verweisungszeichen, *(referring for decision)* Ver-, Überweisung, *(relation)* Beziehung, Bezug;
for ~ zur Information; **for ready** ~ zum sofortigen Auffinden; **outside our** ~ außerhalb unserer Zuständigkeit; **with (in)** ~ **to** unter Berufung (mit Bezug) auf; **with further** ~ **to my letter** im Anschluß an mein Schreiben; **with** ~ **to** in Anlehnung an; **without** ~ **to** ohne Verbindung zu;
~**s** Empfehlungen, *(book)* Fußnoten;
banker's ~ Bankauskunft, -referenz; **business** ~ geschäftliche Empfehlung, Geschäftsempfehlung; **character** ~ persönliche Referenzen; **cross** ~ Kreuzverweis; **first-class** ~**s** erstklassige (prima) Referenzen; **footnote** ~ Fußnotenverweis; **good** ~**s** gute Zeugnisse; **our** ~ unser Aktenzeichen; **personal** ~ persönliche Empfehlung; **statutory** ~ gesetzlicher Hinweis; **trade** ~ Kreditauskunft; **your** ~ Ihr Aktenzeichen;
~ **to authorities** Quellenangabe; ~ **back** Rückverweisung; ~ **in case of need** *(bill of exchange)* Notadresse; ~ **to be quoted in all communications** im Schriftwechsel anzugebendes Aktenzeichen;
~ *(v.)* mit Verweis versehen;

to be crowded with ~s von Fußnoten nur so wimmeln; to be outside the ~ of a commission nicht zu den Aufgaben eines Ausschusses gehören; to check s. one's ~s Referenzen überprüfen; to follow up ~s Referenzen überprüfen; to furnish ~s Referenzen angeben; to give ~s in a book Belegstellen in einem Buch aufführen; to give one's last employer as a ~ seinen letzten Arbeitgeber als Referenz angeben; to go for a ~ bei jem. Referenzen einholen; to have ~ to sich beziehen auf; to have good (first-class) ~s gute (prima, erstklassige) Referenzen haben; to look up a ~ einem Verweis nachgehen; to make ~ to a dictionary in einem Wörterbuch nachschlagen; to make ~ to an employer Arbeitgeber um Auskunft bitten; to put a ~ on a document Urkunde mit Aktenzeichen angeben; to quote a ~ Aktenzeichen angeben; to quote ~s Referenzen angeben; to supply a banker's ~ Bankauskunft zur Verfügung stellen; to take up ~s Auskunftgeber anschreiben, Referenzen einholen;
~ annual jährlicher Ergänzungsband; ~-back motion Rückverweisungsantrag; ~ book Nachschlagebuch; ~ card-index system Sicht[loch]kartei; ~ checking Referenzenüberprüfung; ~ feature Nachschlagegebiet; ~ files Handakten; ~ group Bezugsgruppe; ~ initials Diktatzeichen; ~ library Präsenz-, Handbibliothek; ~ mark Geschäftszeichen; ~ medium Nachschlagewerk mit Anzeigenanhang; ~ number (business) Geschäftszeichen, Aktenzeichen, Kennziffer, (bookkeeping) Übertragungsvermerk, (business letter) Geschäftsnummer; ~ pattern zurückbehaltene Warenprobe, Ausfall-, Probemuster; ~ period Ausgangszeitraum, (EC) Referenzzeitraum; ~ price empfohlener Preis, (EC) Bezugs-, Referenzpreis; ~ price system (EC) Bezugspreissystem; ~ room (library) Nachschlageraum; ~ sample Kontrollstichprobe; ~ slip (bank) Brief wegen der Nichteinlösung eines Schecks; ~ statutes Vorschriften über Anwendung anderer Gesetze; ~ value Anhaltszahlen; ~ work Nachschlagewerk.
referendary Berichterstatter.
referendum (pol.) Plebiszit, Volksbefragung, -entscheid;
ad ~ zur Berichterstattung;
compulsory (obligatory) ~ obligatorisches Verfassungsreferendum; constitutional ~ Volksbefragung bei Verfassungsänderungen; facultative (optional) ~ fakultatives Gesetzesreferendum; nation-wide ~ Volksbegehren;
~ in a union große Tarifkommission;
to hold a ~ Volksbefragung duchführen;
~ campaign Plebiszitkampagne; ~ decree Plebisziterlaß; ~ plebiscite (vote) Ergebnis der Volksabstimmung.
referent Verweisstelle.
referential mark Verweiszeichen.
referred benannt, bezeichnet.
referring to unter Bezugnahme (Berufung) auf;
~ your letter auf Ihren Brief Bezug nehmend.
refill Ersatzmine, -füllung;
~ (v.) auffüllen.
refinance (v.) refinanzieren.
refinancing Refinanzierung;
to secure ~ Refinanzierung sicherstellen;
~ agency Refinanzierungsgesellschaft; ~ arrangement Refinanzierungszusage, -vereinbarung; ~ costs Refinanzierungskosten; ~ plan Refinanzierungssystem; ~ task Refinanzierungsaufgabe.
refine (v.) (cause to become cultivated) verfeinern, kultivieren, (goods) veredeln, (sublime) vergeistigen;
~ upon another's invention Erfindung eines anderen vervollkommnen; ~ a language Sprache verfeinern; ~ upon one's methods seine Methoden verfeinern; ~ one's style seinen Stil verfeinern.
refined gebildet, kultiviert, fein, vornehm, (goods) veredelt, (sublimed) vergeistigt;
~ death rate spezifische Sterblichkeitsziffer; ~ distinction feine Unterscheidung; ~ manners feine Manieren; ~ speech kultivierte Aussprache (Rede).
refinement gebildetes Wesen, Kultiviertheit, (goods) Veredelung, (pleading) überflüssige Ausführungen, (subtlety) Spitzfindigkeit, Haarspalterei;
all the ~s of the age die ganze Bildung eines Zeitalters; ~(s) in a language Sprachverfeinerungen; ~ of another's invention Vervollkommnung der Erfindung eines Dritten; ~s of luxury Raffinessen des Luxus;
to introduce ~s into a machine Maschine vervollkommnen.
refiner (fig.) Haarspalter.
refinery Raffinerie;
oil ~ Ölraffinerie;
~ capacity Raffineriekapazität.

refining (fig.) Höherentwicklung, Kultivierung, (goods) Veredelung;
to hire ~ capacity Raffineriekapazität pachten; ~ equipment Raffinerieeinrichtungen; ~ industry Veredelungsindustrie.
refit Wiederinstandsetzung, (ship) Reparatur;
~ (v.) instandsetzen, reparieren;
~ a ship Schiff reparieren.
reflate (v.) the currency Währungsinflation vornehmen.
reflation Wirtschaftsbelebung durch Anhebung des Preisniveaus, Konjunkturbelebung durch Geldvermehrung, expansive Konjunkturpolitik.
reflationary expansiv, stimulierend;
~ measures Reflationsmaßnahmen; ~ package ganzes Bündel erneuter Inflationssteigerungsmaßnahmen, Bündel von Maßnahmen zur Anhebung des Preisniveaus, deflationistische Gesamtmaßnahmen; ~ round Reflationsrunde.
reflect (v.) reflektieren, überlegen, nachdenken;
~ discredit upon s. o. j. in Mißkredit bringen; ~ unfavo(u)rably on s. o. schlechtes Licht auf j. werfen.
reflection Rückstrahlung, (fig.) Nachdenken, Überlegung;
upon ~ nach erneuter Überlegung;
to be a ~ on s. th. schlechtes Licht auf eine Sache werfen; to invite ~ Gedanken aufkommen lassen.
reflector Rückstrahler, (car) Scheinwerfer;
~ stud Straßenleuchtnagel.
reflex Spiegelung;
to be a ~ of public opinion öffentliche Meinung widerspiegeln;
~ camera Spiegelreflexkamera.
refloat (v.) (company) sanieren;
~ a loan Anleihe neu auflegen; ~ a ship Schiff wieder flottmachen;
to be ~ed wieder flott werden.
refloating | of a company Reorganisation (Sanierung) einer Gesellschaft; ~ of a loan Neuauflage einer Anleihe; ~ a ship Wiederflottmachung eines Schiffes.
reflux Zurückströmen, Rückfluß;
~ of capital Kapitalrückfluß, -rückwanderung; ~ of funds Mittelrückfluß;
~ (v.) zurückfluten, -fließen, -strömen.
reforest (v.) wiederaufforsten.
reforestation [Wieder]aufforstung.
reform Umgestaltung, Umbau, Reform;
agrarian ~ Bodenreform; calendar ~ Kalenderreform; civil-service ~ Umbau des Verwaltungsapparates; constitutional ~ Verfassungsreform; currency ~ Währungsreform; depreciation ~ Reform der Abschreibungssätze; financial ~ Steuer-, Finanzreform; land ~ Bodenreform; municipal ~ Kommunalreform; penal ~ Strafrechtsreform; political ~s politische Reformen; radical ~ radikale Reform; sweeping ~s weitgehende Reformen; trenchant ~ einschneidende Reform; welfare ~ Reform der Sozialhilfe;
~ of land tenure Bodenreform; ~ in teaching methods Reform in Unterrichtsmethoden;
~ (v.) umgestalten, umbauen, reformieren;
~ an abuse Mißbrauch abstellen; ~ an administration Verwaltungsreform durchführen; ~ a deed Formfehler einer Urkunde durch Gerichtsbeschluß abändern lassen;
to agitate for social ~s für soziale Reformen eintreten; to carry out a ~ Reformen durchführen; to demand sweeping ~s durchgreifende Reformen verlangen; to introduce ~s Reformen einführen; to originate a ~ Reformbewegung ins Leben rufen;
~ act (Br.) Reformgesetz; ~ bill Reformgesetz; ~ efforts Reformbestrebungen; ~ movement Reformbewegung, Reformismus; ~ package Reformpaket, Bündel von Reformen; ~ society reformierte Gesellschaft; ~ wing Reformflügel.
reformation Neugestaltung, Reformierung, (document) Berichtigung.
reformatory Erziehungs-, Besserungsanstalt;
inebriate ~ Trinkerheilanstalt;
~ school (US) Besserungsanstalt, Jugendgefängnis, Fürsorgeerziehung.
reformed drunkard geheilter Trinker.
reforward (v.) [Brief] nachsenden, -schicken, weiterbefördern;
~ on arrival bei Ankunft weiterbefördern.
refrain (v.) Abstand nehmen, absehen von, unterlassen;
~ from hostile actions von feindseligen Handlungen absehen; ~ from consumption Konsumverzicht treiben.
refreight wieder befrachten, unterbefrachten.
refreighter Unterbefrachter.
refresh (v.) auffrischen, erneuern, (ship) frische Vorräte aufnehmen;

~ o. s. Stärkung zu sich nehmen; **~ a battery** Batterie aufladen; **~ one's memory** *(witness)* sein Gedächtnis auffrischen.

refresher Erfrischung, Stärkungstrunk, *(Br.)* zusätzliches Anwaltshonorar, erneuter Anwaltskostenvorschuß; **~ course** *(US)* Fortbildungs-, Auffrischungs-, Wiederholungskurs.

refreshing the memory Gedächtnisauffrischung.

refreshment Erfrischung, Imbiß, Bewirtung; **light ~s** leichte Erfrischungen; **to provide ~s** Erfrischungen anbieten; **to serve ~s** Erfrischungen reichen; **~ area** Pausenzone; **~ bar** Stehbierhalle; **~ booth** Erfrischungskiosk; **~ car** Speisewagen; **~ counter** Getränkeausschank; **~ house** *(Br.)* Restaurant, Gaststätte; **~ kiosk** Getränkeausschank, Erfrischungskiosk; **~ room** Büfett, Erfrischungsraum; **~ stand** Erfrischungskiosk.

refrigerate *(v.)* kühl aufbewahren, tiefkühlen.

refrigerated kühl aufbewahrt, tiefgekühlt; **~ bar** Kühlschrank zur Getränkeaufbewahrung; **~ cargo** Kühlraumladung; **~ traffic** Kühlwagentransport; **~ truck** Kühlwagen; **~ van** *(Br.)* Kühlwagen; **~ vessel** Kühlschiff.

refrigerating | chamber Kühlraum; **~ plant** Gefrieranlage; **~ process** Tiefkühlverfahren.

refrigeration Kälteerzeugung, Kühlung; **~ industry** Tiefkühlindustrie.

refrigerator Kühlschrank, -raum; **~ car (van)** *(US)* Kühlwagen; **~ vessel** Kühlschiff.

refuel *(v.)* auftanken, nachtanken; **~ in mid-air** im Flug auftanken.

refuelling Brennstoffaufnahme, Tanken; **~ base** Auftankstation; **~ stop** Auftankstation; **~ time** Auftankzeit.

refuge Zuflucht, Unterschlupf, Zufluchtsort, *(mountain hut)* Schutzhütte, *(safety zone, Br.)* Verkehrsinsel; **night ~** Nachtasyl; **street ~** Verkehrsinsel; **to seek ~** Zuflucht suchen; **to take ~ to silence** mit Stillschweigen übergehen; **to take ~ with s. o.** sich in jds. Schutz begeben.

refugee Flüchtling, Emigrant, Aussiedler, Heimatvertriebener; **camp ~** im Lager untergebrachter Flüchtling; **to be recognized as a ~** anerkannter Flüchtling sein; **to take in a ~** Flüchtling bei sich aufnehmen; **~ camp** Flüchtlingslager; **~ capital** heißes Geld; **~ government** Emigrantenregierung; **~ mentality** Flüchtlingsmentalität; **~ problems** Flüchtlingsprobleme; **~ relief** Flüchtlingshilfe; **~ resettlement** Flüchtlingssiedlung; **~ resettling** Eingliederung von Flüchtlingen; **~ status** Flüchtlingsstatus.

refund Rückvergütung, -erstattung, Zurückzahlung, Erstattungsbetrag, Ersatz; **liable to ~** rückerstattungspflichtig; **cash ~** Rückerstattung in bar; **contribution ~** Beitragsrückerstattung; **tax ~** Steuererstattung, -rückzahlung; **~s on exports to nonmember countries** *(EC)* Erstattung bei Ausfuhr in Drittländer; **~ of freight charge** Frachtkostenerstattung; **~ of income tax** Einkommensteuererstattung; **~ of premium** Prämienrückgewähr; **~ of purchase price** Zurückerstattung des Kaufpreises; **~ of travel expenses** Erstattung der Reisekosten, Reisekostenerstattung; **~** *(v.)* *(fund anew)* [Anleihe] neu fundieren, *(pay back)* zurückzahlen, -erstatten, *(indemnity)* schadlos halten, ersetzen; **~ an amount** Betrag wieder zur Verfügung stellen; **~ the cost of postage** Portospesen zurückvergüten; **~ duties** Zölle vergüten; **~ an excess of tax** überzahlte Steuer zurückerstatten; **~ the expenses (disbursements)** Auslagen zurückerstatten; **~ s. o. for all his expenses** jem. alle Unkosten ersetzen; **~ money** Geld zurückerstatten; **to make ~** zurückvergüten; **to obtain a ~ of a deposit (the money deposited)** *(customs)* Zollkaution zurückerhalten; **~ annuity contract** Rentenversicherungsvertrag; **[tax] ~ certificate** Steuerrückvergütungsschein; **~ offer** Rückerstattungsangebot bei Nichtgefallen; **tax ~ proceedings** Steuererstattungsverfahren.

refundable rückerstattungsfähig.

refunding Rückerstattung, -vergütung, *(loan)* Neufundierung; **~ of bonds** Refundierung von Obligationen; **~ of duties** Steuerrückerstattung, -nachlaß; **~ at maturity** Anleihetausch vor Fälligkeit; **~ of postage** Portovergütung; **~ bonds** Ablösungsschuldverschreibungen, Umtauschobligationen; **~ first mortgage bonds** *(US)* erststellig abgesicherte neufundierte Obligationen; **~ mortgage** Ablösungshypothek; **~ offer** Rückerstattungsangebot.

refundment Rückerstattung.

refurbish *(v.)* renovieren.

refurnish *(v.)* neu möblieren.

refusal ablehnende Antwort, Ablehnung, Verweigerung, Absage, abschlägiger Bescheid, *(patent law)* Zurückweisung, *(preemption)* Vorhand, Vorkauf; **in case of ~** im Verweigerungsfall; **arbitrary ~** willkürliche Weigerung; **first ~ of** erstes Anrecht; **flat ~** glatte Ablehnung; **point-blank ~** offene Absage; **clearly worded ~** klare Absage; **~ of acceptance (to accept)** Annahmeverweigerung, Nichtannahme; **~ to accept performance** Annahmeverzug; **~ to deal** *(antitrust law, US)* Abschlußverweigerung, Liefersperre; **concerted ~ to deal** *(US)* abgestimmte Lieferverweigerung, Gruppenboykott; **individual ~ to deal** *(antitrust law, US)* einzelne Abschlußverweigerung; **~ to deliver** Auslieferungsverweigerung; **~ of delivery** Abnahmeverweigerung; **~ to give evidence** Aussageverweigerung; **~ of goods** Ab-, Annahmeverweigerung; **~ of inheritance** Erbausschlagung; **~ to license** Lizenzverweigerung; **~ of an invitation** Absage einer Einladung; **~ of justice** Rechtsverweigerung; **~ of an offer** Ablehnung eines Angebots; **~ to pay** Zahlungsverweigerung; **~ to supply** Lieferablehnung, Auftragsverweigerung; **~ of a visa** Visumablehnung; **~ to work** Arbeitsverweigerung; **to buy the ~** Waren auf Termin kaufen; **to give the ~** freie Wahl lassen; **to give (have) the right of first ~** Vorkaufsrecht einräumen, vorkaufsberechtigt sein; **to meet with a square ~** glatte Absage erfahren, abfällig beschieden werden; **first-~ clause** *(US)* Vorkaufsklausel; **~ rate** *(interview)* Ablehnungsquote.

refuse *(garbage)* Müll, Abfall, Kehrricht, *(job goods)* Ausschuß[ware], Ramsch, *(rubbish)* Schutt; **household ~** Haushaltsabfälle, Hausmüll; **recyclable ~** wiederverwertbare Abfallstoffe; **special ~** Sondermüll; **town ~** *(Br.)* Stadtmüll; **trade ~** *(Br.)* gewerblicher Abfall, Gewerbemüll; **~** *(v.)* aus-, abschlagen, verweigern, ablehnen, zurück-, abweisen, [Gesuch] abfällig bescheiden; **~ the acceptance** Abnahme (Annahme) verweigern; **~ admittance** Zutritt verweigern (verwehren); **~ an appeal** Beschwerde verwerfen; **~ an application** Antrag ablehnen, *(patent law)* Anmeldung zurückweisen; **~ to back a bill** Giro verweigern; **~ a candidate** Kandidaten ablehnen; **~ to confess** Geständnis verweigern; **~ one's consent** seine Zustimmung versagen; **~ [to take] delivery** Annahme verweigern; **~ to be drawn** sich zu keiner Äußerung verleiten lassen; **~ flatly** rundweg abschlagen; **~ a gift** Geschenk nicht annehmen; **~ goods** Warenannahme verweigern; **~ an offer** Angebot ablehnen; **~ s. o. a hearing** j. nicht anhören; **~ help to s. o.** jem. Hilfe verweigern; **~ an invitation** Einladung nicht annehmen; **~ an offer** Angebot ablehnen; **~ an office** Amt nicht annehmen; **~ a patent** Patent versagen; **~ payment** nicht honorieren, Bezahlung verweigern; **~ s. o. permission** jem. die Erlaubnis verweigern; **~ a request** Gesuch abschlagen; **~ with one voice** sich einstimmig weigern; **~ bag** Abfallbeutel; **~ bin** Mülltonne; **~ collection** Müllabfuhr; **~ collector** Müllverwerter; **~ destructor** Abfallvernichtungsanlage; **~ disposal** Abfall-, Müllbeseitigung; **~ disposal site** Müllplatz, Deponie; **~ dump** Müllhalde; **~ material of a building** Bauschutt; **~ parts** Ausfall.

refused acceptance Annahmeverweigerung.

refutable widerlegbar.

refutal, refutation Widerlegung.

refute | (v.) an opponent Gegner widerlegen; **~ a statement** Behauptung widerlegen.

regain *(v.)* wieder-, zurückerlangen; **~ a market** Markt wiedergewinnen.

regaining of a market Wiedergewinnung eines Marktes.

regal | dignity königliche Würde; **to live in ~ splendo(u)r** wie ein Fürst residieren; **~ title** Königstitel.

regalia Krönungsinsignien; **Sunday ~** Sonntagsstaat.

regality königliches Hoheitsrecht.

regard *(consideration)* Rücksicht[nahme], Hinsicht, Bezug, Berücksichtigung, *(estimation)* Wertschätzung, [Be]achtung, *(respect)* Hinsicht, Beziehung, Bezug; **as ~s** bezüglich, mit Beziehung auf, was anbetrifft; **in this ~** in dieser Hinsicht; **with due ~** unter gebührender Berücksichtigung; **with ~ to** bezüglich, unter Berücksichtigung von, in Hinsicht auf; **with kind ~s** mit herzlichen Grüßen; **with kind ~s from the author** mit den besten Empfehlungen des Autors; **without ~ to** ohne Rücksicht auf; **without ~ to cost** ohne Kostenrücksicht;

~ *(v.)* *(concern)* betreffen, angehen, *(consider)* ansehen, betrachten, berücksichtigen;

~ **s. one's advice** jds. Ratschläge befolgen; ~ **a communication as confidential** Mitteilung vertraulich behandeln; ~ **s. th. as a crime** etw. als Verbrechen ansehen; ~ **s. o. highly** große Stücke von jem. halten;

to give one's kind ~s to s. o. jem. Empfehlungen übermitteln; **to have ~ to** berücksichtigen; **to have a high ~ of s. one's judgment** viel von jds. Urteilskraft halten; **to have little ~ for the feelings of others** auf die Gefühle anderer Leute keine Rücksicht nehmen; **to hold s. o. in high ~** Hochschätzung für j. empfinden; **to pay due ~** beachten, berücksichtigen, Rechnung tragen; **to present one's ~s** Grüße übermitteln.

regarded, to be ~ as gelten.

regardful, to be respektieren, berücksichtigen.

regardless ohne Rücksicht (Berücksichtigung) auf;

~ **of expense(s)** ohne Rücksicht auf die Kosten; ~ **of prices** ohne Rücksicht auf die Preise.

regency Regentschaft[srat].

regent Regent, Reichsverweser, *(university, US)* Verwaltungsrat, Kurator;

prince ~ Prinzregent.

regime Regierungsform, Regime, *(matrimonial property rights, US)* Güterstand, [eheliches] Güterrecht;

contractual ~ *(US)* vertragsmäßiges Güterrecht; **matrimonial property ~** *(US)* eheliches Güterrecht; **present ~** bestehende Ordnung; **statutory ~** *(US)* gesetzliches Güterrecht;

to establish a new industrial ~ neues Industriezeitalter heraufführen; **to throw out a corrupt ~** bestechliche Verwaltung zum Teufel jagen.

regimen Diätanweisung.

regiment | of the line *(Br.)* Linienregiment;

~ *(v.)* *(fig.)* eingruppieren, reglementieren, durch amtliche Vorschriften regeln, *(mil.)* einem Regiment zuteilen;

~ **into a system** in eine Ordnung bringen; ~ **the workers of a country** Arbeiterschaft im Land organisieren.

regimental | aid post Truppenverbandschaftsplatz; ~ **debts** Nachlaßverwaltung von Militärpersonen; ~ **officer** Regimentsoffizier.

regimentation *(fig.)* Einteilung, Organisation, Reglementierung.

regimented industries unter staatlicher Aufsicht (Staatsaufsicht) stehende Industrien.

region Bezirk, Distrikt, Bereich, Landstrich, Gegend, Gebiet, Region;

economic ~ Wirtschaftsraum; **forest ~** Waldgebiet; **functional (nodal) ~** Funktionsraum; **industrial ~** Industriegebiet; **infrastructural ~** Infrastrukturraum; **overcrowded ~** übervölkertes Gebiet, Ballungsgebiet; **densely (thinly) populated ~** dicht (dünn) besiedeltes Gebiet; **similar ~** *(statistics)* analoger Bereich; **structural ~** Strukturraum;

~ **of high pressure** Hochdruckgebiet; ~ **of low pressure** Tiefdruckgebiet; ~ **of war** Kriegsgebiet.

regional örtlich, lokal, räumlich, regional, zu einem Bezirk gehörig;

~ **accounts** regionalwirtschaftliche Gesamtrechnung; ~ **ads** *(US)* Regionalanzeigen; ~ **advertising** Regionalwerbung; ~ **advertising campaign** regionaler Werbefeldzug; ~ **agency** Bezirksagentur, Bezirksstelle, regionale Einrichtung; ~ **aid** *(EC)* Regionalhilfe; ~ **aid funds** Regionalhilfsmittel; ~ **analysis** Regionalforschung; ~ **arrangement** Gebietsabkommen; ~ **assembly** Bezirksversammlung; ~ **association** Regionalverband; ~ **authorities** *(Br.)* Verwaltungsregionen; ~ **bank** Regional-, Landes-, Bezirksbank; ~ **basis** regionale Grundlage; ⌂ **Board** *(Br.)* Bezirksbehörde; ~ **boundaries** Bezirksgrenzen; ~ **budget** *(EC)* Regionalhaushalt; ~ **campaign** Kampagne für Regionalanzeigen; ~ **center** *(US)* **(centre, Br.)** Gebietszentrum; ~ **college** Landesuniversität; ~ **commissioner** Bezirksbeauftragter; ~ **committee** Gebietsausschuß; ~ **council** *(Br.)* Bezirksrat; ~ **court** [etwa] Landgericht; ~ **clearinghouse** regionale Scheckverrechnungsstelle; ~ **data bank** regionale Datenbank; ~ **development** regionale Erschließung, Landesplanung; ~ **differential** regionaler Lohnunterschied; ~ **director** Bezirksdirektor, -leiter; ~ **dispersion** regionale Streuung; ~ **division** regionale Aufteilung, Dezentralisierung; ~ **division of labo(u)r** Industriekonzentration; ~ **economic planning board** *(Br.)* Landesplanungsamt; ~ **economic planning council** *(Br.)* Landesplanungsrat; ~ **economic policy** *(EC)* Standortpolitik, regionale Wirtschaftspolitik; ~ **economics** Regionalwirtschaft, -ökonomie; ~ **edition** Bezirksausgabe; ~ **elections** Kommunal-, Bezirks-, Landtagswahlen; ⌂ **Employment Premium** *(Br.)* regionale Arbeitsplatzprämie; ~ **examining body** Landesprü-

fungsausschuß; ~ **exchange** Regionalbörse; ~ **fund** *(EC)* Regionalfonds; ~ **fund spending** *(EC)* Ausgabenwirtschaft des Regionalfonds; ~ **geography** Länderkunde; ~ **government** Provinzial-, Bezirksregierung, örtliche Regierungsbehörde; ~ **help** Regionalhilfe; ⌂ **Industrial Development Board** *(Br.)* regionale Wirtschaftsförderungsstelle; ~ **industrial policy** *(EC)* regionale Wirtschaftspolitik, Standortpolitik; ~ **institution** Regionalinstitut; ~ **line** Nahverkehrslinie; ~ **list system** regionales Listensystem; ~ **meeting** Regionaltreffen, Gebietstreffen; ~ **needs** Regionalbedürfnisse; ~ **neutralization** *(law of nations)* Befriedung; ~ **newspapers** Regionalpresse; ~ **office** Regionalbüro, Bezirksbüro, Zweigstelle, *(US)* Oberfinanzdirektion; ~ **organization** Bezirks-, Regionalgliederung, Regionalorganisation; ~ **origin** örtliche Herkunft; ~ **pact** Regionalabkommen, -pakt; ~ **papers** Regionalzeitungen, -presse; ~ **planning** Landesplanung; ~ **planning consultant** Berater für regionale Planungsvorhaben; ~ **planning program(me)** Raumordnungsprogramm; ~ **policy** Regionalpolitik, Raumordnung; ~ **policy plan** Raumordnungsplan; ~ **representative** Bezirksvertreter; ~ **research** regionale Strukturforschung; ~ **salesman** Bezirksvertreter, Regionalverkaufsleiter; ~ **show** landwirtschaftliche Ausstellung; ~ **specialization** regionale Spezialisierung; ~ **station** *(Br.)* Großrundfunksender; ~ **statistics** Regionalstatistik; ~ **strategics** Raumordnungsprogramm; ~ **structure** regionale Struktur; ~ **study** Regionalstudien, -untersuchung; ~ **survey** räumliche Bestandsaufnahme; ~ **system** regionales Selbstverwaltungssystem; **to be operated under a ~ system** regional geleitet werden; ~ **tax** Regionalsteuer, Erschließungsabgabe; ~ **trade** Regionalhandel; ~ **unit** Raumeinheit; ~ **wage differential** regional bestimmter Lohnunterschied.

regionalism Dezentralismus.

regionalization Aufteilung in Verwaltungsbezirke, Dezentralisierung;

~ **concept** Dezentralisierungsidee.

regionalize *(v.)* in Verwaltungsbezirke aufteilen, dezentralisieren.

register Register, *(ledger)* Journal, Kontobuch, *(minutes)* Protokoll, *(official written record)* [amtliches] Register, [amtliche] Liste (Aufstellung), Verzeichnis, Eintragungsbuch, *(records of landed property, Scot.)* Grundbuch, *(registration)* Registrierung, Eintrag[ung], Aufzeichnung, *(records of landed property)* Grundbuch, *(registration)* Registrierung, Eintrag[ung], Aufzeichnung, *(registrar, US)* Registerführer, Registrator, *(ship's ~)* Schiffsregister, *(official abstract of ship's ~)* Schiffsregisterauszug, *(table of contents)* Register, Inhaltsverzeichnis, Index;

~**s** Jahrbücher;

cash ~ Kontroll-, Registrierkasse; **charges ~** *(Br.)* Grundpfandverzeichnis, [etwa] Abteilung III des Grundbuchs, Hypothekenregister; **check (cheque, Br.) ~** Scheckverzeichnis; **church ~** Kirchenbuch; **colonial ~** *(Br.)* Verzeichnis der in den Dominions eingetragenen Aktiengesellschaften; **debt ~** Schuldbuch; **deposit ~** Register über alle für Einzahlungen auf Depositenkonten ausgegebenen Quittungen; **dominion ~** *(Br.)* Aktionärsverzeichnis im Commonwealth wohnender Mitglieder; **electoral ~** Wählerverzeichnis; **estate ~** Kataster; **Federal ⌂** *(US)* [etwa] Bundesanzeiger; **fixed-assets ~** Anlagenkartei; **general ~** Firmen-, Genossenschaftsregister; **hotel ~** Fremdenbuch; **land ~** *(Br.)* Grundbuch[amt]; **Lloyd's ~** *(Br.)* Schiffsregister; **Official ⌂** *(US)* Amts-, Gesetzblatt; **parish ~** Kirchenbuch; **parliamentary ~** Wählerliste; **passbook ~** *(bank)* Kontobücherverzeichnis; **patent ~** *(US)* Patentrolle; **principal ~** *(trademarks, US)* Hauptregister; **property ~** Grundstücksregister; **proprietorship ~** *(Br.)* Eigentum-, Eigentümerverzeichnis; **public ~** amtliches Register; **public ~s** öffentliche Bücher; **real-estate ~** *(US)* Grundbuch[amt]; **share ~** *(Br.)* Aktionärsverzeichnis; **ship's ~** Schiffszertifikat, Registerbrief; **stock ~** Gesellschaftsregister, Zertifikat; **supplemental ~** *(trademarks, US)* Nebenregister; **trade ~** Handelsregister; **transfer ~** *(Br.)* Umschreiberegister; **unpaid ~** *(checks)* Verzeichnis nicht eingelöster Schecks; **voucher ~** Belegsammlung, -order, Verzeichnis der Buchungsunterlagen;

~ **of pending actions** *(Br.)* amtliches Verzeichnis anhängiger Grundstückssachen und Konkursfälle; ~ **of aircraft** Luftfahrzeugrolle; ~ **of aliens** Fremdenregister; ~ **of annuities** *(Br.)* Register der Staatspapiere; ~ **of apprentices** Lehrlingsliste; ~ **in bankruptcy** *(earlier act of congress, US)* Konkursrichter; ~ **of births, deaths and marriages** *(Br.)* Standesamts-, Personenstandsbücher, -register; ~ **of births, marriages and burials** *(US)* Personenstandsregister; ~ **of charges** *(company, Br.)* Belastungsregister, Grundpfandverzeichnis; ~ **of companies** *(Br.)*

Gesellschaftsregister, Handelsregister; ~ **of convictions** Straf-register; ~ **of condolence** Kondolenzbuch, Trauerliste; ~ **of cooperative societies** Genossenschaftsregister; ~ **of copyrights** Urheberrechtsregister, -rolle; ~ **of corporations** *(US)* Handels-, Gesellschaftsregister; ~ **of deaths** Sterberegister, -liste, -buch; ~ **of debentures (debenture holders)** *(Br.)* Liste der Schuldver-schreibungsinhaber; ~ **of deeds** *(Scot.)* Grundbuchamt, *(some US states)* Urkunds-, Grundbuchbeamter; ~ **of deeds of arrangement affecting land** *(Br.)* Verzeichnis von Vergleichsverein-barungen in Grundstückssachen; ≗ **of Designs** *(Br.)* Geschmacksmusterrolle; ~ **of directors** Vorstandsverzeichnis, Direktorenverzeichnis; ~ **of electors** Wählerliste; ~ **of fares** Fahrpreisverzeichnis; ~ **of goods in bond** Verzeichnis der Zoll-verschlußwaren; ~ **of land charges** *(Br.)* Grundschuld-, Hypo-thekenregister; ~ **of land office** *(US)* Grundbuchrichter; ~ **of marriages** Heiratsbuch, Familienbuch; ~ **of members** Mit-gliederverzeichnis, *(stock exchange, Br.)* Aktionärsregister, -verzeichnis; ~ **of membership corporations** *(US)* Vereinsre-gister; ~ **of mortgages** Hypothekenregister; ~ **of names of owners** namentliches Eigentümerverzeichnis; ~ **of patents** *(US)* Patentverzeichnis, -register, -rolle; ~ **of persons** Personenver-zeichnis; ~ **of probate** *(US)* Nachlaßrichter; ~ **of properties** Grundstücksverzeichnis; ~ **of sasines** *(Scot.)* Grundbuch; ~ **of securities** *(Br.)* lebendes Depot, Effektendepot, -verzeichnis; ~ **of shares** Aktienbuch; ~ **of ships (shipping)** Schiffsregister; **Lloyd's** ≗ **of Shipping** Lloyds Schiffahrtsregister; ~ **of vital statistics** *(US)* Personenstandsbücher, -register; ~ **of taxes** Hebeliste; ~ **of titles** *(Scot.)* Grundbuchamt; ~ **of trademarks** Warenzeichenregister, -rolle; ~ **of transfers** *(Br.)* Register für Aktienverkäufe, Umschreibungsbuch; ≗ **of the Treasury** *(US)* Bundesschatzmeister; ~ **of voters** Wählerliste; ~ **of wills** *(US)* Urkundsbeamter des Nachlaßgerichtes; ~ **of writs** *(Br., for-mer)* Prozeßregister; ~ **of writs and orders affecting land** *(Br.)* Verzeichnis von Zwangsversteigerungsverfahren und Seque-stereinsetzungen;

~ *(v.) (enter in the minutes)* protokollieren, *(hotel register)* sich anmelden, sich in das Fremdenbuch einschreiben, *(letter)* ein-schreiben lassen, *(luggage)* aufgeben, *(patent)* in das Patentre-gister eintragen, *(post office)* einschreiben lassen, *(record in list, books etc.)* registrieren, [amtlich] eintragen, in eine Liste (ein Verzeichnis) eintragen, amtlich erfassen, gesetzlich schüt-zen lassen, *(record in writing)* ver-, aufzeichnen, *(shares)* im Register umschreiben, *(ship)* Schiffszertifikat ausstellen, *(uni-versity)* in die Matrikel einschreiben, immatrikulieren;

~ **o. s.** sich eintragen, *(politics)* sich in die Wahlliste (Wählerli-ste) eintragen; **not** ~ **with s. o.** keinen Eindruck bei jem. machen, j. nicht beeindrucken; ~ **a birth** Geburt beurkunden; ~ **bonds** Obligationen auf den Namen eintragen; ~ **a car** Auto polizeilich anmelden (zulassen); ~ **a caution** Vormerkung im Grundbuch eintragen lassen; ~ **a newborn child (the birth of a child, US)** Kind beim Standesamt anmelden; ~ **a child for school** Kind bei der Schule anmelden; ~ **a company (corpora-tion)** Gesellschaft (Firma) handelsgerichtlich eintragen [las-sen]; ~ **contracts for premises** *(Br.)* Mietverträge mit Mieterschutzbestimmungen registrieren; ~ **for a course of lec-tures** Vorlesung belegen; ~ **a death** Sterbefall beurkunden; ~ **a deed** Urkunde vom Notar aufnehmen lassen; ~ **for a fair** sich zu einer Messe anmelden; ~ **small gains** kleine Gewinne ver-zeichnen; ~ **at a hotel** sich in das Fremdenbuch eintragen, Anmeldezettel im Hotel ausfüllen; ~ **a land charge** Grund-schuld bestellen; ~ **a mortgage** Hypothek bestellen (ins Grund-buch eintragen lassen); ~ **a motor vehicle** Kraftfahrzeug anmelden; ~ **one's name** seinen Namen eintragen; ~ **at an office** sich bei einer Dienststelle melden; ~ **o. s. with the police** sich polizeilich anmelden; ~ **sailors** Matrosen anwerben; ~ **for a school** zu einer Schule anmelden; ~ **a security** Sicherheit bestel-len; ~ **shares** Aktien überschreiben lassen; ~ **a stop** *(check)* sperren lassen; ~ **a new top** neuen Höchstkurs verbuchen; ~ **a trade** Gewerbe anmelden; ~ **with a tradesman** sich in eine Kundenliste eintragen lassen; ~ **a trademark** Warenzeichen anmelden; ~ **a treaty** *(law of nations)* Vertrag registrieren; ~ **o. s. on the voting list** sich in die Wählerliste eintragen; ~ **a will** notarielles Testament errichten;

[not] to be on the ~ [nicht] erfaßt sein; **to enter in the** ~ in ein Register eintragen, registrieren; **to keep the** ~ Protokoll füh-ren; **to keep** ~**s of the government stocks** Staatsanleihenver-zeichnis führen; **to maintain a** ~ **of charities** *(Br.)* Stiftungsregister führen; **to rectify the** ~ Grundbuch berichti-gen; **to refuse to** ~ **a firm** einer Firma die handelsgerichtliche Eintragung versagen; **to remove a firm from the** ~ Firma im Handelsregister löschen; **to rule a** ~ **similar** Parallelregister

führen; **to sign the** ~ *(Br.)* Eintragung im Personenstandsregi-ster unterzeichnen; **to sign the** ~ **of condolence** sich in die Kondolenzliste eintragen; **to strike off the** ~ im Register löschen;

~ **balance** Registerguthaben; ~ **book** Schiffshypothekenregi-ster; ~ **card** Karteikarte; ~ **certificate** *(Br.)* Effektenbesitzbe-scheinigung; ~ **county** *(Br.)* Grafschaft mit Grundbuchrecht; ~ **number** Auftragsnummer; ~ **office** Registerbehörde, Registra-tur, Annahme-, Anmeldestelle, *(court)* Geschäftsstelle, *(Br.)* Standesamt, *(employment* ~*, US)* Stellenvermittlung, *(trade)* Handelsregisteramt; ~ **port** Heimat-, Registerhafen; ~ **ship** Registerschiff; ~ **ton** Bruttoregistertonne, Registertonne.

registered eingetragen, registriert, *(company)* handelsgerichtlich eingetragen, *(letter, parcel)* eingeschrieben, *(securities)* einge-tragen, auf den Namen lautend, *(trademark)* gesetzlich geschützt;

≗! Einschreiben;

officially (duly) ~ handelsgerichtlich eingetragen; **state** ~ staat-lich anerkannt;

to be ~ auf den Namen lauten; **to have one's luggage** ~ *(Br.)* sein Gepäck aufgeben;

~ **address** feststehende Adresse; ~ **agreement** *(cartel law, Br.)* registrierte Absprache; ~ **association** eingetragener Verein; ~ **bond** Namensschuldverschreibung; ~ **capital** autorisiertes (ein-getragenes) [Aktien]kapital, Grundkapital; ~ **certificate** Namenspapier; ~ **charge** *(Br.)* eingetragene Grundstücksbela-stung, eingetragene Reallast, Grundschuld; ~ **club** *(Br.)* Verein mit Alkoholkonzession; ~ **company** handelsgerichtlich einge-tragene Gesellschaft; ~ **coupon bond** *(US)* Namensschuldver-schreibung; ~ **customer** in die Kundenkartei aufgenommener Kunde, Stammkunde; ~ **debenture** Namensschuldverschrei-bung; ~ **design** *(Br.)* eingetragenes Gebrauchsmuster; ~ **dispo-sition** Vormerkung; ~ **gross tonnage** Bruttoregistertonnage; ~ **holder** *(Br.)* eingetragener Wertpapierinhaber; ~ **holding com-pany** *(Securities Commission, US)* registrierte Holdinggesell-schaft; ~ **items** eingeschriebene Postsendungen, Einschreibe-sendungen; ~ **land** grundbuchamtlich erfaßtes Grundstück; ~ **letter** Einschreibebrief, Wertbrief; ~ **luggage** *(Br.)* aufgegebe-nes (großes) Gepäck; ~ **mail** *(US)* Einschreibsendungen; **by** ~ **mail** *(US)* als Einschreiben; ~ **mail insurance** *(US)* Postwertver-sicherung; ~ **mail receipt** *(US)* Posteinlieferungsschein; ~ **mortgage** eingetragene Hypothek; ~ **nurse** *(US)* staatlich geprüfte Krankenschwester; ~ **office** *(Br.)* eingetragener Gesellschafts-, Geschäftssitz, Dienstsitz, Hauptniederlas-sung; ~ **parcel** Einschreibpäckchen; ~ **pattern** Gebrauchsmu-ster, geschütztes Modell; ~ **policy** auf den Namen ausgestellte Police; **by** ~ **post** *(Br.)* per Einschreiben; ~ **port** Heimathafen; ~ **property** grundbuchlich eingetragenes Grundstück; ~ **proprie-tor** *(Br.)* im Grundbuch eingetragener Eigentümer; ~ **repre-sentative** *(US)* Börsenauftragnehmer; ~ **securities** Namenspa-piere, -aktien, auf den Namen lautende Wertpapiere; ~ **share** *(Br.)* Namensaktie, -papier; ~ **shareholder** *(Br.)* Inhaber von Namensaktien; ~ **ship** registriertes Schiff, Registerschiff; ~ **societies** *(Br.)* eingetragene Genossenschaften; ~ **stock** *(US)* Namensaktie, -papier; ~ **tonnage** Registertonnage; ~ **trade-mark** eingetragenes Warenzeichen; ~ **unemployed** gemeldete Arbeitslose; ~ **user** *(trademark, Br.)* eingetragener Lizenzneh-mer (Warenzeichenbenutzer); ~ **value** festgestellter Wert; ~ **voter** eingetragener Wähler.

registerer Registrierer.

registrability Eintragungsfähigkeit.

registrable eintragungsfähig, registrierbar, -fähig;

~ **as to principal only** nur dem Kapitalbetrag nach eintragungsfähig.

registrant Registerführer, Meldepflichtiger, *(trademarks)* Inha-ber eines Warenzeichens, Schutzmarkeninhaber.

registrar *(Br.)* Registrator, Archivar, Registerführer, Urkunds-beamter, Rechtspfleger, *(officer of public records, Br.)* Standes-, Personenstandsbeamter, *(real estate, US)* Grundbuch-beamter, *(of university)* höchster Verwaltungsbeamter;

deputy ~ *(Br.)* stellvertretender Standesbeamter; **district** ~ Lei-ter einer Bezirksgeschäftsstelle; ≗ **General** *(Br.)* Oberster Stan-desbeamter; **stock** ~ *(US)* Überwachungsstelle für Aktien-emissionen; **superintendent** ~ *(Br.)* Hauptstandesbeamter;

~ **in bankruptcy (of a bankruptcy court, Br.)** Konkursrichter; ≗ **of Bills of Sales** *(Br.)* Register für die Eintragung von Siche-rungsübereignungen; ≗ **General of Births, Deaths and Marria-ges** *(Br.)* Oberster Standesbeamter; ≗ **of business names** *(Br.)* Firmen-, Handelsregister; ≗ **of Companies** *(Br.)* Gesellschafts-, Handelsregisterführer; ~ **of Joint Stock Companies** Aktien-rechtsregister; ~ **of the court** Urkundsbeamter der Geschäftsstelle; ~ **of a bankruptcy court** Geschäftsstelle eines Konkursgerichts; ~ **of deeds** *(US)* Grundbuchbeamter; ⬩ **of Friendly Societies** *(Br.)* Aufsichtsamt für das Sparkassenwesen; ⬩ **at the Land Charges department** Grundbuchrichter; ~ **of mortgages** Grundbuchrichter; ~ **of vital statistics** *(US)* Standesbeamter; ⬩ **of Restrictive Trade Practices** *(Br.)* Kartellamt, -behörde; ⬩ **of Restrictive Trading Agreements** *(Br.)* Registrierungsstelle für wettbewerbsbeschränkende Kartellvereinbarungen, Meldestelle für marktbeherrschende Zusammenschlüsse, Kartellamt; ~ **of transfer** *(shares, Br.)* Umschreibungsbeamter; ⬩ **of the Treasury** *(US)* Schiffsregister; ~ **of a university** Universitätssekretariat; ~ **of voters** Wahlamtsleiter, -listenprüfer; **to get married before the** ~ *(Br.)* sich standesamtlich trauen lassen; **to officiate as** ~ *(Br.)* als Standesbeamter fungieren; ~'**s licence** *(Br.)* Heiratslizenz; ~'**s office** Registratur, Geschäftsstelle, *(marriages, Br.)* Standesamt.

registration amtliche Eintragung, Eintragungsvermerk, Registrierung, Erfassung, Protokollierung, Vormerkung, Aufzeichnung, *(enrolment)* Anmeldung, *(luggage, Br.)* Gepäckannahme, *(persons registered)* registrierter Personenkreis, *(with the police)* polizeiliche Anmeldung, *(political science)* Eintragung in die Wählerliste, *(post office)* Einschreiben, *(securities)* Börsenanmeldung von Wertpapieren, *(university, US)* Immatrikulation;

subject to ~ eintragungs-, anmeldepflichtig;

aliens' ~ Registrierung von Ausländern; **compulsory** ~ Eintragungszwang; **copyright** ~ Registrierung des Urheberrechts; **first** ~ Ersteintragung; **general** ~ Eintragung in die Wählerliste; **home** ~ *(trademark)* Ursprungseintragung; **improper** ~ fehlerhafte Eintragung; **land** ~ *(Br.)* Grundbucheintragung; **re-** ~ Wiedereintragung; **temporary** ~ vorläufige Zulassungsgenehmigung;

~ **of aliens** Registrierung von Ausländern, Ausländererfassung, -registrierung; ~ **of bankruptcy proceedings** Erfassung von Konkursverfahren; ~ **as a bill of sale** Eintragung in das Mobiliarpfandregister; **public** ~ **of a birth** standesamtliche Geburteneintragung; ~ **of births, deaths and marriages** Beurkundung des Personenstandes; ~ **of business** Gewerbeanmeldung, Registrierung des Firmennamens, Firmeneintragung; ~ **of business names** *(Br.)* handelsgerichtliche Eintragung, Registrierung des Firmennamens, Firmeneintragung; ~ **of new cars** Anmeldung von Neufahrzeugen; ~ **of charges** *(land registry, Br.)* Eintragung von Belastungen; ~ **of a new-born child** Anmeldung eines Kindes beim Standesamt; ~ **of a company** *(Br.)* **(corporation, US)** handelsgerichtliche Eintragung einer Gesellschaft; ~ **of copyright** Urheberrechtseintragung; ~ **for a course of studies** Belegung von Vorlesungen, Anmeldung zu einem Vorlesungskurs; ~ **of designs** Geschmacksmustereintragung; ~ **of employees** Arbeitnehmerliste; ~ **of land** *(Br.)* Grundbucheintragung; ~ **of a land charge** Eintragung einer Grundstücksbelastung; ~ **with the Land Registry** *(Br.)* Grundbucheintragung; ~ **of a letter** Briefaufgabe per Einschreiben; ~ **of luggage** *(Br.)* Gepäckaufgabe; ~ **of a mortgage** *(Br.)* Hypothekeneintragung; ~ **of a motor vehicle** *(Br.)* Anmeldung eines Kraftfahrzeugs, Kfz-Registrierung; ~ **of foreign nationals** *(Br.)* Ausländererfassung, -registrierung; ~ **of notice** Eintragung einer kommunalen Grundstückslast; ~ **of a patent** Eintragung in die Patentrolle; ~ **with the police** polizeiliche Anmeldung; ~ **of property** Vermögenserfassung; ~ **of satisfaction** *(charges)* Tilgungseintragung, Löschung von Belastungen; ~ **of securities** Anmeldung von Wertpapieren; ~ **of stock** Aktionärsverzeichnis, Eintragung ins Aktionärsregister; ~ **of title to land** Grundstück-, Grundbucheintragung; **compulsory** ~ **of title to land** Grundbuchzwang; ~ **of trademarks** Eintragung eines Warenzeichens, Warenzeicheneintragung; ~ **of the university** Universitätssekretariat; ~ **of voters** Eintragung in die Wählerliste;

to apply for ~ **as citizen** sich um Bürgerrechte bewerben; **to cancel (expunge) a** ~ Eintragung löschen; **to deny a** ~ Eintragungsantrag zurückweisen; **to make** ~ **compulsory** Registrierung verbindlich vorschreiben; **to provide an exemption from** ~ von der Registrierungspflicht ausnehmen; **to report for** ~ sich registrieren lassen; **to require one's** ~ anmelde-, registrierungspflichtig sein; **to search for a particular** ~ nach einer bestimmten Eintragung suchen; **to vacate a** ~ Sperrvermerk [im Grundbuch] eintragen;

Land ⬩ **Act** *(Br.)* Grundbuchordnung; ⬩ **of Business Names Act** *(Br.)* Gesetz über die Eintragung von Firmennamen; **compulsory** ~ **area** *(Br.)* anmelde-, grundbuchpflichtiges Gebiet; ~ **bills** *(trademark)* Warenzeichenrolle; ~ **card** Personalbogen, Stammrolle, Zulassungs-, Registrierungsausweis, Anmeldeschein, *(elections)* Wahlausweis; ~ **certificate** Eintragungsurkunde, *(foreigner, Br.)* Ausländerausweis, *(motor vehicle, US)* Zulassungspapiere, -urkunde, Kraftfahrzeugbrief; ~ **district** Registrierungsbezirk; ~ **fee** Eintragungs-, Einschreibe-, Aufnahme-, Vormerkungs-, Ummelde-, Inskriptions-, Anmeldegebühr, *(post office)* Einschreibegebühr, *(transfer of shares)* Umschreibungs-, Übertragungsgebühr, *(university, US)* Immatrikulationsgebühr; ~ **and transfer fee** *(stock register)* Eintragungs- und Umschreibungsgebühr; ~ **form** Anmeldeformular, Meldeschein, -zettel; ~ **label** Klebezettel für Einschreibesendungen, Einschreibezettel; **date-stamp** ~ **letter** *(car)* Tüv-Plakette; ~ **list** Melde-, Wählerliste; ~ **number** Eintragungsnummer; ~ **number of a car** Zulassungs-, Wagennummer; ~ **office** Einwohnermelde-, Register-, Standesamt, [An]meldestelle, Meldebehörde; ~ **period** Eintragungsdauer; ~ **plate** *(car, Br.)* polizeiliches Kennzeichen; ~ **privilege** *(US)* Berechtigung zu einer auf den Namen lautenden Eintragung, Eintragungsanspruch; ~ **procedure (proceedings)** Eintragungs-, Registrierungsverfahren; ~ **purpose** Registrierungszweck; ~ **requirements** Eintragungsbedingungen; ~ **slip** Wagenpapiere; ~ **statement** Anmeldeerklärung, *(balance sheet)* Gründungs-, Eröffnungsbilanz, *(stock exchange admission, US)* Eintragungsbekanntmachung, Registrierungsunterlagen; ~ **window** Gepäckschalter.

registry *(births, marriages, deaths)* Standesamt, *(employment office)* Arbeitsvermittlungsstelle, -nachweis, Stellenvermittlung, *(law court)* Gerichtskanzlei, Geschäftsstelle, Registratur, Gerichtsschreiberei, *(marine transportation)* Schiffsregisterbrief, *(office)* Eintragungsstelle, Registratur, *(register)* Verzeichnis, Register, Protokoll, *(registration)* Eintragung, Registrierung, *(ship)* Eintragung im Schiffsregister;

married at the ~ standesamtlich getraut;

district ~ *(High Court of Justice, Br.)* Zweiggeschäftsstelle; **district probate** ~ *(US)* Geschäftsstelle des Nachlaßgerichtes; **Land** ⬩ *(Br.)* Kataster-, Grundbuchamt; **servants'** ~ Stellenvermittlung für Hausangestellte, Hausangestelltennachweis;

~ **of deeds** *(US)* Grundbuchamt; ~ **of joint stock companies** Verzeichnis der Aktiengesellschaften, Aktienrechtsregister; ~ **of a ship** Eintragung ins Schiffsregister; ~ **of title** Grundbuch; **to be married at a** ~ standesamtlich getraut sein; ~ **books** Matrikel, Register; ~ **and transfer department** *(US)* Registrier- und Übertragungsabteilung; ~ **fee** *(real estate)* Grundbuchkosten, -gebühren, *(post office)* Einschreibegebühr; ~ **marriage** standesamtliche Trauung; ~ **office** *(Br.)* Standesamt, *(US)* Registerbehörde; **to marry at a** ~ **office** standesamtlich heiraten; **servants'** ~ **office** Stellenvermittlungsbüro; ~ **system** Grundbuchsystem.

reglet *(print.)* Steg, Zeilendurchschuß.

regnal year *(Br.)* Regierungsjahr, Jahr der Thronbesteigung.

regrade *(v.)* [gehaltlich] neu einstufen.

regrading *(of civil servants, Br.)* [gehaltliche] Neueinstufung.

regrant erneute Bewilligung, Wiederverleihung, *(Br.)* Wiederverpachtung;

~ *(v.)* erneut bewilligen, wiederverpachten.

regrate *(v.) (victuals)* auf-, weiterverkaufen.

regrating Lebensmittelan- und -verkauf.

regress Wiederinbesitznahme, *(recourse)* Schadloshaltung.

regression Rückschritt;

true ~ *(statistics)* fehlerfreie Regression;

~ **analysis** Regressionsanalyse; ~ **estimate** Regressionsschätzwert.

regressive *(taxes)* regressiv;

~ **scale of tax rates** regressiver Steuertarif; ~ **taxation** regressive Besteuerung.

regrets Absagebrief;

~ **only** Antwort nur bei Absage erforderlich;

to decline with many ~ mit größtem Bedauern absagen; **to express one's** ~ sein Bedauern aussprechen.

regroup *(v.)* umschichten, umsetzen, -gruppieren.

regrouping *(capital)* Umgruppierung, *(concentration)* Rekonzentration, Umschichtung;

industrial ~ Umgruppierung in der Industrie;

~ **of labo(u)r** Umgruppierung von Arbeitskräften.

regular *(customer)* Stammkunde, *(mil.)* Berufssoldat, *(party politics, US)* treuer Parteianhänger;

~ *(a.)* normal, regelmäßig, regulär, ständig, *(according to established rule)* satzungs-, ordnungs-, vorschriftsmäßig, *(mil.)* regulär, zur Kampftruppe gehörig, *(train)* fahrplanmäßig;

as ~ **as clockwork** pünktlich wie die Uhr;

to be ~ **on its face** *(cheque)* äußerlich in Ordnung sein; **to be** ~ **in one's attendance at one's office** seine Bürostunden pünktlich einhalten;

~ **agent** ständiger Vertreter; ~ **amount of pay rate** Normallohnsatz; ~ **army** reguläre Armee, Berufsheer; ~ **arrangement** übliche Abmachung; ~ **business** laufende Geschäfte; ~ **collateral** *(US)* Sicherheit durch Hinterlegung handelsüblicher Effekten; ~ **course of business** normaler Geschäftsablauf; ~ **customer** Stammkunde, *(restaurant)* Stammgast; ~ **customers** feste Kundschaft, Stammkundschaft; ~ **day** Empfangstag, Jour; ~ **deposit** normaler Hinterlegungsvertrag; ~ **dividend** an festen Terminen zahlbare (normale) Dividende; ~ **doctor** Hausarzt; ~ **election** regelmäßige Wahl; ~ **employee** festangestellter Bediensteter; ~ **employment** feste Anstellung; ~ **fee** übliche Gebühr; ~ **habits** geordnete Lebensweise, feste Gewohnheiten; ~ **hours** Normalarbeitszeit; **to keep** ~ **hours** genauen Stundenplan einhalten; ~ **income** festes (laufendes) Einkommen; ~ **indorsement** gewöhnliches Giro; **at** ~ **intervals** in regelmäßigen Abständen, turnusmäßig; ~ **judge** ordentlicher Richter; ~ **lot** *(stock exchange)* handelbare Größe, *(US)* Normal-, Börsenabschlußeinheit; ~ **marriage** *(Br.)* rechtsgültige Ehe; ~ **meeting** *(board)* Routinesitzung, *(US, stockholders)* ordentliche Hauptversammlung; ~ **member** ordentliches Mitglied; ~ **model** Normalausführung; ~ **money** *(Br.)* ziemlich festes Tagesgeld; ~ **navigation** Linienschiffahrt; ~ **nomination** vorschriftmäßige Ernennung; ~ **occupation** ständiger Beruf; ~ **officer** Berufsoffizier; ~ **pay** Normallohn; ~ **payments** regelmäßig wiederkehrende Zahlungen; ~ **physician** approbierter Arzt; ~ **and established place of business** Betriebsstätte; ~ **price** regulärer Preis, Normalpreis; ~ **procedure** korrektes Verfahren; ~ **process** ständige Einrichtung; **to have no** ~ **profession** keinen festen Beruf ausüben; ~ **rate** *(stock exchange)* feste Valuta, *(wages)* Normaltarif, üblicher Lohnsatz; ~ **reader** Dauerleser; ~ **salary** festes Gehalt, Fixum; ~ **sale** *(stock exchange)* Verkauf für Lieferung am folgenden Tag; ~ **service** turnusmäßiger Dienst, *(railway)* fahrplanmäßiger Verkehr; ~ **session** ordentliche Sitzung; ~ **size** Normalgröße, -format; ~ **soldier** aktiver Soldat, Berufssoldat; ~ **staff** ständiges Personal; ~ **supplier** regelmäßiger Lieferant; ~ **term** richterliche Frist; ~ **ticket** *(US)* offizielles Parteiprogramm; ~ **time** Normalarbeitszeit; ~ **traveller** Dauerkarteninhaber; ~ **troops** reguläre Truppen; ~ **turn** geregelte Reihenfolge, Turnus; ~ **wage** Normallohn; ~ **way** *(stock exchange, US)* Lieferung am nächsten Geschäftstag; ~ **weight** ordentliches Gewicht; **to be in** ~ **work** fest angestellt sein; **to have no** ~ **work** keine feste Anstellung haben, keine bestimmte Tätigkeit ausüben; ~ **workforce** Stammbelegschaft.

regularity Regel-, Ordnungsmäßigkeit;
for ~'**s sake** der Ordnung halber.

regularization Regulierung, Bereinigung.

regularize *(v.)* regulieren, bereinigen, *(fix)* gesetzlich festlegen, regeln;
~ **the proceedings** ordnungsgemäßes Verfahren sicherstellen.

regulate *(v.)* regulieren, regeln, einrichten, lenken, ordnen, *(business)* Geschäft abwickeln, *(rectify)* Rechnung berichtigen;
~ **one's expenditure** seine Ausgabenwirtschaft in Ordnung bringen; ~ **the industries of a country** Wirtschaft eines Landes reglementieren; ~ **the level of demand** Nachfragebedürfnisse steuern; ~ **the speed of a machine** Geschwindigkeit einer Maschine regulieren; ~ **traffic** Verkehr regeln.

regulated│company *(ancient)* privilegierte Handelsgesellschaft;
~ **industries** *(US)* gebundene Industriezweige.

regulation Regelung, Regulierung, Reglement, *(direction)* Bestimmung, Vorschrift, Verordnung, Verfügung, *(Br.)* *(governing precept)* Durch-, Rechts-, Ausführungsverordnung, *(technics)* Dienst-, Betriebsvorschrift;
according to ~s vorschriftsmäßig, statutengemäß; **contrary to** ~s satzungs-, vorschriftswidrig; **in conformity with the** ~s laut Vorschrift;
~s *(statute)* Satzung, Statuten;
additional ~ Zusatzbestimmung; **administrative** ~s Ausführungsbestimmungen; **automatic** ~ Selbststeuerung; **banking** ~ staatliche Ordnung des Kreditwesens; **building** ~s Bauvorschriften; **censor** ~s Zensurvorschriften; **city** ~s städtische Verordnungen; **currency** ~s Devisenbestimmungen; **current** ~s geltende Bestimmungen; **customs** ~s Zollvorschriften; **domestic** ~s innerstaatliche Vorschriften; **economic** ~s wirtschaftliche Maßnahmen; **exchange** ~s *(control)* Devisenbestimmungen, *(stock exchange)* Börsenordnung; **export** ~s Ausfuhrbestimmungen; **factory** ~s gewerbepolizeiliche Anordnungen; **import** ~s Einfuhrbestimmungen; **income-tax** ~s Einkommensteuerbestimmungen; **internal** ~s interne Bestimmungen, Dienstvorschriften; **market** ~s Marktordnung; **monthly** ~ Ultimoliquidation; **official** ~s amtliche Bestimmungen; **pedestrian-crossing** ~ Regelung des Fußgängerverkehrs;

petty ~s engstirnige Bestimmungen; **police** ~s polizeiliche Vorschriften; **postal** ~s postalische Bestimmungen; **price** ~s Preisvorschriften; **provisional** ~ vorläufige Regelung; **restricting marketing** ~ einschränkende Vorschriften über den Marktverkehr; **road** ~s Straßenverkehrsvorschriften; **safety** ~s Sicherheitsbestimmungen; **service** ~s Dienstordnung, *(railway)* Betriebsvorschriften; **specific** ~s nähere Bestimmungen; **speed** ~s Geschwindigkeitsbegrenzung; **staff** ~s Personalstatut, Dienstordnung; **stock-exchange** ~s Börsenordnung; **tax** ~s steuerrechtliche Bestimmungen, Steuervorschriften; **telephone** ~ Bestimmungen über das Führen von Ferngesprächen; **trade** ~s *(US)* Wettbewerbsregeln; **traffic** ~s Verkehrsvorschriften; **withholding** ~s Bestimmungen über die Einbehaltung von Lohnsteuern; **working** ~s Betriebsordnung, -vorschriften;
laws and ~s Gesetze und [Rechts]verordnungen;
~ **of an account** Kontoregulierung; ~ **of an affair** Regelung einer Angelegenheit; ~ **of private carriers** Vorschriften für gewerbliche Transportunternehmen; ~s **of a corporation** Gesellschaftsstatut, Satzung einer Gesellschaft; ~ **of credit** Kreditlenkung, -regulierung; ~ **of an executive department** ministerielle Durch-, Ausführungsverordnung; ~ **under federal law** *(US)* bundesgesetzliche Regelung; ~s **in force** geltende Vorschriften; ~s **governing meetings** Hauptversammlungsrichtlinien; ~ **of the market** Marktregulierung; ~ **of navigation** Schiffahrtsverordnung; ~s **of pay scale** Tarifordnung; ~ **of payments** Regelung des Zahlungsverkehrs; ~ **of production** Produktionslenkung; ~s **for Preventing Collisions at Sea** Seestraßenordnung; ~s **governing prizes** Prisenordnung; ~ **of production** Produktionslenkung; ~s **of the railway** Bahnvorschriften; ~ **of rates** Tarifregulierung; ~s **of a society** Vereinsstatuten;
to act in accordance with the ~s vorschriftsmäßig handeln; **to apply a** ~ **very loosely** Verordnung elastisch handhaben; **to bring under** ~ reglementieren; **to comply with** ~s Vorschriften befolgen; **to evade** ~s Vorschriften umgehen; **to lay down a** ~ Anordnung erlassen; **to put up with** ~s sich mit Vorschriften abfinden; **to suffer from undue** ~s wegen unnötiger Staatseingriffe Schaden erleiden;
it says in the ~s die Bestimmungen besagen;
~ **charge** Gewerbescheingebühr; ~ **dress** offizieller (vorgeschriebener) Anzug; ~ **form** vorgeschriebenes Formular; ~ **mourning** übliche Trauerzeit; ~ **size** Normalgröße, vorschriftsmäßige Größe.

regulator Ordner, *(el.)* Regler, *(office)* Aufsichtsbehörde, Überwachungsstelle, *(Chancellor of the Exchequer, Br.)* Vollmachten zur Veränderung der indirekten Steuersätze;
state ~ staatliche Überwachungsstelle;
~ **of the economy** Konjunkturregulativ.

regulatory regulativ, regelnd, bestimmend;
~ **agency** *(US)* zuständige Behörde, Aufsichtsbehörde, Durchführungsstelle, -behörde; ~ **area** Durchführungsbereich; ~ **body** *(US)* Aufsichtsbehörde, -organ; **to wield the** ~ **club** mit dem Aufsichtsknüppel drohen; **state** ~ **commission** *(US)* staatliche Aufsichtsstelle, -behörde; ~ **function** Zuständigkeit für den Erlaß von Verwaltungsvorschriften; ~ **impact** Aufsichtswirkung; ~ **job** Regulierungsaufgabe, Überwachungstätigkeit, -funktion, Aufsichtstätigkeit; ~ **matters** Aus-, Durchführungsangelegenheiten, Regularien; ~ **maze** wahrer Irrgarten von Durchführungsbestimmungen; ~ **measures** Durchführungsmaßnahmen; ~ **officer** Aufsichtsbeamter; ~ **policies** Durchführungsmethoden; ~ **powers** Überwachungs-, Aufsichts-, Kontrollfunktionen; ~ **process** Regulierungsprozeß, fortschreitende Reglementierung; ~ **statute** Ausführungsbestimmungen, Verwaltungsvorschrift; ~ **tool** Regulativ; ~ **void** Überwachungslücke.

rehabilitate *(v.)* normalisieren, *(old buildings)*, wieder aufbauen, restaurieren, instandsetzen, *(reinstate)* wiedereinsetzen, *(reorganize)* sanieren, *(restore)* rehabilitieren, *(workers)* umschulen, wieder ins Berufsleben eingliedern;
~ **a company financially** Finanzen einer Gesellschaft sanieren; ~ **offenders** Strafentlassene wieder eingliedern; **to be** ~**d in one's former esteem** seine frühere Stellung in der Gesellschaft wiedererlangen.

rehabilitation Normalisierung, *(buildings)* Restaurierung, *(criminal)* Bewährung, *(employee)* Umschulung, Wiedereingliederung in das Berufsleben, *(reinstatement)* Wiedereinsetzung [in frühere Rechte], Rehabilitierung, *(reorganization)* Sanierung;
industrial ~ wirtschaftliche Wiedereingliederung; **monetary** ~ Währungssanierung; **plant** ~ Wiederaufbau eines Betriebes; **postwar** ~ Wiederaufbau in der Nachkriegszeit; **vocational** ~ [berufliche] Umschulung;

~ of disabled men Wiedereingliederung von Berufsunfähigen in das Wirtschaftsleben; **~ and resettlement** berufliche und soziale Wiedereingliederung, Resozialisierung; **~ of occupied territory** Wiederaufbau besetzter Gebiete;

~ center (centre, Br.) Umschulungszentrum; **~ costs** *(house)* Instandsetzungskosten; **~ expenses** Umschulungs-, Wiederherstellungskosten; **~ loan** Wiederaufbauanleihe; **~ plan** Sanierungsplan; **industrial ~ problem** wirtschaftliches Wiederaufbauproblem; **~ relief** Umschulungsbeihilfe; **~ services** berufliche Umschulungsleistungen.

rehash *(fig.)* Aufgewärmtes;

~ *(v.)* auf neu frisieren, *(rediscuss, sl.)* immer wieder durchkauen;

~ last term's lectures for the coming term Vorlesungsstoff für das kommende Semester überarbeiten; **~ old arguments** alte Argumente von neuem vorbringen.

rehear *(v.)* erneut (nochmals) verhandeln, nochmals in die Verhandlung eintreten, Verfahren wiederaufnehmen.

rehearing Wiedereintritt in die Verhandlung, erneute Verhandlung, Wiederaufnahmeverfahren.

rehearsal *(theater)* Generalprobe;

dress ~ Kostümprobe;

~ of grievances Litanei von Beschwerden;

to be in ~ einstudiert werden; **to take the ~s** Proben leiten.

rehearse *(v.)* einstudieren;

~ the events of the day Tagesereignisse Revue passieren lassen.

rehearser Probenleiter.

rehire *(v.)* wieder einstellen (anstellen).

rehiring Wiederanstellung, -einstellung.

rehouse *(v.)* neuen Wohnraum schaffen;

~ people from slums Bevölkerung aus Elendsvierteln umquartieren.

rehousing Umquartierung;

to desperately need ~ dringend eine neue Wohnung benötigen.

rehypothecate *(v.)* nochmals (weiter) verpfänden, erneut lombardieren;

to have securities ~s als Pfand bestellte Effekten lombardieren lassen.

rehypothecation Wieder-, Weiterverpfändung, *(securities)* zweite Lombardierung.

reign Herrschaft, Regierung[szeit];

~ of law Herrschaft des Gesetzes;

~ *(v.)* herrschen, regieren;

~ over a kingdom über ein Königreich herrschen.

reimbursable rückzahlbar, erstattungsfähig.

reimburse *(v.)* *(indemnify)* abgelten, entschädigen, *(repay)* [zurück]vergüten, wiederbezahlen, zurückzahlen, -erstatten;

liable to ~ erstattungspflichtig;

~ o. s. nachnehmen; **~ o. s. upon s. o.** sich bei jem. bezahlt machen (schadlos halten, erholen); **~ s. o. for his costs** jem. die Spesen ersetzen; **~ expenses** Kosten decken, Auslagen erstatten; **~ s. o. for his losses** jds. Verluste übernehmen; **~ for postage incurred** Portoauslagen vergüten.

reimbursed, to be ~ for one's expenses seine Auslagen erstattet bekommen, seine Unkosten decken können.

reimbursement *(indemnification)* Abgeltung, Ersatz[leistung], Entschädigung, Schaden-, Geldersatz, *(repayment)* Wiederbezahlung, Rückzahlung, -erstattung, [Rück]vergütung;

for ~ of out-of-pocket expenses gegen Erstattung der baren Auslagen;

~ of charges Gebühren[rück]erstattung, Spesenvergütung; **~ of expenses incurred** Rückerstattung (Ersatz) von Auslagen, Aufwandsentschädigung, Spesen-, Kostenerstattung, -ersatz; **~ for exports** Rückvergütung für Exporte, Ausfuhrrückvergütung; **~ of fees** Gebührenerstattung; **~ of outlays** Auslagenerstattung; **~ of premium** Prämienrückerstattung; **~ of taxes** Steuerrückvergütung;

to take as ~ als Deckung annehmen;

~ card Nachnahmekarte; **~ charges** Spesenvergütung; **~ claim** Erstattungsanspruch; **~ credit** Rembourskredit; **~ draft** Rembourstratte; **~ fund** Deckungskapital.

reimport *(v.)* wieder einführen.

reimportation Wieder-, Rückeinfuhr.

reimpose *(v.)* **taxes** neue Steuern auferlegen.

reimposition erneute Besteuerung.

reimpression Neudruck, Wiederabdruck.

rein | s of government Zügel der Regierung; **~ of terror** Schreckensherrschaft;

to assume the ~s of government Regierung antreten; **to drop the ~s of government** sein Amt abgeben; **to hold the ~s of government** Regierung leiten; **to hold the ~s of an organization** organi-

satorische Leitung haben; **to keep a tight ~ on s. o.** j. fest an der Kandare haben; **to keep a tight ~ on s. th.** etw. fest im Griff haben; **to take over the ~s** Leitung übernehmen.

reincorporate *(v.)* rückgliedern.

reincorporation Rückgliederung.

reindorse *(v.)* umschreiben, wieder indossieren, zurückgirieren.

reinforce *(v.)* *(mil.)* unterstützen, Nachschub zuführen;

~ an argument Beweisführung untermauern; **~ a fleet** Schlagkraft einer Flotte erhöhen; **~ a garrison** Besatzung einer Garnison verstärken; **~ a guarantee** Bürgschaft verstärken.

reinforced concrete Stahlbeton.

reinforcement *(mil.)* Verstärkung, Nachschub;

~ troops Nachschubkräfte.

reinstall *(v.)* wiedereinsetzen.

reinstal(l)ment Wiedereinsetzung, -einstellung;

~ of an employee Wiedereinstellung eines Angestellten.

reinstate *(v.)* *(restore to proper order)* wieder instandsetzen, wieder einstellen (anstellen), *(to privileges)* wieder einsetzen, wiederzulassen;

~ a case Verfahren in den vorigen Stand wiedereinsetzen, Wiedereinsetzung in den vorigen Stand gewähren; **~ the contents of a parcel** Paketwert ersetzen; **~ an insurance** Versicherung wiederaufleben lassen; **~ s. o. in his former office** j. in sein früheres Amt wiedereinsetzen; **~ s. o. in his rights** j. wieder in seine Rechte einsetzen; **~ workers** Arbeiter wiedereinstellen.

reinstatement Wiederinstandsetzung, Wiedereinsetzung, *(fire insurance)* Wiederaufbau, *(insurance)* Wiederaufnahme von Prämienzahlungen, Wiederaufleben einer Versicherung, *(law court)* Wiedereinsetzung in den vorigen Stand, *(worker)* [bedingungslose] Wiedereinstellung;

~ in civil employment Wiedereinstellung aus dem Wehrverhältnis Entlassener;

~ insurance gleitende Neuwertversicherung; **~ order** *(US)* Wiedereinstellungsverfügung; **~ policy** Wiederaufbaupolice.

reinsurance Rück-, Gegenversicherung;

catastrophe ~ Katastrophenrückversicherung; **excess ~** Rückversicherung für einen Spitzenbetrag, Exzedentenrückversicherung; **excess loss ~** unbegrenzte Rückversicherung; **facultative ~** individuelle Rückversicherung; **flat ~** unkündbare Rückversicherung; **surplus treaty ~** Rückversicherung mit Festlegung des maximalen Selbstbehalts; **treaty ~** automatisch wirksame Rückversicherung;

~ by quota cession Quotenrückversicherung;

to accept ~ automatically Rückversicherung automatisch annehmen; **to take out a ~** sich rückversichern, Rückversicherung abschließen;

~ agreement Rückversicherungsvertrag, Rückversicherungsvereinbarung; **~ broker** Rückversicherungsmakler; **~ broking** Rückversicherungsgeschäft; **~ business** Rückversicherungsgeschäft; **~ carrier** Rückversicherer, Rückversicherungsgesellschaft; **~ company** Rückversicherungsgesellschaft; **~ contract** Rückversicherungsvertrag; **~ group** Rückversicherungskonzern; **~ policy** Rückversicherungspolice; **~ pool** *(Br.)* Rückversicherungsfonds, -pool; **~ premium** Rückversicherungsprämie; **~ protection** Rückversicherungsschutz; **~ recovery** Beziehung der Rückversicherungsbeträge; **~ requirements** Voraussetzungen für den Betrieb von Rückversicherungsgeschäften; **~ share** Rückversicherungsanteil; **~ syndicate** Rückversicherungskonsortium; **~ transaction** einzelnes Rückversicherungsgeschäft; **~ treaty** Rückversicherungsvertrag.

reinsure *(v.)* nach-, rückversichern.

reinsured Rückversicherter;

~ carrier rückversicherte Gesellschaft.

reinsurer, reinsuring carrier Rückversicherer;

specialist ~ reiner Rückversicherer.

reintegrate *(v.)* wiedervereinigen.

reintegration Wiedervereinigung.

reintroduce *(v.)* wiedereinführen.

reintroduction Wiedereinführung.

reinvest *(v.)* [Geld] wieder anlegen, Kapitalumdispositionen vornehmen, reinvestieren.

reinvestment Neu-, Wiederanlage, Kapitalumdisposition, Reinvestition;

automatic ~ of income automatische Wiederanlage der Erträge; **~ of a patent** Neuerteilung eines Patents; **~ of proceeds** Wiederanlage des Erlöses;

~ ratio Wiederanlagequote.

reissuable *(banknotes)* wieder ausgebbar.

reissue *(banknotes)* Wiederausgabe, *(new issue)* Neuemission, *(publishing)* Neuauflage;

~ of a patent *(US)* Neuerteilung eines Patents;

~ *(v.)* *(bank notes)* wieder begeben, *(publishing)* wiederauflegen, neu auflegen;
~ patent Abänderungspatent; **~ stamps** Briefmarken nachdrucken.
reissued *(book, loan)* neu aufgelegt.
reiteration *(print.)* Wiederdruck.
reject *(job goods)* Ausschußware, *(mil.)* Diensttauglicher, *(person)* verwendungsunfähiger Mensch;
~s beanstandete Ware, Ausschußware;
export ~s Exportausschuß; **factory ~** Fabrikausschuß; **manufacturing ~s** Ausschußware;
~ *(v.)* ablehnen, abweisen, zurückweisen, ausschlagen, *(discard)* aussondern, ausmustern, als wertlos ausscheiden, *(sell cheaply)* als Ausschuß[ware] verkaufen;
~ s. o. *(army doctor)* für untauglich erklären;
~ an appeal Rechtsmittel zurückweisen; **~ an application** Bewerbung ablehnen; **~ a bill** Gesetzvorlage verwerfen; **~ a check** *(cheque, Br.)* Scheck zurückweisen; **~ a claim** Anspruch bestreiten, Reklamation zurückweisen; **~ a custom** sich über eine Sitte hinwegsetzen; **~ food** Nahrungsaufnahme verweigern; **~ goods delivered** Warenlieferung beanstanden, Warenlieferung ablehnen; **~ a motion** Antrag ablehnen; **~ an offer** Angebot ablehnen; **~ a request** Gesuch abschlägig bescheiden (ablehnen).
rejected geringwertig;
to be ~ *(theater)* durchfallen;
~ goods zurückgewiesene Ware.
rejection Abweisung, Ablehnung, Zurückweisung, *(refusal of acceptance)* Annahmeverweigerung, *(social interaction)* soziale Abstoßung;
~s *(job goods)* Ausschußware, -stücke;
express ~ ausdrückliche Ablehnung; **implied ~** sich aus den Umständen ergebende Ablehnung, vermutete Ablehnung;
~ of a claim Zurückweisung einer Reklamation; **~ of goods delivered** Beanstandung von Waren; **~ of a motion** Antragsablehnung; **~ of offer** Ablehnung eines Angebots, Angebotsablehnung; **~ of proof** *(bankruptcy proceedings)* Zurückweisung einer Konkursforderung; **~ of proxy** Zurückweisung einer Stimmrechtsermächtigung;
to move the ~ of the proof of a bill Ablehnung eines Gesetzentwurfes beantragen;
~ letter Absagebrief; **~ line** *(statistics)* Ablehnungslinie; **~ number** *(statistics)* Ablehnungszahl; **~ region** *(statistics)* Ablehnungsbereich; **~ slip** Verwerfungsschein.
rejector circuit *(el.)* Sperrkreis.
rejoin *(v.)* *(law)* duplizieren, auf die Replik erwidern;
~ a party sich einer Partei wieder anschließen.
rejoinder Erwiderung, Entgegnung, Duplik.
rejudge *(v.)* neues Urteil fällen.
rekindle *(v.)* neu beleben.
relabel *(v.)* neu etikettieren.
relade *(v.)* wieder beladen.
relapse Rückfall, *(stock exchange)* Rückschlag, -gang;
~ *(v.)* *(bad habit)* rückfällig werden, *(prices)* fallen, Rückschlag erleiden (erfahren).
relapser Rückfälliger.
relapsing rückfällig.
relate *(v.)* Bezug haben, sich auf etw. beziehen;
~ back *(v.)* rückwirkende Kraft haben; **~ losses** Verluste rückwirkend verwenden; **~ a result with a cause** Ergebnis mit einer Ursache in Kausalzusammenhang bringen.
related verwandt, verbunden;
closely ~ näher verwandt;
~ by blood blutsverwandt; **~ to** mit Bezug auf; **~ in the collateral line** in der Seitenlinie verwandt; **~ by marriage** verschwägert; **~ on the mother's side** mütterlicherseits verwandt;
to be ~ to s. o. mit jem. verwandt sein; **to be ~ to s. th.** Beziehung zu etw. haben;
~ company Tochter-, Konzerngesellschaft; **~ cost** notwendige Kosten; **~ enterprises** verbundene Unternehmen; **~-item display** Warenauslage verwandter Artikel; **~ language** verwandte Sprache.
relation [Rechts]beziehung, Zusammenhang, Verhältnis, Bezug, [Ver]bindung, Relation, *(denunciation)* Anzeige, Denunziation, *(pleading)* Vortrag des Sachverhalts, *(to prior date)* Rückwirkung, -beziehung, *(relative)* Verwandter;
in ~ to in Bezug auf;
~s Verwandtschaft;
blood ~ Blutsverwandtschaft; **business ~s** geschäftliche Beziehungen, Geschäftsbeziehungen; **close ~s** enge [Geschäfts]beziehungen; **commercial ~** wirtschaftliche Beziehungen; **confi-**

dential ~(s) Vertrauensverhältnis; **conjugal ~(s)** eheliche Lebensgemeinschaft; **consensual ~s** schuldrechtliche Beziehungen; **contractual ~(s)** Vertragsverhältnis; **customer ~** Beziehungen zur Kundschaft; **diplomatic ~s** diplomatische Beziehungen; **distant ~** entfernter Verwandter; **external ~s** auswärtige Beziehungen; **family ~s** Familienbeziehungen; **fiduciary ~** Vertrauensstellung, -verhältnis; **financial ~** kapitalmäßige Bindung; **friendly ~s** freundschaftliche Beziehungen; **governmental ~s** Beziehungen zu den Behörden; **human ~s** zwischenmenschliche Beziehungen; **industrial ~s** *(US)* Beziehungen zwischen Arbeitgebern und Arbeitnehmern; **intimate ~s** intime Beziehungen; **labo(u)r-management ~s** Beziehungen zwischen Arbeitgebern und -nehmern; **mutual ~** Wechselbeziehung; **near ~** nahe Verwandtschaft; **pleasant business ~** langjährige angenehme Geschäftsbeziehungen; **public ~** Öffentlichkeitsarbeit, Vertrauenswerbung; **strained ~s** gespannte Beziehungen;
parents and ~s Eltern und Verwandte;
~ back *(receiving order)* Rückwirkung, -beziehung; **~ back to the date of filing the petition** Zurückbeziehung auf das Datum des Konkurseröffnungsantrages; **~ back of losses** Verlustrücktrag; **~s by blood** Blutsverwandte; **~ between cause and effect** Kausalzusammenhang; **foreign ~s of a country** diplomatische Beziehungen eines Landes; **~ in the fourth degree** Verwandtschaft im vierten Grad; **~ by lineal descent** Verwandtschaft in gerader Linie; **~ by marriage** Verschwägerung, verschwägerte Verwandtschaft; **~ of master to servant** Verhältnis zwischen Prinzipal und Angestelltem; **~ on the mother's side** Verwandtschaft mütterlicherseits; **~ of place** Lagebeziehung;
to attend to foreign ~s auswärtige Beziehungen pflegen; **to be out of all ~ to s. th.** mit etw. nichts zu tun haben; **to bear no ~ to s. th.** in keiner Beziehung zu etw. stehen; **to bear no ~ to the result** zum Ergebnis in keinem Verhältnis stehen; **to break off ~s** Beziehungen abbrechen; **to enter into ~s with s. o.** mit jem. in Verbindung treten; **to entertain ~s with s. o.** zu jem. Beziehungen unterhalten; **to establish a legal ~** Rechtsverhältnis begründen; **to have ~s with s. o.** sich mit jem. abgeben; **to have ~ to** in Beziehung stehen zu; **to have ~ to March 1st** rückwirkend vom 1. März an gelten; **to have business ~s with s. o.** in Geschäftsbeziehungen mit jem. stehen; **to maintain business ~ with s. o.** Geschäftsbeziehungen mit jem. aufrechterhalten; **to maintain friendly ~s** freundschaftliche Beziehungen unterhalten; **to open up business ~s** Geschäftsbeziehungen anknüpfen;
Foreign ~s Committee *(US)* außenpolitischer Ausschuß.
relationship Beziehung, Verhältnis, *(kinship)* Verwandtschaft, *(relatives)* Verwandschaftsverhältnis, -beziehung;
agency ~ Vertretungsverhältnis; **blood ~** Blutsverwandtschaft; **business (commercial) ~** Vertragsbeziehung, -verhältnis; **quasi-contractual ~** vertragsähnliches Verhältnis; **contractual ~** Vertragsverhältnis; **external ~** Außenverhältnis; **fiduciary ~** Treuhandverhältnis; **healthy ~** gesundes Verhältnis; **internal ~** Innenverhältnis; **legal ~** Rechtsverhältnis; **working ~** funktionierendes Verhältnis;
~ by marriage Verschwägerung;
to have a one-to-one ~ im Verhältnis 1 : 1 stehen.
relationless alleinstehend.
relative *(kinsman)* Verwandte[r], Angehörige[r], *(statistics)* Meßziffer;
dependent ~ unterhaltspflichtiger Angehöriger;
~ by blood Blutsverwandter;
~ *(a.)* relativ, verhältnismäßig;
to be ~ to demand von der Nachfrage abhängen;
~ cost relative Kosten; **to live in ~ ease** verhältnismäßig wohlhabend sein; **~ evidence** sachdienlicher Beweis; **~ frequency** relative Häufigkeit; **~ majority** relative Mehrheit; **~ number** Beziehungszahl; **~ rights** wechselseitige Rechte; **~ value** verhältnismäßiger Wert, *(math.)* Bezugswert.
relator Anzeigeerstatter, Denunziant.
relaunch *(v.)* **the multinational trade negotiations** multinationale Handelsbeziehungen wieder in Gang bringen.
relax *(v.)* entspannen, ausruhen, sich erholen, *(make less firm)* lockern;
~ a blockade Blockade lockern; **~ discipline** Disziplin lockern; **~ [in] one's efforts** in seinen Anstrengungen nachlassen; **~ an hour** Stunde ausspannen; **~ a penalty** Strafe mildern; **~ requirements** Anforderung herabsetzen; **~ restrictions** Beschränkungen abbauen; **~ rules** Bestimmungen lockern; **~ tension** *(pol.)* Lage entspannen; **~ one's tone** sich im Ton mäßigen.
relaxation *(diminution of severity)* Lockerung, Milderung, *(punishment)* Erleichterung, *(recreation)* Erholung, Entspannung;

~ **in credit (of credit squeeze)** Lockerung der Kreditrestriktionen, Krediterleichterungen; ~ **of money rates** Erleichterung des Geldmarktes; ~ **of tension** Entspannung der Lage, Spannungsabnahme;
to seek ~ **in the country** sich auf dem Lande erholen;
~ **allowance** Ruhepause.

relaxed zwanglos, gelöst, entspannt;
~ **atmosphere** zwanglose Atmosphäre.

relay Ablösung[smannschaft], *(broadcasting)* Übertragung, *(el.)* Relais;
~ *(v.)* **a broadcast program(me)** Rundfunkprogramm übertragen; ~ **news** Nachrichten durch Relaisstationen übertragen; ~ **the pavement of a street** Straße neu pflastern;
~ **station** Relaisstation.

relearn *(v.)* umlernen.

release *(conveyance)* Übertragung, *(discharge from responsibility)* Entlastung, Entpflichtung, Entbindung, *(document effecting ~)* Verzichts-, Übertragungsurkunde, *(liberation)* Befreiung, Freistellung, [Haft]entlassung, *(for press)* Freigabe, Veröffentlichung, *(quitclaim)* Verzichtserklärung, -urkunde, Erledigungsschein, *(receipt)* Quittung, *(remission)* Erlaß, *(renunciation)* Verzicht[leistung], Aufgabe, Preisgabe, *(from service)* Entlassung, *(setting free)* Freigabe, Entsperrung, Aufhebung einer Beschlagnahmung, *(technics)* Auslöser, *(ward's certificate)* Entlastungsbescheinigung [für den Vormund];
with immediate ~ mit sofortiger Wirkung;
carriage ~ *(typewriter)* Randauslösungstaste; **conditional** ~ *(criminal, US)* bedingte Entlassung (Freilassung); **day** ~ Freistellung zur beruflichen Fortbildung; **express** ~ formeller Schuldenerlaß, *(mortgage)* besondere Löschungszustimmung; **first** ~ *(film)* Uraufführung; **gear** ~ Freigabe (Auslösung) der Kupplung; **general** ~ Verzicht auf alle gegenwärtigen und zukünftigen Forderungen, *(mil.)* Demobilmachung, *(of taxes)* allgemeine Steueramnestie; **home-town** ~ für die Lokalpresse bestimmte Presseveröffentlichung; **illegal** ~ widerrechtliche Freilassung; **implied** ~ stillschweigend gewährter Schuldenerlaß; **newest** ~**s** neueste Filme; **press** ~ Presseveröffentlichung, -information, -freigabe; **saturation** ~ ausführliche Veröffentlichung; **transitional** ~ *(criminal, US)* Bewährungsfrist; **unconditional** ~ *(principal debtors)* völlige Freistellung;
~ **of a blocked account** Aufhebung einer Kontosperre, Kontenfreigabe, Entsperrung eines Kontos; ~ **on bail** Haftentlassung gegen Kautionsgestellung; ~ **from bond** Zollfreigabe; ~ **of a book** Freigabe eines Buches; ~ **of a claim** Forderungerlaß; ~ **of credit** sinkender Kreditbedarf; ~ **of custody items** Freigabe von Depotstücken; ~ **from debts** Erlaß von Schulden, Schuldenerlaß; ~ **of an easement** Löschung einer Dienstbarkeit; ~ **of expectancy** *(US)* Verzicht auf ein Anwartschaftsrecht, Erbverzicht; ~ **of a film** Freigabe für den Verleih; ~ **of funds** Freigabe von Mitteln; ~ **of liquid funds** Liquiditätsfreisetzung; ~ **on habeas corpus** Entlassung nach richterlicher Haftprüfung; ~ **of hoarded gold** Freigabe von gehortetem Gold; ~ **of goods against payment** Warenfreigabe gegen Bezahlung; ~ **of land** Baulandbeschaffung; ~ **from liability** Haftungsfreistellung; ~ **on licence** *(criminal, Br.)* bedingte Entlassung; ~ **of liquidator** Entlastung des Liquidators; ~ **of mortgage** Hypothekenlöschung, löschungsfähige Quittung; ~ **from nationality** Entlassung aus dem Staatsangehörigkeitsverhältnis; ~ **by operation of law** kraft Gesetzes eintretende Schuldbefreiung; ~ **on parole** bedingte [Straf]entlassung; ~ **from prison** Entlassung aus dem Gefängnis, Haftentlassung; ~ **of prior provisions** Auflösung von Wertberichtigungen und Rückstellungen; ~ **of a reserve** Rücklagenauflösung; ~ **of right** Verzicht auf ein Recht, Rechtsverzicht; ~ **under seal** förmlicher Erlaß; ~ **of security** Freigabe von Sicherheiten; ~ **of surety** Entlastung (Freistellung) eines Bürgen; ~ **of surplus labo(u)r** Freisetzung von Arbeitskräften; ~ **of trustee** Entpflichtung eines Treuhänders; ~ **from work** Arbeitsbefreiung;
~ *(v.)* *(a claim)* Forderung erlassen, *(convey)* [Vermögen] übertragen, *(discharge from responsibility)* entlasten, entbinden, befreien, freistellen, *(from office)* entheben, *(relet)* wieder vermieten, *(remit)* [Schuld (Steuer)] erlassen, Verzicht leisten, *(renounce)* Verzicht leisten, verzichten, [Recht] aufgeben, *(set free)* freilassen, *(spaceship)* abkoppeln;
~ **a blocked account** gesperrtes Konto freigeben, Kontensperre aufheben; ~ **an attachment** Freigabe anordnen; ~ **on bail** gegen Kautionsgestellung freilassen; ~ **a bomb** *(airplane)* Bombe auslösen (ausklinken); ~ **s. o. from bondage** j. aus einer Bürgschaftsverpflichtung entlassen; ~ **capital** Kapital flüssigmachen; ~ **a claim** Forderung erlassen; ~ **from a contract** aus einer vertraglichen Verpflichtung entlassen; ~ **from custody**

aus der treuhänderischen Verwahrung freigeben, *(police)* aus der Haft entlassen; ~ **debts** Schulden erlassen; ~ **the principal debtor** Hauptschuldner freistellen; ~ **special deposits** niedrige Mindestreservensätze festsetzen; ~ **one's equity of redemption** seine Einlösungsrecht verkaufen; ~ **a film** Film zum Verleih freigeben; ~ **funds** gesperrte Gelder freigeben; ~ **goods against payment** Waren gegen Zahlung freigeben; ~ **from a guarantee** aus einer Garantieverpflichtung entlassen; ~ **on habeas corpus** nach dem Haftprüfungsverfahren entlassen; ~ **the hand brake** Handbremse lösen; ~ **an indebtedness** Schuld erlassen; ~ **a mortgage** Hypothek löschen; ~ **from an oath** vom Eid entbinden; ~ **from obligations** von Verpflichtungen befreien; ~ **to the press** für die Presse freigeben; ~ **s. o. from prison** jem. aus dem Gefängnis (aus der Haft) entlassen; ~ **a prisoner** Gefangenen freilassen; ~ **prisoners halfway through their terms** Gefangene nach Verbüßung der Hälfte ihrer Strafzeit entlassen; ~ **on probation** auf Bewährung entlassen; ~ **a property** Vermögen übertragen; ~ **for publication** zur Veröffentlichung freigeben; ~ **a reserve** Reserve (Rücklage) auflösen; ~ **a right** auf Ausübung eines Rechtes verzichten; ~ **securities** Sicherheiten freigeben; ~ **a statute** Satzung aufheben; ~ **surplus labo(u)r** Arbeitskräfte freisetzen; ~ **a text for the public** Pressenotiz herausgeben; ~ **from working** von der Arbeit befreien;
to demand a ~ *(trustee)* Entlastung verlangen; **to grant** ~ Entlastung erteilen; **to grant a** ~ **from a fine** Geldstrafe erlassen; **to obtain a** ~ **from an obligation** aus einer Verpflichtung entlassen werden, von einer Verpflichtung befreit werden; **to order s. one's** ~ **from prison** jds. Haftentlassung anordnen; **to sign a** ~ Verzichtsleistung unterschreiben; **to withhold** ~ Entlastung verweigern;
~ **cord** *(parachute)* Reißleine; ~ **date** Freigabedatum, Veröffentlichungstermin; ~ **number** Freigabenummer.

released|rate *(railroad, US)* ermäßigter Tarif bei beschränkter Haftpflicht des Spediteurs; ~ **valuation** *(railroad, US)* Wertermäßigung.

releasee Begünstigter, Haftentlassener.

releaser *(photo)* Auslöser.

releasor Veräußerer.

relegate *(v.)* verbannen, des Landes verweisen, *(law court)* [an ein niederes Gericht] zurückverweisen;
~ **s. o. j.** zurechtweisen; ~ **for details to footnotes** Einzelheiten in Fußnoten unterbringen; ~ **to the position of a housekeeper** zur reinen Haushälterin degradieren.

relegation *(banishment)* Verbannung, Landesverweisung, *(law court)* Zurückverweisung.

relet *(v.)* wieder (weiter) vermieten.

reletting Weiter-, Wiedervermietung.

relevance, relevancy [Rechts]erheblichkeit, Belang, Relevanz;
~ **of evidence** Beweiserheblichkeit.

relevant [rechts]erheblich, relevant, wichtig, sachdienlich, entsprechend;
legally ~ rechtserheblich; **not** ~ nicht zur Sache gehörig, unerheblich;
~ **in law** rechtserheblich; ~ **in point** einschlägig;
~ **costs** relevante Kosten; ~ **document** rechtserhebliche Urkunde; ~ **evidence** sachdienlicher Beweis; ~ **information** zweckdienliche Auskunft; ~ **market** *(antitrust law, US)* maßgeblicher (relevanter) Markt; ~ **period** steuerlich bedeutsamer Zeitraum.

reliability Zuverlässigkeit, Verlaß, Sicherheit, Vertrauenswürdigkeit, *(financial rating)* Kreditwürdigkeit, Solidität, Bonität;
~ **of operation (service, working)** Betriebssicherheit;
to pass for a man of absolute ~ als absolut zuverlässig gelten;
~ **trial** Zuverlässigkeitsprüfung, -fahrt.

reliable zuverlässig, verläßlich, vertrauenswürdig, sicher, *(solvent)* kreditwürdig, solide, reell;
~ **authority** zuverlässiger Gewährsmann, zuverlässige Quelle; ~ **evidence** glaubhafte Zeugenaussage; ~ **firm** solide (reelle) Firma; ~ **guarantee** sichere Garantie; ~ **list** Liste, auf die man sich verlassen kann; ~ **man** zuverlässiger Mann; ~ **person** Vertrauensperson; ~ **security** ordnungsgemäße Sicherheit; **to have from a** ~ **source** aus zuverlässiger Quelle haben.

reliance Vertrauen, Verlaß;
in ~ **thereon** im guten Glauben daran;
to place ~ [up]**on s. o.** sich auf j. verlassen.

relic Überbleibsel, Relikt;
~**s of the past** Altertümer.

relict überlebender Ehegatte, Hinterbliebene[r], Witwe[r];
~ **of earlier civilizations** Überbleibsel früherer Kulturen.

relief *(assistance to the poor)* Wohlfahrts-, [Gemeinde]unterstützung, Fürsorge, Sozialhilfe, *(discharge)* Entlastung, *(help)* Hilfe, Erleichterung, *(law)* Rechtshilfe, -mittel, *(mil.)* Dienstablösung, Einsatzheer, *(print.)* Reliefdruck, *(reduction of taxes, Br.)* Nachlaß, Ermäßigung, Steuerabzug, -freibetrag, *(relieving party)* Ablösungsmannschaft, *(remedy)* Abhilfe, *(replacing)* Ablösung, *(wages for public work)* Entlohnung für Notstandsarbeiten;

eligible for (entitled to) ~ *(Br.)* fürsorge-, sozialhilfe-, unterstützungsberechtigt;

age ~ *(Br.)* Altersfreibetrag; **alternative** ~ zur Wahl stehendes Rechtsmittel, Alternative, Hilfsantrag; **basic** ~ *(taxation, US)* Grundfreibetrag; **child** ~ *(Br.)* Kinderfreibetrag; **compensatory** ~ *(Br.)* Steuerausgleichsbetrag; **corporation-tax** ~ *(Br.)* körperschaftssteuerfreier Betrag; **dependant-relative** ~ *(Br.)* Freibetrag für Unterstützung abhängiger Verwandter; **direct** ~ *(Br.)* Erteilung der Besteuerungsrechte; **double-taxation** ~ *(Br.)* Anrechnung im Ausland gezahlter Steuern; **earned-income** ~ *(Br.)* Freibetrag für Berufstätige; **excess** ~ unberechtigte Steuervergünstigungen, *(Br.)* steuerliche Anrechnung außergewöhnlicher Belastungen; **general** ~ allgemeines Rechtsschutzbegehren; **group** ~ *(Br.)* konzerninterner Verlustausgleich, Steuernachlaß im Konzernverband; **housekeeper** ~ *(Br.)* Freibetrag (Steuerermäßigung) für eine Hausangestellte (für Beschäftigung einer Haushaltshilfe); **small-income** ~ *(Br.)* gestaffelter Freibetrag für kleine (untere) Einkommen; **income-tax** ~ *(Br.)* Steuervergünstigung, -abzug, Freibetrag; **indoor (institutional)** ~ *(Br.)* anstaltsinterne Unterstützung; **interlocutory** ~ vorläufiger Rechtsschutz; **life-assurance** ~ *(Br.)* Steuerabzug (Freibetrag) für Lebensversicherungsbeiträge; **life-insurance** ~ Abzug (Freibetrag) für Lebensversicherungsbeiträge; **loss** ~ Verlustanrechnung; **machinery and plant** ~ *(estate duty)* Erbschaftssteuernachlaß auf Maschinen und maschinelle Anlagen; **marginal** ~ *(Br.)* ermäßigter Steuersatz für die untersten Einkommenssteuergruppen; **out[door]** ~ *(Br.)* Fürsorgeunterstützung, Sozialhilfe; **parish** ~ Fürsorge-, Gemeindeunterstützung; **pauper** ~ *(US)* öffentliche Unterstützung; **personal** ~ *(Br.)* persönlicher Steuerfreibetrag; **poor** ~ *(Br.)* Armenfürsorge, öffentliche Fürsorge, Sozialhilfe, Wohlfahrt; **public** ~ *(US)* öffentliche Unterstützung, Fürsorgeunterstützung, Sozialhilfe; **reduced-rate** ~ *(Br.)* gestaffelte Steuerermäßigung für kleine Einkommen; **restricted** ~ begrenzte Steuerermäßigung; ~ **sought** Klagebegehren; **tax** ~ steuerliche Entlastung, Steuererleichterung, -vergünstigung; **transitional** ~ vorübergehend gewährte Steuervergünstigung; **wife's earned income** ~ *(Br.)* Steuerermäßigung für die berufstätige Ehefrau; **unemployment** ~ Arbeitslosenunterstützung;

~ **for the aged** Altersunterstützung; ~ **under the business scale** Steuernachlaß für Betriebsanteile; ~ **for capital allowance** *(Br.)* Steuerabzug für Abschreibung auf Anlagegüter; ~ **in chancery** Klage auf Vertragsannullierung; ~ **for excess charges** *(Br.)* steuerliche Anrechnung übermäßiger Belastungen; ~ **for debts** Steuervergünstigungen für Schuldenrückzahlung; ~ **of duty** Steuererleichterung; ~ **from the estate rate** Vergünstigungen bei der Anwendung des Erbschaftssteuersatzes; ~ **to the eye** Wohltat fürs Auge; ~ **against forfeiture** *(tenant)* Mieterschutz, Vollstreckungsschutz; ~ **of a fortress** Entsetzung einer Festung; ~ **by injunction** Abhilfe im Wege einer einstweiligen Verfügung; ~ **allowable in respect of interest paid** Steuervergünstigung für gezahlte Zinsen; ~ **for interest paid to building societies** Steuervergünstigung für bezahlte Bausparzinsen; ~ **from liability** Haftungsbefreiung; **equitable** ~ **for mistake** vom Equity Recht gewährter Rechtsschutz für irrtümlich abgeschlossene Verträge; ~ **to officers** Vorstandsentlastung [durch den Betriebsprüfer]; ~ **of old people** Alterunterstützung, -fürsorge; ~ **of poverty** Linderung der Armut; ~ **against premium received** *(Br.)* Steuererleichterung für gezahlte Abstandsbeträge; ~ **for refugees** Flüchtlingshilfe; ~ **of a sentry** Wachablösung; ~ **for trading losses** Steuernachlaß für Betriebsverluste; ~ **from taxation** Steuererleichterung, -vergünstigung;

to apply to the court for ~ Sachantrag stellen; **to apply for** ~ **under the poor law** Sozialhilfe beantragen; **to be available for** ~ *(taxation)* steuerlich abzugsfähig sein; **to be eligible for** ~ sozialhilfeberechtigt sein, *(income tax, Br.)* Freibetragsvoraussetzungen erfüllen, zu Einkommenssteuervergünstigungen berechtigt sein; **to be on** ~ *(US)* [Fürsorge]unterstützung (Sozialhilfe) beziehen; **to be on local public** ~ Fürsorgeunterstützung (Sozialhilfe) beziehen; **to be a** ~ **for the state** Staat finanziell entlasten; **to be called in for** ~ zur Aushilfe geholt werden; **to bring out the facts in full** ~ Tatsachen scharf herausarbeiten; **to claim** ~ *(Br.)* Steuerermäßigung beantragen; **to claim** ~ **for interest paid** Zinszahlungen steuerlich geltend

machen; **to gain** ~ steuerliche Abschreibungen vornehmen können; **to get** ~ **at law** Rechtshilfe erhalten; **to give** ~ Entlastung erteilen; **to give** ~ **against capital gains in the future** auf zukünftige Kapitalgewinne Steuern anrechnen; **to grant** ~ Unterstützung gewähren; **to grant** ~ **from capital gains tax** Steuerermäßigung bei der Kapitalertragssteuer gewähren; **to grant the** ~ **sought in the petition** dem Klageantrag entsprechen; **to grant stock appreciation** ~ **on its holding of foreign currency notes** *(Br.)* Freibeträge bei der Wertverminderung auf ausländische Sorten gewähren; **to obtain [state]** ~ *(US)* [Fürsorge]unterstützung (bekommen) erhalten; **to provide** ~ **for refugees** Flüchtlinge unterstützen; **to receive state** ~ *(US)* Fürsorgeunterstützung beziehen; **to require** ~ unterstützungsbedürftig werden; **to send** ~ **to people made homeless by floods** Spenden für Flutgeschädigte zur Verfügung stellen; **to stand out in** ~ plastisch hervortreten;

~ **agency** Hilfsorganisation, -werk; ~ **aid** [Hilfs]spenden; ~ **applicant** Unterstützungssuchender; ~ **army** Einsatzheer; **mutual** ~ **association** Unterstützungsverein, Fürsorgeverein, -verband; ~ **attack** *(US)* Entlastungsangriff; **to put on a** ~ **bus** zusätzlichen Omnibus einsetzen; ~ **committee** Hilfskomitee, -ausschuß; ~ **expedition** Hilfsexpedition; ~ **freight railway line** Entlastungsbahn für den Güterverkehr; ~ **fund** Hilfs-, Entschädigungs-, Unterstützungsfonds, -kasse, Härtefonds; ~ **loan** Notstandskredit, -anleihe; ~ **map** Hochbild-, Reliefkarte; **to organize** ~ **measures** Hilfsaktion (Hilfsmaßnahmen) einleiten; ~ **office** *(Br.)* Wohlfahrtsbehörde, Sozial-, Fürsorgeamt; ~ **officer** *(Br.)* Sozialhelfer, Fürsorgebeamter; ~ **operations** Hilfsmaßnahmen; ~ **payments** Unterstützungszahlungen; ~ **population** Gesamtheit der Sozialhilfeempfänger; ~ **printing** Reliefdruck; ~ **program(me)** Unterstützungs-, Hilfs-, Notstandsprogramm; ~ **road** Entlastungsstraße; ~ **roll** *(Br.)* Fürsorge-, Sozialhilfe-, Wohlfahrtsempfängerliste; **to go on** ~ **rolls** *(Br.)* Fürsorge-, Sozialunterstützung empfangen; ~ **secretary** Aushilfssekretärin; ~ **shift** *(US)* zusätzliche Schicht; ~ **standards** *(Br.)* normale Unterstützungssätze; ~ **system** Unterstützungssystem; ~ **telephonist** Aushilfstelefonist; ~ **ticket** *(Br.)* Unterstützungsbescheinigung; ~**train** Entlastungs-, Vorzug; ~ **vessel** Entsatzschiff; ~ **works** Notstandsarbeiten; ~ **worker** Notstandsarbeiter.

relievable sozialhilfe-, unterstützungsberechtigt.

relieve *(v.) (exonerate)* entlasten, Entlastung erteilen, entpflichten, *(help)* helfen, beistehen, *(redress)* abhelfen, wiedergutmachen, Recht verschaffen, *(release)* erlassen, *(subsist)* unterstützen, Unterstützung gewähren, *(taxation)* bei der Steuer in Abzug bringen;

~ **o. s. of s. th.** sich einer Sache entledigen; ~ **the common distress** allgemeine Not lindern; ~ **distress among flood victims** Los der Flutgeschädigten erleichtern; ~ **s. o. of his duties** j. im Dienst ablösen; ~ **an emergency** Notlage beheben; ~ **the enemy** Feindunterstützung (Kriegsverrat) begehen; ~ **the guard** Wache ablösen; ~ **hardships** Härtefälle mildern; ~ **s. o. from a liability** j. von einer Haftung befreien; ~ **the market** Markt entlasten; ~ **s. o. of the necessity of working** j. in die Lage versetzen, nicht mehr arbeiten zu müssen; ~ **the people of a tax** Öffentlichkeit von einer Steuer befreien; ~ **the poor** die Armen unterstützen; ~ **an official of his post** Beamten aus dem Dienst entlassen (seines Postens entheben); ~ **the railway** Eisenbahnverkehr entlasten; ~ **s. o. of all responsibility** jem. jedwede Verantwortung abnehmen; ~ **a sentry** Posten ablösen; ~ **the tension** Lage entspannen; ~ **a besieged town** belagerte Stadt entsetzen.

reliever of the poor *(Br.)* Fürsorgebeamter, Wohlfahrts-, Sozialhelfer.

relieving | the enemy Feindunterstützung, Kriegsverrat; ~ **clause** Entlastungsklausel; ~ **officer** *(Br.)* Fürsorgebeamter, Wohlfahrtspfleger, Sozialhelfer; ~ **party** Ablösungsmannschaft; ~ **troops** Ersatztruppen.

religion Religion, Glaubensbekenntnis; **established** ~ *(Br.)* Staatsreligion; **to be in** ~ einem Orden angehören.

religious | affiliation Religionszugehörigkeit; ~ **belief** Konfession, Glaube; ~ **community** Glaubensgemeinschaft; ~ **freedom** Glaubensfreiheit; ~ **house** kirchlichen Zwecken dienendes Anwesen; ~ **men** Ordensangehörige; ~ **service** Gottesdienst; ~ **society** Religionsgemeinschaft.

relinquish *(v.) (abandon)* verlassen, aufgeben, abandonieren, *(cede)* überlassen, abtreten, *(renounce)* Verzicht leisten, verzichten;

~ **an action** Klage zurücknehmen; ~ **one's appointment** von seinem Posten zurücktreten, seine Stellung aufgeben; ~ **a**

claim von einer Forderung Abstand nehmen; ~ **a debt** Schuld erlassen; ~ **one's duties as chairman** seine Funktionen als Vorstandsvorsitzer abgeben; ~ **an idea** Idee fallen lassen; ~ **an inheritance** *(US)* auf eine Erbschaft verzichten; ~ **office** aus dem Amt ausscheiden; ~ **one's place** seine Tätigkeit beenden; ~ **a plan** Plan aufgeben; ~ **a residence** Wohnsitz aufgeben; ~ **a right** auf sein Recht verzichten; ~ **one's right to part of the income** auf Teileinkünfte verzichten; ~ **a suit** Klage zurücknehmen.

relinquished land aufgegebenes Grundstück.

relinquishment *(abandonment)* Aufgabe, *(cession)* Überlassung, Abtretung, *(relinquished land, US)* aufgegebenes Grundstück, *(renunciation)* Verzicht[leistung];
~ **of authority** Autoritätsverlust; ~ **of a claim** Aufgabe eines Anspruchs; ~ **of one's property** Vermögensaufgabe, Eigentumsverzicht; ~ **of a right** Aufgabe eines Rechtes, Rechtsverzicht; ~ **of succession** Erbschaftsausschlag, -verzicht.

reliquidate *(v.)* wieder liquidieren.

reliquidation abermalige Liquidation.

relish *(v.)* schmecken, *(fig.)* Anstrich haben;
not ~ the prospect einer Sache keinen Geschmack abgewinnen.

reload *(v.)* umladen, wieder beladen, umschlagen, *(stock exchange)* billig kaufen und teuer verkaufen.

reloading Umladung, Umschlag, Wiederverladung;
~ **charges** Umschlagskosten, Umladegebühren.

relocate *(v.)* sich wieder ansiedeln, *(define boundaries, US)* Grenzen neu festlegen, *(plant)* verlagern;
~ **an employee** Angestellten in die Zentrale zurückversetzen; ~ **the population** Bevölkerung umsiedeln (zwangsevakuieren).

relocation Umsiedlung, *(employee)* [Zurück]versetzung in die Zentrale, *(lease, Scot.)* Pachtvertragserneuerung, *(plant)* Verlagerung;
tacit ~ *(lease)* stillschweigende Erneuerung;
~ **of business** Geschäftsverlegung; ~ **of industry** Industrieverlagerung; ~ **of a plant** Betriebsverlagerung; ~ **of the population** Bevölkerungsumsiedlung, Zwangsevakuierung der Bevölkerung;
~ **allowance** Rücksiedlungszuschuß; ~ **assistance** Repatriierungs-, Umzugshilfe; ~ **center** *(US)* Wiederansiedlungsraum; ~ **expenses** Übersiedlungs-, Umzugs-, Versetzungskosten; ~ **grant** *(workers)* Umsetzungszuschuß; ~ **plan** Verlagerungsplan; ~ **specialist** Verlagerungsfachmann.

reluctance Zurückhaltung;
~ **of the state** staatliche Zurückhaltung.

reluctant *(buyer)* zurückhaltend;
to be ~ to commit o. s. sich ungern festlegen; **to be ~ to go into debt** sich ungern verschulden, Verschuldung scheuen;
~ **consent** notgedrungene Zustimmung.

rely *(v.)* **on** sich verlassen (bauen, fußen) auf, auf (mit) etw. rechnen;
~ **upon an award** Schiedsspruch geltend machen; ~ **upon a case** sich auf eine frühere Entscheidung berufen; ~ **s. one's evidence** sich auf jds. Aussage verlassen; ~ **heavily on s. o.** feste Stütze in jem. finden; ~ **upon s. o. for help** auf jds. Hilfe zählen können; ~ **upon a broken reed** *(fig.)* auf Sand bauen.

relying [up]on im Vertrauen auf.

remain *(v.)* übrigbleiben, restieren, *(formula concluding a letter)* verbleiben, *(prices)* stehen, sich halten, *(stay on)* bleiben;
~ **active in business** im Geschäft tätig bleiben; ~ **in arrears** im Rückstand bleiben; ~ **basically the same** im Prinzip gleich sein; ~ **in existence** *(firm)* weiterbestehen; ~ **firm** *(prices)* fest bleiben, sich behaupten; ~ **in force** Geltung behalten, in Kraft bleiben; ~ **on hand (unsold)** unverkauft [liegen]bleiben; ~ **a mystery** noch immer ungelöst sein; ~ **on the shelf** auf Lager bleiben; ~ **steady** *(market)* fest bleiben, *(prices)* sich behaupten; ~ **until called for** postlagernd aufbewahrt werden.

remainder [Rest]bestand, Restbetrag, Überbleibsel, *(arrears)* Rückstand, *(balance)* Saldo, *(books)* Partieartikel, *(estate for life)* beschränktes Eigentum, *(publishing)* Restauflage, *(right of succession)* Erbanwartschaft, Nacherbe;
entitled in ~ anwartschaftsberechtigt; **without a ~** restlos;
contingent (executory) ~ bedingtes Herrschaftsrecht; **cross ~** wechselseitiges Anwartschaftsrecht; **legal ~** gesetzliches Anwartschaftsrecht; **vested ~** unentziehbares Anwartschaftsrecht;
~ **of an account** Rechnungsrückstand, Passivsaldo; ~ **of the day** übrige [Tages]zeit; ~ **of a debt** Restschuld, geschuldeter Restbetrag; ~ **vested subject to being divested** *(real estate)* auflösend bedingtes Anwartschaftsrecht; ~ **in goods** Warenbestand; ~ **of order** Auftragsrest, -bestand; ~ **of stocks** Restbestand;
~ *(v.)* Restauflage billig abstoßen;

to be left to s. o. with ~ to another jem. als nicht befreitem Vorerben zufallen; **to pay the ~** nachschießen;
~ **book trade** Resteauflagen-, Restebuchhandel; ~ **estate** Nacherbschaft; ~ **interest** Anwartschaftsrecht; ~ **line** unverkaufter Restbestand; ~ **man** Nacherbe; ~**s offer** Restauflagenangebot; ~ **rules** Anwartschaftsregeln; ~ **sale** Ausverkauf einer Auflage; ~ **shop** Restauflagen verkaufender Buchladen.

remainderman Anfallberechtigter, Anwärter, Heimfalls-, Anwartschaftsberechtigter, *(inheritance)* Nacherbe;
to pass to the ~ auf den Nacherben übergehen.

remaindership Anwartschaftseigentum, *(inheritance)* Nacherbschaft.

remaining verbleibend, übriggeblieben, restlich, *(unsold)* unverkauft;
~ **amount** Restbetrag; ~ **assets** *(bankruptcy)* Restmasse; ~ **credit balance** verbleibendes Guthaben; ~ **foreign exchange** nicht ausgenutzte Devisenbeträge; ~ **life** Restnutzungsdauer; ~ **margin** Spitze; ~ **stock** Restbestand.

remains Überbleibsel, *(literarian)* literarischer Nachlaß;
mortal ~ sterbliche Überreste (Hülle);
sole ~ of a large family letzte Überlebende einer großen Familie.

remake Umarbeitung, *(film)* Wieder-, Neuverfilmung;
~ *(v.)* umarbeiten, *(film)* neu (wieder) verfilmen.

remand Zurücksendung, *(law court, US)* Zurückverweisung, *(prisoner, Br.)* Untersuchungsgefangener, *(remanding)* Haftanordnung, Anordnung der Haftfortdauer, Untersuchungshaft;
~ **on bail** *(Br.)* Freilassung gegen Kautionsstellung; ~ **in custody** *(Br.)* **(into custody, US)** Haftanordnung, -fortdauer, Anordnung der Untersuchungshaft;
~ *(v.)* zurücksenden, *(law court)* an ein anderes Gericht verweisen, *(US)* vorübergehende Haft anordnen, in die Untersuchungshaft zurückschicken, *(Br.)* gegen Kaution freilassen;
~ **the accused in custody** *(US)* Haftbefehl gegen den Beschuldigten aufrechterhalten; ~ **s. o. on bail** *(Br.)* j. gegen Kaution freilassen; ~ **a case (cause)** *(US)* Sache zurückverweisen; ~ **the accused for a medical report** *(magistrate, Br.)* ärztliche Untersuchung des Angeschuldigten anordnen; ~ **to a mental hospital** *(US)* in eine Heil- und Pflegeanstalt einweisen; ~ **an order** Auftrag zurücknehmen; ~ **for a week** für eine Woche zurückstellen, *(prisoner)* Untersuchungshaft um eine Woche verlängern;
to appear on ~ *(Br.)* im Haftprüfungsverfahren vorgeführt werden; **to be on ~** *(Br.)* in Untersuchungshaft sein; **to be brought up on ~** aus der Untersuchungshaft vorgeführt werden; **to take into ~** verhaften;
~ **center** *(Br.)* Jugendbewahranstalt; ~ **court** Haftungsprüfungsgericht; ~ **home** *(Br.)* Jugendgefängnis, -strafanstalt, Fürsorgeinternat, Arrestanstalt; ~ **prison** Untersuchungsgefängnis; ~ **prisoner** Untersuchungsgefangener, Häftling.

remanded, to be in Haft bleiben;
~ **prisoner** Untersuchungshäftling, -gefangener.

remanding a case Zurückverweisung einer Sache.

remanet Rest, Rückstand, *(parl., Br.)* noch nicht erledigter Gesetzentwurf.

remanufacture Umarbeitung.

remargin *(v.)* *(US)* nachschießen.

remargining *(US)* Nachschuß[zahlung].

remark Be-, Anmerkung;
~**s** Ausführungen;
concluding ~s Schlußbemerkungen; **flippant ~s** leichtfertige Äußerungen; **opening ~s** Einführungsworte; **preliminary ~** Vorbemerkung; **snide ~** geringschätzige Bemerkung;
~ **endorsed on the bill of lading** Konnossementsvermerk;
~ *(v.)* ausführen, bemerken;
~ **merchandise** Warenpreise neu auszeichnen (festsetzen); ~ **in passing** am Rande bemerken;
to make a few ~s kurze Ansprache halten; **to pass without ~s** kommentarlos übergehen; **to take up the ~s of the speaker** an den Vorredner anknüpfen.

remarking of merchandise Neufestsetzung (Neuauszeichnung) von Warenpreisen.

remarriage Wiederverheiratung.

remarry *(v.)* zweite Ehe eingehen, wieder heiraten.

remeasure *(v.)* *(ship)* neu vermessen.

remedial abhelfend, formell;
~ **action** Schadensersatzklage; ~ **education** Hilfsschulunterricht; ~ **instruction** Förderungsunterricht; ~ **loan society** gemeinnütziger Kreditverein, gemeinnützige Pfandleihanstalt; ~ **measures** Abhilfemaßnahmen; ~ **statute** Schutzgesetz; ~ **treatment** Schutzbehandlung.

remedies *(antitrust law, US)* Sanktionen;
~ **of the unpaid seller** Rechtsbehelf des unbezahlt gebliebenen Verkäufers.

remedy Hilfsmittel, *(mintage)* Toleranz, Remedium, *(school, Br.)* freier Nachmittag;
adequate ~ ausreichender Rechtsbehelf, ausreichende Klagemöglichkeit; **civil** ~ Rechtsbehelf in bürgerlichen Rechtstreitigkeiten; **cumulative** ~ zusätzlicher Rechtsbehelf; **domestic** ~ innerstaatliche Rechtshilfe; **extrajudicial** ~ außergerichtlicher Rechtsbehelf; **extraordinary** ~ außerordentlicher Rechtsbehelf; **judicial** ~ Klagemöglichkeit; **legal** ~ Rechtsbehelf, -mittel; **local** ~ innerstaatliches Rechtsmittel; ~ **over** Regreß; **provisional** ~ einstweilige Anordnung, vorläufiger Rechtsbehelf; **speedy** ~ summarischer Rechtsbehelf;
~ **of damages** Schadenersatzanspruch; ~ **of fineness** zulässige Abweichung vom Feingehalt; ~ **of the mint** *(US)* Remedium, Toleranz; ~ **for social evils** Beseitigung sozialen Elends;
~ *(v.)* Abhilfe schaffen, abhelfen, beheben;
~ **a complaint** einer Beschwerde abhelfen; ~ **defects** Mängel beseitigen; ~ **grievances** Beschwerden abstellen (abhelfen); ~ **an omission** etw. nachholen; ~ **an ambiguous passage** undeutliche Stelle klarstellen;
to have no ~ **at law** keine gesetzlichen Abhilfemöglichkeiten haben; **to resort to a** ~ Rechtsmittel einlegen, von einem Rechtsbehelf Gebrauch machen;
~ **allowance** *(Br.)* Toleranz, zulässige Abweichung.

remember *(v.)* sich erinnern, *(convey greetings)* empfehlen, grüßen;
~ **the waiter** dem Ober ein Trinkgeld geben; ~ **in a will** im Testament bedenken.

remembrance Erinnerung, Gedächtnis, *(token)* Erinnerungsstück, Souvenir;
~s Empfehlungen, Grüße;
⁰ Day Waffenstillstandstag.

remembrancer Erinnerungshilfe, Memento.

remigrant Rückwanderer.

remigrate *(v.)* zurückkehren.

remigration Rückwanderung.

remilitarization Remilitarisierung, Wiederbewaffnung.

remilitarize *(v.)* remilitarisieren, wiederbewaffnen.

remind *(v.)* erinnern, mahnen.

reminder Mahnung, Hilfs-, Mahnzettel, -brief;
~ **of due date** Fälligkeitsavis;
~ **advertisement** Erinnerungsanzeige; ~ **advertising** Erinnerungswerbung; ~ **letter** Mahnbrief; ~ **value** *(bookkeeping)* Erinnerungswert, -posten.

reminiscent talk Austausch von Erinnerungen.

remise Aufgabe eines Rechtes, Rechtsverzicht;
~ *(v.)* [Rechts]ansprüche aufgeben (übertragen, abtreten, zedieren);
~ **a claim** sich eines Anspruchs begeben.

remiss säumig, nachlässig;
~ **in paying one's bills** schludrig beim Bezahlen seiner Rechnungen;
to be ~ **in the performance of one's official duties** seine Amtspflichten vernachlässigen;
~ **correspondent** unzuverlässiger Briefschreiber.

remissibility Begnadigungsfähigkeit.

remissible begnadigungsfähig.

remission *(abatement)* Ermäßigung, Nachlaß, *(customs)* Erstattung, *(debts)* Erlaß, *(pardon)* Gnadenerweis, *(penalty)* Erlaß, Nachlaß, *(relaxation)* Entspannung;
conventional ~ ausdrücklicher Schulderlaß; **an hour's** ~ Erholungsstunde; **tacit** ~ stillschweigender Schuldenerlaß;
~ **to arbitration** Verweisung an einen Schiedsrichter; ~ **of charges** Gebührenerlaß, Gebührenbefreiung; ~ **of a claim** Forderungsverzicht; ~ **of a debt** Erlaß einer Schuld; ~ **of duty** Zollerlaß; ~ **of examination fees** Befreiung von den Prüfungsgebühren; ~ **of fees** Gebührenfreiheit; ~ **of money** Geldüberweisung; ~ **of rent** Miet-, Pachtnachlaß; ~ **of a sentence** Strafnachlaß, -ermäßigung; ~ **of taxes** Steuererlaß, -ermäßigung, -milderung; ~ **of taxation** Steuerverkürzung;
to allow a ~ Nachlaß gewähren; **to get a couple of years** ~ **for good conduct** wegen guter Führung vorzeitig entlassen werden.

remit *(v.)* *(cover)* Deckung anschaffen, Rimesse machen, *(to lower court)* [zurück]verweisen, *(make over)* überlassen, vermachen, abtreten, *(postpone)* verschieben, vertagen, *(release)* [Schuld, Steuer] erlassen, *(transmit)* überweisen, Überweisung vornehmen;
~ **$ 1000 for s. one's account** für jds. Rechnung 1000 Dollar überweisen; ~ **arrears of maintenance** Unterhaltsrückstände

erlassen; ~ **an award for the reconsideration of the arbitrators** Schiedsspruch zur nochmaligen Beratung an die Schiedsrichter zurückverweisen; ~ **through a bank** durch eine Bank überweisen; ~ **a bill** Wechsel einlösen (übertragen); ~ **a bill for collection** Wechsel zum Inkasso übersenden; ~ **a candidate's examination fees** Prüfling von den Examensgebühren befreien; ~ **by check (cheque,** *Br.)* mit Scheck bezahlen; ~ **a claim** Forderung nachlassen; ~ **the consideration of a matter until the next session** Erörterung einer Angelegenheit bis zur nächsten Sitzung zurückstellen; ~ **one's efforts** in seinen Anstrengungen nachlassen; ~ **a fee** Gebühr erlassen; ~ **a fine** Geldstrafe erlassen; ~ **home every month** monatlich Geld nach Hause schicken; ~ **s. o. to liberty** j. wieder in Freiheit setzen; ~ **by mail** brieflich überweisen; ~ **a matter to a higher tribunal** Fall an höheres Gericht abgeben; ~ **a penalty** Strafe erlassen; ~ **by return of post** postwendend überweisen; ~ **the proceeds** Gegenwert anschaffen; ~ **samples** Muster vorlegen; ~ **a sentence** Strafe erlassen; ~ **a sum of money to s. o.** jem. einen Geldbetrag überweisen; ~ **a sum to a bank** Betrag bei einer Bank anschaffen; ~ **a tax** Steuer erlassen; ~ **one's work** seine Arbeit einstellen.

remitment Abführen in die Haft.

remittal Überweisung, *(law)* Verweisung [an ein anderes Gericht].

remittance Geldsendung, -anweisung, Überweisung, überwiesene Summe, *(cover)* Anschaffung, *(consignment of valuables)* Wertsendung;
~ **abroad** Überweisung im Ausland, Auslandsüberweisung; ~ **assessed** besteuerte Auslandsüberweisung; **cable** ~ telegraphische Geldüberweisung; **clean** ~s einfache Rimessen; **documentary** ~ dokumentarische Rimesse; **par** ~ *(US)* Überweisung eines Schecks zu Parikurs; **prepaid** ~ portofreie Sendung; **return** ~ Gegenrimesse, -anschaffung, Rücküberweisung; **capital** ~s **abroad** Kapitalausfuhr; ~ **for the amount payable** Überweisung des geschuldeten Betrages; ~ **per appoint** Ausgleichswechsel; ~ **of a bill** Wechselsendung; ~ **of capital** Kapitalüberweisung; ~ **in cash** Barsendung, -anschaffung, Geldsendung; ~ **of commission** Provisionsüberweisung; ~ **in any convertible currency** Geldüberweisung in jeder frei konvertierbaren Währungseinheit; ~ **of cover** Regulierung eines überzogenen Kontos; ~ **of funds** Geldsendung; ~s **of overseas income** Überweisungen in Übersee erzielter Einkünfte; ~ **by post** Zahlung auf dem Postwege, postalische Überweisung; ~ **of proceeds** Überweisung (Anschaffung) des Gegenwertes; ~ **of profits** Gewinntransferierung; ~ **in transit** Durchgangsposten; **to constitute a** ~ steuerlich den Tatbestand einer Auslandsüberweisung erfüllen; **to make (send, provide for)** ~ Rimesse machen, remittieren, Deckung (Gegenwert) anschaffen; **to send s. o. a** ~ jem. Geld überweisen;
~ **account** Rimessen-, Überweisungskonto; ~ **basis** *(income tax, Br.)* Versteuerung nur nach England überwiesener Beträge, beschränkte Besteuerung ins Inland überwiesener Einkünfte; ~ **fee** Übermittlungsgebühr; ~ **form** Überweisungsformular; ~ **letter** Inkassoanweisung; ~ **man** im Ausland lebender Rentner; ~ **order** Überweisungsauftrag; ~ **slip** Überweisungsträger.

remittancer Übersender, Remittent.

remitted case zurückverwiesene Sache.

remittee Empfänger einer Geldsendung, Überweisungsempfänger.

remitter, remittor Geldsender, Übersender, *(bill)* Remittent, *(postal order)* Aufgeber, *(remitting to another court)* Überweisung an ein anderes Gericht;
~ **to an estate** Wiedereinsetzung in einen Besitz;
to be in ~ wieder eingesetzt werden.

remitting bank überweisende Bank.

remittitur of record Aktenrücksendung.

remnant [Über]rest, Überbleibsel, Rückstand;
~s **of a large property** Überbleibsel eines großen Vermögens; ~ **of a state** Reststaat;
~ **buying** *(advertising)* Erwerb übriggebliebenen Anzeigenraums; ~ **sale** Resteverkauf.

remodel *(v.)* umarbeiten, -gestalten;
~ **a corporation** Unternehmen umorganisieren.

remodel(l)ing job Reorganisationsaufgabe.

remonetization Wiederinkurssetzung von Münzen.

remonetize *(v.)* wieder in Kurs setzen, *(US)* als zweites Währungsmetall bestimmen.

remonstrance Protest[kundgebung], Gegenvorstellung;
in ~ **with** vorstellig bei;
~s *(dipl.)* Vorstellungen.

remonstrant Beschwerdeführer.

remonstrate *(v.)* remonstrieren, Protest erheben.

remonstration Gegenvorstellung.

remonstrative letter Protestschreiben.

remorse Gewissensbiß, Reue.

remortgage wieder aufgefüllte (beliehene) Hypothek.

remote *(US, radio, television)* ferngesteuertes Programm, Direkt-übertragung, -aufnahme;

~ *(a.)* abgelegen, entlegen, entfernt, weitläufig, *(damage)* nicht in Kausalzusammenhang stehend, mittelbar;

to be pretty ~ nicht sehr wahrscheinlich sein; **to be** ~ **from a subject** weitab vom Thema liegen; **to be (lie)** ~ **from the road** abseits der Straße liegen; **to live in a house** ~ **from any town or village** in einer gottverlassenen Gegend leben;

~ **ages** unvordenkliche Zeiten; ~ **cause** kein ursächlicher Zusammenhang, mittelbare Ursache; ~ **conception** vage Vorstellung; ~ **consequences** mittelbare Folgen; ~ **control** Fernsteuerung; **to steer by** ~ **control** fernlenken, -steuern; **~-controlled** fernbedient, -gesteuert; **~-controlled aircraft** Fernlenkflugzeug; ~ **damage** nicht voraussehbarer (indirekter, nicht zurechenbarer, entfernter) Schaden; ~ **future** ferne Zukunft; ~ **guided** ferngesteuert, -gelenkt; ~ **kinsman** weitläufiger Verwandter; ~ **party** *(bill of exchange)* mittelbar Beteiligter; ~ **place** abgelegener Platz; ~ **possibility** entfernte Möglichkeit; ~ **recording** Fernregistrierung.

remoteness Abgelegenheit, Entlegenheit, Ferne;

~ **of damages** Grad des Folgeschadens; ~ **of evidence** Beweisunerheblichkeit; ~ **of market** Marktferne, -entlegenheit.

remount *(v.) (map, photo)* neu aufziehen.

removable transportierbar, *(fixture)* entfernbar, *(person)* absetzbar;

~ **bed** Klappbett.

removal Entfernen, Fortschaffen, *(alien)* Zurück-, Abschiebung, *(bankruptcy)* Beiseiteschaffen [von Vermögensgegenständen], *(changing of residence, Br.)* Aus-, Weg-, Umzug, Wohnsitzverlegung, -wechsel, Räumung, *(discharge)* Entlassung, Ver-, Absetzung, *(law of nations)* Herausnahme bestimmter Gebiete, *(murder)* Umbringen, Beseitigung, *(putting an end)* Behebung, Abstellung, *(retrenchment)* Abbau, *(transfer)* [Straf]versetzung;

bulk ~ totale Entfernung; **mandatory** ~ zwangsweise Entlassung;

~ **from the agenda** Absetzung von der Tagesordnung; ~ **to avoid taxes** Verlagerung aus Steuergründen, Beiseiteschaffung zwecks Steuerhinterziehung; ~ **of business** *(Br.)* Geschäftsverlegung; ~ **of a cause** *(US)* Verweisung einer Rechtsstreitigkeit; ~ **without proper cause** unberechtigte Entlassung, willkürliche Amtsenthebung; ~ **of difficulties** Behebung von Schwierigkeiten; ~ **of directors** Abberufung (Absetzung) des Vorstandes; ~ **of disqualification** Wiedererlangung (Rückgabe) des Führerscheins; ~ **of documents** Urkundenbeseitigung; ~ **of an embargo** Embargobeseitigung; ~ **of fixtures** Entfernung von Zubehör; ~ **of furniture** Möbeltransport, Umzug; ~ **of goods** Beiseiteschaffen von Waren, Vollstreckungsvereitelung; ~ **of a landmark** Grenzverrückung; ~ **of liquidator** Abberufung des Abwicklers (Liquidators); ~ **without notice** fristlose Entlassung; ~ **from office** Dienstentlassung, Entfernung aus dem Amt, Amtsenthebung; ~ **of an officer** Beamtenentlassung; ~ **of a pauper** Abschiebung eines Unterstützungsempfängers; ~ **of price ceilings** Beseitigung von Höchstpreisbestimmungen; ~ **of refuse** *(US)* Müllabfuhr; ~ **of a trademark from the register** Löschung in der Warenzeichenrolle; ~ **of restrictions** Aufhebung von Beschränkungen; ~ **from the stock-exchange list** Absetzung von (Streichung in) der amtlichen Notierung; ~ **of stores** Lagerräumung; ~ **of tariff** Zollaufhebung; ~ **of traces** Spurenbeseitigung;

to order the ~ **of disorderly persons** ungehörige Besucher aus dem Sitzungssaal entfernen lassen;

~ **allowance** *(Br.)* Umzugskostenersatz, -beihilfe; ~ **bond** Zollfreigabeschein für Verbringung in ein anderes Waren[lager]; ~ **business** *(Br.)* Umzugs-, Speditionsgeschäft; ~ **contractor** *(Br.)* Möbelspediteur; ~ **expenditure** *(Br.)* Umzugsgeld, -kosten; ~ **firm** *(Br.)* Möbelspeditionsfirma, -spediteur; ~ **goods** *(Br.)* Umzugsgut; ~ **grant** *(enterprise)* Verlagerungszuschuß; ~ **jurisdiction** *(US)* ausschließliche bundesgerichtliche Zuständigkeit; ~ **man** Möbelpacker; ~ **operation** Betriebsverlegung; ~ **proceedings** Verweisungsverfahren; ~ **van** *(Br.)* Möbelwagen.

remove *(change of residence, Br.)* Wohnsitzveränderung, Umzug, *(degree)* Grad, Stufe, Schritt, *(degree of relationship)* Verwandtschaftsgrad, *(departure)* [Ab]reise, *(discharge)* Absetzung, *(print.)* Schriftgradunterschied, *(school, Br.)* Versetzung;

in the first ~ *(cousin)* ersten Grades;

~**s to convertibility** Übergang zur Konvertibilität; ~ **of one's furniture** Möbeltransport;

~ *(v.)* fortschaffen, wegnehmen, *(bankruptcy)* [Vermögensgegenstände] beiseite bringen, *(business)* verlegen, *(change residence, Br.)* aus-, umziehen, räumen, Wohnsitz verlegen, *(discharge)* entlassen;

~ **from the agenda** von der Tagesordnung absetzen; ~ **a blockade** Blockade aufheben; ~ **a book from the shelf** Buch aus dem Regal nehmen; ~ **a business** *(Br.)* Geschäft verlegen; ~ **a cause by appeal** *(US)* Fall durch Berufung an ein anderes Gericht ziehen; ~ **the causes of poverty** Armutsursachen beseitigen; ~ **a child from school** Kind von der Schule nehmen; ~ **into the country** *(Br.)* aufs Land umziehen; ~ **controls** Beschränkungen aufheben; ~ **defects** Mängel beseitigen (beheben); ~ **a director** Vorstandsmitglied abberufen; ~ **the disqualification** eingezogenen Führerschein zurückgeben; ~ **the last doubts** letzte Zweifel beseitigen; ~ **excess white-collar jobs** Überhang an Angestellten entlassen; ~ **furniture** *(Br.)* [Wohnungs]umzüge besorgen; ~ **from the helm** Führung entreißen; ~ **a landmark** Mark-, Grenzstein versetzen; ~ **a manager** Geschäftsführer abberufen; ~ **mountains** *(fig.)* Berge versetzen, Wunder vollbringen; ~ **s. one's name from a list** jds. Namen von einer Liste streichen; ~ **s. o. from office** j. aus dem Amt entfernen, j. aus dem Dienst entlassen; ~ **an obstacle** Hindernis beseitigen; ~ **an official** Beamten absetzen; ~ **patent rights** Patentrechte aufheben; ~ **o. s. from a place** sich wegbegeben; ~ **s. o. from his post** j. seines Postens entheben; ~ **a prisoner** Gefangenen abführen [lassen]; **fraudulently** ~ **property** Vermögensstücke in betrügerischer Absicht beiseite schaffen, Vollstreckung vereiteln; ~ **from the register** *(trademark)* in der Warenzeichenrolle löschen; ~ **restrictions** Beschränkungen aufheben; ~ **the apparent risk barriers** *(credit)* augenscheinliche Kreditrisiken beseitigen; ~ **the seals** Plomben abnehmen; ~ **a civil servant** Staatsbeamten entlassen; ~ **a ship** Schiff überführen; ~ **traces** Spuren verwischen; ~ **troops to the front** Truppen an die Front werfen; ~ **s. o. out of the way** j. umbringen;

to get one's ~ *(school, Br.)* versetzt werden; **to have one's furniture** ~**d** *(Br.)* umziehen, seinen Umzug bewerkstelligen.

remover *(furniture, Br.)* [Möbel]spediteur, -transportgeschäft, *(law)* [Rechtsstreit]verweisung.

removing Beseitigung, Räumung;

furniture ~ Möbeltransport;

~ **cloud from title** Rechtsmängelbeseitigung, Beseitigung von Rechtsmängeln;

~ **expenses** *(Br.)* Umzugskosten; ~ **van** *(Br.)* Möbelwagen.

remunerate *(v.) (pay)* honorieren, dotieren, besolden, *(reimburse)* vergüten, *(reward)* belohnen;

~ **the labo(u)r** Arbeit bezahlen; ~ **s. o. for his services** jem. einen Dienst vergelten, j. für seine Dienste bezahlen; ~ **s. o. for his trouble** j. für seine Bemühungen entschädigen.

remunerated gegen Vergütung, vergütet;

ill ~ schlecht bezahlt;

~ **by commission** mit Provisionszahlungen abgefunden.

remuneration *(fee)* Honorar, Dotierung, Besoldung, *(for labo(u)r)* Arbeitsentgelt, Lohn, Bezahlung, *(reimbursement)* Entgelt, Entschädigung, Entlohnung, Vergütung, *(reward)* Belohnung;

as ~ **for your services** als Bezahlung für Ihre Dienste; **without** ~ unentgeltlich;

adequate ~ entsprechende Belohnung, angemessene Entlohnung; ~ **agreed upon** vereinbartes Entgelt; **fixed** ~ feste Vergütung, Fixum; **gross** ~ Bruttovergütung; **total** ~ Gesamtvergütung;

~ **of auditors** Honoraraufwand für die Wirtschaftsprüfer; ~ **in cash** Barentlohnung; ~ **of directors** Vorstandsvergütung; **normal senior** ~ **into five figures** übliche fünfstellige Gesamtvergütung für leitende Angestellte; ~ **from a profession** freiberufliche Einkünfte, Einkünfte aus freiberuflicher Tätigkeit; ~ **for salvage** Bergelohn; ~ **of staff** Besoldung des Personals; ~ **of trustee** Treuhändervergütung; ~ **for work** Arbeitsentgelt;

to charge ~ Honorar liquidieren; **to receive an adequate** ~ **for one's work** angemessene Vergütung für seine Arbeit erhalten;

~ **package** Gesamtvergütung, Gesamtdotierung.

remunerative vorteilhaft, einträglich, lohnend, Gewinn abwerfend, gewinnbringend, ergiebig, lukrativ;

~ **business** einträgliches (lukratives) Geschäft; ~ **duties** vorteilhafte Gemeindeabgaben; ~ **employment** Erwerbstätigkeit; ~ **investment** lukrative Anlage, gewinnbringende Kapitalanlage; ~ **price** lukrativer Preis; ~ **salary** anständiges Gehalt; ~ **undertaking** rentables Unternehmen.

remunerativeness Einträglichkeit, Rentabilität.

rename *(v.)* neuen Namen geben, umbenennen.

rencontre *(mil.)* Gefecht, Treffen.

rend *(v.)* spalten;
~ **a country into two parts by civil war** Land durch den Bürgerkrieg in zwei Teile zerreißen;
to turn and ~ s. o. j. nach Strich und Faden ausnehmen.

render *(v.) (cede)* auf-, abgeben, *(give back)* zurückgeben, -erstatten, *(pay rents)* bezahlen, *(translate)* übersetzen, -tragen;
~ **account** Rechnung [vor]legen, Rechenschaft ablegen; ~ **an account for one's expenditure** seine Spesenabrechnung einreichen; ~ **legal advice** Rechtsrat erteilen; ~ **aid to the poor** Arme unterstützen; ~ **annual dues** jährliche Abgaben entrichten; ~ **assistance** Hilfe zuteil werden lassen, Beistand leisten; ~ **available** zugänglich (benutzbar) machen; ~ **an award** Schiedsspruch fällen; ~ **English into French** aus dem Englischen ins Französische übertragen; ~ **a fortress to the enemy** Festung dem Feind übergeben; ~ **goods marketable** beschädigte Waren wieder zurechtmachen; ~ **help to those in need** Bedürftige unterstützen; ~ **information** Auskunft erteilen; ~ **judgment** *(US)* Urteil verkünden (fällen); ~ **s. o. liable** j. haftbar machen; ~ **o. s. liable to proceedings** sich strafbar machen; ~ **a message** Botschaft überbringen; ~ **a net statement** netto abrechnen; ~ **an opinion** Gutachten erstatten; ~ **up possession** Besitz zurückgeben; ~ **the price of a purchase** Kaufpreis übersenden (überweisen); ~ **a profit** Gewinn abwerfen; ~ **o. s. liable to prosecution** sich strafbar machen; ~ **a service** Dienstleistung erbringen; ~ **thanks** Dank abstatten; ~ **valid** validieren; ~ **a verdict** *(jury)* Strafurteil fällen; ~ **void** nichtig machen.

rendered, to (per) account laut erteilter (früherer) Rechnung;
to be ~ helpless by an accident durch einen Unfall hilflos werden.

rendering Übertragung, Übersetzung;
~ **of accounts** Rechnungsauflegung, -aufstellung; ~ **a highway dangerous** Gefährdung des Straßenverkehrs; ~ **of services** Dienstleistung; ~ **of thanks** Danksagung.

rendition *(Commonwealth)* Auslieferung, *(judgment, US)* Urteilsfällung, -verhütung;
interstate ~ *(US)* Überstellung von Straftätern;
~ **of services** Dienstleistung; ~ **of a foreign text** Übersetzung eines ausländischen Textes.

renegade Überläufer, Verräter, Renegat.

renegotiate *(v.)* neu aushandeln, *(US)* Bedingungen eines Heereslieferungsvertrages modifizieren;
~ **a contract** Vertrag neu aufsetzen.

renegotiation erneute Verhandlung, Neuverhandlung, *(war contract, US)* Vertragserneuerung;
~ **exercise** Wiederaufnahme von Verhandlungen.

renew *(v.)* wiederherstellen, restaurieren, renovieren, *(extend)* erneuern, verlängern;
~ **an aquaintance** Bekanntschaft erneuern; ~ **an attack** erneuten Angriff starten; ~ **a bill (draft)** Wechsel prolongieren; ~ **one's complaint** seine Beschwerden erneut vorbringen; ~ **a contract** Vertrag erneuern; ~ **a credit** Kredit prolongieren; ~ **one's efforts** erneute Anstrengungen machen; ~ **a lease** Mietvertrag (Pachtvertrag) verlängern; ~ **a licence** einer Lizenzverlängerung zustimmen; ~ **an order** nachbestellen, Nachbestellung vornehmen; ~ **a passport** Paß erneuern; ~ **a policy** Police erneuern; ~ **a stock of goods** Vorräte ergänzen, Warenlager wieder auffüllen; ~ **one's subscription** sein Abonnement erneuern; ~ **one's supplies of coal (oil)** seine(n) Kohlenvorräte (Ölvorrat) ergänzen; ~ **a title** Eigentumsanspruch erneuern; ~ **one's tyres (tires, US)** seine Reifen erneuern.

renewable erneuerungs-, verlängerungsfähig, *(bill)* prolongationsfähig;
~ **insurance** Versicherung mit ermäßigter Anfangsprämie; ~ **term [life] insurance** verlängerungsfähige Risikolebensversicherung, befristete Lebensversicherung mit Verlängerungsrecht.

renewal [Vertrags]verlängerung, Erneuerung, *(bill)* Prolongation, *(country planning, Br.)* Sanierung, *(insurance business)* Fortsetzung des Versicherungsverhältnisses;
~**s** *(balance sheet)* Neuanschaffungen;
automatic ~ automatische Verlängerung; **subsequent** ~ laufende Erneuerungen; **tacit** ~ stillschweigende Verlängerung; **village** ~ Dorferneuerung, -sanierung;
~ **of an agreement** Vertragserneuerung; ~ **of a bill of exchange** Prolongationsakzept, Wechselprolongation; ~ **of a building** Gebäudeerneuerung; ~ **of contract** Vertragserneuerung; ~ **of a copyright** Urheberrechtserneuerung, Erneuerung des Verlagsrechts; ~ **of coupon sheets** Bogenerneuerung; ~ **of credit** Kredit-

prolongation; ~ **of a lease** Pachtverlängerung; ~ **of a licence** Lizenzverlängerung; ~ **of a loan** Verlängerung der Laufzeit eines Darlehns; ~ **of negotiations** Wiederaufnahme von Verhandlungen; ~ **of orders** Auftragserneuerung; ~ **of passport** Paßerneuerung, -verlängerung; ~ **of a subscription** Erneuerung des Abonnements, Abonnementsverlängerung; ~ **of term of office** Verlängerung der Amtsdauer; ~ **of title** Erneuerung eines Eigentumsanspruchs;
to agree (assent) to a ~ einer Prolongation zustimmen; **to grant a ~ of a draft** Wechsel prolongieren; **to put through ~s at 2 per cent** Verlängerungen zum Satz von 2% tätigen;
~ **area** *(country planning, Br.)* Sanierungsgebiet; ~ **bill** Prolongationswechsel; ~ **bonds** *(US)* prolongierte Obligationen; ~ **certificate** Erneuerungsschein, Talon; ~ **clause** automatische Verlängerungsklausel; ~ **commission** Prolongationsprovision, *(insurance)* Erneuerungsprovision; ~ **contract** Erneuerungsvertrag; ~ **costs** Erneuerungs-, Prolongationskosten; ~ **coupon** Talon, Erneuerungsschein; ~ **date** Erneuerungstag, -termin; ~ **fee** *(patent)* Patentverlängerungs-, Erneuerungsgebühr; ~ **fund** Erneuerungsrücklage, Erneuerungsfonds; ~ **instructions** Anweisungen zur Abonnementsverlängerung; ~ **invoice** prolongierte Rechnung; ~ **notice** Prämienrechnung; ~ **order** Erneuerungsauftrag; ~ **papers** *(insurance)* Hinweis auf Fortsetzung des Versicherungsverhältnisses; ~ **period** Verlängerungszeitraum; ~ **policy** Erneuerungspolice; ~ **premium** *(insurance)* Erneuerungsprämie, Folgeprämie; ~ **procedure** *(insurance)* Verfahren zur Festsetzung der Folgeprämie, Erneuerungsverfahren; ~ **rate** Prolongationssatz [für den nächsten Tag], Erneuerungsrate; ~ **receipt** Erneuerungsschein, *(insurance)* Verlängerungsquittung; ~ **reserve** Erneuerungsfonds; **social** ~ **work** soziale Erneuerungsarbeiten.

renewed verlängert, erneuert;
~ **if required** mit Prolongationsrecht;
~ **delivery (supply)** Nachlieferung; ~ **lease** verlängerter Mietvertrag (Pachtvertrag); ~ **note** prolongierter Schuldschein.

renounce *(v.)* aufgeben, verzichten, Verzicht leisten;
~ **activity as an executor of an heir** auf sein Testamentsvollstreckeramt verzichten; ~ **an allotment letter** Bezugsrecht abtreten; ~ **one's citizenship** *(Br.)* seine Staatsangehörigkeit aufgeben; ~ **a claim** auf eine Forderung verzichten; ~ **one's claim to the throne** auf den Thron verzichten; ~ **a debt** Schuld nicht anerkennen; ~ **one's faith (religion)** seinem Glauben abschwören; ~ **an inheritance (one's interest in an estate)** Erbschaft ausschlagen, auf eine Erbschaft verzichten; ~ **one's nationality** *(US)* seine Staatsangehörigkeit aufgeben; ~ **probate** Nachlaßverwaltung ausschlagen; ~ **one's property** auf sein Vermögen verzichten; ~ **one's rights** sich seiner Rechte begeben; ~ **one's rights to the throne** dem Thron entsagen; ~ **one's son** sich von seinem Sohn lossagen; ~ **one's title** auf seinen Anspruch verzichten; ~ **a treaty** Vertrag aufkündigen; ~ **the worlds** Eremitendasein führen.

renounceable verzichtbar.

renouncement Verzicht[leistung];
~ **of one's citizenship (nationality, US)** Aufgabe der Staatsangehörigkeit; ~ **of one's property** Vermögensverzicht, Erbverzicht; ~ **of a succession** Erbschaftsausschlagung.

renouncer Verzichtleistender.

renouncing probate *(US)* Ablehnung einer Testamentsvollstreckertätigkeit.

renovate *(v.)* wiederherstellen, erneuern, renovieren;
~ **a house** an einem Haus Erneuerungen vornehmen.

renovation Erneuerung, Renovierung;
costly ~**s** kostspielige Renovierungsarbeiten;
~ **scheme** Erneuerungsplan, -vorhaben.

renown Name, guter Ruf, Leumund;
to acquire ~ sich einen Namen machen.

renowned angesehen, namhaft, bekannt, berühmt;
~ **banking company** bekanntes (angesehenes) Bankhaus; **world-** ~ **firm** weltweit bekannte Firma.

rent *(periodical payment)* [Wohnungs]miete, Mietzins, Pacht[zins], Pachtgeld, *(return of value)* Einkommen[squelle], Rente, Miet-, Pachteinnahme, *(US)* Pachtbesitz;
for ~ *(US)* zu vermieten (verleihen); **free of** ~ mietfrei; **subject to** ~ mietzinspflichtig;
~**s** Staatsanleihen, Rentenpapiere;
accrued ~ Mietrückstände; **accustomed** ~ übliche Miete; **advanced** ~ Mietvorschuß, -vorauszahlung; **agreed upon** ~ vereinbarte Miete; **annual** ~ Jahresmiete, Grundrente; **apartment** ~ Miete für eine Etagenwohnung; **back** ~ rückständige Miete; **barren** ~ testamentarisch ausgesetzte Rente [unabhängig von der wirtschaftlichen Lage des Empfängers]; **black** ~ ungesetz-

liche Miete; **chief** ~ Hauptmiete, -pacht; **commercial** ~ wirtschaftlich berechtigter Mietzins; **consumers'** ~ Konsumentenrente; **contract** ~ vertraglich vereinbarte Miete (Pacht); **controlled** ~ *(Br.)* bewirtschaftete (dem Mieterschutz unterliegende) Miete; **current market** ~ ortsübliche Miete; **dead** ~ Bergregalabgabe; **double** ~ Pachtzins für die Zeit nach der Aufkündigung; **dry** ~ Naturalzins; ~ **due** fällige Miete (Pacht); **economic** ~ *(Ricardian theory of rent)* Grundrente, *(rental)* Kostenvergleichsmiete, *(special bonus)* besondere Einkünfte aufgrund vorzüglicher Leistungen; ~ **exclusive of ...** reine Miete ohne ...; **fair** ~ angemessene Miete, *(Ireland)* fünfzehnjährig festgelegte Pacht; **farm** ~ Pachtzins; **fee-farm** ~ Erbpachtzins; **fixed** ~ Bergregalabgabe; **flat** ~ Pauschalmiete; **forehand** ~ Mietanzahlung, -vorauszahlung; **garage** ~ Garagenmiete; **ground** ~ Grundabgabe, Reallast, Grundstückspacht, Erbpacht[zins]; **heavy** ~ hohe Miete, *(Maryland)* Nutzungsentgelt; **high** ~ hohe Miete; **imputed** ~ Mietwert der eigengenutzten Wohnung im Einfamilienhaus, Eigennutzungswert; **judicial** ~ gesetzlich festgesetzte Miete, angemessener Pachtzins; **legal** ~ gesetzliche Miete; **low** ~ niedrige Miete; **monthly** ~ Monatsmiete; **net** ~ Grundrente; **nominal** ~ nominelle Rente, Anerkennungsbetrag für ein Mietverhältnis; **office** ~ Büromiete; **open market** ~ verkehrsübliche Miete; **outstroke** ~ *(coal mining)* Bergregalabgabe; **peppercorn** ~ *(Br.)* nomineller, an die Gemeinde zahlbarer, symbolischer Pachtzins; **premium** ~ Supermiete; **prepaid** ~ Mietvorauszahlung; **pre-war** ~ Vorkriegs-, Friedensmiete; **progressive** ~ Miete (Pacht) mit automatischer Steigerungsklausel; **pure** ~ Grundrente; **quarter's** ~ Vierteljahresmiete; **quasi-**~ Produzentenrente; **rack** ~ *(Br.)* jahresübliche Miete, *(Ireland)* Wuchermiete; **receivable** ~ Sollmiete; **received** Mieterträge, -einnahmen; **registered** ~ *(Br.)* bei der Schiedsstelle registriertes Mietverhältnis; **residential** ~ Wohnungsmiete; ~ **seck** testamentarisch ausgesetzte Rente; **situation** ~ Belegenheitsmiete; **sleeping** ~ Bergregalabgabe; **standard** ~ *(Br.)* normale Friedensrente [per 3. 8. 1914]; **true** ~ Grundrente; **uncontrolled** ~ *(Br.)* freie Miete; **warehouse** ~ Speichermiete; **a year's** ~ Jahresmiete;

~ **in advance** Mietvorschuß, Mietvorauszahlung; ~ **paid for business premises** bezahlte Geschäftsmiete; ~ **of dwellings** Wohnungsmiete; ~ **of the furniture** Möbelmiete; ~**s, issues and profits** Einkünfte aus Grundbesitz, Vermögenserträgnisse, -einkünfte; ~**s and profits from land** Einkünfte aus Grundbesitz; ~ **in kind** Naturalrente; ~ **stated in the lease** vertraglich festgesetzte Miete; ~**s from [un]furnished lettings** Einkünfte aus [nicht] möblierten Wohnungen; ~ **of office** Büromiete; ~ **with an option to purchase** Mietkauf; ~ **paid in advance** vorausbezahlte Miete; ~ **of a premise** Wohnungsmiete; ~ **lying in prender** *(Br.)* Mietbringschuld; ~**s from property** Grundstücksrendite, Immobilienerträge; ~ **lying in render** *(Br.)* Mietholschuld; ~ **of a structure** Gebäudemiete;

~ *(v.)* mieten, [ab]pachten, *(borrow, US)* sich etw. leihen, *(let for* ~, *US)* vermieten, verpachten, *(to be let at)* vermietet (verpachtet) werden zu;

~ **temporary accommodation** vorübergehende Unterkunftsräume anmieten; ~ **an appartment** *(US)* Wohnung [ver]mieten; ~ **a building with the option of purchase** Haus mit Vorkaufsrecht mieten; ~ **a farm** Hof pachten; ~ **a field to a farmer** landwirtschaftliche Nutzfläche verpachten; ~ **a film** Film verleihen; ~ **a flat** *(Br.)* Wohnung vermieten; ~ **a flat and take over the furniture** *(Br.)* Wohnung mieten und die Möbel übernehmen; ~ **s. o. high (low)** hohe (niedrige) Miete von jem. verlangen; ~ **a house** Haus mieten; ~ **a house from the tenant** Haus im Wege der Untermiete pachten; ~ **by the month** monatlich mieten; ~ **one's tenants low** seinen Mietern geringe Miete abverlangen; ~ **at £ 900 a year** 900 Pfund an Miete im Jahr erbringen;

to be in arrears with one's ~ im Mietrückstand sein; **to be subject to a controlled** ~ *(Br.)* dem Mieterschutzgesetz unterliegen; **to collect** ~**s** Mieten einziehen (kassieren); **to command a high** ~ hohe Miete erzielen; **to determine** ~**s** *(rent tribunal, Br.)* Mietpreis festlegen; **to distrain s. one's goods for** ~ jds. Sachen wegen Mietschulden pfänden; **to earn no** ~ keine Miete erbringen; **to fall behind with one's** ~ Miete schuldig bleiben; **to fix a** ~ Mietzins festsetzen; **to have a house free of** ~ mietfrei wohnen; **to increase the** ~ Miete erhöhen; **to let one's property at an economic** ~ Hausgrundstücke zu Kostensätzen vermieten; **to let for** ~ verpachten; **to lift** ~**s** *(fam.)* Mieten kassieren; **to lower the** ~**s** Mieten herabsetzen; **to mass** ~**s** Mieten einziehen; **to owe three months'** ~ drei Monate mit der Miete im Rückstand sein; **to pay a heavy (high)** ~ **for farming land** für eine landwirtschaft-

liche Nutzfläche eine hohe Pacht bezahlen; **to pay a** ~ **in untaxed cash** Miete bar und steuerunschädlich entrichten; **to pay one's** ~ **at the end of a quarter** Miete vierteljährig postnumerando bezahlen; **to pay the whole of one's** ~ seine ganze Miete auf einmal bezahlen; **to put up the** ~ Miete erhöhen (heraufsetzen); **to raise a lodger's** ~ j. in der Miete steigern; **to refer the amount of** ~ **to arbitration** Miethöhe schiedsgerichtlich festlegen lassen; **to take a** ~ pachten; **to tender the amount of** ~ Mietschuld zu begleichen anbieten; **to yield a** ~ Miete abwerfen;

~**s have soared** Mieten sind gestiegen;

~ **account** Mietkonto, -rechnung; ⌀ **Act** *(Br.)* Wohnraumbewirtschaftungsgesetz, Mieterschutzgesetz; **to be subject to the** ⌀ **Restriction Act** *(Br.)* den Mieterschutzbestimmungen unterliegen, wohnraumbewirtschaftet sein; **to exploit the** ⌀ **Act dodge** von der Umgehung des Mieterschutzgesetzes profitieren; ⌀ **Act protection** Mieterschutz; ~**-a-car** Mietwagen; ~**-a-car agency (firm, corporation)** Mietwagenverleih, Autovermietungsfirma; ~**-a-car reservation office** Mietwagenverleihbüro; ~**-a-crowd standards** übliche Menschenmengen bei Demonstrationen; ~ **allowance** Wohnungsgeldzuschuß, Mietzuschuß; **perpetual** ~ **annuity** lebenslängliche Rente; ~ **arrears** Miet-, Pachtrückstand, rückständige Miete; ~ **bill** Mietrechnung; ~ **ceiling** Höchstmiete, Miethöchstpreis; ~ **charge** Grunddienstbarkeit, *(Br.)* Erbzins, *(lodgment)* Mietbelastung, -anteil; ~ **charge bonds** Erbzinsobligationen; ~ **charger** Nutznießer (Inhaber) einer Grunddienstbarkeit; ~ **collection** Einziehung der Miete; ~ **collector** Mieteinsammler, -einnehmer; ~ **concession** Entgegenkommen in der Wohnungsmiete; ~ **control** *(Br.)* Mieterschutz, Mietpreisbindung; **to ease** ~ **controls** *(Br.)* Preisbindung bei Wohnungsmieten lockern; **Furnished Houses** ⌀ **Control Act** *(Br.)* Mieterschutzgesetz; ~**-controlled flat** *(Br.)* den Mieterschutzbestimmungen unterliegende Wohnung; ~ **day** Zahlungstermin für die Miete (Pacht), Pachttermin; ~ **deficiency** Mietausfall, -verlust; ~ **expense(s)** Mietaufwendungen; ~**-free** pacht-, mietfrei; **to live** ~**-free in a house** mietfrei wohnen; ~**-free house** mietfreies Haus; **to occupy a house** ~**-free** Haus zur freien Miete bewohnen; ~**-free period** mietfreier Zeitraum; **2-year** ~**-free period** mietfreie Zweijahresperiode; **to lift the** ~ **freeze** Mietpreisstopp aufheben; ~ **income** Pacht-, Mieteinkommen, -erträgnisse; ~ **increase** Mieterhöhung, -anhebung, -steigerung; ~ **insurance** Mietausfall-, Mietverlustversicherung; ~ **money** Pachtgeld, -preis; ⌀ **Officer** *(Br.)* Angestellter einer Mietpreisstelle; ~ **owner** Erbzinsberechtigter; ~ **payer** Mieter, Pächter; ~**-paying** ertragreich; ~ **payment** Rentenauszahlung; ~ **prices** Mietpreise; ~**-raising** miet-, pachterhöhend; ~ **rebate** Mietnachlaß; **local authorities'** ~ **rebate scheme** kommunales Mieterstattungssystem; ~ **receipts** Miet-, Pachteinnahmen; ~**-reducing** gewinnmindernd; ~ **restrictions** Mieterschutzbestimmungen, gesetzlicher Mieterschutz; ⌀ **Restriction Act** *(Br.)* Wohnraumbewirtschaftungsgesetz, Mieterschutzgesetz; ~ **return** Mietertrag; ~ **roll** Zinsbuch, -register, Rentenverzeichnis, *(income from* ~*)* Pacht-, Mietertrag, Einkünfte aus Vermietung und Verpachtung; **total** ~ **roll** Gesamtmiet-, -pachteinnahmen; ~ **schedule** Mietertragstabelle; ~ **subsidy** Mietzuschuß; ~ **supplement** Mietzuschuß; ~ **tribunal** *(Br.)* Mieteinigungsamt.

rental Miet-, Pachteinnahme, [Brutto]mietertrag, *(amount paid as rent)* Miete, Pacht, Miet-, Pachtzins, *(tel., Br.)* Grundgebühr, *(US)* Mietgegenstände;

~**s** Miet-, Pachtsätze;

assessed ~ steuerlicher Mietwert; **car** ~ Automietgebühr, -miete; **fixed** ~ *(tel.)* Pauschalgebühr; **gross** ~ Roh-, Bruttoertrag; **housing** ~ Wohnungsmiete; **management-supervised** ~ zentralüberwachte Vermietung; **net** ~ Nettopacht, -miete, *(real estate)* Nettoertrag; **standing** ~ Naturalpacht; **subscriber's** ~ Fernsprechanschlußgebühr;

to put out on ~ mietweise überlassen;

~ **agent** Häusermakler; ~ **allowance** Wohnungsgeld, Mietzuschuß; ~ **apartment** Mietwohnung; ~ **basis** Mietgrundlage; ~ **charges** Mietpreise; ~ **car company** Mietwagenfirma, -unternehmen, Verleihfirma, -gesellschaft; ~ **commission** Vermietungsprovision; ~ **commitments** Mietverbindlichkeiten; ~ **company** Verleihfirma, -gesellschaft; ~ **deal** Vermietungsgeschäft; ~ **development** Mietpreisentwicklung; ~ **earnings** *(motion picture)* Verleiheinnahmen; ~ **fee** Mietgebühr, Mietkosten; ~ **figure** *(term insurance)* Rentabilitätsziffer, -darstellung; ~ **fleet** Mietwagenflotte; ~ **income** Miet-, Pachteinkommen; **to produce** ~ **income** Mieteinkünfte abwerfen; ~ **instalment** Mietzins, Miete; ~ **library** *(US)* Leihbibliothek, -bücherei; ~ **loss** Mietausfall; ~ **maintenance** Wartung der Mietgegenstände; ~ **market** Mietenmarkt; ~ **payments** Mietzahlungen; ~ **period** Miet-, Pachtzeit; ~ **property** Mietgegenstand; **to employ s. th. as ~ property** Vermögensgegenstand mietweise nutzen; ~ **rate** *(US)* Miet-, Pachtpreis; **to break out its sales-to-~ ratio for public display** Verteilerschlüssel von Verkäufen zu Vermietung öffentlich bekanntgeben; ~ **result** Vermietungsergebnis; ~ **return** Miet-, Pachtertrag; ~ **revenue** Einkünfte aus Vermietung und Verpachtung; ~ **right** *(Br.)* Erbpacht; ~ **schedule** Mietertragstabelle; ~ **space** für Vermietungszwecke zur Verfügung stehende Fläche; ~ **value** Miet[ertrags]wert, Pachtwert; **rent and ~ value insurance** Mietausfallversicherung; ~ **value policy** Mietausfallpolice.

rentcharge Grunddienstbarkeit, *(Br.)* Erbzins.

rented vermietet, verpachtet;
~ **car** Mietauto, Leihwagen; ~ **land** verpachtetes Grundstück, Pachtland.

renter Mieter, Pächter, *(film industry)* Filmverleih;
standing ~ in Naturalien bezahlender Pächter;
~ **of a safe** Safe-, Depotmieter.

renting Mieten, Miete;
~ **of cars** Autovermietung; ~ **of safes** Schrankfachmiete;
to roll into ~ ins Verleihgeschäft einsteigen;
~ **ability** Mieteigenschaft; ~ **department** Miet-, Pachtabteilung; ~ **failure** Mietausfall; ~ **market** Mietenmarkt; ~ **space** Miet-, Pachtfläche; ~ **station** Anmietstelle.

rentless ertrag-, zinslos;
~ **land** unterhalb der Ertragsgrenze liegender Grundbesitz.

rentroll Einkünfte aus Vermietung und Verpachtung.

renumber *(v.)* umnumerieren.

renunciation Verzicht[leistung], -erklärung, Absage;
~ **of an administratorship** Ablehnung eines Testamentvollstreckeramtes; ~ **of agency** Widerruf des Vertretungsverhältnisses; ~ **of citizenship** *(Br.)* Verzicht auf die Staatsangehörigkeit; ~ **of dower** Ausschlagung der Mitgift; ~ **of force** Gewaltverzicht; ~ **of guarantee** Garantieverzicht; ~ **of an inheritance** *(US)* Erbverzicht, Ausschlagung einer Erbschaft; ~ **of nationality** *(US)* Verzichtleistung auf die Staatsangehörigkeit; ~ **of probate** Ausschlagung des Testamentsvollstreckeramtes; ~ **of a right** Rechtsverzicht; ~ **of a succession** *(US)* Ausschlagung einer Erbschaft; ~ **of title** Eigentumsverzicht, -aufgabe; ~ **form** *(Br.)* Verzichtleistungsschreiben [für Bezugsrechte].

renvoi, renvoy *(law of nations)* Ausweisung, Abschiebung.

reoccupation *(mil.)* Wiederbesetzung.

reoccupy *(v.)* wieder besetzen.

reopen *(v.)* wieder eröffnen (in Betrieb setzen), *(school)* wieder anfangen;
~ **a case** Verfahren wiederaufnehmen; ~ **a case of bankruptcy** Konkursverfahren noch einmal aufrollen; ~ **a discussion** Diskussion fortsetzen; ~ **on Monday** Montag wieder beginnen; ~ **a shop** Laden wiedereröffnen.

reopening Wiedereröffnung, -inbetriebnahme; ~ **of a case** Wiederaufnahme eines Verfahrens; ~ **of the securities exchanges** Wiedereröffnung der Effektenbörsen;
to order the ~ of a foreclosure Aussetzung der Zwangsversteigerung anordnen;
~ **clause** *(US)* Vertragsklausel zur Neufassung bestimmter vertraglicher Leistungen, Offenhalteklausel.

reoperate *(v.)* nacharbeiten.

reoperating cost Nacharbeitskosten.

reoperation Nacharbeit.

reorder Nach-, Neubestellung, Erneuerungsauftrag;
~ *(v.)* nach-, neu bestellen;
~ **priorities** Prioritätenliste neu zusammenstellen.

reordering work Nachbestellarbeit.

reorganization Neugestaltung, Neuregelung, Um-, Reorganisation, Umstellung, *(company)* Sanierung, Bereinigung, Veränderung der Kapitalstruktur, *(US)* Gläubigervergleich, *(legal reconstruction)* Neugründung;
company ~ Vergleichs- und Sanierungsverfahren für eine Gesellschaft, Firmensanierung; **local government ~** Reorganisation der Kommunalverwaltung; **tax-free ~** steuerfreie Sanierung;
~ **under Chapter 10** *(US)* Vergleichsverfahren, Liquidation zu Sanierungszwecken; ~ **of a corporation** *(US)* Vergleichs- und Sanierungsverfahren, Sanierungsumgründung, Firmenvergleich; ~ **of finances** finanzielle Sanierung; ~ **of share capital** Änderungen in der Verteilung des Aktienkapitals;
to file the petition for ~ under Chapter 10 *(US)* Antrag auf Eröffnung des Vergleichs- und Sanierungsverfahrens stellen; **to pass through a ~** Sanierungsphase durchlaufen; **to petition for ~** *(US)* Vergleichsantrag stellen;

~ **account** *(US)* Vergleichskonto; ~ **bar** *(US)* Vergleichsverfahrensspezialisten; ~ **bond** *(US)* Gewinnschuldverschreibung; ~ **committee** *(creditors)* Sanierungsausschuß; ~ **fund** Sanierungsfonds; ~ **measures** Sanierungsmaßnahmen; ~ **petition** Vergleichsantrag; **involuntary ~ petition** Zwangsvergleichsantrag; ~ **plan** Sanierungs-, Reorganisations-, wirtschaftlicher Wiederaufbauplan; ~ **proceedings** *(US)* Vergleichsverfahren; ~ **program(me)** Sanierungsprogramm; ~ **report** Sanierungsbericht; ~ **scheme** Sanierungsplan; ~ **trustee** *(US)* Vergleichsverwalter.

reorganize *(v.)* wieder einrichten, reorganisieren, neu regeln (gestalten, umstellen), *(firm)* sanieren, *(economy)* wiederaufbauen;
~ **under Chapter 10** *(US)* Vergleichs- und Sanierungsverfahren durchführen; ~ **the economy on a stable basis** stabile Verhältnisse in der Wirtschaft wieder herstellen; ~ **an industry on commercial lines** Industriezweig nach kaufmännischen Gesichtspunkten sanieren; ~ **the share capital** Änderung in der Verteilung des Aktienkapitals vornehmen;
to apply for permission to ~ under the Bankruptcy Act Antrag auf Eröffnung des Vergleichsverfahrens stellen.

reorganizer Reorganisator.

reorganizing Reorganisation, Umgründung, Sanierung.

reorient *(v.)* *(pol.)* Kursänderung vornehmen.

reorientation *(pol.)* Kursänderung.

repack *(v.)* umpacken, wieder verpacken.

repackage *(v.)* umpacken.

repaid zurückgezahlt.

repair Instandsetzung, Wiederherstellung, Reparatur, Ausbesserung, *(accounting)* Instandhaltungsaufwand, *(house)* baulicher Zustand, *(place of resort)* Zuflucht-, Aufenthaltsort;
~**s** Instandsetzungsarbeiten, Reparaturen, *(costs)* Wiederherstellungs-, Reparaturkosten;
in bad ~ *(house)* baufällig, in schlechtem Zustand; **beyond ~** nicht mehr zu reparieren; **in good ~** *(house)* in gut erhaltenem Zustand; **in need of ~** reparatur-, ausbesserungs-, instandsetzungsbedürftig; **out of ~** in schlechtem Erhaltungszustand, *(house)* baufällig, reparaturbedürftig; **under ~** in Reparatur;
emergency ~s unbedingt notwendige Reparaturen; **major ~s** größere Reparaturen; **minor ~s** geringfügige Reparaturen; **necessary ~s** *(ship)* notwendige Reparaturen; ~ **needed** erforderliche Reparaturen; **ordinary ~s** regelmäßig notwendige Reparaturen; **road (street) ~s** Straßeninstandsetzungsarbeiten; **running ~s** laufende Instandsetzungsarbeiten; **temporary ~s** provisorische Reparaturen; **tenant's ~s** dem Mieter obliegende Reparaturen;
~ **to a building** Gebäudeinstandsetzung; ~**s chargeable to the owner** zu Lasten des Eigentümers gehende Reparaturen; ~ **of premises** am Betriebsgebäude durchgeführte Reparaturen; ~**s of structure** Gebäudereparaturen;
~ *(v.)* erneuern, ausbessern, instandsetzen, reparieren, *(machine)* überholen, in Ordnung bringen, *(make amends)* wiedergutmachen, Verlust ersetzen, entschädigen;
~ **a damage** Schaden beheben; ~ **one's fortune** seine Vermögensverhältnisse neu ordnen; ~ **a house** an einem Haus Reparaturen durchführen (Erneuerungen vornehmen); ~ **a loss** Verlust wettmachen; ~ **a mistake** Fehler berichtigen; ~ **a motor** Motor reparieren; ~ **a puncture** Reifenschaden beheben; ~ **the roads** Straßen instandsetzen; ~ **to the seaside resorts** Seebäder im Sommer frequentieren; ~ **a wrong** Unrecht wiedergutmachen;
to be closed during ~s während der Reparaturarbeiten geschlossen sein; **to be in bad ~** schlecht erhalten sein; **to be in good ~** gut erhalten sein, *(machine)* tadellos in Ordnung sein, in tadellosem Zustand sein; **to be in need of constant ~** laufender Reparaturen bedürfen; **to be in pressing need of ~** dringend reparaturbedürftig sein; **to be out of ~** nicht mehr zu reparieren sein; **not to be ~d** nicht wiederherzustellen sein; **to be under ~** in Reparatur sein, repariert werden, sich in Ausbesserung befinden; **to carry out ~s** Reparaturen durchführen (vornehmen); **to effect ~s on the site** Reparaturen an Ort und Stelle vornehmen; **to estimate for the ~ of a building** Reparaturkosten eines Gebäudes veranschlagen; **to get out of ~** *(house)* baufällig werden; **to hand in for ~** zur Reparatur abgeben; **to keep a building in fair ~** Gebäude in gutem baulichen Zustand erhalten; **to need ~s** reparaturbedürftig sein; **to need putting into ~** dringend reparaturbedürftig sein; **to put s. th. in ~** etw. instand setzen; **to put into port for ~s** zur Vornahme von Reparaturen in den Hafen einlaufen; **to undergo ~s** Reparaturen unterzogen werden;

~ activity Reparaturarbeit; [statutory]**~s allowance (deduction)** [etwa] 7b-Abschreibung; **~ bill** Reparaturrechnung; **~ costs** Reparatur-, Instandsetzungskosten; **~ covenant** Reparaturverpflichtung; **~ crew** Reparaturmannschaft; **~ department** Reparaturabteilung; **~ expenditure** Reparaturaufwand; **~ facilities** Reparaturanlagen, -möglichkeiten; **~ increase** auf Instandsetzungskosten beruhende Mieterhöhung; **~ order** Reparatur-, Instandsetzungsauftrag; **~ permit** Reparaturschein; **~ service** Instandsetzungs-, Reparatur-, Kundendienst; **~ ship** Reparaturschiff; **~ shipyard** Reparaturwerft; **~ shop** Reparaturanstalt, -werkstatt; **~ truck** *(railway)* Eisenbahnausbesserungswagen; **~ vehicle** Reparaturfahrzeug; **~ work** Ausbesserungs-, Instandsetzungsarbeiten; **~ workshop** Reparaturwerkstatt; **~ yard** Ausbesserungs-, Reparaturwerft.

repairable, reparable reparaturfähig, -bedürftig.

repairer Wiederhersteller;
road ~ Straßenarbeiter.

repairing|charges Instandsetzungskosten, Reparaturkosten; **~ covenant** Reparaturvereinbarung, -verpflichtung; **~ lease** Pachtvertrag mit Instandsetzungsklausel; **~ shop** Reparaturwerstatt.

repairman *(US)* Techniker, Mechaniker, Handwerker;
automobile ~ *(US)* Autoschlosser, Kraftfahrzeugmechaniker; **~ shop** Reparaturwerkstatt.

reparation Instandsetzung, Wiederherstellung, *(Scot.)* Wiedergutmachung, Entschädigung, Ersatz;
~s Reparationen, Reparationszahlungen, Kriegsentschädigungen;
war ~s Kriegsreparationen;
~ of the damage *(US)* Schadensersatz;
to be in need of constant ~s laufender Reparaturen bedürfen; **to make ~s** Reparationen leisten; **to make ~s for an injury** *(US, Scot.)* Schadenersatz leisten;
~ account Reparationskonto; **~ agreement** Reparationsabkommen; **~ charges** Reparatur-, Instandsetzungskosten; **~ claims** Reparationsforderungen; **~ commission** *(Br.)* Übertragungsvorschuß [für deutsche Reparationszahlungen]; **~ Committee** Reparationsausschuß, Wiedergutmachungskommission; **~ covenant** *(rent)* Reparaturvereinbarung; **~ demand** Reparationsforderung; **~ levy** *(Br.)* Reparationsabgabe [für deutsche Einfuhr nach England]; **~ list** Reparationsliste; **~ obligations** Reparationsverpflichtungen; **~ payments** Reparationszahlungen; **~ program(me)** Reparationsprogramm.

reparole *(US)* erneute bedingte Entlassung.

repartee schlagfertige Antwort.

repartition [verhältnismäßige] Aufteilung, *(profit)* Gewinnverteilung;
loss ~ Verlustaufteilung, Schadensverteilung;
~ (v.) aufteilen;
~ treaty *(country)* Teilungsvertrag.

repass *(pol.)* nochmals beschließen.

repatriate Heimkehrer, *(resettled person)* Kriegs-, Zivilinterner, Umsiedler;
~ (v.) in die Heimat zurückführen (zurückschaffen), repatriieren, umsiedeln;
~ capital Kapital wieder ausführen (rückführen); **~ earnings from foreign investments** ausländische Anlagenerlöse devisenmäßig vereinnahmen; **~ foreign investment** Auslandsanlagen auflösen; **~ funds** Kapitalien aus dem Ausland zurückholen; **~ gold** Goldabflüsse nach dem Inland zurückbringen; **~ profits** Gewinne transferieren.

repatriated|bonds repatriierte Anleihen; **~ person** Umsiedler; **~ soldier** Heimkehrer.

repatriation Wiedereinbürgerung, *(foreign workers)* Rückführung, Heimaturlaub;
~ of capital Kapitalrückführung; **~ of dividend** Dividendentransfer; **~ of earnings from foreign investments** devisenmäßige Vereinnahmung ausländischer Anlagenerlöse; **~ of foreign exchange** Devisentransfer, -rückfluß; **~ of British funds from US** Rückwanderung englischer Anleihen aus den USA; **~ of prisoners of war** Rückschaffung von Kriegsgefangenen; **~ of profits** Gewinntransfer;
~ agreement Repatriierungsabkommen.

repawn *(v.)* erneut verpfänden.

repay *(v.)* zurück[be]zahlen, nochmals bezahlen, wiederbezahlen, rückerstatten, -vergüten, abdecken, *(make amends)* entschädigen, Ersatz leisten, ersetzen;
liable to ~ erstattungspflichtig;
~ o. s. sich erholen (schadlos halten);
~ s. o. in the same coin *(fig.)* j. mit gleicher Münze heimzahlen;
~ a credit Kredit zurückzahlen; **~ before the expiration of a**

period vor Verfall zurückzahlen; **~ s. o. in full** j. voll befriedigen; **~ a kindness** sich revanchieren; **~ a loan** Kredit zurückzahlen; **~ a mortgage debt** Hypothek tilgen; **~ an obligation** sich von einer Verbindlichkeit frei machen.

repayable rückzahlbar;
~ on demand auf Verlangen rückzahlbar; **~ by annual instalments** in Jahresraten zu tilgen; **~ at par** pari rückzahlbar; **~ at short notice** kurzfristig rückzahlbar.

repayment Rückzahlung, -vergütung, -erstattung, *(redemption)* Tilgung;
due for ~ zur Rückzahlung anstehend;
anticipated ~ Einlösung vor Fälligkeit, vorzeitige Rückzahlung; **part ~** teilweise Rückzahlung, Teilrückzahlung;
~ of advance Zurückzahlung eines Vorschusses, Kreditrückzahlung; **~ of capital** Kapitalrückzahlung; **~ of a credit** Kredittilgung; **~ of debts** Schuldentilgung; **~ of duty** Steuerrückzahlung; **~ by instal(l)ments** Rückzahlung in Raten, Abzahlung, Teilzahlung; **~ of a mortgage debt** Hypothekentilgung; **~ of principal** Kapitalrückzahlung; **~ of tax** Steuerrückzahlung, Steuerrückerstattung;
to demand ~ Kapital kündigen;
~ claim Rückzahlungsanspruch; **~ date** Rückzahlungstermin; **~ due** Rückzahlungsanspruch; **~ method** Rückzahlungsweise; **~ order** Rückzahlungsverfügung; **~ period** Rückzahlungszeitraum, Rückzahlungszeit, *(hire purchase)* Abzahlungsfrist, -periode; **[medium-term] ~ program(me)** [mittelfristiger] Rückzahlungsplan; **~ proposal** Rückzahlungsvorschlag; **~ table** Rückzahlungstabelle; **~ value of a contract** *(saving)* Rückkaufwert eines Sparvertrages.

repeal Aufhebung, Außerkraftsetzung, *(last will)* Widerruf;
~ of a law Aufhebung eines Gesetzes;
~ (v.) aufheben, abschaffen, außer Kraft setzen;
~ a will letztwillige Verfügung aufheben (widerrufen).

repealable widerruflich, aufhebbar.

repeat neue Bestellung, neuer Antrag, Neubestellung, *(advertising)* Ersatz-, Erinnerungs-, Wiederholungsanzeige, *(broadcasting)* Wiederholungssendung;
~ (v.) wiederholen, *(election, US)* mehr als eine Stimme abgeben, *(recover)* irrtümlich erhaltenes Geld zurückzahlen;
~ an article nach-, neu bestellen; **~ back a telegram** Telegramm kollationieren; **~ s. th. heard** etw. weitererzählen; **~ a mistake** Fehler wiederholen; **~ a pattern** Muster vervielfältigen;
~ audience *(advertising)* wiederholt angesprochene Konsumenten; **~ business** Wiederkäufe; **~ order** Neu-, Nachbestellung, *(advertising)* Wiederholungsauftrag; **to place a ~ order** nachbestellen; **~ performance** *(broadcasting)* wiederholte Sendung, Wiederholungssendung; **~ purchases** Nachkäufe, -order; **~ sale** *(US)* Verkauf auf Grund von Erinnerungswerbung.

repeated requests wiederholte Aufforderungen.

repeater *(broadcasting)* Relaisübertragung, *(criminal, US)* Rückfälliger, rückfälliger Täter, Wiederholungstäter, *(elections)* Doppelwähler, *(school)* Repetent, Sitzengebliebener, *(tel.)* Verstärker.

repeating clause Widerrufsklausel.

repel *(v.) (Scot.)* zurückweisen;
~ the enemy Feind vertreiben; **~ an offer** Angebot ausschlagen; **~ a suggestion** Ansinnen von sich weisen.

repentance Reue.

repercussions *(pol.)* Rückwirkungen;
~s of war Kriegsfolgen;
to have ~ weite Kreise ziehen.

repertoire *(theater)* Repertoire, Spielplan.

repertory Auswahl, Vorrat, *(store of collection)* Fundgrube, *(theater)* Spielplan;
~ theater (theatre, Br.) Theater mit stehender Truppe.

repetition Wiederholung, *(recover)* Klage auf Rückerstattung irrtümlich gezahlter Gelder, *(Scot.)* Verlesung einer Zeugenaussage;
~ of an order Auftragswiederholung;
~-paid telegram kollationiertes Telegramm; **~ work** Serienarbeit, -herstellung.

repetitive regelmäßig wiederkehrend;
~ timing Einzelzeitverfahren; **~ work** Routinearbeit.

replace *(v.) (refund)* wieder-, rückerstatten, rückvergüten, *(become subsitute)* als Nachfolger eingesetzt werden, ersetzen, Stelle einnehmen, *(provide substitute)* an die Stelle setzen, ersetzen, erneuern, wiederbeschaffen;
~ s. o. jds. Stelle einnehmen; **~ antiquated equipment** alte Betriebsausstattung ersetzen; **~ fixed assets** Anlagen erneuern; **~ one book against another** zwei Bücher austauschen; **~ capital**

goods Investitionsgüter ersetzen; ~ **coal by oil** Kohle durch Öl ersetzen; ~ **a dictionary on the shelf** Wörterbuch ins Regal zurückstellen; ~ **as much as 20% of its faculty each year** pro Jahr bis zu 20% Abgänge haben; ~ **the receiver** Telefonhörer auflegen; ~ **on the register** wieder im Register eintragen; ~ **stolen money** unterschlagenes Geld ersetzen; ~ **a sum of money borrowed** geliehenen Geldbetrag zurückgeben.

replaceable ersetzbar, austauschbar.

replaced | equipment Ersatzanschaffungen; ~ **parts** ausgewechselte Teile.

replacement *(accounting)* Anlagenerneuerung, *(destroyed building)* Wiederherstellungs-, Wiedererrichtungskosten, *(person)* Ersatzperson, Vertreter, *(substituting)* Ersatz-, Wiederbeschaffung, Ersatzleistung, Ersatzlieferung, Ersetzung, Erneuerung, Ersatz;
~**s** Neueinstellungen;
holiday ~ *(Br.)* Ferien-, Urlaubsvertretung; **machinery** ~ Erneuerung des Maschinenparks; **partial** ~ Teilersatz; **strike** ~ Ersatzkräfte für Streikfälle; **vacation** ~ *(US)* Ferienvertretung, -vertreter, Urlaubsvertretung;
~ **of assets** [Sach]anlagenerneuerung; ~ **of goods** Warenersatz; ~ **of inventories** Bestandsauffüllung, Auffüllung der Lagerbestände; ~ **in kind** Naturalersatz; ~ **of worn-out parts** Ersatz abgenutzter Einzelteile; ~ **of a trustee** Auswechslung eines Treuhänders;
to buy goods in ~ Deckungskauf vornehmen; **to get a** ~ **while one is away on holiday** Ferienvertretung zugeteilt erhalten; **to require goods in** ~ Ersatzlieferung verlangen; **to train a** ~ Ersatzmann anlernen;
~ **aircraft** Ersatzflugzeug; ~ **car** Ersatzfahrzeug; ~ **contract** Ersatzvertrag; ~ **copy** Ersatzstück, Ersatzexemplar; ~ **cost** Ersatz-, Gestehungs-, Wiederbeschaffungskosten, Neuanschaffungskosten, -wert; ~ **cost of real estate** Wiederaufbaukosten; ~ **cost depreciated** tatsächlicher Wert [der Ersatzbeschaffung]; ~ **cost depreciation** Abschreibung der Wiederbeschaffungskosten; ~ **cost new** Neuanschaffungswert; ~ **cost standard** *(balance sheet)* Wiederbeschaffungswert; ~ **delivery** Ersatzlieferung; ~ **demand** Ersatz-, Erneuerungsbedarf; ~ **draft** Ersatzwechsel; ~ **equipment** Ersatzausstattung; ~ **expenditure** Ersatzaufwendungen; ~ **fund** Wiederbeschaffungs-, Erneuerungsrücklage, -fonds; ~ **goods** Ersatzware, Ersatzgüter; ~ **housing** Ersatzwohnung; ~ **investment** Ersatzinvestition; ~ **method of depreciation** Abschreibung auf Basis der Wiederbeschaffungskosten; ~ **needs** Wiederbeschaffungs-, Ersatzbedarf; ~ **outlay** Ersatzaufwand; ~ **parts** Ersatzteile; ~ **practices** Wiederbeschaffungspraxis; ~ **price** Wiederbeschaffungspreis; ~ **program(me)** Ausweichprogramm, *(investing)* Anlagenerneuerungsplan; ~ **rate** Wiederbeschaffungs-, Anlagenerneuerungssatz, *(employees)* Zu- und Abgangsrate; ~ **reserve** Rücklage für Wiederbeschaffung, Wiederbeschaffungsrücklage, Erneuerungsfonds, -rücklage; ~ **ship** Ersatzschiff; ~ **tonnage** Ersatztonnage; ~ **unit** erneuerte Anlage, Ersatzeinheit; ~ **value** Ersatz-, Wiederbeschaffungswert; ~ **warhead** Ersatzsprengkopf.

replacer Ersatzmann.

replant *(v.) (fig.)* wieder einsetzen.

replay Wiederholungsspiel.

replead *(v.)* neuen Schriftsatz einreichen.

repleader Antrag auf Wiederaufnahme des Verfahrens;
to award a ~ erneutes Plädoyer anordnen.

repledge *(v.)* wieder verpfänden, *(collateral securities)* wiederverpfänden.

replenish *(v.)* ergänzen, auffüllen;
~ **one's inventory** sein Lager auffüllen, Lagerergänzungen vornehmen; ~ **a loan** zusätzliche Sicherheit leisten; ~ **the reserves** Reserven auffüllen; ~ **a ship's stores** Schiffsvorräte ergänzen; ~ **one's stocks** sein Lager vervollständigen, seine Bestände auffüllen; ~ **one's wardrobe** seine Garderobe ergänzen.

replenishment Ergänzung, Auffüllung;
~ **of a loan** Gestellung zusätzlicher Sicherheiten; ~ **of stocks** Lagerauffüllung, Lagerergänzung; ~ **of supplies** Ergänzung der Vorräte;
~ **order** Ergänzungsbestellung; ~ **ship** Versorgungsschiff.

replete with all modern conveniences mit dem modernsten Komfort ausgestattet.

repleviable, replevisable der Herausgabe unterliegend.

replevin *(action at law, US)* Herausgabeklage, *(bail)* Pfandauslösung, Selbsthilfeverkauf, Pfandfreigabe gegen Kautionsgestellung;
personal ~ Haftprüfungsverfahren;
~ *(v.)* Pfand auslösen, *(US)* herausverlangen;

to grant a ~ Beschlagnahme (Pfändung) aufheben, Pfandverstrickung lösen;
~ **bond** Sicherheitsleistung bei der Zwangsvollstreckung.

replevisor Pfandschuldner.

replevy Herausgabeverfügung;
~ *(v.) (distraint)* gepfändete Gegenstände gegen Sicherheitsleistung zurückerhalten.

replica Kopie, Nachbildung, Reproduktion;
scaled-down ~ Miniaturausgabe;
~ **of a painting** Kopie eines Gemäldes.

replication Wiederholung, *(law, US)* Replik, *(statistics)* Parallelversuch;
general ~ allgemeines Bestreiten; **special** ~ Bestreiten und Gegenvorbringen;
to deliver a ~ Replik vorbringen.

reply *(letter)* Antwortschreiben, Erwiderung, Rückäußerung, *(law)* Replik;
in ~ **to your letter** in Beantwortung Ihres Briefes; **without** ~ unbeantwortet;
affirmative ~ zusagende Antwort; **condensed immediate** ~ Blitzantwort; **early** ~ baldige Antwort; **evasive** ~ ausweichende Antwort; **favo(u)rable** ~ zusagender Bescheid; **frivolous** ~ unbegründete Replik; **immediate** ~ umgehende Antwort, Eilzuschrift; **interim (intermediate)** ~ Zwischenbescheid; ~ **leaving today** heute abgehende Antwort; **missing** ~ ausstehende Antwort; **negative** ~ abschlägiger (ablehnender) Bescheid; **official** ~ amtlicher Bescheid; ~ **paid** [Rück]antwort bezahlt; **provisional** ~ Zwischenbescheid; ~ **received** eingegangene Antwort; **sham** ~ unbegründete Replik;
~ **to a complaint** Beschwerdeerledigung, Erledigung einer Beschwerde; ~ **by return of post** *(Br.)* **(mail, US)** postwendende Antwort;
~ *(v.)* Antwort erteilen, antworten;
~ **in the affirmative** zustimmend antworten;
~ **card** *(US)* [Rück]antwortkarte; **business** ~ **card** Werbeantwortkarte; **international** ~ **coupon** [Post]antwortschein [für das Ausland], Antwortkupon, Rückschein, *(advertising)* Bestellkupon; ~ **envelope** Beikuvert; **business** ~ **items** Geschäftsantwortsendungen; ~**-paid postcard** *(Br.)* Rückantwortkarte; ~**-paid telegram (wire)** Telegramm mit bezahlter Rückantwort, [Rück]antworttelegramm.

replying to your letter in Beantwortung Ihres Briefes.

repolish *(v.) (fig.)* neuen Glanz verleihen.

repopulation Wiederbevölkerung.

report *(account of occurrence)* Nachricht, Meldung, *(corporation)* Geschäfts-, Rechenschaftsbericht einer Aktiengesellschaft, *(customs, Br.)* Zolldeklaration, *(declaration)* Anzeige, *(mil.)* Meldung, *(opinion)* Untersuchungsbericht, Gutachten, *(formal statement)* dienstliche Mitteilung, [Rechenschafts]bericht, Berichterstattung, Referat, *(statement of judicial opinion)* Urteilsspruch, *(of year)* Jahresbericht;
by mere ~ vom bloßen Hörensagen; **through good and evil** ~ in guten und schlechten Tagen;
administrative ~ Verwaltungsbericht; **annual** ~ *(Br.)* Bericht über das Geschäftsjahr, Jahres-, Geschäftsbericht, -abschluß; **auditors'** ~ Bericht der Buchprüfer, Prüfungs-, Revisionsbericht; **brief** ~ kurzer Bericht; **budget** ~ Haushaltsbericht; **captain's** ~ Verklarung, Seeprotest; **cash** ~ Kassenbericht; ~ **certified** *(publishing business)* Auflagenbestätigung; **change** ~ Ab- und Zugangsbericht, Veränderungsmeldung; **classified** ~ *(US)* Geheimbericht; **colo(u)red** ~ gefärbter Bericht; **commercial** ~ Handelsbericht; **committee** ~ Ausschußbericht; **common** ~ allgemein verbreitetes Gerücht; **completed** ~ abgeschlossener Bericht; **comprehensive** ~ zusammenfassender Bericht; **confidential** ~ vertraulicher Bericht; **consolidated** ~ zusammengefaßter Bericht; ~ **covering half a page** halbseitiger Bericht; **credit** ~ Kreditauskunft; **current** ~**s** laufende Berichterstattung; **daily** ~ Tagesbericht; **damage** ~ *(insurance)* Schadensmeldung, -bericht, *(marine insurance)* Havariebericht; **damaging** ~ negative Beurteilung; **detailed** ~ ausführlicher Bericht; **directors'** ~ Geschäfts-, Rechenschaftsbericht; **efficiency** ~ Leistungsbericht, *(official)* Beamtenbeurteilung; **evil** ~ schlechter Ruf; **examiner's** ~ Prüfungsnoten; **exchange** ~ Kursbericht; **expert's** ~ Sachverständigengutachten; **factual** ~ Tatsachenbericht; **false newspaper** ~ Zeitungsente; **favo(u)rable** ~ befriedigende Auskünfte; **final** ~ Schlußbericht; **financial** ~ Jahres-, Geschäftsbericht, Bericht über die Vermögenslage; **general** ~ Gesamtbericht; **good** ~ guter Ruf; **harvest** ~ Erntebericht; **initial** ~ einleitender Bericht; **interim** ~ vorläufiger Bericht, Zwischenbericht; **introductory** ~ Einführungsbericht; **investigating** ~ Untersuchungsbericht; **joint** ~ gemeinsam ver-

faßter Bericht; **law** ~s Gerichtsentscheidungen, Entscheidungssammlung; **majority** ~ Mehrheitsbericht; **market** ~ Markt-, Preisbericht, *(stock exchange)* Börsen-, Kursbericht; **medical** ~ ärztliches Zeugnis; **minority** ~ Minderheitsbericht; **misleading** ~ irreführender Bericht; **monthly** ~ Monatsbericht; **newspaper** ~ Zeitungsmeldung, -nachricht, -bericht; **official** ~ *(parl.)* amtliches Protokoll, amtliche (dienstliche) Meldung, Parlamentsprotokoll; **overall** ~ Gesamtbericht; **over-the-counter** ~s *(US)* Kursblatt für Freiverkehrswerte; **periodical** ~s Berichtsreihe; **preliminary (preparatory)** ~ Vorbericht; ~ **prepared by** Bericht, erstattet von; **printed** ~ gedrucktes Protokoll; **quarterly** ~ Vierteljahresbericht; **receiving** ~ Wareneingangsmeldung; **referee's** ~ Sachverständigengutachten; **reliable** ~s zuverlässige Berichte; **secretary's** ~ *(association)* Bericht des Schriftführers, Gesellschaftsbericht; **service** ~ Eignungsbericht; **sick** ~ Krankenzustandsmeldung; **special** ~ Sonderbericht; **statutory** ~ *(company)* gesetzlich vorgeschriebener Gründungsbericht; **stock-market** ~ *(US)* Kursblatt; **supplementary** ~ Zusatz-, Ergänzungsbericht; **trading** ~ Gewinnausweis; **treasurer's** ~ Kassenbericht, Bericht des Schatzmeisters; **verbatim** ~ mündlich erstatteter Bericht; **weather** ~ Wetterbericht; **whispered** ~ unbestätigte Nachricht;

~ **from abroad** Bericht aus dem Ausland, Auslandsbericht; ~ **of an accident** Unfallbericht; ~ **and accounts** Geschäfts-, Rechenschaftsbericht; ~ **of the auditors** Revisionsbericht; ~ **of public accountants** Wirtschaftsprüferbericht; ~ **on business [conditions]** Konjunkturbericht; ~ **yet to come** ausstehender Bericht; ~ **of legislative committee** Ausschußbericht; ~ **of compliance** Durchführungsmeldung; ~ **of a conference** Konferenzbericht; ~ **of the directors** Geschäfts-, Vorstandsbericht; ~ **from the front** Frontbericht; ~ **of the group** Geschäftsbericht eines Konzerns; ~ **for induction** *(Selective Service Act, US)* Wehrdienstgestellung; ~ **of a journey** Beschreibung einer Reise, Reisebericht; ~ **of loss** Schadensmeldung; ~ **of the market** Markt-, Preisbericht, *(stock exchange)* Börsen-, Kursbericht; ~ **of the meeting** Sitzungsbericht, Protokoll; ~ **of a public meeting** Versammlungsbericht; ~ **of proceedings** Protokoll, Verhandlungsbericht; **fair and accurate** ~s **of judicial proceedings** sachliche und genaue Berichterstattung über Gerichtsverhandlungen; ~s **of proceedings in Parliament** Parlamentsberichte; ~ **of production** Produktionsbericht; ~ **on the situation** Situationsbericht; ~ **on the state of the roads** Straßenzustandsbericht; ~ **of survey** Havariegutachten; ~ **on title** Eigentumsnachweisbericht; **false** ~ **of weight** falsche Gewichtsangabe;

~ *(v.) (customs)* deklarieren, *(denounce)* [Vergehen] anzeigen, Anzeige erstatten, *(civil law)* Gerichtsentscheidungen zur Veröffentlichung vorbereiten, *(present o. s.)* sich anmelden, *(serve as reporter)* als Berichterstatter tätig sein, *(state a fact)* melden, berichten, Bericht erstatten;

~ **o. s.** sich ausweisen; ~ **s. o. for s. th.** j. wegen etw. anzeigen; ~ **[up]on s. th** über etw. referieren (berichten); ~ **an accident to the police** Unfallmeldung erstatten; ~ **back from leave** sich vom Urlaub zurückmelden; ~ **a bill** *(Br.)* über ein Gesetz referieren, über eine Gesetzesvorlage Bericht erstatten; ~ **a bill with amendments** *(Br.)* Gesetzesvorlage dem Plenum mit Abänderungsvorschlägen vorlegen; ~ **to the court** dem Gericht einen Fall als Berichterstatter vortragen; ~ **a death to the authorities** Todesfall anzeigen; ~ **directly to the President** dem Vorstandsvorsitzenden unmittelbar unterstehen; ~ **for duty [at the office]** sich zum Dienstantritt melden; ~ **an employee for misconduct** Angestellten zur disziplinarischen Bestrafung melden; ~ **on a longer depreciable life basis** bei der Handelsbilanz längere Abschreibungsfristen anwenden; ~ **fully** wortgetreu wiedergeben; ~ **to headquarters** sich beim Hauptquartier melden; ~ **a marked improvement in business** Konjunkturaufschwung feststellen; ~ **[o. s.] to the manager** sich beim Vorstand anmelden lassen; ~ **upon a matter** über eine Sache berichten; ~ **a meeting** über eine Versammlung berichten; ~ **to s. o. in his office** sich bei jem. im Büro melden; ~ **one's operations one way for tax purposes** Gesellschaftsbericht nach Steuerbilanzgründen abfassen; ~ **a parliamentary debate** über eine Debatte im Unterhaus berichten; ~ **s. o. to the police** j. [bei der Polizei] anzeigen; ~ **to the police station** *(Br.)* sich bei der Polizei melden, sich der Polizei melden, sich der Polizei stellen; ~ **an offence to the police** der Polizei eine Straftat melden; ~ **to the port authorities** sich beim Hafenamt melden; ~ **o. s. present** sich zur Stelle melden; ~ **pretty much on the same basis as one's tax form** Handelsbilanz der Steuerbilanz weitgehendst angleichen; ~ **progress** über den Stand einer Angelegenheit berichten, *(parl., Br.)* Schluß der Debatte erklären; ~ **progress to s. o.**

jem. über den Stand einer Arbeit berichten; ~ **the receipts and expenditures** Übersicht über die Finanzverhältnisse geben; ~ **one's return** sich zurückmelden; ~ **for service** sich zum Dienstantritt melden; ~ **o. s. sick** sich krank melden; ~ **a speech** über eine Rede in zusammenfassender Form berichten; ~ **for the "Times"** Berichterstatter der "Times" sein; ~ **s. one's unpunctuality** j. wegen Unpünktlichkeit melden;

to appear from a ~ aus einem Bericht hervorgehen; **to be of good** ~ guten Leumund haben (Ruf besitzen); **to bring a** ~ **up to date** Bericht auf den neuesten Stand bringen; **to circulate a** ~ Bericht in Umlauf setzen, Nachricht verbreiten; **to cook a** ~ *(sl.)* Bericht frisieren; **to draft a** ~ protokollieren, Protokoll aufnehmen; **to draw up a** ~ Bericht abfassen; **to draw up a** ~ **on an accident** Unfallschadensmeldung aufnehmen; **to file a** ~ Bericht einreichen; **to frame a** ~ Bericht formulieren; **to give a** ~ Bericht erstatten; **to give currency to a** ~ Bericht in Umlauf setzen; **to have a** ~ **made** zu Protokoll geben; **to include in a** ~ in einem Bericht aufnehmen, berichten; **to issue a** ~ Bericht veröffentlichen; **to make a** ~ Vortrag halten, referieren, Bericht erstatten; **to make a** ~ **for s. o.** Bericht für j. anfertigen; **to make a** ~ **on the state of the roads** Straßenzustandsbericht erstatten; **to mention in a** ~ in einem Bericht niederlegen; **to move to** ~ **progress** *(parl., Br.)* Unterbrechung der Debatte beantragen (verlangen); **to prepare a** ~ Bericht abfassen; **to present a** ~ **on a plan** über den Fortgang eines Unternehmens berichten; **to publish a** ~ Bericht veröffentlichen; **to receive a** ~ **on a firm** Auskünfte über eine Firma erhalten; **to render a** ~ Bericht erstatten; **to request a** ~ Bericht anfordern; **to spread a** ~ Gerücht verbreiten; **to stifle a** ~ Bericht unterdrücken; **to submit a** ~ Bericht einreichen (vorlegen); **to verify a** ~ Bericht prüfen;

~ **has it** es geht das Gerücht;

~ **card** *(school, US)* Zeugnis; ~ **form** Gewinn- und Verlustrechnung in Staffelform; ~ **preparation** Berichterstattung, -erstellung; ~ **stage** *(parl., Br.)* Berichtsstadium; **to reach the** ~ **stage** *(bill, Br.)* reif zur Diskussion im Plenum sein; ~ **writing** Abfassung eines Berichts.

reportable zur Berichterstattung geeignet, *(disease)* anzeige-, meldepflichtig;

~ **accidents in industries** meldepflichtige Betriebsunfälle.

reported berichtet, gemeldet;

it is ~ es verlautet;

to be ~ **absent** als abwesend gemeldet sein;

~ **area** *(weather)* Vorhersagebereich; ~ **profits** ausgewiesene Gewinne.

reportedly wie gerüchtweise verlautet.

reporter Berichterstatter, Reporter, *(law court, US)* Schrift-, Protokollführer, Referent;

Federal ~ *(US)* Entscheidungssammlung von Bundesgerichtshofentscheidungen; **police** ~ *(US)* Gerichtsreporter; **top-notch** ~ Spitzenjournalist.

reporting Berichterstattung, *(giving accounts)* Rechnungslegung, *(of felony)* Anzeigenerstattung;

corporate ~ Berichterstattung der Aktiengesellschaften; **newspaper** ~ Zeitungsberichterstattung; **parliamentary** ~ Bericht über die Parlamentssitzungen, Parlamentsbericht; **prejudicial** ~ voreingenommene Berichterstattung;

~ **of property** Vermögensanmeldung; ~ **form** Berichtsformular, *(insurance)* Risikoformular; ~ **insurance** Inventarversicherung mit der Auflage von Veränderungsmeldungen; ~ **methods** Bilanzierungsmethoden; ~ **pay** garantierter Mindestlohn für Anwesenheit am Arbeitsplatz, Anwesenheitsgeld; ~ **period** Berichtszeitraum; ~ **policy** *(US)* aufgrund periodisch zu erstattender Wertangabe ausgestellte Feuerversicherungspolice; ~ **requirements** Berichtsauflagen; ~ **role** Berichterstatteraufgabe, Berichtserstattungsaufgabe.

repose *(v.)* **confidence in s. o.** jem. Vertrauen entgegenbringen.

reposit *(v.)* aufbewahren, in Verwahrung geben, deponieren, lagern.

reposition Aufbewahrung, Deponierung.

repository Verwahrungsort, *(fig.)* Zentrum, Hochburg, *(morgue)* Leichenhalle, *(reliable person)* Vertrauter, *(shop)* Laden, *(source)* Quelle, Fundgrube, *(vessel)* Behälter, Behältnis, *(warehouse)* Warenlager, Niederlage, Magazin, Speicher;

central ~ Zentralarchiv; **furniture** ~ [Möbel]speicher;

~ **for old bills** Aufbewahrungsort für alte Rechnungen; ~ **of information** Informationsquelle; ~ **for securities** Depotstelle.

repossess *(v.)* [Besitz] wiedererlangen;

~ **o. s. of a place** seinen Platz wieder einnehmen; ~ **goods** *(hire purchase)* auf Teilzahlung gekaufte Waren wieder in Besitz nehmen.

repossession Wiederinbesitznahme, Wiedergewinnung seines Besitzes, *(instalment business)*, Rücknahme einer auf Teilzahlung gekauften Sache.

reprehend *(v.)* kritisieren.

reprehensible verwerflich.

reprehension Verweis, Rüge, Tadel.

represent *(v.)* vertreten, wieder (erneut) vorlegen, *(act as deputy)* [stell]vertreten, repräsentieren, *(serve as symbol)* verkörpern, *(state)* darlegen, -stellen, erklären, *(theater)* aufführen, geben, spielen;
~ **against** Vorstellungen (Einwendungen) erheben; ~ **to an audience** dem Publikum vorführen; ~ **a bill** Wechsel erneut vorlegen; ~ **a constituency** Wahlkreis vertreten; ~ **o. s. as an expert** sich als Sachverständigen ausgeben; ~ **every facet of business** repräsentativen Querschnitt der gesamten Wirtschaft darstellen; **falsely ~ o. s. to be a person holding office under Her Majesty** *(Br.)* Amtsanmaßung begehen; ~ **a firm** Firma vertreten; ~ **graphically** graphisch darstellen; ~ **one's grievances to the Governor** seine Beschwerden dem Gouverneur vortragen; ~ **the interests of the creditors** Gläubigerinteressen wahrnehmen; ~ **one's urgent needs** seine dringenden Bedürfnisse verdeutlichen; ~ **one tenth of the total voting rights** ein Zehntel der Gesamtstimmrechte vertreten; ~ **the best traditions of one's country** die besten Traditionen seines Landes verkörpern.

representation [Stell]vertretung, Repräsentation, *(accounting)* Vorstandserläuterung über die Geschäftspolitik für Revisionsbeamte, *(description)* Darstellung, -legung, Schilderung, Erklärung, *(law of descent)* Erbrecht (Erbfolge) nach Stämmen, *(parl.)* Volksvertretung, *(protest)* Vorhaltungen, Protest, *(symbolization)* Verkörperung, *(theater)* Aufführung, Vorstellung;
not according to ~s nicht den Angaben entsprechend;
from proportional ~ towards single-member constituencies von der Listen- zur Direktwahl;
~s *(contract)* Zusicherungen, Garantieerklärungen, *(dipl.)* Vorhaltungen, *(insurance)* Anzeige von Gefahrenumständen, Risikobeschreibung;
~s **abroad** Auslandsvertretungen; **board-level ~** Vertretung im Vorstand; **diplomatic ~** diplomatische Vertretung; **employees' ~** Angestelltenvertretung; **false ~s** falsche Vorspiegelungen (Angaben); **fraudulent ~s** irreführende Angaben, Vorspiegelung falscher Tatsachen; **functional ~** berufliche Vertretung in Gremien; **graphic ~** graphische Darstellung; **joint ~** Gesamtvertretung; **labo(u)r ~** Arbeiter-, Gewerkschaftsvertretung; **legal ~** gerichtliche Vertretung, Vertretung bei Gericht; **legal and general ~** gerichtliche und außergerichtliche Vertretung; **managerial ~** Vertretung der Betriebsführung; **material ~** wesentliche Angaben, *(life insurance)* versicherungswichtiger Umstand; **mere ~s** rechtlich unbedeutende Erklärungen; **occupational ~** berufsständische Vertretung; **promissory ~** Zusagen bei Vertragsabschluß; **proportional ~** Proportional-, Verhältniswahlrecht; **universal ~** *(Scot.)* Universalsukzession; **written ~** schriftlicher Vorschlag;
~ **of facts** Sachdarstellung; ~ **of intention** Absichtserklärung; ~ **of interests** Interessenvertretung; ~ **of the majority** Mehrheitsvertretung; ~ **in equal numbers** paritätische Vertretung; ~ **of ownership** Vertretung der Anteilseigner; ~ **of persons** Stellvertretung; ~ **of the workers** Betriebsdelegation;
to have ~ at the bargaining table am Verhandlungstisch vertreten sein; **to inherit the right of ~** als Ersatzerbe berufen werden; **to make ~s** Vorhaltungen machen, Vorstellungen erheben bei; **to make diplomatic ~s to a state** auf diplomatischen Wege bei einem Staat vorstellig werden; **to make written ~s** schriftliche Erklärungen abgeben; **to make ~s to the Inspector of Taxes about an excessive assessment** Einspruch beim Finanzamt gegen zu hohe Veranlagung einlegen; **to take out a ~** Bestallungsurkunde erhalten;
~ of the People Act *(Br.)* Wahlgesetz; ~ **allowance** Aufwandsentschädigung.

representational activity Repräsentationstätigkeit.

representative [Stell]vertreter, Bevollmächtigter, Beauftragter, Repräsentant, Agent, *(typical embodiment)* repräsentativer Querschnitt, *(pol.)* Volksvertreter, Parlamentarier, Parlamentsmitglied, Abgeordneter, Repräsentant, *(successor)* [Rechts]nachfolger, *(type)* Musterbeispiel, Typ, Verkörperung;
~ **abroad** Auslandsvertreter; **authorized ~** bevollmächtigter Vertreter, Bevollmächtigter; **chief ~** Generalbevollmächtigter; **commercial ~** Handelsvertreter; **consular ~** konsularischer Vertreter; **diplomatic ~** diplomatischer Vertreter; **district ~** Bezirksvertreter; **employees' ~** Arbeitnehmervertreter; **em-**

ployers' ~ Arbeitgebervertreter; **foreign ~** Auslandsvertreter; **lawful ~** ordnungsgemäß bevollmächtigter (rechtmäßiger) Vertreter; **legal ~** Stellvertreter, gesetzlicher Vertreter, ordnungsmäßig bestellter Vertreter; **manufacturer's ~** Vertreter, Handlungsreisender; **natural (real) ~** Rechtsnachfolger, Erbe, Vermächtnisnehmer; **nominated ~** bestellter Vertreter; **people's ~** Volksvertreter; **personal ~** persönlicher Referent, *(succession)* Testamentsvollstrecker, Erbschafts-, Nachlaßverwalter; **principal ~** Hauptbevollmächtigter; **public ~** Vertreter öffentlichen Interesses; **real ~** Immobiliarerbe; **sales ~** Vertreter; **sole ~** *(firm)* General-, Alleinvertreter; **special ~** Sonderbeauftragter, *(advertising)* Bezirksvertreter, Repräsentant; **top ~** erster Vertreter; **travelling ~** Untervertreterausbilder; **union ~** Gewerkschaftsvertreter;
~ **of a bank** Bankvertreter; **our ~ in the House of Commons** unser Abgeordneter; **body ~ of the people** Volksvertretung; ~ **of the press** Pressevertreter, Vertreter der Presse;
to appoint a ~ Vertreter benennen; **to be a ~ of s. th.** etw. verkörpern; **to send a ~ to a conference** Delegierten zu einer Konferenz entsenden;
~ *(a.)* vertretungsberechtigt, [stell]vertretend, *(typical)* repräsentativ, typisch, charakteristisch;
~ **action** Musterprozeß, *(shareholder)* Aktionärsklage, Klage in Prozeßstandschaft; ~ **capacity** Vertretereigenschaft; **in a ~ character** als Vertreter; ~ **collection** typische Zusammenstellung; ~ **conglomeration** repräsentativer Querschnitt; ~ **democracy** Volksdemokratie, parlamentarische Demokratie; ~ **district** *(US)* Wahlkreis; ~ **example** typisches Beispiel; ~ **faculty** Vorstellungsvermögen; ~ **firm** Durchschnittsfirma, repräsentatives Unternehmen; ~ **government** parlamentarische Regierung; ~ **heir** Ersatzerbe; ~ **men from all classes** Repräsentanten aller Bevölkerungsschichten; ~ **money** *(US)* Papiergeld, Geldsurrogat; ~ **office** Vertreterbüro, Agentur, Repräsentanz; ~ **offices abroad** Vertretungen im Ausland; ~ **sample** Serienmuster; ~ **sampling** repräsentatives Auswahlverfahren; ~ **selection** repräsentative Auswahl, *(statistics)* repräsentativer Querschnitt; ~ **selection of exports** repräsentative Auswahl von Exportgütern; ~ **stock** *(US)* führende Börsenwerte, Standardwerte; ~ **suit** Klage in Prozeßstandschaft.

representational activity Repräsentationstätigkeit.

representativeness repräsentativer Charakter, Repräsentationsfähigkeit, Symbolcharakter.

represented vertreten, verkörpert;
~ **on the board** im Aufsichtsrat vertreten; ~ **by counsel** *(US)* anwaltlich vertreten;
to be legally ~ anwaltlich vertreten sein.

repress|*(v.)* **a revolt (sedition)** Aufruhr (Aufstand) unterdrücken.

repressed inflation zurückgestaute Inflation.

represser Unterdrücker.

repression Unterdrückung, Dämpfer.

repressive measures Ordnungsstrafen.

reprice *(v.)* neu auszeichnen (bewerten).

repricing *(state)* erneute Preisfestsetzung;
~ **clause** Preisänderungsklausel; ~ **provisions** Klauseln für die Festsetzung neuer Preise.

reprieve Strafvollstreckungs-, Urteilsaufschub, Begnadigung;
~ *(v.)* Strafaufschub gewähren, begnadigen;
to petition for ~ Gnadengesuch einreichen.

reprimand Verwarnung, öffentlicher Verweis, Tadel, Rüge;
severe ~ strenger Verweis;
~ *(v.)* Verweis erteilen, zurechtweisen, rügen, verwarnen.

reprint Wiederab-, Wiederholungsdruck, Neuauflage, -druck, neue, unveränderte Ausgabe, *(number of copies)* Auflageziffer, *(US)* Ab-, Nachdruck;
cheap ~ Volksausgabe; **separate ~** Sonderdruck;
~s **of a talk** vervielfältigter Vortrag;
~ *(v.)* neu auflegen, wieder abdrucken;
~ **edition** Neu-, Volksausgabe; ~ **royalty** Abdrucktantieme.

reprinted neu aufgelegt.

reprinter Nachdrucker.

reprinting, to be in the course of kurz vor der Neuauflage stehen.

reprisal|s Vergeltungsmaßnahmen, Repressalien;
general ~ *(law of nations)* generelle Beschlagnahme; **negative ~** *(law of nations)* unterlassene Vertragserfüllung; **positive ~** *(law of nations)* Beschlagnahme und Inhaftierung; **special ~** *(in times of peace)* Repressalienrecht im Einzelfall;
to make ~s Repressalien ergreifen;
~ **action** Vergeltungsaktion.

reprise *(film)* Wiederaufführung, Reprise, *(Br., quit-rent)* Jahres-, Erbzins, jährliche Nebenabgaben;
above ~s Abgaben abgerechnet.

reprivatization Reprivatisierung.

reprivatize *(v.)* reprivatisieren.

repro proofs Probeabzüge.

reproach Tadel, Vorwurf.

reprobate verkommenes Subjekt, Taugenichts;
~ **of his family** schwarzes Schaf der Familie;
~ *(v.)* mißbilligen, verwerfen.

reprobation Einwendungen.

reprocessing plant Wiederaufbereitungsanlage.

reproduceable assets reproduzierbares Realvermögen.

reproduce *(v.)* vervielfältigen, wieder hervorbringen, *(photo)* reproduzieren, ab-, nachbilden;
~ **a former civilization** frühere Kultur bildlich darstellen; ~ **an extract** auszugsweise wiedergeben; ~ **a letter** Brief abdrucken; ~ **a witness** Zeugen erneut vorführen.

reproducer Vervielfältiger, *(machine)* Reproduktionsapparat, *(phonograph)* Lautsprecher, Tonabnehmer.

reproducible reproduzierbar.

reproduction Abdruck, Wiederherstellung, Reproduktion, Vervielfältigung, *(goods)* Nachbau, *(photo)* Abzug;
mechanical ~ Vervielfältigung auf mechanischem Wege; ~ **of real estate** Wiederaufbaukosten; ~ **on a small scale** Verkleinerung;
~ **not permitted** Nachdruck verboten;
~ **cost** Veredlungskosten, *(print.)* Vervielfältigungskosten, *(replacement)* Wiederbeschaffungskosten; ~ **fee** Abdruckvergütung, -honorar; ~ **standard** *(balance sheet)* Wiederbeschaffungswert; ~ **value** Reproduktionswert.

reproductive | debts werbende Schulden; ~ **proof (pull)** reproduktionsfähiger Abzug; ~ **service** werbende [öffentliche] Dienstleistungen.

reproval Tadel, Mißbilligung.

reprove *(v.)* rügen, Rüge erteilen.

reprovision *(v.)* frisch proviantieren.

reptile *(fig.)* Kriecher;
~ **press** gedungene Presse.

republic Republik;
~ **of letters** literarische Welt;
to proclaim a ~ Republik ausrufen.

republican Republikaner;
~ *(a.)* republikanisch;
~ **government** republikanische Regierungsform; ℗ **Party** *(US)* Republikanische Partei; ~ **ticket** republikanisches Parteiprogramm.

republicanism republikanische Regierungsform.

republication Nachdruck, Neuauflage, Wiederveröffentlichung, *(last will)* Widerruf eines Testamentswiderrufes.

republish *(v.)* neuauflegen, wiedererscheinen lassen, nachdrucken, *(will)* Testamentsnachtrag widerrufen.

repudiate *(v.)* nicht anerkennen, zurückweisen;
~ **an agreement** Vertrag nicht anerkennen (als ungültig behandeln); ~ **authority** Autorität nicht anerkennen; ~ **the authorship of a book** Autorschaft eines Buches leugnen; ~ **a child** Kind nicht anerkennen; ~ **s. one's claims** jds. Forderungen in Abrede stellen; ~ **a contract** Vertragserfüllung ablehnen; ~ **a contract of service** von einem Dienstvertrag zurücktreten; ~ **the national debt** *(US)* Staatsschuld nicht anerkennen; ~ **a gift** Geschenk nicht annehmen (zurückweisen); ~ **one's wife** seine Frau verstoßen.

repudiation Zurückweisung, *(of national debt, US)* Nichtanerkennung, Zahlungsverweigerung, Repudiation, *(of performance)* Leistungs-, Erfüllungsverweigerung, *(of wife)* Verstoßung;
~ **of contract** abgelehnte Vertragserfüllung, Nichtanerkennung eines Vertrages, Rücktritt vom Vertrag, Vertragsaufhebung; ~ **of a debt** Zahlungsverweigerung.

repugnant *(clauses in a deed)* im Widerspruch stehend, widersprechend, unvereinbar;
to be ~ im Widerspruch stehen.

repulse Zurückweisung, *(negative reply)* abschlägige Antwort;
to meet with a ~ Ablehnung erfahren, sich eine Abfuhr holen.

repurchasable rückkauffähig.

repurchase Wieder-, Wiederan-, Rückkauf;
with option of ~ mit Rückkaufsrecht;
~ **of units** *(Br.)* Einlösung (Rückkauf) von Investmentanteilen;
~ *(v.)* zurück-, wiederkaufen;
~ **short sales** Leerabgaben einer Position decken;
~ **agreement** Rückkaufsvertrag; ~ **cost** Wiederbeschaffungskosten; ~ **obligation** *(International Monetary Fund)* Rückkaufsverpflichtung; ~ **price** *(investment company)* Rücknahmepreis; ~ **privilege** *(investment fund)* Rückgaberecht; ~ **rate**

Rückkaufkurs; ~ **rate for money-market papers** Rücknahmesätze für Geldmarktpapiere; ~ **value** Rückkaufswert.

repurchaser Rück-, Wiederkäufer.

reputable angesehen, geachtet;
~ **citizen** angesehener Mitbürger; ~ **employment** angesehene Stellung.

reputation Leumund, guter Ruf, Ansehen, Renommee;
of good ~ angesehen, unbescholten;
bad ~ schlechter Ruf, Mißkredit; **business** ~ geschäftliches Ansehen; **clouded** ~ zweifelhafter Ruf, Bescholtenheit; **general** ~ allgemeine Ansicht; **good** ~ guter Leumund; **international (world-wide)** ~ Weltruf; **stainless** ~ untadeliger Ruf;
~ **of a firm** geschäftliches Ansehen einer Firma;
to damage s. one's ~ jds. Ruf schädigen, Rufmord an jem. begehen; **to earn a** ~ sich einen Namen machen; **to enjoy the highest** ~ höchstes Ansehen genießen; **to gain a good** ~ sich einen guten Ruf erwerben; **to have a good** ~ **as a doctor** anerkannt guter Arzt sein; **to have a** ~ **for courage** für seine Zivilcourage allgemein bekannt sein; **to have the** ~ **of being a miser** allgemein als Geizkragen verschrien sein; **to have a** ~ **of one's own** sich einen Namen gemacht haben; **to injure s. one's** ~ jds. Leumund zerstören; **to live up to one's** ~ standesgemäß leben; **to maintain one's** ~ seinen guten Ruf bewahren; **to save one's** ~ seinen guten Ruf retten;
~ **monopoly** Meinungsmonopol.

repute Ruf, Ansehen, Leumund, Renommee;
by common ~ nach allgemeiner Ansicht; **of good** ~ gut renommiert;
ill ~ übler Leumund.
habit and ~ *(law)* als Tatsache angenommen;
to be in bad ~ in schlechtem Ruf stehen; **to be held in high** ~ hohes Ansehen genießen; **to have a good** ~ guten Ruf haben; **to know s. o. by** ~ jem. dem Namen nach kennen.

reputed angeblich, vermutlich;
highly ~ hoch angesehen;
to be ~ **wealthy** als wohlhabend gelten;
~ **father** mutmaßlicher Kindesvater; ~ **manor** *(Br.)* ehemaliges Rittergut; ~ **owner** vermutlicher Eigentümer; ~ **ownership** *(law of bankruptcy)* vermutliches Eigentum, Eigentumsvermutung.

requalify *(v.)* erneut seine Berechtigung nachweisen.

request *(asking for)* Bitte, [An]ersuchen, Aufforderung, *(demand)* Nachfrage, Anforderung, *(petition)* Gesuch, Eingabe, Antrag, Verlangen, *(statement in plaintiff's declaration)* Nachweis der ordnungsgemäßen Zahlungsaufforderung;
by (on) ~ auf Ansuchen (Vorschlag, Wunsch), bei Bedarf; **in** ~ gefragt, begehrt; **in great** ~ stark gefragt; **in little** ~ wenig gefragt; **on (at) one's own** ~ auf eigenen Wunsch; **dying** ~ letzte Bitte; **formal** ~ förmliche Aufforderung; **urgent** ~ dringendes Anliegen; **vain** ~ Fehlbitte; **vacation** ~ *(US)* Urlaubsgesuch; **written** ~ Aufforderungsschreiben;
~ **for cancellation** Stornierungsgesuch; ~ **for check (cheque,** *Br.***)** Scheckanforderung; ~ **for delivery** Abruf bestellter Ware; ~ **for diminution of taxes** Steuerherabsetzungsantrag; ~ **for extension of time** Fristverlängerungsantrag, Stundungsgesuch; ~ **for extradition** Auslieferungsbegehren; ~ **for help** Hilfsgesuch; ~ **for a holiday** *(Br.)* Urlaubsgesuch; ~ **for further information** angebotsbezogene Rückfrage; ~ **for money (payment)** Zahlungsaufforderung, Mahnbrief; ~ **for an opinion** Einholung eines Gutachtens; ~ **for overtime** Überstundenforderung; ~ **for patterns** Musteranfrage; ~ **for quotation** Preisanfrage; ~ **for repurchase** Rückkaufsantrag; ~ **for respite** Stundungsgesuch; ~ **in writing** schriftliche Aufforderung;
~ *(v.)* bitten, ersuchen;
~ **a brief delay** um eine kurze Fristverlängerung einkommen; ~ **an extension of time** um Fristverlängerung bitten; ~ **s. o. to use his influence** jds. Beziehungen für sich einzusetzen suchen; ~ **information** um Auskunft bitten; ~ **a loan** Kredit beantragen; ~ **an opinion** Gutachten einholen; ~ **payment** Zahlung verlangen; ~ **permission** um Erlaubnis bitten;
to be in great (little) ~ sehr (wenig) gefragt (begehrt, gesucht) sein; **to be very much in** ~ **as lecturer** als Vortragender sehr beliebt sein; **to be issued upon** ~ bei Bedarf ausgegeben werden; **to come at s. one's** ~ auf jds. Veranlassung kommen; **to deal with a** ~ Antrag bearbeiten; **to draw up a** ~ Gesuch aufsetzen; **to grant a** ~ Gesuch bewilligen, Bitte erfüllen; **to grant a** ~ **for better terms** einer Anfrage für bessere Bedingungen entsprechen; **to grow out of** ~ aus der Mode kommen; **to handle written** ~**s** schriftliche Anfragen beantworten; **to make a** ~ Gesuch einreichen; **to refuse a** ~ **for credit** Kreditgesuch ablehnen; **to reject a** ~ Gesuch abschlägig bescheiden; **to send by** ~ auf Bestellung zuschicken; **to stop by** ~ *(bus)* bei Bedarf halten;

~s **book** Bechwerdebuch; ~ **form** Bestellschein; ~ **note** *(Br.)* Genehmigungsantrag für die Verlagerung zollpflichtiger Waren; ~ **program(me)** Wunschkonzert; ~ **slip** Bücherbestellzettel; ~ **stop** *(Br.)* Bedarfshaltestelle.

requested sehr begehrt (gesucht);
as ~ wie gewünscht;
~ **authority** ersuchte Behörde.

requesting state um Auslieferung nachsuchender Staat.

require *(v.)* *(demand)* [an]fordern, verlangen, *(need)* benötigen, Bedarf haben an, brauchen;
~ **all one's authority** seine ganze Authorität aufbieten müssen; ~ **medical care** ärztlicher Behandlung bedürfen; ~ **a great deal of s. o.** hohe Anforderungen an j. stellen; ~ **haste** eilbedürftig sein; ~ **extra help** zusätzliche Arbeitskräfte benötigen; ~ **money** Geld kosten; ~ **at least three years** mindestens drei Jahre in Anspruch nehmen.

required erforderlich, vorgeschrieben, *(advertisement)* zu kaufen gesucht, verlangt;
if ~ bei eintretendem Bedarf; **not much** ~ wenig gefragt, geringer Bedarf; **when** ~ nach Bedarf;
to be ~ **at the business** im Geschäft benötigt werden; **to be** ~ **to hand (send) in a curriculum vitae** Lebenslauf vorzulegen haben; **to have the money** ~ über das erforderliche Kapital verfügen; ~ **idle time** unvermeidliche Verlustzeit; ~ **reserves** *(banking, US)* Pflichtrücklagen, Mindestreserven; **in the** ~ **time** in der vorgeschriebenen Frist.

requirement *(demand)* [An]forderung, *(direction)* Vorschrift, *(need)* Bedarf, Erfordernis, Bedürfnis, *(qualification)* erforderliche Eigenschaft;
for immediate ~s für sofortigen Bedarf; **meeting the** ~s den Anforderungen (Vorschriften) entsprechend;
additional ~ Mehrbedarf, nachträglicher Bedarf; **anticipated** ~s voraussichtlicher Bedarf; **counter** ~s [Zahlungs]anforderungen im Schalterverkehr; **domestic** ~s Inlandsbedarf; **educational** ~s Bildungsvoraussetzungen, -vorschriften; **export** ~s Exportbedarf; **financial (monetary)** ~s Finanzbedarf; **formal** ~s Formerfordernisse; **government-imposed** ~s staatliche Forderungen; **home** ~s Inlandsbedarf; **household** ~s Haushaltsbedarf; **labo(u)r** ~s Arbeitskräftebedarf; **legal** ~s gesetzliche Voraussetzungen, *(banking, US)* gesetzlich vorgeschriebenes Deckungsverhältnis; **licensing** ~s gewerbepolizeiliche Voraussetzungen; **listing** ~s *(US)* Voraussetzungen für die Börseneinführung; **local** ~s Bedarf am Platze; **manufacturing** ~s betriebstechnische Anforderungen; **monthly** ~s Ultimobedürfnisse; **necessary** ~s notwendiger Bedarf; **nonrecurrent** ~s außerordentlicher Bedarf; **number-one** ~ allererste Voraussetzung; **over-the-counter** ~s Anforderungen im Schalterverkehr; **own** ~ Eigenbedarf; **peacetime** ~s Friedensbedarf; **personal** ~ Eigenbedarf, persönlicher Bedarf; **public** ~s öffentlicher Bedarf; **recurrent** ~s ordentlicher Bedarf; **regular** ~ Normalausstattung; **similar credit** ~s Voraussetzung der Gegenseitigkeit; **statutory** ~s Satzungserfordernisse, gesetzlich vorgeschriebene Voraussetzungen; **subsidy** ~ Zuschußbedarf; **total** ~ Gesamtbedarf; **traffic** ~s Verkehrsbedürfnisse; **variable** ~s elastische Bedürfnisse; **over-the-window** ~s Anforderungen im Schalterverkehr; **yearly** ~ Jahresbedarf;
~s **for admission** Zulassungsvoraussetzungen; ~ **for college entrance** Aufnahmebedingungen einer Hochschule; ~ **of form** Formerfordernis; ~s **in goods** Warenbedarf; ~s **of primary importance** lebenswichtiger Bedarf; ~s **of the law** Gesetzesvorschriften; ~s **of raw material(s)** Rohstoffbedarf; ~s **of registration** Eintragungserfordernisse, -voraussetzungen; ~s **for success** Erfolgsvoraussetzungen; ~s **of traffic** Verkehrsbedürfnisse; **constitutional** ~ **of uniformity** von der Verfassung geforderter Gleichheitssatz;
to answer the ~s den Anforderungen entsprechen; **to be exempt from the** ~s **of registration** nicht eintragungspflichtig sein; **to be modest in one's** ~s bescheidene Ansprüche stellen; **to comply with the** ~s den Anforderungen entsprechen, Bedarf decken; **to fall short of the** ~s hinter den Bedarf zurückfallen; **to fill every** ~ allen Anforderungen entsprechen; **to fulfil the** ~s **of the law** den gesetzlichen Erfordernissen genügen; **to meet the** ~s den Anforderungen (Vorschriften) entsprechen; **to meet s. one's** ~s jds. Bedarf decken; **to meet the** ~s **at a competitive price** preisgünstig liegen; **to meet the** ~s **for entrance** Aufnahmebedingungen erfüllen; **to meet the** ~s **of raw material** Rohstoffbedarf decken; **to produce only for its own** ~s um den eigenen Bedarf zu decken; **to record the** ~s Bedarf schriftlich angeben; **to reduce the** ~s **for capital** Investitionsmittelbedarf einschränken; **to set a** ~ Forderung aufstellen;
~ **contract** Bedarfsdeckungsvertrag.

requisite Gebrauchsgegenstand, Bedarfsartikel, -gegenstand, *(condition)* [notwendige] Bedingung, Erfordernis, Voraussetzung;
office ~s Büroartikel; **principal (prime)** ~s Haupt, Grunderfordernisse; **travel(l)ing** ~s Reiseartikel, -utensilien, -bedarf;
~ *(a.)* erforderlich, notwendig;
~ **capital** notwendiges Betriebskapital; **to lack the** ~ **capital** unzureichende Deckungskapitaldecke haben; ~ **cover** Deckungserfordernis; ~ **form** vorgeschriebene Form; ~ **majority** erforderliche Mehrheit; **to take the** ~ **measures** erforderliche Maßnahmen ergreifen.

requisition [gerichtliches] Ersuchen, Auf-, Anforderung, *(formal application)* Anforderung[sschein], *(demand)* Nachfrage, Bedarf, *(international law, US)* Requisition, Auslieferungsersuchen, *(mil.)* Beschlagnahme, Beitreibung, Erfassung, Inanspruchnahme von Sachleistungen, *(notary, Scot.)* Zahlungsaufforderung;
upon ~ auf Verlangen;
~s Anforderungen, Materialanforderungen;
material ~ Materialanforderung; **personnel** ~ Personalanforderung; **purchase** ~ Ermächtigung der Einkaufsabteilung; **stores** ~ Lageranforderung;
~ **of a house** Beschlagnahme eines Hauses; ~ **of material** Materialanforderungen; ~ **for a meeting** *(Br.)* Sitzungseinladung; ~ **for money** Geldanforderung; **notary's** ~ **of payment** notarielle Zahlungsaufforderung; ~ **for the production of accounts** Aufforderung zur Einreichung von Rechnungen; ~ **for a search** Antrag auf Einsichtnahme; ~ **of shareholders** Antragstellung auf Einberufung einer Hauptversammlung; ~ **for supplies** Lieferungsanforderung; ~s **on title** anwaltlicher Fragebogen anstelle einer Grundbucheinsicht; ~s **for a university degree** Voraussetzungen für die Erlangung der Doktorwürde;
~ *(v.)* Sachleistungen in Anspruch nehmen, beschlagnahmen, erfassen, requirieren, beitreiben;
~ **food for the troops** Lebensmittel für die Armee requirieren; ~ **s. one's services** jds. Dienste in Anspruch nehmen; ~ **a town for motor lorries** *(mil.)* einer Stadt die Gestellung von Lastwagen auferlegen;
to be in constant ~ *(bus)* in fortlaufendem Einsatz sein; **to lay under** ~ im Wege der Requisition erheben; **to make** ~s **upon a community** einer Gemeinde Requisitionen auferlegen; **to make a** ~ **on the citizens for stores** Bürgerschaft zur Bevorratung veranlassen; **to put in** ~ beschlagnahmen, requirieren; **to put an orator in** ~ **in a political campaign** Redner in einem Wahlfeldzug einsetzen;
~ **blank** Anforderungsformular; ~ **form** *(Br.)* Bestell-, Auftragszettel; ~ **number** Bestellnummer.

requisitioned unter Beschlagnahme.
~ **meeting** von den Aktionären beantragte Hauptversammlung.

requisitioning Inanspruchnahme von Sachleistungen, Requisition, Requirierung;
~ **authority** Erfassungsstelle; ~ **order** Beschlagnahmeverfügung.

requisitionist *(company meeting)* Antragsteller.

requital Vergütung, Belohnung;
by way of ~ zur Entschädigung;
to get food and lodging in ~ **of one's services** au pair leben.

rerecord *(v.)* *(motion picture)* überspielen.

reregister *(v.)* wieder eintragen.

reregistration Wiedereintragung.

reroll *(v.)* *(film)* umspulen.

reroute *(v.)* umleiten, *(air ticket)* umschreiben.

rerouting Umleitung, *(air ticket)* Umschreibung.

rerun Wiederholung, *(motion picture)* Wiederauf-, Wiedervorführung, *(television)* Wiederholungssendung;
~ **of an election** wiederholte Wahl.

res|derelicta herrenlose Sache; ~ **judicata** *(lat.)* rechtskräftig entschiedene Sache.

resalable wiederverkäuflich.

resale *(by default of payment)* Selbsthilfeverkauf, *(sale at second-hand)* Verkauf aus zweiter Hand, *(second sale)* Weiter-, Wiederverkauf, Weiterveräußerung;
~ **agreement** Wiederverkaufsvereinbarung; ~ **price** Wiederverkauf-, Einzelhandels-, Ladenverkaufs-, Kleinhandelspreis; **[maintained] minimum** ~ **price** gebundener Mindestpreis, Mindestwiederverkaufspreis; **to maintain fixed** ~ **prices** Preisbindung für Markenartikel verlangen; **to sell at a price below the** ~ **price** unter dem Wiederverkaufspreis verkaufen; ~ **Prices Act** *(Br.)* Preisbindungsgesetz; ~ **price agreement** Preisbindungsabkommen, -vereinbarung; ~ **price condition** Preisbindung

[für Markenartikel]; ~ **price fixing (maintenance,** *Canada, Br.*) Preisbindung der zweiten Hand, vertikale Preisbindung, Einhaltung von Wiederverkaufspreisen; ~ **price maintenance agreement** Preisbindungsabkommen; ~ **maintaining** Einhaltung von Wiederverkaufspreisen; ~ **profit** Wiederverkaufsgewinn; ~ **value** Wiederverkaufswert; **to have a better** ~ **value** sich gut weiterverkaufen lassen.

rescale *(advertising)* Formatänderung.

reschedule *(v.)* | **old loans into new ones** alte Anleihen in neue umwandeln; ~ **production** neue Produktionseinteilung vornehmen; ~ **short-term debts** kurzfristige Verbindlichkeiten umschulden.

rescind *(v.) (repeal)* abschaffen, *(make void)* aufheben, annullieren, umstoßen, für ungültig erklären, rückgängig machen; ~ **a bargain** von einem Geschäft zurücktreten; ~ **a contract** von einem Vertrag zurücktreten, Vertrag annullieren; ~ **a contract by mutual consent** Vertrag im gegenseitigen Einvernehmen aufheben; ~ **a decree** Beschluß aufheben; ~ **a guaranty** Garantieversprechen für ungültig erklären; ~ **a judgment** Urteil aufheben (kassieren); ~ **a law** Gesetz aufheben, Gesetz außer Kraft setzen; ~ **a lease on the grounds of mistake** Mietverhältnis wegen Irrtums aufheben; ~ **a resolution** Beschluß (Resolution) ablehnen; ~ **a sale** Kauf rückgängig machen, wandeln.

rescindable aufhebbar, anfechtbar.

rescinder Anfechtungsberechtigter.

rescinding a contract Vertragsannullierung.

rescission Rückgängigmachung, Annullierung, Aufhebung, Anfechtung, Rücktritt, Nichtigkeits-, Ungültigkeitserklärung; **qualified** ~ Vertragsaufhebung unter Beibehaltung von Schadenersatzansprüchen; ~ **for breach of warranty** *(US)* Wandlung wegen Gewährleistungsbruchs; ~ **of a contract** Rücktritt vom Vertrag, Vertragsrücktritt, -anfechtung, -annullierung, -aufhebung; ~ **of duress** Anfechtung wegen Nötigung; ~ **for fraud** Anfechtung wegen Betrugs (arglistiger Täuschung); ~ **for innocent misrepresentation** Anfechtung wegen unabsichtlicher Falschbenennung; ~ **for mistake** Irrtumsanfechtung; - **by one party** einseitiger Rücktritt eines Vertragsteiles; ~ **of a receiving order** Aufhebung einer Konkursanordnung; ~ **of a resolution** Ablehnung einer Resolution, Beschlußaufhebung; ~ **of a sale** Rückgängigmachung eines Kaufes; ~ **of terms** Annullierung und Festlegung neuer Vertragsbestimmungen; **to be subject to** ~ der Anfechtung unterliegen; **to bring an action for** ~ Wandlungsklage erheben; **to claim for** ~ **of a contract** auf Anfechtung eines Vertrages klagen; ~ **bonds** Schuldverschreibungen zur Ablösung ungültig ausgegebener Garantien.

rescissory action *(Scot.)* Wandlungsklage.

rescript Erlaß einer Verordnung, *(US, appellate court)* Entscheidungsgründe, *(law court, US)* prozeßleitende Verfügung.

rescue Rettung, Hilfe, *(law)* Pfandbruch, Vollstreckungsvereitelung, *(international law)* gewaltsame Befreiung, Prisenrückeroberung, *(salvage)* Bergung, Rettungswerk, -wesen; ~ **of goods restrained** Pfand-, Verstrickungsbruch, Vollstreckungsvereitelung; ~ *(v.) (international law)* Prisenschiff aufbringen, *(liberate)* befreien, *(mil.)* entsetzen, *(recover)* retten; ~ **s. o. from arrest** j. gewaltsam aus der Haft befreien; ~ **s. o. from captivity** j. aus der Gefangenschaft befreien; ~ **a bankrupt company** Hilfsmaßnahmen für einen Firmenbankrott einleiten; ~ **the crew of a sinking ship** Mannschaft eines untergehenden Schiffs bergen; ~ **a drunkard** Trinker entwöhnen; ~ **goods restrained** Pfandbruch (Vollstreckungsvereitelung) begehen; ~ **the market** Markt stützen, Stützungsaktionen unternehmen; ~ **s. one's name from oblivion** jds. Namen der Vergessenheit entreißen; ~ **s. o. from poverty** j. vor der Armut bewahren; **to back a** ~ einer Sanierungsaktion Rückenwind geben; **to come to the** ~ zu Hilfe kommen; **to gallop to s. one's** ~ zu jds. Rettung herbeieilen; **to make a** ~ Gefangenen befreien; ~ **attempt** Rettungsversuch; ~ **bid** Bergungsversuch; ~ **case** Schadenersatzprozeß aufgrund geleisteter Nothilfe; ~ **doctrine** Grundsatz der Schadenshaftung im Fall von Rettungsaktionen; ~ **home** Fürsorgeheim; ~ **mission** Rettungsmission; ~ **operation** Rettungs-, Hilfsaktion, Rettungsunternehmen; ~ **package** umfassendes (gekoppeltes) Sanierungsangebot; ~ **party (squad)** Bergungsmannschaft, Hilfstrupp; ~ **plan** Rettungsplan; **last-ditch** ~ **plan** Rettungsplan fünf Minuten vor zwölf; ~ **plane** Rettungsflugzeug; ~ **service** Rettungs-, Nothilfedienst; ~ **ship** Rettungsschiff; ~ **team** Rettungsmannschaft, *(mountaineering)* Bergwacht; ~ **vehicle** Rettungsfahrzeug, -boot; ~ **work** Rettungsarbeiten.

rescuer Retter, Befreier.

research genaue Untersuchung, Nachforschung, *(advertising)* Werbevorbereitung, Markt- und Meinungsforschung, Erhebung, Analyse, *(scientific)* Forschung[sarbeit]; **applied** ~ angewandte Forschung; **audience** ~ *(Br.)* Höreranalyse; **basic** ~ Grundlagenforschung; **business** ~ betriebswissenschaftliche Forschung, Konjunkturforschung; **defense** *(US)* **(defence,** *Br.*) ~ Verteidigungsforschung; **defence-funded** ~ mit Verteidigungsaufträgen finanzierte Forschung; **desk** ~ Sekundärerhebung; **external** ~ außerbetriebliche Forschung; **field** ~ Primärerhebung; **industrial** ~ betriebswissenschaftliche Untersuchung, Konjunkturforschung; **listenership** ~ *(US)* Höreranalyse; **market** ~ Markt-, Absatzforschung, Marktanalyse, -untersuchung; **motivational** ~ Motivforschung; **operational** *(Br.)* **(operations,** *US)* ~ Unternehmensforschung; **opinion** ~ Meinungsbefragung; **original** ~ eigene Forschungstätigkeit; **painstaking scientific** ~ genaue wissenschaftliche Untersuchungen; **product** ~ Marktforschung für ein neues Erzeugnis; **pure** ~ zweckfreie Forschung; **readers' interest** ~ Leserumfrage; **scientific** ~ wissenschaftliche Untersuchung; **subscriber** ~ Abonnentenanalyse; ~ *(v.)* Untersuchungen anstellen, forschen, Forschertätigkeit ausüben, *(advertising)* Meinungsforschung betreiben; **to carry out** ~ **into the causes of a disease** Forschungen nach den Ursachen einer Krankheit betreiben; **to make ~es** Nachforschungen anstellen; ~ **activity** Forschungstätigkeit; ~ **analyst** *(stockbroker)* Effektenberater; ~ **appraisal** Bewertung der Forschungstätigkeit; ~ **arm** *(US)* Forschungsabteilung; ~ **assignment** Forschungsauftrag, -aufgabe; ~ **assistance** Förderung der Forschung; ~ **association** Forschungsgemeinschaft, -gesellschaft; ~ **base** Forschungsobjekt; ~ **board** *(Br.)* Forschungsamt; ~ **budget** Forschungsetat; ~ **center (centre,** *Br.*) Forschungszentrum, -stelle; ~ **consultant** als Forscher tätiger Berater; - **contract** Forschungsauftrag; **National** ⌐ **Council** *(US)* Forschungsrat; ~ **department** Versuchs-, Forschungsabteilung; ~ **design** Anlage einer Untersuchung; ~ **director** *(advertising)* Leiter der Marktforschung; ~ **economist** Wirtschaftsforscher; ~ **engineer** Forschungsingenieur; ~ **establishment** Forschungsinstitut, -stätte; ~ **expenditure** Forschungsaufwand, -ausgaben; ~ **experience** Erfahrungen auf dem Forschungsgebiet; ~ **facilities** Forschungsanlagen; ~ **fellow** Assistent in einem Forschungsinstitut, Forschungsstipendiat; ~ **findings** Forschungsergebnisse; ~ **firm** Meinungsforschungsinstitut; ~ **funds** Mittel für die Forschung; ~ **grant** Forschungsbeihilfe; ~ **group** Forschungsmannschaft, -gruppe; ~ **institute (institution)** Forschungsinstitut; ⌐ **Institute for Consumers' Affairs** Forschungsinstitut für Verbraucherfragen; ~ **laboratory** Forschungslaboratorium; ~ **library** wissenschaftliche Bibliothek; ~ **man** Meinungsbefrager; ~ **material** Forschungsergebnisse, *(marketing)* Informationsmaterial; ~ **minister** Forschungsminister; ~ **organization** Forschungseinrichtung, -organisation; **economic** ~ **organization** Konjunkturinstitut; ~ **plant** Versuchsanlage, -anstalt; ~ **professor** als freier Forscher tätiger Professor; **scientific** ~ **program(me)** Forschungsprogramm; ~ **project** Forschungsprojekt, -vorhaben, -unternehmen; ~ **reactor** Forschungsreaktor; ~ **report** Forschungs-, Untersuchungsbericht; ~ **satellite** Forschungssatellit; ~ **scholarship** Forschungsstipendium; ~ **scientist** Forschungswissenschaftler; ~ **secretariat** Forschungsstelle; ~ **service** *(advertising)* Ausschnittsdienst; ~ **studentship** *(Br.)* Forschungsstipendium; ~ **study** Forschungstätigkeit; ~ **unit** Forschungseinheit, -stelle; ~ **work** Forschungsarbeit, -tätigkeit; **authoritative** ~ **and reference work** maßgebendes Nachschlagewerk; ~ **work on parallel lines** Forschungsarbeit auf dem gleichen Gebiet; **to be engaged in** ~ **work** in einem Forschungsinstitut tätig sein, Forschungsauftrag haben; ~ **worker** Forscher.

researcher Forscher.

reseat *(v.)* wieder einsetzen.

reseize *(v.)* wieder in Besitz nehmen.

resell *(v.)* weiter-, wiederverkaufen.

reseller Wiederverkäufer.

resend *(v.)* zurücksenden.

resentment Verärgerung, Resentiment, *(pol.)* Verstimmung.

reservable *(US)* bestellbar.

reservation *(clause)* Einschränkung, Vorbehalt[sklausel], *(land reserved, US)* Reservat, *(law)* Vorbehalt[srecht], *(reserve)* Rückstellung, *(reserved privilege)* Reservatrecht, *(reserved room)* reserviertes Zimmer, *(of seats)* Vorbestellung, Buchung, Platzkarte, reservierter (belegter) Platz, Reservierung, *(telephone exchange)* reservierte Sprechzeit:

with this ~ mit dieser Einschränkung; **with** ~ **as to** vorbehaltlich; **with the usual** ~s unter üblichem Vorbehalt; **without** ~ ohne Vorbehalt, vorbehaltlos;

confirmed ~ feste Reservierung; **continuing-plane** ~ Anschlußbuchung; **express** ~ ausdrückliche Einschränkung, ausdrücklicher Vorbehalt; **firm** ~ feste Buchung; **flight** ~ Flugplatzreservierung; **Indian** ~s *(US)* Indianerreservate; **mental** ~ geheimer Vorbehalt, Mentalreservation; **provisional** ~s vorsorgliche Buchungen; **return-plane** ~ für den Rückflug vorgenommene Buchung, Rückflugbuchung; **room** ~ Zimmerreservierung; **seat** ~ Platzbelegung, -reservierung;

~ **of berths** Kabinenreservierung; ~ **of ownership** Eigentumsvorbehalt; ~ **of a right** Rechtsvorbehalt; ~ **of all rights** alle Rechte vorbehalten; ~ **of the right to rescind** Rücktrittsvorbehalt; ~ **of right of way** Wegerechtsvorbehalt; ~ **of seats** Platzbestellung, -reservierung; ~ **of space** Platzreservierung; ~ **of earned surplus** Gewinnrückstellung; ~ **of title** Eigentumsvorbehalt;

to accept s. th. without ~ etw. vorbehaltlos (bedingungslos) annehmen; **to agree to a plan with certain** ~s einem Plan mit bestimmten Einschränkungen zustimmen; **to agree without the slightest** ~ vorbehaltlos zustimmen; **to cancel a** ~ [Platz]reservierung rückgängig machen, abbestellen; **to enter a** ~ **in respect of a contract** Vertragsvorbehalt aufnehmen lassen; **to make** ~s Vorbehalte anmelden (vormerken); **to make** ~s **with respect to s. th.** Bedingungen an etw. knüpfen; **to make all the necessary** ~s **for a journey** alle Buchungen für eine Reise erledigen; **to make one's seat** ~ Platzkarte bestellen; **to make one's** ~ **direct with the airline** unmittelbar bei der Fluggesellschaft buchen; **to telegraph to a hotel for a** ~ Hotelzimmer telegrafisch vorbestellen;

~ **agent** Buchungsagent; ~ **clause** Vorbehaltsklausel; ~ **fee** Platzvorbestellungsgebühr, Vormerk-, Reservierungsgebühr; ~ **form** Platzkartenformular; **computer** ~ **network** computergesteuertes Buchungssystem; ~ **office** Buchungsstelle; ~ **officer** Reservierungsstelle; ~ **service** Buchungsservice; ~ **system** Reservierungs-, Buchungssystem.

reserve *(balance sheet)* Reserve, Rücklage, *(US)* Rückstellung, *(currency)* Währungsreserve, *(land reserved, US)* Schutzgebiet, Reservat[ion], *(price)* Vorbehaltspreis, *(reservation)* Einschränkung, Vorbehalt, Ausnahme, Reservation, *(supply)* Vorrat, Reserve;

flush with ~s mit Reserven angereichert; **in** ~ vorrätig, in Reserve; **under** ~ vorbehaltlich; **under the usual** ~ unter üblichem Vorbehalt; **without** ~ rückhaltlos, ohne Ausnahme (Vorbehalt), unbedingt, *(auction sale)* freier Verkauf [ohne Mitbieten des Eigentümers];

~s Reserven, Rücklagen, *(central banking)* Zentralbankreserven, *(mil.)* Reserve[truppen];

accumulated ~s angesammelte Reserven; **actual** ~ Istreserve, *(insurance)* Deckungskapital, Prämienreserve; **adequate** ~ aus-, hinreichende Reserven; **adjusted** ~ *(US)* besondere Rückstellung der Bundes-Reserve-Banken; **amortization** ~ Rücklagen (Rückstellung) zur Abschreibung langfristiger Anlagegüter; **available** ~ freie (frei verfügbare) Reserven; **bad-debts** ~ *(US)* Rücklagen für zweifelhafte Forderungen; **bank** ~ *(US)* Mindestreserve; **Bank of England** ~ Reserven der Bank von England, Zentralbankreserven; **bonus** ~ Dividendenrücklagen; **capital** ~ nicht steuerpflichtiger Kapitalgewinn; **cash** ~ Barbestand; **operating cash** ~ Betriebsmittelrücklage; **catastrophe** ~ *(insurance)* Rücklagen für Katastrophenfälle, Katastrophenrücklage; **claim** ~ *(insurance company)* Rückstellung für Schadensfestsetzungskosten, *(US)* Rückstellungen für strittige Forderungen; **company's** ~ nicht verteilter Gewinn, Betriebsrücklage; **contingency** ~ Sicherheitsrücklage, Eventualreserve, Eventualverbindlichkeiten, Delkredererückstellung, Rücklage für Notfälle; **contingent** ~ Rückstellung für unvorhergesehene Ausgaben; **declared** ~ ausgewiesene (offene) Rücklagen; **deficiency** ~ Rückstellung für Mindereinnahmen, Rückstellungen für Produktionsausfall; **debt reduction (redemption)** ~ Schuldentilgungsrücklage; **doubtful debt** ~ *(Br.)* Rückstellung für Dubiose; **deferred repairs** ~ Rückstellung für aufgeschobene Reparaturen; **depletion** ~ Rückstellung für erschöpfte Bodenschätze; **depreciation** ~ Rückstellung für Abschreibungen, Wertberichtigung für Abnutzung, Entwertungsrücklage; **disclosed** ~ offene Rücklagen; **discretionary** ~ freie Rücklagen; **employee compensation** ~ Rücklage für Arbeitnehmerabfindungen; **equalization** ~ Ausgleichsrücklage; **evaluation** ~s Rückstellungen und Wertberichtigungen; **excess** ~ *(banking, US)* außerordentliche Reserven, freie Rücklagen; **foreign-exchange** ~ Devisenpolster; **extraordinary** ~ außerordentliche

Rücklage, Sonderrückstellung; **fractional** ~s *(US)* vorgeschriebene Mindestreserven; **free** ~s freie Rücklagen, Überflußreserven, *(banking, US)* [etwa] freie Guthaben bei der Landeszentralbank; **funded** ~ in langfristig verzinslichen Wertpapieren angelegte Rücklagen; **general** ~ frei verfügbare Rücklage, Betriebsrücklage; **general-purpose contingency** ~ allgemeine Rücklage; **gold** ~ Goldreserve; **hidden** ~ stille Reserve (Rücklage); **initial** ~ *(life insurance)* Anfangsreserve [für das nächste Jahr]; **inner** ~ stille (innere) Reserve; **inventory** ~ Wertberichtigung des Vorratsvermögens; **labo(u)r** ~ Arbeitskräftereservoir; **latent** ~ stille Reserven; **legal** ~ *(banking, US)* gesetzlich vorgeschriebene Reserve (Rücklagen), Mindestreserve; **liability** ~ Rückstellung für eingegangene Verbindlichkeiten (Eventualverbindlichkeiten), Schadensreserve; **life-insurance** ~ Reservefonds (Rücklagen) einer Lebensversicherungsanstalt; **liquid** ~ sofort realisierbare Rücklage; **loss** ~s Rückstellungen für Verluste, *(insurance)* Rücklage für laufende Risiken, Schadensreserve; **maintenance** ~ Rückstellung für Unterhaltungskosten; ~s **maintained** *(banking)* Ist-, Mindestreserve; **mathematical** ~ *(insurance)* Deckungsrücklage, -kapital; **mental** ~ geheimer Vorbehalt, Mentalreservation; **minimum** ~ *(bank)* Mindestreserven; **minimum cash** ~ Pflicht-, Mindestreserve; **monetary** ~ Liquiditätsüberhang; **naked** ~ *(US)* besondere Rückstellung der Bundes-Reserve-Banken; **net** ~ Nettoreserve; **nonearning** ~ stillgelegte Gelder; **nonstatutory capital** ~s gesetzlich nicht erforderliches Reservekapital, freie Rücklagen; **official** ~ offene Reserven, *(balance of payments)* Währungsreserven; **oil** ~s Erdölreserven; **open** ~s offene Rücklagen; **operating** ~ Rückstellung für Betriebskostenerhöhungen, Betriebsmittelrücklage; **operating-cash** ~ Rücklagen für das Betriebskapital; **passive** ~ stille Reserven; **pension** ~ Rückstellung für Ruhegeldverpflichtungen; **industrial plant** ~ betriebliche Reservekapazität; **primary** ~ *(banking)* Kassenreserve, *(International Monetary Fund)* Primärreserve; **provident** ~ Sonderrückstellung; **published** ~s offene Rücklagen; **qualifying** ~ Wertberichtigung; **ready** ~ *(mil., US)* Reserve; **real** ~ *(banking)* Kassenreserve, -bestand; **redemption** ~ Tilgungsrücklage; **replacement** ~ Rückstellung für Ersatzbeschaffungen; **required** ~s Pflichtrücklagen, *(Federal Reserve System, US)* Mindestreserven, Mindestreservesoll; **return-package** ~ Rückstellung für zurückkommende Verpackung; **revaluation** ~ Rückstellung für Neubewertungen; **revenue** ~ *(balance sheet, Br.)* Ertragsrücklage, steuerpflichtiger Kapitalgewinn; ~ **running short** abnehmende Reserven; **secondary** ~ *(International Monetary Fund)* Sekundärreserve; **secret** ~ stille Reserven (Rücklagen); ~ **set up** eingesetzte Reserve; **sinking-fund** ~ Rückstellungen zur Schuldentilgung; **special** ~ Sonderposten mit Rücklageanteil, Sonderrückstellung, -lage; **special contingency** ~ besondere Rücklage; **special revaluation** ~ Neubewertungsrücklage; **specific** ~s *(insurance)* Sonderrückstellungen; **statutory** ~ gesetzlich vorgeschriebene Reserve, gesetzliche Rücklage, satzungsgemäße Rücklage, Mindestreserve; **sterile** ~s unnütze Reserven; **surplus** ~ *(US)* außerordentliche Reserve (Rücklage), zweckgebundene Rücklage, Gewinnrücklage, *(banking)* über die gesetzlichen Verpflichtungen hinausgehende Reserve, Liquiditätsüberhang; **surplus contingency** ~ Rückstellung für mögliche Verluste am Reingewinn; **taxation** ~ Steuerrückstellung; **technical** ~s *(insurance)* Rückstellungen für drohende Verluste; **terminal** ~ *(insurance)* Prämienreserve; **true** ~ *(US)* außerordentliche Rücklage; **uncommitted** ~s freie Rücklagen; **undisclosed** ~ stille Reserven (Rücklagen); **unearned-premium** ~ *(life insurance)* Prämienreserve, Deckungskapital, -rücklage, -stock, -überhang; **valuation** ~ Wertberichtigung, Bewertungsrücklage; **visible** ~ offene Reserve (Rücklagen); **voluntary** ~ freie Rücklagen; **warranty** ~ Rücklage für Gewährleistungsansprüche; **wild-life** ~ Naturschutzgebiet; **world monetary** ~s Weltwährungsreserven;

~ **for accidents** Unfallrückstellung; **general** ~s **for accounts receivable** Einstellung in die Pauschalwertberichtigung von Forderungen; ~ **for additions, betterments and improvements** Erneuerungsrücklage; ~ **for amortization** Rückstellung für Anlageerneuerung; ~ **provided by the articles** satzungsmäßig vorgesehene Rücklage; ~ **to balance the budget** Ausgleichsrücklage; ~ **of bills** *(Br.)* Gesetzgebungsvorbehalt; ~ **of capital** steuerfreier Kapitalgewinn; ~s **for catastrophes** *(insurance)* Katastrophenreserve; ~ **for outstanding claims** *(insurance company)* Schadensreserve; ~ **for claims in litigation** Rückstellung für schwebende Prozesse; ~ **for claims pending** Rückstellung für schwebende Versicherungsfälle; **workable** ~s **of coal** abbauwürdige Kohlenlager; ~ **for contingencies** Rückstellung für

unvorhergesehene Ausgaben (Eventualverbindlichkeiten, Risiken), Delkredererückstellung; ~ **for contingent liabilities** Rückstellung für zweifelhafte Schulden (Eventualverbindlichkeiten); ~ **required by contract** vertraglich vorgeschriebene Rücklagen, Reserve-, Rücklagensoll; ~ **for currency equalization** Rückstellung für Währungsausgleich; ~ **for bad debts** (US) Rückstellung (Wertberichtigung) für Dubiose (zweifelhafte Forderungen), Delkredere; ~ **for debt redemption** Rückstellung für Schuldentilgung; ~ **for future decline in inventories** Rückstellung für Wertminderung der Vorräte; ~ **for depletion** Wertberichtigungsposten auf Anlagen, Rückstellung für Substanzverzehr; ~ **for depreciation** Rückstellung für Abnutzung, Entwertungs-, Abschreibungsrücklage, Wertberichtigung auf das Anlagevermögen; ~ **depreciation of real estate owned** Rückstellung für Grundstücksentwertungen; ~ **for discounts** Rückstellung für Skontonachlässe; ~ **at disposal** freie Reserven (Rücklagen); ~ **for deferred dividends** Rückstellung für Dividendennachzahlungen; ~ **for dividends voted** Rückstellung für Dividendenausschüttungen; ~ **for encumbrances** Rückstellung für Haushaltsbelastungen; ~ **for expansion** (US) Rücklagen für Erweiterungsbauten; ~ **for authorized expenditures** Rücklage für genehmigte Ausgaben; **net borrowed ~s of Federal Reserve member banks** (US) [etwa] Bruttorediskontlinie der dem Landeszentralbanksystem angeschlossenen Banken; ~ **of grain** Getreidevorräte; ~ **for income tax** Einkommensteuerrückstellungen; ~ **for possible inventory losses** Rückstellungen für mögliche Inventarverluste; ~ **for investment fluctuations** Rückstellungen für Anlageveränderungen; ~ **of labo(u)r** Arbeitskräftereservoir; ~ **of liquidity** Liquiditätsreserve; ~ **for outstanding losses** (insurance company) Schadensreserve; ~ **for possible loan losses** Rückstellung für eventuelle Verluste im Kreditgeschäft; ~ **for loss on investment** Rücklagen für Kursverluste; ~ **of manner** Zurückhaltung; ~ **of orders** zurückhaltende Aufträge; ~ **for overheads** Rückstellung für Generalunkosten; ~ **for payments to be made under a pending lawsuit** Rückstellung für Kosten eines schwebenden Prozesses; ~ **for plant expansion** (US) Rücklage für Betriebserweiterungen; ~ **for uncarned premiums** (balance sheet) Prämiumüberhang; ~ **for purchase of treasury stock** (US) Rücklage für den Ankauf eigener Aktien; ~ **for special purposes** zweckbedingte Reserve (Rücklagen); ~ **for redemption** Tilgungsrücklage; ~ **for renewals and replacements** Erneuerungsrücklage; ~ **for repairs** Rückstellungen für Reparaturen; ~ **for deferred repairs and renewals** Rückstellungen für Reparaturen und Neuanschaffungen; ~ **for replacement** Erneuerungsrücklage; ~ **for high replacement cost** Rückstellung für Anschaffungskosten hochwertiger Wirtschaftsgüter des Anlagevermögens; ~ **for retirement allowances** Rückstellung für Pensionsverpflichtungen; ~ **for retirement of preferred stock** (US) Rücklage für den Rückkauf von Vorzugsaktien; ~ **of rights** Vorbehalt der Rechte, Rechtsvorbehalt; ~ **against shareholding interests in foreign banks** Rücklage für Beteiligung an ausländischen Banken und Bankinstituten; ~ **for sinking fund** Rücklage für den Tilgungsfonds, Tilgungsrücklage; ~ **for surplus contingencies** Delkredererückstellung aus dem Reservefonds; ~ **for taxes (future taxation)** Steuerrückstellungen, Rückstellungen für Steuern; ~ **for wear, tear, obsolescence or inadequacy** Abschreibungsrücklage;
~ (v.) (goods) Waren zurückhalten, (make reservation, US) buchen, (set aside) aufsparen, reservieren, zurückstellen, (by stipulation) vorbehalten, ausbedingen;
~ **a th. to o. s.** sich eine Sache vorbehalten;
~ **one's decision** seine Entscheidung zurückstellen, sich seine Entscheidung vorbehalten; ~ **defence** sich Einwendungen vorbehalten; ~ **judgment** Urteilsverkündung aussetzen; ~ **one's judgment** mit seiner Meinung zurückhalten; ~ **a judgment on appeal** Urteil in der Berufsinstanz aufheben; ~ **money for unforeseen contingencies** Geld für unvorhergesehene Ereignisse zurücklegen; ~ **a part of the profit** Gewinnteil zurücklegen; ~ **a question for further consideration** Frage zwecks weiterer Überlegung zurückstellen; ~ **a right for o. s.** sich ein Recht vorbehalten; ~ **the right of recourse** sich Regreßansprüche vorbehalten; ~ **the right of disposal of goods** sich das Verfügungsrecht an Waren vorbehalten; ~ **all rights in an invention** sich alle Rechte aus einer Erfindung vorbehalten; ~ **the right of regress** sich Regreßansprüche vorbehalten; ~ **rooms at a hotel** Zimmer vorausbestellen; ~ **a seat for s. o.** Sitz (Platz) für j. reservieren; ~ **space** Anzeigenraum belegen; ~ **for special guests** für Ehrengäste reservieren; ~ **for another time** auf ein andermal verschieben; ~ **one's view** sich die Stellungnahme vorbehalten;
to abolish a ~ Vorbehalt aufheben; **to accept s. one's conditions**

to abolish a ~ Vorbehalt aufheben; **to accept s. one's conditions without** ~ jds. Bedingungen vorbehaltlos annehmen; **to accept a statement without** ~ einer Erklärung vollen Glauben schenken; **to accumulate ~s** Reserven ansammeln, Rücklagen bilden; **to appropriate to free ~s** in die freien Rücklagen einstellen; **to be classifiable as** ~ den Reserven (Rücklagen) zugerechnet werden; **to be a draw on one's ~s** Rücklagenabbau verursachen; **to be required to keep legal ~s** (US) Mindestreserven unterhalten müssen; **to be short in one's ~s** unzureichende (unzulängliche) Reserven (Rücklagen) haben; **to be well padded with hidden ~s** über ausreichende stille Reserven verfügen; **to be sold without** ~ auf jeden Fall verkauft werden; **to break through s. one's** ~ j. auflockern, j. zur Aufgabe seiner Zurückhaltung veranlassen; **to build up ~s** Reserven ansammeln, Rücklagen bilden; **to cancel ~s** (International Monetary Fund) Reserven aus dem Verkehr ziehen; **to carry an amount to** ~ Betrag den Rücklagen zuführen; **to create a** ~ Reserve (Rücklagen) bilden; **to dip even deeper into ~s** Reserven (Rücklagen) in immer stärkerem Maße in Anspruch nehmen; **to disclose one's** ~**s** seine Reserven (Rücklagen) offen darlegen; **to disclose a material inadequacy of ~s** Unangemessenheit der Rücklagen offenlegen; **to draw on the** ~ von den Reserven zehren, Rücklagen angreifen, Rücklagenabbau verursachen; **to exercise** ~ Zurückhaltung üben; **to fall back on one's ~s** auf seine Reserven zurückgreifen; **to form ~s** Reserven (Rücklagen) bilden; **to have the character of ~s** Rücklagencharakter haben; **to have a great** ~ **of energy** große Kraftreserven haben; **to have a little money in** ~ etw. Geld zurückgelegt haben; **to have recourse to financial ~s** finanzielle Reserven als Rückhalt haben; **to maintain ~s** Reserven unterhalten; **to maintain legal ~s** (banking, US) Mindestreserven unterhalten; **to overrun one's ~s** seine Rücklagen aufzehren; **to place (put) to** ~ den Rücklagen zuführen (überweisen), auf das Rücklagenkonto überweisen, auf Reservekonto verbuchen; **to place a ~ on a picture** Mindestverkaufspreis für ein Bild festlegen; **to publish news with all ~s** Nachrichten mit allem Vorbehalt veröffentlichen; **to put large sums to** ~ größere Beträge dem Rücklagenfonds zuführen, hohe Rückstellungen vornehmen; **to release a** ~ Reserve[fonds] (Rücklagen) auflösen; **to replenish the ~s** Rücklagen (Reserven) auffüllen; **to set aside as a** ~ zurückstellen, Rückstellungen vornehmen, zur Rücklagenbildung verwenden; **to set up a** ~ Rückstellung bilden; **to shunt undisclosed sums into inner ~s** nicht offengelegte Beträge in den stillen Rücklagen verstecken; **to stipulate a** ~ Vorbehalt formulieren; **to transfer to** ~ den Rücklagen zuführen;
~ **account** Rückstellungs-, Rücklagen-, Delkredere-, Reservekonto, Konto Rückstellungen; **depreciation** ~ **account** Erneuerungskonto; **Federal** ⸠ **Act** (US) Gesetz über die Bundesbank der USA, Bundesnotenbankgesetz; ~ **adequacy** Angemessenheit von Reserven (Rücklagen); ~ **agent** (US) Nationalbank mit der Befugnis zur Verwaltung von Mindestreserven; ~ **allocation** Rücklagenzuweisung; ~ **army of unemployed labo(u)r** industrielle Reservearmee; ~ **assets** Währungsguthaben, -reserven; ~ **asset management** Verwaltung von Währungsguthaben; ~ **balance** Rücklageguthaben; ~ **balance requirements** Mindestreservebestimmungen; ~ **assets** Währungsguthaben; **Federal** ⸠ **Bank** (US) eine der 12 Bundesbanken der USA, [etwa] Landeszentralbank; ~ **bank credit** (US) [etwa] Landeszentralbankkredit, Darlehen der Landeszentralbank; ~ **capacity** Kapazitätsreserve; ~ **capital** Kapitalreserve im Fall einer Liquidation; ~**-carrying** (banking) mindestreservepflichtig; ~ **city** (US) Stadt, in der eine Federal Reserve Bank mehr als 25% Reserven unterhalten muß, Bankplatz zweiter Klasse; ~ **claim** (International Monetary Fund) Reserveforderung; ~ **currency** Reservewährung; ~ **currency balance** Reservewährungsguthaben; ~ **deficiency** nicht ausreichende (unzureichende) Reserven (Rücklagen); ~ **depository** (US) Nationalbank mit der Befugnis der Verwaltung von Mindestreserven; ~ **depot** (mil.) Ersatzteillager; ~ **echelon** (mil.) Reserveeinheit; ~ **forces** (mil., Br.) Reserve[einheiten]; ~**-free base figure** [etwa] landeszentralbankfreie Einlagensumme.
reserve fund Rücklage, Reserve[fonds], Rücklagevermögen;
capital redemption ~ (Br.) Kapitaltilgungsrücklage, Rücklage zum Rückkauf von Vorzugsaktien; **provident** ~ außerordentliche Rücklagen; **specific** ~ (insurance) Reservefonds für drohende Verluste; **statutory** ~ gesetzliche Rücklage;
to add to the ~ den Rücklagen zuführen, dem Reservefonds zuweisen; **to build a secret** ~ stille Reserven schaffen; **to carry to the** ~ den Rücklagen zuführen; **to go to the** ~ dem Reservefonds zugeführt werden; **to increase a** ~ Fonds dotieren; **to transfer to** ~ der Rücklage zuweisen.

reserve│holding *(International Monetary Fund)* Reserveguthaben; ~ **hospital** Ausweichkrankenhaus; ~ **income tax** negative Einkommenssteuer; ~ **item** Rückstellungsposten; **tax-free bad-debt** ~ **level allowed to banks** *(US)* steuerfreie Rücklagen für dubiose Bankkunden; ~ **liability** *(life insurance, Br.)* Nachschußpflicht; **to be on the** ~ **list** *(mil.)* der Reserve angehören; ~ **manager at the Bank of England** Mindestreservepolitiker; **overall** ~ **needs** *(currency)* Gesamtreservenbedarf; ~ **officer** außerplanmäßiger Beamter, *(mil.)* Reserveoffizier; ~ **part (piece)** Ersatzteil; ~ **position** Rücklagenpolster, *(advertising)* Ausweichplazierung, *(International Monetary Fund)* Reserveposition; ~ **pay** Löhnung von Reservisten; ~ **price** Mindestpreis, -gebot, *(auction sale)* Einsatz-, Mindestverkaufs-, Vorbehaltspreis, Preislimit, *(EC)* Rücknahmepreis; **to put a** ~ **price on a house** Mindestverkaufspreis für ein Haus festlegen, mit dem Verkaufspreis eines Hauses zurückhalten; ~ **purpose** Rückstellungszweck; **legal** ~ **ratio** *(US)* Deckungssatz, Flüssigkeitskoeffizient der Bundes-Reserve-Banken, gesetzlicher Mindestreservesatz; **minimum** ~ **ratio** Mindestreservesatz; ~ **ration** *(mil.)* eiserne Ration, Minimum; **legal** ~ **requirements** *(US)* Vorschriften über die Bildung der gesetzlich vorgeschriebenen Reserve, Mindestreservevorschriften; **minimum** ~ **requirements** *(US)* Mindestreservenerfordernisse; **cash** ~ **requirements on deposits** *(US)* Mindestreservevorschriften für Bareinlagen; **to increase the minimum** ~ **requirements** *(US)* Mindestreserven bei der Bundesnotenbank erhöhen; **dollar's** ~ **role** Goldersatzrolle des Dollars; ~ **statement** *(US)* Reserveausweis; ~ **stock** Vorratslager; ~ **strength** Überschuß der Aktiva über die laufenden Verbindlichkeiten; **Federal** ⌀ **System** *(US)* [etwa] Landeszentralbankwesen; **fractional** ~ **banking system** System vorgeschriebener Mindestreserven; ~ **team** Ersatzmannschaft; ~ **unit** Ersatzteil; **collective** ~ **unit** *(International Monetary Fund)* kollektive Reserveeinheit; ~ **value** *(insurance)* Prämienreserve.

reserved *(mil.)* unabkömmlich, u. k. gestellt, *(person)* zurückhaltend, reserviert, *(seat, US)* belegt, *(stock exchange)* zurückhaltend;
all rights ~ alle Rechte vorbehalten, Nachdruck verboten; **all seats** ~ nur gegen Platzkarten; **sum** ~ Rückstellungsbetrag; ~ **bidding** beschränkte Versteigerung; ~**-interest account** Konto zweifelhafter Zinseingänge; ~ **judgment** ausgesetztes Urteil; ~ **land** *(US)* unverkäuflicher staatlicher Grundbesitz; ~ **list** *(Br.)* Verzeichnis pensionierter Seeoffiziere; ~ **material** bereitgestelltes Material; ~ **occupation** *(mil.)* UK-, Unabkömmlichkeitsstellung; ~ **position** *(advertising)* reservierter Anzeigenplatz; ~ **power** Klausel, Vorbehalt; ~ **powers** *(US)* den Einzelstaaten vorbehaltene Rechte; ~ **price** Mindestpreis, -gebot; ~ **prices** bescheidene Preise; ~ **rights** Reservatrechte; ~ **seat** *(US)* bestellter (numerierter, reservierter, belegter) Platz; ~**-seat ticket** *(US)* Platzkarte; ~ **share** *(stock, US)* Vorratsaktie; ~ **sum** ~ Rückstellungsbetrag; ~ **speech** vorbehaltene Wortmeldung; ~ **surplus** Reservebetrag, Gewinnvortrag, zweckgebundene Rücklage; ~ **table** bestellter Tisch.

reservery *(mil.)* Reserveübung.

reserving vorbehaltlich;
~ **due payment** unter Vorbehalt des Eingangs, Eingang vorbehalten.

reservist Reservist.

reservoir Behälter, Reservoir, Talsperre, Staubecken, *(fig.)* Sammelbecken;
~ **of labo(u)r** Arbeitskräftereservoir.

reset│of theft *(Scot.)* Hehlerei von Diebesgut;
~ *(v.) (print.)* neu setzen.

resetter *(Br.)* Hehler.

resetting of the type Neusatz.

resettle *(v.)* wiederbesiedeln, umsiedeln, *(after the war)* wieder eingliedern;
~ **offenders** Straffällige wieder eingliedern; ~ **European refugees** europäische Flüchtlinge ansiedeln.

resettlement Umsiedlung, Wiederbesiedlung, *(after the war)* Zurückführung in den Zivilberuf, Wiedereingliederung;
occupational ~ berufliche Umschulung;
~ **of offenders** Wiedereingliederung von Straftätern, Wiedereingliederung Straffälliger; ~ **of refugees** Ansiedlung von Flüchtlingen;
~ **administration** *(US)* Siedlungsbehörde; ~ **aid** Rücksiedlungsbeihilfe; ~ **allowance** Umsiedlungs-, Wiedereingliederungsbeihilfe; ~ **fund** Wiedereingliederungsfonds; ⌀ **Transfer Scheme** *(Br.)* Programm zur Umsiedlung von Industriearbeitern.

resettler Umsiedler, Wiedereingegliederter.

reshape *(v.)* **a company** Firma umorganisieren.

reship *(v.)* wieder (weiter) verladen, weiterversenden, als Rückfracht senden, *(ship)* umladen.

reshipment erneute Verladung, Umladung, Wiederversendung, -verladung, Weiterversendung, *(re-export)* Wiederausfuhr, *(return freight)* Rück[ver]ladung, -fracht, -sendung.

reshipping cost Weiterversendungskosten.

reshuffle│of the Cabinet (government) Kabinetts-, Regierungsumbildung, Umgruppierung der Regierung (des Kabinetts);
~ *(v.)* umgruppieren, umbilden;
~ **the Cabinet (government)** Regierung umbilden; ~ **the coalition** Koalition umbilden; ~ **its top team** Vorstandsspitze neu besetzen.

reshuffling of top management Umbesetzung der Schlüsselpositionen in der Vorstandsspitze.

reside *(v.) (dwell)* wohnen, seinen Wohnsitz haben, ansässig sein, sich aufhalten, domizilieren, *(be in official residence)* seiner Residenzpflicht nachkommen, *(rest with)* liegen, *(to be vested as a title)* zustehen;
~ **abroad** im Ausland wohnen; ~ **in entrenched interests** in festverwurzeltem Interesse liegen; ~ **in the people** *(power)* beim Volke liegen; ~ **with the plaintiff** *(burden of proof)* dem Kläger obliegen; ~ **in the President** *(power)* beim Präsidenten liegen.

residence *(abode)* ständiger Aufenthalts-, Wohnort, [Wohn]sitz, Ansässigkeit, *(dwelling)* Wohnung, *(duration of abode)* Aufenthaltsdauer, *(fact of being officially present)* Residenzpflicht, *(mansion)* herrschaftliches Wohnhaus, Herrenhaus, Landsitz;
in ~ *(official)* mit einer Dienstwohnung ausgestattet, *(undergraduate)* im College wohnend;
~ **abroad** Auslandsaufenthalt, Wohnort im Ausland; **country** ~ Landsitz; **detached** ~ freistehendes Haus; **family** ~ Einfamilienhaus; **fixed** ~ fester (ständiger) Wohnsitz; **gentleman's** ~ Herrensitz; **habitual** ~ gewöhnlicher Aufenthaltsort; **lawful** ~ ordnungsgemäßer Aufenthalt; **legal** ~ gesetzlicher Wohnsitz, Wohnort; **main** ~ Hauptwohnsitz; **official** ~ Dienstsitz, Amts-, Dienstwohnung; **ordinary** ~ gewöhnlicher Aufenthaltsort, *(Br.)* steuerlicher Wohnsitz; **permanent** ~ [etwa] fester (ständiger) Wohnsitz, Dauerwohnung; **private** ~ Privatwohnung, -besitz; **rent-free** ~ mietfreie Dienstwohnung; **suburban** ~ Vorstadtwohnung; **temporary** ~ vorübergehender Aufenthalt; **town** ~ Stadthaus;
board and ~ Unterkunft und Verpflegung;
temporary ~ **abroad for business** vorübergehender geschäftsbedingter Auslandsaufenthalt; ~ **of a company (corporation)** Gesellschaftssitz; ~ **for tax purposes** steuerlicher Wohnsitz; ~ **[un]limited in time** [un]befristeter Aufenthalt;
to be in ~ residieren, *(undergraduate)* im College wohnen; **to change one's** ~ seinen Wohnsitz verlegen, umziehen; **to choose one's** ~ seinen Wohnsitz begründen; **to determine s. one's** ~ **for exchange-control purposes** jds. Deviseneigenschaft nach seinem Wohnsitz festlegen; **to fix one's** ~ **in a city** sich im Hauptgeschäftsviertel niederlassen, sein Geschäftssitz begründen; **to have one's** ~ **in X** in X wohnen; **to make** ~ **a condition of relief** Wohnsitzeigenschaft zur Unterstützungsvoraussetzung machen; **to occupy a** ~ **rent-free** mietfrei in einem Haus wohnen; **to take up one's** ~ sich ansiedeln, seinen Wohnsitz begründen (aufschlagen); **to take up temporary** ~ **abroad** seinen Wohnsitz vorübergehend im Ausland aufschlagen; **to testify to the foreign** ~ **of a customer** Devisenausländereigenschaft eines Kunden bezeugen;
~ **is required** Residenzpflicht;
~ **address** Privat-, Wohnsitzanschrift; ~ **burglary insurance** Einbruchs-, Diebstahlsversicherung; ~ **certificate** Aufenthaltsgenehmigung; ~ **insurance** Gebäudeversicherung; ~ **and outside theft insurance** Einbruchsdiebstahlversicherung; ~ **permit** Aufenthaltsgenehmigung, -erlaubnis; ~ **qualification (requirement)** Wohnsitzerfordernis; ~ **status for tax purposes** Steuerwohnsitz.

residency Amtssitz, Residenz.

resident Anwohner, Bewohner, *(Br.)* Regierungsvertreter, *(city)* Bürger, ortsansässiger Einwohner, Gebiets-, Ortsansässiger, Inländer, *(dipl.)* ständiger Gesandter, *(hotel)* Dauergast, *(Exchange Control Act, Br.)* Deviseninländer;
~ **General** *(Br.)* Generalresident; **individual** ~ natürliche Person mit Wohnrecht; **minister** ~ Gesandter, Regierungsvertreter; **national** ~ *(US)* Staatsangehöriger; ~**s only** *(traffic sign)* Anliegerverkehr; **U. K. (British)** ~ britischer Staatsangehöriger;
~ **inside the sterling area** *(Br.)* Deviseninländer; ~ **outside the sterling area** *(Br.)* Devisenausländer; ~**s of the suburbs** Vorstadtbevölkerung; ~ **outside the scheduled territories** *(Br.)* Devisenausländer;

~ *(a.)* ortsansässig, im Bezirk wohnend, wohnhaft, beheimatet, angesessen, eingesessen, *(Br.)* in Großbritannien ansässig; **ordinarily** ~ wohnhaft;

~ **abroad** im Ausland wohnend; ~ **at college** *(undergraduate)* im College wohnend;

to be ~ ansässig sein, domizilieren; **to be** ~ **abroad** Auslandswohnsitz haben; **to be** ~ **at college** im College wohnen; **to be** ~ **or established** Wohnsitz oder Geschäftssitz haben; **to be** ~ **for exchange-control purposes inside (outside) the Scheduled Territories** *(Br.)* seinen Wohnsitz außerhalb (innerhalb) eines zum Sterlingblock gehörenden Landes haben, devisenrechtlich Inländer (Ausländer) sein; **to be not** ~ **or ordinarily** ~ **in the United Kingdom** weder seinen gewöhnlichen noch ständigen Aufenthalt in England nehmen; **to be ordinarily** ~ seinen gewöhnlichen Aufenthaltsort haben; **to be permanently** ~ seinen ständigen Wohnsitz haben; **to be regarded as** ~ steuerlich als Deviseninländer behandelt werden; **to be** ~ **of a state** in einem Staat ansässig sein; **to become a** ~ ansässig (einheimisch) werden; **to cease to be** ~ *(Br.)* Status eines in Großbritannien ansässigen Steuerzahlers verlieren, *(US)* Deviseninländereigenschaft verlieren;

~ **account** Deviseninlandskonto; ~ **agent** Empfangsbevollmächtigter, Inlandsvertreter; ~ **alien** ansässiger Ausländer, *(US)* ausländischer Staatsbürger mit Wohnsitz in den USA; ~ **area** Wohnviertel; ~ **buyer** im Ausland ansässiger Einkaufsvertreter, ortsansässiger Einkäufer; ~ **citizen** *(US)* Staatsbürger mit Wohnsitz in den USA, Ortsansässiger; ~ **community** Einwohnerschaft; ~ **company** inländische Handelsgesellschaft; U. K. ~ **company** *(Br.)* Handelsgesellschaft mit Geschäftssitz in Großbritannien; ~ **convertibility** Inländerkonvertierbarkeit; ~ **foreign corporation** *(US)* ausländische Gesellschaft mit Sitz in den USA; ~ **freeholder** ansässiger Grundstückseigentümer; ~ **housekeeper** im Haus wohnende Hausangestellte; ~ **landowner** ortsansässiger Grundstücksbesitzer; ~ **magistrate** Schnellrichter; ~ **minister** Ministerresident; ~ **person** Ortsansässiger; ~ **physician** diensthabender Arzt; ~ **population** Einwohner, ortsansässige Bevölkerung; ~ **porter** ständig anwesender Hausmeister; ~ **status for exchange-control purposes** Devisenstatus; ~ **sterling** *(Br.)* Währungsbestände von Gebietsansässigen, Währungsbestände von Bewohnern des Sterlingblocks; ~ **taxpayer** inländischer Steuerpflichtiger; ~ **tutor** Hauslehrer.

residential für ein Privathaus geeignet;

~ **accommodation** Wohnraumgestellung, Wohnmöglichkeit; ~ **alien** *(US)* Nichtamerikaner; ~ **allowance** Ortszulage; ~ **amenity** Wohnwert; ~ **area** Wohngegend, -viertel; ~ **building** Wohngebäude; ~ **building outlook** Wohnungsbauprognose; ~ **community** Wohnzentrum, -gemeinschaft; ~ **construction** *(US)* Wohnungsbau[wesen]; **private** ~ **construction** *(US)* privater Wohnungsbau; **foreign** ~ **corporation** *(US)* ausländische Gesellschaft mit Sitz in den USA; ~ **course** *(Br.)* Erwachsenenlehrgang für Ortsansässige; ~ **development** Entwicklung zur Wohngegend; ~ **district** Wohngegend, -bezirk, Villenviertel; **low-(high-)rent** ~ **district** billige (teure) Wohnlage; ~ **estate** Wohngrundstück; ~ **financing** Eigenheimfinanzierung; ~ **flat** Privatwohnung; ~ **holdings** Kapitalanlage in Wohngrundstücken; ~ **home** Altenwohnheim; ~ **hotel** Familienpension; ~ **housing construction** Wohnungsbau; ~ **investment** Investitionen auf dem Wohnbausektor; ~ **levy** Grundsteuer; ~ **mortgage** Eigenheimhypothek; ~ **neighbo(u)rhood** Wohngegend; ~ **outlay** Aufwendungen für die Errichtung von Wohnhäusern; ~ **parts of a city** Wohngegend einer Stadt; ~ **premises** Wohngebäude, -grundstück; ~ **property** Wohngrundstück; ~ **qualifications for voters** Wohnsitzerfordernisse für Wahlbeteiligte; ~ **quarter** Wohnviertel, -bezirk, -gegend; ~ **real estate** Wohngrundstück; ~ **refuse** Haushaltsmüll; ~ **rent** Wohnungsmiete; ~ **section** Wohngegend; ~ **segment** Wohnungs-, Eigenheimanteil; ~ **settlement** [Wohn]siedlung; ~ **space** Wohnraum; ~ **status for a tax** Steuerwohnsitz; ~ **street** Wohnblockstraße; ~ **suburb** Vorstadtwohngegend; ~ **taxpayer** unbeschränkt (inländischer) Steuerpflichtiger; ~ **theft coverage** Einbruch-, Diebstahlsversicherungsschutz; ~ **trade** Lokalhandel; ~ **unit** Wohneinheit; ~ **zone** Wohngegend.

residentiary residenzpflichtig.

residing wohnhaft.

residual Rest, *(statistics)* Restgröße;

~ *(a.)* übrigbleibend, übrig;

~ **amount** Restbetrag; ~ **assets** Restvermögen; ~ **claim** Restforderung; ~ **claimant** Anspruchsberechtigter auf den Rest; ~ **cost** Restbuchwert; ~ **debt** Restschuld; ~ **demand** Restnachfrage; ~ **error** *(balance of payments)* ungeklärte Differenz; ~ **estate** *(US)*

Restnachlaß; ~ **fee** Nebeneinkommen; ~ **insurance rates** *(auto insurance)* Tarifsätze für die vom Versicherer nicht akzeptierten Autofahrer; ~ **item** Restposten; ~ **market** *(auto insurance)* nicht versicherungsfähiger Restbestand; ~ **oil** Rückstandsöl; ~ **payment** reiner Unternehmergewinn; ~ **product** Abfall-, Nebenprodukt; ~ **quantity** Differenzbetrag; ~ **term** Restlaufzeit; ~ **unemployment** Restbestand der Arbeitslosigkeit, Bodensatzarbeitslosigkeit; ~ **value** *(balance sheet)* Restbuchwert; ~ **variance** Restvarianz.

residuary Reinnachlaß, Nachlaßvermächtnis;

~ *(sl.)* restlich, übrig, rückständig, *(law)* den Nachlaß betreffend;

~ **account** *(Br.)* Rechnungslegung über den Nachlaß; ~ **beneficiary** auf den Restnachlaß eingesetzter Erbe, Nachlaßbegünstigter; ~ **bequest** letztwillige Zuwendung, Nachvermächtnis; ~ **clause** Testamentsbestimmung über die Einsetzung des Haupterben (Verteilung des Nachlasses nach Abzug der Nachlaßverbindlichkeiten); ~ **devise** letztwillige Verfügung über den Restnachlaß; ~ **devisee** Haupterbe des Grundbesitzes; ~ **estate** *(Br.)* Nachlaß zur Schuldentilgung, Nachlaß nach Zahlung aller Verbindlichkeiten; ~ **gift** Vermächtnis des Vermögensrestes; ~ **legacy** Vermächtnis nach Abzug der Nachlaßverbindlichkeiten, Nachvermächtnis; ~ **legatee** Nachvermächtnisnehmer; **some** ~ **odds and ends** einige Überbleibsel; ~ **property** Nachlaß nach Zahlung aller Verbindlichkeiten.

residue restlicher Teil, Rest[betrag], *(balance)* Rechnungsrest, *(estate)* reiner Nachlaß, Restnachlaß, Nachlaßrest, *(remainder)* [Waren]rest;

~ **of expenditure** Kostenrest; ~ **of profit** Restgewinn;

to fall back into ~ dem Gesamtnachlaß zufallen.

resign *(v.) (relinquish)* verzichten auf, aufgeben, *(retire, US)* zurücktreten, ausscheiden, abdanken;

~ **an agency** Vertretung niederlegen (aufgeben); ~ **in a body** geschlossen zurücktreten; ~ **from the Cabinet** *(minister, Br.)* demissionieren, aus der Regierung ausscheiden; ~ **one's children to s. one's care** jem. seine Kinder anvertrauen; ~ **a claim** auf eine Forderung verzichten; ~ **under a cloud** unter Verdachtsumständen zurücktreten; ~ **from a club** aus einem Verein austreten, Vereinsaustritt erklären; ~ **control of an estate** *(US)* Nachlaßverwaltung abgeben; ~ **from government** *(Br.)* aus der Regierung ausscheiden; ~ **o. s. to doing without domestic help** sich auf den Zustand einer nicht vorhandenen Haushaltshilfe einstellen; ~ **o. s. to one's fate** sich mit seinem Schicksal abfinden; ~ **o. s. to s. one's guidance** sich jds. Führung anvertrauen; ~ **into s. one's hands** in jds. Hände legen; ~ **o. s. to an idea** sich mit einem Gedanken befreunden; ~ **an inheritance** *(US)* Erbschaft ausschlagen; ~ **one's job** seinen Beruf aufgeben; ~ **from management** von der Geschäftsführung zurücktreten; ~ **a managership** Vorstandsamt niederlegen; ~ **from membership** seinen Austritt erklären; ~ **office** aus dem Amt scheiden, Amt aufgeben (niederlegen), *(minister)* sein Portefeuille zur Verfügung stellen; ~ **one's position** seinen Posten (seine Stellung) aufgeben, von seinem Posten zurücktreten; ~ **one's position as a teacher** sein Lehramt aufgeben; ~ **a property to s. o.** jem. einen Besitz überlassen; ~ **the representation** Vertretung niederlegen; ~ **a right** Recht aufgeben; ~ **voluntarily** von sich aus kündigen, seinen Arbeitsplatz aufgeben; ~ **a ward to a new guardian** sein Amt einem neuen Vormund übergeben.

resignation *(giving up a claim)* Verzicht, Verzichtleistung, *(membership)* Austritt[serklärung], *(formal document)* Rücktrittsschreiben, -gesuch, *(office)* [Amts]niederlegung, Rücktritt, Rücktrittsgesuch, -erklärung;

involuntary ~ nahegelegte Kündigung;

~ **of a benefice** *(Br.)* Pfründenaufgabe; ~ **of cabinet** *(Br.)* Regierungsrücktritt; ~ **of membership** Mandatsverzicht; ~ **of one's right** Rechtsverzicht;

to address one's ~ **to X** sein Rücktrittsgesuch an X richten; **to call for s. one's** ~ j. zum Rücktritt auffordern; **to send in (tender) one's** ~ seinen Rücktritt erklären, sein Rücktrittsgesuch einreichen, um seinen Rücktritt einkommen; **to withdraw one's** ~ **from the government** seinen Rücktritt aus dem Kabinett rückgängig machen;

~ **letter** Rücktrittsschreiben, -gesuch; ~ **request** Rücktrittsersuchen.

resigned zurückgetreten, außer Diensten.

resigner Verzichtleistender.

resile *(v.)* **from a contract** von einem Vertrag zurücktreten.

resin, artificial Kunststoff.

resist *(v.)* Widerstand leisten, widerstehen;

~ **[an] arrest** sich der Verhaftung widersetzen; ~ **an attack** Angriff abwehren; ~ **the authority of the court** sich einer richterlichen Verfügung widersetzen; ~ **a claim** Anspruch bestreiten; ~ **the enemy** dem Feind widerstehen; ~ **the evidence** Beweismaterial nicht anerkennen; ~ **an influence** sich einem Einfluß entziehen; ~ **a motion** Antragsgegner sein; ~ **the police** der Polizei Widerstand entgegensetzen; ~ **s. one's will** sich jds. Willen widersetzen.

resistance Widerstand, *(material)* Festigkeit, Beständigkeit; **armed** ~ bewaffneter Widerstand; **last-ditch** ~ Widerstand bis zum letzten Mann; **passive** ~ passiver Widerstand, innere Emigration;
~ **to high prices** Käuferwiderstand; ~ **to taxation** Steuerwiderstand, Steuerstreik; ~ **to wear** Verschleißfestigkeit;
to break down the enemy's ~ feindlichen Widerstand brechen; **to evoke** ~ **in the public** Ablehnung (Auflehnung) in der Öffentlichkeit hervorrufen; **to make no** ~ **to the enemy's advance** dem feindlichen Vorrücken keinen Widerstand entgegensetzen; **to meet with** ~ auf Widerstand stoßen; **to offer** ~ entgegentreten, Widerstand leisten; **to offer armed** ~ bewaffneten Widerstand leisten; **to offer** ~ **in the public** von der Öffentlichkeit nicht positiv aufgenommen werden; **to show strong** ~ *(market)* sehr widerstandsfähig sein, Widerstandsfähigkeit zeigen; **to take the line of least** ~ Weg des geringsten Widerstands einschlagen;
~ **fighter** Widerstandskämpfer; ~ **group** Widerstandsgruppe; ~ **level** *(stock market)* Widerstandsschwelle; **to break a** ~ **level** *(stock market)* Widerstandslinie überwinden; ~ **movement** Widerstandsbewegung; ~ **organization** Widerstandsorganisation; ~ **point** *(US)* abgeschlossener Kursstand.

resistant *(stock exchange)* widerstandsfähig;
~ **to the slowdown** konjunkturunempfindlich.

resister, passive passiver Widerstandskämpfer.

resisting a constable *(Br.)* (officer, *US*) **in the execution of his office (duty)** Widerstand gegen die Staatsgewalt.

resolution [Abfassen einer] Resolution, Beschluß[fassung], Entschließung, *(bankruptcy, Br.)* Gläubigerbeschluß, *(cancellation of contract)* Vertragsaufhebung, *(decision of a court)* Gerichtsbeschluß;
by ~ durch Beschluß, im Beschlußwege;
concurrent ~ *(US)* gemeinsame Resolution durch Senat und Repräsentantenhaus; **corporate** ~ *(US)* Hauptversammlungsbeschluß; **directors'** ~ Aufsichtsratsbeschluß; **draft** ~ Entschließungs-, Resolutionsentwurf; **extraordinary** ~ *(bankruptcy)* qualifizierter Mehrheitsbeschluß, *(company, Br.)* mit 3/4 Mehrheit gefaßter Hauptversammlungsbeschluß; **firm** ~ fester Entschluß; **good** ~s gute Vorsätze; **joint** ~ *(US)* Beschlußfassung durch Senat und Repräsentantenhaus; **majority** ~ mit Stimmenmehrheit verabschiedete Entschließung; **ordinary** ~ *(bankruptcy, company meeting, Br.)* einfacher Mehrheitsbeschluß aller Besitzer nachgewiesener Forderungen; **special** ~ *(company meeting, bankruptcy proceedings)* qualifizierter Mehrheitsbeschluß; **unanimous** ~ einstimmige Entschließung; **valid** ~ rechtsgültiger Beschluß;
~ **for adjournment** Vertagungsbeschluß; ~ **of board of directors** Vorstandsbeschluß; ~ **of creditors** *(Br.)* Gläubigerbeschluß; ~ **of directors** Vorstandsbeschluß; ~ **of a doubt** Behebung eines Zweifels; ~ **of the majority** Mehrheitsbeschluß; ~s **at general meetings** Hauptversammlungsbeschlüsse; ~s **of a public meeting** Versammlungsbeschlüsse; ~ **of a picture** Bildrasterung; ~ **of surrender** Auflösungsbeschluß; ~ **for the winding up** Liquidationsbeschluß; ~ **to wind up voluntarily** Liquidationsbeschluß der Hauptversammlung; ~ **in writing** schriftlicher Beschluß;
to adopt (carry) a ~ Entschließung (Antrag, Resolution) annehmen; **to convert successful** ~s **into draft minutes** verabschiedete Resolutionen in Protokollform übertragen; **to draft a** ~ Resolutionsentwurf vorbereiten; **to get a** ~ **past a committee** Beschluß von einem Ausschuß genehmigen lassen; **to introduce a** ~ Beschluß einbringen; **to lack** ~ entschlußunfreudig sein, keine Entschlußkraft besitzen; **to move a** ~ Entschließung (Resolution) einbringen; **to pass a** ~ annehmen; **to pass a** ~ **in favo(u)r** sich zugunsten eines Vorschlages aussprechen; **to pass a** ~ **of protest** Protest beschließen, Protestbeschluß fassen; **to put a** ~ **to the meeting** Entschließung (Resolution) einbringen; **to put a** ~ **to the vote** Entschließung zur Abstimmung vorlegen; **to reject a** ~ Resolutionsentwurf ablehnen; **to rescind a** ~ Resolution aufheben (umstoßen); **to show great** ~ große Entschlußkraft beweisen; **to table a** ~ Resolution vorlegen; **to vote on a** ~ über eine Entschließung abstimmen;
~s **committee** Resolutionsausschuß.

resolutioner Verfasser einer Resolution.

resolutive | clause Annullierungsbestimmung; ~ **condition** auflösende Bedingung, Resolutionsbedingung.

resolutory condition Resolutivbedingung, auflösende Bedingung.

resolve Vorsatz, Beschluß, Entschluß, *(US)* Entschließung, Beschlußfassung, Resolution;
~ *(v.)* Beschluß fassen, beschließen, *(become void)* nichtig werden;
~ **itself into a commission** *(parl.)* sich zu einem Ausschuß konstituieren; ~ **to hold back nothing** sich zu rücksichtsloser Offenheit durchringen; ~ **an issue against the defendant** gegen den Beklagten entscheiden; ~ **a matter** Angelegenheit entscheiden; ~ **that the meeting is in favo(u)r** Zustimmung einer Versammlung beschließen; ~ **upon s. th.** sich für etw. entscheiden.

resolved fest entschlossen, *(protocol)* es wurde beschlossen.

resort Aufenthaltsort, *(place of popular resort)* Urlaubsort, *(recourse)* Ausweg, *(resource)* Hilfsmittel, Zuflucht, *(stream)* Strom [von Besuchern];
as a last ~ wenn alle Stricke reißen, wenn alles schiefgeht, *(law court)* in letzter Instanz; **without** ~ ohne Berufungsmöglichkeit;
health ~ Bade-, Kurort; **holiday** ~ Ferienaufenthalt; **last** ~ letzte Instanz; **seaside** ~ Seebad; **summer** ~ Sommerkurort; **winter** ~ Winterkurort, -sportplatz;
~ **to court** Inanspruchnahme (Anrufung) des Gerichts; ~ **to force** Anwendung von Gewalt; ~ **to the share (stock) market** Beanspruchung des Aktienmarktes;
~ *(v.)* sich begeben, seine Zuflucht nehmen;
~ **to arbitration** schiedsrichterliche Entscheidung in Anspruch nehmen; ~ **to the capital market** Kapitalmarkt in Anspruch nehmen; ~ **to other counsels** sich anderweitig beraten lassen; ~ **to a court** Gericht anrufen; ~ **to force** zur Gewalt Zuflucht nehmen, Gewaltmaßnahmen ergreifen; ~ **to a fund** auf einen Fonds zurückgreifen; ~ **to an inn** in einem Gasthaus verkehren; ~ **to publicity** in die Öffentlichkeit flüchten; ~ **to a physician** laufend zum Arzt gehen (rennen); ~ **to a remedy** Rechtsmittel ergreifen; ~ **to the springs** Kurort aufsuchen, Kur gebrauchen; ~ **to surety** Bürgen in Anspruch nehmen;
to build ~s **on a monster scale** Erholungsgebiete im Riesenmaßstab errichten;
~ **facilities** Kuranlagen; ~ **hotel** Ferien-, Kurhotel; ~ **project** Ferienprojekt; **last-** ~ **tool** letztes Zufluchtsmittel.

resounding success enormer Erfolg.

resource Ausweg, Hilfsquelle, Behelf, *(accounting, coll.)* Aktivposten, *(means of spending leisure time)* Unterhaltung, Entspannung, Erholung, *(reserve)* Vorrat, Reserve, *(supply)* ständige Bezugsquelle;
without ~ hoffnungslos;
last ~ letzte Instanz, letzter Ausweg;
~ **allocation** Mittelverteilung; ~ **allowance of 25% production income** Steuerfreibetrag zur Stärkung der Eigenmittel in Höhe von 25% des Produktionserlöses; ~ **appraisal** Vorratsbewertung; ~ **center** Unterhaltungszentrum; ~ **conservation** Mittelkonservierung; ~ **hotel** Ferien-, Kurhotel; ~ **policy** auf Erhaltung der Bodenschätze ausgerichtete Politik; ~ **project** Ferienprojekt; ~ **shortage** knappe Bodenschätze; ~ **transfer** Transfer von Vermögenswerten, Mittelüberweisung, Geldüberweisung.

resourceless ohne Hilfsquellen, mittellos.

resourcelessness Mittellosigkeit.

resources Hilfsmittel, -quellen, *(accounting, coll.)* Aktiva, Vermögenswerte, *(company)* Eigenmittel, *(available means of a country)* Reichtümer, ungenutzte Bodenschätze, *(money)* Geldmittel;
out of one's own ~ aus eigenen Mitteln; **without** ~ mittellos; **business** ~ geschäftliche Aktiva; **a company's** ~ Gesellschaftskapital; **covering** ~ Deckungsmittel; **credit** ~ Kreditmittel, -quellen; **financial** ~ finanzielle Mittel; **human** ~ Menschenreserve, Arbeitskräftepotential; **inexhaustible** ~ unerschöpfliche Bodenschätze; **limited** ~ beschränkte Mittel; **liquid** ~ flüssige Mittel; **local** ~ örtliche Hilfsquellen; **natural** ~ Natur-, Bodenschätze, natürliche Vorkommen; **own** ~ Eigenmittel; **real** ~ Güter und Dienstleistungen;
natural ~ **of a country** natürliche Bodenschätze eines Landes; ~ **in men** Arbeitskräfte-, Menschenreserve; ~ **of one's own** eigene Mittel; ~ **of self-employed** Selbständigeneinkommen;
to be at the end of one's ~ alle Mittel aufgebraucht haben, *(fig.)* keinen Ausweg mehr wissen; **to be left to one's own** ~ auf sein eigenes Talent angewiesen sein; **to be thrown upon s. one's** ~ auf sich selbst angewiesen sein; **to be thrown upon s. one's** ~ jem. zur Last fallen; **to bet its own** ~ **fully on a project** Projekt lediglich mit eigenen Mitteln finanzieren; **to draw upon one's** ~ seine Hilfsquellen in Anspruch nehmen; **to exploit the natural**

~ **of a country** Bodenschätze eines Landes ausbeuten; **to have exhausted all** ~ alle Reserven aufgebraucht haben; **to have only limited** ~ nur beschränkte Mittel zur Verfügung haben; **to leave s. o. to his own** ~ j. sich selbst überlassen; **to make the most of one's** ~ sein Kapital schwerpunktartig einsetzen; **to mobilize one's** ~ seine Hilfsquellen mobilisieren; **to open up new** ~ neue Hilfsquellen erschließen; **to pool one's** ~ seine Mittel gemeinsam einsetzen, zusammenschießen; **to throw all one's** ~ **into a job** zur Durchführung eines Auftrags alle Hilfsmittel mobilisieren; **to use one's** ~ seine Hilfsquellen einsetzen; **to withdraw** ~ Mittel entziehen.

resourceless ohne Hilfsquellen.

resourcelessness Mittellosigkeit.

respect *(moral worth)* Ansehen, Achtung, Respekt, Ruf, *(reference)* Hinsicht, Rücksicht, Beziehung, Bezug;
in all ~**s** in jeder Hinsicht; **in all other** ~**s** in allen anderen Bereichen; **with** ~ **to, in** ~ **of** in bezug auf, in betreff, hinsichtlich;
~**s** Grüße, Empfehlungen;
world-wide ~ Weltgeltung;
~ **for the law** Achtung vor dem Gesetz;
~ *(v.)* berücksichtigen, *(have regard)* achten, respektieren, *(relate)* Bezug haben, sich beziehen;
~ **a clause in a contract** Vertragsklausel respektieren; ~ **one's own interests** eigene Interessen berücksichtigen; ~ **the law** dem Gesetz Achtung zollen; ~ **neutrality** Neutralität respektieren; ~ **s. one's opinion** jds. Meinung respektieren;
to be admirable in ~ **of style** stilistisch hervorragend sein; **to be held in the greatest** ~ hoch angesehen sein; **to enforce** ~ **for a decree** einem Beschluß Achtung verschaffen; **to give (present, send) one's** ~ **to s. o.** sich jem. empfehlen, jem. Empfehlungen übermitteln; **to have no** ~ **for one's promises** seine Versprechungen nicht einhalten, sich nicht an sein Versprechen halten; **to pay one's** ~**s to s. o.** jem. seine Aufwartung (einen Anstandsbesuch) machen; **to pay one's** ~**s to the needs of the general reader** auf die Bedürfnisse der Leserschaft Rücksicht nehmen; **to send one's** ~**s to s. o.** jem. Empfehlungen übermitteln; **to speak without** ~ **of persons** auf niemanden Rücksicht nehmen.

respectabilities Honoratioren;
~ **of life** Anstandsregeln;
to maintain the ~ **of life** Regeln des menschlichen Anstands einhalten; **to observe the** ~ Konventionen wahren.

respectability Ehrbarkeit, *(business)* geschäftliches Ansehen, Solidität, *(status)* geachtete Stellung.

respectable angesehen, hochachtbar, solide, reell;
~ **amount** bedeutende (beachtliche) Summe; ~ **attendance** erhebliche (beachtliche) Beteiligung; **to belong to the** ~ **middle class** zum gehobenen Mittelstand gehören; ~ **competence** beachtliches (erhebliches) Vermögen; **to be considered** ~ **in a country** zu den guten Sitten eines Landes zählen; ~ **family** angesehene Familie; **to run to a** ~ **figure** erheblichen Betrag ausmachen; ~ **firm** angesehenes Haus; **to have a** ~ **income** schönes Einkommen haben; **to act from** ~ **motives** aus ehrenwerten Motiven handeln; **to have quite** ~ **talents** über erhebliche Begabung verfügen.

respected, my ~ **colleague** mein geschätzter Kollege.

respectfully yours *(letter)* hochachtungsvoll, ergebenst.

respecting hinsichtlich, betreffend.

respective beziehungsweise, jeweilig;
to give s. o. work ~ **of his abilities** jem. entsprechend seinen Fähigkeiten einsetzen.

respite Aufschub, *(delay permitted in paying, Br.)* Frist, Termin, Nachsicht, Bedenkzeit, Zahlungsaufschub, Stundung, *(temporary suspension, Br.)* Begnadigung, Aussetzung der Todesstrafe, [Straf]vollstreckungsaufschub;
additional (after) ~ Nachfrist; **forced** ~ vorläufige Vollstreckungseinstellung; **voluntary** ~ mit dem Gläubiger abgesprochene Aussetzung der Vollstreckung;
~ **of appeal** Vertagung der Berufungsverhandlung; ~ **of a month** Monatsfrist; ~ **for payment** Zahlungsaufschub, Stundung, Moratorium; ~ **of a sentence** Aussetzung der Vollstreckung;
~ *(v.)* *(Br.)* stunden, Stundung gewähren, Zahlungsaufschub bewilligen (gewähren), *(reprieve)* begnadigen, Strafe aussetzen;
~ **execution of a judgment** Vollstreckungsaufschub gewähren; ~ **a murderer** Mörder begnadigen; ~ **payment** Zahlungsfrist (Stundung) gewähren, stunden;
to accord a ~ Frist zugestehen; **to accord a** ~ **for payment of a draft** Wechsel prolongieren; **to apply for a** ~ Stundung beantragen, Stundungsgesuch stellen; **to ask for a** ~ um Zahlungs-

aufschub bitten; **to grant a** ~ Frist einräumen (gewähren), Zahlungsaufforderung befristen, *(sentence)* Vollstreckung des Urteils aussetzen; **to toil without** ~ unablässig schuften; **to work without** ~ ohne Unterbrechung (Pause) arbeiten;
~ **money** Prolongationsgebühr.

respited freight gestundete Fracht.

respond *(v.)* [be]antworten, *(acknowledge)* bestätigen, Empfang bescheinigen, *(act in response)* reagieren, *(be liable for payment, US)* haften, einstehen, *(pleading)* Klageerwiderung einreichen, *(render satisfaction)* Befriedigung gewähren;
~ **to changing conditions** auf veränderte Verhältnisse reagieren; ~ **for a credit** für einen Kredit einstehen; ~ **in damages** *(US)* schadensersatzpflichtig sein; ~ **to a letter** Brief beantworten; ~ **to a speech of welcome** Begrüßungsansprache erwidern; ~ **well to the controls** *(airplane)* sehr gut auf den Steuerknüppel ansprechen.

respondeat superior Haftung für den Erfüllungsgehilfen.

respondent Auskunftsperson, *(opinion research, Br.)* Befragter, *(divorce case)* Scheidungsbeklagter, *(opponent)* Antragsgegner, *(appellate practice)* Beklagter [im Berufungsverfahren], Berufungsbeklagter;
~ *(a.)* beklagt.

respondentia Verschiffungskredit, Bodmerei auf die Schiffsladung;
~ **bond** Bodmereibrief auf Schiff und Ladung.

responder *(US)* automatischer Anrufbeantworter.

response Antwort, *(advertising)* Reaktion;
in ~ **to your enquiry** in Beantwortung Ihrer Anfrage;
controlled ~ *(mil.)* begrenzter Gegenschlag; **flexible** ~ *(mil.)* Strategie der angemessenen Gegenmaßnahmen;
to meet with a ~ *(fig.)* ein Echo finden; **to meet with no** ~ unbeantwortet (ohne Reaktion) bleiben.

responsibilities Verantwortungsbereich;
to be promoted to heavier ~ in eine Stellung mit höherem Verantwortungsbereich befördert werden; **to fill well one's** ~ seinen Verantwortungsbereich gut ausfüllen, voll gerecht werden; **to get operational** ~ Führung eines Unternehmens übernehmen.

responsibility Kompetenz, Verantwortlichkeit, Verantwortung, Verantwortungsbereich, Verpflichtung, *(ability to contract, US)* Vertragsfähigkeit, *(liability)* Haftung, *(solvency, US)* Zahlungsfähigkeit, Solidität;
on one's own ~ auf eigene Verantwortung, aus eigener Machtvollkommenheit; **without** ~ ohne Verbindlichkeit (Obligo);
additional ~ erhöhte Haftung; **collective** ~ Kollektivschuld; **criminal** ~ strafrechtliche Verantwortlichkeit, Zurechnungsfähigkeit; **international** ~ völkerrechtliche Haftung; **joint** ~ gemeinsame Haftung, Gesamthaftung; **limited** ~ verminderte (eingeschränkte) Zurechnungsfähigkeit; **major** ~ Hauptverantwortung; **ministerial** ~ Ministerverantwortung; **official** ~ Amtshaftung; **personal** ~ persönliche Verantwortung; **reduced** ~ Teilverantwortung;
~ **for an accident** Unfallhaftung; ~ **of the accused** Zurechnungsfähigkeit des Angeklagten; ~ **of eviction** Beweislast bei einer Räumungsklage; ~ **of one seeking a loan** Kreditfähigkeit eines Darlehnsnehmers; ~ **will be to the general manager** unmittelbare Unterstellung unter den Vorstandsvorsitzer; ~ **and accountability of ministers** ministerielle Verantwortlichkeit; **husband's** ~ **for wife's expenditure** ehemännliche Haftung für Ausgaben im Rahmen der Schlüsselgewalt;
to accept ~ **for s. th.** Verantwortung für etw. auf sich nehmen; **to admit one's** ~ seine Verantwortlichkeit zugeben; **to assume** ~ Verantwortung übernehmen; **to assume [the]** ~ **for another's debts** Haftung für j. übernehmen; **to assume** ~ **in the overall operating management** Gesamtverantwortung in einem Vorstandsbereich übernehmen; **to be immune of criminal** ~ strafrechtlich nicht verantwortlich (unzurechnungsfähig) sein; **to bear** ~ Verantwortung tragen; **to decline all** ~ **for an accident** Verantwortung für einen Unfall restlos ablehnen; **to do s. th. on one's [own]** ~ etw. auf eigene Verantwortung übernehmen; **to get rid of a** ~ Verantwortung von sich abschieben; **to incur** ~ Verantwortung übernehmen; **to join together in** ~ Verantwortung gemeinsam übernehmen; **to pass** ~ **down the line** Verantwortungsbereich dezentralisieren; **to pin** ~ **on s. o. for s. th.** j. für etw. verantwortlich machen; **to put** ~ **on s. one's shoulders** jem. Verantwortung auferlegen; **to question the** ~ **of s. one seeking a loan** jds. Kreditfähigkeit in Frage stellen; **to saddle o. s. with a** ~ sich eine Verantwortung aufbürden (aufladen); **to seek relief from one's** ~ Haftungsbefreiung zu erreichen suchen; **to take the** ~ Haftung übernehmen; **to withdraw from a** ~ sich der Verantwortung entziehen;

~ **basis** Verantwortungsbereich; ~ **chart** Schaubild der Verantwortungsbereiche; ~ **costing** verantwortlich aufgeteilte Kostenkalkulation.

responsible *(accountable)* rechnungspflichtig, *(legally accountable)* zurechnungs-, geschäftsfähig, *(answerable)* verantwortlich, *(politically answerable)* rechenschaftspflichtig, *(competent)* zuständig, kompetent, *(liable)* haftpflichtig, haftbar, *(solvent)* zahlungsfähig, solvent, solid, *(trustworthy)* vertrauenswürdig;

jointly and severally ~ solidarisch (gesamtschuldnerisch) haftbar; **not** ~ nicht geschäftsfähig, geschäftsunfähig, *(criminal)* nicht zurechnungsfähig; **primarily** ~ unmittelbar haftpflichtig; ~ **to a limited extent** beschränkt geschäftsfähig; ~ **before public opinion** der öffentlichen Meinung verantwortlich;

to be ~ Verantwortung tragen, verantwortlich zeichnen, aufkommen, einstehen, *(liable)* haften; **to be** ~ **to s. o.** jem. unterstehen; **not to be** ~ unzurechnungsfähig sein; **to be** ~ **for s. one's actions** für j. haften (voll verantwortlich sein); **to be** ~ **to the court** dem Gericht Rechnung zu legen haben; **to be** ~ **for the expenditure** Ausgaben zu verantworten haben; **to be** ~ **for a loss** auf Schadenersatz haften, für einen Verlust aufkommen müssen; **to be** ~ **for maintenance** unterhaltspflichtig sein; **to be** ~ **for the passengers' safety** Verantwortung für die Sicherheit der Passagiere tragen; **to be** ~ **for [the] payment of a debt** für die Rückzahlung einer Schuld einzustehen haben; **to be** ~ **for the petty cash** Portokasse verwalten; **to be primarily** ~ unmittelbar verantwortlich sein (haften); **to hold s. o.** ~ j. verantwortlich machen, sich an j. halten; **to hold the carrier** ~ **for the full value** vollen Schadenersatz vom Spediteur verlangen; **to make o. s.** ~ verantwortlich zeichnen;

~ **age** geschäftsfähiges Alter, Mündigkeit; **[not] to be of** ~ **age** unzurechnungsfähig sein; ~ **bidder** zahlungsfähiger Ersteigerer; ~ **business** zahlungsfähige (solvente) Firma; ~ **cause** Haftungsgrund; ~ **editor** verantwortlicher Redakteur; ~ **government** parlamentarische Regierungsform, *(Br.)* demokratische Regierung; ~ **job** Vertrauensstellung; **to give a task to a** ~ **man** einem vertrauenswürdigen Mann eine Aufgabe übertragen; ~ **office** verantwortungsvolles Amt; ~ **partner** persönlich haftender Gesellschafter (Teilhaber); ~ **position (post)** Vertrauensstellung, -position; **to have a very** ~ **position** sehr verantwortungsreiche Stellung innehaben; ~ **work** verantwortungsvolle Tätigkeit.

responsions *(Br.)* Aufnahmeprüfung.

responsive zugänglich, ansprechbar;
to be ~ **to the government's appeal** dem Wunsch der Regierung nachkommen.

rest Nachtruhe, *(abode)* Wohnstätte, Aufenthalt, *(balance)* Rest, [Rechnungs]saldo, Konto-, Rechnungsabschluß, *(balance sheet, Br.)* Bücherabschluß, Bilanzierung, *(Bank of England balance)* ausgewiesener Bilanzgewinn, Reservefonds, *(remainder)* [Über]rest, *(repose)* Ruhepause, *(reserve fund, Br.)* Reserve[fonds] [der Bank von England];

for the ~ im übrigen; **in need of a** ~ erholungsbedürftig; **without** ~ unverzüglich, ohne aufzuhören;

~**s** Rückstände;

half-yearly ~**s** Halbjahresabschlüsse; **net** ~ Nettoüberschuß; **night's** ~ nächtliche Ruhe; **sailor's** ~ Seemannsheim; **traveller's** ~ Touristenherberge; **well-earned** ~ wohlverdiente Ruhe;

~ **(v.)** *(matter)* unerledigt bleiben, *(be quiet)* feiern, nicht arbeiten, sich ausruhen;

~ **up** *(US)* sich ausruhen; ~ **upon** vertrauen, sich stützen, beruhen; ~ **with** *(burden of proof)* liegen bei, *(title)* gehören zu; ~ **assured** versichert sein können; ~ **one's case** *(US)* sein Plädoyer abschließen; ~ **one's case on equity** seinen Fall auf Treu und Glauben abstellen; ~ **a case on slender evidence** Fall auf schwachen Beweisen aufbauen; ~ **in the churchyard** auf dem Friedhof [begraben] sein; ~ **upon credit** auf Vertrauen beruhen; ~ **with s. o. to decide** jds. Entscheidung überlassen bleiben; ~ **a field a year** Acker ein Jahr brachliegen lassen; ~ **more and more in s. one's hands** immer mehr von jem. abhängen; ~ **a machine** Maschine zum Stillstand bringen; ~ **on one's oars** sich auf seinen Lorbeeren ausruhen; ~ **largely on personal opinion** vorwiegend Ansichtssache sein; ~ **an opinion on proof** seine Meinung auf Beweise stützen;

to be laid to ~ begraben werden; **to have several** ~**s on one's way** mehrere Ruhepausen einlegen; **to let a matter** ~ Sache auf sich beruhen lassen; **to set s. one's mind at** ~ j. beruhigen, auf j. beruhigend einwirken; **to set a question at** ~ Frage entscheiden; **to take a** ~ **[from work]** sich eine Arbeitspause gönnen; **to throw away the** ~ Rest wegwerfen; **to travel with occasional** ~**s** mit Unterbrechungen reisen;

~ **accommodation** Bereitstellung von Freizeiträumen; ~ **account** *(Br.)* Kontoabschluß; **transferred to** ~ **account** *(Br.)* auf das Rücklagenkonto übertragen; ~ **capital** *(Br.)* Kapitalreserve im Fall der Liquidation; ~ **center (centre, Br.)** Erholungsstätte, -zentrum; ~ **day** Ruhetag; ~ **fund** *(banking)* Mindestreserve; ~ **home** Erholungsheim; ~ **house** Rasthaus; ~ **interval** Ruhepause; ~ **pause (period)** Ruhezeit, Arbeits-, Betriebs-, Ruhe-, Werkspause; ~ **room** Aufenthalts-, Tagesraum, *(US)* Waschraum, Toilette, *(public lavatory)* öffentliche Bedürfnisanstalt.

restart *(v.)* wieder in Betrieb setzen;
~ **investing** erneut investieren.

restate *(v.)* erneut darstellen;
~ **a question** Frage erneut formulieren.

restatement Neuformulierung, erneute Darstellung.

restaurant Gastwirtschaft, -stätte, Lokal, Restaurant, Restauration;

de-luxe ~ Luxusrestaurant; **fast-food** ~ Schnellimbißrestaurant; **municipal** ~ städtische Gaststätte; **takeaway** ~ Hauslieferant von Menüs, Buffetdienst;

to operate *(US)* **(run, Br.)** a ~ Restaurant betreiben;

~ **bill** Restaurantrechnung; **hotel and** ~ **business** Gaststättengewerbe; ~ **car** *(US)* Speisewagen; ~ **chain** Restaurantkette; ~ **keeper** Gastwirt; ~ **owner** Restaurantbesitzer; ~ **tax** Schanksteuer; ~ **worker** Gaststättenangestellter.

restaurateur Gastwirt, Restaurantbesitzer.

resting place Ruheplatz, *(dead person)* Ruhe-, Begräbnisstätte.

restitute *(v.)* ersetzen, Ersatz leisten, wiederherstellen, wiedergutmachen, *(refund)* zurückzahlen, rückerstatten.

restitutee Wiedergutmachungs-, Rückerstattungsberechtigter.

restitutio in integrum *(lat.)* Wiederherstellung des ursprünglichen Zustands.

restitution *(maritime law)* Rückgewinnung von Ladungswurfgütern, *(restoration)* Wiedererstattung, *(return)* Rückgabe, -erstattung, -lieferung, Restitution, Herstellung des früheren Zustandes, Wiedergutmachung, -gabe, *(judicial writ)* Wiedereinsetzung in den vorigen Stand;

~ **of stolen goods** Herausgabe gestohlener Gegenstände; ~ **in kind** Naturalrestitution, -herstellung; ~ **of minors** Aufhebung von Verträgen von Minderjährigen; ~ **of the purchase money** Rückerstattung des Kaufpreises; ~ **of property** Vermögensrückgabe, Restitution; ~ **of rights** Wiederherstellung von Rechten; ~ **of conjugal rights** *(Br.)* Wiederherstellung der ehelichen Gemeinschaft;

to be liable to make ~ rückerstattungspflichtig sein; **to demand** ~ Herausgabe verlangen; **to make** ~ rückerstatten, Ersatz leisten;

~ **case** Restitutions-, Rückerstattungsprozeß, -sache, Wiedergutmachungsfall, -prozeß; ~ **costs** Wiederherstellungskosten; ~ **order** *(Br.)* Rückerstattungsbeschluß; ~ **treaty** Wiedergutmachungsabkommen.

restitutor Rückerstattungspflichtiger.

restitutory right Restitutionsrecht, Rückerstattungsanspruch.

restless audience unruhiges Publikum.

restock *(v.)* *(US)* wieder auf Lager nehmen, Lager wieder auffüllen, Vorrat ergänzen.

restocking *(US)* Lagerauffüllung, Vorratsergänzung;
~ **operations** *(US)* Vorratsergänzungsgeschäfte.

restoration *(currency)* Sanierung, *(to office)* Wiedereinsetzung, *(reparation)* Instandsetzung, Wiederherstellung des früheren Zustands, Wiedergutmachung, Restaurierung, *(return)* Wieder-, Rück-, Herausgabe, Rückerstattung, Wiederbringung, Restitution;

closed during ~ während der Instandsetzungsarbeiten geschlossen;

large-scale ~ Restaurationsmaßnahmen im großen Stil;

~ **of a building** Gebäudeinstandsetzung; ~ **to its original condition** Wiederherstellung des ursprünglichen Zustands; ~ **of currency** Sanierung der Währung; ~ **of goods in distraint** Pfandfreigabe; ~ **to health** Wiederherstellung der Gesundheit; ~ **of a painting** Restaurierung eines Gemäldes; ~ **of a lapsed patent** Wiederherstellung eines verfallenen Patents; ~ **of peace** Wiederherstellung des Friedens; ~ **to the original position** Herstellung des ursprünglichen Zustands; ~ **of possession** Wiedereinräumung des Besitzes; ~ **of confiscated property** Vermögensrückgabe, Restitution; ~ **of stolen property** Wiedererlangung gestohlener Gegenstände; ~ **of public order** Wiederherstellung der öffentlichen Sicherheit und Ordnung; ~ **from sickness** Gesundung, Wiederherstellung der Gesundheit; ~ **of supplies** Umlagerung von Vorräten;

~ **project** Gebäudesanierung.

restore *(US) (give back)* zurückgeben, -erstatten, wiederbringen, *(reimburse)* wiedererstatten, ersetzen, *(reinstate)* wiedereinsetzen, *(repair)* instandsetzen, reparieren, *(replace)* wiedereinsetzen, -herstellen, *(supplies)* umlagern;

~ **borrowed books** geliehene Bücher zurückgeben; ~ **a ruin[ed building]** verfallenes Gebäude wiederherstellen (instandsetzen); ~ **the cargo** Ladung neu verstauen; ~ **to its original condition** in den vorherigen Stand wiedereinsetzen; ~ **an employee to his old post** einem Angestellten seine alte Stellung wiedergeben; ~ **stolen goods** gestohlene Gegenstände zurückgeben; ~ **to a level** wieder auf den vorherigen Stand zurückbringen; ~ **s. o. to liberty** jem. die Freiheit wiedergeben; ~ **money to the owner** Geld dem Eigentümer zurückerstatten; ~ **an officer to his command** einem Offizier sein Kommando zurückgeben; ~ **an officer to full pay** Offizier reaktivieren; ~ **a painting** Gemälde restaurieren; ~ **peace** Frieden wieder herstellen; ~ **to possession** wieder in den Besitz setzen; ~ **confiscated property** beschlagnahmtes Vermögen freigeben; ~ **public order (law and order)** öffentliche Sicherheit und Ordnung wiederherstellen; ~ **in status quo ante** ursprünglichen Zustand wiederherstellen; ~ **the state of things** früheren Zustand wiederherstellen; ~ **a text** Text rekonstruieren; ~ **a king to the throne** König wiedereinsetzen; ~ **the real value of income tax allowance** Realwert der Einkommenssteuerfreibeträge den Inflationsauswirkungen anpassen.

restow *(v.)* erneut verstauen.

restrain *(v.)* zurückhalten, ein-, beschränken, *(law)* hemmen.

~ **o. s.** sich Zwang auferlegen (zurückhalten); ~ **s. one's activities** jds. Tätigkeitsbereich einschränken; ~ **one's appetite** seinen Appetit zügeln; ~ **the boom** Konjunktur dämpfen; ~ **competition** Wettbewerb beschränken; ~ **s. one's freedom to work** jem. ein Wettbewerbsverbot auferlegen; ~ **an insane person** Geisteskranken in einer geschlossenen Anstalt unterbringen; ~ **production** Produktion drosseln; ~ **rights** Rechte schmälern; ~ **trade** Wettbewerb beschränken.

restraining Beschränkung, Zurückhaltung;

~ **of trade** Wettbewerbsbeschränkung; ~ **clause** Konkurrenzklausel, einschränkende Bestimmung; ~ **order** *(US)* einstweilige Verfügung, Verfügungsverbot, *(public company)* Verfügungsverbot für Aktienübertragungen; ~ **powers** Vollmachtsbeschränkung; ~ **statute** einschränkende Verordnung.

restraint *(check)* Eindämmung, Hemmung, Verhinderung, *(reserve)* Zurückhaltung, [Verfügungs]beschränkung, *(of liberty)* Freiheitsbeschränkung, Sicherheitsverwahrung;

under ~ unter Gewahrsam; **without** ~ ungehemmt, außer Kontrolle;

ancillary ~ wettbewerbsbeschränkende Nebenabrede; **felonious** ~ *(US)* bösartige Beschränkung der Handelsfreiheit; **monetary** ~ Geldverknappung; **self-**~ Selbstbeherrschung, -beschränkung; **unreasonable** ~ unlauterer Wettbewerb;

~ **on alienation** *(Br.)* Veräußerungsverbot; ~ **upon anticipation** *(US)* Verbot der Vorausverfügung, *(wife)* Verfügungsbeschränkung über Vorbehaltsgut; ~ **of competition** Wettbewerbsbeschränkung; ~ **on disposal** Verfügungsbeschränkung; ~ **upon liberty** Freiheitsbeschränkung; ~ **of marriage** Eheverbot, Heiratsbeschränkung; ~ **of lunatic** Sicherungsverwahrung eines Geisteskranken; ~ **of poverty** Fesseln der Armut; ~ **of princes and rulers** *(marine insurance)* Verfügungen von hoher Hand, hoheitsrechtliche Eingriffe, Embargo, Einwand der Beschlagnahme auf hoher See; ~ **in spending** Einschränkung der Ausgabenwirtschaft; ~ **of trade** Handelserschwerung, -beschränkung, *(competition)* Konkurrenzbeschränkung, -verbot, Einschränkung des freien Wettbewerbs, Wettbewerbsbeschränkung; ~**s of foreign trade** Außenhandelsbeschränkungen;

to act without ~ nach Gutdünken handeln; **to be put under** ~ entmündigt werden; **to break loose from all** ~ alle Hemmungen über Bord werfen; **to fling aside all** ~ alle Hemmungen fahren lassen; **to lay s. o. under** ~ jem. Beschränkungen auferlegen; **to place s. o. under** ~ Sicherungsverwahrung für j. anordnen; **to put a** ~ **upon o. s.** sich zügeln, sich Zurückhaltung auferlegen; **to put a** ~ **on s. one's activities** jds. Betätigungsfeld (Tätigkeitsdrang) einschränken; **to put s. o. under illegal** ~ j. ungesetzlich in Gewahrsam halten; **to put a lunatic under** ~ Geisteskranken entmündigen (in eine Anstalt bringen); **to speak without** ~ rückhaltlos sprechen; **to submit to** ~ sich Zurückhaltung auferlegen; **to uphold a** ~ auf einer Verfügungsbeschränkung bestehen;

~ **agreement** Konkurrenz-, Wettbewerbsvereinbarung; ~ **clause** Konkurrenz-, Wettbewerbsklausel.

restrict *(v.)* ein-, beschränken, *(real estate, US)* Baubeschränkungen erlassen;

~ **competition** Wettbewerb einschränken; ~ **the consumption of alcohol** Alkoholverbrauch einschränken; ~ **cultivation** Anbaubeschränkungen erlassen; ~ **a district** *(US)* Baubeschränkungen für ein bestimmtes Gebiet festsetzen; ~ **the freedom of movement** Freizügigkeit einschränken; ~ **one's investigations** seine Untersuchungen beschränken; ~ **one's matter to two points** sich lediglich auf zwei Punkte beschränken; ~ **to thirty miles an hour in built-up areas** Höchstgeschwindigkeit in geschlossenen Ortschaften auf 50 km beschränken; ~ **s. one's powers within narrow limits** jds. Vollmacht in engen Grenzen halten; ~ **production** Produktion drosseln; ~ **the right to transfer shares** Aktien vinkulieren; ~ **a road** Geschwindigkeitsbeschränkungen für eine Straße festsetzen; ~ **the use of monopoly powers** Ausnutzung einer Monopolstellung einschränken.

restrictable beschränkbar.

restricted beschränkt, begrenzt, eingeschränkt, *(controlled)* bewirtschaftet, *(confidential)* nur für den Dienstgebrauch, *(under reserve)* vorbehaltlich;

to be ~ **to advising** nur beraten dürfen;

~ **account** beschränktes Börsenkonto; ~ **application** begrenzte Anwendung; ~ **area** *(US)* Zone mit Geschwindigkeitsbegrenzung, Sperrgebiet; ~ **cash** Termineinlagen; **to live in a** ~ **circle** sehr kleinen Bekanntenkreis haben; ~ **covenant** Nutzungsbeschränkung; **to enjoy** ~ **credit** bescheidenen Kredit genießen; ~ **data** *(US)* Geheimbestimmungen unterliegende Angaben; **to declassify** ~ **data** *(US)* Geheimmaterial freigeben; ~ **district** *(US)* Gebiet mit Baubeschränkungen; ~ **fund** Thesaurierungsfonds, Spezialfonds; ~ **governmental contract** geheimhaltungsbedürftiger Staatsauftrag; ~ **horizon** beschränkter Horizont; ~ **hours** Parkverbotszeit; ~ **hours tariff** *(el.)* Nachtstromtarif; ~ **indorsement** beschränktes Giro; ~ **information** vertrauliche Information; ~ **information circular** Information für den internen Dienstgebrauch; ~ **lands** *(US)* nur mit Genehmigung verkäufliche Grundstücke; ~ **matter** *(US)* nur für den Dienstgebrauch, Verschlußsache; ~ **ownership** beschränktes Eigentum; ~ **receipts** zweckgebundene Einnahmen; ~ **regulations** einschränkende Bestimmungen; ~ **share** gebundene Aktie; ~ **stock** *(US)* nur an private Abnehmer verkaufsfähige Aktie; ~ **stock option** *(US)* Aktienangebot an die Angestellten; ~ **street** Parkverbotsstraße.

restriction Be-, Einschränkung, *(land register, Br.)* Veräußerungsbeschränkung, *(reservation)* Vorbehalt, *(zoning laws, US)* Baubeschränkung;

without ~**s** uneingeschränkt;

bank ~ Beschränkung der Einwechselungspflicht; **credit** ~ Kreditrestriktion, -einschränkung; **currency (foreign-exchange)** ~ Devisenbeschränkungen, -bewirtschaftung; **customer** ~ *(antitrust law, US)* Kundenbeschränkung; **mental** ~ geheimer Vorbehalt, Mentalreservation; **quantitative** ~**s** Mengenbeschränkungen, mengenmäßige Beschränkungen, *(import)* mengenmäßige Einfuhrbeschränkungen; **quota** ~**s** Kontingentbeschränkungen; **rent** ~**s** *(Br.)* Mieterschutzbestimmungen; **territorial** ~**s** *(antitrust laws, US)* Gebietsbeschränkungen; **zoning** ~**s** *(US)* Baubeschränkungen;

~**s on allotment** Zuteilungsbeschränkungen; ~ **to a certain area** Aufenthaltsbeschränkung auf ein bestimmtes Gebiet; ~ **of armaments** Rüstungsbegrenzung; ~ **on benefit** *(insurance)* Karenz; ~ **of the birth rate** Geburtenbeschränkung; ~**s on business** wirtschaftliche Beschränkungen; ~ **on circulation** Auflagebegrenzung; ~ **of commerce** Handelsbeschränkungen; ~**s set on consumption** Konsumbeschränkungen; ~ **of credit** Kreditverknappung; ~ **of consumer credits** Konsumptivkreditbeschränkung; ~ **on cultivation** Anbaubeschränkung; ~**s on discharge** Entlassungsbeschränkungen; ~ **on freedom of establishment** Niederlassungsbeschränkung; ~ **of expenditure** Ausgabenbeschränkung; ~ **of exports** Ausfuhrbeschränkungen; ~**s on immigration** Einwanderungsbeschränkungen; **quantitative** ~ **of imports** mengenmäßige Einfuhrbeschränkung; ~**s on investment** Investitionsbeschränkung, Anlagebeschränkungen; ~ **on investment of special classes** *(insurance company)* Anlagebeschränkung auf bestimmte Sparten; ~**s on landing** beschränkte Landemöglichkeiten; ~ **of a law** Einengung durch ein Gesetz; ~ **of output** Ertrags-, Ausstoßbeschränkung, Produktionsbegrenzung; ~ **of power** Vollmachtsbeschränkung, Einschränkung einer Vollmacht; ~ **of production** Produktionsdrosselung, -beschränkung; ~**s contrary to the public interest** gegen das allgemeine Wohl verstoßende Beschränkungen; ~**s on residence** Aufenthaltsbeschränkungen; ~ **of a road** Geschwindigkeitsbeschränkung auf einer Straße; ~ **on sales**

Verkaufsbeschränkung; ~ on [the right to transfer] shares Vinkulierung von Aktien; ~ of supply Angebotsbeschränkung; ~ in the use of power Einschränkung des Energieverbrauchs; ~s on travelling Reisebeschränkungen;

to abrogate ~s Beschränkungen aufheben; to be subject to ~s Einschränkungen unterliegen; to lift ~s on instalment buying Beschränkungen auf dem Abzahlungsgebiet aufheben; to place ~s on the sale of s. th. Verkaufsbeschränkungen für etw. festsetzen (anordnen); to plan ~s on imports Einführung von Einfuhrbeschränkungen beabsichtigen; to reimpose ~s on imports Liberalisierung aufheben; to remove ~s Beschränkungen beseitigen; to withdraw ~s Beschränkungen aufheben.

restrictionist *(Canada)* Schutzzollanhänger.

restrictive einschränkend, beschränkend;
to construe ~ly einschränkend (eng) auslegen;
~ **budget policy** restriktive Haushaltspolitik; ~ **business practices** unlauterer Wettbewerb, *(cartel law, Br.)* wettbewerbsbeschränkende Verhaltensweise; ~ **central bank policy** restriktive Notenbankpolitik; ~ **clause** einschränkende Bestimmung; ~ **condition** Unterlassungsverpflichtung; **to hold a ~ economic course** restriktive Wirtschaftspolitik betreiben; ~ **covenant** Nutzungsbeschränkung, *(employee)* Wettbewerbsverbot, -beschränkung, Konkurrenzklausel, *(real estate)* Baubeschränkungsvereinbarung, *(US)* obligatorische Nebenvereinbarung; ~ **credit policy** restriktive Kreditpolitik, Kreditdrosselungspolitik; ~ **elements** zeitlich nicht beeinflußbare Arbeitsgänge; ~ **endorsement** beschränktes Giro (Indossament), Rektagiro, -indossament; ~ **fiscal policy** restriktive steuerpolitische Maßnahmen; ~ **indorsement** *(US)* beschränktes Giro, Rektaindossament; ~ **injunction** Verbotsverfügung, Unterlassungsanordnung; ~ **interpretation** einschränkende (enge) Auslegung; ~ **labo(u)r practices** *(trade union)* Überbesetzung von Arbeitsplätzen; ~ **particle of a tariff** einschränkende Tarifbestimmung; ~ **policy** Restriktionspolitik; ~ **practices** wettbewerbsbeschränkende Verhaltensweisen, *(labo(u)r, Br.)* untaugliche Arbeitsmethoden; ~ **practice agreement** Kartellvertrag; ℗ **Practices Court** *(Br.)* Gericht für Wettbewerbsbeschränkungen, Kartellgericht; ~ **regulations** einschränkende Bestimmungen; ~ **trade agreement** *(Br.)* Kartellvereinbarung; ~ **trade practices** *(Br.)* wettbewerbsbeschränkende Geschäftspraktiken, Kartellmaßnahmen; ℗ **Trade Practices Act** *(Br.)* Kartellgesetz; ~ **trading agreement** *(Br.)* wettbewerbsbeschränkende Kartellvereinbarung (Absprache), Kartellabkommen; ~ **travel clause** *(insurance)* territoriale Einschränkungsklausel.

restrike *(coins)* Neuprägung.
restructure *(v.)* **an industry throughout the community** Industriezweig in der gesamten Europäischen Gemeinschaft völlig umstrukturieren.
restructuring, top-to-bottom Neugliederung von Grund auf;
~ **scheme** Umstellungsschema.
restyle *(v.)* umarbeiten, -ändern.
resubmission Wiedervorlage.
result [End]ergebnis, Auswirkung, Resultat, Folge, Erfolg, Ausfall, *(balance sheet, US)* Jahresergebnis;
~s *(achievement)* Leistung, *(advertising)* Werbeerfolg, *(consequence)* Folge;
approximate ~ annähernd richtiges Ergebnis (Resultat); **audited** ~ *(US)* bilanzgeprüftes Jahresergebnis; **drab** ~ kümmerliches Ergebnis; **election** ~ Wahlergebnis; **examination** ~ Prüfungsergebnis; **favo(u)rable** ~ günstiges Ergebnis; **final** ~ Schlußergebnis; **financial** ~ finanzielles Ergebnis; **operating** ~ Geschäftsergebnis; **physical** ~ praktisches Ergebnis; **poor** ~ mageres Ergebnis; **profit** ~ Gewinnergebnis; **proximate** ~ unmittelbare Folge; **scientific** ~s wissenschaftliche Ausbeute; **tangible** ~s greifbare Ergebnisse; **trading** ~ Geschäftsergebnis; **trustworthy** ~ sicheres Ergebnis; **total** ~ Gesamtergebnis;
~s **of an accident** Unfallfolgen; ~ **of adjudication** Verdingungsergebnis; ~ **of ballot** Abstimmungsergebnis; ~ **of an inquiry** Ermittlungs-, Untersuchungsergebnis; ~ **of a survey** Umfrageergebnis; ~s **for the year** *(US)* Abschluß-, Jahresergebnis; ~ **of the vote** Wahlresultat, Abstimmungsergebnis; ~s **of the war** Kriegsfolgen, -auswirkungen;
~ *(v.)* erwachsen, sich ergeben, hervorgehen, resultieren;
~ **to s. o.** *(estate)* jem. zufallen; ~ **in** zur Folge haben; ~ **from an accident** unfallbedingt sein; ~ **badly** schlechtes Ergebnis zeitigen; ~ **in failure** Mißerfolg sein; ~ **in the fall of the government** Regierungssturz herbeiführen, zum Sturz der Regierung führen; ~ **in a loss** mit Verlust abschließen; ~ **from negligence** auf Fahrlässigkeit zurückzuführen sein; ~ **in nothing** zu nichts führen; ~ **in a profit** Gewinn zeitigen; ~ **in war** Krieg zur Folge haben;

to announce the ~s of a competition Wettbewerbsergebnisse veröffentlichen; **to declare the ~ of a poll** Abstimmungsergebnis veröffentlichen; **not to expect to evaluate ~s until well into calendar 1981** positive Ergebnisse nicht vor Mitte 1981 erwarten; **to get ~s from a new treatment** mit einer neuen Behandlung Erfolge erzielen; **to give out the ~s** Wettbewerbsergebnisse verkünden; **to have a favo(u)rable ~** günstiges Ergebnis zeitigen; **to obtain (show) good ~s** gute Resultate erzielen (Ergebnisse zeitigen); **to suffer from the ~s of the war** an den Kriegsfolgen leiden; **to work with good ~s** mit Gewinn arbeiten; **to work without ~** umsonst arbeiten, kein Ergebnis erzielen; **to yield ~s** gute Ergebnisse zeitigen;
~ **fee** *(Br.)* Erfolgshonorar; ~ **wage** Erfolgslohn.

resulting herrührend;
~ **bank** Nachfolgebank; ~ **powers** resultierende Rechte; ~ **trust** gesetzlich vermutetes Treuhandverhältnis; ~ **use** zeitlich beschränktes Nießbrauchrecht.

resume *(v.)* wiederaufnehmen, *(parl.)* wieder in die Plenarsitzung eintreten, *(recover)* wiedererlangen, *(summarize)* zusammenfassen, resümieren;
~ **one's activities** seine Tätigkeit wieder aufnehmen; ~ **business** Geschäft wiedereröffnen; ~ **a correspondence with s. o.** mit jem. wieder in Briefwechsel treten, Korrespondenz mit jem. wiederaufnehmen; ~ **one's duties** seinen Pflichten wieder nachgehen; ~ **hostilities** Feindseligkeiten wiederaufnehmen; ~ **a journey** Reise fortsetzen; ~ **liberty** Freiheit wiedergewinnen; ~ **one's maiden name** Mädchennamen wieder annehmen; ~ **negotiations** Verhandlungen wiederaufnehmen; ~ **payments** Zahlungen wiederaufnehmen; ~ **possession of s. th.** etw. wieder in Besitz nehmen; ~ **proceedings** Verfahren wiederaufnehmen; ~ **one's seat** seinen Platz wiedereinnehmen; ~ **a speech** in seiner Rede fortfahren; ~ **a territory** Gebiet wiedererobern; ~ **the thread of one's discourse** Faden seiner Erzählung wiederaufnehmen; ~ **work** Arbeit wiederaufnehmen.

resumé Zusammenfassung, Resümee.
resummon *(v.)* erneut (nochmals) laden.
resummons erneute (nochmalige) Ladung.
resumption Wiederaufnahme, -annahme, *(grant)* Zurücknahme einer Bewilligung, Lizenzentzug;
~ **of business** Wiederaufnahme der Geschäftstätigkeit; ~ **of dividends** Wiederaufnahme der Dividendenzahlungen; ~ **of a grant** erneute Gewährung eines Zuschusses; ~ **of inflation** Inflationsrückkehr; ~ **of payments** Wiederaufnahme der Zahlungen; ~ **of specie payments** Wiederaufnahme der Barzahlungen; ~ **of possession** Wiederinbesitznahme; ~ **of residence** Wiederbegründung des Wohnsitzes; ~ **of service of a loan** Wiederaufnahme des Anleihezinsendienstes; ~ **of specie payments** Wiederaufnahme der Barzahlungen; ~ **of a trial** Wiederaufnahme eines Verfahrens; ~ **of work** Wiederaufnahme der Arbeit.

resupply Wiederbelieferung;
~ *(v.)* erneut beliefern.
resurface *(v.)* *(submarine)* wieder auftauchen;
~ **a road** Straßendecke erneuern.
resurgence in earnings wiederauflebende Ertragsstärke.
resurgent nationalism wiederauflebender Nationalismus.
resurrect *(v.)* | **a body** Leiche exhumieren; ~ **an ancient custom** alte Sitte wiederaufleben lassen.
resurrection *(body snatching)* Leichenraub.
resurvey neue Vermessung;
~ *(v.)* erneut vermessen.
resuscitate *(v.)* wiederbeleben.
resuscitation Wiederbelebung.
retail Klein-, Handverkauf, Handel in kleinen Mengen, Detailgeschäft, Einzelverkauf, -handel;
by ~ im einzelnen, en detail, in kleinen Mengen, im Einzelhandel, stückweise; **wholesale and ~** im Groß- und Einzelhandel;
~ *(v.)* im kleinen (en detail) verkaufen, wiederverkaufen, detaillieren, Einzelhandelsgeschäft betreiben;
~ **at five shillings** im Einzelhandel 5 Schilling kosten; ~ **a slander** Verleumdung verbreiten;
to buy ~ en detail kaufen; **to sell [by, *Br.*, at, *US*] ~** einzeln (en detail, im Einzelhandel) verkaufen, wiederverkaufen, im Kleinverkauf absetzen;
~ **account** Einzelhandelskunde; ~ **advertising** Einzelhandelswerbung; ~ **association** *(US)* Einzelhändlerverband, Einzelhändlervereinigung; ~ **book credit** Kundenkredit [des Kaufmanns]; ~ **bookseller** Sortimentsbuchhändler, Sortimenter; ~ **bookseller customer** Sortimenter-Kommittent; ~ **business** Einzelhandels-, Detailgeschäft; **to make ~ calls** Einzelhandelsgeschäfte besuchen; ~ **ceiling price** Verbraucher-

höchstpreis; ~ **chain** *(US)* Einzelhandelskette; ~ **charge account** Kundenkreditkonto; ~ **clientele** Einzelhandelskundschaft; ~ **competitor** Einzelhandelskonkurrenz; ~ **consignments** Einzelsendungen, Stückgut; ~ **co-ops** Einkaufsgenossenschaften des Einzelhandels; ~ **cooperative society** *(Br.)* Konsumgenossenschaft; ~ **cost** *(accounting)* Zuschlagkosten; ~ **credit** *(US)* Kunden-, Konsumptivkredit; **to seek ~ credit** *(US)* Kundenkredit beantragen; ~ **credit [exchange] bureau** *(US)* Kundenkreditauskunftsstelle; ~ **creditor** *(US)* Kundenkreditgeschäft; ~ **customer** Einzelhandelskunde; ~ **dealer** Einzel-, Kleinhändler, Wiederverkäufer, Einzelhandelskaufmann; ~ **dealing** Einzelhandel[sgeschäfte]; ~ **demand** Bedürfnisse des Einzelhandels; ~ **department** Einzelhandelsabteilung; ~ **discount** Einzelhandels-, Kleinhandelsrabatt; ~ **distribution** Einzelhandelsverteilung; ~ **distribution agency** Einzelhandelsverteilungsstelle; ~ **drawing** Stückauszeichnung; ~ **enterprise (establishment, firm)** Einzelhandelsunternehmen, -betrieb, -firma, Ladengeschäft; ~ **function** Einzelhandelsfunktion; ~ **goods** Detailwaren; ~ **group** *(US)* Händlervereinigung; ~ **house** Detail-, Einzelhandelsgeschäft; ~ **issue** Klein-, Einzelhandelsverkauf; ~ **industry** Einzel-, Kleinhandelsindustrie; ~ **issue** Kleinverkauf; ~ **licence** Gewerbeschein für den Einzelhandel, Einzelhandelslizenz, -konzession; ~ **line** Sortiment des Einzelhandels; ~ **margin** Einzelhandelsgewinn-, Kleinverkaufsspanne; ~ **market** Einzelhandel; ~ **markup** Einzelhandelsspanne; ~ **member** Einzelhandelsmitglied; ~ **merchandising** Wareneinzelhandel; ~ **merchant** Einzel-, Klein-, Detailhändler; ~ **method** *(accounting)* Zuschlagsmethode; ~ **method of valuation** Realisationsprinzip; ~ **middleman** Detailzwischenhändler; ~ **operation** Einzelhandelsbetrieb, -unternehmen; ~ **organization** Einzelhandelsorganisation; ~ **outlet** Einzelhandelsgeschäft; **established ~ outlet** anerkannte Verkaufsstelle; ~ **[selling] price** Kleinhandels-, Einzelhandels-, Laden-, Detail-, Konsumenten-, Kleinverkaufspreis; ~ **ceiling price** Verkaufshöchstpreis; **controlled ~ price** *(book trade)* gebundener Ladenpreis; **fixed ~ price** Endverbraucherpreis; **recommended ~ price** empfohlener Ladenpreis; ~ **price determination (fixing, making)** Bestimmung des Einzelhandelspreises; ~ **price index** Einzelhandelspreisindex; ~ **price maintenance** Preisbindung der zweiten Hand; ~ **net profit** Einzelhandelsnettoverdienst; ~ **reduction** Herabsetzung der Einzelhandelspreise; ~ **sale** Ladenverkauf; ~ **sales** Einzelhandelsumsatz; **not made up for ~ sale** nicht in Aufmachungen für den Einzelverkauf; ~ **sales tax** *(US)* Kleinhandels-, Einzelhandelsumsatzsteuer; **to lead the ~ sector** im Einzelhandel führend sein; ~ **shop** *(Br.)* Klein-, Einzelhandelsgeschäft; ~ **shop selling** *(Br.)* Einzelhandelsverkauf; ~ **society** *(Br.)* Konsumgenossenschaft; ~ **spending boom** Einzelhandelskonjunktur; ~ **store** *(US)* Detail-, Laden-, Einzelhandelsgeschäft [eines Konzerns]; ~ **store sales** *(US)* Einzelhandelsumsätze; ~ **structure** Einzelhandelsstruktur; ~ **trade** Einzelhandel[sgewerbe]; ~ **trade demands** Bedürfnisse des Einzelhandels; ~ **trader** Einzelhändler, Einzelhandelskaufmann; ~ **trading** Einzelhandel; ~ **trading zone** zentrumsnahes Geschäftsviertel; ~ **turnover** Einzelhandelsumsätze; ~ **value** Kleinhandelsverkaufspreis.

retailer Klein-, Wiederverkäufer, Detail, Einzelhändler, Detaillist, kleiner Kaufmann;
independent ~ selbständiger Einzelhändler; **limited-line** ~ Inhaber eines Spezialgeschäftes; **mail-order** ~ Einzelhandelsversandgeschäft; **single-store** ~ selbständiger Einzelhändler; **small** ~ Kleinhändler;
~ **of merchandise** Einzelhändler;
~**affiliated** einzelhandelsorientiert; ~ **cooperative** *(US)* Einzelhändlereinkaufsgenossenschaft; ~'**s excise tax** *(US)* Einzelhandels-, Kleingewerbesteuer; ~**-sponsored** vom Einzelhändler gefördert; ~ **survey** Einzelhändlerbefragung.

retailing Detailverkauf, Einzelhandel, -verkauf;
large-scale ~ Massenfilialbetrieb;
to go into ~ ins Einzelhandelsgeschäft einsteigen;
~ **company** Einzelhandelsgesellschaft; ~ **sale** Stückverkauf.

retain *(v.)* behalten, *(book)* [Plätze] belegen, *(keep possession)* zurück-, einbehalten, thesaurieren, *(mil.)* Feindkräfte binden;
~ **for o. s.** sich vorbehalten; ~ **an agent** Vertreter beschäftigen; ~ **an amount out of the pay** Betrag vom Lohn einbehalten; ~ **a barrister** *(Br.)* **(counsel,** *US)* Anwalt bestellen, sich einen Anwalt nehmen; ~ **books** Handelsbücher, Bücher aufbewahren; ~ **in the business** Erträge im Geschäft wieder anlegen, im Geschäft als Rücklage verwenden; ~ **one's citizenship** *(Br.)* seine Staatsangehörigkeit beibehalten; ~ **control of one's car** seinen Wagen in der Gewalt behalten; ~ **an old custom** alten Brauch beibehalten; ~ **on a per-diem-plus-expense basis** auf

Tages- und Unkostenbasis engagieren; ~ **in exercise of one's lien** Eigentumszurückbehaltungsrecht ausüben; ~ **income** Erträge thesaurieren; ~ **a lien on shares** Zurückbehaltungsrecht an Aktien ausüben; ~ **in one's mind** im Gedächtnis behalten; ~ **part of the money** Teil des Geldes einbehalten, Teil des Geldes zurückbehalten; ~ **a clear memory of one's school days** sich bestens an seine Schulzeit erinnern können; ~ **one's nationality** *(US)* seine Staatsangehörigkeit beibehalten; ~ **one's position** seine Stellung behalten (behaupten); ~ **possession** nicht ausziehen; ~ **the power of s. th.** sich das Recht an etw. vorbehalten; ~ **the profit** Gewinn thesaurieren; ~ **profit for expansion** Gewinnrücklage für Erweiterungsinvestitionen bilden; ~ **a right** sich ein Recht vorbehalten; ~ **a sample** Probe entnehmen; ~ **s. one's service** sich jds. Dienste versichern; ~ **s. o. specially** jem. mit einem Sonderauftrag betreuen; ~ **title** sich das Eigentum vorbehalten; ~ **the use of all one's faculties** noch im vollen Besitz seiner geistigen Fähigkeiten sein.

retainable einbehaltungsfähig.

retained | in business im Betrieb stehengelassen;
~ **composition** *(print.)* Stehsatz; ~ **earnings** *(US)* nicht ausgeschüttete Gewinne, thesaurierter Gewinn, Gewinnvortrag; ~ **income** *(US)* nicht entnommener Gewinn, Gewinnrücklage; ~ **profits** *(US)* thesaurierter (nicht entnommener) Gewinn; ~ **risk** *(insurance)* nicht rückversicherter Risikoteil.

retainer Anwaltsbestellung, Inanspruchnahme eines Anwalts, *(fee, Br.)* vorläufiges Anwaltshonorar, Anwaltskostenvorschuß, Gebührenvorschuß, *(flat fee)* Pauschalhonorar, *(power of attorney)* Prozeßvollmacht, *(formal retention)* Zurückbehaltung[srecht], *(vassal)* Vassal;
old family ~ Familienfaktotum; **general** ~ ständige anwaltliche Tätigkeit bei Bedarf, *(fee)* festes Honorar, Pauschalhonorar; **special** ~ Sonderauftrag, *(special fee)* Sonderhonorar;
~ **of debts** *(personal representative)* Vorwegbefriedigungsrecht;
to charge a ~ Kostenvorschuß in Rechnung stellen;
~ **pay** Vergütung für Zeitfreiwillige.

retaining | a cause *(Br.)* Beibehaltung einer Zuständigkeit;
~ **fee** Anwalts-, Gebührenvorschuß; ~ **lien** Zurückbehaltungsrecht des Anwalts; ~ **note** *(US)* Eigentumsvorbehaltsurkunde; ~ **wall** Stützmauer.

retake *(film)* Wiederholungsaufnahme;
~ *(v.)* *(film)* nochmals aufnehmen, *(mil.)* zurückerobern;
~ **a town from the enemy** dem Feind eine Stadt wieder abnehmen.

retaking Wiederinbesitznahme.

retaliate *(v.)* *(customs)* Vergeltungsmaßnahmen treffen, Kampfzölle (Retorsionszölle) erheben;
~ **a charge on the accuser** Beschuldigung auf den Kläger zurückfallen lassen; ~ **upon one's enemy** Vergeltung an seinem Feind üben.

retaliation Vergeltung[smaßnahmen], Repressalien, *(customs)* Retorsion;
by way of ~ im Vergeltungswege;
fiscal ~ Erhebung von Kampfzöllen; **massive** ~ *(mil.)* massive Vergeltung;
to exercise (inflict) ~ Repressalien ergreifen; **to suffer** ~ Vergeltungsmaßnahmen hinnehmen.

retaliatory | action Vergeltungsaktion; ~ **deaths** als Vergeltungsmaßnahme gedachtes Blutvergießen; ~ **duty** Kampf-, Retorsionszoll; ~ **forces** *(mil.)* Schwerststreitkräfte; ~ **measures** Repressalien, Vergeltungsmaßnahmen; ~ **raid** Vergeltungsschlag, Rachefeldzug.

retard *(v.)* verzögern, verschleppen, hinauszögern;
~ **development** Entwicklung behindern; ~ **a pupil** Schüler nicht fördern.

retardation Verzögerung, Verschleppung, Hinauszögern, *(psychology.)* Zurückgebliebensein, Unterentwickeltsein.

retarded, mentally [geistig] zurückgeblieben;
~ **ignition** Spätzündung; ~ **protest** verspäteter Protest.

retell *(v.)* *(news)* durch-, weitergeben.

retent *(v.)* *(reinsurance business)* Teilwagnis selbst behalten.

retention Ein-, Bei-, Zurückbehaltung, *(possessory lien)* Besitzpfand, *(reinsurance business)* Selbstbehalt;
~**s** Nachrechnungen und Gewinne;
net ~ Selbstbehalt; **title** ~ Eigentumsvorbehalt;
~ **of deposit** Einbehaltung von hinterlegtem Geld; ~ **of earnings** Lohneinbehaltung; ~ **of goods** Zurückbehaltung vor Waren, Warenhortung; ~ **of a licence** Konzessionsbelassung; ~ **of name** weitere Namensführung; ~ **of nationality** Beibehaltung der Staatsangehörigkeit; ~ **in office** Belassung im Amt; ~ **of profits** Gewinneinbehaltung, -thesaurierung; ~ **of title** Eigentumsvorbehalt; ~ **of wages** Lohneinbehaltung;

to advise ~ of longer commitments als langfristige Anlage empfehlen;

~-of-title clause Eigentumsvorbehaltsklausel; **~ figure** *(reinsurance)* Selbstbehaltsbetrag; **~ manual** Handbuch über Aufbewahrungspflichten; **~ money** *(Br.)* Sicherheitssumme, einbehaltene Garantiesumme; **~ schedule** Schema für die Aufbewahrung von Akten.

retenue Selbstbeherrschung.

rethink *(v.)* **its policy** Politik überdenken.

rethinking process Umdenkungsprozeß.

reticence Verschwiegenheit.

reticulate netzformig, *(fig.)* verwickelt.

retinue Gefolge, Hofstaat, Suite.

retiral Rückzug, *(bill of exchange)* Einlösung eines Wechsels, *(retirement from business)* Zurückziehen aus dem Geschäft, Rücktritt, Ausscheiden.

retire *(v.)* sich zurückziehen, *(board member)* abwählen, *(bookkeeping)* ausbuchen, *(from circulation)* [Noten] aus dem Verkehr ziehen, *(give up office)* zurücktreten, ausscheiden, Amt niederlegen, sich pensionieren lassen, in Pension gehen, sich zur Ruhe setzen, *(pension off)* pensionieren, in den Ruhestand versetzen, *(troops)* sich zurückziehen;

~ into o. s. sich ganz zurückziehen, sich verschließen; **~ under the age limit** wegen Erreichung der Altersgrenze in den Ruhestand treten, sich aus Altersgründen pensionieren lassen; **~ from an association** aus einem Verband (Verein) ausscheiden; **~ a bill** Wechsel vor Fälligkeit einlösen; **~ bonds** Obligationen aus dem Verkehr ziehen (tilgen); **~ from business** aus dem Geschäft ausscheiden (austreten), sich vom Geschäft zurückziehen, sich zur Ruhe setzen; **~ to one's cabin** sich in seine Kabine zurückziehen; **~ coins from circulation** Münzen aus dem Verkehr ziehen; **~ 5,4 million of debts** Dollarschuld von 5,4 Mio. zurückzahlen; **~ in disorder** *(mil.)* sich ungeordnet zurückziehen; **~ early** sich frühzeitig pensionieren lassen; **~ from a firm** aus einer Firma ausscheiden; **~ gracefully** mit Würde abtreten, sich einen guten Abgang verschaffen; **~ the head clerk** Prokuristen pensionieren; **~ a loan** Anleihestücke zurückzahlen; **~ an officer from the active list** j. aus der Liste der aktiven Offiziere streichen; **~ outstanding issues** fällige Emissionen zurückkaufen; **~ an obligation** einer [Zahlungs-]verpflichtung nachkommen; **~ on a pension** in den Pensionsstand treten, sich pensionieren lassen; **~ on a pension at 60** unter Gewährung eines Ruhegehalts mit 60 Jahren pensioniert werden; **~ from one's full executive responsibility** seine Vorstandstätigkeit beenden; **~ by rotation** turnusgemäß ausscheiden; **~ from active service** sich pensionieren lassen; **~ to consultant status** in Pension gehen, aber noch beratend tätig bleiben; **~ out of turn** außerplanmäßig pensioniert werden; **~ a unit** Anlage außer Betrieb nehmen; **~ from the world** sich ins Privatleben zurückziehen, in ein Kloster eintreten;

to be due to ~ ins Pensionsalter kommen, Altersgrenze erreicht haben; **to sound the ~** *(mil.)* Rückzugssignal blasen.

retired *(abandoned)* ausgebucht, *(bill)* zurückgezogen, eingezogen, *(mil.)* inaktiv, *(from office)* ausgeschieden, zurückgetreten, *(pensioned)* im Ruhestand, pensioniert, in Pension;

to be ~ gegangen werden; **to be hono(u)rably ~** ehrenvollen Abschied erhalten; **to have ~** nicht mehr arbeiten; **to live ~** im Ruhestand leben;

to live a ~ life ganz zurückgezogen leben; **~ list** Pensionärsliste, Liste der Ruhestandsbeamten; **to be on the ~ list** pensioniert (im Ruhestand) sein; **to be placed on the ~ list** seinen Abschied erhalten; **to be placed on the ~ list at one's own request** auf eigenen Wunsch pensioniert werden; **to place (put) s. o. on the ~ list** j. in den Ruhestand versetzen, j. pensionieren; **~ loan** abgelöste Anleihe; **~ partner** ausgeschiedener Gesellschafter; **~ pay** Ruhegehalt, Pension[zahlung]; **~ civil servant** pensionierter Beamter; **in a ~ spot** in einer abgelegenen Gegend.

retiree Ruheständler, -gehaltsempfänger.

retirement *(bill)* Zurück-, Einziehung, *(board member)* Abwahl, *(bookkeeping)* Ausbuchung, buchmäßiger Abgang [eines Anlagegutes], *(club)* Austrittserklärung, *(of jury)* Zurückziehen [zur Beratung], *(mil.)* planmäßige Absetzbewegung, *(from office)* Rück-, Austritt, Ausscheiden, Pensionierung, Amtsniederlegung, Ruhestand, Pension, *(removal of fixed assets)* Außerbetriebnehmen eines Anlagegutes, *(withdrawal from circulation)* Außerkurssetzung;

nearing ~ kurz vor der Pensionierung;

~s *(balance sheet)* Abgänge;

compulsory ~ Zwangspensionierung; **debt ~** Schuldentilgung, Schuldenabbau; **disability ~** Versetzung in den Ruhestand wegen Arbeitsunfähigkeit; **early ~** frühzeitige (vorzeitige)

Pensionierung; **involuntary ~** Zwangspensionierung; **optional ~** Pensionierung auf eigenen Wunsch, freiwillige Pensionierung; **temporary ~** einstweiliger Ruhestand; **voluntary ~** Pensionierung (Versetzung in den Ruhestand) auf eigenen Wunsch, freiwillige Pensionierung;

~ on account of age Alterspensionierung; **~ of a bill** vorzeitige Wechseleinlösung; **~ from business** Aufgabe eines Geschäftes; **~ of the public debt** *(US)* Tilgung der öffentlichen Schuld; **~ of a director** Ausscheiden eines Direktors; **~ of a loan** Anleiherückkauf, -rückzahlung; **~ of a partner** Ausscheiden eines Teilhabers; **~ on full pension** Pensionierung mit vollem Ruhegehalt; **~ by rotation** turnusmäßiges Ausscheiden; **~ of securities** Kraftloserklärung von Wertpapieren; **~ of stock** Kapitaleinziehung; **~ from the world** Eintritt in ein Kloster;

to choose early ~ at sixty sich mit sechzig vorzeitig pensionieren lassen; **to go into ~** sich ins Privatleben zurückziehen, sich zur Ruhe setzen; **to live in ~** im Ruhestand leben; **to provide for one's ~** Altersvorsorge treffen; **to reach ~** pensioniert werden; **to spend an active ~** sich nach seiner Pensionierung noch betätigen;

~ accounting method Abschreibungsmethode; **~ age** Altersgrenze, Renten-, Pensionierungsalter; **to be nearing ~ age** kurz vor der Pensionierung stehen; **to be past ~ age** Pensionsalter überschritten haben; **to reach the ~ age** Altersgrenze erreichen; **to stay on past ~ age** über das pensionspflichtige Alter hinaus tätig bleiben; **~ age limit** Pensionierungsgrenze; **~ allowance** Altersrente, Pensionszuschuß; **~ annuity** bei der Pensionierung ausgezahlte Versicherungsrente, Altersrente; **~ annuity system for the self-employer** Alters- und Hinterbliebenenversorgung für Selbständige; **~ benefits** *(US)* Pensionszuwendung, -bezüge, Altersversorgung, Ruhegeld; **~ benefit system** *(US)* Versorgungssystem; **~ community** Pensionärswohngegend; **~ credit** Anrechnung für die Pensionsanwartschaft, Pensionsanspruch; **~ curve** Sterblichkeitskurve; **~ eligibility** Pensionsberechtigung; **~ fund** Rentenfonds, Pensionsfonds, -kasse; **~ income** Pensionseinkommen, -einkünfte, Ruhegehaltsbezüge; **~ insurance** Ruhestandsversicherung; **~ loss** Ausbuchungs-, Abschreibungsverlust; **~ matters** Pensionsgelegenheiten; **~ pay** Ruhegehalt; **~ pension** bei der Entlassung gewährte Pension, Altersversorgung, -rente, Ruhegehalt, *(National Insurance Act, Br.)* Altersrente; **~ pension expectancy** Renten-, Pensionsanwartschaft; **~ pensioner** Pensionär, Ruhegehaltsempfänger, *(Br.)* Rentner; **~ plan** Pensionssystem; **~ planning** Vorbereitung der Pensionierung; **~ provision** Altersfürsorge, *(loan)* Rückkaufsatz; **~ rate** *(loan)* Rückkaufsatz; **~ reserve fund** Tilgungsrücklage; **~ right** Pensionierungsanspruch; **early ~ scheme** Plan für vorgezogene Pensionierungen; **~ table** Sterbetafel; **~ unit** außer Betrieb genommene (abgeschriebene) Anlage; **~ vacancies** durch Pensionierungen frei gewordene Stellen; **~ years** Pensionsjahre, -zeit, Ruhestandsjahre.

retiring Pensionierung, Versetzung in den Ruhestand;

~ of a bill vorzeitige Wechseleinlösung; **~ from business** Ausscheiden aus einem Geschäft; **~ from office** Amtsniederlegung; **~ age** Pensionierungs-, Pensions-, Renten-, Ruhegehaltsalter; **to abolish the compulsory ~ age of 70** die auf 70 Jahre abgestellte Zwangspensionierung abschaffen; **to reach ~ age** Pensionsalter erreichen; **~ allowance** Ruhegehalt, Pension; **~ board** Pensionsausschuß; **~ date** Pensions-, Rücktrittstermin; **~ director** ausscheidendes Vorstandsmitglied; **~ partner** ausscheidender Gesellschafter; **~ pension** Ruhegehalt; **~ president** bisheriger Präsident; **~ room** Toilette.

retool *(v.)* **industry** Industrie neu ausrüsten.

retooling Neuausstattung, -ausrüstung.

retorsion Retorsion, *(international law)* Retorsion, Vergeltung, Repressalien, Vergeltungsmaßnahmen.

retort scharfe Entgegnung, *(law of nations)* Retorsion üben;

~ *(v.)* vergelten;

~ upon one's accusers Gegenbeschuldigungen gegen seine Ankläger erheben; **~ insult for insult** sich mit einer Gegenbeleidigung revanchieren.

retouch Retusche, Überarbeitung;

~ *(v.)* nacharbeiten, *(essay)* überarbeiten, *(photo)* retuschieren; **~ a photograph** Foto retuschieren.

retouching Retusche.

retour of service *(Scot.)* Erbscheinausfertigung.

retrace *(v.)* **one's family** seinen Stammbaum zurückverfolgen.

retract *(v.)* zurücknehmen, -ziehen, *(accused)* sein Unrecht einsehen;

~ an accusation Anschuldigung zurücknehmen; **~ a bid** Angebot zurückziehen; **~ a confession** Geständnis widerrufen; **~**

~ from an engagement von einer Verbindlichkeit zurücktreten; **~ from a resolve** Entschluß aufgeben; **~ a statement** Erklärung widerrufen; **~ a testimony** Zeugenaussage widerrufen; **~ the undercarriage** Fahrgestell einziehen.

retractable | ball-point pen Druckkugelschreiber; **~ landing gear** einziehbares Fahrgestell.

retraction Zurücknahme, Widerruf;
~ of a deposition Widerruf einer Zeugenaussage; **~ of the undercarriage** *(plane)* Einziehen des Fahrgestells.

retrain *(v.)* umschulen.

retraining Umschulung;
~ scheme Umschulungsprogramm.

retransfer Rücküberweisung, -übertragung;
~ *(v.)* zurückübertragen, -überweisen.

retread *(tyre)* Runderneuerung, runderneuerter Reifen;
~ *(v.)* **a tyre** Reifen runderneuern.

retreat *(asylum)* Zufluchtsort, Zuflucht, Asyl, *(mental hospital)* Trinkerheil-, Heil- und Pflege-, Irrenanstalt, *(mil.)* Rückmarsch, -zug, Zurückziehung, *(seclusion)* Zurückgezogenheit, *(stock exchange)* allgemeiner Kursrückgang;
quiet country ~ abgelegener Landsitz;
~ on the capital *(mil.)* Rückzug auf die Hauptstadt; **~ to the wall** *(self-defence)* extreme Notlage;
~ *(v.)* zurückgehen, sich zurückziehen;
to be in full ~ in vollem Rückzug begriffen sein; **to beat a ~** *(fig.)* Vorhaben aufstecken, Unternehmen abblasen; **to force the enemy to ~** Feind zum Rückzug zwingen; **to make good one's ~** sich erfolgreich absetzen; **to sound the ~** zum Rückzug blasen; **~ house** Freizeitheim.

retrench *(v.)* *(cut down expenses)* Ausgaben einschränken, sparen, *(civil service cut)* Verwaltungsapparat abbauen, *(reduce)* kürzen, schmälern;
~ discussion Diskussionszeit beschränken; **~ one's expenses** sich einschränken, Einsparungen vornehmen; **~ a passage in a book** Buchstelle streichen; **~ a pension** Pension (Ruhegehaltsbezüge) kürzen; **~ privileges** Vorrechte aufheben; **~ this year** in diesem Jahr sehr sparsam leben.

retrenchment Einschränkung, Kürzung, Schmälerung, Verminderung, *(of employees)* [Beamten]abbau, *(mil.)* inneres Verteidigungssystem;
~ of employees Abbau des Personals, Personalabbau; **~ of budgetary expenditure** Haushaltseinsparungen; **~ of expenses** Ausgabenbeschränkung, Kostenverringerung, Sparsamkeit; **~ of salary** Gehaltsabbau, -kürzung;
~ program(me) Sparprogramm.

retrial erneute Verhandlung, Wiederaufnahmeverfahren, neuer Strafprozeß.

retribution Vergeltung.

retributive ausgleichend, vergeltend;
~ damages *(US)* verschärfter Schadensersatz; **~ justice** ausgleichende Gerechtigkeit.

retrievable loss ersetzbarer Verlust.

retrieval Wiederherstellung, -gutmachung;
~ of one's fortune Zurückerlangung seines Vermögens.

retrieve *(v.)* wiedererhalten, -erlangen, -gewinnen;
~ an error Fehler verbessern; **~ one's fortune** sein Vermögen wiederbekommen; **~ a loss** Verlust wieder einbringen, sich für einen Verlust schadlos halten; **~ a lost piece of luggage** *(Br.)* verlorengegangenes Gepäckstück zurückerhalten; **~ one's reputation** seinen Ruf wiederherstellen.

retroact *(v.)* zurückwirken.

retroactive *(law, tax)* rückwirkende Kraft.

retroactive *(law)* rückwirkend;
with ~ effect mit rückwirkender Kraft, rückwirkend; **~ insurance** *(marine insurance)* Haftpflichtversicherung für ein unbekannt abgebliebenes Schiff; **~ law (statute)** rückwirkendes Gesetz; **~ pay** rückwirkende Lohnerhöhung.

retroactively mit rückwirkender Kraft.

retroactivity rückwirkende Kraft.

retrocede *(v.)* wiederab-, zurücktreten, -übertragen, *(insurance)* rückversichern.

retrocession Rück-, Wiederabtretung, Rückübertragung, *(reinsurance)* Folgerückversicherung.

retrocessionary Rückabtretungsempfänger.

retrograde rückgängig;
~ movement *(stock exchange)* rückgängige [Kurs]bewegung; **~ policy** rückschrittliche Politik.

retrorocket Bremsrakete.

retrospect Rückblick.

retrospective *(law)* rückwirkend;
~ appraisal Bewertung für einen bestimmten zurückliegenden

Zeitpunkt; **to have ~ effect** rückwirkende Kraft haben; **~ law** Gesetz mit rückwirkender Kraft; **~ legislation** Gesetzgebung mit rückwirkender Kraft; **~ maintenance** Unterhaltsleistungen für die zurückliegende Zeit; **~ view** Aussicht nach hinten.

retry *(v.)* **a case** Fall erneut verhandeln (aufrollen).

return *(act of reelecting)* Wiederwahl, *(advertising)* Werbeantwort, *(bailiff)* Vollzugsbericht, *(census)* Volkszählung, *(coming back)* Rückkehr, -kunft, Wiederkehr, *(income tax)* [Einkommen]steuererklärung, *(insurance)* Storno, *(journey)* Rückfahrt, -reise, *(parl., Br.)* Kandidatenwahl, *(repayment)* Rückzahlung, -erstattung, *(replacement)* Rückgabe, -lieferung, Wiedergabe, *(report)* Wahlbericht, [amtliche] Meldung, [amtlicher] Bericht, statistischer Ausweis, *(response)* Antwort, Erwiderung, *(sending back)* Rücksendung, -lieferung, *(sending back of writ)* Wiederzustellung der Prozeßakten, *(statement)* [Bank]ausweis, [Ertrags]übersicht, Aufstellung, *(ticket)* Hin- und Rückfahrkarte, *(turnover)* Umsatz, *(yield)* Zinsertrag, Erträgnis, Einnahme, [Anlage]gewinn, -verzinsung, Rendite, [Gewinn]ergebnis;
by ~ [of post] postwendend; **for collections and ~s** zwecks Einziehung und Überweisung; **in ~ for** als Ersatz; **in ~ for his services** als Entgelt für seine Tätigkeit; **on my ~** bei meiner Rückkunft; **on [sale for] ~** in Kommission; **please ~** unter Rückerbittung; **without ~** unentgeltlich, umsonst; **yielding a ~** rentabel, rentierlich;
~s *(balance sheet)* Einkünfte aus Kapitalvermögen, *(bookseller)* Remission, *(circulation of money)* [Geld]umsatz, -verkehr, Wiedereingang von Geldbeträgen, *(goods returned)* Retour-, Rückwaren, -gut, Remittenden, *(receipts)* Gegenwert, Einnahmen, Erträgnisse, *(Brutto]gewinn, *(redrafts, Br.)* retournierte Schecks, Rückwechsel, *(results)* Zählungs-, Wahlergebnis, *(set of tabulated statistics)* Zusammenstellung, statistische Aufstellung, Listen, Angaben, *(unsold copies)* nicht verkaufte Exemplare;
amended ~ Einkommensteuerberichtigung; **annual ~** Jahresausweis, Jahresübersicht, *(company register)* jährliche Meldung, *(taxation, Br.)* jährliche [Einkommen]steuererklärung; **average ~** Durchschnittsertrag; **bank ~** Bankausweis; **Board of Trade ~s** *(US)* Ausweis des Statistischen Bundesamtes, Handelsstatistik; **cheap day ~** verbilligte Rückfahrkarte; **combined ~** *(conglomerate)* zusammengefaßte Bilanz; **consolidated ~** *(US)* Steuererklärung eines Konzerns; **corporate income-tax ~** Körperschaftsteuerformular; **corrected ~** berichtigte Einkommensteuererklärung; **custom ~s** Zollerträge; **daily ~s** Tagesumsatz, -einnahme; **decreasing ~** sinkender Ertrag; **diminishing ~s** Ertragsrückgang; **duty-free ~** zollfreie Wiedereinfuhr; **early ~s** rascher Umsatz; **election ~s** amtlicher Wahlbericht, Wahlresultat; **false ~** *(sheriff)* fehlerhafte Zustellungsbestätigung, *(taxation)* unkorrekte Einkommensteuererklärung; **gross ~s** Bruttoeinnahmen, Bruttoeinkünfte, -ertrag; **income-tax ~** Einkommensteuererklärung; **increment[al] ~** Gewinnertrag; **interim ~** Zwischenausweis; **~s inwards** zurückgenommene Waren; **irregular ~** unregelmäßige Wahl; **joint ~** *(income tax)* gemeinsame [Einkommen]steuererklärung; **large ~s** große Umsätze; **marginal ~** Grenzertrag; **monthly ~** Monatsausweis, -übersicht; **mouth-watering ~s** äußerst attraktive Rendite; **net ~s** Nettoumsatz; **normal ~s** amtliche Ziffern, statistischer Bericht; **official ~s** amtliche Ziffern, statistischer Bericht; **~s outwards** zurückgesandte Waren; **physical ~** Kapitalrelation; **processed ~** bearbeitetes Einkommensteuerformular; **production ~** Produktionsübersicht; **quarterly ~** Vierteljahresbericht, *(taxation)* vierteljährliche Steuererklärung; **quick ~** schneller Absatz (Umsatz); **reasonable ~** angemessener Gewinn; **recurring ~s** wiederkehrende Nutzungen; **~ requested** gegen Rückschein; **sales ~s** Verkaufserlös; **separate ~** *(tax)* getrennte Einkommensteuererklärung; **small ~s** geringer Nutzen; **smaller ~s** Mindererlös, -ertrag; **tax ~** Steuererklärung; **tax-free ~** steuerfreier Ertrag; **token ~** *(bookseller)* körperlose Remission; **trade ~s** Handelsstatistik; **traffic ~s** Verkehrsziffern, *(railway)* Betriebsstatistik; **unopposed ~** konkurrenzlose Wahl; **~ unsatisfied** *(bankruptcy)* Konkursmasse nicht ausreichend, mangels Masse; **week's (weekly) ~** Wochenausweis;
large ~s from agents in the field hohe Umsätze durch die Vertreter im Außendienst; **~ of allotments** Aktienzuteilungsbericht; **~s and allowances** *(balance sheet)* Retouren und Rabatte; **~ of an amount overpaid** Rückerstattung eines zuviel gezahlten Betrages; **~ on assets** Anlagenrendite; **12% ~ on net assets** zwölfprozentige Verzinsung des Nettovermögens (Nettorendite auf das Anlagevermögen); **~ to barracks** Einrücken in die Kaserne; **~ of bill to drawer** Wechselrückgabe

~ **on capital employed** Kapitalverzinsung, -rendite; ~ **of a capital sum** Rückzahlung des Kapitalbetrages; ~ **of car** Wagenrückgabe; ~ **of a charge** *(tel.)* Gebührenerstattung; ~ **of contribution** Beitragsrückerstattung, -gewähr; ~ **of unsold copies** Remittendenrückgabe; ~**s of the day** Tagesumsatz; **many happy ~s of the day** herzliche Glückwünsche zum Geburtstag; ~ **of the death penalty** Wiedereinführung der Todesstrafe; ~ **of duties** Gebührenrückerstattung; ~ **of empties** Rücksendung der Verpackung (des Leergutes); ~ **on common equity** Eigenkapitalverzinsung; **net real ~ on equity** reale Kapitalnettorendite; ~ **in equivalent** Gegenleistung; ~ **of exchange** Rückwechselrechnung; ~ **of expenses** Spesen-, Ausgabenaufstellung, Unkostenetat; ~ **of a gift** Widerruf einer Schenkung, Schenkungswiderruf; ~ **of goods** Warenrückgabe; ~ **of income** Einkommensteuererklärung; ~ **on investment** Ertrag des investierten Kapitals; **fair ~ on an investment** gute Kapitalverzinsung (Rendite); **first-class ~ to Munich** einmal erster Klasse nach München und zurück; ~ **to public order** Wiederherstellung von Ruhe und Ordnung; ~ **to the owner** Rückgabe an den Eigentümer; ~**s of payment** Rimessen, Rückzahlungen; ~ **to plant** wieder aufgenommene Arbeit; ~ **of premium** *(marine insurance)* Prämienrückgewähr, -rückerstattung, Storno; ~ **of process** Wiederaufnahme des Verfahrens; ~ **on sales** Gewinnspanne; ~ **to scale** Skalenertrag, Niveaugrenzprodukt; ~ **of tax** Steuererklärung; ~ **of thanks** Danksagung; ~ **of troops to quarters** Rückkehr der Truppen in ihre Quartiere; ~ **of cold weather** Kälterückfall; ~ **for the week** *(Bank of England)* Bank-, Wochenausweis der Notenbank; ~ **to work** Wiederaufnahme der Arbeit; ~ **of writs** Pfändungsbericht; ~ **during the year** Jahreseinkommen;

~ *(v.) (come back)* zurück-, wiederkommen, zurück-, wiederkehren, *(give back)* zurück-, wiedergeben, wiederbringen, *(send back)* zurückschicken, -senden, wiederzustellen, *(politics, Br.)* Wahlergebnis melden (veröffentlichen), *(remit)* übermachen, retournieren, remittieren, zurückgewähren, *(repay)* zurückerstatten, -zahlen, *(response)* antworten, erwidern, Antwort geben, *(state officially)* melden, [amtlich] berichten, *(turnover)* umsetzen, *(yield)* einbringen, abwerfen;

~ **an overpaid amount** zuviel gezahltes Geld zurückgeben; ~ **an amount by bill of exchange** Betrag durch Wechsel übermachen; ~ **an article** Ware retournieren; ~ **a bill accepted** Wechsel mit Akzept zurückschicken; ~ **a bill to drawer** Wechsel retournieren; ~ **a bill of exchange protested** Wechsel mit Protest zurückschicken; ~ **a bill unpaid** Wechsel unbezahlt zurückgehen lassen; ~ **a book to its place** Buch auf seinen Platz zurückstellen; ~ **a call** Gegenbesuch machen; ~ **a check (cheque,** *Br.)* Scheck zurückweisen; ~ **a commission** Provision zurückvergüten; ~ **from the dead** von den Toten auferstehen; ~ **a denial** Gegendementi abgeben; ~ **the details of one's income** detaillierte Einkommensteuererklärung abgeben; ~ **to the family** *(estate)* an die Familie zurückfallen; ~ **a fine** Geldstrafe bezahlen; ~ **five per cent** sich mit fünf Prozent verzinsen; ~ **guilty** für schuldig erkennen; ~ **to one's old habits** seine Gewohnheiten wiederaufnehmen; ~ **home** in die Heimat zurückkehren; ~ **to one's home** nach Hause zurückkehren; ~ **one's income at $ 15.000** 15.000 Dollar an Einkommen versteuern; ~ **an indictment** Anklage erheben, Anklagebeschluß verkünden; ~ **a good interest** gut verzinslich sein; ~ **from a journey** von einer Reise zurückkehren; ~ **liabilities at £ 10.000** Verbindlichkeiten mit 10.000 Pfund angeben; ~ **a list of jurors** Geschworenenliste veröffentlichen; ~ **to the original owner** zum ursprünglichen Eigentümer zurückkommen; ~ **a member to parliament** Abgeordneten wählen (stellen); ~ **to one's muttons** wieder auf sein Gesprächsthema zurückkommen, seinen Gesprächsknochen wiederaufnehmen; ~ **parts of industry to private hands** Industriebetriebe teilweise reprivatisieren; ~ **to a point later in one's lecture** auf einen Punkt in einem späteren Teil der Vorlesung zurückkommen; ~ **to port** wieder in den Hafen einlaufen; ~ **to a position** auf einen Posten zurückkehren; ~ **a profit** Gewinn abwerfen; ~ **property to its rightful owner** Vermögensgegenstand dem rechtmäßigen Eigentümer zurückgeben; ~ **under protest** unter Protest zurückkommen; ~ **a result** Ergebnis zeitigen; ~ **the results of the poll** Wahlergebnis veröffentlichen; ~ **by settlement date** *(bookseller)* zum Abrechnungstag remittieren; ~ **later to a subject** später noch einmal auf eine Sache zurückkommen; ~ **taxes to the treasury** Steuern bezahlen; ~ **s. o. unfit for duty** *(mil.)* j. als untauglich einstufen; ~ **a verdict of guilty** *(jury)* Schuldspruch fällen; ~ **a warrant** Haftbefehl mit Protokoll wieder zustellen; ~ **the way one came** gleichen Weg zurück benutzen; ~ **a writ of summons** *(sheriff)* Ladung mit Durchführungsbericht vorlegen; ~ **in writing** schriftlich [be]antworten;

to answer by ~ of mail *(US)* postwendend antworten; **to ask for the ~ of a loan** Rückzahlung eines Kredits verlangen; **to be on one's ~** auf der Rückreise sein; **to bring a fair ~** guten Ertrag abgeben, angemessenen Gewinn abwerfen; **to deliver goods on sale and ~** Waren in Kommission geben; **to fail to file a ~** keine Steuererklärung abgeben; **to file a joint ~** gemeinsame [Einkommen]steuererklärung abgeben, sich zusammen veranlagen lassen; **to file separate ~s** getrennte Einkommensteuererklärung abgeben, sich getrennt veranlagen lassen; **to get (give) a good ~ on an investment** gute Verzinsung für seine Kapitalanlage bekommen, gute Rendite erwirtschaften, hohe Rendite abwerfen; **to get a small ~ for one's money** nur wenig Nutzen aus seinem Kapital ziehen; **to have a ~ of an illness** Rückfall in seine Krankheit erleiden; **to make one's income-tax ~** seine [Einkommen]steuererklärung machen; **to make double ~s** das Doppelte einbringen; **to make good ~s** gute Umsätze erzielen; **to make a ~ of nulla bona to the writ of fiere facias** Erfolglosigkeit auf dem Vollstreckungsbefehl vermerken; **to negotiate a ~ to work pending further talks** Arbeit bei Fortsetzung der Lohnverhandlungen wieder aufnehmen; **to owe s. o. some ~** jem. eine Gegenleistung schulden; **to pay in ~** als Gegenleistung gewähren; **to prepare a[n income-] tax ~** [Einkommen]steuererklärung aufsetzen; **to process a ~** Einkommensteuererklärung bearbeiten; **to secure one's ~ to X** als Vertreter des Wahlkreises X ins Parlament einziehen; **to send [goods] on ~** [Waren] in Kommission geben; **to send a reply by ~** umgehend antworten; **to take a first-class ~ to X** Rückfahrkarte erster Klasse nach X lösen; **to transmit the ~** Gegenwert überweisen; **to yield an easy (quick, short) ~** schnell abgehen, rasch umgesetzt werden; **to yield high ~s** reichen Ertrag abwerfen, sich hoch verzinsen;

in case of nondelivery ~ to the sender falls nicht zustellbar bitte an den Absender zurück;

~ **account** Rückrechnung; ~**s account** Retourenkonto; **[missing] ~ address** [fehlender] Absender; ~ **air fare** Rückflugkarte; ~ **air passage** Rückflug, Rückflugbetrag; ~ **book** *(Br.)* Abgeordnetenverzeichnis, Abgeordnetenliste; ~**s book** Retourenbuch; ~ **business** Gegengeschäft; ~ **card** [Rück]antwortkarte, *(advertising)* Bestellkarte; ~ **cargo** Rückfracht, -ladung, Retourfracht; ~ **charge** *(rent-a-car)* Rückführungsgebühr; ~ **charges** Rückfracht, -spesen; ~ **check** *(theater)* Wiedereinlassungskarte; ~ **commission** Provisionsvergütung; ~**-on-investment concept** Renditekonzeption; ~ **copies** *(book trade)* Remittenden; ~ **coupon** Kupon in Form einer Bestellkarte; ~**s credit voucher** Gutschriftsanzeige; ~ **day** *(law court, US)* Tag des persönlichen Erscheinens, Termin für die Rücksendung einer Klageschrift, Verhandlungstermin; **general ~ day** allgemeiner Gerichtstag; ~ **debit** Rückbelastung; ~ **debit voucher** Rückbelastungsaufgabe; ~ **disposal** Rückverfügung; ~ **draft** Rückwechsel; ~ **envelope** Freiumschlag; ~ **fare** Fahrgeld für Hin- und Rückfahrt; ~ **flight** Rückflug; ~ **form** Einkommensteuerformular; **to issue a ~ form** Einkommensteuerformular zusenden; ~ **freight** *(Br.)* Rückfracht; ~ **goods** *(customs)* Rückwaren; ~ **half** *(Br.)* Rückfahrkartenabschnitt; **a ~ home** Heimkehr; ~ **journey** Rückreise, -fahrt, -weg; ~ **load factor** Rückfrachtfaktor; ~ **party** Gegenbesucher; ~ **passage** Rückfahrt; ~ **passenger** Rückreisender; ~ **performance** Gegenleistung; ~ **period** *(income tax)* vierteljährlicher Abgabetermin, *(statistics)* Periode der Wiederkehr; ~ **plane** Rückflugzeug; ~ **plane reservation** für den Rückflug vorgenommene Buchung; ~ **postage** Rückporto; ~ **premium** rückvergütete (stornierte) Prämie, Rückprämie; ~ **privilege** Rückgaberecht; ~ **receipt** Rück-, Empfangsschein; ~ **reference** Wiedervorlage; ~ **remittance** Rücküberweisung, *(US)* Anschaffung mittels Scheck; ~ **request** *(US)* Bitte um Rücksendung eines unbestellten Briefes; ~ **run** *(train)* Rückfahrt; ~ **service** Gegendienst; ~ **shipping order** Rücklieferungsauftrag; ~**signal** *(mil.)* Rückzugssignal; ~ **tag** Rücksendeadresse; ~ **ticket** Rückfahrkarte, Retourbillet, *(worker)* Arbeiterrückfahrkarte; ~ **ticket available for three days** Rückfahrkarte mit dreitägiger Gültigkeit; **to book the ~ ticket** Rückfahrkarte kaufen; ~ **travel fare** Rückfahrkarte; ~ **visit** Gegenbesuch; ~ **voyage** *(Br.)* Rückfahrt, -reise.

returnable rückgabepflichtig, *(able to return)* wählbar, *(law court)* wieder zuzustellen, *(repayable)* rückzahlbar;
not ~ nicht umtauschfähig, Einwegpackung;
~ **fees** zurückzuerstattende Gebühren; ~ **goods** zurückgehende Waren.

returned zurückgesandt, retourniert;
~ **empty** leer zurück;
~ **for want of acceptance** mangels Annahme zurück;
member ~ gewählter Abgeordneter;

to be ~ at $ 200.000 *(liabilities)* auf 200.000 Dollar geschätzt werden; **to be ~ to Parliament** ins Parlament gewählt werden; **to be ~ guilty** für schuldig befunden werden; **to be ~ unfit for work** arbeitsunfähig geschrieben werden;
~ **articles** Remittenden; ~ **bill** Rück-, Retourwechsel; ~ **checks (cheques,** *Br.)* Rück-, Retourschecks; ~ **empties** zurückgesandte Verpackung, Leergut zurück; ~ **goods** *(customs, US)* zurückgehende Waren, Rück-, Retourware; ~ **letter** unzustellbarer Brief; ~**-letter office** Postamt für unbestellte Postsendungen; ~ **note** nicht honorierter Solawechsel; ~ **shipments** Retoursendungen; ~**-shipment rate** *(US)* verbilligter Frachtsatz für Leergut; ~**-stores report** Lagerrückgabemeldung.

returnee Heimkehrer.

returner Remittent.

returning Rückgabe, -erstattung, *(election)* Wahl, *(sending back)* Rücksendung;
on ~ bei Rückgabe;
~ **board** *(US)* Wahlausschuß; ~ **borough** Wahlkreis; ~ **goods** Remittenden; **by ~ mail (post)** postwendend; ~ **officer** *(Br.)* Wahlkommissar, Kreiswahlleiter, *(law court)* Berichterstatter; **deputy ~ officer** *(Br.)* Wahlbeisitzer.

reunification Wiedervereinigung.

reunion Wiedersehentreffen;
family ~ Familientreffen.

reunite *(v.)* wiedervereinigen;
~ **after long years of separation** nach jahrelanger Trennung wieder zusammenfinden.

reunited wiedervereinigt.

reup *(v.) (sl.)* sich erneut zum Wehrdienst verpflichten.

reusable wiederverwendbar.

reuse Wiederverwendung;
~ **package** Mehrwegverpackung, wieder verwendbare Verpackung.

rev *(motor)* Tourenzahl;
~ *(v.)* **up** auf Touren kommen.

revaccination erneute (wiederholte) Impfung, Zweitimpfung.

revalidate erneut in Kraft setzen;

revalidation erneute Inkraftsetzung.

revalorization Neubewertung, Aufwertung.

revalorize *(v.)* neu bewerten, *(currency)* aufwerten.

revaluate *(v.)* neu bewerten, umwerten.

revaluation erneute Schätzung, *(revalorisation)* Neube-, Um-, Aufwertung;
currency ~ Geldverteuerung; **surplus ~** aus Höherbewertung von Anlagegütern gebildete Rücklagen;
~ **of fixed assets** Neubewertung des Anlagevermögens, Re-, Nachaktivierung; ~ **of the currency** Neueinstufung der Währung; ~ **of the pound** Aufwertung des Pfundes; ~ **of property** Neubewertung von Vermögen;
~ **loss** Aufwertungsverlust; **quasi-~ measures** aufwertungsähnliche Maßnahmen; ~ **reserves** Rückstellung für Wertberichtigungen, Neubewertungsreserve; ~ **surplus** Aufwertungsgewinn, *(US)* aus Höherbewertung des Anlagevermögens gebildete Rücklagen.

revalue *(v.)* von neuem schätzen, neu bewerten, *(revalorize)* aufwerten;
~ **assets** Anlagen nach-, reaktivieren; ~ **a currency** Währung aufwerten.

revaluing of gold reserves Goldreservenaufwertung.

revamp *(v.) (coll.)* aufpolieren, reorganisieren;
~ **agriculture in a backward country** Landwirtschaft in einem zurückgebliebenen Land modernisieren; ~ **the cabinet** Kabinett (Regierung) umbilden; ~ **rules** Richtlinien überholen.

revampment *(coll.)* Aufpolierung, Reorganisation.

reveal *(v.)* enthüllen, offenbaren;
~ **a defect** Fehler offenlegen; ~ **one's identity** sich zu erkennen geben; ~ **a secret** Geheimnis enthüllen.

revel | *(v.)* **away money** sein Geld verplempern; ~ **in gossip** in Klatschgeschichten schwelgen.

revendication Herausgabeanspruch;
~ **action** Herausgabeklage, Klage auf Herausgabe des Eigentums.

revenge *(v.)* **on injustice** sich für eine Ungerechtigkeit rächen.

revenue *(government board)* Finanzverwaltung, Fiskus, *(income)* fundiertes Einkommen, Einnahme[n], Einkünfte, Ertrag, *(source of income)* Einnahme-, Einkommensquelle, *(state's annual income)* Staatseinnahmen, -einkünfte, Steueraufkommen, *(periodical yield from investment)* Nutzung, Ertrag, Rendite, Kapitalrente;
annual ~ Jahreseinnahme; **annual gross operating ~** *(motor carrier)* jährlicher Bruttobetriebsertrag; **average ~** Waren-

stückpreis; **continuing ~** Dauereinnahmen, -einkünfte; **current ~s** laufende Erträge; **customs ~** Zolleinnahmen; **government ~** *(Br.)* Staatseinkünfte; **inland** *(Br.)* **(internal,** *US)* ~ Steuereinnahmen, -aufkommen; **land ~** *(Br.)* Domänenerträge; **local ~** Kommunaleinnahmen; **marginal ~** Grenzertrag; **national ~** *(US)* Staatseinnahmen, Nationaleinkommen; **nonoperating ~s** betriebsfremde (außerbetriebliche) Einkünfte; **nontax ~s** nicht aus Steuereingängen herrührende Staatseinnahmen; **operating ~** Betriebseinnahmen; **public ~** Staatseinkommen, -einkünfte, Einkünfte der öffentlichen Hand; **recurring ~s** wiederkehrende Nutzungen; **rental ~** Einkünfte aus Vermietung und Verpachtung; **special ~** Sondereinnahmen, -erträge; **stable ~** feste Einkünfte; **state ~** Staatseinkünfte; **surplus ~** Mehreinkommen; **taxable ~** steuerbares Einkommen; **total ~** Gesamteinkommen; **uncommitted ~** nicht verplante Staatseinkünfte; **unearned ~** *(balance sheet)* transitorische Passiva, *(taxation)* Einkünfte aus Kapitalbesitz, Kapitalrente; **yearly ~** Jahreseinkommen;
~s **of the city council** Kommunaleinnahmen; ~ **from customs and excise** Eingänge aus Zöllen und Verbrauchssteuern; ~s **and expenditure** Staatseinnahmen und -ausgaben; ~ **from income** Einkünfte aus Kapitalvermögen; ~ **of a produce** Nutzungswert; ~ **from taxation** Steueraufkommen;
to be attributable ~ steuerlich als Einkommen behandelt werden; **to defraud the ~** Steuern hinterziehen, Steuerhinterziehung begehen; **to derive ~s from** Einkünfte beziehen; **to feed the ~ back into the economy** Steueraufkommen der Wirtschaft wieder zuführen; **to produce less ~** geringeres Steueraufkommen erzielen;
~ **account** Ertrags-, Gewinn- und Verlustkonto; ~ **Acts** *(US)* Steuergesetze; ~ **agent** *(US)* Steuer-, Finanzbeamter, *(customs)* Zollbeamter; ~ **assets** werbende Betriebsmittel; ~ **authorities** Steuer-, Finanzbehörden, Fiskus; **to widen the ~ base** Fundament seiner Einkommensmöglichkeiten erweitern; ~ **bill** *(US)* Staatshaushaltsgesetz; ~ **board** Steuervorlage; ~ **bonds** *(US)* kurzfristige Schatzanweisungen; ~ **calculation** Einnahmeschätzung; ~ **case** Steuersache, -ermittlungsfall; ~ **charges** Kapitalaufwand [für nicht aus dem Einkommen zu deckende Ausgaben]; ~ **classification** *(balance sheet)* Einnahmenaufgliederung; ~ **Code** Einkommensteuergesetz; ~ **concession** Steuererleichterung; ~ **considerations** Steuerüberlegungen; ~ **cutter** Zollschiff, -kutter, -wachschiff, -boot, -fahrzeug; ~ **cutter service** *(US)* Zolldienst; ~ **deduction** *(municipal accounting)* Erlösschmälerung; ~ **deficit** *(taxes)* Einkommen-, Steuerdefizit; ~ **department** *(Br.)* Finanzverwaltung; ~ **drain** *(budgeting)* steuerlicher Verlustfaktor; ~ **duty** Finanzzoll, fiskalische Gebühr; ~ **earner** Ertragsfaktor, Einkommensfaktor; ~ **earning** einträglich, gewinnbringend; ~ **estimates** Steuervorausschätzungen; ~ **expenditure** Betriebsausgabe, Kapitalaufwand, Investitionen zur Erzielung kurzfristiger Kapitalerträge, erfolgswirksamer Aufwand; **to calculate ~ figures in constant prices** Staatseinnahmen zu konstanten Preisen ansetzen; **to provide ~ figures to measure against the expenditure plans** zum Vergleich mit den Ausgabeplänen geeignetes Ziffernmaterial der Staatseinnahmen zur Verfügung stellen; ~ **forecast** Steueraufkommensschätzung; ~ **fraud** Steuer-, Zollhinterziehung; ~ **gain** Steuergewinn; ~ **increase** Einkommensanstieg, *(taxation)* Erhöhung des Steueraufkommens; ~ **item** Einnahmeposten; ~ **law** *(US)* Einkommensteuergesetz; ~ **loss** Steuerverlust; ~ **minister** *(Canada)* Finanzminister; **to be of a ~ nature** dem Einkommen zuzuschreiben sein; ~ **offence** Finanz-, Steuerdelikt, -vergehen, Zolldelikt; ~ **office** Zollamt; **inland ~ office** Steuerbehörde; ~ **officer** Finanz-, Steuerbeamter, *(customs)* Zollbeamter; **medium-term ~ plans** mittelfristige Finanzplanung; ~ **policy** Steuerpolitik; ~ **principle** Ertragswertberechnung; ~ **producer** *(budgeting)* steuerlicher Gewinnfaktor; ~ **projection** Steuereinnahmenprognose; ~ **raiser** steueraufbringende Maßnahmen, Einkommensteuerzuwachs; ~ **raising** Erhöhung des Steueraufkommens; ~**-raising powers** Besteuerungsbefugnisse; ~ **realization** Einnahmeverbuchung; ~ **receipts** Steueraufkommen, -einnahmen; **additional ~ requirements** zusätzliche Steuerforderungen; ~ **reserve** *(Br., balance sheet)* Ertragsrücklage, steuerpflichtiger Kapitalgewinn; ~ **service** Zolldienst; **Internal ~ Service** *(US)* oberste Steuerbehörde; **to introduce to ~ service** im Zolldienst einsetzen; ~ **sharing** *(government)* Steuer-, Finanzausgleich; ~ **shortage** unzureichende Steueraufkommen; ~ **shortfall** Einnahmenausfall; ~ **side** Einnahmeseite; ~ **side of the Exchequer** Gerichtsabteilung für fiskalische Ansprüche; ~ **sources** Steuerquellen; ~ **stamp** Banderole, Gebührenstempel, Steuermarke, -stempel; ~ **surplus** *(taxes)*

Steuer-, Einnahmeüberschuß; ~ **takeover** Übernahme öffentlicher Unternehmen durch Privatfirmen; ~ **tariff** fiskalische Gebühr, Finanzzoll; ~ **tax** Finanzzoll; **internal** ~ **taxes** inländische Steuern und Abgaben; ~ **traffic** Verkehrseinnahmen; ~ **waybill** Frachtrechnung.

revenuer *(US sl.)* Zollbeamter, -kutter.

reverence Ehrerbietung, Reverenz;
　to regard s. o. with ~ mit Hochachtung auf j. schauen.

reversal Umschwung, Umkehrung, *(counterentry)* Stornierung, Storno-, Gegenbuchung, *(overthrow)* Aufhebung, Umstoßung, *(pol.)* Umschwung;
　~ **of accruals** Auflösung von Rückstellungen; ~ **of the burden of proof** Umkehrung der Beweislast; ~ **of judgment** Urteilsaufhebung [in der Berufungsinstanz]; ~ **in the money market** Liquiditätsumschwung; ~ **of opinion** Meinungsänderung, -umschwung; ~ **of an order of the court** Aufhebung einer richterlichen Verfügung; ~ **of procedure** Verfahrensänderung; ~ **in stockpiling** Umschwung in den Lagerdispositionen; ~ **test** *(statistics)* Umkehrprobe [bei Indexzahlen].

reverse *(check)* Revers, *(coin)* Rückseite, Gegenseite, *(fig.)* Kehrseite, *(gear)* Rückwertsgang, *(setback)* Rückschlag, Schlappe; **in** ~ rückwärtsfahrend; **on the** ~ umstehend, rückseitig, auf der Rückseite; **written in** ~ in Spiegelschrift;
　automatic ribbon ~ automatische Farbbandumspulung; **financial** ~ mißliche Finanzlage;
　~ **of a coin** Rückseite einer Münze; ~ **of fortune** Schicksalsschlag; **the** ~ **of the medal** die Kehrseite der Medaille;
　~ *(v.) (law)* [Urteil] aufheben;
　~ **o. s.** seine Meinung grundlegend ändern; ~ **one's car into the garage** sein Auto rückwärts in die Garage fahren; ~ **the charge** *(tel., US)* R-Gespräch herstellen; ~ **an earlier decision** frühere Entscheidung aufheben; ~ **the decision of a lower court** Entscheidung in der Berufungsinstanz aufheben; ~ **a decree** Beschluß aufheben; ~ **an entry** Buchung stornieren; ~ **the judgment of the court below** Urteil in der Berufungsinstanz aufheben; ~ **a nose-dive in share prices** Sturz der Aktienkurse ins Gegenteil umkehren; ~ **the onus of proof** Beweislast umkehren; ~ **one's opinion** seine Meinung völlig ändern; ~ **one's policy** seine Politik revidieren; ~ **a procedure** Verfahren ändern; ~ **a process** umgekehrtes Verfahren wählen;
　to go in ~ Rückwärtsgang einschalten; **to suffer a slight** ~ *(mil.)* leichte Schlappe erleiden;
　~ *(a.)* umgekehrt, entgegengesetzt;
　~-**charge call** *(tel., US)* R-Gespräch; ~ **curve** S-Kurve; ~ **direction** entgegengesetzte Richtung; ~ **entry** Gegenbuchung, -eintrag; ~ **flying** *(plane)* Rückenflug; ~ **gear** *(car)* Rückwärtsgang; ~ **income tax** vom Staat an niedrige Einkommensgruppen gezahlte Unterstützungen; ~ **motion** Rückwärtsbewegung; **in** ~ **order** in umgekehrter Reihenfolge; ~ **plate** negative Ätzung, Negativklischee; ~ **side** Rückseite [eines Wertpapiers]; ~ **split** *(US)* Aktiensplit, -zusammenlegung; ~ **split-up** Aktiensplit, -zusammenlegung; ~ **yield gap** umgekehrtes Renditegefälle.

reversed *(judgment)* aufgehoben;
　~ **call** *(tel., US)* R-Gespräch; ~ **plate** Negativätzung.

reverser *(Scot.)* Hypothekenschuldner.

reversible *(law)* umstoßbar, rechtsmittelfähig, reversibel;
　~ **error** Revisionsfehler; ~ **film** Umkehrfilm; ~ **judgment** revisionsfähiges Urteil.

reversing of an entry Stornierungseintrag, Wertberichtigungsbuchung, Eintrag einer Gegenbuchung;
　~ **gear** Rückwärtsgang; ~ **lamp** *(light)* Rückfahrscheinwerfer; ~ **switch** *(el.)* Umkehrschalter.

reversion Umkehrung, *(deferred annuity)* Anwartschaftsrente, *(life insurance)* Versicherungssumme, *(return of estate)* An-, Heimfall [einer Erbschaft], Erbschaftsanfall, *(right of reversion)* Heimfall-, Rückfallrecht, *(right of succession)* Anwartschaft;
　immediate ~ unmittelbares Heimfallrecht; **legal** ~ *(Scot.)* gesetzliche Frist zur Ausübung des Rückkaufsrechts; ~ **of an estate** anfallende Erbschaft; ~ **of an inheritance** Anwartschaft auf eine Erbschaft; ~ **to private ownership** *(Br.)* Reprivatisierung; ~ **of a sentence** Nichtigkeitserklärung;
　to come into a ~ mit einem Heimfallrecht belastetes Vermögen erben;
　~ **claim** Anwartschaft[srecht]; ~ **[value] duty** *(Br.)* 10%ige Wertzuwachssteuer für an den Pächter zurückfallenden Besitz; ~ **estate** Rückfallgut.

reversionary anwartschaftlich, heimfällig, mit Aufschub zahlbar;
　~ **additions** *(life insurance)* Summenzuwachs durch stehenge-

lassene Prämien; ~ **annuity** einseitige Überlebensrente, Rente auf den Überlebensfall; ~ **bonus** *(insurance)* Summenzuwachs; ~ **bonus plan** *(life insurance)* Gewinngutschriftssystem; ~ **heir** Nacherbe; ~ **interest** Anwartschaftsrecht, Rückfall-, Heimfallanspruch, Nacherbschaftsrecht, Rückfallanspruch; **to have a** ~ **interest in an estate** Anwartschaftsrecht besitzen; ~ **lease** *(Br.)* zweiter (neu abzuschließender) Pachtvertrag; ~ **patent** Anwartschaftspatent; ~ **potential** Heimfallmöglichkeit; ~ **succession** Nacherbfolge[recht].

reversioner Heimfall-, Anwartschaftsberechtigter, Nacherbe.

revert *(v.)* anfallen, [an den Vorbesitzer] zurückfallen, *(office)* wieder einsetzen;
　~ **to an ascendant** einem Verwandten zufallen; ~ **back to** zurückfallen auf; ~ **to the Crown** *(Br.)* an den Staat fallen; ~ **to a matter in due course** zu gegebener Zeit auf eine Sache zurückkommen; ~ **to private enterprise** *(Br.)* reprivatisieren; ~ **to private status by buying out the quoted minority** durch Aufkauf der an der Börse zugelassenen Fremdaktien wieder zum reinen Privatbetrieb werden; ~ **to a former owner** an den früheren Eigentümer zurückgeben; ~ **property** Eigentum zurückübertragen; ~ **to the state** an den Staat fallen; ~ **to one's original statement** auf seine erste Erklärung zurückkommen; ~ **to one's subject** zu seinem Thema zurückkehren.

reverter Rückfallrecht.

revertibility Belastung mit einem Heimfallrecht.

revertible heimfällig, zurückfallend.

reverting to ours im Verfolg unseres Schreibens.

revest *(v.)* zurückerwerben, *(in office)* wieder einsetzen, *(right)* wieder wirksam werden;
　~ **in a former owner** an den früheren Eigentümer zurückgeben; ~ **property** Eigentum wieder in Besitz nehmen, Eigentum zurückübertragen.

revesting Rückgabe an den früheren Eigentümer.

revet *(airplane)* Splitterbox.

revictual *(v.)* neu verproviantieren.

revictualling Wiederauffüllen der Vorräte.

review *(of book)* Besprechung, Rezension, *(check)* [Nach]prüfung, *(judicial revision)* gerichtliche Überprüfung, Revision, *(mil.)* [Truppen]parade, -schau, Musterung, *(periodical)* Zeitschrift, Magazin, *(school)* Wiederholung, nochmaliges Durchgehen, *(survey)* Über-, Rückblick;
　not subject to ~ nicht revisibel (anfechtbar); **under** ~ zu besprechen;
　annual ~ Jahresübersicht; **critical** ~ kritische Zeitschrift; **judicial** ~ Normenkontrolle; **law** ~ juristische Zeitschrift; **market** ~ Börsen-, Marktbericht; **military** ~ Parade, Truppenschau; **monthly** ~ Monatsbericht; **naval** ~ Flottenparade; **previous** ~ *(book)* Vorbesprechung; **rave** ~ überschwengliche Kritik;
　~ **on appeal** *(US)* Urteilsüberprüfung der Vorinstanz; ~ **of costs** Überprüfung einer Kostenrechnung; ~ **of the fleet** Flottenparade; ~ **of the market** Börsen-, Marktbericht; ~ **of remand cases** Haftprüfungsverfahren; ~ **of taxation** *(Br.)* nochmalige Gebührenüberprüfung der Anwaltsrechnung;
　~ *(v.)* [über]prüfen, revidieren, einer Revision unterziehen, *(pupil)* wiederholen, repetieren, *(write critical examination)* rezensieren, Kritik abgeben (schreiben);
　~ **[copy of] a book** Buch rezensieren (besprechen); ~ **a book favo(u)rably** Buch positiv besprechen, günstige Buchkritik schreiben; ~ **a case** Prozeß im Wege der Revision behandeln; ~ **a judgment** Urteil der Vorinstanz überprüfen; ~ **last week's lesson** Lektion der Vorwoche wiederholen; ~ **one's manuscript** sein Manuskript kritisch durchsehen; ~ **a price list** Preisliste berichtigen; ~ **the proceedings** Verfahren nochmals überprüfen; ~ **the situation** Lage überblicken; ~ **taxation** *(Br.)* Kostenrechnung eines Anwalts überprüfen; ~ **for the „Times"** als Buchkritiker bei der „Times" arbeiten; ~ **troops** Truppen besichtigen, Truppenparade abnehmen;
　to be subject to ~ der Nachprüfung unterliegen, nachprüfungspflichtig sein; **to come under** ~ einer Prüfung unterzogen werden; **to hold a** ~ Parade abnehmen; **to keep a question under** ~ Sache genau verfolgen; **to pass one's life in** ~ sein Leben im Geist Revue passieren lassen; **to petition for** ~ Nachprüfungsantrag stellen; **to refuse to** ~ **a lower court decision** Revision gegen das Urteil einer Vorinstanz ablehnen; **to write** ~**s for monthly magazines** Buchbesprechungen für Monatszeitschriften schreiben;
　~ **board** *(US)* Prüfungsausschuß, -kommission; ~ **committee** Inspektionsausschuß; ~ **copy** *(book)* Rezensions-, Presseexemplar; ~ **course** Wiederholungskurs; ~ **order** *(mil.)* Paradeanzug, -ordnung, *(fig.)* Gala, voller Wichs; ~ **powers** Überprüfungsmöglichkeiten.

reviewability Rechtsmittelfähigkeit.

reviewable *(judgment)* rechtsmittelfähig, revisibel, revisionsfähig, durch Revision anfechtbar.

reviewal Kritik, Rezension, *(law)* Revision.

reviewer Rezensent, Kritiker;
~'s **copy** Rezensionsexemplar.

reviewing, in ~ **our records (books)** bei Durchsicht unserer Bücher;
~ **court** Rechtsmittelgericht; ~ **taxation** *(law court)* Überprüfung von Kostenrechnungen.

revile *(v.)* verunglimpfen, schmähen, öffentlich herabsetzen;
~ **the memory of the dead** Tote verunglimpfen.

revindicate *(v.)* zurückfordern.

revindication Zurückforderung.

revisable revisionsfähig, revisibel.

revisableness Revisibilität, Revisionsfähigkeit.

revisal Prüfung, Durchsicht, *(print.)* zweite Korrektur;
second ~ letzte Korrektur.

revise nochmalige Überprüfung, Revision, *(proof taken after correction)* verbesserter Text, Revisionsbogen;
press ~ druckfertiger Korrekturbogen; **second (final)** ~ letzte Korrektur, Umbruchkorrektur;
~ *(v.)* *(correct)* verbessern, über-, umarbeiten, *(examine)* durchsehen, überprüfen, revidieren, *(print.)* Korrekturen überprüfen (lesen);
~ **an assessment** Steuerberichtigung vornehmen, Einkommensteuerveranlagung berichtigen; ~ **boundaries** Grenzen revidieren; ~ **a decision** Entscheidung abändern; ~ **a dictionary** Wörterbuch neu bearbeiten (überarbeiten); ~ **one's estimates** Neukalkulation vornehmen; ~ **one's lessons** seine Lektionen noch einmal durchnehmen; ~ **one's opinions** of s. o. seine Ansicht über j. revidieren; ~ **a statute** Gesetz neu fassen;
~ **proof** Revisionsbogen.

revised│arrangement Neuregelung; ~ **edition** neubearbeitete (verbesserte) Auflage; ~ **figure** bereinigte (berichtigte) Zahl; ~ **proof** Korrekturbogen, Zweitkorrektur; ~ **statute** geänderte Satzung; ᵉ **Statutes** Sammlung neugefaßter Gesetze.

reviser Korrektor.

revising│assessors *(Br.)* Wahlprüfungsbeamte; ~ **barrister** *(parl.)* Wählerlisten überprüfender Anwalt.

revision Nachprüfung, Revidierung, Revision, Überarbeitung, *(examination)* [Text]durchsicht, *(rehearsal)* erneute Verhandlung, *(revised edition)* Überarbeitung, überarbeitete Auflage, zweite Bearbeitung, Neubearbeitung;
frontier ~ Grenzberichtigung;
~ **of an assessment** Berichtigungsveranlagung, -feststellung; **subsequent** ~ **of books** Betriebsnachkalkulation; ~ **of judgment** Wiederaufnahme des Verfahrens; ~ **of a price** Berichtigung eines Preises, Preisberichtigung; ~ **of statute** Neufassung eines Gesetzes; ~ **of a treaty** Vertragsrevision;
to send a case back to the lower court for ~ Fall zur erneuten Verhandlung zurückverweisen.

revisionary chamber zweite Kammer.

revisionism Revisionismus, Revisionspolitik.

revisionist Revisionist, Revisionspolitiker.

revisory powers Überprüfungsrecht.

revitalization of the capital market Wiederbelebung des Kapitalmarktes.

revitalize *(v.)* wiederbeleben, neue Impulse geben;
~ **the capital market** Kapitalmarkt wiederbeleben.

revival Erneuerung, *(market)* Wiederbelebung, -aufleben, Aufschwung, Erholung, *(law)* Wiederinkrafttreten;
trade ~ Geschäftsbelebung, Konjunkturaufschwung;
~ **of an action** Fortsetzung eines ruhenden Verfahrens; ~ **in business** Geschäftsaufschwung, Konjunkturbelebung; ~ **of consumption** Wiederbelebung des Verbrauchermarktes; ~ **of contract** Wiederauflebenlassen eines Vertrages, Vertragserneuerung; ~ **of an old custom** Wiederbelebung alten Brauchtums; ~ **of a debt barred by the Statute of Limitations** Wiederaufleben einer verjährten Forderung; ~ **of investment** Anlagenerneuerung; ~ **of judgment** Urteilserneuerung; ~ **of the market** Erholung des Marktes; ~ **of a play** Wiederaufnahme eines lange nicht mehr gespielten Stücks; ~ **of sales** Absatzbelebung; ~ **of trade** Geschäftsbelebung, Konjunkturaufschwung, -belebung; ~ **of a restored will** Wiederinkrafttreten eines widerrufenen Testaments.

revive *(v.)* *(debt barred by the statute of limitations)* wiederaufleben lassen, erneuern, *(judgment)* wieder in Kraft treten lassen (setzen), *(stocks)* sich erholen, *(speculation)* wiedereinsetzen, *(trade)* sich wiederbeleben, aufblühen;
~ **economic activity** Konjunktur beleben; ~ **an action** Prozeß

wieder aufnehmen; ~ **an agreement** Vertrag wiederaufleben lassen; ~ **the death penalty** Todesstrafe wieder einführen; ~ **an industry** Industriezweig beleben; ~ **the issue of mergers** Fusionsbestrebungen beleben; ~ **justice** Gerechtigkeit wiederherstellen; ~ **an expired patent** erloschenes Patent wiederherstellen; ~ **a will** widerrufenes Testament wiederaufleben lassen.

revivor Wiederaufnahmeverfahren.

revocability Widerruflichkeit.

revocable widerruflich;
to be ~ **at any time** jederzeit widerruflich sein;
~ **deed** widerrufliche Urkunde; ~ **letter of credit** widerrufliches Akkreditiv; ~ **licence** widerrufliche Genehmigung; ~ **trust** kündbare Stiftung, widerrufliche Treuhandbestellung.

revocation *(decree)* Widerruf, Zurücknahme;
constructive ~ gesetzliche Beendigung; **dependent relative** ~ auslegungsfähiger Testamentswiderruf; **general** ~ allgemeiner Widerruf; **judicial** ~ Widerruf kraft gerichtlicher Verfügung; **special** ~ Sonderwiderruf;
~ **of agency** Widerruf des Vertretungsverhältnisses; ~ **of a contract** Vertrags[auf]kündigung; ~ **of a donation (gift)** Schenkungswiderruf; ~ **of a grant** Konzessionsrücknahme; ~ **of a guarantee** Annullierung einer Bürgschaft; ~ **of a law** Gesetzesaufhebung; ~ **of a legacy** Legatentziehung; ~ **of a letter of credit** Zurückziehung eines Akkreditivs; ~ **of a licence** Entziehung einer Lizenz, Lizenzrücknahme; ~ **of a driving licence** *(Br.)* **(a driver's license,** *US)* Führerscheinentzug; ~ **of an offer** Zurücknahme eines Vertragsangebots; ~ **of a patent** Patententziehung, -rücknahme, -löschung; ~ **of a power of attorney** Vollmachtswiderruf; ~ **of probate** Erbscheinseinziehung; ~ **of a proxy** Widerruf einer Stimmrechtsermächtigung, Vollmachts-, Stimmrechtsermächtigungswiderruf; ~ **of a trust** Rücktritt von einer Treuhanderrichtung; ~ **of a will** Aufhebung (Umstoßung, Widerruf) eines Testaments, Testamentsaufhebung; ~ **by another will** Testamentswiderruf durch Errichtung eines neuen Testaments; ~ **of a will by destruction** Testamentswiderruf durch Vernichtung;
~ **clause** *(will)* Widerrufsklausel.

revocatory action Nichtigkeitsklage.

revoke Annullierung, Widerruf, Aufhebung;
~ **of an authority** Vollmachtswiderruf;
~ *(v.)* widerrufen, *(cancel)* anfechten, rückgängig machen, annullieren, *(licence)* zurückziehen, -ziehen, entziehen;
~ **an agency** Vertretungsverhältnis aufheben; ~ **an authority** Vollmacht widerrufen; ~ **an agent's authority at any time** Vertretungsbefugnis jederzeit widerrufen; ~ **one's consent** seine Genehmigung zurückziehen; ~ **a contract** Vertrag aufkündigen; ~ **a grant** Genehmigung zurückziehen, Schenkung rückgängig machen; ~ **a law** Gesetz aufheben; ~ **a letter of credit** Akkreditiv zurückziehen; ~ **a licence** Lizenz zurücknehmen; ~ **a driving licence** *(Br.)* Führerschein entziehen; ~ **an offer** Vertragsangebot zurücknehmen; ~ **an order** Auftrag stornieren (annullieren); ~ **an order of discharge** Konkursaufhebungsbeschluß annullieren; ~ **a patent** Patent zurücknehmen; ~ **a power of attorney** Vollmacht widerrufen; ~ **a proxy** Stimmrechtsermächtigung zurückziehen; ~ **a will** Testament widerrufen (umstoßen).

revolt Empörung, Aufstand, Aufruhr, Revolte, Erhebung;
servile ~ Sklavenaufstand;
~s **against authority** Aufruhr gegen die Obrigkeit;
~ *(v.)* sich erheben, revoltieren, *(fig.)* Widerwillen empfinden; ~ **against their ruler** sich gegen ihren Herrscher erheben;
to break out in ~ sich erheben, in Aufruhr geraten; **to crush a** ~ Aufruhr niederschlagen; **to stir the people to** ~ Volksmasse zum Aufruhr anstiften.

revolted aufrührerisch, aufständisch.

revolter Rebell, Aufrührer, Aufständischer.

revolution Revolution, Umsturz, Umwälzung;
industrial ~ industrielle Umwälzung; **managerial** ~ Regime der Manager; **world** ~ Weltrevolution;
~s **in our ideas of time and space** Umwälzung unserer Ansichten über Zeit und Raum; ~s **per minute** Tourenzahl pro Minute; ~ **in thought** Umschwung im Denken; ~ **in our ways of travelling** Revolution unseres ganzen Verkehrssystems;
to quell a ~ Aufstand niederschlagen;
~ **counter** Tourenzähler.

revolutionary revolutionär, umstürzlerisch, *(fig.)* epochemachend;
to create a ~ **climate** Klima für die Entwicklung revolutionärer Verhältnisse schaffen; ~ **principles** revolutionäre Prinzipien; ~ **society** revolutionäre Gesellschaft.

revolutionism Revolutionszustand.

revolutionist Revolutionär, Umstürzler.

revolutionize *(v.)* revolutionieren.

revulsion of public feeling Umschwung in der öffentlichen Meinung.

revolve *(v.)* kreisen, sich drehen, rotieren, *(stocks)* umlaufen, sich periodisch erneuern;
~ **in s. one's mind** jem. im Kopf herumgehen; ~ **a problem** Problem wälzen.

revolvement of stocks periodische Lagererneuerung.

revolver Revolver.

revolving revolvierend;
~ **account** revolvierendes Konto; ~ **assets** Umlaufvermögen; ~ **case** drehbares Büchergestell; ~ **[letter of] credit** sich automatisch erneuerndes Akkreditiv, revolvierender Kredit; **secured ~ credit** Warenlombardkredit; ~ **credit agreement (arrangement)** Revolvingabkommen; ~ **fund** *(governmental accounting, US)* rückzahlbare Staatssubvention, Umlauf-, Erneuerungsfonds; ~ **payments** wiederkehrende Zahlungen; ~ **pencil** Drehbleistift; **to be topped with a ~ radar disk** mit einem auf dem Dach angebrachten Radarspiegel ausgestattet sein.

revue *(theater)* Revue, Ausstattungsstück.

reward [Finder]lohn, [Geld]belohnung, *(fee)* Honorar, Vergütung, Entgelt;
as a ~ for als Belohnung (Entgelt) für;
due ~ angemessene Belohnung; **reasonable ~** angemessene Gegenleistung;
~ *(v.)* belohnen, vergüten;
~ **richly** reich belohnen; ~ **s. o. suitably** j. nach Gebühr belohnen;
to advertise a ~ Belohnung aussetzen; **to confer a ~ on s. o.** jem. eine Belohnung gewähren; **to get a fair ~ for one's labo(u)r** angemessen bezahlt werden; **to get very little ~ for one's hard labo(u)r** für seine schwere Arbeit nur geringfügig entlohnt werden; **to hold out ~s** Belohnung aussetzen; **to offer a ~** Belohnung aussetzen, Auslobung vornehmen, ausloben; **to tailor one's ~s to the international value of goods and services one provides** seine Bedürfnisse dem internationalen Gegenwert der eigenen Waren und Dienstleistungen anpassen;
~ **claim** *(Australia)* Mutungsanspruch; ~ **system** Prämienlohnsystem.

rewarding book lesenswertes Buch.

rewarehouse *(v.)* wieder einlagern.

rewarehousing Wiedereinlagerung.

reweigh *(v.)* nachwiegen.

reweight nochmals ermitteltes Gewicht.

rewind *(v.)* **a film** Film umspulen.

reword *(v.)* neu formulieren (fassen).

rework *(v.)* nach-, überarbeiten;
~ **statements into a standard form** Bilanzziffern in das übliche Bilanzformular übertragen;
~ **expense** Nacharbeitungskosten.

rewrite Neufassung, *(US)* Reportage (Bericht) in zeitungsgerechter Form;
~ *(v.)* neufassen, nochmals schreiben, *(journalist)* umschreiben;
~ **man** Redaktionsmitglied.

rezone *(v.)* *(US)* Baubeschränkungen aufheben;
~ **for corporate business** Flächennutzungsplan zugunsten wirtschaftlicher Nutzung abändern.

rezoning *(US)* Aufhebung von Baubeschränkungen, Änderung des Flächennutzungsplans.

rhapsodize *(v.)* **about a new book** voll Begeisterung über ein neues Buch schreiben.

rhapsody *(fig.)* überschwengliche Rede.

rhetoric Beredsamkeit, Redekunst.

rhetorical | efforts rhetorische Bemühungen; ~ **question** rhetorische Frage.

rhetorician Phrasendrescher.

rhino *(Br., sl.)* Moneten, Kies.

rhubarb *(sl.)* Provinznest.

rhyme, without ~ or reason ohne Sinn und Verstand.

ribbon Farbband, *(microphone, sl.)* Mikrophon, *(mil.)* Ordensband;
magnetic ~ Tonband; **typewriter ~** Farbband;
~ **building** *(Br.)* am Stadtrand gelegene Reihenhäuser; ~ **development** *(Br.)* Stadtrandsiedlung; ~ **feed** Farbbandtransport; ~ **microphone** Bandmikrophon; ~ **movement** Farbbandtransport; ~ **reverse** Farbbandumschaltung; ~ **road** Serpentinenstraße; ~ **switch** Farbbandeinsteller; ~ **transmitter** Bandmikrophon.

rich *(abounding)* reichhaltig, ergiebig, *(fertile)* fruchtbar, fett, *(wealthy)* wohlhabend, begütert, reich;
for ~er, for poorer in guten wie in schlechten Zeiten;
the new[ly] vulgar ~ Neureiche;
~ **as a Jew (Croesus, Br.)** steinreich;
to grow ~ reich werden; **to smell ~** Atmosphäre von Reichtum atmen;
~ **allusion** bedeutungsvolle Anspielung; ~ **crop** reiche (ergiebige) Ernte; ~ **gift** kostbares Geschenk; ~ **harvest** ergiebige Ernte; ~ **idea** großartige Idee; **to pass for a ~ man** als reich gelten; ~ **oil** Schweröl; **the ~ people** die Reichen; ~ **reward** hohe Belohnung; ~ **soil** fruchtbarer Boden.

Richard Roe otherwise troublesome fiktiver Beklagter.

riches Reichtum, Ergiebigkeit, Vermögen;
to amass great ~ Reichtümer ansammeln (anhäufen); **to have ~ to spare** gut dotiert sein, *(fig.)* mit einer Fülle von Begabungen ausgestattet sein.

richness Reichtum, Ergiebigkeit.

rick Heuschober.

rid | *(v.)* befreien;
~ **the country of bandits** Land von Banditen säubern; ~ **o. s. of an employee** Angestellten loswerden; ~ **one's estate of debts** seinen Grundbesitz schuldenfrei machen; ~ **o. s. of an obligation** sich von einer Verbindlichkeit befreien;
to get ~ of loswerden, an den Mann bringen; **to get ~ of one's money** sein Geld loswerden; **to get ~ of old stock** alte Bestände abstoßen; **to get ~ of an unwelcome visitor** unerwünschten Besucher loswerden;
hard to get ~ of schwer loszuwerden.

riddance Befreiung, Erlösung.

ridden, police- von der Polizei unterdrückt, unter Polizeiherrschaft.

riddle Rätsel;
~ *(v.)* *(evidence)* sichten, prüfen;
~ **an argument** Beweis zerpflücken; ~ **s. one's reputation** jds. guten Ruf untergraben;
to solve a ~ Rätsel lösen.

ride Fahrt, *(carrousel, coll.)* Karussel, *(anticyclone)* Ausläufer, *(mil.)* Trupp berittener Soldaten;
~ **on a bus** Autobusfahrt; ~ **on a motor cycle** Motorrad-Fahren;
~ *(v.)* *(in examination, sl.)* spicken, pfuschen, *(vehicle)* [in öffentlichem Verkehrsmittel] fahren;
~ **the air** *(sl.)* Hochbauarbeiter sein; ~ **at anchor** *(ship)* vor Anker liegen; ~ **around** *(US)* herumfahren; ~ **a bicycle** Fahrrad fahren; ~ **on a bus** Omnibusfahrt machen, Omnibus fahren; ~ **on s. one's coat-tails** in jds. Schlepptau segeln; ~ **down a fugitive** Flüchtling einholen; ~ **at easy** vor Anker treiben; ~ **for a fall** Schicksal herausfordern; ~ **free** umsonst mitfahren; ~ **the goat** *(US)* in einen Geheimbund aufgenommen werden; ~ **the gravy train** *(sl.)* schnell und bequem Geld verdienen; ~ **hard on s. th.** etw. kontrollieren; ~ **high in the opinion poll** ausgezeichnete Ergebnisse bei Meinungsumfragen verzeichnen; ~ **higher off the ground** *(car)* höhere Straßenlage haben; ~ **a hobby** Steckenpferd haben; ~ **out a contraction of business** mit abnehmendem Geschäftsvolumen fertig werden; ~ **out the steel crisis** Stahlkrise einigermaßen übersehen; ~ **out a storm** stürmische Zeiten überstehen; ~ **out bad times** schlechte Zeiten überstehen; ~ **over all protests** sich über alle Proteste hinwegsetzen; ~ **a pony** *(sl.)* Eselsbrücke (Klatsche) benutzen; ~ **roughshod** rücksichtslos vorgehen; ~ **on a side issue** auf einer Nebenfrage herumreiten; ~ **Shank's mare** *(sl.)* auf Schusters Rappen reiten; ~ **on a wave of popularity** von einer Woge der Begeisterung getragen werden; ~ **to work on a streetcar** *(US)* mit der Straßenbahn zur Arbeit fahren;
to be a twopenny ~ on the bus zwei Pence für den Bus kosten; **to give s. o. a ~** j. [im Auto] mitnehmen; **to give s. o. a rough ~** j. äußerst unmanierlich behandeln; **to go for a ~ in a car** Autofahrt unternehmen; **to go along for the ~** *(sl.)* so eben um mal mitzumachen; **to hitch a ~ on exports** sich allein auf Exportsteigerungen versteifen; **to share a ~** sich die Fahrtkosten teilen; **to steal a ~** ohne Fahrkarte fahren, schwarzfahren; **to take s. o. for a ~** j. im Auto mitnehmen, *(fig.)* j. übers Ohr hauen, *(sl.)* j. kaltmachen, j. begaunern;
~ **officer** berittener Zöllner.

rider Reiter, *(advertisement)* abschließender Kaufappell, *(of a bill)* Verlängerungszettel, Wechselallonge, *(document)* Anlage, Anhang, *(endorsement)* Nachtrag, Zusatz[klausel], *(insurance)* besondere Versicherungsvereinbarung, *(law)* Zusatzklausel, -artikel, Nebenbestimmung, *(to a motion)* Zusatz, *(motor cycle)* Fahrer;
dispatch ~ *(mil.)* Meldefahrer;

~ of a motor-assisted pedal cycle Mopedfahrer;

to add a ~ to a verdict recommending mercy Urteil mit einem Begnadigungsvorschlag versehen.

riding Reiten, Fahren, *(Br.)* Verwaltungsbezirk, *(Canada)* Wahlbezirk;

to be ~ for a fall ins Unglück rennen;

~ **comfort** Fahrkomfort; ~ **gear** Motorradkleidung; ~ **light** *(ship)* Ankerlicht; ~ **school** Reitschule.

rif *(v.) (sl.)* feuern, rausschmeißen.

rife weit verbreitet;

to be ~ grassieren; **to be ~ with rumo(u)rs** gerüchteschwanger sein; **to grow ~** überhandnehmen.

rifle *(v.) for (fam.)* genau durchsuchen.

rig [behelfsmäßige] Vorrichtung, Ausrüstung, Ausstattung, *(fraudulent trick)* abgekartetes Spiel, *(stock exchange)* Börsenmanöver;

queer ~ seltsame Ausstaffierung;

~ *(v.)* durch unlautere Machenschaften beeinflussen, betrügerisch handhaben, *(plane)* montieren;

~ **an election** Wahlresultat manipulieren, Wahlschiebung begehen; ~ **the market** Kursniveau künstlich beeinflussen; ~ **out** ausrüsten, -statten; ~ **o. s. out** sich ausstaffieren; ~ **a ship with new sails** Schiff mit neuen Segeln ausstatten; ~ **up** behelfsmäßig herrichten, zusammenbasteln; ~ **up the prices** Preise (Kurse) heraufschrauben; ~ **up a shelter for the night** Schutzhütte für die Nacht aufschlagen; ~ **up a scaffolding for the workers** Gerüst für die Arbeiter erstellen;

to run a ~ Streich aushecken.

rigged bid Scheingebot.

rigger Preistreiber, *(airplane)* Flugzeugmonteur, *(building)* Schutzgerüst, *(stock exchange)* Kurstreiber.

rigging betrügerische Handhabung, *(airplane)* Verspannung;

~ **the market** Preistreiberei, *(stock exchange)* Kurstreiberei, Börsenmanöver.

right Recht, Anrecht, [Rechts]anspruch, Berechtigung, *(application right)* Bezugsrecht auf neue Aktien, *(privilege)* Vorrecht, *(ship)* Steuerbord;

all ~s reserved alle Rechte vorbehalten, Nachdruck verboten; **as of ~s** von Rechts wegen; **by ~** kraft, aufgrund, de jure; **by good ~s** mit gutem Recht; **cum ~s, ~s on** mit (inklusive) Bezugsrechten; **ex ~s** ohne Bezugsrecht; **in ~ of his wife** im Namen seiner Frau; **in one's own ~** eigenständig, aus eigenem Verdienst; **of ~** rechtmäßig; **with ~s** mit Bezugsrecht; **with ~ of transfer** mit dem Recht der Weitergabe; **with ~ to batch (lot) completion** *(book trade)* mit Recht der Partieergänzung; **without ~** rechtlos; **without prejudice to my ~s** unter Vorbehalt meiner Rechte;

absolute ~ absolutes (uneingeschränktes, ausschließliches) Recht; **~s accrued** erworbene Rechte; **duly acquired ~s** wohlerworbene Rechte; **alienable ~** veräußerliches Recht; **appendant** Nebenrecht; **application ~** *(Br.)* Bezugsrecht; **bare ~** abstraktes Eigentum; **belligerent ~s** kriegsführende Rechte; **birth ~** Geburtsrecht; **bumping ~** Recht auf Beibehaltung des Arbeitsplatzes bei Entlassungen; **chartered ~s** verbriefte Rechte; **civil ~s** Grundrechte, staatsbürgerliche Rechte; **common ~** allgemein anerkanntes Recht; **conditional ~** bedingtes Recht; **conflicting ~s** entgegenstehende Rechte; **conjugal ~s** eheliche Rechte; **constitutional ~** verfassungsmäßig verbürgtes Recht, Grundrecht; **contingent ~** Anwartschaftsrecht; **contractual ~** vertraglich begründetes Recht; **customary ~** Gewohnheitsrecht; **dramatic ~s** Aufführungsrechte; **drawing ~** Auslosungsrecht; **equitable (equity) ~** Billigkeitsanspruch; **exclusive ~** Ausschließlichkeitsrecht; **existing ~** gegenwärtiges Recht; **film ~s** Film[verwertungs]rechte; **forfeited ~** verwirktes Recht; **fundamental ~s** grundlegendes Recht; **future ~** zukünftiges Recht; **homestead ~** *(US)* Heimstättenvollstreckungsschutz; **immaterial ~** unkörperliches Recht; **immediate ~** sofort fälliger Anspuch; **imperfect ~s** unvollkommene (unklare, unbestimmte) Rechte; **inalienable ~** unübertragbares Recht; **inchoate ~** schwach begründetes Recht; **incorporeal ~s** Immaterialgüterrechte; **indefeasible ~** unverzichtbares Recht; **industrial ~** gewerbliches Schutzrecht; **inherent ~** durch Geburt erworbenes Recht; **intangible ~** unkörperliches (immaterielles) Recht; **legal ~** Rechtsanspruch [nach Common Law]; **litigious ~** strittiges Recht; **magazine ~** Nachdruckrechte für Zeitschriften; **majority ~s** Rechte der Mehrheit; **marital ~s** ehe[männ]liche Rechte; **mere ~** besitzloses Eigentum; **mineral ~s** Schürf-, Bergbaurecht; **minority ~** Rechte der Minderheit; **moral ~** moralische Berechtigung; **natural ~** Naturrecht, originäres Recht, Grundrecht; **obligatory ~** Leistungsanspruch; **optional ~** Optionsrecht; **one's own ~** frei verfügbarer Besitz;

participating ~s Gewinnbeteiligungsrechte; **patent ~** Patentrecht, -anspruch; **pauper's ~** *(US)* Armenrecht; **perfect ~** eindeutiges Recht; **performing ~s** Aufführungsrechte; **personal ~** pesönliches (obligatorisches) Recht, Persönlichkeitsrecht; **political ~s** verfassungsmäßige Grundrechte; **possessory ~** Besitzanspruch, -recht; **precarious ~** widerrufliche Gestattung; **preemptive ~** *(stockholder, US)* Bezugsrecht; **preferential ~** Vorzugsrecht; **prescriptive ~** durch Ersitzung erworbenes Recht, Gewohnheitsrecht; **preventive secondary ~** Schutzrecht; **primary ~** anerkanntes Recht (Privileg); **prior ~** älteres Recht; **priority ~** Vorzugsrecht; **private ~** persönliches Recht; **production ~** Herstellungsrecht; **property ~** Vermögens-, Eigentumsrecht; **proprietary ~** Eigentums-, Urheberrecht; **protective secondary ~** Schutzrecht; **qualified ~** eingeschränktes (bedingtes) Recht; **real ~** *(Scot.)* dingliches Recht; **redemption ~** Auslosungsrecht; **relative ~** obligatorisches Recht; **rental ~** Erbpacht; **revisionary ~** Anwartschaftsrecht; **restitutory ~** Rückerstattungsanspruch; **revisionary ~** Anwartschaftsrecht; **riparian ~s** Uferanliegerrechte; **secondary ~** Nebenanspruch, -recht; **selling ~** Verkaufsrecht; **serial ~s** Veröffentlichungsrechte in Zeitungen und Zeitschriften; **shop ~s** Fabrikationsrechte; **stage ~s** Aufführungs-, Bühnenrechte; **sole ~** alleiniges Recht; **stock ~** *(US)* Bezugsrecht; **subscription ~** *(Br.)* Bezugsrecht; **substantial ~** Grundrecht; **trademark ~** Warenzeichen[benutzungs]recht; **transferable ~** abtretbares Recht; **translation ~s** Übersetzungsrechte; **unclaimed ~** nicht geltend gemachtes Recht; **unimpeachable ~** unangreifbares Recht; **union ~s** Gewerkschaftsrechte; **vested ~s** wohlerworbene (verbriefte) Rechte; **visitorial ~** Inspektions-, Aufsichtsrecht; **widow ~** Pflichtteilsanspruch der Witwe; **women's ~s** Frauenrechte;

~ **of access** Zugangs-, Zutrittsrecht; ~ **of access to the books** Recht auf Einsichtnahme in die Geschäftsbücher; ~ **of accrual** Anwachsungsrecht; ~ **to act as a contracting party** Selbsteintrittsrecht; ~ **in action** obligatorischer Anspruch, obligatorisches Forderungsrecht; ~ **to bring action** Klagebefugnis, -recht, einklagbarer Anspruch, *(right to sue)* Prozeßfähigkeit; ~ **to adjourn** Vertagungsrecht, -anspruch; ~ **of admission** Zulassungsanspruch; ~ **to air** Recht auf saubere Luft; ~ **to air space** Recht auf Luftraum; ~ **of alienation** Veräußerungsrecht; ~ **to alimony** Unterhaltsanspruch [der Ehefrau]; ~ **to amend** Abänderungsrecht; ~ **of anchorage** Ankerrecht; ~ **of anticipation** Vorkaufsrecht; ~ **of anticipated arrest** *(law of nations)* vorbeugendes Beschlagnahmerecht; ~ **of appeal** Berufungsrecht, *(income tax)* vorbeugendes Beschlagnahmerecht; ~ **of assembly** Versammlungsrecht; ~ **to assign** Zessionsrecht; ~ **of asylum** Asylrecht; ~ **of approach** Recht auf Flaggenerkundung; ~ **of aubaine** *(law of nations)* Heimfallrecht; ~ **of avoidance** Rücktritts-, Anfechtungsrecht; ~ **to begin** *(law suit)* Anspruch, die Klage als erster zu begründen; ~ **to draw benefits** *(social security)* Leistungsanspruch; ~ **of calling** *(option business)* Abnahmerecht [im Prämiengeschäft]; ~ **of cancellation** Rücktrittsrecht; ~ **of change** *(insurance)* Wahlrecht; ~ **of choice** Wahlrecht; ~ **to choose the place of delivery** Wahl des Lieferortes; ~ **of coinage** Münzhoheit; ~ **to collect** Einziehungsrecht; ~ **of combination** Kartellrecht; ~ **of common** Mitbenutzungsrecht; ~ **of compensation** Schadenersatz-, Entschädigungsanspruch; ~ **to compete** Wettbewerbsrecht; ~ **to complain [of complaint]** Beschwerderecht; ~ **to consolidate** Recht auf Mithaftung des zweiten Pfands; ~ **of contiguity** Angrenzer-, Anrainerrecht; ~ **to compound** Vergleichsanspruch; ~**s and obligations arising under a contract** Rechte und Verpflichtungen aus einem Vertrag; ~ **granted by contract** vertraglich eingeräumtes Recht; ~ **to contribution** *(cosurety)* Ausgleichsanspruch; ~ **of conversion** Umwandlungsrecht; ~ **to convey** Übertragungsanspruch; ~ **to counsel** Beratungsanspruch; ~ **of courtesy** Erbteilsanspruch des Ehemanns am Vorbehaltsgut der Ehefrau; ~**s of creditors** Gläubigerrechte; ~ **of custom** Gewohnheitsrecht; ~ **of disclaim** *(receiver)* Verzichtsrecht; ~ **to dispose (of disposal)** Verfügungsmacht; ~ **of distress** Pfändungsanspruch; ~ **of discussion** Einrede der Vorausklage; ~ **to distrain** Pfändungsanspruch; ~ **to a dividend** Dividendenanspruch; ~ **of division** *(Scot., surety)* Haftungsbeschränkung; ~ **of dowry** Witwenpflichtteilsrecht; ~ **of drip** Abflußrecht über das Nachbargrundstück; ~ **of easement** Grunddienstbarkeit; ~ **to emblements** Recht des Aberntens [auch nach Beendigung der Pachtzeit]; ~ **of eminent domain** Zwangsenteignungsrecht; ~ **of emption** Recht des Kaufvertrages; ~ **to end the agreement** Anspruch auf Vertragsbeendigung; ~ **to enforce** Vollstreckungs-, Durchsetzungsanspruch; ~ **to enjoyment of a property** Nutzungsrecht eines Grundstücks; **present fixed ~ of future** enjoyment in Wirksamkeit getretene Anwartschaft; ~ of entry Inbesitznahmerecht, *(international law)* Einreiserecht; ~ of sole emption alleiniges Erwerbsrecht; ~ of free entry Recht auf ungehinderten Zugang; ~ and equity Recht und Billigkeit; ~ of equity of redemption *(US)* Auslösungsrecht des Hypothekenschuldners; ~ to estovers Holzgerechtigkeit; ~ not to be evicted *(spouse)* Räumungsschutzanspruch; ~ of exploitation Verwertungsrecht; ~ to fish Fischereirecht; ~ to foreclose Zwangsvollstreckungsanspruch; ~ to hold a market Marktrecht; ~ of free entry Recht auf ungehinderten Zugang; ~ in gros grundstücksunabhängiges Recht; ~ of habitation *(Louisiana)* kostenloses Wohnrecht; ~ of indemnity Schadensersatzanspruch; ~ of inheritance Erbberechtigung, Erbrecht, Erbschaftsanspruch; ~s of innocent third parties Rechte gutgläubiger Dritter; ~ to inspect Besichtigungsrecht, Recht auf Einsichtnahme; ~ to intervene Interventionsrecht; ~ to issue bank notes Banknotenprivileg; ~ of labo(u)r Recht auf Arbeit; ~s of a landlord Vermieterrechte; ~s and liabilities Rechte und Pflichten; ~ of lien Zurückbehaltungs-, Pfandrecht; ~ to light Lichtrecht; ~ of maintenance Unterhaltsanspruch; ~ to manufacture Fabrikations-, Herstellungsrecht; ~ to marry and found a family Recht auf Heirat und Familiengründung; ~ of public meeting Versammlungsrecht; ~s in respect of membership Mitgliedschaftsrechte; ~ of mining (to mine) Bergbauberechtigung, Bergregal; ~s of minority groups Minderheitsrechte; ~ to money Geldanspruch; ~ of movement Freizügigkeit; ~ to name Benennungsrecht, Recht der Benennung; ~ of nomination Vorschlagsrecht; ~ of notice Kündigungsrecht; ~ of objection Recht, den Richter abzulehnen; ~ of occupation Mieterschutzrecht; ~ to opt Optionsrecht; ~ to pass through Durchfahrtsrecht; ~ to a patent Patentanspruch; sole ~s to the patent alleinige Patentrechte; ~ to participate in trade-union activities gewerkschaftliches Betätigungsrecht; ~s of innocent third parties Rechte gutgläubiger Dritter; ~ to pension Pensions-, Rentenanspruch; ~ in personam *(lat.)* obligatorisches Recht; ~ of persons höchstpersönliches Recht; ~ to possess (of possession) Besitzrecht, -anspruch, Räumungsanspruch; ~ to exclusive possession Recht auf ausschließlichen Besitz; ~ of preemption Vorkaufsrecht, Option; ~ to retain possession Zurückbehaltungsrecht; ~ of priority Prioritätsrecht, *(creditor)* Recht auf vorzugsweise Befriedigung im Konkursverfahren; ~ of privacy Schutz der Intimsphäre (des Persönlichkeitsrechtes); ~ of property Eigentums-, Vermögensrecht; ~s of innocent purchasers Rechte gutgläubiger Dritter; ~ of recourse Rückgriffsrecht, Regreßrecht, -anspruch; ~ of recovery Schadenersatzanspruch, Regreß, Rückgriffsrecht; ~ to redeem (of redemption) Tilgungs-, Auslösungs-, Rückkaufsrecht; ~ of reentry Recht auf Wiederinbesitznahme; ~ of registration Eintragungsanspruch; ~ of reinstatement *(life insurance)* Erneuerungsanspruch; legal ~ to reinstatement gesetzlicher Anspruch auf Wiedereinstellung; ~ to reject Recht auf Gegendarstellung; ~ of representation Einspruchsrecht; ~ of relief *(Scot.)* Recht auf Inanspruchnahme des Hauptschuldners; ~ in rem dingliches Recht; ~ of renewal Prolongationsanspruch; ~ of reply Recht auf Gegendarstellung; ~ of representation Einspruchsrecht; ~ of representation and performance Aufführungsrecht; ~ of repurchase Wieder-, Rückkaufsrecht; ~ of resale Wiederverkaufsrecht; ~ to rescind (of rescission) Rücktrittsrecht, Annullierungsanspruch, Anfechtungsrecht; ~ of retention Zurückbehaltungsrecht; ~ to return *(bookseller)* Remissionsrecht; ~ in reversion Anwartschaftsrecht; ~ of review Nachprüfungsrecht; ~ of search Durchsuchungsrecht [für Schiffe]; ~ of self-defence Selbstverteidigungsrecht; ~ of self-determination Selbstbestimmungsrecht; ~ of local self-government Selbstverwaltungsrecht; [sole] ~ to sell (of selling) [alleiniges] Verkaufs-, Vertriebsrecht, Universalverkaufsrecht; ~ of separation Absonderungsanspruch; ~ of setoff Aufrechnungsanspruch; ~ of settlement Niederlassungsrecht; ~ to speak (of free speech) Recht auf freie Meinungsäußerung; ~ of staple Niederlassungsrecht; ~ of stoppage in transit (to stoppage in transit) Anhalte-, Rückrufrecht; ~ to strike Streikrecht; ~ to sublet Untervermietungsrecht; ~ of subrogation Recht auf Abtretung des Ersatzanspruches; ~ to subscribe Subskriptions-, Bezugsrecht; ~ to succeed Erbberechtigung; ~ of succession *(Br.)* Erbfolgerecht; ~ to sue (to bring a suit) Klagerecht, Aktivlegitimation, Prozeßführungsbefugnis, -fähigkeit; ~ to support Recht auf Grenzabstützung; ~ to tack *(Br.)* Hypothekenvereinigungsanspruch; ~s of a tenant Mieterrechte; ~ of termination Kündigungsrecht, -anspruch; ~ of things Rechte an Sachen; ~ of translation Übersetzungsrecht; ~ to exclusive use ausschließliches Benutzungs-

recht; ~ of user Benutzungsrecht; full ~ of user uneingeschränktes Gebrauchsrecht; ~ of usufruct Nießbrauch[recht]; ~ to veto Veto-, Einspruchsrecht; ~ of visit[ation] and research Durchsuchungsrecht auf hoher See; ~ to vote Wahlberechtigung, Stimm-, Wahlrecht; ~ of water Wasserrecht; ~ of way Wegerecht, *(to move first)* Vorfahrt, Vorfahrtsrecht, *(railway)* Bahngelände, *(strip of land)* vom Staat beanspruchter Geländestreifen; public ~ of way öffentliches Wegerecht; ~ to withdraw (of withdrawal) Austritts-, Rücktrittsrecht; ~ to work Recht auf Arbeit;
~ *(v.)* in die richtige Lage bringen, *(damage)* wiedergutmachen;
~ o. s. sich rehabilitieren, sich selbst Recht verschaffen; ~ s. o. jem. zu seinem Recht verhelfen; ~ a car quickly after it skidded rutschendes Auto schnell abfangen; ~ an error Fehler berichtigen; ~ a machine Flugzeug abfangen; ~ a wrong Unrecht wiedergutmachen;
to abandon a ~ sich eines Rechtes begeben, auf einen Anspruch verzichten; to acquire a ~ Recht erwerben; to act within one's ~ by claiming seine Forderung zu Recht erheben; to affect the ~s Rechte berühren; to assert ~s Rechte geltend machen; to avail o. s. of a ~ von einem Recht Gebrauch machen; to be in the ~ Recht auf seiner Seite haben; to be within one's ~s im Recht sein; to be subject to an unpaid seller's ~ of lien einem Eigentumsvorbehalt des Verkäufers unterliegen; to belong to s. o. by ~ jem. rechtmäßig gehören; to claim one's ~ sein Recht fordern; to come into one's own ~ zu seinem Recht kommen; to confer a ~ Recht übertragen; to constitute a ~ Recht begründen; to contest s. one's ~s jem. ein Recht streitig machen; to disclaim a ~ auf ein Recht verzichten; to divest s. o. of a ~ jem. ein Recht aberkennen; to encroach upon s. one's ~s in jds. Rechte eingreifen; to enforce one's ~ sein Recht geltend machen; to enjoy a ~ Recht genießen; to exercise a ~ Recht ausüben, von einem Recht Gebrauch machen, *(stock exchange)* Bezugsrecht ausüben; to exercise one's perfectly valid ~ von seinem guten Recht Gebrauch machen; to forego one's ~s sich seiner Rechte entäußern; to forfeit a ~ eines Rechts verlustig gehen; to forfeit the ~ of recourse Regreßanspruch verlieren; to give a ~ to berechtigen, Recht verleihen; to give workers a recognized ~ to a bit of the equity den Arbeitern ein verbrieftes Recht auf Grundkapitalbeteiligung zugestehen; to grant a ~ Recht verleihen; to have a ~ to s. th. Anrecht auf etw. haben; to have the ~s of sole distribution Alleinvertriebsrecht besitzen; to have had s. th. ~ up to here von einer Sache die Nase voll haben; to have the legal ~ to file a claim anspruchsberechtigt sein; to have £ 400 in one's own ~ über eine Jahresrente von 400 Pfund verfügen; to declare to have no ~ of action Einwand der Prozeßunfähigkeit erheben; to hold a ~ Recht innehaben; to infringe a ~ Recht verletzen; to insist on one's ~ sein Recht geltend machen; to know the ~s of a case wahren Sachverhalt (Sache in- und auswendig) kennen; to lose one's ~s under a guaranty seiner Garantieansprüche verlustig gehen; to meet as of ~ automatisch zusammentreten; to possess s. th. in one's own ~ etw. zu Eigentum (als Eigentümer) besitzen; to relinquish a ~ auf ein Recht verzichten; to renounce a ~ auf ein Recht verzichten; to reserve the ~ of Rechtsanspruch vorbehalten; to reserve the ~ of property Eigentums[recht] vorbehalten; to reserve the ~ of recourse sich Regreßansprüche vorbehalten; to restrict the ~ to vote Stimmrecht beschränken; to rule by ~ of conquest mit dem Recht des Eroberers herrschen; to sell the ~s on behalf of the holder Bezugsrechte im Inhaberauftrag verkaufen; to sell one's ~s on the market sein Bezugsrecht auf der Börse verkaufen; to send s. o. to the ~ about *(Br.)* j. kurzerhand entlassen; to succeed to s one's ~s jds. Rechtsstellung einnehmen; to sue in the ~ of a corporation namens einer Aktiengesellschaft klagen; to transfer a ~ Recht übertragen; to trespass on s. one's ~s jds. Rechte verletzen; to use a ~ von einem Recht Gebrauch machen; to vindicate one's ~s seine Ansprüche geltend machen; to waive a ~ auf ein Recht (einen Anspruch) verzichten; to waive one's ~ to immunity auf Immunitätsrechte verzichten; to waive one's ~ of privacy auf seine Geheimhaltungsansprüche verzichten; to warp the ~ Recht verdrehen;
~s dealings *(US)* Handel in Bezugsrechten, Bezugsrechtshandel; ~s earnings Lizenzerträge; ~s issue Bezugsrechtsausgabe, -angebot; to slip in with a £ 200 m ~s issue Bezugsrechtsangebot in Höhe von 200 Mio. Pfund zeitgerecht unterbringen; ~ joint *(sl.)* vorzeigbarer Nachtklub; ~s letter Bezugsrechtsmitteilung; ~s list Bezugsliste; ~s market *(US)* Markt für Bezugsrechte; ~s offering Bezugsrechtsangebot;
~ *(a.)* gerecht, billig, richtig, angemessen, *(immediately)* gleich, sofort, *(politics)* rechtsgerichtet;

to get s. th. ~ etw. richtigstellen; **to keep to the** ~ sich rechts halten; **to owe money** ~ **and left** an allen Ecken und Enden verschuldet sein; **to put** ~ in Ordnung bringen; **to put o. s.** ~ **with the authorities** sich mit den Behörden arrangieren; **to put an account** ~ Rechnung in Ordnung bringen; **to think it** ~ es für angemessen halten;

to give a ~ **account of the facts** wahrheitsgemäßen Bericht über die Tatsachen geben; ~ **arm** *(fig.)* rechte Hand, Hauptstütze; ~**-bank** *(v.)* in eine Rechtskurve gehen; ~ **center** *(pol.)* **(centre,** *Br.)* rechte Mitte, gemäßigte Rechte; ~ **conduct** ordnungsgemäßes Verhalten, gute Führung; ~ **hand** *(fig.)* [jds.] rechte Hand; **to put one's** ~ **hand to the work** Hand an die Arbeit legen; ~**-hand man** *(fig.)* rechte Hand; ~**-hand side** rechte Kontoseite; ~ **heir** rechtmäßiger Erbe; ~ **joint** *(sl.)* passabler Nachtklub; **to be in one's** ~ **mind** bei klarem Verstand sein; **to be out of one's** ~ **mind** nicht ganz normal sein; ~ **money** *(sl.)* Bestechungsgeld; **to know the** ~ **people** Beziehungen haben; ~ **road** richtige Straße; ~ **time** genaue Zeit.

rightful | **action** berechtigter Anspruch; ~ **authority** ordnungsgemäße Vollmacht; ~ **claimant** Anspruchsberechtigter; ~ **heir** Erbberechtigter; ~ **owner** rechtmäßiger Eigentümer; ~ **property** rechtmäßiges Eigentum.

right-wing rechtsgerichtet, nach rechts tendierend, rechtsorientiert;

the ~**s** Konservative;

~ **of a political party** rechter Parteiflügel;

~ **extremist** Rechtextremist; ~ **opposition** Rechtsopposition; ~ **party** Rechtspartei; ~ **political leaning** politischer Rechtsdrall.

right-winger Angehöriger des rechten Flügels; **hardline** ~ Rechtsextremist.

righteous rechtschaffen, redlich; ~ **cause** gerechte Sache.

rightful gerecht, berechtigt, rechtmäßig; ~ **action** berechtigter Anspruch; ~ **authority** ordnungsgemäße Vollmacht; ~ **cause** gerechte Sache; ~ **claim** berechtigter Anspruch; ~ **claimant** Anspruchsberechtigter; ~ **heir** rechtmäßiger Erbe; ~ **inheritance** rechtlich einwandfreie Erbschaft; ~ **king** rechtmäßiger König; ~ **owner** rechtmäßiger Eigentümer; ~ **property** rechtmäßiges Eigentum.

rightfulness Rechtmäßigkeit.

rightist Rechtsradikaler, -eingestellter, Rechtspolitiker, Konservativer, Reaktionär; ~ *(a.)* konservativ, reaktionär; ~ **press** Rechtspresse.

rightness Rechtschaffenheit.

rightward *(pol.)* rechtsgerichtet.

rigid *(supply and demand)* starr, unelastisch, *(technics)* stationär, ortsfest; ~ **airship** starres Luftschiff, Starrluftschiff; ~ **constitution** unabänderliche Verfassung; ~ **disciplinarian** strenger Vorgesetzter; ~ **economy** strengste Sparsamkeit, sparsame Wirtschaftsführung; ~ **helicopter** Tragdrehflügelflugzeug; ~ **obligation** harte Verpflichtung; ~ **parsimony** filziger Geiz; ~ **prices** unelastische Preise; ~ **principles** strenge Grundsätze; ~ **rules** starre Regeln.

rigidity | **of prices** Preisstarrheit; ~ **of supply** Unelastizität des Angebots.

rigmarole Geschwätz, Faselei; **to tell a long** ~ herumfaseln.

rigor mortis *(lat.)* Totenstarre.

rigo(u)r | **of the law** Strenge des Gesetzes; ~**s of the weather** Wetterunbilden; **to put the law into operation in all its** ~ Gesetz mit aller Strenge (Härte) zur Anwendung bringen.

rigorous | **accuracy** peinliche Genauigkeit; ~ **climate** hartes (unfreundliches) Klima; ~ **definition** enge Auslegung; ~ **discipline** strenge Disziplin; ~ **law** strengstes Gesetz; ~ **measures** rigorose Maßnahmen; ~ **search for dutiable goods** rücksichtslose Zolldurchsuchung.

rigout Aufmachung, Aufzug.

rim Rand, *(car)* Felge.

rime Nebelfrost, Reif; **to cover with** ~ sich bereifen.

rimland Rundlandschaft.

ring Ring, Kartell, Syndikat, *(bell)* Klingel, Rufzeichen, *(circus)* Manege, *(gang)* Bande, *(politics)* Kampffeld, *(stock exchange)* Börsenkonsortium, *(tel.)* [Telefon]anruf;

bull ~ *(stock exchange)* Haussepartei; **counterfeiting** ~ Fälscherbande; **key** ~ Schlüsselring; **narcotics** ~ Rauschgiftbande; **spy** ~ Spionagering, -organisation; **the** ~ *(Br.)* Buchmacher; **wedding** ~ Ehering;

~ **of burglars** Einbrechersyndikat; ~ **of dealers at an auction** Händlergruppe (Aufkäuferring) bei einer Versteigerung; ~ *(v.)* Kordon bilden;

~ **an alarm** Alarm schlagen, Alarmknopf drücken; ~ **a bell** *(fig.)* [schöne] Erinnerungen wachrufen; ~ **the bell** Erfolg haben; ~ **the changes** *(US)* etw. auf alle Touren versuchen; ~ **a coin** Echtheit einer Münze prüfen; ~ **down** *(theater)* Vorhang fallen lassen; ~ **the knell of s. th.** *(fig.)* etw. zu Grabe tragen; ~ **in one's mind** im Gedächtnis haften bleiben; ~ **off** *(tel.)* Hörer auflegen; ~ **out** *(US)* Lieferungsgeschäfte erledigen; ~ **through** *(tel.)* durchrufen; ~ **up** *(tel.)* [telefonisch] anrufen, -klingeln, telefonieren, *(theater)* Vorstellung beginnen; ~ **up a telephone exchange** Zentrale anrufen;

to be in the ~ **for the governorship** sich um das Gouverneursamt bewerben; **to enter the** ~ **with most of the advantages** Arena mit größeren Ausgangschancen betreten; **to give a** ~ anrufen, antelefonieren; **to have a good** ~ *(coin)* echt klingen; **to run** ~**s around s. o.** j. einwickeln, j. in die Tasche stecken;

~ **binder** Ringbuch; ~ **defense (defence,** *Br.)* Flaksperrgürtel; ~ **dropping** *(Br.)* Trickdiebstahl; ~ **fence** Einfriedung; ~ **road** Ringstraße; **to have a** ~**-side seat** *(circus)* an der Ballustrade sitzen, guten Platz haben; ~ **settlements** Abmachungen eines Händlerringes; ~ **trading** *(Br.)* Händlerabsprachen.

ringed about with enemies von Feinden umgeben.

ringing Klingeln; ~ **the changes** Wechselgeldbetrug; **to set the whole town** ~ ganze Stadt in Aufruhr versetzen; ~ **cheers** brausende Hochrufe; ~ **frost** klirrender Frost; ~ **tone** *(tel.)* Freizeichen; ~ **up** *(commission merchants)* Abrechnung zwischen Kommissionären und Maklern.

ringleader Banden-, Rädelsführer.

ringman *(Br.)* Buchmacher.

ringmaster Zirkusdirektor, Manegechef.

ringster Bandenmitglied, *(politics)* Cliquenmitglied.

riot Aufstand, Aufruhr, Zusammenrottung, Landfriedensbruch, Unruhe, Krawall;

prison ~ Gefangenenaufstand, -revolte; **racial** ~ Rassenkrawall; **students'** ~ Studentenunruhen;

~ **and civil commotions** Aufruhr und bürgerliche Unruhen; ~ **during the elections** Wahlunruhen; ~ **of sounds** Stimmgewirr; ~ *(v.)* sich zusammenrotten, revoltieren;

~ **away one's money** *(US)* sein Geld verjubeln; ~ **away one's time** *(US)* seine Zeit verplempern; ~ **away one's life** sich ausleben;

to be a ~ *(play)* Riesenerfolg sein; **to cause a** ~ Auflauf verursachen; **to deal with a** ~ mit einem Aufstand fertig werden; **to put down a** ~ **by force** Aufstand gewaltsam unterdrücken; **to quash a** ~ Aufruhr unterdrücken; **to run** ~ sich undiszipliniert verhalten;

~ **area** Aufruhrgebiet; ~ **Act** *(Br.)* Aufruhrakte, Tumultgesetz; **to read the** ~ **Act** Menge öffentlich verwarnen (zu friedlichem Auseinandergehen auffordern); **to read the** ~ **Act to s. o.** jem. die Leviten lesen; **to send a** ~ **call** Überfallkommando rufen; ~**s clause** Aufruhrklausel; ~ **damage** Tumult-, Aufruhrschäden; ~ **Damages Act** *(Br.)* Tumultschädengesetz; ~ **gun** Straßenkampfwaffe; ~ **and civil commotion insurance** Aufstandsversicherung; ~ **leader** Rädelsführer; ~ **police** Bereitschaftspolizei; ~ **shield** polizeilicher Schutzschild; ~ **squad** *(US)* Überfallkommando.

rioter Aufrührer, Meuterer, Unruhestifter.

riotous aufrührerisch, aufständisch, tumultarisch; ~ **assembly** *(Br.)* aufrührerische (gesetzwidrige) Versammlung, Zusammenrottung; **to be charged with** ~ **behavio(u)r** wegen Landfriedensbruch belangt werden; ~ **conduct** aufrührerisches Verhalten; **to lead a** ~ **life** in Saus und Braus leben.

rip Taugenichts; ~ *(v.) (ship)* abwracken; **to let things** ~ den Dingen ihren Lauf lassen.

riparian Uferanlieger, -bewohner; ~ *(a.)* am Ufer gelegen; ~ **nations** Flußanliegerstaaten; ~ **owner (proprietor)** Ufereigentümer, Flußanlieger; ~ **rights** Uferanliegerrecht; ~ **state** Uferstaat; ~ **water** normaler Flußwasserstand.

ripe ausgereift, reif; ~ **for development** entwicklungsfähig, -trächtig, *(land)* baureif; ~ **for execution** ausführungsreif; ~ **for judgment** entscheidungsreif; **to be** ~ **for execution** durchgeführt werden können; **to be** ~ **for revolt** kurz vor dem Aufstand stehen; ~ **age** reifes Alter; ~ **judgment** reifes Urteil; ~ **scholar** vollendeter Gelehrter.

ripple *(water)* Kräuselung, *(US)* kleine Stromschnelle;
~ **of conversation** munter dahinfließende Konversation;
~ *(v.)* **out into more sectors** größeren Bereich erfassen.
rise *(amount of increment)* Zuwachs, Zunahme, *(nation)* Aufstieg, *(extra pay, Br.)* Zulage, Gehaltsaufbesserung, -erhöhung, -zulage, *(in prices)* Anziehen, Steigen, [Preis]steigerung, Preiserhöhung, [Preis]aufschlag, *(occasion)* Anlaß, Grund, *(personal advancement)* Emporkommen, sozialer Aufstieg, *(stock exchange)* Aufschwung, Aufwärtsbewegung, Besserung [der Kurse], Kursanstieg, -steigerung, Hausse;
on the ~ im Steigen begriffen;
abrupt ~ scharfer Kursanstieg; **~s already agreed** *(Br.)* bereits vereinbarte Gehaltserhöhungen; **earnings** ~ Ertragsanstieg; **moderate** ~ leichter Kursanstieg; **salary** ~ *(Br.)* Gehaltserhöhung; **widely spread** ~ Kursanstieg auf breiter Basis; **substantial ~s** beträchtliche Kursteigerungen;
~ **in the bank rate** *(Br.)* Diskonterhöhung; ~ **of postal charges** *(Br.)* Erhöhung der Portogebühren; ~ **in costs (expenditure)** Kostensteigerung, -anstieg; ~ **in real earnings** Reallohnerhöhung; ~ **in exports** Exportsteigerung, Ausfuhrerhöhung; ~ **in food prices** Nahrungsmittelpreissteigerung; ~ **in the ground** Bodenerhebung; ~ **in income** Einkommenssteigerung; ~ **in interest rates** Zinsauftrieb; ~ **in labo(u)r costs** Arbeitskostenanstieg; ~ **in life** sozialer Aufstieg, Emporkommen; ~ **in population** Bevölkerungszuwachs, -zunahme; ~ **in social position** gesellschaftliches Vorwärtskommen; ~ **to power** Machtübernahme; ~ **in prices** Preisanstieg, *(stock exchange)* Kurserhöhung, -anstieg; ~ **in production** Produktionssteigerung; ~ **in profits** Gewinnanstieg; ~ **of railroad rates** *(US)* Erhöhung der Eisenbahntarife; ~ **in sales** Absatz-, Umsatzerhöhung; ~ **of shares** Steigen der Aktienkurse; ~ **in spending** Ausgabenanstieg; ~ **in the standard of living** Erhöhung (Verbesserung) des Lebensstandards; ~ **of stocks** *(US)* Aktienhausse; ~ **in temperature** Temperaturanstieg; ~ **in unemployment** erhöhte Arbeitslosigkeit; ~ **in value** Wertsteigerung, -erhöhung; ~ **of wages** Lohnerhöhung, Anstieg der Löhne;
~ *(v.)* sich erheben, *(adjourn)* auseinandergehen, Sitzung aufheben, sich vertagen, *(amount to)* sich belaufen, betragen, *(curtain)* aufgehen, *(grow up)* heranwachsen, *(mil.)* befördert werden, *(person)* in einer Stellung vorankommen, *(prices)* anziehen, [im Preise steigen], sich aufwärts bewegen, hochgehen, in die Höhe gehen, teurer werden, *(riot)* sich empören, revoltieren, *(stock exchange)* sich bessern, anziehen, steigen;
~ **at 8 p. m.** *(parl.)* Diskussion (Sitzung) um 20 Uhr beenden; ~ **to the bait** auf den Leim gehen; ~ **to be chairman** Vorsitzender werden; ~ **to an emergency** in der Notzeit seinen Mann stehen; ~ **in s. one's esteem** in jds. Achtung steigen; ~ **above events** über den Ereignissen stehen; ~ **into new high ground** neuen Höchstkurs erzielen; ~ **with the lark** mit den Hühnern aufstehen; ~ **above mediocrity** über das Mittelmaß herausragen; ~ **by merit only** seinen Aufstieg allein sich selbst (seinen Leistungen) verdanken; ~ **next Friday** *(parl.)* am nächsten Freitag die Parlamentsferien beginnen; ~ **from nothing** aus kleinsten Verhältnissen stammen; ~ **to the occasion** sich der Lage gewachsen zeigen; ~ **to a difficult occasion** sich in einer schwierigen Situation bewähren; ~ **to order** zur Geschäftsordnung sprechen; ~ **to power** an die Macht gelangen; ~ **from the ranks** von der Pike auf dienen; ~ **to a higher rank** befördert werden; ~ **in revolt** sich erheben, revoltieren; ~ **sharply** *(stock exchange)* hausseartig ansteigen; ~ **from a sickbed** von einer Krankheit genesen; ~ **strongly** *(market)* scharf anziehen; ~ **from a mere trifle** aus nichtigem Anlaß entstehen; ~ **up** *(nation)* sich erheben, *(parl.)* sich zu Wort melden; ~ **up in arms** bewaffneten Aufstand machen; ~ **to wealth** zu einem Vermögen gelangen, wohlhabend werden; ~ **next week** *(parl.)* sich bis zur nächsten Woche vertagen; ~ **widely** *(prices)* auf breiter Front steigen; ~ **in the world** im Leben vorankommen;
to ask one's employer for a ~ *(Br.)* seinen Arbeitgeber auf Gehaltserhöhung ansprechen; **to be on the** ~ [im Preis] steigen, im Steigen begriffen sein, *(person)* vorankommen, *(stock exchange)* Kursteigerung erfahren, im Kurs steigen; **to be back on the** ~ wieder ansteigen; **to buy for a** ~ auf eine Hausse hin Käufe tätigen, auf Hausse spekulieren; **to experience a** ~ **in price** Preiserhöhung erfahren; **to get a** ~ *(Br.)* [Gehalts]zulage bekommen; **to get a** ~ **out of s. o.** j. in Harnisch (hoch) bringen, *(sl.)* Gehaltserhöhung bei jem. herausschlagen; **to give** ~ **to anxiety** Anlaß zu Besorgnis geben; **to give** ~ **to misunderstanding** zu Mißverständnissen führen; **to give** ~ **to a scandal** Ärgernis hervorrufen; **to give in for a** ~ auf Hausse spekulieren; **to have a sudden** ~ plötzlich im Kurs steigen; **to operate for a** ~ auf Hausse spekulieren; **to secure substantial** ~**s** beträchtliche

Kurssteigerungen erzielen; **to show a** ~ Steigerung aufweisen; **to speculate on a** ~ auf Hausse spekulieren; **to undergo a** ~ Steigerung erfahren;
~ **forecast** Kurssteigerungsprognose.
riser Steigrohr, *(el.)* Steigleitung;
early ~ Frühaufsteher.
rising Steigerung, *(prices)* Steigen, Steigerung, Anstieg, Anziehen, Erhöhung, Bodenerhebung, Steigung, *(uproar)* Aufruhr, Erhebung;
upon the ~ **of Parliament** nach Beginn der Parlamentsferien;
~ **of a bridge** Brückenauffahrt; ~ **of a court** Vertagung des Gerichts; ~ **of Parliament** Vertagung des Parlaments;
~ *(a.)* steigend, anziehend, *(fig.)* aufstrebend, *(stock exchange)* kursanziehend;
to be ~ *(prices)* ansteigen, anziehen;
~ **costs** steigende Kosten; ~ **floor** Hebebühne; ~ **generation** heranwachsende Generation; ~ **ground** Rampe, Auffahrt; ~ **gust** Steigbö; ~ **lawyer** aufstrebender Anwalt; ~ **main** Steigrohr; ~ **market** steigende Kurse, Kursanstieg; **to be a** ~ **market** im Kurs steigen, Kursteigerung erfahren; ~ **politician** kommender Politiker; ~ **prices** Preisanstieg; ~ **star** aufgehender Star; ~ **statesman** an Bedeutung zunehmender Staatsmann; ~ **tendency** Preiserhöhungstendenz, *(stock exchange)* Kursaufschwung; **to show a** ~ **tendency** Kursaufschwung nehmen, sich befestigen; ~ **tide** kommende Flut.
risk Verlust, Risiko, Fährnis, *(insurance)* Wagnis, Gefährdung, Verlustgefahr, *(object or person insured)* Gefahrenquelle, versicherte Person, versicherter Gegenstand;
against all ~s (A. A. R.) gegen alle Gefahren; **at all ~s** ohne Rücksicht auf Verluste; **at my** ~ auf mein Risiko; **at one's own** ~ auf eigenes Risiko (eigene Gefahr, Verantwortung); **at company's** ~ auf Gefahr der Bahn; **at consignor's** ~ auf Gefahr des Absenders; **at the** ~ **of one's own life** unter Gefahr seines Lebens, unter Lebensgefahr; **at owner's** ~ auf eigene Gefahr; **at your** ~ auf Ihre Verantwortung; **for your account and** ~ für Ihre Rechnung und Gefahr; **on carrier's** ~ auf Gefahr des Spediteurs;
abnormal ~ erhöhtes Risiko; **accident** ~ Unfallrisiko; **aggravated** ~ erhöhte Gefahr, erhöhtes Risiko; **assigned** ~ zugewiesenes Versicherungsrisiko; **automobile dealer's** ~ Autohändlerhaftpflicht; **aviation** ~ Flugverkehrrisiko; **bad insurance** ~ schlechtes Versicherungsrisiko, unfallhäufiger Versicherungsnehmer; **business** ~ Ausfall-, Geschäftsrisiko; **calculated** ~ wohlabgewogenes Risiko; **catastrophe** ~ Katastrophengefahr; **commercial** ~ wirtschaftliches Risiko, Unternehmerwagnis; **consumer's** ~ Verbraucherrisiko; **contractor's** ~ Unternehmerrisiko; ~ **covered** gedecktes Risiko, versicherte Gefahr; **credit** ~ Kreditrisiko; **current ~s** laufende Versicherungsrisiken; **customary ~s** handelsübliche Risiken; **discernible** ~ erkennbares Risiko; **economic** ~ Konjunkturrisiko; **exchange** ~ Kursrisiko; **excluded** ~ ausgeschlossenes Risiko; **expectable** ~ unkalkulierbares Risiko, nicht abzuschätzendes Risiko; **extraordinary** ~ außerordentliches Risiko; **fair ~s** versicherbare Risiken; **fidelity guarantee** ~ Kautionsversicherungsrisiko; **financial** ~ finanzielles Risiko; **fire** ~ Brand-, Feuersgefahr; **flat** ~ *(insurance)* Pauschalsatz; **fundamental** ~ Katastrophenrisiko, Risiko höherer Gewalt; **imminent** ~ unmittelbar bevorstehende Verlustgefahr; **individual** ~ *(fire insurance)* Eigengefahr; **insurable** ~ versicherbares Risiko; **insolvency** ~ Insolvenzerisiko; **loading** ~ Verladerisiko; **marine (maritime)** ~ Seetransportgefahr; **moral** ~ moralisches Risiko; **normal** ~ normales Risiko; **obvious** ~ offensichtliche Gefahr, klar erkennbares Risiko; **ordinary** ~ übliches Risiko; **own** ~ Selbstbehalt; **owner's** ~ Gefahr beim Eigentümer; **particular** ~ auf einen Einzelfall beschränktes Risiko; **pending ~s** laufende Risiken; **perceivable** ~ erkennbare Gefahr, übersehbares Risiko; **personal** ~ Personenrisiko; **place** ~ Platzrisiko; **price** ~ Kursrisiko; **property** ~ Sachschadenrisiko; **pure** ~ *(insurance business)* Risiko im engeren Sinne; **run** ~ versicherte Gefahr; **sea ~s** Seegefahr; **security** ~ Sicherheitsrisiko; **shifting ~s** durch auswechselbare Bestände gedecktes Risiko; **special** ~ Sonderrisiko; **speculative** ~ *(insurance business)* Spekulationsrisiko; **standard** ~ normales Risiko; **subscribed** ~ versicherte Gefahr; **substandard** ~ *(life insurance)* unterdurchschnittliches (anormales) Risiko; **tenant's** ~ Mieterhaftung; **trading** ~ Geschäftsrisiko; **transport** ~ Transportrisiko; **uncovered** ~ nicht gedecktes Risiko; **undesirable** ~ *(automobile insurance)* unerwünschter Fahrer; **unexpired ~s** *(insurance company)* noch bestehende Risiken; **uninsurable** ~ nicht versicherbares Risiko; **uninsured ~s** ungedeckte Risiken; **unknown** ~ unbekanntes Risiko; **war** ~ Kriegsrisiko;

~ of breakage Bruchgefahr, Bruchrisiko; **~ of business** Geschäftsrisiko; **~s assured by the buyer** vom Käufer übernommene Risiken; **~s of carriage** Beförderungsgefahr, Transportrisiko; **~ of collision** Kollisionsgefahr; **~ of competition** Wettbewerbsrisiko; **~ of conveyance** Transportrisiko; **~ of deterioration** Gefahr der zufälligen Verschlechterung; **~ of death** Sterblichkeitsrisiko; **~ after discharge** Gefahr nach Löschung der Ladung; **~ incident to employment** Berufsrisiko, Haftpflicht; **~ of error** Fehlerrisiko; **~ of exchange** Kursrisiko; **~ of fire** Feuersgefahr; **~ of inflation** Inflationsgefahr, inflationistische Gefahren; **~ of investment** Anlagen-, Investitionsrisiko; **~ of liability** Haftungsrisiko; **~ of loss** Gefahrentragung, Gefahr des Verlustes, Verlustrisiko; **~ of marketing** Absatzrisiko; **~ of mines** Minengefahr; **~ of navigation** Seegefahr; **~ of occupation** berufliches Risiko; **~s and perils** *(insurance)* gedeckte Gefahren; **~s and perils of the sea** Seegefahr; **~ of pilferage** Plünderungsgefahr; **~ of production** Fabrikationsrisiko, Produktionsrisiko; **~ at sea** Seegefahr; **~ of being washed away by the sea** Gefahr des Fortgespültwerdens; **~ of shoplifting** Ladendiebstahlsrisiko; **~s of an undertaking** unternehmerisches Risiko; **~ of war** Kriegsrisiko;

~ *(v.)* wagen, riskieren;

~ defeat Niederlage einkalkulieren; **~ one's fortune** sein Vermögen einsetzen; **~ one's health** seine Gesundheit aufs Spiel setzen; **~ money** Geld wagen (einsetzen); **~ one's neck** seinen Kragen riskieren; **~ one's reputation** seinen guten Ruf riskieren; **~ one's own skin** seine Haut zu Markte tragen; **~ everything on one throw** alles auf eine Kappe (Karte) setzen;

to assume all ~ volles Risiko übernehmen; **to avoid the ~ of incriminating o. s.** Risiko der Selbstbelastung vermeiden; **to be an above-average ~** überdurchschnittliches Risiko darstellen; **to be exposed to considerable ~** erheblichem Risiko ausgesetzt sein; **to be full of ~s** voller Risiken stecken; **to be particularly at ~** besonders gefährdet sein; **to be prepared to take a ~** risikofreudig sein; **to bear a ~** Risiko, Gefahr tragen; **to calculate the ~s** Risiko abwägen; **to chance a high ~** hohes Risiko auf sich nehmen; **to class as high ~** zum besonders hohen Risiko erklären; **to come off ~** *(insurer)* Versicherungsrisiko loswerden; **to cover a ~** für ein Risiko die Versicherung übernehmen; **to cover all ~s** alle Gefahren decken; **to create a serious ~ of public disorder** ernsthafte Gefahren für öffentliche Ruhestörung beschwören; **to expose o. s. to a ~** sich einem Risiko aussetzen; **to do s. th. at one's own ~** etw. auf eigene Gefahr unternehmen; **to relieve of a ~** vom Risiko befreien (entlasten); **to include ~s** mit Gefahr verbunden sein; **to incur a ~** sich einem Risiko aussetzen, Risiko übernehmen (eingehen); **to involve a ~** Gefahren mit sich bringen; **to judge s. o. to be a ~** j. für sittlich gefährdet halten; **to lay off a ~** sich durch Rückversicherung decken; **to put thousands of jobs at ~** Verlust von tausenden von Arbeitsplätzen riskieren; **to relieve of a ~** von einem Risiko befreien; **to run a ~** Gefahr laufen, Risiko eingehen, riskieren; **to run the ~ of losing everything** alles auf eine Karte setzen; **to spread the ~** Risiko verteilen, *(reinsurance)* Rückversicherungsrisiko atomisieren; **to take a ~** Gefahr (Risiko) übernehmen, Risiko eingehen; **to take a ~ on a cargo** Ladung versichern; **to take long-shot ~s** ziemlich aussichtslose Risiken eingehen; **to take no ~s** kein Risiko eingehen; **to undertake a ~** Risiko übernehmen; **to underwrite a ~** Versicherung unter Risikobeteiligung übernehmen; **to vary the ~** versicherte Gefahr in eine andere abändern;

~ analysis Risikoanalyse; **~ appraisal** Risikoabschätzung; **~ assurance** Risikoversicherung; **~-averse** risikoscheu; **~ bearer** Gefahren-, Risikoträger; **~ [-bearing] capital** Spekulations-, Risikokapital; **~ book** Liste übernommener Risiken; **~ capital opportunities** Chancen für den Einsatz von Risikokapital; **co-operative ~ carrying** gemeinschaftliche Risikoübernahme; **~ factor** Risikofaktor; **~-free** risikolos; **~ function** *(statistics)* Risikofunktion; **~ improvement** Risikoverminderung; **all-~s insurance policy** globale Risikoversicherungspolice; **~ limitation** Risikoabgrenzung; **~ management** Verwaltung von Versicherungsrisiken; **~ manager** für Geschäftsrisiken verantwortliche Führungskraft; **~ money** Kaution, *(cashier)* Manko-, Fehlgeld; **~ note** *(railway, Br.)* Haftungsbeschränkung des Transportunternehmers auf eigenes Verschulden der Angestellten; **all-~s policy** *(car)* Universalversicherung; **builder's ~ policy** Gefahrenzulage bei Gebäudeversicherung; **road-~ policy** *(motor trades)* Versicherungspolice für Straßenbenutzung; **~ premium** Gefahrenprämie, Risikoprämie; **~ reserve** Risikorückstellung; **~ taker** Gefahren-, Risikoträger; **~ taking** Risikoübernahme, -bereitschaft, Gefahrtragung, Gefahrenübernahme; **~ venture** Risikoverteilung.

risky mit Gefahr verbunden;

~ business riskante Angelegenheit; **~ fellow** tollkühner Bursche; **~ shifts** *(opinion research)* riskante Veränderung [von Gruppenmitgliedern]; **~ speculation** riskante Spekulation; **~ undertaking** riskantes Unternehmen.

rite Brauch, Ritus, Zeremoniell, formal, ordnungsgemäß;
burial ~s Begräbniszeremonien; **initiation ~s** Einweihungsfeierlichkeiten.

rival Konkurrent, Mitbewerber, Nebenbuhler, Rivale;
without a ~ ohnegleichen;
~s in business Konkurrenten, Konkurrenzunternehmen;
~ *(v.)* rivalisieren, konkurrieren, in Wettbewerb treten;
~ a product mit einem Erzeugnis konkurrieren;
to be ~s rivalisieren;
~ bid Konkurrenzangebot; **~ business concern** Konkurrenzgeschäft, -betrieb, -unternehmen, -firma; **~ candidate** Gegenkandidat; **~ claim** Gegenbehauptung; **~ commodities** Konkurrenzerzeugnisse; **~ company** Konkurrenzfirma; **~ firm** Konkurrenzbetrieb, -unternehmen, -firma; **~ manufacturer** Konkurrenzbetrieb; **~ plant** Konkurrenzbetrieb; **~ product** Konkurrenzerzeugnis; **~ shop** Konkurrenzgeschäft; **~ supply** Konkurrenzangebot; **~ trader** Konkurrent.

rivalries between political parties Rivalitäten zwischen politischen Parteien.

rivalry Rivalität, *(in business)* Konkurrenz, Wettbewerb;
to enter into ~ with s. o. mit jem. in Konkurrenz treten.

rivalship Nebenbuhlerschaft.

river Fluß, Strom, *(fig.)* Flut, Strom;
down the ~ stromab; **up the ~** stromaufwärts;
internationalized ~s internationalisierte Flüsse; **navigable ~** schiffbarer Fluß; **private ~** Privatfluß; **public ~** öffentlicher Wasserweg;
~s defiled by waste from factories vom Fabrikabfall verschmutzte Flüsse; **~s of money** Geldströme;
to be up the ~ *(US sl.)* im Kasten sitzen; **to run along the ~** *(frontier)* sich am Fluß hinziehen, am Fluß verlaufen; **to sell s. o. down the ~** *(sl.)* j. völlig im Stich lassen, j. richtig hereinlegen; **⚓ Authority** *(Br.)* Wasserwirtschaftsamt; **~ bank** Uferbefestigung; **~ basin** Einzugsgebiet; **~ bed** Flußbett; **~ bill of lading** *(Br.)* Flußladeschein, Binnenkonnossement; **⚓ Board** *(Br.)* Binnenschiffahrtsbehörde; **~-borne** auf dem Wasserwege befördert; **~ craft** Flußfahrzeug; **~ dam** Staudamm, Talsperre; **~ driver** *(US)* Flößer; **~ fishery** Binnenfischerei; **~ freight** Binnenschiffahrts-, Flußfrachtgut; **~ freight rate** Binnenschiffahrtsatz; **~ insurance** Flußversicherungen; **~ navigation** *(Br.)* Fluß-, Binnenschiffahrt; **~ police** Strompolizei; **~ rates** Flußfrachtsätze; **~ steamer** Flußdampfer; **~ traffic** Flußschiffahrt, -verkehr, *(Br.)* Beförderung im Binnenschiffahrtsverkehr.

riverain [Fluß]anlieger.

riverman Flößer.

riverside Flußufer;
by the ~ am Ufer gelegen;
~ inn Ausflugslokal am Fluß.

riverway Wasserweg.

road [Land]straße, Verkehrs-, Fahrweg, Strecke, *(mining)* Förderstrecke, *(railroad, US)* Eisenbahnlinie, -strecke, Geleise, Gleisanlage, *(roadstead)* Reede, *(route)* Fahrstrecke, Reiseweg, *(track)* Fahrbahn, Weg, *(theater)* Gastspielgebiet, *(waterway)* Wasserweg;
at the ~ auf der Reede, vor Anker; **by ~** auf dem Straßenweg, per Fahrzeug, mit dem Lastauto, im Straßentransport; **in the ~** auf der Reede; **on the ~** auf der Fahrbahn (Straße), *(theatrical company)* auf Tournee, *(travelling)* auf der Reise, auf Reisen, geschäftlich unterwegs;
~s *(roadstead)* Reede, *(stock exchange, US)* Eisenbahnwerte;
A and B ~s *(Br.)* Bundes- und Landstraßen; **access ~** Zufahrtsstraße, Zubringer; **accommodation ~** Zufahrtsstraße; **adopted ~** *(US)* vom Kommunalverband unterhaltene Straße; **arterial ~** Hauptverkehrsstraße, Verkehrsader; **bumpy ~** holprige Straße; **by-~** Seiten-, Neben-, Umgehungsstraße; **classified ~** *(Br.)* Landstraße erster Ordnung; **~ clear** *(US)* freie Fahrt; **closed ahead** gesperrt für den Durchgangsverkehr; **control ~** Teststrecke; **country ~** Kreis-, Landstraße; **covered ~** feste Straße; **decontrolled ~** Straße ohne Geschwindigkeitsbegrenzung; **derestricted ~** keiner Geschwindigkeitsbegrenzung unterliegende Straße; **dirt ~** ungepflasterte Straße; **first-class ~** erstklassige Straße; **frequented ~** häufig befahrene Straße; **frontage ~** *(US)* parallel zur Autobahn verlaufende Straße; **frozen ~** vereiste Straße; **good ~** geschlossene Reede; **hard-surface ~** staubfreie Straße; **heavy ~** ausgefahrene Straße; **high**

~ Hauptverkehrsstraße; **the high ~s** Straßenwesen; **impassable**
~ nicht befahrbare (unbefahrbare) Straße; **iron ~** Schienenweg; **level ~** ebene Straße; **local ~** Dorf-, Kreis-, Landstraße;
long-distance ~ [etwa] [Bundes]fernstraße; **main ~** Haupt[ver-
kehrs]straße, *(railroad)* Hauptstrecke; **major ~** Hauptver-
kehrs-, Vorfahrtsstraße; **major ~ ahead** Vorfahrt beachten;
motor ~ Auto-, Schnellstraße; **open ~** offene Landstraße; **outward ~** aus der Stadt herausführende Straße; **paved ~** gepflasterte Straße; **post ~** Poststraße; **private ~** nicht öffentliche
Straße, Privatstraße, -weg; **public ~** öffentliche Straße, öffentlicher Weg; **rough ~** unbefestigte Straße; **safe ~** geschlossene
Reede; **service ~** Verkehrsstraße; **side ~** Seitenstraße; **~ inadequately signposted** ungenügend beschilderte Straße; **special ~**
(Br.) Autobahn; **subsidiary ~** Entlastungsstraße; **third-class ~**
Gemeindeverbindungsweg; **through ~** Durchgangsstraße; **no
through ~** Sackgasse; **toll ~** gebührenpflichtige Straße; **township ~** von der Stadt unterhaltene Straße; **trunk ~** Fernverkehrsstraße; **twisty ~** gewundene Straße; **two-lane ~** Straße mit zwei
Fahrbahnen; **two-way ~** Gegenverkehrsstraße; **unadopted ~**
(US) nicht vom Kommunalverband unterhaltene Straße; **
underground ~** unterirdische Straße; **unpaved ~** Schotterstraße; **~ up** Straße gesperrt; **uphill ~** ansteigende Straße; **
vehicular ~** befahrbare Straße, Verkehrsstraße; **winding ~**
(Br.) gewundene Straße;
~ of approach Vormarschstraße; **~ of a bridge** Fahrbahn einer
Brücke; **~ lined with police** von Polizisten umsäumte Straße; **~
and rail** Schiene und Straße; **~ under repair** wegen Instandsetzungsarbeiten gesperrte Straße; **~ versus rail** Wettbewerb zwischen Schiene und Straße; **~ to ruin** Weg ins Verderben; **~ to
salvation** Rettungsweg; **~s and sewers** *(balance sheet)* Anlieger-
und Kanalisationskosten; **~ carrying a great deal of traffic**
verkehrsreiche Straße; **~ carrying fast-moving traffic** *(Br.)*
Schnellverkehrsstraße; **~ closed to motor traffic** für den Autoverkehr gesperrte Straße; **~ fit for traffic** befahrbare Straße; **~
open to traffic** für den öffentlichen Verkehr freigegebene
Straße; **~ passable (practicable) for vehicles** befahrbare Straße;
to be in the ~(s) auf der Reede (vor Anker) liegen; **to be in s.
one's ~** jem. im Wege stehen; **to be off the ~** *(car)* aus dem
Verkehr gezogen sein; **to be on the ~** *(bus)* im Betrieb (eingesetzt) sein, *(traveller)* [geschäftlich] unterwegs (auf Reisen,
Tour) sein; **to be on the ~ about a third of the time** Drittel des
Jahres unterwegs (auf Achse) sein; **to be on the ~ to fortune** im
Begriff sein, ein Vermögen zu machen; **to block (close) a ~**
Straße sperren; **to bond a ~** Straße mit Kommunalobligationen
finanzieren; **to build a ~** Straße bauen; **to clog the ~s leading to
the airport** Zufahrtsstraßen zum Flughafen blockieren; **to
close a ~** Straße sperren; **to construct a ~** Straße anlegen; **to
cross the ~** Fahrbahn überschreiten; **to fit a ~ for traffic** Straße
instandsetzen; **to hit the ~** trampen; **to hit the right ~** auf die
richtige Straße kommen; **to keep a ~ in repair** Straße unterhalten (instandhalten); **to lie in the ~s** auf der Reede liegen; **to lie
remote from the ~** abseits der Straße liegen; **to make a ~** Straße
bauen; **to open a ~ for traffic** Straße für den Verkehr freigeben;
to put out a vessel on the ~s Schiff auf die Reede fahren; **to ride
at the ~** vor Anker (auf der Reede) liegen; **to swerve off the ~ of
profitable growth** Gewinnaufstieg nicht fortsetzen; **to take the
~** Reise antreten, *(theatrical group)* Gastspielreise unternehmen, auf Tournee gehen; **to take off the ~** aus dem Verkehr
ziehen; **to touch a public ~** an eine öffentliche Straße angrenzen; **to wash out a ~** Straße unterspülen; **to widen a ~** Straße
erweitern;
~ accident Auto-, Verkehrsunfall; **~ accident case** Unfallsache;
~ accident figures Verkehrsunfallstatistik; **public ~ administration** *(US)* Straßenverwaltung; **~ agent** *(US)* Straßenräuber; **~
behavio(u)r** Verkehrsdisziplin; **~ bend (curve)** Wegebiegung;
~ Board *(Br.)* örtliches Straßenbauamt; **~-bound** straßenge-
bunden; **~ budget** Straßenbauetat; **~ builder** Straßenbauunternehmer, -meister; **~ building** Straßenbau; **~-building fund** *(Br.)*
Straßenbaufonds; **~-building machine** Straßenbaumaschine; **~
bump** eingelassene Betonschwelle; **~ car** zweistöckiger Omnibus; **~ charge** Anliegergebühr; **~ check** Straßen-, Verkehrskontrolle; **~ company** *(theater)* Gastspieltruppe, Wanderbühne; **~ conditions** Straßenzustand; **~ congestion** Straßen-
verstopfung; **~ construction** Straßenbau[arbeiten]; **~ construction gang** Straßenbautrupp; **~ contractor** Fuhrunternehmer,
Straßenbauunternehmer; **~ district** Straßenbauverband; **~
frontage** Straßenfront; **~ fund** *(Br.)* Straßenbaufonds; **~-fund
tax** *(Br.)* Verkehrssteuer; **~ gang** Straßenbautrupp; **~ grader**
Planiermaschine; **~ grip** *(car)* Straßenlage; **~ haulage** Güterkraftverkehr, Beförderung mit Lastkraftwagen; **long-distance
~ haulage** Transport per Achse, Fernlast-, Güterkraftverkehr;

~ haulage company Güterkraftverkehrsunternehmen; **~ haulage firm** *(Br.)* Fernspediteur; **~ haulage industry** *(Br.)* Kraft-
verkehrsindustrie; **long-distance ~-haulage services** Fernlast-
verkehrsgewerbe; **~ haulier** LKW-Transportunternehmen,
Fernspediteur; **~ hog** Verkehrsrowdy, Straßenschreck; **~-hog
(v.)** rücksichtslos fahren; **~-holding facilities** *(car)* Straßenlage;
~ hole Schlagloch; **~ improvements** Straßenverbesserung; **~
inspector** Straßenaufseher; **~ intersection** *(US)* Weg-, Straßenkreuzung; **~ jam** Verkehrsstockung, -störung; **~ junction** Straßenkreuzung, -spinne; **~ labo(u)r** Straßenarbeiten; **~ labo(u)r-
er** Straßenarbeiter; **~ licence** *(Br.)* Kraftfahrzeugzulassung; **~
machine** Planiermaschine; **~ maintenance** Straßeninstandsetzung, -unterhaltung; **~ map** Straßen-, Wege-, Autokarte; **~
marking** Straßenmarkierung; **~ mender** Straßenarbeiter; **~
mending** Straßenausbesserung, -instandsetzung; **~ metal** Stra-
ßenbeschotterung, -decke; **~ monster** Kilometerfresser; **~ network** Wege-, Straßennetz; **~ number** Bundesstraßennummer; **~
patrol** Straßendienst; **~ post** Wegweiser; **~ program(me)** Stra-
ßenbauprogramm; **~ race (racing)** Straßenrennen; **~-ready**
fahrbereit; **~ regulations** Straßen-, Verkehrsvorschriften; **~
repairs** [Straßen]ausbesserungsarbeiten; **~ repairer** Straßenarbeiter; **~ roller** Straßenwalze; **~ safety** Verkehrssicherheit; **~
Safety Act** *(Br.)* Verkehrssicherheitsgesetz; **~ safety bill** Verkehrssicherheitsgesetz; **~ safety campaign** Verkehrserziehung;
~ safety instruction Verkehrsunterricht; **~ safety poster** Ver-
kehrssicherheitsplakat; **~ sense** Fahrgefühl; **~ services** Straßenverkehrsgewerbe; **~ sign** Wegweiser, Straßenschild,
Verkehrshinweis, -zeichen; **~ speed** Fahrzeuggeschwindigkeit;
~ surface Straßendecke, -belag; **~ and rail system** Straßennetz,
Eisenbahnwesen, Verkehrsnetz; **~ tax** *(Br.)* Straßenbenutzungsgebühr, *(US)* Arbeitsdienstverpflichtung zur Instandhaltung einzelner Landstraßen in den USA; **~ taxes**
Straßenabgaben; **~ test** Straßentauglichkeitsprüfung, *(car)*
Probefahrt, Einfahren; **~ toll** Straßenbenutzungs-, Autobahngebühr; **~ track** Strecke; **~ traffic** Straßenverkehr; **~ Traffic
Act** *(Br.)* Straßenverkehrsgesetz, -ordnung; **~ traffic control**
Verkehrsregelung; **~ transport** *(Br.)* Beförderung mit dem
(Güterverkehr mit) Lastkraftwagen, Straßen-, Güterkraftverkehr; **~-transport service** *(Br.)* Fernlast-, Lastwagenfernver-
kehr, Straßenverkehrsgewerbe; **~-transport undertaking** *(Br.)*
Straßenverkehrsbetrieb; **~ use fee** Straßenbenutzungsgebühr;
~ user Verkehrsteilnehmer; **~ user on foot** Fußgänger; **~
vehicle** Straßenfahrzeug; **~ warning** Straßenverkehrszeichen;
~ widening Straßenerweiterung, -verbreiterung; **~-widening
scheme** Straßenerweiterungsvorhaben; **~ worker** Straßenarbeiter.
roadability *(car)* Fahreigenschaften, Straßenlage.
roadable zum Straßentransport geeignet;
~ **aircraft** Autoflugzeug.
roadbed Bahnkörper, Eisenbahnoberbau, Gleissystem;
~ **maintenance** Bahnkörpererhaltung.
roadblock *(mil.)* Straßensperre, -hindernis.
roadbook Straßenatlas, Reisehandbuch, Autoreiseführer.
roader Straßenkehrer, -arbeiter.
roadhouse Rasthaus, Ausflugslokal, Herberge.
roading *(US)* Fahren auf der Landstraße.
roadman Straßenarbeiter, *(hawker)* Hausierer, Straßenhändler.
roadmaster Streckenmeister.
roadside Straßenseite, *(piece of land)* an der Straße gelegenes
Grundstück;
at the ~ am Wege [gelegen], am Straßenrand;
~ *(a.)* an der Landstraße gelegen;
a year's free ~ assistance from the AA *(Br.)* Straßendienstkarte
des ADAC; **~ crowd** Straßenauflauf; **~ establishment** Straßenrestaurant; **~ inn** Gasthaus an der Landstraße, Rasthaus; **~
repairs** unterwegs erforderlich Reparaturen, behelfsmäßige
Ausbesserung; **~ sign** Hinweisschild; **~ stand** *(US)* Straßen-
verkaufsstand.
roadstead Reede.
roadster Sportzweisitzer, -wagen, offener Wagen.
roadway Fahrstraße, -bahn, -damm, *(mining)* Förderbahn.
roadworthiness Verkehrstauglichkeit, -sicherheit.
roadworthy verkehrstauglich, -sicher.
roar *(v.)* *(motor)* dröhnen.
roaring, to keep on weiterhin seine Stimme erheben;
~ business Bombengeschäft; **to drive a ~ trade** glänzende
Geschäfte machen; **the ~ twenties** die goldenen zwanziger
Jahre.
roast Neckerei;
~ *(v.)* s. o. j. aufziehen;
to stand the ~ als Zielscheibe des Spotts dienen.

rob *(v.)* rauben;
~ **a bank** Bank überfallen; ~ **Peter to pay Paul** ein Loch aufreißen, um ein anderes zu stopfen; ~ **s. o. of the reward of his labo(u)rs** j. um die Früchte seiner Arbeit bringen.
robber, highway Straßenräuber.
robbery Raub, Raubüberfall, räuberischer Diebstahl, Beraubung, Überfall;
aggravated ~ schwerer Raub; **armed** ~ bewaffneter Überfall; **bank** ~ Banküberfall, -raub; **high-class** ~ Hochstapelei; **highway** ~ Straßenraub; **mail** ~ Postdiebstahl;
~ **with violence** Raubüberfall;
to be a highway ~ *(fig.)* unverschämte Forderung darstellen; **to commit** ~ Raub begehen; **to take part in a gang** ~ sich an einem Raubüberfall beteiligen;
~ **insurance** Raubüberfallversicherung.
robe Robe, Amtstracht, Staatskleid;
coronation ~ Krönungsrobe; **long** ~ Juristenberuf.
robot Roboter, *(automation)* Automat, *(mil.)* vollautomatische Waffe, *(traffic sign)* automatisches Verkehrszeichen;
~ **pilot** Selbststeuergerät.
robotize *(v.)* mechanisieren.
rock Felsen, Klippe;
on the ~**s** *(drink)* mit Eiswürfeln, *(ship)* gestrandet, *(stressed conditions)* pleite, in Geldnöten;
~ *(v.)* in den Grundfesten erschüttern;
~ **the boat** *(fig.)* unüberlegte Schritte tun, Plan umschmeißen; ~ **the retail trade by dropping trade stamps** Einzelhandel durch Aufgabe von Rabattmarken zum Wanken bringen; ~ **in security** in Sicherheit wiegen;
to be on the ~**s** in äußerster Geldverlegenheit (pleite) sein, *(fig.)* auf dem letzten Loch pfeifen; **to have** ~**s in one's head** *(sl.)* nicht alle beisammen haben; **to run upon the** ~**s** auf dem letzten Loch pfeifen, Schiffbruch erleiden; **to see** ~**s ahead** große Schwierigkeiten voraussehen.
rock-bottom allerunterst, Allerniedrigstes;
to get down to ~ einer Sache auf den Grund gehen; **to have touched** ~ Tiefstand erreicht haben;
~ **price** äußerst kalkulierter Preis, Schlager-, Schleuderpreis.
rock formation Felsformation.
rocker blotter Wiegelöscher.
rocket Rakete;
anti-aircraft ~ Luftabwehrrakete; **atomic** ~ Atomrakete; **carrier** ~ Trägerrakete; **control** ~ Steuerrakete; **intermediate-range** ~ Mittelstreckenrakete; **intercontinental** ~ Interkontinentalrakete; **long-range** ~ Langstreckenrakete; **multistage** ~ Mehrstufenrakete; **retro-**~ Bremsrakete; **solid-propellant** ~ Feststoffrakete; **step** ~ Stufenrakete; **three-stage** ~ dreistufige Rakete;
~ *(v.) (mil.)* mit Raketen beschießen, *(price)* steil ansteigen;
~ **costs** Unkosten raketenartig ansteigen lassen;
to launch a ~ Rakete abschießen;
~ **[-driven] airplane** Raketenflugzeug; ~ **apparatus** *(ship)* Rettungsgerät; ~ **base** Raketenabschußbasis; ~ **builder** Raketenkonstrukteur; ~ **composition** Raketentreibsatz; ~ **engine** Raketentriebwerk; ~ **field** Raketenabschußgelände; ~ **launching** Raketenabschuß, -feuerung; ~ **launching site** Raketenabschußbasis; ~ **plane** Raketenflugzeug; ~**-powered** mit Raketenantrieb; ~ **propulsion** Raketenantrieb; ~ **range** Raketenversuchsgelände.
rocketeer Raketenforscher.
rocketry Raketenwesen, -technik.
rod *(fig.)* Amtsgewalt, *(revolver, sl.)* Pistole, Knarre;
to hit the ~**s** *(sl.)* umsonst in einem Güterzug mitfahren; **to make a** ~ **for one's own back** sich selbst eine Last aufbürden;
~ **antenna** Stabantenne; ~ **licence** Angelschein.
rodeo Schaukampf, Wildwestschau, Cowboyfest, Autorodeo.
rogatory letters *(US)* Rechtshilfeersuchen zwecks Zeugenvernehmung.
roger *(US sl., radio message)* verstanden.
rogue *(Br.)* Landstreicher, Vagabund, Bettler;
~**s' gallery** *(US)* Verbrecheralbum.
rôle Aufgabe, Funktion, Rolle;
in the ~ **of a prosecutor** in der Anklägerrolle;
central ~ Hauptrolle; **offbeat** ~ außergewöhnliche Funktion; ~ **as debtor** Schuldnerrolle;
to assume the ~ **of a judge** richterliche Funktionen übernehmen; **to have a major** ~ Hauptrolle spielen; **to play a** ~ Rolle spielen, Funktion ausüben; **to play the** ~ **of a martyr** Märtyrerrolle spielen;
~ **performance** Rollendarstellung; ~ **performer** Rollendarsteller.

roll *(of barristers, Br.)* Anwaltsliste, -verzeichnis, *(of court, Scot.)* Terminkalender, Prozeßregister, *(money, US sl.)* zusammengerollter Geldschein, *(register)* Verzeichnis, Liste, Rolle, *(register of names)* Namensverzeichnis, -liste, Anwesenheitsliste, *(sheet)* Gerichtsakte;
~**s** Akten, Urkunden;
the ~**s** Staatsarchiv;
assessment ~ Steuer-, Hebeliste; **bank** ~ Banknotenbündel; **court** ~**s** Gerichtsakten; **death** ~ Verlustliste; **electoral** ~ Wählerliste; **imparlance** ~ Vertagungsliste; **issue** ~**s** Prozeßakten; **judgment** ~ Urteilsverzeichnis; **membership** ~ Mitgliederliste; **muster** ~ *(ship)* Stamm-, Musterrolle; **nominal** ~ Namensverzeichnis, -liste, *(mil.)* Stammrolle; **Parliament** ~**s** *(Br.)* Parlamentsprotokoll; **patent** ~ *(Br.)* Patentregister, -rolle; **process** ~ Prozeßregister; **rent** ~ Pachtaufkommen; **tax** ~ Hebeliste, Verzeichnis der Steuerzahler;
~**s of the exchequer** Abgabenverzeichnis; ~ **of film** *(Br.)* Filmrolle; ~ **of hono(u)r** Gefallenenliste; ~**s of Parliament** höchstrichterliche Entscheidungen; ~ **of printing paper** Rolle Druckpapier; ~ **of solicitors** Anwaltsliste;
~ *(v.)* rollen, fahren, *(paper)* kalandern, *(shift taxes)* Steuern abwälzen;
~ **s. o.** *(US sl.)* Betrunkenen berauben;
~ **along at a pace closer to its capacity** seine Kapazitäten in stärkerem Maße ausfahren; ~ **back** *(US coll.)* Preise durch Subventionsmaßnahmen senken; ~ **back the pay cuts** Gehaltskürzungen rückgängig machen; ~ **a big deal** *(sl.)* großes Ding drehen; ~ **in** *(money)* hereinkommen; ~ **in money** im Geld schwimmen (wühlen); ~ **out the red carpet for s. o.** *(sl.)* großen Bahnhof für j. veranstalten; ~ **out 20.000 trucks a year** jährlich 20.000 LKW's herstellen; ~ **over an advertisement to the next week** nicht plazierte Anzeige in der nächsten Woche bringen; ~ **over bank loans on a continuing basis** Bankkredit revolvierend einsetzen; ~ **past** vorbeifahren; ~ **the price increases back** Preiserhöhung rückgängig machen; ~ **a problem round in one's mind** Problem wälzen; ~ **a road surface** Straße planieren; ~ **up** *(car)* vorfahren, *(debts)* sich summieren; ~ **up like a hedgehog** sich einigen;
to be admitted to the ~ *(Br.)* als Anwalt zugelassen werden; **to be struck off the** ~ *(Br.)* von der Anwaltsliste gestrichen werden; **to call the** ~ Anwesenheitsliste verlesen, namentlich aufrufen; **to keep the** ~ Protokoll führen; **to strike s. o. off the** ~ *(disqualify)* disqualifizieren, *(solicitor, Br.)* Anwalt aus der Anwaltschaft ausschließen;
~**-away ironer** Bügelautomat; ~ **bar** *(car)* Kopfstütze; ~ **call** Namensaufruf, -verlesung, *(mil.)* Anwesenheitsappell; ~**-call** *(v.)* namentlich verlesen (aufrufen); ~**-call note** namentliche Abstimmung; ~ **film** *(photo)* Rollfilm; ~**-front cabinet** Rollschrank; ~ **mill** Walzwerk; ~ **number** *(building society)* Bausparvertrag, -nummer; ~**-on** (~**-off**) **service** Huckepackverkehr; ~**-over bank loans** revolvierend eingesetzte Bankkredite; ~**-over credit** kurzfristig finanzierter langfristiger Kredit; ~ **top** Rolladen; ~**-top desk** Rollschreibtisch; ~**-up map** hochziehbare Filmleinwand.
rollback *(US coll.)* Preisherabsetzung, staatliche Preissenkungsaktion, *(wages)* Lohnkürzung;
~ **of the invading army** Zurückwerfen der Invasionstruppen; ~ **subsidies** *(US)* Subventionen für Preisherabsetzung.
rolled gold Doublégold.
roller Walzwerkarbeiter, *(print.)* Druckwalze;
~ **clutch** Freiluftkupplung; ~ **coaster** *(US)* Berg- und Talbahn; ~ **mill** Walzenstraße; ~ **skate** *(Br., sl.)* Panzerfahrzeug.
rollickings ausgelassene Feste.
rolling *(ship)* Schlingerbewegung;
~ *(a.)* unterwegs, auf dem Transport, fahrbar, auf Rädern;
to be ~ **heavily** *(ship)* schlingern; **to be** ~ **in luxury** Luxusleben führen; **to be** ~ **in money** *(sl.)* im Geld schwimmen; **to start the ball** ~ *(fig.)* Stein ins Rollen bringen;
~ **adjustment** *(US)* allmähliche Konjunkturanpassung, Konjunkturdämpfung auf einzelnen Gebieten; ~ **annuities** steigende Renten; ~ **barrage** *(mil.)* Sperrfeuer, Feuerwalze; ~ **capital** Betriebskapital; ~ **chair** Rollstuhl; ~ **charges** Rollgeld; ~ **freight** Rollgut; ~ **kitchen** Feldküche; ~ **mill** Walzwerk; ~ **mill train** Fertigstraße; ~ **plant** *(railway)* Betriebsmittel, Wagenpark; ~ **press** Kupferdruck, Rotationspresse; ~ **stock** *(railway)* rollendes Material, Eisenbahnbetriebsmittel, Wagenpark; **a** ~ **stone** ewiger Wanderer.
Roman type Antiquaschrift.
Rome Treaties Verträge von Rom.
romp *(v.)* **through one's examination** sein Examen spielend bewältigen.

rood of land Viertelmorgen.
roof Dach;
  out on the ~ *(sl.)* auf einer Sauftour;
  broken ~ *(mansard)* Mansardendach; **flat ~** flaches Dach;
  tuckaway ~ *(car)* abnehmbares Dach;
  ~ of a car Autodach;
  ~ *(v.) (prices)* übermäßig ansteigen;
  ~ a house Haus unter Dach bringen;
  to go through the ~ *(prices)* in die Höhe schießen; **to live under the same ~ with s. o.** mit jem. unter dem gleichen Dach leben (wohnen); **to raise the ~** Riesenkrach machen, Heidenspektakel veranstalten;
  ~ garden Dachgarten; **~ rack** *(car)* Gepäckträger; **~ timbers** Dachsparren; **to shout facts from the ~ tops** Tatsachen lauthals verkünden; **~-top restaurant** Dachrestaurant.
roofer *(Br.)* Dankbrief [für Einladungen].
rook Betrüger;
  ~ *(v.)* übervorteilen, ausspielen.
rookie Novize, Neuling, *(mil.)* Rekrut.
room Zimmer, Raum, Stube, Kammer, *(extent of space)* Raum, Platz, *(mining)* Abbaustrecke, *(occasion)* Gelegenheit, Anlaß, Veranlassung, *(place at Lloyds)* Versicherungsbörse, *(platform)* Bühne, *(stock exchange)* Börsensaal;
  air-conditioned ~ klimatisiertes Zimmer; **auction ~** Auktionslokal; **assembly ~** Versammlungsraum; **bed-sitting ~** Wohnschlafzimmer; **empty ~** Leerzimmer; **furnished ~ [with attendance]** möbliertes Zimmer [mit Bedienung]; **hotel ~** Hotelzimmer; **living ~** Wohnzimmer; **meeting ~** Sitzungssaal; **~ required** Raumbedarf; **shared ~** *(ship)* Dreibettkabine; **show ~** Ausstellungsraum; **single ~** Einzelzimmer; **sitting ~** Wohnzimmer; **standing ~** *(bus)* Stehplatz; **store ~** Lagerraum; **strong ~** Tresor, Stahlkammer; **unfurnished ~** unmöbliertes Zimmer; **vacant ~** freies Zimmer; **waiting ~** Warte-, Vorzimmer;
  ~ and board Kost und Logis; **~ for complaint** Anlaß zur Beschwerde; **~ at the back** rückwärtiges Zimmer; **no ~ for doubts** kein Zweifel; **~ for improvement** Verbesserungsmöglichkeit; **much ~ for improvement** viel zu wünschen übrig lassend; **~s to let** Zimmer zu vermieten; **~ for manoeuvre** Bewegungsfreiheit, Verhandlungsspielraum; **~ for two people** *(hotel)* Doppelzimmer; **~s of good proportions** wohlproportionierte Räume; **~ of adequate size** ausreichend großes Zimmer; **not enough ~ to swing a cat** überhaupt kein Spielraum;
  ~ *(v.) (US)* logieren, als Mieter wohnen;
  ~ together zusammen wohnen;
  to book a hotel ~ Hotelzimmer bestellen; **to cancel a ~ at a hotel** Hotelzimmer abbestellen; **to change one's room** in ein anderes Zimmer ziehen; **to engage a ~** Zimmer mieten; **to find (get) s. o. a ~** jem. ein Zimmer besorgen; **to have a private ~** *(hospital)* erster Klasse liegen; **to hold a ~ in readiness for s. o.** Zimmer für j. bereithalten; **to let furnished ~s** möblierte Zimmer vermieten; **to live in furnished ~s** möbliert wohnen; **to rent a ~** Zimmer mieten; **to reserve a ~** Zimmer bestellen; **to share a ~ with s. o.** mit jem. zusammenziehen; **to take a ~** Zimmer mieten; **to take up too much ~** zuviel Platz beanspruchen;
  ~ clerk *(hotel, US)* Empfangschef; **~ conditioning** Klimatisierung eines Einzelzimmers; **~ fee** Zimmerpreis; **~ heating** Raumheizung; **~ key** Zimmerschlüssel; **~ mate** Zimmergenosse; **~ rate** *(hotel)* Zimmerpreis; **~ service** Zimmerbedienung; **~ telephone** Telefonanschluß auf dem Zimmer; **~ temperature** Zimmertemperatur; **~ trader** *(US)* auf eigene Rechnung spekulierendes Börsenmitglied.
roomer *(US)* Untermieter.
roomette *(US)* Schlafwagen-, Einzelkabine.
rooming house *(US)* Pension, Logiehaus.
roommate Zimmergenosse.
roomy großräumig;
  ~ cabin geräumige Kabine.
Roosa bonds *(US)* einjährige Schatzwechsel.
roost *(coll.)* Schlafstätte.
root Wurzel, Ursache;
  ~ of contract wesentlicher Vertragsinhalt; **~ of descent** Abstammung; **~ of a matter** Kern einer Sache; **~ of title** urkundlicher Eigentumsnachweis, unanfechtbarer Rechtsanspruch; **~ of the trouble** Wurzel des Übels;
  ~ *(v.)* **for a candidate** jds. Wahl betreiben; **~ out a bill from under a pile of letters** Rechnung unter einem Stoß von Briefen hervorziehen;
  to destroy evil practices ~ and branch üble Machenschaften mit der Wurzel ausrotten; **to get to the ~ of a matter** einer Sache auf den Grund gehen; **to go to the ~ of a contract** wesentlichen Inhalt eines Vertrages berühren; **to strike ~** *(fig.)* Wurzeln

schlagen, sich einleben; **to take ~ from** basieren, seinen Ausgang nehmen;
  ~ cause Grundursache; **~ crop** Hackfrucht; **~-and-branch destruction** totale Zerstörung; **~ idea** Grundidee.
rooted angestammt.
rope Strick, Seil, *(fig.)* Bewegungs-, Handlungsfähigkeit, *(punishment by hanging)* Tod durch den Strang;
  on the high ~s von oben herab;
  ~s Kniffe, Schliche;
  ~ of pearls Perlenschnur; **~ of sand** scheinbare Sicherheit;
  ~ *(v.)* **s. o. in for a job** j. für eine Arbeit einspannen; **~ off** absperren; **~ out the spectators** Zuschauer durch Seilabsperrung ausschließen;
  to be on the ~ *(sl.)* in hilfloser Lage sein; **to give s. o. plenty of ~** j. am langen Zügel führen, j. schalten und walten lassen; **to have s. o. on the ~s** *(sl.)* j. fertiggemacht haben; **to know the ~s** sein Handwerk von Grund auf verstehen; **to learn the ~s** Sache von Grund aus lernen; **to show s. o. the ~s** jem. alle Schliche beibringen;
  ~ dancer Seiltänzer; **~ ladder** Strickleiter.
roper *(gambling establishment, US sl.)* Schlepper.
ropeway Drahtseilbahn.
rosa, sub durch die Blume.
roster Liste, Tabelle, Namenliste, Teilnehmerverzeichnis, *(mil.)* Dienstplan;
  advancement (promotion) ~ Beförderungsliste; **duty ~** Dienstplan;
  blue-chip ~ of partners erstklassiges Führungsgremium.
rostrum Rednerbühne, -pult, *(fig.)* Plattform;
  to go up to the ~ Rednertribüne besteigen.
rosy *(sl.)* optimistisch, *(tight)* beschwipst.
rot Fäulnis, Verwesung, *(Br., sl.)* Quatsch, *(house)* Schwamm;
  electoral ~ Wählerschwund; **pretty good ~** *(sl.)* nichts wert;
  ~ *(v.)* **in goal** im Gefängnis schmachten.
rota *(Br.)* regelmäßiger Gang, *(roster)* Dienstplan, Turnus;
  to take the chair according to ~ Vorsitz turnungsmäßig übernehmen.
rotaire bewegliches Werbemittel.
rotary *(construction engineering)* Verkehrskreisel;
  ~ current *(el.)* Drehstrom; **~ duplicator** Drehvervielfältiger; **~ photogravure** Rotationstiefdruck; **~ press** Rotationspresse; **~ printing** Rotationsdruck; **~ printing machine** Rotationsdruckmaschine; **~ traffic** Kreisverkehr; **~-wing aircraft** Drehflügelzeug.
rotate *(v.)* turnusmäßig, auswechseln (ausscheiden);
  ~ advertising executives Umbesetzung der Werbefachleute vornehmen; **~ crops** im Fruchtwechsel anbauen, Wechselwirtschaft treiben; **~ promising executives** erfolgversprechende Nachwuchskräfte turnusmäßig versetzen; **~ in office** sich turnusmäßig abwechseln.
rotating ständig wechselnd;
  ~ beacon Drehfunkfeuer; **~ shift** Wechselschicht.
rotation geregelter (turnusmäßiger) Stellenwechsel, Turnus, *(advertising)* ständig wiederholte Werbeserie;
  in ~ turnusmäßig, im Turnus, abwechselnd; **in strict ~** *(orders)* in der Reihenfolge des Eingangs;
  job ~ *(US)* Arbeitsplatzwechsel; **three-course ~** Dreifelderwirtschaft;
  ~ of crops Fruchtfolge, Wechselwirtschaft; **~ of directors** turnusmäßiger Vorstandswechsel; **~ of the earth** Erdumdrehung; **~ in office** turnusmäßiger Wechsel im Amt; **~ of seasons** Wechsel der Jahreszeiten;
  to practise ~ on a field Wechselwirtschaft treiben; **to retire by ~** turnusmäßig ausscheiden;
  ~ period Turnus; **~ training** Praktikantenausbildung.
rotatory rotierend, *(fig.)* abwechselnd, turnusmäßig;
  ~ assemblies turnusmäßig aufeinander folgende Versammlungen.
rote Routine, Übung;
  by ~ rein mechanisch;
  to learn s. th. by ~ etw. auswendig lernen;
  ~ section *(US)* Kupfertiefdruckbeilage.
rotodyne Tragschrauber.
rotogravure Rastertief-, Rotationstiefdruck.
rotor *(plane)* Drehflügel, Tragschraube.
rotorcraft, rotorplane Drehflügelflugzeug.
rotten *(borough)* korrupt, *(goods)*, verdorben, schlecht, verfault;
  ~ to the core durch und durch korrupt;
  ~ clause *(marine insurance)* Haftungsausschluß [bei Seeuntüchtigkeit]; **~-egg** *(v.)* mit faulen Eiern beschmeißen; **~ play** miserables Stück; **~ weather** Sauwetter.

rotunda Rundbau, Rotunde.
rough Rohzustand, *(advertising)* Faust-, Rohskizze;
~ **and smooth of life** Auf und Ab des Lebens; ~ **and tumble** *(fam.)* wirres Handgemenge;
~ *(v.)* **it** anspruchslos leben;
to be still in the ~ noch im Rohzustand sein; **to cost $ 100 in the** ~ überschläglich (ungefähr) 100 Dollar kosten; **to see a statute only in the** ~ Statut nur im Entwurf sehen; **to take s. o. in the** ~ j. nehmen, wie er ist;
~ *(a.)* roh, rauh, *(fig.)* ungefähr, annähernd, überschläglich, *(print.)* unbeschnitten, *(uncultivated)* ungebildet, unkultiviert;
~ **accommodation at a small country inn** dürftige Unterbringung in einem kleinen Landgasthaus; ~ **average** ungefährer Durchschnitt; ~ **balance** Probe-, Rohbilanz; ~ **book** Vormerkbuch, Kladde; ~ **calculation** flüchtige (ungefähre) Berechnung, Voranschlag, Überschlag; **on a** ~ **calculation** nach ungefährer Berechnung; ~ **coat** Rohputz; ~ **copy** Entwurf, Skizze; ~ **crossing** stürmische Überfahrt; ~ **cut** *(film)* Rohschnitt; ~ **diamond** ungeschliffener Diamant, *(fig.)* guter Kern in einer rauhen Schale; ~ **draft** erster Entwurf, Vorentwurf, Konzept; ~ **element of the population** ungebildate Masse; ~ **estimate** grobe Schätzung; ~ **estimate of expenses** ungefährer Kostenanschlag; ~ **going** schwierige Bedingungen; ~ **guess** ungefähre Schätzung; ~ **guide on** Faustregel für; ~**handle** *(v.)* brutal behandeln; ~ **handling** schlechte Behandlung; ~**hewn** *(fig.)* uneben; ~ **justice** summarisches Verfahren; **to lead a** ~ **life away from civilization** hartes Leben fern aller Zivilisation führen; **in a** ~ **and ready manner** behelfsmäßig, mehr schlecht als recht; ~ **nursing** schlechte Pflege; ~ **passage** stürmische Überfahrt; ~ **quarter of a town** gewalttätiges (unruhiges) Stadtviertel; ~ **sea** rauhe (grobe) See; **to give s. o. a lick with the** ~ **side of one's tongue** mit jem. ein ernstes Wörtchen reden; ~ **sketch** flüchtiger Entwurf, Rohentwurf; ~ **street** holprige Straße; **to have a** ~ **time** scheußliche Zeit durchleben; ~ **translation** annähernde Übersetzung, Rohübertragung; ~**-and-tumble life** draufgängerisches Leben; ~ **welcome** unfreundlicher Empfang; ~ **work** primitive Arbeit.
roughage content *(of flour)* Ausmahlungsquote.
roughdry clothes Trockenwäsche.
roughhouse *(sl.)* Keilerei;
~ **fighting at close quarters** brutaler Nahkampf.
roughly ungefähr, etwa;
to cost ~ überschläglich kosten.
rouleau Geldrolle.
roulette Roulett;
~ **table** Roulettisch.
round Rundung, *(mil.)* Streife, Patrouille, *(police)* Rundgang, Runde, *(tour)* Rundreise, Tour, *(tour of inspection)* Besichtigungs-, Rundgang;
daily ~ tägliche Beschäftigung; **postman's** ~ Bestellgang des Briefträgers; **visiting** ~ Inspektionsfahrt;
~ **of ammunition** Schuß Munition; ~ **of applause** nicht endenwollender Beifall; ~ **of the balloting** Wahlrunde; **tough ~s of collective bargaining** harte Tarifauseinandersetzung; **another** ~ **of wage claims** erneute Lohnrunde; ~ **of drinks** Runde; **another** ~ **of lame duckery** weitere Runde zur Rettung nutzloser Betriebe; ~ **of negotiations** Verhandlungsrunde; ~ **of oratory** Rednerschlacht; ~ **of pay policy** Lohnrunde; ~ **of pleasure** Vergnügungstour; ~ **of visits** Besuchstour; **doctor's** ~ **of visits** tägliche Arztvisite;
~ *(v.)* *(ship)* wenden, *(watchman)* Runde machen;
~ **on s. o.** j. denunzieren; ~ **a curve** Kurve ausfahren; ~ **off** abrunden; ~ **off a bill** Gesetzentwurf abschließend behandeln; ~ **off one's career by being made Minister** seine Karriere mit einem Ministeramt abrunden; ~ **off one's property** sein Gelände arrondieren; ~ **up** aufrunden, *(cattle)* zusammentreiben, *(fig.)* ausfindigmachen; ~ **up a gang of criminals** Verbrecherbande aufrollen; ~ **up tourists** Touristen zusammentrommeln;
to argue ~ **and** ~ **a subject** um eine Sache herumreden; **to be soon passed** ~ schnell bekanntwerden; **to bring s. o.** ~ j. umstimmen; **to come** ~ **to the facts** sich mit den Tatsachen abfinden; **to drive a long way** ~ großen Umweg fahren; **to get** ~ **regulations** *(US)* Bestimmungen umgehen; **to go** ~ [Bestimmungen] umgehen; **to go the** ~ *(doctor)* Visite machen; **to go the** ~ **of the papers** durch alle Zeitungen gehen; **to hand the papers** ~ Zeitungen austragen; **to journey** ~ **the world** Weltreise machen; **to make** ~ arrondieren; **to make a** ~ Umweg, Rundfahrt machen, *(doctor)* Visite machen; **to make one's ~s every hour** alle Stunden seine Runden gehen; **to order one's car** ~ seinen Wagen kommen (vorfahren) lassen; **to pay for a** ~ **of drinks**

Runde (Lage) spendieren (ausgeben); **to pay somewhere** ~ **$ 4000 a year** ungefähr 4000 Dollar im Jahr zahlen; **to serve a** ~ **of drinks** Lage stiften; **to show s. o.** ~ j. herumführen; **to show s. o.** ~ **the factory** j. die Fabrik besichtigen lassen; **to show s. o.** ~ **the house** jem. das Haus zeigen, mit jem. eine Hausbesichtigung machen; **to sleep the clock** ~ zwölf Stunden durchschlafen; **to stand a** ~ Lage ausgeben; **to take the** ~ **of the village** im Dorf schnell die Runde machen; **to walk one's** ~ seinen Rundgang machen; **to win s. o.** ~ *(sl.)* j. herumkriegen;
~ *(a.)* rund, abgerundet, ganz, voll, *(stock exchange)* ungefähr, zirka, etwa;
~ **answer** unverblümte Antwort; ~ **dozen** rundes Dutzend; **in** ~ **figures** in runden Zahlen; ~**-of-wage increase** globale Anhebung des Lohnniveaus; ~ **lot** *(US)* mehrere hundert Aktien umfassendes Aktienpaket; ~ **number** abgerundete Zahl; ~**-the-clock service** vierundzwanzigstündiger Bereitschaftsdienst; **good** ~ **sum** abgerundeter Betrag; ~ **table** Verhandlungs-, Konferenztisch; ~**-table conference** Konferenz am runden Tisch; ~**-table talks** Gespräche am runden Tisch; ~ **tour** Rundreise; ~ **transaction (turn)** abgeschlossenes Börsengeschäft.
round-the-clock im 24-Stundenrythmus;
~ **bombing** ununterbrochenes Bombardement; ~ **service** 24-Stundendienst.
round trip Rundreise, -fahrt, *(US)* Hin- und Rückfahrt;
scheduled economy ~ Touristenrundreise in einer Linienmaschine.
round-trip *(US)* für Hin- und Rückfahrt gültig;
~ **air fare** Rundreiseflugkarte; ~ **discount** Rückfahrtermäßigung; ~ **excursion fare** Rundreise-, Ausflugskarte; ~ **fare** *(US)* Fahrpreis für die Hin- und Rückreise; ~ **jet** Düsenflugzeugrundreise; ~ **ticket** Rundreisefahrkarte.
round voyage Schiffsrundreise.
roundabout *(detour, US)* Umleitung, *(road junction, Br.)* Kreisel-, Rundverkehr, *(merry-go-round)* Karussell;
~ **explanation** umständliche Erklärung; ~ **methods of production** Produktionsumweg; ~ **route** Umwegstrecke, Umleitung; ~ **system of traffic** Kreisverkehr; **in a** ~ **way** durch die Blume, hintenherum; **to hear news in a** ~ **way** Nachrichten auf Umwegen erhalten; **to take a** ~ **way** Umfahrt machen, umfahren.
rounder *(US sl.)* Gewohnheitsverbrecher.
roundhouse *(US)* Lokomotivschuppen.
rounded number aufgerundete Zahl.
rounding *(statistics)* Auf- und Abrundung;
perfect ~ **off** zufriedenstellender Abschluß.
roundly ungefähr, im Überschlag;
to go ~ **to work** ernsthaft an die Arbeit gehen.
roundsman *(Br.)* Laufbursche, Lieferbote, Austräger, *(police, US)* Streifengänger, Polizeistreife;
milk ~ Milchmann.
roundup Zusammentreiben, Razzia, *(survey)* Zusammenfassung, Übersicht;
~ **of criminals** *(US sl.)* Aushebung von Verbrechern;
to conduct a ~ Razzia durchführen.
roup *(Br., fam.)* Versteigerung, Auktion.
rouse Toast, *(mil., Br.)* Werksignal;
~ *(v.)* **o. s. to do** sich zu etw. aufraffen; ~ **to action** zur Tätigkeit bringen; ~ **the masses** Mob aufhetzen;
to give a ~ **to s. o.** Toast auf j. ausbringen.
rouser etw. Aufregendes, *(coll.)* Schwindel.
rousing|campaign aufregender Wahlfeldzug; ~ **trade** blühender Handel.
roustabout *(US)* Schauermann, Werftarbeiter.
rout Auflauf, Tumult, Zusammenrottung, Mob, *(mil.)* zügelloser Rückzug;
~ *(v.)* *(print.)* ausfräsen;
~ **s. o. out of his house** j. aus seinem Haus vertreiben.
route Strecke, Route, [Transport]weg, *(airplane)* Fluglinie, -route, -strecke, *(direction)* Richtung, *(insurance)* Transportweg, *(line)* Linienführung, *(mil.)* Marschbefehl, *(road)* [Reise]route, Weg, [Bundes]straße, *(salesman)* Verkaufstournee, *(ship)* Schiffahrtsweg, Kurs;
en ~ unterwegs;
access ~ Zugangsweg; **agreed** ~ vereinbarte Flugroute; **bus** ~ Omnibusstrecke; **definite** ~ *(salesman)* bestimmte Verkaufstournee; **direct** ~ kürzeste Strecke; **forwarding** ~ *(goods traffic)* Beförderungsweg; **grand** ~ Fernverbindungsstrecke; **high-density** ~ Fluglinie mit hoher Verkehrsdichte; **main** ~ Hauptstrecke; **overland** ~ Landweg; **roundabout** ~ umständlicher Umweg; **sea** ~ Seeweg; **through** ~ Durchgangsstrecke; **top scenic** ~ landschaftlich schönste Strecke; **trade** ~ Handelsstraße;

low-cost ~ to raise capital to finance expansion billiger Finanzierungsweg für Betriebsausweitungen; ~ **to be followed** Reisestrecke; ~ **to be followed by a case of goods** Transportweg einer Warensendung; ~ **of travel** Beförderungsweg;

~ *(v.)* befördern, leiten, dirigieren, *(material)* einer Reihe von Verarbeitungsprozessen unterwerfen, *(post)* mit Postleitvermerk versehen, *(railway)* Route kennzeichnen;

~ **documents** Urkunden auf dem Amtsweg weiterleiten; ~ **a memo** Aktennotiz versenden; ~ **an unauthorized payment through a private company** unberechtigte Geldbeträge über eine Privatfirma schleusen; ~ **in a sales race** im Umsatzwettrennen auf den zweiten Platz verweisen; ~ **shipments** Frachtsendungen leiten (dirigieren); ~ **troops** Truppen in Marsch setzen;

to be en ~ unterwegs sein; **to build regular** ~s feste Verkaufstournee festlegen; **to find a new** ~ neuen Weg finden; **to fly by the** ~ **across the Pole** Polroute befliegen; **to get the** ~ *(mil.)* Marschbefehl erhalten; **to go the** ~ *(fig.)* bis zum Schluß durchhalten; **to pick up** ~ **10** *(US)* der Bundesstraße 10 folgen; **to travel over a new** ~ neue Fahrstrecke ausprobieren;

~ **application** Fluglinienantrag; ~ **army** marschbereite Armee; ~ **award** Fluglinienzuteilung; ~ **card** Arbeitsablaufkarte; ~ **confirmation sign** Vorwegweiser auf der Autobahn; ~ **forecast** Streckenvorhersage, Flugwetterdienst; ~ **instructions** Leitvermerk; ~ **items** *(US)* Boteninkassi; ~ **list** Postleitvermerkeverzeichnis; ~ **man** Sachbearbeiter für bestimmte Kunden; ~ **map** Straßenkarte, *(airplane)* Fluglinienkarte, *(railway)* Streckenkarte; ~ **march** *(mil., Br.)* Übungsmarsch; ~ **marker** Fernverkehrsstraßenschild; ~ **order** *(mil.)* Marschbefehl; ~ **planning** Fluglinienfestlegung.

routed *(postal item)* mit Leitvermerk versehen;
to be ~ **via X** *(letter)* über X gehen.

routine Prozedur, gewohnheitsmäßiger Verlauf, Trott, Schlendrian, Routine[sache], *(business)* [Geschäfts]routine, *(matter of form)* Brauch, Formsache, Dienstweg;
by ~ routinemäßig, nach der Schablone;
business (office) ~ üblicher Arbeitsgang (Geschäftsgang), gewöhnliche Büroarbeiten;
to be ~ Regel (Routine) sein; **to be only** ~ reine Formsache sein; **to do s. th. as a matter of** ~ etw. routinemäßig erledigen; **to make a** ~ **of** es zur Regel werden lassen;
~ *(a.)* alltäglich, üblich, routine-, gewohnheitsmäßig, mechanisch, schablonenhaft;
~ **board** Dienstplan; ~ **business** Routinearbeit, laufende Geschäftsangelegenheiten, *(fig.)* geistlose Beschäftigung; ~ **business letter** üblicher Geschäftsbrief; ~ **chores** Routinearbeit; ~ **contracts** Normverträge; ~ **correspondence** Geschäftskorrespondenz; ~ **duties** Routineaufgaben; ~ **expenditure** tägliche Ausgaben; ~ **flight** Routineflug; ~ **job** mechanische Arbeit (Tätigkeit); ~-**like** schablonenhaft; ~ **maintenance** normaler Erhaltungsaufwand; ~ **matters** übliche Angelegenheiten; ~ **operation** mechanische Tätigkeit; ~ **order** Routineauftrag, *(mil.)* Tages-, Dienstbefehl; ~ **procedure** übliches Verfahren, Routineverfahren; ~ **reply** Routineantwort; **to furnish a** ~ **report** Routinebericht vorlegen; ~ **request** Routineauftrag; ~ **testing** planmäßige Prüfung; ~ **visit** Routinebesuch; ~ **work** tägliches Einerlei, Routinearbeit.

routing Festlegung des Leitvermerks, Leitvermerkbestimmung, *(plant)* Festlegung der Reihenfolge der Arbeitsabläufe;
~ **of salesmen** Festlegung der Verkaufsrouten von Vertretern; ~ **clerk** *(US)* Abfertigungsbeamter; ~ **order** Anordnung eines Leitweges; ~ **plan** Festlegung der Verkaufstournee; ~ **sheet** Arbeitsfolgenplan; ~ **slip** Laufzettel.

routinism Schablonenhaftigkeit.
routinist alter Praktikus, Gewohnheitsmensch.
routinization routinemäßige Erledigung.
routinize *(v.)* routinemäßig erledigen.
rove *(v.)* wandern, umherziehen.
rover Wanderer, Landstreicher, Gammler;
to shoot at ~s *(fig.)* Schuß ins Blaue abgeben.
~ **ticket** Netzkarte.
roving|commission fliegender Ausschuß; ~ **life** Gammler-, Vagabundenleben;
row Reihe, *(building line)* Baufluchtlinie, *(uproar)* Rummel, Krach, Streit, Auseinandersetzung, Krawall;
in ~s reihenweise;
family ~ Familienkrach;
hard ~ **to hoe** schweres Stück Arbeit; **long** ~ **to hoe** *(US)* schwierige Angelegenheit; ~ **of houses** Häuserreihe; ~ **of seats** Sitzreihe;
~ *(v.)* *(fig.)* abkanzeln, Leviten lesen;

~ **in the same boat** *(fig.)* im gleichen Boot sitzen; ~ **with one's neighbo(u)rs** mit seinen Nachbarn Streit anfangen; ~ **against the tide (stream, wind)** gegen den Strom schwimmen;
to be always ready for a ~ Streithammel sein; **to get into a** ~ in Schwierigkeiten geraten; **to have a** ~ **with one's neighbo(u)rs** mit seinen Nachbarn Streit bekommen; **to hoe one's own** ~ *(US)* sich um seine eigenen Angelegenheiten kümmern; **to kick up a** ~ Krach schlagen;
~ **house** *(US)* Reiheneigenheim; **front-**~ **seat** Sitz in der ersten Reihe.
rowdiness rüpelhaftes Benehmen.
rowdy Randalierer.
Royal|assent *(parl.)* königliche Zustimmung; ~ **Charter** *(Br.)* königliche Verleihungsurkunde; ~ **Commission** *(Br.)* Untersuchungsausschuß; ~ **Commissioner** *(Br.)* Staatsbeauftragter; ~ **Corps of Signals** *(Br.)* Fernmeldetruppe; ⯑ **estate** *(Br.)* Staatsdomäne; **The** ~ **Exchange** Londoner Börsengebäude; ~ **Family** königliche Familie, Herrscherfamilie; ⯑ **hono(u)rs** diplomatische Vorrechte gekrönter Häupter; ~ **Humane Society** *(Br.)* Lebensrettungsgesellschaft; ~ **Mint** *(Br.)* Münzprägeanstalt; ~ **Prerogative** königliches Privileg; ⯑ **road** müheloser Weg; ⯑ **road to learning** [etwa] Nürnberger Trichter; ⯑ **speech** Thronrede; ⯑ **warrant** *(Br.)* Hoflieferantendiplom.
royalties königliches Privileg, Regal;
free of ~ frei von Lizenzabgaben; **subject to payment of** ~ lizenz-, tantiemenpflichtig;
author's ~ Autorenanteil; **mining** ~ Förderabgaben;
~ **on patents** Patentertägnisse;
to derive ~ Lizenzgebühren beziehen.
royalty *(copyright)* Autorenanteil, Tantieme, Honorar, *(kingdom)* Königstum, -würde, *(licence)* Lizenzgebühr, -abgabe, Nutzungsabgabe, *(mining)* Bergwerksabgabe, *(patent)* Patentgebühr, *(publisher)* Absatzhonorar, *(royal prerogative)* königliches Privileg, Regal, Schürfrecht, *(share in profit)* Gewinn-, Ertragsanteil, Tantieme, *(tax paid to the Crown)* Grundzehnter, Regal;
accrued ~ Tantiemenforderung; **copyright** ~ Urheberlizenz; **director's** ~ Aufsichtsratstantieme; **inventor's** ~ Patent-, Lizenzgebühr; **minimum** ~ Mindesttantieme; **mining** ~ Bergregal, Bergwerksabgabe; **overriding** ~ *(petrol industry)* Tantiemenanteil;
~ **of 10% on the published price** zehn Prozent vom Ladenverkaufspreis;
to fix a ~ Lizenzgebühr festlegen; **to get a** ~ **on** Tantieme erhalten;
on a ~ **basis** gegen Zahlung einer Lizenzgebühr; ~ **bonus** *(oil and gas lease)* zusätzliche Konzessionsgebühr; ~ **demand** Tantiemenforderung; ~ **department** Honorarabteilung; ~ **fees** Patent-, Lizenzgebühren; ~-**free licence** gebührenfreie Lizenz; ~ **interest** Lizenz-, Tantiemenanteil; ~ **payment** Lizenzzahlung, *(author)* Honorarüberweisung; ~ **remittance** Tantiementransfer; ~ **statement** Lizenzabrechnung, *(author)* Honoraraufstellung; ~ **tax** Tantiemenabgabe; ~ **value** *(mining)* kapitalisierte Bergwerksabgabe.
rub *(difficulty)* Haken, Pferdefuß, *(harsh criticism)* Stichelei, Seitenhieb;
~ *(v.)* **along (on)** gerade so auskommen; ~ **along with one's means of support** sich mit eigenen Mitteln über Wasser halten; ~ **elbows with s. o.** sich mit jem. bekanntmachen; ~ **one's hands** *(fig.)* sich die Hände reiben; ~ **it in** aufs Butterbrot schmieren, unter die Nase reiben, dauernd darauf herumreiten; ~ **off in great style** glänzenden Absatz finden; ~ **off on s. o.** auf j. abfärben; ~ **out pencil marks** Bleistiftnotizen ausradieren; ~ **shoulders with people** zu Gesellschaften gehen; ~ **through the world** sich recht und schlecht durchschlagen; ~ **up one's French** sein Französisch aufpolieren; ~ **s. o. the right way** j. richtig zu nehmen wissen; ~ **s. o. the wrong way** j. irritieren (verschnupfen);
to have a ~ **in it** einen Haken haben;
~ **joint** *(sl.)* schäbige Spelunke.
rubber Kautschuk, Radiergummi, *(fig.)* Stichelei, *(print.)* Farbläufer, *(tire, sl.)* Autoreifen;
~s *(stock exchange)* Gummiwerte, -aktien;
soft ~ Speckgummi;
~ *(v.)* *(US sl.)* Stielaugen machen;
~ **bands** Gummiringe; ~ **boat (dingy)** Schlauchboot; ~ **bumper** Gummistoßstange; ~ **check** *(coll., US)* ungedeckter (geplatzter) Scheck; ~ **estate** Kautschukplantage; ~ **heel** Gummiabsatz, *(detective, sl.)* Privatdetektiv; ~ **industry** Gummiindustrie; ~ **shares** Gummiwerte, -aktien; ~ **stamp** Gummistempel, *(innocent agent)* willenloses Werkzeug, *(stereotyped expres-*

sion) Klischee; ~-**stamp** *(v.)* sich genau nach den Vorschriften richten; ~-**stamp** *(v.)* **a candidate** einem Kandidaten die Zustimmung erteilen; ~-**stamp commitments** *(US sl.)* Zahlungsverpflichtungen routinemäßig erledigen; ~-**stamp parliament** Parlament von Jasagern; ~ **truncheon** Gummiknüppel; ~ **tyre (tire,** *US)* Gummireifen.

rubberneck *(US sl.)* neugieriger Tourist;
~ *(v.)* Stielaugen machen, sich den Hals verrenken;
~ **waggon** *(sl.)* Aussichtsbus.

rubbing strip Schonstreifen.

rubbish Kehrricht, Müll, Schutt, Ramsch, Altmaterial, *(coll.)* Schund, wertloses Zeug;
to shoot ~ Müll abladen;
no ~ **may be dumped here** Schuttabladen verboten;
~ **chute** Müllschlucker; ~ **collection** Müllabfuhr; ~ **dump** Deponie, Müllhalde; ~ **heap** Schutthaufen; ~ **hunter** Lumpensammler.

rubble Trümmer, Schutt;
~ **clearing** Trümmerbeseitigung; ~ **floor** Estrich.

rubric Rubrik, *(heading)* Überschrift, Titelkopf, *(law)* Gesetzestitel, Rubrik;
~ **of a statute** Gesetzestitel;
~ *(a.)* rot angestrichen, gedruckt.

rubricate *(v.)* rubrizieren, mit Rubriken versehen, rot anstreichen.

rubricated mit Rubriken versehen;
~ **letters** Buchstaben in roter Schrift.

rubrication Rubrizierung.

ruck, the common die große Masse;
to get out of the ~ sich hocharbeiten; **to rise out of the** ~ sich über den Durchschnitt erheben.

rucksack Rucksack.

rudder Steuer, Ruder, *(plane)* Seitenruder.

rude ungebildet, primitiv, unzivilisiert, unkultiviert;
~ **classification** grobe Unterteilung; ~ **fare** Rohkost; **to write in a** ~ **hand** ungelenke Handschrift haben; **to be in** ~ **health** vor Gesundheit strotzen; ~ **observer** flüchtiger Beobachter; ~ **ore** Roherz; ~ **produce** Rohprodukt; **to say** ~ **things** unfreundliche Worte gebrauchen.

rudiments Grundlage, Anfangsgründe, Ansätze, Vorkenntnisse.

rudimentary elementar;
~ **knowledge** rudimentäre Kenntnisse.

rue *(v.)* **a bargain** Geschäft rückgängig machen wollen.

ruffle Störung;
without ~ **or excitement** ohne große Aufregung;
~ *(v.)* **a book** Buch flüchtig durchblättern; ~ **paper** Papier zerknüllen.

rug kleiner Teppich, Bettvorlage, Brücke, *(Br.)* Wolldecke;
travelling ~ Reisedecke;
~ *(v.)* **cut** *(sl.)* sich den Eintritt erschleichen;
to sweep under the ~ *(fig.)* unter den Teppich kehren;
~ **joint** *(sl.)* eleganter Nachtklub.

ruin *(building)* Trümmerhaufen, Ruine, *(fig.)* Ruin, finanzieller Zusammenbruch;
~**s** Trümmer;
blue ~ *(sl.)* komplette Pleite;
~ **of a country** Ruin eines Landes;
~ *(v.)* ruinieren, zugrunde richten, zerrütten;
~ **the crop** Ernte zerstören (ruinieren); ~ **good English** englische Sprache verhunzen; ~ **s. one's plans** jds. Pläne zunichte machen; ~ **s. one's prospects** jds. Zukunft ruinieren; ~ **s. one's good reputation** Rufmord an jem. begehen;
to be faced with ~ vor dem Ruin stehen; **to be on the brink of** ~ kurz vor dem Zusammenbruch stehen; **to be in** ~**s** ruiniert sein; **to bring to a total** ~ in Grund und Boden wirtschaften; **to fall into** ~ zur Ruine werden; **to go to** ~ zugrunde gehen; **to lay in** ~**s** in Schutt und Asche legen; **to lie in** ~**s** in Trümmern liegen.

ruined, to be ruiniert sein; **to get** ~ zugrunde gehen.

ruinous *(building)* baufällig;
~ **expenditure** ruinöser Aufwand; ~ **heap** Trümmerhaufen; **to live in a** ~ **old house** in einem alten und zerfallenen Haus wohnen; ~ **price** ruinöser Preis, Schleuder-, Verlustpreis; ~ **project** halsbrecherisches Unternehmen; ~ **sale** Verlustkauf; ~ **state** Baufälligkeit.

ruinously high prices mörderisch hohe Preise.

rule Regal, Richtlinie, *(king)* Herrschaft, Regierung, *(determined method)* Lehrsatz, *(prescription, US)* Ausführungs-, Rechtsverordnung, Vorschrift, Verfügung, Verwaltungsvorschrift, [gesetzliche] Bestimmung, Richtsatz, *(print.)* Kolumnenmaß, *(ruler)* Meßstab, Lineal, *(usage)* Usance, Regel, [Handels]-brauch, Normalfall;

according to the ~**s** bestimmungsgemäß; **against the** ~**s** regel-, vorschriftswidrig; **as a** ~ in der Regel; **by** ~ **of thumb** überschläglich, über den Daumen gepeilt; **contrary to the** ~**s** den Bestimmungen zuwider, bestimmungs-, regelwidrig; **during the** ~ **of** während der Regierung; **to** ~ laut Vorschrift; **under the** ~**s** *(stock exchange)* börsenmäßig;
~**s** Bestimmungen, *(law court)* Geschäftsordnung, Verfahrensregeln, Prozeßvorschriften;
absolute ~ *(Br.)* unanfechtbare (endgültige) Entscheidung, rechtskräftige Verfügung, *(ruler)* unumschränkte Herrschaft; **common** ~**s** Richtlinien; **conflicting** ~**s** widersprechende Vorschriften, Kollisionsnormen; **contra proferentem** ~ Rechtssatz der Auslegung gegen den Urkundenaussteller; ~ **discharged** Verfügung aufgehoben; **fixed** ~ feststehende Regel; **folding** ~ Zollstock; **foreign** ~ Fremdherrschaft; **foreign** ~**s** fremde Usancen; **formal** ~**s** Formal-, Formvorschriften; **fundamental** ~ Grundregel; **general** ~**s** allgemeine Verfahrensvorschriften; **guiding** ~ Richtlinien; **hard and fast** ~ feststehende Regel, absolut bindende Vorschrift, strenger Handelsbrauch; **iron-clad** ~ unumstößliche Regel; **joint** ~ *(parl., US)* gemeinsame Geschäftsordnung; **judge's** ~**s** *(Br.)* Verhörrichtlinien; ~ **laid down** aufgestellter Rechtsgrundsatz; **majority** ~ *(election)* Mehrheitsherrschaft, -system, Grundsatz der Mehrheitsentscheidung; **white minority** ~ alleinige Regierungsherrschaft der weißen Minderheit; **ten-minute** ~ *(parl.)* Kurzdebatte; **mob** ~ Pöbelherrschaft; ~ **nisi** *(law, Br.)* vorläufiger Beschluß, vorläufige gerichtliche Anordnung, Vorbehaltsbeschluß; **optional** ~ Kannvorschrift; ~ **practice** ~**s** Verfahrensvorschriften; **peremptory** ~ zwingende Vorschrift; **procedural** ~**s** Verfahrens-, Prozeßordnung; **shop** ~**s** Betriebssatzung; **slide** ~ Rechenschieber; **special** ~ verfahrensmäßige Sonderregelung, *(law court)* Verweisung an den Einzelrichter; **standing** ~**s** Geschäftsordnung, Satzung;
golden ~ **of accumulation** optimale Investitionsquote; ~ **against accumulation** Thesaurierungsverbot; ~**s of action** Verhaltungsmaßregeln; ~**s for admission** Zulassungsbedingungen; ~ **of agency** Haftung für den Erfüllungsgehilfen; ~**s of the air** Luftverkehrsordnung; ~ **of apportionment** *(subdivided tract)* Ausgleichsbestimmung; ~**s of assessment** Veranlagungsrichtlinien, Steuerrichtlinien; **golden** ~**s of banking** goldene Bankregeln; ~**s of bankruptcy** Konkursvorschriften; ~**s of a brokerage board** Vorschriften des Maklerausschusses; ~**s and byelaws** Satzung, Statuten; ~**s of a cartel** Kartellvorschriften; ~ **of comity** Grundsatz der Gegenseitigkeit; ~**s of Conciliation and Arbitration** *(International Chamber of Commerce)* Vergleichs- und Schiedsgerichtsordnung; ~**s of conduct** Verhaltensmaßregeln; ~**s of courteous conduct** allgemeine Anstandsregeln; ~ **of construction** Auslegungsregel; ~**s of contract** Vertragsvorschriften, -bestimmungen; ~ **of conversion** Umrechnungsregeln; ~ **of course** *(judge)* antragsgemäß erlassene Verfügung; ~ **of court** gerichtliche Entscheidung; **general (standing)** ~**s of court** Verfahrensbestimmungen, Prozeßordnung; ~**s for a credit** Kreditrichtlinien; **liberalized** ~**s on depreciation** günstige Abschreibungsmodalitäten; ~**s of disclosure** Offenlegungsbestimmungen; ~ **of evidence** Beweisregel, Beweisvorschrift; ~**s of exchange** Börsenordnung; ~**s on expense-account spending** Spesenrichtlinien; ~ **of fashion** Tyrannei der Mode; ~ **of force** Gewaltherrschaft; ~**s of good forms** Anstandsregeln; ~**s which govern** Vorschriften über; ~**s of the house** Hausordnung; ~**s of good husbandry** *(Br.)* Regeln einer ordnungsgemäßen Bewirtschaftung; ~**s of interpretation** Auslegungsregeln; ~ **of law** Rechtsnorm, -grundsatz, -vorschrift, -staatlichkeit; **positive** ~ **of law** positive Rechtsvorschrift; ~**s of navigation** internationale Schiffahrtsregeln; ~ **of order** Verhandlungsrichtlinien, *(parl.)* Geschäftsordnung; ~ **of partnership** Gesellschaftsrechnung; ~**s of pension** Pensionsrichtlinien; ~ **of the people** Herrschaft des Volkes; ~ **against perpetuities** Fideikommißverbot; ~ **to plead** prozeßleitende Verfügung; ~**s of practice** Prozeß-, Verfahrensordnung, Verfahrensvorschriften; ~**s of civil practice** Zivilprozeßordnung; ~ **for the prevention of accidents** Unfallverhütungsvorschriften; ~**s of a prison** Außenbezirk eines Gefängnisses; ~**s of procedure** Verfahrensregeln; **standing** ~**s of procedure** Satzung; **Federal** ~**s of Civil Procedure** *(US)* Zivilprozeßordnung; **Federal** ~**s of Criminal Procedure** *(US)* Strafprozeßordnung; ~ **of proof** Beweisregeln; ~ **of property** Eigentumsgrundsatz; ~ **of reason** Vernunftregel, *(antitrust law, US)* Grundsatz wirtschaftlich vernünftiger Regelung; ~**s and regulations** Durchführungsbestimmungen; ~ **of relation back** *(bankruptcy)* Zurückbeziehungsgrundsatz; ~**[s] of the road** *(US)* Verkehrsregeln; **Inland** ~**s of the Road** *(US)* Wasserstraßenverkehrsordnung; **International** ~**s of the Road**

Seestraßenordnung; ~ **to show cause** Ladung mit Aufforderung zur Klagebegründung; ~**s of the stock exchange** Börsenordnung; ~**s of taxation** Besteuerungsvorschriften, Steuerrichtlinien; ~ **of thumb** Faustregel, Erfahrungsmethode, Überschlagsrechnung; ~**s of work** Arbeitsrichtlinien;
~ *(v.) (direct)* anordnen, bestimmen, verfügen, regeln, festsetzen, *(be in force)* gelten, in Kraft sein, *(govern)* regieren, herrschen, *(law)* regeln, entscheiden, Entscheidung treffen, Gerichtsbeschluß verkünden, festsetzen, *(paper)* liniieren, *(prices)* notieren, stehen, sich stellen;
~ **around 7 1/2%** zu etwa 7 1/2% umgehen; ~ **easier** *(prices)* abgeschwächt liegen; ~ **in s. one's favo(u)r** zu jds. Gunsten entscheiden; ~ **in favo(u)r of credits** *(US)* Steuerfreibeträge einräumen; ~ **high** *(prices)* hoch liegen, hohes Kursniveau haben; ~ **higher** sich höher stellen; ~ **low** niedrig liegen; ~ **lower** *(prices)* niedriger stehen; ~ **nominally** nur dem Namen nach Herrscher sein; ~ **off an account** Konto abschließen; ~ **off a column of figures** Zahlenkolonne durch eine Linie abteilen; ~ **out** ausschließen, *(US)* für unzulässig erklären, ablehnen; ~ **s. o. out of order** jem. das Wort entziehen; ~ **s. th. out of order** etw. für regelwidrig erklären; ~ **a motion out of order** Antrag von der Tagesordnung absetzen; ~ **out a possibility** Möglichkeit ausschließen; ~ **out the right to associate** Vereinigungsrecht aufheben; ~ **over a country** Land beherrschen, über ein Land herrschen; ~ **that a question is out of order** *(judge)* Frage nicht zulassen; ~ **the roost** Kommando führen, das Wort haben, tonangebend sein, *(wife)* die Hosen anhaben; ~ **with a rod of iron** mit eiserner Hand regieren; ~ **steady** *(prices)* sich halten; **to adopt** ~**s** Richtlinien aufstellen; **to adopt the** ~**s of procedure** Geschäftsordnung beschließen; **to be the** ~ vorgeschrieben sein; **to become the** ~ zur Regel werden; **to bend the** ~**s** Spielregeln zu seinen Gunsten auslegen; **to break a** ~ Regel verletzen; **to break the** ~ **of a cartel** gegen eine Kartellvereinbarung verstoßen; **to continue to** ~ **high** weiterhin hohe Kurse behaupten (hoch notieren); **to continue to** ~ **low** weiterhin niedrig notieren; **to discharge a** ~ Beschluß aufheben; **to draw up the** ~**s of procedure** Geschäftsordnung aufstellen; **to fix the** ~**s of procedure** sich eine Geschäftsordnung geben; **to grant a** ~ Entscheidung erlassen (fällen); **to lay down** ~**s** Regeln aufstellen; **to loosen** ~**s on depreciation** Abschreibungsmodalitäten lockern; **to make it a** ~ regelmäßig tun; **to obey the** ~**s of the game** Spielregeln befolgen (einhalten); **to observe a** ~ Regel beachten; **to observe the** ~**s of procedure** Geschäftsordnung einhalten; **to operate a crude** ~ **of thumb** über den Daumen kalkulieren; **to revamp** ~**s** Richtlinien überholen; **to serve as a** ~ als Richtschnur dienen; **to state a** ~ Regel festlegen; **to stick to the** ~**s** sich genau an die Vorschriften halten; **to transgress a** ~ gegen eine Regel verstoßen; **to violate** ~**s regarding charter operations** gegen Vorschriften für Charterfluggesellschaften verstoßen; **to work to** ~ *(labo(u)rers)* Bestimmungen übergenau einhalten, genau (streng) nach Vorschrift arbeiten, Dienst nach Vorschrift tun;
~~**book** Kodex, *(plant)* Arbeitsordnung; **approved of trade-union** ~ **book** *(Br.)* anerkanntes Gewerkschaftsstatut; ~ **change** Richtlinienänderung; ~**s committee** *(parl., US)* Geschäftsordnungsausschuß, Ältestenrat; ~**-day** Tag des Inkrafttretens; ~~**of-thumb ratio** über den Daumen gepeilter Verteilungsschlüssel.
ruled liniiert;
to be ~ **by s. o.** unter jds. Einfluß stehen;
~ **case** entschiedene Sache; ~ **frame** Linienumrandung; ~ **paper** liniiertes Papier, Linienpapier.
ruler Herrscher, Machthaber, Regent, Fürst, *(strip of wood)* Lineal.
rulership Regierung, Herrschaft.
ruling Entscheidung, Entschließung, Regelung, Bescheid, *(drawing ruled lines)* Liniierung, *(law court)* richterliche Verfügung (Entscheidung), Bescheid;
court (judicial) ~ gerichtliche Verfügung, gerichtliche Entscheidung, Gerichtsbeschluß;
~ **of the court** Gerichtsentscheidung, -beschluß;
to give a ~ **in favo(u)r of s. o.** [Gerichts]entscheidung zu jds. Gunsten fällen; **to make a** ~ Entscheidung fällen;
~ *(a.)* regierend, herrschend, *(economics)* bestehend, geltend; ~ **case** maßgebliche Entscheidung, Präzedenzfall; ≙ **Case Law** *(US)* Entscheidungssammlung, ~ **classes** privilegierte (herrschende) Klassen; ~ **house** Herrscherhaus; ~ **party** an der Macht befindliche Partei; ~ **pen** Reißfeder; ~ **price** gegenwärtiger (geltender) Preis, Tages-, Markt-, Durchschnittspreis; **to be the** ~ **spirit in a firm** maßgebender Kopf eines Unternehmens sein.

rum Rum, *(US)* Alkohol;
~ *(a.) (Br., sl.)* eigenartig, sonderbar;
~ **customer** gefährlicher Kunde; ~ **go** dumme Sache (Geschichte); ~ **hole** *(sl.)* Destille, Kneipe; ~ **lot** komischer Verein.
rumble *(carriage)* Rattern, *(place for luggage)* Gepäckraum;
~ **of cannon** Kanonendonner;
~ *(v.)* rattern, *(sl.)* auf die Schliche kommen;
~ **seat** *(car)* Not-, Klappsitz.
ruminate *(v.)* **about recent events** letzte Ereignisse Revue passieren lassen.
rummage Ausschuß, Ramsch, Ausschuß-, Restwaren, *(search by customs officials)* zollamtliche Durchsuchung, Zolluntersuchung;
~ *(v.)* durchsuchen;
~ **around** herumstöbern; ~ **a dictionary for a satisfactory word** Wörterbuch nach einem passenden Wort durchstöbern; ~ **out** hervorkramen; ~ **among old papers** in alten Akten (Papieren) herumkramen; ~ **a ship** *(Br.)* Schiff zollamtlich untersuchen; ~ **goods** Ausschußware; ~ **sale** Fundsachenversteigerung, Ramschverkauf, *(sale for charity)* Wohltätigkeitsbasar.
rummaging *(of ship)* Zolluntersuchung.
rumo(u)r Gerücht, Gerede;
persistent ~ hartnäckiges Gerücht; **unfounded** ~**s** haltlose Gerüchte;
~**s of war** Kriegsgerüchte;
~ *(v.)* Gerücht verbreiten, gerüchteweise berichten;
to spread a ~ Gerücht ausstreuen (kolportieren); **to set a** ~ **afloat** Gerücht aufbringen;
~ **has it** dem Vernehmen nach.
rump Überbleibsel, Rest;
~ **cabinet** Rumpfkabinett; ~ **caucus** Rumpfversammlung; ~ **grouping** Rumpfgruppierung; ~ **parliament** Rumpfparlament.
rumple *(complaint, sl.)* Beschwerde bei der Polizei.
rumpus Krawall, Tumult;
to have a ~ **with s. o.** Krach mit jem. haben;
~ **room** *(US)* Hobbyraum.
rumrunner *(US)* [Alkohol]schmuggler, *(ship)* Schmugglerschiff.
rumrunning *(US)* Alkoholschmuggel.
run Lauf, *(airplane)* Rollstrecke, *(circulation)* [Zeitungs]auflage, *(class of goods)* Sorte, Qualität, *(course)* Lauf, Gang, Fortgang, *(great demand)* Absatz, Abgang, Vertrieb, starker Zulauf, starke Nachfrage, Ansturm, Andrang, Run, Zustrom, *(election campaign, US)* Wahlkampf, *(heavy fall)* plötzlicher Sturz, *(licence to make free use)* freies Verfügungsrecht, *(machine)* Arbeitsperiode, -zeit, *(military plane)* Bombenzielanflug, *(office)* Amtsdauer, *(output)* Betriebsleistung, -ausstoß, *(punch-card system)* Durchlauf, *(riot)* Auflauf, Aufruhr, Empörung, *(series)* Folge, Serie, Reihe, *(production series)* Fertigungsserie, *(stockings, US)* Laufmasche, *(in taxi)* Taxifahrt, *(tendency)* Tendenz, *(tenure of office)* Amtszeit, *(short visit)* kurzer Besuch, Abstecher, Flitztour, *(theater)* Aufführungszeitraum, *(validity)* Gültigkeitsdauer, Laufzeit, *(watercourse, US)* Bach-, Strombett;
in the long ~ auf lange Sicht gesehen, langfristig; **on the** ~ immer auf dem Trapp, *(enemy)* auf der Flucht; **still on the** ~ immer noch flüchtig; **with a** ~ plötzlich, auf einmal;
common ~ Durchschnittsklasse; **full-power** ~ Probelauf mit voller Kraft; **general** ~ allgemeine Mode; **great** ~ starke Nachfrage; **inaugural** ~ Jungfernfahrt; **ordinary** ~ Durchschnitt, Allgemeinheit; **net press** ~ Gesamtauflage; **quite a little** ~ recht gute Nachfrage; **trial** ~ Versuchs-, Probefahrt, Probelauf;
~ **on a bank** Ansturm auf eine Bank, Bankpanik; ~ **of business** Geschäftsgang; **ordinary** ~ **of buyers** übliche Käuferschicht; ~ **of creditors** Zudrang (Ansturm) der Gläubiger; ~ **of customers** Kundenansturm; ~ **of disasters** Katastrophenserie; ~ **of events** Gang der Ereignisse; **full** ~ **of figures** gesamtes Zahlenmaterial; **first** ~ **of a film** Filmpremiere; ~ **of a library** Mitbenutzung einer Bibliothek; ~ **of luck** Glückssträhne; ~ **of bad luck** Pechsträhne; **common** ~ **of man** Durchschnittsmensch; **the common** ~ **of mankind** Durchschnittsmenschen; ~ **of the market** Marktverlauf; ~~**of-the-mill** Durchschnittserzeugnis, mittlere Durchschnittsqualität; ~ **of mine** Fördernetz; ~ **of misfortune** Unglücksserie, Pechsträhne; **a** ~ **for one's money** etw. für sein Geld; ~ **in office** Amtsdauer; ~ **of a paper** Ausgabe einer Zeitung; ~ **of paper position** *(advertising)* ohne Platzanweisung, Plazierung erfolgt durch die Redaktion; **trial** ~ **of a plant** Probelauf einer Fabrik; ~ **on oil stocks** ungeheure Nachfrage nach (Sturm auf) Erdölaktien; ~ **of one's teeth** freie Kost; **normal** ~ **of things** üblicher Gang der Dinge; ~ **of validity** Gültigkeitsdauer; ~ **of dry weather** Trockenheitsperiode;

~ *(v.)* *(circulate)* [um]laufen, in Umlauf sein, *(customers)* Run veranstalten, *(become due)* laufen, fällig werden, *(be in force)* gelten, gültig sein, Geltung (Rechtskraft) haben, *(function)* funktionieren, laufen, gehen, arbeiten, im Betrieb sein, *(letter)* lauten, *(operate)* betreiben, *(pass)* verlaufen, *(price)* sich stellen [auf], *(railway)* in Betrieb sein, gehen, [Züge] verkehren lassen, *(rumo(u)r)* umlaufen, zirkulieren, *(time)* verstreichen, verfließen, vergehen, *(train)* fahren, *(to be worded)* lauten.

run *(v.)* **about the streets** sich auf der Straße herumtreiben.

run *(v.)* **across** begegnen;
~ **an old friend** alten Freund wiedertreffen.

run *(v.)* **against** | **s. o.** als jds. Gegenkandidat auftreten; ~ **s. one's interests** jds. Interessen zuwiderlaufen; ~ **the political machine** gegen die Parteiorganisation Sturm laufen; ~ **stock against one's clients** *(Br.)* Aktien seiner Auftraggeber aufkaufen; ~ **one's head the wall** *(fig.)* mit dem Kopf gegen die Wand laufen.

run *(v.)* | **aground** *(ship)* auflaufen, stranden; ~ **at pari** *(shares)* Pari stehen.

run *(v.)* **at** | **about 22% a year** *(inflation)* jährlich um 22% steigen; ~ **less than a third of the early 1970s level** nur noch knapp 1/3 des 1970er Umfangs betragen; ~ **par** *(shares)* Pari stehen; ~ **a profit** mit Gewinn arbeiten.

run *(v.)* **away** flüchten, durchbrennen;
~ **from s. o.** jem. aus dem Wege gehen; ~ **from home** von zu Hause weglaufen; ~ **with a lot of ratepayers' money** erhebliche kommunale Mittel verschlingen; ~ **with the show** *(theater)* größten Publikumserfolg haben; ~ **from a subject** von einem Thema abschweifen.

run *(v.)* **counter** *(interests)* sich kreuzen, gegeneinanderstehen, *(tendency)* entgegenlaufen.

run *(v.)* **down** herunterwirtschaften, *(prices)* drücken;
~ **s. o. down** j. schlecht machen; ~ **a battery** Batterie erschöpfen; ~ **the coast** Küste entlangfahren; ~ **a criminal** Verbrecher aufbringen (in die Enge treiben); ~ **the goods of a competitor** Konkurrenzware anschwärzen; ~ **to rock bottom** absoluten Tiefstand erreichen; **to be** ~ **by a lorry** von einem Lastwagen angefahren werden.

run *(v.)* **for** | **It** ausreißen, sich aus dem Staube machen; ~ **an office** kandidieren; ~ **parliament** für das Unterhaus kandidieren; ~ **a position** sich um einen Posten bewerben; ~ **the presidency** *(US)* als Präsident kandidieren, sich um das Präsidentenamt bewerben; ~ **profit** auf Renditebasis betreiben; ~ **reelection** sich zur Wiederwahl stellen.

run *(v.)* **from** | **... through** *(US)* sich erstrecken von ... bis; ~ **50 p to a Pound** von 50 p bis zu einem Pfund variieren.

run *(v.)* **immediately** *(statute of limitations)* sofort zu laufen beginnen.

run *(v.)* **in** *(car)* einfahren, *(candidate)* durchbringen, *(criminal)* festnehmen, dingfest machen, einsperren, *(manuscript)* kürzer werden, *(motor)* sich einlaufen;
~ **the blood** in der Familie liegen; ~ **a new car** neuen Wagen einfahren.

run *(v.)* **into** sich belaufen;
~ **a car a garage** Auto in die Garage fahren; ~ **a credit crisis** in eine Kreditkrise geraten; ~ **debt** in Schulden geraten, Schulden machen, sich in Schulden stürzen; ~ **debt again** sich erneut verschulden; ~ **six editions** sechs Auflagen erleben; ~ **s. o. into unnecessary expenses** jem. unnötige Ausgaben verursachen; ~ **five figures** fünfstelligen Betrag ausmachen; ~ **an old friend** ganz unerwartet einen alten Freund treffen; ~ **heavy selling** sich schwer verkaufen lassen; ~ **letters into a file** Briefe abheften; ~ **losses** sich in Verluste stürzen; ~ **a lot of money** sehr teuer werden; ~ **money** *(coll.)* ins Geld gehen; ~ **port for supplies of food** zur Verproviantierung in den Hafen einlaufen; ~ **very large sums** sehr ins Geld gehen; ~ **thousands** sich auf Tausende belaufen; ~ **trouble** in Schwierigkeiten geraten.

run *(v.)* **low** auf die Neige gehen, knapp werden, ausgehen.

run *(v.)* **off** weglaufen, sich davonmachen, *(clear)* (Lager) räumen, *(bill of exchange)* ablaufen, fällig werden, *(prices)* im Preis sinken, *(print.)* abdrucken lassen, *(stock exchange)* rückläufig sein;
~ **an article for the local newspaper** Artikel für die Lokalzeitung schreiben; ~ **with the cash** mit der Kasse durchgehen (durchbrennen); ~ **copies** Abschriften herstellen; ~ **copies of a report** Bericht vervielfältigen; ~ **a first printing of 100.000 copies** Erstauflage von 100.000 Stück drucken; ~ **a hundred copies on the duplicating machine** hundert Abzüge mit der Kopiermaschine anfertigen; ~ **with all funds** *(treasurer)* mit der ganzen Kasse durchbrennen; ~ **a letter on the typewriter** Brief auf der Schreibmaschine herunterrasseln; ~ **with s. one's luggage** *(Br.)* jem. das Gepäck stehlen; ~ **the mouth** *(sl.)* zu viel

quasseln; ~ **the rails** entgleisen; ~ **readily** guten Absatz finden; ~ **a speech** Ansprache herunterrasseln; ~ **standard batteries** mit normalen Batterien betrieben werden.

run *(v.)* **on** *(debts)* auflaufen, *(decree)* in Kraft bleiben, *(print.)* ohne Absatz fortlaufen, fortlaufend setzen;
~ **politics** *(conversation)* sich um Politik drehen; ~ **time** pünktlich verkehren; ~ **pretty well time** Fahrplan ziemlich pünktlich einhalten.

run *(v.)* **out** *(contract)* auslaufen, *(lease)* ablaufen, *(loan)* erschöpft werden, *(passport)* ablaufen, *(print.)* mehr Satz als berechnet ergeben, *(stock)* zu Ende gehen, ausgehen, versiegen, alle werden;
~ **of cash** sich ganz verausgabt haben; ~ **of control** außer Rand und Band geraten; ~ **of funds** keine Mittel mehr zur Verfügung haben; ~ **of gas** *(fig.)* in der Wirkung verpuffen; ~ **of gasoline** *(US)* kein Benzin mehr haben; ~ **it out** *(sl.)* sich verdächtig machen; ~ **of port** aus dem Hafen auslaufen; ~ **into the sea** *(pier)* sich in die See erstrecken; ~ **of steam** keine Puste (Energiereserven) mehr haben;
to be ~ ausverkauft sein; **to have** ~ **its strings** abgelaufen (im Abklingen) sein.

run *(v.)* **over** *(examine)* durchsehen, *(print.)* überlaufen, im Druck zu viel ergeben, *(vehicle)* überfahren;
~ **s. o.** *(sl.)* j. überfahren; ~ **one's accounts** seine Konten durchgehen; ~ **to a neighbo(u)r's house** zum Nachbarn herüberlaufen; ~ **one's notes** sich seine Notizen noch einmal ansehen; ~ **one's part again** seine Rolle noch einmal durchgehen;
to be ~ überfahren werden.

run *(v.)* **through** | **an account** Rechnung überfliegen, überrechnen; ~ **one's mail** seine Post durchsehen; ~ **one's property** sein Vermögen durchbringen; ~ **one's work** sich mit einer Arbeit beeilen.

run *(v.)* **to** sich belaufen auf;
~ **a holiday** sich eine Ferienreise leisten; ~ **a pretty penny** anständige Stange Geld kosten.

run *(v.)* **up** sich summieren, auflaufen, *(force up prices)* hinauftreiben, in die Höhe schrauben, überbieten, *(rise in price)* im Preise steigen, anziehen;
~ **an account** auf Rechnung kaufen, *(bill)* anschreiben (Schuldkonto anwachsen) lassen; ~ **against s. o.** mit jem. Streit bekommen; ~ **against difficulties** plötzlich Schwierigkeiten bekommen; ~ **to betragen**, sich beziffern auf; ~ **the bidding** *(auction)* Angebote hinauftreiben; ~ **a big bill in a hotel** große Hotelrechnung machen; ~ **bills in a store** *(US)* in einem Geschäft anschreiben lassen; ~ **the costs** Kosten steigern; ~ **debts** sich in Schulden stürzen, Schulden anwachsen lassen; ~ **a flag** Flagge hissen (aufziehen); ~ **a score** anschreiben lassen; ~ **into thousands** in die Tausende gehen; ~ **s. o. to town** j. zur Stadt fahren;
to let the arrears ~ Rückstände auflaufen lassen.

run *(v.)* **upon thge rocks** *(ship)* auflaufen.

run *(v.)* **with** übereinstimmen, konform gehen;
~ **a heavy hand** mit harter Hand regieren; ~ **the land** dinglich mit dem Grundstück verbunden sein, *(restrictive covenant)* auf einem Grundstück lasten.

run *(v.)* | **an account with a shop** bei einem Laden auf Rechnung einkaufen, anschreiben lassen; ~ **an ad** *(US)* Anzeige laufen haben; ~ **to s. one's aid** jem. zu Hilfe kommen; ~ **ashore** stranden; ~ **the blockade** Blockade durchbrechen; ~ **a book** anschreiben lassen; ~ **a bus company** *(US)* Omnibusunternehmen betreiben; ~ **a business** Gewerbe betreiben; ~ **a candidate** Kandidaten aufstellen; ~ **s. th. on candle ends and bits of string** mit fast Nichts auskommen; ~ **a car** Auto unterhalten; ~ **a car on one's small salary** sich mit seinem kleinen Gehalt ein Auto leisten; ~ **a car at small cost** wenig Geld für sein Auto ausgeben; ~ **a good chance** gute Aussichten haben; ~ **cheaply** billige Fahrpreise haben; ~ **in connection with** *(train)* Anschluß haben; ~ **the country** außer Landes flüchten; ~ **a country's economy** Volkswirtschaft eines Landes steuern; ~ **a country's foreign policy** für die auswärtige Politik eines Landes verantwortlich sein; ~ **its course** seinen Verlauf nehmen; ~ **day and night** *(trains)* Tag und Nacht verkehren; ~ **debts** Schulden machen; ~ **to earth** aufstöbern; ~ **in an election** bei einer Wahl kandidieren; ~ **errands** Botengänge machen; ~ **a factory** Fabrik betreiben; ~ **a factory at a loss** in einer Fabrik mit Verlust arbeiten; ~ **things fine** seine Zeit restlos ausnutzen; ~ **by fits and starts** nur unregelmäßig verkehren; ~ **flat** *(business)* auf niedrigen Touren laufen, auf Sparflamme kochen; ~ **flat-out** auf Hochtouren laufen; ~ **one's fortune** sein Glück versuchen; ~ **foul of each other** *(ships)* miteinander kollidieren; ~ **foul of the police** mit der Polizei in Konflikt geraten; ~ **from 8 - 13** von 8 - 13 Uhr dauern; ~ **in the general election** bei der Wahl

kandidieren; ~ **a group of people** Mitarbeiterstab leiten; ~ **high** *(prices)* gestiegen sein; ~ **a hotel** Hotel leiten; ~ **the hose over a car** Wagen abspritzen; ~ **every hour** *(train)* alle Stunden verkehren; ~ **sixty miles an hour** 100 Kilometer in der Stunde fahren; ~ **s. one's house** jem. den Haushalt führen; ~ **a red light** rotes Licht überfahren, bei Rot über die Kreuzung (Ampel) fahren; ~ **a cheap line** billige Artikel verkaufen; ~ **lines of credit** Kreditlinie in Anspruch nehmen; ~ **low** *(provisions)* knapp werden, ausgehen; ~ **for luck** *(US)* etw. auf gut Glück versuchen; ~ **to meet one's troubles** sich im voraus Sorgen machen; ~ **messages** Botengänge erledigen; ~ **every ten minutes** *(train)* alle 10 Minuten verkehren; ~ **a newspaper** Zeitung herausgeben; ~ **an organization on a sound financial basis** Unternehmen nach gesunden finanzpolitischen Grundsätzen leiten; ~ **properly** *(machine)* gut laufen; ~ **red with ink** *(US)* Defizit aufweisen; ~ **riot** Amok laufen; ~ **a risk** Risiko laufen, Wagnis eingehen; ~ **a rumo(u)r back to its source** Gerücht bis zu seinem Ursprung (seiner Quelle) zurückverfolgen; ~ **a sandy on s. o.** *(US sl.)* j. an der Nase herumführen; ~ **on schedule** *(US)* fahrplanmäßig verkehren; ~ **a score** anschreiben lassen; ~ **a service of trains between two places** Zugverkehr zwischen zwei Plätzen einrichten; ~ **short** knapp werden, zur Neige gehen, ausgehen; ~ **short of cash** schwache Kassenbestände haben; ~ **short of money** sich verausgaben; ~ **the show** *(sl.)* den Boss abgeben, Sache schmeißen; ~ **past a signal** *(train)* Haltesignal überfahren; ~ **smoothly** ruhig verlaufen; ~ **a stand** Kiosk besitzen; ~ **state enterprises on economic lines** Erträge in Staatsbetrieben erwirtschaften; ~ **a stop sign** Haltesignal überfahren; ~ **a temperature** Fieber (Temperatur) haben; ~ **a poor third in the race** gerade noch Dritter werden; ~ **extra trains** Sonderzüge einsetzen; ~ **twice a week** *(train, bus)* zweimal wöchentlich verkehren; ~ **pretty well on time** Fahrplanzeit ziemlich genau einhalten; ~ **from one topic to another** von einem Thema zum anderen überspringen; ~ **true to form** sich konformgerecht verhalten, den Erwartungen entsprechen; ~ **like wildfire** sich blitzschnell (wie ein Lauffeuer) verbreiten; ~ **only a year** *(lease)* nur über ein Jahr laufen; **to be on the** ~ auf der Flucht sein; **to be much (greatly)** ~ **after** großen Zulauf haben; **to be in the** ~ *(US)* im Rennen liegen, kandidieren; **to be always on the** ~ immer auf den Beinen sein; **to be out (outside) of the common** ~ besser als der Durchschnitt sein; **to be** ~ **at small cost** *(car)* billig im Betrieb sein; **to come down with a** ~ *(prices)* ruckartig fallen; **to give a** ~ probieren; **to give a free** ~ freie Hand lassen; **to give s. o. a** ~ **for his money** jem. für sein Geld etw. bieten; **to give s. o. the** ~ **of the garden** j. seinen Garten mitbenutzen lassen; **to have** ~ *(period)* abgelaufen sein; **to have 30 days to** ~ *(bill)* 30 Tage Laufzeit haben; **to have s. o. on the** ~ jem. Beine machen; **to have a great** ~ großen Zulauf haben; **to have come down with a** ~ *(prices)* plötzlich gefallen sein; **to have a good** ~ **of business** gute Geschäfte machen; **to have a great** ~ großen Zulauf haben; **to have a long** ~ lange im Amt bleiben, *(fashion)* lange modern sein, *(play)* lange auf dem Spielplan stehen; **to have a** ~ **for one's money** auf seine Kosten kommen; **to have a** ~ **in the country** Ausflug aufs Land unternehmen (machen); **to have the** ~ **of a house** in einem Haus ein- und ausgehen; **to have the** ~ **of a thing** freien Zugang zu etw. haben; **to have a considerable** ~ sehr gefragt sein; **to have a** ~ **of ill-luck** Pechsträhne haben; **to pay in the long** ~ sich auf die Dauer bezahlt machen; **to live within a few seconds** ~ **of the station** in unmittelbarer Nähe des Bahnhofs wohnen; **to stop a** ~ **on deposits** Einlagensturm abstoppen; **to take off its usual** ~ von der üblichen Fahrtroute abziehen;
~ *(a.)* *(coll.)* geschmuggelt;
efficiently ~ wirkungsvoll geleitet;
~ **by a battery** von einer Batterie angetrieben.

run-down *(mil.)* Verminderung der Truppenstärke, Truppenverminderung, *(personnel)* Personalabbau, -reduzierung;
brief ~ Kurzfassung;
~ **of a naval establishment** Kürzung des Kriegsflottenpotentials;
~ *(a.)* heruntergekommen, abgewirtschaftet, *(battery)* erschöpft, entladen, verbraucht.

run-in fortlaufender Satz, *(cars)* Zusammenstoß, *(print.)* Einschiebsel, *(proofreading)* kein Absatz;
~ *(a.)* eingefügt, geschoben.

run|-of-the-mill guests Durchschnittsgäste; **~-of-the-mill work** *(film)* Durchschnittsfilme; **~-of paper** Anzeigenplazierung nach Wahl des Verlegers.

run-on *(print.)* angehängt, fortlaufend gesetzt;
~ **matter** glatter Satz; ~ **sentence** Bandwurmsatz.

run|-out *(proofreading)* Absatz; ~ **through** *(theater)* kurze (schnelle) Probe.

run-up *(airplane)* Anflug, *(motor car)* Probelauf;
high-cost ~ hoher Kostenaufwand;
~ **to an election** Vorfeld einer Wahl; ~ **in the money supply** Geldbedarfszunahme; ~ **of prices** *(US)* Kursanstieg, -steigerung.

runabout Herumtreiber, Landstreicher, *(car)* Kleinwagen;
~ **car** offener Zweisitzer; ~ **ticket** *(railway, Br.)* Netzkarte; ~ **utility vehicle** Kombiwagen.

runaround *(US)* Herumschicken, verzögerliche Behandlung, *(cliché)* Klischee einschließender Text;
to give s. o. the ~ *(US)* j. pausenlos hinhalten, j. von Pontius zu Pilatus schicken.

runaway Fahrbahn, Piste, Flüchtling, *(mil.)* Überläufer;
~ *(a.)* ausgerissen, fortgelaufen, *(convict)* entsprungen, flüchtig, *(economy)* schnellen Veränderungen unterworfen, *(prices)* schnell steigend;
~ **convict** entlaufender Sträfling; ~ **cost** schnell steigende Kosten; ~ **couple** durchgegangenes Liebespaar; ~ **inflation** zügellose (hemmungslose) Inflation; ~ **marriage (wedding)** Entführungsheirat; ~ **shop** Gewerbe im Umherziehen, Wandergewerbe; ~ **victory** Erdrutschsieg; ~ **visual range** Landebahnsicht.

runic *(print.)* Runenschrift.

runner Bote, Botengänger, Laufbursche, *(agent for steamship line)* Passagiermakler, *(driver, US)* Fahrer, Maschinist, *(manager, US)* Geschäftsführer, Unternehmer, *(mil.)* Meldegänger, *(retail store)* gängiger (glänzend gehender) Artikel, *(running-down action)* Verkehrs-, Unfallsache, *(salesman, US)* Handlungsreisender, Vertreter, *(smuggler, coll.)* Schmuggler[schiff], *(tout, Br.)* Schlepper, Kundenwerber;
bank ~ Bankbote; **blockade** ~ Blockadebrecher;
~-up Nächstplazierter, zweiter Preisträger;
not to be a big ~ kein großer Verkaufsschlager sein.

running *(currency)* Laufzeit, Gültigkeitsdauer, *(function)* Laufen, Lauf, Betrieb, *(lead)* Führung, Verwaltung, Aufsicht, *(operation)* Betreiben, *(trip)* Abstecher, Spritztour;
blockade ~ Blockadedurchbruch;
~ **in** *(car)* Einfahren; ~ **of an account** Kontoabwicklung; ~ **of a benefit** Geltungsdauer eines Nutzungsrechts; ~ **of the blockade** Blockadedurchbruch; ~ **of the border line** Grenzverlauf; ~ **of a burden** Laufzeit einer Belastung; ~ **of a country** Regieren eines Landes; ~ **into debt** Verschuldung; ~ **down** Anfahren; ~ **down of assets** Anlagenabbau, -verringerung; ~ **down the goods of a competitor** Anschwärzung von Konkurrenzerzeugnissen; ~ **down of an industry** Industrieabbau; ~ **down of reserves** rückläufige Reserven, Rücklagenverringerung; ~ **of a fleet** Fahrzeugeinsatz; ~ **the gauntlet** Spießrutenlaufen; ~ **with the land** dingliche Verbindung mit einem Grundstück; ~ **of a machine** Bedienung einer Maschine; ~ **of a period** Lauf einer Frist; ~ **of a risk** Eingehen eines Risikos; ~ **of a school** Leitung einer Schule; ~ **of the Statute of Limitations** Beginn der Verjährungsfrist; ~ **a decent postal system** Bereitstellung ausreichender postalischer Einrichtungen; ~ **of trains** Zugverkehr; ~ **of the universities** Universitätsbetrieb;
~ *(a.)* *(circulating)* zirkulierend, umlaufend, *(current)* laufend, offen, *(working)* in Betrieb;
~ **free** mit vollen Segeln; ~ **in** *(car)* wird eingefahren; ~ **with the land** mit dem Grundstück fest verbunden; ~ **at large** *(animal)* umherstreunend; ~ **with the reversion** mit dem Eigentumsrecht verbunden;
to alter the ~ **of trains** Zugfolge ändern; **to be** ~ im Betrieb sein, *(trains)* verkehren; **to be** ~ **at 60 miles an hour** *(train)* mit einer Geschwindigkeit von 100 km in der Stunde fahren; **to be** ~ **again** *(hotel)* wieder in Betrieb sein; **to be always** ~ **s. o. down** j. laufend anschwärzen; **to be in the** ~ gut im Rennen liegen; **to be out of the** ~ nicht mehr in Betracht kommen, ausgeschieden sein; **to be** ~ **late** nicht fahrplanmäßig sein; **to be** ~ **low** *(fund)* bald erschöpft sein, dem Ende zugehen; **to be out of the** ~ ausgeschieden sein, nicht mehr in Betracht kommen; **not to be** ~ **today** heute ausfallen (nicht verkehren); **to have ceased** ~ *(factory)* Betrieb eingestellt haben, *(hotel)* geschlossen sein; **to keep** ~ im Betrieb halten; **to make the** ~ *(fig.)* Tempo angeben; **to supervise the day-to-day** ~ **of an account** täglichen Kontostand überwachen; **to take the** ~ Führung übernehmen;
~ **account** Kontokorrent[konto], laufende (offene) Rechnung, Verrechnungskonto; **to have a** ~ **account** in Rechnung stehen, Kontokorrentkonto haben; **~-account mortgage** *(Br.)* Höchstbetragshypothek; ~ **bales** nach dem tatsächlichen Gewicht berechnete Ballen; ~ **battle** ständiger Kampf; ~ **board** *(car)* Trittbrett; ~ **body** *(advertising)* Hauptteil einer Anzeige; ~ **cash** umlaufendes Geld; ~ **commentary** Rundfunkkommentar,

Reportage, Hörbericht; ~ **contract** laufender Vertrag; ~ **costs** Betriebs[un]kosten; ~ **course of exchange** laufender Kurs; ~ **days** Liege-, Ladetage; **for three days** ~ drei Tage hintereinander; ~ **debts** laufende (schwebende) Schulden; **~-down action (case)** Verkehrssache; **~-down clause** *(ship)* Kollisionsklausel; ~ **engagements** laufende Verpflichtungen; ~ **expenses** laufende Geschäftsunkosten, *(railway)* Betriebs-, Transportkosten; ~ **fight** *(mil.)* Rückzugsgefecht; ~ **fire** *(fig.)* Kreuzfeuer; ~ **fire of questions** Kreuzfeuer von Fragen; ~ **form** *(insurance)* Risikoformular; ~ **gear** Fahrwerk; ~ **hand** Kurrentschrift, ausgeschriebene Handschrift; ~ **head** durchgehender Titel, lebender Kolumnentitel, -leiste; ~ **idle** *(machine)* Leerlauf; ~ **interest** laufende Zinsen; **to find one's** ~ **legs** seinen eigenen Weg erkennen; ~ **light** *(ship)* Positionslampe; ~ **mate** ständiger Begleiter, *(politics, US)* Mitkandidat; **per** ~ **meter** pro laufenden Meter; ~ **number** laufende Nummer; **in** ~ **order** betriebsfertig; ~ **policy** laufende Police; ~ **powers** Bahnbenutzungsrecht; ~ **repairs** laufende Reparaturen; ~ **shed** *(Br.)* Lokomotivschuppen; **to give s. o. his** ~ **shoes** *(sl.)* j. kurzerhand feuern; ~ **speed** Fahrgeschwindigkeit; ~ **text** Hauptteil einer Anzeige; ~ **time** Fahrzeit, *(film)* Laufzeit; ~ **title** Kolumnentitel; ~ **water** fließendes Gewässer; **to have cold and hot** ~ **water** *(bedroom)* Kalt- und Warmwasseranschluß haben; ~ **yield** *(Br.)* laufende Verzinsung.

runoff *(sport)* Entscheidungsrennen;
~ **election** *(US)* endgültige Vorwahl; ~ **primary** *(US)* endgültige Präsidentschaftsvorwahl; ~ **vote** Entscheidungswahl.

runthrough *(theatre)* Schnellprobe.

runway *(aeronautics)* Lande-, Roll-, Startbahn, *(vehicle)* Fahrbahn, Piste;
~ **visual range** Landebahnsicht.

rupture Abbruch, Unterbrechung;
~ **of an agreement** Vertragsbruch; ~ **of diplomatic relations** Abbruch der diplomatischen Beziehungen;
to come to a ~ zum Bruch kommen.

rural ländlich, landwirtschaftlich;
~ **area** Agrargebiet, landwirtschaftliches Gebiet; ~ **borough** *(Br.)* Landkreis; ~ **bus service** regionaler Omnibusverkehr; ~ **cooperative** *(US)* landwirtschaftliche Genossenschaft; ~ **community** Landgemeinde; ~ **credit** landwirtschaftlicher Kredit, Landwirtschafts-, Agrarkredit; ~ **credit bank** landwirtschaftliche Genossenschaftsbank; ~ **development** Entwicklung der Landwirtschaft; ~ **district** *(Br.)* ländlicher Bezirk, Landkreis; ~ **economy** Landwirtschaft; ~ **excursion** Landpartie; ~ **exodus** Landflucht; **~-free delivery** *(US)* freie Landpostzustellung; ~ **population** Landbevölkerung; ~ **property holder** Eigentümer eines Landwirtschaftsbetriebs; ~ **rehabilitation** Resozialisierung ländlicher Gebiete; **to live in** ~ **seclusion** in ländlicher Abgeschiedenheit leben; ~ **sections** landwirtschaftliche Gebiete; ~ **service** *(post)* Landzustellung; ~ **servitude** Grunddienstbarkeit an einem landwirtschaftlichen Grundstück; ~ **society** Agrarsoziologie; ~ **township** *(US)* Landgemeinde; ~ **worker** Landarbeiter.

ruralization Umstellung auf das Landleben.

ruralize *(v.)* auf das Landleben umstellen.

rush Andrang, Ansturm, Zulauf, Betrieb, *(business)* Geschäftsandrang, *(demand)* äußerst lebhafte Nachfrage, *(traffic)* [Verkehrs]andrang, Hochbetrieb;
not worth a ~ wertlos;

~es *(film)* schnell fertiggestellte Positive;
Christmas ~ vorweihnachtliche Geschäftigkeit; **gold** ~ Goldrausch;
~ **of business** Geschäftsandrang, Drang der Geschäfte; ~ **of city life** Rastlosigkeit des Großstadtlebens; ~ **of imports** lebhafte Einfuhrnachfrage; ~ **of orders** Auftragsstrom; ~ **to the refreshment camp** Ansturm auf das Erfrischungszelt; ~ **for seats** Sturm auf die Sitzplätze; **wild** ~ **on a shop** wilder Ansturm auf einen Laden; ~ **at the stations** Betrieb auf den Bahnhöfen; ~ **on mining stocks** Nachfrage nach Montanaktien;
~ *(v.)* *(business)* sich lebhaft entwickeln;
~ **s. o. for an article** *(sl.)* jem. einen überhöhten Preis für einen Artikel abjagen; ~ **a bill through the house** *(Br.)* Gesetz durchpeitschen; ~ **the boats** Boote stürmen; ~ **one's car into the city** mit dem Auto in die Stadt rasen; ~ **to conclusions** übereilte Schlußfolgerungen ziehen; ~ **into certain death** in den sicheren Tod rennen; ~ **into extremes** in Extreme verfallen; ~ **s. o. to the hospital** j. auf schnellstem Wege ins Krankenhaus bringen; ~ **s. o. for money** j. dringend um Geld bitten; ~ **in with new orders** neuen Auftragsstrom auslösen; ~ **through an order for goods in three days** Warenauftrag in drei Tagen ausliefern; ~ **troops to the front** Truppen an die Front werfen; ~ **o. s. into an undertaking** sich in ein Abenteuer stürzen; ~ **up** *(prices, US)* in die Höhe treiben; ~ **up reinforcements** in aller Eile Verstärkungen heranschaffen;
to keep pace with the ~ **of orders** Auftragseingänge pünktlich erledigen;
~ **hour** verkehrsstarke Zeit, Hauptverkehrszeit, Verkehrsandrang, Stoß-, Hauptgeschäftszeit; **to beat the** ~ **hours** Hauptverkehrszeit umgehen; **~-hour peak** Hauptverkehrs-, Stoßzeit; **~-hour traffic** Verkehrsstoß, Spitzenverkehr; ~ **job (order)** Eilauftrag, vordringlicher Auftrag; ~ **period** Hochbetrieb, Hauptbetriebs-, Stoßzeit; ~ **report** Eilbericht; ~ **wedding** *(fig.)* unsichere Verbindung; ~ **work** schludrige Arbeit, Schnellschuß.

rust Rost, *(inactivity)* Untätigkeit, *(injurious influence)* schädlicher Einfluß;
~ *(v.)* rosten, *(fig.)* einrosten, verkommen;
~ **trap** Rostfänger.

rustic ländlich, rustikal;
~ **entertainment** anspruchslose Unterhaltung; ~ **house** Bauernhaus; ~ **manners** bäuerliches Benehmen; ~ **speech** ungehobelte Rede.

rusticate *(v.)* ländliches Leben führen, *(university)* relegieren;
~ **a student** Studenten vom Universitätsstudium vorübergehend ausschließen.

rustication Leben auf dem Lande, Landaufenthalt, *(university)* Verweisung von der Universität, Ausschluß vom Universitätsstudium, zeitweilige Relegation.

rustle *(v.)* **up** organisieren, hinkriegen;
~ **some food for unexpected guests** etw. zum Essen für unerwarteten Besuch auftreiben.

rustler *(US sl.)* Viehdieb.

rusty rostig, verrostet, *(fig.)* eingerostet, aus der Übung, *(shoddy)* abgetragen, schäbig;
to be a bit ~ ein bißchen der Auffrischung bedürfen.

rut Wagenspur, *(fig.)* üblicher Trott, gewohntes Geleise;
to get into a ~ zur Routine werden; **to lift s. o. out of the** ~ j. aus seinem gewohnten Trott bringen.

S

S curve S-Kurve.
sabbath breaking Verletzung der Sonntagsruhe.
sabbatical, to be on bezahlten Studienurlaub haben;
  ~**funds** Studienmittel; ~ **leave** Studienurlaub.
sabotage Sabotage[akt];
  economic ~ Wirtschaftssabotage;
  ~ (v.) sabotieren, Sabotage treiben;
  to be caused by ~ durch Sabotage verursacht werden; **to prac-**
  tise ~ Sabotage begehen, sabotieren;
  ~ **squad** Sabotagekommando; ~ **threat** Sabotagedrohung.
sabre, the (fig.) das Militär;
  to rattle one's ~ (fig.) mit dem Säbel rasseln;
  ~ **rattling** Säbelrasseln, Machtdemonstration.
saboteur Saboteur;
  ~ **camp** Sabotageausbildungslager.
sack Sack, (dismissal, sl.) Entlassung, Hinauswurf, (pillaging)
  Plünderung;
  coal ~ Kohlensack; **sad** ~ (US) Kompanietrottel;
  ~ (v.) (dismiss, sl.) feuern, hinauswerfen, rausschmeißen, an
  die Luft setzen, entlassen, Laufpaß geben, fristlos kündigen,
  (plunder) plündern;
  ~ **in (out)** (sl.) pennen gehen;
  to get the ~ (sl.) gekündigt (fristlos entlassen, an die Luft
  gesetzt, gefeuert) werden, hinausfliegen; **to give s. o. the** ~ (sl.)
  j. entlassen (herauswerfen, feuern); **to hold the** ~ **for the whole**
  of the balance unpaid (fam., US) Haftung für den unbezahlten
  Rechnungssaldo übernehmen; **to put to** ~ plündern; **to threaten**
  s. o. with the ~ jem. mit Entlassung (dem Hinauswurf) drohen;
  ~ **artist** (rat, sl.) Schlafratte; ~ **duty** (mil., sl.) Schlafzeit; ~ **time**
  (sl.) Bettzeit.
sackable, easily leicht zu entlassen.
sackcloth Sackleinwand;
  to mourn in ~ **and ashes** in Sack und Asche trauern.
sacked (sl.) gefeuert, hinausgeworfen, abgehalftert;
  to be ~ hinausfliegen; **to be promptly** ~ sofort entlassen
  werden.
sacking Sackleinwand, (dismissal, firing, sl.) Hinauswurf,
  Entlassung;
  ~ **of a town** Plünderung einer Stadt.
sacred interests unantastbare Interessen.
sacrifice Verlust, (fig.) Verzicht, Opfer, (marine insurance)
  Aufopferung, (loss) Gewinnverlust, Einbuße;
  at a ~ mit Verlust;
  general average ~**s** Aufopferungen der großen Havarie;
  ~ **of accuracy** Verzicht auf Genauigkeit; ~ **of time**
  Zeitaufwand;
  ~ (v.) mit Verlust verkaufen;
  ~ **one's life** sein Leben hingeben; ~ **one's life to one's husband's**
  welfare sein ganzes Leben seinem Ehegatten widmen;
  to give one's life as a ~ **for one's country** sein Leben für sein
  Vaterland opfern; **to make a** ~ finanzielles Opfer bringen; **to**
  sell at a ~ zu jedem Preis losschlagen;
  ~ **price** Verlustpreis; ~ **sale** Verlustverkauf.
sacrificed goods spottbillige Waren, (marine insurance) aufgeopferte Güter.
sad | apple (sl.) Pessimist; ~ **sack** (US sl.) Kompanietrottel.
saddle (book) Buchrücken;
  in the ~ (fig.) im Amt, an der Macht;
  ~ (v.) **a murder on an innocent person** einem Unschuldigen
  einen Mord anhängen; ~ **s. o. with a responsibility** jem. Verantwortung auferlegen;
  to be in the ~ Heft in der Hand haben; **to put the** ~ **on the wrong**
  horse an die falsche Adresse kommen;
  ~ **horse** Reitpferd; ~ **stitching** Drahtheftung.
safe (bank) Schließ-, Bank-, Stahlkammerfach, Depot, (strong
  box) Tresor, Geldschrank, Safe;
  burglar-proof ~ diebessicherer Geldschrank; **cash** ~ eiserner
  Geldschrank; **fire-proof** ~ feuerfester Geldschrank; **fire pro-**
  tection steel filing ~ feuersicherer Panzerschrank; **fire and**
  burglar-resisting ~ feuer- und diebessicherer Geldschrank;
  ~ (a.) (cautious) solide, zuverlässig, kein Risiko eingehend,
  (secure) wohlbehalten, gefahrlos, sicher, in Sicherheit;
  as ~ **as houses** todsicher, absolut sicher; ~ **to operate** betriebssicher; ~ **and sound** gesund und wohlbehalten;
  to be ~ (criminal) auf Nummer Sicher sein; **to be** ~ **from**
  recognition unerkannt bleiben; **to be** ~ **to win one's seat** sich
  seines Parlamentssitzes sicher sein; **to consider s. o.** ~ **for a**

credit of $ 4000 j. für einen Kredit von 4000 Dollar für gut
(sicher) halten; **to crack a** ~ Geldschrank aufbrechen, Tresor
knacken; **to keep s. th.** ~ etw. sicher aufbewahren; **to play** ~ auf
Nummer Sicher gehen; **to rent a** ~ Tresorfach mieten;
~ **arrival** glückliche Ankunft; ~ **builder** Geldschrankfabrikant;
~ **buster** Geldschrankknacker; **iron** ~ **clause** (insurance business) Safeklausel; ~ **conduct** sicheres Geleit, Schutzgeleit, (letter of safe conduct) Geleit-, Schutzbrief; **to grant s. o.** ~ **conduct**
jem. freies Geleit gewähren; ~ **custodies** (Br.) Depotgeschäft.
safe custody (banking) Verwahrung, Aufbewahrung, (Br.) [Wert-
papier]depot;
in ~ in sicherem Gewahrsam;
~ **of securities** (Br.) Aufbewahrung von Wertpapieren, Effektenverwaltung, -verwahrung; ~ **of shares** (Br.) Aktienver-
waltung;
to assume ~ (Br.) Effekten verwalten; **to deposit securities for** ~
Wertpapiere ins Depot einliefern; **to have** ~ **of the securities of**
a unit trust (Br.) als Depotbank für eine Kapitalanlagegesellschaft fungieren; **to hold in** ~ im Depot aufbewahren; **to keep in**
~ sicher aufbewahren, (Br.) im Depot verwahren; **to leave**
one's jewellery in ~ seinen Schmuck im Tresor lassen; **to place**
shares in ~ Aktien in Depotverwaltung geben; **to provide** ~ **for**
valuables Schließfächer für Wertsachen zur Verfügung stellen;
~ **account** (Br.) Depotkonto, Effektendepot; ~ **business** (Br.)
Depotgeschäft; ~ **charges (fees)** (Br.) Safe-, Depot[verwal-
tungs]gebühr; ~ **contract** Schließfach-, Depotaufbewahrungs-
vertrag; ~ **department** (Br.) Depotabteilung; ~ **items** (Br.)
Depotstücke; ~ **procedure** Depotverwaltungsmethoden; ~
receipt (Br.) Depotempfangsbescheinigung, Aufbewahrungs-
schein, Depotquittung, -schein; ~ **receipt counterfoil** Depot-
quittungs-, Kontrollabschnitt; ~ **register** (Br.) Depotverzeichnis, Effektenstrazze; ~ **transactions** (Br.) Depotgeschäfte.
safe deposit Geldschrank, Tresor, Stahlkammer, -fach, (US)
[Bank]depot, (administration of custodianship account) Aufbewahrung im Tresor, Depotverwahrung, -verwaltung, Schließfachverwahrung.
safe-deposit feuer-, einbruchssicher;
~ **balance** Depotguthaben; ~ **box** Schließ-, Tresor-, Stahl-,
Bankfach, [Geld]safe; **to rent a** ~ **box** Schließ-, Tresorfach
mieten; ~ **box insurance** Depotversicherung; ~ **company** (Br.)
Gesellschaft zur Aufbewahrung von Wertgegenständen, (US)
Schließfachgesellschaft; ~ **department** Tresorabteilung; ~
facilities (banking, US) Aufbewahrung in Stahlkammern
(Schließfächern), Schließfachvermietung; ~ **fee** Schließfach-,
Tresor-, Depot-, Aufbewahrungsgebühr; ~ **institution** Tre-
sorvorrichtung, -anlagen; ~ **insurance** Tresor-, Schließfach-
versicherung; ~ **keeping** (US) Aufbewahrung in Stahlkammern, Stahlfach-, Schließfachaufbewahrung; ~ **register** (US)
Depotbuch; ~ **rent** Schließfach-, Depot-, Tresormiete; ~
vault (US) Stahl-, Schließfach, Stahlkammer.
safe, to be of ~ **discretion** vertrauenswürdig sein; ~ **driver**
zuverlässiger Kraftfahrer; ~ **estimate** vorsichtige Schätzung; ~
guide zuverlässiger Führer; ~ **harbo(u)r** sturmsicherer Hafen;
~ **hiring** Tresor-, Schließfach, Safemiete, Vermietung von
Safes (Schließfächern); ~ **investment** [mündel]sichere [Kapi-
tal]anlage; **perfectly** ~ **investment** todsichere Geldanlage; ~
lifter Tresor-, Geldschrankknacker; ~ **limit of speed** (automobile) ausreichende Bremsgeschwindigkeit; ~ **loading place**
sicherer Verladeplatz; ~ **lock** Tresorschloß; ~ **means of access**
sicherer Zugang zur Arbeitsstelle; ~ **place to work** unfallsiche-
rer Arbeitsplatz; **to put in a** ~ **place** in Sicherheit bringen;
~**-pledge** Kautionsgestellung; ~ **policy** risikolose Politik; **from**
a ~ **quarter** aus zuverlässiger (sicherer) Quelle; ~ **seat** sicherer
Parlamentssitz; **to be on the** ~ **side** auf Nummer Sicher gehen; ~
[limit of] speed ausreichende Bremsgeschwindigkeit; ~ **states-**
man vorsichtiger Staatsmann; ~ **sum in hand** sicherstehender
Betrag; ~ **system of working** Arbeitsschutz; ~ **undertaking**
gefahrloses Unternehmen.
safeblower Geldschrankknacker.
safeblowing Aufbrechen eines Geldschranks.
safebreaker Geldschrankknacker.
safebreaking Geldschrankknackerei.
safecracker Geldschrankknacker.
safecracking Aufbrechen eines Geldschranks, Tresorknacken.
safeguard Sicherung, Schutz, (protection) Schutzvorrichtung,
  (safe conduct) Paß, Schutz-, Geleitbrief;
  ~**s** Sicherungsklauseln;

contractual ~s vertragliche Schutzbestimmungen; **minority** ~s Schutzbestimmungen für Minderheiten;

~ **of the national security** (US) Schutz der nationalen Sicherheit;

~ (v.) sicherstellen, schützen;

~ **an industry** Schutzzölle für einen Industriezweig festsetzen; ~ **s. one's interests** sich für jds. Interessen einsetzen; ~ **against losses** gegen Verluste sicherstellen;

to obtain ~s Garantien erhalten;

~ **clause** Sicherungsklausel; ~ **antimissile system** Raketenabwehrsystem.

safeguarding | of credits Kreditbesicherung; ~ **of the currency** Währungssicherung;

♘ **of Industry Act** (Br.) Gewerbeschutzgesetz; ~ **duty** (Br.) Schutzzoll.

safekeeper Verwahrer.

safekeeping sichere Aufbewahrung, Verwahrung, Gewahrsam, (bank, US) Aufbewahrung in Stahlkammern, Schließfachverwahrung, Depot[aufbewahrung];

~ **of securities** (US) Effektenverwahrung;

to be in ~ in sicherem Gewahrsam sein; **to give money to the bank for** ~ sein Geld einer Bank anvertrauen; **to have jewels in** ~ Schmuck im Tresor haben; **to hold for** ~ (US) im Depot aufbewahren; **to take into** ~ in Verwahrung nehmen;

~ **account** (US) Depotkonto; ~ **contract** (US) Schließfachvertrag; ~ **period** Aufbewahrungsfrist.

safelight (photo) Dunkelkammerlampe.

safemaker Geldschrankfabrikant.

safemaking Geldschrankfabrikation.

safeman Geldschrankfabrikant.

safety Sicherheit, Schutz, Gefahrlosigkeit;

for ~'s **sake** sicherheitshalber;

absolute ~ unbedingte Sicherheit; **domestic** ~ innere Sicherheit; **national** ~ nationale Sicherheit; **public** ~ öffentliche Sicherheit; **road** ~ Verkehrs-, Straßensicherheit; ~ **of capital** sichere Kapitalanlage; ~ **of lives at sea** Schiffssicherheit; ~ **in operation (service)** Betriebssicherheit; ~ **on the roads** Straßen-, Verkehrssicherheit, Sicherheit des Verkehrs; ~ **of traffic** Verkehrssicherheit;

to be in ~ in Sicherheit sein; **to bring into** ~ sichern, in Sicherheit bringen; **to endanger the** ~ **of the workmen** nicht für genügend Schutzvorrichtungen für die Arbeiter sorgen; **to ensure the** ~ **of the state** Sicherheit des Staates gewährleisten; **to play for** ~ Risiken vermeiden; **to seek** ~ **in flight** sein Heil in der Flucht suchen;

~ **appliance (apparatus)** Sicherheitsvorrichtung; **on** ~ **aspects** aus Sicherheitsüberlegungen; ~ **belt** Rettungsgürtel, (car) Sicherheitsgurt, Anschnallgürtel; ~ **bolt** Sicherheitsriegel; ~ **box** Panzerschrank; ~ **buoy** Rettungsboje; ~ **car** den Sicherheitsbestimmungen gerecht werdendes Auto; ~ **card** Sicherheitsausweis; ~ **catch** Sicherheitsvorrichtung; ~ **chain** Sicherheitskette; ~ **clause** (life insurance) Nachschlußklausel bei Versicherungsvereinen auf Gegenseitigkeit; ~ **committee** Ausschuß für Fragen des Industrieschutzes; ~ **committee regulations** Bestimmungen über die Bildung von Ausschüssen in Fragen des Industrieschutzes; ~ **conditions** Sicherheitsbestimmungen; **to be** ~**conscious** Sicherheitsbestimmungen sorgfältig beachten; **to promote** ~ **consciousness** sorgfältige Einhaltung der Sicherheitsbestimmungen gewährleisten; ~ **control zone** Sicherheitszone; ~ **council** (Br.) Beratungsorgan für die Sicherheit am Arbeitsplatz; **National** ♘ **Council** (US) Verkehrssicherheitsrat; ~ **curtain** (theater) eiserner Vorhang; ~ **devices** Sicherheitsvorkehrungen, -einrichtungen; ~ **education** Verkehrserziehung; ~ **engineering** technische Überwachung; ~ **engineering department** technische Überwachungsabteilung; ~ **equipment** Sicherheitseinrichtungen; ~ **factor** Sicherheitsfaktor; ~ **features** Sicherheitseinrichtungen; ~ **film** nicht brennbarer Film; ~ **first** Sicherheit über alles; ~**-first policy** Politik der Klugheit; ~ **fund** Reservefonds, (banking, US) Mindestreserven; ~ **fund rate** (US) Mindestreservesatz; ~ **fund system** (banking, US) Mindestreservensystem; ~ **fuse** (el.) Sicherung; ~ **glass** Sicherheitsglas; ~ **harness** Sicherheitsgurt; ~ **hazard** Sicherheitsrisiko; ~ **hoist** Sicherheitsaufzug; ~ **inspection of factories** gewerbepolizeiliche Überprüfung der Betriebssicherheit; ~ **island (isle)** Fußgänger-, Verkehrsinsel; ~ **lamp** Grubenlampe; ~ **lift** Sicherheitsaufzug; ~ **load** zuverlässige [Höchst]belastung; ~ **lock** Sicherheitsschloß; ~ **margin** Sicherheitsmarge; ~ **measures** Sicherheitsmaßnahmen; ~ **net** Sicherheitsnetz; ~ **pin** Sicherheitsnadel; ~ **precautions** Sicherheitsvorkehrungen, Schutzmaßnahmen; ~ **performance** Sicherheitsausführung; ~ **program(me)** Sicherheitsprogramm; ~

provisions Sicherheitsbestimmungen; ~ **rail** Leitschiene; ~ **razor** Rasierapparat; **to improve one's** ~ **record** sein Renommee verbessern; **to qualify under the new** ~ **regulations** den neuen Sicherheitsvorschriften entsprechen; ~ **representative** Industrieschutzbeauftragter; **for** ~'s **sake** sicherheitshalber; ~ **standards** Sicherheitsnormen; ~ **supervision** Sicherheits-, Unfallschutzüberwachung; ~ **supervisor** Leiter des betrieblichen Unfallschutzes; ~ **switch** Sicherheitsschalter; ~ **testing** Überprüfung von Unfallschutz-, Sicherheitsbestimmungen; ~ **tyre** Sicherheitsreifen; ~ **valve** Überdruckventil, (fig.) Spielraum, Betätigungsfeld; **to sit on the** ~ **valve** Unterdrückungspolitik betreiben; ~ **vault** Panzergewölbe, Stahlschrank, Banktresor; ~ **vehicle** den Sicherheitsbestimmungen voll entsprechendes Fahrzeug; ~ **zone** (pol.) Sicherheitszone, (traffic) Fußgängerüberweg, Zebrastreifen, Fußgänger-, Verkehrsinsel.

sag (airplane) Durchsacken, abgesackte Stelle, (price) vorübergehende Preisdepression, (stock market) Kursdepression;

~ (v.) (prices) nachgeben, gedrückt sein, sinken, abflauen, sich abschwächen;

~ **in price** im Preis fallen.

saga, family Familienroman.

sagging (stock market) Baisse;

~ **of the Franc** Nachgeben des Frank-Kurses; ~ **of the market** Kursabschwächung;

~ (a.) abgeschwächt;

~ **market** abgeschwächter Markt, (stock exchange) nachgebende Kurse; ~ **prices** (sl.) sinkende Preise (Kurse); ~ **spirits** sinkender Mut.

said vorbenannt, vorher erwähnt.

sail [Segel]schiff;

~ (v.) (of goods) zur See befördert werden, (ship) in See stechen, auslaufen, abgehen, (begin voyage) zu Schiff fahren, reisen;

expected to ~ voraussichtliche Abfahrt;

~ **into** (sl.) sich an etw. ranmachen, tüchtig anpacken; ~ **in ballast** mit Ballast fahren; ~ **close (near) to the wind** (fig.) es mit dem Gesetz nicht allzu genau nehmen, sich hart an der Grenze des Erlaubten bewegen; ~ **under false colo(u)rs** unter falscher Flagge segeln, (fig.) seine wahren Motive verbergen; ~ **in company** im geschlossenen Verband fahren; ~ **under convoy** im Konvoy fahren; ~ **on freight** auf Fracht fahren; ~ **serenely through life** gelassen durchs Leben gehen; ~ **to schedule** (US) fahrplanmäßig auslaufen; ~ **through** glatt passieren; ~ **against the wind** (fig.) von der öffentlichen Meinung keine Notiz nehmen; ~ **with every shift of wind** sein Mäntelchen nach dem Winde hängen;

to set ~ in See stechen; **to take in the** ~s (fig.) weniger hohe Ansprüche stellen, zurückstecken; **to take the wind out of s. one's** ~s jem. den Wind aus den Segeln nehmen.

sailing Abfahrt, (ship) Auslaufen, [Segel]schiffahrt, Navigation; **plain** ~ leichte Sache; **not at all plain** ~ keine einfache Sache; **arrival and** ~ Ankunft und Abfahrt;

~ **boat** Segelboot; ~ **card** Verladeanweisung; ~ **date** (ship) Abfahrtszeit, -datum; ~ **instructions** Fahrtanweisungen; ~ **line** Schiffahrtslinie; ~ **list** Fahrplan; ~ **orders** Befehl zum Auslaufen, Marschbefehl; ~ **rules** Fahrregeln; ~ **ship** Segelschiff.

sailor Schiffer, Seemann, Matrose, (sl.) Flaneur; **bad** ~ nicht seefester Reisender; **ordinary** ~ Leichtmatrose; ~s' **home** Seemannsheim.

sailplane Segelflugzeug.

sake, for the ~ **of peace** um des lieben Friedens willen; **for its own** ~ um seiner selbst willen, als Selbstzweck; **for the** ~ **of practice** übungshalber;

to do s. th. for the ~ **of one's family** etw. nur wegen seiner Familie tun.

salaam (v.) tiefe Verbeugung machen.

salable verkäuflich, (marketable) absatz-, marktfähig, umsetzbar, gängig, einschlagend;

highly ~ gut verkäuflich;

~ **price** gängiger Preis; ~ **stock** börsengängige Papiere; ~ **type** gängiger Typ; ~ **value** gewöhnlicher Verkaufswert.

salableness, salability Verkäuflichkeit, Gangbarkeit.

salad days (sl.) Sturm- und Drangzeit.

salaried festes Gehalt beziehend, fest angestellt, besoldet;

high-~ hoch bezahlt, mit einem hohen Gehalt;

~ **basis** Gehaltsbasis; ~ **class** Gehaltsempfänger[schicht]; ~ **clerk** Büroangestellter; ~ **employee** (Br.) Gehaltsempfänger, Angestellter; ~ **group** Angestelltenklasse; ~ **man** Angestellter, Gehaltsempfänger; ~ **office** besoldetes Amt; ~ **officer** Angestellter; **high-**~ **officials** hochbezahlte Angestellte; ~ **personnel** Gehaltsempfänger; ~ **post (position)** Angestelltenposten; ~ **staff** Angestellte, Gehaltsempfänger.

salaries, accrued Gehaltsrückstände; **agreed-scale** ~ Tariflöhne; **actually earned** ~ Effektivbezüge; **executive** ~ Gehälter leitender Angestellter, Vorstandsbezüge;
~ **not covered by the salary scale** Bezüge im außertariflichen Bereich; ~ **to staff** Angestelltengehälter, Belegschaftsgehälter; ~ **and wages** Löhne und Gehälter;
~ **list** Gehaltsliste.

salary Gehalt, Besoldung, Dienstbezüge, Lohn, Salär;
acc rued ~ Gehaltsrückstände; **advance** ~ Gehaltsvorschuß; **agreed-upon** ~ vereinbartes Gehalt; **annual** ~ Jahresgehalt; **appointive** ~ Anfangsgehalt; **basic** ~ Grundgehalt; **commencing** ~ Anfangsgehalt; **competitive** ~ vergleichbares Gehalt; **consular** ~ Bezüge eines Konsuls; ~ **desired** Gehaltswünsche; **expected** ~ *(advertisement)* Gehaltsansprüche; **fat** ~ *(fam.)* dickes Gehalt; **fixed** ~ Fixum, festes Gehalt; **flat** ~ Pauschalgehalt; **government** ~ staatliches Gehalt; **gross** ~ Bruttogehalt; **high** ~ hohes Gehalt; **increasing** ~ steigendes Gehalt; **initial** ~ Anfangsgehalt; **maximum** ~ Höchstgehalt, oberste Gehaltsgrenze; **minimum** ~ unterste Gehaltsgrenze, Mindestgehalt; **miserable** ~ kümmerliches Gehalt; **monthly** ~ Monatsgehalt; ~ **negotiable** Gehalt ist Verhandlungssache; **officer's (official)** ~ Diensteinkommen, Beamtengehalt; ~ **open** *(advertisement)* Gehalt ist Verhandlungssache; **regular** ~ Festgehalt; **remunerative** ~ anständiges Gehalt; ~ **required** *(advertisement)* Gehaltsansprüche, -wünsche angeben; **respectable** ~ anständiges Gehalt; **starting** ~ *(advertisement)* mit Angabe der Gehaltsansprüche; **starting** ~ **negotiable** Anfangsgehalt ist Verhandlungssache; **straight** ~ festes Gehalt ohne Beteiligung; **tax-free** ~ steuerfreies Gehalt; **top[level]** ~ Spitzengehalt; **weekly** ~ Wochenlohn;
~ **by arrangement** Gehalt nach Vereinbarung; **starting** ~ **in the $ 25.000 area plus significant bonus arrangement** Anfangsgehalt in der Größenordnung von 25.000 Dollar und zusätzliche erhebliche Tantiemevereinbarungen; **excellent starting base** ~ **plus unusually generous fringe benefits** erstklassiges Anfangsgehalt und zusätzlich eine ungewöhnlich großzügige Aufwandsentschädigung; ~ **to date** augenblickliches Gehalt; ~ **fully equated to the levels of responsibility** dem Verantwortungsbereich entsprechendes Gehalt; ~ **and other emoluments** Gehalt und andere Bezüge; ~ **of a member of Parliament** Aufwandsentschädigung eines Abgeordneten, Diäten; ~ **no object (is secondary consideration)** *(newspaper)* Gehalt ist Nebensache; ~ **appendant to a position** mit einer Stellung verbundenes Gehalt;
~ *(v.)* Gehalt bezahlen, besolden;
to anticipate one's ~ Gehaltsvorschuß bekommen; **to apply for a boost** *(US)* **(increase, rise, Br.) in** ~ um Gehaltserhöhung einkommen; **to appoint (fix) a** ~ Gehalt auswerfen (festlegen); **to assign a** ~ **for an office** Bezüge für ein Amt festsetzen; **to assure s. o. a definite** ~ jem. ein bestimmtes Gehalt zusichern; **to be on a regular** ~ fest angestellt sein; **to carry an attractive** ~ mit gehobeneren Gehaltsansprüchen verbunden sein; **to command a very substantial** ~ Spitzengehalt beinhalten; **to cut s. one's** ~ jds. Bezüge herabsetzen; **to depend on one's** ~ auf sein Gehalt angewiesen sein; **to draw a** ~ Gehalt beziehen; **to draw on one's** ~ von seinem Gehalt abheben; **to draw a fixed** ~ fest angestellt sein; **to earn a** ~ *(parliament)* Diäten erhalten; **to earn a good** ~ gutes Gehalt haben; **to give s. o. a** ~ jem. Gehalt zahlen, j. besolden; **to have one's** ~ **docked** Gehaltskürzung erfahren; **to increase a** ~ am Gehalt zulegen, Gehalt erhöhen; **to live on a small** ~ von einem kleinen Gehalt leben; **to offer a** ~ Gehaltsangebot machen; **to offer a** ~ **and support for a year** Gehalt und Lebensunterhalt für ein Jahr anbieten; **to offset one's small** ~ mit seinem knappen Gehalt auskommen; **to pay a** ~ besolden, Gehalt zahlen; **to pay s. one's** ~ **in full** jds. Gehalt voll ausbezahlen; **to raise a** ~ [Gehalts]zulage gewähren, am Gehalt zulegen; **to receive a** ~ Gehaltsempfänger (besoldet) sein; **to receive part of one's** ~ **in advance** Gehaltsvorschuß bekommen; **to review a** ~ **annually** Gehaltsrahmen jährlich überprüfen;
~ **account** Gehaltskonto; ~ **adjustment** Gehaltsangleichung; **wage and** ~ **administration** Lohn- und Gehaltswesen; ~ **advance** Gehaltsvorschuß; **within-grade** ~ **advancement** laufbahnmäßige Gehaltserhöhung; ~ **arrears** Gehaltsrückstand; ~ **bonus** Besoldungs-, Gehaltszulage; ~ **book** Lohnbuch; ~ **boost** *(US)* Gehaltsaufbesserung; ~ **bracket** Gehaltsklasse, Besoldungsgruppe, -stufe; ~ **check** *(US)* Gehaltsscheck; ~ **class** Gehalts-, Besoldungsgruppe; ~ **classification** Gehaltseinstufung, -eingruppierung, Besoldungsregelung; ~ **compensation** festes Honorar; ~ **conditions** Besoldungsverhältnisse; **wage and** ~ **control** Lohn- und Gehaltskontrolle; ~ **cut** Gehaltskürzung; ~ **decrease** Gehaltskürzung; **demotional** ~ **decrease**

Gehaltskürzung infolge anderweitiger Einstufung; ~ **demand** Gehaltsansprüche, -forderung; ~ **differential** Sonderzulagen für erschwerte Arbeitsbedingungen; ~ **earner** Gehaltsempfänger; ~ **evolution** Gehaltsentwicklung; ~ **expense** Gehälterunkosten; ~ **expense item** Gehaltsaufwandsposten; ~ **figures** Gehaltsziffern; ~ **fund** Gehälterfonds; ~ **grade** Gehaltsstufe, -klasse, Besoldungsgruppe; ~ **group** Gehaltsklasse, Besoldungsgruppe; ~ **hike (increase)** Gehaltserhöhung, -verbesserung; ~ **history** Gehaltsentwicklung; **automatic** ~ **increase** automatische Gehaltserhöhung; **promotional** ~ **increase** mit einer Beförderung verbundene Gehaltserhöhung; ~ **indicator** Gehaltsrahmen; ~ **inflation** Gehälterinflation; ~ **level** Gehaltsniveau; **present** ~ **level** augenblickliche Bezüge; ~ **list** Besoldungsliste; ~ **open** *(advertising)* Gehalt ist Verhandlungssache; ~ **package** gebündeltes Gehaltsangebot, Gesamtbezüge; ~ **payment** Besoldung, Gehaltszahlung; ~ **problem** Gehaltsfrage; ~ **progression** Gehaltsentwicklung, Gehälterprogression; ~ **progression to date** auf den neuesten Stand gebrachte Gehaltsentwicklung; ~ **promotion** Gehaltsanhebung; ~ **proportion** Gehaltsanteil; ~ **raise** *(US)* Gehaltsaufbesserung; ~ **range** Gehaltsrahmen; ~ **rate** Besoldungssatz; ~ **ratio** Lohnquote; **wage and** ~ **receipts** Lohn- und Gehaltseinnahmen; ~ **reclassification** Besoldungsneuordnung; ~ **record** Gehaltsnachweis; ~ **reduction** Gehaltssenkung, Gehälterabbau; ~ **requirements** Gehaltsansprüche, -forderungen; ~ **research unit** Team zur Ermittlung von Gehältern; ~ **review** Gehaltsübersicht; ~ **rise** *(Br.)* **(raise, US coll.)** Gehaltssteigerung, -aufbesserung, -erhöhung; ~ **roll** Gehälter-, Besoldungsliste, Gehaltsabrechnung; ~ **scale** Gehaltsskala, -rahmen, -stufe, -tabelle, Besoldungsordnung; ~ **a secondary consideration** *(advertisement)* Gehalt ist Nebensache; ~ **slip** Gehaltsstreifen; ~ **structure** Gehaltsrahmen; ~ **supplements (supplementation)** zusätzlich zum Gehalt gewährte Vergütungen; ~ **survey** Gehälterübersicht; ~ **system** Gehaltssystem.

sale Verkauf, *(agreement)* Kaufvertrag, *(alienation)* Veräußerung, *(clearance sale)* Inventur-, Saisonaus-, Saisonschlußverkauf, *(distribution)* Vertrieb, [Markt]absatz, Markt, *(public auction)* [öffentliche] Versteigerung, Auktion;
at the time of ~ beim [Ver]kauf[s]abschluß; **by private** ~ unter der Hand, aus freier Hand; **faked up for** ~ für den Verkauf zurechtgemacht; **free on** ~ frei verkäuflich; **for (on)** ~ zum Verkauf, zu verkaufen, [ver]käuflich, feil; **for** ~ **to the highest bidder** dem Höchstbietenden zustehend; **no longer on** ~ nicht mehr lieferbar; **no** ~s kein Umsatz, umsatzlos; **not for** ~ Muster ohne Wert, unverkäuflich; **on** ~ **and return** mit Rückgaberecht; **slow of** ~ schlecht verkäuflich; **subject to prior** ~ Zwischenverkauf vorbehalten;
~s *(balance sheet)* Abgänge, Umsatzerlöse, *(stock exchange)* Abschlüsse, *(turnover)* Umsatz, Absatz;
absolute ~ bedingungsloser Verkauf, Kaufvertrag ohne Eigentumsvorbehalt; ~ **account** ~s *(US)* **(commission merchant)** Verkaufsabrechnung; **accrued** ~s getätigte Verkäufe; **actual** ~ Verkaufsabschluß; **adjourned** ~ gerichtlich ausgesetzte Auktion; **advance** ~ Vorverkauf; **aggregate** ~s Gesamtverkäufe, -umsatz; **annual** ~s Jahresumsatz; **as-is** ~ Verkauf wie es steht und liegt; **bailment** ~ Kommissionsverkauf mit Selbsteintritt; **bargain** ~ Gelegenheitskauf, Verkauf zu herabgesetzten Preisen, Sonderangebot, *(advertising)* Reklamenverkauf; **bear** ~ *(Br.)* Verkauf auf Baisse; **bearish** ~ *(stock exchange)* Blankoverkauf, Leerabgabe; **bogus** ~ betrügerischer Verkauf; **brisk** ~s gute (flotte) Umsätze; **bulk** ~ Verkauf in Bausch und Bogen; **bulk-seat** ~ Verkauf von Flugplätzen für Gruppenreisen; **cash** ~ Barverkauf, Verkauf gegen Barzahlung ohne Kundendienst, *(stock exchange)* Kassageschäft; **cash-on-delivery** ~ Verkauf gegen Nachnahme; **casual** ~ Gelegenheitsverkauf; **catalog(ue)** ~ Verkauf auf Grund übersandten Katalogs, Versandgeschäft; **certified net** ~ *(newspaper)* tatsächlich verkaufte Auflage; **charge** ~ Verkauf mit Anzahlung, Kreditverkauf; **clearance (cheap)** ~ Ausverkauf; **close-out** ~ Schluß-, Ausverkauf; **closing-down** ~ Totalausverkauf, Räumungsverkauf; **commodity** ~ Warenverkauf; **compulsory** ~ Zwangsversteigerung, -verkauf, Enteignung; **conditional** ~ Verkauf unter Eigentumsvorbehalt; **consignment** ~ Kommissions-, Konsignationsverkauf; **consolidated outside** ~s *(balance sheet)* Umsatz an die Kundschaft; **over-the-counter** ~ Verkauf über den Ladentisch, *(stock exchange)* Verkauf im Freiverkehr, Freiverkehrsverkauf; **under-the-counter** ~ Verkauf unter dem Ladentisch; **countermanded** ~ rückgängig gemachter Kauf; **credit** ~ Kreditverkauf, Verkauf auf Ziel; **cross** ~ *(floor broker)* Selbsteintritt; **dead** ~ flauer Absatz; **deferred payment** ~ *(US)* Verkauf auf Abzahlungsbasis, Abzahlungsgeschäft; **definite** ~

abgeschlossener Verkauf; **deposit** ~ Verkauf mit Lieferung nach Bezahlung; **direct** ~ Verkauf ohne Zwischenhändler, Direktverkauf, *(securities)* Privatabsatz; **distress** ~ Notverkauf gepfändeter Gegenstände, Zwangsvollstreckungsverkauf; **domestic** ~s Inlandsabsatz; **dull** ~s langsamer Verkauf, *(stock exchange)* matte Verkäufe; **duty-paid** ~ Verkauf nach erfolgter Verzollung; **end-of-season** ~ Saisonschlußverkauf; **exclusive** ~ Alleinverkauf; **executed** ~ Handkauf, erfüllter Kaufvertrag, Kauf mit Eigentumsübergang; **execution** ~ *(US)* Zwangsverkauf; **executory** ~ noch zu erfüllender Kaufvertrag; **external** ~s *(balance sheet)* Fremdumsatz; **fair** ~ ordnungsgemäß durchgeführte Zwangsversteigerung; **fictitious** ~s fingierter Umsatz; **all** ~s **final** kein Umtausch; **final liquidation** ~ Zwangsverkauf; **firm** ~ fester Verkauf; **forced** ~ [by order of the court] [gerichtlich angeordnete] Zwangsversteigerung, Vollstreckungsverkauf; **foreclosure** ~ *(US)* Zwangsversteigerung; **foreign** ~s Auslandsumsätze; **forward** ~ *(stock exchange)* Verkauf auf Lieferung, Terminverkauf; **fraudulent** ~ betrügerischer Verkauf [mit der Absicht der Gläubigerschädigung]; **going-out-of-business** ~ Totalausverkauf; **gross** ~s Bruttoumsatz, -erlös; **heavy** ~ schlechter Absatz, *(stock market)* größere Abgaben; **hedging** ~ Verkauf zu Deckungszwecken, Deckungsverkauf; **hire-purchase** ~ *(Br.)* Verkauf auf Abzahlungsbasis, Abzahlungsgeschäft, Abzahlungs-, Ratenkauf; **home** ~s Inlandsverkäufe; **important** ~s Massenabsatz; **instal(l)ment** ~ Abzahlungsgeschäft, Verkauf gegen Ratenzahlung, Verkauf auf Abzahlungsbasis; **intercompany** ~s Umsätze innerhalb eines Konzerns, konzerneigene Verkäufe, Konzernumsatz; **inventory** ~ Inventurausverkauf; **judicial** *(Scot., US)* vom Gericht angeordnete Versteigerung, Zwangsversteigerung; **jumble** ~ Ramschverkauf; **large** ~s großer Absatz, große Umsätze; **long** ~ Effektenverkauf aus eigenen Beständen; **loose-leaf** ~ Verkauf in Bausch und Bogen; **losing** ~ Verlustverkauf; **mail-order** ~ *(US)* Verkauf auf Grund übersandten Katalogs, Versandgeschäft; **matched** ~s *(stock exchange)* gekoppelte Börsengeschäfte; **memorandum** ~ Kauf auf Probe (mit Rückgaberecht), Kommissionsverkauf; **money** ~ Barverkauf; **net** ~s Nettoumsatz; **new-car** ~s Neuwagengeschäft; **no** ~s *(stock market)* ohne Umsatz; **odds-and-ends** ~ *(US)* Abfallverkauf; **offhand** ~ freihändiger Verkauf; **ontrack** ~ Verkaufspreis bei Eingang des Fahrzeuges am Versandort; **open** ~ Blankoverkauf; **open-market** ~s Verkäufe am offenen Markt; **opening** ~ *(stock exchange)* erster Abschluß; **outright** ~ fester Verkaufsabschluß, Abschluß zu einem festen Verkaufspreis; **overall** ~s Gesamtumsatz; **extensive** ~s **overseas** umfangreiche Auslandsumsätze; **panic** ~ Angstverkauf; **partial** ~ Teilverkauf; **priority** ~ *(securities)* Prioritätsverkauf; **private** ~ freihändiger Verkauf, Verkauf unter der Hand; **profit-taking** ~ [Verkauf zwecks] Gewinnrealisierung, Sicherungsverkauf; **pro-forma** ~ Scheinverkauf; **public** ~ öffentliche Versteigerung, Zwangsversteigerung; **qualified** ~ Konditions[ver]kauf; **quick** ~s rascher Umschlag; **rapid** ~s reißender Absatz; **ready** ~ rascher Verkauf, schlanker (schneller) Absatz; **regular** ~ *(stock exchange)* Verkauf auf Lieferung am folgenden Tag; **remainder** ~ Ausverkauf einer Auflage, Verkauf einer Restauflage; **remnant** ~ Restverkauf; **repeat** ~ Kauf auf Grund von Erinnerungswerbung; **retail** ~ Einzelhandelsumsätze; **rising** ~s Umsatzsteigerungen; **ruinous (sacrifice)** ~ Verlustverkauf; **rummage** ~ Verkauf von Ramschware, Ramschverkauf; **seasonal** ~ Saisonschlußverkauf; **secondhand** ~ Kauf aus zweiter Hand; **sham** ~ Schein-, Verkauf pro forma; **sheriff's** ~s *(US)* Zwangsversteigerung; **short** ~s *(stock exchange) (US)* Leerverkauf, Verkauf ohne Deckung, Blankoverkauf, -abgabe; **slow** ~s langsamer Absatz; **short** ~s schneller (schlanker) Absatz; **split** ~ *(stock exchange)* Verkauf zu verschiedenen Zeiten und zu verschiedenen Preisen; **special** ~s Sonderverkaufsveranstaltung; **spot** ~ Barverkauf, *(stock exchange)* Umsätze am Kassamarkt, Kassaumsätze; **spring** ~s Schlußverkauf im Frühling; **summer** ~s Sommerschlußverkauf; **tax** ~s Verkäufe zur Überwindung des Steuertermins, Verkauf zur Bezahlung von Steuern; **tie-in** ~ Koppelungsgeschäft; **time** ~ Kauf auf Zeit, Zeitkauf; **tying-in** ~s *(US)* Koppelungsgeschäfte; **total** ~s Gesamtumsatz, Geschäftsumsatz, Absatzvolumen; **uncovered** ~ Verkauf ohne Deckung; **under-the-counter** ~ Verkauf unter dem Ladentisch; **unrestricted** ~ unbehinderte (unkontrollierte) Verkäufe; **used-car** ~s Gebrauchtwagenverkäufe, -umsatz; **voluntary** ~ Freiverkauf, freihändiger Verkauf; **wash** ~ *(stock exchange)* Simultankauf und -verkauf, Börsenscheingeschäft; **weekend** ~ Wochenendumsätze; **white** ~ weiße Woche; **winter** ~s Winterschlußverkauf;

bargain and ~ Kaufvertrag;

~ **on account** Verkauf auf Rechnung (mit Anzahlung); ~ **for the account** *(stock exchange, Br.)* Verkauf für zukünftige Lieferung, Terminverkauf; ~ **on approval** Kauf auf Probe; ~s **to arrive (on arrival)** Verkauf vorbehaltlich sicherer Ankunft, Transitwarenverkauf; ~ **of assets** Anlagenverkauf; ~ **at** *(US)* **(by,** *Br.)* **auction** Verkauf im Wege der Versteigerung; ~ **per aversionem** *(lat.)* Verkauf in Bausch und Bogen, Pauschalverkauf; ~ **by sealed bids** Submissionsverkauf; ~ **to the highest bidder** Zuschlag an den Meistbietenden; ~ **ex bond** Verkauf ab Zollager; ~ **by the bulk** Verkauf in Bausch und Bogen, Partie-, Bauschverkauf; ~ **of a business** Firmen-, Geschäftsverkauf; ~ **of chattels** Verkauf beweglicher Sachen; ~ **on consignment** Kommissionsverkauf, kommissionsweiser Verkauf, Verkauf auf Kommissionsbasis; **total** ~s **of the consolidated companies** Gesamtumsatz der in den konsolidierten Jahresabschluß einbezogenen Gesellschaften; ~ **by private contract** freihändiger (privatrechtlicher) Verkauf; ~ **per copy** *(newspaper)* Einzelverkauf; ~ **below cost** Schleuderverkauf, Abgabe unter Selbstkostenpreis; ~ **under a court order** gerichtliche Versteigerung; ~ **on credit** Terminverkauf, Lieferkredit; ~ **of foreign currencies** Devisenverkauf; ~ **for prompt delivery** Verkauf zur sofortigen Lieferung; ~ **by description** Verkauf nach Beschreibung; ~s **per employee** Absatz je beschäftigte Person; ~ **with all faults** Verkauf wie es steht und liegt, Verkauf unter Ausschluß von Gewährleistungsansprüchen; ~ **for forward (future) delivery** *(stock exchange)* Verkauf auf Lieferung (Zeit), Termin[ver]kauf; ~ **of goods** Waren-, Güterverkauf, Warenabsatz, Handelskauf; ~ **of ascertained goods** Spezieskauf; ~ **of specific goods** Spezieskauf; ~ **of unascertained goods** Gattungskauf; ~ **in gross** Partieverkauf, Verkauf in Bausch und Bogen; ~ **on inspection** Kauf nach Besichtigung (wie besehen); ~ **of land** Grundstücks[ver]kauf; ~s **transacted at large** Warenvertrieb im großen, ~ **of a licence** Lizenzverkauf; ~s **of loans** Anleiheverkäufe, -absatz; ~ **by lots** Verkäufe in Partien, Partieverkauf; ~ **of luxuries** Luxusgütervertrieb; ~ **of machinery** Maschinenverkauf; ~ **in the open market (in market overt)** freihändiger Verkauf, Laden- und Marktverkauf, Freihandelsverkauf; ~ **with option of repurchase** Verkauf mit Rückkaufsrecht; ~s **to others** *(balance sheet)* Verkäufe an Dritte; ~ **to pattern** Verkauf nach Muster; ~ **of personalty (personal property)** Verkauf beweglicher Sachen; ~ **of plant** Veräußerung eines Betriebes; ~ **of pledge** Pfandverkauf; ~s **from the portfolio** Verkäufe von Nostro-Effekten; ~ **under a special power** Verkauf aufgrund einer Sonderermächtigung; ~ **at giveaway prices** Schleuderverkauf; ~ **of property** Veräußerung von Vermögensgegenständen, Immobilienverkauf; ~ **of provisions** Lebensmittelverkauf; **direct** ~ **to the public** *(stock exchange)* freihändiger [Effekten]verkauf; ~ **of real property (realty)** Grundstücksverkauf, Verkauf von Grundbesitz; ~ **at retail** Einzelhandels- Detail-, Kleinhandelsverkauf, Verkauf zu Einzelhandelspreisen; ~ **and return** Verkauf mit Rückgaberecht, Kommissionsgeschäft, -verkauf; ~ **with right of redemption** Verkauf mit Rückgaberecht; ~ **by sample** Kauf nach Probe (Muster); ~s **made on the basis of samples** auf Grund von Warenproben getätigte Käufe; ~ **of securities** Begebung von Wertpapieren, Wertpapier-, Effektenabsatz; ~s **of savings certificates** Sparbriefabsatz; ~ **of services** Dienstleistungsgeschäft; ~ **for the settlement** *(stock exchange, Br.)* Terminverkauf; ~ **of shares** Vertrieb von Anteilen (Aktien), Aktienverkäufe, -plazierung; ~ **to specification** Spezifikationsverkauf; ~s **on speculation** Meinungsverkäufe; ~s **on the spot** Platzverkauf, Verkauf an Ort und Stelle; ~s **per sq. m. of salesroom** Absatz je qm Verkaufsraum; ~ **on the deferred payment system** *(US)* Abzahlungsgeschäft; ~ **by [sealed] tender** Verkauf aufgrund einer Ausschreibung, Submissionsverkauf; ~ **by test** Kauf nach Erprobung; ~ **by private treaty** freigestalteter Verkauf; ~ **on trial** Verkauf zur Probe; ~ **at a valuation** Spezifikations-, Bestimmungskauf; ~ **of weapons** Waffenverkäufe; ~ **of work** Verkauf zu Wohltätigkeitszwecken;

to achieve world-wide ~ weltweiten Absatz haben; **to advertise a** ~ Verkauf anzeigen; **to annul a** ~ **by paying a fine** Kaufvertrag gegen Zahlung einer Geldbuße annullieren; **to attend a** ~ bei einem Verkauf mitwirken; **to avoid a** ~ Verkauf widerrufen; **to be dull of** ~ sich schwer verkaufen lassen; **to be entrusted with the** ~ **of s. th.** mit dem Verkauf einer Sache beauftragt sein; **to be exposed for** ~ zum Verkauf aufliegen; **to be for** ~ verkäuflich sein, zum Verkauf stehen; **to be left over from a** ~ vom Verkauf übrigbleiben; **to be of quick** ~ schnell (reißend) Absatz finden; **to be of slow** ~ langsam umgesetzt werden; **to be up for** ~ angeboten werden, zum Verkauf stehen; **to become permanent on** ~s **of 250.000 a day** täglich zweihundertfünfzigtausend

Stück verkaufen; **to buy goods at the ~s** Waren auf einer Auktion (im Ausverkauf) kaufen; **to close (consummate) a ~** Verkauf abschließen (tätigen); **to conclude a ~** Handel abschließen (tätigen); **to display for ~** zum Verkauf auslegen (ausstellen); **to effect a ~** realisieren, Kauf abschließen; **to entrust s. o. with the ~** j. mit dem Verkauf betreuen; **to exhibit for ~** zum Verkauf ausstellen; **to expose for ~** zum Verkauf auslegen; **to find a quick (ready) ~** guten (schnellen) Absatz finden; **to find no ~** keinen Absatz finden, nicht untergebracht werden können, sich nicht verkaufen lassen; **to go on ~** zum Verkauf gelangen; **to help ~s** sich umsatzsteigernd auswirken; **to increase ~s** Absatz fördern, Umsatz steigern; **to make more ~s** größere Umsätze tätigen; **to make ~ of a thing** Verkauf einer Sache bewirken; **to make ~s on credit to retail customers** seinen Einzelhandelskunden Warenkredit einräumen; **to meet with a [ready] ~** [guten] Absatz finden, sich leicht (gut) verkaufen [lassen]; **to filter down to ~s** zu Verkäufen führen; **to negotiate a ~** Verkauf abschließen; **to offer for ~** zum Verkauf anbieten; **to pass by ~** (property) beim Verkauf übergehen; **to push ~s** Absatz vorantreiben; **to put to ~** zum Verkauf bringen; **to put up (set out) for ~** feilbieten, meistbietend verkaufen, zum Verkauf stellen; **to rack up big ~s** dick verdienen; **to rescind a ~** Verkauf rückgängig machen; **to ring up the ~** Betrag registrieren; **to roll up the ~s** Umsatz steigern, Umsatzsteigerung erzielen; **to satisfy a ~ made under power of attorney** einem vom bevollmächtigten Vertreter getätigten Verkauf zustimmen; **to suspend the ~** Verkauf einstellen; **to take on ~** zum Verkauf übernehmen; **to take s. th. on ~ and return** etw. in Kommission nehmen; **to take ~s well** (market) Verkäufe gut (glatt) aufnehmen;

on ~, owner retiring from business wegen Geschäftsaufgabe zu verkaufen;

~ of goods Act (Br.) Ladenverkaufsgesetz; **~ application** Verkaufsauftrag; **~ board** Verkaufsschild; **~ catalog(ue)** Auktionsliste; **~ contract** Verkaufsvertrag; **~ goods** Ausverkaufs-, Ramschwaren; **~ invoice** Verkaufsrechnung; **~-lease back** (US) Erwerb von Anlagegütern im Leasingverfahren; **~ note** (broker, US) Schlußnote, -schein; **~ price** [Aus]verkaufspreis; **~ proceeds** Verkaufserlöse; **~ ring** (auction) Käuferring, Aufkäufergruppe; **~ and report system** (travel agency) Buchung bereits verkaufter Flugplätze; **~ terms** (US) Absatz-, Vertriebs-, Liefer-, Verkaufsbedingungen; **~ value** Verkaufswert; **~ wares** Waren.

salegoer Käufer.
saleroom (Br.) Verkaufsraum, (auction) Auktionslokal.
sales|ability Verkaufsbegabung; **~ account** Warenausgangs-, Verkaufskonto, (advertising agency) Kunde, Kundenetat, (commission) Verkaufsrechnung; **~ activity** Verkaufstätigkeit, -aktivität, Umsatzbewegung; **~ administration** Vertriebsapparat; **~ agency** Handels-, Absatzvertretung, Verkaufsagentur, -organisation, -niederlassung; **~ agent** (US) Handels-, [General]vertreter, [Handlungs]reisender; **travelling ~ agent** (US) Handlungs-, Geschäftsreisender; **~ agreement** Kaufvereinbarung, -vertrag; **conditional ~ agreement** Kaufvertrag unter Eigentumsvorbehalt; **~ aid** Verkaufsunterstützung; **~ allowance** [Verkaufs]rabatt, Preisnachlaß; **~ analysis** Verkaufs-, Absatzanalyse; **~ angle** Verkaufsgesichtspunkt; **~ appeal** Kaufappell, -anreiz; **~ approach** Verkaufsgesichtspunkt, -politik; **[narrow] ~ area** [beschränktes] Absatzgebiet (Verkaufsgebiet), **~ argument** Verkaufsargument; **emotional ~ argument** gefühlsbetontes (emotionales) Verkaufsargument; **rational ~ argument** rationell ansprechendes Verkaufsargument; **~ assistant** Aushilfe; **~ association** Vertriebs-, Verkaufsgesellschaft; **industrial ~ background** industrielle Verkaufserfahrungen; **~ ban** Verkaufsverbot; **~ base** Verkaufsbasis, -grundlage; **~ bill [of exchange]** Warenwechsel, Verkaufstratte; **~ book** Ausgangsfakturen-, [Waren]verkaufsbuch; **~ booth** Verkaufsstand, -bude; **~ branch** Verkaufsfiliale, -niederlassung; **manufacturer's ~ branch** fabrikeigenes Ladengeschäft; **~ breakdown** Umsatzanalyse; **~ brochure** Verkaufsprospekt; **~ budget** Umsatzplanung; **~ bulletin** Kundenzeitschrift; **~ call** Vertreter-, Kundenbesuch; **~ call costs** Vertreterbesuchskosten; **~ campaign** Verkaufskampagne, -aktion, -feldzug, Werbe-, Absatzfeldzug; **~ cancellation** Verkaufsstornierung; **~ capacity** Vertreter-, Verkäufertätigkeit; **~ cartel** Absatz-, Rayonierungskartell; **~ catalog(ue)** Verkaufskatalog; **~ channel** Absatzweg, Vertriebweg, -kanal; **~ charge** Abschlußgebühr; **~ chart** Umsatzkurve in graphischer Darstellung, Um-, Absatzstatistik; **~ check** (US) Kassenzettel, -beleg, -quittung, Verkaufsquittung; **~ classification** Absatzgliederung; **~ club** Verkäufervereinigung; **~ combine** Absatz-, Vertriebsgemein-

schaft; **~ commission** Verkaufs-, Absatz-, Abschlußprovision; **~ committee** Absatz-, Vertriebsausschuß; **~ company** Vertriebsgesellschaft; **~ completion** Verkaufsabschluß; **~ conditions** Liefer-, Verkaufsbedingungen; **~ conference** Absatzgremium; **~ considerations** Absatzerwägungen; **~ consultant** Vertriebs-, Verkaufsberater; **~ contest** Verkaufswettbewerb; **~ contract** Liefer-, Kaufvertrag; **conditional ~ contract** Verkaufsvertrag mit Eigentumsvorbehalt; **to rescind a ~ contract** vom Kaufvertrag zurücktreten; **~ control** Verkaufs-, Absatzkontrolle, -lenkung; **~ check control** Kassenzettelkontrolle; **~ convention** Absatztagung; **~ cost** Absatz-, Vertriebskosten; **~ correspondent** Korrespondent; **~ crisis** Absatzkrise, Umsatztief, -krise; **~ curve** Absatzdiagramm, Absatz-, Verkaufs-, Umsatzkurve; **to stem the downward ~ curve** weiteres Absinken der Umsatzkurve verhindern; **~ data** Verkaufsziffern; **~ day book** Warenausgangsbuch; **~ decline** Absatz-, Umsatzrückgang; **~ demonstration** Verkaufsvorführung; **~ department** Verkaufs-, Vertriebsabteilung; **~ devices** Vertriebseinrichtungen; **~ diagram** Absatzdiagramm; **~ difficulties** Verkaufs-, Absatzschwierigkeiten; **~ dip** Verkaufs-, Umsatzrückgang; **~ discount** Kunden-, Verkaufsrabatt; **~ display** [Verkaufs]auslage; **~ drive** Hochdruckverkauf, Verkaufsvorstoß, -kampagne, verstärkter Werbeeinsatz, Absatz-, Vertriebsanstrengungen; **~ efforts** verstärkte Absatzbemühung, Verkaufsanstrengungen; **total ~ effort of a company** gesamter Firmenabsatz; **~ elasticity** Vertriebselastizität; **~ engineer** Verkaufs-, Vertriebsingenieur, technischer Kaufmann, **~ estimate** Vertriebs-, Absatzkalkulation, Umsatzschätzung; **~ etiquette** Berufsethos beim Verkaufen; **~ event** verkaufsförderndes Ereignis, spezieller Verkaufsanlaß; **~ executive** für den Verkauf verantwortliches Vorstandsmitglied, Verkaufsleiter; **~ expansion** Umsatzausweitung; **~ expectancy** erwartete Verkaufserfolge, Umsatz-, Verkaufserwartung; **~ expenses** Verkaufsunkosten, Vertriebskosten; **~ experience** Verkaufserfahrung; **~ figures** Vertriebs-, Verkaufsziffern, Absatzzahlen, -ziffern, Umsatzzahlen, -werte; **foreign ~ figures** Außenhandelsziffern; **~ finance company** (US) Absatzfinanzierungsgesellschaft, Kundenkredit-, Teilzahlungsbank; **~ floor** Verkaufsfläche; **~ fluctuations** Absatz-, Umsatzschwankungen; **~ force** (US) Verkäufer, Verkaufspersonal, -mannschaft, -außendienst, Verkäufer-, Vertreter-, Absatzstab; **~ force participation** Umsatzbeteiligung des Absatzstabes; **~ and service force** Verkaufs- und Kundendienstnetz; **~ forecast[ing]** Absatzprognose, -vorausschätzung, Verkaufsvoraussage; **~ form** (stock exchange) Kaufauftrag; **~ frequency** Umsatz-, Umschlagsgeschwindigkeit; **~ gains** Absatzsteigerungen, Umsatzgewinne; **~ gimmicks** (US sl.) Verkaufstrick; **~ group** Vertriebs-, Verkaufsgemeinschaft; **~ guaranty** Umsatz-, Absatzgarantie; **~ idea** Verkaufs-, Vertriebsidee; **~ impact** (advertising) Wirkungsgrad einer Anzeige; **~ increase** Absatz-, Umsatzsteigerung; **~ index** Absatzindex; **~ inducement** Kaufanreiz; **~ interview** Verkaufsinterview; **~ invoice** Verkaufsrechnung; **~ journal** Warenausgangsbuch, -journal; **~ jump** sprungartiger Umsatz-, Absatzanstieg; **~ kit** (US) Verkaufsausrüstung, Werbematerial [eines Reisenden], Verkaufsförderungsmaßnahmen; **~ lady** (coll.) Verkäuferin; **~ lag** Verkaufslücke; **~ leap** sprungartig angestiegener Umsatz; **~ leasing** Vermietung von Ausrüstungsgütern unter gleichzeitiger Rückmiete; **~ ledger** Warenausgangs-, Debitorenbuch; **~ letter** Werbebrief, -schreiben; **~ licence** Übernahmeschein; **~ limit** Umsatz-, Absatzgrenze; **~ literature** Verkaufsprospekt, -literatur; **~ load** (investment trust) Verkaufsspesen, Vertriebskostenanteil; **~ location** Verkaufsgelände; **~ management** Verkaufsleitung; **~ manager** Verkaufsleiter, -direktor, Direktor der Verkaufsabteilung, Vertriebsleiter, Repräsentant; **aggressive ~ manager** einfallsreicher (aktiver) Verkaufsleiter; **divisional (district) ~ manager** Bezirksverkaufsleiter; **export ~ manager** Exportleiter; **~ manual** Handbuch für Verkäufer, Verkaufshandbuch; **~ marketing conference** Absatzgremium; **~ measures** Verkaufsaktivitäten; **~ meeting** Vertretertagung, Verkäuferschulung; **~ message** Verkaufsaussage, Werbebotschaft; **~ method** Absatz-, Vertriebs-, Verkaufsmethode; **~ minded** umsatz-, absatzbewußt; **~ mindedness** Absatzbewußtsein; **~ mission** Verkaufsdelegation; **~ mix** (US) Verkaufsmischung, Sortiment; **~ monopoly** Absatz-, Vertriebsmonopol; **~ note** (US) Schlußnote, -schein; **conditional ~ note** zur Sicherung des Eigentumsvorbehaltes ausgestellte Urkunde; **~ notice** Verkaufshinweis; **~ objective** Umsatz-, Verkaufsziel; **~ offer** Verkaufsofferte, -angebot; **~ office** Verkaufsbüro, -stelle; **to beef up one's ~ operations** seine Verkaufsanstrengungen verstärken; **~ opportunity** Absatzmöglichkeit, -chance; **~ order** (*stock exchange*) Verkaufsauftrag, -order; ~ **organization** Absatz-, Vertriebsorganisation, Vertriebsapparat, Verkaufsorganisation, (*subsidiary*) Vertriebsgesellschaft; **subsidiary** ~ **organization** Verkaufsorganisation einer Tochtergesellschaft; ~ **organizer** Verkaufsorganisator; ~ **outlet** (*US*) Vertriebs-, Verkaufsstelle, Verkaufsniederlassung, Filiale; ~ **outlook** Verkaufsaussichten; **allocated** ~ **overhead expenses** verrechnete Vertriebsgemeinkosten; ~ **package** Verkaufs[ver]packung; ~ **patter** Verkäuferjargon; ~ **people** (*US*) (**personnel**) Verkaufspersonal, Verkäufer, Absatzstab; **to hire extra** ~ **people** zusätzliches Verkaufspersonal einstellen; ~ **percentage** Umsatzprovision; ~ **performance** Verkaufstätigkeit, -durchführung; ~ **permit** Veräußerungsgenehmigung; ~ **person** Verkäufer[in]; ~ **pitch** Verkaufserfolg eines Verkäufers; ~ **plan** Vertriebsplan; ~ **planning** Verkaufs-, Absatz-, Umsatzplanung; ~ **plus** Verkaufsplus; ~ **policy** Vertriebs-, Absatz-, Verkaufspolitik; ~ **position** Verkaufslage, (*employee*) Verkaufsstellung; ~ **possibilities** Markt-, Absatzchancen; ~ **potential** Absatz-, Verkaufspotential; ~ **premium** Umsatz-, Abschlußprämie; ~ **price** Verkaufs-, Kaufpreis; **to arrive** ~ **price** Verkaufspreis bei Eintreffen der Ware; **special** ~**s price** Ausverkaufspreis; **on-truck** ~ **price** Verkaufspreis bei Eingang des Fahrzeugs am Versandort; **to pay the** ~ **price** Kaufpreis erlegen; **net** ~ **proceeds** Verkaufsreinerlös; ~ **process** Verkaufsvorgang; **to speed up the** ~ **process** Absatzbeschleunigung herbeiführen, für beschleunigten Umsatz Sorge tragen; ~ **profit** Gewinn aus Veräußerungen, Veräußerungsgewinn, Verkaufserlös; ~**-profit ratio** Verhältnis Gewinn zu Umsatz; ~ **progress control** Verkaufskontrolle; ~ **prohibition** Veräußerungsverbot; ~ **projection** Absatzplan; ~ **promoter** Vertriebskaufmann, Verkaufsleiter; ~ **promotion** Förderung des Absatzes, Vertriebs-, Verkaufs-, Absatzförderung, Absatzsteigerung; ~ **promotion agency** Absatzvertretung; ~ **promotion aids** Mittel der Verkaufsförderung; ~ **promotion budget** Verkaufsförderungsetat; ~ **promotion campaign** Verkaufsförderungsaktion; ~ **promotion manager** Leiter der Verkaufsförderung; ~ **promotion techniques** Absatzförderungsverfahren; ~ **promotional efforts** (**practices**) (*US*) Anstrengungen (Maßnahmen) zur Absatzsteigerung; ~ **proportion** Absatzquote; ~ **proposition** Verkaufsvorschlag; ~ **prospects** Vertriebs-, Verkaufs-, Absatzchancen, -erwartungen, Absatz-, Vertriebsaussichten; ~ **psychology** Verkaufspsychologie; ~ **publicity** Verkaufswerbung; ~ **push** Verkaufsanstrengungen; ~ **prospects** Geschäftsaussichten; ~ **quota** (*cartel*) Absatz-, Verkaufskontingent, -quote, Sollvorgaben im Verkauf; ~ **rate** (*forward deal*) Abschlußkurs, -satz; ~ **receipts** Verkaufserlös; ~ **record** Kassenbeleg, Verkaufsunterlage; ~ **records** hervorragende Verkaufsergebnisse; ~ **reduction** Absatz-, Umsatzrückgang; ~ **region** Vertretergebiet; ~ **register** Verkaufsbuch; ~ **report** Absatzbericht; ~ **representation** Verkaufsaktion; **to drive a** ~ **representation** Verkaufsaktion durchführen; **to streamline one's** ~ **representations** nach modernsten Methoden verkaufen; **to tailor one's** ~ **representation** sein Verkaufsprogramm darauf abstellen; ~ **representative** Verkäufer, Handelsvertreter, Handlungsreisender, Reisender; ~ **research** Verkaufs-, Absatzforschung; ~ **resistance** Kaufabneigung, -unlust; **to meet with considerable** ~ **resistance** es mit schwierigen Kunden zu tun zu haben; ~ **restrictions** Verkaufsbeschränkungen; ~ **results** Absatz-, Verkaufs-, Vertriebs-, Umsatzergebnis; ~ **returns** Retourwaren, (*sales receipts*) Verkaufserlös, -ertrag; ~ **revenue** Gesamtverkaufseinnahmen, gesamtes Absatzergebnis, Umsatzerträge; ~ **revenue maximization** Umsatzmaximierung; ~ **section** Verkaufsdezernat; **after-**~ **service** Kundendienst; ~ **sheet** Verkaufszettel, Kassenbeleg, -zettel, Verkaufsbescheinigung; ~ **shipment** Versendungsverkauf; **on the** ~ **side** auf der Verkaufsseite; ~ **situation** Absatz-, Marktlage; ~ **slip** Kassenschein, -beleg, -zettel; ~ **slump** rückläufige Verkaufsergebnisse; **spring** ~ **sprint** frühjahrsbedingter Absatzanstieg; ~ **staff** Verkaufspersonal, Absatzstab; ~ **statistics** Verkaufs-, Umsatz-, Absatzstatistik; **to map out a** ~ **strategy** strategischen Verkaufsplan ausarbeiten; ~ **supervision** Verkaufsüberwachung; ~ **supervisor** Verkaufsleiter, Außenrevisor; ~ **syndicate** Vertriebs-, Verkaufs-, Absatzgemeinschaft, Verkaufssyndikat; ~ **talk** Verkaufsgespräch, unverbindliche Anpreisungen, (*fig.*) Überredungskünste; ~ **target** Verkaufsziel; ~ **tax** (*US*) Verkaufs-, Umsatzsteuer; ~**-tax refund** (*US*) Umsatzsteuerrückvergütung; ~ **tax relief** Umsatzsteuerfreibetrag; ~ **team** Verkaufsgruppe; ~ **techniques** Verkaufspraktiken; ~ **terms** (*US*) Verkaufs-, Absatz-, Lieferungs-, Vertriebsbedingungen; ~ **territory** Absatz-, Vertriebs-, Verkaufsgebiet; ~ **test** Verkaufsschulung; ~ **ticket** (*US*) Kassenschein, -beleg, -zettel, Verkaufszettel; ~ **tool** Ver-

kaufshilfe; ~ **trainee** Verkaufspraktikant; ~ **training** Verkäuferschulung; ~ **training course** Verkaufsausbildungskursus; ~ **training group** Schulungsgruppe für Verkäufer; ~ **training pro-gram(me)** Ausbildungsprogramm für Verkaufsleiter; ~ **transaction** Verkaufstransaktion; ~ **trend** Umsatzentwicklung, Absatztendenz, -bewegungen, -trend; ~ **trip** Verkaufs-, Vertretertour; ~ **turnover** Warenumsatz; ~ **value** Verkaufswert; ~ **vigo(u)r** Verkaufsleistung, Wirksamkeit der Verkaufstätigkeit; ~ **volume** Umsatz-, Absatz-, Verkaufsvolumen, Mengenumsatz, Kapitalumschlag; ~ **volume rate** Umschlagshäufigkeit des Kapitals, Kapitalumschlagshäufigkeit; ~ **voucher** Kassenbon; ~ **warrant** Kassenschein, -beleg; ~ **week** Verkaufswoche; ~ **year** Verkaufsjahr.

salesclerk (*US*) [angestellter] Verkäufer.

salesfolder illustrierter Klappprospekt, Verkäufermerkblatt.

salesgirl Ladenmädchen, Verkäuferin.

salesman Kaufmann, (*US*) [Laden]verkäufer, Ladenangestellter, (*broker*) Effektenmakler, (*wholesaler*) [Groß]händler; **carpet-bagging** ~ unseriöser Vertreter; **distributive** ~ Vertriebsfachmann; **engineer** ~ Vertriebsingenieur, technischer Verkäufer; **high-cost** ~ hochqualifizierter Verkäufer; **missionary** ~ Werbeschulungsleiter; **outside** ~ Verkäufer im Außendienst; **professional** ~ Vertriebsfachmann im Angestelltenverhältnis, festangestellter Reisender; **regional** ~ Bezirksvertreter; **speciality** ~ Spezialitätenverkäufer; **star (top)** ~ Verkaufskanone, Spitzenverkäufer; **travelling** ~ Geschäfts-, Provisionsreisender; **to be a born** ~ der geborene Verkäufer sein; ~'**s advertising portfolio** Angebotsmappe eines Handlungsreisenden; ~'**s basic pay** Vertreterfixum; ~'**s performance** Verkäufer-, Vertreterleistung; ~'**s position** Verkäufer-, Vertreterstellung; ~ **type** Vertretertyp.

salesmanship Verkaufsgewandtheit, -technik, -kunst; **high-pressure** ~ zielbewußte Verkaufsmethode; **unfair** ~ unlautere Verkaufspraktiken, rasante Verkaufstechnik; **to succeed in** ~ Erfolg als Verkäufer haben.

salesmen under my guidance mir unterstehende Verkäufer.

salesperson Verkäufer[in].

salesroom Verkaufs-, Auktionslokal.

saleswoman Verkäuferin.

salient | **characteristics** hervorstechende Merkmale; ~ **figures** ins Auge fallende Zahlen; ~ **point** (*fig.*) springender Punkt.

sally (*brainwave*) Geistesblitz, (*excursion*) Ausflug, Abstecher, (*mil.*) Ausfall; ~ (*v.*) **out** (**forth**) aufbrechen, sich auf den Weg machen; ~ **out against the besiegers** Ausfall gegen die Belagerer machen; **to make a** ~ **into the country** Landpartie machen.

salon Salon, Empfangszimmer, (*exhibition*) Ausstellungsraum, (*reception*) Empfang.

saloon Saal, Halle, (*bar, Br.*) Bar[raum], (*salon*) Salon, Empfangszimmer, (*ship*) Salon, (*US*) Gastwirtschaft, Kneipe, Spelunke; **billiard** ~ (*Br.*) Billardzimmer; **dining** ~ (*ship*) Speisesaal; **luxury-class** ~ Limousine der Luxusklasse; **sawdust** ~ (*US sl.*) billige Kneipe; **seven-seater** ~ siebensitzige Familienkutsche; ~ **bar** (*Br.*) Schankstube, Bar; ~ **car** (*Br.*) Luxuswagen, Limousine, (*railroad, US*) Salonwagen; ~ **carriage** (*Br.*) Salonwagen; ~ **deck** (*ship*) Salondeck; ~ **anti-**~ **league** (*US*) Alkoholgegnerverband, Blaukreuzlerverein; ~ **steamer** Salondampfer; ~ **train** Luxuszug.

saloonkeeper (*US*) Gastwirt, Kneipier.

salt Salz, (*fig.*) Würze, Witz, Esprit, (*money, sl.*) Kies, Moneten; **with a grain of** ~ mit Vorbehalt; ~ (*v.*) **an account** gepfefferte Rechnung ausstellen; ~ **away a lot of money** viel Geld auf die hohe Kante legen; ~ **away part of one's salary** Teil seines Gehaltes sparen; ~ **the books** Geschäftsbücher frisieren; **to be worth one's** ~ etw. taugen; **not to be worth one's** ~ keinen Schuß Pulver wert sein; **to eat s. one's** ~ von jem. abhängig sein; ~ (*a.*) (*account, sl.*) gesalzen, gepfeffert; ~ **duty** Salzsteuer; **back to the** ~ **mines** (*sl.*) in die Tretmühle zurück; ~ **speech** scharfe Rede.

salted (*fig.*) ausgekocht, abgebrüht.

salubrious climate gesundes Klima.

salutation Grußformel, (*letter*) Begrüßungsformel; **in** ~ zur Begrüßung.

salutatory [**oration**] Eröffnungs-, Begrüßungsrede.

salute Begrüßung, (*firing of guns*) Salut[schießen], (*raising of hand*) Ehrenbezeigung; ~ (*v.*) salutieren; **to take the** ~ **of the troops** Vorbeimarsch abnehmen.

salvage *(dues)* Bergelohn, *(fire insurance)* Wert der geretteten Waren, *(motorcar insurance)* Schrottwertanrechnung, *(property saved)* gerettetes (geborgenes) Gut, Bergungsgut, *(recovery of waste)* [Altmaterial-, Abfall]verwertung, Wiedergewinnung, -verwertung, *(residual, US)* Restwert, *(saving)* Bergung, Rettung, *(welfare work)* soziale Rettungsarbeit;
civil ~ Bergeleistung, Schiffsrettung; **military** ~ Einbringung nach Prisenrecht; **recoverable** ~ wiederverwertbares Bergungsgut;
~ *(v.)* bergen, retten, *(recover)* verwerten;
~ **from the debris** aus den Trümmern bergen;
to assess the amount payable as ~ Höhe des Bergelohnes festsetzen; **to collect old newspapers and magazines for** ~ Altpapiersammlung durchführen; **to make** ~ **of a shipwrecked cargo** Bruchlandung bergen; **to make** ~ **of goods** Güter bergen; **to pay a large** ~ hohes Bergegeld zahlen; **to take over the** ~ *(insurer)* Bergungsgut übernehmen;
~ **agreement** Bergungsvertrag; ~ **boat** Bergungsfahrzeug; ~ **bond** Bergungsverpflichtung, -vertrag; ~ **business** Seerettungsdienst; ~ **charges (cost)** *(marine insurance)* Kosten für Rettungsmaßnahmen, Bergungskosten; ~ **claims** Bergelohnforderungen; ~ **company** Bergungsgesellschaft, -unternehmen; ~ **corps** *(US)* Technische Nothilfe [für Brandkatastrophen usw.]; ~ **craft** Bergungsboot; ~ **crane** Abschleppkran; ~ **dues** Bergungsgebühren; ~ **expert** Versicherungsexperte bei Bergungsschäden; ~ **goods** Strandgut; ~ **loss** *(marine insurance)* Versicherungsschaden nach Abzug der geretteten Waren; ~ **money** Bergegeld, -lohn, Rettungslohn; ~ **operations** *(marine insurance)* Bergungs-, Rettungsmaßnahmen; **to mount a** ~ **operation** Rettungsaktion in Gang setzen; ~ **service** Seenotdienst; ~ **ship** Bergungsdampfer; ~ **stocks** [angeblich] aus See- (Brand-) schaden gerettete Waren; ~ **tug** Bergungsschlepper; ~ **value** *(marine insurance)* durch sofortigen Verkauf realisierbarer Wert, Bergungs-, Schrottwert; ~ **vessel** Bergungsschiff; ~ **worker** Bergungsarbeiter.
salvageable items verwertbare Abfälle.
salvaged property gerettetes Vermögen.
salvagee Eigentümer einer geborgenen Ladung.
salvager Bergungsarbeiter.
Salvation Army Heilsarmee.
salve *(v.)* sein Gewissen durch das Stiften gestohlenen Geldes für wohltätige Zwecke beruhigen.
salver Servierbrett.
salvo *(airplane)* Reihenbombenabwurf, *(law)* Vorbehaltsklausel; **with an express** ~ **of their right** unter ausdrücklicher Wahrung ihrer Rechte.
same | invention *(patent law)* die gleiche Erfindung; ~ **offence** dieselbe Straftat; ~ **size** Originalgröße; ~ **text** gleichbleibender Text.
sample *(of commodities)* [Waren]probe, Kost-, Qualitätsprobe, [Stück]muster, Gebrauchs-, Typenmuster, *(opinion poll)* Befragte, Repräsentativerhebung, *(part of population)* zugrunde gelegte Bevölkerungsziffer, *(statistics)* Stichprobe, Querschnitt, [Erhebungs]auswahl;
according to ~ nach Muster (Probe); **inferior to** ~ schlechter als das Muster; **not to** ~ nicht mustergetreu; **on** ~ nach Probe; **strictly up to** ~ streng nach Muster (der Probe); **up to** ~ dem Muster entsprechend; **~s** Auswahlsendung;
annexed ~**s** anhängende Muster; **area** ~ Flächenstichprobe; **attached** ~ beigefügtes Muster; **balanced** ~ angepaßte Stichprobe; **biased** ~ verzerrte (einseitig betonte) Stichprobe; **controlled** ~ kontrollierte Stichprobe; **defective** ~ unvollständige Stichprobe; **displayed** ~ vorgelegte Probe; **duplicate** ~ doppelt erhobene Stichprobe; **fixed** ~ festgelegte Stichprobe; **haphazard** ~ unkontrollierte Stichprobe; **judgment** ~ subjektiv ausgewählte Stichprobe, ins Ermessen des Befragers gestellte Repräsentativauswahl; **linked** ~ verknüpfte Stichproben; **matched** ~ Stichproben mit Parallelfällen; **mixed** ~ gemischte Stichprobe; **multistage** ~ mehrstufige Stichprobe; **~s only** *(mail)* Muster ohne Wert; **pattern** ~ Muster-, Probstück; **picked** ~ entnommene Probe; **probability** ~ zufallsgesteuerte Stichprobenauswahl; **purposive** ~ bewußt gewählte Probe, gezieltes Auswahlverfahren; **quota** ~ Quotenstichprobe, -verfahren bei der Auswahl, Stichprobenanalyse; **random** ~ Zufallsstichprobe; **reference** ~ Probe-, Vergleichs-, Ausfallmuster; **representative** ~ repräsentative Stichprobe, Serien-, Durchschnitts-, Typenmuster; **scientifically selective** ~ wissenschaftlich einwandfreies Auswahlsystem; **sealed** ~ verschlossenes Muster; ~ **shown** vorgezeigte Probe; **simple** ~ ungeschichtete Stichprobe; **stratified** ~ geschichtete Stichprobe, *(marketing)* nach Schichten spezifizierte Marktuntersuchung; **system-**

atic ~ systematische Auswahl; ~ **taken offhand** unvorbereitete Stichprobe; **traveller's** ~**s** Musterkollektion; **two-stage** ~ zweistufige Stichprobe;
~ **of goods** Warenprobe; ~ **of handwriting** Schriftprobe; ~ **of households** Haushaltsbefragung; ~ **for inspection** Ansichtsmuster; ~ **of merchandise** Warenprobe, -muster; ~ **of persons** Stichprobe aus einer Personengesamtheit; ~ **of quality** Qualitätsprobe; ~, **no commercial value** *(US)* Muster ohne Wert;
~ *(v.)* bemustern, *(try quality)* ausprobieren, durch Entnahme von Mustern prüfen, Proben entnehmen, Muster ziehen;
~ **out** ausfallen;
to assort ~**s** Muster zusammenstellen; **to be up to** ~ dem Muster (der Probe) entsprechen, nach Probe (mustergetreu) sein; **to buy s. th. from** ~ etw. nach dem Muster kaufen; **to cut off a** ~ Muster abschneiden; **to draw** ~**s** Probe nehmen, Muster ziehen; **to keep a stock of** ~**s** Musterlager unterhalten; **to make up** ~**s** Warenproben zusammenstellen; **to match the** ~ dem Muster (der Probe) entsprechen, mustergetreu sein; **to order goods from the** ~ nach dem Muster bestellen; **to put** ~**s through a series of tests** mit Mustern verschiedene Versuche anstellen; **to send** ~**s** bemustern; **to send as** ~ **of no value** *(Br.)* als Muster ohne Wert verschicken; **to submit** ~**s** Muster vorlegen; **to take a** ~ Probe entnehmen, Muster ziehen; **to take** ~**s at random** Stichproben entnehmen;
~ **advertising** Werbung durch Ausgabe von Warenproben; ~ **assortment** Musterkollektion; ~ **bag** Musterkoffer; ~ **balance sheet** Bilanzmuster; ~ **book** Musterbuch; ~ **box** Probekiste; ~ **card** Probe-, Musterkarte; ~ **case** Musterkoffer; ~ **census** Stichprobenbasis; ~ **collection** Mustersendung, [Muster]kollektion; ~ **company** Modellfirma; ~ **copy** Ansichtsexemplar; ~ **depot** Musterlager; ~ **design** Auswahl-, Stichprobenplan; ~ **entry** Mustereintragung; ~ **envelope** Musterkuvert; ~ **fair** Mustermesse; ~ **item** Musterstück; ~ **letter** Musterbrief; ~ **lots (parcels)** Mustersendungen; ~ **make-up** *(statistics)* Zusammensetzung der Repräsentativauswahl, Gruppenzusammensetzung; ~ **number** Musternummer; ~ **offer** bemustertes Angebot; ~ **order** Probebestellung, -auftrag; ~ **packet** Mustersendung; **by** ~ **post** als Muster ohne Wert; ~ **pair** Musterpaar; ~ **plan** Auswahl-, Stichprobenplan; **by** ~ **post** als Muster ohne Wert; ~ **rate** Tarif für Mustersendungen; ~ **request card** Musteranforderungskarte; ~ **respondent** Befragter innerhalb der ausgewählten Stichprobe; ~ **roll** Musterrolle; ~ **room** Ausstellungsraum; **random** ~ **selection** Stichprobenauswahl; ~ **signature** Unterschriftsprobe; ~ **size** Mustergröße, *(statistics)* Stichprobenumfang; ~ **statistic** aus Stichproben gewonnene Meßzahl, Teilerhebung; ~ **stock** Musterlager, -kollektion; ~ **survey** Repräsentativ-, Stichprobenerhebung; ~ **testing** Befragung eines beschränkten Personenkreises; ~ **trunk** Musterkoffer; ~ **unit** Stichprobeneinheit.
sampled offer bemustertes Angebot.
sampleman Musterreisender.
sampler Probierer, Musterzieher.
sampling Repräsentativ-, Musterstück, *(collection)* Mustersammlung, *(free trial, US)* Werbung durch Musterverteilung, [Kost]probenverteilung, *(marketing)* Marktforschung durch genaues Studium einer repräsentativen Käuferschicht, *(price fixing, US)* Preisbestimmung nach dem Muster, *(representative investigation)* Auswahl eines repräsentativen Querschnitts, *(sending of samples)* Musterziehung, -nehmen, Bemusterung, *(statistics)* Auswahl-, Stichprobenverfahren;
acceptance ~ Stichprobennahme bei der Abnahme; **accidental** ~ stichprobenartige Marktuntersuchung; **area** ~ Flächenstichprobeverfahren; **bulk** ~ Stichprobenentnahme; **chunk** ~ planlose Stichprobenauswahl; **controlled** ~ statistisches Auswahlverfahren für Marktforschungszwecke; **double** ~ zweistufiges Stichprobenverfahren; **lattice** ~ Stichprobenverfahren im Gittermuster; **lottery** ~ *(statistics)* Auslosungs-, Stichprobenverfahren; **mixed** ~ ungleichartige Stichprobenauswahl; **multiphase** ~ Mehrphasenauswahl; **multistage** ~ mehrstufiges Stichprobenverfahren; **probability** ~ Zufallsstichproben; **quasi-random** ~ zufallsähnliches Stichprobenverfahren; **quota** ~ Quotenauswahlverfahren; **random** ~ Entnahme von Stichproben, Stichprobenentnahme; **simple** ~ einfaches Stichprobenverfahren; **stratified** ~ geschichtetes Stichprobenverfahren;
~ **by taste** Gratiskostprobe;
~ **demonstration** Kostprobe; ~ **distribution** Stichprobenverteilung; ~ **error** Auswahl-, Stichprobenfehler; ~ **fraction (ratio)** *(statistics)* Auswahlsatz; ~ **inspection** Stichproben-, Teilprüfung; ~ **interval** Auswahlabstand; ~ **point** Stichprobenpunkt; ~ **scheme** Stichprobenschema; ~ **survey** Stichprobenerhebung; ~ **unit** *(statistics)* Auswahleinheit.

sanatorium Sanatorium, Erholungsheim.
sanction Sanktion, *(approval)* Genehmigung, Billigung, Bestätigung, *(coercive measure)* Sanktion, Strafandrohung, Zwangsmaßnahme;
with the ~ of the author mit Genehmigung des Autors;
economic ~s wirtschaftliche Sanktionen; **punitive ~s** Strafsanktionen; **remuneratory ~s** einträgliche Strafmaßnahmen; **vindictive ~** *(law)* Strafandrohung;
~ of the court gerichtliche Genehmigung; **~ of custom** *(fam.)* Gewohnheitsrecht; **~ of the liquidator** Genehmigung des Liquidators; **~ by usage** Sanktionierung eines Brauchs;
~ *(v.)* billigen, zustimmen, sanktionieren;
to apply ~s *(United Nations)* Sanktionen zur Anwendung bringen; **to apply ~s against an aggressor country** Sanktionen gegen einen Angreiferstaat verhängen; **to derive its ~ in** gesetzlich begründet sein in; **to give ~** Genehmigung erteilen; **to impose ~s** Sanktionen auferlegen; **to move slowly on ~s** Sanktionsmaßnahmen nur zögernd anwenden; **to put ~s into motion** Sanktionsmaßnahmen in Gang setzen; **to recede from ~s** Sanktionen fallen lassen.
sanctioned by usage durch Herkommen sanktioniert.
sanctioning limit *(bank)* Genehmigungsgrenze.
sanctity | of contracts Heiligkeit der Verträge; **~ of marriage** Heiligkeit der Ehe; **~ of treaties** Heiligkeit der Verträge;
to violate the ~ of an oath Heiligkeit eines Eides verletzen.
sanctuary Freistaat, Zuflucht, Schutzstätte, Asyl;
~ of political refugees Asyl für politische Flüchtlinge;
to seek ~ an einer Freistätte Zuflucht suchen; **to violate ~** Asylrecht verletzen.
sanctum *(fig.)* Arbeits-, Studierzimmer, *(privacy)* Intimsphäre.
sand, built on auf Sand gebaut;
to throw ~ into the works Sand ins Getriebe streuen;
~ and gravel working Kiesgewinnung.
sandbag Sandsack.
sandwich | of good and bad Nebeneinander von Gut und Böse;
to structure a course on a ~ basis Lehrgang in der Form gleichzeitig stattfindender Ausbildungskurse aufziehen; **~ board** Brust- und Rückenplakat; **~ boy** *(Br.)* Schilder-, Plakatträger, Werbeläufer mit Brust- und Rückenplakat; **~ course** Zwischenlehrgang; **~ man** *(Br.)* Schilder-, Plakatträger; **~ student** Werkstudent.
sane geistig normal;
~ criticism vernünftige Kritik; **of ~ memory** zurechnungs-, geschäftsfähig.
sanitarian Gesundheitsapostel, -fanatiker.
sanitarium *(US)* Heil-, Kuranstalt, Sanatorium.
sanitary *(US)* öffentliche Bedürfnisanstalt;
~ *(a.)* sanitär, hygienisch;
~ Act Hygienegesetz; **~ affairs** Gesundheitswesen; **~ arrangements** sanitäre Einrichtungen; **~ authorities** *(US)* Gesundheitsbehörden, -ämter; **~ board** Gesundheitsamt; **~ conditions** sanitäre Bedingungen; **~ control** Gesundheitsüberwachung; **~ convenience** Bedürfnisanstalt; **~ conveniences** sanitäre Einrichtungen; **~ cordon** Quarantänesperre; **~ deficiencies** sanitäre Mängel; **~ department** Abteilung für sanitäre Einrichtungen; **~ engineer** Installateur sanitärer Anlagen; **~ engineering** sanitärer Anlagenbau; **~ inspection** Überwachung durch die Gesundheitsbehörden; **~ inspector** Gesundheitsbeamter; **~ installations** sanitäre Einrichtungen; **~ measures** sanitäre Maßnahmen; **~ police** Gesundheitspolizei; **~ provisions** Gesundheitsvorschriften; **~ regulations** Gesundheitsbestimmungen, -verordnungen, -vorschriften; **~ service** Gesundheitsdienst; **~ services** sanitäre Anlagen; **~ worker** Kanalarbeiter.
sanitate *(v.)* mit gesundheitlichen Einrichtungen versehen, gesundheitliche Vorkehrungen treffen.
sanitation Gesundheitswesen;
~s sanitäre Einrichtungen;
to improve the ~ of a town Stadt kanalisieren;
~ man *(US)* Müllfahrer; **~ van** *(US)* Müllwagen.
sanity normaler Geisteszustand.
sap *(Br., sl.)* Streber, Büffler, *(fig.)* Kraft, Lebenssaft, *(mil.)* Sappe, *(US sl.)* Tölpel, Dussel;
~ *(v.)* *(Br., sl.)* büffeln, ochsen, pauken, *(fig.)* unterminieren, erschöpfen, untergraben.
sasine *(Scot.)* Auflassung.
satellite Satellit, *(politics)* Anhänger, Trabant, Satellit;
anti-~ Killer-Satellit; **communication ~** Fernmeldesatellit; **domestic ~** Inlandssatellit; **earth-surveying ~** Beobachtungssatellit; **meteorological ~** Wettersatellit; **reconnaissance ~** Aufklärungssatellit; **regional ~** Raumsatellit; **stationary ~** feststehender Satellit; **telecommunication ~** Fernmeldesatellit;

~ airfield Ausweich-, Feldflughafen; **~ broadcasting** Satellitenrundfunk; **~ channel** Satellitenkanal; **~ communication** Satellitennachrichtenübermittlung; **communication ~ corporation** Satellitenfernmeldegesellschaft; **~ communications** Satellitenverbindungen; **~ communications system** Satellitennachrichtenwesen; **~ distribution system** Satellitenverteilungssystem; **~ launching** Satellitenabschuß; **~ nation** Satellitenstaat; **~ project** Satellitenprojekt; **~ regime** Satellitenregime; **~ relay** Satellitensender; **~ state** Satellitenstaat; **~ station** Satellitenstation; **~ suburb** Satellitenstadt; **~ system** Satellitensystem; **~ telecommunication system** Satellitenfernmeldesystem; **~ television relay** Satellitenrelaisfernsehsender; **~ terminal** Satellitenkopfstation; **~ town[ship]** Trabanten-, Satellitenstadt.
satiate *(v.)* **the market** Markt sättigen.
satisfaction Zufriedenheit, Genugtuung, *(payment)* Begleichung, Bezahlung, Tilgung, Befriedigung, Erfüllung, *(compensation)* Abfindungssumme, *(revenge for insult)* Ehrenerklärung;
in ~ of als Wiedergutmachung;
job ~ *(US)* Arbeitsfreude; **partial ~** Teilbefriedigung; **prior ~** bevorzugte Befriedigung;
accord and ~ außergerichtlicher Vergleich;
~ of an accord Durchführung einer Vereinbarung; **~ of a claim** Befriedigung eines Anspruchs, Anspruchsbefriedigung; **~ of a condition** Erfüllung einer Bedingung; **~ of creditors** Gläubigerbefriedigung, Befriedigung (Auszahlung) der Gläubiger; **~ of debts** Schuldentilgung; **~ of debts by legacies** Schuldenbegleichung im Legatswege; **~ of a judgment** Befriedigung des Gläubigers auf Grund eines Urteils; **~ of mortgage** Löschungsbewilligung; **~ of record** *(US)* Hypothekenlöschung; **~ with (over) the results of the election** Zufriedenheit mit dem Wahlergebnis; **to demand ~** Genugtuung verlangen; **to enter ~** Löschung einer Hypothek im Grundbuch eintragen lassen, Hypothek im Grundbuch löschen; **to establish to the ~** zufriedenstellenden Nachweis erbringen; **to feel ~ at having one's ability recognized** Genugtuung über die Anerkennung seiner Arbeit empfinden; **to find complete ~ in one's work** volle Befriedigung in seinem Beruf finden; **to make ~** Genugtuung leisten; **to make ~ for a debt** Anspruch voll befriedigen; **to pass an examination to one's own ~** mit seiner Examensnote zufrieden sein; **to show to the ~** glaubhaft machen;
~ piece *(real-estate law, US)* löschungsfähige Quittung.
satisfactory genügend, befriedigend, zufriedenstellend;
mutually ~ arrangement alle Teile befriedigende Abmachung; **to bring negotiations to a ~ conclusion** Verhandlungen zu einem erfolgreichen Abschluß bringen; **~ control** *(statistics)* ausreichende Qualitätskontrolle; **~ evidence** hinlänglicher Beweis; **~ pension** auskömmliche Pension; **~ progress** zufriedenstellende Fortschritte; **~ provisions** ausreichende Bestimmungen.
satisfy *(v.)* *(convince)* überzeugen, *(give compensation)* [Scha-den]ersatz leisten, *(meet expectations)* zufriedenstellen, befriedigen, *(fulfil(l) obligations)* Verpflichtungen nachkommen (erfüllen), Schulden bezahlen;
~ an accord Vergleich durchführen; **~ a call** Einschuß leisten; **~ a claim** Anspruch befriedigen, Forderung erfüllen; **~ a claimant** Forderung des Klägers erfüllen; **~ a condition** Bedingung erfüllen; **~ a contract** Vertrag erfüllen; **~ one's creditors** seine Gläubiger befriedigen; **~ a debt out of a property** sich aus einem Vermögensstück befriedigen; **~ the demand** Nachfrage befriedigen; **~ the examiners** Prüfung mit ausreichend bestehen; **~ an execution** Zwangsvollstreckung durch Zahlung abwenden; **~ a judgment** einem Urteil nachkommen; **~ all requirements** allen Anforderungen Genüge leisten; **~ o. s. of the truth of a report** sich von der Wahrheit eines Berichts überzeugen.
saturate *(v.)* sättigen, *(mil.)* mit einem Bombenteppich belegen.
saturated *(market)* nicht mehr aufnahmefähig, gesättigt.
saturation | of consumer demands Marktsättigung; **~ of the home market** Sättigung des Inlandsmarktes;
~ bombing Belegung mit einem Bombenteppich; **~ coefficient** *(marketing)* Sättigungskoeffizient; **~ point** *(market)* Sättigungspunkt; **~ raid** Vergeltungsschlag.
Saturday | business Wochenendgeschäft; **devil-may-care ~ nights** Sonnabende, bei denen man auf die Pauke haut.
sauce *(gasoline, sl.)* Saft;
to have a ~ keck sein.
saucer, flying fliegende Untertasse.
saunterer Müßiggänger.
sausage Wurst, *(fig.)* undefinierbare Masse.
savage Wilder, *(employee, sl.)* schlecht bezahlter Hilfsarbeiter.
save as you earn (S. A. Y. E.) *(Br.)* steuerfreies Sparen, *(Br.)* automatische Einbehaltung eines Sparbetrages, *(Br.)* indexgekoppeltes Prämiensparsystem.

save *(v.)* retten, schützen, bewahren, *(abstain from expending)* [ein]sparen, Ersparnisse machen, *(keep for future use)* erübrigen, *(reduce requisite amount)* ersparen;

~ **for one's old age** für sein Alter sparen; ~ **alive** lebend bergen; ~ **the appearance** den Schein wahren; ~ **30% on costs versus competitors** Kostenersparnis von 30% gegenüber den Konkurrenzfirmen erzielen, 30% kostengünstiger als die Konkurrenz arbeiten; ~ **from drowning** vom Ertrinken retten; ~ **one's face** sein Gesicht wahren, keinen Gesichtsverlust erleiden; ~ **as you earn** durch automatische Abbuchung vom Lohnkonto sparen; ~ **the full deposit** Bausparvertrag voll ansparen; ~ **expenses** Kosten sparen; ~ **for the future** für später zurücklegen; ~ **half of one's salary each month** Hälfte seines Monatsgehalts zurücklegen; ~ **s. o. hours hanging round** jem. unnützen Zeitaufwand ersparen; ~ **on income taxes** Steuern sparen, Steuerersparnisse machen; ~ **via an insurance scheme** auf dem Versicherungssektor sparen; ~ **labo(u)r** Arbeitskräfte einsparen; ~ **one's life** sein Leben bewahren; ~ **s. one's life** jem. das Leben retten; ~ **little by little** kleine Beträge sparen; ~ **a lot of expense** Haufen Unkosten vermeiden; ~ **middlemen's profit** Provision sparen; ~ **money for a holiday** für den Urlaub sparen; ~ **one's neck** seinen Hals retten; ~ **a packet over the years** im Laufe der Jahre ein Vermögen sparen; ~ **at a higher rate** in größerem Umfang sparen, erhebliche Sparanstrengungen machen; ~ **the situation** Situation retten; ~ **one's skin** seine Haut retten; ~ **spending money for the bus fare** Omnibusfahrkarte sparen; ~ **the statute of limitations** Verjährungsfrist unterbrechen; ~ **time** Zeit sparen (gewinnen); ~ **the train** Zug erreichen; ~ **s. o. a trip to town** jem. einen Gang in die Stadt abnehmen; ~ **up for one's old age** für sein Alter sparen; ~ **up money for a holiday** Geld für eine Reise zusammensparen;

not to know how to ~ money nicht sparen können;

~-**all** Sparbüchse; **government-approved ~-as-you-earn system** *(Br.)* staatlich gefördertes (steuerbegünstigtes) Sparen;

~ *(a.)* außer, ausgenommen, mit Ausnahme von; ~ **as provided** vorbehaltlich; ~ **as provided in paragraph 1** vorbehaltlich Artikel 1; ~ **as provided otherwise** mangels gegenteiliger Vorschrift; ~ **error and omission** Freizeichnungsklausel, Irrtum vorbehalten.

saver Sparer, sparsamer Mensch, *(appliance)* sparsames Gerät, *(rescuer)* Retter;

life ~ Lebensretter; ~ **of labo(u)r** Arbeitskräfteersparnis; ~**s' club** Sparverein; ~**s' surplus** Sparergewinn.

saving *(economizing)* Sparvorgang, Sparen, [Kosten]einsparung, *(material reservations)* [Rechts]vorbehalt, *(rescuing)* Rettung; ~**s** Ersparnis[se], Spartätigkeit, erspartes Geld, Notpfennig, *(deposit)* Spargelder, Spareinlagen, -groschen;

business ~s nicht entnommene Gewinne, Geschäftsersparnisse; **collective ~** Werksparen; **compulsory ~s** Zwangssparen; **considerable ~** beträchtliche Verbilligung; **contractual ~** *(Br.)* [etwa] Prämiensparen; **current ~s** laufende Spartätigkeit; **forced ~** noch nicht angelegtes Sparkapital; **fresh ~** neues Sparkapital; **index-linked ~** inflationssicheres Sparen; **individual ~s** private Spartätigkeit; **labo(u)r ~** Arbeitskräfteeinsparung; **long-term ~s** langfristiges Sparen, langfristiger Sparvorgang; **net ~s** Nettoersparnis; **passbook ~s** Sparleistungen; **personal ~s** private Spartätigkeit; **planned ~s** freiwilliges Sparen; **postal ~s** Postsparguthaben, Postsparen; **school ~s** Schulsparen; **social ~s** kollektives Sparen; **staff ~s** Personaleinsparungen; **tax ~s** Steuerersparnisse; **tax-favo(u)red ~s** steuerbegünstigtes Sparen; **unplanned ~** unsystematisches Sparen; **war ~s** Kriegsersparnisse;

~ **of cash** finanzielle Einsparung; ~**s in handling costs** Einsparungen bei den Bearbeitungskosten; ~ **of duty** Steuerersparnis; ~**s for education** Ausbildungsrücklage; ~ **of expense** Kostenersparnis; ~ **in freight** Frachtkostenersparnis; ~**s in fuel** Treibstoffersparnis, Benzineinsparungen; ~ **of labo(u)r** Arbeits-, Personalersparnis; ~**s placed in loan institutes** Spareinlagenbestand bei den Kreditinstituten; ~ **of raw materials** Werkstoffeinsparung; ~ **of material cost** Sachkostenersparnis; ~ **the statute of limitations** Unterbrechung der Verjährungsfrist; ~**s amounting to a large sum** größere Sparrücklagen; ~ **of time** Zeitersparnis; **useful ~ of time and money** nützliche Zeit- und Geldersparnis;

to be careful of one's small ~s äußerst sparsam wirtschaften; **to cheat s. o. out of his ~s** j. um seine Ersparnisse bringen; **to dig into ~s to pay current debts** seine Ersparnisse zur Schuldenbezahlung angreifen; **to draw on one's ~s** auf seine Ersparnisse zurückgreifen; **to encourage ~** Spartätigkeit fördern, Sparförderungsmaßnahmen ergreifen; **to invest one's ~s in a business**

enterprise seine Ersparnisse in einem Geschäft investieren; **to keep one's ~s in the post office** Postsparguthaben besitzen; **to live on one's ~s** von seinen Ersparnissen leben; **to make ~s** Ersparnisse machen; **to make a large hole in one's ~s** Loch in seine Ersparnisse reißen; **to promote ~s** Spartätigkeit ermutigen (fördern); **to take ~s in deferred form** steuerbegünstigt sparen;

~ *(a.)* sparsam, haushälterisch, *(economical)* wirtschaftlich, sparend, *(rescuing)* rettend;

cost-~ kostensparend; **labo(u)r-~** arbeitssparend; ~ **a dollar** außer einem Dollar;

~ **activity** Spartätigkeit; ~ **bond** Sparbon; ~ **capacity** Sparfähigkeit; ~**s certificate** Sparbon, Rabattmarke; ~ **clause** einschränkende Bestimmungen, Freizeichnungs-, Vorbehaltsklausel; ~ **formula** rettende Formel; ~ **investment** *(US)* sichere [Kapital]anlage, erstklassiges Anlagepapier; ~ **manager** sparsamer Verwalter; ~ **manoeuvre** Rettungsmanöver; ~ **measures** Sparmaßnahmen; ~ **process** Sparvorgang; ~ **proportion** gesamtwirtschaftliche Ersparnisse; ~ **ratio** Sparquote; ~**schedule** Spartabelle; ~ **wage** Ersparnisse gestattender Lohn; ~ **way** Sparmethode.

savingness Sparsamkeit, Wirtschaftlichkeit.

savings account Spar[kassen]guthaben, -anlage, -einlagen-[konto];

life-insured ~ *(US)* mit einer Lebensversicherung gekoppeltes Sparkonto; **post-office (postal, US) ~** Postsparkonto; **to accept ~s** Sparkonten (Spareinlagen) annehmen; **to move an amount into a ~** Betrag auf ein Sparkonto übertragen; ~ **deposit** Sparguthaben; ~ **owner** Sparkassenbuchinhaber; ~ **passbook** Sparkassenbuch.

Savings | Act Sparprämiengesetz; ~ **Association** *(US)* Sparverein, -vereinigung; ~ **and Loan Association** *(US)* Spar- und Kreditvereinigung, Spar- und Darlehnsverein, Baufinanzierungsgenossenschaft; ~ **balance** Sparguthaben.

savings bank Sparkasse;

cooperative ~ *(US)* genossenschaftliche Sparkasse; **municipal ~** Stadtsparkasse; **mutual ~** *(US)* Sparkasse auf Gegenseitigkeit, genossenschaftsähnliche Sparkasse; **post-office** *(Br.)* **(postal, US) ~** Postsparkasse; **school ~** Schulsparkasse; **stock ~** *(US)* Sparkasse nach Art einer Aktiengesellschaft; **trustee ~** *(Br.)* gemeinnützige Sparkasse; **voluntary ~** *(US)* nicht aufsichtspflichtige Sparkasse;

to put money into the ~ Geld zur Sparkasse tragen.

savings-bank | account Sparkassenkonto, -guthaben; **Trustee ~ Act** *(Br.)* Sparkassengesetz; ~ **[deposit] book** Sparkassenbuch; ~ **deposits** Spareinlagen; ~ **depositor** Spareinleger; ~ **investment** *(US)* mündelsicheres Anlagepapier; ~ **interest rates** Sparzinssätze; ~ **legislation** Sparkassengesetzgebung; ~ **life insurance** Lebensversicherungsgeschäft der Sparkassen; ~ **manager** Sparkassenleiter; ~ **money** Sparkassengelder; ~ **official** Sparkassenangestellter; ~ **securities** sparkassenfähige (mündelsichere) Wertpapiere; ~ **stamp** Sparmarke; ~ **system** Sparkassenwesen; ~ **trust** Stiftung zugunsten eines Dritten.

savings | banking Sparkassenwesen; ~ **bonds** *(US)* kleingestückelte Obligationen, Babybonds, Sparbriefe; ~ **box** Sparbüchse; **British ~ Bonds** [etwa] Bundesschätze, -schatzscheine; **premium ~ bonds** Sparprämienanleihe; **post-office** *(Br.)* **(postal, US) ~ book** Postsparkassenbuch; ~ **business** Sparkassengeschäft; **private ~ capital formation** private Sparkapitalbildung; ~ **certificate** *(Br.)* [Post]sparschein, Sparbon; **national ~ certificate** *(Br.)* Sparkassengutschein; **treasury ~ certificate** *(US)* Sparzertifikat; ~ **certificate account** Sparbriefkonto; ~ **commission** Sparkommission; ~-**conscious** sparbewußt; ~ **department** Sparkassenabteilung; ~ **deposits** Spargelder, -einlagen, Sparguthaben; **demand ~ deposits** sofort fällige Spareinlagen; **longer-term ~ deposits** längerfristige Spareinlagen; ~ **deposits at statutory notice** Spargelder mit gesetzlicher Kündigungsfrist; ~ **depositor** Spareinleger; ~ **facilities** Sparkasseneinrichtungen, Sparmöglichkeiten; ~ **formation** Ersparnisbildung; ~ **fund** Spar[kassen]fonds, *(life-insurance fund)* Prämienreserve, Deckungskapital; ~ **industry** Sparkassenbereich; ~ **institution** Sparkasseninstitut; ~ **insurance** Sparprämienversicherung; ~ **standard interest rate** Spareckzins; ~ **loss** Sparanlagenverlust; ~ **ordinary account** Sparkassenkonto; ~ **plan** Prämienplan, Sparvertrag; **company ~ plan** betriebliche Sparförderung; ~ **premium** Sparprämie; ~ **promotion** Sparförderung; ~ **proportion** gesamtwirtschaftliche Ersparnisse; ~ **rate (ratio)** volkswirtschaftliche Sparrate, Sparquote; ~ **schedule** Spartabelle; ~ **scheme** Sparsystem; **tax-favo(u)red (national, Br.) ~ scheme** steuerbegünstigtes Sparen; **to specialize in ~ service** beim Sparvorgang beratend tätig sein; ~ **specialist** Berater für

Sparanlagen; ~ **stamp** *(Br.)* Rabattmarke; **national ~ stamps** *(Br.)* Sparbons; ~ **system** Sparwesen; ~ **volume** Sparaufkommen; ~ **withdrawals** Abhebungen vom Sparkonto, Spareinlagenabgänge.

savo(u)r Würze, Reiz, *(fig.)* Beigeschmack, Anstrich;
 without ~ *(book)* fade, langweilig;
 ~ **of fanatism** Spur von Fanatismus;
 ~ *(v.) (fig.)* Spuren zeigen;
 ~ **of deception** nach Betrug riechen;
 to be in good ~ guten Ruf haben.

savoury roll belegtes Brötchen.

savvy Grips, Köpfchen.

sawbunk *(sl.)* Zehndollarnote.

sawdust parlor *(sl.)* billige Kneipe.

say Ausspruch, Rede, Meinung;
 fair ~ angemessenes Mitspracherecht;
 ~ *(v.)* ausführen, bemerken;
 ~ **one's mind** seine Meinung sagen; ~ **a mouthful** *(sl.)* reine Wahrheit sagen; ~ **a good word for s. o.** gutes Wort für j. einlegen;
 to gain a greater ~ mehr zu sagen haben; **to give the government a greater ~ in steering investment** der Regierung größere Vollmachten für die Investitionssteuerung geben; **to have a ~** etw. zu sagen haben; **to have one's ~** Bemerkung anbringen, seine Meinung kundtun; **to have no ~ in a matter** in einer Sache kein Stimmrecht haben.

say-so *(coll.)* Entscheidungsgewalt;
 to have the ~ on a matter in einer Sache das letzte Wort haben.

saying Ausspruch, Redensart;
 to go without ~ augenscheinlich sein.

scab *(US sl.)* Nichtgewerkschaftler, Streikbrecher;
 ~ *(v.)* **it** *(sl.)* unter Tariflohn arbeiten;
 ~ **work** *(US)* Schwarz-, Streikarbeit, Arbeit unter Tariflohn.

scads of money *(US)* Unmenge von Geld;
 to have ~ haufenweise Geld haben.

scaffold *(building trade)* Baugerüst, *(for criminals)* Schafott, Blutgerüst, *(platform)* Zuschauertribüne;
 ~ *(v.)* [Haus] mit einem Gerüst umgeben;
 to go to the ~ gehängt werden.

scaffolding [Bau]gerüst.

scalage Schwundgeld.

scale Waagschale, *(gradation)* Gradeinteilung, Abstufung, Staffelung, *(map)* Kartenmaßstab, *(measure)* Maßstab, Größenverhältnis, Skala, *(print.)* Kolumnenmaß, *(range)* Umfang, *(tariff)* Tabelle, Staffel, Tarif, Gehaltsordnung;
 drawn to a ~ of 1 : 5 im Maßstab von 1 zu 5 gezeichnet; **in ~** maßstabgetreu; **on a ~** *(stock exchange)* zu verschiedenen Kursen limitiert; **on the ~ of** in der Größenordnung von; **on the collectively agreed ~** tariflich; **on a descending ~** *(tax)* degressiv; **on every ~** in jeder Größenordnung; **on a grand ~** groß angelegt, in großem Zuschnitt; **on a human ~** nach menschlichen Maßstäben; **on a large ~** in einem großen Ausmaß, in großem Maßstab; **on a limited ~** beschränkten Umfangs; **on a small ~** in kleinem Maßstab;
 ~s *(US, money)* Geld;
 age ~ Altersstaffelung; **business ~** *(estate duty)* Steuertarif für Betriebsbeteiligungen; **cost-of-living sliding ~** Gleitlohntarif; **decimal ~s** Dezimalsystem; **enlarged ~** vergrößerter Maßstab; **general ~** *(estate duty)* allgemeiner Steuertarif; **minimum ~s** Mindesttarif; **numbered ~** statistisch erfaßbare Zahlen; **pay ~** *(US)* Lohntabelle, -gruppe, Gehaltsskala; **proportional (proportionate) ~s** Proportionalsystem; **rate ~** *(US)* gestaffelter Tarif, Staffeltarif; **salary ~** gestaffelter Tarif, Gehaltstabelle, -gruppe, Besoldungsgruppe; **sliding ~** Nachlaßstaffel; **sliding ~ [of wages]** gleitende [Lohn]skala, Staffeltarif; **social ~** Gesellschaftsordnung, -stufe; **standard ~** Normalgröße; **taxation ~** Steuersatz; **wage ~** Lohnskala, -staffel, -tabelle, -gruppe;
 ~ **of allowances** Zuteilungsumfang, Zulagestaffel, Zuschußtafel; ~ **of assessment** Bewertungsskala; ~ **of benefits** Unterstützungsumfang; ~ **of charges** Gebührenordnung, -tabelle, Tarif; ~ **of colo(u)rs** Farbskala; ~ **of commission** *(Br.)* Courtagetarif; ~ **of discount** Nachlaß-, Rabattstaffel; **general ~ of estate duty** allgemeiner Erbschaftssteuertarif; **low ~ of existence** niedere Lebensstufe; ~ **of fees** Gebührenordnung, -staffelung; **official ~s of fees** amtliche Gebührensätze; **high ~ of financing** hoher Finanzierungsumfang; ~ **of imports** Einfuhrumfang; **~s of justice** Waage der Gerechtigkeit; ~ **of living** Lebensstandard; **~s of justice** Waage der Gerechtigkeit; ~ **of operations** Betriebsumfang; **low ~ of pay** niedriges Gehaltsniveau; ~ **of preferences** Präferenzordnung, Tabelle der Verbrauchergewohnheiten, *(economics)* persönliche Dringlichkeitsliste; ~ **of**

premiums Prämienleiter, -staffelung, -staffel, Beitragsstaffel; ~ **of prices** Preisskala, -staffel; ~ **of production** Produktionsumfang; ~ **of rebates** Rabattstaffel; ~ **of remuneration** Vergütungs, Lohntabelle; ~ **of salaries** Gehaltsstaffelung, Besoldungsordnung; ~ **of solicitor's charges** Anwaltsgebührentabelle; ~ **of stipends** Stipendiatenstaffel; ~ **to success** Erfolgsleiter; ~ **of taxation** Steuersatz, -klasse; **highest ~ of taxation** höchste Steuerklasse; ~ **of a thermometer** Thermometerskala; ~ **of wages** Lohnskala (Lohntabelle);
 ~ *(v.)* [aus]wiegen, *(form into ~s)* einstufen;
 ~ **a building** Gebäude maßstabsgerecht zeichnen; ~ **credits** Kredite nach ihrer Größenordnung aufführen; ~ **a crowd** *(Scot.)* Volksauflauf zerstreuen; ~ **a debt** Schuld reduzieren, herabsetzen, beschneiden.

scale down *(v.)* proportional verkleinern, *(fig.)* herunterschrauben;
 ~ **an allotment** Zuteilung repartieren; ~ **applications to cut the public in** Bezugsrechtsausübungsanträge zugunsten öffentlicher Beteiligung beschränken; ~ **one's expectations** seine Erwartungen herunterschrauben; ~ **one's liabilities** seine Verbindlichkeiten reduzieren; ~ **wages** Löhne kürzen (senken), Lohnsenkung vornehmen.

scale | up *(v.)* **income tax 10 per cent** Einkommensteuersätze 10% heraufsetzen; ~ **up prices** Preise erhöhen; ~ **up wages by 6 per cent** Löhne um 6% anheben;
 to be high in the social ~ gesellschaftlich hoch eingestuft sein; **to be long in the ~s** lange unentschieden sein; **to be at the top of the ~** Tabelle anführen; **to be upgraded in the ~ of selection** in eine höhere Qualitätsstufe eingereiht werden; **to buy on a ~** Teilkäufe machen, *(stock exchange, US)* seine Zukäufe über eine Baisseperiode erteilen, zu einem Durchschnittskurs zukaufen; **to hold the ~s even** faire Entscheidung treffen, gerecht urteilen; **to keep house on a small ~** einfaches Haus führen, bescheiden leben; **to live on a large ~** auf großem Fuß leben; **to prepare for war on large ~** Kriegsvorbereitungen größten Ausmaßes treffen; **to remove the ~s from s. one's eyes** *(fig.)* jem. die Realitäten des Lebens klarmachen; **to sell on a ~** *(stock exchange, US)* seine Verkäufe über eine Hausseperiode verteilen, zu einem Durchschnittskurs weiter verkaufen; **to sink in the ~** an gesellschaftlichem Ansehen verlieren, im sozialen Niveau sinken, absinken; **to throw one's sword into the ~** seinen Anspruch mit Waffengewalt vertreten; **to tip the ~s** *(fig.)* ins Gewicht fallen; **to turn the ~ in s. one's favo(u)r** Ausschlag zu jds. Gunsten geben; **to vote on a liberal ~** *(parl.)* freizügig genehmigen, großzügige Bewilligungen vornehmen;
 ~ **analysis** *(marketing)* Skalenanalyse; ~ **buying** *(US)* Wertpapierkauf zu verschiedenen Zeiten (Durchschnittskursen); ~ **division** Gradeinteilung; ~ **drawing** maßstabgerechte Zeichnung; ~ **effect** Auswirkungen der Nachfrageentwicklung, Kostendegression der Massenproduktion; ~ **graduation** Tarifstaffelung; ~ **line** Teilstrich; **large-~ map** Karte in großem Maßstab; ~ **model** maßstabgetreues Modell; ~ **rate** Tarifpreis, *(advertising)* Normalsatz für Tiefdruckätzung, Listenpreis; ~ **rule** Maßstock; ~ **salary** *(US)* Tarifgehalt; ~ **selling** *(US)* sukzessiver Verkauf von Wertpapieren; ~ **ticket** Wiegekarte; ~ **tolerance** Toleranz zwischen Waagen; **~-up** Vergrößerung, Änderung des Größenverhältnisses; ~ **wage** *(US)* Tariflohn; ~ **wage increase** *(US)* Tariflohnerhöhung.

scaled-down anteilmäßig reduziert.

scaling Gradeinteilung, *(US, stock exchange)* Aufgabe von Kauf- und Verkaufsorders zu verschiedenen Zeiten;
 ~ **down** proportionale Verkleinerung, *(allotment)* Repartierung; **~-up** proportionale Vergrößerung.

scalp Siegestrophäe, *(stock exchange, US)* kleiner Weiterverkaufsgewinn;
 ~ *(v.)* *(politics, US)* absägen, um den Einfluß bringen, *(stock exchange, US)* mit kleinen Gewinnen spekulieren, mit kleinem Nutzen realisieren;
 to be out for ~s *(fam.)* auf dem Kriegspfad (angriffslustig) sein.

scalper *(US)* Spekulativhändler.

scalping *(stock exchange, US)* Mitnahme kleinster Spekulationsgewinne.

scamp Schurke;
 ~ *(v.)* schludrige Arbeit leisten;
 ~ **through a book** Buch im Galopp lesen.

scamper Pfuscher, schludriger Arbeiter, *(reading)* eilige Lektüre;
 to take the dog for a ~ Hund Gassi führen.

scamping Pfuscharbeit.

scan kritische Prüfung, *(radar)* Abtastung, *(television)* Bildauflösung;
 ~ *(v.)* *(radar)* abtasten, *(television)* Bild auflösen;

~ **the audience** Publikum kritisch betrachten; ~ **a book** Buch flüchtig ansehen; ~ **figures** Zahlen überprüfen; ~ **s. o. from head to foot** j. von Kopf bis Fuß mustern; ~ **the headlines** Überschriften überfliegen; ~ **the horizon** Horizont absuchen; ~ **a newspaper** Zeitung durchblättern.

scandal skandalöses Ereignis, Skandal, öffentliches Ärgernis, *(pleading)* ehrenrührige Behauptung;
grave ~s **on the stock exchange** schwerwiegender Börsenskandal;
to be the ~ **of one's family** dunkler Punkt in seiner Familie sein; **to give rise to a** ~ Skandal verursachen, Anstoß erregen; **to spread** ~ Klatschgeschichten verbreiten; **to talk** ~ **about s. o.** diffamierende Reden über j. führen;
~**-ridden** skandalumwittert; ~ **sheet** *(sl.)* Spesenrechnung.

scandalization Erregung öffentlichen Ärgernisses.

scandalize *(v.)* Skandal (öffentliches Ärgernis) erregen;
~ **an audience** Publikum schockieren; ~ **the court** Gericht beleidigen.

scandalmonger Lästermaul, Klatschbase.

scandalmongering Verbreitung von Klatschgeschichten.

scandalous skandalös, anstößig, Ärgernis erregend, *(disgraceful)* diffamierend;
~ **conditions** skandalöse Zustände; ~ **crime** schamloses Verbrechen; ~ **matter** ehrenrührige Behauptungen; ~ **statement** ärgerniserregende Erklärung; ~ **stories** Skandalgeschichten; ~ **treatment** schimpfliche Behandlung.

scanned area Rasterplatte.

scanner Radarantenne, *(data processing)* Lesegerät.

scanning *(television)* Bildabtastung;
~ **device** Abtasteinrichtung; ~ **disk** Abtastscheibe; ~ **field** Bildfeld, -raster; ~ **line** Abtast-, Bildzeile, Rasterlinie.

scant knapp, spärlich;
~ **of money** nur mit wenig Geld versehen;
~ *(v.)* knausern einschränken;
~ **s. o. in leisure** jem. nur wenig Freizeit lassen;
~ **allowance** knappe Zuteilung; ~ **supply** geringer Vorrat.

scantiness Knappheit;
~ **of resources** Dürftigkeit finanzieller Mittel.

scanty knapp [bemessen], dürftig, ungenügend;
~ **income** kümmerliches Einkommen; ~ **means** unzureichende Geldmittel; ~ **stores of Latin** dürftige Lateinkenntnisse; ~ **supplies** unzulängliche Vorräte.

scapegoat Sündenbock.

scar Narbe, Schramme, *(fig.)* Schandfleck, Makel;
~ **upon s. one's reputation** Fleck auf jds. weißer Weste;
to bear a ~ mit einem Makel behaftet sein.

scarce knapp, spärlich;
to be ~ **of money** über geringe Mittel verfügen; **to make o. s.** ~ sich rar machen;
~ **articles (commodities, goods, materials)** knappe Waren, Mangelwaren; ~ **book** seltenes Buch; ~ **currency** harte Währung.

scarcity Knappheit[serscheinung], Verknappung, Mangel, Teuerung;
owing to the temporary ~ infolge zeitweiliger Verknappung;
~ **of currency** Devisenmangel, -knappheit; ~ **of gold** Goldmangel; ~ **of goods** Güter-, Warenknappheit; ~ **of housing** Wohnungsnot; ~ **of labo(u)r** Mangel an Arbeitskräften; ~ **of material** Materialknappheit; ~ **of raw materials** Rohstoffmangel, -knappheit; ~ **of money** Geldverknappung, -knappheit; ~ **of paper** *(stock exchange)* Stückemangel; ~ **of provisions** Lebensmittelmangel, -knappheit; ~ **of tonnage** Mangel an Schiffsraum; ~ **of workers** Arbeitskräftemangel;
~ **price** Mangelwarenpreis; ~ **value** Seltenheitswert, durch Warenknappheit erhöhter Wert.

scare Panik;
war ~ Kriegspsychose;
~ **on the stock exchange** Börsenpanik;
~ *(v.)* **a thief** Dieb verscheuchen; ~ **up** *(sl.)* Sonderartikel herstellen; ~ **up money** Geld auftreiben;
to cause a war ~ Kriegspsychose hervorrufen; **to create a** ~ Panik verursachen; **to create a** ~ **in a political party** politische Partei in eine Panik versetzen;
~ **buying** Panik-, Angstkäufe; ~ **headline** Schlagzeile, sensationelle [Zeitungs]überschrift; ~ **strap** *(sl.)* Sicherheitsgurt;
to be ~**d running** in Furcht und Unruhe geraten.

scaremonger Panikmacher.

scaremongering Panikmache.

scat *(v.)* abhauen;
to go ~ Bankrott machen.

scathing criticism ätzende Kritik.

scatter Spelunke, Kneipe;
~ *(v.)* **the crowd** *(police)* Menge zerstreuen (auseinandertreiben); ~ **the floor with paper** Fußboden mit Papier bedecken; ~ **gravel on an icy road** Kies auf eine vereiste Straße streuen; ~ **handbills** Flugblätter (Reklamezettel) verteilen; ~ **about the town** *(tourists)* sich über die Stadt ergießen; ~ **troops** Truppen zersplittern;
~ **coefficient** Streuungskoeffizient; ~ **diagram** *(statistics)* Streubild, -diagramm.

scatterbrain zerstreute Person, Wirrkopf.

scatterbrained zerstreut, schusselig.

scattered | in the plain über die Ebene verstreut;
~ **army** zerstreute Armee; ~ **houses** verstreut liegende Häuser; **thinly** ~ **population** dünn gesäte Bevölkerung; ~ **thoughts** konfuse Gedanken.

scattering of followers sehr kleine Gefolgschaft.

scavenger Straßenkehrer, *(machine)* Straßenreinigungsmaschine.

scenario Drehbuch, Filmmanuskript, *(broadcasting)* Funkmanuskript.

scenarist Drehbuchautor.

scenarization Drehbuchbearbeitung.

scenarize *(v.)* zu einem Drehbuch verarbeiten.

scene Szene, Szenerie, Bühne, Schauplatz, *(subdivision of play)* Szene, Auftritt;
behind the ~s hinter den Kulissen; **behind the** ~s **in politics** hinter den politischen Kulissen; **on the** ~ **of the disaster** auf dem Unglückschauplatz;
~ **of an accident** Unfallstelle, -schauplatz; ~ **of action** *(theater)* Ort der Handlung; ~ **of a crime (deed)** Schauplatz eines Verbrechens, Tatort; ~ **of destruction** Bild der Zerstörung; **distressing** ~s **when the earthquake occurred** schreckliche Szenen beim Ausbruch des Erdbebens; ~ **of fire** Brandstelle; ~ **of operations** Operationsgebiet, Kriegsschauplatz;
to arrive on the ~ auf der Bildfläche erscheinen; **to be behind the** ~s hinter den Kulissen wirken; **to be on the** ~ *(fig.)* zur Stelle sein; **to burst on the** ~ schlagartig auf der Bildfläche erscheinen; **to come on the** ~ erscheinen; **to go abroad for a change of** ~ zwecks Tapetenwechsels ins Ausland verreisen; **to know what is going on behind the** ~s hinter die Kulissen schauen; **to lay the** ~ **of a novel in A** Handlung eines Romans nach A verlegen; **to loom over a** ~ **unrivalled** Scenerie konkurrenzlos beherrschen; **to make a** ~ *(fam.)* Szene machen; **to quit the** ~ *(fig.)* von der Bühne abtreten; **to revisit the** ~s **of one's youth** seine alten Jagdgründe wieder aufsuchen; **to streak on the** ~ plötzlich auf der Bildfläche erscheinen; **to take place behind the** ~s hinter den Kulissen geschehen;
~ **dock** Requisitenraum.

scenerical Landschaftsfilm.

scenery Landschaft, Gegend, *(theater)* Bühnenausstattung, -bild.

scenic landschaftlich;
~ **beauties** landschaftliche Schönheiten; ~ **effects** dramatische Effekte, Bühneneffekte; ~ **railway** Modelleisenbahn; ~ **road** *(US)* Touristenstraße.

sceneshifter *(theater)* Kulissenschieber.

scent Fährte, Spur;
false ~ falsche Spur;
~ *(v.)* **a crime** Verbrechen für möglich halten; ~ **a job** Stellung ausfindig machen; ~ **trouble** Unheil wittern;
to be on the right ~ auf der richtigen Fährte sein; **to be on the** ~ **of an important discovery** kurz vor einer bedeutenden Entdeckung stehen; **to have a good** ~ **for young talents** Nase für junge Talente haben; **to lose the** ~ Spur verlieren; **to put s. o. on a false** ~ j. auf die falsche Fährte setzen; **to throw s. o. off the** ~ j. falsch informieren und von der Fährte abbringen; **to throw the police off the** ~ Polizei abschütteln;
~ **bottle** Parfümfläschchen.

schedular tabellarisch.

schedule *(additional clause)* Zusatzartikel, *(advertising)* Werbeplan, *(annex to income tax)* Einkommensteuerverordnung, *(appendix)* Anhang, Zusatzartikel, *(balance sheet)* Aufstellung über die Aktiven und Passiven, *(bankruptcy, US)* Konkursbilanz, -status, *(bill of quantities)* Baukostenvoranschlag, *(broadcasting)* Programmverzeichnis, -zeitplan, *(constitutional law)* Verfassungsanhang, -zusatz, *(covering note)* Begleitschreiben, *(income-tax bracket, Br.)* Gruppe steuerpflichtiger Einkommen, Einkommensteuerklasse, -gruppe, *(income-tax form)* Einkommensteuerformular, *(prescribed form)* Formblatt, Formular, *(insertions)* Datenschema, *(inventory)* Inventar, *(list of operations)* Produktionsverkauf, *(list annexed)*

Anlage, Anhang, *(printing)* Satzvorlage, *(questionnaire)* Fragebogen, *(railroad guide, US)* Zeit-, Fahrplan, *(rider)* Zusatzurkunde, *(statistics)* Fragebogen, *(timetable)* Ablauf-, Zeit-, Stundenplan, *(working plan, US)* Arbeitsplan, fester Plan, Tagesablauf, *(written statement)* Tabelle, Liste, [tabellarisches] Verzeichnis, [Stücke]verzeichnis, erläuterndes Begleitwerk, Aufstellung, Zettel;
according to (on) ~ *(US)* [fahr]planmäßig; **ahead of** ~ früher als vereinbart; **up to** ~ *(US, train)* auf die Minute [genau];
aging ~ Fälligkeitstabelle; **busy** ~ *(US)* gedrängter Zeitplan; **cost** ~ Kostenaufstellung; **demand** ~ Bedarfsliste; **itemized** ~ Einzelaufstellung; **leave** ~ Urlaubsplan; **production** ~ Produktionsprogramm; **supply** ~ Vorratsverzeichnis; **train** ~ Zugfolge; **vacation** ~ *(US)* Urlaubsplan; **wage** ~ Lohntarif;
~ **of accounts payable** *(US)* Kreditorenverzeichnis; ~ **of accounts receivable** *(US)* Debitorenverzeichnis; ~ **of arrivals and departures** *(US)* Tafel der ankommenden und abgehenden Züge; ~ **of assets** Verzeichnis der Aktiven; ~ **to a balance sheet** Bilanzanlage; ~ **of a bankrupt's creditors** Konkurstabelle; ~ **of a bankrupt's debts** *(US)* Konkursabwicklungsbilanz; ~ **of cases** Terminkalender; ~ **of charges** Gebührentarif, -ordnung; ~ **of commissions** Gebührenordnung, Provisionstabelle; ~ **of commission charges** *(US)* Courtagetarif, ~ **of Concessions** *(GATT)* Zollzugeständnisliste; ~ **for the construction of a building** Arbeitsplan für die Errichtung eines Gebäudes; ~ **of contents** Inhaltsaufstellung; ~ **of creditors** Gläubigerverzeichnis, Konkurstabelle; ~ **of dilapidations** Verzeichnis vorzunehmender Reparaturen; ~ **for discount by frequency and volume** Maß- und Mengenstaffel; ~ **of encumbrances** Verzeichnis der hypothekarischen Belastungen; ~ **of expenses** Kostenaufstellung; ~ **of fares** Fahrpreistabelle; ~ **of fees** *(US)* Gebührenordnung; ~ **of freights** Frachtsatzanzeiger; ~ **of insertions** Datenplan der Anzeigen, Zeitplan für eine Insertion, Insertionsplan; ~ **of investments** Verzeichnis der Anlagewerte; ~ **of liabilities** Liste der Verbindlichkeiten, Schuldenverzeichnis; ~ **of planes** Flugplan; ~ **of plights** *(renting)* Mängelliste; ~ **of prices** Preisverzeichnis; ~ **of property** Vermögensaufstellung, -verzeichnis; ~ **of rates** Frachttarif; ~ **of shipments** Versandplan; ~ **of steamers** *(US)* Abfahrtsplan; ~ **of trains** *(US)* Fahrplan; ~ **of wages** Lohnklasse;
~ *(v.)* Liste (tabellarisch) zusammenstellen, in eine Liste eintragen, klassifizieren, *(annex)* beifügen, *(determine, US)* festlegen, ansetzen, bestimmen, planen, projektieren, *(railroad guide, US)* in einen Fahrplan eintragen, *(theatre)* auf den Spielplan setzen;
~ **an employee for organization** Angestellten in seinen neuen Arbeitsbereich einführen; ~ **production** *(US)* Produktionsablauf festlegen, Produktion programmieren; ~ **the publication for November** Veröffentlichung für November planen; ~ **one's time** seine Zeit einteilen; **a new train** ~ *(US)* neuen Zug in den Fahrplan einfügen;
to arrive right on ~ *(US)* fahrplanmäßig eintreffen; **to be finished on** ~ zeitgerecht (termingemäß) fertig werden; **to be running behind** ~ *(US)* nicht fahrplanmäßig laufen; **to be on a tight** ~ feste Reiseroute befolgen; **to catch up with** ~ Terminplan wieder einhalten; **to compile a** ~ Liste aufstellen; **to coordinate one's** ~s Terminkalender aufeinander abstimmen; **to fall behind** ~ hinter einem Plan zurückbleiben, Planziel nicht erreichen; **to file one's** ~ *(US)* Konkursanmeldung vornehmen, Konkursbilanz aufstellen; **to file a** ~ **of assets and liabilities** Vermögensaufstellung einreichen; **to fit s. th. into one's** ~ etw. in seinem Terminkalender unterbringen; **to go off according to** ~ *(fam.)* programmgemäß verlaufen; **to juggle one's** ~ **around** mit seinem Terminkalender herumrangieren; **to keep a** ~ *(US)* fahrplanmäßig fahren (fliegen); **to maintain a** ~ *(US)* Fahrplan einhalten; **to meet a** ~ Terminplan einhalten; **to open on** ~ zur vorgesehenen Zeit eröffnen; **to open five years behind** ~ fünf Jahre nach dem Fertigstellungstermin eröffnen; **to prepare a** ~ Verzeichnis aufstellen; **to run to a fixed** ~ *(US)* fahrplanmäßig verkehren; **to start on** ~ *(US)* nach Plan abfahren;
~ **change** *(US)* Fahrplanänderung; ~ **contract** Regievertrag; ~ **form** *(fire insurance)* Kompensationsklausel; ~ **maintenance** *(US)* Fahrplaneinhaltung; ~ **point** *(US)* Postumschlagsstelle; ~ **tax on an owner-occupied house** Einkommensteuer auf selbstgenutztes Eigenheim; ~ **time** *(US)* fahrplanmäßige Abfahrts-, Ankunftszeit; ~ **work** Regiearbeiten.
scheduled, as planmäßig, *(US)* fahrplanmäßig;
to be ~ anberaumt sein; **to be** ~ **to arrive at noon** *(US)* fahrplanmäßig mittags ankommen; **to be** ~ **for the next week** für die nächste Woche vorgesehen sein; **to be** ~ **to make a speech** als Redner vorgesehen sein;

~ **airline** *(US)* Fluglinie mit fahrplanmäßigem Dienst; ~ **airline service** *(US)* Linienverkehr, planmäßiger Flugverkehr; ~ **business** *(airline, US)* Liniengeschäft; ~ **carriers' cartel** *(US)* Kartell der Linienfluggesellschaften; ~ **cost** vorkalkulierte Kosten; ~ **departure** *(US)* planmäßige Abfahrt, planmäßiger Abflug; ~ **flight** *(US)* Linienflug; ~ **price** Listenpreis; ~ **production** programmierte Produktion; ~ **repayment** Rückzahlung zu den festgelegten Terminen; ~ **ship** *(US)* fahrplanmäßiges Schiff; ~ **taxes** *(Br.)* veranlagte Steuern; ~ **territories** *(Br.)* Länder des Sterlingblocks; ~ **time** *(US)* fahrplanmäßige Abfahrtszeit; **to arrive at the** ~ **time** *(US)* zur fahrplanmäßigen Zeit eintreffen; ~ **train** *(US)* pünktlich einlaufender (pünktlicher, fahrplanmäßiger) Zug; ~ **work** Regiearbeit.
scheduler, production Produktionsprogrammierer.
scheduling *(US)* Erstellung von Terminplänen, Terminplanung, Ablaufs-, Fertigungsplanung, Produktionsprogrammierung, *(voyage)* Reiseplanung;
master ~ Gesamtplanung;
~ **one's time** Zeiteinteilung.
schema Schema, Übersicht, *(printing)* Satzvorlage.
schematic schematisch.
schematism Schematismus.
scheme *(deceased's estate, Br.)* Verteilungsplan, *(intrigue)* Machenschaft, Komplott, Intrige, *(plan)* Plan, Entwurf, Projekt, Vorhaben, Aktionsprogramm, *(statement)* [tabellarische] Aufstellung, Liste, Übersicht, *(systematic arrangement)* systematische Darstellung, Diagramm, Schema;
allocation ~ Zuteilungsplan; **bubble** ~ *(Br.)* Schwindelunternehmen; **business** ~ geschäftliches Unternehmen; **irrigation** ~ *(Br.)* Bewässerungsprojekt; **paper** ~s Pläne auf dem Papier, theoretische Vorschläge; **pension** ~ Pensionsplan, Altersversorgungswerk; **sampling** ~ Stichprobenschema; **shady** ~ übliches Manöver; **Utopian** ~ utopischer Plan; **viable** ~ lebensfähiges Projekt; **watered-down** ~ verwässerter Plan; **common plot and** ~ *(US)* Komplott;
~ **of arrangement** *(Br.)* **(composition)** Schuldenregelungsplan, vergleichsweise Regelung der Schulden, Vergleichsvorschlag; ~ **of colo(u)r** Farb[en]zusammenstellung; ~ **of corporation tax** Körperschaftssteuersystem; ~ **of demobilization** Demobilmachungsplan; ~ **of development** Bau-, Siedlungsprojekt; ~ **of expenditure** Ausgabenschema; ~ **of inheritance** *(Br.)* Teilungsplan; ~ **for insurance** Versicherungsschema; ~ **of a lottery** Lotterie-, Ziehungsplan; ~ **for the mail service** Zustellungsschema; ~ **of manoeuvre** Manöverplan; ~ **of manufacturing** Produktionsplan; ~ **of marking** Zensurenschema; ~ **on paper** theoretischer Vorschlag; ~ **of philosophy** philosophisches Lehrgebäude; ~ **of reconstruction** Sanierungs-, Wiederaufbauplan; ~ **of redemption (repayment)** Amortisationsplan; ~ **for the term's work** Studien-, Semesterplan; ~ **of work** Arbeitsplan;
~ *(v.)* planen, entwerfen, systematisch anordnen;
~ **for the overthrow of the government** Pläne für den Sturz der Regierung ausarbeiten; ~ **for a post** sich eine Stellung erschleichen wollen;
to draw up a ~ Plan ausarbeiten; **to favo(u)r a** ~ Projekt befürworten; **to promote a** ~ Plan unterstützen; **to push a** ~ Projekt vorantreiben; **to run a** ~ Projekt durchführen; **to realize a** ~ Plan verwirklichen; **to step up a** ~ Plan beschleunigen; **to throw a** ~ **overboard** Plan völlig aufgeben; **to thwart s. one's** ~s jds. Pläne zunichtemachen.
schemer Plänemacher, *(plotter)* Intrigant.
scheming Intrigen, Machenschaften;
~ **times** Intrigenzeit.
schlep *(v.)* **along** *(sl.)* mit sich herumschleppen.
schmaltz *(sl.)* kommerziell ausgenutzte Sentimentalität.
schmear *(v.)* *(sl.)* bestechen.
schnorrer Schnorrer, Bettler.
scholar Gelehrter, Wissenschaftler, *(student)* Stipendiat;
British Council ~ *(Br.)* Auslandsstipendiat; **great** ~ Mann mit großem Wissen; **legal** ~ Rechtsgelehrter; **Rhodes** ~ Rhodesstipendiat;
to be an allround ~ umfassendes Wissen haben; ~**'s season ticket** *(Br.)* Schülermonatskarte.
scholarship Stipendium, Freistelle;
close ~ auf bestimmten Personenkreis begrenztes Stipendium; **open** ~ ausgeschriebenes Stipendium; **state** ~ Staatsstipendium;
~ **examination** Stipendiumsprüfung;
to award a ~ Stipendium zuerkennen; **to found a** ~ Stipendium einrichten; **to gain (win) a** ~ Stipendium erhalten; ~ **system** Stipendienwesen.
scholarly translation gekonnte Übersetzung.

scholastic|competition Schulwettkampf; ~ **education** akademische Bildung; ~ **philosophy** Schulweisheit; ~ **position** Lehramtsstelle; ~ **profession** Lehrerberuf.

school Schule, Schulunterricht, *(course of study)* Lehrgang, Kursus, *(faculty)* Fakultät, *(system)* Lehrsystem, Richtung;
in the ~s *(Br.)* im Schlußexamen; for use in ~s für den Schulgebrauch;
aided ~ *(Br.)* staatlich geförderte Privatschule; **all-age** ~ Zwergschule; **approved** ~ *(Br.)* Fürsorgeinternat; **big** ~ *(sl.)* Staatsgefängnis; **boarding** ~ *(Br.)* Internat; **business** ~ Wirtschaftsfachschule; **charity** ~ Waisenschule; **collegiate** ~ *(Br.)* höhere Schule; **commercial** ~ Handelsschule; **common** ~s öffentliche Schulen; **comprehensive** ~ *(Br.)* Gesamtschule; **continuation** ~ Fortbildungsschule; **controlled** ~ anerkannte Ersatzschule; **correspondence** ~ Fernlehrinstitut; **council** ~ Gemeinde-, Kreisschule; **county** ~ *(Br.)* öffentliche (staatliche) Schule; **dame** ~ *(Br.)* Privatschule für Mädchen; **day** ~ Tagesschule; **denominational** ~ Konfessionsschule; **desegregation** ~ *(US)* Gemeinschaftsschule; **direct-grant** ~ *(Br.)* staatlich anerkannte Privatschule; **district** ~ *(US)*Volksschule; **elementary** ~ Grund-, Volksschule; **endowed** ~ Stiftsschule; **evening** ~ Abendschule, -unterricht, Volkshochschulkursus; **foundation** ~ Stiftsschule; **free** ~ unentgeltlicher Schulunterricht; **grade** ~ *(US)* Volks-, Elementar-, Grundschule; **grammar** ~ *(Br.)* höhere Schule, Oberschule; **grant-aided** ~ *(Br.)* staatlich geförderte Schule; **high** ~ *(US)* Mittelschule, höhere Lehranstalt; **independent** ~ Privatschule; **industrial** ~ Fach-, Berufs-, Gewerbeschule; **infant** ~ *(Br.)* Vor-, Kleinstkinderschule; **integrated** ~ *(US)* Schule ohne Rassentrennung; **junior** ~ *(Br.)* Grundschule; **laissez-faire** ~ liberalistische Richtung; **language** ~ Sprachenschule; **law** ~ *(US)* juristische Fakultät; **learn-by-mail** ~ *(US)* Fernlehrinstitut; **maintained** ~ *(Br.)* kommunal unterhaltene Schule; **the middle** ~ mittlere Schulklassen; **mixed** ~ Schule für beide Geschlechter, gemischte Schule; **modern secondary** ~ *(Br.)* praktische Schule; **night** ~ *(Br.)* Abendschule, Fortbildungsschule, [etwa] Volkshochschule; **nonprovided** ~ *(Br.)* Privatschule; **normal** ~ Lehrerbildungsanstalt, -seminar; **nursery** ~ Kindergarten; **parish** ~ Gemeindeschule; **preparatory** ~ *(Br.)* Vor[bereitungs]schule; **primary** ~ *(US)* Volks-, Grundschule; **private** ~ Privatschule, -unterricht; **professional** ~ Fachschule; **provided** ~ *(Br.)* Gemeindeschule; **public** ~ *(Br.)* öffentlich unterhaltene Schule, *(US)* staatliche Lehranstalt, *(boarding school)* Internat, Stiftsschule; **publicly-supported** ~ öffentlich geförderte Schule; **reform** ~ *(US)* Besserungsanstalt, Jugendgefängnis; **reformatory** ~ Erziehungs-, Besserungsanstalt; **secondary** ~ Mittelschule, *(Br.)* höhere Schule, weiterführende Schule; **secondary grammar** ~ humanistisches Gymnasium; **secondary modern** ~ Realgymnasium; **secondary technical** ~ Oberrealschule; **senior high** ~ *(US)* höhere Schule, Gymnasium; **special-agreement** ~ *(Br.)* Privatschule mit staatlichem Lehrereinsetzungsrecht; **state** ~ *(Br.)* staatliche Schule; **summer** ~ Ferienkursus; **technical** ~ Gewerbe-, Fach-, Berufsschule, Polytechnikum; **trade** ~ *(US)* Handels-, Berufsschule; **training** ~ Berufsschule, *(US)* Schule für schwer erziehbare Kinder; **upper** ~ höhere Schule; **vacation** ~ *(US)* Ferienkursus; **vocational** ~ Berufs-, Fach-, Gewerbeschule;
~ **of art** Kunstakademie; ~ **for arts and crafts** Handwerksschule; **special** ~ **for educationally subnormal children** Hilfsschule; ~ **of commerce** Wirtschaftshochschule; ~ **of mines** Bergakademie; ~ **of thought** Denkrichtung, Lehrmeinung;
~ *(v.)* zur Schule schicken, einschulen, *(train)* ausbilden, unterrichten, -weisen, schulen;
~ **one's temper** sein Temperament zügeln; ~ **s. o. in society ways** j. gesellschaftlich schulen;
to attend a ~ Schule besuchen; **to be absent from** ~ in der Schule fehlen; **to be at** ~ in der Schule sein; **to be in for one's** ~s *(Br.)* sich der Abschlußprüfung unterziehen; **to be late (tardy,** US**) for** ~ unpünktlich zur Schule kommen; **to break up** ~ Schule schließen; **to come out of** ~ mit der Schule fertig sein; **to drop out of high** ~ *(US)* von der Mittelschule ohne Abschluß weggehen; **to enrol in a** ~ *(Br.)* einschulen; **to enter a child for** ~ *(Br.)* Kind einschulen; **to expel from** ~ vom Schulunterricht ausschließen; **to found a** ~ Schule stiften; **to go to** ~ zur Schule gehen, Schulbank drücken; **to go to** ~ **to s. o.** *(fig.)* bei jem. in die Schule gehen; **to graduate at** *(Br.)* **(from,** US**) a** ~ an einer Schule das Abschlußexamen ablegen; **to keep** ~ Schule abhalten, Schulunterricht erteilen; **to leave** ~ aus der Schule entlassen werden, von der Schule abgehen; **to pass through the** ~ Schule durchlaufen; **to register for a** ~ zu einer Schule anmelden; **to scrap up the** ~ Schule mit Ach und Krach hinter sich

bringen; **to send a child to** ~ Kind einschulen lassen; **to set up a** ~ neue Schule einrichten; **to take from** ~ von der Schule nehmen; **to tell tales out of** ~ aus der Schule plaudern;
~ **account** Schulkonto; ~ **age** schulpflichtiges Alter, Schulalter; **compulsory** ~ **age** schulpflichtiges Alter; ~~**-age children** schulpflichtige Kinder; ~ **attendance** Schulbesuch; **compulsory** ~ **attendance** Schulzwang; ~ **authorities** Schulbehörde; ~ **badge** Schulabzeichen; ~ **bench** Schulbank; ~ **board** Schulaufsichtsbehörde; ~ **building** Schulgebäude; **new** ~ **buildings** Schulneubauten; ~ **bus** Schulbus; ~ **bussing** Bustransport von Schulkindern; ~ **camp** Schulerholungslager; ~ **career** Schulwerdegang; ~ **catchment area** Schuleinzugsbereich; ~ **certificate** Schulabgangs-, Reifeprüfungszeugnis; ~ **certificate examination** Reife-, Schulabgangsprüfung; ~ **child** Schulkind; ~ **chum** *(coll.)* Schulkamerad; ~ **clock** Schuluhr; ~ **committee** Schulkommission, -ausschuß; ~ **course** Schulkursus; ~ **days** Schulzeit; ~ **director** Schulaufsichtsbeamter; **consolidated** ~ **district** gemeiner Schulzweckverband; ~ **doctor** Schularzt; ~ **dropout** Schulversager; **central** ~ **education** höhere Schulbildung; ~ **enrol(l)ment** Schulanmeldung; ~ **equipment** Schuleinrichtung; ~ **exercise** Schularbeiten; ~ **exhibition** Schulveranstaltung; ~ **fee** Schulgeld; ~ **fellow** Schulkamerad; ~ **form** Schulklasse; ~ **friendship** Schulfreundschaft; ~ **graduate** Schüler; **to be a high-~ graduate** *(US)* abgeschlossene höhere Schulbildung besitzen; ~ **hall** Aula; ~ **health service** ärztliche Schulfürsorge; ~ **hour** Schulstunde; ~ **inspector** Schulrat; ~ **journal** Schülerzeitung; ~ **leaver** *(Br.)* Schulentlassener, -abgänger; ~~**-leaver job creation scheme** Arbeitsplatzbeschaffungsplan für Schulabgänger; ~ **leaving** Schulabgang; ~~**-leaving age** Schulentlassungsalter; **to raise the** ~~**-leaving age** Schulzeit verlängern; ~~**-leaving ceremony** Entlassungsfeier; ~ **library** Schulbibliothek; ~ **life** Schulzeit; ~ **lunch** Schulspeisung; ~ **magazine** Schülerzeitung; ~ **master** Schullehrer; ~ **meals** Schulspeisung; ~ **milk** Schulmilch; ~ **omnibus** Schulomnibus; ~ **party** Schulausflug; **total** ~ **population** Gesamtschülerzahl; ~ **premises** Schulgebäude, -grundstück; ~ **publisher** Schulverlag; ~ **pupil** Schüler; ~ **savings bank** Sparkasse für Schulkinder; ~ **ship** Schulgrundstück; ~ **staff** Lehrerkollegium; **approved** ~ **system** *(Br.)* Fürsorgeerziehung; ~ **term** Schuljahr; ~ **time** Schulzeit; ~ **treat** Schulausflug; ~ **tuition** Schulgeld; ~ **vacation** Schulferien; ~ **year** Schuljahr.

schoolable schulpflichtig, im schulpflichtigen Alter.
schoolbag Schultasche.
schoolbook Schulbuch.
schoolboy Schuljunge, Pennäler;
~ **mischief** Dummerjungenstreich.
schoolchildren Schulkinder, -jugend;
~'s **work** Schularbeiten.
schooldame *(Br.)* Direktorin, Schulvorsteherin.
schoolhouse Schulgebäude.
schooling Erziehung, Ausbildung;
compulsory ~ Schulpflicht;
part-time ~ **alternating with part-time employment** gleichzeitige Hochschulausbildung und Berufsausübung;
to pay for s. one's ~ Kosten von jds. Erziehung tragen, für jds. Ausbildung aufkommen.
schoolmaster Schulmeister, -leiter, Direktor.
schoolmate Klassen-, Schulkamerad, Mitschüler.
schoolmistress Schulleiterin, Direktorin.
schoolroom Klassenzimmer.
schoolteacher Schullehrer.
schoolteaching Schulunterricht.
schooltime Unterrichtzeit.
schoolwork Klassenarbeit.
schooner Schoner.
science Wissenschaft, Forschung;
economic ~ Wirtschaftswissenschaft; **exact** ~s exakte Wissenschaften; **general** ~ Studium generale; **natural** ~ Naturwissenschaft; **political** ~ Staatswissenschaft; **social** ~ Soziologie, Sozialwissenschaft;
~ **of industrial administration** Betriebswirtschaftslehre; ~ **of future** Wissenschaft von der Zukunft, Futurologie; ~ **of journalism** Zeitungswissenschaft; ~ **of law** Rechtswissenschaft;
to study ~ Naturwissenschaften studieren;
~ **adviser** wissenschaftlicher Berater; ~~**-based industries** Wachstumsindustrien; ~ **degree** Universitätsabschluß; ~ **editor** Schriftleiter einer wissenschaftlichen Beilage; ~ **fiction** technischer Zukunftsroman.
scienter *(lat.)* wissentlich.
scientific [natur]wissenschaftlich;
~ **advance** wissenschaftlicher Fortschritt; ~ **advisory work**

beratende wissenschaftliche Tätigkeit; ~ **attachment** wissenschaftliche Bildung; ~ **antiquarian bookselling** wissenschaftliches Antiquariat; ~ **discoveries** wissenschaftliche Entdeckungen; ~ **farming** wissenschaftlich betriebene Landwirtschaft; ~ **information** wissenschaftliche Erkenntnisse; ~ **institution** wissenschaftliches Institut, Forschungsinstitut; ~ **management** wissenschaftliche Betriebsführung; ~ **method** wissenschaftliche Methode; ~ **outpost** Forschungsbasis; ~ **paper** wissenschaftliches Blatt; ~ **periodical** wissenschaftliche Zeitschrift; ~ **research** Forschung; ~ **tariff** nach wissenschaftlichen Grundsätzen aufgestellter Tarif; ~ **treatise** wissenschaftliche Abhandlung.

scientifically trained wissenschaftlich ausgebildet.

scientist Wissenschaftler.

scintilla Spur;
> **a mere ~ of evidence** nur ein Fünkchen von Beweis.

scion Abkömmling.

scissorbill *(sl.)* Kuponschneider, Rentier.

scissors, price Preisschere.

scofflaw Gesetzesübertreter.

scold zänkisches Weib.

scoop *(piece of news)* sensationelle Reportage, Allein-, Erst-, Exklusivmeldung, Knüller, *(special gain)* Sondergewinn, große Gewinnmitnahme;
> ~ *(v.)* **$ 10.000 in a day** 10.000 Dollar an einem Tag kassieren; ~ **the other papers** Sondernachricht allein veröffentlichen; ~ **in a large profit** Sondergewinn einstreichen, guten Schnitt machen; **to earn a lot of money in one ~** auf einen Schlag viel Geld verdienen; **to make a ~** guten Fang machen, Coup landen; **to win £ 100 at a ~** auf einen Schlag 100 Pfund gewinnen.

scope *(law)* Gültigkeitsbereich, Geltungsgebiet, -bereich, *(range)* Bereich, Umfang, Rahmen, *(sphere of action)* Aufgaben-, Wirkungskreis, -bereich, Reichweite, Bezirk, Gebiet, Betätigungsfeld, *(sphere of business)* Geschäftsbereich;
> **ample ~** große Bewegungsfreiheit, großer Spielraum; **free ~** Handlungsfreiheit;
> ~ **of application** Anwendungsbereich; ~ **of audit** Prüfungsumfang; ~ **of [agent's] authority** Umfang der Vertretungsmacht, Vollmachtsumfang; ~ **of business** Geschäftsumfang; **obligatory ~ of a contract** obligatorischer Charakter eines Vertrages; ~ **of a convention** Geltungsbereich eines Abkommens; ~ **of discretion** Ermessensumfang; ~ **of duties** Aufgabenbereich, -kreis; ~ **of insurance** Versicherungsumfang; ~ **of a law** Gesetzesrahmen; ~ **of licence** Umfang des Nutzungsrechtes; ~ **of a patent** Schutzumfang eines Patents; ~ **of policy** Versicherungsausmaß; ~ **of power** Vollmachtsumfang; ~ **for redistribution** Verteilungsspielraum; ~ **for spending** Ausgabenspielraum; ~ **of talks** Gesprächsrahmen;
> **to act within the ~ of one's authority** im Rahmen seiner Vertretungsmacht handeln; **to be beyond s. one's ~** außerhalb von jds. Befugnissen liegen; **to be beyond the ~ of s. one's mind** außerhalb von jds. Fassungsvermögen liegen; **to be of a nation-wide ~** das ganze Land erfassen; **to be outside the ~ of the national insurance system** nicht sozialversicherungspflichtig (sozialversichert) sein; **to be within the ~ of trade union activities** zum Aufgabenbereich einer Gewerkschaft gehören; **to come within the ~ of the law** unter die gesetzlichen Bestimmungen fallen; **to come within the ~ of normal functions** innerhalb des normalen Aufgabenbereiches liegen; **to extend the ~ of one's activities** sein Tätigkeitsfeld ausdehnen; **to fall within the ~ of s. one's work** im Rahmen von jds. Arbeit liegen; **to give s. o. ~ for his activities** jem. volle Handlungsfreiheit einräumen; **to go beyond the ~ of an essay** Rahmen eines Aufsatzes sprengen; **to have free (full) ~ to act** volle Handlungsfreiheit haben; **to lie within the ~ of possible events** im Rahmen des Möglichen liegen.

scorch *(motorist)* Rasen;
> ~ *(v.)* versengen, *(fig.)* heftig kritisieren, *(mil.)* in verbrannte Erde verwandeln, Politik der verbrannten Erde betreiben, *(motorist)* rasen.

scorched-earth policy Politik der verbrannten Erde.

scorcher Sensation, *(motorist)* Raser.

score Punktwert, -zahl, *(debt owing)* Schuldposten, Zeche, *(injury kept in mind)* alte Rechnung, Zeche, *(loot, sl.)* Sore, *(school)* Note, Zensur, Bewertung, *(successful move)* Dusel, Glück;
> **on the ~ of** aufgrund von; **on more ~s than one** aus verschiedenen Gründen;
> **~s of people** Masse von Leuten;
> ~ *(v.)* auf Rechnung setzen, anschreiben, *(make points)* Punkte erzielen, *(at school)* benoten, bewerten;
> ~ **an advance** Kursgewinn verzeichnen; ~ **at s. one's expense** zu

jds. Lasten anschreiben lassen; ~ **off s. o.** *(Br.)* jem. eins auswischen; ~ **a passage in a book** Buchstelle unterstreichen; ~ **a point** Gewinnpunkt machen; ~ **poorly** schlecht abschneiden; ~ **second** zweiten Platz belegen; ~ **a success** Erfolg verzeichnen; ~ **up debts** Schulden machen; ~ **up the drinks** Getränke anschreiben; ~ **up a remark against s. o.** jem. eine Bemerkung verübeln; ~ **out words** Wörter ausstreichen;
> **to be a ~ in s. one's favo(u)r** jem. einen Pluspunkt einbringen; **to be rejected on the ~ of ill health** wegen schlechter Gesundheit abgelehnt werden; **to desert by ~s** haufenweise desertieren; **to go off at ~s** drauflosgehen; **to have been there ~s of times** an einem Ort schon Dutzende von Malen gewesen sein; **to have some old ~ to settle with s. o.** mit jem. noch eine alte Rechnung zu begleichen haben; **to know the ~** immer auf dem Damm sein; **to make ~s off hecklers at public meeting** bei der Abfertigung von Zwischenrufern erhebliche Punkte in öffentlichen Versammlungen verzeichnen; **to pay one's ~** Rechnung völlig ausgleichen; **to quit ~s with s. o.** *(sl.)* alte Rechnungen mit jem. begleichen, es jem. heimzahlen; **to run up a ~** *(Br.)* Schulden machen, sich verschulden, Schuldkonto anwachsen lassen; **to run up a ~ at a public house** *(Br.)* (saloon, *US*) in einer Wirtschaft anschreiben lassen; **to settle (wipe off) ~s** alte Rechnungen erledigen;
> ~ **card** Zählkarte.

scoreboard Anzeigentafel.

scoring up | of debts Anschreibenlassen; ~ **of drinks** Anschreiben von Getränken.

scot Beitrag, Abgabe;
> **to pay for one's ~** seinen Anteil leisten; **to pay ~ and lot** alles auf Heller und Pfennig bezahlen;
> ~ **and lot voter** gemeindesteuerpflichtiger Wähler.

scot-free ungeschoren, unbehelligt, straffrei, *(free from duty)* frei von Abgaben, steuerfrei;
> **to go ~** straffrei ausgehen.

Scotch | marriage formlose Eheschließung; ~ **tape** Tesafilm, -band.

Scotchman Schotte, *(miser, sl.)* Geizkragen.

scour *(river)* ausgehöhltes Flußbett;
> ~ *(v.)* säubern, reinigen;
> ~ **the country for s. o.** ganzes Land nach jem. durchsuchen; ~ **the invaders from the land** Eindringlinge aus dem Land vertreiben; ~ **a town** in der Stadt eine Razzia durchführen.

scourge of war Kriegsgeisel.

scout Späher, Kundschafter, *(airplane)* Erkundungs-, Aufklärungsflug, *(Oxford)* Diener, Aufwärter, *(patrol man, Br.)* Verkehrswacht, Patrouillenfahrer;
> **on the ~** auf der Lauer;
> ~ *(v.)* auskundschaften;
> ~ **car** Patrouillen-, Aufklärungsfahrzeug, Panzerspähwagen, *(traffic, Br.)* Wagen der Verkehrswacht.

scouting plane Aufklärungsflugzeug.

scoutmaster *(radio, sl.)* Patronatsfirma.

scrabble *(v.) | for one's livelihood* sich für seinen Lebensunterhalt abrackern; ~ **the pennies together** Pfennige zusammenkratzen.

scram *(v.) (sl.)* abhauen;
> ~**-bag** Alarm-, Notgepäck; ~ **money** *(sl.)* Notgroschen.

scramble Gedränge, Balgerei;
> ~ **for office** Ämterjagd; ~ **on stocks** Ansturm auf Aktien; ~ **for the best seats** Gedrängel nach den besten Plätzen; ~ **for wealth** Jagd nach dem Reichtum;
> ~ *(v.) (tel.)* verwürfeln, verschlüsseln;
> ~ **for** *(fig.)* jagen nach; ~ **to one's feet** sich aufrappeln; ~ **up money** Geld zusammenscharren; ~ **for money in the street** sich um hingeworfenes Geld auf der Straße balgen; ~ **for wealth** dem Reichtum nachjagen.

scrambled durcheinandergeworfen;
> ~ **telephone** Geheimtelefon.

scrambler *(tel.)* Geheimhaltungs-, Verwürfelungsanlage.

scrambling *(tel.)* Verschlüsselung, Verwürfelung.

scrap Schrott, Abfall, Ausschuß, Altmaterial, *(building)* Abbruch, *(newspaper)* Zeitungsausschnitt, *(literary work)* Fragment;
> ~**s of cloth** Stoffreste; **not a ~ of evidence** nicht die Spur eines Beweises; ~ **of paper** Fetzen Papier;
> ~ *(v.)* verschrotten, *(cast out)* ausrangieren, auf den Schrotthaufen werfen, zum alten Eisen legen, *(dismantle)* abmontieren;
> ~ **a building** Gebäude abreißen; ~ **a ship** Schiff abwracken; ~ **together** *(money)* zusammenkratzen;
> **not to benefit s. o. a ~** jem. nur wenig nutzen; **to catch ~s of a conversation** Gesprächsfetzen auffangen; **to come round to col-**

lect ~ Altmaterial abholen; **to go to** ~ abgewrackt werden; **to have not a** ~ **of debts** keinen roten Heller schulden; **to pick up** ~s **of knowledge** sich einige Kenntnisse aneignen;

~ **company** Schrottfirma; ~ **dealer** Schrotthändler; ~ **drive** Altmaterialsammlung; ~ **heap** Abfall-, Schutthaufen; **to throw s. th. onto the** ~ **heap** etw. zum alten Eisen werfen; **to throw a man on the** ~ **heap** j. als zum alten Eisen gehörig abschieben; ~ **iron** Abfalleisen, Schrott; ~ **material** Abfallmaterial; ~ **merchant** Schrotthändler; ~ **metal** Schrott; ~-**metal market** Schrottmarkt; ~ **price** Schrottpreis; ~ **proceeds** Schrotterlös; ~ **processing** Schrottverarbeitung, -verwertung; ~ **report** Ausschußmeldung; ~ **sales** Schrottverkäufe; ~-**steel dealer** Schrotthändler; ~-**steel market** Schrottmarkt; ~ **trade** Schrotthandel; ~ **value** Schrott-, Abnutzungswert.

scrapbook *(cuttings)* Einklebebuch [für Zeitungsausschnitte].

scrape Kratzer, Schramme, *(fig.)* Klemme, Verlegenheit, Not; **in a** ~ in der Klemme;

~ *(v.)* **an acquaintance with s. o.** sich mit j. anbiedern; ~ **along** sich kümmerlich durchschlagen; ~ **clear of prison** des Gefängnis gerade noch entgehen; ~ **down a speaker** Redner durch Scharren zum Schweigen bringen; **just** ~ **through one's examination** gerade noch durchs Examen rutschen; ~ **a living** sich kümmerlich durchbringen; ~ **together** zusammenraffen; ~ **together a few dollars for the holiday** ein paar Dollars für eine Urlaubsreise zusammenkratzen; ~ **up an acquaintance with s. o.** jem. seine Bekanntschaft aufdrängen; ~ **up a sum of money** Geld zusammenkratzen;

to get into a ~ in eine Klemme (mißliche Lage) geraten.

scrapepenny *(Br.)* Pfennigfuchser, Geizkragen.

scraper Knicker, Knauser; ~ **board** Schabekarton.

scrapman Autoausschlachter.

scrapping Ausrangieren, *(ship)* Verschrotten, *(vessel)* Verschrottung; ~ **facilities** Schrottverwertungsanlage.

scrapyard Schrottplatz.

scratch Gekritzel, *(available cash, sl.)* verfügbare Moneten, *(fig.)* erster Anfang, Nullpunkt, *(mention in a newspaper, sl.)* Erwähnung in der Zeitung; ~ **of the pen** Federzug;

~ *(v.)* *(US)* Wahlzettel durch Streichung abändern; ~ **along** sich mühsam durchschlagen; ~ **around for evidence** Beweise mühselig zusammenstoppeln; ~ **around for funds** auf der Kapitalsuche sein; ~ **s. one's back** jem. um den Bart gehen; ~ **an item from an account** Rechnungsposten streichen; ~ **a few lines to a friend** einem Freund ein paar Zeilen schreiben; ~ **for s. th.** hinter etw. herjagen; ~ **at the last moment** seine Kandidatur im letzten Augenblick zurückziehen; ~ **out s. one's name from a list** jds. Namen von einer Liste streichen; ~ **a note** etw. hinkritzeln; ~ **out** ausstreichen, -radieren; ~ **the surface of a problem** nur den Anfang eines Problems aufzeigen; ~ **the surface of a subject** Thema nur oberflächlich behandeln; ~ **a ticket** *(US)* Parteiwahlliste durch Streichungen abändern; ~ **together** Geld zusammenkratzen;

to be up to ~ auf Draht (in Form) sein; **to bring s. o. to the** ~ j. vor eine Entscheidung stellen; **to bring s. o. up to** ~ j. bei der Stange halten, *(coach)* j. auf ein Examen einpauken; **to come up to** ~ seinen Mann stellen; **to escape without a** ~ unverletzt davonkommen; **to start from** ~ ganz unten (von vorn, vom Nullpunkt) anfangen; **to toe the** ~ seinen Mann stehen;

when it comes to the ~ wenn es zum Schwur kommt;

~ *(a.)* zu Entwürfen gebraucht;

~ **collection** Zufallskollektion; ~ **crew** bunt zusammengewürfelte Mannschaft; ~ **dinner** Restessen; ~ **figure** *(print.)* durchgestrichenes Zeichen; ~ **house** *(sl.)* Absteige, Asyl für Obdachlose; ~ **to make sure of a** ~ **majority** *(government)* sich gegen eine Zufallsmehrheit absichern; ~ **pad** Schmierblock; ~ **paper** *(US)* Notiz-, Schmierpapier; ~-**penny** Geizkragen; ~ **team** bunt zusammengewürfelte Mannschaft; ~ **vote** zufälliges Abstimmungsergebnis.

scratchboard Schabekarton; ~ **drawing** Schabemanier.

scratcher *(coll., US)* Tageskladde.

scratchy crew bunt zusammengewürfelte Mannschaft.

scrawl Gekritzel; **illegible** ~ unleserliches Gekritzel;

~ *(v.)* **a few words** ein paar Worte kritzeln; ~ **all over the paper** Papier vollkritzeln.

scream *(v.)* lautstark fordern.

screamer *(newspaper, US sl.)* sensationelle Schlagzeile.

screaming poster grellfarbiges Plakat.

screech *(v.) (brake)* quietschen, kreischen.

screed langatmige Rede.

screen Wandschirm, *(car)* Windschutzscheibe, *(cinema)* Film-, Kinoleinwand, *(data processing)* Bildschirm, *(mar.)* Geleitschutz, *(mil.)* Maskierzug, Tarnzug, *(photo)* Filter, *(protection)* Schutz, Schirm, *(slides)* Projektionswand, *(television)* Bild-, Fernsehschirm, Raster;

under the ~ **of night** im Schutze der Nacht;

the ~ Film, Kino; **optical** ~ Filter, Blende; **safety** ~ Schutzschild; **smoke** ~ *(mil.)* Rauchschleier;

~ **for newspaper printing** Raster für Zeitungsdruck; ~ **of trees** durch Bäume geschaffene Sichtblende;

~ *(v.)* überprüfen, *(film)* für den Film bearbeiten, *(marketing)* grobe Vorauswahl treffen, verfilmen, *(mil.)* verschleiern, *(slides)* auf die Leinwand bringen, projizieren, *(tel.)* abschirmen, *(televise)* im Fernsehen bringen;

~ **candidates (competitors)** *(US)* ungeeignete Bewerber ausscheiden; ~ **a house from public view** Haus gegen Einsicht abschirmen; ~ **a refugee** Flüchtling sorgfältig überprüfen (durchleuchten); ~ **s. o. from suspicion** Verdachtsmomente gegen j. beseitigen; ~ **well** sich gut für den Film eignen;

to act as a ~ **for a criminal** einem Verbrecher Unterschlupf gewähren; **to be riveted to the** ~ wie gebannt vor dem Fernsehen sitzen; **to project on a** ~ auf die Leinwand bringen; **to put a play on the** ~ Film vorführen; **to put up a** ~ **of indifference** sich hinter einer gleichgültigen Maske verstecken (verschanzen); **to sit before the** ~ vor dem Fernsehschirm sitzen;

~ **actor** Film-, Fernsehschauspieler; ~ **actress** Filmdiva; ~ **adaptation** Filmbearbeitung; ~ **advertising (advertisement)** Kino-, Filmreklame, Filmwerbung; ~ **credit** *(film actors)* Vorspannbenennung; ~ **printing** Siebdruck; ~ **rights** Verfilmungs-, Fernsehrechte; ~ **star** Fernsehstar; ~ **story** Filmstoff; ~ **technician** Filmfachmann; ~ **test** Filmtest; ~ **wash level** Scheibenwasserstand; ~ **width** Rasterbreite; ~ **window** Moskitofenster.

screenable zur Verfilmung geeignet.

screened aerial abgeschirmte Antenne.

screening Überprüfung, Durchsieben, Verhör, *(film)* Verfilmung, *(mil.)* Abschirmung, Tarnung, *(photo)* Projizierung, *(television)* Erscheinen auf dem Fernsehbildschirm;

~ **of candidates (competitors)** Ausscheiden ungeeigneter Bewerber;

~ **device** *(tel.)* Abschirmvorrichtung; ~ **jury (panel)** *(US)* Prüfungsausschuß; ~ **process** *(US)* Prüfungsverfahren; ~ **question** *(interviewer)* Ausscheidungsfrage; ~ **standards** *(US)* Auswahl-, Auslesebedingungen; ~ **test** *(US)* Auslese-, Eignungsprüfung; ~ **version** Filmfassung.

screenland *(US)* Filmwelt.

screenplay *(US)* Fernsehstück, *(film)* Drehbuch.

screenwriter *(US)* Film-, Fernsehautor.

screenwriting *(US)* Drehbuchherstellung.

screeve *(v.)* auf das Pflaster malen.

screever *(sl.)* Pflastermaler.

screw Schraube, *(skinflint)* Geizkragen, *(wages, Br., sl.)* Lohn, Gehalt;

~ *(v.)* Druck ausüben;

~ **o. s. into s. th.** sich in etw. einmischen; ~ **down prices** Preise herunterdrücken; ~ **money out of s. o.** Geld aus jem. herauspressen; ~ **a promise out of s. o.** jem. ein Versprechen abringen; ~ **up one's courage** seinen ganzen Mut zusammenfassen; ~ **up the rents** Mieten unmäßig erhöhen;

to have a ~ **loose** Schraube locker haben, ein bißchen verrückt sein; **to have one's head** ~ed **on the right way** gesunde Urteilskraft haben; **to put the** ~s **on s. o.** jem. die Daumenschrauben anlegen;

~ **steamer** Schraubendampfer.

screwball *(sl.)* exzentrischer Sonderling.

screwy *(US sl.)* verrückt, verdreht;

to be ~ nicht alle Tassen im Schrank haben.

scribal error Schreibfehler.

scribble Gekritzel, Geschmiere, *(advertising)* erster Rohentwurf, Ideenskizze;

~ *(v.)* kritzeln; ~ **a letter** Brief hinhauen; ~ **block** *(Br.)* Notizblock.

scribbler unbedeutender Schriftsteller, Federfuchser.

scribbling|block *(Br.)* Notiz-, Abreißblock; ~ **diary** *(Br.)* Vormerk-, Terminkalender; ~ **paper** *(Br.)* Konzept-, Schmierpapier, Notizzettel.

scribe Kopist, Schreiberling, Kolumnenschreiber.

scrimmage Handgemenge.

scrimp *(v.)* zu knapp bemessen, knausern;
~ **one's household** mit dem Haushaltsgeld geizen; ~ **one's son for money** seinen Sohn kurz halten.

scrimpiness übertriebene Sparsamkeit.

scrimshank *(v.) (mil., Br., sl.)* sich drücken.

scrimshanker *(mil., Br., sl.)* Drückeberger.

scrip Interims-, Zwischen-, Bezugs-, Berechtigungsschein, *(mil.)* Besatzungsgeld, *(money, US)* [früherer] Staatskassenschein unter 1 Dollar;
dollar ~ *(US)* Skripdollar, Besatzungsgeld; **land ~** *(US)* staatlicher Landzuweisungsschein; **military ~** *(US)* Besatzungsgeld; **registered ~** auf den Namen lautender Interimsschein; **stock ~** *(US)* Berechtigungsschein für den Bezug von Aktien;
~ **payable to bearer** Inhaberzwischenschein;
~ **bonus** *(Br.)* Gratisaktie; ~ **certificate** *(US)* Anteilschein einer Aktie, Zertifikat, *(Br.)* Interims-, Zwischenschein; ~ **company** *(US)* Kommanditgesellschaft auf Aktien; ~ **dividend** *(US)* Berechtigungsschein für spätere Dividendenleistung; ~ **holder** Interimsscheininhaber; ~ **issue** *(Br.)* Ausgabe von [Gratis]aktien; ~ **money** *(US)* Not-, Besatzungs-, Schwundgeld.

script [Hand]schrift, *(broadcasting, film)* Drehbuch, Film-, Fernseh-, Funkmanuskript, *(law)* Original-, Urschrift, Erstausfertigung, *(print.)* Schreibschrift, *(school, Br.)* schriftliche Prüfungsarbeit, *(theater)* Manuskript, *(last will, Br.)* Testamentsentwurf;
~ *(v.)* Drehbuch schreiben;
~ **girl** Skriptgirl; ~ **show** feststehende Sendung; ~ **type** Schreibschrift.

scripted discussion programmierte Diskussion.

scripter Funk-, Film-, Fernsehautor.

scriptwriter Funk-, Film-, Fernsehautor, *(advertising)* Werbetexter.

scrivener Schriftsteller, *(notary)* Notar;
money ~ Geldverleiher, -makler, Finanzmakler.

scroll Strazze, Tabelle, *(old books)* Schriftrolle, *(flourish)* Handzeichen, Schnörkel.

scrounge *(v.) (sl.)* organisieren, schnorren, stibitzen, organisieren.

scrounger Schnorrer.

scrub *(v.)* | **for one's living** sich für seinen Lebensunterhalt abplacken; ~ **out an order** *(sl.)* Auftrag widerrufen.

scruff *(v.) (sl.)* sich kümmerlich durchschlagen.

scruple Bedenken, Skrupel, Gewissensnot;
to tell lies without ~ hemmungslos lügen.

scrupulous gewissenhaft, übergenau;
~ **in money matters** in Geldsachen äußerst pingelig;
to act with ~ honesty gewissenhaft und rechtschaffen handeln.

scrutator Untersuchungsbeamter, Stimmenprüfer.

scrutineer Stimmenzähler, -prüfer, Wahlprüfbeamter, -prüfer.

scrutinize *(v.)* [gründlich] prüfen, Untersuchung durchführen;
~ **an electoral list** Wählerliste überprüfen; ~ **votes** Stimmen zählen.

scrutiny eingehende Untersuchung, genaue Prüfung, *(interviewing)* Antwortenkontrolle;
hard-nosed ~ äußerst sorgfältige Prüfung;
~ **of an electoral list** Überprüfung einer Wählerliste; ~ **of votes** Stimmenzählung;
to demand a ~ Nachprüfung des Wahlergebnisses verlangen;
~ **committee** Untersuchungsausschuß.

scuffle Handgemenge.

scullery *(Br.)* Spülküche;
~ **maid** Küchenmädchen.

scum of the earth Abschaum der Menschheit.

scurry *(v.)* **through one's work** seine Arbeit flüchtig erledigen, schludrig arbeiten.

scutage Dienstpflichttaxe.

scuttle plötzliche Abreise, *(politics, US)* Aufgabe eines besetzten Landes;
~ *(v.) (parl.)* Mandat aufgeben;
~ **a ship** Schiff anbohren.

scuttlebutt *(US sl.)* Gerücht, Latrinenparole.

sea See, Seegang, Ozean, Meer;
all at ~ *(fig.)* im Ungewissen, ratlos; **beyond ~** in Übersee, *(Br.)* außerhalb Großbritanniens; **in the open ~** auf hoher See; **ready for ~** seefertig;
[en]**closed ~** Binnenmeer; **heavy ~** schwerer Seegang; **high ~** Hochsee; **landlocked ~** Binnenmeer; **main ~** das offene Meer; **marginal ~** Randmeer; **narrow ~s** Meerengen; **nasty ~** gefährliche See; **the open ~** freies Meer, Hochsee; **rough (troubled) ~** bewegte (grobe) See; **territorial ~** Küstengewässer;
to be all at ~ im Dunkeln tappen, schwimmen; **to be buried at ~** auf hoher See begraben werden; **to bear to ~** in See stechen; **to enter unchartered ~s** Neuland betreten; **to flow into the ~** ins Meer fließen; **to follow the (go to) ~** Seemann werden; **to gain the open ~** offene See gewinnen; **to put to ~** in See stechen, auslaufen; **to set out to ~** in See gehen; **to take out to ~** auslotsen; **to travel by ~** Schiffsreise machen; **to use the ~** Seemannsberuf ergreifen;
half ~s over betrunken; **utterly at ~** vollständig im Unklaren;
~ **access** Zugang zum Meer; ~ **air** Seeluft; ~ **bathing** Baden im Meer; ~ **batteries** *(merchant service)* Matrosenmißhandlungen; ~ **bed** Meeresgrund; ~ **borne** auf dem Seewege [befördert]; ~-**borne commerce** Überseehandel; ~-**borne goods** Seehandelsgüter; ~-**borne supplies** Lieferungen aus Übersee; ~-**borne trade** Überseehandel; ~-**brief** Schiffspaß; ~ **captain** Schiffskapitän; ~ **cargo** Seefrachtgut; ~ **change** *(fig.)* große Wandlung; ~ **damage** Seeschaden, Havarie; ~-**damaged** havariert, seebeschädigt; ~ **fight** Seegefecht, -schlacht; ~ **fishery** Hochseefischerei; ~ **floor** *(US)* Meeresgrund; ~ **fog** Küstennebel; ~ **forces** Seestreitkräfte; ~ **freight** Seefracht; ~-**greens** *(Scot.)* von einer Springflut bedecktes Gelände; ~ **inlet** Meeresarm; ~ **insurance** Seeversicherung; ~ **journey** Seereise; ~ **lane** Seeweg; ~-**laws** Seehandelsrecht; ~ **lawyer** querulierender Matrose; **to get one's ~ legs** seefest werden; ~-**letter** Schiffspaß; ~ **level** Meeresspiegel, -höhe; ~-**level altitude** Meeresspiegelhöhe; ~ **mile** Seemeile; ~ **orders** Reiseinstruktionen; ~-**packed** seeverpackt, in Seeverpackung; ~ **perils** Seegefahr; ~ **power** Seemacht; ~-**proof** seetüchtig; ~-**proof packing** Überseeverpackung; ~ **risks** Seegefahr, -transportrisiko; ~ **road** *(US)* Seeroute; ~ **robber** Seeräuber, Pirat; ~ **route** Seeweg; ~ **rovers** Piraten; ~ **sickness** Seekrankheit; **to be liable to ~ sickness** seekrank werden; ~ **supremacy** Seeherrschaft; ~ **term** Seemannsausdruck; ~ **transport[ation]** Ozeantransport, Seebeförderung; ~ **trial** Probefahrt auf See; ~ **trip (voyage)** Schiffsreise; ~ **warfare** Seekrieg; ~ **water** Salz-, See-, Meerwasser; ~-**water swimming pool** Seewasserschwimmbad.

seabed Meeresboden;
~ **minerals** Mineralvorkommen auf dem Meeresboden.

seaboard Küstenlinie;
~ **city** Hafenstadt; ~ **market** Küstenhandelsplatz.

seadrome Fluginsel.

seafarers Seeleute.

seafaring Fahren zur See, Seefahrt.

seagoing Seereise;
~ *(a.)* seetüchtig;
~ **vessel** Hochseeschiff.

seal Siegel[abdruck], Dienstsiegel, Beglaubigungsstempel, *(assurance)* festes Versprechen, Zusicherung, *(customs)* Plombe, Verschluß;
under ~ gesiegelt unter Verschluß; **under the ~ of secrecy** unter dem Siegel der Verschwiegenheit; **given under my hand and ~** gesiegelt und eigenhändig von mir unterschrieben;
the ~s Amtssiegel;
broken ~ erbrochenes Siegel; **common ~** *(Br.)* **(corporate, US)** Gesellschafts-, Firmensiegel; **customhouse ~** Zollverschluß, -plombe; **great ~** *(Br.)* großes Staatssiegel; **impressed ~** Prägestempel; **notarial ~** Notariatssiegel; **official (public) ~** *(law)* Dienst-, Amtssiegel; **paper ~** Siegelmarke; **private ~** privatrechtliches Siegel; **Privy ~s** *(Br.)* Kabinetts-, Geheimsiegel; **public ~** Amtssiegel; **quarter ~** *(Scot.)* Nebensiegel; **unbroken ~** unverletzte Plombe;
~ **of approval** Prüfsiegel, Bestätigungssiegel; ~ **of a bottle** Flaschenverschluß; ~ **of a company** *(Br.)* Gesellschafts-, Firmensiegel;
~ *(v.)* [ver]siegeln, stempeln, *(customs)* plombieren, *(law)* pfänden;
~ **a deed** Urkunde siegeln; ~ **a letter** Brief verschließen; ~ **off** hermetisch abkapseln; ~ **off an area** Gebiet abriegeln; ~ **off an area of land** Landstück hermetisch abschließen; ~ **up** versiegeln; ~ **weights and measures** Maße und Gewichte stempeln;
to affix a ~ mit einem Siegel versehen, *(customs)* plombieren; **to affix the ~s** pfänden; **to append a ~ to an act** Siegel auf einem Gesetz anbringen; **to break the ~ of a letter** Brief unberechtigt öffnen, Briefgeheimnis verletzen; **to find ~s on the doors** versiegelt vorfinden; **to impress one's ~** sein Siegel aufdrücken; **to place under ~** unter Siegel legen; **to put the ~ of one's approval on s. th.** einer Sache feierlich zustimmen; **to put one's ~ to a document** Urkunde mit seinem Siegel versehen; **to remove the ~s** Pfändung aufheben; **to remove the ~s from a package** Ware aus dem Zoll freigeben; **to return (resign) the ~s** *(Br.)* sein Amt niederlegen, demissionieren; **to set one's ~** sein Siegel aufdrücken; **to take off the ~s** Siegel abnehmen;

~ day *(Br.)* Eingangstag eines Gerichtsantrags; **~ office** *(judicial writ, Br.)* Eingangsstelle; **~-paper** *(Br.)* Geschäftsverteilungsplan; **~ ring** Siegelring.

sealed versiegelt, verschlossen, *(with lead)* plombiert;
hermetically ~ hermetisch abgeschlossen;
~ and delivered unterzeichnet und gesiegelt;
~ agreement förmlicher Vertrag; **~ bargain** fest vereinbarter Handel; **~ bid** *(US)* Submissionsangebot im versiegelten Umschlag; **~ book** Buch mit sieben Siegeln; **~ form** amtlich genehmigte Ausgabe; **~ instrument** förmlicher Vertrag; **~ language** noch unbekannte (nicht entzifferte) Sprache; **~ letter** verschlossener Brief; **~ orders** geheime Instruktionen; **~ sample** Muster unter versiegeltem Verschluß; **~ tender** Submissionsangebot in versiegeltem Umschlag; **~ vehicle** plombiertes Fahrzeug; **~ will** verschlossenes Testament.

sealer Siegelbeamter, *(weights and measures)* Eichmeister.

sealing Versiegeln, Versiegelung, Plombierung, Plombieren;
~ label Verschlußmarke; **~ wax** Siegelwachs.

seaman Seemann, Schiffer, Matrose;
able-bodied ~ Vollmatrose; **leading ~** Maat; **merchant ~** Handelsschiffer; **ordinary ~** Leichtmatrose;
to enter a ~ on the ship's books Seemann anheuern.

seamanship Seemannserfahrung.

seamark Schiffahrts-, Seezeichen, Leuchtturm, -feuer.

seamen Seeleute;
~'s employment agency Heuerbüro; **~'s shore allowance** Landgangsgelder; **~'s wages** Seemannsheuer.

seaplane Wasserflugzeug, Flugboot, *(mil.)* Marineflugzeug;
~ base Seeflughafen; **~ tender** Flugzeugmutterschiff.

seaport Seehafen.

seaquake Seebeben.

search Suche, *(abstract of title)* Eigentumsnachweis, *(criminal law)* [Haus]durchsuchung, *(international law)* Durchsuchungsrecht, *(scrutiny)* Überprüfung, Recherche;
house ~ Haus[durch]suchung; **mad ~** hektische Suche; **official ~** amtliche Einsichtnahme, amtliche Überprüfung; **personal ~** Leibesvisitation; **title ~** *(US)* Rechtstitelüberprüfung; **unlawful ~** unberechtigte Durchsuchung;
~ for a missing aircraft Suchaktion nach einem überfälligen Flugzeug; **~ for capital** Kapitalsuche; **~ for a fugitive** Fahndung; **~ of luggage and seizure** Durchsuchung und Beschlagnahme; **~ of the [land] register** Grundbucheinsicht; **~ at the land charges register** *(Br.)* Einsichtnahme in das Belastungsverzeichnis nicht eingetragener Grundstücke; **~ for new orders** Auftragssuche; **unreasonable ~ and seizure** unberechtigte Durchsuchung und Beschlagnahme; **~ of title** *(US)* Einsichtnahme in das öffentliche Eigentumsregister, Ermittlung der Eigentumsverhältnisse; **~ of trunks** *(Br.)* Gepäckrevision, -durchsuchung; **~ for a lost will** Nachforschungen nach einem verschwundenen Testament;
~ *(v.)* suchen, fahnden, durchsuchen, überprüfen;
~ a criminal nach einem Verbrecher fahnden; **~ one's desk** seinen Schreibtisch durchsuchen; **~ one's heart** mit sich selbst zu Rate gehen; **~ the land register** *(Br.)* Grundbuch einsehen; **~ one's memory** sein Gedächtnis durchforschen; **~ out an old friend** nach einem alten Freund Ausschau halten; **~ a register** Grundbuch einsehen; **~ a ship** Schiff durchsuchen; **~ through a dictionary for a word not included** in einem Wörterbuch vergeblich ein Wort nachschlagen; **~ s. one's trunks** jds. Gepäck durchsuchen, Gepäckrevision durchführen;
to go in ~ of a missing child Suchaktion nach einem verschwundenen Kind durchführen; **to institute a ~** Nachforschungen anstellen; **to make a ~ for contraband** nach Schmuggelware durchsuchen; **to undergo a personal ~** sich einer Leibesvisitation unterziehen;
official ~ certificate *(Br.)* Bescheinigung über die amtsseits erfolgte Grundbucheinsicht; **~ feature** *(data processing)* Sucheinrichtung; **~ fee** Gebühr für die Rechtstitelüberprüfung; **~ form** Einsichtsformular; **~ party** Suchtrupp, Rettungskolonne, -mannschaft; **~ and rescue service** Such- und Rettungsdienst; **~ unemployment** strukturell bedingte Arbeitslosigkeit; **~ warrant** Haus[durch]suchungsbefehl.

searcher Untersucher, Prüfer, *(Br.)* Zollbeamter, -fahnder.

searchlight Scheinwerfer[strahl].

seashore Küste, Küstenstreifen, Strand, Ufer.

seasick seekrank.

seaside Küste, Küstenland;
to go to the ~ for one's summer holidays in den Sommerferien an die See gehen;
~ holiday Ferien an der See; **~ promenade** Seepromenade; **~ resort** Seebad.

season Jahreszeit, Saison, *(increased business activity)* Hauptverkaufs-, -geschäftszeit, *(date of maturity, US)* Fälligkeitstermin, *(theater)* Spielzeit;
in ~ zur rechten Zeit, fristgerecht, *(market)* günstig auf dem Markt zu haben; **in ~ and out of ~** zu jeder Jahreszeit; **in the off ~** außerhalb der Saison; **out of ~** nicht auf dem Markt, *(untimely)* zur Unzeit, ungelegen;
between ~ Zwischensaison; **busy ~** Hauptsaison; **closed ~** *(hunting)* Schon-, Hegezeit; **dead (dull, off) ~** tote Jahreszeit, stille Saison; **dry ~** Trockenzeit; **high ~** Hochsaison; **holiday ~** Ferienzeit; **late ~** Nachsaison; **marketing ~** Verkaufssaison; **open ~** *(hunting)* Jagdzeit; **peak ~** Hochsaison, -konjunktur; **rainy ~** Regenzeit; **theatrical ~** Spielzeit; **tourist ~** Reisezeit; **~ of drought** Dürre-, Trockenperiode;
to be in (out) of ~ (nicht) zu haben sein; **to be shown for a short ~ from October 1st to November 10th** vom 1. Oktober bis 10. November gezeigt werden; **to endure s. th. for a ~** etw. eine Zeitlang ertragen; **to engage o. s. for the ~** sich für die Saison verpflichten; **to rest for a ~** kurze Pause machen;
~ business Saisongeschäft; **early-~ business** Vorsaisongeschäft; **late-~ business** Nachsaisongeschäft; **~'s greetings** Grüße zum Fest; **end-of-~ sale** Saisonschlußverkauf; **~'s stocks** Saisonwerte.

season ticket *(Br.)* Eisenbahnabonnement, Dauer-, Zeit-, Abonnements-, Monatsfahrkarte;
annual ~ Jahresfahrkarte; **monthly ~** Monatsfahrkarte;
to buy a ~ Dauerfahrkarte erwerben, *(theater)* im Theater abonnieren, Theaterabonnement abschließen; **to have a ~** Inhaber einer Dauerfahrkarte (Zeitkarteninhaber) sein; **to take out a ~** Dauerkarte nehmen (lösen);
~ holder Zeit-, Dauerkarteninhaber, Berufsverkehrsteilnehmer, *(theater)* Theaterabonnent.

seasonable für die Saison passend, *(weather)* der Jahreszeit angemessen;
~ arrival rechtzeitige Ankunft.

seasonal saisonbedingt, -üblich, von der Jahreszeit abhängig, jahreszeitlich bedingt, *(temporarily employed)* zeitweilig (vorübergehend) beschäftigt, *(periodical)* periodisch [wiederkehrend];
~ adjustment Konjunkturausgleich; **~ advances** Saisonkredite; **~ advertising** Saisonwerbung; **~ allowance** Frühbezugsrabatt; **~ articles** Saisonartikel; **~ booster** Saisonspritze; **~ business** Saisongeschäft; **~ clearance** *(US)* **(closing-out,** *Br.***) sale** Saisonschlußverkauf; **~ commodity** Saisonartikel; **~ consumption** saisongebundener Verbrauch, Saisonbedarf; **~ demand** saisonbedingte Nachfrage, saisonbedingter Bedarf; **~ demand for cash** saisonbedingter Geldbedarf; **~ display** Saisonauslage; **~ employment** Saisonbeschäftigung; **~ factors** saisonale Faktoren; **to be due to ~ factors** jahreszeitlich bedingt sein; **~ fluctuations** saisonbedingte (saisonale) Schwankungen, Saisonschwankungen; **~ foods** saisonbedingte Nahrungsmittel; **~ goods** Saisonerzeugnisse, -artikel; **on ~ grounds** saisonbedingt; **~ increase** saisonbedingte Erhöhung; **~ industries** saisonbedingte Industrien; **~ influences** Saisoneinflüsse; **~ item** Saisonartikel; **~ labo(u)rer** Saisonarbeiter; **~ layoffs** saisonbedingte Entlassungen, Saisonentlassungen; **~ loan** Saisonkredit; **~ low** Saisontief; **~ nature** *(industry)* Saisonbedingtheit; **~ occupation** Saisonberuf, -beschäftigung; **~ peak** Stoßzeit in der Saison; **~ pressure** Saisonanforderungen; **~ price fluctuations** saisonal bedingte Preisschwankungen; **~ price increase** Saisonaufschlag; **~ products** Saisonerzeugnisse; **~ production** saisonbedingte Produktionstätigkeit; **~ rates** Saisonsätze; **~ requirements** Saisonbedürfnisse; **~ sale** Saisonschlußverkauf; **~ sickness** sommerliche Flaute; **~ slump** saisonbedingter Geschäftsrückgang; **~ supply** saisonbedingter Bedarf; **~ tariff** *(el., Br.)* saisonbedingter Tarif; **~ tolerance** saisonbedingte Nichtbeachtung der Tarifbestimmungen; **~ trade** Saisongewerbe; **~ trend** saisonbedingte Tendenz, saisonbedingter Konjunkturaufschwung; **~ trough** saisonbedingte Absatzmulde; **~ unemployment** saisonbedingte (konjunkturelle) Arbeitslosigkeit; **~ upswing** Saisonaufschwung, saisonbedingter Anstieg; **~ upturn** saisonbedingter Anstieg; **~ upward trend** saisonbedingter Konjunkturaufschwung; **~ variations** Saisonschwankungen, jahreszeitliche Schwankungen; **~ work** Saisonarbeit; **~ worker** Saisonarbeiter.

seasonality Saisonbedingtheit;
~ of work saisonbedingte Arbeit.

seasonally saisonüblich, -bedingt, -gemäß;
~ adjusted unter Berücksichtigung saisonaler Einflüsse, saisonbereinigt; **~ unstable** durch Saisonschwankungen beeinträchtigt.

seasoned│securities Favoriten, renommierte Wertpapiere; ~ **soldiers** fronterfahrene Soldaten;
to be ~ to a climate an ein Klima gewöhnt sein.

seat Sitz, Sitzplatz, -gelegenheit, Bank, *(administration)* Amts-, Regierungssitz, *(in the country)* Wohn-, Landsitz, *(establishment)* [Gesellschafts]sitz, Hauptniederlassung, *(membership)* Mitgliedschaft, *(parliament)* Mandat, Abgeordnetensitz, *(stock exchange)* Börsensitz;
adjustable ~ *(car)* verstellbarer Sitz; **~s available** verfügbare Plätze; **back ~** Rücksitz; **country ~** Landsitz; **county ~** *(US)* Kreishauptstadt; **reclining ~** *(car)* verstellbarer Sitz; **reserved ~** reservierter (numerierter) Platz; **senatorial ~** Senatsmandat; **~ taken** belegter Platz;
~ on a board Vorstands-, Aufsichtsratssitz; **~ in the cabinet** Kabinetts-, Ministerressort; **chief ~ of commerce** Geschäftszentrum; **~ of government** Sitz der Regierung, Regierungssitz; **~ of learning** Wissenszentrum; **~ in Parliament** [Abgeordneten]mandat; **~ on the stock exchange** Börsensitz, -mitgliedschaft; **~ on the top table at the International Monetary Fund** Sitz und Stimme in der Spitze des Internationalen Währungsfonds;
~ (v.) *(hall)* Sitzplätze haben;
~ a candidate jem. einen Parlamentssitz verschaffen; **~ a member of Parliament** Parlamentssitz bestätigen; **~ passengers** Fahrgäste unterbringen; **~ people for dinner** Tischordnung machen;
to bag the best ~s beste Plätze mit Beschlag belegen; **to be entitled to a ~ on a committee** Anspruch auf einen Ausschußsitz haben; **to book ~s** Plätze [vor]bestellen (reservieren lassen); **to canvass for a ~** sich um einen Parlamentssitz bewerben; **to give workers ~s in the boardroom** den Arbeitern Sitz und Stimme im Aufsichtsrat geben; **to have a ~ on a committee** Ausschußsitz innehaben; **to have a ~ in Parliament** Abgeordneter sein; **to hold five ~s** *(car)* über fünf Sitzplätze verfügen; **to keep a ~ for s. o.** jem. einen Platz freihalten; **to keep one's ~** sitzenbleiben; **to lose one's ~ in Parliament** sein Mandat verlieren; **to occupy a ~** Sitz belegen; **to reserve a ~** Platz vorausbestellen; **to resign one's ~** sein Mandat niederlegen; **to show s. o. to a ~** jem. einen Platz anweisen; **to take a ~** Platz nehmen; **to take one's ~** seinen [angestammten] Platz einnehmen; **to take a ~ in a train** Platz im Zug besetzen; **to vacate one's ~** sein Mandat niederlegen; **to win a ~** Mandat erringen;
~ availability verfügbare Plätze; **~ belt** *(aircraft)* Rettungs-, Anschnall-, Sicherheitsgurt; **~ chart** Sitzplan, -ordnung; **~ reservation** Platzbelegung.

seated, to be sitzen;
~ land genutzter Boden.

seater, two- Zweisitzer.

seating Bestuhlung, Sitzgelegenheiten;
~ accommodation Sitzgelegenheit; **~ arrangement (plan)** Tischordnung; **~ capacity** Fassungsvermögen, Sitzfläche; **~ room** Sitzmöglichkeiten.

seatless ohne Sitzplatz.

seatrain Trajektschiff.

seaway Seeweg, Schiffahrtslinie.

seaworthiness Seetüchtigkeit.

seaworthy seetüchtig;
~ packing seegemäße Verpackung.

secede *(v.)* abfallen, sich lossagen;
~ from a party aus einer Partei austreten.

seceder Abtrünniger.

secession Trennung, Abspaltung, Abfall, Sezession.

secessional sentiments Abfallbestrebungen.

secessionist Abtrünniger, *(US)* Südstaatler;
to be in ~ hands in den Händen der Aufständigen sein; **~ threat** Abfalldrohung.

seclude *(v.)* ausschließen, absondern;
~ a prisoner Gefangenen isolieren; **o. s. from society** sich [aus dem öffentlichen Leben] zurückziehen.

secluded weltabgeschieden, entlegen.

seclusion Abgeschiedenheit;
~ of prisoners Isolierung von Gefangenen;
to live in ~ abgeschieden leben.

second Zweiter, Helfer, *(aid in duel)* Sekundant, *(car)* zweiter Gang, *(of exchange)* Sekunda[wechsel], zweite Wechselausfertigung, Zweitausfertigung, -schrift;
~s *(goods)* Mittelsorte, zweite Wahl, Waren mittlerer Art und Güte (zweiter Qualität), *(newspaper)* Zweitausgabe;
~ in command stellvertretender Kommandeur; **~ in course** girierte (umlaufende) Sekunda; **~ of exchange** Sekundawechsel;

~ (v.) *(motion)* Antrag unterstützen (befürworten), *(soldier, Br.)* abstellen, abkommandieren;
~ for the chair für den Vorstand abstellen; **~ an official** *(Br.)* Beamten vorübergehend versetzen; **~ a petition** Gesuch befürworten; **~ s. o. for service in the General Staff** j. in den Generalstab versetzen;
to be ~ nachstehen; **to be ~ to s. o. in seniority** jem. im Range nachstehen; **to get a ~** gutes Examen machen; **to land ~** als Zweiter durchs Ziel gehen; **to stand a close ~** zahlenmäßig dicht hinter dem Spitzenkandidaten liegen; **to trail a distant ~** weit abgeschlagen an zweiter Stelle liegen;
~ (a.) zweitklassig, -rangig, untergeordnet;
~ bail Nachbürge; **~ ballot** Stichwahl, zweiter Wahlgang; **to come off ~ best** den Kürzeren ziehen; **~-best suit** zweitbester Anzug; **~ cabin** Kabine zweiter Klasse; **~ car** Zweitwagen; **~ chamber** *(parl.)* zweite Kammer, Oberhaus; **~ city** zweitgrößte Stadt.

second-class zweitklassig, -rangig, *(railway)* zweite Klasse;
to go (travel) ~ zweiter Klasse reisen;
~ carriage zweiter Klasse Wagen; **~ compartment** Abteil zweiter Klasse; **~ hotel** zweitklassiges Hotel; **~ mail** *(US)* Zeitungspost; **~ papers** zweitklassige Wertpapiere; **~ passenger** Reisender zweiter Klasse; **~ stamp** Drucksachenbriefmarke; **~ ticket** Fahrkarte zweiter Klasse.

second│cousin Vetter zweiten Grades; **~ degree murder** Totschlag; **~ deliverance** Zweitausfertigung; **~ distance** *(landscape, Br.)* Mittelgrund; **~ distress** Anschlußpfändung; **~ edition** *(newspaper)* Zweitausgabe; **to play the ~ fiddle** Nebenrolle (zweite Geige) spielen; **~ floor** *(Br.)* zweite Etage, zweiter Stock, *(US)* dritte Etage, dritter Stock; **~ gear** *(car)* zweiter Gang; **~ home** Zweitwohnung; **~ issue** *(securities)* zweite Ausgabe (Serie); **~ layer treaty** *(catastrophe risk)* zusätzlicher Rückversicherungsvertrag; **~ level** zweitrangig, -klassig; **~ lien** nachrangiges Pfandrecht; **~-line stocks** zweitklassige Aktien; **~ mortgage** zweit[stellig]e (nachstehende) Hypothek; **to have become ~ nature with s. o.** jem. in Fleisch und Blut übergegangen sein; **~ offence** *(US)* Rückfallvergehen; **~ papers** *(US)* letzter Staatsbürgerantrag [eines Ausländers]; **~-rate** zweitrangig, -klassig, minderwertig; **~ raters** zweitklassige Leute; **~ reading** *(parl.)* zweite Lesung; **~ serial right** zweites Abdruckrecht; **~ sheet** Zweitbogen; **~ sight** zweites Gesicht, Hellsehen; **~ speech** zweiter Diskussionsbeitrag; **~ preferred stock** *(US)* Vorzugsaktien zweiter Klasse; **~ stor(e)y** *(Br.)* zweite Etage, zweiter Stock, *(US)* dritte Etage, dritter Stock; **~ teller** zweiter Kassierer, Kassierer für Einzahlungen; **on ~ thoughts** nach reiflicher Überlegung; **~ tier** zweitrangig; **~-tier authority** zweite Verwaltungsebene; **~-tier industries** zweitrangige Industrien; **~ wind** *(fig.)* neuer Antrieb, frischer Wind in den Segeln.

secondarily liable *(US)* mittelbar haftpflichtig, zweitverpflichtet.

secondary Untergeordnetes, Nebensächliches, *(substitute)* [Stell]vertreter, *(weather)* Randtief;
~ (a.) zweitrangig, -klassig, sekundär, nebensächlich;
~ account Nebenbuchkonto; **~ boycott** mittelbarer (indirekter) Boykott; **~ calling** Nebenberuf; **~ cause** Nebensache; **~ childhood** Greisenalter; **~ consequence** Nebeneffekt; **salary a ~ consideration** Gehalt ist Nebensache; **~ conveyance** Zusatzerklärungen bei der Eigentumsübergabe; **~ credit** *(US)* Gegenakkreditiv; **~ creditor** nachstehender (zweitrangiger) Gläubiger; **~ debtor** Zweitschuldner; **~ depression** Randtief; **~ distribution of securities** nachbörslicher Wertpapierhandel, Pakethandel; **~ education** zweiter Bildungsweg; **~ evidence** unterstützendes Beweismaterial; **~ franchise** Konzession für Versorgungsbetriebe; **~ front** *(mil.)* Nebenfront; **~ fuel** Sekundärenergie; **~ group** *(sociology)* Sekundärgruppe; **~ liability** *(US)* sekundäre (subsidäre) Haftung, Eventualverbindlichkeit, -verpflichtung; **~ line** Nebenlinie, Zweigbahn; **~ liquidity** *(EEC)* Sekundärliquidität; **~ market** Nebenmarkt, Markt zweiter Ordnung; **~ market trader** *(securities)* Erwerber aus zweiter Hand; **~ meaning** *(trademark, US)* Nebenbedeutung; **~ object** Nebenzweck; **~ obligation** Nebenleistung; **~ occupations** Beschäftigungszweige des Produktionsbereichs; **~ picketing** Bestreikung eines nur mittelbar beteiligten Betriebes; **~ product** Nebenprodukt; **~ pupil** Mittelschüler; **~ question** Nebenfrage; **~ railway** Neben-, Sekundärbahn; **~ reserves** *(banking)* Sekundärreserven; **~ right** Nebenanspruch; **~ risk** *(EEC)* Investitionsvorhaben mit durchschnittlichem Risiko; **~ school** Mittelschule, *(Br.)* höhere Schule, Oberschule; **~ grammar school** *(Br.)* Oberrealschule; **~ sector** Fertigungssektor; **~ security** Nebenbürgschaft; **~ strike** mittelbarer Streik; **~ use** aufschiebend bedingtes Nutzungsrecht; **~-use package** weiterverwendungsfähige Packung.

secondhand aus zweiter Hand, gebraucht, antiquarisch;
to buy s. th. ~ etw. antiquarisch (gebraucht) kaufen; **to get news ~** keine Eigenkenntnis von einem Ereignis haben;
~ articles gebrauchte Artikel; **~ assets** gebrauchte Wirtschaftsgüter; **~ book** antiquarisches Buch; **~ bookshop** Antiquariat; **~ bookseller** Antiquar; **~ buyer** Käufer aus zweiter Hand; **~ car** gebrauchter Wagen, Gebrauchtwagen; **~ copy** antiquarisches Buch; **~ dealer** Trödler, Altwarenhändler; **~ evidence** Beweis vom Hörensagen; **~ furniture** gebrauchte Möbel; **~ goods** gebrauchte Sachen; **~ hirer** Untermieter; **to have a ~ knowledge** vom Hörensagen wissen; **~ market** Trödlermarkt; **~ shop** Trödlerladen.

seconding a motion Antragsunterstützung, Antragsbefürwortung, Unterstützung eines Antrags.

secrecy Heimlichkeit, *(keeping a secret)* Geheimhaltung, Verschwiegenheit;
bound to ~ zur Verschwiegenheit verpflichtet; **in strict ~** streng geheim;
banking ~ Bankgeheimnis; **official ~** Amtsverschwiegenheit; **professional ~** berufliche Schweigepflicht; **utmost ~** strenge Geheimhaltung;
~ of a ballot geheime Abstimmung, Wahlgeheimnis; **~ correspondence** Post-, Briefgeheimnis; **~ of manufacture** Fabrikationsgeheimnis; **~ of the vote** Wahlgeheimnis;
to be sworn to ~ zur Amtsverschwiegenheit verpflichtet sein; **to bind s. o. to ~** j. zur Geheimhaltung verpflichten; **to do s. o. to ~** j. zur Geheimhaltung verpflichten; **to do s. th. with great ~** etw. äußerst geheim betreiben; **to enjoin strictest ~ upon s. o.** j. zur äußersten Diskretion verpflichten; **to impose ~ on an invention** Erfindung unter Geheimschutz stellen; **to maintain strictest ~** strikte Geheimhaltung bewahren; **to maintain ~ during negotiations** während der Verhandlungen Stillschweigen bewahren; **to observe strict ~** strengste Verschwiegenheit wahren; **to rely on s. one's ~** sich auf jds. Verschwiegenheit verlassen.

secret Geheimnis;
business ~ Geschäftsgeheimnis; **manufacturing ~** Fabrikationsgeheimnis; **official ~** Amtsgeheimnis; **open ~** offenes Geheimnis; **professional ~** Berufsgeheimnis; **trade ~** Betriebs-, Geschäftsgeheimnis;
~ of correspondence Briefgeheimnis; **~ of state** Staatsgeheimnis; **~ of success** Schlüssel zum Erfolg;
to disclose a ~ Geheimnis preisgeben; **to keep a ~** Geheimnis bewahren; **to keep s. th. ~ from one's family** etw. vor seiner Familie geheimhalten; **to let s. o. into the ~** j. ins Vertrauen ziehen;
~ (a.) geheim, verborgen, *(person)* verschwiegen;
top ~ streng geheim, *(mil.)* geheime Kommandosache;
~ account Geheimkonto; **~ agent** Geheimagent; **~ agreement** Geheimvertrag; **~ alliance** Geheimbündnis; **~ assembly** Geheimversammlung; **~ clause** Geheimklausel; **~ cipher** Geheimschrift; **~ commission** *(agent)* verbotene Sonderprovision; **~ committee** *(parl., Br.)* Sonderausschuß; **to keep up a ~ correspondence with s. o.** geheimen Briefwechsel mit jem. führen; **~ detention centre** geheimes Gefangenenlager, Konzentrationslager; **~ diplomacy** Geheimdiplomatie; **~ document** Geheimdokument; **~ drawer** Geheimschublade, -fach; **~ equity** geheimgehaltener Anspruch; **~ house committee** Geheimausschuß des Parlaments; **~ intelligence service** Geheimdienst; **~ lien** *(vendor)* geheimer Eigentumsvorbehalt; **~ [manufacturing] process** geheimes Herstellungsverfahren; **on a ~ mission** in geheimer Mission; **~ meeting** Geheimversammlung; **~ negotiations** im geheimen geführte Verhandlungen; **~ order** Geheimbefehl; **~ organization** Geheimorganisation; **~ papers** Geheimpapiere; **~ partner** stiller Teilhaber; **~ partnership** stille Teilhaberschaft; **~ patent** Geheimpatent; **~ process** Geheimverfahren; **~ protocol** Geheimprotokoll; **~ reserves** stille Reserven; **~ service** staatlicher Geheim-, Nachrichten-, Sicherheitsdienst, Spionageabwehr; **~ service fund** Geheim-, Reptilienfonds; **~ session** Geheimkonferenz, -sitzung; **~ sign** Geheimzeichen; **~ society** Geheimorganisation, -bund; **~ transmitter** Geheimsender; **~ treaty** Geheimabkommen; **~ trust** Entgegennahme eines Vermächtnisses zugunsten eines Dritten; **~ understanding** geheimes Einverständnis; **~ voting** geheime Wahl.

secretarial | area Sekretariatsbereich; **~ assistance** Sekretariatsgestellung; **~ clerk** Büroangestellter; **~ college** Handelsschule; **~ competence** Sekretariatskenntnisse; **~ course** Sekretariatskursus; **~ department** Kanzleiabteilung; **~ duties** Sekretariatsaufgaben; **~ employment agency** Vermittlungsstelle für Sekretariatskräfte; **~ facilities** Büromitbenutzung; **~ help** Schreib-, Bürohilfe, Hilfskraft im Büro, Sekretariatshilfs-

kraft; **~ job** Sekretariatstätigkeit; **~ pool** Gemeinschaftssekretariat; **~ position** Sekretariatsposten, -stellung; **~ practice** Sekretariatserfahrung; **~ service** Bürotätigkeit, -dienst; **~ staff** Sekretariatskräfte; **~ supply** Sekretärinnenangebot; **~ training** Sekretariatsausbildung; **~ work** Büro-, Sekretariatsbereich; **to train for ~ work** Sekretariatsausbildung absolvieren.

secretariat[e] Geschäftsstelle, Sekretariat.

secretary Sekretär[in], *(counsel)* Syndikus, *(official)* Verwaltungsdirektor, *(of society)* Schriftführer, Geschäftsführer, *(US)* Außenminister, *(writing desk)* Sekretär, Schreibschrank;
assistant ~ *(US)* [etwa] Ministerialdirektor; **company ~** *(Br.)* oberster Verwaltungsbeamter; **competent ~** gewandte Sekretärin; **deputy ~** stellvertretender Staatssekretär; **Energy ≗** *(US)* Energieminister; **executive ~** *(US)* Geschäftsführer; **first ~** *(Br.)* Legationsrat erster Klasse, Botschaftsrat, *(government, Br.)* stellvertretender Premierminister; **Foreign ≗** *(US)* Außenminister; **~ general** Generalsekretär; **German-language ~** deutschsprachige Sekretärin; **Home ≗** *(Br.)* Innenminister; **honorary ~** *(society, Br.)* ehrenamtlicher Geschäftsführer; **parliamentary ~** parlamentarischer Staatssekretär; **permanent ~** *(Br.)* ständiger Staatssekretär; **super permanent ~** *(Br.)* ständiger Staatssekretär mit besonderen Befugnissen; **press ~** Presseattache; **private ~** Privatsekretär[in]; **second ~** Legationsrat zweiter Klasse; **third ~** *(Br.)* Legationssekretär; **trade-union ~** Gewerkschaftssekretär; **under ~** *(Br.)* [Unter]staatssekretär;
≗ of Agriculture *(US)* Landwirtschaftsminister; **≗ of the Airforce** *(US)* Luftfahrtminister; **assistant ~ for educational and cultural affairs** Leiter der Kulturabteilung; **≗ of the Army** *(US)* Heeresminister; **≗ of Commerce** *(US)* Handelsminister; **≗ of Defense** *(US)* Verteidigungsminister; **~ of embassy** Botschaftsrat; **≗ of Health, Education and Welfare** *(Br.)* Minister für Gesundheit, Erziehung und Sozialfragen; **≗ of Housing and Urban Development** Wohnungs- und Städtebauminister; **≗ of the Interior** *(US)* Innenminister; **~ with a knowledge of languages** Fremdsprachensekretärin; **≗ of Labor** *(US)* Arbeitsminister; **~ of legation** Legationssekretär, Gesandschaftsrat; **~ of the managing director** Direktionssekretär; **≗ of the Navy** *(US)* Marineminister; **≗ of Senate** *(US)* Geschäftsstellenleiter des Senats; **≗ of State** *(Br.)* [Kabinetts]minister, *(US)* Außenminister; **Parliamentary ≗ of State** *(Br.)* parlamentarischer Staatssekretär; **≗ of State for Air** *(Br.)* Luftfahrtminister; **≗ of State for Commonwealth Relations** *(Br.)* Commonwealthminister; **≗ of State for Defense** *(US)* Verteidigungsminister; **≗ of State for Employment** *(Br.)* Arbeitsminister; **≗ of State for Energy** *(Br.)* Energieminister; **≗ of State for the Environment** Umweltminister; **≗ of State for Foreign Affairs** *(Br.)* Außenminister; **≗ of State for Home Affairs** *(Br.)* Minister des Inneren, Innenminister; **≗ of State for Industry** *(Br.)* Industrieminister; **≗ of State for Social Services** *(Br.)* Sozialminister; **≗ of State for War** *(Br.)* Kriegsminister; **≗ of State for Trade** *(Br.)* Handelsminister; **≗ of State for Transport** *(Br.)* Verkehrsminister; **≗ of State for Transportation** *(US)* Minister für Transport- und Verkehrswesen; **~ for the time being** einstweiliger Schriftführer; **≗ of the Treasury [Department]** *(US)* Finanzminister, Schatzkanzler; **≗ of War** Kriegsminister;
to employ s. o. as ~ j. als Sekretär beschäftigen;
~'s office Geschäftsstelle, Sekretariat; **~-treasurer** Stadtkämmerer; **~ type** Kanzleischrift.

secretaryship Schriftführeramt, *(politics)* Ministeramt.

secrete *(v.)* o. s. sich verbergen.

secretmonger Geheimniskrämer.

sect Sekte, Religionsgemeinschaft;
open to all ~s allen Konfessionen zugänglich.

sectarian Sektierer;
~ feud konfessioneller Streit; **~ school** Konfessionsschule.

section Dezernat, *(compartment)* Abteil, *(sleeping compartment)* Schlafwagenabteil, *(component)* Einzelteil, [Bestand]teil, *(distinct part of country)* Bezirk, *(law)* Abschnitt, Absatz, Paragraph[zeichen], *(mil.)* Gruppe, Halbzug, *(parcel)* [Grundstücks]parzelle, *(part of book)* Abschnitt, *(people)* Gruppe, *(quarter)* Stadtviertel, *(rail, road)* Streckenabschnitt, Teilstrecke, *(stock exchange)* Marktbereich;
agricultural ~ ländlicher Bezirk; **busy ~** belebter Stadtteil; **commercial ~** Geschäftsviertel; **concluding ~** Schlußabschnitt; **cross ~** Querschnitt; **longitudinal ~** Längsschnitt; **polling ~** Wahlbezirk; **Postal ≗** Postdezernat; **residential ~** Wohnviertel; **shopping ~** Einkaufsgegend; **special ~** Sonderabhandlung; **staff ~** *(mil.)* Stabsabteilung; **vertical ~** Aufriß;
~ of the constitution Verfassungsabschnitt; **~ of a copy** Textblock; **~ of industry** Industriezweig; **~ of land** *(US)* Landab-

schnitt; ~ **of a line** Teilstrecke; ~ **of a machine** Einzelteil einer Maschine; ~ **of a party** Parteigruppe; **~s of the population** Bevölkerungsschichten; **female ~ of the population** weiblicher Bevölkerungsanteil; ~ **of a sleeper** *(US)* Schlafwagenabteil; ~ **of a town** *(US)* Stadtviertel;

to affect wide ~s of the population weite Kreise der Bevölkerung betreffen; **to contract in several ~s** *(stock exchange)* in verschiedenen Effektengruppen Abschlüsse tätigen; **to export in ~s** in Teilladungen verschiffen; **to fall into 4 ~s** in 4 Abschnitte zerfallen; **to run in two ~s** *(train)* in zwei Teilzügen verkehren;

~ **boss** *(railroad, US)* Vorarbeiter; ~ **chief (manager)** Abteilungsleiter; ~ **gang (hand, man)** *(US)* Streckenarbeiter; ~ **leader** Dezernatsleiter; ~ **mark** Paragraph, Abschnittszeichen.

sectional zusammengesetzt, aus einzelnen Teilen bestehend, *(US)* lokal, partikularistisch;

~ **furniture** Anbau-, Aufbaumöbel; ~ **interests** Lokalinteressen, lokale Interessen; ~ **jealousies** lokale Eifersüchteleien; ~ **price list** Einzelprospekt; ~ **pride** Lokalpatriotismus; ~ **strike** örtlich (zeitlich) begrenzter Streik, Teilstreik; ~ **view** Teilansicht.

sectionalism *(US)* Partikularismus.

sectionalist *(US)* Partikularist, Lokalpatriot.

sectionalize *(US)* nach lokalen Gesichtspunkten aufteilen.

sector Sektor, Ausschnitt, Abschnitt, Bereich, Bezirk, Geländestreifen, -abschnitt, *(mil.)* Frontabschnitt;

in the industrial ~ im industriellen Bereich;

postal ~ Postbezirk; **private ~** privater (persönlicher) Bereich; **public ~** öffentlicher Bereich;

~ **of economy** Wirtschaftsgebiet, -zweig; ~ **of industry** Industriesektor; **private ~ of industry** im Privatbesitz befindliches Industrievermögen, Privatwirtschaft; **floating rate ~ of the market** Marktbereich der wechselkursfreigegebenen Euroanleihen; ~ **of public expenditure** Ausgabensektor der öffentlichen Hand;

~ *(v.)* in Abschnitte einteilen;

~ **boundary** Sektorengrenze.

sectoral in Sektoren eingeteilt;

on a ~ comparison im Branchenvergleich; ~ **inflation** sektoral induzierte Inflation.

sectoring Sektorbildung.

secular weltlich, profan;

~ **business** *(Sunday laws)* Werktagsbeschäftigung, übliche Geschäftstätigkeit; ~ **day** Werktag; ~ **or business day** Werk- oder Arbeitstag; ~ **rivalry** Erbfeindschaft; ~ **trend** langfristige Entwicklung.

secularization Säkularisierung.

secularize *(v.)* säkularisieren.

secularized church property säkularisiertes Kircheneigentum.

secure sicher, in Sicherheit, gesichert, geschützt, *(confident in opinion)* ruhig, sorglos;

~ *(v.) (acquire)* sich sichern (verschaffen), erwerben, erlangen, *(guarantee)* sicherstellen, Sicherheit geben, gewährleisten, sichern, decken, *(keep)* etwas verwahren, schützen;

~ **an agency** sich eine Vertretung sichern; ~ **an agreement** Zustimmung einholen; ~ **an application** [Versicherungs]antrag entgegennehmen; ~ **a good appointment** gute Stelle erhalten; ~ **the appointment as president** als Vorsitzender nominiert werden; ~ **a business** Abschluß vermitteln, Geschäft zustande bringen; ~ **by charter** Rechte verbriefen; ~ **a contract** Auftrag erhalten; ~ **credit** sich Kredit verschaffen; ~ **a creditor** Gläubiger sicherstellen; ~ **a debt by mortgage** Anspruch hypothekarisch absichern; ~ **an estate** Eigentumsrecht garantieren; ~ **an interest** Beteiligung erwerben; ~ **o. s. against losses** sich vor Verlust schützen; ~ **a majority of votes cast** Mehrheit der abgegebenen Stimmen erhalten (auf sich vereinigen); ~ **by mortgage on real estate** grundpfandrechtlich besichern; ~ **a note by the pledge of collateral security** Schuldschein mit zusätzlicher Sicherheit ausstatten; ~ **an order** Auftrag erhalten; ~ **payment** Zahlung sicherstellen; ~ **possession** sich Besitz verschaffen; ~ **higher prices** bessere Preise erzielen; ~ **special prices** Sonderpreise vereinbaren; ~ **profits** Gewinne erzielen; ~ **a room in a hotel** Hotelzimmer bestellen; ~ **a seat** Platz belegen; ~ **a good seat for s. o.** jem. einen guten Platz besorgen; ~ **s. one's services** sich jds. Dienste versichern; ~ **a better share of the market** sich einen größeren Marktanteil sichern; ~ **valuables** Wertsachen in Sicherheit bringen; ~ **the best value** Höchstpreis erzielen;

to be ~ from interruption ungestört sein; **to feel ~ about s. one's future** sich um seine Zukunft keine Sorgen machen, beruhigt in seine Zukunft schauen;

~**existence** sichere (gesicherte) Existenz; ~ **foundation** feste Grundlage; ~ **investment** sichere Kapitalanlage; **to establish o. s. in a ~ position** sich in einer Stellung verankern.

secured gesichert, sichergestellt, *(privileged)* bevorrechtigt;

~ **by mortgage** hypothekarisch besichert;

~ **account** abgesichertes Konto; ~ **advance** gedecktes (besichertes) Darlehen, Lombardkredit; ~ **bill** durch Wertpapiere (Dokumente) gedeckter Wechsel; ~ **bond** *(US)* hypothekarisch besicherte Obligation; ~ **credit** besicherter Kredit; ~ **creditor** absonderungsberechtigter (dinglich gesicherter) Gläubiger, Vorzugsgläubiger; ~ **debt** bevorrechtigte (dinglich besicherte) Forderung; ~ **debenture** hypothekarisch besicherte Obligation; ~ **liability** durch Verkauf von Schuldnereigentum realisierte Forderung; ~ **loan** besicherter Kredit; ~ **maintenance** *(Br.)* gesicherte Unterhaltszahlungen; ~ **note** lombardbesicherter Schuldschein; ~ **transactions** *(US)* Sicherungsgeschäfte.

securities Sicherheiten, *(bonds)* [Wert]papiere, Effekten[bestände], Stücke;

active ~ Effekten mit täglichen Umsätzen, lebhaft gehandelte Effekten; **approved ~** zentralbankfähige Papiere; **assented ~** im Sammeldepot hinterlegte und im Sanierungsverfahren abgestempelte Effekten; **assessable ~** nachschußpflichtige Wertpapiere; **bearer ~** auf den Inhaber ausgestellte Wert-, Inhaberpapiere; **callable ~** auslosbare Wertpapiere; **collateral ~** lombardierte Wertpapiere (Effekten), Lombardeffekten; **convertible ~** handelbare Wertpapiere; **corporation ~** Industrieobligationen; ~ **deposited** hinterlegte Effekten, Effektendepot; **deferred ~** Wertpapiere mit zeitweilig gesperrter Dividendenauszahlung; **digested ~** *(US)* plazierte Wertpapiere; **dividend-paying ~** börsengängige Dividendenwerte; **drawn ~** ausgeloste Wertpapiere; **dubious ~** unsichere Anlagewerte, schlechte Papiere; **Exchange Control Act ~** *(Br.)* devisenbewirtschaftete Wertpapiere; **exempted ~** von Börsenvorschriften befreite Wertpapiere; **first-class ~** erstklassige Sicherheiten; **fixed-interest (income) -bearing ~** festverzinsliche Werte (Wertpapiere); **foreign ~** ausländische Effekten, Auslandswerte; **gilt-edged ~** *(Br.)* mündelsichere Wertpapiere (Anleihewerte), erstklassige Effekten; **good-delivery ~** lieferbare Effekten; **government ~** *(Br.)* Staatsobligationen, -papiere, -anleihen, *(US)* Bundesanleihen; **guarantee ~** Kautionseffekten; **high-grade ~** hochwertige Effekten (Anlagewerte), erstklassige Wertpapiere; **higher-yield ~** Wertpapiere mit höherer Rendite; **home ~** inländische Wertpapiere; **inactive ~** Effekten mit geringen Umsätzen, selten gehandelte Wertpapiere; **industrial ~** Industrieobligationen; **inscribed ~** *(Br.)* Schuldbuchtitel; **interbourse ~** *(Br.)* international gehandelte Papiere, internationale Werte; **interest-bearing ~** verzinsliche Wertpapiere; **international ~** international gehandelte Werte (Effekten); **investment ~** Anlagepapiere, *(US)* Inhaberschuldverschreibungen; **irredeemable ~** unkündbare Wertpapiere; **junior ~** *(US)* erst an zweiter Stelle dividendenberechtigte Papiere; **landed ~** Grundpfandrechte; **listed ~** *(US)* amtlich notierte Werte, börsengängige Wertpapiere; **local ~** Lokalwerte; **lost ~** abhanden gekommene Effekten; **low-grade ~** niedrigstehende Werte; **marketable ~** börsengängige (fungible, absetzbare) Effekten, *(balance sheet)* Wertpapiere des Umlaufvermögens; **readily marketable ~** leicht realisierbare Wertpapiere; **medium-term ~** Papiere mit mittlerer und längerer Laufzeit; **miscellaneous ~** *(balance sheet)* verschiedene Werte; **municipal ~** Kommunalanleihen; **negotiable ~** marktfähige (begebbare, durch Indossament übertragbare) Effekten; **noninterest-bearing ~** unverzinsliche Werte; **nonmarketable ~** nicht verkehrsfähige (nicht handelbare) Wertpapiere; **nonnegotiable ~** nicht begebbare (verkehrsfähige) Wertpapiere; **nontaxable ~** *(US)* Wertpapiere mit steuerfreien Zinserträgen; **nonvoting ~** stimmrechtlose Wertpapiere; **off-board ~** *(US)* amtlich nicht notierte Wertpapiere; **outside ~** *(US)* [amtlich] nicht notierte Wertpapiere; **outstanding ~** noch nicht fällige Obligationen; **jointly owned ~** gemeinsame Wertpapiere; **pawned ~** lombardierte Effekten; **personal ~** Namenspapiere; **pledged ~** lombardierte Effekten, Lombardeffekten; **public ~** Staatsobligationen, -papiere, -anleihe, Anleihen der öffentlichen Hand; **quoted ~** notierte Werte; **realizable ~** eintreibbare Forderungen; **redeemable ~** auslosbare Wertpapiere; **registered ~** *(Br.)* eingetragene Wertpapiere, Namenspapiere; **restricted ~** gesperrte Wertpapiere; **savings-bank ~** sparkassenfähige [mündelsichere] Wertpapiere; **seasoned ~** gut eingeführte Wertpapiere; **senior ~** Wertpapiere mit Vorzugsrechten; **short-maturing ~** kurzfristige Anlagewerte; **speculative ~** Spekulationswerte, -papiere; **state ~** *(US)* Staatsanleihen; **suffering ~**

notleidende Werte; **sundry ~** *(balance sheet)* verschiedene Werte; **tax-exempt ~** ertragssteuerfreie Wertpapiere; **tax-free fixed-interest ~** steuerfreie festverzinsliche Wertpapiere; **terminable ~** Zeitrenten; **traction ~** Wertpapiere elektrisch betriebener Bahnen; **transferable ~** übertragbare Wertpapiere; **treasury ~** Portefeuille eigener Aktien; **trustee ~** *(Br.)* mündelsichere Wertpapiere, erstklassige Sicherheit; **uncurrent ~** *(US)* selten notierte Werte; **underlying ~** *(Br.)* Portefeuille [eines Investmentfonds]; **undigested ~** *(US)* vom Markt noch nicht aufgenommene (plazierte) Wertpapiere; **unlisted** *(US)* [amtlich] nicht notierte Werte, Freiverkehrswerte; **unquoted ~** nicht notierte Werte; **voting ~** stimmberechtigte Wertpapiere; **wildcat ~** hochspekulative Wertpapiere (Effekten);

~ dealt in for the account Terminpapiere; **~ owned by the bank** bankeigenes Effektenportefeuille; **~ dealt in for cash** Kassapapiere, marktgängige Werte; **~ held (lodged) as collateral** lombardierte Effekten (Wertpapiere); **marketable ~ at cost** börsenfähige Wertpapiere zu Ankaufspreisen; **~ negotiated for future delivery** auf Zeit gehandelte Wertpapiere; **~ on deposit** Wertpapiere im Depot; **~ entitled to a dividend** Effekten mit Dividendenberechtigung; **~ on hand** Effektenbestand, -portefeuille; **~ payable to bearer** Inhaberpapiere; **~ held in pledge** lombardierte Effekten; **~ sold under agreement to repurchase** mit Rückerwerbsverpflichtung veräußerte Wertpapiere; **~ quoted on the spot market** Kassapapiere, -werte; **~ admitted to (listed at,** *US)* **the stock exchange** zur Börsennotierung zugelassene Effekten;

to advance money on ~ Effekten (Wertpapiere) lombardieren; **to afford ~** Sicherheiten bestellen; **to be loaded up with ~** mit Effekten sehr stark eingedeckt sein; **to borrow on ~** Effekten lombardieren (beleihen) lassen; **to call in ~** Papiere aufrufen (einziehen); **to collaterate ~** Effekten lombardieren; **to commute ~** in Kost gegebene Effekten auswechseln; **to convert ~** Wertpapiere einlösen; **to deposit ~** Wertpapiere (Effekten) hinterlegen; **to deposit ~ in safe custody** *(Br.)* Wertpapiere ins Depot einliefern; **to give ~** Sicherheiten bestellen, *(trustee)* Kaution stellen; **to have ~ hypothecated** Effekten lombardieren lassen; **to hold ~ for safekeeping** Effekten im Depot verwahren; **to hypothecate ~** Wertpapiere beleihen, Effekten lombardieren; **to introduce (list,** *US,* **market) ~ on the stock exchange** Effekten an der Börse einführen; **to invest primarily in ~** seine Anlagen hauptsächlich in Wertpapieren decken; **to lend money on ~** Effekten beleihen (lombardieren); **to list ~ on the New York stock exchange** *(US)* Effekten an der New Yorker Börse einführen; **to marshal ~** Sicherheiten aufteilen; **to place ~ in a deposit** *(US)* Wertpapiere ins Depot einliefern; **to pledge ~** Wertpapiere lombardieren, Effekten verpfänden; **to pledge ~ with a bank for payment of a loan** Effekten bei einer Bank zur Kreditsicherung lombardieren lassen; **to qualify ~ for sale to the public** Wertpapiere zur Börsenzulassung anmelden; **to receive ~ for safe custody** Effekten ins Depot nehmen; **to release ~** Sicherheiten freigeben; **to retire ~** Wertpapiere für kraftlos erklären; **to take ~ on a commission basis** Wertpapiere in Kommission nehmen; **to withdraw ~ from a deposit** Wertpapiere aus einem Depot nehmen;

~ account Stückekonto; **~ Exchange Act** *(US)* Wertpapiergesetz; **~ assistant** Sicherheitenbearbeiter; **~ blotter** *(US)* Effektenstrazze; **~ book** *(Br.)* lebendes Depot[konto]; **~ broker** Effektenmakler, -händler; **~ business** Effekten-, Wertpapiergeschäft; **~ clearing bank** Effektengirobank; **~ collateral loan** Lombardkredit; **~ and Exchange Commission** *(US)* Börsenaufsichtsamt; **~ company** *(US)* Effektenverwertungsgesellschaft; **~ custody** Depotverwahrung; **~ dealer** *(US)* Effektenhändler; **~ dealings** Effektenhandel; **~ department (division)** Effektenabteilung, Depotbuchhaltung; **~ force** *(mil.)* Sicherheitskräfte; **~ holdings** Wertpapier-, Effektenbesitz, Wertpapierbestände, Effektenportefeuille; **~ industry** Wertpapierbranche; **~ industry association** *(US)* Effektenmaklerverband; **~ insurance** Wertpapierversicherung; **~ issue** Effektenemission; **~ journal** *(Br.)* Effektenstrazze; **~ ledger** *(Br.)* Effektenkonto, -register, totes Depot, Effektenbuch; **~ Management Trust** *(Br.)* Auffanggesellschaft für notleidende Industriebetriebe; **~ market** Wertpapier-, Effektenmarkt; **~ over-the-counter ~ market** *(US)* außerbörslicher Effektenmarkt; **to rock the ~ market to its foundations** Wertpapiermarkt (Effektenmarkt) bis in seine Grundfesten erschüttern; **~ market transactions** Effektentransaktionen; **~ offerings** Wertpapier-, Effektenangebot; **~ prices** Effektenkurse; **~ quotation** Wertpapiernotierung; **~ rating** Wertpapier-, Effektenbewertung; **~ register** *(US)* Effektenkonto, lebendes Depot; **~ sales blotter (book,** *US)* Effektenausführungsbuch; **~ salesman** Effektenverkäufer; **~ teller**

Effektenkassierer; **~ trading** Effekten-, Wertpapierhandel; **stolen ~ traffic** Handel mit gestohlenen Wertpapieren; **~ transfer tax** *(US)* Börsenumsatzsteuer; **~ underwriter** Emissionsbank, -firma, -haus.

security Sicherheit, Schutz, *(cover)* Sicherheit, -stellung, Sicherheitsleistung, [Kredit]deckung, Darlehnssicherheit, Sicherung, *(guarantee)* Bürgschaft, Kaution, Garantie, *(guarantor)* Bürge, *(pledge)* [Unter]pfand, *(mil., pol.)* Sicherheit, *(negotiable instrument)* Wertpapier;

able to put up ~ kautionsfähig; **against ~** gegen Sicherstellung; **by way of ~** zur Sicherheit, pfandweise; **in ~ for** als Garantie für; **pledged as ~** sicherungsübereignet, zu Sicherungszwecken (sicherungshalber) übereignet; **liable to give ~** kautionspflichtig; **without ~** ungedeckt;

additional ~ zusätzliche Sicherheit (Deckung); **airline ~** Sicherheit des Flugverkehrs; **ample ~** genügende Deckung; **cash ~** Barsicherheit; **collateral ~** [durch Verpfändung geleistete] zusätzliche Deckung, Lombarddeckung; **collective ~** *(pol.)* kollektive Sicherheit; **continuing ~** Dauerbürgschaft; **dead ~** wertlose Sicherheit; **~ deposited** hinterlegte Sicherheit; **direct ~** persönlich gestellte Sicherheit; **eligible ~** geeignete Sicherheit; **employee ~** Sicherung des Arbeitsplatzes; **fair ~** angemessene Sicherheit; **financial ~** Kreditsicherheit; **floating ~** auswechselbare Sicherheit (Kreditbesicherung); **good ~** sichere Bürgschaft; **heritable ~** *(Scot.)* dingliche Sicherheit; **high-grade ~** hochwertige Sicherheit; **joint ~** Solidarbürgschaft; **liquidator's ~** Kaution des Liquidators; **material ~** dingliche Sicherheit; **national ~** nationale Sicherheit; **~ owned** vorhandene Sicherheit; **personal ~** persönliche Sicherheit, nicht durch Dokumente gedeckte Sicherheit, Mobiliarsicherheit; **prior-ranking ~** vorrangige Sicherheit; **property ~** zusätzliche Deckung; **purchase-money ~** *(US)* Sicherungsrecht für eine Restkaufpreisforderung; **real ~** *(US)* dingliche (hypothekarische) Sicherheit, Grundpfandrecht; **reliable ~** ordnungsgemäße Sicherheit; **registered ~** Rektapapier; **secondary ~** Nebensicherheit; **shifting ~** auswechselbare Kreditsicherheit; **social ~** soziale Sicherheit; **substantial ~** sicherer (tauglicher) Bürge; **sufficient ~** ausreichende Deckung (Sicherheit); **third-party ~** von dritter Seite gestellte Sicherheit; **trading ~** kaufmännische Sicherheit; **trustee ~** *(Br.)* mündelsichere Anlage; **underlying ~** dingliche Sicherheit; **valid ~** gültige Sicherheit;

~ against advance Kreditsicherheit; **~ for good behavio(u)r** *(defendant)* Kaution für zukünftiges Wohlverhalten; **~ for borrowing** Darlehnsbesicherung; **~ for costs** *(required by nonresident)* Sicherheitsleistung für Gerichts-, Prozeßkosten, Kostenvorschuß, -hinterlegung, Prozeßkostenkaution; **~ for a debt** Sicherheit für eine Forderung; **~ by mortgage** hypothekarische Sicherstellung; **~ behind paper money** Notendeckung; **~ of person** persönliche Sicherheit; **~ on property** *(US)* dingliche (hypothekarische) Sicherheit; **~ of the state** Staatssicherheit; **~ of tenure** Mieterschutz;

to afford ~ Sicherheit stellen; **to be deposited as underlying ~** als Unterpfand dienen; **to be eligible as ~** lombardfähig sein; **to be ineligible to serve as ~** als Lombardunterlage nicht gewertet werden; **to be subject to ~** kautionspflichtig sein; **to become ~ for s. o.** für j. Bürgschaft leisten; **to charge ~** Sicherheiten bestellen; **to cross the street in ~ at a pedestrian crossing** Straße sicher auf dem Zebrastreifen überqueren; **to deposit as underlying ~** *(US)* als Sicherheit hinterlegen; **to forfeit ~** Sicherheit[sleistung] für verfallen erklären; **to furnish (give) ~** Bürgschaft, (Kaution, Garantie, Sicherheit) leisten, garantieren, sich verbürgen; **to furnish a bill with ~** Wechsel mit Bürgschaft versehen, Wechsel decken; **to give in ~** sicherungsübereignen; **to hold ~** gesichert (gedeckt) sein; **to lend money on ~** Geld gegen Sicherheiten ausleihen; **to lend money without ~** Blankokredit gewähren; **to lodge as ~** als Sicherheit hinterlegen, lombardieren lassen; **to lodge stock as additional ~** Aktien als weitere Lombardsicherheit hinterlegen; **to offer ~** Sicherheit bieten; **to pay in a sum as a ~** Anzahlung leisten; **to pledge as ~** zu Sicherheitszwecken (sicherungshalber) übereignen; **to provide ~** Kaution stellen; **to provide with acceptable ~** geeignete Sicherheiten stellen; **to realize ~** Sicherheit verwerten; **to register ~** Sicherheit bestellen; **to serve as ~** als Lombarddeckung dienen; **to rock in ~** in Sicherheit wiegen; **to stand ~ for s. o.** Bürgschaft für j. leisten, Garantie (Kaution) für j. stellen; **to stand ~ for a debt** Schuld avalieren; **to stand ~ for a signature** Unterschrift avalieren; **to surrender a ~** auf eine Sicherheit verzichten; **to tighten ~** Sicherheitsvorkehrungen verstärken; **to turn over as ~** als Sicherheit übergeben; **to want a ~** Sicherheit[en] verlangen; **to work in tight ~** unter strengen Sicherheitsbestimmungen arbeiten;

~ **account** Effektenkonto, -rechnung; **to offer** ~ **advice** Effektenberatung andienen; **[national]** ~ **adviser** *(pol., US)* Sicherheitsberater; ~ **agreement** *(pol.)* Sicherheitsabkommen; ~ **analyst** Effektenberater, Anlagefachmann; ~ **apparatus** Sicherheitssystem; ~ **arrangements** Sicherheitsvorkehrungen; ~ **aspect** Sicherheitsaspekt; ~ **bill** durch Effekten gesicherter Wechsel, Kautions-, Garantiewechsel; ~ **bond** Sicherheitsleistung, Kautionsurkunde, Bürgschaftsschein; ~ **border** verteidigungsfähige Grenze; **to receive** ~ **briefing** *(mil.)* in die Sicherheitsbestimmungen eingewiesen werden; ~ **classification** *(mil., US)* Geheimhaltungseinstufung; **to upgrade (downgrade) the** ~ **classification of a document** *(mil., US)* Geheimhaltungsstufe eines Schriftstücks heraufsetzen (herabsetzen); ~ **clause** Kreditdeckungsklausel; ~ **clearance** *(pol.)* Sicherheitsüberprüfung; ~ **committee** *(pol.)* Sicherheitsausschuß; ~ **conference** Sicherheitskonferenz; **to be** ~ **conscious** sicherheitsbewußt sein; ~ **considerations** Sicherheitserwägungen; ~ **contract** Bürgschafts-, Garantieversprechen; ~ **Council** *(UN)* Weltsicherheitsrat; **National** ~ **Council** *(US)* Sicherheitsausschuß; ~ **dealer** Effektenhändler; ~ **deposit** Sicherheitsleistung, *(with the landlord)* Mieterkaution; ~ **deposit with the landlord** Mieterkaution; ~ **deposit account** *(US)* Effekten-, Wertpapierdepot; ~ **deposit receipt** *(US)* Depotschein, -quittung; ~ **director** leitender Sicherheitsbeauftragter; ~ **employees** Wachpersonal; ~ **exchange** Wertpapierbörse; ~ **expense** Aufwand für Wertpapierbörse; ~ **floating company** *(US)* Emissionsgesellschaft, -bank; ~ **forces** *(police)* Leibwache; ~ **form** *(bank)* Sicherheitenformular; **to trade in** ~ **futures** Wertpapierterminhandel betreiben; ~ **grading** *(mil., Br.)* Geheimeinstufung; ~ **guarantee** *(pol.)* Sicherheitsgarantie; ~ **guard** Sicherheitsbeamter; ~ **guards** Wach- und Schließgesellschaft, Sicherheitsbeamter, Sicherheitskräfte; ~ **holder** Sicherheitsempfänger, *(stockholder)* Wertpapierbesitzer, -inhaber; ~ **holdings** Bestand an Wertpapieren, Wertpapierbestände, Wertpapier-, Effektenbestand; ~ **income** Erträgnisse aus Wertpapieren; ~ **interest** Sicherheitsbedürfnis, *(Commercial Code, US)* dingliches Sicherheitsrecht; **purchase money** ~ **interest** *(US)* zur Kaufpreissicherung bestelltes Recht; ~ **investment** Wertpapieranlage; ~ **issue** Wertpapieremission; **to comply fully with the state** ~ **laws** den Bestimmungen des Börsenaufsichtsamtes vollauf genügen; ~ **leak** undichte Stelle, Sicherheitsleck; ~ **lock** Sicherheitsschloß; ~ **man** Wachmann; ~ **market** Effekten-, Wertpapiermarkt, Effektenbörse; ~ **matter** *(mil.)* Geheimsache; ~ **measures** *(police)* Sicherheitsmaßnahmen; ~ **office** Sozialversicherungsamt; ~ **officer** Sicherheitsbeamter; ~ **ownership** Wertpapierbesitz; ~ **pact** *(pol.)* Sicherheitspakt; ~ **paper** Wasserzeichenpapier; ~ **pledge** *(pol.)* Sicherheitsversprechen; ~ **police** Sicherheitspolizei; ~ **portfolio** Wertpapier-, Effektenportefeuille; ~ **precautions** Sicherheitsvorkehrungen; ~ **prices** Effektenkurse, -preise; ~ **purchases** Effekten-, Wertpapierkäufe; ~ **rating** *(US)* Geheimhaltungseinstufung; ~ **reasons** Sicherheitsgründe, -erwägungen; ~ **register** *(Br.)* lebendes Depot, Effektendepot, -verzeichnis; ~ **regulations** *(EURATOM)* Verschlußsachenverordnung; ~ **reserve fund** Sicherheitsrücklage; ~ **risk** *(mil.)* Gefahr für die Sicherheit, Sicherheitsrisiko; ~ **sales** Effekten-, Wertpapierverkäufe; **to put its** ~ **services on full alert** seine gesamten Sicherheitskräfte in Alarmzustand versetzen; ~ **situation** *(pol.)* Sicherheitslage; ~ **system** Alarmsystem, -anlage, *(mil.)* Geheimhaltungssystem; ~ **trader** Wertpapierhändler; ~ **trading** Effekten-, Wertpapierhandel; ~ **transactions** *(US)* Effektentransaktionen, Sicherungsgeschäfte, *(for safety)* Sicherungsmaßnahmen; ~ **treaty** *(pol.)* Sicherheitsvertrag; ~ **value** Bürgschaftswert; ~ **yield** Effekten-, Wertpapierrendite.

sedan Limousine;
~ **chair** Sänfte.
sedative Beruhigungsmittel.
sedentary | fishery Grundfischerei; ~ **life** sitzende Lebensweise; ~ **work** sitzende Tätigkeit.
sedition Zersetzung, Aufstand, Aufwiegelung, Staatsgefährdung;
to incite people to ~ Masse zum Aufstand anstacheln; **to quell (throttle) a** ~ Aufstand niederschlagen (unterdrücken).
seditionary Aufrührer, staatsgefährlicher Hetzer.
seditious aufrührerisch, aufständisch;
~ **libel** *(Br.)* aufrührerische Schmähschrift; ~ **literature** staatsgefährdende Schriften; ~ **meeting** staatsgefährdende Versammlung; ~ **speech** Hetzrede; ~ **writing** Hetzartikel.
seduce *(v.)* s. o. **from his duty** j. zur Pflichtverletzung verleiten; ~ **to leave service** Arbeitskräfte abwerben; ~ **into war** zum Krieg verleiten.

seducing to leave service Abwerbung von Arbeitskräften.
seduction Verführung;
~**s of country life** Verlockungen des Landlebens.
seductive offer verführerisches Angebot.
see *(v.)* [ein]sehen, wahrnehmen;
~ **back** siehe Rückseite; ~ **below** *(book)* siehe unten; ~ **overleaf** siehe Rückseite; ~ **safe** *(bookseller)* mit Rückgaberecht;
~ **about** Sorge tragen für; ~ **action** mitkämpfen; ~ **the back of s. o. j.** loswerden; ~ **a business through** Sache gut abwickeln; ~ **s. o. on business** j. geschäftlich sprechen; ~ **into a claim** Anspruchslage prüfen; ~ **clear in a matter** in einer Sache klarsachen; ~ **a doctor** Arzt konsultieren; ~ **fit es für günstig** halten; ~ **for o. s.** sich selbst überzeugen; ~ **s. o. home** j. nach Hause begleiten; ~ **over a house** Haus besichtigen; ~ **to it** sich um etw. kümmern; ~ **the last of a job** mit einer Sache endlich fertig werden; ~ **s. o. for a few minutes** j. für kurze Zeit empfangen; ~ **from a newspaper** einer Zeitung entnehmen; ~ **s. o. off at the airport** j. am Flugplatz verabschieden; ~ **s. o. out (off the premises)** j. bis zur Gartentür begleiten (hinausbegleiten); ~ **a person off** j. an den Zug begleiten; ~ **a play** Theaterstück ansehen; ~ **red** *(sl.)* rot sehen, wütend werden; ~ **service** Kriegsdienst kennen; ~ **the sights** Sehenswürdigkeiten besichtigen; ~ **s. o. socially** j. bei gesellschaftlichen Veranstaltungen treffen; ~ **one's solicitor** zu seinem Anwalt gehen; ~ **a struggle through** Sache durchstehen; ~ **things** Halluzinationen haben; ~ **things together** Dinge im Zusammenhang sehen; ~ **s. o. through a difficulty** jem. über eine Schwierigkeit hinweghelfen; ~ **through s. one's little game** jds. Spiel durchschauen; ~ **one's way clear** wissen, was man zu tun hat.
seeing-eye dog *(US)* Blindenhund.
seek *(v.)* [nach]suchen, begehren, *(apply for)* sich bewerben;
~ **admission** um Zulassung nachsuchen; ~ **legal advice** sich anwaltlich beraten lassen; ~ **s. one's aid** j. um Hilfe bitten; ~ **s. one's approval** jds. Genehmigung einholen; ~ **divorce** Scheidung beantragen; ~ **employment** Arbeit suchen, sich um eine Stellung bewerben; ~ **one's fortune** sein Glück versuchen; ~ **information** Auskünfte einholen; ~ **an injunction** einstweilige Verfügung beantragen; ~ **the good offices of s. o.** um jds. Vermittlung bitten; ~ **out aufs Korn** nehmen; ~ **recovery** Schadenersatz verlangen; ~ **safety in flight** sein Heil in der Flucht suchen; ~ **shelter with conglomerates** großindustrielle Abstützung suchen.
seeker Aspirant.
seen | and approved gesehen und genehmigt;
to have ~ **better days** in besseren Lebensverhältnissen gewesen sein, es früher besser gehabt haben.
seep *(v.)* **out** *(information)* durchsickern.
seesaw policy Schaukelpolitik, Zickzackkurs.
segment Teil, Abschnitt, Stück;
~**s of business community** Wirtschaftskreise; ~**s of the press** Pressekreise; ~ **of time** Zeitabschnitt.
segregate *(v.)* absondern, trennen, isolieren, *(US)* Mutungsanspruch aufteilen;
~ **assets** Anlagegüter aussondern; ~ **people with infectious disease** Infektionskranke isolieren.
segregated | account *(US)* Sonderkonto; ~ **appropriation** *(fund, US)* gesonderte Zweckbestimmung.
segregation Absonderung, Ausscheidung, Trennung, Isolierung;
racial ~ Rassentrennung;
~ **of assets** Aussonderung von Anlagegütern.
seignior Rittergutsbesitzer.
seigniorage *(Br.)* Münzgebühr, -gewinn, *(royalty)* Tantieme, Autorenanteil.
seigniory Feudalherrschaft.
seisin, seizin Inbesitznahme eines Grundstücks;
actual ~ tatsächlicher Grundbesitz, Eigenbesitz;
~ **in deed (fact)** körperliche Inbesitznahme; ~ **in law** symbolische Besitzergreifung, unmittelbares Besitzrecht;
to take ~ Besitz ergreifen.
seizable pfändbar, beschlagnahmefähig, einziehbar.
seize *(v.)* ergreifen, *(confiscate)* beschlagnahmen, mit Beschlag belegen, einziehen, *(take hold)* gefangennehmen, ergreifen, *(put in possession)* Besitzrechte übertragen, *(take possession)* in Besitz nehmen, *(property)* pfänden;
~ **a fortress** Festung erobern; ~ **s. one's goods for payment of debt** jds. Sachen wegen ausstehender Schulden pfänden; ~ **upon an opportunity** Chance (günstige Gelegenheit) wahrnehmen; ~ **a paper** Zeitung beschlagnahmen; ~ **power** Macht an sich reißen (ergreifen); ~ **goods under process of (property on) execution** Zwangsvollstreckung durchführen; ~ **the throne** Thron usurpieren; ~ **the till** Kassenpfändung vornehmen.

seized eingezogen;
to become ~ of s. th. in den Besitz von etw. gelangen.

seizure *(act of seizing)* Beschlagnahme, Einziehung, vorläufige Konfiskation, *(arrest)* Ergreifung, Gefangen-, Festnahme, Verhaftung, *(distraint)* Pfändung, Arrest, *(ship)* Aufbringung, *(taking possession)* Inbesitznahme, Besitzergreifung;
actual ~ Pfändung (Beschlagnahmung) durch Wegnahme;
constructive ~ Beschlagnahme durch Veräußerungsverbot (Verfügungsverbot);
~ under a prior claim Vorpfändung; **~ of contraband by customs officers** Beschlagnahme von Schmuggelware durch den Zoll; **~ of crops** Pfändung der Früchte auf dem Halm; **~ of goods by the sheriff** Zwangsvollstreckung; **~ of movables** Mobiliarpfändung, Pfändung beweglicher Sachen; **~ of power** Machtergreifung; **~ of property** Fahrnispfändung, Vermögensbeschlagnahme [im Arrestverfahren], Vermögenseinziehung; **~ of real estate (property)** Beschlagnahme von Grundstücken (Immobilien), Immobilienpfändung; **~ of a ship** Beschlagnahme und Einbringung eines Schiffes; **~ of a town** Einnahme einer Stadt; **to be subject to ~** der Beschlagnahme unterliegen; **to be exempt from ~** pfändungsfrei (beschlagnahmefrei) sein; **to be under ~** beschlagnahmt (gepfändet) sein; **to effect a ~** beschlagnahmen, Beschlagnahme vornehmen; **to lift the ~** Beschlagnahme (Pfändung) aufheben; **to make ~** pfänden, Pfändung durchführen, konfiszieren; **to order the ~ of s. th.** Beschlagnahme von etw. anordnen (verfügen);
~ note Quittung des Gerichtsvollziehers.

select vorzüglich, auserlesen, exklusiv, auserwählt;
~ (v.) auswählen, aussuchen;
~ a passage of a book Buchpassagen auswählen; **~ a specimen at random** Muster stichprobenartig auswählen;
~ audience geladenes Publikum; **~ chapter** ausgewähltes Kapital; **~ part of a city** bevorzugte Wohngegend; **~ club** exklusiver Klub; **~ committee (House of Commons, Br.)** Sonderausschuß; **~ council** Oberhaus; **~ party** exklusive Gesellschaft; **~ passages** ausgewählte Stellen; **~ table** Sterblichkeitstabelle.

selected | applicant erfolgreicher Bewerber; **~ company** geschlossene Gesellschaft; **~ goods** auserlesene Ware; **~ investments** ausgesuchte Anlagewerte.

selectee *(mil., Br.)* Einberufener.

selection Auslese, Auswahl, Kollektion, *(personnel)* Personalauswahl, Konkurrenzauslese;
in a wide ~ of fields auf verschiedensten Sparten;
adverse ~ *(life insurance)* Ausscheiden der besseren Risiken, negative Auslese; **natural ~** natürliche Auslese; **portfolio ~** optimale Planung einer Wertpapieranlage; **rich ~** reichhaltige Auswahl; **tentative ~** *(US)* bedingte Warenauswahl;
~ on the basis of aptitude Eignungsauslese, Befähigungsauswahl; **~ in common** gemeinsame (gemeinschaftliche) Nominierung; **~ by the company** *(insurance)* von der Versicherungsgesellschaft getroffene Auswahl; **~ of customers** Kundenwahl; **~ against the insurer** für den Versicherer ungünstige Auswahl; **~ of media** *(advertising)* Auswahl der Werbeträger; **~ of personnel** Personenauswahl; **~ of risks** Risikoauslese; **~ of shares** Aktienauswahl; **~ of site** Grundstückswahl;
to make a ~ Auswahl treffen; **to make a ~ of an author's works** Sonderausgabe der Werke eines Autors veranstalten;
~ board Auswahlgremium; **~ committee** Bewerbungsausschuß; **~ consultant** Berater bei der Auswahl von Führungskräften; **~ poll** *(dealer)* Auswahlbefragung; **~ procedure (process)** Auswahlprozeß, -verfahren, Ausleseverfahren; **~ test** Auswahltest; **~ trunk offering (toll, US)** final *(tel.)* Fernleitungswähler.

selective gezielt, nach Bedarf, von Fall zu Fall, *(radio)* trennscharf;
~ advertising gezielte Werbung; **~ appeal** auf einen ausgewählten Personenkreis gerichtete Werbung; **~ credit control** Kreditlenkung; **~ demand** spezifischer Bedarf; **~ device** Auswahlmöglichkeit; **~ distribution** Vertrieb durch einen ausgewählten Händlerkreis; **~ driver plan** *(US)* Versicherungsnachlaß für unfallfreies Fahren, Schadensfreiheitsrabattsystem; **~ employment tax** *(Br.)* Lohnsummensteuer; **~ function** Auswahlfunktion; **~ import restrictions** gezielte Einfuhrbeschränkungen; **~ investing** zielbewußte Anlagepolitik; **~ program(me)** Personenauswahlprogramm; **~ sales policy (selling)** selektive Absatzpolitik; **~ school** Bedarfsschule; **~ service** *(mil., US)* Wehrpflicht, -dienst; **~ Service System** *(US)* Wehrpflichtsystem; **~ strength** *(stock exchange)* auf Spezialwerte beschränkte feste Haltung; **~ transmission** Getriebe mit Druckknopfschaltung.

selectivity *(radio)* Trennschärfe;
more ~ in accepting clients gezieltere Kundenauswahl.

selectman *(US)* Magistratperson, Stadtratsmitglied, -verordneter.

selector Sortierer, *(Australia)* Ansiedler, *(el.)* Wähler.

self Selbst, Ich;
~-accusation Selbstanklage, -beschuldigung; **~-acquired** selbsterworben; **~-action** Automatik; **~-addressed card** Rückantwortkarte; **~-addressed envelope** Freiumschlag; **~-administer** *(v.)* Selbstverwaltung haben; **~-administrated pension plan** eigene Pensionskasse; **~-administration** Selbstverwaltung; **~-advertise** *(v.)* Eigenwerbung treiben; **~-advertisement** Eigenreklame, -werbung; **~-advertiser** Eigenwerbung betreibende Firma; **to be ~-advertising** für sich selbst die Werbetrommel rühren; **~-appeal** eigene Werbewirkung; **~-appointed** selbsternannt; **~-appraisal** *(taxation)* Selbsteinschätzung; **~-assessable** selbst veranlagungspflichtig; **~-assessed** selbstveranlagt; **~-assessment** [steuerliche] Selbsteinschätzung; **~-authority** angemaßte Vollmacht; **~-balancing** *(general ledger)* ausgeglichen; **~-benefit** Eigenvorteil; **~-centred** ichbezogen, egozentrisch; **~-check** *(banking, US)* eigener Scheck; **~-colo(u)r** naturfarben; **~-confidence** Selbstvertrauen; **~-constituted** angemaßt; **~-construction** *(fixed assets)* Eigenleistung; **~-consumption** Eigenverbrauch; **~-contained flat** *(Br.)* abgeschlossene Wohnung, Wohnung mit eigenem Eingang; **~-contained house** *(Br.)* Einfamilienhaus; **~-contained industries** autarke Industriezweige; **~-contradiction** innerer Widerspruch; **~-control** Selbstbeherrschung; **~-convicted** aufgrund eigener Aussagen überführt; **~-cost** Gestehungs-, Selbstkostenpreis; **~-criticism** Selbstkritik; **~-dealing** *(trustee)* Selbstkontrahieren; **to be ~-defeating** Eigentor zur Folge haben; **~-defence** Selbsthilfe, Notwehr; **to kill s. o. in ~-defence** j. in Notwehr töten; **~-defensive** in Notwehr; **~-dependence** Unabhängigkeit; **~-destruction** *(life insurance)* Selbstentleibung; **~-determination** *(international law)* Selbstbestimmung; **~-development** eigene Fortbildung; **to put 400 million phones in 85 countries within ~-dial reach** 400 Millionen Telefonapparate in 85 Ländern an den Selbstwählverkehr anschließen; **~-disengaging fan** selbstabschaltender Kühlerventilator; **~-drive** *(Br.)* für Selbstfahrer; **~-drive car** selbstgefahrener Leihwagen; **~-drive cars for hire** *(Br.)* Autovermietung für Selbstfahrer; **~-driven** automatisch; **~-duplicating paper** selbst durchschreibendes Papier; **~-educated** im Selbstunterricht, autodidaktisch; **~-educated person** Autodidakt; **~-employed** selbständig erwerbstätig, freiberuflich; **~-employed person** selbständiger Erwerbstätiger, freiberuflich Tätiger, Selbständiger, Freiberufler; **~-employer** freiberuflich Tätiger, selbständiger Freiberufler, selbständiger Unternehmer; **~-employment** selbständige Tätigkeit; **~-employment income** Einkünfte aus selbständiger (freiberuflicher) Erwerbstätigkeit; **~-employment retirement plan** Ruhegeldsystem für selbständig Erwerbstätige; **~-examination** Gewissensprüfung; **~-executing** Ausführungsbestimmungen enthaltend; **~-executing constitutional provision** sofort wirksame Verfassungsbestimmung; **~-executing judgment** sofort vollstreckbares Urteil; **~-executing treaty** unmittelbar anzuwendender Völkerrechtsvertrag; **to be ~-explanatory** für sich selbst sprechen; **~-financing** Eigen-, Selbstfinanzierung; **~-governed** selbstverwaltet; **~-government** Selbstverwaltung, -bewirtschaftung; **local ~ government** kommunale Selbstverwaltung; **~-heating** Selbsterhitzung; **~-help** Selbsthilfe; **~-help enterprise** Selbsthilfeunternehmen; **~-help program(me)** Selbsthilfeprogramm; **~-incrimination** Selbstbezichtigung, -belastung; **~-inflicted wound** *(mil.)* Selbstverstümmelung; **~-instruction** Selbstunterricht; **~-insurance** Eigen-, Selbstversicherung; **~-insurer** Selbstversicherer; **~-interest** Eigennutz; **~-justification** Rechtfertigung des eigenen Verhaltens; **~-liquidating** *(US coll.)* sich automatisch abdeckend; **~-liquidating credit** kurzfristiger Warenkredit; **~-liquidating display** Ausstellungsmaterial zum Selbstkostenpreis; **~-liquidating loan** *(US)* kurzfristiger Warenkredit; **~-liquidating premium** Warenprobe zum Selbstkostenpreis; **~-locking** mit automatischem Verschluß; **~-made** handgearbeitet, selbstgemacht; **~-made man** Autodidakt; **~-mailer** Versandprospekt ohne Umschlag, Werbesache mit Rückantwort; **~-murder** Selbstmord; **~-murderer** Selbstmörder; **~-operating** Werbung in eigenen Verkehrsmitteln; **~-possession** Selbstbeherrschung; **~-preservation** Selbsterhaltung; **~-proclaimed** selbsternannt; **~-production** *(stock in trade)* Eigenleistung; **~-protection** Selbstschutz, Notwehr; **~-rating** Selbsteinschätzung; **~-reading** leicht lesbar; **~-redress** Selbsthilfe; **~-reducing clause** *(insurance value)* automatische Anpassungsklausel; **~-regulate** *(v.)* Eigenkontrolle ausüben; **~-reliance** Unabhängigkeit; **to be ~ reliant** sich auf sich selbst verlassen können; **judicial ~-**

restraint *(US)* Selbstbeschränkung des Bundesverfassungsgerichtes; ~-**retention** *(insurance business)* Selbstbehalt; ~-**retention control** Maximalkontrolle; ~-**righteous** selbstgerecht, pharisäerhaft; ~-**righteousness** Selbstgerechtigkeit, Pharisäertum; ~-**seeking** auf den eigenen Vorteil bedacht; ~-**service** Selbstbedienung; ~-**service restaurant** Restaurant mit Selbstbedienung, Automatenrestaurant; ~-**service shop (store,** *US*) Selbstbedienungsladen; ~-**service system** Selbstbedienungssystem; ~-**serving interests** Eigeninteressen; ~-**slaughter** Selbstmord; ~-**starter** Selbstanlasser, automatischer Anlasser; ~-**study** Selbststudium; ~-**styled** selbst ernannt; ~-**sufficiency** Eigen-, Selbstversorgung; **national** ~-**sufficiency** wirtschaftliche Unabhängigkeit, Autarkie; ~ **sufficient** selbstgenügsam, *(country)* autark; **to be** ~-**sufficient** Selbstversorger (autark) sein; ~-**support** Selbstversorgung; ~-**supporter** Selbstversorger; ~-**supporting** autark; **to be** ~-**supporting** sich selbst ernähren; ~-**supporting nation** autarker Staat; ~-**taught** autodidaktisch; ~-**tuition** Selbstunterricht.

sell *(commercial success)* Geschäftserfolg, *(sl., stock exchange)* zu verkaufendes Wertpapier;

hard ~ *(US)* energische Verkaufstechnik; **no end of a** ~ ausgesprochene Pleite; **soft** ~ *(US)* weiche Tour, zwanglose Warenwerbung;

~ *(v.)* verkaufen, [ver]käuflich überlassen, absetzen, abgeben, losschlagen, unter-, anbringen, *(alienate)* veräußern, *(fam.)* an den Mann bringen, *(find purchasers)* Absatz finden, verkauft (abgesetzt) werden, sich verkaufen lassen, *(puff, US)* anpreisen, *(trade)* handeln, vertreiben, *(turn over)* umsetzen; **certain to** ~ mit sicherer Absatzmöglichkeit;

~ **abroad** ausführen, exportieren; ~ **for the account** *(Br.)* auf Termin verkaufen; ~ **for the account of s. o.** auf jds. Rechnung verkaufen; ~ **to advantage** mit Gewinn verkaufen; ~ **at the best advantage** glänzend verkaufen; ~ **again** wiederverkaufen; ~ **ahead** für zukünftige Lieferung verkaufen; ~ **at 5 p a piece** Stück einen Shilling kosten; ~ **by anticipation** *(US)* auf Lieferung verkaufen; ~ **by** *(Br.)* [**public**] (**at,** *US*) **auction** öffentlich versteigern, im Wege öffentlicher Versteigerung verkaufen, versteigern, versteigern, in die Auktion geben; ~ **one's bacon** *(coll.)* auf den Strich gehen; ~ **badly** sich schwer verkaufen lassen, schwer abgehen; ~ **by private bargain** unter der Hand verkaufen; ~ **a bear** *(stock exchange)* ohne Deckung (blanko) verkaufen, auf Baisse spekulieren; ~ **best in the summer** hauptsächlich im Sommer gängig sein, im Sommer am besten gehen; ~ **at best** bestens (zum Bestpreis) verkaufen, *(stock exchange)* zum Höchstkurs verkaufen; ~ **to the highest bidder** meistbietend verkaufen; ~ **by the bottle** flaschenweise verkaufen (abgeben); ~ **without breaking the bulk** ohne zu entladen verkaufen; ~ **by bulk** im Bausch (in Bausch und Bogen) verkaufen; ~ **like hot cakes** reißenden Absatz finden, wie warme Semmeln (heiße Würstchen) weggehen; ~ **for cash** gegen Barzahlung verkaufen; ~ **one's goods cheaply** seine Ware billig abgeben (ablassen); ~ **on commission** auf Kommissionsbasis verkaufen; ~ **below cost price (less than cost)** unter Selbstkostenpreis (Wert, Herstellungskosten) verkaufen; ~ **over the counter** im Laden (über den Ladentisch) verkaufen, *(stock exchange, US)* im Freiverkehr handeln; ~ **on credit** auf Kredit (gegen Ziel) verkaufen; ~ **the crop standing** Ernte auf dem Halm verkaufen; ~ **dear** teuer verkaufen; ~ **dirt-cheap** verschleudern; ~ **at a discount** mit Verlust (Ermäßigung) verkaufen, *(stock exchange)* unter Preis stehen; ~ **at a discount outside the normal advertising channels** Anzeigenraum verbilligt abgeben; ~ **at a discount to its net asset value** zum Inventarwert unter Pari stehen; ~ **at a disadvantage** mit Verlust verkaufen; ~ **divisions to raise cash** einzelne Fertigungszweige zum Zweck der Liquiditätsverbesserung aufgeben; ~ **in dribs and drabs** in kleinen Partien verkaufen; ~ **free from encumbrances** pfandfrei (lastenfrei) verkaufen; ~ **forward** auf Lieferung (Termin) verkaufen; ~ **for future delivery** auf Termin verkaufen; ~ **goods** Waren debitieren (verkaufen); ~ **one's goods** seine Ware verkäuflich machen; ~ **goods easily** Waren leicht absetzen; ~ **goods under a secondary label** als zweitklassige Waren verkaufen; ~ **by hand** aus freier Hand verkaufen; ~ **hard (heavily)** schlechten Absatz finden, sich schwer verkaufen lassen; ~ **insurance** Versicherungsvertreter sein; ~ **an interest** Geschäftsanteil ([Kapital]beteiligung) verkaufen; ~ **an issue en bloc** Emission en bloc begeben; ~ **as a job lot** im Ramsch verkaufen; ~ **one's life dearly** sein Leben teuer verkaufen; ~ **a new line in a market** neuen Artikel auf den Markt bringen; ~ **long stock** Aktien aus einem großen Portefeuille verkaufen; ~ **at a loss** mit Verlust (Schaden, unter Selbstkostenpreis) verkaufen; ~ **out of a loss situation** aus einer Verlustsituation heraus verkaufen; ~ **in lots**

partieweise verkaufen; ~ **at an all-time low** zu den niedrigsten je erzielten Preisen verkaufen; ~ **at a low figure** billig verkaufen (abgeben); ~ **machinery as junk** Maschinen auf Abbruch verkaufen; ~ **on margin** gegen Sicherheitsleistung verkaufen; ~ **on the black market** auf dem schwarzen Markt (schwarz) verkaufen; ~ **as marked-down** mit Rabatt verkaufen; ~ **in the open market** am offenen Markt (aus freier Hand) verkaufen; ~ **for ready money** gegen bar verkaufen; ~ **off** ausverkaufen, Lager räumen, *(stocks)* liquidieren, realisieren, Glattstellungsverkauf vornehmen, glattstellen; ~ **off goods** Waren abstoßen; ~ **off-hand** freihändig verkaufen; ~ **off one's possessions** seinen ganzen Besitz abstoßen; ~ **at option** auf Prämien verkaufen; ~ **by order of the court** gerichtlich versteigern; ~ **out** ausverkaufen, Lager räumen, *(stock exchange)* Wertpapierbestand restlos liquidieren, lombardierte Wertpapiere realisieren, *(sl., become traitor)* verpfeifen, verraten, verkaufen; ~ **out against s. o.** *(Br.)* Exekutionsverkauf gegen j. durchführen; ~ **out against a client** *(stock exchange)* Börsenorder gegen die Interessen des Auftraggebers ausführen; ~ **out of line** Verkäufe unterhalb der abgesprochenen Preisgrenze vornehmen; ~ **out to the Yankees** *(coll., US)* Unfall haben, ins Krankenhaus kommen; ~ **outright** fest (ohne Vorbehalt) verkaufen; ~ **s. o. a packet** j. für dumm verkaufen; ~ **for current payment** gegen bar verkaufen; ~ **by the piece** stückweise (nach dem Stück) verkaufen; ~ **under the point system** auf Punkte verkaufen; ~ **at a premium** mit Gewinn (Vorteil) verkaufen, *(stock exchange)* über Pari stehen, mit einem Agio verkaufen; ~ **at a good price** guten Preis erzielen; ~ **at a low price** preiswert verkaufen; ~ **at reduced prices** mit Abschlag (unter Taxe) verkaufen; ~ **under price** unter Preis verkaufen; ~ **privately** unter der Hand verkaufen; ~ **by private contract (treaty)** aus freier Hand (freihändig) verkaufen; ~ **at a profit** mit Gewinn verkaufen; ~ **s. o. a project** jem. ein Projekt schmackhaft machen; ~ **the public on s. th.** der Öffentlichkeit etw. anpreisen; ~ **publicly** öffentlich versteigern; ~ **s. o. a pup** *(fam.)* jem. einen alten Hut verkaufen; ~ **rapidly** reißend abgehen; ~ **readily** leicht anzubringen sein, leicht verkäuflich sein, reißenden Absatz finden; ~ **at a reduction** mit Rabatt verkaufen; ~ **as rejects** als Ausschuß verkaufen; ~ **retail** *(Br.)* (en detail) im Kleinverkauf abgeben; ~ **down the river** *(sl.)* verraten und verkaufen; ~ **at a sacrifice** mit Verlust verkaufen; ~ **at public sale** *(US)* verauktionieren, versteigern; ~ **by sample** nach Muster verkaufen; ~ **on a scale** *(stock exchange, US)* seine Verkäufe über eine Hausseperiode verteilen; ~ **separately** einzeln verkaufen; ~ **for the settlement** *(stock exchange, Br.)* auf Termin verkaufen; ~ **shares** Papiere verwerten; ~ **out one's share of business** seine Beteiligung verkaufen; ~ **at 5 p a piece** Stück einen Schilling kosten; ~ **short** *(stock exchange)* ohne Deckung verkaufen, Baisseverkauf tätigen, fixen; ~ **on a scale (slice)** seine Verkäufe über eine Hausseperiode verteilen; ~ **at the spear** im Wege der Auktion verkaufen, versteigern; ~ **on a spot basis** auf der Grundlage der Barzahlung verkaufen; ~ **on the street** *(stocks)* im Freiverkauf verkaufen; ~ **by subhastation** im Wege öffentlicher Versteigerung verkaufen; ~ **under the system** auf Punkte verkaufen; ~ **on tick** *(fam.)* auf Kredit verkaufen; ~ **on time** auf Ziel verkaufen; ~ **to** *(US)* für einen Plan werben; ~ **to the trade** an Wiederverkäufer verkaufen; ~ **on trust** auf Kredit verkaufen; ~ **underhand** [Waren] verschieben; ~ **up** Konkursmasse liquidieren; ~ **s. o. up** j. auspfänden; ~ **for value** entgeltlich überlassen, gegen entsprechende Bezahlung verkaufen; ~ **a wide variety of goods** großes Warensortiment haben; ~ **one's vote** seine Stimme verkaufen; ~ **one's way into profit** durch Umsatzsteigerungen zu Gewinnen gelangen; ~ **by weight** dem Gewicht nach verkaufen; ~ **well** sich leicht verkaufen lassen, gut gehen, gefragt sein; ~ **wholesale** *(Br.)* (at wholesale, *US*) en gros verkaufen; ~ **by working through government program(me)s** beim Verkauf staatliche Finanzierungshilfen in Anspruch nehmen;

to be commissioned to ~ **s. th.** etw. an Hand haben; **to be hard to** ~ schwer verkäuflich sein;

~-**and-lease agreement** Grundstücksverkaufsvertrag unter gleichzeitigem Abschluß eines langjährigen Pachtvertrages; ~ **condition** Verkaufssituation; **soft-**~ **material** unterschwelliges Nachrichtenmaterial; ~-**off** *(stock exchange)* Abgaben, Glattstellenverkauf; ~-**off of holdings** Ausverkauf von Beteiligungen; ~ **order** Verkaufsorder, -auftrag; ~-**out** Ausverkauf, *(betrayal)* Verrat; ~ **signal** Verkaufssignal.

seller Verkäufer, Veräußerer, *(stock exchange, Br.)* Abgeber, Verkäufer, Brief, *(thing readily sold)* Verkaufsschlager, gängiger Artikel;

bad ~ *(book)* schlecht verkäufliches Buch; **bear** ~ Baissespekulant; **best** ~ Verkaufsschlager, Jahreserfolg, *(book)* viel verlangtes Buch, Bestseller; **big** ~ Verkaufsschlager; **common** ~ gewerbsmäßiger Verkäufer; **forward** ~ Terminverkäufer; **good** ~ *(book)* leichtverkäufliches Buch; **hot** ~ Verkaufsschlager; **intermediate** ~ Zwischenverkäufer; **mechanical** ~ Warenautomat; **original** ~ Rückkäufer;

~ **of a call option** *(Br.)* Verkäufer einer Vorprämie; ~ **of a put and call** Stellagegeber; ~ **of a spread** Stellagegeber.

seller's | commission Absatzprovision; ~ **duty to deliver** Übergabepflicht des Verkäufers; **unpaid** ~ **lien** Zurückbehaltungsrecht des Verkäufers; ~ **obligation** Verkäuferpflicht; ~ **option** *(stock exchange)* Rückprämie, Verkaufsoption; **to hold subject to the** ~ **order** zur Verfügung des Verkäufers halten.

sellers *(stock exchange)* Brief;

~ **ahead** *(US)* gehandelt und Brief; ~ **only** *(Br.)* Brief; ~ **over** *(Br.)* vorwiegend Brief, mehr Brief als Geld; **would-be** ~ Verkaufsinteressenten;

~ **and buyers** *(Br.)* Brief und Geld; **more buyers than** ~ *(Br.)* mehr Geld als Brief.

sellers' | cartel Absatzsyndikat; ~ **market** Verkäufermarkt, Marktnachfrage, Absatzkonjunktur.

selling Verkauf[en], Absatz, Vertrieb, *(stock exchange)* Verkäufe, Umsätze;

automatic ~ Verkauf durch Selbstbedienung; **bear** ~ Verkauf unter Spekulation auf Baisse, Verkäufe auf Baisse; **catalog(ue)** ~ Versandhausgeschäft; **development** ~ Entwicklung neuer Verkaufsmöglichkeiten; **direct** ~ direkter Absatz, Direktverkauf, Verkauf ohne Zwischenhändler; **direct-to-customer** ~ direkter Kundenverkauf, Beziehungskauf; **direct-to-point** ~ anschauliche Verkaufsmethoden; **discount** ~ Verkäufe im Einkaufszentrum; **effective** ~ erfolgreiche Verkaufstätigkeit; **forward** Lieferungs-, Terminverkäufe; **hard (high-pressure)** ~ aggressive Verkaufspolitik; **heavy** ~ größere Abgaben; **hedge** ~ Deckungs-, Sicherungsverkauf; **house-to-house** ~ Verkauf durch einen Hausierer, Direktverkauf durch Vertreter, Hausierhandel; **low-pressure** ~ unaufdringliche Verkaufsmethodik; **mail-order** ~ *(US)* Versand[haus]geschäft; **maintenance** ~ Erhaltung des gegenwärtigen Abschlußniveaus, Verkäufe im früheren Umfang; ~ **off (out)** Ausverkauf, *(US sl.)* Vertrauensbruch, *(stock exchange)* Exekutionsverkauf; **scattered** ~s vereinzelte Verkäufe; **selective** ~ Vertrieb durch bestimmte Vertreter; **spasmodic** ~ unregelmäßige Verkäufe; **specialty** ~ Verkauf von Spezialartikeln; **stocks short** Verkäufe auf Baisse, Blankoverkäufe, -abgaben, Fixgeschäfte; **suggestion** ~ suggestive Verkaufsmethode; **tax** ~s zur Überwindung des Steuertermins vorgenommene Verkäufe;

~ **by auction** [Verkauf im Wege der] Versteigerung; ~ **a bear** *(Br.)* Baissespekulation; ~ **below cost price** Verkauf unter Selbstkosten; ~ **in bulk** Massenabsatz; ~ **at a loss** Verkauf zu Verlustpreisen, Verlustverkäufe; ~ **by direct mail** Versandhausgeschäft; ~ **public offices** Ämterverkauf; ~ **with premium** Verkauf mit Zugaben, Zugabewesen; ~ **without premium** Verkauf ohne Zugabe; ~ **under price** Verschleuderung; ~ **on a scale** *(US)* Aufgabe von Kauf- und Verkaufsorders zu verschiedenen Zeiten; ~ **[off] of stock** Abstoßen von Aktien, Aktienverkauf; ~ **stocks short** Fixen, Baissespekulation, *(investment fund)* Leerverkäufe; ~ **by wholesale** Engros-, Massen-, Großhandelsverkäufe;

to be ~ **fast** schnell weggehen; **to be entrusted with the** ~ **of s. th.** mit dem Verkauf von etw. beauftragt sein; **to be** ~ **out** ausverkauft (geräumt) werden; **to run into heavy** ~ sich schwer verkaufen lassen; **to settle on** ~ sich zum Verkauf entschließen;

~ *(a.)* gängig, gut verkäuflich;

hottest ~ am meisten gefragt;

~ **account** Vertriebskonto; ~ **accounts receivable outright** *(US)* Debitorenverkauf, Warenbevorschussung; ~ **agency** Vertriebs-, Verkaufsbüro, Verkaufskontor; ~ **agent** Absatz-, [Verkaufs]vertreter, -kommissionär; ~ **aid** Verkaufshilfe; ~ **appeal** Kaufanreiz; ~ **area** Absatzgebiet; **high-pressure** ~ **arguments** aufdringliche Verkaufsargumente; ~ **arrangement** Verkaufs-, Vertriebs-, Absatzvereinbarung; ~ **attitude** Verkaufsverhalten; ~ **brokerage** Verkaufsprovision; ~ **calendar** Absatzkalender; ~ **campaign** Absatz-, Verkaufsfeldzug; ~ **capacity** Absatz-, Vertriebsfähigkeit; ~ **commission** Absatz-, Verkaufsprovision; **[onerous]** ~ **conditions** [erschwerte] Verkaufsbedingungen, Absatzverhältnisse; ~ **conversation** Verkaufsgespräch; ~ **costs** Vertriebs-, Verkaufs-, Selbstkosten; ~ **days** Verkaufstage; ~ **department** Verkaufsabteilung; ~ **efforts** Vertriebs-, Absatzanstrengungen; ~ **expenses** Vertriebsunkosten, Vertriebsgemeinkosten, Verkaufsspesen; **administrative and general** ~ **expenses** *(balance sheet, US)* Verkaufs-, Verwaltungs- und allgemeine Kosten; ~ **function** Verkaufs-

funktion; ~ **group** Absatzgremium, *(banking)* Emissions-, Verkaufskonsortium; ~ **hours** Verkaufszeit; ~ **licence** Verkaufslizenz; ~ **limit** Verkaufslimit; ~ **machine** Verkaufsautomat; ~ **methods** Absatz-, Vertriebsmethoden; ~ **office** Verkaufsbüro; ~ **order** *(stock exchange)* Verkaufsauftrag, -order; **to give a** ~ **order** zum Verkauf aufgeben, Verkaufsauftrag erteilen; ~ **organization** Verkaufsorganisation; ~**-out day** *(stock exchange)* Tag für Exekutionsverkäufe; ~ **plan** Absatz-, Vertriebssystem, Verkaufsplan; **over-all** ~ **plan** globales Verkaufsprogramm; ~ **point** Verkaufsstelle; ~ **points** Verkaufspunkte, -argumente; ~ **policy** Verkaufs-, Absatzpolitik; ~ **possibility** Vertriebs-, Absatzmöglichkeit; ~ **power** Werbekraft; ~ **pressure** Verkaufsdruck, Absatzmangel, *(stock exchange)* drängendes Angebot; **to be under** ~ **pressure** *(market)* durch Verkäufe gedrückt liegen; ~ **price** Laden[verkaufs]preis, *(stock exchange)* Verkaufs-, Briefkurs; **fixed** ~ **price** fester Verkaufspreis; **to mark with a** ~ **price** mit einem Verkaufspreis (preislich) auszeichnen; **to put up one's** ~ **prices** Verkaufspreise heraufsetzen; ~ **process** Verkaufsverfahren; ~ **prospect** Verkaufsprospekt; ~ **rate** *(foreign exchange)* Verkaufs-, Abgabe-, Briefkurs; ~ **right** Vertriebsrecht; **sole** ~ **rights** Alleinvertriebsrecht; ~ **season** Absatz-, Verkaufssaison; ~ **situation** Absatzlage, -situation; ~ **space** Verkaufsfläche; ~ **staff** Verkaufspersonal, Absatzstab; ~ **stop order** *(US)* limitierte Verkaufsorder; ~ **syndicate** [Emissions]konsortium; ~ **talk** Verkaufsgespräch; ~ **technique** Verkaufskunst; ~ **territory** Absatz-, Verkaufsgebiet; ~ **transactions** *(stock exchange)* Abschlüsse; ~ **value** Verkaufswert; ~ **wave** Verkaufswelle; ~ **weight** Verkaufsgewicht.

sellout *(sl.)* Ausverkauf.

semaphore *(railway)* Signalmast.

semblance of credibility Anschein der Glaubwürdigkeit.

semester *(US)* Halbjahr, Semester.

semiannual halbjährlich;

~ **instal(l)ment** Halbjahresrate; ~ **interest** halbjährliche Zinsen, Halbjahreszins; ~ **magazine** Halbjahresschrift.

semiautomatic halbautomatisch;

~ **working** halbautomatischer Betrieb.

semibold *(printing)* halbfett.

semibusiness halbgeschäftlich.

semicivilized halbzivilisiert.

semicolon Semikolon.

semidetached houses alleinstehendes Doppelhaus.

semidurable beschränkt haltbar;

~ **consumer goods** *(US)* kurzlebige Konsumgüter.

semifinal Halbfinale, Vorschlußrunde.

semifinished halbfertig;

~ **goods** Halbfabrikate; ~ **manufactures** Vorerzeugnisse; ~ **products** Halbfabrikate, Halbfertigwaren.

semifixed fund Investmentfonds mit begrenzt auswechselbarem Portefeuille.

semigovernmental corporation halbstaatliche Gesellschaft.

semiliterate halbgebildet.

semiluxuries, heavily-taxed hochbesteuerte Genußmittel.

semifacture, semimanufactured goods (products) halbfertige Erzeugnisse, Halbfabrikate.

semimonopolistic monopolähnlich.

semimonopoly Quasimonopol.

semimonthly halbmonatlich.

semimunicipal bonds *(US)* nicht vollwertige Kommunalanleihen.

seminar[y] Seminar, Erwachsenenbildungsanstalt;

special ~ Fachseminar;

to run a ~ Seminar abhalten;

~ **room** Seminarraum.

seminationalization halbe Verstaatlichung.

semiofficial halbamtlich, -dienstlich, offiziös.

semipostal Wohlfahrtsmarke.

semiprecious stone Halbedelstein.

semiprivate *(hospital)* in der zweiten Klasse.

semipublic halböffentlich.

semirigid *(airship)* halbstarr.

semiskilled worker angelernter Arbeiter.

semisolus *(advertisement, Br.)* halb alleinstehend.

semitropical tropenähnlich.

semivariable cost Sprungkosten.

semiweekly halbwöchentlich erscheinendes Organ;

~ *(a.)* halbwöchentlich.

senate *(US)* Senat;

~ **committee** Senatsausschuß; ~ **Foreign Relations Committee** Senatsausschuß für auswärtige Angelegenheiten; ~ **confirmation** Senatszustimmung; ~ **house** Senatsgebäude; ~ **inquiry** Senatsenquete.

senator *(US)* Senator, Senatsmitglied.
senatorial *(US)* zur Wahl von Senatoren berechtigt;
~ **approval** Senatszustimmung; ~ **committee** Senatsausschuß; ~ **district** *(US)* Wahlbezirk; ~ **election** Senatswahlen; ~ **objections** Widerstand des Senats; ~ **powers** Vollmachten des Senats; ~ **rank** Rang eines Senators, Senatorenrang; ~ **resolution** Senatsbeschluß; ~ **term** Wahlperiode des Senats; ~ **vote** Senatsbeschluß.
senatorship Senatorenwürde.
send *(v.)* schicken, senden, *(forward)* ab-, ver-, übersenden, [zu]schicken, zugehen lassen, versenden, zum Versand bringen, *(into estasy, sl)* enthousiasmieren, *(remit)* überweisen;
~ **after** nachschicken; ~ **along** vorbeischicken; ~ **in an application** Antrag einreichen; ~ **on approval** zur Ansicht schicken; ~ **away** wegschicken, -geben, *(servant)* entlassen; ~ **back** zurückschicken, retournieren; ~ **in one's bill** seine Rechnung vorlegen (schicken); ~ **in bills to an insurance office** Rechnungen bei einer Versicherung einreichen; ~ **up a bill to the Upper House** *(Br.)* Gesetzesantrag dem Oberhaus vorlegen; ~ **a boy to mill** *(coll.)* unzulängliche Maßnahmen ergreifen; ~ **s. o. about his business** j. herausschmeißen; ~ **in one's card** seine Visitenkarte abgeben; ~ **cash on delivery** *(COD)* per Nachnahme schicken; ~ **one's children to school** seine Kinder zur Schule schicken; ~ **out circulars** Rundschreiben verschicken; ~ **to Coventry** gesellschaftlich boykottieren; ~ **for a doctor** nach einem Arzt verlangen; ~ **down** *(Br.)* [von der Universität] relegieren; ~ **an employee away** Angestellten entlassen; ~ **for** schicken nach, abholen lassen, *(order)* bestellen; ~ **for s. o.** j. zu sich bestellen; ~ **goods to a fair** Messe beschicken; ~ **goods to the market** Markt beliefern; ~ **goods every month** monatlich liefern; ~ **goods by rail** Waren mit der Bahn versenden; ~ **goods by fast train** Waren per Express schicken; ~ **goods regularly by surface mail** Warenversand auf dem normalen Postwege durchführen; ~ **in** einreichen, einsenden; ~ **to invite s. o.** jem. eine Einladung schicken; ~ **on one's luggage** *(Br.)* sein Gepäck im voraus aufgeben; ~ **by mail** *(US)* mit der Post schicken; ~ **a member to Parliament** Abgeordneten stellen; ~ **a message** Nachricht übermitteln; ~ **a messenger to s. o.** jem. einen Boten schicken; ~ **money** Geld überweisen; ~ **every month** monatlich liefern; ~ **in (up) one's name** sich anmelden [lassen]; ~ **off** expedieren, fort-, ab-, verschicken, ab-, versenden, abgehen lassen, *(discharge)* entlassen; ~ **s. o. off** jem. bei der Abfahrt auf Wiedersehen sagen; ~ **off by post** zur Post geben, expedieren; ~ **on** nachsenden, weiterschicken; ~ **out** veröffentlichen; ~ **out accounts** Rechnungen verschicken (herausgehen lassen); ~ **s. o. packing** j. kurzerhand herauswerfen; ~ **in one's papers** um seine Entlassung einkommen; ~ **by post** *(Br.)* mit der Post schicken; ~ **to press** in Druck geben; ~ **prices down** Preise herunterdrücken; ~ **prices up** Preise hinaufschrauben, *(stock exchange)* Kurse in die Höhe treiben; ~ **up** *(sl.)* zu einer Gefängnisstrafe verurteilen; ~ **up gate receipts** Kasseneinnahmen ansteigen lassen; ~ **one's kindest regards** schöne Grüße (beste Empfehlungen) bestellen; ~ **in one's resignation** seinen Rücktritt erklären, sein Rücktrittsgesuch einreichen; ~ **s. o. to the right about** jem. eine Abfuhr erteilen; ~ **to school** in die Schule schicken; ~ **by sea** auf dem Seeweg schicken (befördern); ~ **a son to the university** seinen Sohn studieren lassen; ~ **s. o. a sum of money by post** jem. durch Postanweisung Geld zukommen lassen; ~ **a telegram** Telegramm aufgeben; ~ **with** mitschicken; ~ **word to s. o.** jem. eine Nachricht zukommen lassen; ~ **foreign workers home compulsorily** Gastarbeiter zwangsrepatriieren;
to have to ~ away for many things viele Bestellungen aufgeben haben.
send | -in Eingesandt, *(sl.)* Einführung; **~-off** Verabschiedung, Abschiedsfeier.
sender Ab-, Ein-, Ver-, Übersender, Aufgeber, *(shipper)* Befrachter;
return to ~ an den Absender zurück;
~ **of a money order** Einzahler einer Zahlungsanweisung.
sending Absenden, Auflieferung, *(dipl.)* Entsendung, *(forwarding)* Ver-, Übersendung, Versand, Versendung;
~ **away of an employee** Entlassung eines Angestellten; ~ **down** *(university, Br.)* Verweisung von der Universität, Ausschluß vom Universitätsstudium, zeitweilige Relegation; ~ **of goods** Warenversand; **~-in of money** Geldüberweisung; ~ **money abroad** Überweisungen ins Ausland; **~-out of a circular** Rundschreibenversand; ~ **to prison** Gefängniseinweisung; ~ **of vouchers** Versand von Belegexemplaren, Belegversand;
~ **station** Versandstation, Aufgabestelle.
senile altersbedingt, senil;
~ **decay** Altersschwäche; ~ **dementia** Altersblödsinn.

senility Altersschwäche, Senilität.
senior Dienstälterer, -ältester, Rangältester, Vorgesetzter, Senior[chef], *(school, university, US)* Schüler (Student) im letzten Jahr (Semester);
village ~s Dorfälteste;
~ *(a.)* *(advanced in age)* älter, *(privileged)* bevorrechtigt, vorrangberechtigt, *(security market)* bevorzugt, *(service)* rang-, dienstälter, ranghöher, übergeordnet;
~ **accountant** leitender Buchhalter, *(auditing)* selbständiger Revisionsbeamter; ~ **appointment** Spitzenposition; ~ **bonds** Vorzugsobligationen; ~ **capital** *(Br.)* Stammkapital; ~ **citizen** Rentner; ~ **civil servant** *(Br.)* höherer Staatsbeamter; ~ **class** *(US)* oberste (letzte) Schulklasse; ~ **clerk** Bürovorsteher, *(lawyer's office)* Kanzleivorsteher; ~ **counsel** Hauptprozeßbevollmächtigter, *(Br.)* prozeßführender Anwalt; ~ **director** älteres Vorstandsmitglied; ~ **employee** leitender Angestellter; ~ **executive** leitender Angestellter; ~ **executive officer** *(Br.)* höherer Beamter; ~ **executive position** gehobene Führungsposition; ~ **issue** mit Vorrechten ausgestattete Ausgabe (Serie); ~ **judge** vorsitzender Richter; ~ **lien** älteres Pfandrecht, Vorrangspfandrecht, im Range vorgehendes Pfandrecht; ~ **lien bonds** erstrangig besicherte Pfandbriefe; ~ **line manager** leitender Angestellter einer Fachabteilung; ~ **man** *(Br.)* älteres Semester; ~ **mortgage** *(US)* im Range vorgehende Hypothek, Vorrangshypothek; ~ **officer** *(Br.)* höherer Bedienstester (Beamter), *(enterprise, US)* leitender Angestellter, *(mil.)* höherer Offizier, *(US)* leitendes Firmenmitglied; ~ **local government officer** *(Br.)* höherer Kommunalbeamter; **my ~ officer** mein Vorgesetzter; ~ **partner** Hauptinhaber, Seniorpartner, -chef; ~ **position** leitende (gehobene) Stellung; **to fill ~ positions from one's own staff** Führungspositionen aus den eigenen Reihen besetzen; ~ **school** *(Br.)* letzte Grundschulklassen; ~ **high school** *(US)* Oberstufe in der höheren Schule; ~ **securities** Wertpapiere mit Vorzugsrechten; **the ~ service** *(Br.)* Kriegsmarine; ~ **shares** *(Br.)* Stamm-, Vorzugsaktien; ~ **staff** leitende Angestellte; ~ **stock** *(US)* Vorzugsaktien.
seniority Dienstalter, *(enterprise)* Betriebszugehörigkeitsdauer, *(in rank)* Dienst[vor]rang;
in order of ~ nach dem Dienstalter;
company ~ *(US)* Betriebszugehörigkeitsdauer; **job ~** *(US)* Dienstalter; **pay ~** *(US)* Besoldungsdienstalter;
to be chairman by ~ Alterspräsident sein; **to be promoted by ~** nach dem Dienstalter befördert werden; **to rise by ~** nach dem Dienstalter aufrücken;
~ **allowance** *(US)* Dienstalterzulage; ~ **basis** *(US)* Beförderung nach dem Dienstalter; ~ **list** *(US)* Dienstrangliste; ~ **pay** *(US)* Dienstalters-, Beförderungszulage; ~ **principle** *(US)* Dienstaltersprinzip; ~ **problem** Beförderungsproblem; ~ **right** Beförderungsanspruch; ~ **rule** *(parl., US)* Senioritätsprinzip, Dienstaltersbestimmungen; ~ **system** Dienstaltersplan; **to crack the ~ system** mit Anzienitätsrechten aufräumen.
sensation Sensation;
to create a great ~ große Sensation hervorrufen; **to deal largely in ~** vorwiegend Sensationsnachrichten bringen, Sensationshascherei betreiben.
sensational | journalism Sensationsjournalismus; ~ **newspaper** Sensations-, Skandal-, Revolverblatt; ~ **novel** Sensationsroman; ~ **piece of news** sensationelle Nachricht; ~ **writer** reißerisch schreibender Journalist.
sensationalism Gefühlsaufstachelung.
sensay *(sl.)* sensationell.
sense Sinn, Vernunft, Verstand, *(meaning)* Sinn, Bedeutung;
in the figurative ~ im übertragenen Sinn; **in the legal ~** im juristischen Sinn; **in the literal ~** wörtlich genommen; **in one's right ~s** im Besitz seiner fünf Sinne;
auditory ~ Gehörsinn; **common ~** gesunder Menschenverstand; **gustatory ~** Geschmackssinn; **kinesthetic ~** Kraftsinn; **literal ~** buchstäbliche Bedeutung; **narrow ~** eigentliche Bedeutung; **olfactory ~** Geruchssinn; **proper ~** eigentliche Bedeutung; **visual ~** Gesichtssinn;
~ **of balance** *(driver)* Fahrgefühl; ~ **of belonging** Zugehörigkeitsgefühl; ~ **of bewilderment** Gefühl der Verunsicherung; ~ **of decline** Eindruck des Niedergangs; ~ **of direction** Richtungssinn; ~ **of duty** Pflichtgefühl, -bewußtsein; **dry ~ of humo(u)r** trockener Humor; ~ **of justice** Gerechtigkeitsgefühl; ~ **of locality** Ortssinn; ~ **of mission** Sendungsbewußtsein; ~ **of nationhood** Bewußtsein nationaler Einheit; ~ **of power** Machtgefühl; ~ **of responsibility** Verantwortungsgefühl; ~ **of security** Gefühl der Sicherheit;
to appeal to the ~ of the nation Volk um seine Meinung befragen; **to be in the enjoyment of all one's ~s** über alle fünf Sinne

verfügen können; **to be in one's ~s** geistig normal sein; **to be out of one's ~s** geisteskrank sein; **to bring s. o. to his ~s** j. zur Vernunft bringen; **to come to one's ~s** wieder normal werden; **to feel a ~ of human sympathy** Mitgefühl haben; **to give s. o. a ~ of stability** jds. ruhender Pol sein; **to have no ~ of planning** nicht einteilen können, keine Einteilung haben; **to lose all ~ of judgment** jegliches Urteilsvermögen verlieren; **to retain a ~ of measure** auf dem Teppich bleiben; **to seem good ~** vernünftig erscheinen; **to set the ~s afire** Begeisterung auslösen; **to take leave of one's ~s** verrückt werden; **to take the ~ of a public meeting** Meinung einer öffentlichen Versammlung einholen; **~-appeal copy** gefühlsbestimmte Werbung; **~-organ** Sinneswerkzeug.

sensitized paper lichtempfindliches Papier.
sensitive reagibel, heikel, *(film)* lichtempfindlich;
  ~ to business movements (economic fluctuations) konjunkturempfindlich; **~ to criticism** kritikempfindlich; **~ to market influences** marktreagibel; **~ to money-market influences** geldmarktempfindlich;
  to be ~ to political disturbance *(stock exchange)* empfindlich auf politische Unruhen reagieren; **to be ~ to a downturn** auf konjunkturelle Verschlechterungen empfindlich reagieren; **~ area** Sicherheitsbereich, Sperrzone; **~ indicator** zukunftssensibler Frühindikator; **~ market** empfindlich reagierende Börse; **~ material** vertrauliche Unterlage; **~ products** marktempfindliche Erzeugnisse, *(tariff barrier)* zollempfindliche Erzeugnisse.
sensitivity, mechanical technisches Einfühlungsvermögen;
  ~ to economic fluctuations Konjunkturempfindlichkeit; **~ analysis** Sensitivitätsanalyse; **~ data** *(statistics)* Ja-Nein-Beobachtungen; **~ training** Reaktionstraining.
sensory deprivation Isolationsfolter.
sentence Urteil[spruch], *(grammar)* Satz, *(law)* Rechts-, Richterspruch, Entscheidung, Urteil, *(criminal law)* Strafurteil, -maß, Strafe;
  accessory ~ Nebensatz; **adjective ~** Relativsatz; **capital ~** Todesstrafe; **complex ~** Satzgefüge; **concluding ~** Schlußsatz; **concurrent ~** Gesamtstrafe; **cumulative ~** strafhäufendes Urteil, Strafhäufung; **death ~** Todesstrafe; **excessive ~** übermäßig hohe Strafe; **final ~** abschließendes Urteil; **heavy ~** schwere Strafe; **inadequate ~** zu niedriges Strafmaß; **indeterminate ~** Freiheitsstrafe mit unbestimmter Dauer; **jail ~** *(US)* Gefängnisstrafe; **interlocutory ~** *(civil law)* Zwischenurteil; **lenient ~** milde Strafe, mildes Urteil; **life ~** lebenslängliche Freiheitsstrafe; **maximum ~** Höchststrafe; **minimum ~** Mindeststrafe; **severe ~** strenges Urteil; **stringy ~** endlos langer Satz; **subsidiary ~** Nebenstrafe; **suspended ~** zur Bewährung ausgesetztes Strafurteil, auf Bewährung ausgesetzte Strafe; **topical ~** thematische Synthese;
  ~ of a court Gerichtsurteil; **~ of death** Verurteilung zum Tode, Todesurteil; **~ of death recorded** nicht zu vollstreckende Todesstrafe; **~ of imprisonment** Freiheits-, Gefängnisstrafe;
  ~ (v.) Urteil fällen, verurteilen, Strafmaß aussprechen, verdonnern;
  ~ a thief to six months imprisonment Dieb zu einem halben Jahr Gefängnis verurteilen;
  to appeal against a ~ gegen ein Urteil Berufung einlegen; **to award a ~** auf eine Strafe erkennen; **to bind a ~ over on probation** Strafe zur Bewährung aussetzen; **to break up a ~** *(grammar)* Satz auflösen; **to complete one's ~** seine Strafe voll verbüßen; **to determine the ~** Strafhöhe festsetzen; **to execute a ~** Urteil vollstrecken; **to get a life ~** zu lebenslänglichem Zuchthaus verurteilt werden; **to impose a ~ of imprisonment for an extended term** *(US)* auf eine verlängerte Freiheitsstrafe erkennen; **to pass ~ of one month's imprisonment** auf einen Monat Gefängnis erkennen; **to pronounce a ~** Urteil verkünden; **to reduce a ~** Strafe herabsetzen; **to suspend a ~** Urteilsverkündung (Strafvollstreckung) aussetzen; **to serve a ~ of imprisonment** Strafe absitzen (verbüßen); **to uphold a ~** Urteil bestätigen;
  ~ length Satzlänge; **~ style** Satzstil.
sentencing, suspended Strafaussetzung zur Bewährung;
  to reduce a judge's ~ discretion Ermessensspielraum des Strafrichters herabsetzen; **~ policy** Strafmaßpolitik.
sentential entscheidend, rechtskräftig.
sententious | speech prägnante Rede; **~ style** knapper Stil.
sentiment Mitgefühl, *(market)* [Börsen]stimmung, *(opinion)* Meinung, Ansicht;
  noble ~ edle Gesinnung; **well-orchestrated ~** gut abgestimmte Einstellung;
  ~ of electors Wählerstimmung;

to echo a ~ Meinung nochmals bestätigen; **to explain the ~s of one's government** Ansichten seiner Regierung im einzelnen erläutern; **to have the public ~ in one's pocket** öffentliche Meinung auf seiner Seite haben; **to mobilize public ~** öffentliche Meinung mobilisieren.
sentimental | damage *(insurance)* Wertminderung; **~ value** Liebhaberwert.
sentinel Wächter, Wachmann, *(mil.)* Wache, Wachtposten.
sentry *(mil.)* Posten, Wache;
  to stand ~ auf Wache stehen;
  ~ box Wachhäuschen; **~ line** Postenkette.
sentrygo Postengang.
separability Trennbarkeit;
  ~ clause *(union agreement)* Teilnichtigkeitsklausel.
separable trennbar, teilbar;
  ~ controversy abtrennbares Verfahren; **~ costs** Produktionskosten; **~ program(m)ing** getrennte Planungsrechnung.
separate *(print.)* Sonderdruck;
  ~ (v.) [ab]trennen, *(bankruptcy)* aus-, absondern, ausscheiden, *(corporation)* auflösen, *(employee, US)* entlassen;
  ~ a case Verfahren abtrennen; **~ from a church** aus der Kirche austreten; **~ into small fields** in kleine Parzellen aufteilen; **to be living ~** *(married couple)* getrennt leben; **to keep s. th. ~** etw. getrennt aufbewahren; **to live ~** *(married couple)* getrennt leben;
  ~ (a.) einzeln, getrennt, gesondert, *(bankruptcy)* ausgesondert; **~ account** Sonder-, Separatkonto; **~ accounts** *(pension scheme)* getrennte Anlagen; **~ acknowledgment** *(married woman)* getrenntes Schuldanerkenntnis; **~ action** getrenntes Verfahren, selbständige Klage; **~ agreement** Sonderabkommen, -vertrag; **~ book** Nebenbuch; **~ confinement** Einzelhaft; **~ covenant** Sondervereinbarung, -vertrag; **under ~ cover** in besonderem Umschlag; **~ discussion** Einzelbesprechung; **~ edition** Sonderausgabe; **~ estate** Sondervermögen, *(married woman)* eingebrachtes Gut, Vorbehaltsgut; **~ examination** *(married woman)* Einzelvernehmung; **~ loan account** Lohnsonderkonto; **~ maintenance** *(US)* Unterhaltsleistung [an getrennt lebende Ehefrau]; **~ opinion** abweichende Meinung; **~ and common ownership** Privat- und Gesellschaftseigentum; **~ peace** Separatfriede; **~ print** Sonderdruck; **~ property** *(US)* Sondervermögen, *(married woman)* Vorbehaltsgut, *(partner)* Privatvermögen; **~ return** getrennte Steuererklärung; **~ room** Einzelzimmer; **~ satisfaction** *(bankruptcy)* abgesonderte Befriedigung; **~ trade** Proprehandlung, Handlung auf eigene Rechnung; **~ treaty** Sonderabkommen, Separatvertrag; **~ trial** abgetrenntes Verfahren; **~ volume** einzelner Band, Einzelband.
separatee *(US)* entlassener Soldat, Wehrdienstentlassener.
separately, to keep abgesondert (getrennt) verwahren; **to treat as living ~ for tax purposes** aus Steuergründen als getrennt lebend behandeln.
separating post office *(US)* Verteileramt.
separation Trennung, Teilung, *(bankruptcy proceedings)* Absonderung, Aussonderung, *(married couple)* Getrenntleben;
  ~s *(labo(u)r force)* Abgänge in der Belegschaft;
  administrative ~ verwaltungsmäßige Trennung; **judicial ~** gerichtlich angeordnetes Getrenntleben, Aufhebung der ehelichen Gemeinschaft; **notarial ~** notariell abgesprochene eheliche Trennung; **voluntary ~** *(US)* einverständliche Trennung; **~ from bed and board** Trennung von Tisch und Bett, Ehetrennung; **~ of Church and State** Trennung von Kirche und Staat; **~ of claims** *(bankruptcy)* Absonderung; **~ by consent** *(married couple)* einverständliche Trennung; **~ of estate** Gütertrennung; **~ by order of the court** gerichtlich angeordnetes Getrenntleben; **~ of partnership** Auflösung einer Handelsgesellschaft; **~ from a party** Parteiaustritt; **~ of patrimony** *(probate law, Louisiana)* getrennte Verwaltung des Nachlaßvermögens; **~ of property** *(US)* Gütertrennung; **~ from the service** *(US)* Entlassung aus dem Wehrdienstverhältnis;
  ~ agreement Vereinbarung des Getrenntlebens; **~ allowance** *(mil.)* Trennungszulage, -geld; **~ center** *(mil., US)* Entlassungsstelle, -lager, -zentrum; **~ deed** *(married couple, Br.)* schriftliche Trennungsvereinbarung; **~ order** *(Br.)* Gerichtsbeschluß über die Aufhebung der ehelichen Gemeinschaft, gerichtliche Anordnung des Getrenntlebens; **~ rate** *(staff, US)* Abgangsrate; **~ vote** Trennungsplebiszit.
separatism Separatismus.
separatist Separatist;
  ~ sentiment Unabhängigkeitsgefühl; **~ ticket** Separatistenprogramm; **~ urge** separatistische Wünsche.
sepulcher *(US)* **sepulchre** *(Br.)* Grabstätte.

sepulchral customs Bestattungsgebräuche.

sequacious zeal Diensteifer.

sequel Folge[erscheinung], Konsequenz;
 in the ~ in der Folgezeit;
 judicial ~ gerichtliches Nachspiel;
 ~ in court gerichtliches Nachspiel; **~ of war** Kriegsfolge;
 to have a ~ Nachspiel haben.

sequence Reihenfolge, *(data processing)* Folge, *(film)* Szene, Bildfolge;
 according to the order of ~ turnusmäßig;
 alphabetical ~ alphabetische Reihenfolge; **[un]broken ~** *(law of insurance)* [nicht] unterbrochener Kausalzusammenhang;
 ~ of calamities Unglücksserie; **natural ~ of events** Kausalzusammenhang; **~ of growth** Wachstumsfolge; **~ of good harvests** Reihe guter Ernten; **~ of operations** Arbeitsfolge; **~ of priority** Rangfolge; **~ of weather** Wetterentwicklung;
 to deal with events in historical ~ historisch vorgehen;
 ~ switch *(el.)* Serienschalter.

sequential | estimation *(statistics)* Folgeschätzungen; **~ test** *(statistics)* Folgeprüfung.

sequester [Zwangs]Verwalter, Treuhänder, Sequester, *(property)* treuhänderisch verwaltetes Eigentum;
 ~ *(v.)* mit Beschlag belegen, zwangsverwalten, unter Treuhänderschaft stellen, sequestrieren, besonders verwalten lassen, *(international law)* [Feind]gut einziehen, konfiszieren;
 ~ alien property Feindvermögen beschlagnahmen;
 ~ o. s. from the world sich von der Welt zurückziehen;

sequestered | life zurückgezogenes Leben; **~ village** abgelegenes Dorf.

sequestrable beschlagnahmefähig, konfiszierbar.

sequestrate *(v.)* sequestrieren, beschlagnahmen, konfiszieren.

sequestration Beschlagnahme, *(bankruptcy)* Zwangsverwaltung, Sequestrierung des Vermögens, *(international law)* Beschlagnahme, Einziehung, Konfiszierung, *(law of contracts)* Hinterlegung bei Gericht (bei Dritten) [bis zur Prozeßbeendigung];
 judicial ~ Aufbewahrung durch das Gericht, gerichtliche Hinterlegung, Zwangsverwaltung;
 ~ of income Beschlagnahme von Einkünften, Einkommensbeschlagnahme;
 to award ~ of estate Vermögensbeschlagnahme anordnen; **to put under ~** unter Zwangsverwaltung stellen.

sequestrator of land Zwangsverwalter, Sequester.

serenade Ständchen, Serenade.

sergeant Hauptwachtmeister, Feldwebel, *(law court, Br.)* Polizeiwachtmeister, Gerichtsdiener;
 town ~ örtlicher Polizeichef.

serial *(broadcasting)* Sendereihe, *(novel)* Fortsetzungsroman, *(publication)* Serie, Veröffentlichungsreihe, Lieferungswerk;
 ~ *(a.)* serienmäßig, periodisch, *(publication)* periodisch (in Lieferungen, Fortsetzungen) erscheinend, fortlaufend;
 ~ advertisements Serienanzeigen, Anzeigenserie; **~ bonds** Serien-, Tilgungsanleihe, in Serien unterteilte Obligationen; **~ construction** Serienherstellung, Massenfabrikation; **~ house** Reihenhaus; **~ issue of bonds** Emission in Serien; **~ manufacture** Serienherstellung, Massenfabrikation; **~ number** laufende Nummer, Fabrikationsnummer; **~ number of a bank note** Seriennummer einer Banknote; **~ part** Teillieferung; **in ~ parts** in einzelnen Nummern; **~ price** Serienpreis; **~ production** Fließarbeit, Arbeit am laufenden Band, Reihenan-, Serienfertigung, Massenproduktion; **~ publication** Veröffentlichung in Fortsetzungen; **~ rights** Veröffentlichungsrechte in Zeitschriften; **~ story** Fortsetzungsroman; **~ work** Serienarbeit.

serialization serienmäßige Herstellung, Massenproduktion, *(publishing)* Veröffentlichung in Fortsetzungen.

serialize *(v.)* in Fortsetzungen veröffentlichen, *(production)* serienmäßig herstellen, in Massen produzieren;
 ~ a novel Roman in Fortsetzungen abdrucken.

serialized novel Fortsetzungsroman, -geschichte.

seriate *(v.)* serienweise anordnen.

seriatim Punkt für Punkt.

series Zahlenfolge, Serie, Reihe, Kategorie, Gruppe;
 in ~ serienmäßig, reihen-, serienweise;
 new ~ neue Folge; **ordered ~** *(statistics)* geordnete Reihen; **original ~** Originalserie; **test ~** Versuchsreihe;
 ~ of debentures Schuldverschreibungsserie; **~ of documents** Dokumentenkette; **~ of lectures** Vorlesungsreihe, Vortragsfolge; **~ of misfortunes** Pechsträhne; **~ in numbers** Zahlenreihe;
 to purchase the whole ~ ganze Reihe abnehmen;
 ~ discount *(advertising)* Wiederholungsrabatt; **~ posting** Reihenanschlag; **~ production** Serienherstellung, Massenproduktion; **~ rate** [Anzeigen]tarif; **~ stamps** Briefmarkenserie.

serious, to be *(sl.)* ernsthafte Absichten haben; **to look** *(political situation)* ernst aussehen;
 ~ alteration bedeutende Veränderung; **~ attempt** ernsthafter Versuch; **~ bodily harm** schwere Körperverletzung; **~ business** wichtiges Geschäft; **~ buyer** ernsthafter Reflektant; **~ consequences** schwerwiegende Folgen; **to be in ~ doubt** erhebliche Bedenken hegen; **~ illness** gefährliche Krankheit; **~ personal injury** schwere Verletzung; **~ manifestation** schwerwiegendes Symptom; **~ matter** ernsthafte Angelegenheit; **~ and wilful misconduct** schwere vorsätzliche Verfehlung; **~ mistake** schwerer Fehler; **~ offer** ernstgemeintes Angebot; **~ politician** ernst zu nehmender Politiker; **~ worker** ernsthafter Arbeiter.

seriousness of a country's financial affairs schwierige finanzielle Lage eines Landes.

sermon Predigt, *(admonition)* Strafpredigt.

serpentine road Serpentinenstraße.

servant Dienstbote, Diener, Hausangestellter, Bediensteter, *(labo(u)rer)* Arbeitnehmer, *(law)* [Erfüllungs]gehilfe, *(official)* Angestellter;
 ~s Personal;
 civil ~ *(Br.)* Verwaltungs-, Staatsbeamter; **unestablished civil ~** *(Br.)* außerplanmäßiger Beamter; **crown ~** *(Br.)* Bediensteter der Krone, Staatsbeamter; **domestic ~** Hausangestellte[r]; **fellow ~** *(Br.)* Kollege; **hired ~** Lohndiener; **hotel ~s** Hotelpersonal; **your humble ~** *(closing a letter)* Ihr ergebener Diener; **maid ~** Hausangestellte; **man ~** Hausdiener; **menial ~** Hausangestellte; **your obedient ~** *(closing a letter)* Ihr ergebener; **outdoor ~** Angestellter für Außenarbeiten; **post-office ~** *(Br.)* Postbeamter; **public ~** Angestellter im öffentlichen Dienst, [Staats]beamter; **railway company's ~** [Eisen]bahnbeamter; **subordinate ~** untergeordneter Angestellter;
 ~ of a company Firmenangehöriger; **~ of old standing** langjähriger Hausangestellter;
 to become a civil ~ *(Br.)* in den Staatsdienst eintreten, Beamter werden; **to dismiss a ~** Hausangestellten entlassen; **to engage a ~** Hausangestellten einstellen; **to give a ~ the sack** Dienstboten fristlos kündigen; **to keep a ~** Hausangestellten haben;
 ~ girl Hausangestellte; **~ shortage** Knappheit an Hausangestellten; **~'s wages** Dienstbotenlöhne.

serve *(v.)* dienen, im Dienst stehen, Dienst leisten, *(be of use)* dienen, nützen, *(customers)* bedienen, beliefern, *(deliver summons)* [Klage] zustellen, *(be employed)* beschäftigt sein, *(mil.)* Wehrdienst leisten, *(office)* verwalten, amtieren, fungieren, *(public utility)* versorgen, *(Scot.)* zum Erben erklären;
 ~ upon s. o. jem. eine Ladung zustellen; **~ with s. o.** für j. tätig sein;
 ~ one's apprenticeship seine Lehrjahre ableisten, seine Ausbildung absolvieren; **~ in the army** [beim Heer] dienen, Wehrdienst leisten; **~ one's articles** in der Lehre (Ausbildung) sein; **~ with a bankruptcy notice** Konkurseröffnungsbeschluß zustellen; **~ as collateral** als Deckung dienen; **~ with the colo(u)rs** Wehrdienst leisten; **~ on a committee** Ausschußmitglied sein, einem Ausschuß angehören; **~ copies** Abschriften zustellen; **~ one's country** seinem Lande dienen; **~ a customer** Kunden bedienen; **~ a customer with goods** Waren an einen Kunden liefern; **~ upon the debtor** dem Schuldner zustellen; **~ the defendant** Zustellung an den Beklagten vornehmen; **~ one's own ends** seinen eigenen Zwecken dienen; **~ as a gardener and as chauffeur** zugleich als Gärtner und Fahrer Dienst versehen; **~ as a guidance** als Richtlinie dienen; **~ s. o. heir to a property** j. in den Besitz einer Erbschaft setzen; **~ one's own interests** den eigenen Interessen dienen; **~ on a jury** als Geschworener fungieren; **~ a loan** Anleihe bedienen; **~ two masters** zweierlei Herren dienen; **~ as mayor** Bürgermeister sein; **~ notice on s. o.** jem. die Kündigung zustellen; **~ with a notice of a deed of arrangement** von einem Vergleichsabschluß in Kenntnis setzen; **~ notice of contribution and indemnity** Streit wegen mitwirkenden Verschuldens verkünden; **~ on the dependant a notice of discontinuance** dem Beklagten die Klagerücknahme anzeigen; **~ an office** Amt ausfüllen, Dienst tun; **~ s. o. out** es jem. heimzahlen; **~ overseas** im Ausland Dienst tun; **~ in the police** Polizeibeamter sein; **~ as a pretext** als Vorwand dienen; **~ a prison term** Freiheitsstrafe verbüßen; **~ some private ends** privaten Zwecken dienen; **~ a process on s. o.** jem. einen gerichtlichen Eröffnungsbeschluß zustellen; **~ the purpose** Zweck erfüllen; **~ out rations to the troops** Rationen an die Truppe ausgeben; **~ s. o. the same sauce** es jem. mit gleicher Münze heimzahlen; **~ in a shop** im Laden bedienen; **~ a sentence** Strafe absitzen; **~ s. o. with a summons** jem. eine Ladung zustellen; **~ a term under articles** *(Br.)* im Anwaltsbüro arbeiten; **~ a term of imprisonment** Gefängnisstrafe absitzen; **~ time** seine Strafe

verbüßen (absitzen); ~ **one's time** seine Lehrzeit durchmachen, seine Ausbildung absolvieren; ~ **the time** sich der Zeit anpassen; ~ **one's time of imprisonment** seine Freiheitsstrafe verbüßen; ~ **the town with gas** Stadt mit Gas versorgen; ~ **a warrant on s. o.** jem. eine gerichtliche Verfügung zustellen; ~ **with water** mit Wasser versorgen, an die Wasserleitung anschließen; ~ **a writ on s. o.** jem. einen Schriftsatz zustellen; ~ **a writ of attachment upon s. th.** etw. mit Beschlag belegen (pfänden).

served, to have ~ **one's apprenticeship** ausgelernt haben.

server, process Zustellungsbeamter.

service Dienst[leistung], Arbeitsleistung, Amtstätigkeit, *(attendance)* Bedienung, *(delivery of a writ)* Zustellung, *(drug store)* Dienstbereitschaft, *(machine)* Betrieb, *(mil.)* Wehrdienst, Dienstzeit, *(payment of interest)* Zinsendienst, *(public utilities)* Versorgung, *(for purchasers)* Kundendienst, kostenlose Dienstleistung, Service, *(railway)* [Strecken-, Linien-]verkehrsdienst, *(servant)* Stellung, Dienst, *(set of plates)* Gedeck; **15 per cent for** ~ 15% für die Bedienung;
at your ~ **at all times** stets zu Ihren Diensten; **in consideration of your** ~**s** in Berücksichtigung Ihrer Dienste für uns; **exempt from** ~ dienstfrei; **fit for** ~ dienstfähig; **liable for** ~ leistungspflichtig; **on active** ~ beim Bund, im Einsatz; **on Her Majesty's** ~ *(Br.)* portofrei, [etwa] frei durch Ablösung; **out of** ~ außer Betrieb; **ready for** ~ einsatzbereit; **retired from** ~ in Pension, außer Dienst; **unfit for** ~ dienstuntauglich; **within 2 weeks of** ~ binnen zwei Wochen nach Zustellung;
~**s** Dienstleistungsverkehr, *(wife)* Arbeitsleistung, -kraft;
~ **abroad** Auslandsdienst; **accepted** ~ angenommene Ersatzzustellung; **accessorial** ~**s** zusätzliche Dienstleistungen; **accounting** ~ Buchprüfungsdienst, Revisionstätigkeit; **active** ~ Militärdienst; **administrative** ~ Verwaltungstätigkeit; **advisory** ~ beratende Tätigkeit; **after-sales** ~ Kundendienst; **air** ~ Luftverkehr; **air-mail** ~ Luftpostverkehr; **airspeeded** ~ Luftpostbeförderung; **armed** ~**s** *(mil.)* Streitkräfte; **base** ~**s** untergeordnete Dienste; **built-in-maid** ~ Übernahme von Aufgaben des Verbraucherhaushalts; **burial** ~ Begräbnisfeier; **bus** ~ Omnibusverkehr, -verbindung; **car** ~ Wagenpflege; **career** ~ Berufsbeamtentum; **cartage** ~ Rollfuhrdienst; **civil** ~ *(Br.)* Staats-, Verwaltungs-, öffentlicher Dienst; **classified** ~ gehobener Dienst; **clerical** ~ Bürotätigkeit; **collection** ~ Inkassotätigkeit; **conspicuous** ~ hervorragende Dienste; **constructive** ~ *(process)* Ersatzzustellung; **consular** ~ Konsulatsdienst; **contract** ~**s** vertraglich festgelegte Kundendienstleistungen; **contributing** ~ [auf die Pension] anrechnungsfähige Dienstzeit; **curb** ~ Bedienung im Auto; **customer** ~ Kundendienst; **customs** ~ Zolldienst; **debt** ~ Schuldendienst; **delivery** ~ Zustelldienst; **diplomatic** ~ diplomatischer Dienst; **direct** ~**s** Dienstleistungen ohne Zwischenschaltung eines Produktionsbetriebes, *(process)* unmittelbare (persönliche) Zustellung; **divine** ~ Gottesdienst; **door-to-door airport limousine** ~ Flugplatzabholdienst; **due** ~ *(of a writ)* ordnungsgemäße Zustellung; **electric** ~ elektrischer Betrieb; **emergency** ~ Behelfs-, Bereitschaftsdienst; **eminent** ~**s** hervorragende Dienste; **essential** ~**s** lebenswichtige Betriebe, lebenswichtige Versorgungseinrichtungen; **excellent** ~ ausgezeichnete Bedienung; **express delivery** ~ *(Br.)* Eilzustellung; **faithful** ~**s** treue Dienste; **field** ~ Außendienst, *(mil.)* Frontdienst; **the fighting** ~**s** Streitkräfte; **fiscal** ~ Finanztätigkeit; **foreign** ~ *(US)* auswärtiger Dienst; **freight** ~ Frachtverkehr; **full** ~ *(process)* vollständige Zustellung; **funeral** ~ Trauergottesdienst; **gas** ~ Gasversorgung; **government** ~ Staatsdienst; **gratuitous** ~ unentgeltliche Dienste, Kundendienst; **guest-related** ~ auf Gäste eingestellter Dienstleistungsbetrieb; **hard** ~ schwerer Dienst; **honorary** ~ ehrenamtliche Tätigkeit; **24-hour** ~ Vierundzwanzigstunden-, Tag- und Nachtdienst; **indoor** ~ Innendienst; **inferior** ~**s** untergeordnete Dienste; **intelligence** ~ Geheim-, Nachrichtendienst; **intergroup** ~**s** konzerninterne Leistungen; **line** ~ *(railway)* Außendienst; **lip** ~ Lippenbekenntnis; **loan** ~ Anleihedienst; **local line** ~ Zubringerdienst; **long** ~ langjährige Dienstzeit; **mail** ~ Postzustellung; **marriage** ~ Traugottesdienst; **military** ~ *(mil.)* Dienstpflicht; **omnibus** ~ Omnibusverkehr; **municipal** ~**s** städtische Einrichtungen; **national** ~ *(Br.)* Militärdienst, Wehrpflicht; **night** ~ Nachtdienst; **on-the-spot** ~ Kundendienst an Ort und Stelle; **outdoor** ~ Außendienst; **passenger** ~ Personenverkehr; **past** ~**s** geleistete Dienste; **personal** ~ persönliche Dienstleistungen, *(of a writ)* persönliche Zustellung; **dependent personal** ~ *(double taxation agreement)* unselbständige Arbeit; **phone-and-delivery** ~ telefonischer Bestell- und Lieferbetrieb; **pick-up [and delivery]** ~ Rollfuhrdienst; **postal** ~ Postzustellung, -verkehr; **good postal** ~ gute Postverbindungen; **pre-sales** ~ Service vor Verkaufsabschluß; **press** ~ Pressedienst; **professional** ~**s** freiberufliche Tätigkeit; **prompt** ~ schnelle Bedienung; **proper** ~ *(writ)* ordnungsgemäße Zustellung; **public** ~ *(US)* Staatsdienst; **qualified** ~**s** Dienste höherer Art; **poor railroad** ~ *(US)* schlechte Eisenbahnverbindung; **railway** ~ *(Br.)* Eisenbahnverkehr; **regular** ~ turnusmäßiger Dienst, *(transportation)* regelmäßiger Verkehrsdienst; **regular twenty-four-hour** ~ ganztägiger (durchgehender) Betrieb; ~**s rendered** Dienstleistung, geleistete Dienste; **return** ~ Gegendienst; **religious** ~ Gottesdienst; **reproductive** ~ werbende Dienstleistungen; **salvage** ~ Seenotdienst; **scheduled** ~ *(US)* Linienflugdienst; **secretarial** ~ Bürotätigkeit; **self-** Selbstbedienungsrestaurant; **self-supported** ~ sich selbst tragender Dienstleistungsbetrieb; **shipping** ~ Schiffahrtsverkehr; **shuttle** ~ Pendelverkehr; **store-door** ~ Hauszustellung; **substituted** ~ *(of a writ)* Ersatzzustellung; **supervisory** ~ Überwachungstätigkeit; **take-out** ~ Lieferung frei Haus; **tax-supported** ~ durch Steuern mitfinanzierter Dienstleistungsbetrieb; **technical** ~ technischer Dienst; **telegraph** ~ Telegrafenverkehr; **telephone** ~ Telefonverkehr; **train** ~ Zugverkehr, -folge; **twenty-minute** ~ Zwanzig-Minuten-Verkehr; **public utility** ~**s** Dienstleistungen öffentlicher Versorgungsbetriebe; **valuable** ~ wertvolle Dienste; **veteran** ~ langjährige Dienste; **water** ~ Wasserversorgung; ~ **by advertisement in the press** öffentliche Zustellung; ~**s provided by public authorities** öffentliche Dienste und Dienstleistungen im öffentlichen Interesse; ~ **of capital** Kapitaldienst; ~ **with the colo(u)rs** aktive Dienstzeit; ~ **of complaint** Beschwerdezustellung; ~**s to one's country** Verdienste um sein Vaterland; ~ **of custodianship** *(US)* Depotverwaltung; ~ **to customers** Kundendienst; ~ **of debts** Schuldendienst; ~ **of foreign debts** Auslandsschuldendienst; ~ **in the field** Kriegsdienst; ~ **at the front** Frontdienst; ~ **of a garnishee order** Zustellung eines Pfändungs- und Überweisungsbeschlusses; ~ **under a guarantee** Garantieinanspruchnahme; ~ **of an heir** *(Scot.)* Erbenanerkennung; ~ **at home** Inlandsdienst; ~ **of a loan** Anleihedienst; ~ **by mail** *(US)* **(post,** *Br.*) Zustellung durch die Post, Postzustellung; ~ **of notice** Zustellung einer Erklärung, Zustellung einer Kündigung, *(company meeting)* Ladungszustellung; ~ **of legal proceedings** Zustellung im Zivilprozeß; ~ **of process** Zustellung von Gerichtsdokumenten, Klagezustellung; **constructive** ~ **of process** Ersatzzustellung; ~ **by publication** *(US)* öffentliche Zustellung; ~ **to the state** dem Staat geleistete Dienste; ~ **to stockowners** *(US)* Aktionärspflege; ~ **of trains** Zugverkehr; ~ **of value** wertvolle Dienste; ~ **of a writ of summons** Klage-, Ladungszustellung;
~ *(v.)* instandhalten, versorgen, Pflegedienst übernehmen;
~ **over $ 5 m in debts** Schuldendienstverpflichtungen von über 5 Millionen Dollar haben; ~ **its massive debt** massierte Schuldentilgungen vornehmen;
to accept ~ *(Br.)* Ersatzzustellung annehmen; **to add 10 per cent to the bill for** ~ 10% Bedienungszuschlag auf die Rechnung setzen; **to ask s. o. [for] a** ~ jem. um Unterstützung bitten; **to be at s. one's** ~ jem. zur Verfügung stehen; **to be in s. one's** ~ in jds. Diensten stehen; **to be in the civil** ~ *(Br.)* Staatsbeamter (in der öffentlichen Verwaltung tätig) sein, im Beamtenverhältnis stehen; **to be in the customs** ~ Zollbeamter sein, dem Zolldienst angehören; **to be out of** ~ *(car)* aus dem Betrieb gezogen sein; **to be introduced into regular** ~ in den Fahrplan aufgenommen werden; **to begin commercial** ~ Dienstbetrieb aufnehmen; **to build a** ~ **to a peak of efficiency** Dienstleistungsbetrieb zu hundertprozentiger Leistungsfähigkeit bringen; **to buy a television with** ~ **for six months** Fernsehgerät mit halbjähriger Garantie kaufen; **to come into** ~ Dienstbetrieb aufnehmen, **(ship)** in Dienst gestellt werden; **to conduct a** ~ Gottesdienst abhalten; **to contribute one's** ~**s** seine Arbeitskraft einbringen; **to cut back** ~ Dienstbetriebe einschränken; **to do s. o. a** ~ jem. eine Gefälligkeit erweisen; **to do one's national** ~ *(Br.)* seiner Militärpflicht genügen; **to effect** ~ *(writ)* zustellen; **to enter** ~ Dienst antreten; **to enter the diplomatic** ~ ins Auswärtige Amt eintreten; **to extend tailor-made** ~**s** auf den einzelnen Kunden zugeschnittene Dienstleistungen ausweiten; **to give good** ~ gute Arbeit leisten; **to give only lip** ~ nur ein Lippenbekenntnis ablegen; **to give regular** ~ **to ...** Linienflugdienst nach ... unterhalten; **to go into** ~ sich verdingen, Hausangestellte werden, *(bus, ship)* in Dienst gestellt werden, *(machinery)* in Betrieb genommen werden; **to have seen much** ~ altgedient sein; **to have one's car** ~**d regularly** sein Auto laufend zum Kundendienst (zur Inspektion) bringen; **to launch new** ~**s** neue Dienstleistungen übernehmen; **to leave the** ~ [aus dem Amt] ausscheiden; **to make use of s. one's** ~**s** von jds. Angebot Gebrauch machen, jds. Dienste beanspruchen (in Anspruch nehmen); **to market a** ~ Dienstleistung anbieten; **to need the** ~**s of a lawyer** eines

Rechtsanwalts bedürfen; **to offer one's ~s to s. o.** jem. seine Dienste anbieten; **to opt for alternative ~** *(mil.)* sich für den Ersatzdienst entscheiden; **to pay for ~s** Dienste belohnen; **to perform ~s vicariously** Dienstleistung durch einen Erfüllungsgehilfen erbringen; **to place s. th. at s. one's ~** jem. etw. zur Verfügung stellen; **to press into ~** dienstverpflichten; **to price one's ~ freely** seine Dienstleistungsgebühr unabhängig festlegen; **to provide with intelligent ~** nutzbringenden Service leisten, guten Kundendienst haben; **to put a bus (ship) into ~** Omnibus (Schiff) in Dienst stellen; **to reenter s. one's ~** wieder in jds. Dienste eintreten; **to render s. o. a ~** jem. einen Dienst leisten (eine Dienstleistung erbringen); **to render s. o. a ~ in return** jem. einen Gegendienst leisten; **to retire from ~** aus dem Dienst scheiden, in den Ruhestand treten; **to run joint ~s** gemeinsam betreiben; **to see ~** Kriegsdienst tun; **to sell one's ~ country-wide** seine Tätigkeit über das ganze Land ausdehnen; **to send the car in for ~ every 3000 miles** Auto alle 5000 km zur Inspektion bringen; **to take ~** sich verdingen; **to take s. o. into one's ~** j. als Hausangestellte[n] einstellen; **to take out of ~** aus dem Verkehr ziehen; **to remunerate s. o. for his ~s** j. für seine Dienste entlohnen; **to tender one's ~s** jem. seine Dienste anbieten;

~ agreement Dienstvertrag, -vereinbarung, Dienstleistungsabkommen; **~ allowance** *(agency)* Dienstleistungsrabatt; **~ apportionments** Pensionszuschüsse; **~ area** *(broadcasting)* Sendebereich, *(motorway)* Raststättengebiet, *(town gas)* Versorgungs-, Liefergebiet; **~ balance** Dienstleistungsbilanz; **~ box** *(el.)* Hauptanschluß; **personal ~ business** *(US)* Dienstleistungsgeschäft; **~ business undertaking** Dienstleistungsbetrieb; **~ call** *(tel.)* Dienstgespräch; **~ capacity** Leistungs-, Produktionsfähigkeit; **~ carrier** Dienstleistungsträger; **~ center** *(US)* **(centre, Br.)** Reparaturwerkstätte; **~ charge** Forderung für geleistete Dienste, Unkosten-, Dienstleistungsgebühr, *(banking)* Vermittlungs-, Bearbeitungsgebühr, *(investment trust)* Verwaltungsgebühr, *(restaurant)* Bedienungszuschlag, Trinkgeld; **~ club** gemeinnütziger Verein; **~ commitments** Leistungszusagen; **~ company** *(mil.)* Versorgungskompanie; **public ~ company (corporation, enterprise,** US) Dienstleistungsbetrieb; **~ compartment** Dienstabteil; **~ concept** Kundendienstkonzept; **~ contract** Arbeits-, Dienstvertrag; **company ~ contract** *(Br.)* Heuervertrag; **~ control** Dienstaufsicht; **~ costs** Dienstleistungskosten, *(balance)* abschreibungsfähige Kosten; **future ~ cost** *(pension scheme)* in der Zukunft zu erdienende Versorgungsleistungen; **past ~ cost** *(pension scheme)* nicht fundierte Verbindlichkeiten; **to transfer one's ~ credits** seine zusätzlichen Sozialansprüche abtreten; **~ department** Hilfsbetrieb, *(shop)* Kundendienstabteilung; **~ depot** Außen-, Zweig-, Kundendienststelle, *(car)* Reparaturlager; **~ dress** *(mil.)* Dienstanzug; **~ earnings** Erträge des Dienstleistungsbereichs; **~ economy** Dienstleistungsindustrie; **~ elevator** *(hotel)* Gepäckaufzug; **~ employment** Beschäftigung in der Dienstleistungsindustrie; **~ engineer** Wartungsingenieur, *(television)* Fernsehtechniker; **~ enterprise** *(US)* Dienstleistungsbetrieb, -unternehmen; **~ entrance** Dienstboteneingang; **~ establishment** Dienstleistungsbetrieb; **~ expense** Dienstaufwand; **~ families** Militärangehörige; **~ fee** Zustellungsgebühr, *(agency)* Dienstleistungsgebühr, Agenturgütung; **~ field** Dienstleistungsbereich; **~ flat** *(Br.)* Etagenwohnung mit Bedienung; **~ functions** Betreuungsaufgaben; **~ garage** *(car)* Kundendienstzentrum; **~ grade** Lieferbereitschaftsgrad; **~ hatch** Durchreiche; **~ industries** Dienstleistungsbetriebe, -industrien, -gewerbe; **~ institution** Dienstleistungseinrichtung; **~ instructions** Betriebsvorschriften, Bedienungsanweisung; **~ job** Dienstleistungsberuf; **~ lease** *(US)* Maschinen-, Pacht- und Wartungsvertrag; **~ life** Dienstzeit, *(asset, Br.)* Verwendungs-, Nutzungs-, Lebensdauer; **~ line** *(mil.)* Dienstleitung; **~ machine** *(mil.)* Militärflugzeug; **~ mark** *(US)* Dienstleistungsmarke; **~ medal** Dienstauszeichnung; **~ occupations** Dienstleistungsberufe; **~ office** Dienstleistungsfunktion; **~ organization** *(US)* gemeinnütziger Verein; **~ output depreciation method** Abschreibung auf Basis der erbrachten Leistung; **~ packaging** Werbematerial für Dienstleistungsbetriebe; **~ pattern** Dienstleistungsstruktur; **~ pay** *(mil.)* Wehrsold; **~ pension** Beamtenpension; **~ period** Dienstzeit; **~ period for annuities** anrechnungsfähige Dienstzeit für die Pensionsberechnung; **~ potential** Dienstleistungspotential; **~ provisions** Fürsorgebestimmungen; **~ qualifications** Einstellungsvoraussetzungen für den öffentlichen Dienst; **~ rating (review)** Leistungseinstufung, -beurteilung, analyse; **~ record** *(mil.)* Führungszeugnis; **~ regulations** Dienstvorschriften, *(railway)* Betriebsvorschriften, *(mil.)* Dienstordnung; **~ report** Eignungsbericht; **~ re-**

quirements Betriebserfordernisse; **~ retirement allowance** Pensionszuschuß; **~ road** Verkehrsstraße, -weg; **~ sector** Dienstleistungsbereich, -sektor; **~ space (ship)** Wirtschaftsraum; **~ squad** fliegende Arbeitskolonne; **~ staff** Beamtenkörper, Dienstpersonal; **~ station** Autoreparaturwerkstätte, Kundendienstwerkstatt, *(radio)* Reparaturwerkstatt, *(US)* Tankstelle, Hilfsdienst für Autofahrer; **~-station dealer** *(US)* Tankstellenbesitzer; **~ store** Dienstleistungsbetrieb; **~ stripe** *(mil., US)* Dienstalterstreifen; **~ system** Dienstleistungssystem; **~ times** Bedienungszeiten; **~ trade** Dienstleistungsgewerbe; **~ transactions** Dienstleistungsverkehr, -geschäft; **~ undertaking** Dienstleistungsbetrieb; **~ uniform** *(mil.)* Dienstanzug; **~ unit** *(balance sheet)* Gebrauchseinheit; **~ utility** Nutzeffekt persönlicher Dienstleistungen; **~ van** Versorgungsfahrzeug; **~ vehicle** Dienstauto, -wagen; **~ voter** *(Br.)* Wehrdienst leistender Wähler; **~ wholesaler** Effektivgroßhändler; **~ widow** Beamtenwitwe; **~ work** Betriebsfürsorge; **~ workers** in Dienstleistungsbetrieben Beschäftigte; **~-yield basis [of depreciation]** Abschreibungsberechnungsgrundlage.

serviceable *(durable)* dauerhaft, leistungsfähig, *(ready for service)* betriebsfertig, *(useful)* einsatz-, gebrauchsfähig, brauchbar, nutzbar, nützlich, dienlich;
~ clothes for school strapazierfähige Schulkeidung; **in a ~ condition** in gebrauchfähigem Zustand.

serviceableness Verwendbar-, Dienlichkeit.

serviceman Einberufener.

servicing *(US)* Kundendienst, Wartung;
~ of customers Kundenbedienung; **~ one's debt** Schuldentilgungsdienst; **~ of government debt** Staatsschuldendienst; **~ of loans** Anleihedienst;
~ aircraft Flugzeugwartung; **~ arrangement** Kundendienstregelung.

servient *(real estate)* belastet;
~ land (tenement) dienendes Grundstück.

serving Zustellung, *(shop)* Bedienung;
~ of a sentence Verbüßung einer Freiheitsstrafe.

servitude *(coercion)* Zwangsarbeit, *(easement, Scot., US)* Dienstbarkeit, Nutzungsrecht, Nutznießung;
affirmative ~ positive Dienstbarkeit; **international ~s** Staatsdienstbarkeiten; **involuntary ~** Zwangsarbeit; **landed (real) ~** Realservitut, Grunddienstbarkeit; **negative ~** negative Dienstbarkeit; **penal ~** *(Br.)* Zuchthaus; **personal ~** höchstpersönliches Recht, beschränkt persönliche Dienstbarkeit; **positive ~** positive Dienstbarkeit; **real ~** Grunddienstbarkeit; **urban ~** städtische Dienstbarkeit.

servo│-assisted brake Servobremse; **~ control** Servolenkung; **~ control mechanism** Servolenkung; **~ motor** Hilfsmotor.

session Sitzung, Tagung, Versammlung, Konferenz, *(course)* [Unterrichts]stunde, Kursus, *(court of law)* Gerichtssitzung, *(length of sitting)* Sitzungsdauer, *(parliament)* Sitzungsperiode, *(sl.)* gesellschaftliche Veranstaltung, *(stock exchange)* Börsentag, *(term)* Sitzungsperiode, *(university, Br.)* Studienjahr, akademisches Jahr, *(US)* Kurzsemester;
in ~ während der Sitzung; **in full ~** vor dem Plenum;
autumn ~ Sonder-, Herbstsitzung; **budget ~** Haushaltsberatungen; **closed ~** nichtöffentliche Sitzung; **closing ~** Schlußsitzung; **emergency ~** Notstands-, Krisensitzung, Sitzung eines Krisenstabes; **full ~** Plenarsitzung, Plenum; **general ~s** *(Br.)* Strafgericht; **jam ~** *(sl.)* gesellschaftliche Veranstaltung; **joint ~** *(parl.)* gemeinsame Sitzung; **long ~** lange Konferenz; **morning ~** Vormittagssitzung; **on-the-run ~** Sitzung im Vorbeigehen; **opening [day] ~** Eröffnungssitzung; **parliamentary ~** *(Br.)* Legislaturperiode; **permanent ~** Dauersitzung; **petty ~** *(Br.)* Schnellgericht; **plenary ~** Plenarsitzung, Plenum; **post-election ~** Nachwahlperiode; **private ~** Klausurtagung; **quarter ~s** [etwa] Schöffengericht; **recording ~** *(tapes)* Aufnahmedauer; **regular ~** turnusmäßige Sitzung; **secret ~** Geheimsitzung, -konferenz; **special ~** außerordentliche Sitzung, Sondertermin; **summer ~** *(US)* Sommersemester; **tidying-up ~** abschließende Sitzung;
♀ of Cases *(Scot.)* Urteils-, Entscheidungssammlung; **~ of a commission** Ausschußsitzung; **~ of a court** Gerichtssitzung; **~ of legislature** *(US)* Legislaturperiode; **~ of Parliament** Parlamentsitzung; **~ of the peace** *(Br.)* Gerichtstermin von Friedensrichtern;
to attend a ~ an einer Sitzung teilnehmen; **to be in ~** tagen, Sitzung abhalten; **to convoke a ~** Sitzung einberufen; **to go into secret ~** Geheimkonferenz abhalten; **to have a long ~** lange Sitzung abhalten; **to meet in regular ~s** zu regelmäßigen Tagungen zusammenkommen;
the court is in ~ das Gericht tagt.

sessional (*Br.*) für ein akademisches Jahr, (*parl.*) eine Legislaturperiode betreffend;

~ **course** (*Br.*) Jahreskursus für Erwachsene; ~ **expense allowance** Diäten; ~ **order (rule)** (*Br.*) für eine Legislaturperiode geltende Geschäftsordnung.

set (*apparatus*) Apparat, Ausrüstung, (*books*) mehrbändige Ausgabe, (*broadcasting receiver*) Rundfunk-, Fernsehempfänger, (*film*) Filmdekoration, Szenenaufbau, (*of goods*) Serie, Satz, Sortiment, Garnitur, Kollektion, (*machinery*) Aggregat, (*social group*) Gesellschaftsschicht, Kreis, Sippschaft, Klüngel, Clique, (*lease, Scot.*) Pacht, (*print.*) Drucksatz, (*production process*) Maschinenanlage, (*television*) Fernsehdekoration, (*theater*) Bühnenbild;

all-mains ~ Allstromgerät; **best** ~ Elite; **complete** ~ ganze Garnitur; **construction** ~ Baukasten; **elaborate** ~s (*theatre*) aufwendiges Bühnenbild; **fast** ~ Lebewelt; **literary** ~ literarischer Kreis, literarische Welt; **microvision** ~ Minifernseher; **our** ~ unsere Leute;

~ **of accounts** Buchungssystem; ~ **of articles** Artikelserie; ~ **of bills of exchange** Wechselserie, Satz Wechsel; **complete** ~ **of bills of lading** vollständiger Satz Konnossemente; ~ **of books** Büchersammlung; ~ **of circumstances** Tatumstände, -bestand; ~ **of colo(u)rs** Farbensortiment; ~ **of colo(u)r plates** Farbsatz; ~ **of contradictions** Kette von Widersprüchen; ~ **of crooks** Gaunerbande; ~ **of demands** Angebotssortiment; **full** ~ **of documents** vollständiger Satz Dokumente; ~ **of exchange** Satz Wechsel; ~ **of furniture** Möbelgarnitur; ~ **of houses** Häuserkomplex, -gruppe; ~ **of negotiations** Verhandlungsrunde; ~ **of numbers** Nummernserie; ~ **of public opinion** Tendenz der öffentlichen Meinung; ~ **of patterns** Musterkollektion; ~ **of rooms** Zimmerflucht; ~ **of stamps** Satz Briefmarken; ~ **of thieves** Diebesbande; ~ **of the tide** Richtung der öffentlichen Meinung, Meinungsrichtung; ~ **of tools** Handwerkszeug; ~s **in use** eingeschaltete Empfänger; ~ **of works** mehrbändige Ausgabe;

~ (*v.*) (*dating*) anberaumen, festsetzen, festlegen, bestimmen, (*theater*) mit Requisiten ausstatten;

~ **one's affairs in order** seine Angelegenheiten in Ordnung bringen (regeln); ~ **the alarm clock** Wecker stellen; ~ **the axe to** Axt an etw. legen; ~ **one back** (*US sl.*) einen Zahn zurückstecken; ~ **a book on the shelf** Buch aufs Regal stellen; ~ **books to be read** Leselektüre vorschreiben; ~ **books for a certificate** Studium bestimmter Bücher für die Erlangung eines Scheins obligatorisch machen; ~ **a copy** [als Muster] vorschreiben; ~ **an early date** frühes Datum setzen; ~ **a day** Termin anberaumen; ~ **an engine going** Maschine in Gang bringen; ~ **one's face against** heftig opponieren; ~ **s. o. on his feet** (*fig.*) jem. finanziell wieder auf die Beine helfen; ~ **on fire** in Brand setzen, anzünden; ~ **free** (*capital*) flüssig machen; ~ **s. o. free** j. auf freien Fuß setzen; ~ **going** in Gang setzen; ~ **one's hand to a document** Urkunde unterzeichnen; ~ **one's hands to a task** Sache in Angriff nehmen; ~ **s. one's heart at ease** j. beruhigen; ~ **one's heart on becoming an engineer** mit allen Kräften auf den Ingenieurberuf zusteuern; ~ **one's heart on moneymaking** nur ans Geldverdienen denken; ~ **one's house in order** Reformen durchführen; ~ **s. o. a job** jem. eine Aufgabe stellen; ~ **o. s. to finish a job by the end of the month** sich selbst das Monatsende als Schlußtermin für eine Aufgabe setzen; ~ **a judge at defiance** den Anordnungen eines Richters nicht nachkommen; ~ **the law at defiance** Gesetz mißachten; ~ **s. o. at liberty** j. in Freiheit setzen; ~ **one's life on a chance** sein Leben aufs Spiel setzen; ~ **people at loggerheads** Leute durcheinanderbringen; ~ **machinery going** Betrieb beginnen; ~ **one's name to a document** Urkunde unterschreiben; ~ **the pace** Beispiel geben, Marschrichtung angeben; ~ **the papers for an examination** Examensfragen ausarbeiten; ~ **a pattern** Musterbeispiel geben; ~ **pen to paper** mit dem Schreiben beginnen; ~ **a period of time** Frist setzen; ~ **a precedent** Präzedenzfall schaffen; ~ **a price on s. th.** etw. preislich auszeichnen, Preis für etw. festsetzen; ~ **the price of a house** Verkaufspreis für ein Haus festsetzen; ~ **a prisoner free** Gefangenen freilassen; ~ **a prize (price) on s. one's head** Belohnung auf jds. Ergreifung aussetzen; ~ **s. o. a difficult problem** jem. die Lösung einer schwierigen Frage übertragen; ~ **before the public** vor die Öffentlichkeit bringen; **not to** ~ **the river (Thames) on fire** das Pulver nicht erfunden haben; ~ **sail** auslaufen, abfahren; ~ **one's seal** sein Siegel anbringen; ~ **seal to a document** Urkunde siegeln; ~ **solid** kompreß setzen; ~ **spies on s. o.** j. bespitzeln; ~ **one's signature** seine Unterschrift setzen; ~ **store by** für wertvoll halten; ~ **no (little) store by s. th.** einer Sache keinen (geringen) Wert beimessen; ~ **a task** Aufgabe stellen; ~ **one's teeth** (*fig.*) fest zu etw.

entschlossen sein; ~ **the Thames on fire** Wunder vollbringen; ~ **a trap for s. o.** jem. eine Falle stellen; ~ **one's trust in s. o.** Vertrauen in j. setzen; ~ **one's watch by the time signal on the radio** seine Uhr nach dem Rundfunk stellen; ~ **s. o. on his way** j. ein Stück Weges begleiten; ~ **the wedding day** Hochzeitstag festsetzen; ~ **one's wits to** sich an die Lösung eines Problems machen; ~ **to work** sich energisch an die Arbeit machen.

set|**about** (*v.*) **one's packing** mit dem Packen anfangen; ~ **a rumo(u)r about** Gerüchte in die Welt setzen; ~ **s. o. about a task** j. an eine Arbeit setzen.

set apart (*v.*) beiseitelegen, reservieren, bestimmen für, (*bankruptcy*) aussondern;

~ **funds for a purpose** Sonderfonds einrichten; ~ **so much out of one's savings** bestimmten Betrag von seinen Ersparnissen nehmen; ~ **a tenth of one's salary each month** jeden Monat ein Zehntel des Gehalts abzweigen.

set aside (*v.*) (*annul*) außer Kraft setzen, annullieren, für unwirksam (nichtig) erklären, (*exclude*) absondern, (*money*) beiseite legen;

~ **an agreement** Vertrag für ungültig erklären; ~ **an amount** Betrag absetzen; ~ **clearly** absondern; ~ **a claim** Klage abweisen; ~ **a composition** Vergleich aufheben; ~ **all formalities** alle Formalitäten weglassen; ~ **a part of one's income** Teil seines Einkommens zurücklegen; ~ **a judgment** Urteil aufheben; ~ **an offer** Angebot ablehnen; ~ **a will** Testament für ungültig erklären.

set back (*v.*)|**all efforts at reform** alle Reformanstrengungen zunichte machen; ~ **s. o. back a fiver** j. fünf Pfund kosten; ~ **a house from the street** Hausfront von der Straße zurücknehmen; ~ **s. one's interests** jds. Interessen nicht berücksichtigen.

set by (*v.*) zurücklegen, sparen.

set down (*v.*) schriftlich niederlegen, niederschreiben, aufzeichnen;

~ **to s. one's account** auf jds. Rechnung setzen; ~ **a case for hearing (trial)** Termin zur mündlichen Verhandlung anberaumen; ~ **s. o. at the corner of the street** j. an der Straßenecke absetzen; ~ **o. s. down in a hotel register** Berufsangabe bei der Hotelanmeldung vornehmen; ~ **s. o. down for a job** j. für einen Posten vorsehen; ~ **o. s. down as a journalist** als Berufsbezeichnung Journalist angeben; ~ **a meeting for the 15th** Sitzungstermin auf den 15. anberaumen; ~ **a name** Namen eintragen; ~ **passengers** Passagiere aussteigen lassen; ~ **one's success to hard work** seinen Erfolg harter Arbeit zuschreiben; ~ **in writing** schriftlich niederlegen (fixieren).

set forth (*v.*) vortragen, -bringen, dartun, offen darlegen;

~ **conditions in a contract** Vertragsbestimmungen festlegen; ~ **the grounds** Gründe vorbringen; ~ **on a journey** Reise antreten; ~ **a proposal** Vorschlag vorbringen; ~ **reasons** begründen, Gründe vorbringen; ~ **a theory** Theorie darlegen; ~ **one's political views** seine politischen Ansichten vortragen.

set in (*v.*) (*crisis*) sich einstellen, (*merchant*) sich als Kaufmann niederlassen, (*season*) einsetzen, beginnen;

~ **action (into operation)** in Gang setzen, in Betrieb nehmen.

set off (*v.*) (*Br.*) an-, aufrechnen, in Gegenrechnung bringen, gegen einen Anspruch validieren;

~ **a claim in an action** im Prozeß Aufrechnung geltend machen; ~ **a gain against a loss** Gewinn mit einem Verlust verrechnen; ~ **one item against the other** Posten gegen einen anderen aufrechnen; ~ **on a journey round the world** zu einer Weltreise starten; ~ **a portion of an estate** Teil eines Nachlasses zurückbekommen; ~ **s. o. off talking on his pet subject** j. zum Reden über sein Lieblingsthema bringen (bewegen).

set out (*v.*) ausführlich darlegen, auseinandersetzen, detailliert beschreiben, (*goods*) Ware auslegen, (*pleading*) vortragen;

~ **the circumstances in which the insurance is operative** versicherte Gefahrenumstände detailliert festlegen; ~ **goods on a stall** auf einem Stand Waren zur Schau stellen; ~ **on a journey** Reise antreten; ~ **one's reasons** seine Gründe darlegen; ~ **to break a record** Rekord brechen wollen.

set over (*v.*) übertragen, transferieren.

set to (*v.*) sich dranmachen (dahinterklemmen).

set up (*v.*) errichten, ins Leben rufen, (*auction*) zur Auktion bringen, (*in business*) sich etablieren, sich selbständig machen, sich als Kaufmann niederlassen, (*found*) gründen, stiften, (*machine*) zusammenbauen, -setzen, aufstellen, (*in pleading*) geltend machen, vorbringen, einwenden, entgegensetzen, (*print.*) absetzen, (*railway*) Strecke freimachen, (*restore after illness*) Erholung bringen;

~ **for o. s.** sich etablieren (niederlassen); ~ **one's abode** seinen Wohnsitz begründen; ~ **an account** Konto eröffnen; ~ **s. o. up again** j. finanziell wieder auf die Beine helfen; ~ **a false alibi** falsches Alibi vorbringen; ~ **an assembly plant** Montagewerk errichten; ~ **as a bookseller** sich als Buchhändler niederlassen; ~ **a new branch** neue Zweigstelle eröffnen; ~ **breach of contract** sich auf Vertragsbruch berufen; ~ **a building** Gebäude errichten; ~ **a business** Geschäft aufmachen; ~ **o. s. up in business** eigenes Geschäft gründen; ~ **s. o. up in business** j. [geschäftlich] etablieren; ~ **a candidate** Kandidaten aufstellen; ~ **a claim** Forderung erheben, Anspruch erheben; ~ **a committee [of inquiry]** [Untersuchungs]ausschuß einsetzen; ~ **a company** Gesellschaft gründen; ~ **competition** Konkurrenz machen; ~ **a condition** Bedingung stellen; ~ **a counterclaim** Gegenforderung erheben; ~ **a court of inquiry** Untersuchungsausschuß einsetzen; ~ **a day** Termin anberaumen (festsetzen); ~ **a defence** *(pleading)* Einrede geltend machen, Einwendung vorbringen, *(trial)* Verteidigungslinie aufbauen; ~ **a good defence** gute Verteidigung vorbringen; ~ **a fashion** Mode kreieren (einführen); ~ **a new firm** neue Firma gründen; ~ **for o. s.** sich selbständig machen; ~ **s. o. up in funds** j. mit Geldmitteln versehen; ~ **a house** in ein Haus ziehen; ~ **housekeeping** seinen Hausstand gründen; ~ **an inquiry** Untersuchung einleiten; ~ **invalidity** Ungültigkeit geltend machen; ~ **o. s. up as a lawyer** sich als Rechtsanwalt niederlassen; ~ **a manufactory** Fabrikationsbetrieb errichten; ~ **a manuscript** Manuskript absetzen; ~ **a monument** Denkmal errichten; ~ **a new opinion** moderne Ansicht zur Diskussion stellen; ~ **recruits** Rekruten drillen; ~ **a reign of terror** Schreckensherrschaft begründen; ~ **reserves** Rückstellungen bilden (vornehmen); ~ **ridiculous pretensions** groteske Forderungen stellen; ~ **for public sale** zum Verkauf ausstellen; ~ **a school** Schule gründen; ~ **shop** Laden eröffnen, sich niederlassen; ~ **a son in a trade** seinem Sohn ein Geschäft errichten; ~ **the standard of a revolt** zum Bannerträger eines Aufruhrs werden; ~ **the statute of limitations** Verjährung einwenden; ~ **a tribunal** Gericht einsetzen; ~ **type** Satz vorbereiten, satzfertig machen.

set upon being a test pilot auf jeden Fall Einflieger werden wollen.

set, to be all ~ to do *(fam.)* fest entschlossen sein; **to be hard ~ in** bedrängter Lage sein; **to be drawn in ~s of three** in drei Exemplaren ausgestellt sein; **to fit a new ~ of tyres on a car** Auto neu bereifen; **to have ~** *(fame)* Kulminationspunkt überschritten haben; **to issue a bill in a ~ of three** Wechsel in dreifacher Ausfertigung ausstellen;

~ *(a.)* festgesetzt, -stehend, bestimmt, gebräuchlich; **all ~** startklar;

~ **aside** *(US)* [Lebensmittel]reservefonds; **at a ~ date** zu einem bestimmten Termin; **at the ~ day** am festgesetzten Tag; ~ **form** Muster, Formular; ~ **form of an oath** vorgeschriebene Eidesformel; ~ **opinion** feste Meinung; ~ **out** Aufmachung, Ausstattung; ~ **party** konventionelle Gesellschaft; **within the ~ period** fristgemäß; ~ **person** *(US)* sturer Mensch; ~ **phrases** feststehende Redewendungen; ~ **piece** Prunkstück; ~ **prices** feste Preise; ~ **speech** ausgearbeitete Rede; ~**-up man** guter Mann; ~ **visit** förmlicher Besuch; ~ **work** Serienfabrikat.

setback Rückschlag, Rückgang, Rückschritt, *(building code)* zurückgesetzte Gebäudefront, *(stock exchange)* Einbruch, Rückschlag, Verschlechterung;
business ~ Konjunkturrückschlag; **commercial ~** wirtschaftlicher Rückschlag; **temporary ~** vorübergehender Rückschlag; ~ **in production** Produktionsrückgang;
to have (receive) a ~ in one's business geschäftlichen Rückschlag erleiden.

setdown Verweis, Zurechtweisung, *(full meal, sl.)* richtige Mahlzeit.

setoff *(balancing item)* Ausgleichsposten, *(counterclaim)* Gegenforderung, -rechnung, -wert, *(counterpoise)* Ausgleich, *(squaring of accounts)* Aufrechnung;
as a ~ for damaged goods als Ersatz für beschädigte Ware; ~ **for interest purposes** Verrechnung aus Zinsgründen; **to pay a premium as a ~ to a small rental** Prämie zum Ausgleich für geringe Pacht zahlen; **to take as a ~** als Gegenforderung benutzen; ~ **item** Gegenposten; ~ **paper** Makulaturpapier.

setout Arrangement, *(social life)* geselliges Beisammensein, Gesellschaft.

setter Setzer, *(vulgar)* Polizeispitzel; **type ~** Schriftsetzer.

setting Einsetzen, *(jewelry)* Fassung, *(film)* Ausstattung, *(machine)* Sockel, *(novel)* Schauplatz, Situation, Handlungsraum, *(photo)* Blendeneinstellung, *(print.)* Satz, *(scale)* Einstellung, *(surrounding)* Milieu, Umgebung, *(theater)* Bühnenbild; ~ **apart** Bereitstellung; ~ **aside** Absonderung, *(claims)* Zurückweisung, Verwerfung; ~ **aside of a deed** Annullierung einer

Urkunde; ~ **aside of a trust** Aufhebung eines Treuhandverhältnisses; ~ **an award aside** Aufhebung eines Schiedsspruchs; ~ **down a case for trial** Terminanberaumung; ~ **forth the reasons** Angabe der Gründe; ~ **free of capital** Flüssigmachung von Kapital; ~ **off** Abreise; ~ **out** Abreise; **first ~ out** erster Ausflug; ~ **the retail price** Bestimmung des Einzelhandelspreises; ~ **up** Etablierung, Errichtung, Gründung; ~ **up in business** Geschäftsgründung, Selbständigmachung; ~ **up of cells in a factory** Zellenbildung in einem Betrieb; ~**-up of a committee** Ausschußeinsetzung; ~**-up of a trust** Stiftungsvereinbarung;
to be ~ against a proposal *(public opinion)* gegen einen Vorschlag sein; **to give s. o. a ~ down** jem. einen scharfen Verweis erteilen; **to serve as the ~** als Rahmen dienen;

~ **cost** Einrichte-, Einstellungskosten; ~ **mistake** Satzfehler; ~ **rule** *(print.)* Setzlinie; ~**-up cost** Aufstellungskosten; ~ **up-time** Anlauf-, Einrichtezeit;

settle *(v.)* *(agree)* ab-, ausmachen, übereinkommen, vereinbaren, sich einigen, *(bestow)* aussetzen, übertragen, *(business)* erledigen, regeln, abwickeln, abschließen, *(buy plot of land)* sich ankaufen, *(clear)* bereinigen, berichtigen, *(compound with creditors)* sich vergleichen, [Gläubiger] abfinden, *(debt)* abgelten, abdecken, *(establish o. s. in business)* Geschäft gründen, sich geschäftlich niederlassen, sich etablieren, *(establish colonies)* kolonisieren, Kolonie errichten, *(house)* sich setzen, senken, *(insurance)* regulieren, *(liquidate)* abwickeln, liquidieren, *(make over)* übertragen, *(pay bill)* Rechnung bezahlen, begleichen, glattstellen, *(regulate)* regeln, ordnen, erledigen, *(take residence)* sich niederlassen, seinen Wohnsitz begründen;
~ **o. s.** sich ansässig machen; ~ **for s. o.** Rechnung für j. bezahlen;
~ **an account** Konto ausgleichen, Rechnung begleichen; ~ **one's accounts** seine Abrechnung machen; ~ **accounts with s. o.** *(fig.)* mit jem. abrechnen; ~ **an account on time** Rechnung pünktlich begleichen; ~ **one's affairs** seine Angelegenheiten ordnen; ~ **an affair amicably** sich gütlich einigen; ~ **an affair out of court** sich außergerichtlich vergleichen, ~ **an amount of compensation** Abfindung vereinbaren; ~ **an annuity** Rente aussetzen; ~ **by arbitration** schiedsgerichtlich beilegen; ~ **an argument** Streitfrage entscheiden; ~ **the average** Havariekosten (Dispache) aufmachen; ~ **a balance** Saldo ausgleichen; ~ **a bill** Rechnung begleichen (bezahlen); ~ **a bill of exceptions** Beschwerdeschrift billigen; ~ **a bill in full** Rechnung vollständig begleichen; ~ **a business** Geschäft abwickeln; ~ **one's son in business** seinen Sohn in der Wirtschaft unterbringen; ~ **a doubtful case** Zweifelsfall erledigen; ~ **a case out of court** Sache außergerichtlich vergleichen; ~ **one's children** seine Kinder versorgen; ~ **a claim** Anspruch befriedigen, *(insurance)* Versicherungsanspruch regulieren, Forderung (Anspruch) durchsetzen; ~ **commercial colonies** Handelskolonien errichten; ~ **by compromise** durch Vergleich erledigen; ~ **certain conditions** sich auf bestimmte Bedingungen einigen; ~ **a continent** Kontinent besiedeln; ~ **in the country** sich auf dem Lande niederlassen; ~ **[a point] out of court** sich außergerichtlich vergleichen; ~ **with one's creditors** sich mit seinen Gläubigern vergleichen (einigen); ~ **one's daughter** seiner Tochter eine Aussteuer geben; ~ **a day** Termin vereinbaren; ~ **a day for a hearing** Termin zur mündlichen Verhandlung ansetzen; ~ **a day for a meeting** Sitzungstermin festlegen; ~ **a debt** Schuld abführen (bezahlen, begleichen); ~ **a difference** Meinungsverschiedenheit beilegen; ~ **a dispute** Streit schlichten; ~ **a document** Urkunde formgerecht errichten (in eine rechtsgültige Form bringen); ~ **down** *(excitement)* sich legen, *(market)* sich beruhigen, *(price)* sich einpendeln, *(take residence)* seinen Wohnsitz nehmen, *(weather)* beständiger werden; ~ **down in A** seinen Sitz in A aufschlagen; ~ **down in business** Geschäftsmann werden; ~ **down for good** sich für dauernd niederlassen; ~ **down to a new job** sich in einer neuen Stellung einarbeiten, seinen neuen Beruf schätzen lernen; ~ **down to married life** ruhiger Ehemann werden; ~ **down in a locality** sich in einer Gegend niederlassen; ~ **down in a new place** sich eingewöhnen; ~ **down in the practice of law** sich als Anwalt niederlassen; ~ **down to work** sich an die Arbeit machen (auf seine Arbeit konzentrieren); ~ **at the end of the month** am Monatsende abrechnen; ~ **an estate** Nachlaß verteilen (regulieren, abwickeln), sich auseinandersetzen; ~ **for s. th.** sich mit etw. begnügen; ~ **s. one's hash** *(sl.)* jds. Aufgeblasenheit dämpfen; ~ **in** sich [in einem neuen Haus] einrichten; ~ **an issue** *(Br.)* sich einigen; ~ **a lawsuit amicably** *(US)* Rechtssache gütlich beilegen; ~ **one's liabilities** seinen Verpflichtungen nachkommen; ~ **in life** sich seßhaft machen; ~ **by lot** durch Los entscheiden; ~ **a matter** Sache zur Erledigung bringen, Angelegenheit regeln; ~ **a matter amicably** Angelegenheit freund-

schaftlich (gütlich) beilegen (regeln); ~ **s. one's nerves** jds. Nerven beruhigen; ~ **an order** *(lawyer, Br.)* Wortlaut eines Gerichtsbeschlusses aushandeln; ~ **part of one's estate on one's son** seinem Sohn schon bei Lebzeiten sein Erbteil auszahlen; ~ **a patient for the night** Patienten für die Nacht versorgen; ~ **payments in pounds** in Pfund zahlen; ~ **peace** Frieden festigen; ~ **a pension** Ruhegehalt aussetzen; ~ **points of law** Rechtsfragen klären; ~ **population** Bevölkerung ansiedeln; ~ **a price** Preis absprechen; ~ **property** Nacherbschaft festlegen; ~ **all one's property on one's wife** seiner Ehefrau das ganze Vermögen hinterlassen; ~ **on selling** sich zum Verkauf entschließen; ~ **on a rendezvous** Verabredung treffen; ~ **a road** Straße befestigen; ~ **a room** Zimmer herrichten; ~ **into shape** allmählich Gestalt annehmen; ~ **soon into shape** sich bald wieder einrenken; ~ **on selling** sich zum Verkauf entschließen; ~ **a son in his profession** Sohn gut unterbringen; ~ **the succession** Erbfolge festlegen; ~ **the terms** Bedingungen vereinbaren (festlegen); ~ **the terms of freight** Fracht bedingen; ~ **troops in barracks** Truppen in Kasernen stationieren; ~ **on trust** treuhänderisch verwalten lassen; ~ **up** *(estate)* Nachlaß verteilen, sich auseinandersetzen, *(insolvent corporation)* Konkursmasse verteilen; ~ **up with s. o.** Rechnung bei jem. begleichen; ~ **up at the end of the month** am Monatsende bezahlen; ~ **s. th. upon s. o.** jem. etw. überschreiben; ~ **by will** Treuhandvermögen testamentarisch errichten; ~ **$ 500 a year on s. o.** jem. eine jährliche Apanage von 500 Dollar aussetzen;

to have an account to ~ with s. o. sich mit jem. über etw. auseinandersetzen müssen, mit jem. ein Hühnchen zu rupfen haben.

settled *(balanced)* abgerechnet, abgeschlossen, ausgeglichen, *(decided)* bestimmt, festgelegt, *(daughter)* versorgt, verheiratet, *(domiciled)* ansässig, *(done)* erledigt, abgewickelt, abgemacht, *(paid)* beglichen, bezahlt;

as good as ~ so gut wie abgemacht; **not ~** unbezahlt; **not yet ~** noch nicht entschieden;

to be ~ festliegen; **to be all ~** in Ordnung sein;
~ **abode** fester Wohnsitz; ~ **account** beglichene (bezahlte) Rechnung , reguliertes (ausgeglichenes) Konto, *(banking)* schriftlich anerkanntes Kontokorrent; **sparsely ~ area** dünn besiedeltes Gebiet; ~ **claim** *(insurance)* regulierter Schaden; ~ **areas in a colony** schon besiedelte Landstriche in einer Kolonie; ~ **conviction** feste Meinung; ~ **country** besiedeltes Land; ~ **estate** treuhänderisch gebundenes Sondervermögen; ~ **income** festes Einkommen; ~ **insanity** chronische Geisteskrankheit; ~ **intention** fester Entschluß; ~ **land** der Verfügungsfreiheit entzogener (erbrechtlich gebundener) Grundbesitz, Fideikommiß; ~ **Land Act** *(Br.)* Fideikommißgesetz; ~ **law** allgemein anerkannter Rechtssatz; ~ **opinions** feste Ansichten; ~ **price** abgemachter (abgesprochener) Preis; ~ **production** gleichmäßige (stetige) Produktion; ~ **property** erbrechtlich gebundener Besitz, *(Br.)* treuhänderisch gebundenes Sondervermögen; ~ **question** bereits entschiedene Frage; ~ **thing** feststehende Tatsache; ~ **weather** beständiges Wetter.

settlement *(adjustment)* Beilegung, Erledigung, Schlichtung, *(agreement)* Übereinkommen, Vereinbarung, Abkommen, Abmachung, Regelung, *(of annuity)* Aussetzung einer Rente, *(banking)* Ausgleichsoperation, *(colonization)* Kolonisierung, Besiedlung, *(colony)* [An]siedlung, Kolonie, abgesonderte [Fremden]niederlassung, Auswanderungsgebiet, landwirtschaftliches Siedlungsgebiet, *(composition)* Beilegung, Vergleich, Verständigung, Schlichtung, *(decision)* [endgültige] Entscheidung, *(determination)* Festsetzung, Bestimmung, *(establishment)* Niederlassung, *(establishment in life)* Unterbringung, Einstellung, Versorgung, Begründung einer Lebensstelle, *(estate)* Nachlaßregulierung, Auseinandersetzung, *(foundation of business)* [Geschäfts]gründung, Etablierung, *(indemnity)* Abfindung, *(insurance claim)* Schadensregulierung, *(legacy)* Vermächtnis, Stiftung, *(liquidation)* Liquidation, Liquidierung, *(matrimonial causes, Br.)* güterrechtlicher Ausgleich, *(payment)* Begleichung, Bezahlung, *(regulation)* Regelung, Regulierung, Erfüllung einer Forderung, Glattstellung, *(legal residence)* gesetzlicher Aufenthaltsort, Wohnsitz, *(right growing out of residence)* Heimatrecht, -berechtigung, *(settled property)* erbrechtlich gebundener Besitz, *(settling of accounts)* Ver-, Abrechnung, Saldierung, Ausgleichung, Skontierung, Abschluß, *(settling day, Br.)* Abrechnungstermin, *(transfer of property)* Eigentumsübertragung, *(welfare institution)* Wohlfahrtseinrichtung;

in full ~ *(in ~ of all claims)* zum Ausgleich aller Forderungen; **for monthly ~** per Ultimo; **in ~ of your account** zur Begleichung Ihrer Rechnung;

antenuptial ~ vor der Eheschließung abgeschlossener Ehevertrag; **claim ~** Schadensregulierung; **compounded ~** pauschale Abgeltung; **compulsory ~** Zwangsvergleich; **convict ~** Strafkolonie; **daily ~** *(clearinghouse)* tägliche Abrechnung; **discretionary ~** in pflichtgemäßem Ermessen zu verwaltende Vermögensmasse; **end-of-month ~** Ultimoliquidation, -abrechnung; **extra-judicial ~** außergerichtlicher Vergleich; **family ~** *(Br.)* Familienabkommen; **final ~** Schlußabrechnung, Rechnungsabschluß; **formal ~** offizielle Regelung; **fortnightly ~** Medioabrechnung; **global ~** pauschale Abfindung; **gratuitous ~** unentgeltliche Zuwendung; **heavy ~** schwierige Ultimoregulierung; **judicial ~** Liquidationsvergleich; **lasting ~** Dauerabkommen, -regelung; **legal ~** Gläubigervergleich; **loss ~** Schadensregulierung; **lump-sum ~** globale (pauschale) Abfindung; **marriage ~** Ehevertrag; **mid-month ~** Medioliquidation, -abrechnung; **mid-year ~** Halbjahresrechnung, -abschluß; **monthly ~** monatliche Abrechnung, Monatsabschluß, Ultimoabschluß, -abrechnung, -liquidation; **mutual current ~** laufende gegenseitige Rechnung; **negotiated ~** ausgehandelte Lösung; **noninflationary ~** antiinflationistische Lösung; **out-of-court ~** außergerichtlicher Vergleich; **penal ~** Strafkolonie; **periodical ~** periodische Abrechnung; **personal ~** *(Br.)* Verfügung über bewegliches Vermögen; **post-nuptial ~** nach der Eheschließung abgeschlossener Ehevertrag; **pre-trial ~** Vergleichsvereinbarung vor Prozeßbeginn; **prima-facie ~** natürlicher Wohnsitz; **private ~** gütliche Regelung, Einigung (Erledigung), außergerichtlicher Vergleich; **pro-rata ~** anteilige (proratarische) Befriedigung; **scattered ~** Streusiedlung; **separate ~** Sonderregelung; **special ~** Sonderliquidation, *(stock exchange)* Sonderabrechnung; **strict ~** Errichtung eines Treuhandvermögens, Fideikommißbegründung; **surviving spouse ~** Nachlaßverwaltung für die überlebende Ehefrau; **voluntary ~** unentgeltliche Nießbrauchbestellung; **wage ~** Lohnabkommen; **weekly ~** wöchentliche Abrechnung; **yearly ~** Jahresabschluß, -rechnung;

~ **of an account** Rechnungsbegleichung, Begleichung einer Rechnung, Kontoregulierung, -glattstellung; ~ **of accounts** *(Bank for International Settlements)* Zahlungsausgleich; **final ~ of accounts** Schlußabrechnung, Auseinandersetzung; ~ **of an affair** Abwicklung eines Geschäftes, Erledigung einer Angelegenheit; ~ **by agreement** vergleichsweise Regelung; ~ **by arbitration** schiedsrichterliche Entscheidung, schiedsgerichtlicher Vergleich; ~ **of average** Havarieaufmachung, Dispache; ~ **protected against avoidance** *(Bankruptcy Act)* nicht der Konkursanfechtung unterliegende Vermögensübertragungen; ~ **in cash** Abfindung in bar, Kapital-, Barabfindung; ~ **of a claim** Schadensregulierung; ~ **per contra** *(bookkeeping)* Aufrechnung; ~ **of a controversy** Beilegung einer Kontroverse; ~ **out of court** außergerichtlicher Vergleich; ~ **with one's creditors** Gläubigervergleich, -abfindung; ~ **of damage** Schadensfeststellung; ~ **of a date** Bestimmung eines Zeitpunkts; ~ **of interbank debits and credits** interne Abrechnung der Banken; ~ **of debts** Schuldenregulierung, -regelung, Bezahlung (Begleichung) von Schulden; ~ **of a dispute** Beilegung eines Streitfalls (einer Streitigkeit); ~ **at the end of a month** Ultimoabrechnung; ~ **of an estate** Nachlaßregulierung; ~ **in full** vollständige Bezahlung (Begleichung); ~ **of hardship cases** Härteregelung; ~ **of inheritance** Erbvergleich; ~ **of an invoice** Rechnungsbegleichung; ~ **before judgment** vergleichsweise Regelung vor Urteilsverkündigung; ~ **of a loss** Schadensregulierung; ~ **arrived at by the parties inter se** Parteivergleich; ~ **of paupers** Aufenthaltsbeschränkung von Sozialhilfeempfängern; ~ **of payment** Zahlungsausgleich; ~ **of property** Zuwendung von Vermögenswerten, Vermögenszuwendung, Eigentumsübertragung; ~ **of transactions** Ausgleich des Zahlungsverkehrs; ~ **in trust** Güterrechtsvertrag; ~ **for the wife or children** Stiftung zugunsten der Ehefrau oder Kinder; ~ **created by will** testamentarische Errichtung eines Treuhandvermögens;

to arrange a ~ with s. o. Vergleich mit jem. abschließen; **to buy for ~** auf Lieferung kaufen; **to carry on negotiations for a ~** Vergleichverhandlungen führen; **to come to a ~** zu einem Vergleich gelangen; **to draw up a ~** Abschluß aufstellen; **to get a ~** Regelung erzielen; **to have reached a ~** sich vergleichsweise geeinigt haben; **to make a ~ on s. o.** jem. ein Vermächtnis aussetzen; **to make a ~ with s. o.** Vergleich mit jem. abschließen; **to reach a ~** Vergleich erzielen;

~ **account** Verrechnungs-, Abwicklungskonto, *(stock exchange, Br.)* Liquidations-, Regulierungskonto; ~ **action** Vergleichsverfahren; ~ **agreement** Vergleichsvereinbarung; ~ **allowance** Versorgungsvergütung; ~ **area** Besiedlungsgebiet; ~ **assets** Auseinandersetzungsguthaben; ~ **bargain** *(stock* *exchange)* Termingeschäft; ~ **beneficiary** Begünstigter eines treuhänderisch gebundenen Sondervermögens; ~ **capital** Stiftungs-, Treuhandkapital, Kapital einer Vermögensverwaltung; ~ **clerk** *(US)* Abrechnungsbeamter; ~ **date** *(banking)* Ausgleichstermin, *(bookseller)* Abrechnungstermin, *(of controversy)* Vergleichstermin, *(maturity)* Fälligkeitstag, *(stock exchange)* Abwicklungstermin; ~ **day** *(London stock exchange)* Skontierungs-, Liquidationstag, Abrechnungstag, -termin; ~ **deed** Stiftungs-, Gründungsurkunde; ~ **department** *(Br.)* Effektenliquidationsbüro; ~ **development** Siedlungsentwicklung; ~ **discount** Regulierungsdiskont; ~ **estate duty** Vorerbensteuer; ~ **house** Wohlfahrtseinrichtung; ~ **income** Einkünfte aus einer Stiftung; ~ **market** Terminmarkt; ~ **money** Zuwendung aus einer Stiftung, Beträge aus einer Vermögensverwaltung; ~ **offer** Vergleichsangebot; ~ **office** Liquidationskasse, -termin; ~ **option** Optionsrecht zur Festlegung von Lebensversicherungsteilbeträgen; ~ **pattern** Siedlungsnetz; ~ **policy** Besiedlungspolitik; ~ **price** Terminkurs; ~ **project** Besiedlungsplan; ~ **property** treuhänderisch gebundenes Sondervermögen; ~ **proposal** Einigungs-, Lösungsvorschlag; ~ **right** Auseinandersetzungsanspruch; land ~ **scheme** Siedlungsprogramm; ~ **sheet** *(banking)* Abschlußbogen; ~ **structure** Siedlungsgefüge, -struktur; ~ **terms** Zahlungsbedingungen, *(bankruptcy)* Liquidationsbedingungen; ~ **trustee** Stiftungs-, Vermögensverwalter, *(deceased's estate)* Nachlaßtreuhänder; ~ **type** Siedlungsweise; ~ **value** Wert eines Treuhandvermögens; ~ **warrant** Auszahlungsanweisung; ~ **worker** Mitarbeiter in wohltätigen Einrichtungen.

settler Siedler, Kolonist;
~ **community** Siedlergemeinde.

settling Abmachung, Abrechnung, Liquidation, *(annuity)* Aussetzung, *(colonization)* Besiedlung, *(establishment)* Niederlassung;
~ **of accounts** Rechnungsbegleichung; ~ **down** *(stock exchange)* Beruhigung; ~ **of grievances** Beilegung von Arbeitsstreitigkeiten; ~ **interrogations** *(taking a deposition)* Entscheid über die Zulässigkeit einzelner Vernehmungsfragen; ~ **of issues** *(Br.)* Festlegung von für das Verfahren wesentlichen Fragen; ~ **clerk** [Börsen]abrechner; ~ **day** *(clearing day, Br.)* Abschluß-, Abrechnungs-, Skontierungstag, Abrechnungstermin, Liquidationstag, *(pay day)* Zahl-, Erfüllungstag, *(term of delivery, Br.)* [Ab]lieferungstag, -termin; ~**in period** Eingewöhnungszeit; ~ **period** Abrechnungsperiode; ~ **place** Erfüllungsort; ~ **price** Liquidationspreis; ~ **rate** Liquidations-, Regulierungskurs; ~ **week** Zahlungswoche.

settlor *(donor)* Treugeber, *(law)* Stifter.

setup Arbeitsstab, Organisation, *(accounting)* Kapitalstrukturschema, *(machine)* Rüsten, *(setting up)* Einrichtung, Etablierung, *(society)* Gesellschaftsstruktur, *(US sl.)* Schiebung bei Wettbewerben;
economic ~ Wirtschaftssystem;
~ **costs** Gründungskosten; ~ **time** Anlauf-, Leerlaufzeit [beim Produktionswechsel], Einrichte-, Umstellungszeit.

seven-days | notice wöchentliche Kündigung; ~ **operation** durcharbeitender Betrieb.

sever *(v.)* Besitz in Stücke teilen, *(separate)* absondern, -trennen;
~ **o. s. from the church** aus der Kirche austreten; ~ **one's diplomatic connections (connexions, Br., relations)** seine diplomatischen Beziehungen abbrechen; ~ **a contract** Vertrag auflösen; ~ **relations** Beziehungen abbrechen; ~ **a statute** Satzung aufheben; ~ **a joint tenancy** Gesamthandeigentum in Bruchteilseigentum umwandeln.

severable abtrennbar, teilbar, *(law)* getrennt, unabhängig;
~ **contract obligation** unabhängige Vertragsverpflichtung.

several verschieden, einzeln, gesondert, getrennt, unabhängig;
~ **actions** getrennte Klagen; ~ **covenants** Einzelverpflichtungen; ~ **debt** Einzelschuld, -verpflichtung; ~ **debtor** Einzelschuldner; ~ **demand** Einzelforderung; ~ **estate** Sondervermögen; ~ **fishery** ausschließliches Fischereirecht; ~ **inheritance** getrennter Nachlaß; ~ **issues** mehrere zur Entscheidung anstehende Fragen; ~ **liability** Individual-, Einzelhaftung; ~ **matters** diverse Angelegenheiten; ~ **members of a committee** verschiedene Ausschußmitglieder; ~ **note** Zahlungsversprechen; ~ **obligation** Einzelschuldverhältnis; ~ **tenancy** Einzelbesitzrecht; ~ **ways** getrennte Wege.

several, joint and solidarisch, gesamtschuldnerisch;
~ **bond** Solidarverpflichtung; ~ **guarantee** gesamtschuldnerische Bürgschaft; ~ **liability** Gesamtschuld[nerschaft], Gesamtverbindlichkeit; ~ **mortgage** Gesamthypothek; ~ **note** *(US)* gesamtschuldnerisches Zahlungsversprechen; ~ **obligation** Gesamtschuldverhältnis; ~ **right** Gesamtgläubigerschaft.

severally gesondert, einzeln;
~ **liable** einzeln haftbar;
to be liable jointly and ~ gesamtschuldnerisch (als Gesamtschuldner) haften.

severalties, shifting Grundstücke des jeweiligen Eigentümers.

severalty Sondervermögen, Bruchteilseigentum, -vermögen, Eigenbesitz;
~ **owner** Bruchteilseigentümer.

severance [Ab]trennung, Bruch, *(act of severing)* Teilbarkeit, *(detachment of fixtures)* Entfernung des Zubehörs, *(pleading)* gesondertes Verteidigungsvorbringen;
~ **of an action** Abtrennung eines Verfahrens; ~ **of communications** Unterbrechung von Verbindungen; ~ **of diplomatic relations** Abbruch diplomatischer Beziehungen; ~ **of an estate** *(joint tenancy)* Teilung des Mitbesitzes, Auflösung einer Gemeinschaft;
~ **allowance** *(US)* Trennungsentschädigung, Entlassungsabfindung; ~ **benefit** *(US)* Entlassungsabfindung, *(pension plan)* Übergangsentschädigung; ~ **damage** Entschädigung für entferntes Zubehör; ~ **fund** Härtefonds; ~ **pay** *(US)* Entlassungsabfindung, Härteausgleich; ~ **scheme** *(US)* Sozialplan [bei Personalabbau]; ~ **tax** *(US)* Schürfsteuer, Steuer auf Bodenerzeugnisse; ~ **wage** *(US)* Entlassungsgeld.

severe streng, hart;
~ **to the point of cruelty** streng bis zur Grausamkeit;
to be ~ **on** scharf kritisieren;
~ **competition** scharfe Konkurrenz, scharfer Wettbewerb; ~ **criticism** scharfe Kritik; ~ **illness** *(life policy)* schwere Krankheit; ~ **judge** strenger Richter; ~ **loss** schwerer Verlust; ~ **pain** heftiger Schmerz; ~ **punishment** harte Strafe; ~ **reprimand** strenger Verweis; ~ **requirements** schwierige Bedingungen; ~ **sentence** hartes Urteil.

severity Härte, Strenge, Unnachsichtigkeit;
to punish with ~ hart bestrafen.

sew *(v.)* **up** *(sl.)* restlos fertigmachen.

sewage Abwässer, Kloakenwasser;
~ *(v.)* kanalisieren, mit Kanalisation versehen;
~ **cleansing** Abwässerreinigung; ~ **disposal** Abwässerbeseitigung; ~ **disposal works** Kläranlage; ~ **farm (plant)** Kläranlage, Rieselfeld; ~ **sanitation** Abwässerbeseitigung; ~ **system** Abwässersystem; ~ **treatment plant** Abwässerverwertungsanlage; ~ **works** Abwässeranlagen.

sewer [Abwässer]kanal, Abwässerungsanlage;
~**s** Kanalisation;
public (trunk) ~ Hauptkanal;
~ **outlet** Abwässerabfluß; ~ **pipe** Kanalisationsrohr; ~ **system** Kanalisationssystem.

sewerage Abwässerbeseitigung, *(system of sewers)* Kanalisation, Kanalisationsnetz, -system;
~ **committee** Ausschuß für Abwässerbeseitigung; **to have** ~ **service** am Kanalisationsnetz angeschlossen sein.

sewerman Kanalisationsarbeiter.

sewing | press *(print.)* Heftmaschine; ~ **thread** *(bookbinding)* Heftfaden.

shabby *(clothes)* abgetragen, -genutzt;
~ **treatment** elende Behandlung; ~ **genteel** verarmte Schicht; ~ **gentility** verblichene Eleganz.

shack *(Br.)* gemeinsames Weiderecht, *(US coll.)* Bruchbude, Elendsquartier, *(freight train, sl.)* Bremser;
decrepit ~ morsche Bretterbude.

shackles Fesseln, Handschellen;
~ **of convention** Ketten der Konvention, konventionelle Hemmnisse.

shade Schatten, Dunkel, *(small degree)* geringer Grad, Kleinigkeit, Nuance, Spur, Idee, *(stock exchange)* Schattierung, Nuance;
lamp ~ Lampenschirm;
~**s of meaning** Bedeutungsnuancen; **all** ~**s of opinion** verschiedenartigste Meinungen;
~ *(v.)* beschatten, verfolgen, *(change gradually)* nuancieren, abstufen, *(prices)* allmählich sinken, *(stock exchange)* geringfügige Kursabweichung erfahren;
to be in the ~ *(fig.)* wenig bekannt sein; **to throw (put, cast) s. one's merits in the** ~ jds. Verdienste in den Schatten stellen;
~ **temperature** Schattentemperatur; ~ **tree** Schatten spendender Baum.

shaded schattiert;
~ **lamp** abgedunkelte Lampe; ~ **frame** gerasterter Rahmen; ~ **rule** Strichlinie.

shading Nuancierung, Abstufung, *(stock exchange)* geringfügiger Kursrückgang.

shadow Schatten, *(slightest degree)* Spur, Kleinigkeit, Andeutung, *(fig.)* Verfolger, Schatten, Spion, Detektiv, *(gloomy state)* Schatten, Verstimmung, Trübung;
without a ~ of doubt ohne den geringsten Zweifel;
~ (v.) (spy) beschatten, überwachen, verfolgen;
to be afraid of one's own ~ große Angst haben; **to be only a ~ of one's former self** nur ein Schatten seines eigenen Ichs sein; **to be worn to a ~** zum Skelett abgemagert sein; **to cast a ~** langanhaltenden Einfluß ausüben; **to cast their ~s before them** *(events)* sich vorweg ankündigen; **to catch at ~s** Phantomen nachjagen; **to live in the ~** im Verborgenen leben; **to run after a ~** einer Chimäre nachlaufen;
~-boxing Schattenboxen; **~ Cabinet** *(Br.)* Schattenregierung, -kabinett; **~ factory** *(mil.)* Schatten-, Tarn-, Ausweichbetrieb; **~ halftone** flachgeätzte Autotopie; **~ organization** *(intelligence service)* Deck-, Schattenorganisation; **~ portfolio** *(Br.)* Posten (Ressort) im Schattenkabinett; **~ price** Schattenpreis; **~ print advertisement** Schattendruckanzeige; **~ region** Funkschatten; **~ show** Schattenboxen; **~ trade spokesman** *(Br.)* Sprecher auf handelsrechtlichem Gebiet im Schattenkabinett.
shadowland Geisterreich, Schattenland.
shady *(sl.)* Hinweis, Tip;
to keep ~ *(sl.)* verstecken;
~ (a.) zweifelhaft, fragwürdig; **~ business** dunkles (zweifelhaftes) Geschäft; **~ financier** zweifelhafter Finanzier; **~ side** Schattenseite; **~ speculator** windiger Spekulant; **~ transaction** undurchsichtige Transaktion.
shaft Schacht, *(fig.)* Pfeil;
air ~ Luftschacht; **elevator ~** Aufzugsschacht; **ventilating ~** Luftschacht;
to descend into a ~ Schacht befahren;
~ sinker Schachtarbeiter.
shaftsman Schachtarbeiter.
shake *(coll., US)* Erdbeben, *(rent party)* Bottle Partie, *(sl.)* Abwimmeln;
in two ~s of a duck's tail im Handumdrehen; **on the ~** *(sl.)* auf dem Verbrecherpfad;
no great ~s *(sl.)* nichts Weltbewegendes;
~ of the head Kopfschütteln;
~ (v.) down into a job sich an einen Beruf gewöhnen; **~ down nicely** sich gut zurechtfinden; **~ one's ears** sich aufraffen; **~ s. one's faith** jds. Vertrauen erschüttern; **~ the foundations of society** Grundlagen der Gesellschaft erschüttern; **~ a leg (it up)** sich auf die Socken machen; **~ off a bad habit** üble Angewohnheit loswerden; **~ off one's pursuers** seine Verfolger abschütteln; **~ out** *(stock exchange)* Werte abstoßen; **~ in one's shoes** vor Angst zittern; **~ the witness's evidence** Aussagen des Zeugen erschüttern;
to be no great ~s die Welt nicht gerade einreißen; **to give s. o. the ~** *(sl.)* j. abwimmeln; **to put s. o. on the ~** *(sl.)* von jem. Geld erpressen.
shakedown *(improvised bed)* Nachtlager, bescheidenes Lager, *(US sl.)* Geld-aus-der-Tasche-Ziehen;
~ cruise *(ship)* Probefahrt, *(traveller)* Vergnügungsreise; **~ flight** Probeflug.
shaken *(health)* angegriffen;
badly ~ *(credit)* schwer angeschlagen;
to be ~ by the news von den Nachrichten erschüttert sein; **~ confidence** erschüttertes Vertrauen; **~ credit** geschwächter Kredit; **~ monarchy** erschütterte Monarchie.
shakeout *(closing down)* Produktionsaufgabe, *(economic situation)* Nachlassen der wirtschaftlichen Aktivität, Rückkehr zu normalen Verhältnissen, *(stock exchange)* Ausbooten der Konkurrenz;
new ~ in the shipbuilding industry Produktionsschrumpfung in der Schiffahrtsindustrie.
shaker Mixbecher.
shakeup Umbesetzung, -organisation, *(cabinet)* Kabinettsumbildung, *(reorganization)* Personalumbau, Umbesetzung, Umgruppierung.
shakiness *(business)* Unzuverlässigkeit, Wackligkeit.
shaking out *(US)* Börsenmanöver.
shaky hinfällig, gebrechlich, *(business)* windig;
to feel ~ sich unwohl fühlen;
~ arguments schwache Begründung (Argumente); **~ credit** unsicherer Kredit; **~ firm** unzuverlässige (unsichere) Firma, wackliges Unternehmen; **~ hand** zittrige Hand.
shallow Untiefe;
~ argument leere Ausflucht; **~ depression** flaches Tiefdruckgebiet; **~ talk** seichtes Geschwätz; **~ water** seichtes Wasser.

sham Betrug, Schein, fauler Zauber, Schwindel, *(imitation)* Ersatz, Nachahmung;
~ (v.) nachahmen, imitieren, vortäuschen, fingieren;
~ illness simulieren, sich krank stellen;
~ (a.) falsch, fingiert, nachgemacht, unecht;
~ answer unschlüssiges Gegenvorbringen; **~ battle** Scheingefecht; **~ bid** Scheingebot, fingiertes Angebot; **~ boom** Scheinblüte, Scheinkonjunktur; **~ business** Scheingeschäft, fingiertes Geschäft; **~ butler** Lohndiener; **~ committee** Proforma-Ausschuß; **~ contract** fingierter Vertrag, Scheinvertrag; **~ dividend** Scheindividende, fiktive Dividende; **~ elections** Scheinwahlen; **~ jewelry** imitierter Schmuck; **~ marriage** Scheinehe; **~ package** Schaupackung; **~ page** *(print.)* Schmutzseite; **~ payment** Scheinzahlung, fingierte Zahlung; **~ plea** Scheinantrag, Verzögerungsmanöver; **~ pleading** mutwilliges Parteivorbringen; **~ profit** Scheingewinn; **~ purchase** Scheinkauf, fingierter Kauf; **~ sale** Scheinverkauf, -geschäft; **~ title** angenommener Titel; **~ title page** *(print.)* Schmutztitel; **~ transaction** fingiertes Geschäft, Scheingeschäft; **~ trial** Schauprozeß.
shambles *(fig.)* Schlachtfeld, wildes Durcheinander;
to turn a town into a ~ Stadt in einen Trümmerhaufen verwandeln.
shame Schande;
to cry ~ on s. o. sich über j. entrüsten; **to hang one's head for (in) ~** sein Haupt verhüllen.
shamus *(sl.)* Polyp.
shanghai *(v.)* s. o. j. [durch Betrug] herumkriegen, Matrosen pressen.
shank *(print.)* Schriftkegel;
to ride ~s' mare auf Schusters Rappen reisen.
shanty Elendsquartier;
~-town schäbige Vorstadt.
shape Gestalt, Form, *(pattern)* Modell, Muster;
the latest ~ die neueste Mode;
~ (v.) once's course homeward seinen Weg heimwärts richten; **~ out** formen, gestalten; **~ satisfactorily** sich gut entwickeln; **~ a statement** Erklärung formulieren; **~ up** *(coll.)* endgültige Gestalt annehmen; **~ up very well** sich gut machen (entwickeln), vielversprechend sein;
to be in bad ~ in schlechter Verfassung sein; **to be gradually taking ~** allmählich Gestalt gewinnen; **to be in good ~** in Ordnung sein; **to be in pretty good ~** ganz gute Figur abgeben; **to fall into (take) ~** Gestalt annehmen, sich verwirklichen; **to get s. o. s. back into ~** sich wieder fangen; **to get one's ideas into ~** seine Gedanken ordnen; **to give ~ to s. th.** einer Sache feste Form geben; **to put into ~** formen, gestalten;
~-retaining formbeständig.
shaping Formgebung;
to be ~ well sich zufriedenstellend entwickeln.
share *(bankrupt's estate)* [Konkurs]quote, *(of capital)* Kapitalanteil, -anteilsrecht, Anteil am Gesellschaftsvermögen, Gesellschaftsanteil, Einschuß, *(contribution)* Beitrag [bei Geldsammlungen], *(cooperative society)* Genossenschaftsanteil, *(dividend)* Dividende, *(investment company, US)* Fondsanteil, Investmentzertifikat, *(mining ~)* Kux, *(part)* [An]teil, *(partnership)* Teilhaberschaft, Beteiligung, *(of profits)* Beteiligung, [Gewinn]anteil, Geschäfts-, Gewinnbeteiligung, *(quota)* Kontingent, Quote, *(royalty)* Tantieme, *(ship)* Schiffspart, *(stock)* Aktienanteil, Aktie, *(stock certificate)* Anteilschein;
~ and ~ alike zu gleichen Teilen; **for my ~** meinerseits; **in equal ~s** zu gleichen Teilen;
a-~ stimmrechtslose Aktien; **~s allotted** zugeteilte Aktien; **~s applied for** gezeichnete Aktien; **atomic ~s** Atomaktien; **automobile ~s** *(US)* Autoaktien; **baby ~** Kleinaktie; **bank ~s** Bankaktien, *(stock exchange)* Bankwerte; **bearer ~** Inhaberaktie; **bonus ~** *(Br.)* Genußschein, Gratisaktie; **business ~** Geschäftsanteil; **capital ~** Kapitalanteil; **common ~** *(US)* Stammaktie, -anteil, gewöhnliche Aktie; **cumulative ~** kumulative Aktie; **cumulative preference ~** *(Br.)* nachzugsberechtigte Vorzugsaktie, Vorzugsaktie mit Dividendennachzahlungsanspruch; **deferred ~** *(Br.)* an letzter Stelle dividendenberechtigte Aktie, Nachzugsaktie; **definite ~** endgültige Aktie; **deposited ~** hinterlegte Aktie; **dividend ~** Gratisaktie; **domestic ~s** inländische Aktien; **dummy ~** Proformaanteil [eines Vorstandsmitglieds]; **electricity ~s** Elektrowerte; **established ~s** Standardwerte; **fair ~** gerechter Anteil; **foreign ~s** ausländische Aktien; **forfeited ~s** kaduzierte Aktien; **founder's ~** Gründeraktie; **free ~** Freiaktie, -kux; **fresh ~** neue Aktie; **fully paid-up ~** voll eingezahlte Aktie; **gilt-edged ~s** *(Br.)* erstklassige Aktien; **guaranteed ~** Aktie mit garantierter Mindestdividende; **half ~** hälftiger Anteil, gemeinsame Rechnung, Halbpart; **hereditary ~** *(US)*

gesetzliches Erbteil, Erbanteil; **high-grade** ~s erstklassige Aktien; **industrial** ~ Industrieaktie; **initial** ~ Gründeranteil, Einlage; **inscribed** ~ Namensaktie; **interest-bearing** ~ verzinsliche Beteiligung; **issued** ~ begebene Aktie; **lease-line** ~ verpachtete Aktie mit Dividendengarantie; **legal** ~ Pflichtteil; **limited partner's** ~ Kommanditanteil; **the lion's** ~ Löwenanteil; **listed** ~ *(US)* notierte Aktie; **loaned** ~ lombardierte Aktie; **management** ~s *(US)* Vorstandsaktien; **mining** ~ Kux, Montan-, Bergwerksaktie; **motor** ~s Autoaktien; **multiple** ~ Mehrstimmrechtsaktie; **new** ~s junge Aktien; **noncumulative** ~ nicht kumulative Prioritätsaktie (Vorzugsaktie); **nonnegotiated** ~ nicht weitergegebene Aktie; **nonvoting** ~ nicht stimmberechtigte (stimmrechtslose) Aktie; **nonvoting fixed-interest** ~s stimmrechtslose festverzinsliche Aktien; **nonvoting ordinary** ~s *(Br.)* stimmrechtslose Stammaktien; **nonvoting preference** ~ *(Br.)* stimmrechtslose Vorzugsaktie; **no-par value** *(US)* nennwertlose Aktie, Quotenaktie, Aktie ohne Nennwert; **oil** ~s Erdölaktien; **ordinary** ~ *(Br.)* Stammaktie; **original** ~ Stammaktie, -einlage; ~s **outstanding** ausgegebene Aktien; **own** ~ *(Br.)* eigene Aktie, Vorratsaktie; **paid-up** ~ Vollaktie, voll eingezahlte Aktie; **partly paid[-up]** ~ noch nicht voll eingezahlte Aktie; **participating** ~ gewinnberechtigter Anteil, Anteilschein, dividendenberechtigte Aktie; **partnership** ~ Geschäftsanteil, -einlage; **personal** ~ *(Br.)* Namensaktie; **preference** ~ *(Br.)* Vorrechts-, Vorzugsaktie; **participating preference** ~ *(Br.)* mit zusätzlicher Gewinnbeteiligung ausgestattete Vorzugsaktie; **preferential** ~ *(Br.)* Vorzugs-, Prioritätsaktie; **preferred** ~ *(US)* Prioritäts-, Vorzugsaktie; **preferred ordinary** ~ *(US)* gewöhnliche Vorzugsaktie; **primary** ~ Stammaktie, -anteil; **promoter's (promotion)** ~ Gründeraktie; **proportionate** ~ Verhältnisanteil, *(bankruptcy)* [Gläubiger]quote, anteilmäßige Befriedigung; **qualification** ~s *(Br.)* für die Vorstandsstellung erforderlicher Aktienbesitz, Pflichtaktien des Vorstands; **quoted** ~ an der Börse zugelassene Aktie, börsennotierte Aktie; **railroad** ~s *(US)* Eisenbahnaktien; **railway** ~s *(Br.)* Eisenbahnaktien; **recalled** ~ eingezogene Aktie; **redeemable** ~s rückkaufbare Aktien; **redeemable preference** ~ *(Br.)* rückkaufbare Vorzugsaktie; **redeemed** ~ amortisierte Aktie; **registered** ~ auf den Namen lautende Aktie, Namensaktie; **reserved** ~ Vorratsaktie; **restricted** ~ gebundene Aktie; **rubber** ~s *(Br.)* Gummiaktien, -werte; **shipping** ~s *(Br.)* Schiffahrtsaktien, -werte; **speculative** ~s Spekulationsaktien; **staff** ~s *(Br.)* an die Belegschaft ausgegebene Aktien; **statutory** ~ *(US)* gesetzliches Erbteil, Pflichtteil; **stock** ~ Stammaktie; **subscribed** ~ gezeichnete Aktie; **surrendered** ~ zur Einziehung eingelieferte Aktie; **taxdeductible** ~ steuerlich absetzbare Beteiligung; **narrowly traded** ~s nur im kleinsten Kreis gehandelte Aktien; **transferable** ~ Inhaberaktie; **unclaimed** ~ herrenlose Aktie; **underwriting** ~ Konsortialbeteiligung, -anteil; **unissued** ~ unverwertete Aktie; **unquoted** ~ zum Börsenhandel nicht zugelassene (nicht notierte) Aktie; **utility** ~s Versorgungswerte; **voting** ~ Stimmrechtsaktie; **withdrawn** ~ aus dem Verkehr gezogene Aktie; ~s **and amounts owing from subsidiary companies** *(balance sheet, Br.)* Anteile und Geldbeträge von Tochtergesellschaften; ~s **and securities** *(balance sheet)* Kapitalvermögen; ~ **in bank stock** Bankaktie; ~ **of benefit** Nutzanteil; ~ **in a business** Firmen-, Geschäftsanteil; ~ **in capital** Geschäftseinlage, Kapitalanteil; ~ **in capital introduced by a partner** Kapitaleinlage eines Gesellschafters; ~s **lodged as collateral** als Sicherheit hinterlegte Aktien; ~s **traded over the counter** im Freiverkehr gehandelte Aktien; ~s **at a discount** Aktien unter dem Nennwert; ~ **of earnings** Ertragsanteil; ~s **deposited in escrow** treuhänderisch hinterlegte Aktien; ~ **in an estate** Erbanteil; ~ **of the expenses** [Un]kostenanteil; **[allocated]** ~ **of exports** Ausfuhrkontingent; ~ **of export trade** Außenhandelsanteil; ~ **of the finance** Finanzierungsanteil; ~s **of a fund** Fondsanteile; ~ **in an inheritance** *(US)* Erbanteil; ~ **of beneficial interest** *(US)* Treuhandanteilschein; ~ **under an intestacy** gesetzliches Erbteil, Pflichtteil; ~ **in a loss** Verlustanteil; ~ **in the market** Marktanteil; ~ **in a mine** Kux; ~ **of output** Produktionsanteil; ~ **of overheads** Gemeindekostenanteil; **25%** ~ **in the ownership** 25%iger Eigentumsanteil; ~s **issued at par** zum Nennwert ausgegebene Aktien; ~s **of no par value** *(US)* nennwertlose Aktien, Aktien ohne Nennwert; ~ **in a partnership** Gesellschaftsanteil; ~ **payable to bearer** Inhaberaktie; ~s **issued at a premium** über dem Nennwert ausgegebene Aktien; ~ **of proceeds** Gewinnanteil, Tantieme; ~ **of profit** Beteiligung am Gewinn, Gewinnbeteiligung, -anteil, Profitanteil; ~s **ranking pari passu** gleichrangige Aktien; ~ **cum rights** Aktie mit Dividendenschein; ~ **ex rights** Aktie ohne Prämienrechte; ~ **in a ship** Schiffspart; ~s **for staff** *(Br.)* an die Belegschaft ausgegebene

eigene Aktien; ~ **of stock** Aktie, Anteilschein, Anteil am Aktienkapital, Kapitalanteil; ~ **of corporate stock** *(US)* Geschäftsanteil, Aktie; ~s **not admitted (listed,** *US)* **on the stock exchange** zum Börsenhandel nicht zugelassene Aktien; ~s **marketable on a stock exchange** börsengängige Anteile; ~s **quoted on the stock exchange** *(Br.)* börsennotierte Aktien; ~ **in a syndicate** Konsortialanteil; **common** ~s **held in treasury** Bestand an eigenen Aktien; ~ **of turnover** Umsatzanteil;

~s **that show a depreciation** im Wert geminderte Aktien; ~s **that yield high interest** Aktien mit hoher Rendite; ~ **on which one third has been paid** zu einem Drittel eingezahlte Aktie;

~ *(v.)* teilen, gemeinsam besitzen;

~ **in** teilhaben, sich beteiligen; ~ **and** ~ **alike** Gewinne und Verluste zu gleichen Teilen tragen; ~ **equally in the capital** gleiche Kapitalanteile haben; ~ **with s. o. in the costs** sich mit jem. die [Un]kosten teilen; ~ **one's estate between one's heirs** sein Vermögen unter die Erben aufteilen; ~ **the expenses** Kosten teilen (gemeinsam tragen); ~ **a hotel bedroom with a stranger** sich mit einem Fremden ein Hotelzimmer teilen; ~ **one's household** in Familiengemeinschaft (gemeinsamem Haushalt) leben; ~ **jointly** sich gemeinsam beteiligen; ~ **losses** Verluste aufteilen; ~ **in the expanding market** sich an der Marktausweitung beteiligen; ~ **an office with s. o.** Büro mit jem. teilen, Bürogemeinschaft mit jem. haben; ~ **out** aufteilen; ~ **one's last penny with s. o.** seinen letzten Groschen mit jem. teilen; ~ **in profits** am Gewinn beteiligt (gewinnbeteiligt) sein; ~ **a room with s. o.** Zimmergenossen sein; ~ **a thing** etw. teilen; ~ **s. th. together** etw. gemeinsam erleben; ~ **with s. o. in an undertaking** sich mit jem. an einem Unternehmen beteiligen; ~ **a view** Ansicht teilen;

to allot ~ Aktien zuteilen; **to apply for** ~s *(Br.)* Aktien zeichnen; **to be entitled to equal** ~s zu gleichen Anteilen berechtigt sein; **to be entitled to a** ~ **in the estate** erbberechtigt sein; **to bear a** ~ **in** Anteil haben, beitragen; **to buy its own** ~s eigene Aktien erwerben; **to call in** ~s Aktien einziehen; **to cancel lost** ~s verlorengegangene Aktien für kraftlos erklären (kaduzieren); **to claim a** ~ **in s. th.** Anteil an etw. verlangen; **to claim one's proportionate** ~ seinen [vollen] Anteil beanspruchen; **to come in for a full** ~ **of s. th.** seinen vollen Anteil an etw. bekommen; **to consolidate** ~s Aktien zusammenlegen; **to convert** ~s Aktien umwandeln; **to cut s. o. out from a** ~ **in property** j. von einem Vermögensanteil ausschließen; **to deposit** ~s **for the general meeting** Aktien zur Hauptversammlung anmelden; **to divide** ~s Aktien teilen (stückeln); **to fall to s. one's** ~ jem. bei der Teilung zufallen; **to get one's** ~ sein Teil erhalten; **to get one's full** ~ sein gerütteltes Maß bekommen; **to give s. o. a** ~ **in profits** j. am Gewinn beteiligen; **to go** ~s Gewinn und Verlust zu gleichen Teilen tragen; **to go** ~s **in s. th.** sich in etw. teilen; **to go** ~ **and** ~ zu gleichen Teilen beteiligt sein, gleichen Anteil haben; **to go half** ~s **with s. o.** Metageschäfte mit jem. machen; **to go** ~s **with s. o. in the expense of s. th.** sich in die Unkosten von etw. mit jem. teilen; **to have a** ~ **in a bank** an einer Bank beteiligt sein; **to have a** ~ **in a business** an einem Geschäft beteiligt sein; **to have a** ~ **in the profit** Anteil am Gewinn haben, am Gewinn beteiligt sein, Gewinnbeteiligung haben; **to have a** ~ **in an undertaking** an einem Unternehmen beteiligt sein; **to have no** ~ **in** unbeteiligt sein an; **to have no** ~ **in a business** an einem Geschäft nicht beteiligt sein; **to hold** ~s Aktienbesitzer sein, Aktien besitzen; **to hold** ~s **in business enterprises** geschäftlich beteiligt sein, Geschäftsbeteiligungen besitzen; **to hold** ~s **in a company** Aktionär einer Gesellschaft sein; **to hold** ~s **in safe custody** Aktien im Depot verwahren; **to hold 500** ~s **in a shipping company** 500 Anteile einer Schiffahrtsgesellschaft besitzen; **to ignore** ~s *(stock exchange)* Aktien vernachlässigen; **to issue** ~s **at a discount** Aktien unter dem Nennwert ausgeben; **to issue** ~s **at par** Aktien zum Nennwert ausgeben; **to make additional payment on** ~s auf Aktien nachzahlen; **to own control of** ~s Aktienmajorität besitzen; **to pay off** ~s Aktien einziehen; **to pay one's** ~ mitbezahlen, seinen Teil beitragen, seine Quote aufbringen; **to pay** ~ **and** ~ **alike** gleiche Anteile übernehmen; **to pay up** ~s Aktien voll einzahlen; **to pick up** ~s Aktien mitnehmen; **to place** ~s **with the public** Aktien beim Publikum plazieren; **to put the** ~s **at the present price on a p/e ratio of just over five** Aktienrendite beim augenblicklichen Kursstand von 5 zu 1 zum Kapital ergeben; **to recall** ~s Aktien einziehen; **to redeem** ~s Aktien zurückkaufen; **to sell** ~s Aktien abgeben; **to sell** ~s **on its customers' advice** Aktien im Kundenauftrag verkaufen; **to split** ~s Aktien splitten; **to subdivide** ~s Aktien stückeln; **to subscribe to (for,** *Br.)* ~s Aktien zeichnen; **to surrender** ~s Aktien an die Gesellschaft zurückgeben; **to take a** ~ beteiligt sein, teilhaben; **to take a** ~ **in the expenses** sich an den Unkosten beteiligen; **to take much ~ in a conversation** sich an einem Gespräch lebhaft beteiligen; **to take over ~s** Anteile übernehmen; **to take a personal ~ in a work** an einer Sache persönlich Anteil nehmen; **to take up ~s** Aktien beziehen; **to unload a block of ~s** *(Br.)* Aktienpaket abstoßen;

~ account Aktien-, Stücke-, Kapitalkonto; **to open an ordinary ~ account** Bausparvertrag abschließen; **~-acquisition scheme** *(Br.)* Gewinnbeteiligungssystem für Arbeitnehmer; **~s analyst** Aktienfachmann; **~ applicant** *(Br.)* Aktienzeichner; **~ application** *(Br.)* Aktienzeichnung; **~ application money** *(Br.)* gezeichnete Aktienbeträge, -anteile; **~s bonus** Gewinnprämie, Aktienbonus, *(Br., split up)* Split; **~ broker** Fonds-, Effekten-, Börsen-, Aktienmakler; **to opt for a ~-a-cab system** sich für ein System gemeinsam benutzter Taxis entscheiden; **~ capital** *(US)* Geschäfts-, Aktienkapital, *(original capital)* Stamm-, Grund-, Gründungskapital; **authorized ~ capital** genehmigtes Aktienkapital; **nominal ~ capital** *(Br.)* Nominalkapital; **relevant ~ capital** stimmberechtigtes Grundkapital; **to reduce ~ capital** *(Br.)* Zusammenlegung des Aktienkapitals vornehmen, Grundkapital herabsetzen; **~ certificate** *(Br.)* Aktienzertifikat, -urkunde, -promesse, Anteilschein, Globalaktie, Mantel; **to make an underwritten ~ counterbid** konsortiales Übernahmegegenangebot machen; **~ dealings** Aktienhandel; **~ denomination** Aktienstückelung; **~ deposit account** Stückkonto; **~ discount** Emissionsagio; **~ earnings** Aktienerträgnisse; **~-for-~ exchange** *(stock exchange)* Umtauschverhältnis eins zu eins; **~ exchange offer** Aktienumtauschangebot; **~ exchange transaction** Aktienumtauschgeschäft; **~ fund** *(investment trust)* Aktienfonds; **~ index** *(Br.)* Aktienindex; **industrial ordinary ~ index** Industrieaktienindex; **~ interest** Geschäftsanteil; **~ investment** Anlage in Aktien; **~ issue** Aktienausgabe, -emission; **~ ledger** *(Br.)* Aktionärsverzeichnis, -buch; **~ list** *(Br.)* Aktienkursliste, Kurszettel, *(register)* Aktienregister; **~ loan** Effektenlombardkredit; **~ market** Aktienmarkt; **~ market boom** Aktienhausse; **~ movements** Kursbewegungen; **~ option** Bezugsrecht auf junge Aktien; **~-out** Ver-, Aufteilung; **~-the-work plan** *(US)* Kurzarbeitsprogramm zur Vermeidung von Entlassungen, Kurzarbeitsvereinbarung; **~ portfolio** Aktienportefeuille; **~ premium** Emissionsagio; **~ premium account** Sonderkonto für Emissionsagio, Emissionsagiokonto; **~ price** Aktienkurs, -preis, Börsenkurs; **~ price index** *(Br.)* Aktienkursindex; **to boast a poor ~ price performance** sich nur kleiner Erfolge bei der Aktienkurspflege rühmen können; **~ purchase** Aktienkauf; **broadly diversified ~ purchases** breitgestreute Aktienkäufe; **~ pushing** *(Br.)* Aktienschwindel; **~ quotation** Aktiennotierung, -kurs; **~ register** *(Br.)* Aktienregister, -buch; **~ sales** Aktienverkäufe; **~ stake** Aktieneinlage, -beteiligung; **~ tenancy** in Naturalien zahlbare Pacht; **~ tenant** in Naturalien zahlender Pächter; **~ trading** Aktienhandel; **~ trading subsidiary** für den Aktienhandel gegründete Tochtergesellschaft; **~ transfer** Aktienübertragung; **~ valuation** Aktienbewertung; **~ warrant** [to bearer] *(Br.)* [Inhaber]aktienzertifikat, -promesse.

sharecrop system *(US)* Halbpacht.
sharecropper *(US)* Deputant, Naturalpächter.
sharecropping family *(US)* Tagelöhnerfamilie.
shared, broadly in weiten Kreisen geteilt.
shareholder *(Br.)* Aktieninhaber, -besitzer, Aktionär, Anteilscheinbesitzer, Anteilseigner, *(investment fund, US)* Anteilseigner, -scheinbesitzer, *(partner)* Gesellschafter, Teilhaber;

chief (principal) ~ Hauptaktionär; **controlling ~** beherrschender Aktionär, Großaktionär; **dissenting ~** opponierender Aktionär; **infant ~** minderjähriger Aktionär; **main ~** Hauptaktionär; **nominee ~** als Strohmann vorgeschobener Aktionär; **nonresident ~** auswärtiger Aktionär; **ordinary ~** Inhaber von Stammaktien, Stammaktionär; **outside ~s** *(group)* konzernfremde Gesellschaften; **preferential ~** Vorzugsaktionär; **principal ~** Haupt-, Großaktionär; **registered ~** Inhaber von Namensaktien, eingetragener Aktionär, Stammaktionär; **single ~** Einzelaktionär; **~ in a bank** Bankanteilseigner; **~s outside the family** familienfremde Aktionäre, nicht zur Familie gehörige Aktionäre; **~ of record** im Aktienbuch eingetragener Aktionär; **to impute to the ~ in the form of a tax credit** dem Aktionär in Form einer Steuergutschrift anrechnen; **to tap ~s with rights offering** Aktionären mit Bezugsrechten Geld aus der Tasche locken; **~ pressure** Druck der Aktionäre.
shareholder's bill Aktionärsklage gegen seine Gesellschaft.
shareholders' | approval Genehmigung durch die Anteilseigner; **~ body** Aktionärsgremium; **~ committee** Aktionärsausschuß; **~ dividend** Aktionärsdividende; **~ equity** *(balance sheet, US)*

Eigenkapital, Nettoanteil der Aktionäre; **~ group** Aktionärsgruppe; **~ ledger** Aktienbuch; **~ liabilities** Aktionärsverpflichtungen; **~ meeting** Haupt-, Aktionärsversammlung; **~ newsletter** Aktionärsbrief; **~ proposal** Aktionärsvorschlag; **~ register** Aktionärsverzeichnis; **~ rights** Aktionärsrechte; **~ satisfaction** Aktionärszustimmung; **~ suit** Aktionärsklage; **~ support** Unterstützung durch die Aktionäre.
shareholding | interest Aktienbeteiligung, -besitz; **~ member** Anteilseigner.
shareholdings Beteiligungen, Aktienbesitz, -bestände;
~ nominee ~ auf den Namen von Strohmännern lautende Aktienbeteiligungen, Strohmannbeteiligung;
~ in subsidiaries Beteiligungen an Tochtergesellschaften.
sharepusher *(Br.)* Aktienschwindler.
sharepushing *(Br.)* Aktienschwindel, Börsenmanöver.
sharer Mitinhaber, Teilhaber;
to be ~ in beteiligt sein, teilhaben.
sharing Beteiligung, Ver-, Aufteilung;
cost ~ Kostenbeteiligung; **progress ~** Teilnahme am Fortschritt;
fair ~ of burden gerechte Lastenverteilung; **~ of costs** Beteiligung an den Kosten, Kostenbeteiligung; **~ of experience** Erfahrungsaustausch; **~ of loss** Beteiligung am Verlust, Verlustbeteiligung; **~ the market** Marktaufteilung; **~ of profit** Gewinnbeteiligung;
~ plan *(US)* Gewinnbeteiligungssystem.
shark Schwindler, Betrüger, Gauner, Schmarotzer, *(US sl.)* toller Bursche, Kanone, *(student, sl.)* Schwänzer von Vorlesungen;
loan ~ *(US)* Zinswucherer.
sharp *(coll.)* Fachmann, Kenner, Sachverständiger;
~ *(a.)* scharf, deutlich, *(execution)* sofort vollstreckbar, *(punctual)* pünktlich;
to have a mind as ~ as a razor messerscharfen Verstand haben; **~ business** Schwindel, Gaunerei; **~ clause** *(mortgage)* Unterwerfungsklausel; **~ customer** hartgesottener Kunde; **~ curve** scharfe Kurve; **~ dealer** geschäftstüchtiger Kaufmann; **~ distinction** klare Unterscheidung; **~ frost** beißender Frost; **~ lad** gewitzter Bursche; **~ lawyer** skrupelloser Anwalt; **~ practice(s)** dunkle Geschäfte (Machenschaften), Beutelschneiderei, Schmutzkonkurrenz; **to blink at ~ practices** über unerlaubte Geschäftsmethoden hinwegsehen; **~ protest** energischer Protest; **~ rebuke** scharfe Zurückweisung; **~ remark** spitze Bemerkung; **~ swings** *(stock exchange)* starke Kursschwankungen; **~ words** böse Worte; **~ work** schnelle Arbeit.
sharpener Bleistiftspitzer.
sharper Schwindler, Betrüger, Gauner, *(games)* Falschspieler.
sharpshooter Scharfschütze.
shatter *(v.)* **civilian morale** Moral der Zivilbevölkerung erschüttern;
~-proof glass splittersicheres Glas.
shatting on one's uppers *(US sl.)* total pleite.
shave *(examination)* Durchrutschen, *(US sl.)* übermäßiger Diskont, Wucherzins;
clean ~ *(Br.)* glatter Betrug; **close (narrow) ~** knappes Entkommen;
~ *(v.)* ausbeuten, erpressen, *(bill of exchange)* Wechsel zu hohem Diskont aufkaufen;
~ the budget estimates Haushaltsvoranschlag kürzen; **~ a corner** *(car)* Ecke mitnehmen; **~ through an examination** bei einer Prüfung gerade noch durchrutschen;
to have a close ~ mit knapper Not davonkommen.
shaver Beutelschneider, Wucherer;
young ~ Grünschnabel.
sheaf of notes Bündel Notizen.
sheared *(US)* geprellter Börsenspekulant.
shebang *(US sl.)* Bude, Laden;
the whole ~ der ganze Plunder.
shed Hütte, Geräteschuppen, Remise;
bicycle ~ Fahrradschuppen; **building ~** Bauschuppen, -bude, -hütte; **coal ~** Kohlenschuppen; **customs ~** Zollschuppen; **engine ~** Maschinenschuppen; **freight ~** *(US)* Güterhalle;
~ *(v.)* **favo(u)rs** seine Gunst verschenken; **~ bad habits** schlechte Gewohnheiten ablegen; **~ surplus labo(u)r** überflüssige Arbeitskräfte freisetzen.
shedding of surplus labo(u)r Freisetzung überflüssiger Arbeitskräfte.
sheep | farming Schafzucht; **~-heaves** Schafsweide.
sheepskin gesiegelte Urkunde, *(sl.)* Diplom.
sheer | nonsense dummer Unsinn; **~ silk** reine Seide; **~ waste of time** glatter Zeitverlust.

sheet *(advertising)* großformatige Anzeige, *(newspaper, sl.)* Zeitung, *(piece of paper)* Bogen, Blatt, *(portion of metal)* Blech;
between the ~s *(coll.)* ins Bett; **in ~s** ungebunden, geheftet; **~s lose** Blätter; **the ~s** *(sl.)* Moneten;
advance ~**s** vor Veröffentlichung zugesandte Druckbogen; **attendance** ~ Anwesenheitsliste; **balance** ~ Bilanz; **blank** ~ *(fig.)* unbeschriebenes Blatt; **charge-~** *(Br.)* polizeiliche Vernehmungsunterlagen; **clean** ~ Reinkorrektur, *(fig.)* reine Weste; **cost** ~ Kostenaufstellung; **coupon** ~ Kuponbogen; **defective** ~ Defektbogen; **first** ~ Original eines Maschinenmanuskripts; **fly** ~ Flugblatt; **imperfect** ~ Defektbogen; **inventory** ~ Inventuraufstellung; **loose** ~ loses Blatt, *(fly sheet)* Flugblatt; **order** ~ Bestellschein; **pay** ~ Gehalts-, Lohnliste; **proof** ~ Korrekturbogen; **sale** ~ Verkaufsschein; **spoilt** ~ Fehldruck; **supplementary** ~ Extrabogen, Beiblatt; **tear** ~ *(US)* Belegstück, -seite; **time** ~ *(employee)* Arbeitsblatt, -zettel, Regie-, Stundenzettel, *(railway)* Aushängefahrplan; **waste** ~ Makulaturbogen; **~ of coupons** Zinsschein-, Kuponbogen; **~ of iron** Eisenblech; **of note paper** Bogen Briefpapier; **~ of paper** Papierbogen, Blatt Papier; **stamped** ~ **of paper** Stempelbogen; **~ of waste paper** Makulaturbogen; **~ of wrapping paper** Bogen Packpapier; **~ of prints and figures** Bilderbogen;
to be in ~s *(book)* nicht gebunden (ungebunden) sein;
~ almanac Kalenderbeilage; **~ anchor** *(fig.)* Rettungsanker; **~ iron** Feinblech; **~ lightning** Flächenblitz; **~ mill** Blechwalzwerk; **~ pavement** asphaltierter Bürgersteig; **~ size** Bogenformat; **~ writer** Buchmachergehilfe, *(sl.)* Reporter.

shelf Gestellbrett, Sims, Bord, [Waren]fach, Regal, *(bookcase)* Bücherbord;
on the ~ *(fig.)* auf dem Abstellgleis, ausrangiert, *(official)* ohne Amt;
to buy off the ~ direkt beim Hersteller kaufen; **to have on the ~** auf Lager haben; **to put on the ~** auf die lange Bank schieben; **to remain on the ~** auf Lager bleiben;
~ label Regalschild; **longer ~ life** größere Haltbarkeit; **~ space** Stellfläche; **~ strip** Regalstreifen; **~ warmer** Lager-, Ladenhüter.

shell *(building)* Gerippe, Skelett, *(company)* Firmenmantel, *(firework)* Feuerwerksrakete, *(school, Br.)* Mittelstufe, *(ship)* Rumpf,;
in the ~ *(fig.)* noch in der Entwicklung;
~ of a factory Skelett einer Fabrik;
~ *(v.)* out one's money Geld auf den Tisch legen (berappen);
to come out of one's ~ aus seiner Reserve heraustreten; **to retire into one's ~** sich wieder in sein Schneckenhaus zurückziehen;
~ company Verkaufsgesellschaft von Firmenmänteln; **~-proof** beschußsicher; **~ shock** Bombenneurose; **to have never got much beyond the ~ stage** noch nicht aus dem Entwicklungsstadium heraus sein.

shelter Zuflucht, Schutz, Schirm, Obdach, Schutzraum, *(mil.)* Bunker, Unterstand, Deckung;
under ~ unter Dach und Fach;
airraid ~ Luftschutzbunker; **bus ~** Wartehäuschen; **tax ~** Steuerschutz; **taxi-driver's ~** Unterstand für Taxifahrer;
~ *(v.)* an escaped prisoner einem entflohenen Gefangenen Unterschlupf gewähren;
to get under ~ *(airraid)* in den Luftschutzbunker gehen; **to give ~ to s. o.** jem. Obdach gewähren; **to give ~ to a fugitive** einem Flüchtling Herberge geben; **to seek ~** Zuflucht suchen; **to take ~** Zuflucht suchen;
~-proof bombensicher; **~ zone** Windschatten.

sheltered industries (trades) durch Einfuhrzölle geschützte Industriezweige.

sheltering trust *(US)* treuhänderisch hinterlegtes Vermögen zur Bereitstellung einer Witwenrente.

shelve *(v.)* unberücksichtigt lassen, auf die lange Bank schieben, *(discard)* ausrangieren, *(furnish with shelves)* mit Regalen (Fächern) versehen, *(matter in debate)* zurückstellen, *(put away)* zu den Akten legen, beiseitelegen;
~ s. o. j. entlassen; **~ a bill** *(Br.)* Gesetzesvorlage zurückstellen; **~ books** Bücher auf einem Regal unterbringen; **~ an officer** Beamten entlassen.

shepherd *(v.)* **passengers to an airliner** Passagiere zum Flugzeug geleiten; **~ toward ...** in Richtung auf ... dirigieren.

sheriff *(county, Br.)* Verwaltungsbeamter mit gerichtlichen Funktionen, Urkundsbeamter, *(Scot.)* Richter, *(US)* örtlicher Polizeichef, *(county, US)* oberste Vollstreckungsbehörde;
~ clerk *(Scot.)* Urkundsbeamter; **~'s court** *(Scot.)* Amtsgericht; **~'s officer** Gerichtsvollzieher; **~'s order** Pfändungsauftrag; **~'s sale** *(Br.)* Zwangsversteigerung.

Sherman Act *(US)* Antitrustgesetz.

shield Schutz, *(fig.)* Abschirmvorrichtung, *(screen)* Schutzschirm;
~ of a patent Schutzmantel eines Patents;
~ *(v.)* abschirmen;
~ a friend from censure Freund gegen Tadel in Schutz nehmen.

shift Verlagerung, Verschiebung, *(change)* Wechsel, Veränderung, *(change of residence, dial.)* Wohnungswechsel, Umzug, *(makeshift)* Notbehelf, Ausweg, Hilfsmittel, *(politics)* Kursänderung, *(working hours)* [Arbeits]schicht, Tagewerk, *(workmen)* Schicht, Mannschaft;
as a ~ als Notbehelf; **in ~s** umschichtig;
day ~ Tagesschicht; **double ~** Tag- und Nachtarbeit; **dropped ~** Fehl-, Feierschicht; **eight-hour ~** Achtstundenarbeitstag; **extra ~** Sonderschicht; **first ~** Tagesschicht; **fixed ~** gleichbleibende Schicht; **graveyard ~s** *(US)* durchgehende Nachtschicht; **lobster ~** *(US)* Mitternachtsschicht; **midnight ~** Nachtschicht; **relief ~** *(US)* zusätzliche Schicht; **rotating ~** periodische Schicht, Wechselschicht; **split ~** nicht durchgehende Schicht; **swing ~** *(US)* Zusatzschicht, Hilfs-, Spät-, Sonderschicht; **third ~** *(multiple shift operation)* Nachtschicht; **twelve-hour ~** Zwölfstundenschicht;
~ of crops Wechselwirtschaft; **~ of demand** Nachfrageverschiebung; **~ of direction** Richtungsänderung; **~s in the exchange rate** Verschiebungen im Wechselkursgefüge; **~ in fiscal attitudes** geändertes Fiskalverhalten; **~ in the market** Marktverlagerung, -veränderung; **~ in monetary policy** geldmarktpolitische Änderungen; **~ of opinion** Meinungsänderung, -wandel; **leftward ~ in opinion polls** Linksdrall bei Meinungsfragen; **~ of ownership** Eigentumswechsel; **~ in policy** politische Richtungsänderung; **~ in the popular mood** Wandel in der Volksstimmung; **~ of power** Machtverschiebung; **~ of prices** Kursverschiebung; **~ in supply** Angebotsverschiebung; **~ of votes** Stimmenverlagerung, -verschiebung;
~ *(v.)* verändern, verschieben, wechseln, *(burden)* verlagern, *(capital)* umschichten, *(cargo)* verrutschen, *(goods)* über-, umladen, *(move)* umziehen, Wohnung wechseln, *(resort to shifts)* Ausflüchte gebrauchen, lavieren, *(tax)* abwälzen;
~ for o. s. sich selbst helfen, allein zurechtkommen, auf sich selbst gestellt sein; **~ one's attention to other matters** seine Aufmerksamkeit anderen Dingen zuwenden; **~ berth** Ankerplatz wechseln; **~ the blame on s. o.** jem. die Schuld zuschieben; **~ the burden of proof** Beweislast umkehren; **~ the cargo** umlagern; **~ down** *(US)* herunterschalten; **~ furniture about (round)** Möbel umstellen; **~ gears** umschalten; **~ one's ground** Kampfschauplatz verlegen; **~ for a living** sich durchschlagen; **~ one's opinion** seine Meinung ändern; **~ orders** Aufträge verlagern; **~ one's quarters** *(fam.)* umziehen; **~ the responsibility on s. o.** jem. die Verantwortung zuschieben; **~ the scene** Schauplatz verlegen; **~ slightly** *(prices)* sich leicht verändern; **~ from full-time schedules to part-time** vom Status der Vollbeschäftigung zur Kurzarbeit übergehen; **~ the subject** Thema wechseln; **~ a tax** Steuer überwälzen; **~ all the trains one hour forward** alle Züge um eine Stunde vorverlegen; **~ in transit** *(load)* beim Transport verrutschen; **~ up** *(US)* heraufschalten;
to drop ~s Feierschichten einlegen; **to get a ~** *(mil.)* seine Versetzung erhalten, versetzt werden; **to live by ~s** sich durchmogeln; **to make ~ without help** ohne Hilfe auskommen; **to make ~ with the money one has** mit dem einem zur Verfügung stehenden Geld zurechtkommen; **to resort to dubious ~s in order to get some money** sich mit zweifelhaften Methoden etw. Geld zu verschaffen suchen; **to rotate ~s** Schichten auswechseln; **to work in ~s** Schichtarbeit verrichten, mit Ablösung (in Schichten) arbeiten;
~ allowance (differential) Schichtzuschlag, -ausgleich; **~ key** *(typewriter)* Umschalttaste; **~ lock** *(typewriter)* Feststeller; **~ operation** Schichtbetrieb; **multiple ~ operation schedule** mehrschichtiger Betriebsplan; **~ pay (payment)** Schichtlohn; **~ premium** Schichtzulage; **~ transfer** Versetzung von Arbeitskräften in andere Schichten; **~ wage** Schichtlohn; **~ work** Schichtarbeit, *(education)* Schichtunterricht.

shifter *(theater)* Kulissenschieber.

shifting Verlagerung;
tax ~ Steuerüberwälzung;
~ of burden of proof Umkehrung der Beweislast; **~ of cargo** Verschiebung (Verrutschen) der Ladung; **~ of funds** Deckungsaustausch; **~ of income** Einkommensverlagerung; **~ of influence** Schwerpunktverlagerung; **~ of liens** Auswechslung von Sicherheiten; **~ of loans** Kreditverlagerung; **~ of personnel** Personalumsetzungen; **~ of plant** Vermögensverschiebung; **~ of risk** Risikoabwälzung; **~ of taxation** Steuerabwälzung, -überwälzung;

~ ballast *(marine)* übergehender Ballast; **~ boards** Schotten; **~ clause** *(settlement)* Übergangs-, Ersatzvermächtnisklausel; **~ severalty** Grundstück des jeweiligen Eigentümers; **~ stock of merchandise** veränderlicher Warenbestand; **~ use** gestaffeltes Nießbrauchsrecht.

shiftless einfallslos, unbeholfen.

shiftman Schichtarbeiter.

shifty|behavio(u)r raffiniertes Verhalten; **~ customer** unzuverlässiger Kunde.

shill *(sl.)* Schlepper.

shilling, a ~ in the pound 5 Prozent;
  to cut s. o. off with a ~ j. bis auf den letzten Heller enterben; **to pay twenty ~s in the pound** *(Br.)* seine Schuld auf Heller und Pfennig bezahlen; **to take the Queen's ~** sich als Soldat anwerben lassen.

shilly-shally Beschäftigung mit Nichtigkeiten;
  ~ *(v.)* sich nicht entschließen können.

shine Leuchten, Schein;
  ~ *(v.)* **in s. th.** gute Figur bei etw. machen; **not ~ in conversation** keinen guten Gesprächspartner abgeben;
  to take a ~ to s. o. *(US)* Gefallen an jem. finden;
  ~ box *(sl.)* Tanzhalle.

shiner *(coll.)* Zylinderhut, *(sl.)* Goldstück;
  ~s *(sl.)* Moneten, Dukaten.

shingle *(sl.)* gefälschtes Diplom, *(US)* Firmenschild;
  to put up one's ~ *(doctor)* sich niederlassen, seine Praxis eröffnen.

ship Schiff, *(airplane)* Flugzeug, *(airship)* Luftschiff, *(ship's company)* gesamte Schiffsbesatzung, *(one's fortune)* Geldschiff, Glück;
  ex ~ frei ab Schiff, *(contract of sale)* Eigentumsübergang bei Entladung im Hafen; **on board ~** auf dem Schiff;
  abandoned ~ aufgegebenes Schiff; **American-flag-~** unter amerikanischer Flagge fahrendes Schiff; **cargo ~** Frachtschiff; **class ~** Schiff erster Klasse; **clean ~** Reinschiff; **~ collided with** gerammtes Schiff; **partly completed ~** nur teilweise fertiggestelltes Schiff; **convoy ~** Begleitschiff; **derelict ~** aufgegebenes Schiff; **~ dressed overall** beflaggtes Schiff; **enemy ~** feindliches Schiff; **foreign-going ~** im Überseeverkehr eingesetztes Schiff; **free ~** neutrales Schiff; **full (fully laden) ~** beladenes Schiff; **full-rigged ~** Vollschiff; **fully-manned ~** Schiff mit voller Bemannung; **general ~** Frachtschiff; **homeward (inbound) ~** für den Heimathafen bestimmtes Schiff; **leaving ~** abgehendes Schiff; **merchant ~** Kauffahrtei-, Handelsschiff; **neutral ~** neutrales Schiff; **nuclear-powered ~** atomgetriebenes Schiff; **ocean-going ~** Hochseedampfer; **outgoing (auslaufendes) ~** ausfahrendes Schiff; **passenger ~** Fahrgast-, Passagierschiff; **refrigerator ~** Kühlschiff; **register[ed] ~** Registerschiff; **sailing ~** Segelschiff; **scheduled ~** *(US)* fahrplanmäßiges Schiff; **single-cruising ~** alleinfahrendes Schiff; **transient ~** nicht regelmäßig fahrendes Schiff, Tramper; **weather ~** Schiff des Wetterdienstes; **wrecked ~** schiffbrüchiges Schiff;
  ~ under average havariertes Schiff; **~ bound for Y** nach Y bestimmtes Schiff; **~ of burden** Lastschiff; **~ not under control** manövrierunfähiges Schiff; **~ of the desert** Wüstenschiff, Kamel; **~ in difficulties (in distress)** in Gefahr befindliches Schiff, in Seenot geratenes Schiff, Schiff in Seenot; **~ of the line** Linienschiff; **~ in ordinary** abgetakeltes Schiff; **~s that pass in the night** Gelegenheitsbekanntschaften; **~ anchored in a roadstead** auf Reede liegendes Schiff; **~ under the sea** hilflos dem Meer ausgesetztes Schiff; **♀ of State** Staatsschiff;
  ~ *(v.)* *(on board)* verschiffen, laden, [Ware] einnehmen, einladen, *(forward, US)* verfrachten, verladen, ab-, versenden, abschicken, ausliefern, expedieren, *(transport)* durch Schiffe befördern (transportieren);
  ~ in bulk lose (in loser Schüttung) verladen; **~ in carlots (carloads)** *(US)* in Waggonladungen versenden; **~ a crew for a voyage round the world** Schiffsmannschaft für eine Weltreise anheuern; **~ on deck** auf Deck verladen; **~ freight collect** unter Frachtnachnahme versenden; **~ a gangway** Landungssteg einholen; **~ goods** Güter auf dem Wasserwege befördern; **~ goods to the consignation of s. o.** Waren an j. zum Versand bringen; **~ goods by instal(l)ments** Ware in Teilladungen versenden; **~ goods by sea** Waren auf dem Seeweg versenden; **~ goods by express train** Ware als Eilgut schicken; **~ out** verschiffen; **~ passengers** Passagiere an Bord nehmen; **~ as steward on an airliner** Steward auf einem Verkehrsflugzeug sein; **~ a student** *(sl.)* Studenten relegieren;
  to abandon a ~ Schiff aufgeben (verlassen); **to anchor a ~** Schiff vor Anker legen; **to arrest a ~** Schiff mit Beschlag belegen (pfänden); **to beach a ~** Schiff auflaufen lassen; **to blow up a ~**

Schiff sprengen; **to break up a ~** Schiff ausschlachten; **to bring a ~ into dock** Schiff ins Dock bringen; **to bring a ~ to** Schiff beidrehen; **to bring up a ~** Schiff aufbringen; **to build ~s on stock** Schiffe auf Vorrat bauen; **to come alongside a ~** an ein Schiff anlegen; **to disable a ~** Schiff außer Dienst stellen; **to dismantle a ~** Schiff abtakeln; **to document a ~** Schiff mit amtlichen Papieren ausstatten; **to dress a ~** Schiff beflaggen; **to equip (fit) a ~** Schiff ausrüsten; **to fit out a ~ for a long journey** Schiff für eine lange Reise ausrüsten; **to force a ~** Schiff auf Strand laufen lassen; **to freight out a ~** Schiff verchartern; **to handle a ~** Schiff manövrieren; **to insure a ~ out and home** Schiff auf der Hin- und Rückreise versichern; **to launch a ~** Schiff vom Stapel [laufen] lassen; **to lay a ~ on keel (lay down a ~)** Schiff auf Kiel legen; **to lay up a ~** Schiff außer Dienst stellen; **to lay up a ~ for repairs** Schiff in Reparatur nehmen; **to leave the ~** von Bord gehen; **to let a ~ go down the wind** Schiff seinem Schicksal überlassen; **to load a ~ on the berth** Schiff mit Stückgut befrachten; **to make ~ fast** Schiff festmachen; **to mask a ~ under neutral flag** Schiff unter falscher Flagge laufen lassen; **to moor a ~** Schiff vor Anker legen; **to pass a ~ into a dock** Schiff in ein Dock einschleusen; **to post a ~ missing** Schiff als verloren bezeichnen; **to put a ~ in commission** Schiff in Dienst stellen; **to put up a ~ for freight** Schiff zur Verladung vormerken; **to put a ~ into port** Schiff in den Hafen einbringen; **to recommission a ~** Schiff wieder einstellen; **to run a ~ aground** Schiff auflaufen lassen (festfahren) **to scuttle a ~** Schiff anbohren; **to store a ~ with provisions** Schiff verproviantieren; **to strand a ~** Schiff auflaufen lassen; **to surrender a ~** Schiff aufgeben (verlassen); **to take ~** an Bord gehen; **to take a ~ to freight** Schiff befrachten; **to trade with a ~** Schiff gewerblich nutzen; **to unload a ~** Schiff entladen (löschen); **to unload a ~** Schiff entladen; **to unrig a ~** Schiff abtakeln;
  ~'s agent Schiffsmakler, -agent; **~'s articles** Heuervertrag; **~'s bill** Bordkonnossement; **~ biscuit** Schiffszwieback; **~ breaker** Schiffsaufkäufer, Ausschlachter, Verschrotter, Abwrackgeschäft; **~ broker** Schiffs-, Frachtenmakler; **~ brokerage** Frachten-, Schiffsmaklergeschäft; **~ canal** See-, Schiffahrtskanal; **~'s captain** Schiffskapitän; **~'s carpenter** Schiffszimmermann; **~ chandler** Schiffslieferant, Lieferant von Schiffsbedarf; **~ chandlery** Schiffsbedarf, Schiffsbedarfmagazin, -handlung; **~-channel** Schiffahrtskanal; **~'s company** Schiffsbesatzung; **~'s construction** Schiffskonstruktion; **~ damage** Havarie-, Schiffsschaden; **~'s days** Entladetage; **~ deliverer** Auslader, Löscher, *(forwarder)* Schiffsspediteur; **~ destination** Löschplatz; **~'s distress signal** Schiffsnotsignal; **~ financing** Schiffsfinanzierung; **~'s freight** Schiffsfracht; **~'s hold** Schiffs-, Verladeraum; **~'s husband** Korrespondenz-, Mitreeder; **~ insurance** Schiffsversicherung; **~'s inventory** Schiffsinventar; **~'s journal** Schiffstage-, Logbuch; **~ ladder** Schiffsleiter; **~ letter** Schiffsbrief; **~'s log** Schiffslogbuch; **~'s manifest** Lade-, Warenverzeichnis; **~ master** Schiffer, Schiffsführer, Kapitän; **~ mortgage** Schiffshypothek; **~ news** Schiffahrtsnachrichten; **~'s newspaper** Bordzeitung; **~'s option** *(marine insurance)* Wahlrecht des Schiffseigners; **~ order** Schiffsauftrag; **~'s papers** Schiffspapiere, -dokumente; **~'s passport** See-, Schiffsbrief; **~'s policy** Schiffspolice; **~'s protest** Havarieerklärung, Seeprotest, Verklarung; **~'s rail** Reling des Schiffes; **~ railway** Schiffseisenbahn; **~'s receipt** Schiffsempfangsschein; **~'s register** Schiffsregisterbrief, -zertifikat; **~-repairing company** Reparaturwerft; **~'s report** *(at British port)* Schiffsmeldung; **~ reservation** Schiffsreservierung; **~ stores** Schiffsbedarfsmagazin; **~'s stores** Vorräte an Bord; **~ utilization** Schiffsraumausnutzung.

shipboard, on an Bord;
  ~ container Schiffsbehälter.

shipborne aircraft Bordflugzeug.

shipbreaking Schiffsverschrottung, Ausschlachtung eines Schiffes, *(Scot.)* Einbruch in ein Schiff.

shipbuilder Schiffsbauer, -baumeister, *(shipwright)* Werftbesitzer;
  ~'s yard Schiffswerft.

shipbuilding Schiffsbau;
  ~ boom Konjunktur in der Schiffsbauindustrie; **~ capacity** Schiffsbaukapazität; **~ company** Schiffsbaugesellschaft; **~ industry** Schiffsbau[industrie]; **~ market** Schiffsbaumarkt; **~ nationalization** Verstaatlichung der Schiffahrtsindustrie; **~ order** Schiffsbauauftrag; **~ slump** Schiffsbaukrise.

shiphoist Schiffsaufzug.

shipload Schiffsladung, -last, *(document)* Schiffsempfangsschein;
  by the ~ in riesigen Mengen.

shiploading Schiffsbeladung, -verladung.

shipman Seemann, Schiffer, Matrose.

shipmanship Navigationskunst.

shipmaster Schiffsherr, Schiffer, Kapitän.

shipmate Schiffsmaat.

shipment Verschiffung, *(consignment)* [Waren]sendung, Ladung, Frachtgut, *(US, forwarding)* Spedition, Expedition, Ab-, Versendung, Be-, Verfrachtung, Verladung, Versand, *(shipload)* Schiffsladung;

ready for ~ versandbereit; **received for ~** zur Verschiffung empfangen, *(US)* als Frachtgut registriert;

collective ~ Sammelladung; **composite ~** Sammelladung; **consolidated ~** *(Br.)* Sammelladung; **daily ~** Tagesversand; **drop ~** Auftragssendung; **factory ~** Versand ab Fabrik; **general-commodity ~** Sammelgutladung; **gold ~** Goldsendung; **high-cost peak ~** teure Frachtsendungen in Spitzenverkehrszeiten; **individual ~** Einzeltransport; **interstate ~** binnenstaatlicher Versand; **less-than-carload ~** *(US)* Stückgutsendung, -versand; **merchandise ~** Warenversand; **overseas ~** Überseetransport; **partial ~** Teilsendung, -verladung; **pooled ~** Sammelladung; **prompt ~** prompte Verladung; **short ~** Minderlieferung; **single ~** Einzelversand; **split ~** Teilsendung, -verladung; **through ~** Durchgangsfracht, -ladung; **trucking ~** Überlandtransport, -versand; **truckload ~** *(US)* Stückgutversand;

~ on deck Verladung auf Deck; **~ of food [stuffs]** Lebensmittelsendung; **~ of gold** Goldversand; **~ of goods** Warenversand; **~ at less-than-carload** *(US)* Stückgutversand; **incoming (outgoing) ~ of merchandise** ein(aus)gehende Warensendungen; **~ by sea** Seetransport; **~ of spare parts** Ersatzteilsendung;

to call forward a ~ Sendung abrufen; **to expedite ~** Versand beschleunigen; **to handle ~s** Transporte abwickeln;

~ account Versandkonto; **~ invoice** Versandrechnung; **~ operation** Fracht-, Versandbetrieb; **~ weight** Verschiffungs-, Versandgewicht.

shipowner Reeder, Schiffseigentümer, -eigner;

~s' club Reedereiversicherungsverein auf Gegenseitigkeit; **~'s office** Reederei.

shippable verschiffbar.

shipped an Bord gebracht, verladen, verschifft, versandt, abgesandt;

when ~ nach Verladung;

~ in carloads *(US)* in Waggonladung versandt; **~ on consignment** Versand auf eigene Rechnung; **~ for exportation** für Ausfuhrzwecke beladen; **~ by express** per Express [versandt]; **~ in wag(g)onloads** waggonweise verschickt;

~ bill of lading Verschiffungs-, Bordkonnossement; **~ goods** *(US)* Versandwaren.

shipper Verschiffer, Ab-, Verlader, *(US, land transport)* Ab-, Versender, Spediteur, Verfrachter, *(US, railway)* Eisenbahnspediteur;

all-purpose ~ Universalspediteur; **country ~** *(US)* Binnenspediteur;

~'s manifest *(US)* Ausfuhrdeklaration, Zollausfuhrerklärung; **~'s memorandum** Konnossement; **~'s order** *(bill of lading)* Eigentumsvorbehalt des Spediteurs; **~'s papers** Schiffs-, Versandpapiere, Verladepapiere; **~'s representative** Speditionsagent.

shipping Verladung, Verladen, *(dispatch, US)* Versand, Versendung, Spedition, Auflieferung, *(navigation)* [Handels]schiffahrt, *(on board ship)* Anbordnehmen von Gütern, Verschiffung, *(vessels)* Schiffsbestand, Gesamttonnage, Handelsflotte;

ready for ~ zur Verladung bereit;

coastal ~ Küstenschiffahrt; **idle ~** aufgelegte Tonnage; **inland ~** Binnenschiffahrt; **maritime ~** Seeschiffahrt; **merchant ~** Handelsschiffahrt;

~ of goods Güterversendung, Warenversand; **~ by rail** *(US)* Eisenbahnversand;

to be interested in ~ sein Geld in der Schiffsbauindustrie angelegt haben; **to take ~s** laden, an Bord nehmen;

~ Act *(US)* Schiffahrtsgesetz; **~ advice** Verschiffungs-, Versandbenachrichtigung, Versandanzeige; **~ advice note** Versandanzeige, -benachrichtigung; **~ agency** Schiffsagentur, Schiffahrtskontor, *(US)* Speditionsgeschäft, -firma; **~ agent** Schiffsagent, -makler, Reedereivertreter [im Ausland], *(US)* [Seehafen]spediteur; **~ agreement** Schiffsabkommen; **~ announcement** *(US)* Versandanzeige, **~ area** *(US)* Versandgebiet; **~ articles** Heuervertrag, Schiffsmusterrolle; **~ association** *(US)* Versandvereinigung; **~ authorities** Schiffahrtsbehörden; **~ bill** Verzeichnis verschiffter Waren, Warenbegleitschein, Manifest, *(customs)* Zollfreischein; **~ board** Seeamt, Schiffahrtsbehörde; **~ broker** Schiffsmakler; **~ business** Schiffahrt, Seehandel, -transportgeschäft, Reederei, *(US)* Spedition, Spe-

ditionsgeschäft; **to be in the ~ business** im Schiffshandel (Speditionsgewerbe) sein; **~ card** Liste der Abfahrtsdaten; **~ certificate** Verladezeugnis; **~ charges** Verschiffungs-, Verladegebühren, *(US)* Versand-, Transport-, Speditionskosten, -gebühren; **~ clerk** *(Br.)* Expedient, Leiter der Versandabteilung, Versand-, Schiffsangestellter, *(US)* Spediteur; **~ commissioner** *(US)* Seemannsamtsleiter; **~ company** Schiffahrtsgesellschaft, Reederei; **~ concerns** Schiffsangelegenheiten; **suitable ~ conditions** *(US)* angemessene Transportbeschaffenheit; **~ Conference** Schiffahrtskonferenz; **~ container** *(US)* Versandbehälter; **~ contract** *(US)* Frachtvertrag; **~ costs** *(US)* Versandkosten; **~ country** Herkunftsland; **~ crate** *(US)* Versandkiste; **~ date** Verschiffungstag, *(US)* Versandtermin, Absendetag; **~ department** *(US)* Versandabteilung, Expedition; **~ directory** Schiffahrtskalender; **~ documents** Schiffspapiere, *(US, land transport)* Versand-, Verladepapiere; **~ dues** Schiffsabgaben, Schiffahrtsgebühren; **~ exchange** Frachtenbörse; **~ executive** leitender Reedereiangestellter; **~ expenses** Schiffsspesen, *(US)* Verladekosten, Versand-, Fracht-, Transportkosten; **~ expenses account** *(US)* Speditionskonto; **~ experience** *(US)* Transporterfahrung; **~ facilities** *(US)* günstige Versand-, Frachtmöglichkeiten; **~ firm** Reederei; **~ formalities** *(US)* Versandformalitäten; **~ freight** Schiffsfracht; **~ freight services** Schiffsfrachtgewerbe; **~ group** Schiffskonzern; **~ house** Seehandlung, Reederei; **~ industry** Schiffsbau[industrie]; **~ instructions** *(US)* Versandanweisung, -vorschrift; **~ insurance** *(US)* Transportversicherung; **~ intelligence** Schiffahrtsnachrichten; **~ interests** Schiffahrtsinteressen; **~ issues** *(stock exchange)* Schiffahrtswerte; **~ lane** Schiffahrtsroute; **~ law** *(Br.)* Schiffahrts-, Seerecht; **~ line** Schiffahrtslinie; **to be in the ~ line** Reederei betreiben; **~ list** Schiffsverzeichnis, -liste, *(dispatch book, US)* Versandverzeichnis, -liste; **~ manager** *(US)* Leiter der Versandabteilung; **~ marks** *(US)* Versandmarkierung; **~ master** *(Br.)* Heuerbaas, Schiffsmakler, Seeamtsleiter; **~ needs** Schiffahrtsbedürfnisse; **~ news** Schiffahrtsnachrichten, -berichte; **~ note** *(Br.)* Schiffszettel, *(US)* Verzeichnis der versandten Waren, Lade-, Anlieferungs-, Frachtannahme-, Warenbegleitschein; **~ office** *(US)* Speditionsbüro, *(Br.)* Büro eines Schiffsmaklers, Heuerbüro; **~ operator** Reeder; **~ opportunity** Schiffsgelegenheit; **~ order** Schiffszettel, *(US)* Transport-, Speditions-, Versandauftrag; **~ papers** Schiffspapiere, *(US)* Versandpapiere; **~ place** *(US)* Versandort; **~ point** *(US)* Versandort, -station; **~ point inspection** *(US)* Prüfung am Versandort; **~ policy** Schiffahrtspolitik; **~ port** Ausgangs-, Versand-, Ausfuhr-, Verladehafen; **~ prices** *(US)* Verladepreise; **~ and forwarding receipt** *(US)* Spediteurübernahmeschein; **~ report** Versandanzeige, *(US)* Eisenbahntransportbericht; **~ room** *(US)* Versand-, Verpackungsraum; **~ route** Schiffahrtsweg; **~ sample** *(US)* Versandmuster; **~ season** Schiffahrtssaison; **~ section** Markt für Schiffahrtswerte; **~ service** Schiffahrtsverkehr, *(US)* Frachtdienst; **~ shares** *(stocks, US)* Schiffahrtsaktien, -werte; **~ slump** rückläufige Konjunktur der Schiffsbauindustrie; **~ space** Schiffsraum, *(US)* Versand-, Fracht-, Transportraum; **~ stocks** *(US)* Schiffahrtsaktien, -werte; **~ stretch-outs** *(US)* Überstunden im Speditionsgewerbe; **~ subsidy** Schiffahrtssubvention; **~ terms** *(US)* Versandbedingungen; **~ ticket** *(US)* Versand-, Lieferschein; **~ time** *(US)* Versandzeit, -termin; **~ trade** Reedereibetrieb, *(US)* Transport-, Speditionsgeschäft; **~ traffic** Schiffsverkehr; **~ value** Verschiffungswert; **~ weight** Fracht-, Ablade-, Verschiffungsgewicht; **average ~ weight** durchschnittliches Verschiffungs-, Durchschnittsverladegewicht; **~ worker** *(US)* Versandarbeiter, Packer.

shipplane Bordflugzeug.

shipshape in tadelloser Ordnung.

shipside an Schiffsseite;

delivery ~ Anlieferung an Schiffsseite.

shipway Helling, Stapel, *(marine transportation)* Schiffskanal.

shipwreck Schiffbruch, *(wrecked ship)* schiffbrüchiges Schiff, Wrack;

~ of one's hopes Scheitern seiner Hoffnungen;

~ *(v.)* Schiffbruch verursachen, *(fig.)* zum Scheitern bringen, ruinieren;

to be saved from ~ dem Schiffbruch entgehen, gerettet werden;

to suffer ~ Schiffbruch erleiden.

shipwrecked *(v.)* gestrandet, schiffbrüchig;

~ goods Schiffbruchgüter; **~ person** Schiffbrüchiger.

shipwright Schiffbauer, Werftbesitzer.

~'s wharf Werft.

shipyard Schiffswerft;

~ worker Werftarbeiter.

shirk *(v.)* sich [herum]drücken;
  ~ going to the office Aufbruch zum Büro hinauszögern.
shirker arbeitsscheuer Mensch, Drückeberger.
shirt, to get s. one's ~ out *(sl.)* j. aus dem Häuschen bringen; **to keep one's ~ on** *(sl.)* ruhig Blut bewahren; **to lose one's ~** Kopf und Kragen verlieren; **to put one's ~ upon s. th** *(sl.)* alles auf eine Karte setzen;
  ~-sleeve leger, ungeniert, ohne Formalitäten; **~-sleeve diplomacy** hemdsärmelige Diplomatie.
shirttail *(sl.)* Leitartikel.
shiver Schüttelfrost, Gänsehaut;
  to have the ~s jämmerliche Angst haben.
shoal Untiefe, Sandbank;
  ~s of people Menschenmassen.
shock Stoß, Erschütterung;
  earthquake ~ Erdbebenstoß; **great ~** *(fig.)* schwerer Schlag; **traumatizing ~** seelischer Schock;
  to get the ~ of one's life sich zu Tode erschrecken; **to recover from the ~ of the election result** *(stock exchange)* sich von dem durch den Wahlausgang verursachten Schock erholen;
  ~ absorber *(car)* Stoßdämpfer; **~ absorption** Stoßdämpfung; **~ action** *(mil.)* Überraschungsangriff; **~ brigade** *(US)* Stoßbrigade; **~ loss** *(insurance)* Katastrophenschaden; **~ sacking** plötzliche Entlassung; **~ tactics** *(mil.)* Durchbruchtaktik; **~ therapy (treatment)** Schocktherapie, -behandlung; **~ troops** *(mil.)* Stoßtrupp; **~ worker** Straßenarbeiter; **~ workers** *(US)* Stoßbrigade.
shocker *(Br., sl.)* Schundbuch, Schauerroman, -stück.
shocking| behavio(u)r anstößiges Benehmen; **~ handwriting** miserable Handschrift; **~ news** schreckliche Nachrichten.
shockingly expensive schamlos teuer.
shoddy Schund, Kitsch, *(fig., US)* Emporkömmling;
  ~ aristocracy Pseudoaristokratie; **~ literature** Schundliteratur; **~ piece of work** Arbeit von geringer Qualität.
shoe, over the (up to the) ~s bis über die Ohren;
  dead men's ~s ungeduldig erwartetes Erbe;
  ~ *(v.)* the goose Zeit vertrödeln;
  to be in another man's ~s an jds. Stelle (Lage) sein, in jds. Haut stecken; **to die in one's ~** eines gewaltsamen Todes sterben; **to know where the ~ pinches** wissen, wo der Schuh drückt; **not to like to be in s. one's ~s** nicht in jds. Haut stecken wollen; **to put the ~ on the right foot** *(fig.)* Schuld dem wirklichen Schuldigen geben; **to shake in one's ~s** Bammel haben; **to stand in s. one's ~s** in jds. Haut stecken; **to step into s. one's ~s** jds. Stelle einnehmen;
  ~ box Schuhkarton.
shoeblack *(Br.)* Stiefelputzer.
shoelace *(Br.)* Schnürsenkel.
shoestring *(US)* Schnürsenkel, *(US sl.)* völlig unzureichendes Kapital;
  ~ *(a.)* *(US)* völlig unterkapitalisiert;
  to start a business on a ~ Unternehmen mit völlig unzureichenden Mitteln (ein paar Groschen) starten;
  ~ budget unzureichender Etat; **~ campaign** aussichtsloser Werbefeldzug; **~ margin** *(US)* völlig ungenügende Deckung.
shoo-in *(US)* Spitzenkandidat.
shoot *(dumping place)* Schuttabladestelle, *(film)* [Film]aufnahme, *(hunting)* Jagd[gesellschaft, -revier];
  ~ *(v.)* schießen, feuern, erschießen, *(film)* Filmaufnahmen machen, filmen, drehen;
  ~ ahead sich an die Spitze schieben; **~ the amber** *(US sl.)* bei Gelb über die Kreuzung fahren; **~ away all one's ammunition** seine ganze Munition verfeuern; **~ one's bolt** alles in seinen Kräften Stehende tun; **~ the bull** *(sl.)* Unsinn reden, quatschen; **~ craps** *(US)* Würfel spielen; **~ dead** erschießen; **~ down a bomber** Bombenflugzeug abschießen; **~ into new high ground** *(prices)* in rascher Steigerung neue Höchstkurse erzielen; **~ a line** *(sl.)* angeben; **~ on location** Filmaufnahmen im Freien machen; **~ the moon** *(Br., sl.)* mit der Kasse durchbrennen; **~ off one's mouth** *(US sl.)* drauflosreden, quatschen, sich verplappern; **~ questions at s. o.** j. mit Fragen bombardieren; **~ rubbish** Schutt (Müll) abladen; **~ straight** *(sl.)* sich anständig aufführen; **~ the traffic lights** bei Rot über die Ampel fahren; **~ up a town** *(US sl.)* Stadt terrorisieren; **~ up in the last months** in den letzten Monaten enorm steigen; **~ one's wad** *(sl.)* alles auf eine Karte setzen; **~ the works** *(sl.)* nicht auf halbem Wege stehen bleiben;
  to rent a ~ for the season Jagd pachten;
  ~-up Feuergefecht, Schießerei.
shooting Schießerei, Erschießung, *(film)* Dreharbeiten, Filmaufnahmen, *(hunting)* Jagdberechtigung;

to sell the ~ on an estate Jagd auf einem Gelände verpachten; **~ box** Jagdhütte; **~ brake** *(Br.)* Kombiwagen; **~ gallery** Schießstand; **~ ground** Jagdrevier; **~ incident** Schießerei; **~ licence** *(US)* Jagdschein; **~ lodge** Jagdhütte; **~ match** Wettschießen; **to be back on the verge of a ~ match** kurz vor einer militärischen Auseinandersetzung stehen; **~ range** Schießstand; **~ rights** Jagdrecht; **~ script** Drehplan; **~ season** Jagdzeit; **~ war** heißer Krieg.
shootout *(sl.)* Schießerei, Revolverduell.
shop [Kauf]laden, [Laden]geschäft, Handlung, *(occupation)* Geschäft, Gewerbe, Beruf, Fach, *(operational research)* Bearbeitungsstelle, *(plan)* Betrieb, Fabrik, *(premises)* Geschäftslokal, *(school, Br., sl.)* Penne, *(university, Br., sl.)* Uni, *(workshop)* Werkstatt, Werkstätte;
  all over the ~ *(sl.)* in riesiger Unordnung;
  ~s Fabrikwerkstätten;
  anti-union ~ *(US)* gewerkschaftsfeindlicher Betrieb; **approved closed ~** *(Br.)* staatlich genehmigter gewerkschaftspflichtiger Betrieb; **closed anti-union ~** *(US)* Betrieb, der nur nichtorganisierte Arbeiter einstellt; **antique ~** Antiquitätenladen, -geschäft; **china ~** Porzellanwarengeschäft; **bucket ~** Winkelbörse; **closed ~** gewerkschaftspflichtiger (voll gewerkschaftlich organisierter) Betrieb; **closed-union ~ with closed union** *(US)* Betrieb, der nur Gewerkschaftsangehörige einstellt; **closed-union ~ with open union** *(US)* Betrieb, in dem unter der Auflage des Gewerkschaftseintritts auch nicht gewerkschaftlich organisierte Arbeiter eingestellt werden; **confectioner's ~** Süßwarengeschäft; **cut-price ~** Einzelhandelsgeschäft mit Rabattprinzip; **draper's ~** Tuchhandlung; **duty-free ~** zollfreier Laden; **erecting ~** Montagehalle; **fittings ~** Montagewerkstatt; **fruit ~** Obstgeschäft; **ironmonger's ~** Eisenwarenhandlung; **junk ~** Ramschladen; **machine ~** [mechanische] Werkstatt; **maintenance of membership ~** *(US)* Betrieb, der die Aufrechterhaltung der Gewerkschaftszugehörigkeit verlangt; **mobile ~** fahrender [Lebensmittel]laden, fahrbarer Verkaufsstand; **open ~** offener Laden, *(US)* gewerkschaftsfreier Betrieb; **open-union ~** *(US)* Gewerkschaft anerkennender Betrieb; **the other ~** die Konkurrenz; **pattern ~** Modellwerkstätte; **post-entry closed ~** *(Br.)* nach Arbeitsantritt gewerkschaftspflichtiger Betrieb, Beitrittszwang nur Arbeitsanstellung in einem gewerkschaftspflichtigen Betrieb; **preferential nonunion ~** *(US)* Betrieb, der nicht gewerkschaftlich organisierte Arbeiter bevorzugt; **preferential union ~** *(US)* Betrieb, der Gewerkschaftszugehörige bei der Einstellung bevorzugt; **repair ~** Reparaturwerkstatt; **state-run ~** staatliches Einkaufsgeschäft; **stationer's ~** Schreibwarenhandlung; **struck ~** bestreikter Betrieb; **tobacco ~** Zigarrengeschäft, Tabakwarenladen; **union ~** *(US)* gewerkschaftspflichtiger Betrieb; **well-stocked ~** wohlassortierter Laden;
  ~-by-phone telefonische Einkaufserledigung;
  ~ *(v.)* kaufen, einkaufen [gehen], Besorgungen (Einkäufe) machen, *(criminal, sl.)* verpfeifen, auffliegen lassen;
  ~ around Preisvergleiche in den Läden anstellen; **~ near one's home** seine Besorgungen in Wohnungsnähe machen; **~ regularly at A's** regelmäßig bei A einkaufen;
  to be all over the ~ in alle Himmelsrichtungen verstreut sein; **to break and enter a ~** Ladeneinbruch begehen; **to buy a ~ with all fixtures** Laden mit der gesamten Ausstattung erwerben; **to clear a ~** ausverkaufen; **to close down a ~** Geschäft schließen; **to close up a ~** Geschäft schließen; **to come to the wrong ~** an die falsche Adresse geraten; **to fit out a ~** Geschäft einrichten; **to give up one's ~ to one's son** sein Geschäft seinem Sohn übergeben; **to go through the ~s** *(apprentice)* Lehre (Ausbildungszeit) durchmachen; **to keep [a] ~** Laden haben (halten), Ladenbesitzer sein; **to keep ~ for s. o.** j. im Laden kurzfristig vertreten; **to keep a ~ open** Laden offenhalten (aufmachen); **to lease a ~** Laden vermieten; **to manage a ~** Geschäft führen; **to open a ~** Laden eröffnen; **to patronize a ~** regelmäßig in einem Laden einkaufen; **to rent a ~** Laden [ver]mieten; **to round the ~s looking for s. th.** Läden nach etw. abklappern; **to run a ~** Geschäft führen, Ladengeschäft betreiben; **to send s. o. down to the ~s** j. einkaufen schicken; **to set up ~** Einzelhandelsgeschäft eröffnen; **to shut up ~** Laden zuschließen (dichtmachen), *(give up)* Geschäft aufgeben, vom Geschäftsleben zurückziehen, Bude zumachen, *(stop working)* Feierabend machen; **to sink the ~** *(coll.)* nicht vom Geschäft reden; **to smell of the ~** sich nur für seinen Beruf interessieren; **to start a ~** Laden eröffnen; **to take a ~** Laden übernehmen; **to talk ~** fachsimpeln; **to work in the ~s** in der Fabrik arbeiten;
  ~ will open at the beginning of November Geschäftseröffnung Anfang November;

~s and Offices Act (Br.) Arbeitsplatzgesetz; **~ advertising** Ladenwerbung; **~ agreement** Betriebstarifvertrag, -vereinbarung; **agency ~ agreement** (Br.) Betriebstarifvereinbarung mit Beitragszwang; **approved closed-~ agreement** (Br.) Vereinbarung zur Einrichtung eines vollgewerkschaftspflichtigen Betriebs, Tarifvereinbarung zum Zweck der Festlegung von Zwangsbeiträgen; **~ assistant** (Br.) Handlungsgehilfe, Ladenangestellter, Verkäufer[in]; **~ assistants** (Br.) Bedienung[spersonal]; **~ audit** Händlerbefragung [über den Einzelhandelsumsatz]; **~ bell** Ladenklingel, Türglocke; **~ bill** Geschäftsanzeige, Preisliste, Aushängeschild; **~ buying** (stock exchange) Berufskäufe; **~ case** Vitrine; **~ chairman** (US) Betriebsratsvorsitzender; **~ check** Bestandsaufnahme; **~ clerk** Verkäufer, Ladenangestellter; **~ closing** Ladenschluß; **~ club** Sparverein; **~ commercial complex** Ladenverkaufszentrum; **~ committee** (US) Betriebsrat-, ausschuß; **~ conditions** Betriebsbedingungen, -verhältnisse; **~ cost** Fabrikkosten; **~ council** (US) Betriebsrat; **~ council law** (US) Betriebsrätegesetz; **~ course** Betriebskursus; **~ data** Betriebsangaben; **~ deputy** (US) Betriebsratsvorsitzender, Vertrauensmann der Belegschaft; **~ detective** Ladendetektiv; **~ discipline** Betriebsdisziplin; **~ door** Ladentür; **~s Early Closing Act** (Br.) Ladenschlußgesetz; **~ employee** Ladenangestellter, Betriebsangehöriger; **duty-free ~ facilities** zollfreie Einkaufsmöglichkeit; **~ fitter** Ladenausstatter; **~ fittings** (Br.) Ladeneinrichtung; **~-fitting work** (Br.) Ausstattungsarbeiten; **~ foreman** Werkmeister; **~ front** Ladenfront, Schaufenster, Auslage; **~ hours** Verkaufs-, Geschäftszeit; **~ infraction** Betriebsvergehen; **~ lease** Ladenmiete; **~ management** Betriebsleitung; **~ master** Werkmeister; **~ order** innerbetrieblicher Auftrag; **~ paper** Packpapier; **~ porter** Markthelfer; **~ premises** Geschäfts-, Ladenräume; **~ price** Ladenpreis; **~ property** Laden-, Geschäftsgrundstück; **closed ~ provisions** (trade union, US) Migliedschaftszwang; **~ rent** Lokal-, Geschäfts-, Ladenmiete; **~ right** (patent law, US) Herstellungs-, Fabrikationsrecht, Ausnutzung von Betriebserfindungen durch den Firmeninhaber, Arbeitgeberlizenz; **~ rules** Betriebsordnung; **~ selling** (stock exchange) Berufsverkäufe; **~-soiled** angeschmutzt; **~ steward** Gewerkschafts-, Arbeitnehmervertreter, Vertrauens-, Betriebsobmann, Betriebsratsvorsitzender; **~ stewards' demands** Betriebsratsforderungen; **~ superintendent** Betriebsleiter; **~ till** Ladenkasse; **~-training department** Lehrwerkstätte.

shopboard Ladentisch.

shopbook (US) Journal, Geschäfts-, Hauptbuch.

shopboy Laufbursche.

shopbreaker Ladendieb.

shopbreaking Ladeneinbruch, -diebstahl.

shopcraft | settlement betriebsgewerkschaftliches Abkommen; **~ union** Betriebsgewerkschaft.

shopfloor Fabrikarbeiter, Belegschaft;
on the ~ im Betrieb;
~ dissent Ablehnung durch die Betriebe; **~ necessities** betriebsbedingte Notwendigkeiten; **~ job** Fabrikarbeit; **~ participation** Mitbestimmung am Arbeitsplatz; **~ resistance** betrieblicher Widerstand; **~ space** Ladenfläche; **~ staff** Betriebspersonal.

shopgirl (Br.) Ladenmädchen, Verkäuferin.

shopkeeper (Br.) Geschäfts-, Ladeninhaber, Ladenbesitzer, (shelf warmer) Ladenhüter, (small trader) Krämer, Kleinhändler;
~'s smock Ladenkittel.

shopkeeping Ladenbetrieb, Kleinhandel.

shoplifter Laden-, Warenhausdieb.

shoplifting Laden-, Warenhausdiebstahl.

shoplike ladenähnlich.

shopman Ladendiener, -angestellter, -gehilfe, Kommis, Verkäufer, (shopkeeper) Ladeninhaber, (workshop) Werkstattinhaber, Maschinenschlosser.

shopmark Markenzeichen.

shopmobile fahrbare Verkaufsstelle.

shopper Ladenbesucher, Käufer, (buying agent) Einkäufer;
Christmas ~ Weihnachtseinkäufer;
~s on the lookout for a bargain Gelegenheitskäufer.

shopping Einkauf, Einkaufen [in Läden], Einkäufe, Besorgungen, Ladenbesuch;
spring ~ Frühjahrseinkauf;
to do some ~ einige Einkäufe (Besorgungen) erledigen; **to go [out] ~** Einkäufe (Besorgungen) machen, einholen (einkaufen) gehen;
~ arcade Arkadenläden; **~ area** Geschäftsgegend, -viertel; **~ bag** Einkaufstasche, -beutel, (statistics) statistischer Warenkorb; **~-bag items** Posten des statistischen Warenkorbs; **~**

~ basket Einkaufskorb, (statistics) Warenkorb; **~ cart** Einkaufswagen; **~ center** (US) (centre, Br.) Geschäftsviertel, -zentrum, Einkaufszentrum; **~ cheque** (Br.) Warengutschein; **~ day** Einkaufstag; **~ district** Geschäftsgegend, -viertel; **~ expedition** Ladenbesuch; **~ facility** Einkaufserleichterung; **~ goods** (US sl.) Konsum-, Verkehrsgüter, erst nach Preisvergleich gekaufte Waren; **~ guide** Verkaufskatalog; **~ hinterland** Einzugsgebiet; **~ hours** [Laden]verkaufszeit; **~ list** Einkaufsliste, Besorgungszettel; **~ mall** Einkaufszentrum; **~ news** Kundenzeitschrift; **~ note** Einkaufshinweis; **~ parade** Ausstellungsraum; **~ promenade** Laden-, Einkaufsstraße; **~ spree** Einkaufsorgie; **~ stopover** Einkaufszwischenlandung; **~ street** Laden-, Geschäftsstraße.

shoppy voller Geschäfte, (showing petty commercialism) krämer-, philisterhaft;
~ neighbo(u)rhood Geschäftsgegend; **~ part of a city** Geschäftszentrum einer Stadt; **~ street** Laden-, Geschäftsstraße; **~ talk** Fachsimpelei.

shoptalk Fachsimpelei.

shopwalker [Geschäfts]aufsicht im Laden, Empfangschef, Ladenaufseher, aufsichtsführender Abteilungsleiter [im Warenhaus].

shopwear Angeschmutztsein.

shopwindow Laden-, Schaufenster;
to dress a ~ Auslage herrichten, Schaufenster dekorieren; **to have everything in the ~** sehr auf Äußerlichkeiten bedacht sein; **to put all one's goods in the ~** (fig.) für keinerlei Reserven Sorge tragen;
~ advertising Schaufensterwerbung, -reklame; **~ lighting** Schaufensterbeleuchtung.

shopwoman Verkäuferin.

shopwork maschinelle Arbeit, Werkstattarbeit.

shopworker Laden-, Maschinenarbeiter.

shopworn angestaubt, angeschmutzt, beschädigt.

shore Küste, Ufer, Strand, Gestade, (prop) Strebe, Stützbalken;
from ~ to ~ (marine insurance) von Ufer zu Ufer; **in ~** in Küstennähe;
~ (v.) (fig.) unterstützen;
~ up export industries der Exportwirtschaft jedmögliche Unterstützung zuteil werden lassen;
to go on ~ an Land gehen;
~-based (mil.) an der Küste stationiert; **~ lands** Watt; **~ leave** Landurlaub; **~ line** Küstenlinie; **~ patrol** Küstenstreife, -patrouille.

shoreless ohne Landemöglichkeit.

shorn of one's money um sein Geld gebracht.

short (abbreviation) Kurzform, Abkürzung, (bear) Baissespekulant, Baissier, Fixer, (deficit) Manko, Fehlbetrag, Defizit, (film) Bei-, Kurzfilm, (selling short) Verkauf ohne Deckung;
~s (Br., government securities) Papiere mit kürzerer Laufzeit, (print.) Fehlabzüge, (refuse used for inferior production) zur Weiterverarbeitung geeignete Abfallprodukte, (securities) ohne Deckung verkaufte Wertpapiere, (short-dated stocks) Papiere mit bis zu fünfjähriger Laufzeit, (stock exchange, US) Baissespekulanten, -partei;
the ~s Pleite;
hot ~ (sl.) gestohlenes (kurzgeschlossenes) Auto;
~ in [the] cash Kassendefizit, -manko; **~ for** Abkürzung für; **cash ~s and overts** Kassenüberschüsse und Fehlbeträge; **the long and the ~ of it** um es kurz zu sagen, zusammenfassend;
~ (a.) knapp, (securities) blanko, deckungslos, noch anzuschaffen, (at short sight) mit kurzer Sicht, (short-term) kurzfristig, mit kurzer Laufzeit, (suddenly) jäh, abrupt, plötzlich;
~ of liquid assets (funds) liquiditätsbeengt; **~ of cash** knapp (nicht) bei Kasse; **~ of hands** knapp an Arbeitskräften; **~ of means (money)** nicht bei Kasse, knapp an Geld; **~ and to the point** kurz und knapp; **~ of stock** kapitalarm; **~ of war** bis an den Rand eines Krieges;
~ (v.) (stock exchange) ohne Deckung verkaufen, fixen, Baisseverkauf tätigen;
to be ~ fehlen; **to be $ 10 ~** zehn Dollar zu wenig [in der Kasse] haben; **to be ~ of** knapp sein an, (stock exchange, US) noch Aktien einzudecken haben; **to be ~ of an article** Ware im Augenblick nicht vorrätig haben; **to be caught ~** in einer ungünstigen Lage überrascht werden; **to be little ~ of a miracle** beinahe an ein Wunder grenzen; **to be ~ of money** nicht bei Geld sein; **to be ~ in one's payments** verspätet zahlen, säumiger Zahler sein; **to be ~ of petrol** kein Benzin mehr haben; **to be still three miles ~ of one's destination** noch fünf Kilometer zu fahren haben; **to be ~ with s. o.** j. kurz abfertigen; **to be ~ of staff** an Personalmangel leiden; **to be ~ of stock** (US) noch

Aktien einzudecken haben; **to be ~ of trading capital** nicht über ausreichendes Betriebskapital verfügen; **to commit every crime ~ of murder** jedes Verbrechen mit Ausnahme von Mord begehen; **to cut ~ the proceedings** Verfahren rasch beenden; **to enter ~** *(customs)* unter dem Wert (zu wenig) angeben; **to enter** Wert deklarieren; **to fall ~ of expectations** den Erwartungen nicht entsprechen; **to go ~** blanko (in Baisse) verkaufen, fixen; **to go ~ of money** geldknapp sein; **to keep s. o. ~ of money** j. knapp bei Kasse halten; **to make it ~** sich kurz fassen; **to make ~ work of s. th.** kurzen Prozeß mit etw. machen; **to run ~** knapp werden, zur Neige gehen; **to run ~ of provision(s)** knapp an Vorräten werden; **to sell ~** *(stock exchange)* ohne Deckung verkaufen, in Baisse spekulieren, fixen; **to stop ~** plötzlich bremsen; **to take s. o. up ~** j. unterbrechen;

~ account *(Br.)* Baisseposition, *(US)* Baisseengagements; **~ amount** Minderbetrag; **~ answer** barsche Antwort; **~ balance** Unterbilanz; **~ bill** Wechsel auf kurze Sicht, kurzfristiger Wechsel, *(bill of collection, Br.)* Inkassowechsel; **~ call** Stippvisite; **~ cause** Sache im Schnellverfahren; **~ circuit** *(el.)* Kurzschluß; **~-circuit** *(el.)* Kurzschluß verursachen; **~-circuit a system** System vereinfachen; **~-circuit appeal** *(advertising)* Kurzschlußappell; **~-commons** Hungerration; **to be on ~ commons** nicht genug zum Essen haben; **~ covering** *(US)* Deckungskauf; **~ credit** kurzfristiger Kredit; **~ crop** zu knappe Ernte; **~ cut** Abkürzung[sweg], *(fig.)* abgekürztes Verfahren, Schnellverfahren; **~ date** Kurzfristigkeit, kurze Sicht (Frist); **at ~ date** kurzfristig; **~-dated** kurz[fristig]; **~-dated bill** kurzfristiger Wechsel; **~-dated paper** *(Br.)* kurzfristiges Papier; **~ delivery** unvollständige Lieferung, Teil-, Minderlieferung; **to prevent ~ delivery** stets volles Lager haben; **~ deposits** kurzfristige Einlagen; **~ distance** Kurzstrecke; **~-distance goods traffic** *(Br.)* Güternahverkehr; **~-distance transport** *(Br.)* Nahtransport, -verkehr; **~ drink** Apéritif; **~ end of the market** Markt für kurzfristige Papiere; **~ end of the stick** *(sl.)* unerfreuliche Behandlung; **~ engagements** Baisseengagements; **~ entry** *(banking, Br.)* vorläufige Gutschrift, *(customs)* Unterdeklaration; **~ exchange** *(Br.)* kurzfristiger Devisenwechsel; **~ film** Kurzfilm; **~-form agreement** Kurzfassung eines Vertrags; **to have s. o. by the ~ hairs** *(sl.)* j. völlig in seiner Gewalt haben; **~-form report** Revisionsbericht in abgekürzter Form; **to be ~-handed** knapp an Arbeitskräften sein; **~ hauls** *(US)* Nahverkehr; **~-haul business** *(US)* Kurzstreckenfrachtgeschäft; **~-haul freight traffic** *(US)* Güternahverkehr; **~-haul trunk line** *(tel.)* Nahverkehrsleitung; **by a ~ head** *(fig.)* sehr knapp; **~ holiday** kleine Ferienreise, kurzer Urlaub, Kurzurlaub; **low-traffic ~ hop** Kurzstreckenverbindung; **~ hour** knappe Stunde; **~ hours** Kurzarbeit; **~ hundred** kleiner Zentner; **~ interest** fehlende (nicht verladene) Ware, *(insurance)* Überversicherung, *(of the market, US)* Baisseengagements, -position, Baissiers, Deckungsbedürfnis; **~-landed** zu knapp geliefert; **~ lease** kurzfristiger Miet-, Pachtvertrag; **~ leave** Kurzurlaub; **~ lecture** Kurzstunde; **~ letter** kurzer Brief; **~ line** nicht volle Zeile, Kurzzeile; **~ list** Vorauswahl, Auswahlliste, engere Kandidatenliste; **~-list** *(v.)* Kandidaten in die engere Wahl ziehen; **~-lived** von kurzem Bestand, kurzlebig; **~-lived assets** kurzlebige Wirtschaftsgüter; **~-lived success** schnell verpuffter Erfolg; **~ loan** kurzfristiges Darlehn; **~ loan fund** *(Br.)* Tagesgeldmarkt für Börsenmakler; **~ market** Baissemarkt; **~ measure** knappes Maß, Untermaß; **~ money** kurzfristiges Darlehn; **~ note** *(US)* kurzfristige Promesse; **~ notice** kurze Frist; **at ~ notice** kurzfristig kündbar; **to invest [money, capital] at ~ notice** [Geld, Kapital] kurzfristig anlegen; **~-notice charge** Kleinanzeigenzuschlag; **~ number** *(print.)* kleine Auflage; **~ offer** Baisseangebot; **~ order** *(restaurant)* Schnellgericht; **in ~ order** schnell; **~ paper** Wechsel auf kurze Sicht; **~ paragraph** kleine Textanzeige; **~ period** *(changes of demand)* kurzer Zeitraum; **~ position** *(investment fund)* Baisseengagement, Leerverkaufsposition; **~-posted** zu niedrig angesetzt; **~ premium** niedrige Prämie; **~ price** Nettopreis; **~-range aircraft** Kurzstreckenflugzeug; **~-range plan** kurzfristiger Plan; **~ rate** Devisenkurs für kurzfristige Wechsel, *(advertising, US)* ermäßigter Tarif, Rabattrück-, Nachbelastung, *(insurance)* erhöhte Prämie bei einjähriger Versicherung, Überprämie bei Kündigung durch den Versicherungsnehmer; **~ rates** reduzierte (ermäßigte) Preise; **~ rations** knappe Rationen; **~ return of interest** *(insurance)* Rückvergütung; **~-run** kurzfristig; **in the ~ run** auf kurze Sicht, kurzfristig; **used on ~ runs** *(bus)* auf Kurzstrecken eingesetzt; **~-run costs** kurzfristig entstehende Kosten; **~ sale** *(stock exchange, US)* Verkauf ohne Deckung, Leerverkauf, Blankoabgabe, -verkauf, Fixgeschäft, Terminverkauf, *(ready sale)* schneller Umsatz; **~ seller** *(stock*

exchange) Blankoverkäufer, Leerverkäufer, Fixer, Baissier; **~ selling** *(stock exchange)* Blankoabgaben, -verkäufe, Leerabgabe, Fixgeschäfte, Fixen; **~-ship** *(v.)* a consignment by 1 cwt einen Zentner Ware zu wenig liefern; **~-shipped** in ungenügender (nicht hinreichender) Menge verladen, unverladen geblieben; **~ shipment** Minderlieferung; **~ shrift** *(fig.)* kurzer Aufschub, Galgenfrist; **to give ~-shrift of** kurzen Prozeß machen; **~ side** *(stock exchange, US)* Baissepartei; **at ~ sight** mit kurzer Sicht; **~-sighted** kurzsichtig; **~-sighted policy** kurzsichtige Politik; **~ stock** *(US)* Baisseengagements, auf Baisse verkaufte (gefixte) Aktien; **~ story** Kurzgeschichte; **~ street** kurze Straße; **~ subject** Kurzfilm, Beiprogramm; **~ summons** Ladung mit abgekürzter Frist, *(US)* Schnellverfahren; **to be in ~ supply** beschränkt lieferbar sein; **to have a ~ temper** nicht über genügend Selbstbeherrschung verfügen; **~ term** *(advertising)* Abschluß für weniger als ein Jahr.

short-term kurzfristig, *(pol.)* nur der augenblicklichen Lage Rechnung tragend;
~ borrowings kurzfristige Geldaufnahmen; **~ capital gains** spekulationssteuerpflichtige Börsengewinne; **~ credit** kurzfristiger Kredit; **~ employee** kurzfristig Beschäftigter; **~ financing** Zwischen-, kurzfristige Finanzierung; **~ gains** in naher Zukunft zu erzielende Vorteile; **~ imprisonment** *(US)* kurze Freiheitsstrafe; **~ liability** kurzfristige Verbindlichkeit; **~ loan** kurzfristiges Darlehn; **~ loan, unsecured ~ loan** kurzfristiger Blankokredit; **~ measures** kurzfristige Maßnahmen; **~ notes** *(US)* kurzfristige Schuldscheine; **~ prison sentence** kurze Freiheitsstrafe; **~ prospects** Aussichten auf kurze Sicht, kurzfristige Aussichten, Geschäftsaussichten in der näheren Zukunft; **~ rate of interest** Zinssatz für Dreimonatsgeld.

short time verkürzte Arbeitszeit, Kurzarbeit, Arbeitszeitverkürzung;
~ *(v.)* s. o. j. als Kurzarbeiter beschäftigen;
to be on (work) ~ Kurzarbeiter sein, *(factory)* Kurzarbeit eingeführt haben, kurzarbeiten.

short-time | benefit Kurzarbeitgeld; **~ provisions** Kurzarbeitsbestimmungen; **~ treasury bills** unverzinsliche Schatzanweisungen, U-Schätze; **~ work** Kurzarbeit; **~ worker** Kurzarbeiter; **~ working** Kurzarbeit.

short | timed kurzfristig; **~ title** *(law)* Kurztitel; **~ ton** *(US)* Tonne; **~ train** Kurzzug; **to take a ~ view** nur die Gegenwart im Auge haben; **~ wave** Kurzwelle; **~-wave broadcast** Kurzwellensendung; **~-wave transmitter** Kurzwellensender; **~-wave treatment** Kurzwellenbehandlung; **~ way off** kurze Entfernung, nicht weit entfernt; **~ weight** Fehl-, Unter-, Mindergewicht, zu leichtes Gewicht, Manko; **to give ~ weight** knapp abwiegen; **to make ~ work of it** kurzen Prozeß mit etw. machen.

shortage *(bottleneck)* Engpaß, *(deficiency)* Fehl-, Minderbetrag, -menge, -bestand, Defizit, *(scarcity)* Klemme, Mangel, Knappheit[serscheinung], Verknappung, *(weight)* Gewichtsverlust, -abgang, Manko;
food ~ Lebensmittelknappheit; **housing ~** Wohnungsnot; **labo(u)r ~** Arbeitskräftemangel; **manpower ~** fehlende Arbeitskräfte; **merchandise (stock) ~** Warenverknappung; **staff ~** Personalmangel; **wartime ~** kriegsbedingte Verknappung; **~ of liquid assets** Liquiditätsbeengung; **~ of bulk** Sturzgüterverlust; **~ of capital** Kapitalmangel, -knappheit; **~ of cash** Bargeldmangel, Liquiditätsmangel, *(petty cash)* Devisenmangel; **~ in the cash** Kassendefizit, -fehlbetrag; **~ of foreign currency (exchange)** Devisenknappheit; **~ of dollars** Dollarknappheit; **~ of finance** knappe Finanzdecke; **~ of food** Mangel an Lebensmitteln, Lebensmittelknappheit; **~ of goods** Warenverknappung; **~ of housing** Wohnungsnot; **~ of labo(u)r** Mangel an Arbeitskräften, Arbeitskräftemangel; **~ of liquidity** Liquiditätsbeengung; **~ of manpower** Knappheit an Arbeitskräften, Arbeitskräftemangel; **~ of skilled manpower (workers)** Facharbeitermangel; **~ of materials** Materialknappheit; **~ of merchandise** Warenverknappung; **~ of money** Geldverknappung; **~ in money accounts** mangelnde Flüssigkeit, Liquiditätsbeengung; **~ of mortgage money** knappes Hypothekenangebot; **~ of personnel** Personalmangel, -knappheit; **~ of provisions** Lebensmittelknappheit; **~ of rolling stock** unzureichendes Betriebsmaterial; **~ of staff** Personalknappheit, -mangel; **~ of supplies** Angebotsknappheit, Versorgungsengpaß; **~ of teachers** Lehrermangel; **~ of transport** fehlende Transportmittel; **~ in weight** Untergewicht, Gewichtsmanko, -verlust; **~ of work** Auftragsmangel;
to make up a ~ Fehlbetrag ausgleichen.

shortchange *(v.)* *(US coll.)* zu wenig Wechselgeld herausgeben, *(cheat, US)* betrügen, übers Ohr hauen;
to be ~ed economically wirtschaftlich benachteiligt werden.

shortchanger *(US coll.)* Betrüger, beim Geldwechseln.

shortcoming *(defectiveness)* Unzulänglichkeit, Mängel, *(deficiency)* Defizit, Fehlbetrag, *(negligence)* Pflichtversäumnis, *(shortage)* Verknappung;
~s **of a book** Fehler eines Buches; ~s **in the plant** Mängel der Betriebsanlage;
~ **goods** Mangelwaren.

shorten *(v.)* verkürzen, vermindern, reduzieren;
~ **an article** Artikel zusammenstreichen; ~ **commitments** Aufträge zurückziehen; ~ **a period** Frist abkürzen; ~ **a road** Weg abkürzen; ~ **one's working time** Arbeitszeit verkürzen.

shortening Verkürzung;
~ **of policy** Abkürzung der Versicherungsdauer; ~ **of a term** Fristverkürzung; ~ **of working hours** Verkürzung der Arbeitszeit, Arbeitszeitverkürzung; ~ **of one's working time** Arbeitszeitverkürzung.

shorter, in the ~ **term** auf kürzere Sicht.

shortfall Mangel, Fehlbetrag, -menge, Defizit, Unterschuß;
export ~ Exportrückgang;
~ **in production** Produktionsausfall; ~ **in receipts** Mindereinnahmen; ~ **in the recovery** rückläufige Konjunkturerholung; ~ **in tax revenue** vermindertes Steueraufkommen, Steuerausfall.

shorthand Stenographie, Kurzschrift, Schnellschrift;
as ~ **for** als Kurzbeschreibung für; **in** ~ stenografisch;
typed ~ Maschinenstenographie;
to take down in ~ stenografisch (Diktat) aufnehmen, stenographieren; **to take English** ~ englische Kurzschrift beherrschen; **to take notes in** ~ sich stenographische Aufzeichnungen machen; **to transcribe** ~ Stenogramm übertragen; **to write in** ~ stenographieren, in Kurzschrift schreiben;
~ **is advantage but not essential** *(ad.)* Kurzschrift erwünscht aber nicht Bedingung;
~ *(a.)* stenographisch;
~ **clerk** Stenokontoristin; ~ **expression** Kurzschriftzeichen, Kürzel; ~ **notes** stenographische Aufzeichnungen; ~ **notebook** Stenoblock; ~ **pad** Stenoblock; ~ **secretary** Stenosekretärin; ~ **service** Stenographendienst; ~ **typist** Stenotypist[in]; ~ **writer** Stenograph; ~ **writing** Stenographieren.

shorthanded knapp an Arbeitskräften;
to be ~ Mangel an Arbeitskräften haben.

shortness | of memory Gedächtnisschwäche; ~ **of money** Geldnot, -knappheit; ~ **in weight** *(coin)* Gewichtsverlust.

shortstop *(sl.)* fremden Kunden beliefern.

shot Schuß, *(over public address system, sl.)* Ausruf, *(advertising)* Postwerbeexemplar, *(drink, coll.)* Gläschen, *(injection)* Spritze, Schuß, *(film, photograph)* Bild, Aufnahme, Schnappschuß, *(tel., sl.)* telefonischer Weckruf;
at the first ~ beim ersten Versuch; **by a long** ~ *(sl.)* bei weitem; **like a** ~ wie aus der Pistole geschossen, prompt, sofort, bereitwillig;
big ~ großes Tier, Bonze; **establishing** ~ Gesamtaufnahme; **exterior** ~ *(film)* Außenaufnahme; **longish** ~ *(fig.)* kühne Vermutung; **random** ~ Schuß ins Blaue;
~ **in the arm** [Belebungs]spritze, *(business cycle)* Konjunkturspritze; ~ **in the dark** Schuß ins Blaue; ~ **in the locker** *(fig.)* Geld in der Tasche, Rückhalt, letzte Reserve;
to be ~ **out of a coach** aus einem Bus geschleudert werden; **to be nearer the bull's eye at each** ~ seinem Glück immer näher kommen; **to call the** ~s Vorhersage machen; **to make a** ~ **at it** etw. versuchen, Versuch riskieren; **to stand the** ~ Zeche bezahlen.

shotgun *(sl.)* Heiratsvermittler;
~ **approach** Gewaltmethode; ~ **audience** Zwangspublikum; ~ **marriage** *(US)* Mußheirat; ~ **quarantine** ungesetzliche Zwangsquarantäne; ~ **wedding** vom Schwiegervater erzwungene Ehe.

shoulder *(aerodrome)* Übergangsstreifen, *(letter)* Fleisch, *(street)* ungepflasterter Straßenrand, Seitenstreifen, Banquett;
straight from the ~ unverblümt;
~ *(v.)* **one's son's debts** Schulden seines Sohnes übernehmen; ~ **a liability** Verpflichtung auf sich nehmen; ~ **the responsibility** Verantwortung tragen; ~ **one's way through the crowd** sich einen Weg durch die Menge bahnen;
to give s. o. the cold ~ jem. die kalte Schulter zeigen, j. geringschätzig behandeln; **to have a broad** ~ *(fig.)* viel vertragen können, einen breiten Rücken haben; **to put one's** ~ **to the wheel** energisch an der Arbeit sein, sich tüchtig ins Zeug legen; **to shift the blame to other** ~s anderen die Schuld zuschieben; **to stand head and** ~(s) **above** anderen turmhoch überlegen sein; **to take too much on one's** ~ sich zuviel zumuten; **to tap s. o. on the** ~ j. auf die Schulter tippen;
to earn one's ~ **straps** zum Offizier befördert werden.

shout Schrei, Ruf;
~ *(v.)* *(fig.)* spendieren, stiften;
~ **disapproval** laut sein Mißfallen äußern; ~ **down a speaker** Redner niederbrüllen.

shouter *(pol., US)* Propagandist.

shove Anstoß, Schubs;
~ *(v.)* *(sl.)* Falschgeld in den Verkehr bringen;
~**off** *(sl.)* abdampfen; ~ **through a crowd** sich durch die Menge hindurchdrängeln; ~ **money into one's pockets** Geld in die Tasche stopfen;
to give s. o. a ~ jem. weiterhelfen.

shovel *(v.)* **up money** Geld scheffeln.

show *(entertainment)* Vorführung, Vorstellung, Darbietung, Schau, *(exhibition)* Ausstellung, Messe, *(film)* Filmvorstellung, -vorführung, *(mil., sl.)* Kampfhandlung, *(outfit)* Sache, Laden, Kram, *(pomp)* Protzerei, Großtun, Angeben, *(theatrical performance)* Theatervorstellung, -aufführung, *(window display)* Auslage (Aushang) [im Schaufenster];
for ~ um Eindruck zu schinden; **on** ~ zur Besichtigung, ausgestellt; **on** ~ **on our premises** bei uns zu besichtigen; **only for** ~ nur zum Schein; **with some** ~ **of justice** mit einer gewissen Berechtigung;
agricultural ~ Landwirtschaftsausstellung; **automobile** ~ *(US)* Autoausstellung; **cattle** ~ Viehausstellung; **mere** ~ bloße Aufmachung; **motor** ~ *(Br.)* Auto[mobil]ausstellung; **one-man** ~ Alleinunterhaltung; **poor** ~ kümmerliche Sache; **trade** ~ *(Br.)* Gewerbeausstellung; **travelling** ~ Wanderausstellung;
~ **of force** Machtdemonstration; ~ **of goods** Warenmesse; ~ **of hands** Abstimmung durch Handaufheben; ~ **of muscle** Machtdemonstration; ~ **of reason** Spur von Vernunft; ~ **of solidarity** Solidaritätsbeweis; ~ **of left-wing strength** Machtdemonstration linker Kräfte; ~ **of winning** Gewinnchance;
~ *(v.)* zeigen, *(exhibit)* [Waren] austellen, *(make clear)* nachweisen, *(social life)* sich zeigen (sehen lassen), erscheinen, *(theater)* aufführen;
~ **an advance** *(industrials)* Kurssteigerung aufweisen; ~ **balance in s. one's favo(u)r** Saldo zu jds. Gunsten auf-, ausweisen; ~ **one's cards** seine Karten aufdecken; ~ **cause** triftigen Grund angeben, *(law)* Einwendungen vorbringen, Gegenvorstellungen erheben; ~ **clemency** Gnade vor Recht ergehen lassen; ~ **one's colo(u)rs** seine wahren Absichten erkennen lassen; ~ **a decrease** Ausfall ergeben; ~ **a deficit** Defizit aufweisen; ~ **s. o. the door** j. hinausweisen, -werfen; ~ **one's face** erscheinen, aufkreuzen, sich zeigen; ~ **s. o. a favo(u)r** jem. eine Gunst erweisen; ~ **fight** Kampfbereitschaft zeigen; ~ **forth** dokumentieren, bekanntmachen; ~ **small gains** *(stock exchange)* kleine Gewinne verzeichnen; ~ **gratitude to s. o.** sich jem. gegenüber dankbar erweisen; ~ **one's hand** seine Pläne erkennen lassen; ~ **s. o. [over] a house** jem. ein Haus zeigen; ~ **improvement** Besserung zeigen; ~ **great improvement** *(stock exchange)* erhebliche Kurssteigerung aufweisen; ~ **in hereinführen**; ~ **their intangibles at one dollar** immaterielle Güter bilanzmäßig mit nur einem Dollar bewerten; ~ **one's knowledge** seine Kenntnisse zur Schau stellen; ~ **a leg** *(coll.)* aus dem Bett steigen; ~ **a cheap line of goods** billige Waren feilbieten; ~ **a loss** mit Verlust abschließen, Verlust aufweisen; ~ **off** sich in günstigem Licht zeigen, protzen, seine Künste vorführen; ~ **a clean pair of heels** sich hurtig davonmachen; ~ **s. o. his place** j. in seine Schranken verweisen; ~ **one's plans** seine Pläne erläutern; ~ **a profit** Gewinn aufweisen, Nutzen abwerfen; ~ **s. o. in public** sich mit jem. in der Öffentlichkeit sehen lassen; ~ **reasons** Gründe vorbringen; ~ **results** Resultate aufweisen; ~ **one's right** seinen Eigentumsanspruch nachweisen; ~ **a rise** Steigerung aufweisen, steigen; ~ **s. o. round** j. herumführen; ~ **s. o. to his seat** jem. seinen Platz anweisen; ~ **signs of retrenchment** Kostenabbauzeichen erkennen lassen; ~ **sympathy to s.** o. jem. seine Teilnahme bezeigen; ~ **one's teeth** *(fig.)* die Zähne zeigen; ~ **that one cares** seine Anteilnahme bezeigen; ~ **through** durchscheinen, *(print.)* durchschlagen; ~ **one's ticket** seine Fahrkarte vorzeigen; ~ **a good tone** *(stock exchange)* fest liegen (sein); ~ **s. o. about (around the) town** j. in der Stadt herumführen; ~ **the truth of a statement** Wahrheit einer Aussage (Richtigkeit einer Feststellung) beweisen; ~ **up** *(arrive)* aufkreuzen, sich sehen lassen, sich einstellen, *(display)* ausstellen; ~ **up a fraud** Betrug entlarven; ~ **an uptick** Steigerung aufweisen; ~ **what one is made of** seine Leistungsfähigkeit dokumentieren;
to be on ~ zu besichtigen (ausgestellt) sein, *(theater)* gespielt werden; **to be furnished merely for** ~ nur zu Angabezwecken möbliert sein; **to be sick of the whole** ~ ganze Sache satt haben; **to boss a** ~ für eine Sache verantwortlich sein, Sache deichseln; **to claim with some** ~ **of justice** mit einer gewissen Berechtigung

verlangen; **to get a ~ onto the stage** Vorstellung bühnenreif machen; **to give s. o. a fair ~** jem. eine faire Chance geben; **to give the whole ~ away** sich die Schau stehlen lassen; **not to have a ~ of winning** keinerlei Gewinnchancen haben; **to make a good ~** gute Figur machen; **to make a ~ of one's wealth** seinen Reichtum zur Schau stellen; **not to offer even a ~ of resistance** nicht einmal die Andeutung eines Widerstands erkennen lassen; **to pierce beneath the ~ of a thing** zum Kern einer Sache vorstoßen; **to put on a ~** Schauspiel bieten; **to put up a good ~** große Schau abziehen; **to run a ~** *(sl.)* Sache schmeißen, für eine Sache verantwortlich sein; **to set on ~** ausstellen; **to speak with a great ~ of learning** ganzen Umfang seines Wissens erkennen lassen; **to vote by ~ of hands** durch Handaufheben abstimmen;

~ article Paradestück; **~ bill** Verzeichnis der ausgelegten Waren, *(advertising)* Werbeplakat; **~ boat** Vergnügungsdampfer; **~ boy** Musterschüler; **~ business** Vergnügungs-, Unterhaltungsindustrie, Schaugeschäft; **to make a fortune in ~ business** im Schaugeschäft ein Vermögen verdienen; **~ card** Ausstellungs-, Aufstell-, Werbe-, Reklameplakat, *(shopwindow)* Schaufensterplakat, *(business card)* Muster-, Geschäftskarte; **to issue a ~-cause order** einstweilige Verfügung zur Erhebung einer Feststellungsklage erlassen; **~ flat** Modellwohnung; **~ folk** Künstlervolk; **~ girl** Revuegirl; **~ house** Musterhaus; **~-off** Wichtigtuerei; **~-off piece** Schaustück; **~ place** Ausstellungsort; **~ purpose** Reklamezweck; **~ town** Modellstadt; **~ trial** Schauprozeß; **~-up line** *(sl.)* polizeiliche Vorführung von Tatverdächtigen; **~-of-hands vote** *(US)* Abstimmung durch Handaufheben; **~ waggon** Ausstellungswagen; **~ window** *(US)* Schau-, Auslagefenster.

showboard Anschlagtafel, Schwarzes Brett.

showcase Ausstellungs-, Auslagekasten, Schaukasten, Vitrine, *(entertainment business)* Probevorführung;
~ reserve Musterreservat.

showdown entscheidende Kraftprobe, Entscheidungskampf, *(disclosure)* Offenlegung, *(disclosure of resources)* Enthüllung der tatsächlichen Machtmittel.

shower Schauer, *(exhibitor)* Aussteller, *(shower bath)* Dusche, *(US)* Geschenkesegen, Brautgeschenke;
~ of lead Kugelregen; **~ of letters** Flut von Briefen; **~ of stones** Steinhagel;
~ (v.) down *(sl.)* blechen, berappen; **~ gifts upon s. o.** j. reichlichst beschenken; **~ hono(u)rs upon s. o.** j. mit Ehrungen überhäufen; **~ questions upon a new arrival** Neuankömmling mit Fragen überschütten;
to be caught in a ~ von einem Wolkenguß überrascht werden; **~ bath** Dusche; **~ curtain** Duschvorhang; **~ party** *(US)* Hochzeitsempfang.

showing Zurschaustellung, *(film)* Vorführung, *(outdoor advertising)* Anschlagseinheit;
according to his own ~ nach seinen eigenen Aussagen;
financial ~ *(firm)* Status, finanzielle Lage; **first ~** *(film)* Erstaufführung, Filmpremiere; **full ~** Vollbelegung; **poor ~** schlechtes Abschneiden;
to have a poor financial ~ in einer schlechten Finanzlage sein, miserablen Status aufweisen; **to make a mixed ~** *(stock exchange)* uneinheitliches Bild bieten; **to make a very strong ~** erstaunliche Erfolge aufweisen; **to make a ~ on cost** sich kostenmäßig auswirken, kostenmäßig durchschlagen.

showman Schausteller, Manager.

showmanship effektvolles Auftreten, Effekthascherei, effektvolle Attraktion.

shown | in the accompanying picture nebenstehend abgebildet; **as ~ by the books** ausweislich der Geschäftsbücher, buchmäßig; **not ~ separately below** *(balance sheet)* nicht gesondert ausgewiesen.

showpiece Ausstellungsgegenstand, -stück, *(exhibition)* Glanzstück;
~ value Schaufensterwert.

showroom Ausstellungsraum, Außen-, Verkaufs-, Musterlager;
~ model Ausstellungsstück.

showy marktschreierisch.

shred Lappen, Fetzen, Bruchstück;
not one ~ of evidence kein Fetzen eines Beweises; **~s of clouds** Wolkenfetzen;
to tear an argument to ~s Argument gründlich widerlegen (zerpflücken); **to tear s. one's reputation to ~s** jds. guten Ruf systematisch zerstören.

shrewd | businessman kluger Geschäftsmann; **to make a ~ guess** wahrscheinlich zutreffende Vermutungen anstellen; **~ politician** gewitzter Politiker.

shrieks of outrage Entrüstungsschreie.

shrimp *(v.)* **around for government support** fußfällig um staatliche Unterstützung nachsuchen.

shrink *(v.)* zurückweichen, sich zurückziehen, *(income)* zusammenschrumpfen, niedriger werden, *(textiles)* einlaufen;
~ to profitable size sich gesundschrumpfen; **~ from meeting strangers** sich vor neuen Bekanntschaften drücken.

shrinkage Schwund, Verlust, *(allowance)* Refaktie, Nachlaß, *(decrease)* Abnahme, [Wert]minderung, *(textiles)* Einlaufen, *(trade)* Schrumpfen, Schrumpfung;
profit ~ Gewinnschrumpfung;
~ of the export trade Exportrückgang, -schrumpfung; **~ in the price of stocks** Kursverlust; **~ in the profit margin** Schrumpfung der Gewinnmarge; **~ of stocks** Lagerverlust; **~ in value** Wertminderung.

shrinking | of prices Preisherabsetzung;
~ capital schrumpfendes Kapital.

shrivel *(v.)* **| into nothing** völlig bedeutungslos werden; **~ up** verkümmern.

shroud | of mist Nebelschleier;
to be in a ~ of mystery in Geheimnisse gehüllt sein.

shrunk *(textile)* eingegangen.

shrug, with a ~ of one's shoulders mit einem Achselzucken.

shuck Deut, Pfifferling;
not to care ~s (a ~ about) *(Br.)* sich nichts daraus machen, sich keinen Deut darum kümmern.

shuffle schleppende Arbeitsabwicklung, *(subterfuge)* Trick, Schwindel, Ausflucht;
~ of the Cabinet (of government) Kabinetts-, Regierungsumbildung; **~ of holdings** Beteiligungsumstellungen;
~ (v.) (dodge) Winkelzüge machen, lavieren, *(pol.)* umgruppieren;
~ aside beiseiteschaffen; **~ the cards** seine Taktik ändern; **~ the government** Regierungsumbildung vornehmen, Regierung (Kabinett) umbilden; **~ one's notes** mit seinen Aufzeichnungen herumhantieren; **~ out of the responsibility** der Verantwortung ausweichen; **~ out of an awkward situation** sich leidlich aus einer Sache herausziehen; **~ the papers together in a drawer** Schriftstücke in die Schublade schieben; **~ off responsibilities upon others** Verantwortung auf andere abschieben; **~ through one's work** seine Arbeit nachlässig versehen; **~ towards the center** sich der politischen Mitte annähern; **~ them up** *(railroad use)* Waggons rangieren.

shuffler *(sl.)* Wanderarbeiter.

shuffling | answer ausweichende Antwort; **~ excuse** faule Ausrede.

shun *(v.)* **| publicity** Öffentlichkeit scheuen; **~ society** ungern unter Menschen gehen.

shunt *(el.)* Nebenschluß, *(fig.)* Ausweichen, Umschwenken, Schwenkung, *(railway)* Rangieren;
~ (v.) zurückstellen, aufschieben, *(train)* auf ein Nebengleis fahren, rangieren, abstellen;
~ s. o. j. kaltstellen, j. nicht zum Zuge kommen lassen; **quietly ~ aside** stillschweigend beiseitelegen; **~ away** rangieren; **~ the conversation to less dangerous topics** Gespräch auf weniger gefährliche Themen lenken; **~ a subject** Thema zurückstellen; **~ a train on a siding** Zug auf einem Nebengleis abstellen.

shunter *(engine)* Rangierlokomotive, *(railway employee)* Rangierer, Weichensteller, *(stock market, Br.)* Arbitrageur, *(sl.)* geschickter Organisator.

shunting *(railway)* Verschieben, Rangieren, *(stock market, Br.)* Provinzarbitrage;
~ station Rangier-, Verschiebebahnhof; **~ track** Rangiergleis.

shut | for dividends Dividendenschluß;
~ (v.) (business) stillegen, schließen, [Betrieb] einstellen;
~ the door upon s. o. für j. nicht zu sprechen sein, jem. keine Chance geben; **~ the door upon further negotiations** Tür zu weiteren Verhandlungen zumachen; **~ down a factory** Betrieb einstellen (vorübergehend schließen, stillegen); **~ down like a clam** hermetisch abriegeln; **~ down on Sundays for liquorselling** Alkoholausschank am Sonntag einstellen; **~ one's ears to all appeals for help** sich allen Hilfsersuchen verschließen; **~ in** *(fam., US)* Ölförderung einstellen; **~ s. one's mouth** j. zum Stillschweigen verpflichten; **~ off** *(tel.)* auflegen; **~ s. o. off** Telefongespräch mit jem. abbrechen; **~ off steam** *(railway engine)* Dampf ablassen; **~ off water** Wasser abstellen; **~ out competitive goods** Konkurrenzerzeugnisse nicht hereinlassen; **~ out immigrants** Einwanderungsverbot erlassen; **~ out of foreign markets** von Auslandsmärkten ausschließen; **~ out the view** Sicht versperren; **~ a street** Straße blockieren; **~ up** einschließen, einsperren; **~ up a house** Haus abschließen (zusper-

ren, zuschließen); ~ **up one's jewels in a safe** seinen Schmuck im Safe verschließen; ~ **s. o. up in prison** j. einsperren; ~ **up a prisoner** Gefangenen einsperren; ~ **up shop** Laden schließen (dichtmachen), Bude zumachen;

~ *(a.)* geschlossen, zugemacht;

~ **eye** *(sl.)* Nickerchen; ~**-in** ans Bett gefesselt; ~**-outs** aus Raummangel nicht verladene Güter.

shutdown *(closing of plant)* Stillegung, Schließung, vorübergehende Betriebsstillegung, *(interruption of work)* Arbeitsunterbrechung, -einstellung, Betriebsstörung;

plant-wide ~s umfassende Betriebsstillegungen; **seasonal ~** saisonbedingte Betriebsschließung;

~ **in production** vorübergehende Produktionsstillegung; ~ **costs** Kosten der Betriebseinstellung (Betriebsstillegung); ~ **order** Schließungsanweisung; ~ **point** Produktionsschwelle.

shutoff Absperrvorrichtung, *(hunting)* Schonzeit.

shutout Ausschließung.

shutter Fensterladen, *(photo)* Verschluß;

instantaneous ~ Momentverschluß; **rolling ~** Rouleau, Laden, Rolläden;

~ *(v.)* Fensterläden anbringen;

to put up the ~s Laden schließen (dichtmachen); **to set the ~ to delayed action** Selbstauslöser einstellen; **to take down the ~s** Laden eröffnen;

~ **speed** Verschlußgeschwindigkeit.

shutterbug *(US sl.)* Fotonarr.

shutting | down Stillegung; ~ **up shop** Ladenschluß.

shuttle Pendelverkehr, *(shuttle train, US)* Zubringer-, Vorort-, Pendelzug;

~ *(v.)* hin- und herfahren;

~ **s. o.** j. im Pendelverkehr befördern; ~ **back and forth between two countries** zwischen zwei Ländern hin- und herpendeln; ~ **between government and business** vom Staatsdienst in die Wirtschaft hinüberwechseln; ~ **between two professions** zwischen zwei Berufen schwanken;

~ **bus** im Pendelverkehr eingesetzter Bus; ~ **car** Triebwagen; ~ **diplomacy** Reisediplomatie; ~ **service** Pendelverkehr; ~ **train** Zubringer-, Vorort-, Pendelzug.

shuttlecock *(fig.)* Streitgegenstand, Spielball.

shuttling between government and business Berufswechsel vom Staatsdienst in die Wirtschaft.

shy *(fig.)* Stichelei;

~ **of money** *(US sl.)* knapp bei Kasse;

~ *(v.)* **away from s. th.** vor etw. zurückschrecken;

to have a ~ at an examination Examensversuch riskieren.

shyster *(US)* Hamsterer, Schieber, *(legal business)* Winkelkonsulent, -advokat, Rechtsverdreher.

sick krank, *(ship)* ausbesserungsbedürftig;

~ **at failing to pass the examination** ganz krank vor Angst, das Examen nicht zu bestehen; ~ **for home** heimwehkrank;

to be ~ of a matter einer Sache überdrüssig sein, eine Sache satt haben; **to be ~ and tired of s. th.** etw. satt haben; **to be pretty ~ of s. th.** Nase von etw. ziemlich voll haben; **to fall ~** krank werden; **to go (report)** ~ *(mil.)* sich krank melden;

~**-abed** bettlägerig; ~ **allowance** Krankengeld; ~ **bay** *(ship)* Krankenstation; ~ **benefit** *(Br.)* Krankenbeihilfe, -geld; ~ **benefit fund** Krankenkasse; ~ **berth** (ship) Krankenstation; ~ **call** Krankenbesuch, *(mil.)* Revierstunde; ~ **caller** Krankmelder; ~ **certificate** Krankenschein; ~ **club** Krankenunterstützungsverein; ~ **diet** Krankendiät, -kost; ~ **flag** Quarantäneflagge; ~ **fund** Krankenkasse; ~ **insurance** Krankenversicherung; ~ **insured** krankenversichert; ~ **leave** Erholungs-, Genesungs-, Krankheitsurlaub; **to be on ~ leave** wegen Krankheit beurlaubt sein; ~**-list** *(v.)* *(mil.)* sich krank melden; **to be on the ~ list** ins Revier kommen; **to put on the ~ list** krankschreiben; ~ **market** *(US)* uneinheitlicher und lustloser Markt, flaue Börse; ~ **mind** moralisch gefährdeter Mensch; ~ **pay** Krankengeld; ~**-pay rights** Krankengeldansprüche; ~ **person** Kranker; ~ **rate** Prozentsatz der Kranken, Krankheitsziffer; ~ **report** Krankenbericht.

sickbed Krankenlager, -bett.

sicken *(v.)* krank werden, erkranken, *(feel disgust)* Widerwillen empfinden;

~ **to bring about reforms** auf die Herbeiführung von Reformen völlig versessen sein.

sickness Krankheit, Erkrankung;

absent because of ~ wegen Krankheit abwesend; **in the event of ~** im Krankheitsfall;

last ~ Todeskrankheit; **permanent ~** Dauerkrankheit;

to be insured against ~ einer Krankenkasse angehören; **to suffer from air ~** luftkrank sein.

~ **allowance** *(US)* Krankengeld; ~ **benefit** *(US)* Leistungen im Krankheitsfall; **to draw ~ benefits** *(US)* Krankengeld beziehen; ~ **cash benefit** *(Br.)* Krankengeld; ~ **certificate** Kranken-, Kassenschein; ~ **compensation** Krankengeld, -beihilfe; ~ **cover** *(insurance)* Krankheitsschutz; ~ **disability** auf Krankheit beruhende Erwerbsunfähigkeit; ~ **figure** *(firm)* Krankenstand; ~ **fund** Krankenkasse; ~ **indemnity policy** Krankenversicherungspolice; ~ **insurance** Krankenversicherung; ~ **pay** Krankengeld; ~ **rate** Krankheitssatz; ~ **relief** Krankenbeihilfe.

sicknurse Krankenschwester;

~ *(v.)* als Krankenpfleger[in] tätig sein.

sickroom Krankenzimmer, -stube, *(mil.)* Revier.

side Seite, *(district)* Gegend, Bezirk, Nachbarschaft, *(legal department of a court)* Rechtsabteilung, *(line of descent)* Abstammungslinie, Seite, *(party)* Partei, *(school, Br.)* Studienrichtung, -zweig, *(viewpoint)* Stand-, Blickpunkt;

from all ~s von allen Seiten; **on the ~** *(sl.)* zusätzlich, nebenbei, unter der Hand; **on one's father's ~** väterlicherseits; **on the low ~** *(prices)* billig; **on the wrong ~ of fifty** über Fünfzig; **This ⌀ UP!** Nicht stürzen!;

classical ~ *(Br.)* humanistische Bildung; **credit ~** Kreditseite; **criminal-law ~** Strafrechtsabteilung; **dark ~** Schattenseite; **debit ~** Soll-, Debetseite; **long ~** *(stock exchange)* Haussepartei; **the other ~** Gegenpartei; **left[-hand] ~** Passiv-, Debetseite; **plea ~** Zivilgerichtsbarkeit; **right[-hand] ~** Aktiv-, Kreditseite; **many ~s to s. one's character** verschiedene Charakterzüge; **east ~ of a city** Ostteil einer Stadt; **wrong ~ of the pavement** *(US)* falsche Straßenseite; ~ **of the road** Straßenseite; **left-hand ~ of a road** linke Fahrbahn (Straßenseite); **near ~ of the road** nahegelegener Straßenrand; **the other ~ of the shield** Kehrseite der Medaille;

~ *(v.)* **with s. o.** auf jds. Seite treten; ~ **a book** Buch mit Seiten versehen; ~ **with the ministerial party** Partei der Regierung ergreifen; ~ **with the stronger party** sich den stärkeren Bataillonen anschließen; ~ **up a room** Zimmer aufräumen;

to be on s. one's ~ jem. zur Seite stehen; **to be on the same ~** im gleichen Lager stehen; **to be on the debit ~** im Debet stehen; **to be on the high ~** *(prices)* hoch sein; **to be on the winning ~** auf der Gewinnerseite sein; **to change ~s** zu einer anderen Partei übertreten; **to drive on the right ~** rechts fahren; **to get the public on one's ~** öffentliche Meinung für sich gewinnen; **to go over to the other ~** zur Gegenseite übergehen; **to have the law on one's ~** im Recht sein, das Recht auf seiner Seite haben; **to join the ~ of the liberals** sich für die liberale Partei entscheiden; **to look on the bright ~s of life** das Leben optimistisch betrachten; **to put on ~** sich aufblasen, angeben; **to put on too much ~** sich zu sehr aufspielen; **to study all ~s of a question** alle Seiten eines Problems untersuchen; **to take ~s** sich für eine Partei entscheiden; **to take ~s with s. o.** für j. Partei ergreifen; **to take the same ~** gleiche Haltung einnehmen; **to view a question from all ~s** Frage von allen Seiten beleuchten (betrachten); **to vote for a ~** sich für eine Partei entscheiden; **to win s. o. over to one's ~** j. auf seine Seite ziehen; **to work part-time on the ~** Nebenberuf ausüben; **to write on one ~ of the paper only** Blatt Papier nur einseitig beschreiben;

~ **arms** *(mil.)* Seitenwaffen; ~**-bar job** *(sl.)* Nebenbeschäftigung; ~**-bar rules** *(Br.)* prozeßleitende Verfügungen; ~ **bet** Zusatzwette; ~ **box** *(theater)* Seitenloge; ~ **brake** *(car)* Handbremse; ~ **building** Anbau; **to hear through ~ channels** auf Umwegen hören (erfahren); ~ **cousin** entfernter Verwandter; ~ **dish** Zwischengericht; **by a ~ door** *(fig.)* durch die Hintertür; ~ **effect** Rand-, Begleiterscheinung; **to cause ~ effects** *(drug)* Nebenwirkungen hervorrufen; ~ **entrance (entry)** Seiteneingang; ~**-face** im Profil; ~ **glance** *(fig.)* beiläufige Anspielung; ~ **issue** Nebenfrage, Frage von sekundärer Bedeutung; ~ **partner** *(US)* Mitarbeiter; ~ **reglet** Seitensteg; ~ **reports** *(law court)* zusätzliche Entscheidungssammlung; ~ **road** Seitenstraße; ~ **show** Nebenvorstellung, *(subordinate issue)* Frage von nebensächlicher Bedeutung; ~ **shows of life** Zufälle des Lebens; ~ **slip** Seitensprung, Fehltritt, *(motoring)* Rutschen; ~**-step** *(v.)* **a decision** einer Entscheidung ausweichen; ~ **stitching** Querheftung; ~ **street** Seitenstraße; **to turn down a ~ street** in eine Seitenstraße einbiegen; ~ **view** Seitenansicht; ~**-wheeler** Raddampfer; ~ **wind** *(fig.)* indirektes Mittel.

sideboard Serviertisch.

sidecar *(motorcar)* Beiwagen;

~ *(v.)* im Beiwagen mitfahren.

sidekick[er] *(Br., sl.)* Assistent, zweiter Mann, *(US fam.)* Kumpan, Komplice.

sidelight Seitenlampe, -licht, *(fig.)* Streiflicht;

~**s** interessante Aufschlüsse.

sideline Seitenlinie, *(goods, US)* zusätzliche Waren (Verkaufsartikel), Nebenprodukte, *(profession)* Nebenberuf, -beschäftigung, *(railway)* Nebenlinie, -bahn, Anschlußgleis, *(secondary road, Canada)* Nebenstraße, *(traveller)* zusätzliche Vertretung;
  ~ *(v.) (fig.)* auf ein Abstellgleis stellen;
  to sit on the ~s auf seine Chance warten;
  ~ **business** Nebengeschäft; ~ **employment** Nebenbeschäftigung.

sideliner nebenberuflich Beschäftigter.

sidenote *(print.)* Randbemerkung, -glosse;
  ~s Marginalien.

sider Parteigänger.

sidetrack *(US)* totes Gleis, Anschluß-, Fabrik-, Neben-, Abstellgleis, *(fig.)* unbedeutender Posten, Abstellgleis;
  ~ *(v.)* auf einem Nebengleis abstellen, *(fig.)* kaltstellen;
  ~ **s. o.** j. von seinem Vorhaben abbringen;
  to shunt s. o. ~ j. auf ein Abstellgleis abschieben.

sidewalk *(US)* Bürger-, Fußsteig, Trottoir;
  moving ~ fahrender Bürgersteig;
  ~ **and pavement** *(US)* Gehweg und Fahrbahn;
  ~ **cafe** Straßencafe; ~ **journalism** *(US coll.)* Revolverjournalismus.

sideway Seitenweg;
  ~s **movement** Börsenbewegung ohne bestimmte Gesamttendenz.

siding *(railway)* Anschluß-, Fabrikgleis, Ausweich-, Abstell-, Nebengleis, *(taking sides)* Partei-, Stellungnahme;
  ~s Abstellbahnhof;
  private ~ Privatanschluß[gleis].

siege Belagerung[szustand], Zernierung;
  to lay ~ **to a town** Stadt belagern; **to raise the** ~ Belagerung aufheben; **to stand a** ~ einer Belagerung standhalten.

sieve *(old ship, sl.)* Seelenverkäufer;
  to have a memory like a ~ Gedächtnis wie ein Sieb haben.

sifting sorgfältige Untersuchung;
  ~ **process** Ausleseprozeß.

sigh for the country Sehnsucht nach dem Landleben.

sight Anblick, Sehenswürdigkeit, *(bill of exchange)* Sicht, Vorzeigung, Präsentation, *(navigation)* Sicht, *(opinion)* Meinung, Ansicht, *(power of seeing)* Sicht-, Sehvermögen;
  after ~ nach Sicht; **at** ~ bei Sicht (Vorkommen); **at first** ~ prima facie, auf den ersten Blick; **at short (long)** ~ auf kurze (lange) Sicht; **at** ~ **of the police officers** beim Anblick der Polizisten; **in** ~ *(on the market)* vorhanden; **in my own** ~ nach meiner Meinung; **on sale** ~ **unseen** *(US)* ohne Besichtigung zu verkaufen; **payable at** ~ bei Vorzeigung (Sicht) zahlbar; ~ **unseen** ohne Besichtigung; **30 days** ~ 30 Tage nach Sicht; **commercial** ~ Handelsakzept; **imaginary** ~ Phantasiegebilde; ~s **of a city** Sehenswürdigkeiten einer Stadt; **a** ~ **for sore eyes** ein Labsal für die Augen; ~ **of money** Haufen Geld;
  ~ *(v.)* vorzeigen, präsentieren;
  ~ **a bill** Wechsel mit Sicht versehen; ~ **land** Land sichten;
  to be a long ~ **too good for s. o.** für j. viel zu schade sein; **to be intended for your** ~ **only** nur für Sie bestimmt sein; **to be within** ~ **of a task** Ende einer Arbeit absehen können; **to cost s. o. a** ~ **of money** j. ein schönes Stück Geld kosten; **to dip down out of** ~ aus jds. Blickfeld verschwinden; **to get out of** ~ von der Bildfläche verschwinden; **to give s. o.** ~ **into the business** jem. geschäftlichen Einblick gewähren; **to have lost** ~ **of s. o.** j. ganz aus seinem Gesichtskreis verloren haben; **to have no** ~ **against one's opponents** *(US)* keine Chance gegen seine Gegner haben; **to hono(u)r a draft on** ~ Tratte bei Vorzeigung honorieren; **to know s. o. by** ~ j. von Ansehen kennen; **to look a** ~ verboten aussehen; **to see the** ~s **of a town** Sehenswürdigkeiten einer Stadt besichtigen; **to translate at** ~ vom Blatt (sofort) übersetzen;
  ~ **bill** Sichtwechsel, -tratte, Avistawechsel; ~ **deposits** täglich fällige Gelder, Sichteinlagen; ~ **deposit accounts** Sichteinlagekonten; ~ **draft** Sichttratte, -wechsel; ~ **exchange** Sichtwechselkurs; ~ **items** Sichtpapiere; ~ **liabilities** Sichtverbindlichkeiten; ~ **rate** Kurs für Sichtpapiere, Sichtkurs; ~ **translation** Sofortübersetzung.

sighting a bill *(US)* Präsentieren eines Wechsels.

sightseeing Besichtigung, Besuch von Sehenswürdigkeiten;
  to go ~ **in London** London besichtigen;
  ~ **bus** Aussichts-, Rundfahrtautobus; ~ **excursion** Besichtigungstour; ~ **tour** Stadtrund-, Besichtigungsfahrt.

sightseer Tourist.

sign [An]zeichen, *(advertising)* Werbeschild, *(indication)* Ansatz, Spur, *(mark)* Kennzeichen, Merkmal, *(shop)* Laden-, Aushängeschild, *(tel.)* Ruf[zeichen], *(traffic)* Verkehrszeichen;

characteristic ~ charakteristisches Merkmal; **deaf-and-dumb** ~s Taubstummensprache; **derestrictive** ~ *(Br.)* Geschwindigkeitsbeschränkung aufhebendes Verkehrszeichen; **distinctive** ~ Unterscheidungsmerkmal; **informative** ~ Hinweiszeichen; **inn** ~ Wirtshausschild; **mandatory** ~ Gebotszeichen; **manual** ~ Handzeichen, Namenszug, eigenhändige Unterschrift, Handzeichen; **plus** ~ positives Vorzeichen; **prohibitive** ~ Verbotszeichen; **road** ~ Wegweiser, Verkehrszeichen; **shop** ~ Ladenschild; **stop** ~ Haltesignal; **traffic** ~ Verkehrszeichen; **V-~** *(Br.)* Autofahrergruß; **warning** ~ Warnzeichen;
  ~ **of confidence** Vertrauensbeweis; ~ **of correction** Korrekturzeichen; ~ **and countersign** gegenseitige Erkennungszeichen; ~ **of decay** Verfallszeichen; ~s **of distress** Erschöpfungsanzeichen; ~s **of slowdown** Anzeichen konjunktureller Verschlechterung, konjunkturelle Abschwächungshinweise; ~ **of the times** Zeichen der Zeit;
  ~ *(v.)* [unter]zeichnen, unterschreiben, Unterschrift geben, mit Unterschrift versehen, signieren, *(subscribe)* zeichnen;
  ~ **o. s.** sich anmelden; ~ **the agreement (articles)** anmustern; ~ **as attorney-in-fact** in Vollmacht unterschreiben; ~ **away** [Vermögen, Recht] übertragen; ~ **away one's interest in an estate** auf Grundstücksansprüche verzichten; ~ **away all rights to any inventions** von vornherein auf alle Erfinderansprüche verzichten; ~ **a bill** Wechsel unterschreiben; ~ **a bond** Schuldschein ausstellen; ~ **a check** *(US)* **(cheque, Br.)** Scheck unterschreiben; ~ **one's consent** seine Zustimmung zu erkennen geben; ~ **a contract** Vertrag abschließen; ~ **a sales contract** Kaufvertrag unterzeichnen; ~ **a decree of adjudication** Konkurseröffnungsbeschluß erlassen; ~ **a document** Urkunde mit Unterschrift versehen; ~ **up for evening classes** sich zu Kursen für die Erwachsenenbildung anmelden; ~ **on behalf of a firm** für eine Firma zeichnen; ~ **in full** mit vollem Namen unterschreiben; ~ **for s. o.** Vollmacht für j. unterschreiben; ~ **for the goods** Warenempfang bestätigen; ~ **in one's own hand** eigenhändig unterschreiben; ~ **a hire-purchase agreement** *(Br.)* Abzahlungsvertrag abschließen; ~ **on the dotted line** kritiklos (routinemäßig) unterschreiben; ~ **by a mark** durch ein Kreuzchen unterzeichnen; ~ **one's name** unterschreiben, seinen Namen schreiben; ~ **one's name to a letter** seine Unterschrift unter einen Brief setzen; ~ **off** *(radio, US)* Funkstille (Sendepause) ansagen, Schlußmelodie spielen, *(relinquish one's claims)* verzichten, Ansprüche aufgeben, *(society)* seinen Austritt erklären, *(stop work)* Arbeitsschluß registrieren, *(workman, US)* kündigen; ~ **on** *(broadcasting)* Eingangsmelodie spielen, Sendebetrieb eröffnen, *(factory)* anwerben, einstellen, *(return to work)* sich wieder zur Arbeit melden, *(take up a job)* anmustern, -heuern; ~ **on as a sponsor** Patenschaft für ein Rundfunkprogramm übernehmen; ~ **on a hundred workmen last week** in der letzten Woche hundert Arbeiter anstellen (einstellen); ~ **over** übermachen, übertragen, abtreten; ~ **personally** eigenhändig unterschreiben; ~ **for press** Imprimatur erteilen; ~ **the ship's articles** sich anheuern lassen; ~ **s. o. to stop** *(policeman)* j. zum Anhalten veranlassen; ~ **a trade agreement** Handelsvertrag abschließen; ~ **up** sich verpflichten, *(university, US)* Vorlesung belegen; ~ **up a year in advance** Arbeitsvertrag ein Jahr zuvor abschliessen; ~ **the visitors' book** sich ins Gästebuch eintragen; ~ **on for a voyage** *(seaman)* für eine Reise anheuern; ~ **a will and testament** letztwillige Verfügung unterzeichnen; ~ **on workmen** Arbeiter einstellen;
  to be authorized to ~ zeichnungsberechtigt sein; **to show** ~s **of improvement** Besserungstendenzen erkennen lassen;
  ~ **language** Zeichensprache; ~ **manual** Handzeichen, Namenszug; ~ **mast advertising** Mastwerbung; ~ **painter (writer)** Schildermaler; ~**-off** *(broadcasting)* Sendeschluß; ~**-up** *(sl.)* Parteibeitritt; ~ **writing** Schilderbeschriftung.

signal Signal, Zeichen, *(mil.)* Funkspruch;
  ~s **ahead** Verkehrsampel; **bell** ~ Klingelzeichen; **busy** ~ *(tel., US)* Besetztzeichen; **call** ~ Rufzeichen; **cautionary** ~ *(ship)* Warnsignal; **distress** ~ Gefahr-, Not-, Hilfesignal, *(ship)* SOS; **left-turn** ~ Linksabbiegersignal; **light** ~ Leuchtzeichen; **off-~** *(airraid)* Entwarnung; **on** ~ *(airraid)* Warnsignal, Fliegeralarm; **raiders past** ~ *(airraid)* Entwarnung; **railway** ~ Eisenbahnsignal; **time** ~ Zeitzeichen; **traffic** ~ Verkehrszeichen;
  ~ **of danger** Gefahrenzeichen; ~ **of distress** Notsignal; ~s **for inflation** Inflationsanzeichen;
  ~ *(v.)* übermitteln, signalisieren;
  ~ **a message** Funkspruch übermitteln; ~ **an order** Befehl übermitteln; ~ **a taxi** Taxi herbeiwinken; ~ **a train** Zug melden;
  to be the ~ **for a revolt** Aufruhrzeichen sein; **to get one's** ~s **mixed** falsch reagieren; **to give the** ~ **for retreat** zum Rückzug blasen; **to lock a** ~ *(railway)* Signal festlegen;

~ **achievement** bedeutende Leistung; ~ **arm** *(railway)* Signalarm; ~ **beacon** Signalbake; ~ **bell** *(railway)* Läutewerk; ~ **book** Signalcode, -buch; ~ **box** *(railway)* Stellwerk; ~ **communications** *(mil.)* Fernmeldewesen; ≗ **Corps** *(US)* Fernmeldetruppe; ~ **fire** Leuchtfeuer; ~ **flag** Signalflagge; ~ **gun** *(ship)* Signalschuß; ~ **lamp (lantern)** Blink-, Morselampe, Blinkgerät; ~ **letters** *(ship)* Rufzeichen; ~ **light** Verkehrsampel, Signallaterne, *(railway)* Weichenlaterne; ~ **officer** *(US)* Fernmeldeoffizier; ~ **pistol** *(mil.)* Leuchtpistole; ~ **reward** außergewöhnliche Belohnung; ~ **rocket** *(mil.)* Leuchtkugel; ~ **service** Nachrichtenwesen, Signaldienst; ~ **wave** Betriebswelle.

signal(l)er *(mar.)* Blinker, Signalgast.

signal(l)ing Signalisieren, Nachrichtenübermittlung;
~ **apparatus** Signalvorrichtung.

signalman *(railway)* Bahn-, Blockwärter, *(US)* Fernmeldesoldat, Funker, *(ship)* Signalgast.

signatories to a treaty vertragsschließende Teile.

signatory Unterzeichner, Vertragspartner, Signatar[macht];
~ **to an agreement** Unterzeichner eines Vertrages;
~ *(a.)* vertragsschließend;
~ **government** Unterzeichnerregierung; ~ **power** Signatarmacht, Unterzeichnerland; ~ **state** Signatarstaat.

signature Unterschriftsleistung, Signatur, Unterzeichnung, [eigenhändige Namens]unterschrift, Namenszug, *(broadcasting)* Sende-, Pausenzeichen, *(firm)* Firmenunterschrift;
~ **differs** Unterschrift (Wechselvermerk) ungenau;
autographic ~ eigenhändige Unterschrift; **blank** ~ Blankounterschrift; **corporate** ~ *(US)* Firmenunterschrift, -zeichnung; **deferred** ~ nachträgliche Unterschrift; **facsimile** ~ Faksimileunterschrift; **fictitiuous (forged)** ~ gefälschte Unterschrift, Unterschriftsfälschung; **genuine** ~ echte Unterschrift; **incomplete** ~ unvollständige Unterschrift; **joint** ~ Gesamtzeichnungsberechtigung, Kollektivprokura, ~ **missing** Unterschrift fehlt; **multiple** ~ gemeinsame Unterschrift; **per procuration** ~ Prokuraunterschrift; **single** ~ Alleinzeichnungsberechtigung; **specimen** ~ Unterschriftsprobe; **unauthorized** ~ Unterschrift ohne Ermächtigung; ~ **unknown** Unterschrift unbekannt;
~ **on a bill** Wechselunterschrift; ~ **in blank** Blankounterschrift; ~ **on cheques (checks,** *US)* Scheckunterschrift; ~ **of a contract** Vertragsunterschrift; ~ **of a firm** Firmenunterschrift; ~ **by mark** Unterschrift durch Handzeichen; ~ **by procuration** Unterschrift in Vollmacht, Prokuraunterschrift; ~ **by an authorized representative** Unterzeichnung durch einen bevollmächtigten Vertreter; ~ **of a treaty** Vertragsunterzeichnung;
to acknowledge one's ~ seine Unterschrift als echt anerkennen; **to add one's** ~ **to s. th.** seine Unterschrift dazusetzen; **to append one's** ~ unterschreiben; **to attest (authenticate)** a ~ Unterschrift beglaubigen; **to be open to** ~ zur Unterzeichnung ausliegen; **to bear a** ~ Unterschrift tragen; **to certify a** ~ Unterschrift beglaubigen; **to disown one's** ~ seine Unterschrift nicht anerkennen; **to gather** ~s Unterschriften sammeln; **to have one's** ~ **legalized** seine Unterschrift beglaubigen lassen; **to make up a list of authorized** ~ Unterschriftenverzeichnis erstellen; **to put (set) one's** ~ **to a letter** seinen Namen unter einen Brief setzen; **to round up** ~s Unterschriften sammeln; **to submit a decree to s. o. for** ~ jem. eine Verordnung zur Unterschrift vorlegen; **to verify a** ~ Unterschrift beglaubigen;
~ **book** *(bank)* Unterschriftenverzeichnis; ~ **card** *(bank)* Unterschriftsprobe, -karte; ~ **card file** Unterschriftenkartothek; ~ **clause** *(insurance)* Zusicherungsklausel; ~ **mark** *(print.)* Bogenzeichen, Signatur; ~ **stamp** Unterschrifts-, Faksimilestempel; ~ **tune** Erkennungs-, Sendermelodie, Pausenzeichen.

signboard Aushänge-, Gasthaus, Firmenschild.

signed gezeichnet;
duly ~ ordnungsgemäß unterschrieben;
~ **in duplicate** in doppelter Ausfertigung; ~, **sealed and delivered** unterschrieben, gesiegelt und begeben (ausgefertigt).

signer Unterzeichner, Ausfertiger.

signet Petschaft, Siegel, Firmensiegel;
privy ~ königliches Haussiegel;
~ **ring** Siegelring.

significance *(market reserach)* Bewertungsgrad, Stichhaltigkeit der Ergebnisse;
of no ~ ohne jegliche Bedeutung;
~ **level** *(statistics)* Sicherheitsstufe.

significant bedeutsam, bezeichnend;
~ **amount** erheblicher Betrag; ~ **speech** richtungsweisende Rede.

signification Bedeutung, Sinn.

signify *(v.)* bekanntgeben, -machen, mitteilen, *(mean)* bedeuten;
~ **one's consent** seine Zustimmung schriftlich erteilen.

signing Unterzeichnung;
~ **of a contract** Vertragsunterzeichnung; ~ **a document** Unterschriftsleistung; ~ **of a lease** Abschluß eines Mietvertrages; ~ **on** *(labo(u)r)* Einstellung;
~ **authority** Zeichnungsberechtigung; ~ **clerk** *(Br.)* Handlungsbevollmächtigter; ~ **fee** Zeichnungsgebühr; ~ **power** Unterschriftsvollmacht; ~ **table** Unterschriftentisch.

signpost Hinweiszeichen, Wegweiser, Geschwindigkeitsschild, Verkehrszeichen;
~ **maker** Schilderhersteller.

signwriter Reklamezeichner.

silence Stillschweigen, *(machine)* Geräuschlosigkeit;
electric ~ spannungsgeladenes Schweigen; **prudent** ~ weise Zurückhaltung; **a minute's** ~ Gedenkminute;
~ *(v.)* **the batteries of the enemy** feindliche Batterien zum Schweigen bringen; ~ **complaints** Beschwerden abhelfen; ~ **one's critics** seinen Kritikern den Mund stopfen; ~ **all further opposition** jeden weiteren Widerstand unterdrücken;
to impose ~ **upon s. o.** jem. das Wort entziehen; **to pass over an affair with[in]** ~ Sache mit Stillschweigen übergehen; **to reduce s. o. to** ~ j. zum Schweigen bringen; **to wrap o. s. in** ~ sich in Schweigen hüllen;
~ **cloth** Filztuch;
~ **gives (shows) consent** Stillschweigen bedeutet Zustimmung.

silencer *(car)* Auspufftopf, *(mil.)* Schalldämpfer.

silent schweigend, still, stumm;
to be ~ *(terms of a contract)* nichts aussagen, keine Bestimmung treffen;
~ **butler** Abfallgefäß; ~ **consent** stillschweigende Zustimmung; ~ **film** *(movie)* Stummfilm; ~ **march** Schweigemarsch; ~ **partner** *(Br.)* stiller Teilhaber (Gesellschafter); ~ **partnership** *(Br.)* stille Teilhaberschaft; ~ **propaganda** unauffällige Propaganda; ~ **running of an engine** Geräuschlosigkeit eines Motors; ~ **service** *(US)* Unterseebootdienst; ~ **system** *(penal discipline)* Schweigesystem; ~ **vote** geheime Abstimmung.

silhouette half-tone freistehende Autotypie.

silk Seide, *(silk gown, Br.)* Kronanwalt;
artificial ~ Kunstseide;
to hit the ~ *(sl.)* mit dem Fallschirm abspringen; **to take** ~ *(Br.)* Generalstaatsanwalt (Kronanwalt) werden;
~ **gown** Seidentalar, Robe eines Staatsanwalts, *(fig., Br.)* Kronanwalt; ~ **hat** Zylinderhut; ~ **screen printing** Siebdruck; ~-**stocking** *(US)* wohlhabend, aristokratisch; ~-**stocking district (ward,** *US)* politisch einflußreicher Bevölkerungsteil.

silly season *(fam.)* Sauregurkenzeit.

silt *(v.)* **up** versanden.

silver Silber, *(small change)* Kleingeld;
bar ~ Silberbarren; **fine** ~ Feinsilber; **loose** ~ Silberkleingeld; **standard** ~ Münzsilber;
~ **of base alloy** geringhaltiges Silber; ~ **in ingots** Stangensilber;
~ *(v.)* versilbern;
~ **agio** Silberagio; ~ **alloy** Silberlegierung; ~ **bar** Silberbarren; ~ **basis** Silberwährung; ~ **bullion** Barrensilber; ~ **certificate** *(US)* Silberzertifikat; ~ **coin** Silbermünze; ~ **coinage** Silbergeld; ~ **currency** Silberwährung; ~ **handshake** Abfindung; ~ **lining** *(fig.)* Lichtblick, Silberstreifen; ~ **mine** Silberbergwerk; ~ **plate** Tafelsilber; **to make a** ~ **purse out of a sow's ear** aus einem Kieselstein einen Diamanten schleifen; ~ **quotations** Silbernotierungen; ~ **screen** Filmleinwand; **to be born with a** ~ **spoon in one's mouth** als Kind reicher Eltern geboren (Glückskind) sein; ~ **standard** Silberwährung; ~ **thaw** Frostbeschlag; **to have a** ~ **tongue** redegewandt sein; ~ **wedding** Silberhochzeit.

similar ähnlich, gleichartig, *(analogous)* analog;
~ **description** *(tariff act)* ähnliche Beschaffenheit; **on a** ~ **footing** analog; ~ **services** gleichartige Dienstleistungen.

similarity of business *(restraint of trade)* gleichartige Geschäftsbranche.

simile Gleichnis.

simmer *(v.)* *(fig.)* kochen, sieden;
~ **down** *(v.)* sich abregen.

simony Pfründenhandel.

simple einfach, nicht qualifiziert, *(not evidenced by sealed writing)* nicht in gesiegelter Form;
~ **arbitration** *(Br.)* Einfacharbitrage; ~ **average** einfache Havarie; **of** ~ **birth** von einfacher Herkunft; ~ **bond** hypothekarisch nicht besicherte Obligation; ~ **confession** formelles Schuldbekenntnis; ~ **contract** formloser (einfacher) Vertrag; ~ **contract creditor** gewöhnlicher Konkursgläubiger; ~ **contract debt** nicht bevorrechtigte [Konkurs]forderung; ~ **cooking** bürgerliche Küche; ~ **debentures** nicht hypothekarisch besicherte Pfandbriefe; ~ **debts** gewöhnliche Konkursforderungen; ~ **deposit**

Sammelverwahrung; ~ **diet** einfache Kost; ~ **efforts** geringe Anstrengungen; ~ **fact** absolute Tatsache; ~ **forms of life** niedere Lebensformen; ~ **interest** gewöhnliche Zinsen, Kapitalzinsen; ~ **journal** Journal für einfache Buchführung; ~ **larceny** einfacher Diebstahl; ~ **life** einfaches Leben; ~ **majority** einfache Mehrheit; ~ **obligation** einfache Verpflichtung; ~ **person** schlichter Mensch; ~ **sentence** Hauptsatz; ~ **tool** gewöhnliches Werkzeug; ~ **trust** (*income tax, US*) Thesaurierungsfonds, Stiftung, die nur Zinsen ausschüttet; ~ **warrandice** (*Scot., in a charter*) Erklärung über Rechtsmängelgewährleistungen.

simplex printer Fernschreiber.

simplicity, for the sake of aus Vereinfachungsgründen;
    to be ~ itself kinderleicht sein.

simplification Vereinheitlichung, Typenbeschränkung;
    product ~ Fertigungsvereinfachung;
    ~ of designs Konstruktionsvereinfachung;
    ~ movement Vereinheitlichungsbewegung.

simplified spelling vereinfachte Schreibweise.

simplify (*v.*) vereinfachen;
    ~ matters all round Dinge reihum vereinfachen.

simulate (*v.*) fingieren, vorgeben, heucheln, Krankheit simulieren;
    ~ insanity Unzurechnungsfähigkeit vortäuschen.

simulated | account fingierte Rechnung, Proformarechnung, ~ **contract** Scheinvertrag; ~ **debt** fingierte Forderung; ~ **fact** erfundene Tatsache; ~ **judgment** erschlichenes Urteil, Scheinurteil; ~ **sale** Scheinkauf.

simulation Vorspiegelung, Simulierung, (*civil law*) Scheingeschäft, Scheinvertrag, -transaktion.

simulator Simulant.

simulcast (*television*) Simultansendung, Direktübertragung;
    ~ (*v.*) gleichzeitig über Rundfunk und Fernsehen senden.

simultaneous gleichzeitig, simultan;
    ~ death (*US*) gleichzeitiger Tod; ~ **performance** Erfüllung Zug um Zug; ~ **translation** Simultanübersetzung.

sin of ommission Unterlassungssünde.

sincere aufrichtig, ehrlich;
    Yours ~ly (*Br.*) mit freundlichen Grüßen, Ihr ergebener.

sine die (*lat.*) ohne Festlegung eines neuen Termins, auf unbestimmte Zeit;
    to adjourn a meeting ~ Sitzung auf unbestimmte Zeit vertagen.

sinecure Sinekure, einträglicher Posten.

sing (*v.*) (*criminal*) verpfeifen;
    ~ low zurückhaltend sprechen; ~ **on the other side of one's mouth** auf einmal eine völlig andere Meinung vertreten; ~ **s. one's praises** voller Begeisterung über j. sprechen; ~ **small** klein beigeben; ~ **the same song** ins gleiche Horn blasen; ~ **sorrow** jammern; ~ **another tune (song)** zurückstecken, bescheidener werden.

singe (*v.*) **one's feathers** (*fig.*) sich die Finger verbrennen.

singing shoulder (*US*) Straßenbegrenzungsstreifen.

single (*railway, Br.*) Einzelfahrkarte, (*US sl.*) Eindollarnote;
    ~ (*a.*) einzig, allein, einmalig, (*machine*) nur einen Arbeitsgang verrichtend, (*unmarried*) ledig, unverheiratet, alleinstehend;
    ~ (*v.*) **out** aussondern, ausmustern;
    to be (remain) ~ ledig sein;
    ~ **adventure** (*Br.*) Handelsgesellschaft zur Durchführung einer einmaligen Transaktion, Gelegenheitsgesellschaft; ~ **allowance** (*income tax, Br.*) persönlicher Freibetrag; ~ **basing point system** (*US*) Frachtausgangspunktsystem; ~ **bed** Einzelbett; ~ **bedroom** (*hotel*) Einzelzimmer; ~ **bill** Solawechsel, (~ *obligation*) notarielles Schuldversprechen; ~ **bond** persönlicher Verpflichtungsschein; ~ **borrower** Einzelkreditnehmer; ~**breasted** (*coat*) einreihig; ~**carrier service** kombinierte Speditionsleistung; ~ **cell** Einzelzelle; ~**chamber system** (*pol.*) Einkammersystem; ~**colo(u)red** einfarbig, ~ **column** Einzelspalte; ~**column inch** Spaltenmaß; ~ **compartment** Einzelabteil; **in a ~ copy** einfach ausgefertigt; ~**copy price** Einzelheftpreis; ~ **creditor** einseitig (nur einmal) gesicherter Gläubiger; ~ **debenture** Einzelschuldverschreibung; ~**deck aeroplane** Eindecker; ~ **employer bargaining** Einzeltarifverhandlung; ~**engined** einmotorig; ~ **enterprise** Einzelunternehmen; ~ **entry** Eintrag ohne Gegenbuchung; ~**entry bookkeeping** einfache Buchführung; ~ **escheat** Vermögenseinziehung eines Hochverräters; ~ **exchange rate** Deviseneinheitskurs; **to have a ~ eye for** einseitig interessiert sein; ~**eye glass** Monokel; ~**family dwelling (home)** Einfamilienhaus; ~**family ground** Eigenheimgrundstück; ~ **fare** einfacher Fahrpreis; ~ **house** alleinstehendes Haus; ~ **item** Einzelposten, -betrag; ~ **judge** Einzelrichter; ~ **life** Junggesellendasein; ~ **line** eingleisige Bahn, (*tel.*) Einzelanschluß; ~**line** einzeilig, (*railway*) einbahnig, eingleisig; ~**line retail trade** Fachhandel; ~**line store** (*US*) Spezialartikel-,

Fachgeschäft; ~ **list** (*parl.*) Einheitsliste; ~ **loan** einmalige Staatsanleihe; ~ **man** Alleinstehender; ~**minded** einseitig interessiert; ~**name paper** (*US*) nicht girierter Solawechsel; ~ **obligation** Leistungsversprechen; ~ **option** einfaches Prämiengeschäft; ~ **original** nur einmal vorhandene Urkunde; ~**part production** Einzelanfertigung; ~ **parts** Einzelteile; ~ **payment** einmalige Zahlung; ~ **payment annuity** Rente aufgrund einer einmaligen Kapitalzahlung; ~ **person** Einzelperson, (*unmarried*) Unverheirateter; ~ **plant** Einzelbetrieb; ~**plant bargaining** Einzeltarifverhandlung; ~ **premium** (*insurance*) Einmalprämie; ~**premium life insurance** Lebensversicherung durch Abschluß einer Einmalprämie; ~ **price** Einheitspreis; ~**price store** (*US*) Einheitspreisgeschäft; ~ **project** Einzelprojekt; ~ **proprietorship** (*US*) Einzelfirma, -unternehmen; ~**rail** eingleisig, -spurig; ~**rate letter** einfacher Brief; ~ **recovery** angemessene Entschädigung, ~ **residence** (*US*) Einfamilienhaus; ~ **room** Einzelzimmer; ~**schedule tariff** Einheitszolltarif; ~ **seater** (*plane*) Einsitzer; ~ **shareholder (stockholder, US)** Einzelaktionär; ~**shift operation** Einzelschichtbetrieb; ~ **signature** Alleinzeichnungsberechtigung, Einzelunterschrift; ~**stage turnover tax** Einphasenumsatzsteuer; ~ **standard** (*US*) monometallistische Währung; ~ **state** Junggesellenstatus; ~**step income statement** (*US*) Gewinn- und Verlustrechnung in Kontoform; ~**storey** eingeschossig; ~**storey construction** einstöckige Bauweise; ~ **sum** einmalige Zahlung; **to pay in a ~ sum** auf einmal bezahlen; ~ **tariff** autonomer Tarif; ~ **tax** einzige Steuer; ~ **ticket** (*Br.*) einfache Fahrkarte; ~**tier authority** (*Br.*) einstufige Behörde; ~**track** eingleisige Strecke; ~ **track** eingleisig; ~**track** (*v.*) eingleisige Strecke bauen; **to have a ~track mind** einseitig interessiert sein; ~ **trader** (*Br.*) Einzelkaufmann; ~**use goods** kurzlebige Verbrauchsgüter; ~**venture partnership** (*US*) Handelsgesellschaft zur Durchführung einer einmaligen Transaktion, Gelegenheitsgesellschaft; ~ **volume** Einzelexemplar; ~ **woman** alleinstehende (getrennt lebende) Frau.

singleton alleinstehender Mensch, Einspänner.

singular einfach, einzeln;
    ~ **man** Sonderling; ~ **successor** (*estate law*) Einzelrechtsnachfolger.

sink Spülstein, Ausguß, (*fig.*) Sumpf, Pfuhl;
    ~ of iniquity Lasterhöhle;
    ~ (*v.*) (*amortize*) tilgen, amortisieren, (*house*) sich setzen, (*prices*) sinken, fallen, niedriger werden, (*ship*) sinken, untergehen, absaufen, (*tie up capital*) festlegen, fest anlegen;
    ~ a controversy Streit beilegen; ~ **a debt** Schuld abtragen (tilgen); ~ **a difference** Streit begraben; ~ **an important fact** wichtige Tatsache unterdrücken; ~ **fast** (*patient*) zusehends verfallen; ~ **half of one's fortune in a new business undertaking** Hälfte seines Vermögens in einem neuen Geschäft anlegen; ~ **into insignificance** völlig vergessen werden; ~ **the level of prices** Kursniveau vertiefen; ~ **into s. one's mind** jem. eingehen; ~ **money in annuities** Geld in Rentenwerten anlegen; ~ **money in an undertaking** Geld in ein Unternehmen stecken; ~ **into oblivion** in Vergessenheit geraten; ~ **into poverty** verarmen; ~ **prices** Preise herabsetzen; ~ **in the social scale** gesellschaftlich absinken; ~ **a shaft** Schacht abteufen; ~ **a ship** Schiff versenken; ~ **stock in speculation** Aktien durch Fehlspekulation verlieren; ~ **one's title** seinen Titel verschweigen;
    ~ or swim auf Biegen oder Brechen.

sinkable versenkbar.

sinker Senkblei, (*US sl.*) Falschgeld.

sinking Versenkung, (*investment*) Geldanlage, (*redemption*) Tilgung, Amortisierung;
    ~ of debts Schuldentilgung; ~ **of a shaft** Schaftabteufung;
    ~ (*a.*) fallend, nachgebend, heruntergehend;
    ~ feeling Schwächegefühl.

sinking fund Schuldentilgungs-, Anleihetilgungs-, Ablösungsfonds, Amortisationsfonds, -kasse;
    to raid the ~ Tilgungsfonds zweckentfremden;
    ~ **agent** Verwalter eines Amortisationsfonds; ~ **assets** (*US*) Anlagekonto für den Tilgungsfonds; ~ **bonds** Schuldverschreibungen des Amortisationsfonds, Ablösungsanleihe; ~ **contributions** Zuweisungen für den Tilgungsfonds; ~ **income** Erträgnisse des Amortisationsfonds; ~ **instalment** Tilgungsrate; ~ **investment** Kapitalanlage von Tilgungsfondsmitteln; ~ **loan** Tilgungsanleihe, Darlehn mit Tilgungsplan; ~ **method of calculating depreciation** Abschreibungsmethode mit steigenden Quoten; ~ **mortgage loan** Tilgungshypothek; ~ **notice** (*US*) Bekanntgabe über die erfolgte Kündigung von Wertpapieren und deren Tilgung; ~ **operations** Schuldentilgungsmaßnahmen; ~ **payment** Amortisationszahlung; ~ **reserve** Tilgungsrücklage; ~ **table** Tilgungsplan; ~ **tax** Anleihesteuer.

siphon *(v.)* | **off funds** Mittel abschöpfen; ~ **off traffic from an overcrowded motorway** überlastete Autobahn verkehrsmäßig entlasten.
siren Sirene;
  airraid ~ Luftschutzsirene.
sist *(v.) (Scot.)* Verfahren einstellen.
sister *(coll.)* Krankenschwester;
  ~-in-law Schwägerin;
  ~ **company** Schwestergesellschaft; ~ **ship** Schwesterschiff; ~ **state** *(US)* Einzelstaat; ~ **union** Schwesternverband.
sit *(v.)* sitzen, tagen, Sitzung abhalten;
  ~ **for an artist** sich porträtieren lassen; ~ **back** sich zurücklehnen, *(fig.)* sich zurückziehen, Hände in den Schoß legen; ~ **badly on s. o.** mit jem. schlecht stehen; ~ **on the bench** Richter sein; ~ **on various supervising boards** mehreren Aufsichtsgremien angehören; ~ **for a borough** *(Br.)* für einen Wahlkreis kandidieren; ~ **in camera (chambers)** als Einzelrichter tätig sein, unter Ausschluß der Öffentlichkeit verhandeln, in nicht öffentlicher Sitzung tagen; ~ **on a case** *(court)* in einer Sache verhandeln; ~ **on (upon) a committee** Ausschußmitglied sein, einem Ausschuß angehören; ~ **in conclave** geheime Sitzung abhalten; ~ **in a conference** *(US)* Tagung abhalten, tagen; ~ **in Congress** *(US)* Kongreßabgeordneter sein; ~ **for a constituency** Wahlkreis vertreten; ~ **down** Sitzstreik veranstalten; ~ **down under insults** Beleidigungen stillschweigend hinnehmen (einstecken); ~ **down before a town** Belagerung einer Stadt beginnen; ~ **in for s. o.** j. vertreten; ~ **for an examination** sich einer Prüfung unterziehen; ~ **facing the engine** in der Fahrtrichtung sitzen; ~ **at s. one's feet** jds. glühender Anhänger sein; ~ **on the fence** abwartende Haltung einnehmen; ~ **on Fridays** jeden Freitag eine Sitzung abhalten (tagen); ~ **on one's hands** untätig bleiben, *(sl.)* nicht applaudieren; ~ **at home** untätig zu Hause herumsitzen; ~ **in** sich einfinden; ~ **at a high interest** hohe Zinsen zahlen müssen; ~ **a hearing out** einer mündlichen Verhandlung bis zum Schluß beiwohnen; ~ **on a jury** Geschworener sein; ~ **a lecture out** bis zum Schluß des Vortrags bleiben; ~ **on the lid** *(coll.)* Aufregung zügeln; ~ **out a play** bis zum Schluß der Vorstellung bleiben; ~ **in Parliament** Abgeordneter sein; ~ **with a sick person** bei einem Kranken wachen; ~ **for one's portrait** sich porträtieren lassen; ~ **pretty** *(US sl.)* es gut haben; ~ **on a question** sich mit einer Frage beschäftigen; ~ **up and take notice** *(US coll.)* plötzlich Interesse zeigen; ~ **tight** *(fig.)* bei seiner Meinung bleiben, *(fam.)* sich eisern behaupten; ~ **tight on one's principles** auf seinen Prinzipien herumreiten; ~ **on the throne** regieren, *(student)* Schüler [eines Professors] sein; ~ **under an insult** Beleidigung einstecken; ~ **up late** lange aufbleiben; ~ **upon** Tagung abhalten; ~ **upon s. o.** *(sl.)* jem. aufs Dach steigen; ~ **at \$ 120 a week** 120 Dollar wöchentliche Ausgaben haben; ~ **well on s. o.** mit jem. gut stehen; ~ **at work** über der Arbeit sitzen;
  to make s. o. ~ *(coll.)* j. rankriegen;
  ~-down strike (demonstration) Sitzstreik; **~-in** studentische Protestdemonstration.
site Lage (Belegenheit) eines Grundstückes, Örtlichkeit, *(novel)* Schauplatz, *(plot of land)* Bauplatz, -grund, -gelände;
  delivered [on] ~ Lieferung frei Baustelle;
  building ~ Bauplatz, -stelle, gelände; **cleared** ~ abgeräumtes Grundstück, **erection** ~ *(machine)* Aufstellungsort; **fair** ~ Ausstellungs-, Messegelände; **greenfield** ~ Wiesenparzelle; **home** ~ Eigenheimgrundstück; **obstructed** ~ *(posting)* verdeckter Anschlag; **usual used** ~ allgemeine Anschlagstelle;
  ~s under construction im Bau befindliche Anlagen; ~ **of a fracture** *(med.)* Bruchstelle; ~ **of an industry** Sitz einer Industrie; ~ **for a new school** neues Schulgelände;
  ~ *(v.)* stationieren, plazieren;
  ~ **a new factory** neues Fabrikgelände festlegen;
  to be built on the ~ **of an old fort** auf dem Gelände eines alten Forts errichtet werden; **to deliver materials to a building** ~ Baumaterial zum Bauplatz bringen; **to effect repairs on the** ~ Reparaturen am Aufstellungsort vornehmen; **to preserve as a historic** ~ unter Denkmalschutz stellen;
  ~ **classification** Flächenklassifikation; ~ **development** Baulanderschließung; ~ **foreman** Baustellenleiter; ~ **inspection** Anschlagkontrolle; ~ **inspector** Anschlagkontrolleur; ~ **land** Baugelände; ~ **list** Stellen-, Standortverzeichnis; ~ **owner** Grundstückseigentümer; ~ **plan** Lageplan; ~ **planner** Grundstückserschließer; ~ **planning** Grundstückserschließung; ~ **prefabrication** Wohnblockvorfertigungsmethode; ~ **preparation** Geländeaufbereitung; **~-specific** flächenbezogen; ~ **supervisor** *(US)* Bauführer; ~ **survey** Geländevermessung; ~ **value** Bodenwert, [steuerlicher] Einheitswert; ~ **value rating** Baulandbesteuerung.

siting Belegenheit.
sitter *(fig., sl.)* todsichere Sache, *(portrait)* Modell;
  ~-in Babysitter.
sitting Sitzung, Tagung, *(terms of court)* Gerichtstermin, Sitzungsperiode;
  at a (one) ~ in einer Sitzung; **during a long** ~ im Verlauf einer langen Sitzung;
  all-night ~ lange Nachtsitzung; **closing** ~ Schlußsitzung; **open** ~ öffentliche Sitzung; **private** ~ nichtöffentliche Sitzung; ~ **in banc (bank)** vollzähliger Gerichtshof; ~ **in camera (chambers)** Verhandlung vor dem Einzelrichter, nicht öffentliche Sitzung; ~ **of congress** Kongreßtagung; ~ **of a court** Gerichtssitzung, -termin; ~ **of Parliament** Parlamentssitzung; ~ **after term** Feriensitzungen;
  to attend a ~ Tagungs-, Sitzungsteilnehmer sein; **to be** ~ tagen, Sitzung abhalten, *(court)* zu Gericht sitzen; **to be served in one** ~ *(restaurant)* zur gleichen Zeit bedient werden; **to finish reading a book at one** ~ Buch in einem Rutsch zu Ende lesen;
  ~ *(a.)* zu Gericht sitzend;
  ~ **duck** *(mil.)* leicht zerstörbares Ziel; **to be a** ~ **duck for the enemy** dem Feinde wehrlos ausgeliefert sein; ~ **fee** *(Br.)* Verhandlungs-, Sitzungsgebühr, -geld; ~ **judge (magistrate)** amtierender Richter; ~ **member** Sitzungsteilnehmer; ~ **member for A** *(parl.)* Abgeordneter für A; ~ **place** Sitzplatz; ~ **pretty** *(US sl.)* in guten Verhältnissen; ~ **room** Wohnzimmer; ~ **tenant** Pächter; ~ **term** Sitzungsperiode.
situ, in an Ort und Stelle.
situate *(v.)* Platz bestimmen, aufstellen.
situated gelegen, belegen;
  badly ~ schlecht gestellt, *(plot)* ungünstig gelegen; **well** ~ gut gestellt; **similarly** ~ in ähnlichen Umständen;
  to be awkwardly ~ **just now** momentan in einer mißlichen Lage sein; **to be badly** ~ finanziell schlecht gestellt sein;
  well ~ **business** Geschäft in guter Lage.
situation Lage, Zustand, Situation, *(building)* Geschäftslage, Belegenheit, *(employment)* [An]stellung, Stelle, Posten, *(office)* Amt, *(position)* Stand;
  awkward ~ schwierige Lage; **credit** ~ kreditpolitische Lage; **critical** ~ kritische Lage; **temporarily difficult** ~ zeitweilige Schwierigkeit; **economic** ~ wirtschaftliche Situation, Konjunkturlage; **financial** ~ Finanzlage, Status; **fouled-up** ~ *(US)* verfahrene Situation; **general** ~ allgemeine Lage; **good** ~ gute Stelle, Versorgung; **hazardous** ~ gefährlicher Arbeitsplatz; **labo(u)r** ~ Arbeitsmarktlage; **legal** ~ Rechtsposition, -lage; **local political** ~ innenpolitische Lage; **market** ~ Marktlage, Absatzverhältnisse; **monetary** ~ Währungslage, -situation; **patent** ~ Patentlage; **permanent** ~ Lebens-, Dauerstellung; **~s required** *(newspaper)* Stellengesuche; **stock-market** ~ Lage am Effektenmarkt; **sunny** ~ *(house)* sonnige Lage; **tense** ~ gespannte Lage; **strong** ~ *(theater)* dramatischer Höhepunkt; **trying** ~ unangenehme Situation; **~s vacant** *(newspaper)* Stellenangebot; **~s wanted** Stellengesuche;
  ~ **as bookkeeper** Buchhalterstelle; ~ **of danger** *(vehicle)* Gefahrenlage; ~ **under government** Staatsstellung; **strained** ~ **on the labo(u)r market** angespannter Arbeitsmarkt; ~ **full of potentialities** Situation, in der alles möglich ist; ~ **of the registered office** Belegenheit des eingetragenen Firmensitzes; ~ **as teacher** Lehramt;
  to apply for a ~ sich um eine Stelle umtun (bewerben); **to assess a** ~ Lage überblicken; **to be in a** ~ Stelle (Stellung) haben; **to be in an embarrassing** ~ in einer schwierigen Lage sein; **to be in a pleasant** ~ *(house)* schön gelegen sein; **not to be equal to the** ~ der Lage nicht gewachsen sein; **to be out of a** ~ keine Stellung haben; **to be tailor-made to meet a special** ~ auf eine besondere Lage abgestellt sein; **to cope with a** ~ Situation in den Griff bekommen; **to discuss the** ~ Lagebesprechung abhalten; **to fill a** ~ Stelle bekleiden; **to find a** ~ **for s. o.** j. in einer Stellung unterbringen; **to get a** ~ Stellung erhalten; **to hold a** ~ Stelle haben; **to improve one's** ~ seine Stellung verbessern; **to keep a** ~ **under review** Lage laufend einer Überprüfung unterziehen; **to look for a** ~ Stellung suchen; **to make the most of a** ~ Situation ausnutzen; **to master a** ~ Situation beherrschen; **to survey the international** ~ Überblick über die internationale Lage geben; **to take stock of one's** ~ sich über seine Lage klar werden; **to take a new** ~ neue Stellung antreten; **to throw up a** ~ Stelle (Beschäftigung) aufgeben; **to undertake a** ~ Stelle übernehmen;
  ~ **map** *(mil.)* Lagekarte, *(technics)* Situationsplan.
situational judgment Situationserkenntnis.
situs *(lat.)* Belegenheit, Lage[ort], *(plant)* Geschäftssitz;
  business ~ steuerlicher Geschäftssitz; **taxable** ~ Steuersitz.

siwash *(v.)* biwakieren.
six *(retainer)* Honorar, Gebühr;
  ~ to one *(fig.)* totsicher; **~ of one and half a dozen of the other** gehupt wie gesprungen, Jacke wie Hose;
  to be at ~es and sevens kunterbunt (ganz) durcheinander sein;
  ~-day licence Werktagsschankkonzession; **the ~ form** [etwa] Oberprima; **the ~ former** *(Br.)* Primaner; **~-and eight pence** Honorar, Gebühr; **~ ways to Sunday** *(sl.)* gründlich, total.
sixes *(stock exchange)* Sechsprozenter, sechsprozentige Papiere;
  to be at ~ and sevens kunterbunt durcheinander sein.
sixteenth of a page Sechzehntelseite.
sixty-four dollar question *(US)* Gretchenfrage.
sizable beträchtlich;
  ~ fortune beträchtliches Vermögen.
sizar *(Br.)* Stipendiat.
sizarship *(Br.)* Stipendium.
size Größe, Nummer, Maß, Umfang, Format, Volumen;
  of (in) all ~s in allen Größen;
  commercial ~ marktfähige Größe; **full ~** Lebensgröße; **medium ~** Mittelgröße; **next ~** nächstgrößere Nummer; **odd ~** nicht gängige Größe; **out ~** Übergröße; **pocket ~** Taschenformat; **same ~** Originalgröße; **standard ~** Normalgröße; **standardized ~** genormte Größe; **stock ~** Lagergröße; **unusual ~** ungewöhnliches Format;
  ~ of assets Anlagenumfang, -volumen; **~ of business** Betriebsgröße; **~ of cassettes** Kassettengröße; **~ of holding** Beteiligungsumfang; **~ of income** Höhe des Einkommens; **~ of order** Auftragsumfang, -volumen; **~ of page** Seitenformat; **~ of population** Bevölkerungsgröße; **~ of salary** Gehaltsgröße; **~ of type** *(print.)* Schriftgrad, Kegel;
  ~ *(v.)* nach Größen ordnen (sortieren), *(produce)* in einer bestimmten Größe anfertigen;
  ~ up ein-, abschätzen;
  to arrange according to ~ der Größe nach ordnen; **to be about the ~ of it** *(coll.)* in etwa ein richtiger Lagebericht sein; **to reduce the ~ of a class** Schülerzahl in einer Klasse beschränken; **to seek ~ rather than quality** mehr auf Quantität als auf Qualität gehen;
  ~ group Größeneinteilung; **~ limits** Höchstgrößen [im Postverkehr]; **~ range** *(data processing)* Schriftgrößenbereich; **~ restrictions** Größenbeschränkungen.
sized nach Größen geordnet;
  fair-~ in gangbaren Größen; **full-~** von genauen Abmaßen; **large-~** in Großformat; **standard-~** in Normalgröße;
  ~ paper geleimtes Papier.
sizer Sortierer.
sizing Größeneinteilung.
sizzle *(sl.)* Skandalgeschichte;
  ~ spell of weather Hitzeperiode, -einbruch.
skate *(v.)* *(sl.)* seinem Gläubiger entkommen;
  ~ over a difficulty über eine Schwierigkeit hinweggleiten; **~ on thin ice** sich aufs Glatteis begeben.
sked *(US sl.)* Linienfluggesellschaft.
skedaddle *(sl.)* ungeordneter Rückzug;
  ~ *(v.)* *(coll.)* türmen, abhauen.
skeleton Gerüst, Gestell, *(building)* Rohbau, *(draft)* Skizze, Entwurf, *(mil.)* Rahmen, Stamm[truppe], Kader, *(plane)* Flugzeuggerippe, *(plant)* Stammpersonal;
  family ~ dunkler Punkt in der Familie, Familienschande; **steel ~** Stahlgerippe;
  ~ in the cupboard (closet) dunkler Punkt in der Familie, Familienschande, streng gehütetes Geheimnis; **~ at the feast (banquet)** Gespenst der Vergangenheit;
  ~ agenda Rahmentagesordnung; **~ agreement** Rahmenabkommen; **~ bill of** ausgefülltes [Wechsel]formular, Wechselblankett; **~ bill of exceptions** Schriftsatz vorläufiger Verfahrenseinwendungen; **~ company** *(mil.)* Stammkompanie; **~ construction** Skelettbau, Stahlbauweise; **~ contract** Manteltarif; **~ crew** Stammpersonal; **~ due (fee)** Rahmengebühr; **~ enemy** markierter Feind; **~ face** *(print.)* Skelettschrift; **~ key** Nach-, Generalschlüssel, Dietrich; **~ law** Rahmengesetz; **~ letter** Blankoformular; **~ map** Kartenskizze; **~ note** unausgefülltes Wechselformular; **~ organization** Rahmenorganisation; **~ staff** Stammgruppe, Stamm-, Rahmenpersonal, Rumpfbelegung; **~ tariff** Rahmentarif; **~ wage agreement** Mantel-, Rahmentarifvertrag.
skeletonize *(v.)* im Rohbau anfertigen, *(mil.)* Normalbestand reduzieren.
sketch *(account)* Übersicht, *(calculation)* Überschlag, überschlägige Berechnung, *(draft)* [Schmier]skizze, Riß, Rohentwurf, *(short story)* Kurzgeschichte;

first (rough) ~ Rohentwurf; **hot ~** *(sl.)* Energieprotz;
  ~ *(v.)* skizzieren, flüchtig entwerfen;
  ~ out proposals for a new road Pläne für eine neu anzulegende Straße entwerfen;
  to give s. o. a ~ of one's plans jem. seine Pläne kurz andeuten; **to make a ~ of a harbo(u)r** Hafen in groben Umrissen zeichnen; **to make a ~ of a house** Plan (Grundriß) eines Hauses aufzeichnen;
  ~ block Skizzenblock; **~ book** Skizzenbuch, Kladde; **~ design** Entwurfsskizze; **~ map** Lageskizze, -plan, Faustskizze, Kroki.
sketchy lückenhaft, oberflächlich;
  ~ knowledge dürftige Kenntnisse.
skew *(v.)* **facts** Tatsachen verdrehen.
ski | lift Skilift; **~ resort** Wintersportplatz; **~ run** Piste.
skid *(car)* Schleudern, Rutschen, *(plane)* Gleitkufe;
  ~ in profits Gewinnabfall;
  ~ *(v.)* rutschen, schleudern, *(price)* gleiten, rutschen, fallen;
  ~ over details über Details hinweggehen;
  to be on the ~s *(US sl.)* abrutschen, vergammeln; **to get out of a ~** rutschenden Wagen abfangen; **to go into a ~** ins Schleudern geraten; **to put the ~s under s. o.** *(sl.)* jds. Pläne sabotieren;
  ~ chain *(car)* Schneekette; **~-lid** *(Br., sl.)* Sturzhelm; **~ mark** Rutsch-, Brems-, Schleuderspur; **~ pan** *(Br.)* Hemmschuh; **~-proof** *(tyre)* rutschfest, gleitsicher; **~ road** Holzfällerweg; **~ row** *(sl.)* billiges Vergnügungsviertel.
skies, open *(pol.)* gegenseitige Luftüberwachung;
  to extol (laud) s. o. to the ~ j. (überschwenglich) loben.
skill Geschick[lichkeit], Fertigkeit, Fähigkeit, Können, Kenntnis;
  basic ~s Grundkenntnisse; **communication ~s** Kunst der Menschenbehandlung; **negotiating ~** Verhandlungsgeschick; **reasonable ~** durchschnittliches Können; **survival ~** unbedingt notwendige Fähigkeit, Überlebensfähigkeit;
  ~s of negotiations Verhandlungsfähigkeiten, -künste;
  to be trained in the wrong ~s im falschen Beruf ausgebildet sein; **to exercise reasonable ~ and care** gehörige Sorgfalt anwenden; **to exercise one's ~ of leadership** seine Führungseigenschaften unter Beweis stellen.
skilled gelernt, geschickt, bewandert;
  ~ in the art fachlich ausgebildet, fachkundig;
  to be ~ in a business fachlich ausgebildet sein;
  ~ crafts Handwerk; **~ evidence** Sachverständigenbeweis; **~ job** Arbeit für den Fachmann; **~ labo(u)r** ausgebildete Arbeitskräfte, Fachkräfte, -arbeiter; **~ manpower** gelernte (ausgebildete) Arbeitskräfte; **~ occupation** Anlernberuf; **~ personnel** Fachkräfte, -personal; **~ trade** erlernter Beruf, Spezialberuf; **~ witness** sachverständiger Zeuge; **~ work** Facharbeit; **~ worker** Facharbeiter, gelernter Arbeiter, Fachkraft.
skim flüchtiger Überblick;
  ~ *(v.)* abschöpfen;
  ~ through a book Buch überfliegen; **~ the cream off** *(fig.)* Rahm abschöpfen; **~ through a catalog(ue)** Katalog durchblättern; **~ over a letter** Brief überfliegen; **~ through a newspaper** Zeitung flüchtig durchsehen; **~ surplus purchasing power** überflüssige Kaufkraft abschöpfen.
skimmer, to become a ~ in one's reading diagonal zu lesen lernen.
skimming | off excess profits Gewinnabschöpfung; **~ surplus purchasing power** Abschöpfung überschüssiger Kaufkraft.
skimp *(v.)* schludrig arbeiten.
skimpy *(coll.)* knauserig, knickerig.
skin Haut, *(ship)* Außenhaut;
  ~ *(v.)* *(sl.)* Verweis erteilen, *(in examination, sl.)* Klatsche benutzen;
  ~ out *(US sl.)* sich davonmachen;
  to be in s. one's ~ an jds. Stelle sein; **to be only ~ and bone** nur noch aus Haut und Knochen bestehen; **to dig under s. one's ~** j. näher kennen lernen; **to escape by the ~ of one's teeth** mit knapper Not entkommen; **to get under s. one's ~** jem. auf die Nerven gehen; **to have a thick ~** *(fig.)* dicke Haut (dickes Fell) haben; **to have a thin ~** *(fig.)* sehr empfindlich sein; **to leap out of one's ~** aus der Haut fahren; **to save one's ~** seine Haut retten, mit heiler Haut davonkommen;
  ~-deep oberflächlich; **~-diving gear** Taucherausrüstung; **~ game** *(US sl.)* Bauernfängerei; **~ grafting** Hautverpflanzung.
skinflint *(sl.)* Geizkragen.
skinhead *(sl.)* Halbstarker.
skinned of all one's money völlig ausgeplündert.
skinner Bauernfänger.
skip Überspringen, -gehen, Auslassung, *(debtor, US)* unbekannt verzogener Schuldner;
  significant ~ in an account beträchtliche Berichtslücke;
  ~ *(v.)* überspringen, *(school, sl.)* schwänzen;

~ bail Kaution verfallen lassen; **~ the next chapter** nächstes Kapitel überschlagen; **~ a hotel** *(sl.)* Hotelrechnung nicht bezahlen; **~ off without saying anything** sich sang- und klanglos entfernen; **~ out of the way of a bus** sich vor einem Omnibus durch einen Seitensprung retten; **~ over certain items** gewisse Punkte übergehen; **~ the dull parts of a book** langweilige Buchpassagen auslassen; **~ from one subject to another** Thema häufig wechseln; **~ over to Paris** Blitztour nach Paris machen; **~ tracer** *(US)* Schuldnerermittlungsbüro; **~ tracing** *(US)* Ausfindigmachung (Anschriftenermittlung) eines säumigen Schuldners.

skipper Küstenschiffer, Kapitän, *(police, sl.)* Polizeichef, *(reader given to skipping)* flüchtiger Leser.

skippy strike *(sl.)* Fließbandstreik.

skirmish Vorpostengefecht, *(fig.)* Wortgeplänkel.

skirr *(v.)* durchkämmen.

skirt Außenbezirk;
on the ~s of a town am Stadtrandgebiet;
~ *(v.)* am Stadtrand wohnen.

skit sarkastische Bemerkung;
~s of massen-, haufenweise.

skittle | alley (ground) Kegelbahn;
to be not all beer and ~s keine reine Honiglecke sein.

skulk Drückebergerei;
~ *(v.)* sich drücken.

skulker Drückeberger.

skull *(sl.)* ewiger Student;
~ *(v.)* -drag *(student, sl.)* schuften, büffeln;
~ and cross bones Totenkopf.

skunk *(v.)* *(US sl.)* fertigmachen;
~ s. o. out of s. th. *(sl.)* jem. etw. abjagen.

sky *(astronautics)* Luftraum, *(climate)* Klima, Wetter, Witterung;
under the open ~ außerhalb, unter freiem Himmel, im Freien;
mackerel ~ Schäfchenwolken;
~ advertising Luftwerbung; **~ battle** Luftschlacht; **~ garret** *(sl.)* Dachstübchen; **~-hook** *(US sl.)* Höhenballon; **~ pilot** geprüfter Pilot; **~ shade** *(photo)* Gegenlichtblende; **~ sign** Dach-, Leucht-, Lichtreklame, Werbesilhouette; **~ tourist** Touristenfluggast; **walk-on low-price ~ train** *(US)* billiger Airbus mit Fahrkartenverkauf unmittelbar vor dem Abflug; **~ troops** Luftlandetruppen; **~ truck** *(US)* Transportflugzeug; **~ wire** *(sl.)* Antenne.

skyjacker Luftpirat.

skyjacking Flugzeugentführung, Luftpiraterie.

skylab Raumstation, Himmelslaboratorium.

skylift Luftbrücke.

skylight Oberlicht.

skyline of a town Silhouette einer Stadt.

skyman Fallschirmspringer.

skyrocket *(v.)* *(prices, US)* in die Höhe treiben (schnellen).

skyrocketing Emporschnellen, *(US)* raketenartiges [An]steigen [der Kurse].

skyscraper Wolkenkratzer, Hochhaus.

skyscraperitis Hochhaussucht.

skyway Luftverkehrsweg, -linie, -route.

skywrite *(v.)* *(advertising)* Himmelsschrift schreiben.

skywriter Himmelsschreiber.

skywriting Himmelsschrift, Luftwerbung.

slab *(US)* Betonstraße.

slack Nachlassen, Flaute, *(coll.)* Ruhepause;
~ in the economy Konjunkturflaute; **~s and stacks** Riesenstapel;
~ *(v.)* at one's job bei der Arbeit trödeln; **~ off** im Arbeitstempo nachlassen; **~ off a tension** Spannung lockern; **~ off in one's studies** sein Studium vernachlässigen; **~ up** *(train)* Geschwindigkeit verringern; **~ up before one reaches the crossroad** seine Geschwindigkeit vor der Kreuzung drosseln; **~ up one's pace of work** sein Arbeitstempo verlangsamen; **~ at one's work** bei der Arbeit bummeln (trödeln);
to be ~ wenig zu tun haben, *(stock market)* keinen Auftrieb zeigen, lustlos sein, *(trade)* stocken; **to be ~ in one's duties** seine Pflichten vernachlässigen; **to have a good ~** richtig ausspannen; **to take up the ~** Flaute überwinden;
~ *(a.)* *(stock exchange)* unbelebt, geschäftslos, flau, lustlos, still;
~ business ruhiges Geschäft; **~ demand** spärliche (schwache) Nachfrage; **to keep a ~ hand on affairs** die Zügel schleifen lassen; **~ hours** *(railway)* verkehrsarme Stunden, verkehrsschwache Zeit, Pufferzeit; **~ period (season)** stille (tote) Saison, flaue Geschäftszeit, Pufferzeit, *(traffic)* verkehrsschwache

Zeit; **to keep a ~ rein** *(fig.)* Zügel schleifen lassen; **~ rope** lockere Zügelführung; **~ season** Flaute; **~ times in business** geschäftliche Flaute.

slacken *(v.)* *(demand)* nachlassen, *(stock exchange)* flau werden, sich abschwächen, stocken;
~ one's efforts in seinen Anstrengungen nachlassen; **~ speed** Geschwindigkeit verringern.

slackening *(demand)* Abschwächung, Nachlassen, *(stock exchange)* Abbröckeln;
cyclical ~ konjunkturelle Abkühlung;
~ of attention nachlassende Aufmerksamkeit; **~ of the economic trend** Konjunkturabkühlung, -abschwächung; **~ of demand** nachlassende Nachfrage; **~ off** Absinken, Verminderung;
~ *(a.)* *(stock exchange)* abbröckelnd;
~ share prices abbröckelnde Aktienkurse; **~ tendency** Abschwächungstendenz.

slacker Drückeberger, Faulpelz.

slackness *(demand)* Abschwächung, Nachlassen, *(stock exchange)* Unlust, Unbelebtheit, Flaute, Flauheit, Stillstand;
~ of business Geschäftstockung; **~ of the market** Flaute, geschäftslose Zeit, Absatzflaute; **~ of trade** Geschäftsstockung, -stille.

slag Schlacke.

slam *(sharp criticism, US)* scharfe Kritik, Verriß;
~ *(v.)* *(US sl.)* herunterputzen;
~ about one's work lärmend an die Arbeit gehen; **~ the door on new immigrants** Einwanderungssperre beschließen.

slander Beleidigung, Verleumdung, Verunglimpfung, üble Nachrede;
~ of goods Herabsetzung der Qualität einer Ware; **~ of title** Konkurrenzanschwärzung;
~ *(v.)* üble Nachrede verbreiten, beleidigen, verleumden, verunglimpfen;
~ s. o. j. in falschen Verdacht bringen;
to bring a ~ action against s. o. jem. einen Beleidigungsprozeß anhängen.

slanderer Verleumder.

slanderous verleumderisch, beleidigend.

slang [Berufs]jargon, Slang;
artistic ~ Künstlersprache;
~ s. o. *(v.)* *(fam.)* jem. heftige Vorwürfe machen;
~ expression Slangausdruck.

slant Richtung, Linie, *(US)* Ansicht, Meinung, Tendenz;
~ of the roof Dachschräge;
~ *(v.)* news *(US)* Nachrichten frisieren (färben, zurechtstutzen);
to get a new ~ on the political situation ganz neuen politischen Blickpunkt bekommen; **to have a wrong ~ of a problem** falsche Vorstellung von einem Problem haben.

slap Schlag, Ohrfeige;
~ *(v.)* around abkanzeln; **~ s. o. into jail** j. ins Gefängnis werfen;
~-bang shop *(sl.)* zweitklassiges Restaurant, Bumslokal.

slap-up *(Br.)* totschick, mit allen Schikanen;
~ education erstklassige Ausbildung; **~ restaurant** *(sl.)* erstklassiges Restaurant.

slapdash Pfuscherei, Pfusch;
~ *(a.)* Knall und Fall, blindlings;
to do one's work ~ seine Arbeit flüchtig erledigen, bei der Arbeit pfuschen;
~ worker schludriger (flüchtiger) Arbeiter; **~ writing** hastige Schreibweise.

slash [Preis]nachlaß, Abstrich;
10 per cent price ~ in new cars Preisnachlaß von 10% auf Neuwagen;
~ *(v.)* stark reduzieren, *(fig.)* zerpflücken, herunterreißen;
~ a budget Etat zusammenstreichen; **~ a new book** neu erschienenes Buch kritisieren; **~ costs** Unkosten drastisch reduzieren; **~ prices** Preise stark herabsetzen; **~ a price dramatically** Preis drastisch senken; **~ production** Produktion einschränken, Produktionseinschränkung vornehmen; **~ from the public sector's program(me)** Streichungen bei dem Investitionsprogramm der öffentlichen Hand vornehmen; **~ rations** Rationskürzungen durchführen; **~ a salary** Gehalt stark heruntersetzen; **~ taxes** Steuern kräftig ermäßigen;
to sell at ~ed prices zu herabgesetzten Preisen verkaufen.

slasher scharfer Kritiker.

slashing, price Preisherabsetzung;
~ of production Produktionseinschränkung;
~ attack on the government's policy heftige Kritik der Regierungspolitik; **~ criticism** vernichtende Kritik.

slate Schiefer[platte], *(film)* Klappe, *(nomination, US)* provisorische Kandidatenliste, Vorschlagliste, *(school)* Schiefertafel;
~ *(v.)* kritisieren, *(US)* Kandidaten aufstellen;
~ **s. o. for the Presidency** j. zum Präsidenten vorschlagen; ~ **for nomination as treasurer** zur Ernennung zum Schatzmeister vorsehen;
to clean the ~ reinen Tisch machen; **to have a clean** ~ weiße Weste haben; **to have a** ~ **loose** leichten Dachschaden haben; **to start with a clean** ~ völlig neuen Anfang machen;
~ **club** *(Br.)* Unterstützungsverein, Hilfskasse; ~ **pencil** Griffel; ~ **roof** Schieferdach.
slated, to be *(US)* vorgesehen sein.
slating, to give s. o. a sound j. scharf kritisieren.
slaughter Schlachten, *(fig.)* Gemetzel, Blutbad, *(stock exchange, US)* Verschleuderung, Verlustverkauf;
~ **on the road** Schlachtfeld auf den Straßen;
~ *(v.)* schlachten, *(sl.)* massakrieren, *(goods)* mit Verlust verkaufen, *(stock exchange)* verschleudern;
~ **house** Schlachthaus.
slaughtered price Schleuderpreis.
slaughterer Ramschhändler.
slaughtering *(stock exchange)* Verlustverkauf, Verschleuderung.
slave Sklave, Arbeitstier;
~s **to fashion** Modenarren;
~ *(v.)* Schwerarbeit verrichten;
~ **away on one's dictionary for years** jahrelang wie ein Sklave für sein Wörterbuch arbeiten;
to be a ~ **to convention** in sklavischer Abhängigkeit von Konventionen leben; **to be a** ~ **to duty** pflichtbesessen sein; **to be a** ~ **to money** am Geld hängen; **to make o. s. a** ~ **to one's servants** in sklavische Abhängigkeit von seinen Hausangestellten geraten; **to work like a** ~ wie ein Pferd arbeiten;
~ **arm** *(television)* Fernbedienungsgerät; ~ **dealer (trader)** Sklavenhändler; ~ **dealing** Sklavenhandel; ~ **driver** Leuteschinder; ~ **labo(u)r** Zwangsarbeit; ~ **labo(u)r camp** Zwangsarbeiterlager; ~ **labo(u)rer** Arbeitssklave, Zwangsarbeiter; ~ **market** Sklavenmarkt, *(sl.)* Arbeitsmarkt; ~ **trade (trading)** Sklavenhandel; white ~ **trading** Mädchenhandel.
slavery Sklaverei.
slavish imitation sklavische Nachahmung.
slay *(v.)* erschlagen, ermorden.
slayer Totschläger, Mörder.
sled plane Kufenflugzeug.
sledding, smooth gutes Vorankommen;
to have a hard ~ schleppenden Geschäftsgang aufweisen.
sleep Schlaf;
broken ~ gestörter Schlaf;
~ *(v.)* **s. o.** jem. eine Schlafgelegenheit bieten; ~ **on s. th.** etw. überschlafen; ~ **the clock round** zwölf Stunden durchschlafen; ~ **400 guests** *(hotel)* Übernachtungsmöglichkeiten für 400 Gäste haben; ~ **over a question** Problem überschlafen; ~ **like a top** wie ein Murmeltier schlafen; ~ **over one's work** bei der Arbeit einschlafen; ~ **with one eye open** wachsam bleiben.
sleeper *(railway, Br.)* Eisenbahnschwelle, *(sleeping accommodation)* Schlafplatz, -koje, *(US sl.)* langsam verkäufliche Ware, Ladenhüter, *(book, film, US)* unerwarteter Verkaufserfolg, *(sleeping car, US)* Schlafwagen, *(student use)* langweilige Vorlesung;
~ **train** Schlafwagen; ~ **train service** Schlafwagenverkehr.
sleeperette Schlafkoje;
~ **service** Schlafkojeneinrichtung.
sleeping|**accommodation** Schlafgelegenheit, [Hotel]unterkunft;
~ **account** *(coll.)* totes Konto; ~ **bag** Schlafsack; ~ **car** Schlafwagen; **to book a** ~ **car** Schlafwagenplatz bestellen; ~-**car company** Schlafwagengesellschaft; ~-**car ticket** Schlafwagenkarte; ~ **carriage** *(Br.)* Schlafwagen; ~ **compartment** Schlafwagenabteil; ~ **drug (pill)** Schlaftablette; ~ **drug** Schlafmittel; ~ **partner** *(Br.)* stiller Teilhaber (Gesellschafter), Kommanditist; ~ **partnership** *(Br.)* Kommanditgesellschaft; ~ **place** Schlafstelle; ~ **quarters** Schlafquartier; ~ **rent** Bergregalabgabe; ~ **sickness** Schlafkrankheit.
sleepwalker Schlafwandler.
sleepy little village verschlafenes Dörfchen.
sleeve *(record)* Schallplattenhülle;
to chuckle up one's ~ sich ins Fäustchen lachen; **to hang on s. one's** ~ sich nach jds. Meinung richten; **to have s. th. up one's** ~ Geheimplan (etw. in petto) haben; **to laugh in one's** ~ sich ins Fäustchen lachen; **to put the** ~ **on s. o.** *(sl.)* j. auf der Straße anpumpen; **to roll up one's** ~s sich an die Arbeit machen; **to wear one's heart on one's** ~ sein Herz auf der Zunge tragen;
~ **note** Plattenhüllentext.

sleight-of-hand Taschenspielertrick.
slender|**acquaintance with a subject** geringe Vertrautheit mit einem Thema; ~ **diet** karge Kost; ~ **means** unzureichende Mittel; ~ **profit** magerer Gewinn.
sleuth, slewfoot *(sl.)* Detektiv.
slice Stück, Anteil, *(loan)* Abschnitt, Tranche, *(loot)* Beuteanteil;
~ **of budget** Etatsanteil; ~ **of a commission** Provisionsanteil; ~ **of earnings** Verdienstanteil; ~ **of good luck** gute Portion Glück dabei; ~ **of loan** Anleihentranche; **bigger** ~ **of the market** größerer Marktanteil; ~ **of profit** Gewinnanteil; ~ **of property** Vermögensanteil; ~ **of a territory** Stück Land;
~ *(v.)* **an estate into farms** Rittergut in Bauerngüter aufteilen; ~ **a piece of property** Grundstückskomplex aufteilen.
slick *(oil)* Ölfläche, -fleck, *(US sl.)* Hochglanzmagazin, beliebte Zeitschrift;
~ *(a.)* *(fig.)* pfiffig, gekonnt, gerissen, raffiniert, *(road)* schlüpfrig;
~ *(v.)* **up** auf Hochglanz bringen;
~ **business deal** aalglattes Geschäft; ~ **lawyer** raffinierter Anwalt; ~ **paper** *(sl.)* elegante Zeitschrift; ~ **salesman** gerissener Geschäftsmann.
slicker *(coll.)* raffinierter Betrüger;
city ~ *(sl.)* eleganter Großstadtmensch.
slide Dia[positiv], Stehbild, *(film)* Filmband, *(sliding)* Rutschen, Gleiten, Talfahrt, *(stock exchange)* Absinken;
colo(u)r ~ Farbdiapositiv;
~ **in the interest rates** nachlassende Zinssätze; ~ **in values** Absinken der Kurse;
~ *(v.)* *(car)* rutschen;
~ **away** *(sl.)* sich davonstehlen; ~ **down** *(prices)* abgleiten; ~ **into bad habits** schlechte Gewohnheiten annehmen; ~ **below a trading range anchored in a special plateau** vorher festgelegte Kursmarke unterschreiten; ~ **over a subject** Thema nur flüchtig berühren;
to let things ~ Dinge schleifen lassen;
~ **advertising** Diapositivwerbung; ~ **fastener** Reißverschluß; ~ **lecture** Lichtbildervortrag; ~ **rule** Rechenschieber; ~ **window** Schiebefenster.
sliding gleitend, veränderlich;
~ **budget** veränderlicher Etat; ~ **door** Schiebetür; ~ **parity** stufenflexibler Wechselkurs; ~ **rate of interest** Staffelzins; ~ **roof** *(car)* Schiebedach; ~ **scale** gestaffelter Tarif, Staffeltarif, *(advertising)* Nachlaß-, Rabattstaffel, *(prices)* bewegliche (gleitende) Preisskala, *(wages)* bewegliche (gleitende) Lohnskala, gleitender Lohntarif; ~ **scale of commissions** gleitende Provisionsstaffel; ~ **scale differentials** Preiszuschläge und -abschläge; ~-**scale discount** Rabatt-, Nachlaßstaffel; ~-**scale premium** gleitende Prämie; ~-**scale price** Staffelpreis; ~-**scale tariff** Staffeltarif, gleitender Lohntarif, *(customs)* gleitender Zoll, Gleitzoll; ~ **seat** *(car)* verstellbarer Sitz; ~ **stock** fallende Aktie; ~ **wage scale** gleitende Lohnskala.
slight leicht, geringfügig, unbedeutend;
~ *(v.)* auf die leichte Schulter nehmen;
~ **a guest** Gast links liegen lassen;
~ **cold** leichte Erkältung; ~ **decline** *(stock exchange)* geringe Abschwächung; ~ **error** geringfügiger Fehler; ~ **fault** leichte Fahrlässigkeit; ~ **increase** leichte Zunahme; ~ **inquiries** oberflächliche Untersuchung; ~ **negligence** *(US)* leichte (geringe) Fahrlässigkeit; **to take offence at the** ~**est thing** beim geringsten Anlaß beleidigt sein.
slightness Geringfügigkeit.
slim *(sl.)* Polizeispitzel;
~ *(a.)* dürftig, knapp, armselig;
~ *(v.)* Schlankheitskur machen;
~ **the workforce** Belegschaft durchforsten;
~ **audience** spärliche Zuhörerschaft; ~ **chance of success** geringe Gewinnchance; ~ **evidence** dürftiger Beweis; ~ **excuse** wenig überzeugende Entschuldigung.
slimming Schlankwerden;
~ **of the workforce** Belegschaftsdurchforstung;
~ **cure** Schlankheits-, Abmagerungskur; ~ **diet** Abmagerungsdiät.
slimy fellow schleimiger Bursche.
sling Schlinge, [Arm]binde;
~ *(v.)* **the bull** *(sl.)* an einem Herrenessen teilnehmen; ~ **it** *(sl.)* mit Modeworten um sich schmeißen; ~ **ink** sich schriftstellerisch betätigen.
slip *(advertising)* Aufkleber, *(banking)* Formularstreifen, *(bill of exchange)* Anhang, *(evasion)* Entkommen, *(galley proof)* [Druck]fahne, *(mar.)* Schlippe, Helling, *(marine insurance, Br.)* Versicherungsabschlußbeleg, vorläufige Deckungszu-

sage, *(memorandum)* Vortragsniederschrift, *(mistake)* Versehen, Schnitzer, [Flüchtigkeits]fehler, *(police court)* Anklagebank, *(slight offence)* Übertretung, *(of paper)* Zettel, Schein, Blatt Papier, *(securities)* Händlerzettel, *(ship)* Gleitbahn, Helling, *(voucher)* Beleg, Abschnitt, Kupon;
~s *(theater)* Schiebekulissen;
bank ~ Girozettel, -abschnitt; **bathing** ~s Badehose; **betting** ~ Wettschein; **binding** ~ *(insurance law)* vorläufige Deckungszusage; **check** ~ Kontrollabschnitt; **credit** ~ Bon, Gutschein; **deposit** ~ *(US)* Einzahlungsbeleg, Depotquittung; **human** ~ menschliches Versagen; **paying-in** ~ *(Br.)* Einzahlungsbeleg, -formular, -schein; **pillow** ~ Kissenüberzug, -bezug; **release** ~ Entlassungsbescheinigung; **sales** ~ Verkaufsbeleg, Kassenzettel; **wage** ~ Lohn[abrechnungs]zettel;
~ **initial(l)ed by the cashier** abgezeichneter Kassenbeleg; ~ **of the memory** Gedächtnisfehler; ~ **of the pen** Schreibfehler; ~ **in spelling** Rechtschreibefehler; ~ **of the tongue** Sprachschnitzer, Versprecher; **a few** ~s **in the youth** einige jugendliche Fehltritte;
~ *(v.)* Fehler machen, *(stock exchange)* abgleiten, fallen;
~ **anchor** Anker lichten; ~ **s. one's attention** jds. Aufmerksamkeit entgehen; ~ **back** *(stock exchange)* fallen, sinken; ~ **by** *(years)* vergehen; ~ **a cog** Schnitzer machen; ~ **a coin into the waiter's hand** einem Kellner ein Geldstück in die Hand drücken; ~ **in at the back door** durch die Hintertür eindringen; ~ **through one's fingers** einem durch die Finger gleiten; ~ **in one's grammar** grammatikalischen Fehler begehen; ~ **out of s. one's hands** jds. Führung entgleiten; ~ **in** *(computer)* heimlich einspeichern; ~ **into** hineinschlittern; ~ **over some items** einige Punkte übergehen; ~ **from one's memory** dem Gedächtnis entgleiten; ~ **into a text** sich in einen Text einschleichen; ~ **in a word** ein Wort dazwischenwerfen;
to be still on the ~ *(ship)* noch in Reparatur sein; **to give s. o. the** ~ jem. durch die Lappen gehen; **to let** ~ sich verplappern; **to let an opportunity** ~ Chance ungenutzt vorübergehen lassen; **to put s. o. on the** ~ j. auf die Wahlliste setzen; **to watch a performance from the** ~s einer Vorführung hinter den Kulissen zuschauen;
~ **book** *(bank)* Quittungs-, Belegbuch; ~ **carriage** *(coach)* abgekoppelter Waggon; ~ **fuel tank** abwerfbarer Brennstoffbehälter; ~ **law** *(US)* Einzelveröffentlichung eines Gesetzes; ~ **proof** *(print.)* Fahnenabzug, -korrektur; ~ **sheet** Einschießbogen; ~ **sheets** Makulaturpapier; ~ **system** Belegbuchhaltung; ~**-up** Flüchtigkeitsfehler, Schnitzer.
slipcase Kassette.
slipover cover *(book)* Schutzhülle.
slipperiness of the political ground schlüpfriger politischer Boden.
slippery *(fig.)* aalglatt, heikel, *(not secure)* unsicher, nicht stabil;
~ **customer** rüder Bursche; **to be on** ~ **ground** gefährlichen Boden betreten; ~ **road** schlüpfrige Straße; ~ **subject** heikles Thema; ~ **witness** unzuverlässiger Zeuge.
slipping *(stock exchange)* Abgleiten der Kurse.
sliproad Umgehungsstraße.
slipshod work schlampig ausgeführte Arbeit.
slipway *(ship)* Gleitbahn, Helling.
slit Spalt, Schlitz;
~ **of a letter box** Briefkastenschlitz;
~ *(v.)* **an envelope open** Briefhülle aufschlitzen;
~ **trench** *(mil.)* Splitter-, Deckungsgraben.
slob Morast, Schlamm, *(US sl.)* Banause;
soft ~ gefühlsduseliger Mensch.
slobber Salbaderei, Faselei;
~ *(v.)* schlampen, pfuschen;
~ *(v.)* **away with one's work** sich mit seiner Arbeit abplagen; ~ **a bibful** salbadern.
slogan Schlagwort, -zeile, *(advertising)* Werbetext, -spruch, Slogan, *(politics)* Wahlspruch, Motto, Losung;
political ~ politisches Schlagwort.
sloganeer *(coll.)* Werbetexter.
sloganize *(v.)* Schlagworte gebrauchen, *(advertising)* Werbetexte verfassen.
slogger Arbeitspferd.
sloop Schaluppe, *(police)* Polizeiboot.
slop nasser Fleck, Pfütze, *(mar.)* Bettzeug, Klamotten, *(policeman, Br., sl.)* Polyp, *(ready-made clothes)* Konfektionsware, *(cheap saloon, sl.)* Spelunke, billige Kneipe.
slope Böschung, Abhang, *(mining)* Schrägstollen;
~ **of a roof** Dachneigung, -schräge.
sloping | **curve** fallende Kurve; ~ **type** Kursivschrift.
sloppy Joe's *(sl.)* billiger Mittagstisch.
slopseller Konfektionshändler.

slopshop billiger Konfektionsladen.
slopwork Serienarbeit, *(clothes)* Konfektionskleidung, *(slovenly work)* Pfuscherei.
slopworker Konfektionsarbeiter.
slot Spalt, Einwurf[schlitz] für Münzen, Geldschlitz;
high ~ hohe Schlüsselposition;
~ **machine** automatischer Verkaufsapparat, [Verkaufs]automat, Spielautomat.
slouch *(US sl.)* Niete, Versager;
~ *(v.)* herumlungern.
slovenly | **appearance** schlampiges Aussehen; ~ **kept books** nachlässig geführte Bücher; ~ **work** Schluderarbeit.
slow langsam, *(business)* zurückgeblieben, schleppend, flau, *(debtor)* säumig, saumselig, *(party)* langweilig, ohne Stimmung, *(photo)* lange Belichtungszeit erfordernd;
~ **at accounts** langsam im Rechnen; ~ **of payment** nachlässig im Bezahlen;
~ *(v.)* *(prices)* langsamer steigen;
~ **down** langsamer werden, Tempo verlangsamen, Geschwindigkeit verringern, *(economy)* abflauen; ~ **down to a crawl** *(traffic)* fast zum Erliegen kommen; ~ **down dollar outflow** Dollarabfluß drosseln; ~ **down economy** Konjunktur verlangsamen; ~ **down industrial expansion** Wachstum der Industrie verlangsamen; ~ **down the pace of business** Konjunkturtempo verlangsamen; ~ **up** verzögern, verlangsamen;
to be five minutes ~ *(watch)* fünf Minuten nachgehen; **to be** ~ **of wit** schwer von Begriff sein; **to be** ~ **on the uptake** *(draw)* Spätzünder sein, lange Leitung haben; **to go** ~ sich schonen, *(workers)* Bummelstreik durchführen, streng nach Vorschrift arbeiten; **to take it** ~ vorsichtig an etw. herangehen; **to think an entertainment rather** ~ Unterhaltungsprogramm ziemlich langweilig finden;
~ **assets** feste (fixe) Anlagen; ~ **burn** sparsamer Verbrauch; ~**-burning stove** Dauerbrandofen; ~ **child** Spätentwickler; ~ **coach** langweiliger Bursche, Trödelfritze, Tranfunzel; ~ **goods** Frachtgut; ~ **goods traffic** Frachtgutverkehr; ~ **growth** langsames Wachstum; ~ **line** *(railway)* Nebengleis; ~ **match** Lunte; ~ **motion** in Zeitlupe; ~**-motion film** Zeitlupenfilm; ~**-motion picture** Zeitlupenaufnahme; ~**-motion replay** Zeitlupenwiederholung; ~**-moving** *(business)* flau; ~**-moving goods** Waren mit geringer Umsatzgeschwindigkeit; ~ **payer** säumiger Zahler; ~ **train** Personen-, Bummelzug; ~ **worker** bedächtiger Arbeiter.
slowdown *(demand)* Nachlassen, *(speed)* Geschwindigkeitsverringerung, Verlangsamung, *(workers)* Arbeitsverlangsamung, Bummelstreik;
economic ~ verlangsamte Konjunkturbewegung;
~ **in economic activity** verlangsamter Konjunkturablauf, Konjunkturrückschlag; ~ **in business** verlangsamte Konjunktur; ~ **of exports** Exportdämpfung; ~ **in inflation** Verlangsamung des Inflationstempos, verlangsamtes Inflationstempo; ~ **in investment** Investitionsverlangsamung; ~ **in orders** nachlassender Auftragseingang; ~ **in petrol consumption** verringerter Benzinverbrauch; ~ **in prices** Nachgeben der Preise; ~ **in price increase** nachlassender Preisanstieg; ~ **in the rate of inflation** Verlangsamung der Inflationsrate; ~ **in the recovery** verlangsamter Konjunkturanstieg;
to predict a marginal ~ Konjunkturverlangsamung bis zum Stillstand voraussagen;
~ **period** rückläufige Konjunkturperiode; ~ **strike** *(US)* Arbeitsverlangsamung, Bummelstreik.
slowing down | **on the job** Arbeitsverlangsamung; ~ **of the economy** Konjunkturverlangsamung, Abbremsen der Konjunktur; ~ **of inflation** verlangsamtes Inflationstempo; ~ **in prices** verlangsamter Preisanstieg; ~ **in the rate of advance** verzögerter Wachstumsanstieg.
sloyd *(carpenter)* Werkunterricht.
sludge Klärschlamm.
slug *(print.)* Satzmaschinenzeile;
~s Durchschuß.
sluggish *(market)* stagnierend, lustlos, flau;
~ **demand** lustlose Nachfrage.
sluggishness Geschäftsunlust, Flaute, Stagnation.
sluice Schleuse, *(canal)* Nebenkanal, *(mining)* Erzgoldwaschrinne;
to open the ~s **of feeling** seinen Gefühlen Luft machen;
~ **gate** Schleusentor; ~**-gate price** *(EC)* Schleusenpreis.
sluiceway Schleusenkanal.
slum Elendsgasse, -quartier;
~s Armeleute-, Elendsviertel;
~ *(v.)* Elendsgebiet besichtigen;
to live in a ~ in einer Drecksbude leben;

~ area Elendsgebiet; **~ clearance** Beseitigung von Elendsvierteln, Altstadt-, Städtesanierung; **~ clearance campaign** Sanierungsfeldzug; **~ clearance plan** Städtesanierungsplan; **~ family** asoziale Familie; **~ house** Elendsquartier; **~ landlord** Vermieter einer Elendswohnung; **~ property** im Elendsviertel gelegenes Grundstück; **~ resident** Bewohner von Elendsgebieten; **~ school** im Elendsviertel gelegene Schule; **~ worker** Sozialarbeiter.

slumberette Schlafsitz [im Flugzeug].

slummer Slumbesucher.

slump *(of prices)* Fall, [plötzliches] Fallen der Preise, Preissturz, *(stock exchange)* Kurseinbruch, Baisse, Kurssturz, *(trade cycle)* rückläufige Konjunktur, Konjunkturrückgang, -abschwung, Tiefstand, Rezession, Wirtschaftskrise;
world-wide ~ Konjunktureinbruch auf der ganzen Linie;
~ on the bond market Rentenbaisse; **continuing ~ in construction** anhaltender Konjunkturrückgang in der Bauindustrie; **~ in demand** plötzlicher Nachfragerückgang; **~ in the franc** Frankensturz, Sturz des Frankenkurses; **~ in home building** nachlassende Eigenheimbaukonjunktur; **~ in prices** Kurs-, Preissturz; **heavy ~ in cotton prices** scharfer Einbruch der Baumwollpreise; **worst-ever ~ in share prices** größter je gezeitigter Sturz der Aktienkurse; **~ in agricultural produce** Zusammenbruch des landwirtschaftlichen Preisspiegels; **~ in production** [scharfer] Produktionsrückgang; **~ in sales** Absatzkrise, rapider Umsatzrückgang; **~ in stocks** Aktiensturz; **~ in trade** Geschäftsstockung, Depression, Konjunkturrückgang;
~ *(v.) (prices)* stürzen, *(stock market)* plötzlich [im Wert] fallen;
~ in disappointment enttäuscht in sich zusammensacken; **~ heavily** heftigen Kurssturz erfahren; **~ twenty points** zwanzig Punkte fallen; **~ in the recession** rezessionsbedingten Sturz erleben;
~ clause Baisseklausel; **~ merchant** Krisenhändler; **~ period** rückläufige Konjunkturphase; **~-proof** krisenfest; **~ year** Depressionsjahr.

slumpflation Inflation bei gleichzeitigem Produktivitätsrückgang, Zusammentreffen von Inflation und Rezession.

slur Vorwurf, *(print.)* Schmitz;
~ *(v.) (print.)* schmitzen, verwischen;
~ a crime Verbrechen vertuschen; **~ over s. one's faults** jds. Schwächen übergehen;
to cast a ~ on s. one's reputation jds. guten Ruf angreifen; **to keep one's reputation free from all ~s** reine Weste behalten.

slush Schneematsch, *(emotional talk)* Gefühlsduselei, Schwärmerei;
~ fund *(US)* Reptilien-, Geheim-, Bestechungsfonds; **~ money** *(US)* Schmiergelder.

slushy matschig.

slyboot schlauer Fuchs, Pfiffikus.

smack *(fig.)* Beigeschmack, Anflug, Anstrich;
~ in the eye Schlag ins Gesicht; **~ of knowledge** ein bißchen Wissen;
~ *(v.) of* ... Anstrich von ... haben; **~ of cheapness** Beigeschmack des Gewöhnlichen haben; **~ of liberalism** liberalistisch angehaucht sein;
to get a ~ in the eye Rückschlag erleiden; **to have a ~ at s. th.** Versuch riskieren.

smacker *(US sl.)* Dollar.

smacking breeze steife Brise.

smalls kleinere Gebrauchsgegenstände, *(advertising)* rubrizierte Anzeigen, Kleinanzeigen, *(Oxford, sl.)* Aufnahmeprüfung.

small klein, schwach, gering;
great and ~ alle Bevölkerungsgruppen;
~ of means minderbemittelt;
to make o. s. ~ seinen Kopf einziehen; **to think ~ of one's neighbo(u)rs** auf seine Nachbarn herabsehen;
~ ad *(US)* Kleinanzeige; **~ advance** Kleinkredit; **~ arms** Handfeuerwaffen; **~ audience** wenig Zuhörer; **~ beer** *(fig.)* unbedeutende Person; **to chronicle ~ beer** aus einer Mücke einen Elefanten machen; **to think no ~ beer of o. s.** große Stücke von sich halten; **~ beginning** kleiner Anfang; **~ bonds** *(US)* Obligationen in kleinen Stückelungen; **~ bread** *(sl.)* ungenügender Geldbetrag.

small business *(US)* gewerblicher Mittelstand, mittlerer Betrieb, Klein- und Mittelbetriebe;
~ investment credit Mittelstandskredit; **~ man** Klein-, Einzelhändler, Kleingewerbetreibender; **~ manager** Geschäftsführer eines Mittelstandsbetriebs; **~ men** kleine Geschäftsleute; **~ sector** Mittelstandsbereich; **~ venture** Mittelstandsunternehmen; **~ recommendations** Mittelstandsempfehlungen.

small | **capital** geringes Kapital; **~ capitals (caps)** *(print.)* Kapitälchen; **~ car** Kleinwagen; **~-car market** Kleinwagenmarkt; **~-car plant** Kleinwagenfabrik; **~-car sales** Kleinwagenumsätze; **~ cattle** Kleinvieh; **~ change** Wechsel-, Kleingeld, *(fig., US)* Kleinigkeit, Lappalie; **~ charges** kleine Spesen; **~ children** Kleinkinder; **~ claims court** Bagatellgericht, Gericht erster Instanz; **~ coin** Kupfer-, Scheidemünze, Wechsel-, Kleingeld; **~ committee** engerer Ausschuß; **~ companies rate** *(Br.)* ermäßigter Körperschaftssteuersatz für Kleinbetriebe; **~ consignments** Kleinsendungen, Stückgut; **~ debts** *(Br.)* geringfügige Schulden, Bagatell-, Läpperschulden; **~-debts court** *(Br.)* Bagatellgericht; **~ deer** *(fig.)* Klein-, Kroppzeug; **~ denominations** kleine Stücke (Werte); **~-denomination currency** *(US)* Scheidemünze; **~ deposits** kleine Einlagen; **~ eater** schwacher Esser; **to come out at the ~ end of the horn** der Verlierer sein; **~ enterprise** Kleinbetrieb; **~ establishment** Kleinbetrieb; **~ farmer** Kleinbauer, -landwirt; **~ firm** Mittel-, Kleinbetrieb; **~ fry** unbedeutender Mensch, *(children)* Kleinkinder, Jungvolk, *(sl.)* unbedeutende Hilfskräfte; **~-fry writer** unbedeutender Schriftsteller; **~ gift relief** *(Br.)* Schenkungssteuerfreibetrag für Gegenstände unter DM 2000; **~ hand** gewöhnliche Korrespondenzschrift; **~ harvest** magere Ernte; **Smallgift Holdings and Allotments Act** *(Br.)* Kleinland-, Schrebergartengesetz; **~ hours** frühe Morgenstunden; **~ income** mäßige Einkommen; **~-income allowance** *(Br.)* Freibeträge für niedrige Einkommen; **~-income relief** *(Br.)* Steuererleichterung für Kleingewerbe; **~ industry** Kleinbetrieb; **~ item** kleiner Posten; **~ landowner** Kleinlandbesitzer; **~ letter** Kleinbuchstabe; **~ loan** Kleinkredit; **~-loan company** *(US)* genossenschaftliche Darlehnskasse, *(hire purchase)* Abzahlungsbank; **~-lot consignment** Stückgutsendung; **~-lot production** Kleinserienherstellung; **~ master** Kleinhandwerker; **~ matter** Bagatellsache; **~-merchandising unit** Kleingewerbebetrieb; **~-minded** borniert, engstirnig; **~-mindedness** Engstirnigkeit, Borniertheit; **~ money** Klein-, Wechselgeld; **~ one** *(sl.)* unbedeutender (geringfügiger) Verweis; **~ packet** *(Br.)* Päckchen; **~ packet rate** *(Br.)* Päckchengebühr; **~ and early party** kurze Party im kleinen Kreis; **Smallgift Payments Act** *(Br.)* Gesetz zur Regelung geringfügiger Nachlaßwerte; **~ pica** *(print.)* kleine Ciceroschrift; **~ place** kleiner Ort; **~ pot** *(sl.)* kleiner Geist; **~ potatoes** *(US)* kleine Fische, Lappalie; **~ print** Kleingedrucktes; **~ private-sector company** kleiner Privatbetrieb; **~ profit** geringer Gewinn; **~ resources** unbedeutende Mittel; **~ saver** Kleinsparer; **~ savings account** Kleinsparerkonto; **~-scale** in kleinem Rahmen; **medium and ~-scale enterprises** Mittel- und Kleinbetriebe; **~-scale operator** Kleinbetrieb; **~-service business** Kleingewerbe; **~ shareholder** Kleinaktionär; **~ shopkeeper** kleiner Ladenbesitzer; **~ stock of knowledge** geringe Kenntnisse; **~ stores** *(mil.)* Marketenderware; **~ sum of money** kleiner Geldbetrag; **~ talk** leichte Plauderei, Alltagsgespräch; **~ things** Kleinigkeiten; **~ tools** Handwerkszeug; **~ town** Kleinstadt; **~-townish** kleinstädtisch; **~ tradesman** Minderkaufmann, kleiner Gewerbetreibender; **in a ~ way** bescheiden, *(stock exchange)* mit geringem Stammkapital; **to carry on business in a ~ way** kleines Geschäft unterhalten; **to live in ~ ways** in kleinen Verhältnissen leben; **~ worries of life** übliche Alltagssorgen.

smaller | **receipts** Mindereinnahmen; **~ returns** Minderertrag.

smallholder *(Br.)* Kleinbauer, Kleinlandbesitzer, Siedler, *(savings)* Kleinsparer, *(stock ownership)* Kleinaktionär.

smallholding *(piece of land, Br.)* Kleinlandbesitz [unter 12 ha], Siedlung, *(stock market)* Kleinaktionäre.

smallness Geringfügigkeit.

smallpox vaccination Pockenimpfung;
~ certificate Pockenimpfzeugnis.

smalltime *(US)* unwichtig, unbedeutend;
~ affair unbedeutende Angelegenheit; **~ organization** unwichtiger Verband, Schmalspurorganisation; **~ thief** kleiner Dieb.

smallware[s] Schnitt-, Kurzwaren;
~ business Kurzwarenhandel.

smart *(in business)* geschäftsgewandt, -tüchtig, routiniert, *(considerable)* beträchtlich;
~ aleck *(US)* Schlauberger, Neunmalkluger; **~ answer** freche Antwort; **~ bargainer** pfiffiger Geschäftsmann; **~ dealings** gerissene Geschäfte; **~ guy** Alleskönner; **~ money** Reu-, Abstandsgeld, Buße, *(indemnification, US)* Schmerzensgeld; **~ monkey** *(US)* Schlaumeier; **~ motorcar** schickes Auto; **~ price** ganz schöner Preis; **~ punishment** harte Strafe; **the ~ set** die elegante (große) Welt; **~ speaker** geistreicher Redner; **~ student** intelligenter Student.

smarten *(v.)* | **up** sich zurechtmachen; **~ s. th. up** etw. verschönern.

smartness Geschäftsgewandtheit, -tüchtigkeit, Routine.

smash totaler Reinfall, *(banking)* Bankpleite, *(collision)* Zusammenstoß, *(commercial failure)* Zusammenbruch, Bankrott, Pleite, *(movie, sl.)* Kassenschlager;
bank ~ Bankpleite; **railroad ~** Eisenbahnzusammenstoß;
~ with a car Autozusammenstoß;
~ *(v.) (go bankrupt)* zugrunde (bankrott) gehen, zusammenbrechen, *(v./tr.)* finanziell ruinieren, bankrott machen;
~ a door open Tür aufbrechen; **~ into each other** krachend zusammenstoßen; **~ the enemy** Feind besiegen; **~ a record** Rekord brechen; **~ a theory** Theorie über den Haufen werfen; **~ up** bankrott machen; **~ against a wall** *(car)* gegen eine Mauer rasen;
to go ~ umwerfen, Konkurs machen;
~-and-grab raid Schaufenstereinbruch; **~ hit** Erfolgsstück, Knüller; **bona-fide ~ hit** echter Kassenschlager.
smashed ruiniert, bankrott.
smasher Rückschlag, *(Br., sl.)* Geldfälscher, *(extraordinary thing)* tolle Sache, Bombensache, Mordsding.
smashing *(sl.)* überwältigend, enorm, toll, prima;
~ hit Riesenerfolg.
smashup völliger Zusammenbruch, Bankrott, Riesenpleite, *(car)* Totalzusammenstoß, *(plane)* Bruchlandung;
~ on the railway Eisenbahnunglück.
smatter oberflächliche Kenntnis, Halbwissen;
~ *(v.)* radebrechen;
~ law sich ein bißchen mit Jura beschäftigen.
smatterer Halbgebildeter.
smattering oberflächliches Wissen, Halbwissen.
smaze Rauchnebel.
smear Schmutzfleck, *(fig.)* Verunglimpfung;
~ *(v.) (sl.)* bestechen, schmieren;
~ the axle of a car Auto abschmieren; **~ s. one's reputation** Rufmord an jem. begehen;
~ attempt Verleumdungsversuch; **~ word** *(US)* Schimpfwort.
smearathon *(US)* Verleumdungskampagne.
smearing campaign Rufmord, Verleumdungsfeldzug.
smell *(fig.)* Anflug, Anstrich, Spur;
~ of anarchy Anflug von Anarchie; **~ of powder** Kriegserfahrung;
~ *(v.)* **about (round)** herumschnüffeln; **~ of the lamp** in Nachtarbeit entstanden sein; **~ of nepotism** nach Vetternwirtschaft riechen; **~ one's oats** *(fig.)* zum Endspurt ansetzen; **~ out a plot** Komplott entdecken; **~ a rat** Verdacht schöpfen, den Braten riechen; **~ of the shop** nach Fachsimpelei klingen;
to take a ~ at s. th. *(US)* Sache beriechen.
smeller *(sl.)* Schnüffler, Spion.
smelt *(v.)* verhütten.
smelting Verhüttung;
~ plant *(works)* Hüttenwerk.
smidgeon *(fam., US)* ein klein wenig.
smock Arbeitskittel.
smog Dunstglocke, Industriedunst.
smoke Rauch[fahne], *(coll.)* etw. Rauchbares, *(mil.)* künstlicher Nebel;
from ~ to smother vom Regen in die Traufe; **like ~** *(sl.)* im Handumdrehen;
no ~ without fire kein Gerede ohne Hintergrund;
~ *(v.)* **out a plot** Verschwörung wittern;
to end in ~ in Rauch aufgehen, zu nichts führen, sich in Nichts auflösen; **to go up in ~** verbrennen;
~ abatement Maßnahmen gegen die Luftverschmutzung; **~ bomb** *(mil.)* Rauchbombe; **~ break** Zigarettenpause; **~ consumer** Rauchverzehrer; **~ control** Rauchbekämpfungsvorschriften; **~ emission** Rauchentwicklung; **~ filter** Entstaubungsanlage; **~ screen** *(fig.)* Tarn-, Täuschungsmanöver.
smoker *(railway)* Raucherabteil.
smoking | [no-~] area [Nicht]raucherabteil; **~ carriage** *(car)* Raucherwagen; **~ compartment** Raucher[abteil]; **~ room** Herrenzimmer; **~ volcano** rauchender Vulkan.
smooth glatt, ruhig, eben;
~ *(v.) (palliate)* schlichten, *(statistics)* Unregelmäßigkeiten ausgleichen;
~ away obstacles Hindernisse beseitigen; **~ over difficulties** Schwierigkeiten glätten; **~ over a fault** Fehler bemänteln (beschönigen); **~ s. one's rumpled feathers** jds. Zorn besänftigen; **~ one's manners** sich abschleifen; **~ the soil** Boden einebnen;
to make things ~ for s. o. jem. den Weg ebnen; **to take the rough with the ~** Höhen und Tiefen des Lebens zu ertragen wissen;
~ driving angenehmes Fahren; **~ face** katzenfreundliches Gesicht; **~ flight** angenehmer Flug; **~ functioning** reibungslo-

ser Verlauf, reibungsloses Funktionieren; **~ passage** ruhige Überfahrt; **~ steering** ruhige Fahrt; **~ style** flüssiger Stil; **~ tyre casing** abgefahrene Reifendecke; **to be in ~ water** *(fig.)* es geschafft haben.
smoothing iron Bügeleisen.
smoothly reibungslos;
to go off ~ ungestört ablaufen.
smother *(v.)* **up | a rebellion** Aufruhr ersticken; **~ a scandal** Skandal unterdrücken.
smothered with | flowers mit Blumen überschüttet; **~ work in** Arbeit erstickt.
smoulder *(v.) (pol.)* schwelen.
smouldering rebellion schwelender Aufruhr.
smug *(Br., sl.)* Streber, Büffler;
~ *(a.)* blasiert, selbstgefällig.
smuggle *(v.)* schmuggeln;
~ a new clause into a text neue Bestimmung in einen Vertrag hineinpraktizieren; **~ foreign labo(u)rers** ausländische Arbeitskräfte einschleusen; **~ through the customs** durch den Zoll schmuggeln; **~ a letter into prison** Brief ins Gefängnis einschmuggeln; **~ s. th. out of the country** etw. außer Landes schmuggeln.
smuggled goods Schmuggelware.
smuggler Schmuggler, Schieber, *(vessel)* Schmugglerschiff.
smuggling Schmuggel, Schleichhandel;
currency ~ Devisenschmuggel; **narcotics ~** Rauschgifthandel;
~ of intoxicating liquor Alkoholschmuggel;
~ activities Schmuggeltätigkeit; **~ charge** Anklage wegen Schmuggels; **~ run** Schmuggelfahrt.
snack Imbiß[happen], *(underworld use)* leichte Beute;
~s available free of charge kostenlose Erfrischungen;
to go ~s sich in etw. teilen;
~ bar (counter) Imbißstube.
snaffle *(v.)* klauen, organisieren;
to ride s. o. on the ~ j. am Gängelband führen.
snafu *(US sl.)* Chaos, heilloses Durcheinander.
snag *(difficulties)* Schwierigkeiten, Haken;
to come upon (strike) a ~ auf einen Haken stoßen.
snail's pace Schneckentempo.
snake *(fig.)* Schlange, heimtückischer Mensch;
European ~ *(currency)* Europäische Währungsschlange;
~ in the grass Wolf im Schafspelz, verborgene Gefahr, geheimer Feind;
to see ~s weiße Mäuse sehen, Delirium haben; **to wake ~s** ein Wespennest stören;
~ charmer Schlangenbeschwörer; **~ country** Mitglied der europäischen Währungsschlange; **~ currencies** Schlangenwährungen; **~ meeting** Sitzung der Schlangenmitgliedstaaten; **~ ranch** *(sl.)* Spelunke; **~ system** Währungsschlange.
snap *(dispute)* heftiger Wortwechsel, *(easy job, US sl.)* Druckposten, ruhiger Posten, *(lock)* Schnappschloß, *(pep, coll.)* Schmiß, Schwung, *(style)* Frische, *(theater)* Kurzengagement;
in a ~ im Nu;
cold ~ Kältewelle, -einbruch;
~ *(v.)* in gereiztem Ton antworten, fauchen;
~ at s. o. j. anschnauzen; **~ s. one's bag** jem. die Tasche entreißen; **~ a beggar short** Bettler kurz abfertigen; **~ at a chance** Gelegenheit beim Schopf ergreifen; **~ into it** energisch erledigen; **~ one's fingers at s. o.** j. mit einem Achselzucken abtun; **~ s. one's nose (head) off** jem. in die Parade fahren; **~ at an offer** sich auf ein Angebot stürzen; **~ out** in gereiztem Ton äußern; **~ out one's criticism** kritische Bemerkungen von sich geben; **~ s. o. up** j. nicht ausreden lassen; **~ up the cheapest articles** billigste Ware sofort kaufen;
not to care a ~ sich nicht ein bißchen darum kümmern; **to put some ~ in it** etw. Dampf dahintermachen;
~ check Stichprobe, stichprobenartige Überprüfung; **~ course** leichte Vorlesung; **~ division** unvermutete Abstimmung; **~ election** kurzfristig angesetzte Wahlen; **~ judgment** vorschnelles Urteil; **~ lock** Schnappschloß; **~ vote** Blitzabstimmung; **to take a ~ vote** überraschend eine Abstimmung vornehmen.
snapback method Einzelzeitverfahren.
snapper Knallbonbon, *(story)* Pointe.
snappy conversation angeregtes Gespräch.
snapshot *(photo)* Momentaufnahme, Schnappschuß.
snare Falle;
to set a ~ for s. o. jem. eine Falle stellen.
snaring Fallenstellerei.
snatch *(occasional moment)* Augenblick, Periode, *(sl.)* Ladendieb, *(kidnapping, sl.)* Entführung;
~ of a story Bruchstücke einer Geschichte;

~ *(v.)* Schnappschuß machen, *(arrest)* festnehmen, *(kidnap)* entführen;

~ **a letter out of s. one's hand** jem. einen Brief entreißen; ~ **at an offer** Angebot schnell annehmen, sich auf ein Angebot stürzen; ~ **from the sea** dem Meer entreißen; ~ **an hour's sleep** eine Mütze Schlaf nehmen; ~ **up** zusammenraffen;

to make a ~ **at s. th.** etw. ergattern; **to overhear** ~**es of a conversation** Gesprächsfetzen aufschnappen; **to put the** ~ **on s. o.** *(sl.)* j. verhaften (entführen); **to work in** ~**es** Arbeit etappenweise erledigen;

~ **insurance** *(sl.)* Versicherung gegen Entführungen.

snatcher *(sl.)* Taschendieb, *(kidnapper)* Entführer.

sneak Kriecher, Radfahrer, *(Br., sl.)* Petze;

~ *(v.)* katzbuckeln, kriechen, *(school, Br., sl.)* petzen, klatschen;

~ **about** herumschnüffeln; ~ **presents into one's home** Geschenke in sein Haus schmuggeln;

~ **preview** *(film)* inoffizielle Filmpräsentation; ~ **raid** *(mil.)* Überraschungsangriff; ~ **thief** Langfinger, Gelegenheitsdieb.

sneaker Kriecher, Schleicher.

sneaking | respect heimlicher Respekt; **to have a** ~ **suspicion** leisen Verdacht haben.

sneer *(v.)* **away s. one's reputation** jds. Ruf durch höhnische Bemerkungen verunglimpfen.

sneeze *(sl.)* Entführung;

~ *(v.)* entführen.

sneezed, not to be ~ **at** nicht zu verachten.

snide Blüte, Falschgeld.

sniffer dog Spürhund.

snipe *(cigarette)* Kippe.

sniper Scharfschütze.

sniping *(US)* wilder Plakatanschlag.

snitch *(v.)* *(sl.)* klauen.

snob | appeal Ansprechen snobistischer Gefühle, Snobgefühl; ~ **effect** externer Konsumeffekt.

snollygoster *(sl.)* unfähiger Politiker.

snook *(v.)* spionieren, herumschnüffeln.

snooky *(sl.)* aufgeblasen.

snoop *(US)* Schnüffler, Detektiv;

~ *(v.)* *(US)* klauen, mausen;

~ **around** *(US)* auf der Suche nach Übertretung von Vorschriften sein.

snooper Schnüffler.

snooping politische Schnüffeltätigkeit.

snooze | (v.) time away Zeit vertrödeln;

to have a ~ Nickerchen machen.

snorter *(coll.)* tolle Sache.

snow Schnee[decke], *(cocaine)* Kokain, Schnee, *(television)* Flimmern, Schnee;

blowing ~ Schneetreiben; **melted** ~ Schneewasser;

~ **in** *(v.)* *(letters)* massenweise ankommen; ~ **s. o. with invitations** j. mit Einladungen überschütten; ~ **under a candidate** *(US)* Kandidaten mit großer Mehrheit schlagen; ~ **under with work** mit Arbeit überhäufen;

~ **chains** *(car)* Schneeketten; ~ **drift** Schneeverwehung, ~ **flurry** *(US)* **(shower)** Schneeschauer; ~ **job** Überredungskünste; ~ **plough** Schneepflug; ~ **removal** Schneeräumung, -beseitigung; ~ **tyre** Winterreifen.

snowball Schneeball, *(fund, Br.)* durch Mitgliederwerbung stetig vergrößerter Fonds;

~ *(v.)* **into** lawinenartig anwachsen;

~ **chance** fast keine Chance; ~ **growth** Selbstpotenzierung; ~ **letters** *(Br.)* Schneeballsystembriefe; ~ **system** Schneeballsystem.

snowbird *(sl.)* Kokainsüchtiger.

snowed under eingeschneit, *(fig.)* zugedeckt, überlastet;

~ **with applications** mit Anträgen überhäuft; ~ **with work** mit Arbeit zugedeckt.

snowfall Schneefall.

snowmobile Motorschlitten.

snowshoe *(sl.)* Detektiv.

snowstorm Schneesturm, -gestöber.

snub Verweis, schroffe Abfertigung, Brüskierung;

~ *(v.)* abfertigen, abweisen, kalte Schulter zeigen, brüskieren;

~ **s. o. into silence** j. zum Schweigen bringen;

to meet with a ~ kurz abgefertigt werden.

snuff trauriges Überbleibsel;

~ *(v.)* **out all opposition** jeden Widerstand ersticken;

to be up to ~ *(sl.)* mit allen Hunden gehetzt sein, alle Kniffe kennen; **to give s. o.** ~ jem. einen Denkzettel verpassen.

snuffler Scheinheiliger.

snug wohnlich, gemütlich;

as ~ **as a bug in a rug** pudelwohl;

to be as ~ **as a bug in a rug** wie die Made im Speck sitzen; **to keep it nice and** ~ etw. ganz geheim halten;

~ **cabin** behagliche Kabine; ~ **fortune** ganz nettes Vermögen; ~ **little income** ganz schönes Einkommen.

snuggery behagliches Stübchen.

soak *(US sl.)* Schmier-, Bestechungsgeld, *(binge, sl.)* Sauftour;

~ *(v.)* langsam einsinken, durchsickern, *(drink gluttonously)* saufen, *(pawn, sl.)* versetzen;

~ **s. o. for s. th.** jem. etw. abknöpfen; ~ **into s. one's mind** in jds. Bewußtsein eindringen; ~ **the rich** *(US sl.)* die Reichen kräftig besteuern; ~ **up ink** Tinte aufsaugen; ~ **up tax losses** Steuerverluste kompensieren.

soakage Sickerwasser, Schwund durch Einsickern.

soap Seife, *(sl.)* Bestechungsgeld;

~ *(v.)* von einem improvisierten Rednerpult sprechen;

~ **box** *(sl.)* improvisierte Rednertribüne; ~ **derby** Seifenkistenrennen; ~ **opera** *(US, radio)* rührselige (anspruchslose) Fernseh-, Hörfunkserie, Fortsetzungswerbeprogramm.

soar *(v.)* segelfliegen, *(prices)* emporschnellen, *(rent)* rapide (sprunghaft) steigen.

soaring prices sprunghaft steigende Kurse.

sob | sister *(US sl.)* Berichterstatterin in Jugendstrafsachen; ~ **story** *(US)* rührselige Geschichte; ~ **stuff** *(US sl.)* Schnulze, Druck auf die Tränendrüsen.

sober nüchtern, nicht betrunken;

as ~ **as a judge** stocknüchtern;

to be in ~ **earnest** todernst sein; ~ **estimate** gewissenhafte Schätzung; ~ **facts** ungeschminkte Tatsachen; ~ **judgment** abgewogenes Urteil.

socage tenure Erbpacht.

sociable ungezwungen, gesellig.

social sozial, gesellschaftlich, *(politics)* sozialistisch;

~ **accounting** volkswirtschaftliche Gesamtrechnung, Berechnung des Nationaleinkommens; ~ **activist** Vorkämpfer auf sozialem Gebiet; ~ **activities** gesellschaftliche Veranstaltungen; ~ **adaption** gesellschaftliche Assimilation; ~ **adjustment** *(convict)* Resozialisierung; ~ **administration** Sozialverwaltung; ~ **advance** sozialer Fortschritt; ~ **advancement** gesellschaftlicher Aufstieg, soziale Aufwertung; ~ **affair** gesellschaftliche Veranstaltung; ~ **agency** *(US)* Sozialbehörde; ~ **analysis** Sozialdiagnose; ~ **animal** geselliges Wesen; ~ **assessment** soziale Wertschätzung; ~ **assistance** *(US)* Sozialhilfe, Fürsorgeunterstützung; ~ **background** gesellschaftliche Herkunft; ~ **balance** Gleichgewicht zwischen privater Produktion und öffentlichem Leistungsangebot; ~ **benefits** soziale Erträge, Sozialhilfe, -leistungen, Wohlstandssteigerungen; ~ **breach** gesellschaftlicher Verstoß; ~ **budget** Sozialetat; ~ **capital** Vermögen der öffentlichen Hand; ~ **casework** Einzelfallhilfe; ~ **caseworker** Sozialfürsorger; ~ **category** soziale Schicht; ~ **charges** Soziallasten; ~ **class** soziale Schicht, Gesellschaftsschicht; ~ **climber** gesellschaftlicher Ehrgeizling; ~ **club** Geselligkeitsverein; ~ **commentator** Gesellschaftskritiker; ~ **commitments** gesellschaftliche Verpflichtungen; ~ **conditions** soziale Verhältnisse; ~ **conscience** soziales Gewissen; ~ **consciousness** Sozialbewußtsein; ~ **contract (compact)** Gesellschaftsvertrag, *(Br.)* Sozialvereinbarung, freiwillige Selbstbeschränkung; ~ **cost** soziale Aufwendungen, Soziallasten; ~ **credit** Sozialkredit; ~ **Democracy** Sozialdemokratie; ~ **Democrat** Sozialdemokrat; ~ **distinctions** soziale Unterschiede; ~ **dividend** Sozialprodukt; ~ **duties** soziale Aufgaben; ~**-economic balance sheet** Sozialbilanz; ~ **economics (economy)** Sozialwirtschaft, -ökonomie; ~ **engagements** gesellschaftliche Verpflichtungen; ~ **environment** soziale Umwelt, Milieu; **one's** ~ **equals** sozial Gleichgestellte; **to spend a** ~ **evening** Abend in Gesellschaft verbringen; ~ **event** [gesellschaftliche] Veranstaltung; ~ **evil** Prostitution; ~ **evolution** soziale Entwicklung; ~ **expenditure** *(US)* Sozialausgaben, -leistungen, gesetzliche Sozialaufwendungen; **other** ~ **expenditure** *(balance sheet, US)* andere gesetzliche Sozialaufwendungen; ~ **fetters** soziale Fesseln; **in the** ~ **field** auf sozialem Gebiet; ~ **framework** soziales Gefüge; ~ **function** Repräsentationspflicht; **company** ~ **functions** betriebliche Veranstaltungen; **European** ~ **Fund** Europäischer Sozialfonds; ~ **games** Gesellschaftsspiele; ~ **gathering** gesellschaftliche Veranstaltung, geselliges Beisammensein; ~ **goods** öffentliche Güter; ~ **habits** gesellschaftliche Umgangsformen; ~ **history** Kulturgeschichte, Sozialgeschichte; ~ **house** *(Br.)* mit Mitteln des sozialen Wohnungsbaus finanziertes Haus; ~ **ill** soziales Übel; ~ **income** Volkseinkommen; ~ **indifference curve** volkswirtschaftliche Indifferenzkurve.

social insurance *(US)* Sozialversicherung, *(Br.)* Sozialhilfe; ~ **benefits** *(US)* Sozialversicherungsleistungen; ~ **contributions** *(US)* Sozialversicherungsbeiträge; ~ **expenditure** *(US)* Sozialversicherungsausgaben; ~ **institution** *(US)* Sozialversicherungsträger; ~ **services** *(US)* Sozialversicherungsleistungen; ~ **system** *(US)* Sozialversicherungswesen.

social | interaction gesellschaftliches Verhalten; ~ **intercourse** geselliger Verkehr; ~ **investigation** Sozialuntersuchung; ~ **investigator** Sozialforscher; **to spend time in** ~ **involvement** Zeit für die Lösung sozialer Fragen aufwenden; ~ **isolation** gesellschaftliche Isolierung; ~ **justice** soziale Gerechtigkeit; ~ **legislation** Sozialgesetzgebung; ~ **life** Geselligkeit; ~ **lion** Gesellschaftslöwe; ~ **matters** Sozialwesen; ~ **marginal productivity** marginale Sozialproduktivität; ~ **net product** Nettosozialprodukt; ~ **obligations incident to life in the diplomatic service** mit dem Diplomatenleben verbundene gesellschaftliche Verpflichtungen; **to fulfil(l) one's** ~ **obligations** seinen gesellschaftlichen Verpflichtungen nachkommen; ~ **occasion** gesellige Veranstaltung; ~ **order** soziale Ordnung, Sozial-, Gesellschaftsordnung; **free** ~ **order** freiheitliche Gesellschaftsordnung; ~ **organization** Gesellschaftsleben, Geselligkeitsverein; ~ **overhead capital** allgemeines Sozialkapital; ~ **planning** Planungen auf sozialem Gebiet; ~ **philosopher** Sozialwissenschaftler ~ **policy** Sozialpolitik; ~ **position** gesellschaftliche Stellung; ~ **problem** soziale Frage; ~ **process** gesellschaftlicher Vorgang; **to cut** ~ **program(me)s** Sozialprogramme beschneiden; ~ **progress** sozialer Fortschritt; ~, **domestic and pleasure purposes** *(motor-vehicle owner)* private Zwecke; ~ **question** soziale Frage; ~ **rebellion** sozialpolitischer Aufstand; ~ **reform** soziale Reformen; ~ **reformer** Sozialreformer; ~ **register** *(US)* Prominentenalmanach; ~ **relief** Sozialfürsorge; ~ **research** Sozialforschung; ~ **responsibilities** soziale Verantwortlichkeit; ~ **saving** kollektives Sparen; ~ **scale** Gesellschaftsordnung, -stufe; **to sink in the** ~ **scale** Einbußen in seiner gesellschaftlichen Stellung hinnehmen müssen; ~ **science** Sozialwissenschaften, Soziologie; ~ **science research council** *(Br.)* Sozialwirtschaftsrat; ~ **scientist** Sozialwissenschaftler, Soziologe.

social security soziale Sicherheit, *(Br.)* Sozialhilfe, Sozialfürsorge, *(US)* Sozialversicherung; **to claim** ~ *(Br.)* Sozialhilfe beantragen; ℒ **Act** Sozialversicherungsgesetz; ~ **administration** *(Br.)* Sozialverwaltung; ~ **adjustment** *(US)* Anpassung der Sozialversicherungsleistungen; ~ **benefits** *(Br.)* Fürsorgeleistungen, Sozialhilfe, *(US)* Rente aus der Sozialversicherung, Sozialrente, Sozialversicherungsleistungen; **flat-rate** ~ **benefits** pauschale Sozialversicherungsleistungen; ~ **benefit plan** *(US)* betriebliches Sozialversicherungssystem, Sozialzulagesystem; ~ **bill** *(US)* Sozialversicherungsgesetz; ℒ **Board** *(US)* Sozialversicherungsaufsichtsbehörde; ~ **card** *(US)* Sozialversicherungskarte; ~ **check** *(US)* Sozialversicherungszahlung, Auszahlung der Sozialrente; ~ **contribution** *(US)* Beitrag zur Sozialversicherung, Sozialversicherungsbeitrag, -abgabe; ~ **dependency benefits** Sozialzuschläge für Kinder; ~ **fund** *(US)* Sozialversicherungsvermögen; ~ **legislation** *(US)* Sozialversicherungsgesetzgebung; ~ **obligations** *(US)* Sozialversicherungsleistungen; ~ **office** *(Br.)* Sozialamt; ~ **payments** *(US)* Sozialabgaben, -leistungen; **to be relieved from** ~ **payments** *(US)* keine Sozialversicherungsbeiträge zahlen müssen, sozialversicherungsfrei sein; ~ **payroll tax** *(US)* Arbeitgeberanteil zur Sozialversicherung; ~ **pension** *(US)* Sozial[versicherungs]rente; ~ **policy** *(US)* Sozial[versicherungs]politik; ~ **provisions** *(US)* Sozialversicherungsbestimmungen; ~ **recipient** *(US)* Sozialversicherungsempfänger, -rentner; ~ **reform** *(US)* Reform der Sozialversicherung; ~ **rent** *(US)* Sozialrente; ~ **revenues** *(US)* Sozialversicherungseingänge; ~ **service** *(US)* Sozialversorgung; **voluntary** ~ **services** *(US)* freiwillige Sozialleistungen; ~ **spending** *(US)* Ausgaben auf dem Sozialversicherungssektor; ~ **system** *(US)* Sozialversicherungssystem, -wesen; ~ **tax** *(US)* Sozialversicherungsbeitrag, -belastung, Zwangsbeiträge zur Sozialversicherung; ~ **tax payment** *(US)* Bezahlung der Sozialversicherungsbeiträge; ~ **trust fund** *(US)* Sozialversicherungsvermögen.

social service Wohlfahrt, soziale Fürsorge, *(office)* Sozialamt, -behörde, *(philanthropic assistance)* Fürsorgearbeit, -tätigkeit; ~s Sozialleistungen, Sozial-, Wohlfahrts-, Fürsorgeeinrichtungen, Dienstleistungen der öffentlichen Hand; ~ **costs** Soziallasten; ~ **department** Sozialamt; ~ **expenditure** Fürsorgeaufwand, Sozialausgaben, -leistungen; ~ **payments** Sozialeinkommen; ~ **scheme** Fürsorgewesen; ~ **secretary** Sozialminister.

social | settlement Fürsorgeverband; ~ **spending** Fürsorge-, Sozialaufwand; ~ **stability** soziales Gleichgewicht; ~ **standing (status)** gesellschaftliche Stellung, gesellschaftlicher Rang; ~ **stock** Gesellschaftsvermögen; ~ **structure** Sozialstruktur, soziale Gegebenheiten; ~ **student** Soziologe; ~ **survey** Sozialbericht; ~ **system** Sozial-, Gesellschaftsordnung; ~ **unit** bei Sozialuntersuchungen zugrunde gelegte Menschengruppe; ~ **wage** Soziallohn; ~ **wants proper** Kollektivbedürfnisse; ~ **wealth** Vermögen der öffentlichen Hand, Gemeinschaftsvermögen.

social welfare *(US)* Sozialhilfe, -fürsorge, Wohlfahrt; ~ **activity** soziale Tätigkeit, Sozialarbeit, *(US)* Fürsorgetätigkeit; ~ **benefits** *(US)* [Fürsorgeleistungen aus der] Sozialhilfe; ~ **contributions** *(US)* Beiträge zur Sozialhilfe; ~ **expenditure** *(US)* Sozialleistungen, -ausgaben; ~ **function** *(US)* soziale Wohlstandsfunktion; ~ **minister** *(US)* Sozialminister.

social | work soziale Berufe, Sozialarbeit; ~ **worker** Sozialarbeiter, Fürsorger[in], Fürsorgebeamter.

socialism Sozialismus; **state** ~ Staatssozialismus; ~ **of the chair** Kathedersozialismus.

socialist Sozialist; ~ **achievements** sozialistische Errungenschaften; ~-**communist alliance** Volksfrontbündnis; ~ **party** sozialistische Partei.

socialistic camp sozialistisches Lager.

socialite *(US)* Salon-, Gesellschaftslöwe, Prominenter, Angehöriger der oberen Zehntausend, sozial Hochgestellter.

socialization Sozialisierung, Vergesellschaftung, Verstaatlichung.

socialize *(v.)* sozialisieren, verstaatlichen, vergesellschaften; ~ **o. s.** gesellschaftlichen Umgang pflegen.

socialized vergesellschaftet, sozialisiert, verstaatlicht; ~ **medicine** staatlich gelenkter Gesundheitsdienst; ~ **production** vergesellschaftete Produktion.

socially in sozialer Hinsicht.

society Gesellschaftsordnung, *(association)* Gesellschaft, Verein[igung], Verband, *(community)* Gemeinschaft, *(cooperative society)* Genossenschaft, *(partnership)* Gesellschaft, *(people of fashion)* die große Welt, *(trade partnership)* Berufsgenossenschaft; **not fit for good** ~ nicht gesellschaftsfähig; **actual** ~ bestehende Gesellschaft; **affiliated** ~ Zweig-, Tochtergesellschaft; **aligned** ~ formierte Gesellschaft; **approved** ~ *(US)* staatlich anerkannter Wohltätigkeitsverein; **benefit** ~ *(Br.)* Wohltätigkeitsverein, Hilfskasse; **benevolent** ~ *(US)* wohltätiger Verein, *(US)* Versicherungsverein auf Gegenseitigkeit; **building** ~ *(Br.)* Bausparkasse; **charitable** ~ Wohltätigkeitsverein; **cooperative** ~ *(Br.)* Konsumverein, Genossenschaft; **cooperative buying** ~ *(Br.)* Einkaufsgenossenschaft; **cooperative marketing** ~ *(Br.)* Absatzgenossenschaft; **cooperative productive** ~ *(Br.)* Produktionsgenossenschaft; **cooperative wholesale** ~ *(Br.)* Zentralgenossenschaft; **debating** ~ Debattierklub; **deposit** ~ *(Br.)* Sparergenossenschaft, Depositenkasse; **friendly** ~ *(Br.)* Versicherungsverein auf Gegenseitigkeit, Unterstützungskasse; **incorporated** ~ eingetragener (rechtsfähiger) Verein; **industrial** ~ *(US)* Erwerbsgenossenschaft; **industrial and provident** ~ *(Br.)* Produktions- und Konsumverein; **law** ~ *(Br.)* Anwaltsverein; **learned** ~ gelehrte Gesellschaft; **loan** ~ *(Br.)* Darlehnsverein, -kasse; **mutual** ~ Unterstützungsverein auf Gegenseitigkeit; **provident** ~ *(Br.)* Unterstützungsverein auf Gegenseitigkeit, Hilfsverein; **registered** ~ *(Br.)* eingetragener (rechtsfähiger) Verein; **retail** ~ *(Br.)* Konsumgenossenschaft; **secret** ~ Geheimgesellschaft, -bund; **trade protection** ~ Kreditschutzverein; **unregistered** ~ *(Br.)* nicht eingetragener (rechtsunfähiger) Verein; ℒ **of Friends** Quäker; ~ **of lawyers** Anwaltsverein, -vereinigung; ℒ **for the Prevention of Cruelty to Animals** *(Br.)* Tierschutzverein; **Royal** ℒ **of Science (RSPCC)** *(Br.)* Königliche Wissenschaftliche Gesellschaft; **to be cut off from all** ~ keinerlei gesellschaftlichen Umgang haben; **to be a danger to** ~ Gefahr für die menschliche Gesellschaft darstellen; **to enter a** ~ einer Gesellschaft beitreten; **to go very little in** ~ wenig ausgehen; **to join a** ~ sich in einen Verein aufnehmen lassen; **to spend an evening in the** ~ **of friends** Abend in Gesellschaft von Freunden verbringen; **to withdraw from a** ~ aus einer Gesellschaft austreten; ~ **column** Gesellschafts-, Klatschspalte; **to make the** ~ **columns** in den Klatschspalten auftauchen; ~ **funds** Vereinskasse; ~ **goods** Geheimschaftseigentum; ~ **gossip** Gesellschaftsklatsch; ~ **investments** Kapitalanlage einer Bausparkasse; ~ **lady** Dame der großen Gesellschaft; ~ **man** Gesellschaftslöwe; ~ **matron**

Dame der Gesellschaft; ~ **news** Gesellschaftsnachrichten; ~ **reformer** Sozial-, Gesellschaftsreformer; **~'s rules** Gesellschafts-, Vereinssatzung; ~ **scheme** Altersversorgungswerk eines Verbands; ~ **woman** Dame der Gesellschaft.

socio-economic sozialwirtschaftlich.

sociological soziologisch, sozialwissenschaftlich.

sociologist Soziologe;
industrial ~ Betriebssoziologe.

sociology Soziologie, Sozialwissenschaft;
applied ~ Bindestrich-Soziologie; **industrial** ~ Betriebssoziologie;
~ **of work** Arbeitssoziologie.

sociopolitical gesellschaftspolitisch.

sock *(v.) (sl.)* Geld im Strumpf sparen;
to pull up one's ~s *(Br., sl.)* sich in die Hände spucken.

sockdolager *(US sl.)* Volltreffer.

socket *(el.)* Steckdose, Fassung;
~ **joint** Kugelgelenk.

soda Sodawasser;
~ **fountain** *(US)* Erfrischungshalle, Eisbar; ~ **jerker** *(US sl.)* Mixer in einer Eisbar.

sofa | **bed** Bettcouch; ~ **cushion** Sofakissen; ~ **lizard** *(sl.)* knickriger Student.

soft *(sl.)* leicht verdientes Geld;
~ *(a.)* geschmeidig, nachgiebig, *(drink)* alkoholfrei, *(easy, coll.)* leicht, nicht anstrengend, *(negative)* weich, *(stock exchange)* nachgiebig, unstabil, leicht zu beeinflussen;
~ **as velvet** so weich wie Samt;
~ **answer** ruhige Antwort; ~ **climate** mildes Klima; ~ **coal** bituminöse Kohle; ~ **currency** weiche Währung; **~-currency country** währungsschwaches Land; ~ **drink** alkoholfreies Getränk; **~-drink industry** alkoholfreie Getränkeindustrie; **~-drink parlo(u)r** alkoholfreier Getränkeausschank; ~ **finance package** entgegenkommendes Finanzierungsangebot; ~ **goods** kurzlebige Konsumgüter, *(Br.)* Textilien und verwandte Produkte; ~ **goods department** *(Br.)* Textilwarenabteilung; **~-headed** schwachsinnig; ~ **job** leichte Arbeit; ~ **light** gedämpftes Licht; ~ **loan** zinsbegünstigte Anlage; **~-loan fund** Anleihefonds für währungsschwache Länder; ~ **manners** höfliches Benehmen; ~ **market** nicht sehr aufnahmefähiger Markt; ~ **money** Papiergeld; ~ **nothings** Austausch von Nichtigkeiten, Liebesgeflüster; ~ **outlines** verschwommene Konturen; ~ **pedal** *(pol.)* weiche Welle [eines autoritären Regimes], *(US sl.)* Dämpfer, Maulkorb; **~-pedal** *(v.)* vorsichtige Aussage machen; **~-pedal s. o.** *(US sl.)* jem. einen Dämpfer aufsetzen, j. ducken; **~-pedal one's claims** seine Forderung abschwächen; **~-pedal a story** Nachricht herunterspielen; ~ **people** verweichlichtes Volk; ~ **rain** sanfter Regen; ~ **sell** weiche Tour; ~ **sell in advertising** weiche Werbemasche; **~-sell material** unterschwelliges Nachrichtenmaterial; ~ **shoulder** Sommerweg; **~-skinned vehicle** *(mil.)* nicht gepanzertes Fahrzeug; ~ **soap** *(fig., sl.)* Schmeichelei; **~-soap** *(v.)* schmeicheln; ~ **spot** schwache Seite, *(stock exchange, US)* schwaches Papier bei anziehenden Kursen; ~ **thing** *(sl.)* gutbezahlte leichte Arbeit; **~-top** mit abnehmbarem Verdeck; ~ **weather** mildes Wetter.

soften *(v.)* besänftigen, *(business cycle)* sich abschwächen;
~ **a denial** Dementi abschwächen; ~ **up an enemy** Gegner zermürben.

softening | **in business conditions** Konjunkturabschwächung; ~ **of the brain** Gehirnerweichung; ~ **of a denial** Abschwächung eines Dementis; ~ **in the economy** Nachlassen der Konjunktur, Konjunkturabschwächung.

softness *(business cycle)* Abschwächung, Nachlassen;
~ **in demand** Nachfrageschwäche; ~ **in the economy** Konjunkturschwäche, Nachlassen der Konjunktur.

software *(computer)* Programmierhilfe, Programmausrüstung;
~ **packet** Programmpaket.

softy *(fam.)* Weichling.

soil [Erd]boden, Land, Oberfläche;
alluvial ~ Schwemmland; **fertile** ~ fruchtbarer Boden; **fruitful** ~ ertragreicher Boden; **one's native** ~ Heimatland; **poor** ~ armer Boden; **productive** ~ ertragreicher Boden;
~ *(v.)* **easily** *(material)* leicht verschmutzen;
to cultivate the ~ Land urbar machen; **to exhaust the** ~ Raubbau treiben;
~ **analysis** Bodenuntersuchung; ~ **conservation** Maßnahmen gegen Bodenzerstörung; ~ **erosion** Bodenerosion; ~ **fertility** Fruchtbarkeit des Bodens; ~ **improvement** Melioration; ~ **moisture** Bodenfeuchte; ~ **temperature** Erdbodentemperatur; ~ **working** Bodenbearbeitung.

soirée Abendgesellschaft, Soiree.

sojourn kurzer Aufenthalt (Besuch);
foreign ~ Auslandsaufenthalt;
~ *(v.)* sich vorübergehend aufhalten.

solar | **collector** Sonnenkollektor; ~ **cooking** Kochen mit Sonnenenergie; ~ **energy** Sonnenenergie; ~ **energy research** Forschungsunternehmen auf dem Gebiet der Sonnenenergie; **~-heated** durch Sonnenenergie geheizt; ~ **heating system** Sonnenheizungssystem; ~ **power** Sonnenenergie; **~-powered** durch Sonnenenergie betrieben; ~ **radiation** Sonnenstrahlung; ~ **system** Sonnensystem.

sold verkauft;
~ **by auction** in der Auktion verkauft, versteigert; ~ **in bond** aus dem Zoll verkauft; ~ **for cash** gegen bar (Kasse) verkauft; ~ **on credit** auf Kredit verkauft; ~ **on order** auf Vorbestellung verkauft; ~ **out** ausverkauft, nicht mehr vorrätig, *(books)* vergriffen; ~ **temporarily out** zur Zeit ausverkauft; ~ **up** verkauft, *(bankruptcy)* ausgepfändet, fallit, bankrott; ~ **without resort to legal process** im Selbsthilfewege verkauft; ~ **by weight** nach Gewicht verkauft;
to be ~ verkauft werden, zum Verkauf kommen, im Handel sein, zu verkaufen; **to be ~ commercially** auf dem Markt erhältlich sein; **not to be** ~ unverkäuflich sein; **to be ~ on the idea of profit-sharing** *(US)* zu den Anhängern der Gewinnbeteiligung gehören; **to be ~ out** vergriffen sein; **to be ~ out of small sizes** kleine Größen nicht mehr vorrätig haben;
~ **ledger** Verkaufsbuch, -journal; ~ **note** *(broker, Br.)* Schlußschein, -note.

soldier Soldat, *(mar., sl.)* Drückeberger, *(tip, sl.)* großzügiger Trinkgeldgeber;
common (private) ~ einfacher Soldat; **fellow** ~ Kriegskamerad; **old** ~ alter Hase; **professional** ~ Berufssoldat; **regular** ~ Berufssoldat; **undisciplined** ~ undisziplinierter Soldat; **unknown** ~ unbekannter Soldat;
~ **of fortune** Glücksritter;
~ *(v.) (sl.)* sich drücken, krankfeiern;
~ **on** *(fam.)* unbeirrt weitermachen;
to come the old ~ over s. o. *(sl.)* den alten Hasen gegenüber jem. herauskehren;
~s' home *(US)* Versehrtenheim; **~'s medal** *(US)* Tapferkeitsmedaille.

soldiering *(sl.)* Drückebergerei, Krankfeiern.

soldiery Militär;
licentious ~ zügelloser Soldatenhaufen.

sole allein, einzig, *(law)* ledig, unverheiratet;
feme ~ unverheiratete Frau;
~ **account** alleinige Rechnung; **~-actor doctrine** Zurechenbarkeit der Kenntnis des Erfüllungsgehilfen; ~ **advertisement** alleinstehende Anzeige; **~-advertising representation** reine Anzeigenvertretung; ~ **agency** Alleinvertretung; ~ **agent** Alleinvertreter; **to be ~ agent** Alleinvertretung haben; ~ **bargaining agency** Einzeltarifvertragspartner; ~ **bargaining agent** *(Br.)* Alleinverhandlungspartner für Tarifverhandlungen, Einzeltarifvertreter; ~ **author** alleiniger Verfasser; ~ **bill** Solawechsel; ~ **business** Einzelfirma; ~ **buyer** alleiniger Abnehmer; ~ **cause of an accident** alleinige Unfallursache; **to be left in ~ charge of the business** alleinige Geschäftsaufsicht anvertraut bekommen; ~ **corporation** Einmanngesellschaft; ~ **debtor** Einzelschuldner; ~ **distribution rights** Alleinvertretungsrecht; **to be ~ distributor** Alleinvertretung haben; ~ **executor** einziger Testamentsvollstrecker; ~ **heir** Universal-, Alleinerbe; ~ **judge** Einzelrichter; ~ **legatee** alleiniger Vermächtnisnehmer; ~ **management** alleinige Geschäftsführung; ~ **occupation** ausschließliche Beschäftigung; ~ **and unconditional owner** Alleineigentümer, -inhaber, *(ship)* Alleinreeder; ~ **ownership** Alleineigentum; **to have ~ power** allein befugt sein; ~ **product** einziges Erzeugnis; ~ **proprietor** *(US)* Alleineigentümer, Einzelkaufmann, -unternehmer, *(firm, US)* Alleininhaber, alleiniger Leiter einer Firma; ~ **proprietorship** *(US)* Einzelinhaberschaft, -firma, -unternehmen; ~ **representative** Alleinvertreter; ~ **right** Alleinberechtigung; ~ **right of negotiation** Ausschließlichkeitsrecht [bei Anleiheverhandlungen]; ~ **rights of publication** alleinige Publikationsrechte, Alleinveröffentlichungsrecht; ~ **right to sell (of selling)** alleiniges Verkaufsrecht, Alleinverkaufs-, Alleinvertriebsrecht; **his father's ~ support** einzige Stütze seines Vaters; ~ **tenant** Einzelmieter, Alleinpächter; ~ **trade** Monopol; ~ **trader** Einzelkaufmann; **feme ~ trader** Kauffrau; ~ **trustee** Einzeltreuhänder; ~ **use** alleiniges Benutzungsrecht.

solecism Sprachfehler, -schnitzer.

solely responsible allein verantwortlich.

solemn förmlich, feierlich, in feierlicher Form;
~ **agreement** förmlicher Vertrag; ~ **assertion** feierliche Versicherung; ~ **ceremony** Festakt; ~ **declaration** feierliche Erklärung; ~ **form** gesetzliche Form; ~ **moment** feierlicher Augenblick; ~ **oath** feierlicher Eid; ~ **occasion** feierlicher Anlaß; ~ **protest** feierlicher Protest; ~ **state dinner** Bankett; ~ **war** heiliger Krieg; ~ **warning** ernste Warnung.

solemnity Förmlichkeit, Zeremonie.

solemnization of a marriage formelle Vollziehung der Eheschließung.

solemnize *(v.)* **a marriage** Trauung vollziehen.

solicit *(v.)* nachsuchen, sich bemühen, bitten, *(act as solicitor)* anwaltlich tätig sein, *(plead)* bei Gericht plädieren, *(prostitute)* ansprechen, belästigen, *(take charge)* sich kümmern;
~ **for custom** um Kundschaft werben; ~ **donations** um Spenden bitten; ~ **a favo(u)r of s. o.** j. um eine Gefälligkeit bitten; ~ **a government post** sich um eine staatliche Anstellung bewerben; ~ **one's neighbo(u)rs for contributions** seine Nachbarn für wohltätige Zwecke angehen; ~ **an office** sich um eine Stelle bewerben; ~ **orders** Aufträge sammeln, sich um Aufträge bemühen, seine Dienste anbieten; ~ **proxies** *(US)* sich um Stimmrechtsvollmachten bemühen; ~ **subscriptions** Abonnenten werben; ~ **votes** Stimmenwerbung betreiben, Wahlstimmen werben.

solicitant Bittsteller.

solicitation Bitte, Anliegen, Ersuchen, *(criminal, US)* Anstiftung, *(prostitute)* Belästigung, Ansprechen;
~ **for bids** *(US)* Ausschreibung; ~ **to bribery** Bestechungshandlung; ~ **of business** Geschäftsanfrage, Auftragswerbung, Akquisition; ~ **of chastity** Anstiftung zur Unzucht; ~ **of customers** Kundenwerbung; ~ **to larceny** Verleitung zum Diebstahl; ~ **of loan** Kreditkundenwerbung; ~ **of membership** Mitgliederwerbung; ~ **of orders** Auftragsbesorgung.

soliciting | **of loan** Kreditkundenwerbung; ~ **orders** Hereinholen von Aufträgen, Auftragsbesorgung.

solicitor Bittsteller, *(law court, Br.)* [nicht plädierender Rechts]anwalt, Rechtsbeistand, -konsulent, *(for subscriptions, US)* Agent, Akquisiteur, Abonnentenwerber, Inhaber eines Inkassobüros;
adverse ~ *(Br.)* gegnerischer Anwalt; **city** ~ *(US)* Stadtsyndikus; **experienced** ~ *(Br.)* bewährter Anwalt; ⌾ **General** *(US)* stellvertretender Justizminister, *(Br.)* zweiter Kronanwalt; **official** ~ *(Br.)* Amtsanwalt; **patent** ~ Patentanwalt;
~ **at law** *(Br.)* Rechtskonsulent, -berater, -anwalt; ~ **to the suitor's fund** *(court of chancery)* Prozeßpfleger; ~ **of the treasury** *(US)* zum Justizministerium abgestellter Finanzbeamter; ~ **for votes** Stimmenwerber;
to apply to a ~ *(Br.)* sich an einen Anwalt wenden; **to be admitted as** ~ *(Br.)* als Anwalt zugelassen werden; **to consult a** ~ *(Br.)* Anwalt zuziehen; **to employ a** ~ *(Br.)* Anwalt beschäftigen; **to place a matter in the hands of a** ~ *(Br.)* Angelegenheit einem Rechtsanwalt übergeben; **to retain a** ~ *(Br.)* Anwalt betrauen;
no ~s **allowed in this building** Sammeln ist in diesem Hause nicht gestattet;
~s' **account** *(Br.)* Ander-, Anwaltskonto; ⌾s' **Accounts Rules** *(Br.)* Abstimmungen über die Führung von Anderkonten durch Rechtsanwälte; ⌾s **Act** *(Br.)* [etwa] Bundesrechtsanwaltsordnung; ~'s **bill** *(Br.)* Anwalts-, Honorarrechnung; ~'s **charges** *(Br.)* Anwaltsgebühren; ~'s **client account** *(Br.)* [Anwalts]anderkonto; ~'s **clerk** Anwaltsgehilfe; ~'s **costs** *(Br.)* Anwaltskosten; ~'s **department** Rechts-, juristische Abteilung; ~'s **office** *(Br.)* Anwaltsbüro; ~'s **trust account** *(Br.)* [Rechtsanwalts]anderkonto; ⌾s' **Trust Account Rules** *(Br.)* Richtlinien über die Führung von Anderkonten; ~-**trustee** *(Br.)* als Treuhänder fungierender Anwalt.

solicitorship *(Br.)* anwaltliche Tätigkeit, Anwaltstätigkeit.

solicitous bestrebt, bemüht;
~ **for s. one's comfort** um jds. Wohlbefinden besorgt;
to be ~ sich befleißigen; **to be** ~ **to please** zu gefallen bemüht sein.

solicitously mit Anteilnahme.

solid *(bulky)* massig, *(credit rating)* kreditfähig, -würdig, leistungsfähig, *(honest)* gediegen, solide, redlich, *(politics, US)* einmütig, geschlossen, *(print.)* kompreß, ohne Durchschuß, *(pure)* massiv;
~ **set** kompreß;
to be ~ **with a committee** mit der vollen Unterstützung eines Ausschusses rechnen können; **to be** ~ **for peace** entschlossen für den Frieden eintreten; **to go** ~ **for s. o.** geschlossen hinter jem. stehen; **to vote** ~ **for s. th.** etw. einstimmig annehmen;
~ **arguments** handfeste Argumente; ~ **building** massiv gebaut

---

Gebäude; ~ **business firm** solide Firma, solides Unternehmen; ~ **cash** Hartgeld; ~ **consideration** ernstgemeinte Gegenleistung; ~ **foundation** solide Grundlage; ~ **fuel** fester Treibstoff; ~-**fuelled rocket** Feststoffrakete; ~ **gold** gediegenes Gold; ~-**hour** geschlagene (volle) Stunde; ~ **matter** *(print.)* glatter Satz, Fließsatz; ~ **row of buildings** zusammenhängende Gebäudegruppe, Gebäudekomplex; ~ **silver** gediegenes Silber; ~ **tire** *(US)* **(tyre,** *Br.*) Vollgummireifen; ~ **vote** einstimmige Wahl.

solidarity Solidarität, Interessengemeinschaft, *(civil law)* Gesamtschuldnerschaft, -verhältnis;
monetary ~ Währungssolidarität; **national** ~ nationale Solidarität;
~ **campaign** Solidaritätsfeldzug.

solidary gesamtschuldnerisch, solidarisch.

solidify *(v.)* sich festigen (konsolidieren).

solidity Gediegenheit, *(credit rating)* Kreditfähigkeit, -würdigkeit, Bonität, *(of goods)* Haltbarkeit;
~ **of a building** Solidität eines Gebäudes.

solidness of a vote Einstimmigkeit eines Votums.

solitary allein, abgesondert;
~ **confinement** Einzelhaft; ~ **exception** einzige Ausnahme; ~ **life** einsames (zurückgezogenes) Leben; ~ **valley** abgelegenes Tal.

solitude Abgeschiedenheit, Einsamkeit;
to live in ~ zurückgezogen leben.

solo Alleinvorstellung;
to fly ~ allein fliegen;
~ **flight** Alleinflug.

solus *(retailing)* Warenauslieferungslager;
~ *(a.)* *(theater)* allein;
~ **agreement** Ausschließlichkeitsabkommen; ~ **bus site** Rundumschrifting; ~ **position** *(Br.)* alleinstehend; ~ **site** Ganzstelle.

solution Lösung, Behebung;
final ~ Endlösung; **workable** ~ brauchbare Lösung;
~ **of financial troubles** Behebung finanzieller Schwierigkeiten; **to defy** ~ sich nicht lösen lassen.

solve *(v.)* | **a crossword puzzle** Kreuzworträtsel lösen; ~ **a debt** Schuld ablösen.

solvency Zahlungsfähigkeit, Solvenz, Bonität, *(estate)* Flüssigkeit, Gesundheit, Liquidität;
~ **margin** Liquiditätsspielraum, -marge; **to offer a high** ~ **margin** hohen Liquiditätsstatus aufrechterhalten; ~ **rules** Liquiditätsbestimmungen.

solvent *(able to pay)* zahlungsfähig, solvent, liquid, *(credit rating)* kreditfähig, -würdig, *(financially sound)* leistungsfähig, *(solid)* solide;
to be ~ *(estate)* Schulden decken;
~ **debtor** solventer Schuldner; ~ **estate** liquider Nachlaß; ~ **merchant** zahlungsfähige (leistungsfähige) Firma.

sombre prospects trübe Aussichten.

somebody bedeutende Erscheinung.

somersault *(fig.)* völliger Meinungsumschwung.

something on the ball, to have etw. im Kasten haben.

song, for a mere um ein Spottgeld, für einen Spottpreis;
long ~ lange Litanei; **the same old** ~ immer das alte Lied;
~ **and dance** *(sl.)* Lügengewebe; ~ **of a motor** Motorengeräusch; **to make a** ~ **about** Geschichte unendlich auswalzen; **nothing to make a** ~ **about** kein Aufhebens wert sein; **to pick up for a** ~ für ein Butterbrot kaufen.

sonic | **bang** Überschallknall; ~ **barrier** Schallgrenze; ~ **boom** Überschallknall; ~ **depth finder** Echolot.

sonobuoy Geräuschboje.

sonopuss *(sl.)* Miesepeter.

soon in angemessener Zeit.

sooner or later über kurz oder lang.

soot and grime of a manufacturing town Ruß und Schmutz einer Industriestadt.

soothing syrup *(fig.)* Beruhigungsmittel.

sop *(fig.)* Beschwichtigungsmittel, Schmiergeld;
to throw a ~ **to Cerberus** den Zerberus überreden.

sophism Scheinargument, Spitzfindigkeit.

sophistical spitzfindig.

sophisticate *(v.)* verbilden, *(text)* verfälschen, verdrehen;
~ **s. o.** j. weltklug machen.

sophisticated gekünstelt, *(fig.)* raffiniert, bis ins Letzte ausgefeilt, *(person)* geistig differenziert, intellektuell, hoch intelligent, auf zu hohem Niveau stehend, *(technics)* technisch ausgefeilt, hoch entwickelt (differenziert);
~ **method** hochentwickelte Methode; ~ **novel** Roman für gehobenere Ansprüche; ~ **taste** verwöhnter Geschmack.

sophistication geistige Differenziertheit, Intellektualismus, Weltklugheit, *(technics)* Differenziertheit, hochentwickelter Stand der Technik.

sophomore *(US)* Student im zweiten Universitätsjahr.

sordid | gains unerlaubte Gewinne; **to be living in ~ poverty** in drückender Armut leben; **~ slum** jämmerliches Quartier.

sore *(fig.)* beleidigt, gekränkt, eingeschnappt, sauer;
to be pretty ~ at s. o. über j. ganz schön sauer sein;
~ distress große Not; **to be in ~ need of help** sehr hilfsbedürftig sein; **~ point** wunder Punkt; **~ subject** heißes Thema.

sorehead Enttäuschter, *(politics)* grollender durchgefallener Kandidat.

sorority *(US)* weibliche Studentenvereinigung.

sort Sorte, Klasse, *(brand)* Marke, *(kind)* Gattung, Art, *(print.)* Schriftgarnitur, *(quality)* Güte, Qualität;
after a ~ in gewisser Weise; **of ~s** unsortiert, gemischt, *(fig.)* schlecht und recht; **out of ~s** *(coll.)* unwohl, unpäßlich, nicht in Ordnung, *(print.)* ausgegangen;
a good ~ netter Kerl;
new ~ of car neuer Autotyp; **a ~ of stockbroker** eine Art Börsenmakler;
~ (v.) sichten, sortieren, klassifizieren;
~ letters Briefe sortieren; **~ out** auslesen, ausrangieren, sortieren, sieben, *(law of bankruptcy)* aussondern; **~ out the books** *(accounting)* Bücher überprüfen; **~ out letters** Briefe sortieren; **~ over one's stamps** sich mit seiner Briefmarkensammlung beschäftigen; **~ well with s. one's character** mit jem. harmonieren;
to get ~ of frightened irgendwie Angst bekommen.

sortable sortierbar.

sorter *(post office)* Briefsortierer.

sortie Ausfall, *(plane, mil.)* Einzelflug, -einsatz, Feindflug;
to fly nighttime ~s Nachteinsätze fliegen.

sorting Sortieren, Auslesen, Klassifizierung;
~ out *(law of bankruptcy)* Aussonderung;
~ machine Sortiermaschine; **~ office** *(post)* Verteileramt.

sought after *(securities)* gesucht, gefragt;
to be ~ gefragt sein, gehen;
person ~ Gesuchter.

soul *(fig.)* Triebfeder, Seele, Mittelpunkt;
simple ~ schlichter Mensch;
~ of an enterprise Seele eines Geschäfts, Kopf eines Unternehmens; **~ in torment** gequälte Seele;
to be the ~ of hono(u)r durch und durch ein Ehrenmann sein; **to be the life and ~ of a party** absoluter Mittelpunkt einer Gesellschaft sein; **to have a ~ above material pleasures** sich mit anspruchsvolleren Dingen beschäftigen; **to put one's heart and ~ into one's work** mit ganzer Seele bei der Arbeit sein; **to sink with 300 ~s** mit 300 Mann untergehen.

sound Ton, Klang, *(narrow passage)* Meerenge, Sund;
~ of a letter Ton eines Briefes;
~ (v.) sondieren, ausloten, *(railway wheels)* überprüfen;
~ the alarm Alarm auslösen; **~ the alert clear** entwarnen, Entwarnungssignal auslösen; **~ all right** vernünftig klingen; **~ a capitalist with regard to a proposed investment** Kapitalgeber wegen der Finanzierung eines Unternehmens ansprechen; **~ an action on contract** Klage auf Vertrag stützen; **~ in damages** *(action in law)* Schadensersatzansprüche begründen; **~ the manager on the question of holidays** Geschäftsführer wegen der Ferienregelung sondieren; **~ a note of alarm** besorgten Ton anschlagen; **~ off** *(US sl.)* sich beschweren; **~ a man's praises** sich in Lobsprüchen über j. ergehen; **~ the retreat** zum Rückzug blasen; **~ s. o. on a subject** j. über ein Thema aushorchen; **~ in tort** auf unerlaubte Handlung lauten; **~ s. one's views** jds. Ansichten erforschen;
to be ~ on national defence in Fragen der nationalen Sicherheit zuverlässig sein; **to have a sinister ~** *(news)* unheilvoll (beunruhigend) klingen;
~ (a.) gesund, unversehrt, *(credit rating)* kreditfähig, -würdig, *(without fault)* unbeschädigt, fehlerfrei, *(firm)* solide, reell;
~ delivered gesund ausgeliefert; **financially ~** wirtschaftlich gesund, kapitalkräftig, -stark;
safe and ~ wohlbehalten;
~ as a bell (dollar) kerngesund;
consistently maintained ~ accounting practices ständig fehlerfreie Buchführung; **~ advice** guter Rat; **~ argument** stichhaltiges Argument, vernünftige Beweisführung; **~ bank** seriöse Bank; **~ barrier** Schallmauer, -grenze; **~ box** Tonkapsel; **~ broadcasting** *(Br.)* Hörfunk; **~ business house** solide Firma; **~ camera** Magnettonkamera; **~ claim** begründeter Anspruch; **~ commercial credit** geschäftliches Ansehen; **~ condition** Unversehrt-

heit; **in a ~ condition** *(goods)* in tadellosem Zustand; **~ currency** gesunde Währung, sichere Valuta, gutes Geld; **~ drama** Hörspiel; **~ effects** Klangeffekte, Geräuschkulisse; **~ engineer** Toningenieur; **~ film** Tonfilm; **~ of ~ health** *(insurance)* gesund; **~ judicial discretion** vernünftiger Gebrauch richterlicher Ermessensfreiheit; **~ lawyer** angesehener Anwalt; **~ level** Lautstärke; **~ locator** *(mil.)* Horchgerät; **~ man** Tontechniker; **~ mind** Zurechnungsfähigkeit; **of ~ mind** geistig normal; **~ and disposing mind and memory** *(US)* Testierfähigkeit; **of ~ and disposing mind** *(US)* testierfähig; **to be of ~ mind and memory** *(US)* im vollen Besitz seiner geistigen Kräfte sein; **~ motion picture** *(US)* Tonfilm; **~ policy** kluge Politik; **~ position** sichere Stellung; **~ financial position** gesunde Finanzverhältnisse; **~-proof studio** schallsicheres Tonstudio; **~ protection** Lärmschutz; **~-ranging instrument** Schallmeßgerät; **~ reason** stichhaltiger Grund; **~ recording** Tonaufnahme; **~ recording device** Tonaufnahme, -bandgerät; **~ reproducing instrument** Tonwiedergabegerät; **~ shadow** Schallzone; **~ ship** seetüchtiges Schiff; **in a ~ state** wohlerhalten; **~ title** einwandfreier Rechtstitel; **~ track** *(film)* Tonspur, -streifen; **~ truck** Lautsprecher-, Aufnahmewagen; **~ value** voller Wert, Wert in unbeschädigtem Zustand, *(fire policy)* Verkehrs-, Tageswert; **~ wave** Schallwelle.

sounding ausgelotete Wassertiefe, *(fig.)* Auslotung, Sondierung;
out of ~ *(fig.)* ohne sicheren Boden unter den Füßen;
~ in damages Schadenersatzklage; **~ of public opinion** öffentliche Meinungsumfrage;
to take ~s Lotungen vornehmen; **to take diplomatic ~s** diplomatisch sondieren;
~ balloon Versuchsballon; **~ line** Lotleine; **~ rod** *(tank)* Peilstock.

soundness Fehlerfreiheit, gesunder Geisteszustand, *(credit)* Gesundheit, Bonität, Kreditwürdigkeit.

soup *(aero, sl.)* Pferdestärke [des Motors], *(fog)* Waschküche, *(fuel)* hochwertiger Sprit;
in the ~ *(coll.)* in der Patsche (Klemme);
industrially-made ~ Fertigsuppe;
~ (v.) up an engine *(US sl.)* Motor frisieren;
~ job *(sl.)* schneller Wagen; **~ kitchen** Armen-, Wohlfahrtsküche; **~ ticket** Essenmarke.

souped-up car *(US sl.)* frisiertes Auto.

sour sauer, stinkend, ranzig, *(fig.)* verbittert, sauertöpfisch, griesgrämig;
sweet and ~s of life Freud und Leid des Lebens;
~ to turn *(investment)* sich als mißglückt (Fehlinvestition) herausstellen;
~ old man Griesgram, Sauertopf.

source Ursprung, *(authority)* Gewährsmann, Quelle, *(supplier)* Lieferant;
at the (deducted at) ~ *(taxation)* an der Quelle abgezogen; **from a reliable ~** aus sicherer (zuverlässiger) Quelle; **from a well-informed ~** von einer gut unterrichteten Seite; **from a semi-official ~** aus halbamtlichen Quellen;
~s Quellenverzeichnis;
informed ~s informierte Kreise (Stellen); **long-term ~s** langfristige Finanzierungsquellen; **reliable ~** authentische Quelle, sicherer Gewährsmann; **short-term ~s** kurzfristige Finanzierungsquellen; **~s used** Quellenangaben, -verzeichnis; **well-placed ~s** wohlunterrichtete Quellen;
constant ~ of annoyance Quelle ständigen Verdrusses; **~s close to the bank** der Bank nahestehende Kreise; **~s of crude oil** Rohölquellen; **~ of danger** Gefahrenquelle; **~ of earnings** Einkommensquelle; **~ of energy (power)** Energieträger; **~ of error** Fehlerquelle; **~ of evidence** Beweismittel; **~ of financing** Finanzierungsquelle; **~ of funds** Kapitalquelle, Mittelherkunft; **~ of help** Hilfsquelle; **~ of income** Einnahme-, Einkunftsquelle; **~ of information** Informationsquelle; **~ of the law** Rechtsquelle; **~ of money** Geldquelle; **~ of power** Energiequelle; **~ of profit** Einnahmequelle; **~ of refinancing** Refinanzierungsmittel; **~ of requirements** Bedarfsquelle; **~ of revenue** Steuer-, Einnahmequelle; **~ of supply** Liefer-, Versorgungs-, Bezugsstelle; **~ of taxation** Steuerquelle;
to be a ~ of liquidity liquiditätspolitische Möglichkeit darstellen; **to deduct tax at ~** Steuerabzug an der Quelle vornehmen; **to gather (know) s. th. from a good ~** etw. aus sicherer Quelle wissen; **to levy a tax on the ~** Steuer an der Quelle (Quellensteuer) erheben; **to open up new ~s** neue Quellen erschließen; **to pay a tax at the ~** Steuer gleich vom Ertrag abführen, Quellensteuer entrichten; **to tap new ~s of credit** neue Kreditquellen erschließen; **to turn to private ~s of capital** Kapitalmarktpublikum in Anspruch nehmen;

~ **book** Quellenbuch; ~ **documentation** Quellenangabe, -belegung; ~ **language** *(data processing)* vom Menschen lesbares Programm; ~ **material** Quellenmaterial, *(nuclear power)* Ausgangsstoffe; ~ **notes** Quellenangaben; ~ **and disposition statement** Verwendungsnachweis.

South|Americans *(stock exchange, Br.)* südamerikanische Staatsanleihen; ~ **Africans** *(Br.)* südafrikanische Aktien.

Southern Europe Südeuropa.

souvenir Andenken, Souvenir;
memory ~ bleibende Erinnerung;
~ **edition** Festausgabe; ~ **hunter** Andenkenjäger; ~ **shop** Geschenkartikelgeschäft.

sovereign *(gold coin)* Sovereign, Zwanzigshillinggoldstück, *(ruler)* Herrscher, Regent, Monarch, Fürst, Staatsoberhaupt;
to make s. o. ~ jem. unumschränkte Gewalt geben;
~ *(a.)* unumschränkt, souverän;
~ **emblem** Hoheitszeichen; ~ **immunity of state from liability** Haftungsausschluß bei Ausübung von Hoheitsrechten; ~ **people** Volkssouverän; ~ **power (prerogative)** unbeschränkte Hoheitsgewalt, Hoheitsrecht; ~ **rights** Hoheitsrechte; ~ **state** souveräner Staat; **to become a ~ state** Souveränität erlangen; ~ **territory** Hoheitsgebiet.

sovereignty Hoheits-, oberste Staatsgewalt, Staatshoheit, Oberherrschaft, Souveränität;
consumers' ~ Herrschaft der Verbraucherschaft, Verbraucherherrschaft; **financial** ~ Finanzhoheit; **monetary** ~ Währungshoheit; **territorial** ~ Gebietsherrschaft, -hoheit;
~ **of the air** Lufthoheit; ~ **of the consumer** Verbraucherherrschaft.

Soviet Arbeiter- und Soldatenrat, örtliche Selbstverwaltung;
~ **Government** Sowjet-, Räteregierung.

sovietization Sowjetisierung.

sovietize *(v.)* sowjetisieren.

spa Bade-, Erholungs-, Kurort.

space Raum, Platz, *(advertising, US)* Anzeigenraum, -teil, *(data processing)* Wortabstand, *(print.)* Zwischenraum, Spatium, Durchschuß, *(quantity of time)* Zeitraum, *(ship)* Schiffsraum, *(telegraphy)* Abstand, Pause, Zwischenraum, *(universe)* Weltraum, -all;
after a ~ nach einer Weile; **for a** ~ für einen bestimmten Zeitraum; **in the** ~ **of a year** binnen Jahresfrist; **with** ~ *(print.)* durchschossen;
~s *(print.)* Durchschußmaterial;
advertising ~ Reklamefläche, Anzeigenraum; **blank** ~ freie Stelle; **cargo** ~ Laderaum; **charging** ~ Stellfläche; **confined** ~ begrenzter Raum, *(parking)* enge Parklücke; **floor** ~ Bodenfläche; **housing** ~ Wohnfläche, -raum; **interstellar** ~ Tiefen des Weltraums; **living** ~ Lebensraum; **narrow** ~ enger Raum; **occupied** in Anspruch genommener Raum; **office** ~ Bürofläche; **open** ~ freie Fläche, unbebautes Gelände; **outer** ~ Weltraum; ~ **required** Platz-, Raumbedarf; **standing** ~ Stellfläche;
~ **charged against a block booking** *(US)* Anzeigenraumabnahme in Teileinheiten zum Tarif des Gesamtauftrages; ~ **on board a vessel** Schiffsraum; **limited** ~ **at one's disposal** beschränkt zur Verfügung stehender Raum; ~ **in an exhibition** Ausstellungsraum; ~ **of a month** Monatsfrist; **measurable** ~ **of time** absehbarer Zeitraum; ~ **to work** Arbeitsraum; ~ **of ten years** Zeitraum von zehn Jahren;
~ *(v.)* räumlich (zeitlich) einteilen, *(data processing)* sperren;
~ **out** gesperrt drucken, spationieren, durchschießen; ~ **out payment over several years** Zahlungen über mehrere Jahre verteilen; ~ **out the type more** mit größeren Zwischenräumen setzen;
to allow a breathing ~ Frist einräumen; **to apply for** ~ sich zu einer Messe anmelden; **to be cramped for** ~ wenig Platz haben; **to book** ~ Schiffsraum bestellen, *(advertising, US)* Anzeigenraum belegen; **to clear** ~ **on the platform for the speaker** für den Redner auf der Tribüne Platz lassen; **to contract for** ~ *(US sl.)* Anzeigenraum sicherstellen; **to devote** ~ Platz zur Verfügung stellen; **to fill out blank** ~s leere Stellen ausfüllen; **to leave a blank** ~ Zwischenraum lassen; **to put as much** ~ **as possible between the lines** möglichst großen Zwischenraum zwischen den Zeilen lassen; **to reserve** ~ Platz belegen; **to save** ~ Platz sparen; **to take** ~ **at an exhibition** Ausstellungsraum belegen, Ausstellung beschicken; **to travel through** ~ Weltraum befahren; **to word** ~ Zeile ausschließen; **to write one's name in the** ~ **indicated** seinen Namen an die bezeichnete Stelle setzen;
~ **advertisement** *(US sl.)* seitenteilige Anzeige; ~ **age** Raumfahrtzeitalter; ~ **agency** Raumfahrtsbehörde; ~ **bar** *(typewriter)* Leer-, Zwischentaste; ~ **broker** Werbungsmittler, Annoncenexpedition; ~ **budget** Raumfahrtetat; ~ **buyer** *(US*

sl.) Werbungsmittler, Mediadisponent, Anzeigenkäufer; ~ **buying** *(US sl.)* Anzeigenbelegung; ~ **capsule** Raumsonde; ~ **center** Raumfahrtzentrum; ~ **charge** *(US sl.)* Anzeigen-, Anschlags-, Streukosten; ~ **committee** Raumfahrtausschuß; ~ **communications** Weltraumnachrichtenwesen; ~ **contractor** Raumfahrtsunternehmen; ~ **demand** Raumbedarf; ~ **discount** *(advertising, US sl.)* Mengenrabatt; ~ **docking** *(spaceship)* Kopplungsmanöver; ~~-**docking arrangement** Kopplungseinrichtung für Raumfahrzeuge; ~ **expert** Raumfahrtexperte; ~ **exploration** Erforschung des Weltraums, Weltraumforschung; ~ **fee** Zeilenhonorar; ~ **fiction** Weltraumroman; ~ **flight** [bemannter] Raumflug, -fahrt; ~~-**flight center** Weltraumzentrum; ~ **heater** Raumheizgerät; ~ **helmet** Raumfahrerhelm; ~ **hole** *(advertising, US sl.)* nicht verkaufte Anzeigenfläche; ~ **industry** Raumfahrtindustrie; ~ **key** *(typewriter)* Zwischenraumtaste; ~ **lab** Weltraumlabor; ~ **launch** Raumschiffstart; ~ **law** Weltraumrecht; ~ **navigation** Raumfahrt; ~ **odyssey** Weltraumodyssee; ~ **order** *(US sl.)* Anzeigenauftrag; ~ **outlays** Aufwand für die Raumfahrt; ~ **platform** Raumstation; ~ **probe** unbemannte Raumsonde; ~ **program(me)** Raumfahrtprogramm; **unmanned** ~ **project** unbemanntes Raumfahrtvorhaben; ~ **race** Wettrennen im Weltraum; ~ **rates** *(US sl.)* Anzeigentarif, -preisliste, *(exhibition)* Ausstellungsgebühr; ~ **rental** *(exhibition)* Stand-, Platzmiete; ~ **research** Weltraumforschung; ~ **rocket** Weltraumrakete; ~ **rule** *(print.)* Querlinie; ~ **salesman** *(US sl.)* Anzeigenvertreter, -akquisiteur; ~ **satellite** Weltraumsatellit; ~ **schedule** *(US sl.)* Datenschema, Streuplan; ~ **selling** *(US sl.)* Verkauf von Anzeigenraum; ~ **service** *(communication)* Weltraumfunkdienst; ~ **shuttle** wiederverwendbarer Raumtransporter, Raumfähre; ~ **size** *(US sl.)* Anzeigengröße; ~ **station** Weltraumstation; ~ **suit** Raumfahreranzug; ~~-**time continuum** Raum-Zeit-Kontinuum; ~ **travel** Raumfahrt; ~ **travel(l)er** Weltraumfahrer; ~ **treaty** Weltraumvertrag; ~ **trip** Weltraumreise; ~ **tug** Raumtransporter; ~ **type** *(print.)* Sperrdruck; ~ **unit** Raumfahrerschutzanzug; ~ **user** Raumbenutzer; ~ **vehicle** Raumfahrzeug; ~~-**vehicle launcher** Weltraumraketenfahrzeug; ~ **workshop** Raumfahrtstation; ~ **writer** pro Zeile bezahlter Artikelschreiber.

spaceband *(print.)* Spatienkeil.

spacecraft Raumfahrzeug.

spaced durchschossen, gesperrt gesetzt (gedruckt);
double-~ doppelzeilig;
~ **composition** Sperrsatz; ~ **payment** Ratenzahlung; **in** ~ **type** gesperrt gedruckt.

spaceman Astronaut, Raumfahrer.

spaceship Raumschiff.

spacing *(print.)* Zwischenraum;
double ~ doppelter Zeilenabstand; **single-line** ~ einzeiliger Abstand;
~ **of lines** Zeilenabstand; ~ **out** Spationierung.

spacious umfangreich, geräumig, umfassend.

spade, to call a ~ **a** ~ Kind beim Namen nennen, kein Blatt vor den Mund nehmen; **to dig the first** ~ ersten Spatenstich tun.

spadework Pionierarbeit, Vorarbeiten, *(of a branch)* Umstrukturierung.

span Spanne, Spannweite;
~ **of authority (control)** Kontrollbefugnis; ~ **of life** Lebensspanne; **average** ~ **of life** Durchschnittslebenszeit; **short** ~ **of time** kurze Zeitspanne;
~~-**new** brand-, funkelnagelneu; ~~ **roof** Satteldach.

spanking|clean *(sl.)* blitzsauber; ~ **new** brandneu.

spanner Schraubenschlüssel;
to throw a ~ **into the works** Sabotageakt begehen.

spare Reserve-, Ersatzteil, Extrastück, *(sport)* Ersatzmann;
~ *(v.)* [er]sparen, erübrigen, *(abstain from infliction)* jem. etw. ersparen, *(do without)* entbehren;
~ **a defeated adversary** besiegten Gegner schonen; ~ **no expense(s)** keine Kosten scheuen; ~ **neither effort nor expense** weder Mühe noch Kosten scheuen; ~ **s. o. a gallon of petrol** jem. mit etw. Benzin aushelfen; ~ **o. s. grief** sich Kummer ersparen; ~ **s. one's life** jem. das Leben schenken; ~ **no pains** keine Mühe scheuen; ~ **the time** Zeit sparen;
to be ~**d s. th.** sich mit etw. nicht befassen müssen; **to have enough and to** ~ mehr als genug haben;
~ *(a.)* übrig, als Ersatz;
~ **anchor** Reserveanker; ~ **battery** Ersatzbatterie; ~ **bed** Gästebett; ~ **capacity** freie (ungenützte) Kapazität; **to use** ~ **capacity on scheduled flights** *(US)* nicht gebuchte Linienplätze für Teilcharter benutzen; ~ **capital** flüssiges (verfügbares) Kapital; ~ **cash** übriges Geld; ~ **copy** Reserveexemplar; ~ **diet** knappe Diät; ~ **food** überflüssige Nahrungsmittel; ~ **hand** *(man)*

Ersatzmann; **~ man** Ersatzmann; **~ meal** bescheidene Mahlzeit; **~ money** Notgroschen; **to have very little ~ money** kaum Geld erübrigen können; **~ part** Reserve-, Ersatzteil, Ersatzstück; **~-part service** Ersatzteildienst; **~-parts warehouse** Ersatzteillager; **~ room** Besuchs-, Gast-, Gäste-, Fremdenzimmer; **~ time** Freizeit; **~-time activities** Freizeitbeschäftigung, -gestaltung; **~-time job** Neben-, Freizeitbeschäftigung; **~-time work** Nebenarbeit, -beschäftigung, -tätigkeit; **~ tyres** *(Br.)* (tires, *US*) Ersatzbereifung; **~ wheel** Reservereifen, -rad.

spareness of population geringe Bevölkerungsdichte.
sparer Sparer.
sparing Sparsamkeit;
   ~ (a.) sparsam, haushälterisch.
spark Funke, *(diamond)* Diamant, *(engine)* Zündung, *(fig.)* Spur, Rest, Funke;
   ~s (sl.) Schiffsfunker;
   ~ of generosity generöse Anwandlung;
   ~ (v.) off auslösen;
   to advance the ~ Zündung vorstellen; **to strike ~s from s. o.** j. elektrisieren;
   ~ advance Frühzündung; **~ plug** *(US)* Zündkerze.
sparking plug *(Br.)* Zündkerze.
sparkle (v.) Funken sprühen.
sparkler Feuerwerk, *(fig.)* geistsprühende Persönlichkeit, *(criminal, sl.)* Brillant.
sparkling new funkelnagelneu.
sparrow cop *(sl.)* in Ungnade gefallener Polizist.
sparse population dünn gesäte Bevölkerung.
spasmodic dealings *(stock exchange)* vereinzelte Abschlüsse.
spate *(Br.)* Überschwemmung, Hochwasser, *(fig.)* Flut, Schwall, Erguß;
   ~ of new books to review Massensendung zu besprechender Bücher; **~ of orders** Auftragsstrom; **~ of strikes** massierte Streiks; **to have a ~ of work** *(fam.)* massenhaft (unendlich viel) zu tun haben.
spatial | distribution räumliche Verteilung; **~ economics** Raumwirtschaftslehre; **~ mobility of labo(u)r** regionale Arbeitskräftemobilität; **~ structure** räumlicher Zustand, Raumstruktur.
spatter (v.) with mud beschmutzen, bespritzen.
speak (v.) reden, sprechen, vortragen, Wort ergreifen, *(plead)* plädieren;
   ~ for o. s. für sich selbst sprechen, seine eigene Meinung äußern; **~ for s. th.** sich für etw. aussprechen; **~ without accent** akzentfrei sprechen; **~ by the book** vom Manuskript ablesen; **~ without book** frei sprechen; **~ broken English** gebrochen Englisch sprechen; **~ candidly** offen reden; **~ by the card** ganz präzise sein; **~ in s. one's cast** j. unterbrechen; **~ disparagingly about s. o.** sich über j. abfällig äußern; **~ extempore** aus dem Stegreif sprechen; **~ in s. one's favo(u)r** für j. eintreten; **~ highly of s. o.** anerkennend von jem. sprechen; **~ several languages** mehrere Sprachen beherrschen; **~ to s. o. about a matter** Angelegenheit mit jem. bereden; **~ one's mind clearly and to the point** sich klar und offen äußern; **~ without notes** frei sprechen; **~ off the record** sich vertraulich äußern, nicht für die Öffentlichkeit bestimmte Bemerkungen machen; **~ out** sich verbreiten (rückhaltlos aussprechen); **~ out on human rights** sich für die Menschenrechte einsetzen; **~ one's piece** Heiratsantrag machen; **~ to the point** zur Sache sprechen; **~ in public** öffentlich reden; **~ to a passing ship** Flaggenaustausch mit einem vorüberfahrenden Schiff vornehmen; **~ to the subject** beim Thema bleiben; **~ in support of s. th.** sich für etw. aussprechen; **~ out of turn** von der allgemeinen Sprachregelung abweichen; **~ up for s. o.** sich für j. einsetzen; **~ volumes** Bände sprechen; **~ to the wall** gegen eine Wand reden; **~ not a word** keine Silbe reden;
   to call upon s. o. to ~ jem. das Wort erteilen;
   nothing to ~ of nichts Erwähnenswertes.
speakeasy *(US sl.)* unerlaubter Alkoholausschank, Flüsterkneipe.
speaker Sprecher, Redner, Wortführer, *(fig.)* Sprachrohr, *(parl.)* Vorsitzender, Präsident;
   Mr. ~! Herr Vorsitzender!; **previous ~** Vorredner;
   to be a good ~ redegewandt sein; **to be a poor ~** schlechter Redner sein; **to confuse a ~ with interruptions** Redner mit Zwischenrufen aus dem Konzept bringen;
   to try to catch the ~'s eye ums Wort bitten;
   ~'s ruling Entscheidung des Parlamentspräsidenten.
speakership Amt des Sprechers, Sprecherfunktion.
speakie *(sl.)* Tonfilm.
speaking Sprechen, Redekunst;
   generally ~ allgemein genommen; **humanly ~** nach menschlichen Begriffen; **strictly ~** genau genommen;

~ to one present *(law)* mündliche Erklärung unter Anwesenden; **~ with prosecutor** *(defendant, Br.)* Bitte um Strafmilderung;
to be good at ~ in public guter Volksredner sein;
~ (a.) (tel.) am Apparat;
   ~ ability Darlegungsfähigkeit; **~ acquaintance** flüchtige Bekanntschaft; **~ clock** *(tel.)* Gesprächsuhr; **English-~ countries** englisch-sprechende Länder; **~ course in public** Kurs für freies Sprechen; **~ demurrer** Rüge der fehlenden Schlüssigkeit; **~ engagement** Vortragsverpflichtung; **~ fee** Vortragshonorar; **~ order** Erläuterungsbeschluß; **to be not on ~ terms with s. o.** mit jem. nicht auf Gesprächsfuß stehen; **~ tour** Vortragsreise; **~ trumpet** Megaphon; **~ tube** Sprachrohr.
spearhead *(mil.)* Vorausabteilung, Angriffsspitze;
   ~ (v.) an offensive an der Spitze einer Offensive fahren.
spec *(coll.)* Spekulation;
on ~ auf gut Glück.
special Sonderprogramm, *(constable)* Hilfspolizist, *(correspondent)* Sonderberichterstatter, *(examination)* Sonderprüfung, *(newspaper)* Extrablatt, *(railway)* Sonderzug;
   ~ (a.) speziell, ungewöhnlich, eigentümlich, individuell, besonders;
   ~ ability besondere Eignung; **~ acceptance** eingeschränktes Akzept; **~ account** Sonder-, Separatkonto; **~ act** Sondergesetz; **~ action** Sonderaktion; **~ additional charge** Sonderzuschlag; **~ administration** Verwaltung eines bestimmten Nachlaßteils, gegenständlich beschränkte Nachlaßverwaltung; **~ administrator** Sonderbeauftragter; **~ advances** Sondervorschüsse; **~ advice** Separatanzeige; **~ agency** Sonderorganisation; **~ agent** Sonderbevollmächtigter; **~ agreement** Einzelschiedsvertrag; **~ allowance** Sondervergütung; **~ announcement** *(radio)* Sondermeldung; **~ appearance** Einrede der Unzuständigkeit; **~ area** *(Br.)* Förder-, Notstandsgebiet; **~ Areas Scheme** *(Br.)* Notstandsgesetz; **~ argument** Beweisaufnahme für besondere Fälle; **~ arrangement** Sondervereinbarung; **~ assessment** *(municipal accounting, US)* zweckgebundene Abgabe, Sonderumlage, -ausgabe [für Anliegerkosten]; **~ assessment bonds** *(US)* kommunale Schuldverschreibungen; **~ assessment fund** *(municipal accounting, US)* Meliorationsfonds; **~ assignment** Anweisung zur Befriedigung einzelner Gläubiger; **~ assistant** Sonderberater; **~ assumpsit** Schadensersatz wegen Nichterfüllung; **~ audit** außerplanmäßige Revision; **~ authorization** Sondergenehmigung; **~ bail** zugelassene Kaution; **~ bailiff** *(US)* beauftragter Gerichtsvollzieher, Zustellungsbeamter; **~ bargain** Sonderangebot; **~ bastard** nachträglich legitimiertes (für ehelich erklärtes) Kind; **~ benefit** Enteignungsentschädigung; **~ bill** *(Br.)* privater Gesetzentwurf; **~ bond** Sonderschuldverschreibung; **~ bonus** Sonderzulage; **~ branch** *(secret police)* Sonderabteilung, *(trade)* Spezialität, Fachgebiet; **~ business** besonderer Tagesordnungspunkt; **~ buyer** *(Br.)* Beauftragter der Bank von England auf dem Diskontmarkt, Schatzwechselmakler; **~ calendar** Sofortliste; **~ capital** Kommanditkapital; **~ care** besondere Sorgfalt; **~ carrier** Gelegenheitsspediteur; **~ case** Sonderfall, *(law)* Ausnahmefall; **~ charge** Sondergebühr, Sonderabgabe, *(to jurors)* erbetene Rechtsbelehrung; **~ checking account** gebührenpflichtiges Scheckkonto; **~ colo(u)r** Spezialfarbe; **~ commission** *(Br.)* Sonderausschuß; **~ commissioners** Sonderbeauftragter, *(income tax, Br.)* Veranlagungsstelle, Beschwerdestelle in Einkommensteuerangelegenheiten; **~ committee** Sonderausschuß; **~ concessions** Sonderkonzessionen; **~ conditions** Sonderbestimmungen; **~ constable** *(US)* Hilfspolizist; **~ consultant** Fachberater; **~ contingency reserve** Sonderrücklage, besondere Rücklage; **~ contract** gesicherter Vertrag; **~ contribution** Sonderbeitrag, -abgabe, *(Br.)* Sonderumlage der Industrie; **~ correspondent** Spezial-, Sonderberichterstatter; **~ cost** spezifische Kosten; **~ count** substantiierte Klagebegründung; **~ course of study** Sonderstudium; **~ court-martial** Sonderkriegsgericht; **~ covenant** Sondervereinbarung; **~ credit operation** *(International Monetary Fund)* Sonderkredit; **~ crossing** *(cheque, Br.)* besondere Scheckkreuzung; **~ custom** Platzusance; **~ damage** konkreter Schaden, Schaden im Einzelfall; **~ damages** zusätzlicher ([besonders] nachzuweisender) Schadenersatzanspruch; **~ day** bestimmter Tag.
special delivery *(US)* Eilzustellung;
by ~ *(US)* durch Eilboten;
   ~ envelope *(US)* Eilbriefumschlag; **~ fee** *(US)* Eilzustellungsgebühr; **~ letter** *(US)* Eilbrief; **~ mail** *(US)* Eilpostsendungen; **~ mailman** *(US)* Eilpostzusteller.
special | demurrer auf Formfehler gegründeter Einwand, prozessuale Einrede; **~ deposit** festes Depot; **~ deposits with the Bank**

of England vorgeschriebene Mindestreserven; ~ **deputy** Sonderbevollmächtigter; ~ **device** Zusatzeinrichtung; ~ **dictionary** Fach-, Spezialwörterbuch; ~ **discount** Sonderrabatt; ~ **dividend** außerordentliche Dividende, Superdividende, Bonus; ~ **drawing account** *(International Monetary Fund)* Sonderziehungskonto, Konto für Sonderziehungen; ~ **drawing rights** *(International Monetary Fund)* Sonderziehungsrechte; **to allocate** ~ **drawing rights** Sonderziehungsrechte zuteilen; ~ **drawing rights issue** Ausgabe von Sonderziehungsrechten; ~ **duties** *(mil.)* Ersatzdienst; ~ **edition** *(book)* Sonderausgabe, *(newspaper)* Sondernummer, Extrablatt; ~ **election** Nachwahl; ~ **emissary** Sonderbotschafter; ~ **endorsement** Vollgiro, volles Wechselgiro; ~ **equipment** Sonderausrüstung, -ausstattung; ~ **error** Erwiderung im Revisionsverfahren; ~ **event** Veranstaltung; ~ **examiner** beauftragter Vernehmungsrichter; ~ **exception** *(cause of action)* Formalrüge, Formaleinwand; ~ **execution** vollstreckbare Ausfertigung; ~ **executor** Nachlaßverwalter für einen bestimmten Nachlaßteil; ~ **expenditure** Sonderausgaben; ~ **facts rule** *(corporation law)* Offenbarungspflicht in Sonderfällen; ~ **favo(u)r** Sondervergünstigung; ~ **feature** Besonderheit; ~ **fee** Sondergebühr; ~ **finding** Geschworenenurteil in Einzelfragen; ~ **force** *(mil.)* Sondereinheit; ~ **friend** Busenfreund; ~ **fund** Sonderfonds; **to be placed in a** ~ **fund** einem Sonderfonds zufließen; **by** ~ **grace** auf dem Gnadenwege; ~ **guarantee** *(US)* Kreditbürgschaft; ~ **guardian** Mitvormund; ~ **handling** *(US, postal service)* Einschreiben, eigenhändig, persönlich; ~-**handling parcel** *(US)* Schnellpaket; ~ **hardship allowance** Beihilfe in besonderen Härtefällen; ~ **hazard** *(fire insurance)* Sonderrisiko [bei Industrieversicherungen]; ~ **hospital** Spezialkrankenhaus; ~ **hours** Überschreitung der Arbeitszeit; ~ **impression** Separat-, Sonderdruck; ~ **indorsement** Vollgiro; ~ **injunction** einstweilige Verfügung, gerichtliche Verwarnung; ~ **insurance** zusätzliche Transportversicherung; ~ **interests** Sonderinteressen, *(US)* Sonderbegünstigte; ~-**interest department** *(US)* Sparkassenabteilung; ~ **issue** Sondereinwand; ~ **items including reserves** Sonderposten mit Rücklageanteil; ~ **jurisdiction** Sondergerichtsbarkeit; ~ **knowledge required** erforderliche Spezialkenntnisse; ~ **language** Sonder-, Fachsprache; ~ **law** Neben-, Privatgesetz; ~ **leave** Sonderurlaub; ~ **legacy** Sondervermächtnis; ~ **legislation** *(US)* Sondergesetzgebung, Gesetzgebung zur Förderung von Sonderinteressen; ~ **levy** Sonderabgabe, besondere Umlage; ~ **licence** Sondergenehmigung, *(marriage, Br.)* besondere Heiratsgenehmigung; ~ **lien** Pfandrecht an einer bestimmten Sache, Zurückhaltungsrecht; ~ **limitation** selbsttätige Beendigung eines Nutzungsrechtes; ~ **line** Spezialfach; ~ **lines** Spezialartikel; ~ **majority** qualifizierte Mehrheit; ~ **malice** auf eine bestimmte Person gerichtete böse Absicht; ~ **manager** *(company, Br.)* Liquidator; ~ **master** Gerichtsbeauftragter; ~ **matter** *(defendant)* besonderes Beweismaterial; ~ **meeting** außerordentliche Generalversammlung; ~ **messenger** *(US)* Eil-, Expreßbote; ~ **mission** Sondermission; ~ **notice** Mitteilung über die Einberufung zur Hauptversammlung; ~ **number** Sondernummer; ~ **occasion** besondere Gelegenheit; ~ **occupant** *(US)* treuhänderisch besitzender Erbe, Sonderrechtsnachfolger; ~ **offer** Sonderangebot; ~ **offering** *(securities market)* Sonderangebot; ~ **order** Sonder-, Fabrikationsauftrag; ~ **orders** *(mil.)* Routineverfügungen; ~ **owner** vorübergehender Eigentümer, Eigentümer auf Zeit; ~ **package** Sonderpackung; ~ **page** Sonderseite; ~ **paper** *(law court, Br.)* Liste von Sonderterminen; ~ **partner** beschränkt haftender Teilhaber (Gesellschafter), Kommandist; ~ **partnership** Handelsgesellschaft zur Durchführung einer einmaligen Transaktion, Gelegenheitsgesellschaft; ~ **pass** Sonderausweis; ~ **performance** Sondervorstellung; ~ **permission** Sondererlaubnis; ~ **permit** Ausnahmegenehmigung; ~ **place** *(negotiable instrument)* Zahlstelle; ~ **plane** Sonderflugzeug; ~ **plea** besondere Einrede; ~ **pleader** beratender Anwalt; ~ **pleading** qualifizierte Klageleugnung, *(US)* Eintreten für besondere Interessen; ~ **police unit** polizeiliches Sonderkommando, Sonderpolizeieinheit; ~ **position** *(advertising)* bevorzugte Plazierung, Vorzugsplazierung; ~ **power** Sondervollmacht; ~ **price** Vorzugspreis; ~ **privilege** Sondervorrecht; ~ **proceeding** Sonderverfahren; ~ **property** beschränktes Eigentum, eingeschränktes Besitzverhältnis, Fremdbesitz, Sondervermögen, zeitweiliges Verfügungsrecht; ~ **provisions** Sondervorschriften; ~-**purpose financial statement** Finanzstatus für besondere Zwecke; ~ **quota** Sonderkontingent; ~ **rate** *(advertising)* Sonder-, Vorzugstarif; ~ **reasons** *(disqualification)* Ausnahmegründe; ~ **reduction** Sonderrabatt; ~ **register** *(labo(u)r law, Br.)* Sonderverzeichnis [von Arbeitnehmerorganisationen]; ~ **registration** *(voters)* Sondereintragung;

~ **replication** erneutes Vorbringen; ~ **report** Sonderbericht; ~ **representative** *(US)* Sonderbeauftragter; ~ **request** spezifische Bitte; ~ **requirements** Sonderwünsche, -vorschriften; ~ **reserve** Sonderrückstellung, -lage; ~ **resolution** *(bankruptcy, company meeting, Br.)* qualifizierter Mehrheitsbeschluß aller Stimmberechtigter; ~ **restraint of trade** auf bestimmte Gebiete beschränktes (beruflich oder geographisch abgegrenztes) Konkurrenzverbot; ~ **retainer** Sondervollmacht, *(fee)* Sonderhonorar; ~ **revenue** *(state)* Sondereinnahmen; ~ **revenue fund** *(municipal accounting)* Fonds zur Finanzierung von Sonderaufgaben; ~ **risk** tätigkeitsbedingtes Risiko; ~-**risk policy** kurzfristige Versicherungspolice für ein besonderes Risiko; ~ **road** *(Br.)* Autobahn; ~ **rule** Sonderbestimmung; ~ **rules of law** gesetzliche Sonderbestimmungen; ~ **sales price** Ausverkaufspreis; ~ **school** Sonderschule; ~ **section** Sonderabhandlung, *(newspaper)* Rubrik; ♀ **Senate Committee** *(US)* Sonderausschuß des Senats; ~ **service school** *(mil.)* Kampf-, Waffenschule; ~ **service tariff** Sondertarif; ~ **session** *(justice of peace, Br.)* außerordentliche Sitzung; ~ **settlement** *(stock exchange, Br.)* Sonderabrechnung; ~ **settling day** *(Br.)* Sonderliquidationstag; ~ **show** Sonderschau, -ausstellung; ~ **squad** Sonderkommando; ~ **stamp** Sondermarke; ~ **statute** Sonder-, Privatgesetz; ~ **steel** Edelstahl; ~ **stocks** *(US)* Spezialwerte, Favoriten; ~ **subject** Spezialgebiet, Wahlfach; ~ **supplement** Sonderbeilage; ~ **tariff** Ausnahme-, Sondertarif; ~ **tax** Sondersteuer; ~ **term** *(law court, US)* Verhandlung vor dem Einzelrichter; ~ **terms** Sonderbedingungen, *(books)* Partiepreis; ~ **trade** Spezialhandel; ~ **train** Sonder-, Extrazug; **to put on** ~ **trains** Sonderzüge einsetzen; ~ **training** Sonder-, Fachausbildung; ~ **traverse** substantiiertes Bestreiten; ~ **treatment** Sonderbehandlung; ~ **trouble** außergewöhnliche Mühe; ~ **trust** Treuhandverhältnis zur Vornahme einer einmaligen Aufgabe, *(US)* [einfache] Hinterlegungsstelle; ~ **verdict** *(jurors)* Tatsachenfeststellung; ~ **warranty** Einspruchsverzicht des Veräußerers für sich und seine Erben; ~ **window display** *(bookseller)* Sonderfenster; ~ **wrapping** Sonderverpackung.

specialism Spezialistentum, *(special subject)* Spezialgebiet, -fach.

specialist Fachmann, -arbeiter, Spezialist, Sachverständiger, *(doctor)* Fach-, Spezialarzt, *(US, stock exchange)* Börsenmitglied der New Yorker Börse, Kursmakler;
~s Fachkreise;
accounting ~ Buchprüfungsspezialist; **ear-nose-and-throat** ~ Hals-Nasen-Ohren-Arzt; **eye** ~ Augenarzt; **radio and television** ~ Fachgeschäft für Radio und Fernsehen;
~ **in the property field** Immobilienfachmann;
to become a ~ **in s. th.** sich auf etw. spezialisieren;
~ **broker** *(New York stock market)* Börsenmakler; ~ **buyer** Facheinkäufer; ~ **course** Fachlehrgang; ~ **circles** Fachkreise; ~ **staff** Fachkräfte; ~ **staff appointments** Stabstätigkeit für Spezialisten; ~ **teacher** Fachlehrer; ~ **writer** Sonder-, Spezialberichterstatter.

specialistic fachmännisch.

specialities *(stock exchange, Br.)* Spezialwerte.

speciality besonderes Merkmal, Spezialität.

specialization Spezialisierung, Fachrichtung;
commodity ~ Warenspezialisierung; **functional** ~ Aufgabenspezialisierung;
~ **of machines** Maschinentypisierung.

specialize *(v.)* einzeln aufführen, substantiieren, spezialisieren;
~ **in (on)** [sich] spezialisieren, als Spezialfach betreiben, sich auf ein bestimmtes Gebiet beschränken; ~ **an accusation** Anschuldigung präzisieren; ~ **in an article** sich auf einen Artikel spezialisieren; ~ **a check** *(US)* (cheque, Br.) Scheckeinlösung auf einen bestimmten Empfänger beschränken; ~ **one's studies** sein Studium auf ein bestimmtes Gebiet beschränken.

specialized fachkundig, -männisch;
~ **agencies** *(UN)* Sonderorganisationen; ~ **fair** Fachmesse; ~ **industries** Staatsbetriebe; ~ **knowledge** Sonder-, Fach-, Spezialkenntnisse; ~ **study** Fachstudium; ~ **trade** Fachhandel; ~ **ward** *(hospital)* Spezialabteilung; ~ **worker** Facharbeiter.

specialties *(advertising)* Werbegeschenke, *(stock exchange, US)* Spezialwerte.

specialty Besonderheit, *(Br., contract)* formgebundener Vertrag, notarielle Urkunde, *(goods)* Neuheit, Spezialität, Spezialartikel, *(special pursuit)* Spezial-, Fachgebiet, Spezialfach;
~ **contract** formbedürftiger (gesiegelter) Vertrag; ~ **dealer** Novitätenhändler; ~ **debt** verbriefte Forderung; ~ **gift** Werbegeschenk; ~ **goods** Speziesachen, Marken-, Spezialartikel; ~ **manufacturer** Fabrikant von Spezialartikeln; ~ **product** Spezialerzeugnis, -produkt; ~ **salesman** Spezialitätenverkäufer; ~ **selling** Verkauf von Spezialartikeln; ~ **shop (store,** *US)*

Spezial[artikel]-, Spezialitätengeschäft; **departmental ~ store** Gemischtwarengeschäft; **large ~ store** Waren-, Kaufhaus; ~ **value** Neuheitswert; ~ **work** Spezialgebiet.

specie Hart-, Metallgeld, bares Geld, Bargeld, klingende Münze, gemünztes Geld, Münzsorte;
to pay in ~ in klingender (barer) Münze zahlen;
~ **account** Sortenkonto; ~ **consignment** Barsendung; ~ **payment** Zahlung in Gold; ~ **point** Goldpunkt; ~ **remittance** Geldsendung.

species Art, Sorte, Gattung;
vanishing ~ aussterbende Rasse;
~ **of crime** Verbrechenstyp.

specific spezifisch, besonders, ausdrücklich, fest umrissen, bestimmt, genau formuliert, *(grant)* zweckgebunden, *(precise)* präzise, konkret, kennzeichnend;
be ~! Einzelheiten sind anzugeben!;
~ **aim** besonderer Zweck; ~ **amount** bestimmter Betrag; ~ **bequest** Einzelvermächtnis; **in each ~ case** in jedem Einzelfall; ~ **cause** genau angegebener Grund; ~ **cost** direkte Kosten, Einzelkosten; ~ **denial** begründetes Bestreiten; ~ **deposit** Sonderdepot; ~ **devise** Grundstücksvermächtnis; ~ **duty** *(customs)* Mengen-, Maß-, Stück-, Gewichtszoll, *(special fee)* Sondergebühr; ~ **factor of production** nicht auswechselbarer Produktionsfaktor; ~ **gravity** spezifisches Gewicht; ~ **guaranty** *(US)* Einzelbürgschaft; ~ **legacy** Einzelvermächtnis; ~ **legatee** Sondervermächtnisnehmer; ~ **lien** Zurückbehaltungsrecht, Pfandrecht an einer bestimmten Sache; ~ **name** Gattungsname; ~ **obligation** Speziesschuld; ~ **order** Sonderauftrag; ~**-order cost system** Kostenrechnungssystem für auftragsweise Fertigung; ~ **performance** effektive (vertragsgemäße) Erfüllung, Vertragserfüllung, Naturalleistung; ~ **power [of attorney]** Sondervollmacht; ~ **purpose** Sonderzweck; ~ **rate** *(statistics)* spezifische Verhältnisziffer; ~ **restitution of property** Rückgabe eines bestimmten Vermögensgegenstandes; ~ **statement** ausdrückliche Erklärung; ~ **tariff** Mengentarif, Stückzoll; ~ **tax** Mengensteuer.

specification *(bill of specie)* Sortenzettel, *(full particulars)* genaue Angabe, Einzelaufstellung, Spezifikation, *(law of personal property)* Eigentumserwerb durch Verarbeitung, *(military law)* detaillierte Anklageschrift, *(patent)* Patentbeschreibung, -schrift, *(securities)* namentliches Stückeverzeichnis, *(detailed statement)* Einzelnachweis, nähere Bestimmung;
~**s** *(building estimate)* Baukostenvoranschlag, *(conditions of contract)* Ausschreibungsbedingungen, *(inventory)* Stückeverzeichnis, *(tender)* Angebotsunterlagen, Leistungsverzeichnis;
acceptance ~**s** Abnahmebestimmungen; **building** ~**s** Ausschreibungsbedingungen, Baukostenvoranschlag; **complete ~** *(patent law)* komplette Patentbeschreibung; **export ~** *(Br.)* Ausfuhrerklärung; **job ~** *(US)* Arbeitsplatzbeschreibung; **patent ~** Patentbeschreibung;
~**s for building a garage** Kostenvoranschlag für einen Garagenbau; ~**s of a car** technische Daten eines Autos; ~ **of content** Inhaltsangabe; ~**s of a contract** Vertragsbestimmungen; ~ **of disbursements** Spesen-, Auslagenaufstellung; ~ **of errors** Namhaftmachung der Revisionsgründe; ~ **of grounds of opposition to a bankrupt's discharge** Aufführung der Gründe gegen die Entlastung des Konkursschuldners; ~ **of merchandise** Warendeklaration; ~ **of numbers** Nummernverzeichnis; ~ **of a patent** Patentbeschreibung; ~ **of the points of issue** Aufführung der strittigen Punkte; ~ **as to quantity, weight, measurement and size** Spezifikationen nach Menge, Gewicht sowie Maß und Größe; ~ **of weight** Gewichtsnota; ~ **of witnesses** Zeugenbenennung; ~**s of work to be done** Submissions-, Ausschreibungsbedingungen;
to manufacture by customer's ~ einzeln anfertigen;
~ **bias** systematischer Ansatzfehler; ~ **cost** Standardkosten.

specified vorgesehen, bestimmt;
~ **below** nachstehend aufgeführt;
~ **account** detaillierte (spezifizierte) Rechnung; ~ **currencies** *(exchange control regulations, Br.)* spezifizierte Währungen; ~ **date** bestimmter Zeitpunkt; ~ **goods** Speziessachen; ~ **in instalments** in festgesetzten Raten; ~ **period** vereinbarte Frist; **for a ~ purpose** für einen bestimmten Zweck; ~ **reserve assets** vorgeschriebene liquide Anlageformen.

specify | *(v.)* näher (einzeln) angeben, spezifizieren, detaillieren, detailliert aufführen, stückweise benennen, genau bezeichnen, *(condition)* zur Bedingung machen;
~ **in an arrangement** vertraglich vorsehen; ~ **items** Posten einzeln aufführen; ~ **a place of payment** Zahlungsort angeben; ~ **red tiles for a roof** rote Dachziegel im Bauauftrag vorschreiben; ~ **a time** Zeitpunkt festsetzen.

specimen Muster, Muster-, Probestück, -exemplar, *(print.)* Probe, *(of raw material)* Rohstoff-, Materialprobe;
type ~ *(data processing)* Schriftmuster;
~ **of [one's] handwriting** Schrift-, Handschriftenprobe; ~ **of signature** Unterschriftsprobe; ~ **of type** Schrift-, Satzprobe;
~ **book** Musterbuch; **type ~ book** *(data processing)* Schriftmusterbuch; ~ **copy** Probe-, Ansichts-, Gratis-, Belegexemplar, Probenummer; ~ **form** Formularmuster; ~ **form of notice** Benachrichtigungsmuster; ~ **letter** Musterbrief; ~ **number** Probenummer; ~ **page** Probeseite, -druck; ~ **rate** Vorzugssatz; ~ **signature** Unterschriftsprobe; ~ **volume** Probedruck.

specious scheinbar, trügerisch;
~ **argument** Scheinargument; ~ **claim** plausibler Anspruch; ~ **person** Blender; ~ **reasoning** bestehende Begründung.

spectacle Schauspiel, Sehenswürdigkeit;
~**s** Brille;
to make a ~ of o. s. unangenehm auffallen; **to see everything through rose-colo(u)red ~s** alles durch eine rosarote Brille sehen;
~ **case** Brillenfutteral.

spectacular *(advertising)* Werbegroßanlage, bewegliche Leuchtwerbung, *(newspaper advertisement)* großformatige Anzeige, *(television)* Superfernsehschau, *(theater)* Ausstattungsstück;
~ *(a.)* grandios, pompös;
~ **display of fireworks** phantastisches Feuerwerk.

spectator Zuschauer, Beobachter, Besucher;
unconcerned ~ unbeteiligter Zuschauer;
~ **who pays** zahlender Zuschauer.

spectre *(Br.)* **specter** *(US)* Phantom, Geist, *(fig.)* Schreckgespenst;
to raise the ~ of redundancies Gespenst der Arbeitslosigkeit heraufbeschwören.

spectrum Spektrum, *(fig.)* Bereich, Skala;
whole ~ of demands ganze Palette von Forderungen;
to span the entire left-right ~ gesamtes Spektrum von links bis rechts umfassen.

speculate *(v.)* *(business)* spekulieren, gewagte Geschäfte machen;
~ **in atomic shares** mit Atomaktien spekulieren; ~ **for differences** *(Br.)* mit Kursunterschieden spekulieren, Spekulations-, Differenzgeschäfte machen; ~ **on (for) a fall (rise)** auf Baisse (Hausse) spekulieren; ~ **about the future of humanity** über die Zukunft der menschlichen Rasse nachgrübeln; ~ **on the stock exchange** an der Börse spekulieren; ~ **on the wrong side** falsch spekulieren.

speculating spekulierend;
~ **in contangos** Reportgeschäft;
~ **manoeuvre** Spekulationsmanöver; ~ **transactions** Spekulationsgeschäfte.

speculation Betrachtung, Grübeln, *(business)* Spekulation, gewagtes Unternehmen;
on ~ spekulationsweise;
bad ~ Fehlspekulation; **bear[ish] ~** Baissespekulation; **bull ~** Haussespekulation; **currency (exchange) ~** Währungsspekulation; **good ~** Börsencoup; **hazardous ~** gewagte Spekulation; **profitable ~** gewinnbringende Spekulation; **unbridled ~** zügellose Spekulation; **unlucky ~** verfehlte Spekulation, Fehlspekulation; **wrong ~** Fehlspekulation;
~ **for a fall** Baissespekulation; ~ **in futures** Terminspekulation; ~ **in gold** Goldspekulation; ~ **on price** Preis-, Kursspekulation; ~ **in real estate (land)** Grundstücks-, Terrainspekulation; ~ **for a rise** Haussespekulation; ~ **in stocks** *(US)* Aktienspekulation; ~ **on the stock exchange** Börsenspekulation;
to be given to ~ zum Grübeln neigen; **to buy s. th. on (as a) ~** etw. zu Spekulationszwecken kaufen; **to finance ~** Spekulationsgeschäfte finanzieren; **to lose by ~** durch Spekulationen verlieren; **to make some bad ~s** einige Fehlspekulationen vornehmen; **to turn out a good ~** sich als erfolgreiche Spekulation erweisen.

speculative spekulativ, *(enterprising)* unternehmend, *(theoretical)* theoretisch;
to buy for a ~ account auf Spekulation kaufen; ~ **builder** unseriöser Bauunternehmer; ~ **buying** Spekulations-, Meinungskäufe; ~ **credit** Spekulationskredit; ~ **cycle** Kreislauf der Spekulation; ~ **damages** vorausberechneter Schadensersatz, Ersatz für vermeintliche Folgeschäden; ~ **dealer** Spekulant; ~ **descriptions** Spekulationspapiere; ~ **enterprise** Risikogeschäft, riskantes Unternehmen; ~ **gain** Spekulationsgewinn; ~ **interest** Spekulationsinteresse; ~ **investments** spekulative Kapitalanlagen; ~ **merchant** wagemütiger Kaufmann; ~ **money** Spekulationsgelder; ~ **motive** Spekulationsmoment, *(cash management)* Spekulationsmotiv; ~ **operation** Spekulationsge-

schäft; ~ **pressure** Spekulationsdruck; ~ **price** Spekulationskurs, -preis; ~ **profit** Spekulationsgewinn; ~ **purchases** Spekulations-, Meinungskäufe; ~ **purpose** Spekulationszweck; ~ **sales (selling)** Meinungsverkäufe; ~ **security** Spekulationspapier; ~ **spirit** Spekulationslust; ~ **stock** *(US)* Spekulationsaktie, -papier; ~ **transaction** Spekulationsgeschäft; ~ **underwriting** Spekulationsversicherung; ~ **value** Spekulationswert; ~ **venture** riskantes (gewagtes) Unternehmen.

speculativeness Spekulationslust, *(enterprising spirit)* Unternehmungsgeist.

speculator [Börsen]spekulant, *(ticket seller)* Schwarzhändler; **currency (exchange)** ~ Währungsspekulant; **land** ~ Grundstücksspekulant; **professional** ~ berufsmäßiger Spekulant; ~ **for a fall** Baissespekulant; ~ **in property** Grundstücksspekulant; ~ **for a rise** Haussespekulant; ~ **outside the stock exchange** Winkelbörsenspekulant.

speech Rede, Ansprache, Darlegungen, Ausführungen; ~es *(Br.)* Entscheidungen des Oberhauses; **after-dinner** ~ Tischrede; **attorney's** ~ *(US)* [Anwalts]plädoyer; **bombastic** ~ schwülstige Rede; **canned** ~ auf Band aufgenommene Rede; **capital** ~ ausgezeichnete Rede; **closing** ~ Schlußansprache; **counsel's** ~ *(Br.)* [Anwalts]plädoyer; **defence** ~ Plädoyer des Strafverteidigers; **election** ~ Wahlrede; **extemporaneous** ~ unvorbereitete Ansprache, Stegreifansprache, -rede; **farewell** ~ Abschiedsrede; **flat** ~ inhaltslose Rede; **high-flown** ~ bombastische (schwülstige) Rede; **inaugural** ~ Antrittsrede; **inflammatory** ~ aufrührerische Ansprache, Hetzrede; **keynote** ~ grundlegende (programmatische) Rede; **maiden** ~ *(parl.)* Jungfernrede; **morale-boosting** ~ Durchhalterede; **opening** ~ Eröffnungsrede, -ansprache; **postprandial** ~ Rede nach Tisch; **salt** ~ scharfe Rede; **spread-eagle** ~ *(US)* chauvinistische Rede; **stirring** ~ mitreißende Rede; **undelivered** ~ nicht gehaltene Rede; **virulent** ~ Hetzrede; ~ **for the defence** Plädoyer des Strafverteidigers, Anwaltsplädoyer; **Queen's** ~ **from the throne** Thronrede; **to broadcast a** ~ Rede durch Rundfunk übertragen; **to deliver a** ~ Ansprache (Rede) halten; **to frame a** ~ Rede aufsetzen (entwerfen); **to get stuck in the middle of a** ~ mitten in einer Rede steckenbleiben; **to give s. one's** ~ **a hostile reception** jds. Rede ungünstig aufnehmen; **to have** ~ **with s. o.** mit jem. Rücksprache nehmen; **to interrupt s. o. in his** ~ jds. Rede unterbrechen; **to know s. o. by his** ~ j. an seiner Sprache erkennen; **to lay an embargo on free** ~ Redefreiheit beschränken; **to make a** ~ Rede (Ansprache) halten; **to open a** ~ Rede beginnen; **to pad a** ~ Rede aufbauschen; **to pitch a** ~ **on s. th.** Rede auf etw. abstimmen; **to proceed with one's** ~ mit seiner Rede fortfahren; **to recover one's** ~ Sprache wiedergewinnen; **to run off a** ~ Rede herunterrasseln; **to tag one's** ~ **with verses** in seine Rede Verse einflechten; **to take down a** ~ **in shorthand** Ansprache mit stenographieren; **to wind up one's** ~ seine Rede beschließen; ~ **area** Sprachraum-, gebiet; ~ **balloon** Sprechblase; ~ **center** *(US)* **(centre,** *Br.)* sprachlicher Mittelpunkt; ~ **circuit** *(tel.)* Sprechkreis; ~ **clinic** Sprachklinik; ~ **community** Sprachgruppe; ~ **correction** Sprachkorrektur; ~ **course** Rednerkursus; ~ **day** *(school, Br.)* Jahresschlußfeier; ~ **defect** Sprachfehler; ~ **island** Sprachinsel; ~ **map** Sprachenkarte; ~ **technique** Fertigkeiten des mündlichen Vortrags, Vortragskunst; ~ **tempo** Redetempo; ~ **writer** Ansprachenverfasser, Dichter.

speechify *(v.)* große Reden schwingen.

speechless, to be keine Worte finden, sprachlos sein.

speed Schnelligkeit, Geschwindigkeit, Eile, Tempo, *(photo)* Verschlußgeschwindigkeit, *(railway)* Streckengeschwindigkeit; **at a** ~ **of 30 miles an hour** mit einer Geschwindigkeit von 50 Stundenkilometern; **at a great** ~ in schnellem Tempo; **average** ~ Durchschnittsgeschwindigkeit; **average day-time** ~ tagsüber durchschnittlich erzielte Geschwindigkeit; **breakneck** ~ halsbrecherisches Tempo, halsbrecherische Geschwindigkeit; **cruising** ~ *(airplane, car)* Dauer-, Reisegeschwindigkeit; **excessive** ~ überhöhte Geschwindigkeit; **full** ~ **ahead** volle Kraft voraus; **ground** ~ Geschwindigkeit über Grund; **high** ~ hohe Geschwindigkeit; **less** ~ geringe Geschwindigkeit; **low** ~ geringe Geschwindigkeit; **maximum** ~ Höchstgeschwindigkeit; **permissible** ~ zulässige Höchstgeschwindigkeit; **stalling** ~ *(airplane)* kritische Geschwindigkeit; **scheduled** ~ *(train, US)* fahrplanmäßige Geschwindigkeit; **top** ~ Höchstgeschwindigkeit; ~ **of loading** Ladetempo; **twice the** ~ **of sound** doppelte Schallgeschwindigkeit; ~ **of turnover** Umsatzgeschwindigkeit, Umschlagshäufigkeit;

~ *(v.)* **a parting guest** Gast verabschieden; ~ **down a street** Straße herunterrasen; ~ **up** Geschwindigkeit erhöhen, Tempo steigern, *(engine)* auf Touren bringen, *(increase performance)* zur höchsten Leistung anspornen; ~ **up production** Produktionsausstoß erhöhen, beschleunigen; ~ **up the train service** Zugverbindungen beschleunigen; **to be going at top** ~ in voller Fahrt sein; **to corner at** ~ um die Ecke flitzen; **to cut** ~ Geschwindigkeit herabsetzen; **to gain (gather)** ~ schneller werden; **to go at full** ~ mit höchster Geschwindigkeit fahren; **to increase** ~ Geschwindigkeit erhöhen, *(ship)* Fahrt vermehren; **to lessen (lower)** ~ Geschwindigkeit verlangsamen (herabsetzen); **to maintain a** ~ Durchschnittsgeschwindigkeit beibehalten; **to resume** ~ Geschwindigkeit wiederaufnehmen; **to run at full** ~ auf Hochtouren laufen; **to shift to low** ~ kleinen Gang einschalten; **to slacken** ~ *(ship)* Fahrt vermindern, *(train)* Geschwindigkeit vermindern; **to test the** ~ **over a measured mile** Geschwindigkeit auf einer kontrollierten Strecke feststellen; **to travel at full (top)** ~ mit höchster Geschwindigkeit fahren; ~ **calling** *(tel.)* Schnellwählsystem; ~ **check** Geschwindigkeitskontrolle; ~ **control** Geschwindigkeitskontrolle; ~ **cop** *(sl.)* motorisierter Verkehrspolizist; ~ **counter** Drehzahlmesser, Tourenzähler; ~ **factor** Plannutzungsziffer; ~ **filing** Schnellablage; ~ **goods** *(Br.)* Eilgut; ~ **indicator** Geschwindigkeitsmesser, Tachometer; ~ **limit** Geschwindigkeitsbeschränkung, -begrenzung, Höchstgeschwindigkeit; **to exceed the** ~ **limit** zulässige Geschwindigkeit (Höchstgeschwindigkeit) überschreiten; ~-**limit sign** Geschwindigkeitsbegrenzungsschild; ~ **merchant** Kilometerfresser; **high-** ~ **operation** Schnellverkehr; **high-** ~ **rail car** Schnelltriebwagen; **high-** ~ **railway** Schnellbahn; ~ **range** Geschwindigkeitsbereich; ~ **reading** Schnelllesen; ~ **record** Geschwindigkeitsrekord; ~ **recorder** Fahrtenschreiber; ~ **regulations** Geschwindigkeitsvorschriften; ~ **restriction** Geschwindigkeitsbegrenzung; ~ **service** Schnellbetrieb; ~ **spectrum** Geschwindigkeitsskala; ~ **test** Geschwindigkeitstest; ~ **track** Rennstrecke; ~ **trap** *(police)* Autofalle, Radar-, Straßenfalle; ~ **trial** Schnellverfahren; ~ **wiper** Schnellscheibenwischer.

speedball *(coll.)* Schnellarbeiter.
speedboat Renn-, Schnellboot.
speeder Schnellfahrer.
speeding zu schnelles Fahren, Überschreitung der Höchstgeschwindigkeit; **to be booked (fined) for** ~ wegen Geschwindigkeitsüberschreitung bestraft werden, Strafzettel wegen zu hoher Geschwindigkeit erhalten; ~ **violation** *(US)* Geschwindigkeitsüberschreitung.
speedlink *(Br.)* auf Mittelbetriebe zugeschnittener Frachtbetrieb.
speedometer Geschwindigkeitsanzeiger, Tachometer.
speedster *(US)* Schnellfahrer; ~ **violation** *(US)* Überschreiten der Geschwindigkeitsgrenze.
speedup beschleunigtes Verfahren, Beschleunigung; ~ **in concentration** beschleunigter Konzentrationsvorgang; ~ **of production** beschleunigter Produktionsausstoß, beschleunigte Produktionserhöhung; ~ **of tax collection** beschleunigtes Steuereintreibungsverfahren.
speedway Rennstrecke, *(US)* Schnellstraße, -weg, Autobahn.
speedwalk mobiler Fußgängerweg.
speedy *(sl.)* Eilbrief; ~ **delivery** prompte Lieferung; ~ **execution** sofortige Vollstreckung; ~ **recovery** rasche Erholung; ~ **reference** Schnellnachweis, -hinweis; ~ **remedy** summarischer Rechtsbehelf; ~ **reply** schnelle Antwort; ~ **trial** unverzüglich anberaumte Hauptversammlung.
spell *(fascination)* Zauber, Faszination, *(period of time)* Zeitfolge, -abschnitt, *(leisure time, Australia)* Freizeit, Ruhepause, *(period of work)* Arbeitszeit, Beschäftigung, *(short way, coll., US)* kurze Strecke, Katzensprung; **cold** ~ Kältewelle; **sinking** ~ *(export)* rückläufige Periode; ~ **of depression** vorübergehende Depression; ~ **in opposition** kurze Zeit in der Opposition; ~ **down the road** kleines Stück die Straße herunter; **cold** ~ **in spring** Kälterückfall; ~ **of fine weather** Schönwetterperiode; **continuous** ~ **of warm weather** ganze Reihe warmer Tage; **continuous** ~ **of work** ununterbrochene Arbeitszeit; ~ *(v.)* buchstabieren, [orthographisch] richtig schreiben, *(fig.)* ins Gegenteil verkehren, *(shift, US)* Schicht übernehmen; ~ **backward** keine Schwierigkeiten mit der Rechtschreibung haben; ~ **failure** zu Fehlern führen; ~ **out (over)** mühsam buchstabieren; **to be under the** ~ **of s. o.** von jem. fasziniert sein; **to break the** ~

Mißklang beheben; **to cast a ~ over s. o.** magische Gewalt über j. ausüben; **to give s. o. a ~** j. bei der Arbeit ablösen; **to rest for a [short] ~** kurz pausieren; **to take ~s at the wheel** sich bei einer langen Autoreise am Steuer ablösen.

spellbind *(v.)* faszinieren, *(orator)* fesselnd sprechen.

spellbinder faszinierender Redner.

speller Buchstabierer, *(US)* Fibel.

spelling Buchstabieren, Orthographie, Rechtschreibung;
   simplified ~ vereinfachte Schreibweise;
   ~ bee Rechtschreibewettbewerb; **~ pronunciation** buchstabengetreue Aussprache.

spend *(v.)* *(employ)* aufwenden, *(money)* verausgaben, ausgeben, *(squander)* verschwenden, *(time)* verleben, *(use up)* verbrauchen;
   ~ on advertising für Werbungszwecke ausgeben; **~ one's breath in den Wind reden; ~ on consumption goods** für den Konsum ausgeben; **~ a great deal** großen Aufwand treiben, große Ausgaben vornehmen; **~ all one's energies** sich mit aller Energie an etw. machen, sich mit ganzer Kraft dahintersetzen; **~ an estate in gaming** Vermögen verwetten (verspielen); **~ one's fortune** sein Vermögen durchbringen; **~ freely** freigiebig sein; **~ one's leisure time** seine Freizeit verbringen; **~ most of one's life in politics** größten Teil seines Lebens Berufspolitiker sein; **~ a lot of time on s. th.** viel Zeit für etw. aufwenden; **~ money for s. o.** Geld für j. anderen aufwenden; **~ money with a free hand** Geld leicht ausgeben; **~ all one's money** sein ganzes Geld ausgeben; **~ money like water** Geld mit vollen Händen ausgeben; **~ a penny** *(coll.)* auf die Toilette gehen; **~ up to plan** Ausgabenwirtschaft im festgelegten Rahmen halten; **~ a weekend** ein Wochenende verbringen; **~ one's way into deficit** Defizitwirtschaft betreiben; **~ one's way out of unemployment** Arbeitslosigkeit durch weitere Staatsverschuldung beseitigen; **~ the winter abroad** Winter im Ausland verbringen; **~ £ 10.000 a year** 10.000 Pfund im Jahr ausgeben.

spendable|earnings ausgezahltes Gehalt, Nettoeinkommen; **~ income** Nettoeinkommen.

spender Geldausgeber, Verschwender;
   ~s of foreign exchange Devisenverbraucher.

spending Ausgabe[n], Ausgabenwirtschaft;
   business ~ Gesamtaufwand der Volkswirtschaft; **capital ~** Kapitalaufwand; **consumer ~** Verbraucherausgaben; **deficit ~** öffentliche Verschuldung durch Anleiheaufnahme; **excessive ~** Ausgabenüberschüsse; **government ~** Aufwand der öffentlichen Hand, Staatsausgaben; **personal ~** Privatausgaben; **state ~** Staatsausgaben;
   ~ to automate (for automation) Investitionen für den Automatisierungsprozeß; **~ on housing** Wohnungsbauetat; **~ of leisure time** Freizeitgestaltung; **~ on research** Forschungsaufwand;
   to boost military ~ Verteidigungsetat erhöhen; **to hold ~ down** Ausgabenwirtschaft einschränken; **to hold public ~ level during a period of prolonged growth** öffentliche Ausgabenwirtschaft während einer längeren Wachstumsperiode auf gleichem Niveau halten; **to impose tight cash limits on its own ~** seine Ausgabenwirtschaft in engen Grenzen halten; **to increase one's ~** seine Ausgabenwirtschaft ankurbeln; **to increase its ~ on plant** Betriebsinvestitionen erhöhen; **to keep s. th. for one's own ~** etw. zum eigenen Gebrauch behalten; **to oversee the ~ of all government departments** Ausgabenwirtschaft des gesamten Regierungsapparates überwachen;
   ~ axe Ausgabenbeschneidung, -streichung; **~ behavio(u)r of consumers** Ausgabenverhalten der Verbraucher; **~ bill** Ausgabengesetz; **~ binge** Kauforgie; **to be on a big ~ binge** Geld mit vollen Händen ausgeben; **~ capacity** [Verbraucher]kaufkraft; **~ ceiling** Ausgabenbegrenzug; **public ~ curb** Einschränkung der öffentlichen Ausgabenwirtschaft; **~ cut** Ausgabenkürzung; **~ decision** Ausgabenentscheidung; **~ estimate** Ausgabenschätzung; **to show ~ forbearance** sich in den Ausgaben Beschränkungen auferlegen; **~ group** Käuferschicht; **~ habit** Verbraucher-, Ausgabengewohnheit; **~ income** verfügbares Einkommen; **~ item** Ausgabeposten; **~ leisure** Freizeitausgaben; **to hold ~ level during a period of prolonged growth** öffentliche Ausgabenwirtschaft während einer längeren Wachstumsperiode auf gleichem Niveau halten; **~ mood** Ausgabenstimmung; **~ period** Budgetperiode; **~ plans** geplante Ausgaben, Aufwandsprogramm, Investitionsplan; **~ power** Ausgabenvollmacht, Dispositionsfähigkeit, Kaufkraft; **~ priorities** vordringliche Ausgabeposten, Ausgabeprioritäten; **government's ~ program(me)** Ausgabenprogramm der Regierung; **to keep the program(me) short of its target** Ausgabenetat nicht völlig ausschöpfen; **~ rate** Ausgabenquote; **~ revival** wiederbelebte Ausgabenneigung; **~ shortfall** Ausgabenrück-

gang; **~ side** Ausgabenseite; **~ splurge** rapider Ausgabenanstieg; **~ spree** *(government)* hemmungslose Ausgabenwirtschaft; **to be off (go) on a ~ spree** Geld mit vollen Händen ausschütten, auf einer Bierreise sein; **~ trend** Aufwandsentwicklung; **~ unit** Verbrauchereinheit.

spendthrift Verschwender;
   ~ (a.) verschwenderisch;
   ~ trust *(US)* für einen Verschwender eingesetzte Vermögensverwaltung, Unterhaltsfonds.

spent verbraucht;
   ~ bill of lading erloschener Frachtbrief.

sphere Bereich, Bezirk, Feld, Gebiet, Wirkungskreis;
   ~ of activity (action) Tätigkeits-, Arbeits-, Geschäfts-, Wirkungskreis; **~ of business** Geschäftsrahmen, -zweig, -bereich; **~ of duties** Aufgabenbereich; **~ of influence** *(law of nations)* Interessenssphäre, Einflußgebiet, -sphäre, -zone; **~ of interest** Interessenssphäre, -gebiet; **~ of jurisdiction** Kompetenzbereich, Zuständigkeit; **~ of operation** Wirkungsbereich; **~ of responsibility** Zuständigkeitsbereich;
   to be outside the ~ of s. one's activities außerhalb von jds. Tätigkeitsbereich liegen; **to be distinguished in many ~s** hervorragende Leistungen auf den verschiedensten Gebieten aufweisen; **to extend one's ~ of activities** Erweiterung seines Wirkungskreises vornehmen, seinen Wirkungsbereich ausdehnen; **to keep within one's proper ~** innerhalb seiner Befugnisse bleiben; **to lie outside the ~ of s. one's activities** nicht in jds. Aufgabenbereich fallen, für j. nicht in Frage kommen; **to take s. o. out of his ~** j. aus seiner gewohnten Umgebung herausnehmen.

spice *(fig.)* Würze, Beigeschmack;
   to lack ~ *(story)* keine Pointe haben.

spick and span wie aus dem Ei gepellt.

spiel *(US sl.)* Geschwätz;
   ~ (v.) *(US sl.)* lange Rede halten, schwätzen.

spieler *(US sl.)* routinierter Betrüger.

spiff *(sl.)* Verkaufsprämie.

spiffed up *(sl.)* herausgeputzt, piekfein.

spiffy *(sl.)* hochmodern, piekfein.

spike *(fence)* Eisenspitze;
   ~ (v.) s. one's guns *(US)* jds. Pläne vereiteln.

spill Regenguß, *(out of carriage)* Sturz;
   ~ (v.) *(let out, sl.)* ausplaudern, *(waste, US)* verschleudern;
   ~ the beans *(coll.)* versehentlich rauslassen; **~ one's guts** *(sl.)* alles verraten; **~ money** *(sl.)* Geld ausspucken; **~ over** *(town)* überquellen; **~ a secret** Geheimnis verraten; **~ stocks** *(coll.)* Aktien auf den Markt werfen.

spillage Auslaufen.

spillover *(population)* überquellende Bevölkerung.

spin *(aircraft)* Trudeln, *(travel(l)ing)* Spritztour;
   ~ (v.) *(airplane)* trudeln, *(fail in an examination, sl.)* durchrasseln, *(promise, sl.)* Versprechen brechen, *(vehicle)* sich drehen;
   ~ away *(time)* schnell vergehen; **~ a coin** Geldmünze prüfen; **~ off some of its areas of jurisdiction** etw. von seinem Zuständigkeitsbereich abgeben; **~ out the time by talking** Zeit mit Plaudern verbringen; **~ plots** Pläne aushecken; **~ a yarn** Seemannsgarn spinnen;
   to get out of a ~ Flugzeug abfangen; **to go for (have) a ~** auf eine Spritztour gehen; **to make one's money ~ out until next payday** sich mit seinem Geld bis zur nächsten Gehaltszahlung durchmogeln;
   ~ drier Wäscheschleuder.

spindrift clouds Federwolken.

spine Buchrücken, *(fig.)* Rückgrat, Mut.

spinner *(narrator)* Geschichtenerzähler.

spinning Trudeln;
   to send a car ~ across the road mit dem Auto über die ganze Straße schleudern;
   ~ mill Spinnerei.

spinnoff Abstoßen von Geschäftszweigen, *(US, corporation)* Aktienausschüttung einer Tochtergesellschaft an die Aktionäre der Muttergesellschaft, *(income tax, US)* Aktientausch;
   ~ products anfallende Nebenprodukte, Abfallerzeugnisse.

spinster unverheiratete Frau, alte Jungfer, *(in documents, Br.)* ledig;
   to remain a ~ ledig bleiben.

spiral Spirale, Schraube, *(airplane)* Spiralflug;
   inflationary ~ Inflationsschraube; **wage-price ~** Lohn-Preis-Spirale;
   vicious ~ of rising prices and wages verhängnisvolle Lohn-Preis-Spirale;
   ~ nebula Spiralnebel; **~ staircase** Wendeltreppe.

spiral(l)ing | **of costs** Kostenspirale;
~ **wage costs** spiralartig ansteigende Lohnkosten.
spirit Geist, Gesinnung, *(alcohol)* Spiritus, *(law)* Wesen, *(mood)* Stimmung, *(pep)* Elan, Schwung, *(soul)* treibende Kraft, Seele;
in ~ dem Sinne nach; **in high** ~**s** in gehobener Stimmung; **in a** ~ **of mischief** in böser Absicht; **out of** ~**s** deprimiert;
~**s** geistige (alkoholische) Getränke, Spirituosen;
business (commercial) ~ Geschäftssinn, Handelsgeist; **choice** ~**s** erlesene Geister; **noble** ~ vornehmer Charakter; **public** ~ Gemeinsinn;
~ **of caste** Kastengeist; ~ **of the constitution** Geist der Verfassung; ~ **of an enterprise** Geist eines Unternehmens; ~ **of faction** Parteigeist; ~ **of the law** Sinn des Gesetzes; **animating** ~ **of the rebellion** treibende Kraft hinter dem Aufruhr; **leading** ~ **of the reform movement** führende Persönlichkeit der Reformbewegung; ~ **of tolerance** Geist der Toleranz;
~ *(v.)* inspirieren, ermutigen;
~ **away large quantities of the bank's deposits** Bankeinlagen in größeren Mengen verschwinden lassen;
to be in high ~**s** glänzender Laune (in fröhlicher [gehobener] Stimmung) sein; **to be in** ~ **with s. o.** jem. im Geist verbunden sein; **to be one of the most excellent** ~**s of one's time** zu den hervorragendsten Geistern seiner Epoche zählen; **to buoy up** ~**s** Stimmung aufbessern; **to circumvent the** ~ **of a law** gegen den Geist eines Gesetzes verstoßen; **to flout the** ~ **of the law** Sinn eines Gesetzes verhöhnen; **to follow out the** ~ **of s. one's instructions** jds. Anweisungen sinnvoll befolgen; **to license the sale of** ~**s** Schankkonzession erteilen; **to obey the** ~ **not the letter of a law** Geist eines Gesetzes und nicht seine Buchstaben befolgen; **to put** ~ **in one's work** Schwung hinter seine Arbeit setzen; **to take s. th. in the wrong** ~ etw. falsch auffassen;
~ **lamp** Spirituslampe; ~**s monopoly** Branntweinmonopol; ~ **rapper** Spiritist; ~ **rapping** Tischklopfen, -rücken; ~ **room** *(mar., sl.)* Zahlmeisterbüro; ~ **stove** Spiritusofen.
spirited conversation angeregte Unterhaltung.
spiritual geistig, seelisch;
~ **corporation** kirchliche Körperschaft; ~ **relationship** geistige Verwandtschaft; **to be concerned about one's** ~ **welfare** um sein geistiges Wohl besorgt sein.
spirituous liquors alkoholische Getränke, Spirituosen.
spit Landzunge, *(rod)* Bratspieß;
~ **and polish** *(mil.)* Putz- und Flickstunde;
the very ~ **of s. o.** das genaue Ebenbild jds.;
~ *(v.) (engine)* spucken;
~ **it out** seine wahre Meinung sagen;
to make s. o. ~ j. zum Kochen bringen;
~ **fence** schikanöser Zaun.
spital, spittle Spital.
spiv *(Br., sl.)* Schwarzhändler, Schieber, Tagedieb, Nichtstuer.
splash Spritzer, *(coll.)* Aufsehen, Sensation;
front-page ~ ganzseitig fettgedruckte Schlagzeile;
~ **of mud** Schmutzfleck;
~ *(v.)* **one's money** *(sl.)* mit dem Geld nur so um sich werfen; ~ **a piece of news** *(Br.)* Nachricht in großer Aufmachung bringen (groß herausbringen);
to make a ~ Furore machen;
~**down** *(airplane)* Wasserung.
splashboard *(car)* Schutzblech, *(mar.)* Wellenbrecher.
splice *(film)* Klebestelle, *(marriage, coll.)* Hochzeit.
splinter Splitter, Span, Bruchstück;
bomb ~ Bombensplitter;
~ *(v.) (party)* zersplittern;
to go into ~**s** in tausend Stücke gehen;
~ **group** Splittergruppe; ~ **operation** Kleinbetrieb; ~ **party** Splitterpartei, -gruppe.
splinterproof splittersicher.
split Aufteilung, *(informer, sl.)* Polizeispitzel, Denunziant, *(married couple)* Gütertrennung, *(mixed drink)* Mischgetränk, *(politics)* geteilte Stimmabgabe, *(party politics)* Spaltung, *(splinter party)* abgespaltene Gruppe, Splittergruppe, *(shares, US)* Aktiensplit, *(stock exchange)* Ausführung eines Börsenauftrages in zwei Abschnitten (zu verschiedenen Preisen), *(taxation)* Einkommensaufteilung;
~ **in a party** Parteispaltung;
~ *(v.)* aufteilen, zerlegen, spalten, *(fig.)* Schiffbruch erleiden, *(party)* sich spalten (aufsplittern), *(ship)* zerschellen;
~ **on s. o.** j. denunzieren; ~ **a cause of action** Klageanspruch auf mehrere Klagen verteilen, Teilanspruch einklagen; ~ **the costs of a dinner party** Kosten eines Abendessens aufteilen; ~ **the difference** auf halbem Wege entgegenkommen, sich den [Preis]-unterschied teilen; ~ **the fee** Anwaltshonorar teilen; ~ **the gold**

market into a free and an official market Goldmarkt in einen freien und offiziellen Markt aufspalten; ~ **hairs** Haarspalterei betreiben; ~ **the income** *(US)* Steuereinkommen aufspalten, sich getrennt veranlagen lassen; ~ **a party** Partei spalten; ~ **a party on a question** in einer Frage in einer Partei verschiedener Meinung sein; ~ **the profits** Gewinn untereinander aufteilen; ~ **shares (stocks, US)** Aktien splitten; ~ **straws** pedantisch sein; ~ **a sum into equal shares** Betrag gleichmäßig aufteilen; ~ **even on the swag** sich gleichmäßig die Beute teilen; ~ **one's ticket** *(US)* seine Stimmen auf mehrere Kandidaten verteilen; ~ **up** *(into small amounts)* zerlegen, aufspalten; ~ **up among** aufteilen unter; ~ **up into** auf-, untergliedern; ~ **up into small groups** *(party)* sich in kleine Gesprächsgruppen auflösen; ~ **up into several parties** sich in mehrere Lager spalten; ~ **one's vote** seine Stimmen auf mehrere Kandidaten verteilen;
~ *(a.) (stock exchange)* geteilt;
~ **ballot** gegabelte Befragung; ~ **commission** *(agency)* geteilte Provision; ~ **dollar insurance** *(US)* Arbeitnehmerversicherung durch den Arbeitgeber; ~**half (-test) method** *(statistics)* Halbierungsmethode; ~**level** bessere Hälfte, *(building)* über zwei Ebenen gebaut; ~**level** *(v.)* mit Zwischenstockwerken versehen; ~ **off** *(US)* Aktientausch [zwischen Mutter- und Tochtergesellschaft]; ~ **opening** *(US)* Eröffnungsnotierung mit stark abweichenden Kursen; ~ **order** *(US)* Kaufauftrag für Abschnitte zu verschiedenen Kursen; ~ **personality** *(mind)* gespaltene Persönlichkeit; ~**proof system** *(US)* beschleunigtes Prüfungsverfahren für Kasseneingänge; ~ **quotation** in Sechzehnteln gegebene Notierung, *(US)* Notierung in Bruchteilen; ~ **run** Anzeigenwerbung in Teilauflagen; Anzeigensplit; ~ **second** Sekundenbruchteil, Nu; ~ **sentence** *(fine and imprisonment)* ausgesetzte Haftstrafe; ~ **shift** unterbrochene Arbeitsschicht, Arbeit in wechselnden Schichten; ~ **ticket** *(US)* Wahlzettel mit Kandidaten mehrerer Parteien; ~ **transaction** Börsengeschäft mit verschiedenen Kursen; **[reserve]** ~**up** *(stocks)* Aktienzusammenlegung, [Aktien]split; ~**up** *(legal separation)* Trennung; ~**ups** *(US)* Bonus in Form aufgeteilter Aktien; ~ **vote** geteilte Stimmabgabe; ~ **week** *(theatre)* halbwöchentliches Auftreten in getrennten Städten.
splitting Spaltung, Teilung, Zerlegung, *(advertising)* Auflagenteilung, *(income tax, US)* getrennte Veranlagung, Splitting, *(shares)* Aktiensplit, -teilung;
fee ~ Honorarteilung; **hair** ~ Haarspalterei;
~ **the allowance** Freibetragsaufteilung; ~ **a cause of action** Einklagung eines Teilanspruchs; ~ **of the gold market** Spaltung des Goldmarktes; ~ **up a party** Parteispaltung;
not to hold with ~ **the party** Aufsplitterung der Partei nicht zulassen;
~ **system** *(taxation, US)* getrenntes Veranlagungssystem, Haushaltsbesteuerung.
splotch Schmutzfleck, *(ink)* Tintenklecks.
splurge *(coll.)* Wichtigtuerei, Angeberei, Angabe, *(luxury)* Extravaganz;
~ *(v.)* sich aufspielen (wichtig tun), *(indulge in expense)* über seine Verhältnisse leben.
spoil *(acquisition)* Gewinn, Schatz, Errungenschaft, *(paper)* Makulatur, *(stolen goods)* Beutestück, Diebesgut;
~ *(v.)* ruinieren, verderben;
~ **one's appetite by eating sweets** sich den Appetit durch Süßigkeiten verderben; ~ **s. o. of his goods** j. seiner Habe berauben; ~ **materials** Material vergeuden; ~ **a sheet of paper** Blatt Papier vermanschen;
to divide up the ~**(s)** Beute teilen;
~ **bank** Schutthalde.
spoilage *(goods)* Verderb, Verlust, *(print.)* Ausschuß, Makulatur.
spoiled, spoilt *(goods)* schadhaft, beschädigt, *(food)* verdorben;
to be ~ **of one's money** um sein Geld gebracht werden;
~ **child** verzogenes Kind; ~ **child of fortune** Glückskind; ~ **goods** verdorbene Ware; ~ **stamps** ungültige Briefmarken; ~ **voting paper** ungültige Stimme; ~ **work** Ausschuß.
spoiler Plünderer.
spoils Ausbeute, *(US)* materielle Vorteile des Wahlsieges, Schiebung;
~ **of office** Sporteln; ~ **of war** Kriegsbeute;
~ **system** *(US)* parteipolitische Ämterpatronage, Futterkrippenwirtschaft, [politischer] Kuhhandel.
spoilsman *(US)* Pöstchenjäger, Ämterverteiler.
spoilsmonger *(US)* Ämterverteiler.
spoilsport Spielverderber.
spoke Radspeiche;
to put a ~ **in s. one's wheel** jem. einen Knüppel zwischen die Beine werfen.

spokesman Sprecher, Sprachrohr, Wortführer, Vertrauensmann;
  Foreign Ministry ~ Sprecher des Auswärtigen Amtes;
  to appoint o. s. ~ of a group sich zum Dolmetscher einer Gruppe machen.
spoliate *(v.)* plündern, rauben.
spoliation Plünderung [neutraler Schiffe], *(torts)* Urkundenbeseitigung, *(ecclesiastical law, Br.)* Pfründenentzug;
  ~ of the soil Raubbau; **~ of towns** Städteverschmutzung.
spondulics *(US sl.)* Moneten, Zaster.
sponge *(fam., parasite)* Schmarotzer, Nassauer, Parasit;
  ~ *(v.)* ergattern, schnorren, nassauern;
  ~ on s. o. j. ausnutzen, auf jds. Kosten leben, jem. etw. abknöpfen, bei jem. schmarotzen; **~ out a debt** Schuld begleichen; **~ a dinner** Abendbroteinladung herausschlagen; **~ a fiver from an old acquaintance** einem alten Bekannten einen Hunderter abluchsen; **~ upon one's friends** auf Kosten seiner Freunde nassauern;
  to pass the ~ over aus dem Gedächtnis löschen; **to throw up (in) the ~** *(sl.)* Handtuch (Flinte ins Korn) werfen;
  ~ rubber Schaumgummi.
sponger Schmarotzer, Nassauer, Schnorrer, Parasit.
sponsor *(advertising, US)* Auftraggeber [einer Rundfunkwerbung], *(furtherer, US)* Gönner, Förderer, Schirmherr, Stifter, Geldgeber, *(guarantor)* Bürge, *(radio)* Pate, Patronatsfirma;
  commercial ~ *(US)* Rundfunkwerbung betreibende Firma, Patronatsfirma; **identified ~** *(US)* namentlich genannte Patronatsfirma;
  ~ for a certain legislation treibende Kraft für eine bestimmte Gesetztigkeit;
  ~ *(v.)* fördern, unterstützen, bürgen, Bürgschaft übernehmen, *(advertising)* Auftrag für eine Sendung erteilen, Sendeprogramm fördern (finanzieren);
  ~ for a new employee *(US)* neuen Betriebsangehörigen einweisen (einarbeiten); **~ a radio program(me)** *(US)* Patronatssendung übernehmen, Rundfunkprogramm finanzieren;
  to stand ~ Pate stehen.
sponsored gefördert, unter Schirmherrschaft;
  government-~ staatlich unterstützt (gefördert);
  ~ broadcast program(me) *(US)* Patronatssendung.
sponsoring body Fördergremium.
sponsorship Bürgschaft, *(broadcasting)* Patenstelle, -schaft, Fördertätigkeit, Patronat, *(furthering)* Gönnerschaft;
  ~ announcement Mitteilung über den Programmförderer.
spontaneous spontan, aus eigenem Antrieb, freiwillig;
  ~ act Willensakt; **~ combustion** Selbstentzündung; **~ gift** unerwartetes Geschenk; **~ offer of help** spontanes Hilfsangebot; **~ statement** spontane Erklärung.
spoof *(Br., sl.)* Humbug, Schwindel;
  ~ *(v.)* verkohlen.
spook Spuk, *(reckless driver)* rücksichtsloser Fahrer, Chausseeschreck, *(US sl.)* Sicherheitsoffizier, Geheimdienstbeamter.
spooky house Spukhaus.
spool of film *(US)* Filmrolle.
spoon-fed students gegängelte Studenten.
spoon-feed *(v.)* unselbständig machen, *(industry)* künstlich hochbringen, hochpäppeln.
spoon-feeding Hochpäppelung.
sport Sport, *(amusement)* Zeitvertreib, Zerstreuung, *(bon vivant, US coll.)* Lebemann, Genießer, Geck, *(chap)* Pfundskerl;
  inter-university ~s Universitätswettkämpfe; **track-and-field ~s** Leichtathletik;
  ~ of fortune Spielball des Schicksals;
  ~ *(v.)* zur Schau stellen;
  ~ a beard sich einen Bart zulegen; **~ one's oak** *(Br.)* seine Wohnungstür schließen;
  to be a good ~ kein Spielverderber sein; **to use s. o. for ~** j. zur Zielscheibe für grobe Scherze machen;
  ~s car Sportwagen; **~ clothes** Sportkleidung; **~s columnist** Sportredakteur; **~s coverage (reporting) in television** Sportberichte im Fernsehen; **~s editor** Sportredakteur; **~s event** Sportveranstaltung; **~s gear (goods)** Sportartikel; **~s ground** Sportplatz; **~s stadium** Sportstadion; **~s-wear department** Sportartikelabteilung; **~s writer** Sportjournalist.
sportcast Sportreportage.
sporting, to go *(sl.)* Vergnügungsbummel machen;
  ~ chance mit Risiko verbundene Chance; **~ conduct** faires (anständiges) Verhalten; **~ equipment** Sportausrüstung; **~ goods shop** Sportwarengeschäft; **~ gun** Jagdgewehr; **~ house** *(sl.)* Bordell; **~ plane** Sportflugzeug; **~ rights** Jagdrecht; **~ spectacular** spektakuläres Sportereignis.

spot Ort, Platz, Fleck, Stelle, *(advertising)* kurze Werbeeinblendung, *(dirt)* Schmutzfleck, *(fig.)* Schandfleck, *(film)* Kurzszene, *(local goods)* Lokowaren, *(place of entertainment, sl.)* Vergnügungsstätte, *(radio, US)* Durchsage, *(theater, Br., coll.)* Auftritt, Engagement;
  at the same ~ an derselben Stelle; **in a ~** *(sl.)* in schwieriger Lage (der Klemme); **in ~s** *(US)* stellenweise; **on the ~** am Platze, an Ort und Stelle, *(sl.)* auf Draht, *(US sl.)* in Lebensgefahr;
  ~s sofort lieferbare Ware, Lokowaren, *(stock exchange)* lieferbare Aktien;
  celebrated ~ berühmter Ort; **dark ~** Schandfleck; **hot ~** Touristenattraktion; **one-~** *(sl.)* einjährige Gefängnisstrafe; **over ~** *(stock exchange, Br.)* Report; **tender ~** *(fig.)* weiche Stelle, wunder Punkt, Achillesferse; **under ~** *(stock exchange, Br.)* Deport;
  ~ of land Fleckchen Erde, Stück Land; **~s of mud** Schmutzflecken; **~ on s. one's reputation** Flecken auf jds. weißer Weste;
  ~ *(v.)* beflecken, beschmutzen, *(fig.)* in den Schmutz ziehen, besudeln, *(mil.)* Land- oder Schiffsziele erkunden;
  ~ a criminal Verbrecher aufspüren; **~ easily** *(fabric)* schmutzempfindlich sein; **~ a freight car** Waggon zur Be-, Entladestelle dirigieren; **~ a friend in the crowd** Freund in der Menge entdecken; **~ the optimum moment for raising cash** Barmittel zum günstigsten Augenblick aufnehmen; **~ s. o. at once as German** j. sofort als Deutschen erkennen; **~ the winner in a race** Gewinnvoraussage machen;
  to arrive on the ~ pünktlich zur Stelle sein; **to be killed on the ~** sofort tot sein; **to be without a ~ on one's reputation** makellosen Ruf (blütenweiße Weste) haben; **to be on the ~ within ten minutes** binnen zehn Minuten zur Stelle sein; **to be put on the ~** in die Enge getrieben sein; **to bring to the ~** an Ort und Stelle schaffen; **to deal with a supplier on the ~** Platzgeschäfte machen; **to do a ~ of work** ein bißchen arbeiten; **to find s. one's weak ~** jds. Achillesferse entdecken; **to have a soft ~ for s. o.** Schwäche für j. haben; **to leave the decision to the men on the ~** Entscheidung den Lokalgrößen überlassen; **to put s. o. on the ~** jds. Widerstand herausfordern, *(US)* j. aufs Korn nehmen, *(gangsters)* j. auf die Abschußliste setzen; **to put s. o. in a bad ~** j. in eine schiefe Lage bringen; **to put one's finger on s. one's weak ~** jds. Schwächen herausstellen;
  ~ *(a.)* sofort lieferbar, *(to be paid immediately)* sofort zahlbar; **~ aid** Soforthilfe; **~ announcement** *(US)* Werbedurchsage, -einblendung, -spot; **~ audit** sofortige Teilrevision; **~ bargain** Lokogeschäft; **to buy on a ~ basis** gegen bare Kasse kaufen; **to sell on a ~ basis** auf der Grundlage der Barzahlung verkaufen; **~ broadcasting** regional begrenzte Rundfunkwerbung; **~ broker** Kassa-, Platzmakler; **~ business** Platz-, Lokogeschäft; **~ buy** *(v.)* Sofortkäufe tätigen; **~ cash** *(US)* bares Geld, Barzahlung, sofortige Kasse (Zahlung), *(balance sheet)* sofort verfügbare liquide Mittel, *(stock exchange)* sofortige Kasse; **~ check** Stichprobe, Prüfung an Ort und Stelle; **~-check** *(v.)* **the shipment** Warensendung stichprobenartig überprüfen; **~-check system** Stichprobenverfahren; **~ checking** stichprobenartige Überprüfung; **~ commodities** Kassaware; **~ conditions** Bedingungen bei sofortiger Barzahlung, Barzahlungsbedingungen; **~ contract** Platzgeschäft, -abschluß; **~-credit approval** sofort erteilte Kreditgenehmigung; **~ deal** Kassageschäft; **~ delivery** sofortige Lieferung, Kassalieferung; **to sell for ~ delivery** loko verkaufen; **~ drawing** Streuzeichnung; **~ exchange** Bardevisen; **~ exchange rate** Bardevisen-, Devisenkassakurs; **~ exchange transaction** Kassageschäft in Devisen, Devisenkassageschäft; **~ film** Werbekurzfilm; **~ firm** Barzahlungsgeschäft; **~ foreign currency** Kassadevisen; **~ goods** sofort lieferbare Ware, Kassa-, Lokowaren; **~ market** Loko-, Kassamarkt; **~-market price** Platzkurs; **~ needs** örtliche Bedürfnisse; **~ news reporter** *(US)* Lokalreporter; **~ offer** Platzangebot; **~ parcels** sofort lieferbare Stücke; **~ payment** Barzahlung; **~ price** Lokopreis *(stock exchange)* Kassapreis, -kurs; **~ purchase** Platz-, Lokokauf; **~ quotations** Kassakurs; **~ radio** schwerpunktartige Funkwerbung; **~ rate** Platzkurs, *(freight)* Frachttarif für Expreßversand, *(stock exchange)* Kassakurs; **~ sale** Barverkauf, *(stock exchange)* Umsatz am Kassamarkt, Kassaumsatz; **~ selling rate of the pound** Abgabekurs für Kassapfunde; **on ~ terms** per Kasse; **~ test** Stichprobe; **~ trading** *(US)* Verkäufe gegen sofortige Kasse und Lieferung; **~ transactions** Kassa, Loko-, Effektivgeschäfte, *(commodity exchange)* Spotgeschäfte; **~ transfer** Platzüberweisung.
spotless unbescholten;
  to keep s. th. ~ etw. tadellos in Ordnung halten;
  ~ reputation makelloser Ruf, blütenweiße Weste.

spotlight Punktlicht, *(US)* Scheinwerfer, *(fig.)* Rampenlicht;
~ *(v.)* anstrahlen, ausstrahlen, *(fam.)* in den Blickpunkt der Öffentlichkeit rücken;
to be in (hold) the ~ im Scheinwerferlicht (Mittelpunkt) der Öffentlichkeit stehen.

spotted beschmutzt, *(stock exchange, US)* mit wenigen Ausnahmen unverändert, *(under suspicion)* verdächtig;
quickly ~ schnell festgestellt;
~ **fever** Fleckfieber.

spotter *(railroad, US)* Streckenprüfer, *(passive air defence, Br.)* Flugmeldeposten, -melder, *(US coll.)* Haus-, Privatdetektiv, *(police)* Polizeispitzel.

spouse Ehegatte, -gattin;
complaining ~ *(divorce suit)* Kläger[in]; **surviving** ~ überlebender Ehegatte.

spouseless unverehelicht.

spout Pfand-, Leihhaus;
up the ~ *(coll.)* versetzt, verpfändet;
to be up the ~ beim Pfandleiher (im Pfandhaus) sein; **to go up the** ~ versetzt werden.

sprawl *(v.) (handwriting)* kritzlig sein;
~ **out into the countryside** sich tief ins Land erstrecken.

spraygun Spritzpistole.

spread Ausdehnung, -breitung, Verbreitung, *(advertising)* Streuung, *(advertisement)* ganzseitige (doppelseitige) Werbeanzeige, *(banquet, coll.)* Gelage, Schlemmermahlzeit, *(underwriters' commission)* Konsortialprovision, *(investments)* Streuung, *(first page)* Aufschlagseite, *(margin, US)* Marge, [Kurs]spanne, -differenz, *(put and call, Br.)* Prämien-, Stellage[geschäft], *(statistics)* Abweichung, *(writeup, sl.)* günstiger Zeitungsartikel;
center ~ *(ad, US)* doppelseitige Blattmitte; **double-page** ~ doppelseitige Anzeige; **price** ~ *(US)* Kursdifferenz; **small** ~ kleine Gewinnspanne; **two-page black and white** ~ doppelseitige Schwarzweißanzeige;
~ **of assets** Anlagenstreuung; ~ **of business** weitgestreute Geschäftstätigkeit; ~ **of disease** Verbreitung einer Krankheit; ~ **of education** breitangelegte Ausbildung; ~ **of exchange rates** *(US)* Schwankungsbreite (Bandbreite) der Wechselkurse; ~ **between the intervention points** *(US)* Wechselkursbandbreite; ~ **of knowledge** Wissensumfang; ~ **of land** Stück Land; ~ **of risk** Gefahren-, Risikoverteilung;
~ *(v.)* an Boden gewinnen, verbreiten, sich ausbreiten, verteilen, *(ads)* streuen, *(rumo(u)r)* umlaufen, *(town)* sich ausdehnen; ~ **o. s.** sich ausbreiten, ausführlich zu etw. Stellung nehmen, *(be generous)* gastfrei sein; ~ **about** zirkulieren; ~ **the cost of an asset over its useful life** Anschaffungskosten eines Wirtschaftsguts auf seine Nutzungsdauer verteilen; ~ **a course of studies over twelve months** Kursus über ein Jahr verteilen; ~ **the financial losses of insured members over the whole of the insuring community** finanzielle Verluste des einzelnen Versicherungsunternehmers auf alle verteilen; ~ **the impact of a tax loss over five years** Steuerverlust über fünf Jahre verteilen; ~ **a map on the floor** Karte auf dem Boden ausbreiten; ~ **over several months** *(negotiations)* sich über mehrere Monate hinziehen; ~ **instal(l)ments over several months** Abzahlungsraten auf mehrere Monate verteilen; ~ **a lump sum over three years** einmalige Einnahmen steuerlich über drei Jahre verteilen; ~ **throughout the month** auf den ganzen Monat verteilen; ~ **from mouth to mouth** sich von Mund zu Mund verbreiten; ~ **out** Börse zum Verkauf zwingen; ~ **out goods for sale** Waren zum Verkauf ausbreiten; ~ **out for a hundred miles** sich über 100 Meilen ausdehnen (erstrecken); ~ **out income** Einkommen steuerlich verteilen; ~ **over a variety of shares** sich auf eine Vielzahl von Aktien erstrecken; ~ **on the record** *(US)* aktenmäßig festhalten; ~ **a risk** Risiko verteilen; ~ **a rumo(u)r** Gerücht verbreiten; ~ **the table** Tisch decken; ~ **it thick** *(fig.)* dick auftragen; ~ **payments over the entire taxable year** Zahlungen steuerlich über das ganze Jahr verteilen; ~ **like wildfire** sich wie ein Lauffeuer verbreiten; ~ **throughout the town** sich über die ganze Stadt verbreiten; ~ **work more evenly throughout the year** gleichmäßigen Arbeitseinsatz im ganzen Jahr gewährleisten;
~ *(a.) (advertisement)* mehrspaltig;
to be ~ **about** verlauten;
~ **eagle** Angeber, *(US coll.)* Hurrapatriot, Chauvinist; ~-**eagle** *(v.)* patriotische Rede halten; ~-**eagle on the sand** sich im Sand aalen; ~-**eagle** *(a.) (pretentious)* angeberhaft, *(US coll.)* chauvinistisch; ~-**eagle orator** aufgeblasener Redner; ~ **eagleism** *(US coll.)* Hurrapatriotismus, Chauvinismus; ~-**eagleist** aufgeblasen; ~ **sheet** Verteilungsbogen; ~-**work system** Arbeitsstreckungsverfahren.

spreadhead Zweispaltenüberschrift.

spreading | false news Verbreitung von Falschnachrichten; ~ **the risk** Risikoverteilung, -ausgleich, -streuung; ~ **of work** Arbeitsstreckung;
~ **operations** *(Br.)* Transaktionen in verschiedenen Effekten.

spreadover *(advertising)* Streuplan, *(industry)* Arbeitsstundenanpassung.

spree Bummel, *(drinking bout)* Zechgelage, Sauftour, *(frolic)* lustiger Abend, Vergnügen;
to be on a ~ auf einer Bierreise sein; **to go on a** ~ bummeln (auf den Bummel) gehen.

spring Frühling, *(fig.)* geistige Spannkraft, *(fountain of water)* Springbrunnen, *(motive)* Triebkraft, Antrieb, Beweggrund, *(origin)* Herkunft, Quelle, Ursprung, *(watch)* Feder;
mineral ~ Mineralquelle; **oil** ~ Ölquelle; **thermal** ~ Thermalquelle;
~**s of a motor car** Autofederung;
~ **from** stammen, hervorgehen;
~ **to s. one's assistance** jem. zu Hilfe eilen; ~ *(v.)* **from jail** *(sl.)* aus dem Gefängnis loseisen; ~ **money** *(Br., coll.)* Geld locker machen; ~ **a mine** Mine hochgehen lassen; ~ **s. o. for a quid** *(Br.)* jem. ein Pfund abluchsen; ~ **from a noble stock** aus einer guten Familie stammen; ~ **a surprise on s. o.** jem. eine Überraschung bereiten; ~ **a new theory on s. o.** j. mit einer neuen Theorie überfallen; ~ **up** *(breeze)* aufkommen;
~ **cleaning** Frühjahrsputz; ~ **cultivation** Frühjahrsbestellung; ~ **fair** Frühjahrsmesse; ~ **fever** *(coll.)* Frühjahrsmüdigkeit; ~ **goods** Frühjahrsbedarf; ~ **gun** Selbstschuß; ~ **openings** Frühjahrseröffnung; ~ **resort** Kurort; ~ **sales (shopping)** Frühjahrseinkäufe, -besorgungen; ~ **tide** Springflut.

springboard *(fig.)* Sprungbrett.

springtime Frühlingszeit.

springtraps Fußangeln.

sprinkler Rasensprenger;
~ **leakage policy** Versicherungspolice für automatische Sprinkleranlagen; ~ **system** Sprinkleranlage.

sprinkling mechanism *(estate)* Nachlaßverteilungssystem mit freiem Verfügungsrecht.

sprout Sproß, Sprößling, *(sl.)* junger Krauter.

spruce *(v.)* **up** *(sl.)* sich feinmachen.

spur Sporn, *(fig.)* An-, Auftrieb, Ansporn;
on the ~ **of the moment** spontan, einer momentanen Eingebung folgend, ohne Überlegung;
to win one's ~**s** sich die Sporen verdienen;
~ **track** Nebengleis.

spurred on by ambition vom Ehrgeiz angestachelt.

spurious falsch, gefälscht, unecht, *(child)* unehelich, *(document)* untergeschoben;
~ **bank bill** Falschgeldschein; ~ **bill of exchange** Kellerwechsel; ~ **coin** falsche Münze; ~ **note** Kellerwechsel.

spurt plötzliches Anziehen der Preise (Kurse);
upward ~**s** Kurssprünge;
~ **in prices** plötzlicher Preisanstieg (Kursanstieg);
~ *(v.)* plötzlich steigen;
to put on a ~ zum Endspurt ansetzen.

spy Spion, Schnüffler;
police ~ Polizeispitzel;
~ *(v.)* Spionage betreiben, spionieren;
~ **upon s. o.** hinter jem. herspionieren; ~ **into other people's affairs** anderer Leute Geheimnisse ausspionieren; ~ **out** *(mil.)* auskundschaften; ~ **out a land** Land mit einem Spionagenetz überziehen; ~ **strangers** Ausschluß der Öffentlichkeit beantragen;
to be a ~ **on s. o.** jem. nachspionieren;
~-**catching operations** Spionagebekämpfung; ~ **center** *(US)* (**centre**, *Br.*) Spionagezentrum; ~ **charge** Spionagebeschuldigung; ~ **film** Spionagefilm; ~ **network** Spionagenetz; ~ **plane** Spionageflugzeug; ~ **ring** Spionagering, -organisation; **to smash a** ~ **ring** Spionagering auffliegen lassen; ~ **satellite** Überwachungs-, Kontrollsatellit, Spionsatellit; ~ **scandal** Spionageskandal; ~ **serial** Spionagegeschichte; ~ **ship** Spionageschiff; ~ **system** Spionagewesen, -system; ~ **thriller** Spionageroman; ~ **trial** Spionageverfahren, -prozeß.

spyglass Fernglas.

spyhole *(door)* Guckloch, Spion.

spying Ausspionieren;
~ **activities** Spionagetätigkeit; ~ **charge** Spionageverfahren.

squab *(car, Br.)* Rückenlehne.

squad Gruppe, Trupp, Mannschaft, *(aviation)* Flugzeugstaffel, Geschwader;
assault ~ Stoßtrupp; **awkward** ~ *(fig.)* noch nicht eingearbei-

tete Gruppe; **emergency** ~ Bereitsschaftspolizei, Einsatzkommando; **firing** ~ Hinrichtungskommando; **flying** ~ Einsatzgruppe, *(police)* Überfallkommando, fliegende Feuerwehr; **homicide** ~ Mordkommission; **police** ~ Polizeiabteilung; **rescue** ~ Rettungs-, Bergungsmannschaft; **sanitary** ~ Sanitätskolonne, -trupp; **traffic-control** ~s *(US)* Verkehrspolizei;
~ *(v.)* einer Gruppe zuteilen;
~ **car** *(US)* Streifenwagen, Funkstreife.

squadron Geschwader, Gruppe, Staffel;
bombardment ~ Bomberstaffel; **flying** ~ Eingreifgeschwader;
~ **leader** Geschwaderführer.

squall Bö, Windstoß;
to look out for ~s sich auf ein Donnerwetter gefaßt machen;
~ **front** Böenfront.

squalor of the slums Schmutz der Elendsviertel.

squander *(v.)* [Geld] durchbringen, verschwenden, vergeuden, verbuttern;
~ **one's estate** sein väterliches Erbteil verschleudern; ~ **money** scheffelweise Geld ausgeben.

squandermania Verschwendungssucht.

square unbebaute Fläche, Platz, Viertel, *(block of buildings, US)* Häuserblock, -komplex, *(math.)* Quadrat[zahl], *(meal)* volle Mahlzeit, *(mil.)* Kasernenhof, Manövergebiet, *(naive Person)* primitiver Zeitgenosse, *(philistine, sl.)* altmodischer Spießer, Spießbürger;
by the ~ genau, exakt; **on the** ~ *(coll.)* ehrlich, redlich; **out of** ~ *(fig.)* nicht in Ordnung (im Lot);
public ~ öffentlicher Platz; **town** ~ Rathausplatz;
~ *(a.)* (even) ausgeglichen, quitt, *(honest)* ehrlich, anständig, *(philistine)* altmodisch, spießig, spießbürgerlich;
~ *(v.)* in Ordnung bringen, skontieren, ausgleichen, saldieren, *(math.)* ins Quadrat erheben;
~ **o. s. with s. o.** sich wieder mit jem. vertragen; ~ **accounts** Konten ausgleichen (abrechnen, abgleichen), *(fig.)* Revanche an jem. nehmen; ~ **the circle** *(fig.)* Unmögliches Wirklichkeit werden lassen; ~ **s. o. to hold his tongue** jds. Stillschweigen durch Bestechung erkaufen; ~ **an official** Beamten bestechen; ~ **a number** Zahl zur zweiten Potenz erheben; ~ **one's shoulders** hartnäckig bleiben; ~ **up to s. o.** sich vor jem. aufpflanzen; ~ **up an account with s. o.** mit jem. abrechnen; ~ **up to a problem** zu einem Problem Stellung nehmen;
to act on the ~ sich anständig benehmen; **to be all** ~ quitt sein; **to be on the** ~ Freimaurer sein, *(business)* in Ordnung sein; **to be** ~ **with all the world** mit der Welt im Einklang leben; **to get one's accounts** ~ seine Konten in Ordnung bringen; **to get things** ~ seine Sachen in Ordnung bringen; **to get** ~ **with s. o.** sich mit jem. vergleichen, mit jem. quitt werden;
~ **area** quadratische Fläche; ~ **block** Straßenblock; ~ **brackets** *(print.)* eckige Klammern; ~-**built** vierschrötig; ~ **dance** Quadrille, Volkstanz; ~ **deal** reeller Handel, faire Abmachung; **to get a** ~ **deal** anständig behandelt werden; ~ **dealings** anständiges Verhalten; ~ **denial** glattes Dementi; ~ **half-tone** rechteckige Vollautotypie; ~ **meal** ausreichende (handfeste) Mahlzeit; ~ **measure** Flächenmaß; ~ **mile** Quadratmeile, *(London)* Börsenviertel; ~ **number** Quadratzahl; **to meet with a** ~ **refusal** glatte Ablehnung erfahren; ~ **root** Quadratwurzel; ~ **shooter** *(US)* anständiger Kerl; ~ **unit** Flächeneinheit.

squared paper *(Br.)* Millimeterpapier.

squaring of accounts Kontenabstimmung, -ausgleich.

squash *(at gate)* zusammengequetschte Menschenmenge, Gedrängel, Ansturm, *(fruit, Br.)* ausgepreßter Fruchtsaft;
orange ~ *(Br.)* Orangensaft;
~ *(v.)* unterdrücken;
~ **o. s. into a bus** sich durchzwängen; ~ **people into a bus** Leute in einen Bus stopfen; ~ **through a gate** sich durch ein Tor drängeln; ~ **s. one's hopes** jds. Hoffnungen zunichte machen; ~ **into a lift** sich in einem Aufzug zusammenpressen; ~ **a riot** Aufruhr niederschlagen.

squat *(v.)* herumdösen, *(Br.)* unberechtigte Hausbesetzung durchführen, *(US)* ohne Rechtstitel ansiedeln.

squatter *(Australia)* Siedler auf regierungseigenem Land, *(Br.)* Hausbesetzer, *(US)* Ansiedler ohne Rechtstitel.

squawk *(sl.)* Gekeife, Meckerei;
~ *(v.)* *(sl.)* meckern.

squeak, narrow knappes Entkommen;
~ *(v.)* *(criminal, sl.)* singen, verpfeifen.

squeaker *(sl.)* Verräter.

squeal *(v.)* *(turn informer)* singen, verpfeifen, auspacken;
to make s. o. ~ Geständnis von jem. erpressen.

squealer *(sl.)* Petze, Informant.

squeeze Druck, Klemme, Geldverlegenheit, *(blackmail)* Erpres-

sung, *(commission, East Asia)* unerlaubte Provision, *(extortion, sl.)* erpreßtes Geständnis, *(scarcity)* Knappheit, wirtschaftlicher Engpaß, *(stock exchange)* Zwang zu Deckungskäufen;
bear ~ Zwang zu Deckungskäufen; **close (narrow)** ~ knappes Entkommen; **credit** ~ Kreditbeschränkung, -restriktion; **liquidity** ~ Liquiditätsklemme; **money** ~ geldmarkttechnische Zwangslage, Liquiditätsbeengung;
~ **on profits** Druck auf die Unternehmergewinne;
~ *(v.)* unter Druck setzen, in die Enge treiben, *(tax)* bedrücken; ~ **the bears** *(stock exchange)* zu Deckungskäufen zwingen; ~ **o. s. into a crowded bus** sich in einen Omnibus hineindrängeln; ~ **down prices** Preise (Kurse) herunterdrücken; ~ **money out of s. o.** Geld aus jem. herauspressen; ~ **more money out of the public** der Öffentlichkeit weiteres Geld abjagen; ~ **out** [Börse] zum Verkauf zwingen; ~ **out of business** aus einem Geschäft herausdrängen; ~ **the last penny out of a victim** sein Opfer bis zum letzten Pfennig erpressen; ~ **the shorts** *(stock exchange)* zu Deckungskäufen zwingen; ~ **one's way through the crowd** sich einen Weg durch die Menge bahnen;
to be in a tight ~ tüchtig in der Klemme sitzen;
~ **box** *(sl.)* Quetschkommode; ~ **pricing** *(US)* Über(Unter)bieten aus Konkurrenzgründen.

squeezed for cash mit hohen Bargeldbedürfnissen.

squeezing Erpressung;
~ **the shorts** *(stock exchange)* Zwang zu Deckungskäufen.

squib *(Br.)* Feuerwerkskörper, Knallerbse, *(in newspapers, sl.)* spritzige Kurznotiz.

squint, to have a ~ **at s. th.** kurzen Blick auf etw. werfen.

squire Großgrundbesitzer, Gutsherr, Junker;
~ **of dames** Salonlöwe;
~ *(v.)* **a lady** Dame nach Hause begleiten.

squireling Krautjunker.

squirm *(v.)* herumdrucksen;
~ **out of it** sich aus der Affäre ziehen; ~ **with embarrassment** vor Verlegenheit nicht aus noch ein wissen.

stab Dolchstoß, *(fig.)* Verleumdung, *(try, sl.)* Chance, Versuch;
occasional lucky ~ gelegentlicher glücklicher Ansatz;
~ **in the back** hinterhältiger Angriff, Verleumdung;
~ *(v.)* erdolchen;
~ **s. o. in the back** jem. in den Rücken fallen.

stabber Meuchelmörder.

stability *(goods)* Haltbarkeit, *(prices)* Beständigkeit, Stabilität; **monetary (exchange)** ~ Währungsstabilität;
~ **of cartels** Kartellstabilität, Beständigkeit von Kartellverbindungen; ~ **of the currency** Währungsstabilität, Stabilität der Wechselkurse; ~ **of government** feste Regierung; ~ **of money** Geldwertstabilität; ~ **of prices** Kurs-, Preisstabilität; ~ **of price levels** stabiles Preis-, Kursniveau; ~ **of value** Wertbeständigkeit;
~ **advantage** Stabilitätsvorsprung; ~-**oriented** stabilitätsorientiert.

stabilization Stabilisierung, Festigung;
employment ~ Stabilisierung der Beschäftigungslage; **monetary** ~ Währungsstabilisierung; **population** ~ Stabilisierung der Bevölkerungszunahme; **price** ~ Kurs-, Preisstabilisierung; **raw-material price** ~ Stabilisierung der Rohstoffpreise;
~ **of the currency** Währungsstabilisierung; ~ **of the exchange rate** Stabilität der Wechselkurse; ~ **of value** Wertbeständigkeit;
wage ~ **board** *(US)* Lohnausgleichsstelle; ~ **fund** Stabilisierungs-, Währungsausgleichsfonds; ~ **law** Stabilisierungsgesetz; ~ **levy** Stabilitätsabgabe; ~ **loan** Stabilisierungs-, Aufwertungsanleihe; ~ **policy** Stabilisierungs-, Konjunkturpolitik; ~ **program(me)** Preisstabilisierungsprogramm.

stabilize *(v.)* stabil halten, stabilisieren, festigen;
~ **an airplane** Flugzeug stabilisieren; ~ **prices** Preise stabilisieren (stabil halten).

stabilized | loan Stabilisierungsanleihe; ~ **standard** stabilisierte Währung.

stabilizing | device Stabilisator; ~ **factors of the market** Kursstützungsfaktoren; **to serve as** ~ **force** stabilisierende Tätigkeit (Wirkung) ausüben; ~ **policy** Stabilisierungspolitik.

stable Pferde-, Rennstall, *(management)* fest angestellte Beratergruppe, *(dirty place, sl.)* Dreckecke;
~ *(a.)* beständig, fest, gleichbleibend, stabil, *(goods)* haltbar, dauerhaft, *(in value)* gleichbleibend, wertbeständig, unveränderlich;
~ **in price** preisstabil;
to become ~ sich stabilisieren (beruhigen); **to keep** ~ unveränderlich halten;

~ **companion** Stallgefährte, *(fig., Br., coll.)* Schul-, Klubkamerad; ~ **currency** stabile Währung; **to bolt the ~ door after the horse has bolted** Brunnen zudecken, wenn das Kind hereingefallen ist; ~ **force** gleichbleibende Belegschaft; ~ **government** stabile Regierungsverhältnisse; ~ **income** festes Einkommen; ~ **job** Dauerbeschäftigung; ~ **position** Dauerstellung; ~ **price** stabiler Preis; **of ~ value** wertbeständig.

stableboy Stalljunge.

stack Stapel, Stoß, *(airplane)* Flugzeug auf Wartebahn, *(books, US)* Regal, Büchergestell, *(game)* Haufen Spielmarken, *(hay)* Schober;

~s **of work** *(fam.)* Haufen Arbeit;

~ *(v.) (college use)* Zimmer durcheinanderbringen;

~ **cards** *(sl.)* abgekartetes Spiel treiben; ~ **up** aufstapeln, -schichten, *(car)* Autounfall haben; ~ **up an airplane** Flugzeug auf die Wartebahn schicken; ~ **wood** Holz stapeln;

~ **room** Büchersaal; ~~-**up** *(car, sl.)* Autounfall, *(plane, sl.)* Flugzeugunfall.

stackyard Tenne, Schober.

stadium Stadion, Sportplatz.

staff [Geschäfts]personal, Betriebspersonal, Angestellte, Belegschaft, Gefolgschaft, Personalbestand, Mitarbeiterstab, Stab, Stabskräfte, *(of flag)* Flaggenstock, *(hotel)* Hotelpersonal, *(mil.)* Stab, Kommandostelle, Stabskräfte, *(of civil servants)* Beamtenkörper, *(school)* Lehrkörper, Lehrerschaft, Kollegium, *(surveying)* Meßstab;

on the regular ~ fest angestellt;

administrative ~ Verwaltungspersonal; **branch ~** Filialbelegschaft; **clerical ~** Schreibkräfte, -personal, Büropersonal; **counter ~** Schalterpersonal; **diplomatic ~** diplomatischer Stab; **domestic ~** [Haus]personal, **editorial ~** Redaktion[sstab], Schriftleitung; **efficient ~** gut geschultes Personal; **field ~** Mitarbeiter im Außendienst, Außenorganisation, Außenkräfte; **general ~** *(mil.)* Generalstab; **ground ~** *(airplane)* Bodenpersonal; **home-based ~** aus der Heimat stammendes Betriebspersonal; **hospital ~** ärztliches Personal; **hotel ~** Hotelpersonal; **local ~** ortsansässiges Personal; **managerial ~** Betriebs-, Geschäftsleitung; **nursing ~** Pflegepersonal; **pastoral ~** Bischofstab; **permanent ~** ständige Belegschaft; **postal ~** Postangestellte; **salaried ~** Gehaltsempfänger; **sales ~** Verkaufspersonal, Absatzstab; **senior ~** leitende Angestellte; **shop ~** Belegschaft, Betriebspersonal; **skilled (specialized, trained) ~** Fachpersonal, -kräfte; **superintendence ~** Aufsichtspersonal; **technical ~** Fachkräfte, -personal, **temporary ~** Aushilfspersonal; **workroom ~** Belegschaft;

~ **of s. one's old age** Stütze in jds. Alter; **competent ~ of men** fähiger Mitarbeiterstab; ~ **of a newspaper** Redaktionsstab; ~ **of readers** Lektorenstab; **large ~ of servants** viel Personal;

~ *(v.)* mit Personal versorgen, *(mil.)* Stab bilden;

~ **an office** Büropersonal engagieren, Büro mit Personal besetzen; ~ **overseas posts** Stabspersonal ausländischer Vertretungen stellen; ~ **a new school** Lehrkörper für eine neue Schule zusammenstellen;

to appoint ~ Personal einstellen; **to be on the ~** zum Personal (zur Belegschaft) gehören, beschäftigt sein, *(of a newspaper)* bei einer Zeitung mitarbeiten; **to be on the regular ~** im festen Angestelltenverhältnis stehen; **to be on the ~ of the Times** Mitarbeiter des Times sein; **to be short of ~** Personalmangel haben; **to dismiss one's ~** sein Personal (die Belegschaft) entlassen; **to employ (engage) ~** Personal einstellen; **to handle an efficient ~** leistungsfähiges Mitarbeitergremium haben; **to reduce the ~** Personalbestand verringern, Personal abbauen; **to trim one's ~** seine Stabskräfte reduzieren;

~ **activity** Stabstätigkeit, -arbeit; ~ **agency** Betriebsberatungsstelle; ~ **amenities** Belegschaftseinrichtungen; ~ **association** Personalvertretung, Angestelltenverband; ~ **auditor** Betriebsrevisor; ~ **bonus** Belegschaftstantieme, Gratifikationen für (Extrazahlung an) die Belegschaft; ~ **bonus system** Gewinnbeteiligungsplan für die Angestellten; ~ **canteen** Betriebskantine; ~ **capital formation** betriebliche Vermögensbildung; ~ **Christmas party** betriebliche Weihnachtsfeier; ~ **college** *(mil.)* Führungs-, Kriegsakademie; ~ **conference** Stabsbesprechung; ~ **cooperation** betriebliche Zusammenarbeit; ~ **correspondent** ständiger Korrespondent; ~ **costs** Personalaufwendungen; ~ **council** Betriebsrat; **to be selected for the ~ course** *(mil.)* Generalstäbler werden; ~ **cut** Belegschafts-, Personalabbau; ~ **department** Personal-, Stabs-, Betriebsabteilung, *(mil.)* Stabsabteilung; ~ **director** Stableiter; ~ **division** Stabsabteilung; ~ **duties** Stabsaufgaben; ~ **executive** Leiter der Personalabteilung, Personalchef; ~ **and material expenditure** Verwaltungsaufwand; ~ **expenses** Personalkosten, -aufwand; ~ **functions**

Stabsfunktionen; ~ **fund** Belegschaftsfonds; ~ **group** Stabsgruppe; ~ **guarantee fund** *(Br.)* Belegschaftsfonds gegen evtl. Unterschlagungen; ~ **herding** Rinderweidung im Wald; ~ **lines** Stabsrichtlinien; ~ **magazine** Werkszeitschrift; ~ **manager** Personalchef, -referent, Stableiter; ~ **member** Betriebsangehöriger, Belegschaftsmitglied; ~ **members** *(embassy)* Bedienstete; **middle-echelon ~ member** zu den mittleren Führungskräften gehörendes Stabsmitglied; ~ **morale** Betriebsmoral; ~ **officer** Berater des Vorstandes, Betriebsberater, *(mil.)* Stabsoffizier; ~ **outing** Betriebsausflug; ~ **pension fund** *(Br.)* [Angestellten-]pensionskasse; ~ **planning** Stellenplan; ~ **planning system** Personalplanung; ~ **position** Stabsposition, -stelle; ~ **productivity bonus** Leistungsprämie für die Belegschaft; ~ **provident fund** Unterstützungsfonds für die Belegschaft, Belegschaftsfonds, betriebliche Unterstützungskasse; ~ **reduction** Personalabbau; ~ **register** Personalverzeichnis, *(Br.)* Personalkonto; ~ **regulations** Personalstatut; **to stand for good ~ relations** Wahrzeichen guten Betriebsklimas sein; ~ **relationship** Beziehungen zwischen leitenden Angestellten und dem Personalchef; ~ **representative** *(US)* Mitarbeiter, Vertreter, *(council)* Personalvertreter; ~ **responsibility** Arbeitsbereich einer Stabskraft; ~ **ride** *(mil.)* Geländefahrt; ~ **salaries** Angestelltengehälter; ~ **secretariat** Stabssekretariat; ~ **selection** Personalauswahl; ~ **sergeant** *(mil., Br.)* Oberfeldwebel; ~ **session** Stabssitzung; ~ **severance fund** betrieblicher Abfindungsfonds, Sozialfonds; ~ **shares** *(Br.)* an Betriebsangehörige ausgegebene Aktien, Belegschaftsaktien; ~ **shareholder** *(Br.)* Belegschaftsaktionär; ~ **shortage** Personalknappheit, -mangel; ~ **solidarity** Solidarität der Belegschaft; ~ **structure** Personalstruktur; ~ **superintendent department** *(Br.)* Personalabteilung; ~ **time** Bearbeitungszeit; ~ **training** Personalausbildung, *(mil.)* Generalstabsausbildung; ~ **training department** Ausbildungsabteilung; ~ **transfers** Personalumsetzungen, innerbetriebliche Umsetzungen; ~ **turnover** Belegschaftswechsel, Personalfluktuation; ~ **vacations** Betriebsferien; ~ **walk** *(mil.)* Geländebesprechung; ~ **welfare** Belegschaftsunterstützungen, Sozialleistungen für die Belegschaft; ~ **work** Stabsarbeit, -tätigkeit; ~ **writer** fest angestellter Journalist, *(cinema)* fest bezahlter Autor.

staffed, well gut mit Personal versehen, gut besetzt, personalmäßig gut versorgt.

staffer Stabsmitglied, -angehöriger, *(editorial board)* Redaktionsmitglied.

staffing Stellen-, Personalbesetzung;

~ **schedule** *(US)* Stellenbesetzungsplan.

stag *(irregular dealer, Br.)* nicht an der Börse zugelassener Makler, Spekulant, *(el.)* Verstärkerstufe, *(informer, sl.)* Denunziant, Verräter, *(social gathering)* Herrenabend, *(stock exchange, Br.)* Konzertzeichner, *(US coll.)* Unbeweibter, Herr ohne Damenbegleitung;

~ *(v.) (Br.)* in Aktien spekulieren, Differenzgeschäfte machen; ~ **the market** *(Br.)* Börsenkurse durch Konzertzeichnungen beeinflussen;

to come ~ ohne Ehefrau kommen;

~ **dinner** Herrenessen; ~ **party** Herrenabend, -gesellschaft.

stage Abschnitt, Stadium, Stufe, [Entwicklungs]phase, Etappe, *(rocket)* Stufe, *(theater)* Bühne, Theaterwelt, -beruf, *(EC)* Integrationsstufe, *(traffic)* Abschnitt, Halte-, Teilstrecke, *(works)* Arbeitsstufe;

at an early ~ of our history in der Frühzeit unserer Geschichte; **by ~s** etappenweise; **by easy ~s** mit häufigen Unterbrechungen;

committee ~ Ausschußstadium; **crucial ~** kritisches Stadium; **experimental ~** Versuchsstadium; **fare ~** *(bus)* Tarif-, Teilstrecke; **initial ~** Anfangsstadium; **intermediate ~** Zwischenstufe, -zustand, -stadium; **landing ~** Anlegeplatz, Landungsbrücke; **manufactured ~** abgeschlossenes Produktionsstadium; **matriarchal ~** Matriarchat; **one-man ~** Einmannbetrieb; **operational ~** Betriebsstadium, -abschnitt; **political ~** politische Bühne; **primary ~** Anfangsstadium; **raw-material ~** Rohstoffstadium; **report ~** *(parl.)* Berichtsstadium; **trust ~** Zeitalter der Industriekonzerne;

~s **of appeal (approach)** Instanzenweg, Revisionsinstanz; ~ **of a conference** Konferenzstadium; ~ **of development** Entwicklungsstadium, -zustand; ~s **of growth** Wachstumsstadium; ~ **of s. one's life** Etappe im Leben eines Menschen; ~ **of negotiations** Stand der Verhandlungen; ~ **of proceedings** Prozeßlage; ~s **of processing** Verarbeitungsstufen; ~s **of production** Produktionsstufen; ~ **of recession** Rezessionsphase; ~ **of a rocket** Raketenstufe; ~ **in upswing** Aufschwungsphase;

~ *(v.) (theater)* auf die Bühne bringen, inszenieren;

~ **a come-back** Rehabilitierung vorbereiten;

to be in the earliest ~s of preparation noch ganz im Anfangsstadium sein (stecken); to be on the ~ Schauspieler sein; to be in the last ~ of appeal in der letzten Instanz sein; to enter a critical ~ in ein kritisches Stadium eintreten; to go on the ~ zum Theater gehen; to hold the ~ (theatrical) sich halten; to proceed by ~s schrittweise vorgehen; to quit the ~ of politics politische Bühne verlassen; to reach a certain ~ bis zu einem bestimmten Punkt gedeihen; to reach the ~ inszeniert werden; to study for the ~ Bühnenausbildung erhalten; to travel by brief ~s Reise in Etappen zurücklegen;

~ affair hochoffizielle Angelegenheit; ~ box (theater) Proszeniumsloge; ~ coach (hist.) Postkutsche; ~ directions Bühnenanweisung; ~ director Regisseur; ~ door Bühneneingang; ~ effect Bühnenwirkung; ~ fright Lampenfieber; ~ legislation Gesetzesvorlage; ~-manage (v.) inszenieren, arrangieren; ~ manager Spielleiter, Regisseur, Intendant; ~ management Spielleitung; ~ managing Regieführung; ~ name Künstlername; ~ play Bühnenstück; ~ player Schauspieler; ~ production Bühnenaufführung; ~ properties Theaterrequisiten; ~ rights Aufführungsrechte; three-~ rocket dreistufige Rakete; ~ service Linienverkehr; ~ setter Bühnenbildner; ~ setting Bühnenbild; ~-struck theaterbesessen; ~ whisper weithin hörbares Geflüster.

stagecraft Bühnentechnik.
stager, old erfahrener Praktikus.
stageworthy bühnengerecht.
stagflation mit langsamem Wachstum des Sozialprodukts gekoppelte Inflation.
stagger (prices) Schwanken, (working time) Staffelung;
~ (v.) staffeln, (news) erschüttern, (working time) abwechseln lassen;
~ one's employees' office hours (starting hours) verschiedene Zeiten für den Arbeitsbeginn festlegen; ~ the annual holidays Zeit der großen Ferien aufteilen.
staggered (working time) gestaffelt;
~ schedule (advertising) Wechselstreuung, Würfeln.
staggering| of holidays Aufteilung des Urlaubs, Urlaubsaufteilung; ~ of hours Staffelung der Arbeitszeit; ~ of shifts Schichtverkürzung zur [Arbeitslosenbekämpfung], Kurzarbeit, (traffic) Schichtstaffelung.
stagging| of new issues (Br.) Konzertzeichnungen von neu aufgelegten Wertpapieren; ~ the market (Br.) Beeinflussung der Börsenkurse durch Konzertzeichnungen.
staging Baugerüst, (mar.) Hellinggerüst, (theater) Inszenierung, Bühnenbearbeitung;
~ area (mil.) Bereitstellungsraum; ~ post Zwischenlandestation.
stagnancy (stock exchange) Mattheit, Lustlosigkeit, Stockung, Stagnation, Flaute;
to produce ~ Lustlosigkeit hervorrufen.
stagnant flau, lustlos, stockend, stagnierend;
to be ~ stagnieren, Flaute durchmachen;
~ market stagnierender Markt, matte Börse; ~ state of business (trade) Flaute, Geschäftsstockung.
stagnate (v.) stocken, stagnieren, flau sein (werden), darniederliegen.
stagnation Stillstand, Stagnation, Stockung, Leb-, Lustlosigkeit, Flaute;
cyclical ~ konjunkturelle Flaute;
~ of business Geschäftsstille, Geschäftsflaute, -stockung; ~ of orders Auftragsflaute; ~ of trade Absatzstockung, -flaute.
stain [Schmutz]fleck, (character) Makel;
without a ~ von untadeligem Ruf;
ink ~ Tintenklecks;
~ on s. one's reputation Fleck auf jds. weißer Weste;
~ (v.) easily (fabric) schmutzempfindlich sein; ~ s. one's name jds. Namen besudeln.
stainless| reputation untadeliger Ruf; ~ steel rostfreier Stahl.
stair Treppe, Stiege, (fig.) Stufenleiter;
below ~s (fig.) beim Hauspersonal;
~s Landungssteg;
~ carpet Treppenläufer.
staircase Treppenhaus;
grand ~ Freitreppe; moving ~ Rolltreppe.
stairway Treppenaufgang.
stake [Renn]einsatz, Wetteinsatz, (capital) Einschuß, [Kapital]einlage, (risk) Wagnis, (share) Anteil, Interesse;
at the ~ auf dem Scheiterhaufen;
consolation ~ Trostpreis;
~ in a business geschäftliches Interesse; ~ in ownership Eigentumsanteil;

~ (v.) riskieren, Wetteinsatz vornehmen, aufs Spiel setzen;
~ s. o. (US) jem. unter die Arme greifen; ~ off a mining claim Mutungsrecht abstecken; ~ out abstecken, (sl.) polizeilich überwachen; ~ out a claim Grundstück abstecken, (fig.) Forderung umreißen; ~ 5 on the favo(u)rite 5 Pfund auf den Favoriten setzen; ~ all one's life on it hundertprozentiges Vertrauen haben;
to be at ~ auf dem Spiel stehen; to draw ~s Einsatz zurückerhalten; to go to it like the bear to the ~ ungern an etw. herangehen; to have a ~ in s. th. materielles Interesse an etw. haben; to have a ~ in the country Interesse am Wohlergehen des Landes haben; to have a ~ in the lottery Geld in der Lotterie einsetzen, in der Lotterie spielen; to have large sums at ~ in an enterprise große Beträge in einem Unternehmen investiert haben; to have much at ~ viel zu verlieren haben; to move one's ~s seine Grenzpfähle verrücken; to perish at the ~ Märtyrertod erleiden; to pull up ~s with s. o. (US) j. scharf zurechtweisen; to put to the ~ aufs Spiel setzen; to stick one's ~s Stellung einnehmen; to sweep ~s ganzen Gewinn einstreichen; to withdraw one's ~ seinen Einsatz zurückziehen;
~ money Einsatz, Wettgebühr.
stakeholder Einsatzhalter, (landowner) Parzelleninhaber, (trustee) Sequester, Verwalter, Verweser, treuhändischer Verwahrer.
stale schal, abgestanden, (fig.) veraltet, abgestanden, abgedroschen, (impaired in legal force) verjährt, unwirksam;
to become ~ (power of attorney) ungültig werden;
~ affidavit verjährte eidesstattliche Erklärung; ~ articles unmoderne Waren; ~ bear (bull) geschlagener Baissier (Haussier); ~ beer abgestandenes Bier; ~ bread altbackenes Brot; ~ check (US) (cheque, Br.) verjährter Scheck; ~ claim ungültige Forderung; ~ debt verjährte Schuld; ~ demand verjährter Anspruch; ~ market flaue Börse; ~ news abgestandene Neuigkeiten.
stalemate Patt, (fig.) Sackgasse, toter Punkt;
~ in progress Fortschrittsstillstand;
~ (v.) in die Enge treiben, matt setzen.
stalk würdevoller Gang, (chimney) hoher Schornstein, (hunting) Pirschgang;
~ (v.) einherstolzieren, (illness) umgehen.
stalking horse Deckmantel, Vorwand, (politics) Strohmann, Marionettenfigur;
to make s. o. a ~ j. vorschieben.
stall Verkaufsstand, -bude, Marktstand, Budike, (airplane) überzogener Flug, (for animal) Stall, Box, (criminal use, sl.) Verbrechergehilfe, (mining) Arbeitsplatz, (parking, US) Parkplatz, (theater, Br.) Sperrsitz im Parkett, (US sl.) Hinhaltemanöver;
newspaper ~ Zeitungsstand;
~ (v.) in einer Box unterbringen, (airplane) überziehen, abrutschen, durchsacken, (car) steckenbleiben, sich festfahren, (engine) blockieren, abwürgen, (fig.) frustriert sein, (US sl.) sich stur stellen, sich herumdrücken;
~ a debt Schuld in Raten abtragen; ~ off (US sl.) abwimmeln; ~ for time Zeit zu gewinnen trachten;
to keep a ~ an einem Stand feilhalten;
~ rent Standgeld, -gebühr.
stallage (Br.) Stand-, Marktgeld.
stalling (airplane) Überziehen, Geschwindigkeitsverlust;
~ speed kritische Geschwindigkeit; ~ tactics Verzögerungstaktik.
stallkeeper Budiker, Budenbesitzer.
stalk (v.) (hunt) pirschen, auf die Pirsch gehen.
stalking Pirsch[recht];
~ grounds Jagdgründe.
stalwart (pol.) unnachsichtiger Verfechter;
~s of the market führende Marktwerte;
~ (a.) unerschütterlich, unentwegt;
~ supporter zuverlässiger Anhänger.
stalwartism unentwegte Parteigängerschaft.
stamina Stehvermögen, Widerstandskraft.
stamp (brand) Firmenzeichen, Etikette, (evidence of quality) Qualitätsstempel, (mark) behördlicher Stempel, (postage) Frei-, Briefmarke, Postwertzeichen, (on receipted bill) Stempel[steuer]marke;
free of ~ (stock exchange) börsenumsatzsteuerfrei;
~s Stempelabgaben;
adhesive ~ Stempel-, Klebemarke; affixed ~ aufgeklebte Briefmarke, Aufklebemarke; airmail ~ Luftpostmarke; bill ~ Wechselstempel, -steuermarke; cancelling ~ Entwertungsstempel; coil ~s Briefmarken in perforierten Bogen; ~ collect-

ed Stempelgebühr bezahlt; **commemorative** ~ Gedenkmarke; **contract** ~ Vertragsstempelmarke, *(stock exchange)* Schlußnotenstempel; **date** ~ Eingangs-, Datums-, Tagesstempel; **deed** ~ Urkundenstempel; **defaced** ~ entwertete Briefmarke; **defacing** ~ Entwertungsstempel; **embossed** ~ Trockenstempel; **facsimile** ~ Namens-, Faksimilestempel; **finance** ~ Stempelmarke; **firm** ~ Firmenstempel; **green** ~ *(US)* Rabattmarke; **hand** ~ Handstempel; **imitation** ~ nachgemachte Briefmarke; **impressed** ~ eingedruckte Briefmarke, eingedruckter Stempel, Prägestempel; **inland-revenue** ~ *(Br.)* Steuer-, Gebührenmarke; **jubilee** ~ Jubiläumsmarke; **marking** ~ *(US)* Aufgabe-, Entwertungsstempel; **official** ~ Dienstsiegel, Amtsstempel; **postage** ~ Postzeichen, Briefmarkenstempel; **postage-due** ~ Nachportostempel; **receipt** ~ Quittungsmarke, -stempel; **received** ~ Eingangsstempel; **revenue** ~ Steuermarke, -stempel; **rubber** ~ Gummistempel; **savings** ~ *(Br.)* Sparmarke; **signature** ~ Unterschrifts-, Faksimilestempel; **special-delivery** ~ Aufkleber für Eilzustellung; **subscription** ~ Beitragsmarke; **trading** ~ Rabatt-, Prämienmarke; **unused** ~ nicht benutzte Freimarke; **ad-valorem** ~ Wertmarke; ~ **of social approval** Stempel der gesellschaftlichen Anerkennung; ~ **on securities** *(US)* Effektenstempel, Tagesstempel; ~ **on a warrant** Lagerhausstempel;

~ *(v.)* ver-, abstempeln, *(coin)* prägen, *(mail)* freimachen, frankieren, *(pay taxes)* Stempelsteuer bezahlen; ~ **a document** Stempel auf eine Urkunde setzen, Urkunde verstempeln; ~ **an epidemic disease out** Seuche ausrotten; ~ **the employed person's card** Sozialversicherungskarte abstempeln; ~ **an address on an envelope** Adresse auf den Briefumschlag stempeln; ~ **s. o. a man of high principles** j. als Mann fester Grundsätze prägen; ~ **a manufacturer's name (trademark) on his goods** Warenzeichen auf Waren anbringen; ~ **s. th. on s. one's mind** jem. etw. fest einprägen; ~ **money** Geld drucken; ~ **one's name and address on an envelope** seinen Namen und seine Adresse auf ein Briefkuvert stempeln; ~ **out a rebellion** Aufruhr unterdrücken; **to affix a** ~ Stempel aufdrücken; **to get some green ~s** *(US sl.)* Strafzettel für Geschwindigkeitsüberschreitung bekommen; **to make a claim for allowance of spoiled ~s** Antrag auf Erstattung beschädigter Stempelmarken stellen; **to carry the personal** ~ **of s. o.** jds. persönliche Einwirkung erkennen lassen; **to put a democratic** ~ **on a bill** einen Gesetzentwurf mit dem Stempel der demokratischen Partei versehen; **to put on a** ~ Briefmarke aufkleben; **to put one's personal** ~ **on a company** einer Firma seinen Persönlichkeitsstempel aufdrücken; **to remove (unstick) a** ~ **from an envelope** Briefmarke vom Umschlag ablösen; ~ **Act** *(Br.)* Stempelsteuergesetz; ~ **album** Briefmarkenalbum; ~ **auction** Briefmarkenversteigerung; ~ **book** Portobuch; ~ **booklet** Briefmarkenheft; ~ **boom** Briefmarkenhausse; ~ **collecting** Briefmarkensammeln; ~ **collection** Briefmarkensammlung; ~ **collector** Briefmarkensammler; ~ **dealer** Briefmarkenhändler; **~-dispensing machine** Wertzeichenautomat; ~ **distributor** Verkäufer von Stempelmarken.

stamp duty Stempelsteuer, -gebühr, -abgabe, *(bill of exchange)* Wechsel-, Urkundensteuer;
exempt from ~ stempelsteuerfrei, nicht stempelpflichtig; **subject to** ~ stempelpflichtig;
receipt ~ *(Br.)* Quittungsstempelgebühr;
~ **on cheques** *(Br.)* Schecksteuer; ~ **on securities** Effektensteuer; **to dodge** ~ Effektensteuer umgehen; **to incur** ~ stempelsteuerpflichtig sein.

stamp, special ~ **issue** Briefmarkensonderausgabe; ~ **law** Stempelsteuergesetz; ~ **machine** Briefmarkenautomat; ~ **note** *(Br.)* Zollfreigabeschein; ~ **office** *(US)* Stempelamt; ~ **pad** Stempelkissen; ~ **paper** Briefmarken-, Stempelpapier, Stempelbogen; ~ **rack** Stempelständer; ~ **tax** *(US)* Stempelsteuer, -abgabe; ~ **type** Typendruckerei.

stamped abgestempelt, verstempelt, *(with affixed postage)* freigemacht, frankiert;
duly ~ richtig abgestempelt; **insufficiently** ~ ungenügend frankiert;
to get a deed ~ Stempelsteuer bezahlen;
~ **envelope** Freiumschlag, -kuvert; ~ **paper** Stempelpapier; ~ **receipt** gestempelte Quittung; ~ **shares** abgestempelte Aktien; ~ **signature** gestempelte Unterschrift, Namensstempel; ~ **weight** geeichtes Gewicht.

stampede hektisches Gedränge, Ansturm, Panik, *(pol., US)* Meinungsumschwung;
~ *(v.)* in Panikstimmung versetzen;
~ **s. o. into doing s. th.** j. zu überstürzten Handlungen verleiten.
stampeder Goldsucher.
stamper *(post office)* Briefmarkenentwerter.

stamping Abstempelung, Freimachung, Verstempeln, *(mail)* Frankierung, *(paying duty)* Versteuerung;
~ **ground** *(US coll.)* Tummelplatz, Revier; ~ **machine** Stempel-, Frankiermaschine; ~ **office** *(insurance company)* Genehmigungsstelle für neue Versicherungsverträge.
stance Standpunkt, Haltung, Stellung.
stand Stand, Verkaufsbude, -stand, *(advertising, US)* Fläche für Plakatanschlag, Plakatständer, *(business situation, US)* Geschäftslage, *(for files)* Aktenbock, *(gallery)* Tribüne, *(industrial show)* Messestand, *(point of view)* Standpunkt, *(politics)* politische Haltung, *(theater)* Gastspieldauer, *(till money)* Ladenkasse, *(witness box, US)* Zeugenstand;
on the ~ *(US)* bei der Zeugenvernehmung;
fair ~ Messestand; **market** ~ Marktbude, Stand; **one-night** ~ *(theatrical company)* einmalige Vorstellung, einmaliges Gastspiel; **taxi** ~ Taxistand, -haltestelle; **umbrella** ~ Schirmständer; ~ **at a fair** Messestand; ~ **for ten taxicabs** Haltestelle für zehn Taxis; ~ **in a trade exhibition** Ausstellungsstand; **good** ~ **of wheat** gute Weizenernte;
~ *(v.)* *(agreement)* nicht mehr abgeändert werden können, *(make appearance)* vor Gericht erscheinen, *(law)* in Kraft sein, *(matter)* sich verhalten, *(objection)* bestehenbleiben, *(run)* sich bewerben, kandidieren;
~ **accused** angeklagt sein; ~ **by an agreement** sich an eine Vereinbarung halten; ~ **alone** mit einer Ansicht allein dastehen; ~ **aloof** *(fig.)* sich distanzieren; ~ **bail for s. o.** für jem. Kaution stellen; ~ **aside in favo(u)r of s. o.** zu jds. Gunsten zurücktreten (verzichten); ~ **by** beistehen, *(mil.)* sich in [Alarm]bereitschaft halten, *(radio station)* sendebereit sein, *(receiver)* auf Empfang stehen; ~ **as a candidate** kandidieren; ~ **on ceremony** auf Etikette halten; ~ **on ceremony with s. o.** zurückhaltend mit jem. verkehren; ~ **one's chance** es darauf ankommen lassen; ~ **a poor chance** schlechte Chancen haben; ~ **to one's colo(u)rs** *(mil.)* seine Stellung halten; ~ **in competition with s. o.** mit jem. konkurrieren; ~ **for a constituency** *(Br.)* sich als Kandidat für einen Wahlkreis aufstellen lassen; ~ **convicted** überführt sein; ~ **at cost at ...** *(balance sheet)* mit einem Herstellungspreis von ... zu Buch stehen; ~ **to s. one's credit** als jds. Guthaben ausgewiesen sein; ~ **in cure** in ärztlicher Behandlung sein; ~ **on the defensive** Verteidigungsstellung beziehen; ~ **delcredere** Delkredere übernehmen; ~ **to one's demands** auf seinen Forderungen bestehen; ~ **s. o. a dinner** j. zum Essen einladen (ausführen); ~ **down** *(assign)* abtreten, seine Kandidatur zurückziehen, *(partner)* Beteiligung aufgeben, *(witness)* vom Zeugenstand abtreten; ~ **a drink** einen ausgeben; ~ **to one's duty** treu seine Pflicht tun; ~ **empty** *(dwelling)* leer stehen; ~ **out against an enemy** dem Feind Widerstand leisten; ~ **in s. one's favo(u)r** günstig für j. sein; ~ **fire** Feuertaufe erhalten; ~ **firm** fest bleiben; ~ **for** *(office)* sich um ein Amt bewerben, als Kandidat auftreten, *(signify)* bedeuten, *(support)* eintreten für, verantworten; ~ **for s. th.** Symbol für etw. sein, etw. repräsentieren; ~ **for birth control** für Geburtenbeschränkung eintreten; ~ **clear from the gates** Eingang freihalten; ~ **s. o. a glass of beer** jem. ein Glas Bier spendieren; ~ **good in law** rechtsgültig sein; ~ **one's ground** *(fig.)* sich behaupten, bei seiner Meinung (Aussage) bleiben; ~ **guarantee for s. o.** als Bürge für j. haften; ~ **to one's guns** sich von seiner Ansicht nicht abbringen lassen; ~ **idle** *(factory)* stilliegen, nicht arbeiten; ~ **in for s. o.** für j. einspringen; ~ **in with s. o.** sich mit jem. die Rechnung teilen, sich an jds. Unkosten beteiligen, *(fig.)* sich j. warm halten, *(be in profitable alliance, US sl.)* mit jem. unter einer Decke stecken; ~ **indebted** verschuldet sein; ~ **for justice** für die Gerechtigkeit eintreten; ~ **on one's own legs** *(fam.)* unabhängig sein; ~ **in line** *(US)* Schlange stehen; ~ **first on the list** Liste anführen; ~ **to lose $ 10** zehn Dollar riskieren; ~ **a loss** Verlust tragen; ~ **over until the next meeting** bis zur nächsten Sitzung vertagen; ~ **for ready money** über Bargeld verfügen; ~ **under s. one's name** *(house)* auf jds. Namen eingetragen sein; ~ **in the name of s. o.** *(motion)* in jds. Namen eingebracht sein; ~ **in need of help** der Hilfe bedürfen, Hilfe benötigen; ~ **neutral** neutral bleiben; ~ **off** *(employees)* vorübergehend entlassen, *(fig.)* Abstand halten; ~ **for an office** sich um ein Amt bewerben; ~ **for the offing** in See stechen; ~ **open** offenstehen; ~ **out** nicht teilnehmen, *(ship)* auf Auslandskurs liegen; ~ **out for one's claim** auf seinen Forderungen bestehen; ~ **out of line** nicht mitziehen; ~ **out to the sea** in See gehen; ~ **over** sich vertagen; ~ **over till next week** bis zur nächsten Woche liegen bleiben; ~ **for Parliament** sich um einen Abgeordnetensitz bemühen; ~ **pat** reaktionären Parteistandpunkt vertreten; ~ **a plane on its nose** bei der Landung Kopfstand machen; ~ **to a policy** Politik unterstützen; ~ **in an**

awkward position in einer mißlichen Lage sein; ~ **to one's principles** an seinen Grundsätzen festhalten; ~ **the racket** Feuerprobe bestehen, *(US sl.)* hohe Spesen aushalten können; ~ **the racket of the London season** Wochen gesellschaftlicher Veranstaltungen in London überstehen; ~ **on the record** aufgezeichnet (im Protokoll vermerkt, protokolliert) sein; ~ **on one's right** auf seinem Recht beharren; ~ **a round** Runde (Lage) ausgeben; ~ **security for s. o.** jem. Sicherheit (Garantie) stellen (leisten), sich für j. verbürgen; ~ **as security for a debt** für eine Schuld bürgen; ~ **s. o. 5 shillings** jem. fünf Schillinge zu stehen kommen; ~ **for the shore** auf den Einlaufkurs liegen; ~ **shot to s. o.** j. freihalten; ~ **shoulder to shoulder** Kopf an Kopf stehen; ~ **surety** Aval geben; ~ **by the terms of a contract** sich an die Vertragsbedingungen halten; ~ **the test** sich bewähren; ~ **for racial tolerance** für Rassentoleranz eintreten; ~ **for free trade** Anhänger des Freihandels sein; ~ **treat** Rechnung übernehmen, Zeche (Runde) bezahlen; ~ **one's trial** sich einer Gerichtsverhandlung unterziehen, vor Gericht (unter Anklage) stehen; ~ **up** *(US sl.)* freihalten; ~ **up for o. s.** sich für die eigenen Belange einsetzen; ~ **up for s. o.** für j. eintreten, sich für jds. Anständigkeit einsetzen, *(best man)* jds. Trauzeuge sein; ~ **s. o. up** j. sitzen lassen (versetzen), Verabredung mit jem. nicht einhalten; ~ **up to s. o.** jem. Paroli bieten; ~ **up and be counted** *(US)* sich für etw. einsetzen, seine Meinung äußern; ~ **up straight** *(fig.)* Rückgrat zeigen; ~ **for more wages** auf höheren Löhnen bestehen, Lohnerhöhung fordern; ~ **all the way back in a bus** ganzen Rückweg im Bus stehen; ~ **well with one's chief** sich mit seinem Vorgesetzten gut stehen; ~ **by one's words** zu seinen Worten stehen;

to adopt as it ~s unverändert annehmen; **to be brought to a ~** gestoppt werden, *(mil.)* zum Stehen gebracht werden; **to have a good ~-in with s. o.** gute Nummer bei jem. haben, bei jem. gut angeschrieben sein; **to let an account ~ over** Konto unausgeglichen lassen; **to let a question ~ over** Frage offen (in der Schwebe, ungeklärt) lassen; **to make ~ for one's principles** für seine Grundsätze eintreten; **to make a ~ against the enemy** dem Feind Widerstand leisten; **to put s. o. on the ~** *(US)* j. als Zeugen vernehmen; **to take a ~** Haltung einnehmen; **to take the ~** *(US)* Zeugenstand betreten, Zeugenstuhl einnehmen, als Zeuge aussagen; **to take a ~ in favo(u)r of s. o.** sich für j. einsetzen; **to take a unique ~** individuellen Standpunkt einnehmen; **to take one's ~ on a letter** sich auf einen Brief stützen; **to take one's ~ upon sound precedents** sich an soliden Präzedenzfällen ausrichten;

~-by tariff *(hire service)* Tarif mit begrenztem Sonderangebot (für Sofortflüge); ~ **camera** *(Br.)* Atelier-, Stativkamera; **~-in** *(film, US)* Double, Ersatzschauspieler; ~ **design** Standgestaltung; **~-in charge** stellvertretender Geschäftsführer; ~ **space** Ausstellungsfläche; **~-to** erhöhte Gefechtsbereitschaft; **~-up** *(photograph)* Ganzaufnahme; **~-up buffet** kaltes Buffet; **~-up comedian** aufgeplusterter Komödiant; **~-up guy** *(sl.)* gestandenes Mannsbild; **~-up lunch** im Stehen eingenommener Imbiß.

standard Standard, [Güte]grad, *(average)* Durchschnitt, *(banner)* Banner, Fahne, Standarte, *(coinage)* gesetzlicher Feingehalt, Feingewicht, Münzfuß, -einheit, *(currency)* Währung[sstandard], [feste] Valuta, *(measure)* Maßstab, -einheit, Richt-, Eichmaß, Einheitsform, *(of newspaper)* Niveau, *(norm)* Norm, Normentyp, Richtwert, -linie, *(quality)* Standardqualität, -ausführung, Leistungs-, Qualitätsniveau, *(price)* Normalpreis, *(rule)* Regel, Richtschnur, *(sample)* Muster, *(school, Br.)* Stufe, Klasse, *(time study)* Vorgabeleistung, *(unification)* Vereinheitlichung, *(value)* Wert, Wertmesser, -einheit, *(weight)* Normalgewicht;

above ~ überdurchschnittlich; **below ~** unterdurchschnittlich, *(alloy)* geringhaltig, nicht vollwichtig; **hopelessly below ~** unter aller Kritik; **by European ~s** nach europäischen Maßstäben; **by present day ~s** nach heutigen Maßstäben;

alternative ~ Alternativwährung; **bimetallic (double) ~** Doppelwährung; **commercial ~** handelsübliche Qualität; **commodity ~** *(US)* auf dem Grundsatz Mark gleich Mark aufgebaute Währung; **cotton ~** Durchschnittsbaumwollqualität; **credit ~s** Kreditrichtlinien, -normen; **descriptive ~s** äußerliche Warenmerkmale; **established ~s** anerkannte Normen; **fiduciary ~** Papiergeldwährung; **fixed ~** unveränderliche (feste) Valuta; **fluctuating ~** unbeständige Valuta; **foreign ~** ausländische Valuta; **full ~** *(of a coin)* Vollgehalt; **gold ~** Goldstandard; **gold-bullion ~** Goldkernwährung; **gold-exchange ~** Golddevisenwährung; **gold-specie ~** Goldumlaufwährung; **governmental ~** staatlich festgelegte Norm; **high moral ~s** hohes moralisches Niveau; **ideal ~s** optimale Standardkosten; **industry ~s** Industrienormen; **international ~** internationales Währungssystem, *(law of nations)* völkerrechtliche Verhaltensnormen; **legal ~** gesetzliche Währung; **limping ~** hinkende Währung; **metallic ~** Metallwährung; **monetary ~** Münzstandard, -fuß, Währungseinheit; **multiple ~** Indexwährung; **paper ~** Papierwährung; **performance ~** Leistungskennzahlen; **product ~s** Warennormen; **production ~s** Richtwerte für die Fertigung; **professional ~s** berufsethische Grundsätze; **silver ~** Silberstandard, -währung; **single ~** monometallische Währung; **tabular ~** Währungsstandard nach Kaufkrafttabellen, Indexwährung; **trade ~s** Wirtschaftsnormen;

~ **of alloy** Münzgehalt; **low ~ of attainments** niedriger Bildungsstand; **~s of benefits** Normalsätze des Krankengeldes; **~s of business contracts** einheitliche Grundsätze über den Abschluß von Geschäftsverträgen; **~s of business forms** einheitliche Geschäftsmethoden; **high ~ of care** strenge Anforderungen an die Sorgfaltspflicht; ~ **of coinage** Münzfuß; ~ **of coins** Feingehalt; ~ **of comfort** Wohlstandsniveau; ~ **of conduct** Verhaltensnormen; ~ **of currency** Münzeinheit; **high ~ of diligence** hoher Sorgfaltsgrad; **~s of dimensions, designs or quality** Abmessungs-, Konstruktions- oder Qualitätsnormen; **general ~ of education** allgemeines Bildungsniveau; **~s of efficiency** Leistungsnormen; **high ~ of ethics** hohes sittliches Niveau; **high ~s of an examination** hohe Prüfungsanforderungen; ~ **of fineness** Feingehalt; **~s of height** Qualitätsansprüche; **~s in industry** Industrienormen; ~ **of intelligence** Intelligenzgrad; **normal ~ of interest** üblicher Zinsfuß, -satz; ~ **of knowledge** Bildungsgrad; ~ **established by law** gesetzlich gesetzte Norm; ~ **of learning** Bildungsgrad; **~s of literacy and numeracy** Grundkenntnisse in Lesen, Schreiben und Rechnen; ~ **of living (life)** durchschnittliche Lebenshaltung, Lebensstandard; ~ **of measure** Maßeinheit; ~ **of deferred payments** *(US)* Wertmaß für aufgeschobene Zahlungen; **~s of performance** Leistungskennzahlen, -niveau, Solleistung; ~ **of prices** Preisniveau, -spiegel; ~ **of production** Produktionsstandard; **ethical ~s of a profession** Standespflichten eines Berufs; **prewar ~ of profits** Vorkriegsgewinndurchschnitt; ~ **of pronunciation** Standardaussprache; **exacting ~s of quality** hohe Güte-, Qualitätsanforderungen; **high ~s of quality** hohe Qualitätsnormen, -ansprüche; **national basis ~s of relief** bundeseinheitlich festgelegte Unterstützungsnormen; **~s of safety** Sicherheitsnormen; **~s of selectivity** Auswahlmaßstäbe; ~ **of technology** Leistungsstand; ~ **of value** Wertmesser, -maßstab; ~ **of wages** Lohnniveau; ~ **of weight** Gewichtseinheit;

to apply another ~ anderen Maßstab anlegen; **to apply a new legal ~** neue Rechtsnormen zur Anwendung bringen; **to be below ~** den Anforderungen nicht genügen; **to be up to ~** den Anforderungen (Güteerfordernissen) genügen; **to be up to ~ in every way** allen Qualitätsansprüchen genügen; **to be of high ~** hohes Niveau haben; **not to come up to ~** den Anforderungen nicht Genüge leisten; **to conform to the ~s of society** den gesellschaftlichen Regeln Folge leisten; **to correspond to the ~s of quality** Gütebestimmungen (Qualitätsnormen) entsprechen; **to create ~s of official conduct** berufsethische Richtlinien festlegen; **to establish ~s of quality** Qualitätsnormen festlegen; **to impose highest ~s on s. o.** höchste Qualitätsansprüche an j. stellen; **to maintain ~s** hohen Stand halten; **to meet the ~s for clean air** den festgelegten Werten für saubere Luft entsprechen; **to promote high ~s** hohe Qualitätsansprüche stellen; **to raise the ~ of living** Lebensstandard anheben; **to raise the ~ of free trade** Banner des Freihandels hochhalten; **to reach a high ~ of efficiency** hohen Leistungsgrad erreichen; **to serve as a ~** als Norm gelten; **to set the ~ for** Maßstab abgeben; **to set ~s** Richtlinien aufstellen; **to set a high ~ of business morality** hohe Anforderungen an die Geschäftsmoral stellen; **to set a high ~ for candidates in an examination** hohe Qualitätsansprüche an Examenskandidaten stellen;

~ *(a.)* normal, vorschriftsmäßig, *(classical)* klassisch, *(leading)* führend, maßgebend, musterhaft, *(stable)* stabil, wertbeständig;

~ **account form** Einheitskontoblatt; ~ **advertising register** *(US)* Nachschlagewerk für die Werbung; ~ **amount** *(EC)* Pauschbetrag; ~ **application form** übliches Antragsformular; ~ **articles** Einheitsware; **American ~s Association** Amerikanischer Normenverband; ~ **author** anerkannter Schriftsteller; ~ **automobile public liability policy** *(US)* allgemeine Kraftfahrzeughaftpflichtpolice; ~ **balance sheet** Einheitsbilanzformular; ~ **bearer** *(fig.)* Anführer, Bannerträger; ~ **benefit** Einheitsunterstützung[ssatz]; ~ **book number** Bestellnummer; ~ **book slip** Standardbücherzettel; ~ **broadcast** Mittelwellenfunk; ~ **bullion** Münzgold, -silber; ~ **calculation** Normalkalkulation; ~ **capacity** Normal-, Durchschnittsleistung; ~ **car** Standardtyp,

-ausführung, Normalausführung; ~ **chart of accounts** Kontenrahmen; ~ **claim** Valutaschuld; ~ **International Trade Classification** Internationales Warenverzeichnis für den Außenhandel; ~ **clause** Grundbedingung, *(currency)* Währungsklausel; ~ **coin** Münze mit gesetzlich vorgeschriebenem Feingehalt; ~ **coinage** Münzfuß, -tarif; ~ **commercial article** auf dem Warenmarkt eingeführter Artikel; ~ **condition** Standardklausel; ~ **conditions** normale Arbeitsbedingungen; ~ **contract** Norm-, Muster-, Modellvertrag; ~ **cost** Einheits-, Standard[herstellungs]-, Plan-, Richt-, Normalkosten, vorkalkulierte Kosten; ~ **cost budgeting** Normalkostenplan; ~**cost system** Einheitspreissystem, Kostenindex, Normalkostenrechnung; ~ **costing** Normalkostenrechnung; **gold-~ country** Land mit Goldwährung, Goldwährungsland; **silver-~ country** Land mit Silberwährung, Silberwährungsland; ~ **currency** Einheitswährung; ~ **data** *(time study)* Richtwerte; ~ **deduction for expenses** *(income tax, US)* Pauschalabzug für Geschäftsunkosten, Sonderausgabenpauschale, Werbekostenpauschale; ~ **design** Normal-, Regelausführung; ~ **deviation** *(statistics)* Normal-, Standardabweichung; ~ **distance** Einheitsstrecke; ~ **dictionary** klassisches Wörterbuch; ~ **dividend rate** Einheitsdividendensatz; ~ **dollar** Golddollar; ~ **earnings** Tarifverdienst; ~ **edition** Standardausgabe; ~ **eight-hour day** achtstündiger Normalarbeitstag; ~ **elemental times** Elementarzeiten; ~ **equipment** Normal-, Standardausführung, Standardausstattung; ~ **error** *(statistics)* Standardfehler; ~ **family** Normalfamilie; ~ **figures of distribution** Kennzahlen des Absatzes, Normalabsatzzahlen; ~ **[gauge] film** Normalfilm; ~ **fire policy** Feuerversicherungs-, Einheitspolice; ~ **form** Einheitsformular; ~ **form of application** übliches Antragsformular; ~ **form of bank guarantee** Bürgschaftsformular einer Bank; ~ **form contract** Standard-, Einheits-, Mustervertrag; ~ **form contract conditions** allgemeine Geschäftsbedingungen; ~ **freight** Einheitsfracht; ~ **gauge** Normaleichmaß, *(railway)* Normalspurweite, Vollspur; ~ **German** Hochdeutsch; ~ **gold** Probe-, Münzgold; ~ **grade** Einheitssorte, -qualität; ~ **hours** Tarifstunden, *(time study)* Vorgabestunden; ~ **hourly wage** Tarifstundenlohn; ~ **and Poor's Indices** *(US)* Indexziffern der Börsenkurse; ~ **Industrial Classification** *(Br.)* amtliche Systematik der Betriebsstätten; **British ~s Institution** Britischer Normenverband; ~ **interest** üblicher Zinsfuß, -satz; ~ **international size** internationale Standardgröße; ~ **International Trade Classification** Internationales Warenverzeichnis für den Außenhandel; ~ **item** Serienerzeugnis; ~ **labo(u)r cost** Tariflohnkosten; ~ **labo(u)r rate** Grundlohn einschließlich der Normalzuschläge, Grundlohnsatz plus Prämien; ~ **labo(u)r time (man hours)** Sollfertigungszeit, Normalarbeitszeit, durchschnittliche Arbeitszeit; ~ **lamp** Stehlampe; ~ **letter** Standardbrief; ~ **life** durchschnittliche Lebensdauer; ~ **line** Standardartikel; **to follow** ~ **lines** normales Leben führen; ~ **machine time** Normalleistung; ~ **make** Normalausführung; ~ **mark** Feingehaltsstempel; ~ **market** tonangebende Börse; ~ **measure** Eich-, Originalmaß, Normalmaß; ~ **media rates** Standardwerbetarif; ~ **model** Serienausführung, Standard-, Einheits-, Serienmodell; ~ **money** *(coin)* vollgewichtige Münze, *(currency)* Währungsgeld, Geldeinheit; ~ **mortgage clause** *(fire policy)* Auszahlungsklausel bei der Hypothekengewährung; ~ **novel** klassischer Roman; ~ **order form** übliches Auftragsformular; ~ **organization** Einheitsorganisation; ~ **output** Soll-, Normalleistung; ~ **paper** Normalpapier; ~ **pattern** Einheitsmuster; ~ **payment clause** übliche Zahlungsbedingungen; ~ **performance** Vorgabeleistung; ~ **piece wage** Einheitsstücklohn; ~ **policy** Normal-, Einheitspolice; ~ **population** Standardbevölkerung; ~ **poster board** Litfaßsäule; ~ **practice** übliches Verfahren; **to follow one's** ~ **practice** sein übliches Verfahren anwenden; ~ **price** einheitlicher Preis, Normal-, Richt-, Grund-, Einheitspreis; ~ **production** Normalleistung, Durchschnittsproduktion; ~ **production price** Erzeugerrichtpreis; ~ **profit** Bruttoverdienst; ~ **provisions** allgemeine Versicherungsbedingungen; ~ **purchase price** Normal-, Richt-, Grundpreis; ~ **quality** Einheitsqualität, durchschnittliche Güte (Qualität); ~ **quotation** Einheitskurs; ~ **rate** Grundpreis, Einheitsgebühr, -satz, *(advertising)* Grund-, Standardtarif, *(stock exchange)* Normalkurs, *(taxation, Br.)* [Steuer]normalsatz; ~ **rates** *(wage)* Normaltarif, -lohn, Tariflohn; ~ **rate of income tax** unterer Proportionalsatz des Einkommenssteuertarifs, Eingangssteuersatz; **to pay in excess of** ~ **rates** übertariflich bezahlen; ~ **ratio** Normalbezugsgröße; ~ **reaction** übliche Reaktion; ~ **rent** *(Br.)* normale Friedensmiete *(per 03. 08. 1914)*; ~ **report** Musterbericht; ~ **return form** genormtes Bestellformular; ~**run quantity** wirtschaftliche Losgröße; ~

sample Einheitsmuster; ~ **scheme of account** Normalkontenplan; ~**s setting** Normenfestsetzung; ~ **silver** Münzsilber; ~ **size** Einheitsformat, -größe, Normalgröße, *(advertising)* Standardformat; ~ **specifications** Normalbedingungen; ~ **stock** Normalgröße; ~ **stocks** *(stock exchange)* Spitzen-, Standardwerte, Favoriten; ~ **subscription** Normalbezug; ~ **tax** *(income tax, Br.)* Basissteuer; ~ **tax deduction** *(income tax, US)* abzugsfähiger Tarifbetrag, pauschaler Freibetrag; ~ **text** Mustertext; ~ **time** Normalzeit, *(US)* Zeitnorm [im Arbeitsprozeß]; ~ **time for a given job** Vorgabe-, Normalarbeitszeit; ~**time data** Richtwerte; ~ **type** *(print.)* normale Schrift[form]; ~ **type of form** Einheitsformular; ~ **unit** *(advertising)* Normaleinheit, Standardformat; ~ **unit cost** Normalkosten pro Einheit; ~ **value** *(cost system)* Normal-, Durchschnitts-, Einheits-, Festwert; ~ **values** *(cost system)* Normalwerte; ~ **wage** Tariflohn; ~ **wage rates** Tariflohnsätze; ~ **weight** Nominal-, Normal-, Eichgewicht; ~ **weight and fineness** *(coinage)* Gewichts- und Feingehaltseinheit; ~ **work** Standardwerk; ~ **working day** Normalarbeitstag; ~ **working week** Normalarbeitswoche; ~ **writer** Klassiker.

standardization Normung, Standardisierung, Eichung, Typisierung, Vereinheitlichung;
commercial ~ Warennormung; **monetary** ~ Währungsangleichung;
~ **of commodities** Warennormung; ~ **of factories** Betriebsvereinheitlichung; ~ **of freight charges** Angleichung der Frachtsätze; ~ **of gauge** *(railway)* Spurenvereinheitlichung; ~ **in marketing** Absatznormung; ~ **of sizes** einheitliche Größenregelung; ~ **of tariffs** Tarifangleichung, -vereinheitlichung; ~ **of wages** Lohnangleichung;
~ **committee** Normenausschuß; **International ~ Organization** Internationaler Normenausschuß.

standardize *(v.)* auf eine Norm bringen, in Normwerten ausdrücken, standardisieren, norm[ier]en, festsetzen, vereinheitlichen, typisieren;
~ **freight charges** Frachtsätze angleichen.

standardized vereinheitlicht, genormt, typisiert, übersichtlich; ~ **invoice** Normalrechnung; ~ **product** Einheitserzeugnis; ~ **production** genormte Produktion; ~ **sheet size** Standardformat.

standby Helfer, Hilfe, Beistand, Bereitschaft, *(airline)* Warte-, Bereitstellungsliste, *(mil.)* Abwehrbereitschaft, *(technics)* Not-, Zusatz-, Reservegerät;
to have a sum in reserve as ~ Notpfennig zurückgelegt haben;
~ **agreement** *(underwriting)* Garantie des Direktabsatzes, *(credit line)* Bereitstellungsvereinbarung; ~ **arrangement** *(International Monetary Fund)* Beistandsabkommen, Stillhaltevereinbarung; ~ **charges** Bereitstellungskosten; ~ **cost** fixe Kosten; ~ **credit** Beistandskredit, Kreditzusage; ~ **credit arrangement** für Investitionszwecke im voraus vereinbarter langfristiger Kreditvertrag; ~ **duty** *(mil.)* Dienstbereitschaft, Bereitschaftsdienst; ~ **equipment** Reserveausstattung; ~ **facilities** Stillhaltezusagen; ~ **order** *(mil.)* Bereitschaftsbefehl; ~ **passenger** Fahrgast auf Abruf, Fluggast auf der Warteliste; ~ **position** *(mil.)* Wartestellung; ~ **service** Bereitschaftsdienst; ~ **supply** *(electricity)* Spitzenversorgung; ~ **time** Wartezeit; ~ **underwriting** Übernahmekonsortium für nicht abgesetzte Bezugsrechte; ~ **unit** *(el.)* Notaggregat.

standee *(US)* stehender Zuschauer, Stehplatzinhaber.

stander-by Zuschauer.

standing *(rank)* Rang[dienstalter], Stand, *(repute)* Stellung, Position, Bonität, Ruf, Ansehen, *(right to sue, US)* Klageberechtigung, *(standing place)* Stehplatz;
of equal ~ gleichrangig; **of good** ~ hochangesehen; **of long** ~ langjährig; **of ten years'** ~ mit zehnjähriger Berufszeit;
business ~ wirtschaftliche Stellung; **credit** ~ Kreditwürdigkeit; **doubtful** ~ zweifelhafter Ruf; **financial** ~ *(firm)* Finanzlage, finanzielle Lage, Status, Kreditfähigkeit, -würdigkeit; ~ **idle** *(factory)* Stilliegen; **legal** ~ gesetzlicher Status; **social** ~ soziale Stellung; **sound** ~ Bonität;
general ~ **of a business** wirtschaftlicher Wert eines Geschäftes; ~ **by** Mitwisserschaft; ~ **of a commercial house** bewährter Ruf einer Firma; ~ **in contempt** Nichtbefolgung einer richterlichen Auflage; **high** ~ **of a firm** hohes Ansehen einer Firma; ~ **in industry** kaufmännisches Ansehen, Ruf in der Geschäftswelt; **to be of good** ~ angesehen sein, angesehene Stellung haben; **to be of recognized** ~ sehr angesehen sein; **to be of the same** ~ gleichrangig sein; **to be** ~ **for the shore** auf die Küste zuhalten; **to belong to a family of good** ~ zu einer angesehenen Familie gehören; **to finish a work at one** ~ in einem Arbeitsgang erledigen; **to get official** ~ offiziell anerkannt werden; **to keep** ~

(printing trade) Satz (Druckform) stehen lassen; **to sell the crop ~** Ernte auf dem Halm verkaufen;

~ *(a.)* beständig, dauerhaft, fortbestehend, *(upright)* stehend; **~ army** stehendes Heer; **~ audience** Stehempfang; **~ body** ständiges Organ; **~ charges** konstante Kosten, laufende Unkosten, Dauerlasten; **~ committee** ständiger Ausschuß; **~ contract** fester Vertrag; **~ cost** konstante (feste) Kosten; **~ credit** laufender Kredit; **~ crop** Ernte auf dem Halm; **~ custom** althergebrachter Brauch, Usance; **~ customer** Dauerkunde, langjähriger Kunde; **~ desk** Stehpult; **~ detail** *(advertising)* wiederkehrendes Anzeigenelement; **~ engine** stillstehende Maschine; **~ expenses** laufende (feste) Unkosten; **~ grain** Getreide auf dem Halm; **~ group** *(UNO)* ständige Gruppe; **~ instructions** *(to bank)* Dauerauftrag; **~ invitation** Dauereinladung; **~ matter** *(print.)* Stehsatz; **~ mortgage** Festhypothek; **~ nuisance** Dauerbelästigung; **~ offer** gleichbleibendes (ständig aufrechterhaltenes) Angebot; **~ order** allgemeine Anordnung, fester Auftrag, Dauerauftrag, *(banking)* Dauerauftrag an die Bank, Dauerüberweisungsauftrag, *(magazine)* Abonnement, *(mil.)* ständige Dienstanweisung; **~ orders** *(local government, Br.)* [etwa] Hauptsatzung, *(parl.)* Geschäftsordnung; **with a ~ order** bei regelmäßigem Bezug; **~ order for a newspaper** festes Zeitungsabonnement; **to have a ~ order for an article** bestimmten Artikel regelmäßig beziehen; **~ orders committee** Geschäftsordnungsausschuß; **~ order payment** Dauerzahlung, -auftrag; **~ ovation** im Stehen dargebrachte Ovation; **~ passengers** Fahrgäste ohne Sitzplatz; **~ place** Stehplatz; **~ room** Stehplatz; **~ room only** nur Stehplätze; **~ rule** unabänderliche (feststehende) Regel; **~ rules** Geschäftsordnung, Satzung, *(parl.)* Verfahrensordnung; **~ to sue doctrine** *(US)* Lehrsatz vom Prozeßführungsrecht bei Staatshaftung; **~ type** *(print.)* Stehsatz; **~ wages** festes Gehalt.

standish Schreibtischgarnitur.

standoff *(US)* Distanzierung.

standoffish reserviert, zurückhaltend, distanziert.

standout Außenseiter, *(workers)* Arbeitsverweigerung.

standpat *(politics, US)* verkrusteter Konservativer; **~** *(a.)* reaktionär, gegen jede Änderung eingestellt.

standpatter reaktionärer Parteipolitiker.

stannary *(Br.)* Zinngrube; **~ court** *(Br.)* Bergwerksgericht.

standpoint Standpunkt.

standstill Stillstand, Stockung; **to be at a ~** stocken, *(factory)* nicht in Betrieb sein; **to be at an absolute ~** *(trade)* vollständig zum Erliegen gekommen sein; **to bring to a ~** zum Stillstand bringen; **to have come to a ~** *(conference)* toten Punkt erreicht haben, festgefahren sein; **~ agreement** Stillhalteabkommen; **~ commission** Stillhalteausschuß; **~ credit** Stillhaltekredit; **~ debts** Stillhalteschulden; **~ order** Stillhalteverfügung.

staple *(chief product)* Haupterzeugnis, -produkt, *(clip)* Heftklammer, *(emporium)* Markt-, Stapelplatz, Handelszentrum, *(fig.)* Hauptthema, -gegenstand, *(international laws)* Handelserlaubnis für Ausländer, *(loop of iron)* Öse, Krampe, *(raw material)* Rohstoff, -material; **~s** Hauptartikel, -produkte, -handelsware, Stapelgut, -waren, Massenartikel, -ware; **foreign ~** Ausfuhrmonopol; **~ of news** Nachrichtenzentrum; **~** *(v.)* Handelsniederlage errichten, *(paper)* [fest]klammern, [mit Draht] heften; **to form the ~ of a conversation** hauptsächlichen Gesprächsgegenstand abgeben; **~** *(a.)* marktgängig; **~ articles (commodities, goods)** Massen-, Hauptartikel, Hauptprodukte, Stapelware; **~ earner** Haupteinnahmequelle; **~ fibre** Zellwolle; **~ flavo(u)r** Hauptgeschmacksrichtung; **~ food** Hauptnahrungsmittel; **~ house** Lagerhaus, Niederlage; **~ industries** Hauptindustriezweige; **~ merchandise** Massenartikel; **~ place** Hauptniederlage; **~ port** Stapelhafen; **~ product** Hauptprodukt; **~ right** Marktgerechtigkeit; **~ subject of conversation** Hauptgesprächsthema; **~ town** Haupthandelsplatz; **~ trade** Stapelhandel; **~ ware** Stapelware.

stapler *(dealer in staple goods)* Stapelkaufmann, Sortierer, *(machine)* Heftapparat, -maschine.

stapling machine Heftmaschine.

star Stern, *(film)* Star, *(fig.)* Größe, Berühmtheit, *(print.)* Sternchen; **film ~** Filmstar; **literary ~** literarische Größe; **shooting ~** Sternschnuppe; **unlucky ~** Unglücksstern, Unstern; **~s and stripes** *(US)* Sternenbanner;

~ *(v.)* als Star herausbringen, *(v./i.)* als Hauptdarsteller auftreten; **~ in a new film** Hauptdarsteller in einem neuen Film sein; **to be born under a lucky ~** unter einem glücklichen Stern geboren sein; **to be through with one's ~s** kein Glück mehr haben; **to follow one's ~** seinem guten Stern vertrauen; **~** *(a.)* erstklassig; **~ aerial** Sternantenne; **~ billing** *(US)* Starnummer, -reklame; **all-~ cast** Starbesetzung; **~-chamber proceedings** Kabinettsjustiz; **~ map** Sterntafel; **~ performance** Glanzleistung, *(theater)* Vorstellung mit erster Besetzung; **~ performer** *(stock exchange)* Spitzenreiter; **~ prosecution witness** Hauptbelastungszeuge; **~ quality** Spitzenqualität; **to give ~ rating** erstklassig beurteilen; **~-Spangled Banner** *(US)* Sternenbanner; **~ system** Starunwesen; **~ trappings** Starallüren; **~ turn** Starauftritt, Hauptattraktion, -nummer.

starboard Steuerbord.

starboarder *(US coll.)* Stammkunde.

starch *(US sl.)* Mumm, Energie.

stare decisis *(lat.)* nach herrschender Rechtsprechung.

stargazer Sterndeuter, Astrologe, *(sl.)* Romantiker.

starlet Filmsternchen.

starred als Filmstar herausgebracht.

starry-eyed reformers unrealistische Reformer.

start Start, Aufbruch, *(airplane)* Abflug, *(departure)* Abfahrt, Abreise, *(machine)* Inbetriebsetzung; **after several false ~s** nach einigen Fehlstarts; **from ~ to finish** vom Anfang bis zum Ende; **ready to ~** abfahrbereit; **rum ~** große Überraschung; **~ in life** Startmöglichkeit; **~ of printing** Druckbeginn; **~** *(v.)* anfangen, in Angriff nehmen, starten, *(airplane)* abfliegen, starten, *(depart)* abreisen, abfahren, *(production)* anlaufen, *(set going)* in Gang (Betrieb) setzen, in die Wege leiten, einleiten, *(ship)* auslaufen, *(train)* ab-, anfahren; **~ again** von neuem beginnen; **~ all over again** noch einmal ganz von vorn anfangen; **~ agitation** Unruhe stiften; **~ the ball rolling** Stein ins Rollen bringen; **~ on a book** Buch zu lesen (schreiben) anfangen; **~ in a business** in ein Geschäft einsteigen; **~ s. o. in business** j. etablieren, jem. zu einer selbständigen Existenz verhelfen; **~ a new business enterprise** neues Geschäft eröffnen; **~ a car** Auto starten; **~ s. o. on a career** j. lancieren; **~ a company** Gesellschaft gründen; **~ a drive** Aktion starten; **~ at the wrong end** am falschen Ende anfangen; **~ from the fact** von der Tatsache ausgehen; **~ a new fashion** neue Mode einführen; **~ a fund** Kapital aufbringen, Geldsammlung veranstalten; **~ a hare** etw. ins Spiel bringen; **~ on a journey** Reise antreten, abreisen; **~ on a low key** ganz harmlos anfangen; **~ in life** ins Berufsleben eintreten; **~ negotiations** Verhandlungen beginnen (aufnehmen); **~ a newspaper** neue Zeitung herausbringen; **~ an objection** Einwendung erheben (machen); **~ the price** erstes Gebot abgeben; **~ from reality** sich auf den Boden der Wirklichkeit stellen; **~ a rumo(u)r** Gerücht in Umlauf setzen; **~ running** in Betrieb setzen, anlaufen lassen; **~ after schedule** *(US)* fahrplanmäßig abfahren; **~ from scratch** klein (mit Null) anfangen; **~ from scratch again** wieder von vorn anfangen; **~ a shop** Laden eröffnen; **~ s. o. thinking** j. zum Nachdenken anregen; **~ on time** fahrplanmäßig abfahren; **~ a train** Zug einsetzen; **~ up** *(difficulties)* sich einstellen; **~ on one's way** sich aufmachen; **~ at $ 140 a week** mit 140 Dollar Lohn in der Woche anfangen; **~ well** *(sales)* gut gehen; **~ work** mit der Arbeit anfangen; **~ out to write a novel** sich an die Abfassung eines Romans machen; **to be off to a slow ~** langsam in Gang kommen; **to get a head ~ on s. o.** Vorsprung vor jem. erhalten; **to get a ~ in business** lanciert werden; **to get the ~ of one's competitors (rivals)** seine Konkurrenten überflügeln; **to get a good ~ in life** gute Berufschance bekommen; **to get a slow ~** nur langsam in Gang kommen; **to give s. o. a ~** beim Eintritt ins Leben helfen; **to have made a good ~** gut vorangekommen sein; **to make an early ~** früh aufbrechen; **to make a fresh ~** noch einmal von vorn anfangen; **to muddle at the ~** *(business)* schlechten Start haben; **to work by fits and ~s** ungleichmäßig arbeiten.

starter *(car)* Anlasser, *(founder)* Begründer, *(originator)* Veranlasser, Urheber, *(railway)* Fahrdienstleiter, *(sport)* Teilnehmer; **~ choke (knob, lever, Br.)** Starterklappe; **~ fund** Startfonds.

starting Aufbruch, *(set going)* Inbetriebsetzung; **~ in business** Geschäftseröffnung, -beginn; **~ of an enterprise** Geschäftsbeginn; **~ of production** Anlauf der Erzeugung, Produktionsbeginn, -anlauf; **~ July 1** *(US)* ab 1. Juli;

~ **base** Ausgangsbasis; ~ **credit** Anlaufkredit; ~ **date** Anfangs-datum, *(employee)* Einstellungstermin; ~-**load cost** Vorproduktionskosten, Kosten vor Anlauf der Fertigung; ~ **period** Anfangs-, Anlaufzeit; ~ **place** Abfahrtsort; ~ **platform** Abfahrtsbahnsteig; ~ **point** Anfangs-, Ausgangspunkt; ~ **price** Eröffnungs-, Anfangskurs, *(auction)* Einsatzpreis; ~ **rate** *(employee)* Anfangstarif, -lohn; ~ **salary** Anfangsgehalt; ~ **salary differential** anfängliche Gehaltsunterschiede; ~ **stake** Ersteinlage; ~ **station** Abgangsbahnhof; ~ **time** Abfahrtszeit, *(plant)* Arbeitsbeginn; ~ **trouble** Anlasserschwierigkeiten.

startling news alarmierende Nachrichten.

startup Anlauf, Beginn;
~ **cost** Start-, Anlaufkosten; ~ **money** Startkapital; ~ **problem** Anfangs-, Startproblem; ~ **year** Startjahr.

starvation Hungertod;
to die of ~ verhungern;
to be on a ~ **diet** Abmagerungskur durchführen; ~ **wage** Hungerlohn.

starve *(v.)* hungern, vor Hunger fast umkommen;
~ **to death** verhungern; ~ **a garrison into surrender** Besatzung aushungern.

stash Versteck, geheimes Lager;
~ *(v.)* horten, verstecken, nicht an die Öffentlichkeit kommen lassen.

state *(book)* Erhaltungszustand, *(condition)* [Zu]stand, Lage, *(financial situation, Br.)* Status, *(government)* Staat[swesen], Land, *(mil.)* Stärkemeldung, *(rank)* Stand, Rang, Stellung, *(Br., weekly return)* wöchentlicher [Bank]ausweis, *(stock exchange)* Haltung, *(US)* Einzelstaat;
in a bad ~ in schlechtem Zustand; **in a good** ~ in gutem Zustand; **in the native** ~ *(product)* unbearbeitet;
associated ~ assoziierter Staat; **authoritarian** ~ autoritärer Staat; **banner** ~ führender Staat; **coastal** ~ Küstenland; **confederated** ~ Staat eines Staatenbundes; **contracting** ~ Vertragsstaat; **creditor** ~ Gläubigerstaat; **daily** ~ tägliche Geschäftsübersicht; **deliverable** ~ lieferfähiger Zustand; **drugged** ~ Rauschzustand; **enemy** ~ Feindstaat; **federal** ~ Bundesstaat; **financial** ~ Finanzlage, Status; **first-class** ~ erstklassige Beschaffenheit; **foreign** ~ ausländischer Staat; **free** ~ Freistaat; **friendly** ~ befreundeter Staat; **inchoate** ~ in der Entstehung befindlicher Staat; **individual** ~ Einzelstaat; **injured** ~ geschädigter Staat; **interim** ~ vorübergehendes Staatsgebilde; **landlocked** ~ Binnenstaat; **low** ~ Tiefstand; **married** ~ Ehestand; **medium-ranking** ~ Staat mittlerer Größe; **member** ~ Gliedstaat, Mitgliedsland; **mental** ~ Geisteszustand; **multinational** ~ Nationalitätenstaat; **neighbo(u)ring** ~ Nachbarstaat; **nonaccredited** ~ nicht akkreditiertes Land; **nonaligned** ~ blockfreier Staat; **noncontracting** ~ Nichtvertragsstaat; **one-party** ~ Einparteienstaat; **peripheral** ~ Randstaat; **police** ~ Polizeistaat; **protected** ~ beschützter Staat; **push-button** ~ Druckknopfstaat; **receiving** ~ Empfangsstaat; **riparian** ~ Ufer-, Anliegerstaat; **satellite** ~ Satellitenstaat; **semisovereign** ~ halbsouveräner Staat; **sending** ~ Entsendestaat; **signatory** ~ Unterzeichnerstaat; **single** ~ lediger Stand; **social** ~ Sozialstaat; **sovereign** ~ souveräner Staat; **trading** ~ Handelsstaat; **treaty-breaking** ~ vertragsbrüchiger Staat; **unitary** ~ Einheits-, Zentralstaat; **unrecognized** ~ nicht anerkannter Staat; **welfare** ~ Wohlfahrtsstaat;
~ **of an account** Kontostand; ~ **of affairs** Sachlage, -verhalt, Tatbestand, Lage der Dinge, *(business)* Geschäftslage, Konjunktur; **present** ~ **of affairs** gegenwärtige Lage; **proper** ~ **of affairs** geordnete Zustände; ~ **of the art** *(patent law)* Stand der Technik; ~ **of blockade** Blockadezustand; ~ **of business** Geschäftslage; ~ **of the case** Sachverhalt, Darstellung des Sachverhalts, Begründung der Klage; ~ **of a commercial house** Vermögensverhältnisse einer Firma; ~ **of credit** Kreditsituation; ~ **of decacy** Verfallzustand; ~ **of defence** Verteidigungszustand; ~ **of demand** Bedarfslage; ~ **of destination** Bestimmungsland; **present** ~ **of the economy** gegenwärtige Konjunkturlage, wirtschaftliche Situation; ~ **of national emergency** Ausnahmezustand, Notstand, *(US)* Staatsnotstand; ~ **of employment** Beschäftigungslage; ~ **of facts and proposals** *(lunacy practice, Br.)* Entmündigungsbericht; ~ **of flux** *(stock exchange)* Fließzustand; **radical** ~ **of flux** tiefgreifender beständiger Wechsel; ~ **of health** Gesundheitszustand; ~ **of insolvency** Zustand der Zahlungsunfähigkeit; ~ **of intoxation** Betrunkenheit; **every** ~ **of life** jeder Lebensbereich; **s. one's** ~ **of life** jds. gesellschaftliche Stellung; ~ **of the market** Konjunktur, Marktlage, Absatzklima; **confident** ~ **of the market** zuversichtliche Börsenstimmung; **depressed** ~ **of the market** stagnierende Börse; ~ **of mind** Geisteszustand, -haltung; ~ **of**

need Notlage; **bad** ~ **of the packing** schlechter Verpackungszustand; ~ **of preservation** Erhaltungszustand; ~ **of production** Fertigungs-, Produktionsstand; ~ **of repair** Erhaltungszustand, *(house)* baulicher Zustand; ~ **of residence** *(double taxation agreement)* Wohnsitzstaat; ~ **of the roads** Straßenzustand; ~ **of shock** Schockzustand; ~ **of siege** Belagerungszustand; ~ **of source** *(double taxation agreement)* Quellenstaat; ~ **of trade** Konjunktur-, Geschäftslage; ~ **of the Union** Einzelstaat der USA; ~ **of war** Kriegszustand; ~ **of the world** Weltlage;
~ *(v.)* *(declare)* angeben, erklären, darlegen, ausführen, *(fix)* bestimmen, festlegen, -stellen;
~ **an account** Rechnung spezifizieren; ~ **the average** Dispache (Seeschadensberechnung) aufmachen, dispachieren; ~ **a case** seine Klage vorbringen, *(defendant)* seine Verteidigung vortragen; ~ **the cause of death** Todesursache angeben; ~ **s. th. in one's defence** etw. zu seiner Verteidigung vorbringen; ~ **in detail** genau bezeichnen; ~ **expressly** ausdrücklich festlegen; ~ **facts** Tatsachen anführen (vorbringen); ~ **fully** voll angeben, detaillieren, substantiieren; ~ **one's grievances** Beschwerde führen; ~ **higher (lower)** höher (niedriger) bewerten; ~ **an issue** Frage aufwerfen; ~ **on oath** unter Eid erklären; ~ **one's opinion** seine Meinung sagen; ~ **full particulars** genaue Einzelheiten angeben, substantiieren; ~ **positively** mit Bestimmtheit erklären; ~ **precisely** präzisieren; ~ **a rule** Regel aufstellen; ~ **the tare** tarieren; ~ **a precise time** genaue Zeit angeben; ~ **one's views** seine Meinung äußern, seine Ansichten darlegen;
to award the costs against the ~ Kosten der Staatskasse aufbürden; **to be received in** ~ Staatsempfang erhalten; **to be in a** ~ **of commotion** im Aufruhr sein; **to be in a** ~ **of distress** in bedrängter Lage sein; **to be in a poor** ~ **of health** gesundheitlich schlecht dran sein; **to be in a bad** ~ **of repair** instandsetzungsbedürftig sein; **to be in a good** ~ **of repair** in gut erhaltenem Zustand sein; **to be forfeited by the** ~ vom Staat konfisziert werden; **to be subsidized by the** ~ staatlich subventioniert sein; **to befit s. one's** ~ jds. Position angemessen sein; **to belong to the** ~ Staatseigentum sein; **to detach a** ~ **from a confederation** Staat von einem Staatenbund abtrennen; **to get into a** ~ sich künstlich aufregen; **to hold** ~ residieren; **to incorporate a** ~ **into another** Staat einem anderen einverleiben; **to lie in** ~ öffentlich aufgebahrt sein; **live in** ~ großen Aufwand treiben; **to produce a** ~ **of deadlock in a firm** Unternehmen fast zum Stillstand bringen (praktisch zur Arbeitsunfähigkeit verurteilen);
~ *(a.)* politisch;
~ **account system** Gefangenenarbeitswesen; ~ **affair** Staatsangelegenheit; ~ **agreement** Staatsabkommen; ~ **aid** staatliche Unterstützung, Staatsunterstützung, -hilfe; ~-**aid program(me)** staatliches Unterstützungsprogramm; ~-**aided** staatlich unterstützt, mit Unterstützung aus staatlichen Mitteln, subventioniert; ~ **apartment** Staatsgemach, Prunkzimmer; ~ **archives** Staatsarchiv; ~ **assembly** [etwa] Landtag; ~ **assistance** *(US)* Sozialhilfe; ~**'s attorney** *(US)* Staatsanwalt; ~ **auditor** staatlicher Rechnungsprüfer; ~ **award** staatlicher Schiedsspruch; ~ **bank** Staatsbank, *(US)* staatlich konzessionierte Bank, Landesbank; ~ **bank examiner** *(US)* Bankenkommissar; ~ **banking department** *(US)* Bankenaufsicht; ~ **bonds** *(US)* Staatsobligationen der einzelnen Bundesstaaten; ~ **borrowing** Staatsschuldenaufnahme; ~ **budget** *(US)* Staatshaushalt; ~-**buying organization** staatliche Einkaufsgesellschaft; ~ **cabin** Luxuskabine; ~ **call** formeller Besuch, Höflichkeits-, Anstandsbesuch; ~ **capitalism** Staatskapitalismus; ~ **car** Salonwagen; ~ **carriage** Staatskarosse; ~ **ceremony** feierlicher Staatsakt; ~ **citizenship** *(US)* Staatsangehörigkeit eines Einzelstaats; ~ **clothes** Gala; ~ **coach** Staatskutsche, -karosse; ~ **coffers** Staatsschatz; ~ **conglomerate** Staatskonzern; ~ **conciliation** staatliche Schlichtung; ~ **control** Staatsaufsicht; **to bring industries under** ~ **control** Industriezweige unter Staatsaufsicht stellen; ~-**controlled** unter Staatsaufsicht, bewirtschaftet; ~-**controlled economy** Zwangswirtschaft; ~ **corporation** staatliche Aktiengesellschaft, Staatsunternehmen; ~ **courts** *(US)* Gerichte der Einzelstaaten; ~ **creditor** Staatsgläubiger; ~ **criminal** Staatsverbrecher, *(US)* Straftäter nach einzelstaatlichem Recht; ~ **Department** *(US)* Außenministerium, Auswärtiges Amt; ~ **department Beavers** *(US)* Befürworter einer konzilianten Auslandspolitik im Außenministerium; ~ **documents** Staatspapiere, amtliche Schriftstücke; ~ **election** Landtagswahlen; ~ **employee** Staatsangestellter, Beamter; ~ **employment** Beschäftigung im Staatsdienst; ~-**enforced** staatlichem Zwang unterworfen; ~ **enterprise** Wirtschaftsbetrieb der öffentlichen Hand, Regie-, Staatsbetrieb; ~**'s evidence** *(US)* belastendes Beweismaterial, *(person)* Kronzeuge; ~ **examination** Staatsexamen, -prüfung; ~ **expansion** Erweiterung der

Staatsbefugnisse; ~ **expenditures** *(US)* Ausgaben der Einzelstaaten; ~ **facilities** staatliche Einrichtungen; ~**-fed** subventioniert, staatlich unterstützt; ~ **finance** Staatsfinanzen; ~**-financed** staatlich finanziert; ~ **flower** *(US)* Wappenblume; ~ **forest** Staatsforst; ~ **funds** Staatsgelder, -guthaben, Regierungskonten; ~ **funeral** *(Br.)* Staatsbegräbnis; ~ **government** *(US)* Landesregierung; ~ **governor** Gouverneur; ~ **grant** staatlicher Zuschuß, Staatszuschuß; ~ **highway** *(US)* Bundesstraße; ~ **house** *(US)* Parlamentsgebäude; ~ **indebtedness** Staatsverschuldung; ~ **inebriate reformatory** staatliche Entziehungsanstalt; ~ **inspectorship** Staatsaufsicht; ~ **insurance** staatliche Versicherung, Staatsversicherung; ~ **insurance commission** *(US)* Aufsichtsamt für das Versicherungswesen; ~ **interference** Staatseingriff (staatliche Einmischung) in die Wirtschaft; ~ **intervention** Eingreifen des Staates, staatliche Intervention; ~ **labor law** *(US)* Bundesarbeitsgesetz; ~ **lands** *(US)* staatlicher Grundbesitz; ~ **law** *(US)* Landesrecht; ~ **liability** Staatshaftung; ~ **life insurance fund** staatlicher Lebensversicherungsfonds; ~ **line** Staatsgrenze; ~ **loans** Kreditmittel; ~ **managing** *(theatre)* Regieführung; ~ **lottery** Staatslotterie; ~ **machinery** Staatsapparat; ~ **medicine** staatliches Gesundheitswesen; ~ **of the Union message** *(US)* Regierungserklärung, Rechenschaftsbericht für die Nation; ~ **monopoly** Staatsmonopol; ~ **mourning** Staatstrauer; ~ **note** Staatsschuldschein; ~ **occasion** feierliche (besondere) Gelegenheit; ~ **officer** *(US)* Landesbeamter; **key** ~ **official** erster Staatsdiener; ~**-owned** im Staatseigentum, staatseigen; ~**-owned enterprise** *(US)* staatseigener (volkseigener) Betrieb, Staatsunternehmen; ~ **ownership** *(US)* Staatseigentum; **to transfer to** ~ **ownership** *(US)* verstaatlichen; ~**-paid** staatlich finanziert; ~ **paper** politisches Aktenstück; ~ **papers** Staatsakten, -urkunde; ~ **pension** Staatspension; **to integrate with the** ~ **pension system** *(company)* staatliche Altersversorgung im Betrieb einführen; ~**-pensioned** pensioniert; ~ **planning** *(communist state)* Produktionsplanung, staatliche Planungspolitik, staatliche Planung; ~ **planning agency** staatliche Planungsbehörde; ~ **policy** Staatspolitik; ~ **prison** Staatsgefängnis; ~ **prisoner** politischer Häftling, Staatsgefangener; ~ **property** *(US)* fiskalisches Vermögen, öffentliches Eigentum, Staatseigentum, -besitz; ~ **purchase** Ankauf durch den Staat; ~ **radio** Staatsrundfunk; ~ **railway** Staatsbahn; ~ **reception** Staatsempfang; ~ **recognition** staatliche Anerkennung; ~ **records** Staatsurkunden; ~**-registered** staatlich anerkannt; ~ **regulations** stattlicher Dirigismus; ~ **regulator** staatliche Überwachungsstelle, *(US)* Beamter des Versicherungsaufsichtsamtes; ~ **rescue** staatliche Hilfsaktion; ~ **retirement pension** staatliche Altersrente; ~ **revenue** Staatseinnahmen, -einkünfte; ~ **rights** *(US)* den Einzelstaaten vorbehaltene Rechte; ~ **room** Prunksaal; ~ **scheme** staatliche Altersversorgung; ~ **scholarship** Staatsstipendium; ~ **school** vom Staat unterhaltene Schule; ~ **secret** Staatsgeheimnis; ~ **sector** öffentliche Hand; ~ **securities** *(US)* Staatsanleihe; ~ **security** Staatssicherheit; ~ **security branch** Staatssicherheitsdienst; ~ **security court** Staatssicherheitsgerichtshof; ~ **security organization** Staatssicherheitsdienst; ~ **service** *(US)* Staatsdienst; ~ **servitude** staatliche Dienstbarkeit; ~**'s share** Staatsquote; ~ **shareholding** Aktienbesitz des Staates; ~ **shipyard** Staatswerft; ~ **sickness benefit** staatliches Krankengeld; ~ **socialism** Staatssozialismus; ~ **socialist** Staatssozialist; ~ **spending** Staatsausgaben; ~ **subsidy** Staatsunterstützung, -zuschuß; ~ **superintendant of banks** *(US)* Bankenkommissar, -aufsicht; ~ **supervision** Staatsaufsicht; ~ **supreme court** *(US)* oberstes Gericht eines Einzelstaates; ~ **takeover** Betriebsübernahme durch den Staat; ~ **tax** Staatsabgabe, *(US)* einzelstaatliche Steuer; ~ **tax commission** *(US)* Landessteuerausschuß in den USA; ~ **taxation** *(US)* Besteuerung (steuerliche Erfassung) durch die Länder; ~**-taxed** besteuert; ~ **trading** Regiebetrieb; ~**-trading company** staatliche Handelsgesellschaft; ~ **trading countries** Staatshandelsländer; ~ **trading enterprise** staatliches Handelsunternehmen; ~**-trading nations** Staatshandelsländer; ~ **transfer tax** *(US)* Börsenumsatzsteuer; ~ **trial** politischer Prozeß, Staatsprozeß, Prozeß vor dem Verfassungsgericht; ~ **unemployment insurance tax** Arbeitslosenversicherungsbeitrag; ~ **university** *(US)* Landesuniversität; ~ **use system** *(US, prison work)* System der Gefangenenarbeit, Regiebetrieb; ~ **visit** Staatsbesuch; ~**-wide** *(US)* über den ganzen Staat verbreitet, überregional; ~ **workmen's compensation insurance fund** *(US)* staatlicher Arbeiterunfallversicherungsfonds.

statecraft Staatskunst, -führung, politisches Handwerk.

stated festgelegt, festgesetzt, *(US)* amtlich anerkannt;
as ~ **above** wie oben angeführt (erwähnt); **as** ~ **overleaf** laut umstehender Aufstellung;

to have been ~ **in the newspaper** in der Zeitung gestanden haben;
~ **account** spezifizierte Rechnung; ~ **amount** angegebener Betrag; ~ **capital** *(balance sheet, US)* ausgewiesenes Grund-, Gesellschaftskapital; ~ **case** Sachdarstellung; ~ **date** angegebenes Datum; **on** ~ **days** an festgesetzten Tagen; ~ **hours of business** bestimmte Geschäftsstunden; **by** ~ **instalments** in festgesetzten Raten; **at** ~ **intervals** in regelmäßigen Abständen; ~ **liabilities** buchmäßig ausgewiesene Verbindlichkeiten, Buchschulden; ~ **meeting** satzungsgemäße Hauptversammlung, Aufsichtsratssitzung; ~ **period** angegebene Frist; **at** ~ **periods** regelmäßig; ~ **position** *(ad)* vorgeschriebene Plazierung; ~ **salary** festes Gehalt; ~ **sum** bestimmter Betrag; ~ **term** *(law court)* Routinesitzung; **for a** ~ **term** für eine bestimmte Zeit; **at the** ~ **time** zur festgesetzten Zeit, zum vorgesehenen Termin; ~ **value** festgestellter Wert.

statehood Souveränität, Eigenstaatlichkeit.

statehouse *(US)* Parlamentsgebäude.

stateless staatenlos;
~ **person** Staatenloser.

statelessness Staatenlosigkeit.

statement *(abstract of account)* [Konto]auszug, *(account rendered)* [Rechenschafts]bericht, [Rechnungs]aufstellung, -ablage, *(attorney)* Anklagerede, *(balance sheet, US)* Bilanz, *(bank)* Bankausweis, *(Br., counterfoil)* Abstimmungsblatt, *(declaration)* Angabe, Erklärung, Verlautbarung, Feststellung, *(dictum)* Ausspruch, *(estimate)* Überschlag, Übersicht, Veranschlagung, Vor-, Kostenanschlag, *(of property)* Status, Vermögensstand, Bestandsübersicht, *(report)* Aufstellung, Bericht[erstattung], *(return)* Ausweis, *(report)* Verzeichnis, Liste, *(speaker)* Ausführungen, Darlegungen, Auslassungen, Referat, *(of wages)* Lohn, Tarif;
according to ~ laut Bericht (Angabe); **according to his own** ~ nach seinen eigenen Erklärungen (Angaben, Behauptungen); **as per enclosed** ~ laut anliegendem Verzeichnis; **as per** ~ **below** laut untenstehender Aufstellung;
accounting ~ Revisionsbericht; **admitted** ~ Geständnis; **annexed** ~ beiliegende Aufstellung; **annual** ~**s** Jahresausweis, -abschluß, -bericht; **application of funds** ~ Ausweis über die Verwendung des Grundkapitals; **assets and liabilities** ~ Vermögens- und Schuldenaufstellung; **audited** ~ mit Prüfungsvermerk versehene Gewinn- und Verlustrechnung; **average** ~ Havarieaufmachung, -rechnung, Dispache; **bank** ~ Kontoausweis, -auszug, *(report of bank)* Bankausweis, Geschäftsbericht einer Bank; **cash** ~ Kassenbericht, -ausweis; **certified** ~ bewiesene Feststellung; **clearinghouse** ~ Ausweis einer Girozentrale; **closing** ~ [Ab]schlußbericht; **common size or percentage** ~ *(US)* vergleichende Betriebsbilanz; **comparative** ~ vergleichende Aufstellung, *(US)* Jahresbilanz mit Vergleichsziffern aus dem Vorjahr; **comparative income** ~ *(US)* vergleichende Gewinnrechnung; **condensed** ~ *(US)* Bilanzauszug; **conflicting** ~**s** widersprechende Erklärungen; **consolidated** ~**s** konsolidierte Bilanz, Konzernbilanz; **consolidated profit and loss** ~**s** *(US)* konsolidierte Gewinn- und Verlustrechnung nebst Bilanz; **corporate** ~**s** *(US)* Bilanz (Jahresabschluß) einer Aktiengesellschaft; **daily** ~ Tagesauszug; **declaratory** ~ deklaratorische Erklärung; **detailed** ~ Spezifikation, Einzelaufstellung, ausführlicher Bericht; **earnings** ~ Gewinnausweis, Gewinn- und Verlustrechnung; **explicit** ~ formelle Erklärung; **factual** ~ Tatsachenbericht; **false** ~ falsche (betrügerische) Angaben; **faulty** ~ fehlerhafter Rechnungsauszug; **final** ~ abschließende Feststellung; **financial** ~ Gewinn- und Verlustrechnung, *(US)* Status, Bilanz, Jahresabschluß; **financing** ~ *(political party, US)* Finanzierungsnachweis; **full** ~ umfassende Erklärung; **funds flow** ~ *(US)* Auszug über die Verwendung des Grundkapitals, Bewegungsbilanz, Finanzflußrechnung; **illegitimate** ~ unberechtigte Erklärung; **immaterial** ~ rechtlich unerhebliche Erklärung; **inaccurate** ~ falsche Erklärung; **income** ~ Perioden-, Gewinn- und Verlustrechnung; **income-tax** ~ *(US)* Einkommensteuererklärung; **individual** ~ *(US)* Einzelbilanz; **interest** ~ Zinsaufstellung; **interim** ~ Zwischenabschluß, *(US)* Zwischenbilanz; **joint** ~ gemeinsame Erklärung; **libel(l)ous** ~ verleumderische Behauptung; **material** ~ rechtserhebliche Erklärung; **monthly** ~ monatliche Abrechnung, *(banking)* Monatsausweis, -bericht, monatlicher Ausweis; **official** ~ Kommuniqué, amtliche Erklärung; **opening** ~ einleitende Erklärung; **operating** ~ *(US)* Erfolgsbilanz, Gewinn- und Verlustrechnung; **periodic** ~ *(US)* Periodenbilanz; **periodical** ~ *(bank)* regelmäßiger Auszug; **policy** ~ Grundsatzerklärung; **cumulative profit and loss** ~ *(US)* zusammengesetzte Gewinn- und Verlustrechnung; **public** ~ öffentliche Erklärung (Verlaut-

barung); **registration** ~ *(US)* Gründungs-, Eröffnungsbilanz; ~ **rendered** Rechnungsaufstellung; **royalty** ~ Lizenzabrechnung; **scandalous** ~ ärgerniserregende Erklärung; **source and disposition** ~ *(US)* Verwendungsnachweis, finanzwirtschaftliche Bilanz; **statistical** ~ statistische Aufstellung; **summary** ~ summarische Übersicht; **supplementary** ~ *(US)* Ergänzungsbilanz; **surplus** ~ *(US)* [Rein]gewinnaufstellung, Verwendungsrechnung, Erfolgsbilanz; **sworn** ~ beeidigte Aussage; **tabular** ~ tabellarische Aufstellung; **tax** ~ *(US)* steuerliche Aufstellung, Steuerbilanz, -status; **true** ~ wahrheitsgetreue Angaben; **unsworn** ~ nichteidliche Aussage; **untrue** ~ wissentlich falsche Angabe, unwahre Zeugenaussage; **verbal** ~ mündliche Darlegung des Tatbestandes; **voluntary** ~ aus freiem Willen abgegebene Erklärung; **weekly** ~ Wochenausweis; **well-reasoned** ~ wohlbegründete Erklärung; **working** ~ Geschäftsbericht; **written** ~ schriftliche Erklärung;

~ **of account** *(bank)* Konto[korrent]auszug, Rechnungsauszug, -aufstellung; ~ **of accounts** Jahresbericht; **affixed** ~ **of account** nebenstehender Kontoauszug; ~ **of account closed per December 31st** Kontoauszug per 31. Dezember; **annual** ~ **of accounts** Jahresabschluß; **consolidated annual** ~ **of accounts** Konzernabschluß; **daily** ~ **of accounts** Tagesauszug; **established** ~ **of accounts** festgestellter Jahresabschluß; **statutory** ~ **of affairs** *(Br.)* Bericht über die Vermögenslage, Vermögensaufstellung, Status, *(bankruptcy)* Liquidationsbilanz, Konkursstatus, -bericht, -abwicklungsbilanz; ~ **of application of funds** *(US)* Ausweis über die Verwendung von Barmitteln, Verwendungsnachweis, Bewegungsbilanz, finanzwirtschaftliche Bilanz; ~ **of assets and liabilities** Vermögensaufstellung; ~ **of average** Havarieschadensaufstellung, -aufmachung, Dispache; ~ **of a bank** [Noten]bankbericht; ~ **of bankruptcy** *(US)* Konkursbilanz; ~ **of a business enterprise** *(US)* Geschäftsbilanz; ~ **of capital** Kapitalangabe; ~ **of nominal capital** Erklärung über das ausgewiesene Grundkapital; ~ **of a case** Sachvortrag, Vorlagebericht; **written** ~ **of a case** Schriftsatz; ~ **of charges** Aufstellung der Kosten, Kostenaufstellung, Kostenrechnung, -liquidation; ~ **of claim** *(Br.)* Klageschrift, -begründung, -substantiierung, Schriftsatz; ~ **of [financial] condition** *(US)* Bilanzaufstellung, Finanzstatus; ~ **of confession** *(debtor)* Unterwerfungserklärung; ~ **of contents** Inhaltsverzeichnis, -angabe; ~ **to the contrary** Gegenaussage; ~ **of costs** Kostenrechnung, -aufstellung; ~ **of cost of sales** Verkaufs-, Umsatzbilanz; ~ **of custodianship account** *(US)* Depotauszug; ~ **of damage** Schadensrechnung, -aufstellung; ~ **of debt** Forderungsnachweis; ~ **of defence** *(Br.)* Klagebeantwortung, -erwiderung; ~ **of distribution of income** Aufstellung für die Einkommensteuererklärung; ~ **of duties** Zolltarif; ~s **made in discharge of a legal, moral or social duty** in Erfüllung rechtlicher, moralischer oder sozialer Pflichten abgegebene Erklärungen; **consolidated** ~ **of earnings** *(US)* konsolidierte Gewinn- und Verlustrechnung; ~ **of retained earnings** *(US)* Gewinnverwendungsaufstellung; ~ **of exchanges** Kursbericht; ~ **of expenses** Kosten-, Spesenaufstellung; ~ **of exports** *(company meeting)* Exportaufstellung; ~ **of facts** *(US)* Sachdarstellung, -angabe, -verhalt, Tatbestand; **bare** ~ **of the facts** *(US)* einfache Aufzählung der Tatumstände; **official** ~ **of facts** offizielle Sachdarstellung; ~ **of fees** Gebührentarif; ~ **of financial conditions** *(US)* Finanzstatus; ~ **of goods** Lagerbestand; ~ **of grounds of appeal** Berufungsschriftsatz; ~ **of income** *(US)* Gewinn- und Verlustrechnung, Periodengewinnrechnung, -erfolgsausweis; ~ **of consolidated income** *(US)* Gewinn- und Verlustrechnung eines Konzerns; ~ **of income and accumulated earnings** *(US)* Gesamtergebnisrechnung; ~ **of income and expenses** *(US)* Gewinn- und Verlustrechnung; ~ **of income and surplus** *(corporation, US)* Jahresbericht nebst Bilanz sowie Gewinn- und Verlustrechnung; ~ **of the insured** Angaben des Versicherten; ~ **of interest** Zinsenaufstellung; ~ **of interest paid** Nachweis gezahlter Zinsen; ~ **of investment** Erklärung über die Entwicklung des Eigenkapitals; ~ **of open items** Liste offenstehender Posten; ~ **of law** Rechtserklärung, -darstellung; ~ **in lieu of prospectus** *(public company, Br.)* Vorgründungsbericht [an das Handelsregister], Prospektersatzerklärung; ~ **of loss and gain** *(US)* Gewinn- und Verlustrechnung; ~ **of the market** Marktbericht; ~ **made during the course of negotiations** im Laufe der Verhandlungen abgegebene Erklärung; **material** ~s **made during negotiations** rechtserhebliche, während der Verhandlungen abgegebene Erklärungen; ~ **on oath** eidliche Erklärung; ~ **of opinion** Meinungsäußerung; ~ **of ownership** Eigentumsnachweis; ~ **of particulars** *(Br.)* Spezifikation, *(pleading)* Klagesubstantiierung, *(in case of nonappearance)* Beantragung eines Versäumnisurteils; ~ **on policy** politische

Grundsatzerklärung; ~ **of financial position** *(US)* Finanzstatus; ~ **to the press** Erklärung an die Presse, Presseerklärung; ~ **of price** Preisangabe; ~ **of prices** Preisliste, -verzeichnis; ~ **by prisoner** Gefangenenaussage; ~s **privileged without explanations or contradiction** Äußerungen, zu denen keine Erklärungen oder Berichtigungen veröffentlicht werden müssen; ~ **of proceedings** Bericht über die Konkursabwicklung; ~ **of net proceeds** Reinertragsübersicht; ~ **of profit and loss** *(US)* Gewinn- und Verlustrechnung; ~ **of proof** *(Br.)* anwaltliche Vernehmung von Zeugen; ~ **of the prosecution** Vortrag der Anklagebehörde; ~ **of realization and liquidation** Liquidationsbilanz; ~ **of resources and their application** Verwendungsnachweis, Bewegungsbilanz; ~ **of resources and liabilities** Bilanzauszug; ~ **of responsibility** Verantwortungsbericht; ~ **of operating results** *(US)* Betriebsergebnisrechnung, Gewinnverwendungsaufstellung; ~ **of revenue and expenditure** Gewinn- und Verlustrechnung; ~ **of sales done** Umsatzbilanz; ~ **of securities** Depotauszug, -aufstellung; ~ **of size** Größenangabe; ~ **of sources and application of funds** *(US)* Ausweis über die Verwendung des Grundkapitals; ~ **of specie** Geldkurszettel; ~ **of stockholder's equity** *(investment net worth)* Ausweis über die Verwendung des Grundkapitals, Erklärung über die Entwicklung des Eigenkapitals; ~ **of surplus** *(US)* Erfolgsbilanz; ~ **of earned surplus** *(US)* Kapitalzuwachsbilanz, Darstellung der Veränderungen im Gewinnvortrag, Posten für die Veränderung des Gewinnvortrags, Gewinnübersicht, -veränderungsaufstellung, -ertragsrechnung; ~ **of turnover** Umsatzaufstellung; ~ **of understanding** Einvernehmlichkeitserklärung; ~ **of value** Wertangabe; ~ **of wages** Lohnsummenaufstellung; ~ **made by a witness** Zeugenaussage; ~ **of net worth** *(US)* Ausweis über die Entwicklung des Eigenkapitals;

to be more explicit in one's ~s seine Behauptungen substantiieren; **to bring a** ~ **up to date** Aufstellung auf den neuesten Stand bringen; **to call s. one's** ~ **in question** jds. Erklärung in Zweifel ziehen; **to certify its financial** ~ Bestätigungsvermerk erteilen; **to confine itself to a simple** ~ nur eine Darstellung registrieren; **to contradict a** ~ Gegenerklärung (Dementi) veröffentlichen; **to deny a** ~ Erklärung dementieren; **to disapprove a** ~ Unrichtigkeit einer Behauptung beweisen; **to draw up a** ~ Erklärung aufsetzen; **to hand in a** ~ Bericht erstatten; **to issue a formal** ~ offizielle Erklärung herausgeben; **to make a** ~ Behauptung aufstellen, Aussage machen, Erklärung abgeben, *(budget)* Etat aufstellen; **to make knowingly false** ~s wissentlich falsche Angaben machen; **to make an official** ~ amtliche Erklärung abgeben, amtlich verlautbaren; **to make a personal** ~ persönliche Erklärung abgeben; **to make a** ~ **in a privileged occasion** Äußerungen in Wahrnehmung berechtigter Interessen machen; **to make a** ~ **on oath** unter Eid erklären; **to mishandle the financial** ~s Jahresabschlüsse manipulieren; **to produce testimony to a** ~ Erklärung durch Zeugenaussage untermauern; **to publish a** ~ Erklärung veröffentlichen; **to qualify a** ~ einschränkende Erklärung abgeben; **to refuse to certify its financial** ~ Bestätigungsvermerk verweigern; **to rely upon** ~s sich auf Angaben verlassen; **to send s. o. a** ~ **of the amount owing to him** jem. ein Schuldanerkenntnis schicken; **to verify a** ~ Richtigkeit einer Aufstellung bestätigen;

~ **analysis** *(US)* Bilanzanalyse, -untersuchung, -kritik; ~ **date** *(US)* Bilanzierungstag; ~ **department** *(US)* Kontoauszugsabteilung; ~ **form** Gewinn- und Verlustrechnung in Staffelform; ~ **heading** *(US)* Bilanzschema; ~ **price** Akkordpreis; ~ **purpose** *(US)* Bilanzzweck; ~ **wages** Akkordlohn.

stater, average Dispacheur.

stateroom *(railroad, US)* Privatabteil, *(ship)* Passagierkabine.

stateside die Vereinigten Staaten betreffend.

statesman Politiker, Staatsmann;

elderly ~ erfahrener Staatsmann, Politiker im Ruhestand; **forward** ~ aufgeschlossener Politiker; **front-rank** ~ Staatsmann der ersten Garnitur; **leading** ~ führender Staatsmann.

static *(wireless, US)* atmosphärische Störungen, Empfangsstörung;

~s Statik;

~ *(a.)* statisch, *(tel.)* elektrostatisch, *(wireless)* atmosphärisch; **to be about** ~ fast gleichbleiben;

~ **budget** starrer Etat; ~ **calculation** statische Berechnung; ~**-free** *(wireless, US)* störungsfrei; ~ **ratio** *(analysis sheet)* statische Verhältnisziffer.

stating | an account Spezifizierung einer Rechnung; ~ **a case** Sachdarstellung;

~ **part of a bill** Klagebegründung.

station Station, Stelle, *(broadcasting)* Funkstation, Sender, *(occupation)* Beruf, Stand, Stellung, *(office)* Amt, Stellung,

Posten, Position, Rang, *(official place)* Dienstort, *(police)* Polizeirevier, -wache, *(railway)* Haltestelle, Bahnhof, *(rank)* Rang, Stand;

according to one's ~ in life standesgemäß; **[delivered] free ~** bahnfrei; **left at ~ till called for** bahnlagernd; **suitable to s. one's ~** jds. Lebensstandard entsprechend;

ambulance ~ Unfallstation; **auxiliary ~** Vorbahnhof; **baby ~** Mütterberatungsstelle; **broadcasting ~** Rundfunkstation, -sender; **call ~** *(tel.)* Sprechstelle; **central ~** Hauptbahnhof; **coastguard ~** Küstenwachstation; **collecting ~** *(mil., US)* Feldverbandplatz; **combination ~** vereinigter Kopf- und Durchgangsbahnhof; **daytime ~** Tagessender; **duty ~** *(mil.)* Dienststelle; **filling ~** Tankstelle; **fire ~** *(Br.)* Brand-, Feuerwache; **firstaid ~** Unfallstation; **forwarding ~** Versandbahnhof; **freight ~** Güterbahnhof; **frontier ~** Grenzbahnhof, -posten; **full-time ~** Tag- und Nachtsender; **goods ~** *(Br.)* Güterbahnhof; **harbo(u)r ~** Hafenbahnhof; **health ~** *(US)* Mütterberatungsstelle; **high-power ~** Großkraftwerk, *(broadcasting)* Großsender; **hospital ~** *(mil., US)* Feldlazarett; **intermediate ~** Durchgangs-, Zwischenstation; **jamming ~** Störsender; **key ~** Hauptsender; **lifeboat ~** *(Br.)* Rettungsstation; **local ~** Ortssender; **main ~** Hauptbahnhof; **main dressing ~** *(mil.)* Hauptverbandsplatz; **naval ~** Flottenstützpunkt; **noncommercial ~** Sender ohne Werbeprogramm; **[omni]bus ~** Omnibusbahnhof; **part-time ~** *(US)* Stundensender; **passenger ~** Bahnhof für den Personenverkehr; **petrol ~** *(US)* Tankstelle; **police ~** Polizeiwache, -revier; **polling ~** Wahllokal; **postal ~** *(US)* Postnebenstelle; **power ~** Kraft-, Elektrizitätswerk; **private ~** nichtamtliche Stellung; **radio ~** Rundfunksender, -station; **railway ~** *(Br.)* Bahnhof, -station; **railroad ~** *(US)* Bahnhof; **receiving ~** Annahme-, Empfangsstation; **seismological ~** Erdbebenwarte; **shunting ~** Verschiebebahnhof; **social ~** gesellschaftliche Stellung; **stub ~** Keilbahnhof; **telegraph ~** Telegrafenamt; **terminal ~** Kopf-, End-, Sackbahnhof; **through ~** Durchgangsbahnhof; **trading ~** Handelsniederlassung; **train-order ~** Verschiebe-, Rangierbahnhof; **wireless ~** Rundfunksender;

~ of arrival Ankunftsbahnhof; **~ of attachment** Heimatbahnhof; **~ in business** geschäftliche Position; **~ of departure** Abgangsstation; **~ of destination** Empfangs-, Bestimmungsbahnhof; **~ in life** gesellschaftliche Stellung; **all ~s of life** alle Lebensbereiche;

~ (v.) postieren, aufstellen;

~ o. s. seinen Platz einnehmen; **~ a sentinel** Wachposten aufstellen; **~ troops** Truppen stationieren;

to bring to the ~ zur Bahn schaffen; **to come into the ~** in den Bahnhof einlaufen; **to have one's luggage taken to the ~** *(Br.)* seine Koffer zum Bahnhof bringen lassen; **to jam a ~** Rundfunkempfang stören; **to jam the enemy's ~ during the war** feindliche Rundfunksender im Krieg stören; **to leave the ~** ausfahren; **to marry below one's ~** unter seinem Stand heiraten; **to occupy a high ~ in life** bedeutende Stellung im Leben ausfüllen; **to occupy a humble ~** bescheidene Stellung einnehmen; **to take up one's ~** seinen Platz einnehmen;

~ announcement (break) *(radio)* Pausen-, Sendezeichen; **~ commander** Standortältester; **~ hall** Bahnhofshalle; **~ hospital** *(US)* Standortlazarett; **~ hotel** Bahnhofshotel; **~ house** Polizeiwache; **~ identification** Senderansage; **~ master** Fahrdienstleiter; **~ memory** Senderwahl; **~ office** Dienstraum des Fahrdienstleiters; **~ premises** Bahnhofsanlagen; **at-~ price** Preis ab Versandbahnhof; **~ representative** Werbefunkvertreter; **~ selector** Sendereinstellung; **~ wagon** *(US)* Kombiwagen.

stationary lokal auftretend, *(fixed)* feststehend, ortsfest, stationär, *(sedentary)* seßhaft, *(stable)* unverändert, beständig;

to be (remain) ~ stagnieren, unverändert (fest) bleiben;

~ demand stagnierende Nachfrage; **~ disease** lokal auftretende Krankheit; **~ economy** stationäre Wirtschaft; **~ engine** Standmotor; **~ population** gleichbleibende Bevölkerungszahl; **~ prices** stabile Preise; **~ screen** *(mil.)* Vorpostenkette; **~ sum** feste Summe, Fixum; **~ temperature** gleichbleibende Temperatur; **~ treatment** *(med.)* stationäre Behandlung; **to collide with a ~ vehicle** mit einem stehenden Fahrzeug zusammenstoßen.

stationer Schreibwarenhändler;

~s' Company *(Br.)* Börsenverein der Buchhändler; **to enter at ~s' Company** *(Br.)* Buch gegen unerlaubten Nachdruck registrieren lassen; **~s' company gazette** Börsenblatt für den Buchhandel; **~s' Hall** *(Br.)* Buchbörse; **~s' register** *(Br.)* Verzeichnis von Neuerscheinungen; **~'s shop** *(Br.)* Schreibwarenhandlung.

stationery Bürobedarf, -material, Schreib-, Papierwaren, Schreibmaterialien, *(letter paper)* Briefpapier;

fancy-boxed ~ Briefpapierkassette; **office ~** Büromaterial;

~ cupboard Regal mit Schreib- und Korrespondenzunterlagen; **~ department** Materialverwaltung; **~ goods** Bürogegenstände; **H.M. ~ Office** *(Br.)* Staatsdruckerei, -verlag; **~ shop (store, US)** Schreibwarenhandlung, Papierwarengeschäft.

stationing *(mil.)* Stationierung.

statism Planwirtschaft, Dirigismus.

statist Statistiker, *(politics)* Anhänger der Planwirtschaft, Planwirtschaftler;

~ (a.) dirigistisch, planwirtschaftlich.

statistical statistisch;

~ abstract Statistisches Jahrbuch; **~ bureau** Amt für Statistik; **~ code number** Nummer des statistischen Warenverzeichnisses; **~ commission** statistischer Ausschuß; **~ compilation** statistische Zusammenstellung; **~ data** statistische Angaben; **~ department** statische Abteilung, Abteilung Statistik; **~ discrepancy** statistische Abweichung; **~ evaluation** statistische Wertermittlung; **~ expert** Statistiker; **~ fee** Gebühr für statistische Berechnungen; **~ independence** statistische Unabhängigkeit; **~ index** *(Br.)* langfristiger Preisindex für ausgewählte Produkte; **~ information** statistische Zusammenstellung; **to collect ~ information** statistisches Material zusammenstellen; **~ inquiries** statistische Erhebungen; **~ method** theoretische Statistik; **~ number** *(export trade)* Ausfuhrnummer des statistischen Warenverzeichnisses; **Central ~ Office** *(Br.)* [etwa] Bundesamt für Statistik; **~ quality control** Qualitätskontrolle; **~ returns** Statistiken, statistische Berichte (Ausweise); **~ sampling** Markt- und Meinungsforschung; **~ statement (table)** statistische Aufstellung, Statistik; **~ unit** statistische Einheit, Erhebungseinheit; **~ universe** statistische Gesamtmasse.

statistically | adjusted statistisch bereinigt;

to record statistisch erfassen.

statistician, trained Berufsstatistiker.

statisticize *(v.)* statistisch erfassen.

statistics Statistik, statistische Unterlagen;

business ~ Betriebsstatistik; **commercial ~** Handelsstatistik; **criminal ~** Kriminalstatistik; **demographic ~** Bevölkerungsstatistik; **distribution ~** Absatzkennzahlen; **economic ~** Wirtschaftsstatistik; **foreign trade ~** Außenhandelsstatistik; **government ~** amtliche Statistik; **operational ~** Betriebsstatistik; **popular ~** Bevölkerungsstatistik; **sales ~** Umsatzstatistik; **trade ~** Handelsstatistik; **vital ~** Bevölkerungsstatistik; **wage ~** Lohnstatistik;

~ of employment Beschäftigungszahlen;

to compile ~ statistische Unterlagen zusammenstellen; **to interpret ~** Statistik auswerten, statistische Ergebnisse auswerten.

statuable gesetzlich.

Statue of Liberty Freiheitsstatue.

status [geschäftliche] Lage, Geschäftslage, Status, *(capacity to sue)* Aktivlegitimation, *(legal position)* Rechtsstellung, *(mil.)* Wehrdienstverhältnis, *(position of affairs)* Finanz-, Vermögenslage, *(rank)* Stellung, [Personen]stand, Rang, *(social position)* soziale Stellung;

without any official ~ ohne offiziellen Auftrag;

achieved ~ erworbener Status; **civil ~** Familien-, Personenstand; **dominion ~** Dominiumsstatus; **financial ~** Vermögenslage, Finanzlage, -status, Status; **legal ~** rechtliche Stellung, Rechtslage, -position, -fähigkeit; **marital ~** Familienstand; **marriage ~** Familienstand; **national ~** Staatsangehörigkeit; **nutritional ~** Ernährungszustand; **personal ~** Familien-, Personenstand; **~ quo** *(lat.)* Status quo, gegenwärtiger Zustand; **~ quo ante** *(lat.)* früherer (vorheriger) Zustand; **social ~** soziale (gesellschaftliche) Stellung; **special ~** Sonderstatus; **trustee ~** Treuhänderstatus;

~ of aliens Ausländereigenschaft, -status; **~ of irremovability** *(pauper, Br.)* Recht auf Seßhaftigkeit; **~ of legitimacy** ehelicher Status; **~ of members** Zugehörigkeit zu einer Aktiengattung; **~ of ownership** Eigentumsverhältnisse; **~ of a person** Personenstand; **~ of a professor** Charakter eines Professors; **~ quo restored** erfolgte Herstellung des früheren Zustandes;

to claim one's ~ auf Anerkennung der Vaterschaft klagen; **to desire ~ and security** nach einer gesicherten Stellung trachten; **to have no official ~** keinen beamteten Rang haben; **to raise a colony to the ~ of a substantive nation** einer Kolonie die Unabhängigkeit gewähren;

to use facilities as ~ conveniences Einrichtungen zur Festigung der sozialen Stellung benutzen; **~ enquiry** Statusprüfung, Untersuchung der finanziellen Verhältnisse, Vermögensauskunft; **~ enquiry agency** Finanzauskunftei; **~ plus** Statusgewinn, Verstärkung der gesellschaftlichen Stellung; **~ report** Auskunft über die Finanzlage, Finanzauskunft; **~ symbol** Statussymbol, Standeskennzeichen, Symbolfigur.

statute *(corporation)* Satzung, Statut, Gesellschaftsvertrag, *(law)* gesetztes Recht, Gesetz[esbestimmung], -vorschrift, *(politics)* Parlamentsakte;

according to ~ satzungsgemäß; **contrary to** ~[s] statutenwidrig; **not subject to the** ~ **of limitations** unverjährbar;

affirmative ~ Gebotsgesetz; **criminal** ~ Strafgesetz; **declaratory** ~ Ausführungsgesetz; **enabling** ~ *(US)* Ermächtigungsgesetz; **expository** ~ Erläuterungsgesetz; **general** ~ allgemein verbindliches Gesetz; **local** ~ Ortsstatut; **mandatory** ~ Mandatsstatut; **negative** ~ Verbotsgesetz; **penal** ~ Strafbestimmung, -gesetz; **perpetual** ~ unbeschränkt geltendes Gesetz; **personal** ~ Personalstatut; **private** ~ interne Bestimmung; **public** ~ allgemein verbindliches Gesetz; **punitive** ~ Strafgesetz; **real** ~ Realstatut; Grundstücksrecht; **reference** ~ Gesetz über die Anwendung anderer Gesetzesvorschriften; **regulatory** ~ Ausführungsbestimmungen; **remedial** ~ Abhilfe-, Schlußgesetz; **revised** ~s bereinigte Gesetzessammlung; **special** ~ Sondergesetz; **temporary** ~ befristetes Gesetz, Übergangsgesetz; **university** ~ Universitätssatzung; **validating** ~ Übergangsgesetz, Gesetz zur Heilung fehlerhafter Verwaltungsmaßnahmen;

~ **of amendments and jeofailes** Verordnung über die Berichtigungsmöglichkeit des Sachvortrags; ~s **of an association** Gesellschaftsvertrag; ~ **of bankruptcy** Konkursordnung; ~ **in blank** Blankettgesetz; ~ **of descent** Erbfolgeordnung; ~ **of distribution** Nachlaßordnung, *(US)* gesetzliche Erbfolge; ~s **at Large** *(US)* Bundesgesetzblatt, amtliche Gesetzessammlung; ~ **of limitations** gesetzliche Verjährungsvorschriften, -recht, -gesetz; ~ **of minorities** Minderheitenstatut; ~ **of Monopolies** *(Br.)* Kartellgesetz; ~s **of a party** Parteistatuten;

to apply the ~ **of limitations** Verjährungsvorschriften anwenden; **to bar a debt by the** ~ **of limitations** Verjährungseinwand gegen eine Forderung erheben; **to be barred by the** ~ **of limitations** von den Verjährungsvorschriften betroffen werden; **to comply with the** ~ Satzungserfordernisse erfüllen; **to extend the** ~ **of limitations** Verjährungsvorschriften verlängern; **to pass a** ~ Gesetz verabschieden; **to plead the** ~ **of limitations** Verjährung einwenden, Verjährungseinwand erheben; **to satisfy the** ~ dem Gesetz Genüge tun; **to secure the immunities of a** ~ Vorzüge eines Gesetzes erlangen; **to take a case out of the operation of the** ~ **of limitations** in einem bestimmten Fall die Folgen der Verjährung vermeiden; **to toll the** ~ **of limitations** *(US)* Verjährungsvorschriften unterbrechen, Verjährung unterbrechen (hemmen); **to waive the** ~ **of limitations** auf Geltendmachung der Verjährung verzichten;

~**-barred** *(Br.)* erloschen, verjährt; **to become** ~**-barred** verjähren; ~**-barred right** verjährter Rechtsanspruch; ~ **book** Gesetzessammlung, Gesetzbuch; ~**-of-limitation issue** Verjährungsstreitfrage; ~ **labo(u)r** Frondienst; ~ **law** Gesetzesrecht, geschriebenes Recht; ~ **mile** gesetzliche Meile; ~ **roll** Gesetzesrolle; ~**-run** verjährt.

statutory *(according to statutes of associations)* statuten-, satzungsgemäß, *(according to statute law)* gesetzlich [vorgeschrieben], gesetzlich bestimmt;

~ **action** gesetzliche Maßnahmen; **under** ~ **age** minderjährig; ~ **agency** gesetzliche Vertretungsmacht; ~ **agent** gesetzlicher Vertreter; ~ **alien** *(Br.)* in Großbritannien geborener Ausländer; ~ **authority** gesetzliche Ermächtigung (Befugnis); ~ **basis** gesetzliche Grundlage; ~ **bond** Schuldurkunde in der gesetzlich vorgeschriebenen Form; ~ **books** *(Br.)* gesetzlich vorgeschriebene Geschäftsbücher; ~ **capital reserve** Sonderrücklage für Emissionsagio; ~ **company (corporation, US)** Körperschaft des öffentlichen Rechts; ~ **control** gesetzliche Aufsichtspflicht; ~ **crime** normierter Straftatbestand; ~ **damages** Vertragsstrafe; ~ **declaration** *(Br.)* Erklärung an Eides Statt, schriftliche, eidesstattliche Erklärung; ~ **dedication** gesetzlich vorgesehene Widmung; ~ **deductions** Lohn- und Sozialabzüge; ~ **dividend** satzungsmäßige Dividende; ~ **duty** gesetzliche Verpflichtung, Rechtspflicht, *(local government)* kommunale Pflichtaufgabe; ~ **exception** gesetzliche Ausnahme; ~ **exposition** amtliche Auslegung; ~ **factor's lien** *(US)* Sicherungseigentum an einem Warenlager mit wechselndem Bestand; **on a** ~ **footing** auf gesetzlicher Grundlage; ~**-forced share** *(US)* Pflichtteil; ~ **foreclosure** Betreibung der Zwangsvollstreckung aus einer vollstreckbaren Urkunde; ~ **form** gesetzliche Form; ~ **guardian** gesetzlicher Vormund; ~ **heir** Gesetzeserbe, gesetzlicher Erbe; ~ **holiday** gesetzlicher Feiertag; ~ **instrument** *(Br.)* Aus-, Durchführungs-, Rechtsverordnung, Regierungserlaß; ~ **interest** gesetzliche Zinsen; ~ **interpretation** Auslegung von Gesetzen; ~ **law** geschriebenes (gesetztes) Recht, Gesetzesrecht; ~ **levies** gesetzliche Abgaben; ~ **liability** gesetzliche Haftung, Verpflichtung; ~ **lien** gesetzliches Pfandrecht; ~ **limita-**

tion Verjährung[sbestimmungen], Verjährungsfrist; **to interrupt a** ~ **limitation** gesetzliche Verjährungsfrist unterbrechen; ~ **meeting** *(Br.)* erste Generalversammlung [nach Gesellschaftsgründung], gesetzlich vorgeschriebene Generalversammlung; ~ **minimum** gesetzliches Minimum; ~ **minute book** vorgeschriebenes Protokollbuch; ~ **negligence** *(US)* Verletzung der gesetzlich vorgeschriebenen Sorgfaltspflicht; ~ **notice** gesetzliche Kündigungsfrist; ~ **object** Satzungsziel; ~ **obligation** gesetzliche Verpflichtung; ~ **offence** gesetzlicher Straftatbestand; ~ **office** *(corporation, US)* Büroadresse; ~ **order** Anordnung mit Gesetzeskraft; ~ **owner** Treuhandeigentümer einer Liegenschaft; ~ **period** gesetzliche Frist; ~ **period of limitations** gesetzliche Verjährungsfrist, -zeitraum; **to favo(u)r** ~ **policy** für staatliche Interventionen eintreten; ~ **post** Planstelle; ~ **provisions** gesetzliche Bedingungen (Bestimmungen); ~ **provisions regarding liability** gesetzliche Haftungsbestimmungen; ~ **receipt** löschungsfähige Quittung; ~ **redundancy scheme** *(Br.)* Projekt zur Unterbringung entlassener Arbeiter; ~ **referendum** Volksabstimmung über ein verabschiedetes Gesetz; ~ **regime** *(US)* gesetzlicher Güterstand; ~ **register of mortgages** Hypothekenverzeichnis; ~ **release** Auflassung in gesetzlicher Form; ~ **report** *(Br.)* gesetzlich vorgeschriebener Gründungsbericht, *(joint stock company)* Hauptversammlungsbericht; ~ **requirements** Satzungserfordernisse, gesetzlich vorgeschriebene Voraussetzungen; ~ **reserve** satzungsmäßig vorgeschriebene Reserve (Rücklagen); ~ **reserve of bank notes** Banknotenreserve; ~ **rule** *(Br.)* rechtskräftiger Regierungserlaß, Regierungsverordnung; ~ **share** *(US)* Pflichtteil; ~ **tenancy** *(Br.)* dem Mieterschutz unterliegendes Mietverhältnis; ~ **tenant** *(Br.)* unter Kündigungsschutz stehender Mieter, Zwangsmieter; ~ **trust** *(Br.)* gesetzlich vorgeschriebenes Treuhandeigentum; ~ **undertakers** *(Br.)* öffentliches Versorgungsunternehmen.

stave Faßdaube;

~ *(v.)* *(ship)* leck schlagen;

~ **off trouble** Ärger fernhalten.

stay Halt, *(fig.)* Stütze, Halt, *(suspension of judicial proceedings)* Aussetzung, Einstellung[sbeschluß], *(sojourn)* vorübergehender Aufenthalt, Besuch;

~ **abroad** Auslandsaufenthalt; **a fortnight's** ~ vierzehntägiger Besuch; **temporary** ~ *(arresting judicial proceedings)* einstweilige, vorübergehende Aussetzung;

~ **of action** Aussetzung des Verfahrens; ~ **of his old age** Stütze seines Alters; **main** ~ **of a business** Rückgrat eines Geschäfts; ~ **of execution** Vollstreckungsaufschub, Einstellung der Zwangsvollstreckung; **chief** ~ **of one's family** Rückhalt seiner Familie; ~ **of foreclosure of a mortgage** Einstellung der Zwangsversteigerung; ~ **at a health resort** Kuraufenthalt; ~ **in hospital** Krankenhausaufenthalt; ~ **in a port** Hafenaufenthalt; ~ **of a petition** Aussetzung der Entscheidung über eine Konkursanordnung; ~ **of proceedings** Aussetzung (Einstellung, Ruhen) des Verfahrens;

~ *(v.)* sich aufhalten, bleiben, Reise unterbrechen, *(judicial proceedings)* einstellen;

~ **abroad** im Ausland leben; ~ **an action** Verfahren aussetzen; ~ **around** sich in der Nähe aufhalten; ~ **away** fernbleiben; ~ **the course** *(fig.)* durchhalten; ~ **down in a class** Klasse wiederholen; ~ **execution** Zwangsvollstreckung aussetzen; ~ **with friends** bei Freunden wohnen; ~ **at a hotel** in einem Hotel wohnen (logieren); ~ **in the house** zu Hause bleiben; ~ **judgment** Vollstreckung eines Urteils aussetzen; ~ **only a few minutes** nur ein paar Minuten bleiben; ~ **proceedings** Verfahren aussetzen; ~ **put** sich nicht vom Fleck rühren; ~ **in room No. 312** Nummer (Zimmer) 312 haben; ~ **for supper** zum Abendessen bleiben; ~ **tuned** in empfangsbereit sein; ~ **up** aufbleiben; ~ **with s. o.** bei jem. sein Absteigequartier nehmen (wohnen); ~ **with relations** bei Verwandten absteigen; ~ **with it** dabeibleiben;

to apply for a ~ **of court proceedings** Aussetzung des Verfahrens beantragen; **to be liable to** ~ **of execution** nicht der Zwangsvollstreckung unterliegen; **to come to** ~ sich einbürgern; **to grant a** ~ **of execution** Urteilsaussetzung verfügen; **to make a boy** ~ **in** Jungen nachsitzen lassen; **to make a short** ~ kurz unterbrechen, sich vorübergehend aufhalten; **to make a** ~ **a success** Aufenthalt angenehm gestalten;

~**-at-home** Stubenhocker; ~ **laws** Vollstreckungsschutzgesetze; ~**-down strike** *(miners, Br.)* Untertagestreik; ~**-in strike** *(Br.)* mehrtägiger Sitzstreik.

staying power Standfestigkeit.

stead Statt, Stelle;

to stand s. o. in good ~ jem. von Nutzen sein (zustatten kommen).

steadfast unerschütterlich;
  to be ~ to one's principles an seinen Prinzipien festhalten.
steadiness *(market)* Festigkeit, Stabilität;
  ~ of prices Kursbeständigkeit.
steady ständig, *(price)* fest[stehend], sich behauptend, stabil, *(reliable)* pflichtbewußt, zuverlässig;
  ~ *(v.)* *(ship)* auf Kurs halten, *(stock exchange)* sich festigen;
  to go ~ festen Freund (feste Freundin) haben; **to grow ~** *(market)* stabil werden, sich stabilisieren (befestigen); **to hold fairly ~** *(pound)* sich gut behaupten; **to keep (remain) ~** *(prices)* sich behaupten, fest bleiben;
  ~ climate ausgeglichenes Klima; **~ customer** Stammkunde; **~ demand** gleichbleibende Nachfrage; **on a ~ foundation** auf sicherer Grundlage; **~ increase** ständige Zunahme, stetige Anzeigen; **to lead a ~ life** solides Leben führen; **~ market** feste Börse; **~ prices** stabile Preise; **~ rate of growth (progress)** gleichbleibender Progressionssatz; **~-state growth** konstante Wachstumsrate; **~ work** regelmäßige (feste) Arbeit; **~ worker** fleißiger Arbeiter.
steal *(bargain, coll.)* wohlfeiler Kauf;
  ~ *(v.)* stehlen, entwenden, sich an fremdem Eigentum vergreifen;
  with intent to ~ in der Absicht rechtswidriger Zueignung;
  ~ business at any price Geschäft um jeden Preis abnehmen; **~ a competitor's market** jem. absatzmäßig Konkurrenz machen; **~ electricity** elektrischen Strom widerrechtlich entnehmen; **~ into** sich einschleichen; **~ a march on s. o.** jem. die Schau stehlen; **~ the show** alle anderen an die Wand spielen, allen die Schau stehlen; **~ s. one's thunder** sich mit fremden Federn schmücken, *(advertising)* jem. mit einer Überraschungsreklame zuvorkommen.
stealing Stehlen, Entwendung, Diebstahl;
  ~ of a car Autodiebstahl; **~ of children** Kindesentführung; **~ by finding** Fundunterschlagung.
steam Dampf, *(fig.)* Energie;
  ~ *(v.)* *(of persons)* mit einem Dampfer fahren;
  ~ ahead *(coll.)* sich ins Zeug legen; **~ easily** *(sl.)* sich leicht aufregen; **~ out of the harbo(u)r** Hafen verlassen; **~ open an envelope** Briefhülle mittels Dampfeinwirkung öffnen; **~ into the station** in den Bahnhof einfahren;
  to be heated by ~ Dampfheizung haben; **to let off ~** *(fig.)* sich Luft machen; **to make good under one's own ~** sich aus eigener Kraft hocharbeiten; **to put on ~** *(fig.)* Dampf dahinter machen;
  ~ boiler Dampfkessel; **~-boiler insurance** Dampfkesselversicherung; **~ coal** Bunkerkohle; **~ engine** Lokomotive; **~ ferry boat** Trajektschiff; **~-heated** mit Dampfheizung versehen; **~ heating** Dampfheizung; **~ locomotive** Dampflokomotive; **~ navigation** Dampfschiffahrt; **~ radio** *(coll.)* Tagesprogramm für die Hausfrau, Hausfrauenprogramm; **~ vessel** Dampfschiff.
steamboat Dampfer.
steamer Dampfer;
  mail ~ Postdampfer;
  ~ date Abgangsdatum eines Schiffes; **~ trunk** Kabinenkoffer, Überseekoffer.
steamroller Dampf-, Straßenwalze;
  ~ *(v.)* glattwalzen;
  ~ a conference *(coll.)* Konferenzteilnehmer überfahren.
steamship Dampfschiff, Dampfer;
  ~ company Schiffahrtgesellschaft; **~ line** Dampfschiff; **~ vessel** Dampfschiff.
steel Stahl;
  as true as ~ treu wie Gold;
  ~s *(stock exchange)* Stahlaktien;
  ~ automobile body Stahlkarosserie; **~ boom** Stahlkonjunktur; **~ cartel** Stahlkartell; **~ concern** Stahlkonzern; **~ consortium** Stahlkonsortium; **~ consumption** Stahlverbrauch; **~ crisis** Stahlkrise; **~ demand** Stahlbedarf; **~ engraving** Stahlstich; **~ expansion** Stahlexpansion; **~ export restraint** Zurückhaltung bei Stahlausfuhren; **~ foundry** Stahlhütte; **~ frame** Stahlkonstruktion; **~ group** *(stock exchange report)* Stahl- und Montanindustrie; **~ hedging** Vorratskäufe auf dem Stahlmarkt; **~ imports** Stahleinfuhren; **~-import surge** Stahleinfuhrstrom; **~ importer** Stahleinfuhrunternehmer; **~ industry** Eisen- und Stahlindustrie; **~ manufacturer** Stahlproduzent; **~-making capacity** Stahlkapazität; **~ nationalization** Verstaatlichung der Stahlindustrie; **~ output** Stahlproduktion; **rolled ~ output** Walzstahlerzeugung; **~ plant** Stahlwerk; **~ price** Stahlpreis; **~-price structure** Stahlpreisgefüge; **~ probe** Stahlsonde; **~ processing** Stahlweiterverarbeitung; **~-processing plant** Blechstahlwerk; **~ producer** Stahlfirma, -produzent; **~ production**

Stahlproduktion; **~ quota** Stahlkontingent; **~ recession** Stahlrezession; **~ service center** *(US)* Stahlgroßhandel, -lagerhaus; **~ shipments** Stahllieferungen; **~ shortage** Stahlknappheit; **~ stocks** *(US)* Montan-, Stahlaktien; **~ stähler** stählerner Rolladen; **~ strapping** Bandeisenverschluß; **~ stocks** *(US)* Montan-, Stahlaktien; **~ technician** Stahlfachmann; **~ trust** Stahlkonzern; **~ usage** Stahlverbrauch; **~ user** Stahlverbraucher; **~-using industry** stahlverarbeitende Industrie; **~ vault** Stahlkammer.
steelmaker Stahlfirma, -fabrikant.
steelmaking capacity Stahlkapazität.
steelwork Stahlkonstruktion;
  ~s Hütte, Stahlwerk.
steelworker Stahlarbeiter;
  ~s union Stahlarbeitergewerkschaft.
steep|demand *(coll.)* unverschämte Forderung; **~ fall** jäher Preissturz; **~ price** unverschämter Preis; **~ roof** steiles Dach; **~ story** unwahrscheinliche Geschichte.
steer *(v.)* steuern, lenken, *(fig.)* lenken, leiten, steuern, dirigieren, *(solicit, sl.)* Schlepperdienste leisten;
  ~ an automobile Auto steuern; **~ clear of** sich fernhalten; **~ clear of s. o.** jem. aus dem Wege gehen; **~ a middle course** sich durchmogeln, lavieren; **~ private investments into less developed countries** privates Investitionskapital in Entwicklungsländern zum Einsatz bringen; **~ s. o. through the ranks** j. systematisch zur Nachwuchskraft ausbilden; **~ near receivership** auf den Konkurs zusteuern.
steerage Mittel-, Zwischendeck;
  to go (travel) ~ als Zwischendeckpassagier reisen;
  ~ passenger Passagier dritter Klasse, Zwischendeckpassagier.
steerageway Steuerfähigkeit;
  to maintain ~ steuerfähig bleiben.
steerer *(sl.)* Schlepper;
  ~ automatic Selbststeuergerät.
steering Steuern, Steuerung, Lenkung;
  power-assisted ~ Servolenkung;
  ~ column *(car)* Lenksäule; **~ committee** Lenkungs-, Organisationsausschuß; **~ gear** *(car)* Lenkung; **~ wheel** Lenkrad, *(ship)* Steuerrad.
steersman *(car)* Kraftfahrer.
stellar führend, hervorragend;
  ~ performance *(stocks)* raketenartiger Auftrieb.
stellionate mehrfache Veräußerung ein und derselben Sache;
  ~ paper Matrizenpapier.
stem Baumstamm, *(print.)* Grundstrich, *(ship)* Steven, *(stock)* Stamm, Zweig, Seitenlinie;
  of noble ~ von edler Herkunft;
  ~ *(v.)* abstammen, herrühren, *(river)* stauen;
  ~ from an agreement in einer Vereinbarung begründet sein; **~ back liberalism** Liberalismus eindämmen; **~ the temptations of public life** gegen die Versuchungen des Lebens im Scheinwerferlicht ankämpfen; **~ the tide of popular indignation** gegen die öffentliche Protestwelle angehen.
stencil Matrize, Schablone, *(pattern)* Matrizenabzug;
  ~ *(v.)* Matrize schreiben, durch Matrize vervielfältigen, mittels Schablone aufmalen;
  to cut a ~ Matrize anfertigen, auf eine Matrize schreiben;
  ~ duplicator Schablonenvervielfältiger.
stenograph stenografische Aufzeichnung, Stenogramm.
stenographer *(US)* Schreibkraft, Stenograf;
  court ~ Protokollführer.
stenographic[al] stenografisch, in Kurzschrift;
  ~ service *(US)* Stenografendienst.
stenography Kurzschrift, Stenografie.
stenotype Stenografiermaschine.
stenotypist Stenotypist;
  female ~ Stenotypistin.
step Stufe, Schritt, Maßnahme, *(car)* Trittbrett, *(dipl.)* Demarche, *(mil., rank)* Rangstufe, Grad, *(promotion, mil.)* Beförderung, *(salary)* Gehaltsstufe;
  ~ by ~ vorsichtig; **by ~s** stufen-, schrittweise; **in ~ with** in Einklang mit;
  appropriate ~s geeignete Maßnahmen; **common ~s** *(pol.)* gemeinsame Schritte; **~ forward** Fortschritt; **major ~ forward** wesentlicher Schritt nach vorn; **introductory ~s** einleitende Schritte; **rash ~** übereilte Maßnahme; **stern ~s** scharfe Maßnahmen;
  ~ in the right direction richtige Maßnahme; **~ in the proceedings** Prozeßhandlung; **~s in the social scale** Stufen in der gesellschaftlichen Rangordnung;
  ~ *(v.)* across the road Straße überqueren; **~ aside** abtreten,

(fig.) für einen anderen zurücktreten; ~ **down** *(minister)* zurücktreten, in Pension gehen; ~ **on the gas** *(coll.)* Gaspedal heruntertreten, *(fig.)* Druck dahintermachen; ~ **gingerly around s. o.** j. wie ein rohes Ei behandeln; ~ **in** intervenieren, einschreiten, sich einschalten; ~ **in for s. o.** für j. einspringen; ~ **in with massive aid** massive finanzielle Hilfen gewähren; ~ **into a fortune** spielend zu einem Vermögen gelangen; ~ **into a good job** durch Zufall zu einer guten Stellung kommen; ~ **into s. one's shoes** in jds. Fußstapfen treten; ~ **off** *(distance)* abschreiten; ~ **off the carpet** verheiratet werden; ~ **off the deep end** sich unüberlegt engagieren; ~ **off a train** aus einem Zug aussteigen; ~ **on it** Druck dahintermachen; ~ **onto the platform** Rednertribüne betreten; ~ **out** *(US)* seine Stellung aufgeben, *(sl.)* ausgehen; ~ **up production** Produktion steigern (erhöhen); ~ **up production of a fast-moving line** Produktionsausstoß eines Verkaufsschlagers erhöhen; ~ **up a scheme** Plan beschleunigen; **to be out of** ~ Tritt verloren haben; **to be out of** ~ **with the mainstream of the party** mit den Hauptströmungen der Partei nicht mehr ganz übereinstimmen; **to get one** ~ *(mil.)* befördert werden; **to have a** ~ **in mind** Schritt planen; **to make a long** ~ **towards success** dem Erfolg ein gutes Stück näherrücken; **to retrace one's** ~s seine Maßnahmen rückgängig machen; **to take** ~s Maßnahmen ergreifen; **to take decisive** ~s entscheidende Schritte tun; **to take immediate** ~s umgehende Schritte ergreifen; **to take legal** ~s **against s. o.** j. gerichtlich belangen; **to take the necessary** ~s erforderliche Maßnahmen treffen, erforderliche Schritte veranlassen, Demarche unternehmen; **to take positive** ~s aktiv werden; **to take short** ~s *(diplomacy)* Politik der kleinen Schritte betreiben; **to tread in s. one's** ~ in jds. Fußstapfen treten;
~ **bonus** Leistungsprämie, Stufenakkord; ~-**child** Stiefkind; ~-**by-**~ **deals** schrittweise erzielte Vereinbarungen; ~-**father** Stiefvater; ~ **ladder system** innerbetriebliche Leistungsverrechnung, Stufenleiterverfahren; ~-**mother** Stiefmutter; ~ **rate** *(insurance)* Stufensatz, -tarif, *(el.)* Verbrauchertarif; ~-**rate premium** *(insurance)* jährlich steigende Prämie; ~ **rocket** Stufenrakete.

stepping stone *(fig.)* Sprungbrett;
first ~ **to success** erster Schritt zum Erfolg;
~ **method** *(programming)* vereinfachte Rechenmethode.

stepup Zunahme, Erhöhung;
~ **in inventory growth** lagerzyklischer Aufschwung; ~ **in output** Ausstoßsteigerung.

stepwise schrittweise.

stereo stereophonische Wiedergabe, Stereo;
multichannel ~ Stereoempfang auf mehreren Kanälen;
~ *(v.)* auf Stereo aufnehmen;
~ **compatible headphone** Stereokopfhörer; ~ **illusion** Stereoeindruck; ~ **plate** Druckstock; ~ **tape recorder** Stereobandgerät; ~ **unit** Stereogerät.

stereogram Raumbild.

stereograph stereoskopisches Bild;
~ *(v.)* stereografisch fotografieren.

stereophonic sound Raumton, dreidimensionaler Klang.

stereoscopic camera Stereokamera.

stereotype Druckplatte, *(fig.)* Gemeinplatz, Schablone, Klischee;
~ *(v.)* stereotyp wiederholen.

stereotyped *(fig.)* klischee-, schablonenhaft, stereotyp, *(print.)* stereotypiert.

stereotypography Stereotypdruckverfahren.

sterile *(fig.)* unproduktiv, *(land)* unfruchtbar, *(med.)* keimfrei, steril;
~ **discussion** unfruchtbare Diskussion; ~ **reserves** unnütze Reserven.

sterilization Sterilisierung;
forced ~ Zwangssterilisierung.

sterilize *(v.)* sterilisieren, unfruchtbar machen.

sterling englisches Pfund;
external ~ *(Br.)* mit Fremdwährungsmitteln erworbene Pfunde;
~ *(a.)* echt, unverfälscht, vollgültig, *(coin)* vollwertig;
~ **account** Pfundkonto, -guthaben, ~ **area** Sterlinggebiet, -block; ~ **balance** Sterling-, Pfundguthaben, -saldo; ~ **bill** auf englische Pfund lautender Wechsel; ~ **bloc** Sterlingblock; ~ **bonds** Sterlingobligationen; ~ **book** wertvolles Buch; ~ **certificate of deposit** Guthabenbescheinigung über ein Sterlingkonto; ~ **collapse** Zusammenbruch des Pfundes; ~ **cost** Einkaufspreis; ~ **credit** auf englische Pfund lautender Kreditbrief; ~ **crisis** Pfund-, Sterlingkrise; ~ **equivalent** Gegenwert in Pfunden; **to peg the** ~ **exchange rate** Wechselkurssatz des Pfun-

des stützen; ~ **gold** echtes Gold; ~ **invoice** in Pfund zahlbare Rechnung; ~ **loan** Pfundanleihe; ~ **merit** hervorragender Vedienst; ~ **money** vollwertiges Geld; ~ **notes** Pfunddevisen; ~ **price** Einkaufspreis; ~ **qualities** hervorragende Eigenschaften; ~ **securities** in Pfund notierte Wertpapiere; ~ **value** ursprünglicher Wert.

stern Heck, Achterschiff;
~ *(a.)* starr, streng, strikt;
~ **discipline** strenge Disziplin; ~ **penalty** strenge Haft; ~ **resolve** fester Entschluß; ~ **taskmaster** strenger Vorarbeiter; ~ **wheeler** Heckraddampfer.

stet *(print.)* bleibt!

stevedore Ab-, Belader, Stauer, Schauermann, Güterpacker;
~ *(v.)* ver-, entladen, stauen.

stevedoring cost Verladekosten.

stew Eintopfgericht;
~ *(v.)* *(coll.)* sich aufregen, *(school, sl.)* büffeln, ochsen;
let s. o. ~ **in his own juice** j. in seinem eigenen Saft schmoren lassen;
to be in a ~ in Schwulitäten sein.

steward *(agriculture)* Ökonom, Inspektor, *(bailiff)* Vogt, *(festival)* Helfer, Ordner, *(mar.)* Proviantmeister, *(property)* [Vermögens]verwalter, Administrator, *(of real estate)* Guts-, Grundstücksverwalter, *(ship)* Steward, Kellner;
baggage ~ *(US)* Gepäcksteward; **land** ~ *(Br.)* Guts-, Güterverwalter; **shop** ~ Betriebs-, Vertrauensrat; **union** ~ *(US)* Betriebsobmann;
~ **of a manor** Gerichtsbeamter.

stewardess Flugbegleiterin, Stewardess.

stewardship Vermögensverwaltung, Geschäftsleitung, *(office of steward)* Verwalteramt;
to give an account of one's ~ Rechenschaft über seine Vermögensverwaltung ablegen;
~ **account** Vermögensverwaltungskonto.

stick *(airplane)* Steuerknüppel, *(croupier, sl.)* Croupier, *(dull person)* Stockfisch, *(impediment)* Verzögerungsgrund, *(labour strike, Br., dial.)* Arbeiterstreik, *(mil.)* Bombenladung für Reihenwurf, *(print.)* Winkelhaken, *(scale of social standing)* Rangstufe;
in a cleft ~ in der Klemme;
the ~s *(US)* unerschlossene Gebiete, hinterste Provinz;
control (joy, *sl.)* ~ *(airplane)* Steuerknüppel; **odd** ~ komischer Kauz;
the ~ **and the carrot** Zuckerbrot und Peitsche; ~-**in-the-mud** unbeweglicher Mensch, Schlafmütze, *(pol.)* Ultra-Konservativer, Reaktionär; ~s **and stones** unbelebte Dinge;
~ *(a.)* nicht fortschrittlich, reaktionär, ultrakonservativ;
~-**at-nothing** skrupellos, vor nichts zurückschreckend;
~ *(v.)* *(overcharge, sl.)* übervorteilen;
~ **s. o.** *(US sl.)* j. anpumpen; ~ **s. th. on s. o.** jem. etw. in die Schuhe schieben; ~ **around** *(coll.)* sich verfügbar halten, herumlungern; ~ **bills** Zettel ankleben, Maueranschlag machen, plakatieren, anschlagen; ~ **like a bur to s. o.** sich wie eine Klette an j. hängen; ~ **in a few commas** ein paar Kommata einsetzen; ~ **s. th. down** *(coll.)* etw. aufschreiben; ~ **down an envelope** Briefumschlag (Kuvert) verschließen (zukleben); ~ **s. o. for the drinks** j. blechen lassen; ~ **fast** hoffnungslos festsitzen; ~ **to one's guns** auf seiner Meinung bestehenbleiben; ~ **on a label** Etikett aufkleben; ~ **in the mud** *(car)* festgefahren sein; ~ **one's neck out** Kopf und Kragen riskieren; ~ **at nothing** sich durch nichts aufhalten lassen, vor nichts zurückschrecken; ~ **out like a sore thumb** lästig auffallen; ~ **papers in a drawer** Papiere in eine Schublade stopfen; ~ **out for higher pay** auf höherem Lohn bestehen; ~ **in photographs** Fotografien einkleben; ~ **a placard on a hoarding** Plakat an einem Bauzaun anbringen; ~ **to one's post** an seinem Posten kleben; ~ **to a resolve** an einem Entschluß festhalten; ~ **on a sandbank** auf einer Sandbank auflaufen; ~ **it on during the busy season** während der Saison enorm hohe Preise verlangen; ~ **a stamp on an envelope** Briefmarke auf ein Kuvert kleben; ~ **to one's statement** bei seiner Aussage bleiben; ~ **to the text** sich genau an den Wortlaut halten; ~ **in one's throat** *(proposal)* schwer zu verdauen sein; ~ **together** zusammenhalten, zusammenklucken; ~ **at trifles** sich mit Kleinigkeiten aufhalten; ~ **up for s. o.** für j. eintreten (Partei ergreifen), sich für j. einsetzen; ~ **up a bank** *(sl.)* Bank ausrauben; ~ **up for one's rights** sich nicht die Butter vom Brot nehmen lassen; ~ **out for higher wages** höhere Löhne verlangen; ~ **to one's word** zu seinem Wort stehen;
to be up the ~ *(sl.)* bekloppt sein; **to be high up the** ~ hohe Position innehaben; **to gather dry** ~s trockenes Holz sammeln; **to get hold of the wrong end of the** ~ Sache völlig mißverstehen;

to leave not a ~ standing keinen Stein auf dem anderen lassen; **to make no ~s with a task** mit einer Sache gar nicht vorankommen; **to own only a few ~s** nur ein paar Möbel besitzen; **~ bombing** Reihenwurf; **~-on label** gummiertes Etikett, Aufklebezettel; **~-up** *(US sl.)* bewaffneter Überfall, Raubüberfall; **~-up man** *(sl.)* Bandit.

sticker *(US)* Klebestreifen, Aufklebezettel, Aufkleber, *(drug)* Ladenhüter, *(price tag)* Preisschild; **bill ~** Zettelankleber.

sticking, bill Zettelankleben; **~ plaster** Heftpflaster.

stickler Kleinigkeitskrämer, Nörgler, Pedant; **to be a ~ for details** sich um jede Einzelheit selbst kümmern; **to be no ~ for formality** sich völlig unformell geben, nicht auf Formalitäten bestehen.

sticky *(fig.)* kritisch, *(weather)* stickig, schwül; **to be ~ about letting s. o. have an overdraft** Kontoüberziehungen nur sehr zögernd zugestehen; **~ assets** nur schwer realisierbare Aktiva; **to come to a ~ end** ein schlimmes Ende nehmen; **~ road** schmierige Straße.

stiff steif, formell, *(alcoholic drink)* scharf, stark, *(drunk, sl.)* besoffen, *(glass)* gut eingeschenkt, *(prices)* hoch, fest, versteift; **~ as a poker** stocksteif; **to be scared ~** zu Tode erschrocken sein; **~ adversary** hartnäckiger Gegner; **~ bill** überhöhte Rechnung; **~ breeze** steife Brise; **~ card** *(sl.)* formelle Einladung; **~ course of reading** schwerer Text; **~ denial** glattes Dementi; **to meet a charge with a ~ denial** Anklage glatt ableugnen; **~ examination** schweres Examen; **to keep a ~ upper lip** die Ohren steif halten, Durchhaltevermögen zeigen, sich tapfer halten; **~ market** stabile Marktlage; **~-neck** selbstgerechter Mensch; **~-necked** obstinat, halsstarrig; **~ opposition** hartnäckiger Widerstand; **~ price** *(fam.)* überhöhter Preis; **~ reading** schwere Lektüre; **~ reception** steifer Empfang; **to get a ~ reception** sehr formell empfangen werden; **to keep a ~ rein** Zügel straff in der Hand halten.

stiffen *(v.)* *(prices)* sich festigen (versteifen), Versteifung erfahren, anziehen, fester werden; **~ s. o.** jem. den Rücken stärken; **~ again** wieder anziehen; **~ up slightly** angespannt aufhorchen.

stiffener *(book)* Rückeneinlage.

stiffening | of the attitude Versteifung der politischen Haltung; **~ of prices** Anziehen der Preise (Kurse), *(capital market)* Versteifung am Geldmarkt.

stiffish examination ziemlich schwere Prüfung.

stifle *(v.) | a prosecution** Strafverfolgung gegen Entgelt niederschlagen (einstellen); **~ a report** Bericht unterdrücken; **~ a revolt** Aufruhr ersticken.

stifling a prosecution Niederschlagung einer Strafverfolgung.

stigma of illegitimacy Brandmal der Unehelichkeit.

still Standfoto, Einzelfotografie, *(distillery)* Brennerei; **illicit ~** Schwarzbrennerei; **~ alarm** *(US)* stiller Feueralarm; **~ life** Stilleben.

stillbirth Totgeburt.

stillborn totgeboren; **~ child** Totgeburt; **~ remark** geistlose Bemerkung.

stillhouse Schnapsbrennerei.

stillroom Vorrats-, Abstellkammer.

stillstand Stillstand.

stilts, on auf Stelzen, bombastisch.

stilted style hochtrabender Stil.

stimulant alkoholisches Getränk, *(med.)* Belebungsmittel, Stimulans, *(stock exchange)* anregender Moment.

stimulate *(v.)* anregen, ankurbeln, fördern; **~ *(v.)* business activity** Konjunktur anregen; **~ s. o. to greater efforts** j. zu größeren Anstrengungen ermutigen; **~ industry** Wirtschaft ankurbeln; **~ production** Produktion beleben.

stimulating factors Auftriebsfaktoren.

stimulation, cyclical Konjunkturanregung, -förderung; **~ of business activity** Konjunkturanregung, -förderung, **-stimulus**; **~ of industry** Ankurbelung der Wirtschaft; **~ of production** Produktionsbelebung.

stimulatory measures konjunkturfördernde Maßnahmen.

stimulus *(med.)* anregendes Mittel, Belebungsmittel, Stimulans; **under the ~ of hunger** vom Hunger getrieben; **~ response** Anreizreaktion; **~ threshold** Reizschwelle.

sting *(pep)* Schwung, Pfiff, *(fig.)* Ansporn; **~ of conscience** Gewissensbiß; **~ of hunger** nagender Hunger; **~ *(v.)* *(sl.)* neppen, übervorteilen; **~ s. o. with s. th.** j. mit etw. schockieren; **to have no ~ in it** keinen Schwung haben.

stinging | cold beißende (schneidende) Kälte; **~ rebuke** scharfer Tadel.

stingy knauserig, knickrig, geizig.

stink *(v.)* schlechten Ruf haben; **~ of money** *(sl.)* nach Geld stinken.

stinker Stinkbombe, *(sl.)* Widerling; **to write s. o. a ~** jem. einen beleidigenden Brief schreiben.

stint *(mining)* Schicht, Tagewerk, *(restriction)* Einschränkung, *(Br., task prescribed)* bestimmtes Arbeitspensum; **without ~** rückhaltslos; **~ *(v.)* begrenzen, Beschränkungen auferlegen; **~ o. s.** sich einschränken; **~ money** mit dem Geld knausern; **to do one's daily ~** seiner täglichen Beschäftigung nachgehen, sein Tagespensum erledigen; **to exceed one's ~** seinen Anteil überschreiten; **to spend money without ~** Geld hemmungslos ausgeben; **to work by ~s** auf Schicht arbeiten.

stipend Gehalt, Besoldung, feste Bezüge.

stipendiary Gehalts-, Pensionsempfänger, *(US)* Stipendiat; **~ *(a.)* besoldet, bezahlt, vergütet, honoriert; **~ magistrate** *(Br.)* Richter am Schnellgericht.

stipital *(succession)* nach Stämmen; **~ distribution of property** Nachlaßverteilung nach Stämmen.

stipulate *(v.)* ausbedingen, -machen, vereinbaren, übereinkommen, vorsehen, festsetzen; **~ conditions** Bedingungen stellen; **~ by contract** vertraglich festlegen (abmachen); **~ expressly** ausdrücklich festlegen; **~ for the best material to be used** erstklassige Materialverwendung vereinbaren; **~ payments in gold** Zahlungen auf Goldbasis vereinbaren; **~ that payment should be quarterly** vierteljährliche Zahlungen festsetzen; **~ with the plaintiff** mit dem Kläger ein Abkommen treffen; **~ a reserve** Vorbehalt formulieren; **~ for a reward** Belohnung vereinbaren; **~ tacitly** stillschweigend vereinbaren; **~ the terms of a contract** Bedingungen eines Vertrages fixieren, Vertragsbedingungen festsetzen; **~ a time** Termin anberaumen; **~ a time for delivery** Lieferfrist festsetzen; **~ in writing** schriftlich vereinbaren.

stipulated festgesetzt, ausgemacht, *(contractual)* vertragsgemäß; **as ~** wie vereinbart; **~ by agreement** vertraglich vereinbart; **at the date ~** zur vereinbarten Zeit; **~ damages** Konventionalstrafe; **at the ~ place** am vereinbarten Ort; **~ premium** *(insurance law)* Vertragsprämie; **~ quality** ausbedungene (vereinbarte) Qualität; **to deliver within the ~ time** fristgerecht liefern.

stipulation Abmachung, Ausbedingung, Vereinbarung, *(antitrust law, US)* förmliches Besserungsversprechen, *(condition)* Bedingung, Klausel, [Vertrags]bestimmung, *(stipulating)* Formulierung, [Vertrags]festsetzung, *(written memorandum, US)* Vereinbarung unter den Prozeßanwälten; **by ~** einverständlich; **on the ~ that** unter der Bedingung, daß; **on the express ~** mit der ausdrücklichen Bestimmung; **exclusivity ~** Ausschluß des Wettbewerbs, Wettbewerbsausschluß; **reciprocity ~** Gegenseitigkeitsklausel; **~s of a bill of lading** Konnossementsbestimmungen; **~ of conditions** Festlegung von Bedingungen (Vertragsbestimmungen); **~ to the contrary** gegenteilige Bestimmung; **~s of the parties** Parteiabmachungen; **~ of payment** Zahlungsvereinbarung; **~ in restraint of trade** Konkurrenzklausel; **~ of the terms of an agreement** Festlegung der Vertragsbedingungen; **~ as to time** Zeitbestimmung, -festlegung; **~ proceedings** *(US)* Einigungsverfahren.

stipulator Vertragspartei, Kontrahent.

stir Aufruhr, Lärm, Getümmel, *(prison, sl.)* Kasten; **in ~ for six months** ein halbes Jahr eingebuchtet; **~ *(v.)* aufreizen, schüren; **~ the blood** böses Blut machen; **~ the crew to mutiny** Schiffsmannschaft zur Meuterei veranlassen; **not ~ a finger** keinen Finger rühren; **not ~ an eyelid** nicht mit der Wimper zucken; **~ the pot** *(fig.)* Wirbel machen; **~ one's stumps** *(coll.)* sich auf die Socken machen; **~ up** aufwiegeln, -hetzen, anstiften; **~ up a people to rebellion** Volksaufruhr anzetteln; **~ things up** böses Blut machen.

stirabout Geschäftigkeit, Betriebsamkeit.

stirrer Aufrührer, -wiegler, -hetzer.

stirring | up to boycott Boykotthetze; **~ speech** mitreißende Rede; **~ tales of adventure** aufregende Abenteuergeschichten; **~ times** aufregende Zeitläufe, bewegte Zeit.

stirpes [Familien]stamm, *(ancestor)* Stammvater; **per ~** *(law of inheritance)* nach Stämmen.

stitched *(book)* broschiert.

stitcher *(bookbinding)* Heftmaschine.

stitching, Dutch Holländern; **English** ~ Engländern; **faulty** ~ verheftet.

stiver Heller, Pfennig;
  not to care a ~ sich keinen Deut kümmern.

stock *(Br., capital stock)* Grundstock, Geschäfts-, Stamm-, Grundkapital, *(capital stock, US)* Anfangskapital [einer Aktiengesellschaft], Aktienkapital, *(inventory)* Inventar, *(funded debt, Br.)* Anleiheschuld, *(lineage)* Herkunft, Abstammung, Abkunft, Stamm, Familie, *(ling.)* Sprachengruppe, *(livestock)* Vieh, *(mar.)* Helling, Stapel, *(provisions)* Vorrat, *(ready money)* bares Vermögen, Barschaft, Summe, *(share)* Aktie, *(share paid in)* Einlage, [Gesellschafts]anteil, *(shipping)* Stapel, *(store)* Lagerbestand, -vorrat, Warenbestand, -vorrat, -lager, *(theater)* Repertoire, *(working capital)* Betriebskapital, -mittel;
  carried in ~ lagervorrätig; **ex** ~ ab Lager; **in (on)** ~ auf Lager, vorrätig, vorhanden; **of farming** ~ vom Lande; **on the ~s** *(under construction)* im Bau; **out of** ~ nicht vorrätig, ausverkauft, nicht mehr auf Lager (gefragt); **out of one's own** ~ aus dem eigenen Geldbeutel;
  ~s *(Br., bonds)* Obligationen, Schuldverschreibungen, Pfandbriefe, *(government fund, Br.)* [fundierte] Staatsschuld, Staatspapiere, -anleihen, -renten, *(securities, Br.)* Effekten, Wert-, Börsenpapiere, Aktien, *(store)* Lagerbestände, Warenvorräte;
  accumulative ~ kumulative Vorzugsaktien; **active** ~ *(US)* lebhaft gehandelte Aktien; **actual** ~ Istbestand; **adjustment preferred ~s** *(US)* im Sanierungsverfahren ausgegebene Vorzugsaktien; **advancing** ~s steigende Aktien; **assented** ~s *(US)* im Sammeldepot hinterlegte Aktien; **assessable** ~ *(US)* nachschußpflichtige Aktien; **assigned ~s** Namensaktien mit Übertragungsvermerk, zedierte Papiere; **authorized** ~ *(US)* genehmigtes (autorisiertes) Kapital; **no** ~ **available** leerer Markt; **average** ~ durchschnittlicher Lagerbestand, Lagerbestandsdurchschnitt; **bank** ~ Bankaktien; **barometer ~s** *(US)* Standardwerte; **bearer** ~ Inhaberaktien; **bonus** ~ *(US)* Gratisaktie; **buffer** ~ beweglich geführtes Lager; **callable** ~ kündbare Vorzugsaktie; **capital** ~ *(US)* Grundkapital einer Aktiengesellschaft; **authorized capital** ~ *(US)* genehmigtes Aktienkapital; **[non]voting capital** ~ *(US)* [nicht] stimmberechtigtes Aktienkapital; **unissued capital** ~ *(US)* nicht ausgegebenes Aktienkapital; **carriage** ~ Warenbestand; **classified** ~ *(US)* Vorrangaktien, in verschiedenen Serien ausgegebene Aktien, klassifizierte Aktien; **clearinghouse** ~ *(US)* zum Clearingverkehr zugelassene (börsenfähige) Aktie, im Clearingverkehr abgerechnete Aktie; **closing** ~ Schlußbestand; **common** ~ *(US)* Stammaktie; **consent ~s** dividendenberechtigte Stammaktien; **considerable** ~ bedeutendes Lager; **consignment** ~ Konsignationsware; **consolidated** ~s *(Br.)* konsolidierte Schuldverschreibungen; **convertible** ~ umtauschfähige (umwandelbare) Vorzugsaktie; **cooperative** ~ Genossenschaftskapital; **corporate ~s** *(US)* Kapitalanteile, Effekten, Aktien; **corporation** ~ *(Br.)* kommunale Schuldverschreibungen, Kommunalobligationen; **over-the-counter** ~ *(US)* Freiverkehrswerte; **cumulative** ~ *(US)* Aktie mit rückwirkender Dividendenberechtigung; **cumulative preferred** ~ *(US)* Vorzugsaktie mit Dividendennachzahlungsverpflichtung, kumulative Vorzugsaktie; **curb ~s** *(US)* im Freiverkehr gehandelte (an der Freiverkaufsbörse notierte) Aktien, Freiverkaufswerte; **dated ~s** kündbare Wertpapiere; **dead** ~ unverkäufliche Ware, Partieware, *(bookshop)* unverkaufte Exemplare, *(farming)* totes Inventar; **debenture** ~ Vorzugsaktie, *(Br.)* Schuldverschreibungskapital, [meist hypothekarisch (dinglich) gesicherte] Obligationen (Schuldverschreibungen), *(bonded debt)* Anleihekapital, -schuld, *(US)* Vorzugsaktien; **declining** ~s fallende Aktien; **deferred** ~ *(US)* nicht sofort dividendenberechtigte (bevorrechtigte) Aktie, Nachzugsaktie; **depleted** ~s erschöpfte Vorräte; **deposited** ~ hinterlegte Aktie, Garantieaktie; **distributing** ~ Auslieferungslager; **donated** ~ *(US)* zurückgegebene Gründeraktien; **dormant** ~ Ladenhüter; **double liability** ~ *(US)* in voller Höhe nachschußpflichtige Aktie; **dummy ~s** *(US)* an Strohmänner ausgegebene Aktien; **eight** ~s *(US)* nicht zum regulären Kurs gehandelte kleinere Aktienposten; **employee** ~s *(US)* an die Belegschaft ausgegebene Aktien; **equity** ~ Aktienkapital; **exhausted** ~ erschöpfte Vorräte; **existing** ~ Aktienbestände; **fancy** ~ *(US)* unsichere Spekulationspapiere; **farm** ~ landwirtschaftliches Inventar, Viehbestand; **fictitious** ~ verwässerte Aktie; **finished** ~ *(insurance business)* Fertigwarenlager; **firm** ~ *(Br.)* feste Werte; **first** ~ Stamm-, Grundkapital; **first preferred** ~ *(US)* erste Vorzugsaktien; **first-rate** ~ sicheres (erstklassiges) Papier; **floating** ~ Spekulationspapiere; **food ~s** Lebensmittel-

vorräte; **foreign** ~s *(Br.)* Valutapapiere, Auslandswerte; **founder's** ~s *(US)* Gründeraktien; **fresh** ~ *(US)* neue Aktie; **full[y]-paid** ~ eingezahltes Aktienkapital, *(share)* voll bezahlte Aktie, Aktie mit vollem Nennwert, *(US)* Hundertdollaraktie; **giltedged** ~ *(Br.)* mündelsichere (erstklassige) Wertpapiere, Anlagewerte; **gold** ~ Goldbestand; **government** ~s *(Br.)* Staatspapiere, -anleihen; **growth** ~s Wachstumswerte; **guaranteed** ~s Aktien mit von anderen Gesellschaften garantierter Dividende; **half-** ~ *(US)* Fünfzigdollaraktie, Aktie mit einem Pariwert von 50; **heavy** ~ hohe Lagerinvestitionen; **high-coupon** ~s *(Br.)* hochverzinsbare Staatsanleihen; **high-quality** ~ Spitzenwerte; **imported** ~s Importware; **inactive** ~[s] *(US)* Aktien mit geringen Börsenumsätzen, vernachlässigte Wertpapiere; **income-producing** ~s ertragbringende Wertpapiere; **incoming** ~ Wareneingänge; **incomplete** ~ unvollständiges Lager; **industrial** ~ *(US)* Sicherheit in Form von an der New Yorker Börse gehandelten Industrieaktien; **inscribed** ~ *(Br.)* Schuldbuchgiroforderungen, -titel, Aktien ohne Besitzschein, börsenmäßig gehandelte Buchwerte; **interest-bearing** ~ zinstragende Aktie; **interest-rate sensitive** ~ *(US)* zinsempfindliche Aktien; **international** ~s international gehandelte Papiere, an Auslandsbörsen zugelassene Aktien; **issued** ~ *(US)* effektiv ausgegebenes (emittiertes) Aktienkapital, begebene Aktien; **joint** ~ *(of joint stock company, Br.)* Aktien-, Stammkapital, *(common fund)* Gemeinschafts-, Gesellschaftsfonds, Gesellschaftskapital; **junior** ~ junge Emission; **junior issue** ~s *(US)* junge Aktien; **left-over** ~s Lagerbestand; **letter** ~s *(US)* Aktien mit beschränkter Verwendungsfähigkeit; **listed** ~s *(US)* an der Börse notierte (börsennotierte, eingeführte) Aktien; ~s **loaned** lombardierte Effekten; **local [authority]** ~ *(Br.)* Kommunalpapiere; **long** ~s *(US)* effektiv im Besitz befindliche Aktien; **low** ~ geringer Vorrat; **majority** ~ *(US)* Aktienmehrheit; **management** ~ mehrstimmige Aktie im Besitz der Direktion, Verwaltungsaktie; **merchandise** ~ Warenlager; **slow-moving** ~ Waren mit langer Umschlagzeit; **motor** ~s Automobilaktien; **municipal** ~ *(Br.)* Kommunalschuldverschreibungen, Kommunalobligationen; **negotiable** ~s übertragbare Aktien; ~s **negotiable on the** ~ **exchange** börsenfähige Aktien; **negotiated** ~s gehandelte Werte; **new** ~ frische Vorräte; **new** ~s *(US)* junge Aktien; **no-par [value]** ~ *(US)* nennwertlose Aktie, Aktie ohne Nennwert, Quotenaktie; **nonassessable** ~ nachschuß- und umlagefreie Aktie; **nonassessable preferred** ~ *(US)* nicht nachschußpflichtige Vorschußaktie, im Clearingverkehr abgerechnete Aktie; **nonassented** ~s am Sanierungsverfahren nicht beteiligte (im Einzeldepot verwahrte) Aktien; **noncumulative preferred** ~ *(US)* Vorzugsaktie ohne Dividendenbezugsrecht; **nondividend paying** ~s nicht zinstragende (notleidende) Papiere; **nonvoting** ~ nicht stimmberechtigtes Aktienkapital, Aktien ohne Stimmrecht; ~ **offered** *(stock exchange)* Abgabematerial; **old** ~ zurückgesetzte Waren; **open** ~ ständig vorrätige Ware; **opening** ~ Anfangsbestand; **option** ~s *(Br.)* Prämienwerte; **ordinary** ~ *(US)* gewöhnliche Aktie, Stammaktie; **original** ~ *(US)* Grund-, Stammkapital, Stammaktie; **original-issue** ~ *(US)* Gründeraktie; **outgoing** ~ [Waren]ausgänge; **outstanding** ~ ausgegebenes Aktienkapital, *(shares)* Aktien im Publikumsbesitz; **overissue** ~ übermittierte [ungültige] Aktie; **paid-up** ~ voll bezahlte (voll eingezahlte) Aktie; **par-value** ~ *(US)* Nennwertaktie; **participating preferred** ~ *(US)* mit besonderer (zusätzlicher) Dividendenberechtigung ausgestattete Vorzugsaktie; **partly-paid** ~ teilbezahlte Aktie, Teilzahlungsaktie; **pawned** ~s lombardierte Effekten; **penny** ~s *(US)* unter einem Dollar gehandelte Aktien, Kleinaktien, billige Spekulationsaktien; **permanent** ~ eiserner [Geld-, Waren]bestand; **phantom** ~s nur buchmäßig [von einem Unternehmen Führungskräften] gutgeschriebene Aktien; **pithead** ~s Haldenbestände; **potential** ~ Emissionsreserve; **preference** ~ *(Br.)* Vorzugsaktie, Prioritätspapiere; **preferred** ~ *(US)* Vorzugs-, Prioritätsaktien; **callable preferred** ~s *(US)* kündbare Vorzugsaktien; **cumulative preferred** ~ *(US)* zusätzliche Vorzugsaktie; **premium** ~ *(US)* zu einem Agio ausgegebene Aktie; **prior** ~ Vorzugsaktie; **prior preference (preferred)** ~ *(US)* Sondervorzugsaktie; **profit-sharing** ~ gewinnberechtigte Aktie; **promoters'** ~ *(US)* Gründeraktie; **public** ~s Staatspapiere, Staatsobligationen, -anleihen; **punched-card** ~ gelochtes Aktienzertifikat; **high-quality** ~ erstklassige Papiere; **quarter-** ~ *(US)* Fünfundzwanzigdollaraktie, mit nur ein Viertel des Pariwerts gehandelte Aktie; **quoted** ~s zur Börsennotierung zugelassene (notierte) Aktien; **railroad** *(US)* **(railway, Br.)** ~s Eisenbahnaktien, -werte; **raw** ~ *(insurance business)* Zustand vor der Verarbeitung; **reacquired capital** ~ Portefeuille eigener Aktien; **real** ~ *(US)* Istbestand, effektiv im Besitz befindliche

Aktien; **redeemable preferred** ~s *(US)* rückkaufbare Vorzugsaktien; **registered** ~ *(Br.)* Namenspapier, *(US)* auf den Namen eingetragene Aktie, Namensaktie; **replenishing** ~ Ergänzungslager; **representative** ~s *(US)* führende Börsenwerte, Standardwerte; **reserve** ~ Reservelager; **restricted** ~s *(US)* nur an private Abnehmer verkäufliche (noch nicht zum Börsenhandel zugelassene) Aktien; **rolling** ~ [Eisenbahn]betriebsmaterial, rollendes Material, Wagenpark; **salable** ~s gangbare Werte; **second preferred** ~ *(US)* Vorzugsaktien zweiter Klasse; **short** ~ *(US)* auf Baisse verkaufte Aktien; **sliding** ~s *(US)* fallende Aktien; **sound** ~s sichere Werte; **special** ~s *(US)* Spezialwerte, -papiere, Favoriten; **speculative** ~s *(US)* spekulative Aktien; **splitup** ~s gesplittete Aktien; **steel** ~s *(US)* Stahl-, Montanaktien; **summer** ~ Sommerlager; **surplus** ~ Inventarüberschuß, überschüssige Vorräte; **subscribed** ~s *(US)* gezeichnete Aktien; ~ **taken in** *(Br.)* in Report genommene Effekten; **total** ~ Gesamtkapital; **treasury** ~ *(US)* eigener Aktienbestand, Portefeuille eigener Aktien, *(Br.)* Staatsanleihe; **trust company** ~s *(US)* Aktien einer Treuhandgesellschaft; **trustee** ~s *(US)* mündelsichere Anlagepapiere (Aktien); **unclaimed** ~ herrenlose Aktie; **unified** ~ *(Br.)* konsolidierte Anleihe; **unissued** ~s *(US)* unverwertete Aktien; **unissued capital** ~ *(US)* genehmigtes, noch nicht ausgegebenes Aktienkapital; **unlisted** ~ *(US)* an der Börse nicht notierte (eingeführte) Aktien; **unrestricted** ~s *(US)* jederzeit verkäufliche Aktien; **unsubscribed** ~ nicht gezeichnete Aktie; **unvalued** ~s *(US)* Aktien ohne Nennwert, nennwertlose Aktien, Quotenaktien; **voting** ~ stimmberechtigte Aktie, Stimmrechtsaktie; **voting capital** ~ *(US)* stimmberechtigtes Aktienkapital; **voting-pool** ~ beschränkt stimmberechtigter Kapitalanteil; **voting preferred** ~s *(US)* stimmberechtigte Vorzugsaktien; **wag(g)on** ~ Wagenbestand; ~s **wanted** verlangte Werte; **watered** ~ verwässertes Aktienkapital; **well-assorted (-selected)** ~ wohlassortiertes (wohlversehenes) Lager; **widow and orphan** ~ *(US)* mündelsichere Wertpapiere; **winter** ~ Winterlager; **wholesale** ~ Großhandelslager;

~s **and shares** Aktien und Obligationen; ~s **of ammunition** Munitionsvorräte; ~s **preferred as to assets** Aktien mit bevorzugter Liquidationsberechtigung; ~ **in bank** Bankguthaben; ~ **of bills of exchange** Wechselbestand; ~s **and bonds** Wert-, Börsenpapiere, Effekten; ~ **of books** Büchervorrat; ~ **on commission** Kommissionslager; ~ **in a company** Aktienanteil an einem Unternehmen; **voting** ~ **of a company** *(US)* stimmberechtigtes Aktienkapital; ~ **preferred as to dividends** Aktie mit Dividendenvorzugsberechtigung; ~ **of food** Lebensmittelvorräte; ~ **of gold** Goldvorrat; ~ **of monetary gold** Währungsgold; ~ **of goods** Warenlager; ~ **of finished goods** Fertigwarenlager; ~ **in (on) hand** Vorrat auf Lager, Lagerbestand, Warenbestand, -vorrat; **total** ~ **on hand** Gesamtbestand; **good** ~ **of information** gute Nachrichtenquelle; ~ **and inventory** Lager und Lagerbestand; ~ **of all kinds** Lager in allen Sorten; ~ **of labo(u)r** Arbeitsvorrat; ~ **of a manufactory** gesamter Apparat einer Fabrik; ~ **in the market** Marktvorrat; ~ **of merchandise** Warenvorrat, -lager; ~ **of money** *(US)* gesamter Geldbestand [eines Landes]; ~ **on option** *(Br.)* Prämienwerte; ~ **in process** *(US)* **(progress,** *Br.)* in der Verarbeitung befindliches Material, Ware in Arbeit; ~ **of provisions** Vorratslager; ~ **of raw materials** Rohstofflager; ~ **of regular readers** Leserstamm; ~s **in reserve** Effektenreserven; ~ **carrying rights** *(US)* mit Bezugsrecht ausgestattete Aktien; ~ **of spare parts** Ersatzteillager; ~ **negotiable on the stock exchange** *(US)* börsengängige Aktie; ~ **quoted on the stock exchange** kursfähiges Wertpapier; ~s **in till** *(bank)* Kassenbestand; ~ **in trade** Vorratsvermögen *(capital)* Betriebsmaterial, -mittel, -vorrat, -kapital, -ausstattung, *(goods)* Warenbestand, -vorrat, Handelsvorrat, Fertigwarenlager, *(tools)* Arbeitsmaterial, Werkzeug; ~s **held in treasury** *(US)* Aktien in Eigenbesitz, Portefeuille eigener Aktien;

~ *(v.)* auf Lager nehmen, *(have in stock)* Waren auf Lager halten (haben, führen), vorrätig haben, Vorrat besitzen, *(provide with a stock)* mit einem Lager ausstatten, versorgen, ausrüsten, beliefern, *(store)* aufspeichern, sammeln;

~ **an article** auf Lager haben, Ware führen; **not** ~ **an article** Ware nicht führen (auf Lager haben); ~ **varied goods** alle Arten von Waren (verschiedenste Warengattungen) führen; ~ **a shop with goods** Ladengeschäft assortieren; **not** ~ **outsizes** keine Übergrößen führen; ~ **with provisions** mit Lebensmitteln versehen; ~ **up on** sich eindecken (einen Vorrat zulegen), Lager auffüllen, bevorraten; ~ **up for the holiday trade** sich vorratsmäßig auf die Touristenzeit einstellen; ~ **up for the winter** sich mit Vorräten für den Winter eindecken; ~ **a warehouse with goods** Kaufhaus mit Waren versehen;

to allot ~s *(US)* Aktien nach erfolgter Zeichnung zuteilen; **to be in** ~ vorrätig (auf Lager) sein, *(cash)* bei Kasse sein, Geld haben; **to be long of** ~ *(US)* mit Aktien eingedeckt sein, *(Br.)* mit Wertpapieren eingedeckt sein; **to be out of** ~ nicht auf Lager haben, nicht vorrätig (vergriffen) sein; **to be short of** ~ *(US)* Aktien gefixt (noch einzudecken) haben; **to boom a** ~ Preise (Kurse) hinauftreiben; **to borrow** ~ *(stock exchange, US)* Aktien hereinnehmen (in Prolongation nehmen); **to breed** ~ Viehzucht betreiben; **to build up** ~s Vorräte anlegen, Lager aufstocken; **to build up** ~s **2 1/4 points to 178** *(US)* Aktien von 2 1/4 Punkte auf 178 in die Höhe treiben; **to buy the whole** ~ **of a business** Geschäft in Bausch und Bogen kaufen; **to carry** ~s *(agent)* Konsignationslager unterhalten, *(stock exchange, US)* Aktien hereinnehmen (in Prolongation nehmen); **to carry in** ~ auf Lager (vorrätig) haben; **to carry heavy** ~ umfangreiche Lagervorräte haben; **to clear off old** ~ Lager räumen; **to come of good** ~ aus einer guten Familie stammen; **to come of Puritan** ~ von einer puritanischen Familie abstammen; **to dabble in the** ~s an der Börse spekulieren; **to draw on** ~s auf Lagerbestände zurückgreifen, Vorräte angreifen; **to exchange old** ~s **for new ones** *(US)* alte Aktien in neue umtauschen; **to exercise the right to subscribe to [acquire] new** ~ *(US)* Bezugsrecht auf junge Aktien ausüben; **to get in** ~s **of coal and coke for the winter** sich mit Heizmaterial für den Winter eindecken; **to give on** ~ *(Br.)* in Prolongation geben, hineingeben; **to have in (on,** *US)* ~ auf Lager (vorrätig) haben; **to have an average of six weeks'** ~s **in hand** über Vorräte für durchschnittlich sechs Wochen verfügen; **to have all one's fortune in** ~s *(US)* sein ganzes Vermögen in Aktien angelegt haben; **to have goods in** ~ Waren führen; **to have £ 10.000 in** ~s 10.000 Pfund in Obligationen angelegt haben; **to have no available** ~ nicht lieferfähig sein; **to have only conventional designs in** ~ nur gängige Sorten auf Lager haben; **to have a good** ~ **of wine** gute Weinbestände haben; **to have a great** ~ **of information** sehr gut informiert sein; **to have a lot of unsalable** ~ unverkäufliches Lager am Halse haben; **to have one's money in** ~s *(Br.)* sein Geld in Staatspapieren angelegt haben; **to have** ~s **listed at the stock exchange** *(US)* Aktien an der Börse einführen; **to have a play on the** ~s an einem Theaterstück schreiben; **to hold** ~s *(US)* Aktien besitzen, Aktionär sein; **to hold** ~s **for a rise** *(US)* Aktien für eine Haussebewegung zurückhalten; **to hold** ~s **as security** *(US)* Aktien als Sicherheit halten; **to improve one's** ~ **at home** innenpolitische Position festigen; **to invest one's money in safe** ~ sein Geld in mündelsicheren Papieren anlegen; **to invest £ 1000 in government** ~ tausend Pfund in Staatspapieren anlegen; **to keep in** ~ auf Lager haben, in Vorrat halten; **to keep an article in** ~ Artikel führen; **to lay in** ~ sich eindecken, auf Lager nehmen, sich assortieren; **to lay in fresh** ~s Neuanschaffungen machen (vornehmen); **to lay in** ~s **pretty heavily** erhebliche Lageraufkäufe tätigen; **to lay in a** ~ **of provisions** sich mit einem Lebensmittelvorrat eindecken; **to lay a ship on the** ~s Schiff auf Kiel legen; **to liquidate one's** ~ **of goods** sein Lager abstoßen; **to lodge** ~s **as cover** *(US)* Aktien als Deckung hinterlegen; **to lodge** ~s **as an additional security** *(US)* Aktien als zusätzliche Sicherheit hinterlegen; **to make for** ~ auf Vorrat produzieren, lagermäßig herstellen; **to make further payment on** ~s Nachschußzahlung auf Aktien leisten; **to manipulate** ~s *(US)* Aktien manipulieren, Aktienspekulation durchführen; **to own** ~ **in a paper** an einer Zeitung finanziell beteiligt sein; **to pay a call on** ~ Einzahlung auf Aktien leisten; **to put on the** ~s in Arbeit nehmen; **to put goods into** ~ Waren auf Lager nehmen (einlagern); **to put** ~s **at a certain price** *(US)* Aktien zu einem zugesicherten Preis liefern; **to raise** ~ *(US)* Viehzucht betreiben; **to refill the** ~ Lager wieder auffüllen, Lagerbestand ergänzen; **to renew one's** ~ sein Lager auffrischen; **to replace the** ~ Lager wieder auffüllen, Lagerbestand ergänzen; **to replenish one's** ~ sein Lager wieder auffüllen, Lagerergänzungen vornehmen; **to run down** ~s Lager abbauen; **to run** ~s **against one's client** *(US)* Aktien seines Auftraggebers aufkaufen; **to sell** ~ **registered with the Department of National Savings** *(Br.)* bei der Postsparkassenbehörde registrierte Staatspapiere verkaufen; **to send the** ~ **skyward** *(US)* Aktienkurse raketenartig hochtreiben; **to set a low value on a** ~ *(US)* Aktie (Aktienwert) niedrig ansetzen; **to slaughter** ~s Bestände verschleudern; **to spin** ~s *(US)* Aktien auf den Markt werfen; **to split a** ~ Aktie splitten (unterteilen); **to spring from humble** ~ aus kleinen Verhältnissen stammen; **to subscribe to (for) new** ~ *(US)* junge Aktien beziehen, neue Aktien zeichnen; **to switch out of** ~s **into high-yielding bonds** *(US)* aus Aktien in hochverzinsliche Obligationen umsteigen; **to take** ~ Inventar (Lagerbestand) aufnehmen, Inventur machen, inventarisieren, *(fig.)* Bestandsaufnahme machen, sich Rechenschaft ablegen; **to take in** ~ Anteile nehmen, beteiligt sein, *(goods)* auf Lager nehmen, sich mit Waren eindecken, *(Br., stock exchange)* in Prolongation nehmen, hereinnehmen; **to take in** ~ **for a borrower** *(US)* Aktien hereinnehmen; **to take delivery of** ~ *(US)* Aktien in Zahlung nehmen; **to take** ~ **of a situation** sich über eine Lage klar werden; **to take in** ~ **without charging contango** *(Br.)* Effekten glatt hereinnehmen; **to take up** ~ *(US)* Aktien beziehen, gekaufte Aktien bezahlen; **to tie up in** ~ im Warenlager festlegen; **to unload** ~**s** Aktien abstoßen; **to vote the** ~ *(US)* Aktienstimmrecht ausüben; **to water the** ~ *(US)* Aktienkapital verwässern; **to withdraw from** ~ Bestand nicht mehr ergänzen; **to work on** ~ auf Lager (Vorrat) arbeiten, lagermäßig herstellen; **to work up all the** ~ ganzes Lager verbrauchen;

~ *(a.) (commonplace)* abgedroschen, platt, banal, *(employed in handling stock)* mit der Lagerhaltung beauftragt, *(ready for sale)* vorrätig, auf Lager, *(stereotyped)* oft verwendet, stereotyp, stehend;

~ **account** *(capital, Br.)* Kapitalkonto, -rechnung, *(goods)* Lager-, Waren[bestands]konto, *(securities)* Effektenrechnung, -konto, Aktien-, Stückekonto; ~ **accounting** Lagerbuchhaltung; ~ **accumulation** Lagerauffüllung; ~ **actor** zum ständigen Ensemble gehörender Schauspieler; ~ **adventure** *(Br.)* Aktien-, Fonds-, Effektenspekulation; ~ **adventurer** *(Br.)* Aktien-, Fonds-, Effektenspekulant; ~ **agency** Effektenkommission; ~ **allotment warrant** *(US)* Aktienbezugsschein; ~ **analyst** Effektenberater; ~ **answer** stereotype Antwort; ~ **appeal** *(US)* Aktienanreiz; ~ **appreciation** erhöhte Lagerbewertung; ~ **appreciation relief** *(Br.)* Freibeträge bei der Wertzuwachssteuer, Steuerermäßigung bei Werterhöhungen; ~ **arbitration (arbitrage)** *(Br.)* Effektenarbitrage, *(committee)* Börsenschiedsgericht; ~ **argument** übliches Argument; ~ **arrangement** *(bookseller)* Lagerordnung; ~ **articles** Serienware, stets vorrätige Artikel, Lagerartikel, -ware; ~ **assessment** *(US)* Zuzahlung auf Aktien, Aufforderung zur Nachschußzahlung, Nachschußverpflichtung; ~ **availability** Lagerfähigkeit, -disponibilität; ~ **beer** Lagerbier; ~ **bill** *(US)* bei Aktienauslieferung zahlbarer Wechsel; **to sell a** ~ **bloc to an acquisitive conglomerate** *(US)* Aktien en bloc an einen marktaufkaufenden Konzern veräußern; ~ **book** *(shares, US)* Hauptbuch der Aktionäre, Aktionärsverzeichnis, Aktienbuch, *(Br.)* Effektenbuch, *(store)* Bestands-, Inventar-, Lagerbuch, Warenverzeichnis; ~ **bookkeeping of unpaid items** *(bookseller)* Lagerbuchhaltung in Form offener Posten; ~ **boom** Aktienhausse; ~ **boy** Lagerbursche, -arbeiter; ~ **breeder** Viehzüchter; ~ **breeding** Viehzucht; ~ **bubbling** *(US)* Aktienschwindel; ~ **building** Lageraufstockung, -aufbau; ~**-building cycle** Lagerzyklus; ~ **and share business** *(Br.)* Effektenverkehr, -geschäft, Börsengeschäft, *(US)* Aktiengeschäft; ~ **call** Terminkaufoption; ~ **capital** *(US)* Grund-, Stammkapital; **to increase the** ~ **capital** *(US)* Aktienkapital erhöhen; ~ **capitalization** *(US)* Aktienkapital; ~ **car** Serienwagen, -modell; ~ **card** Inventarkarte; ~ **carrier** Viehtransporteur; ~ **catalog(ue)** Lagerkatalog; ~ **certificate** *(Br.)* Kapitalanteilschein, *(US)* Globalaktie, Aktienzertifikat, -anteilschein, -mantel, -urkunde, Sammelkunde; **punch-card** ~ **certificate** *(US)* gelochtes Aktienzertifikat; ~ **certificate to bearer** Inhaberaktie; **to split** ~ **certificates** *(US)* Aktien unterteilen; ~ **check** Bestandsaufnahme; ~ **Clearing Corporation** *(US)* New Yorker Effektenabrechnungsstelle; ~ **clerk** Lagerverwalter, -kontrollführer; ~ **company** Wanderbühne, *(actors)* ständiges Ensemble, *(corporation)* Aktiengesellschaft; ~ **accepting and negotiating company** Effektenübernahmegesellschaft; ~ **comparison** üblicher Vergleich.

stock control Lagerkontrolle, *(capital, US)* Kapitalkontrolle; ~ **clerk** Lagerverwalter; ~ **register** Lagerkontrollverzeichnis.

stock|corporation *(US)* Kapital-, Aktiengesellschaft; ~ **custom** Börsenusance; ~ **cut** Lagerabbau, *(advertising)* Lagerklischee; ~ **dealer** *(US)* Viehhändler; ~ **deals** Aktiengeschäfte; **phantom** ~ **deals** *(US)* nur buchmäßig erfaßte Aktiengeschäfte; ~ **department** *(bank, Br.)* Effekten-, Börsen-, Wertpapierabteilung; ~ **deposit** *(Br.)* Wertpapierdepot; ~ **depreciation** Herabsetzung des Aktienkapitals; ~ **discount** Agio; ~ **dividend** *(US)* Berichtigungs-, Gratisaktie; **to declare a** ~ **dividend** *(US)* Ausgabe von Gratisaktien beschließen; ~ **evaluation** Bewertung des Lagerbestandes.

stock exchange [Wertpapier]börse, Effekten-, Aktien-, Fondsbörse, Fondsmarkt, Börsenplatz; **listed on the** ~ *(US)* börsengängig, -fähig; **depressed** ~ gedrückte Börse; **local** *(US) (provincial, Br.)* ~ Regionalbörse;

to admit for quotations on the ~ zur Börsennotierung zulassen; **to be on the** ~ an der Börse (Börsenmitglied) sein; **to be dealt in on the** ~ an der Börse gehandelt werden; **to deal on the** ~ Börsengeschäfte machen; **to list on the** ~ *(US)* an der Börse einführen (notieren); **to meet with losses on the** ~ Verluste an der Börse erleiden; **to play on the** ~ auf dem Aktienmarkt spekulieren; **to sell on the** ~ an der Börse verkaufen; **to visit the** ~ zur Börse gehen.

stock-exchange| abbreviation Börsenabkürzung; ~ **account** Börsenbericht; ~ **agent** Börsenvertreter; ~ **approval** Börsengenehmigung, -zulassung; ~ **bank** *(US)* Effektenbank; ~ **broker** Börsen-, Effekten-, Fondsmakler; ~ **business** Effektenhandel, -geschäft, Börsengeschäft; ~ **certificates** *(US)* Börsenpapiere; ~ **circles** Börsenkreis; ~ **clearinghouse** Effektenabrechnungsstelle, -liquidationsbüro; ~ **collateral** *(US)* Sicherheit in Form von an der New Yorker Börse gehandelten Effekten; ~ **commission** Effektenprovision; ~ **committee** *(Br.)* Börsenmaklervereinigung, Börsenausschuß, -vorstand; ~ **commitment** Börsenengagement; ~ **contract** Börsengeschäft in Effekten; ~ **creditor** Börsengläubiger; ~ **custom** Börsenusance, -gebrauch; ~ **customer** Börsenbesucher; ~ **daily official list** *(Br.)* amtliches Kursblatt; ~ **dealings** Börsengeschäfte, -handel; ~ **expression** Börsenausdruck; ~ **gazette** Börsenblatt; ~ **holiday** *(Br.)* Börsenfeiertag; ~ **hours** Börsenstunden; ~ **index** Börsenindex; ~ **intelligence** *(Br.)* Börsennachrichten; ~ **introduction** *(Br.)* Börsenzulassung von Aktien, Börseneinführung; ~ **list** *(Br.)* Börsen-, Kurszettel, Kursblatt; **to remove shares from the** ~ **list** *(Br.)* Aktien von der Notierung absetzen; ~**-listed company** *(US)* an der Börse notierte Aktiengesellschaft; ~ **loan** kurzfristiges Maklerdarlehen (Börsengeld), Tagesgeld; ~ **manoeuvre** Börsenmanöver; ~ **name** Börsenname [eines Wertpapieres]; ~ **news** Börsen-, Fondsbericht, Börsennachrichten, Börseninformation; **capital** ~ **offer** Aktienumtauschangebot; ~ **operations** Effektengeschäfte, -handel, Börsengeschäfte; ~ **operator** Agioteur, Börsenhändler, -spekulant, Börsianer; ~ **order** Börsenorder, -auftrag; ~ **parlance** Börsensprache; ~ **practices** Börsenusancen, -gepflogenheiten; ~ **price** Börsenkurs; ~ **quotation** Börsenkurs, -notierung; ~ **regulations** Börsenordnung; ~ **report** Börsenbericht; ~ **rules** Börsenvorschriften; ~ **seat** Börsensitz, -mitgliedschaft; ~ **securities** börsengängige Wertpapiere, Börsenwerte, an der Börse gehandelte Werte; ~ **settlement** *(Br.)* Liquidation [an der Londoner Börse], Börsenabrechnung; ~ **slang** Börsenjargon; ~ **tax** Börsenumsatzsteuer; ~ **terminology** Börsensprache; ~ **transactions** Börsenabschlüsse, -geschäfte, -handel, Effekten[kommissions]geschäfte, Börsenumsätze; ~ **value** Börsenwert; ~ **venturer** Börsenschwindler; ~ **Year Book** *(Br.)* Börsenjahrbuch.

stock|farm Zuchtfarm; ~ **farmer** Viehzüchter; ~ **farming** Viehzucht; ~ **figure** Lagerwert; ~ **girl** Lagerarbeiterin; ~ **growth** Lagerwachstum; ~ **indicator** Börsentelegraf; ~ **insurance company** Versicherungsgesellschaft auf Aktien; ~ **insurance corporation** *(US)* Versicherungsgesellschaft auf Aktien; ~ **investment** Lagervorrat, *(capital stock)* Kapitalanlage; ~ **issue** *(US)* Aktienausgabe, -emission; ~ **juggling** *(US)* Kursbeeinflussung, -treiberei; ~ **ledger** *(inventory)* Inventarbuch, *(shares, US)* Aktienregister, -buch, Aktionärsverzeichnis; ~**-ledger account** Lagerbuchkonto; ~ **ledger card** Lagerbestandskarte; ~ **limit** Lagerbegrenzung; ~ **list** *(US)* [Aktien]kurszettel, amtliches Börsenkursblatt; ~ **loan** Effektenlombard; ~ **majority** *(US)* Aktienmajorität; ~ **manager** Lagerverwalter; ~ **manipulation** *(US)* Aktienmanipulierung.

stock market Effekten-, Wertpapierbörse, Aktien-, Börsen-, Wertpapier-, Effektenmarkt, [Fonds]börse, *(quotations)* Börsenkurse; **dull** ~ Börsenflaute, schwache Börsenkurse; **to dabble (play) the** ~ auf dem Aktienmarkt spekulieren; **to remain shy of the** ~ sich von der Börse fernhalten; **to shoot up in the** ~ großer Börsenerfolg sein; ~ **activities** Börsengeschehen; ~ **boom** *(US)* Aktienhausse; ~ **collapse** Börsenkollaps, -zusammenbruch; ~ **crash** Börsenzusammenbruch, Zusammenbruch des Aktienmarktes; ~ **credit** Lombardkredit; ~ **decline** Rückgang der Börsenkurse; ~ **favo(u)rite** Kursfavorit; ~ **flotation** Börseneinführung; ~ **gain** Börsengewinn; ~ **judgment** Börsenbeurteilung; ~ **level** Effektenkursniveau; ~ **literature** Börsenliteratur; ~ **loss** Börsenverlust; ~ **observer** Marktkenner, Börsenfachmann; ~ **parlance** Börsenterminologie, -jargon; ~ **prediction** Voraussage der Börsenentwicklung; ~ **report** *(US)* amtliches Börsenkursblatt; ~ **rise** Anstieg der Aktienkurse, Aktienkursanstieg; ~ **sentiment** Börsenstimmung; ~ **setback** Kursrückschlag; ~ **situation** Börsenlage, Lage am Effektenmarkt; ~ **slide** Absinken der

Aktienkurse; ~ **slump** Kurseinbruch; ~ **speculation** Aktien-, Effektenspekulation; ~ **tactics** Börsenstrategie; ~ **trading** Effektenverkehr; ~ **trend** Börsen-, Aktienmarktentwicklung, Börsentendenz; ~ **turnover** Börsenumsatz; ~ **worker** Börsenangestelter.

stock | **model** *(car)* Serienmodell, Normaltyp, Standardfabrikat; ~ **note** *(US)* durch Lombardierung von Wertpapieren gesicherter Schuldschein; ~ **office** Effektenabteilung; ~ **option** *(US)* Aktienbezugsrecht [für Betriebsangehörige]; ~-**option plan** *(US)* Belegschaftsaktiensystem; ~ **order** Lagerauftrag, *(securities)* Effektenauftrag, -order; ~ **owner** Effekteninhaber, -besitzer; ~ **ownership** *(US)* Aktienbesitz [eines Unternehmens]; ~ **peak** Lagerhöchststand; ~ **phrase** feste Redensart; ~ **pile** *(road maintenance)* Schotterhaufen; **phantom** ~ **plan** *(US)* zur zu Verrechnungszwecken vorgenommene Aktiengutschrift; **qualified** ~ **plan** *(US)* steuerlich begünstigter Gewinnbeteiligungsplan; ~ **pooling agreement** Aktienpoolvereinbarung; ~ **portfolio** *(US)* Aktienportefeuille; ~ **position** Vorratslage; ~**post** *(US)* Maklerstand; ~ **power** *(US)* [unwiderruflich erteilte] Effektenverkaufsbefugnis, -vollmacht, Börsenvollmacht; ~ **price** *(US)* Aktienagio; ~ **price** Aktienkurs, -preis; ~-**price average** *(US)* Effekten-, Börsenindex; ~-**price index** Index der Aktienkurse, Aktienkursindex; ~ **printer** Börsentelegraf; [**selective**] ~ **purchases** *(US)* [selektive] Aktienkäufe; ~-**purchase plan** *(US)* Belegschaftsaktiensystem; ~-**purchase right** Aktienbezugsrecht; ~-**purchase warrant** *(US)* Options-, Bezugsberechtigungsschein für den Bezug von Aktien; ~ **purse** Gemeinschaftskasse, gemeinsamer Fonds; ~ **quotation** Aktiennotierung; ~ **raiser** Viehzüchter; ~ **raising** Viehzucht; ~ **rate** Prämiensatz einer nicht gewinnberechtigten Lebensversicherungspolice; ~ **rebate** Lagerrabatt; ~ **receipt** *(US)* Buchungsbescheinigung über Aktienverkauf, Aktienzertifikatsquittung, *(Br.)* Effektenquittung, *(goods)* Wareneingangsquittung; ~ **record** *(US)* Aktionärsverzeichnis, Aktienregister, *(stores ledger)* Lagerhauptbuch; ~ **record card** Lagerbestandskarte; ~-**record division** Lagerbuchhaltung; ~ **reduction** Abbau der Bestände, Lagerabbau; ~ **register** *(US)* Gesellschafter-, Aktienverzeichnis, Aktienregister, Aktienbuch, *(debentures)* Obligationenverzeichnis, *(mutual fund)* Anteilsregister, *(store)* Lagerliste, Inventarverzeichnis; ~ **registrar** *(US)* Überwachungsstelle für die Ausgabe von Aktien; ~ **replacement** Lagerauffüllung; ~ **repurchase** *(US)* Aktienrückkauf; ~ **requirements** Lagerbedarf; ~ **requisition** Lagerbezugs-, -entnahmeschein; ~ **requisitions** Lageranforderungen; ~ **right** *(US)* [Aktien]bezugsrecht; ~ **robbery** *(US)* Aktienschwindel; ~ **room** Vorrats-, Lagerraum, Warenlager, *(hotel)* Ausstellungsraum; ~-**room clerk** Lagerverwalter; ~-**sales ratio** Lagerumsatz; ~ **savings bank** *(Br.)* Sparkasse nach Art einer Aktiengesellschaft; ~ **scrip** *(US)* Berechtigungsschein für den Bezug von Aktien, Interimsaktie; ~ **securities** börsengängige Werte; ~ **selection** Lagerauswahl; ~ **shakeout** Lagerschrumpfung; ~ **share** Kapitalanteil; ~ **sheet** Bestands-, Lagerliste, Inventurblatt; ~ **shortage** Warenverknappung, *(capital stock)* Kapitalfehlbetrag; ~ **shots** Filmarchivmaterial; ~ **shrinkage** Lagerabnahme; [coal] ~**s situation** Kohlenvorratslage; ~ **size** lagergängige (stets vorrätige) Größe, Normal-, Standardgröße; ~ **split** *(US)* Aktiensplit, -aufteilung; ~ **splitdown** Aktienzusammenlegung; ~ **subscription** *(US)* Aktienkapitalzeichnung; ~-**subscription record** *(US)* [Kapital]zeichnungsliste; ~-**subscription right** *(US)* Aktienbezugsrecht; ~ **subscription warrant** *(Br.)* Aktienbezugsschein; ~ **switch** *(US)* Aktientausch; ~ **tag** Lagerpreiszettel; ~ **ticker** Börsentelegraf, -fernschreiber, Ticker; ~ **tip** *(US)* Aktien-, Börsentip; ~ **touting** *(US)* Werbung bei Aktienkunden; ~ **trading** *(US)* Aktien-, Effektenhandel; ~ **trading without transfer** *(US)* stückeloser Effektenverkehr; ~ **transactions** Börsengeschäft, -handel; ~ **transaction for third account** Börsenkommissionsgeschäft.

stock **transfer** *(Br.)* Wertpapier-, Aktienübertragung, Übertragung von Anteilen am Gesellschaftsvermögen; ~ **Act** *(Br.)* Aktienübertragungsgesetz, Wertpapierumschreibungsgesetz; ~ **agent** *(US)* Transferagent für Aktien; ~ **deal** *(US)* Abschlußgeschäft beim Aktienkauf; ~ **form** *(US)* Formular zur Aktienübertragung; ~ **journal** *(US)* Aktienbuch; ~ **office** Aktienumschreibungsstelle; ~ **tax** *(US)* Börsenumsatzsteuer.

stock | **trend** *(US)* Tendenz der Aktienbörse, Börsentendenz; ~-**trial order** Lagerprobeauftrag, probeweise erteilter Lagerauftrag; ~ **trust** *(US)* Dachgesellschaft; ~ **turnover** Lagerumsatz, -umschlag; ~ **usages** Börsenusancen; ~ **valuation** Lagerbewertung; ~ **value** *(US)* Aktienwert; ~ **variable** Bestandsgröße; ~ **voucher** Bestandsbeleg; ~ **warehouse** Warenlager; ~ **warrant**

(US) Aktienbezugsrechtsschein, *(Br.)* Aktienzertifikat; ~-**allotment warrant** *(US)* Optionsschein; ~ **watering** *(US)* Kapitalverwässerung; ~ **work** Lagerarbeit.

stockbreeder *(Br.)* Viehzüchter.

stockbreeding *(Br.)* Viehzucht.

stockbroker Aktien-, Effekten-, Börsen-, Fonds-, Kursmakler, Effektenhändler; ~s Börsenkommissionsgeschäft, Maklerfirma; **outside** ~ Freiverkehrsmakler.

stockbroker's | **bargain book** Schlußnotenbuch; ~ **clerk** Maklergehilfe; ~ **contract** *(Br.)* Schlußnote; ~ **loan** *(Br.)* Maklerdarlehen [unter Beleihung von Wertpapieren].

stockbrokerage Aktien-, Börsen-, Effktenhandel.

stockbroking *(Br.)* Effektengeschäft, -transaktion, Börsenkommissionsgeschäft, *(US)* Aktiengeschäft; **to take up** ~ ins Effektengeschäft gehen, Makler werden; ~ **experience** Effektenerfahrung; ~ **firm** Maklerfirma; ~ **transaction** Effektentransaktion, -geschäft.

stockcar *(railroad, US)* Viehwagen.

stocked geführt, auf Lager, lagerhaltig, vorrätig; **heavily** ~ hinlänglich mit Vorräten versehen; ~ **by all retailers** durch den Einzelhandel zu beziehen; **to be heavily** ~ reichhaltiges Lager haben; **to be well** ~ großes Lager (großen Vorrat) haben; **shoes** ~ **here** Schuhe hier erhältlich; ~ **goods** Warenvorräte, -bestände; **well-**~ **memory** geschultes Gedächtnis.

stockholder *(US)* Aktionär, Effekten-, Aktieninhaber, *(Br.)* Effekten-, Fondsbesitzer, Anteilseigner, *(capitalist)* Kapitalist; **common** ~ *(US)* einfacher Aktionär, Stammaktionär; **controlling** ~ *(US)* Aktienmajoritätsbesitzer; **majority** ~ *(US)* Mehrheitsaktionär; **minority** ~ *(US)* Minderheitsaktionär; **nonresident** ~ *(US)* auswärtiger Aktionär; **ordinary** ~ *(US)* Stammaktionär; **preferred** ~ *(US)* Vorzugsaktionär; **principal** ~ *(US)* Hauptaktionär; ~ **of record** *(US)* im Hauptbuch eingetragener (registrierter) Aktionär, Inhaber von Namensaktien; **to address the** ~s Ansprache an die Aktionäre halten; **to give notice to** ~s **of a general meeting** *(US)* Aktionäre zu einer Hauptversammlung einberufen; ~ **action** *(US)* Aktionärsklage; ~'s **derivative action** *(US)* Aktionärsklage für die Gesellschaft, Prozeßstandschaftsklage eines Gesellschafters; ~ **approval** Zustimmung der Aktionäre; ~ **communication** Verbindung zu den Aktionären, Aktionärspflege; ~ **correspondence** *(US)* Aktionärskorrespondenz; ~ **discontent** *(US)* Mißvergnügen der Aktionäre; ~ **relations** *(US)* Aktionärspflege; ~ **suit** *(US)* Aktionärsklage [für die Gesellschaft].

stockholders' | **equity** *(US)* Eigen-, Gesellschaftskapital; ~ **ledger** *(US)* Hauptbuch der Aktionäre, Aktienbuch; ~ **liability** *(US)* Einzahlungsverpflichtung (Nachschußhaftung) der Aktionäre; ~ **majority** Aktienmajorität; ~ **meeting** *(US)* Aktionär-, General-, Hauptversammlung; ~ **representative action** *(US)* Klage auf Anfechtung von Hauptversammlungsbeschlüssen; ~ **rights** *(US)* Aktionärsrechte.

stockholding *(US)* Aktien-, Effektenbesitz, [Aktien]beteiligungen; **intercorporate** ~s wechselseitige Aktienbeteiligungen; ~ **costs** Lagerhaltungskosten; ~ **elements** Anlagepublikum; ~ **interests in foreign banks at cost** *(balance sheet)* Aktien auswärtiger Banken zum Anschaffungspreis.

stocking Lagerung; ~s Ersparnisse; **increased** ~ vermehrte Lagerhaltung; ~ **in advance** Vorratslagerung; ~ **finance** Lagerfinanzierung.

stockist *(Br.)* einschlägiges Geschäft, Fachgeschäft, -händler.

stockjobber *(Br.)* Börsenmann, -jobber, -händler, -spekulant, *(US)* Fondsmakler, Effektenhändler.

stockjobbery *(Br.)* Aktien-, Effektenspekulation, Börsenmanöver, -spekulation, -schwindel, Effektenten-, Spekulationsgeschäfte, *(US)* Kurstreiberei, -beeinflussung.

stockjobbing *(Br.)* Aktien-, Effekten-, Spekulationsgeschäft, Aktien-, Effektenhandel, Börsenspekulation, Agiotage, *(US)* Kursbeeinflussung, -treiberei.

stockkeeper Lagerhalter.

stockkeeping Lagerhaltung.

stockman *(Australia)* Viehhüter, *(US)* Lagerist, Lagerhalter, -verwalter.

stockmaster Kursaufzeichnungsgerät.

stockowner *(US)* Aktien-, Effektenbesitzer, Aktionär.

stockpile Vorrat, Reserve, [Vorrats]lager, Waren-, Lagerbestand;

surplus ~s Lagerüberschüsse;

~ *(v.)* horten, Vorrat anlegen, aufstapeln, anhäufen, auf Lager nehmen;

~ ships Schiffe auf Halde legen;

to cut back drastically on the ~s drastischen Lagerabbau durchführen; **to sit on ~s** mit einem Lager (auf Lagervorräten) festsitzen;

~ dispositions Lagerdispositionen.

stockpiling Bevorratung, Lager-, Vorratswirtschaft, -bildung, -haltung, Einlagerung, Lageraufstockung;

~ behavio(u)r Lagerdispositionen; **to step up one's ~ pace** Tempo der Lageranreicherung beschleunigen; **~ policy** Lagerpolitik, Vorratspolitik; **~ purchase** Vorratskäufe; **~ target** Lagerplanziel.

stocksshedding Lagerfreisetzung, -abbau.

stocktaking Aufnehmen der Bestände, Lager-, Bestands-, Warenbestandsaufnahme, Inventur[aufnahme];

actual ~ tatsächliche Bestandsaufnahme; **annual ~** Jahresinventur; **departmental ~** Teilinventur; **final ~** Schlußinventur; **physical ~** tatsächliche Inventuraufnahme; **~ sale** Inventurausverkauf.

stockturn Umsatz.

stockyard Schlachthof.

stolen property Diebesgut.

stolid teilnahmslos, stumpf.

stolidity Teilnahmslosigkeit, Phlegma.

stomach Appetit, Hunger;

to have no ~ for a fight keine Lust zu einer Auseinandersetzung haben;

~ upset Magenverstimmung.

stone *(lithography)* Stein, *(print.)* Schließplatte;

to leave no ~ unturned nichts unversucht lassen, alle Hebel in Bewegung setzen;

~ blind *(sl.)* total betrunken; **~-broke** abgebrannt, blank, pleite; **~ broker** *(US)* Kulissenmakler; **~ proof** Bürstenabzug; **~ rich** *(sl.)* steinreich; **~'s throw** Steinwurf, Katzensprung; **within a ~'s throw** in allernächster Nähe.

stonewall *(v.) (politics)* Obstruktion treiben.

stonewaller *(politics, Australia)* Verschleppungstaktiker, Obstruktionist.

stonewalling *(pol., Australia)* Verschleppungstaktik, Obstruktion;

to run up against ~ Verzögerungstaktik konterkarieren.

stony|**-broke** *(sl.)* pleite, abgebrannt; **~ road** steiniger Weg.

stooge Handlager, *(airplane)* Flugschüler, Kopilot, *(broadcasting, US)* Stichwortgeber, *(criminal law, sl.)* Ersttäter, *(one toading a superior)* Jasager, *(subordinate)* Helfershelfer;

~ *(v.)* Handlangerdienste leisten, *(theater, sl.)* dem Konferencier Pointen zuspielen;

~ around herumschleppen, *(airplane)* auf Landeerlaubnis warten.

stool Stuhl, *(plain-clothesman, sl.)* Kriminalbeamter, Privatdetektiv, *(stool pigeon, sl.)* Lockspitzel;

office ~ Bürostuhl;

to fall between two ~s sich zwischen zwei Stühle setzen;

~ pigeon Lockvogel, Köder, *(sl.)* [Polizei]spitzel, Schnüffler, Denunziant.

stoop *(US)* Vorplatz, -halle.

stop Halt, Stillstand, Aufenthalt, *(blockade)* Sperrung, Sperre, Stopp, *(for check)* Sperre, Sperrauftrag, *(inn)* Absteigequartier, Gasthaus, *(pause)* Pause, *(punctuation)* Interpunktionszeichen, Punkt, *(receiver, sl.)* Hehler, *(ship)* Anlegestelle, *(stop order)* limitierter Börsenauftrag, *(station)* Haltepunkt, -stelle, Station;

bus ~ [Omni]bushaltestelle; **conditional ~** Bedarfshaltestelle; **five minutes' ~** Fünf-Minuten-Aufenthalt; **price ~** Preisstopp; **traffic ~** Verkehrsstillstand; **wage ~** Lohnstopp;

~ and go konjunkturpolitischer Zickzackkurs; **~ by telephone** telefonisch angeordnete Sperre;

~ *(v.)* aufhören ,einstellen, *(check)* sperren, *(close down)* stilllegen, beend[ig]en, *(issues ~ order)* Zahlungsverbot erwirken, *(stock exchange)* limitierten Börsenauftrag geben, *(traffic)* abstoppen, anhalten, *(train)* halten;

~ an account Konto sperren; **~ s. one's allowance** jem. den Unterhaltszuschuß streichen (wegnehmen); **~ bankruptcy proceedings** Konkursverfahren einstellen; **~ bankruptcy proceedings for lack of assets** Konkursverfahren mangels Masse einstellen; **~ a bill** Wechsel sperren; **~ bonds** Wertpapiere mit Sperre belegen; **~ business** Betrieb einstellen; **~ a car** Auto anhalten; **~ a case** Prozeß aussetzen; **~ a check** *(US)* (cheque, *Br.*) Scheck sperren; **~ the cost of s. th. out of s. one's wages** jem. die entstandenen Kosten vom Lohn abhalten (abziehen); **~ dead** plötzlich anhalten; **~ s. th. dead in its tracks** etw. abrupt zum Stillstand bringen; **~ one's ears** nichts hören wollen; **~ the execution of a decree** Durchführung einer Verordnung aussetzen; **~ a factory** Betrieb stillegen; **~ a gap** Lücke schließen; **~ at home** *(coll.)* zu Haus bleiben; **~ at an inn** in einem Gasthaus einkehren (absteigen); **~ a leak in a pipe** Leck in einer Rohrleitung abdichten; **~ s. o. in mid-career** j. in seiner Karriere (Laufbahn) behindern; **~ s. one's mouth** jem. den Mund stopfen; **~ a neighbo(u)r's light** dem Nachbarn die Aussicht verbauen; **~ the noise in the street** Straßenlärm unterbinden; **~ at nothing** vor nichts zurückschrecken; **~ off** *(US)* kurzen Aufenthalt einlegen; **~ all operations on an account** gesamten Kontoverkehr untersagen; **~ over at ...** *(US)* Reise in ... unterbrechen; **~ payment** Zahlung sistieren, Auszahlung sperren; **~ payments** *(declare o. s. insolvent)* Zahlungen einstellen; **~ payment of a check** *(US)* (cheque, *Br.*) Scheck sperren lassen, Scheckauszahlung sperren; **~ s. one's pension** Pensionszahlungen an j. einstellen; **~ the period of limitation running** Verjährung hemmen; **~ at a port** Hafen anlaufen; **~ sharp practices on transfer pricing** steuerlich bedingten mißbräuchlichen Preiskalkulationen Einhalt gebieten; **~ the proceedings** Verfahren einstellen; **~ progress** Fortschritt aufhalten; **~ a quotation** Kursnotierung aussetzen; **~ by request** bei Bedarf anhalten; **~ selling** Verkauf einstellen; **~ short** plötzlich anhalten; **~ supplies** Lieferung einstellen; **~ a speaker** Redner unterbrechen; **~ s. one's supply of electricity** jem. den Strom absperren; **~ and think** sich etw. genau überlegen; **~ a train** Zug anhalten; **~ up late** lange aufbleiben; **~ one's visit** seine Besuche einstellen; **~ wages** Lohn einbehalten; **~ so much out of s. one's wages** bestimmten Lohnanteil von jem. einbehalten; **~ 10% from the wages** 10% vom Lohn in Abzug bringen; **~ work** Arbeit aussetzen, in Streik treten;

to be at a ~ *(business)* darniederliegen; **to come to a dead ~** *(term)* Verkehr steckenbleiben; **to go with only three ~s** *(train)* dreimal halten; **to pull out all the ~s to save s. o.** j. mit allen Mitteln zu retten versuchen; **to put a ~ to** beenden, einstellen; **to put a ~ to expenses** Unkosten abbremsen, Spesenaufwand begrenzen; **to put a ~ upon s. th.** etw. beschlagnahmen; **to run without a ~** *(train)* durchfahren;

~ card *(checks)* Sperrliste; **~-go** *(Br.)* Kreditpolitik; **to buck the ~-go business cycle** zyklische Konjunkturbewegungen abschaffen; **~ light** *(car)* Bremsleuchte, *(traffic light, US)* Verkehrsampel; **~ limit** *(stock exchange)* Interventionsgrenze; **~ list** *(trade association)* schwarze Liste, Boykottliste; **~-loss** zur Vermeidung weiterer Verluste bestimmt; **~-loss order** limitierter [Börsen]auftrag; **~-loss premium** Sonderprämie; **~-loss treaty** *(reinsurance)* Rückversicherungsvertrag zur verhältnismäßigen Begrenzung des Versicherungsrisikos; **~ motion** *(photo)* Zeitraffer; **~-off tariff** besondere Speditionsgebühr bei abgeändertem Frachtziel; **~ order** Verkaufsstopp, *(account book)* Anweisung der Kontosperrung, *(check)* Schecksperre, *(stock exchange, US)* limitierter Börsenauftrag; **to issue a ~ order against s. o.** Zahlungsverbot gegen j. erwirken; **~ payment** Stornierung eines Zahlungsauftrags, Zahlungssperre, -einstellung; **~-payment order** Schecksperre; **~-and-go policy** antizyklische Steuerung der Konjunktur durch Staat und Notenbank; **~ press** *(Br.)* [Spalte für] nach Redaktionsschluß einlaufende (letzte) Nachrichten; **~-press news** *(Br.)* letzte (neueste) Nachrichten; **~ price** gestopter Preis, Stopppreis; **~ profit limit** *(stock exchange)* Profitgrenze; **~ sign** Haltezeichen; **~ street** Stopp-, Haltestraße; **~-transfer order** *(US)* Auftrag zur Sperrung einer Aktie.

stopgap Notbehelf, -maßnahme, Lückenbüßer, Aushilfe, Ersatz;

to come as a ~ aushilfsweise kommen;

~ advertisement (advertising) Füllanzeige, Füller; **~ loan** Überbrückungskredit; **~ politics** behelfsmäßige politische Maßnahmen.

stopover *(US)* Fahrtunterbrechung, *(plane)* Zwischenlandung, Flugunterbrechung;

~ place Zwischenlandestelle; **~ ticket** Rundreisefahrkarte.

stoppage Anhalten, Unterbrechung, Sperre, *(civil law)* Aufrechnung, *(closing down)* [Betriebs]stillegung, *(criminal law)* Festnahme eines Reisenden, *(deduction of salary)* Gehaltsabzug, *(stopping payment)* Zahlungseinstellung, *(stopping work)* Arbeitseinstellung, *(traffic jam)* Blockierung, Betriebsstörung, Verkehrsstockung, *(wages)* Gehalts-, Lohnabzug;

~ of business Stillstand der Geschäfte, Betriebseinstellung; ~

of credit Kreditsperre, -entziehung; **~ of leave** Urlaubssperre; **~ of lending** Kreditsperre; **~ of pay** Einbehaltung des Lohns, Lohneinbehaltung; **~ of payment[s]** Zahlungseinstellung, Auszahlungssperre; **~ at source** *(taxation)* Quellenbesteuerung; **~ of trade** Handelsstockung, -sperre, -verbot; **~ of traffic** Verkehrsunterbrechung, -stockung; **~ in transit[u]** Ausübung des Zurückhaltungsrechts an unterwegs befindlichen Waren; **~ of wages** Lohneinbehaltung; **~ of work** Arbeitsunterbrechung, -einstellung;

to put under ~ mit Beschlag belegen.

stopped eingestellt, *(check)* gesperrt.

stopper *(advertising)* Blickfang.

stopping Einstellung der Zahlung;

~ an account Kontosperre; **~ a check** *(US)* **(cheque,** *Br.***)** Sperrung eines Schecks, Schecksperre; **~ payment** Auszahlungssperre; **~ of a road** Straßensperre;

~ distance *(car)* Bremsstrecke, -weg; **~ place** Haltestelle, *(airplane)* Zwischenlandestelle; **legal ~ place** gesetzlich zugelassener Aufenthaltsort; **~ time** Arbeitsschluß; **~ train** Bummelzug.

stopwatch Stoppuhr.

storage *(cost)* Lagergeld, -miete, -spesen, -zins, Speichergeld, Niederlagegebühren, *(data processing)* Speicherung, *(space)* Speicher-, Lagerraum, *(storing)* [Ein]lagerung, Einlagern, [Auf]speicherung;

careless ~ unsachgemäße Lagerung; **cold ~** Kühlraum-, Kühlhauslagerung; **commercial ~** Warenlagerung; **dead ~** vorübergehend nicht zugängliche Einlagerung;

~ of cycles Fahrradaufbewahrung; **~ of goods** Warenlagerung; **~ on hand** Menge der Waren auf Lager; **~ in transit** Zwischenlagerung;

to put into cold ~ [Plan] auf Eis legen; **to put furniture in ~** Möbel auf den Speicher bringen; **to take a car out of ~** Wagen wieder in Betrieb nehmen; **to take goods out of ~** Waren sortieren;

~ accommodation Lagereinrichtungen, -vorrichtungen, Lagerungsmöglichkeit; **~ agency** Lagervertretung; **~ area** Lagerräume; **~ audit** Inventurüberprüfung; **~ battery** Akku[mulator], Sammler; **~ building** Lagergebäude; **~ business** Lagergeschäft, -hausgewerbe; **~ cabinet** Büroschrank mit Fächern; **~ capacity** Lageraufnahme, Lagerungsfähigkeit, Lagervermögen; **~ charges (costs)** Lager[ungs]gebühren, -kosten; **~ check** Lagerschein; **~ company** Lagerhausgesellschaft; **~ credit** Lagerhaltungskredit; **~ depot** Lagerhaus; **~ devices** Lagereinrichtungen; **~ facilities** Lagermöglichkeiten, -einrichtungen; **~ filing cabinet** Kombinations-, Akten- und Büroschrank; **~ function** Lagerfunktion; **~ goods** Lagerwaren; **cold-~ house** Kühlhaus; **~ interest** Lagerzinsen; **~ model** platzsparendes Modell; **~ operation** Lagerbetrieb; **~ period** Lagerdauer; **~ rack** Regal, Gestell; **~ rent** Lagermiete; **~ risk** Lagerrisiko; **~ room** Aufbewahrungs-, Lagerraum, *(ship)* Schiffspackraum; **~ service** Lagerhaltungsdienst, Lagerei; **~ space** Lagerraum; **to let ~ space** Lagerraum vermieten; **~ system** *(tape)* Speichersystem; **~ tank** Reservetank; **~ track** Abstellgleis; **cold-~ vessel** Gefrierschiff; **~ warehouse** [Möbel]speicher, Zollager; **~ yard** Lagerhof.

store *(abundance)* Überfluß, Fülle, *(Br.)* Aufbewahrungsort, Lager[haus], -halle, Magazin, [Waren]speicher, Depot, Niederlage, *(business office)* Büro, *(department store, US)* Kauf-, Warenhaus, *(shop, US)* Geschäft, Laden[geschäft], Handlung, *(supply)* [Waren]vorrat, Warenlager, -bestand;

ex ~ ab Lager[haus]; **for ~** zum Aufbewahren; **in ~** vorrätig, auf Lager;

~s Bestand, Materialvorrat, Vorräte, Proviant, *(mil.)* Ausrüstungsgegenstände, Magazin, *(ship)* Schiffsvorräte;

the ⌂ *(Br.)* Konsumverein;

appraiser's ~ *(US)* Zollspeicher; **army surplus ~** Verkaufsstelle für ausrangiertes Heeresgut; **associated ~** Verbandsgeschäft; **basement ~** *(US)* Laden im Parterre; **bonded ~** Entrepot, Zollniederlage, -freilager; **branch ~** *(US)* Zweiggeschäft, Filiale; **candy ~** *(US)* Süßwarengeschäft; **chain ~** Kettenladen; **cigar ~** *(US)* Tabakwarengeschäft; **clothing ~** *(US)* Kleidergeschäft; **cold ~** Kühllager; **company ~** *(US)* betriebseigenes Geschäft, Werks-, Betriebsladen; **contractor's ~** Materiallager; **cooperative ~** *(US)* Konsumgenossenschaft, -verein, Konsum; **corner ~** *(US)* Laden um die Ecke; **cut-price ~** *(US)* preisdrückendes Geschäft; **department ~** *(US)* Kauf-, Warenhaus; **departmental ~** *(Br.)* Waren-, Kaufhaus; **downtown ~** *(US)* im Stadtzentrum gelegener Laden; **drygoods ~** *(US)* Tuchhandlung; **feed ~** *(US)* Futtermittelhandlung; **general ~** *(US)* Gemischtwarenhandlung; **general-order ~** Zollniederlage; **grocery ~** *(US)* Lebensmittel-, Kolonialwarengeschäft,

Kramladen; **hardware ~** *(US)* Eisenwarenhandlung; **high-class service ~** *(US)* Geschäft mit erstklassiger Bedienung; **high-class speciality ~** *(US)* hochwertiges Spezial[artikel]geschäft; **independent ~** *(US)* selbständiges Einzelhandelsgeschäft; **inner-city ~** *(US)* im Stadtzentrum gelegenes Geschäft; **industrial ~** *(US)* betriebseigener Laden; **integrated ~** *(US)* Kettenladen; **intermediate ~** Zwischenlager für Halbfabrikate; **jewelry** *(US)* **(jewellery,** *Br.***) ~** Juweliergeschäft; **liquor ~** *(US)* Spirituosengeschäft; **marine ~s** Schiffsbedarf, -ausrüstung, Marinebedarf; **medium-sized ~** *(US)* Mittelbetrieb, mittelgroßes Geschäft; **military ~s** Depot, Magazin; **multiple ~** *(Br.)* Kettenladenunternehmen; **naval ~s** Marinedepot; **neighbo(u)rhood ~** *(US)* Laden in der Nachbarschaft; **one-price ~** Einheitspreisgeschäft; **out-of-town ~** *(US)* Stadtrandgeschäft; **parent ~** Hauptgeschäft; **principal ~** Hauptniederlage; **public ~** *(US)* öffentliches Zollager, staatliches Magazin, öffentlicher Speicher; **retail ~** *(US)* Einzelhandelsgeschäft; **rough (raw-material) ~** Rohstofflager; **ship's ~s** Bord-, Schiffsvorräte; **single-line ~** *(US)* Sortimentsgeschäft; **single-line retail ~** *(US)* Einzelhandelsfachgeschäft; **small ~s** *(marine)* persönliche Bedarfsartikel für die Schiffsmannschaft; **speciality ~** *(US)* Spezial[artikel]geschäft; **sporting goods ~** *(US)* Sportartikelgeschäft; **utility-operated ~** *(US)* betriebseigener Laden eines Versorgungsbetriebs; **limited-price variety ~** billiges Warenhaus, „Woolworth"; **variety chain ~** Kaufhaus, -hof; **village ~** Dorfladen; **war ~s** Kriegsvorräte;

~ of energy Energiereserve; **great ~ of knowledge** großes Wissen; **~ of money** Geldreserve; **~ for rent** vermieteter Laden; **~s of natural resources** natürliches Vorratslager; **~ of value** Wertspeicherung, -aufbewahrungsmittel;

~ *(v.)* aufbewahren, [ein]lagern, auf Lager haben, aufs Lager bringen, auf Lager nehmen, *(data processing)* speichern, *(hold)* fassen, *(ship)* verproviantieren;

~ away einlagern, auf Lager nehmen; **~ furniture** Möbel ins Depot (auf den Speicher) geben (speichern); **~ goods** Waren einlagern; **~ the harvest** Ernte einbringen; **~ in** einlagern; **~ one's mind with facts** seinen Kopf mit Tatsachenmaterial füllen; **~ a ship with provisions** Schiff verproviantieren; **~ frequently called phone numbers on tape** häufig gebrauchte Telefonnummern auf einem Band speichern; **~ up** ansammeln, anhäufen, *(take in stock)* einlagern, auf Lager nehmen, aufspeichern, -stapeln, *(money)* thesaurieren;

to be in ~ bevorstehen; **to condemn ~s** Lager beschlagnahmen; **to create a ~** Depot errichten; **to have in ~** vorrätig haben; **to have in ~ for s. o.** für j. bereithalten; **to have s. th. in ~ with s. o.** bei jem. etw. eingelagert haben; **to have a good ~ of provisions in the house** ausreichende Vorräte im Haus haben; **to hold in ~** auf Lager haben; **to keep in ~** auf Lager (vorrätig) haben, lagern lassen; **to lay in ~** Vorrat anlegen; **to lay in ~ for the winter** Wintervorräte anlegen (einlagern); **to mind the ~** *(US)* auf den Laden aufpassen, *(politics)* Regierungsgeschäfte führen; **to put in ~** einlagern; **to run a ~** *(US)* Ladengeschäft betreiben; **to set little ~ by** einer Sache geringen Wert beimessen; **to take out of ~** dem Lager entnehmen, auslagern; **to tend ~** *(US)* Ladenaufsicht innehaben;

~ *(a.)* *(US)* im Laden gekauft;

~ account Lagerkonto, -rechnung; **~ accounting** Lagerbuchführung, -haltung, -rechnung; **~ advertising** *(US)* Ladenwerbung, Geschäftsreklame; **~ boat** Proviantboot; **~ book** Lager-, Bestandsbuch; **~-brand items** *(US)* ladeneigene Erzeugnisse; **~ building** Lageraufstockung; **~ buyer** *(US)* Käufer, Kunde; **~ card** *(US)* Reklamekärtchen [zur Beschreibung der Ware]; **~ cellar** Lagerkeller; **~ charges** Lagergebühren; **~ clerk** *(Br.)* Lagerist, Lagerhalter, *(US)* Warenhausverkäufer; **~ clothes** *(US coll.)* Konfektionskleider; **~ control** Lagerkontrolle; **~ credit** *(US)* kurzfristiger Kundenkredit; **marine ~ dealer** Schiffsartikelgeschäft; **~ decoration** *(US)* Ladendekoration, -ausstattung; **~ department** Beschaffungsabteilung; **~ detective** *(US)* Ladendetektiv; **~ display** *(US)* Ladenauslage; **~-door delivery, ~-door service** *(US)* Zustellung frei Haus, Hauszustellung; **~ employee** *(US)* Ladenangestellter; **~ equipment** *(US)* Ladenausstattung, Geschäftseinrichtung, -ausrüstung; **~ farm** *(Australia)* Viehwirtschaft; **~ farmer** *(Scot.)* Viehzüchter; **~ finance** Geschäftsfinanzen; **~ furniture** *(US)* Speichermöbel; **~s group** Warenhauskonzern; **~ hire** *(US)* Lagermiete; **~ layout** *(US)* Ladenauslage; **~ lease** *(US)* Ladenmiete; **~s ledger** Lagerhauptbuch; **~s ledger account** Lagerbuchkonto; **~s ledger card** Lagerkarte; **~s ledger clerk** Lagerbuchhalter; **~ location** *(US)* Geschäftslage; **~ management** *(US)* Geschäftsleitung, -führung; **~ manager** Lagerverwalter, *(US)* Geschäftsführer, -leiter; **~ mark** Lagermarke; **~ number** Lagernummer; **~ office**

Proviantamt; **new ~ opening** *(US)* Eröffnung eines neuen Ladens; **Sunday ~ opening** *(US)* Ladenverkauf am Sonntag; **~ operation** Geschäftsbetrieb; **~ order** Lagerbestellung, -auftrag, *(US)* Lieferauftrag [für eigene Waren an Angestellte]; **~ order act** *(US)* Barzahlungsgesetz für Löhne; **~ organization** Geschäftsorganisation; **~ owner** *(US)* Ladenbesitzer, Geschäfts-, Ladeninhaber; **~ paper** Werkzeitung; **~ pay** *(US)* Entlohnung in Waren; **~ premises** *(US)* Ladenraum, -grundstück; **~ property** *(US)* Laden-, Geschäftsgrundstück; **~ rent** *(US)* Laden-, Lagermiete; **~ rental** *(US)* Ladenmiete; **returned ~s report** Lagerrückgabemeldung; **~s requisition** Materialbezugsschein, Lageranforderung; **~ robbery** *(US)* Ladenüberfall; **~ sale** *(US)* Ladenverkauf; **~ shares** *(Br.)* Warenhausaktien; **~ shed** Lager-, Materialschuppen; **~ show** *(US)* Ladenausstellung; **~ sign** *(US)* Reklamekärtchen [zur Beschreibung der Ware]; **~ space** *(US)* Laden-, Geschäftsraum; **~ superintendent** *(US)* Geschäftsaufsicht im Laden; **~ supplies** Lageranlieferung; **~ teeth** *(US coll.)* falsche Zähne; **~ visit** *(US)* Ladenbesuch; **~ warehouse** Lager-, Packhaus, Magazin; **~ window** *(US)* Schaufenster; **~ worker** *(US)* Ladenarbeiter.

storecasting *(US)* Lautsprecherwerbung (Werbedurchsage) im Laden.

stored program(me) *(data processing)* Speicherprogramm.

storefront Ladenfront;
~ center *(US)* Ladenstadt, -verkaufszentrum.

storehouse Lagerhaus, [Waren]niederlage, Magazin, Speicher, Warenlager;
~ of information *(book)* wahre Fundgrube.

storehouseman Lagervorarbeiter.

storekeep *(v.) (US)* Laden führen (haben), Ladenbesitzer sein.

storekeeper *(Br.)* Lagerhalter, -verwalter, -aufseher, Magazinverwalter, *(shop, US)* Ladenbesitzer, -inhaber, Händler, Kaufmann;
~'s certificate Lager-, Auslieferungsanweisung.

storekeeping Lagerhaltung, Magazinverwaltung.

storeman Lageraufseher, *(worker)* Lagerarbeiter, Packer.

storemaster *(Scot.)* Viehzüchter.

storer Lageraufseher.

storeroom Vorrats-, Abstell-, Proviant-, Lagerraum, Behältnis, *(theatre)* Fundus;
~ clerk Lagerverwalter.

storeship Proviant, Versorgungs-, Magazinschiff.

storey *(Br.)* Stockwerk, Etage.

storeyed, storied geschossig, *(fig.)* in die Geschichte eingegangen;
six-~ building sechsstöckiges Gebäude.

storiette kleine Erzählung.

storing [Ein]lagern, [Ein]lagerung, Lagerhaltung, Speicherung, *(ship)* Verproviantierung;
while ~ während der Lagerung;
~ in a warehouse Lagerung unter Zollverschluß;
~ business Lagergeschäft; **~ charges** Lagergebühren, -geld; **~ conditions** Lagerbedingungen; **~ expenses** Lagerspesen; **~ facilities** Lagereinrichtungen; **~ number** Lagernummer; **~ place** Lagerplatz; **~ time** Lagerzeit.

storm Sturm, Unwetter, *(mil.)* Ansturm;
~ of anger Entrüstungssturm; **~ of applause** Beifallssturm; **~ of protest** Proteststurm; **~ and stress** Sturm und Drang; **~ in a teacup** Sturm im Wasserglas;
to ride out a ~ das Schlimmste hinter sich haben; **to stir a political ~ in a country** Sturm in einem Lande entfachen; **to take by ~** *(mil.)* im Sturm nehmen; **to weather a ~** schlechte Zeiten gut überstehen;
~ area Sturmfeld, Wetterwinkel; **~ bell** Sturmglocke; **~ center** *(US)* **(centre, Br.)** Sturmzentrum, Auge eines Sturms, *(pol.)* Gefahren-, Krisenherd; **~ clouds** *(fig.)* Gewitterwolken; **~ door** Doppeltür; **~ lantern** Sturmlaterne; **~ signal** Sturmsignal; **~ troops** *(mil.)* Elite-, Sturmtruppen; **~ window** Doppelfenster; **~ zone** Sturmzone.

storming party *(mil.)* Sturmtrupp.

stormy|crossing stürmische Überfahrt; **~ debate** heftige Diskussion; **~ life** bewegtes Leben; **~ meeting** stürmische Versammlung; **~ petrel** *(fig.)* Unglücksbote.

story *(account)* Darstellung, Bericht, *(advertising)* Quintessenz eines Werbetextes, *(film)* Filmgeschichte, *(newspaper report)* Zeitungsbericht, *(novel)* Geschichte, Erzählung, *(US)* Stockwerk, Etage;
according to his own ~ nach seiner eigenen Darstellung;
attic ~ Mansarde; **first ~** erste *(US, zweite)* Etage; **intermediate ~** Zwischenstock; **lower ~** Untergeschoß; **upper ~** Obergeschoß, *(sl.)* Oberstübchen;

~ in the basement hohes Kellergeschoß; **~ of unionism** Gewerkschaftsgeschichte, Geschichte der Gewerkschaftsbewegung;
to add a ~ to a house neues Stockwerk aufsetzen; **to be a little wrong in the upper ~** *(sl.)* nicht ganz richtig im Oberstübchen sein; **to run a big ~** Geschichte groß aufmachen;
~ board Entwurfskizze einer Werbesendung; **three-~ house** drei-, *(US, vierstöckiges)* Haus; **to get in the way of a ~ line** sich hemmend auf den Fortgang einer Geschichte auswirken; **~ rights** Drehbuchrechte.

storybook Märchenbuch;
children's ~ Kinderbuch;
a ~ ending glücklicher Ausgang; **to follow a ~ mould** einem Märchenklischee folgen.

stout resistance hartnäckiger Widerstand.

stove Ofen, *(glasshouse, Br.)* Treibhaus.

stow *(v.)* im Schiffsraum verstauen, packen;
~ away sicher verwahren, *(deadhead)* als blinder Passagier mitreisen; **~ things away in the attic** Sachen auf dem Dachboden schaffen; **~ cargo in a ship's hold** Ladung im Schiff verstauen; **~ a trunk with clothes** Koffer mit Kleidern vollpacken; **~ a wag(g)on** Waggon beladen.

stowage *(charges)* Stauerlohn, *(storeroom)* Laderaum, -tonnage, Nutzraum, *(stored goods)* aufgestaute Güter, *(stowing)* [Schiffs]verpackung, Verstauung, Verstauen;
broken ~ Staulücken; **improper ~** fehlerhafte Verstauung;
to shift the ~ umstauen;
~ certificate Stauattest; **~ plan** Stauplan.

stowaway *(deadhead)* blinder Passagier, *(place where is stored)* Abstellraum;
~ *(v.)* [on board a ship] als blinder Passagier mitfahren.

stowdown verstaute Güter, Ladung.

stower *(ship)* Stauer, Packer.

straddle unentschlossene Haltung, *(stock exchange)* Gegentransaktion, Stellagegeschäft;
~ *(v.)* unentschlossen sein, *(arbitrate)* Arbitrage treiben, *(be noncommittal)* sich noch nicht entschieden haben, *(politics, US)* es mit beiden Parteien halten;
~ an issue einer Frage ausweichen; **~ the lane** Fahrbahn wechseln; **~ the market** *(US)* in einem Wertpapier auf Baisse und in einem anderen auf Hausse spekulieren.

straddling, lane Inanspruchnahme zweier Fahrbahnen, Fahrbahnwechsel;
~ the market *(US)* gleichzeitiger An- und Verkauf von Effekten auf Terminbasis.

strafe *(v.) (sl.)* abweichen, *(spread scatteringly)* verstreut liegen.

straggler Nachzügler, *(mil.)* Versprengter;
~ post Versprengtensammelstelle.

straggling|houses verstreut liegende Häuser; **~ money** *(mil.)* Geldstrafe für unerlaubte Abwesenheit.

straight rechtschaffen, ehrlich, gerade, reell, *(account)* geordnet, in Ordnung, *(direct)* gerade, unmittelbar, *(without discount, US)* ohne Mengenrabatt, mit festem Preis, *(without compromise, US)* rückhaltlos, durch und durch, *(theater)* konventionell;
as ~ as a die grundehrlich; **as ~ as a line** schnurgerade; **~ from the horse's mouth** *(sl.)* aus erster Quelle; **~ from the shoulder** unverblümt, ehrlich, ganz offen gesagt; **~ off** im ersten Ansatz; **~ out** ohne Umschweife, klipp und klar; **~ to the point** ohne Umwege;
~ *(v.)* to be perfectly ~ in all one's dealings sich immer äußerst korrekt verhalten; **to come ~ from A** direkt aus A kommen; **to come ~ to the point** gleich zur Sache kommen; **to find the accounts ~** Bücher in Ordnung befinden; **to go ~** keine krummen Sachen mehr machen; **to go ~ from school into one's father's business** von der Schule aus sofort ins väterliche Geschäft eintreten; **to have everything dead ~ and in order** alles peinlich genau in Ordnung haben; **to keep ~** sich ordentlich halten; **to keep s. o. ~** jem. sich zurechtfinden helfen; **to put ~** [Ansprüche] ausgleichen; **to put one's desk ~** seinen Schreibtisch aufräumen; **to set a room ~** Zimmer in Ordnung bringen; **to tell s. o. ~ out (the ~ of it, US)** jem. etw. ganz offen (die Wahrheit) sagen;
~ accounts sorgfältig geführte Konten; **~ acting** Darstellung ohne Effekthascherei; **to give a ~ answer to a question** Frage ganz klar beantworten; **~ bill of lading** Direktkonnossement, *(US)* auf den Namen ausgestelltes Konnossement, Rektakonnossement, nicht übertragbarer Ladeschein; **~ commercial** *(broadcasting)* eingeblendete Werbedurchsage; **~ commission** vorbehaltlose Provision; **~-commission arrangement** üblicher Provisionsvertrag; **~ credit** *(US)* nur bei bestimmten Banken benutzbares Akkreditiv; **~ dealings** korrektes Geschäftsgeba-

ren; ~ **democrat** unentwegter Demokrat; ~ **fight** *(pol.)* Direktkampf zwischen zwei Kandidaten; ~ **income** Normaleinkommen; ~ **jet** Düsenflugzeug [ohne Propeller]; ~ **job** *(truck driver use)* Lastwagen ohne Anhänger; ~ **life insurance** *(US)* Versicherung auf den Todesfall, Großlebensversicherung; ~ **life policy** *(US)* Lebensversicherungspolice auf den Todesfall; ~ **line** kürzeste Verbindung; ~**-line depreciation** *(income statement, US)* gleichmäßige Abschreibung vom Anschaffungswert, lineare Abschreibung; ~**-line function** lineare Funktion; ~**-line method of calculating depreciation** *(US)* Abschreibungsmethode nach Quoten, lineare Abschreibungsmethode; ~**-line rate** *(el.)* vom Verbrauch unabhängiger Tarif, *(US)* linearer Abschreibungssatz; ~ **loan** auf einmal in voller Höhe fälliges Darlehn, *(US)* unbesicherte Anleihe; ~ **man of business** reeller Geschäftsmann; ~ **matter** *(data processing)* glatter Satz; ~ **note** *(US)* auf den Namen ausgestelltes Papier, Namenspapier; ~ **novel** gewöhnlicher Roman; ~**-out democrat** kompromißloser Demokrat; ~ **paper** *(US)* ungesichertes Papier; ~ **piece-rate plan** Stücklohnsystem; ~ **printing** Flachdruck; ~ **road** gerade Straße; ~ **salary** festes Gehalt [ohne Beteiligung]; ~ **shipment** Versand an einen bestimmten Empfänger; ~ **shoot** *(US)* gerade Eisenbahnlinie (Fluglinie); ~ **thinking** folgerichtiges Denken; **to vote the ~ ticket** *(US)* vorgeschriebene Kandidatenliste wählen; ~ **time** *(US)* normale Arbeitszeit; ~**-time hourly earnings** Durchschnittsstundenlohn; ~**-time pay** reiner Zeit-, Durchschnittslohn; ~ **tip** zuverlässige Auskunft.

straighten|*(v.)* **accounts** Rechnungen in Ordnung bringen; ~ **affairs** Geschäfte abwickeln; ~ **one's face** ernste Miene aufsetzen; ~ **a line** Zeile halten; ~ **out** in Ordnung bringen; ~ **up** *(US)* anständiges Leben beginnen.

straightforward freimütig, direkt;
~ **language** einfache Sprache; ~ **purchase of goods** Direktkauf von Gütern.

strain Anstrengung, -spannung, Bemühung, Kraftaufwand, Beanspruchung, *(distortion)* Verdrehung, forcierte Auslegung, *(streak)* Spur, Anflug;
to the ~s of the national anthem unter den Klängen der Nationalhymne; **under a ~** mitgenommen;
mental ~ seelische Belastung; **social ~s** soziale Spannungen;
~ **of competition** Wettbewerbskampf; ~ **on credit** Kreditanspannung, -beanspruchung; ~ **on the economy** Anspannung der gesamten Wirtschaft; ~ **of fanatism** Spur von Fanatismus; ~ **of insanity** Anlage zur Geisteskrankheit; ~ **of the law** Rechtsverdrehung; ~ **of modern life** Belastungen (Streß) des modernen Lebens; ~ **on liquidity** Liquiditätsanspannung; ~ **in the money market** Anspannungen am Geldmarkt; **great ~ on s. one's resources** gewaltige Anspannung finanzieller Mittel; ~ **of responsibility** Bürde der Verantwortung; ~ **upon the text** Textverdrehung;
~ *(v.) (fig.)* forcieren, vergewaltigen, anspannen;
~ **one's authority** seine Vollmacht überschreiten; ~ **one's credit** seinen Kredit überschreiten; ~ **one's eyes** seine Augen überanstrengen; ~ **at a gnat** bei Kleinigkeiten Umstände machen; ~ **the law** dem Gesetz Gewalt antun; ~ **the meaning of a passage** Stelle in unberechtigter Weise auslegen; ~ **every nerve** alle Kräfte anspannen; ~ **a point** zu weit gehen; ~ **a point in s. one's favo(u)r** sich zu jds. Gunsten zu weit vorwagen; ~ **one's powers** seine Befugnisse überschreiten; ~ **relations** Beziehungen einer Belastung aussetzen; ~ **one's rights** seine Rechte mißbrauchen; **to be a great ~ on s. o.** große Belastung für j. sein; **to be a ~ on s. one's resources** j. finanziell sehr in Anspruch nehmen; **to calculate the ~s and stresses of a bridge** Brückenspannung berechnen; **to place great ~s on the economy** Wirtschaft großen Belastungen aussetzen; **to speak of s. o. in lofty ~s** von jem. in den höchsten Tönen sprechen; **to suffer from the ~ of modern life** den Anforderungen der modernen Zeit kaum gewachsen sein.

strained|**interpretation** gezwungene Auslegung; ~ **relations** gespannte Beziehungen; ~ **situation on the labo(u)r market** angespannte Arbeitsmarktlage.

strait jacket Zwangsjacke.
straiten *(v.)* in Schwierigkeiten bringen.
straitened, to be in ~ circumstances in bedrängten Verhältnissen leben.
straits Meerenge, *(fig.)* Verlegenheit, Klemme;
reduced to great ~s in Schwierigkeiten;
financial (narrow) ~ Finanzklemme, finanzielle Bedrängnisse;
to be in low ~ sich in finanziellen Schwierigkeiten befinden; **to be reduced to great ~** in großer Bedrängnis sein.
strake of planks *(ship)* Plankengang.
strand *(v.)* stranden, auf Grund laufen.

stranded hilflos ausgesetzt, *(fig.)* ohne Mittel;
to be ~ festliegen, -sitzen, festgefahren sein, *(fig.)* auf dem Trockenen sitzen; **to be ~ in a foreign country** hilflos im Ausland festsitzen; **to be ~ through lack of fuel** wegen Benzinmangels festliegen; **to be ~ on the ocean floor** auf dem Meeresgrund liegen;
~ **property** Strandgut, -güter; ~ **sailor** arbeitsloser Matrose.
stranding *(ship)* Schiffbruch, Strandung, Stranden.
strange fremdländisch, *(peculiar)* sonderbar;
to be ~ to city life sich an das Stadtleben noch nicht gewöhnt haben; **to be ~ to the work** sich noch nicht eingearbeitet haben; **to feel ~** sich komisch fühlen;
~ **remark** eigenartige Bedeutung; ~ **surroundings** fremde Umgebung.
stranger Fremder, Ausländer, Außenstehender, Fremdling, Neuling, *(law of contract)* am Vertrag unbeteiligter Dritter;
~ **in blood** nicht verwandte Person;
to be a ~ to a town in einer Stadt fremd sein; **to spy ~s** *(parl., Br.)* Räumung der Galerie (Ausschluß der Öffentlichkeit) beantragen;
distinguished ~s' gallery Prominenten-, Diplomatenbühne.
strangle *(v.)* strangulieren, erwürgen, erdrosseln;
~ **a bill** Gesetzesvorlage abwürgen.
stranglehold *(fig.)* Würgegriff, Umklammerung;
~ **of restrictions** Verbotsmechanismus;
to keep a ~ on the money supply Geldversorgung im Würgegriff halten; **to loosen its ~ on the money supply** Geldhahn wieder aufdrehen; **to put a ~ on trade** für den Handel tödliche Maßnahmen treffen, tödlich für den Handel sein.
strangulation Erwürgung, Erdrosselung, Strangulierung.
strap Riemen, *(packing)* Metallband;
~**-on** anschnallbar.
straphanger stehender Fahrgast.
strapped *(sl.)* ohne einen Pfennig, pleite.
strategic *(mil.)* strategisch;
~ **Air Command** strategisches Luftwaffenkommando; ~ **arms agreement** Begrenzungsabkommen auf dem Gebiet strategischer Waffen; ~ **bomber force** strategische Bomberflotte; ~ **bombing** Bombardierung kriegswichtiger Objekte; ~ **goods** Waren strategischer Bedeutung, kriegswichtige Güter; ~ **items** strategisch wichtige Erzeugnisse; ~ **material** kriegswichtiges (kriegsentscheidendes) Material; ~ **plan** Rahmenplan; ~ **planning** strategische Führung; ~ **point** strategisch wichtiger Punkt; ~ **retreat** strategischer Rückzug; ~ **trade control** Kontrolle strategisch wichtiger Handelsgüter.
strategy Strategie;
~ **of ambiguity** *(mil.)* Verschleierungsstrategie; ~ **of deterrence** Abschreckungsstrategie;
to settle ~ for election Wahlstrategie festlegen.
strategist Stratege.
stratification, social gesellschaftliche Schichtung.
stratified|**sample** nach Schichten spezifizierte Probeentnahme; ~ **sampling** geschichtetes Stichprobenverfahren.
stratocracy Militärdiktatur.
stratocruiser Stratosphärenflugzeug.
stratosphere Stratosphäre.
stratum gesellschaftliche Schichtung, Gesellschaftsschicht.
straw Strohhalm;
not worth a ~ keinen Strohhalm wert;
the last ~ das Allerletzte;
~ **in the wind** zarter Hinweis;
not to care a ~ sich keinen Pfifferling kümmern (nichts daraus machen); **to catch at a ~** sich an einem Strohhalm festhalten; **to make bricks without ~** ohne Werkzeuge arbeiten;
~ *(a.)* fingiert, unecht, *(politics)* inoffiziell;
~ **bail** wertlose Bürgschaft; ~ **bid** *(US)* Scheingebot; ~ **bidder** *(US)* Scheinbieter; ~ **bond** wertloser Verpflichtungsschein; ~ **boss** *(US coll.)* untergeordneter Vorgesetzter, Vorarbeiter; ~ **hat** *(coll., US)* Freilichttheater; ~ **man** Strohmann, vorgeschobene Person, *(perjured witness)* meineidiger Zeuge; ~ **mattress** Strohsack; ~ **vote** *(US)* Probeabstimmung.
strawboard Spanplatte.
stray herrenloses Gut, *(animal)* herrenloses Tier;
~**s** *(wireless)* atmosphärische Störungen;
waifs and ~s verwahrloste (heimatlose) Kinder;
~ *(v.)* herumstreunen;
~ **from the point** nicht beim Thema bleiben;
~ **cattle** verirrte Tiere; ~ **customer** gelegentlicher Kunde; ~ **taxi** vereinzeltes Taxi.
strayaway Streuner.

streak Strich, *(vein)* Spur, Anflug, Anwandlung, *(wood)* Maser;
like a ~ of lightning blitzschnell, wie der Blitz;
generous ~ Anwandlung von Großzügigkeit;
~ of cruelty in s. one's character grausamer Charakterzug; ~ of good luck Glückssträhne; ~ of lightning Blitzschlag.

stream Strom, Wasserlauf, Gewässer, Fluß, Strömung, *(multitude)* Menge, Masse;
down ~ stromabwärts; with the ~ *(fig.)* mit dem Strom, wie alle; A-~ *(education, Br.)* beste Klassengruppe; private ~ Privatfluß; ~ of abuse Flut von Verwünschungen; ~ of air Luftstrom; ~ of cars Autokette, lange Reihe von Autos; ~ of dividends Dividendenstrom; ~ of emigration Auswandererstrom; ~ of goods Güterstrom; ~ of history Lauf der Geschichte; ~ of passengers Fahrgastfluß; ~s of people Menschenfluten, -massen; ~ of protests Flut von Protesten; ~ of refugees Flüchtlingsstrom; ~ of traffic Verkehrsstrom; ~ of visitors Besucherstrom; ~ of words Wortschwall;
~ *(v.) (flag)* flattern, *(light)* fluten, *(people)* strömen, fluten;
~ s. o. *(school, Br.)* j. in verschiedene Leistungsstufen einteilen;
~ a buoy Boje über Bord werfen;
to come on ~ Auswirkungen zeigen; to go with the ~ sich der Mehrheit anschließen.

streamer Wimpel, *(banner)* Streifenanzeige, Dachschild, *(newspaper)* Balkenüberschrift, -schlagzeile.

streaming *(mar.)* Schleppgeld.

streamline Stromlinienform;
~ *(v.)* stromlinienförmig gestalten, *(fig.)* modernen Verhältnissen anpassen, rationalisieren, modernisieren;
~ administration and paperwork Verwaltungs- und Schreibarbeiten modernisieren; ~ one's sales representation seine Verkaufsaktion neuesten Erkenntnissen des Verkaufens anpassen; ~ a tax-collection system Steuereintreibungsverfahren modernisieren;
~ shape Stromlinienform.

streamlined modernisiert, modernen Verhältnissen angepaßt, fortschrittlich, *(car)* windschlüpfig, stromlinienförmig;
~ body Stromlinienkarosserie; ~ car stromlinienförmiges Auto; ~ control hochmoderne Kontrollmethode; ~ superstructure *(ship)* windschlüpfige Aufbauten.

streamliner *(US)* Stromlinienzug, -bus.

streamlining Modernisierung.

street Straße, Gasse, *(stock exchange, Br.)* Nachbörse, nachbörsliches Geschäft, *(curb market)* Freiverkehr;
[done] in the ~ *(stock exchange, Br.)* nach Börsenschluß, nachbörslich; in the open ~ auf offener Straße; not in the same ~ längst nicht so gut, unvergleichlich schlechter; on the ~s *(prostitute)* auf dem Strich; on easy ~ *(US)* in guten Verhältnissen; over the ~ auf der anderen Straßenseite;
~s ahead weit überlegen;
⌾ *(US)* Wallstreet;
the ⌾ *(entertainment centre)* Vergnügungsviertel, *(public)* die Öffentlichkeit, *(stock exchange)* Hauptgeschäfts-, Börsenstraße, -viertel;
adopted ~ Kommunalstraße; back ~ abgelegene Straße; commercial ~ Geschäftsstraße; congested ~ verkehrsreiche Straße; crowded ~s überfüllte Straßen; favo(u)red ~ Vorfahrtsstraße; Fleet ⌾ *(Br.)* Zeitungsviertel in London; high ~ Hauptstraße; scantily lighted ~ kümmerlich beleuchtete Straße; main ~ Hauptstraße; mean ~s armselige Straßen; no-waiting ~ Parkverbotsstraße; off ~ Nebenstraße; one-sided ~ nur auf einer Seite bebaute Straße; one-way ~ Einbahnstraße; quiet ~ ruhige Straße; residential ~ Wohnstraße; restricted ~ Parkverbotsstraße; rough ~ holprige Straße; side ~ Seitenstraße; inadequately signposted ~ schlecht ausgeschilderte Straße; surface ~ gepflasterte Straße; unrestricted ~ parkfähige Straße; two-way ~ Straße mit Gegenverkehr; Wall ⌾ New Yorker Börse (Hochfinanz); well-laid-out ~ schön angelegte Straße;
~ through which there is much traffic verkehrsreiche Straße;
to bar a ~ Straße absperren; to be ~s ahead weit überlegen sein; to be on easy ~ reich (wohlhabend) sein; to be rumo(u)red on the ~ *(US sl.)* auf der Börse erörtert werden; to be up s. one's ~ jds. Kragenweite sein; to beset a ~ Straße blockieren; to clear the ~ Straße frei machen; to cross the ~ Straße überqueren; to line the ~ Spalier bilden; to live on a busy ~ in einer belebten Straße wohnen; to live on main ~ in der Hauptstraße wohnen; to live in the ~ ständig unterwegs (auf Reisen) sein; to put it on the ~ öffentlich ausplaudern; to put workers on the ~ Arbeiter auf die Straße setzen; to sell on the ~ *(Br.)* an der Nachbörse verkaufen, *(curb market)* im Freiverkehr verkaufen; to stop the noise in the ~ Straßenlärm unterbinden; to stroll the ~s durch die Straße schlendern, Straßenbummel machen; to take to the ~s

auf die Straße gehen, um zu demonstrieren; to turn s. o. out into the ~ j. auf die Straße setzen;
~ *(a.) (Br.)* nach Börsenschluß, nachbörslich, *(on the curb market)* im Freiverkehr;
~ accident [Straßen]verkehrsunfall; ~ arab Straßenkind; ~ battle Straßenschlacht; ~ boy *(Br.)* Gassenjunge; ~ brawl Straßenauflauf; ~ broker *(US)* freier Makler, Winkelmakler; ~ certificate *(US)* formlos übertragene Aktie; ~ cleaner *(US)* Straßenkehrer, -kehrmaschine; ~ cleaning Straßenreinigung; ~ collection Straßensammlung; ~ corner Straßenecke; ~ crossing Straßenkreuzung; ~ demonstration Straßendemonstration; ~ door Haus-, Eingangstür; ~ fighting Straßenkämpfe; ~ girl Prostituierte, Straßenmädchen; ~ hawker ambulanter Händler, Straßenhändler; ~ illumination Straßenbeleuchtung; ~ improvement bonds *(US)* kommunale Schuldverschreibungen zur Finanzierung des Straßenbaues; ~ industry Wandergewerbe, Gewerbe im Umherziehen, Hausiergewerbe; ~ island Verkehrsinsel, Inselbahnsteig; ~ lamp (lantern) Straßenlampe; ~ level Straßenniveau; ~ lighting Straßenbeleuchtung; ~ loan *(US)* kurzfristiges Maklerdarlehen; ~ main Hauptrohr; ~ map Straßenkarte; ~ market *(Br.)* Freiverkehrsmarkt, Nachbörse; ~ market price *(Br.)* Freiverkehrskurs; ~ mugging gewaltsamer Straßenraub; ~ number Hausnummer; ~ orderly *(Br.)* Straßenkehrer; ~ organ Leierkasten, Drehorgel; ~ paper *(US)* kurzfristiger, durch einen Makler verkaufter Schuldschein; ~ parking Parken in Ortschaften; ~ patrol Straßenstreife, Verkehrsstreife; ~ pattern Straßensystem; ~ plan Straßenplan; ~ porter Dienstmann; ~ prices *(Br.)* nachbörsliche Kurse, *(curb market)* Freiverkehrskurse; ~ railway Straßenbahn; ~ railway bonds Straßenbahnobligationen; ~ refuge *(Br.)* Verkehrsinsel; ~ repairs Straßeninstandsetzung; ~ rioting Straßenschlacht; ~ roller Straßenwalze; ~ sale Straßenverkauf, -handel; ~ seller (trader, vendor) Straßenhändler, Wandergewerbetreibender; ~ sign Straßenschild; ~ singer Bänkelsänger; ~ sprinkler *(US)* Sprengwagen; ~ sweeper *(Br.)* Straßenkehrer; ~ system Straßensystem; ~ tidy Abfallbehälter; ~ trading Straßenhandel; ~ traffic Straßenverkehr; ~ violence öffentliche Gewaltakte.

streetage Straßengebühr.

streetcar *(US)* Straßenbahnwagen;
~ accident *(US)* Straßenbahnunglück; ~ advertising *(US)* Straßenbahnreklame; ~ line *(US)* Straßenbahnlinie.

streeted von Straßen durchzogen.

streetwalker Prostituierte.

streetwalking Dirnenunwesen, Prostitution.

strength Kraft, Stärke, *(market)* feste Haltung, *(mil.)* Kopfstärke, Truppen-, Schiffsmacht, Bestand, *(personnel)* Personalbestand, *(stock exchange)* feste Haltung, Festigkeit;
below ~ unter Normalstärke; in ~ mit einem großen Aufgebot; in full ~ vollzählig; on the ~ auf den Verdacht hin, im Vertrauen auf, *(mil., Br.)* in der Stammrolle eingetragen;
actual ~ Iststärke; competitive ~ Wettbewerbsfähigkeit; economic ~ Wirtschaftskraft; effective ~ *(mil.)* Präsenzstärke, Sollstärke; enrolled ~ *(party)* Mitgliederzahl; maximum ~ *(mil.)* Höchststärke; overall ~ Gesamtstärke; personnel ~ Belegschaftsstärke; required ~ Sollstärke; selective ~ *(stock exchange)* auf Spezialwerte beschränkte feste Haltung; total ~ Gesamtstärke;
~ of an argument überzeugende Beweiskraft; ~ of a candidate Hausmacht eines Kandidaten (Bewerbers); ~ of character Charakterstärke; ~ of electric current Stromstärke; ~ of the economy anhaltende Konjunktur, Konjunkturwelle; ~ of the establishment *(Br.)* Personalbestand [des Beamtenkörpers]; ~ of judgment Urteilsvermögen; ~ of law Gesetzeskraft; ~ in the market Steigen der Kurse; ~ of memory Gedächtnisstärke; ~ of mind Willensstärke; ~ of public opinion Macht der öffentlichen Meinung; ~ of the police Polizeikräfte; ~ of purpose Entschlußkraft; ~ of the staff Personalbestand; ~ of a statement (testimony) Beweiskraft einer Aussage;
to be below ~ Sollstärke nicht erreichen; to bring the police force up to ~ Polizeikräfte auf ihre Sollstärke auffüllen; to employ s. o. on the ~ of s. one's recommendation j. auf Grund seiner Empfehlungen einstellen; to negotiate on the ~ of samples auf Grund der Vorlage von Mustern verhandeln; to show greater ~ *(prices)* sich gefestigt haben;
~ return Stärkemeldung.

strengthen *(v.)* bestärken, bekräftigen, verstärken, *(market)* sich festigen, sich versteifen;
~ a case Argument erhärten; ~ the dollar price Dollarkurs festigen; ~ its own funds Eigenmittel [ver]stärken; ~ s. one's hand jem. Mut machen; ~ friendly relations Freundschaftsbeziehungen enger gestalten.

strengthening Verstärkung, Befestigung [der Kurse];
~ **of the dollar price** Festigung des Dollarkurses; ~ **of patrols** verstärkte Polizeistreife.

strenuous tatkräftig;
to make ~ efforts erhebliche Anstrengungen machen; **to lead a ~ life** anstrengendes Leben führen; ~ **reformer** eifriger Reformanhänger; ~ **work** anstrengende Arbeit.

stress Anspannung, Beanspruchung, Belastung, Druck, *(accent)* Betonung, Akzent, *(fig.)* Nachdruck, Gewicht, Betonung;
under the ~ of circumstances unter dem Druck der Verhältnisse; **under the ~ of poverty** in drückender Armut;
allowable ~ zulässige Beanspruchung; **highest ~** Höchstbeanspruchung; **static ~** statische Beanspruchung;
~ **of competition** Wettbewerbsdruck; ~ **of money** Geldanspannung; ~ **of weather** Unbilden der Witterung;
to be driven by the ~ of circumstances unter dem Druck der Verhältnisse stehen; **to lay ~ on** Gewicht (Nachdruck) darauf legen; **to lay ~ on foreign languages** auf Fremdsprachen Wert legen;
~ **disease** Managerkrankheit; ~ **mark** Betonungsakzent.

stressed, to be beansprucht werden.

stretch Grundriß, Abriß, *(criminal, coll.)* Strafzeit, *(land)* Strich, Land, *(road)* Strecke, Streckenabschnitt, *(strain)* Anspannung, -strengung;
in (at) a ~ in einer Tour; **with every faculty on the ~** unter Anspannung aller Fähigkeiten;
~ **of authority** Vollmachtsmißbrauch, -überschreitung; ~ **of a road** Wegstrecke;
~ *(v.)* überschreiten, -spannen, *(road)* sich ausdehnen;
~ **one's credit** seine Kreditlinie überschreiten, seinen Kredit übermäßig in Anspruch nehmen; ~ **a law** Gesetz in unberechtigter Weise auslegen; ~ **for miles** sich kilometerweit hinziehen; ~ **the patience of s. o. to its limits** jds. Geduld aufs äußerste strapazieren; ~ **a point** fünf gerade sein lassen; ~ **a point in s. one's favo(u)r** Punkt zu jds. Gunsten auslegen; ~ **one's power** sich übernehmen (überarbeiten); ~ **a principle** es nicht allzu genau nehmen; ~ **a privilege** Vorrecht mißbrauchen; ~ **a rule** Vorschrift zu weit auslegen; ~ **to the sea** sich bis ans Meer ausdehnen; ~ **the truth** es mit der Wahrheit nicht so genau nehmen;
to be at full ~ *(factory)* voll beschäftigt (ausgelastet) sein; **to do a ~** *(Br., sl.)* ein Jahr brummen (im Knast sitzen); **to work for 8 hours at a ~** acht Stunden hintereinander arbeiten;
~**-out** *(US)* Arbeitsintensivierung (Überstundenzeit) ohne Lohnerhöhung; ~**-out of program(me)** Programmstreckung.

stretched, to be fully völlig ausgelastet sein.

stretcher Tragbahre;
~ **case** nicht gehfähiger Verletzter; ~ **bearer** *(mil., US)* Krankenträger.

stricken getroffen;
~ **in years** vom Alter gebeugt;
~ **ship** angeschlagenes Schiff.

strict streng, strikt, genau;
~ **censorship** strenge Zensur; **in ~ confidence** streng vertraulich; ~ **construction** strenge Auslegung; ~ **constructionist** Befürworter einer engen Verfassungsauslegung; ~ **cost price** scharf kalkulierter Herstellerpreis; ~ **discipline** strenge Disziplin; ~ **foreclosure** endgültiger Pfandverfall nach einer Ausschlußfrist; ~ **law** strenges Gesetz; ~ **liability** Gefährdungshaftung; ~ **observance** strenge Einhaltung; ~ **order** genaue Anweisung; ~ **rule** striktes Verbot; ~ **seclusion** völlige Abgeschlossenheit; **in the ~ sense** im strengen Sinn; **to keep ~ silence** absolute Stille bewahren; ~ **settlement** Begründung eines Fideikommisses; ~ **statement of facts** exakte Tatsachenangabe; ~ **time limit** Not-, Ausschlußfrist;
to keep a ~ watch on s. o. j. streng bewachen.

strictly | confidential streng vertraulich;
~ **construed** eng ausgelegt; ~ **off the record** streng vertraulich; ~ **prohibited** streng verboten;
to adhere ~ to a clause Bestimmungen genau beachten;
~ **ministerial duty** strenge Amtspflicht.

stride Ausschreiten, *(coll.)* Schwung;
with rapid ~s mit Riesenschritten;
to hit one's ~ richtig auf Touren kommen; **to make great ~s** rasche Fortschritte machen; **to take s. th. in one's ~** mühelos überwinden, spielend bewältigen, etw. als selbstverständlich hinnehmen.

strike Streik, [Arbeits]ausstand, Arbeitseinstellung, -niederlegung, *(attack)* [Flieger]angriff, *(finding of oil)* Ölfund, *(politics, US sl.)* Erpressungsmanöver;
attack ~ Angriffsstreik; **buyer's ~** Käuferstreik; **civil ~** bürger-

licher Ungehorsam, Steuerstreik; **coal ~** Bergarbeiterstreik; **contract ~** aufgrund von Lohnverhandlungen entstandener Streik; **defence ~** Defensivstreik; **flash ~** wilder Streik; **general ~** General-, Massenstreik, Massenarbeitsniederlegung; **go-slow ~** Arbeitsverlangsamung, Dienst nach Vorschrift; **hit-and-run ~** wilder Streik; **hunger ~** Hungerstreik; **illegal ~** von der Gewerkschaft nicht genehmigter Streik; **industry-wide ~** Streik innerhalb eines ganzen Industriezweiges; **legal ~** ordnungsgemäß durchgeführter Streik; **lightning ~** Streik ohne vorherige Ankündigung, Spontanstreik; **local ~** örtlicher Streik; **lucky ~** *(US)* Glückstreffer; **management ~** Streik der Führungskräfte; **negative ~** Defensivstreik; **one-man ~** Streik zwecks Wiedereinstellung eines entlassenen Arbeiters; **outlaw ~** wilder Streik; **political ~** aus politischen Gründen begonnener Streik; **positive ~** Angriffsstreik; **preemptive ~** *(mil.)* Präventivangriff, -aktionen; **protest ~** Proteststreik; **public-sector ~** Streik der im öffentlichen Dienst Beschäftigten; **public-utility ~** Streik der öffentlichen Versorgungsbetriebe; **quickie ~** *(US)* wilder (unangekündigter) Streik, Kurzstreik; **secondary ~** mittelbarer Boykottstreik; **sectional ~** regional begrenzter Streik, Regionalstreik; **selective ~** schwerpunktartig durchgeführter Streik; **sitdown ~** Sitzstreik; **slowdown ~** Streik durch Verlangsamung der Arbeit, Bummelstreik; **stay-down ~** *(mining)* Sitzstreik; **stay-in ~** *(Br.)* mehrtägiger Sitzstreik; **sympathy (sympathetic) ~** Sympathiestreik; **token ~** symbolischer Streik; **unofficial ~** *(Br.)* wilder Streik; **warning ~** Warnstreik; **wildcat ~** wilder Streik; **work-to-rule ~** Bummelstreik;
~**s, riots and civil commotions** Streik, Aufruhr und bürgerliche Unruhen; ~ **of bus drivers** Autobusfahrerstreik; ~ **in the coal mines** Bergarbeiterstreik; ~ **against bad working conditions** Streik wegen schlechter Arbeitsbedingungen; ~ **with due notice** rechtzeitig angekündigter Streik; ~ **for higher pay** Streik für höhere Löhne; ~ **of stevedores** Hafenarbeiterstreik; ~ **of transport workers** Transportarbeiterstreik;
~ *(v.)* in einen Streik eintreten, streiken, *(cease working)* Feierabend machen, *(coin)* münzen, prägen, *(find oil)* auf ein Öllager stoßen, *(theater)* Kulissen wechseln;
~ **s. o. j.** anpumpen;
~ **up an acquaintance** Bekanntschaft machen; ~ **against** bestreiken; ~ **with the approval of the union** von der Gewerkschaft genehmigten Streik durchführen; ~ **an average** Durchschnitt nehmen; ~ **back** sich revanchieren; ~ **a balance** bilanzieren, *(account)* Rechnung ausgleichen, Saldo ziehen; ~ **a bargain** Handel (Geschäft, Vertrag) [ab]schließen; ~ **on a nation-wide basis** bundesweiten Streik durchführen; ~ **bottom** *(ship)* auf Grund laufen; ~ **camp** sein Lager abbrechen; ~ **coins** Münzen schlagen; ~ **one's colo(u)rs** seine Flagge streichen; ~ **a committee** Ausschuß bilden (konstituieren); ~ **against bad working conditions** wegen schlechter Arbeitsbedingungen in den Streik treten; ~ **dead (dumb)** die Sprache verschlagen; ~ **a dividend** Dividende ausschütten; ~ **a docket** *(bankruptcy proceeding, Br.)* Antrag auf Konkurseröffnung stellen; ~ **off entries** Eintragungen im Buch löschen; ~ **one's flag** seine Flagge einziehen; ~ **up a friendship** Freundschaft schließen; ~ **ground** mit dem Lot auftreffen; ~ **all of a heap** größte Überraschung hervorrufen; ~ **home** seine Wirkung nicht verfehlen; ~ **while the iron is hot** das Eisen schmieden solange es heiß ist; ~ **upon an idea** auf eine Idee stoßen; ~ **in on a problem** bei einer Frage mitreden; ~ **in with a suggestion** sich mit einem Vorschlag einmischen; ~ **into a subject** sich einem Thema zuwenden; ~ **on the job** durch Arbeitsverlangsamung streiken; ~ **a lead** *(fig.)* zu Geld kommen, Geldquelle entdecken; ~ **out a line for o. s.** etw. Neues erfinden; ~ **upon s. one's name in the newspaper** in der Zeitung auf jds. Namen stoßen; ~ **a note of warning** warnenden Ton anschlagen; ~ **a jury** *(US)* Geschworenenliste zusammenstellen; ~ **off** *(auction)* zuschlagen, Zuschlag erteilen, *(cancel an entry)* Eintragung löschen, *(pay a debt)* Schuld tilgen; ~ **off 2%** 2 Prozent abziehen, zweiprozentigen Abzug vornehmen; ~ **off 5000 copies of a book** Auflage von 5000 Stück drucken; ~ **off an item** Posten streichen; ~ **off a man's head** jem. den Kopf abschlagen; ~ **off the register** im Register löschen; ~ **off the medical register** Lizenz als Arzt (ärztliche Approbation) entziehen; ~ **s. o. off the roll** *(Br.)* j. in der Mitgliederliste streichen, *(lawyer)* j. aus der Anwaltskammer ausschließen; ~ **an action off the roll** Verfahren einstellen; ~ **a ship off the list** Schiff abwracken; ~ **oil** *(US)* auf Öl stoßen, fündig werden, *(fig., US sl.)* Geld scheffeln, reich werden; ~ **out** aus-, durchstreichen; ~ **out a new course of life** seinem Leben eine völlig neue Richtung geben; ~ **out a new fashion** neue Mode aufbringen; ~ **out untrodden paths** neue Wege gehen; ~ **a passage out of a book** Buchstelle streichen (herauslassen); ~ **out a new plan of finance**

neuen Finanzierungsplan ersinnen; ~ **out words not applicable** Nichtzutreffendes streichen; ~ **for higher pay** für höhere Löhne in den Streik treten; ~ **it rich** *(US)* auf eine Goldader stoßen, reiche Geldquelle entdecken, gutes Geschäft machen; ~ **roots** Wurzeln schlagen; ~ **at the root of evil** Wurzel eines Übels bloßlegen; ~ **sail** *(fig.)* klein beigeben; ~ **the sands** stranden; ~ **in sympathy** in einen Sympathiestreik treten; ~ **tents** Lager abbrechen; ~ **terror into the people** Volk verängstigen; ~ **through** *(type)* durchschlagen; ~ **the track of s. o.** jem. auf die Spur kommen; ~ **twelve** durchschlagenden Erfolg haben; ~ **between wind and water** bis ins Mark treffen; ~ **a word through** Wort durchstreichen; ~ **a work** Fabrik bestreiken;

to avoid a ~ Streik vermeiden; **to bar a** ~ Streik verbieten; **to be on** ~ streiken, ausständig sein; **to be on** ~ **for more pay** für Gehaltserhöhung streiken; **to break a** ~ Streik brechen; **to call a** ~ Streik ausrufen; **to call off a** ~ Streik abbrechen; **to come out on** ~ streiken; **to declare a** ~ Streik proklamieren; **to go on** ~ in den Streik treten; **to make a** ~ Glück haben; **to proclaim a** ~ Streik ausrufen; **to prohibit a** ~ **by government decree** Streik durch Regierungsbeschluß verbieten; **to stage a** ~ Streik organisieren; **to trigger a** ~ Streik vom Zaun brechen;

~ **action** Streikaktion; **constitutional** ~ **action** verfassungmäßig erlaubte Streikmaßnahmen; **to take** ~ **action** Streikmaßnahmen einleiten; ~ **activity** Streiktätigkeit; ~ **aid** Streikbeihilfe; ~ **ballot** Streikabstimmung; ~ **benefits** Streikgelder, -unterstützung; ~ **benefit money** Streikfonds; ~ **bill** *(US)* erpresserischer Gesetzesantrag; ~**-bound** vom Streik betroffen, bestreikt; **to be ~-bound for a week** eine Woche lang bestreikt werden; ~**-bound factory** bestreikte Fabrik; ~ **call** Streikausruf; ~ **campaign** Streikaktion; ~ **cancellation** Streikbeendigung; ~ **clause** Streikklausel; **no-~ clause** Streikverbotsklausel; ~ **committee** Streikausschuß, -leitung; ~ **date** Streiktermin; ~ **deadline** Streikende, -beendigung; ~ **deterrent** Streikverhütungsmittel; ~ **director** Streikleiter; ~**-free labo(u)r** am Streik unbeteiligte Arbeitskräfte; ~ **forces** *(NATO)* Eingreif- und Unterstützungskräfte; **to beef up the ~ fund** Streikfonds auffüllen; ~ **instruction** Streikanweisung; ~ **insurance** Streikversicherung; ~ **leader** Streikführer; **to victimize a ~ leader** Streikanführer durch Entlassung bestrafen; ~**-like tactics** streikähnliche Maßnahmen; ~ **movement** Streikbewegung; ~ **notice** Streikankündigung; ~ **orders** Streikbefehl, -anweisungen; ~ **outlook** Streikaussichten; ~ **pact** Streikabkommen; ~ **pay** Streikgeld[er], -lohn; ~ **picket** Streikposten; ~ **plan** Streikplan; ~**-prone** streikanfällig, -lustig; ~ **protection forces** Streikschutzkräfte; ~ **provisions** Streikbestimmungen; ~ **record** Streikstatistik, -bilanz; ~ **replacement** Ersatz für Streikausfälle; ~ **settlement** Abkommen zur Streikbeendigung, Streikvereinbarung; ~ **target** Streikziel; ~ **threat** Streikdrohung; ~ **toll** Streiknachteile; ~**-vote meeting** Urabstimmungs-, Streikversammlung; ~ **year** Streikjahr.

strikebreaker Streikbrecher.

strikebreaking Zwangsmaßnahmen zur Streikbeendigung; ~ *(a.)* streikbrechend.

strikemonger Streikhetzer.

striker Streikender, Ausständiger.

striking Streiken;
~ **a balance** Saldierung, Bilanzziehung; ~ **a docket** *(Br.)* Beantragung des Konkursverfahrens, Konkursanmeldung; ~ **a jury** *(US)* Zusammenstellung einer Geschworenenliste; ~ **off the roll** *(Br.)* Streichung von der Anwaltsliste, Ausschluß aus der Anwaltskammer; ~ **out** *(protocol)* gerichtlich angeordnete Entfernung;
~ **clock** Schlaguhr; ~ **employee** streikender Arbeiter; ~ **facts** nicht zu übersehende Tatsachen; ~ **force** *(mil.)* Streitmacht, Eingreifsverband; ~ **headline** knallende Überschrift; ~ **likeness** verblüffende Ähnlichkeit; ~ **member** streikendes Gewerkschaftsmitglied; ~ **power** *(mil.)* Schlagkraft.

string Bindfaden, Schnur, *(clause, US)* Geheimklausel, *(fig.)* Faden, Band, *(US sl.)* Flunkerei, Lügengeschichte, *(telegraph wire, sl.)* Telegraphenlinie;
no ~s attached ohne Klauseln, nicht verklausuliert; **without ~s** *(fam.)* pleite;
purse ~s Finanzkontrolle;
~ **of by-election failures** Kette von Nachwahlmißerfolgen; ~ **of cars** Autokette, -strom, Strom von Fahrzeugen; ~ **of disasters** Katastrophenserie; ~ **easy to untie** Buchhändlerknoten; ~ **of islands** Inselkette; ~ **and brown paper** Schnur und Packpapier; ~ **of lawsuits** Prozeßserie, -lawine; ~ **of pearls** Perlenschnur; ~ **of questions** Reihe von Fragen, Fragenstrom; ~ **of vehicles** Kette von Fahrzeugen;

~ *(v.)* **s. o. along** j. an der Nase herumführen; ~ **along with s. o.** Verbindung zu jem. halten, solang er nützlich ist;
~ **a room with festoons** Zimmer mit Girlanden behängen; ~ **up** *(coll.)* [auf]hängen, *(sl.)* an der Nase herumführen; ~ **up lanterns** Lampions aufhängen; ~ **up to a deed** zu einer Tat ermuntern;

to be second ~ zweite Geige spielen, zur zweiten Garnitur gehören; **to harp on the same** ~ immer das gleiche Thema behandeln, dauernd auf einer Sache herumreiten; **to have a ~ to it** Haken haben, an eine Klausel gebunden sein; **to have s. o. on a** ~ j. am Gängelband haben, j. zappeln lassen; **to have two ~s to one's bow** mehrere Eisen im Feuer haben; **to pull the ~s** hinter den Kulissen agieren, die Strippen (alle Register) ziehen, Fäden in der Hand haben, den Drahtzieher abgeben; **to touch a** ~ Gefühl ansprechen; ~ **alphabet** Blindenschriftsystem; ~ **bag** Einkaufsnetz; ~ **development** Stadtrandsiedlung; ~ **orchestra** Streichorchester.

stringency Knappheit, *(argument)* zwingende Kraft, Schärfe, *(money market)* Angespanntsein, Gedrücktheit;
credit ~ Kreditverknappung; **fiscal** ~ staatlich gesteuerte Geldverknappung; **foreign-exchange** ~ Devisenknappheit; **money** ~ Verknappung am Geldmarkt;
~ **of credit** Kreditverknappung, -knappheit.

stringent *(clause)* bindend, *(law)* streng, hart, *(market)* gedrückt, *(money market)* knapp, angespannt;
to be very ~ *(money market)* unter größter Verknappung leiden;
~ **argument** eindrucksvolle Beweisführung; ~ **code of procedure** strenge Verfahrensordnung; ~ **necessity** zwingende Notwendigkeit; ~ **regulation** strenge Verordnung; ~ **rule against smoking** absolutes Rauchverbot; ~ **stock market** angespannte Börse.

stringer freiberuflicher Mitarbeiter, freier Korrespondent.

strip Streifen, *(advertising)* Streifenanzeige, Bildgeschichte, *(mutilation, US)* Verwüstung, Zerstörung, *(philat.)* Reihe Briefmarken, *(steel)* Bandeisen, -stahl;
flight ~ Notlandebahn; **landing** ~ Start- und Landebahn;
~ **of garden** Gartenland; ~ **of land** schmales Stück Land; ~ **of paper** Stück Papier; ~ **of runway** Start- und Landebahn;
~ *(v.)* ausziehen, entkleiden, *(mining, US)* im Tagebau abbauen, *(techn.)* demontieren, auseinandernehmen, *(tenant)* wiederrechtlich entfernen;
~ **a bed** Bett abziehen; ~ **down an engine** Maschine (Motor) auseinandernehmen; ~ **a factory** Fabrik demontieren; ~ **of funds** Mittel entziehen; ~ **a liar** Lügner bloßstellen; ~ **s. o. of his office** j. seines Amtes entkleiden; ~ **a peg** Anzug von der Stange kaufen; ~ **s. o. of his possessions** jem. seinen ganzen Besitz wegnehmen; ~ **a ship** Schiff abtakeln; ~ **s. o. of a title** jem. seinen Titel aberkennen;
~ **cartoon** Bildgeschichte; ~ **cropping** Hangschutzbepflanzung; ~ **lighting** Neonbeleuchtung; ~ **mine** *(US)* im Tagebau betriebene Grube; ~ **mining** *(US)* Bergbau im Tagebaubetrieb; ~ **tease** Entkleidungsnummer, Striptease.

stripe *(mil.)* Tresse, Ärmelstreifen, *(fig., US)* Art, Sorte;
of quite different ~ von ganz anderem Schlag;
zebra ~ Zebrastreifen;
~ **of land** schmales Stück Land;
to be of the same political ~ derselben politischen Richtung angehören; **to get one's** *(mil.)* befördert werden; **to lose one's ~s** *(mil.)* degradiert werden.

stripped ausgeplündert.

stripper Schönheits-, Nackttänzerin.

striptease Entkleidungsnummer.

stripteaser Schönheits-, Nackttänzerin.

stripping Fotomontage.

strive *(v.)* | **for** sich befleißigen; ~ **against the stream** *(fig.)* gegen den Strom schwimmen.

stroke Strich, *(duct)* Schriftzug, *(engine)* Kolbenhub, *(med.)* Schlaganfall, *(mil.)* Manöver, Handstreich, *(performance)* Errungenschaft, Leistung;
on the ~ pünktlich;
clever ~ [**of policy**] geschickter [politischer] Schachzug; **first** ~ Vorschuß;
good ~ **of business** gutes Geschäft; ~ **of genius** Geistesblitz; ~ **of lightning** Blitzschlag; ~ **of luck** günstiger Zufall, Glücksfall; ~ **of the pen** Federzug;
~ *(v.)* **s. o. the wrong way** j. auf die Palme bringen;
to add the finishing ~ den Garaus machen; **to be on the** ~ absolut (auf die Sekunde) pünktlich sein; **not to have done a** ~ **of work** keinen Strich Arbeit getan haben;
~ **width** *(terminal)* Strichstärke.

stroll Spaziergang;

~ *(v.)* bummeln;

~ **around an exhibition** Ausstellung besichtigen; ~ **the streets** durch die Straßen schlendern;

to go for a ~ Bummel machen.

stroller Bummler, Spaziergänger.

strolling actor Dorfkomödiant.

strong stark, kräftig, *(stock exchange)* fest, widerstandsfähig; **financially** ~ kapitalkräftig, -stark;

to be ~ *(market)* festliegen; **to be** ~ **against s. th.** entschieden gegen etw. sein; **to be going** ~ gut im Schuß sein; **to feel quite** ~ **again** sich völlig erholt haben; **to go it rather** ~ ein bißchen übertreiben;

~ **argument** zwingender Beweis; ~**-arm act** Kraftakt; ~**-arm man** *(US)* Rausschmeißer; ~**-arm methods** *(US)* Zwangsmethoden; ~**-arm treatment** tatkräftige Unterstützung; ~**-arm work** *(US)* Keilerei; ~ **army** starke Armee; ~ **candidate** seriöser (aussichtsreicher) Kandidat; ~ **currency** harte Währung; ~-**currency countries** Hartwährungsländer, währungsstarke Länder; ~ **custom** tief eingewurzelte Sitte; ~ **demand** lebhafte Nachfrage; **to have a** ~ **hold upon s. o.** große Macht über j. haben; ~ **language** starke Ausdrücke; **to be the** ~ **man in the organization** starker Mann in einem Verband sein; ~ **market** feste Börse; ~ **measures** drastische Maßnahmen; ~ **mind** kluger Kopf; ~ **nation** reiches Volk; **to have** ~ **nerves** starke Nerven haben; ~ **partisan** glühender Anhänger; ~ **point** Stärke; ~ **point of s. o.** jds. starke Seite; ~ **point in an argument** Schwerpunkt einer Beweisführung; ~ **prejudice** ausgeprägtes Vorurteil; ~ **suspicion** dringender Verdacht; **to write in** ~ **terms to s. o.** jem. einen energischen Brief schreiben.

strongbox Geldschrank, Stahlkassette, -fach, Tresorfach.

stronghand Gewaltanwendung.

stronghold *(fig.)* Bollwerk, Hochburg, *(mil.)* Festung.

strongroom Panzergewölbe, *(bank)* Stahlkammer, Depot, [Bank]tresor.

struck *(indictment for murder)* tödlich getroffen;

~ **balance** *(Br.)* Zwischenbilanz; ~ **jury** zusammengestellte Geschworenenliste.

structural baulich, strukturell;

~ **adaptation** strukturelle Anpassung; ~ **adjustment** Strukturanpassung; ~ **aid** Strukturhilfe; ~ **alteration or change** Strukturveränderung, *(building)* bauliche Veränderungen, Umbau; **to carry out** ~ **alterations** Umbauten vornehmen, umbauen; **to have a** ~ **basis of about half a million unemployed** über ein strukturell bedingtes Arbeitslosenheer von etwa 1/2 Million verfügen; ~ **beam** Tragebalken; ~ **change** Strukturwandel, -veränderung; ~ **condition** bauliche Beschaffenheit, Bauzustand; ~ **crisis** Strukturkrise; ~ **damage** Substanz-, Bauschäden; ~ **defect** Konstruktionsfehler; ~ **disease** organische Krankheit; ~ **disparities** strukturelle Unterschiede; ~ **distortion** strukturelle Fehlentwicklung; ~ **engineering** Bautechnik; ~ **error** Konstruktionsfehler; ~ **improvements** Strukturverbesserung, bauliche Verbesserungen; ~ **interdependence** strukturelle industrielle Abhängigkeit; ~ **iron** Profileisen; ~ **shifts** strukturelle Verschiebungen; ~ **steel** Baustahl; ~ **unemployment** strukturelle Arbeitslosigkeit; ~ **work** Bauarbeiten.

structure Beschaffenheit, Aufbau, Struktur, Gefüge, *(building)* Gebäude, Bauwerk;

cost ~ Kostengefüge; **divisionalized** ~ Regionalstruktur; **economic** ~ Wirtschaftssystem; **financial** ~ Kapitalstruktur; **market** ~ Marktgefüge, -struktur; **monetary** ~ Geldgefüge; **nonqualifying** ~ nicht abschreibungsfähiges Gebäude; **preliminary** ~ vorläufiger Aufbau; **price** ~ Preisgefüge, -struktur; **social** ~ soziales Gefüge;

~ **of agriculture** Agrarstruktur; ~ **of business** Wirtschaftsstruktur; ~ **of costs** Kostengefüge; ~ **of distribution** Vertriebsstruktur; ~ **of a house** Bauart eines Hauses; ~ **of housing tenure** Strukturwandel im Wohnungsbau; ~ **of interest rates** Zinsgefüge; ~ **in the nature of a building** gebäudeähnliche Anlage; ~ **of an organization** Aufbau einer Organisation; ~ **of population** Bevölkerungsschichtung; ~ **of a sentence** Satzkonstruktion; ~ **of society** Gesellschaftsstruktur; ~ **of trade unions** Gewerkschaftsstruktur;

~ **area** *(Br.)* interkommunaler Planungsraum; ~ **map** Strukturkarte, Struktur-, Flächennutzungsplan; ~ **plan** *(Br.)* Struktur-, Flächennutzungsplan; **agricultural** ~ **policy** Agrarstrukturpolitik.

struggle Kampf;

domestic ~**s** innenpolitische Machtkämpfe;

~ **for existence** Existenzkampf; ~ **for freedom (liberty)** Freiheitskampf; ~ **for life** Lebenskampf; ~ **with poverty** Kampf

gegen die Armut; ~ **for power** Machtkampf; ~ **for redistribution** Verteilungskampf; ~ **to survive** Überlebenskampf; ~ **of wills** auseinandergehende Bestrebungen;

~ *(v.)* **against difficulties** mit Schwierigkeiten zu kämpfen haben; ~ **for influence** Einfluß zu gewinnen suchen; ~ **again over a lot of ground** sich erneut über einen größeren Komplex von Sachfragen auseinandersetzen; ~ **for power** nach Macht streben; ~ **to** sich durchringen zu.

strumpet Hure.

stub Zigarettenstummel, *(check book, US)* Kontrollabschnitt, Talon, *(railroad, US)* kurze Nebenstrecke, *(statement of account)* [anhängendes] Bestätigungsformular;

~ *(v.)* **one's toe** sich die Finger verbrennen;

~ **card** perforierte Karte.

stubborn **resistance** hartnäckiger Widerstand; ~ **soil** schwer zu bearbeitender Boden.

stuck, to be *(car)* festsitzen;

to be ~**-up** *(fam.)* hochnäsig sein.

studded überhäuft;

~ **with jewels** juwelenbesetzt.

student Student, *(course)* Kursusteilnehmer, *(Oxford)* Stipendiat; **the** ~**s** Studentenschaft;

close ~ fleißiger Student; **elementary** ~ *(US)* Grundschüler; **exchange** ~ Austauschstudent; **fellow** ~ Kommilitone; **law** ~ Rechtsstudent; **full-time** ~ Ganztagsstudent;

~ **on full grant** [etwa] Student mit Baföghöchstsatz; ~ **in receipt of a grant from public funds** mit Mitteln des Bundesausbildungsgesetzes geförderter Student, Bafög-Student; ~ **of law** Rechtsgelehrter, -student;

to send a ~ **down** *(Br.)* Studenten vorübergehend relegieren;

~ **adviser** Studienberater; ~ **aid** Studienbeihilfe; ~ **body** Studentenschaft; ~ **council** Schülerrat; ~ **demonstration** Studentendemonstration; ~ **disturbances** Studentenunruhen; ~ **employee** Gastarbeiter; ~ **exchange** Studentenaustausch; ~ **expenses** Studienkosten; ~**-faculty ratio** Schüler-Lehrerverhältnisziffer; ~ **grant** Studienbeihilfe, Bafög; ~**'s hall of residence** Studentenwohnheim; ~ **hostel** Studentenheim; ~ **interpreter** *(Br.)* Attaché; ~ **life** Studentenleben; ~ **protest** Studentenprotest; ~ **riots (unrest)** Studentenunruhen; ~ **subscription** Studentenabonnement; ~ **violence** studentische Gewalttätigkeiten.

studentship Studentenzeit, *(Br.)* Studienbeihilfe, Stipendium.

studied bewandert, belesen, beschlagen.

studies, to continue one's sein Studium fortsetzen;

to fall behind in one's ~ in seinen Leistungen nachlassen; **to finish one's** ~ seine Studien beenden; **to resume one's** ~ sein Studium fortsetzen.

studio Studio, *(film, photo)* Aufnahmeraum, Atelier, *(television)* Fernsehstudio;

broadcasting ~ Senderaum; **sound-proof broadcasting** ~ schalldichtes Rundfunkstudio;

~ **audience** Statistenpublikum; ~ **facilities** Studioeinrichtungen; ~ **flat** Atelierwohnung; ~ **real estate** Studiogelände; ~ **research** *(film company)* Popularitätsumfrage; ~ **shot** Atelieraufnahme.

study Studie, sorgsame (wissenschaftliche) Untersuchung, *(learning)* Studieren, Lernen, *(room)* Arbeits-, Herren-, Studierzimmer, *(studying)* Studium, Studienfach, -zweig, -objekt;

brown ~ Gedankenverlorenheit; **comprehensive** ~ eingehendes Studium; **detailed** ~ gründliches Studium; **formal** ~ regelrechtes Studium; **market** ~ Marktanalyse; **preliminary** ~ Vorstudie; ~ **of foreign trade** Außenhandelsanalyse; ~ **of languages** Sprachstudium; ~ **in manners** Sittenroman; ~ **of planning** Planungsstudie; ~ **of productivity** Produktivitätsstudie;

~ *(v.)* lernen, studieren, Studien betreiben;

~ **for the bar** Rechtswissenschaft (Jura) studieren; ~ **economy** zu sparen versuchen; ~ **for an examination** sich auf ein Examen vorbereiten; ~ **only one's own interests** nur sein eigenes Interesse im Auge haben, nur auf seinen Vorteil bedacht sein; ~ **at one's leisure** in aller Ruhe prüfen; ~ **the relevant literature** Fachliteratur einsehen; ~ **a map** Karte lesen; ~ **one's part** seine Rolle auswendig lernen; ~ **for the teaching profession** sich auf den Lehrerberuf vorbereiten; ~ **the pros and cons** Für und Wider erwägen; ~ **and research** wissenschaftliche Forschungsarbeit betreiben; ~ **up** gründlich studieren;

to give one's time to ~ sich seinem Studium widmen; **to give all one's leisure time to** ~ sich in seiner Freizeit laufend weiterbilden; **to make a** ~ **of s. th.** etw. sorgfältig beobachten; **to make a** ~ **of a country's foreign trade** Außenhandel eines Landes untersuchen; **to pinch and spare for one's** ~ sich sein Studium vom Munde absparen;

~ commission Arbeits-, Studienausschuß; **~ grant** Studienbeihilfe, *(dt.)* Bafög; **~ group** Studiengruppe, Arbeitsausschuß, -gemeinschaft; **to have the ~ habits** Lerndisziplin haben; **~ hall** Arbeitszimmer, *(school)* Lesesaal; **~ hour** Übungsstunde; **~ leave** Bildungsurlaub; **~ panel** Untersuchungsausschuß; **~ reform** Bildungsreform; **~ resolution** Resolutionsentwurf; **~ tour** Studienreise.

stuff *(article)* Ware, *(cash, coll.)* Bargeld, *(journalism)* Manuskript, Artikel, *(material)* Material, *(narcotics)* Stoff, *(refuse)* Gerümpel, wertloses Zeug, Plunder, *(stolen goods)* Hehlerware, *(things, coll.)* Gepäck, eigene Sachen;
grandstand ~ *(sl.)* hochtrabendes Gerede; **household ~** Einrichtungsgegenstände; **strong ~** starker Tobak;
~ *(v.)* vollstopfen, *(electioneering, US sl.)* mit gefälschen Stimmzetteln füllen, *(thieves, sl.)* Hehlerware verkloppen;
~ one's belongings into a small bag seine Habseligkeiten in eine kleine Tasche stopfen; **~ a car with people** Auto überladen;
to be made of sterner ~ aus härterem Holz geschnitzt sein; **to be short of ~** *(fam.)* kein Geld haben; **to be sorry ~** ganz erbärmlich sein; **to have good ~ in one** das Zeug dafür haben; **to know one's ~** sich auskennen, Bescheid wissen, sein Metier beherrschen;
~ gown *(Br.)* Anwaltsrobe; **~ gownsman** jüngerer plädierender Anwalt.

stuffed überfüllt;
~ shirt *(US sl.)* aufgeblasene Null.

stuffer *(cheque, Br., sl.)* ungedeckter Scheck, *(advertising, US)* Reklame-, Werbebeilage, Beilagematerial, *(stolen goods, sl.)* Verkäufer von Hehlerware.

stuffing Polstermaterial, *(writers' cant)* Füllmaterial, Füllsel;
to knock the ~ out of s. o. jem. seine Aufgeblasenheit abgewöhnen.

stuffy verknöchert, verstaubt, spießig, *(book)* fade.

stultification Unzurechnungsfähigkeitserklärung.

stultify *(v.) (law)* für unzurechnungsfähig erklären.

stumble *(fig.)* Fehltritt, Schnitzer;
~ *(v.)* Bock schießen;
~ upon s. th. über etw. stolpern; **~ through an apology** Entschuldigung stottern; **~ at a straw** an allem Anstoß nehmen.

stumblebum *(sl.)* arbeitsloser Bettler.

stumbling block (stone) Stein des Anstoßes.

stumer *(cheque, Br., sl.)* ungedeckter Scheck, *(fabrication)* falsche Banknote.

stump *(politics, US)* Wahlpropaganda;
on the ~ *(coll.)* auf der Wahlreise; **up a ~** *(US sl.)* in der Klemme, in einer verzwickten Lage;
~ of a cigarette Zigarettenstummel; **~ of a tree** Baumstumpf;
~ *(v.) (coll.)* aus der Fassung bringen, *(electioneering)* Wahlreise unternehmen, Wahlrede halten;
~ through the country *(US)* als Wahlredner durchs Land ziehen; **~ it** *(sl.)* zu Fuß gehen; **~ up for one's son's debts** Geld für die Bezahlung der Schulden seines Sohnes aufbringen;
to buy timber on the ~ Holz auf dem Stamm kaufen; **to go on the ~** öffentliche Reden halten, politische Propagandareise unternehmen; **to stir one's ~s** *(coll.)* sich auf die Socken machen; **to be ~ed at a question** von einer Frage überrascht sein;
~ orator *(US)* Wahlredner; **~ oratory (speech)** *(US)* Wahlrede; **~ speaker** *(US)* Volks-, Wahlredner; **~ speaking** *(US)* Wahlreden, politische Propaganda.

stumpage *(US)* Holzpreis.

stumper *(US)* Wahl-, Propagandaredner, politischer Agitator.

stumpy *(Br., sl.)* Zaster, Moneten.

stunned | with one's good fortune von seinem Glück überwältigt; **~ by the news** von einer Nachricht wie gelähmt.

stunner Bombensache, Prachtexemplar.

stunt Glanz-, Bravourstück, *(advertising)* Reklameschlager, aufsehenerregender Trick, *(airplane)* Flugkunststück, *(mil.)* Unternehmen;
~s Kunstflug;
advertising ~s Reklamemätzchen; **good ~** gute Werbeidee; **publicity ~** Werbefeldzug;
~ *(v.)* **an airplane** Flugkunststücke vorführen; **~ the growth of a nation's power** Machtzuwachs einer Nation hemmen;
~ flying Kunstflug; **~ man** *(film, US)* Double [für gefährliche Szenen]; **~ pilot** Kunstflieger.

stunter Kunstflieger.

sturdy resistance heftiger Widerstand.

style Art, Stil, Typ, *(firm)* Firma, Firmenname, -bezeichnung, *(manner of life)* Lebensart, Stil, Manier, *(mode)* Mode, Zuschnitt, *(plant)* Fabrikationsname, Fabrikzeichen, *(print.)* Schriftstil, *(title)* Titel, Anrede, Name, Bezeichnung;

in ~ in gutem Stil; **in all sizes and ~s** in allen Größen und Ausführungen; **in bad ~** geschmacklos; **in a great ~** in großem Zuschnitt; **in the ~ of** in der Manier von; **under the ~ of** unter der Firma (dem Namen) von;
business (commercial) ~ Geschäftsstil; **clever ~** gewandter Stil; **fast-selling ~** schnell verkäuflicher Modeartikel; **flowery ~** blumenreiche Sprache; **juridical ~** Kanzleistil; **latest ~** neueste Mode; **new ~** Neuschöpfung; **stilted ~** geschraubter Stil; **terse ~** knapper Stil;
~ of address Anredeform; **editorial ~ of advertisement** redaktionell gestaltete Anzeige; **~ of architecture** Baustil; **~ of a business firm** Firmenname; **~ of a court of justice** Gerichtsverfahren; **~ of living** Lebensstil; **open ~ of punctuation** moderne Interpunktionszeichenverwendung;
~ *(v.)* anreden, [be]nennen, betiteln, bezeichnen, *(US, boost)* anpreisen, dem Käufer schmackhaft machen, *(fashion)* nach der neuesten Mode entwerfen, Mode kreieren;
~ a new car neues Auto herausbringen;
to be back in ~ wieder in Mode sein; **to do things in ~** die Dinge stilvoll zu erledigen wissen; **to drive up in ~** in einem schicken Auto vorfahren; **to go under the ~ of** Firmennamen tragen (führen); **to have no ~** keine Ausdruckskraft haben; **to have neither ~ nor the stomach for political strifes** weder Zuschnitt noch die Nerven für politische Auseinandersetzungen haben; **to live in great ~** auf großem Fuße leben; **to live in European ~** wie ein Europäer leben; **to live in a ~ beyond one's means** über seine Verhältnisse leben; **to make in three ~s** in drei Ausfertigungen liefern; **to put on ~** vornehm tun; **to trade under the ~** firmieren unter; **to write in conversational ~** im Unterhaltungston schreiben;
~ change Stilveränderung, Modewechsel; **~ name** Fabrikations-, Geschäftsname; **~ show** Modeschau; **~ trend** Modewechsel.

stylebook Handbuch der Stilistik.

styler *(US)* Modezeichner.

styling industrielle Formgebung, *(car)* Karosseriebau, *(goods, US)* Warenanpreisung.

stylish modisch, fesch, flott.

stylus Kopierstift, *(pickup)* Saphirstift.

stymie *(v.) (fig.)* lahmlegen.

suability *(US)* Einklag-, Prozeßfähigkeit;
~ provision *(US)* Prozeßklausel.

suable einklagbar, *(of persons)* prozeßfähig.

suasion Überredung;
moral ~ gütliches Zureden.

sub *(sl.)* Subalterner;
~ *(v.)* vor der Veröffentlichung durchsehen;
~ finem am Ende des Kapitals; **~ judice** *(law case)* noch anhängig, noch nicht entschieden, rechtshängig; **~ rosa** *(lat.)* im Vertrauen, unter der Hand; **~ silentio** vertraulich; **~ voce** *(dictionary)* unter dem angegebenen Wort.

subaccount Unterkonto.

subagency Untervertretung, Spezialagentur, *(power of attorney)* Untervollmacht.

subagent Untervertreter, -bevollmächtigter, *(forwarding business)* Zwischenspediteur.

subagreement Nebenabrede.

subaltern Untergebener;
~ *(a.)* untergeordnet, unselbständig, subaltern.

subarea Gebietseinheit.

subassembly Teilmontage.

subassociation Unter-, Fachverband.

subaudition Lesen zwischen den Zeilen.

subbasement Kellergeschoß.

subbranch *(office)* Zweigstelle, *(organization)* Fachgruppe.

subcase *(railway)* Unterbau.

subcategory Unterabteilung.

subclaim Unteranspruch.

subclass *(patent)* Unterklasse.

subclause Unterabschnitt, Absatz.

subcommittee Unterausschuß.

subcompact Kleinwagen.

subcompany *(US)* Tochtergesellschaft.

subconsciously, to feel im Unterbewußtsein ahnen.

subcontinent Subkontinent.

subcontract Unter-, Nebenvertrag, Vertrag mit einem Zulieferanten (Subunternehmer), Zulieferungsvertrag;
~ *(v.)* Nebenvertrag abschließen, als Zulieferer übernehmen, an einen Subunternehmer vergeben;
~ out Zulieferungsauftrag übernehmen;
~ work Unterlieferantentätigkeit.

subcontracting, to carry out ~ work Arbeiten als Zulieferant ausführen.

subcontractor Zulieferant, Unterlieferant, Subunternehmer.

subdelegate Unterdelegierter.

subdelegation Weiterübertragung.

subdirector stellvertretender Direktor.

subdistrict Unterbezirk.

subdivide *(v.)* auf-, untergliedern, *(real estate, US)* parzellieren; ~ **shares** Aktien stückeln.

subdivision Unterabteilung, *(breakdown)* Aufschlüsselung, Gliederung, *(ledger)* Unterspalte, *(real estate, US)* Parzellierung; **political** ~ Gebietskörperschaft; ~ **of land** *(US)* Aufteilung von Grundstücken in Bauplätze; ~ **of shares** Aktienstückelung.

subduct *(v.)* *(caveat, Br.)* zurückziehen.

subdue *(v.)* *(land)* kultivieren, urbar machen; ~ **wild tribes** wilde Stämme unterwerfen.

subedit *(v.)* vor Veröffentlichung durchsehen.

subedition Nebenausgabe.

subeditor Hilfsredakteur, *(book)* Mitherausgeber.

subfluvial cable Unterwasserkabel.

subfolder Beiakte.

subgroup Untergruppe.

subheading Unterüberschrift, -titel, *(book)* Unterabteilung.

subitem *(agreement)* Nummer, Ziffer.

subjacent unterliegend.

subject [Gesprächs]thema, Gesprächsgegenstand, -stoff, *(constitutional law)* Untertan, Landes-, Staatsangehöriger, *(discipline)* Lehrgegenstand, Fachgebiet, *(province)* Sachgebiet, *(Scot. law)* Vertragsgegenstand; ~**s** *(Scot.)* Grundbesitz, Vermögen; **allied** ~ verwandtes Gebiet; **British [-born]** ~ britischer Untertan durch Geburt; **compulsory** ~ Pflichtfach; **foreign** ~ Ausländer; **hysterical** ~ hysterische Person; **legal** ~ Rechtssubjekt; **natural-born** ~ Staatsangehöriger kraft Geburt; ~**s prescribed** vorgesehene Themen; **British** ~**s resident abroad** Britische Staatsangehörige mit Auslandswohnsitz; ~ **of the action** Prozeßgegenstand; **proper** ~ **for action** geeigneter Klagegrund; ~ **to Britain** britischer Untertan; ~**s to come** in Vorbereitung befindliche Themen; ~ **of complaint** Beschwerdegegenstand, -punkt; **interesting** ~ **of conversation** interessantes Gesprächsthema; ~ **under debate** Gegenstand der Diskussion, Diskussionsgegenstand; ~ **of deliberation** Beratungsgegenstand; ~ **for an essay** Aufsatzthema; ~ **under investigation** untersuchter Gegenstand; ~ **of international law** Völkerrechtssubjekt; ~ **of litigation** Prozeßgegenstand; ~ **of our negotiations** Gegenstand unserer Verhandlungen; ~ **of records** Aktenvorgang; ~ **of rights and duties** Träger von Rechten und Pflichten; ~ **of sale** Verkaufsobjekt; ~ **of a tax (for taxation)** Steuerträger, Steuersubjekt; ~ *(a.) (state)* unselbständig; ~ **to** vorbehaltlich, unterworfen, in Abhängigkeit von; ~ **to alterations** Änderungen vorbehalten; ~ **to s. one's approval** genehmigungspflichtig; ~ **to authorization** genehmigungspflichtig; ~ **to average** *(insurance)* proportionaler Schadensbeteiligung bei Unterversicherung unterworfen; ~ **to call** *(deposits)* täglich kündbar; ~ **to change without notice** freibleibend; ~ **to commission** provisionspflichtig; ~ **to confirmation** gültig nur bei Bestätigung; ~ **to s. one's consent** genehmigungspflichtig; ~ **to contract** im Fall des Vertragsabschlusses; ~ **to control** weisungsgebunden; ~ **to the control of excise** der Zollkontrolle unterliegend; ~ **to correction** Irrtum vorbehalten, ohne Gewähr; ~ **to death duties** erbschaftssteuerpflichtig; ~ **to denunciation** *(international law)* kündbar; ~ **to the deposit of collateral security consisting of first stocks** *(US)* gegen Hinterlegung erstklassiger Aktien; ~ **to a disciplinary action** einem Diziplinarverfahren unterworfen; ~ **to duty** zollpflichtig; ~ **to execution** pfändbar, vollstreckbar, der Zwangsvollstreckung unterliegend; ~ **to a fee** gebührenpflichtig; ~ **as hereafter provided** gemäß nachstehenden Bestimmungen; ~ **to inspection** Besichtigung vorbehalten; ~ **to licence** genehmigungspflichtig, *(trade)* gewerbesteuerpflichtig; ~ **to modification** Änderungen vorbehalten; ~ **to notice** kündbar; ~ **to your order** entsprechend Ihrem Auftrag; ~ **to price fluctuations** Preisschwankungen unterliegend; ~ **to ratification** vorbehaltlich nachträglicher Genehmigung; ~ **to redemption** tilgbar; ~ **to rent** mietzinspflichtig; ~ **to reservation** unter Vorbehalt; ~ **to revision** verbesserungsfähig, vorbehaltlich von Änderungen; ~ **to prior sale** Zwischenverkauf vorbehalten; ~ **to shipment** falls diese Ware versandt wird; ~ **to stamp duty** stempelsteuerpflichtig; ~ **to tax[ation]** steuerpflichtig; ~ **to the terms of the contract**

vorbehaltlich der Vertragsbestimmungen; ~ **to a term of two weeks** unter Einhaltung einer vierzehntägigen Frist; ~ **to** in Abhängigkeit von; ~ **to war clause** der Kriegsrisikoklausel unterworfen;

~ *(v.)* unterwerfen, -jochen, dienstbar (abhängig) machen; **to be ~ to a convention** unter ein Abkommen fallen; ~ **o. s. to criticism** sich der Kritik aussetzen; ~ **s. o. to an examination** j. einer Prüfung unterziehen; **to be a ~ of law** Rechtspersönlichkeit haben; ~ **s. o. to torture** j. der Folter unterwerfen; ~ **to tax** besteuern; ~ **s. o. to a test** j. prüfen, j. einem Test unterziehen; **to be ~ to an appeal** einem Rechtsmittel unterliegen; **to be ~ to confirmation** zustimmungsbedürftig sein; **to be ~ to delay** *(train)* Verzögerungen unterworfen sein; **to be ~ to 4% discount** 4% Rabatt genießen; **to be the ~ of a discussion** Gegenstand einer Aussprache sein; **to be ~ to jurisdiction** der Gerichtsbarkeit unterworfen sein; **to be a ~ of law** Rechtspersönlichkeit haben; **to be ~ to the law of the land** sich nach den Landesgesetzen richten müssen; **to be ~ to modifications** noch Veränderungen unterworfen sein; **to be on the ~ of money** vom Geld sprechen; **to be ~ to ratification** erst nach Ratifizierung gültig sein; **to be well up in one's ~** in seinem Fach gut Bescheid wissen; **to be held ~** abhängig sein; **to broach a ~** Thema anschneiden; **to change the ~** Gesprächsstoff wechseln; **to deviate from the ~** sich weit vom Thema entfernen; **to have ceased to be the ~ of trust** nicht mehr zum Treuhandvermögen gehören; **to keep one ~ distinct from another** Themata abgrenzen; **to master a ~** Angelegenheit (seinen Stoff) voll beherrschen; **to raise a ~** Thema zur Sprache bringen, Frage erörtern; **to speak at some length about (on) a ~** ausführlich über etw. berichten; **to treat a ~ cursorily** Thema flüchtig behandeln; **to waive the ~** Thema wechseln;

~ **area** Sachgebiet, ~ **catalog(ue)** systematischer Katalog, Sach-, Schlagwörterkatalog; ~ **dictionary** Fachwörterbuch; ~ **entry** *(catalog(ue))* Stichworteintragung; ~ **examination** Fachprüfung; ~ **filing** Ablage nach Sachgebieten; ~ **heading** Unterteilung in Sachgebiete, Sachgebietsaufteilung, -rubrik, Rubrik in einem Sachregister; ~ **index** Sachregister, -index, -katalog; ~ **label** Bezeichnung des Sachgebiets, Sachgebietsbezeichnung.

subject matter Stoff, behandelter Gegenstand, [Verhandlungs]-gegenstand, *(performance)* Leistungsgegenstand; ~ **of the action** Streitgegenstand; ~ **of the agency** Gegenstand des Vertretungsverhältnisses; ~ **of the agreement** Vertragsgegenstand; ~ **of the complaint** Beschwerdegegenstand; ~ **insured** *(of insurance)* versicherter Gegenstand, Gegenstand der Versicherung, Versicherungsgegenstand; ~ **of invention** Gegenstand der Erfindung, Erfindungsgegenstand; ~ **of patent** patentfähiger Gegenstand; ~ **of sale** Verkaufsgegenstand.

subject|province abhängige Provinz; ~ **reference** Sachverweis; ~ **section** *(school)* Fachgruppe.

subjection Unterwerfung, -ordnung; ~ **of the rebels** Niederwerfung der Aufständischen; **to be in ~ to s. o.** von jem. abhängig sein; **to live in a state of ~** in einem völligen Abhängigkeitsverhältnis existieren.

subjective subjektiv, unsachlich; ~ **judgment** subjektives Urteil; ~ **value** subjektiver Wert.

subjoin *(v.)* beifügen; ~ **to the files** zu den Akten legen.

subjoined bei-, inliegend, beigefügt, bei-, eingeschlossen, in der Anlage.

subjoinder Anhang.

subjugate *(v.)* unterjochen, -werfen.

subjugation Unterwerfung.

subjunction Beilage.

sublessee Untermieter, -pächter.

sublease Unterpacht, -miete, -vermietung; ~ *(v.)* weiterverpachten, untervermieten; ~ **part of its production** Produktionsaufträge teilweise bei Fremdbetrieben unterbringen.

sublessor Untervermieter.

sublet *(v.)* weiter-, untervermieten; **to write up a ~** Untermieter vermitteln.

sublettee Untermieter.

subletter Untervermieter.

subletting Untervermieten.

sublibrarian Unterbibliothekar, bibliothekarischer Helfer.

sublicence Unterlizenz.

sublicensee Unterlizenznehmer.

sublicenser, sublicensor Unterlizenzgeber.

subliminal|advertising unterschwellige Werbung; ~ **perception** unterschwellige Wahrnehmung.

subliterature Vervielfältigungen für den internen Gebrauch.

submachine gun Maschinenpistole.

submanager stellvertretender Direktor.

submarginal *(land)* nicht mehr rentabel, unrentabel.

submarine Unterseeboot, U-Boot;
missile ~ Raketen-U-Boot; **nuclear** ~ Atom-U-Boot;
~ *(a.)* unterseeisch;
~ **base** U-Boot-Stützpunkt; ~ **cable** Tief-, Seekabel; ~ **chaser** U-Bootjäger; ~ **force** U-Bootstreitmacht; ~**s' missiles** von U-Booten abgefeuerte Raketen; ~ **pen** Unterseebootbunker; ~ **tracking system** U-Bootortungssystem; ~ **warfare** U-Bootkriegsführung.

submaster *(Br.)* stellvertretender Schulleiter.

submerge *(v.)* versenken, *(submarine)* tauchen.

submerged verelendet, *(mine)* ersoffen.

submergence Überflutung;
~ **rescue ship** U-Bootrettungsschiff.

submersible tauchfähig.

submersion Versenkung.

subminimum *(a.)* unter dem Minimum;
~ **rate** untertariflicher Lohn.

submission *(acceptance of power)* Unterwerfung, *(act of submitting)* Eingabe, Vorlage, *(to arbitration)* freiwillige Unterwerfung unter ein Schiedsgericht, Schiedsgerichtsvereinbarung, *(bidding)* Submission, *(theory)* Rechtstheorie;
for ~ **to** zur Vorlage bei; **on** ~ bei Einreichung; **with all due** ~ mit allem gebührenden Respekt;
alternative ~ Hilfsvorbringen;
~ **of account** Rechnungsvorlage; ~ **on approval** Ansichtssendung; ~ **to arbitration** schriftliche Schiedsgerichtsvereinbarung; ~ **of evidence** Vorlage von Beweisen, Beweisantritt; ~ **of the facts** Tatsachenvortrag; ~ **of an offer** Vorlage einer Offerte; ~ **of one's passport** Paßvorlage; ~ **of proof of identity** Identitätsnachweis; ~ **of a question to arbitration** Unterbreitung einer Frage zur schiedsrichterlichen Entscheidung; ~ **of samples** Vorlage von Mustern;
to be starved into ~ durch Aushungerung zur Unterwerfung gebracht werden; **to make** ~**s to the law** Rechtsschlüsse ziehen; **to make a** ~ **to the President** sich dem Präsidenten unterwerfen; ~ **bond** Schiedsgerichtsverpflichtung, -klausel; ~ **date** Submissionstermin.

submit *(v.)* *(counsel)* vortragen, Ansicht vertreten, *(commit to discretion)* anheimstellen, *(present)* vorlegen, einreichen, unterbreiten, *(surrender)* sich unterwerfen;
~ **an application** Gesuch einreichen; ~ **for s. one's approval** jem. zur Genehmigung vorlegen; ~ **to arbitration** Schiedsgericht anrufen; ~ **an article to a newspaper** Zeitungsartikel einsenden; ~ **the case to the court** Fall dem Gericht vortragen; ~ **to conditions** auf Bedingungen eingehen, sich Bedingungen unterwerfen; ~ **for decision** zur Entscheidung vorlegen; ~ **to a decision** sich mit einer Entscheidung abfinden; ~ **a difference to the arbitrator** Streitfall einem Schiedsrichter unterbreiten; ~ **o. s. to discipline** sich disziplinieren; ~ **to the enemy** sich dem Feind ergeben; ~ **evidence** Beweis vorbringen; ~ **goods to a careful examination** Waren einer genauen Untersuchung unterwerfen; ~ **o. s. to the law** sich dem Gesetz unterwerfen; ~ **an offer** Angebot abgeben; ~ **a plan** Plan vorlegen; ~ **a plan to the city council** um Baugenehmigung nachsuchen; ~ **proof of identity** Identitätsnachweis führen; ~ **a proposal** Vorschlag unterbreiten; ~ **a proposition** Gesichtspunkte vortragen; ~ **a question to the court** Frage dem Gericht vorlegen; ~ **a railway to traffic** Eisenbahnlinie dem Verkehr übergeben; ~ **a report** Bericht vorlegen; ~ **one's resignation** seine Entlassung einreichen; ~ **to public sale** zur Versteigerung bringen; ~ **to the separation of one's family** sich mit der Trennung von seiner Familie abfinden; ~ **for signature** zur Unterschrift vorlegen; ~ **a statement of one's affairs** Liquidationsbilanz aufstellen (vorlegen); ~ **a tender** Offerte unterbreiten.

submittal Sach- und Rechtsvortrag.

submitter Antragsteller.

submortgage Unterverpfändung, nachrangige Hypothek;
~ *(v.)* unterverpfänden, nachrangiges Pfandrecht (nachrangige Hypothek) bestellen.

subnormal geistig minderwertig.

suboffice Zweig-, Außenstelle, *(bank)* Depositenkasse, Nebenstelle, *(post office)* Posthilfsstelle.

suboptimal nicht optimal.

subordinate Untergeordnetes, Zweitrangiges, *(person)* Untergebener;
managerial ~ unterstellte Führungskraft;
~ *(v.)* nach-, unterordnen, zurückstellen;
~ **o. s.** sich unterordnen;

~ *(a.)* nach-, untergeordnet, *(of inferior importance)* nebensächlich, zweitrangig;
~ **bodies** untergeordnete Stellen; ~ **clause** Nebenbedingung; ~ **committee** nachgeordneter Ausschuß; ~ **interests** untergeordnete Interessen; ~ **legislation** delegierte Gesetzgebung; ~ **officer** mittlerer Beamter; ~ **partner** *(Br.)* nicht persönlich haftender Gesellschafter; ~ **position** untergeordnete Stellung; ~ **question** nebengeordnete Frage.

subordinated, to be unterstellt sein; **to be** ~ **to a claim of the Inland Revenue** einem Einkommensteuerrückstand nachgeordnet sein;
~ **debt** nachrangige Schuld, im Range nachgehende Forderung; ~ **offer** verstecktes Angebot.

subordination Unterstellung, -ordnung;
~ **to the law** Bindung an das Gesetz.

suborn *(v.)* zur falschen Aussage verleiten;
~ **s. o. to commit perjury** j. zum Meineid anstiften; ~ **a witness** Zeugen bestechen.

subornation Anstiftung, Verleitung;
~ **of perjury** Verleitung (Anstiftung) zum Meineid; ~ **of witness** Zeugenbestechung.

suborner of perjury Anstifter zum Meineid.

subparagraph Unterabschnitt, -absatz.

subpart *(organization, US)* Unterabteilung.

subpartnership Unterbeteiligung.

subpoena Ladung unter Strafandrohung, Zwangsvorladung;
~ *(v.)* **s. o. to appear** j. unter Strafandrohung vorladen; ~ **s. o. as a witness** j. als Zeugen vorladen; ~ **a company's record on quality control** Fabrik auf Vorlage ihrer Unterlagen über Qualitätskontrollen verklagen;
to hand out ~**s** Vorladungen unter Strafandrohung ergehen lassen; **to serve a** ~ Vorladung zustellen;
to grant ~ **powers** Vorladungsvollmachten einräumen.

subpurchaser Käufer aus zweiter Hand, mittelbarer Käufer.

subregion Teilgebiet, -region.

subreptilious erschlichen.

subreption Erschleichung.

subrogate | *(v.)* **s. o. on the place of another** j. an eines anderen Stelle setzen; ~ **s. o. to the rights of another** auf j. die Rechte eines anderen übertragen.

subrogation Sonderrechtsnachfolge, Rechtsübertragung, Gläubigerwechsel, *(law of insurance)* Rechtsübergang auf den Versicherer;
convential ~ vertraglich vereinbarte Rechtsnachfolge, vereinbarte (gewillkürte) Sonderrechtsnachfolge; **legal** ~ gesetzlicher Forderungsübergang, Rechtsübergang kraft Gesetzes;
~ **arising out of contract** gewillkürte Sonderrechtsnachfolge; ~ **of a creditor** Gläubigerauswechslung; ~ **of rights** Rechtsübertragung; ~ **arising from statute** gesetzlicher Rechtsübergang; ~ **act** Rechtseintritt; ~ **assignment** Abtretungserklärung, Abtretung des Ersatzanspruches; ~ **clause** Rechtsnachfolge-, Rechtsübergangsklausel; ~ **rights** Subrogations-, Abtretungsrechte.

subrogee Sonderrechtsnachfolger.

subsample *(market research)* Teilstichprobe.

subscribe *(v.)* *(contribute)* beitragen, -steuern, *(loan, shares)* zeichnen, *(membership, US)* Mitgliedsbeitrag zahlen, *(newspaper)* abonnieren, vorbestellen, subskribieren, halten, *(raise by fees)* durch Beiträge aufbringen, *(sign)* unterzeichnen;
~ **absolutely** *(undertaker)* sich zur festen Übernahme verpflichten; ~ **an affidavit** eidesstattliche Erklärung abgeben; ~ **an amount** Geldsumme aussetzen; ~ **for a book** Buch im Subkriptionswege erwerben; ~ **to charity** zu einer mildtätigen Stiftung beitragen; ~ **liberally to charities** auf dem Wohltätigkeitsgebiet beispielgebend sein; ~ **conditionally** sich nur zur Übernahme nicht plazierter Aktien verpflichten; ~ **to a course of lectures** Vorlesung belegen; ~ **to a club** einem Klub beitreten; ~ **100 dollars** 100 Dollar stiften; ~ **20 dollars to a club** *(US)* Mitgliedsbeitrag von 20 Dollar zahlen; ~ **for** vorausbestellen; ~ **to an issue** auf eine Ausgabe zeichnen; ~ **to a loan** Anleihe zeichnen; ~ **a loan in excess** Anleihe überzeichnen; ~ **the memorandum** Aktien unmittelbar bei der Gesellschaft beziehen; ~ **one's name to a document** Urkunde unterfertigen; ~ **one's name to a petition** seinen Namen auf eine Bittschrift setzen; ~ **a false name** mit einem falschen Namen unterschreiben; ~ **to an opinion** Meinung teilen; ~ **to a proposal** Vorschlag annehmen; ~ **for a publication** Veröffentlichung im voraus bestellen; ~ **to a relief fund** für einen Unterstützungsfonds Geld stiften; ~ **to a resolution** sich einer Entschließung anschließen; ~ **for five shares in a company** fünf Gesellschaftsanteile übernehmen;

to (for) new shares (stock, *US*) neue (junge) Aktien zeichnen; ~ a sum to charity Betrag für wohltätige Zwecke zur Verfügung stellen; ~ to s. one's views sich jds. Ansichten anschließen.

subscribed gezeichnet;
amount ~ Zeichnungsbetrag; fully ~ voll gezeichnet; important sums ~ bedeutende Zeichnungen;
to be ~ several times mehrfach überzeichnet sein;
~ capital [stock] ausstehende Einlagen auf das Grundkapital, Nominalkapital; ~ demand tariff *(el.)* gemischter Stromtarif; ~ risk *(insurance)* übernommene Gefahr.

subscriber *(furtherer)* Befürworter, Förderer, *(newspaper)* Abonnement, Bezieher, Subskribent, *(loan)* Zeichner, *(signer)* Unterzeichner, Signatar, *(tel.)* Fernsprechteilnehmer;
individual ~ *(health insurance)* Einzelmitglied; intending ~ Abonnementsreflektant; loan ~ Anleihezeichner; original ~ Ersterwerber, Stammaktionär; paid ~ Abonnent der mindestens 50% bezahlt hat; telephone ~ Fernsprechteilnehmer;
~ to charity Spender; ~ to a document Signatar, Unterschriftsleistender; ~ to a loan Zeichner einer Anleihe, Anleihezeichner; ~ to the memorandum Erstbezieher von Aktien; ~ to a newspaper Zeitungsabonnent; ~ to a periodical Zeitschriftenabonnent; ~ for shares (stocks, *US*) Aktienzeichner;
to enrol(l) as ~ sich in eine Subskriptionsliste eintragen;
~ analysis Abonnentenanalyse; international ~ dialling *(Br.)* internationaler Selbstwählverkehr; ~'s extension station Nebenanschluß; ~ firm abonnierende Firma; ~ goodwill Abonnentenkreis; ~s' insurance Abonnentenversicherung; ~s' ledger Zeichnungsbuch, -liste, Aktionärsbuch; ~'s line Anschlußleitung, Telefon-, Fernsprechanschluß; ~'s main station Telefonzentrale; ~'s meter Gebührenzähler; ~'s number Teilnehmernummer; ~ research Abonnentenanalyse; ~'s set fest installierter Telefonapparat; ~'s ticket Abonnements-, Dauerkarte; ~ trunk dialling *(Br.)* Selbstwählfernverkehr.

subscribing | the memorandum Erstbezug von Aktien;
to give up ~ Abonnement abbestellen;
~ member förderndes Mitglied; ~ witness Urkundenzeuge.

subscription *(amount subscribed)* Subskriptionssumme, gezeichneter Betrag, Zeichnungsbetrag, *(contribution)* Beitrag, Spende, Gebühr, *(for shares)* [Anteils]zeichnung, *(member)* Mitgliedsbeitrag, *(newspaper)* Bezug, Abonnement, Subskription, *(ordering in advance)* Vor[aus]bestellung, *(price)* Bezugs-, Abonnentenpreis, *(signature)* Unterzeichnung, -schrift;
by ~ im Abonnement; by public ~ im Wege einer öffentlichen Sammlung; open for ~ zur Zeichnung aufgelegt;
annual ~ jährlicher Beitrag, Jahresabonnement, -beitrag; capital-stock ~ Zeichnung von Kapitalanteilen; charitable ~ Spende für wohltätige Zwecke; club ~ Mitglieds-, Klubbeitrag; deductible ~ steuerabzugsfähiger Beitrag; initial ~ Erstzeichnung; lapsed ~ abgelaufenes Abonnement; life ~ einmaliger Beitrag auf Lebenszeit; minimum ~ Mindestzeichnung [einer Wertpapieremission]; political ~ Beiträge für politische Zwecke, politische Spende; popular ~ öffentliche Sammlung; public ~ Freizeichnung; quarterly ~ Vierteljahresbezug, -abonnement; ~ receivables *(US)* ausstehende Zeichnungsbeträge; subsequent ~ Nachzeichnung; total ~ Gesamteinlage; yearly ~ Jahresbeitrag;
~s to be paid in advance im voraus zu bezahlende Abonnements; ~ in cash Barzeichnung; ~ to charity wohltätige Spende; ~ to a club Vereinsbeitrag; ~ by conversion of securities Bezugsrecht bei Anleiheumwandlung; ~ to a document Namensunterschrift; ~ in excess *(loan)* Anleiheüberzeichnung; ~ for (to, *Br.*) a loan Anleihezeichnung; ~s sold by mail Postbezieher; ~ to a newspaper Zeitungsabonnement; ~s to a political party für eine politische Partei aufgewendete Beträge, Spenden für eine politische Partei, direkte Parteizuwendungen; ~ to shares *(Br.)* (stocks, *US*) Aktienzeichnung; ~ for new shares *(Br.)* Bezug junger Aktien; ~s to professional societies Beiträge für Berufsverbände; ~ to a trade association Verbandsbeitrag; ~ to a trade union Gewerkschaftsbeitrag;
to be offered (open) for ~ zur Zeichnung aufliegen; to discontinue ~ to a paper Zeitung[sabonnement] abbestellen; to drop one's ~ sein Abonnement aufgeben (kündigen); to enter a ~ to abonnieren auf; to erect a monument by public ~ Denkmalserrichtung im Wege einer öffentlichen Sammlung finanzieren; to finance by private ~s durch Spenden finanzieren; to get up a ~ Sammlung ins Leben rufen; to invite ~s for a loan Anleihe [zur Zeichnung] auflegen; to invite ~ for shares *(Br.)* (stocks, *US*) Aktien zur Zeichnung auflegen; to issue for public ~ zur öffentlichen Zeichnung auflegen; to offer a loan for ~ Anleihe zur Zeichnung auflegen; to pay a ~ Beitrag zu einer Sammlung leisten; to pay one's ~ seinen Beitrag bezahlen; to raise the ~

Beitrag erhöhen, Beitragserhöhung vornehmen; to renew a ~ Abonnement erneuern; to solicit ~s Abonnementswerbung betreiben, Abonnenten werben; to stop one's ~ sein Abonnement abbestellen; to take out a ~ to (for, *US*) a newspaper Zeitung abonnieren (bestellen); to take out a year's ~ Jahresabonnement nehmen; to take out a ~ to a paper in favo(u)r of s. o. Patenschaftsabonnement für j. übernehmen; to withdraw one's ~ Abonnement aufgeben (abbestellen);
~ agent *(US)* Abonnentenwerber, *(bank)* Annahmestelle; ~ blank *(US)* Subskriptionsvordruck, Zeichnungsformular; ~ book Subskriptionsbuch, Zeichnungsliste; ~ charge Subskriptionsgebühr; ~ check *(US)* (cheque, *Br.*) Subskriptionsscheck; ~ concert Wohltätigkeitskonzert; ~ contract Zeichnungs-, Subskriptionsvertrag; ~ copy Abonnementsexemplar; ~ costs Bezugsgebühren; ~ department Abonnentenabteilung; ~ edition Subskriptionsausgabe; ~ fee Abonnements-, Subskriptionspreis, Bezugs-, Abonnementsgebühr; ~ form Zeichnungs-, Subskriptions-, Abonnementsformular, *(order form)* Bestellschein; ~ income Beitragseinnahmen; ~ ledger *(US)* Aktienzeichnungsbuch; ~ letter Abonnentenbrief; ~ level Zeichnungsergebnis; ~ library Leihbibliothek; ~ list *(newspaper)* Subskribenten-, Subskriptionsliste, Zeichnungsliste, *(shares)* Zeichnungsbogen; to close a ~ list Aktienzeichnung [ab]schließen; to open a ~ list Subskriptionsliste auflegen; ~ method Subskriptionsverfahren; ~ money Bezugspreis, *(loan)* Zeichnungsbetrag; ~ offer Zeichnungsangebot, Subskriptionsaufforderung; ~ order Subskriptions-, Abonnementsauftrag, Bestellung; ~ order form Bestellformular; ~ period Bezugsdauer, *(shares)* Zeichnungsfrist; ~ price Subskriptions-, Abonnements-, Bezugspreis; ~ privilege *(US)* Options-, Bezugsrecht, Zeichnungsberechtigung; ~ quota Beitragsanteil, *(stock exchange)* Übernahmebetrag; ~ rate Abonnements-, Bezugspreis, Tarif, *(loans)* Zeichnungskurs; ~ rate by surface mail normaler Drucksachenbezugspreis; ~ receivables *(US)* ausstehende Zeichnungsbeträge; ~ receipt Zeichnungsbescheinigung; ~ records Zeichnungsunterlagen; ~ renewal Abonnementserneuerung; ~ rental *(Br. tel.)* Grundgebühr; ~ reservation Voraussubskription; ~ right *(shares)* Bezugs-, Optionsrecht; ~ sale Abonnementsverkauf; ~ service Subskriptionsdienst; ~ share Subskriptionsanteil; ~ shares (building society) auf Raten gekaufte Aktien; ~ solicitation Subskriptionsangebot; ~ stamp Beitragsmarke; ~ ticket Abonnement[skarte]; ~ tickets not available Vorbestellungen nicht erhältlich; ~ warrant *(US)* Bezugsrecht, Subskriptionsschein, Optionsschein.

subscriptionist *(US)* Abonnentenwerber.
subscriptive im Subskriptionswege.
subsection Unterabschnitt, Absatz, Ziffer.
subsecurity Nebensicherheit.
subsequency Folgeerscheinung.
subsequent [nach]folgend, nachher, später, nachträglich;
~ additions *(balance sheet)* Zugänge; ~ applicant *(patent law)* späterer Anmelder; ~ assessment Nachveranlagung; ~ charges nachträglich entstandene Kosten; ~ claims spätere (nachträgliche) Ansprüche; ~ clause Zusatzartikel; ~ condition auflösende Bedingung; ~ creditor nachrangiger Gläubiger; ~ delivery Nachlieferung; ~ endorser späterer Girant, Nach-, Hintermann; ~ entry *(bookkeeping)* Nachtragsbuchung; ~ events nachfolgende Ereignisse; ~ holder nachfolgender Inhaber, späterer Besitzer; ~ impossibility nachträgliche Unmöglichkeit; ~ indorser Nachmann, Hintermann; ~ insurance Nachversicherung; ~ levy of duties Nacherhebung von Zöllen; ~ mortgage nachrangiges Pfandrecht, im Range nachfolgende (nachrangige) Hypothek; ~ order Nachbestellung; to give a ~ order nachbestellen; ~ owner nachfolgender Besitzer; to make a ~ order nachbestellen; ~ patent später angemeldetes Patent; ~ payment Nachzahlung, -schuß; ~ policy Nachtragspolice; ~ ratification nachfolgende Ratifizierung; ~ subscription Nachzeichnung von Aktien.

subservient unterwürfig.
subside *(v.)* nachlasssen, abflauen, *(ship)* absacken.
subsidence Bodensenkung, *(fig.)* Nachlassen, Abflauen, *(mining)* Grubensenkung.
subsidiary Konzern-, Tochtergesellschaft, Ableger, Filiale, *(assistant)* Gehilfe, Stütze;
domestic ~ inländische Tochtergesellschaft; foreign ~ ausländische Tochtergesellschaft, Auslandstochter; loss-making ~ Verlusttochter; major ~ Hauptniederlassung; majority-owned ~ durch Mehrheitsbesitz kontrollierte Tochtergesellschaft; operating ~ Betriebsgesellschaft; partly-owned ~ Kommandite; wholly-owned ~ hundertprozentige Tochtergesellschaft;

to own a ~ outright Tochtergesellschaft hundertprozentig besitzen;

~ (a.) subsidiär, untergeordnet, ergänzend;

~ account Hilfs-, Nebenkonto; **~ activity** Nebentätigkeit; **~ agreement** Nebenabkommen, -abrede; **~ bodies** nachgeordnete Stellen; **~ coin** *(US)* Scheidemünze; **~ coins** Hilfsgeld; **~ coinage** *(US)* Wechselgeld, Scheidemünzen; **~ committee** Nebenausschuß; **[wholly owned] ~ company (corporation)** [hundertprozentige] Tochter-, Organgesellschaft; **~-company accounting** Buchführung einer Tochtergesellschaft; **~ contract** Neben-, Untervertrag; **~ costs** Nebenkosten; **~ earnings** Nebenverdienst; **~ employment** Nebenbeschäftigung; **~ firm** Filialbetrieb, -unternehmen; **~ income** Nebeneinkommen; **~ industries** industrielle Hilfsbetriebe; **~ journal** Hilfskontobuch; **~ law** subsidiär geltendes Recht; **~ ledger** Neben-, Hilfsbuch; **~ money** Scheidemünzen; **~ nature** *(employment)* Aushilfscharakter; **~ organ** nachgeordnetes Organ, Hilfsorgan; **~ payments** Hilfeleistungen auf finanziellem Gebiet, *(politics)* Subsidien; **~ plant** Zweigbetrieb, Tochterunternehmen; **~ provisions** Aushilfsbestimmungen; **~ records** Hilfsaufzeichnungen; **~ retail business** Zweiggeschäft; **~ sentence** Nebenstrafe; **~ services** zusätzlicher Kundendienst; **~ source of income** zusätzliche Einkommensquelle, Nebenverdienst; **~ treaty** Subsidien-, Hilfsvertrag; **~ troops** Hilfstruppen; **~ undertaking** Tochterunternehmen; **~ worker** Hilfskraft, -arbeiter.

subsidies *(state)* Subsidien, Hilfsgelder;

agricultural ~ Agrarsubventionen; **food ~** Nahrungsmittelzuschüsse; **industrial ~** Industriesubventionen; **interest-rate ~** Zinszuschüsse;

~ for foreign forces Stationierungskosten; **~ for interest and redemption** Zins- und Tilgungszuschüsse.

subsidizable zuschuß-, subventionsbedürftig.

subsidization Bezuschussung, Subventionierung.

subsidize *(v.)* durch Staatsgelder unterstützen, subventionieren, aus öffentlichen Geldern fördern, Zuschuß gewähren, bezuschussen, *(bribe)* durch Bestechung gewinnen, kaufen;

~ an army Heer unterhalten; **~ farm surpluses** landwirtschaftliche Überschußprodukte subventionieren; **~ the press** Presse bestechen; **~ a steamship line** Schiffahrtslinie subventionieren.

subsidized subventioniert, durch staatliche Zuschüsse unterstützt;

government-~ staatlich subventioniert;

to be ~ by the state staatlich subventioniert sein, Staatszuschüsse erhalten;

~ agent bezahlter Agent; **~ export** subventionierter Export; **~ housing** Wohnungsbauhilfe; **~ industry** subventionierte Industrie; **~ lunch** subventioniertes Mittagsessen, Verpflegungszuschuß.

subsidizing Subventionierung, Unterstützung, Bezuschussung;

~ of exports Exportsubventionierung.

subsidy *(allowance)* Zuschuß, *(international law)* finanzielle Unterstützung von Verbündeten, *(levy, Br.)* Umlage, *(subvention, US)* [Staats]subvention, Subsidien, staatliche Unterstützung, Beihilfe aus öffentlichen Geldern, öffentlicher Zuschuß;

agricultural ~ Agrarsubvention; **construction differential ~** *(US, shipping industry)* Subvention zum Ausgleich für höhere Konstruktionskosten; **under-the-counter ~** versteckte Subventionen; **export ~** Ausfuhrprämie, Exportsubvention; **governmental ~** Staatszuschuß; **nonasset-creating ~** nichtvermögenswirksame Zuschüsse; **operating ~** Betriebszuschuß; **operating differential ~** *(US)* Subvention zum Ausgleich für höhere Unterhaltungskosten; **price ~** Subventionierung von Preisen; **rent ~** Mietzuschuß;

~ on exports Exportsubvention, Ausfuhrprämie, -zuschuß; **~ on interest** Zinssubvention, -zuschuß;

to grant a ~ to an ally einem Verbündeten finanzielle Hilfe gewähren; **to pay (give) a ~** subventionieren, mit öffentlichen Mitteln (durch Staatszuschüsse) unterstützen;

to foot the ~ bill Kosten für Subventionen zu tragen haben; **~ fund** Subventions-, Unterstützungsfonds, -kasse; **~ program(m)e** Hilfsprogramm; **competitive ~ race** Wettlauf um Subventionen zur Erhaltung der Wettbewerbsposition; **~ requirements** Subventions-, Zuschußbedarf; **~ system** Subventionssystem, -wesen.

subsist *(v.)* [fort]bestehen, leben, existieren;

~ s. o. j. unterhalten; **~ on [other men's] charity** von der Wohltätigkeit seiner Mitmenschen leben.

subsistence Dasein, Existenz, [Lebens]unterhalt, Aus-, Fortkommen, *(food)* Nahrung, *(~ money)* Unterhaltungszuschuß, *(provisioning)* Versorgung, Verpflegung;

reasonable ~ angemessener Unterhalt;

~ of troops Truppenversorgung;

to earn a bare ~ das nackte Dasein fristen; **to gain one's ~** sein Auskommen haben;

~ allowance Unterhaltungszuschuß; **~ benefit** Unterhaltsbeihilfe; **~ economy** Versorgungswirtschaft, Bedarfdeckungswirtschaft; **~ expenses** Aufenthaltskosten, Tagegelder; **~ farm** Kleinbauernhof, bäuerlicher Familienbetrieb; **~ level** Existenzminimum; **~ money** *(allowance for expenses)* Unterhaltszuschuß; **~ stores** *(mil.)* Verpflegungslager; **~ theory of wages** Existenzminimum-, Lohnfonds-, Produktionskostentheorie; **~ wage** Mindest-, Existenzlohn; **bare ~ wage** *(US)* das Existenzminimum gerade deckender Lohn, Lohnminimum.

subsisting bill gültiger Wechsel.

subsize Unterformat.

subsoil [Meeres]untergrund.

subsonic speed Unterschallgeschwindigkeit.

substance Stoff, *(essence)* Wesen, Hauptsache, Kern, *(material)* Substanz, Material, *(property)* Vermögen, Mittel, Kapital, *(purport)* Inhalt, Tenor;

fissionable ~ spaltbarer Stoff;

~ of an action Klagegegenstand; **~ of an essay** Gegenstand einer Abhandlung; **~ of a speech** Hauptbedeutung einer Ansprache; **~ of a testimony** Kern einer Aussage;

to agree in ~ im wesentlichen zustimmen; **to be of little ~** wenig Substanz haben; **to lose one's entire ~** seine Existenzgrundlage verlieren; **to waste one's ~** sein Geld sinnlos ausgeben, sein Vermögen verschleudern.

substandard unter der [gesetzlich] vorgeschriebenen Norm, unterdurchschnittlich, *(US)* unter der gesetzlich festgelegten Mindestqualität, nicht vollwertig;

~ business *(life insurance)* Risikogeschäft; **~ goods** Ausschußware; **~ housing** Elendsquartier; **~ risk** *(insurance business)* anomales Risiko; **~ worker** unterdurchschnittlich ausgebildeter Arbeiter.

substantial wesentlich, nennenswert, erheblich, *(commercially sound)* zahlungsfähig, kapitalkräftig, -stark, *(essential)* wesentlich, erheblich, wirklich, real, solide, *(law)* materiellrechtlich, *(well-to-do)* wohlhabend, reich;

to be in ~ agreement sich in den wesentlichen Punkten geeinigt haben; **~ amount** erheblicher Betrag; **~ business firm** solide (kapitalkräftige) Firma; **~ compliance** satzungsgemäße Erfüllung (Erledigung); **~ compliance rule** *(insurance law)* notwendige Mitwirkung bei der Auswechslung des Begünstigten; **~ contribution** wesentlicher Beitrag; **~ damages** Schadenersatz für tatsächlich eingetretenen Schaden; **~ endorser** potenter Girant; **~ equivalent of patented devices** Gleichwertigkeit mehrerer patentierter Erfindungen; **~ evidence** ausreichender (hinreichender) Beweis; **~ gain** beachtlicher Gewinn; **~ harm** beträchtlicher Schaden; **~ improvement** bedeutsame (beträchtliche) Verbesserung; **~ justice** Gerechtigkeit in der Sache selbst; **~ landlord** Großgrundbesitzer; **~ meal** solide, herzhafte Mahlzeit; **~ middle class** Großbürgertum; **~ part** wesentlicher Teil; **~ performance of a contract** annähernde Vertragserfüllung; **~ proof** schlüssiger Beweis; **~ right** materielles Recht; **~ risk** erhebliches Risiko; **~ victory** entscheidender Sieg.

substantiate *(v.)* glaubhaft machen;

~ an action Klage substantiieren; **~ a charge** Anklage begründen; **~ a claim** Anspruch näher begründen; **~ one's opinion by facts** seine Meinung durch Tatsachen erhärten; **~ a statement** Behauptung beweisen; **~ one's statement with documents** seine Aussage urkundlich belegen.

substantiated damage nachgewiesener Schaden.

substantiation nähere Begründung, Glaubhaftmachung, Substantiierung;

in ~ zum Beweis;

~ of appeal Beschwerdebegründung; **~ of claim** Klagebegründung; **~ of a statement** Beweis für eine Behauptung.

substantive wesentlich, *(self-subsistent)* selbständig, unabhängig;

~ evidence erhebliches Beweismaterial; **~ felony** selbständiges Verbrechen; **~ law** materielles Recht; **~ motion** *(parl.)* Antrag zur Sache; **~ nation** selbständiges Land; **~ rank** *(mil.)* Dienstgrad mit Patent; **~ requirements** materielle Voraussetzungen.

substation Neben-, Außenstelle, *(electricity)* Verteilerstation;

post-office ~ Zweigpostamt.

substitute *(imitation)* Nachahmung, *(material)* Ersatz[mittel], Surrogat, Austauschwerkstoff, *(mil.)* Ersatzmann, *(person)* [Stell]vertreter, Substitut, Ersatzmann, Bevollmächtigter, *(Scot.)* Ersatzerbe;

adequate ~ gleichwertiger Ersatz; **money ~** Geld-, Zahlungssurrogat;

~s in an entail Nacherben; ~ for a rights issue Bezugsrechtersatz; ~ to a legatee Ersatzvermächtnisnehmer; ~ for travel Reisekostenersatz, -spesen;

~ (v.) for s. o. j. vertreten;

~ a debt Schuld auswechseln; ~ an heir (Scot.) Ersatzerben bestellen; ~ s. o. in his shoes jds. Platz einnehmen; ~ a word an Stelle eines Wortes ein anderes setzen;

to act as a ~ for s. o. als jds. Stellvertreter fungieren; to be appointed s. one's ~ zu jds. Stellvertreter bestimmt (ernannt) werden; to step in as s. one's ~ als Ersatzmann für j. einspringen;

~ articles Ersatzware, -artikel; ~ commodity Ersatzstoff; ~ cover Ersatzdeckung, -sicherheit; ~ delegate Ersatzdelegierter; ~ judge Ersatzrichter; ~ performance Ersatzvornahme, -leistung; ~ powers Untervollmacht; ~ teacher Hilfslehrer.

substituted | contract neuer Vertrag, Novation; ~ debtor Schuldübernehmer; ~ executor Ersatztestamentsvollstrecker; ~ expenses (average) stellvertretende Kosten; ~ heir (US) Ersatzerbe; ~ legacy Ersatzvermächtnis; ~ legatee Ersatzvermächtnisnehmer; ~ service (US) öffentliche Zustellung, (Br.) Ersatzzustellung.

substitution [Stell]vertretung, Substitution, Substitiierung, (replacement) Ersetzung, Ersatz;

in ~ for an Stelle von;

fideicommissionary (quasi-pupillary) ~ Errichtung eines Fideikommisses;

~ of a child Kindesunterschiebung; ~ of a debt (Scot.) Novation, Schuldenauswechselung; ~ of one debtor for another Schuldübernahme; ~ of an heir (Scot., US) Einsetzung eines Ersatzerben;

~ effect Substitutionseffekt.

substitutional stellvertretend, (inheritance) Ersatzerbschaft betreffend;

~ gift Ersatzvermächtnis; ~ legacy Ersatzvermächtnis.

substitutionary | evidence hilfsweise angebotenes Beweismaterial; ~ executor Ersatztestamentsvollstrecker.

substratum Untergrund, -lage, Basis;

~ of a company Daseinszweck (Gewerbezweck) einer Firma, Geschäftsgrundlage eines Unternehmens;

to have a ~ of truth erheblichen Wahrheitsgehalt haben.

substructure Unterbau, Fundament, (railway) Unterbau.

subsume (v.) subsumieren, zusammenfassen.

subsumption Zusammenfassung.

subsurface torpedo Unterwassertorpedo.

subtenancy Unterpacht, -miete.

subtenant Untermieter, -pächter.

subterfuge (excuse) Ausflucht, -rede, (hiding) Versteck, Zuflucht;

to lower o. s. to a ~ zu einer Ausrede greifen.

subterranean unterirdisch;

~ diplomacy Geheimdiplomatie; ~ passage Unterführung; ~ waters unterirdische Gewässer.

subtlety Finesse.

subtitle Unter-, Zwischentitel;

~ (v.) a film Film mit Zwischentiteln versehen.

subtopia Randgebiet einer Großstadt, zersiedelte Landschaft.

subtotal Zwischen-, Teilsumme, (accounting) Übertrag.

subtract (v.) abziehen, subtrahieren.

subtraction Abzug, Subtraktion, (legal sense) Unterschlagung;

~ of legacies Einbehaltung von Legaten, Nachlaßveruntreuung; ~ of conjugal rights (US) Getrenntleben ohne Berechtigung.

subtropical (climate) subtropisch.

subunderwriter Unterversicherer.

subunderwriting (insurance company) Übernahme einer Versicherung als Unterversicherer, (securities) Unterbeteiligung bei einem Emissionsgeschäft;

~ agreement Vereinbarung einer Unterbeteiligung; ~ commission Unterversicherungs-, Beteiligungsprovision.

suburb Vorstadt, Außenbezirk, (confines) Grenzbezirk, -bereich;

garden ~ Gartenvorstadt; high-income ~ wohlhabendes Viertel; outer ~ Stadtrandvorort; residential ~ Vorstadtwohngegend;

~s of a town Stadtrandgebiete, Randbezirke einer Stadt.

suburban vorstädtisch, (fig.) engstirnig, provinziell, kleinstädtisch, -kariert, spießig;

to go ~ Betrieb in ein Vorstadtgebiet verlegen;

~ apartment Vorstadtwohnung; ~ area Vorstadtgebiet; leafy ~ backwaters grüne und schläfrige Vororte; ~ [housing] estate Stadtrandgebiet; ~ expansion Vorstadtausdehnung; ~ home (house) Vorstadthaus; ~ inhabitant Vorstadtbewohner; ~ line Vorortbahn; ~ locality Vorstadtbelegenheit; ~ railway Vor

ortbahn; ~ residence Vorstadtwohnung; ~ restaurant Vorstadtrestaurant; ~ section (railway) Vorortstrecke; ~ shop (store, US) Vorstadtgeschäft; ~ traffic Nah-, Berufsverkehr, Vorortverkehr; ~ train Vorortzug; ~ traveller Berufsverkehrsteilnehmer; ~ zoning housing (US) Stadtrandsiedlung.

suburbanite Vorstadtbewohner, Kleinstädter.

suburbanity Kleinstädtertum, kleinstädtisches Wesen.

suburbanization Eingemeindung.

suburbanize (v.) eingemeinden, zum Vorort machen.

suburbia Vorstadt, Stadtrand, (fig.) Vorstadtwelt, die Spießer, (inhabitants) Vorstadtbewohner;

to reflect ~ strongly Vorstadtherkunft von weitem erkennen lassen;

~ locality Vorstadtbelegenheit.

subvention staatliche Unterstützung, Subvention;

~ payments Subventionszahlungen.

subventionize (v.) staatlich unterstützen, subventionieren.

subversion Umsturz, gewaltsame Beseitigung;

~ of the constitution Aufhebung der Verfassung; ~ of the government Regierungssturz.

subversive umstürzlerisch, subversiv, aufrührerisch;

to be ~ of peace and order gegen die öffentliche Sicherheit und Ordnung gerichtet sein;

~ activity subversive Tätigkeit, staatsfeindliche Umtriebe; ~ literature Hetzschriften; ~ movement staatsgefährdende Bewegung; ~ speech aufrührerische Rede.

subvert (v.) stürzen;

~ the law Gesetz umstoßen; ~ the monarchy Monarchie stürzen.

subverter Umstürzler.

subway Straßenunterführung, (Br.) Fußgängertunnel, (underground, US) Untergrund-, U-, Unterpflasterbahn;

~ car (US) U-Bahnwagen; ~ platform (US) U-Bahnsteig; ~ rider (US) U-Bahnbenutzer; ~ station (US) U-Bahnstation; ~ system (US) U-, Untergrundbahnnetz.

subworker Handlanger, Gehilfe.

subzone Teilzone.

succeed (v.) (follow in office) [in Amt (Stellung)] nachfolgen, (have success) Erfolg haben, erfolgreich sein, obsiegen;

~ s. o. an jds. Stelle treten; ~ in an action mit einer Klage durchdringen; ~ to a business Geschäft übernehmen; ~ to an estate Grundbesitz erben; ~ in passing an examination Examen erfolgreich bestehen; ~ to a fortune Vermögen erben; ~ a minister jds. Nachfolger im Ministerium werden; ~ to an office Amt antreten; ~ to s. one's property j. beerben; ~ to s. one's rights in jds. Rechte eintreten; ~ to the throne auf dem Throne folgen.

succeeding nachfolgend, aufeinanderfolgend;

each ~ year jedes darauffolgende Jahr.

success Gelingen, Erfolg;

flushed with ~ erfolgstrunken; showing ~ erfolgswirksam; box-office ~ (US) Kassenschlager; financial ~ finanzieller Erfolg, Kassenerfolg; ill ~ Mißerfolg; short-lived ~ schnell vorübergehender Erfolg;

to have ~ with s. o. bei jem. etw. erreichen; to have great ~ in life es im Leben zu etw. bringen; to meet with ~ Erfolg haben; to turn out a ~ sich zu einem Erfolg gestalten, sich erfolgreich entwickeln;

~ fee Erfolgshonorar; ~ story Erfolgsbericht.

successful erfolgreich;

to be ~ all along the line überall Erfolg haben;

~ candidate gewählter Kandidat; ~ party obsiegende Partei.

succession (estate of deceased person) Nachlaß, Erbfall, [Reihen]folge, (office) Nachfolge im Amt, (order of succeeding) Erbfolge, -ordnung, (right of heir to take possession) Erbrecht, Rechtsnachfolge;

by way of ~ im Wege der Erbfolge; in ~ nacheinander; in due ~ in der richtigen Reihenfolge;

artificial ~ (corporation law) gesetzlich fingierte Dauerexistenz; collateral ~ Erbfolge in der Seitenlinie; escheated ~ dem Staat verfallene Erbschaft; hereditary (intestate) ~ gesetzliche Erbfolge; irregular ~ Ersatzerbfolge, Erbanfall an den Staat; legal ~ gesetzliche Erbfolge; linear ~ Erbfolge in gerader Linie; natural ~ gesetzliche Erbfolge; partial ~ Teilrechtsnachfolge; reversionary ~ Nacherbfolge; singular ~ Einzelerbfolge; testamentary ~ testamentarische (gewillkürte) Erbfolge; universal ~ Universalerbschaft, -folge, Gesamtrechtsnachfolge; vacant ~ herrenloser Nachlaß;

~ of crops Fruchtwechsel; ~ of defeats Reihe von Niederlagen; ~ to an estate Erbantritt; ~ of houses Häuserreihe; ~ by inheritance (US) Erbfolge; ~ to an office Amtsnachfolge,

-übernahme; ~ **to property** Vermögensnachfolge; ~ **of states** Staatennachfolge; ~ **per stirpes** Erbfolge nach Stämmen; ~ **to the throne** Thronfolge; ~ **in title** Rechtsnachfolge;

to accrue by way of ~ im Erbgang anfallen; **to bar from** ~ von der Erbfolge ausschließen; **to renounce a** ~ auf sein Erbe verzichten; **to settle the** ~ Erbfolge bestimmen (festlegen);

~ **duty** *(US)* Erbschafts-, Erbanfallsteuer, *(Br.)* Erbschaftssteuer für unbewegliches Vermögen; ~ **relief** Nachlässe bei Veranlagung zur Erbschaftssteuer; ~ **sale** *(US)* Nachlaßversteigerung; ~ **states** *(pol.)* Nachfolgestaaten; ~ **tax** Erbschafts-, Nachlaßsteuer.

successive nachfolgend, suksessiv;

~ **collection of coins** entwicklungsgeschichtliche Münzsammlung.

successively nach und nach.

successor Rechtsnachfolger, *(heir)* Erbe, *(corporation law)* Rechtsnachfolgerin, *(in office)* Amtsnachfolger;

legal ~ Rechtsnachfolger; **singular** ~ Erbe eines einzelnen Nachlaßgegenstandes, Einzelrechtsnachfolger; **universal** ~ *(US)* Universalerbe, Gesamtrechtsnachfolger;

~ **in interest** Rechtsnachfolger; ~ **to an office** Amtsnachfolger; ~ **to the Presidency** Präsidentsschaftsnachfolger; ~ **to the throne** Thronfolger;

to appoint a ~ Nachfolger bestimmen;

~ **company** Nachfolgegesellschaft, Rechtsnachfolgerin.

successorship Nachfolgerschaft.

succinct *(style)* bündig, knapp.

succour Hilfe, *(mil.)* Entsatz;

~s Hilfstruppen;

~ *(v.)* entsetzen.

succourer *(Br.)* Beistand.

succumb *(v.)* **to one's injuries** seinen Verletzungen erliegen.

suck | *(v.)* **advantage of** Vorteil ziehen aus; ~ **around** *(sl.)* herumlungern; ~ **s. one's brains** jem. seine Ideen stehlen, j. aushorchen; ~ **s. one's lifeblood** j. bis aufs letzte ausnutzen; ~ **up to s. o.** *(sl.)* sich bei jem. einschmeicheln;

~-**egg** *(fig.)* Erpresser, Parasit.

sucker *(coll.)* gutgläubiger Trottel;

to play s. o. for a ~ j. für dumm verkaufen;

~ **list** *(sl.)* Liste potentieller Kunden.

sucking barrister angehender Rechtsanwalt.

suckling *(fig.)* Anfänger, Grünschnabel.

sudden plötzlich, unvermutet, überraschend;

~ **action** überstürzte Aktion; ~ **chance** *(stock exchange)* Umschwung; ~ **death** plötzlicher Tod; ~ **heat or passion** *(manslaughter)* Affekthandlung; ~ **or violent injury** unfallbedingte Verletzung; ~ **peril rule** Grundsatz der Nichthaftung bei Verschulden der Gegenseite; ~ **turn** plötzliche Straßenbiegung.

sue *(v.)* gerichtlich belangen (vorgehen), verklagen, [ein]klagen, Klage anstrengen, (einreichen) prozessieren;

~ **s. o.** gerichtlich gegen j. vorgehen (einschreiten); ~ **for admittance** seine Ansprüche auf die Konkursmasse anmelden; ~ **on a bill** Wechselforderung einklagen, Wechselrechtsklage erheben; ~ **for breach of contract[ual] obligations** wegen Nichterfüllung verklagen; ~ **for breach of promise** wegen Bruchs des Eheversprechens verklagen; ~ **for claims on bills of exchange** Wechselforderungen einklagen; ~ **on a contract** aus einem Vertrag klagen; ~ **for conversion** wegen Unterschlagung (auf Herausgabe) verklagen; ~ **in court** bei Gericht Klage erheben; ~ **[in court] for damages** bei einem Gericht auf Schadenersatz [ver]klagen, Schadenersatzklage anstrengen; ~ **for liquidated damages** Konventionalstrafe einklagen; ~ **for unliquidated damages** Schadensersatz dem Grund nach einklagen; ~ **for damages in tort for deceit** vor Gericht Schadensersatz wegen Betruges verlangen; ~ **on a debt in one's own name** Forderung im eigenen Namen einklagen; ~ **for a decree of specific performance** Leistungsurteil klageweise fordern; ~ **for a divorce** Scheidungsklage einreichen; ~ **the enemy for peace** Feind um Frieden bitten; ~ **for one's fees** seine Gebühren einklagen; ~ **in the firm's name** im Firmennamen klagen; ~ **s. o. for infringement of a patent** Patentverletzungsklage gegen j. erheben; ~ **s. o. for civil injury** j. wegen Körperverletzung zivilrechtlich belangen; ~ **s. o. at law** j. verklagen (gerichtlich belangen), Klage gegen j. erheben; ~ **s. one for libel** Klage wegen Verleumdung gegen j. anstrengen, Beleidigungsklage gegen j. erheben; ~ **for mercy** um Gnade bitten; ~ **in its corporate name** unter seinem handelsgerichtlichen Namen klagen; ~ **in one's name** im eigenen Namen klagen; ~ **out** einklagen; ~ **out a commission of bankruptcy** Konkursverfahren erwirken; ~ **in forma pauperis** im Armenrecht klagen; ~ **for performance** auf Erfüllung klagen; ~ **as plaintiff to their next friends** Prozeß im Namen eines

Prozeßbeistandes führen; ~ **on a policy** Versicherungsansprüche einklagen; ~ **for a reasonable price of goods** angemessenen Warenpreis einklagen; ~ **on a quantum meruit** angemessenen Teilbetrag einklagen, auf angemessene Vergütung klagen; ~ **for the return of a deposit** Rückzahlung einer Anzahlung im Klagewege fordern; ~ **for one's salary under a contract** sein vertraglich vereinbartes Gehalt einklagen; ~ **for torts** Schadenersatz aus unerlaubter Handlung verlangen; ~ **in tort for conversion** Schadenersatz wegen Unterschlagung verlangen; ~ **[out] for a writ** gerichtliche Verfügung erwirken, Gerichtsbeschluß beantragen;

~ **and labo(u)r clause** *(marine insurance, Br.)* Schadensminderungsklausel.

suer Antragsteller, *(proceedings)* [Prozeß]partei, Kläger.

suffer *(v.)* dulden, zulassen, gestatten, *(business)* Schaden nehmen (erleiden);

~ **in an accident** bei einem Unfall zu Schaden kommen; ~ **a change** Veränderung erfahren; ~ **death** Tod erleiden; ~ **a slight decline** *(stock exchange)* leichten Rückgang erfahren; ~ **a default** Versäumnisurteil gegen sich ergehen lassen; ~ **defeat** Niederlage erleiden; ~ **a depreciation** Wertminderung erfahren; ~ **the same fate as his predecessors** Schicksal seiner Vorgänger erfahren; ~ **a fool gladly** große Geduld mit einem Narren haben; ~ **one's grief in private** im stillen Kämmerlein trauern; ~ **from labo(u)r troubles** unter Arbeiterunruhen zu leiden haben; ~ **a loss** Verlust erleiden; ~ **a loss in exchange up to 10%** Kurseinbuße bis zu 10% hinnehmen müssen (erleiden); ~ **from loss of memory** an Gedächtnisschwäche leiden; ~ **next morning** *(criminal)* am nächsten Morgen hingerichtet werden; ~ **pain of body** Schmerzen ertragen; ~ **penalty** bestraft werden; ~ **judicial proceedings** Prozeß einfach hinnehmen; ~ **s. one's presence** jds. Anwesenheit dulden; ~ **severely** *(engine)* stark mitgenommen werden.

sufferance [stillschweigende] Duldung, Erlaubnis, Einwilligung, *(customs, Br.)* Zollvergüngstigung;

at ~ *(lease)* stillschweigend geduldet; **through** ~ unter stillschweigender Duldung;

to be here on ~ hier nur geduldet werden; **to leave in** ~ [Wechsel] nicht honorieren; **to remain in** ~ *(bill of exchange)* weiter Not leiden, uneingelöst bleiben;

~ **wharf** *(Br.)* Freihafenniederlage.

sufferer *(fire insurance)* Geschädigter, *(bill of exchange)* Notleidender;

principal ~ Hauptleidtragender.

suffice *(v.)* [aus]reichen;

~ **for s. one's needs** jds. Bedürfnisse befriedigen.

sufficiency Angemessenheit, *(sufficient subsistence)* hinlängliches Auskommen, angemessener Komfort, auskömmlicher Unterhalt;

~ **of fuel** genügend Betriebsstoff; ~ **of funds** ausreichendes Guthaben; ~ **of present laws** ausreichende Grundlage in den bestehenden Gesetzen; ~ **of money** ausreichende finanzielle Mittel;

to have a ~ sein Auskommen haben; **to have money in** ~ Geld zur Genüge haben.

sufficient genügend, hinlänglich, ausreichend;

not ~ *(bill, check)* ungenügende Deckung; **self-**~ selbstgenügsam, selbstversorgend, autark;

~ **in law** rechtlich zulässig; ~ **in numbers** *(quorum)* beschlußfähig;

to be ~ ausreichen, genügen; **to be** ~ **for the expenses of a journey** Reiseunkosten decken;

~ **cause** triftiger Grund, *(notice)* Entlassungsgrund; ~ **consideration** hinlänglicher Gegenwert; ~ **evidence** hinlänglicher Beweis; ~ **funds** *(cheque)* ausreichendes Guthaben; ~ **income** ausreichendes Einkommen; ~ **memorandum (note)** *(unenforceable contract)* Zulässigkeitsvermerk; ~ **security** hinreichende Sicherheit.

suffix Zusatz;

complimentary ~es Höflichkeitszusätze;

~ *(v.)* anfügen.

suffrage Wahlrecht, -berechtigung, Stimmrecht, *(vote)* [Wahl]stimme, *(voting)* Abstimmung, Wahl;

adult ~ Wahlrecht für alle Erwachsenen; **female** ~ Frauenwahlrecht; **limited** ~ beschränktes Wahlrecht; **manhood** ~ Männerwahlrecht; **restricted** ~ beschränktes Wahlrecht; **universal** ~ allgemeines Wahlrecht; **woman** ~ Frauenwahlrecht;

to extend ~ **to women** Wahlrecht auf die Frauen ausdehnen; **to give one's** ~ **to a candidate** einem Kandidaten seine Wahlstimme zukommen lassen.

suffragette Frauenrechtlerin.

sugar *(sl.)* Moneten, Kies;
~ **bag** Zuckersack; ~ **coating** Schönfärberei; ~ **daddy** Geldonkel; ~ **exchange** Zuckerbörse; ~ **hill** *(sl.)* reiche Wohngegend; ~ **refinery** Zuckerraffinerie; ~ **report** *(coll.)* Liebesbrief; ~ **works** Zuckerfabrik.

suggest *(v.)* vorschlagen, anregen, empfehlen, *(lawyer)* behaupten, unterstellen;
~ **s. o. for a position** j. für eine Stelle in Vorschlag bringen.

suggested price empfohlener Richtpreis.

suggestion Rat, Anregung, Empfehlung, Vorschlag, *(lawyer)* Sach-, Rechtsvorbringen, *(trace)* Spur, Idee, Hauch, Anflug; **upon** ~ **of** auf Anregung von;
credit ~ Kreditvorschlag; **hypnotic** ~ hypnotische Beeinflussung; **mere** ~ reine Hypothese; **selling** ~ Verkaufsmethode;
~ **of error** Wiederaufnahmeantrag; ~**s for improvement** Verbesserungsvorschläge; ~ **upon record** schriftliche Eingabe;
to make a ~ in die Debatte werfen; **to speak English with a** ~ **of French** Englisch mit einem leichten französischen Akzent sprechen;
~ **award** Vorschlagsprämie; ~ **box** Briefkasten für Verbesserungsvorschläge, Beschwerdebriefkasten; ~ **program(me)** Vorschlagswesen; ~ **scheme** *(US)* betriebliches Vorschlagswesen; ~ **selling** *(US)* Kundenbeeinflussung; ~ **system** betriebliches Vorschlagswesen.

suggestive, to be auf Suggestivwirkung beruhen;
~ **interrogation** Vernehmung durch Stellen von Suggestivfragen; ~ **writer** anregender Schriftsteller; ~ **speech** gehaltvolle Rede.

sui juris *(lat.)* geschäftsfähig, mündig.

suicidal selbstmörderisch;
~ **intent** *(insurance)* Selbstmordabsicht; ~ **policy** selbstmörderische Politik.

suicide Selbstmord, Freitod, *(self-murder)* Selbstmörder;
attempted ~ Selbstmordversuch; **economic** ~ wirtschaftlicher Selbstmord; **political** ~ politischer Selbstmord; **race** ~ völkischer Selbstmord; **sane or insane** ~ *(life insurance)* Selbstmordklausel;
~ *(v.)* Selbstmord begehen;
to commit ~ Selbstmord begehen; **to commit political** ~ seine Karriere als Politiker zerstören;
~ **clause** Selbstmordklausel; ~ **club** *(mil., sl.)* Selbstmörderklub; ~ **pact** Selbstmordvereinbarung; ~ **prevention** Selbstmordverhütung.

suing and laboring clause *(marine insurance, US)* Schadensminderungsklausel.

suit *(action in law court)* Rechtsstreitigkeit, [Zivil]prozeß, Klage[erhebung], *(dress)* Anzug, *(petition)* Anliegen, Gesuch, Bewerbung, *(set)* Garnitur, Satz, Serie;
before ~ **was brought** vor Klageerhebung; **during the pendency of the** ~ für die Dauer des Verfahrens; **in** ~ **with** im Einverständnis mit; **since the commencement of the** ~ seit Klageeinleitung;
administration ~ Nachlaßverfahren; **adversary** ~ streitiger Prozeß; **civil** ~ bürgerliche Rechtsstreitigkeit, Zivilprozeß; **criminal** ~ Strafverfahren; **damages** ~ Klage auf Schadensersatz; **divorce** ~ Ehescheidungsprozeß, Scheidungsklage; **dress** ~ Abendanzug; **equity** ~ Klage nach Billigkeitsrecht; **foreclosure** ~ *(US)* Zwangsvollstreckungsklage; **formal** ~ Gesellschaftsanzug; **fresh** ~ sofort (neue) angestrengte Klage; **infringement** ~ Schadensersatzprozeß wegen Patentverletzung, Patentklage; **injunction** ~ Unterlassungsklage; **lounge** ~ *(Br.)* Straßenanzug; **nullity** ~ *(marriage)* Anfechtungs-, Nichtigkeitsverfahren, Eheaufhebungsklage; **pending** ~ anhängiger (schwebender) Prozeß; **worsted** ~ Kammgarnanzug;
~ **in chancery** *(Br.)* Klage vor dem Gericht des Lordkanzlers; ~ **for a debt** Einklagen einer Schuld; ~ **on dumping** Dumpingverfahren; ~ **in equity** Forderungsklage; **civil** ~ **for injunction** Verfahren zwecks Erlasses einer einstweiligen Verfügung; ~ **of the king's peace** Hochverratsverfahren; ~ **at law** *(US)* Klagesache, Rechtsstreit, Verfahren, Zivilprozeß; ~ **of a civil nature** zivilrechtliches Verfahren; ~ **of nullity of marriage** Eheaufhebungsklage, -nichtigkeitsantrag; ~ **against state** Klage gegen den Staat;
~ *(v.)* **s. o.** jem. bekömmlich sein; ~ **o. s.** sich keinen Zwang antun; ~ **the action to the word** seinen Worten Taten folgen lassen; ~ **s. one's book** jem. passen (recht sein); ~ **one's style to the audience** sich dem Publikum anpassen;
to be a party to a ~ Prozeßstandschaftsklage, Prozeßpartei sein; **to bring a** ~ **against s. o.** *(US)* mit jem. prozessieren, j. zivilrechtlich verfolgen, Klage gegen j. anstrengen; **to carry on a** ~ *(US)* Prozeß führen; **to commence a** ~ Klage erheben,

klagen; to conduct a ~ Prozeß führen; **to defend a** ~ *(US)* Klageanspruch bestreiten; **to drop a** ~ Klage fallen lassen, Prozeß aufgeben; **to file a** ~ gerichtlich vorgehen, Klage einreichen; **to follow** ~ jds. Beispiel folgen; **to forbear a** ~ Klage unterlassen; **to grant s. one's** ~ jds. Gesuch stattgeben; **to institute a** ~ **against s. o.** Klage gegen j. einreichen; **to maintain a** ~ Rechtsstreit (Prozeß) fortsetzen; **to prosecute a** ~ *(US)* Prozeß führen; **to push one's** ~ seine Belange durchsetzen; **to refuse a** ~ Klage nicht zulassen (abweisen); **to threaten a** ~ Prozeß androhen; **to undertake the defence of a** ~ Prozeßführung übernehmen;
~ **money** *(divorce suit)* Prozeßkostenvorschuß [für die Ehefrau].

suitable sachgemäß, verwendbar, gebührend, geeignet, angemessen, passend, [sach]dienlich;
~ **for investment** zur Kapitalanlage geeignet; **to be** ~ **for** passend sein für, sich qualifizieren (eignen); ~ **alternative employment** angemessene Ersatzbeschäftigung; ~ **replacement housing** geeignete Ersatzwohnung.

suitcase Handkoffer;
to fit into a ~ in einem Koffer Platz haben.

suite Suite, [Reise]gefolge, Stab, *(apartment)* Wohnung, Apartment, *(furniture)* Möbelsatz;
bedroom ~ Schlafzimmereinrichtung; ~ **of rooms** Zimmerflucht.

suitor Bewerber, Freier, *(law, US)* Kläger, Prozeßpartei;
~'**s deposit account** *(US)* Hinterlegungskonto für Sicherheitsleistungen; ~'**s fee fund** Gerichtskasse.

sulks, to be in the schlechte Laune haben.

sum Summe, [Geld]betrag, Posten, *(column)* Zahlen-, Additionsreihe, *(task)* Rechenaufgabe;
~**s** Geldmittel, -beträge;
in ~ insgesamt; **within the** ~ **of human experience** innerhalb der gesamten menschlichen Erfahrungen;
additional ~ Zusatzbetrag; ~ **adjudged** Urteilsbetrag; ~ **allowed** zugebilligte Vergütung; ~ **arrived at** errechnete Summe; ~ **assured** Versicherungssumme; **average** ~ Durchschnittssumme, Pauschalbetrag; ~ **claimed** eingeklagter Betrag; **definite (given)** ~ bestimmte Summe; ~ **due** Schuldposten, geschuldeter (fälliger) Betrag; ~ **employed** verwendeter Betrag; **entire** ~ volle Summe; **even** ~ runde Summe; ~ **exceeding** Betrag von mehr als; **fixed** ~ Fixum; **flat (global)** ~ Pauschalbetrag; **good round** ~ glatte (runde) Summe; **gross** ~ runde Summe; ~ **insured** Versicherungssumme, Deckungssumme; **inadequate** ~ **insured** ungenügende Versicherungssumme; **lump** ~ Pauschalsumme; **nice little** ~ schönes Stück Geld; ~ **owing** geschuldeter Betrag; ~ **paid in** Einlage; **paltry** ~ Bagatelle; ~ **payable** Schuldbetrag, *(bill of exchange)* Wechselbetrag; ~ **received** Einnahmeposten; ~ **reserved** Rückstellungsbetrag; **round** ~ abgerundeter Betrag; **total** ~ Gesamtbetrag, -summe, Totalbetrag; ~ **withdrawn** abgehobener Betrag;
~ **at the bank** Bankguthaben; ~**s due from banks** *(balance sheet)* Bankguthaben; ~ **withdrawn from the bank** von der Bank abgehobener Betrag; ~ **and substance of a complaint** wesentlicher Teil einer Beschwerde; ~ **of the digits** digitale Abschreibung; ~ **available for dividend** für die Dividendenausschüttung verfügbarer Betrag; ~ **in excess** überschießender (zuviel gezahlter) Betrag; ~ **safe in hand** sicherstehender Posten; ~ **certain in money** bestimmte Geldsumme; ~ **of money due and owing** *(balance sheet)* Außenstände; ~ **invested at 5% interest** mit 5% Zinsen angelegter Geldbetrag; ~ **paid as compensation** Abfindungssumme; **small** ~ **for relief** kleiner Unterstützungsbetrag; ~ **chargeable to reserve** aus der Rücklage zu deckender Betrag; ~ **in full settlement of all claims** Abfindungsbetrag; ~ **of a statement** Etatsposten; ~ **in words** Betrag in Worten;
~ *(v.)* **one's cash account** sein Guthaben zusammenrechnen; ~ **up** *(summarize)* zusammenfassen, resümieren, *(add up)* addieren, zusammenrechnen, *(lawyer)* Schlußplädoyer halten; ~ **up the evidence** Beweisergebnis zusammenfassen, Beweiswürdigung vornehmen; ~ **up the items** Rechnungsposten addieren; ~ **up in note form** in Kurzform zusammenfassen; ~ **up the situation at a glance** Situation mit einem Blick überschauen; ~ **up all one's strength** seine ganzen Kräfte zusammenfassen;
to advance a ~ Betrag vorschießen; **to allocate a** ~ **among several people** Betrag unter verschiedene Leute aufteilen; **to be deducted from a** ~ von einer Summe abgehen; **to be in excess of the** ~ **required** benötigten Betrag überschreiten; **to call in a** ~ Betrag kündigen; **to charge a** ~ **to the debit** Betrag zu Lasten eines Kontos vortragen; **to compute a** ~ Summe zusammenrechnen; **to deduct a** ~ Betrag in Abzug bringen; **to deposit a** ~ **in the hands of a third party** Summe hinterlegen; **to do** ~**s**

Aufgaben rechnen; **to do a ~ in one's head** Betrag im Kopf ausrechnen; **to get one's ~s wrong** mit seinen Finanzen durcheinanderkommen; **to invest a ~ at 6 per cent interest** Geldbetrag zu 6% anlegen; **to lend small ~s** kleine Beträge ausleihen; **to make up a ~** Summe vollmachen; **to make up the requisite ~** fehlende Summe vollmachen (ergänzen); **to mount up to the ~ of ...** zum Betrag von ... auflaufen; **to pay in a ~ to s. one's credit** Betrag auf jds. Konto einzahlen; **to pay over a ~** Summe abführen; **to place a ~ against** Summe validieren; **to place a ~ to s. one's debit** jds. Konto mit einem Betrag belasten; **to place a ~ at the disposal of s. o.** jem. einen Geldbetrag zur Verfügung stellen; **to round off a ~** Betrag abrunden; **to save a nice little ~ out of one's wage each week** wöchentlich ganz ansehnlich vom Lohn zurücklegen; **to subscribe a ~ to charity** Betrag für wohltätige Zwecke zur Verfügung stellen; **to vote a ~** Mittel abstimmungsweise bewilligen; **to win a large ~ at the casino** großen Spielbankgewinn machen;

~-of-the-year digits depreciation (US) digitale Abschreibung; **~-of-years digits method** (US) digitale (arithmetisch degressive) Abschreibungsmethode.

summarist Kompendienschreiber.

summarization Zusammenfassung.

summarize (v.) zusammenfassende Darstellung geben, kurz zusammenfassen, resümieren;
~ a discussion Aussprache zusammenfassen.

summarized|balance sheet Bilanzauszug; **~ budget** Gesamthaushaltsplan.

summarizing|account Sammelkonto; **~ sheet** [tabellarische] Zusammenstellung.

summarily, to dismiss fristlos entlassen;
~ sentenced im Schnellverfahren abgeurteilt.

summary (abridged account) kurze Inhaltsangabe, Abriß, Kompendium, (abstract) Auszug, (statement) zusammenfassende Darstellung, Zusammenfassung, [tabellarische] Zusammenstellung, Übersicht;
complete ~ Gesamtaufstellung; **periodic ~** periodischer Bilanzauszug;
~ of assets and liabilities Bilanzauszug; **~ of balance-sheet changes** Ausweis über die Verwendung des Grundkapitals; **~ of contents** Inhaltsangabe; **~ of the debate** zusammengefaßter Verhandlungsbericht; **~ of one's education** zusammengefaßter Ausbildungsgang; **~ of forms** Angebotsgegenüberstellung; **~ of leading cases and decisions** Sammlung höchstrichterlicher Entscheidungen; **~ of the facts** kurze Darstellung des Sachverhalts;
to take a ~ of evidence Beweisergebnis zusammenfassen;
~ (a.) kurz zusammengefaßt, abgekürzt, (with less formality) summarisch;
~ account Übersichts-, Sammelkonto, (report) zusammenfassender Bericht, Schlußbericht; **~ action** (Scot.) summarisches Verfahren; **~ administration** Verwaltung von Bagatellnachlässen, (bankruptcy) Verwaltung von Bagatellkonkursen; **~ case** Bagatellnachlaß, (bankruptcy) Bagatellkonkurs; **~ conviction** Verurteilung im Schnellverfahren; **~ court of jurisdiction** Schnellgericht; **~ court martial** Standgericht; **~ departure** fristlose Arbeitsniederlegung; **~ dismissal** fristlose (sofortige) Entlassung; **~ expulsion** (party politics) Parteiausschluß im Schnellverfahren; **~ judgment** Urteil im Urkundenprozeß, abgekürztes Urteil, Mahnverfahren; **~ judgment with leave to defend** Vorbehaltsurteil im Urkundenprozeß; **~ jurisdiction** amtsgerichtliche Zuständigkeit; **~ justice** Schnell-, Bagatellgerichtsbarkeit, (lower courts) niedere Gerichtsbarkeit; **~ methods** summarisches Verfahren; **~ offence** (US) Übertretung, Bagatellsache; **~ powers** Vollmachten zur Aburteilung im Schnellverfahren; **~ proceedings** abgekürztes (summarisches) Verfahren, Schnellverfahren; **~ procedure** Schnellverfahren; **~ procedure on bills of exchange** (Br.) Wechselprozeß; **~ process** Schnellverfahren; **~ reception order** vorläufige Einweisung in eine Nervenheilanstalt; **~ record** Kurzprotokoll; **~ schedule** kurze Aufstellung; **~ sheet** Abrechnungsblatt; **~ statement** kurze Übersicht; **~ termination** fristlose Kündigung; **~ treatment** abgekürztes Verfahren.

summation Zusammenfassung, -zählung, Addition, (attorney, US) Schlußplädoyer, (law court) Resümee, (sum total) Endergebnis, Gesamtsumme;
~ method (appraisal) Summierungsmethode; **~ value** Wert einer Summe.

summer, late Spätsommer;
~ (v.) Sommer verbringen;
~ stock on upland pasture Vieh übersommern lassen; **~ and winter** das ganze Jahr verbringen;

~ camp Sommer-, Ferienlager; **to run a ~ camp** (university) Ferienkurse durchführen; **~ campus** Sommerlager; **~ capital** Sommerresidenz; **~ cottage** Sommerhaus; **~ holidays** große Ferien, Sommerferien; **~ house** Sommer-, Ferienhaus; **to catch the ~'s Jaguars** wohlhabende Touristen anlocken; **~ job** Sommer-, Ferienbeschäftigung; **~ outing** Sommerausflug, Fahrt ins Grüne; **~ recess** Sommerferien; **~ residence** Sommerwohnsitz; **~ resort** Sommerfrische, Sommeraufenthalt, Ferienort; **~ sale** (US) Sommerschlußverkauf; **~ school** Ferienkurse; **~ session** (US) Sommersemester; **~ stay** Sommeraufenthalt; **~ stock** Sommerlager; **~ time** Sommerzeit; **~ timetable** Sommerfahrplan; **~ visitors** Feriengäste; **~ weather** Sommerwetter.

summerhouse Sommer-, Ferien-, Gartenhaus, Laube, Pavillon.

summing up Zusammenfassung, (adding up) Addition, (court) Zusammenstellung des Beweisergebnisses, (jury) Rechtsbelehrung, (lawyer), [Schluß]plädoyer.

summit Gipfel;
~ of power Gipfel der Macht;
~ agreement Gipfelabkommen; **~ conference** Gipfelkonferenz; **~ meeting** Gipfeltreffen; **~-meeting agenda** Tagesordnung einer Gipfelkonferenz; **~ organization** Spitzenverband.

summitry Gipfeldiplomatie, -politik.

summitteer Gipfelkonferenzteilnehmer.

summon (v.) auffordern, beauftragen, (defendant, witness) vorladen, vor Gericht zitieren;
~ s. o. j. zu sich bestellen; **~ a conference** Sitzung (Konferenz) einberufen; **~ coupons** Zinsscheine aufbieten; **~ s. o. for debt** j. auf Bezahlung einer Schuld verklagen; **~ a debtor** Schuldner vor Gericht laden; **~ up one's energy** seine ganze Energie aufbieten; **~ a garrison of a fort to surrender** Besatzung einer Festung zur Übergabe auffordern; **~ a meeting** Sitzung anberaumen; **~ Parliament** Parlament einberufen; **~ the parties** Beteiligte laden; **~ s. o. to perform a contract** j. zur Vertragserfüllung auffordern; **~ reservists** Reservisten einberufen; **~ shareholders** Aktionäre zur Hauptversammlung einberufen; **~ s. o. by telephone** j. telefonisch beordern; **~ up** zusammennehmen, aufbieten; **~ s. o. to appear as a witness** j. als Zeugen vorladen.

summoned|personally persönlich zugestellt;
to be ~ to appear on the next day am nächsten Tag Termin haben.

summoner Bote, (law court) Gerichtsdiener.

summoning Aufforderung, Einberufung, (summons) [Vor]ladung;
~ of a meeting Anberaumung einer Sitzung;
to be beyond ~ distance sich für eine rechtzeitige Ladung zu weit entfernt aufhalten.

summons (calling) Ruf, Berufung, (court) Ladung, gerichtliche Vorladung, (convocation) Einberufung, (mil.) Aufforderung zur Übergabe, (parl., Br.) Parlamentseinberufung, (subpoena of witness) Zeugenladung unter Strafandrohung;
interpleader ~ Ladung im Zwangsvollstreckungsaussetzungsverfahren; **judgment ~** (Br.) Antrag auf Beugehaft; **originating ~** Ladung zur Hauptversammlung; **short ~** abgekürzte Ladungsfrist, (US) Schnellverfahren;
~ for directions (Br.) Klageantrag auf prozeßleitende Anordnungen; **~ to garnishee** Vorladung eines Drittschuldners; **~ and order** (Br.) Einzelrichterbeschluß auf Antrag; **~ to pay** Aufforderung zur Zahlung, Zahlungsbefehl; **~ ad respondendum** Ladung zur mündlichen Verhandlung und zur Klageerwiderung; **~ and severance** Zwischenverfügung für abgetrennte Verfahren; **~ to surrender** Übergabeaufforderung;
to answer a ~ einer gerichtlicher Ladung Folge leisten; **to be served with a ~** gerichtliche Vorladung erhalten; **to become liable for a ~** sich einer Vertragsverletzung schuldig machen; **to issue a ~** Vorladung ergehen lassen; **to serve a ~** Ladung zustellen; **to take out a ~ against s. o.** j. vorladen lassen, Vorladung gegen j. erwirken;
~ case (criminal case, Br.) Übertretungssache.

sump Senkgrube, (car) Ölwanne.

sumptuary|principle (taxation) Aufwandsprinzip; **~ tax** Aufwand-, Luxussteuer.

sumptuous living aufwendige Lebenshaltung.

sun (fig.) Glück, Wohlstand;
to adore the rising ~ dem neuen Machthaber huldigen; **can't hold a candle to the ~** unvergleichbar sein;
~ blind (Br.) Markise; **~ deck** Sonnendeck; **~ roof** (car) Schiebedach; **~ spots** Sonnenflecken; **~ visor** (car) Sonnenblende.

Sunday|closing (shops) Sonntagsruhe; **~ clothes** Sonntagsstaat; **~ collection** sonntägliche Briefkastenleerung; **~ driver** (sl.)

Sonntagsfahrer; ~ **edition** Sonntagsausgabe; **~s and public holidays** Sonn- und Feiertage; ~ **newspaper** Sonntagszeitung; ~ **Observance Act** Gesetz zur Einhaltung der Sonntagsruhe; ~ **opening** Offenhalten am Sonntag; ~ **paper** Sonntagszeitung; ₂ **run** (sl.) große Entfernung; ~ **school** Sonntagsschule; ~ **store opening** (US) Ladenverkauf am Sonntag; ~ **supplement** Sonntagsbeilage; ~ **trading** Verkauf am Sonntag; ~ **working** Sonntagsarbeit.

sundowner Abendschoppen.

sundries Verschiedenes, Diverses, (expenses) diverse Unkosten, verschiedene Ausgaben, diverse Forderungen;
~ **account** Spesenkonto, Konto für Diverse; ~ **debit form** Spesenbelastungsformular; ~ **journal** Konto Verschiedenes.

sundry verschiedene, diverse;
~ **creditors** diverse Forderungen (Verbindlichkeiten); ~ **creditors account** (Br.) diverse Kreditoren; ~ **debtors** diverse Debitoren, verschiedene Forderungen; ~ **expenditure** außerordentlicher Aufwand; ~ **expenses** verschiedene Unkosten, **goods** Diverses; ~ **money owing** verschiedene Schuldbeträge; ~ **money owing to the estate** verschiedene Nachlaßforderungen; ~ **receipts** verschiedene Einnahmen; ~ **samples** verschiedene Muster, Musterauswahl; ~ **securities** (market report) Nebenwerte.

sundryman Krämer, Kurz-, Gemischtwarenhändler.

sunk cost einmalige Produktionskosten.

sunken | ship gesunkenes Schiff; ~ **treasure** versunkener Schatz.

sunray lamp Höhensonne.

super (quality, sl.) Qualitätsware, erstklassige Qualität, (theater) Statist;
~ **American** hundertprozentiger Amerikaner; **~-duper** (US) phantastisch.

superaddition Hinzufügung, Zusatz.

superannuable pensionsfähig.

superannuate (v.) (reach age limit) Pensionierungsalter erreichen, pensioniert werden, in den Ruhestand treten, (power of attorney) erlöschen, verjähren, (send into retirement) in den Ruhestand versetzen, pensionieren;
~ **s. o.** jem. den Abschied bewilligen.

superannuated (person) altersschwach, überjährig, pensioniert, in den Ruhestand versetzt, (thing) überaltert, veraltet, unmodern;
to be ~ pensioniert (in den Ruhestand versetzt) werden;
~ **management** pensionsreifer Vorstand; ~ **power of attorney** erloschene Vollmacht.

superannuation (pension) Ruhegehalt, Pension, Alterszulage, (power of attorney) Erlöschen, (sending into retirement) Pensionierung [wegen Erreichung der Altersgrenze], Versetzung in den Ruhestand;
entitled to ~ ruhegeld-, pensionsberechtigt;
₂ **Act** (Br.) Altersversorgungsgesetz; ~ **allowance** Pension, Ruhegehalt; ~ **benefits** Versorgungsbezüge; ~ **contribution** Altersversicherungsbeitrag, Beitrag zur Pensionskasse, Pensionszuschuß; ~ **fund** Pensionskasse, -fonds; ~ **money** Pensionsbeitrag; ~ **payments to pension fund** Beiträge zu einer Pensionskasse; ~ **provisions** Ruhegehalts-, Pensionsbestimmungen, -regelung; ~ **scheme** Alterversorgungswerk; ~ **security** Pensionssicherung.

superatomic bomb Wasserstoffbombe.

supercalendered hochsatiniert.

supercargo Ladungs-, Frachtaufseher, Supercargo.

supercharged engine Kompressormotor.

supercharger, to let in the Schnellgang einschalten.

supercivilized überzivilisiert.

supercommission Superprovision.

superdividend Super-, Zusatzdividende, Bonus.

superelevated (curve) überhöht.

superette (US) kleiner Selbstbedienungsladen.

superficial knowledge oberflächliche Kenntnisse.

superficiary Erbbauberechtigter.

superficies (lat.) Erbbaurecht.

superfilm Monumental-, Kolossalfilm.

superfluities of life Entbehrlichkeiten des Lebens.

superfluity of money Geldüberhang.

superfluous land (railway company, Br.) nicht mehr benötigtes enteignetes Land.

superhet Überlagerungsempfänger.

superhighway (US) Autobahn.

superhuman effort übermenschliche Anstrengung.

superimpose (v.) hinzufügen, (ad) einkopieren, (television) überlagern;
~ **a punishment** zusätzliche Strafe verhängen.

superimposed clause Zusatzklausel.

superimposition (television) Überlagerung.

superintend (v.) beaufsichtigen, überwachen, Oberaufsicht führen;
~ **an election** Stimmenabgabe überwachen; ~ **the opening of the letters** beim Öffnen der Briefpost anwesend sein; ~ **work personally** Arbeiten persönlich beaufsichtigen.

superintendence Oberaufsicht, Überwachung, Betriebsleitung;
under the personal ~ of the manager vom Geschäftsführer persönlich überwacht.

superintendency Verwaltungsbezirk, Aufsichtsbereich.

superintendent [Betriebs]leiter, Vorsteher, Aufsichtsbeamter, (police, Br.) Polizeichef, -direktor, (prison, US) Gefängnisdirektor;
medical ~ Chefarzt; **railway ~** Aufsichtsbeamter; **shop ~** Werksführer;
~ **of agents** (insurance) Bezirksdirektor; ~ **of police** (Br.) Polizeichef, -präsident; ~ **of schools** (US) Oberschulrat; ~ **of public works** Bauaufsichtsbehörde;
~ (a.) aufsichtsführend, leitend, kontrollierend;
~'s office (Br.) Kommissariat; ~ **registrar** (Br.) Hauptstandesbeamter; **to get married before the ~ registrar** (Br.) sich standesamtlich trauen lassen.

superintendentship Aufsichtsamt, Oberaufsicht.

superintending committee Beirat.

superior [Dienst]vorgesetzter;
immediate ~ unmittelbarer Vorgesetzter; **ranking ~** Dienstvorgesetzter;
~ **to flattery** gegen Schmeicheleien gefeit; ~ **in rank** Dienstvorgesetzter;
~ (a.) vorzüglich, überlegen, überdurchschnittlich, (index number) hochstehend, (print.) hochgestellt, (railroad) vorrangig, (in rank) rangälter, vorgesetzt, höherstehend;
to be ~ in numbers zahlenmäßig überlegen sein; **to be ~ in rank** höhergestellt (unmittelbarer Vorgesetzter) sein; **to think o. s. ~** sich für etw. besseres halten;
~ **articles** erstklassige Ware, Qualitätsware; ~ **authority** vorgesetzte Behörde; ~ **court** übergeordnetes Gericht, höhere Instanz, Obergericht, (US) höchster Gerichtshof; ~ **estate** (easement) herrschendes Grundstück; ~ **fellow servant** (law of negligence) übergeordneter Erfüllungsgehilfe; ~ **force** (law of negligence) unwiderstehliche (höhere) Gewalt; ~ **forces** (mil.) überlegene Streitkräfte, Übermacht; **to attack with ~ forces** mit überlegenen Kräften angreifen; ~ **grades** Qualitätssorten; ~ **intelligence** überragende Intelligenz; ~ **knowledge** überragendes Wissen; ~ **officer** Dienstvorgesetzter; ~ **person** überragende Persönlichkeit; ~ **quality** vorzügliche Beschaffenheit, beste Qualität; ~ **title** besserer Rechtsanspruch.

superiority Überlegenheit, (mil.) Übermacht;
air ~ Luftüberlegenheit; **economic ~** wirtschaftliche Überlegenheit;
~ **in material** Materialüberlegenheit;
~ **complex** (coll.) Überlegenheitskomplex.

superlative | s, to speak in in Superlativen sprechen;
~ **wisdom** überragende Klugheit.

superman Übermensch.

supermarine (navy) Wasserflugzeug.

supermarket (US) Supermarkt, großes Lebensmittelgeschäft mit Selbstbedienung, Lebensmittelgroßgeschäft, Selbstbedienungsladen;
~ **chain** Warenhauskette; ~ **shopping** Großmarkteinkauf.

supernormal überdurchschnittlich.

supernumerary Hilfsarbeiter, -angestellter, -beamter, (officer) außerplanmäßiger Beamter;
~ (a.) überzählig, (exceeding a required number) außeretats-, überplanmäßig;
~ **clerk** (US) Volontär; ~ **post** außerplanmäßige Stelle.

superordinate übergeordnet.

superpowers überstaatliche Macht, Supermacht.

superprinting (film) Doppelbelichtung.

superride (v.) außer Kraft setzen.

supersaturation Übersättigung.

superscribe (v.) beschriften, adressieren, mit einer Adresse versehen.

superscription Aufschrift, Adresse, (title) Überschrift.

supersede (v.) (cease to employ) aus dem Amt entfernen, kassieren, (pass in promotion) bei der Beförderung übergehen, (set aside) aufheben, abschaffen, außer Kraft setzen, (take the place of) im Amt ablösen, Nachfolger werden, ersetzen;
~ **by a new contract** durch einen neuen Vertrag ersetzen; ~ **previous issues** an die Stelle früherer Aufgaben treten; ~ **a**

judgment Urteil aufheben; ~ **an old machine** alte Maschine ersetzen; ~ **an official** Beamten ablösen; ~ **ordinary roads** gewöhnliche Landstraßen ersetzen; ~ **a system** neues System einführen.

supersedeas Einstellung des Verfahrens, *(execution)* vorläufige Einstellung der Vollstreckbarkeit.

superseding cause *(liability)* Kausalzusammenhang unterbrechendes Ereignis.

superserviceable dienstbeflissen.

supersession Absetzung, *(annulment)* Aufhebung, Umstoßung, *(procedure)* Aussetzung, Einstellung, *(replacement)* Ersetzung; ~ **from office** Amtsenthebung.

supersonic Ultra-, Überschall..., *(el.)* hochfrequent; ~ **age** Überschallzeitalter; ~ **aircraft** Überschallflugzeug; ~ **airline** Überschallfluglinie; ~ **airliner** Überschallflugzeug; ~ **nuclear bomber** Überschallatombomber; ~ **commercial service** planmäßiger Überschall-Linienflugverkehr; ~ **speed** Überschallgeschwindigkeit; **to fly at ~ speed** mit Überschallgeschwindigkeit fliegen; ~ **transport** Überschallverkehr, *(airliner)* Überschallverkehrsflugzeug; ~ **wave** Ultraschallwelle; ~ **wind tunnel** Überschallwindkanal.

supersound Über-, Ultraschall.

superstate überstaatliche Regierungsgewalt, Superstaat.

superstition Aberglaube.

superstructure Überbau, *(railway)* Oberbau.

supertanker Supertanker.

supertare zusätzliche Taravergütung, Übertara.

supertax *(Br.)* Zusatz-, Über-, Mehrgewinnsteuer, *(income tax)* Einkommensteuerzuschlag, Ergänzungszuschlag.

superterrestial überirdisch.

supervene *(v.)* sich plötzlich einstellen.

supervening|cause *(accident)* entscheidende Unfallursache; ~ **impossibility** nachträgliche Unmöglichkeit; ~ **negligence** nicht ins Gewicht fallendes Eigenverschulden.

supervention unvermutetes Eintreten.

supervise *(v.)* überwachen, beaufsichtigen, kontrollieren; ~ **the printing** Druckvorgang überwachen.

supervising|authority aufsichtsführende Behörde, Aufsichtsbehörde, -instanz; ~ **duty** Aufsichtspflicht; ~ **judge** *(US)* aufsichtsführender Richter; ~ **official** Aufsichtsbeamter.

supervision Überwachung, Aufsichtsführung, [Ober]aufsicht, Beaufsichtigung, Kontrolle; **under the ~ of** unter Aufsicht von; **close ~** scharfe Überwachung; **compulsory ~** gerichtlich angeordnete Überwachung; **disciplinary ~** Dienstaufsicht; **factory ~** Betriebskontrolle; **government ~** Staatsaufsicht; **medical ~** ärztliche Aufsicht; **police ~** *(Br.)* Polizeiaufsicht; ~ **of calls** *(tel.)* Gesprächsüberwachung; ~ **of cartels** Kartellaufsicht; ~ **of a class** *(US)* Beaufsichtigung einer Schulklasse; ~ **of guardianship of infants** Beaufsichtigung der für Minderjährige bestehenden Vormundschaften; ~ **of manufacture** Fertigungskontrolle; ~ **of spending** Ausgabenkontrolle; ~ **of the stock exchange** Börsenaufsicht; **to be subject to ~** der Aufsicht unterstehen, aufsichtspflichtig sein; **to be under police ~** unter Polizeiaufsicht stehen; **to be placed under the ~ of a probation officer** unter Bewährungshilfe gestellt werden; ~ **order** *(liquidation)* Überwachungsverfügung, *(police, Br.)* Anordnung der Polizeiaufsicht.

supervisor Aufseher, Inspekteur, Kontrolleur, Aufsichtsbeamter, -person, Nachprüfer, *(school)* Fachbeauftragter, *(US)* städtischer Beamter; ~ **of elections** *(US)* Wahlprüfer; ~ **in a factory** Betriebsaufseher, Werksleiter; **to act as a ~** Überwachungsfunktionen ausüben.

supervisorship Aufsichtsamt.

supervisory aufsichtsführend; ~ **agency** Überwachungsstelle; ~ **authority** Aufsichtsbehörde; ~ **board** *(Br.)* Aufsichtsamt; ~ **body** Aufsichts-, Kontrollorgan; **in a ~ capacity** als Aufsichtsperson (Aufsichtsbehörde); **bank ~ commission** Bankaufsichtsbehörde; ~ **committee** Überwachungsausschuß; ~ **control** Oberaufsicht, *(court)* Zuständigkeit als Rechtsmittelinstanz; **to exercise ~ control** Aufsichtstätigkeit ausüben; ~ **costs** [Betriebs]überwachungskosten; ~ **duty** Aufsichtspflicht; ~ **duties** Überwachungsfunktionen, -aufgaben; ~ **jurisdiction** Aufsichtsinstanz; ~ **organ** Überwachungs-, Aufsichtsorgan; ~ **personnel** *(US)* leitende Angestellte; ~ **position** Aufsichtsstellung; ~ **post** Überwachungsposition; ~ **power** Aufsichtskompetenz; ~ **service** Überwachungstätigkeit; ~ **staff** *(Br.)* leitende Angestellte; ~ **system** Überwachungssystem; ~ **training** Vorgesetztenschulung.

supper Abendessen, -brot; ~ **dance** Abendbrot mit Tanz.

supplant *(v.)* **s. o.** an jds. Stelle einrücken; ~ **the tram** *(bus)* Straßenbahn verdrängen.

supplanted by a rival firm von einem Konkurrenzbetrieb ausgestochen.

supplantation widerrechtliche Besitzergreifung.

supplement Zusatz, Ergänzung, Nachtrag, Anhang, *(book)* Ergänzungsband, *(extra charge)* Preisaufschlag, *(newspaper)* [Gratis]beilage; **commercial ~** Handelsbeilage; **earnings-related ~** *(national insurance, Br.)* lohnabhängiges Kurzarbeitergeld; **Exchequer ~s** *(Br.)* Staatszuschüsse zur Sozialversicherung; **free ~** Gratisbeilage; **income ~** *(US)* Staatszuschuß zum Einkommen; **literary ~** Literaturbeilage, literarischer Teil [einer Zeitung]; **wage ~s** zusätzliche Lohnzahlungen, Zusatzleistungen; **women's ~** Frauenbeilage; ~ *(v.)* ergänzen, Nachtrag liefern; ~ **a book** Nachträge zu einem Buch liefern; ~ **a budget** Nachtragshaushalt vorlegen; ~ **one's ordinary income by journalism** seine Normaleinkünfte durch journalistische Beiträge aufbessern; ~ **a loan** Ergänzungskredit gewähren.

supplemental *(airline)* Charterfluggesellschaft; ~ *(a.)* ergänzend, zusätzlich; ~ **act** Zusatz-, Ergänzungsgesetz, *(law court)* ergänzende Antwort; ~ **affidavit** eidliche Zusatzerklärung; ~ **answer** zusätzliche Klageerwiderung, ergänzender Schriftsatz; ~ **appropriation** Nachtragsbewilligung; ~ **bill** *(equity pleading)* Zusatz-, Ergänzungsantrag; ~ **claim** Nachforderung, zusätzlicher Anspruch; ~ **compensation** Zusatzvergütung; ~ **complaint** *(US)* Klageergänzung; ~ **cost** Preisaufschlag, -zuschlag; ~ **data** zusätzliche Angaben; ~ **deed** Nachtragsurkunde; ~ **election** Nachwahl; ~ **instrument** Zusatzdokument; ~ **patent** Zusatzpatent; ~ **plea** zusätzliche Einwendungen; ~ **pleading** *(US)* zusätzliches Parteivorbringen, ergänzender Schriftsatz; ~ **question** *(parl.)* Zusatzfrage; ~ **register** *(US)* Nebenregister; ~ **statement** Zusatzerklärung; ~ **wages** Lohnzulage, -zuschlag.

supplementary als Nachtrag, nachträglich, ergänzend; **to be ~** Nachtrag darstellen; ~ **advertising** zusätzliche Werbung, Ergänzungswerbung; ~ **agreement** Ergänzungs-, Zusatzabkommen; ~ **allowance** Nachbewilligung, *(Br.)* Zusatz-, Sozialrente; ~ **appropriation** *(US)* Nachtragsbewilligung; ~ **banking functions** irreguläre Bankgeschäfte; ~ **benefit** *(Br.)* Sozialhilfe, staatliche Fürsorge; ⚖ **Benefits Act** *(Br.)* Sozialhilfegesetz; ⚖ **Benefits Commission** *(Br.)* Fürsorgebehörde, Sozialhilfeabteilung, -amt; ~ **benefit level** *(Br.)* Sozialhilfeniveau; ~ **budget** Nachtragshaushalt; ~ **charge** nachträgliche Belastung, Mehrbelastung, Zuschlag; ~ **claim** Nachforderung; ~ **colo(u)r** Zusatzfarbe; ~ **compensation** zusätzliche Vergütung; ~ **contract** Zusatzvertrag; ~ **convention** Zusatzabkommen, -vereinbarung; ~ **costs** zusätzliche Kosten, Preisaufschlag, Fix- und Gemeinkosten; ~ **course** Nachhilfekursus; ~ **credit** Nachtrags-, Ergänzungskredit; ~ **engine** Hilfsmotor; ~ **entry** Nachtragsbuchung; ~ **estimates** Nachtragsetat, -haushalt; ~ **fee** *(post)* Zusatz-, Nachgebühr; ~ **files** Beiakten; ~ **grant** Nachbewilligung; ~ **income** Nebenverdienst, -einkommen, -einnahmen, -bezüge; ~ **insurance** Zusatzversicherung; ~ **list** *(Br.)* Beilage zum amtlichen Kursblatt; ~ **load** Beiladung; ~ **order** Nachbestellung; ~ **ordinance** Zusatzbestimmung; ~ **patent** Zusatzpatent; ~ **payment** Nachzahlung, *(relief)* Zusatzunterstützung; ~ **pension** *(Br.)* Zusatzrente; ~ **pension insurance** *(Br.)* Zusatzrentenversicherung; ~ **policy** Zusatz-, Nachtragspolice; ~ **premium** Zusatzprämie; ~ **proceedings** *(US)* Offenbarungs-, [Zwangs]vollstreckungsverfahren; ~ **protocol** Zusatzprotokoll; ~ **provisions** Ergänzungsbestimmungen; ~ **question** Zusatzfrage; ~ **regulations** Ergänzungsvorschriften; ~ **relief** Zusatzunterstützung; ~ **report** Ergänzungsbericht; ~ **security income** *(US)* Sozialhilfe; ~ **sheet** Beiblatt, Extrabogen; ~ **sickness insurance** Krankenzusatzversicherung; ~ **tax** Nachsteuer; ~ **taxation** Nachbesteuerung; ~ **unemployment insurance** zusätzliche Arbeitslosenunterstützung; ~ **volume** Nachtrags-, Ergänzungsband; ~ **vote** *(credit)* Nachtragsbewilligung.

supplementation Ergänzung, Vervollständigung, Zusatz, Nachtrag; ~ **of salaries** Gehaltsaufbesserung.

suppletory oath Erfüllungseid.

suppliant Bittsteller.

supplication, supplicatory letter Bittschrift, -brief.

supplied|daily täglich beliefert; ~ **to trade only** Lieferung nur an Wiederverkäufer;

to be ~ with goods from abroad Waren aus dem Ausland beziehen; **to be ~ only until stocks run out** nur lieferbar sein, solange der Vorrat reicht;

can be ~ lieferbar.

supplier Auslieferer, Lieferant, Lieferer;

~s *(balance sheet)* Lieferantenschulden, Verbindlichkeiten aus Warenlieferungen;

foreign ~ ausländische Lieferfirma; **main (major) ~** Hauptlieferant; **regular ~** regelmäßiger Lieferant, Stammlieferant; **~ of addresses** Adressenverlag; **~ of goods** Warenlieferant; **~ of power** Energieträger; **~ of services** Erbringer von Dienstleistungen;

to stay with a present ~ augenblicklichen Lieferanten beibehalten;

~s' account Lieferantenkonto; **~ choice** Lieferantenwahl; **~ company** Zulieferungsbetrieb; **~'s costs** Lieferantenkredit; **~'s country** Lieferland; **~'s credit** Lieferantenkredit; **~'s financing** Lieferantenfinanzierung; **~'s instruction** Lieferantenanweisung; **~'s invoice** Lieferantenrechnung; **~'s ledger** Wareneingangsbuch; **~ number** Lieferantennummer; **~'s offer** Lieferantenangebot; **~'s price** Lieferantenpreis; **~ relations** Lieferantenbeziehungen.

supplies *(allowance)* Unterhaltungszuschuß, *(balance sheet, US)* [Hilfs]material, Hilfs- und Betriebsstoffe, *(goods furnished)* Lieferungen, Belieferung, *(grant of money, Br.)* gesondert zu bewilligende Beträge, bewilligter Etat, [Ausgaben]budget, *(mil.)* Nachschub, *(stores)* Vorräte;

adequate ~ ausreichende Vorräte; **common ~** gemeinschaftliche Versorgungsgüter; **continuous ~** geregelte Zufuhr, *(mil.)* Nachschub, Proviant; **food ~** Lebensmittel; **fresh ~** zusätzliche Lieferungen; **limited ~** begrenzte Liefermöglichkeit; **money ~** Geldangebot; **operating ~** Betriebsstoffe; **post-office ~** Postamtsbedarf; **typewriting ~** Schreibmaschinenartikel; **war ~** Kriegslieferungen;

~ in a factory Materiallager; **~ on hand** vorhandene Vorräte; **~ of money** Kapitalquellen; **~ on a deferred payment basis** *(US)* Warenlieferungen auf Abzahlungsbasis; **~ in transit** unterwegs befindliches Material; **~ of wheat** Weizenlieferungen;

to cut off s. one's ~ jem. keinen Unterhaltszuschuß mehr gewähren (die Zufuhr sperren); **to depend on foreign ~** auf ausländische Lieferanten angewiesen sein; **to lay in ~ for the winter** sich mit Wintervorräten eindecken; **to obtain one's ~ from A** sich von A beliefern lassen; **to order ~** Vorräte bestellen; **to receive new ~ of books** neue Büchersendung erhalten; **to refuse ~** Mittel verweigern; **to run short of ~** knapp an Vorräten werden; **to take in ~** sich verproviantieren; **to touch ~** Vorräte angreifen; **to use up all one's ~** seine ganzen Vorräte aufbrauchen; **to vote ~** *(Br.)* Etat (Haushaltsmittel) bewilligen;

~ industry Zulieferungsindustrie.

supply *(allowance)* Zuschuß, Beitrag, *(demand)* [Waren]angebot, *(mil.)* Proviant, Nachschub, Versorgungsmaterial, *(parliament, Br.)* Haushaltsbewilligung, *(additional payment)* Nachzahlung, *(provision)* [Be]lieferung, Eindeckung, Beschaffung, Versorgung, Zu-, Anfuhr, *(store)* Vorrat, Lager, Bestand, *(substitute)* Vertretung, Stellvertreter, Ersatzmann;

in short ~ nur beschränkt lieferbar; **on ~** in Vertretung, als Ersatzmann;

additional ~ Zuschuß; **aggregate ~** Gesamtangebot; **assured ~** gesicherte Zufuhr; **capital ~** Kapitalangebot, -versorgung, Angebote auf dem Kapitalmarkt; **competitive ~** Konkurrenzangebot; **composite ~** zusammengesetztes Angebot; **continuous ~** geregelte (ständige) Zufuhr; **copious ~** reichlicher Vorrat; **credit ~** Kreditbeschaffung; **current ~** laufendes Angebot, *(electricity)* Netzanschluß; **elastic ~** Preiselastizität des Angebotes; **essential ~** lebenswichtiger Bedarf; **excessive ~** Überangebot, Angebotsüberhang; **floating ~** laufendes Angebot; **food ~** Nahrungsmittelversorgung; **fresh ~** Nachschub; **fuel ~** Benzinversorgung, Treibstoffvorrat; **inexhaustible ~** unerschöpfliche Vorräte; **labo(u)r ~** verfügbare Arbeitskräfte, Arbeitskräfteangebot; **large ~** große Auswahl; **marginal ~** Spitzenangebot; **market ~** Marktbeschickung; **minimum ~** Mindestbedarf; **money ~** Geldbedarf, -versorgung; **a month's ~** Monatsbedarf, Monatsvorrat; **plentiful ~** reichlicher Überfluß; **power ~** Energie-, Stromversorgung; **regular ~** Normalbezug; **rival ~** Konkurrenzangebot; **scanty ~** schwache Zufuhr; **seasonal ~** Saisonbedarf; **visible ~** dem Markt zur Verfügung stehende Warenmenge; **water ~** Wasserversorgung;

~ and demand Angebot und Nachfrage;

~ of the agenda paper Bereitstellung der Tagesordnung; **~ of capital** Kapitalbereitstellung, -angebot; **~ of cash** Liquiditäts-

angebot; **~ of credit** zur Verfügung stehender Kredit, Kreditvolumen, -versorgung, -angebot; **excessive ~ over demand** Angebotsüberhang; **~ of energy** Energieversorgung; **daily ~ of food** täglicher Bedarf an Lebensmitteln; **~ of fuel** Brennstoffversorgung; **~ of gold** Goldversorgung; **~ of goods** Güterversorgung, -angebot, Waren[be]lieferung, -zufuhr; **~ on hand** vorhandene Vorräte; **~ of information** Erteilung von Auskünften; **~ of technical knowhow** Zurverfügungstellung industrieller Produktionserfahrungen; **~ of labo(u)r** verfügbare Arbeitskräfte; **excessive ~ of labo(u)r** Überangebot an Arbeitskräften; **~ of land** Grundstücksangebot; **ample ~ of liquid funds** reichliche Liquiditätsversorgung; **~ of machinery** Maschinenlieferung; **~ of materials** Materiallieferung, -versorgung; **~ of raw materials** Rohstoffversorgung; **~ of money** Geldangebot, -versorgung, Angebot am Geldmarkt; **~ of power** Stromversorgung; **sufficient ~ of provisions** ausreichende Versorgung; **~ of reading matter** [Vorrat an] Lesestoff; **~ of scrap** Schrottangebot;

~ *(v.)* *(fill as substitute)* Stelle ausfüllen, vertreten, als Ersatzmann einspringen, *(pay additionally)* nachzahlen, nachschießen, *(procure)* be-, verschaffen, liefern, beliefern, Lieferant sein, ver-, besorgen, *(provision)* mit Proviant versehen, *(replace)* ausgleichen, ersetzen, *(sell)* abgeben, verkaufen;

~ an army Armee beliefern; **~ o. s. with an article from abroad** Ware von außerhalb beziehen; **~ the bulk** Löwenanteil liefern; **~ the capital for s. th.** etw. finanzieren; **~ collateral** Sicherheiten stellen (anschaffen); **~ a defect in a manufacture** Fabrikationsfehler beseitigen; **~ the deficiency** Defizit decken, Fehlbetrag ausgleichen; **~ the public demand** einem öffentlichen Bedürfnis genügen; **~ a document** Urkunde beschaffen; **~ electricity to a town** Stromversorgung einer Stadt übernehmen; **~ evidence** Beweismaterial beibringen; **~ a family** Familie unterhalten; **~ s. o. with a fund** Deckung für jem. anschaffen, j. mit Geldmitteln versehen; **~ o. s. with goods** sich mit Waren eindecken; **~ goods on credit** Waren auf Kredit liefern; **~ information** Auskunft geben (erteilen); **~ an interpreter** Dolmetscher stellen; **~ a loss** Verlust ausgleichen; **~ the market** Markt mit Waren versehen (beliefern); **~ the needs** Bedarf decken; **~ s. one's needs** jds. Lebensunterhalt sicherstellen; **~ to order** auf Bestellung liefern; **~ proof** Beweise liefern; **~ a ship with provisions** Schiff verproviantieren; **~ to the trade** an Wiederverkäufer liefern; **~ a vacancy** freie Stelle besetzen; **~ a want** ein Bedürfnis befriedigen; **~ a want that has long been felt** um einem langempfundenen Bedürfnis abzuhelfen; **~ only to wholesalers** nur den Großhandel beliefern; **~ a missing word** fehlendes Wort ergänzen;

to assure o. s. of adequate ~ seine ausreichende Versorgung sicherstellen; **to be in short ~** knapp sein, beschränkt lieferbar sein; **to cut off ~** Zufuhr abschneiden; **disconnect the ~** Hauptanschluß stillegen; **to draw one's ~ from ...** seinen Bedarf von ... decken; **to exceed the ~** Angebot übersteigen; **to hold a post on ~** Stelle vorübergehend innehaben; **to lay (take) in a ~ of s. th.** Vorrat von etw. anlegen; **to refuse to ~ goods** Lieferung verweigern; **to stay well ahead of ~** Nachfrage nicht befriedigen können; **to tender for a ~ of goods** sich um einen Liefervertrag bemühen; **to withhold ~ of goods from a dealer** Warenlieferungen zurückhalten;

~ agreement Lieferungsvertrag, Lieferabkommen, -vertrag; **~ area** Versorgungsgebiet; **~ base** Nachschub-, Versorgungsbasis, Lieferstelle; **~ bomb** Verpflegungsbombe; **~ bottleneck** Lieferengpaß, Versorgungsengpaß; **~ business** Zulieferungsindustrie; **~ capacity** Bedarfsdeckungsmöglichkeit; **~ center** *(US)* **(centre, Br.)** Versorgungsstelle; **~ chain** Versorgungskette; **~ column** Proviant-, Wagen-, Verpflegungskolonne, *(mil.)* Train[kolonne]; **to convoy a ~ column** einer Nachschubkolonne Geleit geben; **~ conditions** Lieferungs-, Versorgungsbedingungen; **~ contract** Lieferabkommen, Liefervertrag; **to award public ~ contracts** öffentliche Lieferaufträge vergeben; **to defer fulfilment of ~ contracts** Erfüllung von Lieferungsverträgen aussetzen; **~ curve** Angebotskurve; **~ days** *(Br.)* Sitzungen des Haushaltsausschusses; **~ delays** Lieferverzögerungen; **~ department** Proviantamt; **~ depot** Proviantamt, -lager; **~ difficulties** Versorgungsschwierigkeiten; **~ guarantee** Lieferkaution, -garantie; **~ house** Lieferfirma; **~ index figure** Lieferziffer; **gas ~ industry** Gaswirtschaft; **~ line** Versorgungs-, Nachschublinie, Nachschubweg; **~ network** *(electricity)* Leitungsnetz; **~ note** Lieferschein; **~ office** Beschaffungsamt; **~ plant** Lieferwerk; **~ position** Versorgungslage, *(retail shop)* Lieferstellung; **~ price** äußerster (niederster) Preis, Angebotspreis; **~ problem** Versorgungsproblem; **~ requirements** Versorgungsbedarf; **~ schedule** Angebotstabelle, Angebotsfunktion,

Lieferumfang; ~ **service** Lieferdienst; ~ **services** *(Br.)* jährlich neu finanzierte Ausgaben des ordentlichen Haushalts; **electric** ~ **service** Stromversorgung; ~ **shift** Angebotsverschiebung; ~ **ship** Versorgungsschiff; ~ **situation** Liefersituation, Versorgungslage; **tight** ~ **situation** angespannte Versorgungslage; ~ **source** Lieferquelle; **local** ~ **station** Auslieferungslager; ~ **store** Auslieferungslager; ~ **system** Versorgungssystem; ~ **teacher** Aushilfslehrer; ~ **train** Proviantzug; ~ **undertaking** Zuschußbetrieb; ~ **vote** Etatsbewilligung; ~ **waggon** Versorgungswagen.

supplying Versorgung, Belieferung, *(substitution)* vorübergehende Vertretung;

~ **electricity or gas to tenants** Strom- und Gasberechnung für Mieter; ~ **of goods** Warenlieferung; ~ **with provisions** Verproviantierung, Lebensmittelversorgung;

~ **firm** Lieferfirma; ~ **industry** Zulieferungsindustrie.

support *(assistance)* Unterstützung, Hilfe[stellung], Beistand, *(confirmation)* Bestätigung, Bekräftigung, Erhärtung, *(mil.)* Reserve, Verstärkung, Nachtrupp, *(stock exchange)* Stützung, Stützungsaktion, -käufe, *(subsistence)* [Lebens]unterhalt, Mittel, Auskommen, *(technical)* Abstützung, *(theater)* Ensemble; **depending on you for** ~ auf Ihre Unterstützung angewiesen; **deserving** ~ unterstützungsbedürftig; **in** ~ zur Unterstützung, *(mil.)* in Reserve; **in** ~ **of** zur Bestätigung von, als Beleg für; **in** ~ **of a motion** zur Begründung eines Antrages; **with the** ~ **of** mit Unterstützung von; **without government** ~ ohne Staatszuschuß;

advertiser ~ Unterstützung der Werbewirtschaft; **air** ~ Unterstützung durch die Luftwaffe; **banking** ~ Stützungsaktion durch die Banken, Bankenintervention; **bipartisan** ~ Unterstützung beider Parteien; **bull** ~ Stützungskäufe der Haussepartei; **community** ~ von der Gemeinde gewährte Unterstützung; **dollar** ~ Dollarstützung; **government** ~ staatliche Unterstützung; **majority** ~ Unterstützung der Mehrheit; **material** ~ wesentliche Unterstützung; **minority** ~ Unterstützung der Minderheit; **pool** ~ Stützungskäufe durch ein Konsortium; **price** ~ [staatliche] Preisunterstützung;

~ **for economic activity** Stützpfeiler der Konjunktur; ~ **of a church** Unterhaltung einer Kirche; ~ **of credit** Kreditgewährung; ~ **in the election** Wahlunterstützung, -hilfe; **chief** ~ **of one's family** Hauptstütze seiner Familie; ~ **of prices** Preis-, Kursstützung;

~ *(v.)* unterstützen, unterhalten, *(finance)* aufkommen für, finanzieren, *(petition)* befürworten, *(price)* sich halten; ~ **o. s.** seinen Lebensunterhalt selbst verdienen, seine eigenen Ausgaben bestreiten; ~ **s. o.** jem. zur Seite stehen; ~ **a candidate** Kandidaten unterstützen; ~ **a charge** Anklage erhärten; ~ **one's claim** Anspruch begründen, Forderung beweisen; ~ **a conversation** Gespräch im Gang halten; ~ **a currency** Währung stützen; ~ **by documents** mit Urkunden (urkundlich) belegen; ~ **a family** Lebensunterhalt einer Familie sicherstellen; ~ **the gold standard** für Aufrechterhaltung des Goldstandardes eintreten; ~ **an idea** für eine Idee eintreten; ~ **the notes in circulation** im Umlauf befindliche Banknoten decken; ~ **a political party** politische Partei finanziell unterstützen; ~ **a petition** Bittschrift (Eingabe) befürworten; ~ **a resolution** sich für eine Entschließung aussprechen; ~ **the sterling rate of exchange** Stützungsaktion für den Pfundkurs durchführen; ~ **stocks** Stützungskäufe für Aktien durchführen; ~ **by taxes** aus Steuern finanzieren; ~ **a theory** Theorie vertreten;

to be dependent upon s. one's ~ auf jds. Unterstützung angewiesen sein; **to be one's family's sole** ~ alleiniger Ernährer (Versorger) seiner Familie sein; **to be liable for** ~ *(US)* unterhaltspflichtig sein; **to enjoy popular** ~ allgemeine Unterstützung genießen; **to give** ~ **to** unterstützen; **to give** ~ **to the franc** Franken stützen; **to give** ~ **to a proposal** Vorschlag unterstützen; **to have a wife and seven children to** ~ Frau und sieben Kinder zu ernähren haben; **to have s. one's** ~ **in an election** von jem. bei einer Wahl unterstützt werden; **to obtain little** ~ *(proposal)* nur geringe Unterstützung finden; **to offer a salary and** ~ **for the year** Gehalt sowie freie Unterkunft und Verpflegung für ein Jahr anbieten; **to pledge one's** ~ sich zur Unterstützung verpflichten; **to produce documents in** ~ [of an allegation] beweisstützende Unterlagen vorlegen; **to receive financial** ~ finanziell unterstützt werden; **to respond to more** ~ *(market report)* sich größerer Beachtung erfreuen; **to speak in** ~ **of a motion** Antrag unterstützen; **to speak in** ~ **of s. one's policy** sich für jds. Politik aussprechen;

~ **buying** *(stock exchange)* Stützungs-, Interessenkäufe; **compulsory** ~ **commitments** Unterstützungsverpflichtungen; ~ **costs** Unterhaltungskosten; ~ **facilities** Hilfseinrichtungen; ~

law Unterhaltsgeld; ~ **measures** Stützungsaktion; ~ **payments** Unterhaltszahlungen; ~ **policy** Stützungspolitik; ~ **price** *(EC)* Stützungspreis; ~ **purchases** Stützungskäufe; ~ **team** Hilfsstab; ~ **vessel** Reserveschiff.

supportable halt-, vertretbar.

supported unterstützt, *(market)* durch Käufe gehalten;

to be ~ **by voluntary contributions** *(hospital)* durch freiwillige Beiträge (Spenden) unterhalten werden;

~ **price** Stützungspreis; ~ **stocks** durch Käufe gestützte Aktien

supporter Unterstützer, Befürworter, Anhänger;

~ **of a family** Ernährer einer Familie.

supporting | actor Nebendarsteller, Mitspieler; ~ **authorities** Belegstellen; ~ **documents** Nebenurkunden, Belege, Unterlagen; ~ **film** Beifilm; ~ **group** Auftraggebergruppe; ~ **orders** Interventionsauftrag, Stützungskäufe; ~ **program(me)** Beiprogramm; ~ **purchases** Stützungs-, Interventionskäufe; ~ **record** Nachweis, Beweisunterlage; ~ **schedule** erläuternde Aufstellung [für die Steuererklärung]; ~ **structure** Trägergerüst; ~ **syndicate** Stützungssyndikat; ~ **troops** Reservetruppen.

supposal Annahme, Hypothese.

suppose *(v.)* annehmen, vermuten.

supposed vermutet, angeblich;

~ **deceased** *(US)* Verschollener; ~ **insult** eingebildete Beleidigung.

supposition Annahme, Vermutung, Vorraussetzung;

mere ~ bloße Vermutung;

to be based on ~**s** nur auf Vermutungen basieren.

suppositional hypothetisch.

supposititious *(child)* untergeschoben;

~ **name** angenommener Name.

suppress *(v.)* unterdrücken, *(abolish)* abschaffen, abstellen, *(conceal)* verheimlichen, verbergen, *(el.)* entstören, *(text)* streichen;

~ **a book** Buch verbieten; ~ **a document** Urkunde unterdrücken; ~ **evidence** Beweise unterschlagen; ~ **a fact** Tatsache verschweigen; ~ **freedom of speech** Redefreiheit behindern; ~ **information** Informationsmaterial nicht zugänglich machen; ~ **a letter** Brief unterschlagen; ~ **a paper** Zeitung beschlagnahmen; ~ **s. one's pension** jem. seine Pension vorenthalten; ~ **a publication** Veröffentlichung untersagen; ~ **a revolt** Aufruhr niederschlagen; ~ **a scandal** Skandal vertuschen; ~ **the truth** Wahrheit unterdrücken (verschweigen); ~ **a will** Testament unterschlagen.

suppressed unterdrückt, niedergeschlagen, *(abolished)* abgeschafft, *(book)* verboten, *(scandal)* vertuscht;

~ **demand** Nachfragerückstau; ~ **inflation** vorübergehend unterdrückte (zurückgestaute) Inflation.

suppression *(abolition)* Abschaffung, Beseitigung, Aufhebung, *(crushing)* Niederwerfung, Unterdrückung, *(documents)* Verheimlichung, *(el.)* Entstörung;

~ **of crime** Verbrechensbekämpfung; ~ **of deeds (documents)** Urkundenunterdrückung; ~ **of evidence** Beweisunterschlagung; ~ **of facts** Verschweigen von Tatsachen; ~ **of information** Verheimlichung von Informationsmaterial; ~ **of a newspaper** Beschlagnahme einer Zeitung; ~ **of a scandal** Vertuschung eines Skandals; ~ **of the truth** Vertuschung (Verschweigen) der Wahrheit; ~ **of a will** Unterschlagung eines Testamentes.

suppressor Unterdrücker, *(el.)* Entstörungskondensator.

supralocal überörtlich.

supranational überstaatlich, supranational;

~ **institution** supranationale Einrichtung; ~ **organization** supranationale Organisation.

supranationality Supranationalität.

supraprotest per Intervention;

~ **acceptance** Interventionsakzept, Ehrenannahme.

supraregional überregional.

supremacy Oberhoheit, -herrschaft, Souveränität, *(predominance)* Vorherrschaft, Übergewicht;

air ~ Luftherrschaft; **naval** ~ Vorherrschaft zur See, Seeherrschaft.

supreme höchst, oberst;

to be ~ höchste Gewalt haben, herrschen;

⌾ **Allied Commander Europe** oberster alliierter Befehlshaber in Europa; ~ **authority** Regierungsgewalt; ~ **command** Oberbefehl, -kommando; ~ **commander** Oberbefehlshaber; ~ **council** *(Versailles)* Zehnerrat; ⌾ **Court** *(US)* Oberstes Bundesgericht; ⌾ **Court of Appeal** *(Br.)* **(of Errors, US)** Revisionsgericht; ⌾ **Court of Judicature** *(Br.)* Oberster Gerichtshof; ⌾ **Court of the United States** Oberster Bundesgerichtshof der Vereinigten Staaten von Amerika; ~ **court practice** höchstrichterliche Rechtsprechung; ~ **hours in the history of a nation** entscheidende Stunden im Leben einer Nation; ~ **penalty** Todesstrafe; ~ **power** oberste Staatsgewalt; **of ~ quality** von erstklassiger Qualität; **to make the ~ sacrifice** sein Leben hingeben; ⚭ **Soviet** Oberster Sowjet.

surcharge *(advertising)* Preisaufschlag für Plazierungswünsche, Plazierungsaufschlag, *(excessive charge)* Überforderung, -teuerung, zuviel berechnete Gebühr, *(extra charge)* Zuschlag[sgebühr], Gebührenzuschlag, Abgabe, *(freight)* Frachtaufschlag, *(second mortgage)* nachstellige Hypothek, *(fine)* Steuerstrafe, *(overload)* Überlastung, -ladung, *(postage)* Straf-, Zuschlags-, Nachporto, -gebühr, *(stamp)* Überdruck, *(taxation)* Steuerzuschlag, -strafe;

subject to ~ *(postal items, Br.)* nachgebührenpflichtig; **without ~** zuschlagsfrei;

investment income ~ *(Br.)* Steuerzuschlag für Einkünfte aus Kapitalvermögen;

~ of electricity Mehrverbrauch an Strom; **~ and falsify** *(of accounts)* Nachprüfungs- und Berichtigungsbeschluß; **~ on goods** Tarifaufschlag; **~ on imports** Einfuhrabgabe, Sonderzoll; **~ on a letter** Portozuschlag; **~ for special position** Plazierungsaufschlag;

~ *(v.)* überfordern, -teuern, *(extra charge)* aufschlagen, zu viel belasten, mit Zuschlag belegen, *(fine)* mit Geldstrafe belegen, *(postage)* Strafgebühr (Nachporto) erheben, *(print surcharge upon)* [Postwertzeichen] überdrucken;

~ an account Konto belasten.

sure *(reliable)* zuverlässig, vertrauenswürdig;

~ as eggs is eggs mit tödlicher Sicherheit;

to feel ~ of o. s. Selbstvertrauen haben;

~ fire *(fam.)* garantiert hundertprozentig; **to send a letter by a ~ messenger** Brief einem zuverlässigen Boten anvertrauen; **~ proof** untrüglicher Beweis; **~ thing** *(sl.)* totsichere Sache.

surety *(bail)* Bürgschaft[sleistung], *(bond)* Verpflichtungs-, Garantie-, Bürgschaftsschein, *(del credere)* Delkredere, *(guaranty)* Sicherheit, Pfand, Kaution, Garantie[leistung], *(person acting as surety)* [Ausfall]bürge, Bürgschaftsgeber, Garant;

bill ~ Wechselbürge; **good ~** sichere Bürgschaft; **joint ~** Solidarbürgschaft, -bürge; **paying ~** selbstschuldnerischer Bürge; **substantial ~** tauglicher (sicherer) Bürge;

~ for a debt Bürge für eine Schuld; **~ created by operation of law** gesetzliche Garantie; **~ for the payment of a bill** Wechselbürgschaft; **~ for the peace** Kaution für Wohlverhalten; **~ for a ~** Rückbürge, -bürgschaft;

to act as ~ Bürgschaft übernehmen, bürgen; **to act as ~ for a bill** für einen Wechsel bürgen, Wechselbürgschaft übernehmen; **to apply to one's ~** seinen Bürgen in Anspruch nehmen; **to become (go) ~** bürgen, Bürgschaft übernehmen, Sicherheit leisten; **to come forward as a ~** sich als Bürge anbieten; **to find ~** Bürgen stellen; **to stand ~** Bürgschaft eingehen, Delkredere stehen; **to stand ~ for the payment of a bill** für den Eingang eines Wechsels bürgen; **to stand ~ for s. o.** als Bürge für j. haften;

~ acceptance Avalakzept; **~ bond** Bürgschaftserklärung, Kautions-, Garantieverpflichtung, Garantievertrag, -urkunde, -schein; **to enter into a ~ bond** Garantieverpflichtung eingehen; **~ business** Kautionsversicherungsgeschäft; **~ commission** *(US)* Garantie-, Kautionsversicherungsgesellschaft; **~ credit** Avalkredit; **~ insurance** Kautionsversicherungsgesellschaft; **~'s liability** Bürgenhaftung; **~-like** wie ein Bürge, bürgschaftsähnlich; **~ losses** *(balance sheet)* Verluste aus Bürgschaftsverpflichtungen; **~ warrant** Bürgschaftserklärung.

suretyship Bürgschafts[leistung], Garantie[leistung], Bürgschaftsvertrag;

corporate ~ Bürgschaftsleistung einer Aktiengesellschaft;

to enter into a ~ Bürgschaft eingehen;

~ contract vom Hauptschuldner unabhängiger Bürgschaftsvertrag, Bürgschaft.

surf | boat Brandungsboot; **~ risk** Brandungsrisiko.

surface [Ober]fläche, *(airplane)* Tragfläche, *(earth)* Grundfläche, *(fig.)* Außenseite, Äußeres, *(road)* Belag;

on the ~ *(fig.)* oberflächlich betrachtet, *(mining)* im Tagebau;

~ of water Wasseroberfläche;

~ *(v.)* **a road with gravel** Straße mit Kies bestreuen;

to look only on the ~ of men Menschen nur nach dem Äußeren beurteilen; **to rise to the ~** *(submarine)* auftauchen;

~ craft Überwasserstreitkräfte, -fahrzeug; **~ damage** Oberflächenschaden; **~ engineering** Hochbau; **~ forecast chart** Bodenvorhersagekarte; **~ friendship** vorübergehende Freundschaft; **~ hand** Übertagearbeiter; **~ letters** *(Br.)* normale Briefpost, Standardbriefe; **~ mail** *(Br.)* gewöhnliche Post, Brief-, Standardsendungen, Gesamtpost außer Luftpost, Bahnpost; **by ~**

mail *(Br.)* mit gewöhnlicher Post; **~-mail categories** *(Br.)* Bahnpostklassen; **~ mail-printed-paper full rate** *(Br.)* Gebühr für Standardbriefdrucksachen; **~ map** Bodenwetterkarte; **~ marking** Fahrbahnmarkierung; **~-mine** *(v.)* im Tagebau gewinnen; **~-to-air missile** Boden-Luft-Flugkörper; **~ officer** auf einem Überwasserfahrzeug dienttuender Offizier; **~ owner** Grundeigentümer; **~ parcels** *(Br.)* [gewöhnliche] Paketsendungen; **~ politeness** unaufrichtige Höflichkeit; **~ printed papers** *(Br.)* Briefdrucksachen, Standardbriefdrucksachen; **~ printing** Flachdruck; **~ raider** Überwasserfahrzeug; **~ rights** Abbaurechte; **~ road** Hochbaustraße; **~ ship** Überwasserfahrzeug; **~ speed** Überwassergeschwindigkeit; **~ street** gepflasterte Straße; **~ traffic** Land- und Binnenwasserverkehr; **~ transportation** Transport auf dem Land- und Seeweg, *(mail)* normale Postbeförderung; **~ value** Augenschein; **~ vessel** Überwasserfahrzeug; **~ waters** Oberflächenwasser; **~ working** Tagebau.

surfaceman Übertagearbeiter, Arbeiter im Tagebau, *(railroad)* Streckenarbeiter, -wärter.

surge Woge, Sturzsee;

~ of capacity Kapazitätszunahme; **~ in costs** rasanter Kostenanstieg; **~ in earnings** erheblicher Ertragsanstieg; **~ in orders** Auftragsflut, -strom; **~ upward ~ of prices** steigende Preistendenz; **~ in sales** Verkaufsanstieg, -welle;

~ *(v.)* **ahead (forward)** *(prices)* plötzlich steigen; **~ into a building** in ein Gebäude eindringen; **~ forward** *(prices)* steigen auf; **~ out of a sports stadium** aus einem Sportstadion herausdrängen, -quellen.

surgical | insurance *(US)* Operationskostenversicherung; **~ operation** Operation; **~ ward** chirurgische Abteilung.

surname Zu-, Nach-, Familienname;

~ *(v.)* beim Familiennamen nennen.

surpass *(v.)* überflügeln, *(account)* überschreiten, -ziehen;

~ all description jeder Beschreibung spotten; **~ s. one's expectations** jds. Erwartung übertreffen.

surplus *(abundance)* Überfluß, *(balance sheet, US)* Überschuß der Aktiva über Grundkapital und Verbindlichkeiten, unverteilter Reingewinn und Rücklagen, *(exceeding amount)* Überschuß, Aktivsaldo, Mehrertrag, -betrag, überschießender Betrag, Plus, *(excess value)* Mehrwert, *(print.)* Überdruck, *(public finance)* haushaltsrechtliche Überschüsse, *(residue of estate)* Nachlaß nach Abzug aller Verbindlichkeiten, *(weight)* Zulage, Zugabe;

accumulated ~ Gewinnvortrag; **acquired ~** unverteilter Reingewinn bei Geschäftsübernahme; **agriculture ~s** Überschüsse der Landwirtschaft; **appraisal ~** *(US)* aus Höherbewertung von Anlagegütern gebildete Rücklage; **appreciation ~** Kapitalzuwachs aus Werterhöhungen; **appropriated ~** *(US)* zweckgebundene Rücklage, Gewinnrückstellung, -rücklage; **available ~** verfügbarer Reingewinn; **balance-of-payments ~** Zahlungsbilanzüberschuß; **book ~** buchmäßiger Überschuß; **~ brought forward** Gewinnvortrag; **budget ~** Haushalts-, Etats-, Budgetüberschuß; **budget ~es** haushaltsrechtliche Überschüsse; **capital ~** *(US)* in den Rücklagen steckendes zusätzliches Eigenkapital; **capitalized ~** im Zwangsversteigerungsverfahren erzielter Überschuß; **catastrophe ~** *(insurance)* Katastrophenrücklage; **company's ~** Reingewinn einer [Aktien]gesellschaft; **contributed ~** Emissionsgewinn; **corporate ~** *(US)* Gesellschaftsreingewinn; **current-account ~** Leistungsbilanzüberschuß; **dated unearned ~** *(US)* Geschäftsgewinn ab Sanierung; **disposable ~** *(budget)* frei verfügbare Überschüsse; **divisible ~** *(life insurance)* Dividendenguthaben; **donated ~** *(US)* Portefeuille eigener Aktien; **earned ~** *(US)* Rein-, Geschäftsgewinn, den Rücklagen zugeteilter Gewinn, unverteilter (thesaurierter) Gewinn, [etwa] gesetzliche Rücklage; **consolidated earned ~** *(US)* Konzernrücklagen; **unappropriated earned ~** *(US)* unverteilter (ausschüttungsfähiger) Reingewinn, *(balance sheet, US)* Gewinnvortrag, -rücklage; **economic ~** Differentialrente; **export ~** Ausfuhrüberschuß; **external ~** Zahlungsbilanzüberschuß, Aktivsaldo der Zahlungsbilanz; **farm ~es** landwirtschaftliche Überschußprodukte; **foreign-trade ~** Außenhandelsüberschuß; **free ~** frei verfügbarer Reingewinn, *(insurance)* freie Reserve (Rücklage); **gross ~** Bruttoüberschuß, *(balance sheet)* ausweispflichtiger Rohüberschuß; **import ~** Einfuhrüberschuß; **initial ~** *(corporation, US)* Reingewinn vor Eintragung ins Handelsregister, Überschußvortrag; **labo(u)r ~** überschüssige Arbeitskräfte; **life-insurance ~** Prämien-, Dividendenguthaben; **net ~** *(corporation)* nach Rückstellung auf das Rücklagenkonto verfügbarer Gewinn, *(fire insurance)* Schadensreserve; **operating ~** Betriebsüberschuß, Reingewinn eines Geschäftsjahres; **paid-in ~** Emissions-, Agiogewinn, *(US)* stehengelassener (nicht entnommener) Gewinn, [etwa] gesetzliche Rücklagen; **producer's ~** Herstellergewinn; **profit-and loss ~** Reingewinn; **reappraisal ~** aus Höherbewertung von Anlagen gebildete Rücklagen, Wertänderungsgewinn; **recapitalization ~** *(US)* aus Geschäftssanierung entstandene Rücklagen; **reduction ~** stehengelassener Gewinn, *(US)* aus Kapitalherabsetzungen entstandener Gewinn; **revaluation ~** *(US)* durch Wertsteigerung des Anlagevermögens erzielte Rücklagen, aus Höherbewertung des Anlagevermögens entstandene Rücklagen; **total ~** Gesamtgewinn; **trade ~es** Handelsbilanzüberschüsse, Aktivsaldo im Außenhandel; **unappropriated ~** *(US)* unverteilter Reingewinn; **worker's ~** Arbeiterrente;

~ at date of acquisition unverteilter Reingewinn bei Geschäftsübernahme; **~ of appreciation** Gewinn aus einer Buchwerterhöhung; **~ of assets over liabilities** Bilanzüberschuß; **~ in the balance of payments** Zahlungsbilanzüberschuß, Aktivsaldo der Zahlungsbilanz; **~ in the balance of trade** Handelsbilanzüberschuß, Aktivsaldo im Außenhandel; **~ of births over deaths** Geburtenüberschuß; **~ in the cash** Kassenüberschuß; **~ from consolidation** Konsolidierungsgewinn; **~ of a corporation** Nettovermögen eines Unternehmens; **~ on current account** Leistungsbilanzüberschuß, positive Leistungsbilanz; **~ of exports** Export-, Ausfuhrüberschuß; **~ of goods** Warenüberfluß; **~ of imports** Einfuhrüberschuß; **~ on invisibles** Überschuß der Leistungsbilanz; **~ to offer** Überschußangebot; **~ transferred to general reserves** den allgemeinen Rücklagen zugewiesener Gewinn; **~ arising from revaluation** *(US)* auf Neubewertung des Anlagevermögens beruhender Reingewinn; **~ in the service balance** Aktivsaldo in der Dienstleistungsbilanz; **~ of spending power** überschüssige Kaufkraft; **~ in taxes** Steuerüberschuß; **~ on foreign trade** Außenhandelsüberschuß; **~ on trade and services** Aktivsaldo im Waren- und Dienstleistungsverkehr;

~ *(a.)* überschüssig, überzählig;

to distribute a ~ Gewinn ausschütten; **to have a ~ of s. th.** Überschuß an etw. haben; **to shore up the overall ~** Globalüberschuß anreichern; **to show a ~** Aktivsaldo aufweisen.

surplus account Gewinn-, Überschußkonto;
capital ~ Kapitalgewinnkonto; **earned ~** Reingewinnkonto.

surplus | accumulation Gewinnansammlung; **~ adjustment** Gewinnberichtigung; **~ amount** Mehrertrag; **~ analysis** Gewinnanalyse; **~ area** [wirtschaftliches] Überschußgebiet; **~ assets** *(Br.)* Liquidationswert einer Gesellschaft; **~ balance** *(balance of payments)* positive (Aktivsaldo der) Zahlungsbilanz; **~ capacity** freie Kapazität, Kapazitätsüberschuß; **~ charge** Gewinnbelastung; **~ charges** Abzüge vor Verteilung des Reingewinnes; **~ commodities** über den Eigenbedarf hinaus hergestellte Güter; **~ contingency reserve** Rückstellung für mögliche Verluste, Verlustreserve, -rücklage; **~ copies** überschüssige Durchschläge, *(book trade)* Remittenden; **~ countries** Überschußländer; **~ coverage** *(insurance business)* durch Rückversicherung beschaffte fehlende Deckung; **~ crop** Überschußernte; **~ dividend** *(US)* außerordentliche Dividende, Superdividende, Bonus, *(bankruptcy)* übermäßige Konkursquote; **~ earnings** *(US)* Gewinnüberschuß, unverteilter Reingewinn; **~ estate** Nachlaßüberschuß; **~ fund** *(budgeting)* nicht verbrauchte Etatstitel, *(US)* außerordentlicher Reservefonds; **~ fund warrant** Anweisung zur Auflösung nicht verbrauchter Etatstitel; **~ goods** Überschußerzeugnisse; **~ [of] franked investment income** *(Br.)* nicht verbrauchte körperschaftssteuerfreie Beträge; **~ interest** Zinseszinsen; **~ item** Reserveposten; **~ labo(u)r** Mehrarbeit; **~ labo(u)r (manpower)** Überschuß an Arbeitskräften, überschüssige Arbeitskräfte; **~ line** *(insurance business)* für Rückversicherung vorgesehene Versicherungssumme; **~ line broker** *(insurance business)* im Rückversicherungsgeschäft tätiger Makler; **~ line market** Rückversicherungsmarkt; **~ lot of fuel oil** zusätzliche Ölmengen; **~ marketing** Absatzüberschuß; **~ money** nicht ausgegebenes Geld, Geldüberhang; **~ nation** Überschußland; **~ net profit** Reingewinn; **~ population** Überschußbevölkerung, Bevölkerungsüberschuß; **~ price** Mehrpreis; **~ problem** Überschußproblem; **~ proceeds on sale** *(mortgage)* überschüssiger Verwertungserlös; **~ product (produce)** Mehrprodukt, Überschußprodukt; **~ production** Überproduktion, Produktionsüberschuß; **~ profit** Mehr-, Übergewinn, überschießender Gewinn, Gewinnüberschuß, *(US)* unverteilter Reingewinn; **~ property** Überschußgüter; **~ receipts** Einnahmeüberschuß, Mehreinnahmen; **~ reinsurance** Exzedentenrückversicherung; **~ reserve** *(US)* zweckgebundene, offene Rücklagen, Gewinnrückstellung, -lage, *(banking)* über die gesetzlichen Verpflichtungen hinausgehende Reserve, Liquiditätsüberhang; **~ revenues** Einnahmeüberschuß; **~ settlement** Spitzenausgleich;

~ sheets *(print.)* Makulatur; **~ situation** Überschußsituation; **~ state** Überschußgebiet; **~ statement** *(US)* Erfolgsbilanz, Gewinnverwendungsrechnung, -übersicht; **~ stocks** *(stock exchange)* Überangebot; **~ supply** Überschußangebot; **~ supply of labo(u)r** Überangebot an Arbeitskräften; **~ treaty** *(reinsurance)* Vertrag zur Festlegung des maximalen Selbstbehalts; **~ value** Mehrwert, *(taxation)* freies Einkommen über dem Existenzminimum; **~ war property** überschüssiges Kriegsmaterial; **~ weight** Über-, Mehrgewicht, Gewichtsüberschuß; **~ wheat** Getreide-, Weizenüberschuß; **~ workers** Überschuß an Arbeitskräften.

surplusage Überschuß, -fülle, *(law court)* unwesentlicher Umstand, überflüssiges Vorbringen.

surprint Überdruck, *(ad.)* Aufdruck auf fertige Anzeigen;
~ *(v.)* überdrucken.

surprise Überraschung[smoment], Überrumpelung;
~ a burglar in the act Einbrecher auf frischer Tat ertappen; **~ the facts from a witness** Tatsachen durch überraschendes Befragen eines Zeugen herausbekommen; **~ s. o. to unwonted generosity** j. zur ungewohnter Freigiebigkeit verleiten;
~ attack Überraschungsangriff; **~ jump** überraschender Anstieg; **~ military action** Überraschungsangriff; **~ packet** *(Br.)* Überraschungspaket; **to pay s. o. a ~ visit** jem. auf die Bude rücken.

surrebut *(US)* *(v.)* *(law)* Quintuplik vorbringen.

surrebutter *(US)* *(law)* Quintuplik.

surrejoin *(v.)* auf die Duplik antworten.

surrejoinder *(law)* Triplik.

surrender Aufgabe, Preisabgabe, Verzicht, *(delivery)* Heraus-, Übergabe, Aushändigung, Überantwortung, *(insurance business)* Versicherungsrückkauf, *(mil.)* Übergabe, *(real estate)* Auflassung, *(of a right)* Abtretung;
compulsory ~ *(Scot.)* Enteignung; **unconditional ~** *(mil.)* bedingungslose Kapitulation;
~ by bail Übergabe des Beschuldigten zwecks Kautionsfreigabe; **~ of a bankrupt's property** Übertragung der Konkursmasse auf die Gläubiger; **~ of a charter** Konzessionsverzicht; **~ of criminals** Auslieferung von Straftätern; **~ of foreign currency** Devisenabführung; **~ of fugitives** Auslieferung flüchtiger Straftäter; **~ of lease** Räumung, Verzicht auf ein Mietrecht; **~ of a fort to the enemy** Übergabe einer Festung an den Feind; **~ by operation of law** gesetzlich vermutete Pachtübertragung; **~ of a patent** Patentverzicht; **~ of possession** Besitzaufgabe; **~ of preference** *(US)* Aufgabe einer [Konkurs]vorzugsstellung; **~ of prisoners** Überstellung von Gefangenen; **~ of a privilege** Verzicht auf ein Vorrecht; **~ of profits** Gewinnabführung; **~ of a right** Aufgabe eines Rechtes, Rechtsverzicht; **~ of securities** Bestellung von Sicherheiten; **~ of shares** *(Br.)* Aktienrückgabe an die Gesellschaft, Aktienverzicht; **~ of surplus** Abführung des Überschusses, Gewinnabführung;
~ *(v.)* übergeben, aushändigen, verabfolgen, überantworten, *(cede)* abtreten, *(law of nations)* ausliefern, *(mil.)* kapitulieren; **~ s. th. to s. o.** jem. etw. herausgeben; **~ an advantage** Vorteil nicht ausnutzen; **~ o. s. to bail** sich dem Gericht wieder stellen; **~ bonuses** *(Br.)* Gewinnanteile zurückkaufen; **~ a criminal** Straftäter überstellen; **~ at discretion** bedingungslos kapitulieren; **~ to the enemy** sich dem Feind ergeben; **~ an estate** Grundstück auflassen; **~ for exchange** zwecks Umtausch übergeben; **~ foreign currency** Devisen abführen; **~ one's goods to one's creditors** sein Vermögen auf seine Gläubiger übertragen; **~ o. s. to bad influence** sich nachteilig beeinflussen lassen; **~ an insurance [policy]** Lebensversicherungspolice zurückkaufen; **~ the lease** räumen, *(US)* sich der Gerechtigkeit anheimgeben; **~ to justice** sich der Gerechtigkeit anheimgeben; **~ the leasehold estate** Pachtrecht übertragen; **~ one's liberty** auf seine Freiheit verzichten; **~ one's office** seine Entlassung einreichen, demissionieren; **~ a patent** auf ein unberechtigtes Patent verzichten; **~ o. s. to the police** sich der Polizei stellen; **~ a policy** *(life insurance)* Lebensversicherung zurückkaufen; **~ possession** Besitz[recht] aufgeben, *(tenant)* räumen; **~ a privilege** auf ein Vorrecht verzichten; **~ a profit** Gewinn abführen; **~ a right** sich eines Rechtes begeben; **~ one's role as a leading producer** führende Produktionsstellung aufgeben; **~ a ship** Schiff aufgeben (verlassen); **~ upon terms** unter gewissen Bedingungen kapitulieren; **~ unconditionally** sich auf Gnade und Ungnade (bedingungslos) ergeben, bedingungslos kapitulieren;
to demand the ~ of a town Kapitulation einer Stadt verlangen; **~-of-profit agreement** Ergebnisabführungsvertrag, Gewinnabführungsvertrag; **~ charge** *(life insurance)* Verwaltungsgebühr bei Rückkauf einer Lebensversicherung; **~ penalty** *(life insurance)* Rückkaufgebühr; **~ privilege** *(life insurance)* Rück-

kaufsrecht; ~ **rule** (overseas shares, Br.) 25%ige Ablieferungs-
verpflichtung; ~ **terms** (mil.) Kapitulationsbedingungen; ~
value (life insurance) Rückkaufswert [einer Police].

surrenderee Erwerber, [Grundstücks]übernehmer.

surrenderer, surrenderor Veräußerer, Abtretender, Zedent.

surrendering of bonuses (Br.) Rückkauf von Gewinnanteilen; ~
of a town Übergabe einer Stadt.

surreptitious erschlichen, heimlich, durch Betrug erlangt,
betrügerisch;
~ **edition** Raubdruck; ~ **entry** unerlaubtes Eindringen; ~ **management** betrügerische Verwaltung; ~ **obtainment of a patent**
Patenterschleichung; ~ **passage in a manuscript** interpolierte
Manuskriptstelle; ~ **pleasures** heimliche Vergnügen; ~ **removal
of goods** betrügerisches Beiseiteschaffen; ~ **will** gefälschtes
Testament.

surrogate Ersatz[mittel], Surrogat, (deputy) Stellvertreter, (probate court, US) Vormundschafts-, Nachlaßrichter;
~ (v.) als Ersatzmittel verwenden, (US) als Stellvertreter einsetzen (bestimmen);
~'s **court** (New York) Nachlaßgericht; ~ **guardian** gerichtlich
ernannter Gegenvormund.

surrogation Stellvertretung.

surround (Br.) Umrandung;
~ (v.) umgeben, (mil.) umzingeln;
~ **a fort** Festung einschließen; ~ **the speaker** Sprecher
umringen.

surrounded by luxury vom Luxus umgeben.

surrounding umliegend, umgebend;
~ **area** benachbarte Gegend; ~ **circumstances** (culpability)
Begleitumstände; ~ **countryside** umliegende Gegend, Umgebung; ~ **risk** (fire insurance) gefahrerhöhende Nachbarschaft,
Nachbargefahr.

surroundings [Um]gegend, Umweltbedingungen, Begleitumstände;
near ~ nähere Umgebung;
to be in ~ **one** knows sich in vertrauten Gefilden (auf vertrautem Gelände) befinden.

surtax Zusatz-, Zuschlagsteuer, Steuerzuschlag, -aufschlag,
Ergänzungsabgabe, (Br.) progressive Gesamteinkommen-
steuer, zusätzliche Einkommensteuer auf Einkommen über
20.000 Pfund;
~ (v.) Zuschlagsteuer erheben, (income tax, Br.) mit einem
Einkommensteuerzuschlag belegen;
~ **brackets** (Br.) Mehreinkommensteuerstufe; ~ **directions** (Br.)
Richtlinien zur Berechnung der zusätzlichen Einkommensteuer (Ergänzungsabgabe); ~ **net income** (US) Nettoeinkommen nach Abzug der Steuerfreibeträge; ~ **payment** Zahlung
einer Zusatzsteuer; ~ **reduction** Herabsetzung der Ergänzungsabgabe; ~ **surcharge** (Br.) Verbrauchssteuererhöhung.

surveillance Aufsicht, Beaufsichtigung, Überwachung, Kontrolle;
under police ~ unter Polizeiaufsicht;
electronic ~ Überwachung durch eingebaute Abhörgeräte;
~ **file** Polizeiakte; ~ **role** Überwachungsfunktion; ~ **squad**
polizeiliches Überwachungsfahrzeug.

surveillant Aufseher, Überwacher.

survey (account given of inspection) Grundstücks-, Geschäfts-
bewertung, Sachverständigengutachten, Expertise, (inspection) Besichtigung, Begutachtung, Inspektion, (marine insurance) Schiffsbesichtigung durch das Aufsichtsamt, (market
research) Marktuntersuchung, -analyse, -forschung, Umfrage,
Erhebung, Befragung, (measured plan) Lageplan, (study) Fra-
gebogenaktion, Testbericht, Studie, (surveying) Vermessung,
(view) Überblick, -sicht;
cadastral ~ Katasterplan; **consumer** ~ Verbraucherumfrage;
damage ~ Schadensbesichtigung; **dealer** ~ Händlerbefragung;
election ~ Wählerbefragung; **employee-attitude** ~ Betriebsumfrage; **factual** ~ Untersuchung von Tatsachen; **Federal Reserve
⌾** (US) Bundesreserveausweis; **field** ~ Marktforschung an Ort
und Stelle; **fresh** ~ Neu-, Nachvermessung; **general** ~ allgemeiner Überblick; **judicial** ~ (court) Ortsbesichtigung, Augenscheinseinnahme; **mail** ~ Befragung auf dem Postwege;
marketing ~ Marktuntersuchung, -forschung; **mine** ~ Markscheidung; **Ordnance ⌾** (Br.) amtliche Landesvermessung;
political ~ Übersicht über die politische Lage;
~ **of land** Grundstücksvermessung; ~ **of productivity** Rentabili-
tätsbild; ~ **of a school** Schulinspektion; ~ **of a vessel** Schiffsbesichtigung [vor der Ausreise], Schiffszeugnis;
~ (v.) sorgfältig prüfen, (insurance business) begutachten,
sachverständig beurteilen, (marketing) testen, (ship) besichtigen, inspizieren, (real estate) vermessen;

~ **a building** Gebäude amtlich abnehmen; ~ **a building for
quantities** (Br.) Baukostenkalkulation durchführen; ~ **a
district** Gebiet topographisch aufnehmen; ~ **an estate** Grund-
stücksabschätzung vornehmen; ~ **a house** Hausschätzung
durchführen; ~ **and value a parish** Einheitswerte in einer
Gemeinde festlegen; ~ **a railway** Eisenbahnlinie vermessen; ~
the international situation Überblick über die internationale
Lage geben; ~ **a vessel** Schiff [vor der Ausreise] besichtigen;
to carry through a ~ Expertise machen; **to conduct a** ~ Umfrage
durchführen; **to make a** ~ **of an estate** Grundstücksbewertung
vornehmen; **to make a general** ~ **of the international situation**
Überblick über die internationale Lage geben;
~ **answer** Umfrageantwort; ~ **certificate** (ship) Besichtigungs-
schein; ~ **charges** Vermessungsgebühren; ~ **company** Vermes-
sungsgesellschaft; ~ **course** Einführungskursus; ~ **crew**
Vermessungsgruppe; ~ **design** (statistics) Erhebungsplan; ~
fee Besichtigungsgebühr, (expert) Gutachtergebühr; ~ **prices
of 1981** Vergleichspreise im Jahr 1981; ~ **report** Gutachterbe-
richt, (of ship) Havarie-, Schadenszertifikat; ~ **sheet** Fragebogen; ~ **taker** Zusammensteller einer Übersicht.

surveyed firm untersuchte Firma;
to have goods officially ~ **by order of the court** gerichtlich ein
Sachverständigengutachten veranlassen.

surveying Bodenvermessung, [Land]vermessung, Terrainauf-
nahme, Besichtigung, Inspektion, (land) Vermessungswesen;
aerial ~ Luftvermessung; **quantity** ~ Baukosten-, Preiskalkulation;
~ **officer** Vermessungsbeamter; ~ **project** Vermessungsvorha-
ben; ~ **ship** Vermessungsschiff.

surveyor (architect, Br.) [ausführender] Architekt, Baumeister,
(clerk of works) Bauleiter, (customs, US) Zollaufseher, -in-
spektor, (inspector) Aufsichtsbeamter, Aufseher, (insurance
business) Schadensexperte, Gutachter, Sachverständiger,
(land) Vermessungsbeamter, Land-, Feldmesser, (of ships)
amtlich bestellter Schiffssachverständiger, Havariekommis-
sar, (valuer) Sachverständiger, Gutachter, Schätzer;
district ~ (London) Baupolizei; ~ **general** (Br.) [etwa] Generalinspekteur; **land** ~ Vermessungsbeamter; **quantity** ~ (Br.)
Preiskalkulator, Bausachverständiger; **road** ~ Aufsichtsbeamter der Straßenbauverwaltung; **town** ~ Stadtbaurat;
~ **of buildings** Bauamtsleiter; ~ **of the customs** (US) Zollaufseher, -inspektor; ~ **of highways** (Br.) Aufsichtsbeamter der Bauaufsichtsbehörde, Straßenmeister; ~ **of the mines** Bergwerks-
inspektor; ~ **of the port** Leiter des Hafenamtes, (US)
Zollbeamter; **land** ~ **and valuer** Katasterbeamter; ~ **of weights
and measures** (Br.) Eichmeister;
~'s **fees** Architektengebühr, Bauabnahmegebühren; ~s' **office**
Hochbau-, Bauaufsichts-, Bauordnungsamt; ~'s **report**
Gutachter-, Sachverständigenbericht.

survival Überleben;
in case of ~ im Überlebensfalle;
~ **of action** Weiterbestehen des Klageanspruchs; ~ **of the fittest**
Überleben des Tüchtigsten; ~ **of joint liability** Haftung des
überlebenden Schuldners; ~ **of rights** Rechte überlebender
Gläubiger;
~ **equipment** Überlebensausrüstung; ~ **powers** Durchhaltevermögen; ~ **rate** Geburtenüberschuß; ~ **tables** Sterbetafeln; ~
value Erhaltungswert.

survive (v.) über-, weiterleben, (goods) erhalten bleiben;
~ **to s. o.** (estate) in jds. Hände übergehen; ~ **one's children**
seine Kinder überleben; ~ **an earthquake** Erdbeben überleben
(überstehen); ~ **intact** immer noch gültig sein; ~ **in an office**
sich in einem Amt halten können; ~ **on one's own** eigenständig
fortbestehen; ~ **one's usefulness** sich an seine Position
klammern.

surviving überlebend;
~ **company** übernehmende Gesellschaft; ~ **debt** Restschuld; ~
dependants Hinterbliebene; ~ **dependants' allowances** (US)
Hinterbliebenenbezüge; ~ **spouse** überlebender Ehegatte.

survivor Überlebender, Hinterbliebener;
sole ~ **of a shipwreck** einziger Überlebender eines Schiffbruchs;
~s' **benefit** (US) Leistungen an Hinterbliebene, Hinterbliebenenrente; ~s' **insurance** (US) Hinterbliebenenversicherung;
Old Age and ⌾s and Disability Insurance (US) Hinterblie-
benen- und Invalidenversicherung; ~ **life curve** Sterblichkeitskurve.

survivorship Überlebensfall, Anwartschaft des Hinterbliebenen;
~ **account** Gemeinschaftskonto mit Verfügungsrecht des
Überlebenden; ~ **annuity** Überlebensrente; ~**annuity policy**
Rentenversicherungspolice zugunsten eines überlebenden
Dritten; ~ **table** Überlebenstafel.

susceptibility of proof Beweisfähigkeit.
susceptible|of development entwicklungsfähig; ~ **of proof** beweisfähig;
   to be ~ of another interpretation andere Deutung zulassen; **to be ~ of revision** der Revision unterliegen, revisionsfähig (revisibel) sein.
suspect Verdachtsperson, Verdächtiger;
   political ~ politisch Verdächtiger;
   ~ (v.) s. o. of a murder j. des Mordes verdächtigen; ~ **a plot** Verschwörung befürchten; ~ **the truth of the evidence** Wahrheit des Beweismaterials anzweifeln;
   to hold s. o. ~ until his innocence is proved j. bis zum Beweis seiner Unschuld verdächtigen.
suspectable verdächtig.
suspected verdächtig;
   ~ **of an escape** fluchtverdächtig;
   to be ~ im Verdacht stehen;
   ~ **bill of health** Gesundheitspaß mit dem Vermerk „Ansteckungsverdächtig"; ~ **carcase** krankheitsverdächtiger Tierkörper; ~ **person under police surveillance** Verdächtiger unter Polizeiaufsicht.
suspend (v.) aussetzen, einstellen, unterbrechen, sistieren, außer Kraft setzen, [zeitweilig] aufheben, (bank) Zahlungen einstellen, (from office) suspendieren;
   ~ **a cashier pending investigation** Kassierer während der Untersuchung beurlauben; ~ **an employee with full pay** Angestellten mit vollen Bezügen beurlauben; ~ **employment** Beschäftigung zeitweise aussetzen, Beschäftigungsverhältnis ruhen lassen; ~ **the execution** Urteilsvollstreckung aussetzen; ~ **the gold standard** Goldstandard aufheben; ~ **the Habeas Corpus Act** Haftprüfungstermin suspendieren; ~ **a hearing** Verhandlung aussetzen; ~ **hostilities** Feindseligkeiten einstellen; ~ **s. o. indefinitely** j. auf unbestimmte Zeit beurlauben; ~ **a judgment** Vollstreckung eines Urteils aussetzen; ~ **a licence** Konzession suspendieren, (US) Führerschein zeitweilig einziehen; ~ **a member of a club** Vereinsmitglied vorübergehend ausschließen; ~ **a memeber of parliament** Immunität eines Abgeordneten aufheben; ~ **a newspaper** Herausgabe einer Zeitung vorübergehend untersagen; ~ **from office** vorläufig des Amtes entheben, vom Amt suspendieren; ~ **one's opinion** sich noch nicht festlegen; ~ **operations** Betrieb einstellen; ~ **an order of possession** Räumungsbeschluß aussetzen; ~ **payment of one's debts** seine Zahlungen einstellen (aussetzen); ~ **proceedings** Verfahren unterbrechen (aussetzen); ~ **a quotation** Notierung aussetzen; ~ **a regulation** Verordnung zeitweilig aufheben; ~ **a rule** Anordnung außer Kraft setzen; ~ **the sale** mit dem Verkauf warten; ~ **a sentence** (criminal law) Strafaussetzung gewähren, Strafvollzug aussetzen, (legal proceedings) Urteilsverkündung aussetzen; ~ **a student** Studenten relegieren; ~ **the traffic** Verkehr anhalten; ~ **work** Arbeit vorübergehend einstellen, (walk out) in einen Streik treten.
suspended aufgeschoben, -hoben, (law) außer Kraft gesetzt, (statute of limitations) gehemmt;
   to be ~, (officer) seines Dienstes enthoben (dienstenthoben) sein; **to be fined £ 50 with ~ execution of sentence** Geldstrafe von 50 Pfund mit Bewährung erhalten; **to be ~ from practice** Anwaltsberuf vorübergehend nicht ausüben dürfen;
   ~ **account** transitorisches Konto; ~ **animation** Scheintod; ~ **ceiling** Hängedecke; ~ **execution of sentence** Gefängnis mit Bewährung; ~ **officer** suspendierter Beamter; ~**-pocket filing** Hängeregistratur; ~ **prison sentence** auf Bewährung ausgesetzte Gefängnisstrafe; ~ **sentence** zur Bewährung ausgesetzte Gefängnisstrafe; **flat-top ~ system** (filing) Hängeablagesystem.
suspense Ungewißheit, Unentschiedenheit, Aufschub, Schwebe, (law) Ruhen, (stay of execution) Vollstreckungsaufschub;
   in ~ schwebend;
   anxious ~ Hangen und Bangen;
   ~ **of mind** Nervenanspannung;
   to be (hang) in ~ in der Schwebe (unentschieden) sein, ruhen; **to hold in ~** in der Schwebe (unentschieden) lassen; **to keep in ~** [Gläubiger] hinhalten; **to keep a bill in ~** Wechsel Not leiden lassen; **to remain in ~** unentschieden bleiben;
   ~ **account** vorläufiges (transitorisches) Konto, Zwischen-, Berichtigungs-, Interimskonto; ~ **entries** Zwischeneintragungen, transitorische Buchungen, Übergangsposten; ~ **file** Terminmappe; ~ **interest account** (Br.) Konto zweifelhafte Zinseingänge; ~ **item** offenstehender (vorläufiger) Posten, (balance sheet) Rechnungsabgrenzungsposten, transitorischer Posten; ~ **ledger** Hauptbuch für vorläufige Eintragungen; ~ **liabilities** transitorische Passiva.

suspensible aufschiebbar.
suspension Aufschub, einstweilige Aufhebung, vorläufige Einstellung, Aussetzung, Außerkraftsetzung, (from office) vorübergehende Entlassung (Absetzung), Suspendierung, Suspension, (stay of execution) Vollstreckungsaufschub;
   cardanic ~ (car) Kardanaufhängung; **independent ~** Einzelradaufhängung; **independent front-wheel ~** Vorderradaufhängung; **permanent ~** unbefristete Strafaussetzung; **temporary ~** vorübergehende [Straf]aussetzung;
   ~ **of air service** Einstellung des Flugverkehrs; ~ **of arms** Einstellung der Feindseligkeiten, Waffenruhe; ~ **of an automobile** Abmeldung eines Kraftfahrzeugs; ~ **of a bank** Liquidation einer Bank; ~ **of business** Einstellung des Geschäftsbetriebes, Geschäftsschließung; ~ **of the commission of lunacy** Aufhebung eines Entmündigungsbeschlusses; ~ **of dealings** Ruhen der Geschäfte; ~ **of earnings** (US) Verdienstausfall; ~ **of employment** Arbeitsunterbrechung; ~ **of execution** Aussetzung der Zwangsvollstreckung, (criminal) Vollstreckungs-, Strafaufschub; ~ **of the gold standard** Aufhebung des Goldstandards; ~ **of hostilities** Einstellung der Feindseligkeiten; ~ **of an insurance** Ruhen einer Versicherung; ~ **of a judgment** Urteilsaussetzung; ~ **of a law** zeitweises Außerkrafttreten eines Gesetzes; ~ **of a driver's licence** (US) vorübergehender Führerscheinentzug; ~ **of mail** (US) Postsperre; ~ **of a member** vorübergehender Mitgliedsausschluß; ~ **of a member of Parliament** Immunitätsaufhebung; ~ **from office** Dienstenthebung, Beurlaubung; ~ **of s. o. in office** vorläufige Entlassung, einstweilige Dienstenthebung, Beurlaubung; ~ **of operations** Einstellung der Geschäftstätigkeit, Betriebsstillegung, -einstellung; ~ **of military operations** Einstellung der Kampfhandlungen; ~ **of nuclear tests** Einstellung der Atomwaffenversuche, Atomwaffenversuchsstopp; ~ **of payments** Zahlungseinstellung; ~ **of specie payment** (US) Aufhebung der Goldeinlösungspflicht; ~ **of proceedings** Aussetzung des Verfahrens; ~ **of quotas** Kontingentsaufhebung; ~ **of the quotation** (stock exchange) Aussetzung der Kursnotierung; ~ **of diplomatic relations** Unterbrechung der diplomatischen Beziehungen; ~ **of a right** vorübergehende Nichtausübung eines Rechts; ~ **of rules** Suspendierung von Satzungsbestimmungen; ~ **of salary** (US) Verdienstausfall; ~ **of a sentence on probation** Strafaufschub zur Bewährung; **total ~ of all public services** Einstellung der Tätigkeit aller öffentlichen Dienste; ~ **of standing orders** Aufhebung der Geschäftsordnung; ~ **of a statute** zeitweiliges Außerkrafttreten eines Gesetzes; ~ **of the statute of limitations** Hemmung (Unterbrechung) der Verjährung; ~ **of a student** Relegation eines Studenten; ~ **from university** Ausschluß vom Universitätsstudium; ~ **of work** vorübergehende Arbeitseinstellung; ~ **of the writ of habeas corpus** Aussetzung des Rechts auf richterliche Haftprüfung;
   to apply for ~ sich beurlauben lassen; **to force a ~ of the negotiations** Verhandlungsaufschub erzwingen; **to grant ~ on probation** Strafaufschub gegen Bewährungsfrist gewähren;
   ~ **agreement** Aufschubsvereinbarung; ~ **bridge** Hängebrücke; ~ **railway** Schwebebahn.
suspensive|condition (US) aufschiebende Wirkung, Suspensivwirkung; ~ **veto** aufschiebendes Vetorecht.
suspensory|condition aufschiebende Wirkung, Suspensivwirkung; ~ **veto** aufschiebendes Veto.
suspicion Argwohn, Verdacht, Verdächtigung, Mißtrauen, (grain) Anflug;
   above ~ über alle Zweifelsfälle erhaben; **on strong ~** wegen dringenden Tatverdachts; **under ~ of murder** unter Mordverdacht;
   gratuitous ~ grundloser Verdacht; **unfounded ~** unbegründeter Verdacht;
   to arouse (be looked upon with) ~ Verdacht erregen; **to arrest on ~** als Verdächtigen verhaften; **to be arrested on ~ of fraudulent bankruptcy** wegen betrügerischen Bankrotts verhaftet werden; **to be clear of any ~** von jedem Verdacht befreit sein; **to be under ~** verdächtigt werden, unter Verdacht stehen; **to cast (throw) ~ on** verdächtigen, Verdacht lenken; **to dispel a ~** Verdacht zerstreuen; **to fall under ~** verdächtigt werden; **to have a sneaking ~** heimlichen Verdacht hegen; **to verify a ~** Verdacht bestätigen.
suspicious|character verdächtiger Gewohnheitsverbrecher; ~ **circumstances** verdächtige Umstände; ~ **fact** Verdachtsmoment; ~ **person** verdächtige Person, Verdächtiger, Verdachtsperson.
sustain aufrechterhalten, fortsetzen, (suffer) erleiden, ertragen;
   ~ **(v.) an action** einer Klage stattgeben; ~ **an allegation** Behauptung rechtfertigen; ~ **an army** Heer verproviantieren; ~ **burdens** Belastungen ertragen; ~ **the burden of proof** obliegenden

Beweis erbringen; ~ a claim Anspruch aufrechterhalten; ~ s. o. in a claim jds. Anspruch anerkennen; ~ a comparison Vergleich aushalten; ~ competition es mit der Konkurrenz aufnehmen, sich gegen die Konkurrenz durchsetzen; ~ a conversation for hours stundenlange Gespräche führen; ~ damage Schaden erleiden; ~ s. o. in demand jds. Forderung voll anerkennen; ~ a demurrer Einspruch aufrecht erhalten; ~ a family (US) Familie unterhalten; ~ an injury verletzt werden; ~ an industrial injury Arbeitsunfall erleiden; ~ a loss Verlust erleiden; ~ losses (prices) zurückgehen; ~ a motion einem Antrag stattgeben; ~ an objection einem Widerspruch stattgeben; ~ a political party politische Partei finanziell unterstützen; ~ friendly relations freundschaftliche Beziehungen unterhalten; ~ the shock of the enemy's troops dem Angriff der feindlichen Truppen standhalten; ~ a statement Aussage bekräftigen; ~ a suit einem Klagebegehren stattgeben; ~ a theory Theorie erhärten.

sustainable (suit) haltbar.

sustained, reasonably ~ **costs** vernünftigerweise entstandene Kosten; ~ **interest** anhaltendes Interesse.

sustainer (US) Rundfunkprogramm ohne Reklamespots.

sustaining | **program(m)e** (US) rundfunkeigene Sendung; ~ **wall** Stützmauer.

sustainment Lebensmittel, -unterhalt.

sustenance Unterhalt[ung], Versorgung, Lebensunterhalt; **scanty** ~ kärgliches Auskommen.

sustentation Unterhaltung; ~ **of peace** Erhaltung des Friedens; ~ **fund** (strike) Unterstützungsfonds.

sutler (mil.) Kantinenwirt.

suttle weight Nettogewicht.

suzerain Oberherr, souveräner Oberstaat.

suzerainty Oberhoheit, Oberherrschaft, Schutzhoheit, Protektorat.

swab (marine, sl.) Matrose der Handelsmarine.

swad Menschenmasse.

swaddling clothes Windeln; **to be still in its** ~ noch in den ersten Anfängen stecken.

swag Schwanken, (politics, sl.) Schiebergewinn, Hehlerware; ~ (v.) (Australia) trampen, tippeln.

swagger forsches Auftreten.

swagshop Kram-, Trödelladen.

swallow (v.) | **the anchor** (sl.) Stellung (Arbeit) an Land annehmen; ~ **the bait** auf ein Angebot hereinfallen, auf den Leim kriechen; ~ **a book** Buch verschlingen; ~ **a camel** sich einen Bären aufbinden lassen; ~ **up more than one's earnings** mehr als die Einkünfte verschlingen; ~ **it hook, line and sinker** Lügengeschichte hundertprozentig glauben; ~ **an insult** Beleidigung schlucken; ~ **up property portfolios** Grundstücksverwaltungen en bloc übernehmen; ~ **a story** einer Geschichte aufsitzen; ~ **one's words** seine Aussage widerrufen; ~-**tailed coat** Schwalbenschwanz, Frack.

swallowed by a lawyer's bill (earnings) von Anwaltsrechnungen aufgezehrt.

swamp Morast, Sumpf; ~ (v.) überschwemmen, -häufen, (fig.) in Schwierigkeiten geraten; ~ **the market** Markt überschwemmen; ~ **and overflowed land** Überschwemmungsgebiet.

swamped | **with orders** mit Aufträgen überschüttet; ~ **with work** mit Arbeit zugedeckt; **to be** ~ **with debts** bis über die Ohren in Schulden stecken.

swamper (sl.) Beifahrer.

swan song Schwanengesang.

swank Angabe, auffällige Eleganz, Protzerei.

swap [Devisen]swap, Tausch-, Swapgeschäft; ~ (v.) [ver]tauschen, (fire, sl.) hinauswerfen, feuern, (foreign exchange) Swapgeschäfte machen; ~ **horses while crossing a stream** während einer Krise die Regierung wechseln; ~ **politics for business in mid-career** aus dem politischen Bereich in der Lebensmitte in die Wirtschaft überwechseln; **to borrow on** ~**s** zu Swapbedingungen Geld aufnehmen; ~ **arrangement** Swapabkommen, -vereinbarung; ~ **commitment** Swapengagement; ~ **facilities** Swapfazilitäten; ~ **lines** Swaplinien; ~ **rate** Swapsatz; ~ **terms** Swapbedingungen; ~ **transactions** Swapgeschäfte.

swapped, to be den Laufpaß erhalten.

swarm Haufen, Gewimmel; ~ **of bills** Haufen Rechnungen; ~ (v.) **into a cinema** in ein Kino einströmen; ~ **with people** von Menschen wimmeln.

swarming tenement übervölkerte Mietskaserne.

swash Säbelgerassel, Renommieren, Schwadronieren; ~ (v.) **about with one's sword** mit dem Säbel rasseln; ~ **buckler** Säbelrassler, Renommist, Schwadroneur; ~ **buckling** Schwadronieren, Säbelrasseln, Renommieren; ~ **letter** Zierbuchstabe.

swatch (advertising) Farbmuster.

sway Herrschaft[sbereich], Macht, Einfluß; **under the** ~ **of a dictator** in der Gewalt eines Diktators; ~ (v.) herrschen, regieren; ~ **s. o.** j. beeinflussen; ~ **the elections** Einfluß auf die Wahlen haben, Wahlen beeinflussen; ~ **to s. one's side** (public opinion) sich zu jds. Gunsten wenden; ~ **the voters** Wähler beeinflussen; ~ **the world** Welt beherrschen; **to be a man with** ~ einflußreiche Persönlichkeit sein; **to be under a** ~ unter einer Herrschaft stehen; **to have great** ~ **in the House** im Parlament großen Einfluß haben; **to hold** ~ **over the world** Welt beherrschen.

swear (v.) schwören, Eid leisten; ~ **an affidavit** Versicherung durch Eid bekräftigen; ~ **all by that's holy** Stein und Bein schwören; ~ **to a cause** sich feierlich auf etw. festlegen; ~ **a charge against s. o.** Anzeige gegen j. beschwören; ~ **to one's doctor** seinem Arzt voll vertrauen; ~ **an estate at $ 100.000** Nachlaßwert mit 100.000 Dollar angeben; ~ **falsely** Falscheid schwören; ~ **in** vereidigen; ~ **an oath** Eid leisten; ~ **a solemn oath** feierlich geloben; ~ **in an official** einem Beamten den Diensteid abnehmen; ~ **out a warrant of arrest** (US) Haftbefehl durch eidliche Aussage erwirken; ~ **to secrecy** zur Verschwiegenheit verpflichten; ~ **like a trooper** wie ein Landsknecht fluchen; ~ **a witness** Zeugen vereidigen.

swearing Eidesleistung; **false** ~ Falscheid leisten; ~ **an affidavit** Versicherung an Eides Statt; ~ **the peace** Schutzersuchen wegen Bedrohung; ~ **[in] of a witness** Zeugenvereidigung.

sweat (fig.) anstrengende Arbeit, (ship) Schiffsdunst, (sl.) Soldat; **all of a** ~ (coll.) in Schweiß gebadet; ~ (v.) (extort, sl.) bluten lassen, (labo(u)rers) ausbeuten, schinden, schlecht bezahlen, (third degree, sl.) schwitzen lassen, foltern, (work) für Hungerlohn arbeiten, ausgebeutet werden; ~ **blood** Blut und Wasser schwitzen, wie ein Sklave schuften; ~ **it out** (sl.) voller Angst auf etw. warten; ~ **s. th. out** (sl.) durch Folter erpressen; ~ **a practitioner** Praktikanten ausnutzen; ~ **damage** Schiffsdunstschaden.

sweated für Hungerlohn hergestellt; ~ **goods** unter Hungerlöhnen erstellte Ware; ~ **industries** unterbezahlte Industriezweige; ~ **labo(u)rer** ausgebeuteter Arbeiter; ~ **money** Hungerlohn.

sweatee ausgebeuteter Arbeiter.

sweater Ausbeuter, Leuteschinder.

sweating Lohndrückerei, Ausbeutung, Leuteschinderei; ~ **system** Ausbeutungs-, Akkordmeistersystem.

sweatshop (US sl.) Fabrik mit sehr schlechten Arbeitsbedingungen, Ausbeutungsbetrieb.

sweep (fig.) Einflußsphäre, Reichweite, Flut, (mil.) Vorstoß, Kampfhandlung; **at one** ~ mit einem Schlag; **within the** ~ **of human intelligence** im Bereich menschlichen Verstandes; ~ (v.) **all before one** von Erfolg zu Erfolg schreiten; ~ **one's audience along with one** seine Zuhörerschaft mitreißen; ~ **away a bridge** (river) Brücke fortreißen; ~ **away secrecy from committee votes** mit geheimen Ausschußabstimmungen aufräumen; ~ **the board** ganzen Gewinn einstreichen, (fig.) hundertprozentigen Sieg davontragen; ~ **a channel** Fahrwasser räumen; ~ **a constituency** fast alle Stimmen in einem Wahlbezirk erhalten; ~ **some gloomy facts under the bonnet** unerfreuliche Tatsachen unter den Teppich kehren; ~ **s. o. off his feet** j. völlig überwältigen; ~ **all obstacles from one's path** alle Hindernisse aus dem Wege räumen; ~ **the seas of pirates** Seeräuber vertreiben; ~ **coins into one's pockets** Münzen einstreichen; ~ **the sky** (searchlight) Himmel absuchen; ~ **over the enemy's trenches** feindliche Schützengräben überrollen; **to make a clean** ~ **of it** reinen Tisch machen; **to make a clean** ~ **of one's staff** sein gesamtes Personal auswechseln.

sweeper Kehrmaschine, (marine) Räumboot; **street** ~ Straßenkehrer.

sweeping | **changes** umfassende Änderungen; ~ **reduction in prices** zu bedeutend ermäßigten Preisen; ~ **reform** durchgreifende Reform; ~ **statement** weitreichende Erklärung.

sweepstake [etwa] Toto; ~ **ticket** Totoschein.

sweet, as ~ **as a nut** wie aus dem Ei gepellt;
~-**talk** *(v.) (sl.)* jem. schmeicheln;
~ **department** Süßwarenabteilung; ~ **job** *(sl.)* bequeme und lukrative Arbeit.
sweeten *(v.) (fig.)* mundgerecht machen;
~ **a loan** *(US)* hochwertige Aktien lombardieren.
sweetheart agreement *(US)* auf enge Zusammenarbeit abgestellter Tarifvertrag.
sweetener Bestechung, Schmiergeld.
sweetness | **of temper** Liebenswürdigkeit;
to have been all ~ **and light** sich äußerst angenehm entwickelt haben.
sweetshop *(Br.)* Süßwarengeschäft.
swell *(a.) (US)* ausgezeichnet, erstklassig, bombig, pfundig, großartig;
~ **in the population** Anwachsen der Bevölkerung, Bevölkerungsanstieg; ~ **in politics** hohes Tier in der Politik;
~ *(v.)* **into a major political controversy** sich zu einer größeren politischen Kontroverse entwickeln;
to come the heavy ~ **over s. o.** *(sl.)* j. von seiner Bedeutung zu überzeugen versuchen;
to take s. o. to a ~ **dinner party** j. zu einem feudalen Essen ausführen; ~ **hotel** feudales Hotel; ~ **time** wunderbare Zeit.
swellhead *(sl.)* aufgeblasener Bursche.
swerve *(v.)* **from one's duty** Pfad der Pflicht verlassen; **not** ~ **a jot** kein Jota nachgeben.
swift | **witness** parteiischer Zeuge; ~ **worker** flinker Arbeiter.
swim *(coll.)* Lauf der Ereignisse;
in the ~ vertraut sein mit;
~ *(v.)* **against the tide** gegen den Strom schwimmen; ~ **with the tide** *(stream)* sich der Mehrheit anschließen;
to be out of the ~ nicht auf dem Laufenden sein.
swimming | **bath** Schwimmbad; ~ **market** glattes (sich glatt abwickelndes) Geschäft; ~ **pool** Schwimmbecken; ~-**pool attendant** Bademeister.
swimmingly, to go völlig glatt über die Bühne gehen.
swindle Betrug, Schwindel;
~ *(v.)* betrügen, mogeln;
~ **money out of s. o.** jem. sein Geld abjagen;
~ **sheet** gefälschter Spesenbeleg.
swindler Betrüger, Schwindler, Hochstapler.
swindling Betrug, Betrügerei, *(stock exchange)* schwindelhafte Effektengeschäfte;
insurance ~ Versicherungsbetrug;
~ **firm** Schwindelunternehmen.
swing Spielraum, Kreditmarge, -spielraum, *(fig.)* Schwung, Bewegung, *(cyclical movement, US sl.)* Konjunkturperiode, *(parl., US)* Wahlrundreise, *(pol.)* Umschwung, *(shift, coll.)* Schicht, Arbeitsperiode, *(trade agreement)* Überziehungskredit, Swing;
at full ~ in voller Fahrt (Tätigkeit), *(vehicle)* mit Volldampf; **in full** ~ in vollem Betrieb (Gang); **off one's** ~ nicht auf der Höhe;
anti-government (anti-the-men-in-power) ~ Meinungsumschwung zu Ungunsten der Regierung; **free** ~ Bewegungsfreiheit, Spielraum; **local election** ~ Umschwung bei den Kommunalwahlen; **market** ~ Konjunkturumschwung;
~ **away** Abwendung, ~**s in the balance of payments** Zahlungsbilanzschwankungen; ~ **in the economic cycle** Konjunkturperiode; ~ **to the left** Ruck nach links, Linksruck; ~ **of the pendulum** Schwankung der öffentlichen Meinung; ~ **of public opinion** Umschwung der öffentlichen Meinung; ~ **in taxes** schwankende Steuererträge;
~ *(v.)* um eine Kurve fahren, *(US)* erfolgreich durchführen;
~ **into action** auf den Plan treten; ~ **from the chandeliers** wie im siebenten Himmel sein; ~ **round the circle** häufig seine Meinung wechseln, *(parl., US)* Wahlkreise bereisen; ~ **round the corner** *(car)* um die Ecke sausen; ~ **round into clear disapproval** sich klar und deutlich dagegen aussprechen; ~ **a district during the election** Wählerschaft in einem Wahlkreis auf seine Seite ziehen; ~ **elections** zu Veränderungen den bei Wahlen führen; ~ **a gate open** Tor aufstoßen; ~ **it** *(fam.)* etw. hinschaukeln; ~ **the lead** *(sl.)* sich drücken; ~ **the propeller** Flugzeugmotor anwerfen; ~ **sharply to the right** kräftigen Rechtsdruck machen; ~ **out of a side street** *(car)* aus einer Seitenstraße herausschießen;
to be in full ~ sich voll auswirken, in voller Blüte stehen; **to be given full** ~ **in the conduct of business** voll in die Geschäftsführung eingeschaltet werden; **to get into full** ~ sich einspielen, auf Hochtouren laufen; **to give full** ~ **to s. th.** einer Sache freien Lauf lassen; **to go with a** ~ reibungslos ablaufen, glatt verlaufen; **to have one's** ~ seinen Lauf nehmen; **to live in the full** ~ **of**

prosperity im größten Wohlstand leben, *(trade cycle)* Hochkonjunktur erleben; **to need but a small** ~ **to win a clear majority** schon bei einem kleinen Wählerumschwung eine glatte Mehrheit erreichen; **to tip the balance in the** ~ Ausschlag des Meinungsbarometers verändern;
~ **bridge** Drehbrücke; ~ **credit** kurzfristiger Auslandskredit; ~ **door** Pendeltür, Drehtür; ~ **figures** ziffernmäßig erfaßter Meinungsumschwung, Zahlen des Meinungsumschwungs; ~ **room** *(factory, sl.)* Aufenthaltsraum; ~ **shift** *(coll., US)* Hilfs-, Spät-, Sonder-, Zusatzschicht; ~ **shifter** *(US coll.)* Spät-, Schichtarbeiter.
swingback *(politics, US)* Umschlag, Rückschlag.
swingeing | **damages** zuerkannter Schadensersatz; ~ **majority** überwältigende Mehrheit.
swinger modern eingestellter Mensch.
swinging *(fading)* Frequenzschwankungen;
~ **temperature** Temperaturschwankungen; ~ **voter** Wechselwähler.
switch *(change)* Wechsel, Übergang, Umstellung, -schichtung, *(economy)* Umstellung, Umleitung, Umschichtung, *(el.)* Schalter, *(exchange trade)* Kompensationsgeschäft, Switchgeschäft, *(fig.)* Umstellung, Wechsel, Übergang, Weichenstellung, *(railway)* Weiche;
policy ~ politische Umstellung;
~ **of loyalties** Abwanderung von Stammgästen; ~ **from rail to bus** Übergang von der Bahn- auf die Busbenutzung; ~ **from direct to indirect taxation** Umstellung von direkter auf indirekte Besteuerung;
~ *(v.)* umlenken, umleiten, *(el.)* schalten, *(export trade)* Switchgeschäfte machen, *(gear)* umschalten, *(give information, sl.)* verpfeifen, *(railway)* rangieren, umstellen, *(securities, US)* Effektenengagements umstellen, *(tel.)* Anschluß herstellen;
~ **political alliances** Bündnisse auswechseln; ~ **the conversation** Gesprächsthema wechseln; ~ **to shorter-term forms of financing** auf kurzfristigere Finanzierungsformen umschalten; ~ **into growth stock** in Wachstumswerte umsteigen; ~ **off** *(radio)* abschalten, *(tel.)* Anschluß (Verbindung) unterbrechen; ~ **off on energy sav-ing** sich auf Energieeinsparungen einstellen; ~ **on** ein-, anschalten; ~ **out** *(securities)* herausgehen; ~ **out of foreign assets** aus ausländischen Anlagewerten aussteigen; ~ **out of stocks into highyielding bonds** aus Aktien in hochverzinsliche Obligationen umsteigen; ~ **over to the offensive** offensiv werden; ~ **over production** Produktion umstellen; ~ **one's portfolio of assets into gilts at current rates of interest** *(bank)* sein Wertpapierdepot zu Tageskursen in mündelsicheren Papieren anlegen; ~ **to the Republicans** zur republikanischen Partei übergehen; ~ **sides** Lager wechseln; ~ **the talk to another topic** auf ein anderes Thema überleiten; ~ **from sweet talk to arm twisting** vom Zuckerbrot zur Peitsche übergehen; ~ **a train into a siding** Zug auf ein Nebengleis rangieren;
to flick a ~ Schalter betätigen;
~ **hook** *(tel.)* Hakenumschalter; ~ **limits** *(railway)* Rangiergelände; ~ **plug** Schaltstöpsel; ~ **stand** Stellwerk; ~ **tender** *(US)* Weichensteller.
switchback Serpentinenstraße, *(Br.)* Achter-, Berg- und Talbahn;
~ *(v.)* **up** in Serpentinen heraufführen.
switchboard *(el.)* Schalttafel, *(tel.)* Telefonzentrale, Klappenschrank;
to set up a ~ Telefonzentrale einrichten;
~ **operator** *(US)* Telefonist.
switched, to be ~ **over** sich verlagern.
switcher Rangierlokomotive.
switching *(el.)* Umschalten, *(railway)* Rangieren, *(securities)* Umstellung des Effektenportefeuilles;
anomaly ~ *(securities)* durch anormale Kursentwicklungen ausgelöste Gewinnrealisierung; **coupon** ~ *(securities)* Umdisposition in kurzfristig angelegten Werten; **policy** ~ Änderung der langfristigen Anlagepolitik;
~ **political alliances** Bündnisaustausch; ~ **off** Abschaltung; ~ **on** Anschalten, Einstellen, Einschaltung;
~ **carrier** Umladespediteur; ~ **charge** *(carrier)* Rangiergebühr; ~ **crew** Rangiermannschaft; ~ **engine** Rangierlokomotive; **movement** Rangierbetrieb; ~ **operations** Rangierbetrieb, *(carrier)* Umladegeschäft; ~ **service** Rangierdienst, ~ **track** Rangiergleis.
switchman Weichensteller.
switchyard Verschiebe-, Rangierbahnhof.
swivel | **bookrest** drehbare Bücherstütze; ~ **chair** Drehstuhl.
swoop *(v.)* **down on the enemy** sich auf den Feind stürzen.
swop *(v.)* **places with s. o.** Platz mit jem. tauschen; ~ **foreign stamps** ausländische Briefmarken austauschen.

sword of Damocles Damoklesschwert.
sworn vereidigt;
  being duly ~ nach ordnungsgemäßer Vereidigung;
  to be ~ in vereidigt werden;
  ~ appraiser vereidigter Sachverständiger, beeidigter Schätzer;
  ~ broker vereidigter Makler; **~ declaration** eidliche Aussage; **~
  enemies** Todfeinde; **~ expert** vereidigter Sachverständiger; **~
  statement** eidliche Erklärung; **~ translator** beeidigter Übersetzer; **~ witness** vereidigter Zeuge.
swot *(school)* Streber, Büffler, Musterschüler;
  ~ *(v.)* pauken, büffeln, ochsen;
  ~ up *(fam.)* büffeln.
syllabus Lehr-, Stundenplan, *(summary)* Zusammenfassung,
  (symbol) Symbol, Kennzeichen.
symbol of status Statussymbol.
symbolic delivery fingierte (fiktive) Übergabe.
sympathetic│audience sympathisches Publikum; **~ clock** syn-
  chronisierte Uhr; **~ ink** Geheimtinte; **~ lockout** Sympathieaus-
  sperrung; **~ strike** Solidaritäts-, Sympathiestreik; **~ words**
  teilnehmende Worte.
sympathizer Sympathisierender, Sympathisant, Anhänger,
  Mitläufer.
sympathy Mitgefühl, Beileid;
  to offer one's ~ to s. o. jem. kondolieren; **to strike in ~** aus
  Solidarität streiken;
  ~ effect Suggestivwirkung; **~ strike** Solidaritäts-, Sympathiestreik.
symphony hall Konzerthalle.
symposium Tagung, Konferenz, *(account of gathering)* Sitzungs-,
  Tagungsbericht, *(exchange of ideas)* Meinungsaustausch.
symptom Ansatz, Anzeichen;
  ~ of discontent Anzeichen von Unzufriedenheit; **~s of inflation**
  Inflationssymptome.
synallagmatic contract zweiseitiger (gegenseitiger) Vertrag.
synchroflash *(camera)* mit Synchronblitzlicht.
synchromesh geräuschlos schaltbar;
  ~ gear Synchrongetriebe.
synchronization *(film)* Synchronisierung.
synchronize *(film)* synchronisieren.
synchronized shifting Synchronschaltung.
synchronizing Synchronisierung.
syndic Rechtsberater, Syndikus, *(bankruptcy)* Masseverwalter,
  (Cambridge) Senatsmitglied.
syndicalism Syndikalismus;
  criminal ~ Bewegung zur gewaltsamen Veränderung bestehender Wirtschaftsformen.
syndicalist Anhänger des Syndikalismus, Syndikalist.
syndicate Konsortium, Syndikat, Verband, Förderungs-,
  Interessengemeinschaft, *(corner)* Ring, Sammelverkaufsstelle,
  (criminals, US) Verbrecherorganisation, *(journalism)* Nachrichtenagentur, Pressezentrale, *(for issue of a loan)* Anleihe,
  Übernahmekonsortium;
  banking ~ Bankenkonsortium; **distributing ~** *(US)* ausgeben-
  des Konsortium; **financial ~** Finanzkonsortium; **issuing ~**
  Begebungskonsortium; **market ~** Börsensyndikat; **original ~**
  (US) übernehmendes Konsortium, Übernahmekonsortium,
  Ankaufssyndikat; **promoting ~** Gründerkonsortium; **purchase
  (selling) ~** Emissionskonsortium; **supporting ~** Stützungssyn-
  dikat; **underlying ~** *(US)* Gründungskonsortium; **underwriting
  ~** Emissionskonsortium;
  ~ of bankers Bankenkonsortium; **~ on original terms** *(US)*
  Gründerkonsortium; **~ of underwriters** Emissionskonsortium,
  (insurance) Versicherungskonsortium;
  ~ *(v.)* sich zu einem Syndikat zusammenschließen, Konsortium bilden, *(serve as syndic)* als Syndikus tätig sein;
  ~ an article Artikel in verschiedenen Zeitungen gleichzeitig
  veröffentlichen; **~ newspapers** zu einem Zeitungskonzern
  zusammenschließen;
  to form a ~ Konsortium bilden; **to lead a ~** Federführung
  haben, Konsortium leiten; **to put a loan into the hands of a ~**
  Anleiheausgabe einem Konsortium übertragen;
  ~ account Beteiligungs-, Konsortialkonto, Konto „Beteiligungen"; **~ advertising** Werbung für Grundstücksbeteiligungen; **~
  agreement** Konsortialvertrag; **~ bank** Konsortialbank; **~ business** Konsortialgeschäft; **~ buying office** *(US)* Zentraleinkaufs-
  büro eines Konzerns; **~ company** Immobilienbeteiligungs-
  gesellschaft; **~ credit (loan)** Konsortialkredit; **~ holdings**
  Konsortialbeteiligungen; **~ management** Feder-, Konsortialführung; **~ manager** federführende Bank [eines Konsortiums],
  Konsortialführer; **~ member** Mitglied eines Konsortiums,
  Konsortial-, Verbandsmitglied; **~ offering** Angebot eines Kon-

sortiums; **~ operation** [einzelnes] Konsortialgeschäft; **~ participation** Konsortialbeteiligung; **~ profit** Konsortialgewinn; **~
quota** Konsortialanteil, -quote; **~ transaction** Konsortialgeschäft.
syndicated│article in mehreren Zeitungen gleichzeitig erscheinender Artikel; **~ bid** *(discount banks, Br.)* vorher abgesprochenes Angebot; **~ columnist** Korrespondent für mehrere
  Zeitungen, Kolumnenschreiber; **~ loan** Konsortialanleihe.
syndicatee führendes Konsortialmitglied.
syndicating Agenturdienst;
  ~ business Immobilienbeteiligungsgeschäft.
syndication Konsortial-, Syndikatsbildung;
  in ~ *(television)* auf mehreren Kanälen gleichzeitig;
  international multibank ~s multinationale internationale Konsortialgeschäfte; **national ~** überregionale Ausstrahlung;
  ~ of loans Zusammenstellung von Anleihekonsorten, konsor-
  tiale Anleihenbegebung.
syndicator Konsortial-, Syndikatsmitglied.
syndrom Symptonkomplex.
synod Synode, Kirchentag, *(assembly)* beratende Versammlung,
  (council) Konzil, *(in general)* Treffen, Tagung.
synopsis Zusammenfassung, vergleichende Übersicht, Inhalts-
  übersicht.
synoptic weather chart Karte der Großwetterlage.
synoptical übersichtlich;
  ~ table Übersichtstafel.
syntax Satzlehre.
synthesis Synthese.
synthetic synthetisch, künstlich;
  ~ fibre Kunstfaser; **~ fibre producer** Kunstfaserproduzent; **~
  fibre production** Kunstfaserproduktion; **~ resin** Kunstharz; **~
  rubber** synthetisches (künstliches) Gummi, Kunstgummi.
syntonization *(el.)* Frequenzabstimmung.
system System, Gefüge, Plan, Schema, *(arrangement)* Anordnung, *(method)* Verfahren, Methode, *(railway)* Eisenbahnnetz;
  accounting ~ Buchführungswesen; **airmail ~** Luftpostdienst;
  banking ~ Bankwesen; **basing-point pricing ~** System der differenzierten Preisfestsetzung für Auslieferungsstellen; **batch ~**
  System zur beschleunigten Prüfung von Eingängen am Kassenschalter; **capitalistic ~** kapitalistisches System; **cash ~** Barzahlungssystem; **clearing ~** Verrechnungssystem; **contract ~**
  System der Gefangenenarbeit; **credit ~** Kreditwesen; **currency
  ~** Währungssystem; **deferred-payment ~** *(US)* Abzahlungssystem, -wesen; **dial ~** Selbstwählverkehr; **domestic ~** Haus-,
  Heimindustrie; **economic ~** Wirtschaftssystem; **filing ~** Ablagesystem; **fiscal ~** Steuersystem; **flexible exchange-rate ~** System
  flexibler Wechselkurse; **four-course ~** Vierfelderwirtschaft;
  government ~ Regierungssystem; **hire-purchase ~** *(Br.)* Abzahlungswesen, -system; **image-rating ~** System zur Erforschung
  der Kundenmeinung; **inland-transport ~** Binnentransportwe-
  sen; **intercommunication ~** Binnennachrichtennetz; **legal ~**
  Rechtssystem, -ordnung; **manifold ~** Vervielfältigungsme-
  thode; **mercantile ~** Handelssystem; **monetary ~** Währungssystem; **multiple rate ~** System flexibler Wechselkurse; **piecework
  ~** Akkordlohnsystem; **prohibitory ~** Schutzzollsystem; **quota
  ~** Kontingentierungswesen; **railway ~** *(Br.)* Eisenbahn-, Schienennetz; **road ~** Straßennetz; **social ~** Gesellschaftsordnung,
  -form, soziale Ordnung; **standard-cost ~** Kostenindex; **state-
  use ~** System der Gefangenenarbeit; **tally ~** *(Br.)* Abzahlungssystem; **telephone ~** Fernsprechnetz; **ticket-of-leave ~** bedingte
  Strafentlassung; **two-price ~** System der gespaltenen Preise;
  working ~ Arbeitsmethode;
  ~ of abbreviations Abkürzungssystem; **~ of accounts** Buchführungssystem; **uniform ~ of accounts** Gemeinschafts-, Einheits-
  kontenrahmen; **~ of legal aid** Rechtshilfesystem; **~ of
  arbitration** Schlichtungswesen; **~ of first, second and third tier
  authorities** dreistufiges Behördensystem; **~ of bounties** Prämiensystem; **~ of canals** Kanalsystem; **~ of shorthand characters** Kurzschriftsystem; **~ of check and balance** *(pol., US)*
  gegenseitiges Überwachungssystem; **~ of cities** Siedlungs-
  struktur; **~ of classifications** Einteilungs-, Klassifikationssy-
  stem; **~ of collection of tax at source** Quellen[besteuerungs]-
  prinzip; **~ of compensation** Abfindungswesen; **continuing ~ of
  consultation** laufendes Konsultationsverfahren; **~ of control**
  (mil.) Kommandosystem; **~ of coordinates** Koordinatensystem; **~ of drainage** Entwässerungsnetz, -system; **~ of government** Regierungs-, Staatssystem; **parliamentary ~ of government** parlamentarische Regierungsform; **~ of insurance**
  Versicherungssystem; **multiple-line ~ of insurance** System der
  Zulassung aller Versicherungssparten bei einer Gesellschaft; **~
  of intimidation** Einschüchterungspolitik; **~ of justice** Rechtssy-

stem; **automatic ~ of pay settlements** automatisches Lohnangleichungssystem; **~ of payment by results** Akkordlohnsystem; **~ of pipelines** Rohrleitungsnetz; **~ of postcoding** Postleitzahlensystem; **~ of material property** *(US)* Güterstand; **~ of railways (railroads,** *US***)** Eisenbahnnetz; **~ of rating** *(fire insurance)* Prämienfestsetzungssystem; **[graduated] ~ of rationing** [abgestuftes] Rationierungssystem; **~ of roads** Straßennetz; **~ of service** Überprüfungsdienst für Buchhaltungssysteme; **~ of supply** Beschaffungswesen; **~ of support** Unterstützungssystem, -wesen; **of taxation** Steuerwesen, -ordnung; **~ of voting** Wahlsystem;
to follow a ~ System befolgen; **to have ~ in one's work** nach einem System arbeiten; **to lack ~** kein System haben; **to organize into a uniform ~** einheitlich erfassen; **to preside over a ~** Aufsicht über etw. haben; **to provide a safe ~ of work** sichere Arbeitsbedingungen gewährleisten; **to reduce to a ~** in ein System bringen; **to supersede a ~** neues System einführen; **to work without a ~** unsystematisch arbeiten;
~s analysis Kostenanalyse; **~-building concept** Baukastensystem; **~s engineer** Systemanalytiker, -berater; **~s engineering (research)** Systemforschung, -analytik, -beratung; **~-wide** sich über das ganze Verkehrsnetz erstreckend.

systematic planmäßig, systematisch;
~ advertising zielbewußte Werbung; **~ investigation** systematische Untersuchung; **~ sample** systematische Stichprobe; **~ sampling** systematische Marktuntersuchung; **~ soldiering** planmäßige Produktionseinschränkung.

systematize *(v.)* in ein System bringen, systematisieren, planmäßig ordnen.

systematizer Systematiker, Organisator.

T

T *(technics)* T-Stück;
to a ~ haargenau, bis aufs I-Tüpfelchen;
landing ~ Landekreuz;
to cross the ~'s äußerst pingelig sein, auf etw. herumhacken (herumreiten); **to suit a ~** haargenau passen.
tab Etikett, Schildchen, Anhänger, Karteireiter, *(US, account)* Konto, Rechnung, *(control)* Beaufsichtigung, Kontrolle, *(mil.)* Aufschlag, Abzeichen, *(print.)* Indexstanzung, *(IOU, sl.)* Schuldschein, *(theater)* Zwischenvorhang;
to foot the ~ Rechnung bezahlen; **to keep ~s on s. th.** *(Br.)* etw. unter Kontrolle haben; **to keep ~s on the expenses** Spesenwirtschaft im Auge behalten; **to keep close ~s on daily sales** *(Br.)* Tagesumsätze genau kontrollieren; **to keep ~s on the state of the economy** Konjunkturpolitik im Griff behalten; **to pick up the ~** *(US sl.)* Rechnung bezahlen.
tabby *(coll.)* alte Jungfer, Klatschbase.
tabernacle *(shed)* Hütte, Unterschlupf, Behausung, Bleibe;
~ *(v.)* vorübergehend (eine Zeitlang) wohnen.
table Verzeichnis, Liste, *(politics)* Tisch des Hauses, *(printing)* Tabellensatz, *(schedule)* Tabelle, Tafel, Übersicht, Register, Schema, *(technical)* Planke, Diele, Brett;
~ A *(stock company law, Br.)* Mustersatzung;
adjoining ~ nachstehende Tabelle; **alphabetical ~** alphabetisches Inhaltsverzeichnis; **American Experience ♀ *(US)*** amtliche Sterblichkeitstafel; **basic ~** Grundtabelle; **bond-value ~** Tabelle zur Berechnung des Nettoertrages von festverzinslichen Papieren; **card ~** *(gaming)* Spieltisch; **comparison ~** vergleichende Übersicht; **conversion ~** Umrechnungstabelle; **dining ~** Eßtisch; **dressing ~** Frisierkommode; **interest ~** Zinstabelle; **genealogical ~** Familienstammbaum; **mathematical ~s** mathematische Tabellen; **mortality ~** Sterblichkeitstabelle; **multiplication ~** Einmaleins; **negotiating ~** Verhandlungstisch; **quarterly ~** Vierteljahrestabelle; **redemption ~** Tilgungsplan; **Round ♀** Tafelrunde; **sliding ~** Ausziehtisch; **spelling ~** Buchstabiertafel; **synoptic ~** synoptische Tabelle, Übersichtstabelle; **tax ~** Steuertabelle; **wage-tax ~** Tabelle zur Berechnung der Lohnsteuer; **writing ~** Schreibtisch;
~ of authorities consulted Verzeichnis der benutzten Quellen; **~ of birth** Geburtenregister, -tafel; **the regulars' ~ in a cafe** Stammtisch; **~ of cases** Fallsammlung, Sammlung von Gerichtsentscheidungen (Präzedenzfällen); **~ of charges** Preistabelle, Gebührenverzeichnis, -tabelle; **~ of contents** Inhaltsverzeichnis, -anzeige, Register; **~ of depreciation rates** Abschreibungstabelle; **~ of descent** Stammtafel; **~ of estate-duty rates** Erbschaftssteuertabelle; **~ of exchange** Umrechnungstabelle; **~ of fares** Eisenbahntarif; **~ of fees** Gebührentabelle; **~ of insurance** Versicherungstarif; **~ of interest** Zinstabelle; **~ of organization** Organisationsplan; **~ of parities** Paritätentafel; **~ of precedence** *(Br.)* Rangordnung; **~ of rates** Steuertabelle; **~ of retentions** Maximaltabelle; **~ of wages** Lohntabelle; **~ of weights** Gewichtstabelle;
~ *(v.)* Tabelle anlegen, in eine Liste eintragen, in ein Verzeichnis aufnehmen, *(put off, US)* vertagen, verschieben, auf die lange Bank schieben, Behandlung zurückstellen, auf Eis legen;
~ an amendment *(Br.)* Zusatz-, Abänderungsantrag einbringen; **~ a bill** Gesetzentwurf einbringen, *(US)* Beratung eines Gesetzentwurfes vertagen, Gesetzesvorlage aufs tote Gleis schieben; **~ a motion** *(Br.)* Antrag einreichen (einbringen, vorlegen), *(US)* Antrag fallenlassen (zurückstellen); **~ a motion of confidence** *(parl.)* Vertrauensantrag stellen;
to allow a bill to lie on the ~ Gesetzentwurf liegenlassen; **to compile (dress) a ~** Tabelle aufstellen; **to head a ~** Tabelle anführen; **to keep the ~ amused** ganze Tafelrunde unterhalten; **to keep a good ~** gute Küche führen; **to lay on the ~** *(adjourn, US)* zurückstellen, vertagen; **to lay papers on the ~** Urkunden bei Gericht einreichen; **to lead a ~** Tabelle anführen; **to learn one's ~s** rechnen lernen; **to lie on the ~** vertagt werden; **to make a ~ of statistics** statistische Tabelle aufstellen; **to prepare ~s** Tabellen aufbereiten; **to select one's own ~ of benefits** sich die gewünschten Versicherungsleistungen selbst zusammenstellen; **to turn the ~s** Rollen vertauschen, Spieß umdrehen;
~ beer *(Br.)* leichtes Bier, Tafelbier; **~ board** *(US)* Verpflegung, Kost; **~ book** Tabellenbuch; **~ calendar** Tischkalender; **~ cloth** Tischdecke; **~ cover** Tischdecke; **~ lamp** Tischlampe; **~ leaf** Auszieh-, Zwischenplatte; **~ lifting (rapping, turning)** Tischrücken; **~ linen** Tischwäsche; **~ d'hôte lunch** Essen à la carte; **~ method** Tafelmethode; **~ money** *(mil.)* Aufwandsent-

schädigung, Repräsentationsgelder; **~ mountain** Tafelberg; **~ plan** Tischordnung; **~ plate** Tafelsilber; **~ radio** Kofferradio; **~ stake** *(gaming)* Einsatz; **~ talk** Tischgespräch; **~ water** Mineralwasser; **~ work** *(print.)* Tafelsatz.
tableau amtliches Verzeichnis, Register;
~ curtains *(theater)* geteilter Vorhang.
tableland Hochebene.
tablet Notizbuch;
~ of chocolate Tafel Schokolade; **~ of soap** Stück Seife.
tableware Besteck, Eßgeschirr.
tabling | of a bill Einbringung eines Gesetzentwurfes, *(US)* Vertagung der Beratung eines Gesetzentwurfes.
tabloid *(US)* Zeitung im Kleinformat, Boulevardzeitung, Sensations-, Revolverblatt;
popular right-wing ~ volkstümlich aufgemachte nach rechts tendierende Boulevardzeitung;
~ criticism kurze (knappe) Kritik; **in ~ form** in konzentrierter Form; **~ journalism** Sensationspresse; **~ paper** Boulevardblatt.
taboo Tabu, Verbot;
to put s. th. under ~ etw. für tabu erklären;
~ *(a.)* tabu, verboten.
tabula rasa *(fig.)* unbeschriebenes Blatt.
tabular tabellarisch, *(print.)* in Tabellenform angeordnet;
~ bookkeeping *(US)* amerikanische Buchführung; **~ composition** Tabellensatz; **~ copy** *(data processing)* Tabellensatz; **~ form** Tabellenform; **to arrange in ~ form** tabellarisch anordnen; **~ matter** *(print.)* Tabellensatz; **~ method of bookkeeping** amerikanische Buchführungsmethode; **~ premium** Tarifprämie; **~ standard** Preisindexwährung; **~ statement** Aufstellung in Tabellenform, tabellarische Aufstellung; **~ summary** Übersichtstabelle; **~ value** Tabellenwert.
tabularization Tabellierung, Tabelle, tabellarische Aufstellung.
tabularize *(v.)* tabellarisieren, tabellarisch anordnen.
tabulate tabellarisch (in Tabellenform) ordnen, tabellarisieren.
tabulated tabellenförmig [angeordnet].
tabulating | card Lochkarte; **~ machine** Tabellenmaschine.
tabulation tabellarische Darstellung, Tabellisierung;
~ of the expenditure Ausgabenaufstellung; **~ of expenses** Ausgabenaufstellung, Spesenzusammenstellung.
tabulator Tabelliermaschine, *(typewriter)* Tabulator;
~ matter *(print.)* Tabellensatz.
tachograph Drehzahlschreiber, Tachograph.
tachometer Tachometer, Geschwindigkeitsmesser.
tacit | acceptance stillschweigende Annahme; **~ agreement** stillschweigend geschlossener Vertrag, stillschweigende Vereinbarung; **~ approval (consent)** stillschweigend erteilte Zustimmung (Genehmigung); **~ dedication** *(of property)* Widmung; **~ hypothecation** gesetzlich entstandenes Pfandrecht; **~ law** Gewohnheitsrecht; **~ mortgage** gesetzlich entstandene [Sicherungs]hypothek; **~ relocation** stillschweigende Miet-, Pachtverlängerung; **~ renewal of a contract** stillschweigende Erneuerung (Vertragsverlängerung); **~ renovation** stillschweigend vorgenommene Vertragserneuerung; **~ tack** *(Scot.)* stillschweigende Pachtverlängerung; **~ understanding** stillschweigendes Einverständnis.
tack Zwecke, Reißnagel, *(course)* Richtung, Weg, Kurs, Handlungsweise, *(lease, Scot.)* Pachtvertrag, *(pol.)* Lavieren, Zickzackkurs, *(school, sl.)* Rektor, *(supplemental bill)* Zusatzantrag;
on the right ~ auf dem richtigen Wege;
new ~ neuer Kurs;
~ *(v.)* anheften, hinzufügen, *(lien)* Rangvorrang erreichen, *(pol.)* lavieren;
~ an appeal for money onto a speech Rede mit einem Spendenappell abschließen; **~ mortgages** *(Br.)* Hypotheken verschiedenen Ranges zusammenschreiben; **~ a rider to a bill** *(Br.)* Gesetzesvorlage mit einem Zusatzantrag koppeln; **~ securities** *(Br.)* Sicherheiten zusammenfassen; **~ together** zusammenfassen, aneinanderfügen;
to be on the wrong ~ auf dem Holzweg sein; **to change one's ~** andere Maßnahmen ergreifen, andere Richtung einschlagen; **to try another ~** anderen Weg versuchen;
~ duty *(Scot.)* Pachtrente, -zins.
tacking *(different mortgages, Br.)* Hypothekenvereinigung, *(securities)* Zusammenfassung, *(supplemental bill, Br.)* Einreichung eines mit einer Gesetzesvorlage gekoppelten Zusatzantrags.

tackle Gerät, Ausrüstung, Werkzeug;
writing ~ Schreibzeug;
~ *(v.)* in Angriff nehmen, herangehen, sich befassen;
~ **the boss for a raise** *(US)* **(rise,** *Br.)* Chef um Gehaltserhöhung angehen; ~ **s. o. about a matter** ganz offen mit jem. über eine Sache sprechen; ~ **a piece of work** an eine Arbeit herangehen; ~ **a problem** mit einem Problem fertig werden; ~ **a difficult task** schwierige Aufgabe bewältigen; ~ **a thief** Dieb stellen.
tacksman *(Scot.)* Pächter.
tacky verwahrloster Mensch;
~ **party** Lumpenball.
tact Anstandsgefühl, Takt;
to show ~ in dealing with people taktvoll mit den Leuten umgehen.
tactical taktisch, *(fig.)* planvoll;
~ **unit** Kampfeinheit; ~ **atomic weapons** taktische Atomwaffen.
tactician Taktiker.
tactics *(fig.)* planvolles Vorgehen, Taktik, *(mil.)* Taktik;
surprise ~ Überraschungstaktik.
tag Band, Anhängsel, Zipfel, *(dog licence, US)* Hundemarke, *(epilogue)* Nach-, Schlußwort, Epilog, *(added flourish)* Schnörkel, *(label)* Etikett, Anhänger, [Bezeichnungs]schild, *(label indicating price)* Preisauszeichnung, -zettel, *(luggage)* Gepäckanhänger, Anhängeradresse, -schildchen, -zettel, *(mil.)* Kennmarke, *(moral added to a story)* Pointe, Moral, *(hackneyed quotation)* abgedroschenes Zitat, stehende Redensart, *(theater)* Stichwort, *(warrant of arrest, sl.)* Haftbefehl;
dog ~ Hundemarke; **identification ~** *(mil.)* Erkennungsmarke; **licence ~** Steuermarke; **price ~** Preisschild, -zettel;
~, rag and bobtail Krethi und Plethi;
~ *(v.) (arrest, sl.)* verhaften, *(furnish with label)* auszeichnen, etikettieren, mit Preiszetteln versehen, *(luggage)* mit einem Anhänger versehen;
~ **after s. o.** jem. überall nachlaufen; ~ **s. o. alright** j. festnageln;
~ **old articles together to make a book** Buch aus früheren Zeitungsartikeln zusammenstellen; ~ **a speech with verses** Verse in seine Rede einflechten; ~ **together** zusammenschustern;
~ **addresser** Gepäckanhänger; ~ **boat** *(US coll.)* Leichter, Schleppboot; ~ **day** *(US)* Sammeltag; ~ **end** *(coll.)* letzter Rest; ~ **fastener** Etiketthalter; ~ **label** Anhängezettel; ~ **line** stehende Redensart.
tagger dünnes Weißblech;
~ *(v.)* mit einem Anhänger versehen.
tail *(coin)* Rück-, Kehrseite, *(estate law)* beschränktes Erbrecht, *(issue)* Nachkommenschaft, *(plane)* Heck, Rumpfende, Schwanz, *(queue)* Schlange, *(retinue)* Gefolge, Anhang, *(state of entailment)* beschränktes Besitzrecht [an Grundstücken], Vorerbschaft;
in one's ~ *(fig.)* im Rücken; **with one's ~ between one's legs** mit eingezogenem Schwanz, *(fig.)* wie ein begossener Pudel, wie ein geprügelter Hund;
~s Gesellschaftsanzug, Frack, Schwalbenschwanz;
~ **female** auf die weiblichen Nachkommen beschränkte Erbfolge; ~ **general** auf die leiblichen Nachkommen beschränkte Erbfolge; ~ **male** auf männliche Nachkommen beschränkte Erbfolge; **several ~** *(land)* geteilter Fideikommiß für zwei Stämme; **special ~** auf einzelne Erben beschränkte Erbfolge, Erbfolgebeschränkung;
~ **of a marching army** Schluß einer marschierenden Armee; ~ **of the class** Schlechteste der Klasse; ~ **of a comet** Kometenschweif; ~ **of journalists** journalistisches Gefolge, Schwarm von Journalisten; ~ **of a letter** Briefschluß; ~ **of page** unterer Seitenrand; ~ **of a storm** abklingender Sturm; ~ **of the trenches** *(mil.)* hintere Schützengräben;
~ *(v.)* **s. o.** j. beschatten; ~ **after s. o.** jem. auf Schritt und Tritt folgen; ~ **away** *(column)* sich auseinanderziehen, *(storm)* abflauen, verebben; ~ **a ship to a dock** Schiff mit dem Heck am Kai festmachen;
to attack under the ~ von rückwärts angreifen; **not to be able to make head or ~ of it** sich keinen Vers daraus machen können; **to have s. th. by the ~** *(sl.)* Sache im Griff haben; **to have one's ~ between one's legs** Schwanz einziehen, klein beigeben; **to have one's ~ up** sehr fidel sein; **to have the police on one's ~** Polizei dicht auf den Fersen haben; **to keep one's ~ down** niedergeschlagen sein; **to keep one's ~ up** guter Laune bleiben; **to turn ~** Fersengeld geben; **to watch s. o. out of the ~ of one's eye** j. verstohlen betrachten;
~ *(a.)* beschränkt, *(estate in fee)* erbrechtlich begrenzt, mit Vorerbschaft behaftet;
~ **coat** Frack; ~ **chute** Bremsfallschirm; ~ **end of a discourse**

Schuß einer Diskussion; **to come at the ~ end** als Letzter durchs Ziel gehen; ~ **ender** *(competition, US coll.)* Schlußlicht, Allerletzter; ~ **group** *(airplane)* Leitwerk; ~ **lamp** *(car)* Rück-, Schlußlicht; ~ **male** Majorat; ~ **pipe** Auspuffrohr; ~ **plane** Höhenflosse; ~ **spin** *(airplane)* Trudeln; ~**-steering airplane** schwanzgesteuertes Flugzeug; ~ **twisting** *(sl.)* Schikanieren; ~ **unit** *(airplane)* Leitwerk; ~ **wind** *(airplane)* Rückenwind.
tailboard *(car)* Ladeklappe.
tailfirst plane Entenflugzeug.
tailgate *(car)* aufklappbare Hecktür.
tailless airplane Nurflügelflugzeug.
taillight *(car)* Schlußlicht, *(plane)* Hecklicht.
tailor Schneider;
~ **to the trade** Lohnschneider;
~ *(v.) (fig.)* abstellen auf, passend machen für;
~ **output to the market** Ausstoß den Aufnahmemöglichkeiten des Marktes anpassen; ~ **a play for the audience** Theaterstück auf den Publikumsgeschmack abstellen;
to go to the ~'s to be measured for a suit sich beim Schneider Maß nehmen lassen.
tailor-made maßgeschneidert, nach Maß, *(made in a factory)* industriell hergestellt;
~ **for** *(fig.)* nach Maß, zugeschnitten auf;
to be ~ for a job für eine Aufgabe wie geschaffen sein; **to be ~ to meet a special situation** auf eine besondere Lage abgestellt sein.
tailored | for a special purpose für einen besonderen Zweck hergestellt;
to be sharply ~ auf Figur gearbeitet sein;
well-~ suit erstklassig sitzender Maßanzug.
tailoring of pension policy maßgeschneidertes Altersversorgungssystem.
tailpiece Anhang, *(print.)* Schlußvignette, -leiste, -stück.
taint Fleck, *(conviction of felony)* Vorstrafe, Vorbestrafter, *(fig.)* Makel, Schandfleck, *(med.)* Belastung, verborgene Anlage, *(trace)* Spur, Anflug;
free from ~ *(meat)* unverdorben;
hereditary ~ erbliche Belastung;
~ **of insanity** Anlage zur Geistesgestörtheit; ~ **of morbidness** morbider Zug; ~ **of suspicion** Anflug von Mißtrauen;
~ *(v.)* verpesten, verderben, *(fig.)* schädlich beeinflussen, verderben, *(med.)* anstecken.
tainted | air verpestete Luft; ~ **goods** *(Br.)* von Nichtgewerkschaftsmitgliedern hergestellte Waren; ~ **meat** verdorbenes Fleisch.
take Wegnehmen, *(film)* Szenenaufnahme, Filmszene, -abschnitt, *(Br., leasing)* Pachtland, Pachtung, *(mining)* gepachtete Anbaufläche, *(print.)* Manuskript, Portion, *(recording)* Ton-, Probeaufnahme, *(theater)* Kasse, Einnahme;
tax ~ Steuereinnahmen; **total ~** Gesamtausbeute;
~ *(v.)* [weg]nehmen, ergreifen, *(book)* ankommen, einschlagen, *(legal sense)* Besitzrecht erlangen, Eigentum erwerben, *(mil.)* gefangennehmen, *(taxes)* einnehmen, erheben, *(theater)* Anklang finden;
~ **s. o. for s. th.** *(US)* jem. etw. abluchsen; ~ **account of (into account)** in Erwägung (Betracht) ziehen; ~ **s. o. in the act** j. auf frischer Tat ertappen; ~ **action** Schritte unternehmen; ~ **little by an action** durch seine Maßnahmen wenig erreichen; ~ **action against s. o.** Gerichtsverfahren gegen j. einleiten; ~ **in advance** im Vorverkauf erwerben; ~ **advantage** ausnutzen; ~ **undue advantage** in sittenwidriger Weise ausnutzen; ~ **legal advice** sich anwaltlich beraten lassen; ~ **medical advice** Arzt aufsuchen; ~ **the air** Luft schnappen; ~ **amiss** Anstoß nehmen; ~ **an argument from false premises** Behauptung von falschen Voraussetzungen herleiten, von falschen Voraussetzungen ausgehen; ~ **arms** Feindseligkeiten beginnen; ~ **a back seat** *(fig., coll.)* sich im Hintergrund halten, zu jds. Gunsten verzichten; ~ **the back track** Rückzug (Rückmarsch) antreten; ~ **a benefit under a will** testamentarisch bedacht werden; ~ **a bow** *(theater)* sich vor dem Publikum zeigen; ~ **a broadcast on tape** Rundfunksendung auf Band aufnehmen; ~ **the bull by the horns** *(fig.)* Stier bei den Hörnern packen; ~ **to business** an die Arbeit gehen; ~ **the cake** *(sl.)* Preis davontragen; ~ **a call** Anruf entgegennehmen; ~ **for the call** Vorprämie verkaufen; ~ **things calmy** Dinge mit Gelassenheit aufnehmen; ~ **care of s. o.** für j. sorgen; ~ **care of a debt** Schuld bezahlen; ~ **a census** Volkszählung durchführen; ~ **the chair** Präsidium (Vorsitz) übernehmen; ~ **one's chance** seine Chancen wahrnehmen; ~ **one's chance with all applicants for the job** alle Bewerber ausprobieren; ~ **charge of** Leitung (Verantwortung) übernehmen, *(goods)* in Verwahrung nehmen; ~ **charge of the luggage** *(Br.)* sich um das Gepäck kümmern; ~ **to the cinema** *(US)* **(theatre,**

Br.) ins Kino ausführen; ~ **a class** Unterricht in einer Klasse übernehmen; ~ **s. o. into one's confidence** j. ins Vertrauen ziehen; ~ **the consequences** Folgen auf sich nehmen; ~ **into consideration** in Erwägung ziehen; ~ **counsel** sich beraten lassen; ~ **courage** sich ein Herz fassen; ~ **a course** an einem Kurs[us] teilnehmen; ~ **on credit** auf Kredit (Konto) nehmen, anschreiben lassen; ~ **the credit for** sich als Verdienst anrechnen; ~ **a day off** sich einen Tag frei nehmen; ~ **one's degree** sein Doktorexamen machen; ~ **delivery** in Empfang nehmen, abnehmen; ~ **delivery of stock** *(US)* Aktien abnehmen; ~ **a denial** abschlägige Antwort bekommen; ~ **by descent** aufgrund gesetzlicher Erbfolge erben; ~ **s. o. at a disadvantage** j. in einer unangenehmen Situation antreffen; ~ **on discount** Diskont in Anspruch nehmen, diskontieren, in Diskont nehmen; ~ **a disease in time** Krankheit rechtzeitig behandeln; ~ **driving lessons** Fahrunterricht nehmen; ~ **to s. th. like a duck to water** für etw. sofort Feuer und Flamme sein; ~ **to earth** *(fig.)* sich verstecken; ~ **effect** wirksam werden, in Kraft treten; ~ **employment** Arbeit annehmen; ~ **evasive action** *(sl.)* kneifen, sich verdünnisieren, sich drücken; ~ **evidence** Beweis erheben; ~ **s. one's evidence** j. vernehmen; ~ **an examination** Prüfung bestehen; ~ **the fall** *(US sl.)* Suppe auslöffeln, etw. ausbaden; ~ **the public's fancy** beim Publikum sehr gut aufgenommen werden; ~ **one's farewell** Abschied nehmen; ~ **one's father in his old age** seinen Vater im Alter bei sich aufnehmen; ~ **the field** *(mil.)* ausrücken; ~ **fire** brennen, *(fig.)* sich begeistern; ~ **firm** fest übernehmen; ~ **five** *(sl.)* fünf Minuten ausruhen; ~ **a flier** *(US)* spekulative Effektentransaktion durchführen; ~ **French** *(Br.)* Examen in Französisch machen; ~ **a painting for genuine** Gemälde für echt halten; ~ **the goods** Ware abnehmen; ~ **for granted** als selbstverständlich annehmen; ~ **paying guests** Gäste gegen Bezahlung aufnehmen; ~ **s. o. in hand** Verantwortung für j. übernehmen; ~ **s. th. in hand** etw. in Angriff nehmen; ~ **heart** sich ein Herz fassen; ~ **fresh heart** neuen Mut fassen; ~ **as heir** sein Erbe antreten, in die Erbrechte eintreten; ~ **a hint** es sich gesagt sein lassen; ~ **a holiday** in Urlaub gehen, Ferien (Urlaub) machen; ~ **home** netto verdienen; ~ **s. o. home** j. nach Hause bringen; ~ **s. o. for an honest man** j. für anständig halten; ~ **four hours** vier Stunden beanspruchen; ~ **a house for a year** Haus auf ein Jahr mieten; ~ **other people's ideas** sich anderer Leute Ideen zunutze machen; ~ **information** Auskunft einholen; ~ **the initiative** Initiative ergreifen; ~ **an interest** sich interessieren, Interesse zeigen; ~ **an interest in an enterprise** sich an einem Unternehmen finanziell beteiligen; ~ **an interest in politics** sich für Politik interessieren, politisch interessiert sein; ~ **inventory** inventarisieren, Inventur machen; ~ **issue with s. o.** sich jds. Meinung nicht anschließen; ~ **it on the chin** etw. schlucken; ~ **it easy** sich nicht darüber aufregen; ~ **the lead** Führung übernehmen; ~ **one's leave** weggehen, auf Wiedersehen sagen; ~ **lessons** Unterricht nehmen; ~ **a letter** sich einen Brief diktieren lassen; ~ **letters to the post office** Briefe aufgeben (postieren); ~ **the liberty** sich die Freiheit nehmen; ~ **liberties with s. o.** sich Freiheiten gegenüber jem. herausnehmen; ~ **one's life into one's hands** sein Leben aufs Spiel setzen; ~ **a liking** Sympathie empfinden; ~ **to literature** sich mit Literatur befassen; ~ **lodging** sich einmieten, Zimmer mieten; ~ **a loss** Verlust in Kauf nehmen; ~ **a lot of doing** schwer zu bewerkstelligen sein; ~ **in matrimony** ehelichen; ~ **a new meaning** neue Bedeutung gewinnen; ~ **legal measures** gerichtliche Schritte ergreifen, Rechtsweg einschlagen; ~ **the measurements** ausmessen; ~ **medical treatment** sich ärztlich behandeln lassen (in ärztliche Behandlung begeben); ~ **one's medicine** seine Strafe hinnehmen; ~ **a message to s. o.** jem. etw. ausrichten; ~ **a mortgage [on real estate]** Hypothek [auf ein Grundstück] aufnehmen; ~ **a motion from the table** Antrag zur Beratung einbringen; ~ **s. one's name and address** jds. Namen und Adresse feststellen; ~ **a newspaper** Zeitung halten; **not to ~** *(smallpox injection)* nicht angehen; ~ **notes in a lecture** Vorlesung mitschreiben; ~ **notice of s. th.** Kenntnis von etw. nehmen; ~ **no notice of** ignorieren; ~ **an oath from s. o.** jem. einen Eid abnehmen; ~ **an oath upon s. th.** Eid auf etw. ablegen (schwören); ~ **office** Amt antreten, Büroräume mieten; ~ **an order for s. th.** Auftrag für etw. hereinnehmen, Bestellung auf etw. erhalten; ~ **great pains over s. th.** sich große Mühe bei etw. geben; ~ **part** sich beteiligen, teilnehmen; ~ **a part** Rolle übernehmen; ~ **a partner into business** als Teilhaber in sein Geschäft aufnehmen; ~ **s. o. into partnership** j. als Teilhaber aufnehmen (hereinnehmen); ~ **as payment** an Zahlungs Statt annehmen; ~ **a photograph** Aufnahme (Foto) machen; ~ **to pieces** zerlegen, auseinandernehmen; ~ **place** stattfinden; ~ **a place (position)** Stelle (Stellung) einnehmen; **to ~ s. one's place** j. ersetzen; ~ **a**

poll Abstimmung vornehmen; ~ **possession** in Besitz nehmen; ~ **power** Macht ergreifen; ~ **precedence over** Vorrang haben; ~ **priority** Vorrang haben; ~ **s. o. prisoner** j. gefangennehmen; ~ **the first prize** ersten Preis gewinnen; ~ **problems one by one** Probleme der Reihe nach lösen (behandeln); ~ **profits** Gewinne mitnehmen (realisieren); ~ **for public use** für Bedürfnisse der Öffentlichkeit enteignen; ~ **by purchase** käuflich erwerben; ~ **for the put** Rückprämie kaufen; ~ **the rap** *(sl.)* seine Strafe abbüßen; ~ **as read** *(protocol)* auf die Lesung verzichten; ~ **one's readers with one** seine Leser mitreißen; ~ **readily** gern abnehmen; ~ **record of a speech** Rede mitschreiben; ~ **one's recreations** in Erholung gehen; ~ **refuge** Zuflucht nehmen; ~ **s. th. as a reparation** etw. im Wege der Wiedergutmachung erhalten; ~ **all responsibility** volle Verantwortung übernehmen; ~ **as reward** als Belohnung erhalten; ~ **s. o. for a ride** mit jem. eine Autofahrt machen, *(sl.)* j. um die Ecke bringen; ~ **the risk** Risiko auf sich nehmen; ~ **the road to the left** linke Abzweigung wählen; ~ **a room** Zimmer mieten; ~ **little room** wenig Platz beanspruchen; ~ **root** Wurzeln schlagen; ~ **a secretary** Sekretärin engagieren; ~ **the sense of the Senate** Meinung des Senats einholen; ~ **shape** Gestalt annehmen; ~ **shelter** Zuflucht nehmen; ~ **ship** sich einschiffen; ~ **silk** *(Br.)* Kronanwalt werden; ~ **one's stand** *(fig.)* Stellung nehmen; ~ **by stealth** Diebstahl begehen, stehlen; ~ **stock** Lagerbestand (Inventar) aufnehmen; ~ **stock in** Aktien zeichnen; ~ **no stock in s. one's promises** von jds. Versprechungen nichts halten; ~ **by storm** stürmen, im Sturm nehmen, *(audience)* sein Publikum mit sich reißen; ~ **a sum out of one's income** Betrag von seinen Einkünften abzweigen; ~ **from the table** *(parl.)* [Antrag] zur Debatte stellen; ~ **to task** zur Rede stellen; ~ **a taxi** Taxi nehmen; ~ **a thief** Dieb ergreifen; ~ **a ticket** Fahrkarte lösen; ~ **time over a job** sich bei der Arbeit Zeit lassen; ~ **title to property** *(US)* Eigentum erwerben; ~ **a town** Stadt einnehmen; ~ **the train** Bahn benutzen; ~ **a turn** gute (schlechte) Wendung nehmen; ~ **a trial balance** Rohbilanz aufstellen; ~ **under a will** aufgrund testamentarischer Verfügung erben; ~ **s. o. unawares** j. völlig überraschen; ~ **a view of s. th.** Stellung zu etw. nehmen; ~ **views** Aufnahmen machen; ~ **a different view** anderer Ansicht sein; ~ **a vote** abstimmen lassen; ~ **s. o. for a walk** mit jem. spazieren gehen; ~ **water** *(ship)* Wasser übernehmen, *(US sl.)* kneifen; ~ **the water** vom Stapel laufen, ~ **to the waters** Heilkurort aufsuchen; ~ **£ 400 a week** wöchentlich 400 Pfund verdienen; ~ **whatever one can lay hand on** nehmen, was man in die Finger bekommt; ~ **the wind out of s. one's sails** jem. den Wind aus den Segeln nehmen; ~ **s. one at his word** j. beim Wort nehmen;

to be able to ~ it mit etw. fertig werden.
take about *(coll.)* öffentlich begleiten.
take after his father seinem Vater ähneln.
take aside beiseitenehmen.
take away *(v.)* wegnehmen;
~ **s. one's breath away** jem. den Atem benehmen; ~ **from one's public image** Gesichtsverlust in der Öffentlichkeit erleiden; ~ **and carry away** sich in rechtswidriger Absicht zueignen; ~ **customers** Kunden abfangen; ~ **s. one's pension** jem. keine Pension mehr zahlen; ~ **the right to vote** Stimmrecht entziehen; ~ **from school** von der Schule [herunter]nehmen.
take back *(v.) (goods)* zurücknehmen;
~ **s. o. back to his childhood days** j. in die Kindheitstage zurückversetzen.
take down *(v.)* aufschreiben, notieren, *(building)* abreißen, *(engine)* abmontieren, zerlegen, *(the minutes)* niederschreiben, zu Protokoll nehmen, protokollieren, Protokoll führen, *(pledge)* zurücknehmen, *(print.)* Typenmaterial verteilen;
~ **a broadcast on tape** Rundfunksendung mitschneiden; ~ **a building** Gebäude abreißen; ~ **s. one's deposition** jds. Aussage protokollieren; ~ **s. one's name and address** sich jds. Namen und Anschrift notieren; ~ **a peg or two** zurückstecken; ~ **pictures from the wall** Bilder abhängen; ~ **the scaffolding** Gerüst abnehmen; ~ **a speech in shorthand** Rede mitstenografieren; ~ **in writing** zu Protokoll nehmen.
take for *(v.)* annehmen;
~ **s. o. for a fool** j. für einen Narren halten; ~ **granted** als selbstverständlich annehmen.
take in *(v.) (accept)* Aufnahme gewähren, *(deceive)* betrügen, übers Ohr hauen, hereinlegen, *(goods)* hereinnehmen, einkaufen, *(guest)* aufnehmen, *(hotel)* beherbergen, *(lecture)* begreifen, *(newspaper, Br.)* beziehen, halten, abonnieren, *(receive)* empfangen, erhalten, bekommen, *(stock exchange, Br.)* in Report (Prolongation) nehmen, hereinnehmen, *(touring, US)* mitnehmen, noch besuchen;

~ **six European capitals** *(motor-coach tour)* sechs europäische Hauptstädte einschließen; ~ **cargo** Ladung einnehmen; ~ **continuation** in Report nehmen; ~ **contract** auf Akkordbasis anstellen; ~ **s. o. in to dinner** j. zum Essen ausführen; ~ **execution** pfänden; ~ **hand** in Arbeit nehmen; ~ **the harvest** Ernte einbringen; ~ **a lady in** Dame zu Tisch führen; ~ **lodgers** vermieten, Mieter aufnehmen; ~ **a magazine** *(Br.)* Zeitschrift abonnieren; ~ **money** *(US)* Geld kassieren; ~ **[as] payment** an Zahlungs Statt annehmen; ~ **part payment** sich mit Teilzahlungen einverstanden erklären; ~ **pawn** als Pfand annehmen; ~ **petrol** *(Br.)* **(gas,** *US)* Benzin tanken; ~ **a reef** *(fig.)* vorsichtiger vorgehen, *(make economies)* sich in seinen Ausgaben einschränken, Kürzungen vornehmen, kurztreten; ~ **the scene at a glance** Situation sofort erfassen; ~ **a situation** Lage in allen Auswirkungen begreifen; ~ **stock** in Aktien zeichnen, *(Br.)* Wertpapiere hereinnehmen (in Prolongation nehmen); ~ **a traveller in for the night** einem Reisenden ein Nachtquartier geben; ~ **washing** für fremde Leute waschen.

take into *(v.)* [Mitglieder] aufnehmen;

~ **account** einberechnen, -kalkulieren, in Betracht ziehen; ~ **confidence** ins Vertrauen ziehen; ~ **a clerk into the firm** Kommis einstellen; ~ **consideration** in Betracht ziehen, berücksichtigen; ~ **custody** in Verwahrung nehmen; ~ **one's head** sich in den Kopf setzen.

take off *(v.)* wegnehmen, *(airplane)* abfliegen, starten, *(bus)* aus dem Verkehr ziehen, *(deduct)* abziehen, in Abrechnung bringen, *(deduct part of price)* [Preis]senken um, Skonto abziehen, *(market)* aus dem Markt nehmen, *(passengers)* von Bord bringen, *(rest, sl.)* kurze Arbeitspause machen, *(tax)* aufheben, beseitigen;

~ **4%** 4% abrechnen, Rabatt von 4% in Anrechnung bringen, 4% Skonto abziehen; ~ **200 copies** zweihundert Kopien anfertigen; ~ **the crew** *(shipwreck)* Mannschaft retten; ~ **easily** *(plane)* leicht abheben; ~ **an embargo** Beschlagnahme aufheben; ~ **a ship off the active list** Schiff außer Dienst stellen; ~ **so much off the price** soundso viel vom Preis nachlassen; ~ **a proof** Korrekturbogen abziehen; ~ **s. one's name off a list** j. von einer Liste streichen; ~ **the seals** Siegel abnehmen; ~ **s. o. off to the station** j. zum Bahnhof bringen; ~ **a train** Zug aus dem Verkehr ziehen; ~ **a trial balance** Rohbilanz erstellen; ~ **the whips** *(Br.)* Fraktionszwang aufheben, Abstimmung freistellen.

take on *(v.)* in Dienst treten, *(find acceptance, Br.)* Anklang finden, *(bus)* aufnehmen, *(coll.)* großes Getue machen, sich haben, *(goods)* an Bord nehmen, *(labo(u)rers)* einstellen, engagieren, *(members)* aufnehmen;

~ **s. th.** Sache in Angriff nehmen; ~ **a bet** Wette annehmen; ~ **a character of dignity** sich einen würdigen Anstrich geben; ~ **charter** chartern, mieten; ~ **among all classes** *(fashion)* sich in allen Bevölkerungssparten durchsetzen; ~ **all comers** es mit allen aufnehmen; ~ **credit** anschreiben lassen, auf Pump kaufen; ~ **extra work** zusätzliche Arbeiten übernehmen; ~ **extra workers** zusätzliche Arbeitskräfte einstellen; ~ **hire** mieten; ~ **a lease** Pachtvertrag erneuern; ~ **office** Amt übernehmen; ~ **heavy responsibilty** schwere Verantwortung übernehmen.

take out *(v.)* herausholen, -nehmen, wegnehmen, *(pawn)* auslösen;

~ **s. o. out to dinner** j. zum Essen ausführen; ~ **it out** sich schadlos halten; ~ **of bond** aus dem Zollverschluß nehmen; ~ **books out of a library** Bücher aus einer Bibliothek entfernen; ~ **citizen papers** *(US)* Einbürgerung erreichen; ~ **an insurance policy** Versicherung abschließen, Versicherungspolice erwerben; ~ **it out in drinks** sich an Getränken schadlos halten; ~ **it out on one's wife** seine schlechte Laune an der Ehefrau auslassen; ~ **an item** Posten ausziehen; ~ **a licence** sich eine Lizenz geben lassen; ~ **a driving licence** Führerschein erwerben (machen); ~ **a patent for s. th.** sich etw. patentieren lassen, Patent für etw. erwirken; ~ **a passport** sich einen Paß verschaffen; ~ **of pawn** Pfand einlösen; ~ **a summons** Zahlungsbefehl erwirken.

take over *(v.)* übernehmen, *(capital)* Aktienkapital übernehmen, *(pol.)* Macht übernehmen, *(tel.)* verbinden;

~ **accounts receivable and accounts payable** *(US)* Aktiva und Passiva übernehmen; ~ **the assets and liabilities** mit Aktiven und Passiven übernehmen; ~ **a business** Geschäft übernehmen; ~ **a car** Auto von der Fabrik übernehmen; ~ **s. o. over to an island** j. zu einer Insel herüberfahren; ~ **the management** Leitung übernehmen; ~ **s. one's obligations** in jds. Pflichtenkreis eintreten; ~ **the railways** Eisenbahn verstaatlichen; ~ **under a will** aufgrund eines Testaments (testamentarisch) erben.

take to *(v.)*|**the boats** in die Boote gehen, sich in den Booten retten; ~ **business** an die Arbeit gehen; ~ **s. th. like ducks to** water für etw. Feuer und Flamme sein; ~ **gardening when one retires** sich nach der Pensionierung um den Garten kümmern; ~ **bad habits** schlechte Gewohnheiten annehmen; ~ **one's heels** sein Heil in der Flucht suchen; ~ **literature** sich literarisch betätigen; ~ **the road** trampen, *(circus)* auswärts gastieren; ~ **the stage** zur Bühne gehen; ~ **the woods** in die Wälder flüchten; ~ **work** an die Arbeit gehen; ~ **writing** sich für die Schriftstellerei entschließen.

take together *(v.)* *(fig.)* miteinander vergleichen.

take under |*(v.)* **a will** testamentarisch erben; ~ **a benefit under a will** testamentarisch bedacht werden.

take up *(v.)* über-, aufnehmen, sich befassen mit, *(enter upon)* ergreifen, beginnen, *(lodgings)* Wohnung nehmen (beziehen), *(orator)* unterbrechen, verbessern, *(passengers)* aufnehmen, übernehmen;

~ **s. o. up** j. protegieren; ~ **with s. o.** mit jem. besprechen; ~ **an agency** Vertretung übernehmen; ~ **a matter up with a higher authority** Angelegenheit mit einer höheren Instanz besprechen; ~ **a bill** Wechsel honorieren; ~ **a bill when due** Wechsel bei Fälligkeit einlösen; ~ **new capital** neues Kapital aufnehmen; ~ **six columns** sechs Spalten einnehmen; ~ **the documents** Dokumente übernehmen; ~ **a line of goods** Vertrieb verschiedener Erzeugnisse übernehmen; ~ **modern languages** neue Sprachen studieren; ~ **a loan** Darlehn aufnehmen; ~ **money** Geld aufnehmen; ~ **s. th. with one's M.P.** sich wegen einer Sache an seinen Abgeordneten wenden; ~ **current opinions** sich die augenblicklichen Ansichten zu eigen machen; ~ **an option** sich ein Bezugsrecht sichern, Bezugsrecht (Kaufoption) ausüben; ~ **passengers** Passagiere aufnehmen; ~ **photography** sich in der Freizeit mit Fotografieren beschäftigen; ~ **a profession** Beruf ergreifen; ~ **the quarrels of one's neighbo(u)rs** in die nachbarlichen Streitigkeiten eingreifen; ~ **under rebate** *(Br.)* Wechsel diskontieren; ~ **the reins of government** Zügel der Regierung ergreifen; ~ **one's residence** seinen Wohnsitz aufschlagen; ~ **shares** Aktien beziehen (zeichnen); ~ **s. o. up sharp (short)** j. sofort unterbrechen; ~ **taxes** Steuern einziehen (erheben); ~ **a thief** Dieb ergreifen; ~ **time** Zeit beanspruchen.

take upon *(v.)* | **o. s.** Verantwortung für etw. übernehmen; ~ **o. s. risk** Risiko auf sich nehmen; ~ **o. s. to speak for the whole town** sich berufen fühlen, für die ganze Stadt (im Namen der ganzen Stadt) zu sprechen.

take-|**along gift** Mitbringsel; ~**-away meals** Fertigmahlzeiten; ~**-home pay (pay packet, income, wages)** *(coll.)* Lohntüte, effektiv ausgezahlter Lohn, Netto-, Effektivlohn, Nettoverdienst; ~**-home gift** Mitbringsel; ~**-in** *(coll.)* Prellerei, Gaunertrick; ~**-up spool** *(film)* Aufwickelspule.

take-off, takeoff Wegnehmen, *(airplane)* Abflug, [Flugzeug]start, *(fig.)* Start, Sprungbrett, Ausgangspunkt, *(imitation, coll.)* Zerrbild, Karikatur;

assisted ~ Abflug mit Starthilfe; **catapult** ~ Schleuderstart; **smooth** ~ glatter Start;

to wait for ~ auf Starterlaubnis warten;

~ **distance** Startbahnlänge; ~ **phase** Wiederbelebungsphase; ~ **point** Startplatz, Startposition; ~ **position** Abflugstelle; ~ **run** Startstrecke.

take-out *(sl.)* Mittagessen zum Mitnehmen.

take-over, takeover Abnahme, Übernahme, *(management)* Übernahme der Geschäftsführung, *(stock majority)* Übernahme der Aktienmajorität;

~ **agreement** Übernahmevertrag; ~ **bid (offer)** Übernahmeangebot; **to prevent a** ~ **bid on antitrust grounds** Übernahmeangebot aus kartellrechtlichen Gründen verhindern; ~ **consortium** Übernahmekonsortium; ~ **manoeuvres** zweifelhafte Übernahmegeschäfte; ~ **price** Übernahmepreis; ~ **prospect** erwartete Übernahme.

takedown Auseinandernehmen, zerlegen;

~ *(a.)* zerlegbar.

taken *(seat)* besetzt, belegt;

~ **in** *(Br., securities)* hereingenommen; ~ **up by the police** von der Polizei festgenommen; ~ **up outright** *(bookseller)* fest übernommen; **to be** ~ **aback by the news** von den Nachrichten ganz verwirrt sein.

taker Abnehmer, Käufer, Kunde, *(of a bet)* Wetteilnehmer, *(collector)* Einnehmer, -sammler, *(of estate by devise, US)* Vermächtnisnehmer, *(stock exchange, Br.)* Hereinnehmer; **first** ~ erster Anwartschaftsberechtigter; **lowest** ~ Wenigstfordernder; ~**-off** *(print., Br.)* Bogenfänger; **ticket** ~ Fahrkartenkontrolleur;

~ **of a bill** Wechselnehmer; ~ **on bottomry** Bodmereinehmer; ~ **for a call** Verkäufer einer Vorprämie; ~ **of an option** Optionsnehmer, Optant; ~ **of option money** *(Br.)* Prämienverkäufer.

taker | -in Heimarbeiter, *(factory)* Faktor, *(print.)* Bogenfänger, *(stock exchange, Br.)* Hereinnehmer, Kostnehmer, *(swindler)* Betrüger, Gauner; **~-off** Abnahmebeamter, *(print., Br.)* Bogenfänger; **~-out of a patent** Patentinhaber.

taking Wegnahme, Entnehmen, Entnahme, *(criminal law)* Wegnahme, *(mil.)* Eroberung, Einnahme, *(photo)* Aufnahme, *(possession)* Inbesitznahme, *(sexual offence)* Beischlaf mit einer Minderjährigen, *(ship)* Aufbringung;
in a great ~ ganz aus dem Häuschen; **on** ~ bei Entnahme; **~s** Kasseneinnahmen;
inventory ~ Bestandsaufnahme, Inventur; **profit** ~ Gewinnmitnahme, -realisation; **surreptitious** ~ heimliche Wegnahme; **unlawful** ~ unrechtmäßige (widerrechtliche) Wegnahme;
~ of an account Entgegennahme eines Berichtes; **~ on board** Übernahme an Bord; **~ delivery** Abnahme einer Lieferung; **~ effect** Inkrafttreten; **~ of evidence** Beweisaufnahme, -erhebung; **~ an inventory** Bestandsaufnahme, Inventur; **~ of oath** Eidesleistung, -ablegung; **~ an order** Entgegennahme eines Auftrags, Auftragsannahme; **~-to pieces** Auseinandernehmen; **possession** Inbesitznahme; **~ of foreign property** Beschlagnahme ausländischen Vermögens; **~ a risk** Eingehen eines Risikos, Risikoübernahme; **~ samples** Musterziehung; **~ stock** Aktienabnahme, *(inventory taking)* Inventur; **~ of testimony** Zeugenvernehmung;
to reopen the ~ of evidence wieder ins Beweisverfahren eintreten.

taking away Wegnahme, Entnahme, *(airplane)* Abflug.

taking | back Rücknahme; **~ in** Einnahme, Eingang, *(coll.)* hereinlegen.

taking off Wegnahme, *(airplane)* Abflug, *(print.)* Auslegen [des Bogens];
~ the seals Siegelabnahme.

taking out | an insurance contract Abschluß einer Versicherung; **~ of naturalization papers** Einbürgerung; **~ a patent** Erlangung eines Patents; **~ of pawn** Pfandeinlösung.

taking over Ab-, Übernahme;
delayed ~ Abnahmeverzug;
~ a business Geschäftsübernahme; **~ of a debt** Schuldübernahme;
~ price Übernahmekurs.

taking up Auf-, Übernahme;
~ bills under rebate *(Br.)* Wechseldiskontierung; **~ of capital** Kapitalaufnahme; **~ of a discussion** Beginn einer Diskussion; **~ a loan** Darlehnsaufnahme, Aufnahme einer Anleihe.

takings Einnahmen, Eingänge, Einkünfte, [Kassen]einnahmen;
day's ~ Tageseinnahme;
to check the day's ~ Kassensturz machen.

tale Erzählung, Bericht, Darstellung, *(counting of money)* Geldzählen, *(gossip)* Klatsch, Skandalgeschichte, *(plaintiff's narrative)* Parteivortrag;
by ~ dem nominellen Wert entsprechend;
~s *(jury)* Ersatzgeschworene, -männer;
fairy-~ Märchen; **old-wives'** ~s Ammenmärchen; **tall** ~ Münchhausiade;
~s of adventure Abenteuergeschichten; **~ of woe** Leidensgeschichte;
to sell by ~s stückweise verkaufen; **to tell one's own** ~ für sich selbst sprechen; **to tell ~s out of school** aus der Schule plaudern.

talebearer Zwischen-, Zuträger.

talebearing Zuträgerei, Ohrenbläserei.

talent Begabung, Talent, *(agency costs)* künstlerische Gestaltung;
all the ~s gesamte Intelligenz; **local** ~ Lokalgröße; **unexploited ~s** Begabtenreserve;
~s of the first order hervorragende Talente; **~ for organization** Organisationstalent;
to engage the best ~s beste Kräfte verpflichten;
~ hunt Talentsuche; **~ money** *(sport)* Leistungsvergütung; **~ scout** Talentsucher.

talesman Ersatz-, Hilfsgeschworener.

taleteller Märchenerzähler, Flunkerer.

taletelling Flunkerei.

talisman Glücksbringer, Talisman.

talk Reden, Gespräch, Unterhaltung, Besprechung, *(address)* Ansprache, *(conference)* Unterredung, *(gossip)* Geschwätz, Klatsch, *(lecture)* Vortrag, Plauderei, *(mode of speaking)* Sprache, Redeweise, *(object of talking)* Gesprächsgegenstand;
~s Beratungen;
clandestine ~s Geheimverhandlungen; **confidential** ~ vertrauliches Gespräch; **economic ~s** Wirtschaftsbesprechungen; **exploratory ~s** Sondierungen; **harmless** ~ harmloses Ge-

spräch; **face-to-face** ~ Gespräch unter vier Augen; **high-level ~s** Besprechung auf höchster Ebene; **idle** ~ Geschwätz; **informal** ~ zwangloses Gespräch; **organized** ~ vorbereitetes Gespräch; **opening ~s** einleitende Besprechungen; **preliminary ~s** Vorbesprechungen, -verhandlungen; **private** ~ vertrautes Gespräch; **round table ~s** Gespräche am runden Tisch; **small** ~ seichte Unterhaltung; **stand-up** ~ Gespräch im Stehen; **Strategic Arms Limitation ~s (SALT)** Verhandlungen über die Begrenzung strategischer Kernwaffen; **summit ~s** Gipfelverhandlungen; **wireless** ~ Rundfunkstunde;
~s about entry Beitrittsverhandlungen; **~ over the radio** Rundfunkvortrag; **~ prepared for salesmen** für die Vertretertagung vorbereitete Ansprache; **~s about ~s** *(US)* Sondierungsgespräche; **~ of the town** Tages-, Stadtgespräch, Gespräch der ganzen Stadt, Stadtklatsch; **~s under way** im Gang befindliche Besprechungen; **~ on the wireless** Rundfunkansprache;
~ (v.) reden, sprechen, äußern;
~ about *(coll.)* sich Skandalgeschichten erzählen; **~ at s. o.** j. mit einem Wortschwall überschütten; **~ away the time** Zeit verplaudern; **~ big** *(coll.)* großsprecherische Reden führen; **~ business** über Geschäfte sprechen; **~ s. o. into buying s. th.** jem. etw. aufschwatzen; **~ down** unter den Tisch reden, *(airplane)* herunterreden; **~ down to s. o.** in herablassendem Ton mit j. sprechen; **~ down to an audience** sich dem Publikumsniveau anpassen; **~ by exchange of wireless messages** sich durch Funksprüche verständigen; **~ one's head off** sich den Mund fusselig reden; **~ through one's hat** *(sl.)* dummes Zeug quatschen; **~ the hind leg off a donkey** *(fam.)* j. in Grund und Boden reden; **~ s. o. into having a holiday in Italy** j. zu einer Ferienreise nach Italien überreden; **~ for hours together** stundenlang sprechen; **~ ill of s. o.** schlecht über j. sprechen; **~ a matter over** Sache besprechen; **~ into the microphone** ins Mikrophon sprechen; **~ nineteen to the dozen** wie ein Wasserfall reden; **~ it out** sein Herz ausschütten; **~ out of the back of one's neck** *(fam.)* Quatsch reden; **~ out a bill** *(Br., politics)* Gesetzantrag bis zur Vertagung diskutieren; **~ out of the corner of one's mouth** heimliche Bemerkungen machen; **~ o. s. out** sich aussprechen; **~ politics** sich politisch (über Politik) unterhalten; **~ over** besprechen; **~ over an opponent** Widersacher schließlich überzeugen; **~ over plans** Pläne in allen Einzelheiten erörtern; **~ to the purpose** zur Sache reden; **~ round s. th.** um etw. herumreden; **~ s. o. round** j. zu etw. überreden; **~ rubbish** Blech reden; **~ sense** vernünftig reden; **~ shop** *(coll.)* mit Fachausdrücken um sich werfen, fachsimpeln; **~ by signals** sich der Zeichensprache bedienen; **~ in light terms** leicht dahinreden; **~ to o. s.** Selbstgespräche führen; **~ to s. o.** *(coll.)* j. zurechtweisen; **~ treason** landesverräterische Reden führen; **~ [cold] turkey** *(US)* kein Blatt vor den Mund nehmen, reinen Wein einschenken; **~ up** *(praise)* in den Himmel heben, *(US)* j. ins Gespräch bringen; **~ s. th. up** etw. frei heraus sagen; **~ wisdom** vernünftig reden;
to be all ~ alles nur Gerede sein; **to end in ~** im Sande verlaufen; **to give a ~ on s. th.** *(broadcasting)* Vortrag über etw. halten; **to have a ~ with** sich mit jem. unterhalten, mit jem. plaudern; **to hear much ~ about a company's solvency** allerlei Gerüchte über die Liquiditätsschwierigkeiten einer Firma hören;
to hear ~ of war Kriegsgerede hören; **to hold ~s with** Besprechungen abhalten; **to resume political ~s** politische Besprechungen wieder aufnehmen; **in order to squelch ~ of a liquidity pinch** um das Liquiditätsgerede zu beenden;
~ film Tonfilm; **high-level ~-in** Gespräche im engsten Kreis (auf höchster Ebene).

talkathon *(US sl.)* Marathondebatte, -sitzung.

talked about, to be ins Gerede kommen.

talker Redner;
poor ~ schlechter Redner.

talkfest *(US sl.)* Schwatzveranstaltung.

talkie *(US coll.)* Tonfilm, *(mil.)* Funksprechtelefon.

talking Unterhaltung, *(gossip)* Geschwätz;
~ of taxes da man gerade über Steuern spricht;
~ film Tonfilm; **~ machine** Phonograph, Sprechmaschine; **~ point** Gesprächsgegenstand, -stoff, -thema; **~ stage** Gesprächsstadium; **~-to** Standpauke, Schelte; **to give s. o. a ~-to** jem. eine Standpauke halten, j. abkanzeln.

talky Tonfilm.

tall groß, hochgewachsen, *(sl.)* großsprecherisch;
to talk ~ große Reden führen, angeben, renommieren;
~ order starke Zumutung, *(sl.)* Riesenauftrag.

tallage Abgaben.

tally *(account)* Rechnung, [monatliche] Abrechnung, *(coupon)* kleiner Schein, Kupon, *(duplicate)* Seiten-, Gegenstück, Duplikat, *(label)* Etikett, Schild, Anhänger, Kennzeichen, *(list* of goods) Warenliste, (mark) Identifizierungszeichen, Kontrollzeichen, (pass book) Kontobuch, Gegenbuch [des Kunden], (stroke) Zählstrich, Strichmarkierung;

by the ~ nach dem Stück;

~ (v.) kontrollieren, abhaken, (Br., accounts) übereinstimmen, (count by the piece) [Ladung] stückweise nachzählen, (label) Waren bezeichnen, etikettieren, (register) registrieren, buchen;

to buy by the 100 ~ hundertstückweise kaufen; **to keep** ~ **of s. th.** Buch über etw. führen; **to keep** ~ **of goods** Waren auf einer Liste abhaken; **to take the** ~ Abstimmungsergebnis ausrechnen;

~ **business** (Br.) [einzelnes] Abzahlungsgeschäft; ~ **clerk** Fracht-, Ladungskontrolleur, (US) Stimmenzähler; ~ **keeper** Kontrolleur; ~ **out** (US) Lieferschein; ~ **room** (elections, Ireland) Wahlausschußzimmer; ~ **sheet** (US) Kontrolliste, Zahl-, Abrechnungsbogen; ~**sheet method** (US) Strichelverfahren; ~ **shop** (Br.) Abzahlungsgeschäft; ~ **system** (Br.) Abzahlungssystem; ~ **trade** (Br.) Abzahlungsgeschäft.

tallying Abhaken.

tallyman [Ladungs]kontrolleur, (Br., hire purchase) Inhaber eines Abzahlungsgeschäftes, (travel(l)er) Musterreisender.

tallywoman (Br.) Inhaberin eines Abzahlungsgeschäftes.

talon (Br.) Erneuerungsschein, Talon, Zinskupon;

~ **tax** (Br.) Talonsteuer.

tame (animal) zahm, gezähmt, (land, US) bebaut, kultiviert;

~ **cat (pussy)** dummer Kerl; ~ **ending** (story) langweiliger Schluß.

tamer, lion Löwenbändiger.

tamper (v.) (balance sheet) fälschen, frisieren;

~ **with** betrügerische Veränderungen vornehmen, (balance sheet) fälschen, frisieren;

~ **with s. th.** mit etw. herumspielen; ~ **with the cash** sich an der Kasse vergreifen; ~ **with a disease** Krankheit unsachgemäß behandeln; ~ **with a document** Inhalt einer Urkunde verfälschen; ~ **with the seal of a letter** an einem Briefsiegel manipulieren; ~ **with a text** Text verfälschen; ~ **with a witness** Zeugen beeinflussen.

tamperer Pfuscher, Stümper.

tampering | **of a balance sheet** Bilanzfrisur; ~ **with documents** Urkundenverfälschung; ~ **with records** falsche Eintragung; ~ **with a witness** Zeugenbeeinflussung.

tandem | **bicycle** Fahrrad mit zwei Sitzen hintereinander; ~ **connection** Kaskadenschaltung; ~ **office** (tel.) Knotenamt.

tangent (fig.) plötzliches Umschwenken, (US, railroad) gradlinige Eisenbahnstrecke;

upon a ~ mit plötzlich geändertem Kurs;

to fly off at a ~ weit vom Thema abschweifen.

tangible | **s** Sachvermögen;

~ (a.) greifbar, materiell, real, dinglich;

~ **assets** körperliche Wirtschaftsgüter, greifbare Vermögenswerte, Sachanlagevermögen, -anlagen; ~ **goods** materielle Güter; ~ **proof** handfester Beweis; ~ **property** Sachanlagevermögen, greifbares Vermögen, reales Kapital; ~ **result** greifbares Ergebnis; ~ **value** greifbarer (materieller) Wert, Substanzwert, (going concern) Betriebswert.

tank Kanister, Tank, Behälter, Kessel, (coll.) Brotbeutel, (jail, sl.) Untersuchungsgefängnis, (mil.) Panzer, Tank, Kampfwagen, (photo) Wanne, Bad;

fish ~ (sl.) Ausnüchterungszelle; **gasoline (petrol)** ~ Benzintank; **rain-water** ~ Zisterne; **ship's** ~ Schiffstank;

~ (v.) tanken, Tank auffüllen, (sl.) sich besaufen;

~ **armo(u)r** Panzerarmierung; ~ **attack** Panzerangriff; ~ **buster** (mil.) panzerbrechende Waffe, Panzerknacker, (plane) Jagdbomber zur Panzerbekämpfung; ~ **car** (railway) Kessel-, Behälter-, Tankwagen; ~ **crew** Panzerbesatzung; ~ **dozer** (mil.) Räumpanzer; ~ **drama** (theater) Sensationsstück; ~ **driver** Tankerfahrer; ~ **engine** (railway) Tenderlokomotive; ~ **farm** (mil.) Öltanklager; ~ **formation** Panzerverband; ~ **iron** mittelstarkes Eisenblech; ~ **ship** Tanker; ~ **transporter** Panzertransportfahrzeug; ~ **town** (sl.) Provinznest; ~ **trap** Panzerfalle; ~ **truck** Tankwagen; ~ **waggon** (railway) Kessel-, Behälter-, Tankwagen.

tankage Aufbewahrung in Kanistern, (capacity) Fassungsvermögen eines Tanks.

tanked-up, to get (sl.) sich vollaufen lassen.

tanker Tanker, Tankdampfer, -flugzeug;

American-flag ~ unter amerikanischer Flagge fahrender Tanker; **giant** ~ Großraumtanker; **road** ~ Tankwagen;

~ **fleet** Tankerflotte; ~ **lorry** Tankwagen; ~ **market** Tankermarkt; ~ **order** Tankerauftrag; ~ **owner** Tankreeder.

tantrum (coll.) schlechte Laune;

to fly into a ~ Koller kriegen.

tap Zapfen, Spund, (bookbinding) Heftrand, (brand, fam.) Sorte, Marke, (drink) Getränk, Getränkesorte, (el.) Stromabnehmer, (gas, water, Br.) Hahn, (mil., US) Zapfenstreich, (pub) Schankwirtschaft, Schenke, (tel.) Anzapfen, Anzapfung;

on ~ auf Lager, immer verfügbar, vorhanden, zum sofortigen Gebrauch bereit, (beer) vom Faß, (securities) jederzeit unbegrenzt lieferbar; **through the** ~ (treasury bills, Br.) zu einem festgesetzten Abschlag;

excellent ~ hervorragende Getränkesorte; **fresh** ~ frisch angestochenes Faß; **gas** ~ Gashahn; **hot-water** ~ (Br.) Warmwasserhahn; **wire** ~ Telefonanzapfung, Mithöreinrichtung;

~ **of the gilt-edged market** (Br.) Inanspruchnahme des Rentenmarktes;

~ (v.) (fig.) anzapfen, angehen, nutzbar machen, beschließen, (pipeline) abzweigen, (act as a tapster) als Schankkellner arbeiten, (tel.) unberechtigt anzapfen, mithören;

~ **s. o. for $ 20** (coll.) j. um 20 Dollar anpumpen; ~ **the admiral** (marine, sl.) Faß heimlich anzapfen; ~ **capital** Kapital angreifen; ~ **at the door** an die Tür klopfen; ~ **s. o. for information** j. aushorchen wollen; ~ **a line** Telefonleitung anzapfen; ~ **a market** auf einem Markt in Erscheinung treten, Markt erschließen; ~ **the money market heavily** Geldmarkt stark in Anspruch nehmen; ~ **off from the barrel** aus einem Faß abfüllen; ~ **out** (sl.) sein ganzes Geld verlieren; ~ **s. o. on the shoulder** j. auf die Schulter klopfen; ~ **alternative sources of credit** verschiedene Kreditquellen erschließen; ~ **new sources of energy** neue Energiequellen erschließen; ~ **telegraph wires** Telegramme abfangen; ~ **telephone wires** Telefongespräche mithören, Telefonleitung anzapfen;

to open the ~**s** (sl.) auf die Tube drücken; **to turn the** ~ **on** (Br.) Hahn aufdrehen;

~ **cinder** Schlacke; ~ **feeder** (railway) Industriegleis; ~ **issue** (treasury bills, Br.) Plazierung außerhalb des Publikumsverkehrs; ~ **line** Industriebahn, -anschluß; ~ **rate** (Br.) Diskontsatz für kurzfristige Schatzwechsel; ~ **stock** (Br.) von der Regierung in kleinen Tranchen unmittelbar begebene Anleihestücke; ~ **treasury bills** (Br.) unmittelbar (laufend) ausgegebene Schatzwechsel; ~ **water** Leitungswasser.

tape Papierband [des Börsentelegrafs], (bookbinding) Heftband, (data processing) Band, (intoxicating liquor, sl.) Fusel, Schnaps, (print.) Auslegerband, (recording) Ton-, Magnetophonband, (telegraphy) Papierstreifen, -band, (teletype) Lochstreifen;

blank ~ Leerband; **electrician's** ~ Isolierband; **insulating** ~ Isolierband; **magnetic (recording)** ~ Magnetband; **punched** ~ (teletype) Lochstreifen; **red** ~ Bürokratismus, Amtsschimmel; **Scotch** ~ Tesafilm; **sound** ~ (film) Tonband; **ticker** ~ (telegraph) Papierstreifen; **unjustified** ~ (data processing) Endlosband;

composite national ~ **for all markets** zusammenfassende Notierung aller Einzelbörsen der Länder; ~**s for television broadcastings** Bänder für Fernsehsendungen;

~ (v.) (book) heften, (measure) mit einer Meßschnur (einem Bandmaß) messen, (take on record) auf Band sprechen, Tonband aufnehmen;

~ **s. o.** jds. Stimme auf Tonband aufnehmen;

to breast the ~ (fig.) das Rennen machen; **to cut the** ~ (ceremonies) Band zerschneiden; **to have s. o. on the** ~ (sl.) über j. genauestens im Bilde sein; **to punch (record) on** ~ auf Band aufnehmen, Bandaufnahme machen;

~ **abbreviations** Börsenabkürzungen; ~ **cartridge** Magnetbandkassette; **recording** ~ **cassette** Tonbandkassette; ~**controlled** lochstreifengesteuert; ~ **line (measure)** Bandmaß; ~ **machine** (Br.) [Börsen]fernschreiber; ~ **measure** Maßband, Bandmaß; ~ **player** Tonbandgerät; ~ **price** notierter Kurs; ~ **punch** (data processing) Streifenlocher; ~ **quotations** Börsentickernotierungen; ~ **reading** Kursinterpretierung; ~**record** (v.) auf Tonband aufnehmen; ~ **recorder** Tonbandgerät; **to turn on a** ~ **recorder** Tonbandgerät einschalten; **to switch off a** ~ **recorder** Tonbandgerät ausschalten; ~ **recording** [Ton]bandaufnahme; ~ **relay** Lochstreifenbetrieb; **recording** ~ **spool** Tonbandspule; **to be available as monthly** ~ **subscription** im Datenfernverkehr monatlich bezogen werden können; ~ **transcript** Tonbandkopie; ~ **watcher** Börsenbeobachter.

taped auf Band aufgenommen, (US sl.) im Bilde;

~ **music** Tonbandmusik.

taper (estate duty) Staffel;

~ (v.) **off** allmählich abnehmen (aufhören);

~ **relief** (taxation) Staffelvergünstigung.

tapering|provisions *(taxation)* degressive Bestimmungen, Staffelbestimmungen; **~ rate** *(income tax)* Staffeltarif.

tapestry Dekorationsstoff, Wandteppich;
~ **carpet** Wandteppich.

taphouse Schenke, Wirtshaus, Kneipe.

taping session Bandaufnahmeproduktion.

tapis, to bring upon the aufs Tapet bringen.

tapped *(tel.)* angezapft;
~ **out** pleite.

tapper Schankwirt, *(telegraph)* Morsetaste.

tapping, wire Anzapfen von Telefonleitungen, Mithören von Telefongesprächen;
~ **of natural resources** Erschließung von Bodenschätzen;
~ **circuit** Abhörstromkreis.

taproom Schankstube, Wirtsstube.

tapster Schankkellner.

tar Teer, *(sailor, coll.)* Teerjacke.

taradiddle Flausenmacher, Flunkerei;
~ *(v.)* s. o. jem. einen Bären aufbinden (etw. vorflunkern).

tardiness *(US)* Verspätung [im Betrieb];
~ **rate** Verspätungsprozentsatz.

tardy *(US)* verspätet, säumig;
~ **in offering help** wenig hilfsbereit;
~ **progress** langsame Fortschritte.

tare tote Last, Tara, Verpackungsgewicht, *(allowance for tare)* Taravergütung;
actual ~ reines Verpackungsgewicht; **average** ~ Durchschnittsgewicht, -tara; **converted** ~ am Empfangsort umgerechnete Tara; **customary** ~ übliche Tara; **customs** ~ Zollgewicht, -tara; **estimated** ~ geschätzte Tara; **original** ~ Abgangsgewicht; **real** ~ Nettotara; **super** ~ zusätzliche Taravergütung;
~ **assumed by the customs** Zolltara; ~ **and tret** Tara und Gutgewicht;
~ *(v.)* Tara in Abzug bringen (vergüten), tarieren;
to ascertain (allow for) the ~ tarieren, Verpackungsgewicht bestimmen;
~ **account (note, rate)** Abgangs-, Tararechnung; ~ **weight** Taragewicht.

target Ziel, Zielsetzung, *(economics)* wirtschaftliches Planziel, Soll, Vorgabe, *(mil.)* Scheibe, *(production)* Förderungsplan, Produktionssoll, *(radar)* Meßobjekt, Reflektor;
~ **A** *(sl.)* Kriegsministerium; **favo(u)rite** ~ bevorzugtes Objekt; **No. 1** ~ vordringliches Ziel; **output** ~ Produktionsziel; **principal** ~ Hauptangriffsziel, Hauptzielscheibe;
~ **of bitter criticism** Angriffspunkt heftiger Kritik;
~ *(v.)* **for** *(US)* Termin ansetzen;
to be the ~ **of competitive discounting** Ziel wettbewerbsbedingter Preisnachlässe sein; **to fall short of one's** ~ das gesteckte Ziel nicht erreichen;
~ **area** Planziel, *(mil.)* luftgefährdetes Gebiet; ~ **audience** Zielgruppe; ~ **cost** vorkalkulierte Kosten; ~ **country for capital investment** bevorzugtes Anlageland für Investitionskapital; ~ **date** angesetzter Zeitpunkt, letzter (planmäßiger angestrebter) Termin, Abschlußtermin, Stichtag; ~ **destruction** Zielvernichtung; ~ **exchange rate** angestrebte Wechselkurssätze; ~ **figures** projektierte Zahlen; ~ **group** Zielgruppe; ~ **indicator** *(mil.)* Bombenmarkierung; ~ **industries** Planzielindustrien; ~ **lamp** *(railway)* Signallampe; ~ **model** Entscheidungsprogramm; ~ **practice** *(mil.)* Scheiben-, Übungsschießen; ~ **price** *(EC)* Übernahme-, Richt-, Vertragspreis; **national** ~ **price** *(EC)* einzelstaatlicher Richtpreis; ~ **pricing** Zuschlagskalkulation; ~ **rate of return** Sollspanne.

tariff *(customs)* Zoll[tarif], Zollverzeichnis, -satz, Zölle, *(list of charges)* Taxe, Tarif, Gebührenverzeichnis, *(Br., prices in restaurant, hotel)* Preisliste, -verzeichnis, *(railway ~)* Fahrpreistabelle, Eisenbahntarif, *(telephone call)* Gesprächsgebühr;
as per ~ laut Tarif; **in accordance with (by) the** ~ tarifmäßig;
~**s** Tarifwesen;
advance booking charter (ABC) ~ Vorausbuchungstarif für Charterflüge; **advanced purchasing excursion** ~ *(airline)* 45 Tage vorausbezahlter Ferientarif; **agricultural** ~ Zoll auf landwirtschaftliche Erzeugnisse, Agrarzoll; **alternative** ~ Ausweichfrachtsatz; **apex** ~ *(airline)* Vorausbuchungstarif; ~ **applicable** anzuwendender Tarif; **autonomous** ~ autonomer Zolltarif, Zollautonomie; **bargaining** ~ Verhandlungstarif; **basing** ~ einheitlicher Frachtsatz; **block** ~ degressiv gestaffelter Tarif; **budget** ~ *(airline)* Billigtarif; **bulk-supply** ~ Mengentarif; **which-is-cheaper** ~ *(rent-a-car)* Wunschtarif; **class** ~ Tariftabelle; **combination** ~ kombinierter Tarif; **compound** ~ gemischter (kombinierter) Zolltarif; **contractual** ~ Vertrags-

zoll; **conventional** ~ vereinbarter (ausgehandelter) Zolltarif; **countervailing** ~ Ausgleichszoll; **customs** ~ Zolltarif, -satz; **differential** ~ Staffel-, Differentialtarif, Differentialzoll; **discriminating** ~ diskriminierender Zoll; **educational** ~ Erziehungszoll; **electricity** ~ Stromtarif; **exceptional** ~ *(Br.)* Ausnahmetarif; **export** ~ Ausfuhrzoll; **external** ~ Außentarif, Ausfuhrzoll; **flat-rate** ~ Kleinabnehmertarif; **flexible** ~ Staffel-, Stufentarif, gleitender Zoll; **foreign** ~ Auslandszoll, ausländischer Zoll; **freight** ~ Fracht-, Gütertarif; **full** ~ ungekürzter Tarif; **fundamental** ~ Grundtaxe; **gas** ~ Gastarif; **general** ~ allgemeingültiger Tarif, Normaltarif, -zoll, Einheitstarif; **goods** ~ Gütertarif; **graded** ~ Stufentarif; **graduated** ~ gestaffelter Tarif, Staffeltarif; **holiday** ~ *(airplane)* Ferientarif; **homeward** ~ hereinkommender Tarif [in der Seeschiffahrt]; **hotel** ~ *(Br.)* Zimmerpreise; **import** ~ Einfuhrzoll; **insurance** ~ Prämien-, Versicherungstarif; **internal** ~ Binnenzoll; **load-rate** ~ Tarif nach normalem Verbrauch; **local** ~ Binnentarif; **maximum** ~ *(customs)* Maximal-, Höchstzoll, *(insurance)* Höchsttarif; **minimum** ~ *(customs)* Mindestzoll, *(insurance)* Minimaltarif; **mixed** ~ gemischter (kombinierter) Zolltarif; **most-favo(u)red-nation** ~ Meistbegünstigungstarif; **multilinear (multiple)** ~ Mehrfachzoll; **night** ~ Nachttarif; **off-peak** ~ *(el.)* Nachtstromtarif; **outward** ~ ausgehender Tarif [in der Seeschiffahrt]; **passenger** ~ Personentarif; **postal** ~ Porto-, Posttarif; **preferential** ~ Präferenztarif, Begünstigungstarif, Vorzugszoll; **protective** ~ Schutzzoll; **railway (railroad, US)** ~ Fracht-, [Eisen]bahn-, Gütertarif; **reduced** ~ ermäßigter Tarif; **restricted-hours** ~ *(tel.)* Mondscheintarif; **retaliatory** ~ Kampf-, Vergeltungszoll; **revenue** ~ Finanz-, Einfuhrzoll, Finanztarif; **scientific** ~ nach wissenschaftlichen Prinzipien aufgestellter Tarif; **seasonal** ~ jahreszeitlich verschiedener Tarif; **separate** ~ eigener Zolltarif; **single** ~ autonomer Tarif; **single-column** ~ Einspaltentarif; **single-schedule** ~ Einheitstarif; **sliding-scale** ~ degressiver Tarif, Staffeltarif, Gleitzoll, *(wages)* gleitender Lohntarif; **specific** ~ Mengen-, Sondertarif, *(customs)* spezifischer Zolltarif; **standard** ~ Einheitstarif, -satz; **superapex** ~ *(airline)* Ausfülltarif, billiger vorauszuzahlender Ferientarif; **suspended** ~ suspendierter (ausgesetzter) Zoll; **through (transit)** ~ Durchtarif [in der Seeschiffahrt]; **time-of-the-day** ~ *(Br.)* Nachtstromtarif; **time and unlimited mileage** ~ *(rent-a-car)* Pauschaltarif; **two-column** ~ zweispaltiger Tarif, Zweispaltentarif; **two-part** ~ *(gas, electricity)* Grundgebühr plus Verbrauchertarif; **uniform** ~ Einheitstarif; **unilinear** ~ Einspalten-, Einheitstarif; **ad valorem** ~ Wertzoll; **valuation** ~ Wertberechnungsskala;
~ **of coins** Münztabelle; ~ **of fares** Fahrpreistabelle; ~ **in force** gültiger Tarif; ~ **at a hotel** *(Br.)* Zimmerpreise in einem Hotel; ~ **on imports** Einfuhrzoll; ~ **of revenue** Finanztarif; ~ **for revenue only** Finanzzoll;
~ *(v.)* Tarifwert festsetzen, taxieren, *(customs)* mit Zoll belegen, *(fix a price)* Preis festsetzen, *(make a ~)* Tarif aufstellen, tarifieren;
to fix the ~ tarifieren, Tarif festsetzen; **to increase the** ~ Zölle erhöhen; **to lower the** ~ Zölle (Tarif) senken; **to raise a** ~ Tariferhöhung vornehmen; **to rate in the** ~ tarifieren, *(customs)* mit Zoll belegen; **to reduce** ~**s** Zölle abbauen; **to subject to** ~ den Zollbestimmungen (Tarifbestimmungen) unterwerfen;
~ **abandonment** Aufgabe der Tarifbindungen; ~ **abolition** *(motor insurance, Br.)* Abschaffung des Tarifzwangs; **⌐ Act** *(US)* Zollgesetz; ~ **adjustment** Zollangleichung, Tarifanpassung; ~ **advantage** Zollvorteil; ~ **advocate** Tarifanhänger; ~ **agreement** Zollvereinbarung, -abkommen; **⌐ Amendment Act** *(US)* Zolländerungsgesetz; ~ **association** Tarifverband; ~ **barriers** Zollschranken; ~ **battle** Zollkrieg; ~ **bill** Zollgesetz, -vorlage; ~ **board** *(US)* Zollamt; ~**-bound** tarifgebunden, zollpflichtig; ~ **bureau** Tarifverband; ~ **card** Preistarif; ~ **category** Tarifklasse; ~ **changes** [Zoll]tarifänderungen; ~ **charge for calls** Gesprächsgebühr; ~ **charges** [Zoll]tarifsätze; ~ **classification** Tarifierung; ~ **commission (committee)** Tarifausschuß, -kommission, *(US)* Prüfungsausschuß für Zollfragen; ~ **commitments** Tarifbindungen; ~ **companies** *(Br.)* in einem Kartellsystem zusammengeschlossene Versicherungsgesellschaften, tarifgebundene Kraftfahrzeugversicherungsgesellschaften; ~ **concession** Zugeständnis auf dem Gebiet des Zollwesens, Zoll-, Tarifzugeständnis; ~ **conference** Zollkonferenz; ~ **cut** Tarif-, Zollsenkung; ~ **cutback** Zollsenkung; ~ **cutting** Zollabbau; ~**-cutting agreement** Zollsenkungsabkommen; ~**-cutting formula** Zollsenkungsformel; ~**-cutting process** Zollabbauprozeß; **deeper-than-formula** ~ **deductions** über die ausgehandelte Formel hinausgehende Zollsenkung; ~ **development** Entwick-

lung der Zollpolitik, zollpolitische Entwicklung; ~ **differential** Zollunterschied; ~ **discrimination** benachteiligende Zollbehandlung; ~ **duty** Zolltarif, Tarifzoll; ~**fed** durch Zölle geschützt, zollgeschützt; ~ **formula** Tarifformel; ~**free access** zollfreier Zugang; ~**free country** zollfreier Staat; ~ **heading** Position des Zolltarifs, Tarifposition; ~ **hike** Zollerhöhung; ~ **increase** Zollerhöhung, -anhebung; ~ **information** Auskunft in Zollangelegenheiten, Zollauskunft; ~ **information catalog(ue)** Zolltarif, -katalog; ~ **issue** Tarifstreit; ~ **item** Zollposition, Zoll-, Tarifnummer, Tarifposition; **to classify under a ~ item** unter eine Tarifposition einreihen; ~ **law** Zollgesetz; ~ **laws** Zoll-, Tarifgesetzgebung; ~ **legislation** Zollgesetzgebung; ~ **level** Tarifhöhe; ~ **line** Tarifposten; ~ **maker** (US) Zoll festsetzende Stelle, Zollgesetzgeber; ~ **making** (US) Zoll-, Tariffestsetzung; ~ **matters** Zollfragen, -angelegenheiten; ~ **negotiations** Zollverhandlungen; ~ **nomenclature** Zolltarifschema; ~ **office** (motor insurance, Br.) Tarifbüro; ~ **organization** (motor insurance, Br.) Tarifverband; ~ **plank** Tarifgrundsätze; ~ **platform** zollpolitische Forderungen; ~ **policy** Zoll-, Tarifpolitik; ~ **preference** Tarifbegünstigung, Zollpräferenz; ~ **preference agreement** Präferenz-, Zollvorzugsabkommen; ~ **procedure** Zolltarifverfahren; ~**protected** durch Schutzzölle abgesichert, zollgeschützt; ~ **protection** Schutzzollsystem, Zollschutz; **to benefit from incidental ~ protection** mittelbaren Zollschutz genießen; ~ **question** Tariffrage; ~ **quota** Zollkontingent; ~**raised** durch Zölle im Preis erhöht; ~ **raising** Tariferhöhung, (a.) Zoll erhebend; ~ **rate** Gebühren-, Zollsatz, Tarifsatz; ~ **reduction** Zollsenkung, -abbau, Tarifermäßigung, -senkung; ~ **reform** Tarifreform, (Br.) Schutzzollpolitik, (US) Freihandelspolitik; ~ **reformer** Zollreformer; (US) Freihandelspolitiker; ~**regulating** tarifbestimmend, zollregelnd; ~ **regulations** Tarif-, Zollbestimmungen, -vorschriften; ~ **request** Tarifforderung; ~ **revenue** fiskalische Gebühr, Finanzzoll; ~ **revision** Änderung des Zolltarifs, Tarifrevision, -änderung; ~**ridden** mit hohen Zöllen (tariflich) belastet; ~ **rollback** Tarif-, Zollsenkung; ~ **scheme** Tarifschema; ~ **session** Zolltarifsitzung; ~ **structure** Zollgefüge, -konstruktion; ~ **system** Tarif-, Zollsystem; **autonomous ~ system** autonomer Zolltarif, Zollautonomie; **conventional ~ system** Zolltarifvereinbarung; ~ **treaty** Tarifabkommen-, Tarif-, Zollvertrag; ~ **union** Zollverband, -verein; ~ **value** Tarif-, Zollwert; **to schedule the ~ value** (Br.) Tarifwert festsetzen; ~ **wall** Zollmauer, -schranke; **to abolish the ~ walls** Zollschranken beseitigen; **to raise ~ walls against foreign goods** Tarifmauern gegen ausländische Produkte errichten; ~ **war** Tarif-, Zollkrieg; ~**wise** tarifmäßig.

tariffication Tarifierung, Zoll-, Tariffestsetzung.

tariffing Tarifierung.

tariffist Zollanhänger.

tariffize (v.) den Zollbestimmungen unterwerfen.

tarpaulin Persenning, (truck) Wagenplane.

tarred with the same brush (fig.) vom gleichen Kaliber, mit den gleichen Fehlern.

tartar Hitzkopf;
  to catch a ~ an den Falschen geraten.

task Aufgabe, auferlegte Arbeit, (mil.) Kampfauftrag, (piece rate) Mindestleistung, Tagewerk, (school) Schularbeit, -aufgabe, (work) [Arbeits]pensum;
  by (to) ~ stückweise;
  assigned ~ zugewiesene Aufgabe; **priority ~** vordringliche Aufgabe;
  ~ at hand im Augenblick gestellte Aufgabe; **~ at hour** im Augenblick gestellte Aufgabe;
  ~ (v.) s. o. jem. eine Arbeit aufbürden; **~ one's memory** sein Gedächtnis strapazieren; **~ s. one's mind with details** j. mit Einzelheiten behelligen;
  to assign a ~ to s. o. jem. eine Aufgabe zuweisen; **to be adequate to a ~** einer Aufgabe gewachsen sein; **to finish one's ~** seine Schicht verfahren; **to get on a new ~** neuen Plan aushecken; **to perform a ~** Aufgabe lösen (erfüllen); **to set s. o. a ~** jem. eine Arbeit aufgeben; **to take s. o. to ~** j. ins Gebet nehmen, j. zur Rede stellen;
  ~ bonus system Prämienakkordsystem; **~ distribution** Aufgabenverteilung; **~ force** (US) Arbeitsstab, -ausschuß, (plant) im Akkord arbeitende Belegschaft; **~ force report** (US) Bericht des Arbeitsstabs; **~ group** Akkordklasse; **~ time** (US) Zeitnorm im Arbeitsprozeß; **~ wage** Arbeit im Akkord, Akkord-, Stücklohn.

tasker (sl.) Deputant.

taskmaster Vorarbeiter, Aufseher, (fig.) strenger Arbeitgeber.

taskwork Arbeit im Akkord, Stück-, Akkordarbeit.

taskworker Akkordarbeiter.

taste Geschmack, (fig.) Vorgeschmack, Kostprobe, (fashion) Geschmacksrichtung, Mode;
  bad ~ Taktlosigkeit;
  ~ (v.) schmecken, kosten, probieren;
  ~ blood (fig.) auf den Geschmack kommen; **~ the joys of freedom** Freiheit in vollen Zügen genießen;
  to be a matter of ~ Geschmackssache sein; **not to be the ~ of everyone** nicht nach jedermanns Geschmack sein; **to be in bad ~ to refuse an invitation** Einladung nicht gut absagen können; **to have a ~ of a cake** Stück Kuchen versuchen; **to have excellent ~ in dress** sich hervorragend anzuziehen wissen; **to have expensive ~s in clothes** kostspielige Kleider bevorzugen; **to have no ~ for study** dem Studium nichts abgewinnen können; **to leave a bad ~ in the mouth** (fig.) üblen Nachgeschmack hinterlassen.

tastefully decorated with flowers geschmackvoll mit Blumen dekoriert.

tatter Lumpen, Fetzen, (Br., sl.) Lumpensammler;
  to tear s. one's reputation to ~s jds. guten Ruf restlos zerstören.

tattered zerlumpt, abgerissen.

tattler Klatschbase, Schwätzer[in].

tattoo (mil.) Zapfenstreich.

tavern Kneipe, Schenke, Schankwirtschaft, Gast-, Wirtshaus;
  ~ token Getränkemarke.

tax [Staats]steuer, Abgabe, (assessment) Besteuerung, (contribution) Beitrag, Abgabe, (fee) Gebühr, Taxe, (fig.) Bürde, (strain) Anspannung, Belastung, Beanspruchung, Inanspruchnahme;
  after [deduction for] ~es nach Abzug der Steuern; **before ~es** vor Steuerabzug; **free from ~es** (US) steuer-, abgaben-, gebührenfrei; **less ~es** vor Abzug (Berücksichtigung) von Steuern; **liable to ~** steuerpflichtig; **~ paid** nach Bezahlung der Steuern, versteuert; **prior to deduction of ~es** vor Berücksichtigung der Steuern;
  the ~es (Br.) Finanzamt; **accumulated-earnings ~** (US) Körperschaftssteuer für nicht ausgeschüttete Erträge; **accrued ~ [payable]** fällige Steuer[forderung]; **accrued ~es** (balance sheet) Steuerschulden; **additional ~** Steuerzuschlag, Nach-, Ergänzungs-, Zusatzsteuer; **amusement ~** Lustbarkeits-, Vergnügungssteuer; **annual ~** jährliche Abgabe, jährlich erhobene Steuer; **anti-chainstore ~** (US) kettenladenfeindliche Steuer; **apportioned ~** aufgeteilte Steuer, Repartitionssteuer; **assessed ~** direkte (veranlagte, im Veranlagungswege erhobene) Steuer; **automobile ~** (US) Kraftfahrzeugsteuer; **bachelor's ~** Junggesellensteuer; **back ~es** Steuerrückstände; **bank-deposit ~** Depotsteuer; **betterment ~** (Br.) Wertzuwachssteuer; **beverage ~** Getränkesteuer; **alcoholic beverage ~** (US) Getränkesteuer; **blanket ~** umfassende Steuer; **branch-office ~** Filialsteuer; **building ~** Bauabgabe; **business ~** Gewerbesteuer; **capital-gains ~** Spekulations-, Kapitalzuwachssteuer; **capital-stock ~** (US) Aktiensteuer; **capital transfer ~** (Br.) Erbschafts- und Schenkungssteuer; **capital-yields ~** (Br.) Kapitalertragssteuer; **capitation ~** Kopfsteuer; **chain-store ~** (US) Steuer auf Filialgeschäfte, Kettenladensteuer; **cigarette ~** Tabak-, Zigarettensteuer; **circulation ~** (US) Geldverkehrssteuer; **city ~es** städtische Abgaben; **collateral inheritance ~** (US) Nachlaßsteuer für Verwandte in der Nebenlinie; **composition ~** pauschalierte Steuer; **consumption ~** Verbrauchssteuer, -abgabe; **corporate ~** (Br.) Körperschaftssteuer; **corporation [income] ~** (US) Körperschaftssteuer; **advance corporation ~** (US) Körperschaftssteuervorauszahlung; **death ~** (US) Erbschaftssteuer; **~ to be deducted** abzuziehende Steuer; **deferred ~es** (balance sheet) zurückgestellte Steuerzahlungen; **defrauded ~** hinterzogene Steuer; **degressive ~** degressive (nach unten gestaffelte) Steuer; **delinquent ~es** (US) rückständige Steuern, Steuerrückstände; **direct ~** direkte Steuer; **disposal ~** Abfallbeseitigungsgebühr; **dividends ~** Dividendensteuer; **dog ~** Hundesteuer; **~ due** Steuersoll, -schuld; **dues ~** (US) Mitgliedschaftssteuer, Steuer auf Mitgliedschaftsbeiträge; **earned-income ~** (US) Gewerbeertragssteuer; **selective employment ~** (Br.) Lohnsummensteuer; **entertainment ~** Vergnügungssteuer; **equalization ~** Ausgleichfolgesteuer; **estate ~** (US) Nachlaß-, Erbschaftssteuer; **estimated ~es** geschätzte Steuereingänge; **excess ~** zuviel gezahlte Steuer; **excess-profits ~** (US) Kriegs-, Übergewinn-, Sondergewinnsteuer; **excise ~** Verbrauchsabgabe, Gewerbe-, Sonderumsatzsteuer; **excise lien property ~** (US) [etwa] Versicherungssteuer; **export ~** Ausfuhr-, Exportabgabe; **farmer's ~** (Br.) Grundertragssteuer; **federal ~** (US) Bundessteuer; **Federal income ~** (US) Einkommensteuer; **fire-protection ~** Brandkassenbeitrag, Feuerschutzabgabe; **floor ~** (warehouse) Lagervorratssteuer; **franchise ~** (US) Konzessionsabgabe, -gebühr; **gasoline ~** (US)

Treibstoff-, Benzinsteuer; **general** ~es allgemeine Steuern; **general property** ~ *(US)* Vermögenssteuer [auf Grundbesitz], Grundsteuer; **gift** ~ *(US)* Schenkungssteuer; **government** ~es staatliche Abgaben; **graded** ~ stufenweise gewährte Steuervergünstigung; **graduated** ~ gestaffelte (progressive) Steuer, Staffel-, Klassensteuer; **grievous** ~es hohe Steuern; **harmonized** ~ *(EC)* angeglichene Steuer; **head** ~ *(US)* Einwanderungssteuer; **heavy** ~es hohe Abgaben, drückende Steuern; **hidden** ~ versteckte (verschleierte) Steuer; **higher-rate** ~ mit einem höheren Satz berechnete Steuer, Steuer mit höherem Satz; **illegal** ~es völkerrechtswidrige Steuern; **hospital** ~ *(US, navy)* monatliche Abgabe zur Erhaltung von Krankenhäusern; **imperial** ~es *(Br.)* Staatssteuern; **import equalization** ~ *(US)* Einfuhrausgleichsabgabe; **[assessed] income** ~ [veranlagte] Einkommensteuer; **incorporation** ~ Körperschaftsgründungssteuer; **increment income (property increment)** ~ Wertzuwachssteuer; **indirect** ~ indirekte Steuer, Akzise, Verbrauchersteuer; **individual income** ~ *(US)* Einkommensteuer; **industrial** ~ Gewerbesteuer; **inheritance** ~ *(US)* Erbschafts-, Nachlaßsteuer; **initiation fees** ~ Aufnahmegebühr [bei Vereinseintritt]; **interest equalization** ~ *(US)* Zinsausgleichssteuer; **internal revenue** ~es inländische Steuern und Abgaben; **land** ~ *(US)* Grundsteuer, -abgabe; **land and building** ~ *(US)* Grund- und Gebäudesteuer; **land-value** ~ Wertzuwachssteuer für Grundstücke; **landed property** ~ Grundsteuer; **legacy** ~ Vermächtnissteuer; **licence** ~ Lizenzgebühr, -abgabe, *(US)* Gewerbesteuer; **local** ~es *(US)* Gemeinde-, Kommunalabgaben, -steuern; **local authority ad-valorem bed** ~ kommunale Verkehrssteuer pro Hotelbett; **luxury** ~ Luxussteuer; **manufacturer's excise** ~ *(US)* Produzentenumsatz-, Fabrikatsteuer; **maximum** ~ Höchstgebühr; **matured** ~es fällige Steuern; **mileage** ~ *(US)* Güterverkehrssteuer; **mineral-oil** ~ Mineralölsteuer; **motor** *(Br.)* **(motor-vehicle,** *US)* ~ Auto-, Kraftfahrzeugsteuer; **municipal** ~es *(US)* Gemeindeabgaben, Kommunalabgaben; **national** ~ Staatssteuer; **nonresident** ~ Steuer für Devisenausländer; **normal** ~ *(income* ~, *US)* Basissteuer; **nuisance** ~ unwirtschaftliche Steuer; **occupation** ~ Gewerbesteuer; **oleomargarine** ~ Margarinesteuer; **operating** ~ Betriebsabgabe, -steuer; **oppressive** ~es drückende Abgaben (Steuern); **ordinary** ~ normaler Steuersatz; **organization** ~ *(US)* Gründungssteuer; **overdue** ~ rückständige Steuer; **parliamentary** ~es vom Parlament beschlossene Steuern; **pay-as-you-go** ~ *(US)* Lohnsteuerabzug, -einbehaltung; ~es **payable** *(balance sheet)* fällige Steuern; ~ **payable direct** direkte Steuer; **payroll** ~ *(US)* Lohnsummensteuer, Arbeitgeberbeiträge zur Arbeiterrentenversicherung; **percentage** ~ *(insurance)* Umsatzsteuer; **perpetual** ~es feststehende Abgaben; **personal** ~ *(US)* Personensteuer, Steuer auf das bewegliche Vermögen; **personal income** ~ *(US)* Einkommensteuer; **petrol** ~ *(Br.)* Treibstoff-, Benzinsteuer; **poll** ~ Bürger-, Kopfsteuer; **premium** ~ Versicherungssteuer; **private expenditure** ~es Steuern für Ausgaben im privaten Bereich; **privilege** ~ *(US)* Konzessionsabgabe, -gebühr; **processing** ~ *(US)* Verarbeitungssteuer; **profits** ~ *(Br.)* Gewinn-, Ertragssteuer; **proportional** ~es proportional erhobene Vermögenssteuern; **progressive** ~ nach oben gestaffelte Steuer, Progressionssteuer; **property** ~ *(Br.)* Grund- und Gebäude-, Besitzsteuer, *(US)* Vermögenssteuer; **personal-property** ~ *(US)* Vermögenssteuer auf bewegliches Vermögen, Mobiliarvermögenssteuer; **public** ~es staatliche Abgaben; **purchase** ~ *(Br.)* [Einphasenwaren]umsatzsteuer, Umsatzsteuer auf die Güter des gehobeneren Bedarfs; **race-betting** ~ Wettgewinnsteuer, Rennwettsteuer; **real-estate** ~ *(US)* Grundsteuer; **regressive** ~ *(assessed value)* regressive (rückwirkende) Steuer; **resident** ~ Steuer für Deviseninländer; **retail sales (retailers' excise)** ~ Warenverkaufs-, Umsatzsteuer im Einzelhandel, Einzelhandelsumsatzsteuer; **road** ~ *(Br.)* Straßennutzungsgebühr; **road-fund** ~ *(Br.)* Verkehrssteuer; **sales** ~ *(US)* [Waren]umsatzsteuer; **scheduled** ~ veranlagte Steuer; **school** ~ Schulabgabe, -geld; **securities transfer** ~ Börsenumsatzsteuer; **severance** ~ Steuer auf Bodenerzeugnisse, Mineralien-, Schürfsteuer; **shared** ~ Anteilsteuer; **single** ~ einzige Steuer, Globalsteuer; **sinking-fund** ~ Anleihesteuer; **social security** ~ *(US)* Zwangsbeitrag zur Sozialversicherung, Sozialversicherungsbeitrag; **special** ~ Sondersteuer; **specific** ~ Mengen-, Stücksteuer; **stamp** ~ *(US)* Stempelsteuer, -gebühr; **standard** ~ *(Br.)* Basissteuer; **state** ~ *(US)* einzelstaatliche Steuer; **stock-transfer** ~ *(US)* Börsenumsatzsteuer; **succession** ~ Erbschaftssteuer [für unbewegliches Vermögen]; ~ **suffered** vereinnahmte Steuer; **foreign** ~ **suffered** bezahlte Auslandssteuer; **sugar** ~ Zuckersteuer; **takeover** ~ Übernahmegebühr; **talon** ~ Zinsbogensteuer; **tobacco [manufacturer's]** ~ Tabaksteuer;

tonnage ~ *(US)* Tonnagesteuer; **trade** ~ Gewerbeertragssteuer; **transactions** ~ *(Br.)* [Börsen]umsatzsteuer; **transfer stamp** ~ *(Br.)* [etwa] Kapitalverkehrssteuer; **transportation** ~ *(US)* [Personen]beförderungssteuer; **turnover** ~ *(Br.)* Umsatzsteuer; **Federal unemployment** ~ *(US)* Arbeitslosenversicherungsbeitrag; **uniform** ~ einheitliche Steuer, Einheitssteuer; **unit** ~ Einheitssteuer; **user** ~ Benutzungsgebühr; **ad-valorem** ~ *(US)* Wertsteuer; **value-added** ~ Mehrwertsteuer; **vehicle** ~ *(US)* Kraftfahrzeugsteuer; **visitors** ~ Fremdensteuer, Kurtaxe; **wage** ~ Lohnsteuer; **war-profits** ~ *(US)* Rüstungsgewinnsteuer; **wealth** ~ Vermögenssteuer; **wheeled** ~ Fahrzeugsteuer; **window** ~ Fenstersteuer; **withheld** ~es einbehaltene Steuern; **withholding** ~ *(US)* Quellen-, einbehaltene Kapitalertragssteuer, *(wage earner)* Steuerabzug von Dienstbezügen, Lohnsteuer; **rates and** ~es Kommunalsteuern und Abgaben; ~es, **duties, imposts and excises** *(US)* Steuern, Zölle und Abgaben; ~es **and fees** Steuern und Gebühren; ~ **on s. o.** Besteuerung einer Person; ~ **on advertising** Reklamesteuer; ~ **on alcohol (alcoholic beverages,** *US)* Getränkesteuer; ~ **in arrears** rückständige Steuer; ~ **on racing bets** Rennwettsteuer, Wettgewinnsteuer; ~ **on business receipts** *(US)* Umsatzsteuer; ~ **on capital** *(double taxation agreement)* Steuern vom Vermögen, Kapital-, Vermögensteuer; ~es **on capital appreciation** *(double taxation)* Steuern auf den Wertzuwachs; ~ **on capital gains** Kapitalzuwachssteuer; ~ **on cigarettes** Tabaksteuer; ~ **shifted onto the consumer** auf den Verbraucher abgewälzte Steuer; ~ **on consumption** Verbrauchs-, Aufwandsteuer; ~ **on the conveyance of real estate** Grunderwerbssteuer; ~ **on corporations** *(US)* Körperschaftssteuer; ~ **on coupons** Kuponsteuer; ~ **payable by deduction** im Abzugswege zahlbare Steuer; ~ **on directorships** Aufsichtsratssteuer; **withholding** ~ **on dividends** Dividendensteuer; ~ **on earnings** Ertragssteuer; ~ **on foreign earnings** Steuer auf ins Ausland angefallene Erträge; ~es **on expenditure** Aufwandsteuern; ~ **on exports** Exportabgabe; ~ **on freight transportation** *(US)* Verkehrssteuer; ~ **on gasoline** *(US)* Benzinsteuer; ~ **on s. one's health** Belastung seiner Gesundheit; ~ **on income** Einkommensteuer; ~ **on inhabited houses** *(Br.)* Hauszinssteuer; ~es **on income and property** Steuern vom Einkommen, vom Ertrag und vom Vermögen, Einkommens- und Vermögenssteuern; ~es **other than federal income** *(US)* sonstige Steuern; ~ **on income or profits from trades, profession or vocation** Steuern auf Einkünfte aus selbständiger Arbeit; ~ **paid in kind** Naturalabgabe; ~ **on land** *(US)* Grundsteuer, -abgabe; ~ **on lighting material** Zündwarensteuer; ~ **on allocated portion of profits** Tantiemesteuer; ~ **on inherited property** *(US)* Erbschaftssteuer; ~ **on real estate** *(US)* Grund[stücks]steuer; ~ **in respect of any profession or vocation** Steuer auf Einkünfte aus selbständiger Tätigkeit; ~ **on sales** Umsatzsteuer; ~ **on a descending scale** regressive Steuer; **U.K.** ~ **at source** *(dividends)* britische Quellensteuer; ~ **on stock-exchange dealings** *(Br.)* Börsenumsatzsteuer; ~ **on stock sales** *(US)* Aktien-, Börsenumsatzsteuer; ~es **payable by the tenant** vom Pächter zu tragende Steuern; **heavy** ~ **on time** starke Zeitbeanspruchung; ~ **on trades** Gewerbesteuer; ~es **in respect of any trade** *(Br.)* Gewerbesteuern jeglicher Art; ~ **on turnover** *(Br.)* Umsatzsteuer; ~ **shilling** ~ **on wireless sets** *(Br.)* Rundfunkgebühr; ~ **unpaid for earlier years** rückständige Steuerzahlungen;

~ *(v.)* *(US, ask for)* als Preis fordern, *(assess)* steuerlich veranlagen, zu einer Steuer heranziehen, Steuer festsetzen, taxieren, abschätzen, ansetzen, *(examine costs)* Kosten nachprüfen, *(exert)* in Anspruch nehmen, anstrengen, -spannen, *(impose a tax)* mit Abgaben (Steuern) belegen, besteuern, Steuern ausschreiben (erheben);

~ **away** wegsteuern; ~ **the bill of costs** *(law court, US)* Prozeßkosten festsetzen, *(Br.)* Kostenrechnung eines Anwalts feststellen; ~ **the costs** *(Br.)* Gebührenrechnung überprüfen und anerkennen; ~ **a country** Land mit Steuern belegen; ~ **s. o. with a crime** j. eines Verbrechens beschuldigen; ~ **foreign earnings** im Ausland erzielte Einkünfte besteuern; ~ **income** Einkommen versteuern, Einkommensteuer erheben; ~ **income at the source** Einkünfte an der Quelle steuerlich erfassen, Quellensteuer erheben; ~ **luxuries** Luxusgeräte besteuern; ~ **one's memory** sein Gedächtnis anstrengen; ~ **s. o. with neglect of his work** jem. Pflichtversäumnis vorwerfen; ~ **s. one's patience** jds. Geduld ausnutzen; ~ **with a higher rate** mit einem höheren Satz versteuern;

to abate a ~ Steuer herabsetzen; **to abandon a** ~ Steuer aufheben; **to allow for** ~ Steuerrückstellung vornehmen; **to allow United States** ~es **as credit against Federal Republic** ~es in USA gezahlte Steuern in der Bundesrepublik anrechnen; **to**

assess ~es upon besteuern, Höhe einer Steuer berechnen, Steuern festsetzen; **to avoid a ~** Steuer umgehen (vermeiden); **to back down a ~** Steuer wiederaufheben; **to be a ~ on s. o.** Belastung für j. darstellen; **to be a ~ on s. one's attention** jds. Aufmerksamkeit ablenken; **to be exempt from ~es** von Steuerzahlungen befreit sein; **to be liable for income ~** einkommensteuerpflichtig sein; **to be liable to a ~ at a higher rate** höhere Steuersätze bezahlen müssen, höher besteuert werden; **to be subject to ~** steuerpflichtig sein; **to be written off against ~es** steuerlich voll abgeschrieben sein; **to burden ~es upon** mit Steuern belegen; **to charge too little ~** steuerlich zu niedrig veranlagen; **to charge back ~es** nachträglichen Steuerbescheid erlassen; **to charge a ~ at a lower rate** niedrigeren Steuersatz anwenden; **to collect ~es** Steuern eintreiben (beitreiben); **to compound for a ~** Steuer pauschalieren; **to compute the amount of a ~** Steuerbetrag berechnen; **to credit ~es** *(double taxation agreement)* Steuern anrechnen; **to cut down ~es** Steuern ermäßigen; **to deduct ~ at the basic rate** Steuer zum Satz des unteren Proportionalbereichs berechnen; **to defer American ~ on income from abroad until it is repatriated** in Amerika fällige Steuern auf ausländische Einkünfte bis zur Transfermöglichkeit zurückstellen; **to dodge a ~** Steuer umgehen; **to drop a ~** Steuer niederschlagen; **to eliminate a ~** Steuer aufheben; **to evade a ~** Steuer hinterziehen, Steuerhinterziehung begehen; **to exact ~es** Steuern erheben (eintreiben); **to exempt from ~es** von Steuern befreien; **to farm out ~es** Steuern verpachten; **to fight for lower ~es** sich für niedrigere Steuern einsetzen; **to fix the amount of a ~** Steuer berechnen; **to free from ~es** von Steuern befreien, Steuerfreiheit gewähren; **to get in ~es** Steuern hereinholen; **to graduate ~es** Steuersätze staffeln; **to hand over a ~ to the Commissioners of Inland Revenue** *(Br.)* Steuer an die Finanzverwaltung abführen; **to have suffered ~** von der Steuer schon erfaßt sein; **to impose (lay, levy) a ~ on s. th.** etw. mit Steuer belegen (besteuern); **to increase ~es** Steuern erhöhen, Steuererhöhung vornehmen; **to levy ~ on a declining scale on gifts made within two years of death** Geschenke bis zwei Jahre vom Tode des Schenkers degressiv besteuern; **to levy a ~ on dividend distribution** Kapitalertragssteuer erheben; **to levy a ~ at the source** Steuer an der Quelle erheben; **to lighten ~es** Steuern senken; **to lower a ~** Steuer ermäßigen (herabsetzen, senken); **to pass on a ~** Steuer abwälzen; **to pay ~es** versteuern, Steuer zahlen; **to pay $ 2000 in ~es** 2000 Dollar an Steuern bezahlen; **to pay ~ at the basic rate** normale Einkommensteuersätze zahlen; **to pay ~es on income earned abroad** im Ausland erzielte Einkünfte versteuern; **to pay a ~ at the source** Steuer gleich vom Ertrag abführen; **to put a ~ upon** besteuern; **to raise ~es** Steuern erhöhen; **to receive ~es** Steuern einnehmen; **to reclaim paid ~es on all purchases necessary for the output of a business** gezahlte Vorsteuerbeträge zurückverlangen; **to reduce a ~** Steuer ermäßigen (herabsetzen); **to reimpose ~es** neue Steuern auferlegen; **to relieve from ~es** Steuerfreiheit gewähren; **to remit a ~** Steuer erlassen; **to repay a ~** Steuer erstatten, Steuererstattung vornehmen; **to retain a ~** Steuer einbehalten; **to return ~es to the revenue** Steuern bezahlen (abführen); **to save ~** Steuer sparen, Steuerersparnis erzielen; **to shift a ~** Steuer abwälzen; **to suffer ~ at the basic rate** zum Grundtarif besteuert werden; **to suffer ~ at source** der Quellenbesteuerung unterliegen; **to treat ~es simply as business expense** Steuern einfach als Geschäftsunkosten behandeln; **to underpay ~es** zu niedrige Steuern zahlen; **to withdraw a ~** Steuer wiederaufheben; **to withhold a ~** *(US)* Quellensteuer erheben; **to withhold a ~ from wage payment** *(US)* Steuer bei der Lohnzahlung einbehalten;

~ **abatement** Steuernachlaß, -herabsetzung, -milderung; ~ **accounting** Steuerbuchhaltung, -buchführung; ~ **accruals** *(US)* fällige Steuerforderungen; ~ **administration** Steuerverwaltung; ~ **advantage** Steuervorteil; ~ **adviser** Steuerberater; **to hand over one's ~ affairs to s. o.** jem. seine Steuerunterlagen zur Erledigung übergeben.

tax allowance *(Br.)* Steuervergünstigung, -freibetrag;

age ~ *(Br.)* Altersfreibetrag; **child ~** *(Br.)* Kinderfreibetrag; **100% first-year ~** hundertprozentige steuerliche Abschreibung im ersten Jahr;

~ **for children** Steuerfreibetrag für Kinder;

to set ~ short of full indexation Steuerfreibeträge praktisch voll indexieren.

tax|amendment Steueränderung; ~ **amnesty** Steueramnestie; ~ **amount** Steuerbetrag; ~ **angle** Steuergesichtspunkt; ~ **anticipation certificate** *(Br.)* Steuergutschein; ~ **anticipation notes** *(US)* kleingestückelte Steuergutscheine; ~ **appeal** Steuereinspruch; ~ **argument** Steuerstreitfrage; ~ **arrears** Steuerrückstände; **to**

ease ~ **arrears** Steuerrückstände mit Nachsicht eintreiben; ~ **assessing (assessment)** *(Br.)* Festsetzung der Steuer, Steuereinschätzung, -veranlagung, -festsetzung, -bescheid; **to appeal against a ~ assessment** gegen einen Steuerbescheid Einspruch einlegen; ~-**assessment note** *(Br.)* **(notice,** *US*) Veranlagungs-, Steuerbescheid; ~ **assessor** *(US)* Veranlagungsstelle, Finanzbeamter; **National ≗ Association** *(US)* Verband der Steuerzahler; ~ **attorney** *(US)* Anwalt für Steuersachen, Steueranwalt; ~ **audit** *(US)* Steuerprüfung, -revision; ~ **auditor** *(US)* Steuerprüfer, -revisor; ~ **authority** Steuerbehörde; **to declare money to the ~ authorities** Einkünfte versteuern; ~ **avoidance** Steuerumgehung, -vermeidung, -flucht; **top ~-avoidance experts** Spitzenkräfte auf dem Gebiet der Steuerumgehung; ~-**avoidance industry** Gewerbe der Steuerumgehungen; ~-**avoidance scheme** Steuerumgehungsprojekt-, wesen; ~ **avoider** Steuerumgeher; ~-**avoiding** steuerumgehend; ~ **balance sheet** *(US)* Steuerbilanz; ~ **band** Steuerbandbreite, Tarifstufe, steuerliche Progressionszone; **higher-rate ~ bands** höher besteuerte Progressionszonen; **to lift ~ bands in line with inflation** Tarifstufen der inflationellen Entwicklung anpassen; ~ **base** Steuerbemessungs-, Besteuerungsgrundlage, -basis, Veranlagungsgrundlage, Steuerobjekt; ~ **battle** Steuerschlacht; ~ **bearer** Steuerträger; ~ **benefit** Steuererleichterung, steuerliche Vergünstigung; ~ **bill** *(parl.)* Steuergesetz, -vorlage, *(US, taxpayer)* Steuerbescheid, -zettel; ~ **bite** Steuerbelastung; **to put the ~ bite on** Steuerschraube anziehen; ~ **bond** Steuergutschein, *(US)* Steuerquittung; ~ **book** *(US)* Veranlagungs-, [Steuer]hebeliste; ~-**bought** *(US)* aus Steuergründen erworben; ~ **bracket** Steuergruppe, -stufe, -klasse; **to put s. o. in a higher ~ bracket** j. in eine höhere Steuerklasse einstufen; **to shove more of the earned income into the ordinary ~ bracket** größeren Teil des Erwerbseinkommens der normalen Besteuerung unterwerfen; ~ **break** *(US)* Steuervergünstigung, steuerlicher Vorteil; **to cut back drastically on the ~ breaks for capital gains** *(US)* Steuervergünstigungen für Kapitalgewinne drastisch einschränken; ~ **burden** Steuerlast, -belastung, steuerliche Belastung; ~-**burdened** besteuert, steuerlich belastet; ~ **business** Steuerberatung; ~ **calculation** Steuerberechnung; ~ **calendar** Steuerkalender; ~ **certificate** *(US)* Zuschlagsbescheid bei Steuerzwangsvollstreckungen; ~ **changes** steuerliche Veränderungen, Steueränderungen; ~ **charge** steuerliche Belastung, Steuerbelastung; **to write bigger ~ checks** *(US)* **(cheques,** *Br.*) höhere Steuern zahlen; ~ **claim** Steuerforderung, -anspruch; ~ **class** Steuerklasse; ~ **classification** steuerliche Einstufung, Steuereinstufung; ~ **code** Abgabenordnung; ~ **collecting** Steuereinziehung, -erhebung.

tax collection Steuererhebung, -einziehung, Steuereingänge; ~ **office** Steuereinziehungsstelle; ~ **procedure** Steuereinziehungsverfahren; ~ **regulations** Steuereinziehungsbestimmungen; ~ **shortages** nicht eingegangene Steuern, Steuerminderaufkommen; ~ **speedup** beschleunigtes Steuereinziehungsverfahren; ~ **system** Steuereintreibungsverfahren.

tax collector Steuereinnehmer, -beamter, -einzieher; **city ~** Stadtsteueramt; ~'**s district** Steuerbezirk.

tax|commission *(US)* Veranlagungs-, Steuerausschuß; ~ **commissioner** *(Br.)* [Steuer]veranlagungsbehörde; ~ **comparison** Steuervergleich; ~ **compliance** Steuerwilligkeit; ~ **computation** Steuerberechnung; ~ **concession** Steuerbegünstigung, Steuererleichterung, steuerliches Zugeständnis; ~ **concession period** steuerlicher Begünstigungszeitraum; ~ **confidence** Steuerwilligkeit; ~ **consequences** Steuerauswirkungen; ~ **considerations** steuerliche Überlegungen; ~ **consultant** Berater in Steuerfragen, Steuerberater; ~ **consulting (consultation)** Steuerberatung; ~ **and exchange controller** Leiter der Steuer- und Devisenabteilung; ~ **controversy** Steuerverfahren; ~ **convention (conventional treaty,** *US*) Steuerabkommen; ~ **counsel[lor]** Helfer in Steuersachen, Steuersachverständiger; ~ **court** Finanzhof; ≗ **Court of the United States** Bundessteuergericht, Oberster Finanzgerichtshof; ~-**court case** Finanzhofverfahren; ~-**court judge** Finanzrichter.

tax credit *(US)* Steuergutschrift, -freibetrag, -vergünstigung [für Investitionen], Gutschrift für ausländische Steuern und bezahlte Kapitalertragssteuern;

foreign ~ *(US)* Anrechnung ausländischer Steuern; **indirect ~** *(US)* indirekte Steueranrechnung; **10% investment ~** *(US)* 10%iger Steuerzuschuß für Investitionsvorhaben;

~ **method** *(US)* Steueranrechnungsmethode; ~ **relief** *(US)* angerechnete Steuervergünstigung, angerechneter Steuerfreibetrag; ~ **rules** *(US)* Steuervergünstigungsrichtlinien; ~ **system** *(US)* Steueranrechnungsmethode.

tax | cut Steuerherabsetzung, Steuersenkung; ~-cut proposal Steuersenkungsvorschlag; ~ deadline Steuertermin; ~ debacle Steuerkatastrophe; ~ debate Steuerdebatte; ~ debtor Steuerschuldner; ~ declaration Steuererklärung; ~-deductible steuerlich absetzbar, steuerabzugsfähig; ~ deductibles steuerabzugsfähige Beträge; ~ deduction Steuerabzug; ~ deduction at source Quellenbesteuerung, Steuerabzugsverfahren; ~-deduction card (US) Lohnsteuerkarte; ~ deed (US) Grunderwerbsurkunde beim Erwerb eines wegen Steuerrückständen zwangsversteigerten Grundstücks; ~-deferral (US) Steuerstundung, -aufschub, -verlagerung; ~ deferral system Steuerverlagerungssystem; ~ deficit Steuerausfall, -fehlbetrag; ~ delinquency (US) Steuerschuld, -säumnis, verspätete Steuerzahlung; ~ demand (US) Steuerbescheid; to pay a ~ demand under protest (US) Steuerforderung unter Einlegung von Widerspruch zahlen; ~ department Steuerabteilung; ~ depreciation steuerlich anerkannte Abschreibung; ~ difference Steuerunterschied; ~ digest (fiscal office) Steuerunterlagen beim Finanzamt; unsettled ~ dispute unerledigte Steuerfrage; ~ distribution Steueraufteilung; ~ division Steuerabteilung; ~ dodge (dodging) Steuerumgehung, -hinterziehung, -abwehr, -ausweichung; ~ dodger Steuerhinterzieher, -drückeberger; ~-dodging steuerumgehend; ~ dollars (US) Steuergelder, -mittel; delinquent-~ due Säumniszuschlag für verspätet gezahlte Steuern; after-~ earnings Erträge nach Steuern; ~ effects Steuerauswirkungen, steuerliche Auswirkungen; to make a strong ~ effort auf dem Steuergebiet große Anstrengungen machen; ~ equalization item steuerliche Ausgleichsposten; ~ evader (US) Steuerhinterzieher; ~ evasion (US) Steuerhinterziehung, -flucht; to crack down on ~ evasions Steuerumgehungen einen Riegel vorschieben; ~ evasion directive (US) Direktiven zur Verhinderung von Steuerhinterziehungen; ~ evasion offence (US) Steuervergehen; ~-exempt (US) steuerbefreit, steuerfrei, -abgabenfrei, von der Besteuerung ausgenommen, (free of Federal income tax, US) einkommensteuerfrei; ~ -exempts (US) Einkommensteuerfreibeträge; ~-exempt amount (US) Einkommensteuerfreibetrag; ~-exempt bonds (US) steuerfreie Wertpapiere; ~-exempt income (US) steuerfreies Einkommen; ~-exempt note (US) steuerfreier Schuldschein; ~-exempt securities steuerfreie Wertpapiere; ~-exempt status (US) steuerfreie Stellung.

tax exemption Steuerbefreiung, -freiheit, (US) Steuerfreibetrag; excise ~ (US) Verbrauchssteuerfreibetrag; ~ to employers for training Steuerfreibeträge für Arbeitgeber bei Abhaltung von Ausbildungslehrgängen; ~ to encourage research and development (US) Steuerfreibeträge zur Förderung von Forschungs- und Entwicklungsarbeiten; ~ on equipment or machinery Steuervergünstigungen bei Maschinenanschaffungen; ~ on capital improvement (US) Steuerfreibetrag für werterhöhende technische Verbesserungen; ~ on land improvement (US) Steuerfreibetrag für Grundstücksmeliorationen.

tax | exile Steuerflüchtling; ~ expense steuerlich absetzbare Unkosten; ~ experience Erfahrung in Steuersachen; ~ expert Steuerberater, -fachmann, -helfer, -sachverständiger; ~ farmer (hist.) Steuerpächter; ~ favo(u)r Steuervergünstigung; attractive ~ features attraktive Steuervorteile; ~ ferret Steuerfahnder; ~ ferrets Steuerfahndung; ~ file Steuerakte; ~-filing date (US) Steuertermin; ~ foreclosure Steuerpfändung; ~ forgiveness Steuernachlaß; ~ form Steuerformular, Steuererklärungsvordruck; ~ fraud Steuerhinterziehung.

tax-free steuerfrei; ~ allowance (Br.) Steuerfreibetrag; ~ bonds steuerfreie Obligationen; ~ covenant (US) Vereinbarung der Steuerfreiheit; ~ element steuerfreier Gehaltsanteil; ~ gift steuerfreie Schenkung; ~ interests steuerfreie Zinsen; ~ loan steuerfreie Anleihe; ~ shop zollfreier Laden (Verkauf); ~ transaction steuerfreies Wertpapiergeschäft.

tax | function steuerliches Aufgabengebiet; ~ gathering Steuererhebung; ~-gathering season hauptsächliche Steuereinnahmezeit; ~ grab unberechtigte Steuerbelastung; ~ group Steuerklasse; ~ guide Steuerberatungsheft, steuerlicher Ratgeber; ~ haven Steuerparadies, -oase; ~ holiday steuerfreier Tag; ~ impact (Br.) Steuerbelastung; ~ implications Steuerfolgen, steuerliche Folgewirkungen, steuerliche Auswirkungen; ~ incentive Steueranreiz, ~-incentive steuerlich attraktiv; ~ incentive program Steuerbegünstigungsprogramm; ~ incidence Steueranfall, -effekt, -wirkung; ~ increase Steuererhöhung; ~ indexation Steuerindexierung; ~ inflation Steuerinflation; ~ information Steuerauskunft; ~ inspection Betriebs-, Steuerprüfung; ~ inspector Betriebs-, Steuerprüfer, Steuerrevisor; ~

instalment (US) Steuerrate, (income tax) Einkommensteuervorauszahlung; ~ instruction Steueranordnung, Steuerverfügung; ~ investigation steuerliche Untersuchung; ~ investment steuerbegünstigte Kapitalinvestition; ~ item Steuerposten; personal income ~ job (US) einkommensteuerliche Aufgabe; ~ judgment Steuerurteil, -entscheidung; ~ jurisdiction steuerliche Zuständigkeit; ~ justice Steuergerechtigkeit; ~ knowledge Steuerkenntnisse; ~-laden (US) steuerlich belastet; Federal Income ⬩ Law (US) Einkommensteuergesetz; under ~ law laut den steuerrechtlichen Bestimmungen; to simplify the ~ laws applicable to companies Körperschaftssteuergesetzgebung vereinfachen; ~-law provisions Steuerbestimmungen; ~ lawyer (US) Steueranwalt, Anwalt für Steuersachen; ~ lawyers relief clauses Entlastungsbestimmungen für Steueranwälte; ~ layer Steuererheber; ~ lease Pachtrechtübertragung bei Zwangsveräußerungen wegen rückständiger Steuern; [income] ~ legislation [Einkommen]steuergesetzgebung; ~ levy Steuererhebung, Steuerumlage, (total sum raised by a tax) gesamtes Steueraufkommen; ~ liability Steuerschuld, -pflicht; subject to unlimited ~ liability (double taxation agreement) unbeschränkt steuerpflichtig; actual ~ liability tatsächliche Steuerschuld; limited ~ liability beschränkte Steuerpflicht; income ~ liability, ~ liability based on income Einkommensteuerschuld, -pflicht; ~ lien (US) Steuerpfandrecht, steuerliche Haftung des Grundbesitzers; deemed ~ life steuerlich geschätzte Nutzungsdauer; useful ~ life steuerlich festgesetzte Nutzungsdauer; ~ limit Steuerhöchstgrenze; ~ list Hebeliste, -rolle, (real-estate tax) Liste säumiger Steuerzahler; ~ load Steuerlast, -belastung, steuerliche Belastung; ~ loophole steuerliches Hintertürchen, Steuerlücke; to plug ~ loopholes steuerliche Hintertürchen dichtmachen; ~ loss Steuerverlust; to declare a ~ loss against future earnings Steuerverlust vortragen; to spread the impact of a ~ loss over five years Steuerverlust über fünf Jahre verteilen; ~ loss carryover Steuerverlustvortrag; ~-loss selling steuerliches Verlustgeschäft; ~ man Steuerfachmann; ~es management Finanz-, Steuerverwaltung, (corporation) Verwaltung des Steuerressorts; ⬩ Management Act (Br.) Steuerdurchführungsgesetz; ~ manager Vorstandsmitglied für Steuerfragen; ~ matters Steuersache; ~ measures steuerpolitische Maßnahmen, Steuermaßnahmen; ~ mitigation Steuermilderung, -vermeidung; ~ money Steuermittel, -gelder; ~ morale Steuermoral; deferred ~ needs Steuerstundungserfordernisse; to be in the ~ net von der Steuer erfaßt sein; ~ notice Steuerbenachrichtigung, -bescheid, Abgabenbescheid; ~ obligations Steuerverbindlichkeiten, steuerliche Verpflichtungen; ~ offence Übertretung der Steuerbestimmungen; ~ and revenue office (US) Finanzamt; ~ office reference number Steuernummer; ~ official Finanz-, Steuerbeamter; ~ package Steuerpaket; ~-paid versteuert; ~ papers Steuerakten, -unterlagen; ~ paper bill (US) Steuerzettel; ~-paying public der Steuerzahler; ~ payments Steuerzahlungen; advance ~ payment Steuervorauszahlung; ~ payment date Steuertermin; ~ penalty Steuerstrafe, -säumniszuschlag; ~ penalty rate Steuerstrafsatz; to remove ~ perks Steuervergünstigungen beseitigen; ~ pile Steuersäule; ~ plan Steuersystem; ~ planner Steuersystematiker, Steuerberater; ~ planning Steuersystematik; ~ policies Steuerpolitik; ~ position Steuerlage, -position; [local] ~ power [kommunales] Besteuerungsrecht; ~ practices steuerliche Maßnahmen, Steuerpolitik; debatable ~ practices zweifelhafte Steuerverfahren; ~ practitioner (Br.) Steuerberater; ~ preference income steuerlich begünstigte (steuerbegünstigte) Einkünfte; ~ preference items steuerlich begünstigte Einkommenspositionen; ~ preparation Ausfüllung eines Steuerformulars; ~-preparation business Steuerberatungsgewerbe, -wesen; ~ -preparation service Steuerberatungsdienst; ~ preparer Ausfüller eines Steuerformulars, Steuerberater, -helfer, Helfer in Steuersachen; ~ prepayment Steuervorauszahlung; ~ privilege Steuervergünstigung, steuerliche Vergünstigung; with ~ privileges steuerbegünstigt; to enjoy ~ privileges steuerbegünstigt sein; ~-privileged steuergünstig; ~ probe (US) Steueruntersuchung; ~ procedure Steuerrechtsverfahren; ~ proceeds Steuerertrag; after-~ profit Gewinn nach [Abzug von] Steuern; ~ program(me) Steuerprogramm; ~ progression Steuerprogression; to raise a hue and cry against new ~ proposals gegen neue Steuervorschläge Sturm laufen; ~ provisions Steuerbestimmungen; deferred ~ provision Rückstellung für Steuerzahlungen, Steuerrückstellung; ~ purchaser (US) Ersteigerer bei zum Zwecke der Bezahlung von Steuern vorgenommener Zwangsversteigerung; to allocate only receipts from sales within the city for ~ purposes nur in der Stadt selbst getätigte Umsätze der Steuer unterwerfen; to be treated as a corporate body for ~ **purposes** steuerlich wie eine juristische Person behandelt werden; **to be treated as separated for ~ purposes** aus steuerlichen Gründen getrennt veranlagt werden; ~ **query** Steuereinspruch; ~ **question** Steuerfrage.

tax rate Steuermeßbetrag, -satz;
basic ~ Normalsteuersatz; **income** ~ Einkommensteuersatz, -fuß; **marginal** ~ Steuerhöchstsatz; **maximum** ~ Steuerhöchstsatz; **top** ~ steuerlicher Spitzensatz, höchster Steuersatz;
to apply the ~ **to** Steuersatz anwenden auf; **to face the highest marginal** ~ mit den höchsten Einkommensteuersatz konfrontiert sein; **to raise the** ~ Steuern erhöhen; **to reduce the** ~ Steuersatz senken;
~ **limit** Steuerhöchstsatz; ~ **schedule** Steuertabelle.

tax|reappraisal Steuernachveranlagung; ~ **reasons** steuerliche Gründe, Steuergründe; ~ **rebate** Steuerrabatt, -rückvergütung, -nachlaß; **rebate for exporters** Ausfuhrsteuerrückvergütung; ~ **receipts** Steueraufkommen, -einnahmen; ~ **receivables** (balance sheet, US) Steuerrückstände; ~ **receiver** (US) Steuereinnehmer; ~ **recovery** Steuerbeitreibung.

tax reduction Steuererleichterung, -herabsetzung, -kürzung, -senkung, -ermäßigung, -minderung, -nachlaß;
flat-rate ~ lineare Steuersenkung; **graduated** ~ gestaffelte Steuersenkung; **income-~** Einkommensteuersenkung.

tax reform Steuerreform.
~ **bill** (act, US) Steuerreformvorlage; ~ **legislation** Steuerreformgesetzgebung; ~ **package** Steuerreformbündel; ~ **proposal** Steuerreformvorschlag.

tax refund Steuererstattung, -rückvergütung, -rückzahlung;
on-the-spot ~ sofortige Steuererstattung;
~ **certificate** verzinslicher Steuervergütungsschein; ~ **check** (US) (cheque, Br.) Steuererstattungsscheck; ~ **proceedings** Steuererstattungsverfahren.

tax regulations steuerrechtliche Bestimmungen.

tax relief Steuererleichterung, -vergünstigung, steuerliche Entlastung, steuerliche Erleichterungen, (Br.) Steuerfreibetrag;
entitled to ~ steuerbegünstigt;
100% first-year ~ **on new machinery and plant** hundertprozentige steuerliche Abschreibung für Maschinen und Betriebsausrüstung im Anlaufjahr; ~ **on interest payments** Steuervergünstigungen für bezahlte Zinsen;
to derive less than full benefit of ~s and allowances Steuervergünstigungen und -erleichterungen nicht voll ausschöpfen; **to qualify for** ~ (Br.) Steuerfreibeträge in Anspruch nehmen können;
~ **advantage** Steuervorteil; ~ **bonds** (US) Steuervorgriffsscheine; ~ **measures** steuerliche Erleichterungen.

tax|reminder Steuermahnung, -mahnzettel; ~ **remission** Steuererlaß; ~ **remission bill** (certificate) Steuergutschein; ~ **payment** Steuererstattung; ~ **repayment** Steuererstattung; **repayment due** Steuererstattungsanspruch; ~ **replacement** Steuerrückvergütung, -erstattung; ~ **report** Steuerbilanz; **for** ~ **reporting** für Steuerbilanzzwecke; ~ **representative** Steuerbeauftragter, -bevollmächtigter; ~ **reserve** Steuerrückstellung, -rücklage, Veranlagungsrücklage; ~ **reserve certificate** (Br.) für Steuerrücklagen erworbene Wertpapiere mit steuerfreien Zinserträgen; ~ **result** Steuerergebnis; ~ **return** Steuererklärung; **to prepare an income-~ return** Einkommensteuerformular ausfüllen; ~ **return form** Einkommensteuerformular; ~ **revenue** Steuereinkommen, -aufkommen, -ertrag, -einnahmen [des Staates]; ~ **revenue per capita** Steueraufkommen pro Kopf der Bevölkerung; ~ **revenue gains** erhöhte Steuereinnahmen; **~-ridden** (US) steuerlich belastet, steuerbelastet; ~ **rise** Steuererhöhung; ~ **roll** (US) [Steuer]hebeliste, -kataster; ~ **rules** Steuerrichtlinien; ~ **sale of property** (US) Zwangsvollstreckung zwecks Bezahlung von Steuerrückständen; ~ **savings** Steuerersparnisse; **estate** ~ **saving** Nachlaßsteuerersparnis; **potential** ~ **saving** Steuereinsparungsmöglichkeit; **~-saving pattern** übliches steuersparendes Verfahren; **~-saving service** steuersparende Tätigkeit, steuerliche Beratungstätigkeit; ~ **scale** Steuertarif; ~ **scandal** Steuerskandal; ~ **schedule** Steuertabelle; ~ **scheme** Steuerschema, -system; **to put the** ~ **screw on** Steuerschraube ansetzen; ~ **selling** Wertpapierverkäufe zwecks Bezahlung der Einkommensteuer, Steuerzwangsverkauf; ~ **service** Steuerprüfdienst, Steuerberatung, Beratung in Steuerangelegenheiten; **to offer** ~ **service** seine Dienste als Steuerberater anbieten; **to reinforce its ~ services at senior management level** höhere Angestellte im verstärktem Maße steuerlich beraten; ~ **service business** Steuerberatungsgewerbe; **~-service wholesaler** Steuerberatungsfirma; ~ **sharing** (US) Finanzausgleich; **~-sharing formula** (US) Finanzausgleichsformel; ~ **sheet** Steuerkarte; ~ **shelter** Verhinderung

steuerlicher Belastungen; **to create a** ~ **shelter** einer steuerlichen Belastung ausweichen; **to exploit** ~ **shelters** von Steuererleichterungsbestimmungen Gebrauch machen; **~-shelter deal** steuerbegünstigtes Geschäft; ~ **shifting** Steuerabwälzung, -überwälzung; ~ **source** Steuerquelle; ~ **sovereignty** Steuerhoheit; ~ **stamp** Steuerzeichen; ~ **statement** (status) Steuerbilanz, -status, -aufstellung, steuerliche Aufstellung; **long-range** ~ **strategy** langfristige Einkommensteuerpolitik; ~ **structure** Steuersystem, -gefüge; **unified** ~ **structure** vereinheitlichtes Steuersystem; **[income] ~-supported** steuerlich begünstigt, steuerbegünstigt; ~ **surcharge** Einkommensteuerzuschlag, -zusatzsteuer; ~ **switch** Änderung des Besteuerungssystems; ~ **system** [Einkommen]steuersystem; **local** ~ **system** (US) Kommunalsteuerwesen; ~ **table** [Lohn]steuertabelle; **optional** ~ **table** wahlweise Steuerveranlagung nach der Steuertabelle; ~ **take** Steuereinnahmen, fiskalische Abschöpfung; ~ **taker** Steuereinnehmer; ~ **taper for five-to-seven year deferral** auf 5 - 7 Jahre beschränkte Steuervergünstigung; ~ **tapering to zero after five years** nach fünf Jahren auslaufende Steuervergünstigung; ~ **technician** Steuerfachmann; ~ **theory** Steuertheorie; ~ **threshold** (income tax) Steuerschwelle, -anfangsbetrag, steuerpflichtiges Anfangseinkommen, unterer Proportionalbereich; ~ **title** bei der zu steuerlichen Zwecken vorgenommenen Zwangsversteigerung erworbenes Eigentumsrecht; ~ **treatment** steuerliche Behandlung; **to campaign for more favo(u)rable** ~ **treatment** Feldzug für günstigere Steuersätze führen; **to qualify for a charity's favo(u)rable** ~ **treatment** steuerliche Vergünstigungen für wohltätige Stiftungen in Anspruch nehmen können; ~ **treaty** (US) Steuerabkommen, -vereinbarung; **anti-double** ~ **treaty** (US) Doppelbesteuerungsabkommen; ~ **warrant** Ausweis des Steuereinnehmers; **to benefit ~-wise** steuerlich profitieren; ~ **withholding** Steuereinbehaltung, -abzug; ~ **withholding on dividends** im Abzugswege erhobene Kapitalertragssteuer; ~ **work** Bearbeitung von Steuerunterlagen; ~ **wrinkles** Steuerkniffe; ~ **writeoffs** (US) steuerlich zulässige Abschreibungen; ~ **writer** Steuergesetzgeber; **~-writing committee** Steuerveranlagungsausschuß, -behörde; ~ **yield** Steueranfall, -erträgnisse, -aufkommen.

taxability [Be]steuerbarkeit, Steuerpflichtigkeit, (fee) Gebührenpflichtigkeit, (plaintiff) Erstattungspflicht;
limited ~ beschränkte Steuerpflicht.

taxable Steuerpflichtiger;
~ (a.) [be]steuerbar, steuer-, abgaben-, veranlagungs-, gebührenpflichtig, besteuerungsfähig, (charged against the plaintiff) erstattungspflichtig;
to be ~ **as ordinary income** als normales Einkommen versteuerbar (normal zu versteuern) sein; **to make** ~ steuerpflichtig machen, Veranlagungspflicht begründen;
~ **article** Steuerobjekt; ~ **base** Steuerbemessungsgrundlage; **capacity** Besteuerungsfähigkeit, Steuerkraft, Steuerleistungsfähigkeit; ~ **class of goods** steuerpflichtige Waren; ~ **costs** [zu erstattende, erstattungsfähige] Gerichtskosten; ~ **estate** steuerpflichtige Erbschaftsmasse; ~ **gain** Steuergewinn; ~ **income** Steuereinkommen, versteuerbares (steuerpflichtiges) Einkommen darstellen; **to constitute** ~ **income** steuerpflichtiges Einkommen darstellen; **to reach the** ~ **level** für die Besteuerung in Frage kommen, steuerbar (steuerpflichtig) sein; ~ **loss** Steuerverlust; ~ **period** Steuerperiode, Veranlagungszeitraum; ~ **person** Steuer-, Veranlagungspflichtiger; ~ **persons** veranlagungsfähiger Personenkreis; ~ **portion** steuerpflichtiger Betrag; ~ **profit** steuerpflichtiger (veranlagungspflichtiger) Gewinn, Steuergewinn; ~ **property** steuerpflichtiges (veranlagungspflichtiges) Vermögen; ~ **transaction** steuerpflichtiger Vorgang; ~ **transactions** versteuerbarer (steuerpflichtiger) Umsatz; ~ **unit** Steuergegenstand, -objekt; ~ **value** Steuerwert; **to assess for** ~ **value** nach dem Steuerwert abschätzen; ~ **year** Veranlagungs-, Steuerjahr, steuerpflichtiges Jahr.

taxableness Besteuerbarkeit.

taxation Besteuerung, Steuerwesen, (appraisal) Abschätzung, steuerehrliche Erfassung, [Steuer]veranlagung, (law, Br.) Gerichtskostenfestsetzung, (revenue from taxes) Steuereinnahmen, -einkünfte, -aufkommen;
adjusted for ~ steuerlich berichtigt, steuerbereinigt; **exempt from** ~ steuer-, gebühren-, abgabenfrei; **for the purpose of** ~ zu Steuerzwecken, aus steuerlichen Gründen, aus Veranlagungsgründen; **subject to** ~ veranlagungs-, steuerpflichtig;
commensurate ~ maßvolle Besteuerung; **company** ~ Firmenbesteuerung; **confiscatory** ~ konfiskatorische Besteuerung; **direct** ~ direkte Steuern (Besteuerung), Direktbesteuerung; **discriminative** ~ Steuerdiskriminierung; **double** ~ Doppelbesteuerung; **excessive** ~ Überbesteuerung; **flat-rate** ~ pauschale

Besteuerung, Pauschalbesteuerung; **foreign** ~ ausländische Steuergesetzgebung; **future** ~ *(balance sheet, Br.)* Steuerrückstellung; **graduated** ~ abgestuftes Steuersystem; **harsh** ~ hohe Besteuerung; **heavy** ~ Auferlegung hoher Steuern; **incentive** ~ zyklisches Steuersystem; **increased** ~ erhöhte Steuerbelastung; **indirect** ~ indirekte Besteuerung (Steuern); **light** ~ geringe Besteuerung; **local** ~ Kommunalsteueraufkommen; **marginal** ~ Eingangsbesteuerung, Besteuerung im unteren Proportionalbereich; **maximum** ~ Steuerhöchstsatz; **minimum** ~ Steuermindestsatz; **multiple** ~ *(different states)* mehrfache Besteuerung, Mehrfachbesteuerung; **municipal** ~ Kommunalabgaben, Gemeindesteuern; **negative** ~ Negativbesteuerung; **oppressive** ~ Steuerschraube; **personal** ~ *(US)* Einkommensbesteuerung; **progressive** ~ progressive Besteuerung, Staffelbesteuerung; **property** ~ Vermögensbesteuerung; **proportional** ~ anteilsmäßige Besteuerung, Proportionalbesteuerung; **reasonable** ~ erträgliche Steuern; **reduced** ~ verminderte Steuerlast; **regressive** ~ regressives Besteuerungssystem; **state** ~ *(US)* Besteuerung durch die Einzelstaaten; **subsequent** ~ Nachversteuerung; **supplementary** ~ zusätzliche Besteuerung; **U.K.** ~ *(Br.)* laufende Steuern; **war-time** ~ Kriegsbesteuerung;

~ **of capital** Vermögensbesteuerung; ~ **of costs** *(court, Br.)* Überprüfung der Gebührenrechnung [eines Anwalts], *(US)* Festsetzung der Prozeßkosten, Kostenfestsetzung; ~ **of party-to-party costs** *(US)* Festsetzung erstattungsfähiger Kosten; ~ **of an estate** Erbschaftsbesteuerung; ~ **on income** Einkommenbesteuerung; ~ **of rents** Rentenbesteuerung; ~ **at the source** Quellenbesteuerung; ~ **by stages** fortlaufend erhobene Steuer; **to allow (make provision) for** ~ Steuerrückstellung vornehmen, für Steuern zurückstellen; **to assess property for** ~ zur Vermögenssteuer veranlagen; **to cut marginal** ~ **at the bottom** Eingangssteuersätze (Sätze im unteren Proportionalbereich) senken; **to grumble at high** ~ sich über hohe Steuersätze beklagen; **to increase** ~ Steuerschraube anziehen; **to offer beneficial** ~ Steuervergünstigungen gewähren; **to reduce** ~ Steuersenkung vornehmen, Steuern senken; **to review** ~ über eine Erinnerung gegen einen Kostenfestsetzungsbeschluß entscheiden, Kostenentscheidung überprüfen;

~ **affairs** Steuerangelegenheiten; **double** ~ **agreement** *(Br.)* Doppelbesteuerungsabkommen; ~ **allowances** Steuerfreibeträge; ~ **aspects** Steueraspekte; ~ **assistant** Mitarbeiter in der Steuerabteilung; ~ **authority** Steuerbehörde, Veranlagungsstelle; ~ **benefits** steuerliche Vergünstigungen; ~ **charge** Steuerbelastung; ~ **concession** Steuervergünstigung; ~ **consequences** steuerliche Auswirkungen; ~ **cut** Steuersenkung; ~ **disadvantage** Steuernachteil; ~ **discrimination** steuerliche Diskriminierung; ~ **equalization reserve** *(balance sheet, Br.)* Steuerausgleichsrücklage; ~ **law** Steuergesetz; ~ **legislation** Steuergesetzgebung; ~ **matters** Steuerangelegenheiten; ~ **method** Veranlagungsmethode; ~ **policy** Steuerpolitik; ~ **position** Steuerlage, steuerliche Lage; ~ **powers** Besteuerungsvollmachten; ~ **primer** Steuer-ABC; ~ **purpose** Steuerzweck; ~ **relief** *(Br.)* Steuervergünstigung; **double-**~ **relief** *(Br.)* Befreiung von der Doppelbesteuerung, Doppelbesteuerungsvergünstigung, Anrechnung im Ausland gezahlter Steuern; ~ **reserve** Rückstellung für Steuern, Steuerrücklage, -rückstellung; ~ **specialist** Steuerfachmann, -experte, -spezialist; ~ **system** Steuerwesen, Besteuerungssystem; ~ **treatment** steuerliche Behandlung.

taxational Steuern betreffend.
taxeater Wohlfahrts-, Unterstützungsempfänger, *(plant)* staatlich (steuerlich) subventionierter Betrieb.
taxeating staatlich (steuerlich) subventioniert.
taxed besteuert;
heavily ~ hochbesteuert; ~ **off** *(US)* bei der Kostenfestsetzung gekürzt;
to be ~ besteuert (veranlagt) werden, der Steuerpflicht unterliegen, steuerpflichtig (veranlagungspflichtig) sein; **to be** ~ **heavily** schwer besteuert werden; **to be** ~ **at lower income rates** zu niedrigeren Einkommensteuersätzen veranlagt werden; **to be** ~ **separately** getrennt veranlagt werden; **to be** ~ **to the utmost** außerordentlich in Anspruch genommen werden;
~ **bill of costs** *(US)* Prozeßkostenaufstellung, Kostenfestsetzungsbeschluß, *(Br.)* Gebührenrechnung [für den Anwalt]; ~ **costs** *(US)* festgesetzte Prozeßkosten.
taxer [Ab]schätzer, Taxator.
taxgatherer Steuereinnehmer.
taxgathering Steuererhebung, -einziehung;
~ **season** hauptsächliche Steuereingangszeit.
taxi [Auto]taxe, Taxi, Kraftdroschke;
~ **with the flag up** freie Taxe;

~ *(v.)* Taxe benutzen (nehmen), mit dem Taxi fahren, *(airplane)* rollen;
~ **to the station** Taxe zum Bahnhof nehmen;
to take a ~ mit dem Taxi fahren, Droschke mieten;
~ **aircraft** Flugtaxi; ~ **dancer (girl)** Animierdame; ~ **driver** Taxichauffeur, -fahrer; ~ **driver plying for hire** auf Kundschaft wartender Taxifahrer; ~ **drivers' union** Taxifahrergewerkschaft; ~ **return fare** Taxipreis für hin und zurück; ~**-holding position** *(airplane)* Haltepunkt; ~ **operator** Taxibesitzer; ~ **ride** Taxifahrt; ~ **stand (rank, Br.)** Halteplatz für Taxen, Taxistand, -haltestelle; ~ **strip** Rollbahn.
taxibus gemieteter Bus.
taxicab Taxe, Taxi, Mietauto.
taxiing Taxi fahren.
taximan *(Br.)* Taxifahrer.
taximeter *(taxi)* Fahrpreisanzeiger, Taxameter, Zähler, Zähluhr.
taxing Festsetzung der Steuer, Steuerfestsetzung;
~ **away** steuerliche Abschöpfung;
~ **of costs** *(law court, US)* Kostenfestsetzung;
~ **area** Steuer-, Veranlagungsbezirk; ~ **authority** Steuerbehörde, Veranlagungsstelle; ~ **capacity** Steuerleistungsfähigkeit, -kraft; ~ **district** *(US)* Veranlagungs-, Steuerbezirk; ~ **feature** Steuermerkmal; ~ **jurisdiction** Steuer[verwaltungs]bezirk; ~ **master** *(law)* Kostenbeamter, Kostenfestsetzungsbeamter; ~ **officer** *(parl.)* Schätzer des für private Gesetzesvorlagen erforderlichen Geldbedarfs; ~ **power** *(US)* Besteuerungs-, Steuerrecht, -hoheit; ~ **provisions** Besteuerungsbestimmungen; **not to be within the** ~ **sections** nicht den Steuerbestimmungen unterliegen; ~ **state** veranlagender (besteuernder) Staat; ~ **statute** *(US)* Steuergesetz; ~ **unit** Steuereinheit, -objekt, -subjekt.
taxiplane *(US)* Mietflugzeug, Lufttaxi.
taxless steuerfrei.
taxpayer Steuerzahler, -pflichtiger, Besteuerter, Veranlagter *(real estate)* vorübergehend errichtetes Gebäude;
basic-rate ~ Normalversteuerer, Steuerpflichtiger im unteren Proportionalbereich; **dilatory** ~ säumiger Steuerzahler; **low-income** ~ Steuerzahler mit niedrigem Einkommen; **nonresident** ~ beschränkt Steuerpflichtiger; **resident** ~ unbeschränkt Steuerpflichtiger; **standard-rate** ~ normaler Steuerzahler; **top-rate** ~ Steuerzahler in der Spitzenklasse;
~ **in arrears** rückständiger (säumiger) Steuerpflichtiger;
~**s' cash** Steuergelder; ~ **corporation** steuerpflichtiges Unternehmen, steuerpflichtiger Betrieb; ~**s' files** Steuerakten; ~**'s pocket** Taschen des Steuerzahlers.
taxpayers' | **code** Einkommenssteuertarif; ~ **list** Veranlagungs-, Hebeliste; ~ **money** Geld der Steuerzahler, Steuergelder; **to view a matter from the** ~ **standpoint** Angelegenheit aus der Sicht des Steuerzahlers sehen; ~ **strike** Steuerstreik.
taxpaying Steuerzahlungen;
~ *(a.)* steuerlich leistungsfähig.
tea Tee, Teemahlzeit;
beef ~ Kraftbrühe; **five-o-clock** ~ Fünfuhrtee; **not my cup of** ~ nicht nach meinem Geschmack;
~**-bag** Teebeutel; ~ **biscuit** Teegebäck; ~ **break** *(Br.)* Frühstückspause; ~ **chest** *(export business)* Teekiste; ~ **dance** Tanztee; ~ **fight** *(sl.)* Teegesellschaft; ~ **gown** Nachmittagskleid; ~ **garden** Gartenrestaurant, *(plantation)* Teepflanzung; ~**-hound** *(coll.)* Salonlöwe; ~ **house** Teehaus; ~ **merchant** Teehändler; ~ **party** Kaffeetafel, *(sl.)* Marijuanaraucher; ~**-room** Teestube; ~**-service set** Teeservice; ~ **shop** *(Br.)* Imbißstube; ~**-stick** *(sl.)* Marijuanazigarette; ~**-things** Teegeschirr; ~**-time** Teezeit; ~ **trolley** Teewagen.
teach *(v.)* unterrichten, Unterricht erteilen, lehren;
~ **s. o. better** j. eines Besseren belehren; ~ **for a living** sich mit Stundengeben durchbringen; ~ **s. o. manners** jem. Manieren beibringen; ~ **in a school** an einer Schule unterrichten; ~ **well** guten Unterricht geben.
teach-in *(coll.)* Podiumsdiskussion, *(students)* Protestdemonstration.
teacher Lehrer, *(university)* Dozent, Hochschullehrer;
~**s' college** *(US)* Lehrerbildungsanstalt, Pädagogische Hochschule; ~ **edition** Ausgabe nur für Lehrer; ~**'s examination** Lehramtsprüfung; ~ **glut** Lehrerüberschuß; ~ **pupil ratio** Lehrer-Schülerprozentsatz; ~ **shortage** Lehrerknappheit; ~ **training** Lehrerausbildung; ~ **training college** *(Br.)* Lehrerbildungsanstalt.
teaching Unterricht, Lehre, *(profession)* Lehrberuf;
to earn a living by ~ sich durch Stundengeben Geld verdienen;
~ **aid** Hilfslehrmittel; ~ **appointment** Berufung auf einen Lehrstuhl; ~ **discipline** Lehrfach; ~ **fellow** Lehrkraft; ~ **hospital**

Lehrkrankenanstalt; ~ **job** Lehrerberuf, *(university)* Dozentenstellung; ~ **load** Belastung durch eine Lehrfunktion; ~ **machine** Lehrmaschine; ~ **method** Lehrmethode; ~ **program(me)** Lehrprogramm, -plan; ~ **staff** Lehrkörper, *(university)* Dozentenschaft; ~ **techniques** Unterrichtsmethoden.

teahouse Teehaus.

teakettle Tee-, Wasserkessel.

team Arbeitsgemeinschaft, -gruppe, Mannschaft, *(animals)* Gespann, *(shift)* Schicht, Abteilung, Gruppe, *(sport)* Mannschaft;
   hand-picked ~ sorgfältig zusammengestellte Arbeitsgruppe; **management** ~ Führungsgruppe; **scratch** ~ zusammengewürfelte Mannschaft;
   ~ **of canvassers** Werbekolonne; ~ **of workmen** [Arbeits]schicht; ~ *(v.) (let out to subcontractors, sl.)* an Unterlieferanten vergeben;
   ~ **up** *(US)* sich zu einer Gruppe zusammenschließen (zusammentun), zusammenarbeiten;
   to play on the wrong ~ auf der falschen Seite mitwirken;
   ~ **member** Mannschaftsmitglied; ~ **spirit** Gemeinschaftsgeist; ~ **thinking** Gruppendenken; ~ **track** Entladegleis.

teaming Arbeitsteilung.

teammate Mannschafts-, Arbeitskamerad.

teamster Fuhrmann, *(US)* Lastwagenfahrer.

teamwork koordinierte Zusammenarbeit, Gruppenarbeit.

tear Zerreißen, *(spree, US sl.)* Zechgelage;
   at full ~ in vollem Schwung;
   ~ *(v.)* **o. s. away** sich losreißen; ~ **a check (cheque,** *Br.)* **out of the book** Scheck vom Scheckheft abtrennen; ~ **the foundation of a state** Staatsgefüge unterwühlen; ~ **up a letter** Brief zerreißen; ~ **a page out of a book** Buchseite herausreißen;
   to go on a ~ auf den Rummel gehen;
   that ~**s it** *(sl.)* damit ist alles vermasselt;
   ~ **bomb** Tränengasbombe; ~ **gas** Tränengas; ~**-gas grenade** Tränengasgranate; ~ **off** *(ticket)* Abriß; ~**-off calendar** Block-, Abreißkalender; ~**-open wrapper** Aufreißpackung; ~ **sheet** Belegseite, -stück.

tearing | **of will** Zerreißen eines Testaments;
   ~ **strength** Zerreißfestigkeit.

tearjerker *(US coll.)* Schnulze, Schmachtfetzen.

tease Foppen, Stichelei, Necken;
   ~ *(v.)* hänseln, foppen, necken, *(vex)* in den Ohren liegen.

teaser Plagegeist, Quälgeist, *(problem, coll.)* harte Nuß, schwieriges Problem;
   ~ **advertisement** *(US sl.)* Neugier erregende Anzeige, Rätselreklame; ~ **campaign** *(US sl.)* Neckwerbung.

technical handwerksmäßig, technisch, fachlich, fachgemäß, *(immaterial)* unwesentlich, *(legal sense)* regelrecht, *(skilled)* fachlich ausgebildet, *(not stable)* nicht stabil, *(stock exchange)* durch Manipulationen beeinflußt, manipuliert;
   ~ **adviser** technischer Berater, Fachberater; ~ **aid** technische Hilfeleistungen; ⚲ **Assistance Board** *(UNO)* Amt für Technische Hilfe; ~ **assault** regelrechter Angriff; ~ **body** Fachgremium; ~ **bonus** Erfinderprämie; ~ **book** Fachbuch; ~ **bureau** Konstruktionsbüro; ~ **class** Berufsschulklasse; ~ **collaboration** technische Zusammenarbeit; ~ **college** Technische Hochschule; ~ **committee** Fachausschuß; ~ **consultant** technischer Berater; ~ **course** Fachlehrgang; ~ **data** Fachangaben, technische Unterlagen; ~ **department** technische Betriebsabteilung; ~ **details** technische Einzelheiten; ~ **dictionary** Fachwörterbuch; ~ **difficulties** technische Schwierigkeiten; ~ **director** technischer Leiter; ~ **education** Fachausbildung, Ausbildung an einer technischen Hochschule; ~ **estoppel** Unzulässigkeit einer Prozeßeinrede; ~ **expression** Fachausdruck; ~ **feat** technische Errungenschaft; ~ **high school** [etwa] Gewerbeschule; ~ **improvements** technische Verbesserungen; ~ **inducement** Fachzulage; ~ **innovations** technische Neuerungen; ~ **instruction** Fachunterricht; ~ **instructor** Gewerbelehrer; ~ **knowledge** Fachkenntnisse, -wissen, Spezialkenntnisse; ~ **language** Fachterminologie; ~ **library** Fachbücherei; ~ **magazine** Fachzeitschrift, -blatt; ~ **man** Fachmann; ~ **manager** technischer Direktor (Leiter); ~ **market** manipulierter Markt; ~ **meaning** fachliche Bedeutung; ~ **mortgage** formgerechte Hypothek; ~ **offence** Formaldelikt; ~ **office** technisches Büro; ~ **personnel** Fachkräfte; **to quash a judgment on a** ~ **point** Urteil aus formellen Gründen aufheben; ~ **potential** technische Dimensionen; ~ **prerequisites** technische Voraussetzungen; ~ **press** Fachpresse; ~ **price** durch Manipulationen beeinflußter (manipulierter) Preis (Kurs); ~ **profession** technischer Beruf; ~ **progress** technischer (technologischer) Fortschritt; ~ **publication** Fachzeitschrift; ~ **question** verfahrensrechtliche Frage, Verfahrens-

frage; ~ **sales representative** technischer Verkäufer; ~ **school** Berufs-, Fach-, Gewerbeschule, Polytechnikum, *(US)* Jugendstrafanstalt; ~ **service** *(tel.)* Betriebsdienst; ~ **skill** technisches Geschick; ~ **staff** Fachpersonal; ~ **term** Fachausdruck, -wort, technischer Ausdruck; ~ **training** Fachschul-, Berufsausbildung; ~ **translation** Fachübersetzung; ~ **traverse** Formaleinwand, formeller Einwand; ~ **word** Fachwort.

technicalities technische Einzelheiten;
   building ~ bautechnische Probleme; **legal** ~ Förmlichkeiten eines Verfahrens.

technicality technischer Zustand, technische Beschaffenheit, *(technical word)* Fachausdruck.

technician technischer Fachmann, Techniker, *(worker)* Facharbeiter;
   to be an excellent ~ über eine brillante Technik verfügen.

technicolo(u)r Technikolorverfahren.

technics Technik, Ingenieurwissenschaft, *(terms)* technische Ausdrücke, Fachausdrücke.

technique Technik, Methode, technische Ausführung, *(skill)* technisches Geschick, Kunstfertigkeit;
   industrial ~ industrielles Herstellungsverfahren; ~ **of production** Produktionsverfahren.

technochemistry Industriechemie.

technocracy Technokratie.

technocrat Technokrat.

technocratic technokratisch.

technography Beschreibung technischer Fertigkeiten.

technological technologisch, technisch, gewerbekundig;
   ~ **advance** technologischer Fortschritt; ~ **backwardness** technologischer Rückstand; ~ **dictionary** technisches Fachwörterbuch; ~ **forecasting** *(US)* technische Vorschau; ~ **gap** technischer Rückstand, technologische Lücke; ~ **improvements** entwicklungsbedingte Verbesserungen; ~ **obsolescence** *(product)* entwicklungsbedingtes Überholtsein; ~ **progress** technologische Entwicklung, technischer Fortschritt; ~ **revolution** Revolution der Technik; ~ **school** Technikum; ~ **unemployment** technologisch bedingte Arbeitslosigkeit.

technologist Technologe, Gewerbekundiger.

technology Gewerbekunde, Technologie, *(nomenclature)* technische Fachterminologie, *(applied science)* angewandte Naturwissenschaft.

Teddy boy *(Br.)* Halbstarker.

tedious | **lecture** langweilige Vorlesung; ~ **work** ermüdende Arbeit.

tee T-Stück, T-Eisen, *(fig.)* genauer Zeitpunkt;
   to a ~ aufs I-Tüpfelchen, haargenau.

teem *(v.)* reichlich vorhanden sein, wimmeln;
   ~ **with mistakes** von Fehlern strotzen; ~ **with people** von Menschen wimmeln.

teeming, to ~ **with bright ideas** voller hervorragender Ideen stecken;
   ~ **rain** strömender Regen.

teenage Jugendalter;
   ~ **crime** Jugendkriminalität; ~ **offender** jugendlicher Verbrecher.

teenager Jugendlicher.

teens, in one's early als Halbwüchsiger;
   to be in one's ~ in den Jugendjahren sein.

teetering on the edge of disaster kurz vor einer Katastrophe.

teeth, to be armed to the ~ bis an die Zähne bewaffnet sein; **to be fed to the** ~ **with a business** Sache bis oben hin stehen haben; **to get one's** ~ **into s. th.** an einer Sache herumzukauen haben; **to have no** ~ *(fig.)* sich nicht durchsetzen können; **to have one's** ~ **capped** Zähne mit Jacketkronen versehen lassen; **to set s. one's** ~ **on edge** j. total nervös machen; **to take the bit between one's** ~ sich jeder Kontrolle entziehen.

teething troubles Anfangsschwierigkeiten.

teetotal abstinent, *(US coll.)* vollständig, total;
   to be strictly ~ völlig abstinent sein;
   ~ **meeting** Blaukreuzlerversammlung.

teetotalism Abstinenzlertum.

teetotaller Mäßigkeitsapostel, Abstinenzler.

tel quel rate *(Br.)* Telquelkurs.

tele-tourist scheme telefonischer Kundendienst für Touristen.

telearchics *(plane)* [drahtlose] Fernsteuerung.

teleautogram Bildbrief, -telegramm, Faksimile.

teleautograph Bildbriefsender.

teleautomatics [drahtlose] Fernsteuerung.

telebarometer Fernbarometer.

telecamera Kamera mit Teleobjektiv, *(television)* Fernsehkamera.

telecar Telegrammfahrzeug.
telecast *(US)* Fernsehsendung, -übertragung;
  closed-circuit ~ *(US)* betriebliche Fernsehsendung;
  ~ *(v.)* *(US)* im Fernsehen übertragen, Fernsehübertragung bringen, Fernsehprogramm senden.
telecaster Fernsehsprecher, -schauspieler.
teleceiver Fernsehempfänger.
telecine Fernsehfilm.
telecommunication Fernverbindung;
  ~s Fernmeldewesen, -verkehr, -verbindungen, -dienst, -technik;
  ~s business Fernmeldewirtschaft; **~ division** Fernmeldeeinheit; **~ facilities** Fernmeldeanlagen, -einrichtungen; **~ industry** Fernmeldeindustrie; **~ installation** Fernmeldeanlage; **~ network** Fernmeldenetz; **~ satellite** Fernmelde-, Nachrichtensatellit; **~ service** Fernmeldedienst, -verkehr; **~ side** Fernmeldesektor; **~s technology** Fernmeldetechnologie; **~ traffic** Fernmeldeverkehr; **International ~ Treaty** Internationaler Fernmeldevertrag.
telecon *(US)* Telefongespräch.
telecontrol Fernsteuerung, -lenkung.
telecopier Telekopiergerät.
telecourse Fernsehlehrgang.
teledictation unit Telefondiktieranlage.
teledynamic cable Fernsehkabel.
telefilm Fernsehfilm.
telegenic telegen, für Fernsehsendungen besonders geeignet.
telegram Telegramm, Drahtnachricht, Depesche;
  by ~ telegrafisch;
  cash-on-delivery ~ Telegramm zu Lasten des Empfängers; **cipher (code) ~** Chiffretelegramm, verschlüsseltes Telegramm; **collated ~** verglichenes Telegramm; **decorative ~** Schmuckblatt-Telegramm; **deferred ~** gewöhnliches Telegramm; **exchange ~** Kursdepesche; **fast ~** Blitztelegramm; **forwarded ~** nachgesandtes Telegramm; **government ~** Staatstelegramm; **greetings ~** Glückwunschtelegramm; **international ~** Auslandstelegramm; **interurban ~** Telegramm im Fernverkehr; **letter ~** Brieftelegramm; **local ~** Telegramm im Ortsverkehr; **money-order ~** telegrafische Geldüberweisung; **multiple ~** vervielfältigtes Telegramm; **mutilated ~** verstümmeltes Telegramm; **ordinary ~** gewöhnliches Telegramm; **picture ~** Bildtelegramm; **prepaid ~** Telegramm mit bezahlter Rückantwort; **radio ~** Funktelegramm; **repetition-paid ~** Telegramm mit bezahlter Wiederholung, kollationiertes Telegramm; **reply-paid ~** Telegramm mit bezahlter Rückantwort; **~ sent collect** *(US)* vom Empfänger bezahltes Telegramm; **service ~** Diensttelegramm; **unrouted ~** Telegramm ohne Leitvermerk; **urgent ~** dringendes Telegramm; **wireless ~** Funktelegramm; **wordy ~** langatmiges Telegramm;
  ~ to be called for postlagerndes Telegramm; **~ in cipher** verschlüsseltes Telegramm; **~ of condolence** Beileidstelegramm; **~ in plain language** unchiffriertes (offenes) Telegramm; **~ delivered by mail** *(Br.)* Brieftelegramm; **~ with notice of delivery** mit Empfangsbenachrichtigung; **~ addressed poste restante** postlagerndes Telegramm; **~ with repetition** Telegramm mit Wiederholung; **~ by telephone** zugesprochenes Telegramm;
  ~ *(v.)* telegrafieren, telegrafisch benachrichtigen, Telegramm absenden;
  to code a ~ Telegramm chiffrieren; **to deliver a ~** Telegramm aufgeben; **to deliver a ~ by telephone** Telegramm telefonisch aufgeben; **to dispatch (file, US, hand in) a ~** Telegramm aufgeben; **to inquire by ~** telegrafisch anfragen; **to intercept a ~** Telegramm abfangen; **to kill a ~** Telegramm widerrufen; **to recall a ~** Telegramm widerrufen; **to repeat back a ~** Telegramm kollationieren; **to send [off] a ~** Telegramm aufgeben; **to translate a ~** Telegramm dechiffrieren;
  ~ address Telegrammadresse; **~s counter** *(Br.)* Telegrammschalter; **~ form** Telegrammformular; **~ rate** Wort-, Telegrammgebühr; **~ reception** Telegrammannahme.
telegraph Telegraph, *(telegram)* Telegramm;
  page-printing ~ Blattdrucker;
  ~ *(v.)* telegrafieren, telegrafisch benachrichtigen, drahten, depeschieren, *(signal)* signalisieren, Zeichen geben;
  ~ boy Depeschen-, Telegrafenbote; **~ cable** Kabel; **~ clerk** Angestellter des Telegrafenamtes; **~ code** Telegrammschlüssel; **~ form** Depeschen-, Telegrammformular; **~ key** Morsetaste; **~ line** Telegrafenleitung, -linie; **~ lineman** Telegrafenarbeiter; **~ messenger** Telegramm-, Depeschenbote; **~ office** Telegrafenamt, Telegramm[annahme]schalter; **~ operator** Angestellter des Telegrafenamtes; **money ~ order** telegrafische Geldüberweisung; **~ post (pole, Br.)** Telegrafenstange, -mast;

~ repeater Telegrammübertragung; **[commercial] ~ service** Telegrammverkehr [der Wirtschaft]; **~ wire** Telegrafenleitung, -draht; **~ wireman** Telegrafenarbeiter.
telegraphese Telegrammstil.
telegraphic telegrafisch, im Telegrammstil, telegrammartig;
  ~ acceptance Drahtakzept; **~ address** Telegrammadresse, Drahtanschrift; **~ answer** Drahtantwort; **~ brevity** telegrammartige Kürze; **~ charges** Telegrammgebühren; **~ code** Telegrammschlüssel; **~ communication** telegrafische Mitteilung; **~ English** Telegrammsprache; **~ message** telegrafische Mitteilung; **~ money order** telegrafische Überanweisung; **~ news** Drahtbericht; **~ order** Drahtauftrag; **~ remittance** telegrafische Geldüberweisung; **to speak in ~ sentences** im Telegrammstil sprechen; **~ transfer** Telegrammübermittlung, *(money)* telegrafische Auszahlung, Kabelüberweisung, telegrafische Überweisung; **~ transfer rate** Kabelkurs.
telegraphy Telegrafie, telegrafische Übermittlung.
teleimage Fernsehbild.
telemechanics mechanische Fernsteuerung, *(el.)* drahtlose Übertragung elektrischer Energie.
telemeter Entfernungsmesser, *(el.)* Fernmeßgerät.
telemeterograph Fernmeßanlage.
telemetry Fernmessung, Fernmeßtechnik;
  ~ data Fernmeßdaten.
telepathy Gedankenübertragung.
telephone Fernsprecher, Telefon, *(letterhead)* Fernruf;
  by ~ telefonisch, fernmündlich; **connected by ~** mit Telefonanschluß; **on the ~** durch Fernsprecher, telefonisch;
  automatic ~ Selbstanschluß[betrieb]; **desk ~** Tischtelefon; **inter-office ~** Hausanlage; **plug-in ~** umsteckbarer Telefonapparat; **public ~** öffentliche Fernsprechstelle; **coin-operated public ~** öffentlicher Münzfernsprecher; **room ~** *(hotel)* Telefonanschluß auf dem Zimmer; **subscriber's ~** Telefonanschluß; **unlisted ~** *(US)* Geheimanschluß, -nummer; **video ~** Fernsehtelefon; **wall ~** Wandtelefon;
  ~ *(v.)* [an]telefonieren, Ferngespräch führen, fernmündlich sprechen, anrufen, *(install a telephone)* Telefonanschluß einrichten;
  ~ ahead telefonisch anmelden; **~ a message** Mitteilung telefonisch durchgeben; **~ a wire** Telegramm telefonisch durchsagen;
  to answer the ~ Telefonanruf entgegennehmen, Telefon[zentrale] bedienen; **to be on the ~** Telefon haben [besitzen], telefonisch erreichbar sein, [Fernsprech]teilnehmer sein, *(hold the line)* am Apparat sein (bleiben); **to be wanted on the ~** telefonisch verlangt werden; **to call s. o. to the ~** j. an den Apparat rufen; **to come through on the ~** telefonisch durchkommen; **to inform s. o. by ~** j. fernmündlich benachrichtigen; **to inquire by ~** telefonisch anfragen; **to ring s. o. up on the ~** jem. anrufen; **to send a message by ~** telefonische Nachricht übermitteln;
  ~ alphabet Fernsprechalphabet; **~ amplifier** Leitungsverstärker; **automatic ~ answering machine** Fernsprechaufnahmegerät; **~ answering service** Fernsprechauftragsdienst; **~ area** Anschlußbereich; **~ attendant** Fernsprechbedienung; **~ bill** Fernsprechgebührenrechnung, Telefonrechnung; **home ~ bill paid by the office** von der Firma bezahlte private Telefonrechnung; **~ book** Fernsprechbuch, -verzeichnis; **~ booth (box)** Telefonzelle, Fernsprechhäuschen, -kabine, -zelle; **~ box** *(Br.)* Fernsprechzelle; **~ cable** Fernsprech-, Telefonkabel; **~ call** Telefongespräch, -anruf, fernmündlicher Anruf; **conference ~ call** Telefonkonferenz; **long-distance ~ call** *(US)* Ferngespräch; **~ call per unit** Gesprächseinheit; **to take ~ calls** Telefonzentrale bedienen; **~ call box** Fernsprechzelle; **~ channel** Fernsprechkanal; **~ charges** Fernsprech-, Telefongebühren; **~ circuit** Fernsprechleitung; **ten ~ commandments** zehn Gebote fürs Telefonieren; **~ company** Telefongesellschaft; **~ connection (connexion, Br.)** Telefonverbindung, -anschluß, Fernsprechanschluß; **long-distance ~ connection** Fernvermittlung; **to establish ~ connection** Telefongespräch herstellen; **~ conversation** Telefongespräch, fernmündliche Unterhaltung; **tapped ~ conversation** abgehörtes Telefongespräch; **to be cut off in a ~ conversation** in einem Telefongespräch unterbrochen werden; **~ counter** Telefonschalter; **~ digit** Wählernummer; **~ directory** Fernsprech-, Teilnehmerverzeichnis, Telefonbuch; **~ engineer** Fernmeldeingenieur; **~ engineering** Fernsprech-, Fernmeldetechnik; **~ enquiries service** Telefonauskunftsdienst; **~ equipment** Telefoneinrichtungen; **~ exchange** Fernsprechamt, [Fernsprech]vermittlung, Telefonzentrale; **~ expenses** Telefonspesen; **~ extension** Fernsprechnebenstelle, Nebenschluß; **~ facilities** Fernsprechanlagen; **~ fault(s)man** Störungssucher; **~ hookup** Telefonschaltung; **~ index** Telefon-

verzeichnis; ~ **information service** *(US)* Fernsprechauskunfts-, Fernsprechansagedienst; ~ **inquiries** Fernsprechauskunftsdienst; ~ **installation** Telefon-, Fernsprechanlage; ~ **interview** telefonische Befragung; **ship-to-shore ~ interview** Transatlantikinterview; ~ **kiosk** Telefonzelle, Fernsprechautomat, -kabine, -häuschen, öffentlicher Fernsprecher; ~ **lifeline** telefonischer Seelsorgedienst; ~ **line** Telefonleitung, Anschluß; **voice ~ line** gewöhnliche Sprechleitung; **subscriber's ~ line** Telefonanschluß; ~ **link** Telefonverbindung; **to dismantle direct ~ links** unmittelbare Telefonverbindung abschalten; ~ **manner** Verhalten am Telefon; ~ **message** fernmündliche Mitteilung, Fernspruch, telefonische Benachrichtigung; ~ **network** Fernsprechnetz; ~ **number** Fernsprech-, Ruf-, Telefonnummer; ~ **operator** Telefonist, Telefonfräulein, Zentrale; ~ **order** telefonisch aufgegebene Bestellung; **to confirm a ~ order** telefonische Bestellung bestätigen; ~ **privilege** Telefonmöglichkeit; ~ **rates** *(US)* Fernsprechgebühren; **off-peak ~ rates** *(US)* Telefongebühren in der gesprächsarmen Zeit, Mondscheintarif; ~ **receiver** Telefonhörer; ~ **regulations** Bestimmungen über das Führen von Telefongesprächen; ~ **rental** Grundgebühr; ~ **reservation** Festzeitgespräch, reserviertes Telefongespräch; ~ **reservation agent** Festzeitgesprächsvermittler; ~ **service** Fernsprech-, Telefonverkehr, telefonische Seelsorge; **Overseas ~ Service** *(Br.)* Fernsprechauslandsdienst; ~ **set** Telefonapparat; ~ **shares (stocks,** *US)* telefonisch gehandelte Werte, Telefonaktien; ~ **solicitation** telefonische Kundenwerbung, Telefonwerbung; ~ **stamp scheme** Zeittaktsystem für Ferngespräche; ~ **stand** Telefontischchen; ~~**starved** mit zu wenig Fernsprechanschlüssen ausgestattet; ~ **stocks** *(US)* telefonisch gehandelte Werte, Telefonaktien; ~ **subscriber** Fernsprechteilnehmer; ~ **subscription** Grundgebühr; ~ **switchboard** Telefonschrank, -zentrale, Klappenschrank, Telefonvermittlung; ~ **system** Fernsprech-, Telefonnetz; ~ **table** Telefontischchen; ~ **tapping** Abhören von Telefongesprächen; ~ **tax** Telefongebühr; ~ **trade** *(stock exchange)* Telefonhandel, -verkehr; **[local] ~ traffic** [Orts]fernsprechverkehr; ~ **usage** Telefonbenutzung; ~ **user** Fernsprechteilnehmer; ~ **wire** Fernsprechleitung; **to tap the ~ wire** Telefonleitung anzapfen, Ferngespräch mithören.

telephonic fernmündlich, telefonisch, mittels Fernsprecher; ~ **communication** Telefonverbindung; ~ **connection** Fernsprech-, Telefonanschluß.

telephoning Telefon-, Fernsprechverkehr.

telephonist Telefonist, Telefonierender.

telephonograph Bandaufzeichnungsgerät.

telephony Fernsprechwesen; **video ~** Fernsehtelefonie.

telephote fotoelektrische Fernkamera.

telephoto Fernaufnahme, *(telegram)* telegrafisch übermitteltes Bild, Funkbild, Bildtelegramm; ~ **lens** Teleobjektiv.

telephotographic transmission bildtelegrafische Übertragung.

telephotography Bildtelegraphie.

teleprint durch Fernschreiber übermitteln, fernschreiben.

teleprinter Fernschreiber, -drucker; **by ~** fernschreiblich; ~ **channel** Fernschreibkanal; ~ **connection** Fernschreibanschluß; ~ **communication** Fernschreibverkehr; ~ **installation** Fernschreibanlage; ~ **line** Fernschreibleitung; **direct ~ link** direkte Fernschreibverbindung; ~ **network** Fernschreibnetz; ~ **service** Fernschreibdienst; ~ **transmission** fernschriftliche Übermittlung; ~ **unit** Fernschreibstelle; ~ **user** Fernschreibteilnehmer.

teleprocessing Datenfernübertragung, Datenverarbeitung.

teleprompter Fernsehsouffleur, optisches Souffliergerät.

telerecording Fernsehaufzeichnung, -aufnahme.

telescope Fernrohr, Teleskop; ~ *(v.) (cars of a train)* sich ineinanderschieben; ~ **bag** ausziehbare Reisetasche; ~ **sight** *(mil.)* Richt-, Zielfernrohr; ~ **table** Ausziehtisch.

telescopic | **aerial** herausfahrbare Antenne; ~ **brolly** Taschenschirm.

telescreen Fernseh-, Bildschirm.

telescriptor Fernschreiber.

teleseme *(hotel)* Signaltafel.

telestation Fernsehsender, -station.

teletext service Fernsehnachrichtendienst auf Sonderleitungen.

teletype Fernschreiber, *(network)* Fernschreibnetz; **by ~** fernschriftlich; ~ *(v.)* fernschreiben, durch Fernschreiber übermitteln; ~ **channel** Fernschreibkanal; ~ **communication** Fernschreib-

verkehr; ~ **connection** Fernschreibanschluß; ~ **line** Fernschreibleitung; **[direct] ~ link** [direkte] Fernschreibverbindung; ~ **operator** Fernschreiber; ~ **service** Fernschreibdienst, -verkehr; ~ **terminal** Fernschreibanschluß; ~ **unit** Fernschreibstelle; ~ **user** Fernschreibteilnehmer.

teletypesetter Fernsetzmaschine.

teletypesetting Ferndruck.

teletypewriter *(US)* [Funk]fernschreiber.

teleview *(v.)* im Fernsehen sehen, fernsehen, einer Fernsehübertragung beiwohnen.

televiewer Fernsehteilnehmer, -zuschauer.

televise *(v.)* im Fernsehen bringen, durch Bildfunk (im Fernsehen) übertragen, fernsehsenden.

televised speech Fernsehansprache.

television Fernsehen; **on ~** im Fernsehen; **suppressed for ~** fernsehentstört; **tailored for ~** fernsehgerecht; **cable ~** Kabelfernsehen; **closed-circuit ~** innerbetriebliches Fernsehnetz; **coin ~** Münzfernsehen; **colo(u)r ~** Farbfernsehen; **commercial ~** Werbefernsehen; **educational ~** *(US)* Bildungsfernsehen; **independent ~** privates Werbefernsehen; **open-circuit ~** öffentliches Fernsehen; **pay ~** *(US)* Münzfernsehen; **per-channel pay ~** Münzfernsehen; **per program(me) pay ~** Münzfernsehen; **piped ~** Fernsehdrahtfunk; **portable ~** Fernsehkoffergerät, tragbares Fernsehgerät; **transatlantic ~** transatlantischer Fernsehverkehr; **wide-screen ~** großflächiger Bildschirm; **wired ~** Fernsehdrahtfunk, Drahtfernsehen; **to add ~ to its media** Fernsehwerbung miteinbeziehen; **to appear on the ~** im Fernsehen erscheinen; **to broadcast on ~** im Fernsehen übertragen; **to buy a ~ with service for six months** Fernsehgerät mit halbjährigem Kundendienst kaufen; **to crash ~** Fernsehgerät ohne Gebühr benutzen; **to depend mainly on government-controlled ~ for news** Nachrichten weitgehend nur vom staatlich kontrollierten Fernsehen beziehen; **to do not ordinarily watch ~** kein regelmäßiger Fernsehzuschauer sein; **to go on ~** im Fernsehen sprechen (auftreten); **to have ~** Fernsehen haben, Fernsehgerät besitzen; **to interview s. o. on ~** mit jem. ein Fernsehinterview machen; **to look at the ~** fernsehen; **to speak on ~** Fernsehansprache halten; **to switch the ~ off** Fernsehapparat abschalten; **to switch the ~ on** Fernsehapparat einschalten; ~ **ad ban** *(US)* Fernsehwerbeverbot; ~ **ad revenues** *(US)* Fernsehwerbeeinnahmen; ~ **adaption** Fernsehbearbeitung; ~ **addict** Fernsehfanatiker; ~ **address** Fernsehansprache; ~ **advertisement** Werbefernsehen; ~ **advertisement duty** Steuer für Werbefernsehanzeigen; ~ **advertiser** Fernsehwerbegesellschaft, Fernsehwerbefirma; ~ **advertising** Werbefernsehen, Fernsehwerbung; ~ **announcer** Fernsehansager[in], -kommentator; ~ **antenna** Fernsehantenne; ~ **appearance** Fernsehauftritt; **to cut down one's ~ appearance** seine Fernsehauftritte verringern; ~ **audience** Fernsehzuhörerschaft, Fernsehpublikum; ~ **ban** Fernsehverbot; ~ **booking office** Fernsehbuchungsbüro; ~ **broadcast** Fernsehsendung; ~ **broadcaster** Fernsehsender; ~ **broadcasting** Fernsehsendung; ~ **broadcasting circuit** Fernsehleitung; ~ **cabinet** Fernsehtruhe; ~ **camera** Fernsehkamera; **closed-circuit ~ camera** hauseigene Fernsehüberwachungskamera; ~ **cameraman** Fernsehbildberichterstatter; **home ~ cartridge** Fernsehkassette für das Heimkino; ~ **censorship** Fernsehzensur; ~ **channel** Fernsehkanal; ~ **commentator** Fernsehkommentator; ~ **commercial** Fernsehwerbesendung; ~ **commercial time** Fernsehwerbezeit; ~ **company** Fernsehgesellschaft; **commercial ~ company** Werbefernsehgesellschaft; ~ **conference** Fernsehkonferenz; ~ **contract** Fernsehvertrag; **independent ~ contractor** *(Br.)* unabhängige Fernsehproduktionsgesellschaft, kommerzielle Fernsehgesellschaft; ~ **course** Fernsehkurs, Unterrichtskurs im Fernsehen; ~ **coverage** Fernsehberichterstattung; **live ~ coverage** direkte Fernsehübertragung; ~ **crew** Fernsehmannschaft; ~ **critic** Fernsehkritik; ~ **debate** Fernsehdiskussion; ~ **director** *(US)* Fernsehregisseur; ~ **documentary** dokumentarischer Fernsehfilm, Dokumentarbericht im Fernsehen; ~ **engineer** Fernsehtechniker, -ingenieur; ~ **entertainment** Unterhaltungssendung im Fernsehen; ~ **expenses** Fernsehgebühren; ~ **expert** Fernsehexperte; ~ **eye** Fernsehauge; ~ **factory** Fernsehgerätefabrik; ~ **film** Fernsehfilm; ~ **franchise** Fernsehkonzession; **commercial ~ franchise** Werbefernsehlizenz; ~ **frequency** Fernsehfrequenz; ~ **grants** Fernsehzuschüsse; ~ **image** Fernsehbild; ~ **industry** Fernsehindustrie; ~~**industry trade paper** Verbandszeitschrift der Fernsehindustrie; ~ **interests** Fernsehbeteiligungen; ~ **interference** Fernsehstörung; ~ **interview** Fernsehinterview; ~ **interviewer** Fernsehredakteur; **canned ~**

item Fernsehkonserve; ~ **lecture** Fernsehvortrag; ~ **licence** Fernsehgenehmigung; ~ **linkup** Zusammenschluß von Fernsehstationen, von verschiedenen Fernsehstationen gemeinsam ausgestrahlte Sendung; ~ **looker** Fernsehzuschauer; ~ **manufacturer** Fernsehgerätehersteller; ~ **mast** Fernsehantenne; **recorded** ~ **material** Fernsehbandmaterial; ~ **monitor** Fernsehüberwachung; ~ **network** Fernsehsendergruppe, -netz; ~ **news broadcast (bulletin, show)** Tagesschau[sendung]; **cable** ~ **operation** Kabelfernsehbetrieb, -fernsehen; ~ **organization** Fernsehanstalt; ~ **personality** bekannter Fernsehkommentator; ~ **pickup** Fernsehaufnahme; ~ **pickup van** Fernsehaufnahmewagen; ~ **picture** Fernsehbild; ~ **play** Fernsehstück; ~ **press conference** Fernsehkonferenz; ~ **producer** Fernsehregisseur, -filmproduzent; ~ **production** Fernsehinszenierung, -produktion; ~ **program(me)** Fernsehprogramm; **to record a** ~ **program(me) off the air** Fernsehprogramm auf Band aufnehmen; **to watch a** ~ **program(me)** Fernsehprogramm ansehen, fernsehen; ~ **programmer** Fernsehprogrammierer; ~ **ratings** Bewertung von Fernsehsendungen durch das Publikum, Beliebtheitstest; ~ **receiver** Fernsehapparat, Bildempfänger; **colo(u)r-**~ **receiver** Farbfernsehgerät; ~ **receiving licence** Fernsehgenehmigung; ~ **reception** Fernsehempfang; ~ **recordings** Fernsehaufnahmen; ~ **relay station** Fernsehrelaisstation; ~ **rental** Verleih von Fernsehfilmen; ~ **rental company** Fernsehfilmverleihbetrieb; ~ **report** Fernsehansprache; ~ **rights** Fernsehrechte; ~ **schedule** Fernsehprogramm; ~ **screen** Fernsehschirm, -bild; ~ **script** Fernsehmanuskript; ~ **serial** Fernsehserie; ~ **service** Bereitstellung von Fernsehprogrammen; ~ **set** Fernsehapparat, -empfänger, -gerät; **pocket-sized** ~ **set** Fernsehgerät im Westentaschenformat; **portable** ~ **set** Fernsehkoffergerät; **to install a** ~ **set** Fernsehapparat aufstellen; ~**-set accessory** Fernsehzusatzgerät; ~**-set dealer** Fernsehgerätegeschäft; ~**-set manufacture** Produktionsbetrieb für Fernsehgeräte; ~ **short** kurze Fernsehsendung; **prime-time** ~ **show** günstig gelegene Fernsehsendung; **viewable** ~ **show** Fernsehsendung mit Niveau; ~ **special** hochangelegtes Fernsehsonderprogramm, -sonderserie; ~ **spot** Fernsehwerbespot; ~ **spot commercials** kurze Fernsehwerbesendungen; ~ **station** Fernsehstation, -sender; ~ **station owner** Besitzer eines Fernsehsenders; ~ **studio** Fernsehstudio, Aufnahmeraum; **colo(u)r** ~ **system** Farbfernsehsystem; **talkback** ~ **system** Fernsehsprechsystem; ~ **take** Fernsehaufnahme; ~ **tape** Fernsehband; ~ **technique** Fernsehtechnik; ~ **teleimage** Fernsehbild; **prime** ~ **time** vorrangige Fernsehsendezeit; ~ **tower** Fernsehsendeturm; ~ **transmission** Fernsehübertragung; ~ **transmitter** Fernsehsender; ~ **tube** Bildröhre; ~ **viewer** Fernsehzuschauer; ~ **viewing** Fernsehprogrammauswahl; ~ **violence** Darstellung von Gewaltakten im Fernsehen; ~ **watching hour** Fernsehzeit.

televised chat Fernsehplauderei.

televisor Fernsehgerät, -apparat.

telex *(US)* Fernschreiber, *(network)* Fernschreiberteilnehmernetz, Fernschreibverkehr;
by ~ durch Fernschreiber, fernschriftlich;
~ *(v.)* fernschreiben;
to send a ~ Fernschreiben schicken;
~ **call** hergestellte Fernschreibverbindung; ~ **call charge** Fernschreibgebühr; ~ **communication** Fernschreibverkehr; ~ **connection** Fernschreibanschluß; ~ **exchange** Fernschreibvermittlung; ~ **line** Fernschreibleitung; ~ **message** Fernschreiben, Fernschreibnachricht; ~ **number** Fernschreibnummer; ~ **operator** Fernschreiber; ~ **order** Auftrag per Fernschreiben; ~ **rental** Fernschreibgrundgebühr; ~ **service** Fernschreibdienst; ~ **unit** Fernschreibteilnehmer; ~ **user** Fernschreibteilnehmer.

tell *(v.)* berichten, erzählen, *(reveal a secret, coll.)* ausplaudern;
~ **s. th. abroad** etw. herumerzählen; ~ **fortunes from cards** aus den Karten wahrsagen; ~ **it to the marines** *(sl.)* mir kannst du das nicht verkaufen (weismachen); ~ **one's money** *(US)* sein Geld zählen; ~ **one's name** seinen Namen angeben; ~ **the news to everybody in the village** Neuigkeit im ganzen Dorf bekanntmachen; ~ **off s. o.** verpetzen; ~ **off** abzählen, *(mil.)* abkommandieren; ~ **s. o. off** jem. gründlich die Meinung sagen, j. scharf zurechtweisen, jem. einen Anschiß verpassen; ~ **s. o. where to go (get) off** jem. seine geringfügige Bedeutung klarmachen, j. in seine Schranken weisen; ~ **off s. o. for a special duty** j. zu einer Sonderarbeit einteilen; ~ **on s. o.** Spuren bei jem. hinterlassen; ~ **on the economy** sich konjunkturell auswirken; ~ **the plain truth** die reine Wahrheit sagen; ~ **the reasons** Grund angeben; ~ **s. o. a secret** jem. ein Geheimnis anvertrauen; ~ **s. o. to start at once** jem. den sofortigen Aufbruch befehlen; ~ **the tale** *(coll.)* Mitleid zu erregen suchen; ~ **tales about s. o.** j. ins Gerede bringen; ~ **tales out of school** aus der Schule plaudern;

~ **upon** Wirkung erzielen; ~ **the votes** Stimmen zählen; ~ **s. o. what is what** jem. den Kopf zurechtrücken; ~ **the world** felsenfest überzeugt sein.

teller *(bank, US)* Kassierer, Kassen-, Schalterbeamter, *(sl., hit)* Volltreffer, *(informer)* Berichter, *(scrutineer)* Stimmenzähler; **Fifth** ~ *(US)* Staatsbankabrechnung; **paying** ~ erster Kassierer, Kassierer für Auszahlungen; **receiving** ~ Kassierer für Einzahlungen, Beamter am Einzahlungsschalter; ~ **in Parliament** Auszählungsbeamter.

teller's department *(US)* Hauptkasse;
paying ~ Auszahlungskasse; **receiving** ~ Einzahlungskasse.

tellership *(pol.)* Zähleramt, *(US)* Kassiererposten.

telling | effect durchschlagende Wirkung; ~ **speech** beeindruckende Rede.

telstar Fernmeldesatellit.

telltale Zwischenträger, Klatschbase, *(time recorder)* Kontrolluhr.

telly *(Br., coll.)* Fernsehgerät;
~**-familiar face** *(Br.)* aus Fernsehsendungen bekanntes Gesicht.

temper Charakter, Temperament, Naturell, Veranlagung, *(mood)* Stimmung, *(technics)* Zusatz, Beimischung;
in a bad ~ schlecht gelaunt;
~ *(v./i.)* richtigen Härtegrad haben;
~ **justice with mercy** Gnade vor Recht ergehen lassen; ~ **mortar** Mörtel anmachen;
to be in a ~ gereizt sein; **to fly into a** ~ wütend werden; **to keep one's** ~ Ruhe (kühlen Kopf) bewahren; **to show** ~ gereiztes Wesen an den Tag legen.

temperament Gemütsart, Temperament, Naturell.

temperance mäßige Lebensführung, Maßhalten, Mäßigkeit;
~ **drink** alkoholfreies Getränk; ~ **hotel** alkoholfreie Gaststätte; ~ **movement** Abstinenzlerbewegung; ~ **society** Mäßigkeitsverein; ~ **union** Blaues Kreuz, Blaukreuzlerverein.

temperate *(climate)* gemäßigt, milde;
~ **enthusiasm** mäßige Begeisterung; ~ **language** maßvolle Sprache; ~ **zone** gemäßigte Zone.

temperature, inside Zimmertemperatur.

tempo of production Produktionstempo.

temporalities *(law)* zeitliche Güter.

temporality Zeitbedingtheit.

temporarily zeitweilig, vorübergehend, provisorisch;
~ **suspended** zeitweilig außer Kraft.

temporary Zeitbeschäftigter, Angestellter auf Zeit;
~ *(a.)* vorläufig, kommissarisch, einst-, zeitweilig, vorübergehend, provisorisch;
~ **admission** vorübergehende Zulassung, *(customs)* zeitweilig zollfreie Einfuhr; ~ **agreement** Interimsabkommen; ~ **alimony** *(US)* vorläufige Unterhaltsleistung für die Dauer des hierüber anstehenden Prozesses; ~ **annuity** Zeitrente; ~ **appointment** Ernennung auf Widerruf; ~ **arrangement** vorübergehendes Abkommen, Übergangsregelung; ~ **assurance** *(Br.)* abgekürzte Todesfallversicherung, Risikoversicherung; ~ **bonds** vorläufige Obligationen; ~ **bridge** Not-, Behelfsbrücke; ~ **cessation of work** vorübergehende Arbeitsunterbrechung; ~ **chairman** Eröffnungsvorsitzender; ~ **committee** vorläufiger Ausschuß; ~ **contract** befristeter Vertrag; ~ **credit** Zwischenkredit; ~ **denomination** vorläufige Stückelung; ~ **disability** zeitweilige Erwerbsunfähigkeit; ~ **employee** Aushilfskraft, Angestellter auf Zeit; ~ **employer** zeitweiliger Arbeitgeber, *(Br.)* Kurzarbeitgeber; ~ **employment** vorübergehende Erwerbstätigkeit (Beschäftigung), Zwischenbeschäftigung, Kurzarbeit; ~ **employment subsidy** staatliche Unterstützung für die Beschäftigung von Kurzarbeitern, Kurzarbeiterzuschüsse, -geld; ~ **employment subsidy scheme** *(Br.)* Unterstützungsschema für die Zahlung von Kurzarbeiterzuschüssen; ~ **equilibrium price** Ausgleichspreis; ~ **import** Einfuhr im Zollvormerkverfahren; **passed for** ~ **importation** vorübergehend zur Einfuhr zugelassen; ~ **importation papers** Zollpapiere für vorübergehende Einfuhr; ~ **injunction** *(US)* einstweilige Verfügung; ~ **insanity (mental derangement)** vorübergehende Störung der Geistestätigkeit; ~ **investment** Zwischenanlage, *(balance sheet)* Wertpapiere des Umlaufvermögens; ~ **job** Übergangsbeschäftigung; ~ **loan** kurzfristiger Kredit; ~ **lodging** Notquartier, -unterbringung; ~ **measures** vorläufige Maßnahmen; ~ **paper** Notzeitung; ~ **peak** vorläufiger Höchststand; ~ **post (position)** vorübergehende Stellung, Aushilfsstellung; ~ **posting** vorübergehende Einstellung; ~ **postman** Hilfsbriefträger; ~ **provisions** Übergangsbestimmungen; ~ **receipt** vorläufige Empfangsbescheinigung, Zwischenquittung, -schein, Interimsschein; ~ **receiver** vorläufiger Nachlaßverwalter; ~ **relief** vorüberge-

hende Unterstützung; ~ **repairs** provisorische Reparaturen; ~ **scaffolding** Aushilfsgerüst; ~ **staff** Aushilfspersonal, Zeitarbeitskräfte, Angestellte auf Zeit; ~ **statute** befristete Satzung; ~ **suspension** zeitweilige Schließung; ~ **work** Gelegenheitsarbeit.

temporization Zeitgewinn, *(timeserving)* Opportunismus.

temporize *(v.) (contract)* um Zeitgewinn verhandeln, *(yield to the current opinion)* seinen Mantel nach dem Winde hängen, sich opportunistisch verhalten;
~ **between parties** zwischen den Parteien lavieren.

temporizer Opportunist.

temporizing politician Opportunitätspolitiker.

tempt *(v.)* **one's fate** sein Schicksal herausfordern.

temptations | **of easy profit** Versuchungen leichten Verdienstes; ~ **to spend money** Verführung zum Geldausgeben.

tempting offer verlockendes Angebot.

ten | **-percenter** *(sl.)* Theater-, Schriftstelleragent; ~-**strike** *(US)* erfolgreiche Unternehmung, Volltreffer.

tenable *(mil.)* haltbar, *(office)* verliehen;
to be ~ **for ten years** *(office)* für zehn Jahre vergeben werden.

tenacious of one's opinion, to be hartnäckig auf seiner Meinung bestehen.

tenacity of purpose Zielstrebigkeit.

tenancy Pacht[verhältnis], Pachtung, Mietverhältnis, Miete, *(freehold)* [Grund]eigentum, Besitz, *(period)* Pachtdauer;
agricultural ~ landwirtschaftliches Pachtverhältnis; **business** ~ gewerbliches Mietverhältnis; **contractual** ~ vertraglich vereinbartes Mietverhältnis; **controlled** ~ *(US)* Mietverhältnis unter Mieterschutzbestimmungen; **entire** ~ Pachtung in einer Hand, Einzelmietvertrag; **farm** ~ landwirtschaftliche Pachtung; **general** ~ unbefristeter Miet-, Pachtvertrag; **joint** ~ gesamthänderisches Eigentum, Miteigentum, Gesamthandeigentum; **life** ~ lebenslänglicher Nießbrauch [an einem Grundstück]; **month-to-month** ~ sich monatlich verlängerndes Miet-, Pachtverhältnis; **protected** ~ *(Br.)* gesetzlich geschütztes Mietverhältnis, gesetzlicher Räumungsschutz; **several** ~ Einzelmiet-, -pachtverhältnis; **share** ~ in Raten zahlbare Pacht; **statutory** ~ *(Br.)* gesetzlich geschütztes Mietverhältnis, gesetzlicher Räumungsschutz;
~ **in common** Miteigentum nach Bruchteilen, gemeinschaftliche Pachtung; ~ **by the entirety** Gesamthandeigentum [der Ehegatten], Gütergemeinschaft; ~ **for life** lebenslänglicher Nießbrauch an einem Grundstück, Pachtung auf Lebensdauer; ~ **from month to month** monatliche kündbare Mietverträge (Pachtvertrag); ~ **at sufferance** nach Ablauf der Pachtzeit (Mietzeit) jederzeit kündbares Pacht-, Mietverhältnis; ~ **at will** jederzeit kündbares Pacht-, Mietverhältnis; ~ **for years** zeitlich begrenzter Pachtbesitz; ~ **from year to year** jahresweise festgesetztes Mietverhältnis, weiterlaufendes Pachtverhältnis;
to hold a life ~ **of a house** lebenslanges Wohnrecht haben; **to let on an annual agricultural** ~ jahrweise zu landwirtschaftlicher Nutzung verpachten;
~ **agreement** Pacht-, Mietvertrag; ~ **system** Pachtsystem; ~ **year** Pacht-, Mietjahr.

tenant Besitzer, Inhaber, Grundeigentümer, Mieter, Pächter, *(inhabitant)* Insasse, Bewohner;
agricultural ~ landwirtschaftlicher Pächter; **blue-chip** ~ Mieter mit erstklassiger Assiette; **business** ~ gewerblicher Mieter; **cash** ~ *(US)* zur Barzahlung verpflichteter (barzahlender) Pächter; **evicted** ~ exmittierter Mieter; **farm** ~ landwirtschaftlicher Pächter; **game** ~ Jagdpächter; **incoming** ~ neuer Mieter (Pächter); **joint** ~s Miteigentümer, -besitzer, Mitpächter; **land** ~ unmittelbarer Grundstücksbesitzer; **office-building** ~ Mieter eines Bürogebäudes; **outgoing** ~ ausziehender Mieter, weichender Pächter; **permanent** ~ Dauermieter; **prospective** ~ reflektierender Mieter, Mietreflektant; **share** ~ *(US)* Naturalpächter; **sole** ~ alleiniger Mieter, Einzelmieter, -pächter; **statutory** ~ *(Br.)* unter Kündigungsschutz stehender Mieter, Zwangsmieter; **weak** ~ unsicherer Mieter;
landlord and ~ Vermieter und Mieter;
~ **in chief** Kronvasall; ~s **in common** [Grundstücks]eigentümer zu Bruchteilen, Bruchteilseigentümer; ~ **by the courtesy** Witwer mit Nießbrauchrecht am Grundstücksnachlaß der Ehefrau; ~ **of the demesne** Untermieter, -pächter; ~ **of a domain** Domänenpächter; ~ **in dower** Witwe mit einem Pflichtteilsnießbrauch; ~ **in fee simple** unbeschränkter Grundeigentümer; ~ **of the flat above** über uns wohnender Mieter; ~ **for life** Nießbraucher auf Lebenszeit, Nießbrauchbesitzer, Pächter; ~ **by the manner** Pachtbesitzer; ~ **from month to month** monatlich kündbarer Mieter; ~ **in possession** Mieter im Besitz der Mietsa-

che; ~ **in severalty** alleinberechtigter Pächter; **quasi** ~ **at sufferance** gutgläubiger, zur Herausgabe verpflichteter Grundbesitzer, geduldeter Untermieter; ~ **in tail** Grundbesitzer mit Fideikommißbindung, Fideikommißeigentümer; ~ **at will** jederzeit kündbarer Pächter (Mieter); ~ **for years** Pächter auf bestimmte Zeit, Zeitpächter, jährlich kündbarer Mieter; ~ **from year to year** jährlich kündbarer Mieter;
~ *(v.)* gepachtet (gemietet) haben, als Mieter bewohnen, *(lessor)* verpachten, vermieten;
to be a ~ zur Miete wohnen; **to eject a** ~ Mieter zur Räumung zwingen (exmittieren); **to evict a** ~ **for nonpayment of rent** Mieter wegen Mietrückständen exmittieren; **not to get a** ~ **for one's house** keinen Mieter für sein Haus finden; **to let out to** ~s vermieten, verpachten; **to let a farm to a** ~ Hof verpachten; **to protect the** ~ *(Br.)* Mieterschutz gewähren; **to rent one's** ~s **low** seinen Mietern geringe Miete abverlangen; **to turn out a** ~ Mieter exmittieren;
to be ~ed **by a businessman** von einem Geschäftsmann bewohnt werden;
~s' **association** Mieterschutzvereinigung; ~ **farmer** Gutspächter; ~'s **fixtures** Pachtzubehör; ~'s **liability** Mieterschaftspflicht; ~ **list** Mieterliste; ~'s **obligations** Mieterverpflichtungen; ~ **purchase loan** *(US)* Hoferwerbsdarlehen; ~'s **repairs** vom Mieter (Pächter) zu bezahlende Reparaturen; ~ **right** Erstattungsanspruch für Aufwendungen während der Pachtzeit; ~ **righter** Erstattungsberechtigter; ~'s **risk** Mieterhaftung; ~ **scarcity** Mieterknappheit.

tenantable pacht-, mietbar, *(habitable)* bewohnbar, wohnlich;
~ **repair** ordnungsmäßiger Zustand [eines Pachtgrundstückes], *(house)* bewohnbarer (vermietungsfähiger) Zustand.

tenanted by a businessman von einem Geschäftsmann bewohnt.

tenantless unbewohnt, leer, nicht vermietet (verpachtet), unvermietet, leerstehend, unverpachtet.

tenantry gesamte Mieterschaft.

tend Neigung, Tendenz;
~ *(v.)* dazu neigen, Neigung haben, tendieren, Tendenz zeigen, *(be directed)* seine Richtung nehmen, sich richten, streben nach, *(take care)* pflegen, hüten, versorgen, *(serve)* bedienen, aufwarten, sich kümmern;
~ **downwards** fallende Tendenz zeigen; ~ **a flock** Herde hüten; ~ **a machine** Maschine bedienen (in Gang halten); ~ **a patient** Patienten versorgen (pflegen); ~ **to rise** leichte Aufwärtsbewegung erkennen lassen; ~ **a store** Ladenaufsicht haben; ~ **to the success of an enterprise** zum Erfolg eines Unternehmens beitragen; ~ **to undermine morality** zur Untergrabung der Moralbegriffe beitragen, auf eine Unterminierung der Moral hin arbeiten; ~ **upwards** *(prices)* nach oben tendieren.

tendencies of the market Börsenentwicklung, -tendenz.

tendency Vorliebe, Neigung, Hang, Zug, *(economy)* Richtung, Neigung, Tendenz, Strömung, Bewegung, Stimmung, Hinneigung;
bearish (downward) ~ Baissetendenz, Abwärtsbewegung, fallende (rückläufige) Tendenz; **bullish** ~ steigende Tendenz, Haussetendenz; **distinct** ~ ausgeprägte Tendenz; **downward** ~ fallende (rückläufige) Tendenz; **dull** ~ zurückhaltende Stimmung; **falling** ~ Baissetendenz; **firm** ~ feste Tendenz; **general** ~ einheitliche (allgemeine) Tendenz, Grundrichtung; **inflationary** ~ inflationistische Tendenz; **present-day** ~ heutige Tendenz; **price-raising** ~ preissteigernde (kurstreibende) Tendenz, steigende Preistendenz, Preisauftrieb; **rallying** ~ kurserholende Tendenz; **reserved** ~ zurückhaltende Stimmung; **sagging** ~ abschwächende Tendenz; **softening** ~ weichende Tendenz; **unsteady** ~ uneinheitliche Tendenz; **upward** ~ Aufwärtsbewegung [der Kurse], Hochgehen [der Preise], steigende Tendenz; **strong upward** ~ Haussetendenz, -neigung;
~ **to decline** Abschwächungstendenz; ~ **of events** Gang der Ereignisse; ~ **of the money market** Geldmarktentwicklung; ~ **on the stock exchange** Börsenströmung, -tendenz; **stronger** ~ **in prices** Kursbefestigung; **weaker** ~ **in prices** Kursabschwächung; ~ **towards higher prices** Hausseneigung; ~ **for prices to increase** Preis-, Kurssteigerungstendenz; ~ **toward protectionism** protektionistische Strömung;
to have a ~ tendieren; **to show a declining** ~ sich abschwächen; **to show a** ~ **to improve** Aufwärtstendenz erkennen lassen; **to show an irregular (uneven)** ~ uneinheitlich tendieren; **to show a rising** ~ sich festigen.

tendential book Tendenzbuch.

tendentious report tendenziöser Bericht.

tender *(caretaker)* Pfleger, *(estimate of costs)* Kostenanschlag, *(legal* ~*)* Zahlungsmittel, *(of machine)* Maschinenwärter, *(offer)* [Lieferungs]angebot, Offerte, Anerbieten, Antrag,

Submission, *(offer to pay)* Zahlungsangebot, angebotene Geldsumme, *(person who looks after)* Wärter, *(railway)* Begleitwagen, -fahrzeug, Anhänger, Tender, *(ship)* Begleitschiff, Beiboot, Leichter, *(subscription)* Zeichnungsofferte;
by ~ auf dem Submissionswege, durch Ausschreibung;
alternative ~ Alternativangebot; **common ~** gesetzliches Zahlungsmittel; **fluctuating ~** elastisches Angebot; **government ~** staatliche Ausschreibung; **highest ~** Höchstangebot; **lawful (legal,** *Br.***) ~** gesetzliches Zahlungsmittel; **lowest ~** Mindestangebot; **sealed ~** versiegeltes Submissionsangebot; **variable ~** elastisches Angebot; **weekly ~** *(in treasury bills, Br.)* wöchentliche Auktion;
~ of amends Bußeangebot; **~ of bail** Kautionsangebot zwecks Haftverschonung; **~ of delivery** Lieferangebot; **~ of a friendship** Freundschaftsangebot; **~ of goods** Zurverfügungstellung der Ware; **~ of issue** Antrag auf Sachentscheidung; **~ of a loan** Kredit-, Darlehnsofferte; **~ for public loans** Zeichnungsangebot auf öffentliche Anleihen; **~ of money** Rückzahlungsbereitschaft; **~ of payment** Zahlungsangebot; **~ of performance** Leistungsangebot, -andienung; **~ of rent due** Andienung der fälligen Miete; **~ of resignation** Rücktrittsangebot, Entlassungsgesuch; **~ of services** Dienstanerbieten;
~ (v.) (make a ~) [Lieferungs]angebot machen, Lieferung übernehmen, Angebot (Offerte, Anerbieten) machen, andienen, anbieten, offerieren, sich bewerben, *(offer as payment)* als Zahlungsmittel anbieten;
~ the amount of rent Mietschuld zu begleichen anbieten, Miete andienen; **~ one's apologies** seine Entschuldigung vorbringen; **~ an averment in law** Beweis antreten; **~ bail** Kaution zur Haftverschonung anbieten; **~ a bill for discount** Wechsel zur Zahlung einreichen; **~ s. o. a complimentary dinner** zu jds. Ehren ein Essen geben; **~ for the construction of a new motorway** *(Br.)* sich an der Ausschreibung für eine neue Autobahn beteiligen; **~ a contract for supply** Lieferungsvertrag abschließen; **~ for a contract** sich an einer Ausschreibung beteiligen, sich um einen Auftrag bewerben; **~ delivery** Lieferbereitschaft zeigen, Lieferung anbieten; **~ documents** Urkunden vorlegen; **~ evidence** Beweis antreten; **~ to government for a loan** sich um einen Staatskredit bemühen; **~ an issue** Behauptung der Gegenseite bestreiten; **~ for a public loan** Zeichnungsangebot auf eine öffentliche Anleihe abgeben; **~ money in payment of a debt** vernünftiges Angebot zur Schuldenbegleichung machen; **~ an oath** Eid zuschieben; **~ back an oath to s. o.** jem. den Eid zurückschieben; **~ a plea** Einrede erheben; **~ for posting** Paket aufgeben; **~ one's resignation** seine Entlassung einreichen, seinen Rücktritt anbieten; **~ one's services** seine Dienste anbieten; **~ for a supply of goods** sich um einen Liefervertrag bemühen; **~ one's thanks** seinen Dank aussprechen; **~ for work on contract** sich an einer Ausschreibung beteiligen;
to accept the ~ Zuschlag erteilen; **to accept the lowest ~** niedrigstes Angebot annehmen; **to allocate by ~** im Submissionswege vergeben; **to allocate to the lowest ~** an das niedrigste Submissionsangebot vergeben; **to be lawful (legal,** *Br.***) ~** als gesetzliches Zahlungsmittel gelten (Gültigkeit haben) gesetzliches Zahlungsmittel sein; **to call for ~s** *(US)* Ausschreibung veranstalten; **to enclose one's ~** sein Angebot beifügen; **to give out in ~** Submission geben; **to invite ~s for a subscription** Submission ausschreiben; **to invite ~s [for a piece of work]** Ausschreibung veranstalten, Auftrag ausschreiben; **to lodge a ~** Angebot einreichen (abgeben); **to make (put in, send in) a ~** offerieren, Angebot machen, sich um einen Auftrag bewerben; **to make a ~ for a contract** Submissionsangebot machen; **to make a ~ of one's services** seine Dienste anbieten; **to participate in a ~** an einer Ausschreibung teilnehmen; **to place contracts by ~** Aufträge im Submissionswege vergeben; **to put out to ~** ausschreiben, Ausschreibung veranstalten; **to submit ~s** Offerten unterbreiten;
~ (a.) zart, weich, *(mar.)* topplastig, unstabil;
to be ~ of s. th. auf etw. bedacht sein, Rücksicht auf etw. nehmen;
of ~ age im zarten Alter; **~ bills** *(Br.)* Schatzwechsel mit dreimonatiger Laufzeit; **~ care** liebevolle Fürsorge; **to have a ~ conscience** sehr gewissenhaft sein; **~ documents** Submissionsunterlagen; **~ health** schwächliche Gesundheit; **~ heart** mitfühlendes Herz; **~ instructions** Ausschreibungsbestimmungen; **~ offer** *(US)* Übernahmeangebot [an die Aktionäre]; **~ period** Einreichungs-, Bewerbungsfrist; **~ price** Angebots-, Submissionspreis, *(allotment)* Zuteilungskurs; **~ rate** *(public loan, Br.)* Emissionssatz; **to touch s. one's ~ spot** j. an seiner empfindlichen Stelle treffen; **~ subject** heikles (kitzliges) Thema; **~ system** *(Br.)* Angebot mit unbestimmtem Kurs, Tenderverfahren.

tenderee *(US)* Angebotsempfänger, Auftraggeber.
tenderer Angebotsteller, Submittent, Submissionsteilnehmer.
tenderfoot *(US)* Anfänger, *(coll.)* Neuling, Ankömmling.
tenderloin *(US)* zartes Lendenstück, *(New York, sl.)* Verbrecher- und Vergnügungsviertel.
tendering, competitive Ausschreibung.
tenement Wohnhaus, gemietetes Haus, Mietwohnung, *(apartment house, US)* Mietskaserne, Mietshaus, *(labo(u)rer)* Arbeiterwohnung, *(property)* Grundbesitz, Grundstück;
dominant ~ herrschendes Grundstück; **free ~** freier Grundbesitz; **servient ~** dienendes Grundstück;
~ house Mietshaus, -kaserne; **~ lands** Pachtgüter.
tenementization Umbau in ein Mietshaus.
tenementize *(v.)* zum Mietshaus herrichten (umbauen).
tenor *(bill exchange)* Laufzeit, *(copy)* Abschrift, Kopie, *(course)* Fortgang, Verlauf, *(letter, speech)* wesentlicher Inhalt, Gedankengang, *(purport)* Sinn, Inhalt, Wortlaut, Text, Fassung;
of the same ~ gleichlautend, gleichen Inhalts;
~ of a deed genauer Wortlaut einer Urkunde; **~ of a speech** Grundtendenz einer Rede.
tenpence *(Br.)* Zehnpencestück.
tense straff, *(fig.)* gespannt, spannungsgeladen;
to be ~ with expectancy in gespannter Erwartung sein;
~ atmosphere gespannte Atmosphäre; **~ relationship** gespanntes Verhältnis; **~ situation** spannungsgeladene Situation.
tensile drehbar, streckbar;
~ strength Zug-, Dehnfestigkeit.
tension Spannung, *(fig.)* Gespanntheit, gespanntes Verhältnis, nervöse Spannung;
cyclical ~s konjunkturelle Spannungen; **political ~** gespannte politische Lage; **racial ~s** Rassenspannungen; **vapo(u)r ~** Dampfdruck;
to reduce ~ zur Entspannung beitragen;
high-~ battery Anodenbatterie; **high-~ wires** Hochspannungsleitung.
tent Zelt, *(fig.)* Wohnung, Wohnstätte;
~ (v.) in Zelten unterbringen (wohnen), zelten;
to fold up one's ~ sein Zelt abbrechen; **to pitch a ~** Zelt aufschlagen; **to strike a ~** Zelt abbauen; **to withdraw to one's ~** sich von der Öffentlichkeit zurückziehen;
~ bed Feldbett; **~ peg** Zeltpflock, Hering; **~ pole** Zeltstange.
tentacle Fühler;
to stretch out a ~ *(pol.)* Fühler ausstrecken.
tentative zögernd, unentschlossen, versuchsweise, *(provisional)* vorläufig, provisorisch;
~ agreement Vertragsentwurf, vorläufige Abmachung; **~ assent** vorläufige Zusage; **~ balance sheet** vorläufige Bilanz, Bilanzentwurf; **~ budget** vorläufiger Etat; **to come to a ~ conclusion** vorläufige Schlußfolgerung ziehen; **~ draft** Probeentwurf; **~ offer** Verhandlungsangebot; **in a ~ stage** im Versuchsstadium.
tenterhook, to be on ~s aufs höchste gespannt sein, wie auf glühenden Kohlen sitzen; **to keep s. o. on ~s** j. auf die Folter spannen.
tenure Grundbesitz, *(lease)* Besitz[titel] Pacht, Mietkontrakt, *(terms of lease)* Pachtdauer;
communal ~ Gütergemeinschaft; **land ~** Grundstückspacht; **leasehold ~** Pachtbesitz; **life ~** lebenslängliche Anstellung; **multiple ~** gemeinsamer Landbesitz; **permanent ~** unkündbare Stellung; **statutory ~** *(US)* gesetzliche Dienstzeit;
~ of a chair Innehaben eines Lehrstuhls; **~ by the courtesy of England** Nutznießung des Vermögens der verstorbenen Ehefrau; **~ of land** Landpacht; **~ by lease** Pachtbesitz; **~ in office** Amtsführung, Amtsdauer, Dienstzeit; **~ at will** jederzeit kündbarer Pachtbesitz;
~ provision Kündigungsbestimmung.
tenurial relationship Pachtverhältnis.
terce *(Scot.)* Witwenteil, Nießbrauch der Witwe.
tergiversate *(v.)* Ausflüchte gebrauchen, sich herausreden.
tergiversation Ausflucht, Vorwand, Finte, *(shift)* Meinungswechsel.
term Fachausdruck, Wort, Wortlaut, *(appointed day)* Termin, *(condition)* [Vertrags]bedingung, Formel, *(currency)* Laufzeit, *(estate)* Besitzdauer, Gerichtszeit, *(language)* Sprache, Ausdrucksweise, *(law court)* Sitzungsperiode, *(lease)* Miet-, Pachtzeit, *(parl.. US)* Sitzungszeit des Kongresses, Sitzungsperiode, *(quarter, Br.)* Vierteljahresfrist, Quartal, *(rent, Br.)* Quartalstermin, vierteljährlicherzahltag, *(school)* Quartal, *(servants, Br.)* Lohn-, Zahltag, *(space of time granted)* Zahlungsfrist, *(tenure of office, US)* Amtsdauer, -periode, *(time)* Frist, Dauer, Ziel, Zeit, *(university)* Studientrimester;

at ~ zum festgesetzten Termin; **at inclusive** ~**s** zu Pauschalpreisen; **by** ~**s** terminweise; **by the** ~**s of article 2** aufgrund der Bestimmungen von Paragraph 2; **during** ~ während des Semesters; **during his** ~ **of office** in seiner Amtszeit; **for a** ~ **of three years** für die Dauer von drei Jahren; **in** ~**s of** ausgedrückt in, gemessen an, im Bezug auf; **in accordance with the** ~**s** in Übereinstimmung mit den Bedingungen; **in** ~**s of amount** der Höhe nach; **in** ~**s of money** dem Geldwert nach; **in plain** ~**s** unverblümt; **in** ~**s of pounds** in Pfunden ausgedrückt; **in** ~**s of praise** mit lobenden Worten; **in real** ~**s** in reeller Kaufkraft; **in** ~**s of service** an Dienstjahren; **in set** ~**s** festgelegt, -gesetzt; **in** ~**s of approval** beifällig; **in** ~**s of value** wertmäßig; **in** ~**s of volume** mengenmäßig, dem Volumen nach; **on** ~ auf Zeit; **on accommodating** ~**s** zu günstigen Bedingungen; **on bad** ~**s** verfeindet; **on deferred** ~**s** (US) auf Raten (Abzahlung); **on easy** ~**s** unter günstigen Bedingungen; **on equal** ~**s** zu gleichen Bedingungen; **on friendly** ~ in gutem Einvernehmen; **on most moderate** ~**s** bei billigster Berechnung; **on mutual** ~**s** auf Gegenseitigkeit; **on his own** ~**s** zu seinen eigenen Bedingungen; **on reciprocal** ~**s** unter der Bedingung einer Gegenleistung; **on short** ~ auf kurze Frist; **on similar** ~**s** unter ähnlichen Bedingungen; **on strained** ~**s** in gespanntem Verhältnis; **on usual** ~**s** zu den üblichen Bedingungen; **over the long** ~ auf lange Sicht gesehen; **under** ~**s** mit gerichtlichen Auflagen; **under the** ~**s of the clause** nach den Bedingungen dieser Bestimmung; **upon any** ~**s** unter jeder Bedingung;

~**s** (contract) Bestimmungen, Bedingungen, Vertragsformel, (fee) Honorar, (payment) Zahlungsforderungen, Preise, (school) Schulgebühren, (last will) Verfügungen;
~ **agreed upon** vertraglich vereinbarte Frist; **attendant** ~**s** langfristige Verpfändungsbedingungen; **bad** ~**s** gespannte Beziehungen; **best** ~**s** äußerste Bedingungen; **business** ~ Geschäftsausdruck, kaufmännischer Ausdruck; **cash** ~**s** gegen bar; **charge-account** ~**s** Bedingungen für Kundenraten; **commercial** ~ Handelsausdruck, Ausdruck der Handelssprache; **precontractual** ~**s** vorvertragliche Bestimmungen; **conventional** ~**s** übliche Zahlungsfristen; **descriptive** ~ (trademark, US) beschreibende Angabe; **easy** ~**s** (credit) günstige Kreditbedingungen, bequeme Raten, Zahlungserleichterungen; **end-of-month** ~**s** Bedingungen für monatliche Zahlungsweise; **exact** ~ genauer Wortlaut; **expired** ~ abgelaufene Frist; **express** ~**s** ausdrücklich festgelegte Vertragsbedingungen; **extended** ~ (US) verlängerte Strafzeit; **fair** ~**s** annehmbare (angemessene) Bedingungen; **favo(u)rable** ~**s** günstige Bedingungen; **final** ~ äußerster Termin; **financing** ~**s** Finanzierungsbedingungen; **filing** ~ Abgabefrist; **fixed** ~ Frist; **general** ~ (US) vollständige Sitzung des Kongresses, (law court) allgemeine Gerichtszeit; **good** ~**s** gute Beziehungen; **inclusive** ~**s** alles inbegriffen, Inklusivpreis; **implied** ~ mutmaßliche Vertragsbestimmungen; **landed** ~**s** Verkaufspreis einschließlich Fracht- und Entladungskosten, franko Löschung; **legal** ~ juristischer Ausdruck, Rechtsausdruck, -begriff; **local** ~**s** Platzbedingungen; **maximum** ~ Höchststrafe; **minimum** ~ Mindeststrafe; **onerous** ~**s** drückende (erschwerte) Bedingungen; **ordinary** ~ (US) übliche Freiheitsstrafe; **peace** ~**s** Friedensbedingungen; **peremptory** ~ Notfrist; **preferential** ~**s** Vorzugsbedingungen; **presidential** ~ (US) Amtszeit des Präsidenten; **prison** ~ Strafzeit; **reasonable** ~**s** annehmbare Bedingungen, (price) annehmbarer (vernünftiger) Preis; **regular** ~ richterliche Frist; **ruinous** ~**s** mörderische Bedingungen; **satisfactory** ~**s** zufriedenstellende Bedingungen; **scientific** ~ wissenschaftliche Bezeichnung; **special** ~ (US) Verhandlung vor dem Einzelrichter, (criminal proceedings, US) Sonderstrafmaß; **special** ~**s** besondere Bedingungen, Sonderbestimmungen, Sonderbedingungen, (book trade) Partiepreis; **statutory** ~ gesetzlich vorgeschriebene Amtszeit; **strained** ~**s** gespannte Beziehungen, gespanntes Verhältnis; **technical** ~ Fachausdruck, terminus technicus; **trade** ~**s** Wiederverkaufsbestimmungen, handelsübliche Vertragsformen; **trade account** ~**s** Bedingungen für Kundenkonten; **unambiguous** ~**s** präzise Bedingungen;

~ **of acceptance** Annahmefrist, (bill of exchange) Akzeptfrist; ~**s of acceptance** Annahmebedingungen; ~**s of admission** Aufnahme-, Zulassungsbedingungen; ~**s of an agreement** Vertragsbestimmungen; ~**s of amortization** Tilgungsbedingungen; ~ **of apprenticeship** Gesellenzeit; ~**s of an armistice** Waffenstillstandsbedingungen; ~**s of arrangement** Vergleichsbedingungen; ~ **of article** Ausbildungs-, Lehrzeit; ~**s of assignment** Übertragungsbedingungen; ~ **of an award** Inhalt eines Schiedsspruches; ~ **of a bill of exchange** Laufzeit eines Wechsels; ~**s of business** Geschäftsbedingungen; ~**s strictly cash** nur gegen Barzahlung; ~**s strictly net cash** zahlbar sofort ohne Abzug; ~**s**

of collection Einzugsbedingungen; ~**s of composition** Vergleichsvorschläge; ~**s of a concession** Konzessionsbedingungen; ~ **to conclude** (pleading) Schlußfrist für beiderseitiges Parteivorbringen; ~**s of continuation** Verlängerungs-, Prolongationsbedingungen; ~ **of a contract** Laufzeit eines Vertrages, Vertragsdauer; ~**s of a contract** Auftragsbedingungen, Vertragsinhalt; **binding** ~**s of a contract** bindende Vertragsverpflichtungen; ~**s of conveyance** Beförderungsbedingungen; ~ **of copyright** [Urheber]schutzfrist; ~ **of court** (US) Sitzungsperiode eines Gerichts; ~ **of a credit** Laufzeit eines Kredits; ~**s of credit** Akkreditivbedingungen; ~ **for deliberating** Ausschlußfrist des Erben, (heir) Ausschlagungsfrist; ~ **for delivery** Lieferfrist, -termin; ~**s of delivery** Liefer-, Bezugsbedingungen; ~ **of discount** Diskonttag; ~**s are for discussion** (ad) Bedingungen bleiben auszuhandeln; ~**s of employment** Arbeitsbedingungen; ~ **for examination** Examenssemester; ~**s for export** Exportbedingungen; ~**s of financing** Finanzierungsbedingungen; ~**s of freight** Frachtkonditionen; ~ **of gold** Goldeinheiten; ~ **in gross** Zeitpacht; ~ **of guarantee** Garantiefrist; ~**s of guarantee** Garantiebestimmungen; ~**s of hire** Mietbedingungen; **long** ~ **of imprisonment** längere Gefängnisstrafe (Haftdauer); ~**s attendant on the inheritance** langfristige Verpfändungsbedingungen; ~ **of an insurance** Versicherungsdauer; ~**s of interest** Zinskonditionen; ~ **of an issue** Emissionsbedingungen; ~**s and conditions of an issue** Emissionsmodalitäten; ~ **of lease** Miet-, Pachtdauer; ~**s of a lease** Pachtbedingungen; ~ **of a licence** Lizenzdauer; ~**s of a licence** Lizenzbestimmungen; ~ **of life** Lebenszeit, -dauer; ~ **of limitation** Verjährungsfrist; ~ **of a loan** Laufzeit eines Darlehns, Anleihelaufzeit; ~**s of a loan** Darlehns-, Anleihebedingungen, Darlehnsbestimmungen, Anleiheausstattung; ~ **of notice** Kündigungsfrist; ~ **of office** Wahlperiode, Amtsdauer, -zeit; ~**s of partnership** Gesellschaftsvertrag; ~ **of a patent** Schutzdauer eines Patents, Schutzfrist, Patentdauer; ~ **of payment** Zahlungsfrist, -termin; ~**s of payment** Zahlungsbedingungen, -weise, (foreign trade) Zahlungsrelationen; ~**s of pledge** Verpfändungsbestimmungen; ~**s of policy** Versicherungsbedingungen; ~ **of possession** Besitzdauer; ~ **of preclusion** Ausschlußfrist; ~ **of probation** Bewährungsfrist; ~**s of probation** Bewährungsauflagen; ~**s of promotion** Beförderungsbestimmungen; ~**s of redemption** Rückzahlungs-, Tilgungsbestimmungen; ~**s of reference** Richt-, Leitsätze, Richtlinien, (committee) Aufgabengebiet, -bereich; ~**s of renewal** Erneuerungsbedingungen; ~**s of repayment** Rückzahlungsbedingungen; ~ **of sale** Verkaufsziel; ~**s of sale** Verkaufsbedingungen; ~**s inclusive of service** Preise einschließlich Bedienung; ~**s of settlement** Vergleichsbedingungen; ~ **of subscription** Bezugsfrist; ~**s of subscription** Zeichnungsbedingungen; ~**s of supply** Bezugsbedingungen; ~**s of surrender** Kapitulations-, Übergabebedingungen; ~**s of tenancy** Pacht-, Mietbedingungen; ~**s of tender** Ausschreibungsbestimmungen, Submissionsbedingungen; ~**s of termination** Kündigungsbedingungen; ~**s of trade** Meßzahl für Austauschrelationen, Austauschverhältnis, Außenhandelsmeßzahl; ~**s to the trade** Wiederverkaufspreis; ~ **of validity** Gültigkeitsdauer; ~**s under which a ship is chartered** Charterbedingungen; ~**s of a will** Testamentsbestimmungen; ~ **for years** Zeitpacht; ~ **of years** (Br.) zeitlich begrenztes Grundstücksrecht; ~ **of years absolute** (Br.) Erbpacht;

~ (v.) **o. s. professor** sich Professor nennen;
to accept the ~**s** Bedingungen annehmen; **to acquiesce in the** ~**s** den Bedingungen stillschweigend zustimmen; **to adhere to a** ~ Zahlungsfrist einhalten; **to adhere to** ~**s** Bedingungen einhalten; **to be for a** ~ **of 15 years** (loan) auf 15 Jahre zur Verfügung gestellt werden, fünfzehnjährige Laufzeit haben; **to be engaged for a** ~ **of three years** dreijährige feste Anstellung erhalten; **to be on familiar** ~**s with s. o.** auf vertrautem Fuße mit jem. stehen; **to be in the following** ~**s** folgendermaßen lauten; **to be on friendly** ~**s with s. o.** mit jem. befreundet sein; **to be on good** ~**s** auf gutem Fuße stehen, gute Beziehungen haben; **to be outside the** ~**s of s. one's reference** außerhalb von jds. Befugnissen liegen; **to be relieved of the** ~**s of the subpoena** von der Vorladungspflicht entbunden sein; **not to be on speaking** ~**s with s. o.** mit jem. nicht auf Gesprächsfuß stehen; **to bring s. o. to** ~**s** j. zur Annahme von Bedingungen überreden; **to buy s. th. on easy** ~**s** zu erleichterten Zahlungsbedingungen kaufen, (erwerben); **to come to** ~**s** sich vergleichen (einigen) Abkommen treffen, Vergleich schließen, handelseinig werden, paktieren, sich [mit seinen Gläubigern] auseinandersetzen; **to come to** ~**s of a composition** in Vergleichsverhandlungen stehen; **to come to** ~**s with one's creditors** Vergleich mit seinen Gläubigern [ab]schließen; **to come within the** ~**s of a contract** unter die

Vertragsbestimmungen fallen; **to come to ~s with a difficult situation** schwierige Situation meistern; **to comply with a ~** Zahlungsfrist einhalten; **to comply with the ~s** den Bestimmungen entsprechen; **to dictate ~s to s. o.** jem. Bedingungen auferlegen; **to elect to a third ~** für eine dritte Amtsperiode wählen; **to enter one's name for the ~** sich immatrikulieren lassen; **to exceed the ~ of delivery** Lieferfrist überschreiten; **to extend the ~** Zahlungsfrist verlängern; **to facilitate ~s of payment** Zahlungsbedingungen erleichtern, Zahlungserleichterungen gewähren; **to give s. o. special ~s** jem. einen Sonderpreis machen; **to have no right to ~ o. s. a professor** sich zu Unrecht als Professor ausgeben; **to hold ~s with s. o.** gewisses Übereinkommen jem. gegenüber aufrechterhalten; **to inquire about ~s for a stay at a hotel** Zimmerpreise in einem Hotel erfragen; **to keep ~s** Jura studieren; **to keep a ~ at an inn of court** juristische Vorlesung besuchen; **to keep one's ~s** *(university)* Pflichtvorlesungen belegen; **to keep to the ~s of the agreement** der Abrede gemäß handeln; **to lose a ~** Termin versäumen; **to make ~s** handelseinig werden; **to make ~s with s. o.** Einigung mit jem. erzielen; **to make (name) one's ~s** seine Bedingungen nennen; **to make good ~s with s. o.** jem. vorteilhafte Bedingungen gewähren; **to meet s. o. on equal ~s** jem. als Gleichberechtigter gegenübertreten; **to negotiate ~s of peace** Friedensbedingungen aushandeln; **to observe a ~ of notice** Kündigungsfrist einhalten; **to owe a ~ of rent** Vierteljahresmiete schulden; **to postpone a ~** Termin aussetzen; **to refer to s. one's work in ~s of high praise** sich äußerst lobend über jds. Arbeit aussprechen; **to run for a third ~** sich für eine dritte Wahlperiode zur Verfügung stellen; **to set a ~** Frist setzen, Termin festsetzen; **to settle the ~s of a contract** Vertragsbedingungen festlegen; **to shorten a ~** Frist verkürzen; **to state ~s** Bedingungen nennen; **~s and Conditions of Employment Act** *(Br.)* Gesetz zur Regelung von Beschäftigungsbedingungen; **~ assurance** *(Br.)* abgekürzte Todesfall, Risiko-, Kurzversicherung; **~ bonds** gleichzeitig fällig werdende Schuldverschreibungen; **short-~ borrowing** kurzfristige Geldaufnahme; **~ day** festgesetzter Tag, Fälligkeits-, Zahltag, Termin; **~ deposits** Termineinlagen, langfristig angelegte Spargelder; **end-of-~ examination** Zwischen-, Semesterprüfung; **~ fee** *(Br.)* Prozeßgebühr; **~ file** Lieferkartei; **~ insurance** Kurz-, Risikolebensversicherung, Versicherung auf Zeit; **renewable ~ insurance** Risikolebensversicherung mit Verlängerungsmöglichkeit ohne ärztliche Untersuchung; **long- (short)- ~ loan** lang(kurz)fristiges Darlehn; **long-~ movements of capital** kompensatorische (langfristige) Kapitalbewegungen; **~ paper** *(US)* Seminararbeit; **policy** Zeitpolice; **~ settlement** *(stock exchange)* Vierteljahresabrechnung; **long-~ transaction** langfristige Finanztransaktion.

termer Nutznießer auf Zeit.

terminability Befristung, zeitliche Begrenzung.

terminable [zeitlich] begrenzt, *(redeemable)* kündbar, auflösbar, *(repayable)* rückzahlbar, *(timed)* befristet;
~ **at pleasure** jederzeit kündbar;
~ **annuity** *(Br.)* Zeitrente, abgekürzte (befristete) Rente; ~ **association** kündbares Produktionskartell; ~ **contract** kündbarer Vertrag; ~ **mortgage** Amortisationshypothek; ~ **property** zeitlich gebundener Besitz.

terminal *(airport)* Flughafenabfertigungsgebäude, *(charge, Br.)* Zustellgebühr, *(data processing)* Endgerät, Terminal, *(el.)* Anschlußklemme, Endstecker, *(railroad, US)* Endbahnhof, End-, Kopfstation, *(shipping business)* Verteilerstelle, *(university)* Semesterprüfung;
air ~ Flugbahnhof, -abfertigungsgebäude; **bus ~** Autobusstation, -bahnhof; **rail and water ~** Umschlagplatz;
~ *(a.)* termingemäß, -mäßig, -weise;
~ **account** Grenzkonto; ~ **accounts** Schlußrechnung; ~ **aerodrome** Zielflugplatz; ~ **area** Flugplatzgelände; ~ **bonds** *(US)* Eisenbahnobligationen zur Finanzierung eines Bahnhofs; ~ **bonus** Abschlußvergütung, *(life insurance)* Schlußvergütung; ~ **building** Abfertigungs-, Flughafengebäude; ~ **charges** *(freight)* Zustellgebühr; ~ **cooperative commission agency** *(US)* Absatzgenossenschaft auf Provisionsbasis; ~ **costs** End-, Grenzkosten; ~ **course** Abschlußkursus; ~ **date** Frist, Termin; ~ **decision** *(statistics)* Endentscheidung; ~ **design** Flughafenplanung; ~ **examination** Abgangs-, Abschlußprüfung; ~ **facilities** *(railway)* Kopfstationanlagen; ~ **forecast** *(weather)* Flugplatzvorhersage; ~ **job** Beruf ohne Aufstiegsmöglichkeiten; ~ **leave** noch zustehender Urlaub, Resturlaub; ~ **leave pay** Entlassungsgeld, Abschlußzahlung an ausgediente Soldaten; ~ **loss** Abschlußverlust; ~ **market** Schlußbörse, *(products, Br.)* Terminmarkt, Produktenbörse; ~ **payment** *(US)* Schlußzah-

lung, letzte Ratenzahlung; ~ **price** *(Br.)* Preis für künftige Lieferung; ~ **property** Besitz auf Zeit; ~ **quantity** Begriffsumfang; ~ **reserve** *(life insurance)* Prämienreserve zum Jahresschluß; ~ **stage** Endstadium; ~ **[railroad] station** Sack-, Endstation, Kopfbahnhof; ~ **subscription** Grenzsicherungsbetrag; ~ **value** Endwert; ~ **velocity** Endgeschwindigkeit; ~ **wage** *(US)* Entlassungsgeld, -abfindung; ~ **ward** *(hospital)* Sterbepfleger.

terminally semesterweise.

terminate *(v.)* zum Abschluß bringen, beenden, zu Ende führen, abschließen, *(set spatial limit)* [räumlich] begrenzen, *(meeting)* enden, *(give notice)* kündigen;
~ **an agency** Vertretungsverhältnis beenden; ~ **an agreement at any time without notice** Vereinbarung jederzeit fristlos kündigen können; ~ **a contract** Vertragsverhältnis beenden; ~ **a contract by (without) notice** Vertrag [nicht] fristgemäß kündigen; ~ **a controversy** Streit beenden; ~ **a convention** Abkommen kündigen; ~ **s. one's employment** jem. kündigen; ~ **employment without notice** Arbeitsverhältnis fristlos kündigen; ~ **a lease** Mietvertrag (Pachtverhältnis) kündigen; ~ **negotiations** Verhandlungen abschließen;
~ *(a.)* begrenzt.

terminated power of attorney erloschene Vollmacht.

terminating building society *(Br.)* Baugenossenschaft.

termination Ende, Beendigung, Aufhören, Abschluß, Ablauf, Erlöschen, *(notice)* Kündigung;
employment ~ Beendigung des Dienst-, Arbeitsverhältnisses; **satisfactory ~** befriedigender Ausgang; **summary ~** fristlose Kündigung;
~ **of agency** Beendigung eines Vertretungsverhältnisses; ~ **by agreement** einverständliche Vertragsbeendigung; ~ **of an authority** Erlöschen einer Vollmacht; ~ **of a business** Geschäftsaufgabe; ~ **of a contract** Kündigung des Vertragsverhältnisses, Vertragsauflösung; ~ **of a convention** Außerkraftsetzung eines Abkommens; ~ **of the debate** Beendigung der Debatte, Schluß der Diskussion; ~ **of employment** Beendigung des Dienstverhältnisses; ~ **by frustration** Vertragsbeendigung wegen Fortfalls der Geschäftsgrundlagen (objektiver Unmöglichkeit); ~ **of lease** Beendigung eines Mietverhältnisses (Pachtverhältnisses); ~ **of membership** Erlöschen der Mitgliedschaft ~ **by notice** fristgemäße Kündigung; ~ **without notice** fristlose Kündigung; ~ **of offer** Angebotsbegrenzung; ~ **of a power of attorney** Erlöschen einer Vollmacht; ~ **of a speech** Ende einer Rede;
to put a ~ to s. th. einer Sache ein Ende bereiten;
~ **clause** Bestimmung über die Vertragsdauer; ~ **date** Verfalltag; ~ **requirements** *(pension plan)* Auflösungsvoraussetzungen.

terminological terminologisch;
~ **inexactitude** terminologische Ungenauigkeit.

terminology Terminologie, Fachsprache.

terminus Endpunkt, Ende, Ziel, *(boundary stone)* Grenzstein, -zeichen, *(railway, Br.)* Kopfbahnhof, -station, Sack-, Endbahnhof;
~ **hotel** Eisenbahnhotel, *(air terminal)* Flughafenhotel; ~ **station** Flughafenbahnhof.

termly semester-, quartalsweise.

termtime Schul-, Semesterzeit.

terra incognita *(lat.)* unerforschtes Gebiet.

terrace [Garten]terrasse, Geländestufe, *(houses, Br.)* Häuserreihe an erhöhter Straße, *(strip, US, local)* Grünanlage, Rasenstreifen;
irrigation ~s Bewässerungsgelände;
~ *(a.)* terrassenförmig;
~ *(v.)* terrassenförmig anlegen.

terraced house *(Br.)* Reihenhaus.

terrain *(mil.)* Gelände, Terrain;
difficult ~ for heavy armo(u)red vehicles für stark gepanzerte Fahrzeuge schwer passierbares Gelände.

terre-tenant unmittelbarer Grundbesitzer.

terrestrial Erdbewohner, Erdenbürger;
~ *(a.)* irdisch, weltlich;
~ **globe** Erdball; ~ **interests** weltliche Interessen.

territorial *(mil., Br.)* Landwehrmann;
~**s** *(Br.)* Territorialtruppen;
~ *(a.)* territorial, inländisch;
~ **air space** Lufthoheitsraum; ~ **allocation** Marktaufteilung; ~ **application** örtlicher (regionaler) Geltungsbereich; ~ **Army** *(Br.)* Landwehr, Territorialarmee; ~ **bonds** *(US)* von Territorien ausgegebene Obligationen; ~ **change** Gebietsveränderung; ~ **claim** territorialer Gebietsanspruch, Grenzforderung;

to put forward ~ claims Gebietsansprüche geltend machen; **~ courts** *(US)* Gerichte innerhalb der Vereinigten Staaten; **~ division of labo(u)r** industrielle Arbeitsaufteilung; **~ edition** Bezirks-, Regionalausgabe; **~ expansion** territoriale Ausdehnung, Gebietserweiterung, -vergrößerung; **~ gains** *(mil.)* Geländegewinn; **~ government** Territorialregierung; **~ guarantee** Gebietsgarantie; **~ integrity** Unversehrtheit des Staatsgebiets; **~ jurisdiction** Gebietshoheit, örtliche Zuständigkeit, Territorialgerichtsbarkeit; **~ law** *(US)* innerstaatliches Recht; **~ limits** Territorialgrenzen; **~ loss** Gebietsverlust; **~ owner** Grundeigentümer; **~ principle** Territorialitätsprinzip; **~ property** Staatshoheitsgebiet, -territorium, Territorialgebiet; **~ rating** differenzierte Tariffestsetzung nach Gebieten, Gebietstarif; **~ restraint** regional beschränktes Wettbewerbsverbot; **~ restriction** *(cartel law)* Gebietsbeschränkungen, regionale Beschränkungen; **~ right** Territorialrecht; **~ sea** Küstenmeer, Hoheitsgewässer; **~ sovereignty** Gebiets-, Territorialhoheit; **to cement the ~ status** Staatsgrenzen zementieren; **~ system** Territorialsystem; **~ waters** Binnen-, Territorial-, Hoheitsgewässer.

territoriality Status eines Territoriums, Territorialität.

territorialize *(v.)* durch Gebietserwerb vergrößern.

territories, to allocate Märkte aufteilen.

territory Gebiet, Territorium, Landschaft, Region, Landesgebiet, *(fig.)* Bereich, Gebiet, *(law)* Geltungsbereich, *(salesman)* Reisegebiet, Vertreterbezirk, *(sovereignty)* Hoheits-, Staatsgebiet;
in British ~ auf britischem Gebiet;
associated overseas ~ *(EC)* assoziiertes überseeisches Gebiet; **ceded ~** abgetretenes Gebiet; **~ covered** Geltungsbereich; **customs ~** Zollgebiet; **hostile ~** Feindgebiet; **mandated ~** Mandatsgebiet; **metropolitan ~** Einzugsgebiet; **national ~** Staatsgebiet; **neutral ~** neutrales Hoheitsgebiet; **nonself-governing ~** nichtautonomes Gebiet; **protected ~** Protektorat; **sales ~** Absatzgebiet, *(salesman)* Vertreter-, Verkaufsbezirk; **scheduled ~** *(Br.)* zum Sterlingblock gehörendes Gebiet; **self-governing ~** autonomes Gebiet; **specified ~** abgegrenzter Bezirk; **trust ~** Gebiet unter Treuhandverwaltung; **unchartered ~** unerforschtes Gebiet; **United States ~** Hoheitsgebiet der Vereinigten Staaten von Nordamerika;
~ of a judge örtlicher Zuständigkeitsbereich eines Richters; **~ of a state** Staatsgebiet;
~ subject to plebiscite Abstimmungsgebiet;
to cede a ~ Gebiet abtreten; **to enter a ~** in ein Gebiet einmarschieren; **to fly over a ~** Gebiet überfliegen; **to travel over a large ~** *(salesman)* großen Vertreterbezirk haben; **to work one's ~ intensively** seinen Vertreterbezirk gründlich bearbeiten; **~ assignment** Gebietsaufteilung.

terror Terror, Schreckensherrschaft;
to spread ~ Terror hervorrufen; **to suppress ~** Terror unterdrücken;
~ attack Terrorangriff; **~ campaign** Terroraktion; **~ raid** Terrorangriff.

terrorism Gewaltherrschaft, Terrorisierung;
brutal urban guerilla-style ~ stadtguerilla-ähnlicher brutaler Terrorismus.

terrorist Terrorist, *(pol.)* Schwarzseher, Miesmacher;
~ *(a.)* terroristisch;
~ act Terrorakt; **~ action** Terroraktion; **~ band** Terrorbande; **~ group** Terroristengruppe; **~ hideout** Unterschlupf für Terroristen; **~ organization** Terrororganisation; **~ raid** Terroristenangriff; **~ suspect** verdächtiger Terrorist; **~ violence** terroristische Gewaltakte.

terroristic threats *(US)* terroristische Drohungen, Terrordrohungen.

terrorization Terrorisierung, Einschüchterung.

terrorize *(v.)* terrorisieren, Schreckensherrschaft einführen.

terse style knapper Stil.

tertiary|liquidity liquide Mittel dritter Ordnung; **~ risk** *(EC)* Investitionsverfahren mit geringem Risiko.

tessalated pavement Mosaikfußboden.

test *(chem.)* Analyse, *(criterion)* Prüfungsmaßstab, kritischer Prüfstein, *(examination)* Prüfung, Klausur, *(fig.)* Probe, Prüfung, *(method)* Testverfahren, Prüfungsmittel, -verfahren, *(paper)* Examensaufgabe, *(refinery)* Probebohrung, *(sample)* Stichprobe, *(school)* Eignungs-, Leistungsprüfung, *(trial)* Versuch, Probe, Test, Prüfung, Untersuchung, Leistungsprüfung, Bewährungsprobe;
by means of a ~ mittels Stichproben;
acceptance ~ Abnahmeprüfung; **advertising ~** Versuchswerbung; **aptitude ~** Eignungsprüfung; **audit ~** stichprobenartige Prüfung; **blood ~** Blutprobe, *(paternity test)* Blutgruppenun-

tersuchung; **check (control) ~** Gegenprobe; **consumer ~** Warentest; **crucial ~** Feuerprobe; **distribution-free ~** nichtparametrischer Test; **driving ~** *(Br.)* Fahrprüfung; **employment ~** [betriebliche] Eignungsprüfung; **endurance ~** Zerreißprobe; **in-store ~** Test am Verkaufspunkt; **intelligence ~** Intelligenzprüfung; **job ~** berufliche Eignungsprüfung; **launching ~** Testkampagne; **materials ~** Materialprobe; **means ~** Bedürftigungsnachweis; **mental ~** psychologischer Test; **optimum ~** bestmöglicher Test; **oral ~** mündliche Prüfung; **personnel ~** Prüfung des Betriebspersonals; **pilot ~** Probeuntersuchung; **product ~** Warentest; **qualitative ~** qualitative Analyse; **sales ~** Verkaufsschulung; **screening ~** Eignungsprüfung; **severe ~** strenge Prüfung; **short-term ~** kurzfristiger Versuch; **on-side ~** Prüfung am Aufstellungsort; **special ~** Sonderprüfung; **trade ~** Prüfung auf der Handelsschule; **tensile ~** Zerreißprobe; **valid ~** zuverlässiger Test; **weighing ~** Gewichtskontrolle;
~ of apprentice Gesellenprüfung; **~ of aptitude (ability)** Eignungsprüfung; **~ of competence to drive** Fahrtauglichkeitsprüfung; **~ on site** Prüfung am Aufstellungsort;
~ *(v.)* prüfen, versuchen, erproben, einem Test unterziehen, testen, untersuchen;
~ a coin for weight Münze auf das vorschriftmäßige Gewicht prüfen; **~ a line** Telefonleitung überprüfen; **~ out a scheme** Plan ausprobieren; **~ s. one's power of endurance** jds. Geduld auf die Probe stellen;
to conduct a ~ Versuch durchführen; **to make a ~** Stichprobe machen; **to pass a ~** sich mit Erfolg einem Test unterziehen; **to put s. o. to the ~** j. auf die Probe stellen; **to put to the ~ [of experience]** praktisch erproben; **to stand the ~ [Bewährungs-] probe** bestehen, sich bewähren; **to stand a severe ~** durch eine harte Schule gehen; **to stand the ~ of time** *(method)* sich zu allen Zeiten bewährt haben; **to take a driving ~** *(Br.)* Fahrprüfung machen; **to undergo a ~** einer Prüfung unterworfen werden;
~ action Probe-, Musterprozeß; **~ arrangement** Testvereinbarung; **~ audit** stichprobenweise Prüfung; **~ ballot** Probeabstimmung; **~ Ban Treaty** *(atomic weapons)* Atomsperrvertrag; **~ bench** Prüfstand; **~ blank** *(school)* Prüfungsvordruck; **~ bore** Probebohrung; **~ campaign** Testkampagne, *(advertising)* Teststreuung, Versuchsfeld [für Werbezwecke]; **~ car** Versuchswagen, -modell; **~ case** Schulfall, Schul-, Musterbeispiel, *(law)* Grundsatzurteil, *(pol.)* Präzedenzfall; **to fight a ~ case in court** Präzedenzfall vor das Gericht bringen; **~ certificate** Prüfungsprotokoll; **obligatory ~ certificate** *(car)* [etwa] TÜV-Bescheinigung, Bescheinigung des technischen Überwachungsvereins; **~ check** Kontrollprüfung; **~ clerk** Prüfungsbeamter; **~ comparison** Stichprobenvergleich; **~ conditions** Versuchsbedingungen; **~ drive** Probefahrt; **~-drive** *(v.)* Probefahrt unternehmen; **~ facility** Prüfanlage; **~ flight (flying)** Probe-, Versuchsflug; **~-fly** *(v.)* **an aircraft** Maschine einfliegen; **~ market** *(advertising)* Versuchsmarkt; **~-market** *(v.)* versuchsweise auf den Markt bringen; **~ note** Prüfungsvermerk; **~ number** Kontrollnummer, Stichzahl [im Telegrammverkehr]; **~ oath** Treueid; **~ object** Prüf-, Versuchsobjekt, Probestück; **~ paper** Klausurarbeit, *(Br.)* Zulassungsprüfung (schriftliche Prüfungsaufgabe), *(handwriting, US)* Dokument zum Handschriftvergleich, Prüfungsformular, *(jury)* Beweisurkunde; **~ pattern** *(television)* Einstellbild; **~ performance** Prüfungsleistung; **~ piece** Probestück; **~ pilot** Versuchs-, Einflieger, Testpilot; **~ print** Probesatz; **~ result** Versuchs-, Prüfungsergebnis; **~ run** Probe, Probefahrt, -lauf; **to be ~-run** einer Probefahrt unterzogen werden; **~ score** Prüfungsergebnis; **~ series** Versuchsserie; **~ shipment** Probeverzollung; **~ site** Versuchsgelände; **~ specimen** Probe, Muster; **~ town** *(advertising)* Testort; **~ track** Teststrecke; **~ tube** Reagenzglas; **~-tube baby** Retortenkind; **~ weighing** *(customs)* Nachwiegen, Gewichtskontrolle; **~ word** Erkennungswort, Stichwort.

testable prüfbar, *(law)* testierfähig.

testacy Testierfähigkeit.

testament Testament, letzter Wille, letztwillige Verfügung;
closed ~ notariell beglaubigtes Testament; **holographic ~** eigenhändig geschriebenes Testament; **inofficious ~** Pflichtteilsberechtigten ausschließendes (unwirksames) Testament; **military ~** Soldaten-, Militärtestament; **mutual ~** gegenseitiges Testament; **mystic ~** notariell beglaubigtes Testament; **last will and ~** letztwillige Verfügung, Testament;
~ *(v.)* *(Scot.)* Testament errichten;
to contest (dispute) a ~ Testament anfechten, Gültigkeit eines Testaments bestreiten; **to leave in one's ~** testamentarisch hinterlassen; **to make one's ~** testieren, sein Testament machen.

testamentary letztwillig, testamentarisch;
letters ~ Testamentsvollstreckerzeugnis;

~ burden testamentarische Auflage; **~ capacity** Testierfähigkeit; **~ causes** Nachlaßsachen; **~ class** Erbberechtigte; **~ clause** Testamentsbestimmung; **~ contract** Erbvertrag; **~ disposition** Verfügung von Todes wegen, letztwillige Verfügung; **~ executor** Nachlaßverwalter; **~ expenses** Testamentsunkosten, Kosten des Testamentsvollstreckers, Nachlaßkosten; **~ disposition** Verfügung von Todes wegen; **~ gift** letztwillige Zuwendung; **~ guardian** testamentarisch bestellter Vormund; **~ heir** Testamentserbe; **~ incapacity** Testierunfähigkeit; **~ instrument (paper)** Testamentsurkunde, Testament; **~ power** letztwillige Verfügungsmacht; **~ succession** testamentarische Erbfolge; **~ trust** testamentarisch errichtete Stiftung; **~ trustee** *(US)* Testamentsvollstrecker.

testate Testator, Testierender;
~ *(v.)* testieren;
to die ~ unter Hinterlassung eines Testamentes sterben;
~ estate Testamentserbe.

testation testamentarische Verfügung.

testator Erblasser, Testator, Testierender;
~'s capacity Testierfähigkeit.

testatrix Erblasserin.

teste of a writ Beglaubigungsvermerk.

tester Prüfer.

testification Beweis, Zeugnis.

testifier Zeuge.

testify *(v.)* feierliche Erklärung abgeben, *(law)* bezeugen, Zeugnis ablegen, eidlich erhärten;
~ against s. o. gegen j. aussagen; **~ on s. one's behalf** für j. aussagen; **~ before a court** vor Gericht aussagen; **~ to a fact** Tatsache bestätigen; **~ in s. one's favo(u)r** zu jds. Gunsten aussagen; **~ under oath** unter Eid bezeugen; **~ one's regrets** sein Bedauern zum Ausdruck bringen.

testimonial [schriftliches] Zeugnis, Führungs-, Dienstleistungszeugnis, -bescheinigung, *(expert opinion)* Gutachten, *(letter of recommendation)* Empfehlungsschreiben, *(token of regard)* Ehrengabe, öffentliche Anerkennung, *(US)* Ehrenveranstaltung;
to give a ~ to an employee Zeugnis für einen Angestellten ausstellen; **to show one's ~s** seine Zeugnisse vorlegen;
~ dinner Festbankett zu Ehren von, Abschiedsessen; **to give s. o. a ~ dinner** zu jds. Ehren ein Essen geben; **~ proof** Zeugenbeweis.

testimonialize *(v.)* Führungs-, Dienstleistungszeugnis ausstellen, *(give present)* Ehrengeschenk machen.

testimoninum *(clause)* Beglaubigungsvermerk.

testimony Zeugnis, *(law)* [Zeugen]aussage;
according to the ~ nach den Aussagen der Zeugen; **in ~ whereof** urkundlich dessen;
expert ~ Beweis durch Sachverständige, sachverständige Zeugenaussage; **false ~** falsche Zeugenaussage; **negative ~** negative Beweisführung; **perpetuating ~** Beweissicherung; **positive ~** Aussage eines unmittelbaren Zeugen;
~ under oath eidesstattliche Erklärung;
to be called in (to bear) ~ als Zeuge benannt werden; **to bear ~** Zeugnis ablegen; **to call s. o. in ~** j. als Zeugen aufrufen; **to give false ~** als Zeuge falsch aussagen, falsche Zeugenaussage machen; **to have s. one's ~** j. zum Zeugen haben; **to produce ~** Zeugnis ablegen; **to produce ~ to a statement** Erklärung durch Zeugenaussagen untermauern; **to show by ~** durch Zeugen nachweisen; **to take the ~ of s. o.** j. als Zeugen vernehmen; **to withdraw ~** Zeugenaussage widerrufen.

testing Probe, Erprobung, Untersuchung, Prüfung, Probeversuch, *(advertising)* Erfolgskontrolle;
copy ~ Testprüfung, Testen der Werbung; **material ~** Materialprüfung; **routine ~** planmäßige Prüfung;
~ of a product Testen eines Produkts; **~ of vehicles** Fahrzeugüberprüfung; **~ for weight** Gewichtsprüfung;
~ apparatus Prüfgerät; **~ area** Versuchsgebiet; **~ clause** Beglaubigungs-, Gültigkeitsklausel; **~ conditions** Prüfungsbedingungen; **~ engineer** Prüffeldingenieur; **~ engineering** Prüfwesen; **~ facilities** Prüfungseinrichtungen; **~ ground** Prüffeld; **~ instrument** Prüfgerät; **~ load** Probebelastung, -last; **~ method** Test-, Prüfungsmethode; **~ period** Versuchszeit; **~ program(me)** Prüfungsprogramm; **~ service** Durchführung von Testverfahren; **~ stand** Versuchs-, Prüfstand.

tether Haltestrick, Leine, Seil, *(fig.)* Spielraum, geistiger Horizont;
to be at the end of one's ~ mit seinem Latein am Ende sein, nicht mehr weiter wissen; **to be beyond s. one's ~** über jds. Horizont hinausgehen;
~ line Halteseil.

text Text, Wortlaut, Inhalt, *(of book)* textkritische Ausgabe, *(original)* Original[text], *(print.)* Frakturschrift, *(speech)* Thema, Gegenstand, *(subject)* Thema, Gegenstand, *(theater)* Vorlage, *(version)* Fassung, Version, Textausgabe;
abridged ~ gekürzter Text, Kurztext, *(print.)* Schrift; **annotated ~** kommentierter Text; **authentic ~** maßgeblicher Text; **coded ~** verschlüsselter Text; **corrupt ~** entstellter Text, Text voller Fehler; **draft ~** Textentwurf; **illustrated ~** illustrierter Text; **incorrect ~** fehlerhafter Text; **large ~** *(print.)* große Schrift; **official ~** maßgeblicher (amtlicher) Text, amtlicher Wortlaut; **original ~** Urschrift, Original; **revised ~** verbesserter Text; **running ~** gleichbleibender Textteil; **small ~** kleine Schrift; **unjustified ~** *(composition)* Flattersatz;
~ of the law Wortlaut des Gesetzes, Gesetzestext;
to amend a ~ Text kritisch durchsehen; **to annotate a ~** Text kritisch durchsehen; **to comment on a ~** Text mit Anmerkungen versehen (kommentieren); **to open a ~** Text auslegen; **to paraphrase a ~** Text frei wiedergeben; **to read too much into a ~** zu viel in einen Text hineinlesen; **to restore a ~** Text rekonstruieren; **to stick to one's ~** bei der Sache bleiben; **to tamper with a ~** Text verfälschen; **to write notes to a ~** Text kommentieren;
~ edition Studienausgabe; **~ hand** große Kurrentschrift; **~ matter** *(composing)* glatter Satz; **facing ~ matter** Gegenübertext; **~ page** Textseite; **~ writer** Kommentator.

textbook Fach-, Lehrbuch, Leitfaden, *(music)* Libretto;
to stick close to the ~ sich eng ans Lehrbuch halten;
~ coup Theatercoup; **~ edition** Schul-, Studienausgabe; **~ example** Modellbeispiel; **~ writer** Kommentator.

textile Gewebe, Faserstoff, Spinnfaser;
~s Textilwaren;
~ company Textilfirma; **~ finishing** Textilveredlung; **~ goods** Textilien; **~ goods fair** Textilmesse; **~ industry** Textilindustrie; **~ line** Halteseil; **~ maker** Textilfabrikant; **~ mill** Textilfabrik; **~ processing** Textilverarbeitung; **~ shares** Textilwerte; **~ slump** Rezession in der Textilindustrie; **~ worker** Textilarbeiter.

textual dem Text nach, textgemäß, wörtlich, wortgetreu;
~ additions Textzusätze; **~ advertisement** Textanzeige; **~ error** Textfehler; **~ notes on a work** Textanmerkungen; **~ protocol** Wortprotokoll; **~ quotation** wörtliches Zitat.

textural changes strukturelle Veränderungen.

texture Gewebe, Struktur;
~ of a play Aufbau eines Dramas.

Thames, to throw water into the Eulen nach Athen tragen; **not to set the ~ on fire** das Pulver nicht erfunden haben.

thanks Dank, Dankesbezeigung;
~ to his intervention Dank seiner Vermittlung;
~-you card Danksagungskarte; **~ note** Danksagungsbrief.

Thanksgiving Day *(US)* Erntedankfest.

thatch Strohdach.

thatched cottage strohgedecktes Landhaus.

thaw *(politics)* Tauwetter;
~ *(v.)* [auf]tauen, schmelzen, *(fig.)* aus seiner Reserve heraustreten;
~ out one's guests seine Gäste warm werden lassen; **~ out the radiator** Kühler auftauen.

theater *(US)* **(theatre,** *Br.)* Theater[gebäude], Schauspielhaus, *(drama)* Bühnenwerk;
open-air ~ Freilichtbühne; **operating ~** Operationssaal; **picture ~** Filmtheater, Lichtspielhaus, Kino;
~ of life Weltgeschehen; **~ of operations** Operationsgebiet; **~ of war** Kriegsschauplatz;
to be good ~ *(play)* bühnenwirksam sein;
~ capable of seating two thousand Theater mit einem Fassungsvermögen von 2000 Personen;
to play in a ~ in einem Theater auftreten;
~ audience Theaterpublikum; **~ bill** Theaterprogramm; **to make a ~ booking by post** Theaterkarten schriftlich bestellen; **~-curtain advertisement** Vorhangwerbung; **~ owner** Theaterbesitzer; **~ poster** Theaterplakat; **~ publicity** Theaterwerbung; **~ [admission] ticket** Theaterkarte.

theatergoer Theaterbesucher.

theatergoing Theaterbesuch.

theatrical Theateraufführung;
amateur ~ Liebhabervorstellung;
~ *(a.)* theatralisch, übertrieben, gekünstelt;
~ agent Theateragent; **~ company** Schauspielertruppe; **~ performance** Theateraufführung; **~ promoter** Theateragent.

theft *(Br.)* Diebstahl, Entwendung;
aggravated ~ schwerer Diebstahl; **car ~** Autodiebstahl; **mail ~** Postdiebstahl; **partial ~** Teildiebstahl;
~ by false pretext Eigentumserschleichung;

~ **of a car** Autodiebstahl; ~ **of a letter** Briefunterschlagung; ~, **pilferage and nondelivery** Diebstahl und Abhandenkommen; **to charge s. o. with** ~ j. des Diebstahls beschuldigen; **to commit a** ~ Diebstahl begehen;

⌐ **Act** (Br.) Diebstahlsgesetz; ~**-bote** Diebstahlsbegünstigung durch Nichtanzeige; ~ **clause** Diebstahlklausel; ~ **prevention device** Sicherheitsvorrichtung gegen Einbruchsdiebstahl; ~ **insurance** Diebstahlversicherung; ~**-proof** einbruchsicher; ~ **risk** Diebstahlrisiko.

thematic thematisch;

~ **catalog(ue)** thematisches Verzeichnis.

theme Thema, Stoff, Gegenstand, (broadcasting) Pausenzeichen, Kennmelodie, (school, US) Arbeit, Aufsatz;

to have s. th. for ~ etw. zum Thema haben; **to strike a** ~ Thema anschneiden;

~ **song** (film) Titelmelodie, Hauptmelodie, -schlager; ~ **tune** Leitmotiv, Titelmusik.

theorist, price Preistheoretiker.

theory Lehre, Theorie;

in ~ theoretisch;

clear surplus ~ Theorie des reinen Überschusses; **equilibrium** ~ statistische Preistheorie; **pet** ~ Lieblingstheorie;

~ **of case** klagebegründende Tatsachen; ~ **of chances** Wahrscheinlichkeitsrechnung; ~ **of consumer choice** Theorie der Konsumentenentscheidung; ~ **of demand** Konsum-, Nachfragetheorie; ~ **of employment** Beschäftigungstheorie; ~ **of income determination** makroökonomische Beschäftigungstheorie; ~ **of increasing misery** Verelendungstheorie; **quantity** ~ **of money** Quantitätstheorie des Geldes; ~ **of opportunity costs** Substitutionskostentheorie; ~ **of prices** Preistheorie; ~ **of probabilities** Wahrscheinlichkeitsrechnung, -theorie; ~ **of production** Produktionstheorie; ~ **of rent** Lohntheorie; ~ **of economic stages** ökonomische Stufenlehre; ~ **of surplus value** Mehrwerttheorie; ~ **of taxation** allgemeine Steuerlehre; **cost of production** ~ **of value** Produktionskostentheorie; **subsistence** ~ **of wages** Lohn-, Produktionskostentheorie;

to advance a ~ Theorie vortragen; **to advocate a** ~ Theorie verfechten; **to be excellent in** ~ theoretisch hervorragend klingen; **to come up with a** ~ Theorie aufstellen; **to pick a** ~ **to pieces** Theorie zerpflücken; **to put forward a** ~ Theorie aufstellen; **to reduce a** ~ **into practice** Theorie praktisch anwenden; **to set forth a** ~ Theorie darlegen; **to sustain a** ~ Theorie erhärten.

therapy Therapie;

balneo-~ Badekur; **occupational** ~ Beschäftigungstherapie.

there and back (journey, Br.) hin und zurück.

thereinafter nachstehend, im nachstehenden, weiter unten.

thereinbefore vorstehend, im vorstehenden.

thereunder, as ~ **prescribed** wie im nachstehenden vorgeschrieben.

thereupon infolgedessen, unverzüglich.

therm Kilokalorie.

thermal | barrier (high speeds in flying) Hitzebarriere; ~ **conductivity** Wärmeleitfähigkeit; ~ **cutout** (el.) Schmelzsicherung; ~ **energy** Wärmeenergie; ~ **fluctuations** Temperaturschwankungen; ~ **spring** heiße Quelle, Thermalquelle; ~ **value** Heizwert.

thermic | conditions Wärmebedingungen; ~ **protection** Wärmeschutz.

thermionic valve Elektronenröhre.

thermonuclear bomb Wasserstoffbombe.

thermostat Thermostat.

thermostatic control thermostatische Überwachung.

thesaurer Schatzmeister.

thesaurus Wissensschatz, Wörterbuch.

thesis These, Satz, Postulat, (diploma) Doktorarbeit, Inauguraldissertation, Diplomarbeit, (school) Aufsatz;

to write a ~ **upon a subject** über etw. dissertieren;

~ **novel** Tendenzroman; ~ **play** Tendenzstück.

thick (fig.) schwierigster Teil, Brennpunkt, (person, sl.) Dummkopf;

~ **of the crowd** dichtestes Menschengewühl;

~ (a.) (abundant) reichlich, massenhaft, im Überfluß, (letter) breit, (mining) mächtig;

a bit too ~ ein bißchen zu stark aufgetragen; ~ **with dust** staubbedeckt; **in the** ~ **of the fight** im dichtesten Kampfgewühl; **as** ~ **as peas** wie Sand am Meer;

to be pretty ~ **on the ground** zahlreich vertreten sein; **to be as** ~ **as thieves** wie Pech und Schwefel zusammenhalten; **to lay it on** ~ (sl.) dick auftragen;

the ~ **end of the wedge** das dicke Ende; ~ **fog** undurchdringlicher Nebel; ~ **frame** (print.) fette Umrandung, Trauerrand; ~ **print** Fettdruck; ~ **rule** (print.) Balken; **to be** ~**-skinned** dickes

Fell haben; ~ **supporters** zuverlässige Anhänger.

thick-and-thin zuverlässig, ergeben;

through ~ durch dick und dünn;

~ **advocate** unbedingter Befürworter.

thickness | of clouds Wolkendichte; **two** ~**es of silk** zwei Lagen Seide;

to drive through a misty ~ durch undurchsichtigen Nebel fahren.

thickset | with jewels mit Juwelen dicht besetzt;

~ **hedge** dichte Hecke.

thief Dieb;

small-time ~ kleiner Dieb;

to expose a ~ Dieb entlarven; **to scare away a** ~ Dieb verscheuchen; **to set a** ~ **to catch a** ~ den Bock zum Gärtner machen; ~**-proof** diebessicher.

thieves' Latin Gaunersprache.

thin (book) gehaltlos, seicht, (letter) dünn, fein, (photo) undeutlich, kontrastarm, unordentlich, (print.) mager, (soil) mager, arm, unfruchtbar, (theater) schwach besetzt;

~ **in the upper crust** (sl.) leicht bedeppert;

~ (v.) (forest) ausforsten, lichten;

~ [off] (crowd) sich verlaufen; ~ **down the population** Bevölkerung dezimieren;

to vanish into ~ **air** sich in Nichts auflösen; ~ **attendance** spärlicher Besuch, geringe Beteiligung; ~ **audience** geringe Zuhörerschaft; **not worth a** ~ **dime** (US) keinen roten Heller wert; ~ **excuse** kümmerliche (fadenscheinige) Entschuldigung; ~ **house** schwach besetztes Theater; **on** ~ **ice** (fig.) auf gefährlichem Boden, in einer heiklen Lage; ~ **margin** (US) sehr knappe Deckung; ~ **market** (stock exchange, US) schwacher (flauer) Markt; ~**-peopled** dünn bevölkert; ~ **profit** kümmerlicher (geringer) Gewinn; **to have had a** ~ **time** miese Zeit hinter sich haben.

thing Sache, Ding, Gegenstand, (creature) Wesen, Kreatur, Geschöpf, (matter) Angelegenheit, (possession) Habe, Besitz;

for one ~ erstens; **quite the** ~ äußerst fesch; **taking one** ~ **with another** wenn man alles so recht bedenkt;

costly ~ Kostbarkeit; **defective** ~ mangelhafte Sache; **a general** ~ das Übliche;

a ~ **or two** Wissenswertes;

to do the handsome ~ sich großzügig erweisen; **to feel not quite the** ~ sich nicht besonders fühlen, nicht auf dem Posten sein; **to know a** ~ **or two** im Bilde sein, Bescheid wissen; **to let a** ~ **go hang** Sache sich selbst überlassen; **to make a good** ~ **of** (coll.) guten Schnitt machen.

things Sachen, Besitz, (luggage) Reisegepäck, (situation) Sachlage, Verhältnisse;

perfect in all ~ in jeder Hinsicht vollkommen;

~ **corporeal** körperliche Gegenstände; ~ **feminine** Frauenangelegenheiten; **fungible** ~ vertretbare Sachen, Gattungssachen; **immovable** ~ unbewegliche Sachen, Immobilien, Grundstücke; **movable** ~ bewegliche Sachen; ~ **personal** persönliche Habe, bewegliche Sachen; ~ **political** politische Angelegenheiten; ~ **real** unbewegliche Sachen, Grundstücke, Immobilien; ~ **in action** Forderungs-, immaterielle Güterrechte; ~ **in possession** körperliche Gegenstände; ~ **of value** Wertgegenstände; **to be seeing** ~ Halluzinationen haben; **to do great** ~ Großes vollbringen; **to leave** ~ **as they are** Status quo belassen; **to make** ~ **worse** die Situation verschlimmern; **to pack up one's** ~ seine Sachen zusammenpacken; **to put** ~ **into s. one's head** jem. einen Floh ins Ohr setzen.

think (v.) denken, glauben, meinen;

~ **s. th. beneath o. s.** sich für etw. zu fein vorkommen; ~ **better of it** sich eines Besseren besinnen; ~ **better of s. o.** bessere Meinung von jem. haben; ~ **of s. o. as candidate** j. als Kandidaten in Aussicht nehmen; **talk and** ~ **cars** nur Autos im Kopf haben; ~ **fit for tunlich halten; ~ highly of s. o.** hohe Meinung von jem. haben; ~ **a lecture interesting** Vorlesung interessant finden; ~ **nothing of** nichts davon halten; ~ **over** erwägen, überdenken, denken; ~ **of pennies** mit Pfennigen rechnen; ~ **about a scheme** Plan überlegen; ~ **bad thoughts** gemeine Gedanken hegen; ~ **up some routes for a trip** sich ein paar Reiserouten überlegen; ~ **well of s. o.** große Stücke von jem. halten;

~ **piece** (sl.) provozierender Artikel; ~**-tank** Denkfabrik, Planungsstab; ~**-tank parlance** Planungsstabssprache.

thinking Denken, Überlegungen, Gedankengang;

~ (a.) denkend, vernünftig;

cooperatively ~ mitdenkend; **hard-**~ begriffsstutzig;

to be wholly with s. o. in ~ mit jem. in allem gleicher Meinung sein; **to do some hard** ~ scharf nachdenken;

~ **cap** nachdenkliche Stimmung; **to put one's ~ on** über etw. gründlich nachdenken; ~ **machine** *(coll.)* Elektronengehirn; ~ **part** *(theater)* stumme Rolle; ~ **process** Denkvorgang; ~ **shop** *(coll.)* Lehranstalt; ~ **stage** Planungsstadium; ~ **time** Reaktionszeit.

thinly settled (populated) dünn besiedelt.

thinness *(assembly)* geringe Beteiligung;
intellectual ~ geistige Armut.

thinning *(forest)* Ausforsten, Lichten.

third Drittel, *(motor car)* dritter Gang, *(law)* Dritter, dritte Person, *(widow)* Witwengut;
~**s** *(inferior goods)* Waren minderwertiger Qualität (dritter Güte), drittklassige Ware;
~ **of exchange** Wechseldrittausfertigung, Tertialwechsel;
to run a poor ~ gerade noch Dritter werden; **to run a strong ~** sicheren dritten Platz behaupten; **to travel ~ [class]** dritter Klasse reisen;
for ~ account für fremde Rechnung; ~ **arbitrator** Schiedsobmann; ~ **class** *(US, postal service)* Drucksache, *(railway)* dritte Klasse, *(Br., university)* schlechteste Examensgruppe; ~~**class** drittklassig; ~~**class carriage** [Eisenbahn]wagen dritter Klasse; ~~**class compartment** Abteil dritter Klasse; ~~**class mail matter** *(US)* Drucksachen; ~ **copy** dritte Ausfertigung, Drittausfertigung; ~ **country** Drittland; ~ **degree** *(US coll., criminal)* dritter Grad, Folterverhör, polizeiliche Zwangsmaßnahmen; ~ **degree** *(v.)* einem Folterverhör unterwerfen, dritten Grad anwenden; ~~**degree practices** Folterverhör, verschärftes Verhör; ~ **floor** dritter Stock, *(US)* zweiter Stock; ~ **force** *(fig.)* dritte Kraft; ~ **hand** aus dritter Hand erworben; ~ **holder** Drittbesitzer; ~~**largest** drittgrößt; ~ **mortgage bonds** durch dritte Hypothek gesicherte Schuldverschreibungen; ~**s off** *(US, marine insurance)* vom Schiffseigner getragenes Reparaturkostendrittel; ~ **opposition** *(Louisiana)* Drittwiderspruchsklage.

third party dritte Person, Dritter *(insurance law)* unbeteiligter Dritter, *(proceedings)* Nebenintervenient, Streitgenosse;
bona-fide (innocent) ~ gutgläubiger Dritter;
to give notice to a ~ *(US)* einem Dritten den Streit verkünden;
to make payable by a ~ bei einem Dritten zahlbar stellen;
~ **accident insurance** *(Br.)* Unfallhaftpflichtversicherung; ~**arbitrator** Schiedsobmann, *(proceedings)* Nebenintervenient, Streitgenosse; ~ **beneficiary** *(creditor, donee)* *(US)* Begünstigter eines Vertrages zugunsten Dritter; ~ **beneficiary contract** *(US)* Vertrag zugunsten Dritter; ~ **claims** Ansprüche Dritter; ~ **claim proceeding** Nebeninterventionsverfahren; **full ~ cover** voller Unfallversicherungsschutz; ~ **debtor** Drittschuldner; ~ **funds** fremde Gelder, Fremdgelder; ~ **guarantee** Garantie von dritter Seite; ~ **indemnity** Haftpflicht; ~ **indemnity insurance** private Haftpflichtversicherung; ~ **insurance policy** Haftpflichtversicherungspolice; ~ **liability** Haftpflicht; ~ **liability insurance** Haftpflichtversicherung; ~ **notice** Intervention, Streitverkündung; **to serve ~ notice on s. o.** einem Dritten den Streit verkünden; ~ **notice procedure** Streitverkündungsverfahren; ~ **only policy** *(motor insurance, Br.)* reine Haftpflichtversicherung; ~ **order** *(US)* Pfändungs- und Überweisungsbeschluß, Zahlungsverbot (Leistungsverbot) an Drittschuldner; ~ **rights** Rechte Dritter; ~ **risk** *(Br.)* Haftpflichtrisiko; **to insure against ~ risk** *(Br.)* gegen Haftpflicht versichern; ~ **risk policy** *(Br.)* Haftpflichtpolice; ~ **security** von dritter Seite gestellte Sicherheit; ~ **sharing agreement** *(accident insurance)* Vereinbarung über gemeinsame Entschädigungsleistungen an unbeteiligte Dritte.

third | person Dritter; ~ **possessor** *(US)* lastenfreier Grundstückserwerber; ~~**program(me)** *(Br.)* betont intellektuell; ~ **rail** Stromschiene; ~~**rate** drittklassig, -rangig; ~~**rater** kümmerliche Figur; ~~**string** drittrangig; ~ **term** *(US)* dritte Amtsperiode; ~ **wheel** *(fig.)* drittes Rad am Wagen; **the ~ world** Entwicklungsländer.

thirdborough *(Br.)* örtlicher Polizeichef.

thirst for knowledge Wissensdrang, -durst; ~ **for money** Geldgier;
to be parched with ~ am Verdursten sein; **to satisfy one's ~ for adventure** seinem Abenteuerdrang nachgeben.

thirty-two-sheet poster *(advertising)* Riesenplakat.

thorn Dorn, Stachel;
~ **in one's flesh** Pfahl im Fleische, Dorn im Auge;
to sit on ~s wie auf glühenden Kohlen sitzen.

thorny problem heikles (delikates) Problem.

thorough eingehend, gründlich, durchgreifend, völlig, vollkommen, durch und durch;
to be ~ in one's work zuverlässig arbeiten;
to give a room a ~ cleaning Zimmer gründlich reinigen; ~ **command of a language** gute Sprachkenntnisse; ~ **conservative**

eingefleischter Konservativer; **to receive ~ instruction in English** hervorragenden Englischunterricht erhalten; ~ **knowledge** gründliche Kenntnisse; ~ **presentation of a theme** meisterhafte Themendarstellung; ~ **reform** durchgreifende Reform; ~ **training** gründliche Ausbildung; ~ **worker** gründlicher Arbeiter.

thoroughbred reinrassig, *(fig.)* gebildet, kultiviert.

thoroughfare Durchfahrt, -gang, *(frequented way)* Verkehrsader, öffentliche Straße, Hauptverkehrs-, Durchgangsstraße;
in a public ~ auf offener Straße, auf einem öffentlichen Weg; **main ~** Hauptdurchgangsstraße; **no ~** kein Durchgang!, verbotener Weg!, Durchfahrt verboten; **public ~** öffentlicher Verkehrsweg.

thoroughgoing kompromißlos, radikal, durch und durch.

thoroughpaced | egoist Egoist durch und durch; ~ **politician** erfahrener (ausgekochter) Politiker.

those present die Anwesenden.

thought Gedanke, Denken, Trachten, *(consideration)* Erwägung, Überlegung, *(intention)* Absicht, Plan, *(power to conceive)* Vorstellungsvermögen;
after serious ~ nach ernsthafter Erwägung; **on second ~s** bei nochmaligem Nachdenken;
scientific ~ wissenschaftliche Denkweise;
to be a ~ more considerate of other people auf andere Leute etw. mehr Rücksicht nehmen; **to be full of ~s for a patient** um einen Patienten sehr besorgt sein; **to have second ~s** Zweifel bekommen; **to have some ~s of going to Spain this summer** dieses Jahr spanische Ferienpläne haben; **to let o. s. have one's ~s in a matter** sich jem. gegenüber zu einem Thema äußern; **to read s. one's ~s** jds. Gedanken lesen; **to speak one's ~** seine Meinung sagen; **to take no ~ of one's appearance** nicht auf sein Äußeres achten;
~ **reader** Gedankenleser; ~ **transference** Gedankenübertragung.

thoughtful | essay gedankenreiche Abhandlung; ~ **friend** rücksichtsvoller Freund.

thoughtless action unüberlegte Handlung.

thousand, per pro Mille;
a ~ to one [chance] sehr entfernte Möglichkeit; **a ~ apologies** unzählige Entschuldigungen; **the ~ and one worries of life** zahllose Kümmernisse des Lebens.

thrash *(v.)* **out** durchdiskutieren.

thrashing defeat vernichtende Niederlage.

thread Faden, Faser, Fiber, *(fig.)* Faden, *(middle line of river)* Schiffahrtslinie, *(mining)* dünne Kohlenader;
~ **of light** dünner Lichtstrahl;
~ *(v.)* **a film** Film einlegen, Kamera laden; ~ **one's way through a crowd** sich durch die Menschenmenge hindurchzwängen;
to be worn to the last ~ *(suit)* völlig abgetragen sein; **to gather up the ~s of a story** Sache zusammenhängend darlegen; **to hang by a ~** an einem seidenen Faden hängen; **to have no dry ~ on o. s.** keinen trockenen Faden am Leib haben; **to have a ~ of humo(u)r** humorvollen Unterton haben; **to lose the ~ of one's story** Faden der Erzählung verlieren; **to pick up (resume) the ~s** zusammenfassen, Fäden wieder aufnehmen;
~ **mark** *(bank note)* Faserzeichen; ~ **paper** *(fig.)* Bohnenstange; ~ **stitching** Fadenheftung.

threadbare fadenscheinig, *(fig.)* dürftig, schäbig;
~ **arguments** dürftige Beweisführung; ~ **coat** abgetragener Rock; ~ **phrase** abgedroschene Phrase.

threat [Be]drohung;
under the ~ of expulsion *(university)* bei Androhung der Relegierung;
hidden ~ versteckte Drohung; **idle ~s** leere Drohungen; **imminent ~** unmittelbar drohende Gefahr; **terroristic ~s** terroristische Drohungen;
~ **of a coup** drohender Staatsstreich; ~ **of dismissal** Androhung der Entlassung; ~ **to peace** Bedrohung des Friedens, Friedensbedrohung; ~ **of rain** drohender Regen; ~ **of resignation** Rücktrittsdrohung; ~ **of violence** Gewaltanwendung; ~ **of war** Kriegsdrohung;
to be under the ~ of expulsion mit der Relegation rechnen müssen; **to constitute a ~ to security** Bedrohung der Sicherheit darstellen; **to counter a ~** einer drohenden Gefahr entgegentreten; **to pose a serious ~** ernste Gefahr darstellen; **to utter a ~ against s. o.** Drohungen gegen j. ausstoßen;
~**s action** *(patent law, Br.)* Prozeßandrohung.

threaten *(v.)* drohen, bedrohen, bedrohlich aussehen;
~ **legal action** mit einem Prozeß drohen; ~ **an employee with dismissal** einem Angestellten mit Kündigung drohen; ~ **peace** Frieden gefährden; ~ **proceedings** gerichtliche Schritte androhen; ~ **with punishment** Strafe androhen.

threatening| attitude drohende Haltung; **~ behavio(u)r** drohendes Verhalten; **~ letter** Drohbrief.

threes dreiprozentige Papiere.

three| -bottle man ausgekochter Säufer; **~-coat work** dreimaliger Anstrich; **~-colo(u)r printing** Dreifarbendruck; **~-colo(u)r process** Dreifarbendruckverfahren; **~-column article** dreispaltiger Zeitungsartikel; **~-cornered contest** von drei Parteien bestrittener Wahlkampf; **~-cornered trade discussions** dreiseitige Handelsbesprechungen, Diskussion zu Dritt; **~-course system** Dreifelderwirtschaft; **~-d** *(film)* dreidimensional; **~-D-policy** Kautionsversicherung; **~-decker** *(novel, coll.)* dicker Wälzer; **~-dimensional** dreidimensional; **~-dimensional sound** Raumton; **~-figure** dreistellig; **~-fourth majority** Dreiviertelmehrheit; **~-fourth loss clause** *(fire insurance)* Dreiviertelverlustklausel, Ersatz bis zu 3/4 des versicherten Wertes; **~-hour lecture** dreistündige Vorlesung; **~-lane** dreibahnig, -spurig, mit drei Fahrbahnen; **~-mile limit** Dreimeilengrenze; **~-mile zone (belt)** Dreimeilenzone; **~-months' draft** Dreimonatswechsel; **~-months acceptance** Dreimonatsakzept; **~-months deposit (money)** Dreimonatsgeld, Vierteljahreseinlagen; **~-name paper** *(US)* Tratte mit drei Unterschriften; **~-pair** *(Br.)* im dritten Stock gelegen, drei Treppen hoch; **~-per-cents** *(Br.)* dreiprozentige Papiere; **~-phase** *(el.)* dreiphasig; **~-phase current** Drehstrom; **~-point landing** Dreipunktlandung; **~-power conference** Dreimächtekonferenz; **~-sheet** Dreibogenplakat; **~-stage rocket** Dreistufenrakete; **~-volume work** dreibändiges Werk; **~-way switch** *(el.)* Dreifachschalter; **~-weeks holiday** dreiwöchentlicher Urlaub.

threepenny *(fig.)* billig, wertlos.

thresh *(v.)* [Getreide] dreschen;
~ out a matter Sache gründlich besprechen; **~ over straw** leeres Stroh dreschen.

thresher Drescher, Dreschmaschine.

threshing Dreschen;
~ floor Tenne; **~ machine** Dreschmaschine.

threshold Eingang, [Tür]schwelle, Hauseingang, *(fig.)* Beginn, Schwelle, *(income tax)* Anfangsbetrag, unterer Proportionalbereich;
stimulus ~ Reizschwelle;
~ of conscience Bewußtseinsschwelle; **~ of manhood** Schwelle zum Mannesalter;
to be on the ~ of one's career am Beginn seiner Laufbahn stehen;
~ agreement Tarifvertrag mit Indexklausel, Lohnschwellenvereinbarung; **~ dose** kritische Menge; **~ income** einkommensteuerpflichtiges Mindesteinkommen, zu Sätzen des unteren Proportionalbereichs versteuertes Einkommen; **~ increase** Anhebung der Steueranfangsbeträge, Erweiterung des unteren Proportionalbereichs; **~ payment** indexgebundene Lohnerhöhung; **~ price** *(agricultural market, EC)* Eingangs-, Schwellenpreis; **~ tariff** Anfangstarif; **~ worker** *(US)* unerfahrener Arbeiter, Anlernling.

thrift Wirtschaftlichkeit, Sparsamkeit, Ökonomie;
~ account Sparkonto; **~ box** Sparbüchse; **~ department** *(US)* Sparkassenabteilung; **~ deposit** Spargelder, -einlagen; **~ flight** verbilligter Flug; **~ institution** Sparvereinigung; **~ plan** Sparplan; **~ program(m)e** Sparprogramm; **~ society** *(US)* Sparvereinigung; **~ store** Billigpreisladen, Diskontladen.

thriftiness Sparsamkeit, Wirtschaftlichkeit.

thriftless verschwenderisch.

thrifty sparsam, wirtschaftlich, vorsorglich.

thrill Zittern, Beben, *(play)* Erschütterung;
the ~-of-victory-heartbreak-of-defeat himmelhochjauchzend-zu-Tode betrübt;
~ *(v.)* the listeners *(voice)* Zuschauer elektrisieren;
to give s. o. the ~ of one's lifetime jem. das größte Erlebnis seines Lebens vermitteln; **to offer a ~** Nervenkitzel bieten;
~ ride Vergnügungsfahrt.

thriller Reißer, Schauer-, Kriminalroman, Krimi, *(film)* Gruselstück, -film.

thrilling aufregend, reißerisch.

thrillseeker, jaded übersättigter Sensationslustiger.

thrive *(v.)* gedeihen, blühen, prosperieren, florieren;
~ by good husbandry durch gutes Wirtschaften reich werden.

thriving blühend, florierend;
to keep ~ im Gang halten;
~ business blühendes Geschäft.

throat Kehle, Speiseröhre;
~ of a furnace Gicht eines Hochofens;
to be in full ~ lautstark artikulieren; **to cut one's ~** Selbstmord begehen, *(fig.)* sich selbst zugrunde richten; **to force (thrust) s.**

th. down s. one's ~ jem. etw. aufdrängen; **to lie in one's ~** wie gedruckt lügen; **to stick in one's ~** *(words)* im Halse stecken bleiben;
~ microphone Kehlkopfmikrophon.

throne Thron, Regierung, Herrschaft, *(ruler)* Souverän, Herrscher;
**~ *(v.)* ** inthronisieren, auf den Thron erheben;
to ascend the ~ Thron besteigen; **to be called to the ~** auf den Thron berufen werden; **to come to the ~** Regierung antreten; **to lose one's ~** seinen Thron verlieren; **to remain upon one's ~** seinen Thron behaupten; **to renounce one's ~** dem Thron entsagen; **to succeed to the ~** Thron besteigen, in der Regierung folgen; **to usurp the ~** sich den Thron aneignen, sich des Throns bemächtigen.

throng Menschenmasse, Menge, *(rush)* Andrang, Gedränge, Zulauf;
**~ *(v.)* ** sich zusammendrängen;
~ the streets sich in den Straßen drängen;
**~ *(a.)* ** sehr beschäftigt, geschäftig.

throttle Luft-, Speiseröhre, *(car)* Gashebel, -pedal;
with full ~ mit laufendem Motor;
**~ *(v.)* ** erwürgen, erdrosseln, *(fig.)* unterdrücken, ersticken;
~ back the assembly line Produktion verlangsamen; **~ down** *(engine)* verlangsamen; **~ down a car to thirty miles an hour** auf 50 Stundenkilometer heruntergehen; **~ the freedom in a country** Land vergewaltigen; **~ an offensive** Offensive abwürgen; **~ free speech** Redefreiheit unterdrücken;
to cut off the ~ Benzinzufuhr abstellen; **to open out the ~** kräftig Gas geben;
~ lever Gashebel; **~ valve** Drosselklappe, -ventil.

throttling back of assembly lines Produktionsverlangsamung.

through *(high)* Ausläufer;
~ an agent über einen Vertreter; **~ the line** global; **~ the mill** *(coll.)* frustriert;
~ *(a.)* ** durch, *(arrived at the end)* fertig, *(US)* bis einschließlich; **to be ~ with a job Arbeit hinter sich haben; **to come ~** *(US)* den Eindruck erwecken; **to get ~** durchkommen, bestehen; **to go ~ accounts** Konten durchgehen; **to put s. o. ~** *(tel.)* j. verbinden mit, j. durchstellen;
~ bill of lading Transit-, Durchkonnossement; **~ bolt** durchgehender Bolzen; **~ bookings** Pauschalreisen; **~ car** *(US)* *(carriage, coach, Br.)* Kurs-, Durchgangswagen; **~ communication** Durchgangsverkehr, durchgehende Verbindung; **~ connection** direkte Verbindung; **~ freight [business]** Durchgangsfracht[geschäft]; **~ highway** Hauptdurchgangsstraße; **~ fare** Durchgangsfahrkarte; **~ line** Durchgangsgleis, durchgehende Linie; **~ lot** durchgehendes Baugrundstück; **~ passenger** Durchreisender; **~ plane** Direktflugzeug; **~ rate** *(Br.)* Frachtsatz für Ladungen unter einem Zentner, Durchgangssatz, -tarif, Durchfracht; **~ registration of luggage** *(Br.)* Gepäckaufgabe zur durchgehenden Beförderung; **~ road** Durchgangsstraße; **~ route** Durchgangsstrecke, -verbindung; **~ shipment** *(US)* Durch[gangs]fracht, durchgehende Ladung; **~ station** Durchgangsstation; **~ street** *(US)* Vorfahrtstraße, Durchgangsstraße; **~ ticket** Durchgangs-, direkte Fahrkarte, für verschiedene Eisenbahngesellschaften gültige Fahrkarte; **~ traffic** Transit-, Durchgangsverkehr; **~ train** durchgehender Zug, D-Zug; **~ transport** Beförderung im Transitverkehr; **~ transportation** durchgehende Beförderung; **~ waybill** durchgehender Frachtbrief.

throughout in allen Teilen, durchweg;
rotten ~ total verfault; **a sound policy ~** durch und durch vernünftige Politik;
~ the country im ganzen Land; **~ the war** während der ganzen Kriegszeit; **~ the year** das ganze Jahr hindurch.

throughput of traffic Verkehrsbewältigung.

throughway *(US)* Autobahn.

throw Werfen, Schleudern, *(risk)* Wagnis, Risiko, *(sl.)* Stückpreis;
within a stone's ~ in Steinwurfweite;
**~ *(v.)* ** werfen, schleudern, *(gear)* umlegen, ein-, ausschalten, *(racing, US coll.)* in betrügerischer Absicht verlieren;
~ away advice Rat in den Wind schlagen; **~ away a good opportunity** Chance verpassen; **~ into the bargain** drauf-, dazugeben; **~ the book at s. o.** *(sl.)* j. zu einer Höchststrafe verdonnern; **~ a bridge** Brücke schlagen; **~ the bull** *(US sl.)* das Blaue vom Himmel herunterlügen; **~ cold water on** entmutigen; **~ dust in s. one's eyes** jem. blauen Dunst vormachen; **~ down the gauntlet** herausfordern; **~ it into second gear** zweiten Gang einlegen; **~ goods onto the market** Waren auf den Markt werfen; **~ a gun on s. o.** *(US)* Pistole auf j. richten; **~ the hooks** *(sl.)* auf

der Straße betteln; ~ **in** umsonst dazugeben, *(gear)* Gang einschalten; ~ **in one's lot with s. o.** sich mit jem. solidarisch erklären; ~ **in the towel** das Handtuch werfen, sich geschlagen geben; ~ **in with s. o.** *(US coll.)* gemeinsame Sache mit jem. machen; ~ **o. s. into work** sich auf die Arbeit stürzen; ~ **a spanner into the works** Knüppel zwischen die Beine werfen; ~ **light on s. th.** Licht auf etw. werfen; ~ **one's money about** sein Geld verschleudern; ~ **good money after bad** gutes Geld schlechtem hinterherwerfen; ~ **an obligation on s. o.** jem. eine Verpflichtung auferlegen; ~ **off** *(print.)* abziehen; ~ **off a troublesome acquaintance** unangenehme Bekanntschaft loswerden; ~ **off all sense of shame** sich über jegliches Schamgefühl hinwegsetzen; ~ **off one's pursuers** seine Verfolger abschütteln; ~ **open to the public** zur öffentlichen Benutzung freigeben; ~ **out** hinauswerfen; ~ **out a bill** Gesetzentwurf ablehnen (verwerfen); ~ **outs s. o. in his calculations** jds. Kalkulationen durcheinanderbringen; ~ **out a case** Klage abweisen; ~ **out of gear** Gang herausnehmen, *(fig.)* reibungslosen Ablauf der Dinge stören; ~ **out light** Lichtschein verbreiten; ~ **out an orator** Redner aus dem Konzept bringen; ~ **out a new wing to a house** neuen Flügel anbauen; ~ **out of work** arbeitslos machen; ~ **over a friend** Freund im Stich lassen; ~ **overboard a theory** Theorie über Bord werfen; ~ **a party** Gesellschaft geben; ~ **up a post** Posten aufgeben; ~ **s. o. into prison** j. ins Gefängnis stecken; ~ **a regiment into action** Regiment in den Kampf werfen; ~ **a rope to s. o.** *(fig.)* jem. behilflich sein; ~ **into the shade** in den Schatten stellen; ~ **a ship on the rocks** Schiff auf die Felsen werfen; ~ **a sop to s. o.** j. mittels eines kleinen Brockens zum Schweigen bringen; ~ **up the sponge** sich geschlagen geben; ~ **stones at s. o.** *(fig.)* Anschuldigungen gegen j. vorbringen; ~ **a textbook together** Libretto zusammenhauen; ~ **one's thoughts into elegant phrases** seine Gedanken elegant formulieren; ~ **together** zusammenwerfen; ~ **together to build a house** zusammen ein neues Haus bauen; ~ **up** aus dem Boden stampfen, *(print.)* hervorheben; ~ **up a commission** Auftrag zurückgeben; ~ **up one's job** seine Stellung aufgeben; ~ **up the sponge** Flinte ins Korn werfen; ~ **o. s. upon the mercy of the court** sich der Gnade des Gerichts anheimgeben; ~ **one's weight about** seinen Einfluß in die Waagschale bringen; ~ **a [monkey] wrench** *(coll.)* dazwischenfunken, querschießen;
to be s. one's last ~ jds. letzter Coup gewesen sein;
~ **money** Trinkgeld.

throwaway Weggeworfenes, Vergeudetes, *(advertising)* Wurf-, Streusendung, Reklamezettel, -schrift, Flugblatt, Handzettel, *(reduced ticket, sl.)* verbilligte Eintrittskarte;
~ **product** weggeworfenes Erzeugnis.

throwback Rückschlag, -schritt;
~ **to** *(fam.)* Mensch vom alten Schrot und Korn.

thrown|from automobile *(accident policy)* aus dem Auto geworfen; ~ **out of employment** entlassen, arbeitslos;
to be ~ back upon s. o. auf j. angewiesen sein; **to be ~ with bad companions** in schlechte Gesellschaft geraten; **to be ~ into a dilemma** in eine Klemme geraten; **to be ~ down by an earthquake** von einem Erdbeben zerstört (zum Einsturz gebracht) sein; **to be ~ upon one's own resources** auf sich selbst angewiesen sein.

throwout *(print.)* Faltblatt.

thrust Stoß, Hieb, Angriff, *(mil.)* Vorstoß;
~ **for power** Machtstreben;
~ *(v.)* stoßen, schieben;
~ **s. th. upon s. o.** jem. etw. aufdrängen (aufhalsen); ~ **o. s. forward (past into) a bus** sich in einen Bus drängeln; ~ **a coin into a beggar's hand** einem Bettler ein Geldstück in die Hand drücken; ~ **o. s. into a highly paid job** sich mit allen Mitteln eine hochdotierte Stellung verschaffen; ~ **one's nose in** sich einmischen; ~ **s. o. into prison** j. ins Gefängnis werfen; ~ **s. o. from his right** j. aus seinem Recht verdrängen; ~ **a word in now and then** ab und zu ein Wort einwerfen.

thug Bandenmitglied, *(US)* Meuchelmörder.

thuggery Bandenwesen.

thumb Daumen;
as easy as kiss my ~ *(sl.)* ein Kinderspiel, kinderleicht; **on the** ~ per Anhalter; **under s. one's** ~ an jds. Kandare;
~ *(v.)* *(criminal)* Fingerabdrücke machen;
~ **through a book** Buch durchblättern; ~ **a lift (ride)** Auto zum Mitfahren anhalten;
to be under s. one's ~ unter jds. voller Kontrolle sein; **to have s. o. under one's** ~ *(coll.)* j. unter seiner Fuchtel haben; **to have one's** ~ **in s. one's eyes** j. am Kragen haben; **to have fingers all** ~**s** zwei linke Hände haben; **to travel on the** ~**s** per Anhalter reisen; **to turn one's** ~**s down on s. o.** jem. seine Stimme versagen;

a ~**'s breadth** *(fig.)* eine Kleinigkeit; ~ **index** Daumenindex; ~ **lock** Drückerschloß; ~**-print** *(criminal)* Daumenabdruck, *(fig.)* Persönlichkeitsausstrahlung.

thumbed abgegriffen.

thumbmark Daumenabdruck.

thumbmarked schmutzig, abgegriffen.

thumbnail|description knappe Beschreibung; ~ **sketch** kleine Illustrationsskizze.

thumbscrew Flügel-, Klemmschraube.

thumbtack *(US)* Heft-, Reißzwecke.

thump Aufschlag, Plumps;
~ **at the door** Pochen an der Tür;
~ *(v.)* **the cushion** emphatisch reden; ~ **knowledge into s. o.** jem. Kenntnisse einbleuen.

thumper *(coll.)* Wucht.

thunder Donner, *(fig.)* Donnerwetter, Bannstrahl;
~ **of applause** donnernder Beifall; ~ **of cannon** Kanonendonner; ~ **of the church** kirchlicher Bannstrahl; ~ **and lightning** Gewitter, Unwetter;
~ *(v.)* **applause** tosenden Beifall rufen; ~ **through a station** donnernd einen Bahnhof durchfahren;
to steal somebody's ~ jem. mit einer Überraschungsreklame zuvorkommen; **to take the** ~ **out of s. one's approach** jem. den Wind aus den Segeln nehmen.

thunderblast Donnerschlag.

thunderbolt Blitzstrahl, *(fig.)* schreckliche Drohung, Geißel.

thunderclap Donnerschlag.

thundercloud Gewitterwolke.

thundering lie faustdicke Lüge.

thunderous applause donnernder Beifall.

thundershower Gewitterschauer.

thundersquall Gewitterbö.

thunderstorm Gewitter, Unwetter.

thundery|front Gewitterfront; ~ **tendency** Gewitterneigung.

thwack *(v.)* **some sense into s. one's head** jem. etw. Vernunft einbleuen.

thwart *(v.)* **s. one's plans** jds. Pläne durchkreuzen.

tick *(account, fam.)* Rechnung, *(fam., credit)* Kredit, Pump, Anschreibenlassen, *(moment, coll.)* Augenblick, Moment, *(sign of control)* Vermerk, Kontrollzeichen, Haken, Häkchen, *(sum owing)* Schuldposten, Debet;
on ~ auf Pump; **on the** ~ auf die Sekunde [pünktlich]; **not a** ~ **fleid** *(Scot.)* kein bißchen ängstlich;
~ *(v.)* Kredit gewähren, *(exist)* funktionieren, existieren, *(make debts)* Schulden machen, auf Kredit (Pump) kaufen, *(mark with a tick)* abhaken, abstreichen, ankreiden;
~ **away** *(taximeter)* laufen, angestellt sein; ~ **off** an-, abhaken, abzeichnen; ~ **s. o. off** j. abkanzeln, jem. eine Rüge erteilen, jem. gründlich die Meinung sagen; ~ **off items in an account** Rechnungsposten abhaken; ~ **out the news** *(ticker)* Nachrichten drucken; ~ **over** *(engine)* im Leerlauf sein, ausgekuppelt laufen, *(fig.)* gerade noch funktionieren; ~ **up a huge fare** *(taximeter)* hohe Taxirechnung anzeigen;
to buy on ~ *(coll.)* auf Kredit (Borg, Pump) kaufen, anschreiben lassen; **to go** ~ *(coll.)* Schulden machen; **to leave on** ~ stehen lassen, *(coll.)* anschreiben lassen; **to live on** ~ auf Borg leben; **to make s. o.** ~ jem. inneren Antrieb geben, j. in Schwung halten; **to make s. th.** ~ etw. in Gang halten; **to mark with a** ~ abhaken; **to put a** ~ **against an item** Posten abhaken; **to put a** ~ **against a name** Namen abhaken;
to open a ~ **account for s. o.** *(Br.)* Kreditkonto für j. eröffnen.

ticker *(stock exchange, US)* Börsentelegraph, -fernschreiber;
~ **abbreviations** *(US)* Börsenabkürzungen; ~ **firm** *(US)* Börsenmakler; ~ **service** *(US)* Börsenfernschreiber-, Tickerdienst; ~ **tape** Papierstreifen; **to get a** ~**-tape reception** *(New York)* mit einer Konfettiparade geehrt werden.

ticket *(admission)* Einlaß-, Eintrittskarte, -schein, *(air travel)* Flugschein, *(business transaction)* vorläufige Aufzeichnung, *(captain)* Lizenz, *(dismissal, Br., sl.),* Entlassung, *(label)* Etikett, Schildchen, Preiszettel, *(library)* Ausweis, *(list of candidates)* Wahl-, Kandidatenliste, *(local election, US)* offizieller Kandidat, *(lottery)* Lotterielos, *(luggage)* Gepäckschein, *(Br., mil., sl.)* Entlassungsschein, *(party platform)* Wahl-, Parteiprogramm, *(pawn house)* Pfandschein, *(pilot)* Pilotenschein, Fluglizenz, *(police, US)* gebührenpflichtige Verwarnung, Strafzettel, *(price ticket)* Preiszettel, *(railway)* [Eisenbahn]fahrkarte, Fahrschein, *(shingle)* Aushängeschild, *(slip)* Zettel, *(stock exchange, Br.)* Bescheinigung über den Verkauf von Wertpapieren, Skontrozettel;
admission by ~ **only** nur gegen besonderen Einlaßschein;
without a [valid] ~ ohne gültigen Fahrausweis;

additional ~ Zuschlagskarte; admission ~ Eintrittskarte; advance-purchased ~ längerfristig vorausgebuchtes Flugticket; air (airline, aeroplane) ~ Flugschein, -karte; annual ~ Jahresabonnement; baggage ~ (US) Gepäckschein; balance ~ (shares deposited) Depotschein; banker's ~ Retourrechnung; berth ~ Schlafwagenkarte; cheap ~ verbilligte Fahrkarte, Fahrkarte zum zurückgesetzten Preis; circular ~ (Br.) Rundreisebillet; cloakroom ~ Garderobenschein, -marke, (railway, Br.) Gepäckaufbewahrungsschein; collective ~ Sammelfahrschein; combined ~ Fahrscheinheft für Bahn, Bus und Schiff; commutation ~ (US) Zeit-, Dauerfahr-, Abonnementsfahrkarte; complimentary ~ Frei-, Ehrenkarte, (railway) Freifahrschein; coupon ~ Fahrscheinheft, Sammelkarte; day ~ Rückfahrkarte mit eintägiger Gültigkeit; delivery ~ Lieferschein, (stock exchange) Lieferungsanzeige, Schlußnote; democratic ~ (US) demokratische Parteiliste; deposit ~ (US) Einzahlungsbeleg, -schein; excess ~ Zusatzschein, Übergangsfahrkarte; exchange ~ Umtauschfahrschein; excursion ~ [etwa] Sonntagsrückfahrkarte; extra ~ Zuschlagsfahrkarte; first (second) [class-] ~ Fahrkarte erster (zweiter) Klasse; free admission ~ Freikarte, -schein; full-fare ~ Fahrkarte zum vollen Preis; go-as-you-please ~ Netzfahrkarte; half ~ Kinderfahrkarte; half-fare ~ Fahrkarte zum halben Preis; invalid ~ ungültige Fahrkarte; job ~ Arbeitslaufzettel; landing ~ Landungskarte; left-luggage ~ (Br.) Gepäckaufbewahrungsschein; limited ~ Fahrkarte mit beschränkter Gültigkeit; lost ~ verlorengegangene Fahrkarte; lottery ~ Lotterieschein, Los; luggage ~ (Br.) Gepäckschein; meal ~ Essenbon, Gaststättenmarke; mixed ~ (US) Kompromißwahlliste; monthly ~ Monatskarte; one-way ~ (US) Einzelfahrschein, Einzel-, Hinfahrkarte, einfache Fahrkarte; out-of-date ~ verfallene Fahrkarte; parking ~ Strafzettel für ordnungswidriges Parken, gebührenpflichtige Verwarnung; party ~ Fahrkarte für Gruppenreisen, Sammelfahrschein, (politics, US) Kandidatenliste der Partei; pawn ~ Pfandschein; pay ~ Zahlungsanweisung; pilot's ~ Fluglizenz; platform ~ Bahnsteigkarte; point-to-point ~ (airline) Rundreiseflugschein; price ~ Preisauszeichnung, -zettel; privilege ~ verbilligter Fahrschein, Vorzugskarte; Pullman ~ (US) Fahrkarte erster Klasse; railway ~ (Br.) Fahrkarte, -schein; railroad ~ (US) [Eisenbahn]fahrkarte, Fahrschein; reduced-rate ~ (Br.) verbilligte Fahrkarte; reserved-seat ~ reservierter Platz, Platzkarte; return ~ (Br.) Rückfahrkarte; round-trip ~ (US) Hin- und Rückfahrschein, Rückfahrkarte; rover ~ Netzkarte; runabout ~ Netzkarte; scratch ~ (parl.) ungültiger Wahlschein; season ~ [Eisenbahn-] abonnement, Zeit-, Dauer-, Abonnementfahrkarte; monthly season ~ Monatskarte; second-class ~ Fahrkarte zweiter Klasse; single ~ (Br.) Einzelfahrschein, einfache Fahrkarte; sleeping-car ~ Schlafwagenkarte; speeding ~ (US) Strafzettel wegen Überschreitung der Höchstgeschwindigkeit; straight ~ (parl.) Einheits-, Einmannliste; subscription ~ Abonnementsfahrkarte; tear ~ (US) Belegstück; the ~ (coll.) genau das Richtige; through ~ Umsteiger, Umsteigebillet, direkte Fahrkarte; tourist ~ Rundreisebillet, Ferienfahrkarte; transfer ~ Anschlußkarte; transferable ~ übertragbarer Fahrausweis; unused ~ unbenutzte Fahrkarte; weekend ~ Wochenendkarte; weekly ~ Arbeiterwochenkarte; workman's ~ Arbeiterfahrschein;

~ of admission Einlaßkarte, Zulassungsschein; ~ no longer available ungültiger Fahrschein; ~ of leave (prisoner, Br.) Bewährungshilfe, Entlassungsschein eines vorzeitig entlassenen Sträflings, (mil.) Urlaubs-, Entlassungsschein; ~ for speeding Strafzettel für Geschwindigkeitsüberschreitung;

~ (v.) etikettieren, numerieren, mit einem Etikett (Schildchen) versehen, beschriften, [Waren] auszeichnen, (US) als Fahrtteilnehmer eintragen, Fahrkarte aushändigen;

to be the ~ (fam.) genau das Richtige sein; to be out on ~ of leave (Br.) Bewährung haben; to book a ~ in s. one's name eine Fahrkarte auf jds. Namen bestellen; to break one's ~ of leave (Br.) seine Bewährungsauflagen nicht erfüllen; to buy a ~ Fahrkarte lösen; to collect the ~s Fahrkarten abnehmen; to draw a prize-winning ~ Lotteriegewinn ziehen; to get a ~ Strafzettel bekommen; to get one's ~ (prisoner, sl.) entlassen werden; to give s. o. a ~ (policy) Strafzettel (gebührenpflichtige Verwarnung, Protokoll) für j. ausstellen; to issue ~ Fahrkarten ausgeben; to produce one's ~ seine Fahrkarte vorzeigen; to punch a ~ Fahrkarte lochen; to remove s. o. from the ~ (US) j. von der Kandidatenliste streichen; to scratch a ~ (US) Parteiliste durch Streichungen abändern; to show one's ~ seine Fahrkarte vorzeigen; to take a ~ Fahrkarte lösen; to take a ~ at the university sich immatrikulieren lassen; to turn in one's ~ seine Fahrkarte

bei der Sperre abgeben; to vote a ~ (US) Wahlliste wählen; to vote the straight (US) ~ auf die Parteiliste eingeschworen sein, Parteianweisungen bei der Abstimmung befolgen; to work one's ~ Reisekosten abarbeiten; to write one's own ~ sich selbst die Norm setzen; to write s. one's ~ j. entlassen; that's not quite the ~ das gehört sich nicht;

~s please! Fahrkarten vorzeigen!;

~ advertising Fahrscheinwerbung; ~ agent (US) Fahrkartenverkaufsstelle, -büro, (theater) Vorverkauf; ~ book Fahrscheinheft; ~ booking Kartenverkauf; ~ center (US) Fahr-, Flugscheinverkaufsstelle; ~ clerk Fahrkartenverkäufer; ~ collector Fahrkartenabnehmer, -kontrolleur, Bahnsteigschaffner; ~ control Fahrkartenkontrolle; ~ counter Fahrkartenausgabe; ~ day (stock exchange, Br.) Vergleichungs-, Abrechnungs-, Liquidationstag, (London stock exchange) zweiter Liquidationstag; ~ envelope Fahrkartentasche; ~ gate Bahnsteigsperre; ~ holder Fahrkarten-, Fahrscheininhaber; ~ inspector Fahrkartenkontrolleur; ~-of-leave man (Br.) bedingt Entlassener, auf Bewährung vorzeitig entlassener Sträfling; ~ machine Kartenautomat; ~ night Benefizvorstellung; ~ number [Lotterie]losnummer; ~ office (US) [Fahrkarten]schalter, -ausgabe; ~ porter Bahnsteigschaffner, (Br.) Gepäckträger; ~ printer Fahrkartendrucker; ~ punch Fahrkartenlochzange, -locher; ~ puncher Fahrkartenkontrolleur; ~ sales Kartenabsatz; advance ~ sale [Karten]vorverkauf; standby ~ sale Flugscheinverkauf ohne festgelegtes Flugdatum; ~ seller (US) Fahrkartenverkäufer; ~ slot machine Fahrscheinautomat, -apparat; ~ speculator Schwarzhändler von Theaterkarten; airline ~ tax Flugscheingebühr; ~ window (US) Fahrkartenschalter, (theater, US) Kasse.

ticketing Fahrschein-, Flugscheinausstellung, (labelling) Auszeichnung, Etikettierung.

ticking off Abhaken;

to give s. o. a good ~ j. ganz gehörig abkanzeln.

tickle (fig.) Kitzel, (game, sl.) Diebesbeute;

~ s. one's fancy jds. Phantasie anregen; ~ the palate Gaumen kitzeln; ~ s. one's palm (coll.) j. schmieren (bestechen).

tickler (US coll.) Vormerk-, Terminkalender, Mahnkartei;

maturity ~ Wechselverfallbuch;

~ file Wiedervorlagemappe.

ticklish situation kitzlige Lage.

tidal | gauge Gezeitenmesser, Wasserstandsanzeiger; ~ harbo(u)r Gezeitenhafen; ~ power plant Gezeitenkraftwerk; ~ wave Flutwelle.

tide Ebbe und Flut, Gezeiten, (shift) Schicht;

spring ~ Springflut;

~ of events Zeitströmung;

~ (v.) mit dem Gezeitenstrom ein- und auslaufen;

~ it over über die Runden kommen, sich über Wasser halten; ~ s. o. over jem. finanziell unter die Arme greifen; ~ over one's difficulties seiner Schwierigkeiten Herr werden; ~ s. o. over a little longer j. noch etw. über Wasser halten; ~ over a period of unemployment um die arbeitslose Zeit zu überbrücken; ~ over the winter über den Winter hinweghelfen; ~ up the river stromaufwärts treiben;

to ignore the rising ~ of public opinion Umschwung der öffentlichen Meinung mißachten; to work double ~s (Br.) Tag und Nacht arbeiten;

~ day Gezeitentag; ~ gate Schleusentor; ~ gauge Gezeitenpegel; ~ lock Dockschleuse; ~ mark Gezeitenmarke, Pegelstand; ~-over credit Überbrückungskredit; ~ predictor Gezeitenrechner; ~-surveyor Seezollinspektor; ~ table Gezeitentafel.

tideland Watt.

tidemark Gezeitenmarke, Pegelstand.

tidesmen (Br.) Zollpersonal im Hafen.

tidewaiter (ship) Zollaufseher.

tidewater Küstengewässer.

tideway Priel.

tidings, bad schlechte Nachrichten; glad ~ Freudenbotschaft.

tidy sauber, reinlich, ordentlich, akkurat, (not small in size, coll.) anständig, beträchtlich;

~ (v.) o. s. sich zurechtmachen; ~ up aufräumen;

~ day's work ordentliches Tagewerk; ~ farm ganz hübsches Landgut; ~ room aufgeräumtes Zimmer; ~ sum of money hübsches Sümmchen, schöner Batzen Geld.

tie Schlips, Schleife, Masche, (architecture) Bindeglied, Verbindungsstück, (bond, coll.) Fessel, Last, (coll.) Stimmengleichheit, (fig.) Bindung, Verpflichtung, (obligation of a tied house, Br.) festgelegte Abnahmeverpflichtung, (pol.) Punkt-, Stimmengleichheit, Unentschieden, (sleeper, US) Eisenbahnschwelle;

family ~s Familienbande; **marriage** ~s eheliche Bande; ~s **of blood** Bande des Blutes, Blutsbande; ~s **of friendship** Freundschaftsbande; ~s **of matrimonial life** eheliche Bande;
~ (v.) festbinden, (fig.) verknüpfen, zusammenfügen, (pol.) gleichstehen mit;
~ **a bundle** Bündel schnüren; ~ **capital** Kapital festlegen (fest anlegen); ~ **s. o. down** jds. Freizügigkeit einschränken; ~ **s. o. down to a contract** j. vertraglich binden; ~ **s. o. down as to time** j. zeitlich festlegen; ~ **a factory** Fabrik stillegen; ~ **the hands of s. o.** jds. Handlungsfreiheit einschränken; ~ **illustrations with the text** Illustrationen in den Text einbauen; ~ **the knot** Trauung vollziehen; ~ **on a label** Anhänger festmachen; ~ **one's money in land** Immobilienkäufe tätigen; ~ **it off** (sl.) Rest des Tages blau machen; ~ **production** Produktionsstopp vornehmen; ~ **s. o. to the rules** j. zur Einhaltung der Spielregeln zwingen; ~ **s. one's tongue** j. zum Schweigen verpflichten; ~ **up** verschnüren, (business) blockieren, behindern, (estate) unter Verfügungsbeschränkungen vermachen, einer Verfügungsbeschränkung unterwerfen; ~ **up an estate** Vermögen festlegen; ~ **it up** (sl.) zu arbeiten aufhören; ~ **up a parcel** Paket verschnüren; ~ **up a telephone booth** Telefonzelle blockieren; ~ **with s. o.** mit jem. die gleiche Punktzahl haben;
to end in a ~-up stimmengleich sein; **to keep one's ~s with s. o.** seine Verbindungen mit jem. aufrechterhalten.

tie|-break (US) Stichwahl; ~-**break competition** Stichwahlwettbewerb; ~ **division** unentschiedene Abstimmung.

tie-in geheimer Zusammenhang, (advertising) zwei miteinander verbundene Werbungen, aufeinander abgestimmte Werbung; ~s Kopplungsgeschäfte;
~ **advertising** Anknüpfungswerbung; ~ **clause** (US) Kopplungsklausel; ~ **deal** Kopplungsgeschäft; ~ **sale** (US) Kopplungsverkauf, -geschäft.

tie-line installation Direktleitung.

tie-on label Anhängeradresse, -zettel, Anhänger.

tie-up (US) Stillstand, Stockung, Lahmlegung, (strike, US) Ausstand, Streik, Arbeitseinstellung, (traffic jam, US) Verkehrsstockung, (tying up) Vereinigung, Verbindung, Fusion;
general ~ **of industry** Stillegung der gesamten Industrie;
~ **advertising** kombinierte Werbaktion; ~ **shop** an eine Lieferfirma gebundener Verkaufsladen; ~ **quota** (book trade) Bindequota.

tie vote Stimmengleichheit.

tied|to the index indexgebunden; ~ **up** (busy) schwer beschäftigt, (company) zusammengehörig, verbunden;
to be ~ up with another company mit einer anderen Firma geschäftlich verbunden sein; **to be ~ up with other things** anderweitig gebunden (beschäftigt) sein; **to get o. s. ~ up** sich verheddern;
~ **aid** projektgebundene Entwicklungshilfe; ~ **cottage** Werks-, Deputatwohnung; ~-**up capital** festgelegtes Kapital; ~ **garage** Vertragswerkstatt; ~ **house** (Br.) von einer Brauerei gepachtetes Wirtshaus, brauereigebundene Gaststätte, Vertragsgaststätte, -restaurant; ~ **loan** zweckgebundene Anleihe; ~ **sale** (US) Kopplungskauf; ~ **shop** an eine Lieferfirma gebundener Verkaufsladen; ~ **times** knappe Produktionsfristen.

tier Reihe, Stufe, (pol.) Gleichstehender, (theater) Sitzreihe, Rang, (local government, Br.) Verwaltungsebene;
in ~s lagenweise;
upper ~ (Br.) höhere Verwaltungsstufe;
~ **box** (theater) Rangloge; **two-**~ **system** (Br.) zweistufiges Verwaltungssystem.

tiff kleine Meinungsverschiedenheit, Unstimmigkeit;
~ (v.) Unstimmigkeiten haben.

tight fest[sitzend], festgefügt, (argument) hieb- und stichfest, (condensed) zusammengedrängt, komprimiert, (drunk, sl.) total blau, voll, (embarrassed) in Geldverlegenheit, in einer Klemme, (mean) knauserig, knickerig, geizig, (market) angespannt, (money) knapp, angespannt, rar, (in case of default, coll.) sofort vollstreckbar, (secure) unbeweglich, sicher, (ship) nicht leck, abgedichtet, (style) knapp;
packed ~ fest verpackt;
~ **as a drum (lord, tick)** besoffen wie eine Strandhaubitze; **as** ~ **as an owl** total blau;
to get ~ **every payday** an jedem Löhnungstag betrunken sein; ~ **argument** hieb- und stichfestes Argument; ~ **bargain** Geschäft mit kleiner Marge; **to be in a** ~ **corner (place)** in der Klemme sitzen; ~ **credit** gebundener Kredit; ~ **credit policy** restriktive Kreditpolitik; ~-**fisted** geizig; **to need a** ~ **hand** fest angepackt werden müssen; **to get out of a** ~ **hole** sich aus der Klemme ziehen; ~ **job** schlecht bezahlte Arbeit, niedrig bezahlte Akkordarbeit; ~ **knot** fester Knoten; ~ **labo(u)r mar**-

ket leerer (leergepumpter) Arbeitsmarkt; **to be ~-lipped** zugeknöpft sein; ~ **money** knappes Geld, restriktive Kreditpolitik; ~ **money conditions** beengte Liquiditätsverhältnisse; ~ **money market** angespannte Lage auf dem Geldmarkt, angespannter Geldmarkt; **to keep a ~ rein on s. o.** strenges Regiment über j. führen; ~ **rope** straffes Seil; ~ **schedule** übersetzter Zeitplan; ~ **spot** gefährliche Lage; ~ **squeeze** dichtes Gedränge, Schlamassel; ~ **times** Produktionsfristen.

tighten (v.) verstärken, befestigen, (market) sich versteifen;
~ **one's belt** den Riemen enger schnallen, sich einschränken; ~ **a blockade** Blockade verschärfen; ~ **economic bonds** wirtschaftliche Verbindungen verstärken; ~ **a cask** Faß abdichten; ~ **up the censorship** Zensurbestimmungen verschärfen; ~ **credit** Kreditschraube anziehen; ~ **up on one's credit terms** seine Kreditbedingungen verschärfen; ~ **restrictions** Bestimmungen verschärfen; ~ **up the screws** Schrauben anziehen;
to make s. o. ~ his belt jem. den Brotkorb höher hängen.

tightening Anspannung;
~ **of a blockade** Verschärfung einer Blockade, Blockadeverschärfung; ~ **of commission provisions** Verschärfung der Provisionsbestimmungen; **progressive ~ of monetary control** laufende Verstärkung der Geldmarktkontrolle; ~ **of money conditions (the money market)** Anspannung der Liquidität, Versteifung des Geldmarktes, Geldmarktanspannung, Liquiditätsanspannung; ~ **of the money supply** Drosselung der Geldversorgung; ~ **of provisions** Verschärfung von Bestimmungen.

tightly set (print.) kompreß gesetzt.

tightness Knappheitserscheinung, Verknappung, (parsimony) Geiz, Knickrigkeit;
~ **of money** Geldknappheit, -verknappung, angespannter Geldmarkt, Liquiditätsanspannung.

tightrope Drahtseil;
~ **acrobat** Drahtseilakrobat; ~ **dancer** Seiltänzer.

tile [Stein]platte, Fliese, [Ofen]kachel, (roof) Dachziegel, (high silk hat) Zylinder, Angströhre, (pipe) Tonrohr, (tiles collectively) Fliesenvertäfelung;
Dutch (glazed) ~ Kachel; **floor** ~ Fliese, Fußbodenplatte; **paving** ~ Fußbodenfliese; **plain** ~ Flach-, Biberschwanzziegel; **wall** ~ Wandfliese;
to be on the ~s (sl.) liederlich leben, herumsumpfen; **to have a ~ loose** (sl.) nicht ganz richtig im Oberstübchen sein;
~ **burner** Ziegelbrenner; ~ **drain** Tonröhrenkanal; ~ **kiln** Brennofen.

tiler Dachdecker, (tile kiln) Brennofen.

tiling Fliesen-, Platten-, Kachellegen, Kacheln, (roof) Dachdecken.

till Geld-, Ladenkasse, Geldkassette, -lade;
shop ~ Ladenkasse;
~ (v.) kultivieren;
~ **the soil** Boden bestellen;
to break (dip) into (rob) the ~ Kasse angreifen, in die Kasse greifen; **to seize the** ~ Ladenkasse pfänden;
~ **due** bis zur Verfallzeit; ~ **forbid** (advertising) bis auf Widerruf; ~ **now** bis dato;
~ **book** Kassenbuch, -strazze; ~ **money** Geld in der Ladenkasse, (US, banking) Kassenbestand, -reserve.

tillable anbaufähig, bestellbar.

tillage Feld-, Boden-, Ackerbestellung, Kultivierung, (cultivated land) bestelltes Land, Ackerland;
in ~ angebaut, kultiviert.

tiller Landmann, Ackerbauer.

tilt Kippen, Neigung, (lorry) Plane, Verdeck, (mar.) Sonnensegel, (stand) Sonnendach, (television) Schwank;
at full ~ mit voller Wucht;
~ (v.) mit einer Plane überdecken, (ship) krängen;
~ **a cask** Faß kippen; ~ **at windmills** gegen Windmühlen kämpfen;
to have a ~ with s. o. Strauß mit jem. ausfechten;
~ **cart** Kippwagen.

tilter Kippvorrichtung.

timber Bau-, Nutzholz, (forest, US) bewaldetes Land, Wald, (squared piece of wood) Balken, (Br.) Bauholz;
standing ~ Holz auf dem Stamm;
to be of presidential ~ (US) das Zeug zum Präsidenten haben;
~ **cart** Langholzwagen; ~ **culture entry** Aufforstung von Staatsland; ~ **estate** forstwirtschaftlich genutztes Grundstück; ~ **forest** Hochwald; ~ **framing** Holzfachwerk; ~ **group** Konzern der holzverarbeitenden Industrie; ~ **line** (US) Baumgrenze; ~ **merchant** Holzhändler; ~ **supply** Nutzholzversorgung; ~ **trade** Holzhandel; ~ **tree** Nutzholzbaum; ~-**trees** Bauholzbestände.

timbering Verschalung, Holzverkleidung.

timberland *(US)* Waldgebiet.

timberwork of a roof Dachgesparre.

timberyard Bauhof.

time Zeit[punkt], Zeitdauer, -abschnitt, *(apprenticeship)* Ausbildungs-, Lehrzeit, *(broadcasting)* käufliche Werbezeit, *(fuss, US coll.)* Getue, Aufhebens, *(hour)* Stunde, *(prison, coll.)* Gefängnisjahre, *(term)* Frist, *(wages)* Zeit-, Stundenlohn; **against ~** gegen die Uhr, mit größter Geschwindigkeit; **as ~s go** in der heutigen Zeit; **at all ~** stets; **at any ~** zu jeder beliebigen Zeit; **at the appropriate (proper) ~** zum gegebenen Zeitpunkt; **at the fixed ~** zur vorgesehenen Zeit; **at a given ~** zu einer bestimmten Zeit, zu einem festgesetzten Zeitpunkt; **at other ~s** bei anderen Gelegenheiten; **at the same ~** zur gleichen Zeit, zusammen; **at some ~** irgendwann; **at your ~ of life** bei Ihrem Alter; **at the ~ the action is brought** zum Zeitpunkt der Klageerhebung; **at the ~ the claim arose** bei der Anspruchsentstehung; **at the ~ of delivery** bei der Lieferung; **at the ~ of expiration** zur Verfallzeit; **at the ~ of making the will** bei Testamentserrichtung; **at the ~ of marriage** zum Zeitpunkt der Eheschließung; **at the ~ provided by the contract** zum vertraglich vereinbarten Zeitpunkt; **at the ~ of reaching agreement** beim Vertragsschluß; **behind ~** verspätet; **behind the ~s** altmodisch; **by passage of ~** durch Zeitablauf; **for the ~ being** für den Augenblick, vorläufig, unter gegenwärtigen Umständen; **for a certain ~** auf eine im voraus bestimmte Zeit; **for want of ~** aus Zeitmangel; **from this ~** ab jetzt; **from ~ to ~** gelegentlich; **in the course of ~** im Verlauf der Zeit; **in due ~** frist-, termingemäß, rechtzeitig; **in double-quick ~** im Galopp; **in [good] ~** rechtzeitig; **in its ~** seinerzeit; **in the length of ~** auf die Dauer; **in ~s of need** in Notzeiten; **in the nick of ~** zum rechten Augenblick; **in no ~** in kürzester Zeit, im Handumdrehen; **in less than no ~** im Handumdrehen; **in reckoning ~** bei der Fristberechnung; **in one's spare ~** in seiner Freizeit, nach Feierabend; **on ~** pünktlich, rechtzeitig, *(instal(l)ment system)* auf Zeit (Raten); **out of ~** nicht fristgerecht, verspätet, zur Unzeit; **upon expiry of the ~** bei Fristablauf; **within a reasonable ~** innerhalb einer angemessenen Frist; **within the required ~** in der vorgeschriebenen Frist; **within the shortest possible ~** in kürzester Frist; **within the specified ~** fristgemäß; **within the ~ allowed (prescribed) by the law** innerhalb der gesetzlichen Frist; **without any loss of ~** ohne Zeitverlust;

~s *(railway)* Ankunfts- und Abfahrtzeiten, Zeittabelle; **additional ~** zusätzlich gewährte Frist, Zusatzfrist; **~ allowed** Frist; **appointed ~** Termin; **average ~** Zeitdurchschnitt; **broken ~** Arbeitszeitverlust, Verdienstausfall; **Central European ~** Mitteleuropäische Zeit; **certain ~** bestimmter Zeitpunkt; **chargeable ~** *(tel.)* Gebührenminuten; **Christmas ~** Weihnachszeit; **civil ~** Normalzeit; **closing ~** Laden-, Geschäftsschluß, *(hunting)* Schonzeit; **cooling ~** *(strike law)* Abkühlungszeit, Beruhigungsfrist; **dead ~** nicht ausgenutzte (tote) Zeit, *(worker)* Lohnausfall, *(factory)* Verlustzeit; **delay ~** *(factory)* Verlustzeit; **delivery ~** Lieferzeit; **determinable future ~** bestimmbare künftige Zeit; **dull ~** stille Saison, tote Zeit, Flaute; **earliest practicable ~** frühest möglicher Zeitpunkt; **Eastern European ~** Osteuropäische Zeit; **elapsed ~** Fristablauf; **fixed ~** festgesetzte Frist; **free [allowance] ~** standgeldfreie [Lade]zeit; **full ~** volle Arbeitszeit; **gained ~** Zeitgewinn; **the good old ~s** die gute alte Zeit; **~ granted** eingeräumte Frist; **hard ~s** schlechte Zeiten; **idle ~** Verlustzeit, *(production)* verlorene Produktionszeit; **~ immemorial** unvordenkliche Zeit; **individual production ~** Stückzeit; **leisure ~** Freizeit; **limited ~** beschränkte Bezugsdauer; **loading ~** Ladezeit; **local ~** Ortszeit; **local mean ~** mittlere Ortszeit; **machining (operating) ~** Bearbeitungszeit; **off ~** Freizeit; **official ~** Normalzeit; **part ~** Kurzarbeit; **quick ~** *(mil.)* Geschwindschritt; **reasonable ~** angemessene Frist; **record ~** Rekordzeit; **runaround ~** für Botengänge benötigte Zeit; **scheduled ~** *(US)* fahrplanmäßige Zeit; **shipping ~** Versandtermin; **short ~** verkürzte Arbeitszeit, Arbeitszeitverkürzung; **slack ~** harte (schlechte) Zeiten, *(data processing)* Pufferzeit, Flaute; **spare ~** übrige Zeit, Freizeit; **specified (stated) ~** festgesetzte Zeit; **~ spent** Zeitaufwand; **~ spent abroad** Auslandsaufenthalt; **spring ~** Frühling; **standard ~** Normalzeit *(process, US)* Zeitnorm im Arbeitsprozeß; **starting and finishing ~** Arbeitsbeginn und -schluß; **straight ~** regelmäßige Arbeitszeit; **summer ~** Sommerzeit; **~ taken** Istzeit; **task ~** Zeitnorm; **unproductive ~** Verlustzeit; **unquiet ~s** turbulente Zeiten; **valid ~** *(weather forecast)* Gültigkeitsdauer; **waiting ~** Wartezeit, *(production)* Verlustzeit; **~ worked** geleistete Arbeitsstunden; **working ~** Betriebs-, Arbeitszeit;

~ for acceptance *(bill)* Annahmefrist; **~ of accident** Unfallzeitpunkt; **~ of admission** Aufnahmetermin; **~ of adjudication** Zuschlagfrist; **~ and again** immer wieder, wiederholt; **~ of allotment** Zuteilungsfrist; **~ prescribed for appeal** Beschwerde-, Berufungs-, Revisions-, Rechtsmittelfrist; **~ for appealing** Rechtsmittelfrist; **~ for entering an appearance** Einlassungsfrist; **~ of application** Antrags-, Anmeldefrist; **~ of arrival** Ankunftszeit; **~ of bankruptcy** Datum der Konkursanmeldung; **~ of collection** Abholzeit, *(encashment)* Inkassozeit; **~ of conclusion of the contract** Zeitpunkt des Vertragsabschlusses; **~ for consideration (to consider)** Bedenkzeit; **~ as provided in the contract** vertraglich vereinbarter Termin; **~ of contracting** Zeitpunkt des [Vertrags]abschlusses; **~ of crisis** Krisenzeiten; **~ of delivery** Ablieferungsfrist, Liefertermin, -zeit, -frist; **~s of delivery** *(postal service)* Zustellzeiten; **~ of departure** Abflug-, Abfahrtszeit; **~ of depression** Krisen-, Flautezeit; **~ for discussion** Diskussionszeit; **~ of dispatch** Abgangszeit; **~ of disposal** Veräußerungszeitraum; **~ of a draft** Laufzeit eines Wechsels; **~ for entering an appearance** Einlassungsfrist; **~ is the essence of contract** zwingende Lieferfrist; **~ of examination** Prüfungstermin; **~ of a flight** Flugzeit; **~ and a half** 50%iger Lohnzuschlag für Nacht und Feiertagsarbeit; **~ of holding** Sitzungsdauer; **~ of inception** *(claim)* Entstehungszeit; **~ of incorporation** Gründungszeitpunkt; **~ of life** Alter; **~ for loading** Ladezeit, -frist; **~ of maturity** Verfallzeit; **~ out of memory** unvordenkliche Zeit; **~ out of mind** unvordenkliche Zeit; **~ for giving notice** Benachrichtigungsfrist; **~ without number** immer wieder, wiederholt; **~ paid for but not worked** vergütete arbeitsfreie Lohnstunden; **~ to pay** Stundung; **~ off with pay** Urlaubsvergütung; **~ [fixed] for payment** Zahlungstermin, -frist, -ziel, Verfallzeit; **~ of payment of a bill** Fälligkeit eines Wechsels; **~ of performance** Leistungs-, Erfüllungstermin; **~ of posting** Postaufgabezeit; **~ of prescription** Ersitzungs-, Verjährungsfrist; **~ of presentment** Vorlagefrist; **~ of pressure** Krisenzeit; **~ of purchase** Kaufzeit; **~ and a quarter** *(wage)* 25% prozentiger übertariflicher Überstundenzuschlag; **~ in question** fragliche Zeit; **~ of redemption** Tilgungsdauer, Einlösungsfrist; **~ for repayment** Rückzahlungsfrist; **~ to reply** Erwiderungsfrist; **~ to run** *(bill of exchange)* effektive Laufzeit; **~ of sailing** Abgangszeit; **~ of service** Militärzeit; **~ of shipment** *(US)* Versandzeit; **ten ~s the size** zehnmal so groß; **~ limited for speeches** begrenzte Redezeit; **~s of stress** anstrengende Zeiten, Krisenzeiten; **free ~ on television** gebührenfreie Fernsehzeit; **~ of tort** Tatzeit; **~ for unloading** Entladezeit, -frist; **~ of waiting** Wartezeit; **~ for withholding** Einbehaltungszeit; **~ when work begins** Arbeitsbeginn; **~ when work ends** Arbeitsschluß; **dead ~ of the year** geschäftslose Zeit; **the piping ~s of yore** die gute alte Zeit;

~ *(v.)* zur rechten Zeit unternehmen, *(bill of exchange)* effektive Laufzeit feststellen, *(give time)* Frist gewähren, stunden, *(schedule)* zeitlich abstimmen, *(train)* nach Fahrplan fahren lassen;

~ one's arrival rightly richtige Zeit für seine Ankunft wählen; **~ the picture** Spieldauer feststellen; **~ the script** *(film)* Zeitlänge prüfen; **~ the speed** Geschwindigkeit messen; **~ a train** Zug genau nach dem Fahrplan fahren lassen; **to abridge a ~** Frist verkürzen; **to allow ~** Frist gewähren, (einräumen); **to appoint a ~** Termin festsetzen; **to arrange ~ and place for the next meeting** Zeit und Ort für die nächste Sitzung festlegen; **to arrive on ~** *(train)* fahrplanmäßig einlaufen; **to ask for ~** um Aufschub (Fristverlängerung) bitten; **to be abreast of the ~s** mit der Zeit gehen; **to be ahead of one's ~** seinen Zeitgenossen voraus sein; **to be behind ~** Verspätung haben; **to be behind the ~s** *(fig.)* rückständig (altmodisch) sein; **to be always behind ~ with one's payments** seine Zahlungstermine nie einhalten; **to be born before one's ~** seinen Zeitgenossen voraus sein; **to be businessman all the ~** ganze Zeit nur ans Geschäft denken; **to be finished in ~** rechtzeitig fertig sein; **to be on part ~** kurzarbeiten; **to be paid by ~** stundenweise bezahlt werden; **to be living on borrowed ~** nur einen kurzen Zeitgewinn erzielt haben; **to be pinched (pressed) for ~** nicht genug Zeit haben, zeitknapp sein; **to be well past ~** allerhöchste Zeit sein; **to be on ~ and on budget** Fristen und Kostenvoranschläge einhalten; **to begin serving one's ~** seine Strafe antreten; **to bide one's ~** rechten Augenblick (richtigen Zeitpunkt) abwarten; **to buy ~** Zeit gewinnen; **to buy additional ~** auf Zeitgewinn hinarbeiten; **to carry out within a given ~** fristgemäß ausführen; **to come on bad ~s** schlechte Zeiten erleben; **to count ~ and a half** *(overtime)* um die Hälfte erhöhten Lohnsatz erzielen; **to decide on a fit ~** geeigneten Zeitpunkt festsetzen; **to devote one's spare ~** seine Freizeit verwenden; **to dispose of one's ~** über seine Zeit verfügen können; **to do one's ~** *(fam.)* Knast schieben, seine Jahre

absitzen; **to do it in half the ~** in der halben Zeit erledigen; **to drive in double quick ~** auf Tempo fahren; **to expend much ~ on s. th.** viel Zeit auf etw. verwenden; **to extend the ~** Frist verlängern; **to fall on hard ~s** vor einer schweren Zeit stehen; **to fix a ~** Zeit festsetzen, Termin bestimmen; **to gain ~** Zeit gewinnen; **to give s. o. ~** Frist gewähren; **to give ~ off** kurz beurlauben; **not to give s. o. the ~ of day** j. komplett übersehen; **to grant ~** Frist gewähren; **to have a ~ with** *(coll.)* Schwierigkeiten haben; **to have a good ~** sich gut unterhalten; **to have ample ~** reichlich Zeit haben; **to have ~ on one's hands** viel [freie] Zeit haben; **to have no ~ to lose** keine Zeit zu verlieren haben; **to have had one's ~** beste Zeit seines Lebens hinter sich haben; **to have had a hard (thin) ~** schlimme Zeit durchgemacht haben; **to have a rough ~** schwere Zeiten durchmachen; **to have no ~ to spare** keine Zeit übrig haben, völlig ausgebucht sein; **to have the ~ of one's life** sich glänzend amüsieren; **to have no easy ~** keinen leichten Stand haben; **to improve one's ~** seine Zeit gut nutzen; **to keep one's ~** Termin einhalten; **to keep abreast of the ~s** mit der Zeit halten; **to keep good (bad) ~** *(clock)* genau (ungenau) gehen; **to keep up with the ~s** mit der Zeit gehen; **to kill ~** Zeit totschlagen, sich die Zeit vertreiben; **to know the ~ of the day** wissen, was die Glocke geschlagen hat; **to know the ~ of the trains** Zugfahrplan kennen; **to let the appointed ~ pass** Frist verstreichen lassen; **to live through terrible ~s** schlechte Zeiten durchmachen; **to make up ~** aufholen; **to make inroads upon s. one's ~** jem. die Zeit stehlen; **to mark ~** *(fig.)* nicht vom Fleck kommen; **to misemploy one's ~** seine Zeit vergeuden; **to overrun the allotted ~** Redezeit überschreiten; **to overrun the ~ stipulated** festgesetzte Zeit überschreiten; **to pass the ~ of the day with s. o.** jem. seinen Gruß entbieten; **to put s. o. up to the ~ of the day** *(sl.)* jem. wie es gemacht wird; **to save ~** Zeit gewinnen; **to schedule one's ~** seine Zeit einteilen; **to serve ~** seine Strafe absitzen; **to serve one's ~** seine Lehrzeit (Ausbildungszeit) absolvieren, *(mil.)* dienen, seine Zeit abdienen; **to set a ~** Frist setzen; **to snooze ~ away** seine Zeit vertrödeln; **to specify a ~** Zeitpunkt festsetzen; **to spend ~** Zeit verbringen; **to stall for ~** Zeit zu gewinnen trachten; **to stand the test of ~** sich bewähren; **to state a precise ~** genaue Zeit angeben; **to stipulate a ~ for delivery** Lieferfrist festsetzen; **to take ~** sich die Zeit nehmen; **to take ~ by the forelock** Gelegenheit beim Schopf fassen; **to take one's ~** seine Zeit dauern; **to take ~ off** sich freinehmen; **to take ~ out** *(US)* sich eine Ruhepause gönnen; **to waste one's ~** seine Zeit vergeuden; **to watch the ~** häufig nach der Uhr sehen, auf die Zeit aufpassen; **to watch one's ~** seine Chance abwarten; **to work full ~** ganztägig arbeiten;
~ *(a.)* mit bestimmter Zahlungsfrist;
~ account *(stock exchange)* Terminkonto; **~ allowance** Zeitvorgabe, Zeitausgleich; **~ apportionment** Zeitaufteilung; **~ balance** *(stock exchange)* Terminguthaben; **~ bargain** *(option)* Prämiengeschäft, *(stock exchange)* Zeit-, Termin-, Lieferungs-, Differenz-, Fixgeschäft; **~-barred** verjährt; **~ belt** *(US)* Zeitzone; **~ bill** Wechsel mit bestimmter Laufzeit, Zeit-, Nachsichtwechsel, *(railway, Br.)* Fahrplan; **~ bomb** Zeitbombe; **~ book** Arbeits[stunden]buch, *(railway)* Fahrplanbuch; **~ buyer** *(agency)* Sachbearbeiter für Funkwerbung, Funk- und Fernsehreferent; **~ buying** Belegen von Sendezeit; **fixed-~ call** Festzeitgespräch; **~ card** Kontroll-, Lohn-, Stechkarte, *(railway)* Karte mit aufgedrucktem Fahrplan; **~ certificate of deposit** befristeter Depositenschein; **~ charge** *(broadcasting)* Tarif für Werbesendungen; **~ charter** *(ship)* Befrachtung für einen bestimmten Zeitraum, Zeitfracht, -charter; **~ charter party** Zeitcharter; **~ check** Lohnstundennachweis, *(radio)* Zeitansage, *(tel.)* Gesprächsuhr; **~ clauses** Terminbestimmungen; **~ clerk** *(works)* Zeitkontrolleur; **~ clock** Stech-, Kontrolluhr; **~-clock card** Stechkarte; **~-consuming** zeitraubend; **~ cost** *(US)* periodenfremde Aufwendungen; **~-delay relay** Zeitrelais; **~ deposits** *(US)* festliegende (befristete) Gelder, festes (langfristiges) Geld, Einlage mit Kündigungsfrist, Festgeld, Termineinlagen; **one month's ~ deposits** *(US)* Monatsgelder; **two month's ~ deposits** *(US)* Zweimonatsgelder; **~ detector** Kontrolluhr; **~ discount** Bardiskont, *(advertising)* Mengen-, Abschlußrabatt, *(broadcasting)* Funkwerbungsmengenrabatt; **~ draft** Zeitwechsel; **~ efficiency** Zeitausnutzungsgrad; **~ element** Zeitfaktor; **~-expired** *(soldier, Br.)* ausgedient; **~ exposure** *(photo)* Zeitaufnahme; **~ freight** *(US)* Eilfracht; **~ fuse** Zeitzünder; **~ holder** *(advertising)* Komplettierungszeige; **~-hono(u)red** altehrwürdig; **chargeable ~ indicator** *(tel.)* Gesprächsuhr; **built-in ~ indicator scale** eingebaute Zeitablaufskala; **~ interest earned** Festgeldzinsen; **~ interval** Zwischenzeit; **full-~ job** Ganztagsbeschäftigung; **spare-~ job**

Freizeitbeschäftigung; **~ lag** zeitliche Verschiebung, Zeitloch, Zeitverzögerung, Zeitspanne, Phasenunterschied, Nachhinken, *(stock exchange)* Marktanpassungszeit; **~-lapse photography** Zeitrafferaufnahmeverfahren; **~ liabilities** befristete Verbindlichkeiten.

time limit Ausschlußfrist, Termin, Zeitraum, -spanne, -beschränkung, *(pub, Br.)* Öffnungszeiten, *(speaker)* Redezeit;
without ~ ohne zeitliche Begrenzung;
~ for claims Rügefrist;
to adhere to (comply with) a ~ Frist einhalten; **to exceed a ~** Frist überschreiten; **to lay down a ~** Frist setzen; **to lay down a ~ on one's acceptance** für sein Angebot eine Annahmefrist festsetzen; **to observe a ~** Frist einhalten; **to fail to observe a ~** Frist versäumen.

time | limitation *(US)* Verjährung; **~ loan** längerfristiges Darlehn, Monatsgeld; **~ lock** Zeitschloß; **~ management** Zeiteinteilung; **~ method of calculating depreciation** *(US)* Abschreibungsmethode nach Quoten; **~ money** festes Geld, Festgeld, langfristiges Börsengeld; **~ note** Wechsel mit bestimmter Laufzeit, Zeitwechsel; **~-out** *(US)* Arbeitsunterbrechung; **~ paper** Papier mit Laufzeit; **~ path** Verlaufsstruktur; **~ and one half pay** Überstundenbezahlung; **~ payment** *(US)* Ratenzahlung; **~ period** Zeitspanne, -abschnitt; **~ policy** *(marine insurance)* Versicherungspolice für bestimmten Zeitraum, Zeitpolice; **~ poster** Aushängefahrplan; **~ preference** *(economic goods)* Gegenwarts-, Zeitpräferenz; **~ premium** Zeitprämie; **~ purchase** *(stock exchange)* Zeit-, Termin-, Liefergeschäft, Fix-, Zeit-, Terminkauf; **~ rate** *(US)* Zeitlohnsatz, *(advertising)* Serienrabatt innerhalb eines Jahres; **~ recorder** Stech-, Kontrolluhr; **~ report** Stechkarte; **~ sale** Zeit-, Terminverkauf; **~ schedule** Zeitplanung, Terminplanung, Datenschema, *(advertising)* Werbefunkplan; **~ selling** *(US)* Abzahlungsgeschäft; **~ sequence** Zeitfolge; **~ series** zeitliche Anordnung, *(statistics)* Zeitreihe; **~-series diagram** Zeitreihendiagramm; **~-shared** *(data processing)* kurzfristig angemietet; **~ sharing** Verfahren zur besseren Ausnutzung elektronischer Datenverarbeitungsanlagen; **~ sheet** *(US)* Arbeitsblatt, Stundenzettel, Anwesenheitsliste, Arbeits-, Kontroll-, Lohnliste; **~ shutter** *(photo)* Zeitverschluß; **~ signal** Zeitzeichen *(advertising)* mit Werbung verbundene Zeitansage, *(broadcasting)* Zeitansage, -zeichen; **~ slot** *(television)* Fernsehwerbeeinheit; **~ span** Zeitspanne; **~-stained** *(book)* vergilbt; **~ stamp[ing clock]** Zeit-, Eingangsstempel; **~ standard** Lohngrundlage; **~ standards** Vorgabezeiten; **guaranteed ~ standard** garantierte Vorgabezeit; **~-stricken** vom Alter gebeugt, altersschwach; **~ study** Zeitstudie; **~-and-motion study** Rationalisierungs-, Bewegungsstudie; **~-study data** Zeitstudienergebnisse, Rationalisierungsergebnisse; **~-study engineer** Zeitstudieningenieur; **~-study observer** Zeitstudienbeamter; **~-study sheet** Zeitaufnahmebogen; **~ study technique** Zeitstudienmethode; **~ switch** Zeitschalter; **~-of-day tariff** *(el., Br.)* tageszeitlicher Staffeltarif; **~ and mileage tariff** *(rent-a-car)* Normaltarif; **~-tested** altbewährt; **~ ticket** *(US)* Stechkarte; **~ value** Zeitwert; **recorded ~ value** *(performance rating)* festgelegter Zeitfaktor; **~ wage** Zeit-, Stundenlohn; **~-wasting** Zeitvergeudung; **~ and piece wages** Zeit- und Akkordlöhne; **~ zone** Zeitzone.

timed befristet;
ill ~ ungelegen.

timekeeper Zeitmesser, *(factory)* Arbeitszeitkontrolleur;
to be a strict ~ Verabredungen pünktlich einhalten.

timekeeping [Arbeits]zeitkontrolle;
to have a ~ attitude to economic cycles Konjunkturzyklus mit den Augen eines Arbeitszeitkontrolleurs beobachten; **~ check** Kontrollmarke.

timeless ewig, unbegrenzt, zeitlos;
~ art zeitlose Kunst.

timely zur rechten Zeit, rechtzeitig, fristgerecht, günstig, passend;
~ editorial zeitgemäßer (aktueller) Leitartikel.

timeous *(Scot.)* zeitgerecht.

timepiece Chronometer, Zeituhr.

timepleaser Opportunist.

timer *(time study, US)* Zeitstudienbeamter, *(time keeper)* Zeitmesser, Stoppuhr, *(works)* Zeitkontrolleur;
half-~ Halbtagsarbeiter; **part-~** Kurzarbeiter.

timesaver Zeitersparnis.

timesaving zeitsparend.

timeserver Opportunist.

timeserving Opportunismus, Gesinnungslumperei, Liebedienerei;
~ *(a.)* opportunistisch.

timetable Zeit-, Fahrplan, Kursbuch, *(airplane)* Flugplan, Zeitplan, *(tide)* Gezeitentafel;
  airline ~ Flugplan; **crowded** ~ vollbesetzter Stundenplan; **graphic** ~ Bildfahrplan; **service** ~ Dienstfahrplan;
  ~ **that is no longer valid** ungültig gewordener Fahrplan;
  to compile (make out) a ~ Fahrplan aufstellen; **to stick to a** ~ Fahrplan einhalten.
timetaker Arbeitszeitkontrolleur.
timetaking zeitraubend.
timework nach der Zeit bezahlte Arbeit, Stundenlohnarbeit, im Stundenlohn bezahlte Arbeiten.
timeworker im Stundenlohn (nach der Zeit) bezahlter Arbeiter.
timeworn verbraucht, altmodisch, veraltet.
timing Zeitwahl, Terminierung, Abstimmung, Bestimmung (Wahl) des richtigen Zeitpunkts, zeitliche Einteilung (Koordinierung), Synchronisierung, Zeitnahme, Temporegulierung;
  to alter the ~ **of the payment of a tax** steuerliche Zeitphase verschieben;
  continuous ~ **method** Fortschrittzeitverfahren; ~ **problems** Probleme der richtigen Zeitwahl; ~ **switch** *(el.)* Zeitschalter.
timocracy Geldaristokratie.
tin Zinn, *(box)* Blechkanne, -dose, *(can., Br.)* Konservendose, Blechbüchse, -dose, *(sl.)* Zaster, Moos, Moneten, *(policeman)* Polizeimarke;
  ~ **of cigarettes** Zigarettendose;
  ~ *(v.) (Br.)* eindosen;
  ~ **box** Blechbüchse, -dose; ~ **can** Blechbüchse; ~ **foil** Blattzinn, Stanniol; ~-**foil** *(v.)* mit Stanniolpapier ausschlagen; ~ **god** aufgeblasener Mensch, Popanz, Bonze; ~-**lined case** mit Blech ausgeschlagene Kiste; ~ **mine** Zinngrube, -bergwerk; ~ **opener** Büchsenöffner; ~ **ore** Zinnerz; ~ **plate** verzinktes Eisenblech, Weißblech; ~-**plate sign** Blechplakat; ~ **pot** Blechtopf; ~-**pot** drittklassig, kümmerlich, wertlos; ~-**pot Napoleon** *(sl.)* Westentaschendiktator; ~ **shares** Zinnaktien; ~ **sheet** Weißblechplatte; **to get down to** ~ **tacks** zur Sache kommen.
tincture Tinktur, *(fig.)* Spur, Anstrich, Beimischung.
tinge Anstrich, Beigeschmack, *(sl.)* Provisionsreisender schwer verkäuflicher Artikel;
  ~ **of irony** ironischer Unterton;
  ~ *(v.)* tönen, färben.
tingle *(v.)* **with interests** *(story)* spannungsgeladen sein.
tingler *(coll.)* Anpfiff, Zurechtweisung.
tinged with interest spannungsgeladen sein.
tinhorn *(sl.)* ohne finanziellen Rückhalt, kapitalschwach.
tinker Kesselflicker, *(fig.)* Pfuscher, *(art of tinkering)* Pfuscherei, Stümperei, *(pol.)* Stammtischpolitiker;
  ~ *(v.)* Kessel flicken, *(fig.)* pfuschen, schlechte Arbeit leisten, zusammenstoppeln;
  to have an hour's ~ **at the radio set** sich eine Stunde an der Reparatur des Rundfunkgeräts versuchen;
  ~**'s damn** Deut, Pfifferling; **not worth a** ~**'s damn** keinen Pfifferling wert.
tinkle Geklingel, Läuten, *(sl.)* Telefonanruf.
tinner *(Br.)* Konservenfabrikant.
tinning *(Br.)* Konservierung;
  ~ **factory** *(Br.)* Konservenfabrik.
tinny *(Br., sl)* schwerreich.
tinsmith Blechschmied, Klempner.
tint Farbton;
  ~**s** Rastertönungen;
  graded ~**s** verschiedene Farbabstufungen;
  ~ **block** *(print.)* Tonplatte.
tinted getönt;
  ~ **glass** Rauchglas.
tinter farbige Glasscheibe.
tip Spitze, Zipfel, *(cigarette)* Mundstück, *(gratuity)* Trinkgeld, kleines Geldgeschenk, *(crowd of prospective customers)* Zuhörer, *(hint)* Hinweis, Tip, Wink, *(inclination)* Neigung, *(stock exchange)* Börsentip, *(place for rubbish)* Abladeplatz, *(unloaded material)* abgeladenes Material, Schutt, Müll, *(summit)* Gipfel, höchster Punkt, *(tipping device)* Kippvorrichtung, -anlage;
  from ~ **to toe** vom Scheitel bis zur Sohle;
  coal ~ Kohlenhalde; **the straight** ~ der richtige Tip;
  ~ *(v.)* Hinweis (Tip) geben, *(bribe)* spicken, *(shoot rubbish, Br.)* Müll abladen;
  ~ **s. o.** jem. ein Trinkgeld geben; ~ **s. o. for the next Prime Minister** *(coll.)* j. für den nächsten Ministerpräsidenten halten; ~ **s. one's mitt** *(sl.)* Geheimnis versehentlich herauslassen, *(US)* j. bloßstellen; ~ **s. o. off** *(coll.)* j. vorher warnen; ~ **out** durch Kippen entleeren; ~ **over** auskippen, -schütten, umwerfen,

(police, sl.) überraschende Razzia durchführen; ~ **the scale** entscheidenden Ausschlag geben, entscheidend ins Gewicht fallen; ~ **s. o. the wink** jem. verstohlen einen Wink geben; ~ **the winner** auf den Gewinner setzen;
  to give a reporter a ~ **on a no-name basis** einem Journalisten einen anonymen Hinweis zukommen lassen; **to have s. th. at the** ~ **of one's fingers** etw. im kleinen Finger haben; **to have s. th. on the** ~ **of one's tongue** auf der Zunge liegen (haben); **to miss one's** ~ keinen Erfolg haben; **to take the** ~ Ratschlag befolgen;
  ~ **heap** Halde; ~-**in** Beihefter; ~-**off** Fingerzeig, Hinweis, Vorwarnung; ~-**over** *(sl.)* überraschende Razzia; ~-**and-run raid** *(mil.)* blitzschneller Überfall, Überraschungsangriff; ~-**up** aufklappbar; ~-**up seat** Klappsitz; ~ **truck (waggon)** Kippwagen.
tipcart Kippwagen.
tipped mit Mundstück.
tipper Kippwagen.
tipple *(US)* Kipp-, Entladevorrichtung.
tipping Deponie, Müllhalde;
  controlled ~ geordnete Deponie; **no** ~ keine Trinkgelder, *(no dumping)* Schuttabladen verboten;
  ~ **in of insets** Einkleben von Beilagen.
tipstaff *(Br.)* Gerichtsdiener.
tipster *(US)* Tipgeber, Geber eines Börsentips, Wettberater.
tipsy beschwipst, angeheitert.
tiptoe *(fig.)* gespannt.
tiptop Gipfel, Höhepunkt;
  ~ *(a.)* erstklassig, prima, tipptopp;
  ~ **hotel** erstklassiges Hotel.
tirade Wortschwall, Tirade.
tire Ermüdung, *(US)* Reifen;
  off-the-road ~ Geländeprofilreifen; **pneumatic** ~ Luftreifen; **steel radial** ~ Stahlgürtelreifen; **worn-out** ~ abgefahrener Reifen;
  to change a flat ~ Autoreifen wechseln;
  ~ *(v.)* bereifen;
  ~ **the audience** Publikum langweilen; ~ **of doing es** satt haben;
  ~ **casing** Mantel; ~ **chain** Schneekette; ~ **gauge** Reifendruckmesser; ~ **guarantee** Reifengarantie; ~ **lever** Reifenheber; ~ **maker** Reifenhersteller; ~ **plant** Reifenfabrik; ~ **price** Reifenpreis; ~ **pump** Reifenpumpe; ~ **replacement** Reifenersatzbeschaffung, -auswechslung; ~ **store** Reifenlager; ~ **trouble** Reifenpanne; ~ **use** Reifenabnutzung; ~ **vulcanizer** Vulkanisierbetrieb; ~ **wear** Abnutzung durch Gebrauch, Reifenabnutzung.
tired *(Br.)* müde, *(US)* bereift;
  ~ **off** abgenutzt, abgefahren.
tireless *(Br.)* unermüdlich, *(US)* unbereift.
tireman *(US)* Reifenhersteller, -firma, -händler.
tiring room *(theater)* Garderobe.
tiro Neuling.
tit for tat Wurst wider Wurst;
  to give s. o. ~ jem. nichts schuldig bleiben, jem. mit gleicher Münze heimzahlen.
tissue Gewebe, Flor, *(copy, sl.)* Durchschlag, Kopie;
  ~ **of lies** Lügengewebe;
  ~ **paper** Seidenpapier.
titan of industry Industriegigant.
titbit Leckerbissen.
tithe Zehnt.
title Titel, *(book)* Buchrücken, *(claim)* [Rechts]anspruch, Rechtstitel, Anrecht, *(disposition)* Verfügungsrecht, *(division of statute)* Abschnitt, Titel, *(document)* [Eigentums]urkunde, Dokument, *(film)* Untertitel, *(head formula of a document)* Eingangsformel, *(headline)* Titel, Betitlung, [Kapital]überschrift, *(law)* Hauptabschnitt, Titel, *(nomination)* Benennung, Bezeichnung, *(official)* Dienstbezeichnung, *(ownership)* Eigentum[stitel, -recht], *(possession)* Besitzrecht, *(legal procedure)* Prozeßbezeichnung, *(security)* Name [eines Wertpapiers];
  by onerous ~ gegen Entgelt; **under the same** ~ in der gleichen Rubrik; **without lawful** ~ ohne Rechtsgrund;
  absolute ~ dingliches Eigentumsrecht, Grundeigentum; **adverse** ~ Gegenanspruch; **available** ~ *(book trade)* lieferbarer Titel; **bad** ~ fehlendes (nicht einwandfreies) Eigentumsrecht; **bastard** ~ *(print.)* Schmutztitel; **binder's** ~ Buchtitel; **bogus** ~ falscher Titel; **clear** ~ einwandfreier (unangreifbarer) Rechtsanspruch, -titel, lastenfreies Grundeigentum; **clear record** einwandfreier Rechtsanspruch, rechtsmängelfreies Eigentum; **colo(u)rable** ~ unzureichender Eigentumsanspruch, Scheinanspruch; **credit** ~**s** *(film)* Titelaufführung; **defective** ~ mit Mängeln behaftetes Recht, formell nicht einwandfreier (fehler-

hafter) Rechtstitel; **derivative** ~ nicht originärer Rechtstitel, abgeleiteter Rechtsanspruch; **disputed** ~ bestrittenes Eigentumsrecht; **dormant** ~ ruhender Rechtsanspruch; **doubtful** ~ zweifelhafter Rechtsanspruch; **equitable** ~ vorläufiges Eigentum, Eigentumsanwartschaft, Eigentumsrecht nach Billigkeitsrecht; **good** ~ rechtmäßiges Eigentum, rechtsgültiger Anspruch, einwandfreier Rechtsanspruch; **high-sounding** ~ hochtrabender Titel; **honorary** ~ verliehener Titel; **imperfect** ~ aufschiebend bedingtes (vorläufiges) Eigentum; **indefeasible** ~ unverjährbarer Anspruch; **joint** ~ Eigentum zur gesamten Hand; **lawful** ~ rechtmäßiges Eigentum; **legal** ~ Volleigentum; **lucrative** ~ Eigentumserwerb ohne Gegenleistung; **marketable (merchantable)** ~ durchsetzbarer (unangreifbarer) Rechtsanspruch; **official** ~ Amtsbezeichnung; **onerous** ~ entgeltlich erworbenes Eigentum; **outstanding** ~ besseres Recht; **paper** ~ nur auf dem Papier bestehendes Grundstückseigentum; **paramount** stärkeres Recht; **passive** ~ *(Scot.)* Passivlegitimation; **perfect** ~ einwandfreier Rechtstitel; **plaintiff's** ~ klägerischer Rechtsanspruch; **possessory** ~ Besitzanspruch, -recht; **prescriptive** ~ durch Ersitzung erworbenes Eigentum; **presumptive** ~ Besitzvermutung; **qualified** ~ eigentumsähnliches (beschränktes) Recht; **record** ~ verbrieftes (eingetragenes) Grundeigentum; **sham** ~ unberechtigt angenommener Titel; **short** ~ *(law)* Kurztitel; **singular** ~ in Einzelrechtsnachfolge erworbenes Eigentum; **sound** ~ einwandfreier Rechtstitel; **superior** ~ besserer Rechtsanspruch; **tax** ~ bei einer aus Steuergründen vorgenommenen Zwangsversteigerung erworbenes Eigentum; **unmarketable** ~ rechtlich bestrittenes (nicht rechtsmängelfreies) Eigentumsrecht;

~ **by abandonment** Besitzrecht durch Aneignung; ~ **by accession** Eigentumserwerb durch Anwachsung; ~ **of an account** Kontobezeichnung; ~ **of an act** einleitender Teil eines Gesetzes, Gesetztitel; ~ **of an action** Klagerubrum; ~ **to a benefit** *(insurance)* Leistungsanspruch; ~ **by bequest** Eigentumserwerb durch Erbgang; ~ **of a cause** Klagerubrum; ~ **to certificate** Anteilschein; ~ **by courtesy** ehrenhalber verliehener Titel; ~ **of declaration** Klagerubrum; ~ **by descent** Eigentumserwerb durch Erbgang; ~ **by devise** Eigentumserwerb im Vermächtniswege; ~ **by discovery (finding)** Fundeigentum; ~ **of entry** Betretungsrecht; ~ **defective in form** formell nicht einwandfreier Rechtstitel; ~ **by gift** Eigentumserwerb durch Schenkung; ~ **to goods** Eigentum an der Ware; ~ **by increase** Eigentum an Früchten; ~ **to inheritance** Erbanspruch; **[pretended]** ~ **to land** [angebliches] Grundstückseigentum; ~ **of a newspaper** Zeitungstitel; ~ **of nobility** Adelsprädikat; ~ **by occupancy** Besitzrecht durch Aneignung; ~ **by operation of law** Eigentumsübergang kraft Gesetzes; ~ **of ownership** Eigentumstitel; ~ **of a patent** kurze Beschreibung (Kurzfassung) einer Erfindung; ~ **to a pension** Pensionsberechtigung; ~ **of adverse possession** Eigentumserwerb durch Ersitzung; ~ **by prescription** Eigentumserwerb im Wege der Verjährung; ~ **to property** Besitzurkunde, Eigentumsrecht; ~ **in real property** Grundstückseigentum; ~ **by purchase** Eigentumserwerb durch Kauf; **clear** ~ **of record** einwandfreies (rechtsmängelfreies) Eigentum; **only** ~**s held in stock and listed in catalog(ue)** *(bookseller)* nur im Lager und Katalog geführte Titel; ~ **to work a mine** Berechtigung zum Bergbaubetrieb, Bergwerksgerechtigkeit;

~ *(v.)* betiteln, benennen; ~ **a book** Buch mit einem Titel versehen; **to acquire the** ~ Eigentum erwerben; **to acquire a good** ~ fehlerfrei Eigentum erlangen; **to address s. o. by his** ~ j. mit seinem Titel anreden; **to assume a** ~ sich einen Titel beilegen; **to bear a** ~ Titel führen, *(newspaper article)* Überschrift tragen; **to claim** ~ Eigentum beanspruchen; **to clear a** ~ Rechtsanspruch überprüfen, *(land register)* [etwa] Grundbuch einsehen; **to confer a** ~ Titel verleihen; **to confirm s. o. in his** ~ jds. Eigentumsrecht bestätigen; **to constitute** ~ Eigentum schaffen; **to deprive s. o. of his** ~ jem. einen Titel aberkennen; **to derive a** ~ Recht herleiten; **to do** ~**s** Zwischentexte schreiben; **to give s. o. a** ~ **to one's gratitude** jem. zur Dankbarkeit verpflichtet sein; **to have a** ~ **to** [Rechts]anspruch auf etw. haben, rechtmäßiger Eigentümer sein; **to have the** ~ **searched** [etwa] Grundbuch einsehen lassen; **to have the first** ~ nächstberechtigt sein; **to hold a** ~ Titel führen; **to hold the** ~ **to goods** Wareneigentümer sein, Eigentum [an Waren] haben; **to lose a** ~ Titel verlieren; **to lower the** ~ **of the coinage** Währungsstandard senken; **to obtain** ~ **free of the mortgage** unbelastetes Grundeigentum erwerben; **to pass in** ~ in anderes Eigentum übergehen; **to pass** ~ **to s. o.** Eigentum auf j. übertragen; **to recover** ~ sein Eigentum wiedererlangen; **to renew a** ~ Eigentumsanspruch erneuern; **to reserve (retain)** ~ sich das Eigentum vorbehalten; **to search the** ~ *(US)* öffentli-

che Register zur Eigentumsfeststellung einsehen; **to take** ~ **to property** *(US)* Eigentum erwerben; **to transfer (reinvest) a** ~ **back** Eigentum zurückübertragen; **to usurp a** ~ sich einen Titel anmaßen;

~ **bearer** Titelinhaber, -träger; ~ **catalog(ue)** *(library)* Titelkatalog; ~ **company** Rechtstitelversicherungsgesellschaft; ~ **deed** Eigentums-, Besitz-, Erwerbsurkunde, *(real estate)* Grundstücksurkunde, Kaufvertrag; ~ **entry** *(book)* Titelaufführung; ~ **expectant** Titelanwärter; ~ **guarantee** *(US)* Garantie von Rechtsansprüchen [auf Grundeigentum]; ~ **guarantee insurance** *(US)* Rechtstitelversicherung; ~ **offer** *(bookseller)* Titelangebot; ~ **guarantee [insurance] policy** *(US)* Rechtstitelversicherungspolice; ~ **insurance** *(US)* Rechtstitelversicherung, Versicherung gegen Rechtsmängel von Grundbesitz; ~ **insurance company** *(US)* Versicherungsgesellschaft gegen Rechtsmängel im Grundeigentum; ~ **page** Titelseite, -blatt, Kopfseite; ~ **part** Titelrolle; ~ **plant** *(US)* Verzeichnis von Grundstücksurkunden; ~ **protection** *(book trade)* Titelschutz; ~ **registration** *(US)* Grundbucheintragung; ~ **registration office** *(US)* Grundbuchamt; ~-**retaining note** schriftlicher Eigentumsvorbehalt; ~ **retention** Eigentumsvorbehalt; ~ **record** *(US)* [etwa] Grundbuchauszug; ~ **role** Titelrolle; ~ **search** Rechtstitelüberprüfung, [etwa] Grundbucheinsicht; ~ **warranty** Rechtsmängelgewähr.

titled adlig.

titleholder Titelinhaber, Eigentümer.

titling Benennung, *(book)* aufgeprägter Buchtitel.

tittle|**s** Tüpfelchen, Kleinigkeit; **not a** ~ **of it** nicht das geringste davon; **to a** ~ aufs Haar genau; ~-**tattle** Klatsch, Tratsch.

titular nomineller Amtsinhaber; ~ *(a.)* nominell, nur dem Titel nach; ~ **king** Titularkönig.

titularity Titularstellung, nominelle Würde.

titulary nomineller Titelträger.

tizzy [unnötige] Aufregung.

toad *(fig.)* Kröte, Ekel; **to eat s. one's** ~ jem. schmeicheln, vor jem. kriechen.

toadeater, toady Speichellecker.

toadeating Speichelleckerei.

toast Trinkspruch, Toast, *(slice bread)* Toast, geröstete Brotschnitte; **to have s. o. on** ~ *(Br., sl.)* j. völlig in der Hand haben; **to propose a** ~ Trinkspruch ausbringen; ~ **rack** Toaströster.

tobacco Tabak[waren]; ~ **excise (tax)** *(US)* Tabaksteuer.

tobacconist Tabakwarengeschäft.

today's|**newspapers** Tageszeitungen; ~ **rate** *(stock market)* Tageskurs.

toe Zehe, *(shoe)* Kappe; **on one's** ~**s** *(coll.)* auf Draht; ~ *(v.)* **the line** seinen Verpflichtungen nachkommen, *(party politics)* linientreu sein, sich der Parteilinie unterwerfen; **to keep s. o. on his** ~**s** *(fam.)* j. in Spannung halten; **to tread on s. one's** ~**s** jem. auf die Zehen treten.

toehold *(mil.)* Brückenkopf, *(profession)* Ansatzpunkt zum Vorankommen; **to have a** ~ **across the river** Brückenkopf jenseits des Flusses haben; **to offer no** ~ keine beruflichen Chancen bieten.

toft nicht mehr vorhandenes Anwesen; ~ **and croft** Amtstracht; **to don the** ~ **of a judge** Richtertalar anlegen.

togetherness Beisammensein.

togs *(sl.)* Klamotten.

toil mühselige Arbeit, Mühe, Plackerei; **in the** ~**s of debt** in Schulden verstrickt; ~**s and snares** Fallstricke, Schlingen; ~ *(v.)* schuften, sich abplacken; **to be caught in the** ~**s of the law** sich in den Fallstricken des Gesetzes verfangen haben.

toiler Arbeitstier.

toilet Toiletten-, Ankleideraum, *(toilet room, US)* Toilette, Klosett, Badezimmer; ~ **articles** Toilettenartikel; ~ **case** Reisenecessaire, Kulturbeutel; ~ **paper** Toiletten-, Klosettpapier; **public** ~ **room** Bedürfnisanstalt; ~ **table** Frisiertoilette, -tisch.

token Beweis, [An]zeichen, Zeugnis, *(gift)* Andenken, Erinnerungsgeschenk, *(memento)* Erinnerungsgeschenk, Andenken, *(metal fare)* Metallmarke, *(premium)* Gutschein, Bon, *(piece of currency)* Notgeld;

by the same ~ aus dem gleichen Grunde; **in ~** zum Beweis; **book ~** Büchergutschein; **gift ~** Guthabengutschein; **~ of concern** Anteilsbezeugung, Aufmerksamkeit; **~ of surrender** Zeichen der Unterwerfung;

to wear black as a ~ of mourning Schwarz zum Zeichen der Trauer tragen;

~ amount symbolischer Betrag; **~ coin** Scheidemünze; **~ imports** symbolische Einfuhr; **~ money** Geldsurrogat, Ersatz-, Notgeld; **~ payment** Teilzahlung in Anerkenntnis einer Verpflichtung, symbolische Zahlung; **to offer only a ~ resistance** nur scheinbar Widerstand leisten; **~ ring** Freundschaftsring; **~ riot** Scheinangriff; **~ strike** Warnstreik; **~ vote** *(parl.)* Bewilligung einer der Höhe nach nicht festgelegten Geldsumme, Globalbewilligung.

tolerable erträglich, mittelmäßig, leidlich;
in ~ demand ziemlich gesucht; **~ passage** erträgliche Überfahrt.

tolerance Duldung, Toleranz, *(coins)* Nachlaß, Remedium, *(US, customs)* Sperrgeld, Zollabgabe, -gebühr, *(in weight)* zugelassene [Gewichts]abweichung;

subject to any ~ unter Berücksichtigung üblicher Toleranzabweichungen;

racial ~ Rassentoleranz; **~ of cartels** Kartellduldung; **~ of the mint** Münztoleranz; **~ factor** Toleranzfaktor; **~ limit** Toleranzgrenze; **~ requirements** Toleranzgrenzen.

toleration Duldung, Nachsicht, Toleranz.

toll Abgabe, Gebühr, Zoll, *(fig.)* Tribut, *(market)* Markt-, Standgeld, *(right to take toll)* Zollregel, *(road)* Straßenbenutzungsgebühr, Wege-, Brückenzoll, Maut, *(shipping)* Hafengebühr, *(tel.)* Fernsprechgebühr, *(transportation)* Fuhrlohn, Transportgebühr;

canal ~ Kanalgebühr; **intermediate ~** Autobahngebühr, **lighthouse ~** Leuchtfeuergebühr; **port ~** *(US)* Hafengebühr; **railway ~** Frachtgebühr; **town ~** Gemeindeabgabe;
~ of death tödliche Unfallquote; **~ of the road[s]** Verkehrsunfälle, -opfer, Todesopfer der Landstraße;
~ (v.) versperren, *(take toll)* Zoll erheben;
~ the entry Betretungsrecht blockieren; **~ the statute of limitations** *(US)* Verjährungsfrist hemmen;
to pay the ~ Zoll entrichten; **to take ~** Zoll einnehmen (erheben); **to take ~ of s. th.** *(fig.)* etw. einbehalten; **to take ~ of s. o.** j. arg mitnehmen; **to take ~ of s. one's career** jds. Karriere stark beeinträchtigen; **to take heavy ~s of one's income** großen Einkommensteil in Anspruch nehmen; **to take a heavy ~ of a nation** einer Nation hohe Blutopfer abverlangen;
~ bar Zollschranke, Schlagbaum, Sperre; **~ board** Anschlagtafel für Zolltarife; **~ book** Zollquittungsbuch; **~ bridge** mautpflichtige Brücke, Zollbrücke; **~ broadcasting** gebührenpflichtiger Rundfunk; **~ cable** Fernleitungskabel; **~ call** *(tel., Br.)* Schnell-, Nahverkehrsgespräch, Vorortsverkehrsanruf, *(US)* Ferngespräch; **~ charges** Brückenzoll; **~ circuit** *(tel., Br.)* Nahverkehrsleitung, *(US)* Fernleitung; **~ collector** Zolleinnehmer, *(turnstile)* Zählvorrichtung einer Drehkreuzung; **~ exchange** *(tel., Br.)* Schnell-, Nahverkehrsamt, *(US)* Fernamt; **~ final selector** *(US)* Fernleitungswähler; **~-free** abgaben-, zollfrei, *(tel.)* gebührenfrei; **to call a ~-free number** kostenloses Ferngespräch führen; **~ highway** *(US)* gebührenpflichtige Autobahn; **~-less** abgabenfrei; **~ line** *(tel.)* Fernleitung, *(Br.)* Nahverkehrsleitung; **~-line dialing** *(US)* Selbstwählfernverkehr; **~ rate** Passagegebühr; **~ revenues** Benutzungsgebühren; **~ road** Zollstraße, *(US)* gebührenpflichtige Autobahn; **~ service** *(tel.)* Schnelldienst; **~ system** Fernleitungsnetz; **~ through** *(Br.)* Brücken-, Durchgangszoll; **~ traffic** *(tel.)* Schnellamts-, Nahverkehr; **~ traverse** Wegegebühr.

tollable zollpflichtig, verzollbar.

tollage Gebührenerhebung, *(customs)* Zollentrichtung.

tollbooth Gefängnis, *(road tax)* Zahlstation.

toller Zolleinnehmer.

tollgate Zollschranke, Schlagbaum.

tollgatherer Zoll-, Steuernehmer.

tollhouse Zollhaus.

tollkeeper Zolleinnehmer, Zöllner.

tolling the statute of limitations Unterbrechung der Verjährungsfrist.

Tom, Dick and Harry Hinz und Kunz.

tomahawk, to bury the Kriegsbeil begraben, Frieden schließen; **to dig up the ~** Kriegsbeil ausgraben.

tomb Grabmal, Gruft, Mausoleum.

tombola Tombola.

tombstone Grab-, Gedenkstein.

tome Band, *(ponderous volume)* dicker Wälzer.

tomfoolery Affentheater.

tommy *(goods)* Naturalien, *(short rod)* verstellbarer Schraubenschlüssel;
soft ~ *(marine)* weiches Brot;
~ shop (store, US) Werkskantine;
⚥ Atkins *(Br.)* Landser.

tommybag Brot-, Frühstücksbeutel.

ton Tonne[ngehalt], *(capacity)* Trag-, Ladefähigkeit;
by ~s tonnenweise;
displacement ~ *(warship)* Verdrängungstonne, Wasserverdrängung; **freight ~** Frachttonne, Tonnenfracht; **gross register ~** Bruttoregistertonne; **long ~** Tonne (2240 englische Pfund, 1016 kg); **measurement ~** Frachttonne, Raumtonne; **metric ~** metrische Tonne (2204,6 englische Pfund); **~s processed** verarbeitete Tonnenzahl; **net register ~** Nettoregistertonne; **shipping ~** Frachttonne; **short ~** *(US)* Tonne (2000 englische Pfund, 907,2 kg);
~s of people Unmenge Menschen;
to ask s. o. ~s of times j. unzählige Male fragen; **to hit like a ~ of bricks** gewaltig beeindrucken; **to have ~s of money** scheffelweise Geld (Geld wie Heu) haben;
~s deadweight Tragfähigkeit; **~ mile** Tonnenmeile; **~ weight** Gewichtstonne.

tone Ton, Laut, Klang, *(healthy elasticity)* geistige Spannkraft, Elastizität, *(fig.)* Schwung, Elastizität, *(ling.)* Akzent, Betonung, *(shading)* Abstufung, Schattierung, *(stock exchange)* Haltung, Verhalten, Stimmung;
in an angry ~ mit zorniger Stimme; **in a ~ of command** im Kommandoton;
bearish ~ flaue Stimmung; **dial ~** *(tel.)* Freizeichen; **final ~** Schlußhaltung; **prevailing ~** Grundton, Grundhaltung der Börse, vorherrschende Stimmung;
low moral ~ of a city niedriges moralisches Niveau einer Großstadt; **~ of quiet elegance of a room** unaufdringliche Eleganz eines Zimmers; **~ of the market** Börsenstimmung, Börsenklima; **dull ~ in the stock market** flaue Stimmung auf dem Aktienmarkt; **~ of a nation** Haltung einer Nation; **~ of restraint** zurückhaltende Tendenz;
~ (v.) abstufen, tönen, *(picture)* kolorieren;
~ down s. one's anger jds. Zorn dämpfen; **~ down some of the offensive statements in an article** einige aggressive Formulierungen in einem Zeitungsartikel abschwächen; **~ in with the carpet (curtain)** mit dem Teppich (Vorhang) harmonieren;
to adopt the right ~ richtigen Ton anschlagen; **to give a flippant ~ to a debate** Debatte leichtfertig führen; **to lose ~** an Spannkraft verlieren; **to maintain the ~** *(stock exchange)* Grundhaltung beibehalten; **to recover mental ~** geistige Spannkraft wiedererlangen; **to set the ~ of** tonangebend sein; **to set the ~ of a book** Stil eines Buches bestimmen; **to strike the right ~** richtigen Ton anschlagen; **to take on apocalyptic ~s** Weltuntergangstöne anschlagen;
~ arm Tonarm; **~ colo(u)r** Klangfarbe; **~ filter** Tonfilter; **~ painting** Tonmalerei; **~ picture** Tongemälde; **~ poetry** Tondichtung; **~ quality** Tonqualität, Klangfarbe, -charakter.

tongs Zange;
wire-~ Drahtzange;
to go at it hammer and ~ mit aller Kraft darauf losgehen.

tongue Zunge, *(fig.)* Ausdrucks-, Redeweise, *(technics)* Lauf-, Führungsschiene;
one's mother ~ seine Muttersprache; **slanderous ~s** Verleumder; **wagging ~s** Lästerzungen;
~ in cheek ironisch vorgebracht; **~ of land** Landzunge;
to be on the ~s of men in aller Munde sein; **to find one's ~** sich fassen; **to guard one's ~** seine Zunge hüten; **to have a fluent ~** beredt sein; **to have a long ~** geschwätzig sein; **to have lost one's ~** aus Schüchternheit nicht reden; **to have s. th. on the tip of one's ~** etw. auf der Zunge liegen haben; **to hold one's ~** seinen Mund halten; **to keep a civil ~ in one's head** höflich bleiben; **to know a hypocrite by his ~** Heuchler an seiner Redeweise erkennen; **to speak with forked ~** mit doppelter Zunge reden, doppelzüngig reden; **to speak with one's ~ in one's cheek** ironisch sprechen; **to wag one's ~** tratschen;
~ twister Zungenbrecher.

tonic water Sprudel.

toning bath *(photo)* Tonbad.

tonnage Tonnage, Tonnengehalt, Wasserverdrängung, *(cubic capacity)* Lade-, Ladungsfähigkeit, *(ancient customs)* Schiffszoll, Tonnengeld, *(freight charge)* Last[gebühr], *(freight carrying capacity)* Rauminhalt, Tragfähigkeit, Fracht-, Schiffsraum, *(merchant fleet)* Gesamttonnage, *(weight of cargo)* Ladungsgewicht;

cargo ~ Ladefähigkeit; **deadweight** ~ Lade-, Tragfähigkeit; **displacement** ~ Verdrängungstonnage; **gross** ~ Bruttotonnage; **idle** ~ aufgelegte Tonnage, Leertonnage; **net** ~ Nettotonnage, nutzbarer Schiffsraum; **parcels** ~ *(Br.)* Paketfahrttonnage; **registered** ~ [Netto]registertonnage, Registerschiffsraum; **short** ~ Ladungsmanko; **surplus** ~ Ladungsüberschuß; **total** ~ Gesamttonnage; **war-lost** ~ im Krieg verlorene Tonnage; **waste** ~ ungenutzter Schiffsraum;

~ **car** *(US)* Güterwagen; ~ **certificate** Meßbrief, Schiffsmeßschein; ~ **deck** Vermeßungsdeck; ~ **duty** *(Br.)* Tonnengeld, Schiffssteuer; ~ **length** Vermessungslänge; ~ **mark** Vermessungsmarke; ~ **opening** Ladeluke; ~ **quota** *(steel imports)* Tonnagekontingent; ~ **rate** *(US, mining)* Lohnsatz pro Tonne; ~ **record** Tonnagerekord; ~ **rent** *(US)* Tonnengeld, *(mining)* nach der Fördermenge berechnete Fracht.

tontine *(insurance business)* Erbklassenrente.

tony *(sl.)* höchst modern, „in“.

too-too *(coll.)* überspannt, -trieben;

~ **radical** extremer Radikaler.

tool Gerät, Werkzeug, Instrument, *(bookbinding)* [Präge]stempel, *(machine)* Werk-, Arbeitsstück, Werkzeugmaschine, Drehbank;

~s Handwerkszeug, Arbeitszeug, -gerät, *(mil.)* Kriegsgerät; **burglar's** ~s Einbruchwerkzeuge; **gardener's** ~s Gartengerät; **literary** ~s literarische Hilfsmittel, Fachliteratur; **machine** ~ Werkzeugmaschine; **perishable** ~s Verschleißwerkzeuge; **simple** ~s berufsübliche Werkzeuge;

~s **and machinery** technisches Zubehör; ~s **of monetary policy** geldmarktpolitisches Instrumentarium; ~s **of trade** Rüstzeug zur Berufsausbildung;

~ *(v.)* mit Werkzeugen bearbeiten, *(bookbinding)* prägen, mit einem Stempel verzieren;

~ **a factory** Fabrik mit den notwendigen Maschinen (mit dem erforderlichen Maschinenpark) ausstatten; ~ **up a plant** notwendige Fabrikmaschinen aufstellen;

to be a mere ~ **in the hands of a criminal** bloßes Werkzeug eines Verbrechers sein; **to lay down** ~s Arbeit einstellen, streiken;

~ **car** Gerätewagen; ~ **case** *(car)* Werkzeugkasten, -tasche; ~ **control** *(US)* Werkzeugsteuerung; **simple** ~s **doctrine** *(employer)* Haftungsfreiheit für Schäden durch berufsübliche Werkzeuge; ~ **engineer** Arbeitsvorbereiter; ~ **engineering** Arbeitsvorbereitung; ~ **house** Geräteschuppen; ~ **kit** Werkzeugausstattung; **machine** ~ *(industry)* Werkzeugmaschinenindustrie; ~s **insurance** Werkzeugversicherung; ~s **rent** Werkzeugmiete; ~ **shed** Geräteschuppen; ~ **steel** Werkzeugstahl; ~ **subject** *(US)* notwendiges Nebenfach.

toolbox Werkzeugkasten.

toolbuilder, toolmaker Werkzeugmacher, -maschinenspezialist, Feinmechaniker.

tooling Werkzeugausrüstung, -ausstattung, *(book)* Prägung, Prägedruck, *(mechanical operation)* Bearbeitung;

blind ~ Blindprägung;

~s, **furniture and fixtures** *(balance sheet)* Werkzeug, Betriebs- und Geschäftsausstattung; ~ **and implements** Werkzeuge, Instrumente und Geräte;

~ **costs** Bearbeitungskosten; ~ **method** Bearbeitungsverfahren.

toot Tüten, *(spree, sl.)* Sauftour;

~ *(v.)* hupen;

~ **one's own horn** sich beweihräuchern.

tooter Autohupe.

tooth *(technics)* Zahn, Zacken;

the ~ **of time** der Zahn der Zeit;

to fight s. th. ~ **and nail** etw. aufs Messer bekämpfen; **to have a sweet** ~ Leckermaul sein; **to have a great** ~ **for chocolate** Vorliebe für Schokolade haben;

to go over (through) s. th. with a fine ~**-comb** etw. sorgfältig überprüfen; ~ **system** Verzahnung.

toothed wheel gearing Zahnradgetriebe.

top Spitze, Gipfel, höchster Punkt, Krone, *(board, sl.)* Vorstandsmitglied, Boß, *(car)* Verdeck, *(highest degree)* höchster Grad, *(upper end)* Kopfende, *(furniture)* Aufsatz, *(gear)* höchster Gang, *(maximum)* Höchststand, *(position)* Spitzenstellung, Spitzenposition, *(selection)* Auslese, -wahl, Creme;

at the ~ **of affairs** an der Spitze; **at the** ~ **of the ladder (tree)** auf dem Gipfel der beruflichen Möglichkeiten, auf der höchsten Stufe, an oberster Stelle; **at the** ~ **of page 40** auf Seite 40 oben; **at the** ~ **of one's speed** mit höchster Geschwindigkeit; **at the** ~ **of one's voice** aus vollem Hals; **from** ~ **to bottom** vollständig, vom Scheitel bis zur Sohle; **in** ~ im höchsten Gang; **off one's** ~ *(sl.)* verrückt; **on** ~ mit Höchstgeschwindigkeit; **on** ~ **of the world** in allerbester Stimmung, quietschvergnügt;

the big ~ riesengroßes Zirkuszelt; **old** ~ *(coll.)* alter Knabe, altes Haus;

~ **of s. one's ambition** jds. höchster Ehrgeiz; ~ **of one's career** Höhepunkt seiner Laufbahn; ~ **of the class** Klassenprimus; **the** ~ **of all creation** Krone der Schöpfung; ~ **of a cylinder** Zylinderdeckel; ~ **of the pops** *(television, Br.)* Hitparade; ~ **of one's power** Zenith seiner Machtstellung; ~ **of ranks** Spitzenklasse; ~ **of the tide** Höchststand der Flut; ~ **of the water** Wasseroberfläche;

~ *(v.)* übersteigen, übertreffen, *(kill)* umbringen;

~ **it all** um dem Ganzen die Krone aufzusetzen; ~ **the class** Klassenbester sein; ~ **the hill** Gipfel erreichen; ~ **the horizon** *(sun)* am Horizont aufsteigen; ~ **a list** Liste anführen; ~ **the $ 40.000.000 mark** *(sales)* 40 Millionengrenze überschreiten; ~ **off** vervollständigen; ~ **off a dinner with coffee** Essen mit Kaffee abschließen; ~ **one's part** *(theater)* sich selbst übertreffen; ~ **up a car battery** Autobatterie aufladen;

to be on ~ Heft in der Hand haben; **to be on** ~ **of one's form** auf der Höhe sein; **to be back at the** ~ **of the popularity table** Beliebtheitsliste wieder anführen; **to be at the** ~ **of the turnover list** Umsatzspitzenreiter sein; **to blow one's** ~s *(sl.)* aus dem Häuschen geraten; **to buy at the** ~ **of the market** zu Höchstkursen kaufen; **to come to the** ~ sich durchsetzen, Erfolg haben; **to come out on** ~ als Sieger (Bester) hervorgehen; **to do in** ~ *(car)* an Höchstgeschwindigkeit erreichen; **to have got on** ~ **of s. o.** über jds. Kopf gewachsen sein; **to lift the** ~ *(stock exchange)* Höchstkurs heraufsetzen; **to put the luggage on the** ~ **of the car** Gepäck auf dem Wagendach unterbringen; **to reach the** ~ **of the ladder** Spitzenstellung (höchste Position) erreichen; **to register a new** ~ neuen Höchstkurs verbuchen; **to remain** ~ **of the table** obenan bleiben; **to sleep like a** ~ wie ein Murmeltier schlafen; **to take the** ~ **off** *(beer)* Blume abtrinken; **to take the** ~ **of the table** Vorsitz führen; **to zoom to the** ~ an die Spitze gelangen;

~ *(a.)* erstklassig, prima, *(case)* oben, oberst;

~ **aide** Spitzenkraft; ~ **adviser** Spitzenberater; ~ **ale** erstklassiges Bier; ~ **analyst** Spitzenkraft für Wertpapieranlagen; ~ **appointment** Spitzenstellung; ~ **audience** Spitzenpublikum; ~ **board** Spitzenaufsichtsrat; ~ **boots** Stulpenstiefel, Langschäfter; ~ **brackets** höchste Steuerstufen; ~ **brass** oberster Vorgesetzter; ~ **business executives** Spitzkräfte der Wirtschaft; ~ **candidate** Spitzenkandidat; ~ **conditions** erstklassige Bedingungen; ~ **dog** sozial Stärkerer; **to be** ~ **dog** Vorrang haben; ~ **drawer** oberste Schublade, *(fig.)* obere Zehntausend, Oberschicht; ~ **earner** Spitzenverdiener; ~ **echelons** Spitzenpositionen; **to form the** ~ **echelons in civic activities** zu den Spitzen der Behörden zählen; ~ **efficiency** Spitzenleistung; ~ **end of the market** Markt für qualifizierte Erzeugnisse; ~ **executive** *(US)* Spitzenkraft, leitender Angestellter; ~ **executive job (position)** Spitzenposition; ~ **executive management** Vorstand einer Firma; ~ **executive team** Führungsgruppe; ~ **financial expert** führender Finanzfachmann; ~ **floor** oberstes Stockwerk; ~ **gains** *(stock exchange)* Spitzengewinne; ~ **gallery** Gichtbühne; ~ **gear** *(car)* höchster Gang; **to get into** ~ **gear** auf volle Touren kommen; ~ **grade** Spitzenklasse, feinste Sorte; ~**-grade** *(US)* hochwertig; ~**-grade civil servant** höherer Beamter; ~**-grade quality** erste Wahl; ~**-hampered** kopflastig, topplastig; ~ **hat** Zylinder[hut]; **to have to pay for all those** ~ **hats** Drum und Dran einer konventionellen Beerdigung zu zahlen haben; ~**-hat insurance policy** erstklassige Versicherungspolice; ~**-hat pension** Vorstandspension; ~**-hat policy** Versicherungspolice für leitende Angestellte; ~**-hat scheme** Bonussystem für leitende Angestellte; ~ **heaviness** *(plane)* Kopflastigkeit, *(securities)* Überbewertung; ~**-heavy** *(administration)* kopflastig, *(economics)* überkapitalisiert, *(nation)* finanziell überlastet, *(overorganized)* überorganisiert, *(plane)* kopflastig, *(securities)* überbewertet; **to be** ~**-heavy** *(administration)* Wasserkopf haben; ~**-heavy market** zu hohe Aktienkurse; ~**-hole** *(Br., sl.)* prima, glänzend; **to win the** ~ **hono(u)rs in a competition** höchsten Preis in einem Wettbewerb gewinnen; ~ **industrials** industrielle Spitzenwerte; ~ **industrialist** führender Industrieller; ~ **interest rates** Höchstzinssätze; ~ **issue** Hauptproblem; ~ **job** Spitzenstellung; ~ **kick** *(mil., US sl.)* Spieß; **administration's** ~ **leaders** Spitzen der Ministerialbürokratie; ~ **left-hand corner** *(newspaper)* links oben; ~ **level** auf höchster Ebene; ~ **levels** Spitzenkräfte; ~**-level benefits associated with appointments of this nature** mit Spitzenpositionen dieser Art verbundene übliche Sondervergünstigungen; ~**-level conference** Besprechung auf höchster Ebene; ~**-level executive** Spitzenkraft; ~**-level government decision** auf höchster Ebene getroffene Staatsentscheidung; ~**-level management status** Spitzenposition in der

Vorstandsebene; ~-level manager *(US)* oberster Betriebsleiter; ~-level negotiations Verhandlungen auf höchster Ebene; ~-level official Spitzenfunktionär; ~ light *(ship)* Positionslicht; ~ line *(ship)* Positionslicht, *(newspaper)* Kopf-, Titelzeile; ~ liner *(coll.)* Prominenter, Star; ~-loading clause *(shipping)* Obenaufklausel; ~ management *(US)* oberste Betriebsführung, Spitzenkräfte, Unternehmens-, Führungsspitze; ~ management official Vorstandsmitglied; ~ management post *(US)* Spitzenposition; ~ management team *(US)* Spitzengremium; ~ manager *(US)* oberster Betriebsleiter; to be too thin in its ~ managerial ranks *(US)* über zu wenig Spitzenkräfte verfügen; ~ mandarin post Spitzenposition in der Beamtenhierachie; ~ margin Außenrand; ~-of-the-line model Spitzenmodell; ~ negotiator Spitzenunterhändler; ~ notch höchst erreichbares Ziel; ~-notch *(a.)* wunderbar, erstklassig, prima; ~-notch job herrlicher Beruf; ~ organization Spitzenverband; ~ output Höchstleistung, -produktion; ~ pay Spitzengehalt; ~ people Prominenz, Spitzenkräfte; ~-performing mutual funds Spitzenreiter unter den Investmentfonds; ~ place erster Platz; ~ plant Spitzenbetrieb; ~ point Höchstpunkt; ~ position Spitzenstellung; ~ price Höchstpreis, *(stock exchange)* Höchstkurs, -stand; to pay ~ prices Höchstpreise bezahlen; ~ priority höchste Dringlichkeitsstufe; ~-priority job vordringliche Aufgabe; ~-priority needs vordringlicher Spitzenbedarf; ~ producer Spitzenproduzent; ~ quality Spitzenqualität; ~-ranking official *(US)* leitender Angestellter, Spitzenbeamter; ~ rate Höchstsatz; ~ rate of income tax Einkommensteuerhöchstsatz; to hit ~ ratings Spitzenbewertung (höchste Bewertung) erzielen; ~-rating list *(book trade)* Bestsellerliste; ~ reglet Kopfsteg; ~ right position *(advertising)* Plazierung oben rechts; to carry ~-running priority over any other train Vorfahrtsberechtigung vor jedem anderen Zug haben; ~ salary Spitzengehalt; ~ sales Spitzenumsatz; ~ salesman Spitzenverkäufer, Verkaufskanone; ~ sawyer *(coll.)* hohes Tier, Prominenter; ~ secret streng geheim, geheime Kommandosache; ~ seller position Spitzenposition im Verkäufermarkt; ~-selling brand Spitzenerzeugnis der Markenindustrie; ~ sergeant *(US coll.)* Hauptfeldwebel, Spieß; ~ shelf oberstes Fach; ~ speed Höchstgeschwindigkeit; ~ spot Spitzenposition; ~ state people Spitzenmanager von Staatsbetrieben; ~ table Ehrenplatz; ~ talent Spitzenkraft; ~ tax rate höchster Steuersatz, Steuerhöchstsatz, Spitzensteuersatz; ~ earned tax rate höchster Einkommensteuersatz; ~ marginal tax rate Steuerhöchstsatz für Spitzenverdiener, Spitzentarif; ~ team Spitzenmannschaft; ~-of-the-head thinking einsame Entschlüsse; ~ ticket teuerste Eintrittskarte; to rate ~-secret treatment mit größter Geheimhaltung behandelt werden; ~-up cover against inflation zusätzliche Inflationssicherung; ~ value Höchstwert; ~ wages Spitzenlohn; ~ work Spitzenleistung.
topflight erstklassig, prima.
topic [Gesprächs]thema, -stoff, -gegenstand;
chosen ~ Wahlthema; most important single ~ wichtigstes Einzelthema;
~s of conversation Gesprächsthemen; ~ of the day Tagesgespräch; ~ of discussion Gesprächsthema; ~ of a speech Inhalt einer Rede;
to constitute the main ~ of the conversation Hauptgesprächsgegenstand abgeben (bilden); to provide a ~ for discussion Diskussionsthema abgeben.
topical Aktualitätenschau, -film, *(broadcasting)* Zeitpunkt;
~ *(a.)* örtlich, lokal, *(pertaining to a topic)* zeitgemäß, [hoch]aktuell;
~ allusions aktuelle Anspielungen; ~ film aktueller Film; ~ news film Aktualitätenschau; suggested ~ outline vorgeschlagenes Gesprächsthema; ~ subject aktuelles Thema; ~ talk Gespräch von aktuellem Interesse.
topicality lokale Bedeutung, Aktualität.
toploftiness Arroganz, Aufgeblasenheit, Hochnäsigkeit.
toplofty anmaßend, hochnäsig, hochtrabend.
topman *(mining)* Übertagearbeiter.
topmost cost Spitzenkosten.
topography Landesbeschreibung, Topografie.
topped, to be den Kürzeren ziehen.
topper *(coll.)* Mordsding, tolle Sache, *(silk hat)* Angströhre.
topping *(coll.)* famos, prima, erstklassig, fabelhaft, tipptopp.
topside auf Deck, *(fig.)* an leitender Stellung.
topsoil Ackerkrume, Mutterboden.
topsy|-turvification Durcheinanderbringen; ~-turvy Kopfüber, Durcheinander; to turn everything ~-turvy alles auf den Kopf stellen; ~ turvydom ~ Durcheinander, polnische Wirtschaft, Kuddelmuddel.

torch [Pech]fackel, *(fig.)* Fackel, Feuer, Flamme, *(professional incendiary)* Brandstifter;
electric ~ *(Br.)* Taschenlampe;
to carry a ~ for s. o. j. ohne Gegenliebe zu finden bewundern; to hand on the ~ of knowledge Fackel des Wissens weitergeben;
~ battery *(Br.)* Stabbatterie; ~ lamp Lötlampe; ~ song *(US)* sentimentales Liebeslied.
torchbearer Fackelträger.
torchlight Fackelschein, -beleuchtung;
~ procession Fackelzug.
torment Qual, Pein, Schmerz, *(torture)* Folter[ung];
positive ~ of his parents Quälgeist seiner Eltern;
~ *(v.)* quälen, *(stir up)* in Aufregung versetzen;
~ a text Text verzerren.
tormentor *(film)* schallabsorbierende Wand.
tornadic wirbelsturmartig.
tornado Wirbelsturm, Windhose, Tornado.
torpedo *(mar.)* Torpedo, Seemine, *(for bored oil well)* Sprengpatrone;
~ *(v.)* torpedieren, verminen;
~ a disarmament conference Abrüstungskonferenz torpedieren;
~ boat Torpedoboot; ~ body stromlinienförmige Karosserie; ~ bomber Torpedoflugzeug; ~ doctrine Grundsatz der Gefahrenquelle für Kinder; ~ net Torpedonetz; ~ tube Torpedorohr.
torpedoplane Torpedoflugzeug.
torque Drehkraft, -leistung, -moment.
torrent reißender Strom, Wild-, Sturzbach;
~ of abuse Schimpfkanonade; ~ of protests Flut von Protesten; ~ of rain Wolkenbruch; ~ of words Wortschwall.
torrential wolkenbruchartig, *(fig.)* überwältigend;
~ rain Wolkenbruch.
torrid|heat sengende Hitze; ~ plain ausgedörrte Ebene.
torso Torso, Bruchstück.
tort unerlaubte Handlung, Schaden, *(criminal law)* Delikt, Vergehen, Straftat;
actionable ~ unerlaubte Handlung; joint ~ gemeinsam begangene unerlaubte Handlung; maritime ~ auf schiffbaren Gewässern begangene unerlaubte Handlung; personal ~ Verletzung von Persönlichkeitsrechten; property ~ Vermögensschaden, -verletzung; quasi ~ deliktsähnliche Handlung; wilful ~ vorsätzlich begangene unerlaubte Handlung;
~ of conspiracy Delikt der unerlaubten Handlung; ~ of fraud (deceit) Betrugsdelikt; ~ of negligence Fahrlässigkeitsdelikt; ~s subject to penalty strafbare Handlungen;
to be liable in ~ aus unerlaubter Handlung haften; to commit a ~ unerlaubte Handlung begehen; to obtain damages in ~ Schadenersatz wegen unerlaubter Handlungen erlangen; to sue for ~ aus unerlaubter Handlung klagen;
~ action Klage wegen unerlaubter Handlungen; ~ claim Schadenersatz aus unerlaubter Handlung; ~ liability Haftung aus unerlaubter Handlung.
tortfeasor Übertreter, Täter, Schadenersatzpflichtiger;
joint ~ Mittäter.
tortious unerlaubt, deliktisch;
~ act unerlaubte (rechtswidrige) Handlung, Straftat, Delikt; ~ liability Haftung aus unerlaubter Handlung, Deliktshaftung.
tortuous *(fig.)* umständlich, gewunden, *(river)* gewunden, geschlängelt;
~ argument umständliche Beweisführung; ~ policy krumme Touren; ~ politician intriganter (gerissener) Politiker; ~ road kurvenreiche Straße.
torture Folter, Tortur, *(text)* Entstellung, Verdrehung;
~ of a text Textentstellung;
~ *(v.)* foltern, auf die Folter spannen;
~ s. o. to make him confess s. th. jem. durch Folterungen ein Geständnis abpressen; ~ a text Text entstellen;
to put to the ~ auf die Folter spannen;
~ charge Folterbeschuldigung.
torturer Folterknecht.
tory Konservativer;
~ *(a.)* reaktionär;
~ government konservative Regierung.
toss Werfen, Wurf, *(lottery)* Loswurf, *(ship)* Schlingern;
~-up *(Br.)* ungewisse Sache;
~ *(v.)* [hoch]werfen, schleudern, *(coin)* durch Hochwerfen einer Münze losen, *(ship)* schlingern;
~ a coin to a beggar einem Bettler eine Münze zuwerfen; ~ up a newspaper article Zeitungsartikel zusammenschustern; ~ up a party *(sl.)* Gesellschaft geben; ~ up a question Frage aufwerfen;
~ in the towel das Handtuch werfen, aufgeben.

tot *(Br.)* Additionsaufgabe;
~ *(v.)* zusammenzählen, addieren;
~ **up** sich summieren.
total Gesamtleistung, Gesamtsumme, -betrag, Summa, Summe, Betrag;
grand ~ Gesamtsumme, **net** ~ Reinertrag;
~ **of a statement** Etatssumme;
~ *(v.)* im ganzen betragen, sich belaufen auf, ergeben, ausmachen, *(add up)* zusammenrechnen, -zählen;
~ **up** zusammenrechnen, *(fig.)* Fazit ziehen;
to reach a ~ **of £ 100** Gesamtbetrag von 100 Pfund erreichen;
~ *(a.)* gesamt, ganz, *(complete)* alle Hilfsmittel anwendend;
~ **actual hours worked** tatsächlich geleistete Arbeitsstunden; ~ **amount** Gesamtbetrag, -summe, Hauptbetrag; ~ **assets** Gesamtwert der Aktiva, Gesamtvermögen; ~ **average** Gesamtdurchschnitt; ~ **balance of trade** Gesamthandelsbilanz; ~ **capacity** Gesamtleistungsvermögen; ~ **capitalization** vollständige Kapitalausstattung; ~ **casualties** *(mil.)* Gesamtverluste; ~ **circulation** *(newspaper)* Gesamtauflage; ~ **claim** Gesamtforderung; ~ **costs** Gesamtkosten; ~ **current assets** Gesamtumlaufvermögen; ~ **debts** Gesamtschulden; ~ **demand** Gesamtbedarf; ~ **demand curve** Gesamtnachfragekurve; ~ **dependency** *(Workmen's Compensation Act, US)* vollständige Abhängigkeit; ~ **deposits** Gesamteinzahlungen; ~ **disability** vollständige [hundertprozentige] Erwerbsunfähigkeit, Vollinvalidität; ~ **disbursements** Gesamtaufwendungen; ~ **earnings** Gesamtverdienst; ~ **estate** Gesamtmasse; ~ **evaluation** Gesamtbewertung; ~ **eviction** vollständiger Besitzentzug; ~ **expenses (expenditure)** Gesamtausgaben, Ausgabenvolumen; ~ **exports** Gesamtausfuhr; ~ **failure** völliger Fehlschlag; ~ **field under survey** Universum; ~ **fixed costs** gesamte fixe Kosten; ~ **haul** Gesamtausbeute; ~ **hours of work** Gesamtarbeitszeit; ~ **imports** Gesamteinfuhr; ~ **income** Gesamteinkommen; ~ **and permanent disability insurance** Versicherung gegen Vollinvalidität; ~ **investments** Gesamtinvestitionen; ~ **liabilities** Gesamtverpflichtungen, -verbindlichkeiten; ~ **life** Gesamtlebensdauer; ~ **load** Rohlast; ~ **loss** Total-, Gesamtverlust, *(fire insurance)* Totalschaden; **constructive** ~ **loss** *(marine insurance)* fingierter Gesamtschaden; ~ **loss only** *(insurance law)* nur bei Totalverlust; ~ **marketing** Gesamtabsatz; ~ **merger** hundertprozentige Fusion, Totalfusion; ~ **net income** Gesamtnettoeinkommen; ~ **net paid** *(newspaper)* verkaufte Auflage; ~ **number** Gesamtzahl; ~ **outlay** Gesamtaufwand; ~ **output** *(mining)* Gesamtertrag; ~ **population** Gesamtbevölkerung; ~ **possible labo(u)r force** Arbeitskräftereservoir; ~ **power** *(el.)* Gesamtleistung; ~ **premium** Gesamtprämie; ~ **print run** Gesamtauflage; ~ **proceeds** Gesamterlös; ~ **production** Gesamtproduktion; ~ **production costs** volle Produktionskosten; ~ **proprietorship** Gesamteigenkapital; ~ **receipts** Gesamteinnahmen; ~ **recovery** Gesamtausbeute; ~ **rentroll** gesamte Mieteinnahmen; ~ **requirements** Gesamtbedarf; ~ **reserve** Gesamtrücklage; ~ **result** Gesamtergebnis; ~ **revenue** Gesamtaufkommen, *(firm)* Gesamterträge; ~ **sales** Absatzvolumen, Gesamtumsatz; ~ **sales of the consolidated companies** Gesamtumsatz der in den konsolidierten Jahresabschluß einbezogenen Gesellschaften; ~ **saving** Gesamtersparnis; ~ **stock on hand** Gesamtbestand; ~ **subscription** Gesamteinlage; ~ **sum** Gesamtsumme; ~ **supply** Gesamtangebot; ~ **surplus** Gesamtüberschuß; ~ **taxation** gesamtes Steueraufkommen; ~ **tolerance** *(quality control)* zulässige Toleranz; ~ **tonnage** Gesamttonnage; ~ **trade** Gesamtwirtschaft; ~ **transactions** Gesamtumsatz; ~ **turnover** Gesamtumsatz; ~ **value** Gesamtwert; ~ **volume** Gesamtvolumen; ~ **votes [cast]** Gesamtstimmenzahl; ~ **war** totaler Krieg; ~ **weight** Gesamtgewicht; ~ **work in hand** Gesamtaufträge, gesamter Auftragsbestand; ~ **workforce** Gesamtbelegschaft; ~ **wreck** *(ship)* Totalverlust; ~ **yield** Gesamtaufkommen.
totalitarian totalitär;
~ **state** Machtstaat.
totalitarianism totalitäre Staatsform.
totality Gesamtheit.
totalization Zusammenfassung.
totalizator Zählwerk, Registrierapparat, *(racing, Br.)* Totalisator.
totalize *(v.)* zusammenfassen, *(add up)* zusammenzählen, summieren, *(betting)* am Totalisator wetten.
totalizer Addiermaschine.
tote *(Br., sl.)* Toto, *(US coll.)* Schleppen, Tragen;
flourishing ~ **scheme** *(Br., sl.)* blühendes Totogeschäft.
totem Totem.
totted *(debt of the crown, Br.)* beigetrieben.
totten trust *(US)* Stiftung zugunsten eines Dritten.

totter Lumpensammler;
~ *(v.)* schwanken, torkeln, taumeln;
~ **on the verge of bankruptcy** kurz vor dem Konkurs stehen.
tottering | contact *(el.)* Wackelkontakt; ~ **government** wankende Regierung; ~ **state of the money market** schwankender Zustand des Geldmarktes.
totting Lumpensammeln.
touch Berühren, *(act of stealing, sl.)* Organisieren, *(borrowing, sl.)* Anpumpen, *(characteristic)* besondere Note, Charakteristikum, charakteristischer Zug, *(contact)* Fühlungnahme, Verbindung, Kontakt, *(latest detail)* letzte Feinheit, *(metal)* Feingehalts-, Gütestempel, *(borrowed money, sl.)* Pump, gepumptes Geld, *(trace)* Anflug, Anstrich, Spur, Hauch, Stich;
at a ~ beim Berühren; **at the slightest** ~ bei der leichtesten Berührung; **with sure** ~ mit sicherer Hand; **out of** ~ **with** ohne Kontakt zu; **within** ~ in Reichweite;
easy ~ leicht Anzusprechender; **happy** ~ freundliche Note; **near** ~ knappes Entkommen; **the Nelson** ~ sichere Beherrschung einer schwierigen Situation;
~ **in the brain** Geistesschwäche; ~ **of the century** Gepräge eines Jahrhunderts; ~**es of colo(u)r** Farbnuancen; **velvety** ~ **of a fabric** samtartiges Gefühl eines Stoffes; ~ **of fever** kurzer Fieberanfall; ~ **of frost** Anflug von Frost; ~ **and go** kurzes Antippen, *(fig.)* auf der Kippe, auf des Messers Schneide, gewagte Sache, prekäre Situation; **a** ~ **of the macabre** Stich ins Makabre; ~ **of the master** Hand des Meisters; ~ **of romance** Hauch von Romantik;
~ *(v.)* berühren, *(adjoin)* aneinandergrenzen, *(assay)* mit dem Feingehaltsstempel versehen, *(contact)* in Berührung kommen, Kontakt haben, *(delineate with light strokes)* skizzieren, mit wenigen Strichen entwerfen, *(mar.)* anlegen, kurzen Aufenthalt haben, *(steal, sl.)* organisieren, ergaunern, klauen;
~ **s. o.** *(sl.)* j. anpumpen, j. um Geld anhauen; ~ **60 mph** 100 Km pro Stunde erreichen; ~ **35 C** 35 Grad Celsius erreichen;
not ~ **an affair** sich mit einer Angelegenheit nicht befassen; ~ **the bell** Klingelknopf drücken; ~ **the bottom** Grund erreichen, *(fig.)* völlig absinken, *(market)* niedrigsten Kursstand erreichen, *(get at the root)* fündig werden; ~ **the capital** Kapital angreifen; ~ **down** *(plane)* landen, aufsetzen, niedergehen; ~ **elbows** in engem Kontakt sein; ~ **elbows with many sorts of people** mit den verschiedensten Leuten zusammenkommen; ~ **and go** *(ship)* gleich wieder flott werden; ~ **the goal of one's desire** Ziel seiner Wünsche erreichen; ~ **one's heart** j. stärkstens berühren; ~ **s. one's interests closely** jds. Interessen engstens berühren; ~ **for money** *(sl.)* um Geld angehen, anpumpen; ~ **off** auslösen; ~ **off a riot** Aufruhr auslösen; ~ **off a spate of rumo(u)rs** Fülle von Gerüchten auslösen; ~ **each other** *(states)* aneinandergrenzen, gemeinsame Grenze haben; ~ **many points** viele Punkte berühren; ~ **a port** Hafen (Land) anlaufen; ~ **provisions** Vorräte angreifen; ~ **upon a question** Frage nur kurz berühren; ~ **s. o. to the quick** j. empfindlich treffen; ~ **a river** an einen Fluß angrenzen; ~ **shares of armament firms** in Rüstungswerten investieren; ~ **shoulders** in engem Kontakt sein; ~ **the spot** genau das Richtige tun; ~ **and stay** *(fig.)* Hafen anlaufen und dort bleiben; ~ **s. o. on a tender place** j. an einer empfindlichen Stelle treffen; ~ **on treason** an Verrat grenzen; ~ **up** nochmals überarbeiten, *(painting)* retuschieren; ~ **up a program(me)** Programm überarbeiten; ~ **wood** auf Holz klopfen; **to be in** ~ miteinander in Verbindung stehen; **to be in close** ~ **with s. o.** in direkter Verbindung mit jem. stehen; **to be out of** ~ **with s. o.** Verbindung zu jem. verloren haben; **to be out of** ~ **with the political situation** politische Lage im Augenblick nicht überblicken; **to get in** ~ **with s. o.** sich mit jem. ins Benehmen setzen, mit jem. in Verbindung treten, Kontakt mit jem. aufnehmen; **to give the finishing** ~**es** letzten Schliff geben; **to have a** ~ **of a genius** etw. von einem Genie an sich haben; **to have a light** ~ *(typewriter)* leichten Anschlag haben; **to keep in** ~ in Verbindung bleiben; **to lose** ~ Kontakt verlieren; **to put s. th. on the** ~ etw. auf die Probe stellen; **to refuse to** ~ **certain transactions** mit bestimmten Transaktionen nichts zu tun haben wollen;
~ **and go** *(a.)* oberflächlich, unmethodisch, *(risky)* gefährlich, riskant; ~**-and-go business** riskantes Geschäft; ~**-and-go sort of a situation** äußerst riskante Lage; **to be a** ~**-and-go situation** auf des Messers Schneide stehen, höchst riskante Lage sein; ~**-me-not** *(fig.)* heikles Thema, verbotenes Gebiet; ~ **system** Zehnfingersystem, Blindschreiben; **electronic control** ~**-tuning system** computergesteuerte Sensoreinstellung; ~**-type** *(v.)* blindschreiben; ~ **typewriter** Blindschreiber; ~ **typewriting** Blindschreiben.

touchdown *(airplane)* Aufsetzen, Landung.
touched berührt, *(brain)* beeinträchtigt, geschädigt, *(fig.)* bewegt, ergriffen, gerührt;
~ **from the fire** feuerbeschädigt; ~ **by the frost** frostbeschädigt; ~ **in the head** übergeschnappt, nicht mehr ganz richtig; ~ **with pity** von Mitleid erfüllt; ~ **to the quick** empfindlich getroffen; ~ **with rose** rosa getönt; ~ **to tears** zu Tränen gerührt;
to be a bit ~ ein bißchen bekloppt sein; **not to have** ~ **food for two days** seit zwei Tagen keinen Bissen angerührt haben.
toucher, to a haargenau, bis aufs i-Tüpfelchen;
a near ~ knappes Entkommen.
touching|incident ergreifender Vorfall; ~ **the land** mit dinglicher Wirkung; ~ **tale** bewegende Erzählung.
touchstone *(fig.)* Prüfstein, Kriterium.
touchy subject heikles Thema.
tough Draufgänger, *(US)* Flegel, übler Kunde, Rabauke;
~ *(a.)* hart, fest, zäh, *(tenacious)* hartnäckig, unnachgiebig, *(vicious)* verstockt, verderbt, unverbesserlich;
to be ~ **on s. o.** jem. hart ankommen;
~ **bunk** *(sl.)* schwer verdientes Geld; ~ **criminal** hartgesottener Verbrecher; ~ **customer** *(coll.)* unangenehmer Zeitgenosse; ~ **going** saures Stück Arbeit; ~ **guy** *(nut)* harter Brocken; ~ **job** schwierige Arbeit; **to take a** ~ **line against the strikers** energisch gegen Streikende vorgehen; ~ **luck** *(US)* Pech; ~**-minded** illusionslos, realistisch; ~ **neighbo(u)rhood** verrufene Gegend; ~ **offender** verstockter Missetäter; **to adopt a** ~ **policy towards the workers** feste Position bei den Verhandlungen mit den Arbeitnehmern beziehen; ~ **physique** robuste Konstitution; ~ **spot** dicke Luft; **to be in a** ~ **spot with one's boss** bei seinem Chef schlecht angeschrieben sein.
toughen *(v.)* *(pol.)* sich versteifen.
toughening *(pol.)* Versteifung.
tour Reise, Tour, Rundfahrt, -reise, -gang, Ausflug, *(theater)* Tournee, Gastspielreise;
on ~ unterwegs; **on completion of one's** ~ **of duty** nach Beendigung seiner Amtsperiode;
all-expense ~ Pauschalreise, *(US)* kostenlose Besichtigungsreise; **bargain** ~ verbilligte Reise; **business** ~ Geschäftsreise; **circular** ~ *(Br.)* Rundreise; **conducted** ~ zusammengestellte Reise, Gesellschaftsreise; **foreign** ~ Auslandsreise; **guided** ~ Führung, Gesellschaftsreise; **guided package** ~ *(US)* von einem Reiseleiter betreute Gesellschaftsreise; **official** ~ Dienstreise; **motor** ~ Autofahrt; **motor-coach** ~ Omnibusrundfahrt; **mystery** ~ Fahrt ins Blaue; **round-the-world** ~ Weltreise; **organized** ~ Gesellschaftsreise, -fahrt; **overseas** ~ Dienstzeit in Übersee; **packaged** ~ *(US)* Gesellschaftsfahrt, -tour, Pauschalreise;
~ **of the continent** Europareise; **three** ~**s a day** drei Schichten täglich; **one's daily** ~ **of duty** täglicher Pflichtenkreis; ~ **de force** Gewaltstreich, *(ingenious accomplishment)* außerordentliche Leistung, Glanzleistung; ~ **of the garden** Rundgang durch den Garten; ~ **of the house** Hausbesichtigung; ~ **of inspection** Inspektions-, Besichtigungsreise, -rundgang; ~ **round the world** Weltreise; ~ **of three years as a lecturer** dreijährige Dozentenstellung;
~ *(v.)* Tour machen, bereisen, *(inspect)* inspizieren, *(theater)* auf Gastspielreise (Tournee) gehen, Gastspielreise machen;
~ **the fairs** Messen bereisen; ~ **a nation** Rundreise machen; ~ **a play** mit einem Stück auf Tournee gehen;
to be on ~ auf Gastspielreise sein; **to be invited to** ~ zu einer Reise eingeladen werden; **to be on one's** ~ in Geschäften unterwegs (auf Tournee) sein; **to go on** ~ Ausflug machen, *(theatre)* auf Tournee gehen, Gastspielreise machen; **to make the** ~ **of a country** übliche Rundreise machen; **to send s. o. on** ~ j. auf Reisen schicken; **to take a company on** ~ Gastspielreise mit seinem Ensemble machen;
~ **basing fares** auf einheitlicher Berechnungsbasis ausgestellte Flugtickets für Gesellschaftsreisen; ~ **fare** Rundflugkarte; **independently listed** ~ **operator** unabhängig geführtes Touristikunternehmen.
touring Umherreisen, Reiseverkehr;
~ *(a.)* auf Reisen, unterwegs;
to be ~ reisen;
~ **car** Tourenwagen; ~ **company** Gastspielensemble; ~ **exhibition** Wanderausstellung; ~ **information** Reiseauskünfte; ~ **party** Reisegesellschaft; ~ **theater** Wanderbühne.
tourism Reise-, Fremdenverkehr, Tourismus, *(touring parties)* Reisegesellschaften, *(management of tourists)* Fremdenverkehrs-, Touristenwesen;
to be mainly dependent for one's living on ~ hauptsächlich vom Fremdenverkehr leben; **to obtain large sums of foreign**

exchange from ~ große Devisenbeträge dem Fremdenverkehr verdanken;
~ **advertising** Fremdenverkehrswerbung; ~ **business** Fremdenverkehrswesen; ~ **facilities** Fremdenverkehrsmöglichkeiten, -einrichtungen.
tourist [Vergnügungs]reisender, Ausflügler, Tourist;
air ~ Flugreisender, Touristenfluggast; **beginning-of-season** ~**s** Touristen zum Anfang der Saison; **budget-minded** ~ sparbewußter Tourist;
to be full of ~**s** von Touristen überlaufen sein;
~ **accommodation** Touristenquartier; ~ **accommodations** Reiseerleichterungen; ~ **advertising** Fremdenverkehrswerbung; ~ **agency** Reisebüro; ~ **area** Fremdenverkehrsgebiet, Touristenzentrum; ~ **association** Fremdenverkehrsverband; ~ **attraction** Touristenattraktion; ~ **baggage floater insurance** *(US)* globale Reisegepäckversicherung; ~ **bed** Fremdenbett; **~ Board** *(Br.)* Fremdenverkehrsverband; ~ **boom** Touristenkonjunktur; ~ **bureau** *(US)* Reise-, Verkehrsbüro; ~ **cabin** Touristenkabine; ~ **camp** Ferienlager; ~ **car (coach)** Touristenfahrzeug, Reiseomnibus; ~ **center** *(US)* **(centre,** *Br.***)** Touristen-, Fremdenverkehrszentrum, -ort; ~ **class** *(US)* Touristenklasse, zweite Klasse; ~**-class fare** *(US)* Fahrpreis zweiter Klasse; ~ **country** Reise-, Touristenland; ~ **court** Motel; ~ **deficit** Fremdenverkehrsdefizit; ~ **destination** Fremdenverkehrsplatz, Touristenort; ~ **development** Entwicklung des Fremdenverkehrs; ~ **dollar** Touristendollar; ~ **exchange** Reisedevisen; ~ **expenditure** Touristenausgaben; ~ **fare** *(US)* Fahrpreis zweiter Klasse; ~ **floater policy** Reisegepäckversicherungspolice; ~ **guide** Fremdenführer; ~**-haunted (-ridden)** von Touristen überlaufen; ~ **haven** beliebter Touristenort, Touristen-, Ferienparadies; ~ **imbalance** unausgeglichene Fremdenverkehrsbilanz; ~ **industry** Fremden[verkehrs]industrie; ~ **information** Verkehrsauskunft; ~ **inn** Ausflugslokal; ~ **office** *(Br.)* Reisebüro; ~ **officer** Fremdenverkehrsangestellter, Angestellter eines Reisebüros; **government** ~ **organization** staatliche Touristenorganisation; ~ **pamphlet** Reiseprospekt; ~ **passenger** Passagier der Touristenklasse; ~ **promotion** Fremdenverkehrsförderung; ~ **publicity material** Werbematerial für den Fremdenverkehr; ~ **receipts** Einnahmen aus dem Fremdenverkehr; ~ **road** Touristenstraße; ~ **season** Reisezeit; ~ **spending** Ausgaben im Reiseverkehr; ~ **tax** Fremdenverkehrssteuer; ~ **ticket** Rundreisefahrkarte; ~ **trade** Fremdenverkehr[sgewerbe, -swirtschaft]; ~**-trade statistics** Fremdenverkehrsstatistik; ~ **traffic** Reise-, Fremdenverkehr; ~**-traffic propaganda** Fremdenverkehrswerbung; ~ **travel** Reise-, Touristenverkehr; ~ **visa** Touristenvisum; ~ **voucher** Touristengutschein; ~ **weather insurance** Reisewetterversicherung.
touristic growth Tourismuszunahme.
tout Schlepper, Kundenwerber, -schlepper, -fänger, *(insurance agent)* Akquisiteur, Kundenbesucher;
~ *(v.)* Kunden akquirieren (werben), aufdringlich Werbung betreiben, *(canvass for votes)* Stimmenwerbung betreiben, *(spy)* bespitzeln, *(US)* Wettips geben;
~ **s. o. as a friend of the people** j. als Volksfreund hinstellen; ~ **for a hotel** Schlepperdienste für ein Hotel leisten, Hotelgäste werben; ~ **for votes** Stimmen werben.
touting [for customers] Kundenwerbung, *(insurance business)* Akquisition.
tow Schleppen, Schlepparbeit, *(mar.)* Schleppzug, *(rope)* Schleppseil, -tau, -trosse;
~ *(v.)* [ab]schleppen, ins Schlepptau nehmen, *(ship)* bugsieren, ziehen;
~ **a broken car** kaputtes Auto abschleppen; ~ **in** einschleppen; ~ **off** abschleppen;
to have in ~ im Schlepptau haben; **to usually have one's family in** ~ immer gleich die ganze Familie um sich haben; **to take** ~ sich schleppen lassen; **to take into** ~ ins Schlepptau nehmen;
~**-away zone** *(US)* Parkverbotszone, -gebiet; ~ **car** Abschleppwagen; ~**-line** *(a.)* spendabler Zeitgenosse; ~ **rope** Abschleppseil; ~**-row** *(coll.)* Spektakel, Krach; ~ **truck** *(US)* Abschleppfahrzeug, -wagen.
towage Schleppen, Abschleppen, *(ship)* Bugsieren, *(charge)* Schleppgebühr, -lohn;
~ **charges** Abschleppkosten, *(fig.)* Bugsierkosten; ~ **contractor** Abschleppschiffahrtsunternehmen; ~ **service** *(admiralty law)* Abschleppdienst.
towel Handtuch;
to throw in the ~ sich geschlagen geben.
tower Turm, *(aviation)* Kontrollturm, *(stronghold)* Bollwerk, Feste;
water ~ Wasserturm;

~ **of strength** *(fig.)* mächtige Stütze;
~ *(v.)* hochragen, sich hoch erheben;
~ **above s. o.** *(fig.)* j. weit überragen;
~ **block** *(Br.)* Wohnhochhaus; ~ **clock** Turmuhr.

towing Abschleppen, *(fee)* Schleppgebühr, *(ship)* Schleppen, Treideln, Schleppschiffahrt;
~ **charges** Abschleppgebühr; ~ **line (rope)** Abschleppseil; ~ **post** Treidelmast; ~ **service** Abschleppdienst.

towline Schlepp-, Bugsiertau.

town Stadt, Ort, *(Br.)* London, *(business center)* Stadtzentrum, -inneres, *(municipal administration)* Stadt-, Gemeindeverwaltung, *(municipal corporation, US)* Stadtgemeinde, *(university)* Bürgerschaft;
near the ~ in der Nähe der Stadt; **on the** ~ *(US)* auf Stadtrundfahrt, *(sl.)* auf Sauftour, *(social assistance)* auf städtische Unterstützung (Fürsorge) angewiesen; **out of** ~ außerhalb, nicht in der Stadt, *(Br.)* auf dem Lande, verreist, *(sl.)* im Kittchen; **to** ~ in die Stadt, *(Br.)* nach London;
the ~ Stadtbewohner, -bevölkerung;
border ~ Grenzstadt; **commercial** ~ Geschäftsstadt; **commuting** ~ im Nahverkehrsbereich liegende Stadt; **company** ~ *(US)* Firmen-, Werkssiedlung; **county** ~ *(Br.)* Kreisstadt; **country** ~ Provinzstadt; **deserted** ~ entvölkerte Stadt; **fortified** ~ feste Stadt; **front** ~ *(US)* Stadt an der Siedlungsgrenze; **green-belt** ~ Stadt mit Grüngürtel; **host** ~ gastgebende Stadt; **incorporated** ~ *(US)* zur Stadt erhobene Gemeinde; **little** ~ **nearby** benachbartes Städtchen; **manufacturing** ~ Industriestadt; **market** ~ *(Br.)* Marktflecken; **medium-sized** ~ mittlere Stadt; **municipal** ~ *(US)* Stadt mit Selbstverwaltung, Kreisstadt; **native** ~ Geburtsstadt; **new** ~ *(regional planning, Br.)* Entlastungsort, Trabantenstadt; **overspill** ~ überquellende (übervölkerte) Stadt; **rising** ~ aufblühende Stadt; **shanty** ~ Blechbudenstadt; **small** ~ *(US)* Dorf; **trading** ~ Geschäftszentrum, Einkaufsstadt, Handelsplatz; **twinned** ~ Partnerstadt; **undefended** ~ offene Stadt; **well-managed** ~ gut verwaltete Stadt;
~ **on the frontier** Grenzstadt; ~ **possessed of many objects of interest** mit vielen Sehenswürdigkeiten ausgestattete Stadt; ~ **of publication** Verlegerort;
to be defrayable by the ~ von der Stadt getragen werden; **to be all over the** ~ in der ganzen Stadt bekannt sein; **to be a man about** ~ *(Br.)* als Lebemann in London großzügig Geld ausgeben; **to be spending the weekend in** ~ *(Br.)* Wochenende in London verbringen; **to be the talk of the** ~ das Stadtgespräch sein; **to canvass a** ~ Stadt als Vertreter bearbeiten; **to center in a** ~ sich um eine Stadt konzentrieren; **to do one's shopping in** ~ seine Einkäufe in der Stadt erledigen; **to draw the** ~ Alt und Jung anlocken; **to go to** ~ in die Stadt gehen, *(fig.)* Erfolg haben, *(on a spree, sl.)* Stadtbummel (Sauftour) machen; **to go to** ~ **on s. th.** ausführlich über etw. berichten, *(fig.)* sich in etw. stürzen, etw. rückhaltlos tun, sich einer Sache voll und ganz verschreiben; **to go out on the** ~ *(fam.)* ausgehen, sich in der Stadt amüsieren; **to go up to** ~ *(Br.)* in die Innenstadt (nach London) fahren; **to improve the sanitation of a** ~ Stadt kanalisieren; **to incorporate a** ~ Stadt eingemeinden; **to know a** ~ **like the back of one's hand** Stadt wie seine Westentasche kennen; **to live out of** ~ außerhalb (nicht in der Stadt) wohnen; **to manage a** ~ Stadtverwaltung leiten; **to paint the** ~ **red** Stadt unsicher machen, alles auf den Kopf stellen; **to raze a** ~ **to the ground** Stadt völlig einebnen; **to scour the whole** ~ ganze Stadt nach etw. ablaufen (abklappern); **to serve a** ~ **with gas** Stadtgas legen; **to show s. o. around the** ~ jem. die Stadt zeigen; **to start a** ~ **from scratch** Stadt auf einer grünen Wiese errichten; **to take a town** *(mil.)* Stadt einnehmen; **to take to** ~ *(sl.)* völlig verwirren, perplex machen; **to take s. o. all over the** ~ j. in der ganzen Stadt herumführen; **to turn a** ~ **into a shambles** Stadt in einen Trümmerhaufen verwandeln;
~ **agency** Stadtvertretung, Stadtvertreter; ~ **agent** Stadtvertreter, *(prohibition period, US)* Alkoholbeauftragter; ~ **apartment** Stadtwohnung; ~ **book** Stadtgeschichte; ~**-bred** in der Stadt aufgewachsen; ~ **bridge** Stadtbrücke; ~ **car** Limousine mit Trennwand zum Chauffeur; ~ **cause** *(London)* vor dem Stadtrichter verhandelte Sache; ~ **center** *(Br.)* **(centre, US)** Stadtzentrum, -mitte; ~ **cheque** *(Br.)* Scheck auf die Londoner City; ~ **circuit** *(US)* Stadtrichtungsweiser; ~ **circle** Stadtkreis; ~ **clearing** *(Br.)* Scheckabrechnung im Finanzzentrum von London; ~ **clerk** *(Br.)* [Ober]stadtdirektor, *(US)* Gemeindeverwaltungsbeamter, Stadtsyndikus; ~ **clerkship** *(Br.)* Stadtkämmerei; ~ **clothes** Stadtkleidung; ~ **collector** Leiter des Stadtsteueramtes, städtischer Steuereinnehmer; ~**commissioner** Stadtdirektor; ~ **committee** Stadtausschuß; ~ **council** *(Br.)* Gemeinde-, Stadtrat, Magistrat, Stadtverordnetenversamm-

lung; ~ **councillor** Stadtrat[smitglied], Stadtverordneter, Ratsherr, *(US)* Gemeinderatsmitglied; ~ **crier** städtischer Ausrufer, Stadtausrufer; ~ **development** Stadterschließung; ~ **dues** städtische Abgaben; ~ **driving** Stadtfahrt; ~ **dweller** Stadtbewohner; ~ **extension** Stadtausdehnung; ~ **forest** Stadtwald; ~ **gas** städtische Gasversorgung, Stadtgas; ~ **hall** *(Br.)* Rat-, Gemeindehaus; ~ **house** Stadthaus, -wohnung, *(Br.)* Rathaus; ~ **jail** Stadtgefängnis; ~ **library** Stadtbibliothek; ~ **life** Leben in der Stadt; ~ **lot** städtisches Grundstück; ~ **major** *(Br.)* Stadtkommandant; ~ **management** *(US)* Gemeindeverwaltung; ~ **manager** *(US)* Amtsbürgermeister; ~ **major** *(Br.)* Stadtkommandant; ~ **meeting** *(US)* Bürger-, städtische Wählerversammlung, Gemeindeversammlung; ~ **officer** städtischer Beamter; ~ **officers** Stadtrat; ~ **order** Zahlungsanweisung des Stadtkämmerers; ~ **park** Stadtpark; ~ **planner** *(US)* Städteplaner, städtischer Bauamtsleiter, Leiter des Stadtbauamts; ~ **planning** Stadtplanung, -bau, städtebauliche Entwicklung; ~ **and country planning** *(Br.)* Regionalplanung; ~ **and country Planning Act** *(Br.)* [etwa] Gesetz über die Gemeinschaftsaufgabe Verbesserung der regionalen Wirtschaftsstruktur; ~**-planning committee** *(Br.)* städtischer Planungsausschuß; ~**-planning department** *(Br.)* Stadtbauamt; ~**-planning institute** *(US)* Institut für Städteplanung; ~ **planning-system** *(Br.)* Stadtbebauungswesen; ~ **pound** Stadtgefängnis; ~ **property** *(Br.)* Stadtgrundstück, städtisches Grundstück, städtischer Grundbesitz; **for** ~ **purposes** für städtische Zwecke; ~ **rates** *(Br.)* Gemeinde-, Kommunalabgaben; ~ **records** Stadtarchiv; ~ **reeve** *(Canada)* Stadtratsvorsitzender; ~ **refuse** Stadtmüll; ~ **residence** Stadtwohnung; ~**-size group** Ortsgrößenklasse; ~ **surveyor** Stadtbaurat; ~ **talk** Stadtgespräch; ~ **tax** städtische Abgaben, kommunale Abgabe, Kommunalabgabe, -steuer, Bürgersteuer; ~ **traffic** Stadtverkehr; ~ **travel(l)er** *(Br.)* Platzreisender, -vertreter; ~ **treasurer** Stadtkämmerer; ~ **wall** Stadtmauer; ~ **warrant** Zahlungsanweisung des Stadtkämmerers.

towner, small *(US)* Kleinstädter.

townland Gemeindeland.

townlet Städtchen, Kleinstadt.

townscape Stadtbild.

township *(Australia)* Stadtbauplatz, *(Br.)* Stadtgemeinde, städtische Gemeinde, Verwaltungsbezirk, *(South Africa)* nichteuropäisches Viertel, *(US)* Kreis-, Grafschaftsbezirk;
rural ~ *(US)* Landgemeinde;
~ **trustee** kommissarischer Leiter der Stadtverwaltung.

townspeople Stadtbevölkerung, -bewohner.

townwear Stadtkleidung.

towpath Lein-, Treidelpfad, Schleppweg.

toxicant Giftstoff.

toy [Kinder]spielzeug, *(fig.)* Spielerei, Zeitvertreib, Steckenpferd, Liebhaberei, *(knickknack)* Kinkerlitzchen;
~ **dog** Schoßhund; ~ **fair** Spielwarenmesse; ~ **industry** Spielwarenindustrie; ~ **theater** Puppentheater; ~ **train** Spielzeugeisenbahn; ~ **shop** Spielzeugladen, -warengeschäft.

toyman Spielzeugwarenhersteller, -händler.

trace Spur, Fährte, *(car)* Wagen-, Räderspur, *(footprint)* Fußabdruck, *(fortress)* Grundriß, *(mark left behind)* Anzeichen, Spur, Überrest, *(marking made by instrument)* Aufzeichnung, *(path, US)* markierter Weg, Pfad, *(barely detectable quantity)* geringe Menge, Spur, ein bißchen, *(seismograph)* Kurve, *(stock exchange)* durch Giro übertragbarer Lieferschein, *(sketch)* Pausezeichnung, Pause;
no ~ unbekannt verzogen;
~**s of an ancient civilization** Überreste einer alten Kultur; **no** ~ **of humo(u)r** kein bißchen (Funken) Humor; ~**s of Spanish influence** sichtbarer spanischer Einfluß; ~ **of a sleigh** Schlittenspur;
~ *(v.)* *(copy)* durchpausen, *(discover)* feststellen, ausfindig machen, *(investigate)* einer Sache nachgehen, ermitteln, *(letters)* schreiben, ausmalen, *(railway)* trassieren;
~ **back** zurückverfolgen; ~ **back to a childhood experience** auf Kindheitserfahrungen zurückführen; ~ **back a rumo(u)r** einem Gerücht nachgehen; ~ **the causes of a disease** Krankheitsursachen herausfinden; ~ **a check** *(US)* **(cheque, Br.)** Scheck verfolgen; ~ **a copy from the original** Dokument durchpausen; ~ **a criminal to M** Spur eines Verbrechers bis M zurückverfolgen; ~ **one's descent back to an old Norman family** seine Abstammung bis zu einer alten normannischen Familie zurückverfolgen; ~ **the history of a political movement** Geschichte einer politischen Bewegung nachgehen; ~ **a letter** Brief ausfindig machen; ~ **lost goods** verlorene Warenpartie wiederfinden; ~ **the original manuscript** Originalmanuskript auffinden (entdecken); ~ **out**

ausfindig machen; ~ **out the plan of a house** Grundriß eines Hauses entwerfen; ~ **[out] one's route on the map** seine Reiseroute auf der Landkarte einzeichnen; ~ **over** durchzeichnen, -pausen, kopieren; ~ **a plan** Plan entwerfen; ~ **the source of a play** Quelle eines Bühnenstücks erforschen; ~ **a word laboriously** Wort mühselig hinschreiben;
to be unable to find any ~s of a thief keinerlei Spuren eines Diebes auffinden können; **to kick over the ~s** über die Stränge schlagen; **to leave no ~ behind** keine Spur hinterlassen; **to preserve ~s** Spuren sichern; **to remove ~s** Spuren verwischen; ~ **and search department** Fahndungsabteilung; ~ **horse** Zugpferd.
traceability Nachweisbarkeit.
traceable nachweisbar;
~ **costs** direkte (nachweisbare) Kosten.
traceless spurlos, ohne Spuren zu hinterlassen.
tracer *(draftsman)* technischer Zeichner, Entwerfer, Pauser, *(US, collecting business)* Inkassobericht, *(railroad, US)* Laufzettel, Umlauf[schreiben];
~ **blank** *(US)* Inkassoauskunftsformular; ~ **bullet** Leuchtspurgeschoß; ~ **department** *(US)* Inkassoauskunftsabteilung; ~ **information** *(US)* Inkassoauskunft.
tracery on a frosted window Eisblumen an einem Fenster.
tracing Nachforschen, Suchen, *(copy)* Pause, Kopie, *(copying)* Durchpausen, *(right to follow assets, Br.)* Verfolgungsrecht;
~ **file** Suchkartei; ~ **order** Suchauftrag, *(for bank)* Nachforschungsanweisung; ~ **paper** Pauspapier.
track *(airplane)* Kurs über Grund, *(car)* Spurweite, *(film)* Tonspur, *(mar.)* Fahrrinne, -wasser, Kielwasser, *(path)* [Feld]weg, Pfad, Piste, *(railway)* Bahnstrecke, Schienenweg, -strang, Spur, Gleise, Strecke, Fahrgleis, *(ship)* übliche Route, *(satellite)* Flug-, Durchgangsbahn, *(tank)* Raupen-, Gliederkette, *(tyre)* Reifenprofil;
in one's ~ *(sl.)* auf der Stelle, sofort; **off the ~** entgleist, *(fig.)* auf dem Holzweg (der falschen Spur); **on ~** auf der Achse, unterwegs, rollend; **on the ~** dicht auf den Fersen; **on the wrong ~** auf dem Holzweg;
~**s Fahrspur**, *(railway)* Eisenbahngleise, Gleisanlage;
dead ~ totes Gleis; **joint ~** von zwei Spediteuren benutztes Verladegleis; **main ~** Hauptlinie, -strecke, *(railway)* Hauptgleis; **motor-racing ~** Rennstrecke; **North Atlantic ~** Nordatlantikroute; **occupied ~** belegtes Gleis; **single ~** eingleisige Strecke; **team ~** Entladegleis;
~ **of a comet** Kometenbahn; ~ **through the forest** Waldweg; ~ **of a ship** Kurs eines Schiffes; ~ **of a spacecraft** Bahn eines Raumschiffes; ~ **of a storm** Sturmbahn;
~ *(v.)* *(railroad, US)* Schienen verlegen, *(road)* kennzeichnen, ausschildern;
~ **a desert** Wüste durchziehen; ~ **down s. o.** j. ausfindig machen (aufspüren); ~ **down a reference** Referenz überprüfen;
to be born on the wrong side of the ~ *(US)* aus einem asozialen Bezirk stammen; **to be off the ~** auf der falschen Fährte sein; **to be off the beaten ~** vom Normalen abweichen; **to be on s. one's ~** jem. auf der Spur sein; **to be on the wrong ~** auf dem Holzweg sein; **to come round the ~ again** wieder auf der Bildfläche erscheinen; **to cover up one's ~** seine Spur verwischen; **to double an existing ~** Strecke zweigleisig ausbauen; **to follow s. one's ~** in jds. Fußstapfen treten; **to follow s. one's ~ through the snow** jds. Spur im Schnee verfolgen; **to keep s. o. on the ~** j. auf dem laufenden halten; **to keep ~ of a matter** Sache im Auge behalten; **to keep ~ of the current events** Tagesereignisse laufend verfolgen; **to keep ~ of new publications** neue Veröffentlichungen verfolgen; **to keep ~ of reservations** Zimmerreservierungen im Griff behalten; **to leave the ~** *(train)* entgleisen; **to leave the beaten ~** *(fig.)* ausgetretene Gleise verlassen, alten Trott aufgeben; **to lose ~ of** aus den Augen verlieren; **to make ~s** *(US sl.)* davonlaufen, durchbrennen; **to make ~s for s. o.** hinter jem. her sein; **to rebuild ~s** Gleisanlagen erneuern;
~ **clearer** Schienenräumer; ~ **costs** Gleisunterhaltungskosten; ~ **delivery shipment** Massengutabfertigung per Bahn; ~ **improvement** Gleisanlagenausbau, Ausbau der Gleisanlagen; ~ **maintenance** Gleisarbeiten, -unterhaltung; **to have a one-~ mind** eingleisig denken; ~ **record** bisherige Erfolge; **demonstrable effective (proven) record** nachweisbar erfolgreicher Berufsverlauf, nachgewiesener beruflicher Erfolg; **to have a long ~ record** über langjährige Erfahrungen verfügen; ~ **storage** Gleislagergebühr; ~ **suit** Trainingsanzug; ~ **wear** Gleisabnutzung.
trackage Streckenbenutzungsgebühr.
tracked vehicle Ketten-, Raupenfahrzeug.

tracker *(criminal)* Häscher, Verfolger;
~ **dog** Spürhund.
trackhound Spürhund.
tracking Schienenverlegung;
~**-down of criminals** Aufspüren von Verbrechern;
~ **shot** vom fahrenden Kamerawagen gedrehte Szene; ~ **station** *(space vehicle)* Kontaktstation; ~ **system** Fahrspursystem.
tracklayer Schienenleger, Gleisarbeiter, *(tractor)* Raupenschlepper, -fahrzeug.
tracklaying Gleisbau.
trackless trolley Obus.
trackman *(US)* Bahnmeister.
trackwalker *(US)* Streckenwärter.
trackway Fahrbahn, -weg.
tract Grundstücksparzelle, *(region)* Strecke, Landstrich, Gebiet, Gegend, *(treatise)* Broschüre, Traktat, Abhandlung;
pathless ~ unwegsames Gelände; **wooded ~** bewaldetes Gebiet; ~ **of land** Landstrich, Grundstücksparzelle; ~ **of time** Zeitdauer;
~ **number** Katasternummer.
traction Transport, Beförderung, *(treatise)* Traktat, Broschüre; ~ **engine** Zugmaschine, Trecker; ~ **securities** Wertpapiere elektrisch betriebener Bahnen, elektrische Bahnwerte.
tractor Traktor, Trecker, Zugmaschine;
~**-drawn** motorisiert; ~ **plough (plow,** *US)* Motorpflug; ~ **works** Traktorfabrik.
trade Handel, Handelsverkehr, *(business)* [Gewerbe]betrieb, Geschäft, *(business situation)* Geschäftslage, *(business world)* Fach-, Geschäftswelt, Kaufmannschaft, Handelsstand, Berufsschicht, *(customer)* Kundschaft, Kunden, *(exchange)* Austausch, *(futures, US)* [Getreide]termingeschäft, *(guild)* Gilde, Genossenschaft, Zunft, *(handicraft)* Handwerk, handwerklicher Beruf, *(line)* Branche, Fach, Geschäftszweig, *(occupation)* Gewerbe, gewerbliche Tätigkeit, Erwerbszweig, [erlernter] Beruf, Berufsstand, Metier, *(pol., US)* Ämterkauf, Schiebung, *(purchase and sale, US)* Kauf und Verkauf, Geschäft, *(retail trade)* Einzelhandel, *(ship)* Verkehr, Fahrt;
by ~ von Beruf, gelernt; **by way of ~** im Handel; **good for ~** handelsgünstig; **in pursuance of a ~** in Ausübung eines Gewerbes; **in the same ~** im gleichen Metier; **supplied to ~ only** Lieferungen nur an Wiederverkäufer; **without a ~** ohne Beruf; **the ~** *(Br.)* Kaufmannschaft, -stand, *(traffic in liquors, Br.)* Spirituosenhandel, *(sl.)* Dienst auf einem U-Boot;
active ~ Aktivhandel, Export; **aggregate ~** Gesamthandel; **all the ~s** alle Handwerksinnungen; **apprenticeable ~** erlernbares Handwerk; **balanced ~** ausgeglichener Handelsverkehr; **barter ~** Tauschhandel; **basic ~** Schlüsselindustrie; **book ~** Buchhandel, -gewerbe; **brisk ~** flotter Geschäftsgang, Geschäftsaufschwung; **building ~** Bauwirtschaft, -gewerbe; **bullion ~** Handel in Edelmetallen; **business ~** Handelsverkehr; **carrying ~** Transportgewerbe, -geschäft, Frachtgeschäft; **catering ~** Gaststättengewerbe; **chain ~** Kettenhandel; **clandestine ~** Schleich-, Schwarzhandel; **coasting ~** Küstenfahrt; **commodity ~** Rohstoffhandel; **continental ~** *(Br.)* Handel mit dem Festland; **contraband ~** Schmuggel, Schleichhandel; **distributing (distributive) ~** Verteilergewerbe, Absatzwirtschaft; **domestic ~** Binnenhandel[sverkehr], inländischer Handel; **east-west[ern] ~** Ost-West-Handel; **export ~** Export, Außen-, Aktivhandel; **extensive ~** ausgedehnter Handel; **external ~** Außenhandel; **fair ~** *(US)* Lauterkeit (Freihandel auf der Grundlage) des Wettbewerbs, Nichtdiskriminierung im Außenhandel; **fashionable ~** modeabhängiges Gewerbe; **feminine ~** Frauenberuf; **fictitious ~** Scheinverkauf, -geschäft; **flourishing ~** gutgehendes Geschäft, blühendes Geschäft; **foreign ~** Außen-, Überseehandel, Aussenwirtschaft, *(mar.)* große Fahrt; **free ~** Handelsfreiheit, zollfreier Verkehr, Freihandel; **goods ~** Warenverkehr; **handicraft ~** handwerklicher Beruf; **home ~** Binnenhandel, -wirtschaft, *(mar.)* kleine Fahrt; **honest ~** ehrbares Gewerbe; **illicit ~** Schleich-, Schwarzhandel; **immoral ~** sittenwidriges Gewerbe; **import ~** Import, Einfuhr, Passivhandel; **incorporated ~** zünftiges Gewerbe; **inland ~** Binnenhandel, -verkehr; **intercoastal ~** *(US)* Küstenverkehr; **intermediary (intermediate) ~** Zwischenhandel; **internal ~** Binnenhandel; **international ~** Welthandel, -markt; **interstate ~** zwischenstaatlicher Handel; **interzonal ~** Interzonenhandel; **intrastate ~** *(US)* binnenstaatlicher Handel; **invisible ~** Dienstleistungsverkehr; **inward ~** Einfuhr[handel]; **itinerant ~** ambulantes Gewerbe, Hausiergewerbe, Gewerbe im Umherziehen, Wandergewerbe; **jobber ~** Maklerberuf; **languishing ~** darniederliegender Handel; **lawful ~** konzessioniertes Gewerbe; **not lawful ~** verbotenes Gewerbe; **licensed ~** konzessioniertes

Gewerbe; **little ~** *(stock exchange)* geringe Umsätze; **local ~** Platzgeschäft; **lucrative ~** einträgliches Geschäft; **manufacturing ~** gewerbliche Wirtschaft, Industrie; **maritime ~** Seehandel; **metal ~** Metallbranche; **nearby ~** Nahverkehr; **nonestablished retail ~** Wandergewerbe, ambulanter Handel; **ocean ~** *(US)* Überseehandel; **ocean-carrying ~** Hochseeschiffahrt; **offensive ~** gesundheitsschädliches Gewerbe; **over-the-counter ~** *(US)* Schalterverkehr, außerbörslicher Effektenhandel; **overseas ~** überseeischer Handel, Überseehandel; **particular ~** bestimmte Branche; **passive ~** Passiv-, Einfuhrhandel; **petty ~** Ramschhandel, Kurzwarengeschäft; **precarious ~** geduldeter Handel neutraler Staaten; **printing ~** graphisches Gewerbe; **rattling ~** flottes Geschäft; **roaring ~** schwunghafter Handel; **retail ~** Klein-, Einzelhandel; **seaborne ~** Seehandel; **seasonal ~** Saisongeschäft; **~ shown** Einspielergebnis; **skilled ~** erlernter Beruf, Handwerksberuf, Fach-, Spezialberuf; **small ~** Handwerk; **small-scale ~** Kleingewerbe; **sole ~** Einzelgeschäft; **specialized ~** Fachhandel; **stagnant ~** Geschäftsstockung, Flaute; **stepped-up ~** erhöhter Handelsverkehr; **supplier's ~** Zulieferungsbetrieb; **tally ~** *(Br.)* Abzahlungsgeschäft; **telephone ~** *(stock exchange)* Telefonhandel, -verkehr; **total ~** Gesamtwirtschaft; **underhand ~** Schleich-, Schwarzhandel; **unfair ~** unerlaubter Wettbewerb; **useful ~** nützliches Gewerbe; **visible ~** Warenverkehr; **wheat ~** *(mar.)* Weizenfahrt; **wholesale ~** Groß-, Engroshandel; **world ~** Weltwirtschaft;

~ and commerce Handel und Verkehr; **~ and industry** Handel und Wirtschaft;

~ for own account Eigengeschäft, -handel; **~ for third account** Kommissionshandel; **~ in arms** Waffenhandel; **~ in book rights** [Buch]lizenzgeschäft; **~ or business carried on for purpose of profit** *(double taxation agreement)* auf Gewinnerzielung gerichtete gewerbliche Tätigkeit; **~ on cash terms** Bargeldverkehr; **~ in goods** Warenverkehr; **free ~ of goods** freier Warenaustausch; **~ and industry** Handel und Wirtschaft, gewerbliche Wirtschaft; **~ subject to licence** gewerbepolizeipflichtiger Betrieb, genehmigungspflichtiges Gewerbe; **particular ~ of port** Hafenusancen; **~ in [inland] produce (products)** Produkten-, Warenhandel; **~ and services** Waren- und Dienstleistungsverkehr; **~ of storing** Lagerwirtschaft, -gewerbe; **with transit goods** Durchgangs-, Transithandel; **~ and transport** Handel und Verkehr; **~ of war** Kriegshandwerk;

~ (v.) handeln, Handel treiben, verkaufen, *(barter)* [ein]tauschen, Tauschhandel treiben;

~ for own account für eigene Rechnung abschließen; **~ away** verschleudern, -schachern; **~ between London and New York** *(ship)* zwischen London und New York verkehren; **~ at a satisfactory level of turnover** befriedigende Umsätze erzielen.
trade *(v.)* in eintauschen, in Zahlung geben;
~ bills Wechselreiterei treiben; **~ one's 1980 Ford car for a new model** seinen 1980er Ford für das neueste Modell in Zahlung geben; **~ futures** Termingeschäfte abschließen; **~ goods** Warengeschäfte machen; **~ one's political influence** von seinen politischen Beziehungen Gebrauch machen; **~ real estate** Grundstücksmakler sein, Immobiliengeschäfte machen (tätigen), Immobiliengeschäft haben.
trade *(v.)* **off** verschachern, verhandeln, abwägen.
trade *(v.)* **on** spekulieren, reisen auf;
~ the credulity of a client Gutgläubigkeit eines Kunden ausnutzen; **~ the equity** Geschäfte mit geliehenem Kapital betreiben, mit Fremdkapital finanzieren; **~ freight** auf Fracht fahren; **~ one's political influence** von seinen politischen Beziehungen Gebrauch machen.
trade *(v.)* **under the name (style) of ...** unter der Firma ... Handel treiben; **~ under one's own name** Firma unter seinem eigenen Namen betreiben; **~ [up]on s. one's ignorance** jds. Unkenntnis ausnutzen; **~ upon one's past reputation** von seinem guten Namen leben.
trade *(v.)* **with** **s. o.** mit jem. in Geschäftsbeziehungen (Geschäftsverbindung) stehen; **~ borrowed money** mit fremdem Kapital (Fremdkapital) arbeiten; **~ seats with s. o.** mit jem. den Platz wechseln (tauschen).
trade, to be a baker by von Beruf Bäcker sein; **to be in the ~** *(Br.)* Geschäftsmann (Kaufmann) sein, wirtschaftlich (kaufmännisch) tätig sein, Gewerbe betreiben, Geschäft haben, Einzelhändler sein; **to be in the coffee ~** in der Kaffeebranche sein; **to build up ~** Handelsbeziehungen verstärken; **to carry on a ~** Gewerbe betreiben; **to carry on a ~ or business** Gewerbetätigkeit ausüben, gewerblich tätig sein, Geschäft (Gewerbe, Handwerk, Handel) [be]treiben; **to carry on the ~ of s. th.** mit etw. handeln; **to carry 40% per cent of one's ~ in one's own ships** 40% des Handels in eigenen Schiffen befördern; **to carry on a ~**

on a commercial basis Gewerbe nach kaufmännischen Gesichtspunkten betreiben; **to carry on a ~ of plant hire** Gebäude gewerblich vermieten; **to carry on a roaring ~** glänzende Geschäfte machen; **to contemplate ~** Handelsbeziehungen erwägen; **to differ from ~ to ~** je nach Branche verschieden sein; **to divert ~ from a country** Handel ableiten; **to do above the average ~** überdurchschnittliche Umsätze machen; **to do a brisk ~** flott verkaufen; **to do a great (good) ~** gute Geschäfte machen; **to do a lot of ~** bedeutenden Handel treiben; **to drive a good ~** gutgehendes Geschäft haben; **to drive a roaring ~** glänzende Geschäfte (Bombengeschäfte) machen; **to engage in a ~** sich gewerblich betätigen; **to engage in foreign ~** Exportgeschäfte machen; **to exercise a ~** Gewerbetreibender sein, Gewerbe ausüben; **to exercise a useful ~** wirtschaftlich notwendigen Beruf ausüben; **to follow a ~** Gewerbe (Handwerk) ausüben (betreiben); **to foster ~** Wirtschaft ankurbeln; **to give up ~** Geschäft aufgeben; **to go into ~** Beruf ergreifen; **to have learnt a ~** in einem Beruf (beruflich) ausgebildet sein; **to intercept ~** Handelsverkehr unterbrechen, Handel behindern; **to interdict ~ with foreign nations** Handelsverkehr mit dem Ausland untersagen; **to know one's ~** in seinem Fach gut Bescheid wissen; **to learn a ~** Handwerk (Gewerbe) erlernen; **to leave off ~** Geschäft aufgeben; **to open a ~** Geschäft eröffnen, Beruf ausüben, Gewerbe beginnen; **to place restrictions on foreign ~** Exportgeschäfte Handelsbeschränkungen unterwerfen; **to ply a ~** Gewerbe ausüben (betreiben); **to ply one's ~** sein Geschäft besorgen; **to prosecute a ~** einem Gewerbe nachgehen; **to pursue a ~** Gewerbe (Handwerk) ausüben (betreiben); **to put s. o. to a ~** j. in die Lehre geben, j. ein Handwerk (Beruf) lernen (ausbilden) lassen; **to reanimate (revive) ~** Handel wiederbeleben; **to register a ~** Gewerbe anmelden; **to restrain ~** Wettbewerb einschränken; **to sell to the ~** an Wiederverkäufer (Einzelhändler) abgeben; **to set up s. o. in ~** j. geschäftlich etablieren, jem. ein Geschäft einrichten; **to spoil s. one's ~** jem. ins Handwerk pfuschen, jem. das Geschäft verderben; **to talk a fast ~** zu einem raschen Abschluß kommen; **to teach several different ~s** in verschiedenen Fächern unterrichten;
~ (a.) geschäftlich, gewerblich;
~ abuse Handelsmißbrauch; **~ acceptance** Handels-, Kundenakzept, kaufmännische Anweisung, Handels-, Warenwechsel; **~ acceptances receivable** *(balance sheet, US)* ausstehende Handelsakzepte; **~ accord** Wirtschaftsabkommen; **~ accounts** Kundenkonten; **~ accounts payable** *(balance sheet, US)* Verbindlichkeiten aufgrund von Warenlieferungen, Warenschulden; **~ accounts receivable** *(balance sheet, US)* Forderungen aus Warenlieferungen und Leistungen, Warenforderungen; **~ activities** Gewerbetätigkeit; **~ advantage** wirtschaftlicher Vorteil; **~ advertisement** Geschäftsanzeige; **~ advertising** Geschäftsreklame, Händlerwerbung; **~ agency** Handelsagentur; **overseas ~ agency** Außenhandelsstelle; **~ agent** Handelsvertreter.
trade agreement Handelsvertrag, -abkommen, *(trade union, US)* Tarifabkommen, -vertrag;
bilateral ~ zweiseitiges Handelsabkommen; **reciprocal ~** Gegenseitigkeitsabkommen, gegenseitiger Handelsvertrag;
to enter into bilateral ~s zweiseitiges Handelsabkommen abschließen.
trade | allowance Warenskonto, Großhandelsrabatt, Rabatt für Wiederverkäufer; **~ arbitration** gewerbliches Schiedsgerichtswesen; **~ arbitration agreement** Schiedsgerichtabkommen für die gewerbliche Wirtschaft; **~ arbitrator** Wirtschaftsschlichter; **~ area** Handelsgebiet, -zone, Wirtschaftsraum; **free ~ area** Freihandelszone; **~ association** Berufsgenossenschaft, Gewerbeverband, Wirtschaftsverband, -vereinigung, *(employers)* Arbeitgeber-, Unternehmerverband; **~ association directory** Fachverbandsverzeichnis; **~ backsliding** wirtschaftlicher Rückgang.
trade balance Handelsbilanz;
adverse ~ passive Handelsbilanz; **merchandise ~** Warenhandelsbilanz; **negative ~** negative Handelsbilanz; **positive ~** positive Handelsbilanz;
to deteriorate the ~ Handelsbilanz verschlechtern; **to improve the ~** Handelsbilanz verbessern; **to run (show) a favo(u)rable ~** aktive Handelsbilanz aufweisen;
~ deficit Handelsbilanzdefizit, Passivsaldo der Handelsbilanz; **~ surplus** Handelsbilanzüberschuß, Aktivsaldo der Handelsbilanz.
trade | bank Handels- und Gewerbebank; **~ barometer** Wirtschaftsbarometer; **~ barriers** protektionistische Handelsschranken; **to reduce ~ barriers** Handelsschranken abbauen; **~ behavio(u)r** wirtschaftliches Verhalten, Berufseinstellung;

~ **benefits** handelspolitische Vorteile; ~ **bill** Kunden-, Waren-, Handelswechsel; **prime** ~ **bill** erstklassiger Wechsel; ~ **bloc** Wirtschaftsblock; ~ **board** *(Br.)* paritätisch zusammengesetzter Arbeitgeber-Arbeitnehmer-Ausschuß; ⋅≗ **Board Act** *(Br.)* Mindestlohngesetz; ~ **book** im Handel erhältliches Buch; ~ **branch** Wirtschafts-, Gewerbezweig, Branche; ~ **bureau** Wirtschafts-, Handelsbüro; ~ **capitalism** *(US)* Wirtschaftskapitalismus; ~ **card** [geschäftliches] Empfehlungsschreiben; ~ **catalog(ue)** Preisliste, -verzeichnis; ~ **center** *(US)* (**centre,** *Br.)* Wirtschaftszentrum; ~ **channels** Absatzwege, Vertriebskanäle; **to open up new** ~ **channels** neue Handelsbeziehungen anbahnen; ~ **character** *(trade name)* figürlicher Teil; ~ **charge** *(Br.)* Nachnahmebetrag; ~-**charge letter** *(Br.)* Nachnahmebrief; ~-**charge money order** *(Br.)* Nachnahmepostanweisung; ~ **clash** handelspolitische Auseinandersetzung; ~ **club** *(Br.)* Kaufmannsvereinigung; ~ **coin** Handelsmünze; ~ **colony** Handelskolonie; ~ **commission** Handelsausschuß; **Federal** ≗ **Commission** *(US)* Ausschuß zur Bekämpfung unlauteren Wettbewerbs; ≗ **Commissioner** *(Br.)* Wirtschaftsbeauftragter in den Dominions, *(US)* Mitarbeiter des Handelsattaches; ≗ **Commissioner Service** *(Br.)* Handelsdienstorganisation; ~ **committee** Gewerbeausschuß; ~ **competition** Wirtschaftskampf; ~ **composition** *(type setting)* Lohnsatz; ~ **concerns** Belange der Wirtschaft, wirtschaftliche Belange; ~ **conditions** Wirtschaftsverhältnisse, Geschäftsbedingungen; ~ **conference** Wirtschaftsbesprechungen, -verhandlungen, Handelskonferenz; ~ **connections** Handelsbeziehungen, Wirtschaftsverbindungen; ~ **consultant** Wirtschaftsberater; ~ **contract** Wirtschafts-, Handelsvertrag; **foreign** ~ **contract** Außenhandelsvertrag; ~ **control** Gewerbeaufsicht; ~ **convention** Wirtschaftsabkommen; **British** ≗ **Corporation** *(Br.)* Bank für Aussenhandel; ~**s council** Ausschuß der gewerblichen Wirtschaft, *(trade unionism, Br.)* örtlicher Spitzenverband der Gewerkschaft; ~ **credit** Lieferantenkredit; ~ **creditor** Lieferant, Warengläubiger, *(account current)* Gläubiger aus Kontokorrentgeschäften; ~ **crisis** Wirtschaftskrise; ~ **currents** Handels-, Warenströme; ~ **cycle** *(Br.)* Konjunkturzyklus, Kreislauf der Wirtschaft, Konjunkturperiode; ~ **cycle period** Konjunkturphase; ~ **data** Handelsziffern, wirtschaftliche Angaben; ~ **dealer in land** Immobilienmakler; ~ **debts** Lieferantenschulden; ~ **debts recovered** beigetriebene Lieferantenschulden; ~ **debtor** Kontokorrentschuldner; ~ **debtors** *(balance sheet)* Forderungen aus Warenlieferungen, Warenforderungen; ~ **deficit** Passivsaldo im Außenhandel, Handelsdefizit; ~ **delegation** Wirtschaftsabordnung, -delegation, Handelsdelegation; ~ **demand** Handelsbedürfnisse; ~ **department** Auslieferungslager; ~ **depression** Konjunktur-, Wirtschaftskrise, Tiefkonjunktur, Depression; ~ **description** Warenbezeichnung, -beschreibung; ≗ **Description Act** *(Br.)* Warenkennzeichnungsgesetz; ~ **directory** Handels-, Branchenadreßbuch, Firmenverzeichnis, -beschreibung; ~ **discount** Rabatt [an Wiederverkäufer], Wiederverkäuferrabatt, Händlerrabatt, -marge, Warenskonto, *(bookselling)* Kollegenrabatt; **to take one's** ~ **discount** seine Diskontmöglichkeiten ausschöpfen; ~ **discussions** Wirtschaftsverhandlungen; ~ **disease** Berufskrankheit; ~ **disparagement** Anschwärzung der Konkurrenz; ~ **disputes** Auseinandersetzungen mit der Gewerkschaft, Arbeitsstreitigkeiten, Arbeitskämpfe; **to settle** ~ **disputes by arbitration** arbeitsrechtliche Auseinandersetzungen schiedsgerichtlich beilegen; ≗ **Disputes Act** *(Br.)* Gesetz über arbeitsrechtliche Auseinandersetzungen, Gesetz zur Regelung von Arbeitskämpfen; ~ **diversion** Ablenkung des Handels; ~ **dodges** Handelskniffe; ~ **dollar** Silberdollar; ~ **effluent** Abwässer aus Gewerbebetrieben, Industrie-, Betriebsabwässer; ~ **empire** Wirtschaftsimperium; ~ **enquiry** Handelsauskunft; ~ **exchange** Handelsaustausch; ~ **exhibition** Fach-, Gewerbeausstellung, ≗ **Expansion Act** *(US)* Gesetz zur Ausweitung des Handels; ~ **expenses** Handlungsunkosten, Betriebsausgaben; **to charge as** ~ **expenses for tax purposes** steuerlich als Handlungskosten (Betriebsunkosten) behandeln; ~ **facilities** Handelserleichterungen; ~ **factory** Handelsniederlassung; ~ **fair** *(Br.)* [Handels]messe, Fachmesse, Gewerbeausstellung; ~-**fair rebate** Messerabatt; ~ **financing** Geschäftsfinanzierung; ~ **fixtures** fest eingebaute Maschinenanlagen, gewerbliche Einbauten; ~ **flows** Handelsverkehr; ~ **folder** Prospekt für den Handel, Wirtschaftsprospekt; ~ **foothold** wirtschaftliche Festsetzung; **biassed** ~ **freak** handelspolitischer Querkopf; ~ **gain** Außenhandelsüberschuß; ~ **gap** Handelsbilanzdefizit, Außenhandelslücke, -defizit; **to slim its enormous** ~ **gap** sein gewaltiges Handelsdefizit ausgleichen; ~ **goods** Wirtschaftsgüter; ~ **group** Wirtschaftsgruppe, -zweig, Fachgruppe; ~ **group interchange** *(US)* Kundenkreditauskunf-

tei; ~ **guild** Handwerkszunft, Innung, Vereinshaus; ~ **hall** Innungs-, Vereinshaus; ~ **hazard** Handelsrisiko, wirtschaftliches Risiko; ~ **history** Wirtschaftsgeschichte; ~-**in** *(coll.)* in Zahlung gegebene Ware (gegebener Gegenstand); ~-**in allowance** Rabattgewährung bei Inzahlungnahme; ~-**in car** in Zahlung gegebenes Auto, Eintauschwagen; ~-**in value** Eintausch-, Verkehrs-, Verrechnungs, -wert; ~ **information** Informationsdienst; ~ **inspection** Gewerbeaufsicht; ~ **inspector** Gewerbeaufsichtsbeamter; ~ **investments** *(balance sheet, Br.)* Vermögensanlagen im Interesse des Geschäftsbetriebes, geschäftliche Investitionen; ~-**journal** Handelsblatt, Fach-, Wirtschaftszeitschrift; ~-**journal writer** Wirtschaftsjournalist; ~ **kit** Berufskleidung; ~ **knowledge** Wirtschaftskenntnisse, Gewerbekunde; ~ **label** [Waren]etikett; ~ **lead** wirtschaftliche Entwicklung, Wirtschaftsentwicklung; ~ **legislation** Handels-, Wirtschaftsgesetzgebung; ~ **liability** laufende Verpflichtung; ~ **libel** *(US)* Anschwärzung der Konkurrenz; ~ **licence** [Gewerbe]lizenz, -erlaubnis, -schein, -berechtigung, [Betriebs]konzession, Handelsberechtigung; ~ **list** Preisliste [für Großhändler]; ~ **literature** Fachliteratur; ~ **loan** *(US)* Warenkredit; ~ **loss** gewöhnlicher Gewichtsabgang und Schwund; ~ **machinery** fest eingebaute Maschinenanlagen; ~ **magazine** Wirtschafts-, Fach-, Handelszeitschrift; ~ **margin** Handelsspanne; ~-**mark name** Schutz-, Markenname, Schutzmarke; ~ **matters** wirtschaftliche Angelegenheiten, Handelssachen, -fragen; ~ **measures** handelspolitische Maßnahmen; ~ **member** Mitglied eines Berufsverbandes, Verbandsmitglied; ~ **mission** Handelsdelegation, -mission; ~ **monopoly** Handelsmonopol; ~ **name** Firma, Firmenname, Firmen-, Handelsbezeichnung, handelsübliche Bezeichnung, *(trademark)* Warenzeichen; ~-**name** *(v.)* mit einem Firmenzeichen versehen; ~ **negotiations** Wirtschaftsverhandlungen; ~ **negotiator** Wirtschaftsunterhändler; ~ **notes receivable** *(US)* Kundenwechsel; ~ **obligations** geschäftliche Verbindlichkeiten, Geschäftsverpflichtungen; ~-**off** Koordinierungsmaßnahme, Abwägung; ~-**offs** Handelsobjekte; ~-**off of energy** Energieaustausch; ~ **offensive** Handelsoffensive; ~ **offering** Handelsangebot, geschäftliches Angebot; ~ **opportunity** Geschäftsmöglichkeit; ~ **organization** Wirtschaftsverband, Handelsorganisation; **International** ≗ **Organization** Internationale Handelsvereinigung; ~ **package** Bündel handelspolitischer Vorschläge; ~ **pact** Handelsabkommen, -vertrag; **to denounce a** ~ **pact with three months notice** Handelsvertrag mit dreimonatiger Frist kündigen; ~ **paper** *(advertising)* Händlerzeitschrift, *(bill of exchange)* Kunden-, Waren-, Handelswechsel, *(newspaper)* Fachzeitschrift, -zeitung, Verbandsorgan, Wirtschaftszeitung; **fine** ~ **paper** erstklassiger Handelswechsel; **good** ~ **paper** diskontfähiger kurzfristiger Warenwechsel; ~-**paper advertising** Fachzeitschriftenwerbung, Werbung in Fachzeitschriften; ~ **partner** Handels[vertrags]partner.

trade policy Handelspolitik;
free-~ Merkantilsystem, Freihandelspolitik; **government** ~ staatliche Handelspolitik;
~ **effects** handelspolitische Auswirkungen; ~ **initiative** handelspolitische Initiative; ~ **instructions** handelspolitische Instruktionen; ~ **moat** handelspolitischer Graben; ~ **shift** handelspolitische Kursänderung; ~ **solution** handelspolitische Lösung.

trade|position wirtschaftliche Stellung; ~ **practices** Handelsbrauch, -praktiken, -usance; **restrictive** ~ **practices** *(Br.)* wettbewerbsbeschränkende Geschäftspraktiken, *(cartel law)* Kartellmaßnahmen; **unfair** ~ **practices** unlauteres Geschäftsgebaren; **Unfair** ≗ **Practice Acts** *(US)* Gesetzgebung gegen den unlauteren Wettbewerb; ~ **practices submittal** *(US)* Mitwirkung bei einer Vereinbarung über Abstellung von Handelsmißbräuchen; ~ **premises** gewerblich genutzte Räume, Gewerberäume; ~ **premium** Warenrabattprämie, *(export business)* Ausfuhrprämie; ~ **press** Fachpresse; ~ **price** *(coll.)* Großhandels-, Engros-, Wiederverkäuferpreis, Preis ab Werk; ~ **privileges** Handelsprivilegien; ~ **process** Geschäfts-, Betriebsverfahren; ~ **proficiency** handwerkliche Tüchtigkeit, Berufseignung; ~ **program(me)** Wirtschafts-, Handelsprogramm; ~ **promotion** Wirtschafts-, Handelsförderung; ~ **promotional facilities** Handelserleichterungen; ~ **prospects** Handelsaussichten; ~ **protection society** *(Br.)* Kreditschutzverein; ~ **publication** Geschäftsankündigung, geschäftliche Bekanntmachung, *(newspaper)* Fach-, Wirtschaftszeitschrift; ~ **publicity** Wirtschaftspropaganda, Geschäftsreklame; ~ **purchase** Handelskauf; ~ **reasons** wirtschaftliche Überlegungen; ~ **receivables** *(US)* Forderungen aufgrund von Warenlieferungen; ~ **recession** Wirtschaftsflaute, Geschäftsrückgang; ~ **ref-**

erence Geschäftsempfehlung, Kreditauskunft; ~ **refuse** Gewerbe-, Industriemüll; ~ **regulations** *(US)* Wettbewerbsregeln; ~ **relations** Handels-, Wirtschaftsbeziehungen; **three-cornered** **relations** dreiseitige Handelsbeziehungen; ~ **relations with the Far East** fernöstliche Handelsbeziehungen; ~ **report** Handelsbericht; ~ **representative** Handelsvertreter; ~ **research** Marktuntersuchung; ~ **restrictions** Beschränkungen des Handels, Handelsbeschränkungen; ~ **returns** Handelsstatistik; ~ **revival** Wiederbelebung der Wirtschaft, Konjunkturaufschwung; ~ **rights** Firmenrechte; ~ **risk** Geschäftsrisiko; ~ **rivalry** wirtschaftliche (geschäftliche) Konkurrenz; ~ **road (route)** Handelsstraße, -weg; ~ **rule** Handwerksbrauch; **fair ~ rules** *(US)* Wettbewerbsregeln, -bestimmungen; ~ **sale** Bücherauktion; ~ **school** Berufsfach-, Gewerbeschule; ~ **secret** Betriebs-, Gewerbe-, Geschäftsgeheimnis; **to divulge ~ secrets** Betriebsgeheimnisse verraten; ~ **section** Geschäftszweig, Wirtschaftsabteilung, -gruppe, Branche, Gewerbezweig; ~ **service** Handels- und Wirtschaftsabteilung im Auswärtigen Amt; ~ **service diplomat** Handelsattaché; ~ **settlement** Handelsniederlassung; ~ **sharing** Geschäftsbeteiligung; ~ **show** *(distributors)* geschlossene Filmvorstellung; ~ **sign** Gewerbezeichen, Firmenschild; ~ **split** handelspolitische Spaltung; ~ **stamp** *(US)* Rabattmarke; ~ **standards** Wirtschaftsnormen; ~ **standing** handwerkliches Können; ~ **statistics** Handelsstatistik; ~ **stipulation** Handelsklausel; ~ **subscriptions** Beiträge zu Berufsverbänden; ~ **supplies** kaufmännische Bedarfsartikel; ~ **surplus** Außenhandels-, Handelsbilanzüberschuß, Aktivsaldo im Außenhandel; ~ **talks** Handelsbesprechungen, -gespräche; ~ **tax** Gewerbeertragssteuer; ~ **tension** gespannte Handelsbeziehungen; ~ **term** Wirtschaftsausdruck; ~ **terms** Lieferklauseln, handelsübliche Vertragsformen, *(retailing)* Wiederverkaufspreisbestimmungen; ~ **test** berufliche Eignungsprüfung; ~ **training** Fach-, Berufsausbildung; ~ **transaction** geschäftliche Transaktion.

trade union *(Br.)* Gewerkschaft, Arbeitnehmerverband, Berufsgenossenschaft;
building ~ Baugewerkschaft; **free ~** freie Gewerkschaft; **registered ~** *(Br.)* staatlich anerkannte Gewerkschaft;
to form a ~ sich gewerkschaftlich zusammenschließen.

trade union│acts *(Br.)* Gewerkschaftsgesetze; ~ **affiliation** Gewerkschaftszugehörigkeit; ~ **agreement** Vereinbarung mit den Gewerkschaften; **~s' agreement** gewerkschaftliches Einverständnis; ~ **approval** gewerkschaftliche Zustimmung; ~ **block vote** gewerkschaftlicher Abstimmungsblock; ~ **committee** Gewerkschaftsausschuß; **~s Congress** *(TUC, Br.)* Dachorganisation (Dachverband) der britischen Gewerkschaften, Gewerkschaftsbund; ~ **delegate** Gewerkschaftsvertreter; ~ **formation** Gewerkschaftsgründung; ~ **history** Gewerkschaftsgeschichte; ~ **leader** Gewerkschaftsführer; ~ **member** Gewerkschaftsmitglied; ~ **movement** Gewerkschaftsbewegung; ~ **official** Gewerkschaftsfunktionär; ~ **paper** Gewerkschaftszeitung; ~ **policy** Gewerkschaftspolitik; ~ **press** Gewerkschaftspresse; ~ **representative** Gewerkschaftsvertreter; ~ **rules** Richtlinien der Gewerkschaft; ~ **structure** Gewerkschaftsgefüge; ~ **subscription** Gewerkschaftsbeitrag; **to be outside of the ~ system** nicht an Tarifabsprachen gebunden sein; ~ **training centre** gewerkschaftliches Ausbildungszentrum.

trade│unionism Gewerkschaftswesen, -vereinigung, -bewegung; ~ **unionist** Gewerkschaftsangehöriger, Gewerkschaftler; **~ unionist** gewerkschaftlich; ~ **usage** Geschäfts-, Handelsbrauch, Usance; ~ **value** Verkehrs-, Markt-, Handelswert; ~ **volume** Handelsvolumen; ~ **walls** Zollmauern; ~ **war** Handels-, Wirtschaftskrieg; ~ **warranty** *(marine insurance)* Klausel gegen mißbräuchliche Schiffsbenutzung; **~weapon** wirtschaftliche Waffe; ~ **wind** Passat[wind]; ~ **windfall** unerwarteter Handelsgewinn.

traded-in car in Zahlung genommener Wagen.
trademark Waren-, Handels-, Hersteller-, Schutz-, Fabrikzeichen, Fabrik-, Schutz-, Firmen-, Hersteller-, Handelsmarke;
arbitrary ~ willkürlich gewähltes Markenzeichen; **associated ~s** *(Br.)* verbundene Warenzeichen; **certification ~** *(Br.)* Güte-, Verbandszeichen; **collective ~** Kollektivzeichen; **common-law ~** *(US)* nicht eingetragenes Warenzeichen; **defensive ~** *(Br.)* Defensivmarke; **distinctive ~** unterscheidungsfähiges Warenzeichen; **previously existing ~** bereits bestehendes Warenzeichen; **foreign ~** ausländisches Warenzeichen; **pictorial ~** Bildzeichen; **registered ~** eingetragenes (geschütztes) Warenzeichen; **slogan ~** Wortzeichen;
~ with a good name gutes (anerkanntes) Warenzeichen; **~ owned by a subsidiary** im Eigentum einer Tochtergesellschaft stehendes Warenzeichen;

~ *(v.)* gesetzlich schützen lassen, mit einem Warenzeichen versehen, Warenzeichen anbringen, als Warenzeichen eintragen;
to appropriate unlawfully s. one's ~ jds. Warenzeichenrecht verletzen; **to assign a ~** Warenzeichenrecht überschreiben lassen; **to expunge the registration of a ~** Eintragung eines Warenzeichens löschen; **to have a ~ registered at the Board of Trade** Warenzeichen eintragen lassen; **to infringe a ~** Warenzeichen verletzen; **to own a ~** Warenzeichen besitzen; **to pirate a ~** Warenzeichen nachahmen; **to register a ~** Warenzeichen (Handelszeichen) eintragen lassen (anmelden); **to use a ~** Warenzeichen benutzen;
⌾ **[Registration] Act** *(US)* Warenzeichen-, Markenschutzgesetz; ~ **article** Markenartikel; ~ **commodity** Markenware; ~ **infringement** Warenzeichenverletzung, Markenfälschung; ~ **journal** *(Br.)* Warenzeichenblatt; ~ **law** Warenzeichenrecht; ~ **legislation** Schutzmarkengesetzgebung; ~ **licence** Warenzeichenlizenz; ~ **licensing** Lizensierung von Warenzeichen; ~ **name** Schutzmarke; **~s officer** Leiter der Warenprüfungsabteilung; ~ **owner** Warenzeichen-, Schutzmarkeninhaber; ~ **procedure** Verfahren in Warenzeichen; ~ **protection** Warenzeichen-, Musterschutz; **~s register** Warenzeichenrolle; **to remove from the ~ register** in der Warenzeichenrolle löschen; ~ **registration** Warenzeicheneintragung, Eintragung in die Warenzeichenrolle; **to cancel a ~ registration** Warenzeichen im Register löschen lassen; ~ **rights** Warenzeichen-, Schutzmarkenrechte; ~ **section** Warenzeichenabteilung.
trademarked unter Warenzeichenschutz;
~ **commodities (goods)** Markenartikel, -erzeugnisse.
trademaster Gewerbeschullehrer.
trader Händler, Gewerbetreibender, Handeltreibender, Handelsmann, Kaufmann, -herr, Geschäftsmann, *(ship)* Handels-, Kauffahrteischiff, *(stock exchange, US)* freier (selbständiger) Makler, Eigen-, Effekten-, Wertpapierhändler;
~s Wirtschaftskreise, der Handel, Handelsstand;
big-block ~ Pakethändler; **clandestine ~** Schleich-, Schwarzhändler; **coasting ~** Küstenfahrer; **constant ~** auf einer bestimmten Route verkehrendes Schiff; **door-to-door ~** fliegender Händler; **floor ~** *(US)* auf eigene Rechnung spekulierender Makler, zugelassener Börsenhändler; **free ~** *(law)* Kauffrau, selbständige Geschäftsfrau; **illicit ~** Schleich-, Schwarzhändler; **international ~** Außenhandelsfirma; **petty ~** kleiner Geschäftsmann, Kleingewerbetreibender; **pit ~** *(US)* selbständiger Produktenmakler, Terminhändler an der Produktenbörse; **professional ~** *(US)* Berufshändler; **professional ~s** *(stock exchange, US)* Berufshandel, Kulisse; **regular ~** Handelsschiff; **retail ~** Einzelhändler; **room ~** *(US)* auf eigene Rechnung spekulierender Börsenmakler; **small ~** Kleingewerbetreibender, -händler; **sole ~** Einzelkaufmann; **feme-sole ~** Kauffrau, selbständige Geschäftsfrau; **street ~** Straßenhändler; **wholesale ~** Großhändler, Grossist.
trader│s' credits Bankkredite in Form direkt beglichener Kundenrechnungen; **~'s road transport** Werksverkehr; **~s' Road Transport Association** Werksverkehrsverband.
tradesfolk Gewerbetreibende, Geschäftsleute, Händler.
tradesman Gewerbetreibender, [Einzel]händler, Handelsmann, Kaufmann mit offenem Ladengeschäft, *(craftsman, Br.)* Handwerker, Minderkaufmann, *(mil.)* Spezialist;
cutting ~ Preisverderber;
to register with a ~ sich bei einem Geschäft (Laden) als Kunde eintragen lassen.
tradesmen│who supply us unsere Lieferanten;
~'s entrance Eingang für Lieferanten, Lieferanteneingang.
tradespeople Geschäftsleute, Gewerbetreibende, Handelsstand.
tradeswoman selbständige Geschäftsfrau, Ladenbesitzerin, Händlerin.
trading Handel treiben, Handel[n], *(stock exchange)* Börsenhandel;
over-the-counter ~ *(US)* Handel mit nicht notierten Wertpapieren, Schalterverkehr; **under-the-counter ~** Geschäfte unter dem Ladentisch; **equity ~** Geldaufnahme zu niedrigeren Zinsen als der Handelsgewinn, Finanzierung durch Fremdmittel; **fair ~** *(US)* vertikale Preisbildung; **foreign-currency ~** Devisenhandel; **fraudulent ~** betrügerische Geschäftstätigkeit zur Gläubigerbenachteiligung; **heavy ~** *(stock exchange)* hohe Umsätze; **last month's ~** die letzten Monatsumsätze; **light ~** *(stock exchange)* schwache Umsätze; **listless ~** *(US)* Freiverkehr; **municipal ~** Kommunalbetrieb, kommunale Wirtschaftstätigkeit, gemeindliche Gewerbetätigkeit; **mutual ~** gegenseitige Geschäftsbeziehungen; **odd-lot ~** *(US)* Handel in kleineren Effektenstücken; ~ **off** Kuhhandel; **off-board ~**

außerbörslicher Verkehr; **off-floor** ~ *(US)* Handel mit amtlich nicht notierten Werten; **on-floor** ~ *(US)* Börsenhandel auf eigene Rechnung; **push-button** ~ Effektenhandel im Druckknopfverfahren; **speculative** ~ Spekulationsgeschäft; **stock** ~ *(US)* Aktien-, Effektenhandel;

~ **in calls** *(Br.)* Vorprämiengeschäft; ~ **down** *(US)* Handel mit Billigerzeugnissen zwecks Umsatzsteigerung; ~ **with the enemy** geschäftlicher Verkehr mit feindlichen Ausländern; ~ **on the equity** Finanzierung durch Fremdmittel, Fremdmittelfinanzierung; ~ **in futures** *(US)* Termingeschäft; ~ **in commodity futures** Warentermingeschäft; ~-**in** In-Zahlung-Geben (-Nehmen); ~ **on margin** *(US)* Reportgeschäft; ~ **under the name** Firmierung; ~ **in options** Optionshandel; ~ **in puts and calls** Prämiengeschäft; ~ **on rates** Kurshandel, -geschäft; ~ **in securities** Wertpapierhandel; ~ **in security futures** Wertpapiertermingeschäft; ~ **on the short side** Baissetermingeschäft; ~ **in stocks** *(US)* Aktienhandel; ~ **up** *(US)* Handel mit Waren höherer Preislage und größeren Gewinnspannen;

to be accepted for ~ **on the stock exchange** zum Handel an der Börse zugelassen sein; **to be** ~ **on the equity** Fremdfinanzierungsmittel einsetzen; **to carry out foreign** ~ Außenhandelsgeschäfte führen; **to cease** ~ Geschäftsbetrieb einstellen; **to commence** ~ Gewerbebetrieb (Geschäftsbetrieb) beginnen; **to continue** ~ **after knowledge of insolvency** sein Gewerbe bei erkannter Insolvenz fortsetzen; **to dominate** ~ Marktgeschehen beherrschen;

~ *(a.)* gewerbe-, handeltreibend, kaufmännisch, *(to be bribed)* bestechlich, käuflich; ~ **as** firmierend als;

~ **ability** kaufmännische Eigenschaften (Geschicklichkeit); ~ **account** Firmen-, Verkaufskonto, Betriebskonto, -rechnung; ~ **accounts** Geschäftsbücher; ~ **activity** Gewerbetätigkeit, *(stock exchange)* Börsenaktivität; ~ **advantage** Geschäftsvorteil; ~ **adventure** *(taxation)* steuerpflichtiger Umsatz; ~ **agreement** Handelsabkommen; **restrictive** ~ **agreement** *(Br.)* Kartellvereinbarung, -absprache; ~ **area** *(US)* Handelszone, Wirtschaftsgebiet, -raum, Einzugs-, Verkaufsgebiet, Absatzfeld, -bereich, -gebiet; ~ **association** Wirtschafts-, Handelsvereinigung, Berufsverband; ~ **arrangement** Handelsabkommen, Geschäftsvereinbarung; **to enter into a** ~ **arrangement** Handelsabkommen abschließen; ~ **bank** *(Australia)* Handelsbank; ~ **bloc** Wirtschaftsblock; ~ **capital** Gewerbekapital, Betriebskapital, -mittel, -vermögen; ~ **cashflow** für das Börsengeschäft zur Verfügung stehender Reingewinn; ~ **center** *(US)* Handelszentrum, Geschäftszentrum, -gegend; ~ **certificate** *(Br.)* Gewerbegenehmigung, -schein; ~ **cheque** *(Br.)* Warengutschein; ~ **classes** handeltreibende Klassen, Handelsstand; ~ **combine** Kartellvereinigung, -organisation; ~ **community** Handelsgemeinschaft, -welt; ~ **company** kaufmännisches Unternehmen, Handels-, Erwerbsgesellschaft, *(factory)* Faktorei, *(guild)* [Kaufmanns]innung, *(marketing)* Vertriebs-, Absatzgesellschaft, *(purchasing combine)* Einkaufsgesellschaft; **state** ~ **company** staatliche Handelsgesellschaft; ~ **concern** Wirtschafts-, Handelsunternehmen; ~ **conditions** Handels-, Geschäftsbedingungen; ~ **contract** Handels-, Geschäftsvertrag, *(fair)* Ausstellungsvertrag; ~ **corporation** kaufmännisches Unternehmen, Erwerbs-, Handelsgesellschaft; **to pay in all one's** ~ **credits into an account** alle Firmeneinnahmen auf ein Konto einzahlen; ~ **customer** Firmenkunde; ~ **day** Börsentag; ~-**debt collection** Inkasso von Lieferantenschulden; ~ **difference** *(stock exchange)* Aufschlag für kleinere Aktienposten; ~ **enterprise** Handelsunternehmen; **state** ~ **enterprise** staatliches Handelsunternehmen; ~ **estate** *(Br.)* Industriesiedlung; ~ **expenses** Betriebsausgaben; ~ **failure** *(US)* Zahlungseinstellung, Geschäftszusammenbruch, Konkurs; ~ **favo(u)rites** *(stock exchange, Br.)* führende Werte; ~ **figures** Ertragszahlen [im Geschäftsbericht]; ~ **firm** Handelshaus; ~ **group** Konzernunternehmen; ~ **handicap** Geschäftsnachteil; ~ **hazard** Handelsrisiko; ~ **house** Handelshaus; ~ **income** Einkünfte aus Gewerbebetrieb, Geschäftserträgnisse; ~ **interest** Geschäftsinteresse; ~ **item** Handelserzeugnis, Betriebsprodukt; ~ **licence** Gewerbekonzession, Handelsbefugnis, -erlaubnis; ~ **line** Handelszweig; ~ **loss** Geschäfts-, Betriebsverlust; ~ **loss carried forward** vorgetragener Betriebsverlust; **to relate back unrelieved** ~ **losses against the total profits of the preceding accounting period** steuerlich nicht verbrauchte Geschäftsverluste gegen die Gesamteinkünfte des vorausgehenden Veranlagungszeitraums verrechnen; ~ **market** *(US)* flauer und stagnierender Markt; ~ **nation** Handelsnation, -volk; ~ **neighbo(u)r** Handelsnachbar; ~ **operation** Handels-, Tauschgeschäft, Geschäftstransaktion; ~ **operations** geschäftliche Unternehmungen,

Geschäftstätigkeit; ~ **pace** Umsatzgeschwindigkeit; ~ **partner** Handelspartner; ~ **partnership** [offene] Handelsgesellschaft; ~ **performance** Handelsergebnis; ~ **period** Geschäftszeitraum; ~ **place** Handelsplatz; **protectionist** ~ **policies** protektionistische Handelspolitik; ~ **policy** Handels-, Wirtschaftspolitik; ~ **port** Handelshafen; ~ **position** Marktposition; ~ **possibility** Handelsmöglichkeit; ~ **post** Handelsniederlassung, -stützpunkt, -posten, Warenumschlagsstelle, *(stock exchange, US)* Börsen-, Maklerstand, *(New York stock exchange)* Handelsstelle für Freiverkehr; ~ **practice** Handelsbräuche, -usance; ~ **process** Wirtschaftsablauf, -prozeß.

trading profit Geschäfts-, Betriebsgewinn;
gross ~ Warenrohgewinn; **net** ~ Reingewinn nach Versteuerung;
~ **for 1980** Geschäftsgewinn für das Jahr 1980;
to convert a ~ **profit into a loss for tax purposes by means of capital allowance** Geschäftsgewinn mittels Abschreibungen auf das Anlagevermögen steuerlich als Verlust ausweisen;
~ **margin** Betriebshandelsspanne.

trading | radius Geschäftsumkreis; ~ **range** Verkaufsspielraum an der Börse; ~ **rate** *(invisible balance)* Wechselkurs; ~ **receipts** gewerbliche Einnahmen, Betriebseinnahmen, Gewerbeeinkünfte; ~ **report** Erfolgs-, Gewinnausweis, Betriebsbericht; ~ **result** Geschäftsergebnis, Betriebsergebnis; ~ **revenues** Einkünfte aus Gewerbebetrieb, Betriebseinnahmen; ~ **specialist** Börsenfachmann; ~ **settlement** Handelsniederlassung; ~ **stamp** Warenbezugsprämie, Gutschein, Rabattmarke; ᵉ **Stamps Act** *(Br.)* Rabattmarkengesetz; ~ **stamp-scheme** Rabattmarkensystem; ~ **state** Handelsnation; ~ **stocks** Betriebswerte, Lagerbestände; ~ **subsidiaries** Handelstöchter; **net** ~ **surplus** Reingewinn vor Versteuerung; ~ **town** Geschäftszentrum, Handelsplatz; ~ **transactions** Geschäftstransaktionen; ~ **unit** *(stock exchange)* Handelseinheit; ~ **value** Handelswert; ~ **volume** Handelsvolumen; ~ **voyage** Trampschiffahrtsroute; ~ **year** Geschäfts-, Rechnungsjahr.

tradition *(custom)* mündliche Überlieferung, Tradition, Brauchtum, Herkommen, *(delivery)* Besitzverschaffung, *(extradition)* Übergabe, Auslieferung.

traditional herkömmlich, traditionell;
~ **political party** traditionsbewußte politische Partei.

traditionalism Festhalten an der Überlieferung.

traffic *(advertising agency)* termingebundene Arbeiten, *(customers)* Laufkundschaft, *(exchange of goods)* Güteraustausch, -verkehr, *(flow of persons)* Anzahl von Kunden, *(movement of vessels)* Schiffsverkehr, *(railway)* [Bahn]betrieb, Eisenbahnverkehr, *(revenue from ~)* Verkehrseinnahmen, *(total of communications)* Nachrichtenwesen, *(total of passengers transported)* beförderte Personenzahl, Personenverkehr, *(trade)* Handel, Handelsverkehr, *(transportation)* öffentlicher Verkehr, Straßenverkehr, Transport-, Verkehrswesen, Verkehrsverhältnisse, -leben;

air ~ Luftverkehr; **big-city** ~ Großstadtverkehr; **border** ~ Grenzverkehr; **business** ~ Berufsverkehr; **canal** ~ Kanalverkehr; **carrying** ~ Güterverkehr; **charter** ~ Charterverkehr, Verkehr von Chartermaschinen; **city** ~ Stadtverkehr; **coastal** ~ Küstenverkehr; **collective** ~ Sammelgutverkehr; **congested** ~ Verkehrsstauung; **direction** ~ Richtungsverkehr; **downtown** ~ *(coll.)* Verkehr in der Innenstadt (im Stadtzentrum); **illegal drug** ~ Rauschgifthandel; **fast-moving** ~ Schnellverkehr; **freight** ~ *(US)* Güterverkehr; **frontier** ~ Grenzverkehr; **full-truck** ~ Wagenladungs-, Freiladeverkehr; **goods** ~ *(Br.)* Güterverkehr, *(railway)* Einnahmen aus dem Güterverkehr; **grouped** ~ Sammelladungsverkehr; **heavy** ~ starker Verkehr, Verkehrsandrang; **home** ~ Binnenverkehr; **illegal** ~ Schwarzhandel; **inland** ~ Binnenverkehr; **intercity** ~ *(US)* Landesverkehr; **less-than-carload** ~ *(US)* Stückgutverkehr; **local** ~ Nah-, Vorortverkehr; **long-distance** ~ Fern-, Überlandverkehr; **loss-making** ~ *(railway)* Verlustbetrieb; **merchandise** ~ Waren-, Güterverkehr; **motor** ~ Autoverkehr; **narcotics** ~ Rauschgifthandel; **ocean** ~ Hochseeverkehr; **office-hour** ~ Berufsverkehr; **oncoming** ~ Gegenverkehr; **one-way** ~ Einbahnregelung, -verkehr; **passenger** ~ Passagier-, Personenverkehr; **pedestrian** ~ Fußgänger-, Passantenverkehr; **perishable** ~ Handel mit leicht verderblichen Waren; **radio** ~ Funkverkehr; **rail merchandise** ~ [Eisenbahn]güterverkehr; **railroad** ~ *(US)* (**railway,** *Br.*) ~ Eisenbahnverkehr; **recreational** ~ Erholungsverkehr; **retail** ~ Stückgutverkehr; **road** ~ Straßenverkehr; **rush-hour** ~ Spitzen-, Berufsverkehr; **shipping** ~ Schiffsverkehr; **short-distance** [goods] ~ *(Br.)* [Güter]nahverkehr; **short-haul** ~ Nahverkehr; **slave** ~ Sklavenhandel; **street** ~ Straßenverkehr; **suburban** ~ Vorortsverkehr; **telecommunication** ~ Fernmeldewesen;

through (transit) ~ Durchgangsverkehr; **toll** ~ *(tel., Br.)* Nahverkehr; **tourist** ~ Fremdenverkehr; **trunk** ~ *(tel.)* Fernverkehr; **vehicular** ~ Fahrzeugverkehr; **waterborne** ~ Schiffahrtsverkehr; **way** ~ *(US)* Nahverkehr; **white-slave** ~ Mädchenhandel; ~ **in arms** Waffenhandel, -schmuggel; ~ **turning the corner** Einbiegeverkehr; ~ **in goods** Warenverkehr, -handel; ~ **in liquor** Spirituosenhandel; ~ **in the market** Marktverkehr; ~ **on the road** Verkehrsdichte, -stärke; **much** ~ **on the roads** starker Straßenverkehr; ~ **in a town** innerstädtischer Verkehr, Stadtverkehr; ~ **in transit** Durchfuhrverkehr; ~ **in votes** Stimmenkauf, -handel, Wahlschwindel, -schiebung;

~ *(v.)* handeln, Handel treiben, *(haggle)* feilschen, schachern; ~ **away** verschachern, vertauschen; ~ **with other countries** Außenhandel treiben;

to be closed for heavy motor ~ für Lastwagenverkehr gesperrt sein; **to be opened to** ~ in Betrieb genommen werden; **to block** ~ Verkehr behindern (aufhalten); **to by-pass** ~ Verkehr umleiten; **to channelize** ~ Verkehr steuern, in den Verkehr einschleusen; **to control (direct)** ~ Verkehr regeln; **to congest** ~ Verkehrsstau hervorrufen; **to cope with** ~ um den Verkehr bewältigen zu können; **to cream off** ~ *(street)* Verkehr glatt (ohne Schwierigkeiten) aufnehmen; **to direct the** ~ Verkehr regeln; **to disentangle** ~ Verkehrsstau entwirren; **to disturb** ~ zu Verkehrsstörungen führen; **to divert** ~ *(Br.)* Verkehr umleiten; **to dodge** ~ Verkehrsstauungen ausweichen; **to hold up** ~ Verkehr aufhalten (anhalten, hindern); **to inconvenience** ~ Verkehrsfluß behindern; **to intercept** ~ Verkehr unterbrechen; **to move more** ~ mehr Verkehr aufnehmen; **to obstruct the** ~ Verkehr lahmlegen; **to open to** ~ dem Verkehr übergeben; **to pool** ~ gemeinsame Verkehrspolitik betreiben; **to prepare for heavy summer** ~ mit einem großen Verkehrsandrang während der Sommermonate rechnen; **to regulate the** ~ Verkehr regeln; **to stop** ~ Verkehr einstellen; **to suspend** ~ Verkehr anhalten; **to unjam** ~ Verkehrsstockung beheben;

what the ~ **will bear** höhere Gebühren für wertvollere Versandgüter;

Road ⏤ **Act** *(Br.)* Straßenverkehrsgesetz; ~ **accident** Verkehrsunfall; ~ **arrangement** Verkehrsabkommen; ~ **artery** Verkehrsweg; ~ **balances** *(railway)* Verkehrsüberschüsse; ~ **beacon** *(Br.)* Verkehrsampel, Fußgängerampel, -zeichen; ~ **block** Verkehrsstockung, Stau; ~ **case** *(US)* Verkehrsstrafsache, -delikt; ~ **census** Verkehrszählung; ~ **center** *(US)* (**centre**, *Br.*) Verkehrsknotenpunkt; ~ **circle** *(US)* Kreisverkehr; Uniform ⏤ **Code** *(US)* Straßenverkehrsordnung; ~ **commissioner** *(Br.)* Zulassungsstelle; ~-**congested** durch den Verkehr verstopft; ~ **congestion** Verkehrsstauung, Verkehrszusammenballung, -verdichtung; ~ **constable** Verkehrsschutzmann, -polizist; ~ **control** Verkehrsbewältigung, -kontrolle, -regelung; ~ **control squad** Verkehrspolizei; ~ **control tower** *(airport)* Kontrollturm; ~ **cop** Verkehrsschutzmann, Verkehrspolizist; ~ **corridor** Verkehrsweg; ~ **count** Verkehrszählung; ~ **court** Schnellgericht; **morning's** ~ **crush** morgendlicher Verkehrsandrang; ~ **data** *(railway)* Betriebswerte; ~ **delay** Verkehrsstockung; ~ **density** Verkehrsdichte; ~ **department** Verkehrsdezernat, -abteilung, *(advertising)* Terminabteilung, *(department store)* Auslieferungs-, Zustellabteilung; ~ **difficulties** Verkehrsschwierigkeiten; ~ **direction** Verkehrshinweis; ~ **director** Leiter des Verkehrsamtes, Verkehrsdezernent; ~ **discipline** Verkehrsdisziplin; ~ **dislocation** Verkehrsverlagerung; ~ **diversion** *(Br.)* Verkehrsumleitung; ~ **duty** Verkehrsregelung; ~ **education** *(US)* Verkehrserziehung; ~ **engineer** *(US)* Verkehrsingenieur; ~ **explosion** Explosion des Verkehrswesens, explosionsartige Verkehrsentwicklung; ~ **facilities** *(US)* Verkehrseinrichtungen; ~ **fine** gebührenpflichtige Verwarnung; ~ **flow** Verkehrsstrom; ~ **forecast** Verkehrsprognose; ~ **generation** Verkehrsaufkommen; ~ **handling** Verkehrsabwicklung; ~ **hazard** Verkehrsrisiko; ~ **helicopter** Verkehrshubschrauber; ~ **holdup** Verkehrsstockung, -stau; ~ **improvement** Verkehrsverbesserung; ~ **increase** Verkehrszunahme; ~ **indicator** Fahrtrichtungsanzeiger, Winker, Blinker; **self-cancelling** ~ **indicator** automatische Richtungsanzeiger, Blinker; ~ **indicator lights** Blinklicht[anlage]; ~ **infringement** Verkehrsverstoß, -verletzung; ~ **instruction** Verkehrsunterricht; ~ **interests** Verkehrsgewerbe; ~ **island** Verkehrsinsel; ~ **jam** Verkehrsstockung, -stauung; ~ **junction** Verkehrsknotenpunkt; ~-**laden** mit starkem Verkehr belastet; ~ **lane** Fahrstreifen; ~ **law** Verkehrsordnung, Verkehrsgesetz; ~ **vehicle and laws** *(US)* Verkehrsvorschriften; ~ **light** Verkehrsampel, -licht; **mobile** ~ **light** umsetzbare Verkehrsampel; **to be controlled by** ~ **lights** durch Verkehrsampeln gesteuert werden; ~-**light control** Verkehrsampelanlage; ~ **management** Straßenverkehrsaufsicht, *(fac-*

tory) Versandleitung, -wesen; ~ **management system** Verkehrsregelungswesen, Straßenverkehrswesen; ~ **manager** Leiter der Versandabteilung, Versandleiter, Vertriebsdirektor, *(advertising)* für Termine verantwortlicher Sachbearbeiter, Terminbearbeiter, *(local government)* Leiter des Straßenverkehrsamtes, *(railway)* Betriebsleiter, Fahrdienstleiter; ~ **mile** Personenkilometer; **no-delay-~ office** *(tel.)* Schnellverkehrsamt; ~ **offence** Verkehrsdelikt, -verletzung; ~ **offender** Verkehrssünder; ~ **officer** Verkehrsdezernent; ~ **operation** Verkehrsabwicklung; ~ **ordinance** Verkehrsbestimmung; **to stave off** ~ **paralysis** gegen die Lähmung des gesamten Verkehrs angehen; ~ **patrol** Verkehrsstreife; **peak** ~ **period** Verkehrsspitze; ~ **planning** Verkehrsplanung; ~ **police** Verkehrspolizisten; ~ **policeman** Verkehrsschutzmann; ~ **policy** Verkehrspolitik; ~ **post** Verkehrszeichen, -posten; ~ **potential** Verkehrspotential; ~ **problem** Verkehrsproblem; ~ **receipts** Betriebs-, Verkehrseinnahmen; ~ **regulations** Fahrvorschrift, Verkehrsregeln, -vorschriften, Straßenverkehrsordnung; ~ **regulator** Verkehrsschutzmann, -polizist; ~ **requirements** Verkehrsbedürfnisse; ~ **restraints (restrictions)** Verkehrserschwernisse, -beschränkungen; ~ **return** Verkehrsbericht, -ziffern, *(railway)* Betriebs-, Verkehrsstatistik; ~ **road** Fahrstraße; ~ **route** Verkehrsweg; ~ **rules** *(US)* Verkehrsregeln; ~ **safety** *(US)* Verkehrssicherheit; ~ **seizure** Überhandnahme des Verkehrs; ~ **service** Verkehrsgewerbe; ~ **sheet** *(hotel)* Liste geführter Gespräche, Gesprächsbelegzettel, *(railway)* Zugübersicht; ~ **shift** Verkehrsverlagerung; ~ **shifter** Fahrdienstleiter; ~ **sign** Verkehrsschild, -zeichen; **to disobey a** ~ **sign** Verkehrszeichen mißachten; ~ **signal** Verkehrsampel, -zeichen; **to comply with a** ~ **signal** sich nach einer Verkehrsampel richten; **to fail to comply with a** ~ **signal** Verkehrsampel mißachten; ~ **snarl** *(US)* Verkehrschaos, -wirrwarr; ~ **solicitor** Verkehrswerbungsunternehmen; ~ **squad** Überfallkommando, Verkehrsstreife; ~ **statistics** Verkehrsstatistik; ~ **superintendent** Fahrdienstleiter; ~ **taker** Verkehrsstatistiker; ~ **tangle** Verkehrsverstopfung, -stauung; ~ **ticket** *(US)* Strafzettel, Strafmandat, gebührenpflichtige Verwarnung; ~ **tie-up** *(US)* Verkehrsstopfung; ~ **toll** Verkehrsunfallziffer; ~ **tower** Verkehrsturm, -podest; ~ **treaty** Verkehrsvertrag; ~ **use** Verkehrsbenutzung; ~ **violation** Verstoß gegen die Verkehrsvorschriften, Verkehrsübertretung, -verletzung; ~ **violation fine** Knöllchen, Strafzettel; ~ **warden** Straßenwärter, *(Br.)* Parkwächter; ~ **work** Speditionsberuf.

trafficability Passierbarkeit.

trafficable passierbar, für den Verkehr geeignet, *(trade)* für den Handel geeignet, gangbar, gängig.

trafficator *(Br.)* Fahrtrichtungsanzeiger, Winker, Blinker.

trafficker Hausierer, Schleich-, Schwarzmarkthändler; **drug** ~ Rauschgifthändler.

trafficking Hausieren, Schleich-, Schwarzmarkthandel.

trafficway Verkehrsweg, -straße.

tragedy Tragödie, Trauerspiel.

tragic | **actor** Tragöde; ~ **event** tragisches Ereignis.

trail Spur, Fährte, *(path)* ausgetretener Weg, Pfad, Steig; **off the** ~ auf der falschen Fährte; **on the** ~ auf der Spur; **hot on the** ~ auf einer heißen Spur;

vapo(u)r ~**s** Kondensstreifen;

~ **of blood** Blutspur; ~ **of destruction** *(storm)* Vernichtungsbahn; ~ **of meteor** Meteorstreifen; ~ **of smoke** Rauchfahne;

~ *(v.)* *(disparage)* in den Schmutz ziehen, herunterreißen, *(drag)* schleppen, ziehen, *(hunt)* verfolgen, nachspüren, auf den Fersen sein, *(be a trailor)* bahnbrechend wirken; ~ **along** hinterhertrotten, nachhinken; ~ **a criminal** Verbrecher verfolgen; ~ **a flag** Fahne in den Schmutz ziehen; **to be off on the** ~ sich auf die Suche machen; **to be hot on the** ~ **of s. o.** jem. dicht auf den Fersen sein; **to blaze a** ~ bahnbrechend wirken, Pionierarbeit leisten;

~ **blazer** Wegbereiter, Pionier, *(fig.)* Bahnbrecher; ~ **bridge** fliegende Fähre; ~ **drover** Viehtreiber; ~ **rope** Schleppseil.

trailer *(advertising)* Werbedurchsage für ein Nebenprodukt, *(broadcasting)* Vorankündigung, *(car)* Wohnwagen[anhänger], *(film)* Filmvoranzeige, Vorspann, -schau, *(lorry)* Lastwagen-, Kraftfahrzeuganhänger, *(tram)* Beiwagen; ~ **on flat car** *(US)* Huckepackauto; ~ **camp (court, park)** Wohnwagenstadt, -kolonie.

trailerite *(US)* Wohnwagenbenutzer.

trailing | **aerial** Schleppantenne; ~ **wheel** Tragrad.

train [Eisenbahn]zug, *(machine)* Walzenstraße, -strecke, Walzwerk, *(mil.)* Train, Troß, Fahrtruppe, *(mining)* Feuerleitung [für Sprengungen], *(procession)* Reihe, Folge, Kette, Prozession, *(retinue)* Begleitung, Gefolge, *(sleighs, Canada)* Lastschlitten, *(steelworks)* Straße;

by ~ mit der Bahn; **on the** ~ in der Eisenbahn; **on arrival of** ~ bei Zugankunft;

auxiliary ~ Bedarfszug; **baggage** ~ *(mil., Br.)* Troß; **boat-load** ~ *(Br.)* Zug mit Dampferanschluß; **camel** ~ Kamelkarawane; **connecting (corresponding)** ~ Anschlußzug; **corridor** ~ D-Zug; **delayed** ~ verspäteter Zug; **departing** ~ abgehender Zug; **direct** ~ durchgehender Zug; **down** ~ *(Br.)* von London abgehender Zug, *(US)* stadteinwärts fahrender Zug; **drying** ~ Trockenapparat; **early** ~ Frühzug; **emergency-supply** ~ Hilfszug; **excursion** ~ Ausflugszug; **express** ~ Eil-, Schnellzug, Express; **extra-fare** ~ Fern-D-Zug; **fast** ~ Schnell-, D-Zug; **fast goods** ~ *(Br.)* Eilgüterzug; **freight** ~ *(US)* Güterzug; **funeral** ~ Leichenzug; **goods** ~ *(Br.)* Güterzug; **high-speed** ~ Blitzzug; **hospital** ~ Lazarettzug; **in** ~ angekommener Zug; **jam-packed** ~ vollgestopfter Zug; **limited** ~ zuschlagspflichtiger Zug, Zug mit beschränkter Waggon- und Personenzahl, Platzkartenzug; **local** ~ Vorortzug; **local express** ~ im Nahschnellverkehr eingesetzter Zug; **mail** ~ Zug mit Postbeförderung; **main-line** ~ auf einer Hauptstrecke verkehrender Zug, Fernzug; **market** ~ Marktzug; **material** ~ Baumaterialienzug; **mixed** ~ Personen- und Güterzug, gemischter Zug; **morning** ~ Früh-, Morgenzug; **mystery** ~ Fahrt ins Blaue; **nonstop** ~ durchgehender (direkter) Zug; **ordinary** ~ fahrplanmäßiger Zug; **outgoing** ~ abfahrender Zug; **overcrowded (packed)** ~ überfüllter Zug; **parliamentary** ~ *(Br.)* Personenzug mit ermäßigtem Fahrpreis, Bummelzug; **passenger** ~ Personenzug; **advanced passenger** ~ superschneller Zug; **public service** ~ Zug für den öffentlichen Personenverkehr; **Pullman** ~ *(US)* Luxuszug; **raw-goods** ~ Materialzug; **regular** ~ fahrplanmäßiger (pünktlicher) Zug; **relief** ~ Hilfszug; **scheduled** ~ *(US)* fahrplanmäßiger (pünktlicher) Zug; **sleeping-car** ~ Schlafwagenzug; **slow** ~ Personen-, Bummelzug; **special** ~ Vor-, Sonderzug; **stopping** ~ Bummelzug; **through** ~ durchgehender Zug; **vestibule** ~ *(US)* D-Zug; **workmen's** ~ Arbeiterzug; **wrecked** ~ entgleister Zug;

handy ~ **and bus** gute Eisenbahn- und Busverbindungen; ~ **with dining car** Eisenbahnzug mit Kücheneinrichtung; ~ **of camels** Kamelkarawane; ~ **of events** Kette (Folge) von Ereignissen; ~ **of ideas** Gedankengang; ~ **de luxe** Luxus-, Salonzug; **long** ~ **of sightseers** Strom von Schaulustigen; ~ **of thought** Gedankengang; ~ **to town** stadteinwärts fahrender Zug;

~ *(v.)* erziehen, aufziehen, ausbilden, anlernen, unterrichten, schulen, *(animal)* abrichten, dressieren, *(v./i.)* sich üben, sich vorbereiten, trainieren;

~ **s. o.** j. einarbeiten; ~ **in first aid** in erster Hilfe ausbilden; ~ **s. o. to business** j. für das Geschäft anlernen; ~ **for a career** sich auf einen Beruf vorbereiten; ~ **[up] children to be good citizens** Kinder zu guten Staatsbürgern erziehen; ~ **for free** umsonst ausbilden; ~ **it** *(coll.)* mit der Bahn fahren; ~ **off** aus der Übung kommen, *(retire)* sich zur Ruhe setzen; ~ **with well-dressed people** *(sl.)* Umgang mit feinen Leuten haben; ~ **for public service** sich auf den Staatsdienst vorbereiten;

to annul (cancel) a ~ Zug ausfallen lassen; **to be on the** ~ mitfahren; **to be in a fair** ~ gut geregelt sein; **to be part of s. one's** ~ zu jds. Gefolge zählen; **to board a** ~ *(US)* in einen Zug einsteigen; **to bring in its** ~ mit sich bringen; **to change ~s** umsteigen; **to connect with a** ~ Zuganschluß haben; **to dock a** ~ Zug aufs Abstellgleis bringen; **to flag a** ~ Zug ablassen (abwinken); **to follow the** ~ **of one's thoughts** sich seinen Gedanken überlassen; **to forward by mail** ~ als Eilgut befördern; **to get off a** ~ aus einem Zug aussteigen; **to get on the** ~ in den Zug einsteigen; **to go aboard a** ~ in einen Zug einsteigen; **to go by** ~ mit der [Eisen]bahn fahren, Eisenbahn benutzen; **to have in its** ~ nach sich ziehen, mit sich bringen; **to have lunch on the** ~ Mittagessen im Zug einnehmen; **to institute special ~s** Sonderzüge einlegen; **to look up a** ~ **(for a ~ in the timetable)** sich einen Zug heraussuchen; **to make up a** ~ *(of cars)* Zug bereitstellen; **to misroute a** ~ Zug fehlleiten; **to miss one's** ~ seinen Zug verpassen (versäumen); **to put in** ~ in Gang setzen; **to run extra ~s** Sonderzüge einsetzen; **to schedule a new** ~ *(US)* neuen Zug in den Fahrplan einfügen; **to send s. th. by goods** ~ *(Br.)* etw. als Fracht versenden; **to set in** ~ in Gang bringen; **to shift a** ~ **one hour ahead** Zug um eine Stunde vorverlegen; **to shunt a** ~ Zug auf ein Abstellgleis stellen; **to split up a** ~ Zug auflösen; **to start a** ~ Zug abfahren lassen; **to step off a** ~ aus einem Zug aussteigen; **to take a** ~ einen Zug fahren, Zug benutzen; **to travel by** ~ mit dem Zug fahren; **to wreck a** ~ Zug entgleisen lassen;

~ **accident** Eisenbahnunglück; ~ **call** *(tel.)* Zuggespräch; ~ **capacity** Fassungsvermögen eines Eisenbahnzuges; ~ **collision** Zugzusammenstoß; ~ **connections** Eisenbahnverbindungen, Zugverbindungen; **handy** ~ **and bus connections** gute Zug- und Omnibusverbindungen; ~ **container service** Eisenbahnbehäl-

terverkehr; ~ **crew** *(US)* Zugbesatzung, Fahrpersonal; ~ **diagram** graphischer Fahrplan; ~ **disaster** Zugunglück; ~ **dispatch** Zugabfertigung; ~ **dispatcher** Fahrdienstleiter, Zugabfertiger; ~ **driver** Zugführer; ~ **fare** [Eisenbahn]fahrkarte; ~ **ferry** Eisenbahn-, Zugfähre, Fähr-, Trajektschiff; ~ **guard** *(US)* Zugschaffner; ~ **indicator** Zugtafel; ~ **inspector** Zugschaffner; ~ **journey** Eisenbahnfahrt, Eisenbahnreise; ~ **line** Fahrgleis; ~ **mil(e)age** Eisenbahnkilometer; ~ **order** Zugordnung; ~ **reservation** Platzkarte; ~ **ride** Eisenbahnfahrt; ~ **schedule** *(US)* Fahrplan, Zugfolge; ~ **service** [Eisen]bahnverkehr, -verbindung, Zugverkehr, -folge; **passenger** ~ **service** Personenzugverkehr; **to cut** ~ **service** Zugverkehr einschränken; ~ **staff** Zugbesatzung, Fahrpersonal; ~ **telephone** Zugtelefon; ~ **ticket** Eisenbahnfahrkarte, -billet; ~ **warrant** [Fracht]begleitzettel; ~ **wreck** *(accident insurance)* Zugkatastrophe, -entgleisung.

trainbands Miliz.

trained geschult, ausgebildet, beruflich vorgebildet;

well-~ gut erzogen;

to be ~ **full-time for a trade or profession** Ausbildungsvertrag besitzen;

~ **men** Fachkräfte; ~ **nurse** ausgebildete Krankenschwester, Wochenpflegerin.

trainee *(US)* Volontär, Praktikant, Nachwuchskraft, Anlernling, Auszubildender, *(course)* Kursusteilnehmer, *(mil., US)* Rekrut;

business ~ kaufmännischer Lehrling, als Kaufmann Auszubildender; **industrial** ~ Firmenpraktikant; **management** ~ Führungsnachwuchskraft; **on-the-job** ~ *(US)* Firmenpraktikant; ~ **course** Ausbildungslehrgang, -kursus; ~ **pilot** Flugschüler; ~ **teacher** Lehramtskandidat.

trainer Ausbilder, Trainer, *(airplane)* Übungsflugzeug, *(dogs)* Abrichter.

training [Ein]schulung, Ausbildung, Anlernen, Erziehung, Übung, Berufsvorbereitung;

out of ~ aus der Übung;

additional ~ zusätzliche Ausbildung; **advanced** ~ Berufsfortbildung; **apprenticeship** ~ Lehrlingsausbildung; **basic** ~ Grundausbildung; **blitz** ~ *(US)* Ausbildung in Schnellkursen, Schnellkursausbildung; **business** ~ kaufmännische Ausbildung; **cold-storage** ~ *(US)* Ausbildung von Nachwuchskräften; **continuous** ~ Weiter-, Berufsausbildung; **day-release** ~ Bildungsurlaubswesen; **employee** ~ innerbetriebliche Ausbildung; **executive** ~ *(US)* Ausbildung leitender Angestellter, Nachwuchsausbildung; **formal** ~ Pflicht-, regelrechte Berufsausbildung; **further** ~ Weiterbildung; **group** ~ Gruppenausbildung; **in-house** ~ Ausbildung im eigenen Betrieb; **in-plant** ~ *(US)* Ausbildung am Arbeitsplatz; **inservice** ~ betriebliche (berufliche) Förderung, Ausbildung während der Dienstzeit; **individual** ~ Einzelausbildung; **industrial** ~ Berufs-, Fach-, fachliche Ausbildung; **legal** ~ juristische Ausbildung; **management** ~ Managementausbildung, Ausbildung von Führungskräften; **manpower** ~ Ausbildung von Arbeitskräften; **manual** ~ handwerkliche Ausbildung; **mercantile** ~ kaufmännische Ausbildung; **military** ~ militärische Ausbildung; **occupational** ~ Berufs-, Fachausbildung; **[on-the-] job (job instruction)** ~ *(US)* Ausbildung am Arbeitsplatz; **operational** ~ einsatzmäßige Ausbildung; **outside** ~ außerbetriebliche Ausbildung; **pre-employment** ~ Berufsausbildung; **professional** ~ berufliche Ausbildung, Fach-, Berufsausbildung; **re-~** Umschulung; **short-course** ~ Fachausbildung in Kurzlehrgängen; **special** ~ Sonderausbildung; **staff** ~ Personalausbildung; **technical** ~ Fachausbildung; **thorough** ~ gründliche Ausbildung; **vestibule school** ~ *(US)* Werkstattausbildung; **vocational** ~ fachliche Ausbildung, Fach-, Berufsausbildung;

~ **of an apprentice** Lehrlingsausbildung; ~ **for a calling** Berufsausbildung; ~ **in craftsmanship** handwerkliche Ausbildung; ~ **of foremen** Vorarbeiterausbildung; ~ **of guerillas** Partisanenausbildung; ~ **within industry** Berufsausbildung, -schulung; ~ **on the job** *(US)* Ausbildung am Arbeitsplatz; ~ **of management** Ausbildung (Schulung) von Führungskräften; ~ **of nurses** Krankenschwesterausbildung; ~ **of staff** Belegschaftsschulung; ~ **in new technology** Ausbildung in neuen technologischen Verfahren; ~ **for a trade, profession or vocation** *(taxation)* Berufsausbildung;

to be launched into ~ mit der Ausbildung anfangen; **to keep in** ~ in Übung bleiben; **to receive** ~ Ausbildung bekommen;

~ **activity** Ausbildungstätigkeit; ~ **allowance** Umschulungsbeihilfe; ~ **arrangements** Ausbildungsordnung; ~ **area** *(mil.)* Truppenübungsplatz; **business** ~ **background** kaufmännischer Werdegang; ~ **benefit** Ausbildungszuschuß; ~ **benefits** Ausbildungsvorteile; ~ **camp** Schulungslager, Ausbildungslager; ~

camp for saboteurs Sabotageausbildungslager; **~ center** *(US)* **(centre,** *Br.)* Ausbildungszentrum, -zentrale, -stätte, *(mil.)* Lager; **~ college** *(Br.)* Hochschule für Lehrerbildung, Lehrerbildungsanstalt; **~ coordinator** Schulungs-, Ausbildungsleiter; **government ~ contract** staatlicher Ausbildungsvertrag; **shop-~ department** Lehrwerkstatt; **~ costs** Ausbildungskosten; **~ course** [Ausbildungs]kursus, Lehrgang; **advanced ~ course** Aufbau-, Fortbildungskursus; **shop-~ department** Lehrwerkstatt; **~ director** Ausbildungsleiter; **~ facilities** Ausbildungsmöglichkeiten, -stätten; **~ farm** landwirtschaftlicher Lehrbetrieb; **~ film** Ausbildungs-, Lehrfilm; **~ grant** Ausbildungsbeihilfe; **~ ground** Übungsgelände; **~ group** Ausbildungsgruppe; **~ hospital** Lernkrankenhaus; **~ institute** *(US)* Jugendstrafanstalt; **~ instructor** Ausbildender; **~ level** Ausbildungsstufe; **~ location** Ausbildungsstätte; **~ manager** Nachwuchsausbilder; **~ manual** Ausbildungsvorschrift; **~ material** Ausbildungsmaterial; **~ method** Ausbildungsmethode; **~ needs** Ausbildungsmängel; **~ objective** Ausbildungsziel; **basic ~ pattern** Ausbildungsstufen; **~ personnel** Ausbildungspersonal; **~ plane ~** Schulflugzeug; **~ process** Lernvorgang; **job-~ process** berufliches Ausbildungsverfahren; **~ program(me)** Schulungs-, Ausbildungsprogramm; **manpower ~ program** *(unskilled workers, US)* subventioniertes Umschulungsprogramm; **~ record** Ausbildungsnachweis; **~ results** Ausbildungsergebnisse; **~ schedule** Ausbildungsplan; **~ scheme** Ausbildungsprogramm, -plan; **~ school** Berufsschule, *(children, US)* Schule für schwer erziehbare Kinder, Jugendstraf-, Erziehungsanstalt; **additional ~ seminar** Fortbildungsseminar; **~ session** Schulungskursus; **~ ship (vessel)** Schulschiff; **~ shop** Lehrlings-, Anlernwerkstatt; **~ specialist** Ausbildungsfachmann; **~ staff** Lehrpersonal; **~ subsidy** *(US)* Ausbildungsbeihilfe; **~ supervisor** Ausbildungsleiter; **~ time on job** berufliche Ausbildungszeit; **~ tour** Ausbildungsreise.
trainjacking Anhalten zum Ausrauben von Zügen.
trainload Fassungsvermögen eines Eisenbahnzuges.
trainman *(US)* Bahnangestellter.
trainmaster *(US)* Streckenmeister.
traintime Abfahrtszeit.
trainway *(ferry)* Landungsbrücke.
traipse *(v.)* herumlungern.
trait Merkmal, Eigenart, Zug;
~s in character Charaktereigenschaften.
traiteur *(fr.)* Restaurateur.
traitor to his country Landesverräter.
traitorously *(criminal law)* in hochverräterischer Absicht.
traject Eisenbahnfähre, Fähr-, Trajektschiff, *(place for passing across)* Überfahrtsstelle.
trajectory Fluglinie;
~ chart Flugbahnbild.
tram *(Br.)* Straßenbahn, *(mining)* Förderwagen, Laufkarren, Hund, *(tramcar)* Straßenbahnwagen, *(tramway rail)* Schienenstrang;
~ *(v.)* mit der Straßenbahn fahren, *(Br.)* Straßenbahn in Betrieb setzen, *(maintain a tram)* Straßenbahn unterhalten;
to go by ~ Straßenbahn nehmen;
~ shed *(Br.)* Straßenbahnschuppen; **~ shelter** Straßenbahnwartehäuschen.
tramcar *(Br.)* Straßenbahn[wagen], Triebwagen.
tramline *(Br.)* Straßenbahnlinie.
trammelled in prejudices in Vorurteilen befangen.
trammels | of etiquette Hemmschuh der Etikette; **~ of routine** Routinezwang.
trammer *(mining)* Aufladearbeiter.
tramp Vagabund, Tippelbruder, Landstreicher, Strolch, *(act of tramping)* Trampen, Fußreise, Wanderung, *(promiscuous girl, coll.)* Flittchen, *(ship)* Trampschiff, Frachtdampfer auf Trampfahrt;
~ *(v.)* Wanderleben führen, auf der Wanderschaft sein, *(vagabond)* umherstreifen, vagabundieren;
~ it trampen, zu Fuß reisen, wandern; **~ in search of employment** sich unterwegs Arbeit suchen; **~ up and down the platform** auf dem Bahnsteig auf und ab gehen;
to go for (on) a ~ auf Wanderschaft gehen;
~ ship (steamer) Trampschiff, -dampfer; **~ shipping** Trampschiffahrt; **~ shipowner** Trampreeder.
tramper Landstreicher, Vagabund.
tramping Trampschiffahrt.
trample *(v.)* herumtrampeln;
~ down the grass Gras zertrampeln; **~ law and order** öffentliche Ordnung mit den Füßen treten; **~ on s. one's feelings** jem. auf der Seele herumtrampeln; **~ out a fire** Feuer austreten.

tramroad Straßenbahnlinie.
tramstop Straßenbahnhaltestelle.
tramway *(Br.)* Straßenbahnlinie, *(mining)* Gruben-, Förderbahn; **~ advertising** Straßenbahnwerbung; **~ company** Straßenbahngesellschaft; **~ service** Straßenbahnbetrieb; **~ system** Straßenbahnnetz.
tranche Tranche, Abschnitt;
gold ~ *(International Monetary Fund)* in Gold zahlbarer Teilbetrag;
to split a loan in ~s Anleihe in Tranchen aufteilen.
Trans-Europe Express *(T.E.E.)* Transeuropaexpress.
transact *(v.)* durchführen, zustandebringen, abschließen, erledigen, abwickeln, *(negotiate)* ver-, unterhandeln, abmachen;
~ banking business of every description sämtliche Bankgeschäfte ausführen; **~ a bargain** Handel abschließen; **~ business** geschäftliche Tätigkeit ausüben; **~ a business** Geschäft abschließen, Geschäfte machen; **~ business with s. o.** in Geschäftsbeziehungen mit jem. stehen; **~ a deal** Abmachung zustandebringen; **~ with the enemy** mit dem Feind verhandeln; **~ negotiations** Verhandlungen führen und abschließen.
transacting | business Geschäftsbetrieb; **~ foreign business** Devisengeschäft.
transaction *(agreement by mutual concessions)* Übereinkunft, Abmachung, Vergleich, Vertrag, Rechtsgeschäft, *(management of business)* Verrichtung, Durchführung, *(negotiation)* Unter-, Verhandlung, Abwicklung, Erledigung, *(piece of business)* Transaktion, Geschäftsabschluß, -vorgang, -vorfall, Geschäft, Handel, geschäftliches Unternehmen, *(society)* Sitzungsbericht, *(stock exchange)* Umsatz, Abschluß, Transaktion;
for the closing of this ~ zum völligen Ausgleich dieser Sache;
pending the ~ of the business bis zur Abwicklung des Geschäftes;
~s [Geschäfts]umsätze, *(proceedings)* Sitzungs-, Verhandlungsberichte, Verhandlungen, Protokoll, *(stock exchange)* Abschlüsse, Umsätze;
administrative-managerial ~s im Verwaltungswege durchgeführte Transaktionen; **bank's ~** Banktransaktion; **banking ~** bankmäßige (banktechnische) Abwicklung, Banktransaktion; **barter ~** Tausch-, Kompensationsgeschäft; **bear ~** Baissespekulation, -geschäft; **bilateral ~** zweiseitiges Rechtsgeschäft; **break-even ~** Geschäftsabschluß ohne Gewinn und Verlust; **budgeted ~s** im Haushaltsplan vorgesehene Geschäftsabschlüsse; **bull ~** Haussespekulation, -geschäft; **capital ~** Kapitaltransaktion; **capital ~s** Kapitalverkehr; **cash ~** Transaktion gegen sofortige Kasse, Kassageschäft, Barverkauf; **cash ~s** Barumsätze; **commercial ~** Handelsgeschäft; **current ~s** laufende Geschäfte; **dummy (fictitious, pro forma) ~** Scheingeschäft; **evening-up ~** *(US)* Glattstellungsgeschäft; **exchange ~** Devisengeschäft; **executed ~** abgeschlossenes Geschäft; **external ~** Auslandsgeschäft; **few ~s** *(stock exchange)* geringe Umsätze; **financial ~** Geldgeschäft, Finanztransaktion; **foreign ~** Auslandsgeschäft; **foreign exchange ~** Devisengeschäft; **forward ~** Sicht-, Termingeschäft; **illicit ~** unerlaubtes Rechtsgeschäft; **interassociation ~s** *(US)* verbandseigene Geschäfte, konzerneigene Umsätze, Umsätze innerhalb des Konzerns; **invisible ~** unsichtbare Umsätze; **legal ~** Rechtsgeschäft; **long-term ~s** Geschäftsabschlüsse auf lange Sicht; **market ~** Börsengeschäft, -transaktion; **mercantile ~** Handelsgeschäft, geschäftliche Transaktion; **monetary ~s** Geldgeschäfte; **open-market credit ~s** Transaktionen auf dem offenen Markt; **paying ~** rentables Geldgeschäft; **protected ~** *(law of bankruptcy)* nicht der Konkursanfechtung unterliegendes Rechtsgeschäft; **round ~** abgeschlossenes Börsengeschäft; **security ~** *(stock exchange)* Effektentransaktion; **service ~s** Dienstleistungsverkehr; **simulated ~** Scheingeschäft; **speculative ~** Spekulationsgeschäft; **stock-exchange ~s** Börsenumsätze, Effektengeschäfte; **spot ~** Loko-, Effektiv-, Kassa-, Platzgeschäft; **spot exchange ~** Kassageschäft in Devisen; **stockbroking ~** Effektengeschäft; **taxable ~** steuerpflichtiges [Rechts]geschäft; **trade ~** geschäftliche Transaktion; **ultra vires ~** Geschäftstransaktion außerhalb der satzungsmäßigen Befugnisse; **unprotected ~s** *(law of bankruptcy)* der Konkursanfechtung unterliegende Rechtsgeschäfte; **void ~** nichtiges Rechtsgeschäft; **voided ~** angefochtenes Rechtsgeschäft;
~ for the account *(Br.)* [Börsen]termingeschäft; **~ for own account** Geschäft für eigene Rechnung; **~s for third account** Geschäfte für fremde Rechnungen (auf Kommissionsbasis), Kommissionshandel, -geschäfte, Fremdgeschäfte; **~s amounting to several million pounds** Transaktionen in Höhe mehrerer Millionen Pfund; **~ of business** Geschäftsbetrieb; **~ of a socie-**

ty's business Verwaltungsarbeit eines Vereins; ~ **for cash** Bargeschäft; ~ **contra bonus mores** sittenwidriges Rechtsgeschäft; ~ **on credit** Kreditgeschäft; ~ **for future delivery** *(commodity market)* Termingeschäft; ~s **of a firm** Firmenumsatz; ~s **in gold** Goldtransaktionen; ~ **in goods** Warenabschluß; ~s **in goods** Warenverkehr; ~s **at the insurance office** Versicherungsabschlüsse; ~s **contrary to the policy of the law** sittenwidrige Geschäfte; ~s **not protected** konkursrechtlich anfechtbare Rechtsgeschäfte; ~s **in securities** Effekten-, Wertpapierumsätze; ~ **in services** Dienstleistungsverkehr; ~ **for the settlement** *(Br.)* [Börsen]termingeschäft; ~s **at the stock exchange** Börsenabschlüsse, -umsätze; ~s **in syndicate** Konsortialgeschäfte; ~ **for value** entgeltliches Rechtsgeschäft; ~s **inter vivos** Rechtsgeschäfte unter Lebenden;

to avoid a ~ Rechtsgeschäft anfechten; **to become mixed up in shady** ~s in zweifelhafte Geschäfte verwickelt werden; **to carry on illegal** ~s ungesetzlichen Geschäften nachgehen; **to disclose secret** ~s vertrauliche Geschäftsabschlüsse offenlegen; **to effect** ~s Abschlüsse tätigen, Transaktionen durchführen; **to effect exchange** ~s Abschlüsse in Devisen tätigen, Devisengeschäfte machen; **to enter into a** ~ Geschäft abschließen; **to indulge in illicit** ~s unerlaubte Geschäfte machen; **to leave the** ~ **of a matter to s. o.** jem. die Abwicklung einer Angelegenheit überlassen; **to record** ~s Geschäftsvorfälle aufzeichnen; **to set aside a** ~ Geschäft rückgängig machen; **to spend much time on the** ~ **of the society's business** viel Zeit für die Erledigung der Vereinsangelegenheiten aufwenden;

~ **motive** Geschäftsmotiv; ~ **record** Geschäftsbeleg; ~ **reference number** *(bookstore)* Verkehrsnummer; ~ **and sale regulations of the book trade** Verkehrs- und Verkaufsordnung des Buchhandels; ~ **summary** Zusammenstellung der einzelnen Geschäftstransaktionen; ~ **tax** *(Br.)* Umsatzsteuer.

transactional Geschäftsabschlüsse betreffend.

transactor Unterhändler.

transatlantic überseeisch, transatlantisch;
~ **cable** Überseekabel; ~ **flight** Ozeanflug; ~ **liner (ship)** Ozean, Überseedampfer; ~ **rate** Überseetarif; ~ **transport** Überseetransport; ~ **voyage** Überseereise.

transceiver Sende- und Telefongerät, Funktelefon.

transcend *(v.)* | **one's competition** seine Konkurrenten überflügeln; ~ **one's instructions** seine Anweisungen überschreiten.

transcendent quality hervorragende Qualität.

transcribe *(v.)* abschreiben, kopieren, *(bookkeeping)* übertragen, *(broadcasting)* übertragen, aufnehmen, aufzeichnen, *(make abstract)* Abschrift herstellen, *(shorthand notes)* aus dem Stenogramm in Kurrent-, Maschinenschrift übertragen.

transcribe *(v.)* **a program(me)** *(broadcasting)* Programm aufnehmen.

transcript Nieder-, Abschrift, Kopie, *(official copy)* Verhandlungsbericht, -protokoll, *(radio)* Aufzeichnung, Tonaufnahme;
~ **of a bill** Wechselabschrift; ~ **of a legal document** Ausfertigung einer öffentlichen Urkunde; ~ **of evidence** Beweisprotokoll; ~ **of record** Aktenabschrift; **typewritten** ~ **of a speech** Übertragung einer stenografisch aufgenommenen Rede in Schreibmaschinenschrift.

transcription Umschreibung, Abschrift, Kopie, Übertragung, *(broadcasting)* Aufzeichnung, Tonbandaufnahme, *(tape recording)* Tonbandaufnahme;
in ~ in Abschrift;
electrical ~ Elektroaufnahme;
to make ~s Tonbandaufnahmen machen, aufzeichnen;
~ **program(me) library** Schallplatten- und Tonbandarchiv; ~ **service** Aufzeichnungseinrichtung; ~ **turntable** Abspieltisch.

transfer *(amount carried forward)* Übertrag, Umbuchung, *(assignment)* Abtretung, Zession, Zedierung, Übertragung, -lassung, *(business)* [Geschäfts]übergabe, *(changing the train)* Umsteigen, *(conveyance)* Beförderung, *(deed)* Übertragungsurkunde, *(devolution of title)* Eigentumsübergang, *(official)* Versetzung, Überstellung, *(point on railway line, mar.)* Umschlagplatz, *(print.)* Umdruck, Umdrucken, Abzug, *(railroad ticket, US)* Umsteiger, Umsteigefahrschein, *(remittance)* Überweisung, Anweisung, Transfer[ierung], *(removal of business)* Geschäftsverlegung, *(securities)* Umschreibung, Transfer, Übertragung, -schreibung, *(~ company)* Transportgesellschaft;
absolute ~ uneingeschränkte Übertragung; **bank** ~ Banküberweisung; **blank** ~ *(Br.)* Blankoübertragung, Blankoindossament, -giro; **cable** ~ Drahtüberweisung, telegrafische Überweisung, Kabelauszahlung; **cashless money** ~ *(US)* bargeldloser Zahlungsverkehr; **conditional** ~ an Bedingungen

geknüpfte Übertragung; **credit** ~ Überweisung zu Lasten des Kontoinhabers; **currency** ~ Devisentransfer; **forcible** ~ *(law of nations)* Vertreibung; **fraudulent** ~ Vermögensübertragung zwecks Gläubigerbenachteiligung; **improper** ~ ungültige Übertragung; **interbank money** ~ Überweisungsverkehr; **mail** ~ Überweisung durch die Post, Postüberweisung, briefliche Auszahlung; **money** ~ Geldüberweisung; **money** ~s Geldverkehr; **official** ~s staatliche Transferzahlungen; **staff** ~s Versetzungen; **telegraphic** ~ telegraphische Überweisung (Auszahlung);
~ **into an account** Überweisung auf ein Konto; ~ **to another account** Kontoumbuchung; ~ **of assets** Vermögens-, Anlagenübertragung; ~ **of balance** Saldoübertrag; ~ **for the benefit of creditors** Eigentumsumschreibung zugunsten der Gläubiger; ~ **of business** Geschäftsübertragung, -verlegung, Übertragung eines Geschäfts; ~ **of capital** Kapitaltransfer, -übertrag, *(balance sheet)* Überweisung auf das Kapitalkonto; ~ **of capital gains** Übertragung von Veräußerungsgewinnen; ~ **of a case to another court** Verweisung eines Rechtsstreits an ein anderes Gericht; ~ **in contemplation of death** zwecks Erbschaftsregelung vorgenommene Übertragung; ~ **to foreign countries** Transferzahlungen; ~ **on death** Eigentumsübertragung von Todes wegen; ~ **of debentures** *(Br.)* Übertragung von Obligationen; ~ **of a debt** Forderungsabtretung, Abtretung einer Forderung; ~ **for disciplinary reasons** Strafversetzung; ~ **of domicile** Wohnsitzverlegung; ~ **of expectancy** Anwartschaftsübertragung; ~ **of a factory** Fabrikverlagerung, Verlegung einer Fabrik; ~s **by foreign employees** Überweisungen ausländischer Arbeitnehmer; ~ **of foreign exchange** Devisentransfer; ~ **to foreign giro system** Überweisung auf ausländische Postscheckkonten; ~ **of funds** Mittelübertragung; ~ **of funds abroad** Überweisungen ins Ausland; ~ **under hand** Aktienübertragung unter Parteien; ~ **of income** Einkommensübertragung; ~ **to avoid income tax** Eigentumsübertragung zur Umgehung der Einkommensteuer; ~ **of interest** Anteilsübertragung; ~ **of land** Grundstücksübertragung, Auflassung; ~ **of liabilities** Schuldenübertragung; ~ **in lieu of cash** Überweisung an Zahlungs Statt; ~ **on London** Auszahlung London; ~ **of losses from affiliates** Aufwendungen aus Verlustübernahme von Konzerngesellschaften; ~ **by operation of law** gesetzlicher Forderungs-, Rechtsübergang; ~ **of ownership** Eigentumsübertragung; ~ **of personnel** Personalumsetzungen; ~ **of population** Bevölkerungsverschiebungen; ~ **of possession** Besitzverschaffung; ~ **of actual possession** tatsächlicher Besitzübergang; ~ **of power** Machtübergang; ~ **of prisoners** Gefangenenverlegung; ~ **of property** Eigentums-, Vermögensübertragung; **fraudulent** ~ **of property** Gesamtübertragung des Schuldnervermögens zwecks Gläubigerbenachteiligung; ~ **of real estate** *(US)* Grundstücksübertragung; ~ **to reserve** Rückstellung, Rücklagenzuführung; ~ **to special reserves** Einstellungen in Sonderposten mit Rücklageanteil; ~s **from special reserves** Erträge aus der Auflösung von Sonderposten mit Rücklageanteil; ~ **to the reserve fund** Überweisung an den Reservefonds, Rücklagenzuführung; ~s **to surplus reserves** *(balance sheet)* Einstellungen in die offenen Rücklagen; ~s **from surplus reserves** *(balance sheet)* Entnahmen aus den offenen Rücklagen; ~ **of residence** Wohnsitzverlegung; ~ **of resources** Transferierung von Vermögenswerten; ~ **of risk** Gefahrübergang; ~ **of salaries** Gehaltsüberweisung; ~ **under seal** Aktienübertragung mit Gesellschaftssiegel; ~s **of securities** Effektenübertragung; ~ **of shares** *(Br.)* **(stocks,** *US***)** Aktienumschreibung, -übertragung, Depotumbuchung; ~ **of title** Eigentumsübertragung, Übereignung; ~ **of wealth** Vermögensübertragung; ~ **by will** Eigentumsübergang aufgrund einer letztwilligen Verfügung;
~ *(v.)* *(assign)* abtreten, zedieren, übereignen, -tragen, *(convey)* befördern, *(deliver)* übergeben, *(displace employees)* [Angestellte] versetzen, überstellen, *(negotiate)* begeben, *(securities)* umbuchen, *(tel.)* durchverbinden, -stellen, *(title)* auflassen;
~ **to another account (from one account to another)** umbuchen, Umbuchung vornehmen, ristornieren; ~ **back** zurücküberweisen; ~ **baggage from the station** Gepäck vom Bahnhof abholen; ~ **a bank** Geschäftssitz einer Bank verlegen; ~ **a business** Geschäftssitz verlegen; ~ **a case to another court** Sache an ein anderes Gericht verweisen; ~ **foreign currency** Devisen transferieren; ~ **debentures** *(Br.)* Obligationen übertragen; ~ **a debt** Schuldforderung übertragen; ~ **a drawing to a lithographic plate** Zeichnung auf eine lithographische Platte übertragen; ~ **by endorsement (indorsement)** durch Indossament (Giro) übertragen; ~ **entries** umbuchen, Posten [auf einem Konto] austragen; ~ **a factory to a suburb** Fabrik in einen Vorort verlagern; ~ **to the reserve fund** dem Reservefonds zuführen (zuweisen);

land Grundstück auflassen; ~ **a line** *(terminal)* Zeile wegschicken; ~ **money to s. o.** jem. Geld überweisen; ~ **money to an account** Geld auf ein Konto überweisen; ~ **money by cable (telegraph)** telegrafisch Geld überweisen; ~ **an office** Geschäftssitz verlegen; ~ **a passenger from one class to another** Reisenden in eine andere Klasse überwechseln lassen; ~ **to new premises** in neue Geschäftsräume verlegen; ~ **profit to low-tax countries** Gewinne in Länder mit niedrigen Steuersätzen transferieren; ~ **property** Vermögen übertragen; ~ **for disciplinary reasons** strafversetzen; ~ **s. o. to an infantry regiment** j. zur Infanterie versetzen; ~ **to reserves** den Rücklagen zuführen; ~ **one's residence** seinen Wohnsitz verlegen; ~ **a right to s. o.** Recht auf j. übertragen; ~ **a civil servant** Beamten versetzen; ~ **shares** *(Br.)* **(stocks,** *US)* **into the bank's name** Aktien auf den Namen der Bank überschreiben lassen; ~ **a title to land** Grundeigentum übertragen;

to effect a ~ in the books Übertragung in den Büchern vornehmen, umbuchen; **to get a ~** versetzt werden; **to pass up** ~ auf Umsiedlung verzichten; **to stamp up the** ~ Übertragungsurkunde abstempeln;

~ **account** Transferkonto, Girokonto; ~ **agent** *(US)* Transferagent, Umschreibestelle für Aktien; ~ **agreement** Transferabkommen; **bilateral** ~ **agreement** zweiseitiges Verrechnungsabkommen; ~ **allowance** *(US)* Umzugskostenbeihilfe; ~ **balance** Umstellungsbilanz; ~ **bank** Girobank; ~ **book** *(Br.)* Umschreibungsbuch [einer AG]; ~ **business** Überweisungsverkehr; ~ **case** Aktenschrank für abgelegte Korrespondenz; ~ **certificate** *(Br.)* Übertragungsschein, -urkunde; ~ **check** *(US)* **(cheque,** *Br.)* Überweisungsscheck; ~ **commission** Überweisungsprovision; ~ **committee** Reparationsausschuß; ~ **company** Speditionsgesellschaft, Bahnhofspediteur; **local** ~ **company** örtlicher Spediteur; ~ **costs** Verlagerungskosten; ~ **credit** *(US)* Überweisung zu Lasten des Kreditkontos; ~ **day** *(securities)* Eintragungs-, Umschreibungstag; ~ **deed** *(Br.)* Übertragungs-, Zessionsurkunde, Begebungsvertrag, *(title deed)* Auflassungsurkunde; ~ **deposit form** Postscheck. überweisungsformular; ~ **depot** *(US)* Übergangsstation; ~ **duty** Umschreibung-, Stempelgebühr; ~ **earnings** *(factor of production)* Normal-, Opportunitätseinkommen; ~ **entry** Übertragung, Übertrag; ~ **expense** Transfer-, Übertragungsspesen; ~ **fee** Übertragungs-, Transfer-, Umschreibungsgebühr, *(professional footballer)* Auslösungssumme; ~ **form** *(shares, Br.)* Umschreibungs-, Übertragungsformular; ~ **income** Transfereinkommen; ~ **moratorium** Transfermoratorium; ~ **office** Umschreibungsbüro; ~ **order** *(Br.)* Überweisungsauftrag; ~ **paper** *(lithography, Br.)* Umdruck-, Überdruckpapier; ~ **payment** Transfer-, Unterstützungszahlung; ~ **picture** Abziehbild; ~ **point** Umschlagplatz; ~ **price (rate)** *(Br.)* Tages-, Übernahmekurs; ~ **pricing** *(Br.)* Übernahmekursfestsetzung; ~ **problem** Transferproblem; ~ **receipt** *(Br.)* [aktienrechtliche] Übertragungsquittung; ~ **register** *(Br.)* Umschreibungs-, Übertragungsregister; ~ **remittance** telegraphische Vergütung; ~ **restrictions** Transfer-, Überweisungsbeschränkungen; ~ **slip** Überweisungsformular, -träger; ~ **stamp** *(Br.)* Effekten-, Übertragungsstempel; ~ **stamp duty** Umschreibegebühr, *(stock exchange, Br.)* Stempelgebühr; ~ **stamp tax** *(Br.)* [etwa] Kapitalverkehrsteuer; ~ **station** *(railway)* Umladestation; **capital** ~ **tax** *(Br.)* Erbschafts- und Schenkungsteuer; ~ **securities** ~ **tax** *(US)* Börsenumsatzsteuer; ~ **tax mitigation** *(US)* Erbschaftssteuerermäßigung; ~ **theory** Theorie der außerwirtschaftlichen Wertübertragung; ~ **ticket** *(banking)* Verrechnungs-, Überweisungsscheck, Übertragungsschein, Überweisungsformular, -träger [im Verrechnungsverfahren], -schein, *(railway)* Übergangsfahrschein, Anschluß-, Umsteigefahrkarte, Umsteiger; ~ **value** Übergabewert; ~ **voucher** Übertragungsbeleg; ~ **warrant** Umschreibungszertifikat.

transferable übertragbar, abtretbar, *(negotiable)* begebbar, *(share)* umschreibbar;

freely ~ frei (formlos) übertragbar; **not** ~ nicht übertragbar, auf den Namen lautend;

~ **account** *(Br.)* frei transferierbares Devisenkonto; ~ **vote** [auf anderen Kandidaten] übertragbare Wahlstimme.

transferee Zessionar, Transferbegünstigter, Überweisungsempfänger, Übernehmer, Erwerber, Rechtsnachfolger, *(official)* Versetzter, *(securities)* [Erwerber] von Wertpapieren, neuer Empfänger (Käufer), Indossatar;

~ **of a bill of exchange** Wechselübernehmer, Indossatar; ~ **of shares** Aktienerwerber;

~ **company** übernehmende Gesellschaft.

transference Übertragung, Transferierung, *(legacy)* Legatsübertragung, *(stock)* Umschreibung.

transferor Transferent, Übertragender, Abtretender, Weitergeber, Zedent, *(bill)* Indossant;

~ **of shares** Aktienverkäufer;

~ **company** übertragende Gesellschaft.

transferrer Übertragender, *(technical)* Umdrucker.

transform *(v.)* umwandeln, -formen, gestalten, *(el.)* umspannen.

transformation Umwandlung, *(el.)* Umspannung, Umformung.

transformer *(el.)* Transformator.

transfrontier merger grenzüberschreitende Fusion.

transfuse *(v.)* | **blood** Blut übertragen; ~ **principles into s. o.** jem. Grundsätze einprägen.

transfusion, blood Bluttransfusion.

transgress *(v.)* übertreten, -schreiten, verstoßen, verletzen;

~ **the bounds of decency** gegen ungeschriebene Gesetze verstoßen; ~ **one's competence** seine Befugnisse überschreiten; ~ **the law** Gesetz übertreten; ~ **a rule** gegen eine Regel verstoßen; ~ **a treaty** Vertrag verletzten.

transgression Überschreitung, -tretung, Rechtsverletzung.

transgressor Übertreter, Missetäter.

trans(s)hip *(v.)* umschlagen, umladen;

~ **to another vessel** auf ein anderes Schiff umladen.

trans(s)hipment Umladung, Umschlag;

~ **of roll-on, roll-off containers** Umschlag von im Huckepackverkehr eingesetzten Containern;

~ **bill of lading** Umladekonnossement; ~ **bond (delivery note)** Umladeschein, Zolldurchfuhrschein; ~ **centre** Umschlagzentrum; ~ **charge** Umschlag-, Umladegebühr; ~ **harbo(u)r** Umschlaghafen; ~ **point** Umschlagplatz; ~ **traffic** Umlade-, Umschlagverkehr.

trans(s)hipping | **line** Umladegleis; ~ **platform** Umladebühne; ~ **port** Umschlaghafen; ~ **shed** Umladeschuppen; ~ **station** Umschlags-, Umladestation; ~ **traffic** Umschlagverkehr.

transient *(US)* Durchreisender;

~ *(a.)* vorübergehend, *(person)* ohne festen Wohnsitz, transit; ~ **agreement** befristetes Abkommen; ~ **business** *(US)* Transit-, Zwischenhandel; ~ **current** *(el.)* Ausgleichstrom; ~ **foreigner** ausländischer Tourist; ~ **glance** flüchtiger Blick; ~ **guest** *(US)* Durchreisender, Passant; ~ **hotel** *(US)* Passanten-, Durchgangshotel; ~ **interest** vorübergehendes Interesse; ~ **lodger** Durchreisender, vorübergehender Pensionär; ~ **merchant** Wandergewerbetreibender; ~ **periodicals and newspapers** *(US)* einmalig zugesandte Zeitschriften; ~ **person** Person ohne festen Wohnsitz; ~ **rate** *(advertising)* Einzelinsertionstarif; ~ **ship** nicht regelmäßig fahrendes Schiff; ~ **vendor** Zwischenhändler; ~ **visitor** *(US)* durchreisender Passant, Durchreisender.

transire *(Br.)* Zollbegleitschein, -durchlaß-, Passierschein;

to have a permit for ~ mit Zolldurchlaßschein passieren.

transistor Transistor;

~ **radio** Transistorgerät.

transistorize *(v.)* mit Transistoren ausrüsten.

transit *(passage)* Durchfahrt, Überfahrt, Durchfuhr, Durchfuhr verkehr, Durchgang, Transit, Transport, *(air traffic)* Durchflug, Überfliegen, *(route)* Durchgangsstraße, -verkehr, Verkehrsstraße, -weg, *(trade)* Zwischenhandel;

damaged in ~ auf dem Transport (unterwegs) beschädigt; **in** ~ unterwegs, auf dem Transport, *(customs)* im Transit; **lost in** ~ auf dem Transport verlorengegangen;

~**s** Durchgangswaren;

international ~ internationaler Transitverkehr; **overland** ~ Überlandverkehr; **rapid** ~ *(US)* Schnellverkehr; **sea** ~ Überseetransport;

rapid ~ **from city to city** *(US)* Nahschnellverkehr; ~ **of goods** Warentransit; ~ **of persons** Personenverkehr; ~ **by rail** Bahntransport; ~ **by sea** [Über]seetransport;

~ *(v.)* durchschreiten, überqueren; **to be in** ~ durchlaufen, -gehen; **to be delayed in** ~ Transportverzögerungen erfahren; **to convey goods in** ~ Waren im Durchgangsverkehr abfertigen; **to enter goods as** ~ Waren durchdeklarieren, Waren als Durchgangsgut angeben; **to pass in** ~ im Transit durchlaufen, transitieren;

~ **account** Transit-, Übergangskonto; ~ **agent** Durchführ-, Zwischenspediteur; ~ **Authorization Certificate** Durchführ-, Transitschein; ~ **bill** Durchfuhr-, Durchgangsschein; ~ **bond** Transit-, Durchfuhrschein; ~ **call** *(tel.)* Durchgangsgespräch; ~ **camp** Durchfuhr-, Durchgangslager; ~ **car** Kurs-, Durchgangswagen; ~ **cargo** Durchgangsfracht, Transitladung; ~ **certificate** Durchfuhr-, Passierschein; ~ **charges** Transit-, Durchgangsgebühren; ~ **clerk** *(US)* Beamter für Inkassi auf auswärtigen Plätzen; ~ **costs** Transitkosten; ~ **country** Durchfuhrland; ~ **department** *(US)* Abteilung für Inkassi auf auswärtigen Plätzen; ~ **dispatch** Transitversand; ~ **duty** Durchgangs-, Durchfuhr-, Transitzoll, Durchgangs-, Transitabgabe; ~ **entries** durchlaufende Buchungen; ~ **entry** *(customs)* Durchfuhr-, Transiterklärung; ~ **exchange of correspondence** Transitverkehr; ~ **floater** *(marine insurance)* Pauschalversicherungspolice; ~ **freight** Durch[gangs]fracht, Transitladung; ~ **goods** Transitgüter, -waren, Durchfuhrgut; ~ **hall** Durchgangshalle; ~ **hotel** Durchgangs-, Passantenhotel; ~ **insurance** Gütertransportversicherung; ~ **mail service** *(US)* Durchgangspostverkehr; ~ **number** *(banking)* Bankleitzahl; ~ **pass** Passierschein, Durchfahrterlaubnis; ~ **permit** Durchfuhrbescheinigung, -genehmigung, -bewilligung, Transiterlaubnis; ~ **point** Durchgangsplatz; ~ **privilege** Anspruch auf Beförderung zu verbilligten Frachtsätzen, Transitvergünstigung; ~ **rate** verbilligter Frachttarif für Durchgangsgüter, Durchfuhr-, Transittarif; ~ **route** Durchgangsstraße; ~ **shed** Zoll[durchgangs]schuppen; ~ **station** Übergangsbahnhof; ~ **storehouse** Transitlager; ~ **time** Umlaufzeit; ~ **trade** Transit-, Durchgangshandel, Transit-, Durchfuhrverkehr; ~ **traffic** Durchgangs-, Transit-, Übergangsverkehr; ~ **visa** Durchreisevisum; ~ **worker** Transportarbeiter.

transition Übergang, -leitung, *(period)*, Übergangszeit, -periode, -phase, -stadium;

frequent ~ from cold to warm weather häufiger Wechsel von kaltem zu warmem Wetter;

to be in a state of ~ sich in einem Übergangsstadium befinden; **to undergo a** ~ Übergangszeit durchmachen;

~ **period** Übergangszeit, -periode, -phase; ~ **probability** Übergangswahrscheinlichkeit; ~ **provisions** Überleitungs-, Übergangsbestimmungen; ~ **stage (state)** Übergangsstadium.

transitional | arrangement Übergangsregelung; ~ **government** Übergangsregierung; ~ **loan** Überbrückungskredit; ~ **measures** Übergangsmaßnahmen; ~ **payment** *(unemployment insurance)* Überbrückungszahlungen; ~ **period** Übergangsphase, -zeit, -periode; ~ **provisions** Übergangsbestimmungen; ~ **solution** Übergangslösung; ~ **year** Übergangsjahr.

transitive covenant auch für die Nachfolger verbindlicher Vertrag.

transitory vorübergehend, interimistisch, vergänglich, flüchtig, *(balance sheet)* transitorisch, *(passing from place to place)* nicht ortsgebunden;

~ **account** Durchlaufkonto; ~ **action** *(US)* transitorische (an keinen Gerichtsstand gebundene) Klage; ~ **credit** durchlaufender Kredit; ~ **income** transitorisches Einkommen; ~ **item** *(balance sheet)* transitorischer Posten, Durchlauf-, Rechnungsabgrenzungsposten; ~ **period** Übergangsphase, -zeit; ~ **provisions** Übergangsbestimmungen; ~ **stage** Übergangsstadium; ~ **stay** Zwischenaufenthalt; ~ **treaty** Übergangsabkommen.

translatable übersetzbar, übertragbar.

translate *(v.)* übersetzen, -tragen, *(v./i.)* sich zur Übersetzung eignen, *(clothes)* umarbeiten, *(foreign exchange)* Gegenwert bestimmen, *(interpret)* auslegen, erklären, interpretieren;

~ **an English book into French** englisches Buch ins Französische übersetzen; ~ **ideas into actions** Gedanken in die Tat umsetzen; ~ **s. th. as a protest** etw. als Protest auslegen; ~ **without the sanction of the author** ohne Genehmigung des Autors übersetzen; ~ **s. one's silence as refusal** jds. Stillschweigen als Ablehnung auslegen; ~ **talk into action** Worte in Taten umsetzen; ~ **a telegram** Telegramm weiterleiten (dechiffrieren); ~ **well** *(book)* sich sehr gut übersetzen lassen.

translating bureau *(US)* Übersetzungsbüro.

translation Übersetzung, Übertragung, Wiedergabe, *(cable)* Dechiffrierung, *(civil law)* Eigentumsübertragung, *(exercise)* Übersetzungsaufgabe, *(interpretation)* Erklärung, Auslegung; **authentic** ~ maßgebliche Übersetzung; **close** ~ wortgetreue Übersetzung; **free** ~ freie Übersetzung; **literal** ~ wörtliche Übersetzung; **loose** ~ ungenaue Übersetzung; **machine-aided** ~ maschinell unterstützte Übersetzung; **near** ~ sinngetreue Übersetzung; **poor** ~ schlechte Übersetzung; **rough** ~ Rohübersetzung; **word-for-word** ~ [wort]wörtliche Übersetzung;

~ **from German into English** Übertragung vom Deutschen ins Englische; ~ **of a telegram** Weiterleitung eines Telegrammes;

to do (make) a ~ Übersetzung anfertigen;

~ **agency** Übersetzungsbüro; **technical** ~ **aid** maschinelle Übersetzungsschrift; ~ **charge** Übersetzungsgebühr; ~ **exercise** Übersetzungsübung; **official** ~ **expert for the courts** vereidigter Gerichtsdolmetscher.

translator Übersetzer;

free-lance ~ freiberuflicher Übersetzer; **sworn** ~ öffentlich bestellter und vereidigter Übersetzer.

translight *(advertising)* Transparent.
translocate *(v.)* versetzen, *(industry)* aus-, verlagern.
translocation Ortsveränderung, Versetzung;
police ~ Ausweisung;
~ **of industry** Industrieverlagerung.
transmarine überseeisch.
transmigrant Durchreisender.
transmigrate *(v.)* übersiedeln, auswandern.
transmigration Übersiedlung, Auswanderung;
~ **of the soul** Seelenwanderung.
transmigrator Übersiedler, Auswanderer.
transmigratory auswandernd, übersiedelnd.
transmissable übertragbar.
transmission Überbringung, -sendung, -mittlung, Beförderung, Versand, *(heir)* Vererbung des Erbrechts, *(technics)* Transmission, Übersetzung, -tragung, *(television)* Fernsehübertragung, *(wireless)* Rundfunkübertragung, -sendung;
for onward ~ zur Weiterleitung;
automatic ~ automatisches Getriebe; **broadcast** ~ Rundfunkübertragung;
~ **of a claim** Forderungsübergang; ~ **on death** Übergang von Todes wegen; ~ **of disease** Übertragung einer Krankheit; ~ **of documents** Übergabe der Dokumente; ~ **of freight** Frachtgutbeförderung; ~ **of goods** Warenversand, Spedition; ~ **of money** Geldüberweisung; ~ **of news** Nachrichtenübermittlung; ~ **by operation of law** gesetzlicher Rechtsübergang; ~ **by radio** Rundfunkübertragung; ~ **of rights** Rechtsübertragung; ~ **of shares** *(Br.)* Übertragung von Aktien eines Verstorbenen [durch den Nachlaßverwalter]; ~ **of a telegram** Telegrammbeförderung; ~ **of a television program(me)** Übertragung einer Fernsehsendung; ~ **of a text** Textübertragung;
~ **belt** Treibriemen; ~ **business** Speditionsgeschäft, -handel; ~ **cable** Übertragungskabel; ~ **case** Getriebegehäuse; ~ **gear** Wechselgetriebe; ~ **line** Überlandleitung; ~ **loss** *(el.)* Übertragungsverlust; ~ **ratio** Übersetzungsverhältnis; ~ **shaft** Getriebewelle; ~ **system** Übertragungssystem.
transmit *(v.)* *(broadcast)* [durch Rundfunk] übertragen, *(communicate)* mitteilen, weitergeben, überliefern, *(forward)* befördern, schicken, senden, *(remit)* übersenden, transferieren, *(television)* senden, *(transfer)* übertragen, überschreiben;
~ **baggage** *(US)* Gepäck befördern; ~ **a disease** Krankheit übertragen; ~ **electricity** *(metal)* Elektrizität leiten; ~ **a faculty** Fähigkeit vererben; ~ **a message** Botschaft übermitteln; ~ **news** Nachrichten übermitteln; ~ **onward** weiterleiten; ~ **an order** Auftrag übermitteln; ~ **a parcel to s. o.** jem. ein Paket schicken; ~ **property** Besitz übertragen; ~ **one's property by will** sein Vermögen testamentarisch vermachen; ~ **a telegram** Telegramm befördern; ~ **by wireless** durch Funk übertragen.
transmittable übertragbar.
transmittal letter Begleitbrief.
transmitted | credit durchgeleiteter Kredit; ~ **telegram** übermitteltes Telegramm, Durchgangstelegramm.
transmitter Übersender, -mittler, Weitersender, *(broadcasting)* Rundfunksender, -station, *(tel.)* Mikrophon, *(telegraph)* Sendegerät, Sender;
secret ~ Geheimsender;
~ **of goods** Warenabsender;
~ **site** Senderstandort.
transmitting | aerial (antenna) Sendeantenne; ~ **power** Sendestärke; ~ **set** *(broadcasting)* Sendegerät, Sender; ~ **station** Sender, Sendestelle; ~ **studio** Sendestudio.
transnational übernational.
transoceanic überseeisch;
~ **flight** Ozeanflug, Ozeanüberfliegung; ~ **steamer** Überseedampfer.
transom Oberlicht[fenster].
transonic speed Überschallgeschwindigkeit.
transparency Durchsichtigkeit, Transparenz, *(US)* Abziehplakat, *(photo)* Diapositiv;
~ **in business practices** Bilanztransparenz; ~ **of the tax system** Transparenz des Steuersystems.
transparent durchsichtig, transparent, *(fig.)* rein, offen, ehrlich;
~ **colo(u)r** Lasierfarbe; ~ **flattery** leich zu durchschauende Schmeichelei; ~ **style** klarer Stil.
transpire *(v.)* *(fig.)* durchsickern, verlauten, ruchbar werden, verlautbaren.
transplant *(population)* Umsiedlung;
~ *(v.)* umsiedeln, *(med.)* transplantieren.
transplantation Umsiedlung, *(transplanted group)* Umsiedlungsgruppe;
kidney ~ Nierenverpflanzung, -transplation.

transport *(airplane)* Transportflugzeug, *(amount carried forward)* Übertrag, -schreibung, *(on board ship)* Verschiffung, *(convict)* Deportierter, *(forwarding)* Beförderung, Verfrachtung, Verschiffung, Transport, Überführung, Versand, Spedition, *(freighter)* Frachtschiff, Frachter, *(means of conveyance)* Beförderungsmittel, *(mil.)* Truppentransporter, *(traffic)* Verkehr, Verkehrswesen, *(transportation)* Transportwesen;
by public ~ mit öffentlichen Verkehrsmitteln; **without ~** ohne Auto;
air ~ Beförderung auf dem Luftwege, Luftverkehr; **commercial scheduled air ~** *(US)* planmäßiger gewerblicher Luftverkehr; **aircraft ~** Luft-, Frachtverkehr; **collective ~** Sammeltransport; **door-to-door ~** Beförderung von Haus zu Haus; **fare-free ~** Nulltarif; **fixed-track ~** Schienenverkehr; **inland (intercity, US)** Binnenverkehr; **inland water ~** *(US)* Binnenschiffahrtsverkehr; **interstate ~** *(US)* zwischenstaatlicher Güterverkehr; **intrastate ~** *(US)* innerstaatlicher Güterverkehr; **land ~** Beförderungen auf dem Landwege; **long-distance ~** Fernverkehr; **marine (maritime) ~** Beförderung auf dem Seewege, Seetransport; **motor-truck ~** Beförderung mit dem Lastkraftwagen, Lastwagen-, Kraftwagenverkehr; **ocean ~** Transport im Überseeverkehr, Transatlantikverkehr; **passenger ~** Personenbeförderung, -verkehr; **public ~** öffentlicher Verkehr, *(vehicle)* öffentliche Verkehrsmittel; **rail ~** *(Br.)* Eisenbahngüterverkehr; **railway ~** *(Br.)* Bahntransport; **railway passenger ~** *(Br.)* Eisenbahnpersonenverkehr; **road ~** *(Br.)* Beförderung per Achse, Straßentransport, Güterverkehr mit Lastwagen; **sea ~** Beförderung auf dem Seewege, Seetransport; **short-distance ~** Nahverkehr; **subsequent ~** Weiterbeförderung; **troop ~** Truppentransporte, -flugzeug; **waterborne ~** Beförderung auf dem Wasserweg;
~ by air Luftverkehr, Beförderung auf dem Luftwege; **~ in bulk** Massenbeförderung; **~ and communications** Verkehrs- und Nachrichtenwesen; **~ of goods by rail** *(Br.)* Eisenbahngüterverkehr; **~ of goods by road** *(Br.)* Güterverkehr mit Lastwagen, Straßengüterverkehr; **~ of mail** Postbeförderung; **~ of merchandise** Waren-, Gütertransport; **~ by rail** *(Br.)* Transport per Bahn, Bahnbeförderung, Eisenbahnverkehr; **~ of troops by air** Truppenverlegung auf dem Luftwege;
~ (v.) transportieren, befördern, versenden, *(ship)* verschiffen; **~ a criminal** Strafgefangenen (Häftling) deportieren (abschieben); **~ goods by truck (lorry)** Güter verfrachten; **~ mail by airplane** per Luftpost (Post mit dem Flugzeug) befördern; **~ material** Material heranschaffen; **~ troops by boat** Truppen per Schiff befördern;
to be lost in ~ unterwegs verlorengegangen sein; **to provide the necessary ~** notwendige Transportmittel zur Verfügung stellen; **to ride in public ~** öffentliche Verkehrsmittel benutzen; **to suffer in ~** unterwegs beschädigt werden, auf dem Transport Schaden nehmen;
~ Act *(Br.)* Verkehrsgesetz; **~ advertising** *(Br.)* Verkehrsmittelwerbung; **~ agency** Transportagentur, Speditionsfirma; **~ agent** Transportmakler, Transporteur, Spediteur; **~ aircraft** Transportflugzeug; **commercial ~ aircraft** Verkehrsflugzeug; **~ allowance** Fahrgeldzuschuß, Reisekostenentschädigung; **~ authorities** *(US)* Verkehrsbehörden; **~ axis** Verkehrsachse; **~ bill** *(Br.)* Verkehrsgesetz; **~ bottleneck** Verkehrsengpaß; **to run a ~ business** Transportunternehmen leiten; **~ café** Fernfahrerraststätte; **~ capacity** Fahrgastkapazität; **~ charges** Beförderungs-, Transportgebühren, -kosten; **~ Commission** *(Br.)* Eisenbahn- und Binnenschiffahrtsbehörde; **~ company** *(Br.)* Spediteur, Speditionsgesellschaft; **public ~ company** öffentliches Verkehrsunternehmen; **~ contractor** Transportunternehmer; **~ convenience** Transportmöglichkeit; **~ Coordinating Council** *(Br.)* Koordinierungsausschuß für Transportprobleme; **inclusive of all ~ costs** inklusive aller Transportkosten; **~ development** Verkehrsentwicklung; **~ difficulties** Transportschwierigkeiten; **~ document** Transport-, Versanddokument; **~ economics** Verkehrswirtschaft; **~ economist** Verkehrsökonom, Verkehrswirtschaftler; **~ engineer** Verkehrsingenieur; **~ expenses** Versand-, Transportkosten; **~ facilities** Transportmöglichkeiten, Transportgelegenheit, *(installations)* Verkehrsanlagen; **~ holdup** Transport-, Verkehrsstockung; **~ industries** Verkehrsindustrie, Transportgewerbe; **~ installations** Verkehrseinrichtungen; **~ insurance** Transportversicherung; **~ loss** Transportschaden; **~ matters** Beförderungs-, Transportwesen; **~ network** Verkehrsnetz; **public ~ operator** öffentlicher Verkehrsbetrieb; **~ plane** Transportflugzeug; **~ planning** Verkehrsplanung; **~ planning in road sectors** Straßenverkehrsplanung; **~ policy** Verkehrspolitik; **~ provisions** Verkehrsbestimmungen; **~ risk** Beförderungsrisiko, Transport-

risiko, -gefahr; **~ Secretary** *(Br.)* Verkehrsminister; **~ services** Transportleistungen; **public ~ service** Verkehrsbetrieb, öffentliches Transportwesen; **~ ship (vessel)** Frachter, Frachtschiff, *(mil.)* Truppentransporter; **~ system** Transport-, Verkehrssystem; **~ trade** Transportgewerbe; **~ treaty** Verkehrsabkommen; **~ Tribunal** *(Br.)* Aufsichtsamt für Bahn- und andere Beförderungstarife; **~ user** Verkehrsteilnehmer; **~ Users' Consultative Committee** *(Br.)* Beratungsausschuß für Verkehrsbenutzer; **~ unit** Fahrabteilung; **~ vehicle** Fortbewegungsmittel; **~ worker** Transportarbeiter.
transportable transport-, versandfähig.
transportation *(carriage)* Beförderung, Transport, *(charges)* Versand-, Versendungs-, Beförderungs-, Transportkosten, *(forwarding)* Versendung, Versand, Transport, *(forwarding system, US)* Verkehrs-, Transportwesen, *(deportation)* Verbannung, Deportation, *(means of conveyance, US)* Transportmöglichkeiten, -wesen, Verkehrsmittel, Beförderungsmittel, Transportgelegenheiten, *(method of transport)* Transportsystem, -methode, *(ticket)* Fahrschein, -ausweis;
city ~ städtische Verkehrsmittel; **common carrier ~** *(US)* Beförderung durch öffentliche Verkehrsmittel; **highway ~** *(US)* Güterverkehr mit Lastwagen, Landstraßenverkehr; **public ~** *(US)* öffentliches Transportmittel (Verkehrsmittel), öffentliches Transportwesen; **railroad freight ~** *(US)* Eisenbahngüter-, Bahnfrachtverkehr; **reduced-cost ~** verbilligter Transport; **through ~** durchgehende Beförderung; **water-borne ~** *(US)* Transport auf dem Wasserwege;
~ by air Beförderung auf dem Luftwege; **~ of freight** Gütertransport; **~ at ground** Fortbewegung im Bodenverkehr; **~ of passengers** Passagierverkehr; **~ by rail** *(Br.)* Bahnfrachtverkehr;
to be sentenced to ~ for life lebenslänglich verbannt werden; **to control ~** Verkehrswirtschaft steuern;
~ accounting Speditionsbuchführung; **~ advertisement** *(US)* Verkehrsmittelwerbung; **~ agency** Transportagentur, -gesellschaft, Speditions-, Verkehrsgesellschaft; **~ allowance** Fahrkostenzuschuß; **~ bond** Versandkaution; **to cope with the ~ burden** den Belastungen des Transportgewerbes gewachsen sein; **~ carrier** Transport-, Hauptspediteur; **~ charges** Transport-, Versand-, Beförderungskosten; **~ committee** Verkehrsausschuß; **~ company** Speditions-, Verkehrsgesellschaft, Verkehrsbetrieb; **public ~ company** öffentliches Verkehrsunternehmen; **~ consultant** Berater in Verkehrsfragen; **~ contract** Beförderungsvertrag; **~ cost** Fahrt-, Beförderungskosten, Transport-, Frachtunkosten; **~ department** Verkehrsabteilung; **~ Department** *(US)* Verkehrsministerium; **~ economy** Verkehrswirtschaft; **~ enterprise** Verkehrsunternehmen, -betrieb; **~ equipment** Transportausstattung; **~ expenses** Transportkosten; **~ expert** Verkehrssachverständiger; **~ facilities** Verkehrserleichterungen, -anlagen, -einrichtungen; **~ industry** Verkehrswirtschaft; **~ insurance** Transportversicherung; **~ inward costs** Kosten des Abtransportes; **~ line** Verkehrslinie; **to free the entry into the ~ market** staatliche Reglementierung des Verkehrswesens aufheben; **~ means** Transporteinrichtungen, Verkehrsmittel; **~ Minister** *(US)* Verkehrsminister; **~ money** Aufkommen der Verkehrswirtschaft; **~ monopoly** Verkehrsmonopol; **~ needs** Verkehrsbedürfnisse; **~ network** Verkehrsnetz; **~ operation** Transport-, Verkehrsunternehmen; **~ planning** Verkehrsplanung; **~ policy** Verkehrspolitik; **~ problem** Verkehrsproblem; **~ project** Verkehrsprojekt; **~ rate** Transport-, Frachtsatz, -tarif, Verkehrstarif, Beförderungsgebühr; **~ ratio** *(US)* Beförderungs- und Transportverhältnis; **~ receipt** *(US)* Transportempfangsschein; **government ~ request** staatliches Beförderungsersuchen; **~ risk** Transportrisiko; **~ schedule** Frachttabelle; **~ services** Beförderungsleistungen; **~ space** *(US)* Transportraum; **~ system** Transportwesen, Verkehrssystem; **~ tax** *(US)* Beförderungs-, Transportsteuer; **[internal] ~ technician** [Binnen]transportsachverständiger; **~ terminal** Verkehrsendpunkt; **~ ticket** Fahrschein; **~ undertaking** Verkehrsbetrieb; **~ unit** Verkehrsleistung.
transported | to Australia *(criminal)* nach Australien deportiert; **~ with joy** vor Freude außer sich.
transporter Beförderer, *(airplane)* Verkehrs-, Transportflugzeug, *(device)* Transportvorrichtung.
transposal Umstellung, Versetzung, *(proofreader)* Umstellung.
transpose *(proofreading)* Umstellzeichen;
~ (v.) words *(proofreading)* Wörter umstellen.
transposed line umgestellte Zeile.
transposition Übertragung;
~ of words Wortumstellung;
~ cipher *(coding)* Versatzschlüssel.

transumpt *(Scot.)* Urkundenvorlage.

transvaluate *(v.)* neu bewerten, umwerten.

transvaluation Neube-, Umwertung.

trap Falle, Fußangel, -eisen, *(detective, Br.)* Kriminaler, *(mil.)* Falle, Hinterhalt, *(mouth, sl.)* Klappe, Schnauze, *(radio)* Sperrkreis, *(spy, sl.)* Polizeispitzel;
~s *(coll.)* Habseligkeiten, Siebensachen;
night ~ *(sl.)* Nachtlokal;
~ *(v.)* in einer Falle fangen;
~ **s. o.** j. hereinfallen lassen;
to pack up one's ~s seine Sachen packen; **to set a** ~ **for s. o.** jem. eine Falle stellen; **to shut one's** ~ *(sl.)* seine Klappe halten; **to walk into a** ~ in eine Falle gehen;
~ **door** Falltür, *(fig.)* Fußangel, *(theater)* Versenkung.

trapper Fallensteller, Trapper, Pelztierjäger.

trappings Zubehör.

trash unnützer Kram, wertloser Plunder, *(books)* Kitsch, Schund, *(goods)* wertlose Ware, Ausschußware, *(rabble)* leeres Gewäsch, Quatsch, *(refuse, US)* Abfall, Abfälle, Müll;
white ~ *(South America)* arme weiße Bevölkerung;
~ **can** *(US)* Abfalleimer; ~ **disposal** *(US)* Abfallbeseitigung; ~ **dump** *(US)* Schuttabladestelle, Müllkippe, Deponie; ~ **pile** *(US)* Abfallhaufen; ~ **smasher** *(US)* Abfallzerkleinerer.

trashery Plunder, Krimskrams.

trashy minderwertig, *(book)* kitschig;
~ **novel** Schundroman.

trauma Trauma, Gemütserschütterung.

travel Reise[n], Reiseverkehr, *(describing lecture)* Reisebericht;
~ **abroad** Auslandsreise; **air** ~ Flugreise; **business** ~ Geschäftsreise; **foreign** ~ Auslandsreiseverkehr; **intercontinental** ~ Interkontinentalverkehr; **pleasure** ~ Vergnügungsreise; **spare-time** ~ Ferienreise; **tourist** ~ Touristen-, Reiseverkehr;
~ **on official business** Dienstreise; ~ **to clients** Kundenbesuch; ~ **of a piston** Kolbenhub;
~ *(v.)* reisen, Reisen machen, *(salesman)* Reisender sein, bereisen;
fellow-~ mit dem Kommunismus sympathisieren;
~ **about** umherreisen; ~ **abroad** ins Ausland reisen; ~ **by air** per Flugzeug reisen; ~ **around from town to town** von Ort zu Ort reisen; ~ **back** zurückreisen; ~ **by boat** mit dem Dampfer fahren; ~ **on (for the) business** Geschäftsreise unternehmen, geschäftlich unterwegs sein; ~ **for genuine business or professional reasons** aus beruflichen Gründen oder geschäftlich unterwegs sein; ~ **in carpets** Teppichvertreter sein; ~ **second class** zweiter Klasse fahren; ~ **over a country** Land bereisen; ~ **across country** über Land fahren; ~ **a good deal** oft verreisen; ~ **over recent events** sich kürzliche Ereignisse vergegenwärtigen; ~ **on expense account** zu Lasten des Spesenkontos verreisen; ~ **for a firm** Vertreter sein, Firma vertreten; ~ **incognito** unter fremdem Namen reisen; ~ **light** mit wenig Gepäck reisen; ~ **by the map** nach der Karte reisen; ~ **for pleasure** Vergnügungsreise machen; ~ **for a publisher** Verlagsvertreter sein; ~ **Pullman** *(US)* erster Klasse reisen; ~ **by rail** mit der Eisenbahn fahren (reisen); ~ **out of the record** vom Thema abkommen; ~ **by sea** mit dem Schiff reisen, Seeweg benutzen; ~ **faster than sound** sich schneller als das Licht fortpflanzen; ~ **at a speed of ...** sich mit einer Geschwindigkeit von ... bewegen; ~ **at high speed** mit hoher Geschwindigkeit fahren; ~ **over a large territory** großen Vertreterbezirk haben; ~ **through** durchreisen; ~ **against the traffic** dem Verkehrsstrom entgegenfahren; ~ **round the world** Weltreise machen; ~ **the whole world** ganze Welt bereisen;
to spend one's vacation in ~ Ferien auf Reisen verbringen; **to use one's car for personal** ~ sein Auto für Privatfahrten benutzen; **to write a book about one's** ~s seine Reiseerinnerungen in Buchform veröffentlichen;
~ **accident insurance** Reiseunfallversicherung; ~ **account** Tourismuskonto; ~ **advance** *(US)* Reisekostenvorschuß; ~ **agency** Verkehrs-, Reisebüro; ~-**agency business** Tourismusgeschäft; ~ **agent** *(US)* Reiseagentur, -büro, Verkehrsbüro; ~ **agreement** Reiseabkommen; ~ **allowance** Reisekostenzuschuß, *(foreign exchange, Br.)* Devisenfreibetrag (Devisenzuteilung) für Ferienreisende (Auslandsreisen); ~ **arrangements** Reisevorbereitungen; ~ **break** Reiseunterbrechung; ~ **bureau** *(Br.)* Reisebüro; ~ **business** Touristikunternehmen, -branche; ~ **cash** Bargeld auf der Reise; ~ **check** Reisescheck; ~ **checkbook** Reisescheckheft; ~ **clearance** Reisegenehmigung; ~ **costs** Reisespesen; ~ **counter** Verkehrszähler; ~ **counting** Verkehrszählung; ~ **and entertainment diary** Spesennachweisbuch; ~ **display** Werbung in öffentlichen Verkehrsmitteln; ~ **document** Reiseausweis; ~ **editor** Reisejournalist; ~ **expenses** *(US)* Reisekosten, -spesen; ~-**expense report** *(US)* Spesen-, Reisekosten-

abrechnung; ~ **field** Reisewesen; ~ **folder** Reiseprospekt; ~ **funds** Reisegeld; ~ **grant** Reisezuschuß; ~ **growth** Zunahme des Reiseverkehrs; ~ **guide** Reiseführer; ~ **information bureau** Reisebüro; ~ **insurance** Reiseversicherung; ~ **literature** Reiseliteratur; ~ **pass** *(mil.)* Dienstreiseausweis; ~ **permit** Reisegenehmigung; ~ **plan** Reiseplan; ~ **planning** Reiseplanung; ~ **report** *(US)* Spesenabrechnung; ~ **restrictions** Reisebeschränkungen; ~ **season** Saison, Touristenzeit; ~ **service** Reiseverkehr; ~ **souvenir** Reiseandenken, Mitbringsel; ~ **spending** Reiseausgaben; ~ **subsidy (subvention)** Reisekostenzuschuß; ~ **tip** Reisehinweis; ~ **trailer** Reiseanhänger; ~ **urge** Reiselust; ~ **voucher** Fahrausweis.

travelled vielgereist, *(road)* viel befahren;
~ **man** viel gereister Man;; ~ **part of highway** öffentlicher Fußgängerweg; **much-**~ **part of the country** vielbesuchte Gegend, Touristenzentrum.

traveller Reisender, Tourist, Wanderer, *(Br.)* Handlungsreisender, *(sales ticket in retail stores, US)* Einkaufssammelbuch, *(technics)* Laufkatze, Hängekran;
commercial ~ Handlungs-, Geschäftsreisender, Vertreter im Außendienst; **expense-account** ~ Spesenritter; **fellow** ~ Mitreisender, *(fig.)* Gesinnungsgenosse, Kommunistenfreund, Mitläufer, **medium-income** ~ Tourist der mittleren Einkommensklasse; **railway** ~ *(Br.)* Eisenbahnpassagier; **town** ~ Platzvertreter;
~ **on commission** Provisionsvertreter, -reisender;
~ **tip** Reisehinweis.

traveller's | **accident insurance** Reiseunfallversicherung; ~ **aid** Bahnhofsmission; ~ **book** Fremdenbuch; ~ **check** *(US)* (**cheque**, *Br.*) Reisescheck; ~ **guide** Reisehandbuch, „Baedeker"; ~ **hotel** Touristenhotel; ~ **letter of credit** *(US)* Reisekreditbrief; ~ **order** Reiseauftrag; ~ **pass** Reisepass; ~ **rebate for orders placed with publisher's representative** Reiserabatt für Bestellungen beim Verlagsvertreter; ~ **sample** Musterkollektion, Kollektionsmuster; ~ **tale** Lügenmärchen.

travelling Reisen;
~ **to work** Fahrt zum Arbeitsplatz;
to write a book about one's ~ Reiseerinnerungen verfassen;
~ *(a.)* reisend, *(agency)* für Tourneen konzipiert, *(technics)* fahrbar, beweglich;
~ **agent** Handlungs-, Provisionsreisender, Reisevertreter, *(tour)* Reisebegleiter; ~ **allowance** Reisevorschuß, *(parl.)* Reisegeldpauschale; ~ **artisan** Handwerksbursche; ~ **auditor** Außenrevisor; ~ **charges** Reisespesen, -unkosten; ~ **circus** Wanderzirkus; ~ **clerk** Handlungsreisender; ~ **clock** Reisewecker; ~ **companion** Reisebegleiter; ~ **conveniences** Reisekomfort; ~ **dental clinic** fahrbare Zahnklinik; ~ **display** Werbung in öffentlichen Verkehrsmitteln; ~ **dress** Reiseanzug; ~ **equipment** Reiseausrüstung; ~ **exhibition** Wanderausstellung; ~ **expenses** *(Br.)* Geschäftsunkosten, Reisespesen, -kosten; ~ **to get one's** ~ **expenses** *(Br.)* Reisespesen ersetzt bekommen; **to reimburse** ~ **expenses** Reisekosten (Spesen) vergüten (erstatten); ~-**expense account** Spesenkonto; ~ **facilities** Reiseerleichterungen; ~ **fellowship** Auslandsstipendium; ~ **guide** Reiseführer; ~ **inspector** *(insurance)* Reisebeamter, -inspektor; ~ **library** fahrbare Bibliothek, Wanderbibliothek; ~ **money** Zehrpfennig; ~ **platform** Schiebebühne; ~ **post office** fahrbares Postamt, Bahnpost[amt]; ~ **representative** *(US)* Schulungsleiter für Untervertreter, Vertreter, der Untervertreter in ihrem Absatzgebiet schult; ~ **requisites** Reiseutensilien; ~ **salesman** *(US)* [Verkaufs]reisender, Handlungsreisender, Vertreter; ~ **salesman on straight salary** Außendienstmitarbeiter im Angestelltenverhältnis; ~ **scholarship** Auslandsstipendium; ~ **staircase (stairs)** Rolltreppe; ~ **table** fahrbarer Arbeitstisch; ~ **territory** Vertreterbezirk; ~ **vendors** ambulantes Gewerbe, Wandergewerbe; ~ **warrant** Militärfahrschein; ~ **ways** *(coal mining)* Verkehrsstollen.

travelog(ue) Reisebericht, -beschreibung, *(with slides, US)* Lichtbildervortrag.

traveltime Wege-, Reisezeit.

traversable gangbar, *(law)* bestreitbar.

traverse Überquerung, Durchfahren, -reisen, *(architecture)* Querwand, -gang, *(law)* rechtsvernichtende Einwendung, Rechtseinwand, Einrede, Bestreiten, *(criminal law)* Leugnen, Klageleugnung, *(machine)* schwenkbarer Teil, *(mil.)* Traverse, *(pol.)* Zickzackkurs;
common (general) ~ allgemeines Bestreiten; **special** ~ substantiiertes Bestreiten;
~ **of indictment or presentment** Vorbringen gegen wichtige Anklagepunkte; ~ **upon a** ~ Bestreiten des gegnerischen Vorbringens;

~ (v.) durchqueren, -wandern, überqueren, (law) ableugnen, bestreiten, Rechtseinwand (Einrede) erheben, (mil.) auf- und abpatroullieren;
~ **one's beat** (US) seine Runde machen; ~ **a desert** Wüste durchqueren; ~ **the ocean** Ozean überqueren; ~ **s. one's plans** jem. einen Strich durch die Rechnung machen, jds. Pläne durchkreuzen; ~ **a river** (bridge) Fluß überspannen; ~ **the sky** (searchlights) über den Himmel wandern;
~ **jury** Geschworene in der Hauptversammlung; ~ **table** (railway) Schiebebühne.

traversed by canals von Kanälen durchzogen.

traverser Bestreitender.

traversing note allgemeines Bestreiten in der Klageschrift.

travesty Karikatur;
~ **of justice** Zerrbild der Gerechtigkeit; ~ **of s. one's style** Parodie von jds. Stil.

trawl Schleppnetz;
~ (v.) Fische mit dem Schleppnetz fangen.

trawlboat Schleppnetzfischer.

trawler Schleppnetzfischer;
~ **skipper** Schleppfischer.

trawling Schleppfischerei;
~ **industry** Fischfangindustrie.

tray Tablett, Servierbrett, (office) Ablagekorb, (balance) Briefschale, (pedler) Verkaufsbrett, (tramway, Br.) Fangnetz;
developing ~ (photo) Entwicklerschale; **in-**~ Kasten für eingehende Post, Eingangskorb; **out-**~ Kasten für ausgehende Post; **trunk** ~ Koffereinsatz.

treacherous verräterisch, treulos;
~ **ice** trügerisches Eis; ~ **memory** unzuverlässiges Gedächtnis; ~ **weather** trügerisches Wetter.

treachery Verrat, Verräterei, Heimtücke.

tread Schritt, Tritt, (footprint) Spur, (occupation, Scot.) Beschäftigung, Arbeit, (width of step) Spurweite, (tire) Profil, (wheel) Fahr-, Gleitfläche;
~ (v.) **on air** vor Freude außer sich (wie im siebenten Himmel) sein; ~ **the boards** als Schauspieler auftreten; ~ **with caution** vorsichtig vorgehen; ~ **cautiously on the ice** Eis vorsichtig betreten; ~ **on s. one's corns** jem. auf die Hühneraugen treten; ~ **down** niedertrampeln; ~ **on eggs** wie auf Eiern (mit größter Behutsamkeit) gehen; ~ **a fire out** Feuer austreten; ~ **in s. one's footsteps** in jds. Fußstapfen treten; ~ **on s. one's heels** jem. auf dem Fuße folgen; ~ **lightly** vorsichtig zu Werke gehen; ~ **a path** sich einen Weg bahnen; ~ **a dangerous path** gefährlichen Weg beschreiten, risikoreiche Politik betreiben; ~ **the pedals of a bicycle** in die Pedale treten; ~ **the room from end to end** Zimmer von einem zum anderen Ende durchmessen; ~ **the stage** (theater) auftreten; ~ **on s. one's toes** jem. auf die Hühneraugen treten; ~ **under foot** zerstören, vernichten;
do not ~ **on the grass!** bitte den Rasen nicht betreten!;
~ **abrasion** Profilabrieb.

treadle Pedal.

treadmill (fig.) Tretmühle.

treason Verrat, Landes-, Hochverrat, Treubruch;
constructive ~ (Br.) als Hochverrat geltende Verschwörung; **high** ~ (Br.) Hochverrat, (US) Landesverrat, Verbrechen gegen die Staatssicherheit, Majestätsverbrechen; **petit** ~ (Br.) Tötung des Ehemanns;
to commit ~ Landesverrat begehen;
~ **felony** (Br.) Landesverrat; ~ **trial** Landesverratsprozeß.

treasonable [hoch]verräterisch;
~ **act** Hochverratshandlung; ~ **negotiations** hochverräterische Verhandlungen.

treasure Schatz, Hort, (riches) Reichtum, Schätze, (valuable store) Kostbarkeit, seltenes (kostbares) Stück;
art ~s Kunstschätze; **buried** ~ vergrabener Schatz;
~ **of gold** Goldschatz;
~ (v.) **up** (Br.) horten, ansammeln; ~ **s. one's friendship** jds. Freundschaft hoch einschätzen; ~ **up in one's memory** im Gedächtnis bewahren; ~ **s. one's memory** jds. Andenken in Ehren halten;
to dig up a ~ Schatz heben; **to hoard up** ~ Schätze ansammeln;
~ **box (chest)** Schatztruhe, -kasten; ~ **house** (fig.) Fundgrube; ~ **hunt** Schatzsuche; ~ **hunter** Schatzsucher; ~ **issues** Schatzwechselemission; ~ **room** Schatzkammer; ~ **ship** Schatzschiff; ~ **seeker** Schatzgräber, -sucher; ~-**trove** (fig.) Fundgrube, (legal sense) aufgefundener Schatz, Schatzfund.

treasurer (club) Schatzmeister, Kassenverwalter, -wart, -führer, Kassierer, (corporation, US) Finanzdirektor, Leiter der Finanzabteilung, (curator) Rendant, Leiter des Finanzwesens, (local government) Kämmerer;

city ~ (Br.) Stadtkämmerer; **current** ~ augenblicklicher Schatzmeister;
~ **of a corporation** (US) Leiter der Finanzabteilung, Finanzvorstand, -direktor; ~ **of the Royal Household** (Br.) Finanzbeamter des königlichen Haushalts; 2 **of the United States** Schatzminister;
~'**s office** (Br.) Stadtkämmerei.

treasurership Schatzmeisteramt, (club) Amt des Kassenwarts.

treasury (Br.) Schatzamt, Finanzministerium, (book of information) Schatzkästlein, Sammlung, Anthologie, (fisc) Fiskus, (funds of company) Vermögen, (revenue office) Staats-, Finanzkasse, (treasure chest) Schatztruhe, Tresor, (Treasury Department, US) Finanzministerium;
Commissioners (Lords) of 2 (Br.) Finanzministerium; **depleted** ~ leere Kasse; **metallic** ~ Barschatz; **public** ~ Staatskasse, Fiskus;
~ **of a club** Vereinskasse; ~ **of information** Fundgrube für Informationen; ~ **of money** Geldanhäufung;
~ **authorities** Finanzbehörden; ~ **bench** (Br.) Regierungs-, Ministerbank; ~ **bill** (Br.) Schatzanweisung, kurzfristiger Schatzwechsel; **hot** ~ **bills** (Br.) allerneueste Schatzwechsel; **market** ~ **bills** (Br.) wöchentlich ausgegebene Schatzwechsel; **short-time** ~ **bills** (Br.) U-Schätze, unverzinsliche Schatzwechsel; **tap** ~ **bills** (Br.) laufend (unmittelbar) ausgegebene Schatzwechsel; ~ **bill price (rate)** (Br.) Schatzwechselkurs, Satz für Schatzwechsel; 2 **Board** (Br.) Finanzministerium; ~ **bond** (US) Kassen-, langfristige Schatzanweisung, (corporation, US) firmeneigene Schuldverschreibung; **noninterest-bearing** ~ **bonds** unverzinsliche Schatzanweisungen; ~ **cash** Bestand der Staatskasse; ~ **certificate** (US) kurzfristige Schatzanweisung, kurzfristiger Schatzwechsel, (corporation, US) firmeneigene Schuldverschreibung; ~ **chest fund** (Commissioner of the Treasury, Br.) Dispositionsfonds der Staatskasse; ~ **clerk** Finanzbeamter; ~ **coffers** Schatztruhe; ~ **consent** Genehmigung des Finanzministeriums; 2 **Department** (US) Bundesfinanzministerium; ~ **deposit receipts** (Br.) verzinsliche Schatzamtsquittungen für Banken; ~ **directives** (banking, Br.) kreditpolitische Weisungen des Finanzministeriums; ~ **financing** Schatzwechselfinanzierung; ~ **forecasts** Schätzungen des Finanzministeriums; **to overshoot** ~ **forecasts** Prognosen des Finanzministeriums übertreffen; ~ **functions** Finanzamtsaufgaben; ~ **licence** Sondergenehmigung des Finanzministeriums, Devisengenehmigung; ~ **minute** Memorandum des Finanzministeriums; ~ **note** (US) mittelfristiger Schatzwechsel, mittelfristige Schatzanweisung, Kassenanweisung, Darlehnskassenschein; ~ **obligation** Schatzanweisung; ~ **office** Schatzamt; ~ **official** (US) Finanzbeamter; ~ **rate (rating)** Steuerleistung; **total** ~ **receipts** gesamtes Steueraufkommen; ~ **ruling** Verfügung des Finanzministeriums; ~ **savings certificate** Sparzertifikat des US-Schatzamtes; 2 **Secretary** (US) Finanzminister; ~ **securities** Eigenbestand an Wertpapieren, Wertpapierportefeuille [einer AG]; ~ **shares** [Bestand an] eigene[n] Aktien; 2 **Solicitor** (Br.) Justiziar des Finanzministeriums; ~ **special account** (Br.) Marshallplankonto; ~'**s short-term bill borrowings** Schatzwechseldiskontgeschäfte; 2 **Statement** (US) Wochenausweis des Schatzamtes; ~ **stock** (US) Portefeuille (Bestand) eigener Aktien; ~ **stocks** (Br.) britische Staatsanleihen; ~ **subsidy** (Br.) Staatszuschuß; ~'**s target discount rate** angestrebter Schatzwechseldiskontsatz; ~ **tax anticipation certificate** Steuergutschein; ~ **warrant** (Br.) Schatzanweisung.

treat Bewirtung, Festlichkeit, -schmaus, Unterhaltung;
school ~ Schulfest;
~ (v.) behandeln, umgehen mit, zum Gegenstand haben, (defray expenses) freihalten, Kosten tragen, bewirten, (negotiate) verhandeln, Verhandlungen führen;
~ **with** unterhandeln; ~ **s. o. to s. th.** jem. etw. spendieren, j. freihalten; ~ **o. s. to a bottle of wine** sich eine Flasche Wein leisten; ~ **s. o. brutally** brutal mit jem. umgehen; ~ **s. o. with a cake** j. mit einem Kuchen bewirten; ~ **o. s. to a new coat** sich einen neuen Rock zulegen; ~ **of foreign countries** (book) von fremden Ländern handeln; ~ **as delusion** als Phantasiegebilde abtun; ~ **s. o. differently** j. bevorzugt behandeln; ~ **s. o. to dinner** j. zum Essen einladen; ~ **with the French Government** mit der französischen Regierung verhandeln; ~ **s. o. like a lord** j. fürstlich bewirten; ~ **with the enemy for peace** Friedensverhandlungen führen; ~ **of the progress of cancer research** (article) von den Fortschritten in der Krebsforschung handeln (berichten); ~ **exhaustively of a subject** Thema erschöpfend behandeln; ~ **of an interesting topic** interessantes Thema behandeln; ~ **o. s. to a good weekend holiday** sich ein arbeitsfreies Wochenende leisten;

to be a ~ for s. o. Hochgenuß für j. sein, jem. großes Vergnügen bereiten; to be s. one's ~ auf jds. Rechnung gehen; to stand ~ Zeche bezahlen; to stand ~ all round Runde ausgeben, Lage spendieren.

treatable fabric pflegeleichter Stoff.

treated | **as equal** gleichgestellt; ~ **by numerous experts** von zahlreichen Fachleuten behandelt.

treaties, under auf Grund von Staatsverträgen;
unequal ~ *(international law)* ungleiche Verträge.

treating Freihalten, Bewirtung, *(corrupt practices, Br.)* Bewirtung zwecks Wohlbeeinflussung.

treatise [schriftliche] Abhandlung, Bericht, Traktat;
~ **of fundamental importance** grundlegende Abhandlung.

treatment Bearbeitung, Behandlung, Behandlungsmethode, *(film)* schriftliche Fixierung einer Filmidee, *(med.)* Mittel, *(technics)* Bearbeitungsverfahren;
customs ~ zollrechtliche Behandlung; **deferential** ~ rücksichtsvolle Behandlung; **discriminative** ~ diskriminierende Behandlung; **hot-cold** ~ Wechselbadbehandlung; **ill-**~ schlechte Behandlung; **medical** ~ ärztliche Behandlung; **private medical** ~ private Krankenkassenbehandlung; **most-favo(u)red-nation** ~ Meistbegünstigung; **national** ~ Inländerbehandlung; **in-place** ~ Bearbeitung an Ort und Stelle; **preferential** ~ Vorzugsbehandlung; **private medial** ~ private Krankenkassenbehandlung;
~ **of aliens** Ausländerbehandlung; ~ **of capital gains** steuerliche Behandlung von Veräußerungsgewinnen; ~ **of nationals** Inländerbehandlung;
to be under ~ **in hospital** im Krankenhaus behandelt werden; **to recover under a** ~ auf eine Behandlung ansprechen; **to refuse** ~ Krankenbehandlung ablehnen;
~ **center** Entziehungsklinik.

treaty *(act of negotiating)* Unter-, Verhandlung, *(international law)* [Staats]vertrag, Konvention, Abkommen, *(private law)* Übereinkunft, Garantievertrag, *(reinsurance agreement)* Rückversicherungsvertrag;
bound by ~ vertraglich gebunden; **by private** ~ im Verhandlungswege; **by virtue of a** ~ kraft Vertrages; **contrary to** ~ vertragswidrig;
arbitration ~ Schieds[gerichts]vertrag; **basic** ~ Grundvertrag; **binding** ~ völkerrechtlich bindender Vertrag; **bipartite** ~ zweiseitiger Vertrag; **collective** ~ Kollektivvertrag; **commercial** ~ Handelsvertrag, Wirtschaftsabkommen; **contractual** ~ *(international law)* rechtsgeschäftlicher Vertrag; **law (legislative)** ~ *(international law)* normativer Vertrag; **lawmaking** ~ normativer Vertrag; **mixed** ~ gemischter Vertrag; **multilateral** ~ mehrseitiges Abkommen; **naval** ~ Flottenabkommen, -vertrag; **Nonproliferation** ≗ Atomsperrvertrag; **ordinary** ~ rechtsgeschäftlicher Vertrag; **peace** ~ Friedensvertrag; **postal** ~ Postabkommen, -vertrag; **preliminary (provisional)** ~ Vorvertrag; **quota** ~ *(reinsurance)* Quoten-, Schadensteilungsabkommen; **reciprocity** ~ Gegenseitigkeitsvertrag; **self-executing** ~ unmittelbar anzuwendender Völkerrechtsvertrag; **space** ~ Weltraumvertrag; **tariff** ~ Tarifabkommen, Zollvereinbarung, -vertrag; **Test Ban** ≗ Atomsperrvertrag; **ten-line** ~ *(reinsurance)* Rückversicherungsvertrag mit dem Zehnfachen des Selbstbehalts; **transitory** ~ sofort gültiges Völkerrechtsabkommen;
≗ **of Accession** Beitrittsvertrag; ~ **of alliance** Bündnisvertrag; ~ **of arbitration** Schiedsvertrag; ~ **of cession** Abtretungsvertrag; ~ **of commerce** Handelsvertrag, -abkommen, Tarifabkommen, Tarif-, Zollvertrag; ~ **of establishment** Niederlassungsabkommen; ≗ **of Friendship, Commerce and Navigation** *(US)* Freundschafts-, Handels- und Schiffahrtsvertrag; ~ **of guarantee** Garantievertrag; ~ **of limits** Grenzvertrag; ~ **of navigation** Schiffahrtsabkommen, -vertrag; ~ **of neutrality** Neutralitätsvertrag; ~ **of peace** Friedensvertrag; ~ **of protectorate** Protektoratsvertrag; ≗ **of Rome** *(EC)* Römische Verträge;
to be in ~ Verhandlungen pflegen; **to conclude a** ~ Vertrag abschließen; **to denounce a** ~ Vertrag kündigen; **to embody a** ~ **in law** internationalen Vertrag gesetzlich verankern; **to enter into a** ~ **with s. o.** Vertragsvereinbarung mit jem. schließen; **to enter into a** ~ **of commerce** Handelsvertrag abschließen; **to give notice of termination of** ~ Vertrag aufkündigen; **to join a** ~ einem völkerrechtlichen Vertrag beitreten; **to negotiate a** ~ Vertrag aushandeln; **to ratify a** ~ Vertrag bestätigen (ratifizieren) **to register a** ~ Völkerrechtsvertrag registrieren; **to renounce a** ~ Vertrag aufkündigen; **to sell by private** ~ freihändig verkaufen; **to violate a** ~ Vertragsverletzung begehen;
~ **arrangement** vertragliche Vereinbarung; ~ **collection** Vertragssammlung; ~ **commitments** Vertragsverpflichtungen; ~ **duties** Vertragszölle; ~ **makers** Verhandlungsteilnehmer, Vertragsschließende; ~**-making power** Zuständigkeit für völkerrechtliche Vertragsabschlüsse; ~ **obligations** vertragliche Verpflichtungen, Vertragsverpflichtungen; ~ **port** Vertragshafen; ~ **powers** Vertragsmächte; ~ **provisions** Vertragsbestimmungen, *(EC)* Bestimmungen des EG-Vertrages;; ~ **quota** *(reinsurance)* Vertragsanteil; ~ **reinsurance** automatisch wirksame Rückversicherung; ~ **signatory** Vertragsmacht; ~ **system** Vertragssystem.

treble *(v.)* *(prices)* sich verdreifachen;
~ **costs** *(US)* genehmigte erhöhte Kosten.

tree Baum, *(technics)* Schaft, Welle;
at the top of the ~ auf dem Gipfel seiner beruflichen Möglichkeiten; **up the** ~ ruiniert;
Christmas ~ Weihnachtsbaum; **family** ~ Stammbaum;
~ *(v.)* **s. o.** *(coll.)* in die Enge treiben;
to be up a [gum-] ~ in der Klemme sitzen;
~ **population** Baumbestand.

treenail Holznagel, Dübel.

tremble Zittern, Beben;
~ *(v.)* zittern, beben, *(fig.)* in der Schwebe sein.

trembling in the balance in der Schwebe, ungewiß.

tremendous | **explosion** ungeheure Explosion; ~ **performance** hervorragende Leistung; ~ **speed** enorme Geschwindigkeit.

trench *(mil.)* [Schützen]graben;
~**es** *(mil.)* Grabensystem;
~ *(v.)* Gräben ausheben;
~ **upon s. one's property** jds. Eigentumsrechte beeinträchtigen; ~ **upon s. one's rights** in jds. Rechte eingreifen; ~ **upon s. one's spare time** jds. Freizeit in Anspruch nehmen;
to dig ~**es for irrigation** Bewässerungsgräben ziehen; **to mount the** ~**es** *(mil.)* Schützengräben besetzen;
~ **coat** Wettermantel; ~ **companion** Schmarotzer; ~ **mortar** *(mil.)* Granatwerfer; ~ **warfare** Stellungskrieg.

trenchant | **policy** energisches Vorgehen; ~ **speech** energische Rede.

trenching upon s. one's rights Eingriff in jds. Rechte.

trenchwork Schanzarbeit.

trend Lauf, Verlauf, *(inclination)* Neigung, Geneigtheit, *(river)* Verlauf, *(tendency)* Entwicklung, Entwicklungstendenz, Trend, allgemeine Richtung, Tendenz, Neigung;
bonus ~ Tendenz zur Einführung von Tantiemeregelungen; **business** ~ Konjunkturentwicklung; **cost** ~ Kostenentwicklung; **cyclical** ~ Konjunkturverlauf, -entwicklung; **downward** ~ Abwärtsbewegung, Konjunkturrückgang, fallende (rückläufige) Tendenz [des Marktes]; **strong downward** ~ stark fallende Tendenz; **economic** ~ konjunktureller Entwicklungs-, Konjunkturverlauf; **future** ~ zukünftige Entwicklung, Entwicklungstendenz; **longer-term** ~**s** längerfristige Entwicklungen; **market** ~ Konjunktur-, Markt-, Börsenentwicklung, -tendenz, Trend; **governing market** ~ marktbestimmende Entwicklung; **the new** ~ die neue Welle; **present** ~ heutige Tendenz; **regressive business** ~ kontraktive Lageänderung, Konjunkturrückgang; **seasonal** ~ saisonbedingte Tendenz; **secular** ~ langanhaltende Entwicklung; **stock** ~ Tendenz der Aktienkurse; **stock-market** ~ Börsenentwicklung, -tendenz; **upward business** ~ Aufwärtsbewegung, steigende Tendenz, Konjunkturanstieg, -aufstieg, konjunkturelle Aufwärtsbewegung;
~ **of affairs** Geschäftsgang; ~**s in banking** Entwicklungen des Bankwesens; ~ **of births** Entwicklung der Geburtenziffer; ~ **in building trade** Baukonjunktur; ~ **of business** Geschäftsgang; **general** ~ **of business conditions** Konjunkturentwicklung; ~ **of the coastline** Verlauf der Küstenlinie; ~ **to collectivism** kollektivistische Tendenz; ~ **of concentration** Konzentrationsneigung; **decreasing** ~ **in costs** Kostendegression; **increasing** ~ **in costs** Kostenprogression; ~ **of demand** Nachfragetendenz; ~**s in the economy** konjunkturelle Entwicklungstendenzen (Strömungen); ~ **in the domestic economy** binnenwirtschaftliche Entwicklung; ~ **of employment** Beschäftigungsentwicklung; ~ **of events** Gang der Ereignisse, Lauf der Dinge; ~ **of exchanges** Kursentwicklung; ~ **in freights** Frachtkonjunktur; ~ **of interest rates** Zinsentwicklung; **expected** ~**s of the market** Konjunkturerwartungen; ~ **in the population** Bevölkerungsentwicklung; ~ **in prices** Preis-, Kursentwicklung, -tendenz; **upward** ~ **of prices** Preisauftrieb, -konjunktur; ~ **of spending** Ausgabentrend, -entwicklung; ~ **on the stock market** Börsentendenz, -entwicklung; ~ **of thought** Gedankenrichtung; ~ **of the times** Zug der Zeit;
~ *(v.)* Richtung haben, tendieren, *(coast)* sich erstrecken;
~ **away from socialism** Abkehr vom Sozialismus andeuten; ~ **down** in einer Abwärtsbewegung sein;

to buck the ~ der Konjunkturentwicklung entgehen; **to mark the ~ of public opinion** Entwicklung (Trend) der öffentlichen Meinung erkennen lassen; **to set the ~** allgemeine Richtung angeben; **to show an uneven ~** *(prices)* uneinheitlich tendieren; **to take an upward ~** nach oben tendieren;
~ **analysis** Konjunkturanalyse; ~ **breaker** Tendenzveränderer, veränderliches Konjunkturmoment; ~ **extrapolation** Auswertung von Entwicklungslinien; ~ **increase** Konjunkturanstieg; ~ **period** Konjunkturphase, -periode; ~ **rate** Konjunkturrate; ~ **rate of the gross national product growth** entwicklungsbedingte Wachstumsrate des Bruttosozialprodukts; ~**-setter** Richtungsweisender, Trendbestimmer.

trespass Eingriff, Übergriff, *(misfeasance)* Übertretung, Ungesetzlichkeit, Verletzung, Vergehen, Zuwiderhandlung, *(property)* Beeinträchtigung, Eigentumsverletzung, Besitzstörung, Störung im Besitz;
continuing (permanent) ~ fortdauernde Besitzstörung; **criminal** ~ *(US)* strafbares Eindringen, Hausfriedensbruch; **joint** ~ gemeinsam begangene unerlaubte Handlung;
~ **on the case** Schadensersatzklage wegen Verletzung von Rechtsgütern; ~ **for goods carried away** Schadensersatzklage wegen widerrechtlicher Wegnahme von Waren; ~ **on land** unbefugtes Betreten eines Grundstücks; ~ **for mesne profits** *(tenancy)* Schadensersatzklage für Nutzungsentzug; ~ **to try title** *(real property)* Klage auf Herausgabe eines Grundstücks; ~ **wherefore he broke the close** Schadensersatzklage wegen Hausfriedensbruchs; ~ **with force and arms** Schadensersatzklage wegen gewaltsamer und bewaffneter Rechtsverletzung;
~ *(v.) (commit an offence)* übertreten, verletzen, Ungesetzmäßigkeit begehen, *(property)* widerrechtlich betreten, in fremde Rechte eingreifen, Besitz stören;
~ **on s. one's hospitality** jds. Gastfreundschaft mißbrauchen (ausnutzen); ~ **on s. one's land** jds. Grundstück widerrechtlich betreten; ~ **against the law** Gesetz übertreten, sich einer Übertretung schuldig machen; ~ **on s. one's preserves** *(Br.)* jem. ins Gehege kommen; ~ **upon s. one's privacy** jds. Intimsphäre verletzen; ~ **upon s. one's property** widerrechtlich jds. Grundstück betreten, jds. Eigentum verletzen; ~ **on s. one's rights** jds. Rechte verletzen; ~ **upon s. one's time** jds. Zeit in Anspruch nehmen (über Gebühr beanspruchen);
~ **board** Verbotsschild, -tafel.

trespasser Besitzstörer, *(offender)* Übertreter, Zuwiderhandelnder, Rechtsverletzer, *(unauthorized person)* Unbefugter;
defiant ~ *(US)* mutwilliger Rechtsbrecher; **joint** ~**s** Mitbeteiligte bei Begehung einer unerlaubten Handlung;
~ **from the beginning** rückwirkend bestrafter Täter; ~**s will be prosecuted** Zuwiderhandlungen werden strafrechtlich verfolgt, Durchgang (Eintritt) bei Strafe verboten.

trespassing, no Zutritt verboten; **no ~ on railway property** Unbefugten ist das Betreten der Bahnanlagen verboten.

trestle bridge Eisenbahnviadukt.

tret Refaktie, Gewichtsvergütung.

triable verhandlungsreif.

trial *(annoyance)* Belästigung, Nervensäge, *(criminal)* Hauptverhandlung, Strafprozeß, *(hearing)* Gerichtsverhandlung, *(judicial examination)* gerichtliche Untersuchung, [Gerichts]verfahren, Verhör, Vernehmung, mündliche Verhandlung, Prozeß[sache], *(school, Br.)* Versetzungsexamen, *(temptation)* Versuchung, Anfechtung, Schicksalsprüfung, *(test)* Probe, Versuch, Prüfung, Experiment;
by way of ~versuchsweise, *(law court)* vor Gericht; **in one's hour of ~** in der Stunde der Versuchung; **on ~** zur (auf) Probe, *(court)* vor Gericht;
civil ~ Zivilprozeßverfahren; **criminal ~** Strafverfahren, -prozeß; **defended ~** streitige Verhandlung; **duty ~** Leistungsversuch; **fair and impartial ~** gerechtes und objektives Verfahren; **homicide ~** Mordprozeß, -verfahren; **joint ~** gemeinsame Hauptverhandlung; **mock ~** Scheinprozeß, -verfahren; **murder ~** Mordprozeß; **new ~** wiederaufgenommenes Verfahren, Wiederaufnahmeverfahren; **public ~** öffentliche Verhandlung; **separate ~** abgetrenntes Verfahren; **shop ~** Erprobung auf dem Prüfstand; **show ~** Schauprozeß; **speedy ~** Schnellverfahren; **state ~** politischer Prozeß, [etwa] Prozeß vor dem Bundesverfassungsgericht;
~ **of an action** Gerichtsverhandlung; ~ **with assessors** *(Admiralty action)* Verhandlung in Anwesenheit von Sachverständigen; ~ **at bar** Verhandlung vor einem voll besetzten Gericht; ~ **by certificate** schriftliches Verfahren; ~ **by the country** Verhandlung vor den Geschworenen, Schwurgerichtsverfahren; ~ **by court martial** Kriegsgerichtsverfahren; ~ **and error** Herumprobieren; ~ **by inspection or examination** Verhandlung nach

Augenscheinsnahme; ~ **instanter** sofortige Hauptverhandlung; ~ **before a single judge** Verhandlung vor dem Einzelrichter; ~ **by jury** Schwurgerichtsverfahren, Verhandlung vor dem Schwurgericht; ~ **at nisi prius** Verfahren vor dem Einzelrichter; ~ **by the record** Urkundenprozeß; ~ **of strength** Machtprobe;
to adjourn the ~ Verfahren unterbrechen; **to appoint (assign) a day for the ~** Verhandlungstermin ansetzen; **to be on ~** vor Gericht (unter Anklage) stehen, verhört werden; **to be a ~ to s. o.** jem. auf die Nerven gehen; **to be found on ~ to be incompetent** Probezeit nicht bestehen; **to be on one's ~** verhört werden; **to be up for ~** zur Verhandlung kommen; **to bring s. o. up for ~** jem. den Prozeß machen; **to buy s. th. on ~** etw. auf Probe (mit Rückgaberecht) kaufen; **to commit for ~** dem zuständigen Prozeßgericht überstellen; **to conduct a ~** Prozeß leiten; **to demand ~ of a ship before its acceptance** Abnahmeprüfung eines Schiffes verlangen; **to fix a day for the ~** Termin zur Verhandlung ansetzen; **to give s. o. a ~** j. probeweise einstellen; **to go on ~** vor Gericht gestellt werden; **to grant s. o. a new ~** Wiederaufnahme des Verfahrens anordnen; **to have on ~** zur Probe gebrauchen; **to have a ~ of strength with s. o.** seine Kräfte mit jem. messen; **to make a ~** Versuch unternehmen; **to order a new ~** Sache an die Erstinstanz zurückverweisen; **to postpone a ~** Verhandlung vertagen; **to proceed with a ~** Verhandlung fortsetzen; **to put s. o. on ~** j. vernehmen (verhören), jem. den Prozeß machen; **to put a machine to further ~** Maschine weiter ausprobieren; **to resume a ~** Verhandlung wiederaufnehmen; **to send a machine for free ~** Maschine kostenlos zum Ausprobieren zusenden; **to stand ~** Probe bestehen; **to stand on ~** *(law court)* vor Gericht stehen, sich vor Gericht verantworten, Strafverfahren über sich ergehen lassen; **to submit to a ~ by one's fellow members** mit einer Untersuchung durch seine Kollegen einverstanden sein; **to take s. o. on ~** j. auf Probezeit einstellen; **to take one's ~** vor Gericht stehen; **to take a machine on ~** Maschine auf Probe kaufen; **to waive ~** auf ein Verfahren verzichten;
~ **amendment** Änderung des Sachvortrags; ~ **balance** Probe-, Salden-, Roh-, Vorbilanz; **closing ~ balance** bereinigte Probebilanz; ~ **balance book** Zwischenbilanzbuch; ~ **balloon** Versuchsballon; ~ **blackout** Verdunkelungsübung; ~ **case** Probefall; ~ **consignment** Probesendung; ~ **court** *(US)* erstinstanzliches Gericht, Gericht erster Instanz, Prozeß-, Tatsacheninstanz; ~ **date** Verhandlungstermin; ~ **docket** Verhandlungsliste; ~ **engagement** Probeanstellung; ~ **exhibits** Anlagen einer Strafakte; ~ **experience** Gerichtserfahrung, Erfahrung in Strafsachen; ~ **flight** Probeflug, Einfliegen; ~ **issue** Probenummer; ~ **judge** *(US)* erstinstanzlicher Richter; ~ **jury** Schöffengericht in Strafsachen; ~ **lawyer** *(US)* Prozeßanwalt, Strafverteidiger; ~ **lesson** Probelektion; ~ **list** *(US)* Terminkalender des Gerichts, Prozeßverzeichnis; ~ **lot** Probesendung; ~ **membership** Probemitgliedschaft; ~ **offer** Probeangebot; ~ **order** Probeauftrag, -bestellung, Versuchsauftrag; **to place a ~ order** Probeauftrag plazieren; ~ **package** Probesendung, Probepackung; ~ **period** Probezeit; ~ **piece** Muster, Probestück; **to speed up ~ proceedings** Strafverfahrensablauf beschleunigen; ~ **record** Sitzungsprotokoll; ~ **run** Probelauf einer Fabrik, *(ship)* Probe-, Versuchsfahrt; ~ **sample** Muster, Probestück; ~ **shipment** Probesendung, *(customs)* Probeverzollung; ~ **site** Verhandlungsort; ~ **subscription** Probeabonnement, Probezug; ~ **transcript** Sitzungsprotokoll; ~ **trip** *(ship)* Versuchsfahrt; ~ **use** Probebenutzung; ~ **year** Probejahr.

triangular| agreement dreiseitiges Abkommen; ~ **deal** Dreiecksgeschäft; ~ **operation in exchange** Devisenarbitrage in drei verschiedenen Währungen, Dreiecksarbitrage, -geschäft; ~ **talk** *(pol.)* Dreierbesprechungen; ~ **trade** Dreiecksverkehr.

tribal| chief Stammeshäuptling; ~ **customs** Stammesbräuche; ~ **disputes** Stammesstreitigkeiten; ~ **follower** Stammesanhänger; ~ **homeland** Stammesgebiet; ~ **lands** Indianerreservate; ~ **law** Stammesrecht; ~ **strife** Stammesfehde.

tribe Volksstamm, Sippe, *(contemptuously)* Sippschaft; ~ **of politicians** politische Clique.

tribesman Stammesangehöriger.

tribunal Gericht[shof], Tribunal, *(fig.)* Richterstuhl, *(for rents)* Schiedsgericht;
Administrative ~ *(UNO)* Verwaltungsgericht; **arbitral ~** Schiedsgericht; **civil service arbitration ~** Schiedsgericht für Tarifkonflikte im öffentlichen Dienst; **Hague ~** Haager Schiedsgericht; **industrial ~** *(Br.)* Schiedsgerichtshof zur Regelung von Lohnungleichheiten; **lands ~** Enteignungsausschuß; **mental health review ~** Beschwerdeinstanz gegen Einweisung in eine Nervenheilanstalt; **military ~** Militärgerichtshof; **Pen-**

sion $\stackrel{\circ}{-}$ *(Br.)* Gerichtshof zur Regelung abgewiesener Pensions-forderungen, Sozialgericht; **railway rates** ~ *(former, Br.)* Eisenbahntarifschiedsstätte; **rent** ~ *(Br.)* Schiedsgericht für Wohnungsstreitigkeiten, Mieteinigungsamt, Schiedsgericht in Wohnungsstreitigkeiten; **Transport** $\stackrel{\circ}{-}$ *(Br.)* Aufsichtsamt für Bahn- und andere Beförderungstarife;

~ **of commerce** *(US)* Handelsgericht; ~ **of the Hague** Haager Schiedsgerichtshof; ~ **of public opinion** Richterstuhl der öffentlichen Meinung.

to sit upon a ~ einem Schiedsgericht angehören.

tribune Rednerbühne, *(popular leader)* Volksheld;

military ~ Kriegstribun;

~ **of hono(u)r** Ehrentribüne.

tributary Vasallenstaat, *(stream)* Nebenfluß;

~ *(a.)* zins-, steuerpflichtig.

tribute Zins, Abgabe, Zoll, *(mining)* Naturallohn;

to carry a ~ Würdigung vornehmen;

~ **system** *(mining)* Naturallohn.

tricar *(Br.)* Dreiradlieferwagen.

trichromatic process Dreifarbendruck.

trick [Propaganda]trick, Kunstgriff, Winkelzug, Dreh, Schlich, [Kriegs]list, *(characteristic)* Eigentümlichkeit, Zug, Anstrich, *(foolish action)* Spaß, Streich, Posse, *(illusion)* Sinnestäu-schung, Blendwerk, Gaukelheld, *(knack)* [Propaganda]trick, Kunstgriff, Schlich, Dreh;

~s Winkelzüge, Ränke;

card ~ Kartenkunststück; **confidence** ~ Schwindelmethode; **dirty** ~ übler Streich, Gemeinheit; **juggler's** ~ Gauklertrick; **new** ~s Neuerungen;

~ **with cards** Kartenkunsttrick; ~s **of fortune** Tücken des Schicksals; ~ **in a railway dispatch office** Schichtwechsel bei der Bahnabfertigung; ~s **of the trade** Branchenerfahrungen, -kenntnisse; **a** ~ **worth two of it** sehr viel bessere Methode; ~s **of writing** Stilfeinheiten;

~ *(v.)* hereinlegen, hintergehen, in eine Falle locken, prellen;

~ **out (up)** herausputzen; ~ **s. o. out of his property** j. um sein Vermögen bringen; ~ **s. o. into purchasing** j. zum Kauf verlei-ten; ~ **s. o. in a sale** j. beim Verkauf hereinlegen; ~ **the truth out of s. o.** Wahrheit aus jem. herausbekommen; ~ **s. o. out of his wages** j. um seinen Lohn betrügen;

to be up to s. one's ~s jds. Ränke durchschauen; **to be clever at card** ~s Kartenkunststücke beherrschen; **to do the** ~ *(sl.)* Zweck erfüllen; **to get money from s. o. by a** ~ j. in betrügeri-scher Weise um sein Geld bringen; **to know the** ~s **of the trade** sehr guter Kaufmann sein; **to know a** ~ **worth two of that** *(sl.)* raffiniertere Methode kennen; **to learn the** ~ **of it** Bogen bald heraushaben; **to obtain s. th. by** ~ sich etw. erschwindeln; **to play** ~s **upon s. o.** jem. eine Posse (einen Streich) spielen, j. schikanieren; **to pull off the** ~ *(US)* Kunststück zuwegebringen; **to resort to every** ~ **in order** zu jedem Mittel greifen, um; **to resort to** ~s **to gain one's end** sein Ziel durch Tricks zu erreichen suchen; **to try every** ~ **in the book** jeden nur erdenklichen Trick versuchen;

~ **cyclist** *(Br., mil., sl.)* Psychiater; ~ **film** Trickfilm; ~ **flying** Kunstflug; ~ **picture** Trickaufnahme; ~ **scene** *(Br., scene)* Trickszene.

tricker schlauer Gauner, Betrüger.

trickery Kniff, Gaunerei, Betrügerei.

trickily devised raffiniert ausgedacht.

trickiness ränkevolles Wesen, Verschlagenheit.

tricking Gaunerei.

trickle | *(v.)* tröpfeln;

~ **in** in kleinen Gruppen kommen; ~ **out** *(fig.)* durchsickern; ~ **out of the theater** aus dem Theater herausströmen.

tricklet Rinnsal.

trickster Betrüger, Gauner.

tricksy politician durchtriebener Politiker.

tricky verschlagen, durchtrieben, raffiniert, listig.

tricycle Dreirad.

tried | **in open court** öffentlich verhandelt; ~ **and discharged** freigesprochen;

~ **friend** zuverlässiger Freund.

triennial dreijährlich.

trier Prüfgerät, *(fig.)* Prüfstein.

trifle Kleinigkeit, Bagatelle, Lappalie, unbedeutender Gegen-stand, *(small amount)* kleine Geldsumme;

from a ~ aus geringfügigem Anlaß;

a mere ~ nur ein Kinderspiel;

~ *(v.)* leichtfertig umgehen, achtlos behandeln;

~ **with s. o.** j. auf den Arm nehmen wollen; ~ **away with one's food** mit seinem Essen herummanschen; ~ **away one's money**

sein Geld vergeuden (verschleudern, verplempern); ~ **with one's health** mit seiner Gesundheit Raubbau treiben; ~ **away one's time** seine Zeit vertrödeln;

to stand upon ~s Kleinigkeitskrämer sein; **not to stick on** ~s sich nicht mit Kleinigkeiten abgeben; **to waste one's time with** ~s seine Zeit mit Kinkerlitzchen verschwenden;

a ~ **expensive** ein bißchen teuer.

trifler oberflächlicher Mensch.

trifling unbedeutend, -beträchtlich, geringfügig, belanglos;

~ **error** belangloser Fehler; **no** ~ **matter** eine Riesenaffäre, kein Pappenstiel; ~ **value** unerheblicher Wert.

trig steif, formell.

trigger *(gunman)* Revolverheld, *(photo)* Auslöser;

quick on the ~ reaktionsschnell, auf Draht;

price ~ *(steel imports, US)* Mindest-, Bezugs-, Referenzpreis; ~ *(v.) (sl.)* sich an einem Raubüberfall beteiligen;

~ **antidumping measures** gegen internationale Preisunterbie-tung gerichtete Maßnahmen herbeiführen; ~ **off entrepre-neurial investments** Investitionen der Unternehmer auslösen; ~ **off a costly strike** kostspieligen Streik auslösen;

to have one's finger on the ~ Finger am Abzug haben, auf alles vorbereitet sein, *(mil.)* jederzeit einsatzbereit sein; **to pull the** ~ abdrücken;

~**-happy** kriegslüstern; ~ **man** *(underworld use, sl.)* Mörder.

trillion *(US)* Billion.

trim Beschaffenheit, Zustand, *(airplane, ship)* Gleichgewichts-lage, *(car)* Innenausstattung, -ausrüstung, *(gala dress)* Gala-kleidung, Staat, *(mind)* richtige Verfassung, *(window decora-tion, US)* Schaufensterschmuck;

in fighting ~ *(mil.)* gefechtsbereit; **in good** ~ in Ordnung; ~ **of the hold** gute Verstauung der Ladung;

~ *(v.)* in Ordnung bringen, zurechtmachen, *(cheat, coll.)* beschummeln, *(dress up)* sich aufdonnern (auftakeln), *(fig.)* Mittelkurs halten, *(pol.)* lavieren, schwanken, sich anpassen, *(rebuke, sl.)* herunterputzen, abkanzeln, *(ship)* in richtige Schwimmlage bringen, trimmen;

~ **back** beschneiden; ~ **a cabin** Kabine zurechtmachen; ~ **a Christmas tree** Weihnachtsbaum schmücken; ~ **the edges of a book** Buch beschneiden; ~ **the freight** Fracht verstauen; ~ **with fur** mit Pelz garnieren; ~ **off the government's reflationary margin** Möglichkeiten der Regierung zur Wirtschaftsbelebung durch inflationäre Mittel beschneiden; ~ **the hold** Ladung seemäßig verstauen; ~ **s. one's jacket** jem. das Fell versohlen (die Jacke vollhauen); ~ **3% on average off the prices of some 100 basic items** durchschnittlichen Preisabschlag von 3% vom Hundert bei Grundnahrungsmitteln erzwingen; ~ **one's sails to every wind** seinen Mantel stets nach dem Winde hängen; ~ **a shopwindow** Schaufenster dekorieren; ~ **a small slice off the debt** Verschuldung geringfügig abbauen; ~ **with the times** Op-portunitätspolitik betreiben; ~ **up** herausputzen; ~ **o. s. up** sich auftakeln;

to be in ~ **for rough work** sich richtig ausarbeiten wollen.

trimmer Kohlentrimmer, Ladungsarbeiter, Stauer, *(politics, Br.)* Achselträger, Opportunist, Wetterfahne.

trimming *(ship)* Staulage;

~s Besatzartikel, *(car)* Ausstattung, *(dish)* Zutaten, Beilagen, Garnierung;

freight ~ Frachtverstauung; **sound** ~ kräftiger Verweis;

to take a ~ Niederlage hinnehmen;

~s **manufacturer** Posamentierer.

Trinity House *(Br.)* Leuchtturmbehörde, Seeamt.

trip Fahrt, kurze Reise, Ausflug, Tour, Abstecher, Spritzer, *(failure)* Fehler, Irrtum, *(false step)* Fehltritt, *(technics)* Auslösevorrichtung;

air ~ Flug[reise]; **business** ~ Geschäftsreise; **honeymoon** ~ Hochzeitsreise; **pleasure** ~ Vergnügungsreise; **round** ~ Rund-reise; **weekend** ~ Wochenendausflug;

~ **abroad** Auslandsreise; ~ **there and back** *(Br.)* Hin- und Rück-reise; ~ **through a factory** Betriebs-, Fabrikbesichtigung; ~ **to prison** *(sl.)* Festnahme; ~ **to the seaside** Spritztour an die See; ~ **of the tongue** Versprecher;

~ **out** austricksen; ~ **up** stolpern; ~ **a witness by skilful practices** Zeugen durch geschickte Befragung aufs Glatteis führen;

to go for a ~ Ausflug (Spritztour) machen; **to take a** ~ Abste-cher machen; **to take a** ~ **round the world** Weltreise unternehmen;

~ **planning** Reisevorbereitung; ~ **wire** *(mil.)* Stolperdraht.

tripartite dreifach ausgefertigt;

~ **agreement** *(gold and currency)* Dreimächteabkommen; ~ **indenture** Vertragsurkunde in dreifacher Ausfertigung; ~ **treaty** Dreimächtevertrag.

tripe *(sl.)* Plunder, Schund, Mist.
triplicate Drittausfertigung, *(bill of exchange)* Tertiawechsel;
~ *(a.)* dreifach, in dreifacher Ausfertigung;
~ *(v.)* dreifach ausfertigen.
tripod *(photo)* Stativ.
tripper *(Br.)* Ausflügler, Tourist, *(technics)* Auslösevorrichtung;
weekend ~ Wochenendausflügler;
~ **device** Schaltvorrichtung.
triptych Zollpassierschein, internationaler Autopaß, Triptyk.
triumph of science Triumph der Naturwissenschaft.
trivial banal, trivial, alltäglich, gewöhnlich, *(insignificant)* geringfügig, unerheblich, unbedeutend, nichtssagend;
~ **loss** geringfügiger Verlust; ~ **matter** belanglose Angelegenheit; ~ **objections** unerhebliche Einwände; ~ **offence** Bagatellvergehen, -sache; ~ **round** Routineverlauf.
Trojan tüchtiger Mensch;
to work like a ~ wie ein Pferd arbeiten;
~ **horse** *(pol.)* Spionage-, Sabotagegruppe.
trolley *(department store)* Einkaufswagen, *(mining, Br.)* Förderwagen, Laufkatze, Hund, *(Br.)* Hand-, Schubkarren, *(el.)* Stromabnehmerrolle, *(railway, Br.)* Draisine, *(railroad station, US)* Gepäckwagen, *(tram, US)* Straßenbahn[wagen];
off one's ~ ein bißchen verrückt;
~ *(v.)* mit einem Karren befördern;
~ **bus** Omnibus mit elektrischer Oberleitung, Oberleitungsbus, Obus; ~ **car (coach,** *US)* Straßenbahnwagen; ~ **line** Straßenbahn-, Obuslinie; ~ **pole** *(trolley bus)* Kontaktstange; ~ **table** *(Br.)* Tee-, Servierwagen; ~ **wire** Oberleitung.
troop Trupp, Haufe, *(mil.)* Schwadron, Panzereinheit;
~ **of school children** Gruppe von Schulkindern;
~ *(v.) (mil.)* aufstellen, formieren;
~ **away** *(coll.)* sich davonmachen, in einer Marschkolonne marschieren; ~ **the colo(u)rs** *(Br.)* Fahnenparade abnehmen; **up (together)** sich sammeln (scharen).
troops *(mil.)* Truppen;
in ~ truppweise;
fresh ~ neue Truppen; **household** ~ Gardetruppen; **protecting** ~ Sicherungstruppen;
~ **seasoned by battle** kampfgewohnte Truppen; ~ **on manoeuvre** Truppen im Manöver, Manövertruppen;
to assemble ~ Truppen aufmarschieren lassen; **to bring in the** ~ Armee einsetzen; **to concentrate** ~ Truppen ansammeln (konzentrieren); **to march** ~ Truppen in Marsch setzen; **to mass** ~ Truppen massieren, Truppenmassierung vornehmen; **to raise** ~ Truppen ausheben; **to remove** ~ Truppen verlegen; **to shift** ~ Truppen umquartieren.
troop|carrier Truppentransporter; ~ **ceiling** Truppenhöchstgrenze; ~ **commitments** Truppeneinsatz; ~ **cuts** Truppenabbau; ~ **deployment** Truppenverwendung; ~ **detachment** Truppenkontingent; ~ **leader** Truppenführer; ~ **reduction** Truppenreduzierung; ~ **redeployment** Truppenentfaltung; ~ **school** Waffenschule; ~ **withdrawal** Truppenabzug.
trooper *(mil.)* Reiter, Kavallerist, *(transport vessel)* Truppentransporter;
to swear like a ~ wie ein Landsknecht fluchen.
trooping the colours *(Br.)* Fahnenparade.
troopship Truppentransporter.
tropical tropisch, *(fig.)* hitzig, leidenschaftlich;
~ **climate** Tropenklima; ~ **country** Tropengegend; ~ **disease** Tropenkrankheit; ~ **disturbance** tropische Störung; ~ **and subtropical fruits** *(Br.)* Südfrüchte; ~ **heat** tropische Hitze; ~ **kit** Tropenausrüstung.
trot *(fig.)* Trab, schnelle Gangart, *(pony, sl.)* Eselsbrücke, Klatsche;
~ *(v.)* **in** hereinspaziert kommen; ~ **off home** sich nach Hause trollen; ~ **s. o. off his legs** jem. bis zum Umfallen die Sehenswürdigkeiten zeigen; ~ **out** zur Schau stellen, sich produzieren; ~ **out one's knowledge** sich mit seinem Wissen brüsten; ~ **round** Ladenbummel mitnehmen;
to be on the ~ **all day** ganzen Tag auf den Beinen sein; **to go for a** ~ sich die Beine vertreten, kleinen Spaziergang machen; **to go a steady** ~ den ganzen Tag auf den Beinen sein; **to keep s. o. on the** ~ j. in Trab halten; **to proceed at a** ~ schärfere Gangart einschlagen.
trouble Mühe, Beschwerde, Anstrengung, Ungelegenheit, *(annoyance)* Haken, Scherereien, kitzlige (heikle) Lage, Schlamassel, Belästigung, *(distress)* Kummer, Verdruß, Mißgeschick, Schwulitäten, *(el.)* Defekt, Störung, *(data processing)* Fehler, *(pol.)* öffentliche Unruhe, Wirren, Stunk, Skandal, Konflikt, Krawall;
in ~ in der Patsche (Tinte, im Dreck);

children's ~**s** Kinderkrankheiten; **domestic** ~**s** häuslicher Ärger; **gearbox** ~ *(car)* Getriebeschaden; **heart** ~ Herzleiden, -beschwerden; **labo(ur)** ~**s** Arbeiterunruhen;
~**s in the Far East** Unruhen im Fernen Osten;
~ *(v.)* sich beunruhigen (aufregen), *(take pains)* sich die Mühe machen, sich bemühen; ~ **s. o.** jem Umstände machen; ~ **s. o. with a letter** j. mit einem Brief belästigen; ~ **the waters** Frieden stören; ~ **s. o. at work** bei der Arbeit stören;
to ask for ~ sich ins Unglück stürzen, Schicksal herausfordern; **to be causing the most** ~ **on wages** größte Schwierigkeiten bei Lohnverhandlungen machen; **to be in grave** ~ erhebliche Schwierigkeiten haben; **to be a great** ~ **to one's family** große Belastung für seine Familie darstellen; **to be in** ~ **with the law** mit dem Gesetz in Konflikt geraten sein; **to be out looking for** ~ auf Krawall aus sein; **to get into** ~ in Schwierigkeiten geraten, sich Unannehmlichkeiten zuziehen, sich in die Nesseln setzen; **to get a girl into** ~ Mädchen schwängern; **to give s. o.** ~ jem. Sorge bereiten; **to give s. o. much** ~ jem. Umstände machen; **to have a lot of family** ~ ziemliche Schwierigkeiten mit seiner Familie haben; **to have been through much** ~ viel durchgemacht haben; **to look for** ~ sich in die Nesseln setzen; **to make** ~ Schwierigkeiten machen; **to run into** ~ in Schwierigkeiten geraten, geschäftliche Probleme haben; **to save o. s.** ~ sich die Mühe sparen; **to spare s. o.** ~ jem. Unannehmlichkeiten ersparen; **to stir up** ~ Verwirrung (Unruhe) stiften; **to tackle the mounting** ~ mit den wachsenden Schwierigkeiten fertig werden; **to take great** ~ sich große Mühe geben;
~ **area** Krisengebiet, *(engine)* störanfälliges Gebiet; ~**-free** störungsfrei; ~ **man** *(tel., US)* Störungssucher, Entstörer; ~**-shoot** *(tel., US)* Störung auffinden und beseitigen; ~ **shooter** *(mediator)* Schlichter, *(tel., US)* Störungssucher; ~ **shooting** Fehlersuche, *(tel., US)* Störungssuche; ~ **spot** Unruhe-, Krisenherd.
troubled|with a nasty cough von einem hartnäckigen Husten gepeinigt; ~ **about money matters** von Geldsorgen bedrängt; ~ **by bad news** von schlechten Nachrichten aufgeschreckt;
~ **countenance** besorgte Miene; **to be in** ~ **mind** sehr beunruhigt sein; ~ **waters** schwierige Situation, verworrene Situation; **to fish in** ~ **waters** im Trüben fischen; **to pour oil on** ~ **waters** Öl auf die Wogen gießen, *(fig.)* aufgeregte Gemüter beruhigen.
troublous stürmisch;
to live in ~ **times** in einer unruhigen Zeit leben.
troublemaker Unruhestifter, Störenfried.
trough Trog, Mulde, Rinne, Furche, *(business cycle)* Talsohle der Konjunktur, Konjunkturmulde, -tief;
~ **of low barometric pressure** Tiefdruckrinne; ~ **of the sea** Wellental;
to recover from the ~ **in the underwriting cycle** sich von der Konjunkturmulde im Versicherungsgeschäft erholen.
trounce bemängeln, kritisieren.
troupe Schauspielergruppe, *(criminals)* Gangsterbande.
trouper Mitglied einer Schauspielertruppe, Ensemblemitglied.
trousers, to wear the *(fig.)* die Hosen anhaben.
trousseau Aussteuer, Mitgift.
trove Schatzfund.
trover rechtswidrige Aneignung fremder beweglicher Sachen.
trowel Maurerkelle;
to lay it on with a ~ zu dick auftragen.
troy weight Troygewicht.
truancy Müßiggang, Fernbleiben, *(pupil)* Schwänzen;
~ **rate** Prozentsatz der Schulschwänzer.
truant Faulenzer, Bummler, *(school)* Schulschwänzer;
to play ~ Schule schwänzen.
truce Waffenstillstand, -ruhe;
~ **offer** Waffenstillstandsangebot.
truck *(US)* Last[kraft]wagen, LKW, *(small articles)* Gegenstände von geringem Wert, Hausbedarf, Kleinkram, *(barter)* Tausch[handel], -geschäft, -verkehr, Um-, Eintausch, *(flat-topped car)* Hand-, Gepäckwagen, Karren, *(intercourse)* Handel, Umgang, Verkehr, *(mining)* Förderwagen, Lore, Hund, *(payment in goods, Br.)* Warenentlohnung, *(railway, Br.)* [offener] Güter-, Rungenwagen, Waggon, *(rubbish, coll.)* Plunder, Trödel, Abfall;
baggage ~ Handgepäckwagen; **cattle** ~ Viehwagen; **dump** ~ Lastwagen mit Kippvorrichtung; **flat** ~ Pritschenwagen; **freight** ~ *(US)* Güterwagen; **garbage** ~ *(US)* Müllwagen; **garden** ~ *(US)* Gartengemüse; **goods** ~ *(Br.)* offener Güterwagen; **heavy** ~ schwerer Lastkraftwagen (LKW); **industrial** ~ Fernlaster, -lastwagen; **light** ~ *(US)* mittelschwerer LKW; **long-distance** ~ Fernlaster, -lastzug; **motor** ~ Lastkraftwagen, LKW; **pickup** ~ schneller Lastwagen, Kleinlast-, Abholwagen; **poor** ~ *(US)* wertlose Ware; **semitrailer** ~ Sattelschlepper;

~ *(v.)* *(barter)* Tauschhandel treiben, *(barter away)* verschachern, *(be employed as truckman)* Lastwagen fahren, *(railway)* in Güterwagen befördern, *(~ system, Br.)* Lohn in Waren zahlen, *(transport, US)* mit Lastwagen befördern, auf Lastwagen transportieren;

~ **for a living** sich als Lastwagenfahrer sein Geld verdienen; **to drive a ~** Lastwagen fahren; **to have no ~ with s. o.** mit jem. nichts zu tun haben; **to highjack a ~** Lastwagen ausrauben; **to ship by ~** mit Lastwagen (im LKW) befördern; **to stand no ~** sich nichts gefallen lassen;

~ **Acts** *(Br.)* Lohnzahlungsgesetze, Lohnschutzgesetzgebung; ~ **business** Lastwagenfirma; ~ **car** Güterwagen; ~ **carrier** Lastwagentransportfirma, Güterfernverkehrsunternehmen; ~ **charges** Rollgeld; ~ **competition** Lastwagenwettbewerb; ~ **delivery** *(US)* Überlandzustellung; ~ **driver** LKW-, Fernlastfahrer; ~-**driver helper** Beifahrer; ~ **economy** Tauschwirtschaft; ~ **factory** *(US)* Lastwagenfabrik, LKW-Fabrik; ~ **farm (garden)** *(US)* Gemüsegärtnerei; ~ **farmer** *(US)* Gemüsegärtner; ~ **fleet** Lastwagenflotte, Fuhrpark; ~-**leasing business** Lastwagenverleih; ~ **manufacture** Lastwagenherstellung; ~ **manufacturer** Lastwagenhersteller; ~-**manufacturing plant** Lastwagenfabrik; ~ **operation** Transportgeschäft; ~ **plant** *(US)* Lastwagenfabrik; ~ **production** Lastwagenproduktion; ~ **rates** Kilometergeld, Lastwagentarif, Überlandfrachtsatz; ~ **registration** LKW-Zulassung; ~ **rental** LKW-Miete; ~ **requirement** *(Br.)* Waggonbedarf; **to meet ~ requirements** *(Br.)* Waggonanforderungen genügen, Waggons stellen; ~ **service** Lastwagen-, Überlandverkehr; ~ **service distributor** *(US)* Engroshändler ohne eigenes Lager; ~ **shop** *(Br.)* Betrieb mit Entlohnung nach dem Trucksystem, *(US)* Tankstelle mit Restauration, Kraftfahrerraststätte; ~ **stop** Fernlastfahrerhalteplatz; ~ **store** *(US)* Grünkramladen; ~ **supply** *(Br.)* Waggongestellung; ~ **system** *(Br.)* Trucksystem, Bezahlung der Arbeiter in Waren, Warenentlohnung; ~ **trailer** *(US)* Lastwagenanhänger; **motor ~ transport** *(US)* Beförderung mit Lastwagen; ~ **wages** *(Br.)* Warenlohn; ~ **wholesaler** *(US)* Großhändler ohne eigenes Lager.

truckage *(Br.)* Transport auf Güterwagen, Güterwagentransport, *(conveying goods by truck)* Lastwagenbeförderung, Transport auf Lastwagen, LKW-Transport, Güterkraftverkehr, *(exchange)* Tauschsystem, *(money paid, Br.)* Rollgeld.

trucker *(barterer)* Hausierer, *(US)* Fern[last]wagen-, Lastwagen-, Fernfahrer.

trucking Lastwagen-, LKW-Transport, Autospedition, *(Br.)* Beförderung mit Güterwagen, Güterwagentransport, *(barter)* Tauschhandel, *(air freight)* Luftfrachtverkehr;

~ **agency** Rollfuhrunternehmen, Güterspedition, [Straßen]transportunternehmen; **common ~ company** Kraftwagenexpedition, Lastwagentransportunternehmen; ~ **costs** Überlandversandkosten; ~ **depot** Lastwagendepot; ~ **facilities** Landtransporteinrichtungen; ~ **firm** Rollfuhrunternehmen; ~ **fleet** Lastwagenkolonne; ~ **industry** Lastwagenindustrie; ~ **line** Überlandverkehr; ~ **service** Rollfuhrdienst; ~ **shipment** Überlandsendung; ~ **shot** *(film)* vom fahrenden Kamerawagen gedrehte Szene; ~ **strike** Transportarbeiterstreik.

truckle *(v.)* zu Kreuze kriechen.

truckler Kriecher, Speichellecker.

truckload *(US)* Waggon-, Sammelladung;

less-than-~ *(US)* Stückgut;

full ~ shipment Sammeltransport.

truckman Fern-, Fernlast-, Lastwagen-, LKW-Fahrer.

truckster *(US)* Gemüsegärtner.

truckway Straße für Lastwagen.

true wahrheitsgetreu, wahrhaftig, richtig, *(authentic)* echt, getreu, tatsächlich, *(legitimate)* rechtmäßig, legitim, *(pol.)* zuverlässig, *(sincere)* aufrichtig, echt, lauter;

as ~ as gold so treu wie Gold; **out of ~** falsch eingestellt; ~ **to specimen** laut Muster, mit dem Muster übereinstimmend, mustergetreu;

~ *(v.)* **off a bearing** Lager ausrichten; ~ **up a wheel** Rad zentrieren;

to be (hold) ~ zutreffen; **to be ~ only of food prices** nur im Hinblick auf Lebensmittelpreise zutreffen; **to be ~ to one's word** sein Wort (Versprechen) halten; **to come ~** Wirklichkeit werden; **to prove ~** sich als wahr herausstellen;

~ **admission** *(judicial proceedings)* Zugeständnis von Tatsachen; ~ **bill** *(US)* begründete Anklageschrift [des Schwurgerichts]; ~ **blue** *(fig.)* zuverlässiger Mensch, getreuer Anhänger; ~-**blue Tory** waschechter Konservativer; ~-**born American** geborener Amerikaner; ~-**bred** *(fig.)* kultiviert, gebildet; ~ **copy** gleichlautende Abschrift; ~ **discount** *(loan)* offenes Disagio; ~ **exchange** echtes Devisengeschäft; ~-**false test** *(opinion research)* Ja-Nein-Test; ~ **gold** reines Gold; ~ **heir** rechtmäßiger Erbe; ~ **indication** unfehlbares Anzeichen; ~ **interest** reine Zinsen; ~ **interest in s. one's welfare** aufrichtiges Interesse an jds. Wohlergehen; ~ **likeness** sprechende Ähnlichkeit; ~ **name** richtiger Name; ~ **north** geographischer Nordpol; ~ **owner** wirklicher (rechtmäßiger) Eigentümer; ~ **report** wahrheitsgetreuer Bericht; ~ **reserve** *(US)* außerordentliche Reserve; ~ **sign** zuverlässiges Anzeichen; ~ **statesmanship** wahre Staatskunst; ~ **story** wahre Geschichte; ~ **strength** wirkliche Stärke; ~ **value** innerer Wert, Verkehrswert; ~ **value rule** *(issue of shares)* Bareinzahlungspflicht zum Nennwert; ~ **verdict** rechtsgültiger Geschworenenspruch; ~ **weight** genaues Gewicht.

trueborn ehelich;

~ **Englishman** Stockengländer.

truism Binsenwahrheit, Gemeinplatz.

truly, yours *(in a letter)* Ihr sehr ergebener, hochachtungsvoll.

trump Trompetenstoß, *(cards)* Trumpf[karte], *(coll.)* treue Seele, Prachtmensch;

~ *(v.)* übertrumpfen, *(Br., stock exchange,)* Papiere hinauftreiben;

~ *(v.)* **up** sich aus den Fingern saugen;

to come up ~s sich als Trumpfass erweisen; **to keep one's ~s in hand** seine Trümpfe behalten; **to put s. o. to his ~s** j. zur Anwendung seiner letzten Mittel zwingen; **to turn up ~s** sich als das Beste erweisen;

to play one's ~ card seine Trumpfkarte ausspielen.

trumped-up *(coll.)* erdichtet, erlogen;

~ **charge** vorsätzlich falsche Anschuldigung; ~ **excuse** aus den Fingern gesogene Entschuldigung.

trumpery Plunder, Schund, Ramsch[ware], *(rigmarole)* Gewäsch, Geschwätz, Quatsch;

~ **arguments** belanglose Argumente; ~ **furniture** geschmacklose Möbel; ~ **wares** Ausschußware.

trumpet Trompetenstoß, *(fig.)* Ausposauner;

ear ~ Hörrohr; **speaking** ~ Sprachrohr, Schalltrichter;

~ *(v.)* *(fig.)* ausposaunen;

to blow one's own ~ sich beweihräuchern;

~ **call** Trompetensignal.

truncheon *(Br.)* Gummiknüppel, Schlagstock;

~ *(v.)* Gummiknüppel benutzen.

trundle Rolle, Walze, *(car)* kleiner Rollwagen;

~ *(v.)* **a disabled person** Invaliden schieben;

to be on the ~ looking for *(fam.)* auf der Suche sein.

trunk Baumstamm, *(main body)* Stamm, Hauptteil, *(box)* Reise-, Übersee-, Schrankkoffer, *(canal, river)* Hauptfahrrinne, *(railway)* Hauptlinie, -strecke, *(technics)* Rohrleitung, Schacht, *(tel., Br.)* Fernleitung, -verbindung;

~**s** *(Br.)* Fernamt;

~ **of a car** Autokoffer;

~**s please** *(Br.)* Fernamt bitte;

to pack one's ~s seine Koffer packen;

~ **airline** Hauptfluglinie, im Flugverkehr; ~ **cable** Fernkabel; ~ **call** *(Br.)* Ferngespräch, -anruf; **to book a ~ call** *(Br.)* Ferngespräch anmelden; ~ **compartment** *(US)* Kofferraum; ~ **connection** *(tel., US)* Kofferdeck; ~ **deck** *(mar.)* Kofferdeck; ~ **dialling** *(Br.)* Fernwahl; ~ **enquiries** *(Br.)* Fernauskunft; ~ **exchange** *(Br.)* Fernamt; ~ **line** *(US, railroad)* Haupt[eisen]bahn-, Hauptverkehrslinie, Hauptstrecke, Stammlinie, *(tel., Br.)* Stamm-, Fernleitung, Fernverbindung; ~ **line system** *(Br.)* Fernleitungsnetz; ~-**mail** Überseekoffer; ~ **network** *(Br.)* Fernleitungsnetz; ~ **offering final selector** *(Br.)* Fernleitungswähler; ~ **railway** Haupt-, *(road)* Haupt[verkehrs]straße; ⌀ **Roads Act** *(Br.)* Fernverkehrsstraßengesetz; ~ **road investment** zur Erstellung von Fernstraßen aufgewandte Kapitalbeträge; **new ~ road scheme** *(Br.)* fertiggestelltes Fernstraßennetz; ~ **route** Hauptlinie; ~ **telephone service** *(Br.)* Fernleitungswesen; ~ **traffic** Fernverkehr; ~ **wire** Haupttelegraphenlinie; ~ **zone** Fernverkehrsbereich.

trunker Kapitän der Landstraße.

truss *(Br.)* Bündel;

~ *(v.)* **up a criminal** Verbrecher fesseln; ~ **up utensils** Geräte zusammenbinden.

trust *(confidence)* Zu-, Vertrauen, Treu und Glauben, *(US, corner)* Großunternehmen, Trust, Konzern, Ring, Kartell, *(credit)* Kredit, Borg, *(custody)* Treu[pflicht], -verhältnis, Treuhand, Treuhandverhältnis, Pflegschaft, *(depositing)* Aufbewahrung, Obhut, Verwahrung, *(endowment)* Stiftung, *(entail)* Fideikommiß, *(investment trust company)* Kapitalanlage-, Investmentgesellschaft, *(obligation)* Verpflichtung, Pflicht, *(person)* Vertrauensperson, -mann, *(pledge)* anvertrautes Gut, Pfand, *(trust estate)* Treuhandvermögen, -gut;

in ~ zu treuen Händen, treuhänderisch, in treuhänderischer Verwaltung, zur Verwahrung; **on ~** auf Treu und Glauben, zu treuen Händen, *(goods)* auf Kredit (Borg, Pump); **~s** treuhänderische Funktionen;

accessory ~ *(Scot.)* Treuhandverwaltung mit besonderen Vollmachten; **accumulating (accumulation) ~** Wachstums-, Thesaurierungsfonds, Treuhand, Kapitalsammelstelle; **active ~** Treuhandverwaltung mit besonderen Vollmachten; **alimentary ~** Unterhalts-, Rentenfonds, Unterstützungsfonds; **bare ~** *(US)* einfache Hinterlegungsstelle; **brains ~** Beraterstab, Gehirntrust, Expertengruppe, wissenschaftlicher Beirat; **business ~** Trust, Konzern, *(US)* treuhänderisch geleitetes Unternehmen; **business life insurance ~** Treuhandgesellschaft zur Verwaltung einer Teilhaberversicherung; **car ~** *(US)* Finanzierungsgesellschaft für Eisenbahnbedarf; **cash-fund ~** Investmentfonds mit sofortiger Anlage der zufließenden Mittel; **cestui que ~** Nutznießer eines Stiftungsvermögens, Treuhandbegünstigter; **charitable ~** wohltätige (milde) Stiftung, Wohltätigkeitsstiftung; **closed-end [investment] ~** *(Br.)* Kapitalanlagegesellschaft mit konstantem Anlagekapital; **common ~** gemeinsame Treuhandverwaltung; **community ~** Treuhandgesellschaft zur Verwaltung öffentlicher Stiftungen; **complete voluntary (completely constituted) ~** in allen Einzelheiten festgelegte Stiftung, zweckgebundenes Treuhandvermögen, spezifiziertes Treuhandverhältnis; **incompletely constituted ~** Treuhandverhältnis mit noch fehlender Treuhandübertragung; **constructive ~** mittelbares (fingiertes) Treuhandeigentum; **contingent ~** bedingte Stiftung, bedingtes Treuhandverhältnis; **corporate ~** Aktienkonzern; **court ~** *(US)* aufgrund gerichtlicher Anordnung verwaltetes Vermögen; **direct ~** gewillkürtes Treuhandverhältnis; **directory ~** in den Grundzügen festgelegte Stiftung; **discretionary ~** *(Br.)* nach freiem Ermessen verwaltetes Treuhandvermögen, *(investment company)* Kapitalanlagegesellschaft mit breitgestreutem Aktienportefeuille; **dry ~** abstraktes Treuhandverhältnis; **educational ~** Schulstiftung; **executed ~** vollständig festgelegtes Treuhandverhältnis; **executory ~** unvollständige (in das Belieben des Erben gestellte) Stiftung (Treuhanderrichtung); **express ~** ausdrücklich geschaffenes Treuhandverhältnis, gewillkürtes Treuhandverhältnis; **express active ~** Treuhandverwaltung mit voller Freiheit in der Vermögensverwaltung; **family ~** Familienstiftung; **fixed investment ~** *(US)* Kapitalanlagegesellschaft mit festgelegtem Effektenbestand; **flexible ~** *(US)* Kapitalanlagegesellschaft mit wechselndem Portefeuille; **half-secret ~** teilweise verdecktes Treuhandverhältnis; **imperfect ~** unvollständige Treuhandverwaltung; **implied ~** kraft Gesetzes entstandenes (vermutetes) Treuhandverhältnis; **instrumental ~** reines Treuhandverhältnis ohne besondere Verwaltungsaufgaben; **investment ~** Investment-, Kapitalanlagegesellschaft; **involuntary ~** gesetzliches Treuhandverhältnis; **irrevocable ~** unwiderrufliche Treuhandbestellung; **limited ~** für kurze Zeit errichteter Konzern; **living ~** *(US)* lebenslängliche Treuhandverwaltung, Treuhandvermögen zu Lebzeiten des Verfügenden; **managed-list ~** *(US)* Anlagegesellschaft mit Austauschrecht der Investitionseffekten, Kapitalanlagegesellschaft mit Anlagenverwaltung in eigener Regie; **management ~** Kapitalanlagegesellschaft mit freizügiger Anlagepolitik, nach eigenem Ermessen anlegende Kapitalgesellschaft; **Massachusetts ~** *(US)* treuhänderisch geleitetes Unternehmen, gesellschaftsähnlicher Zusammenschluß; **ministerial ~** reines Treuhandverhältnis ohne besondere Verwaltungsaufgaben; **naked ~** einfache (schlichte) Treuhandverwaltung, Treuhandstellung ohne besonderen Aufgabenbereich; **National ~** *(Br.)* Stiftung für Denkmalschutz; **nondiscretionary ~** Investmentfonds mit strengen Anlagevorschriften (festgelegten Anlagewerten); **particular ~** Treuhandverwaltung für Einzelgegenstände; **passive ~** Treuhandstellung ohne besonderen Aufgabenbereich, reine Verwaltung ohne Treuhandfunktionen; **pension ~** Pensionsfonds; **perfect ~** rechtsgültig errichtete Stiftung, detailliert festgelegtes Treuhandverhältnis; **perpetual ~** auf unbegrenzte Zeit errichtete Stiftung (Treuhandverwaltung), Dauertreuhand; **personal ~** Treuhandverwaltung für bestimmte Begünstigte, Familienstiftung; **precatory ~** auf den letzten Wunsch des Erblassers begründete Treuhandverwaltung; **private ~** Treuhandverwaltung für bestimmte Begünstigte, Familienstiftung; **profit-sharing ~** Gewinnbeteiligungsfonds; **proprietary ~** *(Scot.)* schlichte Treuhandverwaltung; **protective ~** *(US)* für einen Verschwender errichtete Stiftung, Treuhandfonds auf Lebenszeit, Unterhaltsfonds; **public ~** öffentlichrechtliche (gemeinnützige) Stiftung, Unterstützungsfonds; **real-estate ~** Terrain-, Immobilienanlagegesell-

schaft, Grundstücksgesellschaft; **resulting ~** gesetzlich vermutetes Treuhandverhältnis, an den ursprünglichen Eigentümer zurückfallende Vermögensmasse; **revocable ~** kündbare Stiftung, widerrufliche Treuhandbestellung; **savings-bank ~** Stiftung zugunsten eines Dritten; **secret ~** verdecktes Treuhandverhältnis; **sheltering ~** für einen Verschwender errichtete Treuhandverwaltung, Stiftung zum Zwecke der Familienversorgung (zur Sicherung eines Verschwenders); **shifting ~** Stiftung (Treuhand) mit festgesetztem Ersatzberechtigten; **simple ~** *(income tax, US)* nur Zinsen ausschüttende Stiftung, schlichte Treuhandverwaltung, Thesaurierungsfonds, einfache Treuhandverwaltung; **special ~** Treuhandverhältnis zur Vornahme eines einmaligen Auftrags, auftragsgebundene Treuhandverwaltung; **spendthrift ~** *(US)* Unterhaltsfonds auf Lebenszeit, für einen Verschwender eingesetzte Treuhandverwaltung; **statutory ~** *(Br.)* gesetzlich begründete Vermögensverwaltung; **steel ~** Stahlkonzern; **testamentary ~** letztwillige Treuhandbestellung, Nachlaßstiftung; **Totten ~** *(US)* Stiftung zugunsten eines Dritten; **transgressive ~** unzulässige Dauertreuhandverwaltung; **uniform ~** von Treuhändern geleiteter Investmentfonds; **registered unit ~** *(Br.)* staatlich anerkannte Kapitalanlagegesellschaft; **vertical ~** Vertikalkonzern; **inter vivos ~** zu Lebzeiten errichtete Stiftung; **voluntary ~** fiduziarische Zuwendung, *(settlement)* rechtsgeschäftliche Stiftung, Unterstützungsfonds; **voting ~** zur Stimmrechtsausübung bestellte Treuhand; **wasting ~** Vermögensverwaltung mit genehmigtem Substanzangriff;

~ for charitable purposes wohltätige Stiftung; **~ of imperfect obligation** Stiftung zwecks Durchführung einer Naturalobligation; **~ of pure personalty to take effect inter vivos** unter Lebenden gültige Fahrnistreuhand; **~ for sale** einem Treuhänder zum Verkauf übertragenes Grundstück, *(Br.)* Veräußerungstreuhand; **ad hoc ~ for sale** für einen Einzelfall vorgesehene Verkaufstreuhänderschaft; **~ for value** entgeltliche Stiftung;

~ (v.) Vertrauen haben, sein Vertrauen setzen, *(allow credit for)* kreditieren, borgen, jem. Kredit geben (einräumen), *(place in trust)* [an]vertrauen;

~ s. o. with s. th. jem. etw. in Verwahrung geben; **~ an account of what has happened** einem Tatsachenbericht Vertrauen schenken; **not ~ s. o. round the corner** jem. nicht über den Weg trauen; **~ one's affairs to a lawyer** seiner Vertretung einen Anwalt betrauen; **~ children out of doors** Kinder aus den Augen verlieren; **~ s. o. to hell and back** mit jem. Pferde stehlen können; **~ one's memory** sich auf sein Gedächtnis verlassen; **~ one's memory too much** sein Gedächtnis überfordern;

to administer a ~ Treu[hand]gut verwalten, treuhänderische Funktionen wahrnehmen; **to be s. one's sole ~** jds. einzige Hoffnung sein; **to be in a position of ~** Vertrauensstellung innehaben; **to be subject to (under) ~** treuhänderisch verwaltet werden; **to buy on ~** auf Kredit (gegen Abzahlung) kaufen; **to commit to the ~ of s. o.** jem. zu treuen Händen (jds. Obhut) anvertrauen; **to create (establish) a ~** Treuhandverhältnis begründen, *(foundation)* Stiftung errichten; **to declare a ~** Treuhandvertrag errichten; **to deliver in ~** in Verwahrung geben, treuhänderisches Eigentum verschaffen; **to enjoy political ~** als Politiker Vertrauen genießen; **to form industries into a vertical ~** Industrien integrieren; **to give [up]on ~** Kredit gewähren, auf Kredit geben; **to hold in ~** treuhänderisch verwalten, [als Treuhänder] verwahren, *(entail)* als Fideikommiß besitzen; **to infringe a ~** Treuverpflichtung verletzen; **to leave (make) a ~** Fideikommiß errichten; **to leave s. th. in ~ with s. o.** jem. etw. anvertrauen; **to place (put) one's ~ in s. o.** Vertrauen in j. setzen; **to release from ~** Sicherungsübereignung aufheben; **to remove from a ~** treuhänderischer Verwaltung entziehen; **to resign from a ~** als Treuhänder zurücktreten; **to supply goods on ~** Waren auf Kredit liefern; **to take in ~** in [treuhänderische] Verwahrung nehmen; **to take it in ~** auf Treu und Glauben hinnehmen; **to take on ~** auf Treu und Glauben hinnehmen; **to take goods on ~** Waren auf Kredit beziehen;

~ account Treuhand-, Treuhänderkonto; **~ administration** Treuhandverwaltung, treuhänderische Verwaltung; **~ agreement** Treuhandvertrag, *(trustee, US)* Sicherungsübereignungs-, Treuhandvertrag; **~ asset** Fonds-, Treuhandvermögen; **~ asset value** Fondswert, Wert eines Treuhandvermögens; **~ bank** Treuhandbank; **~ beneficiary** Nutznießer (Bedachter) einer Stiftung; **~ bond** Schuldverschreibung über eine bevorrechtigte Forderung; **~ buster** *(US sl.)* Beamter des Kartellamtes, Kartelljäger, -entflechter, -brecher; **~ busting** *(US sl.)* Kartellentflechtung; **~ capital** Treuhandeigentum, -gut; **~ capital money** Mittel einer Treuhandverwaltung; **~ cer-**

tificate *(US)* Anteilschein eines treuhänderisch geleiteten Unternehmens; ~ **credit account** kreditorisch geführtes Treuhänderkonto; ~ **company** Kredit-, Treuhandgesellschaft, *(bank, US)* Aktienkredit-, Treuhandbank; ~ **company stocks** *(US)* Aktien einer Treuhandgesellschaft; ~~**controlled** von einer Treuhandgesellschaft verwaltet; ~ **corporation** *(Br.)* öffentlich-rechtliche Treuhandstelle; ~ **debenture** Schuldverschreibung über bevorrechtigte Forderungen; ~ **deed** Treuhandvertrag, *(Br.)* Depotvertrag, *(debentures)* treuhänderische Grundstücksübertragung zur Obligationenbesicherung, *(settlement)* Stiftungsurkunde; ~ **department** *(US)* Abteilung für Vermögensverwaltungen, Treuhandabteilung; ~ **deposit** Treuhänder-, Anderdepot; ~ **division** Treuhandabteilung; ~ **donor** Treugeber; ~ **endorsement** Treuhandindossament; ~ **engagement** Treuhandvertrag, -vereinbarung.

trust estate Treuhandvermögen, -gut, treuhänderisch verwaltetes Vermögen (verwalteter Nachlaß), *(foundation)* Stiftungsvermögen;

to distribute a ~ *(bankruptcy law)* Konkursmasse verteilen; **to pay out of the ~** *(bankruptcy law)* aus der Konkursmasse zahlen; **to wind up a ~** Nachlaß liquidieren.

trust | fund Treuhandmittel, treuhänderisch verwaltetes Vermögen (Geld), Treuhandvermögen, -fonds, *(investment trust)* Investmentfonds, *(foundation)* Stiftungsmittel, *(guardianship)* Mündelgeld, -vermögen, *(receivership)* Massekonto, *(taxation, US)* Sonderfonds für zweckgebundene Steuern; **nonexpendable ~ fund** Thesaurierungsfonds; **personal (private) ~ funds** *(US)* bankverwaltetes Privatvermögen; ~~**and-agency fund** *(municipal accounting)* Zweckvermögen; **to make the ~ fund secure** für die Sicherheit des Treuhandvermögens Sorge tragen; ~ **fund doctrine** Grundsatz der Schuldenhaftung bei Übernahme des Gesamtvermögens; ~ **fund investments** *(US)* mündelsichere Kapitalanlagen; ~ **house** *(Br.)* treuhänderisch geführtes Gasthaus; ~ **income** Treuhand-, Stiftungseinkommen; ~ **indenture** Treuhandurkunde, Treuhandvertrag; ~ **institution** Treuhandgesellschaft; ~ **instrument** Treuhandurkunde; ~ **investment** *(US)* mündelsichere Kapitalanlage; ~ **legacy** von einem Treuhänder verwaltetes Vermächtnis (Legat); ~ **letter** *(Br.)* Sicherungs-, Treuhandschein; ~ **maker** Errichter eines Treuhandverhältnisses, Treugeber; ~ **money** Depositengelder, -einlagen, Treuhand-, Stiftungsgelder, Mündelgeld; ~ **movement** Konzernausdehnung, -entwicklung; ~ **officer** *(US)* Vorsteher der Treuhandabteilung einer Bank, Beamter einer Treuhandgesellschaft, Treuhänder; ~ **patent** Treuhandurkunde; ~ **period** Dauer des Treuhandverhältnisses, Treuhanddauer; ~ **powers** *(bank)* Geschäftserlaubnis für Treuhandgeschäfte; ~ **property** Treugut, -handvermögen, *(foundation)* Stiftungsvermögen; ~ **receipt** *(US)* Treuhandquittung, -bescheinigung, *(banking, US)* [etwa] fiduziarische Übereignung, Sicherungsübereignungsurkunde, *(certificate of deposit)* Hinterlegungsschein; ~ **receipt devise** *(US)* [etwa] Sicherungsübereignungsverfahren; ~ **receipt transaction** *(US)* Sicherungsübereignung; ~ **relation[ship]** Treuhandverhältnis; **to create a ~ relation(ship)** Treuhandverhältnis begründen; ~ **release** Freigabe durch den Treuhänder; ~ **report** Treuhandbericht, Bericht eines Treuhänders; ~ **requirements** Anlagevoraussetzungen für ein Treuhandvermögen; ~ **settlement** treuhänderische Vermögensübertragung, Stiftung[svertrag]; ~ **share** Treuhandzertifikat; ~ **stock** *(US coll.)* mündelsichere Wertpapiere; ~ **territory** Gebiet unter Treuhandverwaltung, Treuhandgebiet; ~ **transaction** fiduziarisches Rechtsgeschäft, Treuhandgeschäft; ~ **undertaking** eingegangene Treuhänderverpflichtung; ~ **woman** Treuhänderin.

trustee Treuhänder, -nehmer, Bevollmächtigter, Vertrauensmann, Beauftragter, *(administrator)* Vermögensverwalter, -pfleger, Kurator, Kuratoriumsmitglied, Administrator, Sequester, Fiduziar, *(bank, Br.)* Depotbank, *(criminal, US)* begünstigter Sträfling, Kalfaktor, *(garnishee, US)* Drittschuldner, *(receiver, US)* Konkursverwalter, *(trust receipt, US)* Sicherungsnehmer;

bare ~ weisungsgebundener Treuhänder; **conventional ~** behördlich bestellter Verwalter (Treuhänder); **court-appointed ~** gerichtlich bestellter Vermögensverwalter (Treuhänder); **custodian ~** Treuhänder (Verwalter) von Mündelvermögen; **constructive ~** als Treuhänder Geltender; **express ~** gewillkürter Treuhänder; **indenture ~** dokumentarisch (urkundlich) bestellter Treuhänder; **joint ~s** Treuhändergremium; **judicial ~** gerichtlich bestellter Pfleger, amtlicher Treuhänder; **managing ~** amtierender Treuhänder; **official ~** amtlich bestellter Treuhänder; **private ~** Vermögensverwalter einer Familienstiftung; **public ~** *(Br.)* amtliche Hinterlegungs-, staatliche Treuhand-

stelle, öffentlich bestellter (staatlich eingesetzter) Treuhänder; **quasi ~** bei einer Unterschlagung wie ein Treuhänder Haftender; **sole ~** Einzeltreuhänder; **solicitor ~** Anwalt als Treuhänder; **successive ~** Ersatztreuhänder; **testamentary ~** *(US)* Testamentsvollstrecker, Treuhänder einer Nachlaßstiftung;

~ for administration Vermögensverwalter; ~ **of a bankrupt's estate** Konkursverwalter; ~ **in bankruptcy** *(Br.)* Masseverwalter, [von den Gläubigern gewählter] Konkursverwalter; ~ **and beneficiary** *(cestui que trust)* Treugeber und Treunehmer; ~ **under bond issue** Treuhandgesellschaft zum Zweck der Aktienausgabe; ~ **under a deed** urkundlich bestellter Treuhänder, Vergleichsverwalter; ~ **of an estate** Nachlaßverwalter; ~ **ex maleficio** unredlicher Verwalter mit zwangsweiser Treuhänderhaftung; ~ **of a pension fund** Ruhegehaltsverwaltung; ~ **under scheme** Vergleichstreuhänder; ~ **of a settlement** Treuhänder, Vermögensverwalter; ~ **in charitable uses** Kurator; ~ **under a will** Nachlaßverwalter, -treuhänder;

~ (v.) *(commit to the care of a ~)* Treuhandverhältnis begründen, einem Treuhänder übergeben, *(serve as ~)* als Treuhänder fungieren, *(~ process, US)* Forderungspfändung durchführen; ~ **an estate** Vermögen auf einen Treuhänder übertragen;

to act as ~ treuhänderisch verwalten, Treuhänder sein; **to appoint a ~** Treuhänder ernennen; **to appoint new ~s** weitere Treuhänder bestimmen; **to authorize a ~ to invest in local authority floating-rate papers** Anlage von Mündelgeldern in mit variablen Zinssätzen ausgestatteten Kommunalanleihen gestatten; **to discharge a ~** Treuhänder entlasten; **to hold a ~ to account** Treuhänder verantwortlich machen; **to remove a ~** Treuhänder abberufen; **to serve as ~** als Treuhänder fungieren; **to vest in a ~** auf einen Treuhänder übertragen;

~s account Treuhänderkonto, Treuhänderabrechnung; ~ **Act** *(Br.)* Treuhändergesetz; **Public ~ Act** *(Br.)* Hinterlegungsordnung; ~ **bank** gemeinnützige Sparkasse; ~ **bonds** *(Br.)* mündelsichere Papiere; ~ **capacity** Qualifikation zum Treuhänder, Treuhändereigenschaft; ~ **business** sicheres Geschäft; ~**'s certificate** Verwahrungs-, Hinterlegungsschein; ~ **character** Treuhandcharakter; ~ **committee** Treuhänderausschuß; ~ **company** Treuhandgesellschaft; ~**'s duties** Treuhänderpflichten; ~ **instrument** *(Br.)* Treuhandurkunde; ~ **investment** *(Br.)* mündelsichere Kapitalanlage; ~ **Investment Act** *(Br.)* Gesetz über mündelsichere Anlagen, Gesetz über die Anlage von Treuhandvermögen; ~**s' meeting** Treuhändersitzung; ~**'s power** Vollmacht eines Treuhänders; ~ **process** *(US)* Zahlungsverbot an den Drittschuldner, Forderungspfändungsverfahren, Beschlagnahme im Ausland; ~ **provisions** Treuhänderbestimmungen; ~ **Reliefs Act** *(US)* Hinterlegungsordnung; ~**'s remuneration** Treuhändervergütung; ~ **savings bank** *(Br.)* gemeinnützige Sparkasse; ~ **Savings Bank Act** *(Br.)* Sparkassengesetz; ~ **securities** *(Br.)* mündelsichere Wertpapiere; ~**'s security** Treuhänderkaution; ~ **shares** Aktien einer Kapitalanlagegesellschaft; ~ **state** Treuhandstaat; ~ **status** Treuhänderstatus; ~ **stock** *(US)* mündelsichere Wertpapiere; **to rank as ~ stock** *(US)* Mündelsicherheit genießen.

trusteeship Treuhandverwaltung, treuhänderische Verwaltung, Treuhänderschaft, Amt des Treuhänders, Kuratorium, *(United Nations)* Treuhandverwaltung;

~ in bankruptcy *(US)* Konkursverwaltung;

to accept the ~ of s. one's property jds. Vermögensverwaltung treuhänderisch übernehmen; **to place under ~** unter Treuhänderschaft stellen;

~ agreement *(UNO)* Treuhandabkommen; ~ **Council** *(United Nations)* Treuhänderrat; ~ **position** Treuhandstellung; ~ **system** Treuhandsystem; ~ **territory** Treuhandgebiet.

trustification Trustbildung, Vertrustung.

trustify *(v.)* Industriesyndikate bilden.

trustman Treuhänder.

trustor Stifter (Begründer) eines Treuhandverhältnisses, Treugeber.

trustwoman Treuhänderin.

trustworthiness Zuverlässigkeit, Sicherheit, Solidität, *(credit rating)* Kreditfähigkeit;

~ in the way of business to the extent of ... geschäftliche Kreditwürdigkeit bis zu ....

trustworthy zuverlässig, vertrauenswürdig, solide, *(credit rating)* kreditfähig;

to consider s. o. ~ to the extent of ... j. bis zur Höhe von ... für kreditfähig halten;

~ guarantee einwandfreie Bürgschaft; ~ **source** sichere (zuverlässige Quelle); ~ **witness** glaubwürdiger Zeuge.

trusty vertrauenswürdig, zuverlässig;

~ business sicheres Geschäft.

truth Wahrheit, Wirklichkeit, *(exactness)* Richtigkeit, Genauigkeit, *(veracity)* Ehrlichkeit, Aufrichtigkeit, Redlichkeit;
contrary to the ~ wahrheitswidrig;
~ **in advertising** Wahrheit in der Werbung; ~ **in lending** *(US)*
ordnungsgemäße Angaben des Darlehnsnehmers; ~ **to nature**
Naturtreue; ~ **of a statement** Richtigkeit einer Aussage;
to admonish to tell the ~ zur Wahrheit ermahnen; **to attest to
the** ~ Wahrheit einer Aussage bestätigen; **to be out of** ~ *(technics)* nicht genau stimmen; **to prove the** ~ **of one's statement**
Wahrheitsbeweis erbringen; **to suppress the** ~ Wahrheit verheimlichen; **to swear the** ~ Wahrheit einer Aussage beschwören; **to take as gospel** ~ für bare Münze nehmen; **to tell s. o. the
plain** ~ jem. reinen Wein einschenken;
~ **drug** Wahrheitsdroge.
try Probe, Versuch, Experiment;
~ *(v.)* versuchen, prüfen, *(conduct a trial)* gerichtlich untersuchen, verhören, verhandeln, [Angeklagten] vor Gericht stellen, *(metals)* raffinieren, scheiden;
~ **s. o.** *(court)* gegen j. verhandeln; ~ **to the best of one's ability**
nach seinen besten Kräften versuchen; ~ **one's best** sein Bestes
tun; ~ **a case** *(law court)* über einen Fall (vor Gericht) verhandeln; ~ **a criminal for murder** Verbrecher wegen Mordes verhören; ~ **it on the dog** j. als Versuchskaninchen benutzen; ~ **one's
hand at editing the staff magazine** sich an die Herausgabe der
Betriebszeitung wagen; ~ **hard for a job** sich ernsthaft um eine
Stellung bemühen; ~ **one's luck with s. o.** sein Glück bei jem.
versuchen; ~ **every possible means** alle erdenklichen Mittel
anwenden; ~ **s. o. for murder** Mordverhandlung gegen j. durchführen; ~ **an offence** in einer Strafsache verhandeln, strafbare
Handlung aburteilen; ~ **on** *(suit)* anprobieren; ~ **it on s. o.** *(sl.)*
j. zu überlisten trachten; ~ **it on with s. o.** *(sl.)* ausprobieren, wie
weit man bei jem. gehen kann, j. übers Ohr zu hauen versuchen; ~ **out an invention** Erfindung ausprobieren; ~ **out a new
method** neue Methode erproben; ~ **for a post** sich um eine
Stellung bewerben; ~ **for a scholarship** sich um ein Stipendium
bemühen; ~ **s. o. separately** gesondert gegen j. verhandeln,
abgetrenntes Verfahren gegen j. durchführen;
to have a ~ **at s. th.** Versuch mit etw. machen, etw.
ausprobieren.
try-on Anprobe, *(coll.)* Überrumpelungs-, Täuschungsversuch.
trying peinlich, mißlich, kritisch;
~ **of a case** Verhandlung einer Sache;
to have a ~ **day** aufreibender (anstrengender) Tag; ~ **person to
deal with** unangenehmer Zeitgenosse; ~ **situation** unangenehme Situation.
tryout Erprobung, *(advertising)* Versuchs-, Werbefeldzug;
~ **campaign** Versuchskampagne.
tryst Verabredung, Stelldichein, Rendezvous;
to break a ~ Verabredung nicht einhalten.
trysting place Rendezvousplatz.
tub Kübel, Zuber, Bottich, Bütte, Wanne, *(small cask)* Fäßchen,
(mining) Förderwagen, -korb, Hund;
bath ~ Badewanne; **rain-water** ~ Regentonne; **washing** ~
Waschbottich, -zuber;
~ **for butter** Butterfaß;
~ **thumper** Volksredner.
tube Rohr, Röhre, *(Br., coll.)* Untergrundbahn, U-Bahn,
(electronics, US) Elektronenröhre;
the ~ *(television, US sl.)* Glotzröhre;
large-diameter ~ Großrohr; **dispatch** *(postal)* ~ Versandrolle;
inner ~ Schlauch; **rubber** ~ Gummischlauch; **torpedo** ~ Torpedorohr, Abschußrohr;
to go (travel) by ~ *(Br.)* mit der U-Bahn fahren, U-Bahn
benutzen;
~ **fare** *(Br.)* U-Bahnfahrschein; ~ **line** *(Br.)* U-Bahnlinie; ~
production Röhrenproduktion; ~ **railway** *(Br.)* Untergrundbahn, U-Bahn; ~ **station** *(Br.)* U-Bahnstation; ~ **ticket** *(Br.)*
U-Bahnfahrschein; ~ **train** *(Br.)* U-Bahnzug.
tubeless tyre *(Br.)* **(tire,** *US)* schlauchloser Autoreifen.
tubing Röhrenherstellung, *(coll.)* Röhrenanlage, Rohrleitung.
tubular röhrenförmig;
~ **furniture** Stahlrohrmöbel; ~ **products** Rohrerzeugnisse.
TUC-Labo(u)r party's liaison committee *(Br.)* Verbindungsausschuß zwischen Gewerkschaften und der Labo(u)rparty.
tuck *(Br., sl.)* Leckereien, *(coll., US)* Schwung, Energie;
~ *(v.)* **away** verstauen, wegstecken; ~ **away under sundry liabilities** unter einem Bilanzposten verschiedene Verpflichtungen
verstecken; ~ **in** *(meal, sl.)* einhauen, verdrücken, wegputzen;
~ **one's tail between one's legs** Schwanz einziehen, ganz klein
und häßlich werden.
tuckshop *(Br., sl.)* Süßwarengeschäft.

tufthunter gesellschaftlicher Ehrgeizling.
tufthunting gesellschaftlicher Ehrgeiz, Snobismus.
tug Ruck, Zug, Zerren, *(fig.)* große Anstrengung, *(mar.)* Schlepper, Schleppdampfer;
salvage ~ Bergungsschlepper;
~ **at s. one's heart strings** Seelenmassage; ~-**of-war** *(fig.)* Tau-
ziehen;
~ *(v.)* schleppen.
tugboat Schleppdampfer, Schlepper.
tuition Unterricht, Unterweisung, Lehre, *(school)* Schulgeld,
(university) Studiengebühr;
group ~ Gruppenunterricht; **postal** ~ Fernunterricht; **private** ~
Privatunterricht, Nachhilfestunden;
to pay ~ **at a university** Universitäts-, Studiengebühren
bezahlen.
tumble Sturz, Purzelbaum, Salto, *(fig.)* Wirrwarr, Unordnung,
Durcheinander;
~ *(v.)* einstürzen, *(prices)* stürzen, fallen, herunterpurzeln,
(idea, US sl.) kapieren, spitzkriegen, über etw. stolpern;
~ **books about** Bücher durcheinanderwerfen; ~ **down** einstürzen; ~ **into an old friend** einem alten Freund in die Arme laufen;
~ **s. o. out of a bus** j. aus einem Bus schleudern; ~ **to pieces** in
Stücke zerfallen; ~ **and toss** *(waves)* hin- und herrollen; ~ **up**
aus den Federn kriechen; ~ **into a war** in einen Krieg
hineinschlittern;
to be all in a ~ kunterbunt durcheinanderliegen; **to give s. o. a** ~
von jem. Notiz nehmen; **not to give s. o. even a** ~ j. wie Luft
behandeln, nicht das geringste Interesse an jem. nehmen;
~-**down** baufällig.
tumbler Trinkglas, *(technics)* Nocken;
~ **switch** Kippschalter.
tumbrel Mistkarren.
tumid *(language)* schwülstig, bombastisch.
tumult Tumult, Getümmel, Aufruhr, Auflauf, Getöse, *(fig.)*
Aufruhr, Erregung;
~ **of battle** Schlachtgetümmel.
tumultuary tumultarisch, undiszipliniert.
tumultuous political meeting erregte politische Versammlung.
tun Tonne, Faß, Fuder;
by ~**s** fuderweise.
tune Melodie, Lied, Weise, *(harmony)* Übereinstimmung, Einklang, *(wireless set)* Fein-, Scharfeinstellung;
in ~ *(airplane)* startbereit; **in** ~ **with** in Übereinstimmung mit,
in gutem Verhältnis; **to the** ~ **of** *(coll.)* im Betrage von;
catchy ~ einschmeichelnde Melodie;
~ *(v.)* **in** *(wireless set)* einschalten, -stellen, auf eine bestimmte
Wellenlänge einstellen; ~ **up** Leistung steigern; ~ **up an aircraft**
(airplane) Flugzeug startbereit machen; ~ **up a car** Auto
frisieren;
to be not in ~ **for** nicht aufgelegt sein; **to be fined to the** ~ **of £ 50**
gebührenpflichtige Verwarnung in Höhe von 200,- DM zahlen
müssen; **to be in** ~ **with one's surroundings** mit seiner Umgebung harmonieren; **to be out of** ~ im Widerspruch stehen; **to be
out of** ~ **with the times** nicht mehr zeitgemäß sein; **to change
one's** ~ *(coll.)* anderen Ton anschlagen; **to dance to s. one's** ~
nach jds. Pfeife tanzen; **to keep the body in** ~ fit bleiben; **to pay
to the** ~ Wucherpreis bezahlen; **to play** ~**s of one's own** seine
eigene Note haben; **to sing another** ~ *(coll.)* anderen Ton
anschlagen.
tuned, broadly unscharf eingestellt.
tuneless piano ausgedientes Klavier.
tuner *(el.)* Abstimmvorrichtung, *(sl.)* Filmmusical.
tungreve Schulze.
tuning *(wireless set)* [genaue] Abstimmung, Einstellen;
~ **eye** magisches Auge.
tunk *(sl.)* informelles geselliges Beisammensein.
tunnel Tunnel, Unterführung, *(mining)* Stollen;
~ *(v.)* untertunneln, *(building)* ausschachten;
~ **out a snowbound house** eingeschneites Haus ausgraben;
to dig a ~ Tunnel graben.
tunnel(l)ing Ausschachtung.
turbary Torfgerechtigkeit.
turbine Turbine;
pressure ~ Druckturbine;
~ **aircraft** Turbinenflugzeug; ~-**powered** mit Turbinenantrieb;
~ **steamer** Turbinendampfer.
turbojet Turbostrahltriebwerk.
turboliner Düsenverkehrsflugzeug.
turboproject engine Propellerturbinentriebwerk.
turbo-ram-jet engine Maschine mit Staustrahltriebwerk.
turbulent mob aufrührerische Menge.

turf Rasen, Grasnarbe, *(fig.)* Pferderennsport, *(track for horses)* Pferderennbahn;
on the ~ *(prostitute, sl.)* auf dem Strich;
~ *(v.)* **out** *(Br., sl.)* herausschmeißen;
to be on the ~ Rennpferde halten;
~ commission agent Buchmacher; **~ cutting** Torfstechen.
turkey *(US sl., theatre)* Versager, Pleite;
to talk ~ *(sl.)* über Grundsätzliches verhandeln; **to talk cold ~** *(US)* kein Blatt vor den Mund nehmen, reinen Wein einschenken;
~ carpet *(Br.)* Orientteppich; **~ day** *(US coll.)* Erntedanktag.
Turks, to come in like young sich wie unabgeführte Jagdhunde aufführen.
turmoil Tumult, Unruhe, Aufruhr.
turn Drehung, *(advantage)* Vorteil, Nutzen, Profit, Schnitt, *(broker)* Courtage, *(change of direction)* Wendung, Drehung, Richtungsänderung, *(crisis)* Umschwung, Krise, *(job)* Arbeit, Beschäftigung, Leistung, *(occasion)* Gelegenheit, Anlaß, *(alternating order)* Reihenfolge, Turnus, *(period of work)* Reihenfolge, Arbeitsgang, Turnus, *(print.)* Fliegenkopf, *(programme, Br.)* Programmnummer, Einlage, *(purpose)* Zweck, Absicht, Bedürfnis, *(road)* Straßenbiegung, Kurve, Kehre, *(screw)* Gang, *(shift, Br.)* [Arbeits]schicht, *(stock exchange)* Umschwung, Wende, Veränderung, *(stock exchange, Br.)* Kursgewinn, *(tour)* Rundfahrt, -gang, *(transaction, US)* vollständig durchgeführte Börsentransaktion, *(turning point)* Umkehr-, Wendepunkt, *(short walk)* kurzer Spaziergang, Rundgang;
at every ~ bei jeder Gelegenheit; **before one's ~** bevor man an der Reihe ist; **by ~s** umschichtig, abwechselnd; **for a ~** *(US)* als ganz kurzfristige Anlage; **full of ~s** kurvenreich; **in ~** umschichtig, der Reihe nach, turnusmäßig, *(successively)* abwechselnd; **out of one's ~** außer der Reihe; **to a ~** vorzüglich, ausgezeichnet;
hand's ~ Handarbeit; **jobber's ~** *(Br.)* Kursgewinn; **no left ~!** Linksabbiegen verboten!; **star ~** Starauftritt; **U-~** hundertprozentige Kehrtwendung;
definite ~ for the better entschiedene Wendung zum Besseren; **~ of the Century** Jahrhundertwende; **~ of the dice** ein Umschwung; **~ of exchange** *(Br.)* Kursaufbesserung; **felicitous ~ of expression** treffliche Formulierung; **~ of life** Lebenswende; **~ of the market** *(jobber, Br.)* Kursgewinn; **~ in the market** Umschwung, Konjunkturumbruch; **~ of mind** Geistesrichtung; **classic ~ of mind** humanistische Denkweise; **~ in policy** politischer Wendepunkt; **sudden ~ in the road** plötzliche Richtungsänderung einer Straße; **~ of the scales** Ausschlagen der Waage; **~ of the tide** Gezeitenwechsel; **~ of Fortune's wheel** Schicksalswende; **~ for the worse** Wendung zum Schlechteren; **~ of the year** Jahreswende;
~ *(v.)* drehen, wenden, verändern, umwandeln, Richtung nehmen, *(divert)* ablenken, *(print.)* blockieren, *(religion)* übertreten, *(stock market)* sich drehen, *(street)* Kurve nehmen;
~ s. one's attention to s. th. jds. Aufmerksamkeit auf etw. lenken; **~ bankrupt** Konkurs machen, bankrott werden; **~ bear** Baissier werden; **~ bull** Haussier werden; **~ the cat in the pan** die Sache schon schaukeln; **~ the channel of a stream** Lauf eines Flusses umleiten; **~ one's coat** die Partei wechseln, überlaufen; **~ around a company** Betrieb völlig umkrempeln; **~ a corner** Kurve nehmen; **~ the corner** *(US)* Umschwung verzeichnen; **~ a deaf ear** *(coll.)* nicht hören wollen; **~ an election** Wahl entscheidend beeinflussen; **~ everything upside down** das Oberste zuunterst kehren; **~ King's** *(Br.)* **(state's,** *US)* **evidence** Kron-, Hauptbelastungszeuge werden; **~ a blind eye** seine Augen vor der Wirklichkeit verschließen; **~ the fashion** der Mode eine andere Richtung geben; **~ firm** *(stock exchange)* fest werden; **~ s. one's flank** *(fig.)* j. überrumpeln; **~ the enemy's flank** feindliche Stellung aufrollen; **~ the hostile forces** feindliche Streitkräfte umgehen; **~ one's hand to s. th.** Hand an etw. legen; **~ one's hand to most jobs** praktisch alles können; **not ~ a hand to help s. o.** keinen Finger für j. rühren; **~ s. one's head** jem. den Kopf verdrehen; **~ one's job in** seine Stellung aufgeben; **~ left** links abbiegen; **~ merchant** Kaufmann werden; **~ one's money three times a year** sein Betriebskapital dreimal jährlich umsetzen; **~ an honest penny** sein Brot ehrlich verdienen; **~ the scale** Ausschlag geben, ausschlaggebend sein; **~ a sentence** Satz abrunden; **~ soft** *(market)* Abschwächung zeigen; **~ one's steps home** seine Schritte heimwärts lenken; **~ a switch** Hebel umlegen; **~ the tables** Lage vollständig verändern; **~ s. th. topsy-turvy** etw. völlig durcheinanderbringen; **~ traitor** zum Verräter werden; **~ turtle** *(sl.)* in eine hilflose Lage versetzen; **~ weak** *(stock exchange)* schwach werden.

turn about *(v.)* herumdrehen, *(fig.)* überdenken, -legen.
turn adrift *(v.)* **in the world** *(v.)* hilflos allein lassen.
turn away *(v.)* entlassen, fortschicken;
~ a beggar Bettler zurückweisen.
turn back *(v.)* *(at border)* zurückweisen.
turn down *(v.)* *(gas)* kleiner drehen, *(law court)* verwerfen, abweisen, *(wireless set)* leiser einstellen;
~ s. o. jem. einen Korb geben, *(US sl.)* jem. Bescheid stoßen; **~ a candidate** Bewerber ablehnen; **~ a chair** Stuhl umlegen; **~ a claim** Forderung zurückweisen; **~ one's thumbs down** ablehnen.
turn in *(v.)* einreichen, -händigen, *(coll.)* zu Bett gehen;
~ s. o. in j. der Polizei übergeben; **~ on o. s.** sich in sich selbst zurückziehen; **~ one's equipment** seine Ausrüstung zurückgeben.
turn into *(v.)* einbiegen;
~ cash (money) flüssig-, zu Geld machen, realisieren, versilbern; **~ a firm into a joint stock company** Firma in eine Aktiengesellschaft umwandeln; **~ one's land into money** sein Grundvermögen flüssig machen; **~ the business of a sole proprietor into a partnership** Einzelunternehmen in eine Gesellschaft umwandeln; **~ a partnership into a limited company** Offene Handelsgesellschaft in eine Gesellschaft mit beschränkter Haftung umwandeln; **~ a passage into English** ins Englische übertragen.
turn off *(v.)* *(gas, water)* abstellen, absperren, *(traffic)* abbiegen;
~ a bank *(sl.)* Bank ausrauben; **~ the faucet of funds** Stiftungszuwendungen einstellen; **~ s. one's water** *(sl.)* jds. Wasserfall stoppen; **~ a wireless set** Radio ausstellen (abschalten).
turn on *(v.)* anstellen, aufdrehen;
~ s. o. on *(fam.)* j. begeistern; **~ the heat** voll aufdrehen, sich hundertprozentig engagieren; **~ a sixpence** sich im Nu wenden; **~ the weather** vom Wetter abhängen.
turn out *(v.)* sich herausstellen (erweisen), *(crop)* ausfallen, werden, *(end up)* ausgehen, enden, *(fire, US)* aus dem Dienst entlassen, *(gas, radio, water)* ausstellen, *(produce)* [Fabrikat] ausstoßen, herstellen, produzieren, *(strike)* Arbeit einstellen;
~ to be an advantage sich als Vorteil auswirken; **~ the attic** Boden ausräumen; **~ a balance** Saldo aufweisen; **~ to be a big city** sich als Großstadt entpuppen; **~ to be an excellent driver** sich als hervorragender Autofahrer entpuppen; **~ for duty** zur Arbeit antreten (erscheinen); **~ goods** Waren herstellen; **~ the government** Regierung stürzen; **~ the guard** Wache heraustreten lassen; **~ s. o. out of his job** j. entlassen; **~ s. o. out of his lodgings** j. zur Räumung zwingen, j. exmittieren; **~ for a meeting** Versammlung besuchen; **~ poorly** *(crop)* schlecht ausfallen; **~ one's pockets inside out** seine Taschen durchsuchen; **~ s. o. out of his position** j. seiner Stellung berauben; **~ large quantities of goods** Waren massenhaft herstellen; **~ a room for the spring cleaning** Zimmer zum Frühjahrsputz ausräumen; **~ satisfactory** befriedigend verlaufen; **~ a tenant** Mieter exmittieren; **~ to be true** sich als wahr herausstellen; **~ to welcome s. o.** zu jds. Begrüßung erscheinen; **~ well** glatt abgehen, guten Ausgang nehmen.
turn over *(v.)* *(book)* umblättern, *(car)* umkippen, *(goods)* Umsatz haben, umsetzen, verkaufen;
~ per annum Jahresumsatz haben; **~ an apprentice to another master** Lehrling an einen anderen Lehrherrn abtreten; **~ the management** Geschäftsführung abgeben; **~ to** [Produktion] umstellen auf; **~ it over ready to a turnkey** schlüsselfertig abliefern; **~ £ 2000 a week** wöchentlich zweitausend Pfund umsetzen, Wochenumsatz von 2000 Pfund haben; **~ to private managers** reprivatisieren; **~ a project over in one's mind** sich einen Plan durch den Kopf gehen lassen; **~ a business to one's successors** Geschäft seinen Nachfolgern übergeben; **~ the stock** Warenlager (Lagerbestand) umschlagen.
turn round *(fig.)* seine Meinung ändern.
turn to *(v.)* | **account** Vorteil ziehen, verwerten, sich zunutze machen, nutzbringend anlegen; **~ a dictionary** Wörterbuch konsultieren, im Wörterbuch nachschlagen; **~ a doctor** sich an einen Arzt wenden; **~ profit** nutzbringend anwenden; **~ another subject** sich einem anderen Thema zuwenden.
turn under *(v.)* unterpflügen.
turn up *(v.)* sich zeigen (einfinden, einstellen), *(appear suddenly)* dazwischenkommen, passieren, *(wireless set)* aufdrehen, lauter stellen, *(work, sl.)* aufstecken;
~ a blank mit einer Niete herauskommen; **~ one's nose at s. th.** verächtlich über etw. die Nase rümpfen; **~ a buried treasure** verborgenen Schatz ausgraben; **~ trumps** zum Vorteil gereichen; **~ a word in a dictionary** Wort im Wörterbuch nachschlagen.

turn | upon *(v.)* **the feasibility of a scheme** sich um die Durchführbarkeit eines Projektes drehen; **~ weak** *(stock exchange)* schwach werden.

turn, to await a ~ of one's luck auf bessere Zeiten warten; **to be on the ~** *(ship)* kentern, *(tide)* sich wenden; **to be one's ~** an der Reihe sein; **to be of a humorous ~** humorvoll sein, Sinn für Humor besitzen; **to be talking out of ~** mit seiner Bemerkung fehl am Platze sein; **to be one's ~ to treat** mit der Bezahlung dran sein; **to continue one's ~ towards ease in money rates** Tendenz in der Politik der Geldmarkterleichterungen fortsetzen; **to do s. o. a good ~** jem. einen Gefallen (guten Dienst) erweisen; **to do s. o. an ill ~** jem. einen schlechten Dienst erweisen; **to get a ~ of work in the harvest** bei der Ernte Arbeit finden; **to give a favo(u)rable ~ to a business** eine Sache richtig in Gang bringen; **to have a ~ for business** kaufmännische Ader (Anlage zum Geschäftsmann) haben; **to have a ~ for languages** sprachbegabt sein; **to have a mechanical ~** sich nur für technische Dinge interessieren; **to have a pretty ~ of speed** *(car)* sehr leistungsfähig sein; **to serve s. one's ~** zweckdienlich für j. sein, jds. Bedürfnissen entsprechen; **to take ~s** einander ablösen, abwechselnd (umschichtig) arbeiten; **to take a ~ at s. th.** sich kurz mit etw. befassen; **to take an interesting ~** interessante Wendung nehmen; **to take a liberal ~** sich liberal verhalten; **to take a ~ for the bad** sich zum Schlechten wenden; **to take a ~ for the better** sich verbessern; **to take a favo(u)rable ~** sich günstig entwickeln; **to wait one's ~** abwarten, bis man (an die Reihe) drankommt;
~ bridge Drehbrücke; **~ indicator** *(plane)* Richtungsanzeiger; **on a ~-key basis** schlüsselfertig; **~-key contract** *(US)* schlüsselfertiger Vertrag; **~-key job** schlüsselfertiger Anlagenvertrag; **~-left signal** Linksabbiegerzeichen; **~-round** Be- und Entladung, *(goods, waggon)* Umlaufzeit; **quick ~ round** *(ship)* rasche Abfertigung.

turnabout *(fig.)* Front-, Gesinnungswechsel, *(merry-go-round, US)* Karussel, *(plane, ship)* Gegenkurs, *(pol.)* Wendepunkt, Umkehr, hundertprozentiger Kurswechsel, *(vehicle)* Generalüberholung;
~ time Abladezeit.

turnaround Wendestelle, *(fig.)* Tendenzwende, *(ship)* Rundreisedauer.

turncoat Abtrünniger, Renegat, Überläufer;
to be a ~ seinen Mantel nach dem Winde hängen.

turndown Abfuhr, Absage;
~ in imports Einfuhrrückgang;
~ (a.) umfaltbar, umlegbar;
~ boots Stulpenstiefel.

turned gestaltet, geformt, *(print.)* umgekehrt, auf dem Kopf stehend;
to be ~ on about s. th. auf etw. scharf sein; **to be ~ right over** *(car)* auf den Kopf gestellt werden; **to have ~ many books in one's life** viel gelesen haben;
~ letter *(print.)* Fliegenkopf; **best ~-out man** bestgekleideter Mann; **~ out to order** auf Bestellung angefertigt.

turning Drehung, *(deviation)* Abbiegen, *(river road)* Krümmung, Biegung;
~ left Linksabbiegen;
~ to account Verwertung; **~ the business of a sole proprietor into a partnership** Umwandlung eines Einzelunternehmens in eine Gesellschaft;
left ~ Linksabbiegen; **second ~ to the right** zweite Abbiegung rechts;
~ knob Abstimmknopf; **~ lathe** Drehbank; **~ point** Wendepunkt, Entscheidung, Krise, Krisis; **~ point in the negotiations** entscheidendes Stadium bei Verhandlungen; **to reach the ~ point** *(business cycle)* umschlagen, *(disease)* in ein kritisches Stadium eintreten; **to reach a ~ point in one's life** Wendepunkt in seinem Leben erreichen.

turnkey Gefängniswärter, Schließer.

turnout Herauskommen, *(audience)* Ansammlung, Menschenmassen, -strom, Publikum, Zuhörer, Besucher, *(book)* Aufmachung, Ausstattung, *(costume)* Kostümierung, Aufzug, *(elections)* Wahlbeteiligung, *(equipage)* Kutsche, Pferdegespann, *(equipment)* Ausstattung, -rüstung, Aufmachung, *(gathering, coll.)* An-, Versammlung, Menschenmasse, Besucher, Zuschauer, *(mil.)* Abmarsch, *(motorway)* Ausweichstelle, *(product)* Erzeugnis, Produkt, *(railway)* Neben-, Ausweichgleis, *(strike, Br.)* Ausstand, Arbeitseinstellung, Streik, *(total output)* Gesamtproduktion;
~ of a book Buchausstattung; **good ~ at the meeting** gut besuchte Versammlung;
to give the room a good ~ Zimmer gründlich aufräumen.

turnover Umschlag, Geschäftsumsatz, *(apprentice, Br.)* überstellter Lehrling, *(employees)* Fluktuation, *(hospital)* Zu- und Abgang, *(leaf of book)* umgeschlagene Seitenecke, *(politics)* Wahlstimmenverschiebung, Verschiebung der Wählerstimmen, *(reorganization)* Umbau-, -organisation, -gruppierung, -besetzung, -schichtung, *(runover, Br.)* auf der nächsten Seite fortgesetzter Zeitungsartikel, *(shakeup)* Umschichtung, -organisation, -gruppierung, Verschiebung, *(of sentiment)* Meinungsumschwung, *(upset)* Umstürzen, Umwerfen;
active ~ reger Umsatz; **annual ~** Jahresumsatz; **average ~** Durchschnittsumsatz; **bank ~** Bankumsatz; **per-capita ~** pro-Kopf-Umsatz; **capital ~** Kapitalumsatz, -umschlag; **contracting ~** schrumpfender Umsatz; **discount ~** Diskontumsatz; **domestic ~** Inlandsumsatz; **external ~** Konzernumsatz, *(foreign trade)* Außenumsatz; **fictitious ~** fingierter Umsatz; **finished-goods ~** Umschlaghäufigkeit des Warenbestandes; **goods ~** Güterumsatz; **gross ~** Bruttoumsatz; **inventory ~** Lagerumschlag; **labo(u)r ~** Arbeitsplatzwechsel, Neu- und Wiedereinstellungsrate; **large ~** großer Umsatz; **management ~** Umbesetzung des Vorstands, Wechsel in der Betriebsführung; **merchandise ~** Warenumsatz; **minimum ~** Mindestumsatz; **mixed ~s** *(stock exchange)* verschiedenartige Umsätze; **new-book ~** Neubücherabsatz; **nonaviation ~** nicht zur Flugzeugindustrie gehörige Geschäftsumsätze; **physical ~** mengenmäßiger Umsatz; **program(me) ~** Rentabilität einer Werbesendung; **quantity ~** mengenmäßiger Umsatz; **quick ~** schneller (rascher) Umsatz; **raw-material ~** Umschlaghäufigkeit des Rohstofflagers; **receivables ~** *(US)* Umschlaghäufigkeit der Forderungen; **stock ~** Lagerumschlag; **taxable ~** steuerpflichtiger Umsatz; **total ~** Gesamt[kassen]umsatz; **total-assets ~** Umschlaghäufigkeit des Kapitals, Kapitalumschlagshäufigkeit; **working-capital ~** Umsatz des Betriebskapitals; **last year's ~** Vorjahresumsatz;
large ~s from agents in the field hohe Umsätze durch die Vertreter im Außendienst; **~ per annum** Jahresumsatz; **bad ~ in a carriage** unangenehmer Fahrzeugunfall; **~ of fifty per cent in a year** Wechsel der halben Belegschaft innerhalb eines Jahres; **thorough ~ of the operating force** komplette Betriebsumstellung, völlige Belegschaftsumschichtung; **~ in gold** Goldumsätze; **rapid ~ of goods** schneller Warenumsatz; **~ of the labo(u)r force** Fluktuation der Arbeitskräfte; **~ of merchandise** Warenumsatz; **~ of money** Geldumsatz; **rapid ~ of patients in a hospital** rascher Patientenwechsel in einem Krankenhaus; **~ of sentiment** Stimmungsumschwung; **~ in shares** Aktienumsätze; **~ in stock** Lagerumschlag; **~ in tenancy** Pachtumsatz; **~ four times a year** viermaliger Umschlag des Warenlagers im Jahr; **~ of seven votes** *(parl.)* Mehrheit von sieben Stimmen; **to do a large ~** *(coll.)* großen Umsatz erzielen; **to need a thorough ~** völlig neu organisiert werden müssen;
~ account Warenverkaufskonto; **~ business** Umschlaggeschäft; **~ commission** Umsatzprovision; **1 m ~ company** Unternehmen mit Milliardenumsatz; **external ~ expansion** Ausweitung des Fremdumsatzes; **~ figures** Umsatzzahlen; **~ gain** Umsatzzuwachs; **~ growth rate** Umsatzwachstumsrate; **~ increase** Umsatzsteigerung, -zunahme; **~ period** Umschlagszeit; **~ proceeds** Umsatzerlös; **~ range** Umsatzumfang; **~ rate** Umsatzziffer, -quote, Umschlagsgeschwindigkeit; **~ ratio** Umsatzquote; **capital ~ ratio** Umschlaghäufigkeit des Eigenkapitals; **inventory ~ ratio** Umschlaghäufigkeit des Warenbestands; **~ situation** Umsatzlage; **~ statistics** Umsatzstatistik; **~ storage** Umschlaglager; **~ tax** *(Br.)* Umsatzsteuer; **~-tax rates** *(Br.)* Umsatzsteuersätze; **~-tax refund** *(Br.)* Umsatzsteuerrückerstattung.

turnpike Zollschranke, Schlagbaum, Übergangs-, Mautstelle, *(freeway, US)* gebührenpflichtige Autobahn;
~ man Gebühreneinnehmer; **~ money** Straßenbenutzungsgebühr, Maut, Wegegeld, Straßenzoll, *(freeway)* Autobahngebühr; **~ road** *(US)* gebührenpflichtige Autobahn.

turnplate *(railway, Br.)* Drehscheibe.

turnround Umschlag, *(airplane, ship)* Abfertigung.

turnscrew Schraubenzieher, -schlüssel.

turnstile *(traffic count)* Drehkreuz.

turntable Wiedergabegerät, *(railway)* Drehscheibe, *(recorder)* Plattenteller;
~ doctrine *(attractive nuisance)* Haftungsprinzip für kindergefährdende Spieleinrichtung.

turnup *(coll.)* Schlägerei, Rauferei;
~ bed Wandklappbett.

turpitude Niederträchtigkeit, Verworfenheit, *(legal sense)* niedere Beweggründe;
moral ~ moralische Verworfenheit.

turret erkerartiger Anbau, *(airplane)* Kanzel, *(mil.)* Panzer-, Gefechtsturm;
~ **lathe** Revolverbank; ~ **ship** Panzerschiff.

turtle *(sl.)* gepanzerter Geldwagen;
to turn ~ *(car)* sich überschlagen, *(ship)* kentern.

tussle Rauferei, *(fig.)* scharfe Kontroverse.

tut *(dial, Br.)* Akkord;
by (upon) the ~ im Akkord;
~ **work** *(mining)* Akkordarbeit.

tutelage *(guardianship)* Vormundschaft, Pflegschaft, Kuratel, *(minor age)* Minderjährigkeit, Unmündigkeit;
dative ~ übertragene Vormundschaft;
to put s. o. under ~ j. entmündigen, j. unter Vormundschaft stellen.

tutelary vormundschaftlich;
~ **authority** *(US)* Gewalt des Vormunds, vormundschaftliche Gewalt; ~ **role** Vormundschaftsrolle.

tutor Privat-, Nachhilfe-, Hauslehrer, Erzieher, *(coach)* Einpauker, Repetitor, *(guardian, Scot.)* Vormund, Pfleger, *(university, Br.)* Studienleiter, *(university, US)* Assistent, Universitätslektor, Lektor;
~ **dative** *(Scot.)* gerichtlich bestellter Vormund; **family (private)** ~ Haus-, Nachhilfe-, Privatlehrer; **individual** ~ Einzellehrer; ~ **nominative** *(Scot.)* von den Eltern bestellter Vormund; **travelling** ~ Reisebegleiter;
~ *(v.)* schulen, erziehen, *(treat sternly)* bevormunden, *(tutelage)* Vormund sein;
~ **s. o.** jem. Privatunterricht (Nachhilfeunterricht) erteilen; ~ **o. s. to be patient** sich zur Geduld zwingen;
to engage a ~ Nachhilfelehrer nehmen.

tutorage Aufsicht, Unterrichtung, *(tutelage)* Vormundschaft, *(charge)* Unterrichtsgebühr.

tutorial Unterrichtsstunde, praktische Übung;
~ *(a.)* vormundschaftlich;
to attend a ~ an praktischen Übungen teilnehmen;
~ **classes** Unterrichtsklassen; ~ **system** Einzelunterricht durch Tutoren.

tutoring Privatunterricht;
~ **experience** Erfahrung als Lektor.

tutorize *(v.)* Hauslehrer sein.

tutorship Hauslehrerstelle, *(Louisiana)* Pflegschaft, Vormundschaft;
~ **by nature** elterliche Gewalt; ~ **by will** testamentarische Vormundseinsetzung.

tutwork *(mining, Br., dial.)* Akkordarbeit.

tuxedo *(US)* Smoking;
~ **junction** *(sl.)* eleganter Treffpunkt.

twaddle Geschwätz, sinnloses Gewäsch.

tweak *(v.)* **s. th. from s. o.** jem. etw. abzwacken.

tweedledum geringfügiger Unterschied.

tween deck Zwischendeck.

tweeter Hochtonlautsprecher.

twenty per cent rule *(banking, US)* System eines zu 20% kreditorisch zu führenden Kontos.

twice | in jeopardy Risiko zweifachen Strafverfahrens; ~ **the sum** doppelte Summe;
to think ~ **about s. th.** sich eine Sache gründlich überlegen.

twiddle *(v.)* **one's thumbs** Hände in den Schoß legen, Daumen drehen.

twig, to work the mit der Wünschelrute gehen;
~ **branch** *(US)* Zweifachgeschäft.

twilight Dämmerung, *(fig.)* Dämmerzustand, Schleier;
in the ~ **of history** im Halbdunkel der Geschichte;
~ **of the gods** Götterdämmerung.

twin-screw steamer Doppelschraubendampfer.

twine Bindfaden, Schnur.

twinkle Flimmern, Flackern, *(fig.)* Augenblick, Nu.

twinkling, in the ~ **of an eye** im Handumdrehen.

twist *(report)* Entstellung, Verdrehung, *(road)* Windung, Biegung, Drehung, Krümmung, *(person)* Verschrobenheit, *(rope)* Seil, Schnur, *(touch)* Anflug, Hauch;
new ~ neue Masche;
~ *(v.)* verschlingen, verflechten, *(fig.)* verdrehen, entstellen, *(insurance business)* zum Versicherungswechsel verleiten, *(river)* sich schlängeln;
~ **o. s. into** sich einschleichen; ~ **an account** Bericht entstellen; ~ **the meaning of a passage** einer Textstelle Zwang antun; ~ **a report** Bericht entstellen; ~ **s. o. round one's little finger** j. um den kleinen Finger wickeln; ~ **the truth** Wahrheit entstellen;
to give s. th. a ~ an einer Sache drehen; **to give a slight** ~ leicht abwandeln.

twister *(coll.)* Gauner, Lügner, *(US)* Wasser-, Sandhose, Tornado;
tongue ~ Zungenbrecher.

twisting *(insurance business, US)* Abspenstigmachung eines Versicherungsnehmers durch einen ausscheidenden Agenten, Verleitung zum Wechsel der Versicherung;
~ **of history** Geschichtsklitterung.

twisty road gewundene Straße.

two, put ~ **and** ~ **together** seine Schlußfolgerungen ziehen;
~~**bit** *(cheap, US)* unbedeutend, billig, wertlos; ~~**bit politician** *(US)* bestechlicher Politiker; ~~**cents worth** *(US coll.)* Scherflein; ~~**colo(u)r process** Zweifarbendruck; ~~**cycle motor** Zweitakter, Zweitaktmotor; ~~**decker** zweistöckiger Omnibus; ~~**dollar broker** *(US)* Auftragsmakler; ~~**engined** *(airplane)* zweimotorig; ~**faced** heuchlerisch; ~~**family house** Zweifamilienhaus; ~~**job man** *(US)* Doppelverdiener; ~~**lane** zweispurig; ~~**line letter** *(print.)* großer Anfangsbuchstabe; ~~**name paper** *(US)* [Sola]wechsel; ~~**party system** Zweiparteiensystem; ~~**part tariff** *(telephone)* kombinierter Tarif; ~~**phase current** Zweiphasenstrom; ~~**piece** Komplet; ~~**price system** System gespaltener Preise; ~~**seater** Zweisitzer; ~ **shakes of a lamb's (duck's) tail** *(coll.)* in Sekunden; ~~**sided** *(fig.)* unaufrichtig, *(law)* beiderseitig, bilateral; ~~**speed gear** Zweiganggetriebe; ~~**spot** *(coll., US)* Grundsatz der Zweidrittelmehrheit; ~~**storey** zweistöckig; ~~**thirds majority** Zweidrittelmehrheit; ~~**third page** *(advertising)* Zweidrittelseite; ~~**thirds rule** *(pol., US)* Grundsatz der Zweidrittelmehrheit; ~~**thousand-hours clause** Überstundenvergütung ab 2000 Arbeitsstunden im Jahr; ~~**tier board** zweistufiges Führungsgremium; ~~**tier bus** Doppeldeckerbus; ~~**tier gold market** gespaltener Goldmarkt; ~~**tier price of gold** gespaltener Goldpreis; ~~**tier scheme of taxation** gespaltenes Steuersystem; ~~**tier system** System des gespaltenen Goldpreises; ~~**time loser** *(sl.)* zweimal Geschiedener; ~~**way** zweibahnig; ~~**way agreement** Austauschabkommen; ~~**way price** *(Br.)* doppelter Kurs; ~~**way radio** Sende- und Empfangsgerät; ~~**way street** Straße mit Gegenverkehr.

twopence *(fig.)* Deut;
not to care ~ sich überhaupt nicht darum kümmern.

twopenny armselig, billig, wertlos.

tycoon, business *(US)* Industriemagnat, -kapitän, Großkapitalist, -industrieller, Bonze.

tying | agreement *(US)* Ausschließlichkeitsabkommen, Kopplungsvertrag; ~ **arrangement** *(antitrust law, US)* Kopplungsvertrag; ~ **clause** *(US)* Kopplungs-, Preisbindungsklausel; ~ **contract** *(US)* Exklusiv-, Kopplungsvertrag; ~~**in sale** *(US)* Kopplungsverkauf; ~~**product** *(US)* gekoppeltes Produkt; ~~**up of capital** Kapitalfestlegung.

type Grundform, Art, Type, Muster, Gattung, *(car)* Bauart, *(machine)* Modell, *(print.)* [Druck]buchstabe, Type, *(typical representative)* typischer Vertreter;
in ~ abgesetzt, gedruckt; **in bold** ~ in Fettdruck, fettgedruckt; **in italic** ~ kursiv, in Kursivdruck; **in large** ~ in Großbuchstaben; **in small** ~ kleingedruckt;
blood ~ Blutgruppe; **condensed** ~ schmallaufende Schrift; **latest** ~ modernste Bauart; **metallic** ~ Bleisatz; **salable** ~ gängiger Typ;
~ **of agreement** Vertragstyp; ~**s of audit** Prüfungsarten; ~ **for bills** Plakatschrift; ~**s of binding** Einbandarten; **all** ~**s of books** alle Buchgattungen; ~ **of business** Geschäftsart; ~ **of construction** Bauart; ~ **of contract** Vertragstyp; ~**s of costs** Kostenart; ~**s of domicile** Wohnsitzarten; ~ **of enterprise** Unternehmensform; ~ **of financing** Finanzierungsweise; **every** ~ **of financing** alle Finanzierungsgeschäfte; ~**s of hazard** Risikoarten; ~**s of income** Einkunftsarten; ~ **of insurance** Versicherungsform; ~ **of investment** Art der Anlage, Anlageform; ~ **of packing** Verpackungsweise; ~ **of promotion** Beförderungsart; ~ **of property** Vermögensgattung; ~ **of rating** Beurteilungsmethode; ~**s of risk** Risikogattungen; ~ **in store** *(print.)* Lagerschriften; ~ **of valuation** Bewertungsmethode; ~ **of wage plan** Lohnzahlungsmethode;
~ *(v.)* maschineschreiben, tippen, *(med.)* Blutgruppe feststellen;
~ **in italics** in Kursivschrift setzen; ~ **a letter** Brief auf der Schreibmaschine schreiben;
to appear in ~ im Druck erscheinen; **to be in** ~ abgesetzt (druckfähig) sein; **to be set in** ~ gesetzt werden; **to be short of certain** ~ bestimmte Drucktypen nicht vorrätig haben; **to get s. th. set up in** ~ etw. absetzen lassen; **to keep the** ~ **standing** Stehsatz anfertigen; **to print in bold (heavy)** ~ fett drucken; **to remain in** ~ im Satz stehenbleiben; **to set** ~ absetzen; **to set** ~ **at high speed** Manuskript äußerst schnell absetzen;

~ **area** Satzspiegel; ~ **bar** *(typewriter)* Typenhebel; ~ **disk** *(terminal)* Schriftscheibe; ~ **face** Schriftart, -bild; ~ **founder** Schriftgießer; ~ **founding** Schriftguß; ~ **foundry** Schriftgießerei; ~**-high** in Schrifthöhe; ~ **layout** Satzanweisung; ~ **master** Schriftscheibe; ~ **measure** Zeilenmesser; ~ **number** Gattungsnummer; ~ **page** Satzspiegel; ~ **sample** Mustertype, Typenmuster; ~ **scale** Zeilenmaß; ~ **size** Druckgröße, *(composing)* Schriftgrad, Kegel; ~ **specifications** Spezifizierung der Schriftart; ~ **style** Schriftcharakter.

typed maschinegeschrieben;
~ **manuscript** Schreibmaschinenmanuskript.

typescript maschinegeschriebenes Schriftstück, Schreibmaschinenmanuskript.

typeset *(v.)* setzen, belichten.

typesetter Schriftsetzer, *(machine)* Satzmaschine;
computer-based ~ computergesteuerte Satzmaschine.

typesetting Schriftsetzen, Satz;
computer-based (computerized) ~ Licht-, Photo-, Computersatz;
~ **machine** Setzmaschine.

typewrite *(v.)* auf der Maschine schreiben, tippen.

typewriter *(machine)* Schreibmaschine, *(person)* Maschineschreiber;
automatic ~ Schreibmaschine mit Lochstreifensteuerung; **electric** ~ elektrische Schreibmaschine; **long-carriage** ~ Breitwagenmaschine; **portable** ~ Reiseschreibmaschine; **silent** ~ geräuschlose Schreibmaschine;
electric ~ **suitable for tabulating** elektrische Schreibmaschine mit Tabulatorvorrichtung;
~ **catalog(ue)** Schreibmaschinenkatalog; ~ **desk** Schreibmaschinentisch; ~ **pad** Schreibmaschinenunterlage; ~ **paper** Schreibmaschinenpapier; ~ **ribbon** Farbband; ~ **table** Schreibmaschinentisch.

typewriting Maschineschreiben;
~ **examination** Schreibmaschinenprüfung; ~ **telegraph** Fernschreibmaschine, Fernschreiber.

typewritten maschinegeschrieben, in Maschinenschrift;
~ **copy** Durchschlag; **to hold four** ~ **pages** vier Schreibmaschinenseiten umfassen.

typhoon Taifun.

typify *(v.)* typisieren, typen, verkörpern, repräsentieren.

typing Schreibmaschineschreiben;
to be good at ~ gut Schreibmaschine schreiben können; **to charge** ~ **by piece rate** Schreibmaschinenseiten pro Seite abrechnen;
~ **batch** Durchschreibsatz; ~ **course** Schreibmaschinenkursus, -lehrgang; ~ **error** Tippfehler; ~ **pool** Gemeinschaftssekretariat, Schreibzentrale; **to save** ~ **time** Zeit beim Schreibmaschineschreiben sparen.

typist Maschinenschreiber, Schreibkraft, Stenotypist;
audio ~ Phonotypistin; **clerk-**~ Schreibkraft; **copy** ~ Schreibkraft; **lady** ~ Maschineschreiberin; **shorthand** ~ Stenotypistin; **to be a quick** ~ flott maschineschreiben;
~**'s chair** Schreibmaschinenstuhl; ~**'s desk** Schreibmaschinentisch.

typograph Satz-, Setzmaschine.

typographer Buchdrucker, Setzer.

typographic typografisch;
~ **design** typografische Gestaltung; ~ **instruction** Satzbefehl; ~ **point** typografischer Punkt.

typographical | error Druck-, Satzfehler; ~ **layout** Satzentwurf.

typography Buchdruckerkunst, Typografie.

tyrannicide Tyrannenmord.

tyrannize *(v.)* unterdrücken, Gewaltherrschaft ausüben.

tyranny Tyrannei, Diktatur, Willkür-, Gewaltherrschaft.

tyrant Tyrann, Despot, Gewaltherrscher.

tyre *(Br.)* Reifen;
~s Bereifung;
off-the-road ~ Geländeprofilreifen; **pneumatic** ~ Luftreifen; ~ *(v.)* bereifen;
to fix a ~ Reifen montieren;
~ **casing** Mantel; ~ **chain** Schneekette; ~ **factory** Reifenfabrik; ~ **gauge** Reifendruckmesser; ~ **guarantee** Reifengarantie; ~ **lever** Reifenheber; ~ **maker** Reifenhersteller; ~ **plant** Reifenfabrik; ~ **price** Reifenpreis; ~ **wear rate** Reifenverschleißwert; ~ **replacement** Reifenersatzbeschaffung, -auswechslung; ~ **store** Reifenlager; ~ **track** Reifenspur; ~ **trouble** Reifenpanne; ~ **use** Reifenabnutzung.

tyro Neuling.

U

U *(Br.)* charakteristisch für die oberen Klassen, vornehm, nobel, *(US sl.)* Uni, Universität;
non-~ unfein, nicht vornehm;
~-boat U-Boot; **~ turn** *(on the street)* Wenden; **~ turns not allowed** *(traffic)* Wenden verboten, Wendeverbot; **~ usage in language** vornehme Ausdrucksweise.
U.N. UNO.
uberrima fides *(lat., life insurance)* höchste Redlichkeit.
udal allodial, erbeigen;
~ tenure Frei-, Allodialgut.
ugly häßlich, abstoßend, *(dirty)* gemein, niederträchtig, *(ill-natured, US coll.)* bösartig;
~ as sin grundhäßlich;
~ crime gemeines Verbrechen; **~ customer** übler Kunde; **~ furniture** geschmacklose Möbel; **~ surroundings** abstoßende Umgebung; **~ symptoms** bedrohliche Anzeichen; **~ weather** bedrohliches Wetter.
ukase Ukas, Erlaß.
ullage Flüssigkeitsverlust [im Faß], Verlust durch Auslaufen, Leckage, *(bags)* Schwund, Gewichtsverlust.
ulterior nachträglich, später folgend, zukünftig;
~ motives Hintergedanken, Nebenabsichten.
ultimate äußerst, allerletzt, *(farthest)* entferntest;
~ in freedom Maximum an Bewegungsfreiheit;
~ balance of an account Abschlußsaldo eines Kontos; **~ buyer** Privatverbraucher; **~ cause** eigentliche Ursache; **~ consumer** End-, Letztverbraucher; **~ consumption** Letztverbrauch; **~ decision** letzte (endgültige, höchstrichterliche) Entscheidung; **~ destination** *(international law)* endgültiger Bestimmungsort; **~ deterrent** Atomwaffe; **~ facts** entscheidungserhebliche Tatsachen; **~ result** Endergebnis; **~ strain** Maximalbelastung; **~ strength** Bruchfestigkeit; **~ taxpayer** Steuerträger.
ultimatum Ultimatum;
to deliver an ~ to a country einem Land ein Ultimatum stellen.
ultimo letzten (vorigen) Monats, Ultimo.
ultimogeniture Erbfolge des jüngsten Sohns.
ultra Extremist, Radikaler;
~ (a.) radikal, extrem;
~-cheap money policy *(Br.)* Politik des ungewöhnlich billigen Geldes, Tiefstzinspolitik; **~ reprisals** nach Spesen-, Rabattabzug; **~-short wave** Ultrakurzwelle.
ultra vires *(Br.)* außerhalb der Vertretungsmacht, vollmachtsüberschreitend, *(law of corporations)* in Überschreitung der Satzungsbefugnisse;
~ action Überschreitung der Vollmacht, Vollmachtsüberschreitung; **~ borrowing** satzungsgemäß nicht gestattete Kreditaufnahme; **~ transaction** außerhalb der Befugnisse vorgenommene Geschäftstransaktion.
ultraconservative erzkonservativ.
ultrahigh frequency Dezimeterwelle.
ultraist Extremist, Radikaler.
ultramodern hypermodern.
ultrasensitve to price increase auf Preiserhöhungen mit äußerster Empfindsamkeit reagierend.
ultrasound Überschall.
ultrasonic Überschall.
ultraviolet rays ultraviolette Strahlen.
umbrella Schirm, *(fig)* Schirm, Schutz, Deckung;
under the ~ of the mayor unter der Schirmherrschaft des Oberbürgermeisters; **under the ~ of the UN** unter dem Schutz der UNO;
aerial ~ *(mil.)* Jagdschutz;
to have s. th. under one's ~ für etw. zuständig sein; **to put up an ~** Schirm aufspannen;
~ barrage Sperrfeuer; **~ case (cover)** Schirmhülle; **~ coverage** *(insurance)* Globaldeckung; **~ holding company** Dachgesellschaft; **~ organization** Spitzen-, Zentralverband, Dachorganisation; **~ stand** Schirmständer.
umpirage schiedsrichterliche Entscheidung.
umpire Preis-, Schiedsrichter, Obmann, *(factory use, sl.)* Gewerbeaufseher;
~ (v.) between two parties als Schiedsrichter zwischen zwei Parteien fungieren.
umpireship Schiedsrichteramt.
un-American activities staatsfeindliche Umtriebe.
unabated interest unvermindertes Interesse.
unabbreviated unverkürzt.

unable unfähig, nicht in der Lage, *(for legal action)* geschäftsunfähig;
~ to earn one's living erwerbsunfähig; **~ to pay [one's debts]** zahlungsunfähig; **~ to testify** als Zeuge ungeeignet; **~ to work** arbeitsunfähig, -untauglich.
unableness Untauglichkeit.
unabbreviated unverkürzt.
unabridged ungekürzt;
~ edition unverkürzte Ausgabe.
unabrogated nicht aufgehoben.
unabsorbed losses steuerlich noch nicht verbrauchte Verluste.
unacceptable unannehmbar.
unaccepted nicht akzeptiert.
unaccommodating unverbindlich, ungefällig, unkulant.
unaccomplishable nicht ausbildungsfähig.
unaccomplished nicht ausgebildet.
unaccountable nicht rechnungspflichtig (haftbar, verantwortlich).
unaccounted for *(balance sheet)* nicht ausgewiesen.
unaccredited nicht beglaubigt (akkreditiert);
~ source unverbürgte Quelle.
unaccrued noch nicht angefallen (fällig);
~ damage noch nicht eingetretener Schadensfall.
unaccustomed ungewohnt;
to be ~ to hardships Entbehrungen nicht gewohnt sein; **to be ~ to speaking in public** über keine Erfahrungen als öffentlicher Redner verfügen.
unacknowledged nicht zugegeben (anerkannt), *(letter)* unbeantwortet, unbestätigt;
~ letter unbestätigter Brief.
unacquainted unerfahren;
to be ~ with s. th. mit einer Sache nicht vertraut sein.
unacquitted *(criminal)* nicht freigesprochen, *(debt)* ungetilgt.
unactable nicht bühnengerecht, unaufführbar.
unaddressed ohne Anschrift (Adresse);
~ mailing *(US)* Postwurfsendung.
unadjudged noch im Streit befangen, streitbefangen, unentschieden.
unadjusted noch nicht vereinbart, *(debt)* noch nicht reguliert, *(statistics)* nicht bereinigt.
unadmitted nicht zugelassen;
~ assets *(insurance)* nicht bewertbare Aktiva.
unadoptable nicht anwendbar.
unadopted nicht angenommen;
~ children nicht adoptierte (elternlose) Kinder; **~ road** nicht unterhaltene Straße.
unadulterated unverfälscht, ohne Beimischung, rein, echt.
unadvanced member *(Br.)* noch nicht zugeteilter Bausparer.
unadvisable nicht empfehlenswert.
unaffiliated nicht eingegliedert;
~ company selbständige Tochtergesellschaft.
unaided *(poor)* ohne Unterstützung.
unalienable unveräußerlich, unverkäuflich.
unallotted nicht verteilt, unverteilt, unverlost;
~ appropriation *(government accounting)* noch nicht zur Verfügung stehende Haushaltsmittel; **~ shares** nicht zugeteilte (unbegebene) Aktien.
unaltered unverändert.
unalloyed unlegiert, unvermischt.
unalterable unabänderlich, unwandelbar.
unaltered unverändert.
unambiguous unzweideutig;
~ terms präzise Bedingungen.
unamenable | to law strafunmündig; **~ to reason** Vernunftgründen nicht zugänglich.
unamendable nicht ergänzungsfähig.
unamended *(law)* ohne Ergänzungen.
unamerican activities staatsfeindliche Umtriebe.
unamortized debt (bond) discount Disagiogewinn.
unanimity Einstimmigkeit;
to reach ~ Einstimmigkeit erzielen.
unanimous einstimmig, ohne Gegenstimme;
to be ~ in their approval of a report Bericht einhellig billigen; **to accept a proposal with ~ approval** Vorschlag einstimmig gutheißen; **~ consent** einhellige Zustimmung; **~ opinion** einhellige Meinung; **~ voice of a jury** einstimmiger Geschworenenspruch; **~ vote** einstimmig gefaßter Beschluß.

unanimously | elected einstimmig gewählt;
to be ~ in support of the government's policy Regierungspolitik einstimmig unterstützen; **to carry a vote ~** Vorschlag einstimmig annehmen; **to vote ~ for a proposal** geschlossen für einen Vorschlag stimmen.

unannounced unangemeldet.

unanswerable nicht bestreitbar, unwiderlegbar, *(not liable)* nicht haftbar.

unanswered unbeantwortet, unerwidert.

unappealable nicht berufungs-, rechtsmittelfähig.

unapplied tot, brachliegend, ungenutzt;
~ for *(position)* ohne Bewerber;
~ cash *(governmental accounting)* frei verfügbare Haushaltsmittel; **~ funds** totes Kapital, tote (brachliegende) Kapitalien.

unapportionable unteilbar, nicht aufteilbar.

unapprehended nicht ergriffen, flüchtig.

unapt ungeeignet, untauglich, *(low)* zurückgeblieben, schwer von Begriff;
~ comparison unpassender Vergleich.

unappropriated herrenlos, nicht in Besitz genommen, *(money)* unausgeschüttet, keiner bestimmten Verwendung zugeführt;
~ budget surplus *(municipal accounting)* Haushaltsüberschuß; **~ earned surplus** *(retained earnings) (US)* nicht verteilter (ausschüttungsfähiger) Reingewinn; **~ funds** *(budgeting)* nicht verwendete [Etats]mittel; **~ income** *(institutional accounting)* nicht vorkalkulierte Ertragsüberschüsse; **~ profit** *(US)* unverteilter Reingewinn.

unapproved nicht genehmigt.

unargued nicht bestritten.

unarranged nicht vereinbart.

unarrested *(property)* nicht beschlagnahmt.

unascertainable nicht feststellbar.

unascertained unbestimmt, nicht festgelegt, *(internal revenue)* nicht ermittelt;
~ duties pauschalierte Steuerzahlungen (Zölle); **~ goods** Gattungssachen; **~ person** nicht ermittelte (unbekannte) Person.

unasked unaufgefordert, ungebeten, unverlangt;
~ contribution freiwillige Spende.

unassailable unanfechtbar, unbestreitbar.

unassented securities *(US)* nicht abgestempelte Effekten.

unassessed *(property)* untaxiert, nicht veranlagt.

unassignable nicht übertragbar (abtretbar), unübertragbar.

unassociated nicht assoziiert.

unassorted unsortiert.

unassured nicht versichert, unversichert.

unattached nicht organisiert, unabhängig, *(mil.)* zur Disposition stehend, *(person, politics)* ungebunden, *(property)* nicht mit Beschlag belegt, *(worker)* nicht organisiert;
~ real-estate agent dem Verband nicht angeschlossener Immobilienmakler.

unattainable unerschwinglich.

unattended *(child)* unversorgt, unbeaufsichtigt, vernachlässigt.

unattested unbeglaubigt, *(Br.)* behördlich nicht überprüft.

unaudited nicht von der Revision erfaßt, nicht überprüft;
~ invoices ungeprüfte Lieferantenrechnungen.

unauthentic nicht authentisch.

unauthenticated unverbürgt, *(not legalized)* unbeglaubigt.

unauthorized unbefugt, -berechtigt, nicht autorisiert (ermächtigt, bevollmächtigt);
~ agency Vertretung ohne Vertretungsmacht; **~ clerk** *(London stock exchange)* unbefugter Maklergehilfe; **~ company** nicht zugelassene Versicherungsgesellschaft; **~ person** Unbefugter, Unberechtigter; **~ reprint** unberechtigter Nachdruck; **~ use** nichtgenehmigte Benutzung.

unavailability Nichtverfügbarkeit.

unavailable nicht verfügbar, *(candidate, US)* ohne Erfolgschancen, *(invalid)* ungültig, *(machine)* unbrauchbar, *(manuscript, US)* ungeeignet;
~ for express trains *(ticket)* berechtigt nicht zur Benutzung von Schnellzügen.

unavailableness Ungültigkeit.

unavailed unbenutzt, nicht ausgenutzt;
~ credit line nicht in Anspruch genommene Kreditlinie.

unavailing nutzlos, vergeblich.

unavoidable unvermeidbar, unvermeidlich, unumgänglich, *(not voidable)* unanfechtbar;
~ accident unvermeidlicher Unfall; **~ casualty** unabwendbares Ereignis; **~ cause** unabwendbare Ursache; **~ cost** feste (notwendige) Kosten, Fixkosten; **~ dangers [of a river]** *(marine policy)* unabwendbare Gefahren; **~ hazards** *(insurance business)* unvermeidbare Risiken.

unavoidably absent unabkömmlich.

unaware in Unkenntnis, *(unexpected)* überraschend;
to come upon s. o. ~s unvermutet auf j. stoßen; **to drop a parcel ~s** Paket versehentlich fallen lassen.

unbacked ungedeckt, ohne Unterstützung;
~ check *(US)* (**cheque**, *Br.*) nicht indossierter Scheck.

unbalance Gleichgewichtsstörung, *(fig.)* Unausgeglichenheit.

unbalanced aus dem Gleichgewicht gebracht, *(fig.)* unausgeglichen, schwankend, unstet;
~ of mind geistesgestört;
~ account nicht ausgeglichenes (saldiertes) Konto; **~ addition** *(national income accounting)* nicht ausgeglichene Wertschöpfung; **~ books** unausgeglichene Bücher; **~ budget** nicht ausgeglichener (unausgeglichener) Haushalt; **~ entry** nicht saldierter Posten; **~ growth** ungleichgewichtiges Wachstum; **~ mind** Störung der Geistestätigkeit; **mentally ~ person** Geistesgestörter; **~ traffic** überwiegender Richtungsverkehr.

unbale *(v.)* Waren [aus dem Ballen] auspacken.

unballasted ohne Ballast, *(fig.)* unbeständig, schwankend, unstet.

unbankable nicht bankfähig (diskontfähig);
~ paper nicht diskontfähiger Wechsel.

unbar *(v.)* aufriegeln.

unbeaten record unangefochtener (unübertroffener) Rekord.

unbecoming ungeziemend, ungebührlich.

unbelievable unglaubhaft.

unbend *(v.) (fig.)* aus sich herausgehen, auftauen;
~ the mind ausspannen; **~ a rope** Tau losmachen.

unbending unbeugsam, hartnäckig, entschlossen;
~ attitude unnachgiebige Haltung.

unbeneficed ohne Pfründe.

unbeneficial nicht vorteilhaft.

unbiassed unvoreingenommen, unparteiisch, objektiv, *(statistics)* erwartungstreu.

unbidden unaufgefordert.

unblemished unbescholten;
~ career makellose Laufbahn; **of ~ character** unbescholten.

unblock *(v.)* **an account** Konto freigeben (entsperren).

unblocking *(of account)* Entsperrung, Freigabe.

unblushing corruption schamlose Korruption.

unborn | child ungeborenes Kind; **~ generation** kommende Geschlechter.

unbosom *(v.)* | **one's heart** sein Herz ausschütten; **~ one's thoughts** seine geheimsten Gedanken enthüllen.

unbought nicht gekauft.

unbound frei, ohne Verpflichtungen, *(book)* broschiert, ungebunden.

unbounded schranken-, zügellos.

unbrace *(v.)* **o. s.** sich entspannen.

unbred ungeschult.

unbribable unbestechlich.

unbridled *(fig.)* ungezügelt, hemmungslos;
~ tongue loses Mundwerk, lose Zunge.

unbroached subject nicht angeschnittenes Thema.

unbroken *(contract)* intakt, unverletzt, *(land)* ungepflügt, *(adverse possession)* ununterbrochen, *(record)* ungebrochen, unübertroffen;
~ account Umsatzkonto; **~ coke** Brechkoks; **~ ground** jungfräulicher Boden; **~ front** *(mil.)* intakte Front; **~ line** durchgezogene Linie; **~ line of authorities** ständige Rechtsprechung; **~ oath** nicht gebrochener Eid; **~ peace** ununterbrochener Friede; **~ record** unübertroffener Rekord; **~ seal** unverletztes Siegel; **~ sleep** Dauerschlaf; **~ spirit** unbeugsamer Geist.

unbuild *(v.)* demolieren, einreißen.

unbuilt unbebaut.

unburden *(v.)* | **one's conscience** sein Gewissen erleichtern; **~ a secret** Geheimnis loswerden; **~ one's troubles** seine Sorgen bei jem. abladen.

unbury *(v.)* exhumieren, ausgraben.

unbusinesslike nicht geschäftsmäßig, unkaufmännisch.

unbuttoned *(fig.)* zwanglos.

uncalculable außerhalb der Berechnung.

uncallable loan unkündbares Darlehn.

uncalled unaufgefordert, *(bonds)* nicht aufgerufen;
~ capital noch nicht eingezahltes (eingefordertes) Kapital; **~-for insult** grundlose Beleidigung; **~-for remark** freche (deplazierte) Bemerkung.

uncancellable unaufhebbar, unwiderruflich.

uncancelled nicht abgesagt, *(stamp)* nicht entwertet.

uncareful unbekümmert, leichtsinnig.

uncatalogued im Katalog nicht aufgeführt, nicht katalogisiert.

uncensored unzensiert, nicht zensiert.

unceremonious formlos, zwanglos, ungezwungen.

uncertain *(debts)* unsicher, zweifelhaft;
  to be ~ of s. th. einer Sache nicht sicher sein; **to be ~ about one's plans** keine bestimmten Pläne haben;
  of ~ age unbestimmtes Alter; ~ **answer** vage Antwort; ~ **arrival** nicht bekannte Ankunft; ~ **quotations** *(Br.)* per Pfund notierte Devisenkurse; ~ **weather** veränderliches Wetter.

uncertainty Unklarheit, Ungewißheit, *(category of risk)* Ungewißheit, Unsicherheit, *(will)* Ungenauigkeit;
  ~ **in a contract** Unbestimmtheit einer Vertragszusage; ~ **of tenure** Widerruflichkeit eines Amtes; ~ **of words** ungenaue Formulierung.

uncertificated ohne amtliche Zulassung (Bescheinigung, Bestätigung), nicht diplomiert;
  ~ **bankrupt** *(Br.)* nicht rehabilitierter Konkursschuldner; ~ **stock** *(Br.)* Schuldbuchgiroforderungen.

uncertified nicht bescheinigt, unbeglaubigt.

unchallengeable unbestreitbar, unanfechtbar, unwiderlegbar.

unchallenged unwidersprochen;
  to let s. th. pass ~ etw. unwidersprochen lassen;
  ~ **evidence** nicht widerlegbares Beweismaterial.

unchanged *(money)* ungewechselt, *(stock exchange)* unverändert.

uncharged *(not debited)* nicht belastet, unbelastet, *(free of charge)* umsonst, franko, unberechnet, wird nicht in Rechnung gestellt, gratis, *(law)* nicht angeklagt, *(ship)* nicht beladen.

unchartered unverbrieft, nicht privilegiert.

unchecked unkontrolliert;
  ~ **advance** *(mil.)* ungehinderter Vormarsch; ~ **baggage** *(US)* nicht aufgegebenes Gepäck, Handgepäck.

uncivility Ungebildetheit, Unhöflichkeit.

uncivilized unzivilisiert.

unclaimed nicht geltend gemacht (beansprucht), *(letter)* nicht abgeholt, unbestellbar;
  ~ **animal** herrenloses Tier; ~ **balance** nicht zurückgefordertes Guthaben; ~ **dividends** nicht abgehobene Dividenden; ~ **funds** nicht abgeholte Geldbeträge; - **letter** nicht abgeholter Brief; ~ **merchandise** nicht abgeholte Ware; ~ **property** herrenloses Gut; ~ **right** nicht geltend gemachtes Recht; ~ **wages** Lohnguthaben; ~ **wreck** herrenloses Wrack.

unclassified nicht eingeordnet, *(mil.)* nicht [mehr] geheim.

unclassify *(mil.)* von der Geheimhaltungsliste streichen, freigeben.

uncle Onkel, *(pawnbroker, sl.)* Pfandleiher;
  ~ **by marriage** angeheirateter Onkel; ᵉ **Sam** *(coll.)* Vereinigte Staaten von Nordamerika;
  to talk to s. o. like a Dutch ~ j. eine Gardinenpredigt halten; ᵉ **Sam's party** *(US sl.)* Löhnungstag.

unclean unsauber, *(fig.)* schmutzig, obszön;
  ~ **bill of lading** unreines Konnossement; ~ **hands principle** Rechtsschutzanerkennung nur für redliche Kläger.

unclear undeutlich.

uncleared nicht abgeschlossen, liegengeblieben, *(criminal)* nicht freigesprochen (entlastet), *(not paid)* unbezahlt, ungetilgt, *(stock exchange, Br.)* nicht verrechnet, nicht abgeschlossen, liegengeblieben;
  ~ **effects** *(Br.)* noch nicht verrechnete Schecks.

unclosed nicht abgeschlossen, offen.

unclouded wolkenlos, unbewölkt, *(fig.)* heiter, unbekümmert;
  ~ **happiness** ungetrübtes Glück.

uncoined ungemünzt, -geprägt.

uncollected nicht eingesammelt, *(fig., tax)* noch nicht erhoben;
  ~ **goods** nicht abgeholte Ware; ~ **items** *(US)* noch nicht eingegangene Abschnitte.

uncollectible nicht beitreibbar (einziehbar), uneinbringlich;
  ~ **items** abgeschriebene Inkassoforderungen; ~ **receivables** uneinbringliche Forderungen, Dubiose; ~ **taxes** uneinbringliche Steuerforderungen.

uncollectibility Uneinbringlichkeit.

uncolo(u)red farblos;
  ~ **account** ungeschminkter Bericht.

uncomfortable beunruhigend, unangenehm;
  to be ~ sich nicht recht wohl fühlen;
  ~ **feeling** ungutes Gefühl.

uncommercial unkaufmännisch, nicht handeltreibend.

uncommissioned ohne Auftrag.

uncommitted *(bill)* noch im Ausschußstadium, *(crime)* nicht begangen, *(pol.)* nicht gebunden, blockfrei;
  ~ **amounts** noch nicht festgelegte Beträge; ~ **countries** blockfreie Länder, Neutrale; ~ **funds** nicht zweckgebundene Mittel.

uncommunicative reserviert, verschlossen, wenig mitteilsam.

uncompensated ohne Entschädigung, unentschädigt.

uncomplaisant ungefällig.

uncompleted transaction unvollständiges Geschäft.

uncomplicated unkompliziert.

uncomplimentary unhöflich, nicht schmeichelhaft.

uncomplying unnachgiebig.

uncompromising zu keinem Kompromiß bereit, kompromißlos.

unconcern Gleichgültigkeit, Interesselosigkeit;
  with ~ gleichmütig, gelassen.

unconcerned | in a business an einer Sache nicht beteiligt;
  to be ~ about the future sich über die Zukunft keine Gedanken machen.

uncondemned nicht verurteilt.

uncondensed *(book)* ungekürzt.

unconditional unbedingt, bedingungslos, vorbehaltlos, ohne Vorbehalt;
  ~ **acceptance** unbedingtes (bedingungsloses) Akzept; ~ **discharge** *(Br., prisoner)* bedingungslose Entlassung; ~ **offer** vorbehaltloses Angebot; ~ **order** unwiderruflich erteilter Zahlungsauftrag; ~ **promise** vorbehaltloses Zahlungsversprechen; ~ **surrender** bedingungslose Kapitulation.

unconditioned ohne Vorbedingung, *(pupil)* ohne Vorbehalt versetzt.

unconfirmed unbestätigt, unverbürgt;
  ~ **letter of credit** unbestätigtes Akkreditiv; ~ **rumo(u)r** unverbürgtes Gerücht.

unconformity Unvereinbarkeit, Nichtübereinstimmung.

unconfutable nicht widerlegbar, unwiderlegbar.

uncongenial | climate ungünstiges Klima; ~ **job** nicht zusagende Arbeit.

unconnected report unzusammenhängender Bericht.

unconscionable unzumutbar, skrupellos;
  ~ **bargain (transaction)** sittenwidriges [Rechts]geschäft, Wuchergeschäft; ~ **conduct** gewissenloses Verhalten; ~ **rascal** skrupelloser Schurke.

unconscious unbewußt, unwissentlich;
  ~ **humo(u)r** unfreiwilliger Humor; ~ **mistake** unbeabsichtigter Fehler.

unconsidered unberücksichtigt.

unconsolidated *(loan)* nicht konsolidiert, unkonsolidiert, unfundiert.

unconstitutional | statute verfassungswidriges Gesetz; ~ **strike** verfassungswidriger Streik.

unconstitutionality Verfassungswidrigkeit.

unconstrained ungezwungen.

unconstricted *(trade)* unbehindert.

unconsumed *(credit)* unverbraucht.

unconsummated marriage nicht vollzogene Ehe.

uncontestable unbestreitbar.

uncontested unbestritten;
  ~ **election** Wahl ohne Gegenkandidaten; ~ **owner** unumstrittener Eigentümer; ~ **seat** *(election)* Parlamentssitz ohne Gegenkandidat.

uncontradicted unwidersprochen, -bestritten, -angefochten.

uncontrollable | divorce unstreitiges Scheidungsverfahren; ~ **expenses** von der Kostenstelle nicht beeinflußbare Kosten; ~ **impulse** *(criminal law)* Affekt; ~ **temper** zügelloses Temperament.

uncontrolled unbeaufsichtigt, ohne Aufsicht;
  ~ **economy** freie Wirtschaft; ~ **rent** *(Br.)* freie (nicht bewirtschaftete) Miete, nicht dem Mieterschutz unterliegendes Mietverhältnis.

uncontrovertible proof unwiderleglicher Beweis.

unconventional ungezwungen, zwanglos, unkonventionell, nicht herkömmlich.

unconverted nicht konvertiert.

unconvertible nicht konvertierbar.

uncooked *(balance sheet)* sauber, einwandfrei, nicht frisiert.

uncopyrighted urheberrechtlich nicht geschützt.

uncorrected unverbessert, -korrigiert.

uncorroborated unbestätigt.

uncorrupted unbestechlich, rechtschaffen.

uncostly von geringem Wert.

uncounted ungezählt.

uncouple *(v.)* auskuppeln, [Waggon] abhängen.

uncovenanted vertraglich nicht vereinbart;
  ~ **benefit** nicht vereinbarter Versicherungsgewinn, *(unemployment insurance, Br.)* ins Ermessen gestellte Arbeitslosenunterstützung.

uncover *(v.)* aufdecken, enthüllen, offenbaren;
  ~ **a plot** Verschwörung aufdecken.

uncovered ungedeckt, ohne Deckung, *(not insured)* unversichert;
  to leave ~ ungedeckt lassen;
  ~ advance Blankovorschuß, ungesicherter (nicht gedeckter) Kontokorrentkredit; **~ balance** ungedeckter Saldo; **~ bill** ungedeckter Wechsel; **~ check** *(US)* **(cheque,** *Br.***)** ungedeckter Scheck; **~ circulation** ungedeckter Notenumlauf; **~ loan** unbesicherter Kredit; **~ paper money** ungedecktes Papiergeld; **~ note** ungedeckter Wechsel; **~ risk** *(insurance)* nicht gedecktes Risiko; **~ sales** Blankoverkäufe, -abgaben, Leerverkäufe.

uncreasable knitterfrei.

uncredited ohne Kredit.

uncritical ohne Urteilsvermögen, unkritisch;
  ~ estimate ungeprüfte Schätzung; **~ reader** unkritischer Leser.

uncrossed cheque *(Br.)* offener Scheck, Barscheck.

uncultivable nicht kultivierbar, unbestellbar.

uncultivated *(fig.)* ungebildet, -kultiviert, *(land)* unbebaut, unangebaut.

unculture Kulturlosigkeit.

uncultured unkultiviert, ungebildet.

uncurrent nicht im Umlauf befindlich, *(order to pay)* ungültig.

uncurtailed unverkürzt, ungeschmälert.

uncustomary ungebräuchlich, nicht üblich.

uncustomed *(custom-free)* zollfrei, unverzollt, *(goodwill)* ohne Kundschaft;
  ~ goods (merchandise) unverzollt eingeführte (zollfreie) Ware.

uncut *(book)* unaufgeschnitten, *(salary)* ungekürzt;
  ~ diamond ungeschliffener Diamant, Rohdiamant; **~ film** ungekürzter Film.

undamaged unbeschädigt, -versehrt;
  ~ reputation makelloser Ruf.

undated ohne Zeitangabe (Datum), undatiert, nicht datiert, *(having no limit)* unbefristet.

undebased unverfälscht, *(not devalued)* nicht entwertet;
  ~ coinage vollwertige Münzen.

undebated *(motion)* ohne Debatte;
  to accept a motion ~ Antrag ohne Debatte annehmen.

undecided unentschieden, *(wavering)* unschlüssig, unentschlossen, schwankend;
  to leave a question ~ Fragen offen lassen.

undecipherable unentzifferbar.

undeclared ohne Angabe, nicht deklariert;
  ~ cargo nicht zur Verzollung angemeldete Ladung; **~ goods** nicht deklarierte Waren; **~ war** Krieg ohne Kriegserklärung.

undedicated ohne Widmung.

undeeded nicht urkundlich übertragen.

undefaced nicht abgestempelt.

undefended unbestritten, *(lawsuit)* ohne Verteidiger;
  ~ suit nichtstreitige Verhandlung; **~ town** offene Stadt.

undeliverable nicht lieferbar;
  ~ letter unzustellbarer Brief.

undelivered *(letter)* unbestellt, nicht zugestellt;
  ~ goods noch nicht gelieferte Waren; **~ speech** nicht gehaltene Rede.

undemocratic undemokratisch.

undeniable unanfechtbar, unbestreitbar.

undenominational konfessionell nicht gebunden, paritätisch;
  ~ school Simultanschule.

undeposable unabsetzbar.

undeposited nicht hinterlegt.

undepreciated nicht entwertet, vollwertig.

undepressed market feste Börse.

under, as wie untenstehend;
  ~ age minderjährig; **~ one's belt** *(fig.)* im Magen; **~ bond** unter Zollverschluß; **~ the castle wall** am Fuß der Schloßmauer; **~ command** manövrierfähig; **~ a contract** vertraglich gebunden; **~ control** unter Aufsicht, *(car)* unter Kontrolle; **~ the counter** unter dem Ladentisch, schwarz; **~ separate cover** in besonderem Umschlag, mit getrennter Post; **~ darkness** im Schutz der Dunkelheit; **~ the hammer** unter dem Hammer, versteigert; **~ my hand** von mir unterschrieben; **~ hand and seal** unterzeichnet und gesiegelt; **~ one's hat** vertraulich; **~ the influence of intoxicating liquor** unter Alkoholeinfluß; **~ protest** unter Vorbehalt; **~ the provisions of the law** nach den gesetzlichen Bestimmungen; **~ quarantine** in Quarantäne; **~ repair** in Reparatur; **~ the rose** vertraulich; **~ the rules** *(stock exchange)* börsenamtlich; **~ one's signature** eigenhändig unterschrieben; **~ and subject** *(conveyancing)* hypothekarisch belastet; **~ suspicion** im Verdacht stehend; **~ the table** *(coll.)* besoffen; **~ water** unterhalb der Wasseroberfläche; **~ way** in Fahrt;
  to be snowed ~ von Arbeit überhäuft sein; **to get out from ~** seine Schulden zurückzahlen; **to go ~** *(firm)* eingehen.

underabsorbed indirect cost Fertigungsgemeinkostenmehranfall.

underachieved *(US)* leistungsschwacher Schüler (Student).

underachiever *(pupil, US)* Schüler mit unterdurchschnittlichen Leistungen.

underage Minderjährigkeit;
  ~ *(a.)* minderjährig, unmündig.

underagent Untervertreter.

underarmed schlecht bewaffnet.

underassessment zu niedrige Veranlagung.

underbanked knapp an Banken.

underbelly *(fig.)* weiche (verwundbare) Stelle.

underbid Unter-, Mindergebot;
  ~ *(v.)* unterbieten, *(public auction)* durch ein niedrigeres Angebot ausstechen.

underbill *(v.)* *(US)* Waren zu niedrig in Rechnung stellen.

underbred unterernährt.

underbuy *(v.)* unter Preis kaufen, billiger einkaufen.

undercapacity zu niedrige (nicht ausreichende) Kapazität.

undercapitalization Unterkapitalisierung.

undercapitalized nicht genügend kapitalisiert, unterkapitalisiert.

undercarriage *(plane)* Fahrgestell;
  ~ wheel Landerad.

undercharge *(low price)* niedriger Preis;
  ~ of tax zu niedrige Steuerzahlung;
  ~ *(v.)* zu wenig berechnen (fordern), zu niedrig in Rechnung stellen;
  ~ a battery Batterie nicht voll aufladen.

underclerk Schreiber.

underclothes Leibwäsche.

underconsumption geringer Verbrauch.

undercover| **activities** Untergrundtätigkeit; **~ agent (man, officer)** *(US)* getarnter Detektiv, Spitzel, Geheimagent; **~ mission** Geheimauftrag; **~ payment** Spitzelgelder.

undercredit *(v.)* zu wenig gutschreiben.

undercroft unterirdisches Gewölbe.

undercurrent Unterströmung, *(fig.)* geheime Gegenströmung, unterschwellige Tendenz;
  political ~ Untergrundbewegung.

undercut| *(v.)* s. o. für niedrigeren Lohn als ein anderer arbeiten, geringere Lohnforderungen stellen; **~ a competitor** Konkurrenz unterbieten; **~ prices** Preise unterbieten; **~ price-wise** preislich unterbieten.

undercutter Preisunterbieter, rücksichtsloser Preisdrücker.

undercutting Preisunterbietung.

underdeduction of tax zu gering angesetzte Steuerabzüge.

underdeveloped rückständig, unterentwickelt, entwicklungsfähig;
  ~ areas unterentwickelte Gebiete, Entwicklungsgebiete; **~ countries** Entwicklungsländer.

underdevelopment Unterentwicklung.

underdiscount *(v.)* **the market** *(US)* erwartete Baisse im voraus berücksichtigen.

underdog Unterprivilegierter, Benachteiligter, zu Unrecht Verfolgter;
  ~ *(v.)* zu kurz kommen;
  to feel for the ~ Mitgefühl mit den Unterlegenen haben.

underdrain *(v.)* durch unterirdische Kanäle entwässern.

underdrainage unterirdische Drainage.

underemployment mangelnde Beschäftigung, Unterbeschäftigung;
  ~ equilibrium Gleichgewicht bei Unterbeschäftigtkeit.

underestimate Unterbewertung, zu niedriger Kostenanschlag;
  ~ *(v.)* unter-, zu niedrig schätzen, unterbewerten;
  ~ the enemy's strength Feindstärke unterschätzen.

underestimation Unterbewertung.

underexpose *(v.)* unterbelichten.

underexposure Unterbelichtung.

underfed unterernährt.

underfeeding Unterernährung.

underfloor heating Fußbodenheizung.

underfreight *(v.)* unter-, weiterbefrachten.

undergarment Leibwäsche.

undergo *(v.)* durchmachen, erfahren;
  ~ a change Wandel durchmachen; **~ changes** *(prices)* Veränderungen erleiden; **~ the city wall** sich unter der Stadtmauer durchgraben; **~ an examination** verhört (vernommen) werden; **~ a loss** Verlust erfahren; **~ an operation** sich einer Operation unterziehen; **~ prescription** verjähren; **~ repairs** in Reparatur sein; **~ a prison sentence** Gefängnisstrafe verbüßen; **~ a test successfully** Prüfungsverfahren gut bestehen; **~ torture** Folterungen ertragen; **~ a trial** vor Gericht gestellt werden.

undergraduate Student;
~ *(a.)* studentisch;
~ **audience** aus Studenten bestehendes Publikum; **in his** ~ **days** in seiner Studentenzeit; **to teach at first year** ~ **level** Vorlesungen für Erstsemester abhalten; ~ **work** Studium.

underground *(railway, Br.)* Untergrundbahn, U-Bahn;
~ *(a.)* unterirdisch, *(mining)* unter Tage, *(secretly)* geheim, verborgen, im Verborgenen;
to go ~ in den Untergrund gehen, zur Untergrundbewegung werden; **to go (travel) by** ~ *(Br.)* mit der U-Bahn fahren;
~ **bistro** Kellerrestaurant; ~ **cable** unterirdisches Kabel; **two-level** ~ **car park** Tiefgarage mit zwei Etagen; ~ **dwelling** Kellerwohnung; ~ **engineering** Tiefbau; ~ **factory** unterirdische Fabrik; ~ **force** Widerstandskräfte; ~ **fortress** geheime Festung; ~ **garage** Tiefgarage; ~ **movement** Widerstands-, Untergrundbewegung; **to belong to an** ~ **movement** sich illegal betätigen; ~ **newssheet** Nachrichtenblatt von Untergrundbewegungen; ~ **parking** unterirdische Parkmöglichkeit, Parken in der Tiefgarage; ~ **passage** unterirdischer Gang; ~ **press** Untergrundpresse; ~ **railroad** *(US)* **(railway,** *Br.)* Untergrundbahn, U-Bahn; ~ **railway advertising** *(Br.)* U-Bahn-, Untergrundbahnwerbung; ~ **road** unterirdische Straße; ~ **rooms** Souterrainräume; ~ **surveyor** *(mining)* Markscheider; ~ **tank** unterirdisches Tanklager; ~ **testing** unterirdische Versuche; ~ **train** U-Bahnzug; ~ **tramway** Unterpflasterbahn; ~ **water** Grundwasser; ~ **work** *(mine)* Untertagearbeit; ~ **worker** Untertagearbeiter; ~ **working** Untertagebau.

undergrounder Anhänger einer Untergrundbewegung, Widerstandskämpfer.

undergrowth Unterholz, Gestrüpp.

underhand heimlich, unreell *(unfair)*, heimtückisch, verstohlen;
~ **dealings** Schiebungen; **to play an** ~ **game** hinterlistiges Spiel betreiben; ~ **methods** unfaire Methoden; ~ **trade** Schleich-, Schwarzhandel.

underhanded mit ungenügenden Arbeitskräften versehen.

underhandedness Mangel an Arbeitskräften.

underinsurance Unterversicherung.

underinsure *(v.)* unterversichern, zu niedrig versichern.

underinsured unterversichert, unter dem Wert versichert.

underissue *(securities)* Minderausgabe.

underlaid verstärkt, unterlegt, gestützt, *(print.)* zugerichtet.

underlay *(print.)* Zurichtbogen;
~ *(v.) (print.)* zurichten, ausgleichen.

underlease Untermiete, -verpachtung;
~ *(v.)* untervermieten, -verpachten.

underlessee Untermieter, -pächter.

underlessor Untervermieter, -verpächter.

underlet *(v.) (let under value)* unter dem Wert vermieten (verpachten), *(sublet)* untervermieten.

underletting Untervermieten.

underlie *(v.)* unterliegen, gebunden sein, *(fig.)* einer Sache zugrundeliegen;
~ **the law** *(Scot., criminal proceeding)* vor Gericht stehen.

underline Unterstreichung, *(illustration)* Bildunterschrift, -text, *(theater)* Vorankündigung [im Theaterzettel];
~ *(v.)* unterstreichen, *(fig.)* betonen.

underling Untergebener, Gehilfe, Handlanger, *(servile person)* Kriecher, unterwürfiger Mensch.

underlying zugrundeliegend;
~ **bonds** *(US)* durch Vorranghypothek gesicherte Obligationen, Prioritätsobligationen; ~ **company** *(US)* [vollständig abhängige] Tochtergesellschaft; ~ **contract** als Grundlage dienender Vertrag; ~ **lien** *(US)* Vorrangpfandrecht; ~ **mortgage** *(US)* Vorranghypothek; ~ **security** dingliche Sicherheit, *(affiliate)* von der Muttergesellschaft verbürgte Wertpapieremission; ~ **syndicate** *(US)* Übernahmekonsortium; ~ **transaction** zugrundeliegendes Geschäft, Grundgeschäft.

undermanned *(ship)* ungenügend bemannt;
~ **industry** unterbesetzte Industrie, unter Arbeitermangel leidende Wirtschaft.

undermine *(v.)* untergraben, unterminieren;
~ **s. one's authority** jds. Autorität untergraben; ~ **a position** Position schwächen; ~ **the power of a state** Staat aushöhlen (unterminieren); ~ **a wall** Mauer unterhöhlen.

undermined by the sea vom Meer unterspült.

underminer heimlicher Feind.

undernourished unterernährt.

undernourishment ungenügende Ernährung, Unterernährung.

underpaid schlecht bezahlt;
postage ~ nicht genügend frankiert.

underpart Nebenrolle, untergeordnete Rolle.

underpass *(US)* Fußgängerunterführung.

underpay *(v.)* schlecht entlohnen, ungenügend bezahlen.

underpayment schlechte (zu niedrige, unzureichende) Bezahlung, Unterbezahlung.

underpin *(v.)* abstützen, *(fig.)* untermauern.

underpinning Untermauerung, Stützwerk;
~ **operations** unterstützende Finanzierungsmaßnahmen.

underplot Nebenhandlung, *(novel)* Episode, *(clandestine plot)* abgekartetes Spiel.

underpopulated unterbevölkert.

underpopulation Unterbevölkerung.

underpossessor Besitzdiener.

underprice *(US)* Schleuderpreis, Preis unter dem Wert.

underprint zu schwach drucken.

underprivileged zu kurz gekommen, sozial (wirtschaftlich) benachteiligt, schlechter gestellt;
the ~ die Schlechtergestellten;
~ **area of a city** Armenviertel einer Stadt; ~ **classes** ärmere (benachteiligte) Bevölkerungsschichten.

underproduction ungenügende Erzeugung (Produktion).

underproof *(alcoholic beverage)* unter Normalstärke.

underprop *(v.)* **one's reputation** seinen guten Ruf bewahren.

underquote *(v.)* [Preise] niedriger berechnen, unterbieten.

underrate Unterbewertung, zu niedrige Bewertung, zu niedriger Ansatz;
~ *(v.)* zu gering ansetzen, unterbewerten, -tarifieren, zu niedrig bewerten;
~ **an opponent** Gegner unterschätzen;
to sell at an ~ unter dem Wert verkaufen, verschleudern.

underrated price zu geringer Preis.

underratement Unterbewertung.

underrent *(v.)* sehr billig vermieten.

underrepresentation Unterrepräsentation.

underrepresented, to be zu wenig Abgeordnete haben.

underrun Minderanfertigung.

underscore *(v.)* unterstreichen, betonen, hervorheben.

undersea unterseeisch;
- **cable** Unterseekabel.

undersealed *(car)* mit Unterbodenschutz.

Undersecretary *(Br.)* [Unter]staatssekretär;
Parliamentary ~ *(Br.)* parlamentarischer Staatssekretär; **permanent** ~ ständiger Unterstaatssekretär.

Undersecretaryship Unterstaatssekretariat.

undersell *(v.)* unter dem Preis (unter dem Wert, billiger) verkaufen, verschleudern, Konkurrenz unterbieten;
~ **the market** *(Br.)* erwartete Baisse am Markt vorausberücksichtigen.

underseller Preisdrücker, -schleuderer.

underselling Preisunterbietung, Dumping;
~ **price** Schleuderpreis.

undershoot *(airplane)* vorzeitiges Aufkommen [auf der Landebahn];
~ *(v.)* **the runway** vor der Landebahn aufkommen; ~ **its target range** Zielgebiet nicht erreichen.

undersign *(v.)* unterschreiben, -zeichnen.

undersigned [Endes]unterzeichner;
~ *(a.)* unterzeichnet, unterschrieben.

undersized unter Normalgröße.

underspend *(v.)* geringe Ausgaben tätigen;
~ **on the budget** Haushaltsmittel nicht voll ausschöpfen.

understaffed zu schwach besetzt, personell unterbesetzt, an Personalmangel leidend;
badly ~ total unterbesetzt;
to be ~ Personalmangel haben;
~ **office** unterbesetztes Büro.

understairs Kellergeschoß.

understand *(v.)* verstehen, begreifen, *(imply tacitly)* stillschweigend, voraussehen;
~ **about s. th.** über etw. Bescheid wissen; ~ **and agree** einverständlich von etw. Kenntnis nehmen; ~ **another** Verständnis für einander aufbringen; ~ **one's business** sein Geschäft verstehen; ~ **driving a car** Auto zu steuern verstehen; ~ **a foreign language** Fremdsprache verstehen; ~ **finance** erfahrener Finanzmann sein; ~ **from a letter** einem Brief entnehmen; ~ **a phrase literally** Satz wörtlich auffassen;
to make s. o. ~ jem. begreiflich machen (zu verstehen geben).

understandable begreiflich, verständlich.

understanding *(agreement)* Absprache, gegenseitiges Übereinkommen, Vereinbarung, Abrede, Übereinkunft, Verständigung, Einvernehmen, -ständnis, *(comprehension)* Verständnis, Begriffsvermögen, *(intelligence)* Verstand, Intelligenz;

entirely without ~ geschäftsunfähig; **on the ~ that** unter der Voraussetzung, daß; **with the implicit ~** unter der stillschweigenden Voraussetzung;

friendly ~ gütliches Einvernehmen; **good ~** gutes Einvernehmen, gute Beziehungen; **real ~** innere Beziehung; **reciprocal ~** Gegenseitigkeitsvereinbarung; **secret ~** geheime Absprache (Abmachung, Übereinkunft), geheimes Einverständnis;

in-depth ~ of retail marketing profunde Kenntnisse auf dem Gebiet des Einzelhandels;

to arrive at an ~ with s. o. etw. mit jem. abmachen; **to come to an ~** sich einigen, übereinkommen, zu einer Verständigung gelangen; **to disturb the good ~** gutes Einvernehmen stören; **to have an excellent ~** ausgezeichneten Verstand besitzen; **to have an ~ of several languages** mehrere Fremdsprachen beherrschen; **to reach an ~** Vereinbarung erzielen;

~ *(a.)* verständnisvoll, intelligent.

understate *(v.)* zu niedrig angeben (ansetzen, bewerten) zu gering angeben, *(mitigate)* abschwächen, mildern, untertreiben;

~ *(v.)* **one's losses** seine Verluste verniedlichen.

understatement zu niedrige Angabe, Unterbewertung, zurückhaltende Darstellung.

understeer *(car)* Leerlauf, toter Gang.

understock *(v.)* ungenügend mit Vorräten versehen, zu kleines Lager unterhalten.

understocked, to be zu wenig Vorräte haben, nicht genügend bevorratet sein.

understood stillschweigend vereinbart;

as is ~ *(law of contract)* es gilt als vereinbart; **readily ~** ohne weiteres verständlich;

at the ~ price zum vereinbarten Preis.

understrapper Kriecher, *(employee)* unbedeutender Mitarbeiter.

understrength *(a.) (mil.)* nicht auf voller Gefechtsstärke.

understudy *(theater)* Ersatzmann;

~ *(v.)* als Ersatzmann einstudieren;

~ **the lead** für den Hauptdarsteller einspringen.

undersubscribed loan nicht in voller Höhe gezeichnete Anleihe.

undertake *(v.)* in die Hand nehmen, sich befassen, unternehmen, besorgen, *(accept an obligation)* Verpflichtung übernehmen, sich verpflichten, übernehmen, dafür einstehen, *(guarantee)* garantieren, sich verbürgen (verpflichten);

~ **for s. one's good behavio(u)r** für jem. gutes Benehmen bürgen; ~ **a business errand** Geschäftsbesorgung übernehmen; ~ **the collection of a bill** Wechsel zum Inkasso (Wechselinkasso) übernehmen; ~ **a guarantee** Gewähr (Garantie, Bürgschaft) übernehmen; ~ **a journey** Reise unternehmen; ~ **the management** Leitung in die Hand nehmen; ~ **an obligation** Verpflichtung eingehen; ~ **an office** Amt übernehmen; ~ **orders** Aufträge annehmen; ~ **not to perform a particular act** sich zur Nichtausübung einer Tätigkeit verpflichten; ~ **a piece of work** Arbeit übernehmen; ~ **a great responsibility** große Verantwortung auf sich nehmen (laden); ~ **a risk** Risiko eingehen (übernehmen); ~ **a task** Aufgabe übernehmen.

undertaker *(book publisher)* Verleger, *(of enterprise)* Unternehmer, *(manager of funerals)* Leichenbestatter, *(organizer of a stage production)* Regisseur, *(speculator)* Spekulant, *(supplier)* Lieferant.

undertakers Beerdigungs-, Bestattungsinstitut, Leichenbestatter.

undertaking Übernahme, -nehmen, Unterfangen, Unternehmen, *(enterprise)* Unternehmen, -nehmung, Betrieb, *(guarantee)* Gewähr, Garantie, Bürgschaft, *(obligation)* Versprechen, Zusage, eingegangene Verpflichtung, Verpflichtungserklärung, Engagement, Sicherheitsleistung;

on the ~ auf die Zusicherung hin;

agricultural ~ landwirtschaftlicher Betrieb; **business ~** Geschäftsunternehmen, Wirtschaftsbetrieb; **charitable ~** wohltätiges Unternehmen; **commercial ~** [Handels]unternehmen, -betrieb; **concerted ~** gemeinschaftliche Unternehmung; **contributory ~** Zuschußbetrieb; **cross ~** Gegenverpflichtung; **governmental ~** Staatsbetrieb; **industrial ~** Gewerbebetrieb, gewerbliches Unternehmen, Industrieunternehmen, -betrieb; **large ~** Großbetrieb, -unternehmen; **private ~** Privatbetrieb, -unternehmen; **public-utility ~** öffentlicher Versorgungsbetrieb; **small ~** Kleinbetrieb; **speculative ~** Spekulationsgeschäft; **subsidiary ~** Tochterunternehmen; **voluntary ~** freiwillige Verpflichtung; **written ~** schriftliche Verpflichtungserklärung;

~ **to pay** Zahlungsversprechen; ~ **as to quality** Zusicherung einer Eigenschaft, Gewährleistung für Sachmängel; ~ **of wide scope** großangelegtes Unternehmen, Großunternehmen; ~ **of a task** Übernahme einer Aufgabe;

to enter into an ~ Verpflichtung eingehen; **to give an ~** Zusage geben; **to operate an ~** *(US)* Unternehmen betreiben; **to set an ~ on its feet** Sache in Gang bringen.

undertenancy Untermiete, Untermietverhältnis, Unterpacht.

undertenant Untermieter, -pächter.

undertone gedämpfter Ton, leise Stimme, *(fig.)* Unterton, Tendenz, *(stock exchange)* Grundton, -stimmung, Tendenz;

~ **of hostility** unterschwellige Feindseligkeit.

undertow Unterströmung, Sog.

undertutor *(Louisiana)* Gegenvormund.

undertrading Umsatzabbau, Verkleinerung des Geschäftsbetriebs.

undervaluation Unterbewertung, -schätzung, Taxe unter dem Wert, zu niedrige Wertangabe, *(customs)* Zollerklärung mit zu niedrigem Wert.

undervalue *(v.)* unterbewerten, zu niedrig bewerten, zu niedrig (gering) ansetzen, zu niedrig (unter dem Wert) schätzen.

undervalued currency unterbewertete Währung.

underwater *(mar.)* unterhalb der Wasserlinie;

~ **explorer** Tiefseeforscher; ~ **growth** Schiffsbewuchs; ~ **resort hotel** Unterwasserkurhotel.

underweight Unter-, Mindergewicht, Gewichtsabgang, knappes (zu leichtes) Gewicht, Gewichtsausfall.

underweight *(a.)* untergewichtig.

underwood Unterholz.

underwork unzureichende Arbeit;

~ *(v.)* billiger arbeiten, pfuschen.

underworld Verbrecher-, Unterwelt.

underwrite *(v.) (document)* unterschreiben, *(guarantee)* bürgen, garantieren, Haftung übernehmen, *(insurance business)* versichern, Versicherung abschließen (unterzeichnen), Versicherungsgeschäfte betreiben (tätigen), Versicherungspolice unterschreiben, assekurieren, *(issue of securities)* Effektenemission garantieren (übernehmen), *(marine insurance)* Transportversicherungsgeschäfte erledigen, *(to do the business of an underwriter)* Konsortialgeschäfte tätigen;

~ **capital** Kapital zeichnen; ~ **the cost of a project** für die Finanzierung eines Projekts geradestehen; ~ **a loan** Übernahme einer Emission garantieren; ~ **a large part of public new issues** Neuemissionen in größerem Ausmaß übernehmen; ~ **a policy** Police unterzeichnen, Versicherung abschließen (übernehmen); ~ **a risk** Versicherung unter Risikoverteilung übernehmen; ~ **marine risk** Seeversicherung unter Risikobeteiligung übernehmen.

underwriter Unterzeichner, *(agent, US)* Versicherungsagent, Prämienfestsetzer, *(banking)* Mitglied eines Emissionskonsortiums, Emissionsgarant, Konsortialmitglied, *(insurance business)* Assekurant, Assekuranzversicherung, Versicherungsgeber, -gesellschaft, -träger, *(marine insurance business)* Seeversicherer, *(issue of securities)* Emissionsfirma, -bank, Anleihegarant, Garantiefondszeichner;

~**s** *(issue of securities)* Übernahmekonsortium, Garantiesyndikat, -konsortium;

cargo ~ Frachtenversicherer; **leading ~** *(banking)* federführende Bank, Konsortialführerin, Federführerin, *(insurance)* Erstversicherer, führende Gesellschaft, Führerin; **life ~** *(US)* Lebensversicherungsvertreter; **local ~** auf Regionalgeschäfte beschränktes Emissionshaus; **Lloyd's ~** *(Br.)* Versicherer bei Lloyds; **marine insurance ~** Seetransportversicherer; **national ~** Emissionshaus für einheimische Werte; **private ~** Privatversicherungsnehmer;

~**'s group** Emissions-, Garantiekonsortium; ~**s' meeting** Konsortialsitzung.

underwriting *(insurance business)* Übernahme von Versicherungen, Abschluß [eines Versicherungsgeschäftes], *(marine insurance business)* [See]versicherungsgeschäft, *(issue of securities)* Emissions-, Effektengarantie, Emissionsübernahmegeschäft;

firm ~ feste Übernahme;

~ **of a policy** Übernahme einer Versicherung; ~ **of a risk** Übernahme eines Versicherungsrisikos;

to invest up to 50% in reserves for future ~ Erlöse bis zu 50% in neuen Versicherungsverträgen steuerverbilligt anlegen;

~ **agency** *(marine insurance, Br.)* Abschlußagent; ~ **agreement** Übernahmeabkommen, Emissions-, Konsortialvertrag; ~ **bank** Konsortialbank; ~ **business** Konsortial-, Effektenemissionsgeschäft, *(insurance)* Versicherungsgeschäft; ~ **capacity** Versicherungsmöglichkeit; **to withdraw ~ capacity** Versicherungsgeschäft einschränken; ~ **commission** Provision aus einer Konsortialbeteiligung, Emissionsprovision; ~ **conditions** *(banking)* Zeichnungsbedingungen; ~ **consortium** Garantiekonsortium; ~ **contract** Emissions-, Konsortialvertrag, Übernahme-

abkommen; ~ **costs** Kapitalemissionskosten; ~ **cycle** Konjunkturverlauf im Versicherungsgeschäft, Versicherungskonjunktur; ~ **deficit** Konsortial-, Versicherungsverlust; ~ **decision** Versicherungsentscheidung; ~ **department** Risikoabteilung einer Versicherungsgesellschaft; ~ **executive** Führungskraft einer Versicherungsgesellschaft; ~ **expenses** Konsortialaufwendungen; ~ **fee** Übernahmespesen; ~ **group** [Emissions]konsortium; ~ **guarantee** *(bond issue)* feste Übernahme, Anlageübernahmegarantie, Effektengarantie; ~ **house** Konsortialmitglied, *(US)* Emissionsfirma; ~ **income** Einkünfte aus Versicherungsgeschäften; ~ **limit** Zeichnungslimit, -grenze; ~ **loss** Emissionsverlust, *(insurance company)* Verlust im Geschäftsjahr; ~ **member** *(Br.)* Mitglied eines Konsortiums, Konsortial-, Syndikatsmitglied, *(insurance business, Br.)* Einzelversicherer; **to take up the remainder of one's ~ obligations** seine Konsortialverpflichtungen voll erfüllen; ~ **participation** Konsortialbeteiligung; ~ **price** Übernahmekurs; ~ **profit** Konsortialgewinn, *(insurance)* Gewinn im Geschäftsjahr, Versicherungsgewinn; ~ **prospectus** Zeichnungs-, Emissionsprospekt; ~ **provision** *(investment fund)* Verkaufsprovision; ~ **reserve** *(insurance company)* ausgewiesene Reserven; ~ **result** *(insurance company)* Abschlußergebnis, Versicherungs-, Geschäftsergebnis; ~ **share** Konsortialanteil, -beteiligung; ~ **staff** Betriebspersonal einer Versicherungsgesellschaft; ~ **syndicate** [Effekten]emissions-, Anlageübernahmekonsortium, Garantiekonsortium, Übernahme-, Beteiligungssyndikat, Konsortialgruppe, Einführungskonsortium; ~ **system** Emissionsgarantiesystem; ~ **transaction** Konsortialgeschäft; ~ **trend** Trend im Versicherungsgeschäft.
underwritten firm *(issue of securities)* fest abgenommen, plaziert.
undeserved unverdient.
underdeserving of mercy eines Gnadenbeweises unwürdig.
undesignated ungezeichnet, nichtangegeben;
~ **cities** *(US)* nicht zum Federal Reserve Board gehörige Städte.
undesigned unbeabsichtigt, unabsichtlich.
undetachable *(coupon)* nicht abtrennbar.
undetached un[ab]getrennt.
undetermined questions offene (unentschiedene) Fragen.
undeveloped unentwickelt, *(land)* unerschlossen, noch nicht baureif;
~ **land** *(Br.)* nicht erschlossenes Baugelände, *(balance sheet)* unbebaute Grundstücke; ~ **land duty** *(Br.)* Bauplatzsteuer.
undigested *(fig.)* unverdaut, unverarbeitet;
~ **securities** *(US)* nicht plazierte (vom Markt noch nicht aufgenommene) Effekten.
undiluted unverdünnt, unverfälscht.
undimished unvermindert, ungeschmälert.
undimmed nicht verdunkelt, *(headlight)* nicht abgeblendet.
undiplomatic undiplomatisch.
undirected unadressiert, ohne Adresse.
undisbursed balance noch nicht ausgezahlter Restbetrag.
undiscerned unbemerkt, unerkannt.
undischarged nicht entlastet, *(ship)* nicht entladen, *(unpaid)* nicht bezahlt, unerledigt;
~ **bankrupt** nicht rehabilitierter (entlasteter) Konkursschuldner; ~ **debt** nicht bezahlte Schuld.
undisciplined undiszipliniert, zuchtlos, *(untrained)* nicht ausgebildet.
undisclosed geheimgehalten, nicht offengelegt (bekanntgeben);
~ **agency** verdeckte Stellvertretung; ~ **buyer** ungenannter (unbekannter) Käufer; ~ **channel(l)ing of profits** *(taxation)* verdeckte Gewinnausschüttung; ~ **principal** ungenannter Auftraggeber; ~ **reserves** stille Reserven, verdeckte Rücklagen.
undiscounted bill nicht diskontierter Wechsel.
undiscoverable unauffindbar.
undiscussed unerörtert.
undisguised unmaskiert, *(fig.)* unverhüllt, offensichtlich.
undispatched unabgefertigt.
undisplay *(US, advertising)* [Anzeigen]fließsatz.
undisposed nicht begeben, unbegeben, *(not sold)* unverkauft.
undisputed unbestritten, unstreitig.
undistributed nicht auf Kosten verteilt;
~ **corporate profits** nicht ausgeschüttete Unternehmensgewinne; ~ **cost** Handlungs-, Generalunkosten; ~ **funds** *(trustee)* nicht ausgeschüttete Vermögensbeträge; ~ **net income** unverteilter Reingewinn; ~ **profit** nicht ausgeschütteter Gewinn, Gewinnvortrag.
undisturbed ungestört, *(ownership)* unbeeinträchtigt.
undiversified nicht aufgefächert (gestreut).

undivided nicht verteilt, unverteilt;
~ **attention** volle (ungeteilte) Aufmerksamkeit; ~ **interest** Nutznießung zur gesamten Hand; ~ **opinion** einhellige Meinung; ~ **profit** nicht ausgeschütteter (nicht entnommener) Gewinn, unverteilter Reingewinn, Gewinnvortrag; ~ **profits tax** Steuer auf stehengelassenen Gewinn; ~ **property** Eigentum zur gesamten Hand; ~ **responsibility** alleinige Verantwortung; ~ **share in land** Liegenschaftsanteil.
undivorced nicht geschieden.
undivulged nicht bekanntgegeben, geheimhalten.
undo *(v.)* ungeschehen (rückgängig) machen, *(contract)* aufheben, annullieren, *(ruin)* ruinieren, zugrunde richten, zerstören, *(unwrap)* auswickeln, auspacken;
~ **a bargain** Handel rückgängig machen, *(London stock exchange)* Effektentransaktion glattstellen; ~ **s. o. hopes** jds. Hoffnungen zunichte machen; ~ **a parcel** Paket aufmachen; ~ **the good work of one's predecessor** seines Vorgängers Leistungen kaputtmachen.
undock *(v.)* entdocken, aus einem Hafen auslaufen.
undoing *(contract)* Rückgängigmachung, Annullierung.
undomesticated unhäuslich.
undone unerledigt, unvollendet, nicht fertiggestellt;
to leave nothing ~ nichts unversucht lassen; **to leave s. th. ~** etw. unausgeführt lassen.
undoubted unbestritten, nicht in Frage gestellt;
~ **improvement** *(patient)* echte Besserung.
undrawn nicht gezeichnet;
to remain ~ unangetastet bleiben;
~ **profit** nicht entnommener Gewinn; ~ **portion of a loan** noch nicht in Anspruch genommener Kreditteil.
undreamed-of possibilities ungeahnte Möglichkeiten.
undress *(ordinary attire)* Straßenanzug, Alltagskleidung, *(informal dress)* Morgenrock, Negligé.
undue *(excessive)* übermäßig, *(not yet due)* noch nicht fällig (geschuldet), *(unlawful)* unzulässig, *(unsuitable)* ungebührlich, -gehörig, unpassend;
to take ~ advantage ausnutzen; ~ **attachment** unberechtigte Pfändung; ~ **behavio(u)r** ungebührliches Benehmen; ~ **debt** nicht geschuldeter Betrag; **without ~ delay** ohne schuldhaftes Zögern; ~ **fee** noch nicht fällige Gebühr; ~ **hardship** unbillige Härte; ~ **haste** übertriebene Eile; ~ **influence** unzulässige Beeinflussung, Einschüchterung, Sittenwidrigkeit; **to exercise ~ influence upon s. o.** j. unzulässig beeinflussen; ~ **preference** *(Br.)* Gläubigerbegünstigung, unzulässige Bevorzugung eines Konkursschuldners; ~ **pressure** Nötigung; ~ **proceedings** unvorschriftsmäßiges Verfahren.
undulating land wellenförmiges Gelände.
undulation wellenförmige Beschaffenheit.
unearned nicht erarbeitet (verdient), unverdient, *(profit)* nicht realisiert;
~ **discount** noch nicht verdienter Wechseldiskont; ~ **income** *(balance sheet)* transitorische Passiva, *(taxation)* Einkünfte aus Kapitalvermögen, Besitz-, Kapitaleinkommen; ~ **increment** *(land)* Bodenwertsteigerung ohne Leistung des Eigentümers, unverdienter Wertzuwachs; ~ **interest** *(balance sheet)* transitorische Zinserträge; ~ **praise** unverdientes Lob; ~ **premium** noch nicht verdiente Prämie; ~ **premium reserve** *(life insurance)* Prämienreserve, Deckungsfonds, -stock; ~ **revenue** *(balance sheet)* transitorische Passiva, *(taxation)* Einkünfte aus Kapitalvermögen.
unearth *(v.)* exhumieren;
~ **new facts** neue Tatsachen ausfindig machen; ~ **a buried treasure** verborgenen Schatz heben.
unearthly überirdisch, *(coll.)* unmöglich;
at an ~ hour zu nachtschlafener Zeit; **to get up at an ~ hour** in aller Herrgottsfrühe aufstehen.
uneasiness Unbehagen, innere Unruhe;
to calm s. one's ~ jds. Unbehagen berücksichtigen.
uneasy innerlich unruhig, beunruhigt;
to be ~ about one's health sich über seine Gesundheit Sorgen machen;
~ **feeling** unbehagliches Gefühl; ~ **suspicion** beunruhigender Verdacht.
uneconomical unökonomisch, unwirtschaftlich, unrentabel, *(not thrifty)* nicht sparsam.
uneducated ungebildet.
unembarrassed ungeniert, *(not in debt)* unverschuldet, schuldenfrei, frei von Geldsorgen, *(real estate)* unbelastet.
unemployability Arbeits-, Beschäftigungsunfähigkeit;
~ **supplement** Zusatzrente für dauernde Beschäftigungsunfähigkeit.

unemployable Arbeitsunfähiger, Nichtarbeitsfähiger;
~ *(a.)* nicht verwendungsfähig, arbeits-, beschäftigungsunfähig;
~ **person** Dauerarbeitsloser, Arbeitsunfähiger, nicht vermittelbarer Arbeitsuchender.

unemployed Arbeitsloser;
university-trained ~ akademische Arbeitslose;
~ **on relief** ausgesteuerter Arbeitsloser;
~ *(a.)* arbeits-, stellen-, erwerbslos, unbeschäftigt, ohne Stellung, *(unused)* unbenutzt, nicht verwendet, brachliegend;
chronically ~ dauerarbeitslos;
to be ~ arbeitslos (ohne Beschäftigung, beschäftigungslos) sein; **to become** ~ erwerbslos werden;
~ **capital** brachliegendes (ungenutztes, totes) Kapital; ~ **person** Arbeitsloser; ₤ **Workmen's Act** *(Br.)* Arbeitslosengesetz.

unemployment Arbeits-, Erwerbs-, Beschäftigungslosigkeit;
chronic ~ Dauerarbeitslosigkeit; **concealed** ~ verdeckte Arbeitslosigkeit; **cyclical** ~ konjunkturbedingte (konjunkturelle) Arbeitslosigkeit; **fractional** ~ temporäre Arbeitslosigkeit, Fluktuationsarbeitslosigkeit; **intermittent** ~ vorübergehende Arbeitslosigkeit; **local** ~ örtlich bedingte (sektionale) Arbeitslosigkeit; **long-run (-term)** ~ langfristige Arbeitslosigkeit; **mass** ~ Massenarbeitslosigkeit; **nonwhite** ~ Negerarbeitslosigkeit; **permanent** ~ Dauerarbeitslosigkeit; **prolonged** ~ anhaltende Arbeitslosigkeit; **recession** ~ rezessionsbedingte Arbeitslosigkeit; **seasonal** ~ saisonbedingte (jahreszeitlich bedingte) Arbeitslosigkeit; **secular** ~ zeitbedingte Arbeitslosigkeit; **structural** ~ strukturelle (strukturbedingte) Arbeitslosigkeit; **sustained** ~ anhaltende Arbeitslosigkeit; **technological** ~ entwicklungsmäßig (technologisch) bedingte Arbeitslosigkeit; **to alleviate** ~ Arbeitslosigkeit beheben (beseitigen); **to be bullish (bearish) about** ~ Arbeitslosenentwicklung positiv (negativ) beurteilen; **to cause a lot of** ~ erhebliche Arbeitslosigkeit hervorrufen; **to focus on reducing** ~ alle Mittel zur Verringerung der Arbeitslosigkeit einsetzen;
~ **advance** Steigerung (Anwachsen) der Arbeitslosigkeit, zunehmende Arbeitslosigkeit; ~ **assistance** *(Br.)* Arbeitslosenhilfe, -fürsorge; **nonmeans-tested** ~ **assistance** nicht von nachgewiesener Mittellosigkeit abhängiges Arbeitslosengeld; ₤ **Assistance Board** *(till 1940, Br.)* Sozialamt; ~**-bedevilled** von Arbeitslosigkeit heimgesucht.

unemployment benefit *(Br.)* Arbeitslosenunterstützung, -geld;
earnings-related ~ *(Br.)* lohn-, gehaltsabhängiges Arbeitslosengeld; **partial** ~ Teilarbeitslosenunterstützung; **plant** ~ betriebliche Arbeitslosenunterstützung; **state** ~ staatliche Arbeitslosenunterstützung, Arbeitslosengeld; **to be disqualified from receiving** ~ keinen Anspruch auf Arbeitslosenunterstützung haben; **to draw (receive)** ~ Arbeitslosenunterstützung (Arbeitslosengeld) beziehen; **to register for** ~ Arbeitslosenunterstützung beanspruchen;
~ **scheme** Arbeitslosenunterstützungswesen.

unemployment | -burdened unter der Arbeitslosigkeit leidend; ~ **certificate** Arbeitslosigkeitsbescheinigung; ~ **claim** Arbeitslosenunterstützungsanspruch.

unemployment compensation *(US)* Arbeitslosenunterstützung, -geld;
to draw (receive) ~ Arbeitslosenunterstützung (Arbeitslosengeld) beziehen;
~ **law** *(US)* Arbeitslosenunterstützungsgesetz; ~ **program(me)** Arbeitslosenunterstützungsprogramm.

unemployment | contributions Arbeitslosenunterstützungsbeiträge; ~ **curve** Arbeitslosenkurve; ~ **disturbances** Arbeitslosenunruhen; ~ **estimates** Arbeitlosenschätzungen; ~ **figures** Erwerbslosen-, Arbeitslosenzahl; ~ **fund** Arbeitslosenunterstützungsfonds; ~ **growth** Arbeitslosenzunahme; ~ **increase** Arbeitslosenzunahme.

unemployment insurance Erwerbslosen-, Arbeitslosenversicherung;
to qualify for ~ Voraussetzungen für die Arbeitslosenunterstützung (Arbeitslosengeld) erfüllen;
₤ **Act** *(Br.)* Arbeitslosenversicherungsgesetz; ~ **contribution** Arbeitslosenversicherungsbeitrag; **supplementary** ~ **credit** Anspruch auf betriebliche Zuschüsse zur Arbeitslosenunterstützung; ~ **tax** *(US)* Arbeitslosenversicherungsbeitrag.

unemployment | level Zahl der Arbeitslosen, Arbeitslosenziffer; ~ **line** *(US)* *(queue, Br.)* Schlangen von Arbeitslosen; **to report to the ~ office** sich beim Arbeitsamt als beschäftigungslos melden; ~ **pay** Arbeitslosenunterstützung, -geld; ~ **peak** Arbeitslosenhöchstziffer; ~ **peaking** Spitzenreiterposition im Arbeitslosenbereich; ~ **problem** Arbeitslosenproblem; ~ **projection** Arbeitslosenschub; ~ **rate** Arbeitslosenprozentsatz, -ziffer,

quote; **crude ~ rate** saisonal nicht bereinigter Arbeitslosenprozentsatz; **seasonally adjusted ~ rate** saisonbedingte Arbeitslosenquote, saisonbedingter Arbeitslosenprozentsatz; **to live with high ~ rates** hohe Arbeitslosenziffern als gegeben hinnehmen; ~ **ratio** Erwerbs-, Arbeitslosenquote, Arbeitslosenprozentsatz; **to swell the ~ register** Arbeitslosenzahl anschwellen lassen; ~ **relief** Maßnahmen zur Bekämpfung der Arbeitslosigkeit, Arbeitslosenfürsorge; ~ **relief project** Notstandsvorhaben; ~ **reserve fund** Arbeitslosenunterstützungsfonds; ~**-ridden** von der Arbeitslosigkeit betroffen; ~ **roll** Arbeitslosenregister, Arbeitslosenkartei; **to be on ~ rolls** Arbeits-, Erwerbslosenunterstützung beziehen; ~ **statistics** Arbeitslosenstatistik; ~ **subsidy fund** Arbeitslosenzuschußfonds; **federal ~ tax** *(US)* Arbeitslosenversicherungsbeitrag; ~ **trend** zunehmende Arbeitslosigkeit; ~ **trust fund** *(US)* Vermögen der Arbeitslosenversicherung.

unenclosed nicht eingefriedet (eingezäunt);
~ **town** *(mil.)* offene Stadt.

unencumbered schuldenfrei, *(lien)* unverpfändet, *(real estate)* unbelastet, hypothekenfrei;
~ **by restriction** ohne irgendwelche Behinderungen;
~ **allotment** *(governmental accounting)* noch nicht ausgegebene und nicht verplante Etatsmittel.

unending grumble pausenloses (unaufhörliches) Gejammer.

unendorsable nicht girierbar.

unendorsed ohne Giro, ungiriert, nicht indossiert.

unendowed nicht ausgestattet (dotiert).

unenforceability Nichteinklagbarkeit, -durchsetzbarkeit.

unenforceable nicht durchsetzbar, nicht [ein]klagbar (vollstreckbar).

unengaged ungebunden, nicht verpflichtet, frei, *(unemployed)* unbeschäftigt, stellenlos, *(unpledged)* nicht verpfändet, unverpfändet.

unentangled unbehindert.

unentered *(bookkeeping)* nicht gebucht, *(customs)* unverzollt, beim Zollamt nicht angegeben, nicht deklariert;
~ **goods** noch unverzollte Waren.

unenterprising man Mann ohne Unternehmungsgeist.

unequal unverhältnismäßig, ungleich, unterschiedlich, *(partial)* ungerecht, parteiisch;
~ **to a task** einer Aufgabe nicht gewachsen.

unequivocal eindeutig, klar, zweifelsfrei.

unessential unwesentlich, unwichtig.

unestablished nicht erwiesen;
~ **civil servant** *(Br.)* außerplanmäßiger Beamter.

unethical sitten-, standeswidrig;
~ **conduct** standeswidriges Verhalten.

uneven ungerade, *(stock exchange)* uneinheitlich, nicht einheitlich;
~ **distribution** ungleichmäßige Verteilung; **to have an ~ temper** Stimmungen unterworfen sein; **to show an ~ tendency** uneinheitlich tendieren.

unexampled success beispielloser Erfolg.

unexchangeable unvertauschbar, nicht austauschbar.

unexceptionable makellos.

unexcised verbrauchssteuerfrei, zollfrei, nicht verbrauchssteuerpflichtig.

unexcused unentschuldigt.

unexecuted *(law)* nicht vollzogen (zustande gekommen).

unexhausted nicht verbraucht;
~ **improvements** noch nicht abgewohnte werterhöhende Leistungen des Mieters.

unexpected unvorhergesehen, unerwartet, unvermutet;
~ **profit** unerwarteter Gewinn.

unexpended nicht ausgegeben (aufgewendet);
~ **appropriation** *(governmental accounting)* noch nicht ausgegebene, jedoch verplante Etatsmittel; ~ **balance** *(governmental accounting)* noch nicht ausgegebener, jedoch bereits verplanter Etatsüberschuß.

unexperienced ohne Erfahrungen, unerfahren, *(equipment)* nicht ausprobiert.

unexpired noch nicht abgelaufen, noch in Kraft;
~ **bill** noch nicht fälliger Wechsel; ~ **expense** transitorische Aktiva; ~ **term** noch nicht abgelaufene Pachtzeit (Mietzeit); ~ **time** nicht abgelaufene Frist.

unexplored unerschlossen.

unexported nicht ausgeführt (exportiert).

unfading *(colo(u)r)* nicht verblassend.

unfailing unfehlbar, sicher, *(unyielding)* unnachgiebig, fest;
~ **patience** unermüdliche Geduld; ~ **resources** unerschöpfliche Reserven.

unfair unreell, unehrlich, unbillig, unlauter, unfair;
~ **to union labo(u)r** gewerkschaftsfeindlich;
~ **advantage** unrechtmäßig erlangter Vorteil, Übervorteilung;
~ **business practices** unlautere Geschäftsmethoden; ~ **competition** unlauterer Wettbewerb; ~ **competitive methods** unlautere Wettbewerbsmethoden; ~ **dismissal** sozial ungerechtfertigte Kündigung; ~ **dismissal provisions** Bestimmungen im Falle sozial ungerechtfertigter Kündigung; ~ **hearing** ungerechtes Verfahren; ~ **industrial practices** *(Br.)* sozialwidriges Verhalten, unlautere Arbeitskampfmethoden; ~ **labor practices** *(US)* unzulässiges Verhalten im Arbeitsleben, diskriminierende Behandlung der Gewerkschaften, Arbeitskampfmethoden; ~ **list** *(trade union, US)* schwarze [Arbeitgeber]liste; ~ **means** unlautere Mittel; ~ **methods of competitious** unlautere Wettbewerbsmethoden; ~ **trade** unlauterer Wettbewerb; ⌐ **Trade Practice Acts** *(US)* Gesetze gegen den unlauteren Wettbewerb; ~ **treatment** ungerechte Behandlung; ~ **wages** unangemessene Löhne.

unfairness Unehrlichkeit, Unredlichkeit.

unfaithful verräterisch, *(bad faith)* bösgläubig, *(husband)* untreu;
~ **copy** ungenaue Abschrift.

unfaltering *(fig.)* unbeugsam, entschlossen.

unfamiliar, to be ~ with a district sich in einer Gegend nicht auskennen.

unfamiliarity mangelnde Vertrautheit.

unfashionable unmodern, altmodisch.

unfathered illegitim, unehelich, *(book)* nicht authentisch.

unfathomed | crime ungelöstes Verbrechen; ~ **ocean depth** unergründliche Meerestiefe.

unfavo(u)rable ungünstig, -vorteilhaft;
~ **balance of trade** passive Handelsbilanz; **to have an ~ effect** sich ungünstig auswirken; ~ **exchange rate** ungünstiger Kurs; **to form an ~ opinion** sich eine ungünstige Meinung bilden; ~ **terms** unvorteilhafte Bedingungen.

unfeasible undurchführbar, nicht ausführbar.

unfeigned satisfaction aufrichtige Befriedigung.

unfertile unfruchtbar.

unfettered unbehindert, unbeschränkt.

unfilled *(blank)* leer, unausgefüllt, *(post)* unbesetzt;
~ **orders** nicht ausgeführte Bestellungen, Auftragsbestand; ~ **orders book** Auftragsbestandsbuch; ~ **post** unbesetzter Posten; ~ **vacancies** offene Stellen.

unfinancial *(sl.)* mit Gewerkschaftsbeiträgen im Rückstand.

unfinished unfertig, *(book)* fragmentarisch, *(house)* unausgebaut, *(style)* nicht ausgefeilt;
~ **business** *(parl.)* unerledigte Punkte [der Tagesordnung], Unerledigtes; ~ **goods** *(Br.)* halbfertige Erzeugnisse, Halbfertigwaren.

unfit *(incapable)* unfähig, ungeeignet, -tauglich, untüchtig, nicht qualifiziert, *(book)* fragmentarisch, *(house)* unausgebaut;
~ **to act** handlungsunfähig; ~ **for business** geschäftsuntüchtig; ~ **to drive** fahruntüchtig; ~ **for human consumption** für die menschliche Ernährung nicht geeignet; ~ **for human habitation** für Wohnzwecke ungeeignet, unbewohnbar; ~ **for motor traffic** für Kraftfahrzeuge nicht zu benutzen; ~ **for a position of trust** einer Vertrauensstellung nicht gewachsen; ~ **for publication** nicht zur Veröffentlichung geeignet; ~ **for service** *(mil.)* dienstuntauglich; ~ **for use as a beverage** als Getränk ungeeignet; ~ **for work** arbeitsunfähig;
to be ~ to do s. th. nicht in der Lage sein, etw. zu tun; **to be ~ for one's job** für seinen Beruf ungeeignet sein; **to be ~ for heavy traffic** dem Verkehrsandrang nicht gewachsen sein; **to be statutorily ~** *(house)* den Wohnungsbestimmungen nicht genügen.

unfitness Untauglichkeit, Untüchtigkeit;
physical ~ schwache Körperkonstitution;
~ **to drive** Fahruntüchtigkeit; ~ **for work** Arbeitsunfähigkeit.

unfitted unausgestattet;
to be ~ for s. th. für etw. ungeeignet sein.

unfitting unschicklich, unangebracht.

unflattering wenig schmeichelhaft.

unflyable weather kein Flugwetter.

unfold *(v.)* unterbreiten, vorlegen, *(ideas)* enthüllen, offenbaren;
~ **one's designs** seine Pläne entwickeln; ~ **a newspaper** Zeitung entfalten; ~ **one's plans for the future** Zukunftspläne enthüllen.

unforced *(fig.)* ungezwungen, natürlich.

unforeseen unvorhergesehen;
~ **calamity** Katastrophenfall; ~ **cause** *(Workmen's Compensation Act)* nicht vorausgesehene Ursache; ~ **circumstances** unvorhergesehene Umstände, höhere Gewalt; ~ **event** *(civil law)* unvorhergesehenes Ereignis; ~ **expense (expenditure)** unvorhergesehene Ausgaben.

unfortunate Prostituierte, *(Irish)* Geisteskranker;
~ **day** schwarzer Tag; ~ **expedition** vom Unglück verfolgte Expedition; ~ **lack of good manners** bedauerlich schlechte Manieren; ~ **man** Pechvogel, Unglücksrabe.

unfounded unbegründet, grundlos, gegenstandslos;
to be ~ völlig aus der Luft gegriffen sein;
~ **hopes** unbegründete Hoffnungen; ~ **rumo(u)rs** gegenstandslose Gerüchte; ~ **suspicion** unbegründeter Verdacht.

unfranked investment income *(Br.)* der Körperschaftssteuer unterliegende Kapitalerträge.

unfree unfrei.

unfreeze *(v.)* **funds** Guthaben zur Auszahlung freigeben.

unfrequented wenig besucht, abgelegen.

unfriendly nicht entgegenkommend (wohlwollend);
~ **act** *(pol.)* unfreundlicher Akt; ~ **fire** *(insurance)* Schadenfeuer.

unfrocked *(sl.)* aus seinem Berufsverband rausgeschmissen.

unfunded *(debt)* unfundiert, nicht fundiert, schwebend;
~ **debt** schwebende (unfundierte) Schuld; ~ **liability** *(pension scheme)* nicht fundierte Verbindlichkeiten.

unfurl *(v.)* **a flag** Flagge entrollen.

unfurnished nicht ausgestattet, *(room)* unmöbliert, leer;
~ **room** Leerzimmer.

ungarbled report nicht entstellter Bericht.

ungated level crossing unbewachter (unbeschrankter) Bahnübergang.

ungenerous knauserig, kleinlich.

ungenial *(weather)* rau, unbekömmlich.

ungentlemanliness unanständiges Benehmen.

ungifted unbegabt.

unglazed unverglast.

ungodly hour, at an zu einer unmenschlichen Zeit.

ungovernable unregierbar.

ungrammatical grammatisch nicht korrekt.

ungranted nicht bewilligt (zugestanden).

ungrounded unbegründet, *(el.)* nicht geerdet.

unguarded unbewacht, *(fig.)* unvorsichtig.

unguided führungslos.

unhampered ungehindert.

unhappy remark ungeschickte Bemerkung.

unhealthy ungesund, gesundheitswidrig, -schädlich.

unheard *(before court)* nicht vernommen.

unheatable unheizbar.

unhelped ohne Unterstützung.

unhesitating ohne Zögern, *(fig.)* anstandslos, bereitwillig.

unhinge *(v.)* s. o. j. aus der Fassung bringen.

unhinged *(mind)* verwirrt.

unhono(u)red *(bill)* nicht akzeptiert (honoriert).

unhook *(v.)* **the pound from the dollar** Pfund vom Dollarkurs lösen (von der Abhängigkeit von der Dollarparität befreien).

unhoped-for piece of good fortune unverhofftes Glück.

unhouse *(v.)* obdachlos machen.

unhoused obdachlos, heimatvertrieben.

unhurt unverletzt, unbeschädigt.

uni-tap contraption Mischbatterie.

unicameral system *(parl.)* Einkammersystem.

unicameralism Einkammersystem.

unidentified nicht identifiziert;
~ **flying object** *(UFO)* unbekanntes Flugobjekt, Ufo.

unifactoral obligation einseitige Verpflichtung.

unification Vereinheitlichung, Eingang;
~ **of Europe** Vereinigtes Europa; ~ **of law** Rechtsvereinheitlichung; ~ **of different loans** Zusammenfassung verschieden ausgestatteter Staatsanleihen;
~ **movement** Einigungsbewegung; ~ **work** Einigungswerk.

unified vereinheitlicht, vereinigt;
~ **bonds** Ablösungsschuldverschreibungen; ~ **debt** konsolidierte (fundierte) Schuld; ~ **mortgage bonds** durch eine Gesamthypothek besicherte Schuldverschreibungen; ~ **stock** *(Br.)* konsolidierte Anleihe.

uniform *(mil.)* Uniform, gleichmäßig, -förmig, einheitlich;
~ **acceleration** gleichmäßige Beschleunigung; ~ **accounting system** einheitliches Buchführungssystem; ⌐ **Acts** *(US)* Modellkodifikationen; ⌐ **Bills of Lading Act** *(Br.)* vereinheitlichtes Konnossementsgesetz; ~ **clothes** einheitliche Kleidung; ⌐ **Commercial Code** *(US)* vereinheitlichtes Handelsrecht; ~ **customs and practices for documentary credits** einheitliche Richtlinien und Gebräuche für Dokumentenakkreditive; ~ **deduction** gleichmäßiger Abzug; ~ **grade** Einheitssorte; ~ **law** *(US)* Vereinheitlichungsgesetz; ⌐ **Law of Bills of Exchange** *(Hague)* einheitliche Wechselordnung; ⌐ **Negotiable Instrument Act** *(US)*

Modellkodifikation des Wertpapierrechtes; ⍟ **Partnership Act** *(US)* vereinheitlichtes Gesetz über Handelsgesellschaften; ~ **price** Einheitspreis; ~ **delivered price** *(US)* vom Lieferort unabhängiger Preis; ~ **quotation** *(securities)* Einheitskurs; ~ **rate** Einheitssatz; ~ **rules for the collection of commercial papers** einheitliche Richtlinien für das Inkassogeschäft; ~ **system of accounts** *(US)* Kontenrahmen für Verkehrsbetriebe; ~ **tariff** Einheitstarif; ~ **tax** einheitliche Steuer, Einheitssteuer; ~ **temperature** gleichbleibende (konstante) Temperatur; ~ **trust** von Treuhändern geleiteter Investmentfonds; ~ **value** einheitlicher Wert.

uniformed branch of the police uniformierter Teil der Polizei.

uniformity *(conformity)* Übereinstimmung, *(not changing in form)* Einheitlichkeit, Gleichförmigkeit, -mäßigkeit;
~ **of prices** Preisübereinstimmung; ~ **in taxation** gleichmäßige (einheitliche) Besteuerung;
~ **clause** Gleichmäßigkeitsklausel.

unify *(v.)* vereinheitlichen, vereinigen, konsolidieren;
~ **a country** Land einigen.

unigeniture alleinige Nachkommenschaft.

unilateral *(law of court)* einseitig;
~ **contract** einseitig bindender Vertrag; ~ **declaration** Einseitigkeitserklärung; ~ **declaration of independence** einseitige Unabhängigkeit; ~ **mistake** einseitiger Irrtum; ~ **obligation** einseitige Verpflichtung; ~ **parking** auf eine Straßenseite beschränkte Parkerlaubnis; ~ **record** einseitige Beweisurkunde; ~ **repudiation of a treaty** einseitige Vertragsaufkündigung; ~ **transaction** einseitiges Rechtsgeschäft; ~ **transfers** unentgeltliche Leistungen.

unilinear tariff Einheitstarif.

unimpaired ungeschmälert, unbeeinträchtigt;
with faculties ~ im vollen Besitz seiner geistigen Kräfte;
~ **fortune** voll erhaltenes Vermögen.

unimpeachable unanfechtbar, nicht einklagbar;
~ **reputation** tadelloser Ruf; ~ **right** unangreifbares Recht; **from an** ~ **source** aus völlig einwandfreier Quelle; ~ **witness** verläßlicher Zeuge.

unimpeded ungehindert.

unimproved unveredelt, *(illness)* unverändert, *(land)* unkultiviert, -bebaut, *(real estate)* nicht im Wert gestiegen;
~ **land** *(US)* nicht erschlossenes Baugelände; ~ **value** *(US)* Verkehrswert nicht erschlossenen Geländes.

unincorporated | association nicht eingetragener rechtsfähiger Verein; ~ **business** nicht eingetragene Firma; ~ **enterprise** Unternehmen ohne eigene Rechtspersönlichkeit.

unincumbered schuldenfrei, *(real estate)* unbeladen, hypothekenfrei.

unindebted schuldenfrei, frei von Schulden, nicht verschuldet.

unindemnified unentschädigt, unvergütet.

unindorsed ungiriert, ohne Giro.

uninflammable nicht brennbar (feuergefährlich).

uninflated nicht inflatorisch.

uninfluenced unvoreingenommen.

uninformed on a subject über eine Angelegenheit nicht unterrichtet.

uninhabitable unbewohnbar.

uninhabited unbewohnt, leer.

uninhibited völlig unkonventionell.

uninjured unbeschädigt, unverletzt, unbeeinträchtigt.

uninominal *(ballot)* nur auf einen Namen lautend.

uninstructed ohne Verhaltungsmaßregeln.

uninsurable nicht versicherungsfähig;
~ **risk** nicht versicherungsfähiges (versicherbares) Risiko.

uninsured | employment versicherungsfreie Beschäftigung; ~ **parcel** nicht versichertes Paket; ~ **risk** ungedecktes Risiko.

unintelligible unverständlich.

unintended unbeabsichtigt, nicht vorsätzlich;
~ **victim** zufälliges Opfer.

unintentional unbeabsichtigt.

uninterested unbeteiligt, gleichgültig, uninteressiert.

uninterpretable unübersetzbar.

uninterrupted ununterbrochen, kontinuierlich.

uninterruptedly in einer Schicht.

uninvested *(capital)* nicht angelegt, brachliegend.

union Verbindung, *(of forms)* Zusammenschluß, *(harmony)* Übereinstimmung, Eintracht, Harmonie, *(machine)* [Rohr]verbindung, Kupplung, *(mar.)* Gösch, *(poor law, Br.)* Gemeindezweckverband, *(pol.)* Anschluß, Vereinigung, Staatenbund, Union, *(society)* Verein, Verband, Körperschaft, Vereinigung, *(trade ~)* Gewerkschaft, *(United States)* Vereinigte Staaten, *(university life)* Debattierklub;

amalgamated craft ~ Fachgewerkschaft; **builders' and construction workers'** ~ [etwa] IG Bau, Steine, Erden; **central labor** ~ *(US)* Landesverband einer Gewerkschaft; **certified** ~ als Vertragspartner anerkannte Gewerkschaft; **closed** ~ *(US)* Gewerkschaft mit Mitgliedersperre; **company** ~ *(US)* Betriebsgewerkschaft; **construction** ~ Industriegewerkschaft Bau; **craft** ~ Fachgewerkschaft; **company craft** ~ erweiterte Berufsorganisation; **credit** ~ Kreditgenossenschaft; **customs** ~ Zollunion; **denominational** ~ konfessionelle Gewerkschaft; **dual** ~ Gegengewerkschaft; **economic** ~ Wirtschaftsunion; **ensign hoisted down** ~ Notflagge; **free trade** ~ freie Gewerkschaft; **happy** ~ glückliche Ehe; **horizontal** ~ fachliche Einheitsgewerkschaft, Fachgewerkschaft; **house** ~ Betriebsgewerkschaft; **independent** ~ unabhängige Fachgewerkschaft; **industrial** ~ Industriegewerkschaft; **international** ~ internationaler Verband, *(US)* Gewerkschaft mit Mitgliedern in USA und Kanada; **labor** ~ *(US)* Gewerkschaft; **local** ~ *(US)* Ortsverein, -verband; **modified shop** ~ Gewerkschaft mit Mitgliedszwang für neue Betriebsmitglieder; **monetary** ~ Währungsunion; **multicraft** ~ mehrere Berufsgruppen umfassende Gewerkschaft; **national** ~ Zentralverband, *(US)* Zentralgewerk[schaftsverband]; **open** ~ Gewerkschaft mit jederzeitiger Mitgliederaufnahme; **outside** ~ betriebsfremde Gewerkschaft; **peaceful** ~ *(US)* wirtschaftsfriedliche Gewerkschaft; **personal** ~ *(law of nations)* Personalunion; **picketing** ~ Streikposten aufstellende Gewerkschaft; **print** ~ Druckergewerkschaft; **public-employee** ~ Angestelltengewerkschaft; **real** ~ *(law of nations)* Realunion; **resident** ~ ortsansässige Gewerkschaft; **single-branch** ~ *(Br.)* Ortsgewerkschaft; **trade** ~ *(Br.)* Gewerkschaft; **Transport and General Workers'** ⍟ *(Br.)* [etwa] Transportarbeitergewerkschaft; **trade** ~ *(Br.)* Gewerkschaft; **universal postal** ~ Weltpostverein; **vertical** ~ Fachgewerkschaft; **yellow** ~ *(US)* wirtschaftsfriedlicher Gewerkschaftsverband;
~ **of local administrations** Gemeindezweckverband; ~ **of international fairs** Internationaler Messeverband; ~ **of shop distributive and allied workers** *(Br.)* [etwa] Gewerkschaft kaufmännischer Angestellter; ⍟ **of Soviet Socialist Republics** *(USSR)* Sowjetunion;
to address the ~ *(US, President)* Ansprache an das Volk der Vereinigten Staaten halten; **to establish a** ~ Gewerkschaft gründen; **to join a** ~ einer Gewerkschaft als Mitglied beitreten; **to keep a** ~ **out of one's plant** Gewerkschaftstätigkeit in seinem Betrieb nicht zulassen; **to live in perfect** ~ in völliger Eintracht leben; **to quit the** ~ aus der Gewerkschaft austreten;
to sack for ~ **activities** wegen gewerkschaftlicher Betätigung feuern; ~ **activity** gewerkschaftliche Tätigkeit, Gewerkschaftstätigkeit; ~ **affiliation** Gewerkschaftszugehörigkeit; ~ **agent** Gewerkschaftsvertreter; ~ **agreement** Tarifvertrag, Gewerkschaftsvereinbarung, Abkommen mit der Gewerkschaft; ~ **assessments** Gewerkschaftsbeiträge, -umlage; ~ **baiter** *(US)* Arbeitgeber, der mit allen Mitteln keine Gewerkschaft zuläßt; ~ **bank** Gemeinwirtschaftsbank; ~ **benefit** von der Gewerkschaft gewährte Unterstützung; ~ **branch** Einzelgewerkschaft; ~ **building** Gewerkschaftshaus; ~ **business** Tätigkeit für die Gewerkschaft; ~ **card** Mitglieds-, Gewerkschaftsausweis; ~ **catalog** *(library, US)* Gesamt-, Zentralkatalog; ~ **certificate** *(US)* gewerkschaftlicher Unbedenklichkeitsvermerk; ~ **claim** Gewerkschaftsforderung; ~ **combative measures** gewerkschaftliche Kampfmaßnahmen; ~ **committee** Gewerkschaftsausschuß; ~ **committeeman** Betriebsratsmitglied; ~ **conference** Gewerkschaftskongreß; ~ **contract** Tarifvertrag; ~ **contribution** Gewerkschaftsbeitrag; ⍟ **Convention** Pariser Verbandsübereinkunft; ~ **crusade** Gewerkschaftsfeldzug; ~ **demands** gewerkschaftliche Forderungen, Gewerkschaftsforderungen; **rival** ~ **dispute** Konkurrenzkampf zweier Gewerkschaften; ~ **dues** Gewerkschaftsbeiträge; ~ **duties** Aufgaben einer Gewerkschaft; ~ **enterprise** gewerkschaftseigenes Unternehmen; ~ **finances** Gewerkschaftsfinanzen; ~ **funds** Gewerkschaftskasse, -gelder, -mittel, -vermögen; ~ **grievance committee** gewerkschaftlicher Beschwerdeausschuß; ~ **headquarters** Gewerkschaftszentrale; ~ **hours** gewerkschaftlich (tariflich) vorgeschriebene Arbeitsstunden; ~ **house** *(Br.)* Armenasyl; **to apply to the** ~ **house** *(Br.)* sich an die Fürsorgebehörden wenden; ~ **institutions** gewerkschaftliche Einrichtungen; ~ **interests** Gewerkschaftsinteressen; ⍟ **Jack** *(Br.)* Nationalflagge, *(marine)* Hoheitsabzeichen, Gösch; ~ **joint** Röhrenkupplung; ~ **jurisdiction** Fachgruppenabgrenzung; ~ **label** *(US)* Gewerkschaftsetikett; ~-**label goods** *(US)* mit Gewerkschaftsetikett versehene Ware; ~ **labo(u)r** gewerkschaftlich organisierte Arbeitskräfte; ~ **leader** Gewerkschaftsführer; ~ **leadership** Gewerkschaftsführung; ~ **man** *(US)*

Gewerkschaftsangehöriger, -mitglied, gewerkschaftlich organisierter Arbeiter, Gewerkschaftler; **~-management cooperation** Zusammenarbeit zwischen Gewerkschaften und Unternehmertum; **~ meeting** Gewerkschaftsversammlung, Gewerkschaftskongreß; **mandatory ~ meeting** gewerkschaftliche Zwangsveranstaltung; **~ member** Gewerkschaftsmitglied; **~ membership** Zugehörigkeit zu einer Gewerkschaft, Gewerkschaftszugehörigkeit, -mitgliedschaft; **compulsory ~ membership** Zwangsmitgliedschaft bei einer Gewerkschaft; **~ message** *(US)* Rede zur Lage der Nation; **~ mortgage clause** *(fire insurance)* Klausel zugunsten des Grundpfandgläubigers; **trade-~ movement** Gewerkschaftsbewegung; **to have the ~ muscle to wreck the economy** mit Hilfe der Gewerkschaften die Konjunktur zugrunderichten können; **~ negotiations** Verhandlungen mit der Gewerkschaft, Tarifverhandlungen; **~ negotiator** Gewerkschaftsunterhändler, Tarifvertragspartner; **~ news service** *(US)* Gewerkschaftsnachrichtendienst; **~ office** Gewerkschaftsbüro; **~ officer** *(US)* Gewerkschaftsfunktionär, -angestellter, -beamter; **national ~ officer** Zentralgewerkschaftsfunktionär; **~ official** Gewerkschaftsangestellter; **~ policy** Gewerkschaftspolitik; **trade-~ press** Gewerkschaftspresse; **~ pressure** von der Gewerkschaft ausgeübter Druck; **~ publication** Gewerkschaftsorgan; **~ racketeering** Gewerkschaftsbereicherung; **~ rate** tariflicher Mindestsatz, Tariflohn; **~ recognition** Anerkennung einer Gewerkschaft; **~ regulations** Gewerkschaftsvorschriften; **~ representation** gewerkschaftliche Vertretung; **~ representative** Gewerkschaftsvertreter; **~-representative election** Gewerkschaftsvertreterwahl; **~ resignation** Gewerkschaftsaustritt; **~ rights** Rechte der Gewerkschaft, Gewerkschaftsrecht; **~ rivalry** Gewerkschaftskonkurrenz; **~ scale** *(US)* gewerkschaftlich festgesetzter Lohntarif; **trade-~ secretary** Gewerkschaftssekretär; **~ section** Gewerkschaftsbezirk; **~ security clause** *(wage contract)* Schutzklausel gegen Mitgliederverlust; **~ shop** *(US)* gewerkschaftlich gebundener (gewerkschaftspflichtiger) Betrieb; **~ shop card** *(US)* Ausweiskarte für gewerkschaftspflichtige Betriebe; **~ shop system** *(US)* Gewerkschaftsmonopol; **~ solidarity** gewerkschaftliche Solidarität; **~ spokesman** Gewerkschaftssprecher; **~ station** *(US)* Zentral-, Hauptbahnhof; **~ steward** *(US)* Betriebsrat, -obmann; **~ termination** Tarifkündigung durch die Gewerkschaft; **~ treasury** Gewerkschaftskasse; **~ victory** Gewerkschaftssieg; **to lose the trade-~ voice** Gewerkschaftsstimmen verlieren; **~ wages** gewerkschaftlich anerkannte Löhne, Tariflöhne; **~ workhouse** *(Br.)* Armenhaus, regionales Armenasyl.

unionism *(US)* Gewerkschaftswesen, -vereinigung;
   industrial ~ fachliche Gewerkschaftsvereinigung; **uplift ~** konservative Gewerkschaftsbewegung.

unionist *(member of trade union)* gewerkschaftlich organisierter Arbeiter, Gewerkschaftsmitglied;
   fellow ~ Mitglied der gleichen Gewerkschaft; **rank-and-file ~s** einfache Gewerkschaftsmitglieder;
   to be an active ~ sich gewerkschaftlich betätigen;
   ~ *(a.)* *(trade union)* gewerkschaftlich;
   ~ worker gewerkschaftlich organisierter Arbeiter.

unionization gewerkschaftliche Zusammenfassung.

unionize *(v.)* gewerkschaftlich organisieren, Gewerkschaftsvorschriften unterwerfen, *(become member)* einer Gewerkschaft beitreten;
   ~ employees Arbeitnehmer zum Eintritt in die Gewerkschaft veranlassen.

unionized gewerkschaftlich organisiert;
   ~ labo(u)r gewerkschaftlich organisierte Arbeitskräfte; **~ plant** unter Gewerkschaftseinfluß stehender Betrieb; **~ worker** gewerkschaftlich organisierter Arbeiter.

unionship Gewerkschaftszugehörigkeit;
   compulsory ~ Zwangsmitgliedschaft in einer Gewerkschaft.

unique einmalig, einzigartig, *(coll.)* großartig, toll.

unissued | capital *(Br.)* **(capital stock**, *US*) nicht ausgegebenes (emittiertes) Aktienkapital; **~ debentures** noch nicht ausgegebene Schuldverschreibungen; **~ shares** **(stock**, *US*) noch nicht ausgegebene Aktien.

unit Einheit, Stück, *(block of securities)* Effektenbündel, *(building)* Bauelement, *(component)* Bestandteil, *(group, US)* Gruppe Gleichgesinnter, *(investment trust, Br.)* Fondsanteil, Investmentanteil, -zertifikat, *(med.)* Dosis, Menge, *(mil.)* Truppenverband, Einheit, Truppenteil, *(physics)* Grundmaßstab, Grundeinheit, Standard, *(rationing)* Marke, *(school, US)* Schul-, Lehrjahr, *(university, US)* Semesterwochenstunde;
   towards the bigger ~ Zug zur größeren Einheit;
   accumulation ~ *(Br.)* Anteilschein mit Wiederanlage der Erträge, Kapitalansammlungsschein; **amo(u)red ~** Panzerver

band; **bargaining ~** Tarifvertragspartei; **board-of-trade ~** Kilowattstunde; **bread ~** Brotmarke; **cost ~** Kosteneinheit; **decision-making ~** entscheidende Stelle; **dwelling ~** Wohnungseinheit; **first-stage ~** *(statistics)* Einheit der ersten Auswahlstufe; **fixed-asset ~** *(accounting)* Anlageneinheit; **income ~** *(Br.)* Investmentzertifikat (Anteilschein) mit Ausschüttung von Erträgen; **local ~** Gemeindeeinheit; **low-rent ~** *(US)* billiges Mietshaus; **manageable ~** dirigierbare Betriebseinheit; **maximum odd linage ~** *(advertising)* größte nicht reguläre Zeileneinheit; **monetary ~** Münz-, Währungseinheit; **primary ~** *(statistics)* Einheit der ersten Auswahlstufe; **regional ~** Raumeinheit; **second ~** *(film)* zweites Aufnahmeteam; **second-stage ~** *(statistics)* Einheit der zweiten Auswahlstufe; **self-contained ~** unabhängige (in sich abgeschlossene) Einheit; **separate ~** selbständige Einheit; **spatial ~** Raumelement; **strategic ~** strategische Einheit; **tactical ~** taktische Einheit; **taxable ~** Steuergegenstand, -objekt;
   ~ of account [Ver]rechnungseinheit; **~ of administration** Verwaltungseinheit; **~ of assessment** Veranlagungsobjekt; **~ of cost** Kostenträger; **~ of currency** Währungseinheit; **~ of electricity** *(Br.)* Kilowattstunde; **~ of employment** Beschäftigungseinheit; **~s in issue** *(Br.)* im Umlauf befindliche Investmentanteile; **~ of labo(u)r** Arbeitseinheit; **~ of length** Längenmaß; **~ of material** Materialeinheit; **~ of measurement** Maßeinheit; **~ of output (production)** Produktionseinheit; **~ of power** Leistungseinheit; **~ of quantity** Mengeneinheit; **~ of sampling** *(population statistics)* Einheit der Stichprobenauswahl; **~ of satisfaction** Genußeinheit; **~ of society** Grundeinheit der Gesellschaft; **~ of taxation** Veranlagungsobjekt; **~ of time** Zeiteinheit **~ of trade** *(stock exchange)* Handelseinheit; **~s in unit trusts** *(Br.)* Investmentanteile, -zertifikate; **~ of wage** Lohneinheit; **~ of work** Arbeitseinheit;
   to hold up to 150 ~s of an issue bis zu 150 Investmentzertifikate einer Serie besitzen; **to join one's ~** *(mil.)* sich zu seiner Einheit begeben; **to put ~s in issue** *(Br.)* Investmentanteile ausgeben; **to repurchase ~s** Investmentzertifikate zurücknehmen;
   ~ amount Betrag pro Einheit; **~ assurance** *(Br.)* mit einem Kapitalanlagegesellschaftsvertrag gekoppelte Lebensversicherung; **~ bank** *(US)* unabhängige Einzelbank; **~ banking** *(US)* Einzelbankwesen; **~ calculation** Einzelkalkulation; **~ certificate** *(Br.)* Anteilschein, Investmentzertifikat; **~ charge** *(tel.)* Gebühr pro Einheit, Gebühreneinheit; **~ company** Einheitsgesellschaft; **~ control** *(US)* Lagerkontrolle nach Wareneinheiten, buchmäßige Mengenkontrolle; **~ costs** Einheitskosten, Stückkosten; **~ standard cost** Normalkosten pro Einheit; **~ evaluation** *(investment fund)* Anteilsbewertung; **present ~ of account exchange rate** Wechselkurs der augenblicklichen Verrechnungseinheit; **~ furniture** Anbaumöbel; **~ head** Abteilungsleiter; **~ holder** *(Br.)* Investment-, Anteilscheinbesitzer; **~ holdings** Portefeuille von Anteilsscheinen; **~ investment trust** *(Br.)* Kapitalanlage-, Investmentgesellschaft; **~ labo(u)r cost** Arbeitsaufwand (Lohnkosten) pro Produktionseinheit, Lohnstückkosten; **~ load** Verladeeinheit; **~-of-sales method** Verkaufssoll-Quotenmethode; **~ power** Leistungseinheit; **~ price** Stück-, Einzel-, Einheitspreis; **~ price labelling** Einheitspreisauszeichnung; **~ pricing** Einheitspreisfestsetzung; **~ pricing store** Einheitspreisgeschäft; **~ quotation** Stücknotiz; **~ rate** Einheitssatz; **~ replacement** Ersatz- und Austauschverfahren; **~ sale** Einheitspreisgeschäft; **~ trust** *(Br.)* Investment-, Kapitalanlagegesellschaft; **fixed-~ trust** *(Br.)* Kapitalanlagegesellschaft mit festgelegtem Wertpapierbestand; **flexible-~ trust** *(Br.)* Kapitalanlagegesellschaft mit auswechselbarem Portefeuille; **registered ~ trust** *(Br.)* zugelassene Kapitalanlagegesellschaft; **~ trust funds** *(Br.)* Kapitalanlagefonds; **~ trust holdings** Investment-, Kapitalanlagezertifikate; **~-trust plan** *(Br.)* Kapitalanlagevertrag; **~-trust unit** *(Br.)* Anteilschein einer Kapitalanlagegesellschaft; **~ valuation** Einzelbewertung; **~ value** *(investment fund)* Wertzuwachs pro Anteil; **~ voting** gleiches Mitgliederstimmrecht; **~ wage** Stück-, Akkordlohn; **~-wage costs** Lohnkosten je Produktionseinheit, Lohnstückkosten.

unitary einheitlich, zentralisiert;
   ~ action Einheitsbestrebung; **~ country (state)** Einheitsstaat; **~ movement** Einheitsbewegung; **~ tendency** Einheitsbestrebung.

unite *(v./t.)* verbinden, vereinigen, geschlossen einsetzen, *(amalgamate)* zusammenlegen, *(v./i.)* sich vereinigen (liieren, zusammenschließen, zusammentun), *(come together)* zusammentreffen, *(marry)* sich verheiraten;
   ~ companies Gesellschaften fusionieren; **~ one country with another** zwei Länder miteinander vereinigen; **~ in signing a petition** Gesuch geschlossen unterzeichnen.

united vereinigt, verbunden;
~ **in interests** interessensverbunden;
~ **efforts** Zusammenwirken; ~ **front** Einheitsfront.
United Auto Workers *(US)* Autoarbeitergewerkschaft; ~ **General Assembly** Vollversammlung der Vereinigten Nationen; ~ **Kingdom of Great Britain and Ireland** *(Br.)* Vereinigtes Königreich von Großbritannien und Irland.
United Nations Vereinigte Nationen;
~ **Charter** Satzung der Vereinten Nationen; ~ **Conference on Trade and Development** Welthandels- und Entwicklungskonferenz; ~ **Economic and Social Council** Wirtschafts- und Sozialrat der Vereinten Nationen; ~ **General Assembly** Vollversammlung der Vereinten Nationen; ~ **Educational, Scientific and Cultural Organization** Organisation der Vereinten Nationen für Erziehung, Wissenschaft und Kultur; ~ **Emergency Forces** Einsatzkräfte der UNO; ~ **High Commissioner** Hochkommissar der UNO für Flüchtlinge; ~ **Industrial Development Organization** Organisation der Vereinten Nationen für industrielle Entwicklung; ~ **Organization** *(UNO)* Organisation der Vereinten Nationen; ~ **peacekeeping force** Sicherheitstruppen der UN; ~ **Relief and Rehabilitation Administration** Wohlfahrts- und Wiedergutmachungsorganisation der UNO.
United | Secretariat Generalsekretariat der Vereinten Nationen; ~ **Security Council** Weltsicherheitsrat.
United States Vereinigte Staaten von Amerika, USA;
to talk ~ deutliche Sprache mit jem. sprechen;
~ **bonds** Schuldverschreibungen der USA; ~ **Chamber of Commerce** *(US)* Industrie- und Handelskammer der USA; ~ **citizenship** amerikanische Staatsangehörigkeit; ~ **Code** Bundesgesetzsammlung; ~ **Commissioner** Beauftragter in Bundesstrafsachen; ~ **courts** Bundesgerichte der USA; ~ **currency** US-Währung; ~ **Employment Service** Arbeitsvermittlungsdienst in den USA; ~ **notes** Bundesschatzwechsel; ~ **officer** amerikanischer Bundesbeamter; ~ **postal savings banks** *(US)* Postsparkassen der USA; ~ **postal savings bonds** *(US)* 2 1/2%ige Postsparkassenschuldverschreibungen; ~ **Tariff Commission** Zollkommission der USA; ~ **Treasurer** Finanzminister der USA; ~ **Treasury Certificates of Indebtedness** kurzfristige Schatzanweisungen der USA; ~ **Treasury Department** Finanzministerium (Schatzamt) der USA; ~ **value** *(customs)* Binnenwert.
unitholder *(Br.)* Investment-, Anteilscheinbesitzer.
unitization Umwandlung in eine Kapitalanlagegesellschaft.
unitize *(v.)* in eine Kapitalanlagegesellschaft umwandeln.
unities of place, time and action Einheit des Ortes, der Zeit und der Handlung.
unity Einheit, *(concord)* Eintracht, Einmütigkeit, Übereinstimmung, Solidarität, *(joint tenancy)* Gesamthandseigentum;
economic ~ Wirtschaftseinheit; **national** ~ nationale Einheit; **political** ~ politische Einheit;
~ **of command** Alleinzuständigkeit; ~ **of interest** Rechtsgemeinschaft, Gleichheit der Beteiligung; ~ **of possession** Mitbesitz; ~ **of joint property** Gesamthandseigentum; ~ **of seizin** *(real estate)* Miteigentum; ~ **of sentiment** Einmütigkeit; ~ **of title** einheitlicher Rechtsgrund;
to dwell in ~ einträchtig beisammenleben.
universal allumfassend, allgemein, universal, weltumfassend, ganz, *(for use of all)* allgemeinverständlich, allgemein üblich;
~ **acclaim** weltweite Anerkennung; ~ **adjustment** *(instrument)* Universaleinstellung; ~ **agent** Generalvertreter, -bevollmächtigter; **to meet with** ~ **applause** allgemeinen Beifall finden; ~ **Copyright Convention** Welturheberrechtsabkommen; ~ **coupling** Kardangelenk; ~ **declaration of human rights** allgemeine Erklärung der Menschenrechte; ~ **entertainment** Massenbelustigung; ~ **genius** Universalgenie; ~ **history** Weltgeschichte; ~ **joint** Kardangelenk; ~ **knowledge** umfassendes Wissen; ~ **language** Weltsprache; ~ **legacy** Universalvermächtnis; ~ **legatee** Alleinvermächtnisnehmer; ~ **military camp** allgemeine Wehrpflicht; ~ **partnership** allgemeine Gütergemeinschaft; ~ **patent** Weltpatent; ~ **Postal Union** Weltpostverein; ~ **provider** *(Br.)* Gemischtwarenhändler, -handlung; ~ **providers** *(Br.)* Waren-, Kaufhaus; ~ **Standard Workmen's Compensation Policy** *(US)* Einheitspolice für die Arbeiterunfallversicherung; ~ **representation** *(Scot.)* Universal-, Gesamtnachfolge; ~ **rule** ausnahmslos geltende Regel; ~ **succession** Universal-, Gesamtnachfolge; ~ **successor** Universalerbe; ~ **suffrage** allgemeines Wahlrecht; ~ **numerical system** *(US, banking)* einheitliches Nummernsystem.
universe Weltall, Universum, Makrokosmos.
Universities Central Council on Admission *(Br.)* zentrale Studienplatzvergabe.

university Universität, Hochschule;
degree-granting ~ Universität mit dem Recht der Promovierung; **land-grant** ~ staatlich geförderte Universität; **red-brick** ~ *(Br.)* Ersatzuniversität;
to be at the ~ Universität besuchen, studieren; **to be admitted to a** ~ *(Br.)* sich immatrikulieren lassen; **to enrol(l) at a** ~ *(US)* sich immatrikulieren lassen; **to enter the** ~ zur Universität gehen; **to go down from the** ~ *(Br.)* Universität verlassen, in die Ferien gehen; **to go up to the** ~ *(Br.)* Universität beziehen; **to have been through the** ~ studiert (akademische Ausbildung) haben; **to have been trained in the** ~ **of** ... aus der Universität ... hervorgegangen sein; **to register at a** ~ *(US)* sich immatrikulieren lassen;
~ *(a.)* akademisch;
~ **administrator** Universitätsbeamter; ~ **appointment** Hochschulanstellung; ~ **authorities** Universitätsbehörden; ~ **bookshop** Universitätsbuchhandlung; ~ **calendar** *(Br.)* (**catalog**, *US*) Hochschulordnung; ~ **campus** *(US)* Universitätsgelände; ~ **course** Universitätsstudium; ~ **degree** akademischer Grad, Doktorgrad; ~ **don** Hochschullehrer; ~-**educated** akademisch ausgebildet, mit Universitätsausbildung, -abschluß; ~ **education** Universitätsausbildung, Hochschulbildung; **with a** ~ **education** akademisch gebildet (ausgebildet); **free** ~ **education** kostenloses Universitätsstudium; **to have had a** ~ **education** [an der Universität] studiert haben, Akademiker sein; ~ **entrance** Aufnahme in eine Universität; ~ **entrance examination** Universitätsaufnahmeprüfung; ~ **examination** Universitätsexamen, Hochschulabschluß; ~ **extension** Erwachsenenbildung, Volksbildungswerk, Volkshochschule; ~ **extension class** Volkshochschulkursus; ~ **extension lectures** Vorlesungen auf der Volkshochschule; ~ **fees** Studiengebühren; **to meet** ~ **fees** Kosten einer Universitätsausbildung decken; ~ **graduate** Hochschulabsolvent; ~ **lecture** [Universitäts]vorlesung; ~ **lecturer** Dozent; ~ **level** Hochschulqualifikation; ~ **library** Universitätsbibliothek; **to be a** ~ **man** Akademiker; **to be a** ~ **man** studiert haben, Akademiker sein; ~ **professor** Universitätsprofessor; ~ **recruiting** *(US)* Anwerbung von Nachwuchskräften auf der Universität; ~ **statute** Universitätssatzung; ~ **student** Student; ~ **teacher** Hochschullehrer; ~ **teaching experience** Erfahrungen als Hochschullehrer; ~ **town** Universitätsstadt; ~-**trained** mit Universitätsabschluß; ~ **training** Hochschul-, Universitätsausbildung; ~ **work forces** bei der Universität angestellte Arbeitskräfte.
univocal unzweideutig, eindeutig.
unjust ungerecht, unbillig;
~ **enrichment** ungerechtfertigte Bereicherung.
unjustified ungerechtfertigt, unberechtigt;
~ **matter** *(print.)* Plattensatz.
unknowingly ahnungslos.
unknown unbekannt, fremd, nicht vertraut;
a great ~ großer Unbekannter;
~ **risk** unbekanntes Risiko; ~ **soldier** unbekannter Soldat.
unlabelled nicht gekennzeichnet, ohne Etikett, nicht beschriftet, *(luggage)* ohne Gepäckzettel.
unlabo(u)red unbearbeitet, *(style)* ungezwungen, natürlich;
~ **field** unbebautes Feld.
unlade *(v.)* Ladung löschen, ent-, ab-, ausladen.
unladen unbeladen, *(fig.)* unbelastet.
unlawful ungesetzlich, widerrechtlich, gesetz-, rechtswidrig, illegal, *(illegitimate)* unehelich;
~ **act** unerlaubte (rechtswidrige) Handlung; ~ **assembly** Auflauf, Zusammenrottung; ~ **belligerents** *(US)* völkerrechtswidrige Teilnehmer an Kampfhandlungen; ~ **combination** ungesetzliche Vereinigung (Konzernbildung); ~ **detainer** *(tenant)* widerrechtlich verweigerte Räumung; ~ **detention** ungesetzliche Haft, Freiheitsberaubung; ~ **dog** wildernder Hund; ~ **entry** widerrechtliche Besitznahme; ~ **game** verbotenes Glücksspiel; ~ **picketing** unerlaubtes Streikpostenstehen; ~ **profits** Gewinne aus einem nicht genehmigten Gewerbe.
unlawfully widerrechtlich.
unleaded *(print.)* ohne Durchschuß (Zwischenräume).
unlearned nicht einstudiert.
unless | countermanded Abbestellung vorbehalten; ~ **lease** *(oil, gas)* auflösend bedingter Bohrvertrag; ~ **otherwise provided** mangels anderweitiger Bestimmung.
unlettered ungebildet, unbelesen, analphabetisch.
unlevied nicht besteuert.
unlicenced unerlaubt, unberechtigt, nicht konzessioniert, ohne Lizenz, *(book)* ohne Erlaubnis gedruckt, *(unauthorized)* ohne Ermächtigung, unbefugt, wild, *(victualler, Br.)* ohne Schankkonzession;

~ broker freier Makler; **~ personnel** Belegschaftsangehörige ohne Arbeitserlaubnis.

unlicked cub *(fig.)* unabgeführter Jagdhund.

unlikelihood Unwahrscheinlichkeit.

unlikely | to win ohne Gewinnchance; **~ tale** unglaubwürdige Geschichte; **~ venture** aussichtsloses Vorhaben.

unlimited unbegrenzt, grenzenlos, uferlos, *(liability)* unein-, unbeschränkt, *(stock exchange)* nicht limitiert, unlimitiert; **~ authority** unumschränkte Vollmacht; **~ cheque** *(Br.)* der Höhe nach unbegrenzter Scheck; **~ claim** ziffernmäßig nicht begrenzte Forderung; **~ company** *(Br.)* Gesellschaft mit unbeschränkter Haftung; **~ credit** Blankokredit; **~ expanse of the ocean** grenzenlose Weite des Ozeans; **~ field of knowledge** uferloses Wissensgebiet; **~ liability** unbeschränkte Haftung; **~ mortgage** Globalhypothek; **~ order** unlimitierte Order, *(stock exchange)* unlimitierter Börsenauftrag; **~ partner** persönlich haftender Gesellschafter, Komplementär; **~ partnership** [etwa] BGB-Gesellschaft; **for an ~ period** auf unbegrenzte Zeit, unbefristet; **~ policy** Generalpolice; **~ power of attorney** unbeschränkte Vollmacht, Blankovollmacht; **~ price** unlimitierter Kurs; **~ railway ticket** unbegrenzt gültige Eisenbahnfahrkarte; **for an ~ time** unbefristet.

unlined nicht liniert.

unliquidated *(not liquidated)* unliquidiert, *(uncertain as to amount)* nicht festgestellt, unbestimmt, *(unpaid)* unbezahlt, unbeglichen, offenstehend, nicht ausgeglichen; **~ damages** vertraglich nicht festgesetzter (schätzungsbedürftiger) Schadensersatzanspruch; **~ demand** der Höhe nach unbestimmte Forderung; **~ encumbrance** *(governmental accounting)* noch nicht bewilligte Umlage.

unlisted nicht eingetragen (aufgeführt), *(US, stock exchange)* unnotiert, nicht notiert (börsenfähig); **~ securities** *(US)* Freiverkehrswerte; **~ securities market** *(US)* Freiverkehrsmarkt.

unlit unbeleuchtet;

unlive *(v.)* **one's reputation** neuen Ruf durch besseren Lebenswandel gewinnen.

unlivery *(maritime law)* Löschen.

unload *(v.)* entladen, abladen, ausladen, -schiffen, [Schiffs]ladung löschen, *(securities, US)* abstoßen, verkaufen, auf den Markt werfen; **~ the cargo of a vessel** Schiff entladen, Fracht löschen; **~ a cart** aus dem Wagen laden; **~ a firearm** Waffe entladen; **~ a bad note on s. o.** *(fam.)* jem. einen falschen Geldschein andrehen; **~ one's resentment** seine Verstimmung loswerden; **~ a ship** Ladung löschen; **~ stock on the market** Markt mit Aktien überschwemmen.

unloading Ab-, Ausladen, *(stock exchange)* Massenverkauf von Effekten; **loading and ~** Laden und Löschen; **to do the ~** Abladen besorgen; **~ berth** *(ship)* Abladeplatz, Lösch-, Ausladeplatz; **~ charges** Abladegebühr, Ausladekosten, *(ship)* Kosten für die Löschung; **~ equipment** Entladegerät; **~ party** Abladekommando; **~ platform** Ausladebahnsteig; **~ point** Ausladeort; **~ port** Abladeplatz; **~ risk** *(insurance)* Entladerisiko, Abladerisiko, Löschrisiko; **~ siding** Absetzgleis; **~ time** Entladedauer, -zeit.

unlock *(v.)* aufschließen, öffnen, *(capital)* Kapital freisetzen; **~ a flood of emotions** Flut von Empfindungen auslösen.

unlodge *(v.)* exmittieren.

unlooked | at unbesehen; **~ for** unerwartet, unvorhergesehen; **~-for mishap or untoward event** unerwartetes Eintreten eines außergewöhnlichen Ereignisses.

unlucky | efforts fruchtlose Bemühungen; **~ expedition** verhängnisvolle Expedition; **~ fellow** Pechvogel; **~ speech** katastrophale Rede; **to be born under an ~ star** der geborene Pechvogel sein.

unmailable *(US)* nicht zum Postversand zugelassen.

unmaintainable unhaltbar, *(defence)* unzulässig.

unmake *(v.)* aufheben, annullieren, rückgängig machen, widerrufen, für null und nichtig erklären, *(depose from a rank)* seines Postens entheben.

unman *(v.)* **a ship** Schiff seiner Besatzung berauben.

unmanageable unhandlich, *(fig.)* unkontrollierbar; **~ child** schwieriges Kind.

unmanned entvölkert, verlassen, leer, öde, *(ship)* unbemannt; **~ aircraft with remote control** ferngesteuertes Flugzeug; **~ spaceship** unbemanntes Raumschiff.

unmannered schlecht erzogen, unmanierlich.

unmanufactured unverarbeitet; **~ materials** Rohmaterialien.

unmapped noch nicht kartographisch erfaßt.

unmarketable *(loan)* unplazierbar, *(nonnegotiable)* nicht marktgängig (marktfähig), verkehrsunfähig, *(unsalable)* unverkäuflich; **~ assets** nicht verwertbare (realisierbare) Aktien; **~ title** unsicherer Eigentumstitel.

unmarriageable nicht heiratsfähig; **~ facts** nicht miteinander zu vereinbarende Tatsachen.

unmarried ledig, unverheiratet; **~ man** Lediger; **~ mother** ledige Mutter; **~ state** Ehelosigkeit.

unmask *(v.)* demaskieren, *(v./i.)* Maske fallen lassen; **~ a traitor** Verräter entlarven.

unmaterial immateriell, geistig.

unmatured noch nicht fällig.

unmeasured abuse grenzenloser Mißbrauch.

unmechanical nicht mechanisch, *(fig.)* nicht maschinenmäßig.

unmentionable nicht erwähnenswert.

unmerchantable nicht marktfähig, unverkäuflich.

unmetal(l)ed *(road)* unbefestigt, unbeschottert.

unmingled unvermengt, unverfälscht, rein.

unmistakable sign of rain unverkennbares Anzeichen für Regen.

unmistaken untrüglich.

unmitigated | liar unverbesserlicher Lügner; **~ scoundrel** Schurke durch und durch.

unmixed unvermischt, rein, pur.

unmodulated *(el.)* nicht ausgesteuert.

unmolested unbelästigt, ungestört; **to live ~** in Frieden leben.

unmoor *(v.)* vom Ankergrund abbringen.

unmortgaged unverpfändet, *(real estate)* nicht hypothekarisch belastet, unbelastet.

unmounted block unmontiertes Klischee.

unmutilated unverstümmelt.

unmuzzle *(v.)* *(fig.)* freie Meinungsäußerung gewähren.

unnatural unnatürlich, *(fig.)* gekünstelt, geschraubt, affektiert; **~ will** ungewöhnliche letztwillige Verfügung.

unnaturalized nicht eingebürgert (naturalisiert).

unnavigable nicht schiffbar.

unnecessary nutzlos, unnötig, überflüssig; **to be ~** entfallen; **~ danger** unnötige Gefährdung; **~ hardship** unnötiger Härtefall; **~ labo(u)r** überflüssige Arbeit.

unnegotiable nicht begebbar (negoziierbar).

unneutral service neutralitätswidrige Dienste.

unnoticed unbemerkt.

unnotified ohne vorherige Benachrichtigung.

unnumbered nicht numeriert, unnumeriert.

unobliging ungefällig, nicht hilfsbereit.

unobnoxious *(candidate)* annehmbar, tragbar; **~ to any party** für alle Parteien tragbar.

unobstructed | policy reibungslos durchgeführte Politik; **~ view** unverbaubare Sicht.

unobtrusive unauffällig, diskret.

unoccupancy Leerstehen, Unbewohntsein.

unoccupied *(unemployed)* unbeschäftigt, frei, *(untilled)* unbestellt, *(unused)* unbenutzt, *(vacant)* unbewohnt, leer[stehend], vakant; **to be ~** leerstehen, unbewohnt sein; **~ dwelling** *(fire insurance)* leerstehende Wohnung.

unoffending nicht anstößig.

unofficial nicht amtlich, inoffiziell, außerdienstlich, offiziös, nicht bestätigt, *(medicine)* den gesetzlichen Vorschriften entsprechend, *(stock exchange, Br.)* außerbörslich; **~ broker** *(Br.)* Freiverkehrs-, Kulissenmakler; **in an ~ capacity** nicht amtlich; **~ dealings** *(Br.)* Freiverkehr; **~ market** *(Br.)* Nachbörse, *(curb market, Br.)* Freiverkehrsmarkt; **~ news** unbestätigte Nachricht; **~ strike** *(Br.)* wilder (nicht von der Gewerkschaft getragener) Streik; **~ trading** *(Br.)* inoffizieller Handel.

unopened | book nicht aufgeschnittenes Buch; **~ letter** nicht geöffneter Brief; **~ market** unerschlossener Markt.

unopposed unbeanstandet, *(parl.)* ohne Gegenkandidat; **to be returned ~** ohne Gegenstimmen gewählt werden; **~ business** unwidersprochen gebliebene Anträge zur Tagesordnung; **~ candidate** einziger (alleiniger) Kandidat.

unorganized unorganisiert, ungegliedert, *(trade union)* nicht gewerkschaftlich organisiert; **~ industry** gewerkschaftsfreie Wirtschaft; **~ labo(u)r** gewerkschaftlich nicht organisierte Arbeitskräfte.

unoriginal aus zweiter Hand.
unowned herrenlos, ohne Eigentümer;
~ **child** [vom Vater] nicht anerkanntes Kind.
unpack *(v.)* **a trunk** Koffer auspacken.
unpacked lose, unverpackt.
unpaged ohne Seitenzahlen, nicht paginiert.
unpaid unbezahlt, nicht bezahlt, unbeglichen, rückständig, *(not prepaid)* unfrankiert, nicht freigemacht;
to leave an account ~ Rechnung nicht bezahlen; **to return a bill** ~ Wechsel nicht honorieren;
~ **agent** ehrenamtlicher Vertreter; ~ **balance** Restschuld; ~ **bill** unbezahlter (nicht eingelöster) Wechsel; ~ **capital** noch nicht eingezahltes [Grund]kapital; ~ **dividend** fällige (noch nicht ausgezahlte) Dividende; ~ **interest** rückständige Zinsen; ~ **letter** nicht freigemachter (frankierter) Brief; ~ **letter stamp** Nachgebührmarke; ~ **position** ehrenamtliche Stellung; ~ **purchase money** Restkaufgeld; ~ **seller** [teilweise] noch unbezahlter Verkäufer; ~ **services** *(national income)* bei der Berechnung des Sozialproduktes außer Ansatz gelassene Dienstleistungen.
unparalleled | achievement unvergleichliche Leistung; ~ **disaster** einmalige Katastrophe.
unparliamentary unparlamentarisch;
~ **language** unhöfliche Ausdrucksweise, unparlamentarische Redeweise.
unpatented nicht patentiert.
unpatronized ohne Kunden.
unpaved ungepflastert, unbefestigt.
unpayable *(yielding no profit)* unrentabel.
unpegged *(currency)* [von der Goldwährung] losgelöst, *(stock exchange)* ohne Kursbindung.
unpeopled unbewohnt, entvölkert, öde, leer.
unperforated *(stamp)* nicht perforiert.
unperformed unerledigt, unverrichtet.
unpicked samples nicht ausgewählte Stichproben.
unpiloted ohne Lotsen, *(fig.)* führerlos.
unplaced unplaziert, ohne Stellung, stellenlos.
unplanned unvorhergesehen.
unplanted nicht bepflanzt, *(country)* unbesiedelt, unkolonisiert.
unpledged unverpfändet.
unplumbed ohne Installation, *(customs)* umplombiert;
~ **depth** unergründliche Tiefe.
unploughed, unplowed *(US)* unbeackert, ungepflügt.
unpointed ohne Interpunktion.
unpolished ungeschliffen, *(manners)* ungehobelt, ungebildet, *(style)* unausgefeilt.
unpolitical unpolitisch, an Politik nicht interessiert.
unpolled | elector Nichtwähler; ~ **vote** ungezählte Stimme.
unpolluted nicht verschmutzt (verseucht), *(water)* sauber.
unpopular nicht volkstümlich, unpopulär;
to prove ~ keinen Anklang finden.
unpopulated unbevölkert, unbewohnt.
unpossessed ohne Besitz, herrenlos.
unposted *(Br.)* nicht aufgegeben, nicht in den Briefkasten eingeworfen, *(not up to date)* uninformiert, nicht unterrichtet.
unpractical unbeholfen, ungeschickt, unpraktisch.
unpractised in business geschäftlich unerfahren.
unprecedented beispiellos, nie dagewesen, *(legal sense)* ohne Präzedenzfall;
~ **rainfall** bisher nie aufgetretene Regenmenge.
unprejudiced sachlich, unbefangen, vorurteilsfrei, unvoreingenommen.
unpremeditated unvorbereitet, nicht im voraus geplant, aus dem Stegreif.
unprepared speech unvorbereitete Rede.
unpresentable nicht gesellschaftsfähig.
unpriced *(goods)* nicht [im Schaufenster] ausgezeichnet, ohne Preisangabe, *(priceless)* unschätzbar.
unpretending anspruchslos, bescheiden, schlicht.
unprincipled gewissenlos, charakterlos.
unprintable nicht bevorrechtigt (privilegiert), *(US)* auf niedrigster gesellschaftlicher Stufe, nicht zur Veröffentlichung geeignet.
unprivileged creditor Massegläubiger.
unprizable unschätzbar.
unprized nicht taxiert (geschätzt).
unprofessional language Laiensprache.
unproductive unproduktiv, unergiebig;
~ **capital** totes Kapital; ~ **consumption** unproduktiver Verbrauch; ~ **expenditure** *(Adam Smith)* unproduktiver Aufwand [des Staates]; ~ **labo(u)r** unproduktive Arbeitskräfte; ~ **wages** Gemeinkostenlöhne.

unproductiveness Unproduktivität.
unprofessional *(contrary to professional etiquette)* standeswidrig, *(not belonging to a profession)* keinem Beruf (keiner Berufsgruppe) zugehörig, nicht berufsmäßig, *(not pertaining to one's profession)* nicht fachmännisch, unfachmännisch, laienhaft;
~ **advertising** stümperhafte Reklame; ~ **conduct** standeswidriges Verhalten; ~ **language** Laiensprache; ~ **work** unstandesgemäße (unfachgemäße) Arbeitsweise.
unprofitable *(not benefited)* unvorteilhaft, ungünstig, nutzlos, zwecklos, *(not yielding any profit)* nicht einträglich, gewinnlos, unrentabel;
~ **servants** überflüssige Bedienstete.
unprofitableness Uneinträglichkeit.
unprogressive rückständig, reaktionär.
unprogressiveness rückschrittliche (reaktionäre) Einstellung.
unprompted spontan.
unpropertied besitzlos.
unproportional unverhältnismäßig, nicht proportional.
unprotected ungeschützt, schutzlos, *(mil.)* ungepanzert;
~ **bill of exchange** nicht eingelöster (honorierter) Wechsel.
unprovided | for unversorgt;
to be left ~ mittellos sein (zurückbleiben), ohne Mittel dastehen.
unprovoked nicht provoziert, ohne Veranlassung.
unpublished nicht veröffentlicht;
~ **memoirs** unveröffentlichte Memoiren.
unpunctual unpünktlich.
unpunishable nicht strafbar.
unpunished unbestraft;
to go ~ straflos ausgehen.
unpurchasable unkäuflich, nicht käuflich.
unqualified ungeeignet, untauglich, unqualifiziert, *(balance sheet approval)* uneingeschränkt, nicht qualifiziert, *(not competent)* nicht zuständig, *(without restriction)* uneingeschränkt;
~ **to serve** wehrdienstuntauglich; ~ **to vote** nicht stimmberechtigt;
to be ~ **for s. th.** für etw. nicht die notwendige Vorbildung haben;
~ **acceptance** *(bill of exchange)* uneingeschränkte Annahme; ~ **assent** uneingeschränkte Zustimmung; ~ **denial** glattes Dementi; ~ **practitioner** Heilpraktiker.
unquestionable unstreitig, nicht zu beanstanden.
unquestioned nicht gefragt, unbestritten.
unquestioning obedience blinder Gehorsam.
unquiet ruhelos, unruhig;
~ **times** turbulente Zeiten.
unquotable nicht zitierbar.
unquote *(v.)* *(telegram message)* Ende des Zitats.
unquoted *(stock exchange)* ohne Notierung, unnotiert, nicht notiert (börsengängig);
~ **list** *(Br.)* Freiverkehrsnotierung; ~ **securities** zur amtlichen Notierung nicht zugelassene Wertpapiere; ~ **shares** amtlich nicht notierte Aktien.
unrated untaxiert, nicht abgeschätzt (taxiert).
unratified noch nicht ratifiziert.
unrationed nicht bewirtschaftet, frei erhältlich, punktfrei.
unravel *(v.)* entwirren;
~ **a plot** Verschwörung aufdecken.
unravelment of the plot Lösung des Knotens.
unreadable unleserlich, unlesbar, *(book)* nicht lesenswert.
unreadiness mangelnde Einsatzbereitschaft.
unready nicht einsatzbereit.
unreal unreal, wirklichkeitsfremd.
unrealizable *(impracticable)* unerfüllbar, *(unsalable)* unverwertbar, -verkäuflich, nicht realisierbar.
unrealized | profit nicht realisierter Gewinn; ~ **revenue** in der Bilanz noch nicht in Erscheinung tretender Einnahmeposten.
unreason Unvernunft, Torheit.
unreasonable unvernünftig, *(claim)* unbillig, unangemessen, *(price)* überhöht, unbescheiden, unverschämt, übermäßig, maßlos, *(restraint of trade, Br.)* Wettbewerb unzulässig einschränkend;
~ **demands** unverschämte (maßlose) Forderungen; ~ **length of time** unangemessene Frist; ~ **refusal to submit to operation** *(injured employee)* unbegründete Operationsverweigerung; ~ **restraint of alienation** unzumutbare Veräußerungsbehinderung; ~ **restraint of trade** *(US)* unberechtigte Preisbindung, Preiskartell zur Wettbewerbeinschränkung; ~ **search** rechtswidrige Hausdurchsuchung.
unreasonably withheld unbegründet vorenthalten.
unreasoning obedience blinder Gehorsam.

unrebuttable unwiderlegbar.
unrecallable unwiderruflich.
unreceipted unquittiert, nicht quittiert, ohne Quittung.
unreceptive nicht aufnahmefähig;
~ **attitude** wenig entgegenkommende Haltung.
unreciprocated nicht auf Gegenseitigkeit beruhend.
unreclaimed nicht zurückgefordert, *(land)* unkultiviertes Land.
unrecognizable, to render unkenntlich machen.
unrecognized unerkannt;
~ **state** nicht anerkannter Staat.
unrecompensed nicht entschädigt, unbelohnt.
unreconstructed *(US)* erzkonservativ, ewig gestrig.
unrecorded nicht amtlich eingetragen, *(not taken on record)* nicht auf dem Tonband aufgenommen;
~ **mortgage** *(US)* nicht eingetragene Hypothek.
unrecoverable nicht beitreibbar.
unrecovered nicht beigetrieben;
~ **cost** *(balance sheet)* nicht abschreibungsfähige Investitionskosten, *(insurance)* nicht versicherter Schaden, Schadensrestwert.
unrectified unberechtigt, *(alcohol)* nicht destilliert.
unredeemable uneinbringlich, untilgbar, unkündbar;
~ **bonds** unkündbare Obligationen.
unredeemed *(bill)* uneingelöst, *(debt)* ungetilgt, nicht eingelöst (zurückbezahlt);
~ **blackguard** Erzschurke; ~ **pledge** uneingelöstes Pfand.
unreduced nicht herabgesetzt.
unreel *(v./i.)* ablaufen, abrollen;
~ **a film** Film ablaufen lassen; ~ **a long story** nicht endenwollende Geschichte vom Stapel lassen.
unrefined ungereinigt, nicht raffiniert, *(fig.)* ungebildet, raubeinig;
~ **manners** unfeines Benehmen; ~ **sugar** Rohzucker.
unrefinement Bildungsmangel.
unrefuted unwiderlegt.
unregistered nicht eingetragen (registriert), *(securities)* nicht auf den Namen lautend, *(trademark)* nicht angemeldet (eingetragen);
~ **company** nicht im Grundbuch eingetragene Gesellschaft; ~ **land** *(Br.)* im Grundbuch nicht eingetragener Grundbesitz; ~ **letter** gewöhnlicher (einfacher) Brief; ~ **society** nicht eingetragener Verein.
unregulated unreguliert.
unrelated ohne Bezug;
~ **business income** *(income tax)* steuerpflichtiger Einkommensteil einer Stiftung.
unrelenting|attacks rigorose Attacken; ~ **pressure** nicht nachlassender Druck; ~ **speed** unverminderte Geschwindigkeit.
unreliable unzuverlässig, *(business firm)* unsolide, unreell;
from an ~ source aus unzuverlässiger Quelle.
unrelieved ohne Unterstützung, *(mil.)* nicht abgelöst, *(taxation)* steuerlich noch nicht in Abzug gebracht.
unremitting unaufhörlich, ausdauernd, beharrlich;
to be ~ in one's attention to a case *(doctor)* sich um einen Krankheitsfall unablässig kümmern;
~ **exertions (efforts)** unermüdliche Anstrengungen.
unremovable unabsetzbar.
unremunerative unwirtschaftlich, brotlos, unrentabel;
to be ~ wenig einbringen (eintragen);
~ **work** unbezahlte Arbeit.
unrepaid nicht zurückgezahlt.
unrepair Reparaturbedürftigkeit, *(building)* Baufälligkeit.
unrepealed nicht aufgehoben (widerrufen).
unrepeated *(law)* noch in Kraft.
unreplaceable unersetzbar.
unrepresentative nicht representativ, *(pol.)* nicht den Wählerwillen repräsentierend.
unrepresented *(in parliament)* nicht vertreten.
unreprievable ohne Gnadenfrist.
unrequested receipts *(balance of payment)* einseitige Transferleistungen.
unrequited unbelohnt;
~ **exports** zur Begleichung von Auslandsschulden dienende Exporte.
unrescinded *(contract)* noch in Kraft, unwiderrufen.
unreserve Freimütigkeit, Offenheit.
unreserved rückhaltlos, uneingeschränkt, *(seat)* nicht im voraus bestellt;
~ **assent** uneingeschränkte Zustimmung; ~ **compliance** volle Zustimmung.

unreservedly ohne Einschränkung;
to speak ~ völlig offen reden; **to trust s. o. ~** jem. uneingeschränktes Vertrauen schenken.
unresisted widerstandslos.
unresolved problem ungelöstes Problem.
unrest innerer Aufruhr, Unruhe, *(industry)* Unzufriedenheit, Unruhen;
articulate ~ spürbare Unruhe; **labo(u)r ~** Arbeiterunruhen; **political ~** politische Unruhen; **student ~** Studentenunruhen; **~ on the foreign currency markets** Unruhe an den Devisenmärkten;
to create social ~ soziale Unruhen hervorrufen.
unrestored nicht zurückerstattet (zurückgegeben).
unrestrained hemmungslos, zügellos.
unrestraint Zügellosigkeit, Hemmungslosigkeit.
unrestricted unbeschränkt, freizügig, *(without speed limit)* ohne Geschwindigkeitsbeschränkung;
~ **sampling** unbegrenzte Zufallsstichprobe.
unreturned nicht zurückgekehrt, *(parl.)* nicht wieder gewählt.
unrevised nicht durchgesehen (revidiert).
unrevoked nicht widerrufen (aufgehoben).
unrewarded unbelohnt.
unrighteous sentence ungerechtfertigtes Urteil.
unripe unreif, unausgereift, *(US sl.)* noch nicht trocken hinter den Ohren.
unrivalled konkurrenzlos.
unroadworthy *(car)* nicht fahrbereit (verkehrssicher), verkehrsuntüchtig.
unrouted telegram Telegramm ohne Leitvermerk.
unruled *(paper)* unliniert.
unruly and dangerous *(animal)* wild und gefährlich.
unsafe *(enterprise)* unsolide;
~ **paper** *(stock exchange)* dubioses Papier.
unsaid unausgesprochen.
unsalable unverkäuflich, nicht einschlagend, *(nonnegotiable)* nicht börsenfähig;
to be ~ liegenbleiben;
~ **article** Ladenhüter; ~ **goods** schwer verkäufliche Waren.
unsalaried unbesoldet, ehrenamtlich;
~ **clerk** Volontär; ~ **employment** unbezahlte Beschäftigung.
unsal(e)able unverkäuflich, nicht einschlagend, *(nonnegotiable)* nicht börsenfähig;
to be ~ liegenbleiben;
~ **article** Ladenhüter.
unsaleableness Unverkäuflichkeit.
unsanctioned nicht genehmigt.
unsanitary unhygienisch.
unsatisfactory unbefriedigend, ungenügend, unzulänglich;
~ **quality** unzureichende Qualität.
unsatisfied *(creditor)* nicht befriedigt, *(unpaid)* unbezahlt;
~ **debts** unbezahlte Schulden; ~ **execution** erfolglose Zwangsvollstreckung; ~ **judgment** noch nicht vollstrecktes Urteil.
unsatisfying letter unbefriedigender Brief.
unsavo(u)ry|reputation miserabler Ruf; ~ **scandal** widerlicher Skandal; ~ **story** Skandalgeschichte.
unsay *(v.)* widerrufen, sich distanzieren;
say and ~ bald ja, bald nein sagen.
unscathed völlig unversehrt.
unscheduled *(train, US)* außerplanmäßig.
unscholarly unwissenschaftlich.
unschooled nicht ausgebildet.
unscientific unwissenschaftlich.
unscramble *(v.)* in seine Bestandteile zerlegen, *(telegram)* entschlüsseln, dechiffrieren;
~ **a business concern** Konzern entflechten; ~ **the steel industry** Verstaatlichung der Stahlindustrie wieder aufheben.
unscreened ungeschützt, *(el.)* nicht abgeschirmt.
unseal *(v.)* entsiegeln, Siegel erbrechen, *(fig.)* freien Lauf lassen;
~ **s. one's eyes** jem. die Augen öffnen; ~ **a letter** Brief öffnen; ~ **s. one's lips** j. zum Sprechen bringen; ~ **a mystery** Geheimnis enthüllen.
unsealed *(fig.)* unverbindlich, unversiegelt, offen.
unsealing Siegelabnahme.
unsearched *(luggage)* nicht durchsucht.
unseasonable nicht der Jahreszeit entsprechend, *(fig.)* unangebracht, ungünstig;
at an ~ hour zu unpassender Zeit.
unseasonableness of a discussion Unangebrachtheit einer Diskussion.
unseasoned nicht ausgereift, *(fig.)* grün, unerfahren, *(wood)* nicht abgelagert.

unseat (v.) | a minister Minister stürzen; ~ an official Beamten von seinem Posten entfernen, (parliamentary seat) des Abgeordnetensitzes für verlustig erklären;

unseated (pol.) aus dem Parlament ausgeschlossen, ohne Mandat;
to be ~ at the general election seinen Sitz bei den Parlamentswahlen verlieren;
~ land (US) ungenutztes Grundstück.

unseaworthiness Seeuntüchtigkeit.

unseaworthy seeuntüchtig, nicht seetüchtig.

unseconded motion nicht unterstützter Antrag.

unsecured unbefestigt, (loan) unbesichert, nicht abgesichert (sichergestellt), ohne Deckung;
~ account unbesichertes Kontokorrentkonto; ~ claim (bankruptcy) Masseanspruch; ~ credit Personal-, Blankokredit, offener Kredit; ~ creditor nicht sichergestellter Gläubiger, Massegläubiger; ~ debentures nicht besicherte Obligationen; ~ debt nicht bevorrechtigte Konkursforderung, Masseschuld; ~ liability unbesicherte Verbindlichkeit, (bankruptcy) gewöhnliche Konkursforderung; ~ loan unbesichertes Darlehn, Blankokredit, nicht garantierte Anleihe; ~ note unbesicherter Schuldschein; ~ overdraft unbesicherter Kontokorrentkredit.

unseemly ungebührlich, unziemlich.

unseen nicht vorbereiteter Prüfungstext;
~ (a.) ground uneinsehbares Gelände, toter Winkel; ~ radio audience unsichtbare Rundfunkhörer.

unseizable unpfändbar.

unseized nicht gepfändet.

unseparated ungeteilt.

unserviceable gebrauchsunfähig, untauglich, unzweckmäßig.

unset (precious stone) ungefaßt, (time) unbestimmt.

unsettle (v.) aus dem gewohnten Gleis bringen.

unsettled (account) nicht ausgeglichen (abgerechnet, abgeschlossen, abgewickelt), (without domicile) ohne festen Wohnsitz, (land) unbesiedelt, (market) uneinheitlich, schwankend, unbeständig, veränderlich, (not fixed in position) in unsicherer Stellung, noch nicht selbständig, unversorgt, (pol.) schwankend, (undecided) unerledigt, (unpaid) unbezahlt, unbeglichen;
~ bill unbezahlte (unerledigte) Rechnung; ~ estate noch nicht regulierte (auseinandergesetzte) Erbschaft; ~ region unbesiedelte Gegend; ~ state of the market Unsicherheit der Börse; ~ weather unbeständiges (veränderliches) Wetter.

unshaded nicht verdunkelt.

unshaken unerschütterlich, standhaft.

unsharp impression unscharfer Druck.

unsheathe (v.) one's sword vom Leder ziehen.

unsheltered schutzlos, obdachlos;
~ industry zollpolitisch nicht geschützte Industriezweige.

unship (v.) ausladen, löschen, (passengers) ausbooten;
~ s. o. (fig.) j. ausbooten.

unshipping, unshipment Ausladen, Löschen.

unshrinkable (material) nicht einlaufend.

unsight, to buy s. th. etw. unbesehen kaufen.

unsighted, still (ship) noch nicht in Sicht.

unsightly advertisements in the country die Landschaft verschandelnde Reklame.

unsigned nicht unterschrieben, ungezeichnet, ohne Unterschrift.

unsilt (v.) ausbaggern.

unsinkable nicht sinkend, (not to be amortized) untilgbar.

unsized nicht nach Größen sortiert.

unskilled ungelernt, ungeschickt;
~ labo(u)r Handarbeit, mechanische Arbeit; ~ labo(u)rer ungelernter Arbeiter, Hilfsarbeiter; ~ manpower ungelernte Arbeitskräfte; ~ workman ungelernter Arbeiter, Hilfsarbeiter.

unskimmed milk Vollmilch.

unsnarl (v.) entwirren.

unsociable ungesellig, nicht umgänglich, reserviert, ungastlich, unwirtlich.

unsocial unsozial, asozial, gesellschaftsfeindlich.

unsold nicht verkauft, unverkauft;
subject to being ~ Zwischenverkauf vorbehalten;
~ copies Remittenden.

unsolemn formlos, schlicht;
~ war ohne Kriegserklärung begonnener Krieg; ~ will Testament ohne Bestellung eines Testamentsvollstreckers.

unsolicited freiwillig, unaufgefordert, unverlangt;
~ testimonial kostenlose Werbeaussage.

unsolid unsicher, (fig.) unbegründet.

unsophisticated ungekünstelt, nicht affektiert, einfach.

unsorted unsortiert.

unsought, to come unvermutet erscheinen.

unsound unzuverlässig, unsolide, unreell, (fruit) verdorben, verfault, (goods) fehlerhaft, schlecht, (unhealthy) ungesund, krank;
~ argument nicht stichhaltiges Argument; ~ credit zweifelhafter Ruf; ~ doctrine Irrlehre; ~ finance finanzielle Mißwirtschaft; ~ financial conditions ungesunde Finanzlage; ~ food ungesunde Nahrungsmittel; ~ ice brüchiges Eis; ~ investment Fehlanlage, -investition; of ~ mind (US) geistesgestört, -schwach, -krank; incurably of ~ mind (US) unheilbar geisteskrank; ~ reason nicht stichhaltiger Grund; ~ sleep unruhiger Schlaf.

unsounded nicht ausgelotet.

unsoundness Unzuverlässigkeit;
~ of mind (US) Unzurechnungsfähigkeit, Geistesschwäche;
incurable ~ of mind (US) unheilbare Geisteskrankheit.

unsparing reichlich, uneingeschränkt;
to be ~ in one's efforts keine Mühe scheuen.

unsparingly nicht kleinlich.

unspecialized nicht [fachlich] ausgebildet.

unspecified nicht spezifiziert.

unspeculative zuverlässig, ohne Risiko.

unspent nicht verausgabt, nicht ausgegeben.

unspoilt unverdorben, unbeschädigt.

unspoken of unerwähnt.

unspotted reputation fleckenloser Ruf.

unstable unsicher, nicht fest, (fig.) schwankend, labil;
seasonally ~ industries saisonabhängige Industriezweige.

unstamped ungestempelt, nicht verstempelt, (not prepaid) unfrankiert, unfrei.

unstatesmanlike eines Staatsmannes unwürdig, politisch unklug.

unstatutable satzungs-, verfassungswidrig.

unsteadfast wankelmütig, flatterhaft.

unsteadiness (market) Unbeständigkeit.

unsteady unstet, schwankend, (market) unbeständig, schwankend;
~ output schwankende Produktionsziffern.

unstinting help großzügige Hilfe.

unstock (v.) a store Lager räumen.

unstocked ohne Lagerbestand.

unstored nicht auf Lager, (without supply) ohne Vorräte, nicht verproviantiert.

unstrained (fig.) ungezwungen, natürlich.

unstring (v.) one's purse seinen Geldbeutel zücken.

unstuck (envelope) aufgegangen;
to have come ~ sich nicht realisiert haben.

unstudied unbewandert, nicht einstudiert, (fig.) ungezwungen, ungekünstelt.

unstylish unmodern.

unsubscribed nicht unterschrieben, (magazine) nicht abonniert, (new issue) ungezeichnet.

unsubsidized nicht subventioniert, ohne Staatszuschuß.

unsubstantial unwesentlich, unwichtig.

unsubstantiated aus der Luft gegriffen, unbegründet;
~ claim nicht substantiierte Forderung.

unsuccessful ohne Erfolg, erfolglos, fruchtlos, (election) nicht gewählt;
to be ~ (lawsuit) verlieren;
~ applicant zurückgewiesener Bewerber; ~ candidate durchgefallener Prüfling; ~ party unterlegene (unterliegende) Prozeßpartei; ~ takeoff Fehlstart.

unsuitable unzulässig, unangemessen, ungeeignet, unpassend, zweckwidrig, nicht verwendbar;
to be ~ for a post für eine Stellung nicht in Betracht kommen.

unsuitableness Unangemessenheit, Ungeeignetheit.

unsuited ungeeignet.

unsummoned nicht vorgeladen.

unsupplied unversorgt, (mil.) ohne Nachschub;
~ remedy nicht abgestellter Mangel.

unsupported unbestätigt.

unsuspected nicht unter Verdacht stehend, unverdächtig.

unsuspecting arglos.

unsustainable (argument) unhaltbar.

unswerving loyalty unerschütterliche Loyalität.

unsworn (witness) nicht vereidigt, unvereidigt;
~ testimony unbeeidigte Zeugenaussage.

untainted fehlerlos, fleckenlos, (food) unverdorben.

untalented unbegabt, untalentiert.

untangle (v.) aus einer schwierigen Lage befreien.

untapped unerschlossen, unangezapft;
~ resources noch nicht in Anspruch genommene Hilfsquellen (Bodenschätze).

untarnished makellos.

untasted book noch nicht gelesenes Buch.

untaxable nicht besteuerungsfähig, steuerfrei;
~ **costs** vom Gericht noch nicht festgesetzte Kosten.

untaxed unbesteuert, steuerfrei;
~ **reserves** steuerfreie Rückstellungen.

untenable | theory unhaltbare Theorie; ~ **view** nicht vertretbare Ansicht.

untenantable unbewohnbar, unvermietbar.

untenanted *(not inhabited)* unbewohnt, *(not let)* unvermietet, unverpachtet.

untested nicht überprüft;
~ **prices** *(stock exchange)* bei fast keinem Umsatz verzeichnete Kurse.

unthrift Unwirtschaftlichkeit, Verschwendung.

unthrifty unwirtschaftlich, verschwenderisch.

untidy room unaufgeräumtes Zimmer.

untied nicht gebunden.

untimely unzeitgemäß, zur Unzeit;
~ **remark** unangebrachte Bemerkung.

untitled unberechtigt, ohne Rechtsanspruch.

untold wealth märchenhafter Reichtum.

untouched unangerührt, unangetastet, unversehrt, *(photo)* unretuschiert;
~ **provisions** unangetastete Vorräte; ~-**upon subject** nicht angeschnittenes Thema.

untraceable nicht ausfindig zu machen, unauffindbar.

untrained unausgebildet, ungeübt;
~ **labor** *(Br.)* ungelernte Arbeitskräfte.

untrammel(l)ed ungehindert.

untransferable nicht übertragbar, unübertragbar.

untranslated nicht übersetzt.

untransportable nicht transportfähig.

untravel(l)ed nicht weit herumgekommen, *(fig.)* mit engem Horizont.

untried unerprobt, ungeprüft, *(legal sense)* nicht verhört (abgeurteilt, entschieden), nicht vor Gericht gestellt;
~ **on** nicht anprobiert.

untrue unrichtig, unwahr, *(not faithful)* unehrlich, falsch;
~ **statement** wissentlich falsche Angaben, falsche Aussage.

untrustworthiness Unzuverlässigkeit, Unsolidität, mangelnde Glaubwürdigkeit.

untrustworthy unzuverlässig, unsolide.

untutored ungeschult, ungebildet.

unused unausgenutzt, nicht gebraucht;
~ **capacity** brachliegende Kapazitäten; ~ **capital** brachliegendes Kapital; ~ **portion of a credit** nicht in Anspruch genommener Teil eines Kredits; ~ **room** unbenutztes Zimmer; ~ **ticket** nicht benutzte Fahrkarte.

unusual | circumstance ungewöhnliche Umstände; ~ **danger** Gefahrenquelle; ~ **size** ungewöhnliches Format.

unvaccinated nicht schutzgeimpft.

unvaluable unschätzbar.

unvalued unbewertet, nicht bewertet (geschätzt), *(policy)* untaxiert, ohne Wertangabe;
~ **policy** Police ohne Wertangabe; ~ **shares (stocks,** *US)* Aktien ohne Nennwert, Quotenaktien.

unvarnished | account ungeschminkter Bericht; ~ **truth** unverblümte (ungeschminkte) Wahrheit.

unveil *(v.)* **a monument** Denkmal enthüllen.

unveiling ceremony Enthüllungsfeier.

unveilment of a monument Enthüllung eines Denkmals, Denkmalsenthüllung.

unventilated nicht gelüftet, ungelüftet, *(fig.)* unbesprochen, nicht zur Sprache gebracht.

unverified unbestätigt.

unversed unbewandert.

unvictual(l)ed ohne Proviant, nicht mit Lebensmitteln versorgt.

unvote *(v.)* durch spätere Abstimmung aufheben.

unvouched unverbürgt, unbestätigt.

unwarrantable untragbar, unhaltbar, nicht vertretbar.

unwarranted unberechtigt, ungerechtfertigt, *(without guarantee)*, unverbürgt, ohne Gewähr (Garantie).

unwashed unsauber, schmutzig;
the great ~ *(coll.)* der Pöbel.

unwatered trocken, *(alcohol)* unverdünnt, *(capital)* unverwässert.

unweighted ungewogen, *(fig.)* unüberlegt;
~ **index** unbewerteter Index.

unwholesome ungesund, gesundheitsschädlich;
~ **food** nicht zum Verzehr geeignete Lebensmittel.

unwilling widerwillig;
to become an ~ **witness** ungewollt Zeuge werden.

unwillingness to invest Investitionsunlust.

unwitnessed unbeobachtet, *(document)* ohne Zeugenunterschriften.

unwittingly unwissentlich, unbeabsichtigt.

unworkable nicht verwendungsfähig, *(machine)* nicht betriebsfähig, *(plan)* undurchführbar.

unworked nicht bearbeitet;
~ **coal** anstehende Kohle.

unworn ungetragen.

unworthy unwürdig, ohne Wert;
~ **of credit** unglaubwürdig;
to be ~ **of respect** keine Achtung verdienen.

unwrap *(v.)* **a parcel** Paket auspacken.

unwritten nicht schriftlich niedergelegt;
~ **agreement** mündliche Abmachung; ~ **constitution** ungeschriebene Verfassung; ~ **law** ungeschriebenes Gesetz, Gewohnheitsrecht.

unwrought unbearbeitet, unverarbeitet, roh;
~ **goods** Rohstoffe.

unyielding unnachgiebig, unbeugsam.

up *(bus)* in die Stadt fahrender Bus, *(elevation)* Bodenerhebung, Anhöhe, *(prospective buyer, sl.)* Kaufinteressent, *(rising price)* Preisanstieg, *(stock exchange)* Kursanstieg, steigender Kurs, *(upstart, coll.)* Glückspilz, Emporkömmling, *(upward course)* Aufwärtsbewegung, Aufstieg;
on the ~ **and** ~ *(coll.)* immer weiter vorankommend, in unaufhörlichem Aufstieg;
~ **in business activity** Konjunkturanstieg; ~ **in the cost of money** Geldverteuerung; ~**s and downs** Glanzzeiten und Tiefpunkte, Steigen und Fallen; ~**s and downs of employment** Schwankungen der Beschäftigungsziffer; ~ **in inflation** Inflationszunahme; ~**s and downs in life** das Auf und Ab im Leben, Höhen und Tiefen eines Lebens; ~**s and downs of the market** Kursschwankungen; **the** ~ **and** ~ der ständige Fortschritt;
~ *(a.)* vorankommend, *(balloon)* aufgeflogen, *(college, Br.)* im College, am Studienort, *(mar.)* luvwärts, gegen den Wind, *(mind)* erregt, durcheinander, *(river)* angeschwollen, *(stock exchange)* hoch [im Kurs], *(time)* abgelaufen, zu Ende;
2 P ~ *(stock exchange)* 2 Pence höher; ~ **and about** *(patient)* wieder auf dem Damm; ~ **in the bucks** *(sl.)* stinkreich; ~ **the country** landeinwärts; ~ **the creek** *(sl.)* glücklos, in Schwierigkeiten; ~ **and doing before day** *(coll.)* schon vor Tagesanbruch auf den Beinen; ~-**and-down** *(US coll.)* offen, ehrlich; ~ **from the ground** von Grund auf; ~ **from my youth** seit meiner Jugend; **from 5 dollars** ~ von fünf Dollar aufwärts; **gone** ~ *(sl.)* pleite; ~ **hill and down dale** über Berg und Tal; ~ **the river** flußaufwärts, *(coll.)* im Kittchen; ~ **the street** die Straße hinauf; ~ **to ...** *(account)* abgeschlossen am ...; ~ **to the chin** bis ans Kinn; **not** ~ **to expectations** nicht den Erwartungen entsprechend; ~ **to and including 1st March** bis einschließlich 1. März; ~ **to the knocker** *(sl.)* prima; ~ **to par** *(fig.)* auf dem Posten, auf der Höhe; ~ **the road** in der Nähe; **not yet** ~ **to the ropes** noch nicht im Bilde; ~ **to standard** vollwertig; ~ **to strength** in voller Stärke; ~ **to town** *(Br.)* nach London; ~ **a tree** *(sl.)* in der Klemme; ~ **and** ~ *(sl.)* äußerst ehrenwert; ~ **for a week** *(Br.)* eine Woche in London;
~ *(v.)* *(price, production)* erhöhen;
~ **one's share of the market** seinen Marktanteil erhöhen; ~ **and ask s. o.** j. plötzlich fragen;
to act ~ **to** sich danach richten; **to add** ~ zusammenzählen; **to be** ~ hoch im Kurse stehen, *(fig.)* an der Spitze sein, *(parl.)* Ferien machen, *(in uproars)* sich in Aufruhr befinden; **to be brought** ~ *(case)* vor Gericht kommen; **to be** ~ **again** wieder obenauf sein; **to be** ~ **against bankruptcy** vom völligen Bankrott bedroht sein; **to be** ~ **against a hard job** vor einer schwierigen Aufgabe stehen; **to be** ~ **against the law** mit dem Gesetz in Konflikt geraten sein; **to be** ~ **against opposition** auf Widerstand stoßen; **to be** ~ **one's alley** in einer Sache ganz zu Hause (ganz in seinem Fach) sein; **to be** ~ **for** vorgeladen sein; **to be** ~ **for auction** zur Versteigerung anstehen; **to be** ~ **for cash** [voll] bei Kasse sein; **to be** ~ **before the High Court of Admiralty** vor dem Seegerichtshof verhandelt werden; **to be** ~ **for discussions** zur Diskussion anstehen; **to be** ~ **for election** auf der Wahlliste stehen; **to be** ~ **for examination** sich einer Prüfung unterziehen; **to be** ~ **before the magistrate** vor den Schnellrichter kommen; **to be** ~ **for sale** zum Verkauf stehen; **to be** ~ **for trial** vor Gericht stehen, *(case)* verhandelt werden, *(person)* vor Gericht kommen; **to be** ~ **on a subject** *(coll.)* in einem Fach auf der Höhe (beschlagen) sein; **to be** ~ **to s. th.** etw. vorhaben (im Schilde

führen); **not to be ~ to his last book** mit seinem letzten Buch nicht zu vergleichen sein; **to be ~ to no good** überhaupt nichts taugen; **not to be ~ to a job** sich für eine Arbeit nicht eignen; **not to be ~ to much** nicht viel taugen; **to be ~ to s. one's tricks** jem. auf die Schliche kommen; **to be right ~ there** ganz oben auf der Liste stehen; **to be still going ~** *(prices)* immer noch steigen; **to be still ~ with one's competitors** seinen Konkurrenten noch immer gewachsen sein; **to be high ~ in school** *(Br.)* in der Schule zu den Besten gehören; **to be well ~** weit fortgeschritten sein; **to draw ~** vorfahren; **to feel ~ to** sich in der Lage fühlen; **to get ~ in the world** im Leben vorankommen; **to get ~ to s. o.** mit jem. Schritt halten; **to go ~** *(prices)* steigen, in die Höhe gehen; **to go ~ to Oxford** die Universität in Oxford beziehen; **to hunt ~ a new room** neues Zimmer ausfinding machen; **to live ~ to** einer Vorschrift entsprechend handeln; **to live ~ to a promise** einem Versprechen nachkommen; **to live three floors ~** im dritten Stock wohnen; **to look ~ and down for it** in allen Ecken und Winkeln danach suchen; **to sail ~ as near as possible** so nahe wie möglich heranfahren; **to spend ~** verbrauchen; **to stay ~ for the vacations** *(Br.)* in den Ferien am Studienort bleiben; **to walk ~ the road** Straße entlangmarschieren; **to walk ~ and down the station platform** auf dem Bahnsteig herumlaufen; **to work one's way ~** sich hocharbeiten;
parliament is ~ das Parlament hat sich vertagt;
~ line in die Stadt führende Bahnlinie; **~ platform** Bahnsteig für Stadtzüge; **~ stroke** Aufwärtsstrich.
up-and-coming *(US)* unternehmenslustig, rührig, auf Draht;
~ young M.P. vielversprechender Nachwuchsparlamentarier.
un-and-doing *(Br.)* unternehmend, agil, aktiv.
up-and-down looks kritisch musternde Blicke.
up-to-date bis zum heutigen Tag, den neuesten Erkenntnissen entsprechend, *(books)* auf dem laufenden, *(fashion)* fortschrittlich, zeitgemäß, modern, *(subject)* aktuell;
highly ~ hochmodern;
to bring ~ auf den neusten Stand (à jour) bringen, *(fashion)* modernisieren;
~ house modernes Haus.
up-to-dateness Modernität, Aktualität.
up-to-the-minute sehr modern.
upbear *(fig.)* hochhalten, unterstützen.
upbeat optimistisch *(book, film)* mit Happy-End.
upborne unterstützt.
upbraid *(v.)* s. o. jem. Vorwürfe machen.
upbraiding Vorwurf, Tadel.
upbringing, good gute Erziehung.
upbuild *(v.)* aufbauen.
upcast shaft Wetter-, Luftschacht.
upcoming plays bevorstehende Aufführungen.
upcountry Landesinnere;
~ (a.) binnenländisch, landeinwärts;
~ district im Landesinnern gelegener Bezirk.
upcurrent Aufwind.
update *(v.)* auf den neusten Stand bringen;
~ the sales forces Verkaufsstab mit den neuesten Informationen versehen;
~ dictionary Wörterbuch auf dem neuesten Stand.
updating of inventory Lagerwirtschaft.
updraft Aufwind.
upend *(v.)* hochkant stellen.
upgrade Aufsteigen, Aufstieg, Steigung;
~ (v.) *(US)* höher einstufen, befördern, *(interchange inferior product)* minderwertiges Erzeugnis ersetzen;
~ economically auf einen wirtschaftlichen Höchststand bringen; **~ slum housing** Elendsgebiete sanieren;
to be on the ~ im Aufstieg sein, *(business)* sich erholen, *(price)* steigen, zur Hausse tendieren.
upgraded area saniertes Baugebiet.
upgrading Höhereinstufung;
~ of income Einkommensanstieg; **~ of management development efforts** erhöhte Anstrengungen zur Verbesserung der Führungsmethoden; **~ of talented students** Begabtenförderung;
~ course *(US)* Förderungskursus.
upgrowth Entwicklung, Wachstum, Wachstumsprozeß.
upheaval vulkanische Bodenerhebung, *(fig.)* Erhebung, Aufstand, Umsturz;
political ~ politischer Aufstand; **social ~** soziale Umwälzung.
uphill bergauf, aufwärts;
~ road ansteigende Straße; **~ struggle** harter Kampf; **~ task** schwierige Aufgabe.

uphold *(v.)* aufrechterhalten, behaupten, bestätigen, billigen, *(building, Br.)* instand halten, *(prices)* stützen;
~ a cause Sache vertreten; **~ a conduct** Verhalten billigen; **~ a conviction** Schuldspruch (Strafurteil) bestätigen; **~ a decision on appeal** Entscheidung in zweiter Instanz (als Berufungsinstanz) bestätigen; **~ an objection** einem Widerspruch stattgeben; **~ opposition** Widerstand fortsetzen; **~ a right** Recht geltend machen; **~ a sentence** Urteil bestätigen.
upholder Verteidiger, Hüter, Stütze;
~ of civilization Kulturträger; **~ of public order** Hüter der öffentlichen Ordnung.
upholster *(v.)* aufpolstern, *(furnish with hangings)* tapezieren.
upholstered goods Polsterwaren.
upholsterer Polsterer, Tapezierer, Dekorateur.
upholstery furniture Polstermöbel.
upkeep [Aufrecht]erhaltung, Instandhaltung, Unterhaltung, *(cost of repair)* Instandsetzungs-, Unterhaltungskosten;
current ~ laufende Unterhaltung;
~ of furniture Instandhaltung des Mobiliars; **~ and improvements** Unterhaltungsaufwendungen und Instandhaltungskosten; **~ of roads** Straßenunterhaltung;
~ (v.) instand halten.
upland Hochland, höher gelegenes Land;
~s Ufergrundstücke.
uplift Bodenerhebung, *(economics)* Konjunkturanstieg, *(fig., US)* moralischer Auftrieb;
~ (v.) s. o. *(US)* j. moralisch aufrichten.
uplifted hand Schwurhand.
upmarket | regions höher entwickelte Marktgebiete;
to move ~ sich spezialisierte Märkte suchen.
upper *(sleeping car)* oberes Bett;
~ (a.) höhergelegen, *(fig.)* höherstehend, übergeordnet;
to be on one's ~s *(coll.)* total abgebrannt sein;
~ beds *(mining)* Hangendschichten; **~-bracket** in der höheren Einkommensklasse; **~-case** *(print.)* in Versalien; **~-case letters** Groß-, Versalbuchstaben, Versalien; **~ circle** *(theater)* zweiter Rang; **the ~ classes** Oberschicht; **~ classman** *(US)* Student im 3. oder 4. Jahr, höheres Semester; **~ coat** Überrock, Oberkleidung; **~ corner** obere Ecke; **~ crust** *(coll.)* Spitzen der Gesellschaft; **~-crust** vornehm, aristokratisch; **~ deck** Oberdeck; **~ dog** *(sl.)* Überlegener; **to get the ~ hand** Oberhand gewinnen; **~ House** *(parl.)* Oberhaus; **~-income section of a city** höhere Einkommensgegend einer Stadt; **~ intervention point** oberer Interventionspunkt; **~ limit** Obergrenze; **~ price limit** Höchstpreis[grenze]; **~ school** Oberschule; **~ side** *(print.)* Schöndruckseite; **~ stor(e)y** obere Etage, Oberstock, *(fig.)* Oberstübchen; **~ ten** *(fig.)* die oberen Zehntausend; **~ world** Erdoberfläche.
uppermost am höchsten gelegen, *(highest in rank)* höchststehend;
to come ~ Oberhand gewinnen.
uprate *(v.)* **a pension regularly in line with earnings** Rente automatisch den Bruttolöhnen anpassen.
upright senkrechte Stellung, *(fig.)* Aufrichtigkeit, Redlichkeit;
~ (a.) aufrecht, senkrecht, hoch aufgerichtet, gerade, *(fig.)* aufrichtig, ehrlich, anständig;
to be ~ in one's business dealings sich in Geschäftsdingen anständig verhalten;
keep ~! *(on a case)* nicht stürzen!;
~ sight and across Hochformat; **~ size** Hochformat.
uprise Anstieg, Aufstieg;
~ (v.) sich erheben;
~ in arms bewaffneten Aufstand machen.
uprising Volkserhebung, Aufstand, Putsch;
to touch off a national ~ zu einer nationalen Erhebung führen.
uproar Aufruhr, Tumult, Krawall, Durcheinander;
to end in an ~ tumultarisches Ende finden; **to make an ~** Aufruhr anstiften.
uproarious tumultarisch, *(applause)* tosend.
uproot *(v.) s. o.* j. aus seiner gewohnten Umgebung reißen.
upset Umstoßen, Umwerfen, *(boat)* Kentern, *(car)* Umfallen, -stürzen, *(difference of opinion)* Meinungsverschiedenheit, Streit, *(topsy-turvydom)* Durcheinander, Verwirrung;
stomach ~ Magenverstimmung;
~ (v.) umwerfen, umkippen, *(fig.)* vereiteln, zunichtemachen;
~ s. one's applecart *(coll.)* jds. Pläne zum Scheitern bringen; **~ a boat** Boot zum Kentern bringen; **~ a car** Auto umkippen; **~ the government** Regierung stürzen; **~ the enemy's plans** feindliche Pläne durcheinanderbringen; **~ one's stomach** sich den Magen verderben;
~ (a.) umgeworfen, umgekippt, umgestürzt, *(fig.)* verwirrt, aufgebracht, durcheinander, *(price)* festgesetzt;
to be easily ~ emotionally sich leicht aufregen;

~ price *(auction)* Mindest-, Ausgangsgebot, *(bankruptcy proceedings)* niedrigster Zuschlagswert, *(foreclosure proceedings)* Anschlagspreis, *(salesman)* Preisuntergrenze.

upshift *(car)* Hochschalten.

upshot Schlußergebnis, Ausgang, Fazit.

upside obere Seite, Oberseite, *(Br.)* Bahnsteig für nach London fahrende Züge;

to be **~ with** s. o. mit jem. quitt sein;

~-down verkehrt herum, drunter und drüber, vollkommen durcheinander; **to turn a house ~ down** alles auf den Kopf stellen; **~-down position** *(airplane)* Rückenlage; **~-down world** verkehrte Welt; **~ potential** Aufstiegsmöglichkeit, *(stock exchange)* Kursauftriebsmöglichkeiten.

upsides *(Br., coll.)* quitt;

to get **~ with** s. o. mit jem. abrechnen.

upspring *(v.)* in die Höhe schießen.

upstage *(US)* Hinterland;

~ *(a.) (backward, coll.)* rückständig, *(snobby)* hochnäsig, *(theater)* im Hintergrund der Bühne.

upstairs Obergeschoß, oberes Stockwerk;

~ *(a.)* in einem oberen Stockwerk, oben;

to go ~ *(plane, sl.)* steigen; **to have got nothing ~** *(sl.)* nichts im Gehirnkasten haben; **to kick** s. o. **~** j. befördern, wegloben;

~ corridor oberer Flur; **~ room** oben gelegenes Zimmer, Zimmer im oberen Stock.

upstart Parvenü, Emporkömmling, Neureicher, *(newcomer)* Neuling;

~ *(a.)* emporgekommen, arrogant;

~ official von unten hochgestiegener Beamter; **~ pride** Bauernstolz.

upstate *(US)* Hinterland.

upstater *(US)* Provinzbewohner, Hinterwäldler.

upstream loan Darlehn der Tochter- an die Muttergesellschaft.

upstroke of a piston Kolbenhub.

upsurge steiler Anstieg, Ansteigen, Auftriebstendenz;

~ in consumption Verbrauchswelle; **~ in housing** Auftrieb in der Wohnungsbauwirtschaft, Wohnungsbaukonjunktur; **~ in imports** rasanter Einfuhranstieg; **~ of interest in** erhöhtes Interesse an; **~ in population** rapide Bevölkerungszunahme; **~ in prices** Preisanstieg, -auftrieb; **~ in production** rasanter Produktionsanstieg; **~ in rates** kräftige Tariferhöhung; **~ in sales** steiler Umsatzanstieg.

upswing Aufstieg, wirtschaftlicher Aufschwung, konjunktureller Auftrieb (Aufschwung), Auftriebstendenz, Konjunkturauftrieb;

cyclical ~ Konjunkturaufschwung; **economic ~** Konjunkturanstieg; **home-made ~** selbstbewirkter Konjunkturaufschwung; **seasonal ~** Saisonaufschwung;

to be on the ~ Hochkonjunktur haben, wirtschaftlichen Aufschwung erleben;

~ phase Aufschwungsperiode; **~ years** Jahre wirtschaftlichen Aufschwungs.

uptake Auffassung, Begreifen, *(ventilation)* Steigrohr, -leitung;

to be quick on (in) the ~ schnell begreifen, rasche Auffassungsgabe haben; **to be slow in the ~** schwer von Begriff sein.

upthrow Umwälzung.

uptick in production Produktionsanstieg.

uptown im oberen Stadtteil, *(US)* im Wohnviertel gelegen.

uptrain *(Br.)* nach London fahrender Zug.

uptrend steigende Tendenz, Aufschwung, Aufwärtsentwicklung, konjunktureller Auftrieb, Aufwärtsbewegung;

cyclical ~ konjunktureller Auftrieb, Konjunkturaufschwung; **~ in cost** Kostenauftrieb; **~ of imports** Einfuhrbelebung; **~ in prices** Preisauftrieb, *(stock exchange)* Kursanstieg.

upturn Besserung, konjunktureller Aufschwung (Auftrieb), *(prices)* Aufwärtsbewegung, *(stock market)* Kursanstieg;

~ in business (in the business cycle) Geschäftsbelebung, Konjunkturanstieg, -aufschwung; **seasonal ~ in demand** saisonbedingter Auftragsanstieg; **~ in exports** Ausfuhrbelebung; **~ in prices** Preisauftrieb; **~ in quotations** Kursauftrieb, -steigerung; **~ in wages** Lohnanstieg.

upvaluation Aufwertung.

upvalue *(v.)* aufwerten.

upvaluer Aufwertungsanhänger.

upward *(fig.)* aufwärts, nach oben, *(up the hill)* bergauf, *(towards the interior)* in das Landesinnere, landeinwärts, *(prices)* steigend, anziehend, *(river)* stromaufwärts;

to climb ~ sich weiter entwickeln; **to go ~s** *(prices)* in die Höhe gehen;

to continue its ~ advance Aufwärtsbewegung fortsetzen; **~ business trend** konjunktureller Aufschwung, konjunkturelle

Aufwärtsbewegung, Konjunkturaufschwung, -anstieg; **sterling's ~ float** Aufwärtsbewegung des Pfundes; **~ movement** Aufwärtsbewegung, *(stock exchange)* Kursanstieg, -auftrieb, Steigen der Kurse; **cyclical ~ movement** konjunkturelle Aufwärtsbewegung; **~ movement of stocks** Anstieg der Aktienkurse; **~ phase** Konjunkturauftrieb, Auftriebstendenz; **~ pressure on wages** zunehmende Lohnbelastung; **to relieve the ~ pressure on sterling** Auftriebstendenz des Pfundes abschwächen; **~ price movement** Preisauftriebstendenz; **to slow down the ~ price trend** Preisauftrieb verlangsamen; **~ push** *(market)* Aufwärtsbewegung; **~ revaluation** Aufwertung; **~ spurts** Kurssprünge; **~ surge** Aufwärtsentwicklung; **~ surge of prices** preissteigernde Tendenz; **~ tendency** Aufwärtstendenz, Auftriebs-, Aufschwungs-, steigende [Kurs]tendenz; **~ tendency in prices** Preisauftrieb; **~ tendency of wages** Lohnauftrieb; **~ trend** steigende Konjunkturtendenz, konjunkturelle Auftriebstendenz; **to show hardly any further ~ trend** sich konjunkturell kaum ausweiten; **to slow down the ~ price trend** Preisauftrieb bremsen; **to take an ~ trend** *(prices)* nach oben tendieren.

upwind Gegenwind.

urban Stadtbewohner;

~ *(a.)* städtisch, verstädtert;

~ administration Stadtverwaltung; **~ affairs** städtische Angelegenheiten; **~ area** Stadtgebiet; **~ center** *(US)* **(centre, Br.)** städtisches Ballungsgebiet; **~ counsellor** Berater der Stadtverwaltung; **~ development** städtebauliche Entwicklung, Stadtsanierung; **~ district** [etwa] kreisangehörige Stadt, *(Br.)* Stadtbezirk; **~ district council** *(Br.)* Gemeinderat; **~ dweller** Stadtbewohner, Städter; **~ economics** industrielle Entwicklung einer Stadt; **~ expressway** *(US)* Stadtautobahn; **~ freeway** Stadtautobahn; **~ growth** Städtewachstum; **to control ~ growth** städtebauliche Entwicklung steuern; **~ guerrilla** Stadtguerilla; **~ homestead** *(US)* vollstreckungsgeschützte Heimstätte; **~ landscape** städtische Szenerie; **~ lighting** städtische Beleuchtung; **~ modernization** Städtemodernisierung; **~ motorway** *(Br.)* Stadtautobahn; **~ nation** Stadtvolk; **~ outmigration** *(US)* Stadtflucht; **~ planner** Städteplaner; **~ planning** Städteplanung; **~ population** Stadtbevölkerung; **~ program(me)** Städteprogramm; **~ rates** städtische Abgaben; **~ redevelopment** städtebauliche Erneuerung; **~ renewal** Städteerneuerung; **~ sanitary district** *(Br.)* dem Gesundheitsamt unterstehender Bezirk; **~ servitude** städtische Dienstbarkeit; **~ sprawl** Stadtausbreitung, Siedlungsbrei; **~ terrorism** Stadtguerillawesen; **~ terrorists** Stadtguerilla; **~ tramway** städtische Straßenbahn.

urbane weltmännisch, höflich, *(courteous)* liebenswürdig, verbindlich.

urbanity Weltgewandtheit, gute Umgangsformen.

urbanization Verstädterung, *(fig.)* Verfeinerung;

~ process Verstädterungsprozeß.

urbanize *(v.)* verstädtern, städtischen Charakter verleihen, *(manners)* verfeinern.

urbiculture Stadtplanung.

urge Drang, Antrieb;

creative ~ Schaffensdrang;

~ to buy Kaufwut; **~ to merge** Fusionsneigung; **~ to write** Schreibwut;

~ *(v.)* drängen, [an]mahnen, dringend auffordern, beschleunigen, dringend ersuchen, *(excite)* anspornen, erregen, *(insist)* hartnäckig darauf bestehen, nachdrücklich betonen, *(press hard)* drängen, treiben;

~ s. o. to accept an offer j. zur Annahme eines Angebots drängen; **~ every argument one can think of** jeden erdenklichen Einwand ins Treffen führen; **~ to buy** zum Kauf zureden; **~ fire** Feuer anfachen; **~ the necessity of a case** Dringlichkeit eines Falles hervorheben; **~ the need for economy** auf die Notwendigkeit zu sparen hinweisen; **~ payment** auf Zahlung drängen; **~ a petition** Petition überreichen; **~ on one's pupils the importance of hard work** seinen Schülern die Notwendigkeit, hart zu arbeiten, eindringlich darlegen; **~ s. o. to keep his promise** j. mahnen, sein Versprechen zu halten; **~ to revolt** zum Aufruhr anstacheln; **~ the workmen on** Arbeiter antreiben.

urged by necessity der Not gehorchend.

urgencies dringende Vorstellungen.

urgency Beschleunigung, dringende Notwendigkeit, [Vor]dringlichkeit, *(entreaty)* dringende Bitte (Aufforderung), *(parl., Br.)* Dringlichkeitsantrag;

in case of ~ im Dringlichkeitsfall; **of the utmost ~** äußerst dringend;

~ of a petitioner Hartnäckigkeit eines Bittstellers; **~ of poverty** drückende Armut;

to be a matter of great ~ äußerst dringlich sein.

urgent dringend, dringlich, eilig, unaufschiebbar, *(solicitous)* aufdringlich;

to be ~ with s. o. in j. dringen, j. drängen; **to be reported as ~** Dringlichkeitsvermerk tragen;

~ appeal dringender Appell; **to give ~ attention** vordringlich behandeln; **~ case** Dringlichkeitsfall; **~ creditor** drängender Gläubiger; **~ item** Eilsendung; **~ letter** eiliger Brief; **memorandum (note)** Dringlichkeitsvermerk; **~ message** eilige Nachricht; **~ need** vordringlicher Bedarf, dringende Notwendigkeit; **to be in ~ need of medical supplies** dringend der ärztlichen Versorgung bedürfen; **to be in ~ need of money** dringend Geld benötigen; **~ rate** *(telegraphic money order)* Eilzuschlag; **~ request** dringende Bitte; **at s. one's ~ request** auf jds. dringende Vorstellungen; **to deal with the most ~ things first** zuerst die dringendsten Fälle erledigen.

urn Urne.

usability [Gebrauchs]eignung, Brauchbarkeit.

usable brauchbar, benutzbar.

usage Brauch, Sitte, Gepflogenheit, Gewohnheit, *(customary mode of procedure)* übliches (herkömmliches) Verfahren, *(customary practice)* [Handels]brauch, Herkommen, Praxis, Usance, *(language)* Sprachgebrauch, *(manner of using)* Gebrauch, *(treatment)* Behandlung, Behandlungsweise;

in accordance with ~ handelsüblich;

business ~ kaufmännische Gepflogenheiten; **commercial ~** Handelsbrauch; **compulsory ~** Benutzungszwang; **English ~** englischer Sprachgebrauch; **fair ~** *(copyright)* zulässige Benutzung; **general ~** allgemeiner Brauch; **immemorial ~** Brauch seit Menschengedenken; **local ~** Ortsgebrauch; **mercantile ~** Kaufmannsbrauch; **ordinary ~** Verkehrssitte;

~ of the place Platzusance; **~ of the port** Hafenusance; **~ of trade** Handelsbrauch, Usance;

to be out of ~ nicht mehr gebräuchlich sein; **to influence social ~** gesellschaftliche Gepflogenheiten beeinflussen; **to meet with a harsh ~** grob behandelt werden; **to wear out under rough ~** *(machine)* bei unsachgemäßer Behandlung schnell kaputt gehen.

usance Usance, *(bill of exchange)* Zahlungs-, Wechselfrist, *(income)* Erträge;

according to ~ börsen-, handels-, usancenmäßig;

local ~ Ortsgebrauch.

use *(advantage)* Nutzen, Vorteil, *(capability of being used)* Brauchbarkeit, Verwendbarkeit, Verwendungszweck, *(custom)* Gewohnheit, Herkommen, Brauch, *(el.)* Entnahme, *(employment)* Gebrauch, Benutzung, Nutzbarmachung, Inanspruchnahme, Anwendung, Verwendung, *(realization)* Verwertung, *(usufruct)* Nutzung, Nutznießung, Nießbrauch, Nutzungsrecht;

fit for ~ betriebsfähig; **for ~** zum Gebrauch; **for daily ~** zum täglichen Gebrauch; **for home ~** zum Verbrauch im Inland; **for private ~** zum eigenen Gebrauch; **for the ~ and benefit of** zugunsten von; **for ~ or consumption** zum Ge- oder Verbrauch; **for ~ only in case of fire** nur bei Feuerausbruch zu benutzen; **for ~ of industrialization** für Industrialisierungszwecke; **for ~ in schools** für den Schulgebrauch; **for the ~ of teachers only** nur für Lehrer bestimmt; **in ~** üblich, gebräuchlich, in Mode; **in common ~** allgemein üblich (gebräuchlich); **no longer ~** nicht mehr gebräuchlich; **of no ~** unbrauchbar, zwecklos; **out of ~** veraltet, aus der Mode; **ready for ~** gebrauchsfertig; **under proper ~** bei ordnungsgemäßem Gebrauch;

adverse ~ mißbräuchliche Benutzung; **agricultural ~** landwirtschaftliche Nutzung; **cestui que ~** Treuhandbegünstigter auf Lebenszeit eines Dritten; **charitable ~** Wohltätigkeitszweck; **common ~** Gemeingebrauch; **constant ~** dauernder Gebrauch; **contingent ~** Anspruch auf zukünftige Nutzung, zukünftiger Nießbrauch; **continued ~** *(patent)* Weiterbenutzung; **cost-effective ~** kostensparende Benutzung; **daily ~** täglicher Gebrauch, *(book)* Handgebrauch; **domestic ~** Hausgebrauch; **economic ~** Nutzungsdauer; **exclusive ~** ausschließliche Benutzung, alleiniges Nutzungsrecht; **executed ~** gesetzlich berechtigter Gebrauch, *(conveyancing)* Besitz- und Nutzungseinräumung; **executory ~** aufschiebend bedingtes Nutzungsrecht; **existing ~** derzeitiger Verwendungszweck; **future ~** zukünftige Verwertung (Verwendung); **improper ~** unzulässiger Gebrauch; **industrial ~** gewerbliche Verwertung (Verwendung); **intended ~** vorgesehener Verwendungszweck; **joint ~** Mitbenutzung; **official ~** Dienstgebrauch; **ordinary ~** gewöhnlicher Gebrauch; **personal ~** persönlicher Bedarf, *(tenant)* Eigenbedarf; **pious ~s** seelsorgische Zwecke; **prior ~** vorherige Benutzung, Vorbenutzung; **productive ~** Gebrauchsüberlassung; **public ~** *(US)* Verwendung im öffentlichen Interesse; **resulting**

~ zeitlich beschränktes Nießbrauchrecht; **secondary ~** nachrangiges Nutzungsrecht; **shifting ~** gestaffeltes Nießbrauchrecht; **sole ~** alleiniges Benutzungsrecht; **springing ~** aufschiebend bedingtes Nutzungsrecht; **unauthorized ~** unbefugte Benutzung, widerrechtlicher Gebrauch;

~ of airfreight in delivery Auslieferung auf dem Luftfrachtwege; **~ of assets** Anlagennutzung; **~ of undue authority** Amtsmißbrauch; **~ of capacity** Kapazitätsausnutzung; **~ of capital** Kapitaleinsatz; **~ of a car for business** Autobenutzung für Geschäftszwecke; **~ of a company's car** Benutzung eines Dienstwagens; **~ of code** Kodebenutzung; **~ on a collective basis** gemeinwirtschaftliche Verwendung; **~ of company resources for the private gain of senior officials** Inanspruchnahme von Firmenmitteln für die privaten Bedürfnisse leitender Angestellter; **~ of credit** Kreditinanspruchnahme; **improper ~ of a firm's name** unbefugter Firmennamengebrauch; **~ of a fund** Inanspruchnahme eines Fonds; **~ of armed forces** Anwendung von Waffengewalt; **~ of force in self-protection** *(US)* Gewaltanwendung im Notwehrfall; **~ of funds** Mittelverwendung, Grundkapitalverwendung; **~ and habitation** Benutzung und Aufenthaltsrecht; **~ of land** Bodennutzung; **~ and occupancy** Gebrauch und Innehabung; **~ and occupation** Nutzung und Besitz; **~ of property** Grundstücks-, Eigentumsnutzung; **~ of a right** Ausübung eines Rechts; **~ of a road** Straßenbenutzung; **~s and customs of the sea** Seegewohnheiten, -gebräuche; **~ of streets** Straßenbenutzung; **~ of a sum of money** Verwendung einer Geldsumme; **~ of a title** Führung eines Titels; **~ of registered trademark** Warenzeichenbenutzung; **~ of troops** Einsatz von Truppen; **~ of one's voice** Stimmrechtsgebrauch; **~ and wont** Sitte und Gewohnheit, Verkehrssitte;

~ (v.) [ge]brauchen, benutzen, verwenden, *(employ)* anwenden, *(follow a practice)* gewohnheitsmäßig gebrauchen, *(raw material)* verarbeiten;

~ to good advantage nützlich (vorteilhaft) verwenden; **~ one's brains** seinen Verstand gebrauchen; **~ care** Sorgfalt anwenden; **~ a credit** Kredit in Anspruch nehmen; **~ diligence** sich Mühe geben; **~ diligence in business** sich gehöriger Sorgfalt in geschäftlichen Dingen befleißigen; **~ with discretion** vorsichtigen Gebrauch machen; **~ one's discretion** nach eigenem Ermessen handeln (entscheiden); **~ to good effect** wirksam einsetzen; **~ force** Gewalt anwenden; **~ one's head** nachdenken; **~ s. o. ill** j. schlecht behandeln; **~ one's influence** seine Beziehungen ausnutzen, seinen Einfluß geltend machen; **~ land for agricultural purposes** Grund und Boden landwirtschaftlich nutzen; **~ bad language** fluchen; **~ a name as reference** j. als Referenz angeben; **~ an opportunity** Gelegenheit benutzen; **~ a patented product** Patent verwerten; **not ~ for any purposes connected with business** keinen gewerblichen Gebrauch von etw. machen; **~ a right** von einem Recht Gebrauch machen, Recht ausüben; **~ the sea** Seemannsberuf ergreifen; **~ one's seashore cottage** sich in seinem Wochenendhaus an der See aufhalten; **~ a sum of money** Geldbetrag verwenden; **~ up all one's provisions** seine ganzen Vorräte aufbrauchen; **~ one's wits** seinen Geist anstrengen;

to alter the ~ of premises Wohnung zweckentfremden; **to be in daily ~** täglich gebraucht werden; **to be out of ~** außer Gebrauch kommen; **to be a room for the ~ of teachers only** lediglich den Lehrern als Aufenthaltsraum dienen; **to come into ~** gebräuchlich werden; **to fall out of ~** ungebräuchlich werden; **to get out of ~** veralten; **to give s. o. the ~ of one's library** j. seine Bibliothek mitbenutzen lassen; **to go out of ~** ungebräuchlich werden; **to have different ~s** verschiedene Verwendungszwecke haben; **to have no ~** keine Verwendung (Verwertung) haben für; **to have little or no ~ for** keinen oder nur geringen Wert beimessen; **to have lost the ~ of one's left eye** auf dem linken Auge nicht mehr sehen können; **to have nonindustrial ~** nicht gewerblich genutzt werden; **to make ~ of** [Hilfe] in Anspruch nehmen; **to make ~ of s. th.** von etw. Gebrauch machen; **to make bad ~ of** mißbrauchen; **to make bad ~ of one's money** sein Geld schlecht anlegen; **to make full ~ of** voll auswerten (ausnutzen, verwerten); **to make good ~ of one's money** sein Geld gut verwenden; **to make good ~ of an opportunity** Chance zu nutzen wissen; **to make great ~ of a dictionary** Wörterbuch viel benutzen; **to make improper ~ of a monopoly** Monopol mißbrauchen; **to make ~ of s. one's name** sich auf j. berufen; **to make ~ of a right** von einem Recht Gebrauch machen; **to pass out of ~** ungebräuchlich werden; **to put to good ~** nutzbringend verwenden; **to put out of ~** *(coins)* außer Kurs setzen; **to put advice to ~** Ratschlag befolgen; **to reserve the ~ of s. th.** sich die Nutznießung einer Sache vorbehalten; **to spread a thing's ~ too thinly** von den vorhandenen Nützlichkeiten zu wenig konzentrierten Gebrauch machen; **to take for one's own ~** für sich verwenden;

~ charge Benutzungsgebühr; **~ classes** *(town planning)* Gebrauchskategorien; **~ district** Bezirk mit Ortsstatut; **home-~ entry** *(customs)* Einfuhr zum eigenen Gebrauch; **~ and occupancy insurance** *(US)* Betriebsunterbrechungsversicherung; **~ life** Nutzungswert; **~ money** *(Br., sl.)* Zins, Zinsen; **~ plaintiff** *(in action)* Drittbegünstigter; **~ value** Nutz-, Gebrauchswert; **established ~ value** anerkannter Nutzungswert.

used gebraucht, ausgenutzt, *(clothes)* getragen, *(customary)* gebräuchlich;

hardly ~ *(marine insurance)* fast neuwertig; **~ for business purposes** gewerblich genutzt; **~ for illegal conveying of liquor** *(automobile)* zum illegalen Alkoholtransport benutzt; **~ on short runs** *(bus)* auf Kurzstrecken eingesetzt; **~ up** verbraucht, aufgebraucht; **~ up by one's toil** total erledigt; **to be quite ~ to hard work** an harte Arbeit gewöhnt sein; **to have grown ~ to s. th.** sich an etw. gewöhnt haben; **to think o. s. ill ~** sich schlecht behandelt fühlen;

~ car Gebrauchtwagen; **~ car with a small mileage** wenig gefahrener Gebrauchtwagen; **~-car lot** Gebrauchtwagenverkauf; **~ stamp** entwertete Marke.

useful nützlich, brauchbar, praktisch, zweckmäßig;

to come in very ~ sich als sehr nützlich erweisen; **to make o. s. ~** sich nützlich machen, sich nützlich betätigen; **~ area** Nutzfläche; **~ life** Nutzungsdauer, -wert; **~ load** Nutzlast; **~ member of the society** nützliches Mitglied der menschlichen Gesellschaft; **~ plant** Nutzpflanze; **~ work** Nutzeffekt, -leistung.

usefulness Nützlichkeit, Verwendbarkeit, Zweckmäßigkeit, *(asset)* Dauerwert.

useless zwecklos, sinnlos, *(inefficient)* nicht zu verwenden, unbrauchbar, nutzlos, *(valueless)* wertlos.

uselessness Unbrauchbarkeit, Wertlosigkeit.

user Benutzer, Verbraucher, *(buyer)* Abnehmer, Konsument, Bedarfsträger, *(electricity)* Entnehmer, *(enjoyment of right)* Benutzungsrecht, Besitzstand, *(usufruct)* Nießbraucher, Nutznießer;

adverse ~ mißbräuchliche Benutzung; **concurrent ~** Mitbenutzer, Mitbenutzung; **crown ~** Benutzung durch den Staat; **joint ~** Mitbenutzer; **large ~** Großabnehmer, -verbraucher; **outsider ~** *(library)* außerbetrieblicher Benutzer; **previous (prior) ~** Vorbenutzer, Vorbenutzung; **registered ~** *(Br.)* eingetragener Warenzeichenbesitzer; **road ~** Verkehrsteilnehmer; **ultimate ~** End-, Letztverbraucher;

individual ~ of the mail service einzelner Postbezieher; **~ of a right** Rechtsausübung;

to reserve the ~ of s. th. sich die Nutznießung einer Sache vorbehalten;

~ cost *(Keynes)* Abschreibungskosten und Erhaltungsaufwand; **~ fee (tax)** Benutzungsgebühr.

usher Platzanweiser[in], *(court)* Gerichtsdiener, *(house)* Türhüter, Pförtner;

~s Saaldienst;

court ~ Gerichtsdiener, -wachtmeister;

~ (v.) hineinführen, -geleiten;

~ in a period of prosperity zu einer konjunkturellen Blütezeit führen.

using | mail to defraud *(US)* Postmißbrauch zu Betrugszwecken; **~ the service of another for pay** *(Compensation Act)* entgeltliche Beschäftigung eines anderen.

usual üblich, gebräuchlich, gewöhnlich, herkömmlich, *(habitual)* gewohnheitsmäßig;

~ agency terms *(solicitor)* übliche Honorarregelung; **my ~ café** mein Stammcafé; **~ charge** *(banking)* übliche Gebühr (Provision); **~ conditions** übliche Bedingungen; **~ Lloyd's conditions** allgemeine Versicherungsbedingungen bei Lloyds; **~ course of employer's trade** *(Compensation Act)* üblicher Geschäftsablauf, -betrieb; **~ covenants** *(conveyancing)* übliche Rechtsmängelgewährhaftung; **~ convenants for title** normale Übertragungsurkunde; **~ contrary to one's ~ habit** ganz gegen seine Gewohnheit; **~ meeting** Routinesitzung; **~ occupation** gewöhnliche Beschäftigung; **~ place of abode** gewöhnlicher Aufenthaltsort; **~ rate of exchange** üblicher Wechselkurs; **under the ~ reserve** unter dem üblichen Vorbehalt; **~ terms** übliche Bedingungen; **to have become the ~ thing** gang und gäbe geworden sein;

business as ~ das Geschäft geht weiter.

usucaption *(law)* Ersitzung.

usucapt *(v.)* ersitzen.

usufruct Fruchtgenuß, Nutznießung, Nießbrauch;

imperfect ~ Nießbrauch an verbrauchbaren Sachen; **legal ~** gesetzliches Nießbrauchrecht; **perfect ~** Naturalnießbrauch; **quasi-~** nießbrauchähnliches Verhältnis;

~ of an investment Nutznießung des angelegten Kapitals;

~ (v.) Nießbrauch (Nutznießung) haben;

to hold in ~ Nießbrauch (Nutznießung) haben.

usufructuary Nießbraucher, -berechtigter, Nutznießer;

~ right Nießbrauch-, Nutznießungsrecht.

usurer Wucherer.

usurious wucherisch;

~ contract Wuchervertrag; **~ discounting of bills** Wechselwucher; **~ interest** Wucherzinsen; **to lend on ~ interest** zu Wucherzinsen [aus]leihen; **~ loan** Wucherdarlehn; **~ price** Wucherpreis; **~ rate of interest** gesetzlich erlaubter Höchstzinssatz; **~ trade** wucherisches Gewerbe, Wuchergeschäft; **~ transaction** Wuchergeschäft.

usurp *(v.)* an sich reißen, sich widerrechtlich aneignen, widerrechtlich in Besitz nehmen, usurpieren, *(employ wrongfully)* sich anmaßen, unrechtmäßig beanspruchen;

~ authority sich amtliche Befugnisse anmaßen, Amtsanmaßung begehen; **~ an office** Amtsanmaßung begehen; **~ power** Macht an sich reißen (ergreifen); **~ s. one's rights** sich jds. Rechte anmaßen; **~ a role** sich eine Rolle anmaßen; **~ the throne** sich des Thrones bemächtigen.

usurpation widerrechtliche Besitzergreifung, widerrechtlicher Nutzungsentzug;

~ of franchise Rechtsanmaßung; **the ocean's steady ~ of the land** ständige Landnahme durch das Meer; **~ of office** Amtsanmaßung; **~ of power** Machtergreifung; **~ of the throne** Thronraub.

usurper widerrechtlicher Besitzergreifer, *(politics)* unrechtmäßiger Machthaber, Usurpator, Thronräuber;

~ of a public office Begeher einer Amtsanmaßung.

usurpingly widerrechtlich, eigenmächtig.

usury Wucher[ei], Kredit-, Zinswucher, Geldschneiderei, *(usurious interest)* Wucherzinsen;

to practise ~ Wucher betreiben; **to return with ~** *(fig.)* mit Zinseszins zurückzahlen;

~ law Wuchergesetz; **~ legislation** Wuchergesetzgebung; **~ limit** Wuchergrenze.

utensil Werkzeug, [Arbeits]gerät, Gebrauchsgegenstand;

farming ~s landwirtschaftliche Geräte; **household ~** Haushaltsgegenstände; **kitchen ~** Küchengeräte; **writing ~s** Schreibwerkzeug.

uterine brother Halbbruder.

utero-gestation Schwangerschaft.

utilitarian | considerations Nützlichkeitserwägungen; **~ principles** Nützlichkeitsprinzip.

utilitarianism Nützlichkeitssystem.

utilities Betriebsmittelanlagen, *(US)* Versorgungsindustrie, Dienstleistungsgewerbe, *(stock exchange, US)* Versorgungswerte;

in the field of public ~ auf dem Gebiet der öffentlichen Versorgungsbetriebe;

~ area Dienstleistungssektor, Versorgungsbereich; **~ expansion** Ausweitungen auf dem Gebiet der Dienstleistungggsbetriebe; **public ~ field** Versorgungsgebiet.

utility Nutzen, Nützlichkeit, *(architecture)* Sachlichkeit, *(corporation US)* gemeinnützige Gesellschaft, Dienstleistungs-, Versorgungsbetrieb, *(patent law)* Nützlichkeits-, Nutzungswert, *(useful thing)* nützliche Einrichtung (Sache);

of no ~ nutzlos; **of public ~** gemeinnützig; **expired ~** Nutzungsunwert; **final (marginal) ~** Grenznutzen; **municipally owned ~** kommunaler Versorgungs-, Dienstleistungsbetrieb; **public ~** Gemeinnützigkeit, gemeinnützige Einrichtung, *(company)* Versorgungsbetrieb; **real-estate ~** Nutzungswert eines Grundstücks; **subjective ~** persönlicher Nutzen; **total ~** Gesamtnutzen, *(economy)* vollkommene Konsumentenbefriedigung;

~ article [einfacher] Gebrauchsgegenstand; **~ bill** Stromrechnung; **~ bonds** Versorgungswerte; **~ car** Gebrauchtwagen; **public ~ company (corporation, US)** gemeinnütziger Betrieb, öffentliches Versorgungsunternehmen, Dienstleistungsbetrieb; **~ department** Versorgungsdezernat; **~ equipment** Versorgungseinrichtungen; **public-~ establishment** Dienstleistungs-, Versorgungsunternehmen; **public-~ field** Versorgungs-, Dienstleistungsgebiet; **~ fund** Sondervermögen für Versorgungswerte; **~ goods** einfache Gebrauchsgüter, *(Br.)* Güter mit sozialem Preis; **~ holding company** Dachunternehmen von Versorgungsbetrieben; **~ man** *(US)* Gelegenheitsar-

beiter, Faktotum, *(theater)* Gelegenheitsschauspieler; ~
merger Fusion von Versorgungsbetrieben; ~**-operated stores**
betriebseigene Läden von Dienstleistungs-, Versorgungsbetrieben; ~ **optimum** höchstmöglicher Nutzen; **patent** *(US)*
Verwertungspatent, Gebrauchsmuster; ~ **rates** Dienstlei-
stungs-, Versorgungstarif; ~ **service** Dienstleistungsgewerbe,
Versorgungswirtschaft; ~ **shares (stocks,** *US*) Versorgungswerte; ~ **squad** fliegende Kolonne; **marginal** ~ **theory** Grenznutzentheorie; ~ **type** einfache Gebrauchsausführung; **public-**
~ **undertaking** öffentlicher Dienstleistungs-, Versorgungsbetrieb; ~ **van (truck, wag(g)on)** Mehrzweckfahrzeug.
utilizable verwendbar, verwertbar, nutzbar, gebrauchsfähig;
~ **circuit** *(el.)* Nutzstromkreis.
utilization Verwendung, Auswertung, Nutzbarmachung, Verwertung;
effective ~ rationelle Ausnutzung (Auslastung);
~ **of a credit** Inanspruchnahme eines Kredits; ~ **of a patent**
Patentverwertung; **full** ~ **of plant [capacity]** volle Ausnutzung
der Betriebskapazität, Kapazitätsausnutzung, -auslastung;
economic ~ **of raw materials** wirtschaftliche Rohstoffverwer-
tung; ~ **of resources** Nutzbarmachung von Bodenschätzen; ~
of waste products Abfallverwertung;
~ **company** *(copyright)* Verwertungsgesellschaft; ~ **rate**
Nutzbarmachungskoeffizient.
utilize *(v.)* zunutze machen, nutzbar machen, verwerten;
~ **a credit** Kredit in Anspruch nehmen; ~ **s. one's name** jds.
Namen benutzen; ~ **an opportunity** Gelegenheit wahrnehmen;
~ **waste products** Abfallprodukte verwerten; ~ **workers** Arbeitskräfte einsetzen.

utilizing plant Verwertungsanlage.
utmost *(limit)* äußerst, entlegenst;
to do one's ~ sich bis zum letzten einsetzen;
~ **care** höchste (größtmögliche) Sorgfalt; **in the** ~ **danger** in der
größten Gefahr; **to the** ~ **ends of the earth** bis ans Ende der
Welt; ~ **good faith** *(insurance principle)* höchste Stufe der Gutgläubigkeit, ohne etw. zu verschweigen; **of** ~ **importance**
von äußerster Wichtigkeit; **with** ~ **reluctance** mit größtem
Widerwillen; ~ **secrecy** strengste Geheimhaltung.
Utopia Utopie, Luftschloß, *(state)* Idealstaat.
utopian Utopist, Weltverbesserer;
~ *(a.)* utopisch, phantastisch, visionär;
~ **scheme** Utopie, utopischer Plan.
utopianism Utopismus, politische Träumerei.
utopianist Utopist, politischer Schwärmer.
utter *(v.)* äußern, ausdrücken, aussprechen, *(crimimal law)*
Falschgeld in Umlauf setzen (in Verkehr bringen);
~ **calumnies** verleumden; ~ **a forged document** Falschurkunde
in Umlauf setzen;
~ *(a.)* äußerst, *(legal sense)* außerhalb befindlich;
~ **bar** jüngere Anwälte; ~ **barrister** *(Br.)* außerhalb des
Gerichts plädierender Anwalt; ~ **denial** entschiedenes
Dementi; ~ **fool** total Verrückter; **to be an** ~ **stranger to s. o.** jem.
völlig unbekannt sein.
utterance Äußerung, *(putting in circulation)* Inumlaufsetzen;
to give ~ **to one's feelings** seinen Gefühlen Ausdruck verleihen;
to give ~ **to one's rage** seiner Wut Luft machen.
uttering false notes Falschgeldverbreitung, Inverkehrbringen
von Falschgeld.

V

v.i.p. hochgestellte Persönlichkeit.
vac *(Br., coll.)* Ferien.
vacancies *(newspaper)* Stellenangebote;
  unfilled ~ *(labo(u)r market)* freie Stellen, Stellenangebote;
  three ~ in an apartment house drei leerstehende Wohnungen in
  einem Mietshaus; ~ to fill freie Stellen; good ~ for typists and
  clerks freie Plätze für Stenotypisten und Kontoristen.
vacancy Vakanz, unbesetzter Platz, unbesetzte (unerledigte,
  offene, freie, frei werdende, leere) Stelle, *(absence of mind)*
  Gedankenlosigkeit, Geistesabwesenheit, *(fire insurance, US)*
  zeitweiliges Unbewohntsein, Leerstehen, *(hotel, US)* Zimmer
  frei, *(leisure time)* Erholungs-, Freizeit, *(mil.)* Fehlstelle,
  (empty space) Vakuum, Nichts, leerer Raum, *(unbuilt area)*
  unbebautes (freies) Gelände, *(vacation of office)* Freiwerden;
  in case of ~ of a property im Fall des Unbewohntseins eines
  Hauses;
  casual ~ Vakanz infolge Todesfalls;
  ~ in the board of directors nicht besetztes Vorstandsressort; ~
  of a city Verlassenheit einer Stadt; ~ on the staff Vakanz in der
  Belegschaft;
  to advertise a ~ freie Stelle ausschreiben; to cause a ~ Lücke
  entstehen lassen; to fill [up] a ~ freie Stelle (freien Posten) [neu]
  besetzen; to fill a ~ in Congress freigewordenen Abgeordnetensitz neu besetzen;
  ~ clause *(insurance, US)* Vertragsbestimmung, die das Leerstehen eines Hauses gestattet; ~ rate Vakanzrate; ~ ratio *(US)*
  Prozentsatz leerstehender Wohnungen.
vacant frei, unbesetzt, leer, *(abandoned)* herrenlos, *(absent-
  minded)* geistesabwesend, gedankenlos, *(house)* leerstehend,
  unbewohnt, frei, unvermietet, *(lot)* unbebaut, *(of persons)*
  untätig, müßig;
  situations ~ *(ad)* Stellenangebot;
  to be ~ unbewohnt sein, leer stehen; to fall ~ frei werden;
  to declare a professional chair ~ Professur ausschreiben;
  ~ estate herrenloser Nachlaß; ~ hour freie Stunde, Muße-
  stunde; ~ house leerstehendes Haus; ~ lot *(US)* unbebautes
  Grundstück; ~ office freie Stelle; to apply for a ~ position sich
  um eine freie Stelle bewerben; ~ possession *(advertisement)*
  freie Verfügbarkeit, sofort beziehbar; ~ post offene Stelle; ~
  room(s) Leerzimmer, *(hotel)* Zimmer frei; ~ seat freier (unbe-
  nutzter) Sitz; ~ situation unbesetzte (offene) Stelle; ~ stare
  ausdrucksloser Blick; ~ succession herrenlose Erbschaft, herrenloser Nachlaß.
vacate *(v.) (annul)* für ungültig erklären, aufheben, annullieren,
  (empty) Zimmer räumen, ausziehen, *(job)* Stelle aufgeben,
  (leave, sl.) abhauen, *(resign)* kündigen, zurücktreten;
  ~ a charter Satzung zurücknehmen; ~ the civilians from the city
  Zivilbevölkerung aus der Stadt evakuieren; ~ an entry of
  record Eintragung löschen; ~ a house Haus räumen; ~ a judgment *(US)* Urteil in der Berufungsinstanz aufheben; ~ office
  Amt niederlegen, von einem Amt zurücktreten; ~ one's place
  of business seinen Geschäftssitz verlegen; ~ a policy Versicherung annullieren; ~ the premises Lokal räumen; ~ a professorship Professur niederlegen; ~ rented rooms Mietwohnung
  räumen; ~ one's residence seinen Wohnsitz aufgeben, ausziehen; ~ a seat Sitz (Platz) freimachen; ~ one's seat sein Mandat
  niederlegen; ~ one's seat in Congress by resignation seinen
  Kongreßsitz aufgeben und sich zurückziehen.
vacating an office Amtsniederlegung, Demission, Rücktritt.
vacation *(court, Br.)* Gerichtsferien, *(holiday)* Urlaub, Ferien-
  [zeit], *(US)* [Erholungs]urlaub, Ferien, *(leaving)* Räumung,
  Verlassen, *(prison term, sl.)* Gefängnisstrafe, *(recreation)*
  Erholung, Erholungsaufenthalt, *(rest)* Pause, *(school, US)*
  Universitäts-, Schulferien;
  eligible for ~s *(US)* urlaubsberechtigt; on ~ *(US)* auf Urlaub;
  Christmas ~ *(US)* Weihnachtsferien; long ~ *(US)* große Ferien,
  (law court, Br.) Gerichtsferien; paid ~ *(US)* bezahlter Urlaub;
  payless ~ *(US)* unbezahlter Urlaub; ski ~ *(US)* Skiurlaub;
  summer ~ *(US)* Sommerferien;
  ~ of a charter Satzungsrücknahme; ~ of the court *(Br.)*
  Gerichtsferien; ~ of an entry of record Löschung einer Eintragung; ~ of a house Räumung eines Hauses; ~ of office Aufgabe
  eines Amtes, Amtsniederlegung; ~ with pay *(US)* bezahlter
  Urlaub; ~ without pay *(US)* unbezahlter Urlaub; ~ of a good
  position Aufgabe einer guten Stellung; ~ of one's seat *(parl.)*
  Mandatsniederlegung;
  to be on ~ *(US)* Urlaub machen, im (auf) Urlaub sein; to have

no ~ from business geschäftlich ununterbrochen in Anspruch
  genommen sein; to spend ~s abroad *(US)* Ferien im Ausland
  verbringen; to split ~ *(US)* Urlaubszeit aufteilen; to take a ~
  (US) Urlaub machen;
  ~ adventure *(US)* Ferienerlebnis; ~ allowance *(US)* Urlaubsabgeltung; ~ barrister *(Br.)* Ferienvertreter; ~ bonus *(US)* Ferien-
  zulage; ~ budget *(US)* Urlaubs-, Ferienetat; ~ bureau *(US)*
  Reisebüro; ~ compensation *(US)* Urlaubsentschädigung; ~
  condominium *(US)* Ferieneigentumswohnung; ~ court *(Br.)*
  Ferienkammer; ~ eligibility *(US)* Urlaubsberechtigung; ~
  expense *(US)* Ferienaufwand; ~ facilities *(US)* Ferienmöglich-
  keiten, -einrichtungen; ~ home *(US)* Ferienheim, -haus; ~
  information *(US)* Reiseprospekte; ~ information service *(US)*
  Reiseberatungsdienst; ~ job Ferienstellung, -beruf; ~ judge
  (Br.) Richter während der Gerichtsferien, Ferienrichter; ~
  land *(US)* Urlaubsland; ~ paradise *(US)* Ferienparadies; ~ pay
  (US) bezahlter Urlaub; ~ period *(US)* Urlaubs-, Ferienzeit; ~
  planner *(US)* Ferienplaner; ~ policy *(US)* Urlaubspolitik; ~
  privilege (right) *(US)* Urlaubsanspruch; ~ procedure *(US)*
  Urlaubsverfahren; ~ provisions *(US)* Urlaubsbestimmungen;
  ~ replacement *(US)* Ferien-, Urlaubsvertretung; ~ request
  (US) Urlaubsgesuch; ~ retreat Ruhesitz; ~ schedule *(US)*
  Urlaubs-, Ferienplan; ~ school *(US)* Ferienkurs; ~ season *(US)*
  Urlaubs-, Ferienzeit; ~ section *(US)* Urlaubs-, Ferienabtei-
  lung; ~ shutdown *(US)* ferienbedingte Schließung, Werks-
  ferien; ~ site *(Br.)* Feriensitz; ~ spot *(US)* Urlaubs-, Ferienort; ~
  system *(US)* Urlaubswesen; ~ time *(US)* Ferien-, Urlaubszeit;
  ~ time allotment *(US)* Urlaubszulage; government ~ travel
  bureau *(US)* staatliches Reisebüro; ~ village *(US)* Feriendorf;
  ~ and welfare features of a contract *(US)* Urlaubs- und Fürsorgebestimmungen eines Vertrages; ~ work *(US)* Ferienarbeit.
vacationeer, vacationist *(US)* Feriengast, Sommerfrischler,
  Erholungssuchender, Urlauber.
vaccination Schutzimpfung;
  compulsory ~ Zwangsimpfung, Impfzwang, -pflicht; preventive ~ Schutzimpfung;
  ~ certificate Impfzeugnis, -schein.
vaccinator, vaccinist Impfarzt.
vaccine Impfstoff;
  ~ institute Impfanstalt.
vaccinee Impfling.
vacuities Belanglosigkeiten.
vacuity *(fig.)* geistige Leere, Ausdruckslosigkeit.
vacuous life müßiges Leben.
vacuum leerer Raum, Leere, Vakuum;
  ~ bottle Thermosflasche; ~ brake Unterdruckbremse; ~ cleaner Staubsauger; ~ fan Ventilator; ~ gauge Manometer, Unter-
  druckmesser; ~ lamp Vakuumlampe; ~ tank Unterdruck-
  förderer; ~ tube Vakuumröhre.
vademecum Handbuch, Leitfaden, Führer.
vagabond Landstreicher, Vagabund;
  ~ *(v.)* herumstreunen, vagabundieren;
  ~ *(a.)* nicht seßhaft, vagabundenhaft;
  ~ habits Vagabundenmanieren; ~ life unstetes Leben; ~ wage
  Hungerlohn.
vagabondage Vagabundentum, -leben, Landstreicherei.
vagabondish vagabundenhaft.
vagabondize *(v.)* vagabundieren.
vagrancy Landstreicherei, Herumstreunen, Vagabundentum.
vagrant Landstreicher, Vagabund, *(pedlar)* Hausierer, Wandergewerbetreibender;
  ~ *(a.)* wandernd, fahrend, vagabundierend;
  ⌐ Act *(Br.)* Gesetz gegen Landstreicherei; to lead a ~ life Vaga-
  bundenleben führen.
vague undeutlich, unbestimmt, vage, *(nebulous)* nebelhaft, verschwommen, unscharf;
  ~ answer unklare (nicht präzise) Antwort; ~ demands unklare
  Forderungen; ~ idea nebelhafte Vorstellung; ~ information
  ungenaue Auskunft; ~ outlines verschwommene Umrisse; ~
  threats unbestimmte Drohungen.
vaguely familiar irgendwie bekannt.
vail Geldgeschenk, Trinkgeld.
vain wertlos, unwesentlich, *(conceited)* eitel, nichtig, hohl;
  to take s. one's name in ~ ein bißchen respektlos von jem.
  sprechen;
  ~ attempt nutzloser Versuch; ~ efforts vergebliche Bemühungen; ~ promise leeres Versprechen.

valediction Abschiedsworte, -rede.
valedictory [speech] *(US)* Abschiedsrede.
valet Kammerdiener, *(hotel)* Hausdiener.
valeting service, good *(hotel)* [gut] geschultes Personal.
valetudinarian Rekonvaleszent;
~ *(a.)* kränkelnd, *(fig.)* hypochonderisch.
valentine *(sl.)* Entlassungswarnung.
valid [rechts]gültig, rechtskräftig, vollgültig, triftig, *(enforceable)* durchsetzbar, vollstreckbar, *(passport)* in Ordnung befindlich, *(ticket)* gültig;
~ **for** bindend für; ~ **in form and fact** formell und materiell gültig; ~ **for three months** drei Monate gültig; ~ **until recalled** *(stock exchange)* gültig bis auf Widerruf;
to be ~ gelten, Geltung haben, gültig sein; **to be** ~ **in law** *(equity)* volle Rechtsgültigkeit haben; **to become** ~ Rechtskraft erlangen; **to make** ~ für gültig erklären; **to remain** ~ Geltung behalten; **to render** ~ validieren, gültig machen, legalisieren;
~ **argument** stichhaltiges Argument; ~ **claim** berechtigter Anspruch; ~ **consideration** rechtswirksame Gegenleistung; ~ **contract** rechtsgültiger Vertrag; ~ **deed** [rechts]gültige Urkunde; ~ **defence** durchgreifende Einrede; ~ **instrument** rechtsgültiger Vertrag; ~ **marriage** gültige Eheschließung; ~ **objection** rechtserhebliche Einwendung; ~ **method** wirksame Methode; ~ **objection** wohlbegründeter Einwand; **to raise** ~ **objections to a scheme** stichhaltige Einwände gegen einen Plan erheben; ~ **proof** triftiger (gültiger) Beweis; ~ **reason** *(statute)* stichhaltiger Grund; ~ **test** zuverlässiger Test; ~ **ticket** gültiger Fahrschein; ~ **title** gültiger Rechtsanspruch; ~ **will** gültiges Testament.
validate | *(v.)* für [rechts]gültig erklären, *(confirm)* bestätigen, legalisieren, validieren;
~ **a claim** Anspruch anerkennen; ~ **an election** Wahlergebnis bestätigen; ~ **securities** Wertpapiere bereinigen.
validating statute Ratifizierungsgesetz.
validation *(act of validating)* Gültigkeitserklärung, Validierung, *(confirmation)* Bestätigung, Legalisierung;
~ **of a fund** *(investment company)* Errechnung des Fondswertes; ~ **of securities** Wertpapierbereinigung;
~ **period** Gültigkeitsdauer.
validity [Rechts]gültigkeit, Rechtswirksamkeit, Geltung, Legalität, *(judicial proceedings)* Rechtmäßigkeit, Berechtigung, *(patent law)* Rechtsbeständigkeit, *(term of ~)* Laufzeit, *(of a ticket)* Gültigkeitsdauer;
of general ~ allgemeingültig;
external ~ Außengeltung; **particular** ~ teilweise Gültigkeit; **universal** ~ Allgemeinverbindlichkeit, -gültigkeit;
~ **of an argument** Stichhaltigkeit eines Arguments; ~ **of a claim** Rechtsgültigkeit einer Forderung; ~ **of a deed** Rechtsgültigkeit eines Vertrages; ~ **of an election** Gültigkeit einer Wahl; ~ **of a patent** Patentgültigkeit; ~ **of a policy** Gültigkeitsdauer einer Police; ~ **of judicial proceedings** rechtsgültiges Verfahren; ~ **of a statute** Verfassungsmäßigkeit eines Gesetzes; ~ **of testimony** Beweiskraft einer Zeugenaussage; ~ **of a treaty** Verfassungsmäßigkeit eines Vertrages; ~ **of a will** Gültigkeit eines Testamentes;
to be deprived of ~ Gültigkeit verlieren; **to dispute the** ~ **of a document** Rechtsgültigkeit einer Urkunde bestreiten; **to extend the** ~ Gültigkeitsdauer verlängern.
valise kleiner Handkoffer, *(mil.)* Tornister.
valley, down the talabwärts.
valorem, ad *(lat.)* nach dem Wert;
~ **[rate of] duty** Wertzoll; ~ **rate** Wertfracht; ~ **stamp** Wertmarke; ~ **tax** *(US)* Wertsteuer.
valorization Aufwertung, Valorisierung, *(US)* Preisstabilisierung, -stützung, *(government scheme)* staatliche Erzeugerpreisstützung;
~ **scheme** Preisstützungsmaßnahme, angebotsbeschränkende Preisstützungspolitik.
valorize *(v.)* aufwerten, valorisieren;
~ **prices** *(US)* Preise stützen (stabilisieren).
valuable Wertgegenstand, -sache;
~s Wertsachen, -gegenstände, Kostbarkeiten;
~s **for safe custody** im Depot verwahrte Wertsachen;
to deposit ~s **in safe custody** Wertsachen zur Aufbewahrung ins Depot geben; **to deposit** ~s **with the manager for safe keeping** Wertsachen dem Hotelgeschäftsführer zur Aufbewahrung übergeben; **to place one's** ~s **in the bank** seine Wertsachen ins Depot geben;
~ *(a.)* *(assessable)* abschätzbar, bewertbar, mit Verkehrswert, *(plot of land)* mit Verkehrswert, *(of great value)* wertvoll, kostbar;

~ **articles** Wertsachen; ~ **cargo** wertvolle Ladung; ~ **consideration** Vertragsinteresse, entgeltliche Gegenleistung; **for** ~ **consideration** entgeltlich, gegen Entgelt; ~ **discovery** wertvolle Entdeckung; ~ **furniture** wertvolle Möbel; ~ **improvements** werterhöhende Aufwendungen, Wertsteigerungen; ~ **information** nützliche Information; ~ **items** Wertgegenstände; ~ **papers** wichtige Urkunden; ~ **property** Vermögensgegenstand; ~ **security** *(Larceny Act)* Wertpapier; ~ **service** nützlicher (wertvoller) Dienst; ~ **thing** Wertgegenstand; ~ **things** Wertsachen.
valuableness Wert, Kostbarkeit.
valuate *(v.)* abschätzen, bewerten.
valuation *(estimation)* [Ab]schätzung, Ansatz, Wertschätzung, Einschätzung, Taxe, Taxierung, Wertung, Veranschlagung, *(personal estimation)* Würdigung, Wertschätzung, *(fixed value)* [festgesetzter, geschätzter] Wert, Schätzwert, *(fixing of value)* Wertbestimmung, -ansetzung, -ansatz, Bewertung, *(insurance business)* Reservenberechnung, *(life insurance)* Rückkaufswert, *(mintage)* Valvation;
at a ~ **of** zu einem Taxpreis (Wert) von;
actuarial ~ Aufstellung einer versicherungstechnischen Bilanz; **added** ~ *(national product)* Wertschöpfung; **American** ~ *(customs)* amerikanischer Inlandswert; **assessed** *(US)* *(assessor's)* ~ steuerliche Bewertung, Steuerbewertung, -veranlagung, Veranlagungswert; **bond** ~ Wertbezeichnung einer Obligation; **breakup** ~ Bewertung im Fall einer Liquidation; **conservative** ~ vorsichtige Bewertung; **declared** ~ *(customs)* Wertangabe, -deklaration; **domestic** ~ Inlandswert; **excess** ~ Mehrbewertung; **fixed-asset** ~ Bewertung fester Anlagen, Anlagenbewertung; **foreign** ~ *(customs)* Auslandswert; **going-concern** ~ Betriebsbewertung; **gross** ~ Reservenberechnung nach dem Bruttowert der Prämie; **index-number** ~ Bewertung anhand des Wirtschaftsindex; **individual** ~ Einzelbewertung; **insurance** ~ *(life insurance)* Festsetzung des Rückkaufswertes; **inventory** ~ Inventar-, Bestands-, Lagerbewertung; **judicial** ~ gerichtliche Schätzung (Taxe); **market** ~ marktgemäße Bewertung, Bewertung des Verkehrswertes; **net** ~ *(insurance)* Reservenberechnung nach dem Nettowert der Prämie; **new** ~ Neubewertung; **official** ~ zollamtliche Bewertung; **professional** ~ amtliche Schätzung; **released** ~ Wertermäßigung; **retrospective** ~ Rückvalutierung; **unit** ~ Einzelbewertung;
~ **of assets** Bewertung der Aktiva, Anlagenbewertung; ~ **of buildings** Baukostenvoranschlag; ~ **of charges** Kostenüberschlag; ~ **of a claim** Bewertung einer Forderung; **false** ~ **of one's environment** falsche Einschätzung seiner Umwelt; ~ **of an estate** Nachlaß-, Grundstücksschätzung; ~ **in exchange** Tauschwert; ~ **of goods** Warenbewertung; ~ **of a house** Hausbewertung, -schätzung; ~ **of inventory** Inventarbewertung; ~ **of probate** Bewertung für Nachlaßzwecke, Nachlaßschätzung, -bewertung; ~ **of profit** Nutzenberechnung; ~ **of property** Vermögensaufnahme; **new** ~ **for rating purposes** *(Br.)* Grundsteuerneufestsetzung; ~ **of real estate** Grundstücksbewertung; ~ **of securities** Bewertung von Sicherheiten; ~ **of shares** Aktienbewertung;
to arrive at different ~s zu verschiedenen Wertansätzen gelangen; **to disagree about a** ~ sich über die Höhe einer Taxe nicht einigen können; **to dispose at a** ~ nach Taxe verkaufen; **to draw up a** ~ Taxe aufstellen; **to make a** ~ **of the goods** Waren abschätzen (taxieren); **to sell at a figure above** ~ über Taxpreis verkaufen; **to set too high a** ~ **on a building** zu hohe Gebäudebewertung vornehmen; **to set a low** ~ niedrig bewerten; **to set too low a** ~ **on goods** Waren unterbewerten; **to take s. o. at his own** ~ jds. hohe Eigenbewertung akzeptieren;
~ **account** Wertberichtigungskonto; ~ **adjustments of plant property and investments** *(balance sheet)* Erträge aus Zuschreibungen; ~ **adjustments on current assets other than inventories** Wertberichtigungen aus Wertminderungen oder dem Abgang von Gegenständen des Umlaufvermögens außer Vorräten; ~ **assessment** Wertfestsetzung; ~ **basis** Bewertungsgrundlage; ~ **board** Taxamt; ~ **case** Schätzungssache; ~ **charge** *(airfreight bill)* Wertzuschlag; ~ **clause** Wertklausel; ~ **committee** Bewertungsausschuß; ~ **constant** *(insurance business)* Hilfszahl für die Prämienreservenberechnung; ~ **contract** Wertbestimmungsvertrag; **local** ~ **court** *(Br.)* Grundsteuerausschuß, Einspruchstelle gegen zu hohe Einheitsbewertung; ~ **criterium** Bewertungsmaßstab; ~ **date** Wertfeststellungstag; ~ **deficit** Bewertungsausfall; ~ **expense** Schätzungskosten; ~ **expert** Bewertungsfachmann; ~ **fee** Schätz-, Abschätzungsgebühr, Taxe; ~ **function** Bewertungsfunktion; ~ **item** Wertberichtigungsposten, -größe, Wertkorrekturposten; ~ **level** Bewertungsniveau; ~ **list** *(Br.)* Einheitswerttabelle, [etwa] Kataster;

~ **matters** Bewertungsfragen; ~ **method** Bewertungsmethode; ~ **officer** Abschätzungsbeamter, Taxator; ~ **point of view** Bewertungsstandpunkt; ~ **privilege** Bewertungsfreiheit; ~ **process** Bewertungsverfahren; **declared** ~ **rate** Werttarif; ~ **report** Bewertungsbericht; ~ **reserve** Bewertungsreserve, Rückstellung für Wertberichtigungen; **asset** ~ **reserve** *(balance sheet)* Wertberichtigung für Wertänderung; ~ **roll** *(Scot.)* Kataster; ~ **rules** Bewertungsrichtlinien; ~ **sheet** Kreditblatt; ~ **table** Valvationstabelle.

valuational bewertungsmäßig.

valuator Taxator, Schätzer.

value Wert, wertvolle Eigenschaft, *(appraisal)* Einschätzung, *(assessed value)* Verkehrswert, *(bill of exchange)* [Wechsel]summe, Betrag, *(buying power)* Kaufkraft, *(currency, Br.)* Währung, Valuta, Münzwert, *(equivalent)* Gegenwert, -leistung, *(market price)* Preis, [Tax]wert, *(quality goods)* preiswerte (reelle) Ware, Qualitätsware, *(rationalization)* Leistungsanalyse, *(validity)* Geltung, Wirksamkeit, *(valuation)* Wertschätzung, *(value of material)* Materialwert, *(value date, Br.)* Tag der Wertstellung, *(weight)* Wert, Bedeutung, Gewicht, *(worth)* [Vermögens]wert;

above ~ über Wert; **according to the** ~ ad valorem; **at** ~ *(stock exchange)* zum Tageskurs; **at full** ~ vollgültig; **below** ~ unter Wert; **fixed in** ~ wertbeständig; **for** ~ entgeltlich, gegen Entgelt; **for** ~ **received** Wert (Betrag) erhalten; **in** ~ an Wert; **fixed in** ~ wertbeständig; **in terms of the technical** ~ nach dem formellen Wertbegriff; **of good** ~ vollwertig; **of great** ~ von großem Wert; **of higher** ~ höher bewertet; **of inferior** ~ minderwertig; **of no** ~ wertlos, unnütz; **of the same** ~ gleichwertig; **of small** ~ geringwertig; **of stable** ~ ~ wertbeständig; **to the** ~ **of** im Betrage von; **~s** Wertvorstellungen;

absolute ~ absoluter Wert; **absorption** ~ berichtigter Wert; **accounting** ~ buchmäßiger Wert, Buch[ungs]wert; **acquisition** ~ Anschaffungswert; **actual** ~ Verkaufs-, Real-, Effektivwert, realer (effektiver, tatsächlicher, wahrer) Wert; **actual cash** ~ *(insurance)* Istwert; **actuarial** ~ *(insurance)* rechnungsmäßiger (versicherungsmathematischer) Wert, Versicherungswert; **net added** ~ *(national accounting)* Mehrwert, Wertschöpfung, -erhöhung; **adjusted declared** ~ berichtigter, erklärter Wert des Aktienkapitals [für Berechnung der Kapital- und Übergewinnsteuer]; **advertising** ~ Werbewert; **aggregate** ~ Gesamtwert; **aggregate sales** ~ Gesamtverkaufswert; **agreed** ~ *(policy)* festgelegter (frei vereinbarter) Wert; **amenity** ~ Annehmlichkeitswert [eines Grundstücks]; **amortized** ~ Amortisationswert; **annual** ~ *(Br.)* jährlicher Ertragswert, Jahresertrag; **apparent** ~ Scheinwert; **appraised** ~ Schätz-, Taxwert, Taxkurs; **approximate** ~ ungefährer Wert, Richt-, [An]näherungswert; **arbitrary** ~ *(customs)* willkürlich angenommener Wert; **artistic** ~ künstlerischer Wert; **ascertainable** ~ feststellbarer Wert; **assay-office (assayed)** ~ Feingehalt; **assemblage** ~ Sammelwert; **assessable** ~ *(Br.)* Steuerwert; **assessed** ~ Steuer-, Tax-, Einheitswert; **asset** ~ Wert des Aktivvermögens (Anlagevermögens), Substanzwert; **assumed** ~ angenommener (fiktiver) Wert; **attached business** ~ Verkehrswert; **average** ~ Mittel-, Durchschnittswert; **balance-sheet** ~ Bilanzwert; **base** ~ Vergleichswert; **basic** ~ Einheitswert; **book** ~ Buchwert; **breakup** ~ Altmaterialwert; **buying** ~ Kaufwert; **caloric** ~ Kaloriengehalt; **capital** ~ Kapitalwert; **capitalized** ~ kapitalisierter Wert, Ertragswert; **caprice** ~ Liebhaberwert, -preis; **carrying** ~ Buchwert; **cash** ~ Bar[ablösungs]wert, Kassafluß; **fair cash** ~ Verkehrswert; **cash market** ~ *(housing)* Verkehrs-, Verkaufswert; **cash-surrender** ~ *(life insurance)* Effektiv-, Geld-, Kapital-, Rückkaufswert; **certified** ~ bestätigter Wert; **circulating** ~ *(banknotes)* Umlaufwert; **clear** ~ *(inheritance tax)* reiner Nachlaßwert; **clear annual** ~ Jahresreingewinn; **commercial** ~ Markt-, Handelswert, *(ore)* Verkehrswert; **comparative** ~ Vergleichswert; ~ **compensated** Valuta kompensiert; **condemnation** ~ Beschlagnahmewert; **contributing** ~ umlagepflichtiger Vermögenswert, Sammelsteuerwert; **cost** ~ Anschaffungs-, Herstellungs-, Einkaufs-, Erwerbswert; **critical** ~ Grenzwert; **currency** ~ Devisenwert; **current** ~ [gegenwärtiger] Marktwert, Gegenwartswert; **declared current** ~ Emissionswert; **customs** ~ Zollwert; **damaged** ~ *(insurance)* Wert im beschädigten Zustand; **declared** ~ *(customs)* angegebener (zollpflichtiger) Wert, Wertangabe; **denominational** ~ Nennwert; **depreciated** ~ abgeschriebener Wert; **diminishing** ~ abnehmender Wert; **discounted** ~ Diskontwert; **domestic** ~ *(of currency)* innerer [Tausch]wert des Geldes; **double** ~ zweifacher Wert; ~ **when due** Wert bei Verfall; **dutiable** ~ zollpflichtiger Wert, Zollwert; **earning-capacity** ~ Ertragswert, kapitali-

sierter Wert; **economic** ~ wirtschaftlicher Wert, Handels-, Marktwert; **enhanced** ~ erhöhter Wert; **enterprise** ~ Firmenwert; **equivalent** ~ Äquivalenzwert; **equity** ~ Forderungs-, Billigkeitswert; **established-use** ~ festgelegter Gebrauchswert; **estimated** ~ Anschlags-, Tax-, Schätzwert; **exaggerated** ~ zu hoch angesetzter Wert; **exchange (exchangeable)** ~ Tauschwert; **expert** ~ Tax-, Schätzwert; **export** ~ Ausfuhr-, Exportwert; **extended** ~ gerichtlich festgesetzter Wert; **extrinsic** ~ äußerer Wert; **face** ~ Nominal-, Nennwert; **fair** ~ Wiederbeschaffungswert, *(of capital stock)* Kapitalwert, *(rate purposes)* Verkehrswert; **fair and equitable** ~ der Billigkeit entsprechender Wert; **fair and reasonable** ~ angemessener Wert; **fair market** ~ gängiger Wert, *(housing)* Verkehrs-, Verkaufswert; **fair cash market** ~ *(housing)* Verkehrs-, Verkaufswert; **fictitious** ~ Scheinwert, fiktiver (willkürlich angenommener) Wert; **firm** ~ Geschäftswert; **fixed** ~ Festwert; **flat** ~ Pauschalwert; **fluctuating** ~ unbeständige Valuta; **food** ~ Nährwert; **forced-sale** ~ Zwangsversteigerungs-, Zwangsverkaufswert; **foreign** ~ Außen-, Auslandswert; **foreign ~s** ausländische Vermögenswerte; **foreign-exchange** ~ Devisenwert; **fractional** ~ Bruchteilswert; **full** ~ *(coin)* Vollgehalt, *(insurance business)* Versicherungs-, Ersatzwert; **future** ~ zukünftiger Wert; **going** ~ Betriebs-, Gebrauchswert; **going-concern** ~ Betriebswert; **good** ~ Qualitätsware; **great** ~ große Bedeutung; **gross** ~ Bruttowert; **home** ~ Inlandswert; **hypothetical** ~ hypothekarischer Wert; **illustrative** ~ Illustrationswert; **imaginary** ~ Scheinwert; **improved** ~ steigender Nutzertrag; **imputed** ~ *(income-tax return)* steuerlich angerechneter Wert; **income** ~ Ertragswert; **increment** ~ Wertzuwachs; **industrial** ~ wirtschaftlicher Wert; **insurable** ~ versicherbarer Wert; **insurance** ~ festgesetzter Versicherungswert, Versicherungstaxe; **intangible** ~ immaterieller Wert, Firmenwert, *(mortgage)* Geldwert; **intrinsic** ~ innerer Wert, *(stock exchange)* Anlagewert; **inventory** ~ Inventar-, Lagerwert; **investment** ~ Investitions-, Anlagewert; **invoice** ~ Faktura-, Rechnungswert; **junk** ~ Schrottwert; **justified** ~ berechtigter Wert; **land** ~ Grundstückswert; **lasting** ~ bleibender Wert, Dauerwert; **leading ~s** *(stock exchange)* führende Werte; **letting** ~ Miet-, Pachtwert; **liquidation** ~ Liquidationswert; **loan** ~ Beleihungs-, Lombardwert; **market** ~ Markt-, Tages-, Verkehrswert, gemeiner (gegenwärtiger) Wert; **common market** ~ gemeiner Handelswert; **fair and reasonable market** ~ gemeiner Marktwert; **lower market** ~ niedrigerer Zeitwert; **marketable** ~ Verkaufswert, Kaufpreis; **maturity** ~ Fälligkeitswert; **maximum** ~ oberste Wertgrenze; **mean** ~ Durchschnitts-, Mittelwert; **memory** ~ *(bookkeeping)* Erinnerungswert; **minimum** ~ Mindestwert, *(law)* Revisionssumme; **monetary** ~ finanzieller Wert, Geldwert; **moral** ~ moralischer Wert; **net** ~ Nettowert, reiner Wert, *(life insurance)* Deckungskapital, Prämienreserve; **net annual** ~ *(income-tax statement, Br.)* Nutzungswert des eigengenutzten Einfamilienhauses; **net asset** ~ *(investment fund)* Liquidations-, Inventarwert; **net realizable** ~ *(Br.)* realisierbarer Verkaufswert; **nonforfeiture** ~ Rückkaufswert einer Versicherungspolice; **nominal** ~ Nominalwert, *(balance sheet, US)* Erinnerungswert; **normal** ~ Normalwert; **nuisance** ~ Ablösungswert; **numerical** ~ Zahlenwert; **original** ~ Neu-, Stamm-, Anschaffungswert; **paid-up** ~ *(life insurance)* Umwandlungs-, Rückkaufswert; **par** ~ Pariwert; **actuarially computed part** ~ versicherungsmathematisch ermittelter Teilwert; **patent** ~ Wert eines Patents; **peak** ~ Höchstwert; **physical** ~ körperlicher Wert; **plottage** ~ Grundstückswert; **present** ~ jetziger Wert, Tages-, Gegenwarts-, Zeit-, Bar-, Gebrauchswert, *(annuity)* Kapitalwert, *(stock exchange)* Wert bei aufgehobener Zahlung; **present-use** ~ augenblicklicher Gebrauchswert; **pre-war** ~ Vorkriegs-, Friedenswert; **principal** ~ *(Br.)* gemeiner Wert; **production** ~ Produktions-, Herstellungswert; **productive** ~ Ertragswert; **productivity** ~ Produktivitätswert; **promotional** ~ Werbewert; **proper** ~ Eigenwert; **property** ~ Vermögenswert, *(Br.)* Grundstückswert; **prospective** ~ entgangener Gewinn; **prudent** ~ vernünftiger Wert; **publicity** ~ Werbewert; **purchase** ~ Erwerbswert; **purchasing** ~ Kaufkraftwert; **quoted** ~ *(Br.)* Kurswert; **rat(e)able** ~ *(Br.)* steuerbarer Wert, Einheitswert; **real** ~ effektiver Wert, Sachwert; **real-estate** ~ Grundstückswert; **realization** ~ Veräußerungs-, Liquidationswert; **reappraisal** ~ Neuschätzungswert; **reasonable** ~ angemessener Gegenwert; ~ **received** *(bill of exchange)* Betrag erhalten; ~ **received in cash** Wert in bar erhalten; **redemption** ~ Rückkaufswert; **registered** ~ deklarierter Wert; **reminder** ~ *(bookkeeping)* Erinnerungswert, -posten; **rental** ~ Mietertragswert, Pachtwert; **replacement (reproduction cost)** ~ Wiederbeschaffungs-, Ersatzwert; **repossession** ~ Wert bei Wiedererlan-

gung; **repurchase** ~ Rückkaufswert; **resale** ~ Wiederverkaufswert; **residual** ~ *(balance sheet)* Restbuchwert; **retail** ~ Einzelhandelspreis; **salable** ~ Verkehrs-, Verkaufswert; **sale** ~ Verkaufswert; **salvage** ~ *(marine insurance)* Bergungs-, Schrottwert, Realisierungswert [bei sofortigem Verkauf]; **scarcity** ~ durch Warenknappheit erhöhter Wert, Seltenheitswert; **scrap** ~ Wert im beschädigten Zustand, Rest-, Schrott-, Abschreibungswert; **security** ~ Bürgschafts-, Garantiewert; **sentimental** ~ Liebhaberwert; **service** ~ Eignungs-, Gebrauchswert; **site** ~ [steuerlicher] Einheitswert [eines Grundstücks]; **sound** ~ *(insurance)* Wert in unbeschädigtem Zustand, *(fire insurance)* Verkehrs-, Tageswert; **speculative** ~ Spekulationswert; **stable** ~ fester Wert; **standard** ~ Normal-, Durchschnitts-, Richt-, Festwert; **starting** ~ Ausgangswert; **stated** ~ festgestellter (erklärter) Wert; **statistical** ~ statistischer Wert; **statutory** ~ gesetzlich festgesetzter Wert; **stock-exchange** ~ Börsenwert; **summation** ~ Wert einer Summe; **surplus** ~ Mehrwert, Überschuß, *(income above subsistence)* freies Einkommen, *(production)* Mehrwert; **cash surrender** ~ *(life insurance)* Rückkaufswert; **tangible** ~ greifbarer (materieller) Wert, Vermögenswert, *(going concern)* Betriebswert; **tax** ~ Steuerwert; **taxable** ~ steuerbarer (steuerpflichtiger) Wert, Versteuerungs-, Einheitswert; **today's** ~ Tageswert, gegenwärtiger Wert; **top** ~ Höchstwert; **total** ~ Gesamtwert; **trade** ~ Verkehrs-, Handelswert; **trading** ~ Handelswert; **transfer** ~ Übergabewert; **true** ~ innerer (echter) Wert, Istwert; **unimproved** ~ Verkehrswert nicht erschlossenen Geländes; **use** ~ anerkannter Nutzungswert, Gebrauchswert; **utility** ~ Nutzungs-, Gebrauchswert; **warranted** ~ garantierter Wert; **written-down** ~ steuerlich voll abgeschriebener Wert, Abschreibungswert;
~ **in account** Wert in Rechnung; **net** ~ **added** *(national income accounting)* Wertschöpfung; ~ **added by zoning** durch Bebauungsbestimmungen hervorgerufene Wertsteigerung; ~ **in account** Wert in Rechnung; ~ **of assets on a gone-concern basis** Anlagenbewertung im Licht des Liquidationstermins; ~ **of fixed assets** Wert des Anlagevermögens; ~ **of the total assets of a company** Gesamtbetriebswert; ~ **of business** Geschäfts-, Firmenwert; ~ **of capital stock** Anlagenwert; ~ **of cargo** Ladungswert; ~ **in cash** Barwert; ~ **of colo(u)r** Farbwert; ~ **of comparison** Vergleichswert; ~ **of complaint** Beschwerdesumme; [**fair**] ~ **as going concern** [angemessener] Betriebswert; ~ **of contents** Inhaltswert; ~ **at cost** Herstellungs-, Einkaufs-, Anschaffungswert, Wertansatz nach Anschaffungskosten; ~ **in damages** [Schaden]ersatz-, Versicherungswert; **total** ~ **of discounts outstanding** Gesamtwert des Wechselobligos; ~ **when due** Wert bei Verfall; **objective** ~ **of education** Wert einer guten Erziehung; ~ **of an estate** Grundstücks-, Nachlaßwert; ~ **in exchange** Tauschwert; ~ **on expiration** Wert bei Verfall; ~ **of the goods ordered** Auftragswert; **ratable** ~ **of a house** *(Br.)* Einheitswert eines Hauses; ~ **of imports** Einfuhrwert; ~ **of inventory** Lagerbestands-, Inventarwert; ~ **as per invoice** Rechnungswert, Wert laut Faktura; ~ **at issue** Kurswert; ~ **of land** Grundstückswert; **current use** ~ **of land** Verkehrswert eines Grundstücks; **developed** ~ **of land** Wert erschlossenen Baulands; ~ **of matter in controversy** Streitwert der befangenen Sache, Wert des Streitgegenstandes; ~ **on maturity** Wert bei Verfall; ~ **of money** Kaufkraft des Geldes; ~ **of mortgage** Hypothekenwert; ~ **as new** Neuwert; ~ **of plant in successful operation** wirtschaftlicher Wert eines gut beschäftigten Unternehmens, Betriebswert; ~ **at point of entry** Deklarationswert; ~ **based on price increment** Teuerungswert; ~ **of production** Produktionswert; ~ **of property** Grundstückswert; ~ **of a reversion** Nacherbschaftswert; ~ **of returns** Ertragswert; ~ **in silver** Valuta in Silber; ~ **in use** Nutzungs-, Gebrauchswert; **cost or market** ~ **whichever is lower** *(balance sheet)* Niederstwert;
~ *(v.)* *(appraise)* [ab]schätzen, einschätzen, *(assets)* taxieren, *(banking)* valutieren, *(draw bill)* ziehen, trassieren, abgeben, *(esteem)* schätzen, achten, *(estimate)* bewerten, Preis (Wert) bestimmen (festsetzen), Bewertung vornehmen, *(negotiate)* begeben, verkaufen;
~ **s. one's advice** jds. Rat hoch einschätzen, viel auf jds. Ratschläge geben; ~ **at 100 per cent** *(balance sheet)* mit 100% bewerten; ~ **assets on a gone-concern basis** Anlagen im Licht des Liquidationstermins bewerten; ~ **on a net asset basis** nach dem Nettoinventarwert ansetzen (veranschlagen); ~ **a bill upon s. o.** Wechsel auf j. ziehen; ~ **cheques on London** *(Br.)* Schecks auf London ausschreiben; ~ **at cost** zum Einkaufswert einsetzen; ~ **the damage [done] at five pounds** Schaden auf fünf Pfund abschätzen; ~ **an estate** Einheitswert [eines Grundstücks] festsetzen; ~ **goods** Waren bewerten (abschätzen); ~ **hono(u)r above right** Ehre vor Reichtum setzen; ~ **a house at $ 80.000**

Hauswert mit 80.000 Dollar festsetzen; ~ **an income** Einkommensteuer festsetzen; ~ **individually** einzeln bewerten; ~ **o. s. on a keen intellect** sich eines scharfen Verstandes rühmen; ~ **each object** jeden Gegenstand einzeln taxieren; ~ **for probate purposes** zur Nachlaßabwicklung schätzen; ~ **a property** Grundstücksschätzung vornehmen; ~ **s. o. as a secretary** j. für eine gute Sekretärin halten; ~ **o. s. on being successful** sich für erfolgreich halten;
to appreciate in ~ an Wert zunehmen; **to arrange in order of** ~ wertmäßig anordnen; **to assess the** ~ Wert ermitteln (festsetzen); **to attch** ~ **to s. th.** einer Sache Wert beimessen; **to be of great** ~ **to s. o. in his studies** für jds. Studium äußerst wertvoll sein; **to be a poor judge of** ~ Vorzüge schlecht beurteilen können; **to be appreciably in excess of book** ~**s** Buchwerte erheblich übersteigen; **to be of** ~ **to s. o.** jem. wertvoll (nützlich) sein; **to be of great** ~ hohen Wert besitzen, wertvoll sein; **to be of little** ~ geringwertig sein; **to be appreciably in excess of book** ~**s** Buchwerte erheblich übersteigen; **to be liable to deteriorate in** ~ einer Wertminderung ausgesetzt sein; **to compute the** ~ Wert berechnen; **to declare the** ~ **of a parcel** Paketwert bei der Verzollung angeben; **to decline in** ~ Wertminderung erfahren; **to deflate the** ~ niedriger bewerten; **to deprive of all** ~ völlig wertlos machen; **to determine the** ~ **of evidence** Beweiswürdigung vornehmen; **to drop in** ~ Wertverlust erleiden; **to establish the** ~ Wert festsetzen; **to fall in** ~ an Wert verlieren, Wertminderung erfahren; **to fluctuate in** ~ im Wert schwanken, Wertschwankungen unterliegen; **to get the full** ~ **of a th.** vollen Wert aus einer Sache herausholen; **to get at a good** ~ preiswert kaufen, gute Ware für sein Geld bekommen; **to get good** ~ **for one's money** sein Geld gut anlegen, gute Ware für sein Geld bekommen, preiswert kaufen; **to give** ~ **for** Gegenleistung erbringen; **to give good** ~ reell bedienen; **to go down in** ~ **all the time** fortgesetzten Wertverlusten ausgesetzt sein; **to have a certain** ~ seinen Preis haben, seinen (einen bestimmten) Wert haben; **to have a fixed** ~ wertbeständig sein; **to impair the** ~ Wert beeinträchtigen; **to improve (increase) in** ~ an Wert zunehmen, Wertsteigerungen erfahren, im Wert steigen, sich im Wert erhöhen; **to inflate the** ~ höher bewerten; **to lose in** ~ an Wert verlieren; **to lose its** ~ wertlos werden; **to offer good** ~ **for long-range investment purposes** für langfristige Anlagezwecke billig liegen; **to pay double the** ~ doppelten Wert bezahlen; **to pay s. o. the lost** ~ **of s. th.** jem. den Verlust einer Sache ersetzen; **to pay off** ~ **received** für Valuta zahlen; **to place [a]** ~ **on s. th.** Wert auf etw. legen; **to purchase for** ~ als Eigentum erwerben; **to raise the face** ~ [Aktien] zum Nennwert berechnen; **to rate one's services at a high** ~ seine Leistungen sehr hoch einstufen; **to recover the** ~ **of lost merchandise** verlorene Ware wertmäßig ersetzt bekommen; **to reduce in** ~ Wert vermindern, entwerten; **to rent below the** ~ zu billig vermieten; **to represent the true** ~ **of the assets** wirklichen Anlagenwert darstellen; **to sell for** ~ gegen Bezahlung (dem Wert entsprechend) verkaufen; **to sell under the** ~ unter dem Preis ablassen; **to set a high** ~ **on** hoch bewerten; **to set a high** ~ **upon s. one's advice** viel auf jds. Ratschlag geben; **to set too high a** ~ **on s. th.** etw. überbewerten, einer Sache zu hohen Wert beimessen; **to set a high** ~ **on one's time** den Wert seines Zeitaufwands sehr hoch einschätzen; **to set a low** ~ **on** niedriger bewerten, geringen Wert beimessen; **to set a low** ~ **on a stock** *(US)* Aktie niedrig ansetzen (bewerten); **to state the** ~ valvieren; **to take for** ~ an Zahlungs Statt annehmen; **to take an instrument for** ~ *(US)* Papier entgeltlich erwerben; **to transfer for** ~ zur Gutschrift überweisen; **to write up the** ~ **of an asset** Anlagewert heraufsetzen;
~-**added tax (VAT)** Mehrwertsteuer; ~-**added tax rebate** Mehrwertsteuererstattung; ~-**added tax receipts** Mehrwertsteuererträge; ~-**added taxation** Mehrwertbesteuerung; ~ **adjustment** Zuschreibung, Einzelwertberichtigung; **global** ~ **adjustment** Sammelwertberichtigung; ~ **analysis** Wertanalyse, *(rationalization)* Leistungsanalyse; ~ **appreciation** Wertsteigerung; ~ **assessment** Wertfestsetzung; ~ **bill** Wechsel gegen Abtretung der Warenforderung, Warenwechsel; ~ **date** *(bookkeeping, Br.)* Wertstellungstermin, Valuta, Verbuchungsdatum, *(check)* Eingangsdatum, *(foreign exchange)* Abrechnungstag; **average** ~ **date** Durchschnittsvaluta; **original** ~ **date** Originalvaluta; ~ **decrease** Wertminderung; ~ **depreciation** Wertverschlechterung, -verminderung; ~ **increment** ~ **duty** Wertzuwachssteuer; ~ **engineering** kostengünstige Entscheidung, Wertgestaltung; ~ **fluctuations** Wertschwankungen; ~-**given clause** Valutaklausel; ~ **guarantee** Wertsicherung; ~ **increase** Werterhöhung, -steigerung; **fixed percentage** ~ **increment** prozentual festgelegte Wertsteigerung; ~ **judgment** Werturteil;

diminishing ~ method gleichmäßige Abschreibung vom Buchwert; **~ payment** *(war damages)* Wertausgleichszahlung; **~ rationing** preisbezogene Rationierung; **~ relief** *(estate duty)* Wertnachlaß; **no par ~ stock** Aktie ohne Nennwert, Quotenaktie; **~ surcharge** *(air freight bill)* Wertzuschlag II; **cash ~ table** *(insurance)* Kapitalwerttabelle; **land ~ tax** Wertzuwachssteuer für Grundstücke; **in ~ terms** wertmäßig; **~ variance** Preisveränderung.

valued geschätzt, veranschlagt, taxiert;
~ at im Wert von; **~ at £ 10** zehn Pfund wert; **~ at the lower of cost or market** *(balancing method)* zum Einstands- oder Marktwert bewertet;
~ policy *(marine insurance)* taxierte Versicherungspolice; **~ possessions** Kostbarkeiten.

valueless nutz-, wertlos;
to render ~ völlig entwerten.

valuer *(Br.)* Schätzer, Taxator;
licensed ~ *(Br.)* beeidigter Schätzer; **professional ~** amtlicher Schätzer, amtlicher Taxator;
~'s charges Taxgebühren; **~'s report** Schätzgutachten.

valuing Abschätzung, Bewertung, *(banking)* Wertannahme für Schecks;
~ real estate Grundstücksschätzung, -bewertung.

valuta Valuta.

valve Ventil, Klappe, Absperrvorrichtung, *(Br.)* Vakuumröhre;
radio ~ Rundfunkröhre; **safety ~** Sicherheitsventil;
~ of a bicycle tyre Fahrradschlauchventil;
~ (v.) mit Ventilen versehen (kontrollieren);
~ box Ventilgehäuse; **~ gear** Ventilsteuerung; **six-~ set** Sechsröhrenempfänger.

vamp *(coll.)* Verführerin, Vamp, *(shoe)* aufgesetzter Flicken, *(fig.)* Flickwerk;
~ up *(v.)* flicken, reparieren, *(newspaper article)* zusammenschustern, stückeln; **~ up some lectures out of old notes** aus alten Aufzeichnungen eine Vorlesungsreihe zusammenschustern.

vamper Flickschuster, Stümper.

vampire Vampir, Ausbeuter, Erpresser.

van *(Br.)* Last-, Lastkraft-, Liefer-, Roll-, Transportwagen, *(Br.)* [geschlossener] Güter-, G-Wagen, *(closed railway car for luggage)* Gepäckwagen, *(fig.)* Avantgarde, *(light waggon, Br.)* Roll-, Lieferwagen, *(marine)* Vorgeschwader, *(mil.)* Vorhut, *(used for wild beasts, US)* Ausstellungswagen;
in the ~ of scientific progress führend im technischen Fortschritt;
delivery ~ *(Br.)* Lieferwagen; **furniture ~** *(Br.)* Möbelwagen; **guard's ~** Dienstwagen; **lift ~** [Möbel]transportbehälter; **luggage ~** *(railway, Br.)* Gepäckwagen; **motor ~** Last[kraft]wagen; **moving ~** *(US)* Möbelwagen; **police loudspeaker ~** Lautsprecherwagen der Polizei; **removal ~** *(Br.)* Möbelwagen; **~ (v.)** in Güterwagen befördern (verschicken);
~ attendant Beifahrer; **~ builder** Wagenbauer; **~ driver** Lastkraftfahrer; **~ load** Waggonladung; **~ loader** Verlader; **~ owner** Lastwagenbesitzer; **~ salesman** fliegender Händler.

vandal Vandale, Rowdy, Barbar.

vandalism mutwillige [Sach]beschädigung, Zerstörungswut, Vandalismus, Rowdytum.

vane Wetterfahne, -hahn;
~ of a fan blower Ventilatorflügel; **~ of a propeller** Propellerflügel.

vangee *(Br.)* Pumpenantrieb.

vanguard *(mil.)* Vorhut, -trupp;
to be in the ~ of Avantgardist sein.

vanish *(v.)* verschwinden, unsichtbar werden, *(boom)* abklingen;
~ into thin air sich in Nichts auflösen; **~ in space** in der Versenkung verschwinden.

vanishing | cream Tagescreme; **~ line** *(perspective)* Fluchtlinie; **~ point** Fluchtpunkt.

vanity Ehrgeiz, Eitelkeit, Selbstgefälligkeit, Arroganz, *(emptiness)* Hohlheit, Leere;
~ bag (case) Kosmetikköfferchen; **~ Fair** Jahrmarkt der Eitelkeiten; **~ table** *(US)* Frisiertisch.

vanman Lieferwagenfahrer, Rollwagenführer.

vantage günstige Gelegenheit, Vorteil;
~ point günstiger Standort.

vapo(u)r Dampf, Dunst, Rauch, *(engine)* Abgase, *(fig.)* Hirngespinst, Phantom;
~ (v.) verdampfen;
~ bath Dampfbad; **~ engine** Gasmotor; **~ pressure** Dampfdruck; **~ trails** *(airplane)* Kondensstreifen.

vapo(u)rise *(v.)* verdampfen, verdunsten.

variable *(statistics)* quantitatives Merkmal;
~ (a.) *(market)* veränderlich, wechselnd, schwankend, *(person)* wankelmütig, schwankend, *(weather)* unbeständig, *(wind)* aus wechselnden Richtungen;
~ annuity von Kursschwankungen abhängige Rentenzahlung, *(pension scheme)* auf den Lebenshaltungsindex (Anlagenwertzuwachs) abgestellte Rente; **~ budget** den Produktionsschwankungen angepaßter Etat; **~ capital** variables Kapital; **~ condensor** Drehkondensator; **~ cost (expenses)** veränderliche (bewegliche, leistungsabhängige, variable) Kosten; **~ deductions** variable (bewegliche leistungsabhängige) Lohnabzüge; **~ exchange** variabler Kurs; **~ fee** schwankender Betrag; **~ geometry aeroplane** *(Br.)* Flugzeug mit veränderlicher Tragflächenstellung; **~ interest bonds** variable Gratisobligationen; **~ premium** veränderliche Prämie; **~ resources** variable Produktionsfaktoren; **~ standards** schwankende Normen; **~ yield securities** Papiere mit schwankendem Ertrag, **~ zone** gemäßigte Zone.

variance Abweichung, Veränderung, *(in cost)* Kostenabweichung, *(criminal case)* Diskrepanz zwischen Anklage und Nachweis der Straftat, *(disagreement)* Unstimmigkeit, Uneinigkeit, Streit, *(fluctuation)* Schwankung, *(patent law)* Patentänderung, *(pleading)* Abweichung des mündlichen Vorbringens vom Schriftsatz (Beweisergebnis), widersprüchlicher Vortrag, *(statistics)* Standardabweichung;
at ~ im Gegensatz zu;
gross ~ Gesamtabweichung der Ist- von den Standardkosten; **price ~** Preisveränderung; **quantity ~** Mengenabweichung; **slight ~** kleine Unstimmigkeit; **zoning ~** *(US)* Ausnahmegenehmigung von den Bebauungsvorschriften;
~ between reports Widersprüche verschiedener Berichte;
to be at ~ with *(witness)* im Widerspruch zueinander stehen, abweichen von; **to be at ~ for years** seit Jahren im Streit miteinander liegen;
~ account Ausgleichskonto; **~ analysis** Varianzanalyse.

variant | in writing Variante;
~ (a.) abweichend;
~ spelling of word andere Schreibweise eines Wortes.

variation Abweichung, Veränderung, Wechsel, *(dispersion)* Streuung, *(machine)* Schwankungsbereich, Variationsbreite, *(pole)* Polabweichung, *(prices)* Schwankung;
allowed ~ zulässige Abweichung; **plus or minus ~** Abweichung nach oben oder unten; **seasonal ~s** saisonbedingte Schwankungen;
~ of guaranty Garantieänderung; **~ in income** Einkommensveränderungen; **~ of offer** Angebotsabänderung; **~ of the order [of business]** Änderung der Tagesordnung; **~s of pressure** Druckschwankungen; **~s in prices** Kurs-, Preisschwankungen; **~s in public opinion** Schwankungen in der öffentlichen Meinung; **~ in quality** Qualitätsabweichung; **~ in quantity** Mengentoleranz; **~ of two pence in the pound** *(stock exchange)* Schwankungen von zwei Pence auf das Pfund; **~ from standard** Normabweichung; **~ of the tax rate** Veränderung des Steuersatzes; **~s in temperature** Temperaturschwankungen; **~s in the weather** Wetteränderung; **~ of a will** gerichtliche Testamentsänderung;
to be a latter-day ~ Variante der jüngsten Zeit sein; **to undergo ~s** Schwankungen unterworfen sein;
~ chart *(mar.)* Variationskarte; **~ compass** *(mar.)* Deklinationskompaß.

varied mannigfaltig, verschiedenartig, abwechslungsreich, bunt;
~ assortment reiche Auswahl, breites Sortiment, breite Palette.

variety Mannigfaltigkeit, Verschiedenheit, Abwechslung, Buntheit, *(limited class)* Sorte, Art, *(collection)* Auswahl, reiches Angebot, breite Palette, Sortimentsbreite, *(show, Br.)* Varieté;
for a ~ of reasons aus verschiedensten Gründen;
climatic ~ klimatisch bedingte Variante;
~ of fashion Modevariationen; **~ of goods** Sortiment; **~ of patterns** Mustersortiment; **wide ~ of product lines** weit gestreutes Warensortiment;
~ actor *(Br.)* Varietékünstler; **~ chain store** Kaufhaus, -hof; **~ entertainment** *(Br.)* Varietéunterhaltung; **~ hour** *(Br.)* *(television)* Varietéstunde; **~ performance** *(Br.)* Kleinkunst-, Varietévorstellung; **~ shop** *(US)* Gemischtwarenhandlung, Kramladen; **~ show** *(Br.)* Kleinkunst-, Varietévorstellung; **~ store** *(Br.)* Billigwarengeschäft, Kleinpreis-, Gemischtwarenhandlung, *(dry goods)* Galanteriewarengeschäft; **~ theater** *(US)* *(theatre, Br.)* Varietétheater.

various verschiedenartig, bunt, vielfältig;
to be known to the police under ~ names unter verschiedensten Namen polizeibekannt sein.

varnish Firnis, Lack, Möbelpolitur, *(fig.)* Tünche, äußerer Glanz;
~ **of good manners** scheinbar gute Manieren;
~ **remover** *(sl.)* sehr starker Kaffee.
varsity *(coll.)* Uni.
vary *(v.)* abweichen, abändern, unterschiedlich gestalten, variieren, *(market)* sich ändern, schwanken;
~ **one's diet** Diätänderung vornehmen; ~ **from the law** vom Gesetz abgehen; ~ **the risk** versicherte Gefahr in eine andere abändern; ~ **with the season** *(prices)* saisonalen Schwankungen unterworfen sein; ~ **one's style** seinen Stil variieren; ~ **the terms of a contract** Vertragsbestimmungen abändern; ~ **the terms of a will** Testament gerichtlich abändern.
varying wechselnd, unterschiedlich;
~ **prices** schwankende Preise.
vassal Untertan, Untergebener, Vasall;
~ **state** Vasallenstaat.
vassalage Vasallenschaft, -tum, Vasallen-, Unterordnungsverhältnis.
vast ausgedehnt, weit, unermeßlich, *(numerous)* zahlreich, zahllos, riesig, ungeheuer;
~ **amount of money** enorme Geldsumme; ~ **majority** überwältigende Mehrheit; ~ **quantities of snow** riesige Schneemassen.
vat Tonne, Faß, Bottich, *(value-added tax, Br.)* Mehrwertsteuer;
~ **borne** bezahlte Mehrwertsteuer;
~ *(v.)* in ein Faß füllen;
registered ~ **business** *(Br.)* vorsteuerbegünstigtes Unternehmen; ~-**exempt** *(Br.)* mehrwertsteuerfrei; ~ **harmonization** *(Br.)* Harmonisierung der Mehrwertsteuer; ~ **increase** *(Br.)* Mehrwertsteuererhöhung; ~ **proposal** *(Br.)* Mehrwertsteuervorschlag; ~ **rate** *(Br.)* Mehrwertsteuersatz; ~ **receipts** *(Br.)* Mehrwertsteuererträge; ~ **register number** *(Br.)* Mehrwertsteuernummer; ~ **zero-rated** *(Br.)* ohne Mehrwertsteuer.
vaudeville *(US)* Varieté;
~ **show** Varietévorstellung, -veranstaltung.
vaudevillist *(US)* Varietékünstler.
vault Gewölbe, *(burial chamber)* Gruft, *(safe, US)* Stahlkammer, Tresor;
bank ~ Banktresor; **family** ~ Familiengruft; **safe-deposit** ~ *(US)* Stahlkammer, Tresor; **safety** ~ Banktresor, Stahlkammer, Panzergewölbe; **wine** ~ Weinkeller;
~ **of heaven** Himmelsgewölbe;
to keep one's jewels in the ~ seinen Schmuck im Banktresor verwahren;
~ **cash** Barbestand (Geldvorrat) einer Bank; ~ **deposit** Verwahrstück; ~ **deposit scrip** Depotschein.
veep *(US coll.)* Vizepräsident.
veer Richtungswechsel, *(fig.)* Meinungsänderung;
~ *(v.)* Richtung ändern, *(fig.)* seine Meinung (Verhalten) ändern;
~ **round to North** *(wind)* nach Norden umspringen.
vegetable Gemüse, Gemüse-, Futterpflanze;
~ *(a.)* pflanzlich, *(fig.)* eintönig, stumpfsinnig;
~ **diet** vegetarische Kost; ~ **growing** Gemüseanbau; ~ **life** eintöniges Leben; ~ **oil** Pflanzenöl.
vegetarian Vegetarier.
vegetate *(v.)* *(agr.)* brachliegen, *(fig.)* vegetieren.
vegetation Vegetation, Pflanzenwelt, *(fig.)* Vegetieren.
vegetative stage Wachstumszustand.
vehicle Fahrzeug, Gefährt, Wagen, Beförderungsmittel, Vehikel, *(fig.)* Ausdrucksmittel, Vehikel, Gefäß, *(mediator)* Vermittler, Medium, Mittel, Träger;
agricultural ~ landwirtschaftlich genutztes Fahrzeug; **all-purpose** ~ Mehrzweckfahrzeug; **all-terrain** ~ geländegängiges Fahrzeug; **armo(u)red** ~ gepanzertes Fahrzeug; **articulated** ~ Gelenkfahrzeug; **commercial** ~ gewerblich genutztes Fahrzeug, Nutzfahrzeug; **deadline** ~ in Reparatur befindliches Fahrzeug; **fighting** ~ Kampffahrzeug; **for-hire** ~ Mietfahrzeug; **foreign-made** ~ ausländisches Fahrzeug; **forestry** ~ Forstfahrzeug; **goods** ~ Lastfahrzeug; **heavy commercial** ~ Schwerlastwagen; **motor** ~ Kraftfahrzeug; **overtaking** ~ überholendes Fahrzeug; **public** ~ öffentliches Verkehrsmittel; **railway's collecting** ~ Zubringerfahrzeug der Eisenbahn; **sealed** ~ plombiertes Fahrzeug; **tracked** ~ Raupen-, Kettenfahrzeug; **would-be get-away** ~ Fluchtauto;
~ **for advertising** Werbemittel, -träger; ~**s belonging to the police** Polizeifahrzeuge; ~ **of (for) propaganda** Propagandamittel;
to assign ~**s** Transportmittel zuteilen; **to exempt a** ~ **from the obligation to register** Fahrzeug von der Zulassungspflicht befreien; **to leave a** ~ **in a dangerous position** Fahrzeug nicht

ordnungsgemäß abstellen; **to use a** ~ Kraftfahrzeughalter sein; **to use a** ~ **for propaganda** als Propagandamittel benutzen; **to use the press as a** ~ **for one's political opinions** sich der Presse als Medium für die Verbreitung seiner politischen Anschauungen bedienen;
~ **bay** Fahrzeughalle; ~ **building** Fahrzeugbau; ~ **business** Fahrzeugindustrie; ~ **damage** Fahrzeugschäden; **damaged** ~ **inspection service** Besichtigung und Schadenabschätzung eines Unfallfahrzeuges; ~ **insurance** Fahrzeugversicherung, *(own damage, US)* Kaskoversicherung; ~ **and traffic laws** *(US)* Verkehrsvorschriften; ~ **licence** Kraftfahrzeugzulassung; ~ **licence duty** [Kraftfahrzeug]zulassungsgebühr; **to run on own operation** eigenes Fuhrparkunternehmen betreiben; ~ **output** Fahrzeugausstoß; ~ **production** Fahrzeugproduktion; ~ **replacement** Fahrzeugerneuerung; ~ **tank** Fahrzeugtank; ~ **tax** Kraftfahrzeugsteuer; ~ **tunnel** Fahrzeug-, Autotunnel; ~ **user** [Kraft]fahrzeugbenutzer.
vehicular | traffic Fahrzeugverkehr; **to be closed for** ~ **traffic** für Fahrzeuge gesperrt sein; ~ **tunnel** Auto-, Fahrzeugtunnel.
veil Schleier, Maske, *(fig.)* Vorspann, Deckmantel;
under the ~ **of darkness** im Schutz der Dunkelheit;
~ **of mist** Nebelschleier;
~ *(v.)* verschleiern, verbergen, bemänteln;
~ **one's motives** seine Motive verbergen;
to commit murder under the ~ **of patriotism** Mord patriotisch verbrämen; **to draw a** ~ **over what followed** Schleier des Vergessens über das Nachfolgende ziehen; **to lift the** ~ Schleier lüften; **to take the** ~ Nonne werden.
vein Spalt, Riß, *(geol.)* [Erz]ader, Flöz, *(mood)* Stimmung, *(strain)* Anlage, Wesenszug, Ader, *(wood)* Faser, Maser;
in the ~ **of** im Stil von; **in a melancholic** ~ in melancholischer Stimmung;
discovery ~ Ausgangsader;
~ **of gold** Goldader; ~ **of humo(u)r** humoristische Ader;
to be in the right ~ in der richtigen Stimmung sein; **to be thoroughly in the American** ~ ganz und gar amerikanischer Weise entsprechen.
veining Maserung.
vellum Pergamentschrift;
~ **paper** Pergamentpapier.
velocity Geschwindigkeit, Schnelligkeit;
at a ~ **of** mit einer Geschwindigkeit von;
initial ~ Anfangsgeschwindigkeit;
~ **of circulation** *(money)* Umlaufsgeschwindigkeit; ~ **of light** Lichtgeschwindigkeit; ~ **of travel** [Reise]geschwindigkeit.
velvet Samt, *(US)* leicht erzielter [Börsen]gewinn;
cotton ~ Baumwollsamt;
~ *(a.)* aus Samt, samtartig, *(fig.)* katzenfreundlich;
to be (play) on ~ *(sl.)* glänzend dastehen, große Chancen (Gewinnaussichten) haben;
~ **carpet** samtartiger Teppich; ~ **glove** Samthandschuh; **to handle s. o. with** ~ **gloves** j. mit Samthandschuhen anfassen; ~ **paper** Samtpapier; ~ **paws** *(fig.)* gute Manieren; ~ **pile** Teppich mit samtartigem Flor.
velvetwork Samtstickerei.
venal käuflich, bestechlich, korrupt;
~ **judge** bestechlicher Richter; ~ **justice** käufliche Justiz; ~ **period** korrupte Zeit; ~ **politician** korrupter Politiker; ~ **practices** korrupte Methoden.
venality Bestechlichkeit, Käuflichkeit, Korruption.
vend Verkauf, *(mining, Br.)* Gesamtumsatz;
~ *(v.)* verkaufen, hausieren.
vendee *(US)* Käufer, Abnehmer, Erwerber.
vendibility Verkäuflichkeit, Gangbarkeit, Gängigkeit.
vendible verkäuflich, gangbar, feil, absetzbar.
vending Verkauf;
street ~ Verkauf auf offener Straße;
~ **machine** Waren-, Verkaufsautomat, *(tickets)* Ausgabeautomat.
vendition Verkauf.
vendor, vender Verkäufer, *(supplier, US)* Lieferer, Lieferant, *(vending machine)* Verkaufsautomat;
conditional ~ Vorbehaltsverkäufer;
~ **of an estate (a piece of land)** Grundstücksverkäufer;
~ **and purchaser Act** Grundstücksgesetz; ~ **company** veräußernde (einbringende) Gesellschaft; ~ **credit** Ankaufskredit; ~**'s lien** Eigentumsvorbehalt des Verkäufers; ~**'s mortgage** *(Br.)* Restkaufgeldhypothek; ~ **number** Verkaufsnummer; ~**'s shares** bei Umwandlung in eine Kapitalgesellschaft als Kaufpreis übernommene Gesellschaftsanteile, eingebrachte Aktien, Gründeranteile.

vendue *(US)* Versteigerung, Auktion;
~ **master** Auktionator.

veneer Furnierholz, *(fig.)* falscher Glanz, Tünche;
~ **of Western civilization** Tünche westlicher Zivilisation;
~ *(v.)* furnieren, *(fig.)* durch gute Manieren verdecken.

venerable verehrungswürdig;
~ **scholar** ehrfurchtgebietender Gelehrter.

veneration Verehrung, Ehrfurcht.

Venetian|blind Rolladen, Jalousie; ~ **carpet** Treppenläufer; ~ **pearl** Glasperle.

venire *(US)* Geschworenenvorladung.

venomous criticism tödliche Kritik.

vent Öffnung, Loch, *(cask)* Spundloch, *(fig.)* Äußerung, Ausdruck, *(for smoke)* Rauchfang, Abzug;
~ *(v.)* Abzugsöffnung anbringen, *(fig.)* freien Lauf lassen, *(publish)* verbreiten, veröffentlichen;
~ **one's anger on the office boy** seinen Ärger am Büroboten auslassen; ~ **a tale** Gerücht verbreiten;
to find a ~ through the dykes *(flood)* durch eine Dammöffnung abfließen; **to give ~ to one's anger** seinem Ärger Luft machen;
to give ~ to one's feelings in an impassioned speech seinen Gefühlen in einer leidenschaftlichen Ansprache Ausdruck verleihen;
~ **hole** Abzugsloch.

ventilate *(v.)* belüften, *(fig.)* erörtern, diskutieren, ventilieren;
~ **a coal mine** Zeche bewettern; ~ **a room** Zimmer lüften.

ventilating brick Luftziegel.

ventilation Lüftung, Ventilation, *(fig.)* Erörterung, *(mining)* Bewetterung;
~ **of one's grievances** Beschäftigung mit seinen Miseren; ~ **shaft** Belüftungsschacht, *(mining)* Grubenventilator, Wetterschacht.

ventilator Ventilator, Lüftungsanlage, *(mining)* Grubenventilator, Wetterschacht, *(orator)* Redner.

venting pipe Ablaßrohr.

venture *(gaming)* [Spiel]einsatz, *(goods)* schwimmendes Gut (Ware), *(object of speculation)* Spekulationsobjekt, *(risk)* Risiko, Wagnis, *(risky undertaking)* gewagtes (spekulatives) Unternehmen, Wagnis, *(speculation)* [Handels]spekulation;
at a ~ auf gut Glück, *(calculation)* bei roher Schätzung;
business (commercial) ~ geschäftliches Unternehmen; **capital** ~ kapitalistisches Unternehmen; **joint** ~ Gemeinschaftsunternehmen, *(US)* Beteiligungsgeschäft, *(entrepreneurs)* Arbeitsgemeinschaft; **lucky** ~ erfolgreiche Spekulation; **mining** ~ Bergwerksunternehmen; **real-estate** ~ *(US)* Grundstücksspekulation; **speculative** ~ gewagtes (riskantes) Unternehmen;
~ **of exchange** Valutarisiko;
~ *(v.) (forward goods)* Waren auf Spekulation (versuchsweise) übersenden, *(risk)* unternehmen, wagen, riskieren, aufs Spiel setzen;
~ **one's fortune in an enterprise** sein Vermögen in einem Unternehmen anlegen; ~ **a guess** Vermutung äußern; ~ **on a perilous journey** gefahrvolle Reise unternehmen; ~ **a lawsuit** es auf einen Prozeß ankommen lassen; ~ **one's life** sein Leben riskieren; ~ **money in a speculation** Geld spekulativ anlegen; ~ **an opinion** Meinung vorbringen; ~ **a remark** Bemerkung riskieren;
to have a share in a ~ sich an einem Geschäft (Unternehmen) beteiligen; **to put to the** ~ riskieren;
~ **analysis** Risikoanalyse; ~ **capital** Spekulations-, Risikokapital; **to raise fresh** ~ **capital** neues Risikokapital auftreiben; ~ **capital company** Risikounternehmen; ~ **capital field** Spekulationsgebiet; **new** ~ **proposals** Vorschläge für neue Projekte.

venturer Spekulant.

venturesome riskant, gefährlich, gewagt.

venue *(clause in declaration)* Gerichtsstandsklausel, *(law court)* Gerichtsstand, zuständiger Gerichtsort, -stand, Verhandlungsort, *(crime)* Tatort, Schauplatz, *(meeting place)* Versammlungs-, Tagungsort;
classy ~ eleganter Treffpunkt; **local** ~ ausschließlich örtlich zuständiges Gericht; **proper** ~ zuständiger Gerichtsstand;
to change a ~ Gerichtsort verlegen; **to fix a** ~ Gerichtsort bestimmen, örtliche Zuständigkeit begründen;
~ **facts** Tatbestand eines besonderen Gerichtsstandes; ~ **jurisdiction** Zuständigkeit für den Gerichtsstand.

veracious wahrheitsliebend, aufrichtig.

veracity Wahrhaftigkeit, Wahrheitsliebe.

verbal mündlich, auf mündlichem Wege übermittelt, in Worte gefaßt, *(translation)* [wort]wörtlich, wortgetreu;
~ **acts** mündliche Äußerungen; ~ **act doctrine** Grundsatz der Beweiszulässigkeit für mündliche Äußerungen beim Geschäftsabschluß; ~ **agreement (contract)** mündliches Einverständnis, mündliche Vereinbarung; ~ **changes** Änderungen des Wortlauts; ~ **communication** mündliche Mitteilungen; ~ **contract** mündliche Absprache; ~ **copy** wortgetreue Abschrift; ~ **criticism** Textkritik; ~ **error** falsche Wortwahl; ~ **index** Wortverzeichnis; ~ **note** *(dipl.)* Verbalnote; **to have a good ~ memory** Erklärung wortwörtlich wiedergeben können; ~ **offer** mündlich gemachtes Angebot; ~ **order** mündliche Anweisung; ~ **picture of the scene** mündlicher Lagebericht; ~ **process** *(Louisiana)* mündliches Verfahren; ~ **statement** mündliche Erklärung; ~ **tradition** mündliche Überlieferung; ~ **translation** wortwörtliche Übersetzung.

verbalism Wortklauberei, Haarspalterei.

verbalist Wortklauber.

verbalization Formulierung.

verbalize *(v.)* formulieren.

verbally in mündlicher Form.

verbatim wortgetreuer Bericht;
~ *(a.)* wortwörtlich, Wort für Wort;
to quote ~ in vollem Wortlaut zitieren;
~ **confirmation** Wort-für-Wort-Bestätigung; ~ **quotation** wörtliches Zitat; ~ **record** wörtliche Wiedergabe; ~ **report** ausführlicher Bericht; ~ **report of the proceedings** wortwörtlicher Verhandlungsbericht.

verbiage Wortschwall;
to loose o. s. in ~ *(speaker)* sich in einer Fülle von Wörtern verheddern.

verbose geschwätzig, weitschweifig.

verbosity Wortschwall.

verderer, verderor *(Br.)* Forstaufseher.

verdict Entscheidung, gerichtliches Urteil, *(jury)* Urteilsspruch, *(opinion)* Urteil, Meinung;
adverse ~ abweisendes Urteil; **chance** ~ Geschworenenspruch durch das Los; **compromise** ~ Kompromißentscheidung der Geschworenen; **false** ~ Rechtsbeugung durch die Geschworenen; **general** ~ Endurteil der Geschworenen; **majority** ~ von der Jurymehrheit getragenes Urteil; **open** ~ *(coroner)* Todesursache unbekannt; **partial** ~ Teilfreispruch; **popular** ~ Volksmeinung; **public** ~ Geschworenenentscheid in öffentlicher Sitzung; **sealed** ~ Geschworenenspruch im versiegelten Umschlag; **special** ~ Feststellung des Tatbestandes;
~ **of no cause of action** Klageabweisung wegen Unschlüssigkeit; ~ **for the defendant** Urteil zugunsten des Beklagten; ~ **of the electors** Wählermeinung; ~ **of guilty** Schuldspruch; ~ **of guilty but insane** Freispruch wegen Unzurechnungsfähigkeit; ~ **of not guilty** Freispruch; ~ **contrary to law** rechtswidriger Geschworenenspruch; ~ **by lot** Geschworenenurteil durch das Los; ~ **for the plaintiff** Urteil zugunsten des Klägers; ~ **of the public** öffentliche Meinung;
to bring in a ~ **of not guilty** Freispruch verkünden; **to deliver a** ~ **of guilty** auf schuldig erkennen; **to give a** ~ Spruch fällen; **to pronounce a** ~ Urteil fällen; **to return a** ~ Geschworenenurteil fällen; **to stick to one's** ~ sein Urteil aufrechterhalten.

verge Rand, Kante, Saum, Grenze, *(jurisdiction)* Zuständigkeit, Zuständigkeitsbereich, *(Royal court, Br.)* Bannkreis, *(strip of grass)* Grünstreifen, -gürtel;
on the ~ **of tears** den Tränen nahe; **on the** ~ **of a war** am Rande eines Krieges; **within the** ~ **of parliament** innerhalb der Bannmeile des Parlaments;
~ **of a court** Zuständigkeitsbereich eines Gerichts;
~ *(v.)* grenzen;
~ **on bankruptcy** am Rande des Bankrotts stehen; ~ **to the north** sich nach Norden erstrecken; ~ **on the ridiculous** beinahe lächerlich sein;
to be on the ~ **of disaster** vor einer Katastrophe stehen; **to be on the** ~ **of a new war** am Rande eines neuen Krieges stehen.

verger Küster.

verging|on bankruptcy kurz vor dem Bankrott; ~ **on tears** den Tränen nahe.

verification *(attestation, US)* eidliche Beglaubigung, *(auditing)* Bestätigung der Richtigkeit, *(authentication)* Beurkundung, *(averment of proof)* Beweisanerbieten, *(confirmation)* Bestätigung, Feststellung der Richtigkeit, Richtigbefund, *(examination)* Nachprüfung, Überprüfung, Kontrolle, *(pleadings)* eidliche Bestätigung;
after ~ nach Richtigbefund; **in** ~ **of which** urkundlich dessen; **on** ~ nach Richtigbefund;
delivery ~ Wareneingangsbestätigung; **partial** ~ Teilprüfung; ~ **of an account** Bestätigung eines Kontoauszuges; ~ **of the cash** Kassenrevision; ~ **of credentials** Vollmachtenüberprüfung, Prüfung von Vollmachten; ~ **of a flag** *(law of nations)* Prüfung

einer Flagge; ~ **of powers** *(parl.)* Wahlprüfung; ~ **of prices** Preisüberprüfung; ~ **of quality** Qualitätsprüfung; ~ **of quantity** Mengenprüfung; ~ **of signature** Unterschriftsbeglaubigung; ~ **on the spot** Sofortkontrolle;

~ **form** *(shares)* Beglaubigungsformular; ~ **statement** *(banking)* Saldenbestätigung.

verified copy beglaubigte Abschrift.

verify *(v.)* *(attest)* beglaubigen, *(auditing)* Richtigkeit bestätigen, *(authenticate)* beurkunden, *(confirm)* bestätigen, *(confirm by oath, US)* eidesstattliche Erklärung abgeben, eidlich bestätigen (bekräftigen), *(examine)* [nach]prüfen, überprüfen, kontrollieren, *(prove)* beweisen, glaubhaft machen;

~ **an account** Richtigkeit eines Kontoauszuges bestätigen; ~ **the accuracy of a balance sheet** Bestätigungsvermerk abgeben; ~ **a calculation** nachrechnen; ~ **the cash** Kasse revidieren; ~ **dates** Datumsangaben verifizieren; ~ **the figures** Zahlenwerk überprüfen; ~ **by invoices** mit Rechnungen belegen; ~ **the items of a bill** Rechnungsposten kontrollieren; ~ **a narrative** Erzählung bestätigen; ~ **on oath** eidlich bekräftigen, eidesstattliche Erklärung abgeben; ~ **pleadings in an action** Wahrheitsgehalt von Schriftsätzen eidlich bestätigen; ~ **a report** Bericht bestätigen; ~ **a signature** Echtheit einer Unterschrift nachprüfen; ~ **a statement** Erklärung bestätigen, *(banking)* Saldenauszug bestätigen; ~ **a suspicion** Verdacht rechtfertigen.

verily wahrlich.

verities, the simple moralische Grundwerte.

verity Wahrheit, Richtigkeit.

vermeil feuervergoldetes Silber (Kupfer).

vermin Ungeziefer, Schädlinge, Parasiten, *(fig.)* Gesindel, Geschmeiß, Otterngezücht.

vernacular Landes-, Muttersprache, *(language of a trade)* Berufs-, Fachsprache, *(mother tongue)* Landes-, Muttersprache;

~ *(a.)* einheimisch, bodenständig, *(language)* mundartlich; ~ **language** Mutter-, Landessprache; ~ **newspapers** in den Dialekten gedruckte Lokalblätter.

vernacularization Einbürgerung von Wörtern.

vernacularize *(v.)* mundartlich ausdrücken, *(words)* Wörter einbürgern.

versatile vielseitig begabt, beweglich, gewandt;

~ **inventor** begabter Erfinder; ~ **mind** anpassungsfähiger Geist.

versatility vielseitige Verwendbarkeit;

~ **training** Vielseitigkeitsausbildung.

verse Vers[zeile], Versmaß, Gedichtzeile.

versed erfahren, bewandert, sachkundig, gewandt, versiert;

~ **in business [matters]** geschäftserfahren;

to be ~ in a trade branchenerfahren sein; **to be well ~** gründliche Kenntnisse haben.

versedness Sachkunde, Versiertheit, Routine;

~ **in trade** Geschäftserfahrung, Branchenkenntnisse, -erfahrung.

version *(account)* Ausführung, Fassung, Lesart, Version, *(act of translating)* Übersetzen, *(school exercise)* Übersetzungsaufgabe, *(translation)* Übersetzung, *(variant)* Spielart, Abart, Variante;

abridged ~ Kurzfassung; **amended** ~ abgeänderte (ergänzte, berichtigte) Fassung; **authorized** ~ maßgebende (gültige) Fassung; **contradictory** ~s sich widersprechende Versionen (Darstellungen); **earlier** ~ ältere Fassung; **English** ~ englische Fassung; **full-scale** ~ Endversion; **revised** ~ revidierte Fassung; **tape-recorded** ~ auf Band aufgenommene Fassung; **watered-down** ~ abgeschwächte Fassung;

~ **of an accident** Unfalldarstellung, -schilderung; **new ~ of a law** Neufassung eines Gesetzes;

to formulate the final ~ endgültige Fassung formulieren; **to give a quite different** ~ **of the affair** Sache ganz anders darstellen.

verso printing Widerdruck.

versus *(lat.)* *(law court)* gegen, kontra;

A ~ B A gegen B.

vertical Senkrechte, senkrechte Linie;

~ *(a.)* senkrecht, lotrecht, vertikal;

~ **amalgamation** vertikaler Zusammenschluß; ~ **cliff** senkrecht abfallender Felsen; ~ **combination (combine,** *US)* vertikaler Zusammenschluß, vertikale Zusammenfassung (Verflechtung), Vertikalkonzern; ~ **cooperation advertising** Gemeinschaftswerbung von Händlern und Herstellern; ~ **cooperative society** gemeinsame Händler- und Herstellerwerbegesellschaft; ~ **envelopment** *(mil.)* Umfassung aus der Luft; ~ **expansion** Vertikalbund; ~ **hold** *(television set)* Zeilenfeststeller; ~ **integration** vertikaler Zusammenschluß; ~ **line** senkrechte Linie; ~ **merger** vertikaler Zusammenschluß; ~ **price-fixing contract** vertikale Preisvereinbarung, Preisbindung der zwei-

ten Hand; ~ **section** Aufriß; ~ **spacing** *(photocomposing)* Durchschuß; ~ **structure** Vertikalstruktur; ~ **take-off aircraft** Senkrechtstarter; ~ **trust** Vertikaltrust, Verbundwirtschaft.

very high | degree of care besonders hohe Sorgfaltspflicht; ~ **frequency** Ultrakurzwelle, UKW-Frequenz.

vessel Schiff, Seefahrzeug, *(aircraft)* Luftfahrzeug, -schiff, *(engineering)* Druckbehälter, *(hollow receptacle)* Gefäß, Behälter;

cargo ~ Frachtschiff; **coastwise** ~ Küstenschiff; **cold-storage** ~ Kühlschiff; **escort** ~ Geleitschiff; **factory** ~ Fischverarbeitungsschiff; **fishing** ~ Fischereifahrzeug; **foreign** ~ Schiff unter fremder Flagge; **idle** ~ stilliegendes Schiff; **laid-up** ~ außer Dienst gestelltes Schiff; **light** ~ unbeladenes Schiff; **fully loaded** ~ voll beladenes Schiff; **merchant (mercantile)** ~ Handels-, Kauffahrteischiff; **passenger** ~ Passagierschiff; **pilot** ~ Lotsenfahrzeug; **public** ~ Staatsschiff; **roll-on, roll-off** ~ Huckepackschiff; **seagoing** ~ Hochseeschiff; **seaworthy** ~ seetüchtiges Schiff; **single-cruising** ~ alleinfahrendes Schiff; **war** ~ Kriegsschiff; **weak** ~ *(fig.)* unsicherer Kantonist;

~ **of charge** Lastschiff; ~ **on freight** frachtsuchendes Schiff; ~ **of inland navigation** Binnenschiff;

to man a ~ Schiff ausrüsten; **to put a** ~ **out of commission** Schiff außer Dienst stellen; **to put up a** ~ **for freight** Schiff zur Verladung vormerken; **to restore a** ~ Schiff zurückgeben.

vest *(v.)* einkleiden, bekleiden, *(come upon)* zufallen, übertragen werden, *(confer authority)* übertragen, verleihen, *(endow with authority)* mit Vollmacht ausstatten, Vollmacht erteilen, bevollmächtigen, *(into possession)* in Besitz setzen, *(condemn property, US)* beschlagnahmen, *(with rights)* einsetzen in, bestallen;

~ **s. o. with authority** Vollmacht auf j. übertragen, j. ermächtigen; ~ **in the courts** den Gerichten zustehen (obliegen); ~ **a court with power to try cases of life and death** einem Gericht die Aburteilung von Schwurgerichtssachen übertragen; ~ **an estate in s. o.** Grundstücksrechte auf j. übertragen; ~ **s. o. with a function** jem. eine Aufgabe übertragen; ~ **in the heir-at-law** auf den gesetzlichen Erben übergehen; ~ **s. o. with an inheritance** j. in eine Erbschaft einweisen; ~ **in possession** in Besitz übergehen; ~ **property in s. o.** jem. den Besitz eines Vermögens verschaffen; ~ **in the official receiver (trustee in bankruptcy,** *Br.)* auf den Konkursverwalter übergehen; ~ **s. o. with rights in an estate** jem. Grundstücksrechte übertragen; ~ **in the tenant of life** auf den lebenslänglichen Nießbraucher übertragen; ~ **s. o. with title and possession of an estate** jem. Eigentum an einem Grundstück verschaffen; ~ **alien property** *(US)* Feindvermögen beschlagnahmen; ~ **trust property** Treuhandvermögen übertragen;

~-**pocket** im Westentaschenformat; ~-**pocket camera** Kleinbildkamera; ~-**pocket edition** Miniaturausgabe.

vested festbegründet, wohlerworben, unabdingbar, festgesetzt, *(clothed with)* verliehen, bekleidet;

~ **in the governor** *(power of pardon)* dem Gouverneur zustehend; ~ **in interest** mit gegenwärtigem Recht auf zukünftige Nutzungen; ~ **in possession** mit unmittelbarem Besitz- und Nutzungsrecht; ~ **with powers** mit Vollmachten versehen; ~ **by way of sale** käuflich übertragen;

to be ~ in s. o. in jds. Händen liegen; **to be ~ with discretion** nach freiem Ermessen entscheiden können; **to be ~ in the people** dem souveränen Volk obliegen; **to be ~ with power to pardon** Begnadigungsrecht ausüben; **to be ~ with the power to declare war** *(Congress)* zur Abgabe von Kriegserklärungen berechtigt sein; ~ **devise** unbedingte letztwillige Verfügung; ~ **estate** Herrschaftsrecht; ~ **gift** vollzogene Schenkung; ~ **interests** wohlerworbene Rechte, althergebrachte Ansprüche; **to have a ~ interest in a concern** an einem Unternehmen kapitalmäßig beteiligt sein; ~ **legacy** unabdingbares Vermächtnis; ~ **pension plan** unentziehbare Ruhegeldanwartschaft; ~ **remainder** unentziehbare Anwartschaft; ~ **rights** *(constitution, US)* wohlerworbene (unabdingbare) Rechte; ~ **school** *(Ireland)* mit Staatszuschüssen erbaute Schule.

vestibule [Vor]halle, -platz, Flur, *(train, US)* Verbindungs-, Harmonikagang;

~ *(v.)* **passenger cars** Personenwagen durch Übergänge verbinden;

~ **car** *(US)* Eisenbahnwagen mit Verbindungsgang; ~ **school** *(US)* Einführungskursus, *(plant)* Lehrwerkstatt; ~ **train** *(US)* Eisenbahnzug mit Verbindungsgang; ~ **training** *(US)* Anlernen von Arbeitskräften, Werkstattausbildung.

vestige Überrest, Spur;

~**s of an earlier civilization** Reste einer früheren Kultur; **not a ~ of truth** kein Fünkchen Wahrheit.

vestigial restlich, verblieben;
~ **words** gegenstandslos gewordene Worte.
vesting Verleihung, *(pension scheme)* Unverfallbarkeit erdienter Ansprüche bei vorzeitiger Entlassung, *(transfer)* Übertragung, Anfallen;
~ **of trust property** Übertragung des Treuhandvermögens;
to reach ~ age Verfügungsalter erreichen; ~ **assent** *(representative, Br.)* Übertragungsurkunde; ~ **date** Übertragungs-, Anschaffungstag; ~ **day** Anlagetermin; ~ **declaration** *(trust property)* Übertragungserklärung; ~ **deed** Übertragungs-, Bestallungsurkunde; ~ **instrument** *(Br.)* Übertragungsurkunde; ~ **order** *(Br.)* Zwangsübereignungsbeschluß, gerichtliche Auflassungsverfügung; ~ **power** *(court)* Einweisungsvollmacht.
vestment Amtstracht, *(fig.)* Gewand.
vestry *(Br.)* Sakristei, *(US)* Kirchenpflegerausschuß;
common ~ *(Br.)* Gemeindesteuerpflichtiger; ~ **general** *(Br.)* Versammlung der Gemeindesteuerpflichtigen;
~ **clerk** *(Br.)* Rechnungsführer einer Kirchengemeinde.
vestrydom engstirnige Gemeinde-, Kirchtumspolitik.
vestryman Mitglied des Kirchenvorstands.
vet *(veterinary)* Tierarzt;
~ *(v.)* tierärztlich untersuchen (behandeln), *(fig.)* auf Herz und Nieren prüfen, *(mil.)* Sicherheit überprüfen.
veteran *(US)* ehemaliger Kriegsteilnehmer, Veteran, *(car)* Schnauferl;
disabled ~ Kriegsversehrter;
~ *(a.) (official)* im Dienst ergraut, *(soldier)* kampferprobt;
~s' administration *(US)* Versorgungsbehörde (Versorgungswerk) für Kriegsveteranen; ~ **hand** altgedienter (bejahrter) Mitarbeiter; ~ **housing** Wohnraumbeschaffung für Kriegsversehrte; ~ **official** im Dienst ergrauter Beamter; ~ **services** langjährige Dienste; ~ **troops** kampferprobte Truppen.
veterinary Tierarzt, Veterinär;
~ *(a.)* tierärztlich;
~ **college** tierärztliche Hochschule; ~ **hospital** Tierklinik; ~ **medicine** Tierheilkunde; ~ **surgeon** Tierarzt.
veto Veto[recht], Einspruch, Ausübung des Vetos;
absolute ~ absolutes Vetorecht; **limited (negative) ~** eingeschränktes Veto; **pocket ~** *(US, president)* indirektes Veto; **qualified ~** *(US)* überstimmbares (eingeschränktes) Veto; **suspensible (suspensory) ~** aufschiebendes Vetorecht;
~ *(v.)* Veto einlegen, Vetorecht ausüben, Einspruch erheben, *(refuse assent)* ablehnen, Zustimmung verweigern;
~ **a bill** einem Gesetzentwurf die Zustimmung versagen; ~ **a decision** gegen eine Entscheidung sein Veto einlegen;~ **a plan** gegen einen Plan Einspruch einlegen; ~ **a procession** *(police)* Umzug verbieten;
to exercise one's ~ von seinem Vetorecht Gebrauch machen, sein Vetorecht ausüben; **to have the power (right) of ~** Vetorecht haben; **to interpose (impose) one's ~** Einspruch erheben, Veto einlegen; **to override a ~** sich über ein Veto hinwegsetzen; **to put (set) a (one's) ~ on s. th.** sein Veto gegen etw. einlegen; **to reserve a ~** Veto rückgängig machen; **to use one's ~** von seinem Vetorecht Gebrauch machen;
~ **message** *(US)* begründetes Veto, *(US, president)* Einspruchsrecht; ~ **power** Einspruchs-, Vetorecht; **to hold ~ powers** über Vetorechte verfügen.
vetoer Vetoeinlegender.
vetoing stock Sperrminorität.
vetoist Vetoeinlegender.
vetting *(mil.)* Sicherheitsüberprüfung.
vex *(v.) (annoy)* schikanieren, belästigen, *(disturb)* quälen, bedrücken;
~ **a saint** selbst einen Engel zur Verzweiflung bringen.
vexation Schikane, Belästigung, Plage, Qual, Verdruß, Ärgernis, *(harassment by process of law)* gerichtliche Scherereien, *(trouble)* Unruhe, Beunruhigung, Sorge;
the little ~s of life die Widrigkeiten des täglichen Lebens;
constant ~s from one's neighbo(u)rs andauernde nachbarliche Belästigungen;
to be subjected to many ~s allerhand Scherereien haben.
vexatious mutwillig, frivol, *(law suit)* schikanös;
~ **Action Act** *(Br.)* Gesetz gegen mißbräuchliches Prozessieren;
~ **delay** Obstruktion, schikanöse Verzögerung; ~ **neighbo(u)r** leidiger Nachbar; ~ **proceedings** schikanöses Prozeßverfahren, mutwillige Klage; ~ **refusal to pay** schikanöse Zahlungsverweigerung; ~ **suit** schikanöser Prozeß.
vexed question heftig diskutiertes Problem.
via *(postal service)* über;
~ **airmail** per Luftpost.

viability Lebensfähigkeit, *(state)* finanzielle Leistungsfähigkeit;
economic ~ Eigenwirtschaftlichkeit.
viable *(fig.)* entwicklungsfähig, *(foetus)* lebensfähig;
commercially (economically) ~ wirtschaftlich rentabel;
to prove ~ sich als lebensfähig erweisen;
~ **scheme** lebensfähiges Projekt.
viaduct Überführung, -bau, Viadukt, Talüberführung.
viands Lebensmittel, Proviant.
viaticum Reiseproviant, *(allowance)* Reisegeld.
vibrant personality kraftvolle Persönlichkeit.
vibrate *(v.)* zittern, vibrieren, *(v./tr.)* in Schwingungen versetzen;
~ **whenever a heavy lorry passes** durch jeden Lastwagen in Schwingungen versetzt werden; ~ **between two opinions** zwischen zwei Meinungen schwanken.
vibration Schwingung, Vibration, *(fig.)* Schwanken.
vibrator Rüttelapparat, *(el.)* Zerhacker, *(print.)* schwingende Farbwalze.
vicarious beauftragt, stellvertretend, kommissarisch;
~ **act** Handlung eines Erfüllungsgehilfen; ~ **agent** Erfüllungsgehilfe; ~ **authority** stellvertretend ausgeübte Vollmacht; ~ **liability** Haftung für fremdes Verschulden (für den Erfüllungsgehilfen, für Dritte); ~ **officer** Verrichtungs-, Erfüllungsgehilfe; ~ **performance** Vertragserfüllung durch den Erfüllungsgehilfen; ~ **power** stellvertretend ausgeübte Vollmacht.
vicariously vertretungsweise.
vice unmoralischer Lebenswandel, Laster, Schwäche, Untugend, *(defect)* Fehler, Mangel [einer Sache];
constitutional ~ Gebrechen; **inherent ~** verborgener Mangel; **redhibitory ~** *(US)* Gewährleistungsmangel, Wandlungsfehler;
~ **of literary style** literarische Entartung;
to be caught in a ~ in einer Zwickmühle sein;
~ *(a.)* an Stelle (in Vertretung) von, stellvertretend;
~-**chairman** stellvertretender Vorsitzender; ~-**chairmanship** Vizepräsidentschaft; ~-**chancellor** Vizekanzler, *(university)* Protektor; ~ **commercial agent** *(consular service, US)* stellvertretender Handelsreferent; ~ **consul** Vizekonsul; ~-**consulate** Vizekonsulat; ~-**manager** stellvertretender Direktor; ~-**member of the management** stellvertretendes Vorstandsmitglied; ~-**presidency** Vizepräsidentschaft; ~-**president** stellvertretender Vorsitzender, Vizepräsident, *(US)* Abteilungsleiter; **executive ~-president** *(US)* geschäftsführender Vizepräsident; ~ **squad** Sittenpolizei; ~ **versa** *(lat.)* wechselseitig, umgekehrt.
vicinage Nachbarschaft.
vicinal benachbart.
vicinity Nähe, Nachbarschaft, Gegend, nähere Umgebung;
in close ~ in unmittelbarer Nähe von;
~ **of a factory** Fabriknähe.
vicious *(addicted to vice)* verderbt, lasterhaft, *(defective)* fehlerhaft, mangelhaft, *(malignant)* bösartig, tückisch, giftig, *(terrible, coll.)* fürchterlich, schrecklich, furchtbar;
~ **air** unreine (verpestete) Luft; ~ **attack** heimtückischer Angriff; ~ **circle** Teufelskreis; ~ **intromission** *(deseased's estate, Scot.)* unlautere Machenschaften; ~ **life** unmoralische Lebensführung; ~ **manuscript** fehlerhaftes Manuskript; ~ **practices** verwerfliche Methoden; ~ **propensity** *(animal)* bösartige Veranlagung; ~ **remark** ungezogene Bemerkung; ~ **slander** *(coll.)* bösartige Verleumdung; ~ **spiral of prices** stetig steigende Preisspirale; ~ **style** schlechter Stil.
vicissitude Unbeständigkeit;
after many ~s nach mancherlei Schicksalsschlägen;
~ **of fortune** Schicksalsschläge; ~**s of life** Auf und Ab des Lebens.
victim Opfer, Verunglückter, Geschädigter, Leidtragender, *(dupe)* Betrogener, Angeführter, Hereingelegter;
war ~ Kriegsopfer;
~ **of a motor accident** Verkehrsopfer; ~ **of a catastrophe** Katastrophenbetroffener; ~ **of circumstances** Opfer der Verhältnisse; **numerous ~s of a confidence trick** zahlreiche Opfer einer Bauernfängerei; ~ **of an earthquake** Erdbebengeschädigter, -opfer; ~ **of inflation** Inflationsopfer; ~**s of Nazi persecution** Verfolgte des Naziregimes; ~**s of oppression** Opfer der Unterdrückungspolitik; ~ **of a plague** Seuchenopfer;
to fall a ~ to propaganda auf Propaganda hereinfallen.
victimization Schikanierung, Verfolgung, *(industrial strife)* Entlassung von Streikführern.
victimize *(v.)* schikanieren, verfolgen, *(unionism)* [Streikführer] durch Entlassung bestrafen.
victory Sieg, Trumpf, Erfolg;
moral ~ moralischer Erfolg; **pyrrhic ~** Pyrrhussieg;
~ **on points** Sieg nach Punkten;

~ garden in Kriegszeiten angelegter Schrebergarten; **~ loan** *(Br.)* Kriegsanleihe.

victual | s *(Br.)* Lebens-, Nahrungsmittel, Proviant;
  ~ *(v.)* mit Lebensmitteln versehen, als Lieferant verpflegen, *(v./i.)* sich mit Lebensmitteln eindecken;
  ~ a ship Schiff verproviantieren;
  ~ house Speisehaus.

victual[l]er Lebensmittelhändler, [Lebensmittel]lieferant, *(innkeeper)* Gastwirt, *(mar.)* Proviantschiff;
  licensed ~ *(Br.)* Gast-, Schankwirt.

victual[l]ing Versorgung mit Lebensmitteln, Verproviantierung, *(trade)* Lebensmittelhandel;
  ~ bill *(Br.)* Zollschein für Schiffsproviant; **~ house** Gaststätte; **~ note** *(Br.)* Verpflegungsgutschein; **~ office** *(mar., Br.)* Verpflegungsamt; **~ ship** Proviant-, Verpflegungsschiff; **~ station** Verpflegungsstation; **~ yard** *(mar., Br.)* Verpflegungslager.

video *(US)* Fernsehen;
  home ~ Fernsehbandgerät;
  ~ *(a.)* zum Fernsehen (Radarbild) gehörig;
  ~ bus Fernsehaufnahmewagen; **~ cartridge (cassette)** Fernsehkassette; **~ cassette machine** Kassettenfernsehgerät; **~ cassette recording** Fernsehkassettenaufnahmegerät; **~ cast** Fernsehsendung; **~ channel** Fernseh-, Bildfrequenzkanal; **~ display unit** Bildschirm-Terminal; **~ frequency** Bild-, Fernsehfrequenz; **~ [tape] recorder** Fernsehkassettengerät; **electronic ~ recording cartridge** Fernsehkassette; **~ tape** Magnet-, Fernsehband; **~ telephone** Bild-, Fernsehtelefon; **~ telephone service** Fernsehsprechdienst, -telefonverkehr; **~ telephony** Fernsehtelefonie; **~ terminal** Bildschirm; **~ transmitter** Bildsender; **~ transmission set** Bildsendegerät; **~ truck** *(US)* Fernsehaufnahmewagen; **~ vernacular** Fernsehfachsprache.

videotape Magnetbild-, band, Fernsehband;
  ~ *(v.)* auf Magnetband (Dose) aufnehmen;
  ~ lecture auf einem Fernsehband aufgenommene Vorlesung; **~ recorder** Fernsehbandaufnahme-, Fernsehtonbandgerät; **~ recording** Fernsehbandaufnahme.

videotaped fernsehmäßig auf Dose aufgenommen;
  ~ lecture auf Kassette aufgenommene Fernsehvorlesung.

viduage Witwenstand.

vie *(v.)* **with s. o.** mit jem. wetteifern.

view *(inquiry)* Untersuchung, Prüfung, *(opinion)* Ansicht, Anschauung, Auffassung, Blickwinkel, Aspekt, *(photo)* Aufnahme, Bild, Fotografie, *(prospect)* Sicht, Aussicht, *(review)* Überblick, Zusammenschau, *(right of prospect)* Recht auf Aussicht, *(purpose)* Absicht, Zweck, *(range of sight)* Blickweite, Sicht, Gesichtsfeld, *(survey)* Übersicht, kurzes Gutachten, *(visit to the scene)* Lokaltermin, Augenscheinsnahme, Tatortbesichtigung;
  in ~ of in Anbetracht, angesichts; **in ~ of the circumstances** in Berücksichtigung der Umstände; **in ~ of the facts** angesichts der Tatsachen; **in my ~** meines Erachtens; **in the longer ~** auf längere Sicht gesehen; **on ~** zur Besichtigung freigegeben; **on nearer ~** bei näherem Zusehen; **plain to ~** gut sichtbar; **to the ~** öffentlich; **with a ~ to** im Hinblick auf, zwecks, mit dem Zweck (Ziel); **with a ~ to facilitating research** um die Forschungstätigkeit zu erleichtern; **with a ~ to saving trouble** um Schwierigkeiten zu vermeiden; **with a ~ to profit** in Gewinnabsicht;
  aerial ~ Luftbild; **back ~** Hinteransicht; **big-picture ~** Panoramablick; **broad ~s** liberale Ansichten; **extreme ~s** *(politics)* radikale Ansichten; **front ~** Vorderansicht; **modern ~s** moderne Ansichten; **political ~** politische Ansicht (Meinung); **private ~** private Vorführung; **retrospective ~** Aussicht nach hinten, *(fig.)* Rückblick; **side ~** Seitenansicht; **stuffy ~s** rückständige Ansichten; **true and fair ~** *(balance sheet, Br.)* wahres und richtiges Bild; **unrestricted ~** unverbaubare Aussicht;
  ~ and delivery *(right of common)* Almendezuweisung; **~ of an inquest** Ortsbesichtigung durch Geschworene; **~ of life** Lebensanschauung; **~ of a mountain** Aussicht von einem Berg; **general ~ of a plant** Gesamtansicht eines Werkes; **~ of a scene of murder** Besichtigung des Mordschauplatzes; **~s on the situation** Lagebetrachtungen; **general ~ of s. one's works** kritischer Überblick über jds. Gesamtwerk;
  ~ *(v.)* besichtigen, in Augenschein nehmen, prüfen;
  ~ favo(u)rably positiv aufnehmen; **~ the matter in the right light** Sachlage richtig beurteilen; **~ a matter from the taxpayer's standpoint** Angelegenheit mit den Augen des Steuerzahlers sehen; **~ a subject in various ways** Thema auf verschiedene Weise behandeln; **~ the coming year** Vorschau auf das nächste Jahr abgeben;
  to agree with s. one's ~ jds. Ansicht beipflichten; **to be open to all ~s** für alles Verständnis haben; **to be on ~ in the big shops** in

den größeren Läden ausgestellt sein; **to be exposed to the full ~ of the crowd** den Blicken der Menge ausgeliefert sein; **to come into ~** in das Blickfeld geraten; **to exchange ~s** Meinungen austauschen; **to express strong ~s on the subject of equal pay** sich dezidiert zum Thema gleichen Lohns äußern; **to fall in with s. one's ~** sich weitgehend jds. Ansichten anschließen; **to form a ~ on s. o.** sich über j. eine Meinung bilden; **to get one's ~s across** seine Meinung an den Mann bringen; **to give an order to ~** Besichtigungsgenehmigung erteilen; **to give one's own personal ~s** seine persönliche Meinung zum Ausdruck bringen; **to give a general ~ of s. one's works** allgemeinen Überblick über jds. Arbeiten geben; **to have in ~** im Auge haben, beabsichtigen; **to have other ~s for the summer** andere Ferienpläne haben; **to have s. th. in ~** sein Augenmerk auf etw. richten; **to hide one's ~s** mit seiner Ansicht hinter dem Berge halten; **to hold a ~** Ansicht (Standpunkt) vertreten; **to hold extreme ~s** extreme Richtung (Ansichten) vertreten; **to lose ~ of** aus den Augen verlieren; **to put forward one's ~s** seine Meinung zum Ausdruck bringen; **to share s. one's ~s** jds. Meinung teilen; **to signal one's ~s** seine Ansicht zu erkennen geben; **to spoil the ~** Landschaft entstellen; **to stand in full ~ of the crowd** für die Volksmenge gut sichtbar sein; **to stick to one's ~s** seine Behauptungen aufrechterhalten; **to take a ~** sich eine Meinung bilden, auf dem Standpunkt stehen; **to take a different ~** verschiedener Meinung sein, andere Ansicht vertreten; **to take a jaundiced ~** voreingenommen sein; **to take a poor ~ of s. one's conduct** jds. Verhalten miserabel beurteilen; **to take a grave ~ of the situation** Lage ernst beurteilen;
  ~ finder *(photo)* Bildsucher.

viewable sichtbar;
  to be ~ gut sichtbares Fernsehbild aufweisen;
  ~ television show sehenswerte Fernsehsendung.

viewer Beschauer, *(court)* Augenscheinsbeauftragter, *(inspector)* Inspektor, *(inspector of highways)* Fernstraßenbeauftragter, *(looker-on)* Zuschauer, *(spectator)* Fernsehzuschauer;
  television ~ Fernsehzuschauer, -teilnehmer;
  ~ survey Umfrage bei den Fernsehzuschauern.

viewing | of land *(damaged by overflow)* Grundstücksbesichtigung; **~ scene of crime** Tatortbesichtigung;
  ~ guide Fernsehheft; **~ lens** Sehlinse.

viewpoint Aussichtspunkt, *(fig.)* Stand-, Gesichtspunkt;
  legal ~ Rechtsstandpunkt;
  to take a poor ~ of s. one's conduct jds. Verhalten miserabel finden.

vigil Nachtwache;
  sickroom ~ Krankenwache;
  to keep ~ over a sick child Nachwache bei einem kranken Kind halten.

vigilance Wachsamkeit, *(caution)* Umsicht, Vorsicht, *(med.)* Schlaflosigkeit, *(US)* Überwachung, *(promptness in pursuing one's rights)* rechtzeitige Geltendmachung;
  ~ committee *(US)* Bürgerausschuß.

vigilant wachsam, umsichtig;
  ~ treasurer umsichtiger Schatzmeister.

vigilante *(US)* Bürgerwehrmitglied, Hilfspolizist.

vignette *(architecture)* Weinlaubverzierung, *(photo)* verlaufendes Bild, *(print.)* Vignette.

vigo(u)r Körper-, Geisteskraft, *(intensity of action)* Aktivität, Energie, *(law)* Gültigkeit, Wirksamkeit;
  ~ of an argument Durchschlagskraft eines Arguments;
  to be still in ~ *(law)* noch gültig sein.

vigorous kräftig, aktiv, lebhaft, tatkräftig;
  ~ enforcement of the country's law strenge Anwenung der Gesetze; **~ prosecution of a war** energische Kriegsführung; **~ protest** eindringlicher (nachdrücklicher) Protest.

vile abscheulich, *(filthy)* anstößig, schmutzig, *(worthless)* geringfügig;
  ~ acts and gestures obszöne Handlungen; **~ character** niedriger Charakter; **~ creature** elende Kreatur; **~ language** vulgäre Sprache; **~ practices** anstößige Praktiken; **~ thoughts** schändliche Gedanken; **~ use of bribery** üble Bestechungsmethode; **~ weather** miserables Wetter.

vilification Herabsetzung, Verleumdung.

villa Landhaus, Villa;
  ~ owner Villenbesitzer.

villadom Villenviertel, Vorstadtbevölkerung.

village Dorf, Ortschaft, *(US)* ländliche Gemeinde;
  bunched ~ Haufendorf;
  ~ community Dorfgenossenschaft, -gemeinschaft; **~ council** *(US)* Gemeinderat; **~ green** Dorfanger; **~ industry** Dorfbetrieb; **~ inn** Dorfkneipe, -gasthaus; **~ post office** Dorfpostamt.

villager Dorfbewohner.

villagey dorfähnlich.

villain Bösewicht, Schurke, Schuft;
~ **services** schurkische Dienste.

villalike villenähnlich.

villein Leibeigener.

villeinage Leibeigenschaft.

vim Mumm, Elan, Schneid, Schwung;
to feel full of ~ Bäume ausreißen können.

vindicable zu rechtfertigen.

vindicate (v.) schützen, in Schutz nehmen, verteidigen, (claim) Anspruch erheben, etw. beanspruchen;
~ **o. s.** sich rechtfertigen; ~ **a claim** Forderung erheben; ~ **one's judgment** seine Beurteilung rechtfertigen; ~ **one's policy** seine Politik bestätigt finden; ~ **one's rights** seine Rechte geltend machen.

vindication Verteidigung, Behauptung, Beanspruchung, (justification) Rechtfertigung;
~ **of one's rights** Geltendmachung seiner Rechte;
to speak in ~ **of one's conduct** sein Verhalten rechtfertigen.

vindicatory rechtfertigend, (punitive) ahndend, strafend;
~ **parts of a law** Sanktionsbestimmungen eines Gesetzes.

vindictive damages Buß-, Reugeld.

vineyard Weinberg, (fig.) Wirkungsstätte, Arbeitsfeld.

viniculture Weinbau.

vinification Weinkelterung.

vintage Weinernte, -ertrag, (time of gathering) Weinlesezeit, (wine of a particular year) Jahrgang;
rare old ~s kostbare alte Jahrgänge;
~ **conversationalist** hervorragender Unterhalter; ~ **newspaper account** alter Zeitungsbericht; ~ **sports car** Veteran, Schnauferl; ~ **wine** Spitzenwein ~ **year of profits** Spitzenjahr.

vintager Weinhändler.

vintner Weinhändler.

violate (v.) verletzen, brechen, verstoßen, übertreten, (commit rape) vergewaltigen, notzüchtigen;
~ **a church** Gotteshaus entweihen (schänden); ~ **a clause** Vertragsbestimmung verletzen; ~ **a contract** Vertrag brechen (verletzen); ~ **a frontier** Grenze verletzen, Grenzverletzung begehen; ~ **a law** gegen ein Gesetz verstoßen; ~ **one's oath** seinen Eid brechen; ~ **s. one's privacy** in jds. Intimsphäre eindringen, jds. Intimsphäre verletzen; ~ **a treaty** Vertrag verletzen.

violating law clause (life insurance) Haftungsausschluß bei Tod in Folge Teilnahme an rechtswidrigen Unternehmungen.

violation Bruch, Mißachtung, Verstoß, Verletzung, Übertretung, (rape) Vergewaltigung, Notzucht;
moving (Br.) (traffic, US) ~ Verletzung einer Verkehrsvorschrift, Verkehrsverstoß, -widrigkeit;
~ **of airspace** Luftraumverletzung; ~ **of banking regulations** Verstoß gegen die Bestimmungen der Bankaufsichtsbehörde; ~ **of the border** Grenzverletzung; ~ **of a church** Entweihung (Profanierung) einer Kirche; ~ **of a contract** Vertragsverletzung, -bruch; ~ **of the covenant** Verstoß gegen die getroffenen Vereinbarungen; ~ **of currency** Devisenvergehen; ~ **of a frontier** Grenzverletzung; ~ **of a law** Gesetzverstoß, -verletzung; ~ **of an international law** Völkerrechtsverletzung; ~ **of law and order** Landfriedensbruch; ~ **of neutrality** Neutralitätsbruch, -verletzung; ~ **of an oath** Eidbruch; ~ **of the peace** Störung der öffentlichen Ruhe und Ordnung; ~ **of the principles of morality** Verletzung moralischer Prinzipien; ~ **of privacy** Verletzung der Intimsphäre; ~ **of the rights of citizens** Verletzung der Grundrechte, Mißachtung der Bürgerrechte; ~ **of the right of free speech** Mißachtung der Redefreiheit; ~ **of a treaty** Vertragsverletzung; ~ **of trust** Vertrauensbruch;
to act in ~ **of a treaty** Vertragsbruch begehen; **to be in** ~ **of a provision** Bestimmung verletzen; **to commit a** ~ (US) Übertretung begehen.

violator Übertreter.

violence Zwang, gewaltsames Vorgehen, Gewalt[tätigkeit], (vehemence) Ungestüm, Heftigkeit, (violation) Verletzung, Übertretung;
~ **of an attack** Heftigkeit einer Attacke; ~ **of a storm** Heftigkeit eines Unwetters;
to die by ~ eines gewaltsamen Todes sterben; **to do** ~ **to one's principles** in Außerachtlassung seiner Prinzipien handeln; **to do** ~ **to a text** Text entstellen, einem Text Gewalt antun; **to practise** ~ Gewalt anwenden.

violent heftig, gewaltig, (acting by physical force) gewalttätig, handgreiflich;
~ **attack** heftige Attacke; ~ **contrast of colo(u)rs** greller Farb-

kontrast; ~ **controversy** heftige Auseinandersetzung; ~ **death** gewaltsamer Tod; **to lay** ~ **hands on** gewalttätig (handgreiflich) werden, Gewalt antun; ~ **heat** große Hitze; ~ **interpretation** gewaltsame (verzerrende) Auslegung; **by** ~ **means** gewaltsam; ~ **measures** Gewaltmaßnahmen; ~ **pains** heftige (große) Schmerzen; ~ **presumption** an Wahrscheinlichkeit grenzende Vermutung; ~ **profits** (Scot.) Zwischengewinne [des Pächters]; ~ **storm** gewaltiger Sturm; ~ **temper** ungezügeltes Temperament.

VIP (coll.) großes Tier.

viper (fig.) Giftschlange.

virago Mannweib, (termagant) Zankteufel.

virement Befugnis zur Etatstitelübertragung.

vires Aufgabenbereich;
to act intra ~ im Rahmen seiner Vollmachten handeln; **to be intra (within)** ~ im Rahmen der satzungsmäßigen Befugnisse liegen; **to be ultra (outside)** ~ satzungsgemäße Befugnisse überschreiten.

virgin Jungfrau;
~ **(a.)** jungfräulich, züchtig;
~ **cruise** Jungfernfahrt; ~ **forest** Urwald; ~ **soil** jungfräulicher Boden.

virile männlich, kräftig;
to live to a ~ **old age** rüstig ins Greisenalter gehen; ~ **style [of writing]** kraftvoller Stil.

virtual tatsächlich, faktisch;
~ **manager** eigentlicher Geschäftsführer.

virtually praktisch.

virtue Unbescholtenheit, Rechtschaffenheit, Tugend, (law) Rechtskraft, (merit) Vorzug, hoher Wert;
by ~ **of my office** kraft meines Amtes; **in** ~ **whereof** urkundlich dessen; **of great** ~ sehr wirkungsvoll;
cardinal ~s Kardinaltugenden;
~ **made of necessity** aus der Not geborene Tugend; **great** ~ **of a scheme** großer Vorzug eines Planes;
to claim a pension in ~ **of one's long military service** unter Berücksichtigung seiner langen Militärdienstzeit Pensionsansprüche stellen; **to make a** ~ **of necessity** aus der Not eine Tugend machen.

virtuosity Virtuosentum, Virtuosität.

virtuoso Virtuose, Künstler, (one skilled in fine arts) Kunstkenner, -liebhaber.

virulence (fig.) Bitterkeit, Schärfe.

virus disease Viruskrankheit.

visa, visé Sichtvermerk, Einreisegenehmigung, Visum, (signature of approval) Genehmigungsvermerk;
additional ~ Zusatzvisum; **collective** ~ Sammelvisum; **customs** ~ Zollvermerk; **diplomatic** ~ Diplomatenvisum; **entry** ~ Einreisevisum; **exit** ~ Ausreisevisum; **immigration** ~ Einwanderungsvisum; **permanent** ~ Dauervisum; **transit** ~ Durchreisevisum; **visitor's** ~ Besuchervisum, (US) Visum für vorübergehenden Aufenthalt, Besuchervisum;
~ **(v.)** Einreisegenehmigung erteilen, Paß mit Sichtvermerk versehen;
to abolish ~s Visumzwang aufheben; **to issue a** ~ Visum ausstellen; **to mark a passport with a** ~ Paß mit Sichtvermerk versehen; **to refuse a** ~ Visum verweigern;
~ **category** Visumrangklasse; ~ **department** Visumabteilung; ~ **fee** Visumsgebühr; ~ **office** Visumabteilung.

vised passport mit Sichtvermerk versehener Paß.

visibility Sichtweite, Flugsicht;
high ~ gute Sicht; **low** ~ schlechte Sicht;
to turn back because of poor ~ (aircraft) wegen schlechter Sichtverhältnisse zurückfliegen;
~ **conditions** Sichtverhältnisse; ~ **meter** Sichtbarkeitsmesser.

visible sichtbar, wahrnehmbar, (balance sheet) durchsichtig, (discernible) bemerkbar, unterscheidbar;
~ **balance** Handelsbilanz; ~ **difficulties** offensichtliche Schwierigkeiten; ~ **envelope** Fensterumschlag; ~ **exports** Warenausfuhr, sichtbare Ausfuhr; ~ **horizon** (mar.) natürlicher Horizont, Kimm; ~ **imports** sichtbare Einfuhr, Wareneinfuhr; ~ **injury** äußerlich sichtbare Verletzung; ~ **items of trade** sichtbare Ein- und Ausfuhr (Posten der Leistungsbilanz), Posten des Warenverkehrs; **no** ~ **means of support** ersichtlich keine Unterhaltsmittel (mittellos); ~ **reserves** offene Reserven; ~ **supply** dem Markt zur Verfügung stehende Warenmenge; ~ **trade** sichtbare Ausfuhr, sichtbarer Außenhandel, Warenverkehr.

vision Sehvermögen, Gesicht, Gesichtssinn, (fig.) Vorstellungsvermögen, (el.) Bild, (object of imaginative contemplation) Phantasie, Wunschbild;

beyond our ~ außerhalb unseres Gesichtskreises; **haunted by ~s** von Gesichtern verfolgt;
~s *(psych.)* Halluzinationen;
political ~ politische Einsicht; **remarkable** ~ bemerkenswerte Schönheit; **romantic ~s** romantische Vorstellungen;
to have ~s of great wealth and success von großem Reichtum und Erfolg träumen; **to lack political** ~ Mangel an politischer Einsicht haben;
~ service Bildtelefonverkehr.

visionary Hellseher, Phantast, Idealist, Schwärmer;
~ *(a.)* visionär, hellseherisch, *(fig.)* phantastisch;
~ plans (schemes) verstiegene (überspannte) Pläne.

visit [kurzer] Besuch, Besuchsreise, *(chat, coll.)* Plauderei, Schwatz, *(physician)* Krankenbesuch, *(search)* Durch-, Untersuchung, Inspektion, Besichtigung, *(ship)* Durchsuchung eines Schiffes, Flaggenkontrolle;
congratulatory ~ Gratulationsbesuch; **courtesy** ~ Höflichkeitsbesuch; **domiciliary** ~ *(Br.)* Haussuchung; **farewell** ~ Abschiedsbesuch; **first** ~ Antrittsbesuch; **flying** ~ Blitzbesuch; **follow-up** ~ nachfassender Vertreterbesuch; **informal** ~ nicht offizieller Besuch; **leave-taking** ~ Abschiedsbesuch; **low-key** ~ heruntergespielter Besuch;
~ of civility Höflichkeitsbesuch; **~ of condolence** Beileidsbesuch; **~ to the doctor** Arztbesuch, ärztliche Konsultation; **~ to an exhibition** Besichtigung einer Ausstellung; **~ to some friends** Besuch bei Freunden; **~ of several hours** mehrstündiger Besuch; **~ and search** *(law of nations)* Durchsuchung; **~ over the telephone** *(coll.)* telefonischer Schwatz; **~ of a commercial traveller** Vertreterbesuch;
~ *(v.)* besuchen, Besuch abstatten, zu Gast sein, *(chat, coll.)* schwatzen, plaudern, *(search)* besichtigen, inspizieren, in Augenschein nehmen, *(ship)* anhalten und durchsuchen;
~ with s. o. sich mit jem. treffen; **~ a fair** Messe besuchen; **~ a museum** Museum besichtigen; **~ one's patients** Krankenbesuche machen, seine Patienten aufsuchen; **~ the sins of the fathers upon the children** die Kinder mit den Sünden der Väter heimsuchen; **~ troops** Truppen inspizieren;
to cancel a ~ Besuch absagen; **to cut a** ~ **short** Besuch abkürzen; **to go on a** ~ **to the seaside** Ausflug an die See machen; **to pay a** ~ Besuch abstatten; **to pay a** ~ **to a prospective customer** möglichen Kunden aufsuchen; **to pay s. o. a flying** ~ jem. auf einen Sprung besuchen; **to prolong a** ~ Besuch verlängern; **to stop one's ~s** seine Besuche einstellen.

visitable der Durchsuchung unterliegen, inspektionspflichtig.

visitation Besuchemachen, *(inspection)* offizieller Besuch, *(fig.)* Heimsuchung, [gottgesandte] Prüfung, Besichtigung, *(corporation law)* Überprüfung, *(international law)* Durchsuchung, *(official inquiry)* offizieller Besuch, Visitation.

visitatorial | power Aufsichtsbefugnis; **~ right** Inspektionsrecht.

visited regularly häufig inspiziert.

visiting Besuchemachen, Besuchen, *(fig.)* Heimsuchung;
direct ~ Wohlfahrtspflege, soziale Fürsorge;
~ at a new hotel Aufenthalt in einem neu eröffneten Hotel;
~ *(a.)* besichtigend;
to be ~ with one's neighbo(u)rs and having a good gossip seine Nachbarn zu einem kleinen Schwatz aufsuchen;
to have a ~ acquaintance with s. o. mit jem. verkehren; **~ appointment** Gastdozentur; **~ book** Besucherliste; **~ card** Visiten-, Besuchskarte; **~ committee** Untersuchungsausschuß; **~ day** Besuchertag, Besuchstag; **~ fireman** *(sl.)* spendabler Provinzonkel; **~ group** Besuchergruppe; **~ hours** *(hospital)* Besuchszeit; **~ list** Besucherliste; **~ nurse** Gemeindeschwester, Fürsorgerin; **~ patrol** *(mil.)* Patrouille; **~ professor** Gastprofessor; **~ teacher** Hauslehrer, *(school)* Schulfürsorger; **to be on ~ terms with s. o.** j. gut kennen; **not to be on ~ terms with s. o.** nicht mit jem. verkehren.

visitor Besucher, [Kur]gast, Tourist, *(hotel)* Hotelgast, *(inspector of corporation)* Prüfer, Revisor, Inspekteur;
anticipated ~s geschätzte Besucherzahlen; **district** ~ Wohlfahrtspfleger, Fürsorger[in], Sozialhelfer; **foreign ~s** ausländische Besucher; **frequent** ~ häufiger Besucher (Gast); **summer ~s** Sommergäste; **winter ~s** Wintergäste;
~s to the museum Museumsbesucher; **~s of the stock exchange** Börsenbesucher, Börsenpublikum;
to attract foreign ~s Fremdenverkehr heben; **to deny ~** Besucher abweisen; **to have ~s** Besuch haben; **to receive ~s** Besucher empfangen; **to take in ~s** Pensiongäste haben;
no ~s will be received Beileidsbesuche verboten;
~s' book *(hotel)* Fremdenbuch; **to enter one's name in the ~'s book** Anmeldeformular ausfüllen; **~ passport** Besucherpaß; **~'s permit** *(prison)* Sprecherlaubnis.

visor Visier, *(fig.)* Maske;
sun ~ *(car)* Sonnenblende.

vista Durch-, Aussicht, Perspektive, *(corridor)* langer Gang, Korridor;
a ~ à conto;
dim ~s of the future ungewisse Zukunftsträume; **~ between rows of trees** Durchblick durch eine Baumreihe; **~s of bygone times** vage Erinnerung an vergangene Zeiten; **~ of years** Reihe von Jahren;
to open up new ~s neue Perspektiven eröffnen;
~ dome *(railroad car, US)* Aussichtskuppel.

visual *(advertising)* Verkaufshilfe, Sichtbarmachung einer Werbeidee;
~ *(a.)* sichtbar, wahrnehmbar, visuell;
~ aids in teaching Anschauungsmaterial für den Unterricht; **~ angle** Gesichtswinkel; **~ arts** bildende Künste; **~ aural range** *(airplane)* Kreiskursfunkfeuer mit Sicht- und Höranzeige; **~ communication** visuelle Kommunikation; **~ control** optische Fernkontrolle; **~ direction finding** *(aviation)* optische Peilung; **~ field** Gesichtsfeld; **~ homing flight** Sichtzielflug; **~ impact** Schaueffekt; **~ impressions** visuelle Eindrücke; **~ instruction** Anschauungsunterricht; **~ means of communication** optische Nachrichtenmittel; **~ memory** visuelles Gedächtnis; **~ merchandising** optisch wirksame Verkaufsförderung, Verkaufsförderung durch Warenauslage; **~ objects** sichtbare Gegenstände; **~ presentation** bildliche Darstellung; **~ signalling** *(mil.)* Verständigung durch Sichtzeichen; **~ transmitter** Fernseh[bild]sender.

visualization Sichtbarmachung, Veranschaulichung.

visualize *(v.)* veranschaulichen, bildhaft vorstellen.

visualizer *(US, advertising)* graphischer Ideengestalter, Ideenmann.

visualizing Ideengestaltung.

vita *(lat.)* Lebensbeschreibung, -abriß.

vital lebenswichtig, notwendig, *(animated)* vital, lebenssprühend, *(essential)* wichtig, entscheidend;
to become ~ in one's daily life zur vitalen Bedeutung im täglichen Leben werden;
~ error grundlegender Fehler; **~ functions** lebenswichtige Funktionen; **~ index** Bevölkerungsindex; **of ~ importance** von entscheidender Bedeutung; **~ interests** lebenswichtige Interessen; **~ merchandising** Verkaufsförderung durch Warenauslage; **~ necessity** Lebensnotwendigkeit; **~ organs** lebenswichtige Organe; **~ part** lebenswichtiger Teil; **~ personality** kraftvolle (vitale) Persönlichkeit; **~ principle** Lebensprinzip; **~ problem** entscheidendes Problem; **~ registration statistics** Bevölkerungsstatistik; **~ space** Lebensraum; **~ statistics** Bevölkerungsstatistik, *(US)* Standesamtswesen; **~ statistics office** *(US)* Standesamt; **~ wound** lebensgefährliche Wunde.

vitality Lebensfähigkeit, -kraft, Vitalität;
economic ~ wirtschaftliche Leistungsfähigkeit;
~ of an institution Lebensdauer einer Einrichtung.

vitally important lebenswichtig.

vitamin Vitamin;
~ deficiency Vitaminmangel; **~ shot** Vitaminspritze; **~ tablets** Vitamintabletten.

vitaminize *(v.)* mit Vitaminen anreichern.

vitascope *(US)* Filmvorführgerät.

vitiate *(v.)* beeinträchtigen, verderben *(legal sense)* aufheben, annullieren;
~ the air Luft verpesten; **~ a contract** Vertrag annullieren; **~ the style of writing** literarischen Stil verfälschen; **~ public taste** öffentliche Moral zersetzen; **~ a transaction** Geschäft annullieren.

vitiated | by luxury durch Luxus verdorben;
~ air verpestete Luft.

vitiating | the public taste Zersetzung der öffentlichen Moral;
~ factors Ungültigkeitsfaktoren.

vitiation Beeinträchtigung, *(legal sense)* Ungültigmachen, Annullieren;
~ of the air Luftverpestung; **~ of contract** Vertragsanfechtung; **~ of patent** Patentaufhebung.

viticulture Weinbau.

vitiligate *(v.)* prozeßsüchtig sein.

vitious intromission *(estate, Scot.)* unlautere Machenschaften.

vituperate *(v.)* mit Schimpfworten überschütten.

viva voce examination mündliches Examen.

vivary *(Br.)* Fischteich, Wildgehege.

vivid lebhaft, impulsiv, *(colo(u)r)* leuchtend, satt, *(distinct)* klar;
~ description of an event lebendige Schilderung eines Ereignisses; **~ recollections of a holiday** deutliche Ferienerinnerungen.

vivos, inter unter Lebenden.

vocable Vokabel.

vocabulary Wortschatz, Vokabular, *(book)* Wörterbuch, Lexikon;

classified ~ nach Sachgebieten geordnetes Wörterverzeichnis; **to add to one's** ~ seinen Wortschatz vergrößern; **to drop from one's** ~ aus seinem Vokabular streichen; **to have a large** ~ über einen großen Wortschatz verfügen;

~ **entry** Wörterbucheintrag; ~ **list** Wörterverzeichnis, -liste; ~ **section** Vokabelteil.

vocabulist Lexikograph.

vocal mündlich;

the most ~ die Lautstärksten;

to be ~ **about one's assignment** ganz bestimmte Vorstellungen über seine Verwendungsmöglichkeiten haben;

~ **communication** mündliche Mitteilung; ~ **person** hartnäckiger Mensch; ~ **proponent** Sprachrohr.

vocation *(aptitude)* Eignung, Talent, *(call)* Berufung, Neigung, *(members of a particular calling)* Berufsstand, *(occupation)* Beruf, Beschäftigung, Geschäft, Gewerbe;

in pursuance of my ~ in Ausübung meines Berufes;

vitally important ~ lebenswichtiger Beruf; **mechanical** ~ handwerklicher Beruf; **overcrowded** ~s überfüllte (übersetzte) Berufe (Berufszweige); **profession or** ~ *(taxation, Br.)* freie und sonstige selbständige Berufe; **specialized** ~ eigener Berufsstand; **usual** ~ normaler Beruf;

to change one's ~ seinen Beruf wechseln, anderen Beruf ergreifen; **to have little or no** ~ **for teaching** sich zum Lehrer kaum eignen; **to miss (mistake) one's** ~ seinen Beruf verfehlen; **to pursue one's** ~ seinem Beruf nachgehen; **to take up the** ~ **of engineering** Ingenieurslaufbahn einschlagen; **to think of one's** ~ **in terms of a professional status** seinen Beruf als Berufung auffassen.

vocational beruflich, berufsmäßig;

~ **adviser (advisor)** Berufsberater; ~ **adjustment** Einarbeitung; ~ **analysis** Berufsanalyse; ~ **aptitude** Berufseignung, berufliche Eignung; ~ **aptitude test** berufliche Eignungsprüfung; ~ **association** Fach-, Berufsverband; ~ **choice** Berufswahl; ~ **class** Berufsschulklasse; ~ **clinic** Berufsberatungsinstitut; ~ **counsel[ing]** *(US)* Berufsberatung; ~ **counseling interview** *(US)* Berufsberatungsgespräch; ~ **counsellor** Berufsberater; ~ **course** Fachausbildungslehrgang; ~ **data** Berufsangaben; ~ **director** Berufsschulleiter; ~ **disease** Berufskrankheit; ~ **education** Fach-, Berufsausbildung; ~ **education bill** Berufsausbildungsgesetz; ~ **education program(me)** Berufsausbildungsprogramm; ~ **equipment** berufliche Eignung; ~ **expert** Sachverständiger; ~ **guidance** Berufslenkung, -beratung; ~ **guidance adviser** Berufsberater; ~ **guidance center** *(US)* **(centre, Br.)** Berufsberatungsstelle; ~ **institution** *(US)* Jugendstrafanstalt; ~ **investment(s)** berufliche Investitionen; ~ **knowledge** Fachkenntnisse; ~ **league** Berufsgenossenschaft; ~ **psychology** Berufspsychologie; ~ **reeducation** [Berufs]umschulung; ~ **rehabilitation** berufliche Wiedereingliederung; ~ **retraining** Umschulung; ~ **school** Berufsschule, *(US)* Jugendstrafanstalt; ~ **teacher** Berufsschullehrer; ~ **test** Eignungsprüfung; ~ **training** Berufs-, Fachausbildung; **advanced** ~ **training** berufliche Fortbildung; ~ **training relationship** Berufsausbildungsverhältnis; ~ **training school** Berufsschule; ~ **work** Facharbeit.

vogue Mode, *(popularity)* Popularität, Erfolg, Anklang, Beliebtheit;

in ~ beliebt, gesucht;

all the ~ neueste Mode;

to acquire ~ Anklang finden; **to be in** ~ in Mode (beliebt, gesucht) sein; **to be in full** ~ sich großer Beliebtheit erfreuen, große Mode sein; **to be the** ~ gerade modern sein; **to bring into** ~ Mode einführen; **to go out of** ~ unmodern werden, aus der Mode kommen; **to have a short-lived** ~ sich kurzfristiger Beliebtheit erfreuen;

~ **craze** Modemanie; ~ **word** Modewort.

voice Laut, Ton, Stimme, *(expression)* Ausdruck, Äußerung, *(opinion)* Stimme, Meinung, *(speaker)* Sprachrohr, Sprecher, *(voting right)* Stimmrecht, Stimme;

by a majority of ~s mit Stimmenmehrheit; **in a matter-of-fact** ~ in ganz sachlichem Ton; **not in good** ~ nicht gut bei Stimme; **with one** ~ einstimmig; **without a dissentient** ~ ohne Widerspruch;

active ~ *(grammar)* Aktivum; **bigger** ~ größere Stimmrechte; **casting** ~ ausschlaggebende Stimme; **passive** ~ *(grammar)* Passivum;

~ **in some affairs** Mitspracherecht; ~ **of conscience** Stimme des

Gewissens; ~ **of the court** Meinung des Gerichtes; ~ **in the management** Mitsprache-, Mitbestimmungsrecht; ~ **of the people** Stimme des Volkes; ~ **in the wilderness** *(fig.)* vergeblich mahnende Stimme;

~ *(v.)* äußern, in Worte fassen;

~ **the feelings of a crowd** Meinung einer Menschenmenge wiedergeben; ~ **one's gratitude** seiner Dankbarkeit Ausdruck geben;

to demand a ~ **in s. th.** Mitsprache bei etw. fordern; **to find** ~ **in one's words** in seinen Worten zum Ausdruck kommen; **to give** ~ **to one's indignation** seiner Empörung Ausdruck geben; **to have a** ~ Einfluß haben; **to have a** ~ **in the management** im Vorstand vertreten sein, in der Verwaltung mitzureden (Mitspracherecht) haben; **to have a technical 50 - 50** ~ **in the management** ziffernmäßig zu 50% an der Geschäftsführung beteiligt sein; **to have no** ~ **in a matter** keine Entscheidungsbefugnisse in einer Sache haben; **to lend one's** ~ **to s. o.** jem. seine Unterstützung zukommen lassen; **to make o. s. the** ~ **of the poor** sich zum Fürsprecher der Armen machen; **to make use of one's** ~ von seinem Stimmrecht Gebrauch machen; **to recognize s. one's** ~ j. an seiner Stimme erkennen; **to refuse with one** ~ einstimmig ablehnen; **to shout at the top of one's** ~ lauthals rufen; **to speak in a low** ~ mit leiser Stimme sprechen;

~ **communication** mündliche Nachrichtenverbindung; ~**-over** Synchronisation; ~ **range** akustische Reichweite; ~ **recording** Sprechaufnahme; ~ **tube** Sprachrohr.

voiceless sprachlos, *(phonetic)* stimmlos, *(pol.)* nicht stimmberechtigt.

void Lücke, leerer Raum, Leere;

~ *(a.)* *(uninhabited)* unbewohnt, *(invalid)* nichtig, [rechts]unwirksam, rechtsungültig, kraftlos, *(space)* leer, *(vacant)* unbesetzt, frei, *(voidable)* anfechtbar, nicht durchsetzbar;

under pain of being declared ~ bei Gefahr der Nichtigkeit;

absolutely ~, **null and** ~ null und nichtig;

~ **ab initio** von Anfang an nichtig; ~ **in part** teilweise nichtig; ~ **for uncertainty** ungültig wegen unklarer Fassung; ~ **of seizable property** unpfändbar; ~ **of common sense** ohne gesunden Menschenverstand;

~ *(v.)* *(render invalid)* ungültig (unwirksam) machen, aufheben, für nichtig erklären;

to be ~ **of interest** kein Interesse finden, ohne jedes Interesse (völlig) uninteressant sein; **to be** ~ **under statute** Voraussetzungen der gesetzlichen Nichtigkeit erfüllen; **to be wholly** ~ **of fear** gänzlich furchtlos sein, überhaupt keine Angst haben; **to become** ~ wegfallen, erlöschen; **to declare an election** ~ Wahl für ungültig erklären; **to declare null and** ~ für nichtig erklären; **to fall** ~ *(office)* frei (vakant) werden, unbesetzt sein; **to fill the** ~ Lücke ausfüllen; **to leave** ~ unausgefüllt lassen, nicht ausfüllen; **to make** ~ annullieren, für nichtig erklären; **to make a clause** ~ Bestimmung nichtig machen;

~ **contract** ungültiger (nichtiger) Vertrag; ~ **judgment** nichtiges Urteil; ~ **marriage** ungültige Ehe; ~ **money order** verfallene Postanweisung; ~ **period** unbewohnte Zeit; ~ **process** ungültiges (nichtiges) Verfahren; ~ **space** leerer Raum, Lücke; ~ **voting paper** ungültiger Stimmzettel.

voidability Vernicht-, Anfechtbarkeit.

voidable aufhebbar, annullierbar, *(contract)* anfechtbar;

to be ~ **at s. one's option** wahlweise anfechtbar sein;

~ **contract** anfechtbarer Vertrag; ~ **judgment** anfechtbares Urteil; ~ **preference** *(bankruptcy law)* anfechtbare Vermögensübertragung, Gläubigerbevorzugung; ~ **transaction** anfechtbares Rechtsgeschäft.

voidableness Anfechtbarkeit, Annullierbarkeit.

voidance Annullierung, Aufhebung, *(ejection from benefice)* Pfründenentziehung, *(vacancy)* Freiwerden, Vakanz.

voiding *(emptiness)* Leere, *(invalidity)* Nichtigkeit, Ungültigkeit.

voidness *(contract, judgment)* Nichtigkeit, Ungültigkeit.

volatile sich schnell verflüchtigend, *(fickle)* wankelmütig;

~ **oil** ätherische Öle.

volcanic vulkanisch, *(fig.)* aufbrausend;

~ **eruption** Vulkanausbruch; ~ **rock** vulkanisches Gestein.

volcanization Vulkanisierung.

volcanize *(v.)* vulkanisieren.

volcano Vulkan, *(fig.)* Vulkan, Pulverfaß;

active ~ tätiger Vulkan; **dormant** ~ untätiger Vulkan; **extinct** ~ erloschener Vulkan; **smoking** ~ rauchender Vulkan;

to sit on top of a ~ wie auf einem Pulverfaß sitzen.

volition Willensentscheidung, -äußerung, -akt;

to do s. th. of one's own ~ etw. aus freien Stücken tun.

volitional | faculty Willenskraft; ~ **insanity** *(criminal)* Unzurechnungsfähigkeit bei Begehung strafbarer Handlungen.

volley *(burst)* Strom, Flut, Schwall, *(missiles)* Salve, Hagel; ~ **of oaths** Hagel von Flüchen; ~ **of stones** Steinhagel; ~ **of words** Schwall von Worten, Wortschwall.

volplane Gleitflug.

volt *(el.)* Volt.

voltage *(el.)* Spannung.

voltaic | battery galvanische Batterie; ~ **cell** elektrolytische Zelle; ~ **current** galvanischer Strom.

volte-face *(politics)* völlige Meinungsänderung.

volubility Zungenfertigkeit.

volume *(book)* Band, Buch, *(bulk)* Maß, Umfang, *(content)* Rauminhalt, Volumen, Gehalt, Fassungsvermögen, *(data processing)* Datenträger, *(electricity)* Lautstärke, *(quantity)* Masse, Menge, Schwall, Flut;
by ~ mengenmäßig, der Menge nach; **of many ~s** vielbändig;
aggregate ~ Gesamtvolumen; **annual ~** Jahresumsatz; **boxed ~** Kistenmaß; **export ~** Exportvolumen; **interleaved ~** durchschossener Band; **large ~** Großband; **prewar ~** Vorkriegsvolumen; **~s already published** bereits erschienene Bände; ~ **recommended** *(book club)* Vorschlagsband; **total ~** Gesamtumfang;
~ **of advertising** Werbeanteil; ~ **of building** Bauvolumen; ~ **of business** Geschäftsvolumen, -umfang; ~ **of a cask** Faßinhalt; ~ **bound in cloth** Leinenband; ~ **of a container** Behälterumfang; ~ **of credit** Kreditvolumen; ~ **of currency** Zahlungsmittelvolumen; ~ **of imports** Einfuhrvolumen; ~ **of investment** Umfang der vorgenommenen Investitionen, Investitionsvolumen; ~ **of letters** Fülle von Briefen; ~ **of liquidity** Liquiditätsvolumen; ~ **of money** Geldvolumen; ~ **of production** Produktionsvolumen; ~ **of sales** Umsatzvolumen; **total ~ of sales** Gesamtabsatz, -umsatz; ~ **of spending** Ausgabenvolumen; ~ **of trade** Geschäftsumfang, Handelsvolumen; ~ **of foreign trade** Außenhandelsvolumen; ~ **of world trade** Welthandelsvolumen; ~ **of traffic** Streckenbelastung, Verkehrsleistung; ~ **of travel** Reisevolumen; ~ **of work** Arbeitsanfall;
to deal in big ~s große Geschäftsabschlüsse (Umsätze) tätigen; **to order the missing ~s of a periodical** fehlende Jahrgänge einer Zeitschrift bestellen; **to pour out ~s of abuses** Schwall von Beschimpfungen ausstoßen; **to reduce the ~ of lending** Ausleihungsvolumen zurückschrauben; **to speak ~s** Bände sprechen; **to speak ~s of s. one's charity** lebender Beweis von jds. Wohltätigkeit sein;
~ **car** in Massen hergestellter Serienwagen; ~ **control** *(wireless set)* Lautstärkeregelung; ~ **cost** fixe Kosten, Engroskosten; ~ **discount** Mengenrabatt; ~ **increaser** *(wireless set)* Lautstärkeregler; ~ **market** Massenabsatz; **three-~ novel** dreibändiger Roman; ~ **order** Mengen-, Großauftrag; **~-produce** *(v.)* in Massen produzieren, in Mengen erzeugen, serienmäßig herstellen; ~ **production** serienmäßige Herstellung, Mengenerzeugung, Massenproduktion; ~ **purchase** Großeinkauf; **in ~ terms** mengenmäßig; **to fall in ~ terms** volumenmäßig zurückgehen; ~ **variance** Mengenabweichung gegenüber dem Standard; **six-~ work** sechsbändiges Werk.

volumed massig, umfangreich;
seven-~ book siebenbändiges Werk.

voluminious *(book)* bändefüllend, vielbändig.

voluntary freiwillige Arbeit (Leistung), *(sport)* Kür;
~ *(a.)* freiwillig, aus eigenem Antrieb, aus freiem Entschluß, spontan, *(amicable)* gütlich, außergerichtlich, vergleichsweise, *(without consideration)* unentgeltlich, *(deliberate)* absichtlich, vorsätzlich, *(independent)* unabhängig, frei, *(subject)* fakultativ, *(supported by voluntary action)* durch Spenden unterstützt;
~ **abandonment** *(divorce law)* grundloses Verlassen; ~ **act** vorsätzliche Handlung; ~ **agency** freiwillige Hilfsorganisation; ~ **agreement** außergerichtlicher Vergleich; ~ **answer** *(pleading)* spontanes Gegenvorbringen; ~ **arbitration** frei vereinbarte Schiedsgerichtsbarkeit; ~ **assignment** freiwillige Vermögensübertragung auf den Konkursverwalter; ~ **association** *(US)* Idealverein; ~ **assumption of risk** Handeln auf eigene Gefahr; ~ **bankruptcy** *(US)* selbst beantragte Konkurserklärung, Konkurseröffnung auf Antrag der Gemeinschuldner; **on a ~ basis** freiwillig, auf freiwilliger Grundlage; ~ **chain** Gemeinschaftseinkauf [unabhängiger Einzelhändler]; ~ **checkoff** *(trade unionism)* vereinbarte Einbehaltung von Gewerkschaftsbeiträgen; ~ **confession** freiwilliges Geständnis; ~ **contribution** Spende, *(health insurance, Br.)* freiwilliger Beitragszahlung; ~ **contributor** *(health insurance, Br.)* freiwilliger Beitragszahler, freiwillig Versicherter; ~ **conveyance** unentgeltliche Übereignung, Übertragung ohne Gegenleistung; ~ **courtesy** Gefälligkeit; ~ **deposit** vereinbarte Hinterlegung; ~ **discontinuance** freiwillige Klagerücknahme; ~ **disposition** rechtsgeschäftliche Verfü-

gung; ~ **escape** Gefängnisausbruch mit Einverständnis des Wärters; ~ **export-restraint agreement** freiwilliges Exportbegrenzungsabkommen; ~ **exposure to unnecessary danger** unnötig in Kauf genommene Selbstgefährdung; ~ **fund** *(London stock exchange)* Unterstützungsfonds für in Konkurs gegangene Börsenmakler; ~ **gift** unentgeltliche Zuwendung; ~ **grantee** freiwilliger Zedent; ~ **group** Einkaufsvereinigung; ~ **helper** freiwilliger Helfer; ~ **home** durch Spenden unterhaltenes Jugendheim; ~ **hospital** durch Spenden unterhaltenes Krankenhaus; ~ **ignorance** *(US)* schuldhaftes Nichtwissen; ~ **improvements** Verschönerungsarbeiten; ~ **indebtedness** *(county)* Kommunalverpflichtungen bei ausgeglichenem Haushalt; ~ **insurance** freiwillige Versicherung; ~ **continued insurance** freiwillige Weiterversicherung; ~ **jurisdiction** *(Br.)* freiwillige Gerichtsbarkeit; ~ **liquidation** freiwillige Liquidation, Selbstauflösung; ~ **manslaughter** Totschlag im Affekt; ~ **nonsuit** freiwillige Klagerücknahme; ~ **negotiations** Verhandlungen zwischen den Tarifpartnern; ~ **oath** Parteieid; ~ **offer** spontanes Angebot; ~ **organization** privater Fürsorgeverband, Wohltätigkeitsorganisation; ~ **partition** Nachlaßvergleich, -auseinandersetzung; ~ **payment** freiwillige Zahlung; ~ **quit** *(resignation)* freiwilliger Rücktritt; ~ **redemption** Pfandfreigabe; ~ **reserve** freie Rücklagen; ~ **reserve fund** freie Rücklagen; ~ **restriction** [freiwillige] Selbstbeschränkung; ~ **sale** Freiverkauf; ~ **school** *(Br.)* durch Spenden unterhaltene Konfessionsschule, anerkannte Ersatzschule; ~ **separation** *(US)* einverständliche Trennung; ~ **service** freiwilliger Hilfsdienst; ~ **settlement of property** unentgeltliche Eigentumsübertragung; ~ **social contributions** *(US)* freiwillige Sozialleistungen; ~ **staff** ehrenamtliche Mitarbeiter; ~ **statement** aus freien Stücken abgegebene Erklärung; ~ **transfer of personalty** unentgeltliche Übertragung beweglicher Vermögensgegenstände; ~ **transfer of property** unentgeltliche Grundstücksübereignung; ~ **trust** rechtsgeschäftlich errichtete Stiftung; ~ **undertaking** freiwillige Verpflichtung; ~ **unemployment** vorsätzlich herbeigeführte Arbeitslosigkeit; ~ **waste** mutwillige Verschwendung, *(tenant)* vorsätzliche Substanzschädigung; ~ **winding-up** Selbstauflösung; ~ **work** freiwillige Arbeit; ~ **worker** freiwilliger Helfer.

voluntarism Freiwilligkeitsprinzip.

volunteer [Kriegs]freiwilliger, *(acquirer without valuable consideration)* unentgeltlicher Erwerber, *(agent of necessity)* Vertreter ohne Vertretungsmacht, Geschäftsführer ohne Auftrag, *(voluntary conveyor)* freiwilliger Zedent, *(unsalaried clerk)* Volontär, *(in underdeveloped country, Br.)* Entwicklungshelfer;
~ *(v.)* sich freiwillig zur Verfügung stellen (melden, freiwillig mitmachen), *(unsalaried clerk)* als Volontär arbeiten, *(mil.)* als Freiwilliger eintreten (dienen);
~ **for a campaign** freiwillig an einem Feldzug teilnehmen; ~ **information** von sich aus Informationsmaterial zur Verfügung stellen;
~ **committee** Freiwilligenausschuß; ~ **corps** Freiwilligenkorps; ~ **unit** Freiwilligenverband.

vomit *(v.)* *(volcano)* Rauch ausstoßen, Lava auswerfen.

voracious | appetite for scandals unersättliches Interesse an Skandalgeschichten; ~ **reader** unersättlicher Leser.

vortex Wirbel, Strudel, *(whirlwind)* Wirbelsturm, *(fire)* Feuersog;
~ **of flames** Flammensog; ~ **of social life** Flut gesellschaftlicher Veranstaltungen;
to be drawn into the ~ of politics in einen politischen Strudel gezogen werden;
~ **wheel** Turbine.

vostro account Vostrokonto.

votable wahl-, stimmberechtigt.

votary of peace Vorkämpfer des Friedens.

vote *(election result)* Wahlergebnis, *(money granted)* bewilligte Summe, bewilligter Betrag, Geldbewilligung, Budget, *(right to vote)* [Wahl]stimme, Stimmberechtigung, *(voter)* Wähler, Stimmberechtigter, *(voting)* Abstimmung, Stimmabgabe, Votum, *(voting paper)* Stimm-, Wahlzettel;
by ~ durch Beschluß (Abstimmung); **entitled to ~** abstimmungs-, stimmberechtigt; **with 7 ~s against** mit 7 Gegenstimmen; **without a ~** ohne Stimme;
affirmative ~ Jastimme, positives Abstimmungsergebnis; **army ~** Heeresetat; **block ~** geschlossene Stimmabgabe; **~s cast** abgegebene Stimmen; **~s cast against** Stimmen dagegen; **casting ~** ausschlaggebende Stimme; **close ~** knappes Abstimmungsergebnis; **confidence ~** Abstimmung über eine Vertrauensfrage; **confirming ~** *(corporation)* Genehmigungsbeschluß;

cumulative ~s kumulierte Stimmen; **direct ~** unmittelbare Wahl; **dissentient ~** Gegenstimme; **eligible ~s** *(Br.)* wahlberechtigte Stimmen; **final ~** Schlußabstimmung; **floating ~** unsichere Stimmen, schwankender Wähleranteil, Wechselwähler; **floor ~** Abstimmung im Plenum; **free ~** freie Abstimmung ohne Fraktionszwang; **individual ~** Stimmrecht; **invalid ~** ungültige Stimme; **key ~** entscheidende Abstimmung; **labour ~** *(Br.)* Stimmanteil der Labour Partei, Arbeiterstimmen; **majority ~** Stimmenmehrheit, -majorität, Mehrheits-, Majoritätsbeschluß; **minority ~** Stimmenminderheit; **national ~** Gesamtstimmenzahl eines Landes; **negative ~** Neinstimme; **nonconfidence ~** Mißtrauensvotum; **open ~** öffentliche Abstimmung; **original ~** Urabstimmung; **party-line ~** Abstimmung unter Fraktionszwang; **plural ~** Pluralwahl, Mehrstimmrecht; **~s polled** abgegebene Stimmen; **popular ~** Volksbefragung; **prohibition ~s** Prohibitionsanhänger; **proportional ~** Verhältniswahl; **~s recorded** abgegebene Stimmen; **roll-call ~** namentliche Abstimmung; **rural ~** Stimmen der Landbevölkerung; **scattered ~s** zersplitterte Stimmen, Splitterstimmen; **secret ~** geheime Wahl; **solid ~** einstimmige Wahl; **show-of-hands ~** *(US)* Abstimmung durch Handaufheben; **straw ~** inoffizielle Probeabstimmung; **strike ~** Abstimmung über einen Streik; **supplementary ~** *(parl.)* Nachbewilligung; **total ~** Gesamtstimmenzahl; **transferable ~** übertragbares Stimmrecht; **unanimous ~** einstimmiger Beschluß; **written ~** schriftlich abgegebene Stimme; **75-per-cent ~** Dreiviertelmehrheit;

~ by acclamation Abstimmung durch Zuruf; **~ on account** *(parl., Br.)* vorläufige Abschlagsbewilligung; **~ of an assembly** Beratung einer Körperschaft; **~ by open ballot** öffentlich vorgenommene Abstimmung; **~ by secret ballot** geheime Abstimmung; **~ in several ballots** Abstimmung in mehreren Wahlgängen; **~ of censure** Mißtrauensantrag; **~ of confidence** Abstimmung über eine Vertrauensfrage, Vertrauensvotum; **~ by correspondence** schriftliche Stimmabgabe, Briefwahl; **~s of credit subject to delay** verzögerte Kreditbewilligung; **~s and proceedings** *(parl.)* Kurzprotokolle; **~ of $ 100.000 for a project** bewilligter Betrag von 100.000 Dollar für ein Vorhaben; **~ by proxy** Abstimmen durch Stellvertreter; **~ on a resolution** Abstimmung über eine Entschließung; **~ by rising** Abstimmung durch Erheben von den Sitzen; **~ by show of hands** Abstimmung durch Handaufheben; **~ on the shopfloor** Betriebsabstimmung; **~ of thanks** Danksagungsadresse;

~ *(v.)* *(give a vote)* abstimmen, Stimme abgeben, wählen, votieren, *(grant)* bewilligen, *(resolve)* beschließen;

~ s. o. [in] jem. wählen; **~ the adjournment of a meeting** Vertagung einer Sitzung beschließen; **~ in the affirmative** Jastimme abgeben; **~ against s. th.** gegen etw. stimmen; **~ the appropriation** Haushaltsvoranschlag bewilligen; **~ by ballot** ballotieren; **~ a bill through** Gesetzantrag durchbringen; **~ the budget** Haushalt genehmigen; **~ that the budget be accepted** für Verabschiedung des Etats eintreten; **~ a candidate into office** für einen Bewerber stimmen; **~ one's employees** seine Angestellten bei der Wahl beeinflussen; **~ the estimates** Haushalt (Etat) genehmigen; **~ in favo(u)r of s. th.** zugunsten von etw. abstimmen; **~ by rising to one's feet** durch Aufstehen wählen; **~ s. o. a fine fellow** j. für einen anständigen Kerl halten; **~ funds** Geldmittel bewilligen; **~ for the government** für die Regierung stimmen; **~ against the government on confidence motion** Mißtrauensantrag gegen die Regierung unterstützen; **~ by head** nach der Kopfzahl abstimmen; **~ for the independents next election** bei der nächsten Wahl die freie Wählergemeinschaft wählen; **~ off a list** von einer Liste wählen; **~ $ 150 million in extra money** zusätzliche Mittel in Höhe von 150 Mio. Dollar bewilligen; **~ in the negative** Neinstimme abgeben; **~ by nominees** an der Abstimmung indirekt teilnehmen; **~ for a party** seine Stimme einer Partei geben; **~ s. o. out of power** j. abwählen; **~ one's preference on a mail-in coupons scheme** sich für Zugabekupons aussprechen; **~ for the pro-government parties** Stimme für die Regierungsparteien abgeben; **~ by proxy** Stimmrecht durch einen Bevollmächtigen ausüben, sich bei der Abstimmung vertreten lassen; **~ on a question** über eine Frage abstimmen; **~ republican** *(US)* für die Republikanische Partei stimmen; **~ a resolution** Beschluß durch Abstimmung fassen; **~ on a resolution** über eine Entschließung abstimmen; **~ in an uninterrupted sequence** hintereinander wählen; **~ by show of hands** durch Handaufheben abstimmen; **~ solidly for s. th.** geschlossen für etw. stimmen; **~ [on] the stock** Stimmrecht einer Aktie (Aktienstimmrecht) ausüben; **~ $ 100.000 for the sufferers** 100.000 Dollar für die Katastrophengeschädigten bewilligen; **~ a sum of money** abstimmungsweise einen Geldbetrag bewilligen; **~ a sum for travel(l)ing expenses** Reisespesen in

einer bestimmten Höhe bewilligen; **~ the supplies** Haushaltsvoranschlag (Haushaltsmittel) bewilligen; **~ a ticket** Liste wählen; **~ the straight ticket** *(US)* vorgeschriebene Kandidatenliste wählen; **~ unanimously** einstimmig beschließen; **~ to waive an irregularity** Formfehler im Beschlußwege heilen;

~ against dagegen stimmen; **~ away** durch Abstimmungsbeschluß beseitigen; **~ down** dagegen-, überstimmen, niederstimmen, Antrag ablehnen; **~ down a motion** Antrag ablehnen; **~ down a proposal** gegen einen Vorschlag stimmen; **~ in** durch Abstimmung aufnehmen (wählen); **~ into the chair** zum Präsidenten (Vorsitzenden) wählen; **~ out** ausschließen, ablehnen; **to allow a free ~** *(parl.)* Fraktionszwang aufheben; **to ask for a ~ of confidence** *(parl.)* Vertrauensfrage stellen; **to be entitled to ~ and to speak** rede- und stimmberechtigt sein; **to be put to the ~** zur Abstimmung gelangen; **to be qualified to ~** stimmberechtigt sein; **to be rejected by 8 ~s to 5** mit 8 gegen 5 Stimmen abgelehnt werden; **to call for a ~ of urgency** Dringlichkeitsantrag stellen; **to cancel a ~** Abstimmung für ungültig erklären; **to canvass for ~s** um Stimmen werben, Wähler bearbeiten, Stimmenwerbung betreiben; **to carry a ~** Resolution annehmen; **to carry a ~ unanimously** Vorschlag einstimmig annehmen; **to cast one's ~** seine Stimme abgeben, an der Abstimmung teilnehmen; **to cast a tie-breaking ~** bei Stimmengleichheit die Entscheidung haben; **to cast a ~ of acquittal** *(jury)* für Freispruch plädieren; **to cast a ~ for the presidency** seine Stimme für die Vorschläge des Präsidenten abgeben; **to cast the swing ~** on split decisions unentschiedene Wähler bei umkämpften Entscheidungen beeinflussen; **to collect the ~s** Stimmen sammeln; **to come to a full ~** zu einer abschließenden Abstimmung kommen; **to count the ~s** Stimmen zählen, Wahlergebnis zusammenstellen; **to declare the ~ closed** Abstimmung schließen; **to defeat by ~** überstimmen; **to get out the ~** Wähler an die Wahlurne bringen; **to give one's ~** abstimmen; **to give one's ~ for a candidate** für einen Bewerber stimmen; **to have the ~** stimmberechtigt sein, Stimmrecht haben; **to have the casting ~** bei Stimmengleichheit entscheiden; **to have a controlling ~** maßgeblichen Einfluß haben; **to lose the labo(u)r ~** Arbeiterstimmen verlieren; **to lose the trade-union ~** Stimmen der Gewerkschaftsmitglieder verlieren; **to open the ~** Abstimmung eröffnen; **to pass a ~ of censure on s. o.** jem. eine Rüge erteilen; **to pass a ~ of no confidence** Mißtrauensvotum durchbringen; **to pick up ~s** Stimmengewinn verzeichnen; **to poll 8 ~s** acht Stimmen erhalten; **to proceed to a ~** zur Abstimmung schreiten; **to put [a question] to the ~** [über eine Frage] abstimmen lassen, zur Abstimmung bringen; **to receive a ~ of confidence** Vertrauensvotum erhalten; **to record one's ~** abstimmen, seine Stimme abgeben; **to recount ~s** Wahlstimmen überprüfen; **to roll up ~s** Stimmenzuwachs erlangen; **to second a ~** Vorschlag unterstützen; **to solicit ~s** Stimmenwerbung betreiben, Stimmen werben; **to split one's ~** seine Stimme auf mehrere Kandidaten verteilen; **to swing the ~** Wählerumschwung herbeiführen; **to take the ~** Abstimmung vornehmen, zur Abstimmung schreiten; **to take a ~ by calling over the names of the members** namentliche Mitgliederabstimmung durchführen; **to take unrecorded ~s on the floor** Abstimmung im Plenum nicht registrieren lassen; **to tell the ~s** Stimmen zählen; **to tender s. o. a ~ of thanks** jem. eine Dankadresse übermitteln; **to withhold one's ~** sich der Stimme enthalten;

~ catcher Stimmenfänger; **~-catching** Stimmenfang; **~-catching manoeuvre** Wahlmanöver; **~ checking** Wahl-, Stimmenkontrolle; **~-conscious** wählerbewußt; **~ count** Stimmenzählung; **~ counter** Stimmenzähler; **~ counting** Stimmenzählen; **~ cycle** Wahlzyklus; **~ getter** Stimmwerber, -fänger; **~ getting** Stimmenwerbung, -fängerei; **to have the edge in ~-getting terms** günstigere Ausgangsposition für neue Wählerstimmen haben; **~ hunter** Stimmenjäger, -fänger; **~ hunting** Stimmenfang; **~ indicator** Abstimmungstafel, -anzeiger; **~ loser** Wahlstimmenverlustgeschäft; **~ manipulator** Wahlmacher; **four-~ margin** knappe Mehrheit von vier Stimmen; **~ recorder** Abstimmapparat; **~ rigging** Wahlbeeinflussung; **~-switching arrangement** wahlentscheidende Vereinbarung; **~ winner** Gewinner einer Wahl; **~-winning goodies** Wahlkampfgeschenke.

voteless nicht stimm-, nicht wahlberechtigt, ohne Stimmrecht.

votemonger Geschäftemacher bei einer Wahl.

voter Wahl-, Stimmberechtigter, Wähler;

absent ~ *(US)* Briefwähler; **agricultural ~** ländlicher Wähler; **casting ~** ausschlaggebender Stimmberechtigter; **floating ~** parteiloser Wähler; **ordinary ~** Durchschnittswähler; **registered ~** eingetragener Wähler;

to win ~ acceptance Zustimmung der Wähler finden; **~s' association** Wählervereinigung; **~ participation** Wahlbeteiligung; **~ reaction** Wählerreaktion; **~-recognition problem** Wähleridentifizierungsproblem; **~ registration** Wählerregistrierung; **~-registration roll** Wahlverzeichnis; **~ resistance** Widerstand der Wähler; **~ sentiment** Wählerstimmung; **in terms of ~ turnout** was die Wahlbeteiligung angeht.

voting Abstimmen, Abstimmung, Stimmabgabe, Wählen, Wahl[beteiligung];
during the ~ bei (während) der Abstimmung;
absent ~ *(US)* Briefwahl; **compulsory ~** Stimmzwang, Wahlpflicht; **cross ~** *(parl.)* Abstimmung mit der Gegenpartei; **cumulative ~** kumulative Stimmabgabe, Stimmenhäufung, mehrfaches Stimmrecht; **direct ~** direkte Wahl; **open ~** öffentliche Abstimmung; **plural ~** Mehrstimmenwahlrecht; **preferential ~** Vereinigung mehrerer Wahlstimmen auf einen Kandidaten; **proxy ~** Stimmrechtsausübung durch Stellvertretung; **second ~** zweiter Wahlgang; **secret ~** geheime Abstimmung; **service ~** Wahlteilnahme der Streitkräfte; **uninominal ~** Einzelwahl;
~ on amendments Abstimmung über Abänderungsanträge; **~ by ballot** geheime Wahl, Ballotage; **compulsory ~ in local elections** Wahlpflicht bei Kommunalwahlen; **~ by mail** schriftliche Abstimmung, Briefwahl; **~ on a poll** *(company meeting)* schriftliche Abstimmung; **~ by proxy** Abstimmung (Stimmrechtsausübung) durch Stellvertreter; **~ by rising and sitting** Abstimmung durch Erheben von den Sitzen; **~ at shareholders'** *(Br.)* **(stockholders', US) meeting** Abstimmung auf der Hauptversammlung;
to abstain from ~ sich der Stimme enthalten; **to bar s. o. from ~ his stock** j. an der Ausübung seines Stimmrechtes hindern; **to disqualify from ~** Stimmrecht aberkennen;
to come of ~ age wahlmündig werden; **~ agreement** Abstimmungsvereinbarung; **~ area** Abstimmungsgebiet; **good ~ base** gute Ausgangsbasis für die Wahlen; **~ behavio(u)r** Verhalten der Wählerschaft; **~ booth** Wahlzelle; **~ box** Wahlurne; **~ business** Wahlgeschäft; **~ capital stock** stimmberechtigtes Aktienkapital; **~ and tax-paying citizen** Vollbürger; **~ control** Stimmrechtkontrolle, Verfügung über Stimmen; **~ figures** Abstimmungsergebnisse; **to play to the ~ galleries** aus Wahlbeeinflussungsgründen handeln; **~ habits** Wählergewohnheiten; **~ hours** Abstimmungs-, Wahlzeit; **~ instincts** Wählergewohnheiten; **~ list of stockholders** *(US)* Liste der stimmberechtigten Aktionäre; **to register o. s. on the ~ list** sich in die Wählerliste eintragen; **~ machine** Stimmzählapparat, Abstimmungs-, Wahlmaschine; **~ majority** Stimmenmehrheit; **~ margin** Abstimmungsspielraum; **narrow ~ margin** knappes Wahlergebnis; **~ member** stimmenberechtigtes Mitglied; **~ paper** *(Br.)* Stimm-, Wahlzettel; **void ~ paper** ungültiger Stimmzettel; **~ paper left blank** *(Br.)* unausgefüllter Stimmzettel; **to deposit a ~ paper** *(Br.)* Stimmzettel einwerfen; **to return a blank ~ paper** *(Br.)* leeren Stimmzettel abgeben; **~ pattern** Wahlmodell; **~ pool** Stimmrechtsübertragung, -bindung; **~-pool stock** beschränkt stimmberechtigter Kapitalanteil; **~ power** Stimmberechtigung, -recht, Abstimmungsbefugnis; **with ~ power** stimmberechtigt; **contingent ~ power** eingeschränkte Stimmberechtigung; **total ~ power** Gesamtstimmenzahl; **to be deprived of ~ power** ohne Stimmrecht sein, seines Stimmrechts verlustig gehen; **to control 10% of the ~ power** 10% des Aktienkapitals kontrollieren; **~ privilege** Abstimmungsbefugnis; **~ procedure** Abstimmungsverfahren; **~ procedure by proxy** Stimmrechtsausübung durch Stellvertreter; **~ registration** Wahlregistrierung, -aufzeichnung; **~ residence** zuständiger Wahlbezirk [eines Wählers]; **~ right** Wahl-, Stimmrecht; **weighted ~ rights** *(shareholder)* erhöhtes Stimmrecht; **to carry ~ rights** *(shares)* stimmberechtigt sein; **to exercise ~ rights** Stimmrecht (Wahlrecht) ausüben; **to exercise ~ rights viva voce** durch Zuruf abstimmen; **to forfeit one's ~ rights** sein Stimmrecht verwirken; **~ rules** Abstimmungsregeln, -richtlinien, -vorschriften; **~ securities** stimmberechtigte Wertpapiere; **~ shares** *(US)* stimmberechtigte Anteile, Stimmrechtsaktien; **to transfer one's ~ shares** *(Br.)* seine Stimmrechte übertragen; **~ share capital** *(Br.)* stimmberechtigtes Aktienkapital; **~ slip** Abstimmungszettel, Stimmkarte; **~ steward** Wahlleiter; **~ stock** *(US)* Stimmrechtsaktie; **~ stock of a company** *(US)* stimmberechtigtes Aktienkapital; **~ strength** Stimmenzahl, Stimmanteil, parlamentarisches Stärkeverhältnis; **to obtain ~ support** Stimmenunterstützung erlangen; **~ system** Wahlsystem; **~ ticket** Wahlkarte; **~ trust** *(US)* Stimmrechtsausübung durch bestellte Treuhänder; **~-trust agreement** *(US)* Stimmenrechtsvereinbarung, -bindungsvertrag; **~-trust certificate** *(US)* Stimmberech-

tigungsschein, -bindungszertifikat; **~ trust certificate holder** *(US)* stimmgebundener Aktionär; **~ trust record** *(US)* Stimmrechtsnachweis; **~ trustee** *(US)* Stimmenvertreter, Stimmrechtstreuhänder.

vouch *(coll.)* Beteuerung, Bestätigung;
~ *(v.)* *(affirm)* bekräftigen, beteuern, *(confirm)* bestätigen, bezeugen, *(corroborate)* belegen, durch Urkunden erhärten, mit einem Stempel bestätigen, *(be surety for)* [sich ver]bürgen, garantieren;
~ for einstehen für; **~ for s. o.** sich für j. verbürgen; **~ for s. one's ability to pay** sich für jds. Zahlungsfähigkeit verbürgen; **~ an authority** anerkannten Fachmann als Beleg zitieren; **~ for s. one's good conduct** für jds. Verhalten die Garantie übernehmen; **~ s. o. as a fit successor** j. als geeigneten Nachfolger erklären; **~ for the truth of one's statement** sich für die Richtigkeit seiner Angaben verbürgen; **~ s. o. to warranty** j. als Gewährsmann vorladen, j. zur Bekräftigung anrufen.
vouched verbürgt;
not ~ unverbürgt.
vouchee in Anspruch genommener Bürge, Gewährsmann.
voucher *(accounting)* [Buchungs]beleg, Buchungsunterlage, Belegschein, -zettel, *(admission ticket)* Eintrittskarte, *(advertising)* Durchführungsbeleg, *(authority)* Zeuge, Gewährsmann, Bürge, *(document)* Urkunde, Dokument, Zeugnis, *(evidence to disburse cash)* [Aus]zahlungsbeleg, *(proof)* [Berechtigungs-]schein, *(receipt)* Gutschein, Bon, Quittung, Rechnungsbeleg, Bon, *(testimony)* Zeugnis, Beweisstück, *(ticket)* Nachweis, Zulassungsmarke, Eintrittsmarke;
approved ~ anerkannter Beleg; **~ attached** Beleg anliegend; **audited ~** geprüfter und zur Zahlung angewiesener Beleg; **bookkeeping ~** Buchungsbeleg; **cash ~** Kassenanweisung-, beleg; **check ~** *(US)* Belegabschnitt am Scheck; **disbursement ~** Kassen-, Zahlungsanweisung; **expense ~** Spesen-, Ausgabenbeleg; **external ~** Fremdbeleg; **gift ~** Geschenkgutschein; **hotel ~** Hotelgutschein; **internal ~** Eigenbeleg; **journal ~** Buchungs-, Journal-, Kassenbeleg; **luggage ~** *(Br.)* Gepäckschein; **luncheon (meal) ~** Essensbon, Verpflegungsmarke; **original ~** Originalbeleg; **pay ~** Kassenanweisung, *(wage earner)* Lohnzettel; **~s payable** zur Zahlung freigegebene Beträge, Auszahlungsbelege; **payment ~** Zahlungs-, Kassenanweisung; **payroll ~** Lohnauszahlungsbeleg, -zettel; **petty-cash ~** Portokassenbeleg; **purchase ~** Einkaufsbeleg; **receipt ~** Quittung, Empfangsbescheinigung;
~ for dividends Dividendenkupon; **~ exchangeable for goods** Warengutschein; **~ for payment** Zahlungs-, Ausgabenbeleg; **~ for receipt** Quittungsbeleg; **~s in support of an account** Rechnungsbelege;
to file a ~ Beleg abheften; **to prepare a ~ for a bill** Rechnungsbeleg anfertigen; **to submit ~s** Belege einreichen; **to support by ~s** dokumentarisch belegen;
~ audit Prüfung der Auszahlungsbelege, *(governmental accounting)* Belegprüfung, Prüfung der Buchungsunterlagen; **~ book** Juxtabuch; **~ bookkeeping** Belegbuchhaltung; **~ check** *(US)* **(cheque, Br.)** Scheck mit anhängendem Zahlungsnachweis, Verrechnungsscheck, *(cloakroom)* Garderobenmarke; **~ clerk** Kreditorenbuchhalter; **~ copy** Belegdoppel, -exemplar, *(advertising, Br.)* Anzeigenbeleg; **~ complete ~ copy** *(Br.)* Belegdoppel, vollständiges Belegduplikat; **~ files** Belegablage; **~ form** Belegformular; **~ index** alphabetisches Empfängerverzeichnis; **cost-~ inventory** Beleginventur; **~ jacket** Ausgabeformular, -beleg; **~ number** Belegnummer; **~ register** Ausgabenbuchführung, Zahlungsnachweisbuch, Belegeverzeichnis, -sammlung, Verzeichnis der Buchungsunterlagen; **~ stamp** abgestempelter Originalbeleg; **~ system** Beleg-, Buchungssystem, Belegbuchhaltung.
vouchsafe *(v.)* sich herablassen, gnädig gewähren;
~ s. o. no reply j. keiner Antwort würdigen.
vow Versprechen, *(religion)* Gelübde;
under a ~ of silence zur Geheimhaltung verpflichtet;
~ of secrecy Geheimhaltungsversprechen;
to be under a ~ not to smoke sich zur Aufgabe des Rauchens verpflichtet haben; **to break one's ~** Versprechen nicht halten.
vox populi *(lat.)* Stimme des Volkes, öffentliche Meinung.
voyage Seereise, *(account of voyage)* Reisebeschreibung, *(journey)* Reise;
on a ~ auf Reisen;
broken ~ unterbrochene Reise; **foreign ~** Auslands-, Überseereise; **home ~** Rück-, Heimreise; **inaugural ~** Jungfernfahrt; **insured ~** versicherte Reise; **~ out** Hinreise; **return ~** *(Br.)* Rückreise;
~ out and home Hin- und Rückfahrt;

~ **of discovery** Entdeckungsreise; ~ **of exploration** Entdekkungs-, Forschungsreise;

~ *(v.)* Seereise unternehmen, Seeweg nehmen;

to send s. o. on a ~ j. auf Reisen schicken; **to share a** ~ vom Reiseergebnis profitieren;

~ **charter** Chartern eines Schiffs; ~ **charterparty** Seefrachtvertrag; ~ **freight** Fracht für die ganze Reise; ~ **insurance** Reiseversicherung; ~ **policy** Reiseversicherungspolice; ~ **premium** Reiseversicherungsprämie.

voyageable befahrbar.

voyager Reisender;

~ **spacecraft** Weltraumsonde.

vulcanite Hartgummi.

vulcanizable vulkanisierbar.

vulcanization Vulkanisierung.

vulcanize *(v.)* vulkanisieren, *(v./i.)* vulkanisiert werden.

vulcanizer Vulkanisierapparat;

tire (tyre, *Br.*) ~ Vulkanisierbetrieb.

vulgar allgemein üblich (verbreitet), landesüblich, volkstümlich, *(obscene)* unanständig, vulgär, *(plebeian)* ordinär, gemein, *(unrefined)* ungebildet, ungehobelt, schlecht erzogen;

~ **behavio(u)r** ungehobeltes Benehmen; ~ **display of wealth** aufdringliche Zurschaustellung seines Reichtums; ~ **fraction** gemeiner (gewöhnlicher) Bruch; **the** ~ **herd** der Pöbel; ~ **language** vulgäre Sprache, Volkssprache; ~ **superstition** volkstümlicher Aberglaube.

vulgarity Roheit, Pöbelhaftigkeit, Unsitte.

vulgarization Verbreitung, Popularisierung, *(making coarse)* Herabwürdigung.

vulgarize *(v.)* popularisieren, unter das Volk bringen.

vulnerable verwundbar, verletzbar, *(liable to be affected)* anfällig, *(mil.)* ungeschützt, offen;

~ **to attack** Angriffen ausgesetzt; ~ **to criticism** kritikempfindlich; ~ **to depreciation** auf Abschreibungsmöglichkeiten stark reagierend; ~ **to inflation** inflationsempfindlich; ~ **to recession** rezessionsempfindlich; ~ **to sabotage** sabotageanfällig;

to be at s. one's most ~ jds. Achillesferse darstellen; **to be** ~ **to betrayal** dem Verrat gegenüber anfällig sein; **to prove** ~ sich als gefährdet erweisen;

~ **heel of Achilles** Achillesferse; ~ **reputation** angreifbarer Ruf; **to find s. one's** ~ **spot** jds. Achillesferse ausfindig machen.

vulture *(fig.)* Aasgeier.

W

wad Bausch, Polster, *(collection of documents)* Rolle von Dokumenten, *(of money, US sl.)* Haufen Geld, Moos, *(of paper)* Papierknäuel, zerknülltes Papier;
~ of bank notes Bündel von Geldnoten, Geldscheinbündel; ~ *(v.)* zusammenknüllen.

waddle *(v.) (clothes)* wattieren;
~ across the road über die Straße watscheln; ~ out of the alley *(Br., sl.)* sich von der Börse zurückziehen, Zahlungen einstellen.

wadding Polsterung, Wattierung.

wade Furt, seichte Stelle;
~ *(v.)* waten;
~ into a problem Problem angehen; ~ through a dull textbook sich durch ein langwieriges Lehrbuch durcharbeiten; ~ through the weeds of a bank Unkraut der Böschung durchqueren.

wadset *(Scot.)* Grundstücksbelastung, -pfand, Hypothek.

wadsetter *(Scot.)* Grundpfand, Hypothekengläubiger.

wafer *(document)* Oblate, Siegelmarke.

waff *(Br.)* Windstoß.

waffle *(sl.)* Geschwafel;
~ *(v.)* quatschen.

wag *(joker)* Spaßvogel, *(Br., sl.)* Schulschwänzer;
with a ~ of his head *(coll.)* mit einem Kopfnicken;
~ *(v.) (coll.)* eilig aufbrechen, *(Br., sl.)* [von der Schule] unerlaubt fernbleiben, schwänzen.

wage [Arbeits]lohn, Werklohn, Arbeitsentgelt, -einkommen, *(allowance)* Diäten, *(award)* Lohn, Belohnung, *(production cost)* Lohnanteil, *(ship)* Heuer;
at a ~ of zu einem Gehalt von;
above-pay-policy ~ *(Br.)* über der amtlichen Richtlinie liegender Lohn; accrued ~s noch nicht fällige Lohnforderungen; actual ~ Reallohn; advance ~s Lohnvorschüsse; one-month advance ~ einen Monat im voraus gezahlter Lohn; aggregate ~s Lohnsumme; agricultural ~s Landarbeitslöhne; annual ~ garantierter Jahreslohn; apprentice ~ Lehrlingsvergütung; average ~ Durchschnittslohn; back ~s rückständige Löhne, Lohnrückstände; basic ~ Eck-, Grund-, Schichtlohn; beginning ~ Anfangslohn; below-poverty ~ Lohn unterhalb des Existenzminimums; bootleg ~s außertariflich gezahlte Löhne; competitive ~ Konkurrenzlohn; construction ~ Bauarbeiterlohn; contractual ~ vertraglich vereinbarter Lohn; current ~ Lohn nach dem letzten Abrechnungszeitraum; day (daily) ~ Tageslohn; a day's ~ Tageslohn; dismissal ~ Entlassungsausgleich, -zahlung; ~ actually earned Effektivlohn; efficiency ~ *(US)* Leistungslohn; fair ~s angemessene Löhne; family ~ Familienstandslohn; farm ~ Landarbeiterlohn; fortnightly ~ *(Br.)* Halbmonatslohn; going ~ üblicher Lohn; gross ~ Bruttolohn; guaranteed ~ garantierter Jahreslohn; guaranteed minimum ~ garantierter Mindestlohn; half-daily ~ Halbtagslohn; hourly ~ Stundenlohn, -verdienst; steadily increasing ~ ständig steigender Lohn; index ~ Indexlohn; individual ~ Einzellohn; industrial ~s Industriearbeiterlöhne; job ~ Stück-, Akkordlohn; journeyman ~ Gesellenlohn; learner ~ Praktikantenlohn; living ~ auskömmlicher Lohn, gebundenes Einkommen, Existenzminimum; local ~ ortsüblicher Lohn; low ~ geringer Lohn; maintenance ~ das Existenzminimum gerade deckender Lohn; maximum ~ Höchstlohn; medium ~ *(US)* mittlerer Lohn; minimum [weekly] ~ [Wochen]mindestlohn; minimum statutory ~ gesetzlicher Mindestlohn; money ~ Geldlohn; monopolistic ~ Monopollohn; monthly ~ Monatslohn; net ~ Nettolohn; nominal ~ Nettolohn; occupational ~ Facharbeiterlohn; peak ~ Spitzen-, Höchstlohn; pegged ~ künstlich gehaltener Lohn, Indexlohn; piece ~ Stück-, Akkordlohn; prevailing ~ gültiger (gängiger, branchenüblicher) Lohn; productive ~s Fertigungslöhne; productivity ~s auf die Produktivität abgestellte Löhne; progressive ~ progressiver (mit der Produktion steigender) Lohn; real ~ Reallohn; regular ~ Normallohn; result ~ Akkordlohn; saving ~ Ersparnisse gestattender Lohn; sliding ~ gleitender Lohn; standard ~ ortsüblicher Lohn, Tariflohn; standard hourly ~ tariflicher Stundenlohn; starvation ~s Hungerlöhne; stipulated ~ festgesetzter (vereinbarter) Lohn; subminimum ~ untertariflicher Lohn; bare subsistence ~ *(US)* das Existenzminimum gerade deckender Lohn; superannuated ~ untertariflicher Lohn; supplemental ~ Zusatzlohn; supplementary ~ Lohnzulage; take-home ~ Nettolohn, Lohntüte; task ~ Akkordlohn; time ~ Zeit-, Stundenlohn;

unclaimed ~s Lohnguthaben; unfair ~s unangemessene Löhne; union ~ gewerkschaftlich ausgehandelter Tariflohn; wartime ~ Kriegslohn; weekly ~ Wochenlohn;
~ paid in cash Barlohn; ~ per hour Stundenlohn; ~s paid to outside labo(u)r Fremdlöhne; ~s of management (superintendence) Gehalt leitender Angestellter, *(owner-manager)* Unternehmergewinn; ~ based on the output Leistungslohn; ~ on piecework basis Stücklohn; ~s and salaries Löhne und Gehälter;
~ *(v.)* a dogfight Luftkampf ausfechten; ~ war Krieg führen; ~ effective war on s. th. einer Sache wirksam zu Leibe gehen;
to assign specified amounts of earned ~s bestimmte Lohnbeträge abtreten; to attach ~s *(Br.)* Lohn pfänden; to curb ~s Löhne drosseln; to cut ~s Löhne kürzen (senken); to deduct from the ~ vom Lohn abziehen; to detain ~s Löhne einbehalten; to earn good ~s gut verdienen, schönes Gehalt haben; to equalize ~s Löhne angleichen; to freeze ~s Lohnstop durchführen; to garnishee ~s Lohn pfänden; to get good ~s gut verdienen; to increase ~s Löhne erhöhen; to pay ~ Lohn auszahlen, entlohnen; to pay bad ~s niedrige Löhne zahlen; to pay out the ~s Lohnzahlungen vornehmen; to peg the ~s at Löhne stoppen bei; to put up ~s Löhne erhöhen; to raise ~s Lohnerhöhung vornehmen; to realign the ~s Löhne angleichen; to receive one's week's ~(s) seinen Wochenlohn erhalten; to reduce ~s Löhne herabsetzen, Lohnkürzungen vornehmen; to retain ~s Lohn einbehalten; to scale down ~s Löhne kürzen, Lohnkürzung vornehmen; to stand (stick out) for higher ~s Lohnerhöhung fordern; to stop ~s Löhne einbehalten; to undercut ~s für zu niedrigen Lohn arbeiten; to withhold so much out of s. one's ~ soundsoviel von jds. Lohn einbehalten; ~s account Lohnkonto; ~ accounting Lohnabrechnung; ~ adequacy Lohnausgleich; ~ adjustment Lohnangleichung, -anpassung; automatic ~ adjustment automatische Lohnregulierung; ~ and salary administration Lohn- und Gehaltswesen; ~ advance Lohnvorschuß, -vorauszahlung; collective ~ agreement Lohnabkommen, Tarifvertrag; ~ arbitration Schiedsgerichtswesen in Lohnstreitigkeiten; ~ assignment Lohnabtretung; ~ avalanche Lohnlawine; ~ award Lohnschiedsspruch; ~ bargaining Tarif-, Lohnverhandlungen, ~ bargaining machinery (system) Tariflohnwesen; ~s bill Lohnliste, *(Br.)* Lohnetat; ~ board *(US)* [Lohn]schlichtungsstelle; National ~s Board *(US)* staatliches Schlichtungsamt, Landesschlichter; ~ book Lohnbuch; ~ boom Lohnkonjunktur; ~ boost *(US)* Lohnanstieg; to tie ~ boosts to productivity gains Lohnanstieg mit Produktivitätszuwachs koppeln; ~ bracket Tarifklasse, Lohngruppe; ~ capital Lohnkapital; ~ ceilings Höchstlöhne; ~ challenge Lohnforderung; ~ changes Lohnveränderungen; ~ check *(US)* (cheque, *Br.*) Lohnscheck; ~ claims Lohnansprüche, -forderungen; ~ class Lohnstufe, Tarifklasse, -gruppe; ~ classification Tarifeinstufung, Lohngruppierung; ~ clause Tarifklausel; ~ clerk Lohnbuchhalter; ~ comparison Lohnvergleich; ~ compensation rate Lohntarif; ~ concessions Lohnzugeständnisse; ~ conditions Lohnbedingungen; ~ and salary control Lohn- und Gehaltsüberwachung, -reglementierung; ~ and price controls Lohn- und Preisüberwachung; ~-control agreement Lohnbegrenzungsabkommen; ~ controversy Lohnstreitigkeiten; ~ costs Lohnaufwand; direct ~ costs unmittelbare Lohnkosten; spiralling ~ costs spiralartig ansteigende Lohnkosten; ~s Council *(Br.)* Tarifkommission; ~s Councils Act *(Br.)* Gesetz zur Berufung von Tarifkommissionen; ~ curb Lohnbremse; ~ curve Lohnkurve; ~ cut[ting] Lohnkürzung, -herabsetzung; ~ data Lohnabgaben; ~s declaration *(insurance)* Jahresmeldung über bezahlte Löhne und Gehälter; ~ deflation Lohnabbau, Absinken der Löhne; ~ demands Forderung nach Lohnerhöhungen, Lohnforderungen, -ansprüche; ~ determination Lohnbestimmung, -festsetzung; automatic ~ determination automatische Lohnfestsetzung; ~ development Entwicklung der Löhne, Lohnentwicklung; ~ differentials Lohngefälle, -differenz, Tarifunterschiede; intercity ~ differential Ortsklassenunterschied; ~ disparity Lohnverschiedenheit; ~ disputes Lohnkämpfe, -streitigkeiten, Tarifstreitigkeiten; ~ distraint Lohneinbehaltung; ~ distribution Lohnverteilung; ~ dividend Lohnprämie; ~ docket Lohntüte; ~ drift durch übertarifliche Bezahlung verursachter Lohnauftrieb; ~ drive Lohnbewegung; ~ earner Lohn-, Gehaltsempfänger, Arbeitnehmer; standard ~ earner Tarifangestellter; weekly ~ earner Wochenlohnempfänger; ~ and salary earners abhängig

Beschäftigte, Erwerbspersonen, lohnsteuerpflichtige Beschäftigte; ~-**earner group (class)** Lohnempfängerklasse; ~ **earnings** Arbeitsverdienst, Gehalts-, Lohneinnahmen; ~-**earning employment** nicht selbständige (lohnsteuerpflichtige) Beschäftigung; ~-**earning man** Lohn-, Gehaltsempfänger; ~-**earning work** Lohnarbeit; ~ **escalation** Lohngleitregelung, gleitende Lohnregelung; ~-**examining bureau** Lohnprüfstelle; ~ **expenses** Lohnaufwand; ~ **exploitation** Lohnausbeutung; ~ **explosion** Lohnexplosion; **public-sector-led** ~ **explosion** im Bereich der öffentlichen Hände gestartete Lohnexplosion; ~ **factor in cost** Lohnkostenfaktor; ~ **fixing** Lohn-, Gehaltsfestsetzung; ~ **floor** Lohnminimum; ~ **formula** Lohn-, Tarifformel; ~ **freeze** Lohnstop; **one-year** ~ **freeze** einjähriges Lohnstillhalteabkommen; ~ **and price freeze** Lohn- und Preisstopp; ~-**freezing policy** Lohnstoppolitik; ~-**freezing and price-lowering policy** auf Lohnstabilisierung und Preissenkung gerichtete Politik; ~ **front** Lohnfront; ~ **fund** Lohnfonds; ~-**fund theory (Ricardo)** Lohnfondstheorie; ~ **gain** Lohnzuwachs; ~ **garnishment (US)** Lohnpfändung; ~ **group** Tarifgruppe; **real** ~ **growth** Anstieg der Reallöhne; ~ **guidelines** Lohnleitsätze; ~ **guidepost** Lohneckpfeiler; ~ **hike** Lohnanstieg, -erhöhung; ~-**hour law (US)** Arbeitszeitgesetz; ~ **incentive** Lohn-, Leistungsanreiz; ~ **incentive payment plan** Leistungs-, Akkordlohnsystem; ~ **income** Lohn-, Erwerbseinkommen; ~ **increase** Erhöhung der Löhne, Lohnerhöhung, -steigerung, -aufbesserung; **across-the-board (round-of-)** ~ **increase** umfassender Lohnanstieg, Lohnwelle; **to hold** ~ **increase to 15%** Lohnerhöhungen auf 15% begrenzen; **to pass on** ~ **increases to the consumer** Lohnerhöhungen auf den Verbraucher abwälzen; ~ **increment (Br.)** Lohnanstieg, -steigerung, -aufbesserung, Lohnerhöhung; ~ **index** Lohnindex; **national** ~ **index corrected to take out inflationary effects** inflationsbereinigter Lohnkostenindex; ~-**indexation** Lohnindexierung; **highest-**~ **industry** lohnintensivster Industriezweig; ~ **inequality** Lohnungleichheit, -ungerechtigkeit, unberechtigter Lohnunterschied; ~ **inflation** inflationäre Löhne, Lohninflation; ~-**intensive** lohnintensiv; ~ **labo(u)r** Lohnarbeit, (pl., US) Lohnempfänger; ~ **leadership** Beeinflussung des Lohnniveaus, tarifpolitische Führerstellung, Lohnführerschaft; ~ **level** Lohnniveau, -stand, -durchschnitt, -höhe; ~ **and salary level** Lohn- und Gehaltsniveau; ~ **line** Lohnkurve; ~ **loss** Lohnausfall; ~ **market** Arbeitsmarkt; ~ **matters** Lohn-, Tariffragen; ~ **mediation** Lohnschlichtung; ~ **minimum** Lohnminimum; ~ **negotiations** Lohn-, Tarifverhandlungen; ~ **objective** Lohnziel; ~ **office** Lohnbüro; ~s **order (Br.)** Tarifordnung; ~ **packet** Lohntüte; ~ **parity** Lohnparität; ~ **pattern** Tarifordnung; ~ **pause** Lohnpause; ~ **paying (payment)** Lohn[aus]zahlung; **advance** ~ **payment** Lohnvorauszahlung; **contract** ~ **payment** ausgehandelte Tariflöhne; ~-**payment plan** Lohnauszahlungssystem, -zahlungsmethode; ~ **plan** Lohnfestsetzungsverfahren, Lohn-, Tarifsystem; **guaranteed** ~ **plan** Lohnabkommen mit garantierter Mindestbeschäftigungszeit; ~ **policy** Lohnpolitik; **leading** ~ **policy** Tarifpolitik; ~ **pressure** Lohndruck; ~-**price control** Lohn-Preiskontrolle; ~-**price guidelines** Richtwerte für die Lohn- und Preisentwicklung, Lohn-Preisrichtzahlen; ~-**price guidepost** Orientierungsdaten zur Lohnfestsetzung; **statutory** ~-**price policy** gesetzlich vorgeschriebene Lohn- und Preiskontrollen; ~-**price spiral** Preis-, Lohnspirale; ~-**price structure** Lohn-Preis-Gefüge; ~ **problem** Lohnproblem; **automatic** ~ **progression** automatische Lohnprogression; **index-number** ~ **provisions** auf den Lebenshaltungsindex abgestimmte Lohnanstiege; ~ **push** Lohndruck, Durchsetzung von Lohnforderungen; ~-**push inflation** Lohninflation; ~ **qualification** [höherer] Lohnanspruch; ~ **raise (US)** Lohnsteigerung; ~ **range** Lohnspanne; ~ **rate** Grundlohntarif, Entlohnungs-, Tariflohnsatz; **base** ~ **rate** Grundlohntarif; **hourly** ~ **rate** Stundenlohn; **learner's** ~ **rate** Anlernlohn; **standard** ~ **rate** Tarif-, Lohnsatz; **to peg the** ~ **rates** Lohnniveau einfrieren; ~-**rate brackets** Tariflohngruppen; ~-**rate change** Lohntarifänderungen; ~ **rate cutting** Lohnkürzung; ~-**rate determination process** Lohnfestsetzungsverfahren; ~-**rate group** Tarif-, Lohngruppe; ~-**ratio** Lohnquote; ~ **and salary receipts** Lohn- und Gehaltseinkommen; ~ **recommendations** Lohnempfehlungen; ~ **reduction** Lohnsenkung; ~s **regulation** Tarif-, Lohnregelung; ~s **regulation proposal** Tarifvorschlag; ~ **relationship** Lohnverhältnis; ~ **reopening** Vereinbarung über erneute Tarifverhandlungen, neue Lohnverhandlungen; ~-**reopening clause** Wiederaufnahmeklausel für Lohnverhandlungen; ~ **request** Lohnforderung; ~ **restraint** Verhinderung von Lohnsteigerungen; **voluntary** ~ **restraint** Selbstbeschränkung bei Lohnforderungen; **weekly** ~ **return (Br.)** wöchentliche Lohnliste; ~ **review** Überprüfung der Tarif-

einstufung; ~ **rise (Br.)** Lohnerhöhung, -anstieg, -aufbesserung, Gehaltserhöhung; ~ **rise pegged to the rate of inflation** mit dem Inflationssatz gekoppelte Lohnerhöhungen; ~ **round** Tarif-, Lohnrunde; ~ **savings** Lohnkostenersparnisse; ~ **scale** Lohnskala, -tarif; **in excess of the** ~ **scale** übertariflich; **sliding** ~ **scale** gleitende Lohnskala, gleitender Lohntarif; ~ **schedule** Lohntabelle; ~ **scramble** Lohngerangel; ~ **setting** Lohnberechnungsverfahren, Tarifsystem; ~ **settlement** Lohnregelung, Lohn-, Tarifabkommen, Tarifabschluß; ~ **share** Lohnquote; ~ **sheet** Lohnliste; ~ **slave** Arbeitssklave; ~ **slip** Lohnabrechnungszettel, -streifen; ~ **solidarity** Tarifsolidarität; ~ **spiral** Lohnspirale; ~ **spread** Lohnspanne; **to go on a** ~ **spree** in überhöhten Lohnforderungen schwelgen; ~ **stabilization** Lohnausgleich; ~ **stabilization board (US)** Lohnausgleichsamt; ~ **and prices standstill** Lohn- und Preisstopp; ~ **statistics** Lohnstatistik; ~ **stop** Lohnstopp; ~ **structure** Lohngefüge; ~ **supplement** Lohn-, Gehaltszulage; **community** ~ **survey** Überblick über die allgemeinen Lohnverhältnisse; ~ **system** Tarifvertragswesen; ~ **table** Lohntabelle; ~ **talks** Lohnverhandlungen; ~ **tariff** Lohntarif; ~ **tax** Lohnsteuer; ~ **theory** Lohntheorie; ~ **tribunal** Lohninstanz.

wager Wette, Wettvertrag, *(stake)* Einsatz;
~ *(v.)* einsetzen, setzen, wetten;
to lay (make) a ~ Wette anbieten, wetten; **to take up a** ~ Wette annehmen;
~ **policy** Wettpolice.

wagering | contract Spielvertrag; ~ **gain** Gewinnanteil; ~ **transaction** [gemeinsame] Wette.

wagework Lohnarbeit.

wageworker *(US)* Lohnempfänger.

wag(g)on Fuhrwerk, [Last]wagen, *(perambulator, coll.)* Kinderwagen, *(railroad, US)* Gepäck-, Güterwagen, Waggon;
by ~ per Achse; **free on the** ~ frei auf den Wagen; **off the [water]**~ *(coll.)* nicht mehr abstinent;
ambulance ~ Unfallwagen; ~s **available** Wagenbestand; **box (covered)** ~ Planwagen, *(Br.)* Frachtwaggon, Güterwagen, *(US)* Lore, Blockwagen; **closed** ~ geschlossener-, G-Wagen; **express** ~ Eilgutwagen; **goods** ~ (Br.) Güterwagen, -waggon; **open** ~ offener Güterwagen, Rungenwagen; **paddy** ~ *(sl.)* Grüne Minna; **patrol** ~ *(US)* Gefangenentransportwagen, Grüne Minna; **station** ~ *(US)* Kombiwagen; **tea** ~ Teewagen; ~ *(v.)* im Waggon befördern, Güter transportieren;
to be on the water ~ *(sl.)* Abstinenzler sein; **to hitch one's** ~ **to a star** sich ein hohes Ziel stecken, sich j. als leuchtendes Vorbild nehmen; **to stow a** ~ Waggon beladen;
~ **distributor (jobber)** *(US)* Großhändler ohne eigenes Lager; ~-**lit (Br.)** Schlafwagen; ~ **lock** Wagenbremse; ~ **lot** *(US)* Waggonladung; ~ **manifest** Ladeverzeichnis, Wagenladeschein; ~ **master** *(railway)* Wagenmeister, *(mil.)* Nachschuboffizier; ~ **stock** Waggonbestand; ~ **track** Fahrgleis; ~ **traffic** Fuhrwesen; ~ **train** Planwagenzug, *(US)* Güterzug, *(mil.)* Dienstzug; ~ **wheel** Wagenrad.

wag(g)onable im Wagen transportierbar.

wag(g)onage Waggonbeförderung, *(charge, US)* Frachtgeld, Fuhrlohn, Transportkosten, *(collection of wag(g)ons)* Wagenpark.

wag(g)oner Fuhrmann.

wag(g)onload Wagenladung, Fuhre, *(fig.)* Menge, *(railway, Br.)* Waggonladung;
by the ~ waggonweise, in Waggonladungen.

wag(g)onway Fahrbahn.

waif herrenlose Sache, herrenloses Gut, *(animal)* streunendes Tier *(stolen goods thrown away, Br.)* weggeworfenes Diebesgut, *(person)* Heimat-, Obdachloser, *(on shore)* Strandgut;
~s weggeworfenes Diebesgut;
~s **and strays** verwahrloste Kinder;
~ *(a.)* entlaufen, streunend, *(Scot.)* nicht seßhaft;
~ **word** geläufiges Wort.

wail Klagen, Jammern, Wimmern;
~ *(v.)* klagen, jammern;
~ **[over] one's fortune** sein Unglück beklagen; ~ **with pain** vor Schmerzen wimmern.

wailing | s of despair Verzweiflungsschreie;
~ *(a.)* jammernd, wimmernd;
to race through the streets with ~ **sirens** mit heulenden Sirenen durch die Straßen rasen; ~ **Wall** Klagemauer.

wainscot Wandtäfelung, Holzverkleidung, Paneelwerk;
tile ~ Kachelverkleidung.

wainscoting Paneelieren, Verkleidungsbretter.

waist Taille, Leibesumfang;
~ **belt** Gürtel, *(airplane)* Anschnallgurt, *(mil.)* Koppel.

waistline Gürtellinie, Taille;
to watch one's ~ auf die schlanke Linie achten.

wait Wartezeit, Verzögerung, *(railway)* Aufenthalt, *(theater)* Pause, Zwischenakt;
~ *(v.)* aufwarten, bedienen, *(rest)* unerledigt bleiben, liegenbleiben;
~ **for** warten auf, zuwarten; ~ **on s. o.** jem. zur Hand gehen;
~ **to be collected** auf seine Abholung warten, abgeholt werden;
~ **s. one's convenience** für jds. Bequemlichkeit sorgen; ~ **dinner for s. o.** mit dem Mittagessen auf j. warten; ~ **a funeral** einer Beerdigung beiwohnen; ~ **two hours on end** geschlagene zwei Stunden warten; ~ **out the market** *(sl.)* durch Zurückhaltung die Marktpreise beeinflussen; ~ **one's opportunity** günstige Gelegenheit abwarten; ~ **on with patterns** Muster vorführen; ~ **and see** sich abwartend verhalten, abwartende Haltung einnehmen; ~ **for a dead man's shoes** auf eine Erbschaft warten; ~ **on the table** bei Tisch bedienen; ~ **one's time** günstige Gelegenheit abwarten; ~ **one's turn** warten bis man drankommt; ~ **up until 11 o'clock** bis 11 Uhr aufbleiben; ~ **upon** seine Aufwartung machen, bedienen; ~ **upon s. o.** *(commercial agent)* jem. einen Besuch abstatten; ~ **upon her husband hand and foot** ihren Ehemann von hinten bis vorn bedienen;
to have a long ~ **for the bus** lange auf den Bus warten müssen; to have a long ~ **at the station** längeren Aufenthalt auf dem Bahnhof haben; to lie in ~ im Hinterhalt liegen;
~ **order** *(advertising)* zu bestimmtem Zeitpunkt abgerufener Anzeigenauftrag, Terminauftrag; ~-**and-see attitude** abwartende Haltung; ~-**and-see policy** abwartende Politik (Haltung).

waiter Ober, Kellner, *(stock exchange, Br.)* Börsendiener.

waiting Warten, *(attendance)* Aufwartung, Bedienen;
in ~ dienstbereit, -tuend, *(mil., Br.)* in Bereitschaft;
no ~ Halteverbot;
~ **at a dinner** Servieren eines Abendessens;
to be in ~ Dienst haben, dienstbereit sein; **to keep s. o.** ~ seine Verabredung nicht einhalten;
no-~ area Halteverbotszone; ~ **course** abwartender Kurs; ~ **gentlewoman** Hofdame; ~ **girl** Zofe; ~ **guard** *(mil.)* Ersatzwache; ~ **line** Warteschlange; ~-**line theory** Warteschlangentheorie; ~ **list** Warteliste, Vormerk-, Anwärterliste; **to put s. o. on the** ~ **list** j. auf die Warteliste setzen; ~ **maid** Dienstmädchen, Zofe; ~ **man** Kammerdiener, Lakai; ~ **period** *(insurance law)* Karenzzeit, *(securities commission, US)* Wartezeit; **initial** ~ **period** Anfangswartezeit; ~ **policy** abwartende Politik; ~ **restriction** Halteverbot; ~ **room** *(doctor)* Warte-, Vorzimmer, *(railway)* Wartesaal; ~ **table** Anrichtetisch; ~ **time** Anwartschaftzeit, *(technical defect)* Warte-, Verlustzeit.

waitress Aufwärterin.

waive *(v.)* Verzicht leisten, verzichten, [Ansprüche] aufgeben, *(postpone)* aufschieben, zurückstellen;
~ **the age limit** über die Altersgrenze hinaus tätig bleiben, Altersdispens erteilen; ~ **the breach** über eine Vertragsverletzung hinwegsehen; ~ **a chance** Chance nicht wahrnehmen; ~ **a claim** sich eines Rechtsanspruches begeben, auf einen Rechtsanspruch verzichten; ~ **debts** Schulden erlassen; ~ **a defence** auf die Geltendmachung einer Einrede verzichten; ~ **hono(u)rs** auf Ehrungen verzichten; ~ **a privilege** auf ein Vorrecht verzichten; ~ **a question till later** Frage zurückstellen; ~ **a question until later in the meeting** Frage auf einen späteren Zeitpunkt in der Sitzung verschieben; ~ **one's right** auf ein Recht (seinen Anspruch) verzichten; ~ **one's right to speak** auf das Wort verzichten; ~ **one's scruples** seine Bedenken fallenlassen.

waiver Aufgabe, Verzicht, *(declaration)* Verzichtleistung, -erklärung, *(insurance law)* Verzicht auf Haftungsbeschränkung;
binding ~ bindende Verzichtserklärung; **express** ~ ausdrücklicher Verzicht; **implied** ~ konkludenter (stillschweigender) Verzicht;
~ **of claims** Anspruchsverzicht; ~ **of demand, notice and protest** Verzichtleistung auf Wechselprotest; ~ **by election of remedies** Verzicht auf Einrede der Vorausklage; ~ **of exemption** schriftlicher Verzicht auf Pfändungsschutz; ~ **of a fee** Gebührenerlaß; ~ **of immunity** *(witness in criminal case)* Verzicht auf die Aussageverweigerung im Falle der Selbstbeschuldigung; ~ **of liability** Haftungsausschluß; ~ **of notice** Benachrichtigungsverzicht, Mitteilungsverzicht; ~ **of premiums** Prämienbefreiung; ~ **of presentation** Verzicht auf Vorlage von Unterlagen; ~ **of privilege** Verzicht auf das Zeugnisverweigerungsrecht; ~ **of protest** *(bill of exchange)* Protestverzicht, Verzicht auf Wechselprotest; ~ **of right** Rechtsaufgabe, -verzicht; ~ **of the statute of limitations** Verzicht auf die Einrede der Verjährung; ~ **of**

tort *(injured party)* Stützung des Klagevorbringens auf Vertrag anstelle von unerlaubter Handlung;
to sign a ~ **of claim** Anspruchsverzicht unterschreiben;
~ **clause** Verzichtsleistungsklausel.

waiving Verzicht[sleistung];
~ **of age limits** Altersdispens; ~ **of presentment** Vorlageverzicht.

wake Wache, Wachen, *(mar.)* Schiffs-, Blasenspur, *(plane)* Luftschraubenstrahl, *(Irish)* Totenwache, Leichenschmaus;
in the ~ **of** unmittelbar nach; **in the** ~ **of s. o.** in jds. Fußstapfen, auf jds. Spur; **in the** ~ **of a ship** im Kielwasser eines Schiffes;
~ *(v.)* wachen, wach bleiben, *(fig.)* sich regen (rühren);
~ **ambition** Ehrgeiz anspornen; ~ **controversy** Meinungsverschiedenheit hervorrufen; ~ **a corpse** Totenwache halten; ~ **memories** Erinnerungen wachrufen; ~ **echoes in a mountain valley** Echo in einem Gebirgstal hervorrufen;
to be in the ~ **of s. o.** in jds. Kielwasser segeln; **to bring trouble in its** ~ unangenehme Folgen nach sich ziehen; **to come in the** ~ **of explorers** den Entdeckern auf dem Fuße folgen; **to get into the** ~ in den Sog geraten.

wakening *(Scot.)* Wiederaufnahme eines Verfahrens.

walk Spaziergang, *(aisle)* Wandelgang, -halle, *(avenue)* Allee, Promenade, *(conduct)* Betragen, Benehmen, Lebenswandel, *(forest, Br.)* Revier, Waldbereich, *(line of business)* Distrikt, Route, *(policeman)* Runde, *(postman)* Zustellbezirk, *(profession)* Beruf[szweig], Fach, Laufbahn, Lebensweg, Stellung, *(scope of work)* Arbeitsgebiet, -kreis, -bereich, Betätigungsfeld, *(sidewalk)* Fußsteig, Spazierweg, *(social status)* soziale Stellung (Schicht), Gesellschaftskreis, *(tour)* Wanderung, Reise, Tour;
from all ~s **of life** aus allen Schichten der Bevölkerung; **in his** ~ **through the world** auf seinen Reisen durch die Welt;
~s *(Br.)* durch Boten eingezogene Wechsel;
conducted ~ Fußtour zur Stadtbesichtigung; **evening** ~ Abendspaziergang; **ten minutes'** ~ zehn Minuten zu Fuß; **quite a** ~ ganz ordentliche Strecke;
~ **of life** Lebensstellung, -gebiet, soziale Stellung; **all** ~s **of life** alle Berufssparten; **highest** ~s **of life** *(Br.)* höchste Gesellschaftskreise; **favo(u)rite** ~s **in the neighbo(u)rhood** beliebte Spaziergänge; **daily** ~ **into town** täglicher Gang in die Stadt;
~ *(v.)* gehen, spazierengehen, *(fig.)* wandeln, leben;
~ **on air** sich wie im siebenten Himmel fühlen; ~ **an airship into the shed** Luftschiff in die Halle befördern; ~ **into an ambush** in einen Hinterhalt geraten; ~ **away from s. o.** j. mühelos schlagen; ~ **back** *(fig.)* Rückzieher machen, früheren Standpunkt aufgeben; ~ **the boards** Schauspieler sein; ~ **one's chalks** *(sl.)* sich auf französisch empfehlen; ~ **the chalk line** ehrbares Leben führen, *(not tight)* nüchtern sein; ~ **over the course** leichten Sieg davontragen; ~ **the deck** auf dem Deck auf und ab gehen; ~ **the whole district** ganzen Bezirk durchwandern; ~ **on eggshells** Eiertanz aufführen; ~ **with God** wohlgefälliges Leben führen; ~ **the hospital** in der Klinik famulieren; ~ **into s. o.** über j. herfallen (herziehen); ~ **in the middle of the road** mitten auf dem Fahrdamm gehen; ~ **the last mile** *(fig.)* seinen Weg zu Ende gehen; ~ **s. o. off** j. polizeilich abführen; ~ **off with s. one's umbrella** aus Versehen jds. Regenschirm mitnehmen; ~ **out** *(US)* Arbeit niederlegen, streiken, *(in protest)* Saal verlassen; ~ **out on s. o.** *(US)* j. in der Not im Stich lassen, j. sitzenlassen; ~ **out with a tradesman** *(cook)* mit einem Lieferanten ein Verhältnis haben; ~ **s. o. over to the neighbo(u)r's house** j. zum Nachbarn begleiten; ~ **round s. o.** *(US)* über's Ohr hauen; ~ **through one's part** *(theater)* seine Rolle herunterspielen; ~ **the plank** zur Aufgabe seines Amtes gezwungen sein; ~ **in one's sleep** nachtwandeln; ~ **on golden slippers** im Gelde schwimmen; ~ **s. o. Spanish** *(sl.)* j. am Schlafittchen nehmen, *(US)* gefeuert werden; ~ **into one's stock of money** gehörigen Griff in seine Brieftasche tun; ~ **the streets** auf den Strich gehen; ~ **out in sympathy** *(US)* in einen Sympathiestreik treten; ~ **a thief off** Dieb abführen; ~ **the ties** *(US sl.)* am Bahndamm entlanglaufen; ~ **the tightrope** auf Distanz halten; ~ **the tracks** den Spuren nachgehen; ~ **the wards** in der Klinik famulieren;
to go for a ~ Spaziergang machen (unternehmen);
~ **bill** *(Br.)* Platzwechsel; ~ **charges** *(Br.)* Inkassospesen; ~ **cheque** *(Br.)* Platzscheck; ~ **clerk** *(banking, Br.)* Bank-, Inkassobote; ~ **collection** *(Br.)* Boteninkasso; ~ **department** *(Br.)* Stadtinkassoabteilung; ~-**in closet** begehbarer Schrank; ~s **items** *(Br.)* Inkassoposten; ~-**up** *(US)* Miethaus ohne Aufzug.

walkable betretbar, begehbar.

walker Spaziergänger, *(guard, Br.)* Kontrolle, Wache.

walkie|-lookie tragbare Fernsehkamera; ~-**pushie** tragbarer Fernsehsender; ~-**talkie** tragbares Funksprechgerät.

walking Wanderung, Tour;
~ **boot** Marschstiefel; ~ **charges** Einziehungskosten, -spesen; ~ **crane** Laufkatze, -kran; ~ **delegate** Branchen-, Geschäftsbevollmächtigter, *(trade union)* Gewerkschaftsvertreter, -funktionär; ~ **dress** Straßenkleid; ~ **gentleman** *(theater)* Statist; ~ **inspector** Reiseinspektor; ~ **papers** *(coll.)* Entlassungspapiere; **to have a ~-on part** Statistenrolle spielen; ~ **possession agreement** *(sheriff)* Lageraufstockungsvereinbarung; ~ **staff** Wanderstab; ~ **ticket** *(coll.)* Entlassungspapiere; ~ **tour** *(Br.)* Fußwanderung.

walkout *(coll.)* Arbeitsniederlegung, [Arbeiter]ausstand, Streik, *(political protest)* Verlassen des Saals;
~ **threat** Streikdrohung.

walkover leichtes Spiel, leichter Sieg.

walkway *(US)* Gehweg, Promenade;
covered ~ überdeckter Gehweg.

wall Wand, Mauer, *(bankruptcy, Br.)* Bankrott, Konkurs, *(fig.)* Schranke, Trennwand, Barriere, *(mining, Br.)* Sohle, Grundstrecke;
up against a ~ in die Enge getrieben; **with one's back to the** ~ allein gegen eine Übermacht, in verzweifelter Lage; **within the ~s** innerhalb einer Stadt;
~**s** *(mil.)* Befestigungswerk, -anlagen;
blank ~ blinde Wand; **common** ~ Brandmauer; **customs ~s** Zollschranken; **dead** ~ freistehende Mauer; **dry-stone** ~ Trockenmauer; **fire-proof** ~ Brandmauer; **partition** ~ Trennwand, Brandmauer; **party** ~ Grenz-, Trennmauer; **tariff** ~ Zollmauer;
~ **of partition** Trennungslinie; ~ **of prejudice** Mauer von Vorurteilen;
~ *(v.)* mit einer Mauer umgeben, ummauern;
~ **around** mit einem Wall umschließen; ~ **off part of a room** Zwischenwand ziehen; ~ **up a window** Fenster zumauern;
to drive to the ~ *(Br.)* zum Konkurs treiben; **to get the** ~ *(Br.)* bankrott machen; **to give s. o. the** ~ *(fig.)* jem. den Vorrang lassen; **to go over the** ~ *(sl.)* aus dem Kittchen entweichen; **to go to the** ~ an die Wand gedrückt werden, *(go bankrupt, Br.)* Konkurs machen; **to push s. o. to the** ~ j. in die Enge treiben, j. übervorteilen; **to run one's head against the** ~ mit dem Kopf durch die Wand wollen; **to see through a brick** ~ das Gras wachsen hören; **to take the** ~ **of s. o.** Vorrang vor jem. beanspruchen;
~ **advertisement** Maueranschlag; ~ **banner** Spannplakat; ~ **box** *(el.)* Wandschalter; ~ **bracket** Mauerkonsole, Wandarm; ~ **calendar** Wandkalender; ~ **flower** *(fig.)* Mauerblümchen; ~ **newspaper** Wandzeitung; ~ **painting** Wandmalerei; ~ **publicity** Giebelwerbung; ~ **sign** Wandschild; ⌖ **Street** *(US)* Wallstreet, *(fig.)* amerikanischer Geld- und Kapitalmarkt, New Yorker Hochfinanz; ⌖ **Street loan** *(US)* Lombardkredit; ~ **telephone** Wandapparat.

wallboard Wandbretter.

walled | -in eingemauert, -geschlossen; ~ **towns** befestigte Städte; ~**-up** zugemauert.

wallet Geldschein-, Brieftasche, *(bag)* Reisetasche, Tornister, Schnappsack, *(flat leather bag)* kleine Werkzeugtasche;
bill ~ Wechselportefeuille;
to join ~s for gemeinsam finanzieren; **to unclutch one's** ~ in die Brieftasche greifen.

walling Ummauerung.

wallow *(v.)* sich wälzen;
~ **in luxury** in größtem Luxus schwelgen; ~ **in pleasure** im Vergnügen schwelgen; ~ **in vice** dem Laster frönen; ~ **in the water** *(boat)* schlingern;
to be ~ing in money *(coll.)* im Geld wühlen, stinkreich sein.

wallpaper Tapete, *(counterfeit paper money)* Falschgeld;
~ *(v.)* tapezieren;
~ **litho** Hifi-Endlosfarbanzeige.

walnut shell *(fig.)* leichtes Boot, Nußschale.

wampum *(US sl.)* Gala, Wichs, Staat.

wand of peace *(Scot.)* Amtsstab des Gerichtsvollziehers.

wander Streifzug, Bummel;
~ *(v.)* wandern, streifen, *(rove at pleasure)* schlendern, bummeln;
~ **from the subject** vom Thema abkommen (abschweifen); ~ **in the wilderness** *(politics)* aus der Regierung ausscheiden, abserviert werden.

wandering Wanderung, -schaft, *(fever)* Fieberphantasie;
~ **in the wilderness** *(politics)* Ausscheiden aus der Regierung, Abserviertwerden;
~ *(a.)* umherschweifend, *(fig.)* ruhelos, unstet;
~ **star** Planet; ~ **tribe** Nomadenstab.

wane Abnehmen, Nachlassen;
in the ~ **of the moon** bei abnehmendem Mond; **on the** ~ im Aussterben;
~ *(v.)* abnehmen, *(colo(u)r)* verblassen, *(prosperity)* abklingen, abflauen, schwinden, nachlassen;
to be on the ~ unter einer Flaute leiden, *(year)* zu Ende gehen.

wangle Kniff, Schwindel, Trick, Machenschaft, Mogelei;
~ *(v.)* hintenherum ergattern, organisieren, schieben, deichseln, durch einen Kniff zustandebringen;
~ **accounts** bei der Kontenführung Betrügereien begehen, Konten frisieren (zurechtmachen, fälschen); ~ **an extra week's holiday** zusätzliche Urlaubswoche herausschinden; ~ **a matter** Sache deichseln; ~ **through somehow** sich irgendwie herauswinden; ~ **one's way through the crowd** sich durch eine Menge hindurchschlängeln;
to get s. th. by a ~ durch einen Trick (Mogelei, Machenschaften) erreichen.

wangler Schieber, Gauner, Mogler.

wangling Schiebung.

want *(deficiency)* Mangel, *(need)* Notwendigkeit, Erfordernis, Bedarf, Bedürfnis, Bedürftigkeit, Not, *(scarcity)* Knappheit;
for ~ **of acceptance** mangels Annahme; **for** ~ **of advice** mangels Bericht; **for** ~ **of consideration** mangels Gegenleistung; **for** ~ **of cover (funds)** mangels Deckung; **for** ~ **of payment** mangels Zahlung; **for** ~ **of time** aus Zeitmangel; **from** ~ **of** aus Mangel; **through** ~ **of care** durch Fahrlässigkeit;
daily ~s tägliche Bedürfnisse; **local ~s** Platzbedarf; **long-felt** ~ längst spürbarer Mangel; **personal ~s** persönlicher Bedarf;
~ **of assent** fehlende Zustimmung; ~ **of capital** Kapitalmangel; ~ **of care** Sorgfaltsmangel, Achtlosigkeit; ~ **of ordinary care** Fehlen der erforderlichen Sorgfalt; ~ **of confidence** mangelndes Vertrauen; ~ **of consideration** fehlende Gegenleistung; ~ **of delivery** Mangel des Erfüllungsgeschäftes; ~ **of economy** mangelnde Sparsamkeit, Unwirtschaftlichkeit; ~ **of facilities** mangelnde Möglichkeiten; ~ **of funds** Kapital-, Geldmangel; ~ **of goods** Warenmangel; ~ **of judgment** mangelnde Urteilskraft; ~ **of jurisdiction** fehlende (mangelnde) Zuständigkeit, Unzuständigkeit; ~**s of life** Lebensbedürfnisse; ~ **of money** Geld-, Kapitalbedarf; ~ **of provisions** mangelnde (fehlende) Vorräte; ~ **of repair** *(highway)* notwendige [Straßen]reparaturen; ~ **of service** nicht erfolgte Zustellung, Zustellungsmangel; ~ **of thought** Gedankenlosigkeit; ~ **of value** Unwert;
~ *(v.)* Mangel haben, *(require)* brauchen, nötig haben, benötigen, bedürfen;
~ **s. th. badly** etw. dringend benötigen; ~ **careful consideration** sorgfältiger Überlegung bedürfen; ~ **a holiday** Urlaub dringend nötig haben; ~ **judgment** nicht genügend Urteilsvermögen besitzen; ~ **for nothing** keinerlei Bedürfnisse haben; ~ **repair** repariert werden müssen;
to be in ~ bedürftig sein, mangeln, Not leiden; **to be in great** ~ **of s. th.** etw. dringend benötigen; **to be living in** ~ in ärmlichen Verhältnissen leben; **to be in** ~ **of money** nicht genügend Geld haben, keine Mittel zur Verfügung haben; **to be in** ~ **of repair** reparaturbedürftig sein; **to be suffering for** ~ **of food and medical supplies** dringend der Nahrungsmittel und ärztlicher Versorgung bedürfen; **to be a man of few ~s** nur geringe Bedürfnisse haben (Ansprüche stellen); **to fall in** ~ in Not geraten; **to meet a** ~ Bedürfnis befriedigen; **to show** ~ **of care** mangelnde Sorgfalt erkennen lassen; **to supply a much-felt** ~ einem dringenden Mangel abhelfen;
~ **ads** *(US)* kleine Anzeigen, Klein-, Suchanzeigen, Stellengesuche; ~ **creation** Bedarfsweckung, Bedürfniserregung; ~ **list** Wunschliste, *(US)* Bestelliste; ~ **slip** [Kunden]bestellschein.

wantage Fehlendes, Fehlmenge, -betrag, Defizit, Manko, *(US)* Fehlgewicht.

wanted verlangt, gesucht, *(criminal)* steckbrieflich gesucht, *(advertisement)* Kaufgesuch, *(stock exchange)* Geld gesucht;
help ~ offene Stelle; ~ **immediately** für sofort gesucht; **situation** ~ Stelle gesucht; **stocks** ~ *(stock exchange)* verlangte (gesuchte) Papiere (Werte);
~ **by the police** steckbrieflich (von der Polizei) gesucht; ~ **persons file** Fahndungsbuch; ~ **list** *(philately)* Fehlliste.

wanting | pages of a book fehlende Buchseiten;
to be found ~ sich als unnütz erweisen; **to be** ~ **in courtesy** es an Höflichkeit fehlen lassen.

wanton mutwillig, *(lewd)* ausschweifend, zügellos, *(without restraint)* leichtfertig, verantwortungslos, rücksichtslos, böswillig;
~ **act** mutwillige Handlung; ~ **child** verspieltes Kind; ~ **cruelty** unmenschliche Grausamkeit; ~ **damage (destruction)** sinnlose Zerstörung; ~ **and furious driving** rücksichtslose (verkehrsge-

fährdende) Fahrweise; ~ **imagination** blühende Phantasie; ~ **looks** lüsterne Blicke; ~ **and reckless misconduct** rücksichtsloses und unsinniges Verhalten; ~ **mood** übermütige Stimmung; ~ **negligence** grobe Fahrlässigkeit; ~ **novel** obszöner Roman; ~ **strike** wilder Streik; ~ **vegetation** wuchernder Pflanzenwuchs; ~ **woman** liederliches Frauenzimmer.

wantonness *(legal sense)* Mutwilligkeit.

war Krieg, Kampf, Streit, *(military profession)* Kriegs-, Waffenhandwerk, Kriegskunst;
after the ~ nach Beendigung des Krieges; **at** ~ im Kriegszustand; **due to the** ~ kriegsbedingt; **embroiled in a** ~ in einen Krieg verwickelt; **for the duration of war** auf Kriegsdauer; **in case of** ~ im Kriegsfalle;
aggressive ~ Angriffskrieg; **aerial** ~ Luftkrieg; **broken-back** ~ nachnukleare Kriegsphase; **bushfire** ~ Steppenbrandkrieg; **civil** ~ Bürgerkrieg; **cold** *(politics)* kalter Krieg; **conventional** ~ Krieg mit konventionellen Waffen; **counterguerilla** ~ Partisanenbekämpfung; **counterinsurgency** ~ Bekämpfung subversiver Elemente; **defensive** ~ Verteidigungskrieg; **guerilla** ~ Partisanenkrieg; **hot** ~ heißer Krieg; **imperfect** ~ begrenzter Krieg; **industrial** ~ Wirtschaftskrieg; **insurgency** ~ subversiver Krieg; **lightning** ~ Blitzkrieg; **international** ~ Völkerkrieg; **major** ~ großer Krieg; **minor** ~ kleiner Krieg; **nuclear** ~ Atom-, Nuklearkrieg; **perfect** ~ allgemeiner Krieg, Volkskrieg; **preventive** ~ Präventivkrieg; **private** ~ Privatfehde; **public** ~ Völkerkrieg; **solemn** ~ völkerrechtlich erklärter Krieg; **tariff** ~ Zoll-, Handelskrieg; **total** ~ totaler Krieg; **trade** ~ Handelskrieg; **undeclared** ~ Krieg ohne Kriegserklärung; **widening** ~ Kriegsausweitung; **World** ~ Weltkrieg;
~ **of aggression** Angriffskrieg; ~ **of the airwaves** Ätherkrieg; ~ **of attrition** Zermürbungs-, Abnutzungskrieg; ~ **of conquest** Eroberungskrieg; ~ **to the death** Krieg bis aufs Messer; ~ **against diseases** Bekämpfung von Seuchen; ~ **of the elements** Aufruhr der Elemente; ~ **of extermination** Vernichtungskrieg; ~ **on two fronts** Zweifrontenkrieg; ~ **of independence** Befreiungs-, Unabhängigkeitskrieg; ~ **of invasion** Invasionskrieg; ~ **to the knife** Krieg bis aufs Messer; ~ **of liberation** Befreiungskrieg; ~ **of nerves** Nervenkrieg, kalter Krieg; ~ **of offence** Offensivkrieg; ~ **and rumo(u)rs of** ~ Krieg und Kriegsgeschrei; ~ **on a large scale** Krieg auf allen Fronten; ~ **of words** Wortgefecht;
~ *(v.)* zum Krieg schreiten, Krieg führen;
to avoid a ~ Krieg vermeiden (verhindern); **to be at** ~ **with** sich im Kriegszustand befinden, Krieg führen; **to be in a** ~ in einen Krieg verwickelt sein; **to be engaged in a** ~ in einen Krieg verwickelt sein; **to be killed in the** ~ im Krieg umkommen; **to bring** ~ **to an end** Krieg beenden; **to carry the** ~ **into the enemy's country (camp)** Krieg in ein feindliches Land tragen; **to date from the** ~ auf den Krieg zurückzuführen sein; **to declare** ~ **upon a country** einem Land den Krieg erklären; **to drift into** ~ in den Krieg hineingezogen werden (hineinschlittern); **to enter into [the]** ~ in den Krieg eintreten; **to go to** ~ **with** Krieg beginnen mit; **to have been in the** ~**s** *(Br., coll.)* arg mitgenommen worden sein; **to levy** ~ **on a country** Krieg gegen ein Land führen; **to levy** ~ **against the King** *(Br.)* Hochverrat begehen; **to lose a** ~ Krieg verlieren; **to maintain a** ~ Krieg führen; **to make** ~ Krieg führen; **to menace with** ~ Kriegsdrohungen ausstoßen; **to outlaw** ~ Krieg ächten; **to plan (prepare) for a** ~ Krieg vorbereiten, Kriegsvorbereitungen treffen; **to prevent a** ~ Krieg verhindern; **to quarantine a** ~ Krieg lokalisieren; **to rebound from the** ~ sich vom Krieg erholen; **to recover from the effects of a** ~ sich von den Kriegsauswirkungen erholen; **to resort to** ~ es auf einen Krieg ankommen lassen, zum Krieg schreiten; **to wage** ~ Krieg führen;
~ **aims** Kriegsziel; ~ **arsenal** Kriegsarsenal; ~ **baby** *(coll.)* Kriegskind, *(US)* durch den Krieg begünstigter Industriezweig; ~**battered** vom Krieg stark mitgenommen; ~ **bonds** Kriegsanleihe, -schuldverschreibungen; ~ **bonus** Kriegszuschlag; ~ **book** Kriegsbuch; ~ **boom** Rüstungshausse; ~ **bride** Soldatenbraut, *(US sl.)* durch den Krieg profitierendes Unternehmen; ~ **burden** Kriegslasten; ~ **cabinet** Kriegskabinett; ~ **casualties** Kriegsverluste; ~ **cemetery** Gefallenenfriedhof; ~ **charities** *(Br.)* Wohltätigkeit zur Linderung der Kriegsnot; ~ **chemicals** Gaskampfstoffe; ~ **chest** Kriegsschatz, -kasse; ~ **circumstances** kriegsbedingte Umstände; **institute**~ **clauses** Kriegsklauseln; ~ **cloud** Kriegsdrohung, -gefahr; ~ **college** *(US)* Kriegsakademie; ~**conditioned** kriegsbedingt; ~ **contract** Rüstungsauftrag; ~ **contribution** Kriegsabgabe; ~ **control commission** Kriegskontrollkommission; ~ **correspondent** Kriegsberichterstatter; ~ **crime** Kriegsverbrechen; ~ **criminal** Kriegsverbrecher; ~ **cry** Feldgeschrei; ~ **damage** Kriegsschaden; ~**damage**

assistance Kriegsschadenhilfe; ~ **damages bill** Kriegsschadensgesetz; ~ **damage compensation** Kriegsentschädigung; ~ **debt** Kriegsschulden [eines Staates]; ~ **debtor** Kriegsschuldner; ~ **Department** *(US)* Kriegsministerium; ~ **disabled** Kriegsbeschädigter; ~**disabled** kriegsversehrt, -beschädigt; ~ **disablement** Kriegsbeschädigung; ~ **economy** Kriegswirtschaft; ~ **efforts** Kriegsanstrengungen; ~ **equipment** Kriegsausrüstung; ~ **establishment** Kriegsstärke; ~ **expenses (expenditure)** Rüstungs-, Kriegskosten; ~ **factory** Rüstungsfabrik; ~ **financing** Rüstungs-, Kriegsfinanzierung; ~ **footing** Kriegsstärke, -bereitschaft; **on a** ~ **footing** kriegsstark; **to keep the army on a** ~ **footing** Armee in Kriegsbereitschaft halten; ~ **game** Kriegs-, Planspiel; ~ **goods** Rüstungsgüter; ~ **grade (of product)** Kriegsausführung; ~ **grant** Rüstungszuschuß; ~ **grave** Soldatengrab; ~**graves commission** Kriegsgräberkommission; ~ **guilt** Kriegsschuld; ~ **hero** Kriegsheld; ~ **hirings** kriegsbedingte Einstellungen, Kriegseinstellungen; ~ **horse** alter Haudegen; ~ **increase** Kriegszuschlag; ~ **indemnity** Kriegsentschädigung; ~ **industry** Rüstungsindustrie; ~ **injury** Kriegsverletzung; ~ **insurance** Versicherung gegen Kriegsgefahr; ~ **loan** Kriegsanleihe; ~ **loss** Kriegsverlust, -schaden; ~ **machine** Kriegsmaschinerie; ~ **Manpower Commission** *(US)* Kriegseinsatzkommission; ~ **material** Kriegsgerät, -bedarf, -material; ~ **medal** Kriegsauszeichnung; ~ **memorial** Kriegerdenkmal; ~ **nose** *(torpedo)* Gefechtskopf; ~ **Office** *(Br.)* Kriegsministerium; ~ **order** Rüstungsauftrag; ~ **orphan** Kriegswaise; ~ **paint** *(fam.)* volle Kriegsbemalung, großer Wichs, Galauniform; ~ **party** Kriegspartei, chauvinistische Partei; ~ **pension** Hinterbliebenenpension; ~ **pensioner** Kriegsinvalide; ~ **plane** Kriegsflugzeug; ~ **planning** Kriegsrüstung; ~ **plant** Kriegs-, Rüstungsbetrieb; ~**making potential** Rüstungs-, Kriegspotential; **presidential** ~ **powers** *(US)* Machtbefugnisse des Präsidenten im Kriege.

war production Kriegs-, Rüstungsproduktion;
~ **area** Rüstungsgebiet; ~ **Board** *(US)* Rüstungsministerium; ~ **center** *(US)* (centre, *Br.*) Rüstungszentrum.

war | profit Kriegs-, Rüstungsgewinn; ~ **profits tax** *(US)* Rüstungsgewinnsteuer; ~ **profiteer** Kriegsgewinnler; ~**proof** kriegserprobt; ~ **propaganda** Kriegspropaganda; ~ **protester** Kriegsgegner; ~ **refugee** Flüchtling, Heimatvertriebener; ~ **report** Kriegsbericht; ~ **reporter** Kriegsberichterstatter; ~ **reserve** *(insurance)* Kriegsrücklage; ~ **resister** Kriegsdienstverweigerer; ~ **risk** Kriegsrisiko, -gefahr; ~**risk clause** Kriegsklausel; ~**risk insurance** Versicherung gegen Kriegsgefahr, Kriegsrisikoversicherung; ~**risk policy** Kriegsrisikopolice; ~ **savings** Kriegsersparnisse; ~**savings certificates** *(Br.)* Kriegsanleihe; ~ **scare** Kriegsfurcht, -neurose; ~ **Secretary** *(US)* Kriegsminister; ~ **service** Kriegsdienst; ~ **stocks (stores)** Kriegsvorräte; ~ **supplies** Kriegslieferungen; ~ **tax** *(US)* Kriegssteuer; ~ **taxation** Rüstungsbesteuerung; ~ **toll** Kriegslasten; ~ **traitor** Landesverräter; ~ **vessel** Kriegsschiff; ~ **veteran** Kriegsteilnehmer; ~ **veterans' bonus** Kriegsteilnehmerabfindung; ~ **victim** Kriegsopfer; ~ **weariness** Kriegsmüdigkeit; ~**weary** kriegsmüde; ~ **widow** Kriegerwitwe; ~ **widow's pension** Kriegerwitwenpension; ~ **work** Rüstungsarbeiten; ~ **worker** Rüstungsarbeiter; ~**worn countries** kriegszerstörte Länder; ~ **year** Kriegsjahrgang; ~ **zone** Kriegsgebiet, -zone, Sperrgebiet.

ward Mündel, Minderjähriger, *(confinement under guard)* Schutzhaft, Gewahrsam, *(custody)* Obhut, Aufsicht, Verwahrung, *(guardianship)* Vormundschaft, *(local elections, Br.)* kommunaler Wahlbezirk, *(hospital)* Anstaltsabteilung, Station, Krankensaal, -[haus]station, *(prison)* Gefängniszelle, *(territorial division)* Stadtviertel, -bezirk, Distrikt, Revier;
in ~ unter Vormundschaft;
casual ~ Asyl für Obdachlose; **casualty** ~ Unfallstation; **childrens'** ~ Kinderstation; **isolation** ~ Isolierstation; **prison** ~ Gefängnisabteilung;
~ **in chancery** Mündel (Minderjähriger) unter Amtsvormundschaft; ~**s of court** Pfleglinge, Kinder und Unzurechnungsfähige, vormundschaftlich betreute Personen;
~ *(v.)* *(asylum)* in ein Obdachlosenasyl aufnehmen, *(hospital)* in eine Krankenhausstation einweisen, auf eine Station legen, *(take in prison)* inhaftieren, in Haft nehmen;
~ **off a danger** Gefahr abwenden;
to be in ~ unter Vormundschaft stehen; **to be under** ~ sich in Haft befinden; **to put s. o. in** ~ j. unter Aufsicht stellen, j. gefangensetzen; **to put a child in** ~ Kind unter Vormundschaft stellen;
~ **heeler** *(US coll.)* blind ergebener Anhänger, Wahlmacher; ~ **mote** *(London)* Bezirksgericht; ~ **orderly** Krankenwärter.

warden Vormund, *(college)* Präsident, *(guardianship)* Mündelverhältnis, *(guild, Br.)* Zunftmeister, *(hostel)* Heimleiter, *(insti-*

tution) Kustos, Kurator, Vorsteher, Präsident, Direktor, *(person under guard)* Schutzbefohlener, Schützling, *(porter, US)* Pförtner, Portier, Türhüter, *(prison, US)* Gefängniswärter, -direktor, Aufseher, *(safeguard)* Schutz, Abwehr;
in ~ unter Vormundschaft;
air-raid ~ Luftschutzwart; **chief** ~ Hauptaufseher; **fire** ~ *(US)* Brandmeister, Feuerwache; **game** ~ Jagdaufseher; **port** ~ *(US)* Hafenaufseher; **prison** ~ *(US)* Gefängnisdirektor; **traffic** ~ Parkkontrolleur;
⚲ **of the Mint** *(Br.)* Direktor der staatlichen Münze, Münzwardein; ~ **of the poor** *(Br.)* Sozialfürsorger; ~ **of a port** *(US)* Hafenmeister; ~ **of a prison** *(US)* Gefangenenaufseher, Kerkermeister; ~ **of the standards** *(Br.)* Vorsteher des Eichamtes.
wardency Vormundschaftsamt.
wardenship Vorsteher, Kuratoramt.
warder Wachmann, Wächter, *(mil.)* Posten, Wache, *(museum, Br.)* Diener, *(prison)* Gefängnisaufseher, Gefangenenwärter.
wardmote *(Br.)* Bezirksversammlung.
wardrobe Garderobe, Kleiderbestand, *(clothes closet)* Kleiderschrank, *(theater)* Requisitenkammer;
built-in ~ eingebauter Garderobenschrank;
~ **bed** Bettschrank; ~ **dealer** Trödler; ~ **trunk** Schrankkoffer.
wardroom *(Br.)* Wachstube, -lokal, *(elections)* Wahllokal, *(mar.)* Offiziersmesse.
wardship Aufseheramt, *(fig.)* Bevormundung, *(tutelage)* Vormundschaft, *(under-age)* Minderjährigkeit;
to be under ~ unter Vormundschaft stehen.
wardsman Wärter.
ware Ware, [Handels]artikel, *(pottery)* Geschirr, Keramik, Porzellan;
~**s** Erzeugnisse, Artikel, Produkte;
literary ~ literarisches Machwerk; **trumpery** ~**s** Ausschußware, -güter;
to advertise one's ~**s** für seine Erzeugnisse werben (Reklame machen); **to peddle one's gossipy** ~**s** mit seinen Klatschgeschichten hausieren gehen; **to puff one's** ~**s** seine Ware anpreisen; **to sell one's** ~**s cheaply** seine Produkte billig abgeben.
warehouse *(storehouse)* Lager[haus], Waren-, Auslieferungslager, Magazin, Speicher, [Waren]niederlage, *(wholesale business, Br.)* Kauf-, Warenhaus, Großhandlung, Großhandels-, Engrosgeschäft;
ex ~ ab Lager;
~ **to** ~ von Haus zu Haus;
bonded ~ *(US)* Transitlager, zollfreies Lagerhaus, Packhaus, Entrepot, Zollspeicher, -[gut]lager, -niederlage; **branch** ~ Nebenspeicher; **buffer** ~ Reservelager; **commercial** ~ Warenspeicher; **custodian** ~ *(US)* Lagerung sicherungsübereigneter Waren, Konsignationslager; **customs** ~ Zollniederlage; **field** ~ Außenlager; **floating** ~ schwimmendes Magazin; **licensed** ~ *(US)* Lagerhaus für zollpflichtige Güter; **merchandise** ~ Warenspeicher; **public** ~ öffentlicher Speicher; **Queen's** ~ *(Br.)* öffentliches Zollager; **storage** ~ Zollniederlage, -lager; **unbonded** ~ *(Br.)* Zollfreilager; **up-town** ~ Stadtlager;
~ *(v.)* *(customs)* unter Zollverschluß bringen (einlagern), *(deposit)* zur Aufbewahrung übergeben, *(goods)* [Güter] [ein-] lagern, [Waren] deponieren, auf Lager (den Speicher) nehmen, speichern;
~ **in the bank's name** für Rechnung der Bank einlagern; ~ **furniture** Möbel auf einen öffentlichen Speicher verbringen;
to be stored in a ~ eingelagert sein; **to deposit in a** ~ in ein Lager (auf den Speicher) bringen, einlagern; **to keep in** ~ lagern lassen; **to lie in a** ~ im Lager liegen, lagern; **to place in a** ~ aufspeichern; **to store in a** ~ in einem Lagerhaus einlagern, auf den Speicher verbringen, *(customs)* unter Zollverschluß einlagern; **to withdraw from a** ~ aus dem Lager entnehmen;
~ **account** Lagerkonto; ~ **bill** Einlagerungswechsel; ~ **bond** Lagerschein, Kaution eines Lagerinhabers, *(customs)* Zollverschlußschein, -bescheinigung; ~ **book** Bestands-, Lagerbuch; ~ **boy** Lagerarbeiter, Lagerist; ~ **business** Lagerungsgeschäft; ~ **capacity** Lagerkapazität; ~ **certificate** *(US)* Lagerschein; ~ **charges** Lagergebühren, -kosten, -miete, -geld, -spesen; ~**-to-~ clause** *(marine insurance)* von Haus zu Haus Klausel, Transportversicherungsklausel; ~ **clerk** Lagerist, Lagerhalter; ~ **company (concern)** Lagerhausgesellschaft; ~ **facilities** Lagereinrichtungen; **to share** ~ **facilities** gemeinsam über Lagermöglichkeiten verfügen; ~ **floor** Lagerbühne, Güterboden; ~ **foreman** Lagervorarbeiter; ~ **goods** Lagerwaren, -gut, Waren auf Lager; **bonded** ~ **goods** Lagergut (Güter) unter Zollverschluß; ~ **hand** Lagerarbeiter; ~**-to-~ insurance** Versicherung[sdeckung] von Haus zu Haus, vollständige Transportversicherung; ~ **keeper** Lageraufseher, -halter, Lager-,

Speicher-, Magazinverwalter; ~**-keeper's certificate** *(Br.)* Quittung über eingelagerte Güter, [nicht begebbarer] Lagerschein; ~ **keeper's receipt** *(Br.)* Lagerpfandschein; ~**-keeper's warrant** *(Br.)* [begebbarer] Lagerschein, Lagerpfandschein; ~ **labo(u)rer** Speicher-, Lagerarbeiter; ~ **line** Lagerungsgeschäft; ~ **loan** Warenbevorschussung, Einlagerungskredit; ~ **manager** Lagerverwalter, Auslieferungsleiter; ~ **owner** Lagerhausbesitzer; ~ **period** Lagerdauer, Zollagerfrist; ~ **porter** Markthelfer; ~ **rates** Speichergebühren; ~ **receipt** *(US)* Lagerpfandschein, Lagerschein, -empfangsbescheinigung; **field** ~ **receipt** *(US)* Lagerschein für sicherungsübereignete [beim Eigentümer verbliebene] Waren; **negotiable** ~ **receipt** *(US)* Namenslagerschein; **to use a** ~ **receipt as security for a loan** *(US)* Lagerpfandschein als Kreditsicherheit verwenden; ⚲ **Receipt Act** *(US)* Gesetz über das Lagerhauswesen; ~ **rent** Lagermiete, -spesen, -geld, Speichermiete, Niederlagegebühren; ~**-rent account** Lagermietenkonto; ~ **room** Lager-, Speicher-, Verkaufsraum; **cooperative** ~ **society** Lagergenossenschaft; ~ **sorter** Lagersortierer; ~ **space** Speicher-, Lagerraum; ~ **surplus** Lagerhausüberschüsse; ~ **system** Zollverschlußwesen; ~ **track** Lagergleisanschluß; ~ **truck** Lagerfahrzeug; ~ **warrant** *(Br.)* Lagerschein.
warehouseman *(clerk)* Lagerist, Lagerverwalter, -aufseher, -halter, Magazinverwalter, *(moving man)* Möbelspediteur, *(trader)* gewerblicher Lagerhalter, *(wholesale trader, Br.)* Großkaufmann, *(worker)* Lager-, Speicherarbeiter;
~**'s lien** Lagerhalterpfandrecht.
warehousing [Ein]lagerung, Lagern, Lagerhaltung, -hausgewerbe, Lagereigewerbe, Lagergeschäft, Magazinverwaltung, *(under bond)* Lagerung unter Zollverschluß;
field ~ *(US)* Lagerung sicherungsübereigneter Waren, Sicherungsübereignung; **transit** ~ Einlagerung von Durchgangsgütern;
~ **business** Lagerungsgeschäft; ~ **charges (expenses)** Lagergeld, Speichergebühren; ~ **company** Lagerhausgesellschaft; ~ **costs** Lagerkosten; ~ **entry** Deklaration zur Einlagerung unter Zollverschluß; ~ **port** Lagerhafen; ~ **surcharges** Zuschläge zu Lagerhauskosten; ~ **system** *(US)* Zollverschlußwesen.
wareroom Lager-, Verkaufs-, Warenraum.
warfare Kriegführung, *(war)* Krieg, *(fig.)* Fehde, Streit, Kampf;
aerial ~ Luftkrieg; **bacteriological** ~ biologische Kriegsführung; **economic** ~ Wirtschaftskrieg; **germ** ~ Kriegsführung mit Bakterien; **global** ~ weltweiter Krieg; **ideological** ~ ideologische Kriegsführung; **large-scale** ~ Kriegsführung großen Ausmaßes; **maritime** ~ Seekrieg; **nuclear** ~ Atomkrieg; **psychological** ~ psychologische Kriegsführung (Kampfführung); **radioactive** ~ radioaktive Kriegsführung; **static** ~ Stellungskrieg; **total** ~ totaler Krieg, totale Kriegsführung;
to be at ~ **with s. o.** mit jem. im Streit leben.
warhead Spreng-, Gefechtskopf;
nuclear ~ Atomsprengkopf.
warlike kriegsmäßig, kriegerisch, kampflustig;
~ **operations** kriegerische Handlungen.
warlock Zauberkünstler, Taschenspieler.
warm warm, *(imparting heat)* erhitzt, glühend, heiß, *(disagreeable)* unangenehm, gefährlich, *(warming)* Aufwärmen;
~ *(v.)* **o. s. at the fire** sich am Feuer wärmen; ~ **on a subject** sich an einem Thema erhitzen; ~ **up to s. o.** sich für j. erwärmen; ~ **up a meal** Mahlzeit aufwärmen; ~ **wise** *(sl.)* zu Verstand kommen; ~ **to one's work** an seiner Arbeit Interesse bekommen; **to grow** ~ **over an argument** sich über eine Streitfrage erhitzen; **to keep a business prospect** ~ sich eine geschäftliche Aussicht warmhalten; **to make things** ~ **for s. o.** jem. die Hölle heiß machen;
~ **advocate** leidenschaftlicher Befürworter; ~ **air** Warmluft; ~ **climate** mildes Klima; ~ **clothes** warme Kleidung; ~ **corner** *(fig.)* gefährliche Lage; ~ **debate** hitzige Debatte; ~ **existence** gesicherte Existenz; ~ **friends** intime Freunde; ~ **front** *(weather)* Warmluftfront; ~ **interest** reges Interesse; ~ **reception** saftiger Empfang; ~ **scene in a play** unanständige Stelle in einem Theaterstück; ~ **supporter** leidenschaftlicher Anhänger; ~ **thanks** herzlicher Dank; ~ **[-water] tap** Warmwasserhahn; ~ **welcome** herzlicher Empfang; ~ **work** schwere Arbeit.
warmed-over *(US)* aufgewärmt;
~ **cabbage** *(fig.)* aufgewärmte alte Geschichte.
warming Erwärmung, Erhitzung, *(heating)* Beheizung, *(sl.)* Tracht Prügel.
to give s. o. a ~ j. verdreschen;
~ **pad** *(el.)* Heizkissen; ~ **pan** Bett-, Wärmflasche; **all chintz and** ~ **pans** alles antik gemütlich; ~**-up time** *(production)* Anlaufzeit.

warmonger Kriegstreiber, -hetzer;
  trigger-happy ~ Kriegslüsterner, Kriegshetzer;
  ~ *(v.)* zum Kriege hetzen.
warmongering Kriegshetze.
warmup *(advertising)* Eisbrecher, Werbevorspann einer Sendung, *(motor)* Warmlaufen.
warn *(v.)* warnen, zur Vorsicht mahnen, warnend aufmerksam machen, *(cite)* vorladen, bescheiden, *(notify)* im voraus benachrichtigen, in Kenntnis setzen;
  ~ **s. o. away** jem. den Dienst aufsagen; ~ **s. o. to appear in court** j. vorladen, jem. eine Vorladung schicken; ~ **for duty** zum Rapport bestellen; ~ **s. o. off** j. zum Verlassen seines Grundstücks auffordern; ~ **a tenant out of the house** Räumungsurteil gegen einen Mieter erwirken.
warner Warnvorrichtung.
warning [Vor]warnung, *(fee)* polizeiliche (gebührenpflichtige) Verwarnung, *(giving notice)* Kündigung, *(previous notice)* Vorausbenachrichtigung, Bescheid, Wink, *(term of notice)* Kündigungsfrist, *(warning signal)* Warnsignal, *(summons)* Vorladung, Aufforderung;
  at a minute's ~ auf jederzeitige Kündigung, in kürzester Frist, fristlos, auf Abruf; **without further** ~ ohne weitere Androhung; **advance** ~ Vorausbenachrichtigung; **air-raid** ~ Fliegeralarm; **early** ~ *(atomic weapons)* Voralarm, Vor-, Frühwarnung; **gale** ~ Sturmwarnung; **a month's** ~ *(Br.)* monatliche Kündigung; **road** ~ Straßenverkehrszeichen;
  ~ **and fee** *(Br.)* gebührenpflichtige Verwarnung;
  to attack without any ~ überraschend angreifen; **to be a** ~ **to others** als abschreckendes Beispiel dienen; **to give** ~ [Arbeitsverhältnis] kündigen; **to give s. o. a fair** ~ j. rechtzeitig kündigen; **to give an employee** ~ einem Angestellten kündigen; **to give s. o. a formal** ~ j. offiziell verwarnen; **to give the tenant** ~ *(landlord)* Mieter kündigen; **to give one's master** ~ seinem Arbeitgeber kündigen; **to give a month's** ~ mit Monatsfrist kündigen; **to ignore the** ~ Warnung in den Wind schlagen; **to issue a** ~ **to pay taxes** rückständige Steuern anmahnen; **to sound a note of** ~ *(speaker)* mit warnendem Unterton sprechen;
  ~ **bell** Signalglocke; ~ **and fee** gebührenpflichtige Verwarnung; ~ **light** *(mar.)* Warnfeuer; ~ **period** Warnzeit; **to fire some** ~ **shots** einige Warnschüsse abgeben; ~ **sign** Warnzeichen, Alarmsignal; ~ **strike** Warnstreik.
warp *(agr.)* Schlammschicht, Schlick, *(fig.)* Verzerrung, Entstellung, *(mar.)* Bugsierleine, Warptrosse, *(wood)* Verwerfung;
  ~ *(v.)* beeinflussen, *(distort)* entstellen, verdrehen, verzerren, *(ship)* bugsieren, verholen, am Warpanker fortziehen, *(wood)* sich verziehen (werfen);
  ~ **s. one's judgment** jds. Urteil verzerren; ~ **s. one's mind** j. verschroben machen; ~ **the sense of a passage** Textstelle verdrehen.
warpage Tonnengeld.
warpath Kriegspfad, *(fig.)* kriegerisches Unternehmen;
  to be on the ~ auf dem Kriegspfad sein, *(fig.)* in gereizter Stimmung sein.
warped | in political principles politisch voreingenommen;
  ~ **judgment** Vorurteil.
warplane Kriegs-, Kampfflugzeug.
warrandice *(real estate, Scot.)* Rechtsmängelgewähr.
warrant *(of attorney)* Prozeßvollmacht, *(authority)* Befugnis, Berechtigung, Ermächtigung, Mandat, Vollmacht, Bevollmächtigung, *(authority to collector of taxes)* Inkassovollmacht, *(bond note)* Zollbegleitschein, *(governmental accounting)* Schatzanweisung, *(guarantor)* Bürge, Gewährsmann, Garant, *(guaranty)* Bürgschaft[svertrag], Gewähr, Garantie, Sicherheit, *(justification)* Berechtigung, Rechtfertigung, Begründung, Grund, *(mil.)* Beförderungs-, Bestallungsurkunde, Patent, *(municipal accounting)* kommunale Auszahlungsanweisung, *(option business, US)* Optionsschein, *(order to pay)* Zahlungsanweisung, *(promissory note, US)* Schuldschein, *(qualifying certificate)* [Berechtigungs]ausweis, -schein, Beleg, Bescheinigung, Urkunde, Zertifikat, *(security)* Sicherheit, *(to stockowner, US)* Bezugsberechtigungsschein, Bezugsrecht, *(warehouse receipt, Br.)* Lager[pfand]-, Warenschein, *(witness)* Anordnung der zwangsweisen Vorführung, *(writ of court)* Haft-, Haussuchungs-, Vollziehungsbefehl;
  bench ~ richterlicher Haftbefehl; **bond** ~ *(Br.)* Zollbegleitschein; **county** ~ Zahlungsanweisung an die Kreisverwaltung, kommunales Schuldscheindarlehn; **death** ~ Hinrichtungsbefehl, Befehl zur Vollstreckung der Todesstrafe; **deposit** ~ Lagerpfand-, Depotschein; **distress** ~ Pfändungsbeschluß, -auftrag, Zwangsvollstreckungsbefehl, Beschlagnahmeverfügung; **dividend** ~ *(Br.)* Aktienabschnitt, Dividendenscheck-,

Gewinnanteilschein; **dock** ~ *(Br.)* Waren-, Docklagerschein; **escape** ~ Haftbefehl für entsprungenen Häftling; **fractional** ~ Berechtigungsschein zum Erwerb gestückelter neuer Aktien; **interest** ~ Zinsschein, -abschnitt; **land** ~ *(US)* Landzuweisungsurkunde; **landlord's** ~ Vermieterpfandrecht; **municipal** ~ kommunale Zahlungsanweisung, Kommunalschuldschein; **part** ~ Teillagerschein; ~**s payable** fällige Zahlungsanweisungen; **produce** ~ Lagerschein über eingelagerte Waren; **registered** ~ *(municipal accounting)* kommunales Schuldscheindarlehn, kommunale Zahlungsanweisung; **Royal** ~ *(Br.)* Hoflieferantendiplom; **search** ~ Haussuchungsbefehl; **share** ~ *(Br.)* Aktienzertifikat, -urkunde; **stock** ~ *(Br.)* Aktienzertifikat, [etwa] Inhaberaktie; **stock-allotment** *(US)* **(subscription,** *Br.)* ~ Berechtigungsschein zum Erwerb neuer Aktien, [Aktien]bezugsrechtsschein; **stock-purchase** ~ *(US)* Bezugsberechtigungsschein; **tax** ~ Ausweis des Steuereinnehmers; **tax-anticipation** ~ *(US)* Steuergutschein; **town** ~ Zahlungsanweisung des Stadtkämmerers; **transferable** ~ begebbarer Lagerschein; **treasury** ~ *(Br.)* Schatzanweisung; **warehouse** ~ *(Br.)* Lager-, Depotschein; **withdrawal** ~ Auszahlungsvollmacht, -ermächtigung;
  ~ **of apprehension** Steckbrief, Haftbefehl; ~ **of arrest** Haftbefehl; ~ **of attachment** Beschlagnahmeverfügung, Pfändungs-, Zwangsvollstreckungsbeschluß; ~ **of attorney** Prozeßvollmacht, Mandat; ~ **in bankruptcy** Konkursbeschlagnahme, Beschlagnahmeverfügung im Konkursverfahren; **share** ~ **to bearer** *(Br.)* Aktienurkunde für eine Inhaberaktie; ~ **on a city treasurer** Auszahlungsanweisung an den Stadtkämmerer; ~ **of commitment** *(US)* Einlieferungs-, Haftbefehl; ~ **of distress** Zwangsvollstreckungs-, Pfändungsbeschluß, Beschlagnahmeverfügung; ~ **for goods** Lagerschein; ~ **of merchantability** Gewährleistung einer Durchschnittsqualität; ~ **for payment** Zahlungsanweisung; ~ **to sue and defend** Prozeßvollmacht;
  ~ *(v.) (acknowledge)* anerkennen, *(assure)* bestätigen, bescheinigen, bezeugen, *(authorize)* befugen, bevollmächtigen, berechtigen, autorisieren, *(guarantee)* gewährleisten, garantieren, zusichern, *(justify)* begründen, rechtfertigen, *(secure)* sicherstellen, bewahren, *(stand bail)* Bürgschaft leisten, [ver-]bürgen, gutsagen;
  ~ **to arrest of a suspected criminal** Haftbefehl gegen einen verdächtigten Verbrecher erlassen; ~ **punctual delivery** für pünktliche Lieferung garantieren; ~ **the genuineness of a text** Echtheit eines Textes verbürgen; ~ **s. o. an honest and reliable person** sich für jds. Ehrlichkeit und Zuverlässigkeit verbürgen; ~ **a title to property** für einwandfreies Eigentum einstehen; ~ **a report to be true** sich für einen Bericht verbürgen;
  to have a ~ **out against one** steckbrieflich gesucht werden; **to have no** ~ **for saying so** zu einer Behauptung keinerlei Veranlassung haben; **to issue a** ~ **of arrest for s. o.** Haftbefehl gegen j. erlassen; **to issue a warehouse** ~ **for goods** Lagerschein für eingelagerte Waren ausstellen; **to represent and** ~ ausdrücklich erklären, zusichern, Gewähr übernehmen; **to return a** ~ Haftbefehl mit Protokoll wiederzustellen; **to secure by** ~ durch Lagerschein sichern; **to sign a death** ~ Todesurteil unterzeichnen; **to take out a** ~ **against s. o.** Haftbefehl gegen j. erwirken; **I** ~ **that the above answers are true** Ich versichere die Richtigkeit obiger Angaben;
  ~ **check** Schatzanweisung; ~ **clerk** Lagerhausverwalter; ~ **creditor** *(municipal accounting)* Schuldscheininhaber, -besitzer; ~ **holder** *(Br.)* königlicher Hoflieferant; ~ **officer** Deckoffizier, *(US)* Zustellungsbeamter.
warrantable vertretbar, gerechtfertigt, berechtigt;
  ~ **by law** gesetzlich erlaubt;
  ~ **outlay** zu rechtfertigende Ausgaben.
warranted garantiert, mit Garantie, verbürgt, echt, *(authorized)* ermächtigt, bevollmächtigt;
  ~ **free** Versicherungshaftung ausgeschlossen; ~ **free from adulteration** Reinheit garantiert; ~ **free of all average** haftet nur bei Totalschaden; ~ **free from capture** Haftungsausschluß der Beschlagnahme; ~ **for three years** mit dreijähriger Garantie.
warrantee Bürgschafts-, Garantieempfänger.
warranter, warrantor Sicherheitsgeber, Bürge, Gewährleistender, Gewährsmann, Garant.
warranty *(authority)* Berechtigung, Ermächtigung, *(for bill)* Wechselbürgschaft, *(guaranty)* Gewähr[leistung], [Mängel-]garantie, Zusicherung, *(justification)* Rechtfertigung, *(insurance)* Versicherung der Richtigkeit der Angaben, *(marine insurance)* Garantie der Seetüchtigkeit, *(power)* Vollmacht, *(real property law)* Gewährleistung für den Bestand des Eigentums, Zusicherungsabrede, *(surety)* Bürgschaft, *(voucher)* Bürgschaftsschein;

in lieu of any ~ **condition or liability implied by law** unter Ausschluß jeder gesetzlichen Haftung;

affirmative ~ *(law of insurance)* Zusicherung der Richtigkeit der gemachten Angaben; **continuing** ~ Dauergarantie; **executive** ~ *(governor of asylum state)* jederzeit widerrufliche Aufenthaltsgenehmigung; **executory** ~ *(insurance)* Zusicherung über Vornahme bestimmter Handlungen; **express** ~ *(US)* vertragliche Gewährleistung für zugesicherte Eigenschaften, Sachmängelhaftung; **general** ~ **[to one's heirs]** Sicherung gegen Rechte Dritter; **implied** ~ *(US)* gesetzliche Gewährleistung (Gewährleistungspflicht), *(insurance)* stillschweigend miteingeschlossene Versicherungsbedingungen; **insurance** ~ Wahrheitsversicherung; **joint** ~ Solidarverpflichtung; **12 months unlimited mileage** ~ von der gefahrenen Kilometerzahl unabhängige Jahresgarantie; **personal** ~ Bürgschaft; **promissory** ~ *(insurance)* besondere Zusicherung der Durchführung oder Unterlassung bestimmter Handlungen; **special** ~ *(deed of land)* Freistellung von etwaigen Ansprüchen gegen den Käufer; **title** ~ Rechtsmängelhaftung, Gewährleistung wegen Rechtsmängeln;

~ **of authority** Vollmachtsnachweis; ~ **in the contract** vertraglich zugesicherte Garantie, Sachmängelgewähr; ~ **against defects** Sachmängelhaftung; ~ **of quiet enjoyment** Zusicherung des ungestörten Besitzes; ~ **of fitness** *(US)* vereinbarte Gewährleistungspflicht, Eignungsgarantie, Garantie der Herstellerfirma; ~ **of genuineness** Echtheitsbürgschaft; ~ **of goods** *(US)* Sachmängelhaftung; ~ **of merchantabilty** *(Br.)* Garantie der Durchschnittsqualität, Gewährleistung durchschnittlicher Qualität; ~ **of quality** Mängelgewähr, Sachmängelhaftung, Garantie durchschnittlicher Qualität; ~ **of title** Rechtsmangelgewähr, -haftung;

to break a ~ gegebene Zusicherung nicht einhalten; **to fill the** ~ Garantieansprüche erfüllen; **to give a** ~ Gewährleistung übernehmen; **to give s. o. a** ~ **of quality of goods** jem. eine Qualitätsgarantie für gelieferte Waren geben; **to perform a** ~ Sicherheit bestellen;

~ **claim** Gewährleistungs-, Garantieanspruch; ~ **clause** Gewährleistungs-, Garantieklausel; ~ **cost** Gewährleistungs-, Garantieunkosten; ~ **deed** Gewährleistungsvertrag, *(US)* Grundstückskaufvertrag mit Rechtsgarantie; ~ **promise** Garantiezusage; ~ **responsibility** Gewährleistungspflicht; ~ **rules** Garantiebestimmungen; ~ **work** Garantiearbeiten, *(auto dealer)* Garantiereparaturen.

warren *(Br.)* Wildgehege, Kaninchengehege, *(city)* Straßengewirr, *(tenement)* Mietskaserne;

free ~ Wildgehegeprivileg; **run-down people** ~ heruntergewirtschaftetes Mietshaus.

warring principles widerstreitende Grundsätze.

warship Kriegsschiff.

wartime Kriegszeiten;

~ **boom** Rüstungshausse; ~ **control commission** Kriegskontroll-, Rüstungskommission; ~ **earnings** Kriegseinkommen; ~ **economy** Kriegswirtschaft; ~ **emergency** kriegsbedingte Notwendigkeit; ~ **expenditure** Kriegsausgaben; ~ **experiences** Kriegserlebnisse; ~ **hysteria** Kriegshysterie; ~ **industry** Industrie der Kriegszeit, Kriegsindustrie; ~ **phenomenon** Kriegserscheinung; **to invoke** ~ **powers** Kriegsrecht verhängen; ~ **production** Kriegsproduktion; ~ **propaganda** Kriegspropaganda; ~ **rationing** kriegsbedingte Rationierungen; ~ **regulations** Kriegsbestimmungen; ~ **taxation** Kriegsbesteuerung; ~ **wages** Kriegslöhne.

warworker Rüstungsarbeiter.

wary wachsam, vorsichtig, umsichtig;

to be ~ **of** auf der Hut sein, mit Skepsis betrachten; **to be** ~ **of doing** Bedenken bei etw. haben.

wash Waschen, Wäsche, *(aeronautics)* Luftstrudel, Sog, *(architecture)* Anstrich, Tünche, *(drawing)* Tuschzeichnung, *(estuary, Br.)* Morast, Sumpf, *(housewife)* [große] Wäsche, *(mar.)* Kielwasser, *(sea)* Wellenschlag, Brandung, *(stock exchange, US)* Börsenscheinverkauf, -geschäft, Scheinkauf von Börsenpapieren, Simultankauf und -verkauf, *(waste liquid)* Spülwasser, *(wishy-washy)* Gewäsch, leeres Gerede;

at the ~ in der Wäscherei;

~ *(v.)* waschen, spülen, reinigen, *(ore)* schlämmen, waschen, *(paint)* tünchen, dünn anstreichen;

~ **ashore** an Land schwemmen; ~ **away** fortspülen, -schwemmen; ~ **a car** Auto abspritzen (waschen); ~ **a carpet** Teppich chemisch reinigen; ~ **20% out of costs in freight** Frachtkosten um 20% kürzen; **not** ~ **in all dangers** allen Gefahren standhalten; ~ **the deck** Deck schrubben; ~ **down a car** Auto abspritzen; ~ **[up] dishes** Geschirr spülen; ~ **away the**

embankment Damm unterspülen; ~ **its face** *(Br., sl.)* sich gerade noch rentieren; ~ **gravel for gold** Gold auswaschen; ~ **one's hands of pay bargaining** sich aus Lohnverhandlungen völlig heraushalten; ~ **one's hands of it** seine Hände in Unschuld waschen; ~ **one's dirty linen in public** *(fig.)* seine schmutzige Wäsche in aller Öffentlichkeit waschen; ~ **out a road** Straße unterspülen; ~ **over** überstreichen; ~ **over the deck** Deck überspülen; ~ **overboard** über Bord spülen; ~ **up a contract automatically** Vertrag automatisch annullieren; ~ **sales of stock** *(US)* Börsenmanöver durchführen, Scheinverkauf vornehmen;

to give the car a ~ Auto waschen; **to send s. th. to the** ~ etw. zum Waschen (in die Wäscherei) geben;

~ **boiler** Waschkessel; ~ **dirt** Goldstand; ~ **drawing** Halbton-, Schwarzweißzeichnung; ~ **glove** Waschlederhandschuh; ~ **goods** waschbares Material, waschechte Stoffe; ~ **rag** *(US)* Waschlappen; ~ **sale** *(US)* Scheinkauf und Scheinverkauf, *(stock exchange)* Simultankauf und -verkauf, Börsenscheinverkauf; ~ **transaction** *(US)* Börsenscheingeschäft.

washboard Waschbrett, *(room)* Scheuerleiste.

washbowl Waschschüssel, -becken.

washed | -out (-up) verwaschen, verblaßt, *(sl.)* erledigt, ruiniert;

~ **out by the sea** vom Meer ausgehöhlt; ~ **by the waves** von den Wellen überspült;

to be ~ **overboard** über Bord gespült werden; **to be** ~ **ashore** an Land getrieben (geschwemmt) werden; **to feel** ~ **out** sich völlig erschöpft fühlen.

washer Wäscher[in], *(apparatus)* Waschmaschine;

dish ~ Geschirrspüler, -spülmaschine; ~ **bottle** Waschflüssigkeitsbehälter.

washing Waschen, Wäsche, *(gold)* Goldwäscherei, *(painting)* Farbüberzug, Tünche, *(stock market, US)* Börsenscheinverkauf, -geschäft;

~ **overboard** Überbordspülen;

to take in one's another ~ *(fig.)* sich gegenseitig helfen;

~ **bay** Wagenwaschraum, -anlage; ~ **day** Waschtag; ~ **facilities** Waschgelegenheit; ~ **machine** Waschmaschine; ~ **place** Waschmöglichkeit; ~ **powder** Waschpulver, -mittel.

washhand basin (stand, *Br.***)** Waschbecken.

washhouse Waschküche, -anstalt.

washout Auswaschung, *(sl.)* Reinfall, Fiasko, Pleite, *(examination)* Durchfallen, *(mil., sl.)* Fahrkarte, Fehltreffer, *(person)* Versager, Niete, Flasche, *(personnel, US sl.)* Ablösung, Aussieben ungeeigneten Personals, *(road)* Einbruch, Unterspülung; ~ **signal** *(railroad parlance)* Notsignal.

washroom Waschraum, Toilette.

washy | coffee dünner Kaffee; ~ **colo(u)r** ausgewaschene Farbe; ~ **style** seichter Stil.

waspish letter gereizter Brief.

wassail Gelage, Umtrunk.

wastage Verschwendung, Vergeudung, *(loss)* Verlust, Abgang, Materialschwund, *(refuse)* Ausschuß, *(wear and tear)* Verschleiß, Abnutzung;

~ **of coal** Kohlenvergeudung; ~ **of energy** Energieverschwendung, *(fig.)* Leerlauf; ~ **of time** Zeitverschwendung.

waste *(cargo)* Abgang, Verlust, Spillage, Schwund, *(extravagance)* übermäßiger Verbrauch, ungenützte Aufwendungen, Verschwendung, Vergeudung, Wertverschleuderung, -verlust, *(leasehold)* Verfallenlassen, Wertverlust durch Vernachlässigung, *(gradual loss)* Verfall, Abnutzung, Verschleiß, Abgang, Verlust, *(mining)* taubes Gestein, Abraum, Alter Mann, *(real estate)* Wertminderung, Verschlechterung, *(refuse)* Ausschuß, Abfall, Schutt, Müll, *(wilderness)* Wüste, Ödland, öde Fläche;

active ~ vorsätzliche Substanzbeschädigung; **ameliorating** ~ *(real estate)* werterhöhende Veränderung an der Grundstückssubstanz, werterhöhende Substanzveränderungen; **atomic** ~ Atommüll; **commissive** ~ Substanzbeschädigung; **double** ~ *(tenant)* durch Holzfällen für das reparaturbedürftige Pachtgebäude verursachte Substanzverschlechterung; **equitable** ~ normaler Verschleiß, *(land)* zulässige Substanzbeschädigung; **natural** ~ gewöhnliche Verschlechterung, üblicher Verschleiß; **permissive** ~ mangelnde Obsorge für die Erhaltung, übliche Abnutzung, Vernachlässigung notwendiger Gebäudereparaturen, Wertminderung durch Nichtstun; **positive** ~ *(tenant)* vorsätzliche Substanzbeschädigung; **voluntary** ~ absichtlich herbeigeführte Wertminderung, vorsätzliche Substanzschädigung;

~ **of energy** Energieverschwendung; ~ **of labo(u)r** unnützer Arbeitsaufwand; ~ **of money** Geldverschwendung; ~ **of snow** Schneewüste; ~ **of time** Zeitverlust, -verschwendung; ~ **of water** Wasserwüste;

~ *(v.)* brachliegen (ungenutzt) lassen, vernachlässigen, in Verfall geraten lassen, Substanzverschlechterung herbeiführen (eintreten lassen), *(decay)* abgenutzt werden, verfallen, *(lose in value)* Wertminderung (Vermögensschaden) erleiden, *(squander)* [übermäßig] verbrauchen, verschwenden, vergeuden, verschleudern, *(wear)* sich verbrauchen, verschleißen, abnutzen;
~ **away** schwächer werden, sich verzehren, hinsiechen; ~ **one's labo(u)r** umsonst arbeiten; ~ **money** Geld durchbringen; one's ~ **property** sein Vermögen verprassen; ~ **in routine work** sich mit routinemäßiger Arbeit verzetteln; ~ **one's time** sich vergeblich bemühen, seine Zeit verschwenden (vertrödeln, vergeuden);
to be [un]impeachable for ~ *(tenant)* für Substanzschäden [nicht] haften; **to lay** ~ verheeren, in Schutt und Asche liegen; **to lie** ~ brachliegen; **to run to** ~ verschwendet werden;
~ *(a.)* öde, wüst, unfruchtbar, *(land)* unbebaut;
~ **accounting** Abfallverrechnung; ~ **book** Strazze, Kladde, Memorial; ~ **circulation** *(advertising)* Fehlstreuung; ~ **coal** Abfallkohle; ~ **coke** Abfallkoks; ~ **disposal** Abfallbeseitigung; ~ **drain** Abflußrinne; ~ **energy** ungenutzte Energie; ~ **expanse of water** Wasserwüste; ~ **handling** Abfallaufbereitung; ~ **heat** Abwärme, verlorene Hitze; ~ **incineration** Müllverbrennung; ~ **materials** Abfallstoffe; ~ **paper** Abfall-, Ausschuß-, Makulatur-, Altpapier, Makulatur; ~-**paper basket** Papierkorb; ~-**paper drive** Altpapiersammlung; ~-**paper salvage campaign** Altpapieraktion; ~ **pipe** Abzugs-, Auslauf-, Ausgußrohr; ~ **product** Abfallprodukt, -erzeugnis; ~ **sheet** *(print.)* Außschußbogen; ~ **stowage (tonnage)** leerer Schiffsraum; ~ **substances** Abfallstoffe; ~ **trap** Wasserverschluß; **municipal** ~ **treatment** kommunale Abfallverwertung; ~-**treatment facilities** Abfallverwertungsanlage; ~-**treatment plant** Abfallverwertungsunternehmen; ~ **utilization** Abfallverwertung; ~ **valve** Absperrventil; ~ **well** Senkgrube.
wastebasket *(US)* Papierkorb.
wasted brachliegend, ungenutzt;
~ **with grief** vom Kummer verzehrt;
to be ~ nutzlos sein, *(person)* am falschen Platz stehen; ~ **money** hinausgeworfenes Geld; ~ **talent** ungenutztes Talent; ~ **time** verlorene Zeit.
wasteful kostspielig, unrentabel, verschwenderisch;
to be ~ **of** verschwenderisch umgehen;
~ **administration** aufwendige Verwaltung; **to do away with** ~ **expenditure** unsinnige Ausgabenwirtschaft einschränken; ~ **process** kostspieliges Verfahren; ~ **system** verschwenderisches System.
wastefulness Unrentabilität.
wasteland Ödland[fläche], nicht angebautes Land.
wasteless ohne Abfall (Verlust).
waster Verschwender, Taugenichts, *(unmarketable piece)* Ausschuß, Abfall-, Ausschußstück, -ware.
wasteway Abflußkanal.
wasting Verschwenden, Vergeudung, *(wearing away)* Schwund, Verlust;
~ *(a.)* kurzlebig, schwindend;
to be ~ **away** immer schwächer werden, dahinsiechen;
~ **assets** kurzlebige Wirtschaftsgüter; **to be of a** ~ **character** der Abnutzung (dem Substanzverzehr) unterliegen; ~ **fortune** schwindendes Vermögen; ~ **property** dem Substanzverzehr unterliegende Vermögenswerte; ~ **trust** Vermögensverwaltung mit genehmigtem Substanzanbruch.
wastrel *(land, Br.)* nicht bebautes Land, Gemeindeland, *(production)* minderwertige Ware, Ausschußware, *(spendthrift)* Verschwender, *(vagabond)* Taugenichts, liederlicher Mensch, Tunichtgut.
watch Wachsamkeit, Hut, Wache, *(body of constables)* Polizeistreife, *(chronometer)* Seechronometer, *(clock)* Armbanduhr, *(hill, Scot.)* Aussichtshügel, *(sentinel)* [Schild]wache, Wachposten, Wächter, *(set of watchmen)* Wache, Wachkommando, Wachmannschaft, *(ship)* Schiffswache;
on ~ auf Wacht;
~ **below** *(ship)* Wachkommando, Freiwache; **first** ~ 1. Wache; **mid (middle,** *US)* ~ Hunde-, Mittelwache; **morning** ~ Morgenwache; **pocket** ~ Taschenuhr; **wrist** ~ Armbanduhr;
~ **and ward** Wachpflicht bei Tag und Nacht;
~ *(v.)* beobachten, achtgeben, Ausschau halten, *(assign watches)* Wachen einteilen, *(mil.)* Wache halten, Posten stehen, *(overlook)* Aufsicht führen, *(police, Br.)* Wache[n] aufstellen, *(follow the trail of an action)* Prozeßverlauf beobachten;
~ **a case for s. o.** für j. in einem Prozeß als Beobachter fungieren; ~ **all night at the bedside of a sick child** Nachtwache bei einem kranken Kind halten; ~ **out** *(coll.)* aufpassen, auf der

Hut sein; ~ **the spread of socialism** Ausbreitung sozialistischer Ideen genauestens verfolgen; ~ **one's step** sich vor Fehlern hüten; ~ **one's time** auf seine Chance warten;
to be on the ~ auf der Hut sein; **to always be on the** ~ **for discrepancies** Ungenauigkeiten scharf im Auge behalten; **to call out the** ~ Wache herausrufen; **to have the** ~ Wache haben; **to have s. o.** ~-**ed by a detective** j. von einem Detektiv überwachen lassen; **to keep [a]** ~ **on (over)** Wache halten, aufpassen; **to keep a better** ~ **over a prisoner** Gefangenen schärfer bewachen; **to keep a close** ~ **on one's interests** sehr auf seine Interessen bedacht sein; **to pass as a** ~ **in the night** schnell vergangen und vergessen sein; **to set a** ~ **upon s. o.** j. heimlich beobachten lassen;
~ **bell** Schiffsglocke; ~ **box** Wärterhäuschen, *(mil.)* Schilderhaus, *(police)* Unterstand; ~ **candle** Totenlicht; ~ **chain** Uhrkette; ~ **change** Wachwechsel; ~ **committee** *(Br.)* städtischer Ordnungsdienst; ~ **fire** *(mil.)* Signalfeuer; ~ **hand** Uhrzeiger; ~ **header** *(mar.)* Wachhabender; ~ **mastiff** Wachhund; ~ **officer** *(mar.)* Wachoffizier; ~ **rate** *(town)* Bewachungs- und Beleuchtungsabgabe; ~ **and Ward Society** *(US)* Zensurstelle für Neuveröffentlichungen; ~ **and warning service** Kreditinformationsaustausch.
watchband Uhrarmband.
watchboat Wach-, Streifenboot.
watchdog Wachhund, *(fig.)* Aufpasser, Anstandswauwau;
~ **committee** Beschwerde-, Überwachungsausschuß; ~ **role** Wachhundfunktion.
watcher Wachhabender, *(elections)* Beobachter, *(hospital)* Krankenwärter, *(lawyer)* Beobachtungsauftrag [im Prozeß];
to hold (keep) a ~ **for s. o.** *(Br.)* Interessen als Beobachter vertreten.
watchful wachsam, achtsam, aufmerksam;
to keep a ~ **eye upon s. o.** wachsames Auge auf j. haben.
watchglass *(mar.)* Glas.
watchhouse Wachstube, *(police station)* Wache.
watching Wachen;
to be ~ **outside** draußen Wache halten.
watchmaker Uhrmacher.
watchman Nachtwächter, Wachmann;
~**'s clock** Stech-, Kontrolluhr.
watchtower Wachturm, *(mar.)* Leuchtturm.
watchword Kennwort, Losung, Parole.
water Wasser, *(level)* Wasserstand;
above ~ über dem Wasserspiegel schwimmend, *(fig.)* finanziell gesichert; **below** ~ unter dem Wasserspiegel; **by** ~ auf dem Wasserwege; **in low** ~ *(fig.)* knapp bei Kasse; **in Chinese** ~s in chinesischen Gewässern; **like** ~ *(fig.)* reichlich, verschwenderisch; **like a fish out of** ~ ungemütlich; **of the first** ~ *(diamond)* von reinstem Wasser, *(quality)* erster Güte; **on the** ~ zur See, auf den Wasserwege (Meer); **under** ~ überflutet; **written on** ~ in den Wind geschrieben, vergänglich;
~s Gewässer, *(flood)* Hochwasser, Flut, *(mineral spring)* Brunnen, Mineralwasser; **the** ~s *(dial.)* Heilquellen, Kurort;
coast ~s Küstengewässer; **developed** ~s an die Oberfläche gebrachtes Wasser; **flood** ~s Überschwemmung; **foreign** ~s ausländische Hoheitsgewässer; **fresh** ~ Süß-, Trinkwasser; **ground** ~ Grundwasser; **inland** ~ Eigen-, Binnengewässer; **melted** ~ Schmelzwasser; **mineral** ~ Mineralwasser; **national** ~s Hoheitsgewässer; **navigable** ~s schiffbare Gewässer; **percolating** ~s Sickerwasser; **private** ~s Privatgewässer; **public** ~s öffentliche Gewässer; **shallow** ~ seichtes Wasser; **subterranean** ~s unterirdische Gewässer; **surface** ~ Oberflächenwasser; **surplus** ~ Überschußwasser; **table** ~ Tafelwasser; **territorial** ~s Territorial-, Hoheitsgewässer; **thermal** ~ Thermalbrunnen; **tide** ~s Flutgebiet, Gezeitenwasser;
~s **of the United States** Binnengewässer der USA;
~ *(v.)* [be]wässern, sprengen, *(airplane)* wassern, *(cattle)* zur Tränke führen, tränken, *(ship)* Wasser einnehmen;
~ **down** *(fig.)* verwässern, abschwächen, mildern; ~ **down a bill** Gesetzentwurf verwässern; ~ **down a country's influence abroad** Einfluß eines Landes im Ausland schwächen; ~ **down provisions** Bestimmungen verwässern; ~ **one's lecture** seinen Vortrag in die Länge ziehen; ~ **the stock** Aktienkapital verwässern;
to be on the ~ verschifft werden; **to be in deep** ~s das Wasser bis zum Halse stehen haben; **to be in low** ~ *(fig.)* auf dem Trockenen sitzen; **to be in smooth** ~s *(fig.)* es geschafft haben; **to bring the** ~ **to s. one's mouth** jem. das Wasser im Munde zusammenlaufen lassen; **to cast one's bread upon the** ~s sein Vermögen aufs Spiel setzen; **to cross the** ~s Meer überqueren; **to draw 15 feet of** ~ 15 Fuß Tiefgang haben; **to drink the** ~s Brunnenkur

machen; **to draw much** ~ *(ship)* tief gehen; **to get into hot** ~ sich Unannehmlichkeiten zuziehen, sich in die Nesseln setzen; **to get into hot** ~ **with s. o.** es mit jem. zu tun bekommen; **to go through fire and** ~ den größten Gefahren trotzen; **to have** ~ **on tap** über Leitungswasser verfügen; **to hold** ~ *(theory)* Probe bestehen; **to keep one's head above** ~ sich über Wasser halten; **to make foul** ~ in seichtem Gewässer segeln; **to make s. one's mouth** ~ jem. das Wasser im Munde zusammenlaufen lassen; **to send by** ~ auf dem Wasserwege befördern, verschiffen; **to spend money like** ~ Geld mit vollen Händen ausgeben; **to take the** ~**s at Bath** Kur in Bath machen; **to take s. o. into dangerous** ~**s** j. einen gefährlichen Weg führen; **to throw cold** ~**s on s. th.** jds. Begeisterung für etw. dämpfen; **to throw one's bread upon the** ~**s** etw. mit der linken Hand tun;

~ **authority** Wasseramt, Amt für Wasserwirtschaft; ~ **bailiff** *(Br.)* Fischereiaufseher, Strom-, Wasserpolizei; ~ **balance** Wasserhaushalt; ~**-bearer** Wasserträger; ~ **bed** Grundwasserschicht; ~**-borne** auf dem Wasserwege befördert; ~**-borne transport** Wasserfracht; ~ **bonds** Obligationen kommunaler Wasserwerke; ~ **bottle** Feldflasche; ~**-bound** vom Wasser eingeschlossen; ~ **butt** Regentonne; ~ **cannon** Wasserwerfer; ~ **carriage** Beförderung auf dem Wasserwege, Wassertransport, Verschiffung; ~ **carrier** Wassertankwagen, *(hauler)* Fluß-, Seespediteur, Wasserfrachtführer; ~ **cart** Wasserwagen; ~ **cask** Wasserfaß; ~ **charges** *(US)* Wassergeld; ~ **cistern** Wasserbehälter, Zisterne; ~ **clock** Wasseruhr; ~ **closet** WC; ~ **cock** Wasserhahn; ~ **colo(u)r** Aquarellmalerei; ~ **colo(u)r pencil** Farbstift; ~ **company** Wasserwerk; ~ **consumption** Wasserverbrauch; ~**-cool** *(v.)* mit Wasser kühlen; ~**-cooled** wassergekühlt; ~**-cooler** Wasserkühltank; ~ **course** Wasser-, Bach-, Stromlauf; ~ **craft** Wasserfahrzeug; ~ **damage** Wasserschaden; ~**-damage insurance** Wasserschadenversicherung; ~ **deck** Regenplane; ~ **depot** *(railway)* Wasserdepot; ~ **divide** Wasserscheide; ~ **drinker** Antialkoholiker, Abstinenzler; ~ **economy** Wasserhaushalt; ~ **engineering** Wasserwirtschaft; ~ **feeder** Wasserzufluß; ~ **finder** Wünschelrutengänger; ~ **flow** strömende Wassermasse; ~ **gang** Wassergraben, Kanal; ~ **gauge** Wasserstandsmesser; ~ **guard** Hafenpolizei, -zollwache, Flußpolizei; ~ **heater** Wasserbereiter, Badeofen; ~ **hole** Pfütze; ~ **house** Wasserturm; ~ **jacket** Wasserkühlmantel; ~ **lane** *(amid ice)* Fahrrinne; ~ **level** Grundwasserspiegel; ~ **line** Ladelinie; ~**-lined** *(paper)* mit Wasserlinien versehen; ~**-logged** manövrierunfähig wegen einer undichten Stelle; ~ **lot** *(US)* unter Wasser stehendes Gelände; ~ **main** Hauptwasserrohr; ~ **meter** Wasserzähler; **inland** ~ **navigation** Binnenschiffahrt; ~ **pipe** Wasserrohr; ~ **pocket** Wassersack; ~ **pollution** Gewässerverunreinigung, -verschmutzung; ~ **power company** Wasserkraftwerk; ~ **power** Wasserkraft, *(mill)* Wassernutzungsrecht; ~ **power company bonds** Schuldverschreibungen von Wasserkraftwerken; ~ **press** hydraulische Presse; ~ **pressure** Wasserdruck; ~ **privilege** Wassernutzungsrecht; ~ **pump** Wasserpumpe; ~ **quality** Gewässergüte; ~ **rate** *(Br.)* Wassergeld; ~ **resources** Wasserhaushalt; ⌾ **Resources Act** Wasserversorgungsgesetz; ⌾ **Resources Board** *(Br.)* Wasserwirtschaftsbehörde; ~ **right** Wassernutzungsrecht, Wasserentnahmerecht; ~ **route** Wasserweg; ~ **service** Wasserversorgung; ~ **shortage** Wasserknappheit, -mangel; ~**-skiing** Wasserski; ~ **snake** *(foreign exchange)* floatende Schlange; ~ **supply** natürliche Bewässerung, Wasserversorgung, -lieferung; **long-distance** ~ **supply** Fernwasserversorgung; ~**-supply engineer** Wasserbauingenieur; ~**-supply engineering** Wasserbauwesen; ~**-supply industry** Wasserwirtschaft; ~ **surface** Wasseroberfläche; ~ **system** Stromgebiet, *(water supply)* Wasserleitung; ~ **table** Grundwasserspiegel; ~ **tank** Wasserbehälter, Tank; ~ **tower** Wasserturm; ~ **transportation** Beförderung auf dem Wasserweg; ~ **tube** Wasserrohr, -röhre; ~ **undertaking** Wasserwirtschaftsunternehmen; ~ **user** Wasserverbraucher; ~ **vapo(u)r** Wasserdunst; ~ **wag(g)on** Wasser[versorgungs]wagen; **to be on the** ~ **waggon** *(Br.)* Abstinenzler sein; ~ **wave** Wasserturbine, *(ship)* Schaufelrad; ~ **wheel** Wasserturbine, *(ship)* Schaufelrad; ~ **witch** *(US)* Wünschelrutengänger; ~ **works** Wasserwerk, Wasserversorgungsanlage.

waterage Beförderung auf dem Wasserweg, Wasserfracht.

watercraft Wasserfahrzeug.

watered capital (stock, *US)* verwässertes Aktienkapital; ~**-down liberalism** verwässerter Liberalismus.

waterfall Wasserfall, Kaskade.

waterfog Tröpfchennebel.

waterfront Uferbezirk, -gelände;
~ **facilities** Kaianlagen für den Warenumschlag; ~ **property** Flußgrundstück, am Wasser gelegenes Grundstück.

watering Bewässerung, Berieselung, Sprengen, *(cattle)* Tränken, *(ship)* Wassernehmen;
~ **of stock** Kapitalverwässerung;
~ **can** Gießkanne; ~ **depot** *(railroad, US)* Wasserdepot; ~ **hole** *(fig.)* Rastplatz; ~ **place** Wasserstelle, *(Br.)* Kurort, Seebad; ~ **pot** Gießkanne.

waterman Binnenschiffer, Bootsmann.

watermark Wasserstand, *(note paper)* Papier-, Wasserzeichen, *(ship)* Tiefgangsmarke;
high ~ Flutmarke, Hochwasserstandszeichen, *(ship)* Lademarke; **low** ~ niedrigster Wasserstand, *(fig.)* Tiefstand;
~ *(v.)* mit einem Wasserzeichen versehen.

watermarked paper Wasserzeichenpapier.

waterplane Wasserflugzeug.

waterproof wasserdicht, -undurchlässig;
~ *(v.)* imprägnieren.

waterproofing Imprägnierung.

waterquake Seebeben.

watershed *(Br.)* Wasserscheide, *(Br.)* Einzugsgebiet.

watersite Wasserkante, Küste, See-, Flußufer;
~ **police** Strom-, Wasserschutzpolizei.

waterskin Wasserschlauch.

waterspout Dachrinne, *(cloudburst)* Wasserhose.

watertight wasserdicht, -undurchlässig, *(fig.)* stichhaltig, unanfechtbar;
~ **compartment** *(mar.)* wasserdichte Abteilung, Schott; **to keep s. th. in a** ~ **compartment** *(fig.)* etw. isoliert betrachten; ~ **document** unanfechtbare Urkunde.

waterway Schiffahrts-, Wasserweg, Wasserstraße;
inland ~**s** Binnengewässer;
⌾**s Board** *(Br.)* Wasserstraßenamt; ~ **operator** Binnenschiffahrtsunternehmen, -spediteur; **inland** ~ **system** Binnenwasserstraßennetz.

waterworker Kanalarbeiter.

waterworks Wasserwerk, -versorgungsanlage, *(stock exchange)* Wertpapiere von Wasserwerken;
town ~ städtische Wasserversorgung.

watery | sky Regenhimmel; ~ **waste** Wasserwüste.

wave Woge, Welle, *(print.)* Guilloche, Zierlinie [auf Wertpapieren], *(salient curved unevenness)* wellenförmige Unebenheit;
in ~**s** wellenförmig;
heat ~ Hitzewelle; **long** ~ Langwelle; **medium** ~ *(radio)* Mittelwelle; **short** ~ *(radio)* Kurzwelle; **white-crested** ~**s** schaumgekrönte Wellen;
~ **of crimes** Flut von Verbrechen; ~ **of demand** Nachfragewelle; ~ **of depression** Krisenwelle; ~ **of a flag** Wink mit einer Flagge; ~ **of the hand** Wink mit der Hand; ~ **of immigrants** Einwandererstrom; ~ **of indignation** Entrüstungsstrom; ~ **of inflation** Inflationswelle; ~ **of mergers** Fusionswelle; ~ **of prosperity** Prosperitätszeit, Hochkonjunktur; ~ **of selling** steigende Kauflust; ~ **of strikes** massierte Streiks, Streikwelle; ~ **of terror** Terrorwelle;
~ *(v.)* sich wellenartig bewegen, *(flag)* wehen, flattern, *(securities)* mit Zierlinien versehen;
~ **aside** mit einer Handbewegung abtun; ~ **s. o. away** j. abweisen; ~ **a train to a halt** Zug mit Winkzeichen anhalten; **to attack in** ~**s** in einander folgenden Wellen angreifen;
~ **band** *(sl.)* Frequenz-, Wellenband; ~**-band coverage** Wellenbereich; ~**-breaker** Wellenbrecher; ~ **changer** *(radio)* Wellenschalter; ~**-damage insurance** Hochwasserversicherung; ~ **guide** *(el.)* Hohlleiter; ~ **length** *(radio)* Wellenlänge; ~ **meter** Frequenzmesser.

wavelike wellenförmig.

waver *(v.)* unschlüssig sein, schwanken, zögern, *(stock exchange)* schwanken;
~ **between two opinions** zwischen zwei Meinungen schwanken; ~ **in one's resolution** in seinem Entschluß schwankend werden.

wavering schwankend, unschlüssig;
~ **lines of the enemy** schwankende feindliche Linien;
to be ~ **on the edge of collapse** *(government)* kurz vor dem Rücktritt.

wax Wachs, *(candle)* Wachskerze, *(record)* Schallplatte;
sealing ~ Siegelwachs;
~ *(v.)* *(record)* auf Schallplatte aufnehmen, *(US)* Oberhand bekommen (gewinnen);
to be ~ **in s. one's hands** Wachs in jds. Händen sein; **to be as close (tight) as** ~ dicht halten, verschwiegen sein; **to fit like** ~ wie angegossen passen (sitzen); **to stick like** ~ **to s. o.** jem. wie eine Klette anhängen;
~ **record** Wachsmatrize.

waxworks Wachsfigurenkabinett.

waxy wachshaltig, *(fig.)* leicht zu beeinflussen, nachgiebig.

way [Verkehrs]weg, Pfad, Bahn, Straße, *(condition of health)* Gesundheitszustand, Verfassung, *(course)* Gang, [Ver]lauf, *(distance)* Entfernung, Weite, *(means)* Mittel, Art und Weise, Weg, *(method)* Verfahren, Methode, *(peculiarity)* Eigenheit, persönliche (eigene) Art, *(profession, coll.)* Fach-, Geschäfts-, Berufszweig, Tätigkeitsbereich, *(progress)* Fortschritt, Fortgang, Vorankommen, *(region)* Umkreis, Umgebung, *(right of way)* Vorfahrtsrecht, *(room to advance)* Entwicklungsmöglichkeit, *(route)* Strecke, *(ship)* Fahrt[geschwindigkeit], *(shipbuilding)* Helling, *(surroundings)* Umgebung, Umkreis, Gegend;
by the ~ im Vorbeigehen; **by ~ of excuse** als Entschuldigung; **by ~ of gift** schenkungsweise; **by ~ of introduction** als Einführung; **by ~ of negotiation(s)** im Verhandlungswege; **by ~ of regulation** im Wege der Verordnung; **from the ~** abseits, abgelegen; **in a ~** gewissermaßen; **in a bad ~** in einer schlimmen Lage; **in a big ~** in großem Stil; **in every ~** in jeder Hinsicht; **in one ~** in einer Beziehung; **in several ~s** in mancherlei Hinsicht; **in the ~** hinderlich, störend; **in the ~ of business** auf dem üblichen Geschäftsweg; **not a great ~ away** nicht sehr weit entfernt; **on my ~ back** auf meiner Rückreise (Rückfahrt); **on the ~** unterwegs; **on the ~ out** *(coll.)* bald ganz unmodern; **on the ~ to business** *(insurance)* auf dem Wege zur Arbeit; **well on one's ~** schon weit vorangekommen; **out of the ~** abseits, abgelegen, abgeschieden, *(fig.)* ungewöhnlich, außergewöhnlich, ausgefallen, auf dem Holzweg; **to my ~ of thinking** nach meiner Meinung; **under ~** im Gang, *(ship)* auf Fahrt, unterwegs; **~ back** Rückweg; **funny ~s** komische Manieren; **a good ~** ein gutes Stück Weg; **~ home** Heimweg; **~ in** *(Br.)* Einfahrt, -gang; **~ out** Ausfahrt, -gang, *(fig.)* Ausweg; **permanent ~** *(Br.)* Bahngleis-, Bahnkörper; **private ~** verbotener Weg; **proper ~** vorschriftsmäßige Art und Weise; **proven ~** erprobte Methode; **public ~** öffentlicher Weg; **~through** Durchreise;
one ~ or another irgendwie; **~ of business** Geschäfts-, Berufszweig; **~ of computing** Berechnungsmethode; **~ to diversify** Auffächerungsmöglichkeiten; **~ of escape** Fluchtweg; **~ of life** Lebensverhältnisse; **~ of living** Lebensart; **~ of necessity** gesetzlich begründetes Wegerecht, Notweg; **~ of operating** Verfahrensweise; **easier ~ to pay** erleichterte Zahlungsmodalitäten; **~ of saving** Sparmöglichkeit; **~ of thinking** Denkweise; **~ of transportation** Transport-, Beförderungsweg; **~ of treating** Behandlungsweise; **~ of the world** Lauf der Welt; **~ of writing** Schreibweise;
to be in one's ~ jem. im Wege (hinderlich) sein; **to be in a fair ~** die besten Möglichkeiten haben, gut dastehen; **to be in a great ~** *(Br., coll.)* völlig außer sich sein; **to be a long ~ off** weit entfernt sein; **to be a long ~ off perfection** keineswegs vollkommen sein; **to be in a terrible ~** in trauriger Verfassung sein; **to be on its ~ out** *(production)* auslaufen; **to be on the ~** *(stock exchange)* erhältlich sein; **to be on their ~** auf Achse (unterwegs) sein; **to be on the ~ up** im Aufstieg begriffen sein; **to be in a bad ~** *(business)* schlecht gehen; **to be in a bad ~ of business** schlechte Geschäfte machen; **to be in a fair ~ to becoming a millionaire** auf dem besten Wege sein, Millionär zu werden; **to be in a good ~ of business** gut verdienen, gute Geschäfte machen; **to be in a large ~ of business** bedeutendes Geschäft haben; **to be in a small ~ of business** kleines Geschäft haben; **to be only 6 miles out of the ~** nur ein Umweg von 10 Kilometern sein; **to be in the shipping ~** im Schiffshandel sein; **to be on the ~ to success** die Erfolgsleiter emporklettern; **to be under ~** *(meeting)* im Gang sein, schon angefangen haben, *(ship)* fahren; **to be on one's ~ up** beruflich vorankommen; **to be in the shipping ~** im Schiffshandel sein; **to beg one's ~** sich durchbetteln; **to contribute to scientific progress in a small ~** nur einen kleinen Beitrag für die Zukunft der Wissenschaft leisten; **to entertain in a large ~** äußerst gastfreundlich (gesellig) sein; **not to fall in s. one's ~** nicht in jds. Fach fallen; **to feel one's ~** vorsichtig zu Werke gehen; **to find a ~** Ausweg finden; **to force one's ~ into** sich Eingang verschaffen; **to gather ~** *(ship)* Fahrt aufnehmen; **to get one's own ~** sich durchsetzen; **to get one's ~ with s. o.** sich bei jem. durchsetzen; **to get s. th. out of the ~** etw. erledigen; **to get out of the ~** ausweichen; **to get under ~** in Gang kommen, *(ship)* in Fahrt kommen; **to give ~** *(price)* sinken, nachgeben; **to give ~ to** Platz machen; **to give s. o. ~ to work his will** jem. seinen Willen lassen; **to go one's ~** seinen Lauf nehmen; **to go on one's ~** sich auf den Weg machen; **to go one's own ~** für sich selbst entscheiden, seinen eigenen Weg gehen; **to go out of one's ~** von seiner gewohnten (der üblichen) Tour seiner Politik) abweichen; **to go the ~ of all the earth** den Weg allen Fleisches gehen; **to go the wrong ~ about s. th.** falsche Methode anwenden, Sache am verkehrten Ende anfassen; **to have**

~ on *(ship)* in Fahrt (unterwegs) sein; **to have the right of ~** Vorfahrt haben; **to have one's ~** sein Konzept durchsetzen; **to have a ~ with s. o.** mit jem. gut zurechtkommen; **to have it both ~s** sich je nach Bedarf aussuchen, sich beide Möglichkeiten offenhalten; **to have a winning ~ with people** mit den Leuten gut zurechtkommen; **to hold one's ~ in spite of all obstacles** sich gegen alle Widerstände durchsetzen; **to inquire the ~** sich nach dem Weg erkundigen; **to lead the ~** Anführer abgeben; **not to lie in s. one's ~** nicht in jds. Fach fallen; **to live across the ~** auf der anderen Straßenseite wohnen; **to live in a great ~** auf großem Fuße leben; **to live in a small ~** sehr bescheiden (in kleinen Verhältnissen) leben, sehr bescheidenes Leben führen, keinen Aufwand treiben; **to live somewhere London ~** irgendwo in der Gegend von London wohnen; **to lose ~** *(ship)* Fahrt verlieren; **to lose one's ~** vom Weg abkommen, sich verfahren; **to make ~** *(ship)* Fahrt machen, *(mar.)* vorwärtskommen; **to make inquiries by ~ of learning the facts of a case** Untersuchungen anstellen, um den Tatbestand zu ermitteln; **to make one's ~ in life** seinen Weg gehen, erfolgreich sein, sein Glück machen; **to make ~ for the fire engine** der Feuerwehr Platz machen; **to make one's ~** seinen Weg machen; **to make one's ~ into** eindringen; **to make a penny go a long ~** sich sein Geld sehr genau einteilen, jeden Groschen dreimal umdrehen; **to make the best of one's ~** so schnell als möglich machen; **to mend one's ~s** sich bessern; **to open a ~ through the crowd** sich einen Weg durch die Menge bahnen; **to pave the ~** Weg ebnen; **to pay it's ~** sich rentieren, seine Unkosten decken; **to pay one's ~** seinen Verbindlichkeiten nachkommen, genug zum Lebensunterhalt verdienen, *(pay one's share)* seinen Kostenanteil tragen; **to plough (plow, US) one's ~ through the mud** sich durch den Schlamm einen Weg bahnen; **to push one's ~ through the crowd** sich rücksichtslos durchdrängen; **to put o. s. out of the ~** sich Unannehmlichkeiten zuziehen; **to put s. o. out of the ~** j. unschädlich machen; **to put s. th. out of harm's ~** etw. an einen sicheren Ort bringen; **to put s. o. in the ~ of earning a living** jem. zu einem Lebensunterhalt verhelfen; **to put s. o. in the ~** jem. etw. zuschustern; **to see one's ~** genau wissen, welchen Weg man einschlagen muß; **not to see one's ~ clear to recommending s. o. for a job** sich nicht für berechtigt halten, j. für eine Stellung zu empfehlen; **to slip back into one's old ~s** in die alten Fehler verfallen; **to stand in the ancient ~s** am Alten festhalten; **to stand in the ~ of justice** der Gerechtigkeit in den Arm fallen; **to strike out a line on one's own ~** seinen eigenen Weg gehen; **to take one's ~ to** ... sich nach ... aufmachen; **to take another's own ~** fremde Ratschläge nicht befolgen; **to take s. o. out of his ~** j. einen Umweg machen lassen; **to twist one's ~ through** sich durchschlängeln; **to work one's ~ up** sich hocharbeiten; **to work one's ~ through college** sich sein Studium als Werkstudent verdienen; **to yield right of ~** Vorfahrt lassen;
~ car *(railroad, sl.)* Dienstwagenabteil; **~ freight** *(US)* für einen Lokalbahnhof bestimmtes Frachtgut; **permanent-~ man** *(Br.)* Streckenarbeiter; **~-out** Ausgang, Ausweg; **~-out clothes** extravagante Kleidung; **out-of-the-~ place** abgelegener Ort; **~ rate** *(US)* Ortstarif; **~ station** Zwischenstation, Klein-, Lokalbahnhof, Durchgangsbahnhof, -station; **~ traffic** *(US)* Nah, Ortsverkehr; **~ train** *(US)* Vorort-, Bummelzug, Nahverkehrszug.

ways and means Mittel und Wege, *(financing)* Geldbeschaffung, Deckungsmittel;
~ advance *(Br.)* offene Buchkredite (Kassenkredite) der Bank von England an die öffentlichen Hände; **~ committee** Haushaltsausschuß; **~ resolution** *(Br.)* Resolution des Haushaltsausschusses.

waybill *(US)* Frachtbrief, -zettel, Beförderungsschein, *(advice of dispatch)* Versandanzeige, *(freight car, US)* Beförderungs-, Begleitschein bei Waggons, Frachtbrief, Abfertigungs-, Warenbegleitschein, *(list of passengers)* Passagierliste;
air ~ Luftfrachtbrief; **duplicate ~** Frachtbriefduplikat; **original ~** Urschrift des Frachtbriefes;
~ (v.) mit Warenbegleitschein verschicken;
~ number Frachtbriefnummer.

waybilling weight Frachtgewicht.

wayfaring Wandern;
~ man Wandersmann.

waygoing|crop nach Pachtablauf reifende Ernte, Ernterecht des gekündigten Pächters; **~ tenant** ausziehender Mieter, abgebender Pächter.

waylayer Wegelagerer.

wayleave *(Br.)* Durchgangs-, Wegerecht, *(airplane)* Überfliegungsrecht;
~ rent Wege[rechts]gebühr.

waymaker Wegbereiter, Bahnbrecher.
waymark Wegzeichen, Meilenstein.
waypost Wegweiser.
wayside Straßenrand, -seite;
  by the ~ am Straßenrand (Wege);
  to fall by the ~ der Mißachtung anheimfallen; **to go by the** ~
  (fig.) baden gehen;
  ~ **inn** Gasthaus an der Landstraße; ~ **station** Haltepunkt.
wayward unberechenbar, launisch, schwankend;
  ~ **child** *(US)* moralisch gefährdetes Kind.
waywarden *(Br.)* Straßenwart.
weak schwach, anfällig, empfindlich, kränklich, nicht gesund,
  (character) haltlos, labil, charakterschwach, *(photo)* weich,
  (stock exchange) schwach, flau;
  financially ~ finanzschwach;
  ~ **in mind** geistesschwach; ~ **of purpose** ohne Entschlußkraft; ~
  as water ganz schwach;
  to hold ~ *(market)* flau liegen; **to turn** ~ *(market)* schwach
  werden;
  ~ **crew** zahlenmäßig geringe Besatzung; ~ **currency** schwache
  Währung; ~**-currency country** währungsschwaches Land; **to
  have** ~ **knees** kein Rückgrat haben; ~ **market** schwacher Markt;
  ~**-minded** geistesschwach; ~**-mindedness** Geistesschwäche; ~
  point schwache Stelle, wunder Punkt; ~ **side** schwache Seite;
  ~**-spirited** verzagt, kleinmütig; **to put one's finger on s. one's** ~
  spot jds. Schwäche erkennen; ~ **stomach** empfindlicher Magen;
  ~ **tea** dünner Tee.
weaken *(v.)* in einem Entschluß schwankend werden, *(stock
  exchange)* nachgeben, abschwächen, schwächer werden.
weakening *(stock exchange)* Abschwächung, Nachgeben;
  ~ **of economic activity** Konjunkturabschwächung.
weaker *(stock exchange)* abgeschwächt;
  ~ **tendency in prices** Kursabschwächung.
weakling Schwächling.
weakly schwächlich.
weakness *(market)* schwache Marktlage, Schwäche, *(object of
  special desire, coll.)* Schwäche, Vorliebe;
  ~ **of old age** Altersschwäche; ~ **of constitution** *(med.)* Konstitu-
  tionsschwäche; ~ **of a country's defences** schwache Stelle in der
  Landesverteidigung; ~ **in the market** Marktschwäche, Abgleiten der Kurse; ~ **of mind** Geistesschwäche; ~ **of prices** Kursabschwächung; ~ **in sterling (of the pound)** Schwäche des
  Pfundes, Pfundschwäche;
  to be inclined to ~ *(market)* zur Schwäche neigen; **to develop** ~
  schwach werden; **to have a** ~ **for s. th.** Schwäche für etw. haben.
weal, common (general, public) Allgemeinwohl.
wealth Vermögen, Besitz, *(abundance)* Fülle, *(riches)* Reichtum,
  Wohlhabenheit, große Besitzungen;
  active ~ flüssiges Kapital; **national** ~ Volksvermögen;
  ~ **of examples** Fülle von Beispielen; ~ **of experience** Erfah-
  rungsschatz; ~ **of illustrations** Vielzahl von Abbildungen; **all
  the** ~ **of the Indies** alle Reichtümer dieser Welt; ~ **of a nation**
  Volksvermögen;
  to acquire (amass) great ~ großes Vermögen erwerben; **to be
  rolling in** ~ im Gelde schwimmen; **to come to** ~ zu Vermögen
  gelangen, vermögend werden; **to create** ~ Vermögen bilden; **to
  gamble away half one's** ~ sein halbes Vermögen verspekulieren; **to rake together** ~ Reichtümer sammeln;
  ~**-creating sector** produktiver Sektor; ~ **creation** Vermögensbildung; ~ **flow** Vermögensertrag; ~ **formation** Vermögensbildung; ~ **fund** Kapitalvermögen; ~ **tax** Besteuerung großen
  Vermögens, Vermögenssteuer.
wealthy vermögend, reich, wohlhabend, gut situiert, kapitalkräftig;
  to make ~ bereichern.
weapon Waffe, Kampfmittel;
  close-range ~ Nahbereichswaffe; **conventional** ~**s** konventionelle Waffen; **deadly** ~ tödliche Waffe; **multipurpose** ~ Mehrzweckwaffe; **nuclear** ~**s** Atomwaffen; **tailored-effect** ~ Waffe
  mit maßgerecht begrenztem Wirkungskreis;
  ~ **of defence** Verteidigungswaffe; ~**s of mass destruction** Mas-
  senvernichtungswaffen; ~ **of offence** Angriffswaffe;
  ~**s activities** Waffengeschäft; ~ **budget** Waffenetat; ~**s development** Waffenentwicklung; ~**s production** Waffenproduktion; ~
  stock Waffenlager; ~**s system** Waffensystem.
weaponeer Atombombenschärfer.
weaponry Waffensystem.
wear Bekleidung, Mode, *(wearing quality)* Haltbarkeit;
  allowing for ~ **and tear** unter Berücksichtigung der Abnutzung; **in general** ~ modern, in Mode; **subject to** ~ abnutzbar,
  dem Verschleiß unterworfen;

household ~ Hauskleidung; **machine** ~ maschinelle Abnutzung; **tire (tyre,** *Br.***)** ~ Reifenabnutzung;
  fair ~ **and tear** [natürliche] Abnutzung, Abnutzung durch
  Gebrauch; **[natural]** ~ **and tear** Verschleiß, Abnutzung durch
  Gebrauch, *(balance sheet)* Abschreibung für Wertminderung;
  ~ *(v.)* tragen, bekleidet sein, *(impair)* abnutzen, sich abnützen;
  ~ **away** langsam vergehen, *(inscription)* verblassen, *(v./i.)* sich
  abtragen, abgenutzt werden, *(rocks)* auswaschen, erodieren,
  (time) schleichen; ~ **away the steps** Stufen abtreten; ~ **the
  breeches** das Regiment führen, die Hosen anhaben; ~ **the
  crown** Krone tragen, König sein, *(fig.)* zum Märtyrer werden; ~
  down the enemy's resistance feindlichen Widerstand brechen; ~ **down the opposition** Widerstand überwinden; ~ **the
  steps down** Treppenstufen austreten; ~ **to an end** langsam zu
  Ende gehen; **s. o. into stubbornness** j. abstumpfen lassen; ~
  the mantle of the poor sich als arm ausgeben; ~ **a neglected look**
  vernachlässigt aussehen; ~ **off** sich abtragen (verbrauchen),
  (impression) sich verlieren, *(goods)* sich verschleißen, *(novelty)*
  Neuheitswert verlieren, verblassen; ~ **on** *(story)* sich in die
  Länge ziehen, *(time)* sich dahinschleppen; ~ **on s. o.** jem. auf
  die Nerven gehen; ~ **out** zermürben, *(goods)* sich verschleißen;
  ~ **out s. one's patience** jds. Geduld erschöpfen; ~ **out one's
  welcome** seinen Besuch zu lange ausdehnen; ~ **the petticoat**
  unter dem Pantoffel stehen; ~ **thin** fadenscheinig werden; ~
  through the day Tag mit Mühe überstehen; ~ **towards its close**
  sich dem Ende zuneigen; ~ **well** sich gut halten; ~ **for years**
  viele Jahre halten; ~ **one's years well** für seine Jahre jung
  aussehen;
  to be apt to ~ **out** sich leicht abnutzen; **to begin to look the worse
  for** ~ allmählich schäbig werden; **to look the worse for** ~
  ziemlich abgenutzt aussehen; **to show signs of** ~ Abnutzungser-
  scheinungen aufweisen; **to specialize in children's** ~ sich auf
  Kinderkleidung spezialisiert haben; **to stand any amount of
  hard** ~ äußerst haltbar sein.
weariful ermüdend, anstrengend.
wearing| **of uniform** Uniform tragen;
  ~ *(a.)* abnützend, verschleißend;
  ~ **apparel** [unpfändbare] Kleidungsstücke; ~ **day** anstrengender Tag; ~ **journey** anstrengende Reise.
wearisome mühsam, beschwerlich;
  ~ **task** langweilige Aufgabe.
weary müde, matt, schlapp, schlaff, *(fig.)* überdrüssig,
  mißmutig;
  ~ **of living all alone** verbittert über das ständige Alleinsein;
  ~ *(v.)* **out** erschöpfen, *(time)* sich hinquälen; ~ **s. o. with
  requests** jem. mit ständigen Bitten auf den Wecker fallen;.
  to be ~ **of s. one's constant grumble** jds. ständige Nörgeleien
  nicht mehr ertragen können; **to be** ~ **of writing letters of thank**
  das Schreiben von Danksagungsbriefen satt haben.
weasel *(fig.)* hinterhältiger Mensch, Schleicher, *(mil.)* geländegängiges Amphibienfahrzeug;
  ~ *(v.)* **out** *(coll.)* sich um etw. herumdrücken;
  to catch a ~ **asleep** jds. Wachsamkeit hintergehen;
  ~ **phrase** doppelsinnige Phrase; **allpurpose** ~ **power** universale
  Verwendbarkeit einer doppelsinnigen Ausdrucksweise; ~
  word *(US)* doppelsinniges Wort.
weather Wetter, Witterung, *(meteorological change)* Wetterveränderung, Witterungswechsel, *(storm)* Unwetter;
  above the ~ *(plane)* über der Wetterzone, sehr hoch, *(sober)*
  wieder nüchtern; **in the** ~ im Freien, der Witterung ausgesetzt;
  in sub-zero ~ bei Temperaturen unter Null; ~ **permitting** falls
  das Wetter es zuläßt; **under the** ~ *(coll.)* in Geldschwierigkeiten, *(tipsy)* beschwipst; **under stress of the** ~ wetterabhängig;
  ~**s** *(vicissitude of fortune)* Wechselfälle;
  April ~ Aprilwetter; **bad** ~ Schlechtwetter; **fair (fine)** ~ Schön-
  wetter; **frosty** ~ Frostwetter; **queen's** ~ Sonnenschein, schönes
  Wetter, Kaiserwetter; **rainy** ~ Regenwetter; **showery** ~ Schau-
  erwetter; **sultry** ~ Schwüle;
  ~ *(v.)* dem Wetter aussetzen, austrocknen lassen, *(v./i.)* verwit-
  tern, *(fig.)* Klippe umschiffen;
  ~ **along** *(mar.)* trotz ungünstigen Wetters vorwärtskommen; ~
  a cape Kap passieren; ~ **a crisis** Krise überstehen (überwinden); ~ **a roof** Dach abschrägen; ~ **a storm** Sturm überstehen;
  ~ **upon s. o.** j. ausnutzen; ~ **many bitter winters** *(house)* viele
  harte Winter überstehen;
  to be under the ~ in schlechter Verfassung sein; **to be still under
  the** ~ Geldschwierigkeiten noch nicht überwunden haben; **to
  feel under the** ~ *(coll.)* wetterabhängig (wetterfühlig) sein; **to
  forecast the** ~ Wettervorhersage machen; **to go out in all** ~**s** bei
  jeder Witterung spazierengehen; **to hope for a break in the** ~ auf
  eine Wetterveränderung hoffen; **to make fair** ~ sich von seiner

freundlichsten Seite zeigen; **to make heavy ~ of s. th.** viel Umstände (Wirbel) wegen etw. machen; **to make good ~** *(mar.)* auf gutes Wetter stoßen;
the ~ will continue changeable Fortdauer des veränderlichen Wetters;
~ analysis Wetteranalyse; **~ anomaly** Wetteranomalie; **~-beaten** verwittert; **~-bound** *(ship)* am Auslaufen verhindert; **~ box** Wetterhäuschen; **~ bureau** Wetteramt, amtliche Wettervorhersagestätte; **~ cast** *(US)* Wettervorhersage; **~ caster** *(US)* Wetteransager, -prophet, Meteorologe; **~ center** *(US)* **(centre,** *Br.***)** Wettervorhersagezentrum; **~ change** Wetterwechsel; **~ chart** Wetterkarte; **~ conditions** Witterungseinflüsse, Wetterverhältnisse, -bedingungen; **~ data** Wetterergebnisse; **~ deck** Sturm-, Wetterdeck; **to keep one's ~ eye open** *(fig.)* auf der Hut sein; **~ forecast** Wetterbericht, -meldung, -ansage; **long-sighted ~ forecast** langfristige Wettervorhersage; **to carry a ~ forecast** Wetterbericht bringen; **~ gauge** *(fig.)* vorteilhafte Stellung (Lage); **~ improvement** Wetterbesserung; **~ insurance** Reisewetterversicherung; **~ map** Wetterkarte; **~ modification** Wetterbeeinflussung; **~ patterns** Witterungsverhältnisse; **general ~ pattern** Großwetterlage; **~ plane** Wetterflugzeug; **~ prophet** Wetterprophet; **~ report** Wetternachrichten, -bericht; **~ satellite** Wettersatellit; **~ service** Wetterdienst; **ocean ~ ship** Schiff des Wetterdienstes; **~ side** *(mar.)* Wetterseite, *(ship)* Windseite; **~ situation** Wetterlage; **~ station** Wetterstation, -warte; **~ strip** *(window)* Dichtungsleiste; **~ working days** wetterabhängige Arbeitstage.
weathercock Wetterhahn.
weatherdrome schwimmende Wetterstation.
weathered verwittert.
weatherglass Barometer.
weatherize *(v.)* **a building** Gebäude wetterfest machen.
weatherman Meteorologe, Wetteransager.
weatherproof wetterfest.
weathertight wetterfest, -dicht.
weave *(v.)* weben, wirken, *(fig.)* ersinnen, erfinden;
~ baskets Körbe flechten; **~ a plot** Komplott schmieden; **~ a story** Geschichte erfinden; **~ one's way through the traffic** sich durch den Verkehr schlängeln; **~ through a valley** *(road)* sich durch ein Tal winden.
web *(broadcasting, sl.)* Sendenetz, *(iron construction)* Tragrippe, *(network)* Gewebe, Netzwerk, *(papermaking)* Papierbahn, *(print.)* Rotationsdruck, *(wheel)* Radscheibe;
~ of business wirtschaftliche Verflechtung; **~ of intrigues** Intrigennetz; **~ of lies** Lügengewebe; **~ of railroads** *(US)* **(railway lines,** *Br.***)** Schienennetz;
to escape the ~ durch die Maschen schlüpfen;
~ defence *(mil.)* gestaffelte Verteidigung; **~ press** Rotationspresse.
wedded verheiratet;
~ to one's own opinions nur mit sich selbst beschäftigt;
~ life Eheleben.
wedding Hochzeitsfeier;
golden ~ goldene Hochzeit;
~ anniversary Hochzeitstag; **~ announcement** Heiratsanzeige; **~ breakfast** Hochzeitsessen; **~ cake** Hochzeitskuchen; **~ card** Vermählungsanzeige; **~ ceremony** Trauung; **~ day** Hochzeitstag; **~ party** Hochzeitsgesellschaft; **~ present** Hochzeitsgeschenk; **~ reception** Hochzeitsempfang; **~ tour (trip)** Hochzeitsreise.
wedge *(fig., mil.)* Keil, *(strip of land)* keilförmiges Stück Land, *(met.)* Hochdruckkeil, *(mil.)* Keilformation;
~ of cold air Kaltluftkeil; **~ of a cake** Kuchenstück;
~ *(v.)* **o. s. in** sich hineinzwängen; **~ off** abspalten, abtrennen; **~ a door open** Tür durch einen Keil aufbrechen;
to get in at the thin end of the ~ *(fig.)* Anfang machen.
wedlock Verheiratung, Trauung, *(state of marriage)* Ehe[stand];
born lawful in ~ ehelich [geboren]; **born out of ~** außer-, unehelich.
wee ein Weilchen;
to wait a ~ Augenblick warten.
weed Unkraut, *(fig.)* Schwächling, *(cheap cigar, coll.)* Glimmstengel;
~ *(v.)* jäten, von Unkraut befreien, *(fig.)* von unerfreulichen Elementen befreien, ausmisten, *(organization)* durchforsten;
~ a garden Unkraut jäten, *(fig.)* Betrieb durchforsten; **~ off** *(sl.)* einem Banknotenbündel entnehmen; **~ a stock of goods** Warenlager räumen; **~ out** ausmerzen, aussondern; **~ out a crime** Verbrechen ausrotten; **~ out the surplus plant and manpower** betriebliche und personelle Überkapazitäten abbauen; **~ out dead wood** Überflüssiges ausrangieren;

to be running to ~s vom Unkraut überwuchert sein;
~ killer Unkrautvernichtungsmittel.
weeding Unkrautjäten, *(organization)* Durchforstung.
week Woche;
by the ~ wochenweise; **for ~s on end** wochenlang hintereinander;
40-hour ~ Vierzigstundenwoche; **working ~** Arbeitswoche; **~ of delay** Verzugswoche; **~ under review** Berichtswoche; **~ of Sundays** lange Zeit;
to take a ~ off sich eine Woche freimachen (-nehmen);
~'s notice wöchentliche Kündigung; **~ order** *(stock exchange, US)* eine Woche gültiger Börsenauftrag.
weekday Wochentag, Werktag;
on ~s werktäglich;
~ service Fahrplan für Werktage; **~ traffic** Berufsverkehr.
weekend, away over the ~ übers Wochenende verreist;
~ *(v.)* Wochenende verbringen;
to spend the ~ with friends Wochenende mit Freunden verbringen;
~ cottage Ferien-, Wochenendhaus; **~ entertainment** Wochenendprogramm; **~ order** Wochenendauftrag; **~ paper** Wochenendzeitung; **special ~ rates** günstiger Wochenendtarif; **~ recreation** Wochenenderholung; **~ retreat** Wochenendasyl; **~ sale** Wochenendverkauf; **~ shack** Wochenendhaus; **occasional ~ shift** gelegentlich am Wochenende erforderliche Arbeitstätigkeit; **~ stay** Wochenendausflug; **~ ticket** Wochenendfahrkarte; **~ visit to the country** Wochenendausflug aufs Land.
weekender Wochenendausflügler.
weekly Wochenblatt, -zeitung, -zeitschrift;
~ *(a.)* wöchentlich;
~ account of work done wöchentliche Arbeitsfortschrittsabrechnung; **~ allowance** wöchentliches Taschengeld; **~ benefit** wöchentlich gezahlte Unterstützung; **~ bill** Wochenrechnung; **~ delivery** wöchentliche Lieferung; **overall ~ earnings** durchschnittlicher Wochenverdienst; **~ fixture** *(banking)* Geld auf eine Woche; **~ gazette** wöchentlich erscheinende Zeitung, Wochenblatt; **~ instal(l)ment** wöchentliche Rate, Wochenrate; **~ magazine** Wochenzeitschrift; **~ market** Wochenmarkt; **~ newspaper** Wochenblatt, -zeitung; **~ paper** wöchentlich erscheinende Zeitschrift, Wochenblatt; **~ pay** Wochenlohn; **~ report** Wochenbericht, wöchentlicher Bericht; **~ return** *(Br.)* **(statement)** Wochenausweis; **~ wages** Wochenlohn; **~ wages return** *(Br.)* wöchentliche Lohnliste.
weeper Trauerflor, -binde, *(movie, sl.)* Schmachtfetzen.
weeping cross, to return by the zu Kreuze kriechen müssen.
weigh *(v.)* Gewicht feststellen, wiegen, *(fig.)* von Bedeutung sein, Gewicht haben;
~ against Gegengewicht bilden; **~ anchor** Anker lichten; **~ the claims** Ansprüche abwägen; **~ down** niederdrücken; **~ evidence** Beweis würdigen; **~ in** *(luggage)* abwiegen; **~ in at 12 tons** 12 Tonnen brutto wiegen; **~ in the gross** Bruttogewicht feststellen, brutto wiegen; **~ with the judge** *(evidence)* Richter beeinflussen; **~ heavy on s. one's mind** j. bedrücken; **~ out** ab-, ver-, auswiegen, *(sell by the weight)* nach [dem] Gewicht verkaufen; **~ one plan against the other** verschiedene Pläne gegeneinander abwiegen; **~ the pros and cons** das Für und Wider gegeneinander abwägen; **~ up the consequences of an action** Folgen einer Handlung bedenken; **~ with s. o.** bei jem. ausschlaggebend sein; **~ one's words** seine Worte abwägen.
weighage Wiegegeld, -gebühr.
weighed down niedergedrückt;
~ with cares von Sorgen bedrückt.
weighhouse öffentliche Waage, Stadtwaage.
weighing Wiegen;
check ~ Nachwiegen;
~ debt drückende Schuld; **~ machine** Waage.
weighmaster Wiegemeister.
weight Gewicht, Schwere, *(burden)* Gewicht, Druck, Bürde, Last, *(importance)* Bedeutung, Gewicht, Wichtigkeit, Ansehen, Einfluß, *(market research)* Bewerten, Bewertung, *(statistics)* relative Bedeutung, *(unit of weight)* Gewichtseinheit;
by ~ nach Gewicht; **of no ~** ohne Bedeutung; **of great ~** von großer Bedeutung; **superior in ~** schwerer; **under ~** zu leicht, untergewichtig, zu geringes Gewicht;
additional ~ Gewichtszuschlag; **agreed ~** *(carrier)* einverständlich festgelegtes Gewicht; **allowed free ~** Frei-, Reingewicht; **apothecary's ~** Apothekergewicht; **carload minimum ~** *(railroad, US)* Mindestgewicht einer Stückgutladung; **chargeable ~** frachtpflichtiges Gewicht; **commercial ~** handelsübliches Gewicht, Handelsgewicht; **dead ~** Leer-, Eigengewicht, Gewichtsfracht; **~ delivered** Eingangsgewicht, Abladegewicht;

dutiable ~ zollpflichtiges Gewicht; **excess** ~ Mehr-, Übergewicht; **false** ~ falsches Gewicht; **freight** ~ Ladungsgewicht, Gewicht der Ladung; **full** ~ reelles (volles) Gewicht; **gross** ~ Bruttogewicht [incl. Verpackung]; **honest** ~ volles Gewicht; **invoice** ~ Rechnungsgewicht; **live** ~ lebendes Gewicht; **maximum** ~ Höchstgewicht; **maximum permissible** ~ höchstzulässiges Gewicht; **miner's** ~ vereinbarte Fördermengen; **minimum** ~ Mindestgewicht; **net** ~ Rein-, Leer-, Eigen-, Trocken-, Nettogewicht; **permissible** ~ zulässiges Gewicht; **shipping** ~ Frachtgewicht, Gewicht einer Ladung; **short** ~ Minder-, Untergewicht, knappes (fehlendes) Gewicht; **specific** ~ spezifisches Gewicht; **stamped** ~ geeichtes Gewicht, Eichgewicht; **standard** ~ Normal-, gesetzliches Gewicht; **surplus** ~ Mehr-, Übergewicht; **ton** ~ Gewichtstonne; **total** ~ Gesamtgewicht; **troy** ~ Goldgewicht; **true** ~ genaues Gewicht;

~ **of age** Bürde des Alters; ~ **of authority** überwiegende (herrschende) Meinung; ~ **of evidence** Last des Beweismaterials; ~ **when empty** Leergewicht; ~ **of fine gold** Feingoldgehalt; ~**s and measures** Maße und Gewichte; **great** ~ **off one's mind** große Last von der Seele; ~ **of packing** Verpackungsgewicht; **great** ~ **of responsibility** große Verantwortungslast; ~ **of** ~ (mil.) volle Breitseite;

~ (v.) wiegen, (load with weight) mit einem Gewicht belasten, (market research) bewerten, (increase by adding inferior quantities) durch Beimischungen schwerer machen, (statistics) relative Bedeutung geben;

~ (v.) **the scales in favo(u)r of s. o.** jem. einen [unerlaubten] Vorteil verschaffen;

to add to the ~ Bedeutung einer Sache erhöhen; **to be a** ~ **off one's mind** Stein vom Herzen haben; **to be deficient in** ~ kein volles Gewicht haben; **to be worth one's** ~ **in gold** nicht mit Gold zu bezahlen sein; **to buy by [the]** ~ nach dem Gewicht kaufen; **to carry** ~s Lasten tragen; **to carry** ~ **with s. o.** großen Einfluß bei jem. haben; **to exceed the** ~ Gewicht überschreiten; **to fall short of** ~ nicht das notwendige Gewicht haben; **to gauge** ~ Gewicht eichen; **to give** ~ **to s. th.** einer Sache große Bedeutung beimessen; **to give full** ~ gutes Gewicht geben; **to have a great** ~ **of responsibility** schwere Verantwortung tragen müssen; **to have to support the** ~ **of the roof** Dach mit tragen müssen; **to keep papers down with a** ~ Papiere mit einem Gewicht beschweren; **to lose** ~ abnehmen; **to make one's** ~ den Gewichtsanforderungen entsprechen; **to pull one's** ~ seinen Teil dazu beitragen, (fig.) aktiv mitarbeiten; **to seal** ~s **and measures** Maße und Gewichte stempeln; **to sell by** ~ nach [dem] Gewicht verkaufen; **to throw one's** ~ **about** seinen Einfluß (seine Position) geltend machen;

~ **cargo** Schwergut; **to be a** ~ **catcher** Abmagerungskur durchführen; ~ **certificate** Gewichtsbescheinigung; ~ **deficiency** Fehlgewicht, Gewichtsmanko; ~ **goods** Schwergut; ~ **limit** (postal service) Gewichtsgrenze, Höchstgewicht; ~ **note** Wiegeschein, Gewichtsnota; ~ **stamp** Wiegestempel; **first** ~ **step** (mail) erste Gewichtserhöhung.

weighted beladen, belastet;
to be ~ **in favo(u)r of s. o.** zu jds. Gunsten gewürdigt werden;
~ **average** Bewertungsdurchschnitt; ~ **index** gewogener Index, Bewertungsindex; ~ **mean** gewogener Mittelwert (Durchschnitt); ~ **voting** Mehrfachstimmrecht.

weighting (index number) Ausgewogenheit.

weightless ohne Gewicht, leicht, (fig.) unbedeutend, (in spacecraft) schwerelos.

weightlessness Gewichtslosigkeit, Leichtheit;
to become accustomed to ~ **in a spacecraft** sich an die Schwerelosigkeit in einem Raumschiff gewöhnen.

weighty triftig, (heavy) schwer, (having influence) einflußreich, angesehen, (momentous) gewichtig, schwerwiegend;
~ **considerations** bedeutsame Überlegungen; ~ **matter** vorrangiges Problem.

weir Wehr;
~ **system** Prämienlohnsystem.

welch (v.) sich seinen Zahlungsverpflichtungen entziehen.

welcome Willkommen, Willkommensgruß, Empfang, Begrüßung;
enthusiastic ~ begeisterter Empfang;
~ **as snow in the harvest** völlig unerwünscht; **and** ~ **to it** es kann mir gestohlen bleiben;
~ (v.) begrüßen, willkommen heißen, freundlich aufnehmen;
~ **a proposal** Vorschlag gern annehmen; ~ **a suggestion coldly** Vorschlag sehr kühl aufnehmen;
to be ~ **to the use of a library** Bibliothek benutzen dürfen; **to bid s. o.** ~ j. willkommen heißen; **to make s. o.** ~ j. willkommen heißen, j. freundlich aufnehmen.

~ **address** Begrüßungsansprache; ~ **guest** willkommener Gast; ~ **letter** Begrüßungsbrief; ~ **mat** roter Teppich; **to spread out the** ~ **mat for s. o.** für j. den roten Teppich ausrollen; ~ **news** angenehme Nachrichten.

weld (v.) zusammenschweißen, (fig.) eng verbinden, -schmelzen.

welfare Wohlergehen, Wohlfahrt, Wohlstand, (US, assistance) Sozialhilfe, (~ work) soziale Einrichtungen, Fürsorgearbeit, -tätigkeit, Sozialhilfe;
child ~ Jugendfürsorge; **common (general)** ~ Gemeinnutzen, -wohl; **compulsory** ~ soziale Abgaben; **industrial** ~ betriebliche Sozial-, Betriebsfürsorge; **infant** ~ Säuglingsfürsorge; **maternity** ~ Fürsorge für Mutter und Kind; **public** ~ (US) öffentliche Wohlfahrt (Fürsorge), Sozialhilfe; **social** ~ soziale Fürsorge;
~ **of children** Jugendfürsorge; ~ **of the handicapped** Behindertenfürsorge; ~ **of troops in the field** Truppenbetreuung;
to be on ~ (US) Fürsorgeunterstützung (Sozialhilfe) beziehen; **to be eligible for** ~ sozialhilfe-, fürsorgeberechtigt sein; **to be solicitous for s. one's** ~ um jds. Wohlbefinden besorgt sein; **to go off** ~ (US) keine Sozialhilfe mehr bekommen; **to work for the** ~ **of the nation** sich um die öffentliche Wohlfahrt verdient machen;
~ **activity** Fürsorge, Wohlfahrtstätigkeit; ~ **agency** (US) Fürsorge-, Sozial-, Wohlfahrtsamt, Fürsorgebehörde; ~ **aid** (US) Sozialhilfe; ~ **assistant** Sozialpfleger; ~ **association** soziales Hilfswerk, Fürsorgeverband; ~ **beneficiary** Wohlfahrts-, Sozialhilfe-, Unterstützungsempfänger; ~ **benefits** Sozialhilfe-, Fürsorgeleistungen, (US) Sozialausgaben; ~ **branch** (US) Fürsorgebehörde; ~ **budget** Sozialbudget; **to save $ 10,8 m last year on the** ~ **budget** im Vorjahr 10,8 Mio Dollar geringere Sozialausgaben haben; ~ **caseworker** Sozialfürsorger; ~ **center** (US) Wohlfahrts-, Fürsorgeeinrichtung, Fürsorgestelle, -amt; **to crack down on** ~ **cheats** Betrügereien beim Bezug von Sozialhilfe den Garaus machen; ~ **check** (US) (cheque, Br.) Wohlfahrtsunterstützung, Sozialhilfe; ~ **client** Sozial-, Fürsorgeempfänger; **public** ~ **committee** Wohlfahrts-, Fürsorge-, Sozialausschuß, Sozialbeirat; ~ **costs** Fürsorgelasten, Sozialaufwand; ~ **department** Sozialabteilung; ~ **economics** Wohlfahrtstheorie; ~ **expenditure** soziale Kosten, Fürsorgeausgaben, -lasten, (US) Sozialaufwand; ~ **expert** Sozialpädagoge, Fürsorgeexperte; ~ **facilities** Sozialeinrichtungen; ~ **family** von der Sozialhilfe lebende Familie, von der Fürsorge unterstützte Familie, Fürsorgefamilie; ~ **features** Merkmale der Fürsorge, Fürsorgemerkmale; ~ **functions** soziale Fürsorge-, Wohlfahrtsfunktionen, Wohlfahrtsaufgaben; ~ **fund** Unterstützungsfonds, Sozialfonds; **public** ~ **funds** Wohlfahrts-, Unterstützungsfonds; ~ **grant** Sozialzuschuß; ~ **home** Fürsorgeanstalt; ~ **housing** Unterbringung in Fürsorgeanstalten; ~ **indicator** Wohlfahrtsindikator; ~ **institutions** Sozialeinrichtungen, soziales Hilfswerk; ~ **legislation** Fürsorge-, Sozialgesetzgebung; ~ **load** soziale Belastungen, Belastungen des Sozialbudgets (Fürsorgeetats); ~ **management** betriebliche Sozialfürsorge; ~ **meals** kostenlos ausgegebene Mahlzeiten [der Wohlfahrt]; ~**-minded** sozial eingestellt; ~ **officer** Sozialfürsorger, Fürsorgebeamter, Wohlfahrtpfleger, Fürsorgerin; ~ **organization** Fürsorge-, Wohlfahrtsverband; ~ **payment** Wohlfahrtsunterstützung, Unterstützungszahlung, Sozialzuwendung; ~ **policies** Fürsorge-, Sozialpolitik; ~ **program(me)** Unterstützungs-, Fürsorgeprogramm; ~ **provisions** Sozialbestimmungen, Fürsorgevorkehrungen; ~ **purpose** Unterstützungszweck; ~ **recipient** Sozialhilfe-, Fürsorge-, Wohlfahrtsempfänger; ~ **reform** Reform der Fürsorgetätigkeit, Sozialreform; ~ **reform plan** Pläne zur Reform des Sozialwesens; ~ **roll** Fürsorgeliste, Liste der Sozialhilfeempfänger; **to end up on the** ~ **rolls** schließlich der Fürsorge zur Last fallen; **to expand the** ~ **rolls** Kreis der Fürsorgeberechtigten ausweiten; **to put on the** ~ **rolls** auf die Liste der Sozialhilfeempfänger (Fürsorgeunterstützungsempfänger) setzen; ~ **rules** Fürsorge-, Sozialhilfebestimmungen; ~ **services** Sozial-, Fürsorgeleistungen; **maternity** ~ **service** Mütterberatungsdienst; ~ **spending** Sozialaufwand; ~ **state** Fürsorge-, Wohlfahrtsstaat; ~ **statism** Fürsorge-, Wohlfahrtssystem, Sozialsystem; ~ **supervisor** Aufsichtsbeamter der Fürsorge (Sozialhilfe); ~ **system** Fürsorge-, Sozialsystem, Fürsorgewesen; **to rewrite the** ~ **system** Sozialgesetzgebung neu fassen; ~ **work** fürsorgerische Tätigkeit, soziale Fürsorge[tätigkeit], Sozialarbeit, Wohlfahrtspflege, (factory) betriebliche Sozialfürsorge; **industrial** ~ **work** Arbeiterfürsorge, betriebliche Sozialfürsorge; **public** ~ **work** öffentliche Fürsorge; ~ **work for the unemployed** Arbeitslosenfürsorge; **to do** ~ **work** sich fürsorgerisch betätigen, in der Fürsorge tätig sein; ~ **worker** Fürsorgebeamter, Wohlfahrtpfleger, (factory) Sozialfürsorger, -referent.

welfarism Wohlfahrtspraktiken, Fürsorgesystem, Sozialhilfesystem, wohlfahrtsstaatliche Prinzipien.

welfarist wohlfahrtsstaatlich.

well [Zieh]brunnen, *(architecture)* Licht-, Aufzugsschacht, *(in a car)* Gepäckraum, *(gas, oil, water)* Bohrloch, Bohrung, *(Br., law court)* eingefriedeter Platz [für Anwälte], *(mineral spring)* Heilquelle, Mineralbrunnen, *(mining)* senkrechter Grubenbau, Schacht, *(source)* Wurzel, Ursprung, Quelle;

completed ~ *(oil prospecting)* fündiger Schacht;

~ *(v.)* **over** überfließen; ~ **up** heraussprudeln;

to sink a ~ Brunnen bohren;

~ **drain** Abzugs-, Drainagegraben; **~-drain** *(v.)* durch Drainage trocken legen, entwässern; ~ **house** Brunnenkammer; ~ **room** *(spring resort)* Brunnenhalle; ~ **sinking** Brunnenbau; ~ **spring** Quelle; ~ **staircase** Wendeltreppe; ~ **water** Brunnenwasser;

~ *(a.)* gut, wohl, *(to a suitable degree)* genügend, ordentlich, ganz, völlig, *(easily)* mit Leichtigkeit, *(friendly)* freundlich, freundschaftlich, *(healthy)* wohl, gesund, *(intimately)* gründlich, genau, *(in a proper manner)* passend, geschickt, *(marine insurance)* sicher, seetüchtig, *(profitable)* vorteilhaft, günstig, *(with propriety)* korrekterweise, mit gutem Grund;

to be ~ off gut situiert sein; **to be ~ on in years** schon bejahrt sein; **to be ~ out of s. th.** etw. gut hinter sich gebracht haben; **to be ~ up in s. th.** sattelfest in etw. sein; **to be ~ up in a list** weit oben in einer Liste stehen; **to behave ~** sich richtig benehmen; **to come off ~** es gut haben; **to do ~** recht daran tun, *(make good profit)* gut verdienen; **to feel perfectly ~** sich ausgezeichnet fühlen; **to know s. o. ~** j. gut kennen; **to live ~** in guten Verhältnissen leben; **to remember ~** sich gut erinnern; **to stand ~ with s. o.** sich mit jem. gut stehen; **to think ~ before speaking** erst nachdenken und dann reden; **to treat s. o. ~** j. gut behandeln;

~-acquired wohlerworben; ~ **advanced in years** in fortgeschrittenem Alter; **~-advised** gut überlegt; **~-aimed** gezielt; ~ **appointed** wohl ausgerüstet; ~ **away** weit weg; **~-balanced** im Gleichgewicht, *(fig.)* ausgeglichen; **~-beaten way** ausgetretener Weg; **~-behaved child** wohlerzogenes Kind; **economic ~-being** Wohlstand; **national ~-being** Volkswohlstand; **~-bred** gut erzogen, gesittet; **~-conditioned** in gutem Zustand; **~-conducted** gut geführt, *(of good behavio(u)r)* von musterhaftem Betragen; **~-connected** aus guter Familie, mit guten Beziehungen; **~-deserved** wohlverdient; **~-disposed** gut aufgelegt, ausgeglichen; ~ **drain** Abzugs-, Drainagegraben; ~ **drilling** Bohrlochherstellung; **~-earned** wohlverdient; **~-edited** gut redigiert; **~-established** wohlerworben; **~-financed** mit reichlichen Mitteln ausgestattet; **~-fixed** *(US)* wohlhabend, gut betucht; **~-found** gut versorgt; **~-founded suspicion** wohlbegründeter Verdacht; **~-grounded** gebildet, fundiert, mit einer guten Vorbildung; **~-heeled** *(US sl.)* betucht, wohlhabend, bei Kasse; **~-informed** gut unterrichtet (informiert), bewandert, gut orientiert; **~-judged** wohl berechnet, taktvoll; **~-knowing** *(pleading)* bewußt; **~-known** weithin bekannt; **~-known people** bekannte Leute, Prominente; **~-landed** begütert; **~-mannered** mit guten Manieren, wohlerzogen; ~ **met** du kommst mir wie gerufen; **~-nigh impossible** so gut wie unmöglich; **~-off** bemittelt, gutsituiert, in guten Verhältnissen, wohlhabend; **to be ~-off** sich gut stehen; **~-oiled** *(fig.)* glatt, schmeichlerisch, *(tipsy, sl.)* beschwipst; **~-ordered** gut geführt; **~-organized** gut aufgezogen; **~-paid** gut bezahlt; **until ~ past midnight** bis lange nach Mitternacht; **to be ~-pleased** hocherfreut sein; **~-positioned** in einer guten Stellung; **very ~ possible** durchaus möglich; **~-preserved** gut erhalten; **~-priced** preisgünstig; **~-read** [sehr] belesen; **~-reputed** angesehen; **~-rounded** abgerundet, *(style)* formvollendet, elegant; **~-rounded education** vielseitige Bildung; **~-run** gut geführt; **~-situated business** Geschäft in guter Lage; **~-situated house** schön gelegenes Haus; **~-spent** gut verwendet; **~-stocked** wohlbesetzt, reichhaltig; **~-thought of** in gutem Rufe stehend; **~-thought out** ausgeklügelt; **~-thumbed** *(book)* abgegriffen; **~-timed** zeitgemäß, rechtzeitig; **~-to-do** *(Br.)* bemittelt, begütert, gut situiert, vermögend, wohlhabend; **~-tried method** erprobtes Verfahren; **~-turned** geschickt formuliert; ~ **up in the list** weit oben in der Liste; **to be ~ up in s. th.** sattelfest in etw. sein; **~-versed firm** erfahrene Firma; **~-warranted** einwandfreier Zustand zugesichert; **~-wisher** Gönner, wohlwollender Freund; **~-worn** abgetragen, *(fig.)* abgedroschen.

wellhead Quelle, *(structure built over)* Brunnenhäuschen.

wellhole Bohrloch.

welsh *(v.)* *(sl.)* behumpsen, *(evade payment, sl.)* sich seinen Zahlungsverpflichtungen entziehen.

welsher *(Br., sl.)* betrügerischer Buchmacher, Betrüger.

welshing Wettbetrug.

welter of political beliefs Durcheinander politischer Überzeugungen.

West, the der Westen;

to go ~ in die Brüche gehen, *(die, sl.)* abkratzen;

~ **coast** Westküste; ~ **end** vornehmes Stadtviertel.

western *(film)* Wildwestfilm;

~ *(a.)* westlich, abendländisch;

~ **boundary** Westgrenze; ~ **course** Westkurs; ~ **Europe** Westeuropa; ~ **European Union** Westeuropäische Union; ~ **Powers** Westmächte; **the ~ World** das Abendland.

westernize *(v.)* westlichen Charakter geben.

wet naß, durchnäßt, *(climate)* niederschlagsreich, feucht, regnerisch, *(coll., US)* nicht unter Alkoholverbot stehend, *(crazy, US sl.)* verkehrt, verrückt, *(unfashionable, sl.)* unmodern;

dripping ~ pudelnaß;

~ **behind the ears** noch nicht trocken hinter den Ohren; ~ **to the skin** naß bis auf die Haut;

~ *(v.)* **a bargain** *(sl.)* Ereignis begießen; ~ **one's whistler** *(coll.)* einen heben;

to get ~ to the skin bis auf die Haut durchnäßt werden;

~ **blanket** Dämpfer, kalte Dusche, *(person)* Spielverderber, Miesmacher; **~-blanket** *(v.)* entmutigen; **to be like a ~ blanket** wie eine kalte Dusche wirken; **to throw a ~ blanket on s. th.** einer Sache einen Dämpfer aufsetzen; ~ **dock** Flutbecken, Schleusenhafen; ~ **gas** Naturgas; ~ **goods** flüssige Waren; ~ **ideas** *(sl.)* Schnapsidee; ~ **nurse** Amme; **~-nurse** *(v.)* *(fig.)* verhätscheln, verzärteln; ~ **printing** Naß-in-Naß-Druck; ~ **process** Naßverfahren; ~ **season** Regenzeit; ~ **sock** *(sl.)* langweiliger Bursche; ~ **time** Schlechtwetterzeit; **~-time pay** Schlechtwetterzulage.

wetback *(sl.)* illegaler Einwanderer.

wetting, to get a durchnäßt werden.

whack *(sl.)* Chance;

on ~ *(marine, sl.)* auf niedrigsten Rationen; **out of ~** *(coll.)* kaputt, nicht funktionierend;

~ *(v.)* parzellieren, aufteilen;

~ **up** *(sl.)* Spielgewinne teilen;

to be in a fine ~ in erstklassigem Zustand sein; **to be out of ~** nicht in Ordnung sein; **to have had one's ~ of pleasure** sich köstlich amüsiert haben.

whacker *(sl.)* Mordsding.

whacking great lie faustdicke Lüge.

whale Wal[fisch];

a ~ of a time herrliche Zeit; ~ **of a lot** Riesenmenge;

to be a ~ at Kanone auf einem Gebiet sein; **to be a ~ for s. th.** auf etw. ganz versessen sein;

~ **fishing (fishery)** Walfang; ~ **oil** Walfischtran.

whaler Walfangschiff.

whalery *(US)* Walfangindustrie.

whaling Walfang;

~ **industry** Walfangindustrie; ~ **port** Walfanghafen; ~ **station** Walfangstation.

wharf Lande-, Lösch-, Ladeplatz, *(quay)* Kai, Dock, Pier, Anlegestelle, *(warehouse)* Lagerhaus [für nicht zollpflichtige Güter];

ex ~ ab Kai;

approved ~ amtlich genehmigter Löschplatz zollpflichtiger Waren; **private ~** Privatpier; **public ~** öffentlicher Anlegeplatz (Kai); **sufferance ~** Freihafen;

~ *(v.)* am Kai festmachen (anlegen), ausladen, Güter löschen, *(furnish with a wharf)* mit einem Kai versehen;

~ **dues** Dockgebühren, Kaigeld; ~ **duty** Kaigeld; ~ **labo(u)rer** Hafen-, Dockarbeiter; ~ **owner** Werftbesitzer; ~ **porter** Dock-, Hafenarbeiter; ~ **worker** Hafen-, Dockarbeiter.

wharfage Kaibenutzung, Lade-, Löschgelegenheit, *(charge)* Umschlaggebühr, Kai-, Löschgeld, Kaigebühr, Dockgebühren, *(handling of goods)* Löschen, Einlagern;

~ **charges** Kosten für die Verbringung an Land, Kaigebühren, Löschungskosten.

wharfing Kai-, Lösch-, Werftanlage.

wharfinger Kaiaufseher, -meister, *(owner-manager)* Werft-, Lagerhofbesitzer, Kaibesitzer;

~'s certificate *(Br.)* Kaiablieferungsbescheinigung; **~'s receipt** Lager-, Kaiannahmeschein; **~'s warrant** *(Br.)* Kailagerschein.

wharfman Kai-, Hafen-, Dockarbeiter.

wharfmaster Kaimeister, -aufseher.

wheat, bulk ~ loser Weizen; **sample ~** Musterweizen; **seed ~** Weizensaatgut;

to sift the chaff from the ~ Spreu vom Weizen scheiden;

~ **belt** *(US)* Weizengürtel; ~ **crop** Weizenernte; ~ **flour** Weizenmehl; ~ **glut** Weizenüberschuß; ~ **growing** Weizenanbau; ~ **harvest** Weizenernte; ~ **pitch** *(US)* Weizenbörse; ~ **shipment** Weizensendung, -lieferung; ~ **shortage** Weizenknappheit; ~ **zone** Weizenzone.

wheaten|**flour** Weizenmehl; ~ **straw** Weizenstroh.

wheedle *(v.)* beschwatzen, überreden;
~ **s. o. into buying s. o.** j. zum Kauf von etw. beschwatzen; ~ **s. o. out of his money** jem. Geld aus der Tasche locken (abluchsen).

wheel Wagenrad, *(car)* Steuer-, Lenkrad, *(transaction, sl.)* Geschäftsabschluß, *(US sl.)* Dollar;
at the ~ *(fig.)* an der Spitze, am Ruder; **on the** ~ auf Achse, unterwegs; **on** ~**s** auf Rädern, *(fig.)* wie geschmiert, sehr schnell;
big ~ *(US sl.)* hohes Tier; **Fortune's** ~ Glücksrad;
fifth ~ **of the coach** *(fig.)* fünftes Rad am Wagen, unnütze Person; ~**s of government** Regierungsapparat; ~**s of life** Räderwerk des Lebens; ~**s of thought** Arbeitsweise des Verstandes; ~**s within** ~**s** komplizierter Mechanismus, *(fig.)* komplizierte (verwickelte) Lage;
~ *(v.)* fahren, rollen;
~ **about** seine Meinung ändern; ~ **on an axis** sich um eine Achse drehen; ~ **to the other extreme** ins andere Extrem fallen; ~ **a piece of furniture into place** Möbelstück an seinen Platz schieben; ~ **in one's opinion** seine Meinung ändern;
to break a butterfly on the ~ mit Kanonen auf Spatzen schießen; **to change a** ~ Reifen wechseln; **to keep the** ~**s of production humming** Produktion in Gang halten; **to put one's shoulder to the** ~ sich tüchtig ins Zeug legen;
~ **brake** Radbremse; ~ **chair** Roll-, Krankenfahrstuhl; ~ **horse** Packesel, Arbeitstier.

wheelage Wege-, Rollgeld.

wheelbarrow Schubkarren.

wheelbase Achsabstand.

wheeler *(US sl.)* Verkehrspolizist;
~**s** Speditionspersonal;
~~-**dealer** *(US sl.)* gerissener Geschäftsmann, listenreicher Vorteilnehmer.

wheelhouse *(mar.)* Steuerhaus.

wheelman *(sl.)* Fahrer eines Fluchtautos.

wheelwork Räderwerk, Getriebe.

wheelwright Stellmacher.

wheeze *(sl.)* uralter Witz, *(theater, sl.)* Gag, improvisierter Scherz.

whereabouts Aufenthaltsort, Wohnsitz;
to trace s. one's ~ jds. Aufenthaltsort feststellen.

whereas in Anbetracht (Erwägung);
~ **clause** einleitender Teil einer Urkunde.

wherewithal, the das nötige Kleingeld;
not to have the ~ nicht die erforderlichen Moneten haben.

wherry *(Br.)* Frachtsegler.

whet *(appetizer)* Appetitanreger, Schnäpschen, *(fig.)* Ansporn, Anreiz.

whetstone *(fig.)* Gehirnakrobatik.

whiff Hauch, Luftzug, *(fig.)* Anflug, *(mar.)* Skuller, leichtes Ruderboot, *(small cigar)* Zigarillo;
~ **of fresh air** frischer Luftzug; ~ **of a cigar** Zigarrenrauch; ~ **of prudery** Anflug von Prüderie; ~**s of the slums** Armeleutegeruch;
to stop work to have a few ~**s** Arbeit zum Verpusten unterbrechen.

whiffle *(v.)* *(fig.)* flatterhaft sein, schwanken.

whiffler Windbeutel, wetterwendischer Mensch.

whiffling turn of mind flatterhaftes Wesen.

whig *(Br.)* Liberaler.

whim, whimsy Schrulle, Laune, Grille;
only a passing ~ kurzfristige Marotte.

whimsical schrullenhaft, wunderlich.

whip Geißel, Peitsche, *(coachman)* Kutscher, *(mar.)* Wimpel, *(Br., parl.)* Fraktionsgeschäftsführer, Einpeitscher, *(call made on M.P.)* Fraktionsanweisung, *(party politics)* Rund-, Aufforderungsschreiben, *(plague)* Geißel, Plage;
~ **and spur** spornstreichs;
chief ~ *(Br.)* Fraktionsvorsitzender, Geschäftsführer der Regierungspartei; **Liberal** ~ Sekretär der Liberalen Partei; **one-line** ~ *(parl., Br.)* Aufforderung zu erscheinen; **two-line** ~ *(parl., Br.)* dringende Anwesenheitsaufforderung; **three-line** ~ *(parl., Br.)* unbedingte Anwesenheitsaufforderung;
~ *(v.)* peitschen, klopfen, schlagen, *(party politics)* zur Disziplin bringen;

~ **s. th. in s. o.** jem. etw. einbleuen; ~ **the cat** *(coll., Br.)* stinkgeizig sein; ~ **a coin into one's pocket** Geldstück grabschen und in seine Tasche stecken; ~ **creation** *(coll.)* alles übertreffen; ~ **in** *(parl., Br.)* [zu einer Abstimmung] zusammentrommeln; ~ **into line** vereinheitlichen, auf Vordermann bringen; ~ **the jewels from the counter** *(thief)* Schmuckstücke vom Ladentisch herunterzerren; ~ **a party majority through the lobbies of parliament** Majorität der Partei an allen Klippen der Beeinflussung des Parlaments vorbei zum effektiven Einsatz bringen; ~ **round for subscriptions** Spenden zusammentrommeln; ~ **together** [Parteimitglieder] zusammentrommeln; ~ **up** zusammentrommeln, mobilmachen;
to crack the ~ *(fig.)* mit der Peitsche knallen; **to heel to the party** ~ Fraktionsdisziplin wahren; **to remove the** ~ **from s. o.** *(Br.)* j. aus der Fraktion ausschließen; **to send a** ~ **round** Parteimitglieder zusammentrommeln; **to take off the** ~ *(Br.)* Fraktionszwang aufheben; **to vote by the** ~ unter Fraktionszwang abstimmen;
to hold the ~ **hand** regieren, Regierungszügel halten; ~~-**round for subscriptions** *(Br.)* Spendenrundschreiben, *(fund raising)* eingesammelter Betrag, Sammlung, Kollekte; **to have the** ~ **row of s. o.** *(sl.)* Vorteil vor jem. haben.

whipbelly *(sl.)* Gesöff.

whipcord Peitschenschnur.

whippersnapper Dreikäsehoch, Knirps, Naseweis, *(presumptuous person)* Wichtigtuer, Gernegroß.

whipping Prügelstrafe;
~ **boy** Prügelknabe; ~ **system** Fraktionszwang.

whipsaw *(v.)* sich von beiden Seiten bestechen lassen.

whipsawed, to be *(stock exchange, US)* doppelten Verlust erleiden.

whipstall *(v.)* **an airplane** Flugzeug überziehen.

whipster *(Br.)* Gauner.

whirl Wirbel, wildes Treiben, Tumult;
~ **of modern life in a big city** Hektik des modernen Großstadtlebens; ~ **of social engagements** Trubel gesellschaftlicher Veranstaltungen (Verpflichtungen);
~ *(v.)* **upwards** *(prices)* in die Höhe schnellen;
to give s. th. a ~ *(US)* etw. ausprobieren.

whirlblast Wirbelwind.

whirlicane Hurrican, Wirbelsturm.

whirligig|**of events** Wirbel der Ereignisse; ~ **of time** Karussel der Zeit.

whirlwind Wirbelsturm.

whisky and splash Whisky mit einem Schuß Sodawasser.

whisp Wisch, Büschel.

whisper Wispern, Geflüster, *(secret utterance)* Tuscheln, Getuschel;
in a near ~ fast im Flüsterton;
~ *(v.)* flüstern, wispern, leise sprechen;
~ **against s. o.** über j. tuscheln; ~ **a tale** sich heimlich eine Geschichte erzählen.

whisperer Zuträger, Ohrenbläser.

whispering campaign Flüsterpropaganda;
to start a ~ **against s. one's products** Konkurrenzerzeugnisse madig machen.

whistle Pfeifsignal;
~ **of astonishment** Pfiff des Erstaunens;
~ *(v.)* **one's dog back** seinen Hund zurückpfeifen; ~ **for it** etw. in den Schornstein schreiben; ~ **off** *(coll.)* sich aus dem Staub machen; ~ **before reaching the level-crossing** vor dem Bahnübergang die Lokomotivpfeife betätigen;
to pay for one's ~ seinen Spaß teuer bezahlen; **to wet one's** ~ sich die Kehle anfeuchten.

whistle stop *(little town)* Kleinstadt, *(US)* Bedarfshaltestelle, *(pol.)* kurzes persönliches Auftreten;
~ *(v.)* *(US)* mit vielen Zwischenaufenthalten reisen;
~ **across the country** *(US)* auf Wahlreise sein, Wahlreden halten;
~ **speech** kurze Wahlrede; ~ **tour** *(US)* Wahlkampfreise mit einem Sonderzug.

whistler *(sl.)* Polizeispitzel.

whistling buoy Heulboje.

whit Kleinigkeit, Deut;
not a ~ kein Jota;
not to care a ~ sich keinen Deut darum kümmern.

white Weiß, weiße Farbe, *(man)* Angehöriger der weißen Rasse, Weißer, *(politics)* Reaktionär, Royalist, *(print.)* ausgesparter Raum, Lücke, *(pureness)* Makellosigkeit, Reinheit, *(wine)* Weißwein;
~ *(a.)* weiß, hellfarbig, licht, *(honest, US coll.)* redlich, ehrlich,

rechtschaffen, anständig, *(licensed)* erlaubt, zulässig, *(metal)* verzinkt, silberlegiert, *(pale)* blaß, bleich, *(politics)* reaktionär, *(print.)* blank, leer, unbedruckt, unbeschrieben, *(race)* von der weißen Rasse beherrscht, *(free from spot)* makellos, sauber, rein, *(US)* weißrassig;

~ **as a sheet** kreidebleich;

~ *(v.)* **out** *(print.)* weiße Stellen freilassen, spationieren; ~ **out a matter** Satz strecken;

to bleed ~ *(fig.)* aussaugen, schröpfen;

~ **alloy** Weißmetall; ~ **bonnet** *(Scot.)* Scheinbieter; ⚹ **Book** *(parl.)* Weißbuch; ~ **cap** Schaumkrone; ~ **Christmas** weiße Weihnachten; ~ **coffee** Milchkaffee.

white-collar⎸**crime** *(US)* Wirtschaftsverbrechen; ~ **criminal** *(US)* Wirtschaftsverbrecher; ~ **criminality** *(US)* Wirtschaftsverbrechen; ~ **job** *(US)* Bürotätigkeit; **to have a** ~ **job** *(US)* als Angestellter arbeiten; ~ **man (worker)** *(US)* [Büro]angestellter; ~ **proletariat** *(US)* Stehkragenproletariat; ~ **union** Angestelltengewerkschaft; ~ **work** *(US)* Kopf-, Büro-, Geistesarbeit; ~ **worker** Geistes-, Kopfarbeiter, [Büro]angestellter.

white⎸**-collared employees** Büroangestellte; ~ **elephant** unrentables Geschäft, lästiger Besitz; ~ **flag** Waffenstillstands-, Parlamentärflagge; **to hoist the** ~ **flag** kapitulieren, sich ergeben; ~ **frost** Raureif; ~ **handed** *(fig.)* unschuldig; ~ **hands** *(fig.)* Schuldlosigkeit; ~ **heat** Weißglut, *(fig.)* fieberhafte Eile; **to work at** ~ **heat** fieberhaft arbeiten; ~ **hope** *(sl.)* hoffnungsvoller Nachwuchs; ~**-hot** weißglühend, *(criminal, sl.)* auf der Fahndungsliste, *(fig.)* in höchster Erregung; **to work at** ~**-hot speed** in fieberhaftem Tempo arbeiten; ⚹ **House** *(US)* Residenz, *(coll.)* Bundesexekutive; ⚹ **House Office** *(US)* Mitarbeiterstab des Präsidenten; ~ **iron** Weißblech; ~ **land** *(Br.)* *(regional planning)* [etwa] Außenbereich; ~ **lie** Notlüge; ~ **line** *(print.)* Durchschußlinie; ~ **man** Angehöriger der weißen Rasse; ~ **meat** *(sl.)* Kinderspiel; ~ **metal** Neusilber; ~ **paper** unbeschriebenes Blatt, *(bill of exchange, Br.)* erstklassiger Wechsel, *(parl., Br.)* wirtschafts- und sozialpolitischer Informationsbericht, Dokumentation offizieller Regierungstätigkeit, Weißbuch; ~ **person** *(US)* Angehöriger der weißen Rasse, Weißer; ~ **race** weiße Rasse; ~**-run country** von einer weißen Minderheit regierter Staat; ~ **sale** Weiße Woche, Ausverkauf; ~ **sale ads** Ausverkaufsanzeigen; **to send in** ~ **sheet** seine Sünden beichten; ~ **slave** *(US)* Opfer des Mädchenhandels; ~**-slave traffic** *(slavery)* Mädchenhandel; ~ **slaver** Mädchenhändler; ~ **space** *(composing)* Fleisch, *(print.)* Durchschuß, Weißraum; ~ **space reduction** *(terminal)* Dicktenreduzierung; ~ **squall** Sturmbö, Fallbö; ~ **stuff** Kokain; ~ **trash** *(US)* arme weiße Bevölkerung; ~ **supremacy** Vorherrschaft der weißen Rasse; ~ **war** *(US)* Wirtschaftskrieg.

whitesmith Klempner.

whitewash Tünche, Kalkanstrich, *(coll., Br.)* Ehrenrettung, Rehabilitierung, Schönfärberei, *(debtor)* Schuldnerentlastung;

~ *(v.)* beschönigen, reinwaschen, Persilschein ausstellen, *(bankrupt)* rehabilitieren, von weiteren Schuldenzahlungen entlasten, wieder zahlungsfähig machen.

whitewashed, to be rehabilitiert werden, *(bankrupt)* seine Entlastung als Gemeinschuldner erhalten.

whitewasher Anstreicher.

whitewashing *(Br.)* Rehabilitierung eines Konkursschuldners.

whittle *(v.)*⎸**down expenses** Spesenetat beschneiden; ~ **down salaries** Gehälter kürzen.

whiz Intelligenzbestie;

~**-kid** *(US sl.)* heller Kopf, karriereverdächtiger Bursche.

whodunit *(sl.)* Krimi, Detektivroman.

whole Gesamtheit, Ganzes;

on the ~ im großen und ganzen, im Ganzen gesehen;

economic ~ wirtschaftliche Einheit;

~ **of our resources** alle uns zur Verfügung stehenden Mittel;

to be sold as a ~ **or in sections** als Ganzes oder in Parzellen zu verkaufen; **to be steady on the** ~ *(prices)* im großen und ganzen unverändert sein; **to bequeath to s. o. the** ~ **of one's estate** jem. sein ganzes Vermögen vermachen; **to deal with the** ~ **of the subject matter of a question** Frage sofort in allen Einzelheiten behandeln; **to determine the** ~ **of s. one's career** jds. Berufslaufbahn entscheidend beeinflussen; **to pay the** ~ **of one's rent** seine Miete auf einmal bezahlen; **to sell land as a** ~ Land in einem Stück verkaufen;

~ *(a.)* gesamt, ganz, voll, *(sound)* gesund;

~ **blood** von gleichen Eltern abstammend; ~ **brother** leiblicher Bruder; ~ **chest** *(tea trade)* Kiste Tee; **out of the** ~ **cloth** *(US)* völlig aus der Luft gegriffen, frei erfunden; ~ **country** gesamte Bevölkerung; **to rain for the three** ~ **days** drei Tage hintereinan-

der regnen; **to give one's** ~ **energies to a task** mit seiner ganzen Energie an einer Aufgabe arbeiten; ~ **gale** schwerer Sturm; ~**-hearted work** ernsthafte Arbeit; **to go the** ~ **hog** ganze Arbeit leisten, seine Sache gründlich machen, nicht auf halbem Wege stehen bleiben; ~**-hogger** äußerst konsequenter Mensch; ~ **hoggism** *(sl.)* Aufs-Ganze-Gehen, Konsequenz; ~**-length portrait** lebensgroßes Bild; ~**-life insurance (assurance, Br.)** Lebensversicherung auf den Todesfall, reine Todesfallversicherung; ~**-life policy** Lebensversicherungspolice auf den Todesfall; ~ **milk** Vollmilch; ~ **number** Ganzzahl; ~ **page** ganze Seite; ~**-seas over** sternhagelvoll; ~ **series of books** ganze Bücherreihe; **to be the** ~ **show** den ganzen Laden schmeißen, die Persönlichkeit sein; **to get off with a** ~ **skin** mit heiler Haut davonkommen; ~**-time job** ganztägige Beschäftigung; ~**-timer** ganztägig (hauptberuflich) beschäftigter Arbeitnehmer; **the** ~ **truth** die ganze Wahrheit.

wholesale Großhandel, -verkauf, Engroshandel, Massenabsatz;

at ~ *(US)* **(by,** *Br.***)** en gros, im Großhandel, zum Großhandelspreis, *(fig.)* pauschal, in Bausch und Bogen, ohne Unterschied;

~ **and retail** im Groß- und Einzelhandel;

~ *(v.)* en gros (im Großhandel) verkaufen;

to be ~ **only** nur Großhandelsartikel führen; **to be manufactured** ~ serienmäßig (fabrikmäßig) hergestellt sein; **to buy goods** ~ zu Großhandelspreisen einkaufen; **to sell** ~ im Großhandel verkaufen; **to send out invitations** ~ Einladungen massenweise verschicken;

~ *(a.)* im großen, engros, partienweise, *(extensive)* massenhaft, -weise, bergeweise, *(fig.)* pauschal, in Bausch und Bogen; ~ **association** Großhandelsverband; ~ **bookseller** Großsortimenter, Großbuchhandlung; ~ **secondhand bookseller** Großantiquariat; ~ **borrowing** Schuldenmachen im großen Maßstab; ~ **branch** Großhandelsfiliale; ~ **business** Großhandels-, Engrosgeschäft, Großhandel, -handlung; **to carry on (conduct, do) a** ~ **business** Großhandelsgeschäft (Engrosgeschäft) betreiben; ~ **buyer** Großeinkäufer; ~ **center** *(US)* **(centre,** *Br.***)** Großhandelszentrum; ~ **cooperative** *(US)* Großeinkaufsgenossenschaft; ~ **cost** Großhandels-, Grossisten-, Engrospreis; ~ **dealer** Großkaufmann, -händler, Grossist, Engroshändler; ~ **dealing** Engros-, Großhandel; ~ **dealing in small quantities** Großhandelsverkauf an Einzelhändler; ~ **deliveries** Lieferungen im Großhandel; ~ **discount** Großhandelsrabatt; ~ **distribution** Großhandelsverteilung; ~ **distributor** Großhandelsverteilerstelle; ~ **district** Großhandelsbezirk; ~ **enterprise (establishment)** Großhandelsunternehmen; ~ **firm** Großhandelsfirma, Großhandlung; ~ **functions** Großhandelsaufgaben, -funktionen; ~ **goods** Großhandelserzeugnisse, -artikel; ~ **grocer** Kolonialwarenhändler en gros, Lebensmittelgroßhändler; ~ **group rate** *(insurance)* pauschalierter Gruppentarif; ~ **house** Engros-, Großhandelsfirma, -betrieb; ~ **investment bank** Effektenemissionsbank; ~ **manufacture** Massen-, Serienfabrikation, fabrikmäßige Herstellung; ~ **margin** Großhandelsverdienstspanne; ~ **market** Großhandelsmarkt; ~ **merchant** Grossist, Engros-, Großhändler, Großhandelskaufmann; ~ **middleman** Spekulativ-, Engroszwischenhändler; ~ **operation** [einzelnes] Großhandelsgeschäft; ~ **peddler** Engroshändler mit Wagenverkauf; ~ **price** Engros-, Grossisten-, Großhandels-, Partiepreis; ~ **price index** Großhandelspreisindex; ~ **price level** Großhandelspreisniveau; ~ **purchase** Groß-, Pauschalkauf, Einkauf en gros; ~ **purchaser** Großein-, Engroskäufer; ~**-purchasing company** Großeinkaufsgesellschaft; ~ **quotations** Großhandelspreise-, notierungen; ~ **receiver** *(US)* Zentralmarkthändler; ~ **representative** Großhandelsvertreter; ~ **salesman** Großhandelsverkäufer; ~ **selling** Großhandelsverkauf; ~ **shop** Großhandelsgeschäft; ~ **slaughter** Massenmord, Massaker; ~ **society** *(Br.)* Großeinkaufsgenossenschaft; ~**-sponsored group** vom Großhandel begünstigte Gruppe; ~ **stock** Großhandelslager; ~ **store** Großhandelsgeschäft; ~ **trade** Groß-, Engroshandel; ~ **fashion trade** Großkonfektionshandel; ~ **trader** Grossist, Großhändler, -kaufmann; ~ **trading** Großhandel[sbetrieb]; ~ **warehouse** Großlager-, Großhandelshaus; ~ **writing-down** vollständige Abschreibung.

wholesaler Engroshändler, Großhändler, -kaufmann, Grossist;

cash-and-carry ~ Engrossortimenter; **drop-shipment** ~ auftragsvermittelnder Großhändler; **full-service** ~ Großhandelskaufmann mit eigenem Lager; **functional** ~ Engrosvertreter; **limited-function** ~ Großhändler mit begrenzter Großhandelsfunktion; **mail-order** ~ Versandgroß-, Verlagshändler; **service** ~ Effektivhändler; **truck** ~ *(US)* Engroshändler (Großhändler) ohne eigenes Lager;

to supply only ~**s** nur den Großhandel beliefern.

wholesaling Großhandelsgewerbe, -einkauf;
~ **functions** Großhandelsaufgaben, -funktionen; ~ **network** Großhandelsnetz.
wholesome förderlich, zuträglich, nützlich, zweckmäßig, *(healthy)* gesund[heitsfördernd];
~ **advice** nützlicher (zweckdienlicher) Rat; ~ **experiences** nützliche Erfahrungen; ~ **food** kräftige Nahrung; ~ **surroundings** gesundheitsfördernde Umgebung.
wholly ganz, gänzlich, vollständig;
to agree ~ hundertprozentig übereinstimmen; **to be** ~ **at a loss** völlig konsterniert sein;
~ **dependent** völlig unterhaltsabhängig; ~ **destroyed** *(building)* total zerstört; ~ **and permanently disabled** voll (dauernd) berufsunfähig; ~ **finished** gänzlich erledigt; ~ **given to drinking** völlig dem Alkohol verfallen; ~ **liable** voll verantwortlich, unbeschränkt persönlich haftend; ~ **liable to tax** voll steuerpflichtig; ~**-owned** im Alleineigentum; ~**-owned government corporation** staatseigene Kapitalgesellschaft; ~**-owned subsidiary** hundertprozentige Tochtergesellschaft.
whoop Pfifferling, *(sound)* lauter Ruf, Geschrei;
not worth a ~ keinen roten Heller wert;
~**s** Kriegsgeschrei;
~ *(v.)* **it (things) up** *(US sl.)* großen Lärm (Riesenkrach) machen.
whoopee Rummel;
to make ~ es hoch her gehen lassen, Freudenfest veranstalten.
whopper Mordsding, *(monstrous lie)* krasse (faustdicke) Lüge.
whore Hure, Dirne, Prostituierte.
whorehouse Freudenhaus, Bordell.
whydunit Psychothriller.
wick Meierei, Gehöft.
wicker | flask Korbflasche; ~ **furniture** Korbmöbel.
wicket Türchen, *(grilled window)* Schalterfenster;
on a good ~ *(fig.)* in günstiger Lage.
wide breit, ausgedehnt, *(Br., sl., clever)* hell, aufgeweckt, gerissen, *(fig.)* umfassend, umfangreich, ausgedehnt, weitreichend, *(of large scope)* groß, beträchtlich, *(loose in character)* lax, *(stock exchange)* unterschiedlich, schwankend;
~ **apart** weit auseinander; ~ **open** *(district, sl.)* ohne Polizeischutz;
to be ~ **of the mark** ganz und gar nicht zur Sache gehören; **to be broke to the** ~ *(coll.)* völlig pleite sein;
~ **angle** *(film)* Breitband; ~**-angle lens** Weitwinkelobjektiv; ~**-awake** hellwach, schlau, gewitzt; ~**-branched** weitverzweigt; ~ **choice** große Auswahl, großes Sortiment; ~ **circulation** große Auflage; ~ **culture** umfassende Bildung; ~ **definition** großzügige Auslegung; ~ **distribution** weite Verbreitung, *(photo)* Weitwinkel; ~ **domain** großes Gebiet; ~ **experience** sehr große Erfahrungen; ~ **field of studies** umfassendes Studiengebiet; ~ **gauge** *(railway)* Breitspur; ~ **generalization** große Verallgemeinerung; ~ **interests** vielseitige (weitgespannte) Interessen; ~ **margin** großer Spielraum, *(typewriting)* breiter Rand (Zwischenraum); ~**-open** weit geöffnet, *(US sl.)* lax; ~**-open town** Polizeistunden und Glücksspiele tolerierende Stadt; ~ **opening** *(stock exchange)* stark voneinander abweichende Eröffnungskurse; ~ **place in the road** *(sl.)* Provinznest; ~ **prices** unterschiedliche Preise, *(stock exchange)* Kurse mit großer Spanne zwischen Geld- und Briefkurs; ~ **quotation** *(stock exchange)* große Kursspanne; ~ **range** ausgedehnter Bereich; ~**-ranging** weitreichend; ~ **reading** große Belesenheit; ~ **road** breite Straße; ~ **screen** *(film)* Breitband, Breitwandfilm; ~**-screen film** Breitwandfilm; ~**-screen process** Breitwandverfahren; ~ **selection of new books** großes Sortiment neuer Bücher; ~ **size** Breitformat; ~**-spread phenomenon** weit verbreitete Erscheinung; ~**-stretched** ausgedehnt; ~ **track** *(railway)* Breitspur; **to take** ~ **views** großzügig sein; **the** ~ **world** die weite Welt.
widely weit und breit, in weiten Kreisen;
~ **held** weit verbreitet; ~ **scattered** weit verstreut;
to be ~ **known** in weiten Kreisen bekannt sein; **to be** ~ **read** sehr belesen sein; **to be differing** ~ **in opinions** sehr unterschiedlicher Meinung sein;
~ **read newspaper** weitverbreitete Zeitung.
widen *(v.)* breiter machen, erweitern, ausdehnen;
~ **a breach** *(fig.)* Bruch vertiefen; ~ **a gap** Kluft vertiefen; ~ **one's interests** seinen Interessenkreis ausweiten; ~ **out the lines** *(print.)* Zeilen durchschießen; ~ **a road** Straße verbreitern.
widening, road Straßenverbreiterung.
wider | -band exchange rates größere Bandbreiten der Wechselkurse; **on a** ~ **plane** auf umfassender Ebene; ~ **range investment** größere Anlagenstreuung einer Kapitalanlagengesellschaft.
widespread weitverbreitet.

widow Witwe, *(print.)* Hurenkind;
grass ~ getrennt lebende (geschiedene) Ehefrau;
~**-bench** *(Br.)* Pflichtteil der Ehefrau; ~ **and orphan stock** *(US)* mündelsichere Wertpapiere, Wertpapiere mit hoher Sicherheit.
widow's | annuity Witwenrente; ~ **allowance** *(Br.)* Witwengeld; ~**'s benefit** *(Br.)* Hinterbliebenenbezüge, Witwengeld; ~ **bounty** Witwenpension; ~ **chamber** Dreißigster, Voraus an den Haushaltungsgegenständen; ~ **cruse** *(fig.)* unerschöpflicher Vorrat; ~ **insurance** Witwenversicherung; ~ **insurance benefits** *(social insurance, US)* Hinterbliebenenrente der Witwe, Witwengeld; ~ **mite** kleine Spende; ~ **pension** Witwenpension, -rente; ~ **terce** *(Scot.)* Nießbrauch der Witwe an einem Drittel der Pachterträge; ~ **weeds** Witwentracht.
widowed verwitwet;
to be ~ **of a friend** Freund verlieren.
widower Witwer.
widowhood Witwenstand, -schaft.
width Breite, Weite, *(bridge)* Spannweite, *(tapestry)* Bahn;
~ **of column** Spaltenbreite; ~ **of mind** geistiger Horizont; ~ **of page** Blattbreite; ~ **of a road** Straßenbreite; ~ **of type** Schriftweite;
~ **plug** *(terminal)* Dicktenstecker; ~ **value** *(terminal)* Dicktenwert.
wield | *(v.)* control Kontrolle ausüben; ~ **the pen** schreiben.
wife Ehefrau, Gattin;
house ~ Hausfrau; **lawful [wedded]** ~ rechtmäßig angetraute Ehefrau;
husband and ~ Eheleute; ~ **and children** *(devise by man)* vermutetes lebenslängliches Nießbrauchrecht für die Ehefrau und Vermögensanfall an die Kinder;
~**'s earned income** Erwerbseinkommen der Ehefrau; ~**'s equity** *(court of equity)* Vorbehaltsgut für Ehefrau und Kinder; ~**'s estate** Vermögen der Ehefrau; ~**'s expenditure** Schlüsselgewalt der Ehefrau; ~**'s insurance benefits** *(social insurance, US)* Zusatzrente für die Ehefrau; ~**'s part** Pflichtteil der Witwe; **to be** ~**-ridden** unter dem Pantoffel stehen.
wifehood Stand als Ehefrau.
wifelessness Ledigenstand.
wig Perücke, *(reprimand, Br., coll.)* Schelte, Rüge, *(student use)* Intellektueller;
~**s on the green** *(coll.)* Handgreiflichkeiten.
wiggery *(fig.)* alter Zopf.
wiggle Schlangenlinie;
~ *(v.)* **through a crowd** sich durch eine Menschenmenge winden.
wigwag *(mar.)* Signalisieren, Winken;
~ *(v.)* *(mar.)* signalisieren.
wigwagger Signalgast.
wigwam *(politics, US sl.)* Versammlungshalle, -zelt.
wild Ödland, Wüste, Wildnis;
vast ~ **of sand** ungeheure Sandwüste;
~ *(a.)* *(angry)* aufgebracht, wütend, *(animal)* ungezähmt, wild, *(crazy)* verrückt, toll, *(dangerous)* gefährlich, *(nation)* unzivilisiert, ungesittet, barbarisch, *(ship)* schwer zu steuern;
running ~ wildgeworden;
~ **with rage** wutentbrannt;
to allow one's children to run ~ seine Kinder völlig unkontrolliert aufwachsen lassen; **to be** ~ **about s. th.** *(coll.)* ganz verrückt (versessen) nach etw. sein; **to drive s. o.** ~ j. zur Raserei bringen; **to run** ~ unkontrolliert dahinrasen; **to talk** ~ wirre Reden führen;
~ **animal** wildes Tier; ~ **beast** Raubtier; ~**-beast show** Raubtierschau; ~ **coast** stürmische Küste; ~ **crew** ungezügelte Mannschaft; ~ **disorder** wüste Unordnung; ~ **excitement** wilde Erregung; ~ **fellow** wilder Kerl; ~ **fowl** jagbare Vögel; ~**-goose chase** fruchtloses Unterfangen, vergebliche Liebesmüh; **to run a** ~**-goose chase** Hirngespinsten nachjagen; ~ **guess** reine Vermutung; ~ **honey** Waldhonig; ~ **land** unbebautes Land; ~ **look** verstörter (irrer) Blick; **to sow one's** ~ **oats** sich die Hörner abstoßen; ~ **orgies** wilde Orgien; ~ **pain** rasender Schmerz; ~ **pitch** Vorstoß auf Geratewohl; ~ **remark** vom Thema abschweifende Bemerkung; ~ **scenery** romantische Landschaft; ~ **scheme** unüberlegter Plan; ~ **shot** *(fig.)* Schuß ins Blaue; ~ **times** tolle Zeiten; ~**-West novel** Wildwestroman; ~**-West show** Wildwestschau; ~ **years** bewegte Jahre; ~ **youth** stürmische Jugend.
wildcat *(business)* Schwindel-, unsolides Geschäftsunternehmen, *(coll.)* Spekulant, *(mining)* spekulative Versuchsbohrung, Probeschürfung, *(quicktempered person)* Hitzkopf, Draufgänger, *(railroad, US)* Rangierlok;

~ *(v.) (mining)* auf eigene Faust Versuchsbohrungen machen, *(railroad, US)* außerfahrplanmäßig fahren;

~ *(a.)* unsicher, riskant, spekulativ, *(bogus)* schwindelhaft, *(not as scheduled, US)* nicht fahrplanmäßig, *(unlawful, US)* unrechtmäßig, unreell, ungesetzlich;

~ **bank** *(US)* Schwindelbank; ~ **brand** unerlaubtes Markenzeichen; ~ **brewery** Schwarzbrauerei; ~ **business house** unsolide Firma; ~ **company** Schwindelgesellschaft; ~ **credit market** Parallelmarkt; ~ **currency** *(US)* schlechte Kassenscheine; ~ **enterprise** riskantes Unternehmen; ~ **finance** ungesunde (wilde) Spekulation, unsolide Finanzverhältnisse; ~ **locomotive** Einzel-, Rangierlok; ~ **methods** anrüchige Methoden; ~ **scheme** unsolides Vorhaben; ~ **securities** hochspekulative Effekten; ~ **stocks** unsichere Aktien; ~ **strike** wilder (unorganisierter) Streik, Spontanstreik; ~ **striker** wilder Streiker; ~ **walkout** wilder Streik.

wildcatter *(US)* wilder Spekulant.

wildcatting *(US)* wilde Spekulation, *(oil industry)* spekulative Erdölbohrung.

wilderness Wüste, Wildnis;

~ **of sea** Wasserwüste; ~ **of things** Masse von Dingen;

to be a ~ verwüstet sein; **to be send off into the** ~ in die Wüste geschickt werden; **to wander in the** ~ *(politician)* abserviert sein.

wildfire verheerendes Feuer, *(thunderless lightning)* Wetterleuchten;

~ **of applause** Beifallssturm;

to spread like ~ sich wie ein Lauffeuer verbreiten.

wilding *(fig.)* Außenseiter.

wildlife freie Wildbahn;

World ♀ **Fund** Internationale Naturschutzorganisation; ~ **refuge (reserve)** Wildreservat; ~ **resources** Wildbestände; ~ **sanctuary** Wildschutzgebiet, Wild-, Tierreservat.

wildness Ausgelassenheit, Zügellosigkeit.

wildwind Orkan.

wilful, willful *(US)* absichtlich, bewußt, vorsätzlich, wissentlich, *(obstinate)* halsstarrig, eigensinnig;

~ **and malicions** böswillig;

~ **act** vorsätzliche Handlung; ~ **damage** absichtliche Beschädigung; ~ **deception (deceit)** arglistige, bewußte Täuschung; ~ **disobedience** bewußter Ungehorsam; ~ **homicide** vorsätzliche Tötung; ~ **and malicious (wanton) injury** vorsätzliche Verletzung (Schädigung); ~ **interference with the safety of others** vorsätzliche Gefährdung Dritter; ~ **mischief** vorsätzliche Sachbeschädigung; ~ **misconduct of employee** *(Workmen's Compensation Act)* schwere Verfehlung einem anderen Angestellten gegenüber; ~ **murder** Mord; ~ **or wanton negligence** *(US)* bewußte Fahrlässigkeit; ~ **tort** vorsätzlich begangene unerlaubte Handlung; ~ **trespass** mutwillige Sachbeschädigung.

wilfulness, willfullness Vorsätzlichkeit.

will Wille, Wunsch, Befehl, *(last will)* Testament, letztwillige Verfügung, letzter Wille, *(purpose)* Zweck, Ziel;

at ~ nach Belieben (Wunsch), *(lease)* jederzeit kündbar; **at the time of making the** ~ zur Zeit der Testamentserrichtung; **by** ~ testamentarisch, im Wege letztwilliger Verfügung; **of one's own** ~ aus freien Stücken; **under his father's** ~ nach dem Testament seines Vaters;

alternative ~ entgegenstehendes Testament; **ambulatory** ~ widerrufliches Testament; **attested** ~ von Zeugen unterschriebenes Testament; **cancelled** ~ widerrufenes Testament; **closed** ~ geheimes Testament; **conditional** ~ bedingtes Testament; **conjoint** ~ gemeinsames Testament; **counter (double)** ~ gegenseitiges Testament; **properly executed** ~ ordnungsgemäß errichtetes Testament; **foreign** ~ Testament eines Ausländers; **forged** ~ untergeschobenes (gefälschtes) Testament; **free** ~ freie Willensbestimmung; **good** ~ Wohlwollen, Gunst; **holographic** ~ handschriftliches (eigenhändiges) Testament; **ill** ~ böser Wille; **informal** ~ formloses Testament; **invalid** ~ ungültiges Testament; **iron** ~ eiserner Wille; **joint** ~ gemeinschaftliches (gemeinsames) Testament; **joint and mutual** ~ gemeinsames (gemeinschaftliches, wechselbezügliches) Testament; **later** ~ später abgefaßtes Testament; **little** ~ Testamentsergänzung, -zusatz; **lost** ~ verlorengegangenes (nicht auffindbares) Testament; **mutual** ~ gegenseitiges (wechselbezügliches) Testament; **mystic** ~ geheimes (notariell errichtetes) Testament; **nonintervention** ~ durch völlig freien Testamentsvollstrecker vollzogenes Testament; **notarial** ~ notariell beglaubigtes Testament; **nuncupative** ~ mündlich und vor Zeugen errichtetes Testament; **officious** ~ Testament zugunsten der Familie; ~ **parole** mündliches Testament; **previous** ~ früheres

Testament; **privileged** ~ formloses Testament, Not-, Soldatentestament; **proved** ~ vom Nachlaßgericht eröffnetes und für gültig erklärtes Testament; **reciprocal** ~ *(US)* gegenseitiges Testament; **sealed** ~ geheimes Testament; **third-person** ~ von der Bestätigung durch einen Dritten abhängiges Testament; **unattested** ~ nicht beglaubigtes Testament; **unnatural** ~ ungewöhnliche letztwillige Verfügung; **unofficious** ~ willkürliches (gesetzliche Erbrechte ausschließendes) Testament; **unsolemn** ~ Testament ohne Bestimmung eines Testamentsvollstreckers; **valid** ~ gültiges Testament; **wicked** ~ Boshaftigkeit, Bosheit; **written** ~ schriftliches Testament;

~ **in custody** Depottestament; **last** ~ **and testament** letztwillige Verfügung, letzter Wille, Testament; ~ **to live** Lebenswille; ~ **to peace** Friedenswille; ~ **of the people** Volkswille; ~ **to power** Machtstreben; ~**-of-the-wisp** Irrlicht;

~ *(v.)* wollen, bestimmen, entscheiden, *(bequeath)* testamentarisch hinterlassen (verfügen), vermachen;

~ **a fortune upon s. o.** jem. sein ganzes Vermögen vermachen; ~ **one's money to a hospital** sein Geld einem Krankenhaus hinterlassen (vermachen);

to adminster a ~ Testament zur Ausführung bringen; **to admit a** ~ **to probate** Testament zwecks Erbscheinserteilung vorlegen; **to attest a** ~ als Zeuge bei der Abfassung eines Testaments fungieren; **to be capable of making a** ~ testierfähig sein; **to be incapable of making a** ~ testierunfähig sein; **to benefit by a** ~ in einem Testament bedacht sein; **to break a** ~ Testament durch Gerichtsverfahren aufheben lassen; **to cancel a** ~ Testament widerrufen; **to constitute a** ~ Erfordernisse eines Testaments aufweisen; **to construe an unskilfully drawn** ~ unvollständiges Testament auslegen; **to contest a** ~ Gültigkeit eines Testaments bestreiten; **to countermand a** ~ Testament widerrufen; **to deposit a** ~ Testament hinterlegen; **to devise by** ~ Grundbesitz testamentarisch vermachen; **to die without making a** ~ ohne ein Testament zu hinterlassen sterben; **to dispose by** ~ letztwillig verfügen; **to dispute a** ~ Testament anfechten; **to draw up a** ~ Testament aufsetzen; **to establish a disputed** ~ Gültigkeit eines Testaments nachweisen; **to execute a** ~ Testament errichten; **to exercise powers entirely at** ~ Vollmachten ganz nach Ermessen ausüben; **to fabricate a** ~ Testament fälschen; **to file a** ~ Testament einreichen; **to grant probate of a** ~ auf Grund vorgelegten Testaments einen Erbschein ausstellen; **to have the** ~ **to do** bestrebt sein; **to have s. o. down in one's** ~ **for £ 10.000** jem. im Testament 10.000 Pfund vermachen; **to include s. o. in a** ~ j. in seinem Testament bedenken; **to invalidate a** ~ Testament für kraftlos erklären; **to leave by** ~ testamentarisch vermachen; **to make one's** ~ sein Testament machen; **to mention s. o. in one's** ~ j. in seinem Testament (testamentarisch) bedenken; **to oppose a** ~ Testament anfechten; **to probate a** ~ Testament gerichtlich bestätigen lassen; **to produce a forged** ~ gefälschtes Testament vorlegen; **to propound a** ~ *(executor)* Testament zur Bestätigung vorlegen; **to prove a** ~ Testament nachlaßgerichtlich eröffnen und bestätigen; **to prove a** ~ **in common form** Testamentsvollstreckerzeugnis vorlegen; **to put s. o. in one's** ~ j. in seinem Testament bedenken; **to read out a** ~ Testament eröffnen; **to reduce a** ~ einem Testament richterliche Anerkennung versagen; **to register a** ~ notarielles Testament errichten; **to remember s. o. in one's** ~ j. im Testament bedenken; **to revive a** ~ widerrufenes Testament wiederaufleben lassen; **to revoke a** ~ Testament aufheben (widerrufen, umstoßen); **to set a** ~ **aside** Testament für ungültig erklären; **to suppress a** ~ Testament unterschlagen; **to take by (under) a** ~ auf Grund eines Testaments erben; **to take the** ~ **for the deed** schon den guten Willen anerkennen; **to take out probate of a** ~ sich einen Erbschein auf Grund eines Testaments ausstellen lassen; **to use undue influence with the maker of a** ~ j. bei der Abfassung seines Testaments in unzulässiger Weise beeinflussen; **to work one's** ~ sein Ziel erreichen; **to write one's** ~ sein Testament machen.

will | -call [purchase] *(US)* Anzahlungskauf; ~**-call for lay-away** *(US)* vom Kunden anbezahlter und zurückgelegter Gegenstand; ~ **contest** Testamentsanfechtung, -verfahren; ~ **power** Willenskraft; ~ **and probate department** Nachlaßgericht.

willies *(US)* Anfall von Nervosität;

to give s. o. the ~ j. nervös machen.

willing gewillt, geneigt, *(ready to act)* willfährig, bereitwillig, *(voluntary)* freiwillig, gern gegeben;

~ **to make concessions** konzessionsbereit; ~ **to pay a price** mit einem Preis einverstanden;

to show ~ *(sl.)* guten Willen beweisen;

~ **faculty** Willensfähigkeit; ~ **gift** gern gegebenes Geschenk; ~ **help** gern gewährte Hilfe; ~ **seller** verkaufsbereiter Veräußerer; ~ **worker** willfähiger Arbeiter.

willingly aus freien Stücken, freiwillig.

willingness Geneigtheit;
~ **to contract** Vertragsbereitschaft; ~ **to pay** Zahlungsbereitschaft; ~ **to sell** Abgabebereitschaft; ~ **to serve** Dienst-, Einsatzbereitschaft; ~ **to spend** Ausgabenneigung, Investitionsbereitschaft; ~ **to work** Arbeitswilligkeit;
to show ~ to discuss diskussionsbereit sein.

willow Weide.

willy-nilly *(sl.)* unvorbereitet, ohne Plan.

wily gerissen, verschlagen.

wimple *(fig.)* Winkelzug;
~ *(v.)* **the lake** Wasseroberfläche kräuseln.

win *(v.)* gewinnen, siegen, Sieg davontragen, Erfolg haben, obsiegen, *(acquire)* erwerben, *(earn)* verdienen, *(mil.)* Festung erobern, *(mining)* erschließen, gewinnen, schürfen;
~ **upon s. o.** Einfluß über j. gewinnen; ~ **s. o. over as an ally** j. zum Bundesgenossen gewinnen; ~ **one's audience over** rasch die Herzen der Zuhörer gewinnen; ~ **one's daily bread** sein tägliches Brot verdienen; ~ **in a canter** *(coll.)* mühelos siegen, mit Leichtigkeit gewinnen; ~ **one's case** seinen Prozeß gewinnen; ~ **s. o. over to a cause** j. für eine Sache interessieren; ~ **a competition** Preisausschreiben gewinnen; ~ **the day** siegreich sein; ~ **the elections** Wahlen gewinnen; ~ **the field** Sieg erringen; ~ **a fortune** Reichtum erlangen; ~ **free** sich freimachen; ~ **hands down** spielend gewinnen; ~ **the jury** Geschworene für sich einnehmen; ~ **one's living** seinen Lebensunterhalt verdienen; ~ **loose** sich freimachen; ~ **mineral** Mineralien abbauen; ~ **out** *(US coll.)* erfolgreich sein; ~ **over** für sich einnehmen; ~ **over the jury** Geschworene für sich freundlich stimmen; ~ **s. o. over to one's view** j. zu seiner Meinung bekehren; ~ **the porcelain hairnet** *(sl.)* sich für nichts und wiedernichts engagieren; ~ **a prize** mit einem Gewinn herauskommen, Preis gewinnen; ~ **raves** *(fam.)* begeisterte Zustimmung finden; ~ **a reputation** Ansehen gewinnen; ~ **a scholarship** Stipendium bekommen; ~ **to the shore** ans Ufer gelangen; ~ **one's spurs** sich seine Sporen verdienen; ~ **one's suit** *(US)* seinen Prozeß gewinnen, in seinem Prozeß obsiegen; ~ **the summit** Gipfel erreichen; ~ **support from a farm** vom Ertrag eines Landgutes leben können; ~ **through** sich durchschlagen, sich durchsetzen; ~ **upon s. o.** Einfluß bei jem. erlangen; ~ **a victory** Sieg erringen; ~ **a war** Krieg gewinnen; ~ **one's way by pluck** durch mutige Entschlossenheit weiterkommen; ~ **one's way up from poverty** sich aus kleinsten Verhältnissen emporarbeiten; ~ **a wife** Ehefrau finden.

wind Wind, Luftzug, -strom, *(aeronautics)* Wind[richtung], *(bend)* Biegung, Windung, *(piece of machinery)* Winde, *(storm)* Sturmwind, Hurrikan, *(mere talk)* Geschwätz, leere Worte;
before the ~ in Windrichtung; **between ~ and water** *(fig.)* an einer empfindlichen Stelle; **in the ~** im Anzug, in geheimer Vorbereitung; **into the teeth of the ~** gegen den Wind; **like the ~** flink, schnell; **puffed up with ~** aufgeblasen; **sound in ~ and limb** kerngesund; **under the ~** in Lee; **to profit** Kostenvorteil;
baffling ~ umspringender Wind; **contrary ~** ungünstiger Wind; **fair ~** günstiger Wind; **the four ~s** die vier Himmelsrichtungen; **second ~** *(fig.)* frischer Wind in den Segeln; **variable ~s** wechselnde Winde;
~ **to the left** Linksbiegung; **warm ~s from the south** warme Südwinde; ~ **of a watch** Aufziehen einer Uhr;
~ *(v.)* dem Wind aussetzen, lüften, *(bend)* sich winden (schlängeln), *(board)* sich verziehen (werfen), *(ship)* wenden;
~ **about** sich durchschlängeln; ~ **o. s. into s. one's affection** sich bei jem. einschmeicheln, jds. Zuneigung erschleichen; ~ **a blanket round o. s.** sich in eine Decke einwickeln; ~ **down to a close** allmählich zu Ende gehen; ~ **into s. one's favo(u)r** sich jds. Gunst erschleichen; ~ **a film** Film weiterdrehen; ~ **s. o. round one's little finger** j. um den kleinen Finger wickeln; ~ **one's horses** seine Pferde verschnaufen lassen; ~ **around a pole** sich um einen Pfahl schlängeln; ~ **a ship out of the harbo(u)r** Schiff aus dem Hafen hieven; ~ **a watch** Uhr aufziehen; ~ **its way through congress** verschlungene Wege des Kongresses überwinden;
to be in the ~ in der Luft liegen; **to be blown to the four ~s** in alle Winde verstreut werden; **to be near (close) to the ~** *(fig.)* sich hart an der Grenze des Erlaubten bewegen; **to cast (fling) to the ~s** außer Acht lassen, in den Wind schlagen, jede Vorsicht vergessen; **to get the ~** Witterung aufnehmen; **to get ~ of s. th.** Wind von etw. bekommen; **to get one's second ~** wieder zu Atem kommen, toten Punkt überwunden haben; **to get the ~ of** *(up)* *(sl.)* Manschetten bekommen (kriegen), Bammel haben; **to give s. o. the ~** *(sl.)* j. abblitzen (fallen) lassen; **to have a long ~** langen Atem haben; **to have in the ~** auf der Spur sein; **to have**

the ~ of s. o. Oberhand über j. gewinnen; **to have three sheets in the ~** sternhagelvoll sein; **to know where the ~ blows** wissen, wie der Hase läuft; **to pump ~ into a tyre** Reifen aufpumpen; **to put the ~ up s. o.** j. Angst einjagen; **to raise the ~** *(sl.)* das erforderliche Geld auftreiben; **to recover one's ~** verschnaufen; **to sail near (close) to the ~** *(husband one's money)* äußerst sparsam wirtschaften; **to sail with every shift of the ~** *(fig.)* sein Mäntelchen nach dem Winde hängen; **to take ~** ruchbar werden; **to take the ~ out of s. one's sails** jem. den Wind aus den Segeln nehmen; **to throw the lessons of the past to the ~s** alle bisher gesammelten Erfahrungen außer acht lassen; **to throw propriety to the ~s** allen Anstand fahren lassen; **to throw prudence to the ~s** guten Rat in den Wind schlagen, Klugheit außer acht lassen;
~ **band** Blasorchester; ~**-bound** *(fig.)* verhindert, aufgehalten; ~ **direction** Windrichtung; ~ **drag** Windwiderstand; ~ **force** Windstärke; ~ **gauge** Anemometer, Winddruckmesser; ~ **indicator** *(aerodrome)* Windrichtungsanzeiger; ~ **instrument** Blasinstrument; ~ **pressure** Winddruck; ~ **rose** *(meteorology)* Windrose; ~ **shake** Windbruch; ~ **side** Windseite; ~ **speed** Windstärke; ~ **spout** Wind-, Wasserhose; ~ **storm** Hurrikan; ~ **tunnel** Windkanal; ~ **vane** Wetterfahne.

wind up *(v.)* aufwickeln, aufspulen, *(account)* abschließen, beendigen, erledigen, *(bankruptcy, Br.)* bankrott (Konkurs) machen, *(business)* Geschäft aufgeben, auflösen, abwickeln, auseinandersetzen, liquidieren, in Liquidation gehen, *(get going)* ankurbeln, in Gang bringen;
~ **an account** Rechnung abschließen; ~ **one's affairs** seine Geschäfte abwickeln (erledigen); ~ **the affairs of a partnership** Gesellschaft liquidieren; ~ **behind bars** sich im Gefängnis wiederfinden; ~ **a business company** Handelsgesellschaft auflösen (liquidieren); ~ **a company** Liquidation einer Handelsgesellschaft durchführen; ~ **compulsorily** zwangsliquidieren; ~ **the debate** Diskussion schließen; ~ **the debtor's business** Geschäft des Gemeinschuldners abwickeln (liquidieren); ~ **doing** letzten Endes tun; ~ **o. s. up for an effort** Kraftanstrengung unternehmen; ~ **an estate** *(Br.)* Nachlaß regeln (auseinandersetzen, abwickeln); ~ **the hillside** *(road)* sich am Berghang emporschlängeln; ~ **liabilities** Verbindlichkeiten ordnen; ~ **a meeting** Versammlung für beendet erklären (schließen); ~ **ore from a mine** Grubenerz fördern; ~ **partnership** [Handels]gesellschaft auflösen; ~ **a pension scheme** Betriebspensionskasse auflösen; ~ **in prison** im Gefängnis enden; ~ **by saying** mit den Worten schließen; ~ **one's speech** seine Rede beschließen; ~ **for a summer holiday** sich in den großen Ferien vertagen; ~ **s. one's temper to a pitch** j. in höchste Erregung versetzen; ~ **in a top policy position** höchstmögliche berufliche Position erreichen; ~ **voluntarily** sich selbst auflösen, freiwillig liquidieren; ~ **a watch** Uhr aufziehen.

windbag *(coll.)* Schaumschläger, Schwätzer, Windbeutel.

windbaggery *(sl.)* leeres Gewäsch (Geschätz).

windbill *(Br.)* Keller-, Reit-, Gefälligkeitswechsel.

windbreak Windbruch.

windcheater *(Br.)* Windjacke.

winder Wendeltreppenstufe.

windfall Fallobst, *(forestry)* Windbruch, *(lucky hit)* unverhoffter Glücksfall, unerwarteter Gewinn;
to come into a ~ unverhofft zu einem Gewinn kommen;
~ **profit** unverhoffter Glücksfall, unerwarteter Gewinn; ~ **receipts** nicht vorhergesehene Einkünfte, Zufallseinnahmen, *(oil industry)* Übergewinne; ~ **wealth** vom Himmel gefallener Reichtum.

windfallen windbrüchig.

windflow Bö, heftiger Windstoß.

windhole *(mining)* Wetterschacht.

windiness of the weather stürmisches Wetter.

winding Wickeln, Spulen, Winden, *(bend)* Windung, Biegung, Krümmung, *(el.)* Wickelung;
~ *(a.)* sich windend (schlängelnd);
~ **sheet** Leichentuch; ~ **staircase** Wendeltreppe; ~ **tower** *(mining)* Förderturm; **self-~ watch** automatische Uhr.

winding up Liquidation[sverfahren], Abwicklung (Auflösung) eines Geschäftes, *(company, Br.)* Eröffnung des Konkursverfahrens;
compulsory ~ Zwangsliquidation, -abwicklung, -auflösung; **voluntary ~** freiwillige Liquidation (Abwicklung), Selbstauflösung, außergerichtliche Firmenliquidation; **member's voluntary ~** *(company resolution)* Eigenliquidation;
~ **of an affair** Abschluß einer Angelegenheit; ~ **by arrangement** Liquidationsvergleich; ~ **of a business** Geschäftsauflösung; ~ **the debtor's business** Liquidation der Geschäfte des Gemein-

schuldners; ~ **a clock** Aufziehen einer Uhr; ~ **of companies** *(Br.)* Liquidation von Gesellschaften; ~ **by the court** gerichtliche Liquidation (Abwicklung), Zwangsliquidation, Gesellschaftskonkurs; ~ **of an estate** *(Br.)* Nachlaßliquidierung; ~ **of a fund** Auflösung eines Fonds; ~ **of a speech** Schluß einer Rede; ~ **subject to the supervision of the court** Liquidation (Abwicklung) unter Aufsicht des Gerichtes;
to supervise the ~ Liquidation überwachen;
~ **Act** Liquidationsordnung; ~ **costs** Liquidationskosten; ~ **losses** Insolvenzverluste; ~ **order** gerichtlicher Liquidationsbeschluß, Konkurs-, Auflösungsbeschluß; **compulsory** ~ **order** Anordnung der Zwangsliquidation; ~ **petition** Antrag auf Liquidation der Gesellschaft, Auflösungs-, Abwicklungs-, Liquidationsantrag; ~ **proceeds** Liquidationserlös; ~ **proceedings** Liquidations-, Abwicklungsverfahren; ~ **provisions** Liquidationsbestimmungen; ~ **regulations** Auflösungsbestimmungen; ~ **resolution** Liquidationsbeschluß; ~ **rules** *(Br.)* Abwicklungs-, Liquidationsrichtlinien, -bestimmungen; ~ **sale** Ausverkauf wegen Geschäftsaufgabe, Totalausverkauf; ~ **transaction** Abwicklungsgeschäft.
windjammer Windjammer, Segelschiff.
windmill Windmühle, *(kite, Br.)* Reit-, Gefälligkeitswechsel, *(sl.)* Hubschrauber;
to throw one's cap over the ~ jede Vorsicht außer Acht lassen, sich über alle Konventionen hinwegsetzen; **to tilt at** ~**s** Kampf gegen Windmühlen führen;
~ **sail** Windmühlenflügel.
window Fenster, *(envelope)* Fenster, *(office, US)* [Bank-, Post]-schalter, *(shop)* Schaufenster, *(shutter)* Fensterrahmen, -laden, *(window pane)* Fensterscheibe;
out the ~ *(sl.)* verloren, *(career)* erledigt;
bay ~ Erker; **blind** ~ blindes Fenster; **curtained** ~ mit Vorhängen versehenes (zugezogenes) Fenster; **rear** ~ Rückfenster; **roll-down** ~ *(car)* automatisch versenkbares Fenster; **ticket** ~ Fahrkartenschalter; **view** ~ Panoramafenster;
the ~**s of heaven** die Schleusen des Himmels;
to be a ~ **to the world** der ganzen Welt zugänglich machen; **to block up the** ~ die Sicht verbauen; **to break a** ~ Fensterscheibe zerbrechen; **to display in the** ~ im Schaufenster ausstellen; **to dress a** ~ Schaufenster dekorieren; **to have gone right out of the** ~ völlig verloren sein; **to put all one's knowledge in the** ~ mit seinem Wissen prahlen; **to smash s. one's** ~**s** jem. die Fenster einwerfen;
~ **advertising** Schaufensterreklame; ~ **bar** Fenstersprosse; ~ **blind** Rouleau, Jalousie, Rolladen; ~ **board** Fensterbrett; ~ **box** Fensterstock; ~ **card** Schaufenster-, Aufstellplakat; ~ **clerk** *(post office, US)* Schalterbeamter; ~ **decoration** Schaufensterdekoration, *(material)* Dekorationsmaterial; ~ **delivery** Schalterdienst.
window display Schaufensterdekoration, -reklame;
~ **competition** Schaufensterwettbewerb; ~ **man** Schaufensterdekorateur; ~ **material** Auslagematerial für Schaufenster, Dekorationsmaterial.
window|dresser Schaufensterdekorateur, -gestalter; ~ **dressing** Schaufensterdekoration, Dekorieren, *(balance sheet)* Bilanzverschleierung, Liquiditätsmanipulationen, *(bank statement)* kurzfristige Liquiditätsanhäufung, *(sham)* Aufmachung, Mache, Schönfärberei, Reklame; ~ **envelope** Fensterumschlag, Fensterbriefhülle; ~ **frame** Fensterrahmen; ~ **gardening** Blumenzucht am Fenster; ~~**gaze** *(v.)* Schaufenster ansehen; ~ **glass** Fensterscheibe, -glas; ~ **head** Fenstersturz; ~ **ledge** Fenstersims; ~ **mirror** Spion; ~ **sash** Fensterrahmen, Schiebefenster; ~ **screen** Fliegenfenster; ~ **seat** Fenstersitz; ~ **shade** Jalousie, Rouleau; ~~**shop** *(v.)* Schaufensterbummel machen; ~~**shopper** Schaufensterbummler; **to go** ~~**shopping** Schaufensterauslagen ansehen, Schaufensterbummel machen; ~ **shutter** Fensterladen; ~ **sill** Fensterbank; ~ **sticker** Fensterklebeplakat; ~ **streamer** *(advertising)* Fenster[auf]kleber, Schaufensterstreifen; ~ **trimming** Dekorieren.
windowman Schalterbeamter.
windowpane Fensterscheibe.
windproof windgeschützt, -undurchlässig.
windscreen Windschutz, -fang, *(Br.)* Windschutzscheibe;
safety-laminated ~ Frontscheibe aus Verbundglas;
to demist the ~ Windschutzscheibe belüften;
~ **washer** *(Br.)* Scheibenwaschanlage; ~ **wiper** *(Br.)* Scheibenwischer.
windshield *(US)* Windschutzscheibe;
~ **washer** *(US)* Scheibenwaschanlage; ~ **washer reservoir** *(US)* Druckluftbehälter für die Scheibenwaschanlage; ~ **wiper** *(US)* Scheibenwischer.

windup Ende, Schluß;
~ **of an account** Rechnungsabschluß; ~ **of a business** Abwicklung eines Geschäftes, Liquidation.
windward Windseite;
~ *(a.)* windwärts, luvwärts;
to get to ~ **of s. o.** Vorteil vor jem. erringen.
windway *(mar.)* Windrichtung, *(mining)* Wetterstrecke.
windy windig, stürmisch, *(changeable)* wetterwendisch, unzuverlässig, *(given to boasting)* hochtrabend, angeberisch, *(given to empty talk)* geschwätzig, eitel, leer.
wine Wein, *(intoxication)* Rausch, Trunkenheit, *(social gathering, Br.)* Weinabend;
in ~ betrunken;
Adam's ~ Gänsewein;
new ~ **in old bottles** junger Wein in alten Schläuchen; ~ **from the cask** offener Wein;
~ *(v.)* mit Wein bewirten;
to adulterate ~ Wein panschen;
~ **bottle** Weinflasche; ~ **cask** Weinfaß; ~ **cellar** Weinkeller; ~ **duty** Weinsteuer; ~ **import quotas** *(EC)* Einfuhrkontingente für Weine; ~ **merchant** Weinhändler; ~ **trade** Weinhandel; ~ **vault** Weinkeller, -lager.
winegrower Weinbauer.
winegrowing Weinbau.
winehouse Weinhandlung.
wineshop Weingeschäft, -handlung.
wing Flug, Fliegen, *(airforce, Br.)* Gruppe, *(airplane)* Tragfläche, *(car)* Kotflügel, *(house)* Seitengebäude, Gebäudeteil, Flügel, *(mil.)* Flanke, Flügel, *(theater)* Seitenkulisse;
on the ~ auf Reisen, unterwegs; **under s. one's** ~**s** unter jds. Fittichen;
left ~ *(pol.)* linker Flügel; **new** ~ Anbau; **right** ~ *(pol.)* rechter Flügel; **set-back** ~**s** weit zurückversetzte Tragflächen; **swept-back** ~ Pfeilflügel; **submerged** ~ Unterwassertragflügel;
new ~ **to a hospital** neuer Krankenhausflügel; **militant** ~ **of party** militanter Parteiflügel;
~ *(v.)* mit Tragflächen (Kotflügeln) versehen, *(coll., airplane)* abschießen, *(fig.)* beflügeln, beschwingen, *(theater)* sich ganz auf den Souffleur verlassen;
~ **round Europe on pleasure trips** in ganz Europa zum Vergnügen herumfliegen; ~ **s. one's steps** jds. Schritte beschleunigen;
to add a new ~ **to a hospital** neuen Krankenhausflügel anbauen; **to be on the right** ~ auf dem rechten Flügel stehen, zum rechten Flügel gehören; **to be waiting in the** ~ im Anzug sein; **to build a new** ~ **to a hotel** Hotelflügel anbauen; **to clip s. one's** ~**s** jem. die Flügel stutzen, *(expenses)* jds. Spesenetat beschneiden; **to get one's** ~**s** *(pilot)* sein Pilotenexamen machen; **to lend** ~**s to s. o.** jem. Flügel verleihen; **to place under the** ~ **of** unter jds. Fittiche stellen; **to take under one's** ~**s** unter seine Fittiche nehmen; **to take to itself** ~**s** sich verflüchtigen (in Nichts auflösen); **to throw out a** ~ **to a house** Flügel anbauen; **to wait in the** ~**s** auf seinen Auftritt warten;
right-~ rechtsstehend;
~ **area** *(plane)* tragende Fläche; ~ **chair** Ohrensessel; ~ **commander** *(US)* Geschwaderkommodore; ~ **compass** Bogenzirkel; ~~**footed messenger** beflügelter Bote; ~ **mirror** auf dem Kotflügel installierter Spiegel; ~ **loading** Tragflächenbelastung; ~ **skid** Tragflächenkufe; ~ **wall** Flügelmauer.
wingspread *(plane)* Spannweite.
wink Blinzeln, Zwinkern, *(moment)* Augenblick;
~ *(v.)* blinken, zwinkern, *(fig.)* nichts sehen wollen, *(signal by flashlights)* durch Lichtsignale anzeigen;
~ **at an insult** Beleidigung ignorieren;
to be gone in a ~ im Nu sein; **not to get a** ~ **of sleep** kein Auge zutun; **to have forty** ~**s** Nickerchen machen.
winker Blinker, Blinkleuchte, *(horse)* Scheuklappe.
winking Blinzeln, Zwinkern;
as easy as ~ *(Br., sl.)* kinderleicht; **like** ~ *(coll.)* wie der Blitz, im Nu;
~ **lights** *(car)* Blinklichter.
winner Gewinner;
to be a ~ *(play)* gut ankommen; **to turn a company into a** ~ Ertragsfähigkeit einer Gesellschaft herstellen.
winning Gewinnen, Sieg, *(mining)* Grube, Schacht, *(profit)* Gewinn, Nutzen;
ore ~ Erzabbau, -gewinnung;
~ **of the war** siegreicher Kriegsausgang;
~ *(a.)* siegreich, *(fig.)* anziehend;
~ **formula** Gewinnformel; ~ **number** *(lottery)* Gewinnlos, -nummer; ~ **smile** gewinnendes Lächeln; ~ **ticket** Lotteriegewinn.

winnings Wettgewinn, Gewinn, Gewinst;
  to collect one's ~ from the betting shop seinen Gewinn vom Wettbüro abholen.
winnow *(v.)* | **the chaff from the grain** Spreu vom Weizen trennen; ~ **the truth from falsehood** Wahrheit von der Lüge unterscheiden.
winnowing machine, to run the nicht leeres Stroh dreschen.
winter Winter, *(fig.)* unproduktive Zeitspanne;
  in the dead of ~ mitten im kalten Winter;
  hard ~ strenger Winter;
  ~ abode Winteraufenthalt; ~ **catalog(ue)** Winterkatalog; ~ **crop** Wintergetreide; ~ **garden** Wintergarten; ~ **heyning** *(forests)* Winterschonzeit; ~ **peak in demand** winterlicher Spitzenbedarf; ~ **quarters** *(mil.)* Winterquartier; ~ **resident** Winterbewohner; ~ **resort** Winterkurort, -sportplatz; ~ **sale** *(US)* Winterschlußverkauf; ~ **schedule** *(US)* Winterfahrplan; ~ **season** Wintersaison; ~ **sports** Wintersport; ~ **sports resort** Wintersportplatz; ~ **stock** Winterlager; ~ **term** Wintersemester; ~ **visitors** Wintergäste.
winterfeed *(v.)* durch den Winter füttern.
wintering Stallfütterung im Winter.
winterize *(v.)* **a car** Auto winterfest machen.
wintry | **greeting** eisiges Willkommen; ~ **weather** winterliches Wetter.
wipe Wischen;
  ~ *(v.)* abwischen, sauber (trocken) wischen;
  ~ s. one's eyes *(sl.)* j. in den Schatten stellen; ~ **the floor with s. o.** *(sl.)* mit jem. Schlitten fahren; ~ **the slate clean** neuen Anfang machen, von vorn anfangen.
wipe off *(v.)* ab-, auf-, wegwischen, *(fig.)* tilgen, auslöschen;
  ~ the books voll abschreiben; ~ **a debit balance** Debetsaldo abbuchen, zweifelhafte Forderung abschreiben; ~ **debts** Schulden abtragen; ~ **it off** *(sl.)* sich ganz aufs Geschäft konzentrieren; ~ **a mortgage** Hypothek zurückzahlen; ~ **a score** etw. wieder in Ordnung bringen; ~ **s. th. off the slate** *(fig.)* etw. begraben.
wipe out *(v.)* auswischen;
  ~ a whole army ganze Armee vernichten; ~ **a disgrace** Scharte auswetzen; ~ **an insult** sich für eine Beleidigung rächen; ~ **the population** Bevölkerung hinweggraffen; ~ **old scores** sich wieder vertragen.
wiper Staub-, Wischtuch, *(car)* Scheibenwischer;
  delayed-action ~ langsam laufender Scheibenwischer;
  ~ blade Scheibenwischergummi.
wiping off (out) of debts Schuldentilgung, -abtragung.
wire Draht, Drahtgitter, *(cable)* Kabel, *(coll.)* Telegramm, Depesche, Drahtnachricht, *(el.)* Leitungsdraht, *(network)* Telegrafennetz, *(tel.)* Leitung, *(thieves, sl.)* Langfinger, Taschendieb;
  by (per) ~ telegrafisch; ~ **collect** *(US)* Telegramm mit bezahlter Rückantwort;
  ~s *(fig.)* geheime Fäden (Machenschaften, Beziehungen);
  barbed ~ Stacheldraht; ~ **collect** *(US)* Telegramm mit bezahlter Rückantwort; **copper ~** Kupferdraht; **hot ~** *(politics)* heißer Draht; **live ~** unter Spannung stehende Leitung; **telephone ~s** Telefonleitung; **urgent ~** dringliches Telegramm;
  ~ *(v.)* telegrafieren, telegrafisch benachrichtigen, Telegramm schicken, drahten, *(el.)* elektrische Leitungen verlegen, mit Installationen versehen;
  ~ away *(coll.)* loslegen, mit Eifer an die Arbeit gehen; ~ **back** zurücktelegrafieren; ~ **a house for electricity** elektrische Leitungen in einem Haus verlegen; ~ **in** *(coll.)* sich mit Eifer an die Arbeit machen; ~ **s. o. to sell shares** jem. einen telegrafischen Aktienverkaufsauftrag zukommen lassen;
  to countermand by ~ abtelegrafieren; **to get one's ~s crossed** falsch reagieren; **to hand in a ~** Telegramm aufgeben; **to kill (recall) a ~** Telegramm widerrufen; **to pull the ~s** seine Beziehungen spielen lassen; **to pull the ~s for office** sich durch Beziehungen eine Stellung verschaffen; **to send s. o. a ~** jem. ein Telegramm schicken, jem. telegrafieren; **to send off a ~** Telegramm aufgeben (expedieren); **to send an order by ~** telegraphisch bestellen; **to telephone a ~** Telegramm telefonisch durchsagen; **to transmit by ~** telegraphisch übermitteln;
  ~ acceptance Drahtannahme; ~ **address** Telegrammanschrift, -adresse; ~ **answer** Drahtantwort, telegrafische Antwort; ~ **block stitching** Drahtblockheftung; ~ **bridge** Drahtseilbrücke; ~ **city** *(sl.)* Gefängnis; ~ **cloth** Drahtgeflecht, -gewebe; ~ **cutter** Drahtzange; ~ **entanglement** Drahtverhau; ~ **fate** drahtet ob bezahlt; ~ **nail** Drahtstift, -nagel; ~ **report** Drahtbericht; ~ **rope** Drahtseil; ~ **screen** Maschendrahtzaun; ~ **service tape** Fernschreiberlochstreifen; ~ **staples** *(bookbinding)* Draht-

klammern; **~-stitched** *(book)* broschiert, geheftet; ~ **stitching** Drahtheftung; ~ **transfer** *(US)* telegrafische Geldüberweisung; ~ **walker** Drahtseilakrobat, Seiltänzer; ~ **wool** Topfkratzer.
wired mit einem Drahtzaun umgeben, *(bugged)* mit Abhörvorrichtungen (Wanzen) versehen;
  ~ for electricity elektrisch installiert;
  ~ glass Drahtglas; ~ **radio (wireless)** Drahtfunk.
wiredrawer Drahtzieher.
wiredrawn *(fig.)* ausgeklügelt;
  ~ argument spitzfindige Beweisführung.
wireless drahtlose Telegraphie, Funktelegraphie, *(radio, Br.)* Radio, [Rund]funk, Radio-, Rundfunkapparat;
  by ~ funktelegraphisch, *(Br.)* durch Rundfunk; **on the ~** im Radio (Rundfunk);
  ~ *(v.)* drahten, telegrafieren, *(Br.)* durch Rundfunk (drahtlos) senden, funken;
  ~ *(a.)* drahtlos;
  ~ communications Funkverkehr; **~-controlled** ferngesteuert; **~-equipped** mit Autoradio; ~ **engineer** Rundfunktechniker; ~ **installation** Funkanlage, Rundfunkeinrichtung; ~ **licence** *(Br.)* Rundfunkgenehmigung; ~ **licence fee** *(Br.)* Rundfunkgebühr; ~ **message** Funkspruch, -telegramm; **to send a ~ message** Funkspruch senden; ~ **officer** Funkoffizier; ~ **operator** Funker, *(ship)* Bordfunker; ~ **picture telegraph** Bildfunk; ~ **pirate** Schwarzhörer; ~ **program(me)** Sendefolge, Rundfunkprogramm; ~ **receiver** Rundfunkempfänger, Radioapparat; ~ **room** *(ship)* Bordfunkstelle; ~ **set** Rundfunkapparat; ~ **silence** Funkstille; ~ **station** [Rund]funk-, Radiostation, Sender; ~ **tax** Rundfunkgebühr; ~ **telegram** Funk-, Radiotelegramm; ~ **telegraphy** drahtlose Telegraphie, Funktelegraphie; ~ **telephone** Funkfernsprecher; ~ **telephony** Funk-, Radiotelefonie; ~ **transmitter** Rundfunksender.
wireman Telefonarbeiter.
wirephoto Bildtelegramm.
wirepull *(v.)* Drahtzieher sein.
wirepuller *(fig.)* Drahtzieher, Ränkeschmied, Intrigant.
wirepulling Spielenlassen von Beziehungen, Intrigen, Machenschaften.
wiretap *(v.)* mithören;
  ~ without a court order Telefongespräche ohne richterliche Genehmigung abhören.
wiretapper *(tel.)* geheimer Mithörer, Anzapfer einer Telefonleitung.
wiretapping Mithören von Telefongesprächen, *(installation)* Mithör-, Abhöreinrichtung.
wirework Drahtgeflecht, -gewebe.
wiring elektrische Anlage, Leitungsnetz, Leitungen;
  ~ machine *(bookbinding)* Drahthefter.
wisdom Klugheit, Einsicht;
  conventional ~ says nach herkömmlichen Erfahrungen;
  to cut one's ~ teeth reifer werden.
wise verständig, gescheit, *(sl.)* glänzend unterrichtet;
  ~ after the event um eine Erfahrung reicher; ~ **in the law** rechtkundig;
  to be none the ~r genauso schlau sein wie zuvor; **to get ~ to what's happening** herausbekommen, was los ist; **to get ~ to the ways of businessmen** kaufmännische Erfahrungen sammeln; **to put s. o. ~ to** j. ins Bild setzen;
  ~ guy Besserwisser, Klugscheißer; ~ **idea** kluger Gedanke.
wiseacre Besserwisser, Klugscheißer.
wisecrack witzige Bemerkung, Bonmot;
  ~s Witzeleien;
  ~ *(v.)* Bonmot machen.
wisehead Schlaukopf, Neunmalkluger, Klugscheißer.
wisewoman Hellseherin, Wahrsagerin.
wish Wunsch, Wille, Verlangen, Begehren;
  heart-felt ~ tiefgefühltes Bedürfnis;
  ~ *(v.)* wünschen, ersehnen, Verlangen haben, *(testament)* letztwillig anordnen;
  ~ s. o. well jem. Glück wünschen;
  to comply with s. one's ~ jds. Wünschen Rechnung tragen; **to have a great ~ for s. th.** großes Verlangen nach etw. haben; **to meet one's customers' ~s without delay** Kundenwünsche unverzüglich erledigen; **to send one's best ~es** seine besten Wünsche übermitteln;
  ~ book *(coll.)* Versandhauskatalog; ~ **fulfilment** Wunscherfüllung.
wish-wash dünnes Gesöff, *(fig.)* hohles Geschwätz, Geseich.
wishful thinking Wunschdenken, Zweckoptimismus.
wishy-washy dünn, wässerig, *(person)* unentschlossen, *(style)* fad, seicht.

wisp Wisch, Bündel, *(will-of-the-wisp)* Irrlicht;
  ~s of clouds Schleierwolken; **~ of hay** Heubündel; **~ of paper** Fidibus; **~ of smoke** Rauchfetzen.
wit geistige Fähigkeit, Intelligenz, Urteilskraft, *(mental sharpness)* geistige Wendigkeit, Esprit;
  out of one's ~s völlig außer sich;
  ~s gesunder Menschenverstand;
  to addle s. one's ~s j. verrückt machen; **to be frightened out of one's ~s** Todesangst bekommen; **to have one's ~s about one** seine fünf Sinne beisammen haben; **to have a ready ~** Esprit haben, schlagfertig sein; **to keep one's ~ about** Situation sofort überblicken; **to live on one's ~s** sich mehr oder weniger ehrlich durchs Leben schlagen; **to lose one's ~s** seinen Verstand verlieren; **to match one's ~s with s. o.** es geistig mit jem. aufnehmen; **to sparkle with ~** vor Geist sprühen;
  at one's ~s' end mit seinem Latein (seiner Weisheit) am Ende.
witch Hexe, Zauberin, häßliche Alte, *(Br., coll.)* bezaubernde Frau;
  ~ (v.) verzaubern, verhexen.
witch-hunt *(politics)* Hexenjagd;
  ~ (v.) Jagd auf politisch Verdächtige machen.
witchcraft Hexerei.
with, to be ~ it *(sl.)* auf Draht sein; **to be not quite ~ it** noch nicht ganz wieder da sein.
withdraw *(v.)* zurückziehen, wegnehmen, entfernen, *(loan)* ablösen, *(money)* abheben, entnehmen, *(motion)* zurücknehmen, *(retire)* sich zurückziehen, zurück-, austreten, ausscheiden;
  ~ an action Klage zurücknehmen; **~ aid** Unterstützung entziehen, Hilfe einstellen; **~ an appeal** Berufung (Rechtsmittel) zurücknehmen; **~ from an association** aus einem Verein austreten; **~ an attachment** Beschlagnahme aufheben; **~ from a bank** von der Bank abheben; **~ dirty bank-notes from circulation** unbrauchbare Banknoten aus dem Verkehr ziehen (einziehen); **~ a bill** Wechsel zurückrufen; **~ a pontoon bridge** Schiffsbrücke abbrechen; **~ one's candidature** seine Kandidatur zurückziehen; **~ one's charge** seine Anschuldigungen (seinen Strafantrag) zurücknehmen; **~ a child from school** Kind von der Schule nehmen; **~ money from circulation** Geld aus dem Verkehr ziehen (außer Kurs setzen); **~ one's claims** von seinen Forderungen abgehen; **~ from a company** aus einer Firma ausscheiden; **~ one's confidence from s. o.** jem. sein Vertrauen entziehen; **~ from a contract** von einem Vertrag zurücktreten; **~ a credit** Kredit kündigen; **~ an offending expression** beleidigende Äußerung zurücknehmen; **~ one's favo(u)r** seine Gunst entziehen; **~ in favo(u)r of s. o.** zu jds. Gunsten zurücktreten; **~ one's friendship** seine Freundschaft entziehen; **~ into one's ivory tower** sich in seinen Elfenbeinturm zurückziehen; **~ a juror** Geschworenen abberufen; **~ one's labo(u)r** streiken; **~ a licence** Konzession entziehen; **~ s. one's driving licence** jds. Führerschein einziehen; **~ from a list** von einer Liste streichen; **~ a measure** Maßnahme rückgängig machen; **~ from membership** als Mitglied ausscheiden (austreten); **~ money** Geld abheben; **~ one's money from a business** seine Beteiligung aufgeben; **~ a motion** Antrag zurücknehmen; **~ from office** aus einem Amt ausscheiden; **~ opposition** Einspruch zurücknehmen; **~ an order** Auftrag widerrufen (stornieren, rückgängig machen); **~ from a partnership** aus einer Handelsgesellschaft austreten, als Gesellschafter ausscheiden; **~ a permit** Genehmigung widerrufen; **~ a play** Stück absetzen; **~ from a political project** politisches Projekt aufgeben; **~ restrictions** Beschränkungen aufheben; **~ securities from a deposit** Effekten aus dem Depot nehmen; **~ a statement** Aussage widerrufen; **~ one's subscription** sein Abonnement aufgeben; **~ a sum of money** Geldbetrag abheben; **~ from a treaty** Staatsvertrag aufkündigen; **~ troops from an exposed position** Truppen aus einer vorgeschobenen (unhaltbaren) Stellung zurücknehmen; **~ from an undertaking** sich von einem Unternehmen zurückziehen; **~ from a warehouse** Auslagerung vornehmen; **~ a word** Wort zurücknehmen; **~ from the world** sich aus dem öffentlichen Leben zurückziehen.
withdrawable at one's years notice mit einjähriger Kündigungsfrist abhebbar.
withdrawal Zurücknahme, -ziehung, *(of action)* Klagerücknahme, *(from circulation)* Entwertung, Außerkurssetzung, *(of contract)* Rücktritt, Widerruf, *(money)* Abhebung, Entnahme, *(retirement)* Aus-, Rücktritt, Ausscheiden, *(retreat)* Rückzug; **~s** *(partner)* Privatentnahme;
  day-to-day ~s tägliche Abhebungen; **emergency ~** Geldabhebung in Notfällen; **gold ~s** Goldabzüge; **gradual ~** stufenweiser Abzug; **ordinary ~** Normalabhebung; **savings ~** Abhebungen vom Sparkonto;

~ of action Klagerücknahme; **~ from an agreement** Rücktritt von einer Vereinbarung; **~ of an application** Rücknahme einer Bewerbung; **~ of the authorization to operate** Konzessionsentzug; **~ of bank-notes** Einziehung von Banknoten, Banknoteneinziehung; **~ of a candidate** Zurückziehung eines Kandidaten; **~ from a candidature** Verzicht auf eine Kandidatur; **~ of capital** Kapitalentnahme; **~ of cash** Barentnahme; **~ of a charge** Zurücknahme des Strafantrags; **~ from a company** Ausscheiden aus einer Firma; **~ from a contract** Vertragsrücktritt; **~ of counsel** Mandatsniederlegung; **~ of credit** Kreditzurückziehung, -kündigung, -entziehung; **~ of a deposit account** *(Br.)* Abhebung von Spareinlagen; **~ of a driving licence** *(Br.)* Führerscheinentzug, Entzug des Führerscheins; **~ of an offending expression** Rücknahme einer Beleidigung; **~ of forces** Truppenabzug; **~ of funds** Abhebungen, Mittelabzug; **~ of gold** Goldabzüge; **~ of s. one's immunity** Aufhebung der Immunität, Immunitätsaufhebung; **~ of a licence** Lizenzentzug; **~ of liquidity** Liquiditätsentzug; **~ from a list** Streichung aus einer Liste; **~ of material** Materialentnahme; **~ from membership** Vereinsaustritt; **~ of money** Geldabhebung; **~ of money from circulation** Außerkurssetzung von Banknoten; **~ of a motion** Zurücknahme eines Antrags, Antragsrücknahme; **~ of a notice** Rücknahme einer Kündigung; **~ of opposition** Einspruchsrücknahme; **~ of an order** Rückgängigmachung einer Bestellung, Auftragsstornierung; *(law court)* Aufhebung einer Verfügung; **~ of a partner** Ausscheiden eines Gesellschafters, Firmenaustritt; **~ of a passport** Paßeinziehung; **~ of a patent** Versagen eines Patents; **~ of a permit** Widerruf einer Genehmigung; **~ of a power of attorney** Vollmachtsrücknahme; **~ resources** Entzug von Mitteln; **net ~s from savings accounts** Nettobelastung von Sparguthaben; **~ of services** Dienstleistungsentzug; **~ of a statement** Rücknahme einer Erklärung; **~ of one's suit** *(US)* Klagerücknahme; **~ of a sum of money** Geldabhebung; **~ from a transaction** Rücktritt (Zurücktreten) von einem Geschäft; **~ from a treaty** Aufkündigung eines Staatsvertrages; **~ of troops** Truppenabzug; **~ of wages** Lohnabhebungen; **~ from a warehouse** Auslagerung;
  to declare one's ~ seinen Rücktritt (Austritt) erklären; **to give notice of ~ of bonds** Rückzahlung von Obligationen ankündigen;
  ~ benefit Abgangsregulierung; **~ form** Abhebungsformular; **~ notice** *(banking)* Kreditkündigung; **~ order** *(stock)* Lagerausgabeanweisung; **~ period** Kündigungsfrist; **~ plan** *(warehouse)* Auslagerungsplan; **~ request** Rücknahmeantrag; **~ requirements** Abhebungserfordernisse; **~ restrictions** Abhebungsbeschränkungen; **~ symptoms** Entziehungserscheinungen; **~ warrant** Auszahlungsermächtigung.
withdrawing a juror Abberufung eines Geschworenen.
withdrawn *(isolated)* abgeschnitten, isoliert, *(money)* abgehoben, entnommen, *(unsociable)* introvertiert;
  unless previously ~ sofern nicht vorher widerrufen.
wither *(v.)* **~ away** nachlassen, vergehen.
withhold *(v.)* hindern, entziehen, vorenthalten, *(possession)* ein-, zurückbehalten;
  ~ o. s. from s. th. sich in einer Sache zurückhalten; **~ s. th. from s. o.** jem. etw. vorenthalten; **~ one's consent** seine Zustimmung versagen, seine Einwilligung vorenthalten; **~ a document** Urkunde nicht herausgeben; **~ a patent** Patenterteilung versagen; **~ so much out of s. one's pay** soundsoviel von jds. Lohn einbehalten; **~ payment** Zahlung vorenthalten; **~ s. one's property** jds. Eigentum zurückbehalten; **~ release of property** Vermögen nicht freigeben, Vermögensfreigabe nicht gestatten; **~ supply of goods from a dealer** Lieferung verweigern; **~ a tax** Quellensteuer erheben; **~ income tax** *(US)* Lohnsteuer einbehalten; **~ a tax from wage payment** Steuern bei der Lohnzahlung (Lohnsteuer) einbehalten; **~ the truth from s. o.** jem. die Wahrheit vorenthalten.
withholding Ein-, Zurückbehaltung, Vorenthaltung, *(tax)* Steuereinbehaltung, -abzugsverfahren;
  ~ income tax *(US)* Lohnsteuereinbehaltung; **~ means of support from dependants** Unterhaltsentzug; **~ of a patent** Patentverwehrung, -versagung; **~ of payments** Zurückhaltung von Zahlungen; **~ supply of goods from a dealer** Lieferverweigerung; **~ from wages** Lohneinbehaltung;
  ~ agent *(Br.)* lohnsteuerabzugspflichtige Stelle; **~ authorization** Vollmacht für die Einbehaltung von Lohnbeträgen; **~ employee's exemption** *(US)* Lohnsteuerfreibetrag; **~ exemption certificate** *(US)* Lohnsteuerfreibetragsbescheinigung; **~ rate** *(US, employees)* Lohnsteuersatz, *(dividends)* Kapitalertragssteuersatz; **~ regulations** *(US)* Bestimmung über die Einbehaltung von Lohnsteuern, Lohnsteuerrichtli-

nien; ~ **statement** *(US)* Bescheinigung über einbehaltene Lohnsteuer, Lohnsteuerbescheinigung; ~ **system** Quellenbesteuerungsverfahren; ~ **table** *(US)* Lohnsteuertabelle; ~ **tax** *(US) (dividends)* Quellen-, Kapitalertragssteuer, *(employee)* Steuerabzug von Dienstbezügen, [im Quellenabzugsverfahren erhobene] Lohnsteuer; **personal ~ tax** *(US)* einbehaltene Lohnsteuer; **federal ~ tax law** *(US)* Gesetz über die Einbehaltung von Lohnsteuern; ~ **tax principle** *(US)* [Lohn]steuerabzugsverfahren, Quellenbesteuerungssystem; ~ **tax table** *(US)* Lohnsteuertabelle.

within binnen, innerhalb, *(in the limits)* im Umkreis;
~ **o. s.** im Stillen, im Geiste; ~ **an ace** beinahe; ~ **call** in Rufweite; ~ **the house** im Hause; ~ **the meaning of the Act** innerhalb des gesetzlichen Anwendungsbereichs; ~ **a week of one's arrival** eine Woche nach Ankunft.

without ungerechnet;
~ **advice** ohne Bericht; ~ **extra charge** ohne Preisaufschlag; ~ **charge of any kind** lastenfrei; ~ **day** ohne Fristangabe; ~ **debt** schuldenfrei; ~ **delay** ohne schuldhaftes Zögern, unverzüglich; ~ **dividend** ohne Dividende; ~ **engagement** ohne Obligo, freibleibend; ~ **expenses** ohne Kosten; ~ **extra charge** ohne Preisaufschlag; ~ **giving compensation therefor** ohne Vergütung; ~ **impeachment of waste** *(lease)* mit dem Recht des Substanzeingriffes; ~ **interest** ohne Zinsberechtigung, franko Zinsen; ~ **issue** ohne Nachkommen; ~ **justification** unberechtigt; ~ **notice** fristlos, ohne vorherige Benachrichtigung; ~ **the pale of civilization** jenseits der Zivilisationsgrenze; ~ **prejudice** unbeschadet, ohne Anerkennung einer Rechtspflicht; ~ **recourse** ohne Regreßmöglichkeit (Obligo, Gewähr); ~ **reserve** *(auction sale)* ohne Vorbehalt; ~ **restriction** ohne Einschränkung, uneingeschränkt; ~ **sales** umsatzlos; **to go** ~ **saying** augenscheinlich sein; ~ **stint** unlimitiert, -beziffert; ~ **the state** *(US)* außerhalb amerikanischen Staatsgebiets;
to do ~ **s. th.** ohne etw. auskommen; **to travel** ~ **a ticket** als blinder Passagier mitfahren.

withstand *(v.)* | **a siege** einer Belagerung standhalten; ~ **temptation** der Versuchung widerstehen; ~ **hard wear** starker Beanspruchung standhalten.

witness Zeuge, Gewährsmann, *(bookbinding)* unbeschnittene Seite, *(testimony)* Zeugnis, Bekräftigung, Bestätigung;
according to ~**es** nach Angabe (den Aussagen) der Zeugen; **as** ~ **our hands** laut eigenhändiger Unterschrift, von uns unterzeichnet; **in** ~ **whereof** zu urkund dessen, urkundlich; **in the presence of** ~**es** vor Zeugen;
adverse ~ Gegenzeuge, Zeuge der Gegenpartei, voreingenommener Zeuge; **attesting** ~ Beglaubigungszeuge; **bribed** ~ bezahlter (bestochener) Zeuge; **challengeable** ~ befangener Zeuge; **compellable** ~ Zeuge ohne Aussageverweigerungsrecht; **competent** ~ geschäftsfähiger Zeuge; **contumacious** ~ unentschuldigt ausgebliebener Zeuge; **credible** ~ klassischer (glaubwürdiger) Zeuge; **defaulting** ~ ausgebliebener (nicht erschienener) Zeuge; **ear** ~ Ohrenzeuge; **expert** ~ sachverständiger Zeuge; **eye** ~ Augenzeuge; **false** ~ falsches Zeugnis; **friendly** ~ eigener Zeuge; **hostile** ~ Zeuge der Gegenpartei; **interested** ~ parteiischer Zeuge; **intermediate** ~ mittelbarer Zeuge; **key** ~ Hauptzeuge, wichtigster Zeuge; **still living** ~ noch lebender Zeuge; **material** ~ wichtiger Zeuge; **outside** ~ neutraler Zeuge; **perjured** ~ meineidiger Zeuge; **principal** ~ Hauptzeuge; **privileged** ~ zur Aussageverweigerung berechtigter Zeuge; **prosecuting** ~ Nebenkläger; **reliable** ~ glaubwürdiger Zeuge; **skilled** ~ sachverständiger Zeuge; **slippery** ~ unzuverlässiger Zeuge; **state's** ~ *(US)* Belastungszeuge; **subscribing** ~ Unterschriftszeuge; **swift** ~ voreingenommener Zeuge; **sworn** ~ vereidigter Zeuge; **tampered** ~ beeinflußter Zeuge; **trustworthy** ~ glaubwürdiger Zeuge;
~ **against s. o.** Belastungszeuge; ~ **against himself** zur Selbstbezichtigung gezwungener Zeuge; ~ **of an accident** Unfallzeuge; ~ **in court** Zeuge vor Gericht; ~ **for the Crown** *(Br.)* Belastungszeuge; ~ **to a deed** Unterschriftszeuge; ~ **for the defence** von der beklagten Partei benannter Zeuge, Entlastungszeuge; ~ **to a document** Unterschriftszeuge, *(deed)* Urkundsperson; ~ **to a marriage** Trauzeuge; ~ **on oath** vereidigter Zeuge; ~ **of well-established position** angesehener Zeuge; ~ **from the profession** sachverständiger Zeuge; ~ **for the prosecution** Zeuge der Staatsanwaltschaft, Belastungszeuge; ~ **to will** Testamentszeuge;
~ *(v.)* Zeuge sein, bezeugen, als Zeuge fungieren (aussagen), *(evidence)* bestätigen, bekunden, *(verify)* urkundlich (unterschriftlich) beglaubigen;
~ **against s. o.** gegen j. (zu jds. Nachteil) aussagen; ~ **for s. o.** zu jds. Gunsten (für j.) aussagen; ~ **an accident** bei einem Unfall

zugegen sein; ~ **against an accused person** gegen einen Angeklagten aussagen; ~ **to the truth of a statement** Wahrheit einer Aussage bestätigen; ~ **a will** als Zeuge bei einer Testamentserrichtung mitwirken;
to adduce ~**es** Zeugen beibringen; **to appear as** ~ als Zeuge erscheinen; **to be a** ~ **of s. th.** Zeuge von etw. sein; **to be** ~ **to a deed** Unterschrift unter einer Urkunde beglaubigen; **to be sworn in as a** ~ als Zeuge vereidigt werden; **to bear** ~ **to (of)** Zeugnis ablegen von, als Zeuge aussagen; **to bear false** ~ falsches Zeugnis ablegen; **to bear** ~ **to the same point** übereinstimmend das Gleiche bezeugen; **to bear** ~ **to the quality of a new car** Qualitätsleistungen eines neuen Autos bestätigen; **to bribe a** ~ Zeugen bestechen; **to bring forward a** ~ Zeugen beibringen; **to buy a** ~ Zeugen bestechen; **to call a** ~ Zeugen laden (aufrufen); **to call s. o. to** ~ *(US)* j. als Zeugen benennen; **to challenge a** ~ Einspruch gegen einen Zeugen erheben, Zeugen ablehnen; **to compel the attendance of a** ~ Zeugen zwangsweise vorführen; **to confront** ~**es** Zeugen einander gegenüberstellen; **to corner a** ~ Zeugen in die Enge treiben (verwirren); **to draw out a** ~ Zeugen ausfragen; **to examine a** ~ Zeugen [eidlich] vernehmen; **to examine a** ~ **in a court of law** Zeugen gerichtlich vernehmen; **to get at a** ~ Zeugen bearbeiten; **to give** ~ **on s. one's behalf in [law] court** vor Gericht für j. aussagen; **to hear a** ~ Zeugen vernehmen, in die Zeugenvernehmung eintreten; **to hear a** ~ **on commission** Zeugen kommissarisch vernehmen; **to object to a** ~ Zeugen ablehnen; **to pin a** ~ **down to facts** Zeugen zwingen, sich an die Tatsachen zu halten; **to prime a** ~ Zeugen präparieren; **to produce a** ~ Zeugen stellen; **to prompt a** ~ Zeugen beeinflussen; **to protest a** ~ Zeugen ablehnen; **to question a** ~ Zeugen vernehmen; **to reexamine a** ~ Zeugen ins Gegenkreuzverhör nehmen; **to reimburse a** ~ **for his expenses** einem Zeugen seine Kosten ersetzen, Zeugengeld zahlen; **to reproduce a** ~ Zeugen erneut vorführen; **to suborn a** ~ Zeugen bestechen; **to subpoena s. o. as** ~ j. als Zeugen vorladen, einem Zeugen die Ladung zustellen; **to summon a** ~ Zeugen vorladen; **to swear in a** ~ Zeugen vereidigen; **to take exception to a** ~ Zeugen ablehnen; **to tamper with a** ~ Zeugen beeinflussen;
~ **assembly** *(production)* Probelauf; ~ **box** Zeugenbank, -stand; ~ **boxing** Benehmen im Zeugenstand; ~ **chair** Zeugenstuhl; ~ **expenses** Zeugengebühr; ~ **fee** Zeugengebühr; ~ **mark** *(surveying)* Markierung; ~ **stand** *(US)* Zeugenstand; ~ **summons** *(Br.)* Zeugenvorladung.

witnessed | **by official means** amtlich beglaubigt;
to have a document ~ Urkunde in Zeugengegenwart legalisieren lassen.

witnessing Bekundung durch Zeugen, Zeugenbeweis, *(legalization)* Beurkundung, Bestätigung;
~ **clause** Beglaubigungsklausel.

witticism Bonmot.

witty geistreich, amüsant.

wizard Zauberkünstler, *(sl.)* Intelligenzbestie;
financial ~ Finanzgenie.

wobble *(v.)* schwanken, torkeln, *(tremble, coll.)* schlottern, zittern;
~ **between two opinions** in seiner Meinung hin und her schwanken.

woeful ignorance *(humo(u)r)* entsetzliche Unwissenheit.

woes Schwierigkeiten, Sorgen, Kalamitäten.

woffle *(sl.)* Geschwafel.

wolf Schürzenjäger, *(stock exchange)* gerissener Börsianer;
a ~ **in lamb's skin (sheep's clothing)** Wolf im Schafspelz;
to cry ~ blinden Alarm schlagen; **to cry** ~ **too often** bei jeder Kleinigkeit um Hilfe rufen; **to have the** ~ **by the ears** in der Klemme sitzen; **to have a** ~ **in one's stomach** Bärenhunger haben; **to hold the** ~ **by the ears** nicht ein noch aus wissen, in der Klemme sitzen; **to keep the** ~ **from the door** sich über Wasser halten, sich recht und schlecht durchschlagen.

wolfish appetite Bärenhunger.

woman Frau, Weib, *(female attendant)* Zofe, Dienstmädchen;
business ~ Geschäftsfrau; **career** ~ berufstätige Frau; **employed** ~ berufstätige Frau; **kept** ~ ausgehaltene Frau; **liberated** ~ emanzipierte Frau; **married** ~ Ehefrau; **needle** ~ Näherin; **single** ~ unverheiratete Frau, Ledige;
~ **of full age** volljährige Frau; ~ **with a history** Frau mit Vergangenheit; ~ **of the world** Frau von Welt;
~ **caretaker** Hausmeisterin; ~ **councillor** Rätin; ~ **doctor** Ärztin; ~ **driver** Fahrerin; ~ **executive** Unternehmerin; ~'s **page** Frauenseite; ~'s **program(me)** *(wireless)* Frauenfunk; ~'s **reason** weibliche Logik; ~ **reporter** Berichterstatterin; ~'s **service magazine** Hausfrauenzeitschrift; ~ **student** Studentin; ~ **suffrage** Frauenwahlrecht, -stimmrecht; ~ **writer** Schriftstellerin.

womanish weibisch, verweichlicht.

womankind weibliches Geschlecht.

women's | movement Frauenbewegung; **~ rights** Frauenrechte; **~ vote** Frauenstimmen; **~ wages** Löhne für weibliche Arbeitskräfte.

wonder Wunder;
for a ~ überraschenderweise; **no little ~** kaum glaublich; **a nine days' ~** kurzlebige Sensation; **signs and ~s** Zeichen und Wunder;
to work ~s Wunder vollbringen;
it is not for others to ~ Dritte brauchen sich hierüber nicht die Köpfe zerbrechen.

wonderland Märchenland;
~ of snow märchenhafte Schneelandschaft.

wood Wald[ung], (cask) Holzfaß, -tonne, Kufe, (timber) Bauholz, Nutzholz, Brennholz, (woodland) Waldgrundstück;
drawn from the ~ vom Faß; **out of the ~s** (coll.) aus dem Schlimmsten heraus, über den Berg;
ornamental ~ Edelholz; **soft ~** Weichholz;
~ (v.) (plant trees) aufforsten, (supply with wood) sich mit Brennholz eindecken;
to be unable to see the ~ for the trees den Wald vor lauter Bäumen nicht sehen;
~ alcohol Methanol; **~-based industry** Holzindustrie; **~ carving** Holzschnitzerei; **~-containing paper** holzhaltiges Papier; **~ floor** Holzfußboden; **~ margin** Waldrand; **~ pavement** Holzpflaster; **~ processing** Holzverarbeitung; **~ pulp** Zellulose; **~-pulp industry** Zelluloseindustrie; **~ wool** Holzwolle.

woodcut Holzschnitt.

woodcutting Holzfällerei, (engraving) Holzschneidekunst.

wooden (fig.) hölzern, unbeholfen.

woodland Waldung, -gebiet, Forst, Gehölz;
commercial ~ forstwirtschaftliches Vermögen;
~ proportion Waldanteil.

woodpile Holzstoß.

woodreeve (Br.) Forstaufseher, -wart.

woodshed Holzschuppen.

woodwork Holzarbeiten;
~ and timber industry Holzindustrie.

woodworker Holzarbeiter.

woody waldig, bewaldet.

wool Wolle, (material) Wollstoff, -tuch;
against the ~ gegen den Strich; **dyed in the ~** (fig.) in der Wolle gefärbt, waschecht;
cotton ~ Watte; **glass ~** Glaswolle;
to dye in the ~ waschecht färben; **to lose one's ~** (coll.) ärgerlich werden; **to pull the ~ over s. one's eyes** j. hinters Licht führen;
~ clip jährlicher Wollertrag; **~ merchant** Wollhändler; **~ mill** Reißwolf; **to take the seat on the ~-sack** (Br.) Oberhaussitzung eröffnen; **~ staple** Stapelplatz für Wolle; **~ stapler** Wollhändler; **~ trade** Wollhandel.

wool(l)en Wollstoff, -zeug;
~s wollene Kleidung;
~ blanket Wolldecke; **~ draper** Tuchhändler; **~ drapery** Wollwarengeschäft; **~ goods** Wollwaren.

woolgrower Schafzüchter.

woolgrowing Schafzucht, Wollproduktion.

woolly wollig, wollartig, (US coll.) atemberaubend, spannend;
~ thoughts wirre Gedanken.

woolpack cloud Haufenwolke.

woolsack (pol., Br.) Amt des Lordkanzlers.

word Wort, (message) Bescheid, Botschaft, Nachricht, Meldung, (mil.) Parole, Losung, (promise) Zusage, Versprechen;
at a ~ aufs Wort, sofort; **as last ~** die letzten Meldungen besagen; **by ~ of mouth** in mündlicher Form; **in a ~** kurzum; **in precatory ~s** (last will) als Bitte formuliert; **not only in ~ but also in deed** nicht nur in Worten, sondern auch mit Taten; **upon my ~** bei meiner Ehre;
~s Rede, Äußerung;
big ~s hochtrabende Worte; **blasphemous ~s** gotteslästerliche Sprache; **coined ~** erfundenes Wort, Kunstwort; **comprehensive ~** vielsagendes Wort; **concluding ~s** Schlußwort; **defamatory ~s** beleidigende Ausdrücke; **deleted ~** gestrichenes Wort; **derivative ~** abgeleitetes Wort; **dying ~s** letzte Worte, Worte auf dem Sterbebett; **four-letter (Saxon) ~s** unflätige Ausdrücke; **hot ~s** zornige Worte; **identification ~s** (tel.) Buchstabierwörter; **key ~** Stichwort; **kind ~s** freundliche Worte; **precatory ~** letztwillige Bitte; **seditious ~s** hochverräterische Reden; **sharp ~s** scharfe (böse) Worte; **sympathetic ~s** teilnehmende Worte; **waif ~** geläufiges Wort;
~s actionable in themselves beleidigende Ausdrücke; **~ of art**

Fachausdruck; **~s of description** beschreibende Ausdrücke; **~s of exemption** Immunitätsklausel; **~ of hono(u)r** Ehrenwort; **~s in italics** kursiv gesetzte Wörter; **foreign ~s of recent introduction** gerade in die Sprache aufgenommene Fremdwörter; **~s of limitation** (last will) einschränkende Worte; **~s of procreation** (estate tail) Nachkommensklausel; **~s of purchase** rechtsverbindliche beim Kauf gebrauchte Worte; **a ~ out of season** unangebrachter Ratschlag; **~s of welcome** Begrüßungsworte;
~ for ~ wortwörtlich; **~s and figures differ** (bill of exchange) Text und Kontext stimmen nicht überein;
~ (v.) in Worte fassen, formulieren, (draw up) [Schriftstück] abfassen;
~ carefully sorgfältig formulieren;
to back up one's ~s with action seinen Worten Taten folgen lassen; **to be not the ~ for it** zur Schilderung eines Sachverhalts kaum ausreichen, keine ausreichende Schilderung darstellen; **to be as good as one's ~** absolut zuverlässig sein; **to be too silly for ~s** unsagbar dumm sein; **to be the last ~ in comfort and convenience** modernste Komfortbedürfnisse befriedigen, das Allerneueste auf dem Gebiet des Komforts bringen; **not to believe a ~ of a story** einer Geschichte überhaupt keinen Glauben schenken; **to break one's ~** seine Versprechen nicht halten; **to divorce a ~ from its context** Wort aus dem Zusammenhang reißen; **to eat one's ~s** zu Kreuze kriechen; **to edge a ~ in** Wort einschieben; **not to get a ~ in edgeways** nicht zu Wort kommen; **to give one's ~** sein Ehrenwort geben; **to go back on one's ~** sein Versprechen nicht halten; **to have a ~ with s. o.** kurz mit jem. sprechen; **to have ~s with s. o.** Streit (Auseinandersetzungen) mit jem. haben; **to have the last ~** das letzte Wort behalten; **to keep one's ~** sein Versprechen halten; **to leave ~** Nachricht (Bescheid) hinterlassen; **to make no ~** keine Worte verlieren; **to misinterpret s. one's ~** jem. das Wort im Munde umdrehen; **to misuse a ~** Wort falsch gebrauchen; **to put into ~s** Schriftstück abfassen; **to put in a good ~ for s. o.** für j. sprechen, sich für j. einsetzen; **to receive ~** Bescheid erhalten; **to send ~ to s. o.** j. benachrichtigen, jem. Nachricht geben; **to suit the action to the ~** den Worten Taten folgen lassen; **to take s. one's ~ for it** jem. Glauben schenken; **to take the ~s of s. one's mouth** jem. das Wort aus dem Munde nehmen; **to thrust a ~ in now and than** ab und zu ein Wort dazwischenwerfen; **to translate ~ for ~** wortgetreu (wortwörtlich) übersetzen; **to waste one's ~s** in den Wind reden; **to write a ~ with an initial letter** Wort mit großen Anfangsbuchstaben schreiben;
~ accent Wortbetonung; **~ bank** Wortbank; **~-catcher** Wortklauber; **~-catching** Wortklauberei; **~-for-~ citation** wörtliches Zitat; **~ division** Silbentrennung; **~ flow** Redeschwall; **~ formation** Wortbildung; **~ order** Satzstellung, Wortreihenfolge; **~ painting** Wortmalerei; **~-perfect** (theater) rollenfest; **~ picture** bildhafte Schilderung, Wortgemälde; **~ power** Wortschatz; **~ processing** (data processing) Textverarbeitung; **~ processor** Schreibautomat; **~ rate** (telegram) Worttarif; **~ splitter** Wortklauber; **~ splitting** Wortklauberei, Sophisterei; **~ stress** Wortbetonung, Akzent; **~-for-word translation** wortwörtliche Übersetzung.

wordbook Lexikon, Nachschlagebuch, -werk, (opera) Textbuch.

wordbuilding Wortbildung.

wordcatcher Wortklauber.

wordcatching Wortklauberei.

worded abgefaßt;
well ~ letter gut formulierter Brief.

wording Formulierung, [Ab]fassung von Schriftstücken, Wortlaut, (caption) Überschrift, Bildtext, (tenor) Inhalt, Text;
loose ~ unpräzise Formulierung; **set ~** festgelegter Wortlaut; **standardized ~s** (insurance business) genormte Versicherungssprache;
~ of a bill Wechseltext; **~ of a contract** Wortlaut eines Vertrages; **~ of a draft** Wechseltext; **~ of a law** Gesetzestext; **~ of the oath** Eidesformel; **~ of a resolution** Wortlaut einer Resolution.

wordplay Wortspiel.

wordy (speaker) weitschweifig;
~ telegram langatmiges Telegramm; **~ warfare** Wortgefecht.

work Arbeit, Beschäftigung, (ability to work) Arbeitsfähigkeit, (achievement) fertiggestellte Arbeit, Werk, (act) Tat, Tätigkeit, Schaffen, (building plot) in Arbeit befindlicher Bau, Baustelle, Bauten, Anlagen, (deed) Handlung, (machine) Betrieb, Arbeit, Leistung, (occupation) Beschäftigung, Beruf, Berufsgebiet, -tätigkeit, -leben, Tätigkeit, (performance) Leistung, (product) Erzeugnis, Produkt, (school) Schularbeit, (treatment) Bearbeitung, Behandlung;
all in the day's ~ absolut üblich; **at ~** bei der Arbeit, im Betrieb (Gang); **at the ~s** in der Fabrik; **ex ~s** ab Fabrik (Werk);

exempt from ~ arbeitsbefreit; **fit for** ~ arbeitsfähig; **out of** ~ ohne Arbeit (Stellung), außer Dienst, unbeschäftigt, arbeits-, erwerbslos; **unable to (unfit for)** ~ arbeitsunfähig; **without** ~ beschäftigungslos;

~s bauliche Anlagen, Bauten, Betriebsanlagen, *(building site)* Baustelle, Bau, *(mil.)* Festungswerk, *(mining)* Grube, Zeche, *(plant)* Fabrik-, Fertigungsanlage, Werk, Betrieb;

the ~s *(coll., US)* der ganze Krempel, die ganze Chose; **accomplished** ~ fertiggestellte Arbeit; **artistic** ~ Kunstwerk; **backbreaking** ~ Pferdearbeit; **badly finished** ~ schludrige Arbeit, Schluderarbeit; **black-coated** ~ *(Br.)* geistige Tätigkeit; **by-~** Nebenarbeit; **brick ~s** Ziegelei; **capital ~s** öffentliche Bauten, Großbauten; **casual** ~ Gelegenheitsarbeit; **chemical ~s** chemische Fabrik; **clerical** ~ Bürotätigkeit; **close** ~ anhaltende Arbeiten; **collected ~s** gesammelte Werke; **constructive ~s** Bauarbeiten; **contract** ~ *(US)* Akkordarbeit, im Stücklohn geleistete Arbeit, Lohnakkord; **contributed** ~ Sammelwerk; **day's** ~ Tages-, Lohnarbeit, Tagewerk; **dead** ~ vorbereitete Arbeit; **desk** ~ Büroarbeit, -tätigkeit; **domestic** ~ Heimarbeit, Hausindustrie; ~ **done** Leistung, geleistete Arbeit; **dry** ~ langweilige Arbeit; **earth ~s** Erdarbeiten; **emergency ~s** Notstandsarbeiten; **executive** ~ leitende Tätigkeit; **factory** ~ Fabrikarbeit; **feeble** ~ mäßige Arbeit; **field** ~ auswärtige Tätigkeit; **first-class** ~ vorzügliche Arbeit; **follow-up** ~ vervollständigende Tätigkeit; **gas ~s** Gasanstalt; **good** ~ wohltätiges Werk; **hard** ~ schwere Arbeit; **health** ~ Gesundheitsdienst; **heavy** ~ Schwerarbeit; **holiday** ~ Ferienbeschäftigung; **home** ~ Heimarbeit; **illicit** ~ Schwarzarbeit; **iron ~s** Eisenhütte; **job** ~ Stück-, Akkord-, Handarbeit; **journeyman** ~ schlecht bezahlte Arbeit; **juvenile court** ~ Tätigkeit am Jugendgericht; **light** ~ leichte Arbeit; **literary** ~ schriftstellerische Tätigkeit; **literary, scientific and artistic ~s** Werke der Literatur, der Wissenschaft und der Kunst; **low-profit** ~ Arbeit mit geringer Verdienstspanne; **lump** ~ global übernommene Arbeit; **mental** ~ geistige Tätigkeit; **general maintenance** ~ laufende Instandhaltungsarbeiten; **managerial** ~ Tätigkeit als Führungskraft; **manual** ~ ungelernte (körperliche) Arbeit, Handarbeit; **musical** ~ Werk der Tonkunst; **new ~s** Neubauten; **night** ~ Nachtarbeit; **off-season** ~ Arbeit außerhalb der Saison; **office** ~ Bürotätigkeit, -arbeit; **own** ~ eigene Fertigung; **badly paid** ~ schlecht bezahlte Arbeit; **part-time** ~ Teil-, Kurzarbeit; **postgraduate** ~ wissenschaftliche Tätigkeit nach der Promotion; **previous (preparatory)** ~ Vorarbeit; **productive** ~ produktive Arbeit; **psychological employment** ~ unselbständige psychologische Arbeit; **public ~s** öffentliche (gemeinnützige) Arbeiten, öffentliche Bauten; **qualified** ~ Wert-, Qualitätsarbeit; **relief ~s** Notstandsarbeiten, Arbeitsbeschaffungsprojekt; **research** ~ Forschungstätigkeit; **rough** ~ primitive Tätigkeit; **routine** ~ Routinearbeit, tägliche Kleinarbeit; **rush** ~ Schnellschuß; **scab** ~ untertariflich bezahlte Tätigkeit; **scientific** ~ wissenschaftliches Werk; **seasonal** ~ Saisontätigkeit; **short-time** ~ Kurzarbeit; **skilled** ~ Facharbeit; **sparetime** ~ Nebenarbeit, -beschäftigung; **steel ~s** Stahlwerk; **strike-free** ~ streikfreie Tätigkeit; **sub-contracted** ~ Zuliefertätigkeit; **suitable** ~ angemessene Tätigkeit; **systematic** ~ systematische Arbeit; **supplementary** ~ zusätzliche Arbeit; **tax** ~ Bearbeitung von Steuerunterlagen; **temporary** ~ Aushilfsarbeit; **time** ~ nach Stunden bezahlte Arbeit; **trying** ~ anstrengende Arbeit (Tätigkeit); ~ **underground** Arbeit unter Tage; ~ **undertaken** übernommene Arbeit; **unfinished** ~ unerledigte Arbeit; **unremunerative** ~ unbezahlte Arbeit; **unskilled** ~ ungelernte Arbeit, Hilfsarbeit; **uphill** ~ saure Arbeit; **useful** ~ nützliche Beschäftigung; **valuable** ~ Wert-, Qualitätsarbeit; **voluntary** ~ freiwillige Arbeit; **warm** ~ schwere Arbeit; **white-collar** ~ *(US)* geistige Tätigkeit, Arbeit des Geistesarbeiters, Bürotätigkeit; **whole-hearted** ~ ernsthafte Arbeit;

~ **in arrears** Arbeitsrückstand; ~s **of art bequeathed to the nation** dem Staat hinterlassene Kunstwerke; ~ **on the assembly line** Fließbandarbeit; ~ **on the bonus system** Arbeiten auf Prämienbasis; ~ **according to the book** *(US)* Dienst nach Vorschrift, planmäßiges Langsamarbeiten; ~ **of charity** Werk der Barmherzigkeit; ~s **of construction** Bauarbeiten; ~ **on contract** Akkordarbeit; ~ **of development** Entwicklungsarbeit; ~ **of the devil** Teufelswerk; ~s **with modern equipment** moderne Betriebsanlage; ~ **on hand** in Bearbeitung befindlicher Auftrag, Auftragsbestand; **total** ~ **on hand** Gesamtaufträge; ~ **out of hours** Tätigkeit außerhalb der Dienststunden; ~ **of national importance** staatswichtige Tätigkeit; ~ **that interests** geistig interessierende Aufgabe; ~ **by the job** Akkordarbeit; ~ **and labo(u)r** Arbeit und Material, Leistungen eines Werklieferungsvertrages; ~ **of necessity** *(Sunday statute)* erlaubte Sonntagsarbeiten; ~ **published in parts** Fortsetzungswerk; ~ **against**

payment vergütete Arbeitsleistung, Lohnarbeit; ~ **at piece rates** im Akkord bezahlte Arbeit; ~ **in process** *(Br.)* **(progress,** *US)* laufende Arbeit, *(balance sheet)* halbfertige Erzeugnisse, Erzeugnisse in der Fabrikation, Halbfabrikate; ~ **of high quality** hochwertige Qualitätsarbeit; ~ **of reference** Nachschlagewerk; ~ **for relief** Notstandsarbeit; ~ **of research** Forschungstätigkeit; ~**-to-rule** *(Br.)* Dienst nach Vorschrift, planmäßige Langsamarbeit, Bummelstreik; ~ **that smells of lamp oil** in nächtlicher Tätigkeit entstandene Arbeit; ~ **at time rates** stundenweise bezahlte Arbeit; ~ **of immediate urgency** vordringliche Arbeit;

~ *(v.)* Arbeit haben, arbeiten, bearbeiten, tätig (beschäftigt) sein, schaffen, *(have effect)* wirken, Wirkung haben, *(exert o. s.)* sich anstrengen (bemühen), *(exploit)* ausbeuten, *(factory)* in Betrieb sein, *(influence)* seinen Einfluß geltend machen, *(keep going)* [Maschine] betreiben, in Betrieb halten, betätigen, bedienen, *(manage)* [Geschäft] leiten, betreiben, *(operate)* [Bergwerk, Fabrik] betreiben, *(v./i.)* funktionieren, gehen, laufen, arbeiten, *(prepare)* bearbeiten, *(put in operation)* in Betrieb setzen (Gang bringen), *(sell, sl.)* verkaufen, *(make use of, coll.)* gebrauchen, ausnutzen;

~ **on s. o.** sich j. vornehmen (vorknöpfen); ~ **s. o. for all he is worth** *(sl.)* j. bis zum letzten ausnutzen; ~ **for one's own account** auf eigene Rechnung arbeiten; ~ **against** entgegenwirken; ~ **an area** Bezirk bearbeiten; ~ **on the assembly line** *(US)* am Fließband arbeiten; ~ **on a full-time basis** hauptamtlich arbeiten; ~ **like a beaver** wie ein Kümmeltürke arbeiten; ~ **to board level** Tätigkeit auf der Vorstandsebene ausüben; ~ **through a book** sich durch ein Buch durcharbeiten; ~ **around the year on the budget** Haushalt das ganze Jahr über kontrollieren; ~ **to 75 per cent or less of capacity** Kapazität kaum zu 75% ausnutzen; ~ **a change** Veränderung bewirken; ~ **like a charm** wie ein Zauber wirken, hundertprozentig erfolgreich sein; ~ **in close cooperation with s. o.** mit jem. Hand in Hand arbeiten; ~ **under a written six-month contract** mit halbjähriger Kündigungsfrist angestellt sein; ~ **o. s. to death** sich abschinden, sich zu Tode arbeiten; ~ **a district** *(traveller)* Bezirk arbeiten (bereisen); ~ **like a dog** wie ein Pferd schuften; ~ **double tides** *(Br.)* Tag und Nacht arbeiten; ~ **easily after the rain** *(soil)* sich nach dem Regen leicht bearbeiten lassen; ~ **economically at a lower output** bei geringerer Produktion wirtschaftlicher arbeiten; ~ **by electricity** *(machine)* elektrisch betrieben werden; ~ **a farm** Gut bewirtschaften; ~ **in one's father's firm** im Betrieb seines Vaters mitarbeiten; ~ **one's fingers to the bone** angestrengt arbeiten; ~ **by fits and starts** ungleichmäßig arbeiten; ~ **as flat out as plant permit** Betriebskapazität voll ausfahren; ~ **a forfeiture** Anspruchsverwirkung herbeiführen; ~ **free-lance** freiberuflich arbeiten; ~ **full-time** ganztägig arbeiten; ~ **half-time** halbtags arbeiten; ~ **hand in glove** eng miteinander zusammenarbeiten; ~ **hard** schwer (angestrengt) arbeiten; ~ **too hard** übermäßig arbeiten; ~ **hard for s. o.** sich intensiv für j. einsetzen; ~ **one's head off** *(sl.)* wie verrückt schuften; ~ **like a horse** wie ein Pferd schuften; ~ **fourty hours a week** Vierzigstundenwoche haben; ~ **ten hours without letup** zehn Stunden hintereinander arbeiten; ~ **without intermission** ununterbrochen arbeiten; ~ **it** etw. zustandebringen; ~ **it so that one has a vacation** *(coll.)* sich zu einem Urlaub verhelfen; ~ **by the job** im Akkord arbeiten; ~ **loose** *(screw)* sich lockern; ~ **mechanically** nach der Schablone arbeiten; ~ **men to one's will** sich Menschen gefügig machen; ~ **with method** methodisch arbeiten; ~ **on s. one's mind** j. bearbeiten; ~ **a mine at a profit** Bergwerk ausbeuten (abbauen); ~ **minerals** Bergbau betreiben; ~ **miracles** Wunder bewirken; ~ **like a nigger** wie ein Kümmeltürke arbeiten; ~ **the oracle** *(sl.)* durch Beziehungen erreichen, *(raise money)* Geld auftreiben; ~ **in order to live** für seinen Lebensunterhalt arbeiten; ~ **overtime** Überstunden machen; ~ **on one's own** selbständig sein; ~ **au pair** *(Br.)* gegen freie Station arbeiten; ~ **part time** halbtags arbeiten; ~ **one's passage** seine Überfahrt abarbeiten; ~ **one's passage back** sich seine Rückreise selbst verdienen; ~ **a patent** Patent verwerten; ~ **by the piece** im Akkord arbeiten; ~ **on piece rates** im Akkord arbeiten; ~ **in preparation** vorarbeiten; ~ **under high pressure** mit Hochdruck arbeiten; ~ **at a printer's** in einer Druckerei arbeiten; ~ **professionally on s. th.** sich mit dem Studium von etw. befassen (beschäftigen); ~ **on a large public sale** an größeren Staatsaufträgen mitarbeiten; ~ **against reform** gegen Reformen eingestellt sein; ~ **on social reform** an einer Sozialreform arbeiten; ~ **to rule** *(Br.)* streng nach Vorschrift (planmäßig langsam) arbeiten; ~ **in three shifts** in drei Schichten arbeiten; ~ **in the shops** in der Fabrik arbeiten; ~ **short-time** nicht ganz kurzarbeiten; ~ **smoothly** *(gears)* sich weich schalten lassen; ~ **in snatches** unregelmäßig arbeiten;

at a white-hot speed fieberhaft arbeiten; **~ one's social relations in business** seine gesellschaftlichen Beziehungen geschäftlich ausnutzen; **~ a sum** Berechnung vornehmen; **~ on a system** nach einer Methode arbeiten; **~ one's tail off** *(US)* sich kaputtarbeiten; **~ on even terms** umsonst arbeiten; **~ through to prices in the shops** auf die Ladenverkaufspreise durchschlagen; **~ a free ticket** Freikarte ergattern; **~ against time** mit der Zeit um die Wette arbeiten; **~ one's way forward** vorankommen; **~ one's way up** sich emporarbeiten (in die Höhe arbeiten); **~ one's way through college** sich sein Studium als Werksstudent verdienen; **~ well** gut funktionieren; **~ one's will upon s. o.** sich bei jem. durchsetzen.

work o. s. in sich einarbeiten.

work *(v.)* **in local references in one's speech** auf Lokalangelegenheiten in seiner Rede Bezug nehmen.

work into verarbeiten zu;

~ *(v.)* **cotton into cloth** Baumwolle zu Tuch verarbeiten; **~ o. s. into s. one's favo(u)r** sich in jds. Gunst einschmeicheln; **~ s. o. into a rage** j. in Wut bringen.

work off *(v.)* *(complete)* aufarbeiten, *(find customers)* abstoßen, *(print.)* abdrucken, -ziehen;

~ one's arrears of correspondence seine Briefschulden erledigen; **~ a debt** Schuld abarbeiten; **~ one's feelings** seine Gefühle abreagieren; **~ a poem as one's own** *(sl.)* Gedicht für sein eigenes ausgeben; **~ a stock of goods** Warenposten losschlagen.

work out *(v.)* *(calculate)* aus-, berechnen, *(take effect)* sich auswirken, *(mine)* abbauen, ausbeuten, erschöpfen, *(plan)* ausarbeiten, *(print.)* abdrucken, -ziehen;

~ s. th. out Denkproblem lösen; **~ at** sich belaufen (stellen) auf, ergeben, herauskommen; **~ a debt** Schuld abarbeiten; **~ heavy deficits** mit schweren Verlusten arbeiten; **~ exactly** glatt aufgehen; **~ in one's head** im Kopf ausrechnen; **~ at £ 5 a head** *(cost)* auf 5 Pfund pro Kopf zu stehen kommen; **~ of a hotel room** vom Hotelzimmer aus seiner Beschäftigung nachgehen; **~ interest** Zinsen berechnen; **~ a coded message** verschlüsselten Funkspruch entziffern; **~ a silver mine** Silbermine erschöpfen; **~ a plan** Plan ausarbeiten; **~ a problem** mit einem Problem fertig werden; **~ a program(me) to the last detail** Programm fix und fertig ausarbeiten; **~ one's own salvation** sich selbst aus den Schlamassel helfen; **~ s. one's share of expenses** jds. Unkostenanteil ausrechnen; **~ one's taxes on the road** seine Steuern mit Straßenarbeiten bezahlen; **~ one's time** seine Lehr[lings]zeit (Ausbildungszeit) beenden; **~ the week** ganze Woche durcharbeiten; **~ quite well** sich ganz gut anlassen.

work over *(v.)* überarbeiten, verbessern, revidieren.

work round *(v.)* sich mit Mühe durcharbeiten, *(sick person)* sich wieder erholen;

~ the clock Tag und Nacht arbeiten; **~ to the south** *(wind)* sich nach Süden drehen.

work *(v.)* | **through the roof** *(rain)* durch das Dach durchkommen; **~ under difficult conditions** unter schwierigen Bedingungen arbeiten.

work up *(v.)* *(achieve by continued effort)* in die Höhe bringen *(business)* Geschäft hochbringen, *(elaborate)* entwickeln, ausarbeiten, gestatten, *(incite)* aufregen, -peitschen, -wiegeln, schüren, *(material)* auf-, verarbeiten, *(subject)* sich einarbeiten;

~ a business Betrieb zum Erfolg bringen; **~ a connexion** sich einen Kundenkreis schaffen; **~ the feelings of an audience** Versammlungsteilnehmer zum Kochen bringen; **~ the passions** Leidenschaften schüren; **~ the plot of a novel** Roman in seinen Grundlinien ausarbeiten; **~ o. s. up to a post** sich hocharbeiten; **~ all the stock** das ganze Lager verbrauchen; **~ a practice as a physician** sich eine Praxis schaffen; **~ a rebellion** Aufruhr anstiften; **~ one's way the clerical route** sich im Büro hochdienen; **~ from a train dispatcher to division superintendent** sich vom Zugabfertiger zum Abteilungspräsidenten hocharbeiten.

work upon *(v.)* | **the conscience** Gewissen beeinflussen; **~ a new novel** an einem neuen Roman sitzen.

work, to apply o. s. to one's sich seiner Arbeit widmen; **to be at ~** an der Arbeit (beschäftigt) sein, arbeiten; **to be in ~** im Beruf (Berufsleben) stehen; **to be in the ~s** im Werk (in der Fabrik) sein; **to be completely absorbed in one's ~** völlig in seinem Beruf aufgehen; **to be in arrears (behind) with one's ~** mit seiner Arbeit im Rückstand sein; **to be hard at ~** fleißig arbeiten; **to be immersed in one's ~** in der Arbeit ertrinken; **to be in regular ~** fest angestellt sein; **to be looking for ~** auf Arbeitssuche sein, Arbeit suchen; **to be obliged to ~** arbeiten müssen, arbeitsverpflichtet sein; **to be off ~** nicht am Arbeitsplatz sein; **to be out at ~** auf Arbeit sein; **to be out of ~** keine Arbeit haben, arbeits-, stellenlos sein, *(machine)* nicht in Betrieb sein, stillstehen; **to be**

in regular ~ again wieder einer geregelten Beschäftigung nachgehen; **to be over heels and ears in ~** mit Arbeit überhäuft sein; **to be in regular ~** fest angestellt sein; **to be smothered with work in ~** in Arbeit ersticken; **to be thorough in one's ~** zuverlässig arbeiten; **to be thrown out of ~** arbeitslos werden; **to be utterly devoted to one's ~** ganz in seiner Arbeit aufgehen; **to be on one's way to ~** auf dem Weg zur Arbeit sein; **to be wrapped up in one's ~** in seine Arbeit vertieft sein; **to be the ~ of a moment** im Augenblick (Nu) geschehen sein; **to buckle down to ~** sich an die Arbeit machen; **to burn with love for one's ~** ganz in seiner Arbeit aufgehen, mit Liebe bei der Arbeit sein; **to bury o. s. in ~** sich ganz in die Arbeit vertiefen; **to carry out a ~** Arbeit zu Ende führen; **to cease ~** Arbeit beenden (einstellen, niederlegen); **to collect material for a scientific ~** Material für eine wissenschaftliche Arbeit zusammenstellen; **to devolve ~ on a subordinate** Arbeit an einen Untergebenen abgeben; **to do job ~** im Akkord arbeiten; **to do one's ~** seine Arbeit verrichten; **to do one's ~ in an office** Büroangestellter sein, Büroarbeit verrichten; **to do ~s of charity** sich karitativ betätigen; **to do the ~ of three men (three men's ~)** drei Arbeitskräfte ersetzen, für drei arbeiten; **to do good ~** tüchtig arbeiten; **to do one's ~ with distinction** Hervorragendes bei seiner Arbeit leisten; **to drop one's ~** seine Arbeit niederlegen; **to fall behind with one's ~** unerledigte Arbeit liegen haben; **to fall out of ~** arbeitslos werden; **to fall within the scope of one's ~** im Rahmen seiner Arbeit (Tätigkeit) liegen; **to find s. o. ~** jem. einen Arbeitsplatz verschaffen; **to find no ~ in one's line** in seiner Berufssparte keine Arbeit finden; **to finish ~ in one standing** in einem Arbeitsgang erledigen; **to fit into ~** in Arbeit bringen; **to get ~** Arbeit bekommen; **to get to one's ~** an die Arbeit gehen, sich an die Arbeit machen; **to get the ~s** *(sl.)* sein Fett abbekommen; **to get through a lot of ~** großen Teil der Arbeit hinter sich bringen; **to give s. o. the ~s** jem. sein Fett geben; **to give ~ helpful to the community** nützliche Arbeitsplätze schaffen; **to go about one's ~** sich an die Arbeit machen; **to go about one's usual ~** seiner täglichen Arbeit nachgehen; **to go to ~ on a system** nach einem bestimmten System verfahren; **to go back to ~** Arbeit wiederaufnehmen; **to go roundly to ~** ernsthaft an die Arbeit gehen; **to gum up the ~s** *(sl.)* Chance vorbeigehen lassen; **to have one's heart in one's ~** mit Freude bei der Arbeit sein, arbeitsfreudig sein; **to have been out of ~ for a year** ganzjährig arbeitslos gewesen sein; **to have much ~ on hand** viel zu tun haben; **to have no regular ~** keine bestimmte Tätigkeit ausüben; **to have one's ~ cut out** *(fam.)* genügend zu tun (alle Hände voll) haben; **to have data to ~ on** entsprechendes Zahlenmaterial zur Verfügung haben; **to have ~ started at once** sofort in Arbeit nehmen; **to keep s. o. from ~** j. von der Arbeit abhalten; **to knock off ~** (mit der Arbeit) zu arbeiten aufhören; **to knock off ~ one week out of two** nur jede zweite Woche arbeiten; **to leave off ~** Arbeit einstellen; **to lend one's soul to one's ~** mit ganzer Seele bei der Arbeit sein; **to live within easy (a short) distance of one's ~** in der Nähe seines Arbeitsplatzes wohnen; **to look for ~** auf Arbeitssuche sein; **to make ~** Arbeit verursachen; **to make ~ one's excuse** sich mit der Arbeit entschuldigen; **to make short ~ of it** nicht viel Umstände machen; **to perform ~** Arbeit verrichten; **to perform useful ~** nützliche Arbeit leisten; **to pitch into ~** sich tüchtig an die Arbeit machen, die Ärmel aufkrempeln; **to place into ~** Arbeit zuweisen; **to press on with the ~** Arbeit vorantreiben; **to put in ~** in Arbeit bringen, Arbeit geben; **to put additional ~ on s. o.** j. mit zusätzlicher Arbeit belasten; **to put one's right hand to ~** Hand an die Arbeit legen; **to quit ~** Arbeit einstellen, kündigen; **to reconcile o. s. to one's ~** seine Arbeit liebgewinnen; **to resume ~** Arbeit (Betrieb) wiederaufnehmen; **to return to ~** sich wieder an die Arbeit begeben; **to scurry through one's ~** seine Arbeit flüchtig erledigen; **to seek ~** Arbeit suchen; **to set to ~** an die Arbeit (ans Werk) gehen, sich an die Arbeit machen, *(labo(u)rers)* Arbeiter beschäftigen, *(engine)* in Betrieb setzen; **to settle down to ~** sich an die Arbeit machen; **to sit at ~** über der Arbeit sitzen; **to sleep over one's ~** bei der Arbeit einschlafen; **to slive away with one's ~** sich mit seiner Arbeit abplagen; **to speed up one's ~** seine Arbeit beschleunigen; **to start one's ~** seinen Dienst antreten; **to stop ~** Arbeit einstellen; **to take a hand in the ~ o. s.** selbst mit Hand anlegen; **to take to ~** auf Arbeit gehen; **to take on extra ~** zusätzliche Arbeiten übernehmen; **to take up ~** Arbeit aufnehmen; **to throw out of ~** entlassen; **to turn up early for ~** pünktlich am Arbeitsplatz erscheinen; **to undertake a piece of ~** Arbeit übernehmen;

~ analysis Arbeitsanalyse; **~s area** *(Br.)* Fabrikgelände, Gewerbegebiet; **Public ~s Administration** *(US)* Arbeitsbeschaffungsbehörde; **~ assignment** Arbeitszuweisung; **~ attitude** Einstellung zur Arbeit; ~ **bag (basket, box)** Nähbeutel; ~ **beast** Arbeitspferd; ~ **call** Arbeitsaufruf; ~ **camp** Arbeitslager; ~ **clothes** Arbeits-, Berufsbekleidung; ~**s committee (council)** Betriebsrat; **public ~s committee** Arbeitsbeschaffungsausschuß; ~**s competition** betrieblicher Wettbewerb; ~ **contract** Arbeitsvertrag; ~~**-in-process control** *(Br.)* Produktionskontrolle; ~ **creation** Arbeitsbeschaffung; ~ **cure** Arbeitstherapie; ~ **curve** Ermüdungskurve; ~ **dodger** Arbeitsscheuer, Drückeberger; ~ **effort** Arbeitsanstrengung; ~ **elements** Arbeitselemente; ~ **environment** Umwelteinflüsse des Arbeitsplatzes; ~ **equipment** Bahnausstattungsgegenstände; ~ **experience** Arbeits-, Berufserfahrung; ~~**-in-progress figures** *(US)* Halbfabrikatezahlen; ~ **girl** Fabrikarbeiterin; ~ **habit** Arbeitsmethode; ~**s holiday** Betriebsferien; ~ **horse** Arbeitspferd; ~ **incentive program(me)** Arbeitsprämienprogramm, Arbeitsansporn; ~**s installation** Werksanlagen; ~**s-internal** innerbetrieblich; ~ **journey** Fahrt zur Arbeit; ~ **norms** Arbeitsnormen; ~ **performance** Arbeitsleistung; ~ **layout** Arbeitsplatzgestaltung; ~ **load** Arbeitsbelastung; ~**s manager** Betriebs-, Fabrikleiter; ~ **map** Arbeitskarte; ~ **material** Arbeitsmaterial; ~ **measurement** Arbeitszeitermittlung, [etwa] REFA-System; ~ **measurement specialist** [etwa] REFA-Mann; ~ **order** Arbeitsanweisung, -auftrag; ~ **norms** Arbeitsnormen; ~**s number** Nummer des Arbeitsausweises; ~~**-out of a plan** Ausarbeitung eines Planes; ~**s outing** Betriebsausflug; ~ **period** Arbeitszeit; ~ **permit** Arbeitsgenehmigung, *(trade union)* Arbeitserlaubnis [für Nichtmitglied]; ~ **piece** Werkstück; ~ **plans** Berufspläne; ~**s premises** Arbeitsräume; ~ **preparation** Vorbereitung auf die Arbeitswelt; ~ **print** *(film)* Rohfassung; ~ **privileges** Arbeitsvorrechte; ~ **process** *(Br.)* **(progress,** *US)* **material** Halbfabrikatematerial; ~~**-in-process inventory** *(Br.)* Bestand an Halbfabrikaten; ~ **program(me)** Arbeitsprogramm, -stückliste; ♀**s Progress Administration** *(US)* Dienststelle zur Untersuchung von Arbeitsbedingungen; ~ **release** *(prison)* Arbeitsurlaub; ~ **relief** Arbeitslosenfürsorge; **relief ~ program(me)** Notstandsprogramm; **relief ~ project** Arbeitsbeschaffungsprojekt; ~ **report** Karteiunterlagen über den einzelnen Arbeiter; ~ **requirements** Arbeitsanfall; ~~**-requirement provisions** *(welfare system)* Bestimmungen über notwendige Arbeitsbereitschaft; ~ **restriction** Arbeitsverlangsamung; ~ **rules** Arbeitsrichtlinien; ~**s' rule-book** Arbeitsordnung; ~~**-rules settlement** Arbeitsrichtlinienvereinbarung; ~ **schedule** Arbeitsplan; **to resume normal ~ schedules** wieder im gleichen Arbeitstempo arbeiten; ~**s security** Werksschutz; ~ **session** Arbeitssitzung, -turnus; ~ **sharing** Arbeitsstreckung, Beschäftigung in Kurzarbeit [zwecks Vermeidung von Entlassungen]; ~ **sheet** Arbeitszettel, -unterlage, *(balancing, US)* [Haupt]abschlußbericht, Rohbilanz; ~ **sheet form** Bilanzvorbereitungsbogen; ~ **shift** Arbeitsschicht; ~ **simplification** [etwa] Arbeitsvereinfachung; **spread ~ system** Arbeitsstreckungsverfahren; ~ **spreading** Arbeitsstreckung; ~**s steward** Betriebsobmann; ~ **stoppage** Arbeitsunterbrechung, -niederlegung; ~ **study** REFA-Zeitstudie; ~~**-study arrangement** Vereinbarung über wechselseitiges Studium und Arbeit; ~~**-study program** *(US, universities)* Studentenförderungsprogramm; ~**s superintendent** Betriebsdirektor; ~**s supervision** Betriebsüberwachung; ~**s supervisor** Werks-, Betriebsleiter; ~ **ticket** Arbeitskarte; ~ **train** Baumaterialienzug; ~**s uniform** Betriebs-, Werksuniform; ~ **unit** Berechnungs-, Leistungs-, Maßeinheit; ~~**-up** *(print.)* Spieß; ~ **urge** Arbeitslust, -eifer; ~ **week** Arbeitswoche.

workable *(material)* bearbeitungsfähig, *(constitution)* brauchbar, *(mining)* [ab]baufähig, *(plan)* ausführbar, funktionsfähig, praktisch durchführbar, brauchbar;
   to be no longer ~ *(mine)* ausgebeutet sein;
   ~ **competition** *(US)* funktionsfähiger Wettbewerb.

workaday werktäglich;
   ~ **clothes** Alltagskleider; ~ **life** Alltagsleben.

workaway *(on steamship, sl.)* zusätzliche freiwillige Arbeitskraft.

workbag Arbeitsbeutel, *(needlework)* Nähbeutel.

workbench Werkbank, Arbeitstisch.

workbook Arbeitsbuch, Buch mit Arbeitsanweisungen.

workbox Werkzeugkasten.

workday Werk-, Arbeitstag;
   ~ **of eight hours** Achtstundentag.

worked bearbeitet, *(mining)* befahren, in Betrieb;
   hours ~ geleistete Arbeit; ~ **out** *(mine)* ausgebeutet;
   ~ **by electricity** elektrisch betrieben;
   to get s. o. ~ up j. auf die Palme bringen;
   ~ **material** aufgearbeitetes Material; ~ **off** *(prices)* abgeschwächt; **well-~ scheme** gut ausgearbeiteter Plan; ~~**-up audience** erregte (hysterische) Versammlung.

worker Arbeiter, Arbeitnehmer, Arbeitskraft, *(print.)* Galvano; **able ~** fähiger (gediegener) Arbeiter; **adult ~** erwachsener Arbeiter; **agricultural ~** Landarbeiter; **arduous ~** zäher Arbeiter; **assembly-line ~** *(US)* Fließbandarbeiter; **auxiliary ~** Hilfsarbeiter; **black-coated** *(Br.)* Büroangestellter; **blue-collar ~** *(US)* Fabrik-, Handarbeiter; **building ~** Bauarbeiter; **casual ~** Gelegenheitsarbeiter; **clerical ~** Bürokraft, -angestellter; **construction ~** Bauarbeiter; **deft ~** flinker Arbeiter; **domestic ~** Hausangestellter; **factory ~** geschickter Arbeiter; **factory ~** Fabrikarbeiter; **farm ~** Landarbeiter; **Federal ~** *(US)* Staatsbeamter; **fellow ~** Mitarbeiter, Kollege, Arbeitskamerad; **female ~** weibliche Arbeitskraft, Arbeiterin; **foreign ~** Fremd-, Gastarbeiter; **general ~** ungelernter Arbeiter; **heavy ~** Schwerarbeiter; **home ~** Heimarbeiter; **hourly ~** im Stundenlohn beschäftigter Arbeiter; **industrial ~** Industrie-, Fabrikarbeiter; **infraconstruction ~s** für den Rohbau benötigte Arbeitskräfte; **itinerant ~** Wanderarbeiter; **job ~** Akkord[lohn]arbeiter; **land ~** *(Br.)* Landarbeiter; **locked-out ~** ausgesperrter Arbeiter; **low-salaried ~** niedrig bezahlter Arbeiter; **maintenance ~s** Wartungskräfte; **male ~** männlicher Arbeiter, männliche Arbeitskraft; **managerial ~** leitender Angestellter; **manual ~** ungelernter Arbeiter; **maritime ~** *(US)* Seetransportarbeiter; **mediocre ~** mäßige Arbeitskraft; **migrant ~** Wanderarbeiter; **part-time ~** Kurzarbeiter; **piece ~** Stück-, Akkordlohnarbeiter; **professional ~** freiberufliche Arbeitskraft, Angehöriger der freien Berufe, Akademiker; **qualified ~** qualifizierter Arbeiter, qualifizierte Arbeitskraft, Spezialarbeiter, -kraft; **highly qualified ~s** hochqualifizierte Arbeitskräfte; **quick ~** flotter Arbeiter; **ready ~** flotter Arbeiter; **redundant ~** überzähliger Arbeiter; **~s released** freigesetzte Arbeitskräfte; **reliable ~** zuverlässige Kraft; **relief ~** Notstandsarbeiter; **rural ~** Landarbeiter; **salaried ~** Angestellter, Gehaltsempfänger; **seasonal ~** Saisonarbeiter; **semiskilled ~** angelernter Arbeiter; **short-time ~** Kurzarbeiter; **skilled ~** Facharbeiter; **slow ~** bedächtiger Arbeiter; **specialized ~** Spezialkraft, Spezialist; **steady ~** fleißiger Arbeiter; **substandard ~** unausgebildeter (ungelernter) Arbeiter; **temporary ~** Aushilfsarbeiter, -kraft; **thorough ~** gründlicher Arbeiter; **two-job ~** Arbeiter mit zwei Berufen, Doppelverdiener; **underage ~** *(US)* minderjähriger Arbeiter; **underground ~** Untertagearbeiter; **unskilled ~** Hilfs-, ungelernter Arbeiter; **wage ~** Lohnarbeiter; **war ~** Rüstungsarbeiter; **white-collar ~** *(US)* [Büro]angestellter; **woman ~** Arbeiterin; **~s on the assembly line** Fließbandarbeiter;
   to absorb new ~s in the labo(u)r force neue Kräfte in den Arbeitsprozeß eingliedern; **to be a good ~** tüchtig schaffen; **to call off ~s** Arbeitskräfte abziehen; **to dislocate ~s** Arbeitskräfte umsetzen; **to engage ~s** Arbeiter anwerben; **to enrol(l) ~s** Arbeitskräfte einstellen; **to lay off ~s** Arbeiter vorübergehend entlassen; **to place ~s** Arbeiter unterbringen; **to put ~s on the street** Arbeiter auf die Straße setzen; **to recruit ~s** *(US)* Arbeiter anwerben (einstellen); **to redistribute ~s throughout the company** über das ganze Unternehmen arbeitsmäßig verteilen; **to reinstate a ~** Arbeiter wiedereinstellen; **to take on extra ~s** zusätzliche Arbeitskräfte einstellen;
   ~ **affluence** Wohlhabenheit der Arbeiterklasse; ~ **analysis** Analyse von Arbeitskräften; ~**s' bus** Arbeiterbus; ~**s' campus** Arbeiteruniversität; ~**s' committee** Arbeiterausschuß; ~**s' compensation** Unfallentschädigung; ~**s' compensation program(me)** Betriebshaftpflichtvorschläge; ~**s' council** Betriebsrat; ~ **decline** Arbeitskräfterückgang; ~**s' delegation** Arbeiterabordnung; ~ **director** *(Br.)* Arbeitsdirektor; ~ **dissatisfaction** Unzufriedenheit von Arbeitskräften; ~**'s dwelling** Arbeiterwohnung; ♀**s' Educational Association (WEA)** *(Br.)* [etwa] Volkshochschule; ~ **education program(me)** Fortbildungsprogramm; ~**s' expectations** Arbeitserwartungen; ~**s' housing** Arbeiterwohnung; ~**s' housing estate** Arbeitersiedlung; ~ **management** Betriebsführung durch die Belegschaft; ~ **participation** Gewinnbeteiligung der Arbeitnehmer; ~ **performance** Arbeitsleistung; **to hit ~s' pockets** sich ertragsmäßig beim Arbeiter niederschlagen; ~ **productivity** Arbeitsproduktivität; ~**'s season ticket** Arbeiterrückfahrkarte; ~ **sentiment** Stimmung unter den Arbeitern; ~**'s surplus** Arbeiterrente; ~ **training** Arbeiterausbildung.

workfellow Arbeitskamerad, Mitarbeiter, Kollege.

workflow Arbeitsablauf.

workfolks *(US)* **workfolk** *(Br.)* Arbeiter.

workforce Belegschaft, Arbeitskräfte;
   university ~ bei der Universität tätiger Arbeitsstab;
   to cut back on the ~ Belegschaftsreduzierung vornehmen;
   broad-scale ~ reduction Belegschaftsabbau auf breiter Front.

workgirl Fabrikmädchen, Arbeiterin.

workhouse *(Br.)* Armenhaus, *(US)* Besserungsanstalt, Arbeitshaus;

~ **ins and outs** alle Gepflogenheiten im Armenhaus.

working Arbeiten, Schaffen, Arbeitsweise, *(execution)* Ausführung, *(of material)* Be-, Verarbeitung, *(mining)* Abbau, *(operation)* Gang, Betrieb, Funktionieren, *(patent law)* Verwertung, *(railway)* Betrieb, *(setting into operation)* Inbetriebsetzung;

below-capacity ~ nicht ausgelastete (ausgenutzte) Kapazität; **continuous** ~ Dauerbetrieb; **disused** ~s stillgelegte Schachtanlagen; **efficient** ~ reibungsloser Ablauf; **hard** ~ *(US)* Schwerarbeit; **intermittent** ~ Stoßbetrieb; **open** ~ *(mine)* Tagebau; **overtime** ~ Überstundenarbeit; **short-time** ~ Kurzarbeit; **single-line** ~ Einmannbetrieb; **surface** ~ *(mine)* Tagebau; **underground** ~ Untertagebau;

~ **of an account** Kontoführung; ~ **to board level** Tätigkeit auf Vorstandsebene; ~ **of business** Betrieb eines Unternehmens; ~s **of conscience** Funktionieren des Gewissens; ~ **of a district** *(agent)* Bearbeitung eines Bezirks; ~ **of a farm** Bewirtschaftung eines Gutes; ~ **out of interest** Zinsenberechnung; ~s **of justice** Gang der Gerechtigkeit; ~**-up of material** Materialverarbeitung; ~ **of mines** Bergbau; ~ **in an office** Bürotätigkeit; ~ **overtime** Überstunden; ~ **of a patent** Patentausnutzung, -verwertung; **compulsory** ~ **of a patent** Zwangsverwertung eines Patents; ~**-out of a plan** Ausarbeitung eines Plans; ~**-out of ship's reckoning** Besteckaufnahme;

~ *(a.)* arbeitend, werk-, berufstätig, *(operating)* betriebsfähig, funktionierend, im Gang, in Betrieb;

incapable of ~ [vorübergehend] arbeitsunfähig; **not** ~ außer Betrieb, nicht funktionierend;

~ **to capacity** voll beschäftigt; ~ **in concert with his colleag(ue)s** im Einvernehmen mit seinen Kollegen;

to alter the ~ **of trains** Fahrplan ändern, Fahrplanänderung vornehmen; **to be** ~ im Beruf stehen, *(machine)* im Gang sein, funktionieren; **to be** ~ **again** wieder in Betrieb sein; **to be** ~ **away on one's job since breakfast** seit dem Frühstück ununterbrochen gearbeitet haben; **to be accustomed to** ~ **independently** an selbständige Arbeit gewohnt sein; **to be** ~ **on a novel** an einem Roman arbeiten; **to begin** ~ Betrieb aufnehmen; **to cease** ~ Betrieb einstellen; **to continue** ~ an der Arbeit bleiben; **to have been** ~ **hard all day** ganzen Tag schwer gearbeitet haben; **to keep** ~ in Betrieb halten; **to start (set)** ~ (Produktion) anlaufen lassen, in Betrieb nehmen, Betrieb aufnehmen; **to stop** ~ Arbeit einstellen, streiken;

~ **account** umsatzreiches laufendes Konto, *(plant)* Betriebsabrechnung; ~ **accounts** *(plant)* Betriebsabrechnung; ~ **affiliation** Arbeitsverbindung; ~ **age** arbeitsfähiges Alter; ~ **agreement** Absprache, Interessengemeinschaft, Einigungsformel; **joint** ~ **agreement** Konsortialvertrag; ~ **assets** Betriebs-, Umlaufsvermögen, Betriebsmittel; ~ **atmosphere** Betriebsklima, ~ **balance** Betriebsmittel[guthaben]; ~ **basis** Arbeitsgrundlage, -basis; ~ **breakfast** Arbeitsfrühstück; ~ **budget** Arbeitsetat; ~ **capacity** Arbeitskapazität, -fähigkeit, -kraft; **reduced** ~ **capacity** Erwerbsminderung, verminderte Erwerbsfähigkeit.

working capital Betriebs-, Umlaufkapital, Betriebsmittel, Aktiv-, werbendes Kapital;

cushion ~ zusätzliche Betriebsmittel; **fixed (permanent)** ~ betriebsnotwendiges Kapital; **net** ~ Betriebskapital nach Abzug der Verbindlichkeiten; **regular** ~ normales Umlaufs-, Betriebsvermögen; **reserve-margin** ~ Ergänzungskapital; **short-time** ~ kurzfristige Betriebsmittel;

to beef up ~ Betriebskapital verstärken;

~ **deficit** Betriebsmitteldefizit; ~ **figures** Betriebsmittelhöhe; ~ **fund** Betriebsmittelfonds, *(municipal accounting)* Mittel für Kommunalbetriebe; ~ **needs** Betriebsmittelbedarf, Betriebskapitalerfordernisse; ~ **purpose** Betriebsmittelzweck; ~ **ratio** *(US)* Verhältnis der flüssigen Aktiva zu laufenden Verbindlichkeiten, Liquiditätsgrad, -koeffizient, Betriebsmittelquote, -kapitalverhältnis; ~ **statement** Betriebskapitalnachweis; ~ **surplus** Betriebsmittelüberschuß; ~ **turnover** Verhältnis von Nettoumsatz zu Betriebskapital.

working card *(US)* Gewerkschaftsmitgliedsausweis; ~ **charges** Betriebskosten; ~ **class** Arbeitertum, -klasse; ~ **classes** Arbeiterbevölkerung, -stand; ~**-class area** Arbeitergegend; ~**-class district** Arbeitergegend, -viertel; ~**-class family** Arbeiterfamilie; ~**-class house** Arbeiterhaus; ~**-class quarter** Arbeiterviertel; ~**-class tenant** zur Arbeiterbevölkerung zählender Mieter; ~**-class vote** Arbeiterstimmen; ~ **climate** Betriebs-, Arbeitsklima; ~ **clothes** Arbeitskleidung, -anzug; ~ **coefficient** Betriebskoeffizent; ~ **committee** Arbeitsausschuß; ~ **conditions** Betriebs-, Arbeitsbedingungen, -verhältnisse, *(machine)* Betriebszustand; ~ **contract** Bauvertrag; ~ **control** Betriebs-

kontrolle; ~ **copy** *(book)* Arbeitsexemplar; ~ **costs** Betriebskosten; ~ **day** Arbeits-, Werktag, *(daily hours)* tägliche Arbeitszeit; **ordinary** ~ **day** Normalarbeitstag, gewöhnlicher Werktag; ~ **day of eight hours** Achtstundentag; ~**-day** werktäglich; ~**-day life** Alltagsleben; ~ **dinner** Arbeitsessen; ~**dog** *(plodding)* mühselig, mühsam; ~ **drawing** Werkstatt-, Detail-, Konstruktionszeichnung, Bauplan, -riß; ~ **employer** mitarbeitender Betriebsinhaber; ~ **environment** Arbeitsumwelt; ~ **equipment** Arbeitsausrüstung; ~ **expenses** Betriebsunkosten; ~ **face** *(mining)* Ort; ~ **facilities** Arbeitsbedingungen; ~ **force** [Betriebs]belegschaft; ~ **foreman** Vorarbeiter; ~ **fund** Betriebsmittel; ~ **fund advances** Betriebsmittelvorschüsse; ~ **group** Arbeitsgruppe; ~ **guides** Richtlinien; ~ **hour** Arbeitsstunde; ~ **hours** Arbeitszeit, *(rent-a-car)* Öffnungszeiten; **outside** ~ **hours** außerhalb der Arbeitszeit; **collectively agreed** ~ **hours** tarifliche Arbeitszeit; ~ **hypothesis** Arbeitshypothese; ~ **instructions** Bedienungsanweisungen; ~ **interest** Beteiligungsprozentsatz, *(mine)* Nutzungsvergütung, Ausbeutebeteiligung; **to have a** ~ **knowledge of French** einige Kenntnisse im Französischen haben, hinlänglich Französisch sprechen; ~ **language** *(conference)* Verständigungs-, offizielle Arbeitssprache; ~ **level** *(mining)* Bausohle; ~ **life** Berufsleben; **to have spent one's** ~ **life with a company** beruflich nur bei einer Firma gewesen sein; ~ **load** Höchstgewicht, Maximalbelastung, *(el.)* Betriebsbelastung; ~ **lunch** *(politics)* Arbeitsessen; **to have a** ~ **majority** über eine arbeitsfähige Mehrheit verfügen; ~ **man** Arbeiter, Arbeitnehmer; **hard-** ~ **man** Schwerarbeiter; ~ **management** Betriebsführung; ~ **manager** Betriebsleiter, -führer; ~ **margin** Sicherheitsbetrag für unvorhergesehene Fälle; ~ **mean** *(statistics)* provisorischer Durchschnitt; **International** ⚒ **Men's Association** Internationale Arbeitervereinigung; ~**-men's club** *(Br.)* Arbeiterfreizeitklub; ~ **men's insurance law** Arbeiterversicherungsgesetz; ~ **men's cooperative society** *(Br.)* [Arbeiter]konsumverein; ~ **method** Arbeits-, Fabrikationsverfahren; ~ **model** Modell.

working order betriebsfähiger Zustand, Betriebszustand;

in ~ betriebsfertig, -fähig; **in full** ~ in vollem Betrieb;

to be in good ~ in gutem Betriebszustand (voll betriebsfähig) sein, gut funktionieren; **to put in full** ~ hundertprozentige Betriebsbedingungen schaffen; **to put a watch in good** ~ Uhr genau einstellen.

working organization betriebliche Gliederung, Betriebsgliederung; ~**-out** *(calculation)* Berechnung, *(elaboration of details)* Ausarbeitung; ~ **overtime** Überstundenarbeit; ~ **papers** Arbeitsunterlagen, -papiere, *(accounting)* Prüfungs-, Revisionsbogen, *(worker)* Arbeitsausweis, *(work permit)* Arbeitserlaubnis; **low-level** ~ **paper** von unbedeutenden Mitarbeitern erstellte Arbeitspapier; ~ **part** Verschleißteil; ~ **partner** aktiver Teilhaber (Gesellschafter); ~ **party** *(Br.)* Arbeitsgemeinschaft, Arbeitsausschuß, -gruppe, *(mil.)* Arbeitsabteilung; ~ **people** Arbeiterschaft, Berufstätige; ~ **period** Produktionsperiode, Arbeitszeit; **standard** ~ **period** regelmäßige Arbeitszeit; ~ **person** Erwerbsperson; ~ **pit** *(mining)* Arbeitsschacht; ~ **place** Arbeitsstätte; ~ **plan** Konstruktionszeichnung, *(banking)* Rahmenkreditvertrag; ~ **plant** Betriebsanlage; ~ **platform** Arbeitspodest; ~ **point** *(mining)* Ort; ~ **pool** Arbeitsgemeinschaft; ~ **population** Zahl der Erwerbspersonen, Erwerbs-, Arbeiterbevölkerung, berufstätiger Bevölkerungsteil; ~ **potential** Arbeitskräftepotential; ~ **power** *(machine)* Leistungsfähigkeit; ~ **premises** Arbeitsräume; ~ **process** Arbeitsverfahren; ~ **proceeds** Fabrikationsertrag; ~ **program(me)** Arbeitsprogramm; ~ **quarter** Arbeitsviertel; ~ **regulations** Betriebsvorschriften, -ordnung; **good** ~ **relationship** gutes Arbeitsverhältnis; ~ **result** Betriebsergebnis; ~**-rule agreement** Betriebsordnung; ~ **scheme** Arbeitsplan, Fabrikationsprogramm; ~ **season** Betriebszeit; ~ **sheet** Arbeitsunterlage; ~ **statement** Betriebsaufstellung; ~ **stock** Betriebsmaterial; ~ **storage** *(data processing)* Arbeitsspeicher; ~ **strength (stress)** Materialbeanspruchung; ~ **system** Arbeitssystem, -methode; ~ **theory** Arbeitstheorie; ~ **time** Betriebsstunden, -dauer, [Werk]arbeitszeit; **to reduce** ~ **time** Arbeitszeit verkürzen; ~**-time regulation** Arbeitszeitordnung; ~ **visit** Arbeitsbesuch; ~ **vitality** Arbeitsvitalität; ~ **week** Arbeitswoche; ~ **wife** mitarbeitende (berufstätige) Ehefrau; ~ **woman** berufstätige Frau, Arbeiterin, Arbeitnehmerin; ~ **year** Betriebs-, Rechnungs-, Geschäftsjahr.

workless arbeits-, beschäftigungslos.

workload *(fig.)* Arbeitsbelastung.

workman [Industrie]arbeiter, Arbeitskraft, *(artisan)* Handwerker;

average ~ Durchschnittsarbeiter; **fine** ~ guter Arbeiter; **good** ~

geschickter Arbeiter; **paid ~** Lohnarbeiter; **skilled ~** Facharbeiter; **striking ~** Streikender; **travel(l)ing ~** Wanderarbeiter; **unskilled ~** ungelernter Arbeiter;
  ~ organized into a trade union gewerkschaftlich organisierter Arbeiter;
  to discharge a ~ Arbeiter entlassen;
  ~'s budget Arbeiterhaushalt; **~'s dwelling** Arbeiterwohnung;
  to dock a ~'s wages Arbeitslohn kürzen.

workmanlike fachmännisch, -gemäß;
  to do s. th. in a ~ manner etw. nach allen Regeln der Kunst machen.

workmanship technische Auführung, Arbeitsausführung, Arbeit, *(skill)* Kunstfertigkeit, Geschicklichkeit, *(skilful execution of work)* Qualitätsarbeit, Wertarbeit, Arbeitsqualität, *(work done)* Werk;
  expert ~ Facharbeit; **excellent (exquisite, honest) ~** ausgezeichnete Leistung, feinste Qualitätsarbeit, Präzisionsarbeit, hervorragende Verarbeitung; **faulty ~** fehlerhafte Ausführung; **finest ~** erstklassige Arbeit (Ausführung); **highclass ~** hochwertige Arbeit; **poor ~** mäßige Ausführung, schlechte Arbeit; **sound ~** sorgfältige Arbeit; **superior ~** Qualitätsarbeit;
  to employ the best ~ only nur bestes Material verarbeiten.

workmaster Werkmeister, Faktor.

workmate Arbeitskollege, Berufskamerad.

workmen Arbeiter, Arbeitskräfte, Arbeitnehmer;
  locked-out ~ ausgesperrte Arbeiter;
  ~ organized into trade unions gewerkschaftlich organisierte Arbeiter;
  to drive one's ~ too hard seine Arbeitskräfte zu sehr ausnutzen; **to fire (sack) one's ~** *(fam.)* seine Arbeiter entlassen; **to have the ~ in** Handwerker im Hause haben;
  Unemployed ⁰ Act *(Br.)* Arbeitslosengesetz; **~'s club** Arbeiterverein; **~'s compensation** *(US)* Unfallentschädigung, -vergütung, *(mining)* Bergmannsprämie; **~'s compensation act** *(Br.)* Betriebsunfallgesetz; **~'s compensation insurance** *(US)* Unternehmer-, Betriebshaftpflicht-, Arbeiterunfallversicherung; **~'s compensation law** *(Br.)* Berufsunfall-, Gewerbeunfallversicherungsgesetz; **~-compensation loss** Vergütung für Verdienstausfall; **~'s dwelling** Arbeiterwohnung; **~'s return ticket** Arbeiterrückfahrkarte; **~'s season ticket** Arbeiterwochenkarte; **~'s settlement** Arbeiterkolonie; **~'s ticket** Arbeiterfahrschein, -karte; **~'s train** Arbeiterzug.

workout Kraftprobe, *(training)* Trainingszeit.

workpeople Arbeiter;
  ~'s train Arbeiterzug.

workpiece Arbeits-, Werkstück.

workplace Arbeitsraum, -platz, *(mining)* Ort;
  safe ~ sicherer Arbeitsplatz;
  ~ layout Arbeitsplatzgestaltung.

workroom Arbeitsraum, -saal, Werkstatt;
  ~ costs Werkstattkosten.

workshop [Gewerbe]betrieb, Werkstatt, Werkstätte, Fabrikräume, *(artist)* Arbeitsweise, *(teaching course)* Ferienkurs, Seminar, Arbeitstagung;
  domestic ~ Heimwerkstatt; **mobile (travelling) ~** fahrbare Werkstatt; **special instruction ~** Lehrwerkstätte;
  ~ costs Werkstattkosten; **~ manager** Betriebsleiter, Werkstattleiter; **~ training** Werkstattausbildung.

workshy arbeitsscheu.

worktime price ratio Verhältnis geleisteter Arbeitsstunden zum Preis.

workwoman Arbeiterin.

world Welt, Erde, *(human society)* menschliche Gesellschaft, Menschen, *(sphere of business)* Berufssphäre, *(great multitude)* Masse, große Menge, Unmenge, *(universe)* All, Universum;
  drunk to the ~ total betrunken; **for all the ~** in jeder Hinsicht; **not for all the ~** um keinen Preis; **nothing in the ~** rein gar nichts; **out of this ~** *(coll.)* himmlisch, phantastisch; **throughout the ~** weltweit; **tired to the ~** totmüde; **to the ~'s end** bis ans Ende der Welt;
  animal ~ Tierkreis; **banking ~** Bankwelt; **business ~** Geschäftswelt; **commercial ~** Handelskreise, Kaufleute; **the English-speaking ~** die Englisch sprechenden Länder, angelsächsische Bevölkerung; **financial ~** Finanzleute, -welt; **the great ~** die feine Gesellschaft; **scientific ~** Welt der Wissenschaft; **vegetable ~** Pflanzenreich;
  ~ of business Geschäftswelt; **~ of buyers** Käuferseite; **the ~ beyond** das Jenseits; **~ of difference** weltweiter Unterschied; **~ of difficulties** Unmenge Schwierigkeiten; **~ of high finance** Hochfinanz; **~ at large** Weltöffentlichkeit; **~ of letters** gelehrte Welt; **all the ~ and his wife** alles, was Rang und Namen hat;

to be all the ~ for s. o. jem. alles bedeuten; **to be decanted into the ~** allein und auf sich gestellt in die Welt entlassen werden; **to begin the ~** von vorn anfangen, ins Berufsleben eintreten; **to carry the ~ before one** hundertprozentigen Erfolg haben; **to do s. o. a ~ of good** jem. glänzend bekommen; **to feel on top of the ~** sich phantastisch fühlen; **to foresake the ~** der Welt entsagen; **to know the ~** das Leben kennen; **to let the ~ slide** alles laufen lassen; **to live out of the ~** ganz zurückgezogen leben; **to make the best of both ~s** geistig und materiell auf seine Kosten kommen; **to make a noise in the ~** allgemeiner Gesprächsstoff sein; **to make a journey round the ~** Weltreise unternehmen; **to make one's way in the ~** Erfolg haben; **to police the ~** Ordnung in der Welt aufrechterhalten; **to rise in the ~** hochkommen, aufsteigen; **to see the ~** Land und Leute kennen; **to take the ~ as one finds it** sich mit den Gegebenheiten abfinden; **to withdraw from the ~** sich vom öffentlichen Leben zurückziehen;
  ~ alliance Weltbund; **~ association** Weltverband; **⁰ Association for Public Opinion** Internationaler Verband für Meinungsforschung; **⁰ Association of Travel Agencies** Weltverband der Reisebüros; **~ auto power** Autoweltmacht; **⁰ Bank** Weltbank; **⁰ Bank bond issue** Weltbankanleihe; **~ capital** Weltstadt; **⁰ Court** Ständiger Internationaler Gerichtshof; **to face ~ competition for export markets** auf dem Exportmarkt konkurrenzfähig bleiben; **~ concept** Weltansicht; **~ congress** Weltkongreß; **~ consumption** Weltverbrauch; **⁰ Court** Internationaler Gerichtshof; **~ currency** Weltwährung; **~ demand** Weltbedarf; **~ depression** Weltwirtschaftskrise; **~-dominating** weltbeherrschend; **~ domination** Weltherrschaft.

world-economic weltwirtschaftlich;
  ~ conditions Weltwirtschaftslage; **~ conference** Weltwirtschaftskonferenz; **~ crisis** Weltwirtschaftskrise; **~ recovery** Erholung der Weltwirtschaft; **~ situation** Weltwirtschaftslage; **~ summit** Weltwirtschaftsgipfel; **~ system** Weltwirtschaftssystem.

world│economy Weltwirtschaft; **~ energy consumption** Weltenergieverbrauch; **~ export market** Weltexportmarkt; **~ fair** Weltausstellung; **~-famous** weltberühmt; **⁰ Federation of Trade Unions (WFTU)** Weltgewerkschaftsbund; **~ food program(me)** Welternährungsprogramm; **~ food reserves** Weltnahrungsmittelvorräte; **~ food shortage** Weltnahrungsmittelknappheit; **~ food supply** Weltnahrungsmittelversorgung; **~ government** Weltregierung; **⁰ Health Organization (WHO)** Weltgesundheitsorganisation; **~-historical** weltgeschichtlich; **~ importance** bedeutende Position in der Welt; **⁰ Intellectual Property Organization** Weltorganisation für geistiges Eigentum; **~ language** Weltsprache; **to be a ~ leader** führende Position in der Welt innehaben; **~ liquidity** Weltliquidität; **~ market** Weltmarkt; **~ market of raw materials** Weltrohstoffmarkt; **~ market price** Weltmarktpreis; **~ market requirements** Bedürfnisse des Weltmarktes; **~ monetary system** Weltwährungssystem; **~-old** so alt wie die Welt; **~ politics** Weltpolitik; **~ population** Weltbevölkerung; **~ power** Weltmacht; **~ premiere** Welturaufführung; **~ press** Weltpresse; **~ price** Preis auf dem Weltmarkt, Weltmarktpreis; **~ price collapse** Zusammenbruch der Weltmarktpreise; **~ production** Weltproduktion; **~-renowned** weltbekannt; **~ recession** weltweite Resession; **⁰ Savings Day** Weltspartag; **~ shortage** Weltknappheit; **~ situation** internationale Gesamtsituation; **~ slump** Weltwirtschaftskrise; **~ stage** Weltbühne; **~ state** Weltstaat; **in ~ terms** im Weltmaßstab; **~ trade** Welthandel, -wirtschaft; **~ trade in food** Weltnahrungsmittelhandel; **~ trade center** Welthandelszentrum; **~ trade position** Welthandelsstellung; **~ trader** Welthandelsnation; **~-trading currency** Welthandelswährung; **~-trading pattern** Welthandelslage; **~ turnover** Weltumsatz; **~ view** Weltanschauung; **~ vituperation** weltweite Empörung; **⁰ War I** Erster Weltkrieg; **~-weary** lebensüberdrüssig, -müde.

world-wide weltpolitisch, -weit, über die ganze Welt verbreitet;
  ~ fame Weltruf; **~ financial crisis** weltweite Finanzkrise; **~ letter of credit** überall gültiger Reisekreditbrief; **~ reputation** Weltruf.

wordly weltlich, zeitlich, irdisch;
  ~ employment or business *(Sunday Laws)* Geschäftstätigkeit; **~ goods** irdische Güter; **~ wisdom** Weltklugheit.

worm *(fig.)* minderwertige Kreatur, *(technics)* Schneckengewinde, *(tube twisted into coils)* Kühlschlange;
  ~ of conscience Gewissensbiß;
  ~ (v.) schleichen, sich verstohlen bewegen, kriechen, *(fig.)* auf krummen Wegen erreichen;
  ~ o. s. into s. one's confidence sich in jds. Vertrauen einschleichen; **~ out of s. th.** *(sl.)* sich um etw. drücken; **~ a secret out of s. o.** jem. die Würmer aus der Nase ziehen;

~-eaten wurmstichig, *(fig.)* morsch, veraltet; **~ fence** Zickzackzaun; **~ gear** Schneckengetriebe.

wormwood *(fig.)* Wermutstropfen.

worn abgenutzt, abgetragen, abgewetzt, verbraucht, *(land)* erschöpft, ausgelaugt;
~ at the heels mit schiefen Absätzen; **~ out** erschöpft, fertig, erledigt; **~ by water** vom Wasser angenagt; **~ by the waves** von den Wellen erodiert;
to be a shadow nur noch ein Schatten seines früheren Ichs sein; **to be ~ out by all this work** durch die viele Arbeit völlig erschöpft sein;
~ coin abgegriffene Münze; **~ currency** abgenutztes Geld; **~ joke** abgedroschener Witz; **~-out argument** verbrauchtes Argument; **~-out health** zerrüttete Gesundheit; **~-out type** abgenutzte Schrift; **well-~ volume** ganz zerlesenes Buch.

worried geplagt, bekümmert, besorgt.

worries, money Geldsorgen;
~ of everyday life Kümmernisse des Alltagslebens.

worry Kummer, Sorge;
~ (v.) quälen, belästigen, plagen, *(bother)* unnötig beunruhigen, Sorgen bereiten;
~ about trifles sich über Kleinigkeiten aufregen; **~ along** sich mit knapper Not durchschlagen; **~ o. s. to death** sich zu Tode ängstigen; **~ s. o. into a decision** jem. eine Entscheidung abnötigen; **~ the life out of s. o.** jem. die Hölle heiß machen; **~ s. o. out** j. hinausekeln; **~ out a problem** Problem nicht loslassen; **~ through the work of a day** sich durch die tägliche Arbeit hindurchquälen.

worrying quälend, beunruhigend.

worse schlechter, schlimmer, übler, *(illness)* kränker, *(inferior)* minderwertig, geringer, niedriger, *(worse off)* schlechter gestellt;
for better, for ~ wie man es auch nimmt; **from bad to ~** vom Regen in die Traufe; **if ~ comes to ~** schlimmstenfalls; **so much the ~** umso schlimmer; **~ off** schlechter gestellt;
to be ~ for schlecht wegkommen bei; **to be a change for the ~ of a patient** sich im Krankheitszustand verschlimmert haben; **to be none the ~ for s. th.** sich wegen einer Sache nicht schlechter stehen; **to be 1/2 ~** *(stock exchange)* einen halben Punkt niedriger stehen, halben Punkt gefallen sein;
~ followed schlimmeres folgte.

worsen *(v.)* verschlechtern, verschlimmern;
~ the balance of payment Zahlungsbilanz verschlechtern.

worsening | of the balance of payments Zahlungsbilanzverschlechterung; **~ in business** Konjunkturverschlechterung; **~ of the economic climate** verschlechtertes Konjunkturklima; **~ of the economy** Konjunkturverschlechterung.

worship Anbetung, Verehrung, Kult, *(religious reverence)* Gottesdienst;
hero ~ Heldenverehrung;
~ of wealth Anbetung des Reichtums;
~ (v.) the golden calf Mammon anbeten.

worshipper of idols Götzendiener.

worst *(a.)* übelst, schlechtest;
at its very ~ im allerschlimmsten Fall; **if the ~ comes to the ~** wenn alle Stricke reißen;
the ~ of it das Schlimmste daran;
to be at its ~ *(illness)* auf dem Höhepunkt sein; **to be prepared for the ~** aufs Schlimmste gefaßt sein; **to get the ~ of it** am schlechtesten wegkommen; **to see s. o. at his ~** j. von der schlechtesten Seite sehen.

worsted Kammgarn[stoff];
~ articles Wollwaren.

worth Betrag, *(equivalent)* Gegenwert, *(importance)* Bedeutung, Wert, Wichtigkeit, *(merit)* Verdienst, Ansehen, *(price)* Preis, *(value)* Wert;
for all one's is ~ nach besten Kräften; **for what it is ~** ohne jede Garantie; **not ~ a damn (curse, brass farthing, penny, rap, shuck)** keinen Pfifferling wert; **of great ~** sehr wertvoll, teuer; **net ~** *(US)* *(balance sheet)* Eigenkapital;
~ (a.) wert, würdig;
~ mentioning erwähnenswert; **~ speaking of** der Rede wert;
to be ~ *(cost)* kosten, wert sein, im Preis stehen, *(to be quoted)* im Kurs stehen, notieren, notiert sein mit, *(receive income)* Einkommen haben (beziehen), verdienen, *(have property)* Vermögen besitzen, *(value)* wert sein, gelten; **not to be ~ the candle** nicht der Mühe wert sein; **to be ~ it** der Mühe wert sein; **to be ~ 40.000 $ a year** 40.000 Dollar Jahreseinkommen haben; **to be hardly ~ troubling about** nichts Aufregendes sein; **to be ~ a million** millionenschwer sein, viele Millionen haben; **to be ~ the money** preiswert (preiswürdig) sein; **not to be ~ the paper it is**

printed on nicht das Druckpapier wert sein; **not to be ~ powder and shot** keinen Schuß Pulver wert sein; **to be well ~ reading** wirklich lesenswert sein; **to be ~ while** der Mühe wert (lohnend) sein, sich auszahlen; **to be ~ one's salt** etw. taugen, sein Geld wert sein; **to die ~ a million** Millionenvermögen hinterlassen; **to get the ~ of one's money** für sein Geld etw. Gleichwertiges bekommen; **to offer one's opinion for what it may be ~** seine unmaßgebliche Meinung zum Besten geben; **to pass news on to s. o. for what it is ~** Nachricht an j. unverbürgt weitergeben; **to want one's money's-~** für sein Geld etw. haben wollen;
~-while der Mühe wert, lohnend.

worthiest of blood männliche Nachkommen.

worthily angemessen, nach Verdienst.

worthiness guter Zustand;
air ~ Lufttüchtigkeit.

worthless wertlos, nichts wert;
~ bill fauler Wechsel.

worthlessness Wertlosigkeit.

worthy *(humo(u)rous)* großes Tier, Person von Rang und Würden;
~ (a.) angesehen, ehrenwert, *(suitable)* würdig, angemessen, passend;
~ of credit glaubwürdig, kreditwürdig; **~ of support** unterstützungswürdig;
~ adversary ebenbürtiger Gegner; **to help only the ~ poor** nur den wirklich Hilfsbedürftigen helfen; **~ reward** angemessene Belohnung.

would-be Möchtegern, Gernegroß;
~ (a.) angeblich, scheinbar;
~ borrower kreditsuchendes Unternehmen; **~ heir** Möchtegernerbe; **~ kindness** beabsichtigte Freundlichkeit.

wound Wunde, Verletzung, Verwundung, *(fig.)* Kränkung, Beleidigung;
~ up liquidiert; **~ up to a high pitch** hochgespannt;
to be ~ up to a high pitch of excitement sich in höchster Erregung befinden.

wounded verwundet, verletzt;
~ feelings verletzter Stolz; **~ vanity** verletzte Eitelkeit; **~ veteran** Kriegsbeschädigter, -versehrter.

wounding schwere Körperverletzung.

wrack Strandgut;
~ and ruin Untergang und Verderben;
~ (v.) zugrundegehen;
to go to ~ untergehen.

wrangle Zank, Hader, *(debate)* Debatte, Diskussion;
~ (v.) streiten, hadern, *(debate)* debattieren, diskutieren;
~ over trifles sich über Kleinigkeiten streiten.

wrangler Zänker, *(debator)* Disputant, Debatteteilnehmer.

wrap Umhüllung, Verpackung, *(censor)* Geheimhaltung, Zensur;
capital ~ *(US)* Zusammenfassung des Wichtigsten;
~ of the news *(US)* Kurzfassung der Nachrichten;
~ (v.) about with a string mit einer Schnur umwickeln, verschnüren; **~ o. s. in a blanket** sich in eine Decke einhüllen; **~ into (up)** einwickeln, -packen; **~ o. s. up** sich warm anziehen; **~ up a business deal** Geschäft erfolgreich abschließen; **~ it up** *(sl.)* erfolgreich abschließen; **~ up a case to one's own satisfaction** *(sl.)* Fall erfolgreich abwickeln; **~ up goods** Waren verpacken; **~ up one's meaning in obscure language** seine Meinung völlig unverständlich ausdrücken; **~ in paper** in Papier einschlagen;
to keep under ~ unter Verschluß halten; **to keep carefully under ~s** sorgfältig unter Verschluß halten; **to keep a plan carefully under ~s** Plan sorgfältig geheimhalten.

wrap-up *(customer, sl.)* schnell entschlossener Käufer, *(easy sale)* leichter Verkauf, *(mail business)* Postversandartikel.

wraparound windshield *(US)* Panorama-, Vollsichtscheibe.

wrappage Verpackung, Packmaterial.

wrapped | in mist in Nebel eingehüllt; **~ in paper** in Papier eingeschlagen;
to be ~ in an intrigue in ein Ränkespiel verwickelt sein; **to be ~ up in Anspruch genommen sein; **to be ~ up in mystery** schleierhaft (rätselhaft) sein; **to be ~ up in one's work** in seine Arbeit vertieft sein.

wrapper [Ein]packer, *(book)* Umschlag, Umhüllung, Schutzhülle, *(outer covering)* Kreuz-, Streifband;
under ~ unter Kreuzband;
to post in ~s unter Kreuzband verschicken.

wrapping Verpackung, Hülle;
original ~ Originalverpackung; **special ~** Sonderverpackung;
~ of goods Warenverpackung;
~ material Verpackungsmaterial; **~ paper** Umschlag-, Einwickel-, Packpapier; **~ room** Pack-, Verpackungsraum.

wrath Zorn, Wut.

wreath Kranz, Girlande, Blumengebinde;
~-**laying ceremony** Kranzniederlegung.

wreck *(building)* Ruine, *(fig.)* Trümmerhaufen, Überreste, Untergang, Ruin, *(flotsam)* Strandgut, *(plane, ship)* gestrandetes (verlassenes) Schiff (Flugzeug), Schiffbruch, Wrack, Wrackteil, -gut, *(dilapidated vehicle)* Schrottwagen, Autowrack;
strewn with ~s von Trümmern übersät;
total ~ *(insurance)* Totalverlust; **worthless ~** *(car)* Totalschaden;
~ *(v.)* zugrunde richten, *(fig.)* zum Scheitern bringen, *(ship)* Schiffbruch erleiden, stranden, zerschellen, *(work upon wrecks)* mit Abwracken beschäftigt sein, abwracken;
~ a commercial house Handelsfirma ruinieren; **~ one's plans** jds. Pläne zum Scheitern bringen; **~ off a ship** Wrack abbrechen; **~ a train** Zug zum Entgleisen bringen;
to be saved from ~ dem Schiffbruch entgehen; **to be a mere ~ of one's former self** nur ein Schatten seines früheren Ichs sein; **to be strewn with ~s** mit Trümmern übersät sein; **to collect the ~s of one's fortune** Reste seines Vermögens sammeln; **to go to ~ and ruin** zugrundegehen; **to suffer ~** Schiffbruch erleiden;
~ buoy Wracktonne; **~ cargo** durch Schiffbruch verlorengegangene Ladung; **~ commissioner** *(Br.)* **(master)** Strandvogt, Leiter einer Bergungsaktion, Bergungsleiter.

wreckage *(cast-offs by society)* gescheiterte Existenzen, Strandgut, Abschaum, *(flotsam)* Schiffstrümmer, Wrackgut, -teile, Strandgut, *(wreck)* Schiffbruch, Scheitern, Untergang;
~ of an aircraft Flugzeugtrümmer.

wrecked schiffbrüchig, *(fig.)* gescheitert, gestrandet;
to be ~ Schiffbruch erleiden, stranden, zerschellen, scheitern; **~ bank** ruinierte Bank; **~ building** abgerissenes Gebäude; **~ cargo** Wrackgut; **~ freight** verlorene Fracht; **~ goods** Strandgut; **~ sailor** schiffbrüchiger Seemann; **~ ship** schiffbrüchiges Schiff; **~ train** entgleister Zug.

wrecker *(plunderer)* Strandräuber, *(relief train)* Hilfszug, *(ship)* Bergungsdampfer, -schiff, *(truck, US)* Abschleppwagen, *(worker)* Abbruch-, Bergungsarbeiter, *(wreckmaster)* Strandvogt.

wreckfree frei von Beschlagnahme als Strandgut.

wrecking Strandraub, *(fig.)* Ruinieren, *(piece of wreckage)* Wrackteil, *(ship, US)* Bergung;
~ amendment *(parl., Br.)* Hilfsantrag; **~ company** *(US)* Abbruchgesellschaft; **~ crane** *(US)* Abschleppkran; **~ crew** *(US)* Abschleppmannschaft, *(ship)* Rettungsmannschaft; **~ policy** Sabotagepolitik; **~ service** *(US)* Abschleppdienst; **~ train** Hilfszug; **~ truck** *(US)* Abschleppwagen.

wrench Schraubenschlüssel;
economic ~ Wirtschaftskrise; **terrible ~** schmerzliche Trennung;
~ *(v.)* **the door open** Tür aufbrechen.

wrest *(v.)* zerren, reißen, *(meaning)* verdrehen, verzerren;
~ from s. o. jem. entreißen; **~ a confession of guilt** Geständnis herauspressen; **~ a living from marginal land** dem kargen Boden seinen Lebensunterhalt abringen.

wrestle *(v.)* | **out** durchfechten; **~ with a problem** sich mit einem Problem herumschlagen.

wretch bedauernswerte Existenz;
poor ~ armer Teufel.

wretched elend, unglücklich, *(deeply afflicted)* jämmerlich;
~ accident fürchterlicher Unfall; **~ health** zerrüttete Gesundheit; **~ house** armselige Behausung; **~ inn** miserables Gasthaus; **to live in ~ poverty** in jämmerlichen Verhältnissen leben; **~ stupidity** entsetzliche Dummheit; **~ weather** scheußliches Wetter.

wriggle Windung, Krümmung, Biegung;
~ *(v.)* **out of s. th.** sich vor etw. drücken; **~ o. s. out of a difficulty** sich aus einer Sache herauswinden; **~ through** sich durchwinden.

wring Wringen, Pressen;
~ *(v.)* *(fruits)* auspressen, ausquetschen, *(torment)* quälen, bedrücken;
~ a confession from s. o. jem. ein Geständnis abpressen; **~ one's hands** die Hände ringen; **~ s. one's hand** jem. die Hand drücken; **~ money out of s. o.** Geld aus jem. herauspressen; **~ out wet clothes** nasse Kleider auswringen.

wringer *(extortioner)* Erpresser;
to put through the ~ durch die Mühle drehen.

wringing wet völlig durchnäßt.

wrinkle Runzel, Falte, *(crease)* Unebenheit, *(device)* Kniff, Trick, *(tip, coll.)* Wink, Andeutung;
to give s. o. a ~ jem. einen Tip geben;
~-resistant knitterfrei.

wristwatch Armbanduhr.

writ *(court order)* gerichtliche Verfügung (Anordnung), Eröffnungsbeschluß, *(document, Scot.)* Urkunde, Schriftstück, *(of execution, Br.)* Vollstreckungsbefehl, *(governmental decree)* behördlicher Erlaß, *(parl., Br.)* Wahlausschreibung, *(statement of claim)* Klageschrift, *(summons, Br.)* [Vor]ladung;
alias ~ Zweitausfertigung eines Vollstreckungstitels; **close ~** *(Br.)* königlicher Geheimbefehl; **concurrent ~** Zweitausfertigung eines Haftbefehls (einer Klageschrift); **specially indorsed ~** Vorladung unter Beifügung von Urkunden; **interlocutory ~** Zwischenurteil; **judicial ~** gerichtliche Verfügung; **junior ~** zuerst eingegangene Klage; **original ~** *(US)* Vorladung des Beklagten, Klagezustellung; **peremptory ~** *(US)* gerichtliche Verfügung; **prerogative ~** außerordentliche richterliche Verfügung;
~ for the arrest Haftbefehl; **~ of assistance** Zolldurchsuchungsbefehl, *(possession of land)* Besitzeinweisung; **~ of attachment** *(US)* dringlicher Arrest [im Zwangsvollstreckungsverfahren], Pfändungs- und Überweisungsbeschluß, *(criminal)* Haft-, Vorführungsbefehl; **~ of capias** *(US)* Haftbefehl zur Vorführung des Beklagten; **~ of certoriari** *(US)* Anforderung von Akten; **~ of commission** Rechtshilfeersuchen; **~ of covenant** Klage aus Vertragsverletzung; **~ of debt** *(US)* Vollstreckungsanweisung wegen einer Geldschuld; **~ of deceit** auf arglistige Täuschung gegründete Schadensersatzklage; **~ of delivery** *(Br.)* Vollstreckungsanordnung; **~ of detinue** Herausgabeklage; **~ of dower** Klage auf Herausgabe des Witwenteils; **~ of ejectment** *(US)* Besitzstörungsklage, Räumungsurteil; **~ of elegit (fieri facias)** Zwangsvollstreckungsbefehl; **~ of entry** Räumungsklage; **~ of error** Revisionszulassungsbeschluß; **~ of error coram nobis** Urteilsberichtigungsbeschluß; **~ of execution** Vollstreckungsanordnung, -befehl, -klausel, -titel; **~ of Habeas Corpus** Anordnung eines Haftprüfungstermins, Vorführbefehl; **~ of injunction** gerichtliches Verfügungsverbot; **~ of inquiry** *(after judgment by default)* Verfahren zur Feststellung der Schadenshöhe; **~ of mainprize** *(Br.)* Anordnung der Haftentlassung gegen Kautionsstellung; **~ of mandate** *(US)* Anweisung an ein unteres Gericht; **~ of mandamus** *(US)* gerichtliche Auflage zwecks Vornahme (Unterlassung) einer Handlung; **~ of possession** gerichtliche Besitzeinweisung, Vollstreckungsanordnung im Räumungsverfahren; **~ of prevention** vorbeugende Unterlassungsverfügung; **~ of privilege** *(Br.)* Anordnung der Haftentlassung; **~ of prohibition** *(US)* Einstellungsverfügung [an unteres Gericht]; **~ of probable cause** *(auxiliary process)* einstweilige Aussetzung; **~ of recaption** Herausgabebeschluß bei zweiter unberechtigter Mietpfändung; **~ of replevin** Herausgabeklage; **~ of restitution** Wiedereinweisungsbeschluß; **~ of review** Rechtsmittelzulassung; **~ of revivor** neue Vollstreckungsklausel; **~ of sequestration** *(Br.)* Beschlagnahmeanordnung; **~ of subpoena** Vorladung unter Strafandrohung; **~ of summons** Prozeßeröffnungsbeschluß, Ladung, Zustellungsurkunde; **~ of supersedeas** Einstellungsverfügung; **~ of supervisory control** Beschluß des Revisionsgerichts im Falle unrichtiger Entscheidungen; **~ of trial** *(Br.)* Verweisungsbeschluß an die untere Instanz; **~ of waste** *(against tenant)* Klage wegen Substanzschädigung;
to answer upon a ~ einer Ladung Folge leisten; **to be party to a ~** sich an einer Klage beteiligen; **to clap a ~ upon s. one's back** jem. einen Prozeß anhängen; **to draw up a ~** Schriftsatz vorbereiten; **to frame a ~** Klageschrift anfertigen; **to indorse a ~** Vorladung erlassen; **to issue a ~ against s. o.** jem. einen Schriftsatz mit Ladung zustellen; **to issue a ~ of execution** Vollstreckungsbefehl ausfertigen; **to serve a ~** *(Br.)* Klage (Ladung) zustellen; **to serve a ~ on the other party** dem Prozeßgegner einen Schriftsatz zustellen; **to take out a ~ against s. o.** Vorladung gegen j. erwirken.

write *(v.)* Schriftstück abfassen, schreiben, niederschreiben, aufzeichnen, schriftlich niederlegen, *(insurance)* Versicherung übernehmen, versichern, *(newspaper)* dirigieren;
~ an account of a journey Reisebericht verfassen; **~ an answer** schriftlich beantworten; **~ an application** Bewerbung aufsetzen, Bewerbungsschreiben aufsetzen; **~ articles** schriftliche Beiträge liefern; **~ to ask** schriftlich anfragen; **~ on s. one's behalf** jem. eine Befürwortung schreiben; **~ no new business for the month** im laufenden Monat keine Geschäfte mehr tätigen; **~ a call naked** Leerverkauf tätigen; **~ a certificate** Bescheinigung ausstellen; **~ a check** *(US)* **(cheque,** *Br.)* Scheck ausschreiben; **~ a class of business** bestimmte Versicherungssparte betreiben; **~ in confidence** bei zugesicherter Diskretion schreiben; **~ for one's contemporaries** für die Gegenwart schreiben; **~ a contract** Vertrag aufsetzen; **~ in depth** tiefschürfend schrei-

ben; ~ **in full** seinen Namen voll ausschreiben; ~ **s. th. in one's own hand** etc. eigenhändig schreiben; ~ **home** regularly regelmäßig nach Hause schreiben; ~ **insurance upon s.** one's life Lebensversicherung für jem. abschließen; ~ **legislation** Gesetze abfassen; ~ **s. o. a letter** jem. einen Brief schreiben; ~ **one's life** seine Lebensgeschichte schreiben; ~ **on a list** in eine Liste einschreiben; ~ **o. s. a man** volljährig werden; ~ **without making mistakes** fehlerlos schreiben; ~ **one's name** seinen Namen schreiben; ~ **a novel** Roman verfassen; ~ **orders** Aufträge buchen; ~ **six pages** sechs Seiten vollschreiben; ~ **for a paper** schriftliche Beiträge liefern, Journalist sein; ~ **for the press** journalistisch tätig sein; ~ **with restraint** zurückhaltend schreiben; ~ **the result** Resultat mitteilen; ~ **a sheet full** Seite vollschreiben; ~ **shorthand** stenografieren; ~ **on both sides of a piece of paper** Papier auf beiden Seiten beschreiben; ~ **a statement for the press** Presseerklärung abfassen; ~ **well** gut schreiben; ~ **one's will** sein Testament machen.

write back (v.) zurückschreiben, antworten, (bookkeeping) zurückbuchen, Stornobuchung vornehmen, stornieren;
~ **provisions** Rückstellungen auflösen.

write down (v.) nieder-, aufschreiben, notieren, eintragen, zu Papier bringen, (depreciate) teilweise (vom Wert) abschreiben, Buchwert herabsetzen, abbuchen, (disparage) herziehen über, schlechtmachen;
~ **an asset** Anlage abschreiben; ~ **the capital** Kapitalherabsetzung vornehmen; ~ **from dictation** aus dem Stenogramm übertragen; ~ **s. o. down as a fool** j. als Narren bezeichnen; ~ **property** Grundstück abschreiben.

write for (v.) schriftlich bestellen;
~ **the newspapers** journalistisch tätig sein.

write in (v.) einschreiben, eintragen, einfügen, (US) zwecks Reklamation einschicken.

write into (v.) **the articles** festschreiben.

write off (v.) (balance sheet) herunterschreiben, vollständig abschreiben, ausbuchen;
~ **o. s. off** (sl.) hopps gehen, tödlich abstürzen; ~ **an account of a sports meeting** Bericht über eine Sportveranstaltung verfassen; ~ **capital** Aktienkapital zusammenlegen; ~ **a claim** Forderung abschreiben; ~ **bad debts** (US) zweifelhafte Forderungen abschreiben; ~ **capitalized development cost** kapitalisierte Entwicklungskosten abschreiben; ~ **for depreciation of machinery** für Maschinenabnutzung abschreiben; ~ **exploration and development expenses immediately** Forschungs- und Entwicklungskosten sofort abschreiben; ~ **as a total loss** als Totalverlust (völlig) abschreiben; ~ **heavy start-up costs** hohe Anlaufkosten abschreiben; ~ **against taxes** steuerlich abschreiben; ~ **so much for wear and tear** bestimmten Betrag für Abnutzung absetzen.

write out (v.) ganz ausschreiben, (copy) abschreiben, kopieren;
~ **o. s. out** sich als Schriftsteller erschöpfen; ~ **a check** (US) (cheque, Br.) Scheck ausstellen; ~ **a copy of an agreement** Vertragsabschrift herstellen; ~ **fair** ins Reine schreiben.

write over (v.) **again** noch einmal abschreiben.

write up (v.) eingehend berichten, ausführlich darstellen, (balance sheet) Buchwert heraufsetzen, aufwerten, (write down) aufschreiben, aufzeichnen, (journalism) lobend herausstellen, (praise) Reklame machen, anpreisen;
~ **the acting of the leading players** über die Rollendarstellung der Hauptschauspieler lobend berichten; ~ **an affair for a paper** vollständigen Bericht für eine Zeitung verfassen; ~ **one's diary** sein Tagebuch aufs laufende bringen (vervollständigen); ~ **one's notes on a lecture** seine Vorlesungsaufzeichnungen überarbeiten; ~ **the value of an asset** Wert einer Anlage (Anlagewert) heraufsetzen.

write-up schriftlicher Bericht, ausführliche Artikel, (balance sheet, US) Höherbewertung, (critic) gute Buchbesprechung, (newspaper, sl.) Pressebericht, (property statement) frisierte Vermögensaufstellung;
~ **of stock values** Lageraufwertung.

writedowns (US) **write-downs** (Br.) Abschreibungen;
inventory ~ Abschreibungen auf Warenbestände;
~ **and other valuation adjustments of investments** Abschreibungen auf Finanzanlagen.

writeoff (US) **write-off** (Br.) vollständige Abschreibung, [beschleunigte] Ausbuchung, (sl.) abgestürztes Flugzeug;
accelerated ~s (US) verkürzte Abschreibungen, steuerliche Sonderabschreibungen; **complete** ~ (airliner, car) Totalverlust; **rapid** ~ beschleunigte Abschreibung; **tax** ~ steuerlich zulässige Abschreibungen;
~ **of assets** Anlagenabschreibung; **fast** ~ **for defence facilities** verteidigungsbedingte Schnellabschreibung; ~s **for losses on foreign exchange** Abschreibungen für Devisenverluste;

to accelerate ~ sofort abschreiben; **to be an instant** ~ sofort gänzlich uninteressant sein; **to vary** ~s Abschreibungssätze variieren;
~ **schedule** Abschreibungsschema.

writer Schreiber, (author) Schriftsteller, Autor, Verfasser, (civil service, Br.) Bürogehilfe, (copyist) Kopist, Kanzlist, Sekretär, (newspaper) Berichterstatter, (Scot.) Anwaltsgehilfe;
editorial ~ Leitartikler; **serial** ~ Feuilletonist; **staff** ~ festbezahlter Autor; **text** ~ Kommentator; **well-known** ~ bekannter Schriftsteller; **woman** ~ Schriftstellerin;
~ **of a letter** Briefschreiber, -verfasser; ~ **for the press** Journalist; ~ **of promise** vielversprechender Autor; ~ **to the signet** (Scot.) [etwa] Rechtsanwalt;
to be a ready ~ gute Feder haben;
~'s **cramp** Schreibkrampf; ~ **scholar** Fachautor.

writhe (v.) | **under insults** unter Kränkungen leiden; ~ **through a thicket** sich durch ein Dickicht winden.

writing Schreiben, (document) Schreiben, Geschriebenes, Schriftstück, -werk, Dokument, Urkunde, (handwriting) [Hand]schrift, (inscription) Inschrift, (literary work) schriftstellerische Arbeit, Aufsatz, Werk, Schriftstellerei, (style in composition) Schreibweise, Stil;
in ~ [hand]schriftlich, in Schriftform, brieflich; **in one's own** ~ mit eigener Hand;
illegible ~ unleserliche Schrift; **legal** ~ juristischer Aufsatz; ~ **obligatory** bindende (schriftliche) Abmachung, gesiegelte Schuldverschreibung; **scientific** ~ wissenschaftliche Literatur; ~ **in cipher** Geheimschrift; ~ **difficult to read** schwer lesbare Handschrift; ~ **on the wall** böses Omen, Menetekel;
to be ~ **one's life** seine Lebensgeschichte schreiben; **to be busy with** ~ mit Schreibarbeiten beschäftigt sein; **to make a living by** ~ sich durch die Schriftstellerei seinen Lebensunterhalt verdienen; **to put in** ~ aufschreiben, schriftlich;
~ (a.) schriftstellernd.

writing back (bookkeeping) Storno-, Rückbuchung, Stornierung;
~ **of provisions** Auflösung von Rückstellungen.

writing-down Niederschrift;
~ **of capital** Kapitalabschreibung;
~ **allowance** Vollabschreibung; ~ **period** Abschreibungszeitraum.

writing off (capital) Kapitalabschreibung;
~ **of a bad debt** Abschreibung einer zweifelhaften Forderung; ~ **of depreciation** Abschreibung für Abnutzung.

writing-up Entwurf, (balance sheet) Zuschreibung, Höherbewertung.

writing, to agree to s. th. in etw. schriftlich vereinbaren; **to be busy with** ~ mit Schreibarbeiten beschäftigt sein; **to conform in** ~ schriftlich bestätigen; **to inquire in** ~ schriftlich anfragen; **to make a living by** ~ von der Schriftstellerei leben; **to put [down] in** ~ niederschreiben, schriftlich niederlegen; **to recognize s. one's** ~ jds. Handschrift erkennen; **to reduce to** ~ schriftlich fixieren; **to verify in** ~ durch Unterschrift bestätigen;
~ **ability** schriftstellerische Begabung; ~ **block** Schreibblock; ~ **book** Schreibheft; ~ **case** Schreibzeug, Briefmappe; ~ **chamber** Schreibstube, (Br.) Schreibtisch, -pult; ~ **desk** Schreibtisch, -pult; ~ **duties** Schreibverpflichtungen; ~ **formula** schriftstellerisches Konzept; ~ **hand** Handschrift; ~ **ink** Tinte; ~ **limit** (reinsurance) Zeichnungsgrenze; ~ **material** Schreibmaterial; ~ **obligatory** gesiegelte Schuldurkunde; ~ **orders** Auftragsbuchung; ~ **pad** Schreibunterlage, -block; ~ **paper** Schreibpapier; ~ **profession** Schriftstellerberuf; ~ **room** Schreibzimmer; ~ **staff** Redaktionsstab; ~ **table** Arbeits-, Schreibtisch; ~ **text** Werbetext.

written schriftlich, geschrieben, in Schriftform;
~ **off** abgeschrieben, (plane) abgestürzt, -geschmiert; ~ **all over** ganz vollgeschrieben; ~ **and spoken** in Wort und Schrift; **entirely** ~ **by the hand of the testator** eigenhändig vom Erblasser geschrieben; ~ **on one side** einseitig beschrieben; **to be** ~ eingetragen sein; **to be** ~ **down as a failure** als Mißerfolg dargestellt werden;
~ **agreement** schriftliche Vereinbarung, schriftliche Abmachung; ~ **censure** schriftlicher Verweis; ~ **communication** schriftliche Benachrichtigung; ~ **consent** schriftliche Zustimmung; ~ **contract** schriftlicher Vertrag; ~ **-down value** Abschreibung vom jeweiligen Buchwert; ~ **evidence** Urkundenbeweis; ~ **evidence of debt** schriftliches Schuldanerkenntnis; ~ **examination** schriftliches Examen, schriftliche Prüfung; ~ **instrument** Urkunde, Schriftstück; ~ **language** Literatursprache; ~ **law** geschriebenes (kodifiziertes) Recht; ~ **matter** Schriftsache; ~ **memorandum** schriftliche Vereinbarung; ~ **notice** schriftliche Mitteilung (Kündigung); **to send in a** ~

notice schriftlich berichten; ~ **order** schriftlich erteilter Auftrag; ~ **receipt slip** schriftliche Empfangsbescheinigung; ~ **record** Niederschrift; **carefully** ~ **report** sorgfältig geschriebener Bericht; ~ **statement** schriftliche Erklärung; **to submit a** ~ **statement of a case** Fall schriftlich darlegen.

wrong Unrecht, Irrtum, *(injustice)* Ungerechtigkeit, *(tort)* unerlaubte Handlung, Rechtswidrigkeit, Rechtsverletzung, Delikt, Vergehen;

in the ~ im Irrtum;

actionable ~ einklagbare unerlaubte Handlung; **private** ~ rechtswidrige (unerlaubte) Handlung; **public** ~ strafbare Handlung;

~ *(v.)* ungerecht behandeln, *(do harm)* Schaden zufügen, schaden, benachteiligen;

~ **s. o.** j. benachteiligen, jem. Nachteil zufügen;

to admit that one was in the ~ seinen Fehler zugeben; **to be** ~ unrecht haben, *(watch)* falsch gehen; **to do** ~ **to s. o.** jem. ein Unrecht zufügen; **to get in** ~ **with s. o.** *(US)* sich jds. Gunst verscherzen; **to get s. o. in** ~ *(coll., US)* j. in Mißkredit bringen; **to go** ~ *(machine)* nicht funktionieren, *(person)* auf die schiefe Bahn geraten, *(plan)* fehlschlagen, schiefgehen, *(watch)* nicht funktionieren; **to go** ~ **in early life** frühzeitig auf die falsche Bahn geraten; **to know the difference between right and** ~ Recht und Unrecht unterscheiden können; **to prove s. o.** ~ jem. einen Irrtum nachweisen; **to put s. o. in the** ~ j. ins Unrecht setzen (in Mißkredit bringen); **to right a** ~ Unrecht wieder gutmachen; **to suffer** ~ Unrecht erleiden;

~ *(a.)* falsch, unrichtig, verkehrt, irrig, *(not in order)* in Unordnung;

~ **address** falsche Adresse, Anschrift; ~ **answer** verkehrte Antwort; **to be in the** ~ **box** fehl am Platz sein, *(be in a jam)* in der Klemme sitzen; **to get hold of the** ~ **end of the stick** etw. völlig mißverstehen; ~ **entry** falsche Eintragung; ~ **flag** falsche Flagge; **to be caught on the** ~ **foot** völlig unvorbereitet angetroffen werden; ~ **font (fount)** Zwiebelfisch; ~ **fount** *(print.)* falsche Type; ~ **number** *(tel.)* falsche Nummer, Fehlverbindung, *(sl.)* Psychopath; **to get up on the** ~ **side of the bed** mit dem verkehrten Fuß aufstehen; **to be on the** ~ **side of forty** jenseits von 40 sein; **to do the** ~ **thing in the** ~ **place** genau das Falsche tun; **to take a** ~ **turning** verkehrt (falsch) abbiegen; **to do s. th. in the** ~ **way** etw. am verkehrten Ende anfangen; **to go the** ~ **way** *(coll.)* in die falsche Kehle geraten.

wrongdoer Misse-, Übeltäter, Gesetzesverletzer.

wrongdoing Untat, Missetat, *(transgression of civil law)* Vergehen, Verbrechen.

wrongful ungerecht, unfair, *(legal sense)* unrechtmäßig, ungesetzlich, widerrechtlich;

~ **act** unerlaubte Handlung; ~ **conduct** zum Schadensersatz verpflichtendes Auftreten; ~ **dismissal** unberechtigte Entlassung, Entlassung ohne Einhaltung einer Kündigungsfrist; ~ **levy** unberechtigte Zwangsvollstreckung; ~ **occupation of an estate** unerlaubte Inbesitznahme eines Grundstücks.

wrongfulness Widerrechtlichkeit.

wrongfully | informed falsch unterrichtet; ~ **intending** in böswilliger Absicht.

wronghead Starrkopf, sturer Mensch.

wrongly verkehrt, falsch, unrichtig;

rightly or ~ mit Recht oder Unrecht;

~ **accused** fälschlich beschuldigt; ~ **worded bill** Wechsel mit unrichtigem Wortlaut.

wrongous imprisonment *(Scot.)* Freiheitsberaubung.

wrought verarbeitet;

hand-~ handgearbeitet;

~ **goods** Fertigfabrikate; ~ **iron** Schmiedeeisen; ~ **steel** Schweißstahl.

wry schief, krumm;

to make a ~ **face** schiefes Gesicht ziehen; ~ **notion** verschrobene Vorstellung; ~ **smile** verzerrtes Lächeln.

X Y Z

x *(US coll.)* Zehndollarschein;
  ~ **certificate** *(film, Br.)* Verbot für Jugendliche unter 16 Jahren.
x-ray Röntgenstrahl;
  ~ *(v.)* röntgen;
  to take a ~ Röntgenbild machen;
  ~ **examination** Röntgenuntersuchung; ~ **film** Röntgenfilm.
xenodochy Gastfreundschaft.
xenophobe Fremdenfeind, -hasser.
xenophobia Fremdenfeindlichkeit, -haß.
xenophobic fremdenfeindlich.
xerox Fotokopie, Ablichtung;
  ~ *(v.)* ablichten, fotokopieren.
Xmas *(coll.)* Weihnachten.

y *(railway)* gegabeltes Gleis.
yacht Segel-, Motorboot.
yak Gequatsche, Gequassel;
  ~-~ **city** Klatschstadt.
Yale-blue collar *(US)* Akademikerkragen.
Yankee Amerikaner;
  ~ *(a.)* amerikanisch.
yankees *(stock exchange, Br.)* amerikanische Eisenbahnaktien.
yard *(enclosure)* Hofraum, eingefriedeter Platz, Hof, *(US)* Arbeitsplatz, Werkstätte, *(garden, US)* Garten, *(grounds, US)* Gelände, Grundstück, *(storing)* Lagerplatz, *(textiles)* Elle;
  under ~ unter Vertrag;
  back ~ Hinterhof; **castle** ~ Schloßhof; **coal** ~ Kohlenlager, -halde; **departure** ~ Abgangsstation, -bahnhof; **goods** ~ Warenlager; **lame-duck** ~ leistungsschwache Werft; **marshalling** ~ Verschiebebahnhof; **naval** ~ *(US)* Staatswerft; **navy** ~ Marinewerft; **poultry** ~ Hühnerhof; **prison** ~ Gefängnishof; **railway** ~ *(Br.)* Verschiebe-, Rangierbahnhof; **receiving** ~ Empfangsstation, -bahnhof; **repair** ~ Ausbesserungswerft; **school** ~ Schulhof; **shipbuilding** ~ Schiffswerft; **switching** ~ Verschiebebahnhof;
  ~s **of statistics** nicht endenwollende Statistiken;
  ~ **closure** Werftstillegung; ~ **conductor** *(US)* Rangiermeister.
yardage Lagerkosten, -gebühren.
yardman *(mar.)* Werftarbeiter, *(railway)* Rangierarbeiter.
yardmaster Rangiermeister.
yardstick Zollstock, *(fig.)* Vergleichsmaßstab.
yarn gesponnener Faden, Garn, *(coll.)* Seemannsgarn, Abenteuergeschichte;
  horror ~ Schauergeschichte;
  to spin a ~ Seemannsgarn spinnen, Abenteuergeschichte erzählen.
yaw *(fig.)* Abweichung, *(mar.)* Gierung;
  ~ *(v.)* von einer Überzeugung abweichen, schwanken, *(plane)* scheren, wenden, *(ship)* aus dem Kurs laufen, gieren.
yawn Abgrund, Schlund;
  ~ *(v.)* *(gulf)* klaffen, gähnen.
yea Jastimme;
  ~s **and nays** Stimmen für und wider.
year [Kalender]jahr, Jahreszahl;
  all the ~ **round** ganzjährig; **as from next** ~ vom nächsten Jahre ab; **by the** ~ jährlich; **for a** ~ **and a day** *(law)* auf Jahr und Tag; **in former** ~s in verflossenen Jahren; **in the** ~ **of marriage** im Jahr der Eheschließung; **of several** ~s mehrjährig; **open throughout the** ~ ganzjährig geöffnet;
  academic ~ Schul-, Universitätsjahr; **account** ~ Rechnungsjahr; ~s **ahead** kommende Jahre; **budgetary** ~ Haushaltsjahr; **business** ~ Geschäftsjahr; **cabbatical** ~ *(academic life)* Urlaubsjahr; **calendar** ~ Kalenderjahr; **civil** ~ bürgerliches Jahr, Kalenderjahr; **college** ~ akademisches Jahr; **commercial** ~ Geschäftsjahr; **common** ~ normales (gewöhnliches) Jahr; **company's financial** ~ *(Br.)* Wirtschafts-, Geschäfts-, Gesellschaftsjahr; **current** ~ laufendes Geschäftsjahr; **economically depressing** ~ Jahr konjunkturellen Rückschlags; **financial** ~ staatliches Rechnungs-, Steuerjahr, *(Br.)* Haushaltsjahr; **fiscal** ~ *(Br.)* Steuerjahr, *(US)* Etats-, Haushaltsjahr; **formative** ~s Entwicklungsjahre; **incoming** ~ beginnendes Jahr; **inter-war** ~s Jahre zwischen den Kriegen; **last** ~ abgelaufenes Jahr, Vorjahr; **leap** ~ Schaltjahr; **legal** ~ Kalenderjahr; **the** ~ **after next** übernächstes Jahr; **old (past)** ~ vorangegangenes Jahr;

policy ~ Versicherungsjahr; **preceding** ~ Vorjahr; **preparatory** ~ Vorbereitungsjahr; **present** ~ laufendes Jahr; **presidential** ~ *(US)* Jahr in dem der Präsident gewählt wird, Präsidentschaftsjahr; **previous** ~ Vorjahr; **regent** ~ *(Br.)* Jahr der Thronbesteigung; **reported on** Berichtsjahr; **most financially rewarding** ~ finanziell erfolgreichstes Jahr; ~s **served** Dienstjahre; **taxable** ~ steuerpflichtiges Jahr; **trading** ~ Berichtsjahr; **whole** ~ volles Jahr; **wild** ~s turbulente Jahre;
  first ~ **of apprenticeship** erstes Lehrjahr; ~ **of assessment** Veranlagungsjahr; ~ **of birth** Geburtsjahr; ~ **of cessation** Schließungsjahr; ~ **of coverage** *(social insurance)* anrechnungsfähiges Jahr; ~s **of discretion** zurechnungsfähiges (unterscheidungsfähiges) Alter; **many** ~s **of experience** jahrelange Erfahrungen; ~ **of issue** Ausgabejahr, *(insurance)* Jahr des Versicherungsbeginns; ~ **of manufacture** Baujahr, Herstellungs-, Fabrikationsjahr; ~ **of maturity** Fälligkeitsjahr; ~ **of mourning** Trauerjahr; ~s **of office** Dienstjahre; ~ **of organization** Gründungsjahr; ~s **of practice** jahrelange Erfahrungen; ~ **of probation** Probejahr; ~ **of small profits** gewinnschwaches Jahr; ~ **of publication** Druckjahr; ~ **of recession** Rezessionsjahr; ~ **under report (review)** Berichtsjahr; ~s **to run** *(insurance)* noch nicht abgelaufene Versicherungsdauer; ~s **of service** Dienstjahre; ~s **of study** Studienjahre, Studentenzeit; ~ **under survey** Berichtsjahr; ~ **of good trading** gutes Geschäftsjahr; ~ **of the war** Kriegsjahr;
  to be let by the ~ auf ein Jahr vermietet werden; **to be off from last** ~ hinter dem Vorjahr zurückbleiben; **to come to (reach)** ~s **of discretion** mündig werden; **to finish the** ~ **with liquid funds of £ 32 m** im Jahresabschluß liquide Mittel von 32 Mio Pfund aufweisen; **to get twenty** ~s zwanzig Jahre Gefängnis bekommen, zu zwanzig Jahren Gefängnis verurteilt werden; **to have twenty thousand a** ~ *(Br.)* 20.000 Pfund im Jahre verdienen; **to hire s. th. by the** ~ Mietvertrag auf ein Jahr abschließen;
  ~'s **account** Jahresrechnung; ~ **end** Jahresende, -ultimo.
year-end | adjustment *(US)* Ultimoausgleich; **to dress up the** ~ **books** *(US)* Jahresschlußbilanz verschönern; ~ **closing** *(US)* Jahresabschluß; ~ **closing entry** *(US)* Jahresschlußbuchung; ~ **compensation** *(US)* Jahresschlußvergütung; ~ **dividend** *(Br.)* am Schluß des Geschäftsjahres gezahlte Sonderdividende; ~ **figures** *(US)* Jahresabschlußziffern; ~-**before figures** *(US)* Vorjahreszahlen, Abschlußzahlen des Vorjahres; ~ **need for cash** *(US)* Geldanforderungen zum Jahresultimo; ~ **report** *(US)* Geschäftsbericht, Jahresschlußbericht.
year | -to-~ growth ratio jährliche Wachstumsrate; **previous-~ level** Vorjahresniveau; ~ **model** Jahresmodell; **ten** ~s' **purchase** zehnfacher Jahresertragswert; ~'s **rental** Jahresmiete; ~-**round** ganzjährig.
yearbook Jahrbuch.
yearling bond market *(Br.)* Anleihemarkt für kurzfristige Papiere.
yearly jährlich;
  ~ **account** Jahres[ab]rechnung; ~ **earnings** Jahresgewinn; ~ **income** Jahreseinkommen, -einkünfte; ~ **letting** Jahrespacht, -miete; ~ **output** Jahresproduktion, -leistung, -ertrag; ~ **payment** Jahreszahlung; ~ **receipts** Jahreseinnahme; ~ **requirements** Jahresbedarf; ~ **revenue** jährliche Einnahmen, Jahreseinnahmen; ~ **settlement** Jahresabschluß, -[ab]rechnung; ~ **subscription** Jahresbeitrag, -abonnement; ~ **value of land** Jahresertragswert.
yell *(v.)* keifen, zetern, schreien.
yellow gelb, *(jealous)* neidisch, eifersüchtig, *(journal, coll.)* sensationslüstern, reißerisch aufgemacht;
  ~ **book** *(pol.)* Gelbbuch; ~ **boy** *(Br., sl.)* Goldstück; ~ **dog minderwertige Person; ~ dog contract** *(US sl.)* Arbeitsvertrag mit Gewerkschaftsbeitrittsverbot; ~ **fever** *(sl.)* Goldrausch; ~ **flag** Quarantäneflagge; ~ **jack** *(sl.)* Quarantäneflagge; ~ **journal** *(US)* Revolver-, Boulevardblatt; ~ **journalism** *(US)* Boulevardjournalismus; ~ **metal** Gold; ~ **paper** *(US)* Revolver-, Boulevardblatt; ~ **peril** gelbe Gefahr; ~ **press** *(US)* Sensations-, Asphalt-, Boulevardpresse; ~ **road sign** polizeiliches Straßenschild; ~ **soap** Schmierseife; ~ **streak** feiger Charakterzug; ~ **union** *(US)* wirtschaftsfriedlicher Gewerkschaftsverband.
yellowback *(Br.)* Schmöker.
yellowed vergilbt.
yeoman Pächter, kleiner Grundbesitzer, *(Br.)* freier Bauer;
  ~ **of signals** *(Br.)* Signalmaat;
  ~ **service** treue Hilfe.

yes, to say einwilligen;
~ **man** [rücksichtsloser] Jasager.
yesterday gestriger Tag;
to be caught up in ~ von der Nostalgiewelle erfaßt werden;
~ *(a.)* gestern, *(fig.)* unlängst, vor kurzem;
~'s **paper** gestrige Zeitung.
yield *(breakdown)* Zusammenbruch, *(crop)* Ernte, Bodenertrag, *(fig.)* Nachgeben, Weichen, *(gain)* Ausbeute, Ertrag, Ergebnis, *(interest)* [Effektiv]verzinsung, Zinsertrag, *(metallurgy)* Metallgehalt, *(stocks)* Rendite, Effektivverzinsung;
average ~ durchschnittlicher Ertrag, Durchschnittsertrag;
basic ~ risikofreier Ertrag; **budgeted** ~ Sollaufkommen; **crop** ~ Ernteertrag; **current** ~ laufender Ertrag; **effective interest** ~ Effektivverzinsung; **flat** ~ laufende Verzinsung; **minimum** ~ Mindestertrag, -verzinsung; **net** ~ Nettoerlös, -ertrag, -verzinsung; **peak** ~ Ertragsspitze; **running** ~ *(Br.)* laufende Verzinsung; **estimated running** ~ geschätzter Durchschnittsertrag; **tax** ~ Steueraufkommen; **total** ~ Gesamtaufkommen; **true** ~ *(securities)* Effektivverzinsung;
~ **per acre** Ertrag pro Morgen; ~ **on capital** Kapitalertrag; ~ **of depreciation** Abschreibungsbetrag; ~ **on invested funds** Kapitalertrag; ~ **upon investment** [Kapital]rendite; ~ **of a loan** Anleiheverzinsung; ~ **on shares (stocks)** Aktienrendite; ~ **of taxes** Steueraufkommen, -ertrag; **good** ~ **of wheat** gute Weizenernte; ~ **for year** Jahresertrag;
~ *(v.) (concede)* zugestehen, gestatten, erlauben, *(interest)* Zinsen tragen (bringen, abwerfen), *(produce)* [Ertrag] abwerfen, bringen, abfallen, tragen, *(bring as result)* [er]bringen, *(submit)* sich unterwerfen, *(surrender)* übergeben, -lassen;
~ **5 per cent** sich mit 5% verzinsen; ~ **to s. one's argument** sich jds. Beweisführung nicht verschließen; ~ **to conditions** auf Bedingungen eingehen; ~ **consent** Zustimmung erteilen; ~ **good crops** gute Ernten hervorbringen; ~ **14% dividend** Dividende von 14% bringen; ~ **a fortress** Festung aufgeben; ~ **s. o. due hono(u)rs** jem. die gebührenden Ehren erweisen; ~ **interest** Zinsen einbringen; ~ **high interest** hochverzinslich sein, *(shares)* hohe Rendite bringen; ~ **little** geringe Rendite abwerfen, wenig eintragen; ~ **net** netto abwerfen; ~ **to no one** keinem nachstehen; ~ **the palm** sich geschlagen geben; ~ **passage** Durchfahrt gestatten; ~ **a point to s. o.** jem. in einem Punkt nachgeben; ~ **precedence to s. o.** jem. den Vorrang einräumen; ~ **o. s. prisoner** sich gefangen geben; ~ **one's privilege** auf sein Privileg verzichten; ~ **a profit** Gewinn abwerfen, Ertrag bringen; ~ **a handsome profit** schönen Gewinn einbringen; ~ **a profit over the book value** den Buchwert übersteigenden Erlös abwerfen; ~ **no return** keinen Ertrag bringen; ~ **one's rights** seine Rechte aufgeben; ~ **right of way!** *(US)* Vorfahrt beachten!; ~ **submission** sich unterwerfen; ~ **an effective sum equivalent to 7 per cent** *(loan)* siebenprozentige Effektivverzinsung erbringen; ~ **to temptation** der Versuchung erliegen; ~ **s. o. thanks** jem. Dank zollen; ~ **one's allotted time** seine Redezeit einhalten; ~ **well** gute Erträge abwerfen;
to obtain ~s Rendite erzielen;
to sell on a ~ **basis** unter Berücksichtigung der Ertragsaussichten Absatz finden; ~ **capacity** Ertragsfähigkeit; ~ **curve** Renditekurve; ~ **gap** Ertragslücke; **fixed-** ~ **investment** Anlage mit festem Ertrag, festverzinsliche Anlage; **variable** ~ **investment** Anlage mit schwankendem Ertrag; ~ **mix** Durchschnittsrendite; ~ **spread** Spanne in den Renditen.
yielding *(complying with)* nachgiebig, willfährig, *(producing)* ergiebig, einträglich;
~ **a dividend of** mit einer Dividende von; ~ **interest** verzinslich; ~ **and paying** *(conveyancing)* Pachteinleitungsklausel; **profit-**~ ertragreich;
~ **year** gutes Geschäftsjahr.
yoke *(fig.)* Joch, Knechtschaft, Unterwerfung;
~ **of oxen** Ochsengespann; ~ **of matrimony** Ehejoch;
~ *(v.)* **one's mind** sich geistig anstrengen;
to come under the ~ sich in eine Niederlage fügen; **to throw off the** ~ Fesseln der Knechtschaft abwerfen.
yoked in marriage ehelich verbunden.
yokefellow Arbeitskollege, Mitarbeiter.
yokel Hinterwäldler.
young jung, klein, im Kindesalter, *(without experience)* unerfahren, unwissend, unreif;
~ **in one's job** ohne Berufserfahrung.
~ **animal** Jungtier; ~ **days** Jugendzeit; ~ **institution** neue Institution; ~ **Men's Christian Association (YMCA)** Christlicher Verein Junger Männer; ~ **offender** jugendlicher Täter; ~ **offender court** Jugendstrafgericht; ~ **people** heiratsfähige Leute; ~ **person** *(Br.)* Jugendlicher; ~ **unemployed persons** arbeitslose

Jugendliche; **Children and** ~ **Persons Act** *(Br.)* Jugendschutzgesetz; ~ **Persons Employment Act** *(Br.)* Jugendarbeitschutzgesetz; **to put an old hat on** ~ **shoulders** der Jugend Weisheit lehren wollen; ~ **turk** *(politics, US)* Jungtürke; ~ **worker** Jungarbeiter.
yours truly *(complimentary suffixes)* mit den besten Empfehlungen, hochachtungsvoll.
youth Jugend[zeit], Jugendfrische, Jugendlichkeit, *(early period)* Frühzeit, Anfangsstadium, *(young man)* junger Mensch, Jugendlicher;
draft-weary ~ wehrunwillige Jugend; **gay** ~ unbeschwerte Kindheitstage; **promising** ~ vielversprechender junger Mann; ~ **of good social position** Söhne aus gutem Hause; ~ **of great promise** vielversprechender junger Mann;
~ **activities** Jugendarbeit, -pflege; ~ **center** *(US)* **(centre, Br.)** Jugendzentrum, -klub, -heim; ~ **club** Jugendfreizeitheim; ~ **delinquency** Jugendkriminalität; ~ **employment** Jugendarbeit, Beschäftigung von Jugendlichen; ~ **employment subsidy** *(Br.)* Zuschüsse für die Einstellung von Jugendlichen; ~ **group** Jugendgruppe; ~ **hostel** Jugendherberge; **British** ~ **Hostels Association** *(Br.)* Jugendherbergsverband; ~ **market** Absatzmarkt für jugendliche Käufer; ~ **meeting** Jugendtreffen; ~ **movement** Jugendbewegung; ~ **officer** Sachbearbeiter für Fragen der Jugendarbeit, Jugendpfleger; ~ **organization** Jugendorganisation; ~ **paper** Jugendzeitung; **to be doing one's** ~ **thing** sich einen jugendlichen Kraftakt leisten; ~ **unemployment** Jugendarbeitslosigkeit; ~ **welfare service** Jugendpflege; ~ **worker** Jugendhelfer.
youthful jugendlich, jugendfrisch;
~ **days** Jugendzeit; ~ **indiscretions** Jugendtorheiten; ~ **offender** jugendlicher Täter.

zeal Dienst-, Arbeitseifer;
full of ~ arbeitseifrig.
zealot Fanatiker.
zealous diensteifrig, *(ardent)* hitzig, fanatisch;
to be ~ **to please one's employer** seinen Arbeitgeber auf jeden Fall zufriedenstellen wollen.
zebra crossing Zebrastreifen, Fußgängerüberweg.
zenith Höhe-, Gipfelpunkt;
to have reached the ~ **of one's power** auf dem Gipfel seiner Macht stehen.
zero Null, *(aeronautics)* Höhe unter 300 m, *(fig.)* Null-, Tiefpunkt, *(mil.)* Nulljustierung, *(scale)* Ausgangs-, Nullpunkt, *(thermometer)* Gefrierpunkt;
~ *(v.) (math.)* gleich Null setzen, *(technics)* auf Null einstellen; ~ **in on s. o.** sich auf j. einschießen; ~ **in on the construction industry** mit der Bauindustrie den Anfang machen; ~ **in on appropriate monetary policy** in der Geldpolitik den absoluten Nullpunkt erreichen;
to be close to ~ fast Nullwerte erreichen; **to be down to** ~ gleich Null sein; **to fly a** ~ *(plane)* unter 300 m fliegen; **to reduce to** ~ auf den Nullwert setzen;
~ **altitude** Bodennähe; ~-**base budgeting process** Etatisierungsverfahren vom Ausgangspunkt; ~ **conditions** vertikal und horizontal begrenzte Sicht; ~ **growth** Nullwachstum; ~-**growth rate** keine Zuwachsrate; ~ **hour** *(fig.)* entscheidender Augenblick, *(mil., Br.)* Nullstunde; **to leave a** ~ **net** keinen Reingewinn erzielen; **to show a** ~ **net tax accrual** keinerlei Steueranspruch ausweisen; ~ **productivity of labo(u)r** Grenzproduktivität der Arbeit; **to have produced** ~ **profit to date** bisher noch keinen Gewinn gemacht haben; ~-**rated** abgabenfrei; **to give** ~ **value as strategic weapon** als strategische Waffe völlig nutzlos sein.
zest Geschmack, Würze;
to add ~ **to s. th.** etw. schmackhaft machen; **to enter a plan with** ~ Geschmack an einem Plan bekommen.
zigzag Zickzack[linie], *(road)* Serpentinenstraße, *(traffic)* Ampel-, Druckknopf-Signal-Überweg, Selbstbedienungsampel;
~ *(v.) (road)* in Serpentinen verlaufen;
~ **course** *(pol.)* Zickzackkurs; ~ **line** Zickzacklinie; ~ **road** Serpentinenstraße.
zinc Zink;
~ **block** *(Br.)* Zinkklischee; ~ **works** Zinkhütte.
Zionism Zionismus.
zip *(car, fam.)* Beschleunigungsvermögen, *(pep, coll.)* Schneid, Schmiß, *(post office, US)* Postleitzahl;
~ *(v.)* mit einem Reißverschluß schließen, *(coll.)* Schneid (Schmiß) haben;

~ along at a yearly rate of increase of 6,4% *(gnp)* Bruttosozial-zuwachsrate von etwa 6,4% aufweisen;
to show less ~ geringen Schwung aufweisen;
~ code *(US)* Postleitzahlwesen, -system; **~-code area** *(US)* Postleitzone; **~ fastener** Reißverschluß.
zipper Reißverschluß, *(coll.)* energischer Mensch;
~ bag Reißverschlußtasche.
zonal zonenartig;
~ authorities Zonenbehörde; **~ claim** Gebietsanspruch; **~ frontier** Zonengrenze; **~ organization** Zonengliederung.
zonation Einteilung in Zonen, Zoneneinteilung.
zone [Teil]gebiet, Randgebiet, Zone, Gürtel, Landstrich, Gebietsstreifen, *(city planning, US)* im Wege des Planfeststellungsverfahrens festgelegtes Gebiet, *(geol.)* Schicht, Gürtel, Zone, *(mil.)* Sperrgebiet, *(parcel post, tel., US)* Tarifzone, *(post)* Postzustellbezirk, *(railway, tram)* Tarifzone, -gebiet, -stufe, Teilstrecke, *(region)* Bezirk, Gegend, Randgebiet;
architectural-freedom ~ von Baubeschränkungen freies Gebiet; **atom-free ~** atomwaffenfreie Zone; **bad-weather ~** Schlechtwettergebiet; **business ~** Geschäftsviertel, -bezirk; **collecting ~** Sammelbezirk; **contiguous ~** angrenzende Zone; **danger ~** Gefahrenzone; **demilitarized ~** entmilitarisierte Zone; **denuclearized ~** atomwaffenfreie Zone; **end-cleared ~** *(aerodrome)* hindernisfreie Zone; **evacuated ~** Evakuierungsgebiet; **forbidden ~** Sperrgebiet; **free ~** *(customs)* Zollausschluß-, Freihafengebiet; **frigid ~** kalte Zone; **economically fused ~s** wirtschaftlich vereinigte Zonen; **limited-force ~** militärisch verdünnte Zone; **limited-parking ~** Kurzparkzone; **littoral ~** Küstengebiet; **200-mile ~** Zweihundertmeilenzone; **closed military ~** militärisches Sperrgebiet; **neutral ~** neutrale Zone; **no-parking ~** Parkverbotsgebiet; **no-stopping ~** Halteverbotszone; **occupation ~** Besatzungszone; **operational ~** Sperr-, Kriegsgebiet; **plebiscite ~** Abstimmungsgebiet; **polar ~** Polargebiet; **postal ~** Zustellbezirk; **prohibited ~** Sperrgebiet; **radio quiet ~** Gebiet mit absolutem Sendeverbot; **residential ~** Wohnbezirk, -gegend; **restricted ~** Baubeschränkungen unterworfenes Gebiet; **slow-drive ~** *(US)* 50-km-Gebiet; **spot ~** Baugebiet mit Sondergenehmigung; **temperate ~** gemäßigte Zone; **three-mile ~** Dreimeilenzone; **torrid ~** heiße Zone; **twilight ~** Dämmerzone; **unrestricted ~** Gebiet mit geringen Baubeschränkungen, freies Baugebiet; **war ~** Kriegsgebiet; **wheat ~** Weizengürtel;
~ of action Aktionsgebiet; **~ of attack** *(mil.)* Angriffsraum; **~ of death** Todesstreifen; **~ of defence** *(mil.)* Verteidigungszone; **~ of employment** *(Workmen's Compensation Act)* Unfallversicherungsbereich; **~ of influence** Einflußzone, Interessensphäre, -gebiet; **~ of interior** Heimatkriegsgebiet; **~ of occupation** Besatzungszone; **~ of operations** Einflußzone; **~ for parcels** *(US)* Paketpostzone; **~ of preference** *(statistics)* Bevorzugungsbereich; **~ of responsibility** Verantwortungsbereich; **~ of free trade** Freihandelszone; **~ of war** Kriegsschauplatz;
~ *(v.)* nach (in) Zonen einteilen, *(city planning, US)* in verschiedene Baubezirke (Ortsklassen) einteilen, *(intr.)* in Zonen aufgeteilt sein, *(railway tariff)* Tarif nach Teilstrecken festsetzen; **spot-~** Bauausnahmegenehmigung für Geschäftshäuser erteilen;
~ for business use Grundstück zur Bebauung mit Geschäftshäusern freigeben; **~ for one-family residences** für die Errichtung von Einfamilienhäusern vorsehen;

to be within the ~ of submarine activities im Operationsgebiet der U-Boote liegen;
~ campaign regionaler Werbefeldzug; **~ center** *(tel.)* Durchgangsfernamt; **~ change** *(US)* Änderung der Bebauungsvorschriften; **~ merger** Zonenzusammenschluß; **~ plan** *(advertising campaign)* Zonenplan, Schwerpunktwerbung; **~ price** Einheitstarif, Einheitspreis für eine Zone; **~ pricing** *(US)* regionalabhängige Preisdifferenzierung, Zonenpreisverfahren, Preisfestsetzung nach Zonen; **~ rates** *(public utilities, US)* Zonentarif; **~ selector** *(tel.)* Zonenwähler; **~ system** Zonensystem; **~ system of pricing** regionale Preisdifferenzierung; **~ tariff** Zonentarif; **~ ticket** Teilstreckenfahrkarte; **~ time** Landes-, Ortszeit.
zoned in Zonen (Ortsklassen) eingeteilt;
~ residential-A *(US)* für die Errichtung von Einfamilienhäusern bestimmt;
to be ~ back into its proper economic classification wieder dem normalen Bebauungszweck zugeführt werden; **to be ~ for manufacturing enterprise** für Fabrikgebiete vorgesehen sein; **to be ~ for multiple-dwelling use** für die Errichtung von Wohnblocks freigegeben sein.
zoning Einteilung in Zonen, Flächenaufteilung, Zonen-, Gebietsabgrenzung, *(cartels)* territoriale Machtaufteilung, *(city planning, US)* Planfeststellung, Aufstellung von Flächennutzungsplänen;
flexible ~ *(US)* Beweglichkeit bei der Festsetzung von Bebauungsrichtlinien (Flächennutzung); **incentive ~** *(US)* Planfestsetzung mit Sonderbewilligungen; **spot ~** *(US)* Bauausnahmegenehmigung für die Errichtung von Geschäftshäusern;
to be free from ~ keinen Baubeschränkungen unterliegen; **to enforce ~** *(US)* Fluchtlinienplan durchsetzen;
~ act Aufbaugesetz, Ortsstatut; **~ administration** *(US)* Planfestsetzungsbehörde; **~ board** *(US)* Planfestsetzungs-, Bau-, Fluchtlinienausschuß; **~ case** *(US)* Flächennutzungs-, Planfeststellungsverfahren; **~ classification** *(US)* Bebauungsbestimmungen, Ortsklasseneinteilung; **~ code** *(US)* Generalbebauungsplan; **~ committee** *(US)* Planfeststellungsausschuß; **~ district** *(US)* Bebauungsbezirk; **~ law** *(US)* Aufbaugesetz, Bauordnung, Ortsstatut, Baubestimmungen; **~ legislation** Bebauungsvorschriften; **~ official** Zonenvertreter; **~ ordinance** *(US)* Fluchtlinien-, Flächennutzungs-, Bebauungsplan, Bebauungsvorschriften; **~ practice** *(US)* Fluchtlinienverfahren; **~ regulations** *(US)* Bebauungs-, Flächennutzungs-, Fluchtlinienbestimmungen; **~ restrictions** *(US)* Bebauungsbeschränkungen, Bebauungsstatut; **~ status** Bebauungsstatus; **~ system** *(post)* Leitzahlsystem; **~ variance** *(US)* Abweichung (Ausnahmegenehmigung) vom allgemeinen Bebauungsplan (Flächennutzungsplan).
zoo Zoo[logischer Garten].
zoom *(film, television)* Heranrücken in Großaufnahme, *(plane)* Hochreißen, schnelles Steigen;
~ *(v.)* hochreißen, *(fig.)* schnell ansteigen lassen, *(film)* in Großaufnahme heranrücken, *(plane)* schnell steigen, *(prices)* senkrecht in die Höhe steigen;
~ to the top an die Spitze gelangen; **~ upward** raketenhaft ansteigen;
~ lens *(photo)* Gummilinse.
zooming *(airplane)* Hochziehen.

Pressestimmen

Frankfurter Allgemeine
Sprichwörtlich zu werden, ist auch für ein Wörterbuch nicht einfach.
„Der Eichborn" hat es geschafft

Capital
Eichborn hat Wirtschaftsenglisch zu seinem Lebenswerk gemacht

Austria Presse Agentur
Dreißig Jahre Erfahrung mit der amerikanischen und englischen
Wirtschaftssprache

Canadian German Chamber of Industry and Commerce
. . . dürfte ein Bestseller werden

Die Sekretärin
. . . . ein unentbehrliches Requisit für alle, die mit Wirtschaftsenglisch Tag für Tag umgehen müssen

Neuer Bücherdienst
Schon Stichproben zeigen, daß einen dieses Taschenbuch kaum jemals im
Stich lassen wird

Handelsblatt
Wirtschaftsenglisch im „Eichborn" up to date

Christ und Welt
Was dem Banker sein Bowler Hat, das ist dem Manager von heute der
„Eichborn"

Verkauf und Marketing
. . . eine uneingeschränkt empfehlenswerte Investition

Export Berater
. . . ein für die Praxis der Wirtschaft unentbehrlicher Ratgeber

Curt L. Schmitt
. . . gehört kurioserweise zu den meistgestohlenen Büchern deutscher Bibliotheken

Südwestfunk
Ein Knüller, der alles enthält, was ein im Bereich der Wirtschaft Tätiger wissen
muß

Niedersächsische Wirtschaft
. . . kann für ex- oder importbetriebene Unternehmen sehr empfohlen werden

Tiroler Tageszeitung
Wer auch nur am Rande mit Wirtschaft zu tun hat, braucht dieses Buch

Volkshochschule im Westen
. . . wohl brauchbarste Wörterbuch des wirtschaftlichen Bereiches

Industrie- und Handelskammer
Kein Kaufmann kann auf ein Nachschlagewerk, das den sich ständig ausweiten-
den Fachsprachensatz registriert, verzichten

Aachener Prisma
Die Benutzer des Wörterbuches werden feststellen, daß sie fast alles finden,
was zur Umgangssprache des modernen Menschen gehört

Tapeten-Zeitung
. . . macht sich in jeder Diskussion sofort bezahlt, weil man die im Wirtschaftsleben gebräuchlichen Spezialausdrücke eben nur hier findet

Beruf und Bildung
Das Standardwerk schlechthin, das sich in der Praxis als unentbehrlich erweist

Berliner Morgenpost
Die Zuverlässigkeit der Eichbornschen Wörterbücher ist erwiesen

Fuchsbriefe
Das Lexikon ist im internationalen Geschäftsverkehr unentbehrlich